MAJOR BRITISH WRITERS

WRITERS

SHORTER EDITION

Chaucer	Swift	Coleridge	Browning
Shakespeare	Pope	Byron	Shaw
Bacon	Johnson	Shelley	Conrad
Donne	Boswell	Keats	Yeats
Milton	Wordsworth	Tennyson	Eliot

HARCOURT, BRACE & WORLD, INC.

NEW YORK   CHICAGO   SAN FRANCISCO   ATLANTA   DALLAS

CONTENTS

JOHN MILTON *Edited by* DOUGLAS BUSH

JONATHAN SWIFT *Edited by* HERBERT DAVIS

ALEXANDER POPE *Edited by* GEOFFREY TILLOTSON

SAMUEL JOHNSON & JAMES BOSWELL
Edited by BERTRAND H. BRONSON

WILLIAM WORDSWORTH & SAMUEL TAYLOR COLERIDGE
Edited by GEORGE W. MEYER

GEORGE GORDON, LORD BYRON   Edited by NORTHROP FRYE

PERCY BYSSHE SHELLEY   Edited by I. A. RICHARDS

JOHN KEATS   Edited by WALTER J. BATE

ALFRED, LORD TENNYSON   *Edited by* DOUGLAS BUSH

ROBERT BROWNING   *Edited by* WILLIAM C. DeVANE

PREFACE

Great literature can be studied mainly in two ways. It can be regarded as part of the history and culture of a people; and if so, the student should become acquainted with an extensive collection of many samples and varieties. But it can also be regarded as the product of fine minds; and if so, it is better to study the works of a few major writers with greater intensity.

Either approach has its advantages — and disadvantages. The wide survey gives a nodding acquaintance with many writers and a little of the best of each; but the selections are inevitably too brief and too few for the fuller understanding of any one author. Those who still prefer the study in breadth are well supplied with several good and well-known anthologies. The study in depth, on the other hand, demands selection and concentration. This book is intended for the more intense study.

At the beginning of any literary study, every student needs first a short selection of relatively simple works which serve to distinguish the writer's voice from the garble of other voices out of the past. This stage is soon passed, and the able student, sensing behind the voice the accents of a rich and complex personality, is no longer satisfied with a bare introduction but wishes to go on to deeper intimacy. Such an intimacy is precisely what this anthology seeks to enable. Great literature is not written for the simple minded. In this collection of some of the best works of the greatest writers in the English language, the editors have shunned complexity neither in their introductions nor in their choice of selections. There is substance enough to challenge any student.

Most of the writers chosen belong to the past — even the distant past. Chaucer wrote nearly five hundred years ago and Shakespeare has been dead for more than three hundred and fifty years. Nevertheless, it would be naive to suppose that they have nothing to say to modern readers. The wise student uses his imagination. He tries to understand the essence of each work of literature, that is, what each work meant to its author and to its first readers; and in this way he expands his own sensitivities to the present. He learns also that though trappings and customs of life and ways of expression and of thought vary from age to age, human nature remains largely unchanged. He may even come to realize that the great artists of the past had certain qualities of mind that have since been lost, but which it may be possible to recover — to the profit of his own humanity and understanding. The intelligent study of the literature of past ages reveals that there are more things in heaven and earth than are revealed by a microscope, a telescope, or even a statistical survey.

The Shorter Edition of *Major British Writers* is an abridgment of the larger work in two volumes called MAJOR BRITISH WRITERS (1954, expanded 1959). In that collection, the authors were chosen as great in themselves, representative of their generation and tradition, and still significant to the modern reader. The work of each author was edited by a distinguished modern scholar-critic who contributed an introduction and a commentary. In making this abridgment, we have followed the principles laid down for the original work, but adapted them somewhat for a different kind of reader. Each author is still represented by a considerable selection from his best work, and with few exceptions much of the critical and editorial aid given by the original editors has been kept.

Users of this book will appreciate that the twenty authors herein represented are not the only great British writers, but a select company chosen from among the best. We assume maturity alike in the reader and in the teacher, but we also realize that not everyone, even among intelligent readers, will like everything in our collection. Nor should anyone ever try to force a feigned enthusiasm for what leaves him indifferent or even bored; but he will be a dull reader who refuses to meet the challenge of the past or of the unfamiliar.

The Publisher and the General Editor wish to thank the several editors for their friendly and helpful co-operation in the difficult task of abridging their contributions to the original work to conform to the plan of this present volume. In the early stages of this edition the work of selection was aided by Mr. Robert Hogan, for whose help we now tender grateful acknowledgment.

G. B. H.

Geoffrey Chaucer

1343?–1400

In his lifetime Geoffrey Chaucer was hailed as the greatest poet of his age. And today, after more than five and a half centuries, during which the warmth, color, humor, and humanity of his poetry have endeared him to his readers, his name stands in the annals of English literature second only to that of Shakespeare.

I. CHAUCER'S CIVIL CAREER

Chaucer was by instinct a poet, but he was also a practical man of affairs and earned his living chiefly in what we would now call the civil service. He was born about 1343 of a wealthy bourgeois family and was comfortably reared in London. He probably did not attend either Oxford or Cambridge, though he may have studied civil law and business procedure in London at the law school known as the Inner Temple. Certainly, whatever the source of his education, he acquired a sound knowledge of Latin, French, and Italian and a wide familiarity with the world of letters; and his career gave him an acquaintance with the world of people such as has fallen to the lot of few poets.

He gained his first practical experience by serving variously as page boy, valet, and esquire in the household of Elizabeth of Ulster, a daughter-in-law of King Edward III. His duties probably included humble jobs such as making beds and looking after clothing, but he had the compensations of traveling in Elizabeth's retinue throughout England and perhaps in Ireland and enjoying a valet's-eye view of the ruling aristocracy of his age. He also served as a soldier against the French under Elizabeth and subsequently under King Edward's influential son, John of Gaunt, and thus learned at first hand something of the mingled chivalry and sordidness of the Hundred Years' War. On one occasion, in company with several of Elizabeth's officers, he was captured by the French but returned by one of those ransoms which the French and English always arranged so amicably.

In 1366 he married Philippa Roet, who was lady-in-waiting to her Flemish compatriot Queen Philippa, King Edward's wife, and later to Constance of Castile, John of Gaunt's second wife. By this marriage Chaucer apparently had two sons and a daughter. Both he and his wife throughout their lifetime seem to have found warm friends among the members of the reigning house.

From 1368 on he served occasionally as a royal diplomatic agent in France and, at least twice, in Italy — a duty for which his linguistic ability and his tact suited him and which in turn notably contributed to his own literary development. For the most part, however, he lived a settled life in London. In 1374 he was appointed by King Edward as Controller of Customs and Subsidy of Wools, Skins, and Hides. This was a responsible position, for wool was one of England's most valuable dutiable exports. He discharged his duties personally until 1385 and through a deputy until 1386, when his appointment lapsed.

In 1385 he moved temporarily outside the city of London into the neighboring county of Kent, where he held the office of Justice of the Peace; and in 1386 he represented the county for one session as member of parliament. It was apparently in 1387 that his wife died, and in 1389 he returned to London as Clerk of the Works, to supervise such important matters as construction and repairs around Westminster Abbey, the Tower of London, Windsor Castle, the royal manor at West Sheen (now Richmond on the Thames), and the south bank of the Thames between Greenwich and Woolwich. By 1391 he had been removed, probably at his own request, from this strenuous responsibility and appointed to a less onerous charge as Subforester of the King's forest at North Petherton, 130 miles west of London.

In 1399 he rented a house in the gardens of Westminster Abbey, and in 1400 he died and was buried in the section of the south transept of the Abbey which later came to be known as the Poets' Corner.

Other isolated records of Chaucer's civil career have survived, but they do not add much to our understanding of him, and even those details that have been mentioned are open to various interpretations. In general, however, it may be said that Chaucer lived a busy and comparatively prosperous life throughout a stormy period of English history. In his lifetime the warrior King Edward III died in his dotage (in 1377), the boy King Richard II succeeded his grandfather on the throne, and the bold Henry IV in 1399 deposed the ineffectual Richard. (See Additional Note below, p. 57.) When Richard ascended the throne, Chaucer was apparently on familiar terms with the ten-year-old boy and his mother, the Fair Maid of Kent, for he addressed a fatherly poem of personal advice to the new monarch; and even after Richard had been deposed, Chaucer evidently felt sure of the continuance of royal favor, for he immediately sent the new King Henry a playful request for the replenishment of his purse.

Both Chaucer and his wife were granted annuities and other perquisites by royal employers and patrons. Chaucer received from King Edward at least two lucrative wardships of heirs who had become orphans while not yet of age. He was awarded by Edward a lifetime gift of a daily pitcher of Gascon wine, and by Richard an annual butt of wine — a gift which was renewed by Henry, who also presented him with a scarlet robe trimmed with fur.

Since other civil servants received similar rewards, these may have been bestowed on Chaucer for his usefulness in public affairs, not for his literary achievements. Even his burial in Westminster Abbey may not have been intended as a special honor accorded to a national poet, for Chaucer was living on the grounds and may have been entitled to burial in the Abbey as a tenant. But there can be no doubt that Chaucer was widely acclaimed as a writer in his lifetime, and nowhere more enthusiastically than at the brilliant court of his royal employers.

His works circulated universally in manuscript while he was alive, and after his death new copies continued to appear in profusion until the introduction of printing. Eighty-four different manuscripts of the *Canterbury Tales* actually survive to the present time. And among the first works to appear from Caxton's press in the fifteenth century were the writings of Chaucer, whom England's first printer saluted as " the worshipful father and first founder and embellisher of ornate eloquence in our English " and as a writer who " ought eternally to be remembered."

II. CHAUCER'S LITERARY CAREER

Chaucer was, like Milton, a writer who possessed the energy and inspiration to live laborious days and produce great poetry in the midst of an active career. We know that he had already turned to poetry in his twenties, and there is every indication that he was still at work when he died in his fifties.

His early work is conventional and strongly influenced by contemporary French verse, though even then its voice bears the individuality of Chaucer. His earliest extant poem is a prayer to the Virgin Mary translated freely from Guillaume Deguilleville's *Pilgrimage of the Human Life,* and it is remarkable for both its religious sensitivity and its metrical skill.

Chaucer's other early works include some love lyrics in which he expresses his complete devotion to his beloved lady in the conventionally plaintive tone which was first affected by courtly European poets in the twelfth century and remained popular in England until the appearance of John Donne. " The more I love, the more she makes me smart," he cries in a typically exaggerated passage. "Through which I see that, without remedy, from death I can in no way escape."

His first extensive and original poem, the graceful *Book of the Duchess,* was composed as a tribute to the memory of the charming young Duchess Blanche, John of Gaunt's first wife, who died in 1369. Here too Chaucer imitates his French contemporaries in features such as the conventional description of the lady, but the tone and conception of the work are original; and though some of its phrases may have been borrowed, Chaucer has adapted them ideally to the pathetic circumstances which occasioned its composition.

Later, the great Italian poets of his own century exercised their spell. His uncompleted *House of Fame* was evidently written after his appointment to the Customs (1374), for in it he reports that after doing his daily reckonings he has sat up at his books at home each night, reading till he is dazed and writing till his head aches. This poem proves that Chaucer had already made an acquaintance with Italian literature, perhaps as the result of his diplomatic journeys in Italy. In the poem he dreams that a garrulous eagle has carried him off to show him whether those in the service of Love are really glad or not; and the eagle (whose mission Chaucer unfortunately left unfulfilled) is modeled upon a more modest eagle guide in Dante's *Divine Comedy* (1307–21).

As Chaucer matured, he turned his attention to philosophy and (c. 1380) translated the *Consolation of Philosophy* into English prose. This influential work was written by Boethius, a Roman nobleman, statesman, and scholar unjustly condemned to death in 524 by the Emperor Theodoric. In it the author, imprisoned and awaiting execution, laments that Fortune continually turns her whirling wheel, indifferently changing the lowest to the highest and the highest to the lowest; and Philosophy replies that God, providently aware of man's vicissitudes, makes even adverse Fortune work towards the ultimate good of man. The subtle interplay of argument obviously appealed to Chaucer, in whose later works the words, phrases, and ideas of Boethius reappear in many contexts.

In this same period Chaucer also wrote his brilliant tragic romance, *Troilus and Criseyde,* a masterly reinterpretation of the material used by Boccaccio in his poem, the *Filostrato.* Chaucer was invited to recite his poem in public before the most distinguished members of the English court — an event memorialized in an appropriately splendid, illuminated picture on the frontispiece of one of the *Troilus* manuscripts. His fame was now secure.

In the year 1387 Chaucer began to compile materials for the *Canterbury Tales,* his most original and most characteristically English work. The framework of this collection of tales was provided by a familiar English scene, the journey to Canterbury of a group of pilgrims, whom Chaucer describes in a general prologue and in links connecting the tales.

According to Chaucer's ambitious plan, each of the thirty or more pilgrims was to tell two tales on the road to Canterbury and two on the road back to London. He died before he had completed the poem, but he did write twenty-four tales, consisting of more than two thousand lines of prose and seventeen thousand lines of verse, most of them linked together by animated conversations between the pilgrims and their master of ceremonies, the Host of the Tabard Inn.

III. CHAUCER'S WORLD

The differences between the age of the Canterbury pilgrimages and our own technological era are considerable, though some of the more obvious dissimilarities are superficial. Travel, for example, was slower and more painful than it is today. Thus, while it took Chaucer's pilgrims two or three days of rough riding on horseback over indifferent roads to travel the sixty miles from London to Canterbury, leisurely sightseers now ride the distance by bus in two or three hours. But the vital differences of social and political structure and of religious life, which are much more important in determining the quality of man's behavior, are far from obvious to the casual reader of Chaucer.

In the fourteenth century the government of England was aristocratic rather than democratic, and the efficacy of the monarch's rule depended largely on the strength of his character and on the power of the nobles whom he could rally to his support. Hence the fate of the country was determined by the personality of the king in a manner now quite undreamed of.

Next to the king, the richest and most influential people in England were those, such as John of Gaunt, who controlled vast agricultural areas. These privileged few had feudal possession of the land, in return for which they supplied manpower, equipment, and money for the wars of their overlord. Inevitably their views played a large part in the administration of the internal and external affairs of the realm. A number of lesser landlords of various ranks were dependent upon them. And, at the bottom of the feudal order, the unprivileged many were virtual serfs who worked the land for their masters. Feudal custom varied from locality to locality, and the social structure was not completely fixed. The king might grant lands and title to a commoner, or a needy knight might marry off his aristocratic son to the plebeian daughter of a farmer, provided the farmer was wealthy. But, in general, the people of England accepted as inevitable the rank, whether high or low, to which they were born and the feudal privileges and duties accompanying it.

The workings of the system are mirrored in seven of the Canterbury pilgrims. The Knight held land and in return for it served in the wars of his overlord, the king, and when necessary supplied trained fighting men; his son, the Squire, was learning to follow in his father's footsteps; and the Knight's Yeoman was a family servant trained to uphold the way of life of his master. The Franklin was an independent gentleman farmer who probably supplied military assistance to the country, when necessary, by a payment of some kind rather than by personal service. The Miller by feudal right milled all the grains grown in an area assigned to him and charged a toll for his service. (Chaucer tells us that his Miller contrived to exact a triple toll!) The Reeve managed a large country estate, and the Plowman was a serf bound to employment under the owner of the land on which he had been born.

But in Chaucer's day feudalism did not embrace the entire population, for urban life with its greater social freedom was beginning to play an important role in England. Thirteen of the pilgrims are dependent on the economy of the town, much as they would be today — the Manciple (a purchasing agent), the Merchant (a wholesale importer-exporter), the Shipman (the owner of a merchant ship), the Haber-dasher, the Carpenter, the Weaver, the Dyer, the Tapestry Maker, the Cook, the Clothmaker (the Wife of Bath), the Innkeeper, and, to some extent, the two professional men, the Physician and the Sergeant of the Law.

The influences of religion on human affairs were, in contrast to our own day, omnipresent. There was one Church, and all Christians were Catholics. People might, and did, disobey the teachings of Holy Church, but no one could ignore it. It controlled all education and, in addition to its regular services of worship, played a daily part among all ranks of society and at all stages of a person's life, from the time of baptism through confirmation and marriage to the funeral rites at burial. It held vast areas of land throughout England, and its complex organization included not merely the regular clergy attached to churches, but also a great number of other religious, such as monks and nuns dedicated to the contemplative life and friars devoted to an active life of service to mankind.

Consequently the reader will not be surprised to discover that no fewer than thirteen of Chaucer's pilgrims depend in some manner upon the Church — the Parson, the Summoner (a sort of church policeman), the Monk, the Prioress with her accompanying Nun and three Priests, the Friar, the Pardoner, the Clerk (an ecclesiastical university student), and the Canon and his Yeoman who later join the pilgrimage.

The deeply religious undercurrent of medieval life is clearly apparent in Chaucer's Canterbury pilgrimage. It springs to birth in a common meeting place at the crossroads of England under the inspiration of a worldly innkeeper and commences with a courtly romance told by a knight. But the pilgrims, worldly and unworldly alike, regardless of rank or of wealth, are all directed towards a holy shrine in a solemn cathedral. The last tale they hear is a sermon by a godly parson who points their thoughts towards the "perfect glorious pilgrimage called heavenly Jerusalem"; and at the end of this tale Chaucer adds his personal repudiation of all that is sinful in his writing and a prayer that he "may be one of them at the Day of Judgment that shall be saved."

In one important respect, however, Chaucer's age was closely akin to ours, for just as much as our own it was a prey to all the ills that flesh is heir to. It was troubled by disease, political insecurity, international animosity, religious dissension, social unrest, and economic disasters.

The Black Plague, which ravaged Europe in 1348, entered England and, like "the privy thief called Death" alluded to in the Pardoner's Tale, slew in every town and village "both man and woman, child, and hind, and page." At its first onslaught it is said to have wiped out perhaps half the population of England. In succeeding years it recurred with appalling severity. It bereft parishes of priests, farms of laborers, and towns of workmen. It enriched no one, with the possible exception of fortunate doctors such as Chaucer's shrewd Physician, who "kept what he gained in the pestilence." It spared neither the talented nor the great, killing a profound scholar like Archbishop Bradwardine of Canterbury, yet it passed by corrupt men like Chaucer's Friar and Pardoner, who were enabled by the death of honest churchmen to climb unchecked to power and wealth.

The Black Death affected England's economy more disastrously than did World War II. Surviving laborers were so scarce that they refused to work unless granted excessive wages. Commodities also became scarce and prices high. Under the unfortunate young Richard II the attempts of the king's council to control the economy failed, and the "stormy people, unstable and ever untrue" rebelled. During the Peasant's Revolt of 1381 an unruly mob broke into London and murdered those whom they considered to be their exploiters, including some unhappy Flemish weavers (referred to by the Nun's Priest) whose competition they resented.

Political life was a dangerous struggle for power. Chaucer's Man of Law remarks in his tale that an observer can always recognize the "pale face, among a crowd, of one that is lead toward his death." And Chaucer had every reason to share this disquieting knowledge, for in 1388 Nicholas Brembre, one of his superiors in the Customs, and Thomas Usk, one of his literary disciples, were executed, along with several others, because of their ill-advised support of King Richard during the temporary ascendancy of the Duke of Gloucester's party.

During the reign of King Richard, the Hundred Years' War between France and England took on a less promising complexion than it had in the happy days of Edward III's victories at Crécy and Poitiers. As the French rallied, England began to fear invasion. English merchant ships had to be impressed for naval service; shore defenses were prepared; and everyone experienced at least some kind of inconvenience, including Chaucer's self-interested Merchant, who feared that his shipping lanes between England and Holland would be cut off.

Not even the great power and influence of the Church were able to bring peace between the two most cultured nations of western Europe, for the Church itself suffered the weakness of division. During the Great Schism from 1378 to 1417 the papacy lay divided. The pope at Rome was supported by the allegiance of the Holy Roman Empire and England, while the antipope at Avignon was supported by France, Scotland, and other nations. It is not surprising, therefore, that in England during this period of disorganization many abuses were committed against religion by fraudulent pardoners, mercenary friars, and worldly monks, whom Chaucer and other contemporary writers condemned. Still others went to the heretical length of questioning the very structure of the Church itself.

Despite these tribulations, however, England reached a cultural peak in the latter part of the fourteenth century. The English were warmly sympathetic to the cultural influences of the Continent. French art, architecture, and music, and — as we have seen in the sketch of Chaucer's own literary career — French and Italian literature were widely appreciated in courtly circles. England, moveover, had a distinguished literature of her own. The anonymous *Sir Gawain and the Green Knight,* for instance, represents the acme of the medieval Arthurian romance; and Langland's *Piers Plowman* is a remarkable and powerful satirical vision almost unique of its kind. Chaucer's supreme achievements were, in fact, a glory superadded to the already great attainments of his countrymen.

When we turn from an appraisal of Chaucer's era to the actual reading of his poetry, the distance of time, the differences of material culture, and the divergencies of human belief, custom, and behavior which separate his world from ours seem miraculously to disappear. The only barrier to our appreciation is one of language, and even that can no more hinder us from relishing his work than a foreign accent can prevent us from enjoying a talented actor on the stage or screen. Besides, our unfamiliarity with Chaucer's language is not his fault.

Chaucer, quaintly clad in antique guise,
With unfamiliar mien scares modern eyes.
No doubt he well invented, nobly felt,
But, O ye powers, how monstrously he spelt!

So wrote Hartley Coleridge, but he added an important injunction:

Yet, thou true poet, let no judgment wrong
Thy rich, spontaneous, many-colored song!

Fortunately for the judgment of Chaucer's song, modern readers soon grow accustomed to his antique guise, which was, after all, the living language of his day, and a language which he used with the most effortless grace. And, having once accustomed their ears to its melody, they will readily realize that in the control of meter, rhyme, and verse form Chaucer equals any of the great English poets of later times, just as he immeasurably excels his own contemporaries.

Chaucer, the lover of letters and the practical man of affairs, learned of life from two great teachers — his wide reading and his rich personal experience; and so memorably did he combine the wit and wisdom he had gleaned from the past with his own vital knowledge of the present that his vanished world still survives today, alive perennially in his poetry.

NOTE ON CHAUCER'S LANGUAGE

SOUNDS

The written record of Chaucer's language does not, of course, now tell us precisely how Chaucer would have pronounced what he wrote, but scholars have succeeded in working out what is probably a close approximation. In particular, the quality of certain long, stressed vowels has changed considerably between the fourteenth century and the present, even though the spelling of many of the words in which they occur has not changed at all. The reader who applies even the following three rules will be able to recapture something of the melody of Chaucer's poetry.

(1) *Pronounce all written consonants as we do those in modern English.* Also, pronounce the sound (now foreign to English) represented by *gh* in *night* somewhat as we now pronounce the *h* sound in *how* but with a stronger breathing. (It is like the *ch* in the Scottish pronunciation of *loch* or in the German pronunciation of *Bach*.)

(2) *Pronounce all final syllables*, even those represented by a final *-e* (here written with a dot over it) and no longer pronounced in modern English. Thus, pronounce Chaucer's *damė* with two syllables as *dah-meh*, and his *damės* as *dah-mess*. (The sound of the final *-e* was probably the same as that of the modern English final unstressed vowel, when unemphatic, in words such as *Stella* and *raven*.)

(3) *Give all written vowels (both short and long) their so-called "Continental" sounds,* such as they would receive, for instance, in modern French or Italian or in our modern pronunciation of Latin.

Thus, pronounce the long vowel spelled *a* in Chaucer's *damė* as the *ah* sound of modern French *dame* or modern English *father*, not as the *ay* sound of modern English *dame*. Other instances are *barė, carė, famė, gamė, hatė, lamė, makė, namė, pagė, ragė, savė, takė, wakė*.

Pronounce the long vowel spelled *e* or *ee* in Chaucer's *regioun* as the *ay* sound of modern French *région* or modern English *rage*, not as the *ee* sound of modern English *region*. Other instances are Chaucer's *be, he, me, she, thee*. The reader may ignore the fact that in some words such as Chaucer's *heeth* (modern *heath*) the *e* or *ee* represented a distinctive vowel sound like that in modern English *ebb*, only lengthened.

Pronounce the long vowel spelled *i* or *y* in Chaucer's *finė* as the *ee* sound in modern French *fine* or modern English *machine*, not as the *eye* sound in modern English *fine*. Other instances are Chaucer's *bitė, glidė, kyndė, minė, primė, ridė, strivė, thinė, wyn* (modern *wine*).

Pronounce the long vowel *u* spelled *ou* or *ow* in Chaucer's *doute* as the *ou* sound in modern French *doute* or modern English *soup*, not as the *ow* sound in modern English *doubt*. Instances are *bour* (modern *bower*), *doute* (modern *doubt*), *flour* (modern *flower*), *foul, hous, licour, mous, out, tour* (modern *tower*).

The other long vowels and diphthongs and all the short vowels have passed down into modern English with less notable change, and the reader may therefore rely on his instinct for their pronunciation.

To illustrate the application of these rules, the first four lines of the General Prologue are here represented in a roughly phonetic transcription, in which all long vowels and diphthongs have been marked with a sign of length.

> Whan that Aprill with his shoures soote
> The droghte of March hath perced to the roote
> And bathed every veyne in swich licour
> Of which vertu engendred is the flour, . . .

> Whán that Ahpríll with his shoures sóhte
> The drócht(e) of March hath perced to the róhte
> And bahthed év(e)ry veyn(e) in swich licour
> Of which vertu engéndred is the flour, . . .

FORMS

All obscure words and idioms in the following selections have been interpreted in the footnotes, but a recognition of certain frequently recurring forms and constructions will facilitate the reading of Chaucer's language.

Pronouns are the same as in modern English with the chief exception of two ambiguities which have now disappeared. The word variously spelt *her, here, hir, hire* is Chaucer's equivalent not only of the modern *her* but also of the modern *their*. Similarly Chaucer's *his* is the equivalent not only of modern *his* but also *its*.

Most verb forms resemble their modern counterparts, but the following peculiarities should be noted. Chaucer normally uses the form (*he, she, it*) *lovéth* rather than the modern verb form *loves*. Verbs with stem ending in *-d* or *-t*, however, regularly contract the ending *-eth*, thus appearing as *he bit* (for *biddeth*), *fint* (*findeth*), *holt* (*holdeth*), *rit* (*rideth*), *stant* (*standeth*). Notice also that *hym lest* (for *lesteth*) means "*it pleases him*" and has a past tense *hym leste*, "it pleased him." (In all three forms the root is variously spelled *lest-, list-, lust-*.)

Many verb endings had a final *-n*, now gone, which might be dropped. Thus *we* (*ye, they*) *lové* and *lovén*

are used interchangeably for modern *we love; we lovédé(n)* for modern *we loved;* and *to lové(n)* for modern *to love*. Also optional was the prefix *y-* as a sign of the past participle, so that the modern *I have loved* appears as *I havé lovéd* or *y-lovéd*, and modern *I have drunk* as *I havé dronké(n)* or *y-dronké(n)*.

One sign of the negative was the still familiar *not* or its variants *noght* and *naught*. Another sign, now gone, was *ne* or *n'*, which was often accompanied by other negative words. "He nevere yet no vileynye *ne* sayde / In al his lyf unto no maner wight" (Gen. Prol., ll. 70–71) means literally, "he never yet no villainy didn't say in all his life to no kind of person"; i.e., "he never yet spoke any villainy to any kind of person." *Ne* combines with the following word in the frequently occurring combinations *nadde* (*ne hadde,* "hadn't"), *nere* ("weren't"), *nolde* ("wouldn't"), *noot* (*ne woot,* "know not"), *nyl* ("will not"), *nyste* (*ne wiste,* "knew not").

A variant form of the past tense was provided by the verb *gan*, which was used sometimes with its literal meaning "began" but often conveyed no more than the modern English *did* in a phrase such as *did go*. Thus it is equivalent to "began" in the sentence: "Anon for joye his herte gan to daunce." But it is merely a sign of the past in the sentence: "A thousand tyme . . . he gan hir kisse"; i. e., "a thousand times . . . he kissed her."

The text of the following selections is based, with the kind permission of the University of Chicago Press, upon *The Text of the Canterbury Tales Studied on the Basis of All Known Manuscripts*, 8 vols. (1940), edited by John M. Manly and Edith Rickert. Punctuation has been added, capitalization has been normalized, and a few preferable readings have been selected from the recorded variants. Readers should notice that the spelling of Chaucer's scribes, which has been left unaltered, is not consistent. After only a little practice the reader will soon realize that *heigh, heighe, hey, heye, hy,* and *hye* are simply variant spellings of our modern *high*. (Here and elsewhere there is generally a grammatical reason for the appearance of the final *-e*.)

THE CANTERBURY TALES

THE GENERAL PROLOGUE

The opening scene of the General Prologue is set in the Tabard Inn "beside the Bell" at Southwark on the south side of the River Thames opposite London; to judge from subsequent astronomical allusions, the date is mid-April, 1387, and the innkeeper's name, we later learn, is Harry Bailly. In these details, as in others, the framework which encloses the *Canterbury*

Tales presents a faithful portrait of real life in fourteenth-century England; for, in Chaucer's day, there actually was an inn known as the Tabard in Southwark, and another known as the Bell, and an innkeeper (or possibly more than one) by the name of Henry Bailly.

Chaucer joins up with a group of people numbering "a good nine-and-twenty" (according to l. 24, though the General Prologue in fact describes thirty characters, not counting Chaucer and the innkeeper), who are to ride as pilgrims the sixty miles of much-traveled road to the shrine of St. Thomas à Becket at Canterbury Cathedral. The famous "holy, blissful martyr," Archbishop Becket, had been murdered in 1170 because he championed the Church against the secular power of King Henry II. In 1172 he was canonized as a saint; in 1174 the king did penance at his tomb; and in 1220 his remains were translated to the splendid shrine which became the most popular of all the religious resorts in England. Pilgrims sought there inspiration for their faith, remission of penalties due for their sins, extra merits, healing for their bodies, and incidentally — in some cases — satisfaction for their wanderlust.

Whan that° Aprill with his shoures soote°
The droghte of March hath perced to the roote
And bathed every veyne in swich licour°
Of which vertu° engendred is the flour,
Whan Zephirus° eek° with his sweete breeth
Inspired hath in every holt° and heeth°
The tendre croppes,° and the yonge sonne
Hath in the Ram his half cours y-ronne,°
And smale foweles maken° melodye
That slepen al the nyght with open eye,   10
So priketh hem Nature in hir corages,°
Than longen folk to goon° on pilgrymages,
And palmeres for to seken straunge strondes,°
To ferne halwes kouthe° in sondry londes.
And specially, from every shires ende
Of Engelond, to Caunterbury they wende,
The holy, blisful martir° for to seke
That hem hath holpen° whan that they were seeke°
    Bifel° that in that sesoun on a day
In Southwerk at the Tabard, as I lay   20
Redy to wenden on my pilgrymage
To a Caunterbury with ful devout corage,°
At nyght was come into that hostelrye
Wel nyne-and-twenty in a compaignye
Of sondry folk by aventure y-falle°
In felaweshipe, and pilgrymes were they alle
That toward Caunterbury wolden° ryde.
The chambres and the stables weren wyde,°
And wel we weren esed atte beste;°
And shortly, whan the sonne was to reste,   30

So hadde I spoken with hem everichon°
That I was of hir° felaweshipe anon;
And made forward° erly for to ryse
To take oure wey ther-as° I yow devyse.°
    But, nathelees,° whil I have tyme and space,
Er that° I ferther in this tale pace,°
Me thynketh it° acordant to resoun
To telle yow al the condicioun
Of ech of hem° so as it semed me,
And whiche they weren, and of what degree,   40
And eek in what array that they were inne;
And at a knyght than wol I first bigynne.

    A KNYGHT ther was, and that a worthy man,
That, fro the tyme that he first bigan
To riden out,° he loved chivalrye,
Trouthe and honour, fredom and curteisye.
Ful worthy was he in his lordes werre,°
And ther-to hadde he riden, no man ferre,°
As wel in Cristendom as in hethenesse,°
And evere honoured for his worthyness.   50
    At Alisaundre° he was whan it was wonne.
Ful ofte tyme he hadde the bord bigonne°
Aboven alle nacions in Pruce.°
In Lettow° hadde he reysed,° and in Ruce,°
No Cristen man so ofte of his degree.
In Gernade° at the seege eek° hadde he be°
Of Algezir,° and riden in Belmarye.°
At Lyeys° was he and at Satalye°
Whan they were wonne; and in the Grete° See
At many a noble armee° hadde he be.   60
At mortal batailles hadde he been fiftene,
And foghten for oure feith at Tramyssene°
In lystes thries,° and ay° slayn his foo.
This ilke° worthy Knyght hadde been also
Som tyme with the lord of Palatye°
Agayn° another hethen in Turkye.

31. everichon: everyone.   32. hir: their.   33. made forward: (we) made agreement.   34. ther-as: where. devyse: tell.   35. nathelees: nevertheless.   36. Er that: before. pace: pass.   37. Me . . . it: it seems to me.   39. hem: them.   45. riden out: ride in expeditions.   47. werre: war. As a feudal duty to his overlord, the king, he had fought in "his lord's war," a term presumably referring to the campaigns of the Hundred Years' War between England and France. The subsequent allusions indicate that the Knight must have been a veteran of more than forty years' service, for he had also enlisted voluntarily against the pagan hordes of northeastern Europe and against the Mohammedans in the Moorish realms of the western Mediterranean and in the Turkish realms of the eastern Mediterranean.   48. ferre: farther.   49. hethenesse: heathendom.   51. Alisaundre: Alexandria (Egypt).   52. bord bigonne: table headed.   53. Pruce: Prussia.   54. Lettow: Lithuania. reysed: campaigned. Ruce: Russia.   56. Gernade: Granada (Spain). eek: also. be: been.   57. Algezir: Algeciras. Belmarye: Benmarin (Morocco).   58. Lyeys: Ayas (Armenia). Satalye: Adalia (Turkey).   59. Grete: Mediterranean.   60. armee: sea-borne expedition.   62. Tramyssene: Tlemcen (Algeria).   63. lystes thries: single combats thrice. ay: always.   64. ilke: same.   65. Palatye: Balat (Turkey).   66. Agayn: against.

GENERAL PROLOGUE.   1. Whan that: when.   soote: sweet.   3. swich licour: such liquid.   4. Of . . . vertu: by power of which.   5. Zephirus: the west wind. eek: also.   6. holt: wood. heeth: heath.   7. croppes: shoots.   7-8. yonge . . . y-ronne: The young sun of spring has run its second half-course through the zodiacal sign of the Ram (April 11).   9. foweles maken: birds make.   11. So . . . corages: Nature so stirs them in their hearts.   12. Than . . . goon: Then people long to go.   13. palmeres . . . strondes: pilgrims (long) to seek unfamiliar strands.   14. ferne . . . kouthe: distant shrines known.   17. martir: Thomas Becket. See headnote.   18. holpen: helped. seeke: sick.   19. Bifel: it befell.   22. corage: heart.   25. by . . . y-falle: by chance fallen.   27. wolden: intended to.   28. wyde: spacious.   29. esed . . . beste: entertained at the best.

And evere moore° he hadde a sovereyn prys,°
And, though that he were worthy, he was wys
And of his port° he meke as is a mayde.
He nevere yet no vileynye ne sayde°   70
In al his lyf unto no maner wight.°
He was a verray,° parfit, gentil knyght.
　　But for to tellen yow of his array,
Hise hors° were goode, but he was nat gay.
Of fustian° he wered a gypoun°
Al bismotered° with his habergeoun,°
For he was late y-come from his viage°
And wente for to doon his pilgrymage.

　　With hym ther was his sone, a yong SQUYER,
A lovere and a lusty bacheler,°   80
With lokkes crulle as° they were leyd in presse.°
Of twenty yeer of age he was, I gesse.
　　Of his stature he was of evene° lengthe,
And wonderly delyvere,° and of greet strengthe;
And he hadde been som tyme in chivachye°
In Flaundres, in Artoys, and Picardye,°
And born° hym wel, as of so litel space,°
In hope to stonden° in his lady° grace.
　　Embrouded° was he as it were a meede°
Al ful of fresshe floures white and reede.   90
Syngynge he was or floytynge° al the day.
He was as fressh as is the monthe of May.
Short was his gowne with sleves longe and wyde.
Wel koude he sitte on hors and faire° ryde.
He koude songes make and wel endite,°
Juste,° and eek daunce, and wel purtreye,° and
　　write.
So hoote he lovede that by nyghtertale°
He slepte namoore than dooth a nyghtyngale.
　　Curteys he was, lowely, and servysable,
And carf° biforn his fader at the table.   100
　　A YEMAN° hadde he° and servantz namo°
At that tyme, for hym liste° ryde so,
And he was clad in coote and hood of grene.
A sheef of pecok arwes° bright and kene

Under his belt he bar° ful thriftily.°
Wel koude he dresse° his takel° yemanly;
His arwes drouped noght with fetheres lowe.
And in his hand he bar a myghty bowe.
A not° heed hadde he, with a broun visage.
Of wodecraft wel koude° he al the usage.   110
Upon his arm he bar a gay bracer,°
And by his syde a swerd° and a bokeler,°
And on that° oother syde a gay daggere,
Harneysed° wel, and sharp as poynt of spere,
A Cristofre° on his brest of silver shene.°
An horn he bar, the bawdryk° was of grene.
A forster° was he soothly,° as I gesse.
　　Ther was also a nonne, a PRIORESSE,
That of hir smylyng was ful symple° and coy.°
Hir gretteste ooth was but " By Seint Loy!"°   120
And she was cleped° Madame Eglentyne.
　　Ful wel she soong° the servyce dyvyne,
Entuned° in hir nose ful semely,°
And Frenssh she spak ful faire and fetisly°
After the scole of Stratford atte Bowe,°
For Frenssh of Parys was to hire unknowe.°
　　At mete° wel y-taught was she with alle;
She leet° no morsel from hir lippes falle,
Ne wette hir fyngres in hir sauce depe;
Wel koude she carie a morsel, and wel kepe°   130
That no drope ne fille° upon hir brest.
In curteisie was set ful muchel° hir lest.°
Hir over lippe wyped she so clene
That in hir coppe ther was no ferthyng° sene
Of grece whan she dronken hadde hir draughte.
Ful semely after hir mete she raughte,°
And sikerly° she was of greet desport,°
And ful plesaunt and amyable of port,°
And peyned hire to countrefete cheere°
Of court, and to been estatlich° of manere,   140
And to been holden digne° of reverence.
　　But for to speken of hir conscience,

---

67. evere moore: always. prys: reputation. 69. port: deportment. 70. no . . . sayde: said anything boorish. 71. unto . . .
wight: to any kind of person. 72. verray: true. 74. hors:
horses. 75. fustian: rough cotton. gypoun: blouse. 76. bis-
motered: stained. habergeoun: coat of mail. 77. viage: journey. 80. bacheler: As a "bachelor" or candidate for knighthood, the Squire was an apprentice both in military training
and in courtly love. 81. crulle as: curled as if. presse: curlers.
83. evene: medium. 84. delyvere: agile. 85. in chivachye:
on a raid. 86. In . . . Picardye: Under the pretext of aiding
the Pope against the rival claimant supported by the French,
an English force raided Flanders, Artois, and Picardy in 1383
without opposition. 87. born: conducted. space: time.
88. stonden: stand. lady: lady's. 89. Embrouded: embroidered. meede: meadow. 91. floytynge: fluting or whistling.
94. faire: gracefully. 95. endite: compose (the words).
96. Juste: joust. purtreye: draw. 97. nyghtertale: night-
time. 100. carf: carved. 101. Yeman: yeoman (servant).
he: the Knight. namo: no more. 102. hym liste: he liked
to. 104. arwes: arrows.

105. bar: carried.   thriftily: neatly.   106. dresse: prepare.
takel: equipment.   109. not: close-cropped.   110. koude:
knew.   111. bracer: archer's guard.   112. swerd: sword.
bokeler: buckler (small shield).   113. that: the.   114. Har-
neysed: mounted.   115. Cristofre: a medal of St. Christopher (the forester's and traveler's patron).   shene: bright.
116. bawdryk: carrying-belt.   117. forster: forester.   soothly:
truly.   119. symple: unpretentious.   coy: quiet.   120. Loy:
She swears appropriately by the talented and courtly St. Loy,
who was both a bishop and a goldsmith in seventh-century
France.   121. cleped: called.   122. soong: sang.   123. En-
tuned: intoned.   semely: properly.   124. fetisly: elegantly.
125. Stratford . . . Bowe: Stratford at the Bow outside London.
Presumably the Prioress was connected with the nearby nunnery of St. Leonard's, which served as a sort of finishing school
for the daughters of London burghers.   126. unknowe: unknown.   127. mete: food.   128. leet: let.   130. kepe: take
care.   131. fille: fell.   132. muchel: much.   lest: concern.
134. ferthyng: particle.   136. raughte: reached.   137. sikerly:
certainly.   desport: fun.   138. port: deportment.   139. peyned
. . . cheere: strove to imitate the appearance.   140. estatlich:
stately.   141. holden digne: considered worthy.

She was so charitable and so pitous,°
She wolde wepe if that she sawe a mous
Caught in a trappe, if it were deed or bledde.
Of smale houndes hadde she that she fedde
With rosted flessh, or mylk and wastel° breed;
But soore wepte she if oon of hem were deed,
Or if men° smoot it with a yerde smerte.°
And al was conscience and tendre herte.   150
  Ful semely° hir wympel pynched° was,
Hir nose tretys,° hir eyen° greye° as glas,
Hir mouth ful smal, and there-to softe and reed,
But sikerly she hadde a fair forheed;
It was almoost a spanne° brood, I trowe,°
For hardily° she was nat undergrowe.
Ful fetys° was hir cloke, as I was war;°
Of smal coral aboute hir arm she bar°
A peyre of bedes, gauded al with grene,°
And ther-on heng a brooch of gold ful shene,°   160
On which ther was first written a crowned A,
And after *Amor vincit omnia.*°

Another NONNE with hire hadde she,
That was hir chapeleyne, and PREESTES thre.

  A MONK ther was, a fair for the maistrye,°
An outridere° that lovede venerye,°
A manly man, to been an abbot able.
Ful many a deyntee° hors hadde he in stable,
And whanne he rood, men myghte° his brydel
    heere
Gynglen° in a whistlynge wynd as cleere   170
And eek° as loude as dooth the chapel belle
Ther-as° this lord was kepere of the celle.°
  The reule of Seint Maure or of Seint Beneit,°
Bycause that it was old and somdel streit,° —
This ilke Monk leet olde thynges pace°
And heeld after the newe world, the space.°
He yaf° nat of that text a pulled° hen
That seith that hunters been° nat holy men,
Ne that a monk, whan he is recchelees,°
Is likned til° a fissh that is waterlees,   180

This is to seyn,° a monk out of his cloystre.
But thilke° text heeld he nat worth an oystre;
And I seyde his opinioun was good.
What° sholde he studie and make hymselven
    wood°
Upon a book in cloystre alwey to poure,°
Or swynken° with his handes and laboure
As Austyn bit?° How shal the world be served?°
Lat Austyn have his swynk° to hym reserved.
Therfore he was a prikasour° aright.
Grehoundes he hadde as swift as fowel° in flight.
Of prikyng° and of huntyng for the hare   191
Was al his lust,° for no cost wolde he spare.
  I seigh° his sleves y-purfiled° at the hond
With grys,° and that the fyneste of a lond;
And for to festne his hood under his chyn
He hadde of gold wroght a ful curious pyn;
A love knotte in the gretter° ende ther was.
His heed was balled,° that shoon as any glas,
And eek his face as° he hadde been enoynt.°
He was a lord ful fat and in good poynt,°   200
His eyen stepe° and rollynge in his heed,
That stemed° as a forneys° of a leed,°
His bootes souple, his hors in greet estat.°
  Now certeynly he was a fair prelat.
He was nat pale as a forpyned goost.°
A fat swan loved he best of any roost.
His palfrey was as broun as is a berye.

  A FRERE° ther was, a wantowne° and a merye,
A lymytour,° a ful solempne° man.
In alle the ordres foure° is noon that kan°   210
So muche of daliaunce° and fair langage.
He hadde maad° ful many a mariage

---

181. seyn: say.   182. thilke: that same.   184. What: why.
hymselven wood: himself insane.   185. poure: pore.   186.
swynken: work.   187. Austyn bit: Augustine commands
(biddeth). The widely followed monastic rule established
by St. Augustine of Hippo in the fifth century warned monks
against sloth.   How . . . served?: Who else will perform the
many worldly services which require a cleric's education if monks
withdraw themselves from the world to the life of spiritual contemplation required of them? (Suitably educated laymen were
not sufficiently numerous.)   188. swynk: work.   189. prika-
sour: fast rider.   190. fowel: bird.   191. prikyng: tracking
(the hare).   192. lust: pleasure.   193. seigh: saw.   y-pur-
filed: trimmed.   194. grys: gray fur.   197. gretter: larger.
198. balled: bald.   199. as: as if. enoynt: anointed.   200. poynt:
condition.   201. eyen stepe: eyes prominent.   202. stemed:
glowed.   forneys: furnace.   leed: boiler.   203. greet estat:
splendid condition.   205. forpyned goost: tormented spirit.
208. Frere: friar.   wantowne: gay.   209. lymytour: limiter,
one allotted a limit or district. Unlike monks, friars followed an
active life of preaching and teaching rather than a contemplative
life. When first organized in the thirteenth century, they earned
any necessary money by manual labor. By Chaucer's time, however, they had become mendicants who begged for alms and were
licensed to raise funds within local limits by hearing confessions
and granting absolutions.   solempne: splendid.   210. ordres
foure: The four orders were Carmelites, Augustinians, Francis-
cans, and Dominicans.   kan: knows.   211. daliaunce: flirtation.
212. maad: arranged.

---

143. pitous: sympathetic.   147. wastel: white wheat.   149. men:
someone.   yerde smerte: stick severely.   151. semely: gracefully.   wympel pynched: headdress pleated.   152. tretys:
shapely.   eyen: eyes.   greye: blue.   155. spanne: handspan.
trowe: believe.   156. hardily: undeniably.   157. fetys: graceful.   war: aware.   158. bar: carried.   159. A . . . grene: a set
of beads (a rosary), with every gaud (large bead among smaller
beads) colored green.   160. shene: bright.   162. Amor . . .
omnia: Love conquers all.   165. a fair . . . maistrye: an extremely fine (one).   166. outridere: supervisor.   venerye:
hunting.   168. deyntee: valuable.   169. myghte: could.
170. Gynglen: jingle.   171. eek: also.   172. Ther-as: where.
celle: group.   173. The . . . Beneit: The originator of the Bene-
dictine order, St. Benedict (Beneit), formulated the rule of behavior in Italy in the sixth century, and his disciple St. Maur
brought it to France.   174. somdel streit: somewhat strict.
175. pace: pass by.   176. the space: for the meanwhile.   177.
yaf: gave.   pulled: plucked.   178. been: are.   179. recchelees:
without a care.   180. likned til: comparable to.

Of yonge wommen at his owene cost.
 Unto his ordre he was a noble post.°
Ful wel biloved and famulier was he
With frankeleyns over-al° in his contree
And with worthy wommen of the toun,
For he hadde power of confessioun,
As seyde hymself, moore than a curat,°
For of his ordre he was licenciat.   220
Ful swetely herde he confessioun,
And plesaunt was his absolucioun.
He was an esy man to yeve° penaunce
Ther-as he wiste° to have a good pitaunce.°
For unto a poure ordre for to yive°
Is signe that a man is wel y-shryve;°
For if he yaf, he dorste make avaunt,°
He wiste that a man was repentaunt;
For many a man so hard is of his herte,
He may not wepe, althogh hym° soore smerte.°
Therfore, in stede of wepynge and preyeres,   231
Men moote° yeve silver to the poure freres.
 His typet° was ay farsed° ful of knyves
And pynnes for to yeven faire wyves.
 And certeynly he hadde a murye note.
Wel koude he synge and pleyen on a rote;°
Of yeddynges° he bar outrely° the prys.
His nekke whit was as the flour de lys;°
Ther-to° he strong was as a champioun.
 He knew the tavernes wel in every toun   240
And every hostiler° and tappestere°
Bet° than a lazar° or a beggestere,°
For unto swich° a worthy man as he
Acorded nat,° as by his facultee,°
To have with sike° lazars aqueyntaunce.
It is nat honeste,° it may nat avaunce,°
For to deelen with no swich poraille°
But al with riche and selleres of vitaille.°
And, over-al° ther-as profit sholde arise,
Curteys he was and lowely of servyse.   250
Ther was no man nowher so vertuous.°
He was the beste beggere in his hous,°
For thogh a wydwe° hadde noght a sho,°

So plesant was his *In principio,*°
Yet wolde he have a ferthyng er° he wente.
His purchas was wel bettre than his rente.°
And rage° he koude as it were right° a whelpe.
 In lovedayes° ther koude he muchel° helpe,
For ther he was nat lyk a cloysterer
With a thredbare cope,° as is a poure scoler,   260
But he was lyk a maister° or a pope;
Of double worstede was his semycope,°
That rounded as a belle out of the presse.
 Somwhat he lipsed° for his wantownesse°
To make his Englissh sweete upon his tonge;
And in his harpyng, whan that he hadde songe,
Hise eyen° twynkled in his heed aright
As doon the sterres in the frosty nyght.
This worthy lymytour was cleped° Huberd.

 A MARCHANT° was there with a forked berd,
In motlee,° and hye on hors he sat,   271
Upon his heed a Flaundryssh° bevere hat,
His bootes clasped faire and fetisly.°
 Hise resons° he spak ful solempnely,°
Sownynge° alwey the encrees of his wynnyng.°
He wolde the see were kept° for any thyng
Bitwixe Middelburgh° and Orewelle.°
Wel koude he in eschaunge sheeldes selle.°
 This worthy man ful wel his wit bisette.°
Ther wiste° no wight° that he was in dette,   280
So estatly was he of his governaunce
With his bargaynes and with his chevysaunce.°
 For sothe,° he was a worthy man with alle,
But, sooth to seyn,° I noot° how men hym calle.

 A CLERK° ther was of Oxenford° also
That unto logyk hadde longe y-go.°

254. *In principio:* "In the beginning" — the first words of St. John's Gospel, used in the Middle Ages as a religious and even magic formula. 255. ferthyng er: farthing before. 256. purchas . . . rente: pickings were much better than his regular income. 257. rage: frolic. as . . . right: just like. 258. lovedayes: arbitration days for settling disputes, especially financial disputes. muchel: much. 260. cope: cloak. 261. maister: Master of Arts. 262. semycope: short cloak. 264. lipsed: lisped. wantownesse: playfulness. 267. eyen: eyes. 269. cleped: called. 270. Marchant: merchant, probably a large wholesale importer-exporter. 271. motlee: figured cloth. 272. Flaundryssh: Flemish. 273. fetisly: elegantly. 274. resons: views. solempnely: impressively. 275. Sownynge: relating. wynnyng: profit. 276. wolde . . . kept: wished the sea were guarded, especially against French pirates. 277. Middelburgh: Middelburg in Holland, where English wool was sold. Orewelle: Orwell Harbor in England, through which the Merchant presumably shipped his wares. 278. Wel . . . selle: He knew well how to sell *ecus* (shields) in exchange. Legally, only the royal money-changers were permitted to exchange French funds. 279. bisette: applied. 280. wiste: knew. wight: person. 282. chevysaunce: manipulation. 283. For sothe: truly. 284. seyn: say. noot: don't know. 285. Clerk: student. Oxenford: Oxford. 286. That . . . y-go: who had long since started on the study of logic, one of the subjects required for a B.A.

214. post: pillar. 216. frankeleyns over-al: rich landholders everywhere. 219. curat: parish priest. 223. yeve: give. 224. wiste: knew. pitaunce: gift. 225. yive: give. 226. is . . . y-shryve: has made a good confession. 227. if . . . avaunt: if he (the man) gave, he (the Friar) dared to avow. 230. hym: he. smerte: smart. 232. Men moote: one ought to. 233. typet: cape. ay farsed: always stuffed. 236. rote: stringed instrument. 237. yeddynges: ballads. bar outrely: carried off completely. 238. flour de lys: fleur-de-lis. 239. Ther-to: in addition. 241. hostiler: innkeeper. tappestere: barmaid. 242. Bet: better. lazar: leper. beggestere: female beggar. 243. swich: such. 244. Acorded nat: It was not suitable. facultee: capacity. 245. sike: sick. 246. honeste: proper. avaunce: benefit. 247. swich poraille: such poor folk. 248. vitaille: victuals. 249. over-al: everywhere. 251. vertuous: gifted. 252. hous: friary. 253. wydwe: widow. sho: shoe.

As leene was his hors as is a rake,
And he was nat right° fat, I undertake,°
But looked holwe° and ther-to sobrely.
Ful thredbare was his overeste courtepy,°   290
For he hadde geten hym yet no benefice,°
Ne was so worldly for to have office,°
For hym was levere° have at his beddes heed
Twenty bookes clad in blak or reed
Of Aristotle and his philosophie
Than robes riche or fithele° or gay sautrie.°

But, al be that he was a philosophre,
Yet hadde he but litel gold in cofre,°
But al that he myghte of his frendes hente,°
On bookes and on lernynge he it spente,°   300
And bisily gan for the soules preye°
Of hem that yaf° hym wher-with to scoleye.°

Of studie took he moost cure° and moost heede.
Noght oo° word spak he moore than was neede,
And that was seid in forme and reverence°
And short and quyk and ful of heigh sentence.°
Sownynge in° moral vertu was his speche,
And gladly wolde he lerne and gladly teche.

A Sergeant of the Lawe, war° and wys,
That often hadde been at the Parvys,°   310
Ther was also, ful riche of excellence.
Discreet he was and of greet reverence —
He semed swich,° hise wordes weren° so wyse.
Justice he was ful often in assise°
By patente° and by pleyn° commissioun.
For° his science° and for his heigh renoun,
Of fees and robes hadde he many oon.°
So greet a purchasour° was nowher noon;
Al was fee symple° to hym in effect.
His purchasyng myghte° nat been infect.°   320
Nowher so bisy a man as he ther nas,°
And yet he semed bisier than he was.

In termes° hadde he caas° and doomes° alle
That from the tyme of Kyng William° were falle.
Ther-to° he koude endite° and make a thyng;°
Ther koude no wight pynchen° at his writyng.
And every statut koude° he pleyn by roote.°
He rood but hoomly° in a medlee° coote,
Girt with a ceynt° of silk with barres smale.
Of his array telle I no lenger tale.   330

A Frankeleyn° was in his compaignye.
Whit was his berd as is the dayesye;°
Of his complexioun he was sangwyn.°
Wel loved he by the morwe° a sop° in wyn.
To lyven in delyt was evere his wone,°
For he was Epicurus owene sone,
That heeld opynyoun that pleyn° delit
Was verray° felicitee parfit.°
An housholdere, and that a greet,° was he;
Seint Julyan he was in his contree.°   340
His breed, his ale, was alweys after oon.°
A bettre envyned° man was nevere noon.
Withoute bake-mete° was nevere his hous
Of fissh and flessh,° and that so plentevous°
It snewed° in his hous of mete° and drynke,
Of alle deyntees that men koude thynke,
After° the sondry sesons of the yeer,
So chaunged° he his mete and his soper.°
Ful many a fat partrich hadde he in muwe,°
And many a breem and many a luce° in stuwe.°
Wo was his cook but if° his sauce were   351
Poynaunt° and sharp, and redy al his geere.°
His table dormaunt in his halle° alway
Stood redy covered al the longe day.
At sessions ther he was lord and sire;°
Ful ofte tyme he was knyght of the shire.°

288. right: particularly. undertake: vow. 289. holwe: hollow.
290. overeste courtepy: outer short coat. 291. benefice: ecclesiastical appointment. 292. office: secular position. 293. hym
. . . levere: he would rather. 296. fithele: fiddle. sautrie:
psaltery (harp). 298. cofre: coffer. The Clerk was obviously a
student of moral philosophy rather than of natural philosophy
or science, which included alchemy. Students of the latter hoped
to discover how to transmute base metals into gold. 299. hente:
get. 301. gan preye: prayed. 302. yaf: gave. scoleye: study.
303. cure: care. 304. oo: one. 305. in . . . reverence: formally and respectfully. 306. sentence: significance. 307.
Sownynge in: tending toward. 309. war: wary. 310. Parvys:
the place in London where clients consulted their lawyers. From
what follows we learn that the Sergeant of the Law, one of a
select group of lawyers appointed by the King, has served not
only as a legal counsel but also as a judge in circuit courts outside
London. 313. swich: such. weren: were. 314. assise: local
assize court. 315. patente: royal appointment. pleyn: full.
316. For: in reward for. science: knowledge. 317. oon: a one.
318. purchasour: buyer of land. 319. fee symple: unrestricted
possession. 320. myghte: could. infect: invalidated. 321.
nas: was.

323. In termes: precisely. caas: cases. doomes: judgments.
324. William: William I (1066-87). 325. Ther-to: in addition.
endite: compose. make a thyng: draw up a document. 326.
wight pynchen: person find fault. 327. koude: knew. pleyn
. . . roote: fully by memory. 328. hoomly: plainly. medlee:
striped. 329. ceynt: belt. 331. Frankeleyn: a rich landowner
and householder. 332. dayesye: daisy. 333. sangwyn: blood-
red. 334. morwe: morning. sop: piece of bread. 335. wone:
custom. 337. pleyn: complete. 338. verray: true. parfit:
perfect. 339. greet: great (one). 340. Seint . . . contree: He
was the local counterpart of St. Julian, the traditional patron
saint of hospitality. 341. after oon: consistently good. 342. en-
vyned: wined. 343. bake-mete: pie. 344. flessh: meat.
plentevous: plentiful. 345. snewed: snowed. mete: food.
347. After: according to. 348. chaunged: varied. soper:
supper. 349. muwe: coop. 350. luce: pike. stuwe: pond.
351. but if: unless. 352. Poynaunt: pungent. geere: utensils.
353. His . . . halle: his permanent (dormaunt) table (rather than
a removable board and trestles) in the main room of his house
(halle). 355. At . . . sire: He presided at sessions of the local
justices of the peace. (More serious cases would be brought
before assize courts conducted by justices such as his companion
the Sergeant of the Law.) 356. knyght . . . shire: member of
parliament.

An anlaas° and a gipser° al of silk
Heeng° at his girdel whit as morne° mylk.
A shirreve° hadde he been and a countour;°
Was nowher swich a worthy vavasour.°   360

An Haberdasshere and a Carpenter,
A Webbe,° a Dyere, and a Tapycer° —
And they were clothed alle in oo° lyveree
Of a solempne° and a greet fraternytee.°
Ful fressh and newe hir geere apiked was;°
Hir knyves were chaped° noght with bras
But al with silver; wroght ful clene and wel
Hir girdles and hir pouches everydel.°
Wel semed ech of hem a fair burgeys°
To sitten in a yeldehalle° on a deys.°   370
Everych° for the wisdom that he kan°
Was shaply° for to been an alderman,
For catel° hadde they ynogh and rente,°
And eek hir wyves wolde it wel assente,°
And elles° certeyn they were to blame.
It is ful fair to been y-cleped° " madame "
And goon to vigilies° al bifore
And have a mantel roialliche y-bore.°

A Cook they hadde with hem for the nones°
To boille the chiknes° with the marybones,°   380
And poudre-marchaunt° tart, and galyngale.°
Wel koude he knowe° a draughte of Londoun ale.
He koude rooste and sethe° and broille and frye,
Maken mortreux,° and wel bake a pye.
But greet harm was it, as it thoughte° me,
That on his shyne° a mormal° hadde he.
For blankmanger° that made he with the beste.

A Shipman° was ther wonyng fer by° weste;
For aught I woot,° he was of Dertemouthe.°
He rood upon a rouncy as he kouthe°   390
In a gowne of faldyng° to the knee.
A daggere hangynge on a laas° hadde he

Aboute his nekke, under his arm adoun.
The hoote somer had mad his hewe al broun.
    And certeynly he was a good felawe.°
Ful many a draughte of wyn hadde he drawe
Fro Burdeuxward° whil that the chapman sleep.°
Of nyce° conscience took he no keep;°
If that he faught and had the hyer hond,
By water he sente hem hoom° to every lond.   400
    But of his craft to rekene wel his tydes,
His stremes,° and his daungers hym bisydes,°
His herberwe,° and his moone, his lodemenage,°
Ther nas noon swich° from Hulle to Cartage.°
Hardy he was and wys to undertake.
With many a tempest hadde his berd been shake.
He knew alle the havenes as they were
Fro Gootland° to the cape of Fynystere°
And every cryke° in Britaigne° and in Spayne.
His barge y-cleped was the Mawdelayne.   410

    With us ther was a Doctour of Phisik;°
In al this world ne was ther noon hym lyk,
To speke of phisik and of surgerye,
For he was grounded in astronomye.°
He kepte° his pacient a ful greet deel
In houres° by his magik natureel.°
Wel koude he fortunen the ascendent°
Of hise ymages° for his pacient.
He knew the cause of every maladye,
Were it of hoot or coold or moyste or drye,   420
And where engendred, and of what humour.°
He was a verray,° parfit practisour.°
    The cause y-knowe° and of his harm the roote,
Anon° he yaf° the sike man his boote.°
Ful redy hadde he hise apothecaries
To sende hym drogges and his letuaries,°
For ech of hem made oother for to wynne;°
Hir° friendshipe nas nat° newe to begynne.

395. good felawe: rascal.   397. Fro Burdeuxward: from Bordeaux (which was the exporting center of the French wine trade and was, in Chaucer's day, held by England).   chapman sleep: dealer slept.   398. nyce: tender.   keep: heed.   400. hem hoom: them home (overboard).   402. stremes: currents.   bisydes: around.   403. herberwe: harbor.   lodemenage: pilotage.   404. nas . . . swich: was none such.   Hulle to Cartage: Hull (northern England) to Cartagena (in Spain).   405. undertake: conduct an enterprise.   408. Gootland: Gottland (off Sweden).   Fynystere: Finisterre (in Spain).   409. cryke: creek.   Britaigne: Brittany.   411. Phisik: medicine.   414. astronomye: astrology, or the study of the influence of the planets on the human body.   415. kepte: watched.   416. houres: astrologically important hours, when appropriate conjunctions of the planets might favor his recovery.   magik natureel: natural (not black) magic, by means of which he counteracted malignant influences.   417. fortunen . . . ascendent: determine the correct point of the zodiac.   418. ymages: representations either of the patient or of his astrological circumstances, made in order to study and cure his malady.   421. humour: temperament.   422. verray: true.   practisour: practitioner.   423. y-knowe: known.   424. Anon: immediately.   yaf: gave.   boote: remedy.   426. letuaries: remedies.   427. wynne: gain.   428. Hir: their.   nas nat: was not.

357. anlaas: dagger.   gipser: purse.   358. Heeng: hung.   morne: morning.   359. shirreve: sheriff.   countour: auditor.   360. vavasour: squire.   362. Webbe: weaver.   Tapycer: tapestry maker.   363. oo: one.   364. solempne: important.   fraternytee: religious guild.   365. hir . . . was: their accessories were trimmed.   366. chaped: decorated.   368. everydel: altogether.   369. burgeys: citizen.   370. yeldehalle: guildhall.   deys: platform.   371. Everych: each one.   kan: knows.   372. shaply: suited.   373. catel: property.   rente: income.   374. assente: agree to.   375. elles: otherwise.   376. y-cleped: called.   377. vigilies: festivals on eves of saints' days.   378. roialliche y-bore: royally carried.   379. nones: occasion.   380. chiknes: chickens.   marybones: marrowbones.   381. poudre-marchaunt: flavoring.   galyngale: spice.   382. knowe: judge.   383. sethe: boil.   384. Maken mortreux: make stews.   385. thoughte: seemed to.   386. shyne: shin.   mormal: ulcer.   387. blankmanger: sweet creamed fowl.   388. Shipman: merchant-ship owner.   wonyng . . . by: living far to the.   389. woot: know.   Dertemouthe: Dartmouth (in Devon).   390. rouncy . . . kouthe: nag as best he could.   391. faldyng: serge.   392. laas: lanyard.

Wel° knew he the olde Esculapius,
And Deiscorides, and eek Rufus,   430
Old Ypocras, Haly, and Galyen,
Serapion, Razis, and Avycen,
Averrois, Damascien, and Constantyn,
Bernard, and Gatesden, and Gilbertyn.
  Of his diete mesurable° was he,
For it was of no superfluitee
But of greet norissynge° and digestible.
His studie was but litel on the Bible.
  In sangwyn° and in pers° he clad was al,
Lyned with taffata and with sendal,°   440
And yet he was but esy° of dispence.°
He kepte that he wan in pestilence.°
For° gold in phisik is a cordial,°
Therfore he loved gold in special.

  A good WYF was ther of biside BATHE,
But she was somdel° deef, and that was scathe.°
  Of clooth-makyng she hadde swich an haunt,°
She passed hem° of Ypres and of Gaunt.°
In al the parisshe, wyf ne was ther noon
That to the offrynge bifore hire sholde goon;° 450
And if ther dide, certeyn, so wrooth was she
That she was out of alle charitee.
  Hir coverchiefs° ful fyne were of ground;°
I dorste° swere they weyeden ten pound
That on a Sonday weren upon hir heed.
Hir hosen weren of fyn scarlet reed,
Ful streite y-teyd,° and shoes ful moyste and
    newe.
Boold was hir face and fair and reed of hewe,
She was a worthy womman al hir lyve.
Housbondes at chirche dore° she hadde fyve,   460
Withouten° oother compaignye in youthe —
But ther-of nedeth nat to speke as nouthe.°
  And thries° hadde she been at Jerusalem.
She hadde passed many a straunge° strem.
At Rome she hadde been, and at Boloyne,°

In Galice° at Seint Jame,° and at Coloyne.°
She koude° muche of wandrynge by the weye.
Gat-tothed° was she, soothly° for to seye.
  Upon an amblere esily she sat,
Y-wympled wel,° and on hir heed an hat   470
As brood as is a bokeler° or a targe,°
A foot-mantel° aboute hir hipes large,
And on hir feet a peyre of spores° sharpe.
  In felawshipe wel koude she laughe and carpe;°
Of remedies° of love she knew par chaunce,°
For she koude° of that art the olde daunce.

  A good man was ther of religioun
And was a poure PERSOUN° of a toun,
But riche he was of holy thoght and werk.
He was also a lerned man, a clerk,°   480
That Cristes gospel trewely° wolde preche.
His parisshens° devoutly wolde he teche.
Benygne he was and wonder° diligent,
And in adversitee ful pacient,
And swich he was preved° ofte sithes.°
  Ful looth were hym° to cursen° for his tithes,°
But rather wolde he yeven out of doute°
Unto his poure parisshens aboute
Of his offrynge° and eek of his substaunce.°
He koude in litel thyng have suffisaunce.   490
Wyd was his parisshe and houses fer asonder,
But he ne lafte° nat for reyn ne° thonder,
In siknesse nor in meschief,° to visite
The ferreste° in his parisshe, muche° and lite,°
Upon his feet, and in his hond a staf.
  This noble ensample° to his sheep he yaf,°
That first he wroghte, and afterward he taughte.
Out of the gospel he tho° wordes caughte.°
And this figure° he added eek ther-to,
That if gold ruste, what sholde iren do?   500
For if a preest be foule on whom we truste,
No wonder is a lewed° man to ruste.
And shame it is, if a preest take keep,°
A shiten° shepherde and a clene sheep.
Wel oghte a preest ensample for to yive°
By his clennesse how that his sheep sholde lyve.

429-34. Wel . . . Gilbertyn: He knew all the standard authorities including five Greek writers (ll. 429-31), from the legendary Aesculapius through Hippocrates, Dioscorides, and Rufus, to Galen in the second century A.D.; seven Arabic writers (ll. 431-33) from the ninth to the twelfth century; and three British writers (l. 434) from the mid-thirteenth century up to Gaddesden of Oxford, who died in 1361. **435. mesurable:** moderate. **437. norissynge:** nourishment. **439. sangwyn:** red. **pers:** Persian blue. **440. sendal:** silk. **441. esy:** cautious. **dispence:** spending. **442. that . . . pestilence:** what he gained in time of plagues, which ravaged England in the second half of the fourteenth century. **443. For:** because. **cordial:** heart remedy. **446. somdel:** somewhat. **scathe:** a pity. **447. swich an haunt:** such a skill. **448. passed hem:** surpassed them (the Flemish weavers). **Gaunt:** Ghent. **450. goon:** go. **453. coverchiefs:** head coverings. **ground:** texture. **454. dorste:** would dare. **457. streite y-teyd:** tightly tied. **460. dore:** Medieval marriages took place at the church door, preceding nuptial mass at the altar. **461. Withouten:** not to mention. **462. as nouthe:** now. **463. thries:** thrice. **464. straunge:** foreign. **465. Boloyne:** Boulogne (France).

466. Galice: Galicia, a region in Spain. **Jame:** James of Compostela. **Coloyne:** Cologne. **467. koude:** knew. **468. Gat-tothed:** gap-toothed. **soothly:** truly. **470. Y-wympled wel:** well hooded. **471. bokeler:** buckler. **targe:** shield. **472. foot-mantel:** outer skirt. **473. spores:** spurs (because she rode astride). **474. carpe:** talk. **475. remedies:** restoratives. **par chaunce:** perchance. **476. koude:** knew. **478. Persoun:** parson. **480. clerk:** scholar. **481. trewely:** faithfully. **482. parisshens:** parishioners. **483. wonder:** remarkably. **485. preved:** proved. **sithes:** times. **486. were hym:** was he. **cursen:** excommunicate. **tithes:** church dues. **487. yeven . . . doute:** give without doubt. **489. offrynge:** voluntary gifts. **substaunce:** income. **492. lafte:** neglected. **ne:** nor. **493. meschief:** misfortune. **494. ferreste:** furthest (members). **muche:** great. **lite:** small. **496. ensample:** example. **yaf:** gave. **498. tho:** those. **caughte:** took. **499. figure:** parallel. **502. lewed:** unlearned. **503. keep:** heed. **504. shiten:** defiled. **505. yive:** give.

He sette nat his benefice to hyre
And leet° his sheep encombred in the myre
And ran to Londoun unto Seint Poules°
To seken° hym a chauntrye° for soules,   510
Or with a bretherhede° to been withholde,°
But dwelte at hoom and kepte° wel his folde
So that the wolf ne made it nat myscarye.
He was a shepherde and noght a mercenarye.
  And thogh he hooly were and vertuous,
He was noght to synful men despitous,°
Ne° of his speche daungerous ne digne,°
But in his techyng discreet and benigne.
To drawen folk to hevene by fairnesse,
By good ensample, this was his bisynesse.°   520
But it° were any persone obstinat,
What so° he were of heigh or lowe estat,
Hym wolde he snybben° sharply for the nonys.°
  A bettre preest I trowe° that nowher noon ys.
He wayted after° no pompe and reverence,
Ne maked hym a spiced° conscience,
But Cristes loore° and his apostles twelve
He taughte, but first he folwed it hymselve.

  With hym ther was a PLOWMAN, was his brother,
That hadde y-lad° of donge° ful many a fother.°
A trewe swynkere° and a good was he,   531
Lyvynge in pees and parfit charitee.
God loved he best with al his hoole herte
At alle tymes, thogh hym gamed or smerte,°
And thanne his neighebore right° as hymselve.
He wolde thresshe and ther-to dyke° and delve°
For Cristes sake for every poure wight
Withouten hire,° if it lay in his myght.
His tithes payde he ful faire and wel
Bothe of his propre swynk° and his catel.°   540
In a tabard° he rood, upon a mere.°

  Ther was also a REVE° and a MILLERE,
A SOMNOUR° and a PARDONER also,
A MAUNCIPLE° and myself; ther were namo.°
  The MILLER was a stout carl for the nones.°

Ful big he was of brawn and eek of bones.
That proved wel, for over-al ther° he cam,
At wrastlyng he wolde have alwey the ram.°
He was short-sholdred, brood, a thikke knarre.°
Ther was no dore that he nolde° heve of harre°
Or breke it at a rennyng with his heed.   551
His berd as any sowe or fox was reed°
And ther-to brood° as though it were a spade.
Upon the cop right° of his nose he hade
A werte,° and ther-on stood a tuft of herys,°
Reed as the bristles of a sowes erys.°
His nosethirles° blake were and wyde.
A swerd and a bokeler bar° he by his syde.
  His mouth as greet was as a greet fourneys.°
He was a jangler° and a goliardeys.°   560
And that was moost of synne and harlotries.°
  Wel koude he stelen corn and tollen thries,°
And yet he hadde a thombe of gold,° pardee.°
  A whit cote and a blew hood wered° hee.
A baggepipe wel koude he blowe and sowne,°
And ther-with-al he broghte us out of towne.

  A gentil MAUNCIPLE° was ther of a temple°
Of which achatours° myghte take exemple
For to be wys in byynge of vitaille,°
For wheither that he payde or took by taille,°   570
Algate he wayted so in his achaat°
That he was ay biforn° and in good staat.
  Now, is nat that of God a ful fair grace
That swich a lewed° mannes wit shal pace°
The wisdom of an heep of lerned men!
Of maistres hadde he mo° than thries ten
That weren of° lawe expert and curious,°
Of whiche° ther were a dozeyne in that hous
Worthy to been stywardes° of rente° and lond
Of any lord that is in Engelond,   580
To make hym lyve by his propre good°
In honour detteles, but if° he were wood,°
Or lyve as scarsly° as hym list° desire;
And able for to helpen° al a shire

547. over-al ther: everywhere.   548. ram: ram (as prize).
549. knarre: knot of a fellow.   550. nolde: would not.   of
harre: off its hinges.   552. reed: red.   553. brood: as broad.
554. cop right: very top.   555. werte: wart.   herys: hairs.
556. erys: ears.   557. nosethirles: nostrils.   558. bar: wore.
559. fourneys: furnace.   560. jangler: talker.   goliardeys: jester.   561. harlotries: ribaldries.   562. tollen thries: levy a toll
thrice.   563. he . . . gold: i.e., "For a miller, he was honest,"
in reference to the ironic proverb, "An honest miller has a golden
thumb."   pardee: certainly.   564. wered: wore.   565. sowne:
play.   567. Maunciple: purchasing agent.   temple: one of the
buildings, once owned by the Templars, serving in Chaucer's
day as a law society's residence and college.   568. Of . . . acha-
tours: from whom buyers.   569. vitaille: victuals.   570. by
taille: on credit.   571. Algate . . . achaat: in any case he watched
so in his buying.   572. ay biforn: always ahead.   574. swich
a lewed: such an unlearned.   pace: surpass.   576. mo: more.
577. of: in.   curious: erudite.   578. Of whiche: among whom.
579. been stywardes: be stewards (business managers).   rente:
income.   581. propre good: own resources.   582. but if: unless.
wood: insane.   583. scarsly: sparingly.   hym list: he wishes to.
584. helpen: aid (legally).

508. leet: left. As the result of the Great Plague priests were
scarce, and rural charges were deserted in favor of urban.
509. Seint Poules: St. Paul's (Cathedral).   510. seken: secure.
chauntrye: endowment established by a donor to pay for the
singing of masses for the repose of his own or some other soul.
511. bretherhede: religious guild such as that alluded to in l. 364.
withholde: retained (as chaplain).   512. kepte: watched.
516. despitous: scornful.   517. Ne: nor.   daungerous ne digne:
domineering or pompous.   520. bisynesse: concern.   521. it:
if there.   522. What so: whether.   523. snybben: reprove.
nonys: occasion.   526. wayted after:
expected.   526. Ne . . . spiced: nor assumed an overscrupulous.
527. loore: teaching.   530. y-lad: hauled.   donge: manure.
fother: load.   531. swynkere: laborer.   534. hym . . . smerte:
he rejoiced or grieved.   535. right: just as much.   536. dyke:
ditch.   delve: dig.   538. hire: payment.   540 propre swynk:
own work.   catel: property.   541. tabard: smock.   mere:
mare (an unfashionable mount).   542. Reve: reeve.   543. Somnour: summoner.   544. Maunciple: manciple.   namo: no more.
545. a . . . nones: an especially stout fellow.

In any caas that myghte falle or happe.
And yet this Maunciple sette hir aller cappe.°

The Reve° was a sclendre, colerik man.
His berd was shave as neigh° as ever he kan;
His heer was by his erys° ful round y-shorn;
His top was dokked° lyk a preest byforn.   590
Ful longe were his legges and ful lene;
Ylik a staf,° ther was no calf y-sene.
Wel koude he kepe a gerner° and a bynne;
Ther was noon auditour koude on hym wynne.
Wel wiste° he by the droghte and by the reyn
The yeldynge of his seed and of his greyn.
His lordes sheep, his neet,° his dayerye,
His swyn, his hors, his stoor,° and his pultrye
Was hoolly in this Reves governynge,
And by his covenant yaf° the rekenynge   600
Syn° that his lord was twenty yeer of age.
Ther koude no man brynge hym in arrerage.°
Ther nas baillif,° ne hierde,° ne oother hyne°
That he ne knew his sleighte° and his covyne.°
They were adrad° of hym as of the deeth.
His wonyng° was ful faire upon an heeth;
With grene trees shadwed was his place.
He koude bettre than his lord purchace;
Ful riche he was astored pryvely.°
His lord wel koude he plesen subtilly   610
To yeve° and lene° hym of his owene good°
And have a thank and yet° a coote and hood.
In youthe he hadde lerned a good myster:°
He was a wel good wrighte, a carpenter.
This Reve sat upon a ful good stot,°
That was al pomely° grey and highte° Scot.
A long surcote of pers° upon he hade,
And by his syde he baar° a rusty blade.
Of Northfolk° was this Reve of which I telle,
Biside a toun men clepen Baldeswelle.°   620
Tukked he was as is a frere° aboute;
And evere he rood the hyndreste° of oure route.°

A Somnour° was ther with us in that place,
That hadde a fyr-reed cherubynnes face,°

For saucefleem° he was, with eyen narwe.
As hoot he was and lecherous as a sparwe,°
With scaled° browes blake and piled° berd.
Of his visage children were aferd.
Ther nas quyksilver, lytarge,° ne brymstoon,
Boras,° ceruce,° ne oille° of tartre noon,   630
Ne oynement that wolde clense and byte,
That hym myghte helpen° of his whelkes° white,
Nor of the knobbes sittynge on his chekes.
Wel loved he garlek, oynons, and eek lekes,
And for to drynke strong wyn red as blood;
Thanne wolde he speke and crye as° he were
        wood;°
And whan that he wel dronken hadde the wyn,
Thanne wolde he speke no word but Latyn.
A fewe termes hadde he, two or thre,
That he had lerned out of som decre.   640
No wonder is! He herde it al the day;
And eek ye knowen wel how that a jay
Kan clepen " Watte "° as wel as kan the Pope.
But who so koude in oother thyng hym grope,°
Thanne hadde he spent al his philosophie.
Ay° " Questio, quid juris? "° wolde he crie.
He was a gentil harlot° and a kynde;
A bettre felawe sholde men noght fynde.
He wolde suffre,° for a quart of wyn,
A good felawe° to have his concubyn°   650
A twelf monthe and excuse hym atte fulle.°
Ful pryvely a fynch eek koude he pulle;°
And if he foond owher° a good felawe,
He wolde techen hym to have noon awe
In swich caas of the ercedekenes curs°
But if° a mannes soule were in his purs,
For in his purs he sholde y-punysshed be.
" Purs is the ercedekenes helle," seyde he.
But well I woot° he lyed right in dede;
Of cursyng oghte ech gilty man drede —   660
For curs wol slee,° right as assoillyng° savith —
And also war hym of° a significavit.°
In daunger° hadde he at° his owene gyse°
The yonge gerles° of the diocise,
And knew hir counseil,° and was al hir reed.°

586. sette . . . cappe: set the dunce cap on them all.   587. Reve:
estate manager. 588. neigh: close. 589. erys: ears. 590. dokked:
cropped (because he was a serf).   592. Ylik a staf: like a stick.
593. kepe a gerner: watch a granary.   595. wiste: knew.
597. neet: cattle. 598. stoor: stock. 600. yaf: (he) gave.
601. Syn: since the time. 602. arrerage: arrears. 603. nas
baillif: was not overseer. hierde: shepherd. hyne: servant.
604. That . . . sleighte: whose tricks he didn't know. covyne:
fraud. 605. adrad: afraid. 606. wonyng: dwelling. 609. astored
pryvely: stocked in secret. 611. yeve: give. lene: lend.
good: property. 612. yet: also. 613. myster: trade. 615. stot:
stallion. 616. pomely: dapple. highte: was called. 617. surcote of pers: overcoat of Persian blue. 618. baar: wore.
619. Northfolk: Norfolk. 620. clepen Baldeswelle: call Bawds-
well. 621. frere: friar. 622. hyndreste: hindermost. route:
company. 623. Somnour: constable of the ecclesiastical court,
which punished offenses against religion and morality. 624. cherubynnes face: cherub's face, like the faces of cherubim colored
red in church ornamentation.

625. saucefleem: pimpled. 626. sparwe: sparrow. 627. scaled:
scabby. piled: scanty. 628. aferd: afraid. 629. lytarge:
lead ointment. 630. Boras: borax. ceruce: white lead.
oille: cream. 632. helpen: rid. whelkes: (leprous) sores.
636. as: as if. wood: mad. 643. clepen "watte": call out
"Walter" (as a parrot calls out "Polly"). 644. grope: examine. 646. Ay: always. "Questio . . . juris?": "Query, what
of the law (here)?" That is, "What law applies to this case?"
647. gentil harlot: obliging rascal. 649. suffre: allow. 650. good
felawe: rascal. concubyn: mistress. 651. atte fulle: fully.
652. Ful . . . pulle: He also knew how to fornicate very secre-
tively. 653. foond owher: found anywhere. 655. ercedekenes
curs: archdeacon's curse (of excommunication). 656. But if:
unless. 659. woot: know. 661. slee: slay. assoillyng: abso-
lution. 662. war . . . of: beware. significavit: writ for arrest.
663. daunger: subjection. at: in. gyse: way. 664. gerles:
people (male and female). 665. hir counseil: their secrets.
al . . . reed: adviser of all of them.

A gerland° hadde he set upon his heed,
As greet as it were for an ale stake;°
A bokeler° hadde he maad hym of a cake.

With hym ther rood a gentil PARDONER
Of Rouncival, his freend and his comper,°   670
That streight was comen fro the court of Rome.°
Ful loude he soong,° "Com hider,° love, to me."
This Somnour bar° to hym a stif burdoun,°
Was nevere trompe° of half so greet a soun.°
This Pardoner hadde heer° as yelow as wex,°
But smothe it heeng° as dooth a strike of flex.°
By ounces° henge his lokkes that he hadde,
And ther-with he his shuldres overspradde,
But thynne it lay by colpons oon and oon.°
But hood, for jolitee,° wered° he noon,   680
For it was trussed up in his walet.°
Hym thoughte he rood al of the newe jet.°
Dischevelee,° save his cappe he rood al bare.
Swiche glarynge eyen hadden he as an hare.
A vernycle° hadde he sowed upon his cappe,
His walet biforn hym in his lappe,
Bret° ful of pardoun comen from Rome al hoot.°
A voys he hadde as smal as hath a goot.°
No berd° hadde he, ne nevere sholde have;
As smothe it was as it were late y-shave.°   690
I trowe he were a geldyng° or a mare.
But of his craft fro Berwyk into Ware
Ne was ther swich another pardoner,
For in his male° he hadde a pilwe-beer°
Which that he seyde was Oure Lady veyl.°
He seyde he hadde a gobet° of the seyl°
That Seint Peter hadde whan that he wente°
Upon the see til Jesu Crist hym hente.°
He hadde a croys of latoun° ful of stones,
And in a glas he hadde pigges bones.   700
But with thise relikes, whan that he fond

A poure persoun° dwellyng upon lond,°
Upon a° day he gat hym moore moneye
Than that the persoun gat in monthes tweye.
And thus with feyned flaterye and japes°
He made the persoun and the peple his apes.°
But trewely to tellen, atte laste,
He was in chirche a noble ecclesiaste.
Wel koude he rede a lessoun or a storie,°
But alderbest° he song° an offertorie,   710
For wel he wiste° whan that song was songe,
He moste° preche and wel affile° his tonge
To wynne silver, as he ful wel koude.
Ther-fore he song the murierly° and loude.

Now have I told yow soothly in a clause°
Th' estaat, th' array, the nombre, and eek the cause
Why that assembled was this compaignye
In Southwerk at this gentil hostelrye,
That highte° the Tabard, faste° by the Belle.°
But now is tyme to yow for to telle   720
How that we baren us° that ilke° nyght
Whan we were in that hostelrie alyght;°
And after wol I telle of oure viage°
And al the remenant of oure pilgrymage.
But first I pray yow of youre curteisye
That ye n' arette it nat my vileynye°
Thogh that° I pleynly speke in this matere
To telle yow hir° wordes and hir cheere°
Ne thogh I speke° hir wordes proprely.°
For this ye knowen also° wel as I,   730
Who so shal telle° a tale after a man,
He moot reherce° as neigh° as evere he kan
Everich a° word if it be in his charge,
Al° speke he nevere so rudeliche° and large,°
Or ellis° he moot telle his tale untrewe,
Or feyne thyng,° or fynde wordes newe.
He may nat spare° al thogh he were his brother;
He moot° as wel seye o° word as another.
Crist spak hymself ful brode° in Holy Writ,
And wel ye woot,° no vileynye is it.   740
Eek° Plato seith, who so kan hym rede,
The wordes mote° be cosyn° to the dede.

666. gerland: garland. 667. ale stake: alehouse sign. 668. bokeler: buckler (small shield). 670. comper: comrade. 671. That . . . Rome: Special indulgences (remissions of the temporal punishment still due after a sinner has been absolved) were issued by the Pope through pardoners, who were entitled to collect money for some pious object from penitents who chose to work off the remaining temporal punishment by this additional act of penance. In Chaucer's time, however, some unlicensed swindlers such as the Pardoner of Rouncivalle (a religious hospital near London) took notorious advantage of the system for their own profit. 672. soong: sang. hider: hither. 673. bar: carried. stif burdoun: strong accompaniment. 674. trompe: trumpet. soun: sound. 675. heer: hair. wex: wax. 676. heeng: hung. strike of flex: hank of flax. 677. By ounces: in wisps. 679. by . . . oon: in single strands. 680. jolitee: jauntiness. wered: wore. 681. walet: traveling bag. 682. jet: style. 683. Dischevelee: with loose hair. 685. vernycle: a copy of St. Veronica's handkerchief, which, according to legend, was miraculously imprinted with the image of Christ's face. 687. Bret: cram. hoot: hot. 688. goot: goat. 689. berd: beard. 690. late y-shave: newly shaved. 691. trowe . . . geldyng: believe he must have been a gelding. 694. male: bag. pilwebeer: pillowcase. 695. Oure Lady veyl: Our Lady's veil. 696. gobet: piece. seyl: sail. 697. wente: walked. 698. hente: caught. See Matt. 14:29. 699. latoun: copper alloy.

702. persoun: parson (who would introduce him to the parish). lond: the country. 703. a: one. 705. japes: tricks. 706. apes: fools. 709. storie: Bible story or saint's life. 710. alderbest: best of all. song: sang. 711. wiste: knew. 712. moste: must. affile: make smooth. 714. murierly: more merrily. 715. soothly . . . clause: truly in brief. 719. highte: was called. faste: close. Belle: Bell (Inn). 721. baren us: conducted ourselves. ilke: same. 722. alyght: alighted. 723. viage: journey. 726. n' arette . . . vileynye: won't blame it on my boorishness. 727. Thogh that: even if. 728. hir: their. cheere: behavior. 729. Ne . . . speke: and if I repeat. proprely: literally. 730. also: as. 731. telle: retell. 732. moot reherce: must repeat. neigh: closely. 733. Everich a: every single. 734. Al: even though. rudeliche: rudely. large: broadly. 735. ellis: else. 736. feyne thyng: invent something. 737. spare: hold back. 738. moot: must. o: one. 739. brode: freely. 740. woot: know. 741. Eek: also. 742. mote: must. cosyn: cousin.

Also, I pray yow to foryeve° it me,
Al° have I nat set folk in hir degree°
Here in this tale as that° they sholde stonde.°
My wit is short, ye may° wel understonde.

Greet cheere made oure Hoost us everichon,°
And to the soper sette he us anon.°
He served us with vitaille° at the beste.
Strong was the wyn, and wel to drynke us
  leste.°   750
A semely° man oure Hoost was with alle
For to been a marchal° in an halle.°
A large man he was, with eyen stepe.°
A fairer burgeys° was ther noon in Chepe,°
Boold of his speche, and wys, and wel y-taught,
And of manhode hym° lakked right naught.
Eke ther-to he was right° a murye man,
And after soper pleyen° he bigan
And spak of myrthe,° amonges othere thynges,
Whan that we hadde maad° oure rekenynges,° 760
And seyde thus, "Now, lordynges,° trewely,
Ye been° to me right welcome, hertely,
For by my trouthe, if that I shal not lye,
I saugh nat this yeer so murye a compaignye
At ones° in this herberwe° as is now.
Fayn° wolde I doon° yow myrthe, wiste I° how.
And of a myrthe I am right now bythoght
To doon yow ese,° and it shal coste noght.
"Ye goon° to Canterbury, God yow spede!
The blisful martir quyte° yow youre mede!° 770
And wel I woot as ye goon by the weye,
Ye shapen yow to talen° and to pleye,
For trewely confort ne° myrthe is noon°
To ryde by the weye domb as a stoon.
And ther-fore wol I maken yow disport,°
As I seyde erst,° and doon yow som confort.
And if yow liketh alle by oon° assent
For to stonden at° my juggement
And for to werken° as I shall yow seye,
Tomorwe, whan ye riden by the weye,   780
Now, by my fader° soule, that is deed,
But° ye be murye, I wol yeve yow myn heed.°
Hoold up youre hondes withouten moore speche."
Oure conseil was nat longe for to seche.°

Us thoughte it was nat worth to make it wys,°
And graunted° hym withouten moore avys°
And bad hym seye his voirdit° as hym leste.°
"Lordynges," quod° he, "now herkneth° for the
  beste,
But taketh it not, I pray yow, in desdeyn.°
This is the poynt, to speken short and pleyn, 790
That ech of yow, to shorte with oure weye,°
In this viage° shal telle tales tweye,° —
To Caunterburyward° I mene it so, —
And homward he shal tellen othere two
Of aventures that whilom° have bifalle.
And which° of yow that bereth° hym best of alle,
That is to seyn, that telleth in this caas
Tales of best sentence° and moost solaas,°
Shal have a soper at oure aller cost°
Here in this place, sittyng by this post,   800
Whan that we come agayn fro Caunterbury.
And, for to make yow the moore mury,
I wol myself goodly with yow ryde
Right at myn owene cost and be your gyde;
And who so° wol my juggement withseye°
Shal paye al that we spende by the weye.
And if ye vouchesauf that it be so,
Tel me anoon° withouten wordes mo,°
And I wol erly shape me° ther-fore."
This thyng was graunted, and oure othes swore°
With ful glad herte, and preyden° hym also   811
That he wolde vouchesauf for to do so,
And that he wolde been oure governour,
And of oure tales juge and reportour,°
And sette a soper at a certeyn prys,
And we wol reuled been at his devys°
In heigh and lough.° And thus by oon assent
We been acorded to his juggement;
And ther-upon the wyn was fet° anoon.
We dronken,° and to reste wente echon°   820
Withouten any lenger taryynge.
A morwe,° whan that day bigan to sprynge,
Up roos oure Hoost and was oure aller cok°
And gadred° us togidre° in a flok,
And forth we riden,° a° litel moore than pas,°
Unto the wateryng° of Seint Thomas,

743. foryeve: forgive.   744. Al: even if.   hir degree: their order of rank.   745. as that: just as.   stonde: stand.   746. may: can.   747. us everichon: for each of us.   748. anon: immediately.   749. vitaille: victuals.   750. leste: it pleased.   751. semely: suitable.   752. marchal: marshal to arrange ceremonies.   halle: banquet hall.   753. stepe: prominent.   754. burgeys: citizen.   Chepe: Cheapside (London).   756. hym: he.   757. right: truly.   758. pleyen: to joke.   759. myrthe: amusement.   760. maad: paid.   rekenynges: bills.   761. lordynges: sirs.   762. been: are.   765. ones: once.   herberwe: lodging.   766. Fayn: gladly.   doon: provide.   wiste I: if I knew.   768. ese: comfort.   769. goon: are going.   770. quyte: grant.   mede: reward.   772. shapen . . . talen: intend to tell tales.   773. ne: nor.   noon: none.   775. disport: amusement.   776. erst: before.   777. oon: one.   778. stonden at: abide by.   779. werken: do.   781. fader: father's.   782. But: unless.   heed: head.   784. seche: seek.

785. wys: difficult.   786. graunted: (we) yielded to.   avys: consideration.   787. voirdit: verdict.   leste: it pleased.   788. quod: said.   herkneth: listen.   789. in desdeyn: contemptuously.   791. shorte . . . weye: cut short our way with.   792. viage: journey.   tweye: two.   793. To Caunterburyward: toward Canterbury.   795. whilom: once upon a time.   796. which: whichever.   bereth: conducts.   798. sentence: significance.   solaas: delight.   799. oure . . . cost: the expense of all of us.   805. who so: whosoever.   withseye: resist.   808. anoon: immediately.   mo: more.   809. shape me: prepare.   810. swore: sworn.   811. preyden: (we) begged.   814. reportour: critic.   816. devys: discretion.   817. In . . . lough: in all matters.   819. fet: fetched.   820. dronken: drank.   echon: each one.   822. A morwe: the next morning.   823. oure . . . cok: the cock (who crowed) for us all.   824. gadred: gathered.   togidre: together.   825. riden: rode.   a: at a.   pas: footpace.   826. wateryng: watering place (two miles from Southwark).

And there oure Hoost bigan his hors areste°
And seyde, "Lordynges, herkneth,° if yow leste.°
Ye woot youre forward° and it yow recorde.°
If evensong and morwesong acorde,°   830
Lat se° now who shal telle the firste tale.
As evere moot° I drynke wyn or ale,
Who so be rebel to my juggement
Shal paye for al that by the wey is spent.
Now draweth cut er that we ferrer twynne.°
He which that hath the shorteste shal bigynne.
Sire Knyght," quod he, "my mayster and my lord,
Now draweth° cut, for that is myn acord.°
Cometh neer," quod he, "my lady Prioresse,
And ye, sire Clerk, lat be° your shamefastnesse,°
Ne studieth noght. Ley hond to, every man."   841
Anoon° to drawen every wight bigan,
And shortly for to tellen as it was,
Were it by aventure° or sort° or cas,°
The sothe° is this: the cut fil° to the Knyght,
Of which ful blithe and glad was every wight,°
And telle he moste° his tale, as was resoun°
By forward and by composicioun,°
As ye han° herd. What nedeth wordes mo?
And whan this goode man saugh that it was so,
As he that wys was and obedient   851
To kepe his forward by his free assent,
He seyde, "Syn° I shal bigynne the game,
What,° welcome be the cut, a° Goddes name!
Now lat us ryde, and herkneth what I seye."
And with that word we ryden forth oure weye,
And he bigan with right a murye° cheere
His tale anoon and seyde as ye may heere.

THE PARDONER'S TALE

The source of the Pardoner's Tale is a widely known folk tale, versions of which had been employed by pagan and Christian alike for purposes of edification or entertainment long before Chaucer wrote the *Canterbury Tales*. The Pardoner, however, uses it as the *exemplum,* or illustrative story, for a sermon on the text from I Timothy 6:10: "For the love of money is the root of all evil: which while some coveted after, they have erred from the faith, and pierced themselves through with many sorrows." And then, having demonstrated his manner of preaching, he brazenly turns (l. 453) to the pilgrims and applies his appeal to them.

In Flaundres whilom° was a compaignye
Of yonge folk that haunteden° folye,
As° riot, hasard,° stewes,° and tavernes
Where-as° with harpes, lutes, and gyternes°
They daunce and pleyen at dees° bothe day and
nyght,
And ete also and drynke over hir myght,°
Thurgh which they doon the devel sacrifise
Withinne that develes temple in cursed wise
By superfluytee abhomynable.
Hir othes been° so grete and so dampnable   10
That it is grisly for to heere hem swere;
Oure blissed Lordes body they to-tere;°
Hem thoughte° that Jewes rente hym noght
ynough!
And ech° of hem at otheres synne lough.°
And right anon thanne comen tombesteres,°
Fetys° and smale,° and yonge frutesteres,°
Syngeres with harpes, baudes,° wafereres,°
Whiche been the verray develes officeres,
To kyndle and blowe the fyr of lecherye,
That is annexed unto glotonye.   20
The Holy Writ take I to my witnesse
That luxurie° is in wyn and dronkenesse.
Lo how that dronken Loth° unkyndely°
Lay by his doghtres two unwityngly.°
So dronke he was, he nyste° what he wroghte.°
Herodes,° whoso° wel the stories soghte,
Whan he of wyn was replet° at his feste,
Right at his owene table he yaf° his heste°
To sleen° the Baptist John ful giltelees.
Senec° seith a good word, doutelees.   30
He seith he kan no difference fynde
Bitwix a man that is out of his mynde
And a man which that is dronkelewe,°
But° that woodnesse y-fallen° in a shrewe
Persevereth lenger than dooth dronkenesse.
O glotonye, ful of cursednesse,
O cause first of oure confusioun!°
O original of oure dampnacioun,
Til Crist hadde boght us with his blood agayn!°
Lo how deere,° shortly for to sayn,°   40

PARDONER'S TALE.   1. **Flaundres whilom:** Flanders once.
2. **haunteden:** practiced.   3. **As:** such as.   **hasard:** dicing.
stewes: brothels.   4. **Where-as:** where.   **gyternes:** gitterns, a
type of guitar.   5. **dees:** dice.   6. **over . . . myght:** beyond
their capacity.   10. **Hir . . . been:** their oaths are.   12. **to-
tere:** tear apart, i.e., when they swear by parts of Christ's body.
13. **Hem thoughte:** It seemed to them.   14. **ech:** each.   **lough:**
laughed.   15. **tombesteres:** dancing girls.   16. **Fetys:** trim.
smale: slender.   **frutesteres:** fruit sellers.   17. **baudes:** bawds.
wafereres: confectioners.   22. **luxurie:** excess.   23. **Loth:** Lot
(Gen. 19:33, 35).   **unkyndely:** unnaturally.   24. **unwityngly:**
unknowingly.   25. **nyste:** didn't know.   **wroghte:** was doing.
26. **Herodes:** Herod (Matt. 14).   **whoso:** as one would know
who.   27. **replet:** overfilled.   28. **yaf:** gave.   **heste:** order.
29. **sleen:** slay.   30. **Senec:** Seneca.   33. **dronkelewe:** drunken.
34. **But:** except.   **woodnesse y-fallen:** madness occurring.
37. **confusioun:** ruin.   39. **boght agayn:** redeemed.   40. **deere:**
dearly.   **sayn:** say.

827. **areste:** to halt.   828. **herkneth:** listen.   **leste:** it pleases.
829. **woot . . . forward:** know your agreement.   **it . . . recorde:**
remember it.   830. **morwesong acorde:** morning song agree.
831. **Lat se:** let's see.   832. **moot:** may.   835. **cut . . . twynne:**
lots before we further depart.   838. **draweth:** draw a.   **acord:**
agreement.   840. **lat be:** lay aside.   **shamefastnesse:** modesty.
842. **Anoon:** immediately.   844. **aventure:** chance.   **sort:** lot.
cas: destiny.   845. **sothe:** truth.   **fil:** fell.   846. **wight:** person.
847. **moste:** must.   **resoun:** right.   848. **composicioun:** compact.   849. **han:** have.   853. **Syn:** since.   854. **What:** why.
a: in.   857. **right a murye:** a very merry.

Aboght° was thilke° cursed vileynye.
Corrupt was al this world for glotonye.
  Adam oure fader, and his wyf also,
Fro° Paradys to labour and to wo
Were dryven for that vice, it is no drede.°
For whil that Adam fasted, as I rede,
He was in Paradys; and whan that he
Eet of the fruyt defended° on the tree,
Anon° he was out cast to wo and peyne.
O glotonye, on thee wel oghte us pleyne.°   50
O, wiste° a man how manye maladies
Folwen of° excesse and of glotonyes,
He wolde been the moore mesurable°
Of his diete, sittyng at his table.
Allas, the shorte throte, the tendre mouth,
Maketh that, est and west and north and south,
In erthe, in eyr, in water, men to swynke°
To gete a glotoun deyntee mete and drynke.
Of this matere, O Paul, wel kanstow° trete.
" Mete unto wombe,° and wombe eek° unto mete,
Shal God destroyen bothe," as Paulus seith.   61
Allas, a foul thyng is it, by my feith,
To seye this word, and fouler is the dede,
Whan man so drynketh of the white and rede°
That of his throte he maketh his pryvee°
Thurgh thilke cursed superfluitee.
  The apostle° wepyng seith ful pitously,
" There walken manye of whiche yow toold have
      I, —
I seye it now wepyng with pitous voys —
They been enemys of Cristes croys,   70
Of whiche° the ende is deth; wombe is hir° God."
O wombe, O bely, O stynkyng cod,°
Fulfilled of donge and of corrupcioun,
At either ende of thee foul is the soun!°
How greet labour and cost is thee to fynde!°
Thise cokes,° how they stampe, and streyne, and
      grynde,
And turnen substaunce into accident,°
To fulfillen° al thy likerous talent.°
Out of the harde bones knokke they
The mary,° for they caste noght awey   80
That may go thurgh the golet° softe and soote.°
Of spicerie of leef, and bark, and roote
Shal been his sauce y-maked, by delit°

To make hym yet a newer appetit.
But, certes,° he that haunteth swiche delices°
Is deed whil that° he lyveth in tho° vices.
  A lecherous thyng is wyn, and dronkenesse
Is full of stryvyng° and of wrecchednesse.
O dronke man, disfigured is thy face,
Sour is thy breeth, foul artow° to embrace,   90
And thurgh thy dronke nose semeth the soun
As thogh thou seydest ay,° " Sampsoun, Sampsoun."
And yet, God woot,° Sampsoun° drank nevere no
      wyn.
Thou fallest as it were a stiked swyn,°
Thy tonge is lost, and al thyn honeste cure.°
For dronkenesse is verray sepulture°
Of mannes wit° and his discrecioun.
In whom that drynke hath dominacioun,
He kan no conseil kepe, it is no drede.
Now kepe yow fro the white and fro the rede,   100
And namely° fro the white wyn of Lepe°
That is to selle in Fisshstrete° or in Chepe.°
This wyn of Spaigne crepeth subtilly
In othere wynes growynge faste by,°
Of which ther riseth swich fumositee°
That, whan a man hath dronken draghtes thre,
And weneth° that he be at hoom in Chepe,
He is in Spaigne right at the toune of Lepe,
Nat at the Rochel° ne at Burdeux° toun.   109
And thanne wol he seyn, " Sampsoun, Sampsoun."
  But herkneth, lordynges, o° word, I yow preye,
That alle the sovereyn actes, dar I seye,
Of victories in the Olde Testament,
Thurgh verray God, that is omnipotent,
Were doon in abstinence and in prayere.
Looketh° the Bible, and ther ye may it leere.°
  Looke, Attila,° the grete conquerour,
Deyde in his sleep with shame and dishonour,
Bledyng at his nose in dronkenesse.
A capitayn sholde lyve in sobrenesse.   120
And over al this, avyseth yow° right wel
What was comaunded unto Lamwel° —
Nat Samuel but Lamwel, seye I.
Redeth the Bible, and fynd it expresly

---

41. Aboght: paid for. thilke: that same. 44. Fro: from. 45. drede: doubt. 48. defended: forbidden. 49. Anon: at once. 50. oghte us pleyne: should we complain. 51. wiste: knew. 52. Folwen of: follow. 53. mesurable: moderate. 57. swynke: toil. 59. kanstow: can you. 60. wombe: belly. eek: also. 64. rede: red (wine). 65. pryvee: privy. 67. apostle: Paul. 71. whiche: whom. hir: their. 72. cod: paunch. 74. soun: sound. 75. fynde: provide for. 76. cokes: cooks. 77. turnen ... accident: turn substance into accident — a facetious allusion to the philosophical theory that "substance" only becomes apparent when it takes on the "accidents" of some particular shape, size, color, etc. 78. fulfillen: satisfy. likerous talent: unrestrained appetite. 80. mary: marrow. 81. golet: gullet. soote: sweet. 83. delit: delight.

85. certes: certainly. haunteth ... delices: pursues such delights. 86. deed ... that: dead while. tho: those. 88. stryvyng: strife. 90. artow: are you. 92. ay: always. 93. woot: knows. Sampsoun: Samson, who was bound by his vow as a Nazarite never to drink wine. 94. as ... swyn: like a stuck pig. 95. honeste cure: care for honor. 96. verray sepulture: the very burial. 97. wit: understanding. 101. namely: particularly. Lepe: in Spain. 102. Fisshstrete: Fish Street (London). Chepe: Cheapside. 104. faste by: nearby, that is, the more expensive vintages of France, which were evidently adulterated in England with coarser Spanish wines. 105. swich fumositee: such spirituous vapors. 107. weneth: believes. 109. the Rochel: La Rochelle. Burdeux: Bordeaux (in France). 111. o: one. 116. Looketh: look at. leere: learn. 117. Attila: the invader of Rome, who, according to tradition, died of drunkenness on his wedding night. 121. avyseth yow: consider. 122. Lamwel: Lemuel, an otherwise unknown king enjoined in Prov. 31: 4-7 to avoid wine.

Of wyn-yevyng° to hem that han justise.
Namoore of this, for it may wel suffise.
   And now that I have spoken of glotonye,
Now wol I yow defenden hasardrye.°
Hasard is verray moder of lesynges,°
And of deceite, and cursed forswerynges,°   130
Blaspheme° of Crist, manslaughtre, and wast° also
Of catel° and of tyme; and forther mo
It is repreve° and contrarie of honour
For to ben holde° a commune hasardour.
And evere the hyer he is of estaat,
The moore is he holden desolat.
If that a prynce useth hasardrye,
In alle governaunce and policye
He is, as by° commune opynyoun,
Y-holde the lasse in reputacioun.   140
   Stilbon, that was a wys embassadour,
Was sent to Corynthe in ful gret honour
Fro Lacedomye° to make hire alliaunce;
And whan he cam, hym happed° par chaunce
That alle the gretteste that were of that lond
Pleiynge atte hasard he hem fond.°
For which, as soone as it myghte be,
He stal° hym hoom agayn to his contree,
And seyde, "Ther wol I nat lese° my name,
N' I wol nat° take on me so greet defame   150
Yow for to allie unto none hasardours.
Sendeth othere wise embassadours,
For, by my trouthe, me were levere° dye
Than I yow sholde to hasardours allye.
For ye that been so glorious in honours
Shal nat allye yow with hasardours
As by my wyl ne as by my tretee."°
This wise philosophre thus seyde he.
   Looke eek that to the kyng Demetrius
The kyng of Parthes,° as the book seith us,   160
Sente hym a paire of dees° of gold in scorn,
For° he hadde used hasard ther-biforn;°
For which he heeld his glorie or his renoun
At no value or reputacioun.
Lordes may fynden oother manere° pley
Honeste ynow° to dryve the day awey.
   Now wol I speke of oothes false and grete
A word or two, as olde bokes trete.
Greet sweryng is a thyng abhomynable,
And fals sweryng is yet moore reprevable.°   170

The heighe God forbad sweryng at al.
Witnesse on Mathew; but in special
Of sweryng seith the holy Jeremye,°
"Thow shalt swere sooth° thyne othes and nat lye,
And swere in doom° and eek in rightwisnesse."°
But ydel° sweryng is a cursednesse.
Bihoold and se that, in the firste table
Of heighe Goddes Hestes° honurable,
How that the Seconde Heste of hym is this:
"Take nat my name in ydel° or amys."   180
Lo, rather he forbedeth swich sweryng
Than homycide or many a cursed thyng.
I seye that, as by ordre,° thus it standeth;
This knowen, that hise Hestes understandeth,
How that the Seconde Heste of God is that.
And forther over, I wol thee telle al plat°
That vengeance shal nat parten° from his hous
That of hise othes is to° outrageous.
"By Goddes precious herte," and "By his nayles,"
And "By the blood of Crist that is in Hayles,°   190
Sevene is my chaunce, and thyn is cynk° and
   treye,"°
"By Goddes armes, if thow falsly pleye,
This daggere shal thurgh out thyn herte go,"—
This fruyt cometh of the bicched bones° two,
Forsweryng, ire, falsnesse, homycide.
Now, for the love of Crist, that for us dyde,
Lete° youre othes, bothe grete and smale.
But, sires, now wol I telle forth my tale.
   Thise riotoures° thre of whiche I telle,
Longe erst er pryme rong° of any belle,   200
Were set hem° in a taverne to drynke;
And, as they sat, they herde a belle clynke°
Biforn a cors° was caried to his grave.
That oon° of hem gan callen to his knave:°
"Go bet,"° quod° he, "and axe° redily
What cors is this that passeth heer forby.
And looke that thow reporte his name wel."
   "Sire," quod this boy, "it nedeth° never a del.°
It was me told er ye cam here two houres.
He was, pardee,° an old felawe° of youres,   210
And sodeynly he was y-slayn to-nyght,°
Fordronke,° as he sat on his bench upright.
Ther cam a pryvee° theef, men clepeth° Deeth,

125. wyn-yevyng: wine-giving.   128. defenden hasardrye: forbid
dicing.   129. verray . . . lesynges: the very mother of falsehood.
130. forswerynges: perjuries.   131. Blaspheme: blasphemy.
wast: waste.   132. catel: substance.   133. repreve: reproach.
134. For . . . holde: to be considered.   139. as by: by.   143.
Lacedomye: Lacedaemon (Sparta).   144. hym happed: it happened to him.   146. fond: found.   148. stal: stole.   149. lese:
lose.   150. N' . . . nat: nor will I.   153. me . . . levere: I would
rather.   157. tretee: agreement.   160. Parthes: Parthia.
161. dees: dice.   162. For: because. ther-biforn: previously.
165. manere: sort of.   166. ynow: enough.   170. reprevable:
reprovable.

173. Jeremye: Jeremiah.   174. sooth: truthfully.   175. doom:
judgment. rightwisnesse: righteousness.   176. ydel: vain.
178. Hestes: (Ten) Commandments.   180. in ydel: in vain.
183. as by ordre: in order.   186. plat: plainly.   187. parten:
depart.   188. to: too.   190. in Hayles: (preserved) at Hayles,
Gloucestershire.   191. cynk: five. treye: three.   194. bicched
bones: cursed dice.   197. Lete: restrain.   199. riotoures:
profligates.   200. erst . . . rong: before prime (9 A.M.) rang.
201. set hem: seated.   202. clynke: clang.   203. cors: corpse
(which).   204. That oon: one. knave: boy.   205. Go bet: go
faster, i.e., hurry. quod: said. axe: ask.   208. nedeth: is
necessary. a del: one bit.   210. pardee: certainly. felawe:
companion.   211. to-nyght: last night.   212. Fordronke: very
drunk.   213. pryvee: secretive. men clepeth: (whom) they call.

That in this contree al the peple sleeth,°
And with his spere he smoot his herte a-two,°
And wente his wey withouten wordes mo.
He hath a thousand slayn, this pestilence.
And, maister, er ye come in his presence,
Me thynketh that it were necessarie
For to be war of swich an adversarie.   220
Beth° redy for to meete hym evere moore.°
Thus taughte me my dame.° I sey namoore."

    " By seinte Marie," seyde this taverner,°
" The child seith sooth, for he hath slayn this yer,
Henne over a myle,° withinne a greet village,
Bothe man and womman, child, and hyne,° and
          page.
I trowe° his habitacioun be there.
To been avysed° greet wisdom it were,
Er that he dide a man a dishonour."

    " Ye,° Goddes armes! " quod this riotour.   230
" Is it swich peril with hym for to meete?
I shal hym seke by wey and eek by strete,
I make avow to Goddes digne° bones.
Herkneth, felawes. We thre been al ones.°
Lat ech of us holde up his hand til° oother,
And ech of us bicome otheres brother,°
And we wol sleen this false traytour Deeth.
He shal be slayn, he that so manye sleeth,
By Goddes dignytee, er it be nyght."

    Togidres° han thise thre hir trouthes plight° 240
To lyve and dyen ech of hem for oother,
As thogh he were his owene y-bore° brother.
And up they stirte,° al dronken in this rage,
And forth they goon towardes that village
Of which the taverner hadde spoke biforn.
And many a grisly ooth thanne han they sworn,
And Cristes blessed body they to-rente.°
Deeth shal be deed, if that they may hym hente!°

    Whan they han goon nat fully half a myle,
Right° as they wolde han treden° over a stile, 250
An old man and a poure° with hem mette.
This olde man ful mekely hem grette°
And seyde thus, " Now, lordes, God yow se."°

    The proudeste of thise riotoures thre
Answerde agayn,° " What, carl!° With sory grace!°
Why artow° al forwrapped° save thy face?
Why lyvestow° so longe in so greet age? "

This olde man gan looke° in his visage
And seyde thus: " For I ne kan nat fynde
A man, thogh that I walked into Inde,°   260
Neither in citee ne in no village,
That wolde chaunge his youthe for myn age.
And, therefore, moot I han° myn age stille,
As longe tyme as it is Goddes wille.
    " Ne Deeth, allas, ne wol nat han my lyf.
Thus walke I lyk a restelees caytyf,°
And on the ground, which is my modres° gate,
I knokke with my staf bothe erly and late,
And seye, ' Leeve° moder, leet me in.
Lo, how I vanysshe, flessh, and blood, and skyn. 270
Allas, whan shul my bones been at reste?
Moder, with yow wolde I chaunge my cheste,°
That in my chambre longe tyme hath be,°
Ye, for an heyre clowt° to wrappe me! '
But yet to me she wol nat do that grace,
For which full pale and welked° is my face.
    " But, sires, to yow it is no curteisye
To speken to an old man vileynye
But° he trespase in word or elles° in dede.
In Holy Writ ye may yourself wel rede,   280
' Agayns° an old man, hoor° upon his heed,
Ye sholde arise.' Wherefore I yeve° yow reed:°
Ne dooth° unto an old man noon harm now,
Namoore than that ye wolde men dide to yow
In age, if that ye so longe abyde.
And God be with yow, wher° ye go° or ryde.
I moot° go thider as° I have to go."
    " Nay, olde cherl. By God, thow shalt nat so,"
Seyde this oother hasardour° anon.
" Thow partest° nat so lightly,° by seint John. 290
Thow spak right now of thilke° traytour Deeth,
That in this contree alle oure freendes sleeth.
Have here my trouthe,° as thow art his espye,°
Telle wher he is, or thow shalt it abye,°
By God and by the holy sacrament!
For soothly thow art oon of his assent°
To sleen us yonge folk, thow false theef! "
    " Now, sires," quod he, " if that yow be so leef°
To fynde Deeth, turn up this croked wey.
For in that grove I lafte° hym, by my fey,°   300
Under a tree, and ther he wol abyde.
Nat for youre boost he wol hym° nothyng hyde.
Se ye that ook?° Right ther ye shal hym fynde.

---

214. sleeth: slays.   215. a-two: in two.   221. Beth: be.   evere
moore: always.   222. dame: mother.   223. taverner: innkeeper.   225. Henne . . . myle: within a mile hence.   226.
hyne: servant.   227. trowe: believe.   228. been avysed: be
prepared.   230. Ye: yes.   233. digne: worthy.   234. ones: one.
235. til: to.   236. otheres brother: the other's sworn brother.
240. Togidres: together.   hir . . . plight: pledged their faith.
242. y-bore: born.   243. stirte: sprang.   247. to-rente: tore
to pieces.   248. hente: catch.   250. Right: just.   han
treden: have stepped.   251. poure: poor.   252. grette:
greeted.   253. se: save.   255. agayn: back.   carl: churl.
With . . . grace: curse you.   256. artow: are you.   for-
wrapped: wrapped up.   257. lyvestow: live you.

258. gan looke: looked.   260. Inde: India.   263. moot I han:
must I have.   266. caytyf: wretch.   267. modres: mother's.
269. Leeve: dear.   272. cheste: clothes chest.   273. be: been.
274. heyre clowt: hair rag.   276. welked: withered.   279. But:
unless. elles: else.   281. Agayns: before. hoor: hoar.   282. yeve:
give. reed: advice.   283. Ne dooth: don't do.   286. wher:
whether. go: walk.   287. moot: must. as: where.   289.
hasardour: gambler.   290. partest: depart. lightly: easily.
291. thilke: that same.   293. trouthe: oath. espye: spy.
294. abye: pay for.   296. of . . . assent: in agreement with him.
298. leef: eager.   300. lafte: left. fey: faith.   302. hym:
himself.   303. ook: oak.

God save yow, that boghte agayn° mankynde,
And yow amende." Thus seyde this olde man.
And everich° of thise riotoures ran
Til they came to that tree, and ther they founde
Of floryns° fyne of gold y-coyned rounde
Wel ny an eighte° busshels, as hem thoughte.°
No lenger thanne after Deeth they soughte;   310
But ech of hem so glad was of the sighte,
For that the floryns been so faire and brighte,
That doun they sette hem° by this precious hoord.
The worste of hem he spak the firste word.
   "Brethren," quod he, "taak kepe° what I seye.
My wit° is greet, thogh that I bourde° and pleye.
This tresor hath fortune unto us yeven,°
In myrthe and jolitee oure lyf to lyven.
And lightly as it cometh, so wol we spende.
By Goddes precious dignytee, who wende°   320
Today that we sholde han so fair a grace?
But, myghte this gold be caried fro this place
Hoom to myn hous, or ellis unto youres —
For wel ye woot° that al this gold is oures —
Thanne were we in heigh felicitee.
But, trewely, by daye it may nat be.
Men wolde seyn° that we were theves stronge°
And for oure owene tresor doon us honge.°
This tresor moste y-caried be by nyghte.
As wisly° and as slyly as it myghte.   330
Wherfore I rede° that cut° among us alle
Be drawe, and lat se° wher the cut wol falle.
And he that hath the cut, with herte blithe
Shal renne° to the toune, and that ful swithe,°
And brynge us breed and wyn ful pryvely.
And two of us shul kepen subtilly°
This tresor wel; and if he wol nat tarie,
Whan it is nyght, we wol this tresor carie
By oon assent wher-as us thynketh° best."
   That oon° of hem the cut broghte in his
      fest,°   340
And bad hem drawe and looke wher it wol falle,
And it fil on the youngeste of hem alle,
And forth toward the toun he wente anon.
And also° soone as that he was agon,°
That oon of hem spak thus unto that oother:
"Thow knowest wel, thow art my sworn brother.
Thy profit wol I telle thee anon.
Thow woost° wel that oure felawe is agon,
And heere is gold, and that ful greet plentee,

That shall departed° been among us thre.   350
But, nathelees,° if I kan shape it so
That it departed were among us two,
Hadde I nat doon a freendes torn° to thee?"
   That oother answerde, "I noot° how that may be.
He woot that the gold is with us tweye.°
What shal we doon? What shall we to hym seye?"
   "Shal it be conseil?"° seyde the firste shrewe.°
"And I shal tellen in a wordes fewe
What we shul doon, and brynge it wel aboute."
   "I graunte," quod that oother, "out of doute,   360
That, by my trouthe, I wol thee nat biwreye."°
   "Now," quod the firste, "thow woost wel we be
      tweye,
And two of us shul strenger be than oon.
Looke, whan that he is set, that right anoon
Arys as though thow woldest with hym pleye,
And I shall ryve° hym thurgh the sydes tweye,
Whil that thow strogelest with him as in game.
And with thy daggere looke thow do the same,
And thanne shal al this gold departed be,
My deere freend, bitwixe me and thee.   370
Thanne may we bothe oure lustes al fulfille,
And pleye at dees° right at oure owne wille."
And thus acorded been thise shrewes tweye
To sleen° the thridde, as ye han herd me seye.
   This youngeste, which that wente to the toun,
Ful ofte in herte he rolleth up and doun
The beautee of thise floryns newe and brighte.
"O Lord," quod he, "if so were that I myghte
Have al this tresor to myself allone,
Ther is no man that lyveth under the trone   380
Of God that sholde lyve so myrie as I!"
And atte laste the feend,° oure enemy,
Putte in his thoght that he sholde poyson beye,°
With which he myghte sleen his felawes tweye,
For-why° the feend foond° hym in swich lyvynge
That he hadde leve° hym to sorwe brynge.
For this was outrely° his full entente,
To sleen hem bothe and nevere to repente.
And forth he goth — no lenger wolde he tarie —
Into the toun unto a pothecarie,°   390
And preyed hym that he hym wolde selle
Som poysoun that he myghte his rattes quelle,°
And eek ther was a polcat° in his hawe,°
That, as he seyde, his capouns° hadde y-slawe,°
And fayn° he wolde wreke hym,° if he myghte,
On vermyn that destroyed° hym by nyghte.

304. boghte agayn: redeemed.   306. everich: each.   308. floryns: florins (coins).   309. Wel ... eighte: very nearly eight. hem thoughte: it seemed to them.   313. hem: themselves. 315. kepe: heed to.   316. wit: understanding.   bourde: jest. 317. yeven: given.   320. wende: would have believed.   324. woot: know.   327. seyn: say.   stronge: violent.   328. doon us honge: have us hanged.   330. wisly: cautiously.   331. rede: advise.   cut: cuts.   332. lat se: let see.   334. renne: run. swithe: quickly.   336. kepen subtilly: guard craftily.   339. wher-as us thynketh: where it seems to us.   340. That oon: the one.   fest: fist.   344. also: as.   agon: gone.   348. woost: know.

350. departed: divided.   351. nathelees: nevertheless.   353. torn: turn.   354. noot: don't know.   355. tweye: two.   357. conseil: secret.   shrewe: wretch.   361. biwreye: betray. 366. ryve: stab.   372. dees: dice.   374. sleen: slay.   382. feend: Devil.   383. beye: buy.   385. For-why: because. foond: found.   386. leve: permission (from God).   387. outrely: entirely.   390. pothecarie: apothecary.   392. quelle: kill. 393. polcat: fitchet (member of the weasel family).   hawe: hedge. 394. capouns: capons.   y-slawe: killed.   395. fayn: gladly. wreke hym: avenge himself.   396. destroyed: annoyed.

The pothecarie answerde, " And thow shalt have
A thyng that, also° God my soule save,
In al this world ther is no creature
That ete° or dronke hath of this confiture°   400
Nat but the montaunce° of a corn° of whete,
That he ne shal his lyf anoon forlete.°
Ye,° sterve° he shal, and that in lasse while
Than thow wolt goon a paas° nat but a myle,
The poysoun is so strong and violent."
    This cursed man hath in his hond y-hent°
This poysoun in a box, and sith° he ran
Into the nexte strete unto a man
And borwed of hym large botels thre,
And in the two his poyson poured he.   410
The thridde he kepte clene for his drynke,
For al the nyght he shoop hym for to swynke°
In cariyng of the gold out of that place.
And whan this riotour — with sory grace!° —
Hadde filled with wyn hise grete botels thre,
To hise felawes agayn repaireth he.
    What nedeth it to sermone of it moore?
For right as they hadde cast° his deeth bifore,
Right so they han hym slayn, and that anon.   419
And whan that this was doon, thus spak that
    oon:
"Now lat us sitte, and drynke, and make us
    merye,
And afterward we wol his body berye."
And with that word it happed hym par cas°
To take the botel ther° the poysoun was,
And drank, and yaf° his felawe drynke also,
For which anon they storven° bothe two.
    But, certes,° I suppose that Avycen
Wroot neverre in no canon ne in no fen°
Mo wonder signes° of empoysonyng   429
Than hadde thise wrecches two er hir° endyng.
Thus ended been thise homicides two,
And eek the false empoysonere also.
    O cursed synne of alle cursednesse!
O traytours homicide! O wikkednesse!
O glotonye, luxurie,° and hasardrye!
Thou blasphemour of Crist with vileynye
And othes grete of usage° and of pryde!°
Allas, mankynde, how may it bityde
That to thy Creatour, which that thee wroghte°

And with his precious herte-blood thee boghte, 440
Thow art so fals and so unkynde,° allas?
    Now, goode men, God foryeve° yow youre tres-
    pas,
And ware yow fro° the synne of avarice.
Myn holy pardoun may yow alle warice,°
So° that ye offre nobles° or sterlynges,°
Or elles silver broches, spones, rynges.
Boweth youre heed under this holy bulle!
Cometh up, ye wyves! Offreth of youre wolle!°
Youre name I entre here in my rolle anon;
Into the blisse of hevene shul ye gon.   450
I yow assoille,° by myn heigh power,
Yow that wol offre, as clene and eek as cler
As we were born. — And lo, sires, thus I preche.
And Jesu Crist, that is oure soules leche,°
So graunte yow his pardoun to receyve,
For that is best. I wol yow nat deceyve.

THE CLERK'S TALE

    The source of the Clerk's Tale is one of the stories
in Boccaccio's famous Italian prose work, the *Decameron* (1353), but Chaucer followed a Latin prose
translation made by Petrarch and, side by side, a
French translation of the Latin. So closely, in fact, did
he follow these two versions that it is frequently possible to tell which he was looking at when he wrote
particular passages.
    The story had circulated as an unpretentious folk
tale before Boccaccio made his literary adaptation, and
Chaucer instinctively preserved the remoteness and unreality inherent in the folk tale which made it so
ideally suited to the otherworldly Clerk. But the predominant tone of the tale has been subtly adapted to
the character of the narrator. And Chaucer's version
is further original in its graceful rhyme-royal stanzas
and in the extraordinary tour de force at the end,
where the same set of rhymes (*ababcb*) runs through
six stanzas.

I

    Ther is at the west syde of Ytaille,°
Doun at the roote of Vesulus° the colde,
A lusty° playne habundant of vitaille,°
Wher many a tour° and toun thow mayst biholde
That founded were in tyme of fadres° olde,
And many another delitable° sighte,
And Saluces° this noble contree highte.°

398. also: as.   400. ete: eaten.   confiture: preparation.   401.
montaunce: quantity.   corn: grain.   402. forlete: lose.   403. Ye:
yes.   sterve: die.   404. goon a paas: walk at footpace.   406. y-
hent: taken.   407. sith: then.   412. shoop . . . swynke: intended
to work.   414. with . . . grace: curse him.   418. cast: planned.
423. it . . . cas: he happened by chance.   424. ther: where.
425. yaf: gave.   426. storven: died.   427. certes: certainly.
428. fen: Avicenna's Arabic treatise on medicine was divided
into fens (sections), containing the canons (rules) of procedure
appropriate to various illnesses, including poisoning.   429. Mo
. . . signes: more wonderful symptoms.   430. er hir: before
their.   435. luxurie: lechery.   437. usage: habit.   pryde:
ostentation.   439. wroghte: made.

441. unkynde: unnatural.   442. foryeve: forgive.   443. ware
. . . fro: beware of.   444. warice: cure.   445. So: providing.
nobles: nobles (6s. 8d.).   sterlynges: silver pennies.   448. wolle:
wool.   451. assoille: absolve.   454. leche: leech (physician).
CLERK'S TALE.   1. Ytaille: Italy.   2. Vesulus: Monte Viso.
3. lusty: pleasant.   habundant of vitaille: abundant in food.
4. tour: tower.   5. fadres: ancestors.   6. delitable: delightful.
7. Saluces: Saluzzo.   highte: is called.

A markys whilom° lord was of that lond,
As were his worthy eldres hym bifore,
And obeisant ay° redy to his hond   10
Were alle his liges° bothe lasse and moore.
Thus in delit he lyveth and hath doon yoore,°
Biloved and drad° thurgh favour of Fortune
Bothe of his lordes and of his commune.°

Therwith he was, to speke as of lynage,°
The gentileste y-born of Lumbardye,°
A fair persone, and strong and yong of age,
And ful of honour and of curteisye,
Discret ynogh° his contree for to gye,°
Save° in somme thynges that he was to blame;   20
And Walter was this yonge lordes name.

I blame hym thus that he considered noght
In tyme comynge what myghte hym bityde,°
But on his lust° present was al his thoght,
As for to hauke and hunte on every syde.
Wel neigh alle oothere cures leet° he slyde;
And eek° he nolde° — and that was worst of
alle —
Wedde no wyf for noght that may bifalle.

Oonly that point his peple bar so soore°
That flokmele° on a day they to hym wente;   30
And oon of hem° that wisest was of loore°—
Or ellis° that the lord best wolde assente
That he sholde telle hym what his peple mente,°
Or ellis koude he shewe° wel swich° matere —
He to the markys seyde as ye shal heere:

"O noble markys, youre humanitee
Assureth us and yeveth° us hardynesse,°
As oft as tyme is of necessitee,
That we to yow mowe° telle oure hevynesse.
Accepteth,° lord, now of youre gentillesse°   40
That° we with pitous° herte unto yow pleyne,°
And lat° youre erys° noght my voys desdeyne,

I dar° the bettre aske of yow a space°
Of audience to shewen oure requeste,
And ye, my lord, to doon right as yow leste.°

"For certes,° lord, so wel us liketh° yow   50
And al youre werk, and evere han doon, that we
Ne kouden nat usself devysen° how
We myghte lyven in moore felicitee,
Save o° thyng, lord, if it youre wille be,
That for to been a wedded man yow leste.°
Thanne were youre peple in sovereyn° hertes reste.

"Boweth youre nekke under that blisful yok
Of sovereynetee, noght of servyse,°
Which that men clepe spousaille° or wedlok;
And thenketh, lord, among youre thoghtes wyse
How that oure dayes passe in sondry wyse,°   61
For, thogh we slepe or wake or rome° or ryde,
Ay° fleeth the tyme; it nyl° no man abyde.

"And thogh youre grene youthe floure as yit,
In crepeth age alwey as stille as stoon,
And deth manaceth° every age and smyt°
In ech estat,° for ther escapeth noon;
And, also° certeyn as we knowe echon°
That we shul dye, as uncerteyn we alle
Been° of that day whan deth shal on us falle.   70

"Accepteth thanne of us the trewe entente
That° nevere yet refuseden youre heste,°
And we wol, lord, if that ye wol assente,
Chese° yow a wyf, in short tyme at the leeste,
Born of the gentileste° and of the meeste°
Of al this lond, so that it oghte seme°
Honour to God and yow, as° we kan deme.°

"Delyvere us out of al this bisy drede,°
And tak a wyf, for hye° Goddes sake,
For if it so bifelle — as God forbede!° —   80
...eeth youre lyne sholde slake,°
...' successour sholde take
...o were us° alyve!
...ow hastily to wyve."°

Hir° meke prayere and hir pitous cheere°
Made the markys herte han pitee.
"Ye wol,"° quod° he, "myn owene peple deere,
To that° I nevere erst° thoghte streyne° me.
I me rejoysed of° my libertee,
That selde tyme° is founde in mariage.   90
Ther° I was free, I moot° been in servage.

"But, nathelees,° I se youre trewe entente,
And truste upon youre wit, and have doon ay.
Wherfore of my free wyl I wol assente
To wedde me as soone as evere I may.
But, theras° ye han profred me today
To chese me a wyf, I yow relesse
That choys and pray yow of that profre cesse.°

"For God it woot that children ofte ben
Unlyk hir worthy eldres hem bifore.   100
Bountee° comth al of God, nat of the stren°
Of which they been° engendred and y-bore.°
I truste in Goddes bountee, and therfore
My mariage and myn estat and reste°
I hym bitake;° he may doon as hym leste.°

"Lat me allone in chesyng of my wyf;
That charge upon my bak I wol endure.
But I yow pray and charge, upon youre lyf,
What° wyf that I take, ye me assure
To worshipe hire whil that hir lyf may dure°   110
In word and werk, bothe here and everywhere,
As° she an emperoures doghter were.

"And ferthermoore this shal ye swere, that ye
Agayn° my choys shal neither grucche° ne stryve,
For, sith° I shal forgoon° my libertee
At your requeste, as evere mote° I thryve,
Theras° myn herte is set, ther wol I wyve;
And, but° ye wol assente in swich manere,   118
I pray yow, speketh namoore° of this matere."

With hertly° wyl they sworen and assenten, —
To al this thyng ther seyde no wight° "nay" —
Bisekynge hym of grace, er that° they wenten,
That he wolde graunten hem a certein day
Of his spousaille as soone as evere he may,
For yet alwey the peple somwhat dredde°
Lest that the markys no wyf wolde wedde.

He graunted hem a day swich as hym leste°
On which he wolde be wedded sikerly,°
And seyde he dide al this at hir requeste;
And they with humble entente buxomly°   130
Knelynge upon hir knees ful reverently
Hym thanken alle, and thus they han an ende
Of hir entente, and hom agayn they wende.

And herupon he to his officers
Comaundeth for the feste to purveye,°
And to his pryvee° knyghtes and squyers
Swich charge yaf° as hym liste on hem leye,
And they to his commandement obeye,
And ech of hem dooth al his diligence
To doon unto the feste reverence.   140

II

Noght fer fro thilke° paleys honurable
Wheras this markys shoop° his mariage,
Ther stood a throop° of site delitable°
In which that poure folk of that village
Hadden hir bestes° and hir herbergage°
And of° hir labour toke° hir sustenance
After that° the erthe yaf hem habundance.

Among thise poure folk ther dwelte a man
Which that° was holden° pourest of hem alle,
But hye God somtyme sende can   150
His grace into a litel oxes stalle.
Janicula men of that throop hym calle.
A doghter hadde he fair ynogh to sighte,
And Grisildis this yonge mayden highte.°

But, for to speke of vertuous beautee,°
Thanne was she oon° the faireste under sonne,
For poureliche y-fostred up° was she.
No likerous° lust was thurgh hir herte y-ronne.°
Wel ofter° of the welle than of the tonne°
She drank, and, for she wolde vertu plese,   160
She knew wel labour, but noon ydel ese.

But thogh this mayde tendre were of age,
Yet in the brest of hir virginitee
Ther was enclosed rype and sad corage,°
And in greet reverence and charitee
Hir olde, poure fader fostred she.

85. Hir: their. pitous cheere: pitiful expression. 87. wol:
will. quod: said. 88. that: what. erst: before. streyne:
constrain. 89. me . . . of: rejoiced in. 90. selde tyme: seldom.
91. Ther: where. moot: must. 92. nathelees: nevertheless.
96. theras: whereas. 98. cesse: (to) cease. 101. Bountee:
goodness. stren: strain. 102. been: are. y-bore: born.
104. reste: repose. 105. hym bitake: commit to him. hym
leste: pleases him. 109. What: whatever. 110. dure: endure. 112. As: as if. 114. Agayn: against. grucche: grum-
ble. 115. sith: since. forgoon: forgo. 116. mote: may.
117. Theras: where. 118. but: unless. 119. speketh namoore:
say no more. 120. hertly: cordial. 121. wight: person. 122. er
that: before. 125. dredde: feared.

127. swich . . . leste: such as suited him. 128. sikerly: certainly. 130. buxomly: submissively. 135. purveye: provide.
136. pryvee: personal. 137. yaf: gave. 141. fer . . . thilke:
far from that same. 142. shoop: prepared. 143. throop: village. delitable: delightful. 145. bestes: animals. herbergage: shelter. 146. of: by. toke: won. 147. After that:
according as. 149. Which that: who. holden: considered.
154. highte: was called. 155. vertuous beautee: the beauty of
virtue (rather than the mere beauty of sight). 156. oon: one
of. 157. poureliche y-fostred up: poorly nurtured. 158. likerous: lecherous. y-ronne: run. 159. Wel ofter: much more
often. tonne: barrel. 164. sad corage: serious heart.

A fewe sheep, spynnynge on feld,° she kepte;°
She wolde noght been ydel til she slepte.

And whan she homward cam, she wolde brynge
Wortes° or othere herbes tymes ofte,   170
The whiche she shredde° and seeth° for hir
  lyvynge,°
And made hir bed ful hard and nothyng softe,
And ay she kepte hir fadres lyf on lofte°
With every obeisance° and diligence
That child may doon to fadres reverence.

  Upon Grisilde, this poure creature,
Ful ofte sithe° this markys sette his eye
As he on huntyng rood paraventure,°
And whan it fil° that he myghte hire espye,
He noght with wantowne lookyng of folye   180
His eyen caste on hire, but in sad° wyse
Upon hir cheere° he wolde hym ofte avyse,°

Commendynge in his herte hir wommanhede
And eek hir vertu passyng° any wight
Of so yong age as wel in cheere as dede,
For, thogh the peple have no greet insight
In vertue, he considered ful right
Hir bountee and disposed° that he wolde
Wedde hire oonly, if evere he wedden sholde.

  The day of weddyng cam, but no wight kan
Telle what womman that it sholde be,   191
For which merveille wondred many a man
And seyden, whan they were in pryvetee,
"Wol nat oure lord yet leve his vanytee?°
Wol he nat wedde? Allas, allas, the while!
Why wol he thus hymself and us bigyle?"

  But nathelees this markys hath doon make,°
Of gemmes set in gold and in asure,°
Broches and rynges, for Grisildis sake;
And of hir clothyng took he the mesure   200
Of a mayde lyk to hir stature,
And eek of othere ornamentes alle
That unto swich a weddyng sholde falle.

The tyme of undren° of the same day
Approcheth that this weddyng sholde be,
And al the paleys put was in array,
Bothe halle and chambres ech in his° degree.

Houses of office° stuffed with plentee
Ther maystow° seen of deyntevous° vitaille
That may be founde as fer as last° Ytaille.   210

This roial markys, richely arrayed,
Lordes and ladyes in his compaignye
The whiche that to the feste were y-prayed,°
And of his retenue the bachelrye°
With many a soun of sondry melodye
Unto the village of the which I tolde
In this array the righte wey han holde.

  Grisilde, of this, God woot, ful innocent°
That for hire shapen° was al this array,
To fecchen water at a welle is went,   220
And cometh hoom as soone as ever she may,
For wel she hadde herd seyd that thilke day
The markys sholde wedde; and, if she myghte,
She wolde fayn han seyn° som of that sighte.

She thoghte, "I wole with othere maydens stonde°
That been my felawes° in oure dore and se
The markisesse,° and therfore wol I fonde°
To doon at hoom as soone as it may be
The labour which that longeth° unto me,
And thanne I may at leyser° hir biholde   230
If she this wey unto the castel holde."

And as she wolde over hir thresshfold gon,
The markys cam and gan hire for to calle,°
And she sette doun hir water pot anon
Bisyde the thresshfold in an oxes stalle,
And doun upon hir knees she gan to falle,
And with sad contenance kneleth stille
Til she hadde herd what was the lordes wille.

  This thoghtful markys spak unto this mayde
Ful sobrely and seyde in this manere: 240
"Where is youre fader, O Grisildis," he sayde;
And she with reverence in humble cheere
Answerde, "Lord, he is alredy heere."
And in she goth withouten lenger lette,°
And to the markys she hir fader fette.°

He by the hand than took this olde man
And seyde thus, whan he hym hadde asyde,
"Janicula, I neither may ne kan
Lenger the plesance° of myn herte hyde.
If that thow vouchesauf, what so bityde,   250

---

167. **spynnynge on feld**: (while) spinning (by hand with a spindle) on the field. **kepte**: tended. 170. **Wortes**: roots. 171. **shredde**: shredded. **seeth**: boiled. **lyvynge**: sustenance. 173. **kepte on lofte**: sustained. 174. **obeisance**: obedience. 177. **sithe**: time. 178. **rood paraventure**: rode perchance. 179. **fil**: befell. 181. **sad**: sober. 182. **cheere**: appearance. **hym avyse**: consider. 184. **passyng**: surpassing. 188. **disposed**: determined. 194. **vanytee**: folly. 197. **doon make**: caused to be made. 198. **asure**: azure. 204. **undren**: 9 A.M. 207. **his**: its.

208. **Houses of office**: household storerooms. 209. **maystow**: you may. **deyntevous**: the most dainty. 210. **last**: extends. 213. **y-prayed**: invited. 214. **bachelrye**: bachelor band. 218. **innocent**: unsuspecting. 219. **shapen**: prepared. 224. **wolde ... seyn**: would very much like to see. 225. **stonde**: stand. 226. **felawes**: companions. 227. **markisesse**: marchioness. **fonde**: try. 229. **longeth**: belongs. 230. **leyser**: leisure. 233. **gan ... calle**: called her. 244. **lenger lette**: longer delay. 245. **plesance**: inclination.

Thy doghter wol I take er that I wende°
As for° my wyf unto my lyves ende.

"Thow lovest me, I woot it wel certeyn,
And art my feithful lige° man y-bore,°
And al that liketh° me, I dar wel seyn,
It liketh thee, and specially therfore
Tel me that point that I have seyd bifore,
If that thow wolt unto that purpos drawe°
To take me as for thy sone-in-lawe."

The sodeyn cas° this man astoneyd° so   260
That reed° he wax;° abayst° and al quakyng
He stood; unnethe° seyde he wordes mo°
But oonly thus, "Lord," quod he, "my willyng
Is as ye wole, ne ayeins youre likyng
I wol no thyng, ye be my lord so deere.
Right as yow list, governeth this matere."

"Yet wol I," quod this markys softely,
"That in thy chambre I and thow and she
Have a collacioun,° and wostow° why?
For I wol aske if it hir wille be   270
To be my wyf and rule hire after me,°
And al this shal be doon in thy presence.
I wol noght speke out of thyn audience."°

And in the chambre whil they were aboute
Hir tretys,° which as ye shal after heere,
The peple cam unto the hous withoute
And wondred hem° in how honeste° manere
And tentifly° she kepte hir fader deere.
But outrely° Grisildis wondre myghte,
For nevere erst ne saw she swich a sighte.   280

No wonder is thogh that she were astoned
To see so greet a gest° come in that place.
She nevere was to swiche gestes woned,°
For which she looked with ful pale face.
But, shortly forth this matere for to chace,°
Thise arn° the wordes that the markys sayde
To this benygne, verray,° feithful mayde.

"Grisilde," he seyde, "ye shal wel understonde
It liketh to° youre fader and to me
That I yow wedde, and eek it may so stonde,   290
As I suppose, ye wol that it so be.

But thise demandes aske I first," quod he,
"That sith it shal be doon in hastif° wyse,
Wol ye assente or ellis yow avyse?°

"I sey this. Be ye redy with good herte
To al my lust,° and that I frely may,
As me best thynketh, do yow laughe or smerte,°
And nevere ye to grucche it nyght ne day;
And eek, whan I sey 'ye,' ne sey nat 'nay,'
Neither by word ne frownyng contenance?   300
Swere this, and here I swere oure alliance."

Wondrynge upon this word, quakyng for drede,
She seyde, "Lord, undigne° and unworthy
I am to thilke honour that ye me bede,°
But, as ye wol yourself, right so wol I.
And heere I swere that nevere willyngly
In werk ne thoght I nyl yow disobeye
For to be deed,° thogh me were looth° to deye."

"This is ynogh, Grisilde myn," quod he;
And forth he goth with a ful sobre cheere   310
Out at the dore, and after that cam she;
And to the peple he seyde in this manere:
"This is my wyf," quod he, "that standeth
      heere.
Honureth hire, and loveth hire, I preye,
Whoso me loveth. Ther is namoore to seye."

And, for that nothyng of hir olde gere°
She sholde brynge into his hous, he bad
That wommen sholde dispoylen° hir right there,
Of which this ladyes were noght right glad
To handle hir clothes wherinne she was clad;   320
But nathelees this mayde bright of hewe
Fro foot to heed they clothed han al newe.

Hir herys° han they kembd° that laye untressed
Ful rudely, and with hir fyngres smale°
A corone° on hir heed they han y-dressed,°
And sette hire ful of nowches° grete and smale.
Of hir array what° sholde I make a tale?
Unnethe° the peple hir knew for hir fairnesse
Whan she translated was in swich richesse.

This markys hath hire spoused with a ryng   330
Broght for the same cause, and thanne° hir sette
Upon an hors snow-whit and wel amblyng,
And to his paleys, er he lenger lette,°

251. wende: leave.   252. As for: for.   254. lige: liege.   y-bore:
born.   255. liketh: pleases.   258. wolt drawe: will agree.
260. sodeyn cas: sudden outcome.   astoneyd: astonished.
261. reed: red.   wax: grew.   abayst: abashed.   262. unnethe:
hardly.   mo: more.   269. collacioun: conference.   wostow:
do you know.   271. rule . . . me: conduct herself according to
my will.   273. audience: hearing.   275. tretys: agreement.
277. wondred hem: marveled.   honeste: honorable a.   278. ten-
tifly: attentively.   279. outrely: utterly.   282. gest: guest.
283. woned: accustomed.   285. chace: pursue.   286. arn: are.
287. verray: true.   289. liketh to: pleases.

293. hastif: hasty.   294. yow avyse: consider.   296. lust:
pleasure.   297. As . . . smerte: as seems best to me, make you
laugh or grieve.   303. undigne: unequal.   304. bede: offer.
308. For . . . deed: on pain of death.   me . . . looth: I should
be loath to die.   316. gere: clothing.   318. dispoylen: undress.
323. herys: hair.   kembd: combed.   324. smale: slim.   325. co-
rone: coronet.   y-dressed: arranged.   326. nowches: jewelry.
327. what: why.   328. Unnethe: hardly.   331. thanne: then.
333. lette: delayed.

With joyful peple that hir ladde° and mette
Conveyed hire; and thus the day they spende
In revel til the sonne gan descende.

And shortly forth this tale for to chace,
I seye that to this newe markysesse
God hath swich favour sent hire of his grace
That it ne semed nat by liklynesse°   340
That she was born and fed in rudenesse
As in a cote° or in an oxe stalle
But norissed° in an emperoures halle.

   To every wight she woxen° is so deere
And worshipful that folk ther she was bore
And from hir birthe knewe hire yeer by yeere
Unnethe trowed° they — but dorste han swore° —
That to Janicle, of which I spak bifore,
She doghter were, for as by conjecture
Hem thoughte° she was another creature.   350

For, thogh that evere vertuous was she,
She was encressed° in swich excellence
Of thewes° goode y-set in heigh bountee,
And so discreet and fair of eloquence,
So benygne and so digne° of reverence,
And koude so the peples herte embrace
That ech hir lovede that looked on hir face.

   Noght oonly of Saluces° in the toun
Publissed° was the bountee of hir name,
But eek bisyde° in many a regioun,   360
If oon seyde wel, another seyde the same.
So spradde° of hir heighe bountee the fame
That men and wommen as wel yonge as olde
Goon to Saluce upon hire to biholde.

   Thus Walter, lowely — nay! but roially —
Wedded with fortunat honestetee,°
In Goddes pees lyveth ful esily
At hom, and outward grace ynow° hadde he;
And, for he saugh° that under lowe degree
Was ofte vertu hid, the peple hym helde   370
A prudent man, and that is seyn ful selde.°

   Noght oonly this Grisildis thurgh hir wit
Koude al the feet° of wyfly humblenesse,
But eek, whan that the cas required it,
The commune profit° koude she redresse.

Ther nas discord, rancour, ne hevynesse°
In al that land that she ne koude apese°
And wisly brynge hem alle in reste and ese.

Thogh that hir housbond absent were anon,
If gentilmen or othere of hir contree   380
Were wrothe, she wolde bryngen hem aton.°
So wise and rype° wordes hadde she,
And juggementz of so greet equytee,
That she from Hevene sent was, as men wende,°
Peple to save and every wrong t' amende.

   Nat longe tyme after that this Grisild
Was wedded, she a doghter hath y-bore.
Al had hir levere° have born a knave° child,
Glad was the markys and the folk therfore,
For, thogh a mayde child coome al bifore,°   390
She may unto a knave child atteyne
By liklyhede syn she nys nat bareyne.

III

   Ther fil, as it bifalleth tymes mo,
Whan that this child had souked° but a throwe,°
This markys in his herte longeth so
To tempte° his wyf hir sadnesse° for to knowe
That he ne myghte out of his herte throwe
This merveillous desir his wyf t' assaye.
Nedelees,° God woot, he thoghte hire for
    t' affraye.°

He hadde assayed hire ynow bifore   400
And fond° hire evere good. What neded it
Hir for to tempte and alwey moore and moore,
Thogh som men preyse it for a subtil wit?
But, as for me, I seye that yvele it sit°
T' assaye a wyf whan that it is no nede
And putten hire in angwyssh and in drede.

For which this markys wroghte in this manere:
He cam allone a nyght ther as° she lay
With steerne face and with ful trouble cheere°
And seyde thus: " Grisilde," quod he, " that day
That I yow took out of youre poure array   411
And putte yow in estat of heigh noblesse,
Ye have nat that forgeten, as I gesse.

" I seye, Grisilde, this present dignitee
In which that I have put yow, as I trowe,
Maketh yow nat foryetful for to be

---

334. ladde: led.   340. by liklynesse: in likelihood.   342. cote:
hut.   343. norissed: nurtured.   344. woxen: grown.   347. trowed:
believed.   dorste . . . swore: would have sworn the contrary.
350. Hem thoughte: it seemed to them.   352. encressed:
increased.   353. thewes: customs.   355. digne: worthy.
358. Saluces: Saluzzo, the town.   359. Publissed: made known.
360. bisyde: besides.   362. spradde: spread.   366. honestetee: distinction.   368. ynow: enough.   369. saugh: saw.
371. selde: seldom.   373. feet: art.   375. profit: interest.

376. hevynesse: oppression.   377. apese: appease.   381. aton:
into accord.   382. rype: mature.   384. wende: believed.
388. Al . . . levere: though she would sooner.   knave: boy.
390. coome al bifore: came first.   394. souked: suckled.   throwe:
while.   396. tempte: test.   sadnesse: stability.   399. Nedelees: needlessly.   thoghte . . . t' affraye: decided to alarm her.
401. fond: found.   404. yvele it sit: ill it sits.   408. ther as:
where.   409. trouble cheere: troubled countenance.

That I yow took in poure estat ful lowe
For any wele° ye mote° yourselven knowe.
Tak hede of every word that I yow seye.
Ther is no wight that hereth it but we tweye. 420

"Ye woot yourself wel how that ye cam heere
Into this hous, it is nat longe ago,
And, thogh to me that ye be lief° and deere,
Unto my gentils° ye be nothyng so.
They seyn, to hem it is greet shame and wo
For to be subgetz° and been in servage°
To thee that born art of a smal village.

"And namely sith° thy doghter was y-bore,
Thise wordes han they spoken, doutelees.
But I desire, as I have doon bifore,   430
To lyve my lyf with hem in reste and pees.
I may nat in this cas be recchelees.°
I moot° doon with thy doghter for the beste,
Nat as I wolde, but as my peple leste.°

"And yet, God woot, this is ful looth to me.
But, nathelees,° withouten youre wityng°
I wol nat doon.° But this wol I," quod he,
"That ye to me assente as in this thyng.
Shewe now youre pacience in youre wirkyng°
That ye me highte° and swore in youre village
That day that maked was oure mariage."   441

    Whan she hadde herd al this, she noght ameved°
Neither in word or cheere or contenaunce,
For, as it semed, she was nat agreved.°
She seyde, "Lord, al lith° in youre plesance.
My child and I with hertly obeisance°
Been youres al, and ye mowe° save or spille°
Youre owene thyng. Werketh after° youre wille.

"Ther may nothyng, God so my soule save,
Liken to° yow that may displese me,   450
Ne I desire nothyng for to have
Ne drede for to lese° save oonly ye.
This wyl is in myn herte and ay shal be.
No lengthe of tyme or deth may this deface,
Ne chaunge my corage° to another place."

    Glad was this markys of hir answeryng,
But yet he feyned as° he were nat so.
Al drery° was his cheere and his lookyng

Whan that he sholde out of the chambre go.
Soone after this a furlong wey or two°   460
He pryvely hath told al his entente
Unto a man and to his wyf hym sente.

A maner sergeant° was this pryvee° man
The which that° feithful ofte he founden hadde
In thynges grete, and eek swich folk wel kan
Doon execucioun in thynges badde.
The lord knew wel that he hym loved and dradde.
And whan this sergeant wiste° his lordes wille,
Into the chambre he stalked hym ful stille.

    "Madame," he seyde, "ye mote° foryeve it me
Thogh I do thyng to which I am constreyned. 471
Ye ben so wys that ful wel knowe ye
That lordes hestes° mowe nat ben y-feyned.
They mowe wel been biwailled or compleyned,
But men mote nede° unto hir lust° obeye,
And so wol I. Ther is namoore to seye.

    "This child I am comaunded for to take";
And spak namoore, but out the child he hente°
Despitously° and gan a cheere make°
As thogh he wolde han slayn it er he wente.   480
Grisildis moot al suffren and al consente,
And as a lamb she sitteth meke and stille
And leet this cruel sergeant doon his wille.

    Suspecious° was the diffame° of this man,
Suspect his face, suspect his word also,
Suspect the tyme in which he this bigan.
Allas, hir doghter that she loved so,
She wende he wolde han slawen° it right tho.°
But nathelees she neither weep ne syked,°
Conformynge hire to that the markys liked.   490

But at the laste speken she bigan,
And mekely she to the sergeant preyde,
So as he was a worthy, gentil man,
That she moste kisse hir child er that it deyde;
And in hir barm° this litel child she leyde
With ful sad face, and gan the child to blisse,°
And lulled it, and after gan it kisse.

And thus she seyde in hir benygne voys,
"Farewel, my child. I shal thee nevere see,
But, sith I thee have marked with the croys°   500
Of thilke° Fader — blessed mote he be —

418. wele: happiness.   mote: might.   423. lief: beloved.
424. gentils: nobles.   426. subgetz: subjects.   servage: servitude.   428. namely sith: particularly since.   432. recchelees:
indifferent.   433. moot: must.   434. leste: it would please.
436. nathelees: nevertheless.   wityng: knowledge.   437. doon:
act.   439. wirkyng: behavior.   440. highte: promised.
442. ameved: responded.   444. agreved: distressed.   445. lith:
lies.   446. hertly obeisance: cordial obedience.   447. mowe:
may.   spille: destroy.   448. Werketh after: act according to.
450. Liken to: please.   452. Ne . . . lese: nor dread to lose.
455. corage: feelings.   457. feyned as: pretended that.
458. drery: dreary.

460. a . . . two: in a short time (lit., as long as it takes to walk a
furlong).   463. maner sergeant: sort of retainer.   pryvee:
secretive.   464. The . . . that: whom.   468. wiste: knew.
470. mote: must.   473. hestes: commands.   475. nede: necessarily.   hir lust: their pleasure.   478. hente: seized.   479. De-
spitously: cruelly.   gan . . . make: gave the appearance.
484. Suspecious: suspect.   diffame: infamy.   488. wolde . . .
slawen: intended to have slain.   tho: then.   489. syked:
sighed.   495. barm: bosom.   496. gan to blisse: made a sign
of the cross over.   500. croys: cross.   501. thilke: that same.

That for us deyde upon a croys of tree,°
Thy soule, litel child, I hym bitake,°
For this nyght shaltow dyen for my sake."

I trowe that to a norice° in this cas
It hadde been hard this routhe° for to se;
Wel myghte a moder than han cryd "allas"!
But nathelees, so sad° stedefast was she
That she endured al adversitee,
And to the sergeant mekely she sayde,   510
"Have here agayn youre litel yonge mayde.

"Goth° now," quod she, "and doth my lordes
     heste.
But o thyng wol I pray yow, of youre grace,
That, but° my lord forbad yow, at the leste
Burieth this litel body in som place
That bestes° ne no briddes° it to-race."°
But he no word wol to that purpos seye,
But took the child, and wente upon his weye.

This sergeant cam unto his lord agayn,
And of Grisildis wordes and hir cheere   520
He tolde hym poynt for poynt in short and playn,
And hym presenteth with his doghter deere.
Somwhat this lord hath routhe° in his manere;
But, nathelees, his purpos held he stille,
As lordes doon whan they wol han hir wille,

And bad this sergeant that he pryvely
Sholde this child softe wynde° and wrappe,
With alle circumstances tendrely,
And carie it in a cofre° or in a lappe,°
But, upon peyne his heed of for to swappe,°   530
That no man sholde knowe of his entente,
Ne whennes° he cam, ne whider that he wente,

But at Boloigne° to his suster deere,
That thilke tyme of Panyk° was countesse,
He sholde it take and shewe° hire this matere,
Bisekynge hire to doon hir bisynesse°
This child to fostre in al gentilesse,
And whos child that it was, he bad hire hyde
From every wight for aught that may bityde.

The sergeant goth and hath fulfild this thyng.
But to this markys now retourne we,   541
For now goth he ful faste ymagynyng°
If by his wyves cheere he myghte se,

Or by hir word aperceyve, that she
Were chaunged, but he nevere hir koude fynde
But evere in oon° ylike sad° and kynde.

As glad, as humble, as bisy in servyse
And eek in love as she was wont to be
Was she to hym in every maner wise,°
Ne of hir doghter noght a word spak she.   550
Noon accident,° for noon adversitee,°
Was seyn in hire, ne nevere hir doghter° name
Ne nempned° she in ernest ne in game.

IV

In this estat ther passed ben foure yeer
Er she with childe was, but, as God wolde,
A knave child she bar by this Walter,
Ful gracious and fair for to biholde;
And, whan that folk it to his fader tolde,
Nat oonly he but al his contree merye
Was for this child, and God they thanke and
     herye.°   560

Whan it was two yeer old, and fro the brest
Departed° of his norice, on a day
This markys caughte yet another lest°
To tempte his wyf yet ofter° if he may.
O nedelees was she tempted in assay,
But wedded men ne knowe no mesure
Whan that they fynde a pacient creature!

"Wyf," quod this markys, "ye han herd er this
My peple sikly berth° oure mariage,
And, namely sith° my sone y-born is,   570
Now is it worse than evere in al oure age.
The murmur sleeth° myn herte and my corage,°
For to myn erys comth the voys so smerte°
That it wel neigh destroyed hath myn herte.

"Now sey they thus, 'Whan Walter is agon,°
Thanne shal the blood of Janicle succede
And been oure lord, for oother have we noon.'
Swiche wordes seith my peple out of drede.°
Wel oghte I of swich murmur taken hede,
For certeinly I drede swich sentence,°   580
Though they nat pleyn speke in myn audience.°

"I wolde lyve in pees, if that I myghte;
Wherfore I am disposed outrely,°

---

502. tree: wood.   503. hym bitake: to him commit.   505. no-rice: nurse.   506. routhe: sorrow.   508. sad: soberly.   512. Goth: go.   514. but: unless.   516. bestes: beasts.   briddes: birds. to-race: may (not) destroy.   523. routhe: pity.   527. wynde: swathe.   529. cofre: chest.   lappe: wrapper.   530. upon . . . swappe: on pain of having his head cut off.   532. whennes: whence.   533. Boloigne: Bologna.   534. Panyk: Panico. 535. shewe: explain to.   536. doon . . . bisynesse: exercise her diligence.   542. ymagynyng: wondering.

546. in oon: consistently.   sad: steadfast.   549. maner wise: sort of way.   551. Noon accident: no disturbance.   for . . . adversitee: no matter what the adversity.   552. doghter: daughter's.   553. nempned: named.   560. herye: praise. 562. Departed: taken.   563. caughte . . . lest: was again seized with another desire.   564. ofter: once more.   569. sikly berth: are dissatisfied with.   570. namely sith: particularly since. 572. sleeth: pierces.   corage: spirit.   573. smerte: bitterly. 575. agon: gone.   578. out of drede: without a doubt.   580. sentence: opinion.   581. audience: hearing.   583. outrely: utterly.

As I his suster served by nyghte,
Right so thenke I to serve hym pryvely.
This warne I yow that ye nat sodeynly
Out of yourself for no wo sholde outraye.°
Beth pacient, and therof I yow praye."

"I have," quod she, "seyd thus and evere
    shal:
I wol nothyng, ne nyl° nothyng, certeyn,   590
But as yow list. Noght greveth me at al
Thogh that my doghter and my sone be sleyn —
At youre comandement, this is to seyn.
I have nat had no part of children tweyne°
But first siknesse, and after wo and peyne.

"Ye ben oure lord. Dooth with youre owene thyng
Right as yow list. Axeth no reed° of me,
For, as I lefte at hom al my clothyng
Whan I first cam to yow, right so," quod she,
"Lefte I my wyl and al my libertee   600
And took youre clothyng; wherfore, I yow preye,
Dooth youre plesance. I wol youre lust° obeye.

"And certes if I hadde prescience°
Youre wyl to knowe, er ye youre lust me tolde,
I wolde it doon withouten necligence.
But now I woot° youre lust and what ye wolde.
Al youre plesance° ferme and stable I holde,
For wiste I° that my deeth wolde doon yow ese,°
Right gladly wolde I dyen yow to plese.

"Deeth may nat make no comparisoun   610
Unto youre loue." And whan this markys say°
The constance of his wyf, he caste adoun
His eyen two and wondreth that she may
In pacience suffre al this array;
And forth he goth with drery contenance,
But to his herte it was ful gret plesance.

    This ugly sergeant, in the same wyse
That he hir doghter caughte,° right so he —
Or worse, if men kan worse devyse° —
Hath hent° hir sone that ful was of beautee;   620
And evere in oon so pacient was she
That she no cheere made of hevynesse,
But kiste hir sone and after gan it blesse,

Save this: she preyde hym that, if he myghte,
Hir litel sone he wolde in erthe grave,°
His tendre lymes delicat to sighte
Fro foweles and fro bestes for to save.

But she noon answere of hym mighte have.
He wente his wey as hym nothyng ne roghte,°
But to Boloigne he tendrely it broghte.   630

This markys wondreth ever lenger° the moore
Upon hir pacience; and, if that he
Ne hadde soothly knowen ther bifoore
That parfitly hir childen loved she,
He wolde have wend° that of som subtiltee
And of malice or of cruel corage
That she hadde suffred this with sad visage.

But wel he knew that, next hymself, certayn,
She loved hir children best in every wise.
But now of wommen wolde I asken fayn°   640
If thise assayes myghte nat suffise.
What koude a sturdy housbond moore devyse
To preve° hir wifhod and hir stedfastnesse,
And he contynuynge evere in sturdynesse?°

But ther ben folk of swich condicioun
That, whan they have a certeyn purpos take,
They kan nat stynte of hir entencioun,
But, right as° they were bounden to that stake,
They wol nat of that firste purpos slake.°
Right so this markys fulliche° hath purposed   650
To tempte his wyf as he was first disposed.

He wayteth if by word or contenance
That she to hym was chaunged of corage,
But nevere koude he fynde variance,
She was ay oon in herte and in visage,
And ay the ferther that she was in age,
The moore trewe, if that it were possible,
She was to hym in love and moore penyble.°

For which it semed thus that of hem two
Ther nas but o° wyl, for as Walter leste,   660
The same lust was hir plesance also;
And, God be thanked, al fil° for the beste.
She shewed wel for no° worldly unreste
A wif as of hirself nothyng ne sholde
Wille in effect but as hir housbond wolde.

    The sclaundre° of Walter ofte and wyde spradde
That of a cruel herte he wikkedly,
For° he a poure womman wedded hadde,
Hath mordred bothe his children pryvely.
Swich murmur was among hem comunly.   670
No wonder is,° for to the peples ere
Ther cam no word but that they mordred were.

587. outraye: become overwhelmed.   590. nyl: shall (I) wish.
594. tweyne: two.   597. reed: advice.   602. lust: pleasure.
603. prescience: foreknowledge.   606. woot: know.   607. plesance: pleasure.   608. wiste I: if I knew.   doon yow ese:
satisfy you.   611. say: saw.   618. caughte: seized.   619. devyse: imagine.   620. hent: taken.   625. grave: bury.

629. as . . . roghte: as if he did not care at all.   631. lenger:
the longer.   635. wend: supposed.   640. wolde fayn: would
like to.   643. preve: test.   644. sturdynesse: sternness.
648. right as: just as if.   649. slake: desist.   650. fulliche:
fully.   658. penyble: sacrificing.   660. o: one.   662. fil: befell.
663. for no: despite any.   666. sclaundre: slander.   668. For:
because.   671. is: it is.

For which, wheras his peple ther bifore
Hadde loved hym wel, the sclaundre of his diffame
Made hem that they hym hated therfore.
To ben a mordrere is an hateful name.
But, nathelees, for ernest ne for game
He of his cruel purpos nolde stente.°
To tempte his wyf was set al his entente

   Whan that his doghter twelve yeer was of age,
He to the court of Rome, in subtil° wise   681
Enformed of his wil, sente his message,°
Comaundynge hem swiche bulles° to devyse
As to his cruel purpos may suffise
How that the pope as for his peples reste°
Bad hym to wedde another if hym leste.

I seye, he bad they sholde contrefete°
The popes bulles, makyng mencioun
That he hath leve his firste wyf to lete°
As by the popes dispensacioun   690
To stynte rancour and dissencioun
Bitwixe his peple and hym; thus seyde the bulle
The which they han publissed at the fulle.°

   The rude peple, as it no wonder is,
Wenden ful wel that it hadde ben right so.
But whan thise tidynges cam to Grisildis,
I deme that hir herte was ful wo,
But she, ylike sad° for evere mo,
Disposed was this humble creature
Th' adversitee of fortune al t' endure,   700

Abidynge evere his lust and his plesance
To whom that she was yeven herte and al
As to hir verray worldly suffisance.
But, shortly if this storie telle I shal,
This markys writen hath in special
A lettre in which he sheweth his entente,
And secrely he to Boloigne it sente.

To the erl of Panyk which that hadde tho°
Wedded his suster, preyde he specially
To bryngen hom agayn his children two   710
In honurable estat al openly;
But o thyng he hym prayde outrely
That he to no wight, thogh men wolde enquere,
Sholde nat telle whos children that they were,

But seye the mayden sholde y-wedded be
Unto the markys of Saluce anon.
And as this erl was preyed, so dide he,
For at day set, he on his wey is gon

Toward Saluce, and lordes many oon
In riche array, this mayden for to gyde,   720
Hir yonge brother ridyng hir bisyde.

   Arrayed was toward hir mariage
This fresshe mayde ful of gemmes clere,°
Hir brother, which that seven yeer was of age,
Arrayed eek ful fressh in his manere.
And thus in gret noblesse and with glad cheere
Toward Saluces shapyng hir journey,
Fro day to day they ryden in hir wey.

V

   Among° al this, after his wikke usage,°
This markys, yet his wif to tempte moore   730
To the outreste preve° of hir corage,
Fully to han experience and loore°
If that she were as stedefast as bifore,
He on a day in open audience
Ful boistously° hath seyd hire this sentence:

   "Certes,° Grisilde, I hadde ynogh plesance
To han yow to my wyf for youre goodnesse,
As for your trouthe and for youre obeisance,
Noght for youre lynage ne for youre richesse;
But now knowe I in verray sothfastnesse°   740
That in gret lordshipe, if I wel avyse,°
Ther is gret servitute in sondry wyse.

"I may nat do as every plowman may.
My peple me constreyneth for to take
Another wyf, and crien day by day;
And eek the pope, rancour for to slake,
Consenteth it, that dar I undertake.°
And, trewely, thus muche I wol yow seye,
My newe wyf is comynge by the weye.

"Be strong of herte, and voyde° anon hir place,
And thilke dowere that ye broghten me   751
Tak it agayn, I graunte it of my grace.
Retourneth to youre fadres hous," quod he.
"No man may alwey han prosperitee.
With evene° herte I rede° yow t' endure
The strook of fortune or of aventure."°

   And she agayn answerde in pacience.
"My lord," quod she, "I woot and wiste°
    alwey
How that bitwixen youre magnificence
And my poverte no wight kan ne may   760
Maken comparisoun; it is no nay.°

678. nolde stente: wouldn't desist. 681. subtil: secret. 682. message: messengers. 683. bulles: papal bulls. 685. as . . . reste:
for the pacification of his (Walter's) people. 687. contrefete:
counterfeit. 689. lete: leave. 693. at the fulle: in full.
698. ylike sad: consistently steadfast. 708. tho: then.

723. clere: brilliant. 729. Among: during. wikke usage: cruel
custom. 731. outreste preve: uttermost proof. 732. loore:
knowledge. 735. boistously: roughly. 736. Certes: certainly.
740. sothfastnesse: truth. 741. avyse: consider. 747. undertake: vow. 750. voyde: vacate. 755. evene: steady. rede:
advise. 756. aventure: chance. 758. wiste: knew. 761. it
. . . nay: there's no denying.

I ne heeld° me nevere digne° in no manere
To be youre wyf, no, ne youre chambrere.°

"And in this hous ther° ye me lady made,
The heighe God take I for my witnesse —
And also wisly he my soule glade° —
I nevere heeld me lady ne maistresse
But humble servant to youre worthynesse,
And evere shal, whil that my lyf may dure,°
Aboven every worldly creature.   770

"That ye so longe of youre benygnytee
Han holden° me in honour and nobleye°
Whereas I was noght worthy for to be,
That thonke I God — and yow — to whom I
          preye,
Foryelde° it yow. Ther is namoore to seye.
Unto my fader gladly wol I wende
And with hym dwelle unto my lyves ende.

"Ther I was fostred of a child ful smal,
Til I be deed, my lyf ther wol I lede,
A wydewe clene in body, herte, and al;   780
For, sith I yaf° to yow my maydenhede°
And am youre trewe wyf, it is no drede,°
God shilde° swich a lordes wyf to take
Another man to housbond or to make.°

"And of youre newe wyf, God of his grace
So graunte yow wele° and prosperitee,
For I wol gladly yelden hire my place
In which that I was blisful wont to be;
For, sith it liketh yow, my lord," quod she,
"That whilom° weren al myn hertes reste,   790
That I shal goon, I wol goon whan yow leste.

"But, theras ye me profre swich dowaire
As I first broghte, it is wel in my mynde,
It were my wrecched clothes nothyng faire,
The whiche to me were hard now for to fynde.
O goode God, how gentil and how kynde
Ye semed by youre speche and youre visage
The day that maked was oure mariage.

"But sooth is seyd — algate° I fynde it trewe,
For in effect it proved is on me —   800
Love is noght old° as whan that it is newe.
But certes, lord, for noon° adversitee,
To dyen in the cas,° it shal nat be

That evere in word or werk I shal repente
That I yow yaf myn herte in hool° entente.

"My lord, ye woot that in my fadres place
Ye dide me strepe° out of my poure wede°
And richely me cladden of youre grace.
To yow broght I noght ellis, out of drede,°
But feith° and nakednesse and maydenhede.   810
And here agayn my clothyng I restore,
And eek my weddyng ryng for evere moore.

"The remenant of youre jewels redy be
Inwith youre chambre, dar I saufly sayn.
Naked out of my fadres hous," quod she,
"I cam, and naked moot I turne agayn.
Al youre plesance wol I folwen fayn.
But yet I hope it be nat youre entente
That I smoklees° out of youre paleys wente.

"Ye koude nat doon so dishoneste a thyng   820
That thilke wombe in which youre children leye
Sholde biforn the peple in my walkyng
Be seyn° al bare. Wherfore, I yow preye,
Lat me nat lyk a worm go by the weye.
Remembre yow, myn owene lord so deere,
I was youre wyf, thogh I unworthy weere.

"Wherfore, in gerdoun° of my maydenhede
Which that I broghte and noght agayn I bere,
As voucheth sauf° to yeve me to my mede°
But swich a smok as I was wont to were,   830
That I therwith may wrye° the wombe of here°
That was youre wyf, and here I take my leve
Of yow, myn owene lord, lest I yow greve."

"The smok," quod he, "that thow hast on thy
          bak,
Lat it be stille, and bere it forth with thee."
But wel unnethes° thilke word he spak
But wente his wey for routhe and for pitee.
Biforn the folk hirselven strepeth she,
And in hir smok with heed and foot al bare
Toward hir fader hous forth is she fare.   840

The folk hir folwen wepynge in hir weye,
And Fortune ay they cursen as they goon,
But she fro wepyng kepte hir eyen dreye,
Ne in this tyme word ne spak she noon.
Hir fader, that this tidynge herd anon,
Curseth the day and tyme that nature
Shoop° hym to be a lyves° creature.

---

762. heeld: considered. digne: worthy. 763. chambrere: chambermaid. 764. ther: where. 766. also ... glade: may he truly comfort my soul. 769. dure: last. 772. holden: maintained. nobleye: nobility. 775. Foryelde: repay. 781. yaf: gave. maydenhede: maidenhood. 782. drede: doubt. 783. shilde: forbid. 784. make: mate. 786. wele: welfare. 790. whilom: once. 799. algate: at least. 801. noght old: not the same when it is old. 802. for noon: no matter what the. 803. To ... cas: (even) in case of death.

805. hool: whole. 807. dide me strepe: had me stripped. wede: clothing. 809. out of drede: without doubt. 810. feith: fidelity. 819. smoklees: without a smock. 823. seyn: seen. 827. gerdoun: reward. 829. As ... sauf: vouchsafe. mede: reward. 831. wrye: conceal. here: her. 836. unnethes: hardly. 847. Shoop: shaped. lyves: living.

For, out of doute, this olde poure man
Was evere in suspect° of hir mariage,
For evere he demed sith that it bigan   850
That, whan the lord fulfild hadde his corage,°
Hym wolde thynke it were a disparage°
To his estat so lowe for t' alighte,°
And voyden° hire as soone as evere he myghte.

Agayns° his doghter hastiliche goth he,
For he by noyse of folk knew hir comynge,
And with hir olde cote as° it myghte be
He covered hire, ful sorwefully wepynge.
But on hir body myghte° he it nat brynge,
For rude was the clooth and she moore of age   860
By dayes fele° than at hir mariage.

Thus with hir fader for a certein space
Dwelleth this flour° of wifly pacience,
That neither by hir wordes ne hir face
Biforn the folk, ne eek in hir absence,
Ne shewed she that hir was doon° offence,
Ne of hir heighe estat no remembrance
Ne hadde she, as by° hir contenance.

No wonder is, for in hir grete estat
Hir goost° was evere in pleyn humylitee.   870
No tendre mouth, noon herte delicat,
No pompe, no semblant° of realtee,°
But ful of pacient benygnytee,
Discreet and pridelees, ay honurable,
And to hir housbonde evere meke and stable.

Men speke of Job, and moost for his humblesse,
As clerkes, whan hem lest,° kan wel endite,°
Namely of men; but as in soothfastnesse,°
Thogh clerkes preyse wommen but a lite,°
Ther kan no man in humblesse hym acquite   880
As wommen kan, ne kan be half so trewe
As wommen been, but it be falle of newe.°

VI

Fro Boloigne is this erl of Panyk come,
Of which the fame up sprong to moore and lesse,
And to the peples eres° alle and some
Was kouth° eek that a newe markisesse
He with hym broghte in swich pompe and richesse
That nevere was ther seyn with mannes eye
So noble array in al West Lumbardye.

The markys which that shoop and knew al
          this,
Er that this erl was come, sente his message   891
For thilke sely° poure Grisildis,
And she with humble herte and glad visage,
Nat with no swollen thoght in hir corage,
Cam at his heste° and on hir knees hir sette,
And reverently and wysly she hym grette.°

" Grisilde," quod he, " my wille is outrely°
This mayden that shal wedded been to me
Receyved be tomorwe as really°
As it possible is in myn hous to be,   900
And eek that every wight in his degree°
Have his estat in sittyng° and servyse
And heigh plesance as I kan best devyse.

" I have no wommen suffisant, certayn,
The chambres for t' arraye in ordynance°
After my lust,° and therfore wolde I fayn
That thyn were al swich manere governance.°
Thow knowest eek of old al my plesance.
Though thyn array be badde and yvel biseye,°
Do thow thy devoir at the leeste weye."°   910

" Nat oonly, lord, that I am glad," quod she,
" To doon youre lust, but I desire also
Yow for to serve and plese in my degree
Withouten feyntyng° and shal evere mo,
Ne nevere for no wele ne no wo
Ne shal the goost withinne myn herte stente°
To love yow best with al my trewe entente."

And with that word she gan the hous to dighte,°
And tables for to sette, and beddes make,
And peyned hire° to doon al that she myghte,   920
Preyynge the chambreres, for Goddes sake,
To hasten hem and faste swepe and shake.
And she, the mooste servysable of alle,
Hath every chambre arrayed and his halle.

Abouten undren° gan this erl alighte,°
That with hym broghte thise noble children tweye,
For which the peple ran to seen the sighte
Of hire array so richely biseye;
And thanne at erst° amonges hem° they seye°
That Walter was no fool thogh that hym leste   930
To chaunge his wyf, for it was for the beste.

---

849. in suspect: suspicious.   851. corage: will.   852. disparage: disparagement.   853. for t' alighte: to descend.   854. voy-
den: (would) expel.   855. Agayns: towards.   857. as: as best.
859. myghte: could.   861. fele: many.   863. flour: flower.
866. hir was doon: to her had been done.   868. as by: to judge
by.   870. goost: spirit.   872. semblant: appearance.   realtee:
regality.   877. hem lest: it pleases them.   endite: write.
878. as in soothfastnesse: in truth.   879. lite: little.   882. but
. . . newe: unless it has recently happened.   885. eres: ears.
886. kouth: known.   892. sely: innocent.   895. heste: command.   896. grette:
greeted.   897. outrely: entirely.   899. really: regally.   901. wight
. . . degree: person according to his social rank.   902. sittyng:
seating.   905. arraye in ordynance: arrange in order.   906. After
my lust: according to my pleasure.   907. manere governance:
kind of responsibility.   909. yvel biseye: poorly provided.
910. devoir . . . weye: duty at least.   914. feyntyng: fail.
916. stente: cease.   918. dighte: prepare.   920. peyned hire:
took pains.   925. undren: 9 A.M.   gan alighte: dismounted.
929. erst: first.   hem: themselves.   seye: say.

For she is fairer, as they demen alle,
Than is Grisilde and moore tendre of age,
And fairer fruyt bitwene hem sholde falle
And moore plesant for° hire heigh lynage;
Hir brother eek so fair was of visage,
That hem to seen the peple hath caught plesance,
Commendynge now the markys governance.°

"O stormy peple, unsad° and evere untrewe,
Ay undiscreet and chaungynge as a vane,°   940
Delitynge evere in rumbul° that is newe,
For lyk the moone ay wexe ye and wane,
Ay ful of clappyng deere ynow a jane!°
Youre doom° is fals, youre constance yvele
    preveth.°
A ful greet fool is he that on yow leveth."°

Thus seyden sadde° folk in that citee,
Whan that the peple gazed up and doun
For they were glad right° for the noveltee
To han a newe lady of hir toun.
Namoore of this make I now mencioun,   950
But to Grisilde agayn wol I me dresse°
And telle hir constance and hir bisynesse.°

Ful bisy was Grisilde in every thyng
That to the feste was apertinent.
Right noght was she abayst° of hir clothyng
Thogh it were rude and somdel eek to-rent,°
But with glad cheere she to the yate is went
With oother folk to greete the markysesse,
And after that dooth forth hir bisynesse.

With so glad cheere his gestes she receyveth,   960
And so konnyngly everich° in his degree,
That no defaute° no man aperceyveth,
But ay they wondren what she myghte be
That in so poure array was for to se
And koude° swich honour and reverence,
And worthily they preysen hir prudence.

In al this menewhile she ne stente°
This mayde and eek hir brother to commende
With al hir herte in ful benygne entente
So wel that no man koude hir pris amende.°   970
But at the laste, whan that thise lordes wende
To sitten doun to mete, he gan to calle
Grisilde as she was bisy in his halle.

"Grisilde," quod he, as it were in his pley,
"How liketh thee my wyf and hir beautee?"
"Right wel," quod she, "my lord, for, in good fey,°
A fairer saw I nevere noon than she.
I prey to God, yeve hire prosperitee,
And so hope I that he wol to yow sende
Plesance ynogh unto youre lyves ende.   980

"O thyng biseke° I yow, and warne also,
That ye ne prike° with no tormentynge
This tendre mayden as ye han don mo,°
For she is fostred in hir norissynge°
Moore tendrely, and, to my supposynge,
She koude nat adversitee endure
As koude a poure fostred creature."

And whan this Walter saw hir pacience,
Hir glade cheere, and no malice at al,
And he so ofte had doon to hire offence,   990
And she ay sad and constant as a wal,
Continuynge evere hir innocence over al,
This sturdy markys gan his herte dresse°
To rewen° upon hir wifly stedfastnesse.

"This is ynogh, Grisilde myn," quod he.
"Be now namoore agast ne yvele apayed.°
I have thy feith and thy benygnytee,
As wel as evere womman was, assayed
In greet estat and poureliche arrayed.
Now knowe I, deere wyf, thy stedfastnesse";   1000
And hire in armes took and gan hir kesse.

And she for wonder took of it no keep.°
She herde nat what thyng he to hir seyde.
She ferde as° she hadde stirt out of a sleep,
Til she out of hir mazednesse abreyde.°
"Grisilde," quod he, "by God that for us deyde,
Thow art my wyf, ne noon oother I have,
Ne nevere hadde, as God my soule save.

"This is thy doghter which thow hast supposed
To be my wyf; that oother, feithfully,   1010
Shal be myn heir, as I have ay disposed.
Thow bare hym in thy body, trewely.
At Boloigne have I kept hem pryvely.
Tak hem agayn, for now maistow° nat seye
That thow hast lorn noon° of thy children tweye.

"And folk that oother weys° han seyd of me,
I warne hem wel that I have doon this dede

For no malice ne for no crueltee
But for t' assaye in thee thy wommanhede,
And nat to sleen my children, God forbede,   1020
But for to kepe hem pryvely and stille
Til I thy purpos knewe and al thy wille."

Whan she this herde, aswowne° doun she falleth
For pitous joye, and after hir swownynge
She bothe hir yonge children to hire calleth,
And in hir armes pitously wepynge
Embraceth hem, and tendrely kissynge
Ful lyk a moder with hir salte teres
She bathed both hir visage and hir heres.°

O which° a pitous thyng it was to se   1030
Hir swownyng, and hir humble voys to heere!
"Graunt mercy,° lord. God thanke it yow," quod
    she,
"That ye han saved me my children deere.
Now rekke I nevere to been ded° right heere.
Sith I stonde in youre love and in youre grace,
No fors of° deeth, ne whan my spirit pace.°

"O tendre, o deere, o yonge children myne!
Youre woful moder wende° stedfastly
That cruel houndes or som foul vermyne
Hadde eten yow, but God of his mercy   1040
And youre benygne fader tendrely
Hath doon yow kept."° And in that same stounde°
Al sodeynly she swapte° adoun to grounde.

And in hir swough,° so sadly° holdeth she
Hir children two whan she gan hem t' embrace
That with greet sleighte° and greet difficultee
The children from hir arm they gonne arace.°
O, many a teer on many a pitous face
Doun ran of hem that stoden hir bisyde.
Unnethe° abouten hire myghte they abyde.°   1050

Walter hir gladeth and hir sorwe slaketh.
She riseth up abaysed° from hir traunce,
And every wight hir° joye and feste° maketh
Til she hath caught agayn° hir contenaunce.
Walter hir dooth so feithfully plesaunce
That it was deyntee° for to seen the cheere
Bitwix hem to, now they ben met y-feere.°

Thise ladies, whan that they hir tyme say,°
Han taken hire, and into chambre goon,
And strepen hire out of hir rude array;   1060
And in a clooth of gold that brighte shoon,°
With a coroune° of many a riche stoon
Upon hir hed, they into halle hir broghte,
And ther she was honured as hir oghte.

Thus hath this pitous day a blisful ende,
For every man and womman dooth his myght
This day in murthe and revel to dispende,
Til on the welkne° shoon the sterres lyght,
For moore solempne° in every mannes syght
This feste was and gretter of costage°   1070
Than was the revel of hir mariage.

Ful many a yeer in heigh prosperitee
Lyven thise two in concord and in reste;
And richely his doghter maried he
Unto a lord, oon of the worthieste
Of al Ytaille; and thanne in pees and reste
His wyves fader in his court he kepeth
Til that the soule out of his body crepeth.

His sone succedeth in his heritage
In reste and pees after his fader day,   1080
And fortunat was eek in mariage,
Al° putte he nat his wyf in gret assay.
This world is nat so strong — it is no nay —
As it hath been in olde tymes yore.
And herkneth what this auctour° seith therfore:

This storie is seyd, nat for that wyves sholde
Folwen° Grisilde as in humylitee,
For it were inportable° thogh they wolde,
But for that every wight in his degree
Sholde be constant in adversitee   1090
As was Grisilde; therfore Petrak writeth
This storie, which with heigh stile he enditeth.

For, sith a womman was so pacient
Unto a mortal man, wel moore us oghte
Receyven al in gree° that God us sent.°
For greet skile is,° he preve that he wroghte;°
But he ne tempteth no man that he boghte,°
As seith Seint Jame, if ye his Pistel° rede.
He preveth folk al day, it is no drede,°

And suffreth us as for oure excercise   1100
With sharpe scourges of adversitee

1023. **aswowne**: in a swoon.   1029. **both . . . heres**: the face and hair of both of them.   1030. **which**: what.   1032. **Graunt mercy**: much thanks.   1034. **rekke . . . ded**: I care never even if I were dead.   1036. **No . . . of**: no matter for.   **pace**: pass on.   1038. **wende**: believed.   1042. **doon . . . kept**: caused you to be saved.   **stounde**: moment.   1043. **swapte**: sank.   1044. **swough**: swoon.   **sadly**: firmly.   1046. **sleighte**: care.   1047. **gonne arace**: removed.   1050. **Unnethe**: hardly.   **abyde**: remain.   1052. **abaysed**: abashed.   1053. **hir**: for her.   **feste**: happiness.   1054. **caught agayn**: recovered.   1056. **deyntee**: a delight.   1057. **y-feere**: together.

1058. **hir . . . say**: their opportunity saw.   1061. **shoon**: shone.   1062. **coroune**: coronet.   1068. **welkne**: heavens.   1069. **solempne**: magnificent.   1070. **costage**: expense.   1082. **Al**: even if.   1085. **auctour**: author (Petrarch).   1087. **Folwen**: follow.   1088. **inportable**: intolerable.   1095. **in gree**: submissively.   **sent**: sends.   1096. **skile is**: reason (there) is.   **preve . . . wroghte**: test what he has made.   1097. **boghte**: redeemed.   1098. **Pistel**: St. James's Epistle.   1099. **drede**: doubt.

Ful ofte to be bete° in sondry wise,
Nat for to knowe oure wyl, for certes he,
Er we were born, knew al oure freletee,°
And for oure beste is al his governance.
Lat us thanne lyve in vertuous suffrance.°

THE NUN'S PRIEST'S TALE

In the General Prologue Chaucer did not develop the character of the three priests riding in the Prioress's retinue, perhaps because he felt that their quietness would lend emphasis to the aristocratic stateliness of the Prioress. But, in any case, the one priest for whom Chaucer supplied a tale, though he is not described in the Prologue, amply expresses his personality now.

He tells an ancient animal fable which in France and Germany had been incorporated into the poetic treatment of the life of the wily Reynard the Fox, a popular folk character. But, with a subtlety of wit which foreshadows the poetry of Pope four centuries later, he elevates the fate of Chauntecleer to a mock-heroic level, turning barnyard creatures into caricatures of human beings and their discussions of the validity of dreams into a satire of scientific thought.

As narrator the Priest plays the part of an unpretentious and unlearned man, but his allusions and judgments suggest that of all the pilgrims he is one of the best informed. He is well-read in both secular and religious subjects. He knows the theories of literary composition advocated by Geoffrey de Vinsauf, and he is equally familiar with the authorities who have written on the theological problem of God's foreknowledge and man's freedom of will. And underneath his playful tone, there runs a note of seriousness, for tactfully but firmly he turns his tale at its conclusion into a sermon.

A poure widwe, somdel stape° in age,
Was whilom° dwellynge in a narwe° cotage
Biside a grove, stondyng in a dale.
This widwe of which I telle yow my tale,
Syn thilke° day that she was last a wyf,
In pacience ladde a ful symple lyf,
For litel was hire catel° and hire rente.°
By housbondrye of swich° as God hire sente
She foond° hireself and eek° hire doghtren° two.
Thre large sowes hadde she and namo,°   10
Thre kyn,° and eek a sheep that highte° Malle.
Ful sooty was hire bour° and eek hire halle,
In which she eet ful many a sklendre° meel.
Of poynaunt° sauce hir neded° never a deel.°

No deyntee morsel passed thurgh hir throte;
Hir diet was acordant to hir cote.°
Repleccioun ne made hire nevere syk;
Attempree° diete was al hir phisyk,
And excercise, and hertes suffisaunce.°
The goute lette° hire nothyng° for to daunce,   20
N' apoplexie shente nat hir heed.°
No wyn ne drank she, neither whit ne reed.
Hir bord° was served moost with whit and blak,
Milk and broun breed, in which she foond no lak,°
Seynd° bacoun, and som tyme an ey° or tweye,
For she was, as it were, a maner deye.°
A yeerd she hadde, enclosed al aboute
With stikkes, and a drye dych° withoute,
In which she hadde a cok heet° Chauntecleer.
In al the land of crowyng nas° his peer.   30
His voys was murier° than the myrie orgon
On massedayes that in the chirche gon.°
Wel sikerer° was his crowyng in his logge°
Than is a clokke or any abbey orlogge.°
By° nature° he knew ech ascensioun
Of the equinoxial in thilke toun,
For whan degrees fiftene were ascended,
Thanne krew he that it myghte nat ben amended.°
His comb was redder than the fyn coral
And batailled as° it were a castel wal.   40
His byle° was blak, and as the jeet° it shoon.
Lyk asure° were hise legges and his toon,°
Hise nayles whitter than the lylye flour,
And lyk the burned° gold was his colour.
This gentil cok hadde in his governaunce°
Sevene hennes for to doon al his plesaunce,°
Whiche were hise sustres° and his paramours,
And wonder° lyke to hym as of colours,
Of whiche the faireste hewed on hire throte
Was cleped° faire damoysele Pertelote.   50
Curteys she was, discreet, and debonaire,
And compaignable, and bar° hirself so faire
Syn thilke day that she was seven nyght oold
That, trewely, she hath the herte in hoold
Of Chauntecleer, loken° in every lith.°

16. cote: means.   18. Attempree: temperate.   19. suffisaunce: sufficiency.   20. lette: hindered.   nothyng: in no way.   21. N' apoplexie . . . heed: nor did apoplexy trouble her head.   23. bord: table.   24. foond . . . lak: found no fault.   25. Seynd: broiled. ey: egg.   26. maner deye: sort of dairywoman.   28. dych: ditch.   29. heet: named.   30. nas: (there) was not.   31. murier: merrier.   32. gon: plays.   33. Wel sikerer: much more accurate.   logge: lodge.   34. orlogge: horologe (clock).   35-37. The sphere of the stars was thought of as rotating 360 degrees every twenty-four hours around the earth's equator. The equinoctial circle of the heaven thus turns or "ascends" 15 degrees every hour.   35. nature: instinct.   38. that . . . amended: so that it couldn't be bettered.   40. batailled as: battlemented as if.   41. byle: bill.   jeet: jet.   42. asure: azure.   toon: toes.   44. burned: burnished.   45. governaunce: control.   46. plesaunce: pleasure.   47. sustres: sisters (sweethearts).   48. wonder: wonderfully.   50. cleped: called.   52. bar: conducted.   55. loken: locked.   lith: limb.

1102. bete: beaten.   1104. freletee: frailty.   1106. suffrance: submission.   NUN'S PRIEST'S TALE.   1. widwe . . . stape: widow somewhat advanced.   2. whilom: once.   narwe: small.   5. Syn thilke: since that same.   7. catel: property.   rente: income. 8. swich: such.   9. foond: supported.   eek: also.   doghtren: daughters.   10. namo: no more.   11. kyn: cows.   highte: was called.   12. bour: bedroom.   13. sklendre: slender.   14. poynaunt: pungent.   hir neded: she needed.   deel: bit.

He loved hire so that wel was hym ther-with.°
But swich a joye was it to here hem° synge,
Whan that the brighte sonne gan to sprynge,°
In swete acord "My leef is faren in londe."°
For thilke° tyme, as I have understonde,   60
Beestes and briddes° koude speke and synge.

And so bifel that in a dawenynge,°
As Chauntecleer among hise wyves alle
Sat on his perche, that was in the halle,
And next hym sat this faire Pertelote,
This Chauntecleer gan gronen° in his throte
As man that in his dreem is drecched° soore.

And whan that° Pertelote thus herde hym rore,
She was agast and seyde, "Herte deere,
What eyleth yow to grone in this manere?   70
Ye ben a verray° slepere. Fy, for shame!"

And he answerde and seyde thus: "Madame,
I prey yow that ye take it nat agrief.°
By God, me mette° I was in swich meschief
Right now that yet myn herte is soore afright.
Now God," quod° he, "my swevene recche°
     aright,
And kepe my body out of foul prisoun.
Me mette how that I romed up and doun
Withinne oure yeerd, where-as I say° a beest,
Was lyk an hound and wolde han maad areest°   80
Upon my body and han° had me deed.
His colour was bitwixe yelow and reed,
And tipped was his tayl and bothe hise erys°
With blak unlik the remenaunt° of hise herys,°
His snowte smal, with glowyng eyen° tweye.
Yet of his look for fere almoost I deye.
This caused me my gronyng, doutelees."

"Avoy!"° quod she. "Fy on yow, hertelees!°
Allas," quod she, "for, by that God above,
Now han ye lost myn herte and al my love.   90
I kan nat love a coward, by my feith!
For, certes,° what so° any womman seith,
We alle desiren, if it myghte be,
To han housbondes hardy, wise, and fre,°
And secree,° and no nygard, ne no fool,
Ne hym that is agast of every tool,°
Ne noon avauntour,° by that God above.
How dorste° ye seyn, for shame, unto youre love
That any thyng myghte make yow aferd?
Have ye no mannes herte and han a berd?   100

"Allas, and konne ye ben agast° of swevenys!°
Nothyng, God woot,° but vanytee in swevene is.
Swevenes engendren of replexions,°
And ofte of fume° and of complexions,°
Whan humours ben to habundant in a wight.°

"Certes, this dreem which ye han met to-nyght°
Comth of the grete superfluytee
Of youre rede colera,° pardee,°
Which causeth folk to dreden° in hir° dremes
Of arwes,° and of fyr with rede lemes,°   110
Of rede bestes that they wol hem byte,
Of contek,° and of whelpes grete and lyte,
Right° as the humour of malencolie
Causeth ful many a man in sleep to crie
For fere of blake beres,° or boles° blake,
Or elles blake develes, wol hem° take.
Of othere humours koude I telle also
That werken° many a man in sleep ful wo,°
But I wol passe as lightly as I kan.
Lo Catoun,° which that was so wys a man,   120
Seyde he nat thus: 'Ne do no fors of° dremes'?

"Now sire," quod she, "whan we fle° fro the
     bemes,
For Goddes love, as taak° som laxatif.
Up° peril of my soule and of my lif,
I conseille yow the beste, I wol nat lye,
That bothe of colere and of malencolye
Ye purge yow. And, for° ye shal nat tarye,
Thogh in this toun is noon° apothecarye,
I shall myself to herbes techen° yow
That shul ben for youre heele° and for youre
     prow.°   130
And in oure yerd tho° herbes shal I fynde
The whiche han° of hire propretee by kynde°
To purge yow bynethe and eek° above.
Foryet nat this, for Goddes owene love:
Ye ben ful colerik of complexioun.
Ware° the sonne in his ascensioun,
Ne fynde yow nat replet of° humours hote,
And, if it do, I dar wel leye a grote°
That ye shul have a fevere terciane°

101. agast: afraid.   swevenys: dreams.   102. woot: knows.
103. engendren . . . replexions: are engendered from repletion.
104. fume: vapor.   complexions: temperaments.   105. humours
. . . wight: humors are too abundant in a person. A superabun-
dance of any one of the four humors affected the temperament.
106. han . . . to-nyght: have dreamed this night.   108. rede
colera: red choler.   pardee: certainly.   109. dreden: be
frightened.   hir: their.   110. arwes: arrows.   lemes: flames.
112. contek: strife.   113. Right: just.   115. beres: bears.
boles: bulls.   116. wol hem: (which) will them.   118. werken:
make.   wo: woeful.   120. Catoun: Dionysius Cato, to whom a
well-known collection of Latin maxims was ascribed.   121. Ne
. . . of: pay no attention to.   122. fle: fly down.   123. as taak:
take.   124. Up: upon.   127. for: in order that.   128. noon:
no.   129. techen: direct.   130. heele: healing.   prow: well-
being.   131. tho: those.   132. The . . . han: which have.
kynde: nature.   133. eek: also.   136. Ware: beware that.
137. replet of: overfilled with.   138. grote: groat (4d.).   139.
terciane: tertian (recurring every other day).

56. wel . . . ther-with: he was well contented.   57. hem: them.
58. gan to sprynge: began to rise.   59. leef . . . londe: sweetheart
has gone to the country.   60. thilke: (at) that.   61. briddes:
birds.   62. in a dawenynge: one dawn.   66. gan gronen: began to
groan.   67. drecched: tormented.   68. whan that: when.
71. verray: sound.   73. agrief: ill.   74. me mette: I dreamed.
76. quod: said.   my . . . recche: may my dream work out.
79. where-as . . . say: where I saw.   80. han . . . areest:
have seized.   81. han: have.   83. erys: ears.   84. rem-
enaunt: rest.   herys: hair.   85. eyen: eyes.   88. Avoy:
shame.   hertelees: faintheart.   92. certes: certainly.   what so:
whatever.   94. fre: generous.   95. secree: discreet.   96. tool:
weapon.   97. avauntour: boaster.   98. dorste: dared.

Or an agu that may be youre bane.°   140
A day or two ye shul have digestyves
Of wormes er° ye take youre laxatyves
Of lauriol,° centaure,° and fumetere,°
Or elles of ellebor° that groweth there,
Of katapuce,° or of gaitrys beryis,°
Of herbe yve° growyng in oure yerd, ther merye
    is.°
Pekke hem up right as they growe, and ete hem in.
Be myrie, housbonde, for youre fader kyn!°
Dredeth no dreem. I kan sey yow namoore."
    "Madame," quod he, "graunt mercy of youre
    loore.°   150
But nathelees, as touchyng daun Catoun,°
That hath of wisdom swich° a gret renoun,
Thogh that he bad no dremes for to drede,
By God, men may in olde bokes rede
Of many a man moore of auctoritee
Than evere Catoun was, so mote I thee,°
That al the revers° seyn of his sentence°
And han wel founden by experience
That dremes ben° significaciouns
As wel of joye as of tribulaciouns   160
That folk enduren in this lyf present.
Ther nedeth° make of this noon argument;
The verray preeve° sheweth it in dede.
    "Oon° of the gretteste auctor° that men rede
Seith thus, that whilom° two felawes° wente
On pilgrymage in a ful good entente,
And happed so they coomen in a toun
Where-as ther was swich congregacioun
Of peple and eek so streit of herbergage°
That they ne founde as muche as a cotage   170
In which they bothe myghte y-logged° be.
Wherfore they mosten° of necessitee,
As for° that nyght, departen° compaignye,
And ech of hem gooth to his hostelrye
And took his loggyng as it wolde falle.
That oon of hem was logged in a stalle
Fer in a yeerd° with oxen of the plow.
That oother man was logged wel ynow°
As was his aventure° or his fortune,
That us governeth alle as in commune.°   180

"And so bifel that, longe er it were day,
This man mette° in his bed ther-as° he lay
How that his felawe gan upon hym calle
And seyde, 'Allas, for in an oxes stalle
This nyght I shal be mordred ther° I lye.
Now help me, deere brother, or I dye.
In alle haste com to me,' he sayde.
    "This man out of his sleep for feere
    abrayde,°
But whan that he was wakned of his sleep,
He turned hym and took of this no keep.°   190
Hym thoughte° his dreem nas but° a vanytee.
Thus twies° in his slepyng dremed he,
And atte thridde tyme yet his felawe
Cam, as hym thoughte, and seyde, 'I am now
    slawe.°
Bihoold my blody woundes, depe and wyde.
Arys up erly in the morwe tyde,°
And at the west gate of the toun,' quod he,
'A carte ful of donge ther shaltow se,°
In which my body is hid ful pryvely.°
Do thilke° carte aresten° boldely.   200
My gold caused my mordre, sooth to seyn ';°
And tolde hym every poynt how he was slayn
With a ful pitous face pale of hewe.
And truste wel his dreem he fond° ful trewe,
For on the morwe, as soone as it was day,
To his felawes in° he took the way,
And whan that he cam to this oxes stalle,
After° his felawe he bigan to calle.
    "The hostiler answerde hym anon°
And seyde, 'Sire, youre felawe is agon.   210
As soone as day he wente out of the toun.'
    "This man gan fallen in suspicioun,
Remembrynge on hise dremes that he mette,
And forth he gooth, no lenger wolde he lette,°
Unto the west gate of the toun and fond
A dong carte, wente° as it were to donge° lond,
That was arrayed in the same wise
As ye han herd the dede man devyse,°
And with an hardy herte he gan to crye
Vengeaunce and justice of this felonye.   220
'My felawe mordred in this same nyght,
And in this carte heere he lyth gapyng
    upright.°
I crye out on the mynystres,'° quod he,
'That sholden kepe and reulen this citee.
Harrow,° allas! Heere lyth my felawe slayn!'

---

140. bane: destruction.   142. er: before.   143. lauriol: spurge
laurel. centaure: centaury. fumetere: fumitory.   144. elle-
bor: hellebore.   145. katapuce: caper spurge. gaitrys beryis:
gaiter-tree berries (dogwood).   146. herbe yve: ground ivy.
ther . . . is: where it is pleasant.   148. fader kyn: father's kin.
150. graunt . . . loore: much thanks for your instruction.   151.
daun Catoun: Master Cato.   152. swich: such.   156. mote
I thee: may I prosper.   157. revers: contrary. sentence:
opinion.   159. ben: are.   162. Ther nedeth: there is (no)
need to.   163. verray preeve: very proof.   164. Oon: one.
auctor: author(s).   165. whilom: once. felawes: companions.
169. streit of herbergage: short of lodgings.   171. y-logged:
lodged.   172. mosten: must.   173. As for: for. departen:
part.   177. Fer . . . yeerd: far off in a courtyard.   178. ynow:
enough.   179. aventure: lot.   180. alle . . . commune: all in
common.

182. mette: dreamed. ther-as: where.   185. ther: where.
188. abrayde: awoke.   190. keep: heed.   191. Hym thoughte:
it seemed to him. nas but: was only.   192. twies: twice.
194. slawe: slain.   196. morwe tyde: morning time.   198.
shaltow se: you will see.   199. ful pryvely: very secretly.   200.
Do thilke: have that same. aresten: stopped.   201. sooth to
seyn: truth to tell.   204. fond: found.   206. felawes in: companion's lodging.   208. After: for.   209. anon: at once.
214. lette: stay.   216. wente: (which) went. donge: manure,
fertilize.   218. devyse: describe.   222. upright: face-upward.
223. mynystres: officers.   225. Harrow: help.

What sholde I moore unto this tale sayn?
The peple out sterte° and caste the cart to grounde,
And in the myddel of the dong they founde
The dede man, that mordred was al newe.°
"O blisful God, that art so just and trewe,   230
Lo how that thow biwreyest° mordre alway.
Mordre wol out, that se° we day by day.
Mordre is so wlatsom° and abhomynable
To God, that is so just and resonable,
That he ne wol nat suffre it heled° be,
Thogh it abyde° a yeer, or two, or thre.
Mordre wol out, this is my conclusioun.
And right anon ministres of that toun
Han hent° the cartere and so soore hym pyned°
And eek the hostiler so soore engyned°   240
That they biknewe° hir wikkednesse anon
And were an-hanged by the nekke bon.°
"Heere may men seen that dremes ben to
    drede.°
And, certes, in the same book I rede,
Right in the nexte chapitre after this —
I gabbe° nat, so have I° joye or blys —
Two men that wolde han passed over see
For certeyn cause into a fer contree,
If that the wynd ne hadde ben contrarie,
That made hem in a citee for to tarie,   250
That stood ful myrie° upon an haven° syde.
But on a day, agayn the even tyde,°
The wynd gan chaunge and blew right as hem
    leste.°
Jolif° and glad they wente unto hir° reste
And casten hem° ful erly for to saille.
"But herkneth! To that o° man fil° a greet
    mervaille,
That oon of hem, in slepyng as he lay,
Hym mette a wonder° dreem agayn° the day.
Hym thoughte a man stood by his beddes syde,
And hym comanded that he sholde abyde,   260
And seyde hym thus: 'If thow tomorwe wende,°
Thow shalt be dreynt.° My tale is at an ende.'
He wook, and tolde his felawe what he mette,
And preyde hym his viage° to lette.°
As for that day, he preyde hym to abyde.
His felawe, that lay by his beddes syde,
Gan for to laughe and scorned hym ful faste.
'No dreem,' quod he, 'may so myn herte agaste°

That I wol lette for to do my thynges.°
I sette nat a straw by thy dremynges,   270
For swevenes ben but vanytees and japes.°
Men dreme alday° of owles and of apes
And of many a maze° therwithal;
Men dreme of thyng that nevere was ne shal.°
But, sith I see that thow wolt here abyde,
And thus forslewthen wilfully° thy tyde,°
God woot,° it reweth me,° and have good day!'
And thus he took his leve and wente his way,
But er that° he hadde half his cours y-seyled,
Noot I° nat why ne° what meschaunce it eyled,°
But casuelly° the shippes botme rente,°   281
And ship and man under the water wente
In sighte of othere shippes it bisyde°
That with hem seyled at the same tyde.
And therfore, faire Pertelote so deere,
By swiche ensamples° olde maystow leere°
That no man sholde been to recchelees°
Of dremes, for I sey thee, doutelees,
That many a dreem ful soore is for to dred.°
"Lo, in the lyf of Seint Kenelm I rede,   290
That was Kenulphus sone,° the noble kyng
Of Mercenrike,° how Kenelm mette a thyng.
A lite er° he was mordred on a day,
His mordre in his avysioun° he say.°
His norice° hym expowned every del°
His swevene, and bad hym for to kepe hym° wel
For° traisoun, but he nas but° sevene yeer old,
And therfore litel tale° hath he told°
Of any dreem, so holy was his herte.
By God, I hadde levere than my sherte°   300
That ye hadde rad° his legende as have I.
Dame Pertelote, I sey yow trewely,
Macrobeus,° that writ° the avysioun
In Affrike of the worthy Cipioun,°
Affermeth dremes and seith that they ben
Warnynge of thynges that men after sen.°
And forther-moore, I pray yow, looketh wel

269. lette . . . thynges: stop doing my business.   **271. japes:** follies.   **272. alday:** every day.   **273. maze:** wonder.   **274. ne shal:** nor shall (be).   **276. forslewthen wilfully:** squander willingly.   **tyde:** time.   **277. woot:** knows.   **it . . . me:** I rue it.   **279. er that:** before.   **280. Noot I:** I don't know.   **ne:** nor.   **eyled:** ailed.   **281. casuelly:** by chance.   **rente:** burst.   **it bisyde:** beside it.   **286. ensamples:** examples.   **maystow leere:** you may learn.   **287. to recchelees:** too heedless.   **289. soore . . . dred:** sorely is to be feared.   **291. Kenulphus sone:** Kenulphus' son. Kenelm dreamed that he had to fly to Heaven; subsequently he was murdered by his aunt.   **292. Mercenrike:** Mercia (central England).   **293. lite er:** little before.   **294. avysioun:** vision.   **say:** saw.   **295. norice:** nurse.   **expowned . . . del:** expounded completely.   **296. for . . . hym:** to guard himself.   **297. For:** against.   **nas but:** was only.   **298. tale:** heed.   **told:** paid.   **300. I . . . sherte:** I would (wish) rather than (that I had) my shirt.   **301. rad:** read.   **303. Macrobeus:** The commentary by Macrobius on Cicero's account of the dream of Scipio Africanus Minor was regarded as a standard authority on dream lore.   **writ:** writes.   **304. Cipioun:** Scipio.   **306. after sen:** afterwards see.

227. sterte: sprang.   **229. al newe:** just recently.   **231. biwreyest:** dost reveal.   **232. se:** see.   **233. wlatsom:** foul.   **235. heled:** concealed.   **236. abyde:** await.   **239. hent:** seized.   **pyned:** tortured.   **240. engyned:** racked.   **241. biknewe:** confessed.   **242. bon:** bone.   **243. ben to drede:** are to be feared.   **246. gabbe:** exaggerate.   **have I:** may I have.   **251. myrie:** pleasant.   **haven:** harbor.   **252. agayn . . . tyde:** towards evening time.   **253. hem leste:** they wished.   **254. Jolif:** jolly.   **hir:** their.   **255. casten hem:** decided.   **256. o:** one.   **fil:** befell.   **258. Hym . . . wonder:** dreamed a wonderful.   **agayn:** before.   **261. wende:** travel.   **262. dreynt:** drowned.   **264. viage:** voyage.   **lette:** delay.   **268. agaste:** frighten.

In the Olde Testament, of Daniel,°
If he heeld dremes any vanytee.
Rede eek of Joseph, and there shul ye see   310
Wher° dremes be somtyme, I sey nat alle,
Warnynge of thynges that shul after falle.
Looke of Egipte the kyng, daun Pharao,°
His bakere, and his butiller also,
Wher they ne felte noon effect in dremes.
Who-so° wol seke actes of sondry remes°
May rede of dremes many a wonder thyng.
Lo Cresus,° which that was of Lyde kyng,
Mette he nat° that he sat upon a tree,
Which signified he sholde an-hanged be?   320
Lo heere Andromacha,° Ectores° wyf,
That day that Ector sholde lese° his lyf,
She dremed on the same nyght biforn
How that the lyf of Ector sholde be lorn°
If thilke° day he wente in to bataille.
She warned hym, but it myghte nat availle;
He wente for to fighte, nathelees.°
But he was slayn anon of° Achilles.
But thilke tale is al to° long to telle,
And eek it is ny° day. I may nat dwelle.   330
  " Shortly I seye, as for conclusioun,
That I shal han of this avysioun
Adversitee, and I seye forther-moor
That I ne telle of laxatyves no stoor,°
For they ben venymes,° I woot it wel.
I hem deffye! I love hem never a del!°
  " Now lat us speke of myrthe and stynte° al this.
Madame Pertelote, so have I° blis,
Of o thyng God hath sent me large grace,
For whan I se the beautee of youre face,   340
Ye ben so scarlet reed aboute youre eyen,
It maketh al my drede for to dyen,
For, also siker as *In principio,*°
'*Mulier est hominis confusio.*'°
  " Madame, the sentence° of this Latyn is,
' Womman is mannes joye and al his blis.'
For whan I feele a-nyght youre softe syde,

Al be it that I may nat on yow ryde
For that° oure perche is maad° so narwe,° allas,
I am so ful of joye and of solas°   350
That I deffye bothe swevene° and dreem."
  And with that word he fley° doun fro the beem,
For it was day, and eke hise hennes alle.
And with a chuk he gan hem for to calle,
For he hadde founde a corn,° lay° in the yerd.
Real° he was; he was na moore aferd.°
He fethered Pertelote twenty tyme
And trad° as ofte er that it was pryme.°
He looketh as it were° a grym leoun,°
And on hise toos he rometh up and doun.   360
Hym deyned° nat to sette his foot to grounde.
He chukketh whan he hath a corn y-founde,
And to hym rennen thanne hise wyves alle.
Thus real as a prince is in his halle
Leve I this Chauntecleer in his pasture,
And after wol I telle his aventure.
  Whan that the monthe in which the world bigan,
That highte° March, whan God first maked man,
Was complet, and passed were also,
Syn March bigan, thritty dayes and two,   370
Bifel° that Chauntecler in al his pryde,
Hise sevene wyves walkyng hym bisyde,
Caste up hise eyen to the brighte sonne,
That in the signe of Taurus° hadde y-ronne
Twenty degrees and oon, and som-what moore,
And knew by kynde° and by noon oother loore
That it was pryme, and krew with blisful stevene.°
  " The sonne," he seyde, " is clomben upon hevene
Fourty degrees and oon, and moore ywis.°
Madame Pertelote, my worldes blis,   380
Herkneth° thise blisful briddes, how they synge,
And se the fresshe floures how they sprynge.
Ful is myn herte of revel and solas."
But sodeynly hym fil° a sorweful cas,°
For evere the latter ende of joye is wo.
God woot that worldly joye is soone ago,°
And if a rethor° koude faire endite,°
He in a cronycle saufly myghte it write
As for a sovereyn notabilitee.°
Now every wys man, lat hym herkne° me;   390
This storie is also° trewe, I undertake,°

308. Daniel: The book of Daniel consists almost entirely of dreams and their interpretations. **311. Wher:** whether. **313. daun Pharao:** Lord Pharaoh. Joseph correctly predicted the meaning of dreams both for him and for his butler and baker (Gen. 37, 40, and 41). **316. Who-so:** whoever. **seke . . . remes:** search the history of various realms. **318. Cresus:** Croesus of Lydia, who according to legend was proud of his dream till his daughter told him that the tree signified the gallows. **319. nat:** not. **321. Andromacha:** Andromache. **Ectores:** Hector's. **322. lese:** lose. **324. lorn:** lost. **325. thilke:** that same. **327. nathelees:** nevertheless. **328. anon of:** immediately by. **329. to:** too. **330. ny:** near. **334. ne . . . stoor:** set no store by laxatives. **335. ben venymes:** are venomous. **336. hem . . . del:** them not at all. **337. stynte:** stop. **338. have I:** may I have. **343. also . . . *principio*:** as surely as "In the beginning (was the Word)," i.e., as surely as the Gospel. (See Gen. Prol., l. 254.) **344. '*Mulier . . . confusio*':** "Woman is man's ruin," a widely known Latin proverb carefully mistranslated by Chauntecleer in l. 346. **345. sentence:** meaning.

349. For that: because. **maad:** made. **narwe:** narrow. **350. solas:** pleasure. **351. swevene:** vision. **352. fley:** flew. **355. corn:** grain of corn. **lay:** (which) lay. **356. Real:** regal. **na . . . aferd:** no more afraid. **358. trad:** trod (her). **pryme:** prime (9 A.M.). **359. looketh . . . were:** looks like. **leoun:** lion. **361. Hym deyned:** he deigned. **368. highte:** is called. It was believed that the world was created in March. **371. Bifel:** it befell. **374. Taurus:** The date is May 3. (March, thirty days of April, and two days of May had passed.) **376. kynde:** nature. **377. stevene:** voice. **379. ywis:** indeed. **381. Herkneth:** listen to. **384. hym fil:** befell him. **cas:** happening. **386. ago:** gone. **387. rethor:** rhetorician. **endite:** compose. **389. As . . . notabilitee:** as a supreme observation. **390. herkne:** hearken to. **391. also:** as. **undertake:** vow.

As is the book of *Launcelot de Lake,*°
That wommen holde in ful gret reverence.
Now wol I torne agayn to my sentence.°

A colfox° ful of sly iniquitee,
That in the grove hadde woned° yeres three,
By heigh ymaginacioun forncast,°
The same nyght thurgh-out the hegges brast°
Into the yerd ther Chauntecleer the faire
Was wont, and eek hise wyves, to repaire,   400
And in a bed of wortes° stille he lay
Til it was passed undren° of the day,
Waitynge his tyme on Chauntecleer to falle,
As gladly doon° thise homycides° alle
That in awayt liggen° to mordre men.
O false mordrour, lurkynge in thy den,
O newe Scariot,° newe Genyloun,°
False dissimilour,° O Greek Synoun,°
That broghtest Troye al outrely° to sorwe!
O Chauntecleer, acursed be that morwe°   410
That thow into the yerd flaugh° fro the bemes.
Thow were ful wel y-warned by thy dremes
That thilke day was perilous to thee.
But what that God forwoot moot nedes° be
After° the opynyoun of certeyn clerkis.°
Witnesse on hym that any parfit clerk is,
That in scole is greet altercacioun
In this matere and greet disputisoun,°
And hath ben of an hundred thousand men.
But I ne kan nat bulte it to the bren°   420
As kan the holy doctour Augustyn,°
Or Boece,° or the bisshop Bradwardyn,°
Wheither that Goddes worthy forewityng°
Streyneth° me nedely° for to doon a thyng—
"Nedely" clepe° I symple necessitee—
Or ellis if fre choys be graunted me

To do that same thyng or do it noght,
Though God forwoot° it er that it was wroght;
Or if his wityng streyneth never a del°
But° by necessitee condicionel.   430
I wol nat han° to do of swich° matere.
My tale is of a cok, as ye may heere,
That took his conseil of his wyf with sorwe
To walken in the yerd upon that morwe
That he hadde met° the dreem that I yow tolde.
Wommens conseils ben ful ofte colde.°
Wommanes conseil broghte us first to wo
And made Adam fro Paradys to go,
Ther-as he was ful myrie and wel at ese.
But, for I noot° to whom it myghte displese   440
If I conseil of wommen wolde blame,
Passe over, for I seyde it in my game.°
Rede auctours° where they trete of swich matere,
And what they seyn° of wommen ye may heere.
Thise ben the cokkes wordes and nat myne;
I kan noon harm of no womman devyne.°

Faire in the sond° to bathe hire myrily
Lith° Pertelote, and alle hir sustres by,
Agayn the sonne;° and Chauntecleer so free
Song myrier than the mermayde in the see,   450
For Phisiologus seithe sikerly°
How that they syngen wel and myrily.

And so bifel that, as he caste his eye
Among the wortes° on a boterflye,
He was war° of this fox that lay ful lowe.
Nothyng ne liste hym thanne° for to crowe,
But cryde anon "Cok, cok," and up he sterte°
As man° that was affrayed° in his herte,
For naturelly° a beest desireth flee
Fro his contrarie,° if he may it see,   460
Though he nevere erst° hadde syn° it with his eye.

This Chauntecleer, whan he gan hym espye,°
He wolde han fled but that the fox anon
Seyde, "Gentil sire, allas! Wher wol ye gon?
Be ye affrayed of me that am youre freend?
Now, certes, I were worse than a feend
If I to yow wolde° harm or vileynye.

392. *Launcelot de Lake:* an entirely fictitious romance concerning Lancelot, the lover of Guinevere, King Arthur's wife. **394.** sentence: subject. **395.** colfox: coal fox. **396.** woned: lived. **397.** heigh . . . forncast: divine knowledge foreordained. **398.** hegges brast: hedges burst. **401.** wortes: herbs. **402.** undren: midmorning. **404.** gladly doon: usually do. homycides: murderers. **405.** in . . . liggen: lie in wait. **407.** Scariot: Judas Iscariot, who betrayed Christ. Genyloun: Ganelon, who betrayed Charlemagne's nephew Roland. **408.** dissimilour: deceiver. Synoun: Simon, who persuaded the Trojans to take the Greeks' wooden horse into Troy. **409.** al outrely: utterly. **410.** morwe: morning. **411.** flaugh: flew. **414.** forwoot . . . nedes: foreknows must needs. **415.** After: according to. clerkis: scholars. **418.** disputisoun: disputation. **420.** I . . . bren: I can't sift it to the bran; i.e., I can't reach certainty in this much-disputed theological problem. (If God foreknows the future, to what extent has man free will?) **421.** Augustyn: St. Augustine of Hippo, who discussed the likelihood that man has "free choice" (l. 426) of action despite the infallibility of God's foreknowledge of future events. **422.** Boece: Boethius, the author of the *Consolation of Philosophy,* who distinguished between the simple (l. 425) and the conditional (l. 430) necessity of man's actions. Bradwardyn: Archbishop Bradwardine of Canterbury (d. 1349), who lectured at Oxford on God's foreknowledge. **423.** worthy forewityng: excellent foreknowing. **424.** Streyneth: constrains. nedely: necessarily. **425.** clepe: call.

428. forwoot: foreknows. **429.** wityng . . . del: knowing constrains not at all. **430.** But: except. **431.** han: have (anything). of swich: with such. **435.** met: dreamed. **436.** colde: fatal. **440.** for I noot: since I don't know. **442.** in my game: in jest. **440.** auctours: authors. **444.** seyn: say. **446.** devyne: imagine. **447.** sond: sand. **448.** Lith: lies. **449.** Agayn . . . sonne: in the sun. **451.** Phisiologus . . . sikerly: Physiologus says certainly. He was reputed to be the author of the first *Bestiary,* a compendium of lore about certain natural and supernatural creatures, including mermaids. The extreme popularity of its numerous adaptations arose less from the appended morals than from the fabulous marvels it recounted. **454.** wortes: plants. **455.** war: aware. **456.** Nothyng . . . thanne: not at all did he wish then. **457.** sterte: sprang. **458.** As man: like someone. affrayed: frightened. **459.** naturelly: by nature. **460.** contrarie: opposite. Each thing and being was believed to have its contrary and to feel a natural antipathy to it. **461.** erst: before. syn: seen. **462.** gan . . . espye: noticed him. **467.** wolde: intended.

I am nat come youre conseil for t' espye,°
But trewely the cause of my comynge
Was oonly for to herkne how that ye synge,   470
For trewely ye han as myrie a stevene°
As any aungel hath that is in hevene.
Ther-with ye han in musyk moore feelynge
Than hadde Boece° or any that kan synge.
My lord, youre fader — God his soule blesse! —
And eek youre moder, of hire gentillesse,°
Han in myn hous y-ben° to my greet ese.°
And, certes, sire, ful fayn° wolde I yow plese.
    "But, for° men speke of syngynge, I wol seye —
So mote I brouke° wel myne eyen tweye! —   480
Save yow I herde nevere man so synge
As dide youre fader in the morwenynge.
Certes, it was of herte,° al that he song.
And for to make his voys the moore strong,
He wolde so peyne hym° that with bothe hise eyen
He moste wynke,° so loude he wolde cryen,
And stonden on his tiptoon ther-with-al,
And strecche forth his nekke long and smal.
And eek he was of swich discrecioun
That ther nas no° man in no regioun   490
That hym in song or wisdom myghte passe.
I have wel rad° in *Daun° Burnel the Asse*,
Among his vers, how that ther was a cok,
For° a preestes sone yaf° hym a knok
Upon his leg, whil he was yong and nyce,°
He made hym for to lese° his benefice.
But, certeyn, ther nys no comparisoun
Bitwix the wisdom and discrecioun
Of youre fader and of his subtiltee.
Now syngeth, sire, for seinte° charitee!   500
Lat se, konne ye youre fader countrefete? "°
    This Chauntecleer hise wynges gan to bete
As man that koude his traysoun nat espie,°
So was he ravysshed with° his flaterie.
    Allas, ye lordes, many a fals flatour°
Is in youre court, and many a losengeour,°
That plesen° yow wel moore, by my feith,
Than he that soothfastnesse° unto yow seith.
Redeth Ecclesiaste of° flaterye.
Beth war,° ye lordes, of hir trecherye.   510

This Chauntecler stood hye upon his toos,
Strecchynge his nekke, and heeld hise eyen cloos,°
And gan to crowe loude for the nones.°
And daun Russell the fox stirte up atones,°
And by the gargat hente° Chauntecleer,
And on his bak toward the wode° hym beer,°
For yet ne was ther no man that hym sewed.°
    O destynee, that mayst nat ben eschewed!°
Allas that Chauntecler fleigh° fro the bemes!
Allas, his wif ne roghte nat° of dremes!   520
And on a Friday fil al this meschaunce.
    O Venus, that art goddesse of plesaunce,°
Syn that thy servant was this Chauntecleer,
And in thy servyce dide al his power
Moore for delit° than world to multiplie,
Why woldestow suffre° hym on thy day° to dye?
    O Gaufred,° deere maister soverayn,
That, whan thy worthy kyng Richard was slayn
With shot, compleynedest° his deth so soore,
Why ne hadde I now thy sentence° and thy loore°
The Friday for to chide, as diden ye?   531
For on a Friday, soothly,° slayn was he.
Thanne wolde I shewe yow how that I koude
      pleyne°
For Chauntecleres drede and for his peyne.
    Certes, swich cry ne lamentacioun
Was nevere of ladyes maad° whan Ylioun°
Was wonne, and Pirrus° with his streite swerd°
Whanne he hadde hent° kyng Priam by the berd
And slayn hym, as seith us *Eneydos,*°
As maden alle the hennes in the cloos°   540
Whan they hadde seyn° of Chauntecleer the sighte.
But sovereynly° dame Pertelote shrighte°
Ful louder than dide Hasdrubales° wyf
Whan that hire housbonde hadde lost his lyf
And that the Romayns hadden brend Cartage.°
She was so ful of torment and of rage
That wilfully° into the fyr she sterte°
And brende hirselven° with a stedefast herte.
    O woful hennes, right so cryden ye
As, whan that Nero brende the citee   550

468. conseil . . . espye: secret to discover.   471. stevene: voice.
474. Boece: Boethius also wrote a work entitled *On Music.*
476. gentillesse: gentility.   477. y-ben: been. ese: satisfaction.
478. fayn: gladly.   479. for: since.   480. mote I brouke: may I use.
483. of herte: hearty.   485. peyne hym: strive.   486. moste
wynke: must shut (his eyes).   490. nas no: was no.   492. rad:
read.   *Daun: Master.* According to the twelfth-century poem,
Burnellus the Ass, a young man threw a stone at a cock and
broke its leg. Later, when he was to have been appointed to a
benefice, the cock avenged itself by failing to crow in time
to awaken him for the ordination.   494. For: because.   yaf:
gave.   495. nyce: foolish.   496. lese: lose.   500. seinte: holy.
501. countrefete: imitate.   503. espie: perceive.   504. ravysshed
with: overwhelmed by.   505. flatour: flatterer.   506. losengeour:
deceiver.   507. plesen: please.   508. soothfastnesse: truth.
509. Ecclesiaste of: Ecclesiasticus on.   510. Beth war: beware.

512. cloos: closed.   513. nones: occasion.   514. stirte . . .
atones: sprang up at once.   515. gargat hente: throat seized.
516. wode: wood.   beer: bore.   517. sewed: pursued.   518.
eschewed: avoided.   519. fleigh: flew.   520. ne . . . nat: took
no heed.   522. plesaunce: pleasure.   525. delit: delight.
526. woldestow suffre: would you allow.   thy day: Friday, the
day of Venus.   527. Gaufred: Geoffrey de Vinsauf, who in his
treatise on the composition of poetry offers as a sample of his
highly rhetorical techniques an elegy for King Richard I, who was
mortally wounded on a Friday.   529. compleynedest: lamented.
530. sentence: erudition.   loore: learning.   532. soothly: truly.
533. pleyne: lament.   536. maad: made.   Ylioun: Ilium
(Troy).   537. Pirrus: Pyrrhus.   streite swerd: drawn sword.
538. hent: seized.   539. seith . . . Eneydos: (the) *Aeneid* tells
us.   540. cloos: enclosure.   541. seyn: seen.   542. sovereynly:
especially.   shrighte: shrieked.   543. Hasdrubales: Hasdrubal's.
545. brend Cartage: burned Carthage.   547. wilfully: voluntarily.   sterte: leapt.   548. brende hirselven: burned herself.

Of Rome, cryden senatours wyves
For that° hir housbondes losten alle hire° lyves.
Withouten gilt this Nero hath hem slayn.
Now wol I turne to my tale agayn.
  The sely° widwe and eek hire doghtres two
Herden thise hennes crye and maken wo,
And out atte dores stirten they anon,
And syen° the fox toward the grove gon,
And bar° upon his bak the cok away,
And criden "Out! Harrow!" and "Weilaway!°
Ha, ha, the fox!" And after hym they ran,   561
And eek with staves° many another man.
Ran Colle oure dogge, and Talbot, and Gerland,
And Malkyn, with a distaf in hire hand.
Ran cow, and calf, and eek the verray hogges,
So fered° for the berkyng of the dogges
And showtynge° of the men and wommen eek.
They ronne so, hem thoughte hir herte breek.°
They yelleden as fendes doon° in helle.
The dokes° cryden as men wolde hem quelle.° 570
The gees for feere flowen° over the trees.
Out of the hyve cam the swarm of bees.
So hydous° was the noyse, A, *benedicitee,*
Certes, he Jakke Straw and his meynee°
Ne made nevere shoutes half so shrille
Whan that they wolden any Flemyng kille
As thilke day was maad upon the fox.
Of bras they broghten bemes,° and of box,°
Of horn, of boon,° in whiche they blewe and
    powped,°
And ther-with-al they skryked,° and they howped.°
It semed as that° hevene sholde falle.   581
Now goode men, I prey yow, herkneth alle.
  Low, how Fortune turneth° sodeynly
The hope and pryde eek of hire enemy.
This cok that lay upon the foxes bak
In al his drede unto the fox he spak
And seyde, "Sire, if that I were as ye,
Yit sholde I seyn,° as wys God helpe me,

' Turneth agayn,° ye proude cherles° alle.
A verray pestilence upon yow falle.   590
Now I am come unto this wodes syde,
Maugree youre heed,° the cok shal here abyde.
I wol hym ete, in feith, and that anon.'"
  The fox answerde, "In feith, it shal be don."
And as he spak that word, al sodeynly
This cok brak° from his mouth delyverly,°
And hye upon a tree he fley anon.
And whan the fox say° that he was gon,
"Allas," quod he, "O Chauntecleer, allas!
I have to yow," quod he, "y-doon trespas°   600
In as muche as I maked yow aferd
Whan I yow hente and broghte out the
    yerd.
But, sire, I dide it in no wikke° entente.
Com doun, and I shal tell yow what I mente.
I shal seye sooth to yow, God help me so."
  "Nay thanne," quod he, "I shrewe° us bothe
    two.
And first I shrewe myself, bothe blood and bones,
If thow bigile me any ofter° than ones.
Thow shalt namoore thurgh° thy flaterye
Do° me to synge and wynke with° myn eye,   610
For he that wynketh, whan he sholde see,
Al wilfully,° God lat hym nevere thee."°
  "Nay," quod the fox, "but God yeve° hym
    meschaunce°
That is so undiscreet of governaunce°
That jangleth° whan he sholde holde his pees."
  Lo, swich it is for to be recchelees,°
And necligent, and truste on flaterye.
  But ye that holden this tale a folye°
As of° a fox, or of a cok and hen,
Taketh the moralitee, goode men.   620
For Seint Poul° seith that al that writen is,
To oure doctryne° it is y-write,° ywis.°
Taketh the fruyt, and lat the chaf be stille.
Now goode God, if that it be thy wille,
As seith my lord, so make us alle goode men,
And brynge us to his heye blisse. Amen.

---

552. For that: because. losten . . . hire: all lost their. **555.** sely: poor. **558.** syen: saw. **559.** bar: carry (*lit.*, carried). **560.** Weilaway: alas. **562.** staves: sticks. **566.** fered: frightened. **567.** showtynge: shouting. **568.** hem . . . breek: they thought their heart would break. **569.** fendes doon: fiends do. **570.** dokes: ducks. quelle: kill. **571.** flowen: flew. **573.** hydous: hideous. **574.** meynee: company. During the Peasants' Revolt of 1381 Jack Straw led a group of rioters into London, where they murdered a number of clothmakers from Flanders who had kept their technique secret from the native workers. (See Intro., p. 5.) **578.** bemes: trumpets. box: boxwood. **579.** boon: bone. powped: puffed. **580.** skryked: shrieked. howped: whooped. **581.** as that: as if. **583.** turneth: overturns. **588.** seyn: say.

589. Turneth agayn: turn back. cherles: churls. **592.** Maugree . . . heed: despite all you can do. **596.** brak: broke. delyverly: nimbly. **598.** say: saw. **600.** trespas: offense. **603.** wikke: evil. **606.** shrewe: curse. **608.** ofter: more often. **609.** namoore thurgh: no more through. **610.** Do: persuade. wynke with: close. **612.** wilfully: voluntarily. thee: prosper. **613.** yeve: give. meschaunce: misfortune. **614.** governaunce: self-control. **615.** jangleth: chatters. **616.** recchelees: careless. **618.** folye: idle tale. **619.** As of: concerning. **621.** Poul: Paul (Rom. 15:4). **622.** doctryne: instruction. y-write: written. ywis: indeed.

William Shakespeare

1564–1616

SHAKESPEARE'S LIFE

Every generation approaches Shakespeare in a somewhat different way. His contemporaries first admired him as the author of the poems *Venus and Adonis* and *Lucrece,* and then as a writer of first-rate plays for the stage. In the latter half of the seventeenth century and in the eighteenth century, he was esteemed rather as a genius who wrote irregular poetic dramas. The romantic poets and critics of the early nineteenth century, especially Coleridge, Lamb, and De Quincey, elevated him almost into the Genius of the English Race. Critics of the Victorian period admired his skill in creating character. In the first third of the twentieth century he was regarded as the greatest of all writers for the stage, while the mid-century critics have been more interested in his poetic techniques and ethical undertones. It is a sign of Shakespeare's perennial greatness that he can provide fresh literary experiences for such a diversity of readers and ages.

William Shakespeare was born in April, 1564, at Stratford-on-Avon, a small country town in the county of Warwickshire. He was the third child, and eldest son, of John Shakespeare and Mary Arden. His father was one of the most prosperous men of Stratford, and held in turn the chief offices in the town. His mother was of gentle birth, the daughter of Robert Arden of Wilmcote.

Stratford-on-Avon at that time was a little town of less than 2000 inhabitants, but its community life was vigorous. It had a grammar school, with a succession of competent schoolmasters who provided a good education for the boys of the town. Elizabethan education, though it might appear narrow by modern standards, was thorough in its disciplines of mind and body. Latin was the main subject of instruction. By the time a boy had finished his course, he had read widely in such authors as Cicero, Ovid, Virgil, and Seneca; he had also received considerable training in the use and structure of the Latin language, in rhetoric, and in the making of Latin verses.

Little is known of Shakespeare's early life; but it is unlikely that a writer who dramatized such a wide range and variety of human kinds and experiences should have spent his early manhood entirely in placid pursuits in a country town. There are various traditions about his early manhood which cannot be finally proved or denied. The most persistent is that he fled from Stratford because he was in trouble for deerstealing, and had fallen foul of Sir Thomas Lucy, the local magnate; another tradition declares that he was for some time a schoolmaster. In December, 1582, Shakespeare married Anne Hathaway, daughter of a farmer of Shottery, near Stratford. The records in the church at Stratford note that their first child, Susanna, was baptized on May 6, 1583, and twins, Hamnet and Judith, on February 22, 1585.

From 1592 onward the records are much fuller. In March, 1592, the Lord Strange's players produced a new play at the Rose Theater called *Harry the Sixth,* which was very successful, and was probably the First Part of Shakespeare's

Henry VI. In August, 1592, Robert Greene, the best known of the professional writers, as he was dying wrote a letter to three fellow writers in which he warned them against the ingratitude of players in general, and in particular against an " upstart crow " who " supposes he is as well able to bombast out a blank verse as the best of you: and being an absolute Johannes Factotum [Johnny Do-All] is in his own conceit the only Shake-scene in a country." This is the first known reference to Shakespeare, and the whole passage suggests that to Greene's disgust Shakespeare had become suddenly famous as a playwright. At this time Shakespeare was brought into touch with Edward Alleyn, the great tragedian, and Christopher Marlowe, the poet and dramatist. Alleyn was then acting the thundering parts of Marlowe's *Tamburlaine,* the *Jew of Malta,* and *Dr. Faustus,* as well as Hieronimo, the hero of Kyd's *Spanish Tragedy,* which was the most popular of all Elizabethan plays.

In April, 1593, Shakespeare published his poem *Venus and Adonis,* which was dedicated to the young Earl of Southampton. It was a great and lasting success, and was reprinted nine times in the next few years. In May, 1594, his second poem, *The Rape of Lucrece,* was also dedicated to Southampton; it was almost as popular as *Venus and Adonis.*

There was little playing in 1593, for the theaters were shut during a severe outbreak of the plague, and the players went on tour in the country. But in the autumn of 1594, when the plague ceased, the playing companies were reorganized, and Shakespeare became a sharer in the company patronized by the Lord Chamberlain. This company, the Chamberlain's Men, went to play in the Theater in Shoreditch, north of the city of London. During these months Marlowe and Kyd died, and Shakespeare was thus for a time without a rival. He had already written the three parts of *Henry VI, Richard III, Titus Andronicus, Two Gentlemen of Verona, Love's Labour's Lost, The Comedy of Errors,* and *The Taming of the Shrew.* Soon afterward he wrote the first of his greater plays, *Romeo and Juliet,* and he followed this success in the next three years with *A Midsummer Night's Dream, Richard II,* and *The Merchant of Venice.* The two parts of *Henry IV,* introducing

Falstaff, the most popular of all his comic characters, were probably written in 1597-98.

The company left the Theater in 1597 owing to disputes with the landlord over a renewal of the lease, and went to play at the Curtain in the same neighborhood. These wranglings continued throughout 1598, but during the Christmas holidays the players settled the matter by demolishing the old Theater and erecting a new playhouse on the south bank of the Thames, near London Bridge. This playhouse was named the Globe. The expenses of the new building were shared by the chief members of the company, including Shakespeare, who was now a man of some means. In 1596 he had bought New Place, a large house in the center of Stratford, and through his father purchased a coat of arms from the Heralds, which was official recognition that he and his family were gentlefolk.

By the summer of 1598 Shakespeare was recognized as the greatest of English dramatists. Booksellers were printing his more popular plays, at times even in pirated or stolen versions, and he received a remarkable tribute from a young writer named Francis Meres. In a long catalogue of English authors in his book *Palladis Tamia,* Meres gave Shakespeare more prominence than any other writer, and mentioned by name twelve of his plays.

Shortly before the Globe was opened, Shakespeare had completed a cycle of plays dealing with the story of the Wars of the Roses. The final play in this series was *Henry V.* It was followed by *As You Like It* and by *Julius Caesar,* the first of the maturer tragedies. In the next three years (1599-1602) he wrote *Troilus and Cressida, The Merry Wives of Windsor, Hamlet* (in its present form), and *Twelfth Night.*

On March 24, 1603, Queen Elizabeth died. Shakespeare's company had often performed before her, but they found her successor a far more enthusiastic patron. One of the first acts of King James I was to take over the company and to promote the players to be his own servants; the Lord Chamberlain's Company was henceforward known as the King's Men. They now acted very frequently at court, and prospered accordingly. In the early years of the reign Shakespeare wrote the more somber comedies, *All's Well That Ends Well* and *Measure for Measure,* which were followed by *Othello, King*

Lear, and *Macbeth.* Then he returned to Roman themes with *Antony and Cleopatra* and *Coriolanus.*

Since 1601 Shakespeare had been writing fewer plays each year, and there were now a number of rival dramatists who were introducing new styles of drama, particularly Ben Jonson (whose first successful comedy, *Every Man in his Humour,* was acted by Shakespeare's company in 1598), Chapman, Dekker, Marston, and also Beaumont and Fletcher, who began to write in 1607. In 1608 the King's Men acquired a second playhouse, a private theater in the fashionable quarter of the Blackfriars in the city of London, and again Shakespeare was a sharer in the expenses. At private theaters, plays were performed indoors; the prices charged were higher than in the public playhouses, and the audience consequently was more select. Shakespeare seems to have retired from the stage about this time; his name does not occur in the various lists of players after 1607. Henceforward he lived for the most part at Stratford, where he was regarded as one of the most important citizens. He still wrote a few plays, and he tried his hand at the new form of tragicomedy — a play with tragic incidents but a happy ending — which Beaumont and Fletcher had popularized. He wrote four of these, *Pericles, Cymbeline, The Winter's Tale,* and *The Tempest;* the last two were acted at court in 1611. For the remaining years of his life Shakespeare lived in retirement. His son Hamnet had died in 1596; his two daughters were now married.

Shakespeare died at Stratford-on-Avon on April 23, 1616, and was buried in the chancel of the church, before the high altar. Shortly afterward a memorial tablet, with a portrait bust, was set up on the north wall. His wife survived him till 1623. The known facts of Shakespeare's life are thus considerable; unfortunately they tell us little of his personality.

SHAKESPEARE'S THEATER

The Elizabethan playhouse was small by modern standards. The Globe, the most famous of all Elizabethan theaters (built in 1599 when Shakespeare was reaching the middle period of his activity) was an octagonal building. On the outside each of the eight sides measured approximately thirty-six feet; and the diameter of the whole was eighty-four feet. It was a frame structure, standing on low, brick supports, and the roof was thatched with straw. It was about thirty-three feet high to the eaves. Inside ran three galleries, one above the other, surrounding the yard, which was fifty-six feet in diameter. The galleries looked down upon the stage, which occupied about a third of the yard at one end.

Three sections of the octagon were used for backstage; the remaining five were used for the spectators. The yard was open to the sky, and the stage was lit by daylight.

The Elizabethan acting company was a "fellowship." It consisted of ten to fifteen sharers, three or four boys who would ultimately become full sharers, and perhaps another ten or a dozen extras — money gatherers (who were sometimes women), stagehands, and the like. The boys took the parts of girls or young women, for as yet there were no professional actresses on the English stage.

With the "groundlings," who stood in the yard because they could not afford to pay for a seat, the most popular member of the company was the clown. He was the low comedian, and most plays gave him a chance to play a comic servant or a watchman or a gravedigger or to indulge in some business of his own. In fact, the clown was so important a member of the cast that in stage directions in early texts he is usually designated as "Clown" regardless of the part which he represents. When the Chamberlain's Men were formed in the autumn of 1594, their first clown was Will Kempe. Kempe, who was older than the other chief sharers of the company, had already won a great reputation. He was an individualist and a great favorite. He was particularly famous for his jigs, which he performed after the play was over. But Kempe fell foul of his fellows, and left the company in 1599. Shakespeare's severe remarks on the clown in *Hamlet,* written after Kempe joined a rival company, were clearly directed against him. After Kempe's departure, a more intelligent and refined kind of clown is noticeable in Shakespeare's plays — Touchstone in *As You Like It,* Feste in *Twelfth Night,* and Lear's singing fool. These parts were taken by Robert Armin.

If by some miracle we could be transplanted to a holiday performance at the Globe, we should be surprised in many ways. The play-house would strike us as small, uncomfortably crowded, and far more intimate than any modern theater. The presentation would at first seem noisy and crude, but we should soon become used to the trumpet calls and the lack of scenery. The acting would appear embarrassingly emotional, but very slick and competent. Shakespeare is not the only dramatist to speak of the "two hours' traffic of the stage." Since the average play of that time contains from sixteen thousand to twenty thousand words, there can have been little dawdling; the rate of speech must have been very rapid, and such pace is only possible when the audience is sensitive, keen, and alert. Indeed, the greatest contrast to our modern theater would be in the spectators, who responded quickly and violently, unashamedly demonstrating their grief, pleasure, or amusement, and at times — if dissatisfied with the performance or the play — their anger. Shakespeare was lucky in having to write for the simple conditions of the Elizabethan playhouse. He would doubtless have succeeded even in Hollywood, but, as it happened, the kind of play which best suited his theater and his audiences needed also the highest kind of poetry.

SHAKESPEARE'S PLAYS

PUBLICATION. By the time Shakespeare died, fourteen of his plays had been separately published in booklets of the kind known as quartos.[1] In 1623 his surviving fellow actors, John Heming and Henry Condell, with the co-operation of a number of printers, published a collected edition of thirty-six plays in one folio volume — the famous First Folio — with an engraved portrait, memorial verses by Ben Jonson and others, and an Epistle to the reader in which Heming and Condell make the interesting note that Shakespeare's "hand and mind went together, and what he thought, he uttered with that easiness that we have scarce received from him a blot in his papers."

[1] The terms "quarto" and "folio," used to describe books, denote the foldings in the sheet of paper. The size of the standard piece of paper was about 14 x 18 inches. In a folio the sheet was folded once, thus giving two leaves (or four pages) each of about 14 x 9. In a quarto the sheet was folded again, thus giving four leaves (or eight pages) each of about 9 x 7 inches.

COMEDIES. In the Folio, Shakespeare's plays are divided into Comedies, Histories, and Tragedies. The division is simple and drastic, and yet it denotes certain general principles which he followed.

The main purpose of Shakespearean Comedy is entertainment; "our true intent," as Quince in *A Midsummer Night's Dream* reminds the spectators, "is all for your delight"; and, as Shakespeare knew well enough, the theme which always delights is a love story ending in a wedding. At the end of *Love's Labour's Lost,* which differs from the usual pattern because the ladies leave their lovers to a year's probation, Berowne sighs:

> Our wooing doth not end like an old play.
> Jack hath not Jill. These ladies' courtesy
> Might well have made our sport a comedy.

So the usual theme for Shakespearean comedy is how Jack woos Jill, or — as commonly — how Jill wins Jack.

The common pattern for a Shakespearean comedy — to be found in *Two Gentlemen of Verona, The Taming of the Shrew, A Midsummer Night's Dream, The Merchant of Venice, Much Ado about Nothing, As You Like It, Twelfth Night,* and *The Tempest* — is a story which involves two or three sets of characters. In the main plot of each play the two principal lovers, after various adventures, are happily paired at the end of Act V. A second plot brings together two friends of the principals; and, to add change of mood to the whole mixture, a comic underplot gives the professional clowns a chance for lower but good-humored laughter.

The surprising fact is that after three hundred and fifty years these comedies should still be so actable and delightful. It shows that Shakespeare had a shrewder instinct for what is permanently pleasing than those grimmer playwrights and critics who demand that comedy as well as tragedy shall always present some moral, social, or psychological problem. Most of Shakespeare's comedies are romantic fantasies — stories of pleasant people in impossible situations.

HISTORIES. In writing his Histories Shakespeare had a more serious purpose. The study of history was popular, for it was regarded as useful and essential knowledge for any intelligent man. History recorded the fall of princes and great men who offended against divine and moral law, and it warned those who would follow such evil examples. Besides, Englishmen had every reason to observe the lessons of history. For more than a century before Shakespeare's time England had been in a state of recurring anarchy and civil war because of the crimes committed by and against ambitious princes. Shakespeare amply illustrated the moral lessons of history in a series of five early plays: the three parts of *Henry VI, Richard III,* and, after an interval, *Richard II.* They showed how the crime committed by Henry Bolingbroke, when he deposed Richard II and usurped the crown, ultimately led to the long and bloody civil Wars of the Roses. These first history plays are wordy and earnest. A little later, in rewriting an old play, by another hand, on the troublesome reign of King John, Shakespeare encountered the amusing but unhistorical character of the Bastard Falconbridge; the earthy humanity with which he endowed Falconbridge enlivens a dull Shakespearean play. Thereafter Shakespeare mingled the high notes of sober history with scenes of lively low comedy. In writing *I* and *II Henry IV* he created Falstaff. Falstaff is a wholly fictitious character, and his vast bulk so overshadows the more important persons of real history that in the two plays the Falstaff scenes occupy more space than the historical episodes. *Henry V,* the last play of this series, lacks Falstaff in person — he dies offstage — but the heroics of the siege of Harfleur and the battle of Agincourt are balanced by the "humors" of Ancient Pistol and Henry's bluff wooing of French Kate.

At the end of his career Shakespeare wrote one more history play, *Henry VIII,* in which he presented in a series of pageant-like scenes some episodes of English history which culminated in the birth of the princess who afterward became Queen Elizabeth.

TRAGEDIES. Tragedy to an Elizabethan playgoer denoted a play ending with violent death for most of the principal persons. In his tragedies, Shakespeare usually followed the common pattern; there are three dead in the last scene of *Romeo and Juliet* and *Othello,* four in *Hamlet,* five in *Lear.* But to justify such carnage, tragedy also demanded that the disaster should be caused by some breach of fundamental moral law.

Shakespeare's greatest tragedies all show how the breaking of moral law leads inevitably to destruction. In *Hamlet,* Claudius' original sin of lust for Gertrude leads to the murder of Gertrude's husband, and ultimately to the deaths of Claudius, Gertrude, Laertes, and Hamlet. In *Othello,* Iago, for the basest of motives, persuades Othello to a mad passion of jealousy against his wife Desdemona, which results in the deaths of Othello, Desdemona, and incidentally of Emilia, Iago's wife. In *Lear,* the old king's foolish pride leads him to discard his faithful daughter Cordelia, while the ruthless ambition of the bastard Edmund prompts him to betray his brother Edgar and then his father Gloucester. As a direct result of pride and ambition, Lear, Gloucester, Edmund, Cordelia, and her two sisters Goneril and Regan all perish. In *Macbeth,* the ambition of Macbeth and his wife brings about the murder of Duncan and a whole series of disasters until Macbeth himself is killed in battle. Shakespeare's greatest tragedies reach down to the depths of emotion because his sense of moral law was as acute as his skill in portraying the pathos of human suffering.

SHAKESPEARE'S DRAMATIC TECHNIQUE

PLOT. It is a fashion nowadays with some critics to declare that Shakespeare's plays are "dramatic poems," and should therefore be subjected to the same kinds of minute dissection, analysis, and symbolical interpretation as modern poetry. There is, however, an elementary distinction to be made between a poem (or even a dramatic poem) and a play. A poem is intended primarily as an experience which first comes to us through the *sound* of the words; the *sight* of what is being done as well as the sound of the words is needed by the spectator of a drama. And Shakespeare wrote his plays to be acted on the stage, not to be analyzed in a laboratory nor even to be read privately.

A drama — and the original Greek word means a "doing" or an "acting" — is thus an artistic experience to be shared among dramatist, actors, and spectators. For that experience to be fully achieved, many different elements, including action, movement, speech, and sometimes music must be fused into a unity. Of these the script which the dramatist contributes is the most important, and for the reader all that remains of the original experience.

A good play needs four component parts: theme, plot, character, and speech or language. Many dramatists begin with the theme and then construct a play to illustrate it. This is not Shakespeare's usual method. Instead, he takes an existing and often familiar story and turns it into a play, and in so doing — no matter how improbable the original tale — he makes the people come alive and their adventures credible.

Shakespeare's plots are not always properly appreciated because his construction is apparently so free and artless, but a closer look will soon show that Shakespeare was an expert plot maker who devised his play so that it would not only convey the complete emotional effect he desired but would also keep the audience interested and attentive from beginning to end. *Hamlet* is a good example of subtle and elaborate plotting.

Hamlet opens with a scene intended to create the atmosphere of dread and impending evil. The Ghost appears and by its very silence arouses our curiosity. We sense that however outwardly serene the Danish court, there is something very rotten within. In Scene ii, the new King holds his first court, and in his opening speech tells us quite naturally of recent events: on the death of the late king, his brother, he has succeeded to the throne and married his brother's widow. He also dispatches ambassadors to Norway to deal with the threat of young Fortinbras, gives permission to Laertes to return to his studies in Paris, and, finally, persuades Hamlet not to return to Wittenberg. These actions are all so lifelike that unless we stop to think critically we do not realize that the purpose of this scene is to feed us with the information that we need to understand what follows.

This business being concluded, King, Queen, and courtiers withdraw, and Hamlet at last occupies our full attention. His first soliloquy reveals his frustrated disgust, and when Horatio and the others arrive to tell him of the midnight apparition, we sense that the Ghost will indeed have something to impart. Meanwhile, to increase our interest by delay, Shakespeare next gives us an intimate picture of the Polonius family at home: Laertes, the impetuous and somewhat priggish son; Ophelia, his sister, inexperienced in the intrigues of court life; and the old statesman himself — cunning, experienced, pompous, wordy, and worldly wise. From this delicious comedy, we are taken back to the battlements where Hamlet encounters the Ghost and is told the dread secret of his uncle's crime.

The whole play is planned with a masterly ease, each scene leading into or contrasting with the next, so that we are kept continuously alert and never allowed to tire with too much of the same emotion or the same situation.

One small detail will illustrate the concealed artistry of the whole design. At the end of the play Fortinbras, Prince of Norway, is needed to take over command and restore order to Denmark. Fortinbras's part is small — less than twenty-five lines in all — and yet at the end he dominates the stage as the most important character. Quietly and subtly Fortinbras has been built up throughout the play. His ambitions are the theme of Horatio's talk in I.i. His suspicious actions cause the sending of the ambassadors in I.ii. In II.ii the ambassadors report on their mission, and Claudius agrees that Fortinbras and his army may have passage through Denmark. In IV.iv Fortinbras himself appears very briefly so that we may see him and remember where he is. Finally, when he reappears just after Hamlet's death, his entrance is entirely natural and needs neither introduction nor explanation.

CHARACTER.   Shakespeare's skill in creating character has been recognized from the first. The word "character" originally meant a letter in the Greek alphabet; thence "handwriting"; and so the nature of a man as written in his face. A living person is a compound of many qualities: his past history, his strength and weakness, his habits, morals, and beliefs, his loyalties, friendships, loves, and hates, and this amalgam is revealed most immediately to others in his face, bearing, gestures, clothes, and manner of speech. We learn to understand him further from the attitude and comments of his friends, his critics, and his enemies, from his own behavior in different situations, from the thoughts which he utters, and not less from the way in which he utters them, and even from his vocabulary. In drama, the bodily expressions and manner of speech are conveyed by the actor; the mind is revealed through the words supplied by the dramatist.

A good example of Shakespeare's methods in characterization is Harry Percy, the "Hotspur of the North," in *I Henry IV*. We first hear of young Hotspur in I.i, when Henry IV tells of Hotspur's victory over the Scots and his insolence in keeping the prisoners whom he has captured. Indeed, the weary King laments the contrast between his own son and this dashing Harry. Hotspur himself first appears in I.iii and at once reveals his fiery, impatient mind, darting away as a new thought appears, obsessed with a zeal for military honor which is not far from vanity, roused at a word, and so an easy victim for the unscrupulous King and his crafty uncle, Worcester. Having drawn this side of his nature, Shakespeare next shows Hotspur (II. iii) in a charming little episode at home with his young wife; and to give added point to this episode, Prince Hal in the next scene briefly sums him up:

. . . the Hotspur of the North, he that kills me some six or seven dozen of Scots at a breakfast, washes his hands, and says to his wife, "Fie upon this quiet life! I want work." "O my sweet Harry," says she, "how many hast thou killed today?" "Give my roan horse a drench," says he, and answers, "Some fourteen," an hour after — "a trifle, a trifle."

It is cruel parody, but a sign that Shakespeare was sure of himself, for only an artist who has complete self-confidence dares to make fun of his own serious efforts.

Hotspur is next shown in conference with Glendower, Worcester, and Mortimer, and the contrast between these four very different characters is cleverly drawn. Hotspur has no patience with the Welshman's solemn claims to be extraordinary, is too impetuous to conceal his boredom, and mocks him beyond endurance; it is a tribute to Hotspur's personality, and a piece of subtle artistry, that such a man as Glendower should twice swallow his anger and give way. Hotspur is a blunt and practical young man with no use for poetry or art, natural or supernatural, insisting on his own way until he gets it, and then yielding at once, and very fond of his wife in his own bluff way. He is a perfect specimen of the romantic soldier who filled Shakespeare with admiration and

amusement, for he was careful to set Falstaff beside Hotspur. Falstaff's brief catechism on honor is a mocking echo of Hotspur's heroics. Hotspur dies at the hands of the Prince whom he had despised, lamenting not so much the loss of his hopes as of his honor as a soldier, and when he is dead his body is dishonorably prodded by the live Falstaff.

SPEECH. Shakespeare, like all Elizabethan dramatists, used four kinds of speech in his plays: *blank verse, rhymed verse, prose,* and *song.* Each kind has its uses, and the whole play, especially in his maturity, is conceived as a kind of verbal symphony, each scene or episode being composed as part of a complete harmony. *The Tempest* in its poetical scenes is the finest example of the musical use of words in all Shakespeare's plays.

Blank verse — in the form of unrhymed lines each having five stresses — is the normal form of speech in Shakespearean drama for all scenes and persons whose appeal is mainly to the emotions of the spectator or reader. English blank verse is a very versatile meter, and can be used with great variety of mood and "pressure" — for conversation of all kinds, serious or gay; for description, as in Hotspur's account of the foppish messenger (*I Hen IV*, I.iii.30–68); for exhortation or rebuke, as when Henry IV chides his erring son (III.ii); for passionate denunciation, as when Hamlet chastises his mother (*Haml*, III.iv); for garrulous volubility, as in Polonius' lecture to Reynaldo (II.i); for meditation and introspection, as when Hamlet rebukes himself for inaction or meditates on suicide (II.ii.575–632, III.i.55–88.)

Shakespeare is so subtle in the variation of rhythms, stresses, pauses, and tones in his blank verse that he can convey not only every mood but even the personal peculiarities of the speaker. In the passage between Hotspur and Glendower (*I Hen IV*, IV.i), the Welsh Prince's speeches, with their pompous insistence on his supernatural origin, almost demand to be spoken with a Welsh accent. Again, when Caliban mutters his grievances against Prospero and Miranda, the stress falls naturally on the snarling words:

I must eat my dinner.
This island's *mine*, by *Sycorax* my mother,
Which thou takest from me. When thou camest first,

Thou strokedst me, and madest much of me,
  wouldst give me
Water with berries in't. And teach me how
To name the bigger light, and how the less,
That burn by day and night. And then I loved thee,
And showed thee all the qualities o' th' isle,
The fresh springs, brine pits, barren place and
  fertile.
Cursèd be I that did so! All the charms
Of Sycorax, *toads, beetles, bats,* light on you!
For I am all the subjects that you have,
Which first was mine own king. And here you *sty*
  me
In this *hard* rock whiles you do keep from me
The rest o' th' island.

The rhythm and tone are very different when
Prospero, saddened and angered by the conspiracy against his life, in musing and visionary
mood, comments on the pageant which has just
disappeared:

              Be cheerful, sir.
  Our revels now are ended. These our actors,
  As I foretold you, were all spirits, and
  Are melted into air, into thin air.
  And, like the baseless fabric of this vision,
  The cloud-capped towers, the gorgeous palaces,
  The solemn temples, the great globe itself —
  Yea, all which it inherit — shall dissolve
  And, like this insubstantial pageant faded,
  Leave not a rack behind. We are such stuff
  As dreams are made on, and our little life
  Is rounded with a sleep.

Here rhythm and sound compel the speaker to
go slowly and solemnly until he reaches the climax at "rounded with a sleep."

Rhymed verse in five-stress lines, usually in
couplets, is common in Shakespeare's early plays,
but in the middle period, to which *I Henry IV*
and *Hamlet* belong, he was more sparing and
used it for definite effects. The commonest use
is in the form of a couplet at the end of a scene
or episode. Here the rhyme has sometimes the
practical purpose of warning those behind the
stage of a change — a curtain to be drawn or an
entrance to be made; but a couplet also rounds
out the dialogue aesthetically and brings it to an
effective close before the actors make their exit.
Thus at the end of I.ii, Hamlet, before following
Horatio and Marcellus off stage, turns to the
audience to comment:

My father's spirit in arms! All is not well.
I doubt some foul play. Would the night were
  come!

Till then sit still, my soul. Foul deeds will rise,
Though all the earth o'erwhelm them, to men's
  eyes.

The rhyme effectively shows us that this episode
is ended and that a new set of characters is about
to enter.

Rhymed verse in or after a passage of blank
verse or prose has also the effect of stiffening the
dialogue and heightening the emotion. Thus in
Twelfth Night (III.i.161), when Olivia can no
longer control her feelings for the disguised Viola, whom she supposes to be "Cesario," she
breaks out:

Cesario, by the roses of the spring,
By maidhood, honor, truth, and everything,
I love thee so, that, mauger all thy pride,
Nor wit nor reason can my passion hide.
Do not extort thy reasons from this clause,
For that I woo, thou therefore hast no cause,
But rather reason thus with reason fetter,
Love sought is good, but given unsought is better.

And Viola, whose complex emotions are in an
even greater turmoil, retorts, also in rhyme:

By innocence I swear, and by my youth,
I have one heart, one bosom, and one truth,
And that no woman has; nor never none
Shall mistress be of it, save I alone.
And so adieu, good madam. Nevermore
Will I my master's tears to you deplore.
OLIVIA. Yet come again, for thou perhaps mayst
  move
That heart which now abhors to like his love.

In his later plays, end rhymes are less common, but Shakespeare will often use a single
speech in rhyme for the definite purpose of un-
derlining, as it were, a particularly significant
moment or situation. Thus Coriolanus, writhing
under the indignity of having to beg for the
votes of the despised plebians, comments:

Better it is to die, better to starve,
Than crave the hire which first we do deserve.
Why in this woolvish toge should I stand here,
To beg of Hob and Dick that do appear
Their needless vouches? Custom call me to 't.
What custom wills, in all things should we do
The dust on ántique time would lie unswept,
And mountainous error to be too highly heaped
For truth to o'erpeer. Rather than fool it so,
Let the high office and the honor go
To one that would do thus. I am half-through.
The one part suffered, the other will I do.

The rhyme stresses the resentment which will soon lead Coriolanus to his destruction.

Another use of rhyme is to effect contrast. In the play scene in *Hamlet* (III.ii.165–271), the Player King and Player Queen speak in a stilted rhymed verse while the talk of Hamlet at this moment is notably naturalistic.

Just as rhyme will stiffen the tension, so a passage of *prose* in a play which is mainly in verse inevitably lowers the emotional pitch and increases the pace; it is appropriate for passages of comedy, farce, and repartee. A Shakespearean character usually laughs in prose but he weeps in verse. Prose, too, is the natural speech for lower and more comic persons; verse would be unnatural on the lips of Falstaff, Osric, the gravediggers, Stephano, or Trinculo. Versatile characters will use all forms of speech; Prince Hal talks prose to Falstaff but verse when in the presence of the King. Hamlet addressing the King or his mother, or alone with his own emotions, will normally use blank verse; but he lapses naturally into prose when mocking Polonius, conversing with Guildenstern and Rosencrantz, instructing the players, or questioning the gravedigger.

Songs in Shakespeare's plays are usually intended to create a particular mood. Thus Ophelia's snatches of song emphasize her madness, and the bawdy little song which she sings to the horrified Queen adds greatly to the pathos of her end.

SHAKESPEARE'S POETRY

Poetry, being in the main a means of evoking emotion in the reader, achieves many of its effects indirectly. By the sounds of individual words and the rhythms of words in combination, the poet works through the ears of his hearers; by metaphor, simile, and the broader use of "imagery" he recalls their memories and associations and charms them to respond to his own mood.

Imagery is of many kinds, and Shakespeare's use of it was continually changing and maturing. In his earliest plays, the imagery is direct and simple, intended only to bring out the immediate meaning of a word or passage; later he uses imagery with constantly increasing subtlety. Thus Henry IV expresses and conveys his con-

tempt for Richard II, whom he has supplanted, in these words:

> The skipping King, he ambled up and down,
> With shallow jesters and rash bavin wits,
> Soon kindled and soon burnt . . .

"Skipping" connotes childishness; "ambling" the aimless shuffling of a fool; "bavin" means brushwood for kindling — worthless and soon consumed. All these images are used directly, and they combine to form a general picture of the essential frivolity of Richard.

In the later plays there is a far more elaborate and indirect use of imagery, when the same kind of image is constantly repeated so that the hearer is almost compelled to feel in a certain way toward the persons and events throughout the play. Thus *Hamlet* [1] contains a number of images of corruption and bodily disorder, of ulcers, tumors, and foul diseases, of weeds and rankness: "Something is rotten in the state of Denmark" . . . "the fat weed / That roots itself in ease on Lethe wharf" . . . "So Lust . . . will sate itself in a celestial bed / And prey on garbage" . . . "your husband, like a mildewed ear, / Blasting his wholesome brother" . . . "do not spread the compost on the weeds / To make them ranker." These images in themselves form a very small part of the whole play, but by repetition they create, maintain, and convey the feeling of general rottenness pervading the court of Denmark; it is as if from time to time we smell whiffs of putrefaction.

In *Macbeth* the imagery is less patterned but more concentrated, and at times Shakespeare fuses together several images to create a general effect. Thus, when Lady Macbeth learns that King Duncan is to be her guest that night, she is filled with a kind of devilish ecstasy at the thought of his murder:

> The raven himself is hoarse
> That croaks the fatal entrance of Duncan
> Under my battlements. Come, you spirits
> That tend on mortal thoughts, unsex me here,
> And fill me, from the crown to the toe, topfull
> Of direst cruelty! Make thick my blood,
> Stop up the access and passage to remorse,
> That no compunctious visitings of nature
> Shake my fell purpose, nor keep peace between
> The effect and it! Come to my woman's breasts,

[1] See Caroline Spurgeon, *Shakespeare's Imagery* (1935), pp. 316–17.

And take my milk for gall, you murdering min-
    isters,
Wherever in your sightless substances
You wait on nature's mischief! Come, thick night,
And pall thee in the dunnest smoke of Hell,
That my keen knife see not the wound it makes,
Nor Heaven peep through the blanket of the dark
To cry, "Hold, hold!"

Here the images of the raven (the bird of ill
omen), of blood ceasing to flow and unnaturally
thick, of mother's milk (naturally the symbol
of tender love) turned to bitterness, of the
black smoke of Hell, darkest night, the murderer's knife — all mingle together to form an
atmosphere of horrible foreboding.

SHAKESPEARE'S UNIVERSALITY

There have been many attempts to analyze
Shakespeare's peculiar genius, but none can be
final because the mark of genius in a writer is
that in some undefinable way he evokes individual responses from each reader, who is made to
feel that he has a kind of kinship with the author as if both had shared their secret experiences. This quality exists to some degree in all
great writers. Shakespeare differs from the rest
because he makes a wider appeal to a greater
number of readers of different ages and of different environments; he is more universal. This
power of universality is unpredictable, for it is
seldom if ever possible to say of any new work
that it will be permanent. Yet when an author's
popularity still endures after three and a half
centuries, at least some of the marks of his genius can be isolated. Dr. Johnson, in his own sonorous way, thus expressed it:

Shakespeare is, above all writers, at least above all
modern writers, the poet of nature; the poet that
holds up to his readers a faithful mirror of manners
and of life. His characters are not modified by the
customs of particular places, unpracticed by the rest
of the world; by the peculiarities of studies or professions, which can operate but upon small numbers; or by the accidents of transient fashions or
temporary opinion; they are the genuine progeny
of common humanity, such as the world will always supply, and observation will always find.[1]

Shakespeare has not only an instinctive understanding of humanity but he has also the
power of expressing this understanding in such

[1] For this essay, see p. 509, below.

a way that his creatures — Hamlet, for instance,
or Falstaff or Polonius — are more real to us
than any person of history. They speak, think,
and act not only as Elizabethans but as human
beings always have thought, spoken, and acted.
This requires a most sensitive and sympathetic
power of observation. Shakespeare was fascinated by the infinite varieties of the human species; and Hamlet thus expresses it:

What a piece of work is a man! How noble in
reason! How infinite in faculty! In form and moving how express and admirable! In action how like
an angel! In apprehension how like a god! The
beauty of the world! The paragon of animals!

But Shakespeare did not always look upon man
with such enthusiasm or optimism. In another
mood, Lear, at the beginning of his madness as
he contemplates the naked beggar, exclaims,

Consider him well. Thou owest the worm no silk,
the beast no hide, the sheep no wool, the cat no
perfume. Ha! Here's three on 's are sophisticated.
Thou art the thing itself. Unaccommodated man
[i.e., man without his trappings] is no more but
such a poor, bare, forked animal as thou art.

Another of Shakespeare's qualities is his power to record what he perceived in language that
cannot be bettered, and the range of experience
expressed is so vast that one can find a quotation from Shakespeare to fit almost any occasion
and mood. Indeed we seldom realize how often,
instinctively or deliberately, we turn to Shakespeare to express our thoughts for us:

There are more things in Heaven and earth,
    Horatio,
Than are dreamt of in your philosophy.

All the world's a stage,
And all the men and women merely players.

Dost thou think because thou art virtuous, there
shall be no more cakes and ale?

A little water clears us of this deed.
How easy is it then!

Mark you this, Bassanio,
The Devil can cite Scripture for his purpose.

Yond Cassius has a lean and hungry look.
He thinks too much, such men are dangerous.

And my poor fool is hanged! No, no, no life!
Why should a dog, a horse, a rat have life
And thou no breath at all? Thou'lt come no more,
Never, never, never, never, never!

We are such stuff
As dreams are made on, and our little life
Is rounded with a sleep.

There are hundreds of these incomparable lines which have been woven into the English language.

Above all, Shakespeare's plays have durability. One can read and reread them year after year, and at every reading they reveal new depths and understanding. No author in the English tongue wears so well or lasts so long.

ADDITIONAL NOTE

THE HISTORY BEHIND
I HENRY IV

Eight of Shakespeare's ten history plays are concerned with one central theme — the rise and fall of the House of Lancaster. They cover a period of nearly a century of complex events.

Edward III reigned fifty years (1327–77). He had seven sons, of whom the eldest was Edward, the Black Prince. In his later days, Edward III became senile, but he outlived his eldest son; the Black Prince died in 1376, Edward III a few months later, in 1377. Thereupon the king's eleven-year-old grandson, Richard II, son of the Black Prince, became king, under the regency of John of Gaunt, Duke of Lancaster, the eldest surviving son of Edward III. In 1382, at the age of sixteen, Richard married Anne of Bohemia. By this time, the control of the kingdom had passed to Thomas of Woodstock, Duke of Gloucester, sixth son of Edward III.

Richard was now growing up; to Gloucester's alarm, he formed a court party of his own friends. Gloucester and his supporters (called the Lords Appellant), who included Henry Bolingbroke, Duke of Hereford (son of John of Gaunt), and Thomas Mowbray (afterward Duke of Norfolk), seized Richard's friends by force and executed them. In 1389, Richard suddenly declared that he was now of age, and Gloucester was obliged to resign his regency. Thereafter for some years Richard ruled competently and moderately; he even seemed to be reconciled with the Lords Appellant; but when Gloucester again began his intrigues he was arrested, sent to Calais (then an English possession), and there murdered.

Richard meanwhile had lost his first wife and had married again. His character changed. He became reckless and extravagant, and his court was filled with favorites and parasites. As a result he was constantly in need of money, which he raised by illegal and most unpopular means.

In 1398, Bolingbroke and Norfolk quarreled. At this point, Shakespeare's *Richard II* begins. Richard banished both noblemen — Norfolk for life and Bolingbroke for six years — but with the promise that the great estates which should come to Bolingbroke on the death of his father (John of Gaunt, Duke of Lancaster), should not be violated. Nevertheless, when Gaunt died a few months later, Richard broke his promise and seized the Lancaster estates to pay for his expedition to subdue a rebellion in Ireland. While Richard was away, Bolingbroke landed in Yorkshire, declaring that he had come to recover his rights as Duke of Lancaster. The Percies of Northumberland — the greatest and most powerful family in the northern parts — joined him, together with all Richard's enemies. When Richard returned to England, he found himself deserted. Bolingbroke now claimed the throne, and Richard was obliged to abdicate in favor of Bolingbroke, who became king as Henry IV. Plotting against the new king began almost at once. In 1400 Richard II was murdered. Here the play of *Richard II* ends.

Henry IV is the sequel to *Richard II;* it covers the period of the next two and a half years, that is, 1400–03.

Richard II left no children. The line of the Black Prince being thus extinct, the next heir to the throne by right of birth was therefore the senior surviving descendant of Lionel, Duke of Clarence (second son of Edward III). Lionel's daughter Phillipa had married Edmund Mortimer, third Earl of March. She had three children, Roger (who became fourth Earl of March), Elizabeth (who married Henry Percy, called "Hotspur," son of the Earl of Northumberland, and who is Lady Percy in the play), and Edmund. Roger had died in Ireland in 1398 and *his* son Edmund, fifth Earl of March, was thus the legal heir to the throne.

The reign of Henry IV was full of troubles. The first serious rebellion occurred in 1403 when Owen Glendower, a Welsh chieftain, led a national rising against the English. King Henry went against him, but without success. He therefore left the command to Hotspur and Edmund Mortimer (uncle of Edmund, Earl of March) [1] and returned to London. Mortimer was captured by Glendower, but the two men became

---

[1] Shakespeare confused the two Edmunds. The Edmund who married the Welsh lady was *not* heir to the throne. See Genealogical Table below.

friends, and Mortimer married Glendower's daughter. Hotspur went back to the North, where at Holmedon Hill he defeated a large army of invading Scots under Douglas.

Soon afterward the Percies quarreled with the king. The chief members of the family were Henry, Earl of Northumberland, Henry "Hotspur" (his son), and Thomas Percy, Earl of Worcester (his brother). When the king demanded that the Percies should hand over the valuable ransoms exacted from the prisoners taken at Holmedon, the Percies refused and rebelled. They planned to gather a combined force to meet the king, their allies being Mortimer, Glendower, and Douglas with his Scots. Hotspur and Douglas marched south to join with Glendower. The issue was decided at the Battle of Shrewsbury (1403). Hotspur was killed,

Worcester captured and beheaded, and Douglas captured and ransomed; Northumberland, who was not present at the battle, submitted.

It is difficult nowadays to realize the vast power of these great nobles, most of whom were related by marriage to the royal family. Moreover, by their various intermarriages and alliances they amassed great wealth and owned much land, which meant also the services of those who lived and worked on the land. Their castles were fortified palaces, and it was easy for a nobleman to raise and maintain a private army of retainers from his estates, especially in days when a soldier needed little further equipment than a sword, a helmet, a bow, and a bundle of arrows.

The First Part of Henry IV comes to an end with the Battle of Shrewsbury.

GENEALOGICAL TABLE

THE HOUSE OF LANCASTER

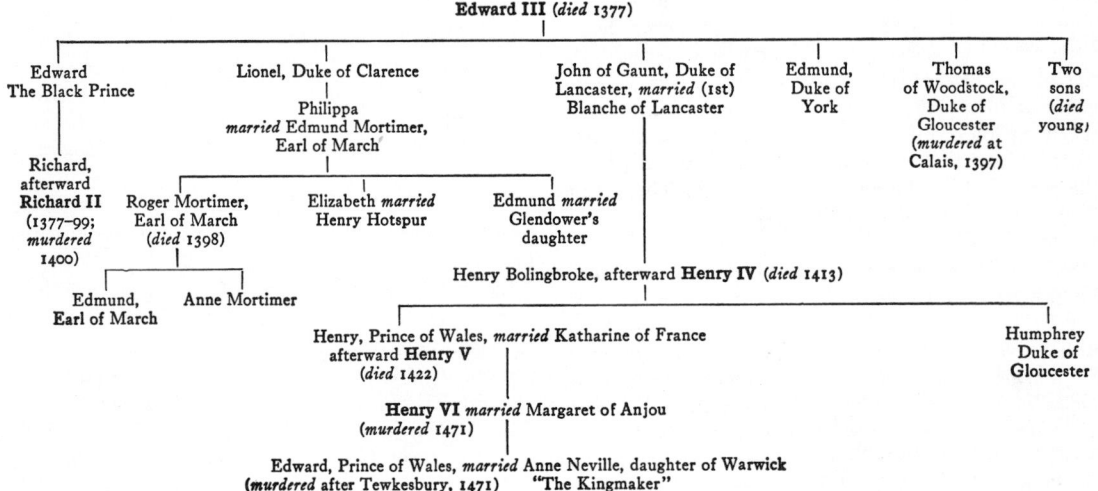

KING HENRY THE FOURTH, Part I

King Henry IV, Part I is the best of Shakespeare's history plays, and the first in which he reached full maturity as a dramatist. The serious scenes are complete in themselves and tell a coherent and moving story — how the unscrupulous king forced the Percies into rebellion so that he might destroy dangerous rivals. The comic scenes of Sir John Falstaff and his disreputable gang contrast and enhance the lessons of sober history. All the persons are alive from the first, for Shakespeare took elaborate care in creating his characters, as has already been suggested in the analysis of Hotspur on p. 53.

But the most notable person in the play is the fat knight, Sir John Falstaff, the supreme comic character in all drama. In creating Falstaff, Shakespeare used principally his own eyes and ears. Falstaff is the gross incarnation of a type of soldier found in any army, and there were many such — though on a lower level of greatness — swarming in London when the play was first written, spending the profits of the last campaign in taverns, brothels, and playhouses, while they intrigued for a new command in the next season's campaign. Some of these captains were of good background and education, younger sons of good family who preferred the excitements and loot of the wars to a quiet, drab life of country pursuits. Many of them were rogues who cheated the government and their own men on all occasions.

There is no need to debate whether Falstaff was a coward. His philosophy, like that of many a better man, was simple: "The better part of valor is discretion" (V.iv.120), and "Honor is a mere scutcheon" (V.i.142–43). "Give me life," he comments over the dead Blunt, "which if I can save, so; if not, honor comes unlooked-for, and there's an end." (V.iii.63–64). Nor can much be said in defense of Falstaff's morals. Though he can quote Scripture on occasion, he is a liar, a drunkard, and a cheat; he robs the poor and flouts every civic virtue; but on the stage at least he redeems his vices by his incomparable wit and his skill in escaping from every tight corner. It is as well not to regard Falstaff too solemnly, for in his own words (*II Hen IV,* I.ii. 10–12), "I am not only witty in myself, but the cause that wit is in other men" — which is justification enough.

As for Prince Henry, he is shown as a young man who is deliberately posing as a waster so that when the time comes he may the more effectively confound the gloomy prophets and begin his reign by surprising his subjects. Herein he is as politic and crafty as his father. Henry IV had deliberately affected modesty, humility, and sobriety in contrast to his cousin, the shallow, pleasure-loving Richard II. Prince Hal purposely mixes with low company to contrast with his father; if his companions in riot do not realize their subordinate parts, the misfortune is theirs. In battle he shows himself the superior of young Harry Hotspur, not only as a soldier but in his far clearer understanding of men and of himself. This calculating self-control in all companies may not make Prince Hal an amiable man, but it is preparing him to become a ruthlessly efficient ruler.

DATE AND SOURCE OF THE PLAY. *I Henry IV* was probably written in the autumn of 1597. The play was entered for printing on February 26, 1598, and a quarto (Q1) was issued soon afterward; this quarto was reprinted in 1599, and in 1604, 1608, 1613, and 1622. Falstaff was the most popular of all Shakespeare's characters and was more often mentioned and quoted than any other. The source of the historical scenes was Raphael Holinshed's *Chronicles of England.* When Shakespeare first wrote the play, the fat knight was called Sir John Oldcastle. The original Oldcastle, sometimes called Lord Cobham, lived in the time of Henry IV and Henry V and was burned for heresy. The name Oldcastle caused Shakespeare considerable trouble. In 1597 the title of Lord Cobham had recently passed to a nobleman called Henry Brooke, who was so greatly offended that his predecessor should be presented on a public stage in such a disreputable guise that Shakespeare was obliged to alter the name. The fat knight was therefore renamed Falstaff, after Sir John Fastolfe, who had already made a brief but discreditable appearance in *I Henry VI.*

The adventures of Sir John Falstaff and Prince Hal are wholly fictitious and mostly Shakespeare's own inventing, though the Prince's wild behavior had long become a stage tradition and had been shown in at least one play which still survives in print. This was a crude piece called *The Famous Victories of Henry the Fifth,* which crams into a succession of short scenes the more popular episodes of the king's life.

King Henry the Fourth, Part I

DRAMATIS PERSONAE

KING HENRY *the Fourth*
HENRY, *Prince of Wales* } *sons to the King*
JOHN *of Lancaster*
EARL OF WESTMORELAND
SIR WALTER BLUNT
THOMAS PERCY, *Earl of Worcester*
HENRY PERCY, *Earl of Northumberland*
HENRY PERCY, *surnamed* HOTSPUR, *his son*
EDMUND MORTIMER, *Earl of March*
RICHARD SCROOP, *Archbishop of York*
ARCHIBALD, *Earl of Douglas*
OWEN GLENDOWER
SIR RICHARD VERNON
SIR JOHN FALSTAFF
SIR MICHAEL, *a friend to the Archbishop of York*

POINS
GADSHILL
PETO
BARDOLPH

LADY PERCY, *wife to Hotspur and sister to Mortimer*
LADY MORTIMER, *daughter to Glendower and wife to Mortimer*
MISTRESS QUICKLY, *hostess of a tavern in Eastcheap*

LORDS, OFFICERS, SHERIFF, VINTNER, CHAMBERLAIN, DRAWERS, *two* CARRIERS, TRAVELERS, *and* ATTENDANTS

SCENE — *England and Wales.*

Act I

SCENE I. *London. The palace.*

[*Enter* KING HENRY, LORD JOHN OF LANCASTER, *the* EARL OF WESTMORELAND, SIR WALTER BLUNT, *and others.*]

KING. So shaken as we are, so wan with care,
Find we° a time for frighted peace to pant,
And breathe short-winded accents of new broils
To be commenced in stronds° afar remote.
No more the thirsty entrance of this soil   5
Shall daub her lips with her own children's blood.
No more shall trenching war° channel her fields,
Nor bruise her flowerets° with the armèd hoofs
Of hostile paces. Those opposèd eyes,
Which, like the meteors° of a troubled heaven,   10
All of one nature, of one substance bred,
Did lately meet in the intestine shock°
And furious close° of civil butchery,
Shall now, in mutual well-beseeming° ranks,
March all one way, and be no more opposed   15
Against acquaintance, kindred, and allies.
The edge of war, like an ill-sheathèd knife,
No more shall cut his master. Therefore, friends,
As far as to the sepulcher of Christ,
Whose soldier now, under whose blessèd cross   20
We are impressèd° and engaged to fight,

Forthwith a power of English shall we levy,
Whose arms were molded in their mothers' womb
To chase these pagans in those holy fields
Over whose acres walked those blessed feet   25
Which fourteen hundred years ago were nailed
For our advantage on the bitter cross.
But this our purpose now is twelvemonth old,
And bootless 'tis to tell you we will go.
Therefore we meet not now.° Then let me hear   30
Of you, my gentle cousin° Westmoreland,
What yesternight our Council did decree
In forwarding this dear expedience.°
    WEST. My liege, this haste was hot in question,°
And many limits of the charge° set down   35
But yesternight, when all athwart° there came
A post° from Wales loaden° with heavy news,
Whose worst was that the noble Mortimer,°
Leading the men of Herefordshire to fight
Against the irregular° and wild Glendower,   40
Was by the rude hands of that Welshman taken,
A thousand of his people butchered.
Upon whose dead corpse there was such misuse,
Such beastly shameless transformation,
By those Welshwomen done as may not be   45
Without much shame retold or spoken of.
    KING. It seems then that the tidings of this broil
Brake off our business for the Holy Land.

Act I, Sc. i: **2. Find we:** let us find.   **4. stronds:** strands, shores.   **7. trenching war:** trench warfare.   **8. flowerets:** little flowers.   **10. meteors:** comets or shooting stars, regarded as terrifying omens.   **12. intestine shock:** clash of civil war.   **13. close:** hand-to-hand battle.   **14. well-beseeming:** seemly.   **21. impressed:** enlisted.

29–30. bootless . . . now: i.e., there is no need to tell you of my decision, which has long been made. Our present meeting is to consider the details. **bootless:** vain.   **31. cousin:** kinsman, used of any near relation.   **33. dear expedience:** urgent enterprise, dear to me.   **34. hot in question:** under eager discussion.   **35. limits . . . charge:** estimates of the cost.   **36. athwart:** cutting across.   **37. post:** messenger. **loaden:** laden.   **38. Mortimer:** See headnote and Genealogical Table, p. 58.   **40. irregular:** unruly.

WEST. This matched with other did, my gracious
  lord;
For more uneven° and unwelcome news   50
Came from the north and thus it did import:
On Holyrood Day,° the gallant Hotspur there,
Young Harry Percy, and brave Archibald,
That ever valiant and approvèd° Scot,
At Holmedon° met,   55
Where they did spend a sad and bloody hour,
As by discharge of their artillery,
And shape of likelihood,° the news was told.
For he that brought them, in the very heat
And pride of their contention° did take horse,   60
Uncertain of the issue° any way.
  KING. Here is a dear, a true industrious friend,
Sir Walter Blunt, new-lighted from his horse,
Stained with the variation of each soil
Betwixt that Holmedon and this seat of ours,   65
And he hath brought us smooth and welcome news.
The Earl of Douglas is discomfited.
Ten thousand bold Scots, two and twenty knights,
Balked° in their own blood did Sir Walter see
On Holmedon's plains. Of prisoners, Hotspur took
Mordake the Earl of Fife, and eldest son   71
To beaten Douglas; and the Earl of Athol,
Of Murray, Angus, and Menteith.
And is not this an honorable spoil?
A gallant prize? Ha, Cousin, is it not?   75
  WEST. In faith,
It is a conquest for a prince to boast of.
  KING. Yea, there thou makest me sad and makest
  me sin
In envy that my Lord Northumberland
Should be the father to so blest a son —   80
A son who is the theme of honor's tongue,
Amongst a grove, the very straightest plant,
Who is sweet Fortune's minion° and her pride —
Whilst I, by looking on the praise of him,
See riot and dishonor stain the brow   85
Of my young Harry. Oh, that it could be proved
That some night-tripping fairy° had exchanged
In cradle clothes our children where they lay,
And called mine Percy, his Plantagenet!
Then would I have his Harry, and he mine.   90
But let him from my thoughts. What think you,
  Coz,°
Of this young Percy's° pride? The prisoners
Which he in this adventure hath surprised

To his own use he keeps, and sends me word
I shall have none but Mordake Earl of Fife.   95
  WEST. This is his uncle's teaching. This is Wor-
  cester,
Malevolent° to you in all aspects,
Which makes him prune° himself, and bristle up
The crest of youth against your dignity.
  KING. But I have sent for him to answer this,   100
And for this cause awhile we must neglect
Our holy purpose to Jerusalem.
Cousin, on Wednesday next our Council we
Will hold at Windsor. So inform the lords,
But come yourself with speed to us again,   105
For more is to be said and to be done
Than out of anger° can be uttered.
  WEST. I will, my liege.   [*Exeunt.*]

SCENE II. *London. An apartment of the
Prince's.*

[*Enter the* PRINCE OF WALES *and* FALSTAFF.]
  FAL. Now, Hal, what time of day is it, lad?
  PRINCE. Thou art so fat-witted, with drinking of
old sack° and unbuttoning thee after supper and
sleeping upon benches after noon, that thou hast forgotten to demand that truly which thou wouldst   5
truly know. What a devil hast thou to do with the
time of the day? Unless hours were cups of sack, and
minutes capons, and clocks the tongues of bawds,
and dials the signs of leaping houses,° and the
blessed sun himself a fair hot wench in flame-colored
taffeta,° I see no reason why thou shouldst be so
superfluous to demand the time of the day.   13
  FAL. Indeed, you come near me now, Hal; for we
that take purses go by the moon and the seven stars,
and not by Phoebus,° he, " that wandering knight so
fair." And I prithee, sweet wag, when thou art King,
as, God save thy Grace — Majesty I should say, for
grace thou wilt have none ——   20
  PRINCE. What, none?
  FAL. No, by my troth,° not so much as will serve
to be prologue to an egg and butter.   24
  PRINCE. Well, how then? Come, roundly, roundly.
  FAL. Marry, then, sweet wag, when thou art King,
let not us that are squires of the night's body be
called thieves of the day's beauty.° Let us be Diana's

---

foresters,° gentlemen of the shade, minions of the moon. And let men say we be men of good government,° being governed, as the sea is, by our noble and chaste mistress the moon, under whose countenance we steal.   33

PRINCE. Thou sayest well, and it holds well too; for the fortune of us that are the moon's men doth ebb and flow like the sea, being governed, as the sea is, by the moon. As for proof, now — a purse of gold most resolutely snatched on Monday night and   39 most dissolutely spent on Tuesday morning; got with swearing "Lay by"° and spent with crying "Bring in"° — now in as low an ebb as the foot of the ladder,° and by and by in as high a flow as the ridge of the gallows.

FAL. By the Lord, thou sayest true, lad. And is not my hostess of the tavern a most sweet wench?   46

PRINCE. As the honey of Hybla,° my old lad of the castle.° And is not a buff jerkin° a most sweet robe of durance?°

FAL. How now, how now, mad wag! What, in thy quips° and thy quiddities?° What a plague have I to do with a buff jerkin?   52

PRINCE. Why, what a pox have I to do with my hostess of the tavern?

FAL. Well, thou hast called her to a reckoning many a time and oft.

PRINCE. Did I ever call for thee to pay thy part?

FAL. No. I'll give thee thy due, thou hast paid all there.   60

PRINCE. Yea, and elsewhere, so far as my coin would stretch. And where it would not, I have used my credit.   63

FAL. Yea, and so used it that, were it not here apparent that thou art heir° apparent —— But I prithee, sweet wag, shall there be gallows standing in England when thou art King? And resolution° thus fobbed° as it is with the rusty curb of old Father Antic° the law? Do not thou, when thou art King, hang a thief.   70

PRINCE. No, thou shalt.

FAL. Shall I? Oh, rare! By the Lord, I'll be a brave judge.

PRINCE. Thou judgest false already. I mean thou shalt have the hanging of the thieves and so become a rare hangman.   76

FAL. Well, Hal, well, and in some sort it jumps° with my humor° as well as waiting in the court, I can tell you.

PRINCE. For obtaining of suits?   80

FAL. Yea, for obtaining of suits,° whereof the hangman° hath no lean wardrobe. 'Sblood,° I am as melancholy as a gib-cat° or a lugged bear.°

PRINCE. Or an old lion, or a lover's lute.   84

FAL. Yea, or the drone of a Lincolnshire bagpipe.

PRINCE. What sayest thou to a hare,° or the melancholy of Moorditch?°   88

FAL. Thou hast the most unsavory similes, and art indeed the most comparative,° rascaliest, sweet young Prince. But, Hal, I prithee trouble me no more with vanity. I would to God thou and I knew where a commodity° of good names were to be bought. An old lord of the Council rated° me the other day   94 in the street about you, sir, but I marked him not; and yet he talked very wisely, but I regarded him not; and yet he talked wisely, and in the street too.

PRINCE. Thou didst well, for wisdom cries out in the streets, and no man regards it.°   100

FAL. Oh, thou hast damnable iteration,° and art indeed able to corrupt a saint. Thou hast done much harm upon me, Hal. God forgive thee for it! Before I knew thee, Hal, I knew nothing; and now am I, if a man should speak truly, little better than one   105 of the wicked. I must give over this life, and I will give it over. By the Lord, an° I do not, I am a villain. I'll be damned for never a king's son in Christendom.

PRINCE. Where shall we take a purse tomorrow, Jack?   111

FAL. 'Zounds,° where thou wilt, lad. I'll make one. An I do not, call me villain and baffle° me.

PRINCE. I see a good amendment of life in thee — from praying to purse-taking.

FAL. Why, Hal, 'tis my vocation, Hal. 'Tis no sin for a man to labor in his vocation.   117 [Enter POINS.] Poins! Now shall we know if Gadshill have set a match.° Oh, if men were to be saved by merit, what hole in Hell were hot enough for him? This is the most omnipotent villain that ever cried "Stand" to a true man.

PRINCE. Good morrow, Ned.   123

POINS. Good morrow, sweet Hal. What says Mon-

28–29. Diana's foresters: thieves who rob by night, Diana being the goddess of the moon.   30–31. good government: well-behaved.   41. Lay by: i.e., "stick 'em up."   42. Bring in: i.e., the drink.   43. ladder: from which a condemned man was thrust off the gallows into space.   47. Hybla: in Sicily, famous for its honey.   47–48. old . . . castle: roisterer, with a pun on Falstaff's original name of Oldcastle.   48. buff jerkin: leather coat worn by the sheriff's sergeant.   49. robe of durance: coat that endures (wears well) and that takes you to *durance* (prison).   51. quips: wisecracks. quiddities: quibbles.   64–65. here . . . heir: a pun, *heir* being pronounced as "hair."   67. resolution: a stout heart.   68. fobbed: fubbed, cheated.   69. Father Antic: i.e., Daddy Buffoon.

77. jumps: agrees.   78. humor: whim.   81. obtaining of suits: with a pun on *suit* — "petitions 'to the sovereign for favor" and "clothes."   82. hangman: The clothes of the executed were the hangman's perquisite. 'Sblood: by God's blood.   83. gib-cat: tomcat. lugged bear: a bear mauled in bearbaiting.   87. hare: regarded as a melancholy creature.   88. melancholy of Moorditch: Moorditch was one of the open sewers of the City of London, proverbial for its stink.   90. comparative: quick at making comparisons.   93. commodity: parcel.   94. rated: rebuked.   90–100. wisdom . . . it: quoted loosely from Proverbs 1:20–24.   101. iteration: ability to quote.   107. an: if.   112. 'Zounds: by God's Wounds.   113. baffle: disgrace; lit., degrade me from my knighthood.   119. set a match: "framed a holdup."

sieur Remorse? What says Sir John Sack and Sugar?
Jack! How agrees the Devil and thee about thy soul,
that thou soldest him on Good Friday last for a cup
of Madeira and a cold capon's leg?°   129

PRINCE. Sir John stands to his word, the Devil
shall have his bargain, for he was never yet a breaker
of proverbs.° He will give the Devil his due.

POINS. Then art thou damned for keeping thy
word with the Devil.   135

PRINCE. Else he had been damned for cozening°
the Devil.

POINS. But, my lads, my lads, tomorrow morning,
by four o'clock, early at Gadshill!° There are pilgrims going to Canterbury with rich offer-   140
ings,° and traders riding to London with fat purses.
I have vizards° for you all, you have horses for yourselves. Gadshill lies tonight in Rochester. I have be-
spoke° supper tomorrow night in Eastcheap. We
may do it as secure as sleep. If you will go, I   145
will stuff your purses full of crowns. If you will not,
tarry at home and be hanged.

FAL. Hear ye, Yedward,° if I tarry at home and go
not, I'll hang you for going.   150

POINS. You will, chops?

FAL. Hal, wilt thou make one?

PRINCE. Who, I rob? I a thief? Not I, by my faith.

FAL. There's neither honesty, manhood, nor good
fellowship in thee, nor thou camest not of the blood
royal, if thou darest not stand for ten shillings.°

PRINCE. Well then, once in my days I'll be a madcap.   160

FAL. Why, that's well said.

PRINCE. Well, come what will, I'll tarry at home.

FAL. By the Lord, I'll be a traitor then, when thou
art King.   165

PRINCE. I care not.

POINS. Sir John, I prithee, leave the Prince and me
alone. I will lay him down such reasons for this adventure that he shall go.   169

FAL. Well, God give thee the spirit of persuasion
and him the ears of profiting, that what thou speak-
est may move and what he hears may be believed,°
that the true Prince may, for recreation sake, prove a
false thief; for the poor abuses of the time want
countenance.° Farewell. You shall find me in Eastcheap.   176

PRINCE. Farewell, thou latter spring!° Farewell,
Allhallown summer!°   [*Exit* FALSTAFF.]

POINS. Now, my good sweet honey lord, ride with
us tomorrow. I have a jest to execute that I can-   180
not manage alone. Falstaff, Bardolph, Peto, and
Gadshill shall rob those men that we have already
waylaid. Yourself and I will not be there, and when
they have the booty, if you and I do not rob them,
cut this head off from my shoulders.

PRINCE. How shall we part with them in setting
forth?   188

POINS. Why, we will set forth before or after them,
and appoint them a place of meeting, wherein it is at
our pleasure to fail, and then will they adventure
upon the exploit themselves; which they shall have
no sooner achieved but we'll set upon them.   194

PRINCE. Yea, but 'tis like that they will know us
by our horses, by our habits,° and by every other
appointment,° to be ourselves.

POINS. Tut! Our horses they shall not see, I'll tie
them in the wood. Our vizards we will change after
we leave them. And, sirrah, I have cases of buck-
ram° for the nonce,° to immask our noted outward
garments.   202

PRINCE. Yea, but I doubt they will be too hard for
us.

POINS. Well, for two of them, I know them to be
as true-bred cowards as ever turned back; and for
the third, if he fight longer than he sees rea-   207
son,° I'll forswear arms. The virtue of this jest will
be the incomprehensible lies that this same fat rogue
will tell us when we meet at supper — how thirty, at
least, he fought with; what wards,° what blows,
what extremities he endured. And in the reproof° of
this lies the jest.   213

PRINCE. Well, I'll go with thee. Provide us all
things necessary and meet me tomorrow night in
Eastcheap. There I'll sup. Farewell.

POINS. Farewell, my lord.   [*Exit.*]

PRINCE. I know you all,° and will a while uphold°
The unyoked humor° of your idleness.
Yet herein will I imitate the sun,   220
Who doth permit the base contagious° clouds
To smother up his beauty from the world,
That, when he please again to be himself,
Being wanted, he may be more wondered at
By breaking through the foul and ugly mists   225
Of vapors that did seem to strangle him.

128–29. Good . . . leg: Good Friday being the Church's most
solemn fast day, to drink Madeira and eat chicken was a damnable sin.   131–32. breaker of proverbs: one to prove proverbs false.
136. cozening: cheating.   139. Gadshill: near Rochester in Kent.
Some slight confusion is caused as the same name is used for
one of the gang. See l. 118, and II.i. 36–106.   140–41. rich
offerings: i.e., for the shrine of Saint Thomas à Becket at Canterbury.   142. vizards: masks.   144. bespoke: ordered.   149. Yedward: a form of Edward, Poins's first name.   157–58. blood . . .
shillings: pun on *royal*, a coin worth 10s.   170–72. God . . .
believed: Falstaff constantly drops into the pious jargon of
professional preachers.   174–75. want countenance: need encouragement.

177. latter spring: late spring; i.e., green autumn.   178. Allhallown summer: Indian summer. Allhallown (All Saints' Day) is
on November 1.   196. habits: clothes.   197. appointment: ac-
couterment.   200–01. cases of buckram: overalls of coarse linen.
201. nonce: occasion.   207–08. fight . . . reason: This is Falstaff's
avowed rule of life. See later V.iv.120.   211. wards: defense.
See II.iv.215.   212. reproof: rebuttal.   218. I . . . all: This
soliloquy is important for the understanding of the Prince's
later treatment of Falstaff and the gang. uphold: tolerate.
219. unyoked humor: unrestrained behavior.   221. contagious:
poisonous.

If all the year were playing holidays,
To sport would be as tedious as to work.
But when they seldom come, they wished-for come,
And nothing pleaseth but rare accidents.   230
So, when this loose behavior I throw off
And pay the debt I never promisèd,
By how much better than my word I am,
By so much shall I falsify men's hopes.
And like bright metal on a sullen° ground,   235
My reformation, glittering o'er my fault,
Shall show more goodly and attract more eyes
Than that which hath no foil° to set it off.
I'll so offend, to make offense a skill,°
Redeeming time° when men think least I will.   240
                                                        [*Exit.*]

SCENE III. *London. The palace.*

[*Enter the* KING, NORTHUMBERLAND, WORCESTER,
    HOTSPUR, SIR WALTER BLUNT, *with others.*]
KING. My blood hath been too cold and temperate,
Unapt to stir at these indignities,
And you have found me;° for accordingly
You tread upon my patience. But be sure
I will from henceforth rather be myself,°   5
Mighty and to be feared, than my condition,°
Which hath been smooth as oil, soft as young down,
And therefore lost that title of respect°
Which the proud soul ne'er pays but to the proud.
WOR. Our house, my sovereign liege, little de-
    serves   10
The scourge of greatness to be used on it,
And that same greatness too which our own hands
Have holp° to make so portly.°
    NORTH. My lord ——
        KING. Worcester, get thee gone, for I do see   15
Danger and disobedience in thine eye.
O sir, your presence is too bold and peremptory,
And Majesty might never yet endure
The moody frontier of a servant brow.°
You have good leave to leave us.° When we need
Your use and counsel, we shall send for you.   21
                                          [*Exit* WORCESTER.]
[*To* NORTHUMBERLAND] You were about to speak.
    NORTH.   Yea, my good lord.
Those prisoners in your Highness' name demanded,°

235. sullen: dull.   238. foil: lit., tin foil set behind a jewel to
give it luster.   239. skill: art.   240. Redeeming time: making
up for the time I have lost.
    Sc. iii: 3. found me: found me out.   5. myself: i.e., King.
6. than my condition: than my naturally mild disposition.   8. title
of respect: claim to be respected.   13. holp: helped. portly: magnificent.   19. moody . . . brow: frowning look on a servant's brow.
20. leave . . . us: a polite phrase of dismissal.   23. prisoners
. . . demanded: In earlier times a prisoner became the property
of his captor, who released him on payment of a ransom according to his rank and wealth.

Which Harry Percy here at Holmedon took,
Were, as he says, not with such strength denied   25
As is delivered to your Majesty.
Either envy,° therefore, or misprision°
Is guilty of this fault, and not my son.
    HOT. My liege, I did deny no prisoners.
But I remember, when the fight was done,   30
When I was dry with rage and éxtreme toil,
Breathless and faint, leaning upon my sword,
Came there a certain lord, neat, and trimly dressed,
Fresh as a bridegroom, and his chin new-reaped°
Showed like a stubble land at harvest home.   35
He was perfumèd like a milliner,
And 'twixt his finger and his thumb he held
A pouncet box,° which ever and anon
He gave his nose and took 't away again;
Who therewith angry, when it next came there,   40
Took it in snuff.° And still he smiled and talked,
And as the soldiers bore dead bodies by,
He called them untaught knaves, unmannerly,
To bring a slovenly unhandsome corse°
Betwixt the wind and his nobility.   45
With many holiday and lady terms°
He questioned me, amongst the rest, demanded
My prisoners in your Majesty's behalf.
I then, all smarting with my wounds being cold,
To be so pestered with a popinjay,°   50
Out of my grief° and my impatience
Answered neglectingly I know not what,
He should, or he should not; for he made me mad
To see him shine so brisk, and smell so sweet,
And talk so like a waiting gentlewoman°   55
Of guns and drums and wounds — God save the
    mark! —°
And telling me the sovereign'st° thing on earth
Was parmaceti° for an inward bruise;
And that it was great pity, so it was,
This villainous saltpeter should be digged   60
Out of the bowels of the harmless earth,
Which many a good tall° fellow had destroyed
So cowardly; and but for these vile guns,
He would himself have been a soldier.
This bald unjointed chat° of his, my lord,   65
I answered indirectly, as I said.
And I beseech you, let not his report
Come current° for an accusation

27. envy: malice—of Hotspur's enemies. misprision: misunderstanding.   34. chin new-reaped: beard closely cut.   38. pouncet
box: small box containing perfume, which the fastidious sniffed
to counteract foul smells.   41. Took . . . snuff: sniffed, with a pun
on the idiomatic meaning "resented."   44. corse: corpse.   46. holiday . . . terms: fancy phrases, as opposed to "working-day" or
plain English.   50. popinjay: parrot.   51. grief: smart (of my
wounds).   55. waiting gentlewoman: lady in waiting, the essence
of fancy femininity.   56. God . . . mark: an impatient apology
for a coarse remark.   57. sovereign'st: most excellent.   58. par-
maceti: spermaceti, a fatty substance found in the whale and
used as an ointment.   62. tall: brave.   65. bald . . . chat: slight
disconnected chatter.   68. Come current: be regarded as valid.

Betwixt my love and your high Majesty.
    BLUNT. The circumstance considered, good my
      lord,   70
Whate'er Lord Harry Percy then had said
To such a person and in such a place,
At such a time, with all the rest retold,
May reasonably die and never rise
To do him wrong, or any way impeach°   75
What then he said, so he unsay it now.
    KING. Why, yet° he doth deny his prisoners,
But with proviso° and exception,
That we at our own charge shall ransom straight
His brother-in-law, the foolish Mortimer,   80
Who, on my soul, hath willfully betrayed
The lives of those that he did lead to fight
Against that great magician,° damned Glendower,
Whose daughter, as we hear, the Earl of March
Hath lately married. Shall our coffers, then,   85
Be emptied to redeem a traitor home?
Shall we buy treason, and indent° with fears,
When they have lost and forfeited themselves?
No, on the barren mountains let him starve.
For I shall never hold that man my friend   90
Whose tongue shall ask me for one penny cost
To ransom home revolted Mortimer.
    HOT. Revolted Mortimer!
He never did fall off,° my sovereign liege,
But by the chance of war. To prove that true   95
Needs no more but one tongue for all those wounds,
Those mouthèd° wounds, which valiantly he took
When on the gentle Severn's sedgy° bank,
In single opposition, hand to hand,
He did confound° the best part of an hour   100
In changing hardiment° with great Glendower.
Three times they breathed and three times did they
    drink,
Upon agreement, of swift Severn's flood;
Who then, affrighted with their bloody looks,
Ran fearfully among the trembling reeds,   105
And hid his crisp head in the hollow bank
Bloodstainèd with these valiant combatants.
Never did base and rotten policy°
Color her working° with such deadly wounds;
Nor never could the noble Mortimer   110
Receive so many, and all willingly.
Then let not him be slandered with revolt.
    KING. Thou dost belie him,° Percy, thou dost belie
    him.
He never did encounter with Glendower.
I tell thee,   115
He durst as well have met the Devil alone

As Owen Glendower for an enemy.
Art thou not ashamed? But, sirrah,° henceforth
Let me not hear you speak of Mortimer.
Send me your prisoners with the speediest means,
Or you shall hear in such a kind from me   121
As will displease you. My Lord Northumberland,
We license your departure with your son.
Send us your prisoners, or you will hear of it.
    [*Exeunt* KING HENRY, BLUNT, *and train.*]
    HOT. An if the Devil come and roar for them,
I will not send them. I will after straight   126
And tell him so, for I will ease my heart,
Albeit I make a hazard° of my head.
    NORTH. What, drunk with choler?° Stay and
    pause awhile.
Here comes your uncle.
    [*Re-enter* WORCESTER.]
    HOT.   Speak of Mortimer!   130
'Zounds, I will speak of him, and let my soul
Want mercy if I do not join with him.
Yea, on his part I'll empty all these veins,
And shed my dear blood drop by drop in the dust,
But I will lift the downtrod Mortimer   135
As high in the air as this unthankful King,
As this ingrate and cankered° Bolingbroke.
    NORTH. Brother, the King hath made your nephew
    mad.
    WOR. Who struck this heat up after I was gone?
    HOT. He will, forsooth, have all my prisoners.
And when I urged the ransom once again   141
Of my wife's brother, then his cheek looked pale,
And on my face he turned an eye of death,
Trembling even at the name of Mortimer.
    WOR. I cannot blame him. Was not he proclaimed
By Richard that dead is the next of blood?   146
    NORTH. He was, I heard the proclamation.
And then it was when the unhappy King—
Whose wrongs in us God pardon!° — did set forth
Upon his Irish expedition,   150
From whence he intercepted° did return
To be deposed and shortly° murderèd.
    WOR. And for whose death we in the world's wide
    mouth
Live scandalized and foully spoken of.
    HOT. But, soft, I pray you. Did King Richard
    then   155
Proclaim my brother° Edmund Mortimer
Heir to the crown?
    NORTH.   He did, myself did hear it.
    HOT. Nay, then I cannot blame his cousin King,
That wished him on the barren mountains starve.
But shall it be that you, that set the crown   160

Upon the head of this forgetful man,
And for his sake wear the detested blot
Of murderous subornation,° shall it be
That you a world of curses undergo,
Being the agents, or base second means,°   165
The cords, the ladder, or the hangman rather?
Oh, pardon me that I descend so low,
To show the line° and the predicament°
Wherein you range° under this subtle King.
Shall it for shame be spoken in these days,   170
Or fill up chronicles in time to come,
That men of your nobility and power
Did gage° them both in an unjust behalf,
As both of you — God pardon it! — have done,
To put down Richard, that sweet lovely rose,   175
And plant this thorn, this canker,° Bolingbroke?
And shall it in more shame be further spoken,
That you are fooled, discarded, and shook off
By him for whom these shames ye underwent?
No, yet time serves wherein you may redeem   180
Your banished honors, and restore yourselves
Into the good thoughts of the world again,
Revenge the jeering and disdained° contempt
Of this proud King, who studies day and night
To answer all the debt he owes to you   185
Even with the bloody payment of your deaths.
Therefore, I say ——
    wor.   Peace, Cousin, say no more.
And now I will unclasp a secret book,
And to your quick-conceiving° discontents
I'll read you matter deep and dangerous,   190
As full of peril and adventurous spirit
As to o'erwalk a current roaring loud
On the unsteadfast footing of a spear.°
    hot. If he fall in, good night! Or sink or swim.
Send danger from the east unto the west,   195
So honor cross it from the north to south,
And let them grapple. Oh, the blood more stirs
To rouse a lion than to start a hare!
    north. Imagination of some great exploit
Drives him beyond the bounds of patience.°   200
    hot. By Heaven, methinks it were an easy leap,
To pluck bright honor from the pale-faced moon,
Or dive into the bottom of the deep,
Where fathom line could never touch the ground,
And pluck up drownèd honor by the locks,   205
So he that doth redeem her thence might wear
Without corrival° all her dignities.
But out upon this half-faced fellowship!°

wor. He apprehends a world of figures here,°
But not the form of what he should attend.   210
Good Cousin, give me audience for a while.
    hot. I cry you mercy.
    wor.   Those same noble Scots
That are your prisoners ——
    hot.   I'll keep them all.
By God, he shall not have a Scot of them.
No, if a Scot would save his soul, he shall not.   215
I'll keep them, by this hand.
    wor.   You start away
And lend no ear unto my purposes.
Those prisoners you shall keep.
    hot.   Nay, I will, that's flat.
He said he would not ransom Mortimer,
Forbade my tongue to speak of Mortimer.   220
But I will find him when he lies asleep,
And in his ear I'll holloa " Mortimer!"
Nay,
I'll have a starling° shall be taught to speak
Nothing but " Mortimer," and give it him,   225
To keep his anger still in motion.
    wor. Hear you, Cousin, a word.
    hot. All studies here I solemnly defy,
Save how to gall° and pinch this Bolingbroke.
And that same sword-and-buckler° Prince of
    Wales,
But that I think his father loves him not   231
And would be glad he met with some mischance,
I would have him poisoned with a pot of ale.
    wor. Farewell, kinsman. I'll talk to you
When you are better tempered to attend.   235
    north. Why, what a wasp-stung and impatient
    fool
Art thou to break into this woman's mood,
Tying thine ear to no tongue but thine own!
    hot. Why, look you, I am whipped and scourged
    with rods,
Nettled,° and stung with pismires,° when I hear
Of this vile politician,° Bolingbroke.   241
In Richard's time — what do you call the place?
A plague upon it, it is in Gloucestershire,
'Twas where the madcap Duke his uncle kept,
His uncle York, where I first bowed my knee   245
Unto this king of smiles, this Bolingbroke —
'Sblood! —
When you and he came back from Ravenspurgh.
    north. At Berkeley Castle.°
    hot. You say true.   250
Why, what a candy deal° of courtesy

162–63. wear . . . subornation: wear the mark of shame as accessories to murder. subornation: procuring someone to commit a crime.   165. second means: assistants.   168. line: disgrace. predicament: class, category.   169. range: rank.   173. gage: pledge, engage.   176. canker: wild rose, contrasted with the garden rose.   183. disdained: disdainful.   189. quick-conceiving: quick-witted.   193. unsteadfast . . . spear: with a spear as unsteady bridge.   200. patience: self-control.   207. corrival: partner.   208. half-faced fellowship: starving partnership; i.e., sharing of honor which is insufficient for two to share.

209. apprehends . . . here: i.e., he is entirely carried away by his imagination. figures: shapes, fantasies.   224. starling: The starling, like the jackdaw and the parrot, can be taught to mimic sound.   229. gall: make sore.   230. sword-and-buckler: swashbuckler.   240. Nettled: whipped with nettles. pismires: ants.   241. politician: schemer.   249. Berkeley Castle: For this episode see *Rich II*, II.iii.41–50.   251. candy deal: deal of candy i.e., hypocritical.

This fawning greyhound then did proffer me!
Look, " when his infant fortune came to age,"
And " gentle Harry Percy," and " kind Cousin."
Oh, the devil take such cozeners! God forgive me!
Good Uncle, tell your tale, I have done.   256
    WOR. Nay, if you have not, to it again.
We will stay° your leisure.
    HOT.   I have done, i' faith.
    WOR. Then once more to your Scottish prisoners.
Deliver them up without their ransom straight,   260
And make the Douglas' son your only mean°
For powers° in Scotland; which, for divers reasons
Which I shall send you written, be assured
Will easily be granted. [To NORTHUMBERLAND] You,
    my lord,
Your son in Scotland being thus employed,   265
Shall secretly into the bosom creep
Of that same noble prelate, well beloved,
The Archbishop.
    HOT. Of York, is it not?
    WOR. True, who bears hard°   270
His brother's death at Bristol, the Lord Scroop.
I speak not this in estimation,°
As what I think might be, but what I know
Is ruminated,° plotted, and set down,
And only stays but to behold the face   275
Of that occasion that shall bring it on.
    HOT. I smell it. Upon my life, it will do well.
    NORTH. Before the game is afoot, thou still° let'st
    slip.°
    HOT. Why, it cannot choose but be a noble plot.
And then the power of Scotland and of York,   280
To join with Mortimer, ha?
    WOR.   And so they shall.
    HOT. In faith, it is exceedingly well aimed.
    WOR. And 'tis no little reason bids us speed,
To save our heads by raising of a head;°
For, bear ourselves as even as we can,°   285
The King will always think him in our debt,
And think we think ourselves unsatisfied,
Till he hath found a time to pay us home.
And see already how he doth begin
To make us strangers to his looks of love.   290
    HOT. He does, he does. We'll be revenged on him.
    WOR. Cousin, farewell. No further go in this
Than I by letters shall direct your course.
When time is ripe, which will be suddenly,
I'll steal to Glendower and Lord Mortimer,   295
Where you and Douglas and our powers at once,
As I will fashion° it, shall happily meet,
To bear our fortunes in our own strong arms,

Which now we hold at much uncertainty.
    NORTH. Farewell, good Brother. We shall thrive,
    I trust.   300
    HOT. Uncle, adieu. Oh, let the hours be short
Till fields and blows and groans applaud our sport!
                                        [Exeunt.]

Act II

SCENE I. *Rochester. An innyard.*

[*Enter a* CARRIER *with a lantern in his hand.*]
    1. CAR. Heigh-ho! An it be not four by the day, I'll
be hanged. Charles's Wain° is over the new chimney, and yet our horse not packed.° What, ostler!   4
    OSTLER. [*Within*] Anon, anon.
    1. CAR. I prithee, Tom, beat° Cut's° saddle, put a
few flocks° in the point.° Poor jade,° is wrung° in
the withers° out of all cess.°   8
                [*Enter another* CARRIER.]
    2. CAR. Peas and beans are as dank here as a dog,
and that is the next way to give poor jades the bots.°
This house is turned upside down since Robin Ostler
died.
    1. CAR. Poor fellow, never joyed since the price of
oats rose. It was the death of him.   14
    2. CAR. I think this be the most villainous house in
all London road for fleas. I am stung like a tench.°
    1. CAR. Like a tench! By the mass, there is ne'er a
king Christen° could be better bit than I have been
since the first cock.   20
    2. CAR. Why, they will allow us ne'er a jordan,°
and then we leak in your chimney, and your chamber lye° breeds fleas like a loach.
    1. CAR. What, ostler! Come away and be hanged!
Come away.   25
    2. CAR. I have a gammon of bacon° and two razes°
of ginger, to be delivered as far as Charing Cross.
    1. CAR. God's body! The turkeys in my pannier°
are quite starved. What, ostler! A plague on thee!
Hast thou never an eye in thy head? Canst not hear?
An 'twere not as good deed as drink to break the pate

---

258. stay: await.   261. mean: means.   262. powers: forces, armies.   270. bears hard: takes hardly.   272. in estimation:
as a guess.   274. ruminated: considered.   278. still: continuously. let'st slip: let loose the greyhound.   284. head: armed
force.   285. bear . . . can: however discreetly we may behave.
297. fashion: contrive.

Act II, Sc. i: 2. Charles's Wain: Charles's Wagon, the constellation of the Great Bear, called also the Great Dipper.
4. horse . . . packed: Carriers at this time used pack horses for
transport.   6. beat: i.e., to make the padding more even. Cut:
name of a horse with a docked tail.   7. flocks: tufts of wool. point:
pommel. jade: horse in poor condition. wrung: galled.   8. withers:
point of the shoulder. out . . . cess: excessively.   10. bots: worms.
16. tench: The tench and the loach (fresh-water fish) are sometimes infested with a form of louse.   19. Christen: Christian.
21. jordan: chamber pot.   23. chamber lye: urine. Elizabethan
sanitary arrangements and domestic habits were crude.   26. gam-
mon of bacon: cured ham. razes: roots.   28. pannier: basket.

on thee, I am a very villain. Come, and be hanged!
Hast no faith in thee?   35

[Enter GADSHILL.*]*

GADS. Good morrow, carriers. What's o'clock?

1. CAR. I think it be two o'clock.

GADS. I prithee lend me thy lantern, to see my gelding in the stable.   39

1. CAR. Nay, by God, soft,° I know a trick worth
two of that, i' faith.

GADS. I pray thee, lend me thine.

2. CAR. Aye, when? Canst tell?° Lend me thy lantern, quoth he? Marry, I'll see thee hanged first.

GADS. Sirrah carrier, what time do you mean to
come to London?   46

2. CAR. Time enough to go to bed with a candle, I
warrant thee. Come, Neighbor Mugs, we'll call up
the gentlemen. They will along with company, for
they have great charge.°   *[Exeunt* CARRIERS.*]*

GADS. What ho! Chamberlain!°   52

CHAM. *[Within]* At hand, quoth pickpurse.

GADS. That's even as fair as — at hand, quoth the
chamberlain; for thou variest no more from picking
of purses than giving direction doth from laboring.
Thou layest the plot° how.   57

[Enter CHAMBERLAIN.*]*

CHAM. Good morrow, Master Gadshill. It holds
current that I told you yesternight. There's a frank-
lin° in the wild° of Kent hath brought three hundred marks° with him in gold. I heard him tell it to
one of his company last night at supper — a kind of
auditor, one that hath abundance of charge too, God
knows what. They are up already, and call for eggs
and butter. They will away presently.   66

GADS. Sirrah, if they meet not with Saint Nicholas'
clerks,° I'll give thee this neck.

CHAM. No, I'll none of it. I pray thee, keep that for
the hangman, for I know thou worshipest Saint
Nicholas as truly as a man of falsehood may.   72

GADS. What talkest thou to me of the hangman?
If I hang, I'll make a fat pair of gallows; for if I hang,
old Sir John hangs with me, and thou knowest he is
no starveling. Tut! There are other Trojans° that
thou dreamest not of, the which for sport sake   77
are content to do the profession some grace; that
would, if matters should be looked into, for their
own credit sake, make all whole. I am joined with no
foot landrakers,° no long-staff sixpenny strikers,°

none of these mad mustachio purple-hued maltworms;° but with nobility and tranquility, burgomasters and great oneyers,° such as can hold in,°
such as will strike sooner than speak, and speak   85
sooner than drink, and drink sooner than pray. And
yet, 'zounds, I lie; for they pray continually to their
saint, the commonwealth; or rather, not pray to her,
but prey on her, for they ride up and down on her
and make her their boots.°   91

CHAM. What, the commonwealth their boots? Will
she hold out water in foul way?

GADS. She will, she will — justice hath liquored°
her. We steal as in a castle, cocksure. We have the
receipt° of fern seed,° we walk invisible.   96

CHAM. Nay, by my faith, I think you are more
beholding to the night than to fern seed for your
walking invisible.

GADS. Give me thy hand. Thou shalt have a share
in our purchase,° as I am a true man.   101

CHAM. Nay, rather let me have it, as you are a
false thief.

GADS. Go to. "Homo" is a common name to all
men. Bid the ostler bring my gelding out of   105
the stable. Farewell, you muddy° knave.   *[Exeunt.]*

SCENE II. *The highway, near* GADSHILL.

[Enter PRINCE HENRY *and* POINS.*]*

POINS. Come, shelter, shelter. I have removed Falstaff's horse, and he frets like a gummed velvet.°

PRINCE. Stand close.

[Enter FALSTAFF.*]*

FAL. Poins! Poins, and be hanged! Poins!   4

PRINCE. Peace, ye fat-kidneyed rascal! What a
brawling dost thou keep!

FAL. Where's Poins, Hal?

PRINCE. He is walked up to the top of the hill. I'll
go seek him.   9

FAL. I am accursed to rob in that thief's company.
The rascal hath removed my horse, and tied him I
know not where. If I travel but four foot by the
squier° further afoot, I shall break my wind. Well, I
doubt not but to die a fair death for all this, if I 'scape
hanging for killing that rogue. I have forsworn°   16
his company hourly any time this two and twenty
years, and yet I am bewitched with the rogue's

---

40. soft: go easy.   43. Canst tell: i.e., "says you!"   51. great
charge: much money.   52. Chamberlain: man in charge of the
bedrooms at an inn.   57. layest . . . plot: It was a common complaint that the chamberlains of inns were in league with highwaymen.   60. franklin: rich farmer. wild: weald; the hilly district
in Kent and adjoining counties.   61. mark: 13s. 4d. (two thirds of
an English pound).   67–68. Saint Nicholas' clerks: thieves,
Saint Nicholas being their patron saint.   76. Trojans: good
lads.   81. foot landrakers: roving footpads; i.e., thieves so poor
that they go on foot. long-staff . . . strikers: robbers who use a
long staff and will hold a man up for a pittance.

82–83. mustachio . . . maltworms: red-faced tipplers with great
mustaches.   84. oneyers: ones. hold in: keep their mouths shut.
91. boots: booty. The chamberlain caps his remark with a pun
on leather boots.   94. liquored: greased.   96. receipt: directions
for using, recipe. fern seed: The seed of the fern is so small that
it was said to be invisible, and if found on Saint John's Day, to
confer invisibility on the finder.   101. purchase: in thieves' language, plunder.   106. muddy: muddleheaded.
Sc. ii: 2. gummed velvet: Cheap velvet (as well as taffeta) was sometimes treated with gum to give it stiffening,
but it frayed sooner.   13. squier: square, rule.   16. forsworn:
sworn off.

company. If the rascal have not given me medicines°
to make me love him, I'll be hanged; it could not be
else, I have drunk medicines. Poins! Hal! A   21
plague upon you both! Bardolph! Peto! I'll starve ere
I'll rob a foot further. An 'twere not as good a deed
as drink, to turn true man and to leave these rogues,
I am the veriest varlet° that ever chewed with a   25
tooth. Eight yards of uneven ground is threescore
and ten miles afoot with me, and the stony-hearted
villains know it well enough. A plague upon it when
thieves cannot be true one to another! [*They*   30
whistle.] Whew! A plague upon you all! Give me
my horse, you rogues, give me my horse, and be
hanged!

   PRINCE. Peace, ye fat-guts! Lie down, lay thine ear
close to the ground and list if thou canst hear the
tread of travelers.   35

   FAL. Have you any levers to lift me up again,
being down? 'Sblood, I'll not bear mine own flesh so
far afoot again for all the coin in thy father's exchequer. What a plague mean ye to colt° me thus?

   PRINCE. Thou liest. Thou art not colted, thou art
uncolted.   42

   FAL. I prithee, good Prince Hal, help me to my
horse, good king's son.

   PRINCE. Out, ye rogue! Shall I be your ostler?   45

   FAL. Go hang thyself in thine own heir-apparent
garters! If I be ta'en, I'll peach for this. An I have
not ballads° made on you all and sung to filthy tunes,
let a cup of sack be my poison. When a jest is so forward, and afoot too! I hate it.   50

[*Enter* GADSHILL, BARDOLPH *and* PETO *with him.*]

   GADS. Stand.

   FAL. So I do, against my will.

   POINS. Oh, 'tis our setter.° I know his voice. Bardolph, what news?   54

   BARD. Case° ye, case ye, on with your vizards.
There's money of the King's coming down the hill,
'tis going to the King's exchequer.

   FAL. You lie, ye rogue, 'tis going to the King's
tavern.

   GADS. There's enough to make us all.   60

   FAL. To be hanged.

   PRINCE. Sirs, you four shall front them in the narrow lane, Ned Poins and I will walk lower. If they
'scape from your encounter, then they light on us.

   PETO. How many be there of them?   66

   GADS. Some eight or ten.

   FAL. 'Zounds, will they not rob us?

   PRINCE. What, a coward, Sir John Paunch?

   FAL. Indeed I am not John of Gaunt, your grandfather, but yet no coward, Hal.   71

   PRINCE. Well, we leave that to the proof.

   POINS. Sirrah Jack, thy horse stands behind the

hedge. When thou needest him, there thou shalt find
him. Farewell, and stand fast.   75

   FAL. Now cannot I strike him, if I should be
hanged.

   PRINCE. Ned, where are our disguises?

   POINS. Here, hard by. Stand close.

[*Exeunt* PRINCE *and* POINS.]

   FAL. Now, my masters, happy man be his dole,°
say I. Every man to his business.   81

[*Enter the* TRAVELERS.]

   1. TRAV. Come, neighbor. The boy shall lead our
horses down the hill. We'll walk afoot awhile, and
ease our legs.

   THIEVES. Stand!

   TRAVS. Jesus bless us!   86

   FAL. Strike, down with them, cut the villains'
throats! Ah, whoreson° caterpillars,° bacon-fed
knaves! They hate us youth. Down with them, fleece
them.

   TRAVS. Oh, we are undone, both we and ours forever!   92

   FAL. Hang ye, gorbellied° knaves, are ye undone?
No, ye fat chuffs,° I would your store were here!°
On, bacons,° on! What, ye knaves! Young men must
live. You are grand jurors,° are ye? We'll jure ye,
'faith.   97

[*Here they rob them and bind them. Exeunt.*]

[*Re-enter* PRINCE HENRY *and* POINS *disguised.*]

   PRINCE. The thieves have bound the true men.
Now could thou and I rob the thieves and go merrily to London, it would be argument° for a week,
laughter for a month, and a good jest forever.

   POINS. Stand close. I hear them coming.   103

[*Enter the* THIEVES *again.*]

   FAL. Come, my masters, let us share, and then to
horse before day. An the Prince and Poins be not
two arrant° cowards, there's no equity stirring.°
There's no more valor in that Poins than in a wild
duck.   108

   PRINCE. Your money!

   POINS. Villains! [*As they are sharing, the* PRINCE
and POINS *set upon them; they all run away; and* FAL-
STAFF, *after a blow or two, runs away too, leaving the
booty behind them.*]

   PRINCE. Got with much ease. Now merrily to
     horse.
The thieves are all scattered and possessed with fear
So strongly that they dare not meet each other.
Each takes his fellow for an officer.
Away, good Ned. Falstaff sweats to death,   115
And lards the lean earth as he walks along.

80. happy . . . dole: i.e., here's luck; lit., may the lucky man have
his reward.   88. whoreson: bastard. caterpillars: parasites
on the public.   93. gorbellied: big-bellied.   94. chuffs: mean
misers. were here: i.e., in your bellies.   95. bacons: fat pigs.
96. grand jurors: i.e., men of highest respectability.   101. argument: matter for talk.   106. arrant: complete. no . . . stirring:
no sound judgment in the world.

19. medicines: love potions.   25. varlet: knave.   40. colt: trick.
48. ballads: popular songs.   53. setter: the accomplice who
brings the victim in.   55. Case: mask.

Were't not for laughing, I should pity him.

POINS. How the rogue roared!   [*Exeunt.*]

SCENE III. *Warkworth Castle.*

[*Enter* HOTSPUR *alone, reading a letter.*]

HOT. " But, for mine own part, my lord, I could
be well contented to be there, in respect of the love I
bear your house." He could be contented. Why is he
not, then? In respect of the love he bears our house.
He shows in this he loves his own barn better 5
than he loves our house. Let me see some more.
" The purpose you undertake is dangerous " — why,
that's certain. 'Tis dangerous to take a cold, to sleep,
to drink; but I tell you, my lord fool, out of this net-
tle danger we pluck this flower safety. " The purpose
you undertake is dangerous; the friends you 10
have named uncertain; the time itself unsorted;° and
your whole plot too light for the counterpoise of so
great an opposition." Say you so, say you so? I say
unto you again, you are a shallow cowardly 15
hind,° and you lie. What a lackbrain is this! By the
Lord, our plot is a good plot as ever was laid, our
friends true and constant — a good plot, good
friends, and full of expectation. An excellent plot,
very good friends. What a frosty-spirited rogue 20
is this! Why, my Lord of York° commends the plot
and the general course of the action. 'Zounds, an I
were now by this rascal, I could brain him with his
lady's fan. Is there not my father, my uncle, and
myself? Lord Edmund Mortimer, my Lord of 25
York, and Owen Glendower? Is there not besides
the Douglas? Have I not all their letters to meet me
in arms by the ninth of the next month? And are
they not some of them set forward already? What a
pagan rascal is this, an infidel! Ha! You shall see 30
now in very sincerity of fear and cold heart, will he
to the King, and lay open all our proceedings. Oh, I
could divide myself, and go to buffets,° for moving°
such a dish of skim milk with so honorable an 35
action! Hang him! Let him tell the King. We are
prepared. I will set forward tonight.

[*Enter* LADY PERCY.] How now, Kate! I must leave
you within these two hours.

LADY P. O my good lord, why are you thus alone?
For what offense have I this fortnight been 41
A banished woman from my Harry's bed?
Tell me, sweet lord, what is't that takes from thee
Thy stomach,° pleasure, and thy golden sleep?
Why dost thou bend thine eyes upon the earth, 45
And start so often when thou sit'st alone?
Why hast thou lost the fresh blood in thy cheeks,

And given my treasures° and my rights of thee
To thick-eyed° musing and cursed melancholy?
In thy faint slumbers I by thee have watched, 50
And heard thee murmur tales of iron wars,
Speak terms of manage° to thy bounding steed,
Cry " Courage! To the field! " And thou hast talked
Of sallies and retires,° of trenches, tents,
Of palisadoes,° frontiers,° parapets, 55
Of basilisks, of cannon, culverin,°
Of prisoners' ransom, and of soldiers slain,
And all the currents° of a heady° fight.
Thy spirit within thee hath been so at war
And thus hath so bestirred thee in thy sleep 60
That beads of sweat have stood upon thy brow,
Like bubbles in a late-disturbèd stream.
And in thy face strange motions have appeared,
Such as we see when men restrain their breath
On some great sudden hest.° Oh, what portènts are
these? 65
Some heavy business hath my lord in hand,
And I must know it, else he loves me not.

HOT. What ho! [*Enter* SERVANT.] Is Gilliams with
the packet gone?

SERV. He is, my lord, an hour ago.

HOT. Hath Butler brought those horses from the
sheriff? 70

SERV. One horse, my lord, he brought even now.

HOT. What horse? A roan, a crop-ear,° is it not?

SERV. It is, my lord.

HOT.   That roan shall be my throne.
Well, I will back him straight. Oh, Esperance!°
Bid Butler lead him forth into the park. 75

[*Exit* SERVANT.]

LADY P. But hear you, my lord.

HOT. What say'st thou, my lady?

LADY P. What is it carries you away?

HOT. Why, my horse, my love, my horse.

LADY P. Out, you mad-headed ape! 80
A weasel hath not such a deal of spleen°
As you are tossed with. In faith,
I'll know your business, Harry, that I will.
I fear my brother Mortimer doth stir
About his title, and hath sent for you 85
To line° his enterprise. But if you go ——

HOT. So far afoot, I shall be weary, love.

LADY P. Come, come, you paraquito,° answer me

---

48. **treasures:** i.e., that ought to be mine.   49. **thick-eyed:** dull-
sighted, because he sees nothing.   52. **manage:** horsemanship.
54. **sallies ... retires:** raids and retreats. 55 **palisadoes:** defensive protection made of pointed stakes. **frontiers:** barricades
56. **basilisks ... culverin:** the heavier pieces of artillery. The
basilisk was of 5-inch caliber and fired a shot of $15\frac{1}{2}$ lbs., the
cannon of 8-inch caliber with a 60-lb. shot, the culverin of $5\frac{1}{2}$-inch
caliber with a 17-lb. shot. Shakespeare is thinking of Elizabethan
ordnance rather than the cannon used in 1400. 58. **currents:**
courses, rapid movement. **heady:** fierce. 65. **hest:** command,
action. 72. **crop-ear:** with short ears. 74. **Esperance:** hope —
the battle cry of the Percies. 81. **spleen:** anger, passion. 86. **line:**
strengthen. 88. **paraquito:** parrot.

Sc. iii: **11. unsorted:** ill-chosen. **16. hind:** female deer, the
essence of timidity. **21. Lord of York:** Richard Scroop, Archbishop of York. **34. go to buffets:** come to blows. **moving:** trying
to move. **44. stomach:** appetite.

Directly unto this question that I ask.
In faith, I'll break thy little finger, Harry,   90
An if thou wilt not tell me all things true.

HOT. Away,
Away, you trifler! Love! I love thee not,
I care not for thee, Kate. This is no world
To play with mammets° and to tilt with lips.°   95
We must have bloody noses and cracked crowns,
And pass them current° too. God's me, my horse!
What say'st thou, Kate? What wouldst thou have
     with me?

LADY P. Do you not love me? Do you not, indeed?
Well, do not, then, for since you love me not,   100
I will not love myself. Do you not love me?
Nay, tell me if you speak in jest or no.

HOT. Come, wilt thou see me ride?
And when I am o' horseback, I will swear
I love thee infinitely. But hark you, Kate,   105
I must not have you henceforth question me
Whither I go, nor reason whereabout.
Whither I must, I must. And, to conclude,
This evening must I leave you, gentle Kate.
I know you wise, but yet no farther wise   110
Than Harry Percy's wife. Constant you are,
But yet a woman. And for secrecy,
No lady closer, for I well believe
Thou wilt not utter what thou dost not know,
And so far will I trust thee, gentle Kate.   115

LADY P. How! So far?

HOT. Not an inch further. But hark you, Kate,
Whither I go, thither shall you go too;
Today will I set forth, tomorrow you.   119
Will this content you, Kate?

LADY P.   It must of force. [*Exeunt.*]

SCENE IV. *The Boar's Head Tavern in Eastcheap.*

[*Enter the* PRINCE, *and* POINS.]

PRINCE. Ned, prithee come out of that fat° room,
and lend me thy hand to laugh a little.

POINS. Where hast been, Hal?

PRINCE. With three or four loggerheads° amongst
three or fourscore hogsheads.° I have sounded   5
the very base string of humility.° Sirrah, I am sworn
brother to a leash° of drawers, and can call them all
by their Christen names, as Tom, Dick, and Francis.
They take it already upon their salvation that though
I be but Prince of Wales, yet I am the king of   10
courtesy; and tell me flatly I am no proud Jack, like

Falstaff, but a Corinthian,° a lad of mettle, a good
boy, by the Lord, so they call me, and when I am
King of England, I shall command all the good lads
in Eastcheap. They call drinking deep, dyeing   15
scarlet, and when you breathe in your watering,°
they cry " hem! "° and bid you play it off.° To conclude, I am so good a proficient in one quarter of an
hour that I can drink with any tinker in his own   20
language during my life. I tell thee, Ned, thou hast
lost much honor that thou wert not with me in this
action. But, sweet Ned — to sweeten which name of
Ned, I give thee this pennyworth of sugar, clapped
even now into my hand by an underskinker,°   25
one that never spake other English in his life than
" Eight shillings and sixpence," and " You are welcome," with this shrill addition, " Anon,° anon, sir!
Score° a pint of bastard° in the Half-Moon,"° or so.
But, Ned, to drive away the time till Falstaff   30
come, I prithee do thou stand in some by-room while
I question my puny° drawer to what end he gave me
the sugar. And do thou never leave calling " Francis," that his tale to me may be nothing but   35
" Anon." Step aside, and I'll show thee a precedent.°

POINS. Francis!

PRINCE. Thou art perfect.

POINS. Francis!   [*Exit* POINS.]

[*Enter* FRANCIS.]

FRAN. Anon, anon, sir. Look down into the Pom
garnet,° Ralph.

PRINCE. Come hither, Francis.

FRAN. My lord?   44

PRINCE. How long hast thou to serve, Francis?°

FRAN. Forsooth, five years, and as much as to ——

POINS. [*Within*] Francis!

FRAN. Anon, anon, sir.   49

PRINCE. Five year! By'r Lady, a long lease for the
clinking of pewter. But, Francis, darest thou be so
valiant as to play the coward with thy indenture°
and show it a fair pair of heels and run from it?   54

FRAN. Oh, Lord, sir, I'll be sworn upon all the
books in England I could find in my heart.°

POINS. [*Within*] Francis!

FRAN. Anon, sir.

PRINCE. How old art thou, Francis?

FRAN. Let me see — about Michaelmas next I shall
be ——   61

---

12. **Corinthian:** a gay lad.   16. **watering:** drinking.   17. **cry
" hem ":** one of those exclamations made by topers, like "Here's
how." **play it off:** get it down.   25. **underskinker:** assistant bar-
tender.   28. **Anon:** at once or by and by, the drawer's cry,
"Coming, sir."   29. **Score:** chalk up, the method of recording
a debt for drink still used in English public houses. **bastard:**
a sweet white wine.   **Half-Moon:** Each room in an inn or a tavern had its own name.   42. **Pomgarnet:** Pomegranate — another room
specimen.   42. **Pomgarnet:** Pomegranate — another room
45. **How . . . Francis:** i.e., how many years of your apprenticeship still remain. As Francis has only served two of his seven
years, he is sixteen.   53. **indenture:** agreement of apprenticeship.
56. **could . . . heart;** i.e., very willlingly.

---

95. **mammets:** dolls. **tilt . . . lips:** kiss.   97. **current:** with a pun
on *cracked crowns;* i.e., broken heads, and crown pieces, cracked
and so not current.

Sc. iv: 1. **fat:** stuffy.   4. **loggerheads:** blockheads.   5. **hogsheads:** casks.   5–6. **sounded . . . humility:** i.e., have sunk to
the lowest depth.   7. **leash:** set of three, properly used of a
leash of greyhounds.

POINS. [*Within*] Francis!

FRAN. Anon, sir. Pray stay a little, my lord.

PRINCE. Nay, but hark you, Francis. For the sugar thou gavest me, 'twas a pennyworth, was't not? 66

FRAN. Oh, Lord, I would it had been two!

PRINCE. I will give thee for it a thousand pound. Ask me when thou wilt, and thou shalt have it. 70

POINS. [*Within*] Francis!

FRAN. Anon, anon.

PRINCE. Anon, Francis? No, Francis, but tomorrow, Francis; or, Francis, o' Thursday; or indeed, Francis, when thou wilt. But Francis!

FRAN. My lord? 76

PRINCE. Wilt thou rob this leathern-jerkin, crystal-button, not-pated, agate-ring, puke-stocking, caddis-garter, smooth-tongue, Spanish-pouch ——° 80

FRAN. Oh, Lord, sir, who do you mean?

PRINCE. Why, then, your brown bastard is your only drink, for look you, Francis, your white canvas doublet will sully. In Barbary,° sir, it cannot come to so much.

FRAN. What, sir? 86

POINS. [*Within*] Francis!

PRINCE. Away, you rogue! Dost thou not hear them call? [*Here they both call him; the* DRAWER *stands amazed, not knowing which way to go.*]
[*Enter* VINTNER.]

VINT. What, standest thou still, and hearest such a calling? Look to the guests within. [*Exit* FRANCIS.] My lord, old Sir John, with half-a-dozen more, are at the door. Shall I let them in? 94

PRINCE. Let them alone awhile, and then open the door. [*Exit* VINTNER.] Poins!
[*Re-enter* POINS.]

POINS. Anon, anon, sir.

PRINCE. Sirrah, Falstaff and the rest of the thieves are at the door. Shall we be merry? 99

POINS. As merry as crickets, my lad. But hark ye, what cunning match° have you made with this jest of the drawer? Come, what's the issue?° 103

PRINCE. I am now of all humors° that have showed themselves humors since the old days of Goodman Adam to the pupilage° of this present twelve o'clock at midnight.
[*Re-enter* FRANCIS.] What's o'clock, Francis? 108

FRAN. Anon, anon, sir. [*Exit.*]

PRINCE. That ever this fellow should have fewer words than a parrot, and yet the son of a woman! His industry is upstairs and downstairs, his elo-

quence the parcel° of a reckoning. I am not yet of Percy's mind, the Hotspur of the North, he that kills 115 me some six or seven dozen of Scots at a breakfast, washes his hands, and says to his wife, " Fie upon this quiet life! I want work." " O my sweet Harry," says she, " how many hast thou killed today? " " Give my roan horse a drench,"° says he, 120 and answers " Some fourteen " an hour after — " a trifle, a trifle." I prithee call in Falstaff. I'll play Percy, and that damned brawn° shall play Dame Mortimer his wife. " Rivo! "° says the drunkard. Call in ribs, call in tallow. 125

[*Enter* FALSTAFF, GADSHILL, BARDOLPH, *and* PETO; FRANCIS *following with wine.*]

POINS. Welcome, Jack. Where hast thou been?

FAL. A plague of all cowards, I say, and a vengeance too! Marry, and amen! Give me a cup of sack, boy. Ere I lead this life long, I'll sew netherstocks° and mend them and foot them too. A plague of all cowards! Give me a cup of sack, rogue. Is there 131 no virtue extant?° [*He drinks.*]

PRINCE. Didst thou never see Titan° kiss a dish of butter? Pitiful-hearted Titan, that melted° at the sweet tale of the sun's! If thou didst, then behold that compound. 136

FAL. You rogue, here's lime° in this sack too. There is nothing but roguery to be found in villainous man. Yet a coward is worse than a cup of sack with lime in it. A villainous coward! Go thy 140 ways, old Jack, die when thou wilt. If manhood, good manhood, be not forgot upon the face of the earth, then am I a shotten° herring. There live not three good men unhanged in England, and one of them is fat, and grows old. God help the while!° A 145 bad world, I say. I would I were a weaver, I 146 could sing psalms° or anything. A plague of all cowards, I say still.

PRINCE. How now, woolsack! What mutter you?

FAL. A king's son! If I do not beat thee out of thy kingdom with a dagger of lath,° and drive all thy subjects afore thee like a flock of wild geese, I'll never wear hair on my face more. You Prince of Wales! 154

PRINCE. Why, you whoreson round man, what's the matter?

FAL. Are not you a coward? Answer me to that. And Poins there?

POINS. 'Zounds, ye fat paunch, an ye call me coward, by the Lord, I'll stab thee. 160

77–80. **leathern-jerkin . . . Spanish-pouch**: This list gives the outward characteristics of a prosperous innkeeper: leather coat (*jerkin*) with crystal buttons, close-cropped head (*not-pated*), large ring, gray (*puke*) stockings, worsted (*caddis*) garters, a *smooth tongue*, and a *pouch* of *Spanish* leather. 84. **In Barbary**: in North Africa — but the Prince's words have passed beyond location. 101. **what . . . match**: what is the game. 103. **issue**: result. 104. **of . . . humors**: i.e., will match my mood with any man's. 106. **pupilage**: boyhood.

113. **parcel**: items. 119. **drench**: purge. 122. **brawn**: fat pig. 124. **Rivo**: another drinkers' exclamation. See l. 17. 129. **netherstocks**: stockings, which at this time were usually cut out of material and sewed, not knitted. 132. **virtue extant**: manhood in existence. 133. **Titan**: the sun. 134. **that melted**: i.e.. the butter. 137. **lime**: used to adulterate wine by giving it a better color and taste. 143. **shotten**: without its roe. 145. **God . . . while**: God help these times. 146–47. **weaver . . . psalms**. Protestant weavers were noted psalm-singers. 151. **lath**: wood.

FAL. I call thee coward! I'll see thee damned ere I call thee coward. But I would give a thousand pound I could run as fast as thou canst. You are straight enough in the shoulders, you care not who sees your back. Call you that backing of your friends? A plague upon such backing! Give me them that will face me. Give me a cup of sack. I am a rogue if I drunk today.   169

PRINCE. O villain! Thy lips are scarce wiped since thou drunkest last.

FAL. All's one for that. [*He drinks.*] A plague of all cowards, still say I.

PRINCE. What's the matter?   174

FAL. What's the matter! There be four of us here have ta'en a thousand pound this day morning.

PRINCE. Where is it, Jack? Where is it?

FAL. Where is it! Taken from us it is — a hundred upon poor four of us.   180

PRINCE. What, a hundred, man?

FAL. I am a rogue if I were not at half-sword° with a dozen of them two hours together. I have 'scaped by miracle. I am eight times thrust through the doublet,° four through the hose;° my buckler°   185 cut through and through; my sword hacked like a handsaw — *ecce signum!*° I never dealt° better since I was a man. All would not do. A plague of all cowards! Let them speak. If they speak more or less than truth, they are villains and the sons of darkness. 191

PRINCE. Speak, sirs, how was it?

GADS. We four set upon some dozen —

FAL. Sixteen at least, my lord.

GADS. And bound them.   195

PETO. No, no, they were not bound.

FAL. You rogue, they were bound, every man of them, or I am a Jew else, an Ebrew° Jew.

GADS. As we were sharing, some six or seven fresh men set upon us —   200

FAL. And unbound the rest, and then come in the other.

PRINCE. What, fought you with them all?   203

FAL. All! I know not what you call all, but if I fought not with fifty of them, I am a bunch of radish. If there were not two or three and fifty upon poor old Jack, then am I no two-legged creature.

PRINCE. Pray God you have not murdered some of them.   210

FAL. Nay, that's past praying for. I have peppered two of them — two I am sure I have paid,° two rogues in buckram suits. I tell thee what, Hal, if I tell thee a lie, spit in my face, call me horse.° Thou knowest my old ward.° Here I lay, and thus I bore

my point. Four rogues in buckram let drive at me ——   217

PRINCE. What, four? Thou saidst but two even now.

FAL. Four, Hal, I told thee four.

POINS. Aye, aye, he said four.   221

FAL. These four came all afront, and mainly° thrust at me. I made me no more ado, but took all their seven points in my target, thus.

PRINCE. Seven? Why, there were but four even now.   226

FAL. In buckram?

POINS. Aye, four, in buckram suits.

FAL. Seven, by these hilts,° or I am a villain else.

PRINCE. Prithee let him alone. We shall have more anon.

FAL. Dost thou hear me, Hal?

PRINCE. Aye, and mark thee too, Jack.   234

FAL. Do so, for it is worth the listening to. These nine in buckram that I told thee of ——

PRINCE. So, two more already.

FAL. Their points being broken ——

POINS. Down fell their hose.°   239

FAL. Began to give me ground. But I followed me close, came in foot and hand, and with a thought seven of the eleven I paid.

PRINCE. Oh, monstrous! Eleven buckram men grown out of two!   244

FAL. But, as the Devil would have it, three misbegotten knaves in Kendal green° came at my back and let drive at me; for it was so dark, Hal, that thou couldst not see thy hand.   248

PRINCE. These lies are like their father that begets them — gross as a mountain, open, palpable. Why, thou clay-brained guts, thou knotty-pated° fool, thou whoreson, obscene, greasy tallow catch ——°   253

FAL. What, art thou mad? Art thou mad? Is not the truth the truth?

PRINCE. Why, how couldst thou know these men in Kendal green when it was so dark thou couldst not see thy hand? Come, tell us your reason. What sayest thou to this?   259

POINS. Come, your reason, Jack, your reason.

FAL. What, upon compulsion? 'Zounds, an I were at the strappado, or all the racks° in the world, I would not tell you on compulsion. Give you a reason

---

182. at half-sword: within half a sword's length. A cautious fighter kept at greater distance.   185. doublet: coat. hose: breeches. buckler: small shield.   187. ecce signum: behold the sign. Here Falstaff displays the dents on his sword. dealt: fought.   198. Ebrew: Hebrew.   212. paid: paid home, done for.   214. horse: Like the ass, the horse was regarded as stupid. 215. ward: stance, position of guard. Here Falstaff re-enacts his heroic exploit.

222. mainly: violently.   229. hilts: sword hilt.   238–39. Their . . . hose: Poins puns on the other meaning of *points*, the laces used for tying the hose to the doublet.   246. Kendal green: cloth made (originally at Kendal in Westmoreland) of the poorest-quality wool, and used by woodmen and servants. 252. knotty-pated: blockhead.   253. tallow catch: the word is variously emended and interpreted. Johnson suggested "keech" — a lump of fat prepared by the butcher for the candlemaker. A *tallow catch* would naturally be "a thing for catching tallow"; i.e., the rim on the candlestick which, when piled up with the drippings of wax, is no bad image for Falstaff.   262. strappado . . . racks: forms of torture.

on compulsion! If reasons were as plentiful as 264
blackberries, I would give no man a reason upon
compulsion, I.

PRINCE. I'll be no longer guilty of this sin — this
sanguine° coward, this bed-presser, this horseback-
breaker, this huge hill of flesh —— 269

FAL. 'Sblood, you starveling,° you elf skin,° you
dried neat's tongue,° you bull's pizzle,° you stockfish!° Oh, for breath to utter what is like thee! You
tailor's yard, you sheath, you bow case, you vile
standing tuck ——° 274

PRINCE. Well, breathe a while, and then to it
again, and when thou hast tired thyself in base comparisons, hear me speak but this.

POINS. Mark, Jack. 278

PRINCE. We two saw you four set on four and
bound them, and were masters of their wealth. Mark
now, how a plain tale shall put you down. Then did
we two set on you four; and, with a word, outfaced
you from your prize, and have it, yea, and can show
it you here in the house. And, Falstaff, you carried
your guts away as nimbly, with as quick dex- 285
terity, and roared for mercy, and still run and roared,
as ever I heard bull calf. What a slave art thou, to
hack thy sword as thou hast done, and then say it
was in fight! What trick, what device, what starting
hole,° canst thou now find out to hide thee from this
open and apparent shame? 292

POINS. Come, let's hear, Jack. What trick hast thou
now?

FAL. By the Lord, I knew ye as well as he that
made ye. Why, hear you, my masters. Was it for me
to kill the heir apparent? Should I turn upon the true
Prince? Why, thou knowest I am as valiant as Hercules. But beware instinct, the lion will not touch the
true prince.° Instinct is a great matter, I was now a
coward on instinct. I shall think the better of 300
myself and thee during my life, I for a valiant lion,
and thou for a true Prince. But, by the Lord, lads, I
am glad you have the money. Hostess, clap to the
doors. Watch tonight, pray tomorrow. Gal- 305
lants, lads, boys, hearts of gold, all the titles of good
fellowship come to you! What, shall we be merry?
Shall we have a play extempore?

PRINCE. Content, and the argument° shall be thy
running away. 311

FAL. Ah, no more of that, Hal, an thou lovest me!

268. **sanguine:** one suffering from an excess of the sanguine
humor. 270. **you starveling:** Falstaff, thoroughly roused,
retorts with a string of images expressing the thinness of the
Prince. **elf skin:** sometimes emended to eelskin, but probably
it meant snakeskin, which as Oberon observed, was "Weed wide
enough to wrap a fairy in." (*M N D*, II.i.256.) 271. **neat's
tongue:** ox tongue. **bull's pizzle:** This portion of the bull's
anatomy was dried and used as a whip. 272. **stockfish:** dried
codfish. 274. **standing tuck:** a rapier stuck in the ground.
290-91. **starting hole:** a hole into which a rabbit bolts for safety.
298-99. **lion . . . prince:** This was very generally believed.
310. **argument:** plot.

[*Enter* HOSTESS.]

HOSTESS. O Jesu, my lord the Prince!

PRINCE. How now, my lady the hostess! What sayest thou to me? 316

HOSTESS. Marry, my lord, there is a nobleman of
the Court at door would speak with you. He says he
comes from your father.

PRINCE. Give him as much as will make him a
royal man,° and send him back again to my mother.

FAL. What manner of man is he? 323

HOSTESS. An old man.

FAL. What doth gravity out of his bed at midnight? Shall I give him his answer? 326

PRINCE. Prithee do, Jack.

FAL. Faith, and I'll send him packing. [*Exit.*]

PRINCE. Now, sirs. By'r Lady, you fought fair; so
did you, Peto; so did you, Bardolph. You are lions
too, you ran away upon instinct, you will not touch
the true prince — no, fie! 332

BARD. Faith, I ran when I saw others run.

PRINCE. Faith, tell me now in earnest, how came
Falstaff's sword so hacked?

PETO. Why, he hacked it with his dagger, and said
he would swear truth out of England but he would
make you believe it was done in fight, and persuaded
us to do the like. 339

BARD. Yea, and to tickle our noses with speargrass
to make them bleed, and then to beslubber° our garments with it and swear it was the blood of true
men. I did that I did not this seven year before, I
blushed to hear his monstrous devices. 344

PRINCE. O villain, thou stolest a cup of sack eighteen years ago, and wert taken with the manner,° and
ever since thou hast blushed° extempore. Thou hadst
fire and sword on thy side, and yet thou rannest
away. What instinct hadst thou for it? 350

BARD. My lord, do you see these meteors? Do you
behold these exhalations?°

PRINCE. I do.

BARD. What think you they portend?

PRINCE. Hot livers and cold purses. 355

BARD. Choler,° my lord, if rightly taken.

PRINCE. No, if rightly taken, halter.

[*Re-enter* FALSTAFF.] Here comes lean Jack, here
comes barebone. How now, my sweet creature of
bombast!° How long is't ago, Jack, since thou sawest
thine own knee? 361

321-22. **as . . . man:** i.e., 3*s*. 4*d*. which is the difference between
a royal (10*s*.) and a noble (6*s*. 8*d*.). It is a manifest sign of Prince
Hal's low behavior that he should make such jokes about
a nobleman of the Court. 341. **beslubber:** smear. 346. **with
. . . manner:** in the act. 347. **blushed:** For Bardolph's permanent blush see III.iii.27-55 and *Hen V*, III.vi.108. 351-52. **meteors . . . exhalations:** Bardolph indicates his own fiery face
which, he claims, is proof that he is a man of wrath. **exhalations:** meteors. 356. **Choler:** anger; pronounced in the same
way as "collar," and so puns on the two words are common.
360. **bombast:** cotton batting, used to stuff garments to make
them appear baggy.

FAL. My own knee! When I was about thy years, Hal, I was not an eagle's talon in the waist, I could have crept into any alderman's thumb ring.° A plague of sighing and grief! It blows a man up like a bladder. There's villainous news abroad. Here 366 was Sir John Bracy from your father; you must to the Court in the morning. That same mad fellow of the North, Percy, and he of Wales, that gave Amamon° the bastinado° and made Lucifer cuckold,° and swore the Devil his true liegeman° upon the cross of a Welsh hook — what a plague call you him? 372

POINS. O, Glendower.°

FAL. Owen, Owen, the same. And his son-in-law Mortimer, and old Northumberland, and that sprightly Scot of Scots, Douglas, that runs o' horseback up a hill perpendicular ——

PRINCE. He that rides at high speed and with his pistol kills a sparrow flying. 380

FAL. You have hit it.

PRINCE. So did he never the sparrow.

FAL. Well, that rascal hath good mettle° in him. He will not run. 384

PRINCE. Why, what a rascal art thou then, to praise him so for running!

FAL. O' horseback, ye cuckoo, but afoot he will not budge a foot.

PRINCE. Yes, Jack, upon instinct. 389

FAL. I grant ye, upon instinct. Well, he is there too, and one Mordake, and a thousand bluecaps° more. Worcester is stolen away tonight; thy father's beard is turned white with the news. You may buy land now as cheap as stinking mackerel. 395

PRINCE. Why, then, it is like, if there come a hot June and this civil buffeting hold, we shall buy maidenheads as they buy hobnails, by the hundreds.

FAL. By the mass, lad, thou sayest true; it is like we shall have good trading that way. But tell me, Hal, art not thou horrible afeard? Thou being heir apparent, could the world pick thee out three such enemies again as that fiend Douglas, that spirit Percy, and that devil Glendower? Art thou not horribly afraid? Doth not thy blood thrill at it? 407

PRINCE. Not a whit, i' faith. I lack some of thy instinct.

FAL. Well, thou wilt be horribly chid tomorrow when thou comest to thy father. If thou love me, practice an answer. 412

PRINCE. Do thou stand for° my father, and examine me upon the particulars of my life.

FAL. Shall I? Content. This chair shall be my state,° this dagger my scepter, and this cushion my crown. 417

PRINCE. Thy state is taken for a joined stool,° thy golden scepter for a leaden° dagger, and thy precious rich crown for a pitiful bald crown! 420

FAL. Well, an the fire of grace be not quite out of thee, now shalt thou be moved. Give me a cup of sack to make my eyes look red, that it may be thought I have wept; for I must speak in passion, and I will do it in King Cambyses'° vein. 426

PRINCE. Well, here is my leg.°

FAL. And here is my speech. Stand aside, nobility.

HOSTESS. Oh Jesu, this is excellent sport, i' faith!

FAL. Weep° not, sweet queen, for trickling tears are vain. 430

HOSTESS. Oh, the father,° how he holds his countenance!°

FAL. For God's sake, lords, convey my tristful° queen,

For tears do stop the floodgates of her eyes. 435

HOSTESS. Oh Jesu, he doth it as like one of these harlotry players° as ever I see!

FAL. Peace, good pint pot; peace, good ticklebrain. Harry, I do not only marvel where thou spendest thy time, but also how thou art accompanied.° For 440 though the camomile,° the more it is trodden on, the faster it grows, yet youth, the more it is wasted, the sooner it wears. That thou art my son, I have partly thy mother's word, partly my own opinion, but chiefly a villainous trick° of thine eye, and a 445 foolish hanging of thy nether° lip, that doth warrant° me. If then thou be son to me, here lies the point; why, being son to me, art thou so pointed at? Shall the blessed sun of heaven prove a micher° 450 and eat blackberries? A question not to be asked. Shall the son of England prove a thief and take purses? A question to be asked. There is a thing, Harry, which thou hast often heard of, and it is known to many in our land by the name of pitch. This pitch, as ancient writers do report, doth 455 defile; so doth the company thou keepest. For, Harry, now I do not speak to thee in drink but in tears, not in pleasure but in passion, not in words only, but in woes also. And yet there is a virtuous man whom I have often noted in thy company, but I know not his name.   461

PRINCE. What manner of man, an it like your Majesty?

FAL. A goodly portly° man, i' faith, and a corpulent; of a cheerful look, a pleasing eye, and a   465 most noble carriage. And, as I think, his age some fifty, or, by'r Lady, inclining to threescore. And now I remember me, his name is Falstaff. If that man should be lewdly given, he deceiveth me, for, Harry, I see virtue in his looks. If then the tree may be   470 known by the fruit, as the fruit by the tree, then, peremptorily° I speak it, there is virtue in that Falstaff. Him keep with, the rest banish. And tell me now, thou naughty varlet, tell me, where hast thou been this month?   475

PRINCE. Dost thou speak like a king? Do thou stand for me, and I'll play my father.

FAL. Depose me? If thou dost it half so gravely, so majestically, both in word and matter, hang me up by the heels for a rabbit-sucker° or a poulter's° hare.

PRINCE. Well, here I am set.   482

FAL. And here I stand. Judge, my masters.

PRINCE. Now, Harry, whence come you?

FAL. My noble lord, from Eastcheap.   485

PRINCE. The complaints I hear of thee are grievous.

FAL. 'Sblood, my lord, they are false. Nay, I'll tickle ye° for a young Prince, i' faith.   489

PRINCE. Swearest thou, ungracious° boy? Henceforth ne'er look on me. Thou art violently carried away from grace. There is a devil haunts thee in the likeness of an old fat man, a tun° of man is thy companion. Why dost thou converse with that trunk of humors,° that bolting hutch° of beastliness,   495 that swollen parcel of dropsies, that huge bombard° of sack, that stuffed cloak bag° of guts, that roasted Manningtree° ox with the pudding in his belly, that reverend vice,° that gray iniquity, that father ruffian, that vanity in years? Wherein is he good,   500 but to taste sack and drink it? Wherein neat and cleanly,° but to carve a capon and eat it? Wherein cunning,° but in craft? Wherein crafty,° but in villainy? Wherein villainous, but in all things? Wherein worthy, but in nothing?   505

FAL. I would your Grace would take me with you.° Whom means your Grace?

PRINCE. That villainous abominable misleader of youth, Falstaff, that old white-bearded Satan.

FAL. My lord, the man I know.   510

PRINCE. I know thou dost.

FAL. But to say I know more harm in him than in myself were to say more than I know. That he is old, the more the pity, his white hairs do witness it; but that he is, saving your reverence, a whore-   515 master, that I utterly deny. If sack and sugar be a fault, God help the wicked! If to be old and merry be a sin, then many an old host that I know is damned. If to be fat be to be hated, then Pharaoh's lean kine are to be loved. No, my good lord. Banish Peto,   520 banish Bardolph, banish Poins. But for sweet Jack Falstaff, kind Jack Falstaff, true Jack Falstaff, valiant Jack Falstaff, and therefore more valiant, being, as he is, old Jack Falstaff, banish not him thy Harry's company, banish not him thy Harry's company.   525 Banish plump Jack, and banish all the world.

PRINCE. I do, I will.   [A knocking heard.
        Exeunt HOSTESS, FRANCIS, and BARDOLPH.]
             [Re-enter BARDOLPH, running.]

BARD. Oh, my lord, my lord! The sheriff with a most monstrous watch° is at the door.   530

FAL. Out, ye rogue! Play out the play. I have much to say in the behalf of that Falstaff.

            [Re-enter the HOSTESS.]

HOSTESS. Oh Jesu, my lord, my lord! —

PRINCE. Heigh, heigh! The Devil rides upon a fiddlestick.° What's the matter?   535

HOSTESS. The sheriff and all the watch are at the door. They are come to search the house. Shall I let them in?

FAL. Dost thou hear, Hal? Never call a true piece of gold a counterfeit. Thou art essentially mad, without seeming so.   541

PRINCE. And thou a natural coward, without instinct.

FAL. I deny your major.° If you will deny the sheriff, so; if not, let him enter. If I become not a cart° as well as another man, a plague on my bringing up! I hope I shall as soon be strangled with a halter as another.   548

PRINCE. Go, hide thee behind the arras,° the rest walk up above. Now, my masters, for a true face and good conscience.

FAL. Both which I have had; but their date is out,° and therefore I'll hide me.   553

PRINCE. Call in the sheriff.

        [Exeunt all except the PRINCE and PETO.]

464. portly: dignified. 472. peremptorily: conclusively. 481. rabbit-sucker: young rabbit. poulter: poulterer.   489. I'll ... ye: I'll show you how to do it.   490. ungracious: graceless.   493. tun: large barrel.   494–95. trunk of humors: great collection of diseases.   495. bolting hutch: round bin into which flour was sifted.   496. bombard: large leather jug used for carrying liquor. 497. cloak bag: for carrying cloaks. 498. Manningtree: a town in Essex where there was a famous cattle market. At fairs it was often a custom to roast an ox whole.   499. vice: the Devil in the old Morality Plays.   502. cleanly: clever.   503. cunning: skillful.   crafty: a craftsman. 506–07. take ... you: explain yourself.

530. watch: citizen police force.   534–35. Devil ... fiddle-stick: what's all the fuss about?   544. I ... major: I deny your major premise, i.e., the main argument on which your conclusion is based; a phrase used in academic arguments. Falstaff puns also on "mayor." "Major" and "mayor" were pronounced alike.   546. cart: which will take him to execution. 549. arras: curtain. 552. date is out: time is expired.

[*Enter* SHERIFF *and the* CARRIER.]
Now, Master Sheriff, what is your will with me?
SHER. First, pardon me, my lord. A hue and
    cry°
Hath followed certain men unto this house.
    PRINCE. What men?
SHER. One of them is well known, my gracious
    lord,
A gross fat man.
    CAR.   As fat as butter.   560
    PRINCE. The man, I do assure you, is not here,
For I myself at this time have employed him.
And, sheriff, I will engage my word to thee
That I will, by tomorrow dinnertime,
Send him to answer thee, or any man,   565
For anything he shall be charged withal.
And so let me entreat you leave the house.
    SHER. I will, my lord. There are two gentlemen
Have in this robbery lost three hundred marks.
    PRINCE. It may be so. If he have robbed these
    men,   570
He shall be answerable. And so farewell.
    SHER. Good night, my noble lord.
    PRINCE. I think it is good morrow, is it not?
    SHER. Indeed, my lord, I think it be two o'clock.
            [*Exeunt* SHERIFF *and* CARRIER.]
    PRINCE. This oily rascal is known as well as   575
Paul's.° Go, call him forth.
    PETO. Falstaff! — Fast asleep behind the arras, and
snorting like a horse.
    PRINCE. Hark how hard he fetches breath. Search
his pockets. [*He searcheth his pockets, and findeth
certain papers.*] What hast thou found?   582
    PETO. Nothing but papers, my lord.
    PRINCE. Let's see what they be. Read them.
    PETO. [*Reads.*]
"Item, A capon, ...   2*s*. 2*d*.
   Item, Sauce, ...   4*d*.
   Item, Sack, two gallons, ... 5*s*. 8*d*.
   Item, Anchovies and sack after supper, 2*s*. 6*d*.
   Item, Bread, ...   ob.°"
    PRINCE. Oh, monstrous! But one halfpenny-   591
worth of bread to this intolerable deal of sack! What
there is else, keep close, we'll read it at more advantage. There let him sleep till day. I'll to the Court in
the morning. We must all to the wars, and thy   595
place shall be honorable. I'll procure this fat rogue a
charge of foot,° and I know his death will be a march
of twelvescore.° The money shall be paid back again
with advantage.° Be with me betimes in the morning. And so good morrow, Peto.   600
    PETO. Good morrow, good my lord.   [*Exeunt.*]

---

556. hue . . . cry: pursuit of a thief.   576. Paul's: St. Paul's,
the largest church in London.   590. ob: one halfpenny.
597. charge of foot: commission as commander of a company
of infantry.   598. twelvescore: i.e., paces. The pace was 60 inches.
599. advantage: interest.

Act III

SCENE I. *Bangor. The* ARCHDEACON'*s house.*

[*Enter* HOTSPUR, WORCESTER, MORTIMER, *and*
             GLENDOWER.]
    MORT. These promises are fair, the parties sure,
And our induction° full of prosperous hope.
    HOT. Lord Mortimer, and Cousin Glendower,
Will you sit down?
And Uncle Worcester. A plague upon it!   5
I have forgot the map.
    GLEND.   No, here it is.
Sit, Cousin Percy. Sit, good Cousin Hotspur,
For by that name as oft as Lancaster
Doth speak of you, his cheek looks pale, and with
A rising sigh he wisheth you in Heaven.   10
    HOT. And you in Hell, as oft as he hears Owen
       Glendower spoke of.
    GLEND. I cannot blame him. At my nativity°
The front° of heaven was full of fiery shapes,
Of burning cressets;° and at my birth   15
The frame and huge foundation of the earth
Shaked like a coward.
    HOT. Why, so it would have done at the same sea-
son if your mother's cat had but kittened, though
yourself had never been born.   20
    GLEND. I say the earth did shake when I was born.
    HOT. And I say the earth was not of my mind
If you suppose as fearing you it shook.
    GLEND. The heavens were all on fire, the earth did
tremble.
    HOT. Oh, then the earth shook to see the heavens
       on fire,   25
And not in fear of your nativity.
Diseasèd nature oftentimes breaks forth
In strange eruptions; oft the teeming° earth
Is with a kind of colic pinched and vexed
By the imprisoning of unruly wind   30
Within her womb; which, for enlargement striving,
Shakes the old beldam° earth and topples down
Steeples and moss-grown towers. At your birth
Our grandam earth, having this distemperature,°
In passion° shook.
    GLEND.   Cousin,° of many men   35
I do not bear these crossings.° Give me leave
To tell you once again that at my birth
The front of heaven was full of fiery shapes,
The goats ran from the mountains, and the herds

Act III, Sc. i: 2. induction: opening.   12. nativity: astrological
moment of birth.   14. front: forehead.   15. cressets: stars
blazing like beacons.   28. teeming: pregnant. This theory of
earthquakes — that they were caused by the expulsion of wind
from within the earth — was generally believed.   32. beldam:
grandmother.   34. distemperature: disorder.   35. passion:
agitation. Cousin: kinsman; used of any relation. Hotspur
is remotely related to Glendower through Lady Percy. See
Genealogical Table, p. 58.   36. crossings: opposition.

Were strangely clamorous to the frighted fields. 40
These signs have marked me extraordinary,
And all the courses of my life do show
I am not in the roll of common men.
Where is he living, clipped in° with the sea
That chides° the banks of England, Scotland, Wales,
Which calls me pupil,° or hath read to me?° 46
And bring him out that is but woman's son
Can trace° me in the tedious ways of art,°
And hold me pace° in deep experiments.
    HOT. I think there's no man speaks better Welsh.
I'll to dinner. 51
    MORT. Peace, Cousin Percy, you will make him
      mad.
    GLEND. I can call spirits from the vasty deep.
    HOT. Why, so can I, or so can any man;
But will they come when you do call for them? 55
    GLEND. Why, I can teach you, Cousin, to command
The Devil.
    HOT. And I can teach thee, Coz, to shame the
      Devil°
By telling truth. Tell truth, and shame the Devil. 59
If thou have power to raise him, bring him hither,
And I'll be sworn I have power to shame him hence.
Oh, while you live, tell truth, and shame the Devil!
    MORT. Come, come, no more of this unprofitable
      chat.
    GLEND. Three times hath Henry Bolingbroke
      made head°
Against my power. Thrice from the banks of Wye
And sandy-bottomed Severn have I sent him 66
Bootless° home and weather-beaten back.
    HOT. Home without boots, and in foul weather
      too!
How 'scapes he agues,° in the Devil's name?
    GLEND. Come, here's the map. Shall we divide our
      right 70
According to our threefold order° ta'en?
    MORT. The Archdeacon hath divided it
Into three limits° very equally.
England, from Trent and Severn hitherto,
By south and east is to my part assigned. 75
All westward, Wales beyond the Severn shore,
And all the fertile land within that bound,
To Owen Glendower. And, dear Coz, to you
The remnant northward, lying off from Trent.
And our indentures tripartite° are drawn; 80
Which being sealed interchangeably,°
A business that this night may execute,

Tomorrow, Cousin Percy, you and I
And my good Lord of Worcester will set forth
To meet your father and the Scottish power, 85
As is appointed us, at Shrewsbury.
My father° Glendower is not ready yet,
Nor shall we need his help these fourteen days.
Within that space you may have drawn together 89
Your tenants, friends, and neighboring gentlemen.
    GLEND. A shorter time shall send me to you, lords.
And in my conduct shall your ladies come,
From whom you now must steal and take no leave;
For there will be a world of water shed
Upon the parting of your wives and you. 95
    HOT. Methinks my moiety,° north from Burton
      here,
In quantity equals not one of yours.
See how this river comes me cranking in,°
And cuts me from the best of all my land
A huge half-moon, a monstrous cantle° out. 100
I'll have the current in this place dammed up,
And here the smug° and silver Trent shall run
In a new channel, fair and evenly.
It shall not wind with such a deep indent,°
To rob me of so rich a bottom° here. 105
    GLEND. Not wind? It shall, it must. You see it
      doth.
    MORT. Yea, but
Mark how he bears his course, and runs me up
With like advantage on the other side,
Gelding the opposèd continent° as much 110
As on the other side it takes from you.
    WOR. Yea, but a little charge° will trench him
      here
And on this north side win this cape of land,
And then he runs straight and even.
    HOT. I'll have it so. A little charge will do it. 115
    GLEND. I'll not have it altered.
    HOT.   Will not you?
    GLEND. No, nor you shall not.
    HOT.   Who shall say me nay?
    GLEND. Why, that will I.
    HOT. Let me not understand you, then. Speak it in
      Welsh. 120
    GLEND. I can speak English, lord, as well as you;
For I was trained up in the English Court,
Where, being but young, I framèd to the harp
Many an English ditty lovely well,
And gave the tongue a helpful ornament,° 125
A virtue that was never seen in you.
    HOT. Marry,°
And I am glad of it with all my heart.

---

44. clipped in: encircled. 45. chides: roars against. 46. calls me pupil: i.e., is my master. hath . . . me: has been my tutor. 48. trace: follow. tedious . . . art: difficult course of magic. 49. hold me pace: keep pace with me. 58. shame . . . Devil: because he is the father of lies. 64. made head: advanced. 67. Bootless: profitless. 69. agues: fever. 71. our . . . order: agreement made between us three. 73. limits: divisions. 80. indentures tripartite: agreement between three parties. 81. interchangeably: each party sealing each copy of the agreement.

87. father: i.e., father-in-law. 96. moiety: share. 98. me . . . in: comes winding into my part. 100. cantle: slice. 102. smug: smooth. 104. indent: indentation. 105. bottom: valley. 110. opposed continent: opposite bank. 112. charge: cost. 125. helpful ornament: i.e., musical accompaniment. 127. Marry: Mary, by the Virgin.

I had rather be a kitten and cry mew
Than one of these same meter balladmongers.°   130
I had rather hear a brazen canstick turned,°
Or a dry wheel grate on the axletree;
And that would set my teeth nothing on edge,
Nothing so much as mincing poetry.
'Tis like the forced gait of a shuffling nag.   135
    GLEND. Come, you shall have Trent turned.
    HOT. I do not care. I'll give thrice so much
      land
To any well-deserving friend.
But in the way of bargain, mark ye me,
I'll cavil° on the ninth part of a hair.   140
Are the indentures drawn? Shall we be gone?
    GLEND. The moon shines fair, you may away by
      night.
I'll haste the writer, and withal
Break with° your wives of your departure hence.
I am afraid my daughter will run mad,   145
So much she doteth on her Mortimer.   [*Exit.*]
    MORT. Fie, Cousin Percy! How you cross my
      father!
    HOT. I cannot choose. Sometime he angers me
With telling me of the moldwarp° and the ant,
Of the dreamer Merlin° and his prophecies,   150
And° of a dragon and a finless fish,
A clip-winged griffin° and a molten raven,
A couching lion and a ramping° cat,
And such a deal of skimble-skamble° stuff
As puts me from my faith. I tell you what —   155
He held me last night at least nine hours
In reckoning up the several° devils' names
That were his lackeys. I cried " hum," and " well, go
      to,"
But marked him not a word. Oh, he is as tedious
As a tired horse, a railing wife,   160
Worse than a smoky house. I had rather live
With cheese and garlic in a windmill, far,
Than feed on cates° and have him talk to me
In any summerhouse° in Christendom.
    MORT. In faith, he is a worthy gentleman,   165
Exceedingly well read, and profited
In strange concealments;° valiant as a lion,
And wondrous affable, and as bountiful
As mines of India. Shall I tell you, Cousin?
He holds your temper° in a high respect,   170
And curbs himself even of his natural scope

130. **meter balladmongers:** doggerel rhymesters. 131. **brazen . . . turned:** brass candlestick being cut out on the lathe. 140. **cavil:** raise objections. 144. **Break with:** break the news to. 149. **moldwarp:** mole. 150. **Merlin:** the old magician at King Arthur's Court. As the Welsh were (more or less) descendants of Arthur's British countrymen, Merlin's prophecies would appeal to Glendower. 151–53. **And . . . cat:** These beasts occur as symbols in ancient prophecies. **griffin:** fabulous beast — half lion, half eagle. 153. **ramping:** on its hind legs. 154. **skimble-skamble:** rambling. 157. **several:** separate, different. 163. **cates:** delicacies. 164. **summerhouse:** country house. 166–67. **profited . . . concealments:** expert in strange mysteries. 170. **temper:** character.

When you come 'cross his humor; faith, he does.
I warrant you that man is not alive
Might so have tempted him as you have done
Without the taste of danger and reproof.   175
But do not use it oft, let me entreat you.
    WOR. In faith, my lord, you are too willful-
      blame;°
And since your coming hither have done enough
To put him quite beside his patience.
You must needs learn, lord, to amend this fault.   180
Though sometimes it show greatness, courage,
      blood —
And that's the dearest° grace it renders you —
Yet oftentimes it doth present harsh rage,
Defect of manners, want of government,°
Pride, haughtiness, opinion,° and disdain;   185
The least of which haunting a nobleman
Loseth men's hearts, and leaves behind a stain
Upon the beauty of all parts besides,
Beguiling° them of commendation.
    HOT. Well, I am schooled. Good manners be your
      speed!°   190
Here come our wives, and let us take our leave.
      [*Re-enter* GLENDOWER *with the* LADIES.]
    MORT. This is the deadly spite° that angers me —
My wife can speak no English, I no Welsh.
    GLEND. My daughter weeps. She will not part with
      you.
She'll be a soldier too, she'll to the wars.   195
    MORT. Good Father, tell her that she and my aunt
      Percy
Shall follow in your conduct speedily.
      [GLENDOWER *speaks to* LADY MORTIMER *in Welsh,
      and she answers him in the same.*]
    GLEND. She is desperate here, a peevish self-willed
harlotry,° one that no persuasion can do good   199
upon.
      [LADY MORTIMER *speaks in Welsh.*]
    MORT. I understand thy looks. That pretty Welsh°
Which thou pour'st down from these swelling
      heavens°
I am too perfect in; and but for shame,
In such a parley° should I answer thee.
      [LADY MORTIMER *speaks again in Welsh.*]
I understand thy kisses and thou mine,   205
And that's a feeling disputation.°
But I will never be a truant, love,
Till I have learned thy language; for thy tongue
Makes Welsh as sweet as ditties highly penned,
Sung by a fair queen in a summer's bower,   210

177. **willful-blame:** to be blamed for willfulness. 182. **dearest:** most valuable. 184. **government:** self-control. 185. **opinion:** conceit. 189. **Beguiling:** causing to lose. 190. **Good . . . speed:** may good manners bring you luck. 192. **spite:** vexation. 199. **harlotry:** silly girl. 201. **pretty Welsh:** i.e., tears. 202. **swelling heavens:** i.e., eyes full of tears. 204. **parley:** manner of speech. 206. **feeling disputation:** conversation by touch.

With ravishing division,° to her lute.

GLEND. Nay, if you melt, then will she run mad.
    [LADY MORTIMER *speaks again in Welsh.*]

MORT. Oh, I am ignorance itself in this!

GLEND. She bids you on the wanton° rushes° lay
you down
And rest your gentle head upon her lap,   215
And she will sing the song that pleaseth you
And on your eyelids crown the god of sleep,
Charming your blood with pleasing heaviness,°
Making such difference 'twixt wake and sleep
As is the difference betwixt day and night   220
The hour before the heavenly-harnessed team°
Begins his golden progress in the east.

MORT. With all my heart I'll sit and hear her sing.
By that time will our book,° I think, be drawn.

GLEND. Do so,   225
And those musicians that shall play to you
Hang in the air a thousand leagues from hence,
And straight they shall be here. Sit, and attend.

HOT. Come, Kate, thou art perfect in lying down.
Come, quick, quick, that I may lay my head in thy
lap.   231

LADY P. Go, ye giddy goose.   [*The music plays.*]

HOT. Now I perceive the Devil understands
Welsh,
And 'tis no marvel he is so humorous.°
By'r Lady, he is a good musician.   235

LADY P. Then should you be nothing but musical,
for you are altogether governed by humors. Lie still,
ye thief, and hear the lady sing in Welsh.

HOT. I had rather hear Lady, my brach,° howl in
Irish.   241

LADY P. Wouldst thou have thy head broken?

HOT. No.

LADY P. Then be still.

HOT. Neither — 'tis a woman's fault.   245

LADY P. Now God help thee!

HOT. To the Welsh lady's bed.

LADY P. What's that?

HOT. Peace! She sings.
    [*Here* LADY MORTIMER *sings a Welsh song.*]
Come, Kate, I'll have your song too.   250

LADY P. Not mine, in good sooth.°

HOT. Not yours, in good sooth! Heart! You swear
like a comfit-maker's° wife. "Not you, in good
sooth," and "as true as I live," and "as God shall
mend me," and "as sure as day,"   255
And givest such sarcenet surety for thy oaths°
As if thou never walk'st further than Finsbury.°
Swear me, Kate, like a lady as thou art,

A good mouth-filling oath, and leave "in sooth"
And such protest of pepper gingerbread°   260
To velvet guards° and Sunday citizens.°
Come, sing.

LADY P. I will not sing.

HOT. 'Tis the next way to turn tailor,° or be red-
breast teacher.° An the indentures be drawn,   265
I'll away within these two hours, and so come in
when ye will.   [*Exit.*]

GLEND. Come, come, Lord Mortimer, you are as
slow
As hot Lord Percy is on fire to go.
By this our book is drawn. We'll but seal,   270
And then to horse immediately.

MORT.   With all my heart.   [*Exeunt.*]

SCENE II. *London. The palace.*

[*Enter the* KING, PRINCE OF WALES, *and others.*]

KING. Lords, give us leave. The Prince of Wales
and I
Must have some private conference. But be near at
hand,
For we shall presently have need of you.
    [*Exeunt* LORDS.]
I know not whether God will have it so,
For some displeasing service I have done,   5
That, in his secret doom,° out of my blood°
He'll breed revengement and a scourge for me;
But thou dost in thy passages of life
Make me believe that thou art only marked
For the hot vengeance and the rod of Heaven   10
To punish my mistreadings. Tell me else,
Could such inordinate° and low desires,
Such poor, such bare, such lewd,° such mean at-
tempts,
Such barren pleasures, rude society,
As thou art matched withal and grafted to,   15
Accompany the greatness of thy blood,
And hold their level with thy princely heart?

PRINCE. So please your Majesty, I would I could
Quit° all offenses with as clear excuse
As well as I am doubtless I can purge   20
Myself of many I am charged withal.
Yet such extenuation let me beg
As, in reproof° of many tales devised,
Which oft the ear of greatness needs must hear,

211. division: melody.   214. wanton: luxuriant. rushes: used to
cover floors.   218. heaviness: drowsiness.   221. team: i.e., the
horses of the sun.   224. book: agreement.   234. humorous: full
of whims.   240. brach: bitch.   251. sooth: truth.   253. comfit-
maker: candymaker.   256. sarcenet . . . oaths: you swear by
such soft things. sarcenet: fine silk.   257. Finsbury: Finsbury
fields, whither London citizens took their Sunday-afternoon walk.

260. pepper gingerbread: a very mild form of heat.   261. velvet
guards: literally bands of velvet used to ornament a gown (and
still used on the gown of a Ph.D.); so "peaceful, timid tradesmen." Sunday citizens: citizens in their Sunday best.   264. turn
tailor: Tailors (before the invention of the sewing machine) used
to sing at their work as they sat cross-legged.   265. redbreast
teacher: one who teaches caged birds to sing. The little English
robin was highly valued as a songbird.
    Sc. ii: 6. doom: judgment. out . . . blood: through one of my
children.   12. inordinate: intemperate.   13. lewd: low.   19. Quit:
acquit myself of.   23. reproof: rebuttal.

By smiling pickthanks° and base newsmongers,   25
I may for some things true wherein my youth
Hath faulty wandered and irregular
Find pardon on my true submission.
   KING. God pardon thee! Yet let me wonder,
     Harry,
At thy affections, which do hold a wing   30
Quite from the flight° of all thy ancestors.
Thy place in Council thou hast rudely lost,
Which by thy younger brother is supplied,
And art almost an alien to the hearts
Of all the Court and princes of my blood.   35
The hope and expectation of thy time°
Is ruined, and the soul of every man
Prophetically doth forethink thy fall.
Had I so lavish of my presence been,
So common-hackneyed° in the eyes of men,   40
So stale and cheap to vulgar company,
Opinion,° that did help me to the crown,
Had still kept loyal to possession,°
And left me in reputeless banishment,
A fellow of no mark nor likelihood.   45
By being seldom seen, I could not stir
But like a comet I was wondered at,
That men would tell their children "This is he."
Others would say, "Where, which is Bolingbroke?"
And then I stole all courtesy from Heaven,   50
And dressed myself in such humility
That I did pluck allegiance from men's hearts,
Loud shouts and salutations from their mouths,
Even in the presence of the crownèd King.
Thus did I keep my person fresh and new,   55
My presence, like a robe pontifical,°
Ne'er seen but wondered at. And so my state,
Seldom but sumptuous, showed like a feast,
And won by rareness such solemnity.
The skipping° King, he ambled up and down,   60
With shallow jesters and rash bavin° wits,
Soon kindled and soon burnt; carded° his state,
Mingled his royalty with capering fools,
Had his great name profanèd with their scorns,
And gave his countenance, against his name,°   65
To laugh at gibing° boys and stand the push°
Of every beardless vain comparative,°
Grew a companion to the common streets,
Enfeoffed° himself to popularity,°

That, being daily swallowed by men's eyes,   70
They surfeited with honey and began
To loathe the taste of sweetness, whereof a little
More than a little is by much too much.
So when he had occasion to be seen,
He was but as the cuckoo is in June,   75
Heard, not regarded; seen, but with such eyes
As, sick and blunted with community,°
Afford no extraordinary gaze,
Such as is bent on sunlike majesty
When it shines seldom in admiring eyes;   80
But rather drowsed and hung their eyelids down,
Slept in his face° and rendered such aspèct°
As cloudy° men use to their adversaries,
Being with his presence glutted, gorged, and full.
And in that very line,° Harry, standest thou;   85
For thou hast lost thy princely privilege
With vile participation.° Not an eye
But is aweary of thy common sight,
Save mine, which hath desired to see thee more,
Which now doth that I would not have it do—   90
Make blind itself with foolish tenderness.
   PRINCE. I shall hereafter, my thrice gracious
     lord,
Be more myself.
   KING.   For all the world
As thou art to this hour° was Richard then
When I from France set foot at Ravenspurgh,   95
And even as I was then is Percy now.
Now, by my scepter and my soul to boot,
He hath more worthy interest to the state
Than thou the shadow of succession;°
For of no right,° nor color like to right,   100
He doth fill fields with harness° in the realm,
Turns head against the lion's armèd jaws,
And being no more in debt to years than thou,°
Leads ancient lords and reverend bishops on
To bloody battles and to bruising arms.   105
What never-dying honor hath he got
Against renownèd Douglas! — whose high deeds,
Whose hot incursions° and great name in arms
Holds from all soldiers chief majority
And military title capital°   110
Through all the kingdoms that acknowledge Christ.
Thrice hath this Hotspur, Mars in swathling°
     clothes,
This infant warrior, in his enterprises
Discomfited great Douglas, ta'en him once,
Enlarged him, and made a friend of him,   115

---

25. pickthanks: men who curry favor by telling tales. 30–31. affections . . . flight: desires, natural inclinations . . . fly a different course. 36. time: lifetime. 40. common-hackneyed: at every man's call. A hackney is a hired horse. 42. Opinion: popular opinion. 43. loyal to possession: loyal to the possessor; i.e., Richard II. 56. robe pontifical: a bishop's robe. 60. skipping: frivolous. 61. bavin: brushwood for kindling, worthless and easily broken. 62. carded: adulterated. 65. against . . . name: contrary to the interest of his reputation. 66. gibing: mocking. stand . . . push: endure the sallies of. 67. beardless . . . comparative: every boy who cared to make jokes at his expense. 69. Enfeoffed: conveyed, made himself over to. popularity: low company, common people.

77. blunted . . . community: satiated by that which is common. 82. in . . . face: in his presence — a gross insult. aspect: look. 83. cloudy: sullen. 85. line: class. 87. vile participation: mixing with low company. 94. to . . . hour: up to now. 99. shadow of succession: shadowy right of succession. 100. of no right: with no right. 101. harness: armor. 103. no . . . thou: See I.i.92,n. 108. incursions: raids. 109–10. Holds . . . capital: keeps from all other soldiers the claim to be considered the greatest. 112. swathling: swaddling.

To fill the mouth of deep defiance up°
And shake the peace and safety of our throne.
And what say you to this? Percy, Northumberland,
The Archbishop's Grace of York, Douglas, Morti-
mer,
Capitulate° against us and are up.   120
But wherefore do I tell these news to thee?
Why, Harry, do I tell thee of my foes,
Which art my near'st and dearest enemy?
Thou that art like enough through vassal° fear,
Base inclination, and the start of spleen°   125
To fight against me under Percy's pay,
To dog his heels and curtsy at his frowns,
To show how much thou art degenerate.
  PRINCE. Do not think so, you shall not find it so.
And God forgive them that so much have swayed
Your Majesty's good thoughts away from me!   131
I will redeem all this on Percy's head,
And in the closing of some glorious day
Be bold to tell you that I am your son;
When I will wear a garment all of blood,   135
And stain my favors° in a bloody mask
Which, washed away, shall scour my shame with it.
And that shall be the day, whene'er it lights,
That this same child of honor and renown,
This gallant Hotspur, this all-praisèd knight,   140
And your unthought-of Harry chance to meet.
For every honor sitting on his helm,
Would they were multitudes, and on my head
My shames redoubled! For the time will come
That I shall make this Northern youth exchange
His glorious deeds for my indignities.   146
Percy is but my factor,° good my lord,
To engross° up glorious deeds on my behalf.
And I will call him to so strict account
That he shall render every glory up —   150
Yea, even the slightest worship° of his time —
Or I will tear the reckoning from his heart.
This, in the name of God, I promise here.
The which if He be pleased I shall perform,
I do beseech your Majesty may salve°   155
The long-grown wounds of my intemperance.
If not, the end of life cancels all bands,°
And I will die a hundred thousand deaths
Ere break the smallest parcel° of this vow.
  KING. A hundred thousand rebels die in this.   160
Thou shalt have charge and sovereign trust herein.
[Enter BLUNT.] How now, good Blunt? Thy looks
  are full of speed.
  BLUNT. So hath the business that I come to speak
  of.
Lord Mortimer of Scotland hath sent word

116. To . . . up: so that defiance may speak with a loud mouth.
120. Capitulate: make agreement. 124. vassal: slavish. 125. start
of spleen: impulse of bad temper. 136. favors: features, face.
147. factor: agent, buyer. 148. engross: buy up wholesale.
151. worship: honor. 155. salve: heal. 157. bands: bonds,
debts. 159. parcel: portion.

That Douglas and the English rebels met   165
The eleventh of this month at Shrewsbury.
A mighty and a fearful head° they are,
If promises be kept on every hand,
As ever offered foul play in a state.
  KING. The Earl of Westmoreland set forth today,
With him my son, Lord John of Lancaster;   171
For this advértisement is five days old.
On Wednesday next, Harry, you shall set forward,
On Thursday we ourselves will march. Our meeting
Is Bridgenorth. And, Harry, you shall march   175
Through Gloucestershire, by which account,
Our business valued,° some twelve days hence
Our general forces at Bridgenorth shall meet.
Our hands are full of business. Let's away.
Advantage feeds him fat° while men delay.   180
                                    [Exeunt.]

SCENE III. *Boar's Head Tavern in Eastcheap.*

[*Enter* FALSTAFF *and* BARDOLPH.]
  FAL. Bardolph, am I not fallen away vilely since
this last action?° Do I not bate?° Do I not dwindle?
Why, my skin hangs about me like an old lady's
loose gown, I am withered like an old applejohn.°
Well, I'll repent, and that suddenly, while I am in   5
some liking.° I shall be out of heart° shortly, and
then I shall have no strength to repent. An I have not
forgotten what the inside of a church is made of, I
am a peppercorn, a brewer's horse° — the inside of a
church! Company, villainous company, hath been
the spoil of me.   11
  BARD. Sir John, you are so fretful you cannot live
long.
  FAL. Why, there is it. Come sing me a bawdy song,
make me merry. I was as virtuously given as a gentleman need to be — virtuous enough; swore little;
diced not above seven times a week; went to a
bawdyhouse not above once in a quarter — of an
hour; paid money that I borrowed, three or four   20
times; lived well, and in good compass.° And now I
live out of all order, out of all compass.
  BARD. Why, you are so fat, Sir John, that you must
needs be out of all compass, out of all reasonable
compass, Sir John.   26
  FAL. Do thou amend thy face, and I'll amend my
life. Thou art our admiral,° thou bearest the lantern

167. head: force. 177. Our . . . valued: considering how much
we have to do. 180. Advantage . . . fat: advantage makes the
most of his opportunities.
  Sc. iii: 2. last action: i.e., the Gadshill affair. bate: grow thin.
applejohn: withered apple, long kept. 6. in . . . liking: in good
condition. out of heart: have no heart for it. 9. brewer's
horse: i.e., old and decrepit. 21. compass: (lit., circumference)
limits, with a pun on Falstaff's girth. 28. admiral: the admiral's ship, which led the way and carried a lighted lantern by
night so that the fleet should keep together.

in the poop,° but 'tis in the nose of thee. Thou art
the Knight of the Burning Lamp.　　　　　30

BARD. Why, Sir John, my face does you no harm.

FAL. No, I'll be sworn, I make as good use of it as
many a man doth of a death's-head° or a memento
mori.° I never see thy face but I think upon　35
Hell-fire and Dives° that lived in purple, for there he
is in his robes, burning, burning. If thou wert anyway given to virtue, I would swear by thy face; my
oath should be " By this fire, that's God's angel."°
But thou art altogether given over, and wert in-　40
deed, but for the light in thy face, the son of utter
darkness. When thou rannest up Gadshill in the
night to catch my horse, if I did not think thou hadst
been an ignis fatuus° or a ball of wildfire,° there's no
purchase in money. Oh, thou art a perpetual tri-　45
umph,° an everlasting bonfire light! Thou hast
saved me a thousand marks in links° and torches,
walking with thee in the night betwixt tavern and
tavern. But the sack that thou hast drunk me would
have bought me lights as good cheap at the dear-　51
est chandler's° in Europe. I have maintained that
salamander° of yours with fire any time this two and
thirty years, God reward me for it!　　　　　55

BARD. 'Sblood, I would my face were in your
belly!

FAL. God-a-mercy! So should I be sure to be heart-
burned. [*Enter* HOSTESS.] How now, Dame Partlet
the hen!° Have you inquired yet who picked my
pocket?　　　　　61

HOSTESS. Why, Sir John, what do you think, Sir
John? Do you think I keep thieves in my house? I
have searched, I have inquired, so has my husband,
man by man, boy by boy, servant by servant.　65
The tithe° of a hair was never lost in my house
before.

FAL. Ye lie, hostess. Bardolph was shaved° and
lost many a hair, and I'll be sworn my pocket was
picked. Go to, you are a woman, go.　　　　　70

HOSTESS. Who, I? No, I defy thee. God's light, I
was never called so in mine own house before!

FAL. Go to, I know you well enough.

HOSTESS. No, Sir John, you do not know me, Sir
John. I know you, Sir John. You owe me money,　75
Sir John, and now you pick a quarrel to beguile me
of it. I bought you a dozen of shirts to your back.

FAL. Dowlas,° filthy dowlas. I have given them

away to bakers' wives, and they have made bolters°
of them.　　　　　81

HOSTESS. Now, as I am a true woman, holland° of
eight shillings an ell.° You owe money here besides,
Sir John, for your diet and by-drinkings,° and
money lent you, four and twenty pound.　86

FAL. He had his part of it. Let him pay.

HOSTESS. He? Alas, he is poor, he hath nothing.

FAL. How! Poor? Look upon his face — what call
you rich? Let them coin his nose, let them coin　90
his cheeks. I'll not pay a denier.° What, will you
make a younker° of me? Shall I not take mine ease
in mine inn but I shall have my pocket picked? I
have lost a seal ring of my grandfather's worth forty
mark.　　　　　95

HOSTESS. Oh Jesu, I have heard the Prince tell
him, I know not how oft, that that ring was copper!°

FAL. How! The Prince is a Jack,° a sneak-cup.°
'Sblood, an he were here, I would cudgel him like a
dog if he would say so.　　　　　101

[*Enter the* PRINCE *and* PETO, *marching, and* FALSTAFF
meets them playing on his truncheon like a fife.]
How now, lad! Is the wind in that door, i' faith?
Must we all march?

BARD. Yea, two and two, Newgate fashion.°

HOSTESS. My lord, I pray you hear me.　　　105

PRINCE. What sayest thou, Mistress Quickly? How
doth thy husband? I love him well, he is an honest
man.

HOSTESS. Good my lord, hear me.

FAL. Prithee let her alone, and list to me.　110

PRINCE. What sayest thou, Jack?

FAL. The other night I fell asleep here behind the
arras, and had my pocket picked. This house is
turned bawdyhouse; they pick pockets.

PRINCE. What didst thou lose, Jack?　　　115

FAL. Wilt thou believe me, Hal? Three or four
bonds of forty pound apiece, and a seal ring of my
grandfather's.

PRINCE. A trifle, some eightpenny matter.

HOSTESS. So I told him, my lord, and I said I　120
heard your Grace say so. And, my lord, he speaks
most vilely of you, like a foul-mouthed man as he is,
and said he would cudgel° you.

PRINCE. What! He did not?

HOSTESS. There's neither faith, truth, nor womanhood in me else.　　　　　126

FAL. There's no more faith in thee than in a
stewed prune, nor no more truth in thee than in a

---

29. poop: stern.　**34. death's-head:** skull.　**34–35. memento
mori:** reminder of death.　**36. Dives:** the rich man in the parable of Dives and Lazarus. See Luke 16:19–31.　**39. By . . .
angel:** a parody of a line in a recent and popular play at the Rose
Theater.　**44. ignis fatuus:** will-o'-the-wisp.　**wildfire:** firework.
46. triumph: rejoicing, celebrated with torches and bonfires.
47. links: torches used to light the way on a dark night.　**52.
chandler:** seller of candles.　**54. salamander:** a kind of lizard,
believed to enjoy fire.　**59–60. Dame . . . hen:** the wife of
Chanticleer the cock in the story of Reynard the Fox.　**66. tithe:**
tenth part.　**68. shaved:** caught venereal disease.　**78. Dowlas:**
coarse linen.

80. bolters: sieves for sifting flour from bran.　**82. holland:** fine
linen.　**83. ell:** 45 inches.　**85. by-drinkings:** drinks between
meals.　**91. denier:** the smallest English coin, worth 1/10*d.*
92. younker: "sucker."　**97. copper:** copper-gilt was the cheap-
est kind of imitation gold.　**99. Jack:** knave. **sneak-cup:** one
who steals cups from taverns, the lowest kind of theft.
104. Newgate fashion: i.e., like the chain gang. **Newgate: the**
London prison for felons.　**123. cudgel:** beat.

drawn fox,° and for womanhood, Maid Marian may be the deputy's wife of the ward to thee.° Go, you thing, go.   131

HOSTESS. Say, what thing? What thing?

FAL. What thing! Why, a thing to thank God on.

HOSTESS. I am no thing to thank God on, I   135 would thou shouldst know it. I am an honest man's wife. And, setting thy knighthood aside, thou art a knave to call me so.

FAL. Setting thy womanhood aside, thou art a beast to say otherwise.   140

HOSTESS. Say, what beast, thou knave, thou?

FAL. What beast! Why, an otter.

PRINCE. An otter, Sir John! Why an otter?

FAL. Why, she's neither fish nor flesh. A man knows not where to have her.   145

HOSTESS. Thou art an unjust man in saying so. Thou or any man knows where to have me, thou knave, thou!

PRINCE. Thou sayest true, hostess, and he slanders thee most grossly.   150

HOSTESS. So he doth you, my lord, and said this other day you ought° him a thousand pound.

PRINCE. Sirrah, do I owe you a thousand pound?

FAL. A thousand pound, Hal! A million!   155 Thy love is worth a million. Thou owest me thy love.

HOSTESS. Nay, my lord, he called you Jack, and said he would cudgel you.

FAL. Did I, Bardolph?   160

BARD. Indeed, Sir John, you said so.

FAL. Yea, if he said my ring was copper.

PRINCE. I say 'tis copper.° Darest thou be as good as thy word now?   164

FAL. Why, Hal, thou knowest, as thou art but man, I dare; but as thou art Prince, I fear thee as I fear the roaring of the lion's whelp.

PRINCE. And why not as the lion?

FAL. The King himself is to be feared as the lion. Dost thou think I'll fear thee as I fear thy   170 father? Nay, an I do, I pray God my girdle break.

PRINCE. Oh, if it should, how would thy guts fall about thy knees! But, sirrah, there's no room for faith, truth, nor honesty in this bosom of thine; it is all filled up with guts and midriff. Charge an   175 honest woman with picking thy pocket! Why, thou whoreson, impudent, embossed° rascal, if there were anything in thy pocket but tavern reckonings, memorandums of bawdyhouses, and one poor penny-

worth of sugar candy to make thee long-   180 winded, if thy pocket were enriched with any other injuries° but these, I am a villain. And yet you will stand to it, you will not pocket up wrong. Art thou not ashamed?   184

FAL. Dost thou hear, Hal? Thou knowest in the state of innocency Adam fell, and what should poor Jack Falstaff do in the days of villainy?° Thou seest I have more flesh than another man, and therefore more frailty. You confess, then, you picked my pocket?   190

PRINCE. It appears so by the story.

FAL. Hostess, I forgive thee. Go, make ready breakfast. Love thy husband, look to thy servants, cherish thy guests. Thou shalt find me tractable° to any honest reason. Thou seest I am pacified   195 still.° Nay, prithee be gone. [Exit HOSTESS.] Now, Hal, to the news at Court. For the robbery, lad, how is that answered?

PRINCE. Oh, my sweet beef,° I must still be good angel to thee. The money is paid back again.   200

FAL. Oh, I do not like that paying back. 'Tis a double labor.

PRINCE. I am good friends with my father, and may do anything.   204

FAL. Rob me the exchequer the first thing thou doest, and do it with unwashed hands° too.

BARD. Do, my lord.

PRINCE. I have procured thee, Jack, a charge of foot.   209

FAL. I would it had been of horse. Where shall I find one that can steal well? Oh for a fine thief, of the age of two and twenty or thereabouts! I am heinously° unprovided. Well, God be thanked for these rebels, they offend none but the virtuous. I laud them, I praise them.   215

PRINCE. Bardolph!

BARD. My lord?

PRINCE. Go bear this letter to Lord John of Lancaster, to my brother John; this to my Lord of Westmoreland. [Exit BARDOLPH.] Go, Peto, to horse,   220 to horse, for thou and I have thirty miles to ride yet ere dinnertime. [Exit PETO.] Jack, meet me tomorrow in the Temple Hall at two o'clock in the afternoon.

There shalt thou know thy charge, and there receive Money and order for their furniture.°   226 The land is burning, Percy stands on high, And either we or they must lower lie.   [Exit.]

FAL. Rare words! Brave world! Hostess, my
   breakfast, come!
Oh, I could wish this tavern were my drum! [Exit.]

---

129. drawn fox: fox driven out from cover, and so cunning.
129-30. Maid . . . thee: Maid Marian, the woman in Robin Hood's gang, was a character in a Whitsun morris dance. She was played by a man as lumpish and awkward. The wife of the deputy of the ward was likely to give herself airs of dignity. Falstaff means "you are more lumpish than Maid Marian compared with a most stately matron."   152. ought: owed. 163. I . . . copper: Here Falstaff gets the "lie direct."   177. embossed: swollen.

181-82. pocket . . . injuries: a pun on the phrase "to pocket up injuries."   187. days of villainy: these wicked times.   194. tractable: agreeable.   196. still: always.   199. beef: ox.   206. unwashed hands: without stopping to wash your hands. 212. heinously: atrociously.   226. furniture: equipment.

Act IV

SCENE I. *The rebel camp near Shrewsbury.*

[*Enter* HOTSPUR, WORCESTER, *and* DOUGLAS.]

HOT. Well said, my noble Scot. If speaking truth
In this fine age were not thought flattery,
Such attribution° should the Douglas have
As not a soldier of this season's stamp°
Should go so general current through the world. 5
By God, I cannot flatter, I do defy
The tongues of soothers;° but a braver place
In my heart's love hath no man than yourself.
Nay, task me to my word.° Approve° me, lord.
DOUG. Thou art the king of honor.   10
No man so potent breathes upon the ground
But I will beard° him.
HOT.   Do so, and 'tis well.

[*Enter a* MESSENGER *with letters.*]

What letters hast thou there? — I can but thank
you.
MESS. These letters come from your father.
HOT. Letters from him! Why comes he not him-
self?   15
MESS. He cannot come, my lord, he is grievous
sick.
HOT. 'Zounds! How has he the leisure to be sick
In such a justling° time? Who leads his power?
Under whose government come they along?
MESS. His letters bear his mind, not I, my lord.
WOR. I prithee tell me, doth he keep his bed? 21
MESS. He did, my lord, four days ere I set forth,
And at the time of my departure thence
He was much feared by his physicians.
WOR. I would the state of time had first been
whole°   25
Ere he by sickness had been visited.
His health was never better worth° than now.
HOT. Sick now! Droop now! This sickness doth
infect
The very lifeblood of our enterprise.
'Tis catching hither, even to our camp.   30
He writes me here that inward sickness —
And that his friends by deputation° could not
So soon be drawn,° nor did he think it meet
To lay so dangerous and dear° a trust
On any soul removed but on his own.   35

Yet doth he give us bold advértisement°
That with our small conjunction° we should on,
To see how fortune is disposed to us;
For, as he writes, there is no quailing now,
Because the King is certainly possessed°   40
Of all our purposes. What say you to it?
WOR. Your father's sickness is a maim to us.
HOT. A perilous gash, a very limb lopped off.
And yet, in faith, it is not; his present want°
Seems more than we shall find it. Were it good 45
To set° the exact° wealth of all our states
All at one cast?° To set so rich a main°
On the nice hazard° of one doubtful hour?
It were not good, for therein should we read
The very bottom and the soul of hope,   50
The very list,° the very utmost bound°
Of all our fortunes.
DOUG.   Faith, and so we should,
Where now remains a sweet reversion.°
We may boldly spend upon the hope of what
Is to come in.   55
A comfort of retirement° lives in this.
HOT. A rendezvous, a home to fly unto,
If that the Devil and mischance look big°
Upon the maidenhead of our affairs.
WOR. But yet I would your father had been here.
The quality and hair° of our attempt   61
Brooks no division. It will be thought
By some, that know not why he is away,
That wisdom, loyalty, and mere dislike
Of our proceedings kept the Earl from hence. 65
And think how such an apprehension
May turn the tide of fearful faction,°
And breed a kind of question in our cause;
For well you know we of the offering° side
Must keep aloof from strict arbitrament,°   70
And stop all sight holes, every loop from whence
The eye of reason may pry in upon us.
This absence of your father's draws° a curtain
That shows the ignorant a kind of fear
Before not dreamed of.
HOT.   You strain too far. 75
I rather of his absence make this use.
It lends a luster and more great opinion,
A larger dare to our great enterprise,
Than if the Earl were here; for men must think
If we without his help can make a head°   80
To push against a kingdom, with his help

Act IV, Sc. i: **3. attribution:** citation of merits.   **4. season's stamp:** of this year's minting. The idea is that Douglas is like a new coin, acceptable (*current*) everywhere as valuable.
7. soothers: flatterers.   **9. task . . . word:** cause me to make my word good. **Approve:** put to the proof.   **12. beard:** dare; lit., pull by the beard.   **18. justling:** jostling, disturbed.   **25. I . . . whole:** I wish the times themselves had first been healthy.
27. better worth: worth more.   **32. deputation:** deputy; i.e., he could not send anyone else.   **33. drawn:** drawn together.
34. dear: important.

36. advertisement: advice.   **37. conjunction:** forces that have joined.   **40. possessed:** informed.   **44. his . . . want:** the need of him at this present time.   **46. set:** hazard. **exact:** entire. **47. cast:** throw of the dice. **main:** stake.   **48. nice hazard:** delicate chance.   **51. list:** limit. **bound:** boundary.   **53. reversion:** portion yet to come.   **56. comfort of retirement:** a place to which we can retire for comfort.   **58. look big:** threaten. **61. hair:** nature.   **67. fearful faction:** timid rebellion.   **69. offering:** challenging.   **70. strict arbitrament:** exact judgment. **73. draws:** draws back.   **80. make a head:** raise an army. See I.iii.284.

We shall o'erturn it topsy-turvy down.
Yet all goes well, yet all our joints are whole.
    DOUG. As heart can think. There is not such a word
Spoke of in Scotland as this term of fear.   85

    [*Enter* SIR RICHARD VERNON.]

    HOT. My cousin Vernon! Welcome, by my soul.
    VER. Pray God my news be worth a welcome, lord.
The Earl of Westmoreland, seven thousand strong,
Is marching hitherward; with him Prince John.
    HOT. No harm. What more?
    VER.   And further, I have learned,   90
The King himself in person is set forth,
Or hitherward intended speedily,
With strong and mighty preparation.
    HOT. He shall be welcome too. Where is his son,
The nimble-footed madcap Prince of Wales,   95
And his comrades, that daffed° the world aside
And bid it pass?°
    VER.   All furnished,° all in arms;
All plumed like estridges that with the wind
Bated like eagles having lately bathed;°
Glittering in golden coats, like images;°   100
As full of spirit as the month of May,
And gorgeous as the sun at midsummer;
Wanton° as youthful goats, wild as young bulls.
I saw young Harry, with his beaver° on,
His cuisses° on his thighs, gallantly armed,   105
Rise from the ground like feathered Mercury,°
And vaulted with such ease into his seat
As if an angel dropped down from the clouds
To turn and wind a fiery Pegasus,°   109
And witch° the world with noble horsemanship.
    HOT. No more, no more. Worse than the sun in
        March,
This praise doth nourish agues. Let them come.
They come like sacrifices in their trim,°
And to the fire-eyed maid of smoky war
All hot and bleeding will we offer them.   115
The mailèd Mars° shall on his altar sit
Up to the ears in blood. I am on fire
To hear this rich reprisal° is so nigh
And yet not ours. Come, let me taste my horse,
Who is to bear me like a thunderbolt   120
Against the bosom of the Prince of Wales.
Harry to Harry shall, hot horse to horse,

Meet and ne'er part till one drop down a corse.
Oh that Glendower were come!
    VER.   There is more news.
I learned in Worcester, as I rode along,   125
He cannot draw his power this fourteen days.
    DOUG. That's the worst tidings that I hear of yet.
    WOR. Aye, by my faith, that bears a frosty sound.
    HOT. What may the King's whole battle° reach
        unto?
    VER. To thirty thousand.
    HOT.   Forty let it be.   130
My father and Glendower being both away,
The powers of us may serve so great a day.
Come, let us take a muster speedily.
Doomsday is near. Die all, die merrily.
    DOUG. Talk not of dying. I am out of° fear   135
Of death or death's hand for this one half-year.
                                        [*Exeunt.*]

SCENE II. *A public road near Coventry.*

    [*Enter* FALSTAFF *and* BARDOLPH.]

    FAL. Bardolph, get thee before to Coventry, fill me
a bottle of sack. Our soldiers shall march through,
we'll to Sutton Co'fil'° tonight.
    BARD. Will you give me money, Captain?
    FAL. Lay out,° lay out.   5
    BARD. This bottle makes an angel.°
    FAL. An if it do, take it for thy labor. And if it
make twenty, take them all, I'll answer the coinage.°
Bid my Lieutenant Peto meet me at town's end.   10
    BARD. I will, Captain. Farewell.   [*Exit.*]
    FAL. If I be not ashamed of my soldiers,° I am a
soused gurnet.° I have misused the King's press°
damnably. I have got, in exchange of a hundred and
fifty soldiers, three hundred and odd pounds. I   15
press me none but good householders, yeomen's°
sons; inquire me out contracted bachelors,° such as
had been asked twice on the banns; such a commod-
ity° of warm slaves as had as lieve° hear the Devil as
a drum; such as fear the report of a caliver°   20
worse than a struck fowl or a hurt wild duck. I
pressed me none but such toasts-and-butter, with

---

129. battle: main army.   135. out of: free from.

Sc. ii: 3. Sutton Co'fil': Sutton Coldfield, a town in Warwickshire.   5. Lay out: pay for it.   6. makes an angel: comes
to an angel (10s) which you owe me.   7–9. take . . . coinage:
Falstaff deliberately misunderstands Bardolph's "make" — "if
the bottle will make angels, I'll guarantee the coins."   12. If . . .
soldiers: Falstaff (see following to l. 52) was typical of many
dishonest captains in the 1590's. His methods of levying recruits (and releasing the best men for bribes) are further shown in
II Hen IV, III.ii.   13. soused gurnet: pickled gurnet (sea
fish with a large head). King's press: the right to conscript
soldiers granted by the King's commission.   16. yeomen: wealthy
farmers.   17. contracted bachelors: bachelors engaged to be
married in a short time.   19. commodity: parcel. lieve: soon.
20. caliver: lighter form of musket or harquebus, used by the
infantry.

96. daffed: waved.   97. bid it pass: cried "let the world pass";
i.e., "who cares a damn?" furnished: in full armor.   97–99. All
. . . bathed: These lines are much annotated. As they stand they
mean: "All wearing plumes like ostriches that flap their wings
(*bate*) in the wind like eagles that have lately bathed." But the
comparison seems hardly apt. Either a line has been omitted
after *wind*, or *with* is a misprint of some such verb as
"wing."   100. images: i.e., of the saints in a Catholic church.
103. Wanton: lusty.   104. beaver: hinged visor of the helmet.
105. cuisses: thigh pieces.   106. feathered Mercury: Mercury,
the messenger of the gods, wore winged sandals.   109. Pegasus:
Perseus's winged horse.   110. witch: bewitch.   113. in . . . trim:
dressed up.   116. mailed Mars: the god of war in his armor.
118. reprisal: prize.

hearts in their bellies no bigger than pins' heads, and they have bought out their services. And now my whole charge consists of ancients, corporals, 25 lieutenants, gentlemen of companies,° slaves as ragged as Lazarus in the painted cloth° where the glutton's dogs licked his sores; and such as indeed were never soldiers, but discarded unjust serv- 30 ingmen,° younger sons to younger brothers,° revolted tapsters, and ostlers trade-fallen;° the cankers of a calm world and a long peace, ten times more dishonorable ragged than an old-faced ancient. And such have I to fill up the rooms of them that 35 have bought out their services that you would think that I had a hundred and fifty tattered prodigals lately come from swine-keeping, from eating draff and husks.° A mad fellow° met me on the way and told me I had unloaded all the gibbets° and 40 pressed the dead bodies. No eye hath seen such scarecrows. I'll not march through Coventry with them, that's flat. Nay, and the villains march wide betwixt the legs, as if they had gyves° on, for indeed I had the most of them out of prison. There's but a shirt and a half in all my company; and the half- 46 shirt is two napkins tacked together and thrown over the shoulders like a herald's coat° without sleeves; and the shirt, to say the truth, stolen from my host at St. Alban's, or the red-nose innkeeper of Daven- 50 try. But that's all one. They'll find linen enough on every hedge.°

[*Enter the* PRINCE *and* WESTMORELAND.]

PRINCE. How now, blown° Jack! How now, quilt!   54

FAL. What, Hal! How now, mad wag! What a devil dost thou in Warwickshire? My good Lord of Westmoreland, I cry you mercy. I thought your honor had already been at Shrewsbury.   59

WEST. Faith, Sir John, 'tis more than time that I were there, and you too; but my powers are there already. The King, I can tell you, looks for us all. We must away all night.

FAL. Tut, never fear me. I am as vigilant as a cat to steal cream.   65

25–26. charge . . . companies: Falstaff has picked up a selection of veterans of various ranks. ancients: ensigns, second lieutenants. gentlemen of companies: gentlemen of good family who served in the ranks of the companies of noblemen. 27. Lazarus . . . cloth: In taverns and less wealthy houses painted cloths showing scenes from Scripture and classical legend were hung on the walls instead of the more costly imported tapestry. 31. servingmen: upper-class servants from some great household. younger . . . brothers: young gentlemen who had no hope of an allowance or a legacy. 32. ostlers trade-fallen: unemployed grooms. 39. draff . . . husks: offal and husks, like the Prodigal Son in the parable who "would fain have filled his belly with the husks that the swine did eat" (Luke, 15:11–32). mad fellow: wit. 40. unloaded . . . gibbets: The bodies of executed felons were often hung up in iron cages near the scene of the crime until they rotted. 44. gyves: fetters on the legs. 48. herald's coat: a sleeveless coat embroidered with the royal coat of arms. 51–52. linen . . . hedge: The washing was laid on the hedges to dry and air. 53. blown: inflated.

PRINCE. I think to steal cream indeed, for thy theft hath already made thee butter. But tell me, Jack, whose fellows are these that come after?

FAL. Mine, Hal, mine.

PRINCE. I did never see such pitiful rascals.   70

FAL. Tut, tut, good enough to toss,° food for powder, food for powder. They'll fill a pit as well as better. Tush, man, mortal men, mortal men.

WEST. Aye, but, Sir John, methinks they are exceeding poor and bare, too beggarly.   75

FAL. Faith, for their poverty, I know not where they had that; and for their bareness, I am sure they never learned that of me.

PRINCE. No, I'll be sworn, unless you call three fingers° on the ribs bare. But, sirrah, make haste. Percy is already in the field.   81

FAL. What, is the King encamped?

WEST. He is, Sir John. I fear we shall stay too long.

FAL. Well,
To the latter end of a fray and the beginning of a
    feast   85
Fits a dull fighter and a keen guest.   [*Exeunt.*]

SCENE III. *The rebel camp near Shrewsbury.*

[*Enter* HOTSPUR, WORCESTER, DOUGLAS, *and* VERNON.]

HOT. We'll fight with him tonight.

WOR.   It may not be.

DOUG. You give him then advantage.

VER.   Not a whit.

HOT. Why say you so? Looks he not for supply?°

VER. So do we.

HOT.   His is certain, ours is doubtful.

WOR. Good Cousin, be advised, stir not tonight.   5

VER. Do not, my lord.

DOUG.   You do not counsel well.
You speak it out of fear and cold heart.

VER. Do me no slander, Douglas. By my life,
And I dare well maintain it with my life,
If well-respected° honor bid me on,   10
I hold as little counsel with weak fear
As you, my lord, or any Scot that this day lives.
Let it be seen tomorrow in the battle
Which of us fears.

DOUG.   Yea, or tonight.

VER.   Content.

HOT. Tonight, say I.   15

VER. Come, come, it may not be. I wonder much,
Being men of such great leading° as you are,
That you foresee not what impediments
Drag back our expedition.° Certain horse°
Of my cousin Vernon's are not yet come up.   20

71. good . . . toss: i.e., on pikes; "good enough for cannon fodder." 79–80. three fingers: i.e., three fingers' thickness of fat. Sc. iii: 3. supply: reinforcements. 10. well-respected: well-considered (not foolhardy). 17. leading: experience in leadership. 19. expedition: haste. horse: cavalry.

Your uncle Worcester's horse came but today,
And now their pride and mettle° is asleep,
Their courage with hard labor tame and dull,
That not a horse is half the half of himself.
    HOT. So are the horses of the enemy   25
In general, journey-bated° and brought low.
The better part of ours are full of rest.
    WOR. The number of the King exceedeth ours.
For God's sake, Cousin, stay till all come in.
            [*The trumpet sounds a parley.*]
          [*Enter* SIR WALTER BLUNT.]
    BLUNT. I come with gracious offers from the King,
If you vouchsafe me hearing and respect.   31
    HOT. Welcome, Sir Walter Blunt, and would to
    God
You were of our determination!°
Some of us love you well, and even those some
Envy your great deservings and good name   35
Because you are not of our quality,°
But stand against us like an enemy.
    BLUNT. And God defend° but still I should stand
    so
So long as out of limit and true rule
You stand against anointed Majesty.   40
But to my charge.° The King hath sent to know
The nature of your griefs, and whereupon
You conjure from the breast of civil peace
Such bold hostility, teaching his duteous land
Audacious cruelty. If that the King   45
Have any way your good deserts forgot,
Which he confesseth to be manifold,
He bids you name your griefs, and with all speed
You shall have your desires with interest,
And pardon absolute for yourself and these   50
Herein misled by your suggestion.°
    HOT. The King is kind, and well we know the
    King
Knows at what time to promise, when to pay.
My father and my uncle and myself
Did give him that same royalty he wears.   55
And when he was not six and twenty strong,
Sick in the world's regard,° wretched and low,
A poor unminded outlaw sneaking home,
My father gave him welcome to the shore.
And when he heard him swear and vow to God   60
He came but to be Duke of Lancaster,
To sue his livery° and beg his peace
With tears of innocency and terms of zeal,°
My father, in kind heart and pity moved,
Swore him assistance, and performed it too.   65
Now when the lords and barons of the realm

Perceived Northumberland did lean to him,
The more and less came in with cap and knee —
Met him in boroughs, cities, villages,
Attended him on bridges, stood in lanes,   70
Laid gifts before him, proffered him their oaths,
Gave him their heirs as pages, followed him
Even at the heels in golden° multitudes.
He presently, as greatness knows itself,
Steps me a little higher than his vow   75
Made to my father while his blood was poor,
Upon the naked shore at Ravenspurgh;
And now, forsooth, takes on him to reform
Some certain edicts and some strait° decrees
That lie too heavy on the commonwealth,   80
Cries out upon abuses, seems to weep
Over his country's wrongs. And by this face,
This seeming brow of justice, did he win
The hearts of all that he did angle for —
Proceeded further, cut me off the heads   85
Of all the favorites that the absent King
In deputation° left behind him here
When he was personal° in the Irish war.
    BLUNT. Tut, I came not to hear this.
    HOT.   Then to the point.
In short time after, he deposed the King,   90
Soon after that, deprived him of his life.
And in the neck° of that, tasked° the whole state.
To make that worse, suffered his kinsman March,
Who is, if every owner were well placed,
Indeed his king, to be engaged° in Wales,   95
There without ransom to lie forfeited;
Disgraced me in my happy victories,
Sought to entrap me by intelligence;°
Rated° mine uncle from the Council board,
In rage dismissed my father from the Court;   100
Broke oath on oath, committed wrong on wrong;
And in conclusion drove us to seek out
This head of safety,° and withal to pry
Into his title, the which we find
Too indirect° for long continuance.   105
    BLUNT. Shall I return this answer to the King?
    HOT. Not so, Sir Walter. We'll withdraw a
    while.
Go to the King, and let there be impawned°
Some surety for a safe return again,
And in the morning early shall mine uncle   110
Bring him our purposes. And so farewell.
    BLUNT. I would you would accept of grace and
    love.
    HOT. And maybe so we shall.
    BLUNT.   Pray God you do. [*Exeunt.*]

---

22. **mettle:** ardor.   26. **journey-bated:** tired by the journey.
33. **determination:** mind.   36. **quality:** fellowship, party.   38. **defend:** forbid.   41. **my charge:** what I have been instructed
(*charged*) to say.   51. **suggestion:** temptation.   57. **Sick ...
regard:** poorly regarded by the world.   62. **sue ... livery:** claim
his inheritance.   63. **terms of zeal:** protestations of loyalty.

73. **golden:** wearing their richest clothes.   79. **strait:** strict.
87. **In deputation:** as his deputies.   88. **was personal:** went in
person.   92. **in ... neck:** on top of. **tasked:** taxed.   95. **engaged:**
held as pledge, hostage.   98. **intelligence:** spies.   99. **Rated:**
dismissed with abuse.   103. **head of safety:** armed force to keep
us safe.   105. **indirect:** not in the straight line of descent.
108. **impawned:** kept as hostage.

SCENE IV. *York. The* ARCHBISHOP'S *palace.*

[*Enter the* ARCHBISHOP OF YORK *and* SIR MICHAEL.°]
ARCH. Hie, good Sir Michael, bear this sealèd
  brief°
With wingèd haste to the Lord Marshal,
This to my cousin Scroop, and all the rest
To whom they are directed. If you knew   4
How much they do import, you would make haste.
    SIR M. My good lord,
I guess their tenor.°
    ARCH.   Like enough you do.
Tomorrow, good Sir Michael, is a day
Wherein the fortune of ten thousand men
Must bide the touch;° for, sir, at Shrewsbury,   10
As I am truly given to understand,
The King with mighty and quick-raisèd power
Meets with Lord Harry. And I fear, Sir Michael —
What with the sickness of Northumberland,
Whose power was in the first proportion,°   15
And what with Owen Glendower's absence thence,
Who with them was a rated sinew° too
And comes not in, o'er-ruled by prophecies —
I fear the power of Percy is too weak
To wage an instant° trial with the King.   20
    SIR M. Why, my good lord, you need not fear.
There is Douglas and Lord Mortimer.
    ARCH. No, Mortimer is not there.
    SIR M. But there is Mordake, Vernon, Lord Harry
  Percy,
And there is my Lord of Worcester and a head   25
Of gallant warriors, noble gentlemen.
    ARCH. And so there is. But yet the King hath
  drawn
The special head° of all the land together —
The Prince of Wales, Lord John of Lancaster,
The noble Westmoreland and warlike Blunt,   30
And many mo° corrivals° and dear men
Of estimation° and command in arms.
    SIR M. Doubt not, my lord, they shall be well op-
  posed.
    ARCH. I hope no less, yet needful 'tis to fear,
And, to prevent° the worst, Sir Michael, speed. 35
For if Lord Percy thrive not ere the King
Dismiss his power, he means to visit us,°
For he hath heard of our confederacy,°
And 'tis but wisdom to make strong against him.
Therefore make haste. I must go write again   40
To other friends. And so farewell, Sir Michael.
                                        [*Exeunt.*]

Sc. iv: s.d., Sir Michael: He has not been identified, presumably a priest or knight in the Archbishop's service.   1. brief:
letter.   7. tenor: import.   10. bide . . . touch: be put to the
test.   15. in . . . proportion: the largest part.   17. rated sinew:
strength highly valued.   20. instant: immediate.   28. special
head: crack troops, "shock troops."   31. mo: more. corrivals:
supporters.   31–32. dear . . . estimation: men highly regarded.
35. prevent: forestall.   37. visit us: come our way.   38. confederacy: conspiracy.

Act V

SCENE I. *The* KING'S *camp near Shrewsbury.*

[*Enter the* KING, PRINCE OF WALES, LORD JOHN OF
LANCASTER, SIR WALTER BLUNT, *and* FALSTAFF.°]
KING. How bloodily the sun begins to peer
Above yon busky° hill! The day looks pale
At his distemperature.°
    PRINCE.   The southern wind
Doth play the trumpet° to his purposes,
And by his hollow whistling in the leaves   5
Foretells a tempest and a blustering day.
    KING. Then with the losers let it sympathize,
For nothing can seem foul to those that win.
        [*The trumpet sounds. Enter* WORCESTER
                and VERNON.]
How now, my Lord of Worcester! 'Tis not well
That you and I should meet upon such terms   10
As now we meet. You have deceived our trust,
And made us doff our easy robes of peace
To crush our old'limbs in ungentle steel.
This is not well, my lord, this is not well.
What say you to it? Will you again unknit   15
This churlish knot° of all-abhorrèd war?
And move in that obedient orb° again
Where you did give a fair and natural light,
And be no more an exhaled meteor,°
A prodigy of fear,° and a portent   20
Of broachèd° mischief to the unborn times?
    WOR. Hear me, my liege.
For mine own part, I could be well content
To entertain the lag end of my life
With quiet hours, for I do protest   25
I have not sought the day of this dislike.
    KING. You have not sought it! How comes it,
  then?
    FAL. Rebellion lay in his way, and he found it.
    PRINCE. Peace, chewet,° peace!
    WOR. It pleased your Majesty to turn your looks
Of favor from myself and all our house.   31
And yet I must remember° you, my lord,
We were the first and dearest of your friends.
For you my staff of office° did I break
In Richard's time, and posted° day and night   35
To meet you on the way, and kiss your hand,
When yet you were in place and in account

Act V, Sc. i: s.d., Falstaff: It is worth noting that Shakespeare
places Falstaff in immediate attendance on the King.   2. busky:
bushy.   3. distemperature: sickness.   4. play . . . trumpet: like
the trumpeter blowing an introductory flourish.   16. churlish
knot: knot which unites men for a brutal purpose.   17. obedient
orb: sphere of obedience, like a planet taking its natural course.
19. meteor: Meteors were believed to be made of vapors drawn
up by the sun.   20. prodigy of fear: a fearful sign of disaster.
21. broached: set loose; lit., tapped (like a cask).   29. chewet:
jackdaw.   32. remember: remind.   34. staff of office: See *Rich
II*, II.iii.26–28.   35. posted: rode hastily.

Nothing so strong and fortunate as I.
It was myself, my brother, and his son
That brought you home, and boldly did outdare   40
The dangers of the time. You swore to us,
And you did swear that oath at Doncaster,
That you did nothing purpose 'gainst the state,
Nor claim no further than your new-fall'n right,°
The seat of Gaunt, Dukedom of Lancaster.   45
To this we swore our aid. But in short space
It rained down fortune showering on your head;
And such a flood of greatness fell on you,
What with our help, what with the absent King,
What with the injuries of a wanton° time,   50
The seeming sufferances° that you had borne,
And the contrarious winds that held the King
So long in his unlucky Irish wars
That all in England did repute him dead.
And from this swarm of fair advantages   55
You took occasion to be quickly wooed
To gripe° the general sway° into your hand;
Forgot your oath to us at Doncaster;
And being fed by us you used us so
As that ungentle gull,° the cuckoo's bird,°   60
Useth the sparrow — did oppress our nest;
Grew by our feeding to so great a bulk
That even our love durst not come near your sight
For fear of swallowing, but with nimble wing
We were enforced, for safety sake, to fly   65
Out of your sight and raise this present head.
Whereby we stand opposèd by such means
As you yourself have forged against yourself,
By unkind usage, dangerous countenance,°
And violation of all faith and troth°   70
Sworn to us in your younger enterprise.
    KING. These things indeed you have articulate,°
Proclaimed at market crosses, read in churches,
To face° the garment of rebellion
With some fine color that may please the eye   75
Of fickle changelings° and poor discontents,
Which gape and rub the elbow at the news
Of hurly-burly innovation.°
And never yet did insurrection want
Such water colors to impaint his cause,   80
Nor moody beggars, starving for a time
Of pell-mell havoc° and confusion.
    PRINCE. In both your armies there is many a soul
Shall pay full dearly for this encounter
If once they join in trial. Tell your nephew,   85
The Prince of Wales doth join with all the world
In praise of Henry Percy. By my hopes,

This present enterprise set off his head,°
I do not think a braver gentleman,
More active-valiant or more valiant-young,   90
More daring or more bold, is now alive
To grace this latter age with noble deeds.
For my part, I may speak it to my shame,
I have a truant been to chivalry,°
And so I hear he doth account me too.   95
Yet this before my father's majesty —
I am content that he shall take the odds°
Of his great name and estimation,
And will, to save the blood on either side,
Try fortune with him in a single fight.   110
    KING. And, Prince of Wales, so dare we venture thee,
Albeit considerations infinite
Do make against it. No, good Worcester, no,
We love our people well, even those we love
That are misled upon your cousin's part.   105
And, will they take the offer of our grace,
Both he and they and you — yea, every man —
Shall be my friend again and I'll be his.
So tell your cousin, and bring me word
What he will do. But if he will not yield,   100
Rebuke and dread correction wait on us°
And they shall do their office. So, be gone.
We will not now be troubled with reply.
We offer fair, take it advisedly.
            [*Exeunt* WORCESTER *and* VERNON.]
    PRINCE. It will not be accepted, on my life.   115
The Douglas and the Hotspur both together
Are confident against the world in arms.
    KING. Hence, therefore, every leader to his charge,°
For on their answer will we set on them.
And God befriend us as our cause is just!   120
[*Exeunt all but the* PRINCE OF WALES *and* FALSTAFF.]
    FAL. Hal, if thou see me down in the battle, and bestride me so, 'tis a point of friendship.
    PRINCE. Nothing but a colossus° can do thee that friendship. Say thy prayers, and farewell.   124
    FAL. I would 'twere bedtime, Hal, and all well.
    PRINCE. Why, thou owest God a death.   [*Exit.*]
    FAL. 'Tis not due yet, I would be loath to pay Him before his day. What need I be so forward with him that calls not on me? Well, 'tis no matter.   130
Honor pricks me on.° Yea, but how if honor prick me off° when I come on? How then? Can honor set to° a leg? No. Or an arm? No. Or take away the grief of a wound? No. Honor hath no skill in surgery, then? No. What is honor? A word. What   135
is in that word honor? What is that honor? Air. A

---

44. new-fall'n right: inheritance which had recently come. **50. wanton:** wild.   **51. sufferances:** injuries.   **57. gripe:** grip. **general sway:** rule of the whole state.   **60. gull:** nestling. **cuckoo's bird:** The cuckoo lays its eggs in the nest of another bird. **69. dangerous countenance:** threatening looks.   **70. troth:** truth.   **72. articulate:** drawn up in schedules.   **74. face:** trim. **76. changelings:** turncoats.   **78. hurly-burly innovation:** confusion and revolution.   **82. havoc:** slaughter.

88. set . . . head: being excepted.   **94. chivalry:** knightly deeds. **97. take . . . odds:** have the advantage.   **111. wait on us:** are our servants.   **118. charge:** command.   **123. colossus:** an enormous statue with its legs apart.   **131. Honor . . . on:** honor spurs me forward to heroism.   **131–32. prick me off:** mark me down on the casualty list.   **132–33. set to:** mend.

trim° reckoning! Who hath it? He that died o' Wednesday. Doth he feel it? No. Doth he hear it? No.
'Tis insensible, then? Yea, to the dead. But will   140
it not live with the living? No. Why? Detraction°
will not suffer it. Therefore I'll none of it. Honor is
a mere scutcheon.° And so ends my catechism.

[Exit.]

SCENE II. The rebel camp.

[Enter WORCESTER and VERNON.]

WOR. Oh, no, my nephew must not know, Sir
    Richard,
The liberal and kind offer of the King.
   VER. 'Twere best he did.
   WOR.   Then are we all undone.
It is not possible, it cannot be
The King should keep his word in loving us.   5
He will suspect us still, and find a time
To punish this offense in other faults.
Suspicion all our lives shall be stuck full of eyes;
For treason is but trusted like the fox,
Who, ne'er so tame, so cherished and locked up,   10
Will have a wild trick° of his ancestors.
Look how we can, or° sad or merrily,
Interpretation will misquote° our looks,
And we shall feed like oxen at a stall,
The better cherished, still the nearer death.   15
My nephew's trespass may be well forgot.
It hath the excuse of youth and heat of blood,
And an adopted name of privilege,°
A harebrained Hotspur, governed by a spleen.°
All his offenses live upon my head   20
And on his father's. We did train° him on,
And, his corruption being ta'en from us,
We, as the spring of all, shall pay for all.
Therefore, good Cousin, let not Harry know,
In any case, the offer of the King.   25
   VER. Deliver° what you will, I'll say 'tis so.
Here comes your cousin.

[Enter HOTSPUR and DOUGLAS.]

   HOT. My uncle is returned.
Deliver up° my Lord of Westmoreland.
Uncle, what news?   30
   WOR. The King will bid you battle presently.°
   DOUG. Defy him by the Lord of Westmoreland.
   HOT. Lord Douglas, go you and tell him so.
   DOUG. Marry, and shall, and very willingly.

[Exit.]

WOR. There is no seeming mercy in the King.   35
   HOT. Did you beg any? God forbid!
   WOR. I told him gently of our grievances,
Of his oath-breaking, which he mended thus,
By now forswearing° that he is forsworn.
He calls us rebels, traitors, and will scourge   40
With haughty arms this hateful name in us.

[Re-enter DOUGLAS.]

   DOUG. Arm, gentlemen, to arms! For I have
    thrown
A brave defiance in King Henry's teeth —
And Westmoreland, that was engaged,° did bear
    it —
Which cannot choose but bring him quickly on.   45
   WOR. The Prince of Wales stepped forth before
    the King
And, Nephew, challenged you to single fight.
   HOT. Oh, would the quarrel lay upon our heads,
And that no man might draw short breath° today
But I and Harry Monmouth! Tell me, tell me,   50
How showed his tasking?° Seem'd it in contempt?
   VER. No, by my soul. I never in my life
Did hear a challenge urged° more modestly,
Unless a brother should a brother dare
To gentle exercise and proof of arms.   55
He gave you all the duties of° a man,
Trimmed up your praises with a princely tongue,
Spoke your deservings like a chronicle,
Making you ever better than his praise
By still dispraising praise valued with you.°   60
And, which became him like a prince indeed,
He made a blushing cital° of himself,
And chid his truant youth with such a grace
As if he mastered there a double spirit
Of teaching and of learning instantly.   65
There did he pause. But let me tell the world,
If he outlive the envy° of this day,
England did never owe° so sweet a hope,
So much misconstrued in his wantonness.
   HOT. Cousin, I think thou art enamored   70
On his follies. Never did I hear
Of any prince so wild a libertine.
But be he as he will, yet once ere night
I will embrace him with a soldier's arm,
That he shall shrink under my courtesy.   75
Arm, arm with speed. And, fellows, soldiers, friends,
Better consider what you have to do
Than I, that have not well the gift of tongue,
Can lift your blood up with persuasion.

[Enter a MESSENGER.]

   MESS. My lord, here are letters for you.   80
   HOT. I cannot read them now.
O gentlemen, the time of life is short!

---

137. trim: neat. 141. Detraction: slander. 143. scutcheon: coat
of arms, painted on boards or cloth, carried in the funeral of a
gentleman and afterward hung up in the church.
   Sc. ii: 11. wild trick: wild habits. 12. or: either. 13. Interpretation . . . misquote: men will deliberately misinterpret.
18. adopted . . . privilege: his nickname Hotspur will be his
excuse. 19. spleen: impetuosity. 21. train: lure. 26. Deliver:
report. 29. Deliver up: release. Westmoreland had been hostage
for Worcester's safe return. 31. presently: immediately.

39. forswearing: falsely denying an oath. 44. engaged: pledged
as hostage. 49. draw . . . breath: i.e., in fighting. 51. tasking:
challenge. 53. urged: put forward. 56. duties of: respect due to.
60. By . . . you: by continuously saying that your praise was
undervalued. 62. cital: recital. 68. envy: malice. 69. owe: own.

To spend that shortness basely were too long
If life did ride upon a dial's point,°
Still° ending at the arrival of an hour.   85
An if we live, we live to tread on kings;
If die, brave death when princes die with us!
Now, for our consciences, the arms are fair
When the intent° of bearing them is just.
    [Enter another MESSENGER.]
MESS. My lord, prepare. The King comes on
    apace.   90
    HOT. I thank him, that he cuts me from my tale,
For I profess not talking, only this —
Let each man do his best. And here draw I
A sword whose temper° I intend to stain
With the best blood that I can meet withal   95
In the adventure of this perilous day.
Now, Esperance! Percy! and set on.
Sound all the lofty instruments of war,
And by that music let us all embrace;
For, heaven to earth, some of us never shall   100
A second time do such a courtesy.
    [The trumpets sound. They embrace, and exeunt.]

SCENE III. *Plain between the camps.*

[The KING *enters with his power. Alarum to the battle.° Then enter* DOUGLAS *and* SIR WALTER BLUNT.]
    BLUNT. What is thy name, that in the battle thus
Thou crossest me? What honor dost thou seek
Upon my head?
    DOUG.   Know then, my name is Douglas,
And I do haunt thee in the battle thus
Because some tell me that thou art a King.   5
    BLUNT. They tell thee true.
    DOUG. The Lord of Stafford dear today hath
    bought
Thy likeness; for instead of thee, King Harry,°
This sword hath ended him. So shall it thee
Unless thou yield thee as my prisoner.   10
    BLUNT. I was not born a yielder, thou proud Scot,
And thou shalt find a King that will revenge
Lord Stafford's death.
    [They fight. DOUGLAS *kills* BLUNT. *Enter* HOTSPUR.]
    HOT. O Douglas, hadst thou fought at Holmedon
    thus,   15
I never had triumphed upon a Scot.
    DOUG. All's done, all's won. Here breathless lies
    the King.
    HOT. Where?
    DOUG. Here.
    HOT. This, Douglas? No. I know this face full
    well.

A gallant knight he was, his name was Blunt,   20
Semblably furnished° like the King himself.
    DOUG. A fool go with thy soul° whither it goes!
A borrowed title hast thou bought too dear.
Why didst thou tell me that thou wert a king?   24
    HOT. The King hath many marching in his coats.°
    DOUG. Now, by my sword, I will kill all his coats.
I'll murder all his wardrobe, piece by piece,
Until I meet the King.
    HOT.   Up, and away!   28
Our soldiers stand full fairly for the day.° *[Exeunt.]*
    [Alarum. Enter FALSTAFF, *alone.]*
    FAL. Though I could 'scape shot-free° at London,
I fear the shot here. Here's no scoring but upon the
pate. Soft! Who are you? Sir Walter Blunt. There's
honor for you! Here's no vanity!° I am as hot as
molten lead, and as heavy too. God keep lead out of
me! I need no more weight than mine own   35
bowels. I have led my ragamuffins where they are
peppered.° There's not three of my hundred and
fifty left alive, and they are for the town's end, to beg
during life. But who comes here?   40
    [Enter the PRINCE.]
    PRINCE. What, stand'st thou idle here? Lend me
    thy sword.
Many a nobleman lies stark and stiff
Under the hoofs of vaunting enemies
Whose deaths are yet unrevenged. I prithee lend me
    thy sword.   44
    FAL. O Hal, I prithee give me leave to breathe a
while. Turk Gregory° never did such deeds in arms
as I have done this day. I have paid Percy, I have
made him sure.
    PRINCE. He is, indeed, and living to kill thee. I
prithee lend me thy sword.   50
    FAL. Nay, before God, Hal, if Percy be alive, thou
get'st not my sword. But take my pistol, if thou wilt.
    PRINCE. Give it me. What, is it in the case?
    FAL. Aye, Hal, 'tis hot, 'tis hot. There's that will
sack a city.   56
    [The PRINCE *draws it out, and finds it*
    to be a bottle of sack.]
    PRINCE. What, is it a time to jest and dally now?
    [He throws the bottle at him. Exit.]
    FAL. Well, if Percy be alive, I'll pierce° him. If he
do come in my way, so. If he do not, if I come in   60
his willingly, let him make a carbonado° of me. I

84. dial's point: hand of a clock. 85. Still: always. 89. intent:
cause. 94. temper: lit., hardness, quality.

Sc. iii: s.d., Alarum . . . battle: battle noises. 8. thee . . .
Harry: Blunt is wearing the King's coat of arms and not his
own, and so is mistaken by Douglas for the King.

21. Semblably furnished: wearing similar armor. 22. A . . .
soul: a proverbial phrase, "you foolish soul." 25. coats: coats
of arms. 29. full . . . day: i.e., are full of fight. 30. shot-free:
without paying the *shot* (the tavern bill) which had been
scored up against him. 33. no vanity: spoken ironically. "Who
said honor was not a vain thing?" 36–37. where . . . peppered:
Falstaff's heroism has a base motive. Until the army is remustered
he will pocket the pay of his dead soldiers. 46. Turk Gregory:
Pope Gregory VII, who had a reputation for ferocity. The Turk
was proverbial for cruelty. 59. pierce: pronounced "perse," a
pun on "Percy." 61. carbonado: piece of meat slashed for
broiling.

like not such grinning honor as Sir Walter hath.
Give me life, which if I can save, so; if not, honor
comes unlooked-for, and there's an end.   [*Exit.*]

SCENE IV. *Another part of the field.*

[*Alarum. Excursions.*° *Enter the* KING, *the* PRINCE,
          LORD JOHN OF LANCASTER, *and*
          EARL OF WESTMORELAND.]

KING. I prithee
Harry, withdraw thyself, thou bleed'st too much.
Lord John of Lancaster, go you with him.
    LANC. Not I, my lord, unless I did bleed too.
    PRINCE. I beseech your Majesty, make up,°   5
Lest your retirement do amaze° your friends.
    KING. I will do so.
My Lord of Westmoreland, lead him to his tent.
    WEST. Come, my lord, I'll lead you to your tent.
    PRINCE. Lead me, my lord? I do not need your
          help.   10
And God forbid a shallow scratch should drive
The Prince of Wales from such a field as this,
Where stained° nobility lies trodden on
And rebels' arms triumph in massacres!
    LANC. We breathe° too long. Come, Cousin West-
          moreland,   15
Our duty this way lies. For God's sake, come.
          [*Exeunt* PRINCE JOHN *and* WESTMORELAND.]
    PRINCE. By God, thou hast deceived me, Lan-
          caster,
I did not think thee lord of such a spirit.
Before, I loved thee as a brother, John,
But now I do respect thee as my soul.   20
    KING. I saw him hold Lord Percy at the point
With lustier maintenance than I did look for
Of such an ungrown warrior.
    PRINCE.   Oh, this boy
Lends mettle° to us all!   [*Exit.*]
          [*Enter* DOUGLAS.]
    DOUG. Another King! They grow like Hydra's
          heads.°   25
I am the Douglas, fatal to all those
That wear those colors on them. What art thou,
That counterfeit'st the person of a king?
    KING. The King himself, who, Douglas, grieves at
          heart
So many of his shadows° thou hast met   30
And not the very King. I have two boys
Seek Percy and thyself about the field.
But, seeing thou fall'st on me so luckily,

I will assay° thee. So defend thyself.
    DOUG. I fear thou art another counterfeit,   35
And yet, in faith, thou bear'st thee like a king.
But mine I am sure thou art, whoe'er thou be,
And thus I win thee.
          [*They fight; the* KING *being in danger, re-enter*
                    PRINCE OF WALES.]
    PRINCE. Hold up thy head, vile Scot, or thou art
          like
Never to hold it up again! The spirits   40
Of valiant Shirley, Stafford, Blunt,° are in my arms.
It is the Prince of Wales that threatens thee,
Who never promiseth but he means to pay.
                    [*They fight:* DOUGLAS *flies.*]
Cheerly, my lord. How fares your Grace?
Sir Nicholas Gawsey hath for succor sent,   45
And so hath Clifton. I'll to Clifton straight.
    KING. Stay, and breathe a while.
Thou hast redeemed thy lost opinion,°
And showed thou makest some tender° of my life,
In this fair rescue thou hast brought to me.   50
    PRINCE. Oh God! They did me too much injury
That ever said I hearkened for° your death.
If it were so, I might have let alone
The insulting° hand of Douglas over you,
Which would have been as speedy in your end   55
As all the poisonous potions in the world,
And saved the treacherous labor of your son.
    KING. Make up to Clifton. I'll to Sir Nicholas
          Gawsey.   [*Exit.*]
          [*Enter* HOTSPUR.]
    HOT. If I mistake not, thou art Harry Monmouth.
    PRINCE. Thou speak'st as if I would deny my
          name.   60
    HOT. My name is Harry Percy.
    PRINCE.   Why, then I see
A very valiant rebel of the name.
I am the Prince of Wales. And think not, Percy,
To share with me in glory any more.
Two stars keep not their motion in one sphere,   65
Nor can one England brook a double reign
Of Harry Percy and the Prince of Wales.
    HOT. Nor shall it, Harry, for the hour is come
To end the one of us. And would to God
Thy name in arms were now as great as mine!   70
    PRINCE. I'll make it greater ere I part from thee,
And all the budding honors on thy crest
I'll crop, to make a garland for my head.
    HOT. I can no longer brook thy vanities.
                    [*They fight.*]
          [*Enter* FALSTAFF.]
    FAL. Well said, Hal! To it, Hal! Nay, you shall
find no boy's play here, I can tell you.   76

Sc. iv: s.d., **Excursions:** noises to indicate rapid movements
in battle. **5. make up:** go up to the front line. **6. amaze:** fill
with dismay. **13. stained:** bloodstained. **15. breathe:** rest.
24. mettle: courage. **25. Hydra's heads:** Hydra was a many-
headed monster slain by Hercules. As soon as one head was cut
off, two others grew in its place. **30. shadows:** imitations.

34. assay: challenge. **41. Shirley . . . Blunt:** who have all fallen
in the battle. **48. opinion:** reputation. **49. makest . . . tender:**
hast some regard for. **52. hearkened for:** desired. **54. insulting:** triumphing.

[*Re-enter* DOUGLAS; *he fights with* FALSTAFF, *who falls down as if he were dead, and exit* DOUGLAS. HOTSPUR *is wounded, and falls.*]

HOT. O Harry, thou hast robbed me of my youth!
I better brook the loss of brittle life
Than those proud titles thou hast won of me.
They wound my thoughts worse than thy sword my
    flesh.   80
But thought's the slave of life, and life Time's fool,
And Time, that takes survèy of all the world,
Must have a stop.° Oh, I could prophesy,
But that the earthy and cold hand of death
Lies on my tongue. No, Percy, thou art dust,   85
And food for ——   [*Dies.*]
    PRINCE. For worms, brave Percy. Fare thee well,
      great heart!
Ill-weaved ambition, how much art thou shrunk!
When that this body did contain a spirit,
A kingdom for it was too small a bound,°   90
But now two paces of the vilest earth
Is room enough. This earth that bears thee dead
Bears not alive so stout a gentleman.
If thou wert sensible° of courtesy,
I should not make so dear a show of zeal.°   95
But let my favors° hide thy mangled face,
And, even in thy behalf, I'll thank myself
For doing these fair rites of tenderness.
Adieu, and take thy praise with thee to Heaven!
Thy ignominy sleep with thee in the grave,   100
But not remembered in thy epitaph!
    [*He spieth* FALSTAFF *on the ground.*]
What, old acquaintance! Could not all this flesh
Keep in a little life? Poor Jack, farewell!
I could have better spared a better man.
Oh, I should have a heavy miss of thee   105
If I were much in love with vanity!°
Death hath not struck so fat a deer today,
Though many dearer, in this bloody fray.
Emboweled° will I see thee by and by.   109
Till then in blood by noble Percy lie.   [*Exit.*]
    FAL. [*Rising up*] Emboweled! If thou embowel
me today, I'll give you leave to powder° me and eat
me too tomorrow. 'Sblood, 'twas time to counterfeit,
or that hot termagant° Scot had paid me scot and
lot° too. Counterfeit? I lie, I am no counterfeit.   115
To die is to be a counterfeit, for he is but the counterfeit of a man who hath not the life of a man. But to
counterfeit dying when a man thereby liveth is to be

no counterfeit, but the true and perfect image of life
indeed. The better part of valor is discretion, in   120
the which better part I have saved my life. 'Zounds,
I am afraid of this gunpowder Percy, though he be
dead. How if he should counterfeit too, and rise? By
my faith, I am afraid he would prove the better   125
counterfeit. Therefore I'll make him sure. Yea, and
I'll swear I killed him. Why may he not rise as well
as I? Nothing confutes me but eyes, and nobody sees
me. Therefore, sirrah [*Stabbing him*], with a   130
new wound in your thigh, come you along with me.
    [*Takes up* HOTSPUR *on his back.*]
  [*Re-enter the* PRINCE OF WALES *and* LORD JOHN
    OF LANCASTER.]
    PRINCE. Come, Brother John, full bravely hast
      thou fleshed
Thy maiden sword.°
    LANC.   But, soft! Whom have we here?
Did you not tell me this fat man was dead?   135
    PRINCE. I did, I saw him dead,
Breathless and bleeding on the ground. Art thou
    alive?
Or is it fantasy° that plays upon our eyesight?
I prithee, speak, we will not trust our eyes   139
Without our ears. Thou art not what thou seem'st.
    FAL. No, that's certain, I am not a double° man.
But if I be not Jack Falstaff, then am I a Jack. There
is Percy [*Throwing the body down*]. If your father
will do me any honor, so; if not, let him kill the next
Percy himself. I look to be either earl or duke, I can
assure you.   146
    PRINCE. Why, Percy I killed myself, and saw thee
    dead.
    FAL. Didst thou? Lord, Lord, how this world is
given to lying! I grant you I was down and out of
breath, and so was he. But we rose both at an   150
instant, and fought a long hour by Shrewsbury
clock. If I may be believed, so; if not, let them that
should reward valor bear the sin upon their own
heads. I'll take it upon my death, I gave him this
wound in the thigh. If the man were alive, and   155
would deny it, 'zounds, I would make him eat a
piece of my sword.
    LANC. This is the strangest tale that ever I heard.
    PRINCE. This is the strangest fellow, Brother John.
Come, bring your luggage nobly on your back.   160
For my part, if a lie may do thee grace,
I'll gild it with the happiest terms° I have.
    [*A retreat is sounded.*]
The trumpet sounds retreat,° the day is ours.
Come, Brother, let us to the highest° of the field,
To see what friends are living, who are dead.   165
    [*Exeunt* PRINCE OF WALES *and* LANCASTER.]

81–83. thought's . . . stop: thought can only exist while there is
life, but life is treated like a fool by Time, and Time itself will
end — a thought in one form or another constantly recurring in
Shakespeare's plays. 90. bound: boundary. 94. sensible: able
to feel. 95. show of zeal: mark of respect. 96. favors: scarf or
handkerchief given to a knight by his lady. 106. vanity: folly.
109. Emboweled: disemboweled. He carries on the metaphor and
pun of deer (l. 107), for the last act in the hunt was the disem-
boweling of the slain deer. 112. powder: pickle. 114. termagant: ferocious. 114–15. paid . . . lot: paid all dues.

133–34. fleshed . . . sword: you have fought bravely in your
first action. 138. fantasy: imagination, illusion. 141. double:
i.e., a double of myself. 162. happiest terms: best phrases.
163. trumpet . . . retreat: i.e., to recall the troops from the
pursuit. 164. highest: i.e., ground.

FAL. I'll follow, as they say, for reward. He that rewards me, God reward him! If I do grow great, I'll grow less; for I'll purge, and leave sack, and live cleanly as a nobleman should do.   [*Exit.*]

SCENE V. *Another part of the field.*

[*The trumpets sound. Enter the* KING, PRINCE OF WALES, LORD JOHN OF LANCASTER, EARL OF WESTMORELAND, *with* WORCESTER *and* VERNON *prisoners.*]

KING. Thus ever did rebellion find rebuke.
Ill-spirited° Worcester! Did not we send grace,
Pardon, and terms of love to all of you?
And wouldst thou turn our offers contrary,
Misuse the tenor of thy kinsman's trust?   5
Three knights upon our party slain today,
A noble Earl and many a creature else
Had been alive this hour
If like a Christian thou hadst truly borne
Betwixt our armies true intelligence.   10
WOR. What I have done my safety urged me to.
And I embrace this fortune patiently,
Since not to be avoided it falls on me.
KING. Bear Worcester to the death, and Vernon too.
Other offenders we will pause upon.   15
          [*Exeunt* WORCESTER *and* VERNON, *guarded.*]
How goes the field?
PRINCE. The noble Scot, Lord Douglas, when he saw

Sc. v: 2. Ill-spirited: evil-spirited.

The fortune of the day quite turned from him,
The noble Percy slain, and all his men
Upon the foot of fear, fled with the rest;   20
And falling from a hill, he was so bruised
That the pursuers took him. At my tent
The Douglas is, and I beseech your Grace
I may dispose of him.
KING.   With all my heart.
PRINCE. Then, Brother John of Lancaster, to you
This honorable bounty shall belong.   26
Go to the Douglas, and deliver him
Up to his pleasure, ransomless and free.
His valor shown upon our crests today
Hath taught us how to cherish such high deeds   30
Even in the bosom of our adversaries.
LANC. I thank your Grace for this high courtesy,
Which I shall give away immediately.
KING. Then this remains, that we divide our power.
You, Son John, and my cousin Westmoreland   35
Toward York shall bend you with your dearest° speed,
To meet Northumberland and the prelate Scroop,
Who, as we hear, are busily in arms.
Myself and you, Son Harry, will toward Wales,
To fight with Glendower and the Earl of March.   40
Rebellion in this land shall lose his sway,
Meeting the check° of such another day.
And since this business so fair is done,
Let us not leave till all our own be won.   [*Exeunt.*]

36. dearest: best.   42. Meeting . . . check: incurring such a disaster.

HAMLET

Hamlet is the most controverted play ever written; even its bibliography fills a large volume. As a drama, its history is long and intricate; the text is full of problems for the scholar; and for the last hundred and fifty years critics of all kinds have competed in offering their key to the heart of Hamlet's mystery. It is the topmost ambition of every serious actor to play the part; and even the doctors, especially the psychiatrists, have taken Hamlet into the clinic to examine his inhibitions.

As for the interpretations of *Hamlet,* discussion is endless, particularly of the problem of why Hamlet delayed in exacting vengeance for his father's death after the Ghost's revelation (I.v) and again when Claudius so clearly revealed his guilt after the play scene (III.ii.276).

There are many answers, none of them wholly satisfactory.

Dr. Johnson, whose comments are always worth pondering, was less puzzled by the play than were many of his successors. He summed it up thus:

If the dramas of Shakespeare were to be characterized, each by the particular excellence which distinguishes it from the rest, we must allow to the tragedy of *Hamlet* the praise of variety. The incidents are so numerous, that the argument of the play would make a long tale. The scenes are interchangeably diversified with merriment and solemnity; with merriment that includes judicious and instructive observations, and solemnity, not strained by poetical violence above the natural sentiments of man. New characters appear from time to time in continual succession, exhibiting various forms of life and particular modes of conversation. The pretended madness of Hamlet causes much mirth, and the mournful distraction of Ophelia fills the heart with tenderness, and every personage produces the effect intended, from the apparition that in the first act chills the blood with horror, to the fop in the last, that exposes affectation to just contempt.

The conduct is perhaps not wholly secure against objections. The action is indeed for the most part in continual progression, but there are some scenes which neither forward nor retard it. Of the feigned madness of Hamlet there appears no adequate cause, for he does nothing which he might not have done with the reputation of sanity. He plays the madman most, when he treats Ophelia with so much rudeness, which seems to be useless and wanton cruelty.

Hamlet is, through the whole play, rather an instrument than an agent. After he has, by the stratagem of the play, convicted the king, he makes no attempt to punish him, and his death is at last effected by an incident which Hamlet has no part in producing.

The catastrophe is not very happily produced; the exchange of weapons is rather an expedient of necessity, than a stroke of art. A scheme might easily have been found to kill Hamlet with the dagger, and Laertes with the bowl.

The poet is accused of having shown little regard to poetical justice, and may be charged with equal neglect of poetical probability. The apparition left the regions of the dead to little purpose; the revenge which he demands is not obtained but by the death of him that was required to take it; and the gratification which would arise from the destruction of an usurper and a murderer, is abated by the untimely death of Ophelia, the young, the beautiful, the harmless, and the pious.

Dr. Johnson's rational analysis of the play was more than compensated for by Goethe's enthusiasm:

To me it is clear that Shakespeare meant, in the present case, to represent the effects of a great action laid upon a soul unfit for the performance of it. In this view the whole piece seems to me to be composed. There is an oak tree planted in a costly jar, which should have borne only pleasant flowers in its bosom; the roots expand, the jar shivered.

A lovely, pure, noble and most moral nature, without the strength of nerve which forms a hero, sinks beneath a burden which it cannot bear and must not cast away. All duties are holy for him; the present is too hard. Impossibilities have been required of him; not in themselves impossibilities, but such for him. He winds, and turns, and torments himself; he advances and recoils; is ever put in mind, ever puts himself in mind; at last does all but lose his purpose from his thoughts; yet still without recovering his peace of mind.

Goethe's judgment has been much quoted, but we may prefer to follow Coleridge, who declared that Shakespeare

> intended to portray a person, in whose view the external world, and all its incidents and objects, were comparatively dim, and of no interest in themselves, and which began to interest only, when they were reflected in the mirror of his mind. Hamlet beheld external things in the same way that a man of vivid imagination, who shuts his eyes, sees what has previously made an impression on his organs.
>
> The poet places him in the most stimulating circumstances that a human being can be placed in. He is the heir apparent of a throne; his father dies suspiciously; his mother excludes her son from his throne by marrying his uncle. This is not enough; but the Ghost of the murdered father is introduced, to assure the son that he was put to death by his own brother. What is the effect upon the son? instant action and pursuit of revenge? No: endless reasoning and hesitating — constant urging and solicitation of the mind to act, and as constant an escape from action; ceaseless reproaches of himself for sloth and negligence, while the whole energy of his resolution evaporates in these reproaches. This, too, not from cowardice, for he is drawn as one of the bravest of his time — not from want of forethought or slowness of apprehension, for he sees through the very souls of all who surround him, but merely from that aversion to action, which prevails among such as have a world in themselves.

Or we may accept the opinion of Bradley, who saw *Hamlet* rather as a " tragedy of moral idealism," for he regarded Hamlet as a young man of the highest ideals who has received a shock so terrible that he is driven into a state of utter melancholy which deprives him of all initiative.

Or we may take the more practical view that Hamlet never has any chance of killing his uncle because he is always closely guarded, except for the brief episode after the play scene when Hamlet comes on him at prayer; and the moment is not suitable for revenge.

Or we may apply modern psychological theories to Hamlet's case and brood over the Oedipus complex, and Hamlet's feelings toward his mother.

Or we may follow the scholars who argue about Elizabethan melancholy and ghost lore and remind us that *Hamlet* is one of many Elizabethan revenge plays which have their regular pattern; and that in most of them the plot is unfolded in stages: (1) the crime, (2) the difficulty in identifying the murderer, (3) the impediments to revenge, and (4) the final bloody slaughter.

No answer is wholly satisfactory; each has some element of truth; and the problem is the more interesting because insoluble. Perhaps Hazlitt has summed it up most neatly: " Hamlet is a name; his speeches and sayings but the ideal coinage of the poet's brain. What then, are they not real? They are as real as our own thoughts. Their reality is in the reader's mind. It is *we* who are Hamlet."

And we may also reflect that when we watch a good performance of *Hamlet* or read the play uncritically, we are so absorbed that we forget all about the problems!

But, problems apart, most readers will agree that *Hamlet* is the most fascinating of all plays; indeed it seems also to have been Shakespeare's favorite, for he revised it more than once. When he wrote it he was, with all the thinking men of his generation, in a period of profound disillusionment and pessimism; and he made *Hamlet* the vessel into which he poured his thoughts on all kinds of topics: on fathers and children, on sex, on drunkenness, on suicide, on loyalty, on acting, on glory and honor, on handwriting even, on fate, on man and the universe. There is more of Shakespeare himself in *Hamlet* than in any other play that he created.

DATE AND SOURCE OF THE PLAY. *Hamlet* in its present form was probably written about 1600 or 1601. An earlier play was being acted in London in 1594, and perhaps in 1589. Shakespeare's play was first printed in a garbled and pirated quarto (Q1) in 1603; a second quarto (Q2), probably set up from Shakespeare's own manuscript, was published in 1604; the version in the first folio omits more than 200 lines to be found in Q2 and adds some new passages of its own. The immediate source was probably the old lost play of 1594, but the Hamlet story goes back in European literature to the twelfth century. The version in François de Belleforest's *Histoires Tragiques,* published in Paris in 1576, was probably the original for English plays on Hamlet.

Hamlet

DRAMATIS PERSONAE

CLAUDIUS, *King of Denmark*
HAMLET, *son to the late, and nephew to the present King*
POLONIUS, *Lord Chamberlain*
HORATIO, *friend to Hamlet*
LAERTES, *son to Polonius*
VOLTIMAND
CORNELIUS
ROSENCRANTZ
GUILDENSTERN } *courtiers*
OSRIC
A GENTLEMAN
A PRIEST
MARCELLUS } *officers*
BERNARDO
FRANCISCO, *a soldier*

REYNALDO, *servant to Polonius*
PLAYERS
TWO CLOWNS, *gravediggers*
FORTINBRAS, *Prince of Norway*
A CAPTAIN
ENGLISH AMBASSADORS

GERTRUDE, *Queen of Denmark, and mother to Hamlet*

OPHELIA, *daughter to Polonius*
LORDS, LADIES, OFFICERS, SOLDIERS, SAILORS, MESSENGERS, *and other* ATTENDANTS

GHOST *of Hamlet's father*

SCENE — *Denmark.*

Act I

SCENE I. *Elsinore. A platform° before the castle.*

[FRANCISCO *at his post. Enter to him* BERNARDO.]
BER. Who's there?
FRAN. Nay, answer me. Stand, and unfold yourself.°
BER. Long live the King!°
FRAN. Bernardo?
BER. He.   5
FRAN. You come most carefully upon your hour.
BER. 'Tis now struck twelve. Get thee to bed, Francisco.
FRAN. For this relief much thanks. 'Tis bitter cold,
And I am sick at heart.
BER. Have you had quiet guard?
FRAN.   Not a mouse stirring.   10
BER. Well, good night.
If you do meet Horatio and Marcellus,
The rivals° of my watch, bid them make haste.
FRAN. I think I hear them. Stand, ho! Who is there?
[*Enter* HORATIO *and* MARCELLUS.]
HOR. Friends to this ground.
MAR.   And liegemen° to the Dane.   15
FRAN. Give you good night.

MAR.   Oh, farewell, honest soldier.
Who hath relieved you?
FRAN.   Bernardo hath my place.
Give you good night.   [*Exit.*]
MAR.   Holloa! Bernardo!
BER.   Say,
What, is Horatio there?
HOR.   A piece of him.
BER. Welcome, Horatio. Welcome, good Marcellus.   20
MAR. What, has this thing appeared again tonight?
BER. I have seen nothing.
MAR. Horatio says 'tis but our fantasy,°
And will not let belief take hold of him
Touching this dreaded sight twice seen of us.   25
Therefore I have entreated him along
With us to watch the minutes of this night,
That if again this apparition come,
He may approve our eyes° and speak to it.
HOR. Tush, tush, 'twill not appear.
BER.   Sit down awhile,   30
And let us once again assail your ears,
That are so fortified against our story,
What we have two nights seen.
HOR.   Well, sit we down,
And let us hear Bernardo speak of this.
BER. Last night of all,   35
When yond same star that's westward from the pole°
Had made his course to illume° that part of heaven

Act I, Sc. i: s.d., **platform**: the level place on the ramparts where the cannon were mounted.   2. **unfold yourself**: reveal who you are.   3. **Long . . . King**: probably the password for the night.   13. **rivals**: partners.   15. **liegemen**: loyal subjects.

23. **fantasy**: imagination.   29. **approve our eyes**: verify what we have seen.   36. **pole**: Polestar.   37. **illume**: light.

Where now it burns, Marcellus and myself,
The bell then beating one ——

              [*Enter* GHOST.]

MAR. Peace, break thee off. Look where it comes
    again!   40
BER. In the same figure, like the King that's
    dead.
MAR. Thou art a scholar.° Speak to it, Horatio.
BER. Looks it not like the King? Mark it, Horatio.
HOR. Most like. It harrows° me with fear and
    wonder.
BER. It would be spoke to.
MAR.   Question it, Horatio.   45
HOR. What art thou that usurp'st this time of
    night,
Together with° that fair and warlike form
In which the majesty of buried Denmark°
Did sometimes march? By Heaven I charge thee,
    speak!
MAR. It is offended.
BER.   See, it stalks away!   50
HOR. Stay! Speak, speak! I charge thee, speak!

               [*Exit* GHOST.]

MAR. 'Tis gone, and will not answer.
BER. How now, Horatio! You tremble and look
    pale.
Is not this something more than fantasy?
What think you on 't?   55
HOR. Before my God, I might not this believe
Without the sensible and true avouch
Of mine own eyes.°
MAR.   Is it not like the King?
HOR. As thou art to thyself.
Such was the very armor he had on   60
When he the ambitious Norway combated.
So frowned he once when, in an angry parle,°
He smote the sledded Polacks° on the ice.
'Tis strange.
MAR. Thus twice before, and jump at this dead
    hour,°   65
With martial stalk hath he gone by our watch.
HOR. In what particular thought to work I know
    not,
But in the gross and scope° of my opinion
This bodes some strange eruption° to our state.

MAR. Good now, sit down and tell me, he that
    knows,   70
Why this same strict and most observant watch
So nightly toils° the subject° of the land;
And why such daily cast of brazen cannon
And foreign mart° for implements of war;
Why° such impress° of shipwrights, whose sore
    task   75
Does not divide the Sunday from the week;
What might be toward,° that this sweaty haste
Doth make the night joint laborer with the day.
Who is 't that can inform me?
HOR.   That can I,
At least the whisper goes so. Our last King,   80
Whose image even but now appeared to us,
Was, as you know, by Fortinbras of Norway,
Thereto pricked° on by a most emulate° pride,
Dared to the combat, in which our valiant Ham-
    let ——
For so this side of our known world esteemed
    him ——   85
Did slay this Fortinbras. Who° by a sealed com-
    pact,°
Well ratified by law and heraldry,°
Did forfeit, with his life, all those his lands
Which he stood seized of° to the conqueror.
Against the which, a moiety competent°   90
Was gagèd° by our King, which had returned
To the inheritance of Fortinbras
Had he been vanquisher, as by the same covenant
And carriage of the article designed°
His fell to Hamlet. Now, sir, young Fortinbras,   95
Of unimprovèd mettle° hot and full,
Hath in the skirts° of Norway here and there
Sharked° up a list of lawless resolutes,°
For food and diet,° to some enterprise   99
That hath a stomach° in 't. Which is no other ——
As it doth well appear unto our state ——
But to recover of us, by strong hand
And terms compulsatory,° those foresaid lands
So by his father lost. And this, I take it,
Is the main motive of our preparations,   105
The source of this our watch and the chief head°

---

42. scholar: As Latin was the proper language in which to address and exorcise evil spirits, a scholar was necessary. **44. harrows:** distresses; lit., plows up. **47. Together with:** i.e., appearing in. **48. majesty . . . Denmark:** the dead King. **57–58. Without . . . eyes:** unless my own eyes had vouched for it. **sensible:** perceived by my senses. **62. parle:** parley. **63. sledded Polacks:** There has been much controversy about this phrase. Q1 and Q2 read "sleaded Pollax," F1 reads "sledded Pollax." Either the late King smote his heavy (leaded) poleax on the ice, or else he attacked the Poles in their sledges. There is no further reference to this incident. **65. jump . . . hour:** just at deep midnight. **68. gross . . . scope:** general conclusion. **69. eruption:** violent disturbance.

72. toils: wearies. **subject:** subjects. **74. foreign mart:** purchase abroad. **75–78. Why . . . day:** i.e., workers in shipyards and munition factories are working night shifts and Sundays. **impress:** conscription. **toward:** in preparation. **83. pricked:** spurred. **emulate:** jealous. **86–95. Who . . . Hamlet:** i.e., before the combat it was agreed that the victor should win the lands of the vanquished. **86. sealed compact:** formal agreement. **87. heraldry:** The heralds were responsible for arranging formal personal combats. **89. seized of:** possessed of, a legal term. **90. moiety competent:** adequate portion. **91. gaged:** pledged. **94. carriage . . . designed:** fulfillment of the clause in the agreement. **96. unimproved mettle:** untutored, wild material, nature. **97. skirts:** outlying parts. **98. Sharked:** collected indiscriminately, as a shark bolts its prey. **lawless resolutes:** gangsters. **99. diet:** maintenance. **100. stomach:** resolution. **103. terms compulsatory:** force. **106. chief head:** main purpose.

Of this posthaste and romage° in the land.

BER. I think it be no other but e'en so.

Well may it sort° that this portentous figure   109
Comes armèd through our watch, so like the King
That was and is the question of these wars.

HOR. A mote° it is to trouble the mind's eye.
In the most high and palmy° state of Rome,
A little ere the mightiest Julius fell,   114
The graves stood tenantless, and the sheeted° dead
Did squeak and gibber° in the Roman streets.
As stars° with trains of fire and dews of blood,
Disasters° in the sun, and the moist star°
Upon whose influence Neptune's empire stands
Was sick almost to doomsday with eclipse.   120
And even the like precurse° of fierce events,
As harbingers° preceding still the fates
And prologue to the omen° coming on,
Have Heaven and earth together demonstrated
Unto our climatures° and countrymen.   125
[Re-enter GHOST.] But soft, behold! Lo where it
    comes again!
I'll cross it,° though it blast me. Stay, illusion!
If thou hast any sound, or use of voice,
Speak to me.
If° there be any good thing to be done   130
That may to thee do ease and grace to me,°
Speak to me.
If thou art privy to° thy country's fate,
Which, happily,° foreknowing may avoid,
Oh, speak!   135
Or if thou hast uphoarded in thy life
Extorted° treasure in the womb of earth,
For which, they say, you spirits oft walk in death,
Speak of it. Stay, and speak! [The cock crows.°]
    Stop it, Marcellus.

MAR. Shall I strike at it with my partisan?°   140

HOR. Do, if it will not stand.

BER.   'Tis here!

HOR.   'Tis here!

MAR. 'Tis gone!   [Exit GHOST.]

We do it wrong, being so majestical,
To offer it the show of violence,
For it is as the air invulnerable,   145
And our vain blows malicious mockery.

BER. It was about to speak when the cock crew.

HOR. And then it started like a guilty thing
Upon a fearful° summons. I have heard
The cock, that is the trumpet to the morn,   150
Doth with his lofty and shrill-sounding throat
Awake the god of day, and at his warning,
Whether in sea or fire, in earth or air,
The extravagant and erring° spirit hies
To his confine.° And of the truth herein   155
This present object made probation.°

MAR. It faded on the crowing of the cock.
Some say that ever 'gainst° that season comes
Wherein Our Saviour's birth is celebrated,
The bird of dawning singeth all night long.   160
And then, they say, no spirit dare stir abroad,
The nights are wholesome, then no planets° strike,
No fairy takes° nor witch hath power to charm,
So hallowed and so gracious is the time.   164

HOR. So have I heard and do in part believe it.
But look, the morn, in russet mantle clad,
Walks o'er the dew of yon high eastward hill.
Break we our watch up, and by my advice
Let us impart what we have seen tonight
Unto young Hamlet, for upon my life,   170
This spirit, dumb to us, will speak to him.
Do you consent we shall acquaint him with it,
As needful in our loves, fitting our duty?

MAR. Let's do 't, I pray. And I this morning know
Where we shall find him most conveniently.   175
                                        [Exeunt.]

SCENE II. A room of state in the castle.

[Flourish.° Enter the KING, QUEEN, HAMLET,
    POLONIUS, LAERTES, VOLTIMAND, CORNELIUS,
        LORDS, and ATTENDANTS.]

KING. Though yet of Hamlet our dear brother's
    death
The memory be green,° and that it us befitted
To bear our hearts in grief and our whole kingdom
To be contracted in one brow of woe,°
Yet so far hath discretion° fought with nature°   5
That we with wisest sorrow think on him,

---

107. posthaste . . . romage: urgency and bustle.   109. Well . . . sort: it would be a natural reason.   112. mote: speck of dust. 113. palmy: flourishing, like a palm.   115. sheeted: in their shrouds.   116. gibber: utter strange sounds.   117. As stars: The sense of the passage is here broken; possibly a line has been omitted after l. 116.   118. Disasters: unlucky signs. moist star: the moon, which influences the tides.   121. precurse: forewarning.   122. harbingers: forerunners. The harbinger was an officer of the Court who was sent ahead to make the arrangements when the Court went on progress.   123. omen: disaster. 125. climatures: regions.   127. cross it: stand in its way. 130–39. If . . . speak: In popular belief there were four reasons why the spirit of a dead man should walk: (a) to reveal a secret, (b) to utter a warning, (c) to reveal concealed treasure, (d) to reveal the manner of its death. Horatio thus adjures the ghost by three potent reasons, but before he can utter the fourth the cock crows.   131. grace to me: bring me into a state of spiritual grace.   133. privy to: have secret knowledge of.   134. happily: by good luck.   137. Extorted: evilly acquired.   139. s.d., cock crows: i.e, a sign that dawn is at hand. See ll. 147–64.   140. partisan: type of spear, used by palace guards.

149. fearful: causing fear.   154. extravagant . . . erring: both words mean "wandering."   155. confine: place of confinement.   156. probation: proof.   158. 'gainst: in anticipation of. 162. planets: Planets were supposed to bring disaster.   163. takes: bewitches.

Sc. ii: s.d., Flourish: fanfare of trumpets.   2. green: fresh. 4. contracted . . . woe: i.e., every subject's forehead should be puckered with grief.   5. discretion: common sense.   nature: natural sorrow.

Together with remembrance of ourselves.
Therefore our sometime sister,° now our Queen,
The imperial jointress° to this warlike state,
Have we, as 'twere with a defeated joy —   10
With an auspicious and a dropping eye,°
With mirth in funeral and with dirge in marriage,
In equal scale weighing delight and dole° —
Taken to wife. Nor have we herein barred
Your better wisdoms,° which have freely gone   15
With this affair along. For all, our thanks.
Now follows that you know. Young Fortinbras,
Holding a weak supposal° of our worth,
Or thinking by our late dear brother's death
Our state to be disjoint and out of frame,   20
Colleagued with the dream of his advantage,°
He hath not failed to pester us with message
Importing the surrender of those lands
Lost by his father, with all bonds of law,°
To our most valiant brother. So much for him. 25
Now for ourself, and for this time of meeting.
Thus much the business is: We have here writ
To Norway, uncle of young Fortinbras —
Who, impotent and bedrid, scarcely hears
Of this his nephew's purpose — to suppress   30
His further gait° herein, in that the levies,
The lists° and full proportions,° are all made
Out of his subject.° And we here dispatch
You, good Cornelius, and you, Voltimand,
For bearers of this greeting to old Norway,   35
Giving to you no further personal power
To business with the King more than the scope°
Of these delated articles° allow.
Farewell, and let your haste commend° your duty.
COR. & VOLT. In that and all things will we show
     our duty.   40
   KING. We doubt it nothing. Heartily farewell.
          [*Exeunt* VOLTIMAND *and* CORNELIUS.]
And now, Laertes, what's the news with you?
You told us of some suit° — what is 't, Laertes?
You cannot speak of reason to the Dane
And lose your voice. What wouldst thou beg,
     Laertes,   45
That shall not be my offer, not thy asking?

The head is not more native° to the heart,
The hand more instrumental° to the mouth,
Than is the throne of Denmark to thy father.
What wouldst thou have, Laertes?
   LAER.   My dread° lord,   50
Your leave and favor to return to France,
From whence though willingly I came to Denmark
To show my duty in your coronation,
Yet now, I must confess, that duty done,   54
My thoughts and wishes bend again toward France
And bow them to your gracious leave and pardon.
   KING. Have you your father's leave? What says
     Polonius?
   POL. He hath, my lord, wrung from me my slow
     leave
By laborsome petition, and at last
Upon his will° I sealed my hard consent.°   60
I do beseech you give him leave to go.
   KING. Take thy fair hour, Laertes, time be thine,
And thy best graces spend° it at thy will!
But now, my cousin° Hamlet, and my son ——
   HAML. [*Aside*] A little more than kin and less
     than kind.°   65
   KING. How is it that the clouds still hang on you?
   HAML. Not so, my lord. I am too much i' the
     sun.
   QUEEN. Good Hamlet, cast thy nighted color° off,
And let thine eye look like a friend on Denmark.
Do not forever with thy vailèd lids°   70
Seek for thy noble father in the dust.
Thou know'st 'tis common — all that lives must die,
Passing through nature to eternity.
   HAML. Aye, madam, it is common.
   QUEEN.   If it be,
Why seems it so particular with thee?   75
   HAML. Seems, madam! Nay, it is. I know not
     " seems."
'Tis not alone my inky cloak, good Mother,
Nor customary suits of solemn black,
Nor windy suspiration of forced breath —
No, nor the fruitful river° in the eye,   80
Nor the dejected havior of the visage,°
Together with all forms, moods, shapes of grief —
That can denote me truly. These indeed seem,
For they are actions that a man might play.°
But I have that within which passeth show,   85
These but the trappings° and the suits of woe.

---

8. sister: i.e., our former sister-in-law.   **9. jointress:** partner
by marriage.   **11. auspicious . . . eye:** an eye at the same time
full of joy and of tears.   **13. dole:** grief.   **14–15. barred . . .
wisdoms:** i.e., in taking this step we have not shut out your
advice. As is obvious throughout the play, the Danes chose
their King by election and not by right of birth. See V.ii.65,
366.   **18. weak supposal:** poor opinion.   **21. Colleagued . . .
advantage:** uniting himself with this dream that here was a
good opportunity.   **24. with . . . law:** legally binding, as already explained in ll. 80–95 above.   **31. gait:** progress.   **32. lists:**
rosters. **proportions:** military establishments.   **33. subject:** subjects.   **37. scope:** limit.   **38. delated articles:** detailed instructions. Claudius is following usual diplomatic procedure. Ambassadors sent on a special mission carried with them a letter
of introduction and greeting to the King of the foreign Court
and detailed instructions to guide them in the negotiations.
29. commend: display; lit., recommend.   **43. suit:** petition.

47. native: closely related.   **48. instrumental:** serviceable.
50. dread: dreaded, much respected.   **60. will:** desire. **sealed
. . . consent:** agreed to, but with great reluctance.   **63. best . . .
spend:** i.e., use your time well.   **64. cousin:** kinsman. The word
was used for any near relation.   **65. A . . . kind:** too near a relation (uncle-father) and too little natural affection. **kind:** affectionate.   **68. nighted color:** black. Hamlet alone is in deep
mourning; the rest of the Court wear gay clothes.   **70. vailed
lids:** lowered eyelids.   **80. fruitful river: stream of tears.**
81. dejected . . . visage: downcast countenance.   **84. play:**
act, as in a play.   **86. trappings: ornaments.**

KING. 'Tis sweet and commendable in your
   nature, Hamlet,
To give these mourning duties to your father.
But you must know your father lost a father,
That father lost, lost his, and the survivor bound   90
In filial obligation for some term
To do obsequious sorrow.° But to perséver
In obstinate condolement° is a course
Of impious stubbornness, 'tis unmanly grief.
It shows a will most incorrect to Heaven,   95
A heart unfortified,° a mind impatient,
An understanding simple and unschooled.
For what we know must be and is as common
As any the most vulgar° thing to sense,
Why should we in our peevish opposition   100
Take it to heart? Fie! 'Tis a fault to Heaven,
A fault against the dead, a fault to nature,
To reason most absurd, whose common theme
Is death of fathers, and who still hath cried,
From the first corse° till he that died today,   105
" This must be so." We pray you throw to earth
This unprevailing° woe, and think of us
As of a father. For let the world take note,
You are the most immediate° to our throne,
And with no less nobility of love   110
Than that which dearest father bears his son
Do I impart toward you. For your intent
In going back to school° in Wittenberg,
It is most retrograde° to our desire.
And we beseech you bend you° to remain   115
Here in the cheer and comfort of our eye,
Our chiefest courtier, cousin, and our son.
   QUEEN. Let not thy mother lose her prayers,
   Hamlet.
I pray thee, stay with us, go not to Wittenberg.   119
   HAML. I shall in all my best obey you, madam.
   KING. Why, 'tis a loving and a fair reply.
Be as ourself in Denmark. Madam, come,
This gentle and unforced accord of Hamlet
Sits smiling to my heart. In grace whereof,
No jocund health that Denmark drinks today   125
But the great cannon° to the clouds shall tell,
And the King's rouse° the Heaven shall bruit°
   again,
Respeaking earthly thunder. Come away.
         [*Flourish. Exeunt all but* HAMLET.]
   HAML. Oh, that this too too solid flesh would melt,
Thaw, and resolve itself into a dew!   130

Or that the Everlasting had not fixed
His canon° 'gainst self-slaughter! Oh, God! God!
How weary, stale, flat, and unprofitable
Seem to me all the uses° of this world!
Fie on 't, ah, fie! 'Tis an unweeded garden,   135
That grows to seed, things rank° and gross in
   nature
Possess it merely.° That it should come to this!
But two months dead! Nay, not so much, not two.
So excellent a King, that was, to this,
Hyperion° to a satyr.° So loving to my mother   140
That he might not beteem° the winds of heaven
Visit her face too roughly. Heaven and earth!
Must I remember? Why, she would hang on him
As if increase of appetite had grown   144
By what it fed on. And yet within a month ——
Let me not think on 't. — Frailty, thy name is
   woman! —
A little month, or ere those shoes were old
With which she followed my poor father's body,
Like Niobe° all tears. — Why she, even she —   149
Oh, God! A beast that wants discourse of reason°
Would have mourned longer — married with my
   uncle,
My father's brother, but no more like my father
Than I to Hercules. Within a month,
Ere yet the salt of most unrighteous tears
Had left the flushing in her gallèd° eyes,   155
She married. Oh, most wicked speed, to post°
With such dexterity° to incestuous sheets!
It is not, nor it cannot, come to good.
But break, my heart, for I must hold my tongue!
       [*Enter* HORATIO, MARCELLUS, *and* BERNARDO.]
   HOR. Hail to your lordship!
   HAML.   I am glad to see you well.   160
Horatio — or I do forget myself.
   HOR. The same, my lord, and your poor servant
   ever.
   HAML. Sir, my good friend — I'll change that
   name° with you.
And what make you from Wittenberg, Horatio?
Marcellus?   165
   MAR. My good lord?
   HAML. I am very glad to see you. [*To* BERNARDO]
   Good even, sir.
But what, in faith, make you from Wittenberg?
   HOR. A truant disposition, good my lord.
   HAML. I would not hear your enemy say so,   170
Nor shall you do my ear that violence

---

92. **obsequious sorrow:** the sorrow usual at funerals.   93. **obstinate condolement:** lamentation disregarding the will of God.
96. **unfortified:** not strengthened with the consolation of religion.
99. **vulgar:** common.   105. **corse:** corpse. There is unconscious
irony in this remark, for the first corpse was that of Abel, also
slain by his brother.   107. **unprevailing:** futile.   109. **most immediate:** next heir.   113. **school:** university.   114. **retrograde:**
contrary.   115. **bend you:** incline.   126. **great cannon:** This
Danish custom of discharging cannon when the King proposed
a toast was much noted by Englishmen.   127. **rouse:** deep
drink. bruit: sound loudly, echo.

132. **canon:** rule, law.   134. **uses:** ways.   136. **rank:** coarse.
137. **merely:** entirely.   140. **Hyperion:** the sun god. **satyr:** a
creature half man, half goat — ugly and lecherous.   141. **beteem:** allow.   149. **Niobe:** She boasted of her children, to the
annoyance of the goddess Artemis, who slew them all. Thereafter
Niobe became so sorrowful that she changed into a rock everlastingly dripping water.   150. **wants . . . reason:** is without ability
to reason.   155. **galled:** sore.   156. **post:** hasten.   157. **dexterity:** nimbleness.   164. **that name:** i.e., friend.

To make it truster of your own report
Against yourself. I know you are no truant.
But what is your affair in Elsinore?
We'll teach you to drink deep° ere you depart.   175
　　HOR. My lord, I came to see your father's funeral.
　　HAML. I pray thee do not mock me, fellow student.
I think it was to see my mother's wedding.
　　HOR. Indeed, my lord, it followed hard upon.
　　HAML. Thrift, thrift, Horatio! The funeral baked
　　　meats   180
Did coldly furnish forth the marriage tables.°
Would I had met my dearest° foe in Heaven
Or ever I had seen that day, Horatio!
My father! — Methinks I see my father.
　　HOR. Oh, where, my lord?
　　HAML.　　　　　　　In my mind's eye, Horatio.   185
　　HOR. I saw him once. He was a goodly King.
　　HAML. He was a man, take him for all in all.
I shall not look upon his like again.
　　HOR. My lord, I think I saw him yesternight.
　　HAML. Saw? Who?   190
　　HOR. My lord, the King your father.
　　HAML.　　　　　　　　　The King my father!
　　HOR. Season your admiration° for a while
With an attent° ear till I may deliver,
Upon the witness of these gentlemen,
This marvel to you.
　　HAML.　　　　　　For God's love, let me hear.   195
　　HOR. Two nights together had these gentlemen,
Marcellus and Bernardo, on their watch
In the dead vast and middle of the night,°
Been thus encountered. A figure like your father,
Armed at point exactly, cap-a-pie,°   200
Appears before them and with solemn march
Goes slow and stately by them. Thrice he walked
By their oppressed and fear-surprisèd eyes
Within his truncheon's° length, whilst they, dis-
　　tilled°
Almost to jelly with the act of fear,   205
Stand dumb, and speak not to him. This to me
In dreadful secrecy impart they did,
And I with them the third night kept the watch.
Where, as they had delivered, both in time,   209
Form of the thing, each word made true and good,
The apparition comes. I knew your father.
These hands are not more like.
　　HAML.　　　　　　　　But where was this?
　　MAR. My lord, upon the platform where we
　　　watched.
　　HAML. Did you not speak to it?

175. drink deep: For more on the drunken habits of the Danes,
see I.iv.8–38.　180–81. Thrift . . . tables: they hurried on the
wedding for economy's sake, so that the remains of food served
at the funeral might be used cold for the wedding. baked meats:
feast.　182. dearest: best-hated.　192. Season . . . admiration:
moderate your wonder.　193. attent: attentive.　198. dead . . .
night: deep, silent midnight.　200. at . . . cap-a-pie: complete
in every detail, head to foot.　204. truncheon: a general's staff.
distilled: melted.

　　HOR.　　　　　　　　　　My lord, I did,
But answer made it none. Yet once methought   215
It lifted up it° head and did address
Itself to motion, like as it would speak.
But even then the morning cock crew loud,
And at the sound it shrunk in haste away
And vanished from our sight.
　　HAML.　　　　　　　　'Tis very strange.   220
　　HOR. As I do live, my honored lord, 'tis true,
And we did think it writ down in our duty
To let you know of it.
　　HAML. Indeed, indeed, sirs, but this troubles me.
Hold you the watch tonight?
　　MAR. & BER.　　　　　　We do, my lord.   225
　　HAML. Armed, say you?
　　MAR. & BER.　　　　　　Armed, my lord.
　　HAML.　　　　　　　　From top to toe?
　　MAR. & BER. My lord, from head to foot.
　　HAML. Then saw you not his face?
　　HOR. Oh yes, my lord, he wore his beaver° up.
　　HAML. What, looked he frowningly?   230
　　HOR. A countenance more in sorrow than in an-
　　ger.
　　HAML. Pale, or red?
　　HOR. Nay, very pale.
　　HAML.　　　　　　　And fixed his eyes upon you?
　　HOR. Most constantly.
　　HAML.　　　　　　I would I had been there.   235
　　HOR. It would have much amazed you.
　　HAML. Very like, very like. Stayed it long?
　　HOR. While one with moderate haste might tell°
　　　a hundred.
　　MAR. & BER. Longer, longer.
　　HOR. Not when I saw 't.
　　HAML.　　　　　His beard was grizzled?° No?   240
　　HOR. It was as I have seen it in his life,
A sable silvered.°
　　HAML.　　　　　　I will watch tonight.
Perchance 'twill walk again.
　　HOR.　　　　　　　　I warrant it will.
　　HAML. If it assume my noble father's person,
I'll speak to it though Hell itself should gape   245
And bid me hold my peace. I pray you all,
If you have hitherto concealed this sight,
Let it be tenable° in your silence still,
And whatsoever else shall hap tonight,
Give it an understanding, but no tongue.   250
I will requite° your loves. So fare you well.
Upon the platform, 'twixt eleven and twelve,
I'll visit you.
　　ALL.　　　Our duty to your Honor.
　　HAML. Your loves, as mine to you. Farewell.
　　　　　　　　　[Exeunt all but HAMLET.]
My father's spirit in arms! All is not well.   255

216. it: its.　229. beaver: front part of the helmet, which could
be raised.　238. tell: count.　240. grizzled: gray.　242. sable
silvered: black mingled with white.　248. tenable: held fast.
251. requite: repay.

I doubt° some foul play. Would the night were
    come!
Till then sit still, my soul. Foul deeds will rise,
Though all the earth o'erwhelm them, to men's
    eyes.   [*Exit.*]

SCENE III. *A room in* POLONIUS'S *house.*

[*Enter* LAERTES *and* OPHELIA.]
LAER. My necessaries° are embarked. Farewell.
And, Sister, as the winds give benefit
And convoy is assistant,° do not sleep,
But let me hear from you.
    OPH.   Do you doubt that?
    LAER. For Hamlet, and the trifling of his favor,°
Hold it a fashion and a toy in blood,°
A violet in the youth of primy° nature,
Forward, not permanent, sweet, not lasting,
The perfume and suppliance of a minute° —
No more.
    OPH. No more but so?
    LAER.   Think it no more.   10
For Nature crescent does not grow alone
In thews and bulk,° but as this temple° waxes
The inward service of the mind and soul
Grows wide withal. Perhaps he loves you now,
And now no soil nor cautel° doth besmirch   15
The virtue of his will.° But you must fear,
His greatness weighed,° his will is not his own,
For he himself is subject to his birth.
He may not, as unvalued persons do,
Carve° for himself, for on his choice depends   20
The safety and health of this whole state,
And therefore must his choice be circumscribed°
Unto the voice and yielding of that body
Whereof he is the head. Then if he says he loves you,
It fits your wisdom so far to believe it   25
As he in his particular act and place
May give his saying deed, which is no further
Than the main voice of Denmark goes withal.
Then weigh what loss your honor may sustain
If with too credent° ear you list his songs,   30
Or lose your heart, or your chaste treasure° open
To his unmastered importunity.
Fear it, Ophelia, fear it, my dear sister,
And keep you in the rear° of your affection,
Out of the shot and danger of desire.   35

The chariest maid is prodigal enough
If she unmask her beauty to the moon.
Virtue itself 'scapes not calumnious strokes.
The canker galls the infants° of the spring
Too oft before their buttons° be disclosed,   40
And in the morn and liquid dew of youth
Contagious blastments° are most imminent.
Be wary, then, best safety lies in fear.
Youth to itself rebels, though none else near.°
    OPH. I shall the effect of this good lesson keep   45
As watchman to my heart. But, good my brother,
Do not, as some ungracious pastors do,
Show me the steep and thorny way to Heaven
Whilst, like a puffed° and reckless libertine,
Himself the primrose path of dalliance° treads   50
And recks not his own rede.°
    LAER.   Oh, fear me not.
I stay too long. But here my father comes.
[*Enter* POLONIUS.] A double blessing is a double
    grace,
Occasion smiles° upon a second leave.
    POL. Yet here, Laertes! Aboard, aboard, for
    shame!   55
The wind sits in the shoulder of your sail
And you are stayed° for. There, my blessing with
    thee!
And these few precepts in thy memory
Look thou cháracter.° Give thy thoughts no tongue,
Nor any unproportioned° thought his act.   60
Be thou familiar, but by no means vulgar.
Those friends thou hast, and their adoption tried,°
Grapple them to thy soul with hoops of steel,
But do not dull thy palm with entertainment°   64
Of each new-hatched unfledged° comrade. Beware
Of entrance to a quarrel, but being in,
Bear 't that the opposèd may beware of thee.
Give every man thy ear, but few thy voice.°
Take each man's censure,° but reserve thy judg-
    ment.
Costly thy habit° as thy purse can buy,   70
But not expressed in fancy° — rich, not gaudy.
For the apparel oft proclaims the man,
And they in France of the best rank and station
Are of a most select and generous chief in that.°

39. canker . . . infants: maggot harms the unopened buds.
40. buttons: buds.   42. Contagious blastments: infectious blasts.
44. though . . . near: without anyone else to encourage it.
49. puffed: panting.   50. primrose . . . dalliance: i.e., the pleasant way of love-making.   51. recks . . . rede: takes no heed of
his own advice.   54. Occasion smiles: i.e., here is a happy
chance.   57. stayed: waited.   59. character: inscribe.   60. un-
proportioned: unsuitable.   62. adoption tried: friendship tested
by experience.   64. dull . . . entertainment: let your hand grow
callous with welcome.   65. unfledged: lit., newly out of the egg,
immature.   68. Give . . . voice: listen to everyone but commit
yourself to few.   69. censure: opinion.   70. habit: dress.
71. expressed in fancy: fantastic.   74. Are . . . that: A disputed
line; this is the F1 reading. Q2 reads "Or of the most select and
generous, chief in that"; i.e., the best noble and gentle families
are very particular in their dress. generous: of gentle birth.

256. doubt: suspect.
    Sc. iii: 1. necessaries: baggage.   3. convoy . . . assistant:
means of conveyance is available.   12. temple: the body.
6. toy in blood: trifling impulse.   7. primy: springtime; i.e.,
youthful.   8. perfume . . . minute: perfume which lasts only
for a minute.   11–12. For . . . bulk: for natural growth is not
only in bodily bulk.   15. cautel: deceit.   16. will: desire.   17. His . . . weighed: when you
consider his high position.   20. Carve: choose.   22. circum-
scribed: restricted.   30. credent: credulous.   31. chaste treasure: the treasure of your chastity.   34. in . . . rear: i.e., farthest from danger.

Neither a borrower nor a lender be,   75
For loan oft loses both itself and friend
And borrowing dulls the edge of husbandry.°
This above all: To thine own self be true,
And it must follow, as the night the day,
Thou canst not then be false to any man.   80
Farewell. My blessing season° this in thee!
   LAER. Most humbly do I take my leave, my lord.
   POL. The time invites you. Go, your servants
     tend.°
   LAER. Farewell, Ophelia, and remember well
What I have said to you.
   OPH.   'Tis in my memory locked,   85
And you yourself shall keep the key of it.
   LAER. Farewell.   [*Exit.*]
   POL. What is 't, Ophelia, he hath said to you?
   OPH. So please you, something touching the Lord
     Hamlet.
   POL. Marry,° well bethought.°   90
'Tis told me he hath very oft of late
Given private time to you, and you yourself
Have of your audience been most free and bounte-
   ous.
If it be so — as so 'tis put on me,
And that in way of caution — I must tell you   95
You do not understand yourself so clearly
As it behooves° my daughter and your honor.
What is between you? Give me up the truth.
   OPH. He hath, my lord, of late made many ten-
     ders°
Of his affection to me.   100
   POL. Affection! Pooh! You speak like a green girl,
Unsifted° in such perilous circumstance.
Do you believe his tenders, as you call them?   103
   OPH. I do not know, my lord, what I should think.
   POL. Marry, I'll teach you. Think yourself a baby
That you have ta'en these tenders° for true pay,
Which are not sterling.° Tender yourself more
   dearly,
Or — not to crack the wind of° the poor phrase,
Running it thus — you'll tender me a fool.   109
   OPH. My lord, he hath importuned me with love
In honorable fashion.
   POL. Aye, fashion° you may call it. Go to, go to.
   OPH. And hath given countenance to his speech,°
   my lord,
With almost all the holy vows of Heaven.
   POL. Aye, springes° to catch woodcocks.° I do
   know,   115
When the blood burns, how prodigal° the soul

Lends the tongue vows. These blazes,° daughter,
Giving more light than heat, extinct in both,
Even in their promise as it is a-making,
You must not take for fire. From this time   120
Be something scanter of your maiden presence,
Set your entreatments at a higher rate
Than a command to parley.° For Lord Hamlet,
Believe so much in him, that he is young,
And with a larger tether° may he walk   125
Than may be given you. In few,° Ophelia,
Do not believe his vows, for they are brokers,°
Not of that dye which their investments° show,
But mere implorators° of unholy suits,
Breathing like sanctified and pious bawds°   130
The better to beguile. This is for all.
I would not, in plain terms, from this time forth
Have you so slander any moment leisure°
As to give words or talk with the Lord Hamlet.
Look to 't, I charge you. Come your ways.   135
   OPH. I shall obey, my lord.   [*Exeunt.*]

SCENE IV. *The platform*

[*Enter* HAMLET, HORATIO, *and* MARCELLUS.]
   HAML. The air bites shrewdly.° It is very cold.
   HOR. It is a nipping and an eager° air.
   HAML. What hour now?
   HOR.   I thinks it lacks of twelve.
   MAR. No, it is struck.
   HOR. Indeed? I heard it not. It then draws near
   the season   5
Wherein the spirit held his wont to walk.
   [*A flourish of trumpets, and ordnance
              shot off within.*°]
What doth this mean, my lord?
   HAML. The King doth wake° tonight and takes
   his rouse,°
Keeps wassail,° and the swaggering upspring reels.°
And as he drains his draughts of Rhenish° down,
The kettledrum and trumpet thus bray out   11
The triumph of his pledge.
   HOR.   Is it a custom?
   HAML. Aye, marry, is 't.

117. blazes: flashes, quickly extinguished (*extinct*). 122–23. Set
... parley: when you are asked to see him do not regard
it as a command to negotiate. parley: meeting to discuss
terms. 125. tether: rope by which a grazing animal is fastened
to its peg. 126. In few: in short. 127. brokers: traveling
salesmen. 128. investments: garments. 129. implorators: men
who solicit. 130. bawds: keepers of brothels. F1 and Q2 read
"bond," an easy misprint for "baud" — the Elizabethan spelling
of "bawd." 133. slander ... leisure: misuse any moment of
leisure.
   Sc. iv: 1. shrewdly: bitterly. 2. eager: sharp. 6. s.d.,
within: off stage. 8. wake: "makes a night of it." rouse: See
I.ii.127,n. 9. wassail: revelry. swaggering ... reels: reel in a
riotous dance. 10. Rhenish: Rhine wine.

77. husbandry: economy. 81. season: bring to fruit. 83. tend:
attend. 90. Marry: Mary, by the Virgin Mary. well bethought:
well remembered. 97. behooves: is the duty of. 99. tenders:
offers. 102. Unsifted: untried. 106-09. tenders ... tender:
Polonius puns on "tenders," counters (used for money in games);
"tender," value; "tender," show. 107. sterling: true currency.
108. crack ... of: i.e., ride to death. 112. fashion: mere show.
113. given ... speech: confirmed his words. 115. springes:
snares. woodcocks: foolish birds. 116. prodigal: extravagantly.

But to my mind, though I am native here
And to the manner born, it is a custom   15
More honored in the breach than the observance.
This heavy-headed revel° east and west
Makes us traduced and taxed of° other nations.
They clepe° us drunkards, and with swinish phrase
Soil our addition,° and indeed it takes   20
From our achievements, though performed at
    height,°
The pith and marrow of our attribute.°
So oft it chances in particular men,
That for some vicious mole° of nature in them,
As in their birth — wherein they are not guilty,   25
Since nature cannot choose his origin —
By the o'ergrowth of some complexion,°
Oft breaking down the pales° and forts of reason,
Or by some habit that too much o'erleavens°   29
The form of plausive° manners, that these men —
Carrying, I say, the stamp of one defect,
Being Nature's livery,° or Fortune's star° —
Their virtues else — be they as pure as grace,
As infinite as man may undergo —
Shall in the general censure take corruption   35
From that particular fault. The dram of eale
Doth all the noble substance of a doubt
To his own scandal.°
               [Enter GHOST.]
    HOR.   Look, my lord, it comes!
    HAML. Angels and ministers of grace defend us!
Be thou a spirit of health or goblin damned,°   40
Bring with thee airs from Heaven or blasts from
    Hell,
Be thy intents wicked or charitable,
Thou comest in such a questionable° shape

That I will speak to thee. I'll call thee Hamlet,
King, Father, royal Dane. Oh, answer me!   45
Let me not burst in ignorance, but tell
Why thy canónized° bones, hearsèd° in death,
Have burst their cerements,° why the sepulcher
Wherein we saw thee quietly inurned°
Hath oped his ponderous and marble jaws   50
To cast thee up again. What may this mean,
That thou, dead corse, again, in complete steel,°
Revisit'st thus the glimpses of the moon,
Making night hideous, and we fools° of nature
So horridly to shake our disposition°   55
With thoughts beyond the reaches of our souls?
Say, why is this? Wherefore? What should we do?
             [GHOST beckons HAMLET.]
    HOR. It beckons you to go away with it,
As if it some impartment° did desire
To you alone.
    MAR.   Look with what courteous action   60
It waves you to a more removèd ground.
But do not go with it.
    HOR.   No, by no means.
    HAML. It will not speak. Then I will follow it.
    HOR. Do not, my lord.
    HAML.   Why, what should be the fear?
I do not set my life at a pin's fee,°   65
And for my soul, what can it do to that,
Being a thing immortal as itself?
It waves me forth again. I'll follow it.
    HOR. What if it tempt you toward the flood, my
    lord,
Or to the dreadful summit of the cliff   70
That beetles o'er° his base into the sea,
And there assume some other horrible form
Which might deprive your sovereignty of reason°
And draw you into madness? Think of it.
The very place puts toys of desperation,°   75
Without more motive, into every brain
That looks so many fathoms to the sea
And hears it roar beneath.
    HAML.   It waves me still.
Go on. I'll follow thee.
    MAR. You shall not go, my lord.
    HAML.   Hold off your hands.   80
    HOR. Be ruled. You shall not go.
    HAML.   My fate cries out,
And makes each petty artery in this body
As hardy as the Nemean lion's nerve.°
Still am I called. Unhand me, gentlemen.   84

---

17. heavy-headed revel: drinking which produces a thick head. **18. traduced . . . of:** disgraced and censured by. **19. clepe:** call. **20. soil . . . addition:** smirch our honor. **addition:** lit., title of honor added to a man's name. **21. though . . . height:** though of the highest merit. **22. pith . . . attribute:** essential part of our honor; i.e., we lose the honor due to our achievements because of our reputation for drunkenness. **24. mole:** blemish. **27. o'ergrowth . . . complexion:** some quality allowed to overbalance the rest. **28. pales:** defenses. **29. o'er-leavens:** mixes with. **30. plausive:** agreeable. **32. Nature's livery:** i.e., inborn. **Fortune's star:** caused by some external misfortune. **36–38. The . . . scandal:** This is the most famous of all disputed passages in Shakespeare's plays. The general meaning is clear: "a small portion of evil brings scandal on the whole substance, however noble." "Eale" is an Elizabethan spelling and pronunciation of "evil," as later in Q2 (II.ii.628); "deale" is the spelling and pronunciation of "Devil." The difficulty lies in "of a doubt," which is obviously a misprint for some such word as "corrupt"; but to be satisfactory it must fit the meter and be a plausible misprint. So far, although many guesses have been made, none is wholly convincing. The best is perhaps "often dout" — often put out. **40. spirit . . . damned:** a holy spirit or damned fiend. Hamlet, until convinced at the end of the play scene (III.ii.298), is perpetually in doubt whether the ghost which he sees is a good spirit sent to warn him, a devil sent to tempt him into some damnable action, or a hallucination created by his own diseased imagination. See II.ii.627–32. **43. questionable:** inviting question.

47. canonized: buried with full rites according to the canon of the Church. **hearsed:** buried. **48. cerements:** waxen shroud, used to wrap the bodies of the illustrious dead. **49. inurned:** buried. **52. complete steel:** full armor. **54. fools:** dupes. **55. disposition:** nature. **59. impartment:** communication. **65. fee:** value. **71. beetles o'er:** juts out over. **73. sovereignty of reason:** control of your reason over your actions. **75. toys of desperation:** desperate fancies. **83. Nemean . . . nerve:** sinew of a fierce beast slain by Hercules.

By Heaven, I'll make a ghost of him that lets° me!
I say, away! Go on. I'll follow thee.
                   [*Exeunt* GHOST *and* HAMLET.]
   HOR. He waxes desperate with imagination.
   MAR. Let's follow. 'Tis not fit thus to obey him.
   HOR. Have after. To what issue will this come?
   MAR. Something is rotten in the state of Den-
     mark.   90
   HOR. Heaven will direct it.
   MAR.   Nay, let's follow him.   [*Exeunt.*]

SCENE V. *Another part of the platform.*

         [*Enter* GHOST *and* HAMLET.]
   HAML. Whither wilt thou lead me? Speak. I'll go
     no further.
   GHOST. Mark me.
   HAML.   I will.
   GHOST.   My hour is almost come
When I to sulphurous and tormenting flames
Must render up myself.
   HAML.   Alas, poor ghost!   4
   GHOST. Pity me not, but lend thy serious hearing
To what I shall unfold.
   HAML.   Speak. I am bound to hear.
   GHOST. So art thou to revenge, when thou shalt
     hear.
   HAML. What?
   GHOST. I am thy father's spirit,
Doomed for a certain term to walk the night   10
And for the day confined to fast in fires
Till the foul crimes done in my days of nature
Are burnt and purged away. But that I am forbid
To tell the secrets of my prison house,
I could a tale unfold whose lightest word   15
Would harrow up thy soul, freeze thy young blood,
Make thy two eyes, like stars,° start from their
    spheres,°
Thy knotted and combinèd° locks to part
And each particular° hair to stand an° end
Like quills upon the fretful porpentine.°   20
But this eternal blazon° must not be
To ears of flesh and blood. List, list, oh, list!
If thou didst ever thy dear father love——
   HAML. Oh, God!
   GHOST. Revenge his foul and most unnatural mur-
     der.   25
   HAML. Murder!
   GHOST. Murder most foul, as in the best° it is,
But this most foul, strange, and unnatural.

   HAML. Haste me to know 't, that I, with wings as
    swift
As meditation or the thoughts of love,   30
May sweep to my revenge.
   GHOST.   I find thee apt,
And duller shouldst thou be than the fat° weed
That roots itself in ease° on Lethe wharf°
Wouldst thou not stir in this. Now, Hamlet, hear.
'Tis given out that, sleeping in my orchard,   35
A serpent stung me — so the whole ear of Denmark
Is by a forgèd process° of my death
Rankly abused. But know, thou noble youth,
The serpent that did sting thy father's life
Now wears his crown.
   HAML.   Oh, my prophetic soul!   40
My uncle!
   GHOST. Aye, that incestuous, that adulterate beast,
With witchcraft of his wit, with traitorous gifts —
O wicked wit and gifts, that have the power
So to seduce! — won to his shameful lust   45
The will of my most seeming-virtuous Queen.
O Hamlet, what a falling-off was there!
From me, whose love was of that dignity
That it went hand in hand even with the vow
I made to her in marriage, and to decline   50
Upon a wretch whose natural gifts were poor
To those of mine!
But virtue, as it never will be moved
Though lewdness court it in a shape of Heaven,°
So Lust, though to a radiant angel linked,   55
Will sate itself° in a celestial bed
And prey on garbage.
But soft! Methinks I scent the morning air.
Brief let me be. Sleeping within my orchard,
My custom always of the afternoon,   60
Upon my secure hour° thy uncle stole
With juice of cursèd hebenon° in a vial,
And in the porches° of my ears did pour
The leperous distillment,° whose effect
Holds such an enmity with blood of man   65
That swift as quicksilver it courses through
The natural gates and alleys of the body,
And with a sudden vigor it doth posset°
And curd, like eager° droppings into milk,
The thin and wholesome blood. So did it mine,   70
And a most instant tetter barked° about,
Most lazarlike,° with vile and loathsome crust,
All my smooth body.
Thus was I, sleeping, by a brother's hand

---

85. lets: hinders.

   Sc. v: 17. stars: planets.   spheres: natural path through the
sky.   18. knotted . . . combined: the hair that lies together in
a mass.   19. particular: individual. an: on. 20. porpentine:
porcupine.   21. eternal blazon: description of eternity.   27. in
. . . best: i.e., murder is foul even when there is a good excuse.

32. fat: thick, slimy, motionless.   33. in ease: undisturbed.
Lethe wharf: the bank of Lethe, the river of forgetfulness in the
underworld.   37. forged process: false account.   54. lewdness
. . . Heaven: though wooed by Lust disguised as an angel.
56. sate itself: gorge.   61. secure hour: time of relaxation.
62. hebenon: probably henbane, a poisonous plant.   63. porches:
entrances.   64. leperous distillment: distillation causing leprosy.
68. posset: curdle.   69. eager: acid.   71. tetter barked: eruption formed a bark.   72. lazarlike: like leprosy.

Of life, of crown, of Queen, at once dispatched —
Cut off even in the blossoms of my sin,°   76
Unhouseled, disappointed, unaneled,°
No reckoning made, but sent to my account
With all my imperfections on my head.
Oh, horrible! Oh, horrible, most horrible!   80
If thou hast nature° in thee, bear it not.
Let not the royal bed of Denmark be
A couch for luxury° and damned incest.
But, howsoever thou pursuest this act,
Taint not thy mind, nor let thy soul contrive   85
Against thy mother aught. Leave her to Heaven
And to those thorns that in her bosom lodge
To prick and sting her. Fare thee well at once!
The glowworm shows the matin° to be near,
And 'gins to pale his uneffectual° fire.   90
Adieu, adieu, adieu! Remember me.   [_Exit._]
      HAML. O all you host of Heaven! O earth! What
      else?
And shall I couple Hell? Oh, fie! Hold, hold, my
      heart,
And you, my sinews, grow not instant old
But bear me stiffly up. Remember thee!   95
Aye, thou poor ghost, while memory holds a seat
In this distracted globe.° Remember thee!
Yea, from the table° of my memory
I'll wipe away all trivial fond° recórds,
All saws° of books, all forms,° all pressures° past,
That youth and observation copied there,   101
And thy commandment all alone shall live
Within the book and volume of my brain,
Unmixed with baser matter. Yes, by Heaven!
O most pernicious woman!   105
O villain, villain, smiling, damnèd villain!
My tables — meet it is I set it down
[_Writing_] That one may smile, and smile, and be a
      villain.
At least I'm sure it may be so in Denmark.
So, Uncle, there you are. Now to my word.°   110
It is " Adieu, adieu! Remember me."
I have sworn 't.
      HOR. & MAR. [_Within_] My lord, my lord!
            [_Enter_ HORATIO _and_ MARCELLUS.]
MAR.   Lord Hamlet!
HOR.   Heaven secure him!
HAML. So be it!
MAR. Illo, ho, ho,° my lord!   115
HAML. Hillo, ho, ho, boy! Come, bird, come.

MAR. How is 't, my noble lord?
HOR.   What news, my lord?
HAML. Oh, wonderful!
HOR. Good my lord, tell it.
HAML.   No, you will reveal it.
HOR. Not I, my lord, by Heaven.
MAR.   Nor I, my lord.   120
HAML. How say you, then, would heart of man
      once think it?
But you'll be secret?
HOR. & MAR.   Aye, by Heaven, my lord.
HAML. There's ne'er a villain dwelling in all Den-
      mark
But he's an arrant° knave.
HOR. There needs no ghost, my lord, come from
      the grave   125
To tell us this.
HAML.   Why, right, you are i' the right.
And so, without more circumstance° at all,
I hold it fit that we shake hands and part —
You as your business and desire shall point you,
For every man hath business and desire,   130
Such as it is. And for my own poor part,
Look you, I'll go pray.
HOR. These are but wild and whirling° words, my
      lord.
HAML. I'm sorry they offend you, heartily,
Yes, faith, heartily.
HOR.   There's no offense, my lord. 135
HAML. Yes, by Saint Patrick, but there is, Horatio,
And much offense too. Touching this vision here,
It is an honest° ghost, that let me tell you.
For your desire to know what is between us,
O'ermaster 't as you may. And now, good friends,
As you are friends, scholars, and soldiers,   141
Give me one poor request.
HOR. What is 't, my lord? We will.
HAML. Never make known what you have seen
      tonight.
HOR. & MAR. My lord, we will not.
HAML.   Nay, but swear 't.
HOR.   In faith,   145
My lord, not I.
MAR.   Nor I, my lord, in faith.
HAML. Upon my sword.
MAR.   We have sworn, my lord, already.
HAML. Indeed, upon my sword,° indeed.
GHOST. [_Beneath_] Swear.
HAML. Ah, ha, boy! Say'st thou so? Art thou
      there, truepenny?°   150
Come on. You hear this fellow in the cellarage.
Consent to swear.

---

76. Cut . . . sin: cut off in a state of sin and so in danger of damnation. See III.iii.80–86.   **77. Unhouseled . . . unaneled:** without receiving the sacrament, not properly prepared, unanointed — without extreme unction.   **81. nature:** natural feelings.   **83. luxury:** lust.   **89. matin:** morning.   **90. uneffectual:** made ineffectual by daylight.   **97. globe:** i.e., head.   **98. table:** notebook. Intellectual young men carried notebooks in which they recorded good sayings and notable observations. See III.ii.42,n.   **99. fond:** trifling.   **100. saws:** wise sayings. **forms:** images in the mind. **pressures:** impressions.   **110. word:** cue.   **115. Illo . . . ho:** the falconer's cry to recall the hawk.

124. arrant: out-and-out.   **127. circumstance:** ceremony.   **133. whirling:** violent.   **138. honest:** true. See I.iv.40,n.   **148. upon . . . sword:** on the cross made by the hilt of the sword; but for soldiers the sword itself was a sacred object.   **150. truepenny:** old boy.

HOR.   Propose the oath, my lord.

HAML. Never to speak of this that you have seen,
Swear by my sword.

GHOST. [*Beneath*] Swear.   155

HAML. *Hic et ubique?*° Then we'll shift our
     ground.
Come hither, gentlemen,
And lay your hands again upon my sword.
Never to speak of this that you have heard,
Swear by my sword.   160

GHOST. [*Beneath*] Swear.

HAML. Well said, old mole! Canst work i' the
     earth so fast?
A worthy pioner!° Once more remove,° good
     friends.

HOR. Oh, day and night, but this is wondrous
     strange!

HAML. And therefore as a stranger give it wel-
     come.   165
There are more things in Heaven and earth, Hora-
     tio,
Than are dreamt of in your philosophy.
But come,
Here, as before, never, so help you mercy,
How strange or odd soe'er I bear myself,   170
As I perchance hereafter shall think meet
To put an antic disposition° on,
That you, at such times seeing me, never shall,
With arms encumbered° thus, or this headshake,
Or by pronouncing of some doubtful phrase,   175
As "Well, well, we know," or "We could an if we
     would,"
Or "If we list to speak," or "There be, an if they
     might,"
Or such ambiguous giving out, to note
That you know aught of me. This not to do,
So grace and mercy at your most need help you,   180
Swear.

GHOST. [*Beneath*] Swear.

HAML. Rest, rest, perturbèd spirit! [*They swear.*]
     So, gentlemen,
With all my love I do commend me to you.
And what so poor a man as Hamlet is   185
May do to express his love and friending° to you,
God willing, shall not lack. Let us go in together.
And still your fingers on your lips, I pray.
The time is out of joint. Oh, cursèd spite
That ever I was born to set it right!   190
Nay, come, let's go together.   [*Exeunt.*]

156. Hic et ubique: here and everywhere.   163. pioner: miner.
remove: move.   172. antic disposition: mad behavior.   174. en-
cumbered: folded.   186. friending: friendship.

Act II

SCENE I. *A room in* POLONIUS's *house.*

[*Enter* POLONIUS *and* REYNALDO.]

POL. Give him this money and these notes, Rey-
     naldo.

REY. I will, my lord.

POL. You shall do marvelous wisely, good Rey-
     naldo,
Before you visit him, to make inquire
Of his behavior.

REY.   My lord, I did intend it.   5

POL. Marry, well said, very well said. Look you,
     sir,
Inquire me first what Danskers° are in Paris,
And how, and who, what means,° and where they
     keep,°
What company, at what expense, and finding
By this encompassment and drift of question°   10
That they do know my son, come you more nearer
Than your particular demands will touch it.°
Take you, as 'twere, some distant knowledge of him,
As thus, "I know his father and his friends,
And in part him." Do you mark this, Reynaldo?   15

REY. Aye, very well, my lord.

POL. "And in part him, but," you may say, "not
     well.
But if 't be he I mean, he's very wild,
Addicted so and so"—and there put on him
What forgeries° you please. Marry, none so rank°
As may dishonor him, take heed of that,   21
But, sir, such wanton, wild, and usual slips
As are companions noted and most known
To youth and liberty.

REY.   As gaming, my lord.

POL. Aye, or drinking, fencing,° swearing, quar-
     reling,   25
Drabbing.° You may go so far.

REY. My lord, that would dishonor him.

POL. Faith, no, as you may season° it in the charge.
You must not put another scandal on him,
That he is open to incontinency.°   30
That's not my meaning. But breathe his faults so
     quaintly°
That they may seem the taints of liberty,
The flash and outbreak of a fiery mind,
A savageness in unreclaimèd° blood,

Act II, Sc. i: 7. Danskers: Danes.   8. what means: what their
income is. keep: live.   10. encompassment . . . question:
roundabout method of questioning.   12. your . . . it: i.e., you
won't get at the truth by straight questions.   20. forgeries:
inventions. rank: gross.   25. fencing: A young man who
haunted fencing schools would be regarded as quarrelsome and
likely to belong to the sporting set.   26. Drabbing: whoring.
28. season: qualify.   30. open . . . incontinency: So long as
Laertes does his drabbing inconspicuously Polonius would not
be disturbed.   31. quaintly: skillfully.   34. unreclaimed:
naturally wild.

Of general assault.°

REY.   But, my good lord ——   35
POL. Wherefore should you do this?
REY.   Aye, my lord,
I would know that.
POL.   Marry, sir, here's my drift,°
And I believe it is a fetch of warrant.°
You laying these slight sullies° on my son,
As 'twere a thing a little soiled i' the working,   40
Mark you,
Your party in converse, him you would sound,
Having ever seen° in the prenominate° crimes
The youth you breathe of guilty, be assured
He closes with you in this consequence° —   45
" Good sir," or so, or " friend," or " gentleman,"
According to the phrase or the addition°
Of man and country.
REY.   Very good, my lord.   49
POL. And then, sir, does he this — he does ——
What was I about to say? By the mass, I was about
to say something. Where did I leave?
REY. At " closes in the consequence," at " friend or
so," and " gentleman."
POL. At " closes in the consequence," aye, marry,
He closes with you thus: " I know the gentleman.
I saw him yesterday, or t'other day,   56
Or then, or then, with such, or such, and, as you
    say,
There was a' gaming, there o'ertook in 's rouse,
There falling out at tennis."° Or perchance,
" I saw him enter such a house of sale,"   60
Videlicet,° a brothel, or so forth.
See you now,
Your bait of falsehood takes this carp of truth.
And thus do we of wisdom and of reach,°
With windlasses° and with assays of bias,°   65
By indirections find directions out.°
So, by my former lecture and advice,
Shall you my son. You have me, have you not?
REY. My lord, I have.
POL.   God be wi' ye, fare ye well.
REY. Good my lord!   70
POL. Observe his inclination in° yourself.
REY. I shall, my lord.
POL. And let him ply his music.
REY.   Well, my lord.
POL. Farewell!   [Exit REYNALDO.]

[Enter OPHELIA.] How now, Ophelia! What's the
    matter?
OPH. Oh, my lord, my lord, I have been so af-
    frighted!   75
POL. With what, i' the name of God?
OPH. My lord, as I was sewing in my closet,°
Lord Hamlet, with his doublet° all unbraced,
No hat upon his head, his stockings fouled,
Ungartered and down-gyved° to his ankle,   80
Pale as his shirt, his knees knocking each other,
And with a look so piteous in purport
As if he had been loosèd out of Hell
To speak of horrors, he comes before me.
POL. Mad for thy love?
OPH.   My lord, I do not know,
But truly I do fear it.   86
POL.   What said he?
OPH. He took me by the wrist and held me hard.
Then goes he to the length of all his arm,
And with his other hand thus o'er his brow,
He falls to such perusal of my face   90
As he would draw it. Long stayed he so.
At last, a little shaking of mine arm,
And thrice his head thus waving up and down,
He raised a sigh so piteous and profound
As it did seem to shatter all his bulk   95
And end his being. That done, he lets me go.
And with his head over his shoulder turned,
He seemed to find his way without his eyes;
For out o' doors he went without their helps,
And to the last bended their light on me.   100
POL. Come, go with me. I will go seek the King.
This is the very ecstasy° of love,
Whose violent property fordoes° itself
And leads the will to desperate undertakings
As oft as any passion under heaven   105
That does afflict our natures. I am sorry.
What, have you given him any hard words of late?
OPH. No, my good lord, but, as you did command,
I did repel his letters and denied
His access to me.
POL.   That hath made him mad. 110
I am sorry that with better heed and judgment
I had not quoted° him. I feared he did but trifle
And meant to wreck thee, but beshrew° my jeal-
    ousy!
By Heaven, it is as proper° to our age
To cast beyond ourselves° in our opinions   115
As it is common for the younger sort
To lack discretion. Come, go we to the King.

35. Of . . . assault: common to all men.   37. drift: intention.
38. fetch . . . warrant: trick warranted to work.   39. sullies:
blemishes.   43. Having . . . seen: if ever he has seen. prenom-
inate: aforementioned.   45. closes . . . consequence: follows
up with this reply.   47. addition: title. See I.iv.20.   59. tennis: Visitors to France were much impressed by the enthusiasm of all classes of Frenchmen for tennis, which in England
was mainly a courtier's game.   61. Videlicet: namely, "viz."
64. wisdom . . . reach: of far-reaching wisdom.   65. windlasses:
roundabout methods. assays of bias: making our bowl (ball) take
a roundabout course.   66. indirections . . . out: by indirect
means come at the direct truth.   71. in: for.

77. closet: private room.   78. doublet: the short close-fitting
coat which was braced to the hose by laces. When a man was relaxing or careless of appearance, he unbraced, as a modern man
takes off his coat. Hamlet behaves like a melancholic lover.
80. down-gyved: hanging around his ankles like fetters.   102.
ecstasy: frenzy.   103. property fordoes: natural quality
destroys.   112. quoted: observed carefully.   113. beshrew:
a plague on.   114. proper: natural.   115. cast . . . ourselves:
be too clever.

This must be known, which, being kept close, might
move
More grief to hide than hate to utter love.°   119
Come.   [*Exeunt.*]

SCENE II. *A room in the castle.*

[*Flourish. Enter* KING, QUEEN, ROSENCRANTZ,
GUILDENSTERN, *and* ATTENDANTS.]
KING. Welcome, dear Rosencrantz and Guilden-
stern!
Moreover° that we much did long to see you,
The need we have to use you did provoke
Our hasty sending. Something have you heard
Of Hamlet's transformation — so call it,   5
Sith° nor the exterior nor the inward man
Resembles that it was. What it should be,
More than his father's death, that thus hath put him
So much from the understanding of himself
I cannot dream of. I entreat you both   10
That, being of so young days brought up with him
And sith so neighbored to his youth and havior°
That you vouchsafe your rest° here in our Court
Some little time, so by your companies
To draw him on to pleasures, and to gather   15
So much as from occasion you may glean,
Whether aught to us unknown afflicts him thus
That opened lies within our remedy.°
QUEEN. Good gentlemen, he hath much talked of
you,
And sure I am two men there art not living   20
To whom he more adheres.° If it will please you
To show us so much gentry° and goodwill
As to expend your time with us a while
For the supply and profit of our hope,°
Your visitation shall receive such thanks   25
As fits a king's remembrance.
ROS.   Both your Majesties
Might, by the sovereign power you have of us,
Put your dread pleasures more into command
Than to entreaty.
GUIL.   But we both obey,
And here give up ourselves, in the full bent°   30
To lay our service freely at your feet,
To be commanded.
KING. Thanks, Rosencrantz and gentle Guilden-
stern.

QUEEN. Thanks, Guildenstern and gentle Rosen-
crantz.
And I beseech you instantly to visit   35
My too-much-changèd son. Go, some of you,
And bring these gentlemen where Hamlet is.
GUIL. Heavens make our presence and our prac-
tices
Pleasant and helpful to him!
QUEEN.   Aye, amen! [*Exeunt* ROSENCRANTZ,
GUILDENSTERN, *and some* ATTENDANTS.]
           [*Enter* POLONIUS.]
POL. The ambassadors from Norway, my good
lord,   40
Are joyfully returned.
KING. Thou still° hast been the father of good
news.
POL. Have I, my lord? I assure my good liege
I hold my duty as I hold my soul,
Both to my God and to my gracious King.   45
And I do think, or else this brain of mine
Hunts not the trail of policy so sure
As it hath used to do,° that I have found
The very cause of Hamlet's lunacy.   49
KING. Oh, speak of that. That do I long to hear.
POL. Give first admittance to the ambassadors.
My news shall be the fruit° to that great feast.
KING. Thyself do grace° to them and bring them
in.   [*Exit* POLONIUS.]
He tells me, my dear Gertrude, he hath found   54
The head and source of all your son's distemper.°
QUEEN. I doubt it is no other but the main,°
His father's death and our o'erhasty marriage.
KING. Well, we shall sift him.
     [*Re-enter* POLONIUS, *with* VOLTIMAND
          and CORNELIUS.]
               Welcome, my good friends!
Say, Voltimand, what from our brother Norway?
VOLT. Most fair return of greetings and desires.
Upon our first,° he sent out to suppress   61
His nephew's levies, which to him appeared
To be a preparation 'gainst the Polack,
But better looked into, he truly found
It was against your Highness, whereat, grieved   65
That so his sickness, age, and impotence
Was falsely borne in hand,° sends out arrests
On Fortinbras; which he, in brief, obeys,
Receives rebuke from Norway, and in fine°
Makes vow before his uncle never more   70
To give the assay of arms° against your Majesty.
Whereon old Norway, overcome with joy,
Gives him three thousand crowns in annual fee

118–19. which . . . love: by being kept secret it may cause more
sorrow than it will cause anger by being revealed; i.e., the King
and Queen may be angry at the thought of the Prince's marrying
beneath his proper rank.

Sc. ii: 2. Moreover: in addition to the fact that. 6. Sith:
since. 12. neighbored . . . havior: so near to his youthful
manner of living. 13. vouchsafe . . . rest: consent to stay.
18. opened . . . remedy: if revealed, might be put right by us.
21. To . . . adheres: whom he regards more highly. 22. gentry: courtesy. 24. supply . . . hope: to bring a profitable conclusion to our hope. 30. in . . . bent: stretched to our uttermost.

42. still: always. 47–48. Hunts . . . do: is not so good at following the scent of political events as it used to be. 52. fruit:
the dessert, which comes at the end of the feast. 53. do grace:
honor; i.e., by escorting them into the royal presence. 55. distemper: mental disturbance. 56. main: principal cause.
61. first: i.e., audience. 67. borne in hand: imposed upon.
69. in fine: in the end. 71. give . . . arms: make an attack.

And his commission to employ those soldiers,
So levied as before, against the Polack.   75
With an entreaty, herein further shown,
                                    [*Giving a paper*]
That it might please you to give quiet pass°
Through your dominions for this enterprise,
On such regards of safety and allowance°
As therein are set down.
    KING.   It likes° us well,   80
And at our more considered time we'll read,
Answer, and think upon this business.
Meantime we thank you for your well-took labor.
Go to your rest. At night we'll feast together.
Most welcome home!
        [*Exeunt* VOLTIMAND *and* CORNELIUS.]
    POL.   This business is well ended.   85
My liege, and madam, to expostulate°
What majesty should be, what duty is,
Why day is day, night night, and time is time,
Were nothing but to waste night, day, and time.
Therefore, since brevity is the soul of wit   90
And tediousness the limbs and outward flourishes,°
I will be brief. Your noble son is mad.
Mad call I it, for to define true madness,
What is 't but to be nothing else but mad?
But let that go.
    QUEEN.   More matter, with less art.°
    POL. Madam, I swear I use no art at all.
That he is mad, 'tis true. 'Tis true 'tis pity,
And pity 'tis 'tis true — a foolish figure,°
But farewell it, for I will use no art.
Mad let us grant him, then. And now remains   100
That we find out the cause of this effect,
Or rather say the cause of this defect,
For this effect defective comes by cause.
Thus it remains and the remainder thus.
Perpend.°   105
I have a daughter — have while she is mine —
Who in her duty and obedience, mark,
Hath given me this. Now gather and surmise.°
[*Reads.*]
" To the celestial, and my soul's idol, the most beau-
    tified° Ophelia — "
That's an ill phrase, a vile phrase, " beautified " is a
vile phrase. But you shall hear. Thus: [*Reads.*]
" In her excellent white bosom, these," and so forth.
    QUEEN. Came this from Hamlet to her?   114
    POL. Good madam, stay awhile, I will be faithful.
[*Reads.*] " Doubt thou the stars are fire,
           Doubt that the sun doth move,
           Doubt truth to be a liar,
           But never doubt I love.   119

" O dear Ophelia, I am ill at these numbers,° I
have not art to reckon my groans, but that I love thee
best, O most best, believe it. Adieu.
    " Thine evermore, most dear lady, whilst this
               machine° is to him, HAMLET."
This in obedience hath my daughter shown me,
And more above, hath his solicitings,   126
As they fell out by time, by means and place,
All given to mine ear.
    KING.   But how hath she
Received his love?
    POL.   What do you think of me?
    KING. As of a man faithful and honorable.   130
    POL. I would fain prove so. But what might you
    think,
When I had seen this hot love on the wing —
As I perceived it, I must tell you that,
Before my daughter told me — what might you
Or my dear Majesty your Queen here think   135
If I had played the desk or table book,°
Or given my heart awinking, mute and dumb,
Or looked upon this love with idle sight —
What might you think? No, I went round° to work,
And my young mistress thus I did bespeak:°   140
" Lord Hamlet is a Prince, out of thy star.°
This must not be." And then I prescripts° gave her
That she should lock herself from his resort,
Admit no messengers, receive no tokens.
Which done, she took the fruits of my advice.   145
And he, repulsèd, a short tale to make,
Fell into a sadness, then into a fast,
Thence to a watch, thence into a weakness,
Thence to a lightness,° and by this declension°
Into the madness wherein now he raves   150
And all we mourn for.
    KING. Do you think this?
    QUEEN.   It may be, very like.
    POL. Hath there been such a time, I'd fain know
    that,
That I have positively said " 'Tis so "
When it proved otherwise?
    KING.   Not that I know.   155
    POL. [*Pointing to his head and shoulder.*] Take
    this from this, if this be otherwise.
If circumstances lead me, I will find
Where truth is hid, though it were hid indeed
Within the center.°

120. numbers: verses. 124. machine: i.e., body, an affected phrase. 136. desk . . . book: i.e., acted as silent go-between (desks and books being natural post offices for a love letter), or been a recipient of secrets but took no action (as desks and notebooks are the natural but inanimate places for keeping secrets). 139. round: straight. 140. bespeak: address. 141. out . . . star: above your destiny. 142. prescripts: instructions. 147-49. Fell . . . lightness: Hamlet's case history, according to Polonius, develops by stages — melancholy, loss of appetite, sleeplessness, physical weakness, mental instability, and finally madness. 149. declension: decline. 159. center: i.e., of the world.

77. quiet pass: unmolested passage. 79. regards . . . allowance: safeguard and conditions. 80. likes: pleases. 86. expostulate: indulge in an academic discussion. 91. flourishes: ornaments. 95. art: ornament. 98. figure: i.e., a figure of speech. 105. Perpend: note carefully. 108. surmise: guess the meaning. 110. beautified: beautiful.

KING. How may we try it further?

POL. You know sometimes he walks four hours together 160
Here in the lobby.

QUEEN. So he does indeed.

POL. At such a time I'll loose° my daughter to him.
Be you and I behind an arras° then.
Mark the encounter. If he love her not,
And be not from his reason fall'n thereon, 165
Let me be no assistant for a state,
But keep a farm and carters.°

KING. We will try it.

QUEEN. But look where sadly the poor wretch comes reading.

POL. Away, I do beseech you, both away. 169
I'll board° him presently. [Exeunt KING, QUEEN, and ATTENDANTS.]
[Enter HAMLET, reading.] Oh, give me leave. How does my good Lord Hamlet?

HAML. Well, God-a-mercy.

POL. Do you know me, my lord?

HAML. Excellent well. You are a fishmonger.°

POL. Not I, my lord. 175

HAML. Then I would you were so honest a man.

POL. Honest, my lord!

HAML. Aye, sir, to be honest, as this world goes, is to be one man picked out of ten thousand.

POL. That's very true, my lord. 180

HAML. For if the sun breed maggots° in a dead dog, being a god° kissing carrion° —— Have you a daughter?

POL. I have, my lord. 184

HAML. Let her not walk i' the sun. Conception is a blessing, but not as your daughter may conceive — friend, look to 't.

POL. [Aside] How say you by that? Still harping on my daughter. Yet he knew me not at first, he said I was a fishmonger. He is far gone, far gone. And truly in my youth I suffered much extremity for love, very near this. I'll speak to him again. — What do you read, my lord? 193

HAML. Words, words, words.

POL. What is the matter, my lord?

HAML. Between who? 196

POL. I mean the matter that you read, my lord.

HAML. Slanders, sir. For the satirical rogue says here that old men have gray beards, that their faces are wrinkled, their eyes purging thick amber and plum-tree gum, and that they have a plentiful lack of wit, together with most weak hams.° All which,

sir, though I most powerfully and potently believe, yet I hold it not honesty to have it thus set down; for yourself, sir, should be old as I am if like a crab you could go backward. 206

POL. [Aside] Though this be madness, yet there is method° in 't. — Will you walk out of the air, my lord?

HAML. Into my grave. 210

POL. Indeed, that's out of the air. [Aside] How pregnant° sometimes his replies are! A happiness° that often madness hits on, which reason and sanity could not so prosperously be delivered of. I will leave him, and suddenly contrive the means of meeting between him and my daughter. — My honorable lord, I will most humbly take my leave of you. 218

HAML. You cannot, sir, take from me anything that I will more willingly part withal — except my life, except my life, except my life.

POL. Fare you well, my lord.

HAML. These tedious old fools!
[Enter ROSENCRANTZ and GUILDENSTERN.]

POL. You go to seek the Lord Hamlet. There he is.

ROS. [To POLONIUS] God save you, sir! 225
[Exit POLONIUS.]

GUIL. My honored lord!

ROS. My most dear lord!

HAML. My excellent good friends!° How dost thou, Guildenstern? Ah, Rosencrantz! Good lads, how do you both? 230

ROS. As the indifferent° children of the earth.

GUIL. Happy in that we are not overhappy.
On Fortune's cap we are not the very button.°

HAML. Nor the soles of her shoe?

ROS. Neither, my lord. 235

HAML. Then you live about her waist, or in the middle of her favors?

GUIL. Faith, her privates° we.

HAML. In the secret parts of Fortune? Oh, most true, she is a strumpet. What's the news? 240

ROS. None, my lord, but that the world's grown honest.

HAML. Then is Doomsday near. But your news is not true. Let me question more in particular. What have you, my good friends, deserved at the hands of Fortune, that she sends you to prison hither? 247

GUIL. Prison, my lord!

HAML. Denmark's a prison.

ROS. Then is the world one.

HAML. A goodly one, in which there are many

---

162. loose: turn loose. 163. arras: tapestry hanging. 167. keep . . . carters: i.e., turn country squire — like Justice Shallow. See II Hen IV. 170. board: accost. 174. fishmonger: Hamlet is now in his "antic disposition," enjoying himself by fooling Polonius. 181. sun . . . maggots: a general belief. 182. god: Q2 and F1 read "good." carrion: flesh. 202. hams: knee joints.

208. method: order, sense. 212. pregnant: apt, full of wit. 212. happiness: good turn of phrase. 228. My . . . friends: As soon as Polonius has gone, Hamlet drops his assumed madness and greets Rosencrantz and Guildenstern naturally. 231. indifferent: neither too great nor too little. 233. button: i.e., at the top. 238. privates: with a pun on "private parts" and "private," not concerned with politics.

confines,° wards,° and dungeons, Denmark being one o' the worst.

ROS. We think not so, my lord. 254

HAML. Why, then 'tis none to you, for there is nothing either good or bad but thinking makes it so. To me it is a prison.

ROS. Why, then your ambition° makes it one. 'Tis too narrow for your mind. 259

HAML. Oh, God, I could be bounded in a nutshell and count myself a king of infinite space were it not that I have bad dreams.

GUIL. Which dreams indeed are ambition, for the very substance of the ambitious° is merely the shadow of a dream. 265

HAML. A dream itself is but a shadow.

ROS. Truly, and I hold ambition of so airy and light a quality that it is but a shadow's shadow.

HAML. Then are our beggars bodies, and our monarchs and outstretched heroes the beggars' shadows.° Shall we to the Court? For, by my fay,° I cannot reason.° 272

ROS. & GUIL. We'll wait upon you.°

HAML. No such matter. I will not sort° you with the rest of my servants, for, to speak to you like an honest man, I am most dreadfully attended.° But in the beaten way of friendship, what make you at Elsinore? 278

ROS. To visit you, my lord, no other occasion.

HAML. Beggar that I am, I am even poor in thanks, but I thank you. And sure, dear friends, my thanks are too dear a halfpenny.° Were you not sent for? Is it your own inclining? Is it a free visitation?° Come, deal justly with me. Come, come. Nay, speak. 285

GUIL. What should we say, my lord?

HAML. Why, anything, but to the purpose.° You were sent for, and there is a kind of confession in your looks which your modesties have not craft enough to color.° I know the good King and Queen have sent for you.

ROS. To what end, my lord? 292

HAML. That you must teach me. But let me conjure° you, by the rights of our fellowship,° by the consonancy° of our youth, by the obligation of our ever preserved love, and by what more dear a better

proposer could charge you withal, be even° and direct with me, whether you were sent for, or no. 299

ROS. [Aside to GUILDENSTERN] What say you?

HAML. [Aside] Nay, then, I have an eye of you. — If you love me, hold not off.

GUIL. My lord, we were sent for. 303

HAML. I will tell you why. So shall my anticipation prevent your discovery, and your secrecy to the King and Queen molt no feather.° I have of late — but wherefore I know not — lost all my mirth, forgone all custom of exercises, and indeed it goes so heavily with my disposition that this goodly frame the earth seems to me a sterile promontory. 310 This most excellent canopy,° the air, look you, this brave o'erhanging firmament,° this majestical roof fretted° with golden fire — why, it appears no other thing to me than a foul and pestilent congregation of vapors. What a piece of work is a man! 315 How noble in reason! How infinite in faculty!° In form and moving° how express° and admirable! In action how like an angel! In apprehension how like a god! The beauty of the world! The paragon of animals! And yet, to me, what is this quintessence° of dust? Man delights not me — no, nor 320 woman neither, though by your smiling you seem to say so.

ROS. My lord, there was no such stuff in my thoughts.

HAML. Why did you laugh, then, when I said " Man delights not me "?

ROS. To think, my lord, if you delight not in man, what lenten entertainment° the players shall receive from you. We coted° them on the way, and hither are they coming to offer you service. 331

HAML. He that plays the King shall be welcome, His Majesty shall have tribute of me. The adventurous knight shall use his foil and target,° the lover shall not sigh gratis, the humorous man° shall end his part in peace, the clown shall make those laugh whose lungs are tickle o' the sere,° and the lady shall say her mind freely or the blank verse shall halt° for 't. What players are they? 340

ROS. Even those you were wont to take such delight in, the tragedians of the city.

HAML. How chances it they travel? Their resi-

252. confines: places of confinement. wards: cells. 258. your ambition: Rosencrantz is feeling after one possible cause of Hamlet's melancholy — thwarted ambition. 264. substance . . . ambitious: that on which an ambitious man feeds his fancies. 269–71. Then . . . shadows: i.e., by your reasoning beggars are the only men of substance, for kings and heroes are by nature ambitious and therefore "the shadows of a dream." outstretched: of exaggerated reputation. 271. fay: faith. 272. reason: argue. 273. wait . . . you: be your servants. 274. sort: class. 276. dreadfully attended: my attendants are a poor crowd. 282. too . . . halfpenny: not worth a halfpenny. 283. free visitation: voluntary visit. 287. anything . . . purpose: anything so long as it is not true. 290. color: conceal. 294. conjure: make solemn appeal to. fellowship: comradeship. 295. consonancy: concord.

298. even: straight. 304–06. So . . . feather: i.e., so by my telling you first you will not be obliged to betray the secrets of the King. prevent: forestall. molt no feather: be undisturbed. 311. canopy: covering. 312. firmament: sky. 313. fretted: ornamented. 316. faculty: power of the mind. 317. moving: movement. express: exact. 319. quintessence: perfection; the fifth essence, which would be left if the four elements were taken away. 329. lenten entertainment: fasting fare, meager welcome. 330. coted: overtook. 334. foil . . . target: rapier and small shield. 335. humorous man: the man who specializes in character parts; e.g., Jaques in As You Like It. 338. are . . . sere: explode at a touch. The sere is part of the trigger mechanism of a gun which if "ticklish" will go off at a touch. 340. halt: limp.

dence, both in reputation and profit, was better both ways.° 345

ROS. I° think their inhibition° comes by the means of the late innovation.°

HAML. Do they hold the same estimation they did when I was in the city? Are they so followed?

ROS. No, indeed are they not. 350

HAML. How comes it? Do they grow rusty?

ROS. Nay, their endeavor keeps in the wonted pace.° But there is, sir, an eyrie° of children, little eyases,° that cry out on the top of question° and are most tyrannically° clapped for 't. These are 355 now the fashion, and so berattle° the common stages° — so they call them — that many wearing rapiers are afraid of goose quills° and dare scarce come thither. 360

HAML. What, are they children? Who maintains 'em? How are they escoted?° Will they pursue the quality° no longer than they can sing? Will they not say afterward, if they should grow themselves to common players — as it is most like if their means are no better — their writers do them wrong to make them exclaim against their own succession?° 368

ROS. Faith, there has been much to-do on both sides, and the nation holds it no sin to tarre° them to controversy. There was for a while no money bid for argument° unless the poet and the player went to cuffs° in the question. 373

HAML. Is 't possible?

GUIL. Oh, there has been much throwing-about of brains.

HAML. Do the boys carry it away?

ROS. Aye, that they do, my lord, Hercules and his load° too. 379

HAML. It is not very strange, for my uncle is King of Denmark, and those that would make mows° at him while my father lived give twenty, forty, fifty, a hundred ducats apiece for his picture in little. 'Sblood,° there is something in this more than natural, if philosophy could find it out. 385

[Flourish of trumpets within.]

GUIL. There are the players.

HAML. Gentlemen, you are welcome to Elsinore. Your hands. Come then. The appurtenance of welcome is fashion and ceremony.° Let me comply° with you in this garb,° lest my extent° to the 390 players — which, I tell you, must show fairly outward — should more appear like entertainment° than yours. You are welcome. But my uncle-father and aunt-mother are deceived.

GUIL. In what, my dear lord? 395

HAML. I am but mad north-northwest.° When the wind is southerly,° I know a hawk from a handsaw.°

[Re-enter POLONIUS.]

POL. Well be with you, gentlemen!

HAML. Hark you, Guildenstern, and you too — at each ear a hearer. That great baby you see there is not yet out of his swaddling clouts.° 401

ROS. Happily he's the second time come to them, for they say an old man is twice a child.

HAML. I will prophesy he comes to tell me of the players, mark it. You say right, sir. O' Monday morning, 'twas so indeed. 407

POL. My lord, I have news to tell you.

HAML. My lord, I have news to tell you. When Roscius° was an actor in Rome ——

POL. The actors are come hither, my lord.

HAML. Buzz, buzz!°

POL. Upon my honor —— 413

HAML. Then came each actor on his ass ——

POL. The° best actors in the world, either for tragedy, comedy, history, pastoral, pastoral-comical, historical-pastoral, tragical-historical, tragical-comical-historical-pastoral, scene individable° or poem unlimited.° Seneca cannot be too heavy, nor Plautus° too light. For the law of writ° and the liberty,° these are the only men. 421

HAML. O Jephthah,° judge of Israel, what a treasure hadst thou!

343-45. Their . . . ways: i.e., if they stayed in the city, it would bring them more profit and fame.   346-79. I . . . too: A reference to the "War of the Theaters," waged between the two Boys' Companies, which greatly excited playgoers in 1600 and 1601.   346. inhibition: formal prohibition.   347. innovation: riot.   352-53. endeavor . . . pace: they try as hard as ever.   353. eyrie: nest.   354. eyases: young hawks.   354 . . . question: either "cry in a shrill voice" or perhaps "cry out the latest detail of the dispute."   355. tyrannically: outrageously.   356. berattle: abuse.   357. common stages: the professional players. The boys acted in "private" playhouses.   359. goose quills: pens—of satirical writers.   362. escoted: paid.   363. quality: acting profession.   368. exclaim . . . succession: abuse the profession to which they will afterward belong.   370. tarre: urge on to fight; generally used of encouraging a dog.   372. argument: plot of a play. See III.ii.242.   372-73. went to cuffs: boxed each other's ears.   378-79. Hercules . . . load: Hercules carrying the globe on his shoulders was the sign of the Globe Playhouse.   381. mows: grimaces.   384. 'Sblood: by God's blood.

388-89. appurtenance . . . ceremony: that which pertains to welcome is formal ceremony.   389. comply: use the formality of welcome; i.e., shake hands with you.   390. garb: fashion. extent: outward behavior.   392. entertainment: welcome.   396. north-northwest: i.e., 327° (out of 360°) of the compass.   397. wind is southerly: The south wind was considered unhealthy.   396-97. hawk . . . handsaw: Either "handsaw" is a corruption of "heronshaw," heron, or a hawk is a tool like a pickax. The phrase means "I'm not so mad as you think."   401. clouts: clothes.   410. Roscius: the most famous of Roman actors.   412. Buzz, buzz: slang for "stale news."   415-21. The . . . men: Polonius reads out the accomplishments of the actors from the license which they have presented him. Playing companies on tour carried a license permitting them to offer all kinds of dramatic entertainment.   418. scene individable: i.e., a play preserving the unities.   418-19. poem unlimited: i.e., a play which disregards the rules.   419-20. Seneca . . . Plautus: the Roman writers of tragedy and comedy with whose plays every educated man was familiar.   420. law of writ: the critical rules; i.e., classical plays. liberty: plays freely written; i.e., "modern" drama.   422. Jephthah: The story of Jephthah is told in Judges, Chapter 11. He vowed that if successful against the Ammonites

POL. What a treasure had he, my lord?

HAML. Why,   425
    " One° fair daughter, and no more,
      The which he lovèd passing well."

POL. [*Aside*] Still° on my daughter.

HAML. Am I not i' the right, old Jephthah?

POL. If you call me Jephthah, my lord, I have a
daughter that I love passing well.   431

HAML. Nay, that follows not.

POL. What follows, then, my lord?

HAML. Why,
    " As by lot, God wot,"°   435
and then you know,
    " It came to pass, as most like it was — "
the first row° of the pious chanson° will show you
more, for look where my abridgement° comes.   439
[*Enter four or five* PLAYERS.] You are welcome, masters, welcome all. I am glad to see thee well. Welcome, good friends. Oh, my old friend!° Why, thy
face is valanced° since I saw thee last. Comest thou
to beard° me in Denmark? What, my young lady°
and mistress! By 'r Lady, your ladyship is nearer to
Heaven than when I saw you last, by the alti-   445
tude of a chopine.° Pray God your voice, like a piece
of uncurrent gold, be not cracked within the ring.°
Masters, you are all welcome. We'll e'en to 't like
French falconers,° fly at anything we see. We'll have
a speech straight. Come, give us a taste of your
quality° — come, a passionate speech.   452

I. PLAY. What speech, my good lord?

HAML. I heard thee speak me a speech once, but
it was never acted, or if it was, not above once; for
the play, I remember, pleased not the million, 'twas
caviar° to the general.° But it was — as I received
it, and others, whose judgments in such matters
cried in the top of mine° — an excellent play, well
digested° in the scenes, set down with as much   460
modesty° as cunning. I remember one said there
were no sallets° in the lines to make the matter
savory, nor no matter in the phrase that might in-
dict the author of affection,° but called it an honest

method, as wholesome as sweet, and by very   465
much more handsome than fine.° One speech in it
I chiefly loved. 'Twas Aeneas' tale to Dido,° and
thereabout of it especially where he speaks of
Priam's° slaughter. If it live in your memory, begin
at this line — let me see, let me see —   471
    " The rugged Pyrrhus,° like th' Hyrcanian
      beast,° — "
It is not so. It begins with " Pyrrhus."
    " The° rugged Pyrrhus, he whose sable° arms,
    Black as his purpose, did the night resemble   475
    When he lay couchèd in the ominous° horse,°
    Hath now this dread and black complexion
      smeared
    With heraldry° more dismal. Head to foot
    Now is he total gules, horridly tricked   479
    With blood of fathers, mothers, daughters, sons,
    Baked and impasted° with the parching streets
    That lend a tyrannous and a damnèd light
    To their lord's murder. Roasted in wrath and
      fire,
    And thus o'ersized with coagulate gore,°   484
    With eyes like carbuncles, the hellish Pyrrhus
    Old grandsire Priam seeks."
So, proceed you.

POL. 'Fore God, my lord, well spoken, with good
accent and good discretion.

I. PLAY.   " Anon he finds him   490
    Striking too short at Greeks. His antique sword,
    Rebellious to his arm, lies where it falls,
    Repugnant to command.° Unequal matched,
    Pyrrhus at Priam drives, in rage strikes wide,
    But with the whiff and wind of his fell sword   495
    The unnerved father falls. Then senseless Ilium,°
    Seeming to feel this blow, with flaming top
    Stoops to his base,° and with a hideous crash
    Takes prisoner Pyrrhus' ear. For, lo! his sword,
    Which was declining° on the milky° head   500
    Of reverend Priam, seemed i' the air to stick.

---

he would sacrifice the first creature to meet him on his return,
which was his daughter.   **426–37. One . . . was:** Quotation from
a ballad of Jephthah.   **428. Still:** always.   **435. wot:** knows.
438. row: line.   **pious chanson:** godly poem.   **439. abridgement:**
entertainment.   **441. old friend:** i.e., the leading player.
442. valanced: bearded.   A valance is a fringe of material
hung round the sides and bottom of a bed.   **443. beard:**
dare, with a pun on "valanced."   **young lady:** i.e., the boy who
takes the woman's parts.   **446. chopine:** lady's shoe with thick
cork sole.   **447. cracked . . . ring:** Before coins were milled on
the rim they were liable to crack. When the crack reached the ring
surrounding the device, the coin was no longer valid currency.
450. French falconers: They were famous for their skill in hawking.   **452. quality:** skill as an actor.   **457. caviar:** sturgeon's
roe, a Russian delicacy not then appreciated (or known) by any
but gourmets.   **general:** common herd.   **459. cried . . . mine:**
surpassed mine.   **460. digested:** composed.   **461. modesty:** moderation.   **462. sallets:** tasty bits.   **463–64. phrase . . . affection:**
nothing in the language which could charge the author with

affection.   **466. fine:** subtle.   **467. Aeneas' . . . Dido:** the
story of the sack of Troy as told by Aeneas to Dido, Queen
of Carthage. The original is in Virgil's *Aeneid*.   **469. Priam:**
the old King of Troy.   **472. Pyrrhus:** the son of Achilles,
one of the Greeks concealed in the Wooden Horse.   **472. Hyr-
canian beast:** the tiger.   **474–541. The . . . gods:** The speech
may be from some lost play of *Dido and Aeneas*, but more
likely it is Shakespeare's own invention. It is written in the
heavy elaborate style still popular in the dramas of the
Admiral's Men. The first player delivers it with excessive
gesture and emotion.   **474. sable:** black.   **476. ominous:** fateful.   **horse:** the Wooden Horse by which a small Greek force
was enabled to make a secret entry into Troy.   **478. heraldry:**
painting. The image of heraldic painting is kept up in *gules* (the
heraldic term for red) and *tricked* (painted like a coat of arms).
481. impasted: turned into a crust by the heat of the burning
city.   **484. o'ersized . . . gore:** covered over with congealed
blood.   **493. Repugnant to command:** refusing to be used.
496. Ilium: the citadel of Troy.   **498. stoops . . . base:** collapses.   **500. declining:** bending toward.   **milky:** milk-white.

So as a painted tyrant° Pyrrhus stood,
And like a neutral to his will and matter,°
Did nothing.
But as we often see, against° some storm 505
A silence in the heavens, the rack° stand still,
The bold winds speechless and the orb° below
As hush as death, anon the dreadful thunder
Doth rend the region° — so after Pyrrhus' pause
Arousèd vengeance sets him new awork. 510
And never did the Cyclops'° hammers fall
On Mars's armor, forged for proof eterne,°
With less remorse° than Pyrrhus' bleeding sword
Now falls on Priam. 514
Out, out, thou strumpet, Fortune! All you gods,
In general synod° take away her power,
Break all the spokes and fellies° from her wheel,
And bowl the round nave° down the hill of Heaven
As low as to the fiends! "
POL. This is too long. 520
HAML. It shall to the barber's, with your beard.
Prithee, say on. He's for a jig° or a tale of bawdry,
or he sleeps. Say on. Come to Hecuba.
 I. PLAY. " But who, oh, who had seen the mobled°
  Queen —"
HAML. " The mobled Queen "?
POL. That's good, " mobled Queen " is good.
 I. PLAY. " Run barefoot up and down, threatening
  the flames
With bisson rheum,° a clout° upon that head
Where late the diadem stood, and for a robe, 530
About her lank and all o'erteemèd° loins
A blanket, in the alarm of fear caught up.
Who this had seen, with tongue in venom steeped
'Gainst Fortune's state would treason have pro-
 nounced.°
But if the gods themselves did see her then, 535
When she saw Pyrrhus make malicious sport
In mincing with his sword her husband's limbs,
The instant burst of clamor that she made,
Unless things mortal move them not at all,
Would have made milch° the burning eyes of
  Heaven 540
And passion in the gods."

POL. Look whether he has not turned his color
and has tears in 's eyes. Prithee, no more.
HAML. 'Tis well; I'll have thee speak out the rest
of this soon. Good my lord, will you see the players
well bestowed?° Do you hear, let them be well used,
for they are the abstract and brief chronicles of the
time.° After your death you were better have a bad
epitaph than their ill report while you live. 551
POL. My lord, I will use them according to their
desert.°
HAML. God's bodykins,° man, much better. Use
every man after his desert and who shall 'scape
whipping? Use them after your own honor and dignity. The less they deserve, the more merit is in your
bounty. Take them in.
POL. Come, sirs. 559
HAML. Follow him, friends. We'll hear a play tomorrow. [*Exit* POLONIUS *with all the* PLAYERS *but the*
FIRST.] Dost thou hear me, old friend? Can you play
The Murder of Gonzago?
 I. PLAY. Aye, my lord. 564
HAML. We'll ha 't tomorrow night. You could, for
a need, study a speech of some dozen or sixteen lines
which I would set down and insert in 't, could you
not?
 I. PLAY. Aye, my lord. 569
HAML. Very well. Follow that lord, and look you
mock him not. [*Exit* FIRST PLAYER.] My good
friends, I'll leave you till night. You are welcome to
Elsinore.
ROS. Good my lord! 574
HAML. Aye, so, God be wi' ye! [*Exeunt* ROSEN-
 CRANTZ *and* GUILDENSTERN.] Now I am alone.
Oh, what a rogue and peasant slave am I!
Is it not monstrous that this player here,
But in a fiction, in a dream of passion,°
Could force his soul so to his own conceit° 579
That from her working° all his visage wanned,°
Tears in his eyes, distraction° in 's aspect,°
A broken voice, and his whole function° suiting
With forms to his conceit? And all for nothing!
For Hecuba!
What's Hecuba to him or he to Hecuba, 585
That he should weep for her? What would he do
Had he the motive and the cue for passion
That I have? He would drown the stage with tears
And cleave the general ear° with horrid speech,
Make mad the guilty and appal the free,° 590

502. painted tyrant: as in the painting of a tyrant. **503. neutral . . . matter:** one midway (*neutral*) between his desire (*will*)
and action (*matter*). **505. against:** just before. **506. rack:**
the clouds in the upper air. **507. orb:** world. **509. region:**
the country round. **511. Cyclops':** of Titans, giants who aided
Vulcan, the blacksmith god, to make armor for Mars, the war god.
512. proof eterne: everlasting protection. **513. remorse:** pity.
516. synod: council. **517. fellies:** the pieces forming the circumference of a wooden wheel. **518. nave:** center of the wheel.
522. jig: pantomimic dance, usually bawdy. **525. mobled:**
muffled. **529. bisson rheum:** blinding moisture. **clout:** rag.
531. o'erteemed: exhausted by bearing children; she had borne
fifty-two. **533-34. Who . . . pronounced:** anyone who had seen
this sight would with bitter words have uttered treason against
the tyranny of Fortune. **540. milch:** milky, i.e., dripping moisture.

548. bestowed: housed. **549-50. abstract . . . time:** they
summarize and record the events of our time. Elizabethan players were often in trouble for too saucily commenting on their betters in plays dealing with history or contemporary events and persons. **552. desert:** rank. **553. God's
bodykins:** by God's little body. **578. dream of passion:** imaginary emotion. **579. conceit:** imagination. **580. her working:**
i.e., the effect of imagination. **wanned:** went pale. **581. distraction:** frenzy. **aspect:** countenance. **582. function:** behavior.
589. general ear: ears of the audience. **590. free:** innocent.

Confound the ignorant, and amaze indeed
The very faculties of eyes and ears.
Yet I,
A dull and muddy-mettled° rascal, peak,°   594
Like John-a-dreams,° unpregnant of my cause,°
And can say nothing — no, not for a King
Upon whose property° and most dear life
A damned defeat° was made. Am I a coward?
Who° calls me villain? Breaks my pate across?
Plucks off my beard and blows it in my face?   600
Tweaks me by the nose? Gives me the lie i' the
    throat
As deep as to the lungs? Who does me this?
Ha!
'Swounds,° I should take it. For it cannot be
But I am pigeon-livered° and lack gall°   605
To make oppression bitter, or ere this
I should have fatted all the region kites
With this slave's offal.° Bloody, bawdy villain!
Remorseless, treacherous, lecherous, kindless° vil-
    lain!
Oh, vengeance!   610
Why, what an ass am I! This is most brave,
That I, the son of a dear father murdered,
Prompted to my revenge by Heaven and Hell,
Must, like a whore, unpack my heart with words
And fall a-cursing like a very drab,°   615
A scullion!°
Fie upon 't! Foh! About, my brain! Hum, I have
    heard
That guilty creatures sitting at a play
Have by the very cunning of the scene
Been struck so to the soul that presently°   620
They have proclaimed their malefactions;°
For murder, though it have no tongue, will speak
With most miraculous organ. I'll have these players
Play something like the murder of my father
Before mine uncle. I'll observe his looks,   625
I'll tent° him to the quick. If he but blench,°
I know my course. The spirit that I have seen
May be the Devil, and the Devil hath power
To assume a pleasing shape. Yea, and perhaps
Out of my weakness and my melancholy,   630
As he is very potent with such spirits,
Abuses me to damn me.° I'll have grounds°

More relative than this.° The play's the thing
Wherein I'll catch the conscience of the King.
                                        [Exit.]

Act III

SCENE I. *A room in the castle.*

[*Enter* KING, QUEEN, POLONIUS, OPHELIA,
    ROSENCRANTZ, *and* GUILDENSTERN.]
    KING. And can you, by no drift of circumstance,°
Get from him why he puts on this confusion,
Grating° so harshly all his days of quiet
With turbulent and dangerous lunacy?   4
    ROS. He does confess he feels himself distracted,
But from what cause he will by no means speak.
    GUIL. Nor do we find him forward to be
    sounded,°
But, with a crafty madness, keeps aloof
When we would bring him on to some confession
Of his true state.
    QUEEN.   Did he receive you well?   10
    ROS. Most like a gentleman.
    GUIL. But with much forcing of his disposition.°
    ROS. Niggard of question,° but of our demands
Most free in his reply.
    QUEEN.   Did you assay him
To any pastime?°   15
    ROS. Madam, it so fell out that certain players
We o'erraught° on the way. Of these we told him,
And there did seem in him a kind of joy
To hear of it. They are about the Court,
And, as I think, they have already order   20
This night to play before him.
    POL.   'Tis most true.
And he beseeched me to entreat your Majesties
To hear and see the matter.
    KING. With all my heart, and it doth much con-
    tent me
To hear him so inclined.   25
Good gentlemen, give him a further edge,°
And drive his purpose on to these delights.
    ROS. We shall, my lord.
        [*Exeunt* ROSENCRANTZ *and* GUILDENSTERN.]
    KING.   Sweet Gertrude, leave us too,
For we have closely° sent for Hamlet hither,
That he, as 'twere by accident, may here   30

594. **muddy-mettled:** made of mud, not iron. **peak:** mope.
595. **John-a-dreams:** "Sleepy Sam." **unpregnant . . . cause:**
barren of plans for vengeance.   597. **property:** personality, life.
598. **defeat:** ruin.   599–602. **Who . . . this:** Hamlet runs through
all the insults which provoked a resolute man to mortal
combat. **pate:** head. **lie . . . throat:** the bitterest of insults.
604. **'Swounds:** by God's wounds.   605. **pigeon-livered:** "as
gentle as a dove." **gall:** spirit.   606–08. **ere . . . offal:** before this
I would have fed this slave's (i.e., the King's) guts to the kites.
fatted: made fat.   609. **kindless:** unnatural.   615. **drab:**
"moll."   616. **scullion:** the lowest of the kitchen servants.
620. **presently:** immediately.   621. **proclaimed . . . malefactions:** shouted out their crimes.   626. **tent:** probe.   **blench:**
flinch.   632. **Abuses . . . me:** i.e., deceives me by thus assuming the appearance of my dead father so that I may commit

the sin of murder which will bring me to damnation. **grounds:**
reasons for action.   633. **relative . . . this:** i.e., more convincing
than the appearance of a ghost.
    Act III, Sc. i: 1. drift of circumstance: circumstantial evi-
dence, hint.   3. **grating:** disturbing.   7. **forward . . . sounded:**
eager to be questioned.   12. **much . . . disposition:** making a
great effort to be civil to us.   13. **Niggard of question:** not asking
many questions.   14–15. **Did . . . pastime:** did you try to interest him in any amusement.   17. **o'erraught:** overtook.
26. **edge:** encouragement.   29. **closely:** secretly.

Affront° Ophelia.
Her father and myself, lawful espials,°
Will so bestow ourselves that, seeing unseen,
We may of their encounter frankly judge
And gather by him, as he is behaved,°   35
If 't be the affliction of his love or no
That thus he suffers for.
     QUEEN.   I shall obey you.
And for your part, Ophelia, I do wish
That your good beauties be the happy cause   39
Of Hamlet's wildness. So shall I hope your virtues
Will bring him to his wonted way° again,
To both your honors.
     OPH..   Madam, I wish it may. [*Exit* QUEEN.]
     POL. Ophelia, walk you here. Gracious,° so please
     you,
We will bestow ourselves. [*To* OPHELIA] Read on
     this book,°
That show of such an exercise may color   45
Your loneliness. We are oft to blame in this —
'Tis too much proved — that with devotion's
     visage°
And pious action we do sugar o'er
The Devil himself.
     KING. [*Aside*] Oh, 'tis too true!
How smart a lash that speech doth give my con-
     science!   50
The harlot's cheek, beautied with plastering art,
Is not more ugly to the thing that helps it°
Than is my deed to my most painted° word.
Oh, heavy burden!   54
     POL. I hear him coming. Let's withdraw, my lord.
               [*Exeunt* KING *and* POLONIUS.
               [*Enter* HAMLET.°]
     HAML. To be, or not to be — that is the question.
Whether 'tis nobler in the mind to suffer
The slings and arrows of outrageous° fortune,
Or to take arms against a sea° of troubles
And by opposing end them. To die, to sleep —   60
No more, and by a sleep to say we end
The heartache and the thousand natural shocks
That flesh is heir to. 'Tis a consummation°
Devoutly to be wished. To die, to sleep,
To sleep — perchance to dream. Aye, there's the
     rub,°   65
For in that sleep of death what dreams may come
When we have shuffled off this mortal coil°

Must give us pause. There's the respect°
That makes calamity of so long life.°   69
For who would bear the whips and scorns of time,
The oppressor's wrong, the proud man's contumely°
The pangs of déspised love, the law's delay,
The insolence of office° and the spurns
That patient merit of the unworthy takes,°
When he himself might his quietus° make   75
With a bare bodkin?° Who would fardels° bear,
To grunt and sweat under a weary life,
But that the dread of something after death,
The undiscovered country from whose bourn°
No traveler returns, puzzles the will,°   80
And makes us rather bear those ills we have
Than fly to others that we know not of?
Thus° conscience does make cowards of us all,
And thus the native hue° of resolution
Is sicklied o'er with the pale cast° of thought,   85
And enterprises of great pitch° and moment
With this regard their currents turn awry
And lose the name of action.° — Soft you now!
The fair Ophelia! Nymph, in thy orisons°
Be all my sins remembered.
     OPH.   Good my lord,   90
How does your Honor for this many a day?
     HAML. I humbly thank you — well, well, well.
     OPH. My lord, I have remembrances of yours
That I have longed long to redeliver.
I pray you now receive them.
     HAML.   No, not I.   95
I never gave you aught.
     OPH. My honored lord, you know right well you
     did,
And with them words of so sweet breath composed
As made the things more rich. Their perfume lost,
Take these again, for to the noble mind   100
Rich gifts wax poor when givers prove unkind.
There, my lord.
     HAML. Ha, ha! Are you honest?°
     OPH. My lord?
     HAML. Are you fair?   105
     OPH. What means your lordship?
     HAML. That if you be honest and fair, your hon-
esty should admit no discourse to your beauty.°

---

31. **Affront:** encounter.   32. **lawful espials:** who are justified in spying on him.   35. **by . . . behaved:** from him, from his behavior.   41. **wonted way:** normal state.   43. **Gracious:** your Majesty — addressed to the King.   44. **book:** i.e., of devotions.   47. **devotion's visage:** an outward appearance of religion.   52. **ugly . . . it:** i.e., lust, which is the cause of its artificial beauty.   53. **painted:** i.e., false.   55 **s.d., Enter Hamlet:** In Q1 the King draws attention to Hamlet's approach with the words "See where he comes poring upon a book." Hamlet is again reading, and is too much absorbed to notice Ophelia.   58. **outrageous:** cruel.   59. **sea:** i.e., an endless turmoil.   63. **consummation:** completion.   65. **rub:** impediment in the bowling green.   67. **shuffled . . . coil:** cast off this fuss of life.

68. **respect:** reason.   69. **makes . . . life:** makes it a calamity to have to live so long.   71. **contumely:** insulting behavior. 73. **insolence of office:** insolent behavior of government officials. 73–74. **spurns . . . takes:** insults which men of merit have patiently to endure from the unworthy.   75. **quietus:** discharge. See Sonnet 126.   76. **bodkin:** dagger. **fardels:** burdens, the coolie's pack.   79. **bourn:** boundary.   80. **will:** resolution, ability to act. 83–88. **Thus . . . action:** the religious fear that death may not be the end makes men shrink from heroic actions.   84. **native hue:** natural color.   85. **cast:** color.   86. **pitch:** height; used of the soaring flight of a hawk.   87–88. **With . . . action:** by continual brooding on this thought great enterprises are diverted from their course and fade away.   89. **orisons:** prayers.   103. **honest:** chaste. 107–08. **That . . . beauty:** if you are chaste and beautiful your chastity should have nothing to do with your beauty — because

OPH. Could beauty, my lord, have better commerce than with honesty?   110

HAML. Aye, truly, for the power of beauty will sooner transform honesty from what it is to a bawd° than the force of honesty can translate beauty into his likeness. This was sometime a paradox,° but now the time gives it proof. I did love you once.   116

OPH. Indeed, my lord, you made me believe so.

HAML. You should not have believed me, for virtue cannot so inoculate our old stock but we shall relish° of it. I loved you not.   120

OPH. I was the more deceived.

HAML. Get thee to a nunnery. Why wouldst thou be a breeder of sinners? I am myself indifferent honest,° but yet I could accuse me of such things that it were better my mother had not borne me. I am   125 very proud, revengeful, ambitious, with more offenses at my beck° than I have thoughts to put them in, imagination to give them shape, or time to act them in. What should such fellows as I do crawling between heaven and earth? We are arrant   130 knaves all. Believe none of us. Go thy ways to a nunnery.° Where's your father?

OPH. At home, my lord.

HAML. Let the doors be shut upon him, that he may play the fool nowhere but in 's own house. Farewell.   137

OPH. Oh, help him, you sweet Heavens!

HAML. If thou dost marry, I'll give thee this plague for thy dowry: Be thou as chaste as ice, as pure as snow — thou shalt not escape calumny.° Get thee to a nunnery, go. Farewell. Or if thou wilt needs marry, marry a fool, for wise men know well enough what monsters° you make of them. To a nunnery, go, and quickly too. Farewell.

OPH. O heavenly powers, restore him!   147

HAML. I have heard of your paintings° too, well enough. God hath given you one face and you make yourselves another. You jig,° you amble,° and you lisp,° and nickname God's creatures, and make your wantonness your ignorance.° Go to, I'll no more on 't — it hath made me mad. I say we will have no more marriages. Those that are married already, all but one, shall live; the rest shall keep as they   156 are. To a nunnery, go.   [Exit.]

OPH. Oh, what a noble mind is here o'erthrown! The courtier's, soldier's, scholar's, eye, tongue, sword —

The expectancy and rose° of the fair state,   160
The glass° of fashion and the mold of form,°
The observed of all observers — quite, quite down!
And I, of ladies most deject and wretched,
That sucked the honey of his music vows,
Now see that noble and most sovereign reason,   165
Like sweet bells jangled, out of tune and harsh,
That unmatched° form and feature of blown° youth
Blasted with ecstasy.° Oh, woe is me,
To have seen what I have seen, see what I see!   169

[Re-enter KING and POLONIUS.]

KING. Love! His affections° do not that way tend,
Nor what he spake, though it lacked form a little,
Was not like madness. There's something in his soul
O'er which his melancholy sits on brood,°
And I do doubt the hatch and the disclose°
Will be some danger. Which for to prevent,   175
I have in quick determination
Thus set it down: He shall with speed to England,
For the demand of our neglected tribute.
Haply° the seas and countries different
With variable objects° shall expel   180
This something-settled° matter in his heart
Whereon his brains still beating puts him thus
From fashion of himself.° What think you on 't?

POL. It shall do well. But yet do I believe
The origin and commencement of his grief   185
Sprung from neglected love. How now, Ophelia!
You need not tell us what Lord Hamlet said,
We heard it all. My lord, do as you please,
But, if you hold it fit, after the play
Let his Queen mother all alone entreat him   190
To show his grief. Let her be round° with him,
And I'll be placed, so please you, in the ear
Of all their conference. If she find him not,
To England send him, or confine him where
Your wisdom best shall think.

KING.   It shall be so.   195
Madness in great ones must not unwatched go.
[Exeunt.]

SCENE II. *A hall in the castle.*

[Enter HAMLET *and* PLAYERS.]

HAML. Speak the speech,° I pray you, as I pro-

(so Hamlet thinks in his bitterness) beautiful women are seldom chaste. **112. bawd:** brothel-keeper. **115. paradox:** statement contrary to accepted opinion. **120. relish:** have some trace. **123–24. indifferent honest:** moderately honorable. **127. at ... beck:** waiting to come when I beckon. **132. nunnery:** i.e., a place where she will be removed from temptation. **141. calumny:** slander. **145. monsters:** horned beasts (deceived husbands). **148. paintings:** using make-up. **150. jig:** dance lecherously. **amble:** walk artificially. **151. lisp:** talk affectedly. **152–53. nickname ... ignorance:** give things indecent names and pretend to be too simple to understand their meanings.

160. expectancy ... rose: bright hope. The rose is used as a symbol for beauty and perfection. Cf. *I Hen IV*, I.iii.175. **161. glass:** mirror. **mold of form:** perfect pattern of manly beauty. **167. unmatched:** unmatchable. **blown:** perfect, like an open flower at its best. **168. Blasted ... ecstasy:** ruined by madness. **170. affections:** state of mind. **173. sits ... brood:** sits hatching. **174. doubt ... disclose:** suspect the brood which will result. **179. Haply:** perhaps. **180. variable objects:** novel sights. **181. something-settled:** somewhat settled; i.e., not yet incurable. **182–83. puts ... himself:** i.e., separates him from his normal self. **191. round:** direct.

Sc. ii: **1. the speech:** which he has written. See ll. 266–67. The whole passage which follows is Shakespeare's own comment

nounced it to you, trippingly° on the tongue. But if you mouth° it, as many of your players do, I had as lief° the town crier spoke my lines. Nor do not saw the air too much with your hand, thus, but use 5 all gently. For in the very torrent, tempest, and, as I may say, whirlwind of passion, you must acquire and beget a temperance that may give it smoothness. Oh, it offends me to the soul to hear a robustious° periwig-pated° fellow tear a passion to tatters, to 10 very rags, to split the ears of the groundlings,° who for the most part are capable of nothing but inexplicable dumb shows° and noise. I would have such a fellow whipped for o'erdoing Termagant° — it out-Herods Herod. Pray you, avoid it. 16

I. PLAY. I warrant your Honor.

HAML. Be not too tame neither, but let your own discretion be your tutor. Suit the action to the word, the word to the action, with this special observ- 20 ance, that you o'erstep not the modesty of nature. For anything so overdone is from° the purpose of playing, whose end, both at the first and now, was and is to hold as 'twere the mirror up to Nature — to show Virtue her own feature, scorn her own 25 image, and the very age and body of the time his form and pressure.° Now this overdone or come tardy off, though it make the unskillful laugh, cannot but make the judicious grieve, the censure of the which one° must in your allowance o'erweigh a 30 whole theater of others. Oh, there be players° that I have seen play, and heard others praise — and that highly, not to speak it profanely — that neither having the accent of Christians nor the gait of Christian, pagan, nor man, have so strutted and bellowed 35 that I have thought some of Nature's journeymen° had made men, and not made them well, they imitated humanity so abominably.

I. PLAY. I hope we have reformed that indifferently° with us, sir. 41

HAML. Oh, reform it altogether. And let those that play your clowns° speak no more than is set down

on the actor's art and states the creed and practice of his company as contrasted with the more violent methods of Edward Alleyn and his fellows at the Rose Playhouse. 2. trippingly: smoothly, easily. 3. mouth: "ham" it. 4. lief: soon. 9. robustious: ranting. 10. periwig-pated: wearing a wig. 11. groundlings: the poorer spectators, who stood in the yard of the playhouse. 14. dumb shows: an old-fashioned dramatic device, still being used by the Admiral's Men: before a tragedy, and sometimes before each act, the characters mimed the action which was to follow. See later l. 145. 15. Termagant: God of the Saracens, who, like Herod, was presented in early stage plays as a roaring tyrant. 22. from: contrary to. 26–27. very . . . pressure: an exact reproduction of the age. form: shape. pressure: imprint (of a seal). 30. the . . . one: i.e., the judicious spectator. 31. there . . . players: An obvious attack on Alleyn. 36. journeymen: hired workmen, not masters of the trade. 41. indifferently: moderately. 42–43. those . . . clowns: A hit at Will Kempe, the former clown of Shakespeare's company. See Intro., p. 49. Q1 adds the passage "And then you have some again that keep one suit of jests, as a man is known by one suit of apparel, and gentlemen quote his

for them. For there be of them that will themselves laugh, to set on some quantity of barren spec- 45 tators to laugh too, though in the meantime some necessary question of the play be then to be considered. That's villainous, and shows a most pitiful° ambition in the fool that uses it. Go, make you 50 ready. [*Exeunt* PLAYERS. *Enter* POLONIUS, ROSENCRANTZ, *and* GUILDENSTERN.] How now, my lord! Will the King hear this piece of work?

POL. And the Queen too, and that presently.

HAML. Bid the players make haste. [*Exit* POLONIUS.] Will you two help to hasten them? 55

ROS. & GUIL. We will, my lord.

    [*Exeunt* ROSENCRANTZ *and* GUILDENSTERN.]

HAML. What ho! Horatio!

    [*Enter* HORATIO.]

HOR. Here, sweet lord, at your service.

HAML. Horatio, thou art e'en as just a man
As e'er my conversation coped° withal. 60

HOR. Oh, my dear lord ——

HAML.   Nay, do not think I flatter,
For what advancement° may I hope from thee,
That no revénue hast but thy good spirits
To feed and clothe thee? Why should the poor be
    flattered?
No, let the candied° tongue lick absurd pomp 65
And crook the pregnant hinges of the knee
Where thrift may follow fawning.° Dost thou
    hear?
Since my dear soul was mistress of her choice
And could of men distinguish, her election
Hath sealed° thee for herself. For thou hast been 70
As one in suffering all that suffers nothing,
A man that fortune's buffets and rewards
Hast ta'en with equal thanks. And blest are those
Whose blood and judgment are so well commingled
That they are not a pipe° for fortune's finger 75
To sound what stop she please. Give me that man
That is not passion's slave, and I will wear him
In my heart's core — aye, in my heart of heart,
As I do thee. Something too much of this.
There is a play tonight before the King. 80
One scene of it comes near the circumstance
Which I have told thee of my father's death.
I prithee when thou seest that act afoot,
Even with the very comment° of thy soul
Observe my uncle. If his occulted° guilt 85

jests down in their tables before they come to the play, as thus: 'Cannot you stay till I eat my porridge?' and 'You owe me a quarter's wages,' and 'My coat wants a cullison,' and 'Your beer is sour,' and blabbering with his lips, and thus keeping in his cinquepace of jests, when God knows the warm clown cannot make a jest unless by chance, as the blind man catcheth a hare. Masters tell him of it." 49. pitiful: contemptible. 60. coped: met. 62. advancement: promotion. 65. candied: sugared over with hypocrisy. 66–67. crook . . . fawning: bend the ready knees whenever gain will follow flattery. 70. sealed: set a mark on. 75. pipe: an instrument that varies its note. 84. comment: close observation. 85. occulted: concealed.

Do not itself unkennel° in one speech
It is a damnèd ghost° that we have seen
And my imaginations are as foul
As Vulcan's° stithy.° Give him heedful note,°
For I mine eyes will rivet to his face,   90
And after we will both our judgments join
In censure of his seeming.°
HOR.   Well, my lord.
If he steal aught the whilst this play is playing,
And 'scape detecting, I will pay the theft.
HAML. They are coming to the play. I must be
idle.°   95
Get you a place.
[*Danish march. A flourish. Enter* KING, QUEEN,
POLONIUS, OPHELIA, ROSENCRANTZ, GUILDENSTERN,
and other LORDS *attendant, with the* GUARD
carrying torches.]
KING. How fares our cousin Hamlet?
HAML. Excellent, i' faith, of the chameleon's dish.
I eat the air, promise-crammed. You cannot feed ca-
pons so.°
KING. I have nothing with this answer,° Hamlet.
These words are not mine.
HAML. No, nor mine now.° [*To* POLONIUS] My
lord, you played once i' the university, you say?
POL. That did I, my lord, and was accounted a
good actor.   106
HAML. What did you enact?
POL. I did enact Julius Caesar. I was killed i' the
Capitol. Brutus killed me.
HAML. It was a brute part of him to kill so capital
a calf there. Be the players ready?   111
ROS. Aye, my lord, they stay upon your patience.°
QUEEN. Come hither, my dear Hamlet, sit by me.
HAML. No, good Mother, here's metal more attrac-
tive.   117
POL. [*To the* KING] Oh ho! Do you mark that?
HAML. Lady, shall I lie in your lap?
[*Lying down at* OPHELIA'*s feet*]
OPH. No, my lord.   120
HAML. I mean, my head upon your lap?
OPH. Aye, my lord.
HAML. Do you think I meant country matters?°
OPH. I think nothing, my lord.
HAML. That's a fair thought to lie between maids'
legs.   126
OPH. What is, my lord?

HAML. Nothing.
OPH. You are merry, my lord.
HAML. Who, I?   130
OPH. Aye, my lord.
HAML. Oh God, your only jig-maker.° What
should a man do but be merry? For look you how
cheerfully my mother looks, and my father died
within 's two hours.   135
OPH. Nay, 'tis twice two months, my lord.
HAML. So long? Nay, then, let the Devil wear
black, for I'll have a suit of sables.° Oh heavens! Die
two months ago, and not forgotten yet? Then there's
hope a great man's memory may outlive his   140
life half a year. But, by 'r Lady, he must build
churches then, or else shall he suffer not thinking on,
with the hobbyhorse,° whose epitaph is " For, oh,
for oh, the hobbyhorse is forgot."   145
[*Hautboys° play. The dumb show enters.° Enter a*
KING *and a* QUEEN *very lovingly, the* QUEEN *embracing him and he her. She kneels, and makes show of
protestation unto him. He takes her up, and declines
his head upon her neck, lays him down upon a bank
of flowers. She, seeing him asleep, leaves him. Anon
comes in a fellow, takes off his crown, kisses it, and
pours poison in the* KING'*s ears, and exit. The* QUEEN
returns, finds the KING *dead, and makes passionate
action. The Poisoner, with some two or three Mutes,
comes in again, seeming to lament with her. The
dead body is carried away. The Poisoner woos the*
QUEEN *with gifts. She seems loath and unwilling
awhile, but in the end accepts his love.   Exeunt.*]
OPH. What means this, my lord?
HAML. Marry, this is miching mallecho.° It means
mischief.
OPH. Belike this show imports the argument° of
the play.   150
[*Enter* PROLOGUE.]
HAML. We shall know by this fellow. The players
cannot keep counsel, they'll tell all.
OPH. Will he tell us what this show meant?
HAML. Aye, or any show that you'll show him. Be
not you ashamed to show, he'll not shame to tell you
what it means.   156
OPH. You are naught,° you are naught. I'll mark
the play.

---

86. unkennel: come to light; lit., force a fox from his hole.
87. damned ghost: See II.ii.627.   89. Vulcan: the blacksmith god. stithy: smithy. heedful note: careful observation.
92. censure . . . seeming: judgment on his looks.   95. be idle:
seem crazy.   98-100. Excellent . . . so: Hamlet takes "fare"
literally as "what food are you eating." The chameleon was supposed to feed on air. promise-crammed: stuffed, like a fattened
chicken (*capon*) — but with empty promises.   101. I . . . answer: I cannot make any sense of your answer.   103. nor . . .
now: i.e., once words have left the lips they cease to belong to
the speaker.   112. stay . . . patience: wait for you to be ready.
123. country matters: something indecent.

132. jig-maker: jigs were dances accompanied by songs.   138. suit
of sables: a quibble on "sable," black, and "sable" gown trimmed
with sable fur, worn by wealthy respectable old gentlemen.
144. hobbyhorse: imitation horse worn by performers in a
morris dance, an amusement much disapproved of by the severer Puritans.   145. s.d., Hautboys: oboes. The dumb show
enters: See III.ii.14n. Critics have been disturbed because the
King is apparently not disturbed by the dumb show. Shakespeare's intention, however, in presenting a play within a play is
to produce something stagy and artificial compared with the play
proper. Moreover, as Hamlet has already complained, dumb
shows were often inexplicable.   147. miching mallecho: slinking
mischief.   149. argument: plot. She too is puzzled by the dumb
show.   157. naught: i.e., disgusting.

PRO.   For us, and for our tragedy,
         Here stooping to your clemency,   160
         We beg your hearing patiently.
HAML.   Is this a prologue, or the posy of a ring?°
OPH.   'Tis brief, my lord.
HAML.   As woman's love.

[*Enter two* PLAYERS, KING *and* QUEEN.]

P. KING. Full° thirty times hath Phoebus' cart°
         gone round   165
Neptune's° salt wash and Tellus'° orbèd ground,
And thirty dozen moons with borrowed sheen°
About the world have times twelve thirties been,
Since love our hearts and Hymen° did our hands
Unite commutual° in most sacred bands.   170
P. QUEEN. So many journeys may the sun and
         moon
Make us again count o'er ere love be done!
But, woe is me, you are so sick of late,
So far from cheer and from your former state,
That I distrust° you. Yet, though I distrust,   175
Discomfort you, my lord, it nothing must.
For women's fear and love holds quantity°
In neither aught or in extremity.°
Now what my love is, proof hath made you know,
And as my love is sized, my fear is so.   180
Where love is great, the littlest doubts are fear,
Where little fears grow great, great love grows there.
P. KING. Faith, I must leave thee,° love, and
         shortly too,
My operant powers° their functions leave to do.
And thou shalt live in this fair world behind,   185
Honored, beloved, and haply one as kind
For husband shalt thou ——
P. QUEEN.   Oh, confound the rest!
Such love must needs be treason in my breast.
In second husband let me be accurst!
None wed the second but who killed the first.   190
HAML.   [*Aside*] Wormwood,° wormwood.
P. QUEEN. The instances° that second marriage
         move
Are base respects of thrift,° but none of love.
A second time I kill my husband dead
When second husband kisses me in bed.   195
P. KING. I do believe you think what now you
         speak,
But what we do determine oft we break.
Purpose is but the slave to memory,

Of violent birth but poor validity,
Which now, like fruit unripe, sticks on the tree   200
But fall unshaken when they mellow be.
Most necessary 'tis that we forget
To pay ourselves what to ourselves is debt.
What to ourselves in passion we propose,
The passion ending, doth the purpose lose.   205
The violence of either grief or joy
Their own enactures° with themselves destroy.
Where joy most revels, grief doth most lament,
Grief joys, joy grieves, on slender accident.   209
This world is not for aye,° nor 'tis not strange
That even our loves should with our fortunes
         change,
For 'tis a question left us yet to prove
Whether love lead fortune or else fortune love.
The great man down, you mark his favorite flies,
The poor advanced makes friends of enemies.   215
And hitherto doth love on fortune tend,
For who not needs shall never lack a friend,
And who in want a hollow friend doth try
Directly seasons° him his enemy.
But, orderly to end where I begun,   220
Our wills and fates do so contráry run
That our devices still are overthrown,
Our thoughts are ours, their ends none of our own.
So think thou wilt no second husband wed,   224
But die thy thoughts when thy first lord is dead.
P. QUEEN. Nor earth to me give food nor Heaven
         light!
Sport and repose lock from me day and night!
To desperation turn my trust and hope!
An anchor's° cheer in prison be my scope!
Each opposite that blanks° the face of joy   230
Meet what I would have well and it destroy!
Both here and hence pursue me lasting strife
If, once a widow, ever I be wife!
HAML.   If she should break it now!
P. KING. 'Tis deeply sworn. Sweet, leave me here
         a while.   235
My spirits grow dull, and fain I would beguile
The tedious day with sleep.   [*Sleeps.*]
P. QUEEN.   Sleep rock thy brain,
And never come mischance between us twain!
                                        [*Exit.*]

HAML.   Madam, how like you this play?
QUEEN.   The lady doth protest too much, methinks.
HAML.   Oh, but she'll keep her word.   241
KING.   Have you heard the argument?° Is there no
         offense in 't?
HAML.   No, no, they do but jest, poison in jest —
         no offense i' the world.   245
KING.   What do you call the play?

---

162. posy . . . ring: It was a pretty custom to inscribe rings with little mottoes or messages, which were necessarily brief. 165–238. Full . . . twain: The play is deliberately written in crude rhyming verse, full of ridiculous and bombastic phrases. 165. Phoebus' cart: the chariot of the sun. 166. Neptune: the sea god. Tellus: the earth goddess. 167. borrowed sheen: light borrowed from the sun. 169. Hymen: god of marriage. 170 commutual: mutually. 175. distrust: am anxious about. 177. quantity: proportion. 178. In . . . extremity: either nothing or too much. 183. leave thee: i.e., die. 184. operant powers: bodily strength. 191. Wormwood: bitterness. 192. instances: arguments. 193. respects of thrift: considerations of gain.

207. enactures: performances. 210. aye: ever. 219. seasons: ripens into. 229. anchor: anchorite, hermit. 230. blanks: makes pale. 242. argument: plot. When performances were given at Court it was sometimes customary to provide a written or printed synopsis of the story for the distinguished spectators.

HAML. *The Mousetrap.*° Marry, how? Tropically.° This play is the image of a murder done in Vienna. Gonzago is the Duke's name, his wife, Baptista. You shall see anon. 'Tis a knavish piece of   250
work, but what o' that? Your Majesty, and we that have free° souls, it touches us not. Let the galled jade wince, our withers are unwrung.°
[*Enter* LUCIANUS.] This is one Lucianus, nephew to the King.

OPH. You are as good as a chorus,° my lord.   255

HAML. I could interpret between you and your love, if I could see the puppets dallying.°

OPH. You are keen, my lord, you are keen.

HAML. It would cost you a groaning to take off my edge.   260

OPH. Still better, and worse.

HAML. So you must take your husbands.° Begin, murderer. Pox, leave thy damnable faces and begin. Come, the croaking raven doth bellow for revenge.

LUC. Thoughts black, hands apt, drugs fit, and time agreeing,   266
Confederate season, else no creature° seeing,
Thou mixture rank of midnight weeds collected,
With Hecate's ban° thrice blasted, thrice infected,
Thy natural magic and dire property°   270
On wholesome life usurp immediately.

[*Pours the poison into the sleeper's ear.*]

HAML. He poisons him i' the garden for his estate.° His name's Gonzago. The story is extant, and written in very choice Italian. You shall see anon how the murderer gets the love of Gonzago's wife.

OPH. The King rises.   276

HAML. What, frighted with false fire!°

QUEEN. How fares my lord?

POL. Give o'er the play.

KING. Give me some light. Away!   280

POL. Lights, lights, lights!

[*Exeunt all but* HAMLET *and* HORATIO.]

HAML. "Why, let the stricken deer go weep,
The hart ungallèd play,
For some must watch while some must sleep.
Thus runs the world away."   285
Would not this, sir, and a forest of feathers° — if the rest of my fortunes turn Turk° with me — with two Provincial roses° on my razed° shoes, get me a fellowship° in a cry° of players, sir?

HOR. Half a share.   290

HAML. A whole one, I.
"For thou dost know, O Damon° dear,
This realm dismantled° was
Of Jove himself, and now reigns here
A very, very — pajock."°   295

HOR. You might have rhymed.

HAML. O good Horatio, I'll take the ghost's word for a thousand pound. Didst perceive?

HOR. Very well, my lord.

HAML. Upon the talk of the poisoning?   300

HOR. I did very well note him.

HAML. Ah, ha! Come, some music! Come, the recorders!°
"For if the King like not the comedy,
Why then, belike, he likes it not, perdy."°   305
Come, some music!

[*Re-enter* ROSENCRANTZ *and* GUILDENSTERN.]

GUIL. Good my lord, vouchsafe me a word with you.

HAML. Sir, a whole history.

GUIL. The King, sir ——   310

HAML. Aye, sir, what of him?

GUIL. Is in his retirement marvelous distempered.°

HAML. With drink, sir?

GUIL. No, my lord, rather with choler.°   315

HAML. Your wisdom should show itself more richer to signify this to the doctor, for for me to put him to his purgation° would perhaps plunge him into far more choler.   319

GUIL. Good my lord, put your discourse into some frame,° and start not so wildly from my affair.

HAML. I am tame, sir. Pronounce.

GUIL. The Queen your mother, in most great affliction of spirit, hath sent me to you.

HAML. You are welcome.   325

GUIL. Nay, good my lord, this courtesy is not of the right breed. If it shall please you to make me a wholesome answer, I will do your mother's commandment. If not, your pardon and my return shall be the end of my business.   330

HAML. Sir, I cannot.

GUIL. What, my lord?

HAML. Make you a wholesome answer, my wit's

---

247. Mousetrap: The phrase was used of a device to entice a person to his own destruction (OED).   **248. Tropically:** figuratively, with a pun on "trap."   **252. free:** innocent.   **252–53. galled . . . unwrung:** let a nag with a sore back flinch when the saddle is put on; our shoulders (being ungalled) feel no pain.   **255. chorus:** the chorus sometimes introduced the characters and commented on what was to follow.   **257. puppets dallying:** Elizabethan puppets were crude marionettes, popular at fairs. While the figures were put through their motions the puppet master explained what was happening.   **262. So . . . husbands:** i.e., as the marriage service expresses it, "for better, for worse."   **267. confederate . . . creature:** the opportunity conspiring with me no other creature.   **269. Hecate's ban:** the curse of Hecate, goddess of witchcraft.   **270. property:** nature.   **273. estate:** kingdom.   **277. false fire:** a mere show.   **286. forest of feathers:** set of plumes, much worn by players.

287. turn Turk: turn heathen, and treat me cruelly.   **288. Provincial roses:** rosettes, worn on the shoes. **razed:** slashed, ornamented with cuts.   **289. fellowship:** partnership, right to a full share. **cry:** pack.   **292. Damon:** Damon and Pythias were types of perfect friends.   **293. dismantled:** robbed.   **295. pajock:** peacock, a strutting, lecherous bird. These verses, and the lines above, may have come from some ballad, otherwise lost.   **303. recorders:** wooden pipes.   **305. perdy:** by God.   **312. distempered:** disturbed; but Hamlet takes the word in its other sense of "drunk."   **315. choler:** anger, which Hamlet again pretends to understand as meaning "biliousness."   **317–18. put . . . purgation:** "give him a dose of salts."   **321. frame:** shape; i.e., "please talk sense."

diseased. But, sir, such answer as I can make you shall command, or rather, as you say, my mother. Therefore no more, but to the matter. My mother, you say —— 337

ROS. Then thus she says. Your behavior hath struck her into amazement and admiration.°

HAML. Oh, wonderful son that can so astonish a mother! But is there no sequel at the heels of this mother's admiration? Impart. 342

ROS. She desires to speak with you in her closet ere you go to bed.

HAML. We shall obey, were she ten times our mother. Have you any further trade with us?

ROS. My lord, you once did love me. 348

HAML. So I do still, by these pickers and stealers.°

ROS. Good my lord, what is your cause of distemper? You do surely bar the door upon your own liberty if you deny your griefs° to your friend.

HAML. Sir, I lack advancement.° 354

ROS. How can that be when you have the voice of the King himself for your succession in Denmark?

HAML. Aye, sir, but " While the grass grows "° — the proverb is something musty. [Re-enter 359 PLAYERS with recorders.] Oh, the recorders! Let me see one. To withdraw° with you —— why do you go about to recover the wind° of me, as if you would drive me into a toil?°

GUIL. O my lord, if my duty be too bold, my love is too unmannerly.° 365

HAML. I do not well understand that. Will you play upon this pipe?

GUIL. My lord, I cannot.

HAML. I pray you.

GUIL. Believe me, I cannot.

HAML. I do beseech you. 371

GUIL. I know no touch of it, my lord.

HAML. It is as easy as lying. Govern these ventages° with your fingers and thumb, give it breath with your mouth, and it will discourse most eloquent music. Look you, these are the stops. 376

GUIL. But these cannot I command to any utterance of harmony, I have not the skill.

HAML. Why, look you now, how unworthy a thing you make of me! You would play upon me, 380 you would seem to know my stops, you would pluck out the heart of my mystery, you would sound me

from my lowest note to the top of my compass — and there is much music, excellent voice, in this little organ — yet cannot you make it speak. 'Sblood, do you think I am easier to be played on than a pipe? Call me what instrument you will, though you can fret° me, you cannot play upon me. [Re-enter PO-LONIUS.] God bless you, sir! 390

POL. My lord, the Queen would speak with you, and presently.

HAML. Do you see yonder cloud that's almost in shape of a camel?

POL. By the mass, and 'tis like a camel indeed.

HAML. Methinks it is like a weasel. 396

POL. It is backed like a weasel.

HAML. Or like a whale?

POL. Very like a whale.

HAML. Then I will come to my mother by 400 and by. They fool me to the top of my bent.° I will come by and by.

POL. I will say so. [Exit POLONIUS.]

HAML. " By and by " is easily said. Leave me, friends. [Exeunt all but HAMLET.]
'Tis now the very witching time° of night, 406
When churchyards yawn and Hell itself breathes out
Contagion° to this world. Now could I drink hot blood,
And do such bitter business as the day 409
Would quake to look on. Soft! Now to my mother.
O heart, lose not thy nature, let not ever
The soul of Nero° enter this firm bosom.
Let me be cruel, not unnatural.
I will speak daggers to her, but use none.
My tongue and soul in this be hypocrites, 415
How in my words soever she be shent,°
To give them seals° never, my soul, consent!
[Exit.]

SCENE III. *A room in the castle.*

[*Enter* KING, ROSENCRANTZ, *and* GUILDENSTERN.]
KING. I like him not, nor stands it safe with us
To let his madness range.° Therefore prepare you.
I your commission will forthwith dispatch,
And he to England shall along with you.
The terms of our estate° may not endure 5
Hazard so near us as doth hourly grow
Out of his lunacies.
GUIL.   We will ourselves provide.°

339. admiration: wonder. 349. pickers . . . stealers: i.e., hands — an echo from the Christian's duty in the catechism to keep his hands "from picking and stealing." 353. deny . . . griefs: refuse to tell your troubles. 354. advancement: promotion. Hamlet harks back to his previous interview with Rosencrantz and Guildenstern. See II.ii.258. 358. While . . . grows: the proverb ends "the steed starves." 361. with-draw: go aside. Hamlet leads Guildenstern to one side of the stage. 362. recover . . . wind: a hunting metaphor; approach me with the wind against you. 363. toil: net. 364-65. if . . . unmannerly: if I exceed my duty by asking these questions, then my affection for you shows lack of manners; i.e., please forgive me if I have been too impertinent. 374. ventages: holes, stops.

389. fret: annoy, with a pun on the frets or bars on stringed in-struments by which the fingering is regulated. 401. top . . . bent: See II.ii.30,n. 406. witching time: deep night, when witches perform their foul rites. 408. Contagion: infection. 412. Nero: Nero killed his own mother. Hamlet is afraid that in the interview to come he will lose all self-control. 416. shent: rebuked. 417. give . . . seals: ratify words by actions, i.e., kill my mother.

Sc. iii:2. range: roam freely. 5. terms . . . estate: i.e., one in my position. 7. ourselves provide: make our preparations.

Most holy and religious fear° it is
To keep those many many bodies safe
That live and feed upon your Majesty.   10
ROS. The single and peculiar° life is bound
With all the strength and armor of the mind
To keep itself from noyance,° but much more
That spirit upon whose weal° depends and rests
The lives of many. The cease of majesty°   15
Dies not alone, but like a gulf° doth draw
What's near it with it. It is a massy° wheel
Fixed on the summit of the highest mount,
To whose huge spokes ten thousand lesser things
Are mortised° and adjoined; which, when it falls,
Each small annexment, petty consequence,°   21
Attends° the boisterous ruin. Never alone
Did the King sigh but with a general groan.
KING. Arm you, I pray you, to this speedy voyage,
For we will fetters put upon this fear,   25
Which now goes too free-footed.
ROS. & GUIL.   We will haste us.
      [*Exeunt* ROSENCRANTZ *and* GUILDENSTERN.]
      [*Enter* POLONIUS.]
POL. My lord, he's going to his mother's closet.
Behind the arras I'll convey myself
To hear the process.° I'll warrant she'll tax° him
      home.
And, as you said,° and wisely was it said,   30
'Tis meet that some more audience than a mother,
Since nature makes them partial, should o'erhear
The speech, of vantage.° Fare you well, my liege.
I'll call upon you ere you go to bed
And tell you what I know.
KING.   Thanks, dear my lord. [*Exit* POLONIUS.]
Oh, my offense is rank,° it smells to Heaven.   36
It hath the primal eldest curse° upon 't,
A brother's murder. Pray can I not,
Though inclination be as sharp as will.°
My stronger guilt defeats my strong intent,   40
And like a man to double business bound,
I stand in pause where I shall first begin,
And both neglect. What if this cursèd hand
Were thicker than itself with brother's blood,
Is there not rain enough in the sweet heavens   45
To wash it white as snow? Whereto serves mercy
But to confront the visage of offense?°
And what's in prayer but this twofold force,
To be forestalled° ere we come to fall

Or pardoned being down? Then I'll look up,   50
My fault is past. But oh, what form of prayer
Can serve my turn? "Forgive me my foul mur-
      der"?
That cannot be, since I am still possessed
Of those effects° for which I did the murder —
My crown, mine own ambition, and my Queen.   55
May one be pardoned and retain the offense?°
In the corrupted currents° of this world
Offense's gilded hand may shove by justice,
And oft 'tis seen the wicked prize° itself
Buys out the law. But 'tis not so above.   60
There is no shuffling, there the action lies
In his true nature,° and we ourselves compelled
Even to the teeth and forehead° of our faults
To give in evidence. What then? What rests?
Try what repentance can. What can it not?   65
Yet what can it when one cannot repent?
Oh, wretched state! Oh, bosom black as death!
Oh, limèd° soul, that struggling to be free
Art more engaged!° Help, angels! Make assay!°
Bow, stubborn knees, and heart with strings of steel,
Be soft as sinews of the newborn babe!   71
All may be well.   [*Retires and kneels.*]
      [*Enter* HAMLET.]
HAML. Now might I do it pat, now he is praying,
And now I'll do 't. And so he goes to Heaven,°
And so am I revenged. That would be scanned: 75
A villain kills my father, and for that
I, his sole son, do this same villain send
To Heaven.
Oh, this is hire and salary,° not revenge.
He took my father grossly,° full of bread,   80
With all his crimes broad blown, as flush° as May,
And how his audit° stands who knows save
      Heaven?
But in our circumstance and course of thought,°
'Tis heavy with him. And am I then revenged,
To take him in the purging of his soul,   85
When he is fit and seasoned,° for his passage?
No.
Up, sword, and know thou a more horrid hent.°
When he is drunk asleep, or in his rage,
Or in the incestuous pleasure of his bed —   90
At gaming, swearing, or about some act
That has no relish of salvation in 't —
Then trip him, that his heels may kick at Heaven
And that his soul may be as damned and black

---

8. fear: anxiety.   11. peculiar: individual.   13. noyance:
injury.   14. weal: welfare.   15. cease of majesty: death of
a king.   16. gulf: whirlpool.   17. massy: massive.   20. mor-
tised: firmly fastened.   21. annexment . . . consequence:
attachment, smallest thing connected with it.   22. Attends:
waits on, is involved in.   29. process: proceeding. tax: censure.   30. as . . . said: Actually Polonius himself had said it
(III.i.189–93).   33. of vantage: from a place of vantage; i.e.,
concealment.   36. rank: foul.   37. primal . . . curse: the curse
laid upon Cain, the first murderer, who also slew his brother.
39. will: desire.   47. confront . . . offense: look crime in the
face.   49. forestalled: prevented.

54. effects: advantages.   56. offense: i.e., that for which he has
offended.   57. currents: courses, ways.   59. wicked prize: the
proceeds of the crime.   61–62. there . . . nature: in Heaven the
case is tried on its own merits.   63. teeth . . . forehead: i.e.,
face to face.   68. limed: caught as in birdlime.   69. engaged:
stuck fast. assay: attempt.   74. And . . . Heaven: satisfactory
vengeance demanded Hell.   79. hire . . . salary: i.e., a kind
action deserving pay.   80. grossly: i.e., in a state of sin. See
I.v.74–80.   81. broad . . . flush: in full blossom, as luxuriant.
82. audit: account.   83. circumstance . . . thought: as it appears
to my mind.   86. seasoned: ripe.   88. hent: opportunity.

As Hell, whereto it goes. My mother stays.   95
This physic but prolongs thy sickly days.   [*Exit.*]
KING. [*Rising*] My words fly up, my thoughts re-
      main below.
Words without thoughts never to Heaven go.
                              [*Exit.*]

SCENE IV. *The* QUEEN's *closet.*

[*Enter* QUEEN *and* POLONIUS.]

POL. He will come straight. Look you lay home
      to° him.
Tell him his pranks have been too broad° to bear
      with,
And that your grace hath screened and stood be-
      tween
Much heat and him. I'll sconce me° even here.
Pray you, be round with him.   5
HAML. [*Within*] Mother, Mother, Mother!
QUEEN.   I'll warrant you,
Fear me not. Withdraw, I hear him coming.
            [POLONIUS *hides behind the arras.*]
                  [*Enter* HAMLET.]
HAML. Now, Mother, what's the matter?
QUEEN. Hamlet, thou hast thy father much of-
      fended.
HAML. Mother, you have my father much of-
      fended.   10
QUEEN. Come, come, you answer with an idle°
      tongue.
HAML. Go, go, you question with a wicked
      tongue.
QUEEN. Why, how now, Hamlet!
HAML.   What's the matter now?
QUEEN. Have you forgot me?
HAML.   No, by the rood,° not so.   14
You are the Queen, your husband's brother's wife,
And — would it were not so! — you are my mother.
QUEEN. Nay, then, I'll set those to you that can
      speak.
HAML. Come, come, and sit you down. You shall
      not budge,
You go not till I set you up a glass°
Where you may see the inmost part of you.   20
QUEEN. What wilt thou do? Thou wilt not mur-
      der me?
Help, help, ho!
POL. [*Behind*] What ho! Help, help, help!
HAML. [*Drawing*] How now! A rat? Dead, for a
      ducat, dead! [*Makes a pass through the arras.*]
POL. [*Behind*] Oh, I am slain!   [*Falls and dies.*]
QUEEN.   Oh me, what hast thou done?
HAML. Nay, I know not. Is it the King?   26
QUEEN. Oh, what a rash and bloody deed is this!

Sc. iv: 1. lay . . . to: be strict with.   2. broad: unrestrained.
Polonius is thinking of the obvious insolence of the remarks about
second marriage in the play scene.   4. sconce me: hide myself.
11. idle: foolish.   14. rood: crucifix.   19. Glass: looking glass.

HAML. A bloody deed! Almost as bad, good
      Mother,
As kill a king and marry with his brother.
QUEEN. As kill a king!
HAML.   Aye, lady, 'twas my word.   30
      [*Lifts up the arras and discovers* POLONIUS.]
Thou wretched, rash, intruding fool, farewell!
I took thee for thy better. Take thy fortune.
Thou find'st to be too busy is some danger.
Leave wringing of your hands. Peace! Sit you down,
And let me wring your heart. For so I shall   35
If it be made of penetrable stuff,
If damnèd custom have not brassed° it so
That it be proof and bulwark against sense.
QUEEN. What have I done that thou darest wag
      thy tongue
In noise so rude against me?
HAML.   Such an act   40
That blurs the grace and blush of modesty,
Calls virtue hypocrite, takes off the rose
From the fair forehead of an innocent love,
And sets a blister° there — makes marriage vows
As false as dicers' oaths. Oh, such a deed   45
As from the body of contraction° plucks
The very soul, and sweet religion makes
A rhapsody of words.° Heaven's face doth glow,
Yea, this solidity and compound mass,°
With tristful visage, as against the doom,°   50
Is thought-sick at the act.
QUEEN.   Aye me, what act
That roars so loud and thunders in the index?°
HAML. Look here upon this picture,° and on this,
The counterfeit presentment° of two brothers.
See what a grace was seated on this brow —   55
Hyperion's curls, the front° of Jove himself,
An eye like Mars, to threaten and command,
A station° like the herald Mercury°
New-lighted° on a heaven-kissing hill,
A combination° and a form indeed   60
Where every god did seem to set his seal°
To give the world assurance of a man.
This was your husband. Look you now what fol-
      lows.
Here is your husband, like a mildewed ear,
Blasting his wholesome brother. Have you eyes?   65
Could you on this fair mountain leave to feed

37. brassed: made brazen; i.e., impenetrable.   44. sets a blister: brands as a harlot.   46. contraction: the marriage contract.
48. rhapsody of words: string of meaningless words.   49. solidity . . . mass: i.e., solid earth.   50. tristful . . . doom: sorrowful
face, as in anticipation of Doomsday.   52. in . . . index: i.e., if
the beginning (*index*, i.e., table of contents) is so noisy, what
will follow?   53. picture: Modern directors usually interpret
the pictures as miniatures, Hamlet wearing one of his father,
Gertrude one of Claudius. In the eighteenth century, wall portraits were used.   54. counterfeit presentment: portrait.
56. front: forehead.   58. station: figure; lit., standing. Mercury:
messenger of the gods, and one of the most beautiful.   59. New-
lighted: newly alighted.   60. combination: i.e., of physical
qualities.   61. set . . . seal: guarantee as a perfect man.

And batten° on this moor? Ha! Have you eyes?
You cannot call it love, for at your age
The heyday° in the blood is tame, it's humble,   69
And waits upon the judgment. And what judgment
Would step from this to this? Sense° sure you have,
Else could you not have motion.° But sure that sense
Is apoplexed;° for madness would not err,
Nor sense to ecstasy° was ne'er so thralled°
But it reserved some quantity of choice   75
To serve in such a difference.° What devil was 't
That thus hath cozened° you at hoodman-blind?°
Eyes without feeling, feeling without sight,
Ears without hands or eyes, smelling sans° all,
Or but a sickly part of one true sense   80
Could not so mope.°
Oh, shame! Where is thy blush? Rebellious° Hell,
If thou canst mutine° in a matron's bones,
To flaming youth let virtue be as wax
And melt in her own fire. Proclaim no shame   85
When the compulsive ardor° gives the charge,
Since frost itself as actively doth burn,
And reason panders° will.
    QUEEN.   O Hamlet, speak no more.
Thou turn'st mine eyes into my very soul,
And there I see such black and grainèd° spots   90
As will not leave their tinct.°
    HAML.   Nay, but to live
In the rank sweat of an enseamèd° bed,
Stewed in corruption, honeying and making love
Over the nasty sty——
    QUEEN.   Oh, speak to me no more,
These words like daggers enter in my ears.   95
No more, sweet Hamlet!
    HAML.   A murderer and a villain,
A slave that is not twentieth part the tithe°
Of your precedent° lord, a vice of kings,°
A cutpurse° of the empire and the rule,
That from a shelf the precious diadem stole   100
And put it in his pocket!
    QUEEN.   No more!
    HAML. A king of shreds and patches——
[Enter GHOST] Save me, and hover o'er me with
    your wings,
You heavenly guards! What would your gracious
    figure?

    QUEEN. Alas, he's mad!   105
    HAML. Do you not come your tardy son to chide
That, lapsed in time and passion, lets go by
The important acting of your dread command?°
Oh, say!
    GHOST. Do not forget. This visitation   110
Is but to whet thy almost blunted purpose.
But look, amazement on thy mother sits.
Oh, step between her and her fighting soul.
Conceit° in weakest bodies strongest works.
Speak to her, Hamlet.
    HAML.   How is it with you, lady?   115
    QUEEN. Alas, how is 't with you
That you do bend your eye on vacancy°
And with the incorporal° air do hold discourse?
Forth at your eyes your spirits wildly peep,
And as the sleeping soldiers in the alarm,   120
Your bedded° hairs, like life in excrements,°
Start up and stand an° end. O gentle son,
Upon the heat and flame of thy distemper°
Sprinkle cool patience. Whereon do you look?
    HAML. On him, on him! Look you how pale he
    glares!   125
His form and cause conjoined,° preaching to stones,
Would make them capable.° Do not look upon
    me,
Lest with this piteous action you convert
My stern effects.° Then what I have to do   129
Will want true color — tears perchance for blood.
    QUEEN. To whom do you speak this?
    HAML.   Do you see nothing there?
    QUEEN. Nothing at all, yet all that is I see.
    HAML. Nor did you nothing hear?
    QUEEN.   No, nothing but ourselves.
    HAML. Why, look you there! Look how it steals
    away!
My father, in his habit as he lived!   135
Look where he goes, even now, out at the portal!
                   [Exit GHOST.]
    QUEEN. This is the very coinage of your brain.
This bodiless creation ecstasy°
Is very cunning in.
    HAML.   Ecstasy!   139
My pulse, as yours, doth temperately keep time,
And makes as healthful music. It is not madness
That I have uttered. Bring me to the test
And I the matter will reword, which madness
Would gambol° from. Mother, for love of grace,

---

67. **batten:** glut yourself. **69. heyday:** excitement. **71. Sense:**
feeling. **72. motion:** desire. **73. apoplexed:** paralyzed. **74. ec-**
stasy: excitement, passion. See II.i.102. **thralled:** enslaved.
76. serve . . . difference: to enable you to see the difference between your former and your present husband. **77. cozened:**
cheated. **hoodman-blind:** blind-man's-buff. **79. sans:** without.
81. mope: be dull. **82–88. Rebellious . . . will:** i.e., if the passion
(*Hell*) of a woman of your age is uncontrollable (*rebellious*), youth
can have no restraints; there is no shame in a young man's lust
when the elderly are just as eager and their reason (which should
control desire) encourages them. **83. mutine:** mutiny. **86. com-**
pulsive ardor: compelling lust. **88. panders:** acts as go-between.
90. grained: dyed in the grain. **91. tinct:** color. **92. enseamed:**
greasy. **97. tithe:** tenth part. **98. precedent:** former. **vice of**
kings: caricature of a king. **99. cutpurse:** thief.

107–08. That . . . command: who has allowed time to pass and
passion to cool, and neglects the urgent duty of obeying your
dread command. **114. Conceit:** imagination. **117. vacancy:**
empty space. **118. incorporal:** bodiless. **121. bedded:** evenly
laid. **excrements:** anything that grows out of the body, such as
hair or fingernails; here hair. **122. an:** on. **123. distemper:**
mental disturbance. **126. form . . . conjoined:** his appearance
and the reason for his appearance joined. **127. capable:** i.e., of
feeling. **128–29. convert . . . effects:** change the stern action
which should follow. **138. ecstasy:** madness. **144. gambol:**
start away.

Lay not that flattering unction° to your soul,   145
That not your trespass but my madness speaks.
It will but skin and film the ulcerous place,
Whiles rank corruption, mining° all within,
Infects unseen. Confess yourself to Heaven,
Repent what's past, avoid what is to come,   150
And do not spread the compost° on the weeds
To make them ranker. Forgive me this my virtue,
For in the fatness° of these pursy° times
Virtue itself of vice must pardon beg —
Yea, curb° and woo for leave to do him good.   155
   QUEEN. O Hamlet, thou hast cleft my heart in
    twain.
   HAML. Oh, throw away the worser part of it,
And live the purer with the other half.
Good night. But go not to my uncle's bed.
Assume a virtue if you have it not.   160
That° monster, custom, who all sense doth eat,
Of habits devil,° is angel yet in this,
That to the use° of actions fair and good
He likewise gives a frock or livery
That aptly° is put on. Refrain tonight,   165
And that shall lend a kind of easiness
To the next abstinence, the next more easy.
For use almost can change the stamp° of nature,
And either the Devil,° or throw him out   169
With wondrous potency. Once more, good night.
And when you are desirous to be blest,
I'll blessing beg of you. For this same lord,
               [*Pointing to* POLONIUS]
I do repent; but Heaven hath pleased it so,
To punish me with this, and this with me,
That I must be their scourge and minister.   175
I will bestow° him, and will answer well
The death I gave him. So again good night.
I must be cruel only to be kind.
Thus bad begins, and worse remains behind.
One word more, good lady.
   QUEEN.   What shall I do?   180
   HAML. Not this, by no means, that I bid you do.
Let the bloat° king tempt you again to bed,
Pinch wanton° on your cheek, call you his mouse,
And let him, for a pair of reechy° kisses   184
Or paddling in your neck with his damned fingers,
Make you to ravel° all this matter out,
That I essentially am not in madness,

But mad in craft. 'Twere good you let him know.
For who that's but a Queen, fair, sober, wise,
Would from a paddock,° from a bat, a gib,°   190
Such dear concernings° hide? Who would do so?
No, in despite° of sense and secrecy,
Unpeg the basket on the house's top,
Let the birds fly, and like the famous ape,°
To try conclusions,° in the basket creep   195
And break your own neck down.
   QUEEN. Be thou assured if words be made of
    breath
And breath of life, I have no life to breathe
What thou hast said to me.
   HAML. I must to England. You know that?
   QUEEN.   Alack,   200
I had forgot. 'Tis so concluded on.
   HAML. There's letters sealed, and my two school-
    fellows,
Whom I will trust as I will adders fanged,
They bear the mandate.° They must sweep my way,
And marshal me to knavery. Let it work,   205
For 'tis the sport to have the enginer°
Hoist with his own petar.° And 't shall go hard
But I will delve one yard below their mines
And blow them at the moon: Oh, 'tis most sweet
When in one line two crafts° directly meet.   210
This man shall set me packing.
I'll lug the guts into the neighbor room.
Mother, good night. Indeed this counselor
Is now most still, most secret, and most grave
Who was in life a foolish prating knave.   215
Come, sir, to draw toward an end with you.
Good night, Mother.   [*Exeunt severally,*°
        HAMLET *dragging in* POLONIUS.]

Act IV

SCENE I. *A room in the castle.*

[*Enter* KING, QUEEN, ROSENCRANTZ, *and*
GUILDENSTERN.]
   KING. There's matter° in these sighs, these pro-
    found heaves,
You must translate. 'Tis fit we understand them.
Where is your son?

---

145. unction: healing ointment.   148. mining: undermining.
151. compost: manure.   153. fatness: grossness. pursy: bloated.
155. curb: bow low.   161–65. That . . . on: i.e., custom (bad
habits) like an evil monster destroys all sense of good and evil, but
yet can become an angel (good habits) when it makes us perform
good actions as mechanically as we put on our clothes.   162. devil:
This is the Q2 reading; the passage is omitted in F1. Probably the
word should be "evil."   163. use: practice.   165. aptly: readily.
168. stamp: impression.   169. either the Devil: some verb such
as "shame" or "curb" has been omitted.   176. bestow: get rid of.
182. bloat: bloated.   183. wanton: lewdly.   184. reechy: foul.
186. ravel: unravel, reveal.

190. paddock: toad. gib: tomcat.   191. dear concernings:
important matters.   192. despite: spite.   194. famous ape:
The story is not known, but evidently told of an ape that
let the birds out of their cage and, seeing them fly, crept
into the cage himself and jumped out, breaking his own neck.
195. try conclusions: repeat the experiment.   204. mandate:
command.   206. enginer: engineer.   207. petar: petard, land
mine.   210. crafts: devices.   217 s.d., Exeunt severally: i.e.,
by separate exits. In F1 there is no break here. The King enters as soon as Hamlet has dragged the body away. Q2 marks the
break. The act division was first inserted in a quarto of 1676.
   Act IV, Sc. i: 1. matter: something serious.

QUEEN. Bestow this place° on us a little while.

    [*Exeunt* ROSENCRANTZ *and* GUILDENSTERN.]

Ah, mine own lord, what have I seen tonight!   5

  KING. What, Gertrude? How does Hamlet?

  QUEEN. Mad as the sea and wind when both contend

Which is the mightier. In his lawless fit,

Behind the arras hearing something stir,

Whips out his rapier, cries " A rat, a rat! "   10

And in this brainish apprehension° kills

The unseen good old man.

    KING.   Oh, heavy deed!

It had been so with us had we been there.

His liberty is full of threats to all,

To you yourself, to us, to everyone.   15

Alas, how shall this bloody deed be answered?

It will be laid to us, whose providence°

Should have kept short,° restrained and out of

    haunt,°

This mad young man. But so much was our love

We would not understand what was most fit,   20

But, like the owner of a foul disease,

To keep it from divulging° let it feed

Even on the pith° of life. Where is he gone?

  QUEEN. To draw apart the body he hath killed,

O'er whom his very madness, like some ore   25

Among a mineral of metals base,

Shows itself pure. He weeps for what is done.

  KING. O Gertrude, come away!

The sun no sooner shall the mountains touch

But we will ship him hence. And this vile deed   30

We must, with all our majesty and skill,

Both countenance° and excuse. Ho, Guildenstern!

    [*Re-enter* ROSENCRANTZ *and* GUILDENSTERN.]

Friends both, go join you with some further aid.

Hamlet in madness hath Polonius slain,   34

And from his mother's closet hath he dragged him.

Go seek him out, speak fair, and bring the body

Into the chapel. I pray you, haste in this.

    [*Exeunt* ROSENCRANTZ *and* GUILDENSTERN.]

Come, Gertrude, we'll call up our wisest friends,

And let them know both what we mean to do

And what's untimely done,°   40

Whose whisper o'er the world's diameter

As level as the cannon to his blank°

Transports his poisoned shot, may miss our name

And hit the woundless air. Oh, come away!

My soul is full of discord and dismay.   [*Exeunt.*]

---

4. **Bestow . . . place:** give place, leave us. 11. **brainish apprehension:** mad imagination. 17. **providence:** foresight. 18. **short:** confined. **out of haunt:** away from others. 22. **divulging:** becoming known. 23. **pith:** marrow. 32. **countenance:** take responsibility for. 40. **done:** A half-line has been omitted. Some editors fill the gap with "So, haply slander." 42. **blank:** target.

SCENE II. *Another room in the castle.*

    [*Enter* HAMLET.]

  HAML. Safely stowed.

  ROS. & GUIL. [*Within*] Hamlet! Lord Hamlet!

  HAML. But soft, what noise? Who calls on Hamlet?

Oh, here they come.

    [*Enter* ROSENCRANTZ *and* GUILDENSTERN.]

  ROS. What have you done, my lord, with the dead

    body?   5

  HAML. Compounded it with dust, whereto 'tis kin.

  ROS. Tell us where 'tis, that we may take it thence

And bear it to the chapel.

  HAML. Do not believe it.

  ROS. Believe what?   10

  HAML. That I can keep your counsel and not mine

own. Besides, to be demanded of a sponge! What

replication° should be made by the son of a king?

  ROS. Take you me for a sponge, my lord?   15

  HAML. Aye, sir, that soaks up the King's countenance,° his rewards, his authorities. But such officers

do the King best service in the end. He keeps them,

like an ape, in the corner of his jaw, first mouthed,

to be last swallowed. When he needs what you have

gleaned, it is but squeezing you and, sponge, you

shall be dry again.   23

  ROS. I understand you not, my lord.

  HAML. I am glad of it. A knavish speech sleeps in

a foolish ear.°

  ROS. My lord, you must tell us where the body is,

and go with us to the King.   28

  HAML. The body is with the King, but the King

is not with the body.° The King is a thing——

  GUIL. A thing, my lord?

  HAML. Of nothing. Bring me to him. Hide   32

fox, and all after.°   [*Exeunt.*]

SCENE III. *Another room in the castle.*

    [*Enter* KING, *attended.*]

  KING. I have sent to seek him, and to find the

    body.

How dangerous is it that this man goes loose!

Yet must not we put the strong law on him.

He's loved of the distracted° multitude,

Who like not in their judgment but their eyes;°   5

And where 'tis so, the offender's scourge° is

    weighed,

Sc. ii: 14. **replication:** answer. 17. **countenance:** favor. 25–26. **A . . . ear:** a fool never understands the point of a sinister speech. 29–30. **The . . . body:** Hamlet deliberately bewilders his companions. 32–33. **Hide . . . after:** a form of the game of hide-and-seek. With these words Hamlet runs away from them.

Sc. iii: 4. **distracted:** bewildered. 5. **like . . . eyes:** whose likings are swayed not by judgment but by looks. 6. **scourge:** punishment.

But never the offense. To bear° all smooth and
    even,
This sudden sending him away must seem
Deliberate pause.° Diseases desperate grown
By desperate appliance are relieved,   10
Or not at all.
[*Enter* ROSENCRANTZ.] How now! What hath be-
    fall'n?
ROS. Where the dead body is bestowed, my lord,
We cannot get from him.
    KING.   But where is he?
ROS. Without, my lord, guarded, to know your
    pleasure.
    KING. Bring him before us.   15
    ROS. Ho, Guildenstern! Bring in my lord.
      [*Enter* HAMLET *and* GUILDENSTERN.]
    KING. Now, Hamlet, where's Polonius?
    HAML. At supper.
    KING. At supper! Where?   19
    HAML. Not where he eats, but where he is eaten.
A certain convocation of politic worms° are e'en at
him. Your worm is your only emperor for diet. We
fat all creatures else to fat us, and we fat ourselves
for maggots. Your fat king and your lean beggar is
but variable service,° two dishes, but to one table.
That's the end.   26
    KING. Alas, alas!
    HAML. A man may fish with the worm that hath
eat of a king, and eat of the fish that hath fed of that
worm.
    KING. What dost thou mean by this?
    HAML. Nothing but to show you how a king may
go a progress° through the guts of a beggar.
    KING. Where is Polonius?   34
    HAML. In Heaven — send thither to see. If your
messenger find him not there, seek him i' the other
place yourself. But indeed if you find him not within this month, you shall nose him as you go up the
stairs into the lobby.   39
    KING. [*To some* ATTENDANTS] Go seek him there.
    HAML. He will stay till you come.
             [*Exeunt* ATTENDANTS.]
    KING. Hamlet, this deed, for thine especial safety,
Which we do tender,° as we dearly grieve
For that which thou hast done, must send thee
    hence
With fiery quickness. Therefore prepare thyself.   45
The bark is ready and the wind at help,°
The associates tend,° and every thing is bent°
For England.
    HAML.   For England?
    KING.   Aye, Hamlet.

    HAML.   Good.
    KING. So is it if thou knew'st our purposes.
    HAML. I see a cherub that sees them. But, come,
for England! Farewell, dear Mother.   51
    KING. Thy loving father, Hamlet.
    HAML. My mother. Father and mother is man and
wife, man and wife is one flesh, and so, my mother.
Come, for England!   [*Exit.*]
    KING. Follow him at foot,° tempt° him with
    speed aboard.   56
Delay it not, I'll have him hence tonight.
Away! For everything is sealed and done
That else leans on the affair. Pray you make haste.
      [*Exeunt* ROSENCRANTZ *and* GUILDENSTERN.]
And, England, if my love thou hold'st at aught —
As my great power thereof may give thee sense,   61
Since yet thy cicatrice° looks raw and red
After the Danish sword, and thy free awe°
Pays homage to us — thou mayst not coldly set
Our sovereign process,° which imports at full,   65
By letters congruing° to that effect,
The present° death of Hamlet. Do it, England,
For like the hectic° in my blood he rages,
And thou must cure me. Till I know 'tis done,
Howe'er my haps,° my joys were ne'er begun.   70
                            [*Exit.*]

SCENE IV. *A plain in Denmark.*

[*Enter* FORTINBRAS, *a* CAPTAIN *and* SOLDIERS,
               marching.]
    FOR. Go, Captain, from me greet the Danish
    King.
Tell him that by his license Fortinbras
Craves the conveyance of a promised march°
Over his kingdom. You know the rendezvous.
If that His Majesty would aught with us,   5
We shall express our duty in his eye,°
And let him know so.
    CAP.   I will do 't, my lord.
    FOR. Go softly on.
             [*Exeunt* FORTINBRAS *and* SOLDIERS.]
[*Enter* HAMLET, ROSENCRANTZ, GUILDENSTERN, *and*
             others.]
    HAML. Good sir, whose powers° are these?
    CAP. They are of Norway, sir.   10
    HAML. How purposed, sir, I pray you?
    CAP. Against some part of Poland.

---

7. **bear:** make.   9. **Deliberate pause:** the result of careful
planning.   21. **convocation . . . worms:** an assembly of political-
minded worms.   25. **variable service:** choice of alternatives.
33. **go a progress:** make a state journey.   43. **tender:** regard
highly.   46. **at help:** favorable.   47. **associates tend:** your
companions are waiting. **bent:** ready.

56. **at foot:** at his heels. **tempt:** entice.   62. **cicatrice:** scar.
There is nothing in the play to explain this incident.   63. **free
awe:** voluntary submission.   64–65. **coldly . . . process:** hesitate to carry out our royal command.   66. **congruing:** agreeing.
67. **present:** immediate.   68. **hectic:** fever.   70. **Howe'er my
haps:** whatever may happen to me.
    Sc. iv: 3. **Craves . . . march:** asks for permission to transport
his army, as had already been promised. See II.ii.76–82.   6. **in
. . . eye:** before his eyes; i.e., in person.   9. **powers:** forces.

HAML. Who commands them, sir?
CAP. The nephew to old Norway, Fortinbras.   14
HAML. Goes it against the main° of Poland, sir,
Or for some frontier?
CAP. Truly to speak, and with no addition,°
We go to gain a little patch of ground
That hath in it no profit but the name.
To pay five ducats, five, I would not farm it,   20
Nor will it yield to Norway or the Pole
A ranker° rate should it be sold in fee.°
HAML. Why, then the Polack never will defend it.
CAP. Yes, it is already garrisoned.
HAML. Two thousand souls and twenty thousand
    ducats   25
Will not debate the question of this straw.
This is the imposthume of° much wealth and peace,
That inward breaks, and shows no cause without
Why the man dies. I humbly thank you, sir.
CAP. God be wi' you, sir.   [Exit.]
ROS.   Will 't please you go, my lord?   30
HAML. I'll be with you straight. Go a little before.
    [Exeunt all but HAMLET.]
How° all occasions do inform against° me
And spur my dull revenge! What is a man
If his chief good and market° of his time
Be but to sleep and feed? A beast, no more.   35
Sure, He that made us with such large discourse,
Looking before and after,° gave us not
That capability and godlike reason
To fust° in us unused. Now whether it be
Bestial oblivion, or some craven scruple   40
Of thinking too precisely on the event —
A thought which, quartered, hath but one part wis-
    dom
And ever three parts coward — I do not know
Why yet I live to say " This thing's to do,"   44
Sith I have cause, and will, and strength, and means
To do 't. Examples gross° as earth exhort me.
Witness this army, of such mass and charge,°
Led by a delicate and tender Prince
Whose spirit with divine ambition puffed
Makes mouths at the invisible event,°   50
Exposing what is mortal and unsure
To all that fortune, death, and danger dare,
Even for an eggshell.° Rightly to be great
Is not to stir without great argument,
But greatly to find quarrel in a straw   55
When honor's at the stake.° How stand I then,

That have a father killed, a mother stained,
Excitements of my reason and my blood,
And let all sleep while to my shame I see
The imminent death of twenty thousand men   60
That for a fantasy and trick° of fame
Go to their graves like beds, fight for a plot
Whereon the numbers cannot try the cause,°
Which is not tomb enough and continent°
To hide the slain? Oh, from this time forth,   65
My thoughts be bloody or be nothing worth!
    [Exit.]

SCENE V. *Elsinore. A room in the castle.*

[*Enter* QUEEN, HORATIO, *and a* GENTLEMAN.]
QUEEN. I will not speak with her.
GEN. She is importunate, indeed distract.°
Her mood will needs be pitied.
QUEEN   What would she have?
GEN. She speaks much of her father, says she hears
There's tricks° i' the world, and hems° and beats
    her heart,   5
Spurns enviously° at straws, speaks things in doubt
That carry but half-sense. Her speech is nothing,
Yet the unshaped use° of it doth move
The hearers to collection.° They aim° at it,   9
And botch° the words up fit to their own thoughts,
Which, as her winks and nods and gestures yield
    them,
Indeed would make one think there might be
    thought,
Though nothing sure, yet much unhappily.
HOR. 'Twere good she were spoken with, for she
    may strew
Dangerous conjectures in ill-breeding minds.   15
QUEEN. Let her come in.   [Exit GENTLEMAN.]
[*Aside*] To my sick soul, as sin's true nature is,
Each toy° seems prologue to some great amiss.°
So full of artless jealousy° is guilt,
It spills itself in fearing to be spilt.°   20
    [*Re-enter* GENTLEMAN, *with* OPHELIA.°]
OPH. Where is the beauteous Majesty of Den-
    mark?
QUEEN. How now, Ophelia!
OPH. [*Sings.*]
    " How should I your truelove know
        From another one?

15. main: mainland.   17. addition: exaggeration.   22. ranker:
richer. in fee: with possession as freehold.   27. imposthume
of: inward swelling caused by.   32–66. How . . . worth: The
soliloquy and all the dialogue after the exit of Fortinbras
are omitted in F1.   32. inform against: accuse.   34. market:
profit.   36–37. such . . . after: intelligence that enables us to consider the future and the past.   39. fust: grow musty.   46. gross:
large.   47. charge: expense.   50. Makes . . . event: mocks at the
unseen risk.   53. eggshell: i.e., worthless trifle.   53–56. Rightly
. . . stake: true greatness is a matter of fighting not for a mighty
cause but for the merest trifle when honor is concerned.

61. fantasy . . . trick: illusion and whim.   63. Whereon . .
cause: a piece of ground so small that it would not hold the
combatants.   64. continent: large enough to contain.
    Sc. v: 2. distract: out of her mind.   5. tricks: trickery. hems:
makes significant noises.   6. Spurns enviously: kicks spitefully.
8. unshaped use: disorder.   9. collection: i.e., attempts to
find a sinister meaning. aim: guess.   10. botch: patch.   18. toy:
trifle. amiss: calamity.   19. artless jealousy: clumsy suspicion.
20. It . . . spilt: guilt reveals itself by its efforts at concealment.
20 s.d., Re-enter . . . Ophelia: Q1 notes "Enter Ophelia playing on a lute, and her hair down, singing."

    By his cockle hat° and staff   25
    And his sandal shoon."°
QUEEN. Alas, sweet lady, what imports this song?
OPH. Say you? nay, pray you, mark. [*Sings.*]
    "He is dead and gone, lady,
      He is dead and gone,   30
    At his head a grass-green turf,
      At his heels a stone."
Oh, oh!
QUEEN. Nay, but, Ophelia ——
OPH.   Pray you, mark. [*Sings.*]
"White his shroud as the mountain snow ——"   35
       [*Enter* KING.]
QUEEN. Alas, look here, my lord.
OPH. [*Sings.*]
    "Larded° with sweet flowers,
    Which bewept to the grave did go
      With truelove showers."°
KING. How do you, pretty lady?   40
OPH. Well, God 'ild° you! They say the owl was
a baker's daughter.° Lord, we know what we are
but know not what we may be. God be at your table!
KING. Conceit upon her father.   45
OPH. Pray you let's have no words of this, but
when they ask you what it means, say you this
[*Sings*]:
    "Tomorrow is Saint Valentine's day,°
    All in the morning betime,
    And I a maid at your window,   50
      To be your Valentine.

    "Then up he rose, and donned his clothes,
      And dupped° the chamber door,
    Let in the maid, that out a maid
      Never departed more."   55
KING. Pretty Ophelia!
OPH. Indeed, la, without an oath, I'll make an end
on 't. [*Sings.*]
    "By Gis° and by Saint Charity,
    Alack, and fie for shame!   60
    Young men will do 't, if they come to 't,
      By cock, they are to blame.
    Quoth she, before you tumbled me,
      You promised me to wed."
He answers:

    "So would I ha' done, by yonder sun,   65
      An thou hadst not come to my bed."
KING. How long hath she been thus?
OPH. I hope all will be well. We must be patient.
But I cannot choose but weep to think they should
lay him i' the cold ground. My brother shall   70
know of it. And so I thank you for your good coun-
sel. Come, my coach! Good night, ladies, good night,
sweet ladies, good night, good night.   [*Exit.*]
KING. Follow her close,° give her good watch, I
pray you.   [*Exit* HORATIO.]
Oh, this is the poison of deep grief. It springs   76
All from her father's death. O Gertrude, Gertrude,
When sorrows come, they come not single spies,°
But in battalions! First, her father slain.
Next, your son gone, and he most violent author°
Of his own just remove. The people muddied,   81
Thick and unwholesome in their thoughts and
    whispers,
For good Polonius' death. And we have done but
    greenly°
In huggermugger° to inter him. Poor Ophelia
Divided from herself and her fair judgment,°   85
Without the which we are pictures,° or mere beasts.
Last, and as much containing as all these,
Her brother is in secret come from France,
Feeds on his wonder, keeps himself in clouds,
And wants not buzzers° to infect his ear   90
With pestilent speeches of his father's death,
Wherein necessity, of matter beggared,
Will nothing stick our person to arraign°
In ear and ear. O my dear Gertrude, this,
Like to a murdering piece,° in many places   95
Gives me superfluous death.   [*A noise within*]
QUEEN.   Alack, what noise is this?
KING. Where are my Switzers?° Let them guard
    the door.
[*Enter another* GENTLEMAN.] What is the matter?
GEN.   Save yourself, my lord.
The ocean, overpeering of his list,°
Eats not the flats° with more impetuous haste   100
Than young Laertes, in a riotous head,°
O'erbears your officers. The rabble call him lord,
And as the world were now but to begin,
Antiquity forgot, custom not known,
The ratifiers and props of every word,°   105

---

25. **cockle hat:** a hat adorned with a cockleshell worn by pilgrims. **26. sandal shoon:** sandals, the proper footwear of pilgrims. **37. Larded:** garnished. **39. truelove showers:** the tears
of his faithful love. **41. 'ild (yield):** reward. **41–42. owl ...
daughter:** An allusion to a legend that Christ once went into a
baker's shop and asked for bread. The baker's wife gave him a
piece but was rebuked by her daughter for giving him too much.
Thereupon the daughter was turned into an owl. **48. Saint ...
day:** February 14, the day when birds are supposed to mate.
According to the old belief the first single man then seen by a
maid is destined to be her husband. **53. dupped:** opened.
59–62. Gis ... cock: for "Jesus" and "God," both words being
used instead of the sacred names, like the modern "Jeez" and
"Gee."

74. **close:** closely.   78. **spies:** scouts.   80. **author:** cause.
83. **done ... greenly:** shown immature judgment.   84. **huggermugger:** secret haste, "any which way."   85. **Divided ... judgment:** no longer able to use her judgment.   86. **pictures:** lifeless
imitations.   90. **buzzers:** scandalmongers.   92–93. **Wherein ...
arraign:** in which, knowing nothing of the true facts, he must
necessarily accuse us.   95. **murdering piece:** cannon loaded with
grapeshot.   97. **Switzers:** Swiss bodyguard.   99. **overpeering
... list:** looking over its boundary; i.e., flooding the mainland.
100. **Eats ... flats:** floods not the flat country.   101. **in ...
head:** with a force of rioters.   104–05. **Antiquity ... word:** forgetting ancient rule and ignoring old custom, by which all promises must be maintained.

They cry " Choose we — Laertes shall be King! "
Caps, hands, and tongues applaud it to the clouds —
" Laertes shall be King, Laertes King! "
   QUEEN. How cheerfully on the false trail they cry!
Oh, this is counter,° you false Danish dogs!   110
                        [Noise within]
   KING. The doors are broke.
    [Enter LAERTES, armed, DANES following.]
   LAER. Where is this King? Sirs, stand you all
    without.
   DANES. No, let's come in.
   LAER.   I pray you, give me leave.
   DANES. We will, we will.
            [They retire without the door.]
   LAER. I thank you. Keep the door. O thou vile
    King,   115
Give me my father!
   QUEEN.   Calmly, good Laertes.
   LAER. That drop of blood that's calm proclaims
    me bastard,
Cries cuckold° to my father, brands the harlot°
Even here, between the chaste unsmirchèd brows
Of my true mother.
   KING.   What is the cause, Laertes,   120
That thy rebellion looks so giantlike?
Let him go, Gertrude. Do not fear° our person.
There's such divinity doth hedge a king°
That treason can but peep° to what it would,
Acts little of his will. Tell me, Laertes,   125
Why thou art thus incensed. Let him go, Gertrude.
Speak, man.
   LAER. Where is my father?
   KING.   Dead.
   QUEEN.   But not by him.
   KING. Let him demand his fill.
   LAER. How came he dead? I'll not be juggled
    with.   130
To Hell, allegiance! Vows, to the blackest devil!
Conscience and grace, to the profoundest pit!
I dare damnation. To this point I stand,
That both the worlds I give to negligence.°
Let come what comes, only I'll be revenged   135
Most throughly° for my father.
   KING.   Who shall stay you?
   LAER. My will, not all the world.
And for my means, I'll husband° them so well
They shall go far with little.
   KING.   Good Laertes,
If you desire to know the certainty   140
Of your dear father's death, is 't writ in your revenge

That, swoopstake,° you will draw both friend and
   foe,
Winner and loser?
   LAER. None but his enemies.
   KING.   Will you know them, then?
   LAER. To his good friends thus wide I'll ope my
    arms,   145
And like the kind life-rendering pelican,°
Repast° them with my blood.
   KING.   Why, now you speak
Like a good child and a true gentleman.
That I am guiltless of your father's death,
And am most sensibly° in grief for it,   150
It shall as level° to your judgment pierce
As day does to your eye.
   DANES.   [Within] Let her come in.
   LAER. How now! What noise is that?
[Re-enter OPHELIA.] O heat, dry up my brains! Tears
    seven times salt
Burn out the sense and virtue of mine eye!   155
By Heaven, thy madness shall be paid with weight
Till our scale turn the beam.° O rose of May!°
Dear maid, kind sister, sweet Ophelia!
Oh heavens! Is 't possible a young maid's wits
Should be as mortal as an old man's life?   160
Nature is fine in love, and where 'tis fine
It sends some precious instance of itself
After the thing it loves.°
   OPH. [Sings.]
    " They bore him barefaced on the bier,
      Hey non nonny, nonny, hey nonny,   165
      And in his grave rained many a tear —— "
Fare you well, my dove!
   LAER. Hadst thou thy wits and didst persuade re-
    venge,
It could not move thus.
   OPH. [Sings.]
    " You must sing down a-down   170
      An you call him a-down-a."
Oh, how the wheel° becomes it! It is the false stew-
ard, that stole his master's daughter.
   LAER. This nothing's more than matter.°   174
   OPH. There's° rosemary, that's for remembrance

---

142. swoopstake: "sweeping the board." 146. life-rendering
pelican: The mother pelican was supposed to feed her young
with blood from her own breast. 147. Repast: feed. 150. sensibly: feelingly. 151. level: clearly. 157. turn . . . beam: weigh
down the beam of the scale. rose of May: perfection of young
beauty. See III.i.160. 161–63. Nature . . . loves: i.e., her love
for her father was so exquisite that she has sent her sanity
after him. Laertes, especially in moments of emotion, is
prone to use highly exaggerated speech. 172. wheel: explained
variously as the spinning wheel, Fortune's wheel, or the refrain.
The likeliest explanation is that she breaks into a little dance
at the words "You must sing," and that the wheel is the turn
as she circles round. 174. This . . . matter: this nonsense means
more than sense. 175–85. There's . . . died: In the language of
flowers, each has its peculiar meaning, and Ophelia distributes
them appropriately: for her brother rosemary (remembrance) and
pansies (thoughts); for the King fennel (flattery) and columbine

---

110. counter: in the wrong direction of the scent. 118. cuckold: a husband deceived by his wife. brands . . . harlot: Convicted harlots were branded with a hot iron. Cf. III.iv.44.
122. fear: fear for. 123. divinity . . . king: divine protection
surrounds a king as with a hedge. 124. peep: look over, not
break through. 134. That . . . negligence: I do not care what
happens to me in this world or the next. 136. throughly: thoroughly. 138. husband: use economically.

— pray you, love, remember. And there is pansies,
that's for thoughts.

LAER. A document° in madness, thoughts and re-
membrance fitted.   179

OPH. There's fennel for you, and columbines.
There's rue for you, and here's some for me — we
may call it herb of grace o' Sundays. Oh, you must
wear your rue with a difference. There's a daisy. I
would give you some violets, but they withered all
when my father died. They say a' made a good
end. [*Sings.*]   186

　"For bonny sweet Robin is all my joy."

LAER. Thought and affliction, passion, Hell itself,
She turns to favor° and to prettiness.

OPH. [*Sings.*]

　　" And will a' not come again?   190
　　And will a' not come again?
　　　No, no, he is dead,
　　　Go to thy deathbed,
　　　He never will come again.

　　" His beard was as white as snow,   195
　　All flaxen was his poll.°
　　　He is gone, he is gone,
　　　And we cast away moan.
　　God ha' mercy on his soul! "

And of all Christian souls, I pray God. God be wi'
you.   [*Exit.*]

LAER. Do you see this, O God?   201

KING. Laertes, I must commune with your grief,
Or you deny me right. Go but apart,
Make choice of whom your wisest friends you will,
And they shall hear and judge 'twixt you and me.
If by direct or by collateral° hand   206
They find us touched,° we will our kingdom give,
Our crown, our life, and all that we call ours,
To you in satisfaction. But if not,
Be you content to lend your patience to us   210
And we shall jointly labor with your soul
To give it due content.

LAER.　　　　　　　　Let this be so.
His means of death, his obscure funeral,°
No trophy, sword, nor hatchment° o'er his bones,
No noble rite nor formal ostentation,°   215
Cry to be heard, as 'twere from Heaven to earth,
That I must call 't in question.

KING.　　　　　　　　So you shall,
And where the offense is let the great ax fall.
I pray you, go with me.   [*Exeunt.*]

(thanklessness); for the Queen rue, called also herb o' grace
(sorrow), and daisy (light of love). Neither is worthy of violets
(faithfulness).　　**178. document:** instruction.　　**189. favor:**
charm.　　**196. flaxen ... poll:** white as flax was his head.
206. collateral: i.e., as an accessory.　　**207. touched:** implicated.
213. obscure funeral: Men of rank were buried with much
ostentation. To bury Polonius "huggermugger" was thus an
insult to his memory and to his surviving family.　　**214. hatch-
ment:** device of the coat of arms carried in a funeral and hung
up over the tomb.　　**215. formal ostentation:** ceremony properly
ordered.

SCENE VI. *Another room in the castle.*

[*Enter* HORATIO *and a* SERVANT.]

HOR. What are they that would speak with me?

SER. Seafaring men, sir. They say they have letters
for you.

HOR. Let them come in.   [*Exit* SERVANT.]
I do not know from what part of the world
I should be greeted, if not from Lord Hamlet.   5

[*Enter* SAILORS.]

I. SAIL. God bless you, sir.

HOR. Let Him bless thee too.

I. SAIL. He shall, sir, an 't please Him. There's a
letter for you, sir. It comes from the ambassador that
was bound for England — if your name be Horatio,
as I am let to know it is.   11

HOR. [*Reads.*] " Horatio, when thou shalt have
overlooked° this, give these fellows some means° to
the King. They have letters for him. Ere we were
two days old at sea, a pirate of very warlike ap-   15
pointment° gave us chase. Finding ourselves too
slow of sail, we put on a compelled valor, and in the
grapple I boarded them. On the instant they got
clear of our ship, so I alone became their prisoner.
They have dealt with me like thieves of mercy;   20
but they knew what they did — I am to do a good
turn for them. Let the King have the letters I have
sent, and repair thou to me with as much speed as
thou wouldest fly death. I have words to speak in
thine ear will make thee dumb, yet are they   25
much too light for the bore of the matter.° These
good fellows will bring thee where I am. Rosencrantz and Guildenstern hold their course for England. Of them I have much to tell thee. Farewell.   30

　　" He that thou knowest thine,
　　　　　　" HAMLET "

Come, I will make you way for these your letters,
And do 't the speedier that you may direct me
To him from whom you brought them.   [*Exeunt.*]

SCENE VII. *Another room in the castle.*

[*Enter* KING *and* LAERTES.]

KING. Now must your conscience my acquittance
seal,°
And you must put me in your heart for friend,
Sith you have heard, and with a knowing ear,
That he which hath your noble father slain
Pursued my life.

LAER.　　　　　　　It well appears. But tell me   5
Why you proceeded not against these feats,°
So crimeful and so capital° in nature,

Sc. vi: **13. overlooked:** read. **means:** access.　　**16. appoint-**
ment: equipment.　　**26. too ... matter:** i.e., words fall short,
like a small shot fired from a cannon with too wide a bore.

Sc. vii: **1. my ... seal:** acquit me.　　**6. feats:** acts.　　**7. capi-**
tal: deserving death.

As by your safety, wisdom, all things else,
You mainly were stirred up.

KING.   Oh, for two special reasons,
Which may to you perhaps seem much unsinewed,°
But yet to me they're strong. The Queen his mother
Lives almost by his looks, and for myself —   12
My virtue or my plague, be it either which —
She's so conjunctive° to my life and soul
That as the star moves not but° in his sphere,   15
I could not but by her. The other motive
Why to a public count° I might not go
Is the great love the general gender° bear him,
Who, dipping all his faults in their affection,°
Would, like the spring that turneth wood to stone,°
Convert his gyves to graces.° So that my arrows, 21
Too slightly timbered° for so loud a wind,
Would have reverted to my bow again
And not where I had aimed them.

LAER. And so have I a noble father lost,   25
A sister driven into desperate terms,°
Whose worth, if praises may go back again,°
Stood challenger on mount of all the age
For her perfections.° But my revenge will come.

KING. Break not your sleeps for that. You must
    not think
That we are made of stuff so flat and dull   31
That we can let our beard be shook with danger
And think it pastime. You shortly shall hear more.°
I loved your father, and we love ourself,
And that, I hope, will teach you to imagine ——   35
[Enter a MESSENGER, with letters.] How now! What
    news?

MESS. Letters, my lord, from Hamlet.
This to your Majesty, this to the Queen.

KING. From Hamlet! Who brought them?

MESS. Sailors, my lord, they say — I saw them
    not.
They were given me by Claudio, he received them
Of him that brought them.   41

KING. Laertes, you shall hear them.
Leave us.   [Exit MESSENGER.]
[Reads] "High and Mighty, you shall know I am
set naked° on your kingdom. Tomorrow shall I beg
leave to see your kingly eyes, when I shall, first asking your pardon thereunto, recount the occasion of
my sudden and more strange return.
                                       "HAMLET"
What should this mean? Are all the rest come
    back?
Or is it some abuse,° and no such thing?   50

LAER. Know you the hand?

KING. 'Tis Hamlet's character.° "Naked!"
And in a postscript here, he says "alone."
Can you advise me?

LAER. I'm lost in it, my lord. But let him come.
It warms the very sickness in my heart   56
That I shall live and tell him to his teeth
"Thus didest thou."

KING.   If it be so, Laertes —
As how should it be so, how otherwise? —
Will you be ruled by me?

LAER.   Aye, my lord,   60
So you will not o'errule° me to a peace.

KING. To thine own peace. If he be now returned,
As checking at° his voyage, and that he means
No more to undertake it, I will work him
To an exploit now ripe in my device,   65
Under the which he shall not choose but fall.
And for his death no wind of blame shall breathe,
But even his mother shall uncharge the practice°
And call it accident.

LAER.   My lord, I will be ruled,
The rather if you could devise it so   70
That I might be the organ.°

KING.   It falls right.
You have been talked of since your travel much,
And that in Hamlet's hearing, for a quality
Wherein they say you shine. Your sum of parts°
Did not together pluck such envy from him   75
As did that one, and that in my regard
Of the unworthiest siege.°

LAER.   What part is that, my lord?

KING. A very ribbon in the cap of youth,
Yet needful too; for youth no less becomes
The light and careless livery that it wears   80
Than settled age his sables and his weeds,°
Importing health and graveness. Two months since,
Here was a gentleman of Normandy.
I've seen myself, and served against, the French,
And they can well° on horseback; but this gallant
Had witchcraft in 't, he grew unto his seat,   86
And to such wondrous doing brought his horse
As had he been incorpsed and deminatured°
With the brave beast. So far he topped my thought°

---

10. unsinewed: weak, flabby.   14. conjunctive: joined inseparably.   15. star: planet. but: only in.   17. count: trial.
18. general gender: common people.   19. dipping . . . affection:
gilding his faults with their love.   20. like . . . stone: In several
places in England there are springs of water so strongly impregnated with lime that they will quickly cover with stone
anything placed under them.   21. Convert . . . graces: regard
his fetters as honorable ornaments.   22. timbered: shafted.
A light arrow is caught by the wind and blown back.   26. terms:
condition.   27. if . . . again: if one may praise her for what
she used to be.   28–29. Stood . . . perfections: i.e., her worth
challenged the whole world to find one as perfect.   33. hear
more: i.e., when news comes from England that Hamlet is dead.
45. naked: destitute.

50. abuse: attempt to deceive.   52. character: handwriting.
61. o'errule: command.   63. checking at: swerving aside from,
like a hawk that leaves the pursuit of his prey.   68. uncharge
. . . practice: not suspect that his death was the result of the
plot.   71. organ: instrument.   74. sum of parts: accomplishments as a whole.   77. siege: seat, place.   81. sables . . .
weeds: dignified robes. See III.ii.138.   85. can well: can do
well.   88. incorpsed . . . deminatured: of one body.   89. topped
my thought: surpassed what I could imagine.

That I, in forgery of shapes and tricks,°   90
Come short of what he did.
    LAER.   A Norman was 't?
    KING. A Norman.
    LAER. Upon my life, Lamond.
    KING.   The very same.
    LAER. I know him well. He is the brooch° indeed
And gem of all the nation.   95
    KING. He made confession° of you,
And gave you such a masterly report
For art and exercise in your defense,
And for your rapier most especial,
That he cried out 'twould be a sight indeed   100
If one could match you. The scrimers° of their na-
    tion,
He swore, had neither motion, guard, nor eye
If you opposed them. Sir, this report of his
Did Hamlet so envenom° with his envy
That he could nothing do but wish and beg   105
Your sudden coming o'er, to play with him.
Now, out of this——
    LAER.   What out of this, my lord?
    KING. Laertes, was your father dear to you?
Or are you like the painting° of a sorrow,
A face without a heart?
    LAER.   Why ask you this?   110
    KING. Not that I think you did not love your
    father,
But that I know love is begun by time,
And that I see, in passages of proof,°
Time qualifies° the spark and fire of it.
There lives within the very flame of love   115
A kind of wick or snuff° that will abate it.
And nothing is at a like goodness still,°
For goodness, growing to a pleurisy,°
Dies in his own too much. That we would do
We should do when we would; for this " would "
    changes   120
And hath abatements and delays as many
As there are tongues, are hands, are accidents,
And then this " should " is like a spendthrift° sigh
That hurts by easing. But to the quick o' the ulcer.°
Hamlet comes back. What would you undertake
To show yourself your father's son in deed   126
More than in words?
    LAER.   To cut his throat i' the church.°

    KING. No place indeed should murder sanctuar-
    ize,°
Revenge should have no bounds. But, good Laertes,
Will you do this, keep close within your chamber.
Hamlet returned shall know you are come home.
We'll put on those° shall praise your excellence   132
And set a double varnish on the fame
The Frenchman gave you, bring you in fine° to-
    gether
And wager on your heads. He, being remiss,°   135
Most generous° and free from all contriving,°
Will not peruse the foils, so that with ease,
Or with a little shuffling, you may choose
A sword unbated,° and in a pass of practice°
Requite him for your father.
    LAER.   I will do 't,   140
And for that purpose I'll anoint my sword.
I bought an unction° of a mountebank°
So mortal that but dip a knife in it,
Where it draws blood no cataplasm° so rare,
Collected from all simples° that have virtue   145
Under the moon,° can save the thing from death
That is but scratched withal. I'll touch my point
With this contagion, that if I gall° him slightly,
It may be death.
    KING.   Let's further think of this,
Weigh what convenience both of time and means
May fit us to our shape.° If this should fail,   151
And that our drift look through our bad perform-
    ance,°
'Twere better not assayed. Therefore this project
Should have a back or second, that might hold
If this did blast in proof.° Soft! Let me see —   155
We'll make a solemn wager on your cunnings.
I ha 't.
When in your motion you are hot and dry —
As make your bouts° more violent to that end —
And that he calls for drink, I'll have prepared him
A chalice° for the nonce,° whereon but sipping,
If he by chance escape your venomed stuck,°   162
Our purpose may hold there. But stay, what noise?
[*Enter* QUEEN.] How now, sweet Queen!
    QUEEN. One woe doth tread upon another's heel,
So fast they follow. Your sister's drowned, Laertes.
    LAER. Drowned! Oh, where?   166

90. forgery . . . tricks: imagination of all kinds of fancy tricks. shapes: fancies.   94. brooch: ornament.   96. confession: report.   101. scrimers: fencers.   104. envenom: poison. 109. painting: i.e., imitation.   113. passages of proof: experiences which prove.   114. qualifies: diminishes.   116. snuff: Before the invention of self-consuming wicks for candles, the wick smoldered and formed a ball of soot which dimmed the light and gave out a foul smoke.   117. still: always. 118. pleurisy: fullness.   123. spendthrift: wasteful, because sighing was supposed to be bad for the blood.   124. quick . . . ulcer: i.e., to come to the real issue. quick: flesh, sensitive part.   127. cut . . . church: i.e., to commit murder in a holy place, which would bring Laertes in danger of everlasting damnation; no crime could be worse.

128. sanctuarize: give sanctuary to.   132. put . . . those: set on some. 134. fine: short. 135. remiss: careless. 136. generous: noble. contriving: plotting.   139. unbated: not blunted, with a sharp point. pass of practice: treacherous thrust. 142. unction: poison. mountebank: quack doctor.   144. cataplasm: poultice.   145. simples: herbs.   146. Under . . . moon: herbs collected by moonlight were regarded as particularly potent.   148. gall: break the skin.   150-51. Weigh . . . shape: consider the best time and method of carrying out our plan. 152. drift . . . performance: intention be revealed through bungling.   155. blast in proof: break in trial, like a cannon which bursts when being tested. 159. bouts: attacks, in the fencing match.   161. chalice: cup. nonce: occasion.   162. stuck: thrust.

QUEEN. There is a willow grows aslant a brook
That shows his hoar° leaves in the glassy stream.
There with fantastic garlands did she come
Of crowflowers, nettles, daisies, and long purples
That liberal° shepherds give a grosser name,   171
But our cold maids do dead-men's-fingers call them.
There on the pendent° boughs her coronet weeds°
Clambering to hang, an envious sliver° broke,
When down her weedy trophies and herself   175
Fell in the weeping brook. Her clothes spread wide,
And mermaidlike awhile they bore her up —
Which time she chanted snatches of old tunes,
As one incapable° of her own distress,
Or like a creature native and indued°   180
Unto that element. But long it could not be
Till that her garments, heavy with their drink,
Pulled the poor wretch from her melodious lay°
To muddy death.
    LAER.   Alas, then, she is drowned!
    QUEEN. Drowned, drowned.   185
    LAER. Too much of water hast thou, poor Ophelia,
And therefore I forbid my tears. But yet
It is our trick° — Nature her custom holds,
Let shame say what it will. When these° are gone,
The woman will be out.° Adieu, my lord.   190
I have a speech of fire that fain° would blaze
But that this folly douts° it.   [Exit.]
    KING.   Let's follow, Gertrude.
How much I had to do to calm his rage!
Now fear I this will give it start again,
Therefore let's follow.   [Exeunt.]

Act V

SCENE I. *A churchyard.*

[*Enter two* CLOWNS,° *with spades, etc.*]
    1. CLO. Is she to be buried in Christian burial°
that willfully seeks her own salvation?

---

168. hoar: gray. The underside of the leaves of the willow
are silver-gray.   171. liberal: coarse-mouthed.   173. pendent:
hanging over the water. coronet weeds: wild flowers woven
into a crown.   174. envious sliver: malicious branch.
179. incapable: not realizing.   180. indued: endowed; i.e.,
a creature whose natural home is the water (*element*).
183. lay: song.   187–88. But . . . trick: it is our habit; i.e., to
break into tears at great sorrow.   189. these: i.e., my tears.
190. woman . . . out: I shall be a man again.   191. fain:
willingly.   192. douts: puts out.
    Act V, Sc. i: s.d., Clowns: countrymen.   1. Christian burial:
Suicides were not allowed burial in consecrated ground, but
were buried at crossroads. The gravediggers and the priest are
professionally scandalized that Ophelia should be allowed
Christian burial solely because she is a lady of the Court.

2. CLO. I tell thee she is, and therefore make her
grave straight.° The crowner° hath sat on her, and
finds it Christian burial.   5
    1. CLO. How can that be, unless she drowned her-
self in her own defense?
    2. CLO. Why, 'tis found so.
    1. CLO. It must be "se offendendo,"° it cannot be
else. For here lies the point. If I drown myself   10
wittingly,° it argues an act, and an act hath three
branches — it is to act, to do, and to perform. Argal,°
she drowned herself wittingly.
    2. CLO. Nay, but hear you, goodman delver.°   15
    1. CLO. Give me leave. Here lies the water, good.
Here stands the man, good. If the man go to this
water and drown himself, it is will he, nill he° he
goes, mark you that; but if the water come to him
and drown him, he drowns not himself. Argal, he
that is not guilty of his own death shortens not his
own life.   22
    2. CLO. But is this law?
    1. CLO. Aye, marry, is 't, crowner's quest° law.
    2. CLO. Will you ha' the truth on 't? If this had
not been a gentlewoman, she should have been
buried out o' Christian burial.   28
    1. CLO. Why, there thou say'st. And the more pity
that great folks should have countenance° in this
world to drown or hang themselves more than their
even° Christian. Come, my spade. There is no ancient gentlemen but gardeners, ditchers, and   34
gravemakers. They hold up° Adam's profession.
    2. CLO. Was he a gentleman?
    1. CLO. A' was the first that ever bore arms.°
    2. CLO. Why, he had none.   39
    1. CLO. What, art a heathen? How dost thou un-
derstand the Scripture? The Scripture says Adam
digged. Could he dig without arms? I'll put another
question to thee. If thou answerest me not to the
purpose, confess thyself ——
    2. CLO. Go to.   45
    1. CLO. What is he that builds stronger than either
the mason, the shipwright, or the carpenter?
    2. CLO. The gallows-maker, for that frame outlives
a thousand tenants.   50
    1. CLO. I like thy wit well, in good faith. The gal-
lows does well, but how does it well? It does well to
those that do ill. Now thou dost ill to say the gallows
is built stronger than the church; argal, the gallows
may do well to thee. To 't again, come.   56
    2. CLO. Who builds stronger than a mason, a ship-
wright, or a carpenter?

---

4. straight: straightway. crowner: coroner who inquired into cases
of suicide.   9. se offendendo: for *defendendo*, in self-defense.
11. wittingly: with full knowledge.   12. Argal: for the Latin
ergo, therefore.   15. delver: digger.   18. will he, nill he:
willy-nilly, whether he wishes or not.   24. quest: inquest.
30. countenance: favor.   33. even: fellow.   35. hold up: support.   38. bore arms: had a coat of arms — the outward sign of
a gentleman.

1. CLO. Aye, tell me that, and unyoke.°

2. CLO. Marry, now I can tell.   60

1. CLO. To 't.

2. CLO. Mass,° I cannot tell.

[*Enter* HAMLET *and* HORATIO, *afar off.*]

1. CLO. Cudgel thy brains no more about it, for your dull ass will not mend his pace with beating, and when you are asked this question next, say "A gravemaker." The houses that he makes last till Doomsday. Go, get thee to Yaughan,° fetch me   67 a stoup° of liquor.   [*Exit* SECOND CLOWN.]

[FIRST CLOWN *digs, and sings.*]

" In youth,° when I did love, did love,
  Methought it was very sweet,
To contract; oh, the time, for-a my behoove,°   71
  Oh, methought, there-a was nothing-a meet."

HAML. Has this fellow no feeling of his business, that he sings at grave-making?

HOR. Custom hath made it in him a property of easiness.°

HAML. 'Tis e'en so. The hand of little employment hath the daintier sense.°   78

1. CLO. [*Sings.*] " But age, with his stealing steps,
    Hath clawed me in his clutch,
  And hath shipped me intil the land°
    As if I had never been such."   82

[*Throws up a skull.*]

HAML. That skull had a tongue in it, and could sing once. How the knave jowls° it to the ground, as if it were Cain's jawbone, that did the first murder! It might be the pate of a politician which this ass now o'erreaches°—one that would circumvent° God, might it not?

HOR. It might, my lord.   89

HAML. Or of a courtier, which could say "Good morrow, sweet lord! How dost thou, good lord?" This might be my lord Such-a-one that praised my lord Such-a-one's horse when he meant to beg it, might it not?

HOR. Aye, my lord.   95

HAML. Why, e'en so. And now my Lady Worm's chapless,° and knocked about the mazzard° with a sexton's spade. Here's fine revolution, an we had the trick to see 't. Did these bones cost no more the breeding but to play at loggats° with 'em? Mine ache to think on 't.   101

---

59. **unyoke:** finish the job, unyoking the plow oxen being the end of the day's work.   62. **Mass:** by the mass. 67. **Yaughan:** apparently the keeper of an inn near the Globe Theatre.   68. **stoup:** large pot.   69–105. **In youth . . . meet:** The song which the gravedigger sings without much care for accuracy or sense was first printed in *Tottel's Miscellany*, 1558. 71. **behoove:** benefit.   75–76. **property of easiness:** careless habit.   77–78. **hand . . . sense:** those who have little to do are the most sensitive.   81. **shipped . . . land:** shoved me into the ground.   84. **jowls:** dashes.   87. **o'erreaches:** gets the better of. **circumvent:** get around.   97. **chapless:** without jaws. **mazzard:** head, a slang word; lit., drinking-bowl.   100. **loggats:** a game in which billets of wood or bones were stuck in the ground and knocked over by throwing at them.

1. CLO. [*Sings.*] " A pickax and a spade, a spade,
    For and a shrouding sheet—
  Oh, a pit of clay for to be made
    For such a guest is meet."   105

[*Throws up another skull.*]

HAML. There's another. Why may not that be the skull of a lawyer?° Where be his quiddities now, his quillets, his cases, his tenures, and his tricks? Why does he suffer this rude knave now to knock him about the sconce° with a dirty shovel, and will   110 not tell him of his action of battery? Hum! This fellow might be in 's time a great buyer of land, with his statutes, his recognizances, his fines, his double vouchers, his recoveries. Is this the fine° of his fines and the recovery of his recoveries, to have his   115 fine pate full of fine dirt? Will his vouchers vouch him no more of his purchases, and double ones too, than the length and breadth of a pair of indentures? The very conveyances of his lands will hardly lie in this box,° and must the inheritor himself have no more, ha?   121

HOR. Not a jot more, my lord.

HAML. Is not parchment made of sheepskins?

HOR. Aye, my lord, and of calfskins too.

HAML. They are sheep and calves which seek out assurance in that. I will speak to this fellow. Whose grave's this, sirrah?

1. CLO. Mine, sir. [*Sings.*]
  " Oh, a pit of clay for to be made
    For such a guest is meet."   129

HAML. I think it be thine indeed, for thou liest in 't.

1. CLO. You lie out on 't, sir, and therefore 'tis not yours. For my part, I do not lie in 't, and yet it is mine.   135

HAML. Thou dost lie in 't, to be in 't and say it is thine. 'Tis for the dead, not for the quick, therefore thou liest.

1. CLO. 'Tis a quick lie, sir, 'twill away again, from me to you.   140

HAML. What man dost thou dig it for?

1. CLO. For no man, sir.

HAML. What woman, then?

1. CLO. For none, neither.

HAML. Who is to be buried in 't?   145

1. CLO. One that was a woman, sir, but, rest her soul, she's dead.

HAML. How absolute° the knave is! We must speak by the card,° or equivocation° will undo us.

107–18. **lawyer . . . indentures:** Hamlet strings out a number of the legal phrases loved by lawyers: *quiddities:* subtle arguments; *quillets:* quibbles; *tenures:* titles to property; *tricks:* knavery; *statutes:* bonds; *recognizances:* obligations; *fines:* conveyances; *vouchers:* guarantors; *recoveries:* transfers; *indentures:* legal agreements to purchase.   110. **sconce:** head; lit., blockhouse.   114. **fine:** ending.   120. **box:** coffin. 148. **absolute:** exact.   149. **by . . . card:** exactly. The card is the mariner's compass. **equivocation:** speaking with a double

By the Lord, Horatio, this three years I have taken note of it — the age is grown so picked° that the toe of the peasant comes so near the heel of the courtier, he galls his kibe.° How long hast thou been a grave-maker?   154

1. CLO. Of all the days i' the year, I came to 't that day that our last King Hamlet o'ercame Fortinbras.

HAML. How long is that since?

1. CLO. Cannot you tell that? Every fool can tell that. It was that very day that young Hamlet was born, he that is mad, and sent into England.   164

HAML. Aye, marry, why was he sent into England?

1. CLO. Why, because a' was mad. A' shall recover his wits there, or, if a' do not, 'tis no great matter there.

HAML. Why?

1. CLO. 'Twill not be seen in him there — there the men are as mad as he.   170

HAML. How came he mad?

1. CLO. Very strangely, they say.

HAML. How " strangely "?

1. CLO. Faith, e'en with losing his wits.

HAML. Upon what ground?

1. CLO. Why, here in Denmark. I have been sexton here, man and boy, thirty years.°

HAML. How long will a man lie i' the earth ere he rot?   179

1. CLO. I' faith, if a' be not rotten before a' die — as we have many pocky° corses nowadays that will scarce hold the laying in — a' will last you some eight year or nine year. A tanner will last you nine year.

HAML. Why he more than another?   185

1. CLO. Why, sir, his hide is so tanned with his trade that a' will keep out water a great while, and your water is a sore decayer of your whoreson° dead body. Here's a skull now. This skull has lain in the earth three and twenty years.   191

HAML. Whose was it?

1. CLO. A whoreson mad fellow's it was. Whose do you think it was?

HAML. Nay, I know not.   195

1. CLO. A pestilence on him for a mad rogue! A' poured a flagon of Rhenish on my head once. This same skull, sir, was Yorick's skull, the King's jester.

HAML. This?

1. CLO. E'en that.

HAML. Let me see. [Takes the skull.] Alas, poor Yorick! I knew him, Horatio — a fellow of infinite jest, of most excellent fancy. He hath borne me on his back a thousand times, and now how ab- 205 horred in my imagination it is! My gorge rises° at it. Here hung those lips that I have kissed I know not how oft. Where be your gibes now? Your gam-bols? Your songs? Your flashes of merriment that were wont to set the table on a roar? Not one 210 now, to mock your own grinning? Quite chop-fallen?° Now get you to my lady's chamber and tell her, let her paint an inch thick, to this favor° she must come — make her laugh at that. Prithee, Hora-tio, tell me one thing.

HOR. What's that, my lord?   217

HAML. Dost thou think Alexander looked o' this fashion i' the earth?

HOR. E'en so.

HAML. And smelt so? Pah!

[Puts down the skull.]

HOR. E'en so, my lord.

HAML. To what base uses we may return, Horatio! Why may not imagination trace the noble dust of Alexander till he find it stopping a bunghole?°

HOR. 'Twere to consider too curiously° to consider so.   228

HAML. No, faith, not a jot, but to follow him thither with modesty° enough and likelihood to lead it. As thus: Alexander died, Alexander was buried, Alexander returneth into dust; the dust is earth; of earth we make loam;° and why of that loam, whereto he was converted, might they not stop a beer barrel?   235

" Imperious Caesar, dead and turned to clay,
    Might stop a hole to keep the wind away.
Oh, that that earth which kept the world in awe
    Should patch a wall to expel the winter's flaw!"°
But soft! But soft! Aside — here comes the King.

[Enter PRIESTS,° etc., in procession; the corpse of
    Ophelia, LAERTES and MOURNERS following;
        KING, QUEEN, their trains, etc.]

The Queen, the courtiers — who is this they follow?
And with such maimèd° rites? This doth betoken°
The corse they follow did with desperate hand   243
Fordo° its own life. 'Twas of some estate.°

206. My . . . rises: I feel sick. gorge: throat.   212. chop-fallen: downcast, with a pun on "chapless," (see l. 97). 213. favor: appearance, especially in the face.   226. bunghole: the hole in a beer barrel.   227. curiously: precisely.   230. with modesty: without exaggeration.   233. loam: mixture of clay and sand, used in plastering walls.   239. flaw: blast.   240. s.d., Enter Priests. The stage directions in early texts are less elaborate. Q2 notes, curtly, Enter K.Q. Laertes and the corse. F1 has Enter King, Queen, Laertes, and a coffin, with Lords attendant. Q1 prints Enter King and Queen, Laertes and other lords, with a Priest after the coffin. This probably was how the scene was originally staged. The modern directions ignore the whole signif-icance of the "maimed rites" — Ophelia's funeral is insult-ingly simple.   242. maimed: curtailed. betoken: indicate. 244. Fordo: destroy. estate: high rank.

sense. The word was being much discussed when Hamlet was being written.   151. picked: refined.   151-53. toe . . . kibe: i.e., the peasant follows the courtier so closely that he rubs the courtier's heel into a blister. From about 1598 onward, writers, especially dramatists, often satirized the practice of yeoman farmers grown rich from war profits in sending their awkward sons to London to learn gentlemanly manners.   177. thirty years: The Clown's chronology has puzzled critics, for the general im-pression is that Hamlet was much younger.   181. pocky: suffer-ing from the pox (venereal disease).   189. whoreson: bastard. Such epithets did not really intend much anger. They were as common and innocuous as similar profane expressions today.

Couch° we awhile, and mark.

                    [Retiring with HORATIO.]

LAER. What ceremony else?

HAML. That is Laertes, a very noble youth. Mark.

LAER. What ceremony else?   248

I. PRIEST. Her obsequies have been as far enlarged
As we have warranty.° Her death was doubtful,
And but that great command o'ersways the order,°
She should in ground unsanctified have lodged
Till the last trumpet; for° charitable prayers,
Shards,° flints, and pebbles should be thrown on her.
Yet here she is allowed her virgin crants,°   255
Her maiden strewments° and the bringing home
Of bell and burial.

LAER. Must there no more be done?

I. PRIEST.   No more be done.
We should profane the service of the dead
To sing a requiem and such rest to her   260
As to peace-parted souls.°

LAER.   Lay her i' the earth.
And from her fair and unpolluted flesh
May violets spring! I tell thee, churlish priest,
A ministering angel shall my sister be
When thou liest howling.

HAML.   What, the fair Ophelia! 265

QUEEN. *[Scattering flowers]* Sweets to the sweet.
Farewell!
I hoped thou shouldst have been my Hamlet's wife,
I thought thy bride bed to have decked, sweet maid,
And not have strewed thy grave.

LAER.   Oh, treble woe
Fall ten times treble on that cursèd head   270
Whose wicked deed thy most ingenious sense°
Deprived thee of! Hold off the earth a while
Till I have caught her once more in mine arms.

                     [Leaps into the grave.]

Now pile your dust upon the quick° and dead
Till of this flat a mountain you have made   275
To o'ertop old Pelion° or the skyish° head
Of blue Olympus.

HAML. *[Advancing]* What is he whose grief
Bears such an emphasis? Whose phrase of sorrow
Conjures the wandering stars and makes them
stand°
Like wonder-wounded hearers? This is I,   280
Hamlet the Dane.   *[Leaps into the grave.]*

LAER. **The Devil take thy soul!**

                    [Grappling with him]

HAML.   Thou pray'st not well.
I prithee, take thy fingers from my throat,
For though I am not splenitive° and rash,
Yet have I in me something dangerous,   285
Which let thy wisdom fear. Hold off thy hand.

KING. Pluck them asunder.

QUEEN.   Hamlet, Hamlet!

ALL.   Gentlemen ——

HOR. Good my lord, be quiet.

              [The ATTENDANTS *part them,
              and they come out of the grave.]*

HAML. Why, I will fight with him upon this
theme
Until my eyelids will no longer wag.   290

QUEEN. O my son, what theme?

HAML. I loved Ophelia. Forty thousand brothers
Could not, with all their quantity of love,
Make up my sum. What wilt thou do for her?

KING. Oh, he is mad, Laertes.   295

QUEEN. For love of God, forbear him.°

HAML. 'Swounds,° show me what thou'lt do.
Woo 't weep? Woo 't fight? Woo 't fast? Woo 't tear
thyself?
Woo 't drink up eisel?° Eat a crocodile?
I'll do 't. Dost thou come here to whine?   300
To outface° me with leaping in her grave?
Be buried quick with her, and so will I.
And if thou prate of mountains, let them throw
Millions of acres on us, till our ground,
Singeing his pate against the burning zone,   305
Make Ossa° like a wart! Nay, an thou 'lt mouth,
I'll rant as well as thou.

QUEEN.   This is mere madness.
And thus awhile the fit will work on him.
Anon, as patient as the female dove
When that her golden couplets° are disclosed,°   310
His silence will sit drooping.

HAML.   Hear you, sir.
What is the reason that you use me thus?
I loved you ever. But it is no matter,
Let Hercules himself do what he may,   314
The cat will mew and dog will have his day.° *[Exit.]*

KING. I pray thee, good Horatio, wait upon him.

                    [Exit HORATIO.]

[To LAERTES] Strengthen your patience in our last
night's speech.
We'll put the matter to the present push.°

---

245. **Couch:** lie down.   249–50. **Her . . . warranty:** the funeral rites have been as complete as may be allowed.   251. **but . . . order:** if the King's command had not overruled the proper procedure.   253. **for:** instead of.   254. **Shards:** pieces of broken crockery.   255. **crants:** wreaths of flowers — a sign that she had died unwed.   256. **maiden strewments:** the flowers strewn on the corpse of a maiden.   261. **peace-parted souls:** souls which departed in peace, fortified with the rites of the Church.   271. **most . . . sense:** lively intelligence.   274. **quick:** living.   276. **Pelion:** When the giants fought against the gods in order to reach Heaven, they tried to pile Mount Pelion and Mount Ossa on Mount Olympus, the highest mountain in Greece. **skyish:** reaching the sky.   279. **stand:** stand still.

284. **splenitive:** hot-tempered.   296. **forbear him:** leave him alone.   297–307. **'Swounds . . . thou:** Hamlet in his excitement cries out that if Laertes wishes to make extravagant boasts of what he will do to show his sorrow, he will be even more extravagant.   299. **eisel:** vinegar.   301. **outface:** browbeat.   306. **Ossa:** See l. 276, n.   310. **couplets:** eggs, of which the dove lays two only. **disclosed:** hatched.   314-15. **Let . . . day:** i.e., let this ranting hero have his turn; mine will come sometime.   318. **push:** test; lit., thrust of a pike.

Good Gertrude, set some watch over your son.
This grave shall have a living monument.° 320
An hour of quiet shortly shall we see,
Till then, in patience our proceeding be. [*Exeunt.*]

SCENE II. *A hall in the castle.*

[*Enter* HAMLET *and* HORATIO.]

HAML. So much for this, sir. Now shall you see
the other.
You do remember all the circumstance?
HOR. Remember it, my lord!
HAML. Sir, in my heart there was a kind of fight-
ing
That would not let me sleep. Methought I lay 5
Worse than the mutines in the bilboes.° Rashly,
And praised be rashness for it, let us know,
Our indiscretion sometime serves us well
When our deep plots do pall.° And that should
learn° us
There's a divinity that shapes our ends, 10
Roughhew them how we will.°
HOR. That is most certain.
HAML. Up from my cabin,
My sea gown° scarfed° about me, in the dark
Groped I to find out them,° had my desire,
Fingered their packet, and in fine withdrew 15
To mine own room again, making so bold,
My fears forgetting manners, to unseal
Their grand commission where I found, Horatio —
Oh royal knavery! — an exact command,
Larded° with many several sorts of reasons, 20
Importing Denmark's health and England's too,
With, ho! such bugs° and goblins in my life°
That, on the supervise,° no leisure bated,°
No, not to stay the grinding of the ax,
My head should be struck off.
HOR. Is 't possible? 25
HAML. Here's the commission. Read it at more
leisure
But wilt thou hear me how I did proceed?
HOR. I beseech you.
HAML. Being thus benetted round with vil-
lainies —
Ere I could make a prologue to my brains, 30
They had begun the play — I sat me down,
Devised a new commission, wrote it fair.
I once did hold it, as our statists° do,

A baseness to write fair, and labored much
How to forget that learning, but, sir, now 35
It did me yeoman's service.° Wilt thou know
The effect of what I wrote?
HOR. Aye, good my lord.
HAML. An earnest conjuration from the King,
As England was his faithful tributary,
As love between them like the palm might flourish,
As peace should still her wheaten garland wear 41
And stand a comma 'tween their amities,°
And many suchlike " Ases "° of great charge,°
That, on the view and knowing of these contents,
Without debatement° further, more or less, 45
He should the bearers put to sudden death,
Not shriving time allowed.°
HOR. How was this sealed?
HAML. Why, even in that was Heaven ordinant.°
I had my father's signet in my purse,
Which was the model° of that Danish seal — 50
Folded the writ° up in the form of the other,
Subscribed° it, gave 't the impression,° placed it
safely,
The changeling° never known. Now the next day
Was our sea fight, and what to this was sequent°
Thou know'st already. 55
HOR. So Guildenstern and Rosencrantz go to 't.
HAML. Why, man, they did make love to this em-
ployment.
They are not near my conscience, their defeat°
Does by their own insinuation° grow.
'Tis dangerous when the baser nature comes 60
Between the pass and fell incensèd points
Of mighty opposites.°
HOR. Why, what a King is this!
HAML. Does it not, think'st thee, stand me now
upon —
He that hath killed my King and whored my
mother,
Popped in between the election and my hopes,° 65

320. **living monument:** with the double meaning of "lifelike
memorial" and "the death of Hamlet."
Sc. ii: 6. **mutines . . . bilboes:** mutineers in the shackles used
on board ship. 9. **pall:** fail. **learn:** teach. 10–11. **There's . . .
will:** though we may make the rough beginning, God finishes our
designs. 13. **sea gown:** a thick coat with a high collar worn by
seamen. **scarfed:** wrapped. 14. **them:** i.e., Rosencrantz and
Guildenstern. 20. **Larded:** garnished. 22. **bugs:** bugbears.
in my life: so long as I was alive. 23. **supervise:** reading. **bated:**
allowed. 33. **statists:** statesmen. As scholars who have had to

read Elizabethan documents know, the more exalted the writer,
the worse his handwriting. As a girl Queen Elizabeth wrote a
beautiful script; as Queen her letters are as illegible as any. All
but the most confidential documents were copied out in a fair
hand by a secretary. 36. **yeoman's service:** faithful service.
The most reliable English soldiers were yeomen — farmers
and their men. 42. **stand . . . amities:** be a connecting
link of their friendship. 43. **"Ases":** Official documents
were written in flowery language full of metaphorical clauses
beginning with "As." Hamlet puns on "asses." **great charge:**
"great weight" and "heavy burden." 45. **debatement:**
argument. 47. **Not . . . allowed:** without giving them time
even to confess their sins. 48. **ordinant:** directing, in control. 50. **model:** copy. 51. **writ:** writing. 52. **Subscribed:**
signed. **impression:** of the seal. 53. **changeling:** lit., an ugly
child exchanged by the fairies for a fair one. 54. **sequent:** following. 58. **defeat:** destruction. 59. **by . . . insinuation:** because they insinuated themselves into this business. 60–62. **'Tis
. . . opposites:** it is dangerous for inferior men to interfere in
a duel between mighty enemies. **pass:** thrust. **fell:** fierce.
65. **Popped . . . hopes:** As is from time to time shown in the play,
the Danes chose their King by election.

Thrown out his angle° for my proper° life,
And with such cozenage° — is 't not perfect con-
   science,
To quit° him with this arm? And is 't not to be
   damned,
To let this canker° of our nature come
In further evil?   70
   HOR. It must be shortly known to him from Eng-
   land
What is the issue of the business there.
   HAML. It will be short. The interim° is mine,
And a man's life's no more than to say " One."
But I am very sorry, good Horatio,   75
That to Laertes I forgot myself,
For by the image of my cause I see
The portraiture of his. I'll court his favors.
But, sure, the bravery° of his grief did put me
Into a towering passion.
   HOR.   Peace! Who comes here?   80
           [*Enter* OSRIC.°]
   OSR. Your lordship is right welcome back to Den-
mark.
   HAML. I humbly thank you, sir. Dost know this
water fly?°
   HOR. No, my good lord.   84
   HAML. Thy state is the more gracious,° for 'tis a
vice to know him. He hath much land, and fertile.
Let a beast be lord of beasts and his crib shall stand
at the King's mess.° 'Tis a chough,° but, as I say,
spacious° in the possession of dirt.   90
   OSR. Sweet lord, if your lordship were at leisure, I should impart a thing to you from His Majesty.
   HAML. I will receive it, sir, with all diligence of
spirit. Put your bonnet to his right use,° 'tis for the
head.
   OSR. I thank your lordship, it is very hot.   97
   HAML. No, believe me, 'tis very cold. The wind is
northerly.
   OSR. It is indifferent° cold, my lord, indeed.   100
   HAML. But yet methinks it is very sultry and hot,
for my complexion ——
   OSR. Exceedingly, my lord. It is very sultry, as
'twere — I cannot tell how. But, my lord, His Majes-

ty bade me signify to you that he has laid a great
wager on your head. Sir, this is the matter ——
   HAML. I beseech you, remember ——   108
       [HAMLET *moves him to put on his hat.*]
   OSR. Nay, good my lord, for mine ease, in good
faith. Sir, here is newly come to Court Laertes — believe me, an absolute° gentleman, full of most excellent differences,° of very soft society° and great
showing.° Indeed, to speak feelingly° of him, he is
the card or calendar of gentry,° for you shall find in
him the continent of what part a gentleman would
see.°   116
   HAML. Sir,° his definement suffers no perdition in
you, though I know to divide him inventorially
would dizzy the arithmetic of memory, and yet but
yaw neither, in respect of his quick sail. But in   120
the verity of extolment, I take him to be a soul of
great article, and his infusion of such dearth and
rareness as, to make true diction of him, his semblable is his mirror, and who else would trace him,
his umbrage — nothing more.   125
   OSR. Your lordship speaks most infallibly of
him.
   HAML. The concernancy,° sir? Why do we wrap
the gentleman in our more rawer breath?°
   OSR. Sir?°   129
   HOR. Is 't not possible to understand in another
tongue? You will do 't, sir, really.
   HAML. What imports the nomination° of this
gentleman?
   OSR. Of Laertes?   135
   HOR. His purse is empty already, all's golden
words are spent.
   HAML. Of him, sir.
   OSR. I know you are not ignorant ——   139
   HAML. I would you did, sir. Yet, in faith, if you
did, it would not much approve° me. Well, sir?

---

111. **absolute:** perfect. 112. **differences:** qualities peculiar to himself. **soft society:** gentle breeding. 112–13. **great showing:** distinguished appearance. 113. **feelingly:** with proper appreciation.
114. **card . . . gentry:** the very fashion plate of what a gentleman
should be. 115–16. **continent . . . see:** all the parts that should be
in a perfect gentleman. 117–25. **Sir . . . more:** Hamlet retorts in
similar but even more extravagant language. This is too much for
Osric (and for most modern readers). Hamlet's words may be paraphrased: "Sir, the description of this perfect gentleman loses
nothing in your account of him; though I realize that if one
were to try to enumerate his excellences, it would exhaust our
arithmetic, and yet" — here he changes the image to one of sailing — "we should still lag behind him as he outsails us. But in
the true vocabulary of praise, I take him to be a soul of the
greatest worth, and his perfume" — i.e., his personal essence —
"so scarce and rare that to speak truly of him, the only thing
like him is his own reflection in his mirror, and everyone else
who tries to follow him merely his shadow." **yaw:** fall off from
the course laid. **verity . . . extolment:** in true praise. **infusion:**
essence. **semblable:** resemblance. **trace:** follow. **umbrage:** shadow.
127. **concernancy:** i.e., what is all this talk about? 127–28. **Why
. . . breath:** why do we discuss the gentleman with our inadequate voices? 129. **Sir:** Osric is completely baffled. 133. **nomi-
nation:** naming. 141. **approve:** commend.

66. **angle:** fishing rod and line. **proper:** own. 67. **cozenage:** cheating. 68. **quit:** pay back. 69. **canker:** maggot. See I.iii.39. 73. **interim:** interval; between now and the news from England.
79. **bravery:** excessive show. 80 s.d., **Osric:** Osric is a specimen
of the fashionable, effeminate courtier. He dresses prettily and
talks the jargon of his class, which at this time affected elaborate
and allusive metaphors and at all costs avoided saying plain things
plainly. 83. **water fly:** a useless little creature that flits about.
85. **Thy . . . gracious:** you are in the better state. 88–89. **Let . . .
mess:** i.e., any man, however low, who has wealth enough will
find a good place at Court. **crib:** manger. **mess:** table.
89. **chough:** jackdaw. 90. **spacious:** wealthy. 95. **Put . . .
use:** i.e., put your hat on your head. Osric is so nice-mannered
that he cannot bring himself to wear his hat in the presence of
the Prince. 100. **indifferent:** moderately.

OSR. You are not ignorant of what excellence Laertes is —— 144

HAML. I dare not confess that, lest I should compare with him in excellence, but to know a man well were to know himself.

OSR. I mean, sir, for his weapon,° but in the imputation° laid on him by them, in his meed° he's unfellowed.° 150

HAML. What's his weapon?

OSR. Rapier and dagger.

HAML. That's two of his weapons, but, well.

OSR. The King, sir, hath wagered with him six Barbary horses, against the which he has imponed,° as I take it, six French rapiers and poniards, with their assigns,° as girdle, hanger,° and so —three of the carriages, in faith, are very dear to fancy,° very responsive to° the hilts, most delicate carriages, and of very liberal conceit.° 160

HAML. What call you the carriages?

HOR. I knew you must be edified by the margent° ere you had done.

OSR. The carriages, sir, are the hangers. 164

HAML. The phrase would be more germane° to the matter if we could carry a cannon by our sides. I would it might be hangers till then. But, on — six Barbary horses against six French swords, their assigns, and three liberal-conceited carriages. That's the French bet against the Danish. Why is this " imponed," as you call it? 171

OSR. The King, sir, hath laid, sir, that in a dozen passes between yourself and him, he shall not exceed you three hits. He hath laid on twelve for nine,° and it would come to immediate trial if your lordship would vouchsafe the answer.

HAML. How if I answer no? 177

OSR. I mean, my lord, the opposition of your person in trial.

HAML. Sir, I will walk here in the hall. If it please His Majesty, it is the breathing-time of day with me.° Let the foils be brought, the gentleman willing, and the King hold his purpose, I will win for him an I can. If not, I will gain nothing but my shame and the odd hits. 185

OSR. Shall I redeliver you e'en so?

HAML. To this effect, sir, after what flourish° your nature will.

OSR. I commend my duty to your lordship. 189

HAML. Yours, yours. [*Exit* OSRIC.] He does well to commend it himself, there are no tongues else for 's turn.

HOR. This lapwing° runs away with the shell on his head.

HAML. He did comply with his dug° before he sucked it. Thus has he — and many more of the same breed that I know the drossy° age dotes on — only got the tune of the time and outward habit of encounter,° a kind of yesty collection° which carries them through and through the most fond° and 200 winnowed° opinions — and do but blow them to their trial, the bubbles are out.°

[*Enter a* LORD.]

LORD. My lord, His Majesty commended him to you by young Osric, who brings back to him that you attend him in the hall. He sends to know if your pleasure hold to play with Laertes, or that you will take longer time. 207

HAML. I am constant to my purposes, they follow the King's pleasure. If his fitness speaks, mine is ready, now or whensoever, provided I be so able as now. 211

LORD. The King and Queen and all are coming down.

HAML. In happy time.°

LORD. The Queen desires you to use some gentle entertainment° to Laertes before you fall to play.

HAML. She well instructs me.   [*Exit* LORD.]

HOR. You will lose this wager, my lord. 219

HAML. I do not think so. Since he went into France I have been in continual practice, I shall win at the odds. But thou wouldst not think how ill all's here about my heart — but it is no matter.

HOR. Nay, good my lord —— 224

HAML It is but foolery, but it is such a kind of gaingiving° as would perhaps trouble a woman.

HOR. If your mind dislike anything, obey it. I will forestall their repair hither and say you are not fit.

HAML. Not a whit, we defy augury.° There's 230 special providence in the fall of a sparrow.° If it be now, 'tis not to come; if it be not to come, it will be now; if it be not now, yet it will come. The read-

148. his weapon: i.e., skill with his weapon.   149. imputation: reputation. meed: merit.   150. unfellowed: without an equal. 156. imponed: laid down as a stake.   157. assigns: that which goes with them. hanger: straps by which the scabbard was hung from the belt.   158–59. dear to fancy: of beautiful design. 159. responsive to: matching.   160. liberal conceit: elaborately artistic.   162. edified ... margent: informed by the notes. In Shakespeare's time the notes were often printed in the margin. 165. germane: related.   174–75. twelve ... nine: the bet is that Laertes will score twelve hits before Hamlet scores nine. 181–82. breathing-time ... me: time when I take exercise. 187. flourish: fanfare, elaborate phrasing.

193. lapwing: a little bird so lively that it can run about the moment it is hatched.   195. did ... dug: was ceremonious with the nipple; i.e., behaved in this fantastic way from his infancy. See II.ii.389.   197. drossy: scummy, frivolous. 198–99. tune ... encounter: i.e., they sing the same tune as everyone else and have the same society manners.   199. yesty collection: frothy catchwords.   200. fond: foolish.   201. winnowed: light as chaff. Winnowing is the process of fanning the chaff from the grain.   201–02. do ... out: force them to make sense of their words and they are deflated, as Hamlet has just deflated Osric.   214. In ... time: at a good moment.   215–16. gentle entertainment: kindly treatment; i.e., be reconciled after the brawl in the churchyard.   226. gaingiving: misgiving.   230. augury: omens.   231. special ... sparrow: The idea comes from Matthew 10:29. "Are not two sparrows sold for a farthing? and one of them shall not fall to the ground without your Father."

iness is all. Since no man has aught of what he leaves,
what is 't to leave betimes? Let be.   235
[*Enter* KING, QUEEN, LAERTES, *and* LORDS, OSRIC *and
other* ATTENDANTS *with foils; a table and flagons of
wine on it.*]
     KING. Come, Hamlet, come, and take this hand
     from me.
        [*The* KING *puts* LAERTES' *hand into* HAMLET'S.]
   HAML. Give me your pardon, sir. I've done you
     wrong,
But pardon 't, as you are a gentleman.
This presence° knows,
And you must needs have heard, how I am pun-
     ished   240
With sore distraction. What I have done
That might your nature, honor, and exception°
Roughly awake, I here proclaim was madness.
Was 't Hamlet wronged Laertes? Never Hamlet.
If Hamlet from himself be ta'en away,°   245
And when he's not himself does wrong Laertes,
Then Hamlet does it not, Hamlet denies it.
Who does it, then? His madness. If 't be so,
Hamlet is of the faction that is wronged,
His madness is poor Hamlet's enemy.   250
Sir, in this audience
Let my disclaiming from a purposed evil°
Free me so far in your most generous thoughts
That I have shot mine arrow o'er the house,
And hurt my brother.
    LAER.   I am satisfied in nature,   255
Whose motive, in this case, should stir me most
To my revenge. But in my terms of honor
I stand aloof, and will no reconcilement
Till by some elder masters of known honor
I have a voice and precedent of peace   260
To keep my name ungored.° But till that time
I do receive your offered love like love
And will not wrong it.
    HAML.   I embrace it freely,
And will this brother's wager frankly play.
Give us the foils. Come on.
    LAER.   Come, one for me.   265
   HAML. I'll be your foil,° Laertes. In mine ignor-
    ance
Your skill shall, like a star i' the darkest night,
Stick° fiery off indeed.
    LAER.   You mock me, sir.
   HAML. No, by this hand.

KING. Give them the foils, young Osric. Cousin
   Hamlet,   270
You know the wager?
   HAML.   Very well, my lord.
Your Grace has laid the odds o' the weaker side.
   KING. I do not fear it, I have seen you both.
But since he is bettered,° we have therefore odds.
   LAER. This is too heavy, let me see another.   275
   HAML. This likes° me well. These foils have all a
length?°   [*They prepare to play.*]
   OSR. Aye, my good lord.
   KING. Set me the stoups° of wine upon that table.
If Hamlet give the first or second hit,
Or quit° in answer of the third exchange,   280
Let all the battlements their ordnance fire.
The King shall drink to Hamlet's better breath,
And in the cup a union° shall he throw
Richer than that which four successive kings   284
In Denmark's crown have worn. Give me the cups,
And let the kettle° to the trumpet speak,
The trumpet to the cannoneer without,
The cannon to the Heavens, the Heaven to earth,
" Now the King drinks to Hamlet." Come, begin,
And you, the judges, bear a wary eye.   290
   HAML. Come on, sir.
   LAER.   Come, my lord.   [*They play.*]
   HAML.   One.
   LAER.   No.
   HAML.   Judgment.
   OSR. A hit, a very palpable° hit.
   LAER.   Well, again.
   KING. Stay, give me drink. Hamlet, this pearl is
   thine° —
Here's to thy health.
     [*Trumpets sound, and cannon shot off within.*]
              Give him the cup.   294
   HAML. I'll play this bout first. Set it by a while.
Come. [*They play.*] Another hit, what say you?
   LAER. A touch, a touch, I do confess.
   KING. Our son shall win.
   QUEEN.   He's fat° and scant of breath.
Here, Hamlet, take my napkin, rub thy brows.
The Queen carouses to thy fortune, Hamlet.   300
   HAML. Good madam!
   KING.   Gertrude, do not drink.
   QUEEN. I will, my lord, I pray you pardon me.
                  [*She drinks.*]
   KING. [*Aside*] It is the poisoned cup, it is too late.
   HAML. I dare not drink yet, madam — by and by.
   QUEEN. Come, let me wipe thy face.   305
   LAER. My lord, I'll hit him now.

---

239. presence: the whole Court.   **242. exception:** resentment.
245. If . . . away: i.e., Hamlet mad is not Hamlet.   **252. Let . . .
evil:** let my declaration that I did not intend any harm.
255–61. I . . . ungored: I bear you no grudge so far as concerns
my personal feelings, which would most readily move me to vengeance; but as this matter touches my honor, I cannot accept
your apology until I have been assured by those expert in matters
of honor that I may so do without loss of reputation.   **266. foil:**
Hamlet puns on the other meaning of foil — tin foil set behind
a gem to give it luster.   **268. Stick . . . off:** Shine out.

274. bettered: considered your superior.   **276. likes:** pleases.
have . . . length: are all of equal length.   **278. stoups:** drinking-
vessels.   **280. quit:** strike back.   **283. union:** a large pearl.
286. kettle: kettledrum.   **292. palpable:** clear.   **293. this . . .
thine:** With these words the King drops the poisoned pearl
into the cup intended for Hamlet.   **298. fat:** out of condition.

KING.   I do not think 't.
LAER. [*Aside*] And yet 'tis almost against my
   conscience.
HAML. Come, for the third, Laertes. You but
   dally.°
I pray you pass with your best violence,
I am afeard you make a wanton of me.°   310
   LAER. Say you so? Come on.   [*They play.*]
   OSR. Nothing, neither way.
   LAER. Have at you now!
   [LAERTES *wounds* HAMLET; *then, in scuffling, they*
      change rapiers,° *and* HAMLET *wounds* LAERTES.]
   KING.   Part them, they are incensed.
   HAML. Nay, come, again.   [*The* QUEEN *falls.*]
   OSR.   Look to the Queen there, ho!
   HOR. They bleed on both sides. How is it, my
      lord?   315
   OSR. How is 't, Laertes?
   LAER. Why, as a woodcock to mine own springe,°
      Osric,
I am justly killed with mine own treachery.
   HAML. How does the Queen?
   KING.   She swounds to see them bleed.
   QUEEN. No, no, the drink, the drink! — O my dear
      Hamlet —   320
The drink, the drink! I am poisoned.   [*Dies.*]
   HAML. Oh, villainy! Ho! Let the door be locked.
Treachery! Seek it out.   [LAERTES *falls.*]
   LAER. It is here, Hamlet. Hamlet, thou art slain.
No medicine in the world can do thee good,   325
In thee there is not half an hour of life.
The treacherous instrument is in thy hand,
Unbated and envenomed. The foul practice
Hath turned itself on me. Lo, here I lie
Never to rise again. Thy mother's poisoned.   330
I can no more. The King, the King's to blame.
   HAML. The point envenomed too!
Then, venom, to thy work.   [*Stabs the* KING.]
   ALL. Treason! Treason!   334
   KING. Oh, yet defend me, friends, I am but hurt.
   HAML. Here, thou incestuous, murderous,
      damnèd Dane,
Drink off this potion. Is thy union° here?
Follow my mother.   [KING *dies.*]
   LAER.   He is justly served.
It is a poison tempered° by himself.
Exchange forgiveness with me, noble Hamlet.   340
Mine and my father's death come not upon thee,°
Nor thine on me!   [*Dies.*]
   HAML. Heaven make thee free of it!° I follow
      thee.
I am dead, Horatio. Wretched Queen, adieu!

You that look pale and tremble at this chance, 345
That are but mutes or audience to this act,
Had I but time — as this fell° sergeant,° Death,
Is strict in his arrest — oh, I could tell you ——
But let it be. Horatio, I am dead,
Thou livest. Report me and my cause aright   350
To the unsatisfied.°
   HOR.   Never believe it.
I am more an antique Roman° than a Dane.
Here's yet some liquor left.
   HAML.   As thou 'rt a man,
Give me the cup. Let go — by Heaven, I'll have 't.
O good Horatio, what a wounded name,   355
Things standing thus unknown, shall live behind
   me!
If thou didst ever hold me in thy heart,
Absent thee from felicity a while,
And in this harsh world draw thy breath in pain
To tell my story. [*March afar off, and shot within*]
               What warlike noise is this?   360
   OSR. Young Fortinbras, with conquest come from
      Poland,
To the ambassadors of England gives
This warlike volley.
   HAML.   Oh, I die, Horatio,
The potent poison quite o'ercrows° my spirit.
I cannot live to hear the news from England,   365
But I do prophesy the election° lights
On Fortinbras. He has my dying voice.°
So tell him, with the occurrents, more and less,
Which have solicited.° The rest is silence. [*Dies.*]
   HOR. Now cracks a noble heart. Good night,
      sweet Prince,   370
And flights of angels sing thee to thy rest!
                           [*March within.*]
Why does the drum come hither?
   [*Enter* FORTINBRAS, *and the* ENGLISH AMBASSADORS,
      with drum, colors, and ATTENDANTS.]
   FOR. Where is this sight?
   HOR.   What is it you would see?
If aught of woe or wonder, cease your search. 374
   FOR. This quarry cries on havoc.° O proud Death,
What feast is toward° in thine eternal cell
That thou so many princes at a shot
So bloodily hast struck?
   I. AMB.   The sight is dismal,
And our affairs from England come too late.   379
The ears are senseless that should give us hearing,

---

347. **fell**: dread. **sergeant**: the officer of the Court who made
arrests.   351. **unsatisfied**: who do not know the truth.
352. **antique Roman**: like Cato and Brutus, who killed themselves
rather than survive in a world which was unpleasing to them.
364. **o'ercrows**: overpowers.   366. **election**: as King of Denmark. See l. 65 above.   367. **voice**: support.   368-69. **occurrents ... solicited**: events great and small which have caused
me to act.   375. **quarry ... havoc**: heap of slain denotes a
pitiless slaughter.   376. **toward**: being prepared.

---

308. **dally**: play.   310. **make ... me**: treat me like a child by
letting me win.   317. **springe**: snare.   337. **union**: pearl, as
in l. 283.   339. **tempered**: mixed.   341. **come ... thee**: are not
on your head.   343. **Heaven ... it**: may God forgive you for it.

To tell him his commandment is fulfilled,
That Rosencrantz and Guildenstern are dead.
Where should we have our thanks?
   HOR.   Not from his mouth
Had it the ability of life to thank you.
He never gave commandment for their death.   385
But since, so jump° upon this bloody question,°
You from the Polack wars, and you from England,
Are here arrived, give order that these bodies
High on a stage be placèd to the view,
And let me speak to the yet unknowing world   390
How these things came about. So shall you hear
Of carnal, bloody, and unnatural acts,
Of accidental judgments, casual slaughters,
Of deaths put on by cunning and forced cause,
And, in this upshot, purposes mistook   395
Fall'n on the inventors' heads.° All this can I
Truly deliver.
   FOR.   Let us haste to hear it,
And call the noblest to the audience.
For me, with sorrow I embrace my fortune.   399

I have some rights of memory° in this kingdom,
Which now to claim my vantage° doth invite me.
   HOR.   Of that I shall have also cause to speak,
And from his mouth whose voice will draw on
   more.°
But let this same be presently performed,
Even while men's minds are wild, lest more mis-
   chance   405
On plots and errors happen.
   FOR.   Let four captains
Bear Hamlet, like a soldier, to the stage.
For he was likely, had he been put on,°
To have proved most royally. And for his passage
The soldiers' music and the rites of war   410
Speak loudly for him.
Take up the bodies. Such a sight as this
Becomes the field, but here shows much amiss.
Go, bid the soldiers shoot.
   [A dead march. Exeunt, bearing off the bodies;
       after which a peal of ordnance is shot off.]

---

386. **jump**: exactly. See I.i.65. **question**: matter. **392–96. carnal ... heads**: These lines sum up the whole tragedy: Claudius' adultery with Gertrude, his murder of his brother, the death of Ophelia due to an accident, that of Polonius by casual chance, Hamlet's device which caused the deaths of Rosencrantz and Guildenstern, the plan which went awry and caused the deaths of Claudius and Laertes.

400. **rights of memory**: rights which will be remembered; i.e., with the disappearance of all the family of the original King Hamlet the situation reverts to what it was before the death of Fortinbras' father. See I.i.80–95.   401. **vantage**: i.e., my advantage, there being none to dispute my claim.   403. **voice ... more**: i.e., Hamlet's dying voice will strengthen your claim.   408. **had ... on**: had he become King.

THE SONNETS

Shakespeare's sonnets are the most discussed and disputed of all collections of poetry in the English language. They first appeared in a small collection, entitled

SHAKE-SPEARES
SONNETS

Neuer before Imprinted.

AT LONDON

By *G. Eld for T. T.* and are
to be solde by *Iohn Wright,* dwelling
at Christ Church gate.
1609.

T. T. (or Thomas Thorpe) dedicated the book TO. THE. ONLIE. BEGETTER. OF. THESE. INSVING. SONNETS. Mr W. H.

There are 154 sonnets in Thorpe's collection, which fall into three groups and tell a kind of fragmentary story. Sonnets 1–17 are addressed to a young man, exhorting him to marry and preserve his beauty in his children. In the second section (18–126) the poet writes to the young man on a variety of topics and in different moods. At first he is shy in the presence of his friend, who is of superior rank. Admiration ripens to love. The poet is an outcast but is comforted by the thought of his love. He warns his friend not to honor him publicly lest he become tainted by scandal. He carries the picture of his friend when traveling on a journey. He grows jealous of another poet, who is seeking the young man's patronage. The young man steals the poet's mistress, and is rebuked for wantonness. He is congratulated on his escape from a "confined doom." There is a separation and a reconciliation. The poet is disgusted by his profession. He defends himself against a charge of ingratitude.

The third series (127–152) is written to a dark woman whom the poet loves and loathes passionately. She is a skillful musician, faithless, unattractive, false to her husband — and yet irresistible. Finally there are two concluding sonnets to Cupid.

Shakespeare's sonnets are written with such an obvious sense of intimacy that it is hard to believe that they are merely poetic exercises; and naturally there have been many attempts to identify "Mr W. H.," the young man, and the dark woman. Unfortunately there are no certain clues, and even those sonnets which seem to point to some particular persons or events are interpreted in quite different ways. Thus Sonnet 107, known as the "Dating Sonnet," obviously refers to certain national events and to some incident in the young man's life; but it has been taken to refer to quite different events which occurred in 1588, 1592, 1596, and 1603! "Sonnet Identification" is a fascinating game, but it belongs to literary detection and not to the study of literature. The serious student does well to ignore it.

As a form, the sonnet was very popular in the sixteenth century and again in the nineteenth. It was first introduced into English through the translations from the Italian of Wyatt and Surrey in the 1530's. Many sonnets were being written in the 1580's, but the sudden popularity of the form was largely due to the publication of Sir Philip Sidney's sonnet sequence known as *Astrophel and Stella* in the spring of 1591. Sidney had then been dead for five years but contemporaries had such veneration for his memory that anything he wrote was eagerly read. *Astrophel and Stella* told of the hopeless love of Sidney for the Lady Penelope Rich and was so personal and sincere that it revealed to English poets possibilities and depths not hitherto realized. In the years following several poets also printed their sonnets, the most important being Michael Drayton's *Idea* and Edmund Spenser's *Amoretti.* It is likely therefore that Shakespeare's sonnets were also written during the vogue, which lasted only for about seven years.

A sonnet is normally a poem of fourteen lines, each carrying five stresses — the meter sometimes called "iambic pentameter." There are two principal forms — the "Petrarchan" and the "Shakespearean." In the Petrarchan, the sonnet is divided into octet (8 lines) and sestet (6 lines). Each section has its own rhyme scheme, though it is usual to have only two rhymes in the octet. English examples of the form will be found in Milton's "How Soon Hath Time" (see p. 215), Wordsworth's "Composed upon Westminster Bridge" (see p. 584), and Keats's "Keen, Fitful Gusts" (see p. 738).

The Shakespearean form, which was not invented by Shakespeare and was in use long before his time, consists of three quatrains with alternate rhymes, followed by a final rhymed couplet.

The sonnet is admirable for saying something short, pretty, effective, or complimentary, but is one of the most difficult forms for sublime utterance, for its rigid and formal pattern can be too cramping. Moreover, Shakespeare chose the more difficult pattern. When successful, the sonnet expresses a single thought, expanded in the quatrains and neatly concluded in the last word of the final couplet; but too often the couplet is a lame conclusion to a twelve-line poem. Nevertheless, in the best of the sonnets Shakespeare displays his own particular gifts. The imagery is fresh and vivid, collected from direct experience and observation and not from examples in a manual of poetics. The thoughts may be old and familiar but never before have they been so well expressed.

An appeal to the young man to marry and beget children.

2

When forty winters shall besiege thy brow
And dig deep trenches in thy beauty's field,
Thy youth's proud livery, so gazed on now,
Will be a tattered weed,° of small worth held.
Then being asked where all thy beauty lies,   5
Where all the treasure of thy lusty days,

Sonnet 2: 4. tattered weed: ragged garment.

To say within thine own deep-sunken eyes
Were an all-eating° shame and thriftless° praise.
How much more praise deserved thy beauty's use
If thou couldst answer, "This fair child of mine 10
Shall sum my count° and make my old excuse,"°
Proving his beauty by succession° thine!
    This were to be new-made when thou art old,
    And see thy blood warm when thou feel'st it cold.

On the young man's beauty, perpetuated in verse.

18

Shall I compare thee to a summer's day?
Thou art more lovely and more temperate.
Rough winds do shake the darling buds of May,
And summer's lease hath all too short a date.
Sometime too hot the eye of heaven° shines,   5
And often is his gold complexion dimmed.
And every fair from fair sometime declines,
By chance or nature's changing course untrimmed.°
But thy eternal summer shall not fade,
Nor lose possession of that fair thou owest,°   10
Nor shall Death brag thou wander'st in his shade
When in eternal lines to time thou grow'st.
    So long as men can breathe, or eyes can see,
    So long lives this, and this gives life to thee.°

33

Full many a glorious morning have I seen
Flatter the mountaintops with sovereign° eye,
Kissing with golden face the meadows green,
Gilding pale streams with heavenly alchemy,°
Anon permit the basest clouds to ride   5
With ugly rack° on his celestial face
And from the forlorn world his visage hide,
Stealing unseen to west with this disgrace.
Even so my sun one early morn did shine
With all-triumphant splendor on my brow.   10
But out, alack! he was but one hour mine,
The region° cloud hath masked him from me now.
    Yet him for this my love no whit disdaineth.
    Suns of the world may stain when heaven's sun
      staineth.

The thought of this sonnet is to be found in most collections: "Everything decays, but you will live forever

in my verse; your memory will last longer than the costly tombs of the mighty or the simple gravestones of the humble."

55

Not marble, nor the gilded monuments
Of princes, shall outlive this powerful rhyme.
But you shall shine more bright in these contents
Than unswept stone,° besmeared with sluttish time.
When wasteful war shall statues overturn,   5
And broils root out the work of masonry,
Nor Mars his sword nor war's quick fire shall burn
The living record of your memory.
'Gainst death and all-oblivious enmity
Shall you pace forth. Your praise shall still find
    room
Even in the eyes of all posterity   11
That wear this world out to the ending doom.
    So, till the judgment° that° yourself arise,
    You live in this, and dwell in lovers' eyes.

This catalog of the social evils that make a man long for death is a good example of Shakespeare's power of turning abstract ideas into vivid human persons.

66

Tired with all these, for restful death I cry,
As, to behold desert a beggar born,°
And needy nothing trimmed in jollity,°
And purest faith unhappily forsworn,
And gilded honor shamefully misplaced,   5
And maiden virtue rudely strumpeted,
And right perfection wrongfully disgraced,
And strength by limping sway disabled,°
And art made tongue-tied by authority,°
And folly, doctorlike,° controlling skill,   10
And simple truth miscalled simplicity,°
And captive good attending captain ill.
    Tired with all these, from these would I be gone,
    Save that, to die I leave my love alone.

I grow old and my end is nearing. The idea of human decay is worked out in three images—an avenue of trees, leafless in the fall of the year; daylight passing into darkness; and a fire dying down into ashes.

73

That time of year thou mayst in me behold
When yellow leaves, or none, or few, do hang

---

8. **all-eating:** devouring. **thriftless:** unprofitable. **11. sum my count:** balance my account with Nature. **old excuse:** justification in old age. **12. succession:** right of succession as your natural heir.
    Sonnet 18: 5. eye of heaven: the sun. **8. untrimmed:** shorn of beauty. **10. fair . . . owest:** beauty you possess. **13-14. So . . . thee:** This sentiment — that the poet is giving immortality to his subject — is a commonplace with sonneteers.
    Sonnet 33: 2. sovereign: supreme, glorious. **4. alchemy:** transmutation of base metal to gold. **6. rack:** mass of clouds. **12. region:** of the air.

    Sonnet 55: 4. unswept stone: the dusty inscribed slab over a grave on the floor in a church. **13. judgment . . . arise:** until you rise again at the Day of Judgment. **that:** when.
    Sonnet 66: 2. desert . . . born: i.e., the deserving man handicapped by being born poor. **3. needy . . . jollity:** i.e., the beggar born clad in gay clothes. **8. strength . . . disabled:** the strong man put down by a puny, lame official. **9. art . . . authority:** the intelligent man silenced by his social superior. **10. doctorlike:** with the airs of a profound scholar. **11. simplicity:** stupidity.

Upon those boughs which shake against the cold,
Bare ruined choirs° where late the sweet birds sang.
In me thou see'st the twilight of such day   5
As after sunset fadeth in the west,
Which by and by black night doth take away,
Death's second self, that seals up° all in rest.
In me thou see'st the glowing of such fire,
That on the ashes of his youth doth lie   10
As the deathbed whereon it must expire,
Consumed with that which it was nourished by.
  This thou perceivest, which makes thy love more
    strong,
  To love that well which thou must leave ere long.

One of the "Rival Poet" sonnets. There are various
candidates for the rival poet, the most popular being
George Chapman and Christopher Marlowe.

86

Was it the proud full sail of his great verse,
Bound for the prize of all too precious you,
That did my ripe thoughts in my brain inhearse,°
Making their tomb the womb wherein they grew?
Was it his spirit, by spirits taught to write   5
Above a mortal pitch,° that struck me dead?
No, neither he, nor his compeers by night°
Giving him aid, my verse astonishèd.°
He, nor that affable familiar ghost°
Which nightly gulls him with intelligence,°   10
As victors, of my silence cannot boast.
I was not sick of any fear from thence.
  But when your countenance filled up his line,°
  Then lacked I matter. That enfeebled mine.

The praises of beauties dead and gone were but feeble
foreshadowings of your beauty, which is beyond praise.

106

When in the chronicle of wasted° time
I see descriptions of the fairest wights,°
And beauty making beautiful old rhyme
In praise of ladies dead and lovely knights,
Then, in the blazon° of sweet beauty's best,   5
Of hand, of foot, of lip, of eye, of brow,
I see their antique pen would have expressed
Even such a beauty as you master now.

So all their praises are but prophecies
Of this our time, all you prefiguring,   10
And, for° they looked but with divining° eyes,
They had not skill enough your worth to sing.
  For we, which now behold these present days,
  Have eyes to wonder, but lack tongues to praise.

The "Dating Sonnet," variously interpreted. The
gloomy prophecies of what would happen when the
moon was eclipsed have been falsified, for peace has
followed.

107

Not mine own fears, nor the prophetic soul
Of the wide world dreaming on things to come,
Can yet the lease of my true love control,
Supposed as forfeit to a cónfined doom.°
The mortal moon hath her eclipse endured,°   5
And the sad augurs° mock their own presage.
Incertainties now crown themselves assured,
And peace proclaims olives° of endless age.
Now with the drops of this most balmy time
My love looks fresh, and Death to me subscribes,°
Since, spite of him, I'll live in this poor rhyme   11
While he insults° o'er dull and speechless° tribes.
  And thou in this shalt find thy monument,
  When tyrants' crests and tombs of brass are spent.

116

Let me not to the marriage of true minds
Admit impediments.° Love is not love
Which alters when it alteration finds,
Or bends with the remover to remove.°
Oh no! It is an ever-fixèd mark°   5
That looks on tempests and is never shaken.
It is the star to every wandering bark,
Whose worth's unknown, although his height be
    taken.°
Love's not Time's fool,° though rosy lips and cheeks
Within his bending sickle's compass come.   10
Love alters not with his brief hours and weeks,
But bears it out even to the edge of doom.°

11. for: except that. **divining:** foreseeing.
    Sonnet 107: 4. Supposed . . . doom: if the *lease* is forfeit, the
meaning of the quatrain is "those who declared that our love
was ended have proved bad prophets." If *love* (i.e., my friend)
is forfeit, the line means "believed to be condemned to imprisonment." **5. The . . . endured:** The mortal moon is Queen Elizabeth, but it is disputable whether the line means "has passed
through an eclipse and emerged safely" or has been permanently
eclipsed; i.e., has died. The Queen died on March 24, 1603.
6. sad augurs: i.e., those who prophesied disaster. **8. olives:**
The olive is the symbol of peace. **10. subscribes:** yields.
12. insults: triumphs. **speechless:** who cannot express themselves.
    Sonnet 116: 2. impediments: a legal word for causes which
invalidate a marriage. **4. Or . . . remove:** or wishes to change
when the loved one is inconstant. **5. ever-fixed mark:** sea
mark — a conspicuous object (such as a tower or hill) by which
seamen check their course. **8. height be taken:** i.e., in reckoning a ship's position by the stars. **9. Love's . . . fool:** i.e.,
mocked by Time, who is symbolized as a reaper with a sickle.
12. edge of doom: doomsday, the end of the world.

Sonnet 73: 4. choirs: that part of a cathedral or large church
in which the services are conducted. The image was suggested
by the roofless choir of a ruined abbey, which resembles a leafless avenue of tall trees. **8. seals up:** concludes.
    Sonnet 86: 3. inhearse: entomb, bury. **6. mortal pitch:**
natural height. **7. compeers by night:** deep fellow scholars.
8. astonished: surprised, subdued. **9. ghost:** spirit. **10. gulls
. . . intelligence:** cheats him with news. **13. your . . . line:**
when your face inspired his verse.
    Sonnet 106: 1. wasted: passed, dead and gone. **2. wights:**
men, a poetic word. **5. blazon:** praise; lit., heraldic description
of a coat of arms.

If this be error and upon me proved,
I never writ, nor no man ever loved.

One of the bitterest sonnets to the dark woman—the
disillusion and remorse that follow the enjoyment of
lust.

129

The expense of spirit in a waste of shame
Is lust in action, and till action, lust
Is perjured, murderous, bloody, full of blame,
Savage, extreme, rude, cruel, not to trust,
Enjoyed no sooner but despisèd straight,   5
Past reason hunted, and no sooner had,
Past reason hated, as a swallowed bait,
On purpose laid to make the taker mad.
Mad in pursuit, and in possession so,
Had, having, and in quest to have, extreme,   10
A bliss in proof, and proved,° a very woe.
Before, a joy proposed, behind, a dream.
    All this the world well knows, yet none knows
        well
    To shun the Heaven that leads men to this Hell.

A mocking parody of the common conventions of
sonneteers praising the divine beauty of their mistresses.

130

My mistress' eyes are nothing like the sun,
Coral is far more red than her lips' red.

Sonnet 129: 11. proved: experienced.

If snow be white, why then her breasts are dun,
If hairs be wires, black wires grow on her head.
I have seen roses damasked,° red and white,   5
But no such roses see I in her cheeks.
And in some perfumes is there more delight
Than in the breath that from my mistress reeks.
I love to hear her speak, yet well I know
That music hath a far more pleasing sound.   10
I grant I never saw a goddess go,°
My mistress, when she walks, treads on the ground.
    And yet, by Heaven, I think my love as rare
    As any she belied with false compare.

143

Lo, as a careful housewife runs to catch
One of her feathered creatures broke away,
Sets down her babe, and makes all swift dispatch
In pursuit of the thing she would have stay
Whilst her neglected child holds her in chase,   5
Cries to catch her whose busy care is bent
To follow that which flies before her face,
Not prizing her poor infant's discontent —
So runn'st thou after that which flies from thee
Whilst I thy babe chase thee afar behind.   10
But if thou catch thy hope, turn back to me,
And play the mother's part, kiss me, be kind.
    So will I pray that thou mayst have thy "Will,"
    If thou turn back and my loud crying still.

Sonnet 130: 5. damasked: variegated pink and white.
11. go: walk.

BASIL WILLEY, *Editor*

Francis Bacon

1561–1626

FRANCIS BACON called himself "the trumpeter of the new age" (*buccinator novi temporis*), and it is as the herald of the modern or Faustian era of Western civilization that he still impresses us. For over three centuries he has remained a symbolical figure, revered throughout Europe as the prophet of science and as a modern Solomon — even if, like his prototype, he combined universal wisdom with certain flaws of character. Shelley classed him among the "poets" in virtue of his prophetic insight, and all down the nineteenth century the chorus of praise went on, tempered only by regrets that such a man could be both "the wisest *and* the meanest of mankind," combining intellectual pre-eminence with corruption and the betrayal of his friend Essex. An examination of the facts of his career tends, I think, to blunt the edges of Pope's epigram, and to show Bacon as neither the wisest nor the meanest, but certainly one of the most distinguished of mankind.

Bacon was born in January, 1561, at York House, Strand, the London residence of his father, Sir Nicholas Bacon, Lord Keeper of the Great Seal. Through his mother (Anne Cooke) he was related to one of the greatest Elizabethan families, for her sister was the wife of William Cecil, Lord Burghley. Next to nothing is known of his early boyhood, except that he seems to have divided his time between London and Gorhambury, his father's stately seat in Hertfordshire, to which Queen Elizabeth paid more than one visit.

His entry to Trinity College, Cambridge, at the age of twelve need not indicate any special precocity (the age of admission was then often absurdly low by our standards), though Rawley[1] records that the queen used to enjoy questioning the boy, and hearing his replies delivered "with that gravity and maturity above his years, that Her Majesty would often term him 'the young Lord Keeper.'" His precocity appears far more strikingly (if we may believe Rawley) in his alleged judgment on the Cambridge curriculum, for it contains already the essence of his contribution to modern thought:

Whilst he was commorant [living] at the University, about sixteen years of age (as his lordship hath been pleased to impart unto myself), he first fell into the dislike of the philosophy of Aristotle; not for the worthlessness of the author, to whom he would ever ascribe all high attributes, but for the unfruitfulness of the way; being a philosophy . . . only strong for disputations and contentions, but barren of the production of works for the benefit of the life of man. . . .

His father planned for him a career of diplomacy or politics, and, after entering him for legal training at Gray's Inn (1570), sent him to Paris with Sir Amyas Paulet, the new ambassador to France. Two years later Sir Nicholas Bacon died, and the young Francis, now and for long afterward thrown upon his own resources, took up residence at Gray's Inn to train as a barrister. Ambitious by nature, and conscious of his great gifts, he now began a long struggle for advance-

---

[1] William Rawley (1588?–1667), Bacon's chaplain and first biographer. After Bacon's death Rawley edited his unpublished writings and translated his English works into Latin.

ment. It was an uphill fight lasting over twenty years, in the course of which he acquired that knowledge of men and affairs which appears in the *Essays*. He tried unsuccessfully to secure the patronage of his powerful uncle Lord Burghley, but the Cecils were perhaps jealous of their clever "poor relation" (by marriage). Soon after being called to the bar (1582), he entered parliament as M.P. for Melcombe Regis, and long remained a prominent House of Commons man, serving on many important committees. His influence was always exerted on the side of moderation: the *via media* between royal prerogative and parliamentary privilege, and unity through toleration in religion. In his defense of parliamentary privilege, however, he had the misfortune to offend the queen, and this for many years stood in the way of his advancement — the Cecils meanwhile fanning the flame of her resentment.

He next attached himself to the ill-fated Earl of Essex, whose importunate zeal on his behalf seems to have annoyed the queen still more. Essex tried, without success, to get him appointed to the Mastership of the Rolls and the office of Attorney General, and finally, in his impulsive friendship, presented him with some land near Twickenham which brought him £1800. It must not be supposed that throughout all this period of intrigue for preferment Bacon had none but wordly ends in view. His was not a simple character. Hungry though he certainly was for wealth and ostentation, he was also a dreamer of dreams and a seer of visions; he had a vast idea to bring to fruition — nothing less than "the knowledge of causes and secret motions of things; and the enlarging of the bounds of human empire, to the effecting of all things possible." In the midst of his poverty and struggle he wrote to Burghley, "I have taken all knowledge for my province." One, at least, of his motives for seeking wealth and honor was to gain leisure for pursuing this great aim. "My mind," he wrote to Elizabeth, "turneth upon other wheels than those of profit." The first fruits of his meditations were given to the world in 1597, when the slender first edition of the *Essays* was published (it contained only ten essays: "Of Studies," "Of Discourse," "Of Ceremonies and Respect," "Of Followers and Friends," "Of Suits" ["Suitors"], "Of Expense," "Of Regiment of Health," "Of Honor

and Reputation," "Of Faction," and "Of Negotiating," all of them enlarged by 1625 into the form in which we now know them). Fine and characteristic as these are, they represent only the more immediate preoccupations of a man of affairs, not Bacon's whole mind in "the wide circuit of its musings."

The disgrace of Essex, following his disastrous campaign in Ireland (1599), involved Bacon in a maze of negotiations too intricate to unfold here. The part he played in the final trial and condemnation of his former friend and patron has left — not quite justly — a slur upon his name. Gardiner [1] the historian said, "That the course Bacon took indicates poverty of moral feeling cannot be denied." Yet it seems clear that in the earlier stages of Essex's downward course, when Bacon did not know the full story of his treasonable plot to seize the queen's person, he consistently tried to restore Essex to favor. Even at the time of his closest intimacy with the Earl, when acknowledging the gift of land at Twickenham, he had with modest dignity reminded him that his first duty was to the sovereign: "My lord, I see I must be your homager and hold land of your gift: but do you know the manner of doing homage in law? Always it is with a saving [reservation] of his faith to the king . . .: and therefore, my lord, I can be no more yours than I was, and it must be with the ancient savings." Later, then, when he discovered the full extent of Essex's treason, was it so blameworthy to carry out this principle of superior loyalty by accepting appointment as one of Essex's minor accusers? We may shrink from the judicial coldness of Bacon's character (it is evident in his *Essays,* especially those on personal relationships), but as a public man he acted with probity, and his contemporaries — even Essex himself — did not censure him.

The accession of James I in 1603 brought no immediate improvement to Bacon's prospects (except a knighthood). Yet it is clear that Bacon had high hopes of benefit from the reign of this learned monarch; to see this it is enough to read the dedication of *The Advancement of Learning,* in which he fulsomely ascribes to James "the power and fortune of a king, and knowl-

---

[1] Samuel Rawson Gardiner (1829–1902), English historian, famous for his lengthy and elaborate histories of England in the seventeenth century (eighteen volumes published over a period of forty years).

edge and illumination of a priest, and the learning and universality of a philosopher." In 1605 he published *The Advancement of Learning,* which he conceived as the first part of his grandiose but never fully completed design, the *Magna Instauratio* (the Great Renewal, or New Foundation). The *Instauratio* was really the name for Bacon's conception of his life's work: laying new and firmer foundations on which science could be securely built. All his philosophical works were, so to speak, fragments of the vast idea which, in its greater part, remained unfulfilled. It would have contained, for example, a survey of the present state of knowledge (realized in the *Advancement*); a method for investigating and interpreting nature (the *Novum Organum*); a huge tabulated list of the phenomena of the universe and of their operations; and an application of the new method to all these phenomena. The *Advancement* was later (1623) published (with important additions) in Latin, then the " universal language " of scholars, so that it might become accessible to learned readers throughout Europe.

Bacon's marriage (1606) at the age of forty-five to Alice Barnham, daughter of a London alderman, appears as only a minor episode in the main drama of his career. This indeed is what one would expect from the writer of the essay " Of Love," in which he says that " the stage is more beholding to love than the life of man," adds that " great spirits and great business do keep out this weak passion," and quotes with approval the saying " that it is impossible to love and to be wise." The wedding itself illustrated one side of Bacon's nature, his passion for display; Carleton [1] reports that " he was clad from top to toe in purple, and hath made himself and his wife such store of fine raiments of cloth of silver and gold that it draws deep into her portion." In the essay " Of Parents and Children " he wrote " the noblest works and foundations have proceeded from childless men, which have sought to express the images of their minds, where those of their bodies have failed "; his own marriage was childless, and there was an estrangement in its later years.

The next ten years saw Bacon rising, first slowly and then with mounting rapidity, to the height of his worldly ambition. He became Solicitor General in 1607, Attorney General in 1613, Lord Keeper in 1617, Lord Chancellor and Baron Verulam in 1618, and Viscount St. Albans in 1621. Meanwhile he produced many writings, of which the best-known are the *De Sapientia Veterum* (Wisdom of the Ancients) (1609), the 1612 enlarged edition of the *Essays,* and his most important philosophical work, the *Novum Organum* (1620), which was the second part (dealing with scientific method) of the *Instauratio.*

Bacon's fall from his pinnacle of glory came with a suddenness unusual even in those days of swift reversals of fortune. It is indeed painfully disturbing to reflect that one so great and so nobly endowed should have been indicted for the sordid offense of taking bribes in the execution of the highest legal office in the country. There was a touch of greatness in his very confession of guilt, but his refusal to defend himself need not prevent his admirers from taking a more lenient view of his behavior. There are palliating considerations, which should not be overlooked. First, one must remember what he himself called the *vitia temporis,* the evil customs of the age; judges did accept gifts in those days. Secondly, he never allowed the gifts to pervert justice; even his accusers admitted that he decided against them in spite of the bribes. " I had no bribe or reward in my eye or thought when I pronounced any sentence or order," he said. Thirdly, gifts received after a case was ended were universally considered to be legitimate. The only fault of which, after close self-examination, he could accuse himself, was that of neglecting to ascertain, when accepting a gift, whether a case were " fully at an end or no." One gets the impression of a luxury-loving man, willing enough to enjoy the full perquisites of office as then understood and condoned, yet essentially incorruptible at heart, and too much preoccupied with his inward life to trouble about observing those punctilios which might have made him safe from his enemies. His own verdict may stand: " I was the justest judge that was in England these fifty years; but it was the justest censure in Parliament that was these two hundred years." His sentence was drastically severe, including an immense fine, imprisonment, and loss of all office. Most of it was soon afterwards remitted, but he never held office again,

[1] Sir Dudley Carleton (1573–1632), afterwards Viscount Dorchester, ambassador at Venice and The Hague. His numerous letters and dispatches are a mine of information on contemporary affairs and personalities.

and spent his few remaining years in retirement. He occupied his leisure in writing his *History of Henry VII* (1622), in the translation of the *Advancement,* in compiling installments of his natural history, and in putting the finishing touches to the final edition of the *Essays* (1625).

The *New Atlantis,* which was first published in 1627, was at one time regarded as a work of Bacon's last years, but it was more probably produced or sketched at least ten years before his death. Bacon had intended to depict here an ideal commonwealth or Utopia, but he got no further than describing (in Rawley's words) " a college instituted for the interpreting of nature and the producing of great and marvelous works for the benefit of men, under the name of Salomon's House." This imaginary college became to some extent a model and inspiration for the foundation of the Royal Society (1662).

The cause of his death has about it more pathos than dignity: it was a chill caught by stuffing a fowl with snow, on a cold spring day, to test its powers of refrigeration. Even in this slightly grotesque experiment there is evidence of a mind careless of outward things, and actively pursuing its own concerns to the last.

II

Bacon stands at the threshold of the seventeenth century as the prophet and chief propagandist of the greatest intellectual revolution of modern times — the scientific movement that changed the traditional world-picture. It was not that he made any of the significant discoveries; that was left to men like Copernicus, Kepler, Galileo, Gilbert, and Harvey. What Bacon did was to seize with fine insight, and proclaim with incomparable literary power, the principles by which alone any scientific advances could be made. Bacon belonged to an age of expansion and exuberant vitality, when unlimited possibilities seemed to be opening up on all sides. The Pillars of Hercules were no longer the boundary of the known world: beyond the Atlantic lay an unexploited America, and beyond the Cape the riches of the gorgeous East. Since the shattering of the medieval cosmography, the very universe had expanded to infinity, and this world, no longer its fixed center, might be but one of innumerable worlds. Marlowe's Faustus spoke for his age when he exclaimed

O what a world of profit and delight
Is promised to the studious artisan!

The vision that had dawned upon Bacon, and that lends excitement to his writings, was a vision of power achieved through knowledge; of nature mastered and controlled in the interests of mankind; of progress and unheard-of glory for humanity. The dreams of the astrologer and the alchemist — dreams of control over fortune and over natural forces — might be realized after all, but only by those who were humble enough to consult Nature herself, not their own imagination or reason: in a word, by the experimental physicist and chemist.

The circumstances of Bacon's age were such that this part of his program necessarily assumed a theological cast. Among the obstacles that blocked the road for the new science were several beliefs or attitudes inherited from the past, of which one of the chief was the idea that natural science was the knowledge forbidden to Adam, its pursuit the re-enactment of the Fall, and its end damnation. This association of science with the Devil and all his works had been vividly expressed in the Faust legend (the first surviving quarto of Marlowe's *Dr. Faustus* was published only the year before the *Advancement*); behind it, too, lay St. Paul's warning against the wisdom of this world and the knowledge that puffeth up (see *Advancement,* I. i. 2 and 3, below). At the very outset, therefore, Bacon had to deal with this fundamental objection. He disposes of it by arguing, first, that God has declared himself to mankind by two kinds of revelation: by Scripture, the book of his word, and by Nature, the book of his works. It is no more impious, then, to study Nature than to read the Bible. The knowledge which caused the Fall was not natural science (symbolized by Adam's naming of the creatures); it was rather that of the Scholastic philosophers themselves: the speculative curiosity that presumes to read the mind of God, and know good and evil, and to make man independent of God. No amount of natural science will harm us, provided it be seasoned with the " corrective spice " of piety or charity; that is to say, it must be directed to " the glory of the Creator and the relief of man's estate." Nor will the study of natural laws (" second causes ") lead to atheism; a little learning may indeed be a dangerous thing, but deeper drafts will bring us back to God, the first of all causes. So long, then, as our knowledge is devoted " to charity, and not to swelling," " to use, and not to ostentation," we cannot be " too well studied . . . in the book of God's works." We must beware, however, not to confuse science and religion; if we do, the result will be a fabulous science on the one hand and a heretical religion on the other. Through Nature we can indeed ascend to God, but we learn there merely of his existence, power, and wisdom; to know his will for us, and how we may be saved, we must turn to revealed religion: " give to faith the things that are faith's."

Among the other hindrances to knowledge that Bacon enumerates are the study of words rather than of things, that is, excessive attention to philology, grammar, and rhetoric and not enough to " weight of matter "; vanity of the matter itself, as in the " subtle, idle, and . . . vermiculate questions " of the Schoolmen; and excessive reverence for antiquity and tradition, leading men to repeat ancient errors from century to century rather than take the trouble of going to Nature for the true answers.

But the deepest sources of error lie within the human mind itself, and it is in his exposure of these " idols " (as he afterwards called them) that Bacon shows his profoundest insight. The mind of man, by its very fabric and constitution, has within it certain radical tendencies to error, which must be recognized and corrected before it can interpret Nature aright. Bacon elaborated his critique on the " idols of the mind " more fully in the *Novum Organum* and the *De Augmentis,* but much of it is already sketched out in the *Advancement* (see II. xiv. 9, 10, and 11, pp. 176–78, below). First, there are the " false appearances that are imposed upon us by the general nature of the mind " — the " idols of the tribe." These spring from our habit of making man the measure of all things, and assuming that Nature must necessarily behave according to our own sense of fitness. We " usually suppose and feign in nature a greater equality and uniformity than is in truth," and thus we distort nature instead of interpreting her. This was the typical fallacy of the ancient and medieval philosophers who, instead of noting how Nature actually behaved, tried to make her conform to preconceived notions. Thus the moon was a celestial body; it is the nature of celestial bodies

to be perfect; the only perfect shape is a sphere; therefore the moon is spherical, and if Galileo's telescope reveals mountains and hollows on its surface, so much the worse for the telescope and for Galileo. Bacon's point is that God's ways are not our ways, neither are his thoughts our thoughts; " if that great workmaster had been of an human disposition, he would have cast the stars into some pleasant and beautiful works and orders, like the frets in the roofs of houses; whereas one can scarce find a posture in square, or triangle, or straight line, amongst such an infinite number; so differing an harmony there is between the spirit of man and the spirit of nature."

Next there are the " idols of the cave," errors arising, not from the general defectiveness of the human mind, but from the limitations of each man's individual upbringing or environment. We must come forth into the light of things, abandon the delusions of sect and coterie, and let Nature be our teacher.

Thirdly, there are the " idols of the market place," the " false appearances that are imposed upon us by words." We may try to think with the wise, but we have to speak with the vulgar — that is, make use of words whose " popular " meanings often conflict with the exact meaning intended. In all discussions we should begin by defining our terms; otherwise we shall find ourselves arguing at cross-purposes, and have to end where we should have begun.

In the *Novum Organum* Bacon added a fourth class of idols, those of the " theater " (i.e., the lecture theater); these are errors that have arisen from various systems of philosophy. There is the "sophistic," which takes certain common observations without reducing them to certainty, and relies for the rest upon meditation and activity of wit. Aristotle is the chief offender here; he decides the nature of things on insufficient evidence, and then "drags experiment along as a captive constrained to accommodate herself to his decisions." There is the " empiric," which does indeed make a few careful experiments, but produces a complete system prematurely, and on an inadequate basis. And there is the " superstitious " type, which mixes up theology with science, some even having tried to build a system of natural philosophy upon the first chapter of the Book of Genesis.

These, in fine, are the idols that must be abjured before the human mind can begin to interpret the divine mind as it is expressed in nature. "The understanding must be completely freed and cleared of them, so that the access to the kingdom of man, which is founded on the sciences, may resemble that to the kingdom of heaven, where no admission is conceded except to children." (*Novum Organum,* I. 68).

The last-quoted remark well illustrates the technique by which Bacon, while always distinguishing clearly between the spheres of religion and science, tries to give a religious sanction to his scientific propaganda. What he means, in this context, is that science, so far from leading to pride of intellect, can only be successfully pursued in that very same spirit of humility which is required of the Christian believer. There is no need to question Bacon's sincerity when, as constantly happens, he exalts revelation above reason, and places the *summum bonum* where religion places it — in salvation and heavenly joy. What is certain, however, is that the emphasis of his interest is steadily upon this world, upon the active rather than the contemplative life, upon becoming rather than upon being. The other world has for ages been sufficiently attended to; it is now this world's turn. This attitude comes out very clearly in the extract printed below (*Advancement,* II. vii. 1–7), where the topic is the inquiry into causes. What need investigating, Bacon urges, are the inward atomic structures, which make things what they are (he calls them "forms" or "formal causes"), and the "efficient" causes, i.e., the physical forces which actually produce motions. But these are just what have been neglected. Men have contented themselves by explaining why or to what purpose things existed and behaved in such and such fashion (the "final causes"), and ignored the "how" almost entirely. The point is not, he characteristically adds, that these "final causes" are not true or not worth considering, but that "their excursions into the limits of physical causes hath bred a vastness and solitude in that tract."

Similarly in morality, the ultimate issues and sanctions lie within the sphere of religion, but there has been a neglect of the humbler details of daily living and the actual technique of self-discipline. The theoretical principles of ethics have been well discussed, and fair copies of the virtues held up for admiration, but the question of "how to attain these excellent marks" has been passed over in silence.

Bacon devotes a section of the *Advancement* to this practical wisdom, which he calls the "Georgics of the mind, concerning the husbandry and tillage thereof." But it is in his *Essays* that he goes farthest toward filling the gap, for they are the distillation of his experience of men and affairs. He himself aptly described them as "certain brief notes, set down rather significantly than curiously . . . of a nature whereof a man shall find much in experience, little in books." In the *Advancement* he had pleaded for rules of self-management, and for a science of psychological types whereby we could manage other men. In the *Essays* we get the wise guidance of an experienced sage on how to manage our own concerns — our health, our wealth, our affections, and our fortunes, on how to govern others, and on the methods of administering public affairs. There is no need to enlarge upon the pungency, the conciseness, the aphoristic brilliance, the vivid imagery, and (especially in the later essays and added passages) the eloquence that have made these *Essays* famous. A point worth remembering, however, is that, though Bacon is justly reputed the father of the English essay, it is the form of this genre, rather than its tone and temper, that we owe to him. The essay properly so called derives from Montaigne rather than from Bacon: it was Montaigne who taught such men as Browne, Cowley, Addison, Lamb, Hazlitt, and R. L. Stevenson how to exploit their own personalities in that intimate, that deliberately informal or carpet-slipper style, which we have come to regard as the essential note of this literary form. The essayists in this succession have mostly been whimsical individualists who preferred byways to highways, and cared little for the things most valued by the first-class passengers through life. Bacon, on the other hand, scorned to be found anywhere but at the metropolis of the world and of the mind; he writes like a lord chancellor, and his essays are the *sententiae* of a worldly-wise man. His advice is nowhere corrupt; its basis is in Christian ethics, but his values are those of the world rather than of the spirit.

Bacon is a prophet, not of the Kingdom of Heaven, but of the Kingdom of Man. What he would have us do is to exploit to the uttermost the brave new world, not to be lookers-on but active workers for the benefit of humanity; then death, when it comes, will come unnoticed:

He that dies in an earnest pursuit is like one that is wounded in hot blood; who, for the time, scarce feels the hurt ("Of Death").

ESSAYS OR COUNSELS

Civil and Moral

Bacon's *Essays* were first published in 1597. This volume contained only the following ten essays (the original titles are given here): "Of Studies," "Of Discourse," "Of Ceremonies and Respects," "Of Followers and Friends," "Of Suits," "Of Expense," "Of Regiment of Health," "Of Honor and Reputation," "Of Faction," and "Of Negotiating."

Revised and enlarged editions appeared in 1612 and 1625, the number of essays being increased to thirty-eight in 1612 and fifty-eight in 1625. In general, the successive revisions took the form of enrichment by added allusions and illustrations, but there was also some transference from one essay to another, and in some essays considerable rewriting.

The essays are given here in their final form of 1625. The date appended to each indicates when the essay first appeared; it does not mean (except where the essay first appeared in 1625) that its original version is here given. As a specimen of the 1597 volume, the essay "Of Studies" is reproduced as it appeared in that edition, as well as in its final form. Readers will thus be able to note the contrast between the concise, aphoristic style of the first essays and the richer, more developed manner of the later ones. A good notion of the development of Bacon's style can be gained by comparing Essay V, "Of Adversity" (1625), with the 1597 version of "Of Studies."

ESSAY I

OF TRUTH

What is truth? said jesting Pilate, and would not stay for an answer. Certainly there be that delight in giddiness, and count it a bondage to fix a belief; affecting free will in thinking, as well as in acting. And though the sects of philosophers of that kind be gone, yet there remain certain discoursing wits which are of the same veins, though there be not so much blood in them as was in those of the ancients. But it is not only the difficulty and labor which men take in finding out of truth, nor again that when it is found it imposeth upon men's thoughts, that doth bring lies in favor; but a natural though corrupt love of the lie itself. One of the later school of the Grecians [1] examineth the matter, and is at a stand to think what should be in it, that men should love lies; where neither they make for pleasure, as with poets; nor for advantage, as with the merchant; but for the lie's sake. But I cannot tell: this same truth is a naked and open daylight, that doth not show the masques and mummeries and triumphs of the world, half so stately and daintily as candlelights. Truth may perhaps come to the price of a pearl, that showeth best by day; but it will not rise to the price of a diamond or carbuncle, that showeth best in varied lights. A mixture of a lie doth ever add pleasure. Doth any man doubt, that if there were taken out of men's minds vain opinions, flattering hopes, false valuations, imaginations as one would, and the like, but it would leave the minds of a number of men poor shrunken things, full of melancholy and indisposition, and unpleasing to themselves? One of the fathers, in great severity, called poesy *vinum daemonum*,[2] because it filleth the imagination, and yet it is but with the shadow of a lie. But it is not the lie that passeth through the mind, but the lie that sinketh in and settleth in it, that doth the hurt, such as we spake of before. But howsoever these things are thus in men's depraved judgments and affections, yet truth, which only doth judge itself, teacheth that the inquiry of truth, which is the love-making or wooing of it, the knowledge of truth, which is the presence of it, and the belief of truth, which is the enjoying of it, is the sovereign good of human nature. The first creature of God, in the works of the days, was the light of the sense; the last was the light of reason; and his sabbath work, ever since, is the illumination of his Spirit. First he breathed light upon the face of the matter or chaos; then he breathed light into the face of man; and still he breatheth and inspireth light into the face of his chosen. The poet that beautified the sect [3] that was otherwise inferior to the rest, saith yet excellently well: *It is a pleasure to stand upon the shore, and to see ships tossed upon the sea: a pleasure to stand in the window of a castle, and to see a battle and the adventures thereof below: but no pleasure is comparable to the standing upon the vantage ground of truth* (a hill not to be commanded, and where the air is always clear and serene), *and to see the errors, and wanderings,*

ESSAYS. 1. Grecians: probably Lucian, who in his *Philopseudes* has a character who asks why men love lying. 2. *vinum daemonum*: "the wine of evil spirits" (epithet applied by Jerome, Augustine, or Tertullian, early Fathers of the Christian Church). 3. The poet . . . sect: Lucretius; the Epicureans.

and mists, and tempests, in the vale below: [4] so always that this prospect be with pity, and not with swelling or pride. Certainly, it is heaven upon earth, to have a man's mind move in charity, rest in Providence, and turn upon the poles of truth.

To pass from theological and philosophical truth, to the truth of civil business: it will be acknowledged, even by those that practice it not, that clear and round dealing is the honor of man's nature; and that mixture of falsehood is like allay [5] in coin of gold and silver; which may make the metal work the better, but it embaseth it. For these winding and crooked courses are the goings of the serpent; which goeth basely upon the belly, and not upon the feet. There is no vice that doth so cover a man with shame as to be found false and perfidious. And therefore Mountaigny [6] saith prettily, when he inquired the reason, why the word of the lie should be such a disgrace and such an odious charge? saith he, If it be well weighed, to say that a man lieth, is as much to say as that he is brave towards God and a coward towards men. For a lie faces God, and shrinks from man. Surely the wickedness of falsehood and breach of faith cannot possibly be so highly expressed, as in that it shall be the last peal to call the judgments of God upon the generations of men; it being foretold, that when Christ cometh, he shall not find faith upon the earth.

1625

ESSAY II

OF DEATH

Men fear death, as children fear to go in the dark; and as that natural fear in children is increased with tales, so is the other. Certainly, the contemplation of death, as the *wages of sin,* and passage to another world, is holy and religious; but the fear of it, as a tribute due unto nature, is weak. Yet in religious meditations there is sometimes mixture of vanity and of superstition. You shall read in some of the friars' books of mortification, that a man should think with himself what the pain is if he have but his finger's end pressed or tortured, and thereby imagine what the pains of death are, when the whole body is corrupted and dissolved: when many times death passeth with less pain than

the torture of a limb; for the most vital parts are not the quickest of sense. And by him, that spake only as a philosopher and natural man,[7] it was well said, *Pompa mortis magis terret quam mors ipsa.*[8] Groans and convulsions, and a discolored face, and friends weeping, and blacks, and obsequies, and the like, show death terrible. It is worthy the observing, that there is no passion in the mind of man so weak, but it mates and masters the fear of death; and therefore death is no such terrible enemy, when a man hath so many attendants about him that can win the combat of him. Revenge triumphs over death; love slights it; honor aspireth to it; grief flieth to it; fear pre-occupateth [9] it; nay, we read, after Otho the emperor had slain himself, pity (which is the tenderest of affections) provoked many to die, out of mere compassion to their sovereign, and as the truest sort of followers. Nay, Seneca adds niceness [10] and satiety: *Cogita quam diu eadem feceris; mori velle, non tantum fortis, aut miser, sed etiam fastidiosus potest.*[11] A man would die, though he were neither valiant nor miserable, only upon a weariness to do the same thing so oft over and over. It is no less worthy to observe, how little alteration, in good spirits, the approaches of death make; for they appear to be the same men till the last instant. Augustus Caesar died in a compliment: *Livia, conjugii nostri memor, vive et vale.*[12] Tiberius in dissimulation, as Tacitus saith of him: *Jam Tiberium vires et corpus, non dissimulatio, deserebant.*[13] Vespasian in a jest, sitting upon the stool: *Ut puto Deus fio.*[14] Galba with a sentence: *Feri, si ex re sit populi Romani,*[15] holding forth his neck. Septimius Severus in dispatch: *Adeste si quid mihi restat agendum.*[16] And the like. Certainly the Stoics bestowed too much cost upon death, and by their great preparations made it appear more fearful. Better saith he, *Qui finem vitae extremum inter munera ponat Naturae.*[17] It is as natural to die as to be born; and to a little infant,

---

4. below: The passage from *De Rerum Natura,* II. 1–10, is freely paraphrased.   5. allay: alloy.   6. Mountaigny: Michel de Montaigne (1533–92), French essayist.

7. him . . . man: Seneca; "natural": pagan.   8. *Pompa . . . ipsa:* "The parade of death frightens more than death itself."   9. pre-occupateth: anticipates [i.e., by suicide].   10. niceness: fastidiousness.   11. *Cogita . . . potest:* "Consider how often you do the same things; a man may wish to die, not only because he is brave, or miserable, but even because he is disgusted with life."   12. *Livia . . . vale:* "Farewell, Livia, and remember our married life."   13. *Jam . . . deserebant:* "At length vitality and bodily strength were deserting Tiberius, not his duplicity."   14. *Ut . . . fio:* "As I think [a pun on *puto,* cleanse], I am becoming a god."   15. *Feri . . . Romani:* "Strike, if it be in the interest of the Roman people."   16. *Adeste . . . agendum:* "Come along, if anything remains for me to do."   17. *Qui . . . Naturae:* "He who reckons the close of life among the boons of nature" (paraphrase of Juvenal).

perhaps, the one is as painful as the other. He that dies in an earnest pursuit is like one that is wounded in hot blood; who, for the time, scarce feels the hurt; and therefore a mind fixed and bent upon somewhat that is good doth avert the dolors of death. But above all, believe it, the sweetest canticle is *Nunc dimittis;* [18] when a man hath obtained worthy ends and expectations. Death hath this also, that it openeth the gate to good fame, and extinguisheth envy. *Extinctus amabitur idem.*[19]

1612

ESSAY V

OF ADVERSITY

It was an high speech of Seneca (after the manner of the Stoics): *That the good things which belong to prosperity are to be wished; but the good things that belong to adversity are to be admired. Bona rerum secundarum optabilia, adversarum mirabilia.* Certainly, if miracles be the command over nature, they appear most in adversity. It is yet a higher speech of his than the other (much too high for a heathen): *It is true greatness to have in one the frailty of a man, and the security of a god. Vere magnum, habere fragilitatem hominis, securitatem dei.* This would have done better in poesy, where transcendences are more allowed. And the poets indeed have been busy with it; for it is in effect the thing which is figured in that strange fiction of the ancient poets, which seemeth not to be without mystery; nay, and to have some approach to the state of a Christian: that *Hercules, when he went to unbind Prometheus* (by whom human nature is represented), *sailed the length of the great ocean in an earthen pot or pitcher:* lively describing Christian resolution, that saileth in the frail bark of the flesh through the waves of the world. But to speak in a mean.[20] The virtue of prosperity is temperance; the virtue of adversity is fortitude; which in morals is the more heroical virtue. Prosperity is the blessing of the Old Testament; adversity is the blessing of the New; which carrieth the greater benediction, and the clearer revelation of God's favor. Yet even in the Old Testament, if you listen to David's harp, you shall hear as many hearse-like airs as carols; and the pencil of the Holy Ghost hath labored more in

describing the afflictions of Job than the felicities of Salomon. Prosperity is not without many fears and distastes; and adversity is not without comforts and hopes. We see in needleworks and embroideries, it is more pleasing to have a lively work upon a sad and solemn ground, than to have a dark and melancholy work upon a lightsome ground: judge therefore of the pleasure of the heart by the pleasure of the eye. Certainly virtue is like precious odors, most fragrant when they are incensed or crushed: for prosperity doth best discover vice; but adversity doth best discover virtue.

1625

ESSAY XI

OF GREAT PLACE [21]

Men in great places are thrice servants: servants of the sovereign or state; servants of fame; and servants of business. So as they have no freedom, neither in their persons, nor in their actions, nor in their times. It is a strange desire, to seek power and to lose liberty; or to seek power over others and to lose power over a man's self. The rising unto place is laborious, and by pains men come to greater pains; and it is sometimes base, and by indignities men come to dignities. The standing is slippery; and the regress is either a downfall, or at least an eclipse, which is a melancholy thing. *Cum non sis qui fueris, non esse cur velis vivere.*[22] Nay, retire men cannot when they would; neither will they when it were reason; but are impatient of privateness,[23] even in age and sickness, which require the shadow: like old townsmen, that will be still sitting at their street door, though thereby they offer age to scorn. Certainly, great persons had need to borrow other men's opinions, to think themselves happy; for if they judge by their own feeling, they cannot find it: but if they think with themselves what other men think of them, and that other men would fain be as they are, then they are happy as it were by report, when perhaps they find the contrary within. For they are the first that find their own griefs, though they be the last that find their own faults. Certainly, men in great fortunes are strangers to themselves, and while they are in the puzzle of business they have

---

18. *Nunc dimittis:* "(Lord) now lettest thou (thy servant) depart (in peace)" (Luke 2:29).   19. *Extinctus . . . idem:* "The same [i.e., the envied] man will be beloved when he is dead."   20. mean: prosaic language, or level terms.

21. Great Place: high office.   22. *Cum . . . vivere:* "When [or since] you are no longer what you were, there is no reason why you should wish to live" (Cicero).   23. are . . . privateness: cannot endure private life [retirement].

no time to tend their health, either of body or mind. *Illi mors gravis incubat, qui notus nimis omnibus, ignotus moritur sibi.*[24] In place there is license to do good and evil; whereof the latter is a curse: for in evil the best condition is not to will, the second not to can. But power to do good is the true and lawful end of aspiring. For good thoughts (though God accept them) yet towards men are little better then good dreams, except they be put in act; and that cannot be without power and place, as the vantage and commanding ground. Merit and good works is the end of man's motion; and conscience of the same is the accomplishment of man's rest. For if a man can be partaker of God's theater,[25] he shall likewise be partaker of God's rest. *Et conversus Deus, ut aspiceret opera quae fecerunt manus suae, vidit quod omnia essent bona nimis;* [26] and then the Sabbath. In the discharge of thy place, set before thee the best examples; for imitation is a globe of precepts. And after a time set before thee thine own example; and examine thyself strictly, whether thou didst not best at first.[27] Neglect not also the examples of those that have carried themselves ill in the same place; not to set off thyself by taxing their memory, but to direct thyself what to avoid. Reform, therefore, without bravery [28] or scandal of former times and persons; but yet set it down to thyself as well to create good precedents as to follow them. Reduce things to the first institution, and observe wherein and how they have degenerate; but yet ask counsel of both times; of the ancient time, what is best; and of the latter time, what is fittest. Seek to make thy course regular, that men may know beforehand what they may expect; but be not too positive and peremptory; and express thyself well when thou digressest from thy rule. Preserve the right of thy place, but stir not questions of jurisdiction: [29] and rather assume thy right in silence and *de facto,*[30] than voice it with claims and challenges. Preserve likewise the rights of inferior places; and think it more honor to direct in chief than to be busy in all. Embrace and invite helps and advices touching the execution of thy place; and do not drive away such as bring thee information as meddlers, but accept of them in good part. The vices of authority are chiefly four: delays, corruption, roughness, and facility.[31] For delays, give easy access; keep times appointed; go through with that which is in hand; and interlace not business but of necessity. For corruption, do not only bind thine own hands or thy servants' hands from taking, but bind the hands of suitors also from offering. For integrity used doth the one; but integrity professed, and with a manifest detestation of bribery, doth the other. And avoid not only the fault, but the suspicion. Whosoever is found variable, and changeth manifestly without manifest cause, giveth suspicion of corruption. Therefore always when thou changest thine opinions of course, profess it plainly and declare it, together with the reasons that move thee to change; and do not think to steal it. A servant or a favorite, if he be inward,[32] and no other apparent cause of esteem, is commonly thought but a byway to close [33] corruption. For roughness, it is a needless cause of discontent: severity breedeth fear, but roughness breedeth hate. Even reproofs from authority ought to be grave, and not taunting. As for facility, it is worse than bribery. For bribes come but now and then; but if importunity or idle respects lead a man, he shall never be without. As Salomon saith: " To respect persons is not good; for such a man will transgress for a piece of bread." [34] It is most true that was anciently spoken, *A place showeth the man:* and it showeth some to the better, and some to the worse. *Omnium consensu capax imperii, nisi imperasset,*[35] saith Tacitus of Galba; but of Vespasian he saith, *Solus imperantium Vespasianus mutatus in melius:* [36] though the one was meant of sufficiency, the other of manners and affection. It is an assured sign of a worthy and generous spirit, whom honor amends. For honor is, or should be, the place of virtue; and as in nature things move violently to their place, and calmly in their place; so virtue in ambition is violent, in authority settled and calm. All rising to great place is by a winding stair; and if there be factions, it is good to side a man's self whilst he is in the rising, and to balance himself when he is placed. Use the memory of thy predecessor fairly and tenderly; for if thou dost not, it is a debt will sure be paid when thou art gone. If thou have colleagues, respect them, and rather call them when

---

24. *Illi . . . sibi:* "Death lies heavily on the man who dies too well known to everyone but ignorant of himself" (Seneca). 25. *God's theater:* the world. 26. *Et . . . nimis:* "And God turned to behold the works which his hands had made, and saw that all things were very good" (Gen. 1:31). 27. *whether . . . first:* to see whether you did not begin better than you have gone on. 28. *bravery:* flouting, defiance. 29. *stir . . . jurisdiction:* Do not raise discussions about the powers of your office. 30. *de facto:* as a matter of course.

31. *facility:* being too easygoing, too easily influenced by others. 32. *inward:* intimate, in your confidence. 33. *close:* secret. 34. *"To . . . bread":* Prov. 28:21. 35. *Omnium . . . imperasset:* "By universal consent he was fit to govern, if only he had not governed." 36. *Solus . . . melius:* "Of all the emperors, Vespasian alone changed for the better" [i.e., after accession].

they look not for it, than exclude them when they have reason to look to be called. Be not too sensible [37] or too remembering of thy place in conversation and private answers to suitors; but let it rather be said, *When he sits in place he is another man.*

1612

ESSAY XVIII
OF TRAVEL

Travel, in the younger sort, is a part of education; in the elder, a part of experience. He that traveleth into a country before he hath some entrance into the language, goeth to school, and not to travel. That young men travel under some tutor, or grave servant, I allow well; so that he be such a one that hath the language and hath been in the country before; whereby he may be able to tell them what things are worthy to be seen in the country where they go; what acquaintances they are to seek; what exercises or discipline the place yieldeth. For else young men shall go hooded, and look abroad little. It is a strange thing that in sea voyages, where there is nothing to be seen but sky and sea, men should make diaries, but in land travel, wherein so much is to be observed, for the most part they omit it; as if chance were fitter to be registered than observation. Let diaries, therefore, be brought in use. The things to be seen and observed are: the courts of princes, specially when they give audience to ambassadors; the courts of justice, while they sit and hear causes, and so of consistories ecclesiastic; [38] the churches and monasteries, with the monuments which are therein extant; the walls and fortifications of cities and towns, and so the havens and harbors; antiquities and ruins; libraries; colleges, disputations, and lectures, where any are; shipping and navies; houses and gardens of state and pleasure, near great cities; armories; arsenals; magazines; exchanges; burses; warehouses; exercises of horsemanship, fencing, training of soldiers, and the like; comedies, such whereunto the better sort of persons do resort; treasuries of jewels and robes; cabinets and rarities; and, to conclude, whatsoever is memorable in the places where they go. After all which the tutors or servants ought to make diligent inquiry. As for triumphs, [39]

masques, feasts, weddings, funerals, capital executions, and such shows, men need not to be put in mind of them; yet are they not to be neglected. If you will have a young man to put his travel into a little room, and in short time to gather much, this you must do. First, as was said, he must have some entrance into the language, before he goeth. Then he must have such a servant, or tutor, as knoweth the country, as was likewise said. Let him carry with him also some card or book describing the country where he traveleth; which will be a good key to his inquiry. Let him keep also a diary. Let him not stay long in one city or town; more or less as the place deserveth, but not long: nay, when he stayeth in one city or town, let him change his lodging from one end and part of the town to another; which is a great adamant [40] of acquaintance. Let him sequester himself from the company of his countrymen, and diet in such places where there is good company of the nation where he traveleth. Let him, upon his removes from one place to another, procure recommendation to some person of quality residing in the place whither he removeth; that he may use his favor in those things he desireth to see or know. Thus he may abridge his travel with much profit. As for the acquaintance which is to be sought in travel, that which is most of all profitable is acquaintance with the secretaries and employed men of ambassadors; for so in traveling in one country he shall suck the experience of many. Let him also see and visit eminent persons in all kinds, which are of great name abroad; that he may be able to tell how the life agreeth with the fame. For quarrels, they are with care and discretion to be avoided: they are commonly for mistresses, healths, [41] place, and words. And let a man beware how he keepeth company with choleric and quarrelsome persons; for they will engage him into their own quarrels. When a traveler returneth home, let him not leave the countries where he hath traveled altogether behind him, but maintain a correspondence by letters with those of his acquaintance which are of most worth. And let his travel appear rather in his discourse than in his apparel or gesture; and in his discourse, let him be rather advised [42] in his answers than forwards to tell stories; and let it appear that he doth not change his country manners [43] for those of foreign parts, but only prick in some

---

37. **sensible:** sensitive, or conscious.   38. **consistories ecclesiastic:** church convocations and courts.   39. **triumphs:** processions, pageants.

40. **adamant:** literally "loadstone"; hence, means of attracting.   41. **healths:** i.e., drinking toasts.   42. **advised:** well informed.   43. **his . . . manners:** the manners of his own country.

flowers of that he hath learned abroad into the customs of his own country.

1625

ESSAY XXII

OF CUNNING

We take cunning for a sinister or crooked wisdom. And certainly there is a great difference between a cunning man and a wise man; not only in point of honesty, but in point of ability. There be that can pack the cards, and yet cannot play well; so there are some that are good in canvasses and factions, that are otherwise weak men. Again, it is one thing to understand persons, and another thing to understand matters; for many are perfect in men's humors, that are not greatly capable of the real part of business; which is the constitution of one that hath studied men more than books. Such men are fitter for practice than for counsel; and they are good but in their own alley: turn them to new men, and they have lost their aim; so as the old rule to know a fool from a wise man, *Mitte ambos nudos ad ignotos et videbis,*[44] doth scarce hold for them. And because these cunning men are like haberdashers of small wares, it is not amiss to set forth their shop.

It is a point of cunning, to wait upon him with whom you speak, with your eye, as the Jesuits give it in precept; for there be many wise men that have secret hearts and transparent countenances. Yet this would be done with a demure abasing of your eye sometimes, as the Jesuits also do use.

Another is, that when you have anything to obtain of present dispatch, you entertain and amuse the party with whom you deal with some other discourse, that he be not too much awake to make objections. I knew a counselor and secretary, that never came to Queen Elizabeth of England with bills to sign, but he would always first put her into some discourse of estate, that she might the less mind the bills.

The like surprise may be made by moving things [45] when the party is in haste, and cannot stay to consider advisedly of that is moved.

If a man would cross a business that he doubts some other would handsomely and effectually move, let him pretend to wish it well, and move it himself in such sort as may foil it.

The breaking off in the midst of that one was about to say, as if he took himself up, breeds a greater appetite in him with whom you confer to know more.

And because it works better when anything seemeth to be gotten from you by question, than if you offer it of yourself, you may lay a bait for a question, by showing another visage and countenance than you are wont; to the end to give occasion for the party to ask what the matter is of the change? As Nehemias did: " And I had not before that time been sad before the king."

In things that are tender and unpleasing, it is good to break the ice by some whose words are of less weight, and to reserve the more weighty voice to come in as by chance, so that he may be asked the question upon the other's speech. As Narcissus did, in relating to Claudius the marriage of Messalina and Silius.

In things that a man would not be seen in himself, it is a point of cunning to borrow the name of the world; as to say, *The world says,* or, *There is a speech abroad.*

I knew one that, when he wrote a letter, he would put that which was most material in the postscript, as if it had been a by-matter.

I knew another that, when he came to have speech, he would pass over that that he intended most, and go forth, and come back again, and speak of it as of a thing that he had almost forgot.

Some procure themselves to be surprised at such times as it is like the party that they work upon will suddenly come upon them, and to be found with a letter in their hand, or doing somewhat which they are not accustomed; to the end they may be apposed of [46] those things which of themselves they are desirous to utter.

It is a point of cunning, to let fall those words in a man's own name, which he would have another man learn and use, and thereupon take advantage. I knew two that were competitors for the secretary's place in Queen Elizabeth's time, and yet kept good quarter between themselves, and would confer one with another upon the business; and the one of them said, That to be a secretary in the *declination of a monarchy* was a ticklish thing, and that he did not affect it: [47] the other straight caught up those

---

44. *Mitte . . . videbis:* "Send both naked amongst strangers, and you will see."   45. **moving things:** bringing up matters for discussion.

46. **apposed of:** questioned about.   47. **affect it:** care for, or favor it.

words, and discoursed with divers of his friends, that he had no reason to desire to be secretary in the *declination of a monarchy*. The first man took hold of it, and found means it was told the Queen; who, hearing of a *declination of a monarchy,* took it so ill, as she would never after hear of the other's suit.

There is a cunning, which we in England call *the turning of the cat in the pan;* which is, when that which a man says to another, he lays [48] it as if another had said it to him. And to say truth, it is not easy, when such a matter passed between two, to make it appear from which of them it first moved and began.

It is a way that some men have, to glance and dart at others by justifying themselves by negatives; as to say, *This I do not:* as Tigellinus did towards Burrhus; *Se non diversas spes, sed incolumitatem imperatoris simpliciter spectare.*[49]

Some have in readiness so many tales and stories, as there is nothing they would insinuate, but they can wrap it into a tale; which serveth both to keep themselves more in guard, and to make others carry it with more pleasure.

It is a good point of cunning, for a man to shape the answer he would have in his own words and propositions; for it makes the other party stick the less.

It is strange how long some men will lie in wait to speak somewhat they desire to say, and how far about they will fetch,[50] and how many other matters they will beat over, to come near it. It is a thing of great patience, but yet of much use.

A sudden, bold, and unexpected question doth many times surprise a man, and lay him open. Like to him, that having changed his name, and walking in Paul's,[51] another suddenly came behind him and called him by his true name, whereat straightways he looked back.

But these small wares and petty points of cunning are infinite; and it were a good deed to make a list of them; for that nothing doth more hurt in a state than that cunning men pass for wise.

But certainly some there are that know the resorts and falls [52] of business, that cannot sink into the main of it; like a house that hath convenient stairs and entries, but never a fair room. Therefore, you shall see them find out pretty looses [53] in the conclusion, but are no ways able to examine or debate matters. And yet commonly they take advantage of their inability, and would be thought wits of direction. Some build rather upon the abusing of others, and (as we now say) *putting tricks upon them,* than upon soundness of their own proceedings. But Salomon saith: *Prudens advertit ad gressus suos: stultus divertit ad dolos.*[54]

1612

ESSAY XXIII

OF WISDOM FOR A MAN'S SELF

An ant is a wise creature for itself, but it is a shrewd [55] thing in an orchard or garden. And certainly men that are great lovers of themselves waste the public. Divide with reason between self-love and society; and be so true to thyself, as thou be not false to others, specially to thy king and country. It is a poor center of a man's actions, himself. It is right earth. For that only stands fast upon his own center; whereas all things that have affinity with the heavens move upon the center of another, which they benefit.[56] The referring of all to a man's self is more tolerable in a sovereign prince; because themselves are not only themselves, but their good and evil is at the peril of the public fortune. But it is a desperate evil in a servant to a prince, or a citizen in a republic. For whatsoever affairs pass such a man's hands, he crooketh them to his own ends; which must needs be often eccentric to [57] the ends of his master or state. Therefore let princes, or states, choose such servants as have not this mark; except they mean their service should be made but the accessory. That which maketh the effect more pernicious is that all proportion is lost. It were disproportion enough for the servant's good to be preferred before the master's; but yet it is a greater extreme, when a little good of the servant shall carry things against a great good of the master's. And yet that is the case of bad officers, treasurers, ambassadors, generals, and other false and corrupt servants; which set a bias upon their bowl, of their own petty ends and envies, to

---

48. lays: represents.   49. *Se . . . spectare:* "That he did not entertain a variety of hopes [hinting that Burrhus did], but simply considered the safety of the emperor" (Tacitus).   50. how . . . fetch: what roundabout ways they will use.   51. Paul's: St. Paul's Cathedral in London.   52. resorts . . . falls: expedients and chances.

53. looses: weak points.   54. *Prudens . . . dolos:* "The wise man looks to his own footsteps: the fool turns aside into deceits [snares]" (Prov. 14:15).   55. shrewd: mischievous.   56. For . . . benefit: Bacon writes here as a believer in the pre-Copernican system (geocentric).   57. eccentric to: having a different center, hence divergent from.

the overthrow of their master's great and important affairs. And for the most part, the good such servants receive is after the model of their own fortune; but the hurt they sell for that good is after the model of their master's fortune. And certainly it is the nature of extreme self-lovers, as they will set an house on fire, and it were but to roast their eggs; and yet these men many times hold credit with their masters, because their study is but to please them and profit themselves; and for either respect they will abandon the good of their affairs.

Wisdom for a man's self is, in many branches thereof, a depraved thing. It is the wisdom of rats, that will be sure to leave a house somewhat before it fall. It is the wisdom of the fox, that thrusts out the badger, who digged and made room for him. It is the wisdom of crocodiles, that shed tears when they would devour. But that which is specially to be noted is, that those which (as Cicero says of Pompey) are *sui amantes sine rivali*,[58] are many times unfortunate. And whereas they have all their time sacrificed to themselves, they become in the end themselves sacrifices to the inconstancy of fortune, whose wings they thought by their self-wisdom to have pinioned.

1612

ESSAY XXXI
OF SUSPICION

Suspicions amongst thoughts are like bats amongst birds, they ever fly by twilight. Certainly they are to be repressed, or at the least well guarded: for they cloud the mind; they lose friends; and they check [59] with business, whereby business cannot go on currently and constantly. They dispose kings to tyranny, husbands to jealousy, wise men to irresolution and melancholy. They are defects, not in the heart, but in the brain; for they take place in the stoutest natures: as in the example of Henry the Seventh of England: there was not a more suspicious man, nor a more stout. And in such a composition they do small hurt. For commonly they are not admitted but with examination, whether they be likely or no? But in fearful natures they gain ground too fast. There is nothing makes a man suspect much, more than to know little; and therefore men should remedy suspicion by procuring to know more, and not to keep their suspicions in smother. What would men have? Do they think those they employ and deal with are saints? Do they not think they will have their own ends, and be truer to themselves than to them? Therefore there is no better way to moderate suspicions, than to account upon such suspicions as true, and yet to bridle them as false. For so far a man ought to make use of suspicions, as to provide as, if that should be true that he suspects, yet it may do him no hurt. Suspicions, that the mind of itself gathers, are but buzzes; [60] but suspicions, that are artificially nourished and put into men's heads by the tales and whisperings of others, have stings. Certainly, the best mean to clear the way in this same wood of suspicions, is frankly to communicate them with the party that he suspects: for thereby he shall be sure to know more of the truth of them than he did before; and withal shall make that party more circumspect not to give further cause of suspicion. But this would not be done to men of base natures; for they, if they find themselves once suspected, will never be true. The Italian says, *Sospetto licentia fede;* [61] as if suspicion did give a passport to faith: but it ought rather to kindle it to discharge itself.

1625

ESSAY XXXII
OF DISCOURSE

Some in their discourse desire rather commendation of wit, in being able to hold all arguments, than of judgment, in discerning what is true; as if it were a praise to know what might be said, and not what should be thought. Some have certain commonplaces and themes wherein they are good, and want variety; which kind of poverty is for the most part tedious, and, when it is once perceived, ridiculous. The honorablest part of talk is to give the occasion; [62] and again to moderate and pass to somewhat else; for then a man leads the dance. It is good, in discourse, and speech of conversation, to vary and intermingle speech of the present occasion with arguments; tales with reasons; asking of questions with telling of opinions; and jest with earnest: for it is a dull thing to tire, and, as we say now, to jade anything too far. As for jest, there be

---

58. *sui . . . rivali:* "lovers of themselves without a rival."
59. check: interfere.

60. buzzes: buzzing beetles, without any sting.
61. *Sospetto . . . fede:* "Suspicion is the passport to faith."
62. give . . . occasion: start the subject.

certain things which ought to be privileged from it; namely, religion, matters of state, great persons, any man's present business of importance, and any case that deserveth pity. Yet there be some that think their wits have been asleep, except they dart out somewhat that is piquant and to the quick: that is a vein which would be bridled:

Parce, puer, stimulis, et fortius utere loris.[63]

And generally, men ought to find the difference between saltness and bitterness. Certainly, he that hath a satirical vein, as he maketh others afraid of his wit, so he had need be afraid of others' memory. He that questioneth much, shall learn much, and content much; but especially if he apply his questions to the skill of the persons whom he asketh: for he shall give them occasion to please themselves in speaking, and himself shall continually gather knowledge. But let his questions not be troublesome; for that is fit for a poser. And let him be sure to leave other men their turns to speak. Nay, if there be any that would reign and take up all the time, let him find means to take them off and to bring others on; as musicians use to do with those that dance too long galliards. If you dissemble sometimes your knowledge of that you are thought to know, you shall be thought another time to know that you know not. Speech of a man's self ought to be seldom, and well chosen. I knew one was wont to say in scorn, *He must needs be a wise man, he speaks so much of himself:* and there is but one case wherein a man may commend himself with good grace, and that is in commending virtue in another, especially if it be such a virtue whereunto himself pretendeth. Speech of touch[64] towards others should be sparingly used; for discourse ought to be as a field,[65] without coming home to any man. I know two noblemen, of the west part of England, whereof the one was given to scoff, but kept ever royal cheer in his house: the other would ask of those that had been at the other's table, *Tell truly, was there never a flout or dry blow*[66] *given?* to which the guest would answer, *Such and such a thing passed:* the lord would say, *I thought he would mar a good dinner.* Discretion of speech is more than eloquence; and to speak agreeably to him with whom we deal, is more than to speak in good words or in good order. A good continued speech,[67] without a good speech of interlocution, shows slowness; and a good reply or second speech, without a good settled speech, showeth shallowness and weakness. As we see in beasts, that those that are weakest in the course, are yet nimblest in the turn; as it is betwixt the greyhound and the hare. To use too many circumstances, ere one come to the matter, is wearisome; to use none at all, is blunt.

1597

ESSAY XXXIII

OF PLANTATIONS

"Plantation" means a settlement or colony in a new country. Bacon was personally interested in colonization, and after the failure of Sir Walter Raleigh's Virginian colony he was one of the new "adventurers" (along with his cousin the Earl of Salisbury, Captain John Smith, and others) in the London or South Virginia Company — chartered by King James I in 1606.

Plantations are amongst ancient, primitive, and heroical works. When the world was young, it begat more children; but now it is old, it begets fewer: for I may justly account new plantations to be the children of former kingdoms. I like a plantation in a pure soil; that is, where people are not displanted to the end to plant in others. For else it is rather an extirpation than a plantation. Planting of countries is like planting of woods; for you must make account to lose almost twenty years' profit, and expect your recompense in the end. For the principal thing that hath been the destruction of most plantations, hath been the base and hasty drawing of profit in the first years. It is true, speedy profit is not to be neglected, as far as may stand with the good of the plantation, but no further. It is a shameful and unblessed thing to take the scum of people, and wicked condemned men, to be the people with whom you plant: and not only so, but it spoileth the plantation; for they will ever live like rogues, and not fall to work, but be lazy, and do mischief, and spend victuals, and be quickly weary, and then certify[68] over to their country to the discredit of the plantation. The people wherewith you plant ought to be gardeners, plowmen, laborers, smiths, carpenters, joiners, fishermen, fowlers, with some

---

63. *Parce . . . loris:* "Boy, spare the whip, and tightlier hold the reins" (Ovid, *Metamorphoses*, II. 127).   64. of touch: personal references which might give offense.   65. be . . . field: i.e., deal with general topics only.   66. flout . . . blow: an insult or sarcastic hit.

67. speech: It should be remembered that Bacon is using "speech" to mean "habit or way of speaking."   68. certify: testify, or send messages.

few apothecaries, surgeons, cooks, and bakers. In a country of plantation, first look about, what kind of victual the country yields of itself to hand; as chestnuts, walnuts, pineapples, olives, dates, plums, cherries, wild honey, and the like; and make use of them. Then consider what victual or esculent things there are, which grow speedily, and within the year; as parsnips, carrots, turnips, onions, radish, artichokes of Jerusalem, maize, and the like. For wheat, barley, and oats, they ask too much labor; but with peas and beans you may begin, both because they ask less labor, and because they serve for meat as well as for bread. And of rice likewise cometh a great increase, and it is a kind of meat. Above all, there ought to be brought store of biscuit, oatmeal, flour, meal, and the like, in the beginning, till bread may be had. For beasts or birds, take chiefly such as are least subject to diseases, and multiply fastest; as swine, goats, cocks, hens, turkeys, geese, house doves, and the like. The victual in plantations ought to be expended almost as in a besieged town; that is, with certain allowance. And let the main part of the ground employed to gardens or corn be to a common stock; and to be laid in, and stored up, and then delivered out in proportion; besides some spots of ground that any particular person will manure for his own private. Consider likewise what commodities the soil where the plantation is doth naturally yield, that they may some way help to defray the charge of the plantation: so it be not, as was said, to the untimely prejudice of the main business; as it hath fared with tobacco in Virginia. Wood commonly aboundeth but too much; and therefore timber is fit to be one. If there be iron ore, and streams whereupon to set the mills, iron is a brave commodity where wood aboundeth. Making of bay salt,[69] if the climate be proper for it, would be put in experience. Growing silk likewise, if any be, is a likely commodity. Pitch and tar, where store of firs and pines are, will not fail. So drugs and sweet woods, where they are, cannot but yield great profit. Soap ashes likewise, and other things that may be thought of. But moil not too much under ground; for the hope of mines is very uncertain, and useth to make the planters lazy in other things. For government, let it be in the hands of one, assisted with some counsel; and let them have commission to exercise martial laws, with some limitation. And above all, let men make

that profit of being in the wilderness, as they have God always, and his service, before their eyes. Let not the government of the plantation depend upon too many counselors and undertakers in the country that planteth, but upon a temperate number: and let those be rather noblemen and gentlemen, than merchants; for they look ever to the present gain. Let there be freedom from custom, till the plantation be of strength; and not only freedom from custom, but freedom to carry their commodities where they may make their best of them, except there be some special cause of caution. Cram not in people, by sending too fast company after company; but rather harken how they waste, and send supplies proportionably; but so as the number may live well in the plantation, and not by surcharge be in penury. It hath been a great endangering to the health of some plantations, that they have built along the sea and rivers, in marish [70] and unwholesome grounds. Therefore, though you begin there, to avoid carriage and other like discommodities, yet build still rather upwards from the streams than along. It concerneth likewise the health of the plantation that they have good store of salt with them, that they may use it in their victuals when it shall be necessary. If you plant where savages are, do not only entertain them with trifles and jingles; but use them justly and graciously, with sufficient guard nevertheless: and do not win their favor by helping them to invade their enemies, but for their defense it is not amiss. And send oft of them over to the country that plants, that they may see a better condition than their own, and commend it when they return. When the plantation grows to strength, then it is time to plant with women as well as with men; that the plantation may spread into generations, and not be ever pieced from without. It is the sinfullest thing in the world to forsake or destitute a plantation once in forwardness: for besides the dishonor, it is the guiltiness of blood of many commiserable persons.

1625

ESSAY L

OF STUDIES

Studies serve for delight, for ornament, and for ability. Their chief use for delight is in privateness

---

69. **bay salt:** salt from evaporation of sea water.

70. **marish:** marshy.

and retiring; for ornament, is in discourse; and for ability, is in the judgment and disposition of business. For expert men can execute, and perhaps judge of particulars, one by one; but the general counsels, and the plots and marshaling of affairs, come best from those that are learned. To spend too much time in studies is sloth; to use them too much for ornament is affectation; to make judgment wholly by their rules is the humor of a scholar. They perfect nature, and are perfected by experience; for natural abilities are like natural plants, that need pruning by study; and studies themselves do give forth directions too much at large, except they be bounded in by experience. Crafty men contemn [71] studies; simple men admire [72] them; and wise men use them: for they teach not their own use; but that is a wisdom without them and above them, won by observation. Read not to contradict and confute; nor to believe and take for granted; nor to find talk and discourse; but to weigh and consider. Some books are to be tasted, others to be swallowed, and some few to be chewed and digested: that is, some books are to be read only in parts; others to be read, but not curiously; and some few to be read wholly, and with diligence and attention. Some books also may be read by deputy, and extracts made of them by others; but that would be only in the less important arguments, and the meaner sort of books; else distilled books are like common distilled waters, flashy [73] things. Reading maketh a full man; conference a ready man; and writing an exact man. And therefore, if a man write little, he had need have a great memory; if he confer little, he had need have a present wit; and if he read little, he had need have much cunning, to seem to know that he doth not. Histories make men wise; poets witty; [74] the mathematics subtle; natural philosophy deep; moral grave; logic and rhetoric able to contend. *Abeunt studia in mores.*[75] Nay, there is no stond [76] or impediment in the wit, but may be wrought out by fit studies: like as diseases of the body may have appropriate exercises. Bowling is good for the stone and reins; [77] shooting for the lungs and breast; gentle walking for the stomach; riding for the head; and the like. So if a man's wit be wandering, let him study the mathematics; for in demonstrations, if his wit be called away never

so little, he must begin again: if his wit be not apt to distinguish or find differences, let him study the Schoolmen; for they are *cymini sectores:* [78] if he be not apt to beat over matters, and to call one thing to prove and illustrate another, let him study the lawyers' cases: so every defect of the mind may have a special receipt.[79]

1597

OF STUDIES (1597)

Here follows the essay "Of Studies" as it appeared in the 1597 volume. The original spelling and paragraphing are retained.

¶ Studies serue for pastimes, for ornaments & for abilities. The chiefe vse for pastime is in priuatenes and retiring; for ornamente is in discourse, and for abilitie is in iudgement. For expert men can execute, but learned men are fittest to iudge or censure.

¶ To spend too much time in them is slouth, to vse them too much for ornament is affectation: to make iudgement wholly by their rules, is the humour of a Scholler.

¶ They perfect *Nature,* and are perfected by experience.

¶ Craftie men contemne them, simple men admire them, wise men vse them: For they teach not their owne vse, but that is a wisedome without them: and aboue them wonne by obseruation.

¶ Reade not to contradict, nor to belieue, but to waigh and consider.

¶ Some bookes are to bee tasted, others to bee swallowed, and some few to bee chewed and disgested: That is, some bookes are to be read only in partes; others to be read, but cursorily, and some few to be read wholly and with diligence and attention.

¶ Reading maketh a full man, conference a readye man, and writing an exacte man. And therefore if a man write little, he had neede haue a great memorie, if he conferre little, he had neede haue a present wit, and if he reade little, he had neede haue much cunning, to seeme to know that he doth not.

¶ Histories make men wise, Poets wittie: the Mathematickes subtle, naturall Philosophie deepe: Morall graue, Logicke and Rhetoricke able to contend.

---

71. **contemn:** despise.   72. **admire:** wonder at (with open mouths).   73. **flashy:** insipid.   74. **witty:** full of nimble fancy.   75. *Abeunt . . . mores:* "Studies influence behavior" (Ovid, *Heroides,* XV. 83).   76. **stond:** stoppage.   77. **reins:** kidneys.

78. **cymini sectores:** "hairsplitters" (literally, "dividers of cumin seed").   79. **receipt:** prescription (in the medical sense), remedy.

THE ADVANCEMENT
OF LEARNING

In this work, published in 1605, Bacon made (as it were) his first sketch map of the intellectual world, noting which territories had already been charted, and which were still insufficiently or wholly unexplored. It was later translated into Latin and published (1623) in a much expanded form as *De Augmentis Scientiarum*.

It should be explained that the extracts given below begin after the preliminary address to the king (James I), in which Bacon explains the purpose of the book. He has just said that his treatise will have two main parts, the first dealing with the true excellence and advancement of knowledge (see note 1), and the second with its previous history and present defects.

THE
FIRST BOOK OF FRANCIS BACON
OF THE PROFICIENCE AND
ADVANCEMENT OF LEARNING
DIVINE AND HUMAN

I. 1. In the entrance to the former of these,[1] to clear the way, and as it were to make silence, to have the true testimonies concerning the dignity of learning to be better heard, without the interruption of tacit objections; I think good to deliver it from the discredits and disgraces which it hath received, all from ignorance; but ignorance severally [2] disguised; appearing sometimes in the zeal and jealousy of divines; sometimes in the severity and arrogancy of politiques,[3] and sometimes in the errors and imperfections of learned men themselves.

[The true dignity of learning vindicated against those who think that knowledge caused the Fall of Man, and that it leads to pride and atheism. Natural science was not the knowledge forbidden to Adam; moreover, through nature we arrive at a knowledge of God's existence and power.]

2. I hear the former sort say, that knowledge is of those things which are to be accepted of with great limitation and caution: that the aspiring to overmuch knowledge was the original temptation and sin whereupon ensued the Fall of Man: that knowledge hath in it somewhat of the serpent, and therefore where it entereth into a man it makes him

swell; *Scientia inflat:* [4] that Salomon gives a censure, "That there is no end of making books, and that much reading is weariness of the flesh"; and again in another place, "That in spacious knowledge there is much contristation,[5] and that he that increaseth knowledge increaseth anxiety": that St. Paul gives a caveat, "That we be not spoiled through vain philosophy": that experience demonstrates how learned men have been archheretics, how learned times have been inclined to atheism, and how the contemplation of second causes [6] doth derogate from our dependence upon God, who is the first cause.[7]

3. To discover then the ignorance and error of this opinion, and the misunderstanding in the grounds thereof, it may well appear these men do not observe or consider that it was not the pure knowledge of nature and universality,[8] a knowledge by the light whereof man did give names unto other creatures in Paradise, as they were brought before him, according unto their proprieties,[9] which gave the occasion to the Fall: but it was the proud knowledge of good and evil, with an intent in man to give law unto himself, and to depend no more upon God's commandments, which was the form of the temptation. Neither is it any quantity of knowledge, how great soever, that can make the mind of man to swell; for nothing can fill, much less extend the soul of man, but God and the contemplation of God; . . .

If then such be the capacity and receipt of the mind of man, it is manifest that there is no danger at all in the proportion or quantity of knowledge, how large soever, lest it should make it swell or outcompass itself; no, but it is merely the quality of knowledge, which, be it in quantity more or less, if it be taken without the true corrective thereof, hath in it some nature of venom or malignity, and some effects of that venom, which is ventosity [10] or swelling. This corrective spice, the mixture whereof maketh knowledge so sovereign, is charity, which the Apostle immediately addeth to the former clause: for so he saith, "Knowledge bloweth up, but charity buildeth up"; not unlike unto that which he delivereth in another place: "If I spake," saith he, "with the tongues of men and angels, and had not charity, it were but as a tinkling cymbal";

ADVANCEMENT OF LEARNING.   1. **former of these:** i.e., "the excellency of learning and knowledge . . . and the . . . merit and true glory in the augmentation and propagation thereof." 2. **severally:** in various ways.   3. **politiques:** politicians.

4. *Scientia inflat:* "Knowledge puffs up."   5. **contristation:** sadness.   6. **second causes:** natural laws or causes.   7. **first cause:** physical or natural causes being second causes.   8. **universality:** general principles.   9. **proprieties:** particular natures. 10. **ventosity:** windiness.

not but that it is an excellent thing to speak with the tongues of men and angels, but because, if it be severed from charity, and not referred to the good of men and mankind, it hath rather a sounding and unworthy glory, than a meriting and substantial virtue. And as for that censure of Salomon, concerning the excess of writing and reading books, and the anxiety of spirit which redoundeth from knowledge, and that admonition of St. Paul, " That we be not seduced by vain philosophy "; let those places be rightly understood, and they do indeed excellently set forth the true bounds and limitations, whereby human knowledge is confined and circumscribed; and yet without any such contracting or coarctation,[11] but that it may comprehend all the universal nature of things; for these limitations are three: the first, That we do not so place our felicity in knowledge, as we forget our mortality: the second, That we make application of our knowledge, to give ourselves repose and contentment, and not distaste or repining: the third, That we do not presume by the contemplation of nature to attain to the mysteries of God. . . .

And as for the conceit that too much knowledge should incline a man to atheism, and that the ignorance of second causes should make a more devout dependence upon God, which is the first cause; first, it is good to ask the question which Job asked of his friends: " Will you lie for God, as one man will do for another, to gratify him? " For certain it is that God worketh nothing in nature but by second causes:[12] and if they would have it otherwise believed, it is mere imposture, as it were in favor towards God; and nothing else but to offer to the author of truth the unclean sacrifice of a lie. But further, it is an assured truth, and a conclusion of experience, that a little or superficial knowledge of philosophy may incline the mind of man to atheism, but a further proceeding therein doth bring the mind back again to religion. For in the entrance of philosophy,[13] when the second causes, which are next unto the senses, do offer themselves to the mind of man, if it dwell and stay there it may induce some oblivion of the highest cause; but when a man passeth on further, and seeth the dependence of causes, and the works of Providence, then, according to the allegory of the poets, he will easily believe that the highest link of nature's chain must

needs be tied to the foot of Jupiter's chair. To conclude therefore, let no man upon a weak conceit of sobriety or an ill-applied moderation think or maintain, that a man can search too far, or be too well studied in the book of God's word, or in the book of God's works, divinity or philosophy; but rather let men endeavor an endless progress or proficience in both; only let men beware that they apply both to charity, and not to swelling; to use, and not to ostentation; and again, that they do not unwisely mingle or confound these learnings together.

[The " vanities " of learning: " vain " imaginations, disputes, and affections. The " distempers " of learning: (a) studying words rather than things; (b) the degenerate learning of the Schoolmen.]

IV. 2. There be therefore chiefly three vanities in studies, whereby learning hath been most traduced: . . . the first, fantastical learning; the second, contentious learning; and the last, delicate[14] learning; vain imaginations, vain altercations, and vain affectations; and with the last I will begin. Martin Luther, conducted (no doubt) by an higher providence, but in discourse of reason, finding what a province he had undertaken against the bishop of Rome and the degenerate traditions of the Church, and finding his own solitude, being no ways aided by the opinions of his own time, was enforced to awake all antiquity, and to call former times to his succors to make a party against the present time: so that the ancient authors, both in divinity and in humanity, which had long time slept in libraries, began generally to be read and revolved. This by consequence did draw on a necessity of a more exquisite travail in the languages original, wherein those authors did write, for the better understanding of those authors, and the better advantage of pressing and applying their words. And thereof grew again a delight in their manner of style and phrase, and an admiration of that kind of writing; which was much furthered and precipitated by the enmity and opposition that the propounders of those primitive but seeming new opinions had against the Schoolmen; who were generally of the contrary part, and whose writings were altogether in a different style and form; taking liberty to coin and frame new terms of art to express their own sense, and to avoid circuit of speech, without regard to the pureness, pleasantness, and (as I may call it) lawfulness of the phrase or word. And again, because the great

---

11. **coarctation:** restriction.   12. **God . . . causes:** all God's operations in nature are carried out through natural laws. 13. **philosophy:** i.e., natural science.

14. **delicate:** affected.

labor then was with the people (of whom the Pharisees were wont to say, *Execrabilis ista turba, quae non novit legem*) [15] for the winning and persuading of them, there grew of necessity in chief price and request eloquence and variety of discourse, as the fittest and forciblest access into the capacity of the vulgar sort: so that these four causes concurring, the admiration of ancient authors, the hate of the Schoolmen, the exact study of languages, and the efficacy of preaching, did bring in an affectionate [16] study of eloquence and copie [17] of speech, which then began to flourish. This grew speedily to an excess; for men began to hunt more after words than matter; more after the choiceness of the phrase, and the round and clean composition of the sentence, and the sweet falling of the clauses, and the varying and illustration of their works with tropes and figures, than after the weight of matter, worth of subject, soundness of argument, life of invention, or depth of judgment. . . .

3. Here therefore is the first distemper of learning, when men study words and not matter; whereof, though I have represented an example of late times, yet it hath been and will be *secundum majus et minus* [18] in all time. . . .

5. The second which followeth is in nature worse than the former: for as substance of matter is better than beauty of words, so contrariwise vain matter is worse than vain words. . . .

Surely, like as many substances in nature which are solid do putrefy and corrupt into worms; so it is the property of good and sound knowledge to putrefy and dissolve into a number of subtle, idle, unwholesome, and (as I may term them) vermiculate [19] questions, which have indeed a kind of quickness and life of spirit, but no soundness of matter or goodness of quality. This kind of degenerate learning did chiefly reign amongst the Schoolmen: who having sharp and strong wits, and abundance of leisure, and small variety of reading, but their wits being shut up in the cells of a few authors (chiefly Aristotle their dictator) as their persons were shut up in the cells of monasteries and colleges, and knowing little history, either of nature or time, did out of no great quantity of matter and infinite agitation of wit spin out unto us those laborious webs of learning which are extant in their books. For the

wit and mind of man, if it work upon matter, which is the contemplation of the creatures of God, worketh according to the stuff and is limited thereby; but if it work upon itself, as the spider worketh his web, then it is endless, and brings forth indeed cobwebs of learning, admirable for the fineness of thread and work, but of no substance or profit. [20]

[The " distempers of learning " (continued): (c) excessive respect for traditional authority.]

V. 6. Another error hath proceeded from too great a reverence, and a kind of adoration of the mind and understanding of man; by means whereof, men have withdrawn themselves too much from the contemplation of nature, and the observations of experience, and have tumbled up and down, in their own reason and conceits. Upon these intellectualists, which are notwithstanding commonly taken for the most sublime and divine philosophers, Heraclitus gave a just censure, saying, " Men sought truth in their own little worlds, and not in the great and common world "; for they disdain to spell, and so by degrees to read in the volume of God's works: and contrariwise by continual meditation and agitation of wit do urge and as it were invocate their own spirits to divine and give oracles unto them, whereby they are deservedly deluded. . . .

[(d) Misconception of the true object of science, namely " the glory of the Creator and the relief of man's estate."]

11. But the greatest error of all the rest is the mistaking or misplacing of the last or furthest end of knowledge. For men have entered into a desire of learning and knowledge, sometimes upon a natural curiosity and inquisitive appetite; sometimes to entertain their minds with variety and delight; sometimes for ornament and reputation; and sometimes to enable them to victory of wit and contradiction; and most times for lucre and profession, [21] and seldom sincerely to give a true account of their gift of reason, to the benefit and use of men: as if there were sought in knowledge a couch whereupon to rest a searching and restless spirit; or a terrace for a wandering and variable mind to walk up and down with a fair prospect; or a tower of state for a proud mind to raise itself upon; or a fort

---

15. *Execrabilis . . . legem:* "This multitude which knoweth not the law are accursed" (John 7:49).   16. **affectionate:** zealous.   17. **copie:** abundance.   18. *secundum . . . minus:* in greater or lesser degree.   19. **vermiculate:** full of worms.

20. The third "vice" or "disease" in learning—not included here—is "deceit or untruth."   21. **profession:** livelihood.

or commanding ground for strife and contention; or a shop for profit or sale; and not a rich storehouse for the glory of the Creator and the relief of man's estate. But this is that which will indeed dignify and exalt knowledge, if contemplation and action may be more nearly and straitly conjoined and united together than they have been; a conjunction like unto that of the two highest planets, Saturn, the planet of rest and contemplation, and Jupiter, the planet of civil society and action. Howbeit, I do not mean, when I speak of use and action, that end beforementioned of the applying of knowledge to lucre and profession; for I am not ignorant how much that diverteth and interrupteth the prosecution and advancement of knowledge, like unto the golden ball thrown before Atalanta, which while she goeth aside and stoopeth to take up, the race is hindered,

Declinat cursus, aurumque volubile tollit.[22]

Neither is my meaning, as was spoken of Socrates, to call philosophy down from Heaven to converse upon the earth; that is, to leave natural philosophy aside, and to apply knowledge only to manners and policy.[23] But as both Heaven and earth do conspire and contribute to the use and benefit of man; so the end ought to be, from both philosophies to separate and reject vain speculations, and whatsoever is empty and void, and to preserve and augment whatsoever is solid and fruitful; that knowledge may not be as a courtesan, for pleasure and vanity only, or as a bondwoman, to acquire and gain to her master's use; but as a spouse, for generation, fruit, and comfort.

[Philosophy serves religion by manifesting God's glory in his own works.]

VI. 16. Wherefore to conclude this part, let it be observed, that there be two principal duties and services, besides ornament and illustration, which philosophy and human learning do perform to faith and religion. The one, because they are an effectual inducement to the exaltation of the glory of God. For as the Psalms and other Scriptures do often invite us to consider and magnify the great and wonderful works of God, so if we should rest only in the contemplation of the exterior of them as they first offer themselves to our senses, we should do a like injury unto the majesty of God, as if we should

judge or construe of the store of some excellent jeweler, by that only which is set out toward the street in his shop. The other, because they minister a singular help and preservative against unbelief and error. For our Savior saith, "You err, not knowing the Scriptures, nor the power of God"; laying before us two books or volumes to study, if we will be secured from error; first the Scriptures, revealing the will of God, and then the creatures expressing his power; whereof the latter is a key unto the former: not only opening our understanding to conceive the true sense of the Scriptures, by the general notions of reason and rules of speech; but chiefly opening our belief, in drawing us into a due meditation of the omnipotency of God, which is chiefly signed and engraven upon his works. Thus much therefore for divine testimony and evidence concerning the true dignity and value of learning.

THE
SECOND BOOK OF FRANCIS BACON
OF THE PROFICIENCE AND
ADVANCEMENT OF LEARNING
DIVINE AND HUMAN

[Poetry as imaginary history.]

IV. 1. Poesy is a part of learning in measure of words for the most part restrained, but in all other points extremely licensed, and doth truly refer to the imagination; which, being not tied to the laws of matter, may at pleasure join that which nature hath severed, and sever that which nature hath joined; and so make unlawful matches and divorces of things; *Pictoribus atque poetis, etc.*[24] It is taken in two senses in respect of words or matter. In the first sense it is but a character of style, and belongeth to arts of speech, and is not pertinent for the present. In the latter it is (as hath been said) one of the principal portions of learning, and is nothing else but feigned history, which may be styled as well in prose as in verse.

2. The use of this feigned history hath been to give some shadow of satisfaction to the mind of man in those points wherein the nature of things doth deny it, the world being in proportion inferior to the soul; by reason whereof there is, agreeable to the spirit of man, a more ample greatness, a more exact goodness, and a more absolute variety, than can be found in the nature of things. Therefore, be-

---

22. *Declinat . . . tollit:* "deserts the race, and picks up the golden ball" (Ovid, *Metamorphoses*, X. 667).   23. **manners . . . policy:** practical affairs, social or political.

24. *Pictoribus . . . poetis:* "Painters and poets [have been still allowed their pencils, and their fancies, unconfined]" (Horace, *Ars Poetica*, IX Roscommon's translation).

cause the acts or events of true history have not that magnitude which satisfieth the mind of man, poesy feigneth acts and events greater and more heroical. Because true history propoundeth the successes and issues of actions not so agreeable to the merits of virtue and vice, therefore poesy feigns them more just in retribution, and more according to revealed providence. Because true history representeth actions and events more ordinary and less interchanged, therefore poesy endueth them with more rareness, and more unexpected and alternative variations. So as it appeareth that poesy serveth and conferreth to magnanimity, morality, and to delectation. And therefore it was ever thought to have some participation of divineness, because it doth raise and erect the mind, by submitting the shows of things to the desires of the mind; whereas reason doth buckle and bow the mind unto the nature of things. And we see that by these insinuations[25] and congruities with man's nature and pleasure, joined also with the agreement and consort it hath with music, it hath had access and estimation in rude times and barbarous regions, where other learning stood excluded.

[Religion and science must be kept separate.]

VI. 1. . . . And as concerning divine philosophy or natural theology, it is that knowledge or rudiment of knowledge concerning God, which may be obtained by the contemplation of his creatures; which knowledge may be truly termed divine in respect of the object, and natural in respect of the light. The bounds of this knowledge are, that it sufficeth to convince atheism, but not to inform religion: and therefore there was never miracle wrought by God to convert an atheist, because the light of nature might have led him to confess a God: but miracles have been wrought to convert idolaters and the superstitious, because no light of nature extendeth to declare the will and true worship of God. For as all works do show forth the power and skill of the workman, and not his image, so it is of the works of God, which do show the omnipotency and wisdom of the maker, but not his image. And therefore therein the heathen opinion differeth from the sacred truth; for they supposed the world to be the image of God, and man to be an extract[26] or compendious image of the world; but the Scriptures never vouchsafe to attribute to the world that honor, as to be the image of God, but only " the work of his hands "; neither do they speak of any other image of God, but man. Wherefore by the contemplation of nature to induce and enforce the acknowledgment of God, and to demonstrate his power, providence, and goodness, is an excellent argument, and hath been excellently handled by divers.[27] But on the other side, out of the contemplation of nature, or ground of human knowledges, to induce any verity or persuasion concerning the points of faith, is in my judgment not safe: *Da fidei quae fidei sunt*.[28] For the heathen themselves conclude as much in that excellent and divine fable of the golden chain: " That men and gods were not able to draw Jupiter down to the earth; but contrariwise Jupiter was able to draw them up to heaven." So as we ought not to attempt to draw down or to submit the mysteries of God to our reason; but contrariwise to raise and advance our reason to the divine truth. So as in this part of knowledge, touching divine philosophy, I am so far from noting any deficience, as I rather note an excess: whereunto I have digressed because of the extreme prejudice which both religion and philosophy hath received and may receive by being commixed together; as that which undoubtedly will make an heretical religion, and an imaginary and fabulous philosophy.

[Natural science divided into " physic," dealing with matter and motion, and "metaphysic," dealing with " formal and final causes," i.e., the inner principles of things and their ultimate purpose. Too much attention has been paid to "purposes" and not enough to investigating the inner natures ("forms") of phenomena.]

VII. 1. Leaving therefore divine philosophy or natural theology (not divinity or inspired theology, which we reserve for the last of all as the haven and sabbath of all man's contemplations) we will now proceed to natural philosophy. . . .

2. Natural science or theory is divided into physic and metaphysic: wherein I desire it may be conceived that I use the word " metaphysic " in a differing sense from that that is received.[29] And in like manner, I doubt not but it will easily appear to men of judgment, that in this and other particulars, wheresoever my conception and notion may differ

---

25. insinuations: intertwinings (hence, close relationship).
26. extract: epitome; miniature reproduction (man as "microcosm").

27. divers: various (writers).   28. Da . . . sunt: "Render unto faith the things that are faith's."   29. received: accepted or understood.

from the ancient, yet I am studious to keep the ancient terms. For hoping well to deliver myself from mistaking, by the order and perspicuous expressing of that I do propound; I am otherwise zealous and affectionate to recede as little from antiquity, either in terms or opinions, as may stand with truth and the proficience of knowledge. . . .

3. To return therefore to the use and acception of the term "metaphysic," as I do now understand the word: it appeareth, by that which hath been already said, that I intend *philosophia prima*,[30] summary [31] philosophy and metaphysic, which heretofore have been confounded as one, to be two distinct things. For the one I have made as a parent or common ancestor to all knowledge; and the other I have now brought in as a branch or descendant of natural science. It appeareth likewise that I have assigned to summary philosophy the common principles and axioms which are promiscuous and indifferent [32] to several sciences: I have assigned unto it likewise the inquiry touching the operation of the relative and adventive characters of essencès,[33] as quantity, similitude, diversity, possibility, and the rest: with this distinction and provision: that they be handled as they have efficacy in nature, and not logically. It appeareth likewise that natural theology, which heretofore hath been handled confusedly with metaphysic, I have enclosed and bounded by itself. It is therefore now a question what is left remaining for metaphysic; wherein I may without prejudice preserve thus much of the conceit of antiquity, that physic should contemplate that which is inherent in matter, and therefore transitory; and metaphysic that which is abstracted and fixed. And again, that physic should handle that which supposeth in nature only a being and moving; and metaphysic should handle that which supposeth further in nature a reason, understanding, and platform.[34] But the difference, perspicuously expressed, is most familiar and sensible. For as we divided natural philosophy in general into the inquiry of causes, and productions of effects: so that part which concerneth the inquiry of causes we do subdivide according to the received and sound division of causes. The one part, which is physic, inquireth and handleth the material and efficient

causes; and the other, which is metaphysic, handleth the formal and final causes.[35]

5. For metaphysic, we have assigned unto it the inquiry of formal and final causes; which assignation, as to the former of them, may seem to be nugatory and void, because of the received and inveterate opinion, that the inquisition of man is not competent to find out essential forms or true differences: of which opinion we will take this hold, that the invention [36] of forms is of all other parts of knowledge the worthiest to be sought, if it be possible to be found. As for the possibility, they are ill discoverers that think there is no land, when they can see nothing but sea. But it is manifest that Plato, in his opinion of ideas,[37] as one that had a wit of elevation situate as upon a cliff,[38] did descry *that forms were the true object of knowledge;* but lost the real fruit of his opinion, by considering of forms as absolutely abstracted from matter, and not confined and determined by matter; and so turning his opinion upon theology, wherewith all his natural philosophy is infected. But if any man shall keep a continual watchful and severe eye upon action, operation, and the use of knowledge, he may advise and take notice what are the forms, the disclosures whereof are fruitful and important to the state of man. For as to the forms of substances [39] (man only except, of whom it is said, *Formavit hominem de limo terrae, et spiravit in faciem eius spiraculum vitae,*[40] and not as of all other creatures, *Producant aquae, producat terra*),[41] the forms of substances I say (as they are now by compounding and transplanting multiplied) are so perplexed, as they are not to be inquired; no more than it were either possible or to purpose to seek in gross the

35. **material . . . causes:** This "division" of causes is Aristotle's (*Metaphysics*): (1) "material," the stuff which is acted upon; (2) "efficient," that which actuates; (3) "formal," the inner individuating principle (*raison d'être*) which makes a thing what it is: often called the "form" (see below); (4) "final," that for the sake of which a thing exists: its end or purpose. For example, take a stone: its "material" cause is simply the stuff it is made of; its "efficient" cause is the force which places it where it is; its "formal" cause is what makes it a particular kind of stone (e.g., flint or quartz) and not another; its "final" cause is the purpose for which it exists (e.g., for throwing at somebody, for ornament.)   Bacon's innovation is to assign "formal causes" in scientific inquiry.   36. **invention:** discovery.   37. **Plato . . . ideas:** Plato's theory of ideal forms existing in heaven, of which earthly things, qualities, etc., were imperfect or shadowy copies.   38. **as . . . cliff:** like a person viewing distant objects from a point of vantage.   39. **substances:** here used to mean complex created things, or creatures, e.g., animals and trees.   40. *Formavit . . . vitae:* "[God] formed man of the dust of the earth, and breathed into his nostrils the breath of life" (Gen. 2:7).   41. *Producant . . . terra:* "Let the waters bring forth, let the earth bring forth" (Gen. 1:20,24).

30. *philosophia prima:* first (primary) philosophy.   31. **summary:** highest (or "basic").   32. **promiscuous . . . indifferent:** generally applicable.   33. **relative . . . essences:** the attributes of things when considered in their relationship with other things; thus, their "adventitious" qualities — qualities arising from outward relations.   34. **platform:** plan, or idea.

forms of those sounds which make words, which by composition and transposition of letters are infinite. But on the other side to inquire the form of those sounds or voices which make simple letters is easily comprehensible; and being known induceth and manifesteth the forms of all words, which consist and are compounded of them. In the same manner to inquire the form of a lion, of an oak, of gold; nay, of water, of air, is a vain pursuit: but to inquire the forms of sense, of voluntary motion, of vegetation, of colors, of gravity and levity, of density, of tenuity, of heat, of cold, and all other natures and qualities, which, like an alphabet, are not many, and of which the essences (upheld by matter) of all creatures do consist; to inquire, I say, the true forms of these, is that part of metaphysic which we now define of. Not but that physic doth make inquiry and take consideration of the same natures: but how? Only as to the material and efficient causes of them, and not as to the forms. For example, if the cause of whiteness in snow or froth be inquired, and it be rendered thus, that the subtle intermixture of air and water is the cause, it is well rendered; but nevertheless is this the form of whiteness? No; but it is the efficient, which is ever but *vehiculum formae*.[42] This part of metaphysic I do not find labored and performed: whereat I marvel not: because I hold it not possible to be invented by that course of invention which hath been used; in regard that men (which is the root of all error) have made too untimely a departure and too remote recess from particulars.

7. The second part of metaphysic is the inquiry of final causes, which I am moved to report not as omitted but as misplaced. And yet if it were but a fault in order, I would not speak of it: for order is matter of illustration, but pertaineth not to the substance of sciences. But this misplacing hath caused a deficience, or at least a great improficience in the sciences themselves. For the handling of final causes, mixed with the rest in physical inquiries, hath intercepted the severe and diligent inquiry of all real and physical causes, and given men the occasion to stay upon these satisfactory and specious causes,[43] to the great arrest and prejudice of further discovery. For this I find done not only by Plato, who ever anchoreth upon that shore, but

by Aristotle, Galen,[44] and others which do usually likewise fall upon these flats of discoursing causes. For to say that "the hairs of the eyelids are for a quickset and fence about the sight"; or that "the firmness of the skins and hides of living creatures is to defend them from the extremities of heat and cold"; or that "the bones are for the columns or beams, whereupon the frames of the bodies of living creatures are built"; or that "the leaves of trees are for protecting of the fruit"; or that "the clouds are for watering of the earth"; or that "the solidness of the earth is for the station and mansion of living creatures," and the like, is well inquired and collected in metaphysic, but in physic they are impertinent. Nay, they are indeed but *remoraes*[45] and hindrances to stay and slug the ship from further sailing; and have brought this to pass, that the search of the physical causes hath been neglected and passed in silence. And therefore the natural philosophy of Democritus[46] and some others, who did not suppose a mind or reason in the frame of things, but attributed the form thereof able to maintain itself to infinite essays or proofs[47] of nature, which they term fortune, seemeth to me (as far as I can judge by the recital and fragments which remain unto us) in particularities of physical causes more real and better inquired than that of Aristotle and Plato; whereof both intermingled final causes, the one as a part of theology, and the other as a part of logic, which were the favorite studies, respectively, of both those persons. Not because those final causes are not true, and worthy to be inquired, being kept within their own province; but because their excursions into the limits of physical causes hath bred a vastness[48] and solitude in that tract. . . .

[The fallacies ("idols") imposed upon us by the human mind itself: (a) making man the measure of all things and assuming that nature must behave according to our own sense of fitness; (b) individual prejudices and delusions; (c) inexact use of words.]

XIV. 9. But lastly, there is yet a much more important and profound kind of fallacies in the mind of man, which I find not observed or inquired at all, and think good to place here, as that which of all others appertaineth most to rectify judgment: the

---

42. *vehiculum formae:* vehicle of the form; that which carries within it the formal principle.   43. stay . . . causes: to be too soon contented with these plausible explanations (in terms of "end" or "purpose"), and so to neglect physical inquiries.

44. Galen: the most celebrated of ancient medical writers, born in Mysia about 130 A.D.   45. *remoraes: remora*, a fabulous fish said to adhere to the hull of a ship, and so impede its motion; thus, a hindrance.   46. Democritus: Greek philosopher who reduced nature to material atoms in a void.   47. proofs: efforts or experiments.   48. vastness: empty wilderness.

force whereof is such, as it does not dazzle or snare the understanding in some particulars, but doth more generally and inwardly infect and corrupt the state thereof. For the mind of man is far from the nature of a clear and equal glass, wherein the beams of things should reflect according to their true incidence; nay, it is rather like an enchanted glass, full of superstition and imposture, if it be not delivered and reduced. For this purpose, let us consider the false appearances [49] that are imposed upon us by the general nature of the mind, beholding them in an example or two; as first, in that instance which is the root of all superstition, namely, that to the nature of the mind of all men it is consonant for the affirmative or active to affect more than the negative or privative. So that a few times hitting or presence, countervails ofttimes failing or absence; as was well answered by Diagoras to him that showed him in Neptune's temple the great number of pictures of such as had scaped shipwreck, and had paid their vows to Neptune, saying, " Advise now, you that think it folly to invocate Neptune in tempest." " Yea, but " (saith Diagoras) " where are they painted that are drowned? " [50] Let us behold it in another instance, namely, that the spirit of man, being of an equal and uniform substance, doth usually suppose and feign in nature a greater equality and uniformity than is in truth. Hence it cometh, that the mathematicians cannot satisfy themselves except they reduce the motions of the celestial bodies to perfect circles, rejecting spiral lines, and laboring to be discharged of eccentrics.[51] Hence it cometh, that whereas there are many things in nature, as it were *monodica, sui juris;* [52] yet the cogitations of man do feign unto them relatives, parallels, and conjugates,[53] whereas no such thing is; as they have feigned an element of fire, to keep square with earth, water, and air, and the like. Nay, it is not credible, till it be opened, what a number of fictions and fantasies the similitude of human actions and arts, together with the making of man *communis mensura,*[54] have brought into natural philosophy; not much better than the heresy of the Anthropomorphites,[55] bred in the cells of gross and solitary monks, and the opinion of Epicurus, answerable to the same in heathenism, who supposed the gods to be of human shape. And therefore Velleius the Epicurean needed not to have asked, why God should have adorned the heavens with stars, as if he had been an *aedilis,*[56] one that should have set forth some magnificent shows or plays. For if that great workmaster had been of an human disposition, he would have cast the stars into some pleasant and beautiful works and orders, like the frets in the roofs of houses; whereas one can scarce find a posture in square, or triangle, or straight line, amongst such an infinite number; so differing an harmony there is between the spirit of man and the spirit of nature.

10. Let us consider again the false appearances imposed upon us by every man's own individual nature and custom,[57] in that feigned supposition that Plato maketh of the cave: for certainly if a child were continued in a grot or cave under the earth until maturity of age, and came suddenly abroad, he would have strange and absurd imaginations. So in like manner, although our persons live in the view of heaven, yet our spirits are included in the caves of our own complexions and customs, which minister unto us infinite errors and vain opinions, if they be not recalled to examination. . . .

11. And lastly, let us consider the false appearances that are imposed upon us by words,[58] which are framed and applied according to the conceit and capacities of the vulgar sort: and although we think we govern our words, and prescribe it well, *Loquendum ut vulgus sentiendum ut sapientes;* [59] yet certain it is that words, as a Tartar's bow,[60] do shoot back upon the understanding of the wisest, and mightily entangle and pervert the judgment. So as it is almost necessary, in all controversies and disputations, to imitate the wisdom of the mathematicians, in setting down in the very beginning the definitions of our words and terms, that others may know how we accept and understand them, and whether they concur with us or no. For it cometh to pass, for want of this, that we are sure to end there where we ought to have begun, which

---

49. false appearances: elsewhere called by Bacon "idols of the mind." This first type he calls the "idols of the tribe." See Intro., p. 157.   50. drowned: The story is told by Cicero (*De Natura Deorum*).   51. eccentrics: irregular orbits.   52. *monodica . . . juris:* unique, obeying no law but their own.   53. relatives . . . conjugates: relationships, analogies and connections.   54. *communis mensura:* the common measure (of all things); the teaching of Protagoras.   55. Anthropomorphites: a branch of the Monophysite heretics, who held that God was of human shape.   56. aedilis: The Roman "aediles" were officers in charge of public decorations, etc.   57. false . . . custom: the "idols of the cave" (or den). Reference is to Plato's parable in the *Republic*. In Book VII Plato describes ordinary men as dwellers in a cave with their backs turned to the light, seeing only shadows on the wall and mistaking them for realities.   58. false . . . words: the "idols of the market place."   59. *Loquendum . . . sapientes:* "Speak like common folk but think like wise men."   60. Tartar's bow: The Tartars, or Parthians, were said to shoot backward in retreat.

is, in questions and differences about words. To conclude therefore, it must be confessed that it is not possible to divorce ourselves from these fallacies and false appearances, because they are inseparable from our nature and condition of life; so yet nevertheless the caution of them (for all *elenches*,[61] as was said, are but cautions) doth extremely import the true conduct of human judgment. The particular *elenches* or cautions against these three false appearances, I find altogether deficient.

[Morality. Philosophers have described the virtues and discussed the theory of ethics, but have not shown us how to attain the good.]

XX. 2. The reason of this omission I suppose to be that hidden rock whereupon both this and many other barks of knowledge have been cast away; which is, that men have despised to be conversant in ordinary and common matters, the judicious direction whereof nevertheless is the wisest doctrine (for life consisteth not in novelties nor subtleties), but contrariwise they have compounded sciences chiefly of a certain resplendent or lustrous mass of matter, chosen to give glory either to the subtlety of disputations, or to the eloquence of discourses. But Seneca giveth an excellent check to eloquence, *Nocet illis eloquentia, quibus non rerum cupiditatem facit, sed sui.*[62] Doctrine should be such as should make men in love with the lesson, and not with the teacher; being directed to the auditor's benefit, and not to the author's commendation. And therefore those are of the right kind which may be concluded as Demosthenes concludes his counsel, *Quae si feceritis, non oratorem duntaxat in praesentia laudabitis, sed vosmetipsos etiam non ita multo post statu rerum vestrarum meliore.*[63]

3. Neither needed men of so excellent parts to have despaired of a fortune, which the poet Virgil promised himself, and indeed obtained, who got as much glory of eloquence, wit, and learning in the expressing of the observations of husbandry, as of the heroical acts of Aeneas:

Nec sum animi dubius, verbis ea vincere magnum
Quam sit, et angustis his addere rebus honorem.[64]

And surely, if the purpose be in good earnest, not to write at leisure that which men may read at leisure, but really to instruct and suborn action and active life, these Georgics of the mind, concerning the husbandry and tillage thereof, are no less worthy than the heroical descriptions of virtue, duty, and felicity. Wherefore the main and primitive division of moral knowledge seemeth to be into the exemplar or platform [65] of good, and the regiment or culture of the mind: the one describing the nature of good, the other prescribing rules how to subdue, apply, and accommodate the will of man thereunto.

[The doctrines of the Christian religion are based on revelation, not on reason or the light of nature.]

XXV. 2. Howbeit (if we will truly consider of it) more worthy it is to believe than to know as we now know. For in knowledge man's mind suffereth from [66] sense; but in belief it suffereth from spirit, such one as it holdeth for more authorized than itself, and so suffereth from the worthier agent. Otherwise it is of the state of man glorified; for then faith shall cease, and we shall know as we are known.

3. Wherefore we conclude that sacred theology (which in our idiom we call divinity) is grounded only upon the word and oracle of God, and not upon the light of nature: for it is written, *Coeli enarrant gloriam Dei;* [67] but it is not written, *Coeli enarrant voluntatem Dei;* [68] but of that it is said, *Ad legem et testimonium: si non fecerint secundum verbum istud, etc.*[69] This holdeth not only in those points of faith which concern the great mysteries of the Deity, of the creation, of the redemption, but likewise those which concern the law moral truly interpreted: " Love your enemies: do good to them that hate you: Be like to your heavenly Father, that suffereth his rain to fall upon the just and unjust." To this it ought to be applauded, *Nec vox hominem sonat:* [70] it is a voice beyond the light of nature. So we see the heathen poets, when they fall upon a libertine passion, do still expostulate with laws and moralities, as if they were opposite and malignant to nature; *Et quod natura remittit, invida jura*

---

61. *elenches:* self-contradictions, or logical refutations.   62. *Nocet . . . sui:* "Eloquence harms those in whom it arouses love, not of the subject, but of itself."   63. *Quae . . . meliore:* "If you do these things, you shall not only praise the orator at the moment, but yourselves also soon after, when your state of affairs has improved."   64. *Nec . . . honorem:* "Well do I know how hard it is to bind words to such use, and add luster even to these mean affairs" (Virgil, *Georgics*, III. 289).

65. **exemplar or platform:** pattern or ground plan.   66. **suffereth from:** receives impressions from.   67. *Coeli . . . Dei:* "The heavens declare the glory of God" (Ps. 19:1).   68. *Coeli . . . Dei:* "The heavens declare the will of God."   69. *Ad . . . etc.:* "To the law and to the testimony: if they speak [act] not according to this word [it is because there is no light in them]" (Isa. 8:20).   70. *Nec . . . sonat:* "Nor does this voice sound [like that of] a man" (Virgil, *Aeneid*, I. 328).

negant.[71] So said Dendamis the Indian unto Alexander's messengers, that he had heard somewhat of Pythagoras, and some other of the wise men of Grecia, and that he held them for excellent men: but that they had a fault, which was that they had in too great reverence and veneration a thing they called law and manners. So it must be confessed, that a great part of the law moral is of that perfection, whereunto the light of nature cannot aspire: how then is it that man is said to have by the light and law of nature, some notions and conceits of virtue and vice, justice and wrong, good and evil? Thus, because the light of nature is used in two several senses; the one, that which springeth from reason, sense, induction, argument, according to the laws of heaven and earth; the other, that which is imprinted upon the spirit of man by an inward instinct, according to the law of conscience, which is a sparkle of the purity of his first estate;[72] in which latter sense only he is participant of some light and discerning touching the perfection of the moral law: but how? sufficient to check the vice, but not to inform the duty. So then the doctrine of religion, as well moral as mystical, is not to be attained but by inspiration and revelation from God.

71. *Et . . . negant:* "And that which nature allows, jealous laws forbid" (Ovid, *Metamorphoses*, X. 330).

72. **first estate:** i.e., in Eden before the Fall.

John Donne

1572–1631

JOHN DONNE is a fascinating figure, whether you think of him as a man, as a poet, or as a divine, and still more when you consider him in all three aspects together. His poetry "went to the head" of many readers and critics in the two decades following World War I, and ever since it has been more read and discussed than at any time since his death. He impressed his contemporaries, first by his wit, learning, and personal charm, and later by the passion and eloquence of his preaching.

One may think of his life as a process in which he gradually turned away from dissipation, cynicism, and worldly ambition and became a devout Christian and a great churchman. Donne was born in London, probably in the early part of 1572, of Roman Catholic parents. His father, a prosperous ironmonger, was a Welshman of high pedigree; his mother was descended from the family of Sir Thomas More. She, left a widow when Donne was an infant, brought up her children strictly as Roman Catholics — in those days a risky thing to do. One of Donne's brothers died in prison for harboring a priest, and he himself not only had to leave Oxford (and perhaps Cambridge as well) without a degree, but later went through agonies of study and inward conflict before he could decide which Church was Christ's true "spouse." After leaving the university about a year younger than most students now enter it, he began to study law, a subject which suited his precise and subtle mind and in which he afterwards became very proficient. But first he had to face the pressing problem of religion, and, in the words of his earliest biographer, Isaak Walton,

About the nineteenth year of his age, he being then unresolved what religion to adhere to, and considering how much it concerned his soul to choose the most orthodox, did therefore . . . lay aside all study of the law . . . , and begun seriously to survey and consider the body of divinity, as it was then controverted between the reformed and the Roman Church.

It was then that he wrote the oft-quoted lines ("Satire III," ll. 79–84):

> On a huge hill,
> Cragged, and steep, Truth stands, and he that will
> Reach her, about must, and about must go;
> And what the hill's suddenness resists, win so;
> Yet strive so, that before age, death's twilight,
> Thy soul rest, for none can work in that night.

But we must not allow Walton to romanticize Donne's turbulent youth for us unduly; he was no pensive Hamlet, no mere "wrestler for the truth" — or if he was, he was a great deal else besides. The Donne who wrote the lines above was also writing the other *Satires,* the *Elegies,* and the early *Songs and Sonnets,* poems coruscating with wit, insolence, cynicism, and sophistication. Walton's obituary piety must be balanced against the realism of Sir Richard Baker,[1] who describes the young Donne as "not dissolute, but very neat, a great visitor of ladies, a great frequenter of plays, a great writer of con-

[1] Sir Richard Baker (1568–1645), historian; Donne's contemporary and friend at Oxford.

ceited verses." No doubt Donne's religious struggle was both genuine and severe, and yet a correct choice concerned his worldly prospects as well as his soul. Walton, describing his final choice of the Reformed Church, complacently remarks that "Truth had too much light about her to be hid from so sharp an inquirer; and he had too much ingenuity not to acknowledge he had found her." We have no right to question Donne's sincerity, and yet we cannot forget that he was ambitious, and that in rejecting Rome he was shaking off a handicap which would have excluded him forever from all public employment, and condemned him to the life of obscurity and danger from which his family had long suffered. He certainly hoped at one time that his skill in theological dispute would win the favor of King James I, and so lead on to some showy and lucrative office like a secretaryship or an ambassadorship rather than — as actually happened — to holy orders.

But no sooner had he cleared the way to advancement by becoming a Protestant, than he condemned himself to years of poverty and struggle by a hasty and (in a worldly sense) imprudent marriage. After voyaging to Cadiz (1596) and the Azores (1597) with Essex (and traveling also, at some undetermined date, in Italy and Spain), he had become private secretary to Sir Thomas Egerton, Keeper of the Great Seal, later Lord Ellesmere and Lord Chancellor of England. This seemed a very promising start, for Egerton (according to Walton) was much impressed by Donne's "learning, languages, and other abilities" and intended the secretaryship to be an introduction to "some more weighty employment in the state; for which, his Lordship did often protest, he thought him very fit." "Nor," Walton adds, "did his Lordship . . . account him to be so much his servant, as to forget he was his friend; and to testify it, did always use him with much courtesy, appointing him a place at his own table, to which he esteemed his company and discourse to be a great ornament." Within a short time, however, Donne had fallen hopelessly in love with Lady Egerton's niece Anne More, who lived with her aunt's family; and she, captivated by his irresistible charm, agreed to a secret engagement. Her father, Sir George More, tried to nip this love affair in the bud by carrying his daughter off home (she was still under seven-

teen). But it was too late, and they were secretly married, Anne being seventeen and Donne twenty-nine.

"This was the remarkable error of his life," says Walton. But was it? It certainly aroused the fury of Anne's father, who not only forced Egerton to dismiss Donne but even had his son-in-law thrown into jail, together with the parson who had performed the wedding ceremony and the friend who had given away the bride. It is true that all this put an end to Donne's worldly advancement; he fell out of the race for promotion and sank into a dim and rather squalid routine of rural domesticity, varied only by constant appeals to this potential patron or that, and by the distracting noise and the sicknesses of an ever-increasing family (there were twelve children in all). When he felt most depressed about his prospects he sometimes allowed himself to ask Hamlet's question, and even wrote a book (*Biathanatos, c.* 1608) justifying suicide. Undoubtedly the marriage, judged by ordinary standards, had been rash. But it had been a love match, and through all the vicissitudes of family life — the ever-recurring cycle of births, illnesses, deaths, and poverty — Donne and his wife remained constant lovers until death parted them. This love steadied and purified Donne's nature (it had needed some purifying), and was a necessary stage in his spiritual progress. Had he not loved Anne so much, he might never have come (as he finally did) to love God still more. The actual dating of the individual *Songs and Sonnets* will probably always remain conjectural, but the contrast between the more outrageous "evaporations" (such as "The Flea," "The Indifferent," "Go and Catch a Falling Star," "Woman's Constancy," and several of the *Elegies*) and such passionate utterances as "The Anniversary," "A Valediction: Forbidding Mourning," etc., is too striking to be without inward significance, and we must believe — with Grierson — that the poems "in which ardor is combined with elevation and delicacy of feeling were addressed to Anne More before and after their marriage."

Meanwhile Donne's destiny — or, as he himself afterwards believed, the guiding hand of Providence — was leading him steadily toward the Church. He helped Thomas Morton, then Dean of Gloucester and one of the King's chaplains, in a task the king had set his heart upon:

the conversion of the English Roman Catholics. And the controversial skill and theological knowledge which he displayed (especially in his *Pseudo-Martyr,* 1610) convinced the king that Donne was marked for ordination. Donne hesitated at first, whether for worldly or for spiritual reasons, or for both; and when Morton offered him a living he declined it on the ground that " some irregularities of his past life " might disgrace the sacred calling. A few years later, however, he was ordained (1615).

Two years after this, as if to wean him from all earthly affections, his wife was taken from him, and the whole force of his impassioned and tormented soul was now turned toward God. Four years after Anne's death, the king appointed him Dean of St. Paul's. To the duties of this responsible and conspicuous post, in spite of recurrent sickness and declining strength, Donne now devoted all the energies of his mind and heart. That personal magnetism which in his youth had won him friends and lovers as by " a strange kind of elegant irresistible art " now held his congregations spellbound.

His *Divine Poems, Devotions,* and *Sermons,* which include some of his finest work and rank high in the devotional literature of all time, show clearly that, although his faith burned strongly, it was seldom free from smoke. He never for long achieved the tranquil poise of one who is assured of salvation and whose conversation is in heaven. Contraries still met in him, and he had to wrestle daily with his God, beseeching him to

break, blow, burn and make me new.

Toward the close of his life, when he felt death approaching, he " prepared to leave the world before life left him." He had a portrait painted of himself in his winding sheet, and this, placed by his bedside, " became his hourly object until his death." A few days before the end, when he had " preached his own funeral sermon," he seems to have attained spiritual tranquillity. Looking back on his past life, he was able to say to an old friend:

I now plainly see that it was his [God's] will I should never settle or thrive till I entered into the ministry; in which I have now lived almost twenty years (I hope to his glory). . . . I cannot plead innocency of life, especially of my youth; but I am to be judged by a merciful God, who is not willing to see what I have done amiss. And though of myself I have nothing to present to him but sins and misery, yet I know he looks not upon me now as I am of myself, but as I am in my Saviour . . . : I am therefore full of inexpressible joy, and shall die in peace.

II

There are certain epochs in the history of poetry when a break has to be made with the past, and a new style devised to meet new needs. This happens when, as a result of complex historical causes — the rise of a new social class, a changed world picture, new scientific theories, religious, social, and economic developments, or a combination of these — a new kind of sensibility appears, which cannot be adequately expressed in the established forms.

Donne, as we shall see, was one of these innovators, the first in a series covering the past three hundred years. In him the intellectual curiosity of the Renaissance and the stimulus and strain of a new world view forced themselves into (nondramatic) verse and changed its quality. Donne is a representative figure in that he, like his age, had been trained along medieval lines and had then had to face the disturbing implications of the Copernican cosmography. Medieval and modern elements were mixed in him, and the result was the " Metaphysical " style. (See below.)

Another break of this kind occurred after 1660, when the era of civil war and religious fanaticism seemed safely over, when the ideas of the Royal Society were in the ascendant, and men aspired above all to be civilized, rational, correct, clear, and classical. In the eyes of men like Dryden the Elizabethan and Metaphysical styles, though admittedly admirable in their own time and for their own purposes, appeared barbarous, pedantic, or " gothic." The heroic couplet, as shaped by Dryden and perfected by Pope, was the medium best suited to an age no longer in love with paradox and mystery, no longer bent upon imaginative or spiritual pioneering, but anxious instead to say as crisply, plainly, and effectively as possible what all reasonable men were thinking. Another such break occurred at the end of the eighteenth century, when Rousseau and the French Revolution had cracked the molds of the *ancien régime* and spread abroad new ferments of enthusiasm, nature worship, and humanitarian sentiment. The couplet, so expressive of fixity and finality in thought and in society, seemed no longer able to contain the new and heady wine, and Wordsworth wrote his Preface and the *Lyrical Ballads*. Another break came (after World War I) in the 1920's, when the tradition started by Wordsworth and developed by the Victorians seemed itself to have lost vitality, and Yeats, Eliot, D. H. Lawrence, and others struggled to free themselves from the nineteenth century in order to speak as men of their own time.

When these breaks and new starts take place, it generally happens that an earlier style or school, long out of favor, enjoys a renewed vogue. This is what happened to Donne in the 1920's. Everyone was then reading and discussing him, and the new poets were learning from him how to talk and argue in verse, how to be tough, subtle, and allusive. In that postwar decade there was a widespread revolt against something called " Victorianism," almost against the nineteenth century as such. The war of 1914–18 seemed to have made nonsense of that century's hopes and ideals; accordingly, it was hastily assumed that the ideals had been bogus all the time, and that the whole period had been wormeaten with sentimentality, progress worship, escapism, and hypocrisy. Those who felt that the world was much harsher, uglier, and more puzzling than their grandfathers had imagined turned with distaste from the whole Wordsworthian and Tennysonian tradition (often without understanding it) and found in Donne something much more to their taste. Here at least was a poet as inquisitive, as cynical, and as disenchanted as themselves, and one who could use his brains as well as his emotions. The very fact that Donne had been neglected for a couple of centuries added zest to the new enthusiasm. The feeling was very much like that expressed three centuries earlier by Thomas Carew in his " Elegy upon the Death of Dr. John Donne":

The Muses' garden, with pedantic weeds
O'erspread, was purged by thee; the lazy seeds
Of servile imitation thrown away,
And fresh invention planted. . . .
Thou hast . . . opened us a mine
Of rich and pregnant fancy, drawn a line
Of masculine expression. . . .

These lines show that Donne was recognized in his own time as an innovator. Although his world picture is essentially Elizabethan, and although witty and " conceited " writing abounds in the poetry that precedes him, nevertheless it is right to think of him as one who deliberately broke with the tradition of the Petrarchan sonneteers and with the classical and pastoral conventions of the mellifluous song writers, and infused into lyric poetry new qualities of psychological realism and intellectual complexity. Instead of sighing or yearning or singing, he often scoffed, analyzed, or argued, and into everything that he wrote he packed a weight of close and clear thinking.

Donne's reputation has always had its ups and downs. His contemporary, Ben Jonson, said that " for not keeping of accent he deserved hanging," but he also " esteemed him the first poet in the world in some things " (he seems to have meant some of the early *Elegies* and *Epistles,* in which Donne's intellectual fireworks appear in their most exuberant and dazzling form). Dryden called him " the greatest wit, though not the greatest poet of our nation." It was Dryden (followed by Samuel Johnson [see his *Life of Cowley,* below]) who fixed upon Donne and his school the label " Metaphysical." " He affects the metaphysics," said Dryden, " and perplexes the minds of the fair sex with nice speculations of philosophy, when he should engage their hearts, and entertain them with the softnesses of love." Dryden meant that Donne appeared to him learned and obscure; he sensed in Donne that medieval-Scholastic cast of mind from which he and his generation were emancipating themselves. The term " Metaphysical " has stuck to Donne and his followers, and it is important to remember, when using it ourselves, that it does not mean simply " philosophical." There is philosophical poetry, poetry dealing with ultimate issues, or the nature of things, even with strictly metaphysical problems, which is not " Metaphysical" in this special sense (one thinks of Milton, Pope, Wordsworth, Tennyson, and others). When we call Donne " Metaphysical " we are not classing him with such poets as these; he seldom writes from a purely philosophical impulse. What he does constantly do, however, is to use philosophical imagery to illustrate and define his emotional and intellectual adventures. And this imagery is mainly drawn from Scholastic sources of the medieval type: astronomy, astrology, alchemy, mathematics, the Aristotelian doctrines of form and matter, soul and body; and of course from the vast reservoir of Christian theology. It was precisely because so much of this was coming to seem obsolete in Dryden's time that Dryden broke with it and changed his notes to "heroic."

Samuel Johnson thought that poetry should deal in sublime or moving generalities, such as find an echo in every heart, and found the Metaphysicals too elaborate, too analytical, and too full of farfetched conceits. "Deficient in the sublime and the pathetic," he wrote, "they abounded in hyperbole, in unnatural thoughts, violent fictions, foolish conceits"; they "yoked heterogeneous ideas by violence together"; "to show their learning was their whole endeavor." He conceded that to write on their plan it was at least necessary to read and to think, but it is not surprising that Johnson, to whom Gray's "Elegy" was a touchstone of poetic excellence, should have found Donne neither "natural" nor "just."

The Romantics, on the whole, had little use for Donne. He was too purely intellectual, cared nothing for nature, and was deficient in color and music. Coleridge, who relished his wit and admired his sermons, wrote of him:

> With Donne, whose Muse on dromedary trots,
> Wreathe iron pokers into true-love knots;
> Rhyme's sturdy cripple, fancy's maze and clue,
> Wit's forge and fire-blast, meaning's press and
>   screw.

And this was the general view of him until about 1920; he was like a fire choked with fuel and smoke, which only seldom flashed into pure flame — that is to say, into lines or images pleasing to a romantic taste.

To say that the poets, critics, and readers of the 1920's found in Donne a model and a stimulus is not to say that his vogue was a passing fashion. It is not likely that he will ever again be omitted, as Arnold omitted him, from the muster roll of our great poets. We no longer instinctively judge poets by nineteenth-century standards; "great" poetry, we now see, can be conceived and composed in the "wits" as well as in what the Victorians meant by the "soul." The distinctive merit of Donne (though some other poets, not all of them of his school or pe-

riod, have it also) is that he can be "witty" — that is, intellectually nimble and alert — without ceasing to be passionate. Sometimes, indeed, his brain seems to be doing all the work and his heart very little; he will at times draw out an argument, expand a metaphor, or exploit a paradox, in a spirit of sheer extravagance. But at his best he thinks and feels simultaneously; his brilliant intellect plays with glancing lights upon a stream of strong emotion. Moreover, he brought the language of lyric poetry much closer than his predecessors had done to that of speech, skillfully counterpointing speech rhythms with metrical patterns and introducing a new bluntness of tone and vocabulary.

Coupled with this tone is a new directness of approach. In his love poetry Donne usually brushes convention aside and explores his feelings — sometimes with curiosity, irony, or cynicism, or again with ardent idealism or intense devotion, but always with subtlety and precision — never with mere profuseness or sentimentality. It is useless, in reading Donne, to sit passively and expect to be charmed, or lulled, or glutted with sound and color. To read him properly is a bracing experience; one's whole self, mind as well as soul, must be on the alert. There is in him no imprecise word or image, no vague suggestiveness; no phrase of his can be slurred over without loss of essential meaning. To read Donne is indeed an excellent preparation for reading "modern" poetry. For although he does not give us the abrupt transitions, the cinematograph technique of some living poets, he yet demands from us, by his high speed and his ever-shifting imagery, a similar kind of vigilance.

With all this in mind, let us consider a few examples of Donne's poetry. First, what about these "conceits" which Dr. Johnson condemned? What is a conceit? We might begin by calling it a farfetched comparison, a bringing together of thoughts or images usually considered to be very remote from each other. In the poem "A Valediction: Of Weeping," where Donne is bidding a tearful farewell to his lady, he first compares his tears to coins bearing her image, and thence deriving their value:

> For thy face coins them, and thy stamp they bear,
> And by this mintage they are something worth, . . .

But this does not satisfy him, and he passes on to a far more extravagant comparison:

> On a round ball
> A workman that hath copies by, can lay
> An Europe, Afric, and an Asia,
> And quickly make that, which was nothing, *All;*
> So doth each tear,
> Which thee doth wear,
> A globe, yea world by that impression grow,
> Till thy tears mixed with mine do overflow
> This world, by waters sent from thee, my heaven
> dissolvèd so.

The shape of the teardrop reminds him first of a globe; then he thinks of a globe on which a map of the world is depicted; the mapmaker has turned the round "O" of the globe — i.e., in another sense, "nothing" — into "everything," because the world is "all." Similarly, each teardrop which bears the lady's image becomes a whole world, because she is everything to him; and lastly, because she is his "heaven," *her* tears are like rain from "dissolving" clouds above, and mixed with his own will overflow the earth. The "world" image is a favorite one with Donne; he often uses it to symbolize the wholeness of perfect love. Thus the lovers in "The Sun Rising" are a world of themselves, and Donne tells the sun:

> Thou sun art half as happy as we,
> In that the world's contracted thus;
> Thine age asks ease, and since thy duties be
> To warm the world, that's done in warming us.

The same image or "conceit" appears again in a very different form and with a quite different meaning, in the "Hymn to God My God, in My Sickness," where his own prone figure, as he lies on his bed sick to death, becomes a map studied by his physicians. This thought at once suggests others: his death will be a "Southwest discovery"; it will be a passing through the straits of death into the Pacific of eternity. Moreover, just as in all flat maps east and west are one, though apparently so far apart, so his west (sunset, death) is really also his east (sunrise, resurrection) because it is the entrance into new life:

> As west and east
> In all flat maps (and I am one) are one,
> So death doth touch the Resurrection.

The best of Donne's prose is in his *Devotions* and *Sermons*, of which some specimens are given below. We saw above how powerfully his sermons affected his hearers, and it is possible to guess why this was so — although by our standards they are too long, and too heavily laden with Scholastic learning and ingenious analogies. But he evidently preached like a man possessed: possessed by the thoughts of God, of eternity, of Heaven, of sin, judgment, mercy, and redemption; and in his passionate yearning to save souls he constantly rose to a richly orchestrated eloquence, often varied, however, and made more telling by a familiar, everyday allusion. Donne's prose unit is the cumulative period (often of enormous length and intricacy), and no short passage can give a true impression of his style. The reader is referred to the extracts which follow; and when he has read these and the *Divine Poems,* and juxtaposed both with the earlier secular verse, he will perhaps begin to see more clearly why Carew ended his "Elegy upon Donne" with these words:

> Here lies a King that ruled as he thought fit
> The universal Monarchy of wit;
> Here lie two Flamens, and both those the best,
> Apollo's first, at last the true God's priest.

SONGS AND SONNETS

First published in 1633 (after Donne's death). It is not possible to date the composition of these poems exactly, but they were probably written before 1600 (Ben Jonson says "ere he was twenty-five years old"). It is usually supposed that the more cynical ones were written before 1598, and the more passionate and heartfelt after his meeting with Anne More in that year.

THE GOOD MORROW

I wonder by my troth, what thou and I
Did, till we loved? were we not weaned till then?
But sucked° on country pleasures, childishly?
Or snorted° we in the seven sleepers'° den?
'Twas so; but this, all pleasures fancies be.
If ever any beauty I did see,
Which I desired, and got, 'twas but a dream of thee.

THE GOOD MORROW. **3. sucked:** suckled. **4. snorted:** snored. **seven sleepers:** seven young men of Ephesus who (according to Gregory of Tours) were walled up in a cave by the persecuting Emperor Decius in A.D. 250, and slept there till they were found alive in A.D. 479.

And now good morrow to our waking souls,
Which watch not one another out of fear;
For love all love of other sights controls,   10
And makes one little room an everywhere.
Let sea-discoverers to new worlds have gone,
Let maps to other, worlds on worlds have shown,
Let us possess one world, each hath one, and is one.

My face in thine eye, thine in mine appears,
And true plain hearts do in the faces rest;
Where can we find two better hemispheres
Without sharp north, without declining west?
Whatever dies, was not mixed equally;°
If our two loves be one, or thou and I   20
Love so alike that none do slacken, none can die.

SONG

Go, and catch a falling star,
   Get with child a mandrake° root,
Tell me, where all past years are,
   Or who cleft the devil's foot,
Teach me to hear mermaids singing,
Or to keep off envy's stinging,
      And find
      What wind
Serves to advance an honest mind.

If thou be'st born to strange sights,   10
   Things invisible to see,
Ride ten thousand days and nights,
   Till age snow white hairs on thee,
Thou, when thou return'st, wilt tell me
All strange wonders that befell thee,
      And swear
      Nowhere
Lives a woman true, and fair.

If thou find'st one, let me know,
   Such a pilgrimage were sweet;   20
Yet do not, I would not go,
   Though at next door we might meet,
Though she were true, when you met her,
And last, till you write your letter,
      Yet she
      Will be
False, ere I come, to two, or three.

WOMAN'S CONSTANCY

Now thou hast loved me one whole day,
Tomorrow when thou leav'st, what wilt thou say?

Wilt thou then antedate some new-made vow?
      Or say that now
We are not just those persons, which we were?
Or, that oaths made in reverential fear
Of Love, and his wrath, any may forswear?
Or, as true deaths true marriages untie,
So lovers' contracts, images of those,
Bind but till sleep, death's image, them unloose?
      Or, your own end to justify,   11
For having purposed change, and falsehood, you
Can have no way but falsehood to be true?
Vain lunatic, against these 'scapes° I could
      Dispute, and conquer, if I would,
      Which I abstain to do,
For by tomorrow, I may think so too.

THE CANONIZATION

For God's sake hold your tongue, and let me
      love;
   Or chide my palsy, or my gout,
My five gray hairs, or ruined fortune flout;
   With wealth your state, your mind with arts im-
      prove,
      Take you a course, get you a place,
      Observe his Honor, or his Grace,
Or the king's real, or his stampèd face°
   Contemplate; what you will, approve,
   So you will let me love.

Alas, alas, who's injured by my love?   10
   What merchant's ships have my sighs drowned?
Who says my tears have overflowed his ground?
   When did my colds a forward spring remove?
      When did the heats which my veins fill
      Add one more to the plaguy bill?°
Soldiers find wars, and lawyers find out still
   Litigious men, which quarrels move,
   Though she and I do love.

Call us what you will, we are made such by love;
   Call her one, me another fly,   20
We're tapers too, and at our own cost die,°
   And we in us find th' eagle and the dove.°
      The Phoenix° riddle hath more wit
      By us; we two being one, are it.
So to one neutral thing both sexes fit,
   We die and rise the same, and prove
   Mysterious by this love.°

19. not . . . equally: not compounded of simple and similar elements, and therefore subject to corruption. Cf. Aquinas: "For there is no corruption save where there is contrariety." SONG. 2. mandrake: the mandragora plant, with a forked root like the lower part of the human body. It was currently supposed to shriek when pulled up.

WOMAN'S CONSTANCY. 14. 'scapes: excuses, evasions. THE CANONIZATION. 7. stampèd face: i.e., on coins. 15. plaguy bill: list of deaths from the plague (issued weekly during epidemics). A big epidemic of plague occurred in 1603. 20-21. Call . . . die: "Call us each midges, which burn in a taper's flame; we are also like the tapers, self-consumed." 22. Eagle . . . dove: symbols of constancy and love. 23-27. Phoenix . . . love: Only one of these fabulous birds ever existed at a time; it died (like the taper) self-consumed in flame, but from its ashes arose a new phoenix.

We can die by it, if not live by love,
  And if unfit for tombs and hearse
Our legend be, it will be fit for verse;   30
  And if no piece of chronicle° we prove,
  We'll build in sonnets pretty rooms;
  As well a well-wrought urn becomes
The greatest ashes, as half-acre tombs,
  And by these hymns, all shall approve
  Us canonized for love;

And thus invoke us: "You whom reverend love
  Made one another's hermitage;
You, to whom love was peace, that now is rage;
  Who° did the whole world's soul contract, and
      drove   40
    Into the glasses of your eyes
    (So made such mirrors, and such spies,
That they did all to you epitomize),
    Countries, towns, courts°: beg from above
    A pattern of your love! "°

SONG

Sweetest love, I do not go,
  For weariness of thee,
Nor in hope the world can show
  A fitter love for me;
    But since that I
Must die at last, 'tis best
To use myself in jest,
    Thus by feigned deaths° to die.

Yesternight the sun went hence,
  And yet is here today;   10
He hath no desire nor sense,
  Nor half so short a way:
    Then fear not me,
But believe that I shall make
Speedier journeys, since I take
    More wings and spurs than he.

O how feeble is man's power,
  That° if good fortune fall,
Cannot add another hour,
  Nor a lost hour recall!   20
    But come bad chance,
And we join to it our strength,
And we teach it art and length,°
    Itself o'er us to advance.

When thou sigh'st, thou sigh'st not wind,
  But sigh'st° my soul away,
When thou weep'st, unkindly kind,
  My life's blood doth decay.
    It cannot be
That thou lov'st me, as thou say'st,   30
If in thine my life thou waste,
    That art the best of me.

Let not thy divining heart
  Forethink me any ill,
Destiny may take thy part,
  And may thy fears fulfill;
    But think that we
Are but turned aside to sleep;
They who one another keep
    Alive, ne'er parted be.   40

THE ANNIVERSARY

All kings, and all their favorites,
  All glory of honors, beauties, wits,
The sun itself, which makes times,° as they pass,
Is elder by a year, now, than it was
When thou and I first one another saw:
All other things to their destruction draw,
  Only our love hath no decay;
This, no tomorrow hath, nor yesterday,
Running it never runs from us away,
But truly keeps his first, last, everlasting day.   10

Two graves must hide thine and my corse,
  If one might, death were no divorce.
Alas, as well as other princes, we
(Who prince enough in one another be)
Must leave at last in death, these eyes, and ears,
Oft fed with true oaths, and with sweet salt tears;
  But souls where nothing dwells but love
(All other thoughts being inmates°) then shall
      prove
This, or a love increasèd there above,
When bodies to their graves, souls from their
      graves remove.   20

And then we shall be throughly blessed,
  But we no more than all the rest;°
Here upon earth, we're kings, and none but we
Can be such kings, nor of such subjects be.
Who is so safe as we? where none can do
Treason to us, except one of us two.
  True and false fears let us refrain,

31. chronicle: prose history or inscription.   **40-44. Who . . . courts:** Cf. "The Good Morrow," l. 14, "Let us possess one world, each hath one, and is one."   **44-45. beg . . . love:** The canonized lovers are asked to pray Heaven for a pattern for others to copy.   **SONG. 8. feigned deaths:** imagined deaths (departure from his mistress being considered as a form of "dying").   **18-23. That . . . length:** "We can make ill luck seem worse and last longer, though we cannot prolong or recover good fortune."

26. sigh'st: Each sigh was supposed to consume a drop of the heart's blood. **THE ANNIVERSARY. 3. times:** seasons. **18. inmates:** transient lodgers (as distinct from the permanent dweller, love). **22. But . . . rest:** In Heaven all are equally happy, whereas here on earth "none but we can be such kings."

Let us love nobly, and live, and add again
Years and years unto years, till we attain   29
To write threescore: this is the second of our reign.

LOVE'S GROWTH

I scarce believe my love to be so pure
     As I had thought it was,
     Because it doth endure
Vicissitude, and season, as the grass;
Methinks I lied all winter, when I swore
My love was infinite, if spring make it more.
But if this medicine, love, which cures all sorrow
With more, not only be no quintessence,°
But mixed of all stuffs, paining soul, or sense,
And of the sun his working vigor borrow,   10
Love's not so pure, and abstract, as they use
To say, which have no mistress but their Muse,
But as all else, being elemented° too,
Love sometimes would contemplate, sometimes do.

And yet no greater, but more eminent,°
     Love by the spring is grown;
     As, in the firmament,
Stars by the sun are not enlarged, but shown,°
Gentle love deeds, as blossoms on a bough,
From love's awakened root do bud out now.   20
If, as in water stirred more circles be
Produced by one, love such additions take,
Those like so many spheres, but one heaven make,
For they are all concentric unto thee.°
And though each spring do add to love new heat,
As princes do in times of action get
New taxes, and remit them not in peace,
No winter shall abate the spring's increase.

THE DREAM

Dear love, for nothing less than thee
Would I have broke this happy dream,
     It was a theme
For reason, much too strong for fantasy,
Therefore thou waked'st me wisely; yet
My dream thou brok'st not, but continued'st it;
Thou art so truth,° that thoughts of thee suffice
To make dreams truths, and fables histories;
Enter these arms, for since thou thought'st it best,
Not to dream all my dream, let's act the rest.   10

As lightning, or a taper's light,
Thine eyes, and not thy noise waked me;
     Yet I thought thee
(For thou lovest truth) an angel, at first sight,
But when I saw thou sawest my heart,
And knew'st my thoughts, beyond an angel's art,°
When thou knew'st what I dreamt, when thou
     knew'st when
Excess of joy would wake me, and cam'st then,
I must confess, it could not choose but be
Profane, to think thee anything but thee.   20

Coming and staying showed thee, thee,
But rising makes me doubt, that now,
     Thou art not thou.
That love is weak, where fear's as strong as he;
'Tis not all spirit, pure, and brave,
If mixture it of *Fear, Shame, Honor,* have.
Perchance as torches which must ready be,
Men light and put out, so thou deal'st with me,
Thou cam'st to kindle, goest to come; then I
Will dream that hope again, but else would die.   30

A VALEDICTION: OF WEEPING

     Let me pour forth
My tears before thy face, whilst I stay here,
For thy face coins them, and thy stamp they bear,°
And by this mintage they are something worth,
     For thus they be
     Pregnant of thee;
Fruits of much grief they are, emblems of more;
When a tear falls, that thou falls which it bore,°
So thou and I are nothing then, when on a diverse
     shore.

     On a round ball   10
A workman that hath copies by, can lay
An Europe, Afric, and an Asia,
And quickly make that, which was nothing, *All;*°
     So doth each tear,
     Which thee doth wear,
A globe, yea world by that impression grow,°
Till thy tears mixed with mine do overflow
This world, by waters sent from thee, my heaven
     dissolvèd so.

---

16. **And . . . art:** She can read his thoughts, which angels cannot do. A VALEDICTION: OF WEEPING. **3. For . . . bear:** in general, because she causes them, but probably also because each (like a tiny mirror) reflects her face. **8. that . . . bore:** "Thou" is probably a noun, thus: "With each tear that falls, there falls also that 'Thou' (image of thee) which it carried upon it." **10-13. On . . . All:** A skilled geographer, with maps at hand, can soon turn a globe (shaped like "O," hence "nothing") into a representation of the world, i.e., "All." **14-16. So . . . grow:** "In the same way each tear of mine, because it has your image in it, becomes a globe, indeed a whole world (because you are all the world to me)."

LOVE'S GROWTH. **8. quintessence:** (in ancient and medieval philosophy) the fifth essence, apart from the "four elements"; a refined extract supposed to have medicinal properties. **13. elemented:** embodied in, or mixed with, material elements (earth, water, air, fire). **15. eminent:** conspicuous. **18. shown:** i.e., made to *seem* larger (said to be the case just before sunrise). **23-24. Those . . . thee:** referring to the medieval world picture of concentric heavenly "spheres" surrounding the earth. THE DREAM. **7. truth:** She is Truth itself (like God himself), hence—

O more than moon,
Draw not up seas to drown me in thy sphere,   20
Weep me not dead, in thine arms, but forbear
To teach the sea, what it may do too soon;
        Let not the wind
        Example find,
To do me more harm, than it purposeth;
Since thou and I sigh one another's breath,
Whoe'er sighs most, is cruelest, and hastes the
        other's death.

THE MESSAGE

Send home my long strayed eyes to me,
Which O! too long have dwelt on thee;
Yet since there they have learned such ill,
        Such forced fashions,
        And false passions,
            That they be
            Made by thee
Fit for no good sight, keep them still.

Send home my harmless heart again,
Which no unworthy thought could stain;   10
But if it be taught by thine
        To make jestings
        Of protestings,
            And cross° both
            Word and oath,
Keep it, for then 'tis none of mine.

Yet send me back my heart and eyes,
That I may know, and see thy lies,
And may laugh and joy, when thou
        Art in anguish   20
        And dost languish
            For someone
            That will none,
Or prove as false as thou art now.

A VALEDICTION:
FORBIDDING MOURNING

As virtuous men pass mildly away,
    And whisper to their souls, to go,
Whilst some of their sad friends do say,
    The breath goes now, and some say, no:

So let us melt, and make no noise,
    No tear-floods, nor sigh-tempests move,
'Twere profanation of our joys
    To tell the laity our love.

Moving° of th' earth brings harms and fears,
    Men reckon what it did and meant,   10
But trepidation of the spheres,
    Though greater far, is innocent.°

Dull sublunary lovers' love
    (Whose soul is sense) cannot admit
Absence, because it doth remove
    Those things which elemented it.°

But we by a love, so much refined,
    That ourselves know not what it is,
Interassurèd of the mind,
    Care less eyes, lips, and hands to miss.   20

Our two souls therefore, which are one,
    Though I must go, endure not yet
A breach, but an expansion,
    Like gold to airy thinness beat.

If they be two, they are two so
    As stiff twin compasses are two,
Thy soul the fixed foot, makes no show
    To move, but doth, if th' other do.

And though it in the center sit,
    Yet when the other far doth roam,   30
It leans, and hearkens after it,
    And grows erect, as that comes home.

Such wilt thou be to me, who must
    Like th' other foot, obliquely run;
Thy firmness makes my circle just,
    And makes me end, where I begun.

THE FUNERAL

Whoever comes to shroud me, do not harm
        Nor question much
That subtle wreath of hair, which crowns my arm;
The mystery, the sign you must not touch,
        For° 'tis my outward soul,
Viceroy to that, which then to heaven being gone,
        Will leave this to control,
And keep these limbs, her provinces, from dissolu-
        tion.°

A VALEDICTION: FORBIDDING MOURNING. **9-12. Moving . . . innocent:** Earthquakes cause alarm and damage, but heavenly
movements (specifically the oscillation of the ecliptic or sun's
orbit, which was supposed to cause the precession of the equinoxes — continuous changes in the time of the equinoxes due
to slow change in the position of the earth's axis) are harmless.
16. which . . . it: in which it was embodied; or simply, which
composed it. THE FUNERAL. **5-8. For . . . dissolution:** "The
soul is what keeps the body intact; when mine has departed,
the wreath of hair must act as its external representative."

THE MESSAGE. **14. cross:** cancel.

For° if the sinewy thread my brain lets fall
    Through every part,   10
Can tie those parts, and make me one of all;
These hairs which upward grew, and strength and
    art
    Have from a better brain,°
Can better do't; except she meant that I
    By this should know my pain,
As prisoners then are manacled, when they're con-
    demned to die.

Whate'er she meant by it, bury it with me,
    For since I am
Love's martyr, it might breed idolatry,
If into others' hands these reliques came;   20
    As 'twas humility
To afford° to it all that a soul can do,
    So, 'tis some bravery,°
That since you would save none of me, I bury some
    of you.

THE PROHIBITION

    Take heed of loving me,
At least remember, I forbade it thee;
Not that I shall repair my unthrifty waste
Of breath and blood, upon thy sighs, and tears,
By being to thee then what to me thou wast;
But so great joy our life at once outwears,
Then, lest thy love, by my death, frustrate be,
If thou love me, take heed of loving me.

    Take heed of hating me,
Or too much triumph in the victory.   10
Not that I shall be mine own officer,°
And hate with hate again retaliate;
But thou wilt lose the style° of conqueror,
If I, thy conquest, perish by thy hate.
Then, lest my being nothing lessen thee,
If thou hate me, take heed of hating me.

    Yet, love and hate me too,
So, these extremes shall neither's office do;°
Love me, that I may die the gentler way;
Hate me, because thy love is too great for
    me;   20
Or let these two, themselves, not me decay;

So shall I, live, thy stage, not triumph be;
Lest thou thy love and hate and me undo,°
To let me live, O love and hate me too.

HOLY SONNETS

The "Holy Sonnets" given here are taken from the series of nineteen composed after the death of Donne's wife, which occurred in 1617, two years after his ordination. These sonnets show all the force of Donne's passionate nature turned toward God. His poetical powers are seen here at their height, for, though his "wit" has not ceased to be active, it is used, not for the sake of "conceit" but as a means of expressing profound and sincere emotion.

I

Thou hast made me, and shall thy work decay?
Repair me now, for now mine end doth haste,
I run to death, and death meets me as fast,
And all my pleasures are like yesterday;
I dare not move my dim eyes any way,
Despair behind, and death before doth cast
Such terror, and my feeble flesh doth waste
By sin in it, which it towards hell doth weigh;
Only thou art above, and when towards thee
By thy leave I can look, I rise again;   10
But our old subtle foe so tempteth me,
That not one hour myself I can sustain;
Thy grace may wing me to prevent his art,
And thou like adamant° draw mine iron heart.

VII

At the round earth's imagined corners, blow
Your trumpets, angels, and arise, arise
From death, you numberless infinities
Of souls, and to your scattered bodies go,
All whom the flood did, and fire shall o'erthrow,
All whom war, dearth, age, agues, tyrannies,
Despair, law, chance, hath slain, and you whose
    eyes
Shall behold God, and never taste death's woe.°
But let them sleep, Lord, and me mourn a space,
For, if above all these, my sins abound,   10
'Tis late to ask abundance of thy grace,
When we are there; here on this lowly ground,
Teach me how to repent; for that's as good
As if thou hadst sealed my pardon, with thy blood.

9–13. **For ... brain:** "If the spinal cord and nerves ('sinewy thread') descending from the brain can unify my bodily parts, surely her hairs, which grew 'upward,' and from a better brain, can do it better still. 22. **afford:** attribute. 23. **some bravery:** a spirited act. THE PROHIBITION. 11. **Not ... officer:** i.e., "not that I shall execute justice in my own person." 13. **style:** title. 18. **So ... do:** In that way, neither of these extremes will perform its proper function.

22–23. **So ... undo:** "Or let these two (love and hate) destroy, not me, but one another. In this way I shall live to show off — as on a stage — your daily victories, whereas if you 'triumphed' over me completely I should be dead." HOLY SONNETS. I. 14. **adamant:** here used in the obsolete sense of "loadstone." VII. 7–8. **you ... woe:** i.e., "you who will be alive at the time of the Last Judgment."

X

Death be not proud, though some have callèd thee
Mighty and dreadful, for thou art not so,
For those whom thou think'st thou dost overthrow,
Die not, poor Death, nor yet canst thou kill me.
From rest and sleep, which but thy pictures be,
Much pleasure, then from thee, much more must
flow,
And soonest our best men with thee do go,
Rest of their bones, and soul's delivery.
Thou art slave to fate, chance, kings, and desperate
men,
And dost with poison, war, and sickness dwell,   10
And poppy, or charms can make us sleep as well,
And better than thy stroke; why swell'st thou then?
One short sleep past, we wake eternally,
And death shall be no more; Death, thou shalt die.

XIII

What if this present were the world's last night?
Mark in my heart, O Soul, where thou dost dwell,
The picture of Christ crucified, and tell
Whether that countenance can thee affright,
Tears in his eyes quench the amazing light,
Blood fills his frowns, which from his pierced head
fell.
And can that tongue adjudge thee unto hell,
Which prayed forgiveness for his foes' fierce spite?
No, no; but as in my idolatry
I said to all my profane mistresses,   10
Beauty, of pity, foulness only is
A sign of rigor:° so I say to thee,
To wicked spirits are horrid shapes assigned,
This beauteous form assures a piteous mind.

XIV

Batter my heart, three-personed God; for, you
As yet but knock, breathe, shine, and seek to mend;
That I may rise and stand, o'erthrow me, and bend
Your force, to break, blow, burn, and make me
new.
I, like an usurped town, to another due,
Labor to admit you, but oh, to no end,
Reason, your viceroy in me, me should defend,
But is captived, and proves weak or untrue.
Yet dearly I love you, and would be lovèd fain,
But am betrothed unto your enemy: 10
Divorce me, untie, or break that knot again,
Take me to you, imprison me, for I
Except you enthrall me, never shall be free,
Nor ever chaste, except you ravish me.

XIII. 11-12. Beauty . . . rigor: Beauty betokens a compassionate heart; ugliness betokens severity.

XVIII

Show me, dear Christ, thy spouse,° so bright and
clear.
What! is it she,° which on the other shore
Goes richly painted? or which robbed and tore
Laments and mourns in Germany and here?°
Sleeps she a thousand, then peeps up one year?
Is she self truth and errs? now new, now outwore?
Doth she, and did she, and shall she evermore
On one, on seven, or on no hill° appear?
Dwells she with us, or like adventuring knights
First travail we to seek and then make love?   10
Betray, kind husband, thy spouse to our sights,
And let mine amorous soul court thy mild dove,
Who is most true, and pleasing to thee, then
When she is embraced and open to most men.

XIX

Oh, to vex me, contraries meet in one;
Inconstancy unnaturally hath begot
A constant habit; that when I would not
I change in vows, and in devotion.
As humorous° is my contrition
As my profane love, and as soon forgot:
As riddlingly distempered, cold and hot,
As praying, as mute; as infinite, as none.
I durst not view heaven yesterday; and today
In prayers, and flattering speeches I court God: 10
Tomorrow I quake with true fear of his rod.
So my devout fits come and go away
Like a fantastic ague: save that here
Those are my best days, when I shake with fear.

DEVOTIONS UPON
EMERGENT OCCASIONS

These meditations, suggested to Donne during a
serious illness by the various stages of the malady as
they arose or developed ("emergent occasions"), were
written in 1623 and published in 1624. They are
prayers, soliloquies, or reflections, and form a sequence
following the course of the disease. Death and sickness always fascinated Donne, and here we see him
extracting spiritual meanings even from his own pain
and grave danger.

The Latin mottoes mark each successive stage: the
onset of the illness, its effects, the coming of the physician, the final crisis, and the recovery; the English sentence opposite each epigraph is Donne's free translation of it. (Readers will understand that only a few
of these stages are represented in the following extracts.)

XVIII. 1. spouse: i.e., the Church. 2. she: the Roman Catholic Church. 3-4. or . . . here: the reformed Church in Germany
and England. 8. one . . . hill: Wittenberg, Rome, and Geneva.
XIX. 5. humorous: fickle, subject to changing "humors."

II

Actio Laesa.[1]   The strength, and the function of the senses, and other faculties change and fail.

The heavens are not the less constant because they move continually, because they move continually one and the same way. The earth is not the more constant because it lies still continually,[2] because continually it changes, and melts in all parts thereof. Man, who is the noblest part of the earth, melts so away, as if he were a statue, not of earth, but of snow. We see his own envy melts him, he grows lean with that; he will say, another's beauty melts him; but he feels that a fever doth not melt him like snow, but pour him out like lead, like iron, like brass melted in a furnace: it doth not only melt him, but calcine him, reduce him to atoms, and to ashes; not to water, but to lime. And how quickly? Sooner than thou canst receive an answer, sooner than thou canst conceive the question; earth is the center of my body, heaven is the center of my soul; these two are the natural places of those two; but those go not to these two in an equal pace: my body falls down without pushing, my soul does not go up without pulling: ascension is my soul's pace and measure, but precipitation my body's: and even angels, whose home is heaven, and who are winged too, yet had a ladder to go to heaven by steps. The sun who goes so many miles in a minute, the stars of the firmament, which go so very many more, go not so fast as my body to the earth. In the same instant that I feel the first attempt of the disease, I feel the victory; in the twinkling of an eye, I can scarce see, instantly the taste is insipid, and fatuous; instantly the appetite is dull and desireless; instantly the knees are sinking and strengthless; and in an instant, sleep, which is the picture, the copy of death, is taken away, that the original, death itself may succeed, and that so I might have death to the life. It was part of Adam's punishment, In the sweat of thy brows thou shalt eat thy bread:[3] it is multiplied to me, I have earned bread in the sweat of my brows, in the labor of my calling, and I have it; and I sweat again and again, from the brow to the sole of the foot, but I eat no bread, I taste no sustenance: miserable distribution of mankind, where one half lacks meat, and the other stomach.

III

Decubitus sequitur tandem.[4] The patient takes his bed.

We attribute but one privilege and advantage to man's body, above other moving creatures, that he is not as others, groveling, but of an erect, of an upright form, naturally built and disposed to the contemplation of heaven. Indeed it is a thankful form, and recompenses that soul which gives it, with carrying that soul so many foot higher towards heaven. Other creatures look to the earth; and even that is no unfit object, no unfit contemplation for man; for thither he must come; but because man is not to stay there, as other creatures are, man in his natural form is carried to the contemplation of that place which is his home, heaven. This is man's prerogative; but what state hath he in this dignity? A fever can fillip him down, a fever can depose him; a fever can bring that head, which yesterday carried a crown of gold five foot towards a crown of glory, as low as his own foot today. When God came to breathe into man the breath of life, he found him flat upon the ground; when he comes to withdraw that breath from him again, he prepares him to it, by laying him flat upon his bed. Scarce any prison so close, that affords not the prisoner two, or three steps. The anchorites[5] that barked themselves up in hollow trees, and immured themselves in hollow walls; that perverse man, that barreled himself in a tub,[6] all could stand, or sit, and enjoy some change of posture. A sick-bed is a grave; and all that the patient says there, is but a varying of his own epitaph. Every night's bed is a type of the grave: at night we tell our servants at what hour we will rise; here we cannot tell ourselves at what day, what week, what month. Here the head lies as low as the foot; the Head of the people, as low as they whom those feet trod upon; and that hand that signed pardons, is too weak to beg his own, if he might have it for lifting up that hand: strange fetters to the feet, strange manacles to the hands, when the feet and hands are bound so much the faster, by how much the cords are slacker; so much the less able to do their offices, by how much more the sinews and ligaments are the looser. In the grave I may speak through the stones in the voice of my friends, and in the accents of those words which their love may afford my memory; here I am mine own ghost, and rather affright my beholders than instruct them; they conceive the

---

DEVOTIONS. **1.** *Actio Laesa:* "[Powers of] action stricken down." **2.** Donne here assumes the truth of the pre-Copernican (geocentric) system. **3. In . . . bread:** Gen. 3:19.

4. *Decubitus . . . tandem:* At length he continues, lying in bed. **5. anchorites:** hermits. **6. perverse . . . tub:** Diogenes.

worst of me now, and yet fear worse; they give me for dead now, and yet wonder how I do, when they wake at midnight, and ask how I do tomorrow. Miserable and (though common to all) inhuman posture, where I must practice my lying in the grave by lying still, and not practice my resurrection by rising any more.

XVI

Et properare meum clamant, è Turre propinqua, Obstreperae Campanae aliorum in funere, funus.[7]

From the bells of the church adjoining, I am daily remembered of my burial in the funerals of others.

We have a convenient author, who writ a discourse of bells, when he was prisoner in Turkey. How would he have enlarged himself if he had been my fellow prisoner in this sick-bed, so near to that steeple which never ceases, no more than the harmony of the spheres, but is more heard.[8] When the Turks took Constantinople, they melted the bells into ordnance; I have heard both bells and ordnance, but never been so much affected with those, as with these bells. I have lain near a steeple, in which there are said to be more than thirty bells; and near another, where there is one so big as that the clapper is said to weigh more than six hundred pound, yet never so affected as here. Here the bells can scarce solemnize the funeral of any person, but that I knew him, or knew that he was my neighbor: we dwelt in houses near to one another before, but now he is gone into that house, into which I must follow him. There is a way of correcting the children of great persons, that other children are corrected in their behalf, and in their names, and this works upon them, who indeed had more deserved it. And when these bells tell me that now one and now another is buried, must not I acknowledge that they have the correction due to me, and paid the debt that I owe? There is a story of a bell in a monastery which, when any of the house was sick to death, rung always voluntarily, and they knew the inevitableness of the danger by that. It rung once, when no man was sick; but the next day one of the house fell from the steeple and

died, and the bell held the reputation of a prophet still. If these bells that warn to a funeral now, were appropriated to none, may not I, by the hour of the funeral, supply? How many men that stand at an execution, if they would ask, for what dies that man, should hear their own faults condemned, and see themselves executed by attorney? We scarce hear of any man preferred, but we think of ourselves, that we might very well have been that man; why might not I have been that man, that is carried to his grave now? Could I fit myself to stand or sit in any man's place, and not to lie in any man's grave? I may lack much of the good parts of the meanest, but I lack nothing of the mortality of the weakest; they may have acquired better abilities than I, but I was born to as many infirmities as they. To be an incumbent[9] by lying down in a grave, to be a doctor by teaching mortification[10] by example, by dying: though I may have seniors, others may be elder than I, yet I have proceeded apace in a good university, and gone a great way in a little time, by the furtherance of a vehement fever; and whomsoever these bells bring to the ground today, if he and I had been compared yesterday, perchance I should have been thought likelier to come to this preferment, then, than he. God hath kept the power of death in his own hands, lest any man should bribe death. If man knew the gain of death, the ease of death, he would solicit, he would provoke death to assist him by any hand which he might use. But as when men see many of their own professions preferred, it ministers a hope that that[11] may light upon them; so when these hourly bells tell me of so many funerals of men like me, it presents, if not a desire that it may, yet a comfort whensoever mine shall come.

XVII

Nunc lento sonitu dicunt, Morieris.[12]

Now, this bell tolling softly for another, says to me, Thou must die.

Perchance he for whom this bell tolls, may be so ill, as that he knows not it tolls for him; and perchance I may think myself so much better than I am, as that they who are about me, and see my state, may have caused it to toll for me, and I know

---

7. *Et . . . funus:* "And it is to hasten my burial that the noisy bells toll from the neighboring tower at the funeral of others."
8. spheres . . . heard: The heavenly spheres, in their revolutions, were thought to make harmonious sounds inaudible to our gross ears. Cf. "ninefold harmony" in Milton's "Nativity," st. 13, below.

9. incumbent: a beneficed clergyman (a play on the Latin meaning of *incumbere*, to lie down).   10. doctor . . . mortification: probably a play on the medical and theological senses of these words.   11. that: i.e., promotion or "preferment."
12. *Nunc . . . Morieris:* Donne's own (free) translation suffices.

not that. The Church is Catholic, universal, so are all her actions; all that she does belongs to all. When she baptizes a child, that action concerns me; for that child is thereby connected to that Head which is my Head too, and engrafted into that body, whereof I am a member. And when she buries a man, that action concerns me: all mankind is of one Author, and is one volume; when one man dies, one chapter is not torn out of the book, but translated into a better language; and every chapter must be so translated; God employs several translators; some pieces are translated by age, some by sickness, some by war, some by justice; but God's hand is in every translation; and his hand shall bind up all our scattered leaves again, for that Library where every book shall lie open to one another: As therefore the bell that rings to a sermon, calls not upon the preacher only, but upon the congregation to come; so this bell calls us all: but how much more me, who am brought so near the door by this sickness. There was a contention as far as a suit (in which both piety and dignity, religion and estimation,[13] were mingled), which of the religious orders should ring to prayers first in the morning; and it was determined, that they should ring first that rose earliest. If we understand aright the dignity of this bell that tolls for our evening prayer, we would be glad to make it ours, by rising early, in that application, that it might be ours, as well as his, whose indeed it is. The bell doth toll for him that thinks it doth; and though it intermit again, yet from that minute, that that occasion wrought upon him, he is united to God. Who casts not up his eye to the sun when it rises? but who takes off his eye from a comet when that breaks out?[14] Who bends not his ear to any bell, which upon any occasion rings? but who can remove it from that bell, which is passing a piece of himself out of this world? No man is an island, entire of itself; every man is a piece of the continent, a part of the main;[15] if a clod be washed away by the sea, Europe is the less, as well as if a promontory were, as well as if a manor of thy friends or of thine own were; any man's death diminishes me, because I am involved in mankind; and therefore never send to know for whom the bell tolls; it tolls for thee. Neither can we call this a begging of misery or a borrowing of misery, as though we were not miserable enough of ourselves, but must fetch in more from the next house, in taking upon us the misery of our neighbors. Truly it

were an excusable covetousness if we did; for affliction is a treasure, and scarce any man hath enough of it. No man hath affliction enough that is not matured, and ripened by it, and made fit for God by that affliction. If a man carry treasure in bullion, or in a wedge of gold, and have none coined into current monies, his treasure will not defray him as he travels. Tribulation is treasure in the nature of it, but it is not current money in the use of it, except we get nearer and nearer our home, Heaven, by it. Another man may be sick too, and sick to death, and this affliction may lie in his bowels, as gold in a mine, and be of no use to him; but this bell, that tells me of his affliction, digs out, and applies that gold to me; if by this consideration of another's danger I take mine own into contemplation, and so secure myself by making my recourse to my God, who is our only security.

XVIII

At inde
Mortuus es, Sonitu celeri,
pulsuque agitato.[16]

The bell rings out, and tells me in him, that I am dead.

The bell rings out; the pulse thereof is changed; the tolling was a faint and intermitting pulse, upon one side; this stronger, and argues more and better life. His soul is gone out; and as a man who had a lease of one thousand years after the expiration of a short one, or an inheritance after the life of a man in a consumption, he is now entered into the possession of his better estate. His soul is gone; whither? Who saw it come in, or who saw it go out? Nobody; yet everybody is sure he had one, and hath none. If I will ask mere philosophers what the soul is, I shall find amongst them that will tell me it is nothing but the temperament and harmony, and just and equal composition of the elements in the body, which produces all those faculties which we ascribe to the soul; and so in itself is nothing, no separable substance that overlives[17] the body. They see the soul is nothing else in other creatures, and they affect an impious humility, to think as low of man. But if my soul were no more than the soul of a beast, I could not think so; that soul that can reflect upon itself, consider itself, is more than so. If I will ask, not mere philosophers, but mixed men, philosophical divines, how the soul, being a separate substance, enters into the man, I shall find

---

13. **estimation:** self-esteem.   14. **comet . . . out:** comets were regarded as portents of disaster.   15. **main:** mainland.

16. *At . . . agitato:* "Then lo! with rapid stroke and uneasy throb [it says], 'Thou art dead.'"   17. **overlives:** survives.

some that will tell me that it is by generation and procreation from parents, because they think it hard to charge the soul with the guiltiness of original sin, if the soul were infused into a body,[18] in which it must necessarily grow foul, and contract original sin, whether it will or no; and I shall find some that will tell me, that it is by immediate infusion from God, because they think it hard, to maintain an immortality in such a soul, as should be begotten, and derived with the body from mortal parents. If I will ask, not a few men, but almost whole bodies, whole Churches, what becomes of the souls of the righteous at the departing thereof from the body, I shall be told by some that they attend an expiation, a purification in a place of torment; by some, that they attend the fruition of the sight of God, in a place of rest but yet of expectation; by some, that they pass to an immediate possession of the presence of God. St. Augustine studied the nature of the soul as much as anything but the salvation of the soul; and he sent an express messenger to St. Jerome, to consult of some things concerning the soul: but he satisfies himself with this: let the departure of my soul to salvation be evident to my faith, and I care the less how dark the entrance of my soul into my body be to my reason. It is the going out, more than the coming in, that concerns us. This soul, this bell tells me, is gone out; whither? Who shall tell me that? I know not who it is; much less what he was; the condition of the man, and the course of his life, which should tell me whither he is gone, I know not. I was not there in his sickness, nor at his death; I saw not his way, nor his end, nor can ask them who did, thereby to conclude or argue whither he is gone. But yet I have one nearer me than all these: mine own charity; I ask that, and that tells me he is gone to everlasting rest, and joy, and glory: I owe him a good opinion; it is but thankful charity in me, because I received benefit and instruction from him when his bell tolled: and I, being made the fitter to pray, by that disposition wherein I was assisted by his occasion, did pray for him; and I pray not without faith; so I do charitably, so I do faithfully believe, that that soul is gone to everlasting rest, and joy, and glory. But for the body, how poor a wretched thing is that? we cannot express it so fast, as it grows worse and worse. That body which scarce three minutes since was such a house, as that that soul, which made but one step from thence to heaven, was

scarce thoroughly content to leave that for heaven: that body hath lost the name of a dwelling house, because none dwells in it, and is making haste to lose the name of a body, and dissolve to putrefaction. Who would not be affected, to see a clear and sweet river in the morning, grow a kennel of muddy land-water by noon, and condemned to the saltness of the sea by night? And how lame a picture, how faint a representation is that, of the precipitation of man's body to dissolution! Now all the parts built up, and knit by a lovely soul, now but a statue of clay, and now these limbs melted off, as if that clay were but snow; and now, the whole house is but a handful of sand, so much dust, and but a peck of rubbish, so much bone. If he who, as this bell tells me, is gone now, were some excellent artificer, who comes to him for a clock or for a garment now? or for counsel, if he were a lawyer? If a magistrate, for justice? Man, before he hath his immortal soul, hath a soul of sense, and a soul of vegetation before that: this immortal soul did not forbid other souls to be in us before,[19] but when this soul departs, it carries all with it; no more vegetation, no more sense: such a mother-in-law [20] is the earth, in respect of our natural mother; in her womb we grew; and when she was delivered of us, we were planted in some place, in some calling in the world; in the womb of the earth, we diminish, and when she is delivered of us, our grave opened for another, we are not transplanted, but transported, our dust blown away with profane dust, with every wind.

LXXX SERMONS, 1640
from SERMON LXVI

January 29, 1625/6

Donne's first surviving sermon dates from 1615; his last was preached at St. Paul's shortly before his death in 1631. The sermons were published posthumously, *LXXX Sermons* in 1640, *Fifty Sermons* in 1649, and *XXVI Sermons* in 1660.

"He preached the word," wrote Walton, "so as showed his own heart was possessed by those very thoughts that he labored to distill into others. A preacher in earnest, weeping sometimes for his auditors, sometimes with them; always preaching to himself like an angel from a cloud, but in none; carrying

18. if . . . body: i.e., as would be the case if the soul were directly infused by God.

19. Man . . . before: The soul was supposed to comprise three parts: the soul of growth (shared with the plants), the soul of sense (shared with the animals), and the rational soul (distinctively human), which was immortal.   20. mother-in-law: probably in the sense of "step-mother."

some, as St. Paul was, to heaven in holy raptures, and enticing others by a sacred art and courtship to amend their lives."

In his sermons we see the whole range of Donne's rhetorical power, from the homely illustration, through reasoned argument, up to impassioned utterance.

If you look upon this world in a map, you find two hemispheres, two half-worlds. If you crush heaven into a map, you may find two hemispheres too, two half-heavens; half will be joy, and half will be glory; for in these two, the joy of heaven, and the glory of heaven, is all heaven often represented unto us. And as of those two hemispheres of the world, the first hath been known long before, but the other (that of America, which is the richer in treasure), God reserved for later discoveries; so though he reserve that hemisphere of heaven, which is the glory thereof, to the resurrection, yet the other hemisphere, the joy of heaven, God opens to our discovery, and delivers for our habitation even whilst we dwell in this world. As God hath cast upon the unrepentant sinner two deaths, a temporal, and a spiritual death, so hath he breathed into us two lives; for so, as the word for death is doubled, *Morte morieris,* "Thou shalt die the death," [1] so is the word for life expressed in the plural, *Chaiim, vitarum,* "God breathed into his nostrils the breath of lives," [2] of divers lives. Though our natural life were no life, but rather a continual dying, yet we have two lives besides that, an eternal life reserved for heaven, but yet a heavenly life too, a spiritual life, even in this world; and as God doth thus inflict two deaths, and infuse two lives, so doth he also pass two judgments upon man, or rather repeats the same judgment twice. For, that which Christ shall say to thy soul then at the Last Judgment, "Enter into thy Master's joy," [3] he says to thy conscience now, "Enter into thy Master's joy." The everlastingness of the joy is the blessedness of the next life, but the entering, the inchoation is afforded here. . . .

Howling is the noise of hell, singing the voice of heaven; sadness the damp of hell, rejoicing the serenity of heaven. And he that hath not this joy here, lacks one of the best pieces of his evidence for the joys of heaven; and hath neglected or refused that earnest, by which God uses to bind his bargain, that true joy in this world shall flow into the joy of heaven, as a river flows into the sea; this joy shall not be put out in death, and a new joy kindled in me in heaven; but as my soul, as soon as it is out of my body, is in heaven, and does not stay for the possession of heaven, nor for the fruition of the sight of God, till it be ascended through air, and fire, and moon, and sun, and planets, and firmament, to that place which we conceive to be heaven, but without the thousandth part of a minute's stop, as soon as it issues, is in a glorious light, which is heaven (for all the way to heaven is heaven; and as those angels, which came from heaven hither, bring heaven with them, and are in heaven here, so that soul that goes to heaven, meets heaven here; and as those angels do not devest [4] heaven by coming, so these souls invest heaven in their going). As my soul shall not go towards heaven, but go by heaven to heaven, to the heaven of heavens, so the true joy of a good soul in this world is the very joy of heaven; and we go thither, not that being without joy, we might have joy infused into us, but that as Christ says, "our joy might be full," [5] perfected, sealed with an everlastingness; for, as he promises that no man shall take our joy from us,[6] so neither shall death itself take it away, nor so much as interrupt it, or discontinue it, but as in the face of death, when he lays hold upon me, and in the face of the Devil, when he attempts me, I shall see the face of God (for everything shall be a glass, to reflect God upon me), so in the agonies of death, in the anguish of that dissolution, in the sorrows of that valediction, in the irreversibleness of that transmigration, I shall have a joy which shall no more evaporate than my soul shall evaporate, a joy that shall pass up, and put on a more glorious garment above, and be joy superinvested [7] in glory. Amen.

---

1. "Thou . . . death": Gen. 2:17.   2. "God . . . lives": Gen. 2:7.   3. "Enter . . . joy": Matt. 25:23.

4. devest: divest, strip.   5. "our . . . full": John 16:24. 6. that . . . us: John 16:22.   7. superinvested: clothed over again.

John Milton

1608–1674

I. BIOGRAPHICAL SKETCH

JOHN MILTON was born in London on December 9, 1608. King James had been on the throne for nearly six years and had lost some of his initial popularity; he had shown his antagonism to two forces that were steadily rising in strength, Puritanism and the authority of parliament. But, as yet, England seemed to be enjoying an era of peace and prosperity.

Milton grew up in an ideal setting. John Milton senior, a well-to-do scrivener (that is, a notary, conveyancer, and private banker), was able and eager to give his talented son the best possible education, and the boy's ardent devotion to the humanities marked him out, in the minds of his elders and in his own mind, for the Church. Then the father was a composer, of some repute even in the richest period of English music, and the son, as many glowing allusions in his verse and prose testify, was a lover of music from youth to old age. And this intellectual and aesthetic cultivation was combined, in family life, with religious and moral training that was an active reality. Although, when the time came, Milton was too convinced of ecclesiastical corruption and tyranny to take holy orders, he always thought of the true poet as a priest.

Milton attended St. Paul's School in London and had additional instruction from tutors at home. From the age of twelve, he records, he hardly ever went to bed before midnight; and, if we think of him reading, by candlelight, the crabbed type of many old classical texts, we may share his opinion that such study was the first cause of his later blindness. In 1625 he went up to Christ's College, Cambridge. The one close friend of his youth and early manhood, Charles Diodati, had already gone to Oxford, and the two exchanged letters in Latin verse. Of Milton's many early Latin poems some of the best reveal elements in his nature that we might not infer from his early English verse, in particular an intense susceptibility to feminine beauty and to the intoxications of springtime. Milton's own feminine fairness of complexion gained him the college nickname " the Lady of Christ's," a nickname further borne out by his dislike of the coarser diversions of his fellows. At Christmas, 1629, when he was just twenty-one, he wrote his first great poem, " On the Morning of Christ's Nativity." " L'Allegro " and " Il Penseroso," which reflect complementary sides of his temperament, may perhaps be assigned to the long vacation of 1631.

Milton's intellectual and idealistic ardor showed itself in some of the Latin speeches that he gave as part of the curriculum: reacting against the academic tradition of scholastic logic, he held up, before himself and his audience, a fervent vision of a great awakening, of man's mastering all problems through humanistic and scientific inquiry. He was already both a Platonist and a Baconian (whether or not he had read Bacon).

Milton received his B.A. degree in 1629, his M.A. in 1632. Since he had decided against taking orders, he retired to his father's country place at Horton, near Windsor, and there set about giving himself the kind of liberal education he believed in—a strenuous and prolonged effort to digest all fruitful knowledge and thought, classical and modern. The chief early literary fruit of that self-consecration was the masque *Comus* (1634), a radiant expression of his Christian Platonism. Toward the end of the Horton period, when he had spent five years in studious obscurity preparing for the unknown future, and had so far, it seemed, accomplished little or nothing, the hint of self-doubt revealed in Sonnet VII became, in "Lycidas" (1637), a vehement questioning of his own destiny and of God's providence and justice.

During 1638–39 Milton spent some fifteeen months abroad, chiefly in Italy, where he richly enjoyed association with Italian men of letters and where, as he says in *Areopagitica,* he visited Galileo in his confinement. His return was hastened, though not unduly, by news of religious and political troubles in England. While abroad, he had learned of the death of his old friend Diodati, whom he later mourned in a heartfelt Latin elegy. Since he was not equipped for any profession, Milton rented a house in London and took in private pupils. The nature of his teaching may be judged from the small tract, *Of Education,* which he wrote in 1644. At the same time Milton followed with close interest the conflicts that were leading toward civil war. He had already, like so many Renaissance poets, planned to write the great modern heroic poem, but he had even more than his share of the Renaissance humanist's sense of civic responsibility, along with a higher religious motive; and—as he explains in *The Reason of Church Government*—he felt obliged to put aside poetic ambition and take part in the struggle for liberty. St. Peter's speech in "Lycidas" had indicated Milton's view of the religious and ecclesiastical situation. The essence of the very complex problem was this: the Elizabethan settlement of the Church of England had been a compromise, a combination of Protestant doctrine with the traditional Catholic hierarchy and the Catholic ritual (this modified and in English), but a growing body of people inside the Church, and some who were splitting off, abhorred these relics of Romanism and insisted that the Reformation be carried on to its logical end, to the pure simplicity of the apostolic church. The majority of Puritans desired a Presbyterian system, while Archbishop Laud, supported by King Charles, insisted that the traditional discipline and hierarchy of the Church of England be rigorously maintained. When in 1641–42 the agitation against the bishops was at its height, Milton wrote five tracts in support of the Presbyterian position. But Presbyterianism, when it got the upper hand, showed itself to be no less uniformitarian and tyrannical than episcopacy had been, as Milton said in *Areopagitica* (1644), and he moved from Presbyterianism (the Right of the revolutionary party) to Independency (the Center), which was liberal, progressive, and tolerant.

In 1642, a few months before war broke out, Milton had married Mary Powell, the seventeen-year-old daughter of a somewhat down-at-heel Royalist squire. The marriage, as everyone knows, turned out unhappily; the bride of a few weeks, going home for a visit, declined to return. (The pair were reconciled in 1645, and Milton took her family into his house as well.) His four pamphlets on divorce (1643–45) were partly inspired by painful experience, but partly also by his prolonged concern with social and public questions. In pleading for divorce on the ground of incompatibility rather than adultery alone, Milton was setting up a high ideal of marriage and of woman as a true companion and helpmate of man.

Milton's greatest work in English prose, *Areopagitica,* one of the classic documents of our civilization, is no less clear than powerful in its eloquence, and only three general remarks on it are offered here. First, there is the principle of "Christian liberty" which Milton, like other men, inherited from the Reformation but which he made peculiarly his own. Whereas the Mosaic law was a largely external and ceremonial code imposed upon the relatively primitive Hebrews, by the Christian gospel man achieved Christian liberty and became, under God, a self-directing agent, free from constraint by any earthly power or institution. Obviously such a doctrine contained revolutionary dynamite, and it inspired Milton's battles for liberty on many fronts; it is one of the central doctrines of *Paradise Lost* (and is expounded in Book XII, ll. 285–306).

But for Milton liberty always presupposes wisdom, goodness, discipline, and responsibility, and *Areopagitica* is not a plea for complete freedom of speech and of the press. Like other

Christian liberals of his time, Milton assumes that certain absolutes of religion and morality must be safeguarded; and, while he attacks censorship before publication, he allows for subsequent censorship of writings that endanger the public good.

Finally, we can measure the despair that Milton had later to overcome if we appreciate the boundless optimism that animates his early tracts in general and — in spite of parliament's effort to suppress free discussion — *Areopagitica* in particular. He sees a whole nation resuming its role as the standard-bearer of religious and civil liberty, a nation of Platonic philosopher-kings and Puritan saints; Christ's kingdom is being established on earth, and Milton himself is to have a share, as both pamphleteer and poet, in the great work. But, as time went on, the " unrealistic " idealist was to learn more and more of human inertia and corruption, to see the grand reformation fading into the light of common day.

The Restoration, though it destroyed all that Milton had hoped and striven for during twenty years, did not make him a sullen or cynical defeatist. His hostility to the new regime flamed out at times in the major works of his later years, *Paradise Lost* (1667), *Paradise Regained* (1671), and *Samson Agonistes* (1671), but a more important effect of his profound disillusionment was a purer and even stronger religious and moral faith, a faith wholly independent of popular movements and founded only on God and the individual soul. If he had written his epic in the early 1640's, it would doubtless have embodied his triumphant confidence in immediate revolution and reformation; as it was, his later works contained a sadder and sterner reading of human experience. They were concerned with individual and inward temptations, defeats, and victories.

Mary Milton had died in 1652; Milton's second wife, Katherine Woodcock, died in 1658, a little more than a year after marriage, and was lamented in the last, and one of the greatest, of his sonnets; in 1663 he married an Elizabeth Minshull, who long outlived him. In his old age Milton suffered from blindness, from gout (not the result of high living), from trouble with his daughters, and from unhappy memories of " the Good Old Cause," but he had some compensations. His quiet routine be-

gan, John Aubrey records, at 4:30 in the morning, when a man came to read him the Hebrew Bible. In addition to hearing books read aloud, there was the dictating and revising of his own compositions. Otherwise, he passed his days in meditation, in walking in his garden (" he always had a garden where he lived," says Aubrey), in playing on the organ and singing, and in talking with friends, old and young, and with the English and foreign visitors who sought him out. It is pleasant to learn that, before going to bed, he took not only the ascetic refreshment of a glass of water but a pipe. He died in 1674.

II. THE MINOR POEMS

English poetry in the early seventeenth century flowed mainly in three channels associated with the names of Spenser, Donne, and Ben Jonson. These three poets — and Milton — all had much the same kind of classical education, which included training in rhetoric and logic, but their instincts and experience led them along partly different roads. When the young Milton began to write, the heirs of Spenser were a minor group, and most rising poets were disciples of Donne or Jonson or, very often, of both. Milton was almost wholly untouched by the influence of Donne and his followers. As we might infer from lines 116–20 of " Il Penseroso," he would be attracted by Spenser's fusion of romance with Christian and Platonic idealism, and his poetic manner was, and for all its originality remained, more or less in the Spenserian tradition; Dryden reported that in his old age Milton named Spenser as his master. But the young scholar-poet was attracted also by the disciplined classical art of Jonson, who prized organic symmetry, rational clarity of thought and image, and impersonal restraint. In his early poems Milton may be said to have begun as a Spenserian and then to have inclined in the Jonsonian direction. " On the Morning of Christ's Nativity " is akin to the work of some Spenserians in its Italianate quality (including its fanciful conceits) and its stanza forms, but it also displays Milton's own concern for symmetrical organization and firm texture, his verbal and rhythmical energy, his instinct for blending the classical and the Christian, and his large imagination that embraces time and space and links earth with heaven. Perhaps a year and a half later, in "L'Allegro" and "Il Penseroso," Milton writes in a very different manner appropriate for very different themes; and, apart from the deliberate extravagance of the ten-line preludes, it is a crisp, polished, and graceful manner that suggests Jonson. The young poet's classicism appears in the impersonal rendering of personal moods, the generalized — but evocative — images, the subordination of particulars to a dominant theme, and the urbane modulation of tone and rhythm.

In "Lycidas" — we are not here concerned with the elaborate and beautiful *Comus* — the poet, now nearly 29, is reacting to the first really dark shadow that has fallen across the bookish and happy serenity of his sheltered life; and, in its complexity and depth, "Lycidas" is his first completely mature poem. Its real theme and its emotional intensity are under such firm artistic control, and are in fact conveyed so often obliquely, that the poem may not make a full immediate impact; some persons, after a too casual first reading, may, like Dr. Johnson,[1] resent both the absence of grief and the presence of the pastoral convention. There was, however, no apparent reason for Milton to feel keen personal sorrow; the drowning of Edward King evokes the poet's impassioned questioning of both his own past, present, and future and the religious meaning of life and death. In a world in which not a sparrow falls to the ground without God's will, and in which an exemplary and promising life is cut off on its threshold, what is to be thought of God's providence and justice, what is the use of man's self-discipline and high aspiration? But the poet's own involvement is barely touched. The pastoral convention becomes — as it had been for Theocritus and Virgil and others — an impersonal vehicle for the most personal utterance, a dramatic mask that enlarges rather than restricts the poet's freedom; and Milton's subtle interweaving of pagan and Christian images and ideas is a central element in his complexity of suggestion. The poem progresses through a series of marked contrasts in theme, imagery, language, tone, and sound which express or veil oscillations of feeling; and everywhere, even in the picture of Lycidas' reception into heaven, de-

tails are concrete and build up a solid whole. "Lycidas" is Milton's first attempt to assert Eternal Providence and justify the ways of God to men, but his acceptance of life is assured only after a struggle with dismay and fear, a struggle that goes on before our eyes and yet below the mainly smooth surface.

III. "PARADISE LOST"

Only portions of *Paradise Lost* can be included in this book, and it may be hoped that readers will look up a complete edition and read the parts omitted, so that they can see the organic structure of the whole and our sections in the right perspective.

The story of the creation and of the fall of man had been told, in narrative or dramatic form, by many medieval and later writers in various European countries, and had also been the subject of much theological commentary, and Milton would know a number of works of both kinds. Like most earlier writers (and like most people for a long time afterward), he seems to have regarded the Biblical story of Adam and Eve as in essence historical, but the degree of the poet's belief in the truth of his fable has no real bearing on the present value of the poem; what matters is that the fable embodies elements of human experience that are true in all ages. Furthermore, Milton felt quite free to amplify the sacred material.

In his beliefs and ideas Milton was the last and greatest poetic exemplar of the Christian humanism of the Renaissance. What we now call Christian humanism was a philosophy of order. Christian faith was of course the central foundation, but that does not need to be outlined: some other general ideas do. The doctrine of Christian liberty has been touched on already. Another and all-embracing set of doctrines we meet in many writers, because these doctrines formed the framework of thought and belief for centuries. The universe was conceived of as a great chain of being, from God the Creator down to plants and stones, in which every creature and thing had its appointed place and function.[1] Man, placed midway between the angels and the beasts, partakes of the character of both; his reason links him with the angels, his appe-

---

[1] See Johnson's *Life of Milton*, below.

[1] See also Pope's *Essay on Man*, below.

tites and passions with the beasts. What God is in the universe, man's reason should be among the discordant elements of his nature. In the good man, reason informs the will and the will obeys reason. Man is, however, prone to sin, and he lives in a world, he is himself a little world, in which evil is at war with good; but he can be saved, here and hereafter, through faith in Christ and through the efficacy of divine grace. At this point the Christian humanist diverges from Luther and Calvin. Whereas they saw man as utterly corrupt and helpless without grace, the Christian humanist insisted on man's rational dignity and free will and power of choice; and Milton was bound to break away from his inherited Calvinism. In *Paradise Lost* and his other late works, it should be added, Milton still exalts reason, but he lays even more stress upon faith, humility, obedience, and grace.

Milton's theme in *Paradise Lost* is the war between good and evil in the individual soul and in the world at large. The root of evil is pride, the pride that violates the law of love and righteousness in order to exalt the unregenerate self, to win power. Satan is, in Milton's presentation, a figure of heroic magnificence, one of the great creations of world literature, and it was almost inevitable that a character great in evil should, in dramatic force, overshadow Christ, the active agent of good; evil characters are always more vivid than good ones. But that should not lead us into misunderstanding of Milton's total design. If Satan's first great speech of defiance (ll. 84-124) wins our applause, then we are quite off the track and in a fair way to misapprehend the whole poem; for the speech is a passionately egoistic defiance of all goodness, love, reason, order, all the highest values we believe in.

Here we must take note of Milton's dramatic and ironic method, because the irony with which Satan is enveloped is the corrective to admiration for grandly heroic qualities (if any corrective be needed when those qualities are continually shown to be perverted and corrupt). The use of a story universally known was for Milton, as for the Greek dramatists, an asset rather than a liability, since the author could therefore use irony and ambiguity with much more certain effect. Also, Milton could rely upon all the beliefs, attitudes, and associations that ages of Christian teaching had made a central part of everyone's consciousness. Thus, at least for Milton's early readers, Satan's defiance of God and his heroic grandeur involved no risk of misunderstanding; it is mainly since the Romantic age that, for many readers, rebellion has appeared altogether laudable, regardless of what is rebelled against.

Apart from some soliloquies, Satan and his followers are treated throughout in terms of irony. Though the poem does embody a tragic reading of human life, its pattern is that of a "divine comedy"; evil can work evil, but it must in the end be overcome by good. (The aging poet no longer dreams, as he had dreamed in his early pamphlets, of a reformation here on earth; the vision of a new world is to be realized only after the day of judgment.) Meanwhile Satan — in his public harangues — and his followers are blind to the true nature of the conflict; they see themselves as temporarily defeated by a superior military force, and they seek victory or revenge. And they use such words as "free," "right," "order," with a false conception of their meaning. On the other hand, the innocent Adam and Eve are likewise enveloped in irony. We witness their first idyllic happiness knowing that it is not to last long, that Satan is already in Paradise, so that everything they say and do has tragic overtones.

In addition to Satan's defiances of Heaven, the modern reader's conditioning may lead him astray from the poet's design on two other points. One is very directly concerned with the main theme of pride. Satan bases his whole campaign against Eve and Adam on their being forbidden to eat the fruit of the tree of knowledge. He instills into Eve the desire to attain superhuman knowledge, to become a goddess, and it is to that motive that she succumbs. Before her fall, in Adam's and Raphael's discussion of the cosmos (Book VIII), the angel enforced the lesson that such remote subjects of inquiry as astronomy may distract man from religious humility and the practice of virtue. The importance in the poem of this principle is underlined by its reappearance at the very end (XII. 557-87). The modern mind may react violently against what perhaps seems to be a condemnation of the pursuit of knowledge (and a repudiation of *Areopagitica*), and may urge that without the pursuit of knowledge we would still be in a state of barbarism. That is true, no doubt, and yet a good many people, including some scientists, would reply that we are now in a state of barbarism, that human pride, with its scientific power, has in the last two decades committed barbaric crime and murder on a colossal scale, and that we are all contemplating the unimaginable horrors of the next war. At any rate Milton is not repudiating *Areopagitica,* where he was concerned with the knowledge that leads to wisdom and goodness, nor is he condemning science in itself; he is insisting that first things must be put first.

There was special need for the imaginative embellishment of the story Milton had to tell. Although, through the centuries, a good deal had been added to the simple brevity of Genesis, it was a story of God, Christ, Satan and other angels, and two earthly characters who were not ordinary human beings and who, in their paradisal garden, were remote from ordinary human life and interests. All this was very far from the solid concreteness of Homer and heroic narratives in general. At every turn Milton faced a problem that did not exist for Homer, though it did in some degree for Virgil — that is, the problem of rendering an abstract theme or idea through the concrete characters and action that the heroic poem required. In the several invocations of *Paradise Lost,* and most explicitly in that of Book IX, Milton speaks of his Christian poem as moving on a higher level than pagan fictions, but he was, as artist, proudly and humbly conscious of being in the succession of Homer and Virgil. While Milton was said to have known the Homeric poems almost by heart, and often echoed Homer, his main pattern was closer to the *Aeneid,* which was the great formal model for the Renaissance epic and which had, moreover, some affinity with Milton's theme: Virgil's hero had been tempted into betrayal of his divinely appointed destiny, and the whole story of the fall of Troy and the founding of a new nation in the west was akin to the fall of man and his being brought to see the way of redemption for himself and his posterity.

The large epic conventions that Milton uses are supernatural agencies (though his assertion of Eternal Providence is of course a main theme, not a mere convention); the roll call and council of leaders; an inset narrative of events preceding that with which the poem opened; and

last, a prophetic revelation of future history.

Along with those large devices that contribute to solidity and concreteness, there was epic simile and allusion, which Milton employed in original ways suited to the needs of his fable. For the substance he drew mainly upon the Old Testament, classical myth and history, and geography; and miscellaneous items range from the romances of Charlemagne to the Turkish sultan, from Shakespeare's English fairies to the lewd hirelings who climb into the English Church. Such similes and allusions — many of them among the richest jewels in the poem — have diverse and often complex effects. For one thing, apropos of the line we have been following, allusions to Biblical and classical history and to geography add elements of concreteness and relate the bare, primitive, remote fable to all subsequent human history. Even classical myth — which Milton, in his sacred context, so often labels as pagan fiction, even while his imagination is inspired by its beauty — had been regarded by many writers as only a corruption of authentic history (the flood of classical myth being identified with Noah's, and so on); and such myths were at any rate so familiar to everyone that even they were a sort of link with actuality.

Similes and allusions are very numerous in the first book, where Milton is setting the stage. Thus in the account of Satan's rising from the lake of fire and moving toward the shore, he is made a solid, grand, and gigantic figure partly through direct description, partly through allusions to the Giants and Titans, the Biblical Leviathan (and a realistic fisherman mistaking a whale for an island), an earthquake in Sicily and the volcano of Etna. A little later Satan's shield is likened to the spotty moon seen by Galileo through his telescope, his spear to a Norwegian pine-tree used for a flagship's mast. His followers are not only innumerable as fallen autumn leaves (a traditional epic simile), but as leaves in the brooks of the Italian Vallombrosa. All these allusions heighten our visual and imaginative response and make Satan and his fellows more real. At the same time such allusions add ideas of immensity, of grandeur, of power, of beauty, of horror.

With all this concreteness, this "material sublime," that belongs to the epic is combined what is perhaps even more distinctive of Milton's imagination and art, namely, vagueness of description. It is an element of technique that accords with the vast scene of the poem, and that is in marked contrast with the precise particularity of Dante's circumscribed world. Milton's world is not merely the so-called Ptolemaic universe of spheres and planets and fixed stars, with the earth at its center, for that large universe hangs from heaven by a golden chain, and all around is the infinite space of Chaos and far below is the huge prison of hell. (While Milton shows his knowledge of the Copernican doctrine, his use of the Ptolemaic world was justified by its traditional familiarity and by the fact that it kept the earth and man in the focal center; but the total universe, containing heaven, Chaos, hell, and the newly created Ptolemaic world, was in part the poet's invention.) We are never allowed to lose our consciousness of vast space. For instance, Satan voyages from the lake of hell to its gates, then through measureless Chaos to the top of the outer shell of the world, then down through the spheres to the sun and finally to the earth. At the same time the vast space, though it reflects the infinite power and universal presence of God, is in a sense only the backdrop for the fateful drama that is enacted on a spot of earth in the souls of Adam and Eve. To come back to the technique of vagueness, the opening descriptions of hell are superlative examples; they afford no basis for any picture that one could draw, but they are richly suggestive to the imagination. Furthermore, if Milton were always vague, the result would be as nebulous as Shelley or Swinburne; it is the fusion and interplay of vagueness and concreteness that is so effective. And to think of Miltonic vagueness is to think of his use of darkness and light, as both physical phenomena and spiritual symbols; there are continual contrasts between the lurid darkness of hell on the one hand and the sunlight of earth and the radiance of heaven on the other. Indeed the whole poem is knit together by innumerable parallels and contrasts, large and minute, concrete and abstract, in scene and action and character — heaven and hell, goodness and evil, order and anarchy, reason and passion, humility and pride, love and hate, creation and destruction, nature and artifice, and so on.

The texture of Milton's style shows a similar blending of the ornate and the plain, the general and the relatively particular. We think, rightly enough, of elevated and generalized grandeur of style and tone as the dominant quality; in writing an epic, above all an epic on such a theme as his, Milton naturally wished to raise the reader's mind above mundane affairs, to create a world and an atmosphere befitting his divine and superhuman characters. In other words, *Paradise Lost* is highly stylized, as the *Iliad, Odyssey,* and *Aeneid* were. The theory and practice of much recent writing have enforced the doctrine that poetry must use the language and rhythms of common speech, but that is a wholly arbitrary dogma which is right for some kinds of poetry and wrong for others. And Milton's grand style is not monotonous because of the continual contrasts and variations (not to mention his unflagging energy) that are possible, for him, within the stylization; examples are found on almost any page. Then Milton's elevation of style and generalizing habit have the effect of keeping action and scene and characters at a requisite aesthetic distance; everything must have a recognizable reality, but not too much. A realistic treatment of Adam and Eve would be quite fatal; as it is, they are both human and superhuman, and their home is both a garden and all ideal gardens — although, in the close-up drama of Book IX, Milton adopts a semidramatic manner. In earlier books Adam and Eve speak with the majestic courtesy and rhetorical amplitude that belong to their nature and situation, but, as temptation and sin reduce them to the ordinary human level, their utterance becomes more colloquial. We might compare, for instance, the beautiful speech (IV. 635–58) in which Eve declares her love for Adam, weaving and unweaving a chain of pastoral images, with the everyday naturalness of her soliloquy (IX. 795–833) after she has eaten the fruit, in which her words come out just as her thoughts occur to her. Finally — to cut short generalities which the reader must apply himself — the ornate splendor of *Paradise Lost* owes something to the many interwoven threads of simplicity (even if this is at times a sophisticated simplicity):

> where peace
> And rest can never dwell, hope never comes
> That comes to all.

> There rest, if any rest can harbor there.

Thus with the year
Seasons return; but not to me returns
Day, or the sweet approach of even or morn,
Or sight of vernal bloom, or summer's rose,
Or flocks, or herds, or human face divine.

In the invocation to Light, from which these last lines come, Milton had created such an atmosphere, such quiet emotional intensity, that he can achieve the most poignant effect by a listing of familiar sights which those who have eyes take for granted; if we want to know what we mean when we talk of classical generality and classical restraint, this is it. And no lines are at once more simple, and more complex than the last ones in the poem, where we see Adam and Eve departing from Paradise to begin life anew in the grim world of history; the lines seem to be only a succession of plain narrative statements, yet every phrase carries ambiguities that play off against one another.

The few lines just quoted remind us that, in all the varied emotional effects Milton creates, the rich complexities of his rhythms have a large share, from the grandiose glamor of sonorous proper names to the subtlest overtones of meaning. But, as T. S. Eliot has said, Milton is never monotonous. While he sticks closely to the ten-syllable line, the number, weight, and position of stresses are open to an infinity of permutations and combinations. For a random example we might take the opening lines (remembering that two signs are not at all adequate for showing differences of stress and tempo):

Ŏf mán's / fírst dis/ŏbéd/iĕnce, // ănd / thĕ frúit
Ŏf thằt / fŏrbíd/dĕn treé, // whŏse mór/tắl tásте
Broúght deáth / ĭntŏ / thĕ wórld, // ănd áll / oŭr
  woe,
Wĭth loss / ŏf Éd/ĕn, // tĭll / óne greát/ĕr Mán
Rĕstóre / ŭs, // ănd / rĕgaín / thĕ blíss/fŭl seát . . .

Whatever particular changes in scansion other readers might make, it is clear that in the first five lines we have not reached the main verb of the sentence, that three of the five lines are run on, and that stresses, falling on important words, reinforce the sense. In the first phrase the consecutive heavy beats underline the heinousness of the sin. The relentless regularity of the second line (the only regular one) leads into

the positive action, and irregular accents, of "Brought death . . . world"; and the two final iambic feet, "and all our woe," with their prolonged monosyllabic stresses, their regularity in the midst of irregularity, and the ensuing pause, deepen the sense of irrevocable doom. In line 4, the weak ending of "Eden," coming at the caesura, contributes to the idea of loss, but the line ends with the strong accents of "one greater Man" that emphasize the note of hope and salvation, a note carried on in the alliterative strength of "Restore . . . regain." These and many other things are best discovered by the individual reader; the analysis of even a few lines will quicken and refine his perceptions and make it impossible to read with the eye alone. And Milton's orchestration is not something added to the text; it is an essential part of its life and meaning.

IV. "SAMSON AGONISTES"

Since we have glanced at metrics, we might follow that road into *Samson Agonistes,* where Milton displays still greater boldness than he had within the more conventional patterns. The bulk of the drama is in blank verse, although this goes beyond the dramatic parts of *Paradise Lost* in semicolloquial and rugged irregularity. A more distinct innovation, which comes closer still to dramatic speech, is the use, in choruses and some parts of the dialogue, of more or less short and irregular lines (much more irregular and less lyrical than those of "Lycidas"). These are not free verse but varied combinations of regular metrical feet. One characteristic principle — which Gerard Hopkins, with reference to this drama, called counterpoint — is the superimposing of one rhythm upon another. To take a simple instance, line 81 may be scanned thus:

Ĭrrĕcóv/ĕrăb/lў dárk, // tótăl / ĕclípse.

The first part of the line is in rising rhythm, each foot ending with a stressed syllable (an anapaest and two iambs); the first foot after the caesura begins with one. Thus a falling (trochaic) rhythm disrupts the basic movement, and the effect — illustrated throughout in rich variety — is both colloquially "prosaic" and strongly emotive. For a somewhat less simple instance we might take lines 631–34:

Thence faínt/ings, // swóon/ings of / despaír,
And sénse / of Heaven's / deser/tion.

Í wás / his núrs/ling once // and choíce / delíght,
His dés/tined from / the womb . . .

Here one cannot miss the contrast in rhythm as well as sense between the first two and the second two lines. The irregularities of the first two, including weak endings, reflect the speaker's despair, while the last two, on his former greatness, are relatively regular, the caesura falling after a stressed syllable and most of the feet ending on strong accents.

Samson, with all its bareness, makes a greater or fuller impact on some readers than *Paradise Lost.* In addition to its obvious brevity, it is much less complex; its hero, except in his physical strength, is an ordinary human being and a sinner; and the theme of sin and regeneration, while religious, has no theological framework, so that the drama remains as universal as the Greek tragedies. *Samson* is indeed the only English drama on the Greek model that can be ranked with them.

Samson had been included in Milton's list of possible heroic subjects, compiled twenty years before the Restoration, so that it had dwelt in his mind a long time. How far the elderly poet, now eyeless in London under Charles II, projected himself into his hero is a question. Certainly at some points (e.g., ll. 692–700) Milton is thinking of the Stuart government and his own situation; and some critics have found topical significance or wishful thinking in Samson's destruction of the Philistines and have even called up the unhappy ghost of Mary Powell. It is probably a mistake to scan these things too closely.

His preface sets forth his classical conception of tragedy and, as we should expect of a scholar-poet in the Renaissance tradition, he follows the formal pattern of classical and neoclassical dramas. But his genius, and his dynamic motives, were far too powerful to produce a tame imitation. While Milton has natural affinities with all three of the Greek tragic dramatists, two plays may have been especially in his mind, Aeschylus' *Prometheus Bound* and Sophocles'

Oedipus at Colonus. One classical device that Milton exploits to the full is dramatic irony, the use of words and ideas that have one meaning for the speaker and persons addressed and another for the reader. Thus even in the title the Greek word *agonistes,* which means a contestant in public games, applies — both literally and ironically — to Samson's last acts in the Philistine temple and applies also to his spiritual wrestlings with himself. In addition to many such particular ambiguities, there is a larger irony in the effect Samson's successive visitors have upon him, an effect contrary to their and our expectation.

In the Bible Samson is a mere barbarian of strength; Milton greatly elevates his character and gives him a conscience wanting in the original. In fact Samson's agonized sense of his personal relation to God — which is partly similar to Job's — is the one, and a central, element in the drama that may be called un-Greek, though it is not altogether so. The chief thing for the reader to realize (as Dr. Johnson did not) is that the action is, until the end, purely psychological. Through a series of encounters with sympathetic or hostile visitors Samson rises from self-centered preoccupation with his miseries and wrongs to a new humility and faith.

What has been said here about Milton's life and character and writings gives at least, or at best, an indication of the greatness of his spirit and of his poetic art. The word " sublime " has dropped out of the modern critical vocabulary, but it has always, and rightly, been attached to Milton, by virtue of both his themes and his poetic quality. Much of the most serious fiction of our day has been concerned with evil and with hell; one difference, no doubt an inevitable difference, between such fiction and Milton's poetry is suggested by one of those incidental sublimities struck out in his prose — " that as no man apprehends what vice is so well as he who is truly virtuous, no man knows hell like him who converses most in heaven."

The publishers of this book and the editor of the selections from Milton make grateful acknowledgment to the Viking Press for the use of the Milton text prepared by the same editor for *The Portable Milton,* 1949 (Viking), which contains all the major poems, *Of Education,* and *Areopagitica,* most of the early poems, and selections from other prose works. In the present text many minute changes, chiefly in punctuation, have been made.

ON THE MORNING OF
CHRIST'S NATIVITY

Milton's first great poem was written at Christmas time, 1629, shortly after his twenty-first birthday; it was printed in his *Poems* (1645). The "Hymn" develops three motifs: peace on earth; the angelic music which links earth and man with heaven (and the birth of Christ with the Creation and Judgment); and the flight of the pagan gods. The triumphant rhythm befits a celebration of divine love, order, and harmony.

1

This is the month, and this the happy morn,
Wherein the Son of Heaven's eternal King,
Of wedded Maid and Virgin Mother born,
Our great redemption from above did bring;
For so the holy sages° once did sing,
   That he our deadly forfeit° should release,
And with his Father work us a perpetual peace.

2

That glorious form, that light unsufferable,
And that far-beaming blaze of majesty,
Wherewith he wont° at Heaven's high council-
   table   10
To sit the midst of Trinal Unity,°
He laid aside; and here with us to be,
   Forsook the courts of everlasting day,
And chose with us a darksome house of mortal clay.

3

Say, Heavenly Muse, shall not thy sacred vein
Afford a present to the infant God?
Hast thou no verse, no hymn, or solemn strain,
To welcome him to this his new abode,
Now while the Heaven, by the sun's team untrod,
   Hath took no print of the approaching light, 20
And all the spangled host keep watch in squadrons
   bright?

4

See how from far upon the eastern road
The star-led wizards° haste with odors sweet!
O run, prevent° them with thy humble ode,
And lay it lowly at his blessed feet;
Have thou the honor first thy Lord to greet,
   And join thy voice unto the angel quire,
From out his secret altar touched with hallowed
   fire.

ON THE MORNING OF CHRIST'S NATIVITY. **5. holy sages:** Old Testament prophets. **6. deadly forfeit:** the penalty of death brought upon man by Adam's sin. Cf. *Paradise Lost*, XII. 395–410. **10. wont:** was wont. **11. Trinal Unity:** the Trinity. **23. wizards:** the three Wise Men (Matt. 2:1–11). **24. prevent:** anticipate.

THE HYMN

1

It was the winter wild
While the Heaven-born child   30
   All meanly wrapped in the rude manger lies;
Nature in awe to him
Had doffed her gaudy trim,
   With her great Master so to sympathize;
It was no season then for her
To wanton with the sun, her lusty paramour.

2

Only with speeches fair
She woos the gentle air
   To hide her guilty front° with innocent snow,
And on her naked shame,   40
Pollute with sinful blame,
   The saintly veil of maiden white to throw,
Confounded that her Maker's eyes
Should look so near upon her foul deformities.

3

But he her fears to cease,
Sent down the meek-eyed Peace;
   She, crowned with olive green, came softly slid-
     ing
Down through the turning sphere,°
His ready harbinger,
   With turtle° wing the amorous clouds dividing,
And waving wide her myrtle wand,   51
She strikes a universal peace through sea and land.

4

No war or battle's sound
Was heard the world around:
   The idle spear and shield were high uphung;
The hookèd° chariot stood
Unstained with hostile blood;
   The trumpet spake not to the armèd throng;
And kings sat still with awful° eye,
As if they surely knew their sovran° Lord was by.

5

But peaceful was the night   61
Wherein the Prince of Light
   His reign of peace upon the earth began:
The winds with wonder whist,°
Smoothly the waters kissed,
   Whispering new joys to the mild ocëan,
Who now hath quite forgot to rave,

39. front: face. **48. turning sphere:** the whole globe of the stars which, in the old, more or less Ptolemaic, astronomy, turned daily about the earth. **50. turtle:** turtledove (an emblem of peace and love). **56. hooked:** armed with projecting blades. **59. awful:** filled with awe. **60. sovran:** sovereign. **64. whist:** hushed.

While birds of calm° sit brooding on the charmèd
    wave.

6

The stars with deep amaze
Stand fixed in steadfast gaze,   70
  Bending one way their precious influence,°
And will not take their flight
For all the morning light,
  Or Lucifer° that often warned them thence;
But in their glimmering orbs did glow,
Until their Lord himself bespake, and bid them go.

7

And though the shady gloom
Had given day her room,
  The sun himself withheld his wonted speed,
And hid his head for shame,   80
As his inferior flame
  The new-enlightened world no more should
    need;
He saw a greater sun appear
Than his bright throne or burning axletree could
    bear.

8

The shepherds on the lawn,
Or ere° the point of dawn,
  Sat simply chatting in a rustic row;
Full little thought they than°
That the mighty Pan°
  Was kindly come to live with them below;   90
Perhaps their loves, or else their sheep,
Was all that did their silly° thoughts so busy keep.

9

When such music sweet
Their hearts and ears did greet,
  As never was by mortal finger strook,
Divinely warbled voice
Answering the stringèd noise,
  As all their souls in blissful rapture took;°
The air, such pleasure loth to lose,
With thousand echoes still prolongs each heavenly
    close.°   100

10

Nature that heard such sound
Beneath the hollow round

Of Cynthia's seat,° the airy region thrilling,
Now was almost won
To think her part was done,
  And that her reign had here its last fulfilling;
She knew such harmony alone
Could hold all Heaven and Earth in happier union.

11

At last surrounds their sight
A globe of circular light,   110
  That with long beams the shame-faced Night ar-
    rayed;
The helmèd Cherubim°
And sworded Seraphim°
  Are seen in glittering ranks with wings displayed,
Harping in loud and solemn quire,
With unexpressive° notes to Heaven's new-born
    Heir.

12

Such music (as 'tis said)
Before was never made,
  But when of old the sons of morning° sung,
While the Creator great   120
His constellations set,
  And the well-balanced world on hinges hung,
And cast the dark foundations deep,
And bid the weltering waves their oozy channel
    keep.

13

Ring out, ye crystal spheres,°
Once bless our human ears
  (If ye have power to touch our senses so),
And let your silver chime
Move in melodious time,
  And let the bass of Heaven's deep organ blow;
And with your ninefold harmony   131
Make up full consort° to the angelic symphony.

14

For if such holy song
Enwrap our fancy long,
  Time will run back and fetch the age of gold,°
And speckled Vanity
Will sicken soon and die,
  And leprous Sin will melt from earthly mold,

102–03. round . . . seat: sphere of the moon.   112–13. Cherubim, Seraphim: See *PL*, I.129n.   116. unexpressive: inexpressible.   119. sons of morning: See Job 38:6–7.   125. spheres:
the celestial spheres of old astronomy, here taken as nine in
number (l. 131); their movements made "the music of the
spheres."   132. consort: harmony.   135–48. age . . . hall:
Ancient poets nostalgically celebrated the golden age, a mythical
time of ideal goodness, peace, and abundance which was followed by progressive corruption. Milton has in mind Virgil's
fourth *Eclogue* and Ps. 85:10–11.

68. birds of calm: halcyons, whose nesting, at the winter solstice
(about December 22), was associated with calm at sea.   71. influence: in astrology, the power exerted over nature and man
by the celestial bodies.   74. Lucifer: the morning star, or the
sun.   86. Or ere: before.   88. than: a variant form of *then*.
89. Pan: the Greek god of shepherds; here Christ.   92. silly:
simple, innocent.   98. took: charmed.   100. close: cadence.

And Hell itself will pass away,
And leave her dolorous mansions to the peering°
   day.   140

15

Yea, Truth and Justice then
Will down return to men,
   Orbed in a rainbow; and, like glories wearing,
Mercy will sit between,
Throned in celestial sheen,
   With radiant feet the tissued clouds down steer-
   ing;
And Heaven, as at some festival,
Will open wide the gates of her high palace hall.

16

But wisest Fate says no,
This must not yet be so;   150
   The Babe lies yet in smiling infancy,
That on the bitter cross
Must redeem our loss,
   So both himself and us to glorify;
Yet first to those ychained in sleep,
The wakeful trump of doom must thunder through
   the deep,

17

With such a horrid clang
As on Mount Sinai rang
   While the red fire and smoldering clouds out-
   brake;°
The aged Earth aghast   160
With terror of that blast
   Shall from the surface to the center shake,
When at the world's last session
The dreadful Judge in middle air° shall spread his
   throne.

18

And then at last our bliss
Full and perfect is,
   But now begins; for from this happy day
The old Dragon° under ground,
In straiter limits bound,
   Not half so far casts his usurpèd sway,   170
And, wroth to see his kingdom fail,
Swinges° the scaly horror of his folded tail.

19

The oracles are dumb,°
No voice or hideous hum

Runs through the archèd roof in words deceiv-
   ing.
Apollo from his shrine
Can no more divine,
   With hollow shriek the steep of Delphos° leav-
   ing.
No nightly trance or breathèd spell
Inspires the pale-eyed priest from the prophetic
   cell.   180

20

The lonely mountains o'er,
And the resounding shore,
   A voice of weeping heard, and loud lament;
From haunted spring and dale,
Edged with poplar pale,
   The parting Genius° is with sighing sent;
With flower-inwoven tresses torn
The nymphs in twilight shade of tangled thickets
   mourn.

21

In consecrated earth,
And on the holy hearth,   190
   The Lars° and Lemures° moan with midnight
   plaint;
In urns and altars round,
A drear and dying sound
   Affrights the flamens° at their service quaint;°
And the chill marble seems to sweat,
While each peculiar power forgoes his wonted seat.

22

Peor° and Baalim°
Forsake their temples dim,
   With that twice-battered god of Palestine;°
And moonèd Ashtaroth,°   200
Heaven's queen and mother both,
   Now sits not girt with tapers' holy shine;
The Libyc Hammon° shrinks his horn,
In vain the Tyrian maids their wounded Tham-
   muz° mourn.

23

And sullen Moloch,° fled,
Hath left in shadows dread
   His burning idol all of blackest hue;
In vain with cymbals' ring

---

140. **peering:** "peer" meant both "peer" and "appear."
157–59. **With . . . outbrake:** Moses' receiving of the Ten Commandments (Exod. 19:16f.).   164. **middle air:** in traditional
theory, one of three regions of the atmosphere, a cold and misty
one.   168. **Dragon:** Satan (Rev. 12:9, 20:2).   172. **Swinges:**
throws about.   173 f.: In Christian tradition the pagan gods,
who supposedly inspired answers given to petitioners at oracular
shrines, were regarded as devils. Cf. *PL*, I. 364 f.

178. **Delphos:** Delphi, the seat of Apollo's oracle.   186. **Genius:**
local divinity.   191. **Lars:** Lares, Roman household gods.
Lemures: spirits of the dead.   194. **flamens:** ancient Roman
priests. **quaint:** elaborate.   197 f.: Peor, Baal (pl. Baalim), and
the rest were heathen gods of Palestine and Egypt; some were
represented in animal form. Cf. *PL*, I. 412, 422, 457–66.   199. **that**
. . . Palestine: Dagon. See *PL*, I. 457n.   200. **Ashtaroth:** See *PL*, I.
438n.   203. **Hammon:** Ammon, an Egyptian god (see *PL*, IV.
275–79n.).   204. **Thammuz:** Adonis. See *PL*, I. 446n.   205. **Mo-**
loch: See *PL*, I. 392n.

They call the grisly king,
    In dismal dance about the furnace blue;   210
The brutish gods of Nile as fast,
    Isis° and Orus, and the dog Anubis,° haste.

24

Nor is Osiris° seen
In Memphian° grove or green,
    Trampling the unshowered grass with lowings
        loud;
Nor can he be at rest
Within his sacred chest,
    Nought but profoundest Hell can be his shroud;
In vain with timbreled° anthems dark
The sable-stolèd sorcerers bear his worshiped ark.

25

He feels from Juda's land   221
The dreaded Infant's hand,
    The rays of Bethlehem blind his dusky eyn;°
Nor all the gods beside
Longer dare abide,
    Not Typhon° huge ending in snaky twine:
Our Babe, to show his Godhead true,
Can in his swaddling bands control the damnèd
    crew.

26

So when the sun in bed,
Curtained with cloudy red,   230
    Pillows his chin upon an orient° wave,
The flocking shadows pale
Troop to the infernal jail;
    Each fettered ghost slips to his several grave,
And the yellow-skirted fays°
Fly after the night-steeds, leaving their moon-loved
    maze.

27

But see, the Virgin blest
Hath laid her Babe to rest.
    Time is our tedious song should here have end-
        ing;
Heaven's youngest-teemèd° star   240
Hath fixed her polished car,
    Her sleeping Lord with handmaid lamp attend-
        ing;
And all about the courtly stable
Bright-harnessed° angels sit in order serviceable.

---

212. Isis: sister and wife of Osiris, mother of Orus, a sun god. **Anubis:** identified with the Greek Hermes, represented with a jackal's head.   **213. Osiris:** the chief Egyptian god, worshiped as a bull.   **214. Memphian:** Egyptian (from the capital, Memphis).   **219. timbreled:** accompanied by tambourines. **223. eyn:** old plural of *eye*.   **226. Typhon:** See *PL*, I. 197n. **231. orient:** eastern.   **235. fays:** fairies.   **240. youngest-teemed:** latest-born, the star that led the Wise Men to Bethlehem.   **244. Bright-harnessed:** in bright armor

---

L'ALLEGRO

"L'Allegro" and "Il Penseroso" were written probably in the long vacation of 1631, when Milton was 22; they were published in the *Poems* of 1645. The twin pieces, which describe ideal days (and nights) in the life of a cheerful and of a contemplative man, are linked by continual and contrasting parallels; the cheerful man is, among other things, a lover of light and the human scene; the thoughtful man loves darkness and solitude. The poems partake of various traditions — the pastoral, the prose "character" (a sketch of an ethical or social type), the academic disputation. There seem to be many echoes of other poets, for example, of Marlowe's lyric, "Come live with me and be my love." The four-stressed lines vary between seven and eight syllables and between trochaic and iambic measures.

Hence, loathèd Melancholy,°
    Of Cerberus° and blackest Midnight born,
In Stygian° cave forlorn
    'Mongst horrid shapes, and shrieks, and sights
        unholy,
Find out some uncouth° cell,
    Where brooding darkness spreads his jealous
        wings,
And the night-raven sings;
    There under ebon° shades and low-browed rocks,
As ragged as thy locks,
    In dark Cimmerian desert ever dwell.   10
But come, thou Goddess fair and free,
In heaven yclept° Euphrosyne,
And by men, heart-easing Mirth,
Whom lovely Venus, at a birth,
With two sister Graces more,
To ivy-crownèd Bacchus bore;
Or whether (as some sager sing)
The frolic wind that breathes the spring,
Zephyr, with Aurora playing,
As he met her once a-Maying,   20
There on beds of violets blue,
And fresh-blown roses washed in dew,
Filled her with thee, a daughter fair,
So buxom,° blithe, and debonair.
Haste thee, Nymph, and bring with thee
Jest and youthful Jollity,
Quips and Cranks° and wanton Wiles,
Nods, and Becks, and wreathèd Smiles,
Such as hang on Hebe's cheek,

L'ALLEGRO.   **1–10.** The melancholy here banished is a disease, not the contemplative mood celebrated in "Il Penseroso" (nor is the folly condemned at the beginning of the latter poem the innocent mirth of "L'Allegro").   **2. Cerberus:** in classical myth, the three-headed dog that guarded the entrance to Hades. **3. Stygian:** relating to the Styx, a river of the mythological underworld; infernal.   **5. uncouth:** strange, desolate.   **8. ebon:** black.   **12. yclept:** called.   **24. buxom:** lively.   **27. Cranks:** odd turns of speech.

And love to live in dimple sleek;
Sport that wrinkled Care derides,
And Laughter holding both his sides.
Come, and trip it as ye go
On the light fantastic toe,
And in thy right hand lead with thee
The mountain nymph, sweet Liberty;
And if I give thee honor due,
Mirth, admit me of thy crew,
To live with her, and live with thee,
In unreprovèd° pleasures free;   40
To hear the lark begin his flight,
And singing startle the dull night,
From his watch-tower in the skies,
Till the dappled dawn doth rise;
Then to come,° in spite of sorrow,
And at my window bid good-morrow,
Through the sweet-briar, or the vine,
Or the twisted eglantine;
While the cock, with lively din,
Scatters the rear of darkness thin,   50
And to the stack or the barn door
Stoutly struts his dames before;
Oft listening how the hounds and horn
Cheerly rouse the slumbering morn,
From the side of some hoar hill,
Through the high wood echoing shrill:
Sometime walking, not unseen,
By hedgerow elms, on hillocks green,
Right against the eastern gate,
Where the great sun begins his state,°   60
Robed in flames and amber light,
The clouds in thousand liveries dight;
While the ploughman, near at hand,
Whistles o'er the furrowed land,
And the milkmaid singeth blithe,
And the mower whets his scythe,
And every shepherd tells his tale°
Under the hawthorn in the dale.
Straight mine eye hath caught new pleasures,
Whilst the lantskip° round it measures: 70
Russet lawns and fallows gray,
Where the nibbling flocks do stray,
Mountains on whose barren breast
The laboring clouds do often rest,
Meadows trim with daisies pied,
Shallow brooks and rivers wide;
Towers and battlements it sees
Bosomed high in tufted trees,
Where perhaps some beauty lies,
The cynosure of neighboring eyes.   80
Hard by, a cottage chimney smokes
From betwixt two aged oaks,

Where Corydon° and Thyrsis° met   30
Are at their savory dinner set
Of herbs and other country messes,
Which the neat-handed Phillis° dresses;
And then in haste her bower she leaves,
With Thestylis° to bind the sheaves;
Or if the earlier season lead,
To the tanned haycock in the mead.   90
Sometimes with secure° delight
The upland hamlets will invite,
When the merry bells ring round,
And the jocund rebecks° sound
To many a youth and many a maid
Dancing in the chequered shade;
And young and old come forth to play
On a sunshine holiday,
Till the livelong daylight fail:
Then to the spicy nut-brown ale,   100
With stories told of many a feat,
How fairy Mab the junkets eat;
She° was pinched and pulled, she said,
And he,° by friar's lantern° led,
Tells how the drudging goblin° sweat
To earn his cream-bowl duly set,
When in one night, ere glimpse of morn,
His shadowy flail hath threshed the corn
That ten day-laborers could not end;
Then lies him down the lubber fiend,°   110
And stretched out all the chimney's length,
Basks at the fire his hairy strength;
And crop-full out of doors he flings,
Ere the first cock his matin rings.
Thus done the tales, to bed they creep,
By whispering winds soon lulled asleep.
Towered cities please us then,
And the busy hum of men,
Where throngs of knights and barons bold
In weeds of peace high triumphs hold,   120
With store of ladies, whose bright eyes
Rain influence,° and judge the prize
Of wit or arms, while both contend
To win her grace whom all commend.
There let Hymen° oft appear
In saffron robe, with taper clear,
And pomp, and feast, and revelry,
With masque and antique pageantry;
Such sights as youthful poets dream
On summer eves by haunted stream.   130
Then to the well-trod stage anon,
If Jonson's learnèd sock° be on,
Or sweetest Shakespeare, Fancy's child,

83, 86, 88. Corydon, Thyrsis, Phillis, Thestylis: traditional names in pastoral literature.   91. secure: carefree.   94. rebecks: fiddles.   103–04. She, he: members of the story-telling group.   104. friar's lantern: will-o'-the-wisp.   105. goblin: Robin Goodfellow, Puck.   110. lubber fiend: drudging spirit.   122. influence: Cf. "Nativity," l. 71n.   125. Hymen: the classical god of marriage.   132. sock: the light shoe of ancient comic actors, a symbol of comedy.

40. unreproved: not deserving reproof.   45. to come: i.e., the poet comes to his window to greet the new day.   60. state: stately progress (compare this image of the sun with those in the "Nativity," st. 7 and 26).   67. tells his tale: counts the number (of his sheep).   70. lantskip: landscape.

Warble his native wood-notes wild;°
And ever against eating cares,
Lap me in soft Lydian° airs,
Married to immortal verse,
Such as the meeting soul may pierce
In notes with many a winding bout°
Of linkèd sweetness long drawn out,   140
With wanton heed and giddy cunning,
The melting voice through mazes running,
Untwisting all the chains that tie
The hidden soul of harmony;
That Orpheus' self may heave his head
From golden slumber on a bed
Of heaped Elysian flowers, and hear
Such strains as would have won the ear
Of Pluto, to have quite set free
His half-regained Eurydice.   150
These delights if thou canst give,
Mirth, with thee I mean to live.

IL PENSEROSO

Hence, vain deluding Joys,
  The brood of Folly without father bred,
How little you bestead,
  Or fill the fixèd mind with all your toys;°
Dwell in some idle brain,
  And fancies fond° with gaudy shapes possess,
As thick and numberless
  As the gay motes that people the sunbeams,
Or likest hovering dreams,
  The fickle pensioners of Morpheus' train.   10
But hail, thou Goddess sage and holy,
Hail, divinest Melancholy,
Whose saintly visage is too bright
To hit the sense of human sight,
And therefore to our weaker view
O'erlaid with black, staid Wisdom's hue;
Black, but such as in esteem
Prince Memnon's° sister might beseem,
Or that starred Ethiop queen° that strove
To set her beauty's praise above   20
The sea nymphs, and their powers offended.
Yet thou art higher far descended:
Thee bright-haired Vesta° long of yore
To solitary Saturn° bore;

His daughter she (in Saturn's reign°
Such mixture was not held a stain).
Oft in glimmering bowers and glades
He met her, and in secret shades
Of woody Ida's° inmost grove,
While yet there was no fear of Jove.   30
Come, pensive Nun, devout and pure,
Sober, steadfast, and demure,
All in a robe of darkest grain,
Flowing with majestic train,
And sable stole of cypress lawn
Over thy decent° shoulders drawn.
Come, but keep thy wonted state,°
With even step and musing gait,
And looks commercing° with the skies,
Thy rapt soul sitting in thine eyes;   40
There held in holy passion still,
Forget thyself to marble, till
With a sad° leaden downward cast
Thou fix them on the earth as fast.
And join with thee calm Peace and Quiet,
Spare Fast, that oft with gods doth diet,
And hears the Muses in a ring
Aye round about Jove's altar sing;
And add to these retired Leisure,
That in trim gardens takes his pleasure;   50
But first, and chiefest, with thee bring
Him that yon soars on golden wing,
Guiding the fiery-wheelèd throne,°
The Cherub Contemplation;
And the mute Silence hist° along,
'Less Philomel° will deign a song,
In her sweetest, saddest plight,
Smoothing the rugged brow of Night,
While Cynthia checks her dragon yoke
Gently o'er the accustomed oak.°   60
Sweet bird, that shunn'st the noise of folly,
Most musical, most melancholy!
Thee, chauntress, oft the woods among
I woo to hear thy even-song;
And missing thee, I walk unseen
On the dry smooth-shaven green,
To behold the wandering moon,
Riding near her highest noon,
Like one that had been led astray
Through the Heaven's wide pathless way;   70
And oft, as if her head she bowed,
Stooping through a fleecy cloud.
Oft on a plat° of rising ground

133–34. Shakespeare is characterized partly in contrast with the learned Jonson, partly in terms of the outdoor comedies which the mirthful man would like.   136. Lydian: delicate, sensuous.   139. bout: a musical "run," passage.   IL PENSEROSO.   4. toys: trifles.   6. fond: foolish.   18. Memnon was a handsome Ethiopian prince who fought in the Trojan War.   19. Ethiop queen: Cassiopeia boasted of her daughter Andromeda's beauty (not her own) and was changed into a constellation. Milton's version is that of some mythographers.   23. Vesta: goddess of the hearth, a symbol of purity.   24. Saturn: father of Jove, here an astrological symbol of contemplative melancholy. Cf. *saturnine*.

25. Saturn's reign: a golden age. See "Nativity," ll. 135–48n.   29. Ida: a mountain in Crete where Jove was born.   36. decent: comely.   37. state: dignity.   39. commercing: communing.   43. sad: serious.   53. fiery-wheeled throne: see Ezek. 10.   55. hist: summon silently.   56. Philomel: the nightingale.   59–60. While . . . oak: Cynthia (Diana, the moon), rising as usual over a particular tree, pauses to listen to the bird's song (the team of dragons was, in classical myth, associated with Diana in another of her threefold functions, as goddess of the underworld).   73. plat: plot.

I hear the far-off curfew sound
Over some wide-watered shore,
Swinging slow with sullen roar;
Or if the air will not permit,
Some still removèd place will fit,
Where glowing embers through the room
Teach light to counterfeit a gloom,   80
Far from all resort of mirth,
Save the cricket on the hearth,
Or the bellman's° drowsy charm,
To bless the doors from nightly harm.
Or let my lamp at midnight hour
Be seen in some high lonely tower,
Where I may oft outwatch the Bear,°
With thrice-great Hermes,° or unsphere°
The spirit of Plato to unfold
What worlds or what vast regions hold   90
The immortal mind that hath forsook
Her mansion in this fleshly nook;
And of those daemons that are found
In fire, air, flood, or under ground,
Whose power hath a true consent
With planet or with element.°
Sometime let gorgeous Tragedy
In sceptered pall come sweeping by,
Presenting Thebes,° or Pelops'° line,
Or the tale of Troy divine,   100
Or what (though rare) of later age
Ennobled hath the buskined° stage.
But, O sad Virgin, that thy power
Might raise Musaeus° from his bower,
Or bid the soul of Orpheus sing
Such notes as, warbled to the string,
Drew iron tears down Pluto's cheek,
And made Hell grant what love did seek;
Or° call up him that left half told
The story of Cambuscan bold,   110
Of Camball, and of Algarsife,
And who had Canace to wife,
That owned the virtuous° ring and glass,
And of the wondrous horse of brass,
On which the Tartar king did ride;
And if aught else great bards° beside
In sage and solemn tunes have sung,
Of tourneys and of trophies hung,

---

83. **bellman:** a watchman who cried the hours.   87. **outwatch...**
Bear: sit up all night (since the constellation of Great Bear
does not set).   88. **thrice-great Hermes:** Hermes Trismegistus,
supposed author of Neoplatonic writings of the third century
A.D. **unsphere:** call down from his sphere.   96. **element:** earth,
water, air, fire. Cf. *PL* II. 275n.   99. **Thebes:** plays concerning
Oedipus and his family. **Pelops:** progenitor of Atreus, Agamemnon, and other Greek tragic figures.   102. **buskined:** tragic
(from the high boot worn by Greek tragic actors).   104. **Musaeus:** a mythical Greek poet.   109–15. **Or ... ride:** Chaucer's
unfinished Squire's Tale.   113. **virtuous:** magical.   116–20. **bards
... ear:** Milton is doubtless thinking especially of Spenser's
The Faerie Queene.

Of forests and enchantments drear,
Where more is meant than meets the ear.   120
Thus, Night, oft see me in thy pale career,
Till civil-suited Morn appear,
Not tricked° and frounced° as she was wont
With the Attic boy° to hunt,
But kerchieft in a comely cloud,
While rocking winds are piping loud,
Or ushered with a shower still,
When the gust hath blown his fill,
Ending on the rustling leaves,
With minute° drops from off the eaves.   130
And when the sun begins to fling
His flaring beams, me, Goddess, bring
To archèd walks of twilight groves,
And shadows brown that Sylvan° loves,
Of pine or monumental oak,
Where the rude axe with heavèd stroke
Was never heard the nymphs to daunt,
Or fright them from their hallowed haunt.
There in close covert by some brook,
Where no profaner eye may look,   140
Hide me from Day's garish eye,
While the bee with honied thigh,
That at her flowery work doth sing,
And the waters murmuring
With such consort° as they keep,
Entice the dewy-feathered Sleep;
And let some strange mysterious dream
Wave at his wings in airy stream
Of lively portraiture displayed,
Softly on my eyelids laid.   150
And as I wake, sweet music breathe
Above, about, or underneath,
Sent by some spirit to mortals good,
Or the unseen Genius of the wood.
But let my due feet never fail
To walk the studious cloister's pale,°
And love the high embowèd roof,
With antic° pillars massy proof,°
And storied windows richly dight,
Casting a dim religious light.   160
There let the pealing organ blow
To the full-voiced quire below,
In service high and anthems clear,
As may with sweetness, through mine ear,
Dissolve me into ecstasies,
And bring all Heaven before mine eyes.
And may at last my weary age
Find out the peaceful hermitage,
The hairy gown and mossy cell,

---

123. **tricked:** adorned. **frounced:** with hair curled.   124. **Attic
boy:** Cephalus, the hunter loved by Aurora ("Morn").
130. **minute:** falling at intervals of a minute.   134. **Sylvan:**
Silvanus, an ancient rural divinity.   145. **consort:** harmony.
156. **pale:** enclosure.   158. **antic:** ornamented, or perhaps old
(antique). **massy proof:** massive and strong.

Where I may sit and rightly spell 170
Of every star that Heaven doth shew,
And every herb that sips the dew,
Till old experience do attain
To something like prophetic strain.
These pleasures, Melancholy, give,
And I with thee will choose to live.

SONNET VII. HOW SOON HATH TIME

This sonnet, written probably on Milton's twenty-fourth birthday (December 9, 1632), is a landmark in his personal and poetic development. He has left Cambridge and academic fame behind him and while contemporaries — like his close friend, Charles Diodati — forge ahead, he is studying, in the obscurity of his father's house at Horton, to fit himself for God's service, in the world if not in the Church (see Introduction, p. 402). It is characteristic that the Christian self-dedication of the sestet should include an echo of Pindar's fourth Nemean ode.

How soon hath Time, the subtle thief of youth,
  Stolen on his wing my three and twentieth
    year!°
My hasting days fly on with full career,
But my late spring no bud or blossom
    shew'th.
Perhaps my semblance might deceive the truth,
  That I to manhood am arrived so near,
  And inward ripeness doth much less appear,
  That some more timely-happy spirits endu'th.
Yet be it less or more, or soon or slow,
  It shall be still° in strictest measure even   10
  To that same lot, however mean or high,
Toward which Time leads me, and the will of
    Heaven;
  All is, if° I have grace to use it so,
  As ever in my great Task-Master's eye.

SONNET VII. 2. three and twentieth year: i.e., twenty-three years   10. still: always.   13. All is, if: all depends on whether I am enabled by divine grace to use my talent.

LYCIDAS

"Lycidas," written in November, 1637, was Milton's contribution to a volume of elegies, published in 1638, in memory of a Cantabrigian, Edward King, who had drowned in a wreck in the Irish Sea. While King was apparently not a close friend of Milton's, he was a virtuous young cleric and, in a small way, a poet, and his death on the threshold of a fruitful life in the Church carried Milton far beyond the usual themes of a pastoral elegy (see Introduction, pp. 404–05). But his personal feeling is masked and controlled by the pastoral conventions: the lament of nature for the shepherd-poet, the procession of mourners, and — as in the Christianized pastoral tradition — the consolation of heavenly immortality. Irregularities of line and rhyme assist expressive flexibility; there are ten unrhymed lines. The text was somewhat revised in Milton's *Poems* of 1645, and the introductory note — printed just below — was added.

In this monody the author bewails a learned friend, unfortunately drowned in his passage from Chester on the Irish Seas, 1637. And by occasion foretells the ruin of our corrupted clergy, then in their height.

Yet once more, O ye laurels, and once more,
Ye myrtles brown, with ivy never sere,°
I come to pluck your berries harsh and crude,°
And with forced fingers rude
Shatter your leaves before the mellowing year.
Bitter constraint, and sad occasion dear,°
Compels me to disturb your season due;
For Lycidas° is dead, dead ere his prime,
Young Lycidas, and hath not left his peer.
Who would not sing for Lycidas? he knew°   10
Himself to sing, and build the lofty rhyme.
He must not float upon his watery bier
Unwept, and welter to the parching wind,
Without the meed of some melodious tear.
  Begin then, Sisters° of the sacred well
That from beneath the seat of Jove doth spring,
Begin, and somewhat loudly sweep the string.
Hence with denial vain, and coy° excuse;
So may some gentle Muse
With lucky words favor my destined urn,   20
And as he passes turn,
And bid fair peace be to my sable shroud.
For we were nursed upon the self-same hill,
Fed the same flock, by fountain, shade, and rill.
  Together both, ere the high lawns appeared

LYCIDAS. 1–2. Crowns of laurel, myrtle, and ivy were classical emblems of poetic achievement. Milton's last notable work had been *Comus* (1634).   3. crude: unripe.   6. dear: costly grievous.   8. Lycidas: a traditional pastoral name.   10. knew: knew how.   15. Sisters: the Muses, who dance about the fountain of Aganippe ("the sacred well") and the altar of Zeus on Mount Helicon.   18. coy: modest, reluctant.

Under the opening eyelids of the morn,
We drove afield, and both together heard
What time the gray-fly winds her sultry horn,
Battening° our flocks with the fresh dews of night,
Oft till the star° that rose, at evening, bright   30
Toward Heaven's descent had sloped his westering
    wheel.
Meanwhile the rural ditties were not mute,
Tempered to the oaten flute;
Rough Satyrs danced, and Fauns with cloven heel
From the glad sound would not be absent long,
And old Damoetas° loved to hear our song.
    But O the heavy change, now thou art gone,
Now thou art gone, and never must return!
Thee, Shepherd, thee the woods and desert caves,
With wild thyme and the gadding vine o'ergrown,
And all their echoes mourn.   41
The willows and the hazel copses green
Shall now no more be seen
Fanning their joyous leaves to thy soft lays.
As killing as the canker to the rose,
Or taint-worm to the weanling herds that graze,
Or frost to flowers, that their gay wardrobe wear,
When first the white-thorn° blows;°
Such, Lycidas, thy loss to shepherd's ear.
    Where were ye, Nymphs, when the remorseless
    deep   50
Closed o'er the head of your loved Lycidas?
For neither were ye playing on the steep
Where your old bards, the famous Druids, lie,°
Nor on the shaggy top of Mona° high,
Nor yet where Deva° spreads her wizard stream.
Ay me, I fondly° dream,
Had ye been there! — for what could that have
    done?
What could the Muse herself that Orpheus° bore,
The Muse herself, for her enchanting son,
Whom universal Nature did lament,   60
When by the rout° that made the hideous roar
His gory visage down the stream was sent,
Down the swift Hebrus to the Lesbian shore?
    Alas! what boots° it with uncessant care
To tend the homely slighted shepherd's trade,
And strictly meditate the thankless Muse?
Were it not better done as others use,°
To sport with Amaryllis° in the shade,

Or with the tangles of Neaera's° hair?
Fame is the spur that the clear spirit doth raise   70
(That last infirmity of noble mind)
To scorn delights, and live laborious days;
But the fair guerdon when we hope to find,
And think to burst out into sudden blaze,
Comes the blind Fury° with the abhorrèd shears,
And slits the thin-spun life. "But not the praise,"
Phoebus° replied, and touched my trembling ears:
"Fame is no plant that grows on mortal soil,
Nor in the glistering foil°
Set off to the world, nor in broad rumor lies,   80
But lives and spreads aloft by those pure eyes
And perfect witness of all-judging Jove;
As he pronounces lastly on each deed,
Of so much fame in Heaven expect thy meed."
    O fountain Arethuse,° and thou honored flood,
Smooth-sliding Mincius,° crowned with vocal
    reeds,
That strain I heard was of a higher mood.
But now my oat° proceeds,
And listens to the Herald of the Sea,°
That came in Neptune's plea.   90
He asked the waves, and asked the felon winds,
What hard mishap hath doomed this gentle swain?
And questioned every gust of rugged wings
That blows from off each beakèd promontory;
They knew not of his story,
And sage Hippotades° their answer brings,
That not a blast was from his dungeon strayed;
The air was calm, and on the level brine
Sleek Panope° with all her sisters played.
It was that fatal and perfidious bark,   100
Built in the eclipse,° and rigged with curses dark,
That sunk so low that sacred head of thine.
    Next Camus,° reverend sire, went footing slow,
His mantle hairy, and his bonnet sedge,
Inwrought with figures dim, and on the edge
Like to that sanguine flower inscribed with woe.°
"Ah, who hath reft," quoth he, "my dearest
    pledge?"
Last came, and last did go,
The Pilot of the Galilean Lake;°
Two massy keys he bore of metals twain   110
(The golden opes, the iron shuts amain°).
He shook his mitered locks, and stern bespake:

---

29. Battening: feeding.   30. star: the evening star, Hesperus or Venus.   36. Damoetas: a pastoral name, presumably for some Cambridge don.   48. white-thorn: hawthorn. blows: blossoms.   52–53. steep . . . lie: a mountain in north Wales where the bardic priests of the early Britons were buried.   54. Mona: the Isle of Man off the Welsh coast.   55. Deva: the river Dee, which flows into the Irish Sea; its changes supposedly foretold good or ill for England and Wales.   56. fondly: foolishly.   58–63. Orpheus, son of the Muse Calliope, was torn to pieces by Thracian Bacchantes; his head was thrown into the river Hebrus and floated to Lesbos.   61. rout: disorderly band.   64. boots: profits.   67. use: are wont to do.   68–69. Amaryllis, Neaera: traditional names of pastoral maidens.

75. Fury: Atropos, that one of the Fates who cut the thread of life.   77. Phoebus: Apollo, god of poetry.   79. glistering foil: glittering setting (of a jewel).   85–86. Arethuse, Mincius: a Sicilian fountain and a north Italian river, associated with Theocritus and Virgil, respectively, as symbols of pastoral poetry.   88. oat: oaten pipe.   89. Herald . . . Sea: Triton.   96. Hippotades: Aeolus, god of the winds.   99. Panope: a sea nymph.   101. eclipse: of evil omen.   103. Camus: god of the river Cam, a symbol of Cambridge University.   106. sanguine . . . woe: the hyacinth, supposedly marked with the Greek cry of lamentation, "aiai."   109 f. Pilot . . . Lake: St. Peter, the fisherman of Galilee, traditionally the first bishop ("mitered locks"), to whom Jesus gave the keys of Heaven.   111. amain: with force.

"How well could I have spared for thee, young
    swain,
Enow° of such as for their bellies' sake
Creep and intrude and climb into the fold!
Of other care they little reckoning make
Than how to scramble at the shearers' feast,
And shove away the worthy bidden guest.
Blind mouths! that scarce themselves know how
    to hold
A sheep-hook, or have learned aught else the least
That to the faithful herdman's art belongs!   121
What recks it° them? What need they? They are
    sped;°
And when they list,° their lean and flashy° songs
Grate on their scrannel° pipes of wretched straw;
The hungry sheep look up, and are not fed,
But swoln with wind and the rank mist they draw,
Rot inwardly, and foul contagion spread;
Besides what the grim wolf° with privy paw
Daily devours apace, and nothing said;
But that two-handed engine° at the door   130
Stands ready to smite once, and smite no more."
   Return, Alpheus,° the dread voice is past
That shrunk thy streams; return, Sicilian Muse,
And call the vales, and bid them hither cast
Their bells and flowerets of a thousand hues.
Ye valleys low where the mild whispers use
Of shades and wanton winds and gushing brooks,
On whose fresh lap the swart star° sparely looks,
Throw hither all your quaint° enameled eyes,
That on the green turf suck the honied showers,
And purple all the ground with vernal flowers.   141
Bring the rathe° primrose that forsaken dies,
The tufted crow-toe, and pale jessamine,
The white pink, and the pansy freaked° with
    jet,
The glowing violet,
The musk-rose, and the well-attired woodbine,
With cowslips wan that hang the pensive head,
And every flower that sad embroidery wears.
Bid amaranthus° all his beauty shed,
And daffadillies fill their cups with tears,   150
To strew the laureate hearse° where Lycid lies.
For so to interpose a little ease,
Let our frail thoughts dally with false surmise;
Ay me! whilst thee the shores and sounding seas
Wash far away, where'er thy bones are hurled,
Whether beyond the stormy Hebrides,°

Where thou perhaps under the whelming
    tide
Visit'st the bottom of the monstrous° world;
Or whether thou, to our moist vows denied,
Sleep'st by the fable of Bellerus° old,   160
Where the great Vision of the guarded mount°
Looks toward Namancos° and Bayona's hold;°
Look homeward, Angel,° now, and melt with
    ruth;°
And, O ye dolphins,° waft the hapless youth.
   Weep no more, woeful shepherds, weep no
    more,
For Lycidas, your sorrow, is not dead,
Sunk though he be beneath the watery floor;
So sinks the day-star° in the ocean bed,
And yet anon repairs his drooping head,
And tricks° his beams, and with new-spangled
    ore°
Flames in the forehead of the morning sky: 171
So Lycidas sunk low, but mounted high,
Through the dear might of him that walked the
    waves,
Where, other groves and other streams along,
With nectar pure his oozy locks he laves,
And hears the unexpressive nuptial song,°
In the blest kingdoms meek of joy and love.
There entertain him all the saints above,
In solemn troops and sweet societies
That sing, and singing in their glory move,   180
And wipe the tears for ever from his eyes.
Now, Lycidas, the shepherds weep no more;
Henceforth thou art the Genius° of the shore,
In thy large recompense, and shalt be good
To all that wander in that perilous flood.
   Thus sang the uncouth° swain to the oaks and
    rills,
While the still morn went out with sandals gray;
He touched the tender stops of various quills,°
With eager thought warbling his Doric° lay.
And now the sun had stretched out all the hills,
And now was dropped into the western bay;   191
At last he rose, and twitched° his mantle blue:
To-morrow to fresh woods, and pastures new.

114. **Enow:** enough.   122. **recks it:** does it matter to. **sped:** well-established.   123. **list:** are inclined. **flashy:** tasteless.   124. **scrannel:** thin, harsh.   128. **wolf:** the Roman Catholic Church.   130. **two-handed engine:** this much-discussed phrase probably means the sword of God's avenging justice.   132. **Alpheus:** the river god who loved Arethusa; a symbol of pastoral poetry.   138. **swart star:** Sirius, associated with the browned herbage of late summer.   139. **quaint:** fanciful.   142. **rathe:** early.   144. **freaked:** spotted.   149. **amaranthus:** an actual flower and also an imaginary unfading one.   151. **hearse:** bier.   156. **Hebrides:** islands west of Scotland.

158. **monstrous:** inhabited by sea monsters.   160. **Bellerus:** a fabled giant from whom Land's End (the tip of Cornwall) supposedly got its Roman name, Bellerium.   161. **Vision . . . mount:** St. Michael's Mount, off the Cornish coast.   162. **Namancos, Bayona:** on the Spanish coast.   163. **Angel:** St. Michael, who is asked to turn his gaze away from Spain to England and pity Lycidas. **ruth:** pity.   164. **dolphins:** a dolphin had carried to shore the dead body of Melicertes, when his mother Ino leaped with him into the sea; he became the sea god Palaemon, whom the Romans identified with Portunus, the protecting god of harbors.   168. **day-star:** the sun.   170. **tricks:** dresses. **ore:** gold.   176. **unexpressive . . . song:** the inexpressible or mystical song for the marriage of the Lamb.   183. **Genius:** local divinity. See l. 164n., above.   186. **uncouth:** rustic, rude.   188. **quills:** the hollow reeds of pastoral pipes.   189. **Doric:** pastoral.   192. **twitched:** pulled up.

from

AREOPAGITICA

A Speech for the Liberty of Unlicensed Printing, to the Parliament of England

From before Shakespeare's time books and pamphlets had to be registered with the Stationers' Company (the guild of London printers) and approved by the Archbishop of Canterbury or the Bishop of London (i.e., by their chaplains). In 1637 a Star Chamber decree reinforced the existing law and restricted printing to twenty printers, but this decree lapsed with the Long Parliament's abolition of that much-hated court in 1641. The years 1641–43 brought a flood of unlicensed pamphlets, Milton's among them, and in June, 1643, the mainly Presbyterian parliament, now more concerned to suppress opposition than to uphold liberty, re-established censorship of books before their publication. Milton's grand protest appeared in November, 1644. (Some comments on his ideas and attitudes are made in the Introduction, pp. 200–01.) The tract was not actually a speech, though it was composed in the form of a classical oration. *Areopagitica* had little or no effect in its own time, partly perhaps because Milton's learning and manner were over the heads of many readers, partly because the main theme of pamphlet debate in 1644–45 was religious toleration (a topic that Milton only touches on in the course of his main argument against censorship).

This is true liberty, when free-born men,
Having to advise the public, may speak free,
Which he who can, and will, deserves high praise;
Who neither can, nor will, may hold his peace:
What can be juster in a state than this?

EURIPIDES, Suppliants

I conceive, therefore, that when God did enlarge the universal diet of man's body, saving ever the rules of temperance, he then also, as before, left arbitrary the dieting and repasting of our minds; as wherein every mature man might have to exercise his own leading capacity. How great a virtue is temperance, how much of moment through the whole life of man! Yet God commits the managing so great a trust, without particular law or prescription, wholly to the demeanor [1] of every grown man. And therefore when he himself tabled the Jews from heaven, that omer,[2] which was every man's daily portion of manna, is computed to have been more than might have well sufficed the heartiest feeder thrice as many meals. For those actions which en-

ter into a man, rather than issue out of him, and therefore defile not, God uses not to captivate under a perpetual childhood of prescription, but trusts him with the gift of reason to be his own chooser; there were but little work left for preaching, if law and compulsion should grow so fast upon those things which heretofore were governed only by exhortation. Solomon [3] informs us that much reading is a weariness to the flesh, but neither he nor other inspired author tells us that such or such reading is unlawful; yet certainly had God thought good to limit us herein, it had been much more expedient to have told us what was unlawful than what was wearisome. As for the burning of those Ephesian books by St. Paul's converts,[4] 'tis replied the books were magic, the Syriac so renders them. It was a private act, a voluntary act, and leaves us to a voluntary imitation: the men in remorse burnt those books which were their own; the magistrate by this example is not appointed; these men practiced the books, another might perhaps have read them in some sort usefully.

Good and evil we know in the field of this world grow up together almost inseparably; and the knowledge of good is so involved and interwoven with the knowledge of evil, and in so many cunning resemblances hardly to be discerned, that those confused seeds which were imposed on Psyche [5] as an incessant labor to cull out and sort asunder, were not more intermixed. It was from out the rind of one apple tasted that the knowledge of good and evil, as two twins cleaving together, leaped forth into the world. And perhaps this is that doom which Adam fell into of knowing good and evil, that is to say, of knowing good by evil. As therefore the state of man now is, what wisdom can there be to choose, what continence to forbear, without the knowledge of evil? He that can apprehend and consider vice with all her baits and seeming pleasures, and yet abstain, and yet distinguish, and yet prefer that which is truly better, he is the true warfaring Christian. I cannot praise a fugitive and cloistered virtue, unexercised and unbreathed, that never sallies out and sees her adversary, but slinks out of the race where that immortal garland is to be run for, not without dust and heat. Assuredly we bring not innocence into the world, we bring impurity much rather; that which purifies us

---

AREOPAGITICA.   1. demeanor: management.   2. omer: See Exod. 16:16.

3. Solomon: Eccles. 12:12.   4. converts: Acts 19:19.   5. Psyche: Apuleius, *The Golden Ass*, VI. Psyche, because she was loved by Venus' son Cupid, was given impossible tasks by Venus.

is trial, and trial is by what is contrary. That virtue therefore which is but a youngling in the contemplation of evil, and knows not the utmost that vice promises to her followers, and rejects it, is but a blank virtue, not a pure; her whiteness is but an excremental [6] whiteness; which was the reason why our sage and serious poet Spenser, whom I dare be known to think a better teacher than Scotus [7] or Aquinas, describing true temperance under the person of Guyon, brings him in with his palmer through the cave of Mammon and the bower of earthly bliss, that he might see and know, and yet abstain. Since therefore the knowledge and survey of vice is in this world so necessary to the constituting of human virtue, and the scanning of error to the confirmation of truth, how can we more safely, and with less danger, scout into the regions of sin and falsity than by reading all manner of tractates and hearing all manner of reason? And this is the benefit which may be had of books promiscuously read.

But of the harm that may result hence, three kinds are usually reckoned. First is feared the infection that may spread; but then all human learning and controversy in religious points must remove out of the world, yea, the Bible itself; for that ofttimes relates blasphemy not nicely, it describes the carnal sense of wicked men not unelegantly, it brings in holiest men passionately murmuring against Providence through all the arguments of Epicurus: in other great disputes it answers dubiously and darkly to the common reader; and ask a Talmudist [8] what ails the modesty of his marginal Keri,[9] that Moses and all the prophets cannot persuade him to pronounce the textual Chetiv. For these causes we all know the Bible itself put by the papist into the first rank of prohibited books. The ancientest fathers must be next removed, as Clement of Alexandria,[10] and that Eusebian book of evangelic preparation,[11] transmitting our ears through a hoard of heathenish obscenities to receive the gospel. Who finds not that Irenaeus, Epiphanius,[12] Jerome, and others discover [13] more

heresies than they well confute, and that oft for heresy which is the truer opinion?

Nor boots it to say for these and all the heathen writers of greatest infection, if it must be thought so, with whom is bound up the life of human learning, that they writ in an unknown tongue, so long as we are sure those languages are known as well to the worst of men, who are both most able and most diligent to instil the poison they suck, first into the courts of princes, acquainting them with the choicest delights and criticisms [14] of sin. As perhaps did that Petronius [15] whom Nero called his arbiter, the master of his revels; and that notorious ribald of Arezzo,[16] dreaded and yet dear to the Italian courtiers. I name not him, for posterity's sake, whom Harry VIII named in merriment his vicar of hell.[17] By which compendious way all the contagion that foreign books can infuse will find a passage to the people far easier and shorter than an Indian voyage, though it could be sailed either by the north of Cataio [18] eastward, or of Canada westward, while our Spanish licensing gags the English press never so severely.

But, on the other side, that infection which is from books of controversy in religion is more doubtful and dangerous to the learned than to the ignorant; and yet those books must be permitted untouched by the licenser. It will be hard to instance where any ignorant man hath been ever seduced by papistical book in English, unless it were commended and expounded to him by some of that clergy; and indeed all such tractates, whether false or true, are as the prophecy of Isaiah was to the eunuch, not to be " understood without a guide." [19] But of our priests and doctors how many have been corrupted by studying the comments of Jesuits and Sorbonists,[20] and how fast they could transfuse that corruption into the people, our experience is both late and sad. It is not forgot, since the acute and distinct Arminius [21] was perverted merely by the perusing of a nameless discourse written at Delft, which at first he took in hand to confute.

Seeing therefore that those books, and those in great abundance, which are likeliest to taint both life and doctrine, cannot be suppressed without the

---

6. **excremental:** external.   7. **Scotus:** Duns Scotus (d. 1308), Scholastic philosopher; Thomas Aquinas (d. 1274), the greatest of the Scholastics.   8. **Talmudist:** an expert in Jewish oral traditions concerning Old Testament law.   9. **Keri:** in the Hebrew Old Testament, a gloss substituting what is to be read in place of a coarser term in the text ("Chetiv").   10. **Clement of Alexandria:** Christian theologian (*fl.* 200) who wrote against paganism.   11. **preparation:** Eusebius' collection of pagan writings designed to turn readers to Christianity.   12. **Irenaeus, Epiphanius:** early bishops who attacked heresies.   13. **discover:** uncover.

14. **criticisms:** refinements.   15. **Petronius:** author of the *Satyricon*, arbiter of taste at Nero's court.   16. **Arezzo:** Pietro Aretino (d. 1556), Italian satirist.   17. **vicar of hell:** Sir Francis Bryan, a courtier and cousin of Anne Boleyn.   18. **Cataio:** Cathay, China.   19. **"understood . . . guide":** Acts 8:28–35.   20. **Sorbonists:** members of the theological school of the University of Paris.   21. **Arminius:** Dutch opponent of Calvinistic predestination and founder of the liberal "Arminian" theology (d. 1609).   Milton later held Arminian views.

fall of learning, and of all ability in disputation; and that these books of either sort are most and soonest catching to the learned (from whom to the common people whatever is heretical or dissolute may quickly be conveyed); and that evil manners are as perfectly learnt without books a thousand other ways which cannot be stopped; and evil doctrine not with books can propagate, except a teacher guide, which he might also do without writing, and so beyond prohibiting; I am not able to unfold how this cautelous [22] enterprise of licensing can be exempted from the number of vain and impossible attempts. And he who were pleasantly disposed could not well avoid to liken it to the exploit of that gallant man who thought to pound up the crows by shutting his park gate.

Besides another inconvenience, if learned men be the first receivers out of books and dispreaders both of vice and error, how shall the licensers themselves be confided in, unless we can confer upon them, or they assume to themselves above all others in the land, the grace of infallibility and uncorruptedness? And again, if it be true that a wise man, like a good refiner, can gather gold out of the drossiest volume, and that a fool will be a fool with the best book, yea, or without book, there is no reason that we should deprive a wise man of any advantage to his wisdom, while we seek to restrain from a fool that which, being restrained, will be no hindrance to his folly. For if there should be so much exactness always used to keep that from him which is unfit for his reading, we should, in the judgment of Aristotle [23] not only, but of Solomon [24] and of our Savior,[25] not vouchsafe him good precepts, and by consequence not willingly admit him to good books; as being certain that a wise man will make better use of an idle pamphlet than a fool will do of sacred Scripture.

'Tis next alleged we must not expose ourselves to temptations without necessity, and next to that, not employ our time in vain things. To both these objections one answer will serve, out of the grounds already laid, that to all men such books are not temptations nor vanities, but useful drugs and materials wherewith to temper and compose effective and strong medicines, which man's life cannot want.[26] The rest, as children and childish men, who have not the art to qualify and prepare these

working minerals, well may be exhorted to forbear, but hindered forcibly they cannot be by all the licensing that sainted Inquisition could ever yet contrive. Which is what I promised to deliver next: that this order of licensing conduces nothing to the end for which it was framed; and hath almost prevented [27] me by being clear already while thus much hath been explaining. See the ingenuity [28] of truth, who, when she gets a free and willing hand, opens herself faster than the pace of method and discourse can overtake her.

It was the task which I began with, to show that no nation, or well instituted state, if they valued books at all, did ever use this way of licensing; and it might be answered that this is a piece of prudence lately discovered. To which I return that, as it was a thing slight and obvious to think on, so if it had been difficult to find out, there wanted not among them long since who suggested such a course; which they not following, leave us a pattern of their judgment that it was not the not knowing, but the not approving, which was the cause of their not using it. Plato, a man of high authority indeed, but least of all for his commonwealth, in the book of his laws,[29] which no city ever yet received, fed his fancy with making many edicts to his airy burgomasters, which they who otherwise admire him wish had been rather buried and excused in the genial cups of an Academic [30] night-sitting. By which laws he seems to tolerate no kind of learning but by unalterable decree, consisting most of practical traditions, to the attainment whereof a library of smaller bulk than his own dialogues would be abundant. And there also enacts that no poet should so much as read to any private man what he had written, until the judges and lawkeepers had seen it and allowed it; but that Plato meant this law peculiarly to that commonwealth which he had imagined, and to no other, is evident. Why was he not else a lawgiver to himself, but a transgressor, and to be expelled by his own magistrates, both for the wanton epigrams and dialogues which he made, and his perpetual reading of Sophron Mimus [31] and Aristophanes, books of grossest infamy; and also for commending the latter of them, though he were the malicious libeler of his chief friends,[32] to be read by the tyrant Diony-

---

22. cautelous: deceitful.   **23. Aristotle** (*Nicomachean Ethics,* I. 3 and X. 9) admits that the discussion of ethics does not affect the mass of mankind.   **24. Solomon:** Prov. 17:2.   **25. Savior:** Matt. 7:6.   **26. want:** do without.

27. prevented: anticipated.   **28. ingenuity:** openness.   **29. laws:** *Laws,* VII. 800–02.   **30. Academic:** pertaining to Plato's Academy.   **31. Sophron Mimus:** author of mimes or dramatic sketches.   **32. friends:** Aristophanes satirized Socrates in *The Clouds.*

sius, who had little need of such trash to spend his time on? But that he knew this licensing of poems had reference and dependence to many other provisos there set down in his fancied republic, which in this world could have no place; and so neither he himself, nor any magistrate or city, ever imitated that course, which, taken apart from those other collateral injunctions, must needs be vain and fruitless.

For if they fell upon one kind of strictness, unless their care were equal to regulate all other things of like aptness to corrupt the mind, that single endeavor they knew would be but a fond [33] labor — to shut and fortify one gate against corruption and be necessitated to leave others round about wide open. If we think to regulate printing, thereby to rectify manners, we must regulate all recreations and pastimes, all that is delightful to man. No music must be heard, no song be set or sung, but what is grave and Doric.[34] There must be licensing dancers, that no gesture, motion, or deportment be taught our youth, but what by their allowance shall be thought honest; for such Plato was provided of. It will ask more than the work of twenty licensers to examine all the lutes, the violins, and the guitars in every house; they must not be suffered to prattle as they do, but must be licensed what they may say. And who shall silence all the airs and madrigals that whisper softness in chambers? The windows also, and the balconies, must be thought on; there are shrewd [35] books, with dangerous frontispieces, set to sale: who shall prohibit them, shall twenty licensers? The villages also must have their visitors [36] to inquire what lectures the bagpipe and the rebeck [37] reads, even to the ballatry [38] and the gamut [39] of every municipal fiddler; for these are the countryman's *Arcadias,* and his *Montemayors.*[40]

Next, what more national corruption, for which England hears ill [41] abroad, than household gluttony? Who shall be the rectors of our daily rioting? And what shall be done to inhibit the multitudes that frequent those houses where drunkenness is sold and harbored? Our garments also should be referred to the licensing of some more sober work-masters, to see them cut into a less

wanton garb. Who shall regulate all the mixed conversation [42] of our youth, male and female together, as is the fashion of this country? Who shall still appoint what shall be discoursed, what presumed, and no further? Lastly, who shall forbid and separate all idle resort, all evil company? These things will be, and must be; but how they shall be least hurtful, how least enticing, herein consists the grave and governing wisdom of a state.

To sequester out of the world into Atlantic and Utopian polities,[43] which never can be drawn into use, will not mend our condition; but to ordain wisely as in this world of evil, in the midst whereof God hath placed us unavoidably. Nor is it Plato's licensing of books will do this, which necessarily pulls along with it so many other kinds of licensing as will make us all both ridiculous and weary, and yet frustrate; but those unwritten or at least unconstraining laws of virtuous education, religious and civil nurture, which Plato there mentions [44] as the bonds and ligaments of the commonwealth, the pillars and the sustainers of every written statute; these they be which will bear chief sway in such matters as these, when all licensing will be easily eluded. Impunity and remissness, for certain, are the bane of a commonwealth; but here the great art lies, to discern in what the law is to bid restraint and punishment, and in what things persuasion only is to work. If every action which is good or evil in man at ripe years were to be under pittance and prescription and compulsion, what were virtue but a name, what praise could be then due to well-doing, what gramercy [45] to be sober, just, or continent?

Many there be that complain of divine Providence for suffering Adam to transgress. Foolish tongues! when God gave him reason, he gave him freedom to choose, for reason is but choosing; he had been else a mere artificial Adam, such an Adam as he is in the motions.[46] We ourselves esteem not of that obedience, or love, or gift, which is of force; God therefore left him free, set before him a provoking object, ever almost in his eyes; herein consisted his merit, herein the right of his reward, the praise of his abstinence. Wherefore did he create passions within us, pleasures round about us, but that these, rightly tempered, are the very ingredients of virtue? They are not skillful con-

---

33. fond: foolish.   **34. Doric:** manly. Cf. Plato, *Republic,* III. 399.   **35. shrewd:** mischievous.   **36. visitors:** a term recalling Laud's much-resented campaign for uniformity in the church. **37. rebeck:** fiddle.   **38. ballatry:** balladry.   **39. gamut:** range of notes.   **40.** *Arcadias ... Montemayors:* romances like Sidney's *Arcadia* and the Spanish Montemayor's *Diana.*   **41. hears ill:** is ill spoken of.

42. conversation: association.   **43. Atlantic ... polities:** ideal states like Bacon's New Atlantis and More's Utopia.   **44. Plato ... mentions:** *Republic,* IV. 424-33, *Laws,* I. 643.   **45. gramercy:** thanks.   **46. motions:** puppet shows.

siderers of human things who imagine to remove sin by removing the matter of sin; for, besides that it is a huge heap increasing under the very act of diminishing, though some part of it may for a time be withdrawn from some persons, it cannot from all, in such a universal thing as books are; and when this is done, yet the sin remains entire. Though ye take from a covetous man all his treasure, he has yet one jewel left — ye cannot bereave him of his covetousness. Banish all objects of lust, shut up all youth into the severest discipline that can be exercised in any hermitage, ye cannot make them chaste that came not thither so: such great care and wisdom is required to the right managing of this point.

Suppose we could expel sin by this means: look how much we thus expel of sin, so much we expel of virtue, for the matter of them both is the same; remove that, and ye remove them both alike. This justifies the high providence of God, who, though he command us temperance, justice, continence, yet pours out before us even to a profuseness all desirable things, and gives us minds that can wander beyond all limit and satiety. Why should we then affect a rigor contrary to the manner of God and of nature, by abridging or scanting those means, which books freely permitted are, both to the trial of virtue and the exercise of truth?

SONNETS

XIX. WHEN I CONSIDER HOW MY LIGHT IS SPENT

This sonnet was probably composed early in 1652, when Milton's blindness became complete.

When I consider how my light is spent,
  Ere half my days° in this dark world and wide,
  And that one talent which is death to hide°
  Lodged with me useless, though my soul more bent
To serve therewith my Maker, and present
  My true account, lest he returning chide,
  "Doth God exact day-labor, light denied?"
  I fondly° ask. But Patience, to prevent
That murmur, soon replies, "God doth not need
  Either man's work or his own gifts; who best

Bear his mild yoke, they serve him best. His state   11
Is kingly: thousands° at his bidding speed,
  And post o'er land and ocean without rest;
  They also serve who only stand and wait."

XVIII. ON THE LATE MASSACRE IN PIEDMONT

In April, 1655, members of the Protestant Vaudois or Waldensian sect, who had long inhabited the mountains of Piedmont, and had been granted freedom of worship, were massacred by Italian soldiers who had been billeted among them. Cromwell sent a protest (written by Milton as secretary) to the Duke of Savoy and addressed appeals (also written by Milton) to the leaders of continental Protestantism; a large fund was raised in England for the surviving refugees.

Avenge, O Lord, thy slaughtered saints, whose bones
  Lie scattered on the Alpine mountains cold,
  Even them who kept thy truth so pure of old
  When all our fathers worshiped stocks and stones,°
Forget not; in thy book record their groans
  Who were thy sheep, and in their ancient fold
  Slain by the bloody Piedmontese, that rolled
  Mother with infant down the rocks. Their moans
The vales redoubled to the hills, and they   9
  To heaven. Their martyred blood and ashes sow
  O'er all the Italian fields, where still doth sway
The triple tyrant,° that from these may grow
  A hundredfold, who, having learnt thy way,
  Early may fly the Babylonian woe.°

XX. LAWRENCE, OF VIRTUOUS FATHER VIRTUOUS SON

Edward Lawrence (1633–57), the young man Milton addresses, was the eldest son of Henry Lawrence, Lord President of the Council under Cromwell. The sonnet was perhaps written in 1655.

Lawrence, of virtuous father virtuous son,
  Now that the fields are dank and ways are mire,
  Where shall we sometimes meet, and by the fire
  Help waste a sullen day, what may be won

SONNET XIX. **2. Ere . . . days:** Milton is presumably thinking, not of his whole life span, but of his fruitful maturity. **3. talent . . . hide:** See the parable of the talents (Matt. 25:14–30) and the early Sonnet VII above. **8. fondly:** foolishly.

12. thousands: of angels. SONNET XVIII. **3–4. who . . . stones:** the Waldensian "heresy" arose in the twelfth century. **12. triple tyrant:** the pope, as claiming authority on earth and in Heaven and Hell. **14. Babylonian woe:** Protestant tradition (and such Catholics as Petrarch) saw an image of papal corruption in the Babylon of Rev. 14:8, 17:5, 18:2.

From the hard season gaining? Time will run
  On smoother, till Favonius° reinspire
  The frozen earth, and clothe in fresh attire
  The lily and rose, that neither sowed nor spun.°
What neat repast shall feast us, light and choice,
  Of Attic taste,° with wine, whence we may rise
  To hear the lute well touched, or artful voice 11
Warble immortal notes and Tuscan° air?
  He who of those delights can judge, and spare°
  To interpose them oft, is not unwise.

XXII. TO MR. CYRIACK SKINNER
UPON HIS BLINDNESS

Skinner was a lawyer who had been Milton's pupil and remained his friend. The title, evidently not Milton's, was used by his nephew, Edward Phillips, when he printed the sonnet in 1694. It was probably written in 1655.

Cyriack, this three years' day° these eyes, though
  clear
  To outward view of blemish or of spot,
  Bereft of light their seeing have forgot;
  Nor to their idle orbs doth sight appear
Of sun or moon or star throughout the year,
  Or man or woman. Yet I argue not
  Against Heaven's hand or will, nor bate a jot
  Of heart or hope, but still bear up° and steer
Right onward. What supports me, dost thou
  ask?
  The conscience,° friend, to have lost them over-
  plied   10

In liberty's defense,° my noble task,
Of which all Europe talks from side to side.
  This thought might lead me through the world's
  vain masque,
  Content though blind, had I no better guide.°

XXIII. METHOUGHT I SAW MY LATE
ESPOUSÈD SAINT

Katherine Woodcock, at the age of 28, became Milton's second wife in November, 1656, and died in February, 1658, some four months after the birth of a child.

Methought I saw my late espousèd saint°
  Brought to me like Alcestis from the grave,
  Whom Jove's great son to her glad husband gave,
  Rescued from death by force, though pale and
  faint.°
Mine, as whom washed from spot of child-bed
  taint
  Purification in the Old Law did save,°
  And such as yet once more I trust to have
  Full sight of her in Heaven without restraint,
Came vested all in white, pure as her mind.
  Her face was veiled,° yet to my fancied sight 10
  Love, sweetness, goodness, in her person
  shined
So clear as in no face with more delight.
  But O as to embrace me she inclined,
  I waked, she fled, and day brought back my
  night.

SONNET XX. **6. Favonius:** the west wind. **8. lily . . . spun:** See Matt. 6-28. **10. Of . . . taste:** as at Athenian banquets. **12. Tuscan:** Florentine, Italian. **13. spare:** the context perhaps favors "spare time," but Milton's usage — and perhaps his character — favor "forbear." SONNET XXII. **1. this . . . day:** these last three years. **8. bear up:** turn the helm so as to put a vessel before the wind. **10. conscience:** consciousness.

11. liberty's defense: See Intro., pp. 200-01. **14. better guide:** God, his conscience. SONNET XXIII. **1. late . . . saint:** the woman I lately married, now a saint in Heaven. **2-4. Alcestis . . . faint:** In the myth dramatized by Euripides, Alcestis, King Admetus' wife, yielded herself to death as a substitute for her husband, but was brought back from Hades by Heracles (Hercules). **5-6.** In Hebrew law (Lev. 12) a woman underwent a ritual of purification after childbirth. **10. Her . . . veiled:** like Alcestis, and because apparently Milton had never seen her.

PARADISE LOST

[General critical comments on *Paradise Lost* are made in the Introduction. Some factual data are given here. As early as 1639 Milton had in mind an epic on King Arthur, the kind of subject that would have been in accord with classical and Renaissance tradition, but he shifted to a subject of higher and more universal significance. He shifted also, for a time, to the idea of dramatic treatment and made some outlines for a drama; he returned, however, to the epic plan. The actual composition of *Paradise Lost* apparently began some time during the years 1655–58; the latter part of the invocation to Book VII obviously belongs to the Restoration period. Day and night were much alike to the blind poet, and, as he says several times, he composed at night. The first edition (1667) contained ten books; in the second edition (1674) the seventh and tenth books were each split into two and some small revisions were made.

Only portions of the poem can be given in this volume, and gaps in the narrative are filled in, after a fashion, by brief editorial summaries. Milton's arguments to the individual books are given for those books reprinted in full (I, II, and IX) and for Book IV; otherwise they are omitted.]

THE VERSE

The measure is English heroic verse without rhyme, as that of Homer in Greek and of Virgil in Latin, rhyme being no necessary adjunct or true ornament of poem or good verse, in longer works especially, but the invention of a barbarous age, to set off wretched matter and lame meter — graced indeed since by the use of some famous modern poets, carried away by custom, but much to their own vexation, hindrance, and constraint to express many things otherwise, and for the most part worse, than else they would have expressed them. Not without cause, therefore, some both Italian and Spanish poets of prime note have rejected rhyme both in longer and shorter works, as have also long since our best English tragedies, as a thing of itself, to all judicious ears, trivial and of no true musical delight; which consists only in apt numbers, fit quantity of syllables, and the sense variously drawn out from one verse into another, not in the jingling sound of like endings, a fault avoided by the learned ancients both in poetry and all good oratory. This neglect then of rhyme so little is to be taken for a defect, though it may seem so perhaps to vulgar readers, that it rather is to be esteemed an example set, the first in English, of ancient liberty recovered to heroic poem from the troublesome and modern bondage of rhyming.

BOOK I

THE ARGUMENT

This first book proposes, first in brief, the whole subject, man's disobedience, and the loss thereupon of Paradise wherein he was placed: then touches the prime cause of his fall, the Serpent, or rather Satan in the Serpent; who, revolting from God, and drawing to his side many legions of angels, was by the command of God driven out of Heaven with all his crew into the great Deep. Which action passed over, the poem hastes into the midst of things, presenting Satan with his angels now fallen into Hell — described here, not in the center (for Heaven and Earth may be supposed as yet not made, certainly not yet accursed), but in a place of utter darkness, fitliest called Chaos. Here Satan with his angels lying on the burning lake, thunderstruck and astonished, after a certain space recovers, as from confusion; calls up him who, next in order and dignity, lay by him; they confer of their miserable fall. Satan awakens all his legions, who lay till then in the same manner confounded. They rise: their numbers, array of battle, their chief leaders named, according to the idols known afterwards in Canaan and the countries adjoining. To these Satan directs his speech, comforts them with hope yet of regaining Heaven, but tells them lastly of a new world and new kind of creature to be created, according to an ancient prophecy or report in Heaven; for that angels were long before this visible creation, was the opinion of many ancient Fathers. To find out the truth of this prophecy, and what to determine thereon, he refers to a full council. What his associates thence attempt. Pandemonium, the palace of Satan, rises, suddenly built out of the Deep; the infernal peers there sit in council.

Of man's first disobedience, and the fruit
Of that forbidden tree, whose mortal° taste
Brought death into the world, and all our woe,
With loss of Eden, till one greater Man°
Restore us, and regain the blissful seat,
Sing, Heavenly Muse,° that on the secret° top
Of Oreb, or of Sinai,° didst inspire
That shepherd, who first taught the chosen seed
In the beginning how the Heavens and Earth
Rose out of Chaos; or if Sion hill°   10
Delight thee more, and Siloa's brook that flowed
Fast by the oracle of God, I thence
Invoke thy aid to my adventurous song,
That with no middle flight intends to soar
Above the Aonian mount,° while it pursues
Things unattempted yet in prose or rhyme.

PARADISE LOST. Book I: 2. **mortal**: the word may combine the sense of "human" with that of "deadly." 4. **one . . . Man**: Christ, traditionally thought of as "the second Adam." 6. **Heavenly Muse**: Milton's invocations are not mere imitations of Homer and Virgil but prayers. See his account, in the *Reason of Church Government*, of the inspiration he craved. Urania, the Muse of astronomy, became for Renaissance writers the Muse of sacred poetry, and Milton associates her with the divine spirit that illuminated Moses ("That shepherd"), the supposed author of the first five books of the Bible, and the later Hebrew prophets. **secret**: remote, mysterious. 7. **Oreb . . . Sinai**: alternative names for the mountain north of the Red Sea, where Moses received the law from God. 10. **Sion hill**: Zion, the hill of Jerusalem on which, later, stood the temple ("the oracle of God"). 15. **Aonian mount**: Helicon, in Boeotia, the haunt of the Muses. As a Christian poet, Milton can hope for more than classical inspiration.

And chiefly thou, O Spirit,° that dost prefer
Before all temples the upright heart and pure,
Instruct me, for thou know'st; thou from the
    first
Wast present, and with mighty wings outspread
Dove-like sat'st brooding on the vast abyss   21
And mad'st it pregnant: what in me is dark
Illumine, what is low raise and support;
That to the highth° of this great argument°
I may assert Eternal Providence,
And justify the ways of God to men.

    Say first, for Heaven hides nothing from thy
    view,
Nor the deep tract of Hell, say first what cause
Moved our grand° parents in that happy state,
Favored of Heaven so highly, to fall off   30
From their Creator, and transgress his will
For one restraint, lords of the world besides?
Who first seduced them to that foul revolt?
The infernal Serpent; he it was, whose guile,
Stirred up with envy and revenge, deceived
The mother of mankind, what time his pride°
Had cast him out from Heaven, with all his host
Of rebel angels, by whose aid aspiring
To set himself in glory above his peers,
He trusted to have equaled the Most High,   40
If he opposed; and with ambitious aim
Against the throne and monarchy of God,
Raised impious war in Heaven and battle proud
With vain attempt. Him the Almighty Power
Hurled headlong flaming from the ethereal sky
With hideous ruin° and combustion down
To bottomless perdition, there to dwell
In adamantine chains and penal fire,
Who durst defy the Omnipotent to arms.
Nine times the space that measures day and night°
To mortal men, he with his horrid crew   51
Lay vanquished, rolling in the fiery gulf,
Confounded though immortal. But his doom
Reserved him to more wrath; for now° the thought
Both of lost happiness and lasting pain
Torments him; round he throws his baleful eyes,
That witnessed huge affliction and dismay
Mixed with obdúrate pride and steadfast hate.
At once as far as angels ken° he views
The dismal situation waste and wild: 60
A dungeon horrible on all sides round
As one great furnace flamed, yet from those flames

No light,° but rather darkness visible
Served only to discover sights of woe,
Regions of sorrow, doleful shades, where peace
And rest can never dwell, hope never comes
That comes to all; but torture without end
Still urges,° and a fiery deluge, fed
With ever-burning sulphur unconsumed:
Such place Eternal Justice had prepared   70
For those rebellious, here their prison ordained
In utter° darkness, and their portion set
As far removed from God and light of Heaven
As from the center° thrice to the utmost pole.°
O how unlike the place from whence they fell!
There the companions of his fall, o'erwhelmed
With floods and whirlwinds of tempestuous fire,
He soon discerns, and weltering by his side
One next himself in power, and next in crime,
Long after known in Palestine, and named   80
Beëlzebub. To whom the Arch-Enemy,
And thence in Heaven called Satan,° with bold
    words
Breaking the horrid silence thus began:
    "If thou beest he — but O how fallen! how
    changed
From him,° who in the happy realms of light
Clothed with transcendent brightness didst outshine
Myriads though bright — if he whom mutual
    league,
United thoughts and counsels, equal hope
And hazard in the glorious enterprise,
Joined with me once, now misery hath joined   90
In equal ruin: into what pit thou seest
From what highth fallen! so much the stronger
    proved
He with his thunder; and till then who knew
The force of those dire arms? Yet not for those,
Nor what the potent Victor in his rage
Can else inflict, do I repent or change,
Though changed in outward luster, that fixed mind
And high disdain, from sense of injured merit,
That with the Mightiest raised me to contend,
And to the fierce contention brought along   100
Innumerable force of spirits armed
That durst dislike his reign, and, me preferring,
His utmost power with adverse power opposed
In dubious battle on the plains of Heaven,
And shook his throne. What though the field be
    lost?
All is not lost; the unconquerable will,

---

17 f. Spirit: the creative spirit of God that "moved upon the face of the waters" (Gen. 1:2) and later inspired his prophets. **24. highth:** Milton preferred this form of the word. **argument:** theme. **29. grand:** first. **36. pride:** the traditional motive of Satan, irreligious and unbridled self-sufficiency and ambition. **46 ruin:** fall (the Latin sense). **50. Nine . . . night:** In the myth of the Titans' war on the gods, the defeated Titans, hurled from heaven by Zeus, fell nine days and nights to earth, and nine more to hell. **54. for now:** the transition from the general statement of the theme to the epic action, which begins *in medias res*. **59. ken:** probably a verb ("see"), perhaps a noun ("angel's ken").

62–63. yet . . . light: In traditional belief the fires of Hell gave no light. **68. urges:** drives, afflicts. **72. utter:** outer. **74. center:** earth. **pole:** either end of the axis of the Ptolemaic universe, pointing toward Heaven and Hell. **82. Satan:** the name means "adversary." **84–85. how . . . him:** These words (to cite one of Milton's countless echoes) seem to combine Isa. 14:12: "How art thou fallen from heaven, O Lucifer, son of the morning," and Virgil's picture of the dead Hector appearing to Aeneas, *"quantum mutatus ab illo Hectore,"* "how changed from that Hector . . ." (*Aeneid*, II. 274). Satan's unfinished phrases (ll. 84–94) reflect his agitation.

And study of revenge, immortal hate,
And courage never to submit or yield:
And what is else not to be overcome?°
That glory never shall his wrath or might   110
Extort from me. To bow and sue for grace
With suppliant knee, and deify his power
Who from the terror of this arm so late
Doubted his empire, that were low indeed,
That were an ignominy° and shame beneath
This downfall; since by fate the strength of gods
And this empyreal substance° cannot fail,
Since through experience of this great event,
In arms not worse, in foresight much advanced,
We may with more successful hope resolve   120
To wage by force or guile eternal war
Irreconcilable to our grand Foe,
Who now triumphs, and in the excess of joy
Sole reigning holds the tyranny of Heaven."
    So spake the apostate Angel, though in pain,
Vaunting aloud, but racked with deep despair;
And him thus answered soon his bold compeer:°
    "O Prince, O Chief of many thronèd Powers,
That led the embattled Seraphim° to war
Under thy conduct, and in dreadful deeds   130
Fearless, endangered Heaven's perpetual King,
And put to proof his high supremacy,
Whether upheld by strength, or chance, or fate;
Too well I see and rue the dire event,°
That with sad overthrow and foul defeat
Hath lost us Heaven, and all this mighty host
In horrible destruction laid thus low,
As far as gods and heavenly essences°
Can perish: for the mind and spirit remains
Invincible, and vigor soon returns,   140
Though all our glory extinct, and happy state
Here swallowed up in endless misery.
But what if he our Conqueror (whom I now
Of force° believe almighty, since no less
Than such could have o'erpowered such force as
          ours)
Have left us this our spirit and strength entire
Strongly to suffer and support our pains,
That we may so suffice his vengeful ire,
Or do him mightier service as his thralls
By right of war, whate'er his business be,   150
Here in the heart of Hell to work in fire,
Or do his errands in the gloomy deep?
What can it then avail, though yet we feel
Strength undiminished, or eternal being
To° undergo eternal punishment?"

Whereto with speedy words the Arch-Fiend re-
          plied:
    "Fallen Cherub, to be weak is miserable,
Doing or suffering: but of this be sure,
To do aught good never will be our task,
But ever to do ill our sole delight,   160
As being the contrary to his high will
Whom we resist. If° then his providence
Out of our evil seek to bring forth good,
Our labor must be to pervert that end,
And out of good still° to find means of evil;
Which ofttimes may succeed, so as perhaps
Shall grieve him, if I fail° not, and disturb
His inmost counsels from their destined aim.
But see the angry Victor hath recalled
His ministers of vengeance and pursuit   170
Back to the gates of Heaven; the sulphurous hail
Shot after us in storm, o'erblown hath laid
The fiery surge, that from the precipice
Of Heaven received us falling, and the thunder,
Winged with red lightning and impetuous rage,
Perhaps hath spent his shafts, and ceases now
To bellow through the vast and boundless deep.
Let us not slip° the occasion, whether scorn
Or satiate fury yield it from our Foe.
Seest thou yon dreary plain, forlorn and wild,   180
The seat of desolation, void of light,
Save what the glimmering of these livid flames
Casts pale and dreadful? Thither let us tend
From off the tossing of these fiery waves,
There rest, if any rest can harbor there,
And reassembling our afflicted powers,°
Consult how we may henceforth most offend
Our Enemy, our own loss how repair,
How overcome this dire calamity,
What reinforcement we may gain from hope,   190
If not, what resolution from despair."
    Thus Satan talking to his nearest mate
With head uplift above the wave, and eyes
That sparkling blazed; his other parts besides,
Prone on the flood, extended long and large,
Lay floating many a rood, in bulk as huge
As whom the fables name of monstrous size,°
Titanian or Earth-born, that warred on Jove,
Briareos° or Typhon,° whom the den
By ancient Tarsus held, or that sea-beast   200
Leviathan,° which God of all his works
Created hugest that swim the ocean stream:
Him haply slumbering on the Norway foam,°

109. And . . . overcome: How can we be said to be overcome if
we still cherish our revengeful hatred and courage?   **115. ignominy:** pronounced "ignomy."   **117. empyreal substance:**
Heaven, the empyrean, and its inhabitants were composed of an
indestructible substance superior to that of man's world and
man.   **127. compeer:** companion.   **129. Seraphim:** In medieval
angelology there were nine orders, which were, from the highest
downward: Seraphim, Cherubim, Thrones; Dominations, Virtues, Powers; Principalities, Archangels, Angels; but Milton uses
the terms loosely.   **134. event:** outcome.   **138. heavenly essences:** See l. 117n.   **144. Of force:** perforce.   **155. To:** so as to.

162–65. If . . . evil: one of Milton's many reminders of his
central theme.   **165. still:** always.   **167. fail:** mistake.
178. slip: lose.   **186. afflicted powers:** overthrown forces.
197 f. See l. 50n. The Titans and Giants ("Earth-born") were often confused. Briareos was a hundred-handed Giant who helped
Zeus (Jove) against the Titans. Typhon or Typhoeus, a son of
Earth, was a hundred-headed serpent-monster of Cilicia (near
Tarsus) who attacked heaven and was imprisoned by Zeus beneath Mount Etna.   **201. Leviathan:** sea monster or whale
(Isa. 27:1).   **203 f.** The story of seamen's mistaking a whale
for an island was widespread in medieval literature; the whale

The pilot of some small night-foundered° skiff,
Deeming some island, oft, as seamen tell,
With fixèd anchor in his scaly rind
Moors by his side under the lee, while night
Invests the sea, and wishèd morn delays:
So stretched out huge in length the Arch-Fiend lay
Chained on the burning lake; nor ever thence   210
Had risen or heaved his head, but that the will
And high permission of all-ruling Heaven
Left him at large to his own dark designs,
That with reiterated crimes he might
Heap on himself damnation, while he sought
Evil to others, and enraged might see
How all his malice served but to bring forth
Infinite goodness, grace and mercy shown
On man by him seduced, but on himself   219
Treble confusion, wrath and vengeance poured.
  Forthwith upright he rears from off the pool
His mighty stature; on each hand the flames
Driven backward slope their pointing spires, and
  rolled
In billows, leave in the midst a horrid vale.
Then with expanded wings he steers his flight
Aloft, incumbent on the dusky air
That felt unusual weight, till on dry land
He lights, if it were land that ever burned
With solid, as the lake with liquid fire;
And such appeared in hue,° as when the force   230
Of subterranean wind transports a hill
Torn from Pelorus,° or the shattered side
Of thundering Etna, whose combustible
And fueled entrails thence conceiving fire,
Sublimed° with mineral fury, aid the winds,
And leave a singèd bottom all involved
With stench and smoke: such resting found the
  sole
Of unblest feet. Him followed his next mate,
Both glorying to have scaped the Stygian flood
As gods, and by their own recovered strength,   240
Not by the sufferance of supernal power.
  "Is this the region, this the soil, the clime,"
Said then the lost Archangel, "this the seat
That we must change for Heaven, this mournful
  gloom
For that celestial light? Be it so, since he
Who now is sovran° can dispose and bid
What shall be right: farthest from him is best,
Whom reason hath equaled, force hath made su-
  preme
Above his equals. Farewell, happy fields,
Where joy for ever dwells! Hail, horrors! hail,   250
Infernal world! and thou, profoundest Hell,
Receive thy new possessor; one who brings
A mind not to be changed by place or time.

The mind is its° own place, and in itself
Can make a Heaven of Hell, a Hell of Heaven.
What matter where, if I be still the same,
And what I should be, all but less than° he
Whom thunder hath made greater? Here° at
  least
We shall be free; the Almighty hath not built
Here for his envy, will not drive us hence: 260
Here we may reign secure, and in my choice
To reign is worth ambition, though in Hell:
Better to reign in Hell than serve in Heaven.
But wherefore let we then our faithful friends,
The associates and copartners of our loss,
Lie thus astonished° on the oblivious° pool,
And call them not to share with us their part
In this unhappy mansion, or once more
With rallied arms to try what may be yet
Regained in Heaven, or what more lost in Hell? "
  So Satan spake, and him Beëlzebub   271
Thus answered: "Leader of those armies bright,
Which but the Omnipotent none could have foiled,
If once they hear that voice, their liveliest pledge
Of hope in fears and dangers, heard so oft
In worst extremes, and on the perilous edge
Of battle when it raged, in all assaults
Their surest signal, they will soon resume
New courage and revive, though now they lie
Groveling and prostrate on yon lake of fire,   280
As we erewhile, astounded and amazed;°
No wonder, fallen such a pernicious° highth! "
  He scarce had ceased when the superior Fiend
Was moving toward the shore; his ponderous
  shield,
Ethereal° temper, massy, large, and round,
Behind him cast; the broad circumference
Hung on his shoulders like the moon, whose orb
Through optic glass° the Tuscan artist° views
At evening from the top of Fesole,°
Or in Valdarno,° to descry new lands,   290
Rivers or mountains in her spotty globe.
His spear, to equal which the tallest pine
Hewn on Norwegian hills, to be the mast
Of some great ammiral,° were but a wand,
He walked with, to support uneasy steps
Over the burning marl,° not like those steps
On Heaven's azure; and the torrid clime
Smote on him sore besides, vaulted with fire.
Nathless° he so endured, till on the beach

---

254. its: one of the three places in Milton's verse (see "Nativity,"
l. 106, and *PL*, IV. 813) where he uses "its"; ordinarily he uses
"her" or "his." Satan's boast in lines 254–55 he later finds to be
untrue (cf. IV. 75).   257. all . . . than: almost equal to.   258–
63. Here . . . Heaven: one of Satan's many revelations of his
false conception of freedom.   266. astonished: dazed.   obvious: causing forgetfulness.   281. amazed: stupefied.   282. pernicious: destructive.   285. Ethereal: heavenly.   288. optic
glass: telescope.   Tuscan artist: Galileo (d. 1642).   289. Fesole:
Fiesole, a hill town near Florence.   290. Valdarno: the valley
of the Arno river, in which Florence is situated.   294. ammiral:
flagship.   296. marl: soil.   299. Nathless: nevertheless.

---

was sometimes allegorized as Satan.   204. night-foundered:
benighted.   230. hue: appearance.   232. Pelorus: a Sicilian
promontory.   235. Sublimed: made incandescent (from alchemy).   246. sovran: sovereign.

Of that inflamèd sea he stood and called   300
His legions, angel forms, who lay entranced,
Thick as autumnal leaves that strow the brooks
In Vallombrosa,° where the Etrurian shades
High over-arched embower; or scattered sedge
Afloat, when with fierce winds Orion° armed
Hath vexed the Red Sea coast, whose waves o'er-
          threw
Busiris° and his Memphian° chivalry,
While with perfidious hatred they pursued
The sojourners of Goshen,° who beheld
From the safe shore their floating carcasses   310
And broken chariot wheels; so thick bestrown,
Abject° and lost lay these, covering the flood,
Under amazement of their hideous change.
He called so loud, that all the hollow deep
Of Hell resounded: " Princes, Potentates,
Warriors, the flower of Heaven, once yours, now
          lost,
If such astonishment as this can seize
Eternal spirits! or have ye chosen this place
After the toil of battle to repose
Your wearied virtue, for the ease you find   320
To slumber here, as in the vales of Heaven?
Or in this abject posture have ye sworn
To adore the Conqueror, who now beholds
Cherub and Seraph rolling in the flood
With scattered arms and ensigns, till anon
His swift pursuers from Heaven gates discern
The advantage, and descending tread us down
Thus drooping, or with linkèd thunderbolts
Transfix us to the bottom of this gulf?
Awake, arise, or be forever fallen! "   330
     They heard, and were abashed, and up they
          sprung
Upon the wing, as when men wont to watch
On duty, sleeping found by whom they dread,
Rouse and bestir themselves ere well awake.
Nor did they not perceive the evil plight
In which they were, or the fierce pains not feel;
Yet to their general's voice they soon obeyed
Innumerable. As when the potent rod
Of Amram's son° in Egypt's evil day
Waved round the coast, up called a pitchy° cloud
Of locusts, warping° on the eastern wind,   341
That o'er the realm of impious Pharaoh hung
Like night, and darkened all the land of Nile:
So numberless were those bad angels seen
Hovering on wing under the cope° of Hell

303. **Vallombrosa**: a "shady valley" (very different from the fires of Hell) eighteen miles from Florence.   305. **Orion**: a constellation associated with storms.   307-11. **Busiris . . . wheels**: for the destruction of the Egyptians who were pursuing the Israelites, see Exod. 14:26-31. The name Busiris for Pharaoh perhaps came (as D. C. Allen suggests) from a universal history by the German theologian Melanchthon. **Memphian**: Egyptian (from the city of Memphis).   309. **Goshen**: the Egyptian home of the Israelites.   312. **Abject**: thrown down.   339. **Amram's son**: Moses (see Exod. 10:12-15).   340. **pitchy**: black as pitch.   341. **warping**: tacking, veering.   345. **cope**: vault.

'Twixt upper, nether, and surrounding fires;
Till, as a signal given, the uplifted spear
Of their great Sultan° waving to direct
Their course, in even balance down they light
On the firm brimstone, and fill all the plain;   350
A multitude like which the populous North
Poured never from her frozen loins, to pass
Rhene or the Danaw,° when her barbarous sons
Came like a deluge on the South, and spread
Beneath Gibraltar to the Libyan sands.
Forthwith from every squadron and each band
The heads and leaders thither haste where stood
Their great commander; godlike shapes and forms
Excelling human, princely dignities,   359
And powers that erst in Heaven sat on thrones;
Though of their names in heavenly records now
Be no memorial, blotted out and rased°
By their rebellion from the Books of Life.
Nor had they yet among the sons of Eve°
Got them new names, till wandering o'er the
          Earth,
Through God's high sufferance for the trial of
          man,
By falsities and lies the greatest part
Of mankind they corrupted to forsake
God their Creator, and the invisible
Glory of him that made them to transform   370
Oft to the image of a brute, adorned
With gay religions° full of pomp and gold,
And devils to adore for deities:
Then were they known to men by various names,
And various idols through the heathen world.
     Say, Muse, their names then known, who first,
          who last,
Roused from the slumber on that fiery couch,
At their great emperor's call, as next in worth
Came singly where he stood on the bare strand,
While the promiscuous crowd stood yet aloof.   380
     The chief were those who from the pit of Hell,
Roaming to seek their prey on Earth, durst fix
Their seats long after next the seat of God,
Their altars by his altar, gods adored
Among the nations round, and durst abide
Jehovah thundering out of Sion, throned
Between the Cherubim; yea, often placed
Within his sanctuary itself their shrines,
Abominations; and with cursèd things
His holy rites and solemn feasts profaned,   390
And with their darkness durst affront his light.
First Moloch,° horrid king besmeared with blood
Of human sacrifice, and parents' tears,
Though for the noise of drums and timbrels loud

348. **Sultan**: the word recalls the age-old European fear of the Turks.   353. **Rhene . . . Danaw**: Rhine, Danube; a reference to the barbarian invasions of the Roman empire.   362. **rased**: erased.   364 f. Milton follows the tradition that the fallen angels became the pagan gods.   372. **religions**: rites.   392. **Moloch**: the name means "king." For the human sacrifices see II

Their children's cries unheard, that passed through
   fire
To his grim idol. Him the Ammonite°
Worshiped in Rabba and her watery plain,
In Argob and in Basan, to the stream
Of utmost Arnon. Nor content with such
Audacious neighborhood, the wisest heart   400
Of Solomon he led by fraud to build
His temple right against the temple of God
On that opprobrious hill,° and made his grove
The pleasant valley of Hinnom,° Tophet thence
And black Gehenna called, the type of Hell.
Next Chemos,° the obscene dread of Moab's sons,
From Aroer to Nebo, and the wild
Of southmost Abarim;° in Heseson
And Horonaim, Seon's° realm, beyond
The flowery dale of Sibma clad with vines,   410
And Elealè to the Asphaltic pool:
Peor his other name, when he enticed
Israel in Sittim on their march from Nile
To do him wanton rites, which cost them woe.
Yet thence his lustful orgies he enlarged
Even to that hill of scandal,° by the grove
Of Moloch homicide, lust hard by hate;
Till good Josiah° drove them thence to Hell.
With these came they, who from the bordering
   flood
Of old Euphrates° to the brook that parts   420
Egypt from Syrian ground, had general names
Of Baalim° and Ashtaroth,° those male,
These feminine. For spirits° when they please
Can either sex assume, or both; so soft
And uncompounded is their essence pure,
Not tied or manacled with joint or limb,
Nor founded on the brittle strength of bones,
Like cumbrous flesh; but in what shape they
   choose,
Dilated or condensed, bright or obscure,
Can execute their aery purposes,   430
And works of love or enmity fulfil.
For those the race of Israel oft forsook
Their Living Strength, and unfrequented left
His righteous altar, bowing lowly down
To bestial gods; for which their heads as low

Bowed down in battle, sunk before the spear
Of despicable foes. With these in troop
Came Astoreth,° whom the Phoenicians called
Astarte, queen of heaven, with crescent horns;
To whose bright image nightly by the moon   440
Sidonian° virgins paid their vows and songs;
In Sion also not unsung, where stood
Her temple on the offensive mountain,° built
By that uxorious king° whose heart though large,
Beguiled by fair idolatresses, fell
To idols foul. Thammuz° came next behind,
Whose annual wound in Lebanon allured
The Syrian damsels to lament his fate
In amorous ditties all a summer's day,
While smooth Adonis° from his native rock   450
Ran purple to the sea, supposed with blood
Of Thammuz yearly wounded: the love-tale
Infected Sion's daughters with like heat,
Whose wanton passions in the sacred porch
Ezekiel saw, when by the vision led
His eye surveyed the dark idolatries
Of alienated Judah.° Next came one°
Who mourned in earnest, when the captive ark
Maimed his brute image, head and hands lopped
   off
In his own temple, on the grunsel° edge,   460
Where he fell flat, and shamed his worshipers:
Dagon his name, sea monster, upward man
And downward fish; yet had his temple high
Reared in Azotus, dreaded through the coast
Of Palestine, in Gath and Ascalon,
And Accaron and Gaza's° frontier bounds.
Him followed Rimmon,° whose delightful seat
Was fair Damascus, on the fertile banks
Of Abbana and Pharphar, lucid streams.
He also against the house of God was bold: 470
A leper° once he lost and gained a king,
Ahaz° his sottish conqueror, whom he drew
God's altar to disparage and displace
For one of Syrian mode, whereon to burn
His odious offerings, and adore the gods
Whom he had vanquished. After these appeared
A crew who under names of old renown,

Kings 23:10, Jer. 7:31, 19:1–6. **396. Ammonite:** The Ammonites were a nation east of the Jordan; Rabba was their capital. **403. opprobrious hill:** the Mount of Olives, where Solomon built heathen shrines (I Kings 11:7, II Kings 23:13). **404. Hinnom:** a valley (in Greek, Gehenna) near Jerusalem, where human sacrifices were offered to Moloch and where later rubbish was burned (see Biblical references in l. 392n., above). **406. Chemos:** a Moabite god, otherwise Baal-Peor (l. 412). See Num. 25. Moab was east of the Dead Sea ("the Asphaltic pool"). **408. Abarim:** hills, including Mount Nebo, east of the Dead Sea. **409. Seon:** Sihon, king of the Amorites, conquered by the Israelites. **416. hill of scandal:** Mount of Olives. See l. 403n., above. **418. Josiah:** See II Kings 23. **420. Euphrates:** the eastern boundary of Palestine. **422. Baalim, Ashtaroth:** See "Nativity," ll. 197–200, and *PL,* I. 438n., below. **423–31. spirits . . . fulfil:** This power possessed by the angels is utilized at later points in the poem.

438. Astoreth: a Phoenician moon goddess (pl. Ashtaroth), identified with Aphrodite and Venus. **441. Sidonian:** Sidon was a city on the Phoenician coast. **443. offensive mountain:** See l. 403n. and l. 416n., above. **444. that . . . king:** Solomon (I Kings 11:1–8). **446. Thammuz:** the Phoenician Adonis, whose annual death was mourned in seasonal rites. **450. Adonis:** the Syrian river, which was reddened by mud in spring floods. **455–57. Ezekiel . . . Judah:** See Ezek. 8:14–15. **457–66: one . . . bounds:** Dagon, a Philistine god, whose image fell before the ark of the Lord, which the Philistines had captured and placed in Dagon's temple (I Sam. 5:1–5). **460. grunsel:** ground sill. **464–66. Azotus . . . Gaza's:** the five main Philistine cities. **467. Rimmon:** a Syrian god. **471–76. A leper . . . vanquished:** Naaman, the Syrian general, when cured of leprosy by Elisha in the water of Jordan, accepted Israel's God (II Kings 5:1–19). **472. Ahaz:** the Jewish king who adopted the Syrian religion (II Kings 16).

Osiris, Isis, Orus,° and their train,
With monstrous shapes and sorceries abused°
Fanatic Egypt and her priests, to seek   480
Their wandering gods disguised in brutish forms
Rather than human. Nor did Israel scape
The infection when their borrowed gold composed
The calf in Oreb;° and the rebel king
Doubled that sin in Bethel and in Dan,°
Likening his Maker to the grazèd ox —
Jehovah, who in one night when he passed
From Egypt marching, equaled with one stroke
Both her first-born and all her bleating gods.°
Belial° came last, than whom a spirit more lewd
Fell not from Heaven, or more gross to love   491
Vice for itself. To him no temple stood
Or altar smoked; yet who more oft than he
In temples and at altars, when the priest
Turns atheist, as did Eli's sons,° who filled
With lust and violence the house of God?
In courts and palaces he also reigns
And in luxurious° cities, where the noise
Of riot ascends above their loftiest towers,
And injury and outrage; and when night   500
Darkens the streets, then wander forth the sons
Of Belial,° flown° with insolence and wine.
Witness the streets of Sodom,° and that night
In Gibeah,° when the hospitable door
Exposed a matron to avoid worse rape.
These were the prime in order and in might;
The rest were long to tell, though far renowned,
The Ionian gods, of Javan's° issue held
Gods, yet confessed later than Heaven° and Earth,
Their boasted parents; Titan, Heaven's first-born,
With his enormous brood, and birthright seized
By younger Saturn; he from mightier Jove,   512
His own and Rhea's son, like measure found;
So Jove usurping reigned. These, first in Crete
And Ida° known, thence on the snowy top
Of cold Olympus ruled the middle air,°

Their highest Heaven; or on the Delphian cliff,°
Or in Dodona,° and through all the bounds
Of Doric° land; or who with Saturn old
Fled over Adria to the Hesperian fields,°   520
And o'er the Celtic° roamed the utmost isles.°
    All these and more came flocking; but with looks
Downcast and damp, yet such wherein appeared
Obscure some glimpse of joy, to have found their
        Chief
Not in despair, to have found themselves not lost
In loss itself; which on his countenance cast
Like doubtful hue. But he, his wonted pride
Soon recollecting, with high words, that bore
Semblance of worth, not substance, gently raised
Their fainting courage, and dispelled their fears.
Then straight commands that, at the warlike sound
Of trumpets loud and clarions, be upreared   532
His mighty standard; that proud honor claimed
Azazel as his right, a Cherub tall;
Who forthwith from the glittering staff unfurled
The imperial ensign, which full high advanced
Shone like a meteor streaming to the wind,
With gems and golden luster rich emblazed,
Seraphic arms and trophies; all the while
Sonorous metal blowing martial sounds;   540
At which the universal host upsent
A shout that tore Hell's concave, and beyond
Frighted the reign° of Chaos° and old Night.°
All in a moment through the gloom were seen
Ten thousand banners rise into the air
With orient° colors waving; with them rose
A forest huge of spears; and thronging helms
Appeared, and serried° shields in thick array
Of depth immeasurable. Anon they move
In perfect phalanx to the Dorian° mood   550
Of flutes and soft recorders; such as raised
To highth of noblest temper heroes old
Arming to battle, and instead of rage
Deliberate valor breathed, firm and unmoved
With dread of death to flight or foul retreat,
Nor wanting power to mitigate and swage°
With solemn touches troubled thoughts, and chase
Anguish and doubt and fear and sorrow and pain
From mortal or immortal minds. Thus they,
Breathing united force with fixèd thought,   560
Moved on in silence to soft pipes that charmed
Their painful steps o'er the burnt soil; and now
Advanced in view they stand, a horrid° front

478. Osiris . . . Orus: See "Nativity," ll. 212–13n. 479. abused:
deceived.   482–84. Nor . . . Oreb: Aaron made a golden calf as
an idol (Exod. 12:35–36, 32:4).   484–85. king . . . Dan: Jere-
boam, leader of ten revolting tribes of Israel, set up two golden
calves for worship (I Kings 12).   487–89. Jehovah . . . gods:
When the Israelites were not allowed to leave Egypt, the Lord
smote the first-born of every Egyptian and of his beasts, and
the Egyptian animal gods (Exod. 12:12).   490. Belial: not
properly a god; the name is an abstract term meaning "worthlessness."   495. Eli's sons: See I Sam. 2:12–25.   498. luxurious: lewd.   500–02. "The sons of Eli were sons of Belial"
(I Sam. 2:12). "Sons of Belial" had often been applied by Puritans to their Cavalier enemies; Milton is thinking of young
roisterers in London.   502. flown: overflowing, swollen.
503–04. Sodom, Gibeah: See Gen. 19:4–11, Judg. 19:22–28.
508. Javan: son of Japheth or Japhet (Gen. 10:2), supposed
progenitor of the Ionians or Greeks.   509–14. Heaven . . .
reigned: Heaven and Earth were the primordial Greek deities
and parents of the Titans; in Milton's version, one, Titan, was
dethroned by his brother Saturn, who in turn was dethroned by
Jove, son of Saturn and Rhea.   515. Ida: Jove was born and
reared on Mount Ida in Crete.   516. middle air: See "Nativity,"
l. 164n.

517–18. Delphian cliff, Dodona: the oracle of Apollo at Delphi
on Mount Parnassus and that of Zeus (Jove) at Dodona in
Epirus.   519. Doric: Greek (strictly the southern half of
Greece).   519–20. Saturn . . . fields: Saturn was said to have
crossed the Adriatic Sea to Italy (the "Hesperian" or "western"
fields), where his reign was a golden age.   521. Celtic: French.
isles: British Isles.   543. reign: realm.   Chaos: for this personification see PL, II. 894–95, 907–09, 959 ff.   Night: a classical
personification.   546. orient: bright.   548. serried: inter-
locked.   550. Dorian: Spartan, manly. Lines 549–60 seem to
be based on Plutarch's account (Lycurgus) of the Spartans marching.   556. swage: assuage.   563. horrid: bristling.

Of dreadful length and dazzling arms, in guise
Of warriors old with ordered spear and shield,
Awaiting what command their mighty Chief
Had to impose. He through the armèd files
Darts his experienced eye, and soon traverse°
The whole battalion views, their order due,
Their visages and stature as of gods;　　　570
Their number last he sums. And now his heart
Distends with pride, and hardening in his strength
Glories; for never, since created man,°
Met such embodied force as named with these
Could merit more than that small infantry°
Warred on by cranes: though all the giant brood
Of Phlegra° with the heroic race were joined
That fought at Thebes and Ilium,° on each side
Mixed with auxiliar gods; and what resounds
In fable or romance of Uther's son°　　　580
Begirt with British and Armoric° knights;
And all who since, baptized or infidel,
Jousted in Aspramont or Montalban,°
Damasco, or Marocco, or Trebisond,°
Or whom Biserta° sent from Afric shore
When Charlemain with all his peerage fell°
By Fontarabbia.° Thus far these beyond
Compare of mortal prowess, yet observed°
Their dread commander. He above the rest
In shape and gesture proudly eminent　　　590
Stood like a tower; his form had yet not lost
All her° original brightness, nor appeared
Less than Archangel ruined, and the excess
Of glory obscured: as when the sun new risen
Looks through the horizontal misty air
Shorn of his beams, or from behind the moon
In dim eclipse disastrous twilight sheds
On half the nations, and with fear of change
Perplexes monarchs. Darkened so, yet shone
Above them all the Archangel; but his face　　600
Deep scars of thunder had intrenched, and care
Sat on his faded cheek, but under brows
Of dauntless courage, and considerate° pride
Waiting revenge. Cruel his eye, but cast
Signs of remorse and passion to behold

The fellows of his crime, the followers rather
(Far other once beheld in bliss), condemned
For ever now to have their lot in pain,
Millions of spirits for his fault amerced°
Of Heaven, and from eternal splendors flung　　610
For his revolt, yet faithful how they stood,
Their glory withered: as when Heaven's fire
Hath scathed° the forest oaks or mountain pines,
With singèd top their stately growth though bare
Stands on the blasted heath. He now prepared
To speak; whereat their doubled ranks they bend
From wing to wing, and half enclose him round
With all his peers: attention held them mute.
Thrice he assayed,° and thrice in spite of scorn,
Tears such as angels weep burst forth; at last　620
Words interwove with sighs found out their way:
" O myriads of immortal spirits, O Powers
Matchless, but with the Almighty, and that strife
Was not inglorious, though the event° was dire,
As this place testifies, and this dire change
Hateful to utter. But what power of mind
Foreseeing or presaging, from the depth
Of knowledge past or present, could have feared
How such united force of gods, how such
As stood like these, could ever know repulse?　630
For who can yet believe, though after loss,
That all these puissant legions, whose exile
Hath emptied Heaven, shall fail to re-ascend
Self-raised, and repossess their native seat?
For me, be witness all the host of Heaven,
If counsels different, or danger shunned
By me, have lost our hopes. But he who reigns
Monarch in Heaven, till then as one secure
Sat on his throne, upheld by old repute,
Consent or custom, and his regal state　　640
Put forth at full, but still his strength concealed,
Which tempted our attempt, and wrought our fall.
Henceforth his might we know, and know our
　　own,
So as not either to provoke, or dread
New war, provoked; our better part remains
To work° in close° design, by fraud or guile,
What force effected not; that he no less
At length from us may find, who overcomes
By force hath overcome but half his foe.　　649
Space may produce new worlds; whereof so rife
There went a fame° in Heaven that he ere long
Intended to create, and therein plant
A generation, whom his choice regard
Should favor equal to the sons of Heaven.
Thither, if but to pry, shall be perhaps
Our first eruption, thither or elsewhere;
For this infernal pit shall never hold
Celestial spirits in bondage, nor the abyss

568. traverse: across.　573. created man: the creation of man
(a Latinism).　575. small infantry: the Pygmies, who were
warred on by cranes (*Iliad*, III. 3–6).　577. Phlegra: the scene,
in Macedonia, of the battle between the Olympian gods and the
Giants.　578. Thebes, Ilium: such warriors as the "seven" who
attacked Thebes and those who fought at Troy.　580. Uther's
son: King Arthur.　581. Armoric: of Brittany, a region important in Arthurian story.　583. Aspramont, Montalban:
places in southern France that figure in romances of Charlemagne (the two names carry transverse rhyme and assonance).
584. Trebisond: on the Black Sea.　585. Biserta: the Tunisian
seaport, where, in romance, Saracens assembled to attack
Charlemagne.　586. Charlemain . . . fell: was utterly defeated
(Charlemagne himself was not killed).　587. Fontarabbia: on
the French-Spanish border where, according to some writers,
the famous Roland was killed (the common tradition put his
death at Roncesvalles).　588. observed: paid reverence to.
592. her: See l 254n., above.　603. considerate: based on deliberation.

609. amerced: punished with the loss of.　613. scathed: damaged.　619. assayed: essayed, tried.　624. event: outcome.
646. work: achieve. close: secret.　651. fame: rumor.

Long under darkness cover. But these thoughts
Full counsel must mature. Peace is despaired,°   660
For who can think submission? War then, war
Open or understood,° must be resolved."
   He spake; and to confirm his words, out flew
Millions of flaming swords, drawn from the thighs
Of mighty Cherubim; the sudden blaze
Far round illumined Hell. Highly they raged
Against the Highest, and fierce with graspèd arms
Clashed on their sounding shields the din of war,
Hurling defiance toward the vault of Heaven.
   There stood a hill not far, whose grisly top   670
Belched fire and rolling smoke; the rest entire
Shone with a glossy scurf, undoubted sign
That in his womb was hid metallic ore,
The work of sulphur.° Thither winged with speed
A numerous brígade hastened: as when bands
Of pioneers° with spade and pickaxe armed
Forerun the royal camp, to trench a field,
Or cast a rampart. Mammon° led them on,
Mammon, the least erected° spirit that fell
From Heaven, for even in Heaven his looks and
    thoughts   680
Were always downward bent, admiring more
The riches of Heaven's pavement, trodden gold,
Than aught divine or holy else enjoyed
In vision beatific. By him first
Men also, and by his suggestion taught,
Ransacked the center,° and with impious hands
Rifled the bowels of their mother Earth
For treasures better hid. Soon had his crew
Opened into the hill a spacious wound
And digged out ribs of gold. Let none admire°
That riches grow in Hell; that soil may best   691
Deserve the precious bane. And here let those
Who boast in mortal things, and wondering tell
Of Babel,° and the works of Memphian kings,°
Learn how their greatest monuments of fame,
And strength and art, are easily outdone
By spirits reprobate, and in an hour
What in an age they with incessant toil
And hands innumerable scarce perform.
Nigh on the plain in many cells prepared,   700
That underneath had veins of liquid fire
Sluiced from the lake, a second multitude
With wondrous art founded the massy ore,°
Severing each kind, and scummed the bullion dross.
A third as soon had formed within the ground
A various mold, and from the boiling cells
By strange conveyance filled each hollow nook,
As in an organ from one blast of wind

To many a row of pipes the sound-board breathes.
Anon out of the earth a fabric huge   710
Rose like an exhalation,° with the sound
Of dulcet symphonies and voices sweet,
Built like a temple, where pilasters round
Were set, and Doric pillars overlaid
With golden architrave; nor did there want
Cornice or frieze, with bossy° sculptures graven;
The roof was fretted gold.° Not Babylon,
Nor great Alcairo° such magnificence
Equaled in all their glories, to enshrine
Belus° or Serapis° their gods, or seat   720
Their kings, when Egypt with Assyria strove
In wealth and luxury. The ascending pile
Stood fixed her stately highth, and straight the
    doors
Opening their brazen folds discover, wide
Within, her ample spaces, o'er the smooth
And level pavement; from the archèd roof,
Pendent by subtle magic, many a row
Of starry lamps and blazing cressets,° fed
With naphtha and asphaltus, yielded light
As from a sky. The hasty multitude   730
Admiring entered, and the work some praise,
And some the architect: his hand was known
In Heaven by many a towered structure high,
Where sceptered angels held their residence,
And sat as princes, whom the supreme King
Exalted to such power, and gave to rule,
Each in his hierarchy, the orders bright.
Nor was his name unheard or unadored
In ancient Greece, and in Ausonian° land
Men called him Mulciber;° and how he fell   740
From Heaven, they fabled, thrown by angry Jove
Sheer o'er the crystal battlements: from morn
To noon he fell, from noon to dewy eve,
A summer's day; and with the setting sun
Dropped from the zenith like a falling star,
On Lemnos the Aegean isle. Thus they relate,
Erring; for he with this rebellious rout°
Fell long before; nor aught availed him now
To have built in Heaven high towers; nor did he
    scape
By all his engines,° but was headlong sent   750
With his industrious crew to build in Hell.
   Meanwhile the wingèd heralds by command
Of sovran power, with awful ceremony
And trumpet's sound, throughout the host proclaim
A solemn council forthwith to be held
At Pandemonium,° the high capitol

---

660. **despaired:** despaired of.   662. **understood:** by us in secret.
674. **sulphur:** In alchemy, metals were believed to be products of
sulphur and mercury.   676. **pioneers:** sappers.   678. **Mammon:** an abstract word meaning "riches" (Matt. 6:24), but
personified in medieval tradition.   679. **erected:** elevated.
686. **center:** earth.   690. **admire:** wonder.   694. **Babel:** See
Gen. 10:10, 11:1-9. **works . . . kings:** Egyptian pyramids.
703. **founded . . . ore:** extracted the heavy or solid metal.

711. **exhalation:** vapor.   716. **bossy:** embossed.   717. **fretted
gold:** gold wrought in designs.   718. **Alcairo:** Cairo (for Memphis, the old capital).   720. **Belus:** a Babylonian god (Baal).
Serapis: the Egyptian Osiris as god of the underworld.
728. **cressets:** hanging lamps.   739. **Ausonian:** Italian.
740. **Mulciber:** the Greek god Hephaestus (Vulcan), whom his
father Zeus threw out of heaven (*Iliad*, I. 590-94).   747. **rout:**
mob.   750. **engines:** contrivances.   756. **Pandemonium:**
"place of all the demons" (apparently a Miltonic coinage)

Of Satan and his peers; their summons called
From every band and squarèd regiment
By place or choice the worthiest; they anon
With hundreds and with thousands trooping came
Attended. All access was thronged, the gates   761
And porches wide, but chief the spacious hall
(Though like a covered field, where champions
     bold
Wont° ride in armed, and at the Soldan's chair
Defied the best of paynim chivalry
To mortal combat or career with lance)
Thick swarmed, both on the ground and in the air,
Brushed with the hiss of rustling wings. As bees
In springtime, when the sun with Taurus° rides,
Pour forth their populous youth about the hive
In clusters; they among fresh dews and flowers
Fly to and fro, or on the smoothèd plank,   772
The suburb of their straw-built citadel,
New rubbed with balm, expatiate° and confer°
Their state affairs. So thick the aery crowd
Swarmed and were straitened;° till the signal given,
Behold a wonder! they but now who seemed
In bigness to surpass Earth's giant sons,
Now less than smallest dwarfs, in narrow room
Throng numberless, like that Pygmean race   780
Beyond the Indian mount,° or fairy elves,°
Whose midnight revels, by a forest side
Or fountain, some belated peasant sees,
Or dreams he sees, while overhead the moon
Sits arbitress,° and nearer to the Earth
Wheels her pale course; they on their mirth and
     dance
Intent, with jocund music charm his ear;
At once with joy and fear his heart rebounds.
Thus incorporeal spirits to smallest forms
Reduced their shapes immense, and were at large,°
Though without number still, amidst the hall   791
Of that infernal court. But far within,
And in their own dimensions like themselves,
The great Seraphic Lords and Cherubim
In close recess and secret conclave sat,
A thousand demi-gods on golden seats,
Frequent° and full. After short silence then
And summons read, the great consult° began.

BOOK II

THE ARGUMENT

The consultation begun, Satan debates whether another battle be to be hazarded for the recovery of
Heaven: some advise it, others dissuade. A third proposal is preferred, mentioned before by Satan, to search
the truth of that prophecy or tradition in Heaven concerning another world, and another kind of creature,
equal or not much inferior to themselves, about this
time to be created. Their doubt who shall be sent on
this difficult search; Satan, their chief, undertakes
alone the voyage; is honored and applauded. The council thus ended, the rest betake them several ways and
to several employments, as their inclinations lead them,
to entertain the time till Satan return. He passes on
his journey to Hell gates, finds them shut, and who
sat there to guard them; by whom at length they are
opened, and discover to him the great gulf between
Hell and Heaven; with what difficulty he passes
through, directed by Chaos, the Power of that place, to
the sight of this new world which he sought.

High on a throne of royal state,° which far
Outshone the wealth of Ormus° and of Ind,°
Or where the gorgeous East with richest hand
Showers on her kings barbaric pearl and gold,
Satan exalted sat, by merit raised
To that bad eminence; and from despair
Thus high uplifted beyond hope, aspires
Beyond thus high, insatiate to pursue
Vain war with Heaven, and by success° untaught,
His proud imaginations thus displayed: 10
"Powers and Dominions, Deities of Heaven,
For since no deep within her gulf can hold
Immortal vigor, though oppressed and fallen,
I give° not Heaven for lost. From this descent
Celestial Virtues° rising will appear
More glorious and more dread than from no fall,
And trust themselves to fear no second fate.
Me though just right and the fixed laws of Heaven
Did first create your leader, next, free choice,
With what besides, in counsel or in fight,   20
Hath been achieved of merit, yet this loss,
Thus far at least recovered, hath much more
Established in a safe unenvied throne
Yielded with full consent. The happier state
In Heaven, which follows dignity,° might draw
Envy from each inferior; but who here
Will envy whom the highest place exposes
Foremost to stand against the Thunderer's° aim
Your bulwark, and condemns to greatest share
Of endless pain? Where there is then no good   30
For which to strive, no strife can grow up there
From faction; for none sure will claim in Hell
Precedence, none whose portion is so small
Of present pain, that with ambitious mind
Will covet more. With this advantage then
To union, and firm faith, and firm accord,

764. Wont: were wont to.   769. Taurus: the sun is in the zodiacal sign of Taurus the Bull in April and May.   774. expatiate:
walk abroad. confer: discuss.   776. straitened: crowded.
780–81. Pygmean . . . mount: the Pygmies were supposed to live
in central Asia.   781–88. fairy elves . . . rebounds: Milton is
recalling *A Midsummer Night's Dream* and Virgil, *Aeneid*,
VI. 450–55.   785. arbitress: witness.   790. at large: not
crowded.   797. Frequent: in a crowd.   798. consult: debate.

Book II: 1–4. Artificial luxury is, as usual, a symbol of evil.
2. Ormus: a famous trading port in the Persian Gulf.   Ind:
India.   9. success: outcome.   14. give: count.   15. Virtues:
the word has both a general and a special sense. See I.129n.
25. dignity: worth.   28. the Thunderer: the epithet, an echo of
the Roman poets' *Jupiter Tonans*, is a crude conception in
keeping with Satan's perverted view of God, "just right,"
"merit," etc.

More than can be in Heaven, we now return
To claim our just inheritance of old,
Surer to prosper than prosperity
Could have assured us; and by what best way,   40
Whether of open war or covert guile,
We now debate; who can advise, may speak."

He ceased, and next him Moloch, sceptered king,
Stood up, the strongest and the fiercest spirit
That fought in Heaven, now fiercer by despair.
His trust was with the Eternal to be deemed
Equal in strength, and rather than be less
Cared not to be at all; with that care lost
Went all his fear: of God, or Hell, or worse
He recked not, and these words thereafter spake:

"My sentence° is for open war. Of wiles,   51
More unexpert,° I boast not: them let those
Contrive who need, or when they need, not now.
For while they sit contriving, shall the rest,
Millions that stand in arms, and longing wait
The signal to ascend, sit lingering here,
Heaven's fugitives, and for their dwelling-place
Accept this dark opprobrious den of shame,
The prison of his tyranny who reigns
By our delay? No, let us rather choose,   60
Armed with Hell flames and fury, all at once
O'er Heaven's high towers to force resistless way,
Turning our tortures into horrid arms
Against the Torturer; when to meet the noise
Of his almighty engine° he shall hear
Infernal thunder, and for lightning see
Black fire and horror shot with equal rage
Among his angels, and his throne itself
Mixed° with Tartarean° sulphur and strange fire,
His own invented torments. But perhaps   70
The way seems difficult and steep to scale
With upright wing against a higher foe.°
Let such bethink them, if the sleepy drench°
Of that forgetful lake° benumb not still,
That in our proper motion we ascend
Up to our native seat; descent and fall
To us is adverse.° Who but felt of late,
When the fierce foe hung on our broken rear
Insulting, and pursued us through the deep,
With what compulsion and laborious flight   80
We sunk thus low? The ascent is easy then;
The event° is feared! Should we again provoke
Our stronger, some worse way his wrath may find
To our destruction, if there be in Hell
Fear to be worse destroyed: what can be worse
Than to dwell here, driven out from bliss, con-
    demned

In this abhorrèd deep to utter woe;
Where pain of unextinguishable fire
Must exercise° us without hope of end
The vassals of his anger, when the scourge   90
Inexorably, and the torturing hour,
Calls us to penance? More destroyed than thus,
We should be quite abolished and expire.
What fear we then? what° doubt we to incense
His utmost ire? which to the highth enraged,
Will either quite consume us, and reduce
To nothing this essential,° happier far
Than miserable to have eternal being;
Or if our substance be indeed divine,
And cannot cease to be, we are at worst   100
On this side nothing; and by proof we feel
Our power sufficient to disturb his Heaven,
And with perpetual inroads to alarm,
Though inaccessible, his fatal° throne;
Which if not victory is yet revenge."

He ended frowning, and his look denounced°
Desperate revenge, and battle dangerous
To less than gods. On the other side up rose
Belial, in act more graceful and humane;°
A fairer person lost not Heaven; he seemed   110
For dignity composed and high exploit:
But all was false and hollow, though his tongue
Dropped manna, and could make the worse appear
The better reason, to perplex and dash°
Maturest counsels: for his thoughts were low;
To vice industrious, but to nobler deeds
Timorous and slothful: yet he pleased the ear,
And with persuasive accent thus began:

"I should be much for open war, O Peers,
As not behind in hate, if what was urged   120
Main reason to persuade immediate war
Did not dissuade me most, and seem to cast
Ominous conjecture on the whole success:
When he who most excels in fact° of arms,
In what he counsels and in what excels
Mistrustful, grounds his courage on despair
And utter dissolution, as the scope
Of all his aim, after some dire revenge.
First, what revenge? The towers of Heaven are
    filled
With armèd watch, that render all access   130
Impregnable; oft on the bordering deep
Encamp their legions, or with obscure wing
Scout far and wide into the realm of Night,
Scorning surprise. Or could we break our way
By force, and at our heels all Hell should rise
With blackest insurrection, to confound
Heaven's purest light, yet our great Enemy
All incorruptible would on his throne
Sit unpolluted, and the ethereal mold°

51. **sentence:** vote.   52. **unexpert:** inexperienced.   65. **engine:**
thunderbolt.   69. **Mixed:** confounded.   **Tartarean:** Tartarus
was one of the classical names for hell.   70–72: **But . . . foe:**
Here, and in ll. 82–85, Moloch anticipates objections.   73. **sleepy
drench:** drink causing sleep.   74. **forgetful lake:** causing forgetfulness, like the mythological river Lethe. Cf. I. 266, II. 583.
77. **adverse:** contrary to our nature.   82. **event:** outcome.

89. **exercise:** torment.   94. **what:** why.   97. **essential:** essence.
104. **fatal:** upheld by fate.   106. **denounced:** threatened.
109. **humane:** urbane.   114. **dash:** frustrate.   124. **fact:** feat.
139. **mold:** substance.

Incapable of stain would soon expel   140
Her mischief, and purge off the baser fire,
Victorious. Thus repulsed, our final hope
Is flat despair; we must exasperate
The almighty Victor to spend all his rage,
And that must end us, that must be our cure,
To be no more. Sad cure! for who would lose,
Though full of pain, this intellectual being,
Those thoughts that wander through eternity,
To perish rather, swallowed up and lost
In the wide womb of uncreated Night,   150
Devoid of sense and motion? And who knows,
Let° this be good, whether our angry Foe
Can give it, or will ever? How he can
Is doubtful; that he never will is sure.
Will he, so wise, let loose at once his ire,
Belike° through impotence, or unaware,
To give his enemies their wish, and end
Them in his anger, whom his anger saves
To punish endless? 'Wherefore cease we then?'
Say they who counsel war; 'we are decreed,   160
Reserved, and destined to eternal woe;
Whatever doing, what can we suffer more,
What can we suffer worse?' Is this then worst,
Thus sitting, thus consulting, thus in arms?
What when we fled amain,° pursued and strook
With Heaven's afflicting thunder, and besought
The deep to shelter us? this Hell then seemed
A refuge from those wounds. Or when we lay
Chained on the burning lake? that sure was worse.
What if the breath that kindled those grim fires,
Awaked, should blow them into sevenfold rage
And plunge us in the flames? or from above   172
Should intermitted vengeance arm again
His red right hand to plague us? What if all
Her stores were opened, and this firmament
Of Hell should spout her cataracts of fire,
Impendent horrors, threatening hideous fall
One day upon our heads; while we perhaps
Designing or exhorting glorious war,
Caught in a fiery tempest shall be hurled   180
Each on his rock transfixed, the sport and prey
Of racking° whirlwinds, or forever sunk
Under yon boiling ocean, wrapped in chains,
There to converse° with everlasting groans,
Unrespited, unpitied, unreprieved,
Ages of hopeless end? this would be worse.
War therefore, open or concealed, alike
My voice dissuades; for what can° force or guile
With him, or who deceive his mind, whose eye
Views all things at one view? He from Heaven's
        highth   190
All these our motions° vain, sees and derides;
Not more almighty to resist our might

Than wise to frustrate all our plots and wiles.
Shall we then live thus vile, the race of Heaven
Thus trampled, thus expelled to suffer here
Chains and these torments? Better these than
        worse,
By my advice; since fate inevitable
Subdues us, and omnipotent decree,
The Victor's will. To suffer, as to do,
Our strength is equal, nor the law unjust   200
That so ordains: this was at first resolved,
If we were wise, against so great a foe
Contending, and so doubtful what might fall.°
I laugh when those who at the spear are bold
And venturous, if that fail them, shrink and fear
What yet they know must follow, to endure
Exile, or ignominy,° or bonds, or pain,
The sentence of their Conqueror. This is now
Our doom; which if we can sustain and bear,
Our supreme Foe in time may much remit   210
His anger, and perhaps, thus far removed,
Not mind us not offending, satisfied
With what is punished; whence these raging fires
Will slacken, if his breath stir not their flames.
Our purer essence then will overcome
Their noxious vapor, or inured not feel,
Or changed at length, and to the place conformed
In temper and in nature, will receive
Familiar the fierce heat, and void of pain;
This horror will grow mild, this darkness light,
Besides what hope the never-ending flight   221
Of future days may bring, what chance, what
        change
Worth waiting, since our present lot appears
For happy° though but ill, for ill not worst,
If we procure not to ourselves more woe."
        Thus Belial with words clothed in reason's garb,
Counseled ignoble ease, and peaceful sloth,
Not peace; and after him thus Mammon spake:
        "Either to disenthrone the King of Heaven
We war, if war be best, or to regain   230
Our own right lost. Him to unthrone we then
May hope, when everlasting Fate shall yield
To fickle Chance, and Chaos judge the strife:
The former,° vain to hope, argues as vain
The latter;° for what place can be for us
Within Heaven's bound, unless Heaven's Lord su-
        preme
We overpower? Suppose he should relent
And publish grace to all, on promise made
Of new subjection; with what eyes could we
Stand in his presence humble, and receive   240
Strict laws imposed, to celebrate his throne
With warbled hymns, and to his Godhead sing
Forced halleluiahs; while he lordly sits

---

152. Let: granted.   156. Belike: doubtless (ironical).
165. amain: with all speed.   182. racking: driving, torturing.
184. converse: live.   188. can: can achieve.   191. motions:
schemes

203. fall: befall.   207. ignominy: see I. 115n.   224. For happy:
in comparison with happiness.   234. The former: to dethrone
God.   235. The latter: to regain our rights.

Our envied Sovran, and his altar breathes
Ambrosial odors and ambrosial flowers,
Our servile offerings? This must be our task
In Heaven, this our delight; how wearisome
Eternity so spent in worship paid
To whom we hate. Let° us not then pursue,
By force impossible, by leave obtained   250
Unácceptable, though in Heaven, our state
Of splendid vassalage, but rather seek
Our own good from ourselves, and from our own
Live to ourselves, though in this vast recess,
Free, and to none accountable, preferring
Hard liberty before the easy yoke
Of servile pomp. Our greatness will appear
Then most conspicuous, when great things of
          small,
Useful of hurtful, prosperous of adverse
We can create, and in what place soe'er   260
Thrive under evil, and work ease out of pain
Through labor and endurance. This deep world
Of darkness do we dread? How oft amidst
Thick clouds and dark doth Heaven's all-ruling
          Sire
Choose to reside, his glory unobscured,
And with the majesty of darkness round
Covers his throne, from whence deep thunders roar,
Mustering their rage, and Heaven resembles Hell!
As he our darkness, cannot we his light
Imitate when we please? This desert soil   270
Wants° not her hidden luster, gems and gold;
Nor want we skill or art, from whence to raise
Magnificence; and what can Heaven show more?
Our torments also may in length of time
Become our elements,° these piercing fires
As soft as now severe, our temper changed
Into their temper; which must needs remove
The sensible° of pain. All things invite
To peaceful counsels, and the settled state
Of order, how in safety best we may   280
Compose our present evils, with regard
Of what we are and where, dismissing quite
All thoughts of war. Ye have what I advise."
     He scarce had finished, when such murmur filled
The assembly, as when hollow rocks retain
The sound of blustering winds, which all night
          long
Had roused the sea, now with hoarse cadence lull
Seafaring men o'erwatched,° whose bark by chance
Or pinnace anchors in a craggy bay
After the tempest. Such applause was heard   290
As Mammon ended, and his sentence pleased,

Advising peace; for such another field°
They dreaded worse than Hell: so much the fear
Of thunder and the sword of Michaël°
Wrought still within them; and no less desire
To found this nether empire, which might rise
By policy, and long process of time,
In emulation opposite to Heaven.
Which when Beëlzebub perceived, than whom,
Satan except, none higher sat, with grave   300
Aspect he rose, and in his rising seemed
A pillar of state; deep on his front° engraven
Deliberation sat and public care;
And princely counsel in his face yet shone,
Majestic though in ruin: sage he stood,
With Atlantean° shoulders fit to bear
The weight of mightiest monarchies; his look
Drew audience and attention still as night
Or summer's noontide air, while thus he spake:
     "Thrones and imperial Powers, offspring of
          Heaven,   310
Ethereal Virtues! or these titles now
Must we renounce, and changing style° be called
Princes of Hell? for so the popular vote
Inclines, here to continue, and build up here
A growing empire; doubtless! while we dream,
And know not that the King of Heaven hath
          doomed
This place our dungeon, not our safe retreat
Beyond his potent arm, to live exempt
From Heaven's high jurisdiction, in new league
Banded against his throne, but to remain   320
In strictest bondage, though thus far removed,
Under the inevitable curb, reserved
His captive multitude. For he, be sure,
In highth or depth, still first and last will reign
Sole king, and of his kingdom lose no part
By our revolt, but over Hell extend
His empire, and with iron scepter rule
Us here, as with his golden those in Heaven.
What° sit we then projecting peace and war?
War hath determined° us, and foiled with loss
Irreparable; terms of peace yet none   331
Vouchsafed or sought; for what peace will be given
To us enslaved, but custody severe,
And stripes, and arbitrary punishment
Inflicted? and what peace can we return,
But to° our power hostility and hate,
Untamed reluctance,° and revenge though slow,
Yet ever plotting how the Conqueror least
May reap his conquest, and may least rejoice
In doing what we most in suffering feel?   340
Nor will occasion want,° nor shall we need

249–52. Let . . . vassalage: Let us not seek to regain our state of
splendid subservience in Heaven; we cannot regain it by force,
and we could not bear to regain it by God's permission.
271. Wants: lacks. **275. elements:** the four elements, earth,
water, air, fire, with which devils were traditionally associated.
278. sensible: sense, sensation. **288. o'erwatched:** weary with
watching.

292. field: battle. **294. Michael:** the leader of God's angelic
army. **302. front:** forehead. **306. Atlantean:** of Atlas, the
Titan who held up the sky. **312. style:** title. **329. What:**
why. **330. determined:** made an end of. **336. to:** to the
utmost of. **337. reluctance:** resistance. **341. want:** be wanting.

With dangerous expedition to invade
Heaven, whose high walls fear no assault or siege,
Or ambush from the deep. What if we find
Some easier enterprise? There is a place
(If ancient and prophetic fame° in Heaven
Err not), another world, the happy seat
Of some new race called man, about this time
To be created like to us, though less
In power and excellence, but favored more   350
Of him who rules above; so was his will
Pronounced among the gods, and by an oath,
That shook Heaven's whole circumference, con-
    firmed.
Thither let us bend all our thoughts, to learn
What creatures there inhabit, of what mold
Or substance, how endued,° and what their power,
And where their weakness, how attempted° best,
By force or subtlety. Though Heaven be shut,
And Heaven's high Arbitrator sit secure
In his own strength, this place may lie exposed,
The utmost border of his kingdom, left   361
To their defense who hold it; here perhaps
Some advantageous act may be achieved
By sudden onset, either with Hell fire
To waste his whole creation, or possess
All as our own, and drive, as we were driven,
The puny habitants; or if not drive,
Seduce them to our party, that their God
May prove their foe, and with repenting hand
Abolish his own works. This would surpass   370
Common revenge, and interrupt his joy
In our confusion, and our joy upraise
In his disturbance; when his darling sons,
Hurled headlong to partake with us, shall curse
Their frail original,° and faded bliss,
Faded so soon. Advise° if this be worth
Attempting, or to sit in darkness here
Hatching vain empires." Thus Beëlzebub
Pleaded his devilish counsel, first devised
By Satan, and in part proposed; for whence,   380
But from the author of all ill, could spring
So deep a malice, to confound the race
Of mankind in one root, and Earth with Hell
To mingle and involve, done all to spite
The great Creator? But their spite still serves
His glory to augment. The bold design
Pleased highly those infernal States,° and joy
Sparkled in all their eyes; with full assent
They vote: whereat his speech he thus renews:
    "Well have ye judged, well ended long debate,
Synod of gods, and like to what ye are,   391
Great things resolved; which from the lowest deep
Will once more lift us up, in spite of Fate,
Nearer our ancient seat; perhaps in view

Of those bright confines, whence with neighboring
    arms
And opportune excursion we may chance
Re-enter Heaven; or else in some mild zone
Dwell not unvisited of Heaven's fair light
Secure, and at the brightening orient beam
Purge off this gloom; the soft delicious air,   400
To heal the scar of these corrosive fires,
Shall breathe her balm. But first whom shall we
    send
In search of this new world, whom shall we find
Sufficient? who shall tempt° with wandering feet
The dark unbottomed infinite abyss°
And through the palpable obscure° find out
His uncouth° way, or spread his aery flight
Upborne with indefatigable wings
Over the vast abrupt,° ere he arrive
The happy isle;° what strength, what art can then
Suffice, or what evasion bear him safe   411
Through the strict senteries° and stations thick
Of angels watching round? Here he had need
All circumspection, and we now no less
Choice in our suffrage;° for on whom we send,
The weight of all and our last hope relies."
    This said, he sat; and expectation held
His look suspense,° awaiting who appeared
To second, or oppose, or undertake
The perilous attempt: but all sat mute,   420
Pondering the danger with deep thoughts; and
    each
In other's countenance read his own dismay
Astonished.° None among the choice and prime
Of those Heaven-warring champions could be
    found
So hardy as to proffer or accept
Alone the dreadful voyage; till at last
Satan, whom now transcendent glory raised
Above his fellows, with monarchal pride
Conscious of highest worth, unmoved thus spake:
    "O Progeny of Heaven, empyreal° Thrones,
With reason hath deep silence and demur°   431
Seized us, though undismayed. Long is the way
And hard, that out of Hell leads up to light;°
Our prison strong, this huge convex° of fire,
Outrageous to devour, immures us round
Ninefold, and gates of burning adamant
Barred over us prohibit all egress.
These passed, if any pass, the void profound
Of unessential° Night receives him next
Wide gaping, and with utter loss of being   440

404. tempt: attempt.   405. abyss: Chaos.   406. palpable obscure: darkness that can be felt (Exod. 10:21).   407. uncouth:
unknown.   409. abrupt: the space between Hell and Heaven,
Chaos.   410. isle: the created universe, in the "ocean" of
Chaos.   412. senteries: sentries.   415. Choice . . . suffrage:
care in our voting.   418. suspense: in suspense.   423. Astonished: dismayed.   430. empyreal: heavenly.   431. demur:
hesitation.   432–33. Long . . . light: See III. 19–21n.   434. convex: vault.   439. unessential: without substance.

346. fame: rumor.   356. endued: endowed (in mind).   357. attempted: attacked.   375. original: progenitor, i.e., Adam.
376. Advise: consider.   387. States: peers.

Threatens him, plunged in that abortive° gulf.
If thence he scape into whatever world,
Or unknown region, what remains° him less
Than unknown dangers and as hard escape?
But I should ill become this throne, O Peers,
And this imperial sovranty, adorned
With splendor, armed with power, if aught pro-
    posed
And judged of public moment, in the shape
Of difficulty or danger could deter
Me from attempting. Wherefore do I assume   450
These royalties, and not refuse to reign,
Refusing° to accept as great a share
Of hazard as of honor, due alike
To him who reigns, and so much to him due
Of hazard more, as he above the rest
High honored sits? Go therefore, mighty Powers,
Terror of Heaven, though fallen; intend° at home,
While here shall be our home, what best may ease
The present misery, and render Hell
More tolerable, if there be cure or charm   460
To respite or deceive,° or slack the pain
Of this ill mansion; intermit no watch
Against a wakeful foe, while I abroad
Through all the coasts of dark destruction seek
Deliverance for us all: this enterprise
None shall partake with me." Thus saying rose
The Monarch, and prevented° all reply;
Prudent,° lest from his resolution raised°
Others among the chief might offer now
(Certain to be refused) what erst they feared;   470
And so refused might in opinion stand
His rivals, winning cheap the high repute
Which he through hazard huge must earn. But
    they
Dreaded not more the adventure than his voice
Forbidding, and at once with him they rose;
Their rising all at once was as the sound
Of thunder heard remote. Towards him they bend
With awful reverence prone; and as a god
Extol him equal to the Highest in Heaven.
Nor failed they to express how much they praised
That for the general safety he despised   481
His own: for° neither do the spirits damned
Lose all their virtue; lest bad men should boast
Their specious deeds on Earth, which glory excites,
Or close° ambition varnished o'er with zeal.
    Thus they their doubtful consultations dark
Ended rejoicing in their matchless Chief:
As when from mountain tops the dusky clouds
Ascending, while the north wind sleeps, o'erspread

Heaven's cheerful face, the louring element°   490
Scowls o'er the darkened lantskip° snow or shower;
If chance° the radiant sun with farewell sweet
Extend his evening beam, the fields revive,
The birds their notes renew, and bleating herds
Attest their joy, that hill and valley rings.
O shame to men! Devil with devil damned
Firm concord holds, men only disagree
Of creatures rational, though under hope
Of heavenly grace; and God proclaiming peace,
Yet live in hatred, enmity, and strife   500
Among themselves, and levy cruel wars,
Wasting the Earth, each other to destroy:
As if (which might induce us to accord)
Man had not hellish foes enow° besides,
That day and night for his destruction wait.
    The Stygian council thus dissolved; and forth
In order came the grand infernal Peers;
Midst came their mighty Paramount,° and seemed
Alone the antagonist of Heaven, nor less
Than Hell's dread Emperor, with pomp supreme,
And god-like imitated state; him round   511
A globe° of fiery Seraphim enclosed
With bright emblazonry and horrent° arms.
Then of their session ended they bid cry
With trumpet's regal sound the great result.
Toward the four winds four speedy Cherubim
Put to their mouths the sounding alchemy°
By herald's voice explained; the hollow abyss
Heard far and wide, and all the host of Hell
With deafening shout returned them loud acclaim.
Thence more at ease their minds and somewhat
    raised   521
By false presumptuous hope, the rangèd powers°
Disband, and wandering each his several way
Pursues, as inclination or sad choice
Leads him perplexed, where he may likeliest find
Truce to his restless thoughts, and entertain
The irksome hours, till his great Chief return.
Part° on the plain, or in the air sublime°
Upon the wing, or in swift race contend,
As at the Olympian° games or Pythian° fields;
Part curb their fiery steeds, or shun the goal   531
With rapid wheels,° or fronted° brígades form:
As when to warn proud cities war appears°
Waged in the troubled sky, and armies rush
To battle in, the clouds; before each van°

441. abortive: monstrous, or destructive.   443. remains: awaits.
452. Refusing: if I refuse.   457. intend: consider.   461. deceive: beguile.   467. prevented: forestalled.   468. Prudent:
shrewd.   raised: made bolder.   482–85. for . . . zeal: Let not
bad men boast of seemingly noble deeds inspired by love of glory
and ambition, since even damned angels retain that degree of
virtue.   485. close: secret.

490. element: sky.   491. lantskip: landscape.   492. If chance:
if it chances that.   504. enow: enough.   508. Paramount: chief.
512. globe: solid troop.   513. horrent: bristling.   517. sounding alchemy: trumpets of material resembling gold.   522. ranged
powers: assembled armies.   528–38. Part . . . burns: Milton
here uses, in his own way, the epic convention of athletic games.
528. sublime: aloft.   530. Olympian: the Olympic Games held
at Olympia in southern Greece.   Pythian: the similar games
held at Delphi.   531–32. shun . . . wheels: chariots turning
close around a mark.   532. fronted: in line.   533 f. Such visions
have been reported, throughout history, in times of crisis or war;
or the reference may be to phenomena like the Northern Lights.
535. van: vanguard.

Prick° forth the aery knights, and couch their
    spears,
Till thickest legions close; with feats of arms
From either end of Heaven the welkin burns.
Others with vast Typhoean° rage more fell
Rend up both rocks and hills, and ride the air   540
In whirlwind; Hell scarce holds the wild uproar;
As° when Alcides, from Oechalia crowned
With conquest, felt the envenomed robe, and tore
Through pain up by the roots Thessalian pines,
And Lichas from the top of Oeta threw
Into the Euboic sea. Others more mild,
Retreated in a silent valley, sing
With notes angelical to many a harp
Their own heroic deeds and hapless fall
By doom of battle; and complain that Fate   550
Free virtue should enthrall to force or chance.
Their song was partial,° but the harmony
(What could it less when spirits immortal sing?)
Suspended Hell, and took° with ravishment
The thronging audience. In discourse more sweet
(For eloquence the soul, song charms the sense)
Others apart sat on a hill retired,
In thoughts more elevate, and reasoned high
Of providence, foreknowledge, will, and fate,
Fixed fate, free will, foreknowledge absolute,   560
And found no end, in wandering mazes lost.
Of good and evil much they argued then,
Of happiness and final misery,
Passion and apathy,° and glory and shame,
Vain wisdom all, and false philosophy;
Yet with a pleasing sorcery could charm
Pain for a while or anguish, and excite
Fallacious hope, or arm the obdured° breast
With stubborn patience as with triple steel.
Another part, in squadrons and gross° bands,   570
On bold adventure to discover wide
That dismal world, if any clime perhaps
Might yield them easier habitation, bend
Four ways their flying march, along the banks
Of four infernal rivers° that disgorge
Into the burning lake their baleful streams:
Abhorrèd Styx, the flood of deadly hate;
Sad Acheron of sorrow, black and deep;
Cocytus, named of lamentation loud   579
Heard on the rueful stream; fierce Phlegethon,
Whose waves of torrent fire inflame with rage.

Far off from these a slow and silent stream,
Lethe, the river of oblivion, rolls
Her watery labyrinth, whereof who drinks
Forthwith his former state and being forgets,
Forgets both joy and grief, pleasure and pain.
Beyond this flood a frozen continent°
Lies dark and wild, beat with perpetual storms
Of whirlwind and dire hail, which on firm land
Thaws not, but gathers heap,° and ruin seems   590
Of ancient pile; all else deep snow and ice,
A gulf profound as that Serbonian bog°
Betwixt Damiata and Mount Casius old,
Where armies whole have sunk; the parching air
Burns frore,° and cold performs the effect of fire.
Thither by harpy-footed Furies° haled,
At certain revolutions° all the damned
Are brought; and feel by turns the bitter change
Of fierce extremes, extremes by change more fierce,
From beds of raging fire to starve° in ice   600
Their soft ethereal warmth, and there to pine
Immovable, infixed, and frozen round,
Periods of time; thence hurried back to fire.
They ferry over this Lethean sound
Both to and fro, their sorrow to augment,
And wish and struggle, as they pass, to reach
The tempting stream, with one small drop to lose
In sweet forgetfulness all pain and woe,
All in one moment, and so near the brink;
But Fate withstands, and to oppose the attempt
Medusa° with Gorgonian terror guards   611
The ford, and of itself the water flies
All taste of living wight, as once it fled
The lip of Tantalus.° Thus roving on
In confused march forlorn, the adventurous bands,
With shuddering horror pale, and eyes aghast,
Viewed first their lamentable lot, and found
No rest. Through many a dark and dreary vale
They passed, and many a region dolorous,
O'er many a frozen, many a fiery Alp,°   620
Rocks, caves, lakes, fens, bogs, dens, and shades of
    death,
A universe of death, which God by curse
Created evil, for evil only good,
Where all life dies, death lives, and Nature breeds,
Perverse, all monstrous, all prodigious things,
Abominable, inutterable, and worse
Than fables yet have feigned, or fear conceived,
Gorgons and Hydras,° and Chimeras° dire.

---

536. Prick: spur, ride.   **539. Typhoean:** See note on I. 197 f.
542–46. As . . . sea: Nessus, a centaur, dying at the hand of
Hercules (Alcides), told Hercules' wife, Deianira, that his blood
would preserve her husband's love. When Hercules, returning
from victory in Oechalia with the captive Iole, prepared to offer
sacrifice on Mount Oeta in Thessaly, he sent home for a fresh
robe. The robe, which Deianira steeped in Nessus' blood, tortured Hercules into frenzy, and he threw Lichas, who had
brought it, into the sea.   **552. partial:** prejudiced.   **554. took:**
captured, charmed.   **564. apathy:** a Stoic term for freedom
from passion.   **568 obdured:** hardened.   **570. gross:** compact.
575 f. The four underworld rivers of classical myth.

587 f. In medieval belief Hell contained a frozen as well as
a fiery region.   **590. gathers heap:** gathers in a heap.   **592.
Serbonian bog:** Lake Serbonis on the east side of the Nile
delta.   **595. frore:** frozen.   **596. harpy-footed Furies:** The
Furies, the avenging spirits of Greek myth, are here given the
claws of the foul bird-women called Harpies.   **597. revolutions:** i.e., of time.   **600. starve:** freeze.   **611. Medusa:**
one of the three Gorgons, whose face turned beholders to stone.
614. Tantalus: was condemned by Zeus to stand in water which
eluded his attempts to drink.   **620. Alp:** any high mountain.
628. Hydras: monsters that sprouted new heads for every
one destroyed. **Chimeras:** The Chimera was a fire-breathing

Meanwhile the Adversary of God and man,   629
Satan, with thoughts inflamed of highest design,
Puts on swift wings, and toward the gates of Hell
Explores his solitary flight; sometimes
He scours the right-hand coast, sometimes the left;
Now shaves with level wing the deep, then soars
Up to the fiery concave° towering high:
As when far off at sea a fleet descried
Hangs in the clouds, by equinoctial winds
Close sailing from Bengala,° or the isles
Of Ternate and Tidore,° whence merchants bring
Their spicy drugs: they on the trading flood,   640
Through the wide Ethiopian° to the Cape,°
Ply stemming nightly toward the pole.° So seemed
Far off the flying Fiend. At last appear
Hell bounds high reaching to the horrid roof,
And thrice threefold the gates; three folds were
     brass,
Three iron, three of adamantine rock,
Impenetrable, impaled° with circling fire,
Yet unconsumed. Before the gates there sat°
On either side a formidable shape;
The one seemed woman to the waist, and fair,
But ended foul in many a scaly fold   651
Voluminous and vast, a serpent armed
With mortal sting. About her middle round
A cry° of Hell-hounds never ceasing barked
With wide Cerberean mouths full loud, and rung
A hideous peal; yet, when they list,° would creep,
If aught disturbed their noise, into her womb,
And kennel there, yet there still barked and
     howled,
Within unseen. Far less abhorred than these
Vexed Scylla, bathing in the sea that parts   660
Calabria° from the hoarse Trinacrian° shore;
Nor uglier follow the night-hag,° when called
In secret, riding through the air she comes,
Lured with the smell of infant blood, to dance
With Lapland° witches, while the laboring° moon
Eclipses at their charms. The other shape —
If shape it might be called that shape had none
Distinguishable in member, joint, or limb,
Or substance might be called that shadow seemed,
For each seemed either — black it stood as Night,

Fierce as ten Furies, terrible as Hell,   671
And shook a dreadful dart; what seemed his head
The likeness of a kingly crown had on.
Satan was now at hand, and from his seat
The monster moving onward came as fast,
With horrid strides; Hell trembled as he strode.
The undaunted Fiend what this might be ad-
     mired,°
Admired, not feared; God and his Son except,
Created thing nought valued he nor shunned;
And with disdainful look thus first began: 680
"Whence and what art thou, execrable Shape,
That dar'st, though grim and terrible, advance
Thy miscreated front athwart my way
To yonder gates? Through them I mean to pass,
That be assured, without leave asked of thee.
Retire, or taste thy folly, and learn by proof,
Hell-born, not to contend with spirits of Heaven."
     To whom the goblin full of wrath replied:
"Art thou that traitor angel, art thou he,
Who first broke peace in Heaven and faith, till
     then   690
Unbroken, and in proud rebellious arms
Drew after him the third part of Heaven's sons
Conjured° against the Highest, for which both
     thou
And they, outcast from God, are here condemned
To waste eternal days in woe and pain?
And reckon'st thou thyself with spirits of Heaven,
Hell-doomed, and breath'st defiance here and scorn
Where I reign king, and to enrage thee more,
Thy king and lord? Back to thy punishment,
False fugitive, and to thy speed add wings,   700
Lest with a whip of scorpions I pursue
Thy lingering, or with one stroke of this dart
Strange horror seize thee, and pangs unfelt before."
     So spake the grisly terror, and in shape,
So speaking and so threatening, grew tenfold
More dreadful and deform.° On the other side,
Incensed° with indignation Satan stood
Unterrified, and like a comet burned,
That fires the length of Ophiuchus° huge
In the arctic sky, and from his horrid hair   710
Shakes pestilence and war. Each at the head
Leveled his deadly aim; their fatal hands
No second stroke intend; and such a frown
Each cast at the other, as when two black clouds,
With Heaven's artillery fraught, come rattling on
Over the Caspian, then stand front to front
Hovering a space, till winds the signal blow
To join their dark encounter in mid-air:
So frowned the mighty combatants, that Hell
Grew darker at their frown, so matched they
     stood;   720

monster killed by Bellerophon. The names are symbols of the
physical and mental hell of the fallen angels.   **635. concave:**
the vault of Hell.   **638. Bengala:** Bengal.   **639. Ternate,
Tidore:** islands of the Moluccas, south of the Philippines.
641. Ethiopian: the Indian Ocean.   **Cape:** Cape of Good Hope.
642. pole: the South Pole.   **647. impaled:** surrounded.
648 f. The allegory of Sin and Death is based on Jas. 1:15: "Then
when lust hath conceived, it bringeth forth sin: and sin, when it
is finished, bringeth forth death." Sin is modeled on Scylla
(l. 660; cf. l. 1020n., below) and similar monsters; Spenser's
Error (*Faerie Queene*, I. i) is one of the family.   **654. cry:** pack.
656. list: pleased.   **661. Calabria:** the "toe" of Italy.   **Trina-
crian:** Sicilian (see l. 1020n., below).   **662. night-hag:** Hecate,
the queen of witches (as in *Macbeth*).   **665. Lapland:** the northern part of Europe, in popular belief a notorious abode of
witches.   **laboring:** eclipsing.

677. admired: wondered.   **693. Conjured:** united by an oath.
706. deform: deformed.   **707. Incensed:** kindled.   **709. Ophiu-
chus:** a large constellation, "the Serpent-Bearer."

For never but once more was either like
To meet so great a foe.° And now great deeds
Had been achieved, whereof all Hell had rung,
Had not the snaky sorceress that sat
Fast by Hell gate, and kept the fatal key,
Risen, and with hideous outcry rushed between.
    "O father, what intends thy hand," she cried,
"Against thy only son?° What fury, O son,
Possesses thee to bend that mortal dart
Against thy father's head? and know'st for whom?
For him who sits above and laughs the while   731
At thee ordained his drudge, to execute
Whate'er his wrath, which he calls justice, bids,
His wrath which one day will destroy ye both."
    She spake, and at her words the hellish pest
Forbore; then these to her Satan returned:
    "So strange thy outcry, and thy words so strange
Thou interposest, that my sudden hand
Prevented spares to tell thee yet by deeds
What it intends; till first I know of thee,   740
What thing thou art, thus double-formed, and why
In this infernal vale first met thou call'st
Me father, and that phantasm call'st my son.
I know thee not, nor ever saw till now
Sight more detestable than him and thee."
    To whom thus the portress of Hell gate replied:
"Hast thou forgot me then, and do I seem
Now in thine eye so foul? once deemed so fair
In Heaven, when at the assembly, and in sight
Of all the Seraphim with thee combined   750
In bold conspiracy against Heaven's King,
All on a sudden miserable pain
Surprised thee; dim thine eyes, and dizzy swum
In darkness, while thy head flames thick and fast
Threw forth, till on the left side opening wide,
Likest to thee in shape and countenance bright,
Then shining heavenly fair, a goddess armed
Out of thy head I sprung.° Amazement seized
All the host of Heaven; back they recoiled afraid
At first, and called me Sin, and for a sign   760
Portentous held me; but familiar grown,
I pleased, and with attractive graces won
The most averse, thee chiefly, who full oft
Thyself in me thy perfect image viewing
Becam'st enamored; and such joy thou took'st
With me in secret, that my womb conceived
A growing burden. Meanwhile war arose,
And fields were fought in Heaven; wherein re-
    mained
(For what could else?) to our almighty Foe
Clear victory, to our part loss and rout   770
Through all the empyrean:° down they fell
Driven headlong from the pitch° of Heaven, down

Into this deep, and in the general fall
I also; at which time this powerful key
Into my hand was given, with charge to keep
These gates for ever shut, which none can pass
Without my opening. Pensive here I sat
Alone, but long I sat not, till my womb,
Pregnant by thee, and now excessive grown,
Prodigious motion felt and rueful throes.   780
At last this odious offspring whom thou seest,
Thine own begotten, breaking violent way
Tore through my entrails, that with fear and pain
Distorted, all my nether shape thus grew
Transformed; but he my inbred enemy
Forth issued, brandishing his fatal dart
Made to destroy. I fled, and cried out Death!
Hell trembled at the hideous name, and sighed
From all her caves, and back resounded Death!
I fled, but he pursued (though more, it seems, 790
Inflamed with lust than rage) and swifter far,
Me overtook, his mother, all dismayed,
And in embraces forcible and foul
Engendering with me, of that rape begot
These yelling monsters that with ceaseless cry
Surround me, as thou saw'st, hourly conceived
And hourly born, with sorrow infinite
To me; for when they list, into the womb
That bred them they return, and howl and gnaw
My bowels, their repast; then bursting forth   800
Afresh, with conscious terrors vex me round,
That rest or intermission none I find.
Before mine eyes in opposition sits
Grim Death my son and foe, who sets them on,
And me his parent would full soon devour
For want of other prey, but that he knows
His end with mine involved; and knows that I
Should prove a bitter morsel, and his bane,
Whenever that shall be; so Fate pronounced.
But thou, O father, I forewarn thee, shun   810
His deadly arrow; neither vainly hope
To be invulnerable in those bright arms,
Though tempered heavenly, for that mortal dint,
Save he who reigns above, none can resist."
    She finished, and the subtle Fiend his lore
Soon learned, now milder, and thus answered
    smooth:
"Dear daughter, since thou claim'st me for thy sire,
And my fair son here show'st me, the dear pledge
Of dalliance had with thee in Heaven, and joys
Then sweet, now sad to mention, through dire
    change   820
Befallen us unforeseen, unthought of, know
I come no enemy, but to set free
From out this dark and dismal house of pain
Both him and thee, and all the heavenly host
Of spirits that in our just pretenses° armed

722. so . . . foe: Christ.   728. thy . . . son: one of several details that make these characters profane counterparts of God
and the Son.   757–58. goddess . . . sprung: like Athene from
the head of Zeus.   771. empyrean: Heaven.   772. pitch: height.

825. pretenses: claims.

Fell with us from on high. From them I go
This uncouth errand sole, and one for all
Myself expose,° with lonely steps to tread
The unfounded° deep, and through the void im-
    mense
To search with wandering quest a place foretold
Should be, and, by concurring signs, ere now   831
Created vast and round, a place of bliss
In the purlieus of Heaven, and therein placed
A race of upstart creatures, to supply
Perhaps our vacant room, though more removed,
Lest Heaven surcharged with potent multitude
Might hap to move new broils.° Be this or aught
Than this more secret now designed, I haste
To know, and this once known, shall soon return,
And bring ye to the place where thou and Death
Shall dwell at ease, and up and down unseen   841
Wing silently the buxom° air, embalmed
With odors; there ye shall be fed and filled
Immeasurably; all things shall be your prey."
He ceased, for both seemed highly pleased, and
    Death
Grinned horrible a ghastly smile, to hear
His famine° should be filled, and blessed his maw
Destined to that good hour. No less rejoiced
His mother bad, and thus bespake her sire:
   " The key of this infernal pit, by due   850
And by command of Heaven's all-powerful King
I keep, by him forbidden to unlock
These adamantine gates; against all force
Death ready stands to interpose his dart,
Fearless to be o'ermatched by living might.
But what owe I to his commands above
Who hates me, and hath hither thrust me down
Into this gloom of Tartarus° profound,
To sit in hateful office here confined,
Inhabitant of Heaven and heavenly-born,   860
Here in perpetual agony and pain,
With terrors and with clamors compassed round
Of mine own brood, that on my bowels feed?
Thou art my father, thou my author, thou
My being gav'st me; whom should I obey
But thee, whom follow? Thou wilt bring me soon
To that new world of light and bliss, among
The gods who live at ease, where I shall reign
At thy right hand voluptuous,° as beseems
Thy daughter and thy darling, without end."   870
   Thus saying, from her side the fatal key,
Sad instrument of all our woe, she took;
And towards the gate rolling her bestial train,
Forthwith the huge portcullis high up drew,
Which but herself not all the Stygian powers

Could once have moved; then in the key-hole turns
The intricate wards, and every bolt and bar
Of massy iron or solid rock with ease
Unfastens. On a sudden open fly
With impetuous recoil and jarring sound   880
The infernal doors, and on their hinges grate
Harsh thunder, that the lowest bottom shook
Of Erebus.° She opened, but to shut
Excelled her power; the gates wide open stood,
That with extended wings a bannered host
Under spread ensigns marching might pass through
With horse and chariots ranked in loose array;
So wide they stood, and like a furnace mouth
Cast forth redounding° smoke and ruddy flame.
Before their eyes in sudden view appear°   890
The secrets of the hoary deep,° a dark
Illimitable ocean without bound,
Without dimension; where length, breadth, and
    highth,
And time and place are lost; where eldest Night
And Chaos, ancestors of Nature, hold
Eternal anarchy, amidst the noise
Of endless wars, and by confusion stand.
For Hot, Cold, Moist, and Dry, four champions
    fierce,°
Strive here for mastery, and to battle bring
Their embryon atoms; they around the flag   900
Of each his faction, in their several clans,
Light-armed or heavy, sharp, smooth, swift or
    slow,
Swarm populous, unnumbered as the sands
Of Barca or Cyrene's° torrid soil,
Levied° to side with warring winds, and poise
Their lighter wings.° To whom these most adhere,
He rules a moment; Chaos umpire sits,
And by decision more embroils the fray
By which he reigns; next him, high arbiter,
Chance governs all. Into this wild abyss,   910
The womb of Nature and perhaps her grave,
Of neither sea, nor shore, nor air, nor fire,
But all these in their pregnant causes mixed
Confusedly, and which thus must ever fight,
Unless the Almighty Maker them ordain
His dark materials to create more worlds,
Into this wild abyss the wary Fiend
Stood on the brink of Hell and looked a while,
Pondering his voyage; for no narrow frith
He had to cross. Nor was his ear less pealed°   920

827–28. one . . . expose: a contrast with the Son's self-sacrifice.
829. unfounded: bottomless.   837. broils: disturbances, tumults.
842. buxom: yielding.   847. famine: hunger.   858. Tartarus:
the classical Hades, or a hell below it.   868–69. where . . .
voluptuous: like the Son at the right hand of the Father, except
for the shock of the final word

883. Erebus: a classical name for hell.   889. redounding:
in rolling clouds.   891. deep: Chaos. The name is used both
for the chaotic sea of warring elements and for the name of
their personified ruler.   898 ff. The strife of the four elements had been familiar since early Greek antiquity,
especially through the opening lines of Ovid's *Metamorphoses.*
904. Barca, Cyrene: cities of Cyrenaica in northern Africa.
905. Levied: raised.   905–06. poise . . . wings: give weight
to the too light wings of the winds.   920. pealed: assailed
by noise.

With noises loud and ruinous (to compare
Great things with small) than when Bellona°
    storms,
With all her battering engines bent to raze
Some capital city; or less than if this frame
Of Heaven were falling, and these elements
In mutiny had from her axle torn
The steadfast Earth. At last his sail-broad vans°
He spreads for flight, and in the surging smoke
Uplifted spurns the ground; thence many a league
As in a cloudy chair ascending rides   930
Audacious, but that seat soon failing, meets
A vast vacuity: all unawares
Fluttering his pennons vain plumb down he drops
Ten thousand fadom° deep, and to this hour
Down had been falling, had not by ill chance
The strong rebuff of some tumultuous cloud
Instinct° with fire and niter hurried him
As many miles aloft. That fury stayed,
Quenched in a boggy Syrtis,° neither sea,
Nor good dry land, nigh foundered on he fares,
Treading the crude consistence, half on foot,   941
Half flying; behoves him now both oar and sail.
As when a gryphon° through the wilderness
With wingèd course o'er hill or moory dale,
Pursues the Arimaspian, who by stealth
Had from his wakeful custody purloined
The guarded gold: so eagerly the Fiend
O'er bog or steep, through strait, rough, dense, or
    rare,
With head, hands, wings, or feet pursues his way,
And swims or sinks, or wades, or creeps, or flies.
At length a universal hubbub wild   951
Of stunning sounds and voices all confused,
Borne through the hollow dark, assaults his ear
With loudest vehemence; thither he plies,
Undaunted to meet there whatever power
Or spirit of the nethermost abyss
Might in that noise reside, of whom to ask
Which way the nearest coast of darkness lies
Bordering on light; when straight behold the
    throne
Of Chaos, and his dark pavilion spread   960
Wide on the wasteful deep; with him enthroned
Sat sable-vested Night, eldest of things,
The consort of his reign; and by them stood
Orcus and Ades,° and the dreaded name
Of Demogorgon;° Rumor next and Chance,
And Tumult and Confusion all embroiled,
And Discord with a thousand various mouths.

922. **Bellona:** the Roman goddess of war.   927. **vans:** wings.
934. **fadom:** fathoms.   937. **Instinct:** filled, charged.   939. **Syr-tis:** two gulfs near Tripoli, notorious for quicksands.   943–47. **gryphon . . . gold:** Gryphons were fabulous Scythian mon-sters whose gold the Arimaspians tried to steal.   964. **Orcus, Ades:** Latin and Greek names for the underworld (Hades) or, as here, its god.   964–65. **dreaded . . . Demogorgon:** i.e., De-mogorgon of dreaded name, a mysterious (and postclassical) infernal deity.

To whom Satan turning boldly, thus: "Ye pow-
    ers
And spirits of this nethermost abyss,
Chaos and ancient Night, I come no spy,   970
With purpose to explore or to disturb
The secrets of your realm, but by constraint
Wandering this darksome desert, as my way
Lies through your spacious empire up to light,
Alone, and without guide, half lost, I seek
What readiest path leads where your gloomy
    bounds
Confine° with Heaven; or if some other place
From your dominion won, the Ethereal° King
Possesses lately, thither to arrive
I travel this profound.° Direct my course;   980
Directed, no mean recompense it brings
To your behoof, if I that region lost,
All usurpation thence expelled, reduce
To her original darkness and your sway
(Which is° my present journey), and once more
Erect the standard there of ancient Night;
Yours be the advantage all, mine the revenge."
    Thus Satan; and him thus the Anarch° old,
With faltering speech and visage incomposed,°
Answered: "I know thee, stranger, who thou art,
That mighty leading angel, who of late   991
Made head against Heaven's King, though over-
    thrown.
I saw and heard, for such a numerous host
Fled not in silence through the frighted deep
With ruin upon ruin,° rout on rout,
Confusion worse confounded; and Heaven gates
Poured out by millions her victorious bands
Pursuing. I upon my frontiers here
Keep residence; if all I can will serve
That little which is left so to defend,   1000
Encroached on still through our intestine broils
Weakening the scepter of old Night: first Hell
Your dungeon stretching far and wide beneath;
Now lately Heaven and Earth, another world°
Hung o'er my realm, linked in a golden chain
To that side Heaven from whence your legions
    fell.
If that way be your walk, you have not far;
So much the nearer danger; go and speed;
Havoc and spoil and ruin are my gain."
    He ceased; and Satan stayed not to reply,   1010
But glad that now his sea should find a shore,
With fresh alacrity and force renewed
Springs upward like a pyramid of fire
Into the wild expanse, and through the shock
Of fighting elements, on all sides round

977. **Confine:** border.   978. **Ethereal:** heavenly.   980. **pro-found:** deep, abyss.   985. **is:** is the motive of.   988. **Anarch:** Chaos (as personified in this passage).   989. **incomposed:** dis-turbed.   995. **ruin:** fall.   1004. **world:** the lately created uni-verse comprising "Heaven" (the sky) and the earth. Cf. ll. 1051–52.

Environed, wins his way; harder beset
And more endangered, than when Argo° passed
Through Bosporus betwixt the justling rocks,
Or when Ulysses on the larboard shunned
Charybdis,° and by the other whirlpool steered.
So he with difficulty and labor hard   1021
Moved on, with difficulty and labor he;
But he once passed, soon after when man fell,
Strange alteration! Sin and Death amain
Following his track, such was the will of Heaven,
Paved after him a broad and beaten way°
Over the dark abyss, whose boiling gulf
Tamely endured a bridge of wondrous length
From Hell continued reaching the utmost orb°
Of this frail world; by which the spirits perverse
With easy intercourse pass to and fro   1031
To tempt or punish mortals, except whom
God and good angels guard by special grace.
    But now at last the sacred influence
Of light appears, and from the walls of Heaven
Shoots far into the bosom of dim Night
A glimmering dawn; here Nature first begins
Her farthest verge,° and Chaos to retire
As from her° outmost works a broken foe,
With tumult less and with less hostile din,   1040
That° Satan with less toil, and now with ease
Wafts° on the calmer wave by dubious light,
And like a weather-beaten vessel holds°
Gladly the port, though shrouds and tackle torn;
Or in the emptier waste, resembling air,
Weighs his spread wings, at leisure to behold
Far off the empyreal° Heaven, extended wide
In circuit, undetermined° square or round,
With opal towers and battlements adorned
Of living sapphire,° once his native seat;   1050
And fast by hanging in a golden chain°
This pendent world,° in bigness as a star
Of smallest magnitude close by the moon.
Thither full fraught with mischievous revenge,
Accurst, and in a cursèd hour, he hies.

1017. Argo: the ship in which Jason and his fellow Argonauts
sailed through the Bosporus (the strait between the Sea of
Marmara and the Black Sea). 1020. Charybdis: the whirlpool
in the strait between Italy and Sicily; Scylla ("the other whirlpool"), opposite, was the other great danger for mariners. The
two were referred to as both whirlpools and rocks (and monsters).
1026 f.: The building of the bridge is described in X. 282–324.
1029. utmost orb: the outermost sphere or shell enclosing the
universe. 1037–38. here . . . verge: Here Nature, the created,
ordered universe, meets the boundary of Chaos. 1039. her: Nature's. 1041. That: so that. 1042. Wafts: sails. 1043. holds:
makes for. 1047. empyreal: See I. 117n., above. 1048. undetermined: it could not be known whether. 1050. sapphire:
See Rev. 21:19. 1051. hanging . . . chain: This image, originally in the *Iliad*, VIII. 18–27, had been used by countless writers
in various symbolic senses. 1052. world: not merely the earth
but the whole Ptolemaic universe with the earth at its center
and outer spheres in which the planets revolved.

from BOOK III

[The invocation to Light, one of the greatest things in
Milton and in all poetry, has its immediate motive in the
change of scene from Hell and Chaos to Heaven. Milton's
lifelong preoccupation with light and its symbolism inspires
reflections, poignant but firmly controlled, on the contrast
between his physical blindness and his inward vision; personal feeling is merged in a dramatic picture of " the blind
poet."]

Hail, holy Light, offspring of Heaven first-born,°
Or° of the Eternal coeternal beam
May I express° thee unblamed? since God is light,
And never but in unapproachèd light
Dwelt from eternity, dwelt then in thee,
Bright effluence of bright essence increate.°
Or hear'st° thou rather pure ethereal stream,
Whose fountain who shall tell?° Before° the sun,
Before the Heavens thou wert, and at the voice
Of God, as with a mantle didst invest   10
The rising world of waters dark and deep,
Won from the void and formless infinite.
Thee I revisit now with bolder wing,
Escaped the Stygian pool, though long detained
In that obscure sojourn, while in my flight,
Through utter and through middle darkness°
     borne,
With other notes than to the Orphean lyre°
I sung of Chaos and eternal Night,
Taught by the Heavenly Muse to venture down
The dark descent, and up to reascend,   20
Though hard and rare.° Thee I revisit safe,
And feel thy sovran vital lamp; but thou
Revisit'st not these eyes, that roll in vain
To find thy piercing ray, and find no dawn;
So thick a drop serene° hath quenched their orbs,
Or dim suffusion veiled. Yet not the more
Cease I to wander° where the Muses haunt
Clear spring, or shady grove, or sunny hill,
Smit with the love of sacred song; but chief
Thee, Sion,° and the flowery brooks beneath   30

Book III: 1. first-born: The first of three theories of light:
that it was the first thing God created.   **2–6. Or . . . increate:**
the second theory, that it was not created but was co-eternal
with God, an emanation of his own essence.   **3. express:** call.
unblamed: without incurring blame for touching a divine mystery.   **6. increate:** uncreated.   **7–8. Or . . . tell:** the third
theory, that light is a divine thing to which man can assign no
origin.   **7. hear'st:** art called (a classicism).   **8–12. Before . . .
infinite:** a recollection of Gen. 1:1–5.   **16. utter and . . . middle
darkness:** Hell and Chaos.   **17. Orphean lyre:** The name of the
mythical bard, Orpheus, who had gone down to Hades in quest
of his wife, was linked with the mystical "Orphic Hymns,"
such as that to Night. Milton distinguishes his own Christian
inspiration from the pagan.   **19–21. Taught . . . rare:** an echo
of the sibyl's words to Aeneas before he visited the underworld
(*Aeneid*, VI. 126–29). Cf. II. 432–33.   **25. drop serene:** a medical
term (*gutta serena*).   **26–27. Yet . . . wander:** yet I wander
none the less. The declaration of attachment to the pagan classical poets (ll. 26–29) echoes Virgil, *Georgics*, II. 475–78, 485–89.
29–32. Sion: As elsewhere in his prose and verse, Milton ranks the
Bible far above the classics. See, e.g., the *Reason of Church
Government*.

That wash thy hallowed feet, and warbling flow,
Nightly I visit;° nor sometimes forget
Those° other two equaled with me in fate,
So were I equaled with them in renown,
Blind Thamyris and blind Maeonides,
And Tiresias and Phineus, prophets old:
Then feed on thoughts, that voluntary move
Harmonious numbers,° as the wakeful bird°
Sings darkling,° and in shadiest covert hid
Tunes her nocturnal note. Thus with the year   40
Seasons return; but not to me returns
Day, or the sweet approach of even or morn,
Or sight of vernal bloom, or summer's rose,
Or flocks, or herds, or human face divine;
But cloud instead, and ever-during dark
Surrounds me, from the cheerful ways of men
Cut off, and for the book of knowledge fair
Presented with a universal blank°
Of Nature's works to me expunged and rased,
And wisdom at one entrance quite shut out.   50
So much the rather thou, celestial Light,
Shine inward, and the mind through all her powers
Irradiate, there plant eyes, all mist from thence
Purge and disperse, that I may see and tell
Of things invisible to mortal sight.

[Book III has two parts, a council in Heaven and Satan's continued journey. The council, a counterpart to the debate in Hell, provides the theological exposition of the poem. God declares that he has endowed man with reason, the power of choice, and that this freedom carries with it the power of sinful choice. God foresees but does not predetermine man's fall, and, since Milton is repudiating Calvinism, salvation shall be open to all believers; but first justice must be satisfied for man's sin. The Son, the agent of love, humility, and goodness (as Satan is of hate, pride, and evil), volunteers to make atonement for man. All Heaven rejoices in the ultimate victory of good and the prospect of an eternity of joy and love and trust.

In the rest of the book Satan, voyaging through Chaos, alights on the outer shell of the universe, at a point where he can look up to Heaven and down to earth and the paradisal home of Adam and Eve; then he flies down to the sun, and from the sun to the top of Mount Niphates in Armenia.]

from BOOK IV

THE ARGUMENT

Satan, now in prospect of Eden, and nigh the place where he must now attempt the bold enterprise which he undertook alone against God and man, falls into many doubts with himself, and many passions, fear, envy, and despair; but at length confirms himself in

32. Nightly I visit: Milton composed chiefly at night and dictated the result. Cf. VII. 28–30, IX. 22–23.   33–36. In his blindness, though not in his degree of fame, Milton links himself with two blind poets, Homer (Maeonides) and Thamyris (mentioned in the *Iliad*, II. 595–600), and two blind prophets, the Theban Tiresias and the Thracian Phineus.   38. numbers: verses.   wakeful bird: the nightingale.   39. darkling: in the dark.   48. blank: the gray-white effect of light apparent to Milton's blind eyes.

evil, journeys on to Paradise, whose outward prospect and situation is described, overleaps the bounds, sits in the shape of a cormorant on the Tree of Life, as highest in the Garden, to look about him. The Garden described; Satan's first sight of Adam and Eve; his wonder at their excellent form and happy state, but with resolution to work their fall; overhears their discourse; thence gathers that the Tree of Knowledge was forbidden them to eat of, under penalty of death; and thereon intends to found his temptation by seducing them to transgress; then leaves them a while, to know further of their state by some other means. Meanwhile Uriel, descending on a sunbeam, warns Gabriel, who had in charge the gate of Paradise, that some evil spirit had escaped the deep, and passed at noon by his sphere, in the shape of a good angel, down to Paradise; discovered after by his furious gestures in the mount. Gabriel promises to find him ere morning. Night coming on, Adam and Eve discourse of going to their rest: their bower described; their evening worship. Gabriel, drawing forth his bands of night-watch to walk the round of Paradise, appoints two strong angels to Adam's bower, lest the evil spirit should be there doing some harm to Adam or Eve sleeping; there they find him at the ear of Eve, tempting her in a dream, and bring him, though unwilling, to Gabriel; by whom questioned, he scornfully answers, prepares resistance, but hindered by a sign from Heaven, flies out of Paradise.

O for that warning voice, which he° who saw
The Apocalypse heard cry in Heaven aloud,
Then when the Dragon,° put to second rout,
Came furious down to be revenged on men,
"Woe to the inhabitants on Earth!" that now,
While time was, our first parents had been warned
The coming of their secret foe, and scaped,
Haply so scaped, his mortal snare; for now
Satan, now first inflamed with rage, came down,
The tempter ere° the accuser of mankind,   10
To wreak on innocent frail man his loss
Of that first battle, and his flight to Hell:
Yet not rejoicing in his speed, though bold,
Far off and fearless, nor with cause to boast,
Begins his dire attempt, which nigh the birth
Now rolling, boils in his tumultuous breast,
And like a devilish engine° back recoils
Upon himself; horror and doubt distract
His troubled thoughts, and from the bottom stir
The Hell within him, for within him Hell   20
He brings, and round about him, nor from Hell
One step no more than from himself can fly
By change of place. Now conscience wakes despair
That slumbered, wakes the bitter memory
Of what he was, what is, and what must be
Worse; of worse deeds worse sufferings must ensue.

Book IV: 1. he: St. John, supposed author of the Apocalypse (Revelation). Lines 1–5 are based on Rev. 12:7–12.   3. the Dragon: the serpent, Satan (Rev. 12:9). Cf. "Nativity," l. 168.   10. ere: before he was. See Rev. 12:10.   17. engine: cannon.

Sometimes towards Eden which now in his view
Lay pleasant, his grieved look he fixes sad,
Sometimes towards Heaven and the full-blazing
    sun,
Which now sat high in his meridian tower.   30
Then much revolving, thus in sighs began:
  "O thou° that with surpassing glory crowned,
Look'st from thy sole dominion like the god
Of this new world; at whose sight all the stars
Hide their diminished heads; to thee I call,
But with no friendly voice, and add thy name,
O sun, to tell thee how I hate thy beams
That bring to my remembrance from what state
I fell, how glorious once above thy sphere;
Till pride and worse ambition threw me down, 40
Warring in Heaven against Heaven's matchless
    King.
Ah wherefore? He deserved no such return
From me, whom he created what I was
In that bright eminence, and with his good
Upbraided none; nor was his service hard.
What could be less than to afford him praise,
The easiest recompense, and pay him thanks,
How due! Yet all his good proved ill in me,
And wrought but malice; lifted up so high
I sdained° subjection, and thought one step higher
Would set me highest, and in a moment quit° 51
The debt immense of endless gratitude,
So burdensome still° paying, still° to owe;
Forgetful what from him I still° received,
And understood not that a grateful mind
By owing owes not, but still° pays, at once
Indebted and discharged; what burden then?
O had his powerful destiny ordained
Me some inferior angel, I had stood
Then happy; no unbounded hope had raised 60
Ambition. Yet why not? some other power
As great might have aspired, and me though mean
Drawn to his part; but other powers as great
Fell not, but stand unshaken, from within
Or from without, to all temptations armed.
Hadst thou the same free will and power to stand?
Thou hadst. Whom hast thou then or what to ac-
    cuse,
But Heaven's free love dealt equally to all?
Be then his love accurst, since love or hate,
To me alike, it deals eternal woe. 70
Nay cursed be thou, since against his thy will
Chose freely what it now so justly rues.
Me miserable! which way shall I fly
Infinite wrath, and infinite despair?
Which way I fly is Hell; myself am Hell;°

And in the lowest deep a lower deep
Still threatening to devour me opens wide,
To which the Hell I suffer seems a Heaven.
O then at last relent: is there no place
Left for repentance, none for pardon left?
None left but by submission; and that word
Disdain forbids me, and my dread of shame
Among the spirits beneath, whom I seduced
With other promises and other vaunts
Than to submit, boasting I could subdue
The Omnipotent. Ay me, they little know
How dearly I abide that boast so vain,
Under what torments inwardly I groan;
While they adore me on the throne of Hell,
With diadem and scepter high advanced, 90
The lower still I fall, only supreme
In misery; such joy ambition finds.
But say I could repent and could obtain
By act of grace° my former state; how soon
Would highth recall high thoughts, how soon un-
    say
What feigned submission swore: ease would recant
Vows made in pain, as violent° and void.
For never can true reconcilement grow
Where wounds of deadly hate have pierced so deep;
Which would but lead me to a worse relapse 100
And heavier fall: so should I purchase dear
Short intermission bought with double smart.
This knows my Punisher; therefore as far
From granting he, as I from begging peace.
All hope excluded thus, behold instead
Of us outcast, exiled, his new delight,
Mankind created, and for him this World.
So farewell hope, and with hope farewell fear,
Farewell remorse! All good to me is lost;
Evil, be thou my good; by thee at least 110
Divided empire with Heaven's King I hold,
By thee, and more than half perhaps will reign;°
As man ere long, and this new World shall know."
  Thus while he spake, each passion dimmed his
    face
Thrice changed with pale,° ire, envy, and despair,
Which marred his borrowed visage,° and betrayed
Him counterfeit, if any eye beheld.
For heavenly minds from such distempers foul
Are ever clear. Whereof he soon aware,
Each perturbation smoothed with outward calm,
Artificer of fraud; and was the first 121
That practiced falsehood under saintly show,
Deep malice to conceal, couched° with revenge:
Yet not enough had practiced to deceive
Uriel once warned, whose eye pursued him down

32–41. O . . . King: Milton's nephew tells us that these lines were written as Lucifer's first speech in the drama that the poet planned in the early 1640's. 50. sdained: disdained. 51. quit: settle. 53, 54, 56. still: always. 75. Which . . . Hell: Cf. Satan's early boast, I. 254–55.

94. act of grace: pardon. 97. violent: made under duress and hence void. 112. reign: rule. 115. pale: paleness. 116. borrowed visage: In III. 634–44, Satan had changed himself into the likeness of a good angel to inquire his way from Uriel, one of God's chief angels. 123. couched: joined in concealment.

The way he went, and on the Assyrian mount°
Saw him disfigured, more than could befall
Spirit of happy sort: his gestures fierce
He° marked and mad demeanor, then alone,
As he° supposed, all unobserved, unseen.   130
So on he fares, and to the border comes
Of Eden, where delicious Paradise,°
Now nearer, crowns with her enclosure green
As with a rural mound the champaign head°
Of a steep wilderness, whose hairy sides
With thicket overgrown, grotesque and wild,
Access denied; and overhead up grew
Insuperable highth of loftiest shade,
Cedar, and pine, and fir, and branching palm,
A sylvan scene, and as the ranks ascend   140
Shade above shade, a woody theater
Of stateliest view. Yet higher than their tops
The verdurous wall of Paradise up sprung;
Which to our general sire° gave prospect large
Into his nether empire neighboring round.
And higher than that wall a circling row
Of goodliest trees loaden with fairest fruit,
Blossoms and fruits at once of golden hue,
Appeared, with gay enameled colors mixed;
On which the sun more glad impressed his beams
Than in fair evening cloud, or humid bow,°   151
When God hath showered the earth; so lovely
     seemed
That lantskip.° And of pure° now purer air
Meets his approach, and to the heart inspires
Vernal delight and joy, able to drive
All sadness but despair; now gentle gales
Fanning their odoriferous wings dispense
Native perfúmes, and whisper whence they stole
Those balmy spoils. As when to them who sail
Beyond the Cape of Hope,° and now are past   160
Mozambic,° off at sea north-east winds blow
Sabaean odors from the spicy shore
Of Araby the Blest, with such delay
Well pleased they slack their course, and many a
     league
Cheered with the grateful smell old ocean smiles;
So entertained those odorous sweets the Fiend
Who came their bane, though with them better
     pleased
Than Asmodëus° with the fishy fume,

126. Assyrian mount: Niphates, where Satan had alighted on earth.   129. He: Uriel.   130. he: Satan.   132. Paradise: the "park" or "garden" which is the home of Adam and Eve, in the eastern part of Eden. See ll. 208–14.   134. champaign head: plateau.   144. our . . . sire: Adam.   151. humid bow: the rainbow.   153. lantskip: landscape. of pure: after pure. 160. Hope: Good Hope.   161. Mozambic: Mozambique, on the east coast of Africa.   162. Sabaean: of Saba (the Biblical Sheba) in Arabia.   168–71. Asmodëus . . . bound: In the Apocryphal Book of Tobit, Asmodëus, an evil spirit, loved a woman and destroyed her seven husbands; her eighth husband, Tobit's son, drove Asmodëus away with the smell of burning fish, as the angel Raphael had advised. Asmodëus "fled into the utmost parts of Egypt, and the angel bound him" (chap. 8).

That drove him, though enamored, from the spouse
Of Tobit's son, and with a vengeance sent   170
From Media post to Egypt, there fast bound.
     Now to the ascent of that steep savage hill
Satan had journeyed on, pensive and slow;
But further way found none, so thick entwined,
As one continued brake, the undergrowth
Of shrubs and tangling bushes had perplexed
All path of man or beast that passed that way.
One gate there only was, and that looked east
On the other side; which when the Arch-Felon
     saw,
Due entrance he disdained, and in contempt,   180
At one slight bound high overleaped all bound
Of hill or highest wall, and sheer within
Lights on his feet. As when a prowling wolf,
Whom hunger drives to seek new haunt for prey,
Watching where shepherds pen their flocks at eve
In hurdled cotes amid the field secure,
Leaps o'er the fence with ease into the fold;
Or as a thief bent to unhoard the cash
Of some rich burgher, whose substantial doors,
Cross-barred and bolted fast, fear no assault,   190
In at the window climbs, or o'er the tiles:
So clomb this first grand thief into God's fold;
So since into his church lewd° hirelings climb.
Thence up he flew, and on the Tree of Life,
The middle tree and highest there that grew,
Sat like a cormorant; yet not true life
Thereby regained, but sat devising death
To them who lived; nor on the virtue thought
Of that life-giving plant, but only used
For prospect,° what well used had been the pledge
Of immortality. So little knows   201
Any, but God alone, to value right
The good before him, but perverts best things
To worst abuse, or to their meanest use.
     Beneath him with new wonder now he views
To all delight of human sense exposed
In narrow room Nature's whole wealth, yea more,
A Heaven on Earth, for blissful Paradise
Of God the garden was, by him in the east
Of Eden planted; Eden stretched her line   210
From Auran° eastward to the royal towers
Of great Seleucia,° built by Grecian kings,
Or where the sons of Eden long before
Dwelt in Telassar.° In this pleasant° soil
His far more pleasant° garden God ordained;
Out of the fertile ground he caused to grow
All trees of noblest kind for sight, smell, taste;
And all amid them stood the Tree of Life,
High eminent, blooming ambrosial fruit

193. lewd: base.   200. For prospect: as a lookout.   211. Auran: probably Auranitis, on the Euphrates.   212. Seleucia: the capital, on the Tigris, of the kingdom founded by Alexander's general, Seleucus.   214. Telassar: a place in Eden, somewhere in Mesopotamia.   214–15. pleasant: The name Eden means "pleasure." Cf. ll 27–28.

Of vegetable gold; and next to life   220
Our death, the Tree of Knowledge, grew fast by,
Knowledge of good bought dear by knowing ill.
Southward through Eden went a river large,
Nor changed his course, but through the shaggy
    hill
Passed underneath ingulfed, for God had thrown
That mountain as his garden mold,° high raised
Upon the rapid current, which through veins
Of porous earth with kindly° thirst up drawn,
Rose a fresh fountain, and with many a rill
Watered the garden; thence united fell   230
Down the steep glade, and met the nether flood,
Which from his darksome passage now appears,
And now divided into four main streams,
Runs díverse, wandering° many a famous realm
And country whereof here needs no account;
But rather to tell how, if art could tell,
How from that sapphire fount the crispèd° brooks,
Rolling on orient pearl and sands of gold,
With mazy error° under pendent shades
Ran nectar, visiting each plant, and fed   240
Flowers worthy of Paradise, which not nice° art
In beds and curious knots, but Nature boon°
Poured forth profuse on hill and dale and plain,
Both where the morning sun first warmly smote
The open field, and where the unpierced shade
Imbrowned° the noontide bowers. Thus was this
    place,
A happy rural seat of various view;°
Groves whose rich trees wept odorous gums and
    balm,
Others whose fruit burnished with golden rind
Hung amiable,° Hesperian fables true,   250
If true, here only,° and of delicious taste.
Betwixt them lawns, or level downs, and flocks
Grazing the tender herb, were interposed,
Or palmy hillock, or the flowery lap
Of some irriguous° valley spread her store,
Flowers of all hue, and without thorn the rose.
Another side, umbrageous grots and caves
Of cool recess, o'er which the mantling vine
Lays forth her purple grape, and gently creeps
Luxuriant; meanwhile murmuring waters fall   260
Down the slope hills, dispersed, or in a lake,
That to the fringèd bank with myrtle crowned
Her crystal mirror holds, unite their streams.
The birds their quire apply;° airs, vernal airs,
Breathing the smell of field and grove, attune

The trembling leaves, while universal Pan,°
Knit with the Graces and the Hours in dance,
Led on the eternal spring. Not that fair field
Of Enna,° where Prosérpine gathering flowers,
Herself a fairer flower, by gloomy Dis   270
Was gathered, which cost Ceres all that pain
To seek her through the world; nor that sweet
    grove
Of Daphne by Orontes, and the inspired
Castalian spring,° might with this Paradise
Of Eden strive; nor that Nyseian isle,°
Girt with the river Triton, where old Cham,
Whom Gentiles° Ammon call and Libyan Jove,
Hid Amalthea and her florid° son,
Young Bacchus, from his stepdame Rhea's eye;
Nor where Abassin kings their issue guard,   280
Mount Amara,° though this by some supposed
True Paradise, under the Ethiop line°
By Nilus' head,° enclosed with shining rock,
A whole day's journey high, but wide remote
From this Assyrian garden,° where the Fiend
Saw undelighted all delight, all kind
Of living creatures new to sight and strange.
    Two of far nobler shape erect and tall,
God-like erect,° with native honor clad
In naked majesty seemed lords of all,   290
And worthy seemed, for in their looks divine
The image of their glorious Maker shone,
Truth, wisdom, sanctitude severe and pure,
Severe but in true filial freedom placed;
Whence true authority in men; though both
Not° equal, as their sex not equal seemed;
For contemplation he and valor formed,
For softness she and sweet attractive grace;
He for God only, she for God in him.
His fair large front° and eye sublime° declared
Absolute rule; and hyacinthine° locks   301

266. universal Pan: "the All," the god of universal nature.
269. Enna: in Sicily, where Pluto (Dis) carried off Ceres' daughter
to be his queen in Hades.   272–74. grove . . . spring: the gardens of Daphne on the river Orontes in Syria; they contained a
spring (named after the Castalian spring at Delphi) which,
through marks on leaves, gave oracular answers to questioners.
275–79. Nyseian isle . . . Rhea's eye: Nysa, an island in the
river Triton in Tunisia, where the Libyan King Ammon, husband of Rhea, hid his mistress Amalthea and their son Bacchus.
Ammon was identified with Cham (Noah's son Ham) and with
the Greek god Zeus Ammon and the Roman Jupiter Ammon.
Cf. "Nativity," l. 203 and note.   277. Gentiles: non-Jewish
peoples, the Greeks and Romans.   278. florid: flushed (Bacchus
being god of wine).   280–81. Abassin . . . Amara: Amara was
a hill with palaces in Abyssinia, where the native princes were
brought up in seclusion.   282. Ethiop line: the equator.
283. Nilus' head: the source of the Nile.   285. this . . . garden:
the home of Adam and Eve.   288–89. erect: Milton follows
tradition in emphasizing the posture that befits creatures endowed "With sanctity of reason" (VII. 508).   296–99. Not
equal . . . him: The idea of woman's inferiority was not a peculiarly Miltonic view; it was traditional orthodoxy and was bound
up with the whole conception of the great chain of being.
300. front: forehead.   sublime: uplifted.   301. hyacinthine:
dark, brown (?) (a Homeric epithet).

226. garden mold: rich topsoil for a garden.   228. kindly:
natural.   234. wandering: traversing.   237. crisped: rippling.
239. error: wandering (the Latin sense).   241. nice: fastidious,
elegant. As elsewhere, Milton contrasts artifice with nature and
nature's fecundity.   242. boon: bounteous.   246. Imbrowned:
darkened.   247. view: appearance.   250. amiable: lovely.
250–51. Hesperian . . . only: like the golden apples of the
Hesperides, the myth being true only in Eden.   255. irriguous:
well-watered.   264. apply: contribute.

Round from his parted forelock manly hung
Clustering, but not beneath his shoulders broad:
She as a veil down to the slender waist
Her unadornèd golden tresses wore
Disheveled, but in wanton ringlets waved
As the vine curls her tendrils, which implied
Subjection, but required with gentle sway,
And by her yielded, by him best received,
Yielded with coy° submission, modest pride,   310
And sweet reluctant amorous delay.
Nor those mysterious parts were then concealed;
Then was not guilty shame; dishonest° shame
Of Nature's works, honor dishonorable,
Sin-bred, how have ye troubled all mankind
With shows instead, mere shows of seeming pure,
And banished from man's life his happiest life,
Simplicity and spotless innocence.°
So passed they naked on, nor shunned the sight
Of God or angel, for they thought no ill;   320
So hand in hand they passed, the loveliest pair
That ever since in love's embraces met,
Adam the goodliest man of men since born
His sons, the fairest of her daughters Eve.
Under a tuft of shade that on a green
Stood whispering soft, by a fresh fountain side
They sat them down; and after no more toil
Of their sweet gardening labor than sufficed
To recommend cool Zephyr,° and made ease
More easy, wholesome thirst and appetite   330
More grateful, to their supper fruits they fell,
Nectarine fruits which the compliant boughs
Yielded them, sidelong as they sat recline°
On the soft downy bank damasked° with flowers.
The savory pulp they chew, and in the rind
Still as they thirsted scoop the brimming stream;
Nor gentle purpose,° nor endearing smiles
Wanted,° nor youthful dalliance, as beseems
Fair couple linked in happy nuptial league,
Alone as they. About them frisking played   340
All beasts of the earth, since wild, and of all chase°
In wood or wilderness, forest or den;
Sporting the lion ramped,° and in his paw
Dandled the kid; bears, tigers, ounces,° pards,°
Gamboled before them; the unwieldy elephant
To make them mirth used all his might, and
    wreathed
His lithe proboscis; close the serpent sly
Insinuating,° wove with Gordian twine
His braided train,° and of his fatal guile

Gave proof unheeded; others on the grass   350
Couched, and now filled with pasture gazing sat,
Or bedward ruminating;° for the sun
Declined was hasting now with prone career
To the ocean isles,° and in the ascending scale
Of Heaven the stars that usher evening rose:
When Satan still in gaze, as first he stood,
Scarce thus at length failed speech° recovered sad:
    "O Hell! what do mine eyes with grief behold!
Into our room of bliss thus high advanced
Creatures of other mold,° earth-born perhaps,   360
Not spirits, yet to heavenly spirits bright
Little inferior; whom my thoughts pursue
With wonder, and could love, so lively shines
In them divine resemblance, and such grace
The hand that formed them on their shape hath
    poured.
Ah gentle pair, ye little think how nigh
Your change approaches, when all these delights
Will vanish and deliver ye to woe,
More woe, the more your taste is now of joy;
Happy, but for so happy ill secured   370
Long to continue, and this high seat your Heaven
Ill fenced for Heaven to keep out such a foe
As now is entered; yet no purposed foe
To you whom I could pity thus forlorn,
Though I unpitied. League° with you I seek,
And mutual amity so strait, so close,
That I with you must dwell, or you with me
Henceforth; my dwelling haply may not please,
Like this fair Paradise, your sense, yet such
Accept your Maker's work; he gave it me,   380
Which I as freely give; Hell shall unfold,
To entertain you two, her widest gates,
And send forth all her kings; there will be room,
Not like these narrow limits, to receive
Your numerous offspring; if no better place,
Thank him who puts me loth to this revenge
On you who wrong me not, for him who wronged.
And should I at your harmless innocence
Melt, as I do, yet public reason just,
Honor and empire with revenge enlarged   390
By conquering this new World, compels me now
To do what else though damned I should abhor."
    So spake the Fiend, and with necessity,
The tyrant's plea, excused his devilish deeds.
Then from his lofty stand on that high tree
Down he alights among the sportful herd
Of those four-footed kinds, himself now one,
Now other, as their shape served best his end
Nearer to view his prey, and unespied   399
To mark what of their state he more might learn
By word or action marked. About them round
A lion now he stalks with fiery glare;

310. coy: shy.   313. dishonest: impure.   317–18. banished
... innocence: Here and elsewhere Milton, for all his stress
on rational choice (Intro., p. 203), cannot subdue his nostalgic
vision of primal innocence.   329. recommend ... Zephyr:
make the cool breeze pleasant.   333. recline: reclining.
334. damasked: richly variegated.   337. purpose: conversation.   338. Wanted: were lacking.   341. all chase: every
habitat.   343. ramped: reared up.   344. ounces: lynxes.
pards: leopards.   348. Insinuating: winding into folds.
349. train: body.

352. bedward ruminating: chewing the cud before sleeping.
354. ocean isles: the Azores. Cf. l. 592.   357. failed speech: speech
that had failed him.   360. mold: substance.   375–85. League ...
offspring: Satan is enjoying his own sardonic irony.

Then as a tiger, who by chance hath spied
In some purlieu two gentle fawns at play,
Straight couches close, then rising, changes oft
His couchant watch, as one who chose his ground
Whence rushing he might surest seize them both
Gripped in each paw; when Adam first of men
To first of women, Eve, thus moving speech,
Turned him all ear to hear new utterance flow:
 " Sole partner and sole part of all these joys,   411
Dearer thyself than all, needs must the Power
That made us, and for us this ample World,
Be infinitely good, and of his good
As liberal and free as infinite,
That raised us from the dust and placed us here
In all this happiness, who at his hand
Have nothing merited, nor can perform
Aught whereof he hath need; he who requires
From us no other service than to keep   420
This one, this easy charge, of all the trees
In Paradise that bear delicious fruit
So various, not to taste that only Tree
Of Knowledge, planted by the Tree of Life,
So near grows death to life, whate'er death is,
Some dreadful thing no doubt; for well thou
    know'st
God hath pronounced it death to taste that Tree,
The only sign of our obedience left
Among so many signs of power and rule
Conferred upon us, and dominion given   430
Over all other creatures that possess
Earth, air, and sea. Then let us not think hard
One easy prohibition, who enjoy
Free leave so large to all things else, and choice
Unlimited of manifold delights;
But let us ever praise him, and extol
His bounty, following our delightful task
To prune these growing plants, and tend these
    flowers,
Which were it toilsome, yet with thee were sweet."
 To whom thus Eve replied: "O thou for whom
And from whom I was formed flesh of thy flesh,
And without whom am to no end, my guide   442
And head, what thou hast said is just and right.
For we to him indeed all praises owe,
And daily thanks, I chiefly who enjoy
So far the happier lot, enjoying thee
Pre-eminent by so much odds, while thou
Like consort to thyself canst nowhere find.
That day I oft remember, when from sleep
I first awaked, and found myself reposed   450
Under a shade on flowers, much wondering where
And what I was, whence thither brought, and how.
Not distant far from thence a murmuring sound
Of waters issued from a cave and spread
Into a liquid plain, then stood unmoved
Pure as the expanse of Heaven; I thither went
With unexperienced thought, and laid me down

On the green bank, to look into the clear
Smooth lake, that to me seemed another sky
As° I bent down to look, just opposite   460
A shape within the watery gleam appeared
Bending to look on me: I started back,
It started back, but pleased I soon returned,
Pleased it returned as soon with answering looks
Of sympathy and love; there I had fixed
Mine eyes till now, and pined with vain desire,
Had not a voice thus warned me: ' What thou seest,
What there thou seest, fair creature, is thyself,
With thee it came and goes; but follow me,
And I will bring thee where no shadow stays°   470
Thy coming, and thy soft embraces, he
Whose image thou art, him thou shalt enjoy
Inseparably thine; to him shalt bear
Multitudes like thyself, and thence be called
Mother of human race.' What could I do
But follow straight, invisibly thus led?
Till I espied thee, fair indeed and tall,
Under a platan; yet methought less fair,
Less winning soft, less amiably mild,   479
Than that smooth watery image; back I turned,
Thou following cried'st aloud, ' Return, fair Eve,
Whom fli'st thou?° whom thou fli'st, of him thou
    art,
His flesh, his bone; to give thee being I lent
Out of my side to thee, nearest my heart,
Substantial life, to have thee by my side
Henceforth an individual° solace dear.
Part of my soul I seek thee, and thee claim
My other half.' With that thy gentle hand
Seized mine, I yielded, and from that time see
How beauty is excelled by manly grace   490
And wisdom, which alone is truly fair."
 So spake our general mother, and with eyes
Of conjugal attraction unreproved,°
And meek surrender, half embracing leaned
On our first father; half her swelling breast
Naked met his under the flowing gold
Of her loose tresses hid. He in delight
Both of her beauty and submissive charms
Smiled with superior love, as Jupiter   499
On Juno° smiles, when he impregns° the clouds
That shed May flowers; and pressed her matron lip
With kisses pure. Aside the Devil turned
For envy, yet with jealous leer malign
Eyed them askance, and to himself thus plained:°

460–66. As . . . desire: Although Eve was at her creation,
and still is, quite innocent, Milton's use of the myth of Narcissus gives a first faint hint of the vanity that is to be her undoing.   470. stays: waits for.   481–82. Thou . . . thou: Both
the action and the language recall Ovid's tale of Apollo's pursuing Daphne, and, in a way parallel to the myth of Narcissus
above, this veiled allusion gives a hint of the extreme devotion
to Eve that is to be Adam's undoing.   486. individual: inseparable.   493. unreproved: not deserving reproof.   499–
500. Jupiter, Juno: here the sky and the air, respectively.
500. impregns: impregnates.   504. plained: complained.

" Sight hateful, sight tormenting! thus these two
Imparadised in one another's arms,
The happier Eden, shall enjoy their fill
Of bliss on bliss, while I to Hell am thrust,
Where neither joy nor love, but fierce desire,
Among our other torments not the least,   510
Still unfulfilled with pain of longing pines;°
Yet let me not forget what I have gained
From their own mouths. All is not theirs, it seems;
One fatal tree there stands, of Knowledge called,
Forbidden them to taste. Knowledge forbidden?
Suspicious, reasonless. Why should their Lord
Envy them that? can it be sin to know,
Can it be death? and do they only stand
By ignorance, is that their happy state,
The proof of their obedience and their faith?   520
O fair foundation laid whereon to build
Their ruin! Hence I will excite their minds
With more desire to know, and to reject
Envious commands, invented with design
To keep them low whom knowledge might exalt
Equal with gods. Aspiring to be such,
They taste and die; what likelier can ensue?
But first with narrow search I must walk round
This garden, and no corner leave unspied;   529
A chance but chance may lead where I may meet
Some wandering spirit of Heaven, by fountain side,
Or in thick shade retired, from him to draw
What further would be learnt. Live while ye may,
Yet happy pair; enjoy, till I return,
Short pleasures, for long woes are to succeed."
   So saying, his proud step he scornful turned,
But with sly circumspection, and began
Through wood, through waste, o'er hill, o'er dale,
      his roam.
Meanwhile in utmost longitude,° where Heaven
With Earth and Ocean meets, the setting sun   540
Slowly descended, and with right aspect°
Against the eastern gate of Paradise
Leveled his evening rays. It was a rock
Of alablaster,° piled up to the clouds,
Conspicuous far, winding with one ascent
Accessible from Earth, one entrance high;
The rest was craggy cliff, that overhung
Still as it rose, impossible to climb.
Betwixt these rocky pillars Gabriel sat,
Chief of the angelic guards, awaiting night;   550
About him exercised heroic games
The unarmed youth of Heaven, but nigh at hand
Celestial armory, shields, helms, and spears,
Hung high, with diamond flaming and with gold.
Thither came Uriel, gliding through the even
On a sunbeam, swift as a shooting star
In autumn thwarts° the night, when vapors fired°

Impress the air, and shows the mariner
From what point of his compass to beware
Impetuous winds. He thus began in haste: 560
" Gabriel, to thee thy course by lot hath given
Charge and strict watch that to this happy place
No evil thing approach or enter in;
This° day at highth of noon came to my sphere
A spirit, zealous, as he seemed, to know
More of the Almighty's works, and chiefly man,
God's latest image. I described° his way
Bent all on speed, and marked his aery gait;°
But in the mount that lies from Eden north,   569
Where he first lighted, soon discerned his looks
Alien from Heaven, with passions foul obscured.
Mine eye pursued him still, but under shade
Lost sight of him; one of the banished crew,
I fear, hath ventured from the deep, to raise
New troubles; him thy care must be to find."
   To whom the wingèd warrior thus returned:
" Uriel, no wonder if thy perfect sight,
Amid the sun's bright circle where thou sitt'st,
See far and wide. In at this gate none pass
The vigilance° here placed, but such as come   580
Well known from Heaven; and since meridian
      hour
No creature thence. If spirit of other sort,
So minded, have o'erleaped these earthy bounds
On purpose, hard thou know'st it to exclude
Spiritual substance with corporeal bar.
But if within the circuit of these walks,
In whatsoever shape he lurk, of whom
Thou tell'st, by morrow dawning I shall know."
   So promised he, and Uriel to his charge
Returned on that bright beam, whose point now
      raised   590
Bore him slope downward to the sun now fallen
Beneath the Azores; whether the prime orb,
Incredible how swift, had thither rolled
Diurnal,° or this less volúble Earth,
By shorter flight to the east,° had left him there
Arraying with reflected purple and gold
The clouds that on his western throne attend.
   Now came still evening on, and twilight gray
Had in her sober livery all things clad;
Silence accompanied, for beast and bird,   600
They to their grassy couch, these to their nests
Were slunk, all but the wakeful nightingale;
She all night long her amorous descant sung;
Silence was pleased. Now glowed the firmament
With living sapphires; Hesperus° that led
The starry host rode brightest, till the moon,

511. pines: makes (me) pine.   539. utmost longitude: farthest
west.   541. right aspect: directly (so as to light up the inner
side of the rock).   544. alablaster: alabaster.   557. thwarts:
crosses.   vapors fired: heat lightning.

564-71. This . . . obscured: The incident occurred in III.
621-735.   567. described: descried. See ll. 114-30 and l. 116n.
568. aery gait: flight through the air.   580. vigilance: guards.
592-94. whether . . . Diurnal: if, as in old astronomy, the sun
had revolved to the west.   594-95. or . . . east: or, as in Copernican astronomy, the earth had made a much smaller rotation
to the east.   605. Hesperus: the evening star.

Rising in clouded majesty, at length
Apparent° queen unveiled her peerless light,
And o'er the dark her silver mantle threw;
   When Adam thus to Eve: " Fair consort, the
     hour   610
Of night, and all things now retired to rest
Mind us of like repose, since God hath set
Labor and rest, as day and night to men
Successive, and the timely dew of sleep
Now falling with soft slumbrous weight inclines
Our eyelids; other creatures all day long
Rove idle, unemployed, and less need rest;
Man hath his daily work of body or mind
Appointed, which declares his dignity,
And the regard of Heaven on all his ways;   620
While other animals unactive range,
And of their doings God takes no account.
To-morrow ere fresh morning streak the east
With first approach of light, we must be risen,
And at our pleasant labor, to reform
Yon flowery arbors, yonder alleys green,
Our walks at noon, with branches overgrown,
That mock our scant manuring,° and require
More hands than ours to lop their wanton growth.
Those blossoms also, and those dropping gums,
That lie bestrown unsightly and unsmooth,   631
Ask riddance, if we mean to tread with ease;
Meanwhile, as Nature wills, night bids us rest."
   To whom thus Eve with perfect beauty adorned:
" My author° and disposer, what thou bidd'st
Unargued I obey; so God ordains.
God is thy law, thou mine; to know no more
Is woman's happiest knowledge and her praise.
With thee conversing° I forget all time,
All seasons° and their change, all please alike.
Sweet is the breath of morn, her rising sweet, 641
With charm° of earliest birds; pleasant the sun
When first on this delightful land he spreads
His orient beams, on herb, tree, fruit, and flower,
Glistering with dew; fragrant the fertile Earth
After soft showers; and sweet the coming on
Of grateful evening mild, then silent night
With this her solemn bird and this fair moon,
And these the gems of Heaven, her starry train:
But neither breath of morn when she ascends 650
With charm of earliest birds, nor rising sun
On this delightful land, nor herb, fruit, flower,
Glistering with dew, nor fragrance after showers,
Nor grateful evening mild, nor silent night
With this her solemn bird, nor walk by moon
Or glittering starlight, without thee is sweet.
But wherefore all night long shine these, for whom
This glorious sight, when sleep hath shut all eyes?"

   To whom our general ancestor replied: 659
" Daughter of God and man, accomplished Eve,
Those have their course to finish, round the Earth,
By morrow evening, and from land to land
In order, though to nations yet unborn,
Ministering light prepared, they set and rise;
Lest total darkness° should by night regain
Her old possession, and extinguish life
In nature and all things; which these soft fires
Not only enlighten, but with kindly° heat
Of various influence° foment and warm,
Temper or nourish, or in part shed down   670
Their stellar virtue on all kinds that grow
On Earth, made hereby apter to receive
Perfection from the sun's more potent ray.
These then, though unbeheld in deep of night,
Shine not in vain, nor think, though men were
    none,
That Heaven would want spectators, God want
    praise;
Millions of spiritual creatures walk the Earth
Unseen, both when we wake, and when we sleep:
All these with ceaseless praise his works behold
Both day and night. How often from the steep
Of echoing hill or thicket have we heard   681
Celestial voices to the midnight air,
Sole, or responsive each to other's note,
Singing their great Creator; oft in bands
While they keep watch, or nightly rounding° walk,
With heavenly touch of instrumental sounds
In full harmonic number joined, their songs
Divide the night,° and lift our thoughts to
    Heaven."
   Thus talking, hand in hand alone they passed
On to their blissful bower; it was a place   690
Chosen by the sovran Planter, when he framed
All things to man's delightful use; the roof
Of thickest covert was inwoven shade,
Laurel and myrtle, and what higher grew
Of firm and fragrant leaf; on either side
Acanthus, and each odorous bushy shrub
Fenced up the verdant wall; each beauteous flower,
Iris all hues, roses, and jessamine
Reared high their flourished heads between, and
    wrought
Mosaic; under foot the violet,   700
Crocus, and hyacinth with rich inlay
Broidered the ground, more colored than with stone
Of costliest emblem.° Other creature here,
Beast, bird, insect, or worm durst enter none;
Such was their awe of man. In shadier bower
More sacred and sequestered, though but feigned,°

---

608. **Apparent**: a manifest.   628. **manuring**: cultivating.
635. **" My author "**: source of my being.   639. **conversing**:
living.   640. **seasons**: times of day (since Eden enjoys eternal
spring).   642. **charm**: song.

665. **total darkness**: the darkness of Chaos.   668. **kindly**:
natural.   669–73. **influence . . . ray**: a limited recognition of
astrological influence.   685. **rounding**: making the rounds, as
sentries.   688. **Divide . . . night**: i.e., into watches (a Roman
military term).   703. **emblem**: inlaid work.   706. **feigned**:
poetical and pagan fictions.

Pan or Silvanus° never slept, nor nymph
Nor Faunus° haunted. Here in close recess
With flowers, garlands, and sweet-smelling herbs
Espousèd Eve decked first her nuptial bed,   710
And heavenly quires the hymenean° sung,
What day the genial° angel to our sire
Brought her in naked beauty more adorned,
More lovely than Pandora,° whom the gods
Endowed with all their gifts, and O too like
In sad event, when to the unwiser son
Of Japhet brought by Hermes, she ensnared
Mankind with her fair looks, to be avenged
On him who had stole Jove's authentic fire.

　　Thus at their shady lodge arrived, both stood,
Both turned, and under open sky adored   721
The God that made both sky, air, Earth, and
　　Heaven,
Which they beheld, the moon's resplendent globe
And starry pole:° " Thou also mad'st the night,
Maker Omnipotent, and thou the day,
Which we in our appointed work employed
Have finished happy in our mutual help
And mutual love, the crown of all our bliss
Ordained by thee, and this delicious place
For us too large, where thy abundance wants   730
Partakers, and uncropped falls to the ground.
But thou hast promised from us two a race
To fill the Earth, who shall with us extol
Thy goodness infinite, both when we wake,
And when we seek, as now, thy gift of sleep."

　　This said unanimous, and other rites
Observing none, but adoration pure
Which God likes best, into their inmost bower
Handed they went; and eased the putting off
These troublesome disguises which we wear,   740
Straight side by side were laid, nor turned, I ween,
Adam from his fair spouse, nor Eve the rites
Mysterious of connubial love refused;
Whatever hypocrites austerely talk
Of purity and place and innocence,
Defaming as impure what God declares
Pure, and commands to some, leaves free to all.
Our Maker bids increase;° who bids abstain
But our destroyer, foe to God and man?
Hail, wedded Love, mysterious law,° true source
Of human offspring, sole propriety°   751
In Paradise of all things common else.
By thee adulterous lust was driven from men

707–08. Silvanus, Faunus: Roman divinities of field and woodland.　711. hymenean: marriage song.　712. genial: nuptial.
714–19. Pandora . . . fire: When Prometheus ("Forethought"),
the son of Japhet, stole fire from Zeus to aid man, Zeus had
Hephaestus make a woman, Pandora (so called because the
gods endowed her with "all gifts"), who should be fatal to man.
She was brought by Hermes to Prometheus' brother, Epimetheus
("Afterthought"), who married her. A box sent with her,
opened, let loose all the evils of life.　724. pole: sky.　748. Our
. . . increase: See Gen. 1:28.　750. mysterious law: See Eph.
5:32.　751. sole propriety: the one thing peculiar to Adam
and Eve.

Among the bestial herds to range; by thee
Founded in reason, loyal, just, and pure,
Relations dear, and all the charities°
Of father, son, and brother first were known.
Far be it that I should write thee sin or blame,
Or think thee unbefitting holiest place,
Perpetual fountain of domestic sweets,   760
Whose bed is undefiled and chaste pronounced,
Present or past, as saints and patriarchs used.
Here Love his golden shafts employs, here lights
His constant lamp, and waves his purple wings,
Reigns here and revels;° not in the bought smile
Of harlots, loveless, joyless, unendeared,
Casual fruition; nor in court amours,
Mixed dance, or wanton mask, or midnight ball,
Or serenate,° which the starved° lover sings
To his proud fair, best quitted° with disdain.   770
These lulled by nightingales, embracing slept,
And on their naked limbs the flowery roof
Showered roses, which the morn repaired.° Sleep
　　on,
Blest pair; and O yet happiest if ye seek
No happier state, and know to know no more.°

[The action of the rest of Book IV is summarized in
Milton's prefatory Argument. The most important thing is
Satan's embarking on his plan of campaign (see IV. 512–
27) by tempting Eve in a dream.]

from BOOK V

[Eve, in great distress, tells Adam of a dream (of Satanic
inspiration): she had been led to the forbidden Tree of
Knowledge and had yielded to the solicitations of a seeming
angel and eaten of the fruit, which, she was told, would
make her a goddess. She is relieved that it was all a dream
and is reassured by Adam. The two utter a grand canticle
in praise of the Creation and the Creator and go about
their daily work. Since temptation is near, God sends down
Raphael to warn the pair of their responsibility. Adam
wishes to know " Of things above his world," and Raphael
begins (ll. 469 ff.) with an account of the great chain of
being, an account which departs from orthodoxy in its
monistic theory of matter and spirit. Then Raphael goes on
to tell of the great example of pride and disobedience, Satan's revolt after God's proclamation of the Son as his
vicegerent.]

　　To whom the wingèd Hierarch° replied:
" O Adam, one° Almighty is, from whom
All things proceed, and up to him return,   470
If not depraved from good, created all
Such to perfection, one first matter all,
Endued with various forms, various degrees

756. charities: affections.　763–65. Here . . . revels: Milton
transfers to pure marital love the romantic, sensual Cupid of
Ovid and other poets. Cupid's golden arrow inspired love, his
leaden one repelled it.　769. serenate: serenade.　starved:
frozen (outside a mistress' door).　770. quitted: repaid.　773. repaired: replaced.　775. know . . . more: are wise enough
not to seek further knowledge (of good and evil).　Book V:
468. the . . . Hierarch: The periphrasis is an apt preliminary to
the account of hierarchical order in the universe.　469–79. one
. . . kind: Milton is far from materialism, since all matter pro-

Of substance, and in things that live, of life;
But more refined, more spiritous, and pure,
As nearer to him placed or nearer tending,
Each in their several active spheres assigned,
Till body up to spirit work, in bounds
Proportioned to each kind. So from the root
Springs lighter the green stalk, from thence the
    leaves   480
More aery, last the bright consummate flower
Spirits odorous breathes: flowers and their fruit,
Man's nourishment, by gradual scale sublimed,°
To vital spirits aspire, to animal,
To intellectual;° give both life and sense,
Fancy and understanding, whence the soul
Reason° receives, and reason is her being,
Discursive, or intuitive; discourse
Is oftest yours, the latter most is ours,
Differing but in degree, of kind the same.   490
Wonder not then, what God for you saw good
If I refuse not, but convert, as you,
To proper° substance. Time may come when
    men
With angels may participate, and find
No inconvenient diet, nor too light fare;
And from these corporal nutriments perhaps
Your bodies may at last turn all to spirit,
Improved by tract of time, and winged ascend
Ethereal, as we, or may at choice
Here or in heavenly paradises dwell;   500
If ye be found obedient, and retain
Unalterably firm his love entire
Whose progeny you are. Meanwhile enjoy
Your fill what happiness this happy state
Can comprehend, incapable of more."
    To whom the patriarch of mankind replied:
"O favorable Spirit, propitious guest,
Well hast thou taught the way that might direct
Our knowledge, and the scale of Nature set

From center to circumference,° whereon   510
In contemplation of created things
By steps we may ascend to God. But say,
What meant that caution joined, *If ye be found
Obedient?* Can we want obedience then
To him, or possibly his love desert
Who formed us from the dust, and placed us here
Full to the utmost measure of what bliss
Human desires can seek or apprehend? "
    To whom the Angel: " Son of Heaven and
      Earth,
Attend: that thou art happy, owe to God;   520
That thou continu'st such, owe to thyself,
That is, to thy obedience; therein stand.
This was that caution given thee; be advised.
God° made thee perfect, not immutable;
And good he made thee, but to persevere
He left it in thy power, ordained thy will
By nature free, not over-ruled by fate
Inextricable, or strict necessity.
Our voluntary service he requires,
Not our necessitated; such with him   530
Finds no acceptance, nor can find, for how
Can hearts not free be tried whether they serve
Willing or no, who will but what they must
By destiny, and can no other choose?
Myself and all the angelic host that stand
In sight of God enthroned, our happy state
Hold, as you yours, while our obedience holds;
On other surety none; freely we serve,
Because we freely love, as in our will
To love or not; in this we stand or fall.   540
And some are fallen, to disobedience fallen,
And so from Heaven to deepest Hell; O fall
From what high state of bliss into what woe! "
    To whom our great progenitor: " Thy words
Attentive, and with more delighted ear,
Divine instructor, I have heard, than when
Cherubic songs by night from neighboring hills
Aerial music send.° Nor knew I not
To be both will and deed created free;
Yet that we never shall forget to love   550
Our Maker, and obey him whose command
Single is yet so just, my constant thoughts
Assured me, and still assure; though what thou
    tell'st
Hath passed in Heaven some doubt within me
    move,
But more desire to hear, if thou consent,
The full relation, which must needs be strange,
Worthy of sacred silence to be heard;

---

ceeds from and returns to God, and since, in various forms and degrees, it is in the process of becoming spirit. And, having such an origin and end, matter is not evil (as in some religions and philosophies), but intrinsically good.   **483. sublimed:** elevated, distilled.   **484–85. vital . . . intellectual:** In traditional physiology and psychology, the soul operated on three levels: the vegetative soul is purely biological and is shared by plants, animals, and men; the sensitive soul, in animals and men, has the faculties of motion, perception, and feeling; the rational soul, in men only, has the higher and peculiarly human faculties. Corresponding to and nourishing these several powers are three kinds of "spirits," distilled from the blood, namely, natural, vital, and animal (this last pertaining to the soul, *anima*).   **487–90. Reason . . . same:** Man's reason is discursive; i.e., it deliberates, while angelic reason has immediate apprehension. But human reason — for Milton and other men — comprehends more than the mere reasoning faculty; it is the whole rational self of man, the highest of creatures (next to the angels), made in the image of God and finding fulfillment in him.   **491–93. Wonder . . . substance:** Adam had been hesitant about offering lunch to an angel, but Raphael had explained that angels require and digest food, and the topic of digestion had led on to the metaphysical account of the chain of being.   **493. proper:** (my) own.

510. From . . . circumference: from the earth to the spheres around it.   **524–34. God . . . choose:** Adam was endowed with "right reason" which was capable of ordering his life rightly in relation to God and Eve, but, as the event was to show, his will would not necessarily obey his reason. Free will, however, could not exist if overruled by fate or necessity; the condition of freedom is freedom to choose wrongly.   **547–48. Cherubic . . . send:** Cf. IV. 680–88.

And we have yet large day, for scarce the sun
Hath finished half his journey, and scarce begins
His other half in the great zone of heaven."   560
   Thus Adam made request, and Raphael,
After short pause assenting, thus began:
  "High matter° thou enjoin'st me, O prime of
     men,
Sad task and hard, for how shall I relate
To human sense the invisible exploits
Of warring spirits; how without remorse°
The ruin of so many glorious once
And perfect while they stood; how last unfold
The secrets of another world, perhaps
Not lawful to reveal? Yet for thy good   570
This is dispensed,° and what surmounts the reach
Of human sense I shall delineate so,
By likening spiritual to corporal forms,
As may express them best, though what if Earth
Be but the shadow of Heaven, and things therein
Each to other like, more than on Earth is
     thought?°
  "As yet this World was not, and Chaos wild
Reigned where these Heavens° now roll, where
     Earth now rests
Upon her center poised, when on a day°
(For time, though in eternity, applied   580
To motion, measures all things durable
By present, past, and future), on such day
As Heaven's great year° brings forth, the empyreal
     host
Of angels by imperial summons called,
Innumerable before the Almighty's throne
Forthwith from all the ends of Heaven appeared
Under their hierarchs in orders bright.
Ten thousand thousand ensigns high advanced,
Standards and gonfalons 'twixt van and rear
Stream in the air, and for distinction serve   590
Of hierarchies, of orders, and degrees;
Or in their glittering tissues bear emblazed°
Holy memorials, acts of zeal and love
Recorded eminent. Thus when in orbs°
Of circuit inexpressible they stood,
Orb within orb, the Father Infinite,

By whom in bliss embosomed sat the Son,
Amidst as from a flaming mount, whose top
Brightness had made invisible, thus spake:
  "'Hear, all ye Angels, progeny of light,   600
Thrones, Dominations, Princedoms, Virtues, Pow-
    ers,°
Hear my decree, which unrevoked shall stand.
This day I have begot° whom I declare
My only Son, and on this holy hill
Him have anointed, whom ye now behold
At my right hand. Your head I him appoint;
And by myself have sworn to him shall bow
All knees in Heaven, and shall confess him Lord.
Under his great vicegerent reign abide
United as one individual° soul   610
Forever happy. Him who disobeys
Me disobeys, breaks union, and that day
Cast out from God and blessed vision,° falls
Into utter darkness, deep engulfed, his place
Ordained without redemption, without end.'
  "So spake the Omnipotent, and with his words
All seemed well pleased; all seemed, but were not
    all.
That day, as other solemn days, they spent
In song and dance about the sacred hill;
Mystical° dance, which yonder starry sphere   620
Of planets and of fixed° in all her wheels
Resembles nearest, mazes intricate,
Eccentric,° intervolved, yet regular
Then most, when most irregular they seem;
And in their motions harmony divine
So smooths her charming tones, that God's own ear
Listens delighted.° Evening now approached
(For we have also our evening and our morn,
We ours for change delectable, not need);
Forthwith from dance to sweet repast they turn
Desirous; all in circles as they stood,   631
Tables are set, and on a sudden piled
With angels' food, and rubied nectar flows
In pearl, in diamond, and massy gold,
Fruit of delicious vines, the growth of Heaven.

563 ff. High matter: Raphael's reference (ll. 541–43) to Satan's fall prompts Adam's query and the angel's long account of preceding events, which fills the rest of this book and Books VI and VII. Such a narrative corresponds, in the epic structure, to Odysseus' story of his wanderings and Aeneas' story of the fall of Troy and his wandering. Lines 563–76 are the first of Raphael's — i.e., Milton's — several apologies for the attempt to render spiritual things in comprehensible terms; thus the subsequent narrative is a mixture of the literal and the symbolic or metaphorical. **566. remorse:** pity. **571. dispensed:** allowed. **574–76. though . . . thought:** a Platonic idea. **577–79. As . . . day:** the chronological beginning of the events treated in the poem. **578. these Heavens:** the sky, not the heaven of God and the angels. **583. Heaven's . . . year:** an allusion to the Platonic "great year," the long period between the times when all the heavenly bodies returned to their original positions. **592. emblazed:** emblazoned. **594. orbs:** circles.

601. Thrones . . . Powers: See I. 129n. **603. begot:** Milton is echoing Ps. 2:6–7. The word is not used literally but means God's designation of his Son as his vicegerent, as king and mediator between himself and the angels and man, as the active force of good in the world. **610. individual:** not to be divided. **613. blessed vision:** the beatific vision, the sight of God in Heaven. **620–27. Mystical . . . delighted:** the starry dance (the planetary system and the music of the spheres) always arouses in the unmystical Milton a half-mystical sense of the beauty of divine order and harmony. **621. fixed:** the eighth sphere, containing the fixed stars. The seven inner spheres or orbits (listed from the earth outward) carried the moon, Mercury, Venus, the sun, Mars, Jupiter, and Saturn; the ninth or crystalline sphere contained water; the tenth or *Primum Mobile* kept the inner spheres in motion. **623. Eccentric:** Technically, the word means the center of a planetary orbit placed, not in the earth, but on a line between the earth and the moving sun, so that the center of the orbit described a circle around the earth. **625–27. harmony . . . delighted:** the music of the spheres. Cf. "Nativity," ll. 125 ff.

On flowers reposed, and with fresh flowerets
    crowned,
They eat, they drink, and in communion sweet
Quaff immortality and joy, secure
Of surfeit where full measure only bounds
Excess, before the all-bounteous King, who show-
    ered   640
With copious hand, rejoicing in their joy.
Now when ambrosial° night, with clouds exhaled
From that high mount of God, whence light and
    shade
Spring both, the face of brightest Heaven had
    changed
To grateful twilight (for night comes not there
In darker veil) and roseate dews disposed
All but the unsleeping eyes of God to rest,
Wide over all the plain, and wider far
Than all this globous Earth in plain outspread
(Such are the courts of God), the angelic throng,
Dispersed in bands and files, their camp extend
By living streams among the trees of life,   652
Pavilions numberless and sudden reared,
Celestial tabernacles, where they slept
Fanned with cool winds, save those who in their
    course
Melodious hymns about the sovran throne
Alternate all night long. But not so waked
Satan° — so call him now, his former name
Is heard no more in Heaven; he of the first,
If not the first Archangel, great in power,   660
In favor, and pre-eminence, yet fraught
With envy against the Son of God, that day
Honored by his great Father, and proclaimed
Messiah,° King anointed, could not bear
Through pride that sight, and thought himself im-
    paired.
Deep malice thence conceiving and disdain,
Soon as midnight brought on the dusky hour
Friendliest to sleep and silence, he resolved
With all his legions to dislodge, and leave
Unworshiped, unobeyed, the throne supreme,   670
Contemptuous, and his next subordinate°
Awakening, thus to him in secret spake:

" 'Sleep'st thou, companion dear, what sleep can
    close
Thy eyelids? and remember'st what decree
Of yesterday, so late hath passed the lips
Of Heaven's Almighty? Thou to me thy thoughts
Wast wont, I mine to thee was wont to impart;
Both waking we were one; how then can now
Thy sleep dissent? New laws thou seest imposed;

New laws from him who reigns, new minds may
    raise   680
In us who serve, new counsels, to debate
What doubtful may ensue. More in this place
To utter is not safe. Assemble thou
Of all those myriads which we lead the chief;
Tell them that by command, ere yet dim night
Her shadowy cloud withdraws, I am to haste,
And all who under me their banners wave,
Homeward with flying march where we possess
The quarters of the north,° there to prepare°
Fit entertainment to receive our King,   690
The great Messiah, and his new commands,
Who speedily through all the hierarchies
Intends to pass triumphant, and give laws.'

" So spake the false Archangel, and infused
Bad influence into the unwary breast
Of his associate; he° together calls,
Or several one by one, the regent powers,
Under him regent, tells, as he was taught,
That the Most High commanding, now ere night,
Now ere dim night had disencumbered Heaven,
The great hierarchal standard was to move;   701
Tells the suggested cause, and casts between
Ambiguous words and jealousies, to sound
Or taint integrity; but all obeyed
The wonted signal, and superior voice
Of their great Potentate; for great indeed
His name, and high was his degree in Heaven;
His countenance, as the morning star° that guides
The starry flock, allured them, and with lies   709
Drew after him the third part of Heaven's host."°

[In the rest of the book Satan, in the north, rouses his
followers to rebellion. Abdiel alone denounces his wicked
course and, "Unshaken, unseduced, unterrified," leaves Satan's host to return to the mount of God.]

BOOK VI

[In Book VI Raphael tells Adam of the war in Heaven
between Satan and his followers and the army of God led
by Michael. The war begins, in Homeric fashion, with
verbal exchanges between Abdiel (who had been welcomed
with praise by God) and Satan: true freedom, Abdiel declares, is found within the divine order, whereas Satan, for
all his boasts, is a slave to himself. The combats between
the angelic hosts, with their mounting violence and havoc,
are an objectification of Satan's pride and passion; and at
the same time a note of tragicomic extravagance suggests
the ultimate futility of war against Good. On the third day
God ordains that the Son shall end the war, and the irresistible strength and splendor of Good are symbolized in
the picture of the Son:

        Forth rushed with whirlwind sound
    The chariot of Paternal Deity,
    Flashing thick flames. . . .

642. ambrosial: fragrant.   658–65. Satan . . . impaired: Milton
is not giving a philosophical explanation of the origin of evil;
he is, in imaginative terms, showing evil in action. Satan's
resentment at the Son's elevation is akin to Macbeth's over
Duncan's naming Malcolm as Prince of Cumberland, but
Satan's pride is irreligious self-assertion against divine order.
664. Messiah: the word means "anointed."   671. his . . .
subordinate: Beelzebub.

689. the north: See Isa. 14:13 (and folklore in general for the
north as the home of evil).   689–93. prepare . . . laws: Satan
gives a false account of his purpose.   696. he: Beelzebub.
708. morning star: Lucifer, "light-bearer." See Isa. 14:12,
quoted above in I. 84–85n.   710. third . . . host: Cf. II. 692
and Rev. 12:4.

Attended with ten thousand thousand saints,
He onward came, far off his coming shone. . . .

Satan and his fellows, overwhelmed, are driven through a
gap in the wall of Heaven and fall through Chaos into Hell
— the point in the action where the poem had begun. In
concluding the story Raphael reminds Adam of the warning
it contains for him.]

from BOOK VII

[The body of Book VII is an expansion of the first two
chapters of Genesis, with details added from a multitude of
sources. In its total effect the account of Creation is a hymn
to the divine glory and wonder of nature and life. Raphael
ends his narrative with a warning of the conditions of man's
continued happiness.]

Descend from Heaven, Urania,° by that name
If rightly thou art called, whose voice divine
Following, above the Olympian hill I soar,°
Above the flight of Pegasean wing.°
The meaning, not the name I call; for thou
Nor of the Muses nine, nor on the top
Of old Olympus dwell'st, but heavenly born,
Before the hills appeared or fountain° flowed,
Thou with eternal Wisdom° didst converse,°
Wisdom thy sister, and with her didst play   10
In presence of the Almighty Father, pleased
With thy celestial song. Up led by thee
Into the Heaven of Heavens I have presumed,
An earthly guest, and drawn empyreal° air,°
Thy tempering;° with like safety guided down,
Return me to my native element,°
Lest° from this flying steed unreined (as once
Bellerophon, though from a lower clime)
Dismounted, on the Aleian field I fall,

Book VII: 1–39. The war in Heaven over, the poet is returning
to earth, which is to be the chief scene of action in the latter
half of the poem; this change, and arrival at the middle point,
invite a new invocation of the poet's Heavenly Muse.   **1–12. Urania . . . song:** See I. 6n. As in I. 6–22 and III. 16–32, Milton
distinguishes between the classical Muse and his own religious
inspiration.   **3. above . . . soar:** Cf. I. 15, "Above the Aonian
mount . . ." Olympus, like Helicon, was a home of the Muses.
4. Pegasean wing: The winged horse Pegasus (which was ridden
by Bellerophon when he killed the Chimera) with a blow from
his hoof started the fountain of Hippocrene, so that he, as well
as the spring, was associated with poetic inspiration.   **8. hills
. . . fountain:** Milton seems to be thinking both of the Muses'
hills and fountains and of the Creation as described in Genesis and
in Prov. 8:24–25.   **9–12. Wisdom . . . song:** Milton associates
his Heavenly Muse with the Wisdom of Prov. 8:27–30 (who
speaks of attending God at the Creation) and of the Apocryphal
Book of Wisdom.   **9. converse:** live.   **12–14. Up . . . air:** In
Books III, V, and VI Milton had described events in Heaven.
14. empyreal: See I. 117n.   **15. Thy tempering:** His Heavenly
Muse had tempered celestial air so that a mortal might breathe
it.   **16. native element:** the air of earth.   **17–20. Lest . . .
forlorn:** Bellerophon, on Pegasus, had tried to reach the heaven
of Zeus ("a lower clime" than the Christian Heaven) and,
thrown off his horse by the offended god, had fallen down to the
Aleian plain in Lycia, where he wandered miserably until he
died.

Erroneous° there to wander and forlorn.   20
Half yet remains unsung, but narrower bound
Within the visible diurnal sphere;°
Standing on Earth, not rapt above the pole,°
More° safe I sing with mortal voice, unchanged
To hoarse or mute, though fallen on evil days,
On evil days though fallen, and evil tongues;°
In darkness, and with dangers compassed round,
And solitude; yet not alone, while thou
Visit'st my slumbers nightly,° or when morn
Purples the east. Still govern thou my song,   30
Urania, and fit audience find, though few.
But drive far off the barbarous dissonance
Of Bacchus and his revelers,° the race
Of that wild rout° that tore the Thracian bard
In Rhodope, where woods and rocks had ears
To rapture,° till the savage clamor drowned
Both harp and voice; nor could the Muse defend
Her son. So fail not thou who thee implores;
For thou art heavenly, she° an empty dream.

[Adam wishes to know of his own world, and Raphael,
who is commissioned to satisfy his desire for knowledge
"within bounds," tells the story of Creation, the great work
of peace that follows the destructive chaos of the war in
Heaven. The evil angels having been expelled, God ordains
the creation of the world and a race of beings who in time
may merit Heaven. The Son, Satan's mightier opposite, is
God's active agent in the work of creation, and the description of his setting forth is a signal example of vague pictorial suggestion and of rhythms that powerfully reflect both
tumultuous disorder and the imposition of order (ll. 205–
21):

> " Heaven opened wide
> Her ever-during gates, harmonious sound
> On golden hinges moving, to let forth
> The King of Glory in his powerful Word
> And Spirit coming to create new worlds.
> On heavenly ground they stood, and from the shore
> They viewed the vast immeasurable abyss
> Outrageous as a sea, dark, wasteful, wild,
> Up from the bottom turned by furious winds
> And surging waves, as mountains to assault
> Heaven's highth, and with the center mix the pole.
> ' Silence, ye troubled waves, and thou deep, peace,'
> Said then the omnific Word, ' your discord end.'
> Nor stayed, but on the wings of Cherubim
> Uplifted, in paternal glory rode
> Far into Chaos and the World unborn;
> For Chaos heard his voice."]

20. Erroneous: in the Latin sense of "wandering" and probably
also in the sense of "having erred."   **21–22. narrower . . .
sphere:** a more limited scene, within man's universe. The "visible diurnal sphere" is the whole firmament which, in the old
astronomy, revolved daily about the earth.   **23. pole:** the top
of the axis of the created universe. See II. 1051–52 and I. 74n.
24–28. More . . . solitude: a poignant picture of the blind republican after the Restoration. Lines 25–26 are a great example
of the Miltonic "turn," the use, with variations, of repeated
phrases.   **26. evil tongues:** the public and private hostility of
Royalists.   **29. Visit'st . . . nightly:** See the note on III. 32.
33. Bacchus . . . revelers: Charles II and his court.   **34–38. rout
. . . son:** See "Lycidas," ll. 58–63n.   **35–36. where . . . rapture:**
Orpheus' song could move stones and trees, if not his human
pursuers.   **39. she:** Calliope, the classical Muse, mother of
Orpheus.

BOOK VIII

[The first part of Book VIII carries on the theme of temperance in the pursuit of knowledge that does not further the true ends of life. The most obvious example is astronomical inquiry, which had since Copernicus become the most conspicuous branch of science, and which over the centuries had led to so much debate and confusion. Adam asks about the relation of the earth to the firmament around it, and Raphael outlines alternative geocentric and heliocentric theories of the universe and also raises old questions that had revived with the new astronomy, such as the possibility of other inhabited worlds. But the lesson he draws is Adam's need of humility and a right scale of values in his view of knowledge. The significance of the discussion is commented upon in the Introduction, p. 407.

In the rest of Book VIII Adam tells of his first experience of life, of his desire for a companion, and of the creation of Eve and their first union. His fervent tribute to Eve's beauty and her power over him draws from Raphael a rebuke that relates this episode to the astronomical discussion and to the occasion of Adam's fall. It is again a question of order and degree. Milton is not condemning Adam's true devotion or his happiness in physical relations (which, in Book IV, ll. 741–70, he goes out of his way to celebrate); he is saying that Adam, through both his senses and the affections of his heart, seems in danger of letting Eve, who is not only a human being but a being of inferior reason, come between himself and God — as he is to do in Book IX.]

BOOK IX

THE ARGUMENT

Satan, having compassed the Earth, with meditated guile returns as a mist by night into Paradise; enters into the Serpent sleeping. Adam and Eve in the morning go forth to their labors, which Eve proposes to divide in several places, each laboring apart: Adam consents not, alleging the danger lest that enemy, of whom they were forewarned, should attempt her found alone. Eve, loth to be thought not circumspect or firm enough, urges her going apart, the rather desirous to make trial of her strength; Adam at last yields. The Serpent finds her alone: his subtle approach, first gazing, then speaking, with much flattery extolling Eve above all other creatures. Eve, wondering to hear the Serpent speak, asks how he attained to human speech and such understanding, not till now; the Serpent answers that by tasting of a certain tree in the garden he attained both to speech and reason, till then void of both. Eve requires him to bring her to that tree, and finds it to be the Tree of Knowledge forbidden. The Serpent, now grown bolder, with many wiles and arguments induces her at length to eat; she, pleased with the taste, deliberates a while whether to impart thereof to Adam or not; at last brings him of the fruit; relates what persuaded her to eat thereof. Adam, at first amazed, but perceiving her lost, resolves through vehemence of love to perish with her, and, extenuating the trespass, eats also of the fruit. The effects thereof in them both; they seek to cover their nakedness; then fall to variance and accusation of one another.

No° more of talk where God or angel guest
With man, as with his friend, familiar used
To sit indulgent, and with him partake
Rural repast, permitting him the while
Venial discourse unblamed. I now must change
Those notes to tragic: foul distrust, and breach
Disloyal on the part of man, revolt,
And disobedience; on the part of Heaven
Now alienated, distance and distaste,
Anger and just rebuke, and judgment given,   10
That brought into this World a world of woe,
Sin and her shadow Death, and misery,°
Death's harbinger. Sad task, yet argument
Not less but more heroic than the wrath
Of stern Achilles on his foe pursued
Thrice fugitive about Troy wall;° or rage
Of Turnus for Lavinia disespoused;°
Or Neptune's ire° or Juno's,° that so long
Perplexed the Greek and Cytherea's son;
If answerable style I can obtain   20
Of my celestial patroness,° who deigns
Her nightly° visitation unimplored,
And dictates to me slumbering, or inspires
Easy my unpremeditated verse,
Since first this subject for heroic song
Pleased me, long choosing and beginning late;°
Not sedulous by nature to indite
Wars, hitherto the only argument
Heroic deemed, chief mastery° to dissect
With long and tedious havoc fabled knights°   30
In battles feigned (the better fortitude
Of patience and heroic martyrdom
Unsung), or to describe races and games,
Or tilting furniture,° emblazoned shields,
Impresses° quaint, caparisons and steeds,
Bases° and tinsel trappings, gorgeous knights
At joust and tournament; then marshaled feast
Served up in hall with sewers and seneschals;
The skill of artifice or office mean,

Book IX: 1–47. This proem — not, like its predecessors, a direct invocation of the Heavenly Muse — introduces the crucial theme of man's sin, a theme that invites comparison with the heroic tradition. In emphasizing the high truth and significance of his own subject Milton does not do justice to his love of Homer and Virgil and the later romances. Cf. his view of poetry in the *Reason of Church Government*. **1–5. No . . . unblamed:** Raphael has returned to Heaven, and the stage is left to Adam and Eve and Satan. **12. misery:** diseases. **14–16. wrath . . . wall:** the subject of the *Iliad*. **16–17. rage . . . disespoused:** the main story of the second half of the *Aeneid*. **18–19. Neptune's ire:** the hostility of Neptune (Poseidon) toward Odysseus ("the Greek"). **Juno:** her enmity toward Aeneas, the son of Venus (Cytherea). These references to the classical epics contrast God's anger (l. 10) with the less significant anger of mythological gods and men. **21. celestial patroness:** Urania, the Heavenly Muse. **22. nightly:** Cf. III. 29–40, VII. 28–30. **25–26. Since . . . late:** See the headnote to *PL* and IV. 32–41n. **29. chief mastery:** the chief mastery being. **30–38. knights . . . seneschals:** the medieval and later romances of chivalry. **34. tilting furniture:** equipment for tournaments. **35. Impresses:** heraldic devices on shields, etc. **36. Bases:** the ornate housings of a horse.

Not that which justly gives heroic name   40
To person or to poem. Me of these
Nor skilled nor studious, higher argument
Remains, sufficient of itself to raise
That name, unless an age too late,° or cold
Climate,° or years damp my intended wing
Depressed, and much they may, if all be mine,
Not hers who brings it nightly to my ear.
    The sun was sunk, and after him the star
Of Hesperus, whose office is to bring
Twilight upon the Earth, short arbiter   50
'Twixt day and night, and now from end to end
Night's hemisphere had veiled the horizon round,
When Satan, who late fled° before the threats
Of Gabriel out of Eden, now improved
In meditated fraud and malice, bent
On man's destruction, maugre° what might hap
Of heavier on himself, fearless returned.
By night he fled, and at midnight returned
From compassing the Earth, cautious of day,
Since Uriel, regent of the sun, descried   60
His entrance, and forewarned the Cherubim
That kept their watch; thence full of anguish
    driven,
The space of seven continued nights he rode
With darkness, thrice the equinoctial line°
He circled, four times crossed the car of Night
From pole to pole, traversing each colure;°
On the eighth returned, and on the coast averse°
From entrance or cherubic watch, by stealth
Found unsuspected way. There was a place —
Now not, though sin, not time, first wrought the
    change —   70
Where Tigris at the foot of Paradise
Into a gulf shot under ground, till part
Rose up a fountain by the Tree of Life;
In with the river sunk, and with it rose
Satan, involved in rising mist, then sought
Where to lie hid; sea he had searched and land
From Eden over Pontus,° and the pool
Maeotis,° up beyond the river Ob;°
Downward as far antarctic; and in length
West from Orontes° to the ocean barred   80
At Darien,° thence to the land where flows
Ganges and Indus. Thus the orb° he roamed
With narrow° search, and with inspection deep

Considered every creature, which of all
Most opportune might serve his wiles, and found
The serpent subtlest beast of all the field.°
Him after long debate, irresolute
Of thoughts revolved,° his final sentence chose
Fit vessel, fittest imp° of fraud, in whom
To enter, and his dark suggestions hide   90
From sharpest sight; for in the wily snake,
Whatever sleights none would suspicious mark,
As from his wit and native subtlety
Proceeding, which, in other beasts observed,
Doubt° might beget of diabolic power
Active within beyond the sense of brute.
Thus he resolved, but first from inward grief
His bursting passion into plaints thus poured:
    "O Earth, how like to Heaven, if not preferred
More justly, seat worthier of gods, as built   100
With second thoughts, reforming what was old!
For what God after better worse would build?
Terrestrial Heaven, danced round by other Heavens
That shine, yet bear their bright officious° lamps,
Light above light, for thee alone, as seems,
In thee concentring all their precious beams
Of sacred influence!° As God in Heaven
Is center, yet extends to all, so thou
Centring receiv'st from all those orbs; in thee,
Not in themselves, all their known virtue appears
Productive in herb, plant, and nobler birth   111
Of creatures animate with gradual life
Of growth, sense, reason, all summed up in man.
With what delight could I have walked thee round,
If I could joy in aught, sweet interchange
Of hill and valley, rivers, woods, and plains,
Now land, now sea, and shores with forest crowned,
Rocks, dens, and caves; but I in none of these
Find place or refuge; and the more I see
Pleasures about me, so much more I feel   120
Torment within me, as from the hateful siege°
Of contraries; all good to me becomes
Bane, and in Heaven much worse would be my
    state.
But neither here seek I, no nor in Heaven
To dwell, unless by mastering Heaven's Supreme;
Nor hope to be myself less miserable
By what I seek, but others to make such
As I, though thereby worse to me redound.
For only in destroying I find ease
To my relentless thoughts; and him destroyed,   130
Or won to what may work his utter loss,
For whom all this° was made, all this will soon
Follow, as to him linked in weal or woe;
In woe then, that destruction wide may range.

---

44. age . . . late: In the earlier seventeenth century there was a widespread idea that all nature, including man, was in process of decay — an idea Milton had opposed in some Cambridge utterances.   44–45. cold Climate: Milton referred elsewhere to the common belief that the cold north was unfavorable to genius (although early biographers report that he composed happily only from autumn to spring).   53. Satan . . . fled: at the end of Book IV.   56. maugre: in spite of.   64. equinoctial line: equator.   66. From . . . colure: from the north pole to the south and back, following the colures (lines drawn around the globe through the poles and the equinoctial and solstitial points).   67. coast averse: side opposite.   77. Pontus: the Black Sea.   77–78. pool Maeotis: Sea of Azov. Ob: in Siberia.   80. Orontes: a Syrian river.   81. Darien: Isthmus of Panama.   82. orb: globe.   83. narrow: close.

86. serpent . . . field: See Gen. 3:1.   88. Of . . . revolved: among thoughts considered.   89. imp: child.   95. Doubt: suspicion.   104. officious: serviceable.   107–13. influence . . . man: On the influence of the stars, see IV. 668–73; on the scale of nature, see V. 484–85n.   121. siege: battle.   132. all this: The world of nature (the result Satan predicts is described in X. 651–714).

To me shall be the glory sole among
The infernal Powers, in one day to have marred
What he, Almighty styled, six nights and days
Continued making, and who knows how long
Before had been contriving? though perhaps
Not longer than since I in one night freed   140
From servitude inglorious well-nigh half
The angelic name, and thinner left the throng
Of his adorers. He to be avenged,
And to repair his numbers thus impaired,
Whether such virtue spent of old now failed
More angels to create, if they at least
Are his created,° or to spite us more,
Determined to advance into our room
A creature formed of earth, and him endow,
Exalted from so base original,   150
With heavenly spoils, our spoils. What he decreed
He effected; man he made, and for him built
Magnificent this World, and Earth his seat,
Him lord pronounced, and, O indignity!
Subjected to his service angel wings,
And flaming ministers to watch and tend
Their earthy charge. Of these the vigilance
I dread, and to elude, thus wrapped in mist
Of midnight vapor glide obscure, and pry
In every bush and brake, where hap may find   160
The serpent sleeping, in whose mazy folds
To hide me, and the dark intent I bring.
O foul descent! that I, who erst contended
With Gods to sit the highest, am now constrained
Into a beast, and mixed with bestial slime,
This essence° to incarnate and imbrute,
That to the height of deity aspired;
But what will not ambition and revenge
Descend to? Who aspires must down as low
As high he soared, obnoxious° first or last   170
To basest things. Revenge, at first though sweet,
Bitter ere long back on itself recoils;
Let it; I reck not, so it light well aimed,
Since higher° I fall short, on him who next
Provokes my envy, this new favorite
Of Heaven, this man of clay, son of despite,
Whom us the more to spite his Maker raised
From dust: spite then with spite is best repaid."
    So saying, through each thicket dank or dry,
Like a black mist low creeping, he held on   180
His midnight search, where soonest he might find
The serpent. Him fast sleeping soon he found
In labyrinth of many a round self-rolled,
His head the midst, well stored with subtle wiles;
Not yet in horrid shade or dismal den,
Nor nocent yet, but on the grassy herb
Fearless, unfeared, he slept. In at his mouth
The Devil entered, and his brutal sense,

In heart or head, possessing soon inspired
With act° intelligential, but his sleep   190
Disturbed not, waiting close° the approach of
    morn.
    Now whenas sacred light began to dawn
In Eden on the humid flowers, that breathed
Their morning incense, when all things that breathe
From the Earth's great altar send up silent praise
To the Creator, and his nostrils fill
With grateful smell, forth came the human pair
And joined their vocal worship to the quire   198
Of creatures wanting voice; that done, partake
The season, prime for sweetest scents and airs;
Then cómmune how that day they best may ply
Their growing work; for much their work outgrew
The hands' dispatch of two gardening so wide.
And Eve first to her husband thus began:
    "Adam, well may we labor still° to dress
This garden, still° to tend plant, herb, and flower,
Our pleasant task enjoined, but till more hands
Aid us, the work under our labor grows,
Luxurious by restraint; what we by day
Lop overgrown, or prune, or prop, or bind,   210
One night or two with wanton growth derides,
Tending to wild.° Thou therefore now advise
Or hear what to my mind first thoughts present:
Let us divide our labors, thou where choice
Leads thee, or where most needs, whether to wind
The woodbine round this arbor, or direct
The clasping ivy where to climb, while I
In yonder spring° of roses intermixed
With myrtle, find what to redress till noon.
For while so near each other thus all day   220
Our task we choose, what wonder if so near
Looks intervene and smiles, or object new
Casual discourse draw on, which intermits
Our day's work, brought to little, though begun
Early, and the hour of supper comes unearned."
    To whom mild answer Adam thus returned:
"Sole Eve, associate sole, to me beyond
Compare above all living creatures dear,
Well hast thou motioned,° well thy thoughts em-
    ployed
How we might best fulfil the work which here
God hath assigned us, nor of me shalt pass   231
Unpraised; for nothing lovelier can be found
In woman, than to study household good,
And good works in her husband to promote.
Yet not so strictly hath our Lord imposed
Labor, as to debar us when we need
Refreshment, whether food, or talk between,
Food of the mind, or this sweet intercourse
Of looks and smiles, for smiles from reason flow,
To brute denied, and are of love the food,   240

146–47. if . . . created: Satan had acknowledged God's creation
of the angels in IV. 43.   166. This essence: See I. 117n. and
I. 138n.   170. obnoxious: liable.   174. higher: aiming higher
(against God).

190. act: activity.   191. close: hidden.   205, 206. still: always.
212. wild: wildness.   218. spring: clump.   229. motioned:
proposed.

Love not the lowest end of human life.
For not to irksome toil, but to delight
He made us, and delight to reason joined.
These paths and bowers doubt not but our joint
    hands
Will keep from wilderness° with ease, as wide
As we need walk, till younger hands ere long
Assist us. But if much converse perhaps
Thee satiate, to short absence I could yield.
For solitude sometimes is best society,
And short retirement urges sweet return.   250
But other doubt possesses me, lest harm
Befall thee severed from me; for thou know'st
What hath been warned us, what malicious foe,
Envying our happiness, and of his own
Despairing, seeks to work us woe and shame
By sly assault; and somewhere nigh at hand
Watches, no doubt, with greedy hope to find
His wish and best advantage, us asunder,
Hopeless to circumvent us joined, where each
To other speedy aid might lend at need;   260
Whether his first design be to withdraw
Our fealty from God, or to disturb
Conjugal love, than which perhaps no bliss
Enjoyed by us excites his envy more;
Or this, or worse,° leave not the faithful side
That gave thee being, still shades thee and protects.
The wife, where danger or dishonor lurks,
Safest and seemliest by her husband stays,
Who guards her, or with her the worst endures."
    To whom the virgin° majesty of Eve,   270
As one who loves, and some unkindness meets,
With sweet austere composure thus replied:
    " Offspring of Heaven and Earth, and all Earth's
    lord,
That such an enemy we have, who seeks
Our ruin, both by thee informed I learn,
And from the parting angel° overheard
As in a shady nook I stood behind,
Just then returned at shut of evening flowers.
But that thou shouldst my firmness therefore doubt
To God or thee, because we have a foe   280
May tempt it, I expected not to hear.°
His violence thou fear'st not, being such
As we, not capable of death or pain,
Can either not receive, or can repel.
His fraud is then thy fear, which plain infers
Thy equal fear that my firm faith and love
Can by his fraud be shaken or seduced;
Thoughts, which how found they harbor in thy
    breast,
Adam, misthought of her to thee so dear? "
    To whom with healing words Adam replied:

"Daughter of God and man, immortal Eve,   291
For such thou art, from sin and blame entire;°
Not diffident of thee do I dissuade
Thy absence from my sight, but to avoid
The attempt itself, intended by our foe.
For he who tempts, though in vain, at least
    asperses°
The tempted with dishonor foul, supposed
Not incorruptible of faith, not proof
Against temptation. Thou thyself with scorn
And anger wouldst resent the offered wrong,   300
Though ineffectual found. Misdeem not then,
If such affront I labor to avert
From thee alone, which on us both at once
The enemy, though bold, will hardly dare,
Or daring, first on me the assault shall light.
Nor thou his malice and false guile contemn;
Subtle he needs must be, who could seduce
Angels, nor think superfluous others' aid.
I from the influence of thy looks receive
Access in every virtue, in thy sight   310
More wise, more watchful, stronger, if need were
Of outward strength; while shame, thou looking
    on,
Shame to be overcome or overreached,
Would utmost vigor raise, and raised unite.°
Why shouldst not thou like sense° within thee feel
When I am present, and thy trial choose
With me, best witness of thy virtue tried? "
    So spake domestic° Adam in his care
And matrimonial love; but Eve, who thought
Less attribúted to her faith sincere,   320
Thus her reply with accent sweet renewed:
    " If this be our condition, thus to dwell
In narrow circuit straitened° by a foe,
Subtle or violent, we not endued
Single with like defense, wherever met,
How are we happy, still in fear of harm?
But harm precedes not sin: only our foe
Tempting affronts us with his foul esteem
Of our integrity; his foul esteem
Sticks no dishonor on our front,° but turns   330
Foul on himself; then wherefore shunned or feared
By us? who rather double honor gain
From his surmise proved false, find peace within,
Favor from Heaven, our witness, from the event.°
And what is faith, love, virtue, unassayed
Alone, without exterior help sustained?°

245. wilderness: wildness.   265. Or . . . worse: whether he
plans this or worse.   270. virgin: sinless, innocent.   276. angel:
Raphael (at the end of Book VIII).   279–81. But . . . hear:
the first note of something like earthly and feminine shrillness
in Eve's utterances.

292. entire: untouched by.   296. asperses: sprinkles, smears.
314. unite: unite the virtues just spoken of.   315. like sense:
a similar feeling.   318. domestic: devoted (with a hint of excess). Throughout this dramatic book, the epithets applied to
Adam and Eve are important indications of Milton's view of
their behavior.   323. straitened: confined.   330. front: forehead.   334. event: outcome.   335–36. unassayed . . . sustained: if not tested by themselves, without external help. Eve
has sometimes been said to express the spirit of *Areopagitica*,
but (as J. S. Diekhoff has shown) she does not. In the tract
Milton wrote of a world containing evil that must be met, while

Let us not then suspect our happy state
Left so imperfect by the Maker wise
As not secure to single or combined.°
Frail is our happiness, if this be so,   340
And Eden were no Eden° thus exposed."
    To whom thus Adam fervently replied:
" O woman, best are all things as the will
Of God ordained them; his creating hand
Nothing imperfect or deficient left
Of all that he created, much less man,
Or aught that might his happy state secure,
Secure from outward force: within himself
The danger lies, yet lies within his power;
Against his will he can receive no harm.   350
But God left free the will,° for what obeys
Reason is free, and reason he made right,
But bid her well beware, and still erect,°
Lest by some fair appearing good surprised
She dictate false, and misinform the will
To do what God expressly hath forbid.°
Not then mistrust, but tender love, enjoins
That I should mind° thee oft, and mind thou me.
Firm we subsist, yet possible to swerve,
Since reason not impossibly may meet   360
Some specious object by the foe suborned,°
And fall into deception unaware,
Not keeping strictest watch, as she was warned.
Seek not temptation then, which to avoid
Were better, and most likely if from me
Thou sever not; trial will come unsought.
Wouldst thou approve thy constancy, approve°
First thy obedience; the other who can know,
Not seeing thee attempted, who attest?
But if thou think trial unsought may find   370
Us both securer° than thus warned thou seem'st,
Go; for thy stay, not free, absents thee more;
Go in thy native innocence, rely
On what thou hast of virtue, summon all,
For God towards thee hath done his part, do
    thine."
    So spake the patriarch of mankind, but Eve
Persisted; yet submiss, though last, replied:°
    " With thy permission then, and thus forewarned,
Chiefly by what thy own last reasoning words
Touched only, that our trial, when least sought,
May find us both perhaps far less prepared,   381

Eve, in a world created perfect, is needlessly courting temptation; and, as Adam points out, she is criticizing God's creation
and not showing obedience. As Milton says in both *Areopagitica*
and *PL*, to know good by evil is a far less happy state than to
know good only. **339. As . . . combined:** as not safe for us
either separate or together. **341. Eden . . . Eden:** See IV. 214–
15n. **351–53.** Adam repeats a central theme of the poem, already affirmed by God and by Raphael, the freedom of man's
will and his rational power of choice. **353. still erect:** (be) always on the alert. **354–56. Lest . . . forbid:** Adam anticipates
exactly what happens to Eve. **358. mind:** remind. **361. suborned:** employed for an evil purpose. **367. approve:** prove.
371. securer: less careful. Cf. ll. 379–81. **377. yet . . . replied:**
spoke, though submissively, the last word.

The willinger I go, nor much expect
A foe so proud will first the weaker seek;
So bent, the more shall shame him his repulse."
Thus saying, from her husband's hand her hand
Soft she withdrew, and like a wood-nymph light,
Oread or Dryad, or of Delia's° train,
Betook her to the groves, but Delia's self
In gait surpassed and goddess-like deport,°
Though not as she with bow and quiver armed,
But with such gardening tools as art yet rude,   391
Guiltless of fire, had formed, or angels brought.
To Pales,° or Pomona,° thus adorned,
Likest she seemed, Pomona when she fled
Vertumnus, or to Ceres in her prime,
Yet virgin of Proserpina from Jove.°
Her long with ardent look his eye pursued
Delighted, but desiring more her stay.
Oft he to her his charge of quick return
Repeated, she to him as oft engaged   400
To be returned by noon amid the bower,
And all things in best order to invite
Noontide repast, or afternoon's repose.
O much deceived, much failing, hapless Eve,
Of thy presumed return! event perverse!
Thou never from that hour in Paradise
Found'st either sweet repast or sound repose;
Such ambush, hid among sweet flowers and shades,
Waited with hellish rancor imminent
To intercept thy way, or send thee back   410
Despoiled of innocence, of faith, of bliss.
For now, and since first break of dawn the Fiend,
Mere° serpent in appearance, forth was come,
And on his quest, where likeliest he might find
The only two of mankind, but in them
The whole included race, his purposed prey.
In bower and field he sought, where any tuft
Of grove or garden-plot more pleasant lay,
Their tendance° or plantation for delight;
By fountain or by shady rivulet   420
He sought them both, but wished his hap might
    find
Eve separate; he wished, but not with hope
Of what so seldom chanced, when to his wish,
Beyond his hope, Eve separate he spies,
Veiled in a cloud of fragrance, where she stood,
Half spied, so thick the roses bushing round
About her glowed, oft stooping to support°
Each flower of slender stalk, whose head, though
    gay

387. Delia: Diana (from her birthplace, Delos). **389. deport:**
bearing. **393. Pales:** a Roman goddess of flocks and shepherds.
Pomona: a Roman goddess of fruit who was loved by Vertumnus, a god of fruit. **395–96. Ceres . . . Jove:** young Ceres
before she became, by Jupiter, the mother of Proserpine.
413. Mere: pure. (Milton puts aside a tradition that made Satan
appear as part serpent, part angel.) **419. Their tendance:**
which they tended. **427–33. support . . . nigh:** a beautiful
variation on the simile of Proserpine (IV. 268–72).

Carnation, purple, azure, or specked with gold,
Hung drooping unsustained; them she upstays
Gently with myrtle band, mindless° the while,   431
Herself, though fairest unsupported flower,
From her best prop so far, and storm so nigh.
Nearer he drew, and many a walk traversed
Of stateliest covert, cedar, pine, or palm,
Then voluble° and bold, now hid, now seen
Among thick-woven arborets° and flowers
Imbordered° on each bank, the hand° of Eve:
Spot more delicious than those gardens feigned
Or° of revived Adonis,° or renowned   440
Alcinous,° host of old Laertes' son,
Or that, not mystic,° where the sapient king
Held dalliance with his fair Egyptian spouse.°
Much he the place admired, the person more.
As one who long in populous city pent,
Where houses thick and sewers annoy° the air,
Forth issuing on a summer's morn to breathe
Among the pleasant villages and farms
Adjoined, from each thing met conceives delight,
The smell of grain, or tedded° grass, or kine,   450
Or dairy, each rural sight, each rural sound;
If chance with nymph-like step fair virgin pass,
What pleasing seemed, for her° now pleases more,
She most, and in her look sums° all delight:
Such pleasure took the Serpent to behold
This flowery plat,° the sweet recess of Eve
Thus early, thus alone; her heavenly form
Angelic, but more soft and feminine,
Her graceful innocence, her every air
Of gesture or least action overawed   460
His malice, and with rapine sweet bereaved
His fierceness of the fierce intent it brought.
That space the Evil One abstracted stood
From his own evil, and for the time remained
Stupidly good,° of enmity disarmed,
Of guile, of hate, of envy, of revenge;
But the hot hell that always in him burns,
Though in mid Heaven, soon ended his delight,
And tortures him now more, the more he sees
Of pleasure not for him ordained; then soon   470
Fierce hate he recollects, and all his thoughts
Of mischief, gratulating,° thus excites:
  " Thoughts, whither have ye led me, with what
    sweet

Compulsion thus transported to forget
What hither brought us? hate, not love, nor hope
Of Paradise for Hell, hope here to taste
Of pleasure, but all pleasure to destroy,
Save what is in destroying; other joy
To me is lost. Then let me not let pass
Occasion which now smiles: behold alone   480
The woman, opportune to all attempts,
Her husband, for I view far round, not nigh,
Whose higher intellectual more I shun,
And strength, of courage haughty, and of limb
Heroic built, though of terrestrial mold,
Foe not informidable, exempt from wound,°
I not; so much hath Hell debased, and pain
Enfeebled me, to what I was in Heaven.
She fair, divinely fair, fit love for gods,
Not terrible, though terror be in love   490
And beauty,° not° approached by stronger hate,
Hate stronger, under show of love well feigned,
The way which to her ruin now I tend."
  So spake the Enemy of mankind, enclosed
In serpent, inmate bad, and toward Eve
Addressed his way, not with indented wave,
Prone on the ground, as since, but on his rear,
Circular base of rising folds, that towered
Fold above fold a surging maze; his head
Crested aloft, and carbuncle° his eyes;   500
With burnished neck of verdant gold, erect
Amidst his circling spires,° that on the grass
Floated redundant. Pleasing was his shape,
And lovely, never since of serpent kind
Lovelier; not those that in Illyria changed
Hermione and Cadmus,° or the god
In Epidaurus;° nor to which transformed
Ammonian Jove,° or Capitoline was seen,
He with Olympias, this with her who bore
Scipio, the highth of Rome.° With tract° oblique
At first, as one who sought access, but feared   511
To interrupt, sidelong he works his way.
As when a ship by skillful steersman wrought
Nigh river's mouth or foreland, where the wind
Veers oft, as oft so steers, and shifts her sail,
So varied he, and of his tortuous train
Curled many a wanton wreath in sight of Eve,
To lure her eye; she busied heard the sound

431. mindless: heedless.   436. voluble: rolling.   437. arborets: shrubs.   438. Imbordered: planted in the form of borders. hand: handiwork.   439–40. gardens . . . Adonis: Milton may be thinking of such descriptions as Spenser's (*Faerie Queene*, III. vi). Cf. *Comus*, 998 f.   440. Or: either.   441. Alcinous: king of Phaeacia, who entertained Odysseus and who had a miraculous garden (*Odyssey*, VII. 112 f.).   442. not mystic: actual, not mythical or allegorical like the preceding.   442–43. sapient king . . . spouse: Solomon married Pharaoh's daughter (I Kings 3:1; Song of Sol. 7:1).   446. annoy: pollute. 450. tedded: spread out to dry.   453. for her: because of her. 454. sums: comprises, completes.   456. plat: plot.   465. Stupidly good: Satan is incapable of positive good, but for the moment his evil nature is blunted.   472 gratulating: rejoicing.

486. exempt . . . wound: See l. 283.   490–91. though . . . beauty: Although put in the mouth of Satan, the idea is a potent indication of Milton's sensuous intensity.   491. not: if not, unless.   500. carbuncle: deep red.   502. spires: coils.   505–06. changed . . . Cadmus: those that Hermione (more commonly Harmonia) and Cadmus became, when metamorphosed at their own desire.   506–07. god . . . Epidaurus: Aesculapius, god of medicine, whose chief shrine was at Epidaurus and who appeared in serpent form.   508–09. Plutarch records the legend that Jupiter Ammon (see IV. 275–79n.) was the father of Alexander the Great by Olympias, the queen of Philip of Macedon. 508–10. Capitoline . . . Rome: according to the tale that Scipio Africanus, the conqueror of Hannibal, was the son of Sempronia and Jupiter (called Capitoline from his temple on the Capitoline hill).   510. tract: course.

Of rustling leaves, but minded not, as used
To such disport before her through the field   520
From every beast, more duteous at her call
Than at Circean call the herd disguised.°
He bolder now, uncalled before her stood,
But as in gaze admiring. Oft he bowed
His turret crest, and sleek enameled neck,
Fawning, and licked the ground whereon she trod.
His gentle dumb expression turned at length
The eye of Eve to mark his play; he glad
Of her attention gained, with serpent tongue
Organic, or impulse of vocal air,°   530
His fraudulent temptation thus began:
    "Wonder° not, sovran mistress, if perhaps
Thou canst, who art sole wonder, much less arm
Thy looks, the heaven of mildness, with disdain,
Displeased that I approach thee thus, and gaze
Insatiate, I thus single, nor have feared
Thy awful brow, more awful thus retired.
Fairest resemblance of thy Maker fair,
Thee all things living gaze on, all things thine
By gift, and thy celestial beauty adore,   540
With ravishment beheld, there best beheld
Where universally admired; but here
In this enclosure wild, these beasts among,
Beholders rude, and shallow to discern
Half what in thee is fair, one man except,
Who sees thee? (and what is one?) who shouldst be
    seen
A goddess among gods, adored and served
By angels numberless, thy daily train."
    So glozed° the Tempter, and his proem tuned;
Into the heart of Eve his words made way,   550
Though at the voice much marveling; at length
Not unamazed she thus in answer spake:
    "What may this mean? Language of man pro-
    nounced
By tongue of brute, and human sense expressed?
The first at least of these I thought denied
To beasts, whom God on their creation-day
Created mute to all articulate sound;
The latter I demur,° for in their looks
Much reason, and in their actions, oft appears.
Thee, Serpent, subtlest beast of all the field   560
I knew, but not with human voice endued;
Redouble then this miracle, and say,
How cam'st thou speakable of° mute, and how
To me so friendly grown above the rest
Of brutal kind, that daily are in sight?
Say, for such wonder claims attention due."
    To whom the guileful Tempter thus replied:

"Empress of this fair World, resplendent Eve,
Easy to me it is to tell thee all
What thou command'st, and right thou shouldst be
    obeyed.   570
I was at first as other beasts that graze
The trodden herb, of abject thoughts and low,
As was my food, nor aught but food discerned
Or sex, and apprehended nothing high:
Till on a day roving the field, I chanced
A goodly tree far distant to behold,
Loaden with fruit of fairest colors mixed,
Ruddy and gold. I nearer drew to gaze;
When from the boughs a savory odor blown,
Grateful to appetite, more pleased my sense   580
Than smell of sweetest fennel, or the teats
Of ewe or goat dropping with milk at even,°
Unsucked of lamb or kid, that tend their play.
To satisfy the sharp desire I had
Of tasting those fair apples, I resolved
Not to defer; hunger and thirst at once,
Powerful persuaders, quickened at the scent
Of that alluring fruit, urged me so keen.
About the mossy trunk I wound me soon,
For high from ground the branches would require
Thy utmost reach or Adam's: round the tree   591
All other beasts that saw, with like desire
Longing and envying stood, but could not reach.
Amid the tree now got, where plenty hung
Tempting so nigh, to pluck and eat my fill
I spared not, for such pleasure till that hour
At feed or fountain never had I found.
Sated at length, ere long I might perceive
Strange alteration in me, to degree
Of reason in my inward powers, and speech   600
Wanted not long, though to this shape retained.
Thenceforth to speculations high or deep
I turned my thoughts, and with capacious mind
Considered all things visible in Heaven,
Or Earth, or middle,° all things fair and good;
But all that fair and good in thy divine
Semblance, and in thy beauty's heavenly ray,
United I beheld; no fair° to thine
Equivalent or second, which compelled
Me thus, though importune perhaps, to come   610
And gaze, and worship thee of right declared
Sovran of creatures, universal dame."°
    So talked the spirited° sly Snake; and Eve
Yet more amazed unwary thus replied:
    "Serpent, thy overpraising leaves in doubt
The virtue of that fruit, in thee first proved.
But say, where grows the tree, from hence how far?
For many are the trees of God that grow
In Paradise, and various, yet unknown

521–22. more . . . disguised: more ready obedience than that of the men Circe transformed into beasts.   **530. Organic . . . air:** by the use of speech organs or producing the effect of speech through vibration of the air.   **532–48. Wonder . . . train:** Satan, in the manner of an amatory poet, appeals to Eve's vanity.   **549. glozed:** flattered.   **558. The . . . demur:** I am doubtful if reason is denied to beasts.   **563. of:** from being.

581–82. fennel . . . even: In popular lore snakes were said to be fond of fennel and to suck the teats of sheep and goats.   **605. middle:** the air.   **608. fair:** fairness, beauty.   **612. dame:** mistress.   **613. spirited:** inspired (by Satan).

To us; in such abundance lies our choice   620
As leaves a greater store of fruit untouched,
Still hanging incorruptible, till men
Grow up to their provision,° and more hands
Help to disburden Nature of her birth."°
    To whom the wily Adder, blithe and glad:
"Empress, the way is ready, and not long,
Beyond a row of myrtles, on a flat,
Fast by a fountain, one small thicket past
Of blowing° myrrh and balm; if thou accept
My conduct, I can bring thee thither soon."   630
    "Lead then," said Eve. He leading swiftly rolled
In tangles, and made intricate seem straight,
To mischief swift. Hope elevates, and joy
Brightens his crest, as when a wandering fire,°
Compact of unctuous° vapor, which the night
Condenses, and the cold environs round,
Kindled through agitation to a flame,
Which oft, they say, some evil spirit attends,
Hovering and blazing with delusive light,   639
Misleads the amazed night-wanderer from his way
To bogs and mires, and oft through pond or pool,
There swallowed up and lost, from succor far.
So glistered the dire Snake, and into fraud
Led Eve our credulous mother, to the tree
Of prohibition, root of all our woe;
Which when she saw, thus to her guide she spake:
    "Serpent, we might have spared our coming
            hither,
Fruitless to me, though fruit be here to excess,
The credit of whose virtue rest with thee,
Wondrous indeed, if cause of such effects.   650
But of this tree we may not taste nor touch;
God so commanded, and left that command
Sole daughter of his voice; the rest,° we live
Law to ourselves, our reason is our law."
    To whom the Tempter guilefully replied:
"Indeed? Hath God then said that of the fruit
Of all these garden trees ye shall not eat,
Yet lords declared of all in Earth or air?"
    To whom thus Eve yet sinless: "Of the fruit
Of each tree in the garden we may eat,   660
But of the fruit of this fair tree amidst
The garden, God hath said, 'Ye shall not eat
Thereof, nor shall ye touch it, lest ye die.'"
    She scarce had said, though brief, when now
            more bold
The Tempter, but with show of zeal and love
To man, and indignation at his wrong,
New part puts on,° and as to passion moved,
Fluctuates disturbed, yet comely, and in act
Raised, as of some great matter to begin.

As when of old some orator renowned   670
In Athens or free Rome, where eloquence
Flourished, since mute, to some great cause ad-
            dressed,
Stood in himself collected, while each part,°
Motion, each act won audience° ere the tongue,
Sometimes in highth° began, as no delay
Of preface brooking through his zeal of right:
So standing, moving, or to highth upgrown,
The Tempter all impassioned thus began:
    "O sacred, wise, and wisdom-giving Plant,
Mother of science,° now I feel thy power   680
Within me clear, not only to discern
Things in their causes, but to trace the ways
Of highest agents, deemed however wise.
Queen of this universe, do not believe
Those rigid threats of death; ye shall not die:
How should ye? by the fruit? it gives you life
To° knowledge; by the Threatener? look on me,
Me who have touched and tasted, yet both live,
And life more perfect have attained than Fate
Meant me, by venturing higher than my lot.   690
Shall that be shut to man, which to the beast
Is open? or will God incense° his ire
For such a petty trespass, and not praise
Rather your dauntless virtue, whom the pain
Of death denounced,° whatever thing death be,
Deterred not from achieving what might lead
To happier life, knowledge of good and evil?
Of good, how just? of evil, if what is evil
Be real, why not known, since easier shunned?
God therefore cannot hurt ye, and be just;   700
Not just, not God; not feared then, nor obeyed:
Your fear itself of death removes the fear.
Why then was this forbid? Why but to awe,
Why but to keep ye low and ignorant,
His worshipers? he knows that in the day
Ye eat thereof, your eyes that seem so clear,
Yet are but dim, shall perfectly be then
Opened and cleared, and ye shall be as gods,°
Knowing both good and evil as they know.
That ye should be as gods, since I as man,   710
Internal man,° is but proportion meet,
I of brute human, ye of human gods.
So ye shall die perhaps, by putting off
Human, to put on gods,° death to be wished,
Though threatened, which no worse than this can
            bring.
And what are gods that man may not become
As they, participating godlike food?

---

623. Grow . . . provision: multiply in proportion to the fruit provided.   624. birth (spelled *bearth* by Milton): the fruit Nature bears.   629. blowing: blossoming.   634. wandering fire: will-o'-the-wisp.   635. Compact of unctuous: composed of oily.   653. the rest: with respect to the rest.   667. New . . . on: assumes a new role, that of sympathy with man.

673. part: of his body.   674. audience: attention.   675. highth: of the subject and of feeling.   680. science: knowledge. 687. To: as well as.   692. incense: kindle.   695. denounced: ordained, threatened.   708. ye . . . gods: Satan is carrying out his original plan. Cf. IV. 522–26, V. 70, IX. 547 (the first and last of these passages are in this book).   711. Internal man: a man in mental powers.   713–14. by . . . gods: rising from the human to a godlike state — a perverting of St. Paul's phrase for religious conversion, putting off the old man and putting on the new.

The gods are first, and that advantage use
On our belief, that all from them proceeds;
I question it, for this fair Earth I see,   720
Warmed by the sun, producing every kind,
Them nothing. If they° all things, who enclosed
Knowledge of good and evil in this tree,
That whoso eats thereof, forthwith attains
Wisdom without their leave? and wherein lies
The offense, that man should thus attain to know?
What can your knowledge hurt him, or this tree
Impart against his will, if all be his?
Or is it envy, and can envy dwell
In heavenly breasts?° These, these and many more
Causes import° your need of this fair fruit.   731
Goddess humane,° reach then, and freely taste!"
   He ended, and his words replete with guile
Into her heart too easy entrance won.
Fixed on the fruit she gazed, which to behold
Might tempt alone, and in her ears the sound
Yet rung of his persuasive words, impregned°
With reason, to her seeming, and with truth;
Meanwhile the hour of noon drew on, and waked
An eager appetite, raised by the smell   740
So savory of that fruit, which with desire,
Inclinable now grown to touch or taste,
Solicited her longing eye; yet first
Pausing a while, thus to herself she mused:
   "Great are thy virtues, doubtless, best of fruits,
Though kept from man, and worthy to be admired,
Whose taste, too long forborne, at first assay°
Gave elocution to the mute, and taught
The tongue not made for speech to speak thy praise.
Thy praise he also who forbids thy use   750
Conceals not from us, naming thee the Tree
Of Knowledge, knowledge both of good and evil;
Forbids us then to taste, but his forbidding
Commends thee more, while it infers° the good
By thee communicated, and our want;
For good unknown sure is not had, or had
And yet unknown, is as not had at all.
In plain° then, what forbids he but to know,
Forbids us good, forbids us to be wise?
Such prohibitions bind not. But if Death   760
Bind us with after-bands, what profits then
Our inward freedom? In the day we eat
Of this fair fruit, our doom is, we shall die.
How dies the Serpent? He hath eaten and lives,
And knows, and speaks, and reasons, and discerns,
Irrational till then. For us alone
Was death invented? or to us denied
This intellectual food, for beasts reserved?
For beasts it seems; yet that one beast which first
Hath tasted, envies not, but brings with joy   770

The good befallen him, author unsuspect,°
Friendly to man, far from deceit or guile.
What fear I then, rather what know to fear
Under this ignorance of good and evil,
Of God or death, of law or penalty?
Here grows the cure of all, this fruit divine,
Fair to the eye, inviting to the taste,
Of virtue to make wise; what hinders then
To reach, and feed at once both body and mind?"
   So saying, her rash hand in evil hour   780
Forth reaching to the fruit, she plucked, she eat.°
Earth felt the wound, and Nature from her seat
Sighing through all her works gave signs of woe,
That all was lost.° Back to the thicket slunk
The guilty Serpent, and well might, for Eve
Intent now wholly on her taste, nought else
Regarded; such delight till then, as seemed,
In fruit she never tasted, whether true
Or fancied so, through expectation high
Of knowledge, nor was Godhead° from her
       thought.   790
Greedily she engorged without restraint,
And knew not eating death.° Satiate at length,
And heightened as with wine, jocund and boon,°
Thus to herself she pleasingly began:
   "O sovran,° virtuous, precious of all trees
In Paradise, of operation blest
To sapience,° hitherto obscured, infamed,°
And thy fair fruit let hang, as to no end
Created; but henceforth my early care,
Not without song, each morning, and due praise,°
Shall tend thee, and the fertile burden ease   801
Of thy full branches offered free to all;
Till dieted by thee I grow mature
In knowledge, as the gods who all things know;
Though others° envy what they cannot give;
For had the gift been theirs, it had not here
Thus grown. Experience, next to thee I owe,
Best guide; not following thee, I had remained
In ignorance; thou open'st wisdom's way,
And giv'st access, though secret she retire.   810
And I perhaps am secret; Heaven is high,
High and remote to see from thence distinct
Each thing on Earth; and other care perhaps
May have diverted from continual watch
Our great Forbidder, safe° with all his spies
About him. But to Adam in what sort

771. author unsuspect: the serpent, whose authority is not to be
doubted — a sample of the reasoning of the "unwary" Eve.
781. eat: the past tense (pronounced *et*).   782–84. Earth . . .
lost: The divine order of Nature has been violated.   790. Godhead: In this and later passages Milton suggests the Greek
tragic sin of *hubris*, infatuated, irreligious self-sufficiency and
pride.   792. knew . . . death: knew not that she was eating
death — in contrast with the angels who "Quaff immortality
and joy" (V. 638).   793. boon: blithe.   795. sovran: most
sovereign.   796–97. of . . . sapience: having the power to confer
wisdom.   797. infamed: defamed.   800. Not . . . praise: In
Eve's mind the tree has replaced God. Cf. l. 835.   805. others:
gods (Eve is recalling Satan's assertion in l. 718 f.).   815. safe:
not dangerous.

722. If they: if they produced.   729–30. can . . . breasts: Cf.
Virgil, *Aeneid*, I. 11.   731. import: prove.   732. humane: gracious.   737. impregned: impregnated.   747. assay: trial.
754. infers: implies.   758. In plain: in plain terms.

Shall I appear? Shall I to him make known
As yet my change, and give him to partake
Full happiness with me, or rather not,
But keep the odds of knowledge in my power   820
Without copartner? so to add what wants
In female sex, the more to draw his love,
And render me more equal, and perhaps,
A thing not undesirable, sometime
Superior; for inferior who is free?°
This may be well. But what if God have seen,
And death ensue? then I shall be no more,
And Adam wedded to another Eve,
Shall live with her enjoying, I extinct;
A death to think. Confirmed then I resolve,   830
Adam shall share with me in bliss or woe.
So dear I love him, that with him all deaths
I could endure, without him live no life."
    So saying, from the tree her step she turned,
But first low reverence done, as to the power
That dwelt within, whose presence had infused
Into the plant sciential° sap, derived
From nectar, drink of gods. Adam the while,
Waiting desirous her return, had wove
Of choicest flowers a garland to adorn   840
Her tresses, and her rural labors crown,
As reapers oft are wont their harvest queen.
Great joy he promised to his thoughts, and new
Solace in her return, so long delayed;
Yet oft his heart, divine of° something ill,
Misgave him; he the faltering measure° felt;
And forth to meet her went, the way she took
That morn when first they parted. By the Tree
Of Knowledge he must pass; there he her met,
Scarce from the tree returning; in her hand   850
A bough of fairest fruit that downy smiled,
New gathered, and ambrosial smell diffused.
To him she hasted; in her face excuse
Came prologue, and apology to prompt,°
Which with bland words at will she thus addressed:
    "Hast thou not wondered, Adam, at my stay?
Thee I have missed, and thought it long,° deprived
Thy presence, agony of love till now
Not felt, nor shall be twice, for never more
Mean I to try what rash untried I sought,°   860
The pain of absence from thy sight. But strange
Hath been the cause, and wonderful to hear:
This tree is not as we are told, a tree
Of danger tasted,° nor to evil unknown
Opening the way, but of divine effect
To open eyes, and make them gods who taste;
And hath been tasted° such. The Serpent wise,

Or not restrained as we, or not obeying,
Hath eaten of the fruit, and is become
Not dead, as we are threatened, but thenceforth
Endued with human voice and human sense,   871
Reasoning to° admiration, and with me
Persuasively hath so prevailed, that I
Have also tasted, and have also found
The effects to correspond, opener mine eyes,
Dim erst, dilated spirits, ampler heart,
And growing up to Godhead; which for thee
Chiefly I sought,° without thee can despise.
For bliss, as thou hast part, to me is bliss;
Tedious, unshared with thee, and odious soon.   880
Thou therefore also taste, that equal lot
May join us, equal joy, as equal love;
Lest thou not tasting, different degree
Disjoin us, and I then too late renounce°
Deity for thee, when Fate will not permit."
    Thus Eve with countenance blithe° her story
        told;
But in her cheek distemper flushing glowed.
On the other side, Adam, soon as he heard
The fatal trespass done by Eve, amazed,
Astonied° stood and blank, while horror chill   890
Ran through his veins, and all his joints relaxed;
From his slack hand the garland wreathed for Eve
Down dropped, and all the faded roses shed.
Speechless he stood and pale, till thus at length
First to himself he inward silence broke:
    "O fairest of creation, last and best
Of all God's works, creature in whom excelled
Whatever can to sight or thought be formed,
Holy, divine, good, amiable, or sweet!
How art thou lost, how on a sudden lost,   900
Defaced, deflowered, and now to death devote!°
Rather how hast thou yielded to transgress
The strict forbiddance, how to violate
The sacred fruit forbidden! Some cursèd fraud
Of enemy hath beguiled thee, yet unknown,
And me with thee hath ruined, for with thee
Certain my resolution is to die;
How can I live without thee, how forgo
Thy sweet converse and love so dearly joined,
To live again in these wild woods forlorn?°   910
Should God create another Eve, and I
Another rib afford, yet loss of thee
Would never from my heart; no, no! I feel
The link of nature draw me: flesh of flesh,
Bone of my bone thou art,° and from thy state
Mine never shall be parted, bliss or woe."
    So having said, as one from sad dismay

825. for . . . free: the corrupted Eve now holds Satan's false
view of freedom.   837. sciential: conferring knowledge.
845. divine of: divining, foreseeing.   846. faltering measure:
irregular beat.   853–54. in . . . prompt: Her expression was a
prologue to the defense she was about to make.   857. Thee . . .
long: Eve's new knowledge seems to be the art of lying.
860. what . . . sought: what, untried, I rashly sought.
864. tasted: if tasted.   867. tasted such: found such by tasting.

872. to: so as to arouse.   877–78. which . . . sought: another
fib.   884. renounce: try to renounce.   886. blithe: an epithet
that sums up Eve's terrible unawareness of what she has done.
890. Astonied: astounded.   901. devote: doomed.   908–
10. How . . . forlorn: a poignant utterance, especially in the sudden vision of Paradise, without Eve, as "these wild woods forlorn."   914–15. flesh . . . art: See Gen. 2:23.

Recomforted, and after thoughts disturbed
Submitting to what seemed remediless,
Thus in calm mood his words to Eve he turned:
  "Bold deed thou hast presumed, adventurous
    Eve,   921
And peril great provoked, who thus hast dared,
Had it been only coveting to eye
That sacred fruit, sacred to abstinence,
Much more to taste it under ban to touch.
But past who can recall, or done undo?
Not God omnipotent, nor Fate. Yet so
Perhaps thou shalt not die; perhaps the fact°
Is not so heinous now, foretasted fruit,°
Profaned first by the Serpent, by him first   930
Made common and unhallowed ere our taste,
Nor yet on him found deadly; he yet lives,
Lives, as thou saidst, and gains to live as man
Higher degree of life, inducement strong
To us, as likely, tasting, to attain
Proportional ascent, which cannot be
But to be gods, or angels, demi-gods.°
Nor can I think that God, Creator wise,
Though threatening, will in earnest so destroy
Us his prime creatures, dignified so high,   940
Set over all his works, which in our fall,
For us created, needs with us must fail,
Dependent made; so God shall uncreate,
Be frustrate, do, undo, and labor lose,
Not well conceived of God,° who though his power
Creation could repeat, yet would be loth
Us to abolish, lest the Adversary
Triumph and say: 'Fickle their state whom God
Most favors, who can please him long? Me first
He ruined, now mankind; whom will he next?'
Matter of scorn not to be given the Foe;   951
However, I with thee have fixed my lot,
Certain to undergo like doom: if death
Consort with thee, death is to me as life;
So forcible within my heart I feel
The bond of nature draw me to my own,
My own in thee, for what thou art is mine;
Our state cannot be severed; we are one,
One flesh; to lose thee were to lose myself."
  So Adam, and thus Eve to him replied: 960
"O glorious trial of exceeding love,°
Illustrious evidence, example high!
Engaging me to emulate, but short
Of thy perfection, how shall I attain,
Adam? from whose dear side I boast me sprung,
And gladly of our union hear thee speak,
One heart, one soul in both; whereof good proof
This day affords, declaring thee resolved,

Rather than death or aught than death more dread
Shall separate us, linked in love so dear,   970
To undergo with me one guilt, one crime,
If any be, of tasting this fair fruit,
Whose virtue (for of good still good proceeds,
Direct, or by occasion) hath presented
This happy trial of thy love, which else
So eminently never had been known.
Were it I thought death menaced would ensue
This my attempt, I would sustain alone
The worst, and not persuade thee, rather die
Deserted, than oblige° thee with a fact   980
Pernicious to thy peace, chiefly assured
Remarkably so late of thy so true,
So faithful love unequaled; but I feel
Far otherwise the event, not death, but life
Augmented, opened eyes, new hopes, new joys,
Taste so divine, that what of sweet before
Hath touched my sense, flat seems to this and harsh.
On my experience, Adam, freely taste,
And fear of death deliver to the winds."
  So saying, she embraced him, and for joy   990
Tenderly wept, much won that he his love
Had so ennobled, as of choice to incur
Divine displeasure for her sake, or death.
In recompense (for such compliance bad
Such recompense best merits) from the bough
She gave him of that fair enticing fruit
With liberal hand. He scrupled not to eat
Against his better knowledge, not deceived,
But fondly overcome with female charm.°
Earth trembled from her entrails, as again   1000
In pangs, and Nature gave a second groan;
Sky loured, and, muttering thunder, some sad drops
Wept at completing of the mortal sin
Original; while Adam took no thought,
Eating his fill, nor Eve to iterate
Her former trespass feared, the more to soothe
Him with her loved society, that now
As with new wine intoxicated both
They swim in mirth, and fancy that they feel
Divinity within them breeding wings   1010
Wherewith to scorn the Earth. But that false fruit
Far other operation first displayed,
Carnal desire inflaming: he on Eve
Began to cast lascivious eyes, she him
As wantonly repaid; in lust they burn,
Till Adam thus 'gan Eve to dalliance move:
  "Eve, now I see thou art exact° of taste,°
And elegant, of sapience no small part;
Since to each meaning savor we apply,
And palate call judicious; I the praise   1020

928. fact: deed.   929. foretasted fruit: the fruit having been
tasted already.   934-37. Higher . . . demi-gods: Adam now
shares the motive of pride.   945. Not . . . God: not a fitting
conception of God.   961. O . . . love: The words suggest
Christ's selfless love for man and hence an ironic contrast with
Eve's and Adam's inadequate conception of love.

980. oblige: involve.   998-99. Against . . . charm: Unlike Eve,
whose inferior reason was deceived, Adam knows what he is
doing, but his will is overswayed by his devotion to Eve. See
the summary of Book VIII, above.   1017. exact: refined.
1017-20. taste . . . judicious: Adam is playing on the double
meaning of "taste" and "savor" as applied to both the mind
and the palate (the Latin sapere means both).

Yield thee, so well this day thou hast purveyed.
Much pleasure we have lost, while we abstained
From this delightful fruit, nor known till now
True relish, tasting; if such pleasure be
In things to us forbidden, it might be wished
For this one tree had been forbidden ten.
But come, so well refreshed, now let us play,
As meet is, after such delicious fare;
For never did thy beauty since the day
I saw thee first and wedded thee, adorned   1030
With all perfections, so inflame my sense
With ardor to enjoy thee,° fairer now
Than ever, bounty of this virtuous tree."
    So said he, and forbore not glance or toy°
Of amorous intent, well understood
Of Eve, whose eye darted contagious fire.
Her hand he seized, and to a shady bank,
Thick overhead with verdant roof embowered,
He led her nothing loth; flowers were the couch,
Pansies, and violets, and asphodel,   1040
And hyacinth, Earth's freshest softest lap.
There they their fill of love and love's disport
Took largely, of their mutual guilt the seal,
The solace of their sin, till dewy sleep
Oppressed them, wearied with their amorous play.
Soon as the force of that fallacious fruit,
That with exhilarating vapor bland
About their spirits had played, and inmost powers
Made err, was now exhaled, and grosser sleep,
Bred of unkindly° fumes, with conscious dreams
Encumbered, now had left them, up they rose
As from unrest, and each the other viewing,   1052
Soon found their eyes how opened, and their minds
How darkened; innocence, that as a veil
Had shadowed them from knowing ill, was gone;
Just confidence, and native righteousness,
And honor from about them, naked left
To guilty Shame; he° covered, but his robe
Uncovered more. So rose the Danite° strong,
Herculean Samson, from the harlot-lap   1060
Of Philistean Dálilah, and waked
Shorn of his strength, they destitute and bare
Of all their virtue. Silent, and in face
Confounded, long they sat, as strucken mute,
Till Adam, though not less than Eve abashed,
At length gave utterance to these words constrained:
    "O Eve, in evil hour thou didst give ear
To that false worm,° of whomsoever taught
To counterfeit man's voice, true in our fall,
False in our promised rising; since our eyes   1070

Opened we find indeed, and find we know
Both good and evil, good lost and evil got,
Bad fruit of knowledge, if this be to know,
Which leaves us naked thus, of honor void,
Of innocence, of faith, of purity,
Our wonted ornaments now soiled and stained,
And in our faces evident the signs
Of foul concupiscence; whence evil store,°
Even shame, the last° of evils; of the first°
Be sure then. How shall I behold the face   1080
Henceforth of God or angel, erst with joy
And rapture so oft beheld? those heavenly shapes
Will dazzle now this earthly, with their blaze
Insufferably bright. O might I here
In solitude live savage, in some glade
Obscured, where highest woods impenetrable
To star or sunlight, spread their umbrage broad,
And brown° as evening! Cover me, ye pines,
Ye cedars, with innumerable boughs
Hide me, where I may never see them more.°
But let us now, as in bad plight, devise   1091
What best may for the present serve to hide
The parts of each from other that seem most
To shame obnoxious,° and unseemliest seen,
Some tree whose broad smooth leaves together
    sewed,
And girded on our loins, may cover round
Those middle parts, that this newcomer, Shame,
There sit not, and reproach us as unclean."
    So counseled he, and both together went   1099
Into the thickest wood; there soon they chose
The fig-tree,° not that kind for fruit renowned,
But such as at this day to Indians known
In Malabar° or Deccan° spreads her arms
Branching so broad and long, that in the ground
The bended twigs take root, and daughters grow
About the mother tree, a pillared shade
High overarched, and echoing walks between;
There oft the Indian herdsman shunning heat
Shelters in cool, and tends his pasturing herds
At loopholes cut through thickest shade. Those
    leaves   1110
They gathered, broad as Amazonian targe,°
And with what skill they had, together sewed,
To gird their waist, vain covering if to hide
Their guilt and dreaded shame, O° how unlike
To that first naked glory! Such of late
Columbus found the American, so girt
With feathered cincture, naked else and wild
Among the trees on isles and woody shores.

1078. evil store: a store of evil.   1079. last: worst.   first:
lesser.   1088. brown: dark.   1088-90. Cover ... more: See
Rev. 6:16.   1094. obnoxious: liable.   1101. fig-tree: the ban-
yan.   1103. Malabar: the southwestern coast of India.   Dec-
can: the whole peninsula of India.   1111. Amazonian targe: the
crescent-shaped shield of the Amazons, the warrior women of
classical myth.   1114-18. O ... shores: The allusions to India
and America suggest that the king and queen of the earth have
become primitive savages.

1029-32. For ... thee: Adam's words recall two amorous scenes
in the *Iliad*, between Paris and Helen (III. 441-47) and Zeus
and Hera (XIV. 292-353). His horrible mixture of levity and lust
is completed by such a phrase as "enjoy thee," which degrades
both Eve and himself so far below their former state.   1034. toy:
caress.   1050. unkindly: unnatural.   1058. he: Shame.   1059-
62. Danite ... strength: See Judg. 16:4-20 and Milton's *Samson*,
ll. 710-996.   1068. worm: serpent.

Thus fenced, and as they thought, their shame in part
Covered, but not at rest or ease of mind,   1120
They sat them down to weep; nor only tears
Rained at their eyes, but high winds worse within
Began to rise, high passions, anger, hate,
Mistrust, suspicion, discord, and shook sore
Their inward state of mind, calm region once
And full of peace, now tossed and turbulent;
For° understanding ruled not, and the will
Heard not her lore, both in subjection now
To sensual appetite, who from beneath
Usurping over sovran reason claimed   1130
Superior sway. From thus distempered breast,
Adam, estranged in look and altered style,
Speech intermitted thus to Eve renewed:
    " Would thou hadst hearkened to my words, and
         stayed
With me, as I besought thee, when that strange
Desire of wandering, this unhappy morn,
I know not whence possessed thee; we had then
Remained still happy, not as now, despoiled
Of all our good, shamed, naked, miserable.
Let none henceforth seek needless cause to ap-
         prove°   1140
The faith they owe;° when earnestly they seek
Such proof, conclude they then begin to fail."
    To whom, soon moved with touch of blame, thus
         Eve:
" What words have passed thy lips, Adam severe!
Imput'st thou that to my default, or will
Of wandering, as thou call'st it, which who knows
But might as ill have happened thou being by,
Or to thyself perhaps? Hadst thou been there,
Or here the attempt, thou couldst not have dis-
         cerned
Fraud in the Serpent, speaking as he spake;   1150
No ground of enmity between us known
Why he should mean me ill, or seek to harm.
Was I to have never parted from thy side?
As good have grown there still a lifeless rib.
Being as I am, why didst not thou, the head,°
Command me absolutely not to go,
Going into such danger as thou saidst?
Too facile then, thou didst not much gainsay,
Nay didst permit, approve, and fair dismiss.   1159
Hadst thou been firm and fixed in thy dissent,
Neither had I transgressed, nor thou with me."
    To whom then first incensed Adam replied:
" Is this the love, is this the recompense
Of mine to thee, ingrateful Eve, expressed
Immutable° when thou wert lost, not I,

Who might have lived and joyed immortal bliss,
Yet willingly chose rather death with thee?
And am I now upbraided, as the cause
Of thy transgressing? not enough severe,
It seems, in thy restraint. What could I more?
I warned thee, I admonished thee, foretold   1171
The danger, and the lurking enemy
That lay in wait; beyond this had been force,
And force upon free will hath here no place.
But confidence then bore thee on, secure°
Either to meet no danger, or to find
Matter of glorious trial; and perhaps
I also erred in overmuch admiring
What seemed in thee so perfect, that I thought
No evil durst attempt thee, but I rue   1180
That error now, which is become my crime,
And thou the accuser. Thus it shall befall
Him who to worth in women overtrusting
Lets her will rule; restraint she will not brook,
And left to herself, if evil thence ensue,
She first his weak indulgence will accuse."
    Thus they in mutual accusation spent
The fruitless hours, but neither self-condemning,
And of their vain contést appeared no end.

BOOK X

[The Son is sent down to pronounce judgment on the guilty pair. Sin and Death build a bridge from Hell to the new world and show it to Satan on his return to Hell. Satan reports to his followers his success, but, in the moment of applause, they all turn into hissing serpents. On earth, the eternal spring of Paradise gives place to heat and cold, and beasts prey on one another; the golden age is over. Adam, outstretched on the cold ground, in a long soliloquy reproaches God for setting impossible conditions, but finally blames himself, and longs for death. When Eve appears, he denounces her bitterly, but he is softened by her remorseful entreaty, and the two are reunited in unselfish love. Eve proposes that they blunt the judgment pronounced on their posterity either by refraining from having children or by killing themselves; but Adam feels that the only remedy is in penitent confession, in the hope of pardon from their compassionate judge. They confess their sin and pray for mercy.]

BOOK XI

[Although Adam and Eve have lost happiness and immortality, God declares that Heaven will still be open to them after a life of trial, and death; he sends Michael down to expel them from Paradise and to unfold to Adam the course of history. Adam and Eve, while feeling new peace and hope after their prayers, are stricken by the sentence Michael delivers. Michael assures them that God is everywhere and will compass them round with goodness and paternal love. Then — after the pattern of the *Aeneid* (Book VI) and stories of the Fall — Michael takes Adam to the top of a hill and shows him, in a series of visions, the history of his descendants, from Cain's murder of Abel to God's covenant with man after the flood. The theme of all these episodes is " supernal grace contending / With sinfulness of men."]

1127–31. For . . . sway: The natural order and sway of the superior faculties have been reversed.   1140. approve: prove, test (cf. ll. 335–36, 367).   1141. owe: own.   1155. head: Eve uses the word in a very different spirit from that of IV. 443. 1164–65. expressed Immutable: shown to be unchangeable (ll. 906–16, 952–59).

1175. secure: rashly confident.

from BOOK XII

[Michael continues his revelation of the future, now in the form of narrative. The story of Moses leads to an exposition of the doctrine of "Christian liberty." Then Michael tells of the birth and crucifixion of Christ, who shall redeem man from the sin of Adam and thus defeat Satan and Sin and Death, and who, at the end of the world, shall return to judge mankind and receive the faithful into bliss far happier than that of Eden.]

So spake the Archangel Michaël, then paused,
As at the World's great period;° and our sire
Replete with joy and wonder thus replied:
  "O goodness° infinite, goodness immense!
That all this good of evil shall produce,   470
And evil turn to good; more wonderful
Than that which by creation first brought forth
Light out of darkness! full of doubt I stand,
Whether I should repent me now of sin
By me done and occasioned, or rejoice
Much more, that much more good thereof shall
      spring,
To God more glory, more good will to men
From God, and over wrath grace shall abound.
But say, if our Deliverer up to Heaven
Must reascend, what will betide the few   480
His faithful, left among the unfaithful herd,
The enemies of truth; who then shall guide
His people, who defend? will they not deal
Worse with his followers than with him they
      dealt?"
  "Be sure they will," said the Angel; "but from
      Heaven
He to his own a Comforter° will send,
The promise of the Father, who shall dwell,
His Spirit, within them, and the law of faith
Working through love, upon their hearts shall
      write,
To guide them in all truth, and also arm   490
With spiritual armor, able to resist
Satan's assaults, and quench his fiery darts,°
What man can do against them, not afraid,
Though to the death, against such cruelties
With inward consolations recompensed,
And oft supported so as shall amaze
Their proudest persecutors. For the Spirit
Poured first on his Apostles, whom he sends
To evangelize the nations, then on all
Baptized, shall them with wondrous gifts endue
To speak all tongues, and do all miracles,   501
As did their Lord before them. Thus they win
Great numbers of each nation to receive

With joy the tidings brought from Heaven: at
      length
Their ministry performed, and race well run,
Their doctrine and their story written left,
They die; but in their room, as they forewarn,
Wolves shall succeed for teachers, grievous wolves,°
Who all the sacred mysteries of Heaven
To their own vile advantages shall turn   510
Of lucre and ambition, and the truth
With superstitions and traditions taint,
Left only in those written records pure,
Though not but by the Spirit understood.
Then shall they seek to avail themselves of names,
Places and titles, and with these to join
Secular power, though feigning still to act
By spiritual, to themselves appropriating
The Spirit of God, promised alike and given
To all believers; and from that pretense,   520
Spiritual laws by carnal power shall force
On every conscience; laws which none shall find
Left them enrolled, or what the Spirit within
Shall on the heart engrave. What will they then
But force the Spirit of Grace itself, and bind
His consort Liberty? what but unbuild
His living temples,° built by faith to stand,
Their own faith, not another's? for on Earth
Who against faith and conscience can be heard
Infallible? yet many will presume: 530
Whence heavy persecution shall arise
On all who in the worship persevere
Of Spirit and Truth; the rest, far greater part,
Will deem in outward rites and·specious forms
Religion satisfied; Truth shall retire
Bestuck with slanderous darts, and works of faith
Rarely be found. So shall the World go on,
To good malignant, to bad men benign,
Under her own weight groaning, till the day
Appear of respiration° to the just,   540
And vengeance to the wicked, at return
Of him so lately promised to thy aid,
The Woman's Seed, obscurely then foretold,
Now amplier known thy Saviour and thy Lord,
Last in the clouds from Heaven to be revealed
In glory of the Father, to dissolve
Satan with his perverted World; then raise
From the conflagrant mass,° purged and refined,
New Heavens, new Earth, ages of endless date
Founded in righteousness and peace and love,   550
To bring forth fruits, joy and eternal bliss."
  He ended; and thus Adam last replied:
  "How soon hath thy prediction, seer blest,

Book XII: 467. period: end. 469–78. goodness . . . abound: The idea of Christ's redemption of man, of the goodness called into action by evil (an idea repeatedly enunciated from the beginning of the poem), is a traditional paradox of theology — *felix culpa*, "the fortunate fall." 486. a Comforter: the Holy Spirit (John 15:26). 491–92. armor . . . darts: The military metaphor is from Eph. 6:11–17.

508. wolves: See Acts 20:29 (and "Lycidas," l. 128). 527. His . . . temples: individual persons (1 Cor. 3:16–17, 6:19). 540. respiration: refreshing. 548. conflagrant mass: the world consumed by fire at the last day. Lines 547–51 are the last of a number of passages (e.g., III. 333–41, VII. 157–61, XI. 898–901) in which Milton's early hope of a speedy reformation on earth is put off to the end of the world.

Measured this transient World, the race of Time,
Till Time stand fixed: beyond is all abyss,
Eternity, whose end no eye can reach.
Greatly instructed I shall hence depart,
Greatly in peace of thought, and have my fill
Of knowledge,° what this vessel° can contain;
Beyond which was my folly to aspire.   560
Henceforth I learn that to obey is best,
And love with fear the only God, to walk
As in his presence, ever to observe
His providence, and on him sole depend,
Merciful over all his works, with good
Still overcoming evil, and by small
Accomplishing great things, by things deemed weak
Subverting worldly strong, and worldly wise
By simply meek; that suffering for truth's sake
Is fortitude to highest victory,   570
And to the faithful death the gate of life;
Taught this by his example whom I now
Acknowledge my Redeemer ever blest."
   To whom thus also the Angel last replied:
"This having learnt, thou hast attained the sum
Of wisdom; hope no higher, though all the stars
Thou knew'st by name, and all the ethereal powers,
All secrets of the deep, all Nature's works,
Or works of God in heaven, air, earth, or sea,
And all the riches of this world enjoy'dst,   580
And all the rule, one empire; only add
Deeds to thy knowledge answerable, add faith,
Add virtue, patience, temperance, add love,
By name to come called charity,° the soul
Of all the rest: then wilt thou not be loth
To leave this Paradise, but shalt possess
A Paradise within thee, happier far.
Let us descend now therefore from this top
Of speculation;° for the hour precise
Exacts our parting hence; and see the guards,   590
By me encamped on yonder hill, expect
Their motion, at whose front a flaming sword,
In signal of remove, waves fiercely round;
We may no longer stay: go, waken Eve;
Her also I with gentle dreams have calmed,
Portending good, and all her spirits composed
To meek submission: thou at season fit
Let her with thee partake what thou hast heard,
Chiefly what may concern her faith to know,
The great deliverance by her seed to come   600
(For by the Woman's Seed) on all mankind:
That ye may live, which will be many days,°

Both in one faith unanimous though sad,
With cause for evils past, yet much more cheered
With meditation on the happy end."
   He ended, and they both descend the hill;
Descended, Adam to the bower where Eve
Lay sleeping ran before, but found her waked;
And thus with words not sad she him received:
   "Whence thou return'st, and whither went'st, I
      know;   610
For God is also in sleep, and dreams advise,
Which he hath sent propitious, some great good
Presaging, since with sorrow and heart's distress
Wearied I fell asleep. But now lead on;°
In me is no delay; with° thee to go,
Is to stay here; without thee here to stay,
Is to go hence unwilling; thou to me
Art all things under Heaven, all places thou,
Who for my willful crime art banished hence.
This further consolation yet secure   620
I carry hence; though all by me is lost,
Such favor I unworthy am vouchsafed,
By me the Promised Seed shall all restore."
   So spake our mother Eve, and Adam heard
Well pleased, but answered not; for now too nigh
The Archangel stood, and from the other hill
To their fixed station, all in bright array
The Cherubim descended; on the ground
Gliding meteorous, as evening mist
Risen from a river o'er the marish° glides,   630
And gathers ground fast at the laborer's heel
Homeward returning. High in front advanced,°
The brandished sword of God before them blazed
Fierce as a comet; which° with torrid heat,
And vapor° as the Libyan air adust,°
Began to parch that temperate clime; whereat
In either hand the hastening Angel caught
Our lingering parents, and to the eastern gate
Led them direct, and down the cliff as fast
To the subjected° plain; then disappeared.   640
They, looking back, all the eastern side beheld
Of Paradise, so late their happy seat,
Waved over by that flaming brand,° the gate
With dreadful faces thronged and fiery arms.
Some° natural tears they dropped, but wiped them
      soon;
The world was all before them, where to choose
Their place of rest, and Providence their guide.
They hand in hand with wandering steps and slow,
Through Eden took their solitary way.

559–79. knowledge . . . sea: Adam's declaration and Michael's reply are a final reiteration of the principle emphasized throughout the poem, in Satan's temptation of Eve and in Raphael's discussion of astronomy (Book VIII) — that is, the priority of the religious and righteous life over mere knowledge of nature (or wealth or power). **559. vessel:** Adam. **584. charity:** Milton anticipates the use of "charity" for "love" in translations of the Bible (I Cor. 13:1–8). **588–89. top . . . speculation:** the hill they are on, from which they had surveyed the world **602. many days:** Adam was to live 930 years (Gen. 5:5).

614. lead on: Contrast Eve's "Lead then" addressed to the serpent (IX. 631). **615–18. with . . . thou:** After her tragic experience Eve can, with a new simplicity and depth of feeling, reaffirm the devotion she had expressed with lyrical richness in IV. 635–56. **630. marish:** marsh. **632. advanced:** raised aloft. **634. which:** the sword. **635. vapor:** heat. **adust:** burnt. **640. subjected:** lying below. **643. brand:** sword. **645–49. Some . . . way:** *PL*, like Milton's other long poems, ends quietly, but — to repeat what was said in the Introduction — no other ending invests such simple narrative statements with so much complexity of feeling.

SAMSON AGONISTES

A Dramatic Poem

Some comment on this drama is made at the end of the Introduction, pp. 411-12.

OF THAT SORT OF DRAMATIC POEM WHICH IS CALLED TRAGEDY

Tragedy, as it was anciently composed, hath been ever held the gravest, moralest, and most profitable of all other poems: therefore said by Aristotle [1] to be of power, by raising pity and fear, or terror, to purge the mind of those and suchlike passions, that is, to temper and reduce them to just measure with a kind of delight, stirred up by reading or seeing those passions well imitated. Nor is Nature wanting in her own effects to make good his assertion; for so in physic, things of melancholic hue and quality are used against melancholy, sour against sour, salt to remove salt humors. Hence philosophers and other gravest writers, as Cicero, Plutarch, and others, frequently cite out of tragic poets, both to adorn and illustrate their discourse. The Apostle Paul [2] himself thought it not unworthy to insert a verse of Euripides into the text of Holy Scripture, I Cor. 15:33; and Pareus,[3] commenting on the Revelation, divides the whole book, as a tragedy, into acts distinguished each by a chorus of heavenly harpings and song between. Heretofore men in highest dignity have labored not a little to be thought able to compose a tragedy. Of that honor Dionysius the elder [4] was no less ambitious than before of his attaining to the tyranny. Augustus Caesar also had begun his *Ajax,* but, unable to please his own judgment with what he had begun, left it unfinished. Seneca [5] the philosopher is by some thought the author of those tragedies (at least the best of them) that go under that name. Gregory Nazianzen, a Father of the Church, thought it not unbeseeming the sanctity of his person to write a tragedy, which he entitled *Christ Suffering.*[6] This is mentioned to vindicate tragedy from the small esteem, or rather infamy, which in the account of many it undergoes at this day, with other common interludes; happening through the poet's error of intermixing comic stuff with tragic sadness and gravity, or introducing trivial and vulgar persons, which by all judicious hath been counted absurd, and brought in without discretion, corruptly to gratify the people. And though ancient tragedy use no prologue, yet using sometimes, in case of self-defense or explanation, that which Martial [7] calls an epistle; in behalf of this tragedy, coming forth after the ancient manner, much different from what among us passes for best, thus much

beforehand may be epistled: that chorus is here introduced after the Greek manner, not ancient only but modern, and still in use among the Italians. In the modeling therefore of this poem, with good reason, the ancients and Italians are rather followed, as of much more authority and fame. The measure of verse used in the chorus is of all sorts, called by the Greeks *monostrophic,*[8] or rather *apolelymenon,* without regard had to strophe, antistrophe, or epode, which were a kind of stanzas framed only for the music, then used with the chorus that sung; not essential to the poem, and therefore not material; or, being divided into stanzas or pauses, they may be called *allœostropha.* Division into act and scene, referring chiefly to the stage (to which this work never was intended), is here omitted.

It suffices if the whole drama be found not produced beyond the fifth act. Of the style and uniformity, and that commonly called the plot, whether intricate or explicit [9] — which is nothing indeed but such economy, or disposition of the fable, as may stand best with verisimilitude and decorum [10] — they only will best judge who are not unacquainted with Aeschylus, Sophocles, and Euripides, the three tragic poets unequaled yet by any, and the best rule to all who endeavor to write tragedy. The circumscription of time wherein the whole drama begins and ends is, according to ancient rule and best example, within the space of twenty-four hours.[11]

THE ARGUMENT

Samson, made captive, blind, and now in the prison at Gaza, there to labor as in a common workhouse, on a festival day, in the general cessation from labor, comes forth into the open air, to a place nigh, somewhat retired, there to sit a while and bemoan his condition. Where he happens at length to be visited by certain friends and equals [12] of his tribe, which make the chorus, who seek to comfort him what they can; then by his old father, Manoa, who endeavors the like, and withal tells him his purpose to procure his liberty by ransom; lastly, that this feast was proclaimed by the Philistines as a day of thanksgiving for their deliverance from the hands of Samson, which yet more troubles him. Manoa then departs to prosecute his endeavor with the Philistian lords for Samson's redemption; who in the meanwhile is visited by other persons; and lastly by a public officer to require his coming to the feast before the lords and people, to play or show his strength in their presence. He at first refuses, dismissing the public officer with absolute denial to come; at length persuaded inwardly that this was from God, he yields to go along with him, who came now the second time with great threatenings to fetch him. The chorus yet re-

---

8. monostrophic: The context sufficiently explains this and other technical terms: Milton's choric odes are continuous, not divided into parts.   **9. intricate or explicit:** complex (in reversals of fortune) or simple.   **10. decorum:** a key word for neoclassical art, meaning fitness and harmony in all the elements of a work.   **11. twenty-four hours:** Aristotle had required only unity of action, but Greek tragedies, acted continuously on an uncurtained stage, were normally confined to one place and a brief period of time; out of such precept and practice Italian critics of the Renaissance codified "the three unities."   **12. equals:** men of his own age.

SAMSON AGONISTES.   **1. Aristotle:** Milton paraphrases Aristotle's definition of tragic catharsis (*Poetics,* VI).   **2. Paul:** Note also his insertions from Aratus (Acts 17:28) and Epimenides (Titus 1:12).   **3. Pareus:** David Pareus (d. 1622), a German theologian.   **4. Dionysius:** the tyrant of Syracuse.   **5.** Seneca's declamatory Latin tragedies had great influence on the Renaissance theater, notably in the development of the "revenge" type. In *Samson* Milton is concerned with Greek and Italian models.   **6. *Christ Suffering:*** In attributing this drama to Gregory, Milton shared an error of his age.   **7. Martial:** the Roman poet (first century A.D.).

maining on the place, Manoà returns full of joyful hope to procure ere long his son's deliverance; in the midst of which discourse an Hebrew comes in haste, confusedly at first, and afterward more distinctly, relating the catastrophe, what Samson had done to the Philistines, and by accident to himself; wherewith the tragedy ends.

THE PERSONS

SAMSON
MANOA, *the father of Samson*
DÁLILA, *his wife*
HARAPHA OF GATH
PUBLIC OFFICER
MESSENGER
CHORUS OF DANITES [13]

The Scene, before the Prison in Gaza

SAMSON. A little onward lend thy guiding hand°
To these dark steps, a little further on;
For yonder bank hath choice of sun or shade;
There I am wont to sit, when any chance
Relieves me from my task of servile toil,
Daily in the common prison else enjoined me,
Where I, a prisoner chained, scarce freely draw
The air imprisoned also, close and damp,
Unwholesome draught. But here I feel amends,
The breath of Heaven fresh-blowing, pure and
    sweet,   10
With day-spring° born; here leave me to respire.
This day a solemn feast the people hold
To Dagon° their sea-idol, and forbid
Laborious works; unwillingly this rest
Their superstition yields me; hence with leave
Retiring from the popular noise, I seek
This unfrequented place to find some ease,
Ease to the body some, none to the mind
From restless thoughts, that like a deadly swarm
Of hornets armed, no sooner found alone,   20
But rush upon me thronging, and present
Times past, what once I was, and what am now.
O wherefore was my birth from Heaven foretold°
Twice by an angel, who at last in sight
Of both my parents all in flames ascended
From off the altar, where an offering burned,
As in a fiery column charioting
His godlike presence, and from some great act
Or benefit revealed to Abraham's race?
Why was my breeding ordered and prescribed   30
As of a person separate to God,

Designed for great exploits, if I must die
Betrayed, captived, and both my eyes put out,
Made of my enemies the scorn and gaze,
To grind in brazen fetters under task
With this Heaven-gifted strength? O glorious
    strength,
Put to the labor of a beast, debased
Lower than bondslave! Promise was that I
Should Israel from Philistian yoke deliver;
Ask for this great deliverer now, and find him   40
Eyeless in Gaza at the mill with slaves,
Himself in bonds under Philistian yoke;
Yet stay, let me not rashly call in doubt
Divine prediction; what if all foretold
Had been fulfilled but through mine own default?
Whom have I to complain of but myself?
Who this high gift of strength committed to me,
In what part lodged, how easily bereft me,
Under the seal of silence could not keep,
But weakly to a woman must reveal it,   50
O'ercome with importunity and tears.
O impotence of mind, in body strong!
But what is strength without a double share
Of wisdom? vast, unwieldy, burdensome,
Proudly secure, yet liable to fall
By weakest subtleties; not made to rule,
But to subserve where wisdom bears command.
God, when he gave me strength, to show withal
How slight the gift was, hung it in my hair.
But peace! I must not quarrel with the will   60
Of highest dispensation, which herein
Haply had ends above my reach to know:
Suffices that to me strength is my bane,
And proves the source of all my miseries,
So many, and so huge, that each apart
Would ask a life to wail; but chief of all,
O loss of sight, of thee I most complain!
Blind among enemies, O worse than chains,
Dungeon, or beggary, or decrepit age!
Light, the prime work of God, to me is extinct,
And all her various objects of delight   71
Annulled, which might in part my grief have eased,
Inferior to the vilest now become
Of man or worm; the vilest here excel me,
They creep, yet see; I, dark in light, exposed
To daily fraud, contempt, abuse and wrong,
Within doors, or without, still° as a fool,
In power of others, never in my own;
Scarce half I seem to live, dead more than half.
O dark, dark, dark, amid the blaze of noon,   80
Irrecoverably dark, total eclipse
Without all° hope of day!
O first-created beam, and thou great Word,
" Let there be light, and light was over all ";°
Why am I thus bereaved thy prime decree?
The sun to me is dark

---

13. Danites: members of the tribe of Dan, to which Manoa belonged.   **1. A . . . hand:** This first line has its literal sense as addressed to the blind hero's attendant; it also suggests God's continued help of his chosen champion during the brief remainder of his life.   **11. day-spring:** dawn. Lines 10–11, along with the literal sense, carry a hint of divine inspiration and aid.   **13. Dagon:** See *PL,* I. 457–66n.   **23. foretold:** See Judg. 13:3–20.

77. still: always.   **82. all:** any.   **83–84. O . . . all:** See Gen. 1:3.

And silent° as the moon,
When she deserts the night,
Hid in her vacant interlunar cave.°
Since light so necessary is to life,   90
And almost life itself, if it be true
That light is in the soul,
She all in every part, why was the sight
To such a tender ball as the eye confined?
So obvious° and so easy to be quenched,
And not, as feeling, through all parts diffused,
That she might look at will through every pore?
Then had I not been thus exiled from light,
As in the land of darkness, yet in light,
To live a life half dead, a living death,   100
And buried; but O yet more miserable!
Myself my sepulcher, a moving grave,
Buried, yet not exempt
By privilege of death and burial
From worst of other evils, pains and wrongs,
But made hereby obnoxious° more
To all the miseries of life,
Life in captivity
Among inhuman foes.
But who are these? for with joint pace I hear   110
The tread of many feet steering this way;
Perhaps my enemies who come to stare
At my affliction, and perhaps to insult,
Their daily practice to afflict me more.
       CHORUS. This, this is he; softly a while;
Let us not break in upon him.
O change beyond report, thought, or belief!
See how he lies at random, carelessly diffused,°
With languished head unpropped,
As one past hope, abandoned,   120
And by himself given over;°
In slavish habit, ill-fitted weeds°
O'er-worn and soiled;
Or do my eyes misrepresent? Can this be he,
That heroic, that renowned,
Irresistible Samson? whom unarmed
No strength of man, or fiercest wild beast could
       withstand;
Who tore the lion as the lion tears the kid,
Ran on embattled armies clad in iron,
And, weaponless himself,°   130
Made arms ridiculous, useless the forgery°
Of brazen shield and spear, the hammered cuirass,
Chalybean°-tempered steel, and frock of mail

Adamantean proof;
But safest he who stood aloof,
When insupportably° his foot advanced,
In scorn of their proud arms and warlike tools,
Spurned them to death by troops. The bold
       Ascalonite°
Fled from his lion ramp,° old warriors turned
Their plated backs under his heel;   140
Or groveling soiled their crested helmets in the
       dust.
Then with what trivial weapon came to hand,
The jaw of a dead ass, his sword of bone,
A thousand foreskins fell, the flower of Palestine,
In Ramath-lechi, famous to this day;°
Then° by main force pulled up, and on his shoul-
       ders bore
The gates of Azza, post and massy bar,
Up to the hill by Hebron, seat of giants old,
No journey of a Sabbath day, and loaded so;
Like whom the Gentiles feign to bear up Heaven.°
Which shall I first bewail,   151
Thy bondage or lost sight,
Prison within prison
Inseparably dark?
Thou art become (O worst imprisonment!)
The dungeon of thyself; thy soul
(Which° men enjoying sight oft without cause
       complain)
Imprisoned now indeed,
In real darkness of the body dwells,
Shut up from outward light   160
To incorporate with gloomy night;
For inward light, alas,
Puts forth no visual beam.
O mirror of our fickle state,
Since man on earth unparalleled!
The° rarer thy example stands,
By how much from the top of wondrous glory,
Strongest of mortal men,
To lowest pitch of abject fortune thou art fallen.
For him I reckon not in high estate   170
Whom long descent of birth
Or the sphere of fortune raises;
But thee whose strength, while virtue was her mate,
Might have subdued the earth,
Universally crowned with highest praises.
       SAMS. I hear the sound of words; their sense the
       air
Dissolves unjointed ere it reach my ear.
       CHOR. He speaks; let us draw nigh. Matchless in
       might,
The glory late of Israel, now the grief!
We come, thy friends and neighbors not unknown,

From Eshtaol and Zora's fruitful vale,   181
To visit or bewail thee, or if better,
Counsel or consolation we may bring,
Salve to thy sores; apt words have power to swage°
The tumors of a troubled mind,
And are as balm to festered wounds.
   SAMS. Your coming, friends, revives me, for I
     learn
Now of my own experience, not by talk,
How counterfeit a coin they are who "friends"
Bear in their superscription (of the most   190
I would be understood). In prosperous days
They swarm, but in adverse withdraw their head,
Not to be found, though sought. Ye see, O friends,
How many evils have enclosed me round;
Yet that which was the worst now least afflicts me,
Blindness, for had I sight, confused with shame,
How could I once look up, or heave the head,
Who like a foolish pilot have shipwracked
My vessel trusted to me from above,
Gloriously rigged; and for a word, a tear,   200
Fool, have divulged the secret gift of God
To a deceitful woman? Tell me, friends,
Am I not sung and proverbed for a fool
In every street, do they not say, "How well
Are come upon him his deserts"? Yet why?
Immeasurable strength they might behold
In me, of wisdom nothing more than mean;
This with the other should, at least, have paired;°
These two, proportioned ill, drove me transverse.°
   CHOR. Tax not divine disposal; wisest men   210
Have erred, and by bad women been deceived;
And shall again, pretend they ne'er so wise.
Deject not then so overmuch thyself,
Who hast of sorrow thy full load besides.
Yet° truth to say, I oft have heard men wonder
Why thou shouldst wed Philistian women rather
Than of thine own tribe fairer, or as fair,
At least of thy own nation, and as noble.
   SAMS. The first I saw at Timna, and she pleased
Me, not my parents, that I sought to wed,   220
The daughter of an infidel: they° knew not
That what I motioned was of God; I knew
From intimate impulse, and therefore urged
The marriage on; that by occasion hence
I might begin Israel's deliverance,
The work to which I was divinely called.
She proving false, the next I took to wife
(O that I never had! fond° wish too late!)
Was in the vale of Sorec, Dálila,
That specious monster, my accomplished snare.
I thought it lawful from my former act,   231
And the same end,° still watching to oppress

Israel's oppressors. Of what now I suffer
She was not the prime cause, but I myself,
Who, vanquished with a peal of words (O weak-
    ness!),
Gave up my fort of silence to a woman.
   CHOR. In seeking just occasion to provoke
The Philistine, thy country's enemy,
Thou never wast remiss, I bear thee witness:
Yet Israel still serves° with all his sons.   240
   SAMS. That fault I take not on me, but transfer
On Israel's governors and heads of tribes,
Who, seeing those great acts which God had done
Singly by me against their conquerors,
Acknowledged not, or not at all considered,
Deliverance offered: I on the other side
Used no ambition° to commend my deeds;
The deeds themselves, though mute, spoke loud the
    doer;
But they persisted deaf, and would not seem   249
To count them things worth notice, till at length
Their lords the Philistines with gathered powers
Entered Judea seeking me, who then
Safe to the rock of Etham was retired,
Not flying, but forecasting in what place
To set upon them, what advantaged best;
Meanwhile° the men of Judah, to prevent
The harass of their land, beset me round;
I willingly on some conditions came
Into their hands, and they as gladly yield me
To the uncircumcised a welcome prey,   260
Bound with two cords; but cords to me were
    threads
Touched with the flame: on their whole host I flew
Unarmed, and with a trivial weapon felled
Their choicest youth; they only lived who fled.
Had Judah that day joined, or one whole tribe,
They had by this possessed the towers of Gath,
And lorded over them whom now they serve;
But° what more oft in nations grown corrupt,
And by their vices brought to servitude,
Than to love bondage more than liberty,   270
Bondage with ease than strenuous liberty;
And to despise, or envy, or suspect
Whom God hath of his special favor raised
As their deliverer; if he aught begin,
How frequent to desert him, and at last
To heap ingratitude on worthiest deeds?
   CHOR. Thy words to my remembrance bring
How Succoth and the fort of Penuel
Their great deliverer contemned,
The matchless Gideon° in pursuit   280
Of Madian and her vanquished kings:
And how ingrateful Ephraim

---

184. swage: assuage.   208. paired: made equal.   209. transverse: off the course.   215–18: Yet . . . noble: The chorus, like
Job's comforters, contrive to turn the knife in Samson's wound.
221–26. they . . . called: See Judg. 14:4.   228. fond: foolish.
231–32. I . . . end: This motive is not in Judg. 16:4.

240. serves: is in servitude.   247. ambition: canvassing for
support.   256–64. Meanwhile . . . fled: See Judg. 15:9–17.
268–71. But . . . liberty: a recurrent idea in Milton, exemplified
for him in the failure of the Puritan Revolution and England's
restoration of the monarchy.   280. Gideon: See Judg. 8:4–12.

Had dealt with Jephtha,° who by argument,
Not worse than by his shield and spear,
Defended Israel from the Ammonite,
Had not his prowess quelled their pride
In that sore battle when so many died
Without reprieve adjudged to death,
For want of well pronouncing *Shibboleth*.

   SAMS. Of such examples add me to the roll;   290
Me easily indeed mine° may neglect,
But God's proposed deliverance not so.

   CHOR. Just° are the ways of God,
And justifiable to men;
Unless there be who think not° God at all:
If any be, they walk obscure;
For of such doctrine never was there school,
But the heart of the fool,
And no man therein doctor but himself.

   Yet more there be who doubt his ways not just,
As to his own edicts, found contradicting,   301
Then give the reins to wandering thought,
Regardless of his glory's diminution;
Till by their own perplexities involved
They ravel° more, still less resolved,
But never find self-satisfying solution.

   As if they would confine the Interminable,°
And tie him to his own prescript,
Who made our laws to bind us, not himself,
And hath full right to exempt   310
Whomso it pleases him by choice
From national obstriction,° without taint
Of sin, or legal debt;
For with his own laws he can best dispense.

   He would not else, who never wanted means,
Nor in respect of the enemy just cause,
To set his people free,
Have prompted this heroic Nazarite,°
Against his vow of strictest purity,
To seek in marriage that fallacious bride,   320
Unclean,° unchaste.

   Down, Reason, then, at least vain reasonings
   down,
Though Reason here aver
That moral verdict quits° her of unclean:
Unchaste was subsequent; her stain, not his.

   But see, here comes thy reverend sire
With careful° step, locks white as down,
Old Manoa: advise°
Forthwith how thou ought'st to receive him.   329
   SAMS. Ay me, another inward grief, awaked

With mention of that name, renews the assault.
   MANOA. Brethren and men of Dan, for such ye
   seem,
Though in this uncouth° place; if old respect,
As I suppose, towards your once gloried friend,
My son now captive, hither hath informed°
Your younger feet, while mine cast back with age
Came lagging after; say if he be here.

   CHOR. As signal° now in low dejected state,
As erst in highest, behold him where he lies.

   MAN. O miserable change! is this the man,   340
That invincible Samson, far renowned,
The dread of Israel's foes, who with a strength
Equivalent to angels' walked their streets,
None offering fight; who, single combatant,
Dueled° their armies ranked in proud array,
Himself an army, now unequal match
To save himself against a coward armed
At one spear's length? O ever-failing trust
In mortal strength! and oh what not in man
Deceivable and vain! Nay, what thing good   350
Prayed for, but often proves our woe, our bane?
I prayed for children, and thought barrenness
In wedlock a reproach; I gained a son,
And such a son as° all men hailed me happy:
Who would be now a father in my stead?
O wherefore did God grant me my request,
And as a blessing with such pomp adorned?
Why are his gifts desirable, to tempt
Our earnest prayers, then, given with solemn hand
As graces, draw a scorpion's tail behind?   360
For this did the angel twice descend? for this
Ordained thy nurture holy, as of a plant;
Select and sacred, glorious for a while,
The miracle of men; then in an hour
Ensnared, assaulted, overcome, led bound,
Thy foes' derision, captive, poor, and blind,
Into a dungeon thrust, to work with slaves?
Alas, methinks whom God hath chosen once
To worthiest deeds, if he through frailty err,
He should not so o'erwhelm, and as a thrall   370
Subject him to so foul indignities,
Be it but for honor's sake of former deeds.

   SAMS. Appoint not heavenly disposition, father.
Nothing of all these evils hath befallen me
But justly; I myself have brought them on,
Sole author I, sole cause: if aught seem vile,
As vile hath been my folly, who have profaned
The mystery of God given me under pledge
Of vow, and have betrayed it to a woman,
A Canaanite,° my faithless enemy.   380
This well I knew, nor was at all surprised,
But warned by oft experience: did° not she

---

283. **Jephtha:** See Judg. 11:12–33.   291. **mine:** my nation.
293 f. : As ll. 315–25 show, the theme of the chorus is Samson's
marriages, which inspire their general reflections.   295. **think
not:** do not believe in.   305. **ravel:** become tangled.
307. **Interminable:** Infinite (God).   312. **national obstriction:**
Jewish law forbidding marriage with Gentiles.   318. **Nazarite:**
a person vowed to the special service of God, to abstinence from
wines and a razor, etc. (Num. 6).   321. **Unclean:** as being a
Gentile.   324. **quits:** acquits.   327. **careful:** full of care.
328. **advise:** consider.

333. **uncouth:** unfamiliar.   335. **informed:** led.   338. **signal:**
notable.   345. **Dueled:** fought singly.   354. **as:** that.   380. **Canaanite:** equivalent to Philistine, since the Philistines had held
Canaan, the coastal region of southern Palestine.   382–87. **did
. . . rivals:** See Judg. 14:11–18.

Of Timna first betray me, and reveal
The secret wrested from me in her highth
Of nuptial love professed, carrying it straight
To them who had corrupted her, my spies,
And rivals? In this other° was there found
More faith? who also in her prime of love,
Spousal embraces, vitiated with gold,
Though offered only, by the scent conceived   390
Her spurious first-born, treason against me.
Thrice she assayed° with flattering prayers and
    sighs,
And amorous reproaches, to win from me
My capital° secret, in what part my strength
Lay stored, in what part summed, that she might
    know:
Thrice I deluded her, and turned to sport
Her importunity, each time perceiving
How openly, and with what impudence,
She purposed to betray me, and (which was worse
Than undissembled hate) with what contempt
She sought to make me traitor to myself;   401
Yet the fourth time, when mustering all her wiles,
With blandished parleys, feminine assaults,
Tongue-batteries, she surceased° not day nor night
To storm me overwatched,° and wearied out:
At times when men seek most repose and rest,
I yielded, and unlocked her all my heart,°
Who with a grain of manhood well resolved
Might easily have shook off all her snares;
But° foul effeminacy held me yoked   410
Her bondslave; O indignity, O blot
To honor and religion! servile mind
Rewarded well with servile punishment!
The base degree to which I now am fallen,
These rags, this grinding, is not yet so base
As was my former servitude, ignoble,
Unmanly, ignominious, infamous,
True slavery, and that blindness worse than this,
That saw not how degenerately I served.   419
    MAN. I cannot praise thy marriage choices, son,
Rather approved them not; but thou didst plead
Divine impulsion prompting how thou might'st
Find some occasion to infest our foes.
I state not that; this I am sure, our foes
Found soon occasion thereby to make thee
Their captive, and their triumph; thou the sooner
Temptation found'st, or overpotent charms,
To violate the sacred trust of silence
Deposited within thee; which to have kept
Tacit was in thy power; true; and thou bear'st   430
Enough, and more, the burden of that fault;
Bitterly hast thou paid, and still art paying,

That rigid score.° A worse thing yet remains:
This day the Philistines a popular feast
Here celebrate in Gaza, and proclaim
Great pomp, and sacrifice, and praises loud
To Dagon, as their god who hath delivered
Thee, Samson, bound and blind, into their hands,
Them out of thine, who slew'st them° many a
    slain.°
So Dagon shall be magnified, and God,   440
Besides whom is no god, compared with idols,
Disglorified, blasphemed, and had in scorn
By the idolatrous rout amidst their wine;
Which to have come to pass by means of thee,
Samson, of all thy sufferings think the heaviest,
Of all reproach the most with shame that ever
Could have befallen thee and thy father's house.
    SAMS. Father,° I do acknowledge and confess
That I this honor, I this pomp, have brought
To Dagon, and advanced his praises high   450
Among the heathen round; to God have brought
Dishonor, obloquy, and oped the mouths
Of idolists and atheists; have brought scandal
To Israel, diffidence° of God, and doubt
In feeble hearts, propense° enough before
To waver, or fall off and join with idols:
Which is my chief affliction, shame and sorrow,
The anguish of my soul, that suffers not
Mine eye to harbor sleep, or thoughts to rest.
This only hope relieves me, that the strife   460
With me hath end; all the contést is now
'Twixt God and Dagon; Dagon hath presumed,
Me overthrown, to enter lists with God,
His deity comparing and preferring
Before the God of Abraham. He, be sure,
Will not connive,° or linger, thus provoked,
But will arise and his great name assert:
Dagon must stoop, and shall ere long receive
Such a discomfit, as shall quite despoil him
Of all these boasted trophies won on° me,   470
And with confusion blank° his worshipers.
    MAN. With cause this hope relieves thee, and
    these words
I as a prophecy receive; for God,
Nothing more certain, will not long defer
To vindicate the glory of his name
Against all competition, nor will long
Endure it doubtful whether God be Lord,
Or Dagon. But for thee what shall be done?
Thou must not in the meanwhile, here forgot,
Lie in this miserable loathsome plight   480

---

387. this other: Dalila.   392. assayed: essayed, tried.   394. capital: fatal (with a pun on *caput*, "head").   404. surceased: ceased.   405. overwatched: weary from keeping awake.   407. I . . . heart: See Judg. 16:5-21.   410-19. But . . . served: These lines, and the whole speech, show that Manoa's reproaching of God rouses Samson to condemn himself more strongly than before.

433. score: record of debts.   439. slew'st . . . slain: redundant, for emphasis.   them: for them, to their hurt.   448-71. Manoa's account of the glorification of Dagon enlarges the significance of Samson's fall and deepens his grief, not now for his personal plight but for the dishonor he has brought on the God of Israel.   454. diffidence: distrust.   455. propense: inclined.   466. connive: let pass, wink at.   470. on: over.   471. blank: confound. Lines 465-71 are one of a number of general premonitions that build toward the climax.

Neglected. I already have made way
To some Philistian lords, with whom to treat
About thy ransom: well they may by this
Have satisfied their utmost of revenge
By pains and slaveries, worse than death, inflicted
On thee, who now no more canst do them harm.
  sams. Spare that proposal, father, spare the
    trouble
Of that solicitation; let me here,
As I deserve, pay on my punishment,
And expiate, if possible, my crime,   490
Shameful garrulity. To have revealed
Secrets of men, the secrets of a friend,
How heinous had the fact° been, how deserving
Contempt, and scorn of all, to be excluded
All friendship, and avoided as a blab,
The mark of fool set on his front!
But I God's counsel have not kept, his holy secret
Presumptuously have published, impiously,
Weakly at least, and shamefully: a sin
That Gentiles in their parables condemn   500
To their abyss and horrid pains confined.°
  man. Be penitent and for thy fault contrite,
But act not in thy own affliction, son;
Repent the sin, but if the punishment
Thou canst avoid, self-preservation bids;
Or the execution leave to high disposal,
And let another hand, not thine, exact
Thy penal forfeit from thyself; perhaps
God will relent, and quit° thee all his debt;
Who ever more approves and more accepts   510
(Best pleased with humble and filial submission)
Him who imploring mercy sues for life,
Than who self-rigorous chooses death as due;
Which argues overjust, and self-displeased
For self-offense, more than for God offended.
Reject not then what offered means who knows
But God hath set before us, to return thee
Home to thy country and his sacred house,
Where thou mayst bring thy offerings, to avert
His further ire, with prayers and vows renewed.
  sams. His pardon I implore; but as for life, 521
To what end should I seek it?° When in strength
All mortals I excelled, and great in hopes
With youthful courage and magnanimous thoughts
Of birth from Heaven foretold and high exploits,
Full of divine instinct, after some proof
Of acts indeed heroic, far beyond
The sons of Anak,° famous now and blazed,
Fearless of danger, like a petty god
I walked about admired of° all and dreaded 530

On hostile ground, none daring my affront.°
Then swollen with pride, into the snare I
    fell
Of fair fallacious looks, venereal trains,°
Softened with pleasure and voluptuous life;
At length to lay my head and hallowed pledge
Of all my strength in the lascivious lap
Of a deceitful concubine, who shore me
Like a tame wether, all my precious fleece,
Then turned me out ridiculous, despoiled,
Shaven, and disarmed among my enemies.   540
  chor. Desire of wine and all delicious drinks,
Which many a famous warrior overturns,
Thou couldst repress, nor did the dancing ruby
Sparkling outpoured, the flavor, or the smell,
Or taste that cheers the heart of gods and men,
Allure thee from the cool crystálline stream.
  sams. Wherever fountain or fresh current flowed
Against the eastern ray, translucent, pure
With touch ethereal of Heaven's fiery rod,°
I drank, from the clear milky juice allaying 550
Thirst, and refreshed; nor envied them the grape
Whose heads that turbulent liquor fills with fumes.
  chor. O madness, to think use of strongest wines
And strongest drinks our chief support of health,
When God with these forbidden made choice to
    rear
His mighty champion, strong above compare,
Whose drink was only from the liquid brook.
  sams. But what availed this temperance, not com-
    plete
Against another object more enticing?
What boots° it at one gate to make defense,   560
And at another to let in the foe,
Effeminately vanquished? by which means,
Now blind, disheartened, shamed, dishonored,
    quelled,
To what can I be useful, wherein serve
My nation, and the work from Heaven imposed,
But to sit idle on the household hearth,
A burdenous drone? to visitants a gaze,
Or pitied object; these redundant° locks,
Robustious° to no purpose, clustering down,
Vain monument of strength; till length of years
And sedentary numbness craze° my limbs   571
To a contemptible old age obscure.
Here rather let me drudge and earn my bread,
Till vermin or the draff of servile food
Consume me, and oft-invocated death
Hasten the welcome end of all my pains.
  man. Wilt thou then serve the Philistines with
    that gift
Which was expressly given thee to annoy them?

---

493. fact: act. 500–01. Gentiles . . . confined: such as Tantalus, who was punished for betraying the secrets of the gods.
509. quit: cancel. 521–22. His . . . it: Samson's reaction, here
and earlier, to Manoa's plan for ransom marks another upward
step in his relations with himself and God. Cf. ll. 410–19, 448–71
and notes. 528. sons of Anak: See l. 1080n. 530. admired of:
wondered at by.

531. my affront: to meet me. 533. venereal trains: sensual
temptations. 549. fiery rod: rays of the sun. 560. boots:
avails. 568. redundant: luxuriantly flowing. 569. Robustious:
strong. 571. craze: weaken.

Better at home lie bed-rid, not only idle,
Inglorious, unemployed, with age outworn.   580
But God, who caused a fountain at thy prayer
From the dry ground to spring, thy thirst to allay
After the brunt of battle,° can as easy
Cause light again within thy eyes to spring,
Wherewith to serve him better than thou hast;
And I persuade me so; why else this strength
Miraculous yet remaining in those locks?
His might continues in thee not for nought,
Nor shall his wondrous gifts be frustrate thus.   589
    SAMS. All otherwise to me my thoughts portend,
That these dark orbs no more shall treat with light,
Nor the other light of life continue long,
But yield to double darkness nigh at hand:
So much I feel my genial° spirits droop,
My hopes all flat; Nature within me seems
In all her functions weary of herself;
My race of glory run, and race of shame,
And I shall shortly be with them that rest.
    MAN. Believe not these suggestions, which pro-
    ceed
From anguish of the mind and humors black,°
That mingle with thy fancy. I however   601
Must not omit a father's timely care
To prosecute the means of thy deliverance
By ransom or how else: meanwhile be calm,
And healing words from these thy friends admit.
    SAMS. O that torment should not be confined
To the body's wounds and sores,
With maladies innumerable
In heart, head, breast, and reins;°
But must secret passage find   610
To the inmost mind,
There exercise all his fierce accidents,°
And on her purest spirits prey,
As on entrails, joints, and limbs,
With answerable pains, but more intense,
Though void of corporal sense.
    My griefs not only pain me
As a lingering disease,
But finding no redress, ferment and rage,
Nor less than wounds immedicable   620
Rankle, and fester, and gangrene,
To black mortification.
Thoughts, my tormentors, armed with deadly stings
Mangle my apprehensive° tenderest parts,
Exasperate, exulcerate, and raise
Dire inflammation which no cooling herb
Or med'cinal liquor can assuage,
Nor breath of vernal air from snowy Alp.°
Sleep hath forsook and given me o'er

To death's benumbing opium as my only cure.
Thence faintings, swoonings of despair,   631
And sense of Heaven's desertion.
    I was his nursling once and choice delight,
His destined from the womb,
Promised by heavenly message° twice descending.
Under his special eye
Abstemious I grew up and thrived amain;
He led me on to mightiest deeds
Above the nerve° of mortal arm
Against the uncircumcised, our enemies.   640
But now hath cast me off as never known,
And to those cruel enemies,
Whom I by his appointment had provoked,
Left me all helpless with the irreparable loss
Of sight, reserved alive to be repeated°
The subject of their cruelty or scorn.
Nor am I in the list of them that hope;
Hopeless are all my evils, all remediless;
This one prayer yet remains, might I be heard,
No long petition — speedy death,   650
The close of all my miseries, and the balm.°
    CHOR. Many are the sayings of the wise
In ancient and in modern books enrolled,
Extolling patience as the truest fortitude;
And to the bearing well of all calamities,
All chances incident to man's frail life,
Consolatories writ
With studied argument, and much persuasion
    sought,
Lenient of° grief and anxious thought;
But with the afflicted in his pangs their sound   660
Little prevails, or rather seems a tune
Harsh and of dissonant mood from his complaint,
Unless he feel within
Some source of consolation from above,
Secret refreshings that repair his strength,
And fainting spirits uphold.
    God of our fathers, what is man!°
That thou towards him with hand so various —
Or might I say contrarious? —
Temper'st thy providence through his short course,
Not evenly, as thou rul'st   671
The angelic orders and inferior creatures mute,
Irrational and brute.
Nor do I name of men the common rout,
That wandering loose about
Grow up and perish, as the summer fly,
Heads without name, no more remembered;
But such as thou hast solemnly elected,

581–83. **God . . . battle:** See Judg. 15:18–19.   **594. genial:** of the essential self.   **600. humors black:** black bile ("melancholy"), one of the four humors of the body which, if in excess, altered the constitution and character.   **609. reins:** kidneys.   **612. accidents:** technically, medical symptoms; here, torments.   **624. apprehensive:** sensitive.   **628. Alp:** any high mountain.

635. message: messenger (cf. ll. 23–24).   **639. nerve:** muscle. **645. repeated:** made repeatedly.   **651.** Lines 590–98 and 606–51 mark the one relapse in Samson's upward progression; the chief enemy he has now to conquer is despair.   **659. Lenient of:** healing. In 652–62 Milton has in mind the essays of consolation written by classical moralists, which are inadequate without divine help.   **667–86.** In these and following lines the bold and bitter questioning of God's justice brings out the parallel between Samson's situation and Job's.

With gifts and graces eminently adorned
To some great work, thy glory, 680
And people's safety, which in part they effect;
Yet toward these thus dignified, thou oft
Amidst their highth of noon
Changest thy countenance and thy hand, with no
 regard
Of highest favors past
From thee on them, or them to thee of service.
 Nor only dost degrade them, or remit
To life obscured, which were a fair dismission,
But throw'st them lower than thou didst exalt them
 high,
Unseemly falls in human eye, 690
Too grievous for the trespass or omission;
Oft° leav'st them to the hostile sword
Of heathen and profane, their carcasses
To dogs and fowls a prey, or else captived,
Or to the unjust tribunals, under change of times,
And condemnation of the ingrateful multitude.
If° these they scape, perhaps in poverty
With sickness and disease thou bow'st them down,
Painful diseases and deformed,
In crude° old age; 700
Though not disordinate, yet causeless suffering
The punishment of dissolute days; in fine,
Just or unjust, alike seem miserable,
For oft alike, both come to evil end.
 So deal not with this once thy glorious cham-
 pion,
The image of thy strength, and mighty minister.
What do I beg? how hast thou dealt already?
Behold him in this state calamitous, and turn
His labors, for thou canst, to peaceful end.
 But who is this, what thing of sea or land? 710
Female of sex it seems,
That so bedecked, ornate, and gay,
Comes this way sailing
Like a stately ship
Of Tarsus,° bound for the isles
Of Javan° or Gadire,°
With all her bravery on, and tackle trim,
Sails filled, and streamers waving,
Courted by all the winds that hold them play,
An amber° scent of odorous perfume 720
Her harbinger, a damsel train behind;
Some rich Philistian matron she may seem,

692–96. Oft . . . multitude: the clearest topical reference in the drama — the treatment of Commonwealth leaders by the Restoration government. 697–702. If . . . days: Milton could hardly write these lines without thinking of his own career, his reduced circumstances, and his suffering from gout, which could afflict the temperate ("not disordinate") as well as the dissolute. 700. crude: premature. 715. Tarsus: a trading city near the coast of Cilicia. 715–16: isles . . . Javan: isles of Greece. See PL, I. 508n. Gadire: Cadiz in Spain. The highly colored picture of Dalila in her luxury — luxury gained through her betrayal of Samson — is contrasted with the captive in his squalor. 720. amber: ambergris.

And now at nearer view, no other certain
Than Dálila thy wife.
 SAMS. My wife, my traitress, let her not come near
 me.
 CHOR. Yet on she moves, now stands and eyes
 thee fixed,
About to have spoke; but now, with head declined
Like a fair flower surcharged with dew, she weeps,
And words addressed seem into tears dissolved,
Wetting the borders of her silken veil; 730
But now again she makes address to speak.
 DAL. With doubtful feet and wavering resolution
I came, still dreading thy displeasure, Samson,
Which to have merited, without excuse,
I cannot but acknowledge; yet if tears
May expiate (though the fact more evil drew
In the perverse event than I foresaw),
My penance hath not slackened, though my pardon
No way assured. But conjugal affection,
Prevailing over fear and timorous doubt, 740
Hath led me on, desirous to behold
Once more thy face, and know of thy estate;
If aught in my ability may serve
To lighten what thou suffer'st, and appease
Thy mind with what amends is in my power,
Though late, yet in some part to recompense
My rash but more unfortunate misdeed.
 SAMS. Out, out, hyena!° these are thy wonted arts,
And arts of every woman false like thee,
To break all faith, all vows, deceive, betray; 750
Then as repentant to submit, beseech,
And reconcilement move with feigned remorse,
Confess, and promise wonders in her change,
Not truly penitent, but chief to try
Her husband, how far urged his patience bears,
His virtue or weakness which way to assail;
Then with more cautious and instructed skill
Again transgresses, and again submits;
That wisest and best men, full oft beguiled,
With goodness principled° not to reject 760
The penitent, but ever to forgive,
Are drawn to wear out miserable days,
Entangled with a poisonous bosom snake,
If not by quick destruction soon cut off,
As I by thee, to ages an example.
 DAL. Yet hear me, Samson; not that I endeavor
To lessen or extenuate my offense,
But that on the other side if it be weighed
By itself, with aggravations not surcharged,
Or else with just allowance counterpoised, 770
I may, if possible, thy pardon find
The easier towards me, or thy hatred less.
First granting, as I do, it was a weakness
In me, but incident to all our sex,
Curiosity, inquisitive, importúne

748. hyena: The hyena was a traditional type of the wily deceiver. 760. With . . . principled: acting on the good principle.

Of secrets, then with like infirmity
To publish them, both common female faults;
Was it not weakness also to make known
For importunity, that is for nought,
Wherein consisted all thy strength and safety?   780
To what I did thou show'dst me first the way.
But I to enemies revealed, and should not!
Nor shouldst thou have trusted that to woman's
    frailty:
Ere I to thee, thou to thyself wast cruel.
Let weakness then with weakness come to parle,°
So near related, or the same of kind;
Thine forgive mine, that men may censure thine
The gentler, if severely thou exact not
More strength from me than in thyself was found.
And what if love, which thou interpret'st hate,
The jealousy of love, powerful of sway   791
In human hearts, nor less in mine towards thee,
Caused what I did? I saw thee mutable
Of fancy, feared lest one day thou wouldst leave
    me
As her at Timna, sought by all means therefore
How to endear, and hold thee to me firmest:
No better way I saw than by importuning
To learn thy secrets, get into my power
Thy key of strength and safety. Thou wilt say,
" Why then revealed? " I was assured by those   800
Who tempted me, that nothing was designed
Against thee but safe custody and hold:
That made for me;° I knew that liberty
Would draw thee forth to perilous enterprises,
While I at home sat full of cares and fears,
Wailing thy absence in my widowed bed;
Here I should still enjoy thee day and night,
Mine and love's prisoner, not the Philistines',
Whole to myself, unhazarded abroad,
Fearless at home of partners in my love.   810
These reasons in love's law have passed for good,
Though fond° and reasonless to some perhaps;
And love hath oft, well meaning, wrought much
    woe,
Yet always pity or pardon hath obtained.
Be not unlike all others, not austere
As thou art strong, inflexible as steel.
If thou in strength all mortals dost exceed,
In uncompassionate anger do not so.
    sams. How cunningly the sorceress displays   819
Her own transgressions, to upbraid me mine!°
That malice, not repentance, brought thee hither,
By this appears: I gave, thou say'st, the example,
I led the way — bitter reproach, but true;
I to myself was false ere thou to me;
Such pardon therefore as I give my folly,
Take to thy wicked deed; which when thou seest
Impartial, self-severe, inexorable,

785. parle: parley.   803. That . . . me: that favored my plan.
812. fond: foolish.   820. mine: with mine.

Thou wilt renounce thy seeking, and much rather
Confess it feigned. Weakness is thy excuse,
And I believe it, weakness to resist   830
Philistian gold; if weakness may excuse,
What murderer, what traitor, parricide,
Incestuous, sacrilegious, but may plead it?
All wickedness is weakness: that plea therefore
With God or man will gain thee no remission.
But love constrained thee! call it furious rage
To satisfy thy lust: love seeks to have love;
My love how couldst thou hope, who took'st the
    way
To raise in me inexpiable hate,
Knowing, as needs I must, by thee betrayed?   840
In vain thou striv'st to cover shame with shame,
Or by evasions thy crime uncover'st more.
    dal. Since thou determin'st weakness for no
    plea
In man or woman, though to thy own condemning,
Hear what assaults I had, what snares besides,
What sieges girt me round, ere I consented;
Which might have awed the best-resolved of men,
The constantest, to have yielded without blame.
It was not gold, as to my charge thou layst,
That wrought with me: thou know'st the magis-
    trates   850
And princes of my country came in person,
Solicited, commanded, threatened, urged,
Adjured by all the bonds of civil duty
And of religion, pressed how just it was,
How honorable, how glorious to entrap
A common enemy, who had destroyed
Such numbers of our nation: and the priest
Was not behind, but ever at my ear,
Preaching how meritorious with the gods
It would be to ensnare an irreligious   860
Dishonorer of Dagon. What had I
To oppose against such powerful arguments?
Only my love of thee held long debate,
And combated in silence all these reasons
With hard contest. At length, that grounded
    maxim,
So rife and celebrated in the mouths
Of wisest men, that to the public good
Private respects must yield, with grave authority
Took full possession of me and prevailed;
Virtue, as I thought, truth, duty, so enjoining.
    sams. I thought where all thy circling wiles
    would end,   871
In feigned religion, smooth hypocrisy.
But had thy love, still odiously pretended,
Been, as it ought, sincere, it would have taught thee
Far other reasonings, brought forth other deeds.
I, before all the daughters of my tribe
And of my nation, chose thee from among
My enemies, loved thee, as too well thou knew'st,
Too well; unbosomed all my secrets to thee,

Not out of levity, but overpowered   880
By thy request, who could deny thee nothing;
Yet now am judged an enemy. Why then
Didst thou at first receive me for thy husband,
Then, as since then, thy country's foe professed?°
Being once a wife, for me thou wast to leave
Parents and country; nor was I their subject,
Nor under their protection, but my own;
Thou mine, not theirs. If aught against my life
Thy country sought of thee, it sought unjustly,
Against the law of nature, law of nations;   890
No more thy country, but an impious crew
Of men conspiring to uphold their state
By worse than hostile deeds, violating the ends
For which our country is a name so dear;
Not therefore to be obeyed. But zeal moved thee;
To please thy gods thou didst it; gods unable
To acquit themselves and prosecute their foes
But by ungodly deeds, the contradiction
Of their own deity, gods cannot be: 899
Less therefore to be pleased, obeyed, or feared.
These false pretexts and varnished colors failing,
Bare in thy guilt how foul must thou appear!
      DAL. In argument with men a woman ever
Goes by° the worse, whatever be her cause.
      SAMS. For want of words, no doubt, or lack of
      breath;
Witness when I was worried with thy peals.
      DAL. I was a fool, too rash, and quite mistaken
In what I thought would have succeeded best.
Let me obtain forgiveness of thee, Samson;
Afford me place to show what recompense   910
Towards thee I intend for what I have misdone,
Misguided; only what remains past cure
Bear not too sensibly,° nor still insist
To afflict thyself in vain. Though sight be lost,
Life yet hath many solaces, enjoyed
Where other senses want° not their delights,
At home in leisure and domestic ease,
Exempt from many a care and chance to which
Eyesight exposes daily men abroad.
I to the lords will intercede, not doubting   920
Their favorable ear, that I may fetch thee
From forth this loathsome prison-house, to abide
With me, where my redoubled love and care
With nursing diligence, to me glad office,
May ever tend about thee to old age
With all things grateful cheered, and so supplied,
That what by me thou hast lost thou least shall
      miss.
      SAMS. No, no, of my condition take no care;
It fits not; thou and I long since are twain;
Nor think me so unwary or accursed°   930

To bring my feet again into the snare
Where once I have been caught; I know thy
      trains,°
Though dearly to my cost, thy gins, and toils;°
Thy fair enchanted cup and warbling charms°
No more on me have power, their force is nulled;
So much of adder's wisdom° I have learned
To fence my ear against thy sorceries.
If in my flower of youth and strength, when all
      men
Loved, honored, feared me, thou alone could hate
      me,
Thy husband, slight me, sell me, and forgo me;
How wouldst thou use me now, blind, and
      thereby   941
Deceivable, in most things as a child
Helpless, thence easily contemned, and scorned,
And last neglected? How wouldst thou insult
When I must live uxorious to thy will
In perfect thraldom, how again betray me,
Bearing my words and doings to the lords
To gloss° upon, and censuring,° frown or smile?
This jail I count the house of liberty
To thine, whose doors my feet shall never enter.
      DAL. Let me approach at least, and touch thy
      hand.   951
      SAMS. Not for thy life, lest fierce remembrance
      wake
My sudden rage to tear thee joint by joint.°
At distance I forgive thee, go with that;
Bewail thy falsehood, and the pious works
It hath brought forth to make thee memorable
Among illustrious women, faithful wives;
Cherish thy hastened widowhood with the gold
Of matrimonial treason: so farewell.
      DAL. I see thou art implacable, more deaf   960
To prayers than winds and seas; yet winds to seas
Are reconciled at length, and sea to shore:
Thy anger, unappeasable, still rages,
Eternal tempest never to be calmed.
Why do I humble thus myself, and suing
For peace, reap nothing but repulse and hate?
Bid go with evil omen° and the brand
Of infamy upon my name denounced?
To mix with thy concernments I desist
Henceforth, nor too much disapprove my own.
Fame,° if not double-faced, is double-mouthed,   971
And with contrary blast proclaims most deeds;
On both his wings, one black, the other white,
Bears greatest names in his wild aery flight.
My name perhaps among the circumcised
In Dan, in Judah, and the bordering tribes,

932. **trains:** schemes.   933. **gins,** . . . **toils:** traps and nets.
934. **Thy** . . . **charms:** Milton is thinking of Circe.   935. **adder's wisdom:** Adders were supposed to stop their ears and refuse to hear a charmer.   948. **gloss:** comment. **censuring:** judging.
952–53. **Not** . . . **joint:** Dalila's pleas have included sensual hints, and Samson's fear of her touch provokes this violent outburst.
967. **evil omen:** Cf. ll. 955–59.   971. **Fame:** rumor, repute.

884. **professed:** openly declared.   904 **Goes by:** comes off.
913. **sensibly:** keenly.   916. **want:** lack.   930. **accursed:** under a curse.

To all posterity may stand defamed,
With malediction mentioned; and the blot
Of falsehood most unconjugal traduced.
But in my country where I most desire,   980
In Ekron, Gaza, Asdod, and in Gath,
I shall be named among the famousest
Of women, sung at solemn festivals,
Living and dead recorded, who, to save
Her country from a fierce destroyer, chose
Above the faith of wedlock bands; my tomb
With odors° visited and annual flowers:
Not less renowned than in Mount Ephraim
Jael,° who with inhospitable guile
Smote Sisera sleeping, through the temples nailed.
Nor shall I count it heinous to enjoy   991
The public marks of honor and reward
Conferred upon me, for the piety
Which to my country I was judged to have shown.
At this whoever envies or repines,
I leave him to his lot, and like my own.
    CHOR. She's gone, a manifest serpent by her sting
Discovered in the end, till now concealed.
    SAMS. So let her go; God sent her to debase me,
And aggravate my folly who committed   1000
To such a viper his most sacred trust
Of secrecy, my safety, and my life.
    CHOR. Yet beauty, though injurious, hath strange
        power,
After offense returning, to regain
Love once possessed, nor can be easily
Repulsed, without much inward passion felt
And secret sting of amorous remorse.°
    SAMS. Love-quarrels oft in pleasing concord end,
Not wedlock-treachery endangering life.
    CHOR. It is not virtue, wisdom, valor, wit,   1010
Strength, comeliness of shape, or amplest merit
That woman's love can win or long inherit;°
But what it is, hard is to say,
Harder to hit,
(Which way soever men refer it),
Much like thy riddle,° Samson, in one day
Or seven, though one should musing sit;
    If any of these,° or all, the Timnian bride
Had not so soon preferred
Thy paranymph,° worthless to thee compared,
Successor in thy bed,   1021
Nor both so loosely disallied
Their nuptials, nor this last so treacherously
Had shorn the fatal harvest of thy head.
Is it for that° such outward ornament
Was lavished on their sex, that inward gifts

Were left for haste unfinished, judgment scant,
Capacity not raised to apprehend
Or value what is best
In choice, but oftest to affect° the wrong?   1030
Or was too much of self-love mixed,
Of constancy no root infixed,
That either they love nothing, or not long?
    Whate'er it be, to wisest men and best
Seeming at first all heavenly under virgin veil,
Soft, modest, meek, demure,
Once joined, the contrary she proves, a thorn
Intestine, far within defensive arms
A cleaving° mischief, in his way to virtue
Adverse and turbulent; or by her charms   1040
Draws him awry, enslaved
With dotage, and his sense depraved
To folly and shameful deeds, which ruin
    ends.
What pilot so expert but needs must wreck,
Embarked with such a steers-mate at the helm?
    Favored of Heaven who finds
One virtuous, rarely found,
That in domestic good combines:°
Happy that house! his way to peace is smooth;
But virtue which breaks through all opposition,
And all temptation can remove,   1051
Most shines and most is acceptable above.
    Therefore God's universal law
Gave to the man despotic power
Over his female in due awe,
Nor from that right to part an hour,
Smile she or lour:
So shall he least confusion draw
On his whole life, not swayed
By female usurpation, nor dismayed.   1060
    But had we best retire? I see a storm.
    SAMS. Fair days have oft contracted° wind and
        rain.
    CHOR. But this another kind of tempest brings.
    SAMS. Be less abtruse, my riddling days are past.
    CHOR. Look now for no enchanting voice, nor
        fear
The bait of honeyed words; a rougher tongue
Draws hitherward; I know him by his stride,
The giant Harapha of Gath, his look
Haughty, as is his pile° high-built and proud.
Comes he in peace? What wind hath blown him
    hither   1070
I less conjecture than when first I saw
The sumptuous Dálila floating this way;
His habit carries peace, his brow defiance.
    SAMS. Or peace or not, alike to me he comes.

987. odors: spices.   989. Jael: Sisera, defeated by the Hebrews, was lured into a tent by Jael, who drove a nail through his head while he slept (Judg. 4:17–21).   1007. remorse: pity. 1012. inherit: possess.   1016. thy riddle: See Judg. 14:5–18. 1018. these: the qualities listed in 1010–11.   1020. paranymph: "best man." Samson having neglected his bride, her father gave her to one of Samson's companions (Judg. 14:20, 15:1–2). 1025. for that: because.

1030. affect: seek.   1039. cleaving: clinging; an allusion to Nessus' robe. See PL, II. 542–46n.   1048. combines: unites with her husband. This whole chorus, as usual a reflection on the preceding scene, is dramatically relevant and does not necessarily embody any special misogynistic view of Milton's, though he would, like other men, support a husband's authority. 1062. contracted: brought along.   1069. pile: huge body.

CHOR. His fraught° we soon shall know, he now
  arrives.
HARAPHA. I come not, Samson, to condole thy
  chance,
As these° perhaps, yet wish it had not been,
Though for no friendly intent. I am of Gath;
Men call me Harapha, of stock renowned
As Og or Anak and the Emims° old   1080
That Kiriathaim held; thou know'st me now,
If thou at all art known. Much I have heard
Of thy prodigious might and feats performed,
Incredible to me, in this displeased,
That I was never present on the place
Of those encounters where we might have tried
Each other's force in camp° or listed° field:
And now am come to see of whom such noise
Hath walked about, and each limb to survey,
If thy appearance answer loud report.   1090
  SAMS. The way to know were not to see, but taste.
  HAR. Dost thou already single° me? I thought
Gyves and the mill had tamed thee. O that for-
  tune
Had brought me to the field where thou art famed
To have wrought such wonders with an ass's
  jaw;
I should have forced thee soon wish° other arms,
Or left thy carcass where the ass lay thrown:
So had the glory of prowess been recovered
To Palestine, won by a Philistine   1099
From the unforeskinned race, of whom thou bear'st
The highest name for valiant acts; that honor,
Certain to have won by mortal duel from thee,
I lose, prevented by thy eyes put out.
  SAMS. Boast not of what thou wouldst have done,
  but do
What then thou wouldst; thou seest it in thy hand.°
  HAR. To combat with a blind man I disdain,
And thou hast need much washing to be touched.
  SAMS. Such usage as your honorable lords
Afford me, assassinated° and betrayed;
Who durst not with their whole united powers
In fight withstand me single and unarmed,   IIII
Nor in the house with chamber ambushes
Close-banded durst attack me, no, not sleeping,
Till they had hired a woman with their gold,
Breaking her marriage faith, to circumvent me.
Therefore without feigned shifts, let be assigned
Some narrow place enclosed, where sight may give
  thee,
Or rather flight, no great advantage on me;
Then put on all thy gorgeous arms, thy helmet
And brigandine° of brass, thy broad habergeon,°

Vant-brace° and greaves, and gauntlet; add thy
  spear,   1121
A weaver's beam,° and seven-times-folded° shield;
I only with an oaken staff will meet thee,
And raise such outcries on thy clattered iron,
Which long shall not withhold me from thy head,
That in a little time, while breath remains thee,
Thou oft shalt wish thyself at Gath, to boast
Again in safety what thou wouldst have done
To Samson, but shalt never see Gath more.
  HAR. Thou durst not thus disparage glorious
  arms,   1130
Which greatest heroes have in battle worn,
Their ornament and safety, had not spells
And black enchantments, some magician's art,
Armed thee or charmed thee strong, which thou
  from Heaven
Feign'dst at thy birth was given thee in thy hair,
Where strength can least abide, though all thy
  hairs
Were bristles ranged like those that ridge the back
Of chafed wild boars, or ruffled porcupines.
  SAMS. I know no spells, use no forbidden arts;
My° trust is in the Living God who gave me   1140
At my nativity this strength, diffused
No less through all my sinews, joints and bones,
Than thine, while I preserved these locks unshorn,
The pledge of my unviolated vow.
For proof hereof, if Dagon be thy god,
Go to his temple, invocate his aid
With solemnest devotion, spread before him
How highly it concerns his glory now
To frustrate and dissolve these magic spells,
Which I to be the power of Israel's God   1150
Avow, and challenge Dagon to the test,
Offering to combat thee, his champion bold,
With the utmost of his godhead seconded:
Then thou shalt see, or rather to thy sorrow
Soon feel, whose God is strongest, thine or mine.
  HAR. Presume not on thy God, whate'er he be;
Thee he regards not, owns not, hath cut off
Quite from his people, and delivered up
Into thy enemies' hand; permitted them
To put out both thine eyes, and fettered send thee
Into the common prison, there to grind   1161
Among the slaves and asses, thy comrades,
As good for nothing else, no better service
With those thy boisterous locks; no worthy match
For valor to assail, nor by the sword
Of noble warrior, so to stain his honor,
But by the barber's razor best subdued.
  SAMS. All° these indignities, for such they are

1075. fraught: freight, purpose.   1077. these: the chorus.
1080. Og, Anak, Emims: giants referred to in Deut. 3:11, Num.
13:33, Deut. 2:10–11.   1087. camp: field of battle. listed: arranged for a tournament.   1092. single: challenge.   1096. wish:
to wish for.   1105. hand: power.   1109. assassinated: treacherously attacked.   1120. brigandine: armor-plated coat. habergeon: coat of mail.

1121. Vant-brace: armor for the arm.   1122. weaver's beam:
wooden roller in a loom.   seven-times-folded: having seven
layers of hide.   1140–55. My . . . mine: Harapha's words
elicit an assertion of Samson's renewed faith; he has overcome
despair and can now again feel himself God's champion.
1168–77. All . . . adore: Samson's humble confession, made before such an enemy, is even better proof of his new state of mind.

From thine,° these evils I deserve and more,
Acknowledge them from God inflicted on me
Justly, yet despair not of his final pardon   1171
Whose ear is ever open, and his eye
Gracious to readmit the suppliant;
In confidence whereof I once again
Defy thee to the trial of mortal fight,
By combat to decide whose god is God,
Thine or whom I with Israel's sons adore.
    HAR. Fair honor that thou dost thy God, in trusting
He will accept thee to defend his cause,
A murderer, a revolter, and a robber.   1180
    SAMS. Tongue-doughty giant, how dost thou
    prove me these?
    HAR. Is not thy nation subject to our lords?
Their° magistrates confessed it, when they took
    thee
As a league-breaker and delivered bound
Into our hands: for hadst thou not committed
Notorious murder on those thirty men
At Ascalon, who never did thee harm,
Then, like a robber, stripp'dst them of their robes?
The Philistines, when thou hadst broke the league,
Went up with armed powers thee only seeking,
To others did no violence nor spoil.   1191
    SAMS. Among the daughters of the Philistines
I chose a wife, which argued me no foe,
And in your city held my nuptial feast;
But your ill-meaning politician lords,
Under pretense of bridal friends and guests,
Appointed to await me thirty spies,
Who threatening cruel death constrained the bride
To wring from me and tell to them my secret,
That solved the riddle which I had proposed.   1200
When I perceived all set on enmity,
As on my enemies, wherever chanced,
I used hostility, and took their spoil
To pay my underminers in their coin.
My nation was subjected to your lords!
It was the force of conquest; force with force
Is well ejected when the conquered can.
But I a private person, whom my country
As a league-breaker gave up bound, presumed
Single rebellion and did hostile acts!   1210
I was no private but a person raised
With strength sufficient and command from
    Heaven
To free my country; if their servile minds
Me, their deliverer sent, would not receive,
But to their masters gave me up for nought,
The unworthier they; whence to this day they
    serve.
I was to do my part from Heaven assigned,
And had performed it if my known offense

Had not disabled me, not all your force.
These shifts° refuted, answer thy appellant,°   1220
Though by his blindness maimed for high attempts,
Who now defies thee thrice to single fight,
As a petty enterprise of small enforce.°
    HAR. With thee, a man condemned, a slave enrolled,
Due by the law to capital punishment?
To fight with thee no man of arms will deign.
    SAMS. Cam'st thou for this, vain boaster, to survey
    me,
To descant on my strength, and give thy verdict?
Come nearer, part not hence so slight informed;
But take good heed my hand survey not thee.   1230
    HAR. O Baal-zebub!° can my ears unused
Hear these dishonors, and not render death?
    SAMS. No man withholds thee, nothing from thy
    hand
Fear I incurable; bring up thy van;°
My heels are fettered, but my fist is free.
    HAR. This insolence other kind of answer fits.
    SAMS. Go, baffled coward, lest I run upon thee,
Though in these chains, bulk without spirit vast,
And with one buffet lay thy structure low,   1239
Or swing thee in the air, then dash thee down
To the hazard of thy brains and shattered sides.
    HAR. By Astaroth,° ere long thou shalt lament
These braveries,° in irons loaden on thee.
    CHOR. His giantship is gone somewhat crestfallen,
Stalking with less unconscionable° strides,
And lower looks, but in a sultry chafe.
    SAMS. I dread him not, nor all his giant brood,
Though fame divulge him father of five sons,
All of gigantic size, Goliah chief.°
    CHOR. He will directly to the lords, I fear,   1250
And with malicious counsel stir them up
Some way or other yet further to afflict thee.
    SAMS. He must allege some cause, and offered
    fight
Will not dare mention, lest a question rise
Whether he durst accept the offer or not,
And that he durst not plain enough appeared.
Much more affliction than already felt
They cannot well impose, nor I sustain,
If they intend advantage of my labors,
The work of many hands, which earns my keeping   1260
With no small profit daily to my owners.
But come what will, my deadliest foe will prove
My speediest friend, by death to rid me hence,
The worst that he can give, to me the best.

1220. shifts: excuses, tricks. appellant: challenger.   1223. enforce: effort.   1231. Baal-zebub: a particular title of the Philistine god Baal.   1234. van: vanguard (i.e., begin to fight).
1242. Astaroth: See *PL*, I. 438n.   1243. braveries: boasts.
1245. unconscionable: unreasonable (i.e., proud).   1248-49. Though . . . chief: See II Sam. 21:19-22.

1169. thine: thy people.   1183-1204. Their . . . coin: See Judg.
14:8-20, 15:9-15.

Yet so it may fall out, because their end
Is hate, not help to me, it may with mine
Draw their own ruin who attempt the deed.
  CHOR. Oh how comely it is and how reviving°
To the spirits of just men long oppressed,
When God into the hands of their deliverer   1270
Puts invincible might
To quell the mighty of the earth, the oppressor,
The brute and boisterous force of violent men,
Hardy and industrious to support
Tyrannic power, but raging to pursue
The righteous and all such as honor truth;
He all their ammunition
And feats of war defeats
With plain heroic magnitude of mind
And celestial vigor armed;   1280
Their armories and magazines contemns,
Renders them useless, while
With winged expedition
Swift as the lightning glance he executes
His errand on the wicked, who surprised
Lose their defense, distracted and amazed.
  But patience is more oft the exercise
Of saints, the trial of their fortitude,
Making them each his own deliverer,
And victor over all   1290
That tyranny or fortune can inflict;
Either of these is in thy lot,
Samson, with might endued
Above the sons of men; but sight bereaved
May chance to number thee with those
Whom patience finally must crown.°
  This Idol's day hath been to thee no day of rest,
Laboring thy mind
More than the working day thy hands;
And yet perhaps more trouble is behind.   1300
For I descry this way
Some other tending; in his hand
A scepter or quaint° staff he bears,
Comes on amain, speed in his look.
By his habit I discern him now
A public officer, and now at hand.
His message will be short and voluble.°
  OFF. Hebrews, the prisoner Samson here I seek.
  CHOR. His manacles remark° him; there he sits.
  OFF. Samson, to thee our lords thus bid me say:
This day to Dagon is a solemn feast,   1311
With sacrifices, triumph, pomp, and games;
Thy strength they know surpassing human rate,
And now some public proof thereof require
To honor this great feast, and great assembly;
Rise therefore with all speed and come along,
Where I will see thee heartened and fresh clad

To appear as fits before the illustrious lords.
  SAMS. Thou know'st I am an Hebrew, therefore tell them
Our Law forbids at their religious rites   1320
My presence; for that cause I cannot come.
  OFF. This answer, be assured, will not content them.
  SAMS. Have they not sword-players, and every sort
Of gymnic artists,° wrestlers, riders, runners,
Jugglers and dancers, antics,° mummers,° mimics,°
But they must pick me out, with shackles tired,
And overlabored at their public mill,
To make them sport with blind activity?
Do they not seek occasion of new quarrels,
On my refusal, to distress me more,   1330
Or make a game of my calamities?
Return the way thou cam'st; I will not come.
  OFF. Regard thyself; this will offend them highly.
  SAMS. Myself? my conscience and internal peace.°
Can they think me so broken, so debased
With corporal servitude, that my mind ever
Will condescend to such absurd commands?
Although their drudge, to be their fool or jester,
And in my midst of sorrow and heart-grief
To show them feats and play before their god,
The worst of all indignities, yet on me   1341
Joined° with extreme contempt? I will not come.
  OFF. My message was imposed on me with speed,
Brooks no delay; is this thy resolution?
  SAMS. So take it with what speed thy message needs.
  OFF. I am sorry what this stoutness will produce.
  SAMS. Perhaps thou shalt have cause to sorrow indeed.
  CHOR. Consider,° Samson; matters now are strained
Up to the highth, whether to hold or break;
He's gone, and who knows how he may report
Thy words by adding fuel to the flame?   1351
Expect another message, more imperious,
More lordly thundering than thou well wilt bear.
  SAMS. Shall I abuse this consecrated gift
Of strength, again returning with my hair
After my great transgression, so requite
Favor renewed, and a greater sin
By prostituting holy things to idols;
A Nazarite, in place abominable,
Vaunting° my strength in honor to their Dagon?
Besides, how vile, contemptible, ridiculous,   1361
What act more execrably unclean,° profane?

1268 f. The chorus underlines the effect of Harapha's visit, which has revived Samson's faith in himself (l. 1279) and in God's favor (l. 1280).   1294–96. but . . . crown: The chorus' forecast is of course wrong.   1303. quaint: decorated.   1307. voluble: rapid, pointed.   1309. remark: distinguish.

1324. gymnic artists: gymnasts.   1325. antics: clowns, buffoons. mummers: masqueraders. mimics: actors.   1334. Myself . . . peace: The distinction measures the distance Samson has come since his opening complaint.   1342. Joined: enjoined.   1348–53. Consider . . . bear: The chorus, representing average sentiment, advise submission; throughout they have no real understanding of Samson's inward struggles.   1360. Vaunting: displaying.   1362. unclean: See l. 321n.

CHOR. Yet with this strength thou serv'st the
    Philistines,
Idolatrous, uncircumcised, unclean.
    SAMS. Not in their idol-worship, but by labor
Honest and lawful to deserve my food
Of those who have me in their civil power.°
    CHOR. Where the heart joins not, outward acts
    defile not.
    SAMS. Where outward force constrains, the sen-
    tence° holds;   1369
But who constrains me to the temple of Dagon,
Not dragging? The Philistian lords command.
Commands are no constraints. If I obey them,
I do it freely, venturing to displease
God for the fear of man, and man prefer,
Set God behind; which in his jealousy
Shall never, unrepented, find forgiveness.
Yet that he may dispense with° me or thee,
Present in temples at idolatrous rites
For some important cause, thou need'st not doubt.
    CHOR. How thou wilt here come off surmounts
    my reach.   1380
    SAMS. Be of good courage; I begin to feel
Some rousing motions in me which dispose
To something extraordinary my thoughts.
I° with this messenger will go along,
Nothing to do, be sure, that may dishonor
Our Law, or stain my vow of Nazarite.
If there be aught of presage in the mind,
This day will be remarkable in my life
By some great act, or of my days the last.
    CHOR. In time thou hast resolved; the man re-
    turns.   1390
    OFF. Samson, this second message from our lords
To thee I am bid say: art thou our slave,
Our captive, at the public mill our drudge,
And dar'st thou at our sending and command
Dispute thy coming? Come without delay;
Or we shall find such engines to assail
And hamper thee, as thou shalt come of force,
Though thou wert firmlier fastened than a rock.
    SAMS. I could be well content to try their art,
Which to no few of them would prove pernicious.
Yet° knowing their advantages too many,   1401
Because° they shall not trail me through their
    streets
Like a wild beast, I am content to go.
Masters' commands come with a power resistless
To such as owe them absolute subjection;
And for a life who will not change his purpose?
(So mutable are all the ways of men.)

1365–67. Not . . . power: an example of the sober reasonableness that is typical of Samson's later state of mind.
1369. sentence: saying.   1377. dispense with: grant a
special dispensation to.   1384. I . . . along: Samson's altered
resolution, foreshortened in accordance with the necessities
of Greek drama, indicates that he feels a divine prompting.
1401–07. Yet . . . men: Samson, his mind made up for other
reasons, pretends obedience.   1402. Because: so that.

Yet this be sure, in nothing to comply
Scandalous or forbidden in our Law.   1409
    OFF. I praise thy resolution; doff these links.
By this compliance thou wilt win the lords
To favor, and perhaps to set thee free.
    SAMS. Brethren, farewell; your company along
I will not wish, lest it perhaps offend them
To see me girt with friends; and how the sight
Of me as of a common enemy,
So dreaded once, may now exasperate them,
I know not. Lords are lordliest in their wine;
And the well-feasted priest then soonest fired
With zeal, if aught religion seem concerned;   1420
No less the people, on their holy-days,
Impetuous, insolent, unquenchable;
Happen what may, of me expect to hear
Nothing dishonorable, impure, unworthy
Our God, our Law, my nation, or myself;
The last of me or no I cannot warrant.
    CHOR. Go, and the Holy One
Of Israel be thy guide
To what may serve his glory best, and spread his
    name
Great among the heathen round;   1430
Send thee the angel° of thy birth, to stand
Fast by thy side, who from thy father's field
Rode up in flames after his message told
Of thy conception, and be now a shield
Of fire; that spirit that first rushed on thee
In the camp of Dan,°
Be efficacious in thee now at need.
For never was from Heaven imparted
Measure of strength so great to mortal seed,
As in thy wondrous actions hath been seen.   1440
But wherefore comes old Manoa in such haste
With youthful steps? Much livelier than erewhile
He seems: supposing here to find his son,
Or of him bringing to us some glad news?
    MAN. Peace with you, brethren; my inducement
    hither
Was not at present here to find my son,
By order of the lords new parted hence
To come and play before them at their feast.
I heard all as I came, the city rings,
And numbers thither flock; I had no will,   1450
Lest I should see him forced to things unseemly.
But that which moved my coming now was chiefly
To give ye part with me what hope I have
With good success to work his liberty.
    CHOR. That hope would much rejoice us to par-
    take
With thee; say, reverend sire; we thirst to hear.
    MAN. I have attempted one by one the lords,
Either at home, or through the high street passing
With supplication prone and father's tears   1459

1431–34. the angel: Cf. ll. 24–28, 361, 635.   1435–36. spirit . . .
Dan: See Judg. 13:25.

To accept of ransom for my son their priso   .
Some° much averse I found and wondrous harsh,
Contemptuous, proud, set on revenge and spite;
That part most reverenced Dagon and his priests;
Others more moderate seeming, but their aim
Private reward, for which both God and State
They easily would set to sale; a third
More generous far and civil, who confessed
They had enough revenged, having reduced
Their foe to misery beneath their fears;
The rest was magnanimity to remit,   1470
If some convenient ransom were proposed.
What noise or shout was that? It tore the sky.
   CHOR. Doubtless the people shouting to behold
Their once great dread, captive and blind before
      them,
Or at some proof of strength before them shown.
   MAN. His ransom, if my whole inheritance
May compass it, shall willingly be paid
And numbered down; much rather I shall choose
To live the poorest in my tribe, than richest,
And he in that calamitous prison left.   1480
No, I am fixed not to part hence without him.
For his redemption all my patrimony,
If need be, I am ready to forgo
And quit; not wanting him, I shall want nothing.
   CHOR. Fathers are wont to lay up for their sons,
Thou for thy son art bent to lay out all;
Sons wont to nurse their parents in old age,
Thou in old age car'st how to nurse thy son,
Made older than thy age through eyesight lost.
   MAN. It° shall be my delight to tend his eyes,
And view him sitting in his house, ennobled
With all those high exploits by him achieved,   1492
And on his shoulders waving down those locks
That of a nation armed the strength contained.
And I persuade me God had not permitted
His strength again to grow up with his hair
Garrisoned round about him like a camp
Of faithful soldiery, were not his purpose
To use him further yet in some great service,
Not to sit idle with so great a gift   1500
Useless, and thence ridiculous, about him.
And since his strength with eyesight was not lost,
God will restore him eyesight to° his strength.
   CHOR. Thy hopes are not ill-founded, nor seem
      vain,
Of his delivery, and thy joy thereon
Conceived, agreeable to a father's love;
In both which we, as next,° participate.
   MAN. I know your friendly minds and — O what
      noise!

1461–71. Some . . . proposed: The details suggest that Milton
may be thinking of Restoration authorities' attitudes toward
his own defenders.   1490–1503. It . . . strength: Manoa's hope
of success is an ironical "false dawn" before the catastrophe.
1503. to: along with.   1507. as next: as members of the same
tribe.

Mercy of Heaven, what hideous noise was that!
Horribly loud, unlike the former shout.   1510
   CHOR. Noise call you it, or universal groan,
As if the whole inhabitation perished?
Blood, death, and deathful deeds are in that noise,
Ruin,° destruction at the utmost point.
   MAN. Of ruin indeed methought I heard the
      noise.
Oh it continues, they have slain my son.
   CHOR. Thy son is rather slaying them; that outcry
From slaughter of one foe could not ascend.
   MAN. Some dismal accident it needs must be;
What shall we do, stay here or run and see?   1520
   CHOR. Best keep together here, lest running
      thither
We unawares run into danger's mouth.
This evil on the Philistines is fallen;
From whom could else a general cry be heard?
The sufferers then will scarce molest us here;
From other hands we need not much to fear.
What if his eyesight (for to Israel's God
Nothing is hard) by miracle restored,
He now be dealing dole among his foes,   1529
And over heaps of slaughtered walk his way?
   MAN. That were a joy presumptuous to be
      thought.
   CHOR. Yet God hath wrought things as incredible
For his people of old; what hinders now?
   MAN. He can, I know, but doubt to think he will;
Yet hope would fain subscribe, and tempts belief.
A little stay will bring some notice hither.
   CHOR. Of good or bad so great, of bad the sooner;
For evil news rides post, while good news baits.°
And to our wish I see one hither speeding,
An Hebrew, as I guess, and of our tribe.   1540
   MESSENGER. O whither shall I run, or which way
      fly
The sight of this so horrid spectacle
Which erst° my eyes beheld and yet behold?
For dire imagination still pursues me.
But providence or instinct of nature seems,
Or reason, though disturbed and scarce consulted,
To have guided me aright, I know not how,
To thee first, reverend Manoa, and to these
My countrymen, whom here I knew remaining,
As at some distance from the place of horror,   1550
So in the sad event too much concerned.
   MAN. The accident was loud, and here before thee
With rueful cry, yet what it was we hear not;
No preface needs, thou seest we long to know.
   MESS. It would burst forth; but I recover breath
And sense distract, to know well what I utter.
   MAN. Tell us the sum, the circumstance defer.
   MESS. Gaza yet stands, but all her sons are fallen,
All in a moment overwhelmed and fallen.

1514, 1515. Ruin: downfall.   1538. baits: delays to take food.
1543. erst: a while ago.

MAN. Sad, but thou know'st to Israelites not sad-
  dest   1560
The desolation of a hostile city.
  MESS. Feed on that first, there may in grief be
  surfeit.
  MAN. Relate by whom.
  MESS.   By Samson.
  MAN.   That still lessens
The sorrow, and converts it nigh to joy.
  MESS. Ah, Manoa, I refrain too suddenly
To utter what will come at last too soon;
Lest evil tidings, with too rude irruption
Hitting thy aged ear, should pierce too deep.
  MAN. Suspense in news is torture, speak them
  out.
  MESS. Then take the worst in brief: Samson is
  dead.   1570
  MAN. The worst indeed! O all my hope's de-
  feated
To free him hence! but Death who sets all free
Hath paid his ransom now and full discharge.
What windy° joy this day had I conceived,
Hopeful of his delivery, which now proves
Abortive as the first-born bloom of spring
Nipped with the lagging rear of winter's frost.
Yet ere I give the reins to grief, say first,
How died he? death to life is crown or shame.
All by him fell, thou say'st; by whom fell he,   1580
What glorious hand gave Samson his death's
  wound?
  MESS. Unwounded of his enemies he fell.
  MAN. Wearied with slaughter then, or how? ex-
  plain.
  MESS. By his own hands.
  MAN.   Self-violence? What cause
Brought him so soon at variance with himself
Among his foes?
  MESS.   Inevitable cause
At once both to destroy and be destroyed;
The edifice where all were met to see him,
Upon their heads and on his own he pulled.
  MAN. O lastly overstrong against thyself!   1590
A dreadful way thou took'st to thy revenge.
More than enough we know; but while things
  yet
Are in confusion, give us, if thou canst,
Eye-witness of what first or last was done,
Relation more particular and distinct.
  MESS. Occasions drew me early to this city,
And, as the gates I entered with sunrise,
The morning trumpets festival proclaimed
Through each high street. Little° I had despatched
When all abroad was rumored that this day   1600
Samson should be brought forth to show the
  people

Proof of his mighty strength in feats and games;
I sorrowed at his captive state, but minded
Not to be absent at that spectacle.
The building was a spacious theater
Half round on two main pillars vaulted high,
With seats where all the lords, and each degree
Of sort,° might sit in order to behold;
The other side was open, where the throng
On banks° and scaffolds under sky might stand;
I among these aloof obscurely stood.   1611
The feast and noon grew high, and sacrifice
Had filled their hearts with mirth, high cheer, and
  wine,
When to their sports they turned. Immediately
Was Samson as a public servant brought,
In their state livery clad; before him pipes
And timbrels; on each side went armèd guards,
Both horse and foot before him and behind,
Archers, and slingers, cataphracts° and spears.°
At sight of him the people with a shout   1620
Rifted the air, clamoring their god with praise,
Who had made their dreadful enemy their thrall.
He, patient but undaunted, where they led him,
Came to the place; and what was set before him,
Which without help of eye might be assayed,°
To heave, pull, draw, or break, he still° performed,
All with incredible, stupendious° force,
None daring to appear antagonist.
At length for intermission sake they led him
Between the pillars; he his guide requested   1630
(For so from such as nearer stood we heard),
As overtired, to let him lean a while
With both his arms on those two massy pillars
That to the archèd roof gave main support.
He unsuspicious led him; which when Samson
Felt in his arms, with head a while inclined,
And eyes fast fixed he stood, as one who prayed,
Or some great matter in his mind revolved.
At last with head erect thus cried aloud:
"Hitherto, Lords, what your commands imposed
I have performed, as reason was,° obeying,   1641
Not without wonder or delight beheld.
Now of my own accord such other trial
I mean to show you of my strength, yet greater,
As with amaze shall strike° all who behold."
This uttered, straining all his nerves he bowed;
As with the force of winds and waters pent
When mountains tremble, those two massy pillars
With horrible convulsion to and fro
He tugged, he shook, till down they came and
  drew   1650
The whole roof after them, with burst of thunder

1608. sort: rank.   1610. banks: benches.   1619. cataphracts:
armored men on armored horses. spears: spearmen. 1625. assayed: attempted.   1626. still: always.   1627. stupendious:
stupendous.   1641. as reason was: See ll. 1365–67n.
1645. strike: Samson, who has moved far beyond personal concerns, and has conceived his plan, can indulge in a pun.

1574. windy: empty.   1599. Little: little business.

Upon the heads of all who sat beneath,
Lords, ladies, captains, counselors, or priests,
Their choice nobility and flower, not only
Of this but each Philistian city round,
Met from all parts to solemnize this feast.
Samson, with these immixed, inevitably
Pulled down the same destruction on himself;
The vulgar only scaped, who stood without.
   CHOR. O dearly bought revenge, yet glorious!
Living or dying thou hast fulfilled   1661
The work for which thou wast foretold
To Israel, and now li'st victorious
Among thy slain self-killed,
Not willingly, but tangled in the fold
Of dire necessity,° whose law in death conjoined
Thee with thy slaughtered foes, in number more
Than all thy life had slain before.
   SEMICHOR. While° their hearts were jocund and
    sublime,°
Drunk with idolatry, drunk with wine,   1670
And fat regorged° of bulls and goats,
Chanting their idol, and preferring
Before our living Dread who dwells
In Silo,° his bright sanctuary,
Among them he a spirit of frenzy sent,
Who hurt their minds,
And urged them on with mad desire
To call in haste for their destroyer;
They only set on sport and play
Unweetingly° importuned   1680
Their own destruction to come speedy upon
   them.
So fond are mortal men
Fallen into° wrath divine,
As their own ruin on themselves to invite,
Insensate left, or to sense reprobate,
And with blindness internal struck.
   SEMICHOR. But he, though blind of sight,
Despised, and thought extinguished quite,
With inward eyes illuminated,
His fiery virtue roused   1690
From under ashes into sudden flame,
And as an evening dragon° came,
Assailant on the perchèd roosts
And nests in order ranged
Of tame villatic° fowl; but as an eagle
His cloudless thunder bolted° on their heads.
So virtue, given for° lost,

Depressed, and overthrown, as seemed,
Like that self-begotten bird°
In the Arabian woods embost,°   1700
That no second knows nor third,°
And lay erewhile a holocaust,°
From out her ashy womb now teemed,°
Revives, reflourishes, then vigorous most
When most unactive deemed,
And though her body die, her fame survives,
A secular° bird, ages of lives.
   MAN. Come, come, no time for lamentation
   now,
Nor much more cause; Samson hath quit° himself
Like Samson, and heroicly hath finished   1710
A life heroic, on his enemies
Fully revenged; hath left them years of mourning,
And lamentation to the sons of Caphtor°
Through all Philistian bounds. To Israel
Honor hath left, and freedom — let but them
Find courage to lay hold on this occasion;
To himself and father's house eternal fame;
And, which is best and happiest yet, all this
With God not parted from him, as was feared,
But favoring and assisting to the end.   1720
Nothing is here for tears, nothing to wail
Or knock the breast, no weakness, no contempt,
Dispraise, or blame; nothing but well and fair,
And what may quiet us in a death so noble.°
Let us go find the body where it lies
Soaked in his enemies' blood, and from the
   stream
With lavers° pure and cleansing herbs wash off
The clotted gore. I with what speed the while
(Gaza is not in plight° to say us nay)
Will send for all my kindred, all my friends,   1730
To fetch him hence and solemnly attend,
With silent obsequy and funeral train,
Home to his father's house: there will I build
   him
A monument, and plant it round with shade
Of laurel ever green, and branching palm,
With all his trophies hung, and acts enrolled
In copious legend,° or sweet lyric song.
Thither shall all the valiant youth resort,
And from his memory inflame their breasts
To matchless valor and adventures high;   1740

1665–66. Not . . . necessity: Samson is exonerated from the sin of suicide. 1669–86. While . . . struck: The description suggests the Greek *hubris*, blind, infatuated confidence. Cf. *PL*, IX. 790–93. 1669. sublime: exalted. 1671. regorged: gorged to surfeit. 1674. Silo: Shiloh, where the Israelites set up their tabernacle (Josh. 18:1). 1680. Unweetingly: unwittingly. 1683. into: under. 1692. dragon: snake. 1695. villatic: belonging to a farmhouse. 1696. bolted: shot. 1697. given for: given up as.

1699. bird: the phoenix, the bird — in classical myth and Christian symbol — which, after five hundred years, builds a spicy nest, is burned, and rises to life again from its ashes. 1700. embost: hidden in the woods. 1701. That . . . third: there was only one phoenix in existence at a time. 1702. holocaust: a sacrifice burned whole. 1703. teemed: born. 1707. secular: living for ages (*saecula*). 1709. quit: acquitted. 1713. Caphtor: the Philistines' original home. 1721–24. Nothing . . . noble: In spite of this great eulogy, Manoa, like the chorus, sees only external evidence; he has not seen Samson's inward struggle and victory. 1727. lavers: basins of water. 1729. plight: condition. 1737. legend: inscription.

The virgins also shall on feastful days
Visit his tomb with flowers, only bewailing
His lot unfortunate in nuptial choice,
From whence captivity and loss of eyes.
  CHOR. All is best, though we oft doubt,
What the unsearchable dispose°
Of Highest Wisdom brings about,
And ever best found in the close.
Oft he seems to hide his face,
But unexpectedly returns,   1750

And to his faithful champion hath in place°
Bore witness gloriously; whence Gaza mourns,
And all that band them to resist
His uncontrollable intent:
His servants he, with new acquist°
Of true experience from this great event,
With peace and consolation hath dismissed,
And calm of mind, all passion° spent.

1746. dispose: disposal.

1751. in place: on the spot.   1755. acquist: acquisition.
1758. passion: See the first sentence of Milton's Preface.

Jonathan Swift

1667–1745

SWIFT himself is in part responsible for the impression that has survived of him as a powerful but frustrated being, who in spite of many triumphs was always ultimately cheated or disappointed. He liked to represent himself as one who, lacking money and titles, had been forced to make his way in the world by using his intelligence and his wit; and as one who had indeed succeeded in making a reputation and gaining the friendship of the outstanding men of his generation. Nevertheless, as he looked back on his life when he was over sixty, he wrote: " I remember when I was a little boy I felt a great fish at the end of my line which I drew up almost on the ground, but it dropped in, . . . it was the type of all my future disappointments."

First he reckoned he had been cheated in the place of his birth. His parents were English and he was proud of his grandfather Swift, a Tory parson who had been passionately devoted to the Royalist cause in the Civil War; but he was born in Dublin in late November, 1667, when his mother had just been left a poor widow and was unable to provide for him. He resented being indebted to the charity of his uncle for his upbringing and his education, though he was sent to the best school in the country, at Kilkenny, and at the age of fourteen went to Trinity College, Dublin, where he stayed for about seven years.

At length, when he was a little more than twenty-one, through his family's influence he was able to go to England and join the household of Sir William Temple. It seemed likely at the time that the new king, William of Orange, who had known and trusted Temple when he was ambassador to Holland, would bring him out of his retirement into public life again. But if Swift had counted on this he was to be disappointed, for Temple refused to do more than offer his advice to William on certain occasions; and a few years later Swift decided to return to Ireland and take orders in the Church there. After a short time in a country parish, however, he was easily persuaded to return to be secretary to Temple, and remained with him until his death in 1699. But the only tangible results of the long service were the legacy of whatever honor and profit he might obtain from the publication of Temple's *Letters* and *Memoirs,* and the slight connection which he had established with the king and some of the leaders of the Whig party. His hopes for political advancement were shattered by the unexpected death of the king in 1702, and he returned to Ireland to wait for preferment in the Church; but in this also he was for a long time disappointed.

Nevertheless, the years that he spent in seclusion with Temple were of the greatest importance in his own development. He read hard, and lived in a ferment of ideas, stimulated by all the controversies that were raging in the literary world, arising out of the clash between the new ideas and the old in philosophy and religion and science and the arts. He emulated Cowley, the successful poet and best-seller of the seventeenth century, by trying his hand at Pindaric odes. But then he turned with disgust from the Muse who had cheated him with dreams and romantic notions, and determined to open his eyes and clear his gaze, and rid himself of all the conventions of the Schools, while being equally cautious and careful not to become a victim of the follies and absurdities of the new enthusiasts, the virtuosos and collectors and projectors who were to be found among the scientists and in the Royal Society.

Swift turned to satire, and amused himself making fun of everybody; parodying the great Mr. Dryden, the acknowledged master in the last years of the century, whether as poet, critic, or playwright; ridiculing Bentley, the greatest classical scholar England had produced, then Master of Trinity College, Cambridge; harrying the freethinkers, with their new enlightened ideas; but, more daring still, satirizing in the boldest fashion the superstitions of the Roman Church and the fanaticism of the Protestant sects. He wrote and tore up, he says, an enormous amount; but he kept enough for a volume, though it was not in any shape to be published, consisting of stories, parodies, critical stuff, and fragmentary jottings. He must have put this material aside until he had finished off his editing of Temple's *Letters,* Volumes I and II appearing in 1700 and Volume III in 1703. He also published in 1701 a very original and dignified paper, *A Discourse of the Contests and Dissensions Between the Nobles and the Commons in Athens and Rome,* which purported to be a discussion of certain matters in classical history, but which bore on the particular political crisis of the moment; in this he hoped to establish, and did establish, a reputation as a promising journalist, who might prove of great use to his party.

But nothing happened; he was still only an Irish parson with a small living, and no way of staying permanently in London and making a place for himself in the literary world.[1] It was probably then that he decided to take a risk, and publish some of the satires he had written; it would be a mad book, but a book whose wit and genius would astonish and mystify the world. He would not of course put his name to it, would just throw it out on the waters, like the tub that he had read whalers throw out to distract the attention of those dangerous leviathans

who turn on the ship; he would just call it *A Tale of a Tub.* It was a satire on all the extravagances of the fanatical sects and of the superstitious practices of the Roman Church, with digressions on the follies of the academic and literary world. It was followed by *The Battle of the Books,* dealing with the controversy between the Ancients and the Moderns, and *A Discourse Concerning the Mechanical Operation of the Spirit,* which made dangerous play with the whole idea of divine inspiration.

The *Tale* made even more of a splash than Swift had expected. It established his position, among those who knew, as the leading wit and genius of the age; and, lacking the reticence expected of a clergyman's writing, it ruined forever his chance of a bishopric in the English Church. That was in 1704. In the next year or two he continued to write in verse and prose, and showed his astonishing versatility of wit and humor, so that when Steele and Addison started their adventures in journalism with the founding of the *Tatler,* Swift had a hand in it, too. But these pleasant friendships were soon to be disturbed by the bitterness of party politics when in 1710 Swift became the leading party writer for the new ministry — the moderate Tory ministry — which was to give him considerable power in public life and a vast acquaintance among the nobility and gentry who were prominent in town society during these last years of Queen Anne's reign.

He started by running the government's weekly newspaper, the *Examiner,* in which he professed to give a sensible moderate view of the political situation, attacked extremists on both sides, undermined the power of Marlborough, the great general, and prepared the public for coming to terms with France and bringing an end to the War of the Spanish Succession, which had been going on since the beginning of the century in an effort to maintain the balance of power in Europe. When, in the summer of 1711, the paper was well launched, Swift turned it over to others and began to work on a very important review of the conduct of the war to justify the negotiations the ministry had already begun with the enemy and were determined to carry on, whatever the attitude of their allies. And when the Peace of Utrecht was finally signed in 1713, Swift set to work to write a history of the whole affair to justify the terms that

---

[1] He seems to have spent the summers of 1701 and 1702 in England and managed to return to London again in November, 1703, for another six months.

had been accepted. He had access to the official papers and provided what was then recognized as an admirable account of the negotiations; but his characterizations of the ministers and their opponents and his comments on the state of affairs and the government's difficulties led them to decide not to print it.[1] Swift was, however, rewarded for all his efforts by being made Dean of St. Patrick's, Dublin, in 1713. He went to Ireland to be installed in June, but was soon recalled to England and remained there during the last months of the queen's reign, entering into a violent controversy with his friend Sir Richard Steele, who had accused the queen and her ministers of wishing to set aside the Protestant succession in favor of her Catholic brother, the so-called Pretender.

On the death of the queen, Swift saw that all his friends would be out of power, and that the new king George I would choose his ministers entirely from among the Whigs. He therefore retired to his deanery in Dublin and for five or six years continued to perform his duties and to work over his memoirs, without taking any part in public life. At first it seemed as if he were living in exile, after his exciting years in London, his friendships with the leading men of his day, and his connections with the great, whom he had deigned to treat as his equals, if he found them worthy of his notice.

But in Dublin he returned to the companionship of Esther Johnson, better known as Stella, who had been a child of eight when he first saw her in the household of Sir William Temple. At the time of his second stay, she was a girl of fifteen, and Swift enjoyed her companionship for the next three years. At Temple's death she was left some property in Ireland and a small legacy. Two years later, when Swift was returning to his parish in Ireland in September, 1701, he suggested that she and her elderly companion, Mrs. Dingley, should accompany him and settle in Dublin, where their small income would go further than in England. They were soon established among the circle of his friends, who came to admire and respect Stella for her wit and good sense and her humor. When Swift was away in London from 1710 to 1713, he wrote

long detailed letters, addressed to both Stella and Mrs. Dingley, giving the most intimate account of his doings from day to day; these were published after his death and are now generally known as the *Journal to Stella*. Among manuscripts which have recently come to light are passages of his memoirs and copies of his poems in the handwriting of Stella; they are proof of the close companionship between them, after he had been made Dean. Though the story of their secret marriage in 1716 cannot be accepted, there is no doubt of the depth and fullness of their friendship, in spite of the rigorous conventions he established between them. In his letters to her, in the verses regularly composed for her birthdays in Dublin, and above all in the account of her which he set down at the moment of her death, he revealed completely his tenderness and devotion and his anguish for her loss.

Yet even this friendship — the greatest solace of his life — was disturbed for a time by the demands made upon him by Hester Vanhomrigh (or Vanessa, as he called her in verse), who as a girl had fallen in love with him, a grave divine of twice her age, a regular visitor to her mother's home in London. Mrs. Vanhomrigh was the widow of a former Commissary-General of Ireland, and Vanessa had been born in Dublin. In 1714, she followed Swift there, and settled in a house that belonged to her at Celbridge a few miles away, craving his sympathy and demanding his help through her remaining years of illness until her early death in 1723. That story may also now be read in their letters and in a long poem called *Cadenus and Vanessa*, in which he tried to turn it into a comedy:

> But what success Vanessa met,
> Is to the world a secret yet:
> Whether the nymph, to please her swain,
> Talks in a high romantic strain:
> Or whether he at last descends
> To like with less seraphic ends;
> Or, to compound the business, whether
> They temper love and books together;
> Must never to mankind be told,
> Nor shall the conscious Muse unfold.

In the meantime his restless spirit had not been content with the affairs of the cathedral and visits to his friends in the country and the writing of occasional verses, but had driven him to interest himself in the affairs of Ireland. Dis-

---

[1] It was printed in 1758 as *The History of the Four Last Years of the Queen*, but its authenticity was doubted until in 1935 Sir Harold Williams found a manuscript copy of it in the Royal Library at Windsor.

gust at the miseries of the tradesmen and coun-
tryfolk led him to enter the struggle against
Ireland's complete political and economic subjugation to the power of England, and brought
him the satisfaction of opposing again his old
enemies, Walpole and the Whigs. He taught
the Irish the use of a formidable weapon, the
boycott, that is to say, the refusal to accept English imported goods that competed with their
own industries; and he went so far in his letters
to the people of Ireland, written under the assumed name of a Dublin draper, as to challenge the authority of the parliament of England
to interfere at all in the affairs of Ireland. As a
result of his triumph, in 1725 he was acclaimed
as the "Hibernian Patriot," the acknowledged
champion of the Irish cause, and for ten years
more he continued to exercise a powerful influence in Dublin.

But Swift's final achievement was to overshadow these local successes and place him
among the few who have been able to write a
book so wide in its appeal that it has become
known throughout the world. For he had
quietly gathered up all his experience of the
ways of the world, of kings and ministers and
courts, all his observation of men and women,
and had put these together into a book of travels,
a sort of parody on the currently popular books
of voyages and accounts of marvels in newly
discovered lands.

In the spring of 1726, after some hesitation,
not being quite sure how he would be received
by the English government, he went to London
to finish *Gulliver's Travels* and to arrange for it
to be published. It came out in November after
his return to Dublin, and was an immediate success; everyone was amused by the story and
could not help being intrigued by the topical
allusions and witty strokes of satire. So, for the
last time, at the height of his fame, Swift spent
the summer of 1727 in London, at the moment
when there seemed to be some chance that his
Tory friends might be in power again under
George II, who had just come to the throne,
and when there was talk once more of his getting an English preferment. But this was to be
another disappointment.

He returned finally to Ireland in the autumn
of 1727, at the age of sixty, to assume again his
role as champion of the oppressed and to attack
in verse and prose those whom he held responsible for the miserable state of the people: the
court and ministers in London, the members of
the Irish parliament in Dublin, the absentee
landlords, and the dishonest tradesmen who
were themselves to blame for the failure of the
campaign to encourage the use of their own
manufactures. He sums up his case against these
people and shows the depths of his bitterness in
his own *Modest Proposal* to solve all the troubles
of the poor people of Ireland; and in his final
gesture, when he leaves a bequest to found a
hospital for the insane ("Verses on the Death
of Dr. Swift," ll. 479–82):

> He gave the little wealth he had,
> To build a house for fools and mad:
> And showed by one satiric touch,
> No nation wanted it so much: . . .

Throughout these years Swift carried on a
long struggle for health against the fits of deafness and giddiness which afflicted him, caused
as we now know by what is called Menière's
disease; until finally, when he was seventy-five,
he suffered the loss of all his powers, and was
condemned to live on without his reason for
three more years, dying in a corner of the deanery "like a rat in a hole."

Yet, in spite of the disappointments and the
sufferings which the years brought him, it
should not be forgotten that he had seemed to
Addison, who knew him well and was a rare
observer and spectator of English life in the
early eighteenth century, to be "the most agreeable companion, the truest friend, and the greatest genius of his age."

It was as Gulliver that Swift showed the fullness of his power to take a character and create
a part. Swift conceived Gulliver at first because
he wanted to write in the form of the popular
travel books of the day and needed an appropriate mouthpiece. Gulliver is an honest and
experienced ship's surgeon who has acquired
some knowledge of navigation. Even when he
gets a ship of his own, he remains an unaffected
seaman. But in the course of his strange travels,
he learns so much that his eyes are opened to the
true state of the world; and as he goes on with
the stories of his voyages one after the other, we
notice his growth in wisdom and sense, in his
understanding of what is good and what is evil,
and in his ability to distinguish between that
which is and that which is not.

In these selections it has not been possible to include the third of the voyages; but the rest is complete, and for the reader today the narrative may even gain somewhat in unity and intensity without that section, which contains so many varied and unrelated incidents that it does not quite fit into the obvious and simple framework of the book. Swift and his friends recognized at the time that it was not as good as the rest. It is probable that some of the incidents there satirizing the new science may have been taken from fragments of earlier work; other incidents seem to refer to matters so very recent that they must have been added during the summer of 1726 when Swift was in London immediately before the book appeared. And other parts of this third voyage probably arose out of Swift's experiences just before in Ireland. Perhaps for these reasons we are less aware of the figure of Gulliver. Swift himself seems almost to forget him sometimes and introduces asides and comments which break down our belief that we are listening to the story as narrated by Gulliver.

But in the other three voyages, Gulliver fits every purpose that Swift has in mind. In narrative style, in the simple framework of each part, with the short paragraphs at the beginning and end describing the voyage out and the return, with the references to actual ships and captains familiar to the readers of contemporary voyages, he is able to convince us of the reality, the simple truth, of his tale. Some of the popular travel books of course contain all sorts of extravagant stories and wild seamen's yarns, but in a short preface, " The Publisher to the Reader," we are given by a supposed editor, Richard Sympson, an intimate friend of the author, a certificate of Mr. Lemuel Gulliver's reliability:

There is an air of truth apparent through the whole; and indeed the author was so distinguished for his veracity, that it became a sort of proverb among his neighbors at Redriff, when any one affirmed a thing, to say it was as true as if Mr. Gulliver had spoke it.

And in a very short sketch of his life before these adventures begin, we are told that Gulliver was a man of considerable reading and had developed a great facility in learning foreign languages. He shows himself in his dealing with the Lilliputians to be a man of a mild and generous disposition, ready to try to win their good

opinion by his patience and discreet behavior. He is rather taken by surprise and shocked when he learns of the plots of his Lilliputian enemies to bring about his destruction, of the articles of impeachment against him in spite of his heroic exploits in capturing the whole fleet of their Blefuscudian enemies, and of the final decision whereby through the leniency of the emperor, he was only condemned to the loss of his eyes:

Yet, as to myself, I must confess, having never been designed for a courtier either by my birth or education, I was so ill a judge of things, that I could not discover the *lenity* and favor of this sentence, but conceived it (perhaps erroneously) rather to be rigorous than gentle.

Here (Part I, Chapter 7) Swift uses the innocence of Gulliver, his inexperience of the ways of courts and ministers, as a means of expressing ironically his own feelings of horror at the way in which his friends, the ministers of the Crown in the last years of Queen Anne's reign, had been treated by their opponents the Whigs as soon as the Whigs had established their power in the new Hanoverian regime. And he gets a further effect by making Gulliver explain, when he comes later to write the story, that he now realizes — after more experience in the ways of courts — how rash he was not to " have submitted to so easy a punishment with great alacrity and readiness! "

It must not be forgotten that Gulliver is never a mere pseudonym, adopted simply as a disguise to protect the real author, should the book bring him into trouble. He is essential as a character whose eyes are opened to reality as a result of his experiences, whose whole standard of values is gradually changed under the influence first of the simple moral grandeur of the Brobdingnagians, and then finally by the benignant effect of his happy sojourn in the land of those perfectly rational and kindly beings, the Houyhnhnms.

For instance, on several occasions Gulliver tried his best to give the king of the Brobdingnagians a favorable account of the history of his own country, and, as he said, made every effort to " hide the frailties and deformities of his political mother and place her virtues and beauties in the most advantageous light," and to use his opportunity to impress his Majesty with the glories of Western civilization. Nevertheless, while listening to Gulliver's panegyrics (II.6) the king grew more and more horrified and astonished until finally —

taking me into his hands, and stroking me gently, he delivered himself in these words, which I shall never forget, nor the manner he spoke them in. " My little friend Grildrig, you have made a most admirable panegyric upon your country. . . . But, by what I have gathered from your own relation, and the answers I have with much pains wringed and extorted from you, I cannot but conclude the bulk of your natives to be the most pernicious race of little odious vermin that nature ever suffered to crawl upon the surface of the earth."

Gulliver confessed that he was so shocked and puzzled by this that he would have liked to omit all account of it from his story, if it had not been for his extreme love of truth. Notice that while he is living among the giants and so often suffering indignities because of his smallness he is still trying to maintain his belief in the superiority of his own race. In spite of the kindness shown him, and his position at court, and the favor of the king and queen, he felt that " it was upon such a foot as ill became the dignity of human kind." And so he tried to vindicate himself by placing at the disposal of his Majesty all his superior political skill and knowledge of the ways of civilized nations and their methods of gaining power and extending their influence over the world, and by revealing to him the secret of gunpowder, which would make him master of the world. But once again (II.7) Gulliver found that he had made a mistake, and had only succeeded in bringing forth another surprising outburst:

He was amazed how so impotent and groveling an insect as I (these were his expressions) could entertain such inhuman ideas, and in so familiar a manner as to appear wholly unmoved at all the scenes of blood and desolation, which I had painted as the common effects of those destructive machines, . . . he would rather lose half his kingdom than be privy to such a secret, which he commanded me, as I valued my life, never to mention any more.

Swift carries the irony even further, by describing how puzzled Gulliver was to explain such narrow principles and short views. He had the utmost admiration for his Majesty, his wisdom

and his talents for government, and was worried at discovering such a defect in him, as to be hindered by " nice unnecessary scruples " from making himself absolute master of the lives, liberties, and fortunes of his people. He could only conclude that it was due to the general state of ignorance of the Brobdingnagians, who had not " reduced politics into a science, as the more acute wits of Europe have done."

But it was the experiences of his last voyage which completed the education of Gulliver, for among those admirable Houyhnhnms he could live in the contemplation and practice of every virtue, and be entirely without any incitement to lie. Swift does not leave us in any doubt about this. He explains how it was that Gulliver was no longer concerned about the dignity of human kind, though in what he said of his countrymen he still tried to extenuate their faults as much as he dared and give as favorable a turn as the matter would bear (IV.7).

But I must freely confess, that the many virtues of those excellent quadrupeds placed in opposite view to human corruptions, had so far opened my eyes and enlarged my understanding, that I began to view the actions and passions of man in a very different light, and to think the honor of my own kind not worth managing . . . I had likewise learned from his example an utter detestation of all falsehood or disguise; and truth appeared so amiable to me, that I determined upon sacrificing everything to it.

Gulliver indeed soon began to plan never to return to his own country, and when he was finally forced to leave, his " heart quite sunk with grief." The account of his return and of the horrors that he endured when he found himself again among his own race, with its dreadful resemblance to the Yahoos, occupies the last chapters of the book. And here (IV.12) Gulliver is allowed to speak, as it were, in the fullness of his enlightenment, of his attempt to reconcile himself again to the Yahoo-kind.

[It] might not be so difficult, if they would be content with those vices and follies only which nature hath entitled them to. . . . but when I behold a lump of deformity, and diseases both in body and mind, smitten with *pride,* it immediately breaks all the measures of my patience; . . .

When the book first appeared, the editor or publisher, Richard Sympson, explained that he had the author's permission to take the advice of "several worthy persons" who recommended that he should venture to send the *Travels* forth into the world in the hope that they would be "a better entertainment to our young noblemen, than the common scribbles of politics and party." When Swift was revising the book for the collected edition of his *Works*, in 1735, and restoring passages which the first printer had changed because he was afraid they might cause trouble, he decided to give us a little further information about Gulliver. This took the form of a prefatory letter from Captain Gulliver to his cousin Sympson, in which after complaining of the liberties taken with his original manuscript, he went on to express his regrets that he had ever allowed the book to be printed:

Pray bring to your mind how often I desired you to consider, when you insisted on the motive of *public good;* that the *Yahoos* were a species of animals utterly incapable of amendment by precepts or examples: and so it hath proved; for instead of seeing a full stop put to all abuses and corruptions, at least in this little island, as I had reason to expect: behold, after above six months' warning, I cannot learn that my book hath produced one single effect according to my intentions: . . .

Instead of the reformation he expected, Gulliver's book has produced nothing but doubts upon his veracity, all sorts of Keys and Reflections and Memoirs, in which he is attacked for degrading human nature and abusing the female sex. Some have even gone so far as to suggest that his book is a mere fiction. Finally, Gulliver confesses that since his return some corruptions of his Yahoo nature have revived in him; "else I should never have attempted so absurd a project as that of reforming the *Yahoo* race in this kingdom; but, I have now done with all such visionary schemes for ever."

But although, like Gulliver, Swift gave up all hope of reforming mankind, he continued to write in verse and in prose, and to give vent to his indignation and his bitterness. Faced by the miserable state of Ireland, he could still indulge in the luxury of satire, and find an escape from unprofitable political activity in pure irony. And so he comes forward once more among those who are putting out all kinds of schemes and projects with a *Modest Proposal,* of his own, something "wholly new," of "no expense and little trouble," *for preventing the children of poor people, . . . from being a burden to their parents or country; and for making them beneficial to the public.*

It is a very simple plan, and he is able to work out the economic and business details of the proposed new industry in a way which demonstrates very clearly that it would be profitable for all concerned. It would provide a new commodity for the rich and a modest living for the poor. It would cost only about two shillings to rear a child to the age of twelve months, and the carcass should then weigh about twenty-eight pounds, and should sell for about ten shillings. Infants' flesh would be always in season, and would make a "most delicious, nourishing and wholesome food." It would be particularly *"proper for landlords,* who, as they have already devoured most of the parents, seem to have the best title to the children." The *Proposal* is a kind of terrible parody of his own earlier proposals for improving the state of Ireland. He has learned now that he has no longer any power to influence the government or rouse the people. But he can still challenge the conscience of his readers to face a desperate situation and to force them, if they have no better alternative to suggest, to share in his passionate protest and his fierce indignation.

In this and his other later Irish pamphlets, though he did not put his name on the title page, Swift assumes no disguise; he speaks directly, in his own person, as the unnamed champion of the people of Ireland, with the experience of the Dean, the Drapier, and Lemuel Gulliver behind him. He shows the fullness of his power as a master of irony and a writer who has attained to the perfection of simplicity in the art of prose.

GULLIVER'S TRAVELS

Swift first speaks of being at work on his *Travels* in April, 1721; and he sounds as if he were then well under way. They were for the most part finished before he went to England in 1726, though it is possible that some additions were made to the Third Voyage at the suggestion of his friends in London, who seem to have provided him with some very recent examples of the kind of scientific experiments he was making fun of. The Four Voyages were published in two volumes before the end of the year, and were an immediate success. Swift may have set out to "vex the world," but he succeeded in amusing it. He had imitated the manner of the stories of the Discoverers, which were the best-sellers of the day. In the First Voyage to Lilliput there are many references to political figures and happenings which would be familiar to his first readers; but even here, though he likes to make fun of his old

enemies, his attitude is not that of the party writer but of the moralist, whose business is to reveal the frailties and vices of human life as they are displayed among courtiers and politicians. In the Second and Fourth Voyages he allows himself more scope for dramatic irony by placing Gulliver as a pygmy among the giants and as a Yahoo among the Houyhnhnms (best pronounced "Whinnims"), where he is much at a disadvantage in trying to uphold the dignity of his race and to explain the glories of Western civilization. Some of the comments which Swift had permitted himself indeed were too much for his first publisher, who omitted and altered so greatly that Swift was careful to have the book printed under his own supervision in 1735 for the Dublin edition of his collected *Works*, with the full text as he intended it, adding the following letter from Captain Gulliver to his Cousin Sympson.

TRAVELS
INTO SEVERAL REMOTE
NATIONS OF THE WORLD

By Lemuel Gulliver, first a Surgeon, and
then a Captain of several Ships

A LETTER FROM CAPTAIN GULLIVER
TO HIS COUSIN SYMPSON [1]

I hope you will be ready to own publicly, whenever you shall be called to it, that by your great and frequent urgency you prevailed on me to publish a very loose and uncorrect account of my travels; with direction to hire some young gentlemen of either university to put them in order, and correct the style, as my cousin Dampier [2] did by my advice, in his book called *A Voyage Round the World*. But I do not remember I gave you power to consent, that anything should be omitted, and much less that anything should be inserted: therefore, as to the latter, I do here renounce everything

of that kind; particularly a paragraph about her Majesty the late Queen Anne, of most pious and glorious memory; although I did reverence and esteem her more than any of human species. But you, or your interpolator, ought to have considered, that as it was not my inclination, so was it not decent to praise any animal of our composition before my master *Houyhnhnm:* and besides, the fact was altogether false; for to my knowledge, being in England during some part of her Majesty's reign, she did govern by a chief minister; nay, even by two successively; the first whereof was the Lord of Godolphin, and the second the Lord of Oxford; [3] so that you have made me *say the thing that was not.*[4] Likewise, in the account of the Academy of Projectors, and several passages of my discourse to my master *Houyhnhnm,* you have either omitted some material circumstances, or minced or changed them in such a manner, that I do hardly know my own work. When I formerly hinted to you something of this in a letter, you were pleased to answer that you were afraid of giving offense; that people in power were very watchful over the press, and apt not only to interpret, but to punish everything

---

GULLIVER'S TRAVELS. **Prefaces.** **1. Letter ... Sympson:** In spite of the date given, it was certainly written by Swift for the Dublin edition of 1735, in which he restored passages which had been omitted or modified in the first edition owing to the fears of the publisher. **2. Dampier:** Swift here draws attention to the famous account of the real voyages of this great explorer, William Dampier, which he had taken as a model for his own fiction.

3. Godolphin ... Oxford: Lord Treasurer, i.e., first minister under Queen Anne until 1710, when replaced by Robert Harley, who was made Earl of Oxford. **4. say ... not:** a phrase coined by Gulliver's Houyhnhnm master to translate the word "lying," for which there was no term in their language.

which looked like an *innuendo* (as I think you called it). But pray, how could that which I spoke so many years ago, and at about five thousand leagues distance, in another reign, be applied to any of the *Yahoos,* who now are said to govern the herd,[5] especially, at a time when I little thought on or feared the unhappiness of living under them? Have not I the most reason to complain, when I see these very *Yahoos* carried by *Houyhnhnms* in a vehicle, as if these were brutes, and those the rational creatures? And indeed, to avoid so monstrous and detestable a sight, was one principal motive of my retirement hither.

Thus much I thought proper to tell you in relation to yourself, and to the trust I reposed in you.

I do in the next place complain of my own great want of judgment, in being prevailed upon by the entreaties and false reasonings of you and some others, very much against my own opinion, to suffer my travels to be published. Pray bring to your mind how often I desired you to consider, when you insisted on the motive of *public good;* that the *Yahoos* were a species of animals utterly incapable of amendment by precepts or examples: and so it hath proved; for instead of seeing a full stop put to all abuses and corruptions, at least in this little island, as I had reason to expect: behold, after above six months' warning, I cannot learn that my book hath produced one single effect according to my intentions: I desired you would let me know by a letter, when party and faction were extinguished; judges learned and upright; pleaders honest and modest, with some tincture of common sense; and Smithfield[6] blazing with pyramids of lawbooks; the young nobility's education entirely changed; the physicians banished; the female *Yahoos* abounding in virtue, honor, truth, and good sense; courts and levees of great ministers thoroughly weeded and swept; wit, merit, and learning rewarded; all disgracers of the press in prose and verse, condemned to eat nothing but their own cotton,[7] and quench their thirst with their own ink. These, and a thousand other reformations, I firmly counted upon by your encouragement; as indeed they were plainly deducible from the precepts delivered in my book. And, it must be owned, that seven months[8] were a sufficient time to correct every vice and folly to which *Yahoos* are subject; if their natures had been capable of the least disposition to virtue or wisdom: yet so far have you been from answering my expectation in any of your letters; that on the contrary, you are loading our carrier every week with libels, and keys, and reflections, and memoirs, and second parts,[9] wherein I see myself accused of reflecting upon great statesfolk; of degrading human nature (for so they have still the confidence to style it), and of abusing the female sex. I find likewise that the writers of those bundles are not agreed among themselves; for some of them will not allow me to be author of my own travels; and others make me author of books to which I am wholly a stranger.

I find likewise, that your printer hath been so careless as to confound the times, and mistake the dates of my several voyages and returns; neither assigning the true year, or the true month, or day of the month: and I hear the original manuscript is all destroyed, since the publication of my book. Neither have I any copy left: however, I have sent you some corrections, which you may insert, if ever there should be a second edition: and yet I cannot stand to them, but shall leave that matter to my judicious and candid readers, to adjust it as they please.

I hear some of our sea *Yahoos* find fault with my sea language, as not proper in many parts, nor now in use. I cannot help it. In my first voyages, while I was young, I was instructed by the oldest mariners,[10] and learned to speak as they did. But I have since found that the sea *Yahoos* are apt, like the land ones, to become newfangled in their words; which the latter change every year; insomuch, as I remember upon each return to my own country, their old dialect was so altered, that I could hardly understand the new. And I observe, when any *Yahoo* comes from London out of curiosity to visit me at my own house, we neither of us are able to deliver our conceptions in a manner intelligible to the other.

If the censure of *Yahoos* could any way affect me, I should have great reason to complain, that some of them are so bold as to think my book of travels a mere fiction out of my own brain; and have gone so far as to drop hints, that the *Houyhnhnms* and *Yahoos* have no more existence than the inhabitants of Utopia.[11]

5. *Yahoos* . . . herd: the court and government of George I.
6. Smithfield: a market place outside the walls of the city of London, where persons and books condemned for heresy used to be burned. 7. cotton: rag paper. 8. seven months: actually only five months before the supposed date of the letter.

9. libels . . . parts: The book was so popular that rubbishy *Keys* and imitations were quickly printed in the hope of an easy sale. 10. oldest mariners: Swift had borrowed some of the sea terms from Sturmy's *Compleat Mariner,* 1669; they were thus a little old-fashioned. 11. Utopia: Sir Thomas More's ideal commonwealth.

Indeed I must confess, that as to the people of *Lilliput, Brobdingrag* [12] (for so the word should have been spelt, and not erroneously *Brobdingnag*), and *Laputa;* I have never yet heard of any *Yahoo* so presumptuous as to dispute their being, or the facts I have related concerning them; because the truth immediately strikes every reader with conviction. And is there less probability in my account of the *Houyhnhnms* or *Yahoos,* when it is manifest as to the latter, there are so many thousands even in this city, who only differ from their brother brutes in *Houyhnhnm-land,* because they use a sort of a jabber, and do not go naked? I wrote for their amendment, and not their approbation. The united praise of the whole race would be of less consequence to me, than the neighing of those two degenerate *Houyhnhnms* I keep in my stable; because, from these, degenerate as they are, I still improve in some virtues, without any mixture of vice.

Do these miserable animals presume to think that I am so far degenerated as to defend my veracity? *Yahoo* as I am, it is well known through all *Houyhnhnm-land,* that by the instructions and example of my illustrious master, I was able in the compass of two years (although I confess with the utmost difficulty) to remove that infernal habit of lying, shuffling, deceiving, and equivocating, so deeply rooted in the very souls of all my species; especially the Europeans.

I have other complaints to make upon this vexatious occasion; but I forbear troubling myself or you any further. I must freely confess, that since my last return, some corruptions of my *Yahoo* nature have revived in me by conversing with a few of your species, and particularly those of my own family, by an unavoidable necessity; else I should never have attempted so absurd a project as that of reforming the *Yahoo* race in this kingdom; but I have now done with all such visionary schemes for ever.

April 2, 1727

THE PUBLISHER TO THE READER

The author of these Travels, Mr. Lemuel Gulliver, is my ancient and intimate friend; there is likewise some relation between us by the mother's side. About three years ago, Mr. Gulliver growing weary of the concourse of curious people coming to him at his house in Redriff, made a small purchase of land, with a convenient house, near Newark, in Nottinghamshire, his native country; where he now lives retired, yet in good esteem among his neighbors.

Although Mr. Gulliver was born in Nottinghamshire, where his father dwelt, yet I have heard him say his family came from Oxfordshire; to confirm which, I have observed in the churchyard at Banbury,[13] in that county, several tombs and monuments of the Gullivers.

Before he quitted Redriff,[14] he left the custody of the following papers in my hands, with the liberty to dispose of them as I should think fit. I have carefully perused them three times: the style is very plain and simple; and the only fault I find is, that the author, after the manner of travelers, is a little too circumstantial. There is an air of truth apparent through the whole; and indeed the author was so distinguished for his veracity, that it became a sort of proverb among his neighbors at Redriff, when any one affirmed a thing, to say it was as true as if Mr. Gulliver had spoke it.

By the advice of several worthy persons, to whom, with the author's permission, I communicated these papers, I now venture to send them into the world, hoping they may be at least, for some time, a better entertainment to our young noblemen, than the common scribbles of politics and party.

This volume would have been at least twice as large, if I had not made bold to strike out innumerable passages relating to the winds and tides, as well as to the variations and bearings in the several voyages; together with the minute descriptions of the management of the ship in storms, in the style of sailors: likewise the account of longitudes and latitudes; wherein I have reason to apprehend that Mr. Gulliver may be a little dissatisfied: but I was resolved to fit the work as much as possible to the general capacity of readers. However, if my own ignorance in sea affairs shall have led me to commit some mistakes, I alone am answerable for them: and if any traveler hath a curiosity to see the whole work at large, as it came from the hand of the author, I will be ready to gratify him.

As for any further particulars relating to the author, the reader will receive satisfaction from the the first pages of the book.

RICHARD SYMPSON [15]

13. *Brobdingrag:* The correction of course is a trick to make the name sound more real.

13. **Banbury:** market town in Oxfordshire, which Swift must have often ridden through on his way from Ireland to London; the family name "Gulliver" is still known there.   14. **Redriff:** or Rotherhithe, a seafaring place near London on the south bank of the Thames.   15. **Richard Sympson:** Gulliver's imaginary cousin and editor, possibly suggested by William Sympson, from *A New Voyage to the East Indies,* 1715.

PART I

A Voyage to Lilliput

CHAPTER I

The Author gives some account of himself and family; his first inducements to travel. He is shipwrecked, and swims for his life, gets safe on shore in the country of Lilliput,[1] is made a prisoner, and carried up the country.

My father had a small estate in Nottinghamshire; I was the third of five sons. He sent me to Emmanuel College in Cambridge, at fourteen years [2] old, where I resided three years, and applied myself close to my studies; but the charge of maintaining me (although I had a very scanty allowance) being too great for a narrow fortune, I was bound apprentice to Mr. James Bates, an eminent surgeon in London, with whom I continued four years; and my father now and then sending me small sums of money, I laid them out in learning navigation, and other parts of the mathematics, useful to those who intend to travel, as I always believed it would be some time or other my fortune to do. When I left Mr. Bates, I went down to my father; where, by the assistance of him and my uncle John, and some other relations, I got forty pounds, and a promise of thirty pounds a year to maintain me at Leyden;[3] there I studied physic two years and seven months, knowing it would be useful in long voyages.

Soon after my return from Leyden, I was recommended by my good master, Mr. Bates, to be surgeon to the *Swallow,* Captain Abraham Pannell, Commander; with whom I continued three years and a half, making a voyage or two into the Levant,[4] and some other parts. When I came back, I resolved to settle in London, to which Mr. Bates, my master, encouraged me, and by him I was recommended to several patients. I took part of a small house in the Old Jury;[5] and being advised to alter my condition, I married Mrs. Mary [6] Burton, second daughter to Mr. Edmund Burton, ho-

sier, in Newgate Street, with whom I received four hundred pounds for a portion.

But, my good master Bates dying in two years after, and I having few friends, my business began to fail; for my conscience would not suffer me to imitate the bad practice of too many among my brethren. Having therefore consulted with my wife, and some of my acquaintance, I determined to go again to sea. I was surgeon successively in two ships, and made several voyages, for six years, to the East and West Indies, by which I got some addition to my fortune. My hours of leisure I spent in reading the best authors, ancient and modern, being always provided with a good number of books; and when I was ashore in observing the manners and dispositions of the people, as well as learning their language, wherein I had a great facility by the strength of my memory.

The last of these voyages not proving very fortunate, I grew weary of the sea, and intended to stay at home with my wife and family. I removed from the Old Jury to Fetter Lane, and from thence to Wapping, hoping to get business among the sailors; but it would not turn to account. After three years' expectation that things would mend, I accepted an advantageous offer from Captain William Prichard, master of the *Antelope,* who was making a voyage to the South Sea. We set sail from Bristol, May 4, 1699, and our voyage at first was very prosperous.

It would not be proper, for some reasons, to trouble the reader with the particulars of our adventures in those seas: let it suffice to inform him, that in our passage from thence to the East Indies, we were driven by a violent storm to the northwest of Van Diemen's Land.[7] By an observation, we found ourselves in the latitude of thirty degrees two minutes south. Twelve of our crew were dead by immoderate labor, and ill food; the rest were in a very weak condition. On the fifth of November, which was the beginning of summer in those parts, the weather being very hazy, the seamen spied a rock, within half a cable's length of the ship; but the wind was so strong, that we were driven directly upon it, and immediately split. Six of the crew, of whom I was one, having let down the boat into the sea, made a shift to get clear of the ship, and the rock. We rowed, by my computation, about three leagues, till we were able to work no longer, being already spent with labor while we were in

A Voyage to Lilliput. **1. Lilliput:** Swift successfully invented suitable-sounding names for the countries visited, and it is not very profitable to attempt to give their derivations.   **2. at . . . years:** Swift himself had entered Trinity College, Dublin, at fourteen.   **3. Leyden:** the center of medical studies then in Holland.   **4. Levant:** eastern part of Mediterranean.   **5. Old Jury:** or Jewry, on the north of Cheapside, which had been the medieval Jewish quarter of the city of London.   **6. Mrs. Mary:** In Swift's day, "Miss" was used only of young girls, "Mrs." of

all adult women.   **7. Van Diemen's Land:** earlier name for Tasmania, then thought to be a part of the mainland of Australia.

the ship. We therefore trusted ourselves to the mercy of the waves, and in about half an hour the boat was overset by a sudden flurry from the north. What became of my companions in the boat, as well as of those who escaped on the rock, or were left in the vessel, I cannot tell; but conclude they were all lost.

For my own part, I swam as fortune directed me, and was pushed forward by wind and tide. I often let my legs drop, and could feel no bottom: but when I was almost gone, and able to struggle no longer, I found myself within my depth; and by this time the storm was much abated. The declivity was so small, that I walked near a mile before I got to the shore, which I conjectured was about eight o'clock in the evening. I then advanced forward near half a mile, but could not discover any sign of houses or inhabitants; at least I was in so weak a condition, that I did not observe them. I was extremely tired, and with that, and the heat of the weather, and about half a pint of brandy that I drank as I left the ship, I found myself much inclined to sleep. I lay down on the grass, which was very short and soft, where I slept sounder than ever I remember to have done in my life, and, as I reckoned, above nine hours; for when I awaked, it was just daylight. I attempted to rise, but was not able to stir: for as I happened to lie on my back, I found my arms and legs were strongly fastened on each side to the ground; and my hair, which was long and thick, tied down in the same manner. I likewise felt several slender ligatures across my body, from my armpits to my thighs. I could only look upwards; the sun began to grow hot, and the light offended my eyes. I heard a confused noise about me, but in the posture I lay, could see nothing except the sky.

In a little time I felt something alive moving on my left leg, which advancing gently forward over my breast, came almost up to my chin; when bending my eyes downwards as much as I could, I perceived it to be a human creature not six inches high,[8] with a bow and arrow in his hands, and a quiver at his back. In the meantime, I felt at least forty more of the same kind (as I conjectured) following the first. I was in the utmost astonishment, and roared so loud, that they all ran back in a fright; and some of them, as I was afterwards told, were hurt with the falls they got by leaping from my sides upon the ground. However, they soon re-

turned, and one of them, who ventured so far as to get a full sight of my face, lifting up his hands and eyes by way of admiration, cried out in a shrill, but distinct voice, *Hekinah degul:* the others repeated the same words several times, but then I knew not what they meant. I lay all this while, as the reader may believe, in great uneasiness: at length, struggling to get loose, I had the fortune to break the strings, and wrench out the pegs that fastened my left arm to the ground; for, by lifting it up to my face, I discovered the methods they had taken to bind me, and at the same time with a violent pull, which gave me excessive pain, I a little loosened the strings that tied down my hair on the left side, so that I was just able to turn my head about two inches. But the creatures ran off a second time, before I could seize them; whereupon there was a great shout in a very shrill accent, and after it ceased, I heard one of them cry aloud, *Tolgo phonac;* when in an instant I felt above an hundred arrows discharged on my left hand, which pricked me like so many needles; and besides, they shot another flight into the air, as we do bombs in Europe, whereof many, I suppose, fell on my body (though I felt them not), and some on my face, which I immediately covered with my left hand. When this shower of arrows was over, I fell a groaning with grief and pain, and then striving again to get loose, they discharged another volley larger than the first, and some of them attempted with spears to stick me in the sides; but, by good luck, I had on me a buff jerkin,[9] which they could not pierce. I thought it the most prudent method to lie still, and my design was to continue so till night, when, my left hand being already loose, I could easily free myself: and as for the inhabitants, I had reason to believe I might be a match for the greatest armies they could bring against me, if they were all of the same size with him that I saw. But fortune disposed otherwise of me.

When the people observed I was quiet, they discharged no more arrows; but, by the noise increasing, I knew their numbers were greater; and about four yards from me, over against my right ear, I heard a knocking for above an hour, like that of people at work; when turning my head that way, as well as the pegs and strings would permit me, I saw a stage erected, about a foot and a half from the ground, capable of holding four of the inhabitants, with two or three ladders to mount it: from whence one of them, who seemed to be a person of

---

8. **six . . . high:** In Lilliput Swift reduces everything roughly to a twelfth, and increases it by the same amount in Brobdingnag.

9. **buff jerkin:** heavy hide waistcoat.

quality, made me a long speech, whereof I understood not one syllable. But I should have mentioned, that before the principal person began his oration, he cried out three times, *Langro dehul san:* (these words and the former were afterwards repeated and explained to me). Whereupon immediately about fifty of the inhabitants came and cut the strings that fastened the left side of my head, which gave me the liberty of turning it to the right, and of observing the person and gesture of him who was to speak. He appeared to be of a middle age, and taller than any of the other three who attended him, whereof one was a page who held up his train, and seemed to be somewhat longer than my middle finger; the other two stood one on each side to support him. He acted every part of an orator, and I could observe many periods of threatenings, and others of promises, pity, and kindness.

I answered in a few words, but in the most submissive manner, lifting up my left hand, and both my eyes to the sun, as calling him for a witness; and being almost famished with hunger, having not eaten a morsel for some hours before I left the ship. I found the demands of nature so strong upon me, that I could not forbear showing my impatience (perhaps against the strict rules of decency) by putting my finger frequently on my mouth, to signify that I wanted food. The *Hurgo* (for so they call a great lord, as I afterwards learnt) understood me very well. He descended from the stage, and commanded that several ladders should be applied to my sides, on which above an hundred of the inhabitants mounted and walked towards my mouth, laden with baskets full of meat, which had been provided and sent thither by the King's orders, upon the first intelligence he received of me. I observed there was the flesh of several animals, but could not distinguish them by the taste. There were shoulders, legs, and loins, shaped like those of mutton, and very well dressed, but smaller than the wings of a lark. I eat them by two or three at a mouthful, and took three loaves at a time, about the bigness of musket bullets. They supplied me as fast as they could, showing a thousand marks of wonder and astonishment at my bulk and appetite.

I then made another sign that I wanted drink. They found by my eating, that a small quantity would not suffice me; and being a most ingenious people, they slung up with great dexterity one of their largest hogsheads, then rolled it towards my hand, and beat out the top; I drank it off at a draught, which I might well do, for it hardly held half a pint, and tasted like a small wine of Burgundy, but much more delicious. They brought me a second hogshead, which I drank in the same manner, and made signs for more, but they had none to give me. When I had performed these wonders, they shouted for joy, and danced upon my breast, repeating several times as they did at first, *Hekinah degul.*[10] They made me a sign that I should throw down the two hogsheads, but first warned the people below to stand out of the way, crying aloud, *Borach mivola,* and when they saw the vessels in the air, there was an universal shout of *Hekinah degul.* I confess I was often tempted, while they were passing backwards and forwards on my body, to seize forty or fifty of the first that came in my reach, and dash them against the ground. But the remembrance of what I had felt, which probably might not be the worst they could do, and the promise of honor I made them, for so I interpreted my submissive behavior, soon drove out those imaginations. Besides, I now considered myself as bound by the laws of hospitality to a people who had treated me with so much expense and magnificence. However, in my thoughts, I could not sufficiently wonder at the intrepidity of these diminutive mortals, who durst venture to mount and walk on my body, while one of my hands was at liberty, without trembling at the very sight of so prodigious a creature as I must appear to them.

After some time, when they observed that I made no more demands for meat, there appeared before me a person of high rank from his Imperial Majesty. His Excellency, having mounted on the small of my right leg, advanced forwards up to my face, with about a dozen of his retinue. And producing his credentials under the Signet Royal, which he applied close to my eyes, spoke about ten minutes, without any signs of anger, but with a kind of determinate resolution; often pointing forwards, which, as I afterwards found, was towards the capital city, about half a mile distant, whither it was agreed by his Majesty in council that I must be conveyed. I answered in few words, but to no purpose, and made a sign with my hand that was loose, putting it to the other (but over his Excellency's head for fear of hurting him or his train) and then to my own head and body, to signify that

10. *Hekinah degul:* possibly imitating Rabelais' method of coining names, or sheer inventions anticipating James Joyce.

I desired my liberty. It appeared that he understood me well enough, for he shook his head by way of disapprobation, and held his hand in a posture to show that I must be carried as a prisoner. However, he made other signs to let me understand that I should have meat and drink enough, and very good treatment. Whereupon I once more thought of attempting to break my bonds; but again, when I felt the smart of their arrows, upon my face and hands, which were all in blisters, and many of the darts still sticking in them, and observing likewise that the number of my enemies increased, I gave tokens to let them know that they might do with me what they pleased. Upon this, the *Hurgo* and his train withdrew, with much civility and cheerful countenances.

Soon after I heard a general shout, with frequent repetitions of the words, *Peplom selan,* and I felt great numbers of people on my left side relaxing the cords to such a degree, that I was able to turn upon my right, and to ease myself with making water; which I very plentifully did, to the great astonishment of the people, who conjecturing by my motions what I was going to do, immediately opened to the right and left on that side, to avoid the torrent which fell with such noise and violence from me. But before this, they had daubed my face and both my hands with a sort of ointment very pleasant to the smell, which in a few minutes removed all the smart of their arrows. These circumstances, added to the refreshment I had received by their victuals and drink, which were very nourishing, disposed me to sleep. I slept about eight hours, as I was afterwards assured; and it was no wonder, for the physicians, by the Emperor's order, had mingled a sleeping potion in the hogsheads of wine.

It seems that upon the first moment I was discovered sleeping on the ground after my landing, the Emperor had early notice of it by an express; and determined in council that I should be tied in the manner I have related (which was done in the night while I slept), that plenty of meat and drink should be sent me, and a machine prepared to carry me to the capital city.

This resolution perhaps may appear very bold and dangerous, and I am confident would not be imitated by any prince in Europe on the like occasion; however, in my opinion, it was extremely prudent, as well as generous: for supposing these people had endeavored to kill me with their spears and arrows while I was asleep, I should certainly have awaked with the first sense of smart, which might so far have roused my rage and strength, as to enable me to break the strings wherewith I was tied; after which, as they were not able to make resistance, so they could expect no mercy.

These people are most excellent mathematicians, and arrived to a great perfection in mechanics, by the countenance and encouragement of the Emperor, who is a renowned patron of learning. This prince hath several machines fixed on wheels, for the carriage of trees and other great weights. He often builds his largest men-of-war, whereof some are nine foot long, in the woods where the timber grows, and has them carried on these engines three or four hundred yards to the sea. Five hundred carpenters and engineers were immediately set at work to prepare the greatest engine they had. It was a frame of wood raised three inches from the ground, about seven foot long and four wide, moving upon twenty-two wheels. The shout I heard was upon the arrival of this engine, which it seems set out in four hours after my landing. It was brought parallel to me as I lay. But the principal difficulty was to raise and place me in this vehicle. Eighty poles, each of one foot high, were erected for this purpose, and very strong cords of the bigness of pack thread were fastened by hooks to many bandages, which the workmen had girt round my neck, my hands, my body, and my legs. Nine hundred of the strongest men were employed to draw up these cords by many pulleys fastened on the poles, and thus, in less than three hours, I was raised and slung into the engine, and there tied fast. All this I was told, for, while the whole operation was performing, I lay in a profound sleep, by the force of that soporiferous medicine infused into my liquor. Fifteen hundred of the Emperor's largest horses, each about four inches and a half high, were employed to draw me towards the metropolis, which, as I said, was half a mile distant.

About four hours after we began our journey, I awaked by a very ridiculous accident; for the carriage being stopped a while to adjust something that was out of order, two or three of the young natives had the curiosity to see how I looked when I was asleep; they climbed up into the engine, and advancing very softly to my face, one of them, an officer in the guards, put the sharp end of his half-pike a good way up into my left nostril, which tickled my nose like a straw, and made me sneeze violently: whereupon they stole off unperceived, and it was three weeks before I knew the cause of my awaking so suddenly. We made a long march the remaining part of the day, and rested at night with five hundred guards on each side of me, half with torches, and half with bows and arrows, ready to shoot me if I should offer to stir. The next morning at sunrise we continued our march, and arrived within two hundred yards of the city gates about noon. The Emperor, and all his court, came out to meet us; but his great officers would by no means suffer his Majesty to endanger his person by mounting on my body.

At the place where the carriage stopped, there stood an ancient temple,[11] esteemed to be the largest in the whole kingdom; which, having been polluted some years before by an unnatural murder, was, according to the zeal of those people, looked upon as profane, and therefore had been applied to common uses, and all the ornaments and furniture carried away. In this edifice it was determined I should lodge. The great gate fronting to the north was about four foot high, and almost two foot wide, through which I could easily creep. On each side of the gate was a small window not above six inches from the ground: into that on the left side, the King's smiths conveyed fourscore and eleven chains, like those that hang to a lady's watch in Europe, and almost as large, which were locked to my left leg with six and thirty padlocks.[12] Over against this temple, on the other side of the great highway, at twenty foot distance, there was a turret at least five foot high. Here the Emperor ascended, with many principal lords of his court, to have an opportunity of viewing me, as I was told, for I could not see them. It was reckoned that above an hundred thousand inhabitants came out of the town upon the same errand; and, in spite of my guards, I believe there could not be fewer than ten thousand at several times, who mounted my body by the help of ladders. But a proclamation was soon issued to forbid it upon pain of death. When the workmen found it was impossible for me to break loose, they cut all the strings that bound me; whereupon I rose up, with as melancholy a disposition as ever I had in my life. But the noise and astonishment of the people at seeing me rise and walk, are not to be expressed. The chains that held my left leg were about two

yards long, and gave me not only the liberty of walking backwards and forwards in a semicircle; but, being fixed within four inches of the gate, allowed me to creep in, and lie at my full length in the temple.

CHAPTER 2

The Emperor of Lilliput, *attended by several of the nobility, comes to see the Author in his confinement. The Emperor's person and habit described. Learned men appointed to teach the Author their language. He gains favor by his mild disposition. His pockets are searched, and his sword and pistols taken from him.*

When I found myself on my feet, I looked about me, and must confess I never beheld a more entertaining prospect. The country round appeared like a continued garden, and the enclosed fields, which were generally forty foot square, resembled so many beds of flowers. These fields were intermingled with woods of half a stang,[13] and the tallest trees, as I could judge, appeared to be seven foot high. I viewed the town on my left hand, which looked like the painted scene of a city in a theater.

I had been for some hours extremely pressed by the necessities of nature; which was no wonder, it being almost two days since I had last disburthened myself. I was under great difficulties between urgency and shame. The best expedient I could think on, was to creep into my house, which I accordingly did; and shutting the gate after me, I went as far as the length of my chain would suffer, and discharged my body of that uneasy load. But this was the only time I was ever guilty of so uncleanly an action; for which I cannot but hope the candid reader will give some allowance, after he hath maturely and impartially considered my case, and the distress I was in. From this time my constant practice was, as soon as I rose, to perform that business in open air, at the full extent of my chain, and due care was taken every morning before company came, that the offensive matter should be carried off in wheelbarrows, by two servants appointed for that purpose. I would not have dwelt so long upon a circumstance, that perhaps at first sight may appear not very momentous, if I had not thought it necessary to justify my character in point of cleanliness to the world;[14]

---

11. **ancient temple:** The description suggests Westminster Hall, where Charles I had been tried.   12. **fourscore . . . padlocks:** a curious echo of the numbers in *A Tale of a Tub* — fourscore and eleven pamphlets for six and thirty factions.

13. **a stang:** obsolete form of rood, about a quarter of an acre.
14. **justify . . . world:** This is, I believe, Swift's best reply to those

which I am told some of my maligners have been pleased, upon this and other occasions, to call in question.

When this adventure was at an end, I came back out of my house, having occasion for fresh air. The Emperor was already descended from the tower, and advancing on horseback towards me, which had like to have cost him dear; for the beast, though very well trained, yet wholly unused to such a sight, which appeared as if a mountain moved before him, reared up on his hinder feet: but that prince, who is an excellent horseman, kept his seat, until his attendants ran in and held the bridle, while his Majesty had time to dismount. When he alighted, he surveyed me round with great admiration, but kept beyond the length of my chains. He ordered his cooks and butlers, who were already prepared, to give me victuals and drink, which they pushed forward in a sort of vehicles upon wheels, until I could reach them. I took these vehicles, and soon emptied them all; twenty of them were filled with meat, and ten with liquor; each of the former afforded me two or three good mouthfuls, and I emptied the liquor of ten vessels, which was contained in earthen vials, into one vehicle, drinking it off at a draught; and so I did with the rest.

The Empress, and young Princes of the blood of both sexes, attended by many ladies, sat at some distance in their chairs; but upon the accident that happened to the Emperor's horse, they alighted, and came near his person, which I am now going to describe. He is taller by almost the breadth of my nail, than any of his court; which alone is enough to strike an awe into the beholders. His features are strong and masculine, with an Austrian lip [15] and arched nose, his complexion olive, his countenance erect, his body and limbs well proportioned, all his motions graceful, and his deportment majestic. He was then past his prime, being twenty-eight years and three-quarters old, of which he had reigned about seven, in great felicity, and generally victorious. For the better convenience of beholding him, I lay on my side, so that my face was parallel to his, and he stood but three yards off: however, I have had him since many times in my

hand, and therefore cannot be deceived in the description. His dress was very plain and simple, the fashion of it between the Asiatic and the European: but he had on his head a light helmet of gold, adorned with jewels, and a plume on the crest. He held his sword drawn in his hand, to defend himself, if I should happen to break loose; it was almost three inches long; the hilt and scabbard were gold enriched with diamonds. His voice was shrill, but very clear and articulate, and I could distinctly hear it when I stood up. The ladies and courtiers were all most magnificently clad, so that the spot they stood upon seemed to resemble a petticoat spread on the ground, embroidered with figures of gold and silver. His Imperial Majesty spoke often to me, and I returned answers, but neither of us could understand a syllable. There were several of his priests and lawyers present (as I conjectured by their habits) who were commanded to address themselves to me, and I spoke to them in as many languages as I had the least smattering of, which were High and Low Dutch,[16] Latin, French, Spanish, Italian, and Lingua Franca;[17] but all to no purpose.

After about two hours the court retired, and I was left with a strong guard, to prevent the impertinence, and probably the malice, of the rabble, who were very impatient to crowd about me as near as they durst, and some of them had the impudence to shoot their arrows at me as I sat on the ground by the door of my house, whereof one very narrowly missed my left eye. But the colonel ordered six of the ringleaders to be seized, and thought no punishment so proper as to deliver them bound into my hands, which some of his soldiers accordingly did, pushing them forwards with the butt ends of their pikes into my reach; I took them all in my right hand, put five of them into my coat pocket, and as to the sixth, I made a countenance as if I would eat him alive. The poor man squalled terribly, and the colonel and his officers were in much pain, especially when they saw me take out my penknife: but I soon put them out of fear: for, looking mildly, and immediately cutting the strings he was bound with, I set him gently on the ground, and away he ran. I treated the rest in the same manner, taking them one by one out of my pocket, and I observed both the soldiers and people were highly obliged at this mark of my clemency, which was

modern critics who find evidence of abnormality in what Aldous Huxley called "the almost insane violence of his 'hatred of bowels.'" It is odd that some squeamish editors have actually omitted this paragraph. Swift was unusually sensitive to personal cleanliness; and he never hesitated to describe in revolting detail the indecencies of contemporary manners, which disgusted him.
15. Austrian lip: A thick lower lip was characteristic of the Hapsburgs. The Emperor's appearance is very unlike that of George I.

16. High . . . Dutch: i.e., German and Dutch.   17. Lingua Franca: a pidgin French or Italian, used by traders in the Mediterranean.

represented very much to my advantage at court.

Towards night I got with some difficulty into my house, where I lay on the ground, and continued to do so about a fortnight; during which time the Emperor gave orders to have a bed prepared for me. Six hundred beds of the common measure were brought in carriages, and worked up in my house; an hundred and fifty of their beds sewn together made up the breadth and length, and these were four double, which, however, kept me but very indifferently from the hardness of the floor, that was of smooth stone. By the same computation they provided me with sheets, blankets, and coverlets, tolerable enough for one who had been so long inured to hardships as I.

As the news of my arrival spread through the kingdom, it brought prodigious numbers of rich, idle, and curious people to see me; so that the villages were almost emptied, and great neglect of tillage and household affairs must have ensued, if his Imperial Majesty had not provided, by several proclamations and orders of state, against this inconveniency. He directed that those who had already beheld me should return home, and not presume to come within fifty yards of my house without license from court; whereby the secretaries of state got considerable fees.

In the meantime, the Emperor held frequent councils to debate what course should be taken with me; and I was afterwards assured by a particular friend, a person of great quality, who was as much in the secret as any, that the court was under many difficulties concerning me. They apprehended my breaking loose, that my diet would be very expensive, and might cause a famine. Sometimes they determined to starve me, or at least to shoot me in the face and hands with poisoned arrows, which would soon dispatch me; but again they considered, that the stench of so large a carcass might produce a plague in the metropolis, and probably spread through the whole kingdom.

In the midst of these consultations, several officers of the army went to the door of the great council chamber; and two of them being admitted, gave an account of my behavior to the six criminals above mentioned, which made so favorable an impression in the breast of his Majesty and the whole board, in my behalf, that an imperial commission was issued out, obliging all the villages nine hundred yards round the city, to deliver in every morning six beeves, forty sheep, and other victuals for my sustenance; together with a pro-portionable quantity of bread, and wine, and other liquors; for the due payment of which his Majesty gave assignments upon his treasury. For this prince lives chiefly upon his own demesnes, seldom, except upon great occasions, raising any subsidies upon his subjects, who are bound to attend him in his wars at their own expense. An establishment was also made of six hundred persons to be my domestics, who had board wages allowed for their maintenance, and tents built for them very conveniently on each side of my door. It was likewise ordered, that three hundred tailors should make me a suit of clothes after the fashion of the country: that six of his Majesty's greatest scholars should be employed to instruct me in their language: and, lastly, that the Emperor's horses, and those of the nobility, and troops of guards, should be exercised in my sight, to accustom themselves to me.

All these orders were duly put in execution, and in about three weeks I made a great progress in learning their language; during which time, the Emperor frequently honored me with his visits, and was pleased to assist my masters in teaching me. We began already to converse together in some sort; and the first words I learnt were to express my desire that he would please give me my liberty, which I every day repeated on my knees. His answer, as I could apprehend, was, that this must be a work of time, not to be thought on without the advice of his council, and that first I must *Lumos kelmin pesso desmar lon Emposo;* that is, swear a peace with him and his kingdom. However, that I should be used with all kindness; and he advised me to acquire, by my patience and discreet behavior, the good opinion of himself and his subjects. He desired I would not take it ill, if he gave orders to certain proper officers to search me; for probably I might carry about me several weapons, which must needs be dangerous things, if they answered the bulk of so prodigious a person. I said, his Majesty should be satisfied, for I was ready to strip myself, and turn up my pockets before him. This I delivered part in words, and part in signs. He replied, that by the laws of the kingdom I must be searched by two of his officers; that he knew this could not be done without my consent and assistance; that he had so good an opinion of my generosity and justice, as to trust their persons in my hands: that whatever they took from me should be returned when I left the country, or paid for at the rate which I would set upon them. I took up the two officers in my hands, put them first into my coat pockets, and then into every other pocket about me, except my two fobs, and another secret pocket which I had no mind should be searched, wherein I had some little necessaries of no consequence to any but myself. In one of my fobs there was a silver watch, and in the other a small quantity of gold in a purse. These gentlemen, having pen, ink, and paper about them, made an exact inventory of everything they saw; and when they had done, desired I would set them down, that they might deliver it to the Emperor. This inventory I afterwards translated into English, and is word for word as follows:

Imprimis, In the right coat pocket of the Great Man-Mountain (for so I interpret the words *Quinbus Flestrin*), after the strictest search, we found only one great piece of coarse cloth, large enough to be a footcloth for your Majesty's chief room of state. In the left pocket we saw a huge silver chest, with a cover of the same metal, which we, the searchers, were not able to lift. We desired it should be opened, and one of us stepping into it, found himself up to the midleg in a sort of dust, some part whereof flying up to our faces, set us both a sneezing for several times together. In his right waistcoat pocket we found a prodigious bundle of white thin substances, folded one over another, about the bigness of three men, tied with a strong cable, and marked with black figures; which we humbly conceive to be writings, every letter almost half as large as the palm of our hands. In the left there was a sort of engine, from the back of which were extended twenty long poles, resembling the pallisados before your Majesty's court; wherewith we conjecture the Man-Mountain combs his head; for we did not always trouble him with questions, because we found it a great difficulty to make him understand us. In the large pocket on the right side of his middle cover (so I translate the word *ranfu-lo,* by which they meant my breeches), we saw a hollow pillar of iron, about the length of a man, fastened to a strong piece of timber, larger than the pillar; and upon one side of the pillar were huge pieces of iron sticking out, cut into strange figures, which we know not what to make of. In the left pocket, another engine of the same kind. In the smaller pocket, on the right side, were several round flat pieces of white and red metal, of different bulk; some of the white, which seemed to be silver, were so large and heavy, that my comrade and I could hardly lift them. In the left pocket were two black pillars irregularly shaped: we could not, without difficulty, reach the top of them as we stood at the bottom of his pocket. One of them was covered,

and seemed all of a piece; but at the upper end of the other, there appeared a white round substance, about twice the bigness of our heads. Within each of these was enclosed a prodigious plate of steel; which, by our orders, we obliged him to show us, because we apprehended they might be dangerous engines. He took them out of their cases, and told us, that in his own country his practice was to shave his beard with one of these, and to cut his meat with the other.

There were two pockets which we could not enter: these he called his fobs; they were two large slits cut into the top of his middle cover, but squeezed close by the pressure of his belly. Out of the right fob hung a great silver chain, with a wonderful kind of engine at the bottom. We directed him to draw out whatever was at the end of that chain; which appeared to be a globe,[18] half silver, and half of some transparent metal; for, on the transparent side, we saw certain strange figures circularly drawn, and thought we could touch them, until we found our fingers stopped with that lucid substance. He put this engine to our ears, which made an incessant noise like that of a water mill. And we conjecture it is either some unknown animal, or the god that he worships; but we are more inclined to the latter opinion, because he assured us (if we understood him right, for he expressed himself very imperfectly), that he seldom did anything without consulting it. He called it his oracle, and said it pointed out the time for every action of his life. From the left fob he took out a net almost large enough for a fisherman, but contrived to open and shut like a purse, and served him for the same use: we found therein several massy pieces of yellow metal, which, if they be of real gold, must be of immense value.

Having thus, in obedience to your Majesty's commands, diligently searched all his pockets, we observed a girdle about his waist made of the hide of some prodigious animal; from which, on the left side, hung a sword of the length of five men; and on the right, a bag or pouch divided into two cells, each cell capable of holding three of your Majesty's subjects. In one of these cells were several globes or balls of a most ponderous metal, about the bigness of our heads, and requiring a strong hand to lift them: the other cell contained a heap of certain black grains, but of no great bulk or weight, for we could hold above fifty of them in the palms of our hands.

This is an exact inventory [19] of what we found about the body of the Man-Mountain, who used us

18. **a globe:** the high convex glass of the old-fashioned watch.
19. **inventory:** satirizes the government investigations of those suspected of Jacobite intrigues at the beginning of George I's reign.

with great civility, and due respect to your Majesty's Commission. Signed and sealed on the fourth day of the eighty-ninth moon of your Majesty's auspicious reign.

CLEFRIN FRELOCK, MARSI FRELOCK

When this inventory was read over to the Emperor, he directed me, although in very gentle terms, to deliver up the several particulars. He first called for my scimitar, which I took out, scabbard and all. In the meantime he ordered three thousand of his choicest troops (who then attended him) to surround me at a distance, with their bows and arrows just ready to discharge: but I did not observe it, for my eyes were wholly fixed upon his Majesty. He then desired me to draw my scimitar, which, although it had got some rust by the sea water, was in most parts exceeding bright. I did so, and immediately all the troops gave a shout between terror and surprise; for the sun shone clear, and the reflection dazzled their eyes, as I waved the scimitar to and fro in my hand. His Majesty, who is a most magnanimous prince, was less daunted than I could expect; he ordered me to return it into the scabbard, and cast it on the ground as gently as I could, about six foot from the end of my chain. The next thing he demanded was one of the hollow iron pillars, by which he meant my pocket pistols. I drew it out, and at his desire, as well as I could, expressed to him the use of it; and charging it only with powder, which, by the closeness of my pouch, happened to escape wetting in the sea (an inconvenience that all prudent mariners take special care to provide against), I first cautioned the Emperor not to be afraid, and then I let it off in the air. The astonishment here was much greater than at the sight of my scimitar. Hundreds fell down as if they had been struck dead; and even the Emperor, although he stood his ground, could not recover himself in some time. I delivered up both my pistols in the same manner as I had done my scimitar, and then my pouch of powder and bullets; begging him that the former might be kept from fire, for it would kindle with the smallest spark, and blow up his imperial palace into the air. I likewise delivered up my watch, which the Emperor was very curious to see, and commanded two of his tallest yeomen of the guards to bear it on a pole upon their shoulders, as draymen in England do a barrel of ale. He was amazed at the continual noise it made, and the motion of the minute hand, which he could easily discern; for their sight is much more acute

than ours: he asked the opinions of his learned men about him, which were various and remote, as the reader may well imagine without my repeating; although, indeed, I could not very perfectly understand them. I then gave up my silver and copper money, my purse, with nine large pieces of gold, and some smaller ones; my knife and razor, my comb and silver snuffbox, my handkerchief and journal book. My scimitar, pistols, and pouch, were conveyed in carriages to his Majesty's stores; but the rest of my goods were returned to me.

I had, as I before observed, one private pocket which escaped their search, wherein there was a pair of spectacles (which I sometimes use for the weakness of my eyes), a pocket perspective, and several other little conveniences; which being of no consequence to the Emperor, I did not think myself bound in honor to discover, and I apprehended they might be lost or spoiled if I ventured them out of my possession.

CHAPTER 3

The Author diverts the Emperor, and his nobility of both sexes, in a very uncommon manner. The diversions of the court of Lilliput described. The Author has his liberty granted him upon certain conditions.

My gentleness and good behavior had gained so far on the Emperor and his court, and indeed upon the army and people in general, that I began to conceive hopes of getting my liberty in a short time. I took all possible methods to cultivate this favorable disposition. The natives came by degrees to be less apprehensive of any danger from me. I would sometimes lie down, and let five or six of them dance on my hand. And at last the boys and girls would venture to come and play at hide-and-seek in my hair. I had now made a good progress in understanding and speaking their language. The Emperor had a mind one day to entertain me with several of the country shows, wherein they exceed all nations I have known, both for dexterity and magnificence. I was diverted with none so much as that of the rope dancers, performed upon a slender white thread, extended about two foot, and twelve inches from the ground. Upon which I shall desire liberty, with the reader's patience, to enlarge a little.

This diversion is only practiced by those persons who are candidates for great employments, and high favor, at court. They are trained in this art from their youth, and are not always of noble birth, or liberal education. When a great office is vacant, either by death or disgrace (which often happens), five or six of those candidates petition the Emperor to entertain his Majesty and the court with a dance on the rope, and whoever jumps the highest without falling, succeeds in the office. Very often the chief ministers themselves are commanded to show their skill, and to convince the Emperor that they have not lost their faculty. Flimnap, the Treasurer,[20] is allowed to cut a caper on the straight rope, at least an inch higher than any other lord in the whole empire. I have seen him do the summerset several times together upon a trencher fixed on the rope, which is no thicker than a common pack thread in England. My friend Reldresal,[21] principal Secretary for Private Affairs, is, in my opinion, if I am not partial, the second after the Treasurer; the rest of the great officers are much upon a par.

These diversions are often attended with fatal accidents, whereof great numbers are on record. I myself have seen two or three candidates break a limb. But the danger is much greater when the ministers themselves are commanded to show their dexterity; for, by contending to excel themselves and their fellows, they strain so far, that there is hardly one of them who hath not received a fall, and some of them two or three. I was assured that a year or two before my arrival, Flimnap would have infallibly broke his neck, if one of the King's cushions,[22] that accidentally lay on the ground, had not weakened the force of his fall.

There is likewise another diversion, which is only shown before the Emperor and Empress, and first minister, upon particular occasions. The Emperor lays on the table three fine silken threads of six inches long. One is blue, the other red, and the third green.[23] These threads are proposed as prizes for those persons whom the Emperor hath a mind to distinguish by a peculiar mark of his favor. The ceremony is performed in his Majesty's great chamber of state, where the candidates are to undergo a trial of dexterity very different from the former, and such as I have not observed the least resemblance of in any other country of the Old or the New World. The Emperor holds a stick in his

hands, both ends parallel to the horizon, while the candidates advancing one by one, sometimes leap over the stick, sometimes creep under it backwards and forwards several times, according as the stick is advanced or depressed. Sometimes the Emperor holds one end of the stick, and his first minister the other; sometimes the minister has it entirely to himself. Whoever performs his part with most agility, and holds out the longest in leaping and creeping, is rewarded with the blue-colored silk; the red is given to the next, and the green to the third, which they all wear girt twice round about the middle; and you see few great persons about this court, who are not adorned with one of these girdles.

The horses of the army, and those of the royal stables, having been daily led before me, were no longer shy, but would come up to my very feet without starting. The riders would leap them over my hand as I held it on the ground, and one of the Emperor's huntsmen, upon a large courser, took my foot, shoe and all; which was indeed a prodigious leap. I had the good fortune to divert the Emperor one day after a very extraordinary manner. I desired he would order several sticks of two foot high, and the thickness of an ordinary cane, to be brought me; whereupon his Majesty commanded the master of his woods to give directions accordingly; and the next morning six woodmen arrived with as many carriages, drawn by eight horses to each. I took nine of these sticks, and fixing them firmly in the ground in a quadrangular figure, two foot and a half square; I took four other sticks, and tied them parallel at each corner, about two foot from the ground; then I fastened my handkerchief to the nine sticks that stood erect, and extended it on all sides, till it was as tight as the top of a drum; and the four parallel sticks rising about five inches higher than the handkerchief, served as ledges on each side. When I had finished my work, I desired the Emperor to let a troop of his best horse, twenty-four in number, come and exercise upon this plain. His Majesty approved of the proposal, and I took them up, one by one, in my hands, ready mounted and armed, with the proper officers to exercise them. As soon as they got into order, they divided into two parties, performed mock skirmishes, discharged blunt arrows, drew their swords, fled and pursued, attacked and retired, and in short discovered the best military discipline I ever beheld. The parallel sticks secured them and their horses from falling over

20. Flimnap . . . Treasurer: The name suggests a cheat, and is applied to Walpole, who was not unwilling to maintain his power by bribery.   21. Reldresal: possibly Walpole's chief ally, Lord Townshend.   22. one . . . cushions: Duchess of Kendal, mistress of the king.   23. three . . . green: the colors of the orders of the Garter, Bath, and Thistle.

the stage; and the Emperor was so much delighted, that he ordered this entertainment to be repeated several days, and once was pleased to be lifted up and give the word of command; and, with great difficulty, persuaded even the Empress herself to let me hold her in her close chair within two yards of the stage, from whence she was able to take a full view of the whole performance. It was my good fortune that no ill accident happened in these entertainments, only once a fiery horse, that belonged to one of the captains, pawing with his hoof, struck a hole in my handkerchief, and his foot slipping, he overthrew his rider and himself; but I immediately relieved them both: for covering the hole with one hand, I set down the troop with the other, in the same manner as I took them up. The horse that fell was strained in the left shoulder, but the rider got no hurt, and I repaired my handkerchief as well as I could: however, I would not trust to the strength of it any more in such dangerous enterprises.

About two or three days before I was set at liberty, as I was entertaining the court with these kinds of feats, there arrived an express to inform his Majesty, that some of his subjects riding near the place where I was first taken up, had seen a great black substance lying on the ground, very oddly shaped, extending its edges round as wide as his Majesty's bedchamber, and rising up in the middle as high as a man; that it was no living creature, as they at first apprehended, for it lay on the grass without motion, and some of them had walked round it several times: that by mounting upon each other's shoulders, they had got to the top, which was flat and even, and stamping upon it they found it was hollow within; that they humbly conceived it might be something belonging to the Man-Mountain; and if his Majesty pleased, they would undertake to bring it with only five horses. I presently knew what they meant, and was glad at heart to receive this intelligence. It seems upon my first reaching the shore after our shipwreck, I was in such confusion, that before I came to the place where I went to sleep, my hat, which I had fastened with a string to my head while I was rowing, and had stuck on all the time I was swimming, fell off after I came to land; the string, as I conjecture, breaking by some accident which I never observed, but thought my hat had been lost at sea. I entreated his Imperial Majesty to give orders it might be brought to me as soon as possible, describing to him the use and the nature of it: and the next day

the wagoners arrived with it, but not in a very good condition; they had bored two holes in the brim, within an inch and a half of the edge, and fastened two hooks in the holes; these hooks were tied by a long cord to the harness, and thus my hat was dragged along for above half an English mile; but the ground in that country being extremely smooth and level, it received less damage than I expected.

Two days after this adventure, the Emperor having ordered that part of his army which quarters in and about his metropolis to be in readiness, took a fancy of diverting himself in a very singular manner. He desired I would stand like a colossus, with my legs as far asunder as I conveniently could. He then commanded his General (who was an old experienced leader, and a great patron of mine) to draw up the troops in close order, and march them under me; the foot by twenty-four in a breast, and the horse by sixteen, with drums beating, colors flying, and pikes advanced. This body consisted of three thousand foot, and a thousand horse. His Majesty gave orders, upon pain of death, that every soldier in his march should observe the strictest decency with regard to my person; which, however, could not prevent some of the younger officers from turning up their eyes as they passed under me. And, to confess the truth, my breeches were at that time in so ill a condition, that they afforded some opportunities for laughter and admiration.

I had sent so many memorials and petitions for my liberty, that his Majesty at length mentioned the matter, first in the cabinet, and then in a full council; where it was opposed by none, except Skyresh Bolgolam,[24] who was pleased, without any provocation, to be my mortal enemy. But it was carried against him by the whole board, and confirmed by the Emperor. That minister was *Galbet*, or Admiral of the Realm, very much in his master's confidence, and a person well versed in affairs, but of a morose and sour complexion. However, he was at length persuaded to comply; but prevailed that the articles and conditions upon which I should be set free, and to which I must swear, should be drawn up by himself. These articles were brought to me by Skyresh Bolgolam in person, attended by two undersecretaries, and several persons of distinction. After they were read, I was demanded to swear to the performance of them; first in the manner of my own country, and afterwards in the

24. **Skyresh Bolgolam:** the Earl of Nottingham, a Tory, often lampooned by Swift as "Dismal."

method prescribed by their laws; which was to hold my right foot in my left hand, to place the middle finger of my right hand on the crown of my head, and my thumb on the tip of my right ear. But because the reader may perhaps be curious to have some idea of the style and manner of expression peculiar to that people, as well as to know the articles upon which I recovered my liberty, I have made a translation of the whole instrument word for word, as near as I was able, which I here offer to the public.

GOLBASTO [25] MOMAREM EVLAME GURDILO SHEFIN MULLY ULLY GUE, most mighty Emperor of Lilliput, delight and terror of the universe, whose dominions extend five thousand *blustrugs* (about twelve miles in circumference) to the extremities of the globe; monarch of all monarchs, taller than the sons of men; whose feet press down to the center, and whose head strikes against the sun; at whose nod the princes of the earth shake their knees; pleasant as the spring, comfortable as the summer, fruitful as autumn, dreadful as winter. His most sublime Majesty proposeth to the Man-Mountain, lately arrived at our celestial dominions, the following articles, which by a solemn oath he shall be obliged to perform.

First, The Man-Mountain shall not depart from our dominions, without our license under our great seal.

Secondly, He shall not presume to come into our metropolis, without our express order; at which time, the inhabitants shall have two hours warning to keep within their doors.

Thirdly, The said Man-Mountain shall confine his walks to our principal high roads, and not offer to walk or lie down in a meadow or field of corn.

Fourthly, As he walks the said roads, he shall take the utmost care not to trample upon the bodies of any of our loving subjects, their horses, or carriages, nor take any of our subjects into his hands, without their own consent.

Fifthly, If an express requires extraordinary dispatch, the Man-Mountain shall be obliged to carry in his pocket the messenger and horse a six days' journey once in every moon, and return the said messenger back (if so required) safe to our Imperial Presence.

Sixthly, He shall be our ally against our enemies in the Island of Blefuscu, and do his utmost to destroy their fleet, which is now preparing to invade us.

Seventhly, That the said Man-Mountain shall, at his times of leisure, be aiding and assisting to our workmen, in helping to raise certain great stones, towards covering the wall of the principal park, and other our royal buildings.

Eighthly, That the said Man-Mountain shall, in two moons time, deliver in an exact survey of the circumference of our dominions by a computation of his own paces round the coast.

Lastly, That upon his solemn oath to observe all the above articles, the said Man-Mountain shall have a daily allowance of meat and drink sufficient for the support of 1728 of our subjects, with free access to our Royal Person, and other marks of our favor. Given at our Palace at Belfaborac the twelfth day of the ninety-first moon of our reign.

I swore and subscribed to these articles with great cheerfulness and content, although some of them were not so honorable as I could have wished; which proceeded wholly from the malice of Skyresh Bolgolam, the High Admiral: whereupon my chains were immediately unlocked, and I was at full liberty; the Emperor himself in person did me the honor to be by at the whole ceremony. I made my acknowledgments by prostrating myself at his Majesty's feet: but he commanded me to rise; and after many gracious expressions, which, to avoid the censure of vanity, I shall not repeat, he added, that he hoped I should prove a useful servant, and well deserve all the favors he had already conferred upon me, or might do for the future.

The reader may please to observe, that in the last article for the recovery of my liberty, the Emperor stipulates to allow me a quantity of meat and drink sufficient for the support of 1728 Lilliputians. Some time after, asking a friend at court how they came to fix on that determinate number, he told me that his Majesty's mathematicians, having taken the height of my body by the help of a quadrant, and finding it to exceed theirs in the proportion of twelve to one, they concluded from the similarity of their bodies, that mine must contain at least 1728 of theirs, and consequently would require as much food as was necessary to support that number of Lilliputians. By which, the reader may conceive an idea of the ingenuity of that people, as well as the prudent and exact economy of so great a prince.

CHAPTER 4

Mildendo, *the metropolis of* Lilliput, *described, together with the Emperor's palace. A conversation between the Author and a principal Secretary, concerning the*

25. Golbasto: This paragraph is a parody of the oriental style found in the popular travel books.

affairs of that empire. The Author's offers to serve the Emperor in his wars.

The first request I made, after I had obtained my liberty, was, that I might have license to see Mildendo, the metropolis; which the Emperor easily granted me, but with a special charge to do no hurt either to the inhabitants or their houses. The people had notice by proclamation of my design to visit the town. The wall which encompassed it, is two foot and an half high, and at least eleven inches broad, so that a coach and horses may be driven very safely round it; and it is flanked with strong towers at ten foot distance. I stepped over the great Western Gate, and passed very gently, and sideling through the two principal streets, only in my short waistcoat, for fear of damaging the roofs and eaves of the houses with the skirts of my coat. I walked with the utmost circumspection, to avoid treading on any stragglers, who might remain in the streets, although the orders were very strict, that all people should keep in their houses, at their own peril. The garret windows and tops of houses were so crowded with spectators, that I thought in all my travels I had not seen a more populous place. The city is an exact square, each side of the wall being five hundred foot long. The two great streets, which run cross and divide it into four quarters, are five foot wide. The lanes and alleys, which I could not enter, but only viewed them as I passed, are from twelve to eighteen inches. The town is capable of holding five hundred thousand souls. The houses are from three to five stories. The shops and markets well provided.

The Emperor's palace is in the center of the city, where the two great streets meet. It is enclosed by a wall of two foot high, and twenty foot distant from the buildings. I had his Majesty's permission to step over this wall; and the space being so wide between that and the palace, I could easily view it on every side. The outward court is a square of forty foot, and includes two other courts: in the inmost are the royal apartments, which I was very desirous to see, but found it extremely difficult; for the great gates, from one square into another, were but eighteen inches high, and seven inches wide. Now the buildings of the outer court were at least five foot high, and it was impossible for me to stride over them without infinite damage to the pile, though the walls were strongly built of hewn stone, and four inches thick. At the same time the Emperor had a great desire that I should see the magnificence of his palace; but this

I was not able to do till three days after, which I spent in cutting down with my knife some of the largest trees in the royal park, about an hundred yards distant from the city. Of these trees I made two stools, each about three foot high, and strong enough to bear my weight. The people having received notice a second time, I went again through the city to the palace, with my two stools in my hands. When I came to the side of the outer court, I stood upon one stool, and took the other in my hand: this I lifted over the roof, and gently set it down on the space between the first and second court, which was eight foot wide. I then stepped over the buildings very conveniently from one stool to the other, and drew up the first after me with a hooked stick. By this contrivance I got into the inmost court; and lying down upon my side, I applied my face to the windows of the middle stories, which were left open on purpose, and discovered the most splendid apartments that can be imagined. There I saw the Empress and the young Princes, in their several lodgings, with their chief attendants about them. Her Imperial Majesty was pleased to smile very graciously upon me, and gave me out of the window her hand to kiss.

But I shall not anticipate the reader with farther descriptions of this kind, because I reserve them for a greater work, which is now almost ready for the press, containing a general description of this empire, from its first erection, through a long series of princes, with a particular account of their wars and politics, laws, learning, and religion: their plants and animals, their peculiar manners and customs, with other matters very curious and useful; my chief design at present being only to relate such events and transactions as happened to the public, or to myself, during a residence of about nine months in that empire.

One morning, about a fortnight after I had obtained my liberty, Reldresal, principal Secretary (as they style him) of Private Affairs, came to my house attended only by one servant. He ordered his coach to wait at a distance, and desired I would give him an hour's audience; which I readily consented to, on account of his quality and personal merits, as well as of the many good offices he had done me during my solicitations at court. I offered to lie down, that he might the more conveniently reach my ear; but he chose rather to let me hold him in my hand during our conversation. He began with compliments on my liberty: said he might pretend to some merit in it: but, however, added, that if it had not been for the present situation of things at court, perhaps I might not have obtained it so soon. " For," said he, " as flourishing a condition as we appear to be in to foreigners, we labor under two mighty evils: a violent faction at home, and the danger of an invasion by a most potent enemy from abroad. As to the first, you are to understand, that for about seventy moons [26] past there have been two struggling parties [27] in this empire, under the names of *Tramecksan* and *Slamecksan,* from the high and low heels on their shoes, by which they distinguish themselves. It is alleged indeed, that the high heels are most agreeable to our ancient constitution: but however this be, his Majesty hath determined to make use of only low heels in the administration of the government, and all offices in the gift of the Crown, as you cannot but observe; and particularly, that his Majesty's Imperial heels are lower [28] at least by a *drurr* than any of his court; (*drurr* is a measure about the fourteenth part of an inch). The animosities between these two parties run so high, that they will neither eat nor drink, nor talk with each other. We compute the *Tramecksan,* or High-Heels, to exceed us in number; but the power is wholly on our side. We apprehend his Imperial Highness, the Heir to the Crown, to have some tendency towards the High-Heels; at least we can plainly discover one of his heels higher than the other, which gives him a hobble [29] in his gait. Now, in the midst of these intestine disquiets, we are threatened with an invasion from the Island of Blefuscu,[30] which is the other great empire of the universe, almost as large and powerful as this of his Majesty. For as to what we have heard you affirm, that there are other kingdoms and states in the world inhabited by human creatures as large as yourself, our philosophers are in much doubt, and would rather conjecture that you dropped from the moon, or one of the stars; because it is certain, that an hundred mortals of your bulk would, in a short time, destroy all the fruits and cattle of his Majesty's dominions. Besides, our histories of six thousand moons make no mention of any other regions, than the two great empires of Lilliput and Blefuscu. Which two mighty powers have, as I was going to tell you, been engaged in a most obstinate war for six and thirty moons [31] past. It began upon the following occasion. It is allowed on all hands, that the primitive way of breaking eggs before we eat them, was upon the larger end: but his present Majesty's grandfather, while he was a boy, going to eat an egg, and breaking it according to the ancient practice, happened to cut one of his fingers. Whereupon the Emperor his father published an edict, commanding all his subjects, upon great penalties, to break the smaller end of their eggs. The people so highly resented this law, that our histories tell us there have been six rebellions raised on that account; wherein one Emperor lost his life, and another his crown. These civil commotions were constantly fomented by the monarchs of Blefuscu; and when they were quelled, the exiles always fled for refuge to that empire. It is computed, that eleven thousand persons have, at several times, suffered death, rather than submit to break their eggs at the smaller end. Many hundred large volumes have been published upon this controversy: but the books of the Big-Endians have been long forbidden,[32] and the whole party rendered incapable by law of holding employments.[33] During the course of these troubles, the Emperors of Blefuscu did frequently expostulate by their ambassadors, accusing us of making a schism in religion, by offending against a fundamental doctrine of our great prophet Lustrog, in the fifty-fourth chapter of the Blundrecal (which is their Alcoran).[34] This, however, is thought to be a mere strain upon the text: for the words are these: *That all true believers shall break their eggs at the convenient end:* and which is the convenient end, seems, in my humble opinion, to be left to every man's conscience, or at least in the power of the chief magistrate to determine. Now the Big-Endian exiles have found so much credit in the Emperor of Blefuscu's court, and so much private assistance and encouragement from their party here at home, that a bloody war has been carried on between the two empires for six and thirty moons with various success; during

---

26. **seventy moons:** As Gulliver is supposed to have arrived in Lilliput at the end of 1699, this may be taken as a reference to 1629, when the troubles began which led to the Civil War. 27. **two . . . parties:** High Church and Low Church, or Tory and Whig. 28. **Majesty's . . . lower:** George I, a Lutheran himself, and a supporter of the Whigs. 29. **a hobble:** By his intrigues with the Tory opposition, the Prince of Wales had made it doubtful which party he would favor. 30. **Blefuscu:** France.

31. **six . . . moons:** The dates and incidents here do not fit the history of the religious struggles since Henry VIII, but they seem intended to refer to Henry VIII's break with the Pope, and to the fate of Charles I and James II resulting from these struggles. The Big-Endians are the Roman Catholics, and the Little-Endians the Protestants. 32. **long forbidden:** since the reign of Edward VI. 33. **incapable . . . employments:** by the Test Acts, after the Restoration. 34. **Alcoran:** or Koran, the Mohammedan scriptures.

which time we have lost forty capital ships, and a much greater number of smaller vessels, together with thirty thousand of our best seamen and soldiers; and the damage received by the enemy is reckoned to be somewhat greater than ours. However, they have now equipped a numerous fleet, and are just preparing to make a descent upon us; and his Imperial Majesty, placing great confidence in your valor and strength, has commanded me to lay this account of his affairs before you."

I desired the Secretary to present my humble duty to the Emperor, and to let him know, that I thought it would not become me, who was a foreigner, to interfere with parties; but I was ready, with the hazard of my life, to defend his person and state against all invaders.

CHAPTER 5

The Author, by an extraordinary stratagem, prevents an invasion. A high title of honor is conferred upon him. Ambassadors arrive from the Emperor of Blefuscu, *and sue for peace. The Empress's apartment on fire by an accident; the Author instrumental in saving the rest of the palace.*

The Empire of Blefuscu is an island situated to the north northeast side of Lilliput, from whence it is parted only by a channel of eight hundred yards wide. I had not yet seen it, and upon this notice of an intended invasion, I avoided appearing on that side of the coast, for fear of being discovered by some of the enemy's ships, who had received no intelligence of me, all intercourse between the two empires having been strictly forbidden during the war, upon pain of death, and an embargo laid by our Emperor upon all vessels whatsoever. I communicated to his Majesty a project I had formed of seizing the enemy's whole fleet: which, as our scouts assured us, lay at anchor in the harbor ready to sail with the first fair wind. I consulted the most experienced seamen, upon the depth of the channel, which they had often plumbed, who told me, that in the middle at high water it was seventy *glumgluffs* deep, which is about six foot of European measure; and the rest of it fifty *glumgluffs* at most. I walked to the northeast coast over against Blefuscu; where, lying down behind a hillock, I took out my small pocket perspective glass, and viewed the enemy's fleet at anchor, consisting of about fifty men-of-war, and a great number of transports: I then came back to my house, and gave order (for which I had a war-

rant) for a great quantity of the strongest cable and bars of iron. The cable was about as thick as pack thread, and the bars of the length and size of a knitting needle. I trebled the cable to make it stronger, and for the same reason I twisted three of the iron bars together, binding the extremities into a hook. Having thus fixed fifty hooks to as many cables, I went back to the northeast coast, and putting off my coat, shoes, and stockings, walked into the sea in my leathern jerkin, about half an hour before high water. I waded with what haste I could, and swam in the middle about thirty yards till I felt ground; I arrived at the fleet in less than half an hour. The enemy was so frighted when they saw me, that they leaped out of their ships, and swam to shore, where there could not be fewer than thirty thousand souls. I then took my tackling, and fastening a hook to the hole at the prow of each, I tied all the cords together at the end. While I was thus employed, the enemy discharged several thousand arrows, many of which stuck in my hands and face; and besides the excessive smart, gave me much disturbance in my work. My greatest apprehension was for my eyes, which I should have infallibly lost, if I had not suddenly thought of an expedient. I kept among other little necessaries a pair of spectacles in a private pocket, which, as I observed before, had escaped the Emperor's searchers. These I took out and fastened as strongly as I could upon my nose, and thus armed went on boldly with my work in spite of the enemy's arrows, many of which struck against the glasses of my spectacles, but without any other effect, further than a little to discompose them. I had now fastened all the hooks, and taking the knot in my hand, began to pull; but not a ship would stir, for they were all too fast held by their anchors, so that the boldest part of my enterprise remained. I therefore let go the cord, and leaving the hooks fixed to the ships, I resolutely cut with my knife the cables that fastened the anchors, receiving above two hundred shots in my face and hands; then I took up the knotted end of the cables, to which my hooks were tied, and with great ease drew fifty of the enemy's largest men-of-war after me.

The Blefuscudians, who had not the least imagination of what I intended, were at first confounded with astonishment. They had seen me cut the cables, and thought my design was only to let the ships run adrift, or fall foul on each other: but when they perceived the whole fleet moving in order, and saw me pulling at the end, they set up such a scream of grief and despair, that it is almost impossible to describe or conceive. When I had got out of danger, I stopped awhile to pick out the arrows that stuck in my hands and face; and rubbed on some of the same ointment that was given me at my first arrival, as I have formerly mentioned. I then took off my spectacles, and waiting about an hour, till the tide was a little fallen, I waded through the middle with my cargo, and arrived safe at the royal port of Lilliput.

The Emperor and his whole court stood on the shore, expecting the issue of this great adventure. They saw the ships move forward in a large half-moon, but could not discern me, who was up to my breast in water. When I advanced to the middle of the channel, they were yet more in pain, because I was under water to my neck. The Emperor concluded me to be drowned, and that the enemy's fleet was approaching in a hostile manner: but he was soon eased of his fears, for the channel growing shallower every step I made, I came in a short time within hearing, and holding up the end of the cable by which the fleet was fastened, I cried in a loud voice, *Long live the most puissant Emperor of Lilliput!* This great prince received me at my landing with all possible encomiums, and created me a *Nardac* upon the spot, which is the highest title of honor among them.

His Majesty desired I would take some other opportunity of bringing all the rest of his enemy's ships into his ports. And so unmeasurable is the ambition of princes, that he seemed to think of nothing less than reducing the whole empire of Blefuscu into a province, and governing it by a viceroy; of destroying the Big-Endian exiles, and compelling that people to break the smaller end of their eggs, by which he would remain sole monarch of the whole world. But I endeavored to divert him from this design, by many arguments drawn from the topics of policy as well as justice; and I plainly protested, that I would never be an instrument of bringing a free and brave people into slavery. And when the matter was debated in council, the wisest part of the ministry were of my opinion.

This open bold declaration of mine was so opposite to the schemes and politics of his Imperial Majesty, that he could never forgive me; he mentioned it in a very artful manner at council, where I was told that some of the wisest appeared, at least by their silence, to be of my opinion; but

others, who were my secret enemies, could not forbear some expressions, which by a side wind [35] reflected on me. And from this time began an intrigue between his Majesty and a junto [36] of ministers maliciously bent against me, which broke out in less than two months, and had like to have ended in my utter destruction. Of so little weight are the greatest services to princes, when put into the balance with a refusal to gratify their passions.

About three weeks after this exploit, there arrived a solemn embassy from Blefuscu, with humble offers of a peace; [37] which was soon concluded upon conditions very advantageous to our Emperor, wherewith I shall not trouble the reader. There were six ambassadors, with a train of about five hundred persons, and their entry was very magnificent, suitable to the grandeur of their master, and the importance of their business. When their treaty was finished, wherein I did them several good offices by the credit I now had, or at least appeared to have at court, their Excellencies, who were privately told how much I had been their friend, made me a visit in form. They began with many compliments upon my valor and generosity, invited me to that kingdom in the Emperor their master's name, and desired me to show them some proofs of my prodigious strength, of which they had heard so many wonders; wherein I readily obliged them, but shall not interrupt the reader with the particulars.

When I had for some time entertained their Excellencies, to their infinite satisfaction and surprise, I desired they would do me the honor to present my most humble respects to the Emperor their master, the renown of whose virtues had so justly filled the whole world with admiration, and whose royal person I resolved to attend before I returned to my own country: accordingly, the next time I had the honor to see our Emperor, I desired his general license to wait on the Blefuscudian monarch, which he was pleased to grant me, as I could plainly perceive, in a very cold manner; but could not guess the reason, till I had a whisper from a certain person, that Flimnap and Bolgolam had represented my intercourse with those ambassadors as a mark of disaffection, from which I am sure my heart was wholly free. And this was the first time I began to conceive some

35. by . . . wind: indirectly.   **36. junto:** a political group, first applied to the leaders of the Whigs after the Revolution of 1688. **37. a peace:** In all this passage Swift has in mind the negotiations for the Treaty of Utrecht, and the criticisms of the arrangements for the peace.

imperfect idea of courts and ministers.

It is to be observed, that these ambassadors spoke to me by an interpreter, the languages of both empires differing as much from each other as any two in Europe, and each nation priding itself upon the antiquity, beauty, and energy of their own tongues, with an avowed contempt for that of their neighbor; yet our Emperor, standing upon the advantage he had got by the seizure of their fleet, obliged them to deliver their credentials, and make their speech in the Lilliputian tongue. And it must be confessed, that from the great intercourse of trade and commerce between both realms, from the continual reception of exiles, which is mutual among them, and from the custom in each empire to send their young nobility and richer gentry to the other, in order to polish themselves by seeing the world, and understanding men and manners; there are few persons of distinction, or merchants, or seamen, who dwell in the maritime parts, but what can hold conversation in both tongues; as I found some weeks after, when I went to pay my respects to the Emperor of Blefuscu, which in the midst of great misfortunes, through the malice of my enemies, proved a very happy adventure to me, as I shall relate in its proper place.

The reader may remember, that when I signed those articles upon which I recovered my liberty, there were some which I disliked upon account of their being too servile, neither could anything but an extreme necessity have forced me to submit. But being now a *Nardac* of the highest rank in that empire, such offices were looked upon as below my dignity, and the Emperor (to do him justice) never once mentioned them to me. However, it was not long before I had an opportunity of doing his Majesty, at least, as I then thought, a most signal service. I was alarmed at midnight with the cries of many hundred people at my door; by which being suddenly awaked, I was in some kind of terror. I heard the word *burglum* repeated incessantly: several of the Emperor's court, making their way through the crowd, entreated me to come immediately to the palace, where her Imperial Majesty's apartment was on fire, by the carelessness of a maid of honor, who fell asleep while she was reading a romance. I got up in an instant; and orders being given to clear the way before me, and it being likewise a moonshine night, I made a shift to get to the palace without trampling on any of the people. I found they had already applied ladders to the walls of the apart-ment, and were well provided with buckets, but the water was at some distance. These buckets were about the size of a large thimble, and the poor people supplied me with them as fast as they could; but the flame was so violent that they did little good. I might easily have stifled it with my coat, which I unfortunately left behind me for haste, and came away only in my leathern jerkin. The case seemed wholly desperate and deplorable; and this magnificent palace would have infallibly been burnt down to the ground, if, by a presence of mind, unusual to me, I had not suddenly thought of an expedient. I had the evening before drunk plentifully of a most delicious wine, called *glimigrim* (the Blefuscudians call it *flunec,* but ours is esteemed the better sort), which is very diuretic. By the luckiest chance in the world, I had not discharged myself of any part of it. The heat I had contracted by coming very near the flames, and by laboring to quench them, made the wine begin to operate by urine; which I voided in such a quantity, and applied so well to the proper places, that in three minutes the fire was wholly extinguished, and the rest of that noble pile, which had cost so many ages in erecting, preserved from destruction.

It was now daylight, and I returned to my house without waiting to congratulate with the Emperor: because, although I had done a very eminent piece of service, yet I could not tell how his Majesty might resent the manner by which I had performed it: for, by the fundamental laws of the realm, it is capital in any person, of what quality soever, to make water within the precincts of the palace. But I was a little comforted by a message from his Majesty, that he would give orders to the Grand Justiciary for passing my pardon in form; which, however, I could not obtain. And I was privately assured, that the Empress, conceiving the greatest abhorrence of what I had done, removed to the most distant side of the court, firmly resolved that those buildings should never be repaired for her use: and, in the presence of her chief confidants could not forbear vowing revenge.[38]

CHAPTER 6

Of the inhabitants of Lilliput; their learning, laws, and customs. The manner of educating their children.

38. abhorrence . . . revenge: The Queen's resentment has been understood as a reference to her dislike of the coarseness of Swift's satire and her unwillingness that he should be made a bishop.

The Author's way of living in that country. His vindication of a great lady.

Although I intend to leave the description of this empire to a particular treatise, yet in the meantime I am content to gratify the curious reader with some general ideas. As the common size of the natives is somewhat under six inches, so there is an exact proportion in all other animals, as well as plants and trees: for instance, the tallest horses and oxen are between four and five inches in height, the sheep [39] an inch and a half, more or less: their geese about the bigness of a sparrow, and so the several gradations downwards till you come to the smallest, which, to my sight, were almost invisible; but nature hath adapted the eyes of the Lilliputians to all objects proper for their view: they see with great exactness, but at no great distance. And to show the sharpness of their sight towards objects that are near, I have been much pleased with observing a cook pulling a lark, which was not so large as a common fly; and a young girl threading an invisible needle with invisible silk. Their tallest trees are about seven foot high: I mean some of those in the great royal park, the tops whereof I could but just reach with my fist clinched. The other vegetables are in the same proportion; but this I leave to the reader's imagination.

I shall say but little at present of their learning, which for many ages hath flourished in all its branches among them: but their manner of writing [40] is very peculiar, being neither from the left to the right, like the Europeans; nor from the right to the left, like the Arabians; nor from up to down, like the Chinese; nor from down to up, like the Cascagians; but aslant from one corner of the paper to the other, like ladies in England.

They bury their dead with their heads directly downwards, because they hold an opinion, that in eleven thousand moons they are all to rise again, in which period the earth (which they conceive to be flat) will turn upside down, and by this means they shall, at their resurrection, be found ready standing on their feet. The learned among them confess the absurdity of this doctrine, but the practice still continues, in compliance to the vulgar.

There are some laws and customs in this empire

very peculiar; and if they were not so directly contrary to those of my own dear country, I should be tempted to say a little in their justification. It is only to be wished that they were as well executed. The first I shall mention, relates to informers. All crimes against the state are punished here with the utmost severity; but if the person accused make his innocence plainly to appear upon his trial, the accuser is immediately put to an ignominious death; and out of his goods or lands, the innocent person is quadruply recompensed for the loss of his time, for the danger he underwent, for the hardship of his imprisonment, and for all the charges he hath been at in making his defense. Or, if that fund be deficient, it is largely supplied by the Crown. The Emperor does also confer on him some public mark of his favor, and proclamation is made of his innocence through the whole city.

They look upon fraud as a greater crime than theft, and therefore seldom fail to punish it with death; for they allege, that care and vigilance, with a very common understanding, may preserve a man's goods from thieves, but honesty has no fence against superior cunning; and since it is necessary that there should be a perpetual intercourse of buying and selling, and dealing upon credit, where fraud is permitted and connived at, or hath no law to punish it, the honest dealer is always undone, and the knave gets the advantage. I remember when I was once interceding with the Emperor for a criminal who had wronged his master of a great sum of money, which he had received by order, and ran away with; and happening to tell his Majesty, by way of extenuation, that it was only a breach of trust; the Emperor thought it monstrous in me to offer, as a defense, the greatest aggravation of the crime: and truly I had little to say in return, farther than the common answer, that different nations had different customs; for, I confess, I was heartily ashamed.

Although we usually call reward and punishment the two hinges upon which all government turns, yet I could never observe this maxim to be put in practice by any nation except that of Lilliput. Whoever can there bring sufficient proof that he hath strictly observed the laws of his country for seventy-three moons, hath a claim to certain privileges, according to his quality and condition of life, with a proportionable sum of money out of a fund appropriated for that use: he likewise acquires the title of *Snilpall,* or Legal, which is added to his name, but does not descend to his

---

39. the sheep: It must be remembered that the average size of sheep in Swift's time was about a quarter of the present size.
40. manner of writing: Swift is here parodying a paragraph from William Sympson's *New Voyage to the East Indies,* adding his own invention of the Cascagians.

posterity. And these people thought it a prodigious defect of policy among us, when I told them that our laws were enforced only by penalties, without any mention of reward. It is upon this account that the image of Justice, in their courts of judicature, is formed with six eyes, two before, as many behind, and on each side one, to signify circumspection; with a bag of gold open in her right hand, and a sword sheathed in her left, to show she is more disposed to reward than to punish.

In choosing persons for all employments, they have more regard to good morals than to great abilities; for, since government is necessary to mankind, they believe that the common size of human understandings is fitted to some station or other, and that Providence never intended to make the management of public affairs a mystery, to be comprehended only by a few persons of sublime genius, of which there seldom are three born in an age: but they suppose truth, justice, temperance, and the like, to be in every man's power; the practice of which virtues, assisted by experience and a good intention, would qualify any man for the service of his country, except where a course of study is required. But they thought the want of moral virtues was so far from being supplied by superior endowments of the mind, that employments could never be put into such dangerous hands as those of persons so qualified; and at least, that the mistakes committed by ignorance in a virtuous disposition, would never be of such fatal consequence to the public weal,[41] as the practices of a man whose inclinations led him to be corrupt, and had great abilities to manage, to multiply, and defend his corruptions.

In like manner, the disbelief of a divine Providence renders a man uncapable of holding any public station; for, since kings avow themselves to be the deputies of Providence, the Lilliputians think nothing can be more absurd than for a prince to employ such men as disown the authority under which he acts.

In relating these and the following laws, I would only be understood to mean the original institutions, and not the most scandalous corruptions into which these people are fallen by the degenerate nature of man. For as to that infamous practice of acquiring great employments by dancing on the ropes, or badges of favor and distinction by leaping over sticks and creeping under them, the reader

is to observe, that they were first introduced by the grandfather of the Emperor now reigning, and grew to the present height,[42] by the gradual increase of party and faction.

Ingratitude is among them a capital crime, as we read it to have been in some other countries: for they reason thus, that whoever makes ill returns to his benefactor, must needs be a common enemy to the rest of mankind, from whom he hath received no obligation, and therefore such a man is not fit to live.

Their notions relating to the duties of parents and children differ extremely from ours. For, since the conjunction of male and female is founded upon the great law of nature, in order to propagate and continue the species, the Lilliputians will needs have it, that men and women are joined together like other animals, by the motives of concupiscence; and that their tenderness towards their young proceeds from the like natural principle: for which reason they will never allow, that a child is under any obligation to his father for begetting him, or to his mother for bringing him into the world, which, considering the miseries of human life, was neither a benefit in itself, nor intended so by his parents, whose thoughts in their love encounters were otherwise employed. Upon these, and the like reasonings, their opinion is, that parents are the last of all others to be trusted with the education of their own children; and therefore they have in every town public nurseries, where all parents, except cottagers and laborers, are obliged to send their infants of both sexes to be reared and educated when they come to the age of twenty moons, at which time they are supposed to have some rudiments of docility. These schools are of several kinds, suited to different qualities, and to both sexes. They have certain professors well skilled in preparing children for such a condition of life as befits the rank of their parents, and their own capacities as well as inclinations. I shall first say something of the male nurseries, and then of the female.

The nurseries for males of noble or eminent birth, are provided with grave and learned professors, and their several deputies. The clothes and food of the children are plain and simple. They are bred up in

---

41. **weal:** well-being.

42. **present height:** The Order of the Bath had just been revived by George I in 1725 as a means of rewarding his loyal supporters. Cf. Swift's verses on "Reviving the Order of the Bath":

> Quoth King Robin, our Ribbands I see are too few
> Of St. Andrew's the Green, and St. George's the Blue
> I must have another of Color more gay
> That will make all my Subjects with Pride to obey.

the principles of honor, justice, courage, modesty, clemency, religion and love of their country; they are always employed in some business, except in the times of eating and sleeping, which are very short, and two hours for diversions, consisting of bodily exercises. They are dressed by men till four years of age, and then are obliged to dress themselves, although their quality be ever so great; and the women attendants, who are aged proportionably to ours at fifty, perform only the most menial offices. They are never suffered to converse with servants, but go together in small or greater numbers to take their diversions, and always in the presence of a professor, or one of his deputies; whereby they avoid those early bad impressions of folly and vice to which our children are subject. Their parents are suffered to see them only twice a year; the visit is not to last above an hour. They are allowed to kiss the child at meeting and parting; but a professor, who always stands by on those occasions, will not suffer them to whisper, or use any fondling expressions, or bring any presents of toys, sweetmeats, and the like.

The pension from each family for the education and entertainment of a child, upon failure of due payment, is levied by the Emperor's officers.

The nurseries for children of ordinary gentlemen, merchants, traders, and handicrafts, are managed proportionably after the same manner; only those designed for trades, are put out apprentices at seven years old, whereas those of persons of quality continue in their exercises till fifteen, which answers to one and twenty with us: but the confinement is gradually lessened for the last three years.

In the female nurseries, the young girls of quality are educated much like the males, only they are dressed by orderly servants of their own sex; but always in the presence of a professor or deputy, till they come to dress themselves, which is at five years old. And if it be found that these nurses ever presume to entertain the girls with frightful or foolish stories, or the common follies practiced by chambermaids among us, they are publicly whipped thrice about the city, imprisoned for a year, and banished for life to the most desolate part of the country. Thus the young ladies there are as much ashamed of being cowards and fools, as the men, and despise all personal ornaments beyond decency and cleanliness: neither did I perceive any difference in their education, made by their difference of sex, only that the exercises of the females were

not altogether so robust; and that some rules were given them relating to domestic life, and a smaller compass of learning was enjoined them: for their maxim is, that among people of quality, a wife should be always a reasonable and agreeable companion, because she cannot always be young. When the girls are twelve years old, which among them is the marriageable age, their parents or guardians take them home, with great expressions of gratitude to the professors, and seldom without tears of the young lady and her companions.

In the nurseries of females of the meaner sort, the children are instructed in all kinds of works proper for their sex, and their several degrees: those intended for apprentices, are dismissed at seven years old, the rest are kept to eleven.

The meaner families who have children at these nurseries, are obliged, besides their annual pension, which is as low as possible, to return to the steward of the nursery a small monthly share of their gettings, to be a portion for the child; and therefore all parents are limited in their expenses by the law. For the Lilliputians think nothing can be more unjust, than that people, in subservience to their own appetites, should bring children into the world, and leave the burthen of supporting them on the public. As to persons of quality, they give security to appropriate a certain sum for each child, suitable to their condition; and these funds are always managed with good husbandry, and the most exact justice.

The cottagers and laborers keep their children at home, their business being only to till and cultivate the earth, and therefore their education is of little consequence to the public; but the old and diseased among them are supported by hospitals: for begging is a trade unknown in this empire.

And here it may perhaps divert the curious reader, to give some account of my domestic, and my manner of living in this country, during a residence of nine months and thirteen days. Having a head mechanically turned, and being likewise forced by necessity, I had made for myself a table and chair convenient enough, out of the largest trees in the royal park. Two hundred sempstresses were employed to make me shirts, and linen for my bed and table, all of the strongest and coarsest kind they could get; which, however, they were forced to quilt together in several folds, for the thickest was some degrees finer than lawn. Their linen is usually three inches wide, and three foot make a piece. The sempstresses took my measure as I lay on the ground, one standing at my neck, and another at my midleg, with a strong cord extended, that each held by the end, while the third measured the length of the cord with a rule of an inch long. Then they measured my right thumb, and desired no more; for by a mathematical computation, that twice round the thumb [43] is once round the wrist, and so on to the neck and the waist, and by the help of my old shirt, which I displayed on the ground before them for a pattern, they fitted me exactly. Three hundred tailors were employed in the same manner to make me clothes; but they had another contrivance for taking my measure. I kneeled down, and they raised a ladder from the ground to my neck; upon this ladder one of them mounted, and let fall a plumb line from my collar to the floor, which just answered the length of my coat: but my waist and arms I measured myself. When my clothes were finished, which was done in my house (for the largest of theirs would not have been able to hold them), they looked like the patchwork made by the ladies in England, only that mine were all of a color.

I had three hundred cooks to dress my victuals, in little convenient huts built about my house, where they and their families lived, and prepared me two dishes apiece. I took up twenty waiters in my hand, and placed them on the table: an hundred more attended below on the ground, some with dishes of meat, and some with barrels of wine, and other liquors, slung on their shoulders; all which the waiters above drew up as I wanted, in a very ingenious manner, by certain cords, as we draw the bucket up a well in Europe. A dish of their meat was a good mouthful, and a barrel of their liquor a reasonable draught. Their mutton yields to ours, but their beef is excellent. I have had a sirloin so large, that I have been forced to make three bits [44] of it; but this is rare. My servants were astonished to see me eat it bones and all, as in our country we do the leg of a lark. Their geese and turkeys I usually eat at a mouthful, and I must confess they far exceed ours. Of their smaller fowl I could take up twenty or thirty at the end of my knife.

One day his Imperial Majesty, being informed of my way of living, desired that himself and his Royal Consort, with the young Princes of the blood of both sexes, might have the happiness (as he was pleased to call it) of dining with me. They came accordingly, and I placed them in chairs of state

on my table, just over against me, with their guards about them, Flimnap, the Lord High Treasurer, attended there likewise with his white staff,[45] and I observed he often looked on me with a sour countenance, which I would not seem to regard, but eat more than usual, in honor to my dear country, as well as to fill the court with admiration. I have some private reasons to believe, that this visit from his Majesty gave Flimnap an opportunity of doing me ill offices to his master. That minister had always been my secret enemy, although he outwardly caressed me more than was usual to the moroseness of his nature. He represented to the Emperor the low condition of his treasury; that he was forced to take up money at great discount; that exchequer bills [46] would not circulate under nine *per cent.* below par; that I had cost his Majesty above a million and a half of *sprugs* (their greatest gold coin, about the bigness of a spangle); and upon the whole, that it would be advisable in the Emperor to take the first occasion of dismissing me.

I am here obliged to vindicate the reputation of an excellent lady, who was an innocent sufferer upon my account. The Treasurer took a fancy to be jealous of his wife,[47] from the malice of some evil tongues, who informed him that her Grace had taken a violent affection for my person; and the court scandal ran for some time, that she once came privately to my lodging. This I solemnly declare to be a most infamous falsehood, without any grounds, farther than that her Grace was pleased to treat me with all innocent marks of freedom and friendship. I own she came often to my house, but always publicly, nor ever without three more in the coach, who were usually her sister and young daughter, and some particular acquaintance; but this was common to many other ladies of the court. And I still appeal to my servants round, whether they at any time saw a coach at my door without knowing what persons were in it. On those occasions, when a servant had given me notice, my custom was to go immediately to the door; and, after paying my respects, to take up the coach and two horses very carefully in my hands (for, if there were six horses, the postillion always unharnessed four) and place them on a table, where I had fixed a movable rim quite round, of five inches high, to prevent accidents. And I have often had four coaches

45. white staff: the symbol of office of the Treasurer in England. 46. exchequer bills: first issued by the Chancellor of the Exchequer in 1696, when he called in the depreciated currency. Swift disliked such Whig methods of public finance. 47. his wife: probably a little joke at Walpole's expense.

43. thumb: a "rule of thumb," a rough calculation among tailors and dressmakers. 44. bits: bites.

and horses at once on my table full of company, while I sat in my chair leaning my face towards them; and when I was engaged with one set, the coachmen would gently drive the others round my table. I have passed many an afternoon very agreeably in these conversations. But I defy the Treasurer, or his two informers (I will name them, and let them make their best of it) Clustril and Drunlo, to prove that any person ever came to me *incognito*,[48] except the secretary Reldresal, who was sent by express command of his Imperial Majesty, as I have before related. I should not have dwelt so long upon this particular, if it had not been a point wherein the reputation of a great lady is so nearly concerned, to say nothing of my own; although I had the honor to be a *Nardac,* which the Treasurer himself is not; for all the world knows he is only a *clumglum,* a title inferior by one degree, as that of a Marquis is to a Duke in England; yet I allow he preceded me in right of his post. These false informations, which I afterwards came to the knowledge of, by an accident not proper to mention, made the Treasurer show his lady for some time an ill countenance, and me a worse; for although he were at last undeceived and reconciled to her, yet I lost all credit with him, and found my interest decline very fast with the Emperor himself, who was indeed too much governed by that favorite.

CHAPTER 7

The Author, being informed of a design to accuse him of high treason, makes his escape to Blefuscu. *His reception there.*

Before I proceed to give an account of my leaving this kingdom, it may be proper to inform the reader of a private intrigue which had been for two months forming against me.

I had been hitherto all my life a stranger to courts, for which I was unqualified by the meanness of my condition. I had indeed heard and read enough of the dispositions of great princes and ministers; but never expected to have found such terrible effects of them in so remote a country, governed, as I thought, by very different maxims from those in Europe.

When I was just preparing to pay my attendance on the Emperor of Blefuscu, a considerable

person at court (to whom I had been very serviceable at a time when he lay under the highest displeasure of his Imperial Majesty) came to my house very privately at night in a close chair, and without sending his name, desired admittance. The chairmen were dismissed; I put the chair, with his Lordship in it, into my coat pocket: and giving orders to a trusty servant to say I was indisposed and gone to sleep, I fastened the door of my house, placed the chair on the table, according to my usual custom, and sat down by it. After the common salutations were over, observing his Lordship's countenance full of concern, and inquiring into the reason, he desired I would hear him with patience in a matter that highly concerned my honor and my life. His speech was to the following effect, for I took notes of it as soon as he left me.

"You are to know," said he, "that several Committees of Council [49] have been lately called in the most private manner on your account; and it but two days since his Majesty came to a full resolution.

"You are very sensible that Skyris Bolgolam (*Galbet,* or High Admiral) hath been your mortal enemy almost ever since your arrival. His original reasons I know not; but his hatred is much increased since your great success against Blefuscu, by which his glory, as Admiral, is obscured. This Lord, in conjunction with Flimnap the High Treasurer, whose enmity against you is notorious on account of his lady, Limtoc the General, Lalcon the Chamberlain, and Balmuff the Grand Justiciary, have prepared articles of impeachment against you, for treason, and other capital crimes."

This preface made me so impatient, being conscious of my own merits and innocence, that I was going to interrupt; when he entreated me to be silent, and thus proceeded.

"Out of gratitude for the favors you have done me, I procured information of the whole proceedings, and a copy of the articles, wherein I venture my head for your service."

ARTICLES OF IMPEACHMENT AGAINST QUINBUS
FLESTRIN (THE MAN-MOUNTAIN)

ARTICLE I

Whereas, by a statute made in the reign of his Imperial Majesty Calin Deffar Plune, it is enacted,

---

48. came . . . *incognito:* Perhaps this refers to incidents in the trial of Bishop Atterbury for Jacobite intrigue.

49. Committees . . . Council: referring to the committee appointed in 1715 to investigate the activities of tne Tory ministers who had been turned out of office on the death of the queen. The impeachments of Oxford and Bolingbroke followed, and are here satirized in the Articles of Impeachment brought against Gulliver.

that whoever shall make water within the precincts of the royal palace, shall be liable to the pains and penalties of high treason; nothwithstanding, the said Quinbus Flestrin, in open breach of the said law, under color of extinguishing the fire kindled in the apartment of his Majesty's most dear Imperial Consort, did maliciously, traitorously, and devilishly, by discharge of his urine, put out the said fire kindled in the said apartment, lying and being within the precincts of the said royal palace, against the statute in that case provided, *etc.* against the duty, *etc.*

ARTICLE II

That the said Quinbus Flestrin having brought the imperial fleet of Blefuscu into the royal port, and being afterwards commanded by his Imperial Majesty to seize all the other ships of the said empire of Blefuscu, and reduce that empire to a province, to be governed by a viceroy from hence, and to destroy and put to death not only all the Big-Endian exiles, but likewise all the people of that empire, who would not immediately forsake the Big-Endian heresy: He, the said Flestrin, like a false traitor against his most Auspicious, Serene, Imperial Majesty, did petition to be excused from the said service, upon pretense of unwillingness to force the consciences, or destroy the liberties and lives of an innocent people.

ARTICLE III

That, whereas certain ambassadors arrived from the court of Blefuscu, to sue for peace in his Majesty's court: He, the said Flestrin, did, like a false traitor, aid, abet, comfort and divert the said ambassadors, although he knew them to be servants to a prince who was lately an open enemy to his Imperial Majesty, and in open war against his said Majesty.

ARTICLE IV

That the said Quinbus Flestrin, contrary to the duty of a faithful subject, is now preparing to make a voyage to the court and empire of Blefuscu, for which he hath received only verbal license from his Imperial Majesty; and under color of the said license, doth falsely and traitorously intend to take the said voyage, and thereby to aid, comfort, and abet the Emperor of Blefuscu, so late an enemy, and in open war with his Imperial Majesty aforesaid.

"There are some other articles, but these are the most important, of which I have read you an abstract.

"In the several debates upon this impeachment, it must be confessed that his Majesty gave many marks of his great lenity, often urging the serv-

ices you had done him, and endeavoring to extenuate your crimes. The Treasurer and Admiral insisted that you should be put to the most painful and ignominious death, by setting fire on your house at night, and the General was to attend with twenty thousand men armed with poisoned arrows to shoot you on the face and hands. Some of your servants were to have private orders to strew a poisonous juice on your shirts and sheets, which would soon make you tear your own flesh, and die in the utmost torture. The General came into the same opinion; so that for a long time there was a majority against you. But his Majesty resolving, if possible, to spare your life, at last brought off the Chamberlain.

"Upon this incident, Reldresal, principal Secretary for Private Affairs, who always approved himself your true friend, was commanded by the Emperor to deliver his opinion, which he accordingly did; and therein justified the good thoughts you have of him. He allowed your crimes to be great, but that still there was room for mercy, the most commendable virtue in a prince, and for which his Majesty was so justly celebrated. He said, the friendship between you and him was so well known to the world, that perhaps the most honorable board might think him partial: however, in obedience to the command he had received, he would freely offer his sentiments. That if his Majesty, in consideration of your services, and pursuant to his own merciful disposition, would please to spare your life, and only give orders to put out both your eyes,[50] he humbly conceived, that by this expedient, justice might in some measure be satisfied, and all the world would applaud the lenity of the Emperor, as well as the fair and generous proceedings of those who have the honor to be his counselors. That the loss of your eyes would be no impediment to your bodily strength, by which you might still be useful to his Majesty. That blindness is an addition to courage, by concealing dangers from us; that the fear you had for your eyes was the greatest difficulty in bringing over the enemy's fleet, and it would be sufficient for you to see by the eyes of the ministers, since the greatest princes do no more.

"This proposal was received with the utmost disapprobation by the whole board. Bolgolam, the Admiral, could not preserve his temper; but rising up in fury, said, he wondered how the Secretary durst presume to give his opinion for preserv-

---

50. would . . . eyes: Some had proposed that it would be enough to deprive Oxford and Bolingbroke of their titles and estates.

ing the life of a traitor: that the services you had performed, were, by all true reasons of state, the great aggravation of your crimes; that you, who were able to extinguish the fire, by discharge of urine in her Majesty's apartment (which he mentioned with horror), might, at another time, raise an inundation by the same means, to drown the whole palace; and the same strength which enabled you to bring over the enemy's fleet, might serve, upon the first discontent, to carry it back: that he had good reasons to think you were a Big-Endian in your heart; and as treason begins in the heart, before it appears in overt acts, so he accused you as a traitor on that account, and therefore insisted you should be put to death.[51]

"The Treasurer was of the same opinion; he showed to what straits his Majesty's revenue was reduced by the charge of maintaining you, which would soon grow insupportable: that the Secretary's expedient of putting out your eyes was so far from being a remedy against this evil, that it would probably increase it, as it is manifest from the common practice of blinding some kind of fowl, after which they fed the faster, and grew sooner fat: that his sacred Majesty and the Council, who are your judges, were in their own consciences fully convinced of your guilt, which was a sufficient argument to condemn you to death, without the *formal proofs required by the strict letter of the law.*

"But his Imperial Majesty, fully determined against capital punishment, was graciously pleased to say, that since the Council thought the loss of your eyes too easy a censure, some other may be inflicted hereafter. And your friend the Secretary humbly desiring to be heard again, in answer to what the Treasurer had objected concerning the great charge his Majesty was at in maintaining you, said, that his Excellency, who had the sole disposal of the Emperor's revenue, might easily provide against the evil, by gradually lessening your establishment; by which, for want of sufficient food, you would grow weak and faint, and lose your appetite, and consequently decay and consume in a few months; neither would the stench of your carcass be then so dangerous, when it should become more than half diminished; and immediately upon your death, five or six thousand of his Majesty's subjects might, in two or three days, cut your flesh

from your bones, take it away by cartloads, and bury it in distant parts to prevent infection, leaving the skeleton as a monument of admiration to posterity.

"Thus by the great friendship of the Secretary, the whole affair was compromised. It was strictly enjoined, that the project of starving you by degrees should be kept a secret, but the sentence of putting out your eyes was entered on the books; none dissenting except Bolgolam the Admiral, who, being a creature of the Empress, was perpetually instigated by her Majesty to insist upon your death, she having borne perpetual malice against you, on account of that infamous and illegal method you took to extinguish the fire in her apartment.

"In three days your friend the Secretary will be directed to come to your house, and read before you the articles of impeachment; and then to signify the great lenity and favor of his Majesty and Council, whereby you are only condemned to the loss of your eyes, which his Majesty doth not question you will gratefully and humbly submit to; and twenty of his Majesty's surgeons will attend, in order to see the operation well performed, by discharging very sharp-pointed arrows into the balls of your eyes, as you lie on the ground.

"I leave to your prudence what measures you will take; and to avoid suspicion, I must immediately return in as private a manner as I came."

His Lordship did so, and I remained alone, under many doubts and perplexities of mind.

It was a custom introduced by this prince and his ministry (very different, as I have been assured, from the practices of former times), that after the court had decreed any cruel execution, either to gratify the monarch's resentment, or the malice of a favorite, the Emperor always made a speech to his whole Council, expressing his *great lenity* [52] *and tenderness, as qualities known and confessed by all the world.* This speech was immediately published through the kingdom; nor did anything terrify the people so much as those encomiums on his Majesty's mercy; because it was observed, that the more these praises were enlarged and insisted on, the more *inhuman* was the punishment, and the *sufferer more innocent.* Yet, as to myself, I must confess, having never been designed for a courtier either by my birth or education, I was so ill a judge of things, that I could not discover the *lenity* and

---

51. death: Swift had in mind the violence of party hatred against his friends, the Tory leaders, whose loyalty he had constantly upheld, but the details of Gulliver's experience do not need to be given an historical interpretation.

52. great lenity: perhaps a reference to the Address of the House of Lords, praising his Majesty's "endearing tenderness and clemency" about the time of the execution of the rebels of 1715.

favor of this sentence, but conceived it (perhaps erroneously) rather to be rigorous than gentle. I sometimes thought of standing my trial; for although I could not deny the facts alleged in the several articles, yet I hoped they would admit of some extenuations. But having in my life perused many state trials, which I ever observed to terminate as the judges thought fit to direct, I durst not rely on so dangerous a decision, in so critical a juncture, and against such powerful enemies. Once I was strongly bent upon resistance, for while I had liberty, the whole strength of that empire could hardly subdue me, and I might easily with stones pelt the metropolis to pieces; but I soon rejected that project with horror, by remembering the oath I had made to the Emperor, the favors I received from him, and the high title of *Nardac* he conferred upon me. Neither had I so soon learned the gratitude of courtiers, to persuade myself that his Majesty's *present severities acquitted me of all past obligations.*

At last I fixed upon a resolution, for which it is probable I may incur some censure, and not unjustly; for I confess I owe the preserving my eyes, and consequently my liberty, to my own great rashness and want of experience: because if I had then known the nature of princes and ministers, which I have since observed in many other courts, and their methods of treating criminals less obnoxious than myself, I should with great alacrity and readiness have submitted to so *easy* a punishment. But hurried on by the precipitancy of youth, and having his Imperial Majesty's license to pay my attendance upon the Emperor of Blefuscu, I took this opportunity, before the three days were elapsed, to send a letter to my friend the Secretary, signifying my resolution of setting out that morning for Blefuscu pursuant to the leave I had got; and without waiting for an answer, I went to that side of the island where our fleet lay. I seized a large man-of-war, tied a cable to the prow, and, lifting up the anchors, I stripped myself, put my clothes (together with my coverlet, which I carried under my arm) into the vessel, and drawing it after me between wading and swimming, arrived at the royal port of Blefuscu, where the people had long expected me: they lent me two guides to direct me to the capital city, which is of the same name. I held them in my hands till I came within two hundred yards of the gate, and desired them to signify my arrival to one of the secretaries, and let him know, I there waited his Majesty's commands. I had an answer

in about an hour, that his Majesty, attended by the Royal Family, and great officers of the court, was coming out to receive me. I advanced a hundred yards. The Emperor and his train alighted from their horses, the Empress and ladies from their coaches, and I did not perceive they were in any fright or concern. I lay on the ground to kiss his Majesty's and the Empress's hands. I told his Majesty, that I was come according to my promise, and with the license of the Emperor my master, to have the honor of seeing so mighty a monarch, and to offer him any service in my power, consistent with my duty to my own prince; not mentioning a word of my disgrace, because I had hitherto no regular information of it, and might suppose myself wholly ignorant of any such design; neither could I reasonably conceive that the Emperor would discover the secret while I was out of his power: wherein, however, it soon appeared I was deceived.

I shall not trouble the reader with the particular account of my reception at this court, which was suitable to the generosity of so great a prince; nor of the difficulties I was in for want of a house and bed, being forced to lie on the ground, wrapped up in my coverlet.

CHAPTER 8

The Author, by a lucky accident, finds means to leave Blefuscu; and, after some difficulties, returns safe to his native country.

Three days after my arrival, walking out of curiosity to the northeast coast of the island, I observed, about half a league off, in the sea, somewhat that looked like a boat overturned. I pulled off my shoes and stockings, and wading two or three hundred yards, I found the object to approach nearer by force of the tide; and then plainly saw it to be a real boat, which I supposed might, by some tempest, have been driven from a ship; whereupon I returned immediately towards the city, and desired his Imperial Majesty to lend me twenty of the tallest vessels he had left after the loss of his fleet, and three thousand seamen under the command of his Vice-Admiral. This fleet sailed round, while I went back the shortest way to the coast where I first discovered the boat; I found the tide had driven it still nearer. The seamen were all provided with cordage, which I had beforehand twisted to a sufficient strength. When the ships came up, I stripped myself, and waded till I came within an hundred yards of the boat, after which

I was forced to swim till I got up to it. The seamen threw me the end of the cord, which I fastened to a hole in the forepart of the boat, and the other end to a man-of-war; but I found all my labor to little purpose; for being out of my depth, I was not able to work. In this necessity, I was forced to swim behind, and push the boat forwards as often as I could, with one of my hands; and the tide favoring me, I advanced so far, that I could just hold up my chin and feel the ground. I rested two or three minutes, and then gave the boat another shove, and so on till the sea was no higher than my armpits; and now the most laborious part being over, I took out my other cables, which were stowed in one of the ships, and fastening them first to the boat, and then to nine of the vessels which attended me; the wind being favorable, the seamen towed, and I shoved till we arrived within forty yards of the shore; and waiting till the tide was out, I got dry to the boat, and by the assistance of two thousand men, with ropes and engines, I made a shift to turn it on its bottom, and found it was but little damaged.

I shall not trouble the reader with the difficulties I was under by the help of certain paddles, which cost me ten days making, to get my boat to the royal port of Blefuscu, where a mighty concourse of people appeared upon my arrival, full of wonder at the sight of so prodigious a vessel. I told the Emperor that my good fortune had thrown this boat in my way, to carry me to some place from whence I might return into my native country, and begged his Majesty's orders for getting materials to fit it up, together with his license to depart; which, after some kind of expostulations, he was pleased to grant.

I did very much wonder, in all this time, not to have heard of any express relating to me from our Emperor to the court of Blefuscu. But I was afterwards given privately to understand, that his Imperial Majesty, never imagining I had the least notice of his designs, believed I was only gone to Blefuscu in performance of my promise, according to the license he had given me, which was well known at our court, and would return in a few days when that ceremony was ended. But he was at last in pain at my long absence; and after consulting with the Treasurer, and the rest of that cabal, a person of quality was dispatched with the copy of the articles against me. This envoy [53] had

instructions to represent to the monarch of Blefuscu, the great lenity of his master, who was content to punish me no farther than with the loss of my eyes; that I had fled from justice, and if I did not return in two hours, I should be deprived of my title of *Nardac,* and declared a traitor. The envoy further added, that in order to maintain the peace and amity between both empires, his master expected, that his brother of Blefuscu would give orders to have me sent back to Lilliput, bound hand and foot, to be punished as a traitor.

The Emperor of Blefuscu having taken three days to consult, returned an answer consisting of many civilities and excuses. He said, that as for sending me bound, his brother knew it was impossible; that although I had deprived him of his fleet, yet he owed great obligations to me for many good offices I had done him in making the peace. That however both their Majesties would soon be made easy; for I had found a prodigious vessel on the shore, able to carry me on the sea, which he had given order to fit up with my own assistance and direction; and he hoped in a few weeks both empires would be freed from so insupportable an encumbrance.

With this answer the envoy returned to Lilliput, and the monarch of Blefuscu related to me all that had passed; offering me at the same time (but under the strictest confidence) his gracious protection, if I would continue in his service; wherein although I believed him sincere, yet I resolved never more to put any confidence in princes or ministers, where I could possibly avoid it; and therefore, with all due acknowledgments for his favorable intentions, I humbly begged to be excused. I told him, that since fortune, whether good or evil, had thrown a vessel in my way, I was resolved to venture myself in the ocean, rather than be an occasion of difference between two such mighty monarchs. Neither did I find the Emperor at all displeased; and I discovered by a certain accident, that he was very glad of my resolution, and so were most of his ministers.

These considerations moved me to hasten my departure somewhat sooner than I intended; to which the court, impatient to have me gone, very readily contributed. Five hundred workmen were employed to make two sails to my boat, according to my directions, by quilting thirteenfold of their strongest linen together. I was at the pains of making ropes and cables, by twisting ten, twenty or thirty of the thickest and strongest of theirs. A great stone that I happened to find, after a long search,

---

53. This envoy: Frequent protests had been sent to the French government on account of its protection of Jacobites.

by the seashore, served me for an anchor. I had the tallow of three hundred cows for greasing my boat, and other uses. I was at incredible pains in cutting down some of the largest timber-trees for oars and masts, wherein I was, however, much assisted by his Majesty's ship carpenters, who helped me in smoothing them, after I had done the rough work.

In about a month, when all was prepared, I sent to receive his Majesty's commands, and to take my leave. The Emperor and Royal Family came out of the palace; I lay down on my face to kiss his hand, which he very graciously gave me: so did the Empress and young Princes of the blood. His Majesty presented me with fifty purses of two hundred *sprugs* apiece, together with his picture at full length, which I put immediately into one of my gloves, to keep it from being hurt. The ceremonies at my departure were too many to trouble the reader with at this time.

I stored the boat with the carcases of an hundred oxen, and three hundred sheep, with bread and drink proportionable, and as much meat ready dressed as four hundred cooks could provide. I took with me six cows and two bulls alive, with as many ewes and rams, intending to carry them into my own country, and propagate the breed. And to feed them on board, I had a good bundle of hay, and a bag of corn. I would gladly have taken a dozen of the natives, but this was a thing the Emperor would by no means permit; and besides a diligent search into my pockets, his Majesty engaged my honor not to carry away any of his subjects, although with their own consent and desire.

Having thus prepared all things as well as I was able, I set sail on the 24th day of September, 1701, at six in the morning; and when I had gone about four leagues to the northward, the wind being at southeast, at six in the evening I descried a small island about half a league to the northwest. I advanced forward, and cast anchor on the lee side of the island, which seemed to be uninhabited. I then took some refreshment, and went to my rest. I slept well, and as I conjecture at least six hours, for I found the day broke in two hours after I awaked. It was a clear night. I eat my breakfast before the sun was up; and heaving anchor, the wind being favorable, I steered the same course that I had done the day before, wherein I was directed by my pocket compass. My intention was to reach, if possible, one of those islands, which I had reason to believe lay to the northeast of Van Diemen's Land. I discovered nothing all that day; but upon the next, about three in the afternoon, when I had by my computation made twenty-four leagues from Blefuscu, I descried a sail steering to the southeast; my course was due east. I hailed her, but could get no answer; yet I found I gained upon her, for the wind slackened. I made all the sail I could, and in half an hour she spied me, then hung out her ancient, and discharged a gun. It is not easy to express the joy I was in upon the unexpected hope of once more seeing my beloved country, and the dear pledges I had left in it. The ship slackened her sails, and I came up with her between five and six in the evening, September 26; but my heart leaped within me to see her English colors. I put my cows and sheep into my coat pockets, and got on board with all my little cargo of provisions. The vessel was an English merchantman, returning from Japan by the North and South Seas;[54] the Captain, Mr. John Biddel of Deptford, a very civil man, and an excellent sailor. We were now in the latitude of thirty degrees south; there were about fifty men in the ship; and here I met an old comrade of mine, one Peter Williams, who gave me a good character to the Captain. This gentleman treated me with kindness, and desired I would let him know what place I came from last, and whither I was bound; which I did in a few words, but he thought I was raving, and that the dangers I underwent had disturbed my head; whereupon I took my black cattle and sheep out of my pocket, which, after great astonishment, clearly convinced him of my veracity. I then showed him the gold given me by the Emperor of Blefuscu, together with his Majesty's picture at full length, and some other rarities of that country. I gave him two purses of two hundred *sprugs* each, and promised, when we arrived in England, to make him a present of a cow and a sheep big with young.

I shall not trouble the reader with a particular account of this voyage, which was very prosperous for the most part. We arrived in the Downs[55] on the 13th of April, 1702. I had only one misfortune, that the rats on board carried away one of my sheep; I found her bones in a hole, picked clean from the flesh. The rest of my cattle I got safe on shore, and set them a grazing in a bowling green at Greenwich, where the fineness of the grass made them feed very heartily, though I had always feared the contrary: neither could I possibly have pre-

---

54. **North . . . Seas:** North and South Pacific.   55. **Downs:** a roadstead in the English Channel between the Goodwin Sands and the Kent coast, opposite the North Downs.

served them in so long a voyage, if the Captain had not allowed me some of his best biscuit, which, rubbed to powder, and mingled with water, was their constant food. The short time I continued in England, I made a considerable profit by showing my cattle to many persons of quality, and others: and before I began my second voyage, I sold them for six undred pounds. Since my last return, I find the breed is considerably increased, especially the sheep; which I hope will prove much to the advantage of the woolen manufacture, by the fineness of the fleeces.

I stayed but two months with my wife and family; for my insatiable desire of seeing foreign countries would suffer me to continue no longer. I left fifteen hundred pounds with my wife, and fixed her in a good house at Redriff. My remaining stock I carried with me, part in money, and part in goods, in hopes to improve my fortunes. My eldest uncle John had left me an estate in land, near Epping, of about thirty pounds a year; and I had a long lease of the Black Bull in Fetter Lane, which yielded me as much more; so that I was not in any danger of leaving my family upon the parish. My son Johnny, named so after his uncle, was at the Grammar School, and a towardly [56] child. My daughter Betty (who is now married, and has children) was then at her needlework. I took leave of my wife, and boy and girl, with tears on both sides, and went on board the *Adventure,* a merchant ship of three hundred tons, bound for Surat,[57] Captain John Nicholas, of Liverpool, Commander. But my account of this voyage must be referred to the second part of my *Travels.*

THE END OF THE FIRST PART

PART II
A Voyage to Brobdingnag [1]

CHAPTER I

A great storm described. The longboat sent to fetch water, the Author goes with it to discover the country. He is left on shore, is seized by one of the natives, and carried to a farmer's house. His reception there, with several accidents that happened there. A description of the inhabitants.

56. **towardly:** promising.   57. **Surat:** an important seaport north of Bombay. **A Voyage to Brobdingnag: 1. Brobdingnag:** It is described as a great island or continent, jutting out into the Pacific from the northwest coast of North America, a region then little known.

Having been condemned by nature and fortune to an active and restless life, in two months after my return, I again left my native country, and took shipping in the Downs on the 20th day of June, 1702, in the *Adventure,* Captain John Nicholas, a Cornish man, Commander, bound for Surat. We had a very prosperous gale till we arrived at the Cape of Good Hope, where we landed for fresh water, but discovering a leak we unshipped our goods and wintered there; for the Captain falling sick of an ague, we could not leave the Cape till the end of March. We then set sail, and had a good voyage till we passed the Straits of Madagascar; but having got northward of that island, and to about five degrees south latitude, the winds, which in those seas are observed to blow a constant equal gale between the north and west from the beginning of December to the beginning of May, on the 19th of April began to blow with much greater violence, and more westerly than usual, continuing so for twenty days together, during which time we were driven a little to the east of the Molucca Islands, and about three degrees northward of the Line, as our Captain found by an observation he took the 2nd of May, at which time the wind ceased, and it was a perfect calm, whereat I was not a little rejoiced. But he, being a man well experienced in the navigation of those seas, bid us all prepare against a storm, which accordingly happened the day following: for a southern wind, called the southern monsoon, began to set in.

Finding it was likely to overblow,[2] we took in our spritsail, and stood by to hand the foresail; but making foul weather we looked the guns were all fast, and handed the mizzen. The ship lay very broad off, so we thought it better spooning before the sea, than trying or hulling. We reefed the foresail and set him, we hauled aft the foresheet; the helm was hard aweather. The ship wore bravely. We belayed the fore-down-haul; but the sail was split, and we hauled down the yard, and got the sail into the ship, and unbound all the things clear of it. It was a very fierce storm; the sea broke strange and dangerous. We hauled off upon the lanyard of the whipstaff, and helped the man at helm. We would not get down our topmast, but let all stand, because she scudded before the sea very well, and we knew that the topmast being aloft, the ship was the wholesomer, and made better way through

2. **to overblow:** This paragraph is a parody of the use of seamen's technical terms in the popular accounts of voyages; it is stolen from Sturmy's *Compleat Mariner,* 1669.

the sea, seeing we had sea room. When the storm was over, we set foresail and mainsail, and brought the ship to. Then we set the mizzen, main topsail, and the fore topsail. Our course was east northeast, the wind was at southwest. We got the starboard tack aboard, we cast off our weather braces and lifts; we set in the lee braces, and hauled forward by the weather bowlines, and hauled them tight, and belayed them, and hauled over the mizzen tack to windward, and kept her full and by as near as she would lie.

During this storm, which was followed by a strong wind west southwest, we were carried by my computation about five hundred leagues to the east, so that the oldest sailor on board could not tell in what part of the world we were. Our provisions held out well, our ship was staunch, and our crew all in good health; but we lay in the utmost distress for water. We thought it best to hold on the same course, rather than turn more northerly, which might have brought us to the northwest parts of Great Tartary, and into the frozen sea.[3]

On the 16th day of June, 1703, a boy on the topmast discovered land. On the 17th we came in full view of a great island or continent (for we knew not whether) on the south side whereof was a small neck of land jutting out into the sea, and a creek too shallow to hold a ship of above one hundred tons. We cast anchor within a league of this creek, and our Captain sent a dozen of his men well armed in the longboat, with vessels for water if any could be found. I desired his leave to go with them, that I might see the country, and make what discoveries I could. When we came to land we saw no river or spring, nor any sign of inhabitants. Our men therefore wandered on the shore to find out some fresh water near the sea, and I walked alone about a mile on the other side, where I observed the country all barren and rocky. I now began to be weary, and seeing nothing to entertain my curiosity, I returned gently down towards the creek; and the sea being full in my view, I saw our men already got into the boat, and rowing for life to the ship. I was going to hollow after them, although it had been to little purpose, when I observed a huge creature walking after them in the sea, as fast as he could: he waded not much deeper than his knees, and took prodigious strides: but our men had the start of him

half a league, and the sea thereabouts being full of sharp-pointed rocks, the monster was not able to overtake the boat. This I was afterwards told, for I durst not stay to see the issue of that adventure; but ran as fast as I could the way I first went, and then climbed up a steep hill, which gave me some prospect of the country. I found it fully cultivated; but that which first surprised me was the length of the grass, which in those grounds that seemed to be kept for hay, was above twenty foot high.[4]

I fell into a highroad, for so I took it to be, though it served to the inhabitants only as a footpath through a field of barley. Here I walked on for some time, but could see little on either side, it being now near harvest, and the corn rising at least forty foot. I was an hour walking to the end of this field, which was fenced in with a hedge of at least one hundred and twenty foot high, and the trees so lofty that I could make no computation of their altitude. There was a stile to pass from this field into the next. It had four steps, and a stone to cross over when you came to the uppermost. It was impossible for me to climb this stile, because every step was six foot high, and the upper stone above twenty. I was endeavoring to find some gap in the hedge, when I discovered one of the inhabitants in the next field, advancing towards the stile, of the same size with him whom I saw in the sea pursuing our boat. He appeared as tall as an ordinary spire steeple, and took about ten yards at every stride, as near as I could guess. I was struck with the utmost fear and astonishment, and ran to hide myself in the corn, from whence I saw him at the top of the stile, looking back into the next field on the right hand, and heard him call in a voice many degrees louder than a speaking trumpet: but the noise was so high in the air, that at first I certainly thought it was thunder. Whereupon seven monsters like himself came towards him with reaping hooks in their hands, each hook about the largeness of six scythes. These people were not so well clad as the first, whose servants or laborers they seemed to be: for, upon some words he spoke, they went to reap the corn in the field where I lay. I kept from them at as great a distance as I could, but was forced to move with extreme difficulty, for the stalks of the corn were sometimes not above a foot distant, so that I could hardly squeeze my

3. **northwest . . . sea:** a curious way of describing the coast of Siberia and the Arctic Ocean.

4. **twenty . . . high:** The scale is not so carefully calculated as in Lilliput, but Swift uses a similar method by increasing sizes twelve times.

body betwixt them. However, I made a shift to go forward till I came to a part of the field where the corn had been laid by the rain and wind. Here it was impossible for me to advance a step; for the stalks were so interwoven that I could not creep through, and the beards of the fallen ears so strong and pointed that they pierced through my clothes into my flesh. At the same time I heard the reapers not above an hundred yards behind me. Being quite dispirited with toil, and wholly overcome by grief and despair, I lay down between two ridges, and heartily wished I might there end my days. I bemoaned my desolate widow, and fatherless children. I lamented my own folly and willfulness in attempting a second voyage against the advice of all my friends and relations. In this terrible agitation of mind I could not forbear thinking of Lilliput, whose inhabitants looked upon me as the greatest prodigy that ever appeared in the world; where I was able to draw an Imperial Fleet in my hand, and perform those other actions which will be recorded forever in the chronicles of that empire, while posterity shall hardly believe them, although attested by millions. I reflected what a mortification it must prove to me to appear as inconsiderable in this nation as one single Lilliputian would be among us. But this I conceived was to be the least of my misfortunes: for, as human creatures are observed to be more savage and cruel in proportion to their bulk, what could I expect but to be a morsel in the mouth of the first among these enormous barbarians who should happen to seize me? Undoubtedly philosophers are in the right when they tell us, that nothing is great or little otherwise than by comparison. It might have pleased fortune to let the Lilliputians find some nation, where the people were as diminutive with respect to them, as they were to me.[5] And who knows but that even this prodigious race of mortals might be equally overmatched in some distant part of the world, whereof we have yet no discovery?

Scared and confounded as I was, I could not forbear going on with these reflections, when one of the reapers approaching within ten yards of the ridge where I lay, made me apprehend that with the next step I should be squashed to death under his foot, or cut in two with his reaping hook. And

5. diminutive . . . me: or, as Swift expresses it in verse —

So, Nat'ralists observe, a Flea
Hath smaller fleas that on him prey,
And these have smaller fleas to bite 'em,
And so proceed *ad infinitum;* . . .

therefore when he was again about to move, I screamed as loud as fear could make me. Whereupon the huge creature trod short, and looking round about under him for some time, at last espied me as I lay on the ground. He considered a while with the caution of one who endeavors to lay hold on a small dangerous animal in such a manner that it shall not be able either to scratch or bite him, as I myself have sometimes done with a weasel in England. At length he ventured to take me up behind by the middle between his forefinger and thumb, and brought me within three yards of his eyes, that he might behold my shape more perfectly. I guessed his meaning, and my good fortune gave me so much presence of mind, that I resolved not to struggle in the least as he held me in the air about sixty foot from the ground, although he grievously pinched my sides, for fear I should slip through his fingers. All I ventured was to raise my eyes towards the sun, and place my hands together in a supplicating posture, and to speak some words in an humble melancholy tone, suitable to the condition I then was in. For I apprehended every moment that he would dash me against the ground, as we usually do any little hateful animal which we have a mind to destroy. But my good star would have it, that he appeared pleased with my voice and gestures, and began to look upon me as a curiosity, much wondering to hear me pronounce articulate words, although he could not understand them. In the meantime I was not able to forbear groaning and shedding tears, and turning my head towards my sides; letting him know, as well as I could, how cruelly I was hurt by the pressure of his thumb and finger. He seemed to apprehend my meaning; for, lifting up the lappet of his coat, he put me gently into it, and immediately ran along with me to his master, who was a substantial farmer, and the same person I had first seen in the field.

The farmer having (as I supposed by their talk) received such an account of me as his servant could give him, took a piece of a small straw, about the size of a walking staff, and therewith lifted up the lappets of my coat; which it seems he thought to be some kind of covering that nature had given me. He blew my hairs aside to take a better view of my face. He called his hinds about him, and asked them (as I afterwards learned) whether they had ever seen in the fields any little creature that resembled me. He then placed me softly on the ground upon all fours, but I got immediately up, and walked slowly backwards and forwards, to let those people see I had no intent to run away. They all sat down in a circle about me, the better to observe my motions. I pulled off my hat, and made a low bow towards the farmer. I fell on my knees, and lifted up my hands and eyes, and spoke several words as loud as I could: I took a purse of gold out of my pocket, and humbly presented it to him. He received it on the palm of his hand, then applied it close to his eye, to see what it was, and afterwards turned it several times with the point of a pin (which he took out of his sleeve), but could make nothing of it. Whereupon I made a sign that he should place his hand on the ground. I then took the purse, and opening it, poured all the gold into his palm. There were six Spanish pieces of four pistoles [6] each, beside twenty or thirty smaller coins. I saw him wet the tip of his little finger upon his tongue, and take up one of my largest pieces, and then another, but he seemed to be wholly ignorant what they were. He made me a sign to put them again into my purse, and the purse again into my pocket, which after offering to him several times, I thought it best to do.

The farmer by this time was convinced I must be a rational creature. He spoke often to me, but the sound of his voice pierced my ears like that of a water mill, yet his words were articulate enough. I answered as loud as I could, in several languages, and he often laid his ear within two yards of me, but all in vain, for we were wholly unintelligible to each other. He then sent his servants to their work, and taking his handkerchief out of his pocket, he doubled and spread it on his hand, which he placed flat on the ground, with the palm upwards, making me a sign to step into it, as I could easily do, for it was not above a foot in thickness. I thought it my part to obey, and for fear of falling, laid myself at full length upon the handkerchief, with the remainder of which he lapped me up to the head for further security, and in this manner carried me home to his house. There he called his wife, and showed me to her; but she screamed and ran back, as women in England do at the sight of a toad or a spider. However, when she had a while seen my behavior, and how well I observed the signs her husband made, she was soon reconciled, and by degrees grew extremely tender of me.

It was about twelve at noon, and a servant brought in dinner. It was only one substantial dish of meat (fit for the plain condition of an husbandman) in a dish of about four-and-twenty foot diameter. The company were the farmer and his wife, three children, and an old grandmother. When they were sat down, the farmer placed me at some distance from him on the table, which was thirty foot high from the floor. I was in a terrible fright, and kept as far as I could from the edge for fear of falling. The wife minced a bit of meat, then crumbled some bread on a trencher, and placed it before me. I made her a low bow, took out my knife and fork, and fell to eat, which gave them exceeding delight. The mistress sent her maid for a small dram cup, which held about two gallons, and filled it with drink; I took up the vessel with much difficulty in both hands, and in a most respectful manner drank to her ladyship's health, expressing the words as loud as I could in English, which made the company laugh so heartily that I was almost deafened with the noise. This liquor tasted like a small cider, and was not unpleasant. Then the master made me a sign to come to his trencher side; but as I walked on the table, being in great surprise all the time, as the indulgent reader will easily conceive and excuse, I happened to stumble against a crust, and fell flat on my face, but received no hurt. I got up immediately, and observing the good people to be in much concern, I took my hat (which I held under my arm out of good manners) and waving it over my head, made three huzzas, to show I had got no mischief by the fall. But advancing forwards toward my master (as I shall henceforth call him), his youngest son who sat next him, an arch boy of about ten years old, took me up by the legs, and held me so high in the air, that I trembled every limb; but his father snatched me from him, and at the same time gave him such a box on the left ear, as would have felled an European troop of horse to the earth, ordering him to be taken from the table. But being afraid the boy might owe me a spite, and well remembering how mischievous all children among us naturally are to sparrows, rabbits, young kittens, and puppy dogs, I fell on my knees, and pointing to the boy, made my master understand, as well as I could, that I desired his son might be pardoned. The father complied, and the lad took his seat again; whereupon I went to him and kissed his hand, which my master took, and made him stroke me gently with it.

In the midst of dinner, my mistress's favorite cat leapt into her lap. I heard a noise behind me like

6. **four pistoles:** the largest gold coins, worth between three and four pounds.

that of a dozen stocking weavers at work; and turning my head, I found it proceeded from the purring of this animal, who seemed to be three times larger than an ox, as I computed by the view of her head, and one of her paws, while her mistress was feeding and stroking her. The fierceness of this creature's countenance altogether discomposed me; though I stood at the farther end of the table, above fifty foot off; and although my mistress held her fast for fear she might give a spring, and seize me in her talons. But it happened there was no danger; for the cat took not the least notice of me when my master placed me within three yards of her. And as I have been always told, and found true by experience in my travels, that flying, or discovering fear before a fierce animal, is a certain way to make it pursue or attack you, so I resolved in this dangerous juncture to show no manner of concern. I walked with intrepidity five or six times before the very head of the cat, and came within half a yard of her; whereupon she drew herself back, as if she were more afraid of me: I had less apprehension concerning the dogs, whereof three or four came into the room, as it is usual in farmers' houses; one of which was a mastiff, equal in bulk to four elephants, and a greyhound, somewhat taller than the mastiff, but not so large.

When dinner was almost done, the nurse came in with a child of a year old in her arms, who immediately spied me, and began a squall that you might have heard from London Bridge to Chelsea, after the usual oratory of infants, to get me for a plaything. The mother out of pure indulgence took me up, and put me towards the child, who presently seized me by the middle, and got my head in his mouth, where I roared so loud that the urchin was frighted, and let me drop; and I should infallibly have broke my neck if the mother had not held her apron under me. The nurse to quiet her babe made use of a rattle, which was a kind of hollow vessel filled with great stones, and fastened by a cable to the child's waist: but all in vain, so that she was forced to apply the last remedy by giving it suck. I must confess no object ever disgusted me so much as the sight of her monstrous breast, which I cannot tell what to compare with, so as to give the curious reader an idea of its bulk, shape and color. It stood prominent six foot, and could not be less than sixteen in circumference. The nipple was about half the bigness of my head, and the hue both of that and the dug so varified with spots, pimples, and freckles, that nothing could appear more nauseous: for I had a near sight of her, she sitting down the more conveniently to give suck, and I standing on the table. This made me reflect upon the fair skins of our English ladies, who appear so beautiful to us, only because they are of our own size, and their defects not to be seen but through a magnifying glass, where we find by experiment that the smoothest and whitest skins look rough and coarse, and ill colored.

I remember when I was at Lilliput, the complexion of those diminutive people appeared to me the fairest in the world; and talking upon this subject with a person of learning there, who was an intimate friend of mine, he said that my face appeared much fairer and smoother when he looked on me from the ground, than it did upon a nearer view when I took him up in my hand and brought him close, which he confessed was at first a very shocking sight. He said he could discover great holes in my skin; that the stumps of my beard were ten times stronger than the bristles of a boar, and my complexion made up of several colors altogether disagreeable: although I must beg leave to say for myself, that I am as fair as most of my sex and country, and very little sunburnt by all my travels. On the other side, discoursing of the ladies in that Emperor's court, he used to tell me, one had freckles, another too wide a mouth, a third too large a nose, nothing of which I was able to distinguish. I confess this reflection was obvious enough; which, however, I could not forbear, lest the reader might think those vast creatures were actually deformed: for I must do them justice to say they are a comely race of people; and particularly the features of my master's countenance, although he were but a farmer, when I beheld him from the height of sixty foot, appeared very well proportioned.

When dinner was done, my master went out to his laborers, and as I could discover by his voice and gesture, gave his wife a strict charge to take care of me. I was very much tired, and disposed to sleep, which my mistress perceiving, she put me on her own bed, and covered me with a clean white handkerchief, but larger and coarser than the mainsail of a man-of-war.

I slept about two hours, and dreamed I was at home with my wife and children, which aggravated my sorrows when I awaked and found myself alone in a vast room, between two and three hundred foot wide, and above two hundred high, lying in a bed twenty yards wide. My mistress was gone about her household affairs, and had locked me in. The bed was eight yards from the floor. Some natural necessities required me to get down; I durst not presume to call, and if I had, it would have been in vain, with such a voice as mine, at so great a distance from the room where I lay to the kitchen where the family kept. While I was under these circumstances, two rats crept up the curtains, and ran smelling backwards and forwards on the bed. One of them came up almost to my face, whereupon I rose in a fright, and drew out my hanger [7] to defend myself. These horrible animals had the boldness to attack me on both sides, and one of them held his forefeet at my collar; but I had the good fortune to rip up his belly before he could do me any mischief. He fell down at my feet, and the other seeing the fate of his comrade, made his escape, but not without one good wound on the back, which I gave him as he fled, and made the blood run trickling from him. After this exploit, I walked gently to and fro on the bed, to recover my breath and loss of spirits. These creatures were of the size of a large mastiff, but infinitely more nimble and fierce, so that if I had taken off my belt before I went to sleep, I must have infallibly been torn to pieces and devoured. I measured the tail of the dead rat, and found it to be two yards long, wanting an inch; but it went against my stomach to drag the carcass off the bed, where it lay still bleeding; I observed it had yet some life, but with a strong slash across the neck, I thoroughly dispatched it.

Soon after my mistress came into the room, who seeing me all bloody, ran and took me up in her hand. I pointed to the dead rat, smiling and making other signs to show I was not hurt, whereat she was extremely rejoiced, calling the maid to take up the dead rat with a pair of tongs, and throw it out of the window. Then she set me on a table, where I showed her my hanger all bloody, and wiping it on the lappet of my coat, returned it to the scabbard. I was pressed to do more than one thing, which another could not do for me, and therefore endeavored to make my mistress understand that I desired to be set down on the floor; which after she had done, my bashfulness would not suffer me to express myself farther than by pointing to the door, and bowing several times. The good woman with much difficulty at last perceived what I would be at, and taking me up again in her hand, walked into the garden, where she set me down. I went on one side about two hundred yards, and beckoning to her not to look or to follow me, I hid myself between two leaves of sorrel, and there discharged the necessities of nature.

I hope the gentle reader will excuse me for dwelling on these and the like particulars, which however insignificant they may appear to groveling vulgar minds, yet will certainly help a philosopher to enlarge his thoughts and imagination, and apply them to the benefit of public as well as private life, which was my sole design in presenting this and other accounts of my travels to the world; wherein I have been chiefly studious of truth, without affecting any ornaments of learning or of style. But the whole scene of this voyage made so strong an impression on my mind, and is so deeply fixed in my memory, that in committing it to paper I did not omit one material circumstance: however, upon a strict review, I blotted out several passages of less moment which were in my first copy, for fear of being censured as tedious and trifling, whereof travelers are often, perhaps not without justice, accused.

CHAPTER 2

A description of the farmer's daughter. The Author carried to a market town, and then to the metropolis. The particulars of his journey.

My mistress had a daughter of nine years old, a child of towardly parts for her age, very dexterous at her needle, and skillful in dressing her baby.[8] Her mother and she contrived to fit up the baby's cradle for me against night: the cradle was put into a small drawer of a cabinet, and the drawer placed upon a hanging shelf for fear of the rats. This was my bed all the time I stayed with those people, although made more convenient by degrees, as I began to learn their language, and make my wants known. This young girl was so handy, that after I had once or twice pulled off my clothes before her, she was able to dress and undress me, although I never gave her that trouble when she would let me do either myself. She made me seven shirts, and some other linen, of as fine cloth as could be got, which indeed was coarser than sackcloth; and these she constantly washed for me with her own hands. She was likewise my schoolmistress to teach me the language: when I pointed

---

7. **hanger**: short sword.

8. **baby**: doll.

to anything she told me the name of it in her own tongue, so that in a few days I was able to call for whatever I had a mind to. She was very good-natured, and not above forty foot high, being little for her age. She gave me the name of *Grildrig,* which the family took up, and afterwards the whole kingdom. The word imports what the Latins call *nanunculus,* the Italians *homunceletino,*[9] and the English *mannikin.* To her I chiefly owe my preservation in that country: we never parted while I was there; I called her my *Glumdalclitch,* or little nurse: and I should be guilty of great ingratitude, if I omitted this honorable mention of her care and affection towards me, which I heartily wish it lay in my power to requite as she deserves, instead of being the innocent but unhappy instrument of her disgrace, as I have too much reason to fear.

It now began to be known and talked of in the neighborhood, that my master had found a strange animal in the field, about the bigness of a *splacknuck,* but exactly shaped in every part like a human creature; which it likewise imitated in all its actions; seemed to speak in a little language of its own, had already learned several words of theirs, went erect upon two legs, was tame and gentle, would come when it was called, do whatever it was bid, had the finest limbs in the world, and a complexion fairer than a nobleman's daughter of three years old. Another farmer who lived hard by, and was a particular friend of my master, came on a visit on purpose to inquire into the truth of this story. I was immediately produced, and placed upon a table, where I walked as I was commanded, drew my hanger, put it up again, made my reverence to my master's guest, asked him in his own language how he did, and told him he was welcome, just as my little nurse had instructed me. This man who was old and dimsighted, put on his spectacles to behold me better, at which I could not forbear laughing very heartily, for his eyes appeared like the full moon shining into a chamber at two windows. Our people, who discovered the cause of my mirth, bore me company in laughing, at which the old fellow was fool enough to be angry and out of countenance. He had the character of a great miser, and to my misfortune he well deserved it, by the cursed advice he gave my master to show me as a sight upon a market day in the next town, which was half an hour's riding, about two and twenty miles from our house. I guessed there was some

mischief contriving, when I observed my master and his friend whispering long together, sometimes pointing at me; and my fears made me fancy that I overheard and understood some of their words. But the next morning Glumdalclitch, my little nurse, told me the whole matter, which she had cunningly picked out from her mother. The poor girl laid me on her bosom, and fell a weeping with shame and grief. She apprehended some mischief would happen to me from rude vulgar folks, who might squeeze me to death, or break one of my limbs by taking me in their hands. She had also observed how modest I was in my nature, how nicely I regarded my honor, and what an indignity I should conceive it to be exposed for money as a public spectacle to the meanest of the people. She said, her papa and mamma had promised that Grildrig should be hers, but now she found they meant to serve her as they did last year, when they pretended to give her a lamb, and yet, as soon as it was fat, sold it to a butcher. For my own part, I may truly affirm that I was less concerned than my nurse. I had a strong hope, which never left me, that I should one day recover my liberty; and as to the ignominy of being carried about for a monster, I considered myself to be a perfect stranger in the country, and that such a misfortune could never be charged upon me as a reproach, if ever I should return to England; since the King of Great Britain himself, in my condition, must have undergone the same distress.

My master, pursuant to the advice of his friend, carried me in a box the next market day to the neighboring town, and took along with him his little daughter, my nurse, upon a pillion behind him. The box was close on every side, with a little door for me to go in and out, and a few gimlet holes to let in air. The girl had been so careful to put the quilt of her baby's bed into it, for me to lie down on. However, I was terribly shaken and discomposed in this journey, though it were but of half an hour. For the horse went about forty foot at every step, and trotted so high, that the agitation was equal to the rising and falling of a ship in a great storm, but much more frequent. Our journey was somewhat further than from London to St. Albans.[10] My master alighted at an inn which he used to frequent; and after consulting a while with the innkeeper, and making some necessary preparations, he hired the *Grultrud,* or crier, to give notice through the town of a strange creature to be seen

9. *nanunculus . . . homunceletino:* coined words perhaps to ridicule such pedantries.

10. St. Albans: about twenty miles from London.

at the Sign of the Green Eagle, not so big as a *splacknuck* (an animal in that country very finely shaped, about six foot long), and in every part of the body resembling an human creature, could speak several words, and perform an hundred diverting tricks.

I was placed upon a table in the largest room of the inn, which might be near three hundred foot square. My little nurse stood on a low stool close to the table, to take care of me, and direct what I should do. My master, to avoid a crowd, would suffer only thirty people at a time to see me. I walked about on the table as the girl commanded: she asked me questions as far as she knew my understanding of the language reached, and I answered them as loud as I could. I turned about several times to the company, paid my humble respects, said they were welcome, and used some other speeches I had been taught. I took up a thimble filled with liquor, which Glumdalclitch had given me for a cup, and drank their health. I drew out my hanger, and flourished with it after the manner of fencers in England. My nurse gave me part of a straw, which I exercised as a pike, having learned the art in my youth. I was that day shown to twelve sets of company, and as often forced to go over again with the same fopperies, till I was half dead with weariness and vexation. For those who had seen me made such wonderful reports, that the people were ready to break down the doors to come in. My master for his own interest would not suffer anyone to touch me except my nurse; and, to prevent danger, benches were set round the table at such a distance as put me out of everybody's reach. However, an unlucky schoolboy aimed a hazelnut directly at my head, which very narrowly missed me; otherwise, it came with so much violence, that it would have infallibly knocked out my brains, for it was almost as large as a small pumpion: [11] but I had the satisfaction to see the young rogue well beaten, and turned out of the room.

My master gave public notice, that he would show me again the next market day, and in the meantime he prepared a more convenient vehicle for me, which he had reason enough to do; for I was so tired with my first journey, and with entertaining company eight hours together, that I could hardly stand upon my legs, or speak a word. It was at least three days before I recovered my strength; and that I might have no rest at home,

11. pumpion: pumpkin.

all the neighboring gentlemen from an hundred miles round, hearing of my fame, came to see me at my master's own house. There could not be fewer than thirty persons with their wives and children (for the country is very populous); and my master demanded the rate of a full room whenever he showed me at home, although it were only to a single family; so that for some time I had but little ease every day of the week (except Wednesday, which is their Sabbath) although I were not carried to the town.

My master finding how profitable I was like to be, resolved to carry me to the most considerable cities of the kingdom. Having therefore provided himself with all things necessary for a long journey, and settled his affairs at home, he took leave of his wife, and upon the 17th of August, 1703, about two months after my arrival, we set out for the metropolis, situated near the middle of that empire, and about three thousand miles distance from our house. My master made his daughter Glumdalclitch ride behind him. She carried me on her lap in a box tied about her waist. The girl had lined it on all sides with the softest cloth she could get, well quilted underneath, furnished it with her baby's bed, provided me with linen and other necessaries, and made everything as convenient as she could. We had no other company but a boy of the house, who rode after us with the luggage.

My master's design was to show me in all the towns by the way, and to step out of the road for fifty or an hundred miles, to any village or person of quality's house where he might expect custom. We made easy journeys of not above seven or eight score miles a day: for Glumdalclitch, on purpose to spare me, complained she was tired with the trotting of the horse. She often took me out of my box, at my own desire, to give me air, and show me the country, but always held me fast by leading strings. We passed over five or six rivers many degrees broader and deeper than the Nile or the Ganges; and there was hardly a rivulet so small as the Thames at London Bridge. We were ten weeks in our journey, and I was shown in eighteen large towns besides many villages and private families.

On the 26th day of October, we arrived at the metropolis, called in their language *Lorbrulgrud,* or Pride of the Universe. My master took a lodging in the principal street of the city, not far from the royal palace, and put out bills in the usual form, containing an exact description of my person and parts. He hired a large room between three and four hundred foot wide. He provided a table sixty foot in diameter, upon which I was to act my part, and pallisadoed it round three foot from the edge, and as many high, to prevent my falling over. I was shown ten times a day to the wonder and satisfaction of all people. I could now speak the language tolerably well, and perfectly understood every word that was spoken to me. Besides, I had learnt their alphabet, and could make a shift to explain a sentence here and there; for Glumdalclitch had been my instructor while we were at home, and at leisure hours during our journey. She carried a little book in her pocket, not much larger than a Sanson's Atlas; [12] it was a common treatise for the use of young girls, giving a short account of their religion: out of this she taught me my letters, and interpreted the words.

CHAPTER 3

The Author sent for to court. The Queen buys him of his master the farmer, and presents him to the King. He disputes with his Majesty's great scholars. An apartment at court provided for the Author. He is in high favor with the Queen. He stands up for the honor of his own country. His quarrels with the Queen's dwarf.

The frequent labors I underwent every day made in a few weeks a very considerable change in my health: the more my master got by me, the more insatiable he grew. I had quite lost my stomach, and was almost reduced to a skeleton. The farmer observed it, and concluding I soon must die, resolved to make as good a hand of me as he could. While he was thus reasoning and resolving with himself, a *Slardral,* or Gentleman Usher, came from court, commanding my master to bring me immediately thither for the diversion of the Queen and her ladies. Some of the latter had already been to see me, and reported strange things of my beauty, behavior, and good sense. Her Majesty and those who attended her were beyond measure delighted with my demeanor. I fell on my knees, and begged the honor of kissing her Imperial foot; but this gracious princess held out her little finger towards me (after I was set on a table), which I embraced in both my arms, and put the tip of it, with the utmost respect, to my lip. She made me some general questions about my country and my travels, which I answered as distinctly and in as few words as I

could. She asked whether I would be content to live at court. I bowed down to the board of the table, and humbly answered, that I was my master's slave, but if I were at my own disposal, I should be proud to devote my life to her Majesty's service. She then asked my master whether he were willing to sell me at a good price. He, who apprehended I could not live a month, was ready enough to part with me, and demanded a thousand pieces of gold, which were ordered him on the spot, each piece being about the bigness of eight hundred moidores; but, allowing for the proportion of all things between that country and Europe, and the high price of gold among them, was hardly so great a sum as a thousand guineas would be in England. I then said to the Queen, since I was now her Majesty's most humble creature and vassal, I must beg the favor, that Glumdalclitch, who had always tended me with so much care and kindness, and understood to do it so well, might be admitted into her service, and continue to be my nurse and instructor. Her Majesty agreed to my petition, and easily got the farmer's consent, who was glad enough to have his daughter preferred at court: and the poor girl herself was not able to hide her joy. My late master withdrew, bidding me farewell, and saying he had left me in a good service; to which I replied not a word, only making him a slight bow.

The Queen observed my coldness, and when the farmer was gone out of the apartment, asked me the reason. I made bold to tell her Majesty that I owed no other obligation to my late master, than his not dashing out the brains of a poor harmless creature found by chance in his field; which obligation was amply recompensed by the gain he had made in showing me through half the kingdom, and the price he had now sold me for. That the life I had since led, was laborious enough to kill an animal of ten times my strength. That my health was much impaired by the continual drudgery of entertaining the rabble every hour of the day, and that if my master had not thought my life in danger, her Majesty perhaps would not have got so cheap a bargain. But as I was out of all fear of being ill treated under the protection of so great and good an Empress, the Ornament of Nature, the Darling of the World, the Delight of her Subjects, the Phoenix [13] of the Creation; so I hoped my late master's apprehensions would appear to be groundless, for I already found my spirits to revive by the influence of her most august presence.

---

12. **Sanson's Atlas:** a large folio, measuring 25 by 20 inches.

13. **Phoenix:** here used in the sense of "paragon."

This was the sum of my speech, delivered with great improprieties and hesitation; the latter part was altogether framed in the style peculiar to that people, whereof I learned some phrases from Glumdalclitch, while she was carrying me to court.

The Queen giving great allowance for my defectiveness in speaking, was however surprised at so much wit and good sense in so diminutive an animal. She took me in her own hand, and carried me to the King, who was then retired to his cabinet. His Majesty, a prince of much gravity, and austere countenance, not well observing my shape at first view, asked the Queen after a cold manner, how long it was since she grew fond of a *splacknuck;* for such it seems he took me to be, as I lay upon my breast in her Majesty's right hand. But this princess, who hath an infinite deal of wit and humor, set me gently on my feet upon the scrutore,[14] and commanded me to give his Majesty an account of myself, which I did in a very few words; and Glumdalclitch, who attended at the cabinet door, and could not endure I should be out of her sight, being admitted, confirmed all that had passed from my arrival at her father's house.

The King, although he be as learned a person as any in his dominions, and had been educated in the study of philosophy, and particularly mathematics; yet when he observed my shape exactly, and saw me walk erect, before I began to speak, conceived I might be a piece of clockwork (which is in that country arrived to a very great perfection), contrived by some ingenious artist. But when he heard my voice, and found what I delivered to be regular and rational, he could not conceal his astonishment. He was by no means satisfied with the relation I gave him of the manner I came into his kingdom, but thought it a story concerted between Glumdalclitch and her father, who had taught me a set of words to make me sell at a higher price. Upon this imagination he put several other questions to me, and still received rational answers, no otherwise defective than by a foreign accent, and an imperfect knowledge in the language, with some rustic phrases which I had learned at the farmer's house, and did not suit the polite style of a court.

His Majesty sent for three great scholars who were then in their weekly waiting, according to the custom in that country. These gentlemen, after they had a while examined my shape with much nicety, were of different opinions concerning me. They all agreed that I could not be produced ac-

cording to the regular laws of nature, because I was not framed with a capacity of preserving my life, either by swiftness, or climbing of trees, or digging holes in the earth. They observed by my teeth, which they viewed with great exactness, that I was a carnivorous animal; yet most quadrupeds being an overmatch for me, and field mice, with some others, too nimble, they could not imagine how I should be able to support myself, unless I fed upon snails and other insects, which they offered, by many learned arguments, to evince that I could not possibly do. One of them seemed to think that I might be an embryo, or abortive birth. But this opinion was rejected by the other two, who observed my limbs to be perfect and finished, and that I had lived several years, as it was manifested from my beard, the stumps whereof they plainly discovered through a magnifying glass. They would not allow me to be a dwarf, because my littleness was beyond all degrees of comparison; for the Queen's favorite dwarf, the smallest ever known in that kingdom, was near thirty foot high. After much debate, they concluded unanimously that I was only *relplum scalcath,* which is interpreted literally, *lusus naturae;*[15] a determination exactly agreeable to the modern philosophy[16] of Europe, whose professors, disdaining the old evasion of *occult causes,* whereby the followers of Aristotle endeavor in vain to disguise their ignorance, have invented this wonderful solution of all difficulties, to the unspeakable advancement of human knowledge.

After this decisive conclusion, I entreated to be heard a word or two. I applied myself to the King, and assured his Majesty, that I came from a country which abounded with several millions of both sexes, and of my own stature; where the animals, trees, and houses were all in proportion, and where by consequence I might be as able to defend myself, and to find sustenance, as any of his Majesty's subjects could do here; which I took for a full answer to those gentlemen's arguments. To this they only replied with a smile of contempt, saying, that the farmer had instructed me very well in my lesson. The King, who had a much better understanding, dismissing his learned men, sent for the farmer, who by good fortune was not yet gone out of town. Having therefore first examined him privately, and then confronted him with

---

14. scrutore: escritoire.

15. *lusus naturae:* a freak of nature.   16. modern philosophy: the new science, with its own special jargon to hide its ignorance.

me and the young girl, his Majesty began to think that what we told him might possibly be true. He desired the Queen to order that a particular care should be taken of me, and was of opinion that Glumdalclitch should still continue in her office of tending me, because he observed we had a great affection for each other. A convenient apartment was provided for her at court: she had a sort of governess appointed to take care of her education, a maid to dress her, and two other servants for menial offices; but the care of me was wholly appropriated to herself. The Queen commanded her own cabinetmaker to contrive a box that might serve me for a bedchamber, after the model that Glumdalclitch and I should agree upon. This man was a most ingenious artist, and according to my directions, in three weeks finished for me a wooden chamber of sixteen foot square, and twelve high, with sash windows, a door, and two closets, like a London bedchamber. The board that made the ceiling was to be lifted up and down by two hinges, to put in a bed ready furnished by her Majesty's upholsterer, which Glumdalclitch took out every day to air, made it with her own hands, and letting it down at night, locked up the roof over me. A nice workman, who was famous for little curiosities, undertook to make me two chairs, with backs and frames, of a substance not unlike ivory, and two tables, with a cabinet to put my things in. The room was quilted on all sides, as well as the floor and the ceiling, to prevent any accident from the carelessness of those who carried me, and to break the force of a jolt when I went in a coach. I desired a lock for my door, to prevent rats and mice from coming in: the smith, after several attempts, made the smallest that was ever seen among them, for I have known a larger at the gate of a gentleman's house in England. I made a shift to keep the key in a pocket of my own, fearing Glumdalclitch might lose it. The Queen likewise ordered the thinnest silks that could be gotten, to make me clothes, not much thicker than an English blanket, very cumbersome till I was accustomed to them. They were after the fashion of the kingdom, partly resembling the Persian, and partly the Chinese, and are a very grave, decent habit.

The Queen became so fond of my company, that she could not dine without me. I had a table placed upon the same at which her Majesty eat, just at her left elbow, and a chair to sit on. Glumdalclitch stood upon a stool on the floor, near my table, to assist and take care of me. I had an entire set of silver dishes and plates, and other necessaries, which, in proportion to those of the Queen, were not much bigger than what I have seen in a London toyshop, for the furniture of a baby-house: these my little nurse kept in her pocket, in a silver box, and gave me at meals as I wanted them, always cleaning them herself. No person dined with the Queen but the two Princesses Royal, the elder sixteen years old, and the younger at that time thirteen and a month. Her Majesty used to put a bit of meat upon one of my dishes, out of which I carved for myself, and her diversion was to see me eat in miniature. For the Queen (who had indeed but a weak stomach) took up at one mouthful, as much as a dozen English farmers could eat at a meal, which to me was for some time a very nauseous sight. She would craunch the wing of a lark, bones and all, between her teeth, although it were nine times as large as that of a full-grown turkey; and put a bit of bread into her mouth, as big as two twelve-penny loaves. She drank out of a golden cup, above a hogshead at a draught. Her knives were twice as long as a scythe set straight upon the handle. The spoons, forks, and other instruments were all in the same proportion. I remember when Glumdalclitch carried me out of curiosity to see some of the tables at court, where ten or a dozen of these enormous knives and forks were lifted up together, I thought I had never till then beheld so terrible a sight.

It is the custom that every Wednesday (which, as I have before observed, was their Sabbath) the King and Queen, with the royal issue of both sexes, dine together in the apartment of his Majesty, to whom I was now become a favorite; and at these times my little chair and table were placed at his left hand, before one of the saltcellars. This prince took a pleasure in conversing with me, inquiring into the manners, religion, laws, government, and learning of Europe; wherein I gave him the best account I was able. His apprehension was so clear, and his judgment so exact, that he made very wise reflections and observations upon all I said. But, I confess, that after I had been a little too copious in talking of my own beloved country, of our trade, and wars by sea and land, of our schisms in religion, and parties in the state; the prejudices of his education prevailed so far, that he could not forbear taking me up in his right hand, and stroking me gently with the other, after an hearty fit of laughing, asked me, whether I were a Whig or a Tory. Then turning to his first minister, who waited behind him with a white staff, near as tall as the mainmast of the *Royal Sovereign*,[17] he observed how contemptible a thing was human grandeur, which could be mimicked by such diminutive insects as I. "And yet," said he, "I dare engage, those creatures have their titles and distinctions of honor, they contrive little nests and burrows, that they call houses and cities; they make a figure in dress and equipage; they love, they fight, they dispute, they cheat, they betray." And thus he continued on, while my color came and went several times, with indignation to hear our noble country, the mistress of arts and arms, the scourge of France, the arbitress of Europe, the seat of virtue, piety, honor, and truth, the pride and envy of the world, so contemptuously treated.

But as I was not in a condition to resent injuries, so, upon mature thoughts, I began to doubt whether I were injured or no. For, after having been accustomed several months to the sight and converse of this people, and observed every object upon which I cast my eyes, to be of proportionable magnitude, the horror I had first conceived from their bulk and aspect was so far worn off, that if I had then beheld a company of English lords and ladies in their finery and birthday clothes, acting their several parts in the most courtly manner, of strutting, and bowing, and prating; to say the truth, I should have been strongly tempted to laugh as much at them as this King and his grandees did at me. Neither indeed could I forbear smiling at myself, when the Queen used to place me upon her hand towards a looking glass, by which both our persons appeared before me in full view together; and there could be nothing more ridiculous than the comparison; so that I really began to imagine myself dwindled many degrees below my usual size.

Nothing angered and mortified me so much as the Queen's dwarf, who being of the lowest stature that was ever in that country (for I verily think he was not full thirty foot high) became so insolent at seeing a creature so much beneath him, that he would always affect to swagger and look big as he passed by me in the Queen's antechamber, while I was standing on some table talking with the lords or ladies of the court, and he seldom failed of a smart word or two upon my littleness; against which I could only revenge myself by

17. *Royal Sovereign:* one of the largest ships in the British navy, launched in 1637, burned 1696.

calling him brother, challenging him to wrestle, and such repartees as are usual in the mouths of court pages. One day at dinner this malicious little cub was so nettled with something I had said to him, that raising himself upon the frame of her Majesty's chair, he took me up by the middle, as I was sitting down, not thinking any harm, and let me drop into a large silver bowl of cream, and then ran away as fast as he could. I fell over head and ears, and if I had not been a good swimmer, it might have gone very hard with me; for Glumdalclitch in that instant happened to be at the other end of the room, and the Queen was in such a fright that she wanted presence of mind to assist me. But my little nurse ran to my relief, and took me out, after I had swallowed above a quart of cream. I was put to bed; however, I received no other damage than the loss of a suit of clothes, which was utterly spoiled. The dwarf was soundly whipped, and as a farther punishment, forced to drink up the bowl of cream, into which he had thrown me: neither was he ever restored to favor: for, soon after the Queen bestowed him on a lady of high quality, so that I saw him no more, to my very great satisfaction; for I could not tell to what extremity such a malicious urchin might have carried his resentment.

He had before served me a scurvy trick, which set the Queen a laughing, although at the same time she was heartily vexed, and would have immediately cashiered him, if I had not been so generous as to intercede. Her Majesty had taken a marrow bone upon her plate, and after knocking out the marrow, placed the bone again in the dish erect as it stood before; the dwarf watching his opportunity, while Glumdalclitch was gone to the sideboard, mounted the stool that she stood on to take care of me at meals, took me up in both hands, and squeezing my legs together, wedged them into the marrow bone above my waist, where I stuck for some time, and made a very ridiculous figure. I believe it was near a minute before anyone knew what was become of me, for I thought it below me to cry out. But, as princes seldom get their meat hot, my legs were not scalded, only my stockings and breeches in a sad condition. The dwarf, at my entreaty, had no other punishment than a sound whipping.

I was frequently rallied by the Queen upon account of my fearfulness, and she used to ask me whether the people of my country were as great cowards as myself. The occasion was this: the kingdom is much pestered with flies in summer; and these odious insects, each of them as big as a Dunstable lark, hardly gave me any rest while I sat at dinner, with their continual humming and buzzing about my ears. They would sometimes alight upon my victuals, and leave their loathsome excrement or spawn behind, which to me was very visible, though not to the natives of that country, whose large optics were not so acute as mine in viewing smaller objects. Sometimes they would fix upon my nose or forehead, where they stung me to the quick, smelling very offensively, and I could easily trace that viscous matter, which our naturalists tell us enables those creatures to walk with their feet upwards upon a ceiling. I had much ado to defend myself against these detestable animals, and could not forbear starting when they came on my face. It was the common practice of the dwarf to catch a number of these insects in his hand, as schoolboys do among us, and let them out suddenly under my nose, on purpose to frighten me, and divert the Queen. My remedy was to cut them in pieces with my knife as they flew in the air, wherein my dexterity was much admired.

I remember one morning when Glumdalclitch had set me in my box upon a window, as she usually did in fair days to give me air (for I durst not venture to let the box be hung on a nail out of the window, as we do with cages in England), after I had lifted up one of my sashes, and sat down at my table to eat a piece of sweet cake for my breakfast, above twenty wasps, allured by the smell, came flying into the room, humming louder than the drones of as many bagpipes. Some of them seized my cake, and carried it piecemeal away, others flew about my head and face, confounding me with the noise, and putting me in the utmost terror of their stings. However I had the courage to rise and draw my hanger, and attack them in the air. I dispatched four of them, but the rest got away, and I presently shut my window. These insects were as large as partridges: I took out their stings, found them an inch and a half long, and as sharp as needles. I carefully preserved them all, and having since shown them with some other curiosities in several parts of Europe; upon my return to England I gave three of them to Gresham College,[18] and kept the fourth for myself.

18. Gresham College: the home of the Royal Society.

CHAPTER 4

The country described. A proposal for correcting modern maps. The King's palace, and some account of the metropolis. The Author's way of traveling. The chief temple described.

I now intend to give the reader a short description of this country, as far as I traveled in it, which was not above two thousand miles round Lorbrulgrud the metropolis. For the Queen, whom I always attended, never went further when she accompanied the King in his progresses, and there stayed till his Majesty returned from viewing his frontiers. The whole extent of this prince's dominions reacheth about six thousand miles in length, and from three to five in breadth. From whence I cannot but conclude that our geographers of Europe are in a great error, by supposing nothing but sea between Japan and California; for it was ever my opinion, that there must be a balance of earth to counterpoise the great continent of Tartary; and therefore they ought to correct their maps and charts, by joining this vast tract of land to the northwest parts of America, wherein I shall be ready to lend them my assistance.

The kingdom is a peninsula, terminated to the northeast by a ridge of mountains thirty miles high, which are altogether impassable by reason of the volcanoes upon the tops. Neither do the most learned know what sort of mortals inhabit beyond those mountains, or whether they be inhabited at all. On the three other sides it is bounded by the ocean. There is not one seaport in the whole kingdom, and those parts of the coasts into which the rivers issue are so full of pointed rocks, and the sea generally so rough, that there is no venturing with the smallest of their boats, so that these people are wholly excluded from any commerce with the rest of the world. But the large rivers are full of vessels, and abound with excellent fish, for they seldom get any from the sea, because the sea fish are of the same size with those in Europe, and consequently not worth catching; whereby it is manifest, that nature, in the production of plants and animals of so extraordinary a bulk, is wholly confined to this continent, of which I leave the reasons to be determined by philosophers. However, now and then they take a whale that happens to be dashed against the rocks, which the common people feed on heartily. These whales I have known so large that a man could hardly carry one upon his shoulders; and sometimes for curiosity they are brought in hampers to Lorbrulgrud: I saw one of them in a dish at the King's table, which passed for a rarity, but I did not observe he was fond of it; for I think indeed the bigness disgusted him, although I have seen one somewhat larger in Greenland.

The country is well inhabited, for it contains fifty-one cities, near an hundred walled towns, and a great number of villages. To satisfy my curious reader, it may be sufficient to describe Lorbrulgrud. This city stands upon almost two equal parts on each side the river that passes through. It contains above eighty thousand houses, and about six hundred thousand inhabitants. It is in length three *glonglungs* (which make about fifty-four English miles) and two and a half in breadth, as I measured it myself in the royal map made by the King's order, which was laid on the ground on purpose for me, and extended an hundred feet: I paced the diameter and circumference several times barefoot, and computing by the scale, measured it pretty exactly.

The King's palace is no regular edifice, but an heap of buildings about seven miles round: the chief rooms are generally two hundred and forty foot high, and broad and long in proportion. A coach was allowed to Glumdalclitch and me, wherein her governess frequently took her out to see the town, or go among the shops; and I was always of the party, carried in my box; although the girl at my own desire would often take me out, and hold me in her hand, that I might more conveniently view the houses and the people, as we passed along the streets. I reckoned our coach to be about a square of Westminster Hall,[19] but not altogether so high; however, I cannot be very exact. One day the governess ordered our coachman to stop at several shops, where the beggars, watching their opportunity, crowded to the sides of the coach, and gave me the most horrible spectacles that ever an European eye beheld. There was a woman with a cancer in her breast, swelled to a monstrous size, full of holes, in two or three of which I could have easily crept, and covered my whole body. There was a fellow with a wen in his neck, larger than five woolpacks, and another with a couple of wooden legs, each about twenty foot high. But the most hateful sight of all was the lice crawling on their clothes. I could see distinctly the

19. **Westminster Hall:** probably means a square of the breadth, i.e., 68 feet; it was 85 feet high.

limbs of these vermin with my naked eye, much better than those of an European louse through a microscope, and their snouts with which they rooted like swine. They were the first I had ever beheld, and I should have been curious enough to dissect one of them, if I had proper instruments (which I unluckily left behind me in the ship), although indeed the sight was so nauseous, that it perfectly turned my stomach.

Besides the large box in which I was usually carried, the Queen ordered a smaller one to be made for me, of about twelve foot square, and ten high, for the convenience of traveling, because the other was somewhat too large for Glumdalclitch's lap, and cumbersome in the coach; it was made by the same artist, whom I directed in the whole contrivance. This traveling closet was an exact square with a window in the middle of three of the squares, and each window was latticed with iron wire on the outside, to prevent accidents in long journeys. On the fourth side, which had no window, two strong staples were fixed, through which the person that carried me, when I had a mind to be on horseback, put in a leathern belt, and buckled it about his waist. This was always the office of some grave trusty servant in whom I could confide, whether I attended the King and Queen in their progresses, or were disposed to see the gardens, or pay a visit to some great lady or minister of state in the court, when Glumdalclitch happened to be out of order: for I soon began to be known and esteemed among the greatest officers, I suppose more upon account of their Majesties' favor, than any merit of my own. In journeys, when I was weary of the coach, a servant on horseback would buckle my box, and place it on a cushion before him; and there I had a full prospect of the country on three sides from my three windows. I had in this closet a field bed and a hammock hung from the ceiling, two chairs and a table, neatly screwed to the floor, to prevent being tossed about by the agitation of the horse or the coach. And having been long used to sea voyages, those motions, although sometimes very violent, did not much discompose me.

Whenever I had a mind to see the town, it was always in my traveling closet, which Glumdalclitch held in her lap in a kind of open sedan, after the fashion of the country, borne by four men, and attended by two others in the Queen's livery. The people who had often heard of me, were very curious to crowd about the sedan, and the girl was complaisant enough to make the bearers stop, and to take me in her hand that I might be more conveniently seen.

I was very desirous to see the chief temple, and particularly the tower belonging to it, which is reckoned the highest in the kingdom. Accordingly one day my nurse carried me thither, but I may truly say I came back disappointed; for the height is not above three thousand foot, reckoning from the ground to the highest pinnacle top; which allowing for the difference between the size of those people, and us in Europe, is no great matter for admiration, nor at all equal in proportion (if I rightly remember) to Salisbury steeple.[20] But, not to detract from a nation to which during my life I shall acknowledge myself extremely obliged, it must be allowed, that whatever this famous tower wants in height is amply made up in beauty and strength. For the walls are near an hundred foot thick, built of hewn stone, whereof each is about forty foot square, and adorned on all sides with statues of gods and emperors cut in marble larger than the life, placed in their several niches. I measured a little finger which had fallen down from one of these statues, and lay unperceived among some rubbish, and found it exactly four foot and an inch in length. Glumdalclitch wrapped it up in a handkerchief, and carried it home in her pocket to keep among other trinkets, of which the girl was very fond, as children at her age usually are.

The King's kitchen is indeed a noble building, vaulted at top, and about six hundred foot high. The great oven is not so wide by ten paces as the cupola at St. Paul's:[21] for I measured the latter on purpose after my return. But if I should describe the kitchen grate, the prodigious pots and kettles, the joints of meat turning on the spits, with many other particulars, perhaps I should be hardly believed; at least a severe critic would be apt to think I enlarged a little, as travelers are often suspected to do. To avoid which censure, I fear I have run too much into the other extreme; and that if this treatise should happen to be translated into the language of Brobdingnag (which is the general name of that kingdom) and transmitted thither, the King and his people would have reason to complain that I had done them an injury by a false and diminutive representation.

His Majesty seldom keeps above six hundred horses in his stables: they are generally from fifty-four to sixty foot high. But when he goes abroad on solemn days, he is attended for state by a militia guard of five hundred horse, which indeed I thought was the most splendid sight that could be ever beheld, till I saw part of his army in battalia, whereof I shall find another occasion to speak.

CHAPTER 5

Several adventures that happened to the Author. The execution of a criminal. The Author shows his skill in navigation.

I should have lived happy enough in that country, if my littleness had not exposed me to several ridiculous and troublesome accidents: some of which I shall venture to relate. Glumdalclitch often carried me into the gardens of the court in my smaller box, and would sometimes take me out of it and hold me in her hand, or set me down to walk. I remember, before the dwarf left the Queen, he followed us one day into those gardens, and my nurse having set me down, he and I being close together, near some dwarf apple trees, I must needs show my wit by a silly allusion between him and the trees, which happens to hold in their language as it doth in ours. Whereupon, the malicious rogue watching his opportunity, when I was walking under one of them, shook it directly over my head, by which a dozen apples, each of them near as large as a Bristol barrel, came tumbling about my ears; one of them hit me on the back as I chanced to stoop, and knocked me down flat on my face, but I received no other hurt, and the dwarf was pardoned at my desire, because I had given the provocation.

Another day Glumdalclitch left me on a smooth grassplot to divert myself while she walked at some distance with her governess. In the meantime there suddenly fell such a violent shower of hail, that I was immediately by the force of it struck to the ground: and when I was down, the hailstones gave me such cruel bangs all over the body, as if I had been pelted with tennis balls;[22] however, I made a shift to creep on all four, and shelter myself by lying flat on my face on the lee side of a border of lemon thyme, but so bruised from head to foot that I could not go abroad in ten days. Neither is this at all to be wondered at, because nature in that country observing the same proportion through

---

20. **Salisbury steeple:** about 400 feet high.   21. **cupola . . . St. Paul's:** 122 feet in diameter.

22. **tennis balls:** the hard balls used in the original game of court tennis.

all her operations, a hailstone is near eighteen hundred times as large as one in Europe, which I can assert upon experience, having been so curious to weigh and measure them.

But a more dangerous accident happened to me in the same garden, when my little nurse believing she had put me in a secure place, which I often entreated her to do, that I might enjoy my own thoughts, and having left my box at home to avoid the trouble of carrying it, went to another part of the garden with her governess and some ladies of her acquaintance. While she was absent, and out of hearing, a small white spaniel belonging to one of the chief gardeners, having got by accident into the garden, happened to range near the place where I lay. The dog following the scent, came directly up, and taking me in his mouth, ran straight to his master, wagging his tail, and set me gently on the ground. By good fortune he had been so well taught, that I was carried between his teeth without the least hurt, or even tearing my clothes. But the poor gardener, who knew me well, and had a great kindness for me, was in a terrible fright. He gently took me up in both his hands, and asked me how I did; but I was so amazed and out of breath, that I could not speak a word. In a few minutes I came to myself, and he carried me safe to my little nurse, who by this time had returned to the place where she left me, and was in cruel agonies when I did not appear, nor answer when she called: she severely reprimanded the gardener on account of his dog. But the thing was hushed up, and never known at court; for the girl was afraid of the Queen's anger, and truly as to myself, I thought it would not be for my reputation that such a story should go about.

This accident absolutely determined Glumdalclitch never to trust me abroad for the future out of her sight. I had been long afraid of this resolution, and therefore concealed from her some little unlucky adventures that happened in those times when I was left by myself. Once a kite hovering over the garden made a stoop [23] at me, and if I had not resolutely drawn my hanger, and run under a thick espalier, he would have certainly carried me away in his talons. Another time walking to the top of a fresh molehill, I fell to my neck in the hole through which that animal had cast up the earth, and coined some lie, not worth remembering, to excuse myself for spoiling my clothes. I likewise broke my right shin against the shell of a snail, which I happened to stumble over, as I was walking alone, and thinking on poor England.

I cannot tell whether I were more pleased or mortified, to observe in those solitary walks, that the smaller birds did not appear to be at all afraid of me, but would hop about within a yard distance, looking for worms, and other food, with as much indifference and security, as if no creature at all were near them. I remember, a thrush had the confidence to snatch out of my hand, with his bill, a piece of cake that Glumdalclitch had just given me for my breakfast. When I attempted to catch any of these birds, they would boldly turn against me, endeavoring to pick my fingers, which I durst not venture within their reach; and then they would hop back unconcerned, to hunt for worms or snails, as they did before. But one day I took a thick cudgel, and threw it with all my strength so luckily at a linnet, that I knocked him down, and seizing him by the neck with both my hands, ran with him in triumph to my nurse. However, the bird, who had only been stunned, recovering himself, gave me so many boxes with his wings on both sides of my head and body, although I held him at arm's length, and was out of the reach of his claws, that I was twenty times thinking to let him go. But I was soon relieved by one of our servants, who wrung off the bird's neck, and I had him next day for dinner, by the Queen's command. This linnet, as near as I can remember, seemed to be somewhat larger than an English swan.

The maids of honor often invited Glumdalclitch to their apartments, and desired she would bring me along with her, on purpose to have the pleasure of seeing and touching me. They would often strip me naked from top to toe, and lay me at full length in their bosoms; wherewith I was much disgusted; because, to say the truth, a very offensive smell came from their skins; which I do not mention or intend to the disadvantage of those excellent ladies, for whom I have all manner of respect; but I conceive that my sense was more acute in proportion to my littleness, and that those illustrious persons were no more disagreeable to their lovers, or to each other, than people of the same quality are with us in England. And, after all, I found their natural smell was much more supportable than when they used perfumes, under which

I immediately swooned away. I cannot forget that an intimate friend of mine in Lilliput took the freedom in a warm day, when I had used a good deal of exercise, to complain of a strong smell about me, although I am as little faulty that way as most of my sex: but I suppose his faculty of smelling was as nice with regard to me, as mine was to that of this people. Upon this point, I cannot forbear doing justice to the Queen my mistress, and Glumdalclitch my nurse, whose persons were as sweet as those of any lady in England.

That which gave me most uneasiness among these maids of honor (when my nurse carried me to visit them) was to see them use me without any manner of ceremony, like a creature who had no sort of consequence. For they would strip themselves to the skin, and put on their smocks in my presence, while I was placed on their toilet directly before their naked bodies, which, I am sure, to me was very far from being a tempting sight, or from giving me any other emotions than those of horror and disgust. Their skins appeared so coarse and uneven, so variously colored, when I saw them near, with a mole here and there as broad as a trencher, and hairs hanging from it thicker than pack threads, to say nothing further concerning the rest of their persons. Neither did they at all scruple, while I was by, to discharge what they had drunk, to the quantity of at least two hogsheads, in a vessel that held above three tuns. The handsomest among these maids of honor, a pleasant frolicsome girl of sixteen, would sometimes set me astride upon one of her nipples, with many other tricks, wherein the reader will excuse me for not being over particular. But I was so much displeased, that I entreated Glumdalclitch to contrive some excuse for not seeing that young lady any more.

One day a young gentleman, who was nephew to my nurse's governess, came and pressed them both to see an execution. It was of a man who had murdered one of that gentleman's intimate acquaintance. Glumdalclitch was prevailed on to be of the company, very much against her inclination, for she was naturally tender-hearted: and as for myself, although I abhorred such kind of spectacles, yet my curiosity tempted me to see something that I thought must be extraordinary. The malefactor was fixed in a chair upon a scaffold erected for the purpose, and his head cut off at one blow with a sword of about forty foot long.

The veins and arteries spouted up such a prodigious quantity of blood, and so high in the air, that the great *jet d'eau* [24] at Versailles was not equal for the time it lasted; and the head, when it fell on the scaffold floor, gave such a bounce, as made me start, although I were at least an English mile distant.

The Queen, who often used to hear me talk of my sea voyages, and took all occasions to divert me when I was melancholy, asked me whether I understood how to handle a sail, or an oar, and whether a little exercise of rowing might not be convenient for my health. I answered, that I understood both very well: for although my proper employment had been to be surgeon or doctor to the ship, yet often, upon a pinch, I was forced to work like a common mariner. But I could not see how this could be done in their country, where the smallest wherry was equal to a first-rate man-of-war among us, and such a boat as I could manage would never live in any of their rivers. Her Majesty said, if I would contrive a boat, her own joiner should make it, and she would provide a place for me to sail in. The fellow was an ingenious workman, and, by my instructions, in ten days finished a pleasure boat, with all its tackling, able conveniently to hold eight Europeans. When it was finished, the Queen was so delighted, that she ran with it in her lap to the King, who ordered it to be put in a cistern full of water, with me in it, by way of trial; where I could not manage my two sculls, or little oars, for want of room. But the Queen had before contrived another project. She ordered the joiner to make a wooden trough of three hundred foot long, fifty broad, and eight deep; which being well pitched to prevent leaking, was placed on the floor along the wall, in an outer room of the palace. It had a cock near the bottom to let out the water when it began to grow stale, and two servants could easily fill it in half an hour. Here I often used to row for my diversion, as well as that of the Queen and her ladies, who thought themselves agreeably entertained with my skill and agility. Sometimes I would put up my sail, and then my business was only to steer, while the ladies gave me a gale with their fans; and when they were weary, some of the pages would blow my sail forward with their breath, while I showed my art by steering starboard or

24. *jet d'eau:* The largest fountain at Versailles rose over 70 feet in the air.

larboard as I pleased. When I had done, Glumdalclitch always carried my boat into her closet, and hung it on a nail to dry.

In this exercise I once met an accident which had like to have cost me my life: for, one of the pages having put my boat into the trough, the governess, who attended Glumdalclitch, very officiously lifted me up to place me in the boat, but I happened to slip through her fingers, and should have infallibly fallen down forty feet upon the floor, if by the luckiest chance in the world, I had not been stopped by a corking pin [25] that stuck in the good gentlewoman's stomacher; the head of the pin passed between my shirt and the waistband of my breeches, and thus I was held by the middle in the air till Glumdalclitch ran to my relief.

Another time, one of the servants, whose office it was to fill my trough every third day with fresh water, was so careless to let a huge frog (not perceiving it) slip out of his pail. The frog lay concealed till I was put into my boat, but then seeing a resting place, climbed up, and made it lean so much on one side, that I was forced to balance it with all my weight on the other, to prevent overturning. When the frog was got in, it hopped at once half the length of the boat, and then over my head, backwards and forwards, daubing my face and clothes with its odious slime. The largeness of its features made it appear the most deformed animal that can be conceived. However, I desired Glumdalclitch to let me deal with it alone. I banged it a good while with one of my sculls, and at last forced it to leap out of the boat.

But the greatest danger I ever underwent in that kingdom, was from a monkey, who belonged to one of the clerks of the kitchen. Glumdalclitch had locked me up in her closet, while she went somewhere upon business, or a visit. The weather being very warm, the closet window was left open, as well as the windows and the door of my bigger box, in which I usually lived, because of its largeness and conveniency. As I sat quietly meditating at my table, I heard something bounce in at the closet window, and skip about from one side to the other; whereat, although I were much alarmed, yet I ventured to look out, but not stirring from my seat; and then I saw this frolicsome animal, frisking and leaping up and down, till at last he came to my box, which he seemed to view with great pleasure and curiosity, peeping in at the door

and every window. I retreated to the farther corner of my room, or box, but the monkey looking in at every side, put me into such a fright, that I wanted presence of mind to conceal myself under the bed, as I might easily have done. After some time spent in peeping, grinning, and chattering, he at last espied me, and reaching one of his paws in at the door, as a cat does when she plays with a mouse, although I often shifted place to avoid him, he at length seized the lappet of my coat (which being made of that country silk, was very thick and strong) and dragged me out. He took me up in his right forefoot, and held me as a nurse does a child she is going to suckle, just as I have seen the same sort of creature do with a kitten in Europe: and when I offered to struggle, he squeezed me so hard, that I thought it more prudent to submit. I have good reason to believe that he took me for a young one of his own species, by his often stroking my face very gently with his other paw. In these diversions he was interrupted by a noise at the closet door, as if somebody were opening it; whereupon he suddenly leaped up to the window, at which he had come in, and thence upon the leads and gutters, walking upon three legs, and holding me in the fourth, till he clambered up to a roof that was next to ours. I heard Glumdalclitch give a shriek at the moment he was carrying me out. The poor girl was almost distracted: that quarter of the palace was all in an uproar; the servants ran for ladders; the monkey was seen by hundreds in the court, sitting upon the ridge of a building, holding me like a baby in one of his forepaws, and feeding me with the other, by cramming into my mouth some victuals he had squeezed out of the bag on one side of his chaps, and patting me when I would not eat; whereat many of the rabble below could not forbear laughing; neither do I think they justly ought to be blamed, for without question the sight was ridiculous enough to everybody but myself. Some of the people threw up stones, hoping to drive the monkey down; but this was strictly forbidden, or else very probably my brains had been dashed out.

The ladders were now applied, and mounted by several men, which the monkey observing, and finding himself almost encompassed; not being able to make speed enough with his three legs, let me drop on a ridge tile, and made his escape. Here I sat for some time, five hundred yards from the ground, expecting every moment to be blown down by the wind, or to fall by my own giddiness, and

---

25. corking pin: or *calkin*, a pin of double the usual size.

come tumbling over and over, from the ridge to the eaves; but an honest lad, one of my nurse's footmen, climbed up, and putting me into his breeches pocket, brought me down safe.

I was almost choked with the filthy stuff the monkey had crammed down my throat: but my dear little nurse picked it out of my mouth with a small needle, and then I fell a vomiting, which gave me great relief. Yet I was so weak and bruised in the sides with the squeezes given me by this odious animal, that I was forced to keep my bed a fortnight. The King, Queen, and all the court, sent every day to inquire after my health, and her Majesty made me several visits during my sickness. The monkey was killed, and an order made that no such animal should be kept about the palace.

When I attended the King after my recovery, to return him thanks for his favors, he was pleased to rally me a good deal upon this adventure. He asked me what my thoughts and speculations were while I lay in the monkey's paw; how I liked the victuals he gave me; his manner of feeding; and whether the fresh air on the roof had sharpened my stomach. He desired to know what I would have done upon such an occasion in my own country. I told his Majesty, that in Europe we had no monkeys, except such as were brought for curiosities from other places, and so small, that I could deal with a dozen of them together, if they presumed to attack me. And as for that monstrous animal with whom I was so lately engaged (it was indeed as large as an elephant), if my fears had suffered me to think so far as to make use of my hanger (looking fiercely and clapping my hand upon the hilt as I spoke), when he poked his paw into my chamber, perhaps I should have given him such a wound, as would have made him glad to withdraw it with more haste than he put it in. This I delivered in a firm tone, like a person who was jealous lest his courage should be called in question. However, my speech produced nothing else besides a loud laughter, which all the respect due to his Majesty from those about him could not make them contain. This made me reflect how vain an attempt it is for a man to endeavor doing himself honor among those who are out of all degree of equality or comparison with him. And yet I have seen the moral of my own behavior very frequent in England since my return, where a little contemptible varlet, without the least title to birth, person, wit, or common sense, shall presume to look with importance, and put himself upon a foot with the greatest persons of the kingdom.

I was every day furnishing the court with some ridiculous story: and Glumdalclitch, although she loved me to excess, yet was arch enough to inform the Queen, whenever I committed any folly that she thought would be diverting to her Majesty. The girl, who had been out of order, was carried by her governess to take the air about an hour's distance, or thirty miles from town. They alighted out of the coach near a small footpath in a field, and Glumdalclitch setting down my traveling box, I went out of it to walk. There was a cow dung in the path, and I must needs try my activity by attempting to leap over it. I took a run, but unfortunately jumped short, and found myself just in the middle up to my knees. I waded through with some difficulty, and one of the footmen wiped me as clean as he could with his handkerchief; for I was filthily bemired, and my nurse confined me to my box till we returned home; where the Queen was soon informed of what had passed, and the footmen spread it about the court: so that all the mirth, for some days, was at my expense.

CHAPTER 6

Several contrivances of the Author to please the King and Queen. He shows his skill in music. The King inquires into the state of Europe, *which the Author relates to him. The King's observation thereon.*

I used to attend the King's levee once or twice a week, and had often seen him under the barber's hand, which indeed was at first very terrible to behold: for the razor was almost twice as long as an ordinary scythe. His Majesty, according to the custom of the country, was only shaved twice a week. I once prevailed on the barber to give me some of the suds or lather, out of which I picked forty or fifty of the strongest stumps of hair. I then took a piece of fine wood, and cut it like the back of a comb, making several holes in it at equal distance with as small a needle as I could get from Glumdalclitch. I fixed in the stumps so artificially, scraping and sloping them with my knife toward the points, that I made a very tolerable comb; which was a seasonable supply, my own being so much broken in the teeth, that it was almost useless: neither did I know any artist in that country so nice and exact, as would undertake to make me another.

And this puts me in mind of an amusement wherein I spent many of my leisure hours. I desired the Queen's woman to save for me the combings of her Majesty's hair, whereof in time I got a good quantity, and consulting with my friend the cabinetmaker, who had received general orders to do little jobs for me, I directed him to make two chair frames, no larger than those I had in my box, and then to bore little holes with a fine awl round those parts where I designed the backs and seats; through these holes I wove the strongest hairs I could pick out, just after the manner of cane chairs in England. When they were finished, I made a present of them to her Majesty, who kept them in her cabinet, and used to show them for curiosities, as indeed they were the wonder of every one who beheld them. The Queen would have had me sit upon one of these chairs, but I absolutely refused to obey her, protesting I would rather die a thousand deaths than place a dishonorable part of my body on those precious hairs that once adorned her Majesty's head. Of these hairs (as I had always a mechanical genius) I likewise made a neat little purse about five foot long, with her Majesty's name deciphered in gold letters, which I gave to Glumdalclitch, by the Queen's consent. To say the truth, it was more for show than use, being not of strength to bear the weight of the larger coins, and therefore she kept nothing in it but some little toys that girls are fond of.

The King, who delighted in music, had frequent consorts [26] at court, to which I was sometimes carried, and set in my box on a table to hear them: but the noise was so great, that I could hardly distinguish the tunes. I am confident that all the drums and trumpets of a royal army, beating and sounding together just at your ears, could not equal it. My practice was to have my box removed from the places where the performers sat, as far as I could, then to shut the doors and windows of it, and draw the window curtains; after which I found their music not disagreeable.

I had learned in my youth to play a little upon the spinet. Glumdalclitch kept one in her chamber, and a master attended twice a week to teach her: I call it a spinet, because it somewhat resembled that instrument, and was played upon in the same manner. A fancy came into my head that I would entertain the King and Queen with an English tune upon this instrument. But this appeared extremely difficult: for the spinet was near sixty

26. consorts: musical entertainments.

foot long, each key being almost a foot wide, so that, with my arms extended, I could not reach to above five keys, and to press them down required a good smart stroke with my fist, which would be too great a labor, and to no purpose. The method I contrived was this. I prepared two round sticks about the bigness of common cudgels; they were thicker at one end than the other, and I covered the thicker end with a piece of a mouse's skin, that by rapping on them I might neither damage the tops of the keys, nor interrupt the sound. Before the spinet a bench was placed, about four foot below the keys, and I was put upon the bench. I ran sideling upon it that way and this, as fast as I could, banging the proper keys with my two sticks, and made a shift to play a jig, to the great satisfaction of both their Majesties: but it was the most violent exercise I ever underwent, and yet I could not strike above sixteen keys, nor, consequently, play the bass and treble together, as other artists do; which was a great disadvantage to my performance.

The King, who, as I before observed, was a prince of excellent understanding, would frequently order that I should be brought in my box, and set upon the table in his closet. He would then command me to bring one of my chairs out of the box, and sit down within three yards distance upon the top of the cabinet, which brought me almost to a level with his face. In this manner I had several conversations with him. I one day took the freedom to tell his Majesty, that the contempt he discovered towards Europe, and the rest of the world, did not seem answerable to those excellent qualities of mind that he was master of. That reason did not extend itself with the bulk of the body: on the contrary, we observed in our country, that the tallest persons were usually least provided with it. That among other animals, bees and ants had the reputation of more industry, art and sagacity, than many of the larger kinds. And that, as inconsiderable as he took me to be, I hoped I might live to do his Majesty some signal service. The King heard me with attention, and began to conceive a much better opinion of me than he had ever before. He desired I would give him as exact an account of the government of England as I possibly could; because, as fond as princes commonly are of their own customs (for so he conjectured of other monarchs, by my former discourses), he should be glad to hear of anything that might deserve imitation.

Imagine with thyself, courteous reader, how often I then wished for the tongue of Demosthenes or Cicero, that might have enabled me to celebrate the praise of my own dear native country in a style equal to its merits and felicity.

I began my discourse by informing his Majesty, that our dominions consisted of two islands, which composed three mighty kingdoms under one sovereign, beside our plantations in America. I dwelt long upon the fertility of our soil, and the temperature [27] of our climate. I then spoke at large upon the constitution of an English parliament, partly made up of an illustrious body called the House of Peers, persons of the noblest blood, and of the most ancient and ample patrimonies. I described that extraordinary care always taken of their education in arts and arms, to qualify them for being counselors born to the king and kingdom; to have a share in the legislature; to be members of the highest court of judicature, from whence there could be no appeal; and to be champions always ready for the defense of their prince and country, by their valor, conduct, and fidelity. That these were the ornament and bulwark of the kingdom, worthy followers of their most renowned ancestors, whose honor had been the reward of their virtue, from which their posterity were never once known to degenerate. To these were joined several holy persons, as part of that assembly, under the title of bishops, whose peculiar business it is to take care of religion, and of those who instruct the people therein. These were searched and sought out through the whole nation, by the prince and wisest counselors, among such of the priesthood as were most deservedly distinguished by the sanctity of their lives, and the depth of their erudition; who were indeed the spiritual fathers of the clergy and the people.

That the other part of the parliament consisted of an assembly called the House of Commons, who were all principal gentlemen, freely picked and culled out by the people themselves, for their great abilities and love of their country, to represent the wisdom of the whole nation. And these two bodies make up the most august assembly in Europe, to whom, in conjunction with the prince, the whole legislature is committed.

I then descended to the courts of justice, over which the judges, those venerable sages and interpreters of the law, presided, for determining the disputed rights and properties of men, as well as for the punishment of vice, and protection of innocence. I mentioned the prudent management of our treasury; the valor and achievements of our forces by sea and land. I computed the number of our people, by reckoning how many millions there might be of each religious sect, or political party among us. I did not omit even our sports and pastimes, or any other particular which I thought might redound to the honor of my country. And I finished all with a brief historical account of affairs and events in England for about an hundred years past.

This conversation was not ended under five audiences, each of several hours, and the King heard the whole with great attention, frequently taking notes of what I spoke, as well as memorandums of what questions he intended to ask me.

When I had put an end to these long discourses, his Majesty in a sixth audience consulting his notes, proposed many doubts, queries, and objections, upon every article. He asked what methods were used to cultivate the minds and bodies of our young nobility, and in what kind of business they commonly spent the first and teachable part of their lives. What course was taken to supply that assembly when any noble family became extinct. What qualifications were necessary in those who are to be created new lords: whether the humor of the prince, a sum of money to a court lady, or a prime minister, or a design of strengthening a party opposite to the public interest, ever happened to be motives in those advancements. What share of knowledge these lords had in the laws of their country, and how they came by it, so as to enable them to decide the properties of their fellow subjects in the last resort. Whether they were always so free from avarice, partialities, or want, that a bribe, or some other sinister view, could have no place among them. Whether those holy lords I spoke of were constantly promoted to that rank upon account of their knowledge in religious matters, and the sanctity of their lives, had never been compliers with the times, while they were common priests, or slavish prostitute chaplains to some nobleman, whose opinions they continued servilely to follow after they were admitted into that assembly.[28]

He then desired to know what arts were practiced in electing those whom I called commoners:

---

27. **temperature:** temperate quality. N.B. This simple comment on the climate gives the reader no warning of the change of tone in the ironic passage immediately following.

28. **that assembly:** aimed at the Low Church bishops appointed by the Whigs under George I.

whether a stranger with a strong purse might not influence the vulgar voters to choose him before their own landlord, or the most considerable gentleman in the neighborhood. How it came to pass, that people were so violently bent upon getting into this assembly, which I allowed to be a great trouble and expense, often to the ruin of their families, without any salary or pension: because this appeared such an exalted strain of virtue and public spirit, that his Majesty seemed to doubt it might possibly not be always sincere: and he desired to know whether such zealous gentlemen could have any views of refunding themselves for the charges and trouble they were at, by sacrificing the public good to the designs of a weak and vicious prince in conjunction with a corrupted ministry. He multiplied his questions, and sifted me thoroughly upon every part of this head, proposing numberless inquiries and objections, which I think it not prudent or convenient to repeat.

Upon what I said in relation to our courts of justice, his Majesty desired to be satisfied in several points: and this I was the better able to do, having been formerly almost ruined by a long suit in chancery,[29] which was decreed for me with costs. He asked, what time was usually spent in determining between right and wrong, and what degree of expense. Whether advocates and orators had liberty to plead in causes manifestly known to be unjust, vexatious, or oppressive. Whether party in religion or politics were observed to be of any weight in the scale of justice. Whether those pleading orators were persons educated in the general knowledge of equity, or only in provincial, national, and other local customs. Whether they or their judges had any part in penning those laws which they assumed the liberty of interpreting and glossing upon at their pleasure. Whether they had ever at different times pleaded for and against the same cause, and cited precedents to prove contrary opinions. Whether they were a rich or a poor corporation. Whether they received any pecuniary reward for pleading or delivering their opinions. And particularly, whether they were ever admitted as members in the lower senate.

He fell next upon the management of our treasury; and said, he thought my memory had failed me, because I computed our taxes at about five or six millions a year, and when I came to mention the issues, he found they sometimes amounted to more than double; for the notes he had taken were very particular in this point, because he hoped, as he told me, that the knowledge of our conduct might be useful to him, and he could not be deceived in his calculations. But, if what I told him were true, he was still at a loss how a kingdom could run out of its estate[30] like a private person. He asked me, who were our creditors; and where we found money to pay them. He wondered to hear me talk of such chargeable and extensive wars; that certainly we must be a quarrelsome people, or live among very bad neighbors, and that our generals must needs be richer than our kings.[31] He asked what business we had out of our own islands, unless upon the score of trade or treaty, or to defend the coasts with our fleet. Above all, he was amazed to hear me talk of a mercenary standing army[32] in the midst of peace, and among a free people. He said, if we were governed by our own consent in the persons of our representatives, he could not imagine of whom we were afraid, or against whom we were to fight; and would hear my opinion, whether a private man's house might not better be defended by himself, his children, and family, than by half a dozen rascals picked up at a venture in the streets, for small wages, who might get an hundred times more by cutting their throats.

He laughed at my odd kind of arithmetic (as he was pleased to call it) in reckoning the numbers of our people by a computation drawn from the several sects among us in religion and politics. He said, he knew no reason, why those who entertain opinions prejudicial to the public, should be obliged to change, or should not be obliged to conceal them. And as it was tyranny in any government to require the first, so it was weakness not to enforce the second: for a man may be allowed to keep poisons in his closet, but not to vend them about as cordials.

He observed, that among the diversions of our nobility and gentry, I had mentioned gaming. He desired to know at what age this entertainment was usually taken up, and when it was laid down; how much of their time it employed; whether it ever went so high as to affect their fortunes; whether mean vicious people, by their dexterity in that art, might not arrive at great riches, and sometimes keep our very nobles in dependence, as well

---

29. suit in chancery: The Court of Chancery was notorious for delays and expense.

30. its estate: Swift held that a nation could not afford to pile up an enormous national debt to pay for foreign wars.   **31. generals . . . kings:** a reference to the fortune Marlborough had made out of the war.   **32. standing army:** constantly opposed by the Tories.

as habituate them to vile companions, wholly take them from the improvement of their minds, and force them, by the losses they received, to learn and practice that infamous dexterity upon others.

He was perfectly astonished with the historical account I gave him of our affairs during the last century, protesting it was only an heap of conspiracies, rebellions, murders, massacres, revolutions, banishments; the very worst effects that avarice, faction, hypocrisy, perfidiousness, cruelty, rage, madness, hatred, envy, lust, malice, and ambition, could produce.

His Majesty, in another audience, was at the pains to recapitulate the sum of all I had spoken; compared the questions he made with the answers I had given; then taking me into his hands, and stroking me gently, delivered himself in these words, which I shall never forget, nor the manner he spoke them in. " My little friend Grildrig, you have made a most admirable panegyric upon your country. You have clearly proved that ignorance, idleness, and vice, are the proper ingredients for qualifying a legislator: that laws are best explained, interpreted, and applied by those whose interest and abilities lie in perverting, confounding, and eluding them. I observe among you some lines of an institution, which in its original might have been tolerable, but these half erased, and the rest wholly blurred and blotted by corruptions. It doth not appear from all you have said, how any one perfection is required towards the procurement of any one station among you; much less that men are ennobled on account of their virtue, that priests are advanced for their piety or learning, soldiers for their conduct or valor, judges for their integrity, senators for the love of their country, or counselors for their wisdom. As for yourself (continued the King), who have spent the greatest part of your life in traveling, I am well disposed to hope you may hitherto have escaped many vices of your country. But by what I have gathered from your own relation, and the answers I have with much pains wringed and extorted from you, I cannot but conclude the bulk of your natives to be the most pernicious race of little odious vermin that nature ever suffered to crawl upon the surface of the earth."

CHAPTER 7

The Author's love of his country. He makes a proposal of much advantage to the King, which is rejected. The King's great ignorance in politics. The learning of that country very imperfect and confined. Their laws, and military affairs, and parties in the State.

Nothing but an extreme love of truth could have hindered me from concealing this part of my story. It was in vain to discover my resentments, which were always turned into ridicule; and I was forced to rest with patience while my noble and most beloved country was so injuriously treated. I am heartily sorry as any of my readers can possibly be, that such an occasion was given: but this prince happened to be so curious and inquisitive upon every particular, that it could not consist either with gratitude or good manners to refuse giving him what satisfaction I was able. Yet thus much I may be allowed to say in my own vindication, that I artfully eluded many of his questions, and gave to every point a more favorable turn by many degrees than the strictness of truth would allow. For I have always borne that laudable partiality to my own country, which Dionysius Halicarnassensis [33] with so much justice recommends to an historian: I would hide the frailties and deformities of my political mother, and place her virtues and beauties in the most advantageous light. This was my sincere endeavor in those many discourses I had with that mighty monarch, although it unfortunately failed of success.

But great allowances should be given to a King who lives wholly secluded from the rest of the world, and must therefore be altogether unacquainted with the manners and customs that most prevail in other nations: the want of which knowledge will ever produce many prejudices, and a certain narrowness of thinking, from which we and the politer countries of Europe are wholly exempted. And it would be hard indeed, if so remote a prince's notions of virtue and vice were to be offered as a standard for all mankind.

To confirm what I have now said, and further, to show the miserable effects of a confined education, I shall here insert a passage which will hardly obtain belief. In hopes to ingratiate myself farther into his Majesty's favor, I told him of an invention discovered between three and four hundred years ago, to make a certain powder, into an heap of which the smallest spark of fire falling, would kindle the whole in a moment, although it were as big as a mountain, and make it all fly up in the air together, with a noise and agitation greater

33. **Dionysius Halicarnassensis:** (54?–7? B.C.) or Halicarnassus, a Greek writer living in Rome under Augustus who upheld the virtues of the Romans and vindicated the power of their empire.

than thunder. That a proper quantity of this powder rammed into an hollow tube of brass or iron, according to its bigness, would drive a ball of iron or lead with such violence and speed, as nothing was able to sustain its force. That the largest balls thus discharged, would not only destroy whole ranks of an army at once, but batter the strongest walls to the ground, sink down ships, with a thousand men in each, to the bottom of the sea; and, when linked together by a chain, would cut through masts and rigging, divide hundreds of bodies in the middle, and lay all waste before them. That we often put this powder into large hollow balls of iron, and discharged them by an engine into some city we were besieging, which would rip up the pavement, tear the houses to pieces, burst and throw splinters on every side, dashing out the brains of all who came near. That I knew the ingredients very well, which were cheap, and common; I understood the manner of compounding them, and could direct his workmen how to make those tubes, of a size proportionable to all other things in his Majesty's kingdom, and the largest need not be above two hundred foot long; twenty or thirty of which tubes, charged with the proper quantity of powder and balls, would batter down the walls of the strongest town in his dominions in a few hours, or destroy the whole metropolis, if ever it should pretend to dispute his absolute commands. This I humbly offered to his Majesty, as a small tribute of acknowledgment in return of so many marks that I had received of his royal favor and protection.

The King was struck with horror at the description I had given of those terrible engines, and the proposal I had made. He was amazed how so impotent and groveling an insect as I (these were his expressions) could entertain such inhuman ideas, and in so familiar a manner as to appear wholly unmoved at all the scenes of blood and desolation, which I had painted as the common effects of those destructive machines, whereof he said, some evil genius, enemy to mankind, must have been the first contriver. As for himself, he protested, that although few things delighted him so much as new discoveries in art or in nature, yet he would rather lose half his kingdom than be privy to such a secret, which he commanded me, as I valued my life, never to mention any more.

A strange effect of *narrow principles* and *short views!* that a prince possessed of every quality which procures veneration, love, and esteem; of strong parts, great wisdom, and profound learning, endued with admirable talents for government, and almost adored by his subjects, should from a *nice unnecessary scruple,* whereof in Europe we can have no conception, let slip an opportunity put into his hands, that would have made him absolute master of the lives, the liberties, and the fortunes of his people. Neither do I say this with the least intention to detract from the many virtues of that excellent King, whose character I am sensible will on this account be very much lessened in the opinion of an English reader: but I take this defect among them to have risen from their ignorance, by not having hitherto reduced politics into a science, as the more acute wits of Europe have done. For, I remember very well, in a discourse one day with the King, when I happened to say there were several thousand books among us written upon the art of government, it gave him (directly contrary to my intention) a very mean opinion of our understandings. He professed both to abominate and despise all *mystery, refinement,* and *intrigue,* either in a prince or a minister. He could not tell what I meant by *secrets of state,* where an enemy or some rival nation were not in the case. He confined the knowledge of governing within very *narrow bounds;* to common sense and reason, to justice and lenity, to the speedy determination of civil and criminal causes; with some other obvious topics, which are not worth considering. And he gave it for his opinion, that whoever could make two ears of corn, or two blades of grass to grow upon a spot of ground where only one grew before, would deserve better of mankind, and do more essential service to his country, than the whole race of politicians put together.

The learning of this people is very defective, consisting only in morality, history, poetry, and mathematics, wherein they must be allowed to excel. But the last of these is wholly applied to what may be useful in life, to the improvement of agriculture, and all mechanical arts; so that among us it would be little esteemed. And as to ideas, entities, abstractions, and transcendentals,[34] I could never drive the least conception into their heads.

No law of that country must exceed in words the number of letters in their alphabet, which consists only of two and twenty. But, indeed, few of them extend even to that length. They are expressed in the most plain and simple terms, wherein those people are not mercurial enough to discover above

---

34. ideas . . . transcendentals: terms of the medieval Schoolmen.

one interpretation: and to write a comment upon any law is a capital crime. As to the decision of civil causes, or proceedings against criminals, their precedents are so few, that they have little reason to boast of any extraordinary skill in either.

They have had the art of printing, as well as the Chinese, time out of mind: but their libraries are not very large; for that of the King's, which is reckoned the largest, doth not amount to above a thousand volumes, placed in a gallery of twelve hundred foot long, from whence I had liberty to borrow what books I pleased. The Queen's joiner had contrived in one of Glumdalclitch's rooms a kind of wooden machine five and twenty foot high, formed like a standing ladder; the steps were each fifty foot long. It was indeed a movable pair of stairs, the lowest end placed at ten foot distance from the wall of the chamber. The book I had a mind to read was put up leaning against the wall. I first mounted to the upper step of the ladder, and turning my face towards the book, began at the top of the page, and so walking to the right and left about eight or ten paces, according to the length of the lines, till I had gotten a little below the level of my eyes, and then descending gradually till I came to the bottom: after which I mounted again, and began the other page in the same manner, and so turned over the leaf, which I could easily do with both my hands, for it was as thick and stiff as a pasteboard, and in the largest folios not above eighteen or twenty foot long.

Their style is clear, masculine, and smooth, but not florid; for they avoid nothing more than multiplying unnecessary words, or using various expressions. I have perused many of their books, especially those in history and morality. Among the latter, I was much diverted with a little old treatise, which always lay in Glumdalclitch's bedchamber, and belonged to her governess, a grave elderly gentlewoman, who dealt in writings of morality and devotion. The book treats of the weakness of human kind, and is in little esteem, except among women and the vulgar. However, I was curious to see what an author of that country could say upon such a subject. This writer went through all the usual topics of European moralists, showing how diminutive, contemptible, and helpless an animal was man in his own nature; how unable to defend himself from the inclemencies of the air, or the fury of wild beasts: how much he was excelled by one creature in strength, by another in speed, by a third in foresight, by a fourth in industry. He added, that nature was degenerated in these latter declining ages of the world, and could now produce only small abortive births in comparison of those in ancient times. He said, it was very reasonable to think, not only that the species of man were originally much larger, but also, that there must have been giants in former ages, which, as it is asserted by history and tradition, so it hath been confirmed by huge bones and skulls casually dug up in several parts of the kingdom, far exceeding the common dwindled race of man in our days. He argued, that the very laws of nature absolutely required we should have been made in the beginning, of a size more large and robust, not so liable to destruction from every little accident of a tile falling from a house, or a stone cast from the hand of a boy, or of being drowned in a little brook. From this way of reasoning the author drew several moral applications useful in the conduct of life, but needless here to repeat. For my own part, I could not avoid reflecting how universally this talent was spread, of drawing lectures in morality, or indeed rather matter of discontent and repining, from the quarrels we raise with nature. And I believe, upon a strict inquiry, those quarrels might be shown as ill grounded among us, as they are among that people.

As to their military affairs, they boast that the King's army consists of an hundred and seventy-six thousand foot, and thirty-two thousand horse: if that may be called an army which is made up of tradesmen in the several cities, and farmers in the country, whose commanders are only the nobility and gentry, without pay or reward. They are indeed perfect enough in their exercises, and under very good discipline, wherein I saw no great merit; for how should it be otherwise, where every farmer is under the command of his own landlord, and every citizen under that of the principal men in his own city, chosen after the manner of Venice by ballot? [35]

I have often seen the militia of Lorbrulgrud drawn out to exercise in a great field near the city of twenty miles square. They were in all not above twenty-five thousand foot, and six thousand horse; but it was impossible for me to compute their number, considering the space of ground they took up. A cavalier mounted on a large steed, might be about ninety foot high. I have seen this whole

35. **by ballot:** the method of secret voting, introduced in Venice, of dropping a *ballotta*, or little ball, into one of the divisions of a box.

body of horse, upon the word of command, draw their swords at once, and brandish them in the air. Imagination can figure nothing so grand, so surprising, and so astonishing! It looked as if ten thousand flashes of lightning were darting at the same time from every quarter of the sky.

I was curious to know how this prince, to whose dominions there is no access from any other country, came to think of armies, or to teach his people the practice of military discipline. But I was soon informed, both by conversation, and reading their histories. For, in the course of many ages they have been troubled with the same disease to which the whole race of mankind is subject; the nobility often contending for power, the people for liberty, and the King for absolute dominion. All which, however happily tempered by the laws of that kingdom, have been sometimes violated by each of the three parties, and have more than once occasioned civil wars, the last whereof was happily put an end to by this prince's grandfather in a general composition; and the militia, then settled with common consent, hath been ever since kept in the strictest duty.

CHAPTER 8

The King and Queen make a progress to the frontiers. The Author attends them. The manner in which he leaves the country very particularly related. He returns to England.

I had always a strong impulse that I should some time recover my liberty, although it was impossible to conjecture by what means, or to form any project with the least hope of succeeding. The ship in which I sailed was the first ever known to be driven within sight of that coast, and the King had given strict orders, that if at any time another appeared, it should be taken ashore, and with all its crew and passengers brought in a tumbril [36] to Lorbrulgrud. He was strongly bent to get me a woman of my own size, by whom I might propagate the breed: but I think I should rather have died than undergone the disgrace of leaving a posterity to be kept in cages like tame canary birds, and perhaps, in time, sold about the kingdom to persons of quality for curiosities. I was, indeed, treated with much kindness: I was the favorite of a great King and Queen, and the delight of the whole court, but it was upon such a foot as ill became the dignity of human kind. I could never forget those domestic pledges I had left behind me. I wanted to be among people with whom I could converse upon even terms, and walk about the streets and fields without fear of being trod to death like a frog or young puppy. But my deliverance came sooner than I expected, and in a manner not very common: the whole story and circumstances of which I shall faithfully relate.

I had now been two years in this country; and about the beginning of the third, Glumdalclitch and I attended the King and Queen in a progress to the south coast of the kingdom. I was carried, as usual, in my traveling box, which, as I have already described, was a very convenient closet of twelve foot wide. I had ordered a hammock to be fixed by silken ropes from the four corners at the top, to break the jolts, when a servant carried me before him on horseback, as I sometimes desired, and would often sleep in my hammock while we were upon the road. On the roof of my closet, set not directly over the middle of the hammock, I ordered the joiner to cut out a hole of a foot square, to give me air in hot weather, as I slept; which hole I shut at pleasure with a board that drew backwards and forwards through a groove.

When we came to our journey's end, the King thought proper to pass a few days at a palace he hath near Flanflasnic, a city within eighteen English miles of the seaside. Glumdalclitch and I were much fatigued; I had gotten a small cold, but the poor girl was so ill as to be confined to her chamber. I longed to see the ocean, which must be the only scene of my escape, if ever it should happen. I pretended to be worse than I really was, and desired leave to take the fresh air of the sea, with a page whom I was very fond of, and who had sometimes been trusted with me. I shall never forget with what unwillingness Glumdalclitch consented, nor the strict charge she gave the page to be careful of me, bursting at the same time into a flood of tears, as if she had some foreboding of what was to happen. The boy took me out in my box about half an hour's walk from the palace, towards the rocks on the seashore. I ordered him to set me down, and lifting up one of my sashes, cast many a wistful melancholy look towards the sea. I found myself not very well, and told the page that I had a mind to take a nap in my hammock, which I hoped would do me good. I got in, and the boy shut the window close down to keep out the cold. I soon fell asleep, and all I can con-

36. tumbril: a tipcart, or dungcart.

jecture is, that while I slept, the page, thinking no danger could happen, went among the rocks to look for birds' eggs, having before observed him from my window searching about, and picking up one or two in the clefts. Be that as it will, I found myself suddenly awaked with a violent pull upon the ring which was fastened at the top of my box for the conveniency of carriage. I felt the box raised very high in the air, and then borne forward with prodigious speed. The first jolt had like to have shaken me out of my hammock, but afterwards the motion was easy enough. I called out several times, as loud as I could raise my voice, but all to no purpose. I looked towards my windows, and could see nothing but the clouds and sky. I heard a noise just over my head like the clapping of wings, and then began to perceive the woeful condition I was in; that some eagle had got the ring of my box in his beak, with an intent to let it fall on a rock like a tortoise in a shell, and then pick out my body, and devour it. For the sagacity and smell of this bird enable him to discover his quarry at a great distance, though better concealed than I could be within a two-inch board.

In a little time I observed the noise and flutter of wings to increase very fast, and my box was tossed up and down, like a signpost in a windy day. I heard several bangs or buffets, as I thought, given to the eagle (for such I am certain it must have been that held the ring of my box in his beak), and then all on a sudden felt myself falling perpendicularly down for above a minute, but with such incredible swiftness that I almost lost my breath. My fall was stopped by a terrible squash, that sounded louder to my ears than the cataract of Niagara; after which I was quite in the dark for another minute, and then my box began to rise so high that I could see light from the tops of my windows. I now perceived that I was fallen into the sea. My box, by the weight of my body, the goods that were in, and the broad plates of iron fixed for strength at the four corners of the top and bottom, floated about five foot deep in water. I did then, and do now suppose that the eagle which flew away with my box was pursued by two or three others, and forced to let me drop while he was defending himself against the rest, who hoped to share in the prey. The plates of iron fastened at the bottom of the box (for those were the strongest) preserved the balance while it fell, and hindered it from being broken on the surface of the water. Every joint of it was well grooved, and the door did not move on hinges, but up and down like a sash, which kept my closet so tight that very little water came in. I got with much difficulty out of my hammock, having first ventured to draw back the slip board on the roof already mentioned, contrived on purpose to let in air, for want of which I found myself almost stifled.

How often did I then wish myself with my dear Glumdalclitch, from whom one single hour had so far divided me! And I may say with truth, that in the midst of my own misfortune I could not forbear lamenting my poor nurse, the grief she would suffer for my loss, the displeasure of the Queen, and the ruin of her fortune. Perhaps many travelers have not been under greater difficulties and distress than I was at this juncture, expecting every moment to see my box dashed in pieces, or at least overset by the first violent blast, or a rising wave. A breach in one single pane of glass would have been immediate death: nor could anything have preserved the windows, but the strong lattice wires placed on the outside against accidents in traveling. I saw the water ooze in at several crannies, although the leaks were not considerable, and I endeavored to stop them as well as I could. I was not able to lift up the roof of my closet, which otherwise I certainly should have done, and sat on the top of it, where I might at least preserve myself from being shut up, as I may call it, in the hold. Or, if I escaped these dangers for a day or two, what could I expect but a miserable death of cold and hunger! I was four hours under these circumstances, expecting and indeed wishing every moment to be my last.

I have already told the reader, that there were two strong staples fixed upon the side of my box which had no window, and into which the servant who used to carry me on horseback would put a leathern belt, and buckle it about his waist. Being in this disconsolate state, I heard or at least thought I heard some kind of grating noise on that side of my box where the staples were fixed, and soon after I began to fancy that the box was pulled or towed along in the sea; for I now and then felt a sort of tugging, which made the waves rise near the tops of my windows, leaving me almost in the dark. This gave me some faint hopes of relief, although I was not able to imagine how it could be brought about. I ventured to unscrew one of my chairs, which were always fastened to the floor; and having made a hard shift to screw it down again directly under the slipping board that I had lately opened, I mounted on the chair, and putting my mouth as near as I could to the hole, I called for help in a loud voice, and in all the languages I understood. I then fastened my handkerchief to a stick I usually carried, and thrusting it up the hole, waved it several times in the air, that if any boat or ship were near, the seamen might conjecture some unhappy mortal to be shut up in the box.

I found no effect from all I could do, but plainly perceived my closet to be moved along; and in the space of an hour, or better, that side of the box where the staples were, and had no window, struck against something that was hard. I apprehended it to be a rock, and found myself tossed more than ever. I plainly heard a noise upon the cover of my closet, like that of a cable, and the grating of it as it passed through the ring. I then found myself hoisted up by degrees at least three foot higher than I was before. Whereupon I again thrust up my stick and handkerchief, calling for help till I was almost hoarse. In return to which, I heard a great shout repeated three times, giving me such transports of joy, as are not to be conceived but by those who feel them. I now heard a trampling over my head, and somebody calling through the hole with a loud voice in the English tongue, If there be anybody below, let them speak. I answered, I was an Englishman, drawn by ill fortune into the greatest calamity that ever any creature underwent, and begged, by all that was moving, to be delivered out of the dungeon I was in. The voice replied, I was safe, for my box was fastened to their ship; and the carpenter should immediately come and saw an hole in the cover, large enough to pull me out. I answered, that was needless, and would take up too much time, for there was no more to be done, but let one of the crew put his finger into the ring, and take the box out of the sea into the ship, and so into the captain's cabin. Some of them upon hearing me talk so wildly thought I was mad; others laughed; for indeed it never came into my head that I was now got among people of my own stature and strength. The carpenter came, and in a few minutes sawed a passage about four foot square, then let down a small ladder, upon which I mounted, and from thence was taken into the ship in a very weak condition.

The sailors were all in amazement, and asked me a thousand questions, which I had no inclination to answer. I was equally confounded at the sight of so many pygmies, for such I took them to be, after having so long accustomed my eyes to the monstrous objects I had left. But the Captain, Mr. Thomas Wilcocks, an honest worthy Shropshire man, observing I was ready to faint, took me into his cabin, gave me a cordial to comfort me, and made me turn in upon his own bed, advising me to take a little rest of which I had great need. Before I went to sleep, I gave him to understand that I had some valuable furniture in my box, too good to be lost; a fine hammock, an handsome field bed, two chairs, a table, and a cabinet: that my closet was hung on all sides, or rather quilted, with silk and cotton: that if he would let one of the crew bring my closet into his cabin, I would open it there before him, and show him my goods. The Captain hearing me utter these absurdities, concluded I was raving: however (I suppose to pacify me), he promised to give order as I desired, and going upon deck sent some of his men down into my closet, from whence (as I afterwards found) they drew up all my goods, and stripped off the quilting; but the chairs, cabinet, and bedstead, being screwed to the floor, were much damaged by the ignorance of the seamen, who tore them up by force. Then they knocked off some of the boards for the use of the ship, and when they had got all they had a mind for, let the hulk drop into the sea, which by reason of many breaches made in the bottom and sides, sunk to rights. And indeed I was glad not to have been a spectator of the havoc they made; because I am confident it would have sensibly touched me, by bringing former passages into my mind, which I had rather forget.

I slept some hours, but perpetually disturbed with dreams of the place I had left, and the dangers I had escaped. However, upon waking I found myself much recovered. It was now about eight o'clock at night, and the Captain ordered supper immediately, thinking I had already fasted too long. He entertained me with great kindness, observing me not to look wildly, or talk inconsistently: and when we were left alone, desired I would give him a relation of my travels, and by what accident I came to be set adrift in that monstrous wooden chest. He said, that about twelve o'clock at noon, as he was looking through his glass, he spied it at a distance, and thought it was a sail, which he had a mind to make, being not much out of his course, in hopes of buying some biscuit, his own beginning to fall short. That upon coming nearer, and finding his error, he sent out his longboat to discover what I was; that his men came back in a fright, swearing they had seen a swimming house. That he laughed at their folly, and went himself in the boat, ordering his men to take a strong cable along with them. That the weather being calm, he rowed round me several times, observed my windows, and the wire lattices that defended them. That he discovered two staples upon one side, which was all of boards, without any passage for light. He then commanded his men to row up to that side, and fastening a cable to one of the staples, ordered them to tow my chest (as he called it) towards the ship. When it was there, he gave directions to fasten another cable to the ring fixed in the cover, and to raise up my chest with pulleys, which all the sailors were not able to do above two or three foot. He said, they saw my stick and handkerchief thrust out of the hole, and concluded that some unhappy man must be shut up in the cavity. I asked whether he or the crew had seen any prodigious birds in the air about the time he first discovered me. To which he answered, that discoursing this matter with the sailors while I was asleep, one of them said he had observed three eagles flying towards the north, but remarked nothing of their being larger than the usual size, which I suppose must be imputed to the great height they were at; and he could not guess the reason of my question. I then asked the Captain how far he reckoned we might be from land; he said, by the best computation he could make, we were at least an hundred leagues. I assured him, that he must be mistaken by almost half, for I had not left the country from whence I came above two hours before I dropped into the sea. Whereupon he began again to think that my brain was disturbed, of which he gave me a hint, and advised me to go to bed in a cabin he had provided. I assured him I was well refreshed with his good entertainment and company, and as much in my senses as ever I was in my life. He then grew serious, and desired to ask me freely whether I were not troubled in mind by the consciousness of some enormous crime, for which I was punished at the command of some prince, by exposing me in that chest, as great criminals in other countries have been forced to sea in a leaky vessel without provisions: for, although he should be sorry to have taken so ill a man into his ship, yet he would engage his word to set me safe on shore in the first port where we arrived. He added, that his suspicions were much increased by some very absurd speeches I had delivered at first to the sailors, and

afterwards to himself, in relation to my closet or chest, as well as by my odd looks and behavior while I was at supper.

I begged his patience to hear me tell my story, which I faithfully did from the last time I left England to the moment he first discovered me. And, as truth always forceth its way into rational minds, so this honest worthy gentleman, who had some tincture of learning, and very good sense, was immediately convinced of my candor and veracity. But further to confirm all I had said, I entreated him to give order that my cabinet should be brought, of which I kept the key in my pocket (for he had already informed me how the seamen disposed of my closet). I opened it in his presence, and showed him the small collection of rarities I made in the country from whence I had been so strangely delivered. There was the comb I had contrived out of the stumps of the King's beard, and another of the same materials, but fixed into a paring of her Majesty's thumbnail, which served for the back. There was a collection of needles and pins from a foot to half a yard long; four wasp stings, like joiners' tacks; some combings of the Queen's hair; a gold ring which one day she made me a present of in a most obliging manner, taking it from her little finger, and throwing it over my head like a collar. I desired the Captain would please to accept this ring in return of his civilities; which he absolutely refused. I showed him a corn that I had cut off with my own hand, from a maid of honor's toe; it was about the bigness of a Kentish pippin, and grown so hard that when I returned to England, I got it hollowed into a cup, and set in silver. Lastly, I desired him to see the breeches I had then on, which were made of a mouse's skin.

I could force nothing on him but a footman's tooth, which I observed him to examine with great curiosity, and found he had a fancy for it. He received it with abundance of thanks, more than such a trifle could deserve. It was drawn by an unskillful surgeon, in a mistake, from one of Glumdalclitch's men, who was afflicted with the toothache, but it was as sound as any in his head. I got it cleaned, and put it into my cabinet. It was about a foot long, and four inches in diameter.

The Captain was very well satisfied with this plain relation I had given him, and said, he hoped when we returned to England, I would oblige the world by putting it in paper, and making it public. My answer was, that I thought we were already overstocked with books of travels: that nothing could now pass which was not extraordinary; wherein I doubted some authors less consulted truth than their own vanity, or interest, or the diversion of ignorant readers. That my story could contain little besides common events, without those ornamental descriptions of strange plants, trees, birds, and other animals, or the barbarous customs and idolatry of savage people, with which most writers abound. However, I thanked him for his good opinion, and promised to take the matter into my thoughts.

He said he wondered at one thing very much, which was, to hear me speak so loud, asking me whether the King or Queen of that country were thick of hearing. I told him, it was what I had been used to for above two years past; and that I admired as much at the voices of him and his men, who seemed to me only to whisper, and yet I could hear them well enough. But when I spoke in that country, it was like a man talking in the street to another looking out from the top of a steeple, unless when I was placed on a table, or held in any person's hand. I told him, I had likewise observed another thing, that when I first got into the ship, and the sailors stood all about me, I thought they were the most little contemptible creatures I had ever beheld. For, indeed, while I was in that prince's country, I could never endure to look in a glass after my eyes had been accustomed to such prodigious objects, because the comparison gave me so despicable a conceit of myself. The Captain said, that while we were at supper, he observed me to look at everything with a sort of wonder, and that I often seemed hardly able to contain my laughter, which he knew not well how to take, but imputed it to some disorder in my brain. I answered, it was very true; and I wondered how I could forbear, when I saw his dishes of the size of a silver threepence, a leg of pork hardly a mouthful, a cup not so big as a nutshell; and so I went on, describing the rest of his household stuff and provisions after the same manner. For, although the Queen had ordered a little equipage of all things necessary for me while I was in her service, yet my ideas were wholly taken up with what I saw on every side of me, and I winked at my own littleness as people do at their own faults. The Captain understood my raillery very well, and merrily replied with the old English proverb, that he doubted my eyes were bigger than my belly, for he did not observe my stomach so good, although I had fasted all day; and continuing in his mirth, protested he would have gladly given an hundred pounds to have seen my closet in the eagle's bill, and afterwards in its fall from so great an height into the sea; which would certainly have been a most astonishing object, worthy to have the description of it transmitted to future ages: and the comparison of Phaeton was so obvious, that he could not forbear applying it, although I did not much admire the conceit.[37]

The Captain having been at Tonquin,[38] was in his return to England driven northeastward to the latitude of forty-four degrees, and of longitude one hundred and forty-three. But meeting a trade wind two days after I came on board him, we sailed southward a long time, and coasting New Holland[39] kept our course west-southwest, and then south-southwest till we doubled the Cape of Good Hope. Our voyage was very prosperous, but I shall not trouble the reader with a journal of it. The Captain called in at one or two ports, and sent in his longboat for provisions and fresh water, but I never went out of the ship till we came into the Downs, which was on the 3rd day of June, 1706, about nine months after my escape. I offered to leave my goods in security for payment of my freight:[40] but the Captain protested he would not receive one farthing. We took kind leave of each other, and I made him promise he would come to see me at my house in Redriff. I hired a horse and guide for five shillings, which I borrowed of the Captain.

As I was on the road, observing the littleness of the houses, the trees, the cattle, and the people, I began to think myself in Lilliput. I was afraid of trampling on every traveler I met, and often called aloud to have them stand out of the way, so that I had like to have gotten one or two broken heads for my impertinence.

When I came to my own house, for which I was forced to inquire, one of the servants opening the door, I bent down to go in (like a goose under a gate) for fear of striking my head. My wife ran out to embrace me, but I stooped lower than her knees, thinking she could otherwise never be able to reach my mouth. My daughter kneeled to ask my blessing, but I could not see her till she arose, having been so long used to stand with my head and eyes erect to above sixty foot; and then I went

---

37. **conceit:** The stale comparison with the fall of Phaëthon is dragged in to ridicule the unnecessary use of classical tags. 38. **Tonquin:** in French Indochina.   39. **New Holland:** the west coast of Australia.   40. **freight:** passage.

to take her up with one hand, by the waist. I looked down upon the servants and one or two friends who were in the house, as if they had been pygmies, and I a giant. I told my wife, she had been too thrifty, for I found she had starved herself and her daughter to nothing. In short, I behaved myself so unaccountably, that they were all of the Captain's opinion when he first saw me, and concluded I had lost my wits. This I mention as an instance of the great power of habit and prejudice.

In a little time I and my family and friends came to a right understanding: but my wife protested I should never go to sea any more; although my evil destiny so ordered that she had not power to hinder me, as the reader may know hereafter. In the meantime I here conclude the second part of my unfortunate voyages.

THE END OF THE SECOND PART

PART IV

A Voyage to the Country of the Houyhnhnms

CHAPTER I

The Author sets out as Captain of a ship. His men conspire against him, confine him a long time to his cabin, set him on shore in an unknown land. He travels up into the country. The Yahoos, *a strange sort of animal, described. The Author meets two Houyhnhnms.*

I continued at home with my wife and children about five months in a very happy condition, if I could have learned the lesson of knowing when I was well. I left my poor wife big with child, and accepted an advantageous offer made me to be Captain of the *Adventurer,* a stout merchantman of 350 tons: for I understood navigation well, and being grown weary of a surgeon's employment at sea, which however I could exercise upon occasion, I took a skillful young man of that calling, one Robert Purefoy, into my ship. We set sail from Portsmouth upon the 7th day of September, 1710; on the 14th we met with Captain Pocock of Bristol, at Teneriffe,[1] who was going to the Bay of Campechy,[2] to cut logwood. On the 16th, he

was parted from us by a storm; I heard since my return, that his ship foundered, and none escaped but one cabin boy. He was an honest man, and a good sailor, but a little too positive in his own opinions, which was the cause of his destruction, as it hath been of several others. For if he had followed my advice, he might at this time have been safe at home with his family, as well as myself.

I had several men died in my ship of calentures,[3] so that I was forced to get recruits out of Barbados, and the Leeward Islands, where I touched by the direction of the merchants who employed me, which I had soon too much cause to repent: for I found afterwards that most of them had been buccaneers. I had fifty hands on board, and my orders were, that I should trade with the Indians in the South Sea,[4] and make what discoveries I could. These rogues whom I had picked up debauched my other men, and they all formed a conspiracy to seize the ship and secure me; which they did one morning, rushing into my cabin, and binding me hand and foot, threatening to throw me overboard, if I offered to stir. I told them, I was their prisoner, and would submit. This they made me swear to do, and then unbound me, only fastening one of my legs with a chain near my bed, and placed a sentry at my door with his piece charged, who was commanded to shoot me dead, if I attempted my liberty. They sent me down victuals and drink, and took the government of the ship to themselves. Their design was to turn pirates, and plunder the Spaniards, which they could not do, till they got more men. But first they resolved to sell the goods in the ship, and then go to Madagascar[5] for recruits, several among them having died since my confinement. They sailed many weeks, and traded with the Indians, but I knew not what course they took, being kept close prisoner in my cabin, and expecting nothing less than to be murdered, as they often threatened me.

Upon the 9th day of May, 1711, one James Welch came down to my cabin; and said he had orders from the Captain to get me ashore. I expostulated with him, but in vain; neither would he so much as tell me who their new Captain was. They forced me into the longboat, letting me put on my best suit of clothes, which were as good as new, and a small bundle of linen, but no arms ex-

---

A Voyage to the Country of the Houyhnhnms: 1. Teneriffe: the largest of the Canary Islands.   2. Campechy: in the Gulf of Mexico where the best quality logwood was obtained for making dyes.

3. calentures: tropical fevers.   4. South Sea: There was great interest in exploring the South Pacific when the South Sea Company got its monopoly in 1711.   5. Madagascar: at the time a favorite haunt of pirates.

cept my hanger; and they were so civil as not to search my pockets, into which I conveyed what money I had, with some other little necessaries. They rowed about a league, and then set me down on a strand. I desired them to tell me what country it was. They all swore, they knew no more than myself, but said, that the Captain (as they called him) was resolved, after they had sold the lading, to get rid of me in the first place where they discovered land. They pushed off immediately, advising me to make haste, for fear of being overtaken by the tide, and bade me farewell.

In this desolate condition I advanced forward, and soon got upon firm ground, where I sat down on a bank to rest myself, and consider what I had best to do. When I was a little refreshed, I went up into the country, resolving to deliver myself to the first savages I should meet, and purchase my life from them by some bracelets, glass rings, and other toys which sailors usually provide themselves with in those voyages, and whereof I had some about me. The land was divided by long rows of trees, not regularly planted, but naturally growing; there was great plenty of grass, and several fields of oats. I walked very circumspectly for fear of being surprised, or suddenly shot with an arrow from behind or on either side. I fell into a beaten road, where I saw many tracks of human feet, and some of cows, but most of horses. At last I beheld several animals in a field, and one or two of the same kind sitting in trees. Their shape was very singular, and deformed, which a little discomposed me, so that I lay down behind a thicket to observe them better. Some of them coming forward near the place where I lay, gave me an opportunity of distinctly marking their form. Their heads and breasts were covered with a thick hair, some frizzled and others lank; they had beards like goats, and a long ridge of hair down their backs and the foreparts of their legs and feet, but the rest of their bodies were bare, so that I might see their skins, which were of a brown buff color. They had no tails, nor any hair at all on their buttocks, except about the anus; which, I presume, nature had placed there to defend them as they sat on the ground; for this posture they used, as well as lying down, and often stood on their hind feet. They climbed high trees, as nimbly as a squirrel, for they had strong extended claws before and behind, terminating in sharp points, hooked. They would often spring, and bound, and leap with prodigious agility. The females were not so large as the males;

they had long lank hair on their heads, and only a sort of down on the rest of their bodies, except about the anus, and pudenda. Their dugs hung between their forefeet, and often reached almost to the ground as they walked. The hair of both sexes was of several colors, brown, red, black, and yellow. Upon the whole, I never beheld in all my travels so disagreeable an animal, nor one against which I naturally conceived so strong an antipathy. So that thinking I had seen enough, full of contempt and aversion, I got up and pursued the beaten road, hoping it might direct me to the cabin of some Indian. I had not got far when I met one of these creatures full in my way, and coming up directly to me. The ugly monster, when he saw me, distorted several ways every feature of his visage, and stared as at an object he had never seen before; then approaching nearer, lifted up his forepaw, whether out of curiosity or mischief, I could not tell. But I drew my hanger, and gave him a good blow with the flat side of it, for I durst not strike with the edge, fearing the inhabitants might be provoked against me, if they should come to know, that I had killed or mained any of their cattle. When the beast felt the smart, he drew back, and roared so loud, that a herd of at least forty came flocking about me from the next field, howling and making odious faces; but I ran to the body of a tree, and leaning my back against it, kept them off by waving my hanger. Several of this cursed brood getting hold of the branches behind, leapt up into the tree, from whence they began to discharge their excrements on my head; however, I escaped pretty well, by sticking close to the stem of the tree, but was almost stifled with the filth, which fell about me on every side.

In the midst of this distress, I observed them all to run away on a sudden as fast as they could, at which I ventured to leave the tree, and pursue the road, wondering what it was that could put them into this fright. But looking on my left hand, I saw a horse walking softly in the field; which my persecutors having sooner discovered, was the cause of their flight. The horse started a little when he came near me, but soon recovering himself, looked full in my face with manifest tokens of wonder: he viewed my hands and feet, walking round me several times. I would have pursued my journey, but he placed himself directly in the way, yet looking with a very mild aspect, never offering the least violence. We stood gazing at each other for some time; at last I took the boldness to reach my hand towards his neck, with a design to stroke it, using the common style and whistle of jockeys when they are going to handle a strange horse. But this animal seeming to receive my civilities with disdain, shook his head, and bent his brows, softly raising up his left forefoot to remove my hand. Then he neighed three or four times, but in so different a cadence, that I almost began to think he was speaking to himself in some language of his own.

While he and I were thus employed, another horse came up; who applying himself to the first in a very formal manner, they gently struck each other's right hoof before, neighing several times by turns, and varying the sound, which seemed to be almost articulate. They went some paces off, as if it were to confer together, walking side by side, backward and forward, like persons deliberating upon some affair of weight, but often turning their eyes towards me, as it were to watch that I might not escape. I was amazed to see such actions and behavior in brute beasts, and concluded with myself, that if the inhabitants of this country were endued with a proportionable degree of reason, they must needs be the wisest people upon earth. This thought gave me so much comfort, that I resolved to go forward until I could discover some house or village, or meet with any of the natives, leaving the two horses to discourse together as they pleased. But the first, who was a dapple gray, observing me to steal off, neighed after me in so expressive a tone, that I fancied myself to understand what he meant; whereupon I turned back, and came near him, to expect his farther commands: but concealing my fear as much as I could, for I began to be in some pain, how this adventure might terminate; and the reader will easily believe I did not much like my present situation.

The two horses came up close to me, looking with great earnestness upon my face and hands. The gray steed rubbed my hat all round with his right forehoof, and discomposed it so much that I was forced to adjust it better, by taking it off, and settling it again; whereat both he and his companion (who was a brown bay) appeared to be much surprised: the latter felt the lappet of my coat, and finding it to hang loose about me, they both looked with new signs of wonder. He stroked my right hand, seeming to admire the softness and color; but he squeezed it so hard between his hoof and his pastern, that I was forced to roar; after which they both touched me with all possible tenderness. They were under great perplexity about my shoes and stockings, which they felt very often, neighing to each other, and using various gestures, not unlike those of a philosopher, when he would attempt to solve some new and difficult phenomenon.

Upon the whole, the behavior of these animals was so orderly and rational, so acute and judicious, that I at last concluded, they must needs be magicians, who had thus metamorphosed themselves upon some design, and seeing a stranger in the way, were resolved to divert themselves with him; or perhaps were really amazed at the sight of a man so very different in habit, feature, and complexion from those who might probably live in so remote a climate. Upon the strength of this reasoning, I ventured to address them in the following manner: "Gentlemen, if you be conjurers, as I have good cause to believe, you can understand any language; therefore I make bold to let your worships know, that I am a poor distressed Englishman, driven by his misfortunes upon your coast, and I entreat one of you, to let me ride upon his back, as if he were a real horse, to some house or village, where I can be relieved. In return of which favor, I will make you a present of this knife and bracelet" (taking them out of my pocket). The two creatures stood silent while I spoke, seeming to listen with great attention; and when I had ended, they neighed frequently towards each other, as if they were engaged in serious conversation. I plainly observed, that their language expressed the passions very well, and the words might with little pains be resolved into an alphabet more easily than the Chinese.

I could frequently distinguish the word *Yahoo*, which was repeated by each of them several times; and although it was impossible for me to conjecture what it meant, yet while the two horses were busy in conversation, I endeavored to practice this word upon my tongue; and as soon as they were silent, I boldly pronounced *Yahoo* in a loud voice, imitating, at the same time, as near as I could, the neighing of a horse; at which they were both visibly surprised, and the gray repeated the same word twice, as if he meant to teach me the right accent, wherein I spoke after him as well as I could, and found myself perceivably to improve every time, though very far from any degree of perfection. Then the bay tried me with a second word, much harder to be pronounced; but reducing it to the English orthography, may be spelt thus,

Houyhnhnm. I did not succeed in this so well as the former, but after two or three farther trials, I had better fortune; and they both appeared amazed at my capacity.

After some further discourse, which I then conjectured might relate to me, the two friends took their leaves, with the same compliment of striking each other's hoof; and the gray made me signs that I should walk before him, wherein I thought it prudent to comply, till I could find a better director. When I offered to slacken my pace, he would cry, *Hhuun, Hhuun;* I guessed his meaning, and gave him to understand, as well as I could, that I was weary, and not able to walk faster; upon which, he would stand a while to let me rest.

CHAPTER 2

The Author conducted by a Houyhnhnm *to his house. The house described. The Author's reception. The food of the* Houyhnhnms. *The Author in distress for want of meat, is at last relieved. His manner of feeding in that country.*

Having traveled about three miles, we came to a long kind of building, made of timber, stuck in the ground, and wattled across; the roof was low, and covered with straw. I now began to be a little comforted, and took out some toys, which travelers usually carry for presents to the savage Indians of America and other parts, in hopes the people of the house would be thereby encouraged to receive me kindly. The horse made me a sign to go in first; it was a large room with a smooth clay floor, and a rack and manger extending the whole length on one side. There were three nags, and two mares, not eating, but some of them sitting down upon their hams, which I very much wondered at; but wondered more to see the rest employed in domestic business. The last seemed but ordinary cattle; however, this confirmed my first opinion, that a people who could so far civilize brute animals, must needs excel in wisdom all the nations of the world. The gray came in just after, and thereby prevented any ill treatment, which the others might have given me. He neighed to them several times in a style of authority, and received answers.

Beyond this room there were three others, reaching the length of the house, to which you passed through three doors, opposite to each other, in the manner of a vista; we went through the second room towards the third; here the gray walked in first, beckoning me to attend: I waited in the second room, and got ready my presents for the master and mistress of the house: they were two knives, three bracelets of false pearl, a small looking glass, and a bead necklace. The horse neighed three or four times, and I waited to hear some answers in a human voice, but I heard no other returns, than in the same dialect, only one or two a little shriller than his. I began to think that this house must belong to some person of great note among them, because there appeared so much ceremony before I could gain admittance. But, that a man of quality should be served all by horses, was beyond my comprehension. I feared my brain was disturbed by my sufferings and misfortunes: I roused myself, and looked about me in the room where I was left alone; this was furnished as the first, only after a more elegant manner. I rubbed my eyes often, but the same objects still occurred. I pinched my arms and sides, to awake myself, hoping I might be in a dream. I then absolutely concluded, that all these appearances could be nothing else but necromancy and magic. But I had no time to pursue these reflections; for the gray horse came to the door, and made me a sign to follow him into the third room, where I saw a very comely mare, together with a colt and foal, sitting on their haunches, upon mats of straw, not unartfully made, and perfectly neat and clean.

The mare soon after my entrance, rose from her mat, and coming up close, after having nicely observed my hands and face, gave me a most contemptuous look; then turning to the horse, I heard the word *Yahoo* often repeated betwixt them; the meaning of which word I could not then comprehend, although it were the first I had learned to pronounce; but I was soon better informed, to my everlasting mortification: for the horse beckoning to me with his head, and repeating the word *Hhuun, Hhuun,* as he did upon the road, which I understood was to attend him, led me out into a kind of court, where was another building at some distance from the house. Here we entered, and I saw three of those detestable creatures, which I first met after my landing, feeding upon roots, and the flesh of some animals, which I afterwards found to be that of asses and dogs, and now and then a cow dead by accident or disease. They were all tied by the neck with strong withes,[6] fastened to a beam; they held their food between the claws

6. **withes:** a halter made of flexible twigs.

of their forefeet, and tore it with their teeth.

The master horse ordered a sorrel nag, one of his servants, to untie the largest of these animals, and take him into the yard. The beast and I were brought close together, and our countenances diligently compared, both by master and servant, who thereupon repeated several times the word *Yahoo.* My horror and astonishment are not to be described, when I observed, in this abominable animal, a perfect human figure: the face of it indeed was flat and broad, the nose depressed, the lips large, and the mouth wide. But these differences are common to all savage nations, where the lineaments of the countenance are distorted by the natives suffering their infants to lie groveling on the earth, or by carrying them on their backs, nuzzling with their face against the mother's shoulders. The forefeet of the *Yahoo* differed from my hands in nothing else but the length of the nails, the coarseness and brownness of the palms, and the hairiness on the backs. There was the same resemblance between our feet, with the same differences, which I knew very well, although the horses did not, because of my shoes and stockings; the same in every part of our bodies, except as to hairiness and color, which I have already described.

The great difficulty that seemed to stick with the two horses, was, to see the rest of my body so very different from that of a *Yahoo,* for which I was obliged to my clothes, whereof they had no conception. The sorrel nag offered me a root, which he held (after their manner, as we shall describe in its proper place) between his hoof and pastern; I took it in my hand, and having smelt it, returned it to him again as civilly as I could. He brought out of the *Yahoo's* kennel a piece of ass's flesh, but it smelt so offensively that I turned from it with loathing: he then threw it to the *Yahoo,* by whom it was greedily devoured. He afterwards showed me a wisp of hay, and a fetlock full of oats; but I shook my head, to signify, that neither of these were food for me. And indeed, I now apprehended that I must absolutely starve, if I did not get to some of my own species; for as to those filthy *Yahoos,* although there were few greater lovers of mankind, at that time, than myself, yet I confess I never saw any sensitive being so detestable on all accounts; and the more I came near them, the more hateful they grew, while I stayed in that country. This the master horse observed by my behavior, and therefore sent the *Yahoo* back to his kennel. He then put his forehoof to his mouth, at which I

was much surprised, although he did it with ease, and with a motion that appeared perfectly natural, and made other signs to know what I would eat; but I could not return him such an answer as he was able to apprehend; and if he had understood me, I did not see how it was possible to contrive any way for finding myself nourishment. While we were thus engaged, I observed a cow passing by, whereupon I pointed to her, and expressed a desire to let me go and milk her. This had its effect; for he led me back into the house, and ordered a mare-servant to open a room, where a good store of milk lay in earthen and wooden vessels, after a very orderly and cleanly manner. She gave me a large bowl full, of which I drank very heartily, and found myself well refreshed.

About noon I saw coming towards the house a kind of vehicle, drawn like a sledge by four *Yahoos.* There was in it an old steed, who seemed to be of quality; he alighted with his hindfeet forward, having by accident got a hurt in his left forefoot. He came to dine with our horse, who received him with great civility. They dined in the best room, and had oats boiled in milk for the second course, which the old horse eat warm, but the rest cold. Their mangers were placed circular in the middle of the room, and divided into several partitions, round which they sat on their haunches upon bosses of straw. In the middle was a large rack with angles answering to every partition of the manger; so that each horse and mare eat their own hay, and their own mash of oats and milk, with much decency and regularity. The behavior of the young colt and foal appeared very modest, and that of the master and mistress extremely cheerful and complaisant to their guest. The gray ordered me to stand by him, and much discourse passed between him and his friend concerning me, as I found by the stranger's often looking on me, and the frequent repetition of the word *Yahoo.*

I happened to wear my gloves, which the master gray observing, seemed perplexed, discovering signs of wonder what I had done to my forefeet; he put his hoof three or four times to them, as if he would signify, that I should reduce them to their former shape, which I presently did, pulling off both my gloves, and putting them into my pocket. This occasioned farther talk, and I saw the company was pleased with my behavior, whereof I soon found the good effects. I was ordered to speak the few words I understood, and while they were at dinner, the master taught me the names for oats, milk, fire, water, and some others; which I could readily pronounce after him, having from my youth a great facility in learning languages.

When dinner was done, the master horse took me aside, and by signs and words made me understand the concern he was in, that I had nothing to eat. Oats in their tongue are called *hlunnh*. This word I pronounced two or three times; for although I had refused them at first, yet upon second thoughts, I considered that I could contrive to make of them a kind of bread, which might be sufficient with milk to keep me alive, till I could make my escape to some other country, and to creatures of my own species. The horse immediately ordered a white mare-servant of his family to bring me a good quantity of oats in a sort of wooden tray. These I heated before the fire as well as I could, and rubbed them till the husks came off, which I made a shift to winnow from the grain; I ground and beat them between two stones, then took water, and made them into a paste or cake, which I toasted at the fire, and ate warm with milk. It was at first a very insipid diet, though common enough in many parts of Europe, but grew tolerable by time; and having been often reduced to hard fare in my life, this was not the first experiment I had made how easily nature is satisfied. And I cannot but observe, that I never had one hour's sickness, while I stayed in this island. 'Tis true, I sometimes made a shift to catch a rabbit, or bird, by springes [7] made of *Yahoos'* hairs; and I often gathered wholesome herbs, which I boiled, and eat as salads with my bread, and now and then, for a rarity, I made a little butter, and drank the whey. I was at first at a great loss for salt; but custom soon reconciled the want of it; and I am confident that the frequent use of salt among us is an effect of luxury, and was first introduced only as a provocative to drink; except where it is necessary for preserving of flesh in long voyages, or in places remote from great markets. For we observe no animal to be fond of it but man: [8] and as to myself, when I left this country, it was a great while before I could endure the taste of it in anything that I eat.

This is enough to say upon the subject of my diet, wherewith other travelers fill their books, as if the readers were personally concerned whether we fare well or ill. However, it was necessary to mention this matter, lest the world should think it impossible that I could find sustenance for three years in such a country, and among such inhabitants.

When it grew towards evening, the master horse ordered a place for me to lodge in; it was but six yards from the house, and separated from the stable of the *Yahoos.* Here I got some straw, and covering myself with my own clothes, slept very sound. But I was in a short time better accommodated, as the reader shall know hereafter, when I come to treat more particularly about my way of living.

CHAPTER 3

The Author studious to learn the language, the Houyhnhnm *his master assists in teaching him. The language described. Several* Houyhnhnms *of quality come out of curiosity to see the Author. He gives his master a short account of his voyage.*

My principal endeavor was to learn the language, which my master (for so I shall henceforth call him), and his children, and every servant of his house, were desirous to teach me. For they looked upon it as a prodigy that a brute animal should discover such marks of a rational creature. I pointed to everything, and inquired the name of it, which I wrote down in my journal book when I was alone, and corrected my bad accent by desiring those of the family to pronounce it often. In this employment, a sorrel nag, one of the underservants, was very ready to assist me.

In speaking, they pronounce through the nose and throat, and their language approaches nearest to the High Dutch, or German, of any I know in Europe; but is much more graceful and significant. The Emperor Charles V made almost the same observation, when he said, that if he were to speak to his horse, it should be in High Dutch. [9]

The curiosity and impatience of my master were so great, that he spent many hours of his leisure to instruct me. He was convinced (as he afterwards told me) that I must be a *Yahoo,* but my teachableness, civility, and cleanliness, astonished him; which were qualities altogether so opposite to those animals. He was most perplexed about my clothes, reasoning sometimes with himself, whether they were a part of my body: for I never pulled them

7. springes: snares. 8. no . . . man: a strange comment, since horses as well as cattle are extremely fond of salt.

9. Charles V: What he is supposed to have said was that he would speak to God in Spanish, to his mistress in Italian, and to his horse in German.

off till the family were asleep, and got them on before they waked in the morning. My master was eager to learn from whence I came, how I acquired those appearances of reason, which I discovered in all my actions, and to know my story from my own mouth, which he hoped he should soon do by the great proficiency I made in learning and pronouncing their words and sentences. To help my memory, I formed all I learned into the English alphabet, and writ the words down with the translations. This last, after some time, I ventured to do in my master's presence. It cost me much trouble to explain to him what I was doing; for the inhabitants have not the least idea of books or literature.

In about ten weeks' time I was able to understand most of his questions, and in three months could give him some tolerable answers. He was extremely curious to know from what part of the country I came, and how I was taught to imitate a rational creature, because the *Yahoos* (whom he saw I exactly resembled in my head, hands, and face, that were only visible), with some appearance of cunning, and the strongest disposition to mischief, were observed to be the most unteachable of all brutes. I answered, that I came over the sea from a far place, with many others of my own kind, in a great hollow vessel made of the bodies of trees. That my companions forced me to land on this coast, and then left me to shift for myself. It was with some difficulty, and by the help of many signs, that I brought him to understand me. He replied, that I must needs be mistaken, or that I *said the thing which was not.* (For they have no word in their language to express lying or falsehood.) He knew it was impossible that there could be a country beyond the sea, or that a parcel of brutes could move a wooden vessel whither they pleased upon water. He was sure no *Houyhnhnm* alive could make such a vessel, nor would trust *Yahoos* to manage it.

The word *Houyhnhnm,* in their tongue, signifies a *horse,* and in its etymology, *the perfection of nature.* I told my master, that I was at a loss for expression, but would improve as fast as I could; and hoped in a short time I should be able to tell him wonders: he was pleased to direct his own mare, his colt and foal, and the servants of the family, to take all opportunities of instructing me, and every day for two or three hours, he was at the same pains himself. Several horses and mares of quality in the neighborhood came often to our house upon the report spread of a wonderful *Yahoo,* that could speak like a *Houyhnhnm,* and seemed in his words and actions to discover some glimmerings of reason. These delighted to converse with me: they put many questions, and received such answers as I was able to return. By all which advantages, I made so great a progress, that in five months from my arrival I understood whatever was spoke, and could express myself tolerably well.

The *Houyhnhnms* who came to visit my master, out of a design of seeing and talking with me, could hardly believe me to be a right *Yahoo,* because my body had a different covering from others of my kind. They were astonished to observe me without the usual hair or skin, except on my head, face, and hands; but I discovered that secret to my master, upon an accident, which happened about a fortnight before.

I have already told the reader, that every night when the family were gone to bed, it was my custom to strip and cover myself with my clothes: it happened one morning early, that my master sent for me, by the sorrel nag, who was his valet; when he came, I was fast asleep, my clothes fallen off on one side and my shirt above my waist. I awaked at the noise he made, and observed him to deliver his message in some disorder; after which he went to my master, and in a great fright gave him a very confused account of what he had seen. This I presently discovered; for going as soon as I was dressed, to pay my attendance upon his Honor, he asked me the meaning of what his servant had reported, that I was not the same thing when I slept as I appeared to be at other times; that his valet assured him, some part of me was white, some yellow, at least not so white, and some brown.

I had hitherto concealed the secret of my dress, in order to distinguish myself, as much as possible, from that cursed race of *Yahoos;* but now I found it in vain to do so any longer. Besides, I considered that my clothes and shoes would soon wear out, which already were in a declining condition, and must be supplied by some contrivance from the hides of *Yahoos* or other brutes; whereby the whole secret would be known. I therefore told my master, that in the country from whence I came, those of my kind always covered their bodies with the hairs of certain animals prepared by art, as well for decency as to avoid the inclemencies of air, both hot and cold; of which, as to my own person, I would give him immediate conviction, if he pleased to command me: only desiring his excuse, if I did not expose those parts that nature taught us to conceal. He said my discourse was all very strange, but especially the last part; for he could not understand why nature should teach us to conceal what nature had given. That neither himself nor family were ashamed of any parts of their bodies; but however I might do as I pleased. Whereupon, I first unbuttoned my coat, and pulled it off. I did the same with my waistcoat; I drew off my shoes, stockings, and breeches. I let my shirt down to my waist, and drew up the bottom, fastening it like a girdle about my middle to hide my nakedness.

My master observed the whole performance with great signs of curiosity and admiration. He took up all my clothes in his pastern, one piece after another, and examined them diligently; he then stroked my body very gently, and looked round me several times, after which he said, it was plain I must be a perfect *Yahoo;* but that I differed very much from the rest of my species, in the whiteness, and smoothness of my skin, my want of hair in several parts of my body, the shape and shortness of my claws behind and before, and my affectation of walking continually on my two hinder feet. He desired to see no more, and gave me leave to put on my clothes again, for I was shuddering with cold.

I expressed my uneasiness at his giving me so often the appellation of *Yahoo,* an odious animal, for which I had so utter a hatred and contempt. I begged he would forbear applying that word to me, and take the same order in his family, and among his friends whom he suffered to see me. I requested likewise, that the secret of my having a false covering to my body might be known to none but himself, at least as long as my present clothing should last; for as to what the sorrel nag his valet had observed, his Honor might command him to conceal it.

All this my master very graciously consented to, and thus the secret was kept till my clothes began to wear out, which I was forced to supply by several contrivances, that shall hereafter be mentioned. In the meantime, he desired I would go on with my utmost diligence to learn their language, because he was more astonished at my capacity for speech and reason, than at the figure of my body, whether it were covered or no; adding, that he waited with some impatience to hear the wonders which I promised to tell him.

From thenceforward he doubled the pains he had been at to instruct me; he brought me into all company, and made them treat me with civility, because, as he told them privately, this would put me into good humor, and make me more diverting.

Every day when I waited on him, beside the trouble he was at in teaching, he would ask me several questions concerning myself, which I answered as well as I could; and by those means he had already received some general ideas, though very imperfect. It would be tedious to relate the several steps by which I advanced to a more regular conversation: but the first account I gave of myself in any order and length, was to this purpose:

That I came from a very far country, as I already had attempted to tell him, with about fifty more of my own species; that we traveled upon the seas, in a great hollow vessel made of wood, and larger than his Honor's house. I described the ship to him in the best terms I could, and explained by the help of my handkerchief displayed, how it was driven forward by the wind. That upon a quarrel among us, I was set on shore on this coast, where I walked forward without knowing whither, till he delivered me from the persecution of those execrable *Yahoos.* He asked me, who made the ship, and how it was possible that the *Houyhnhnms* of my country would leave it to the management of brutes? My answer was, that I durst proceed no further in my relation, unless he would give me his word and honor that he would not be offended, and then I would tell him the wonders I had so often promised. He agreed; and I went on by assuring him, that the ship was made by creatures like myself, who in all the countries I had traveled, as well as in my own, were the only governing, rational animals; and that upon my arrival hither, I was as much astonished to see the *Houyhnhnms* act like rational beings, as he or his friends could be in finding some marks of reason in a creature he was pleased to call a *Yahoo,* to which I owned my resemblance in every part, but could not account for their degenerate and brutal nature. I said farther, that if good fortune ever restored me to my native country, to relate my travels hither, as I resolved to do, everybody would believe that I *said the thing which was not;* that I invented the story out of my own head; and with all possible respect to himself his family and friends, and under his promise of not being offended, our countrymen would hardly think it probable, that a *Houyhnhnm* should be the presiding creature of a nation, and a *Yahoo* the brute.

CHAPTER .4

The Houyhnhnm's *notion of truth and falsehood. The Author's discourse disapproved by his master. The Author gives a more particular account of himself, and the accidents of his voyage.*

My master heard me with great appearances of uneasiness in his countenance, because *doubting,* or *not believing,* are so little known in this country, that the inhabitants cannot tell how to behave themselves under such circumstances. And I remember in frequent discourses with my master concerning the nature of manhood, in other parts of the world, having occasion to talk of *lying* and *false representation,* it was with much difficulty that he comprehended what I meant, although he had otherwise a most acute judgment. For he argued thus: that the use of speech was to make us understand one another, and to receive information of facts; now if anyone *said the thing which was not,* these ends were defeated; because I cannot properly be said to understand him; and I am so far from receiving information, that he leaves me worse than in ignorance, for I am led to believe a thing black when it is white, and short when it is long. And these were all the notions he had concerning that faculty of *lying,* so perfectly well understood, and so universally practiced, among human creatures.

To return from this digression; when I asserted that the *Yahoos* were the only governing animals in my country, which my master said was altogether past his conception; he desired to know, whether we had *Houyhnhnms* among us, and what was their employment: I told him, we had great numbers, that in summer they grazed in the fields, and in winter were kept in houses, with hay and oats, where *Yahoo* servants were employed to rub their skins smooth, comb their manes, pick their feet, serve them with food, and make their beds. I understand you well, said my master, it is now very plain, from all you have spoken, that whatever share of reason the *Yahoos* pretend to, the *Houyhnhnms* are your masters; I heartily wish our *Yahoos* would be so tractable. I begged his Honor would please to excuse me from proceeding any farther, because I was very certain that the account he expected from me would be highly displeasing. But he insisted in commanding me to let him know the best and the worst: I told him, he should be obeyed. I owned, that the *Houyhnhnms* among us, whom we called horses, were the most generous and comely animals we had, that they excelled in strength and swiftness; and when they belonged to persons of quality, employed in traveling, racing, and drawing chariots, they were treated with much kindness and care till they fell into diseases, or became foundered in the feet; but then they were sold, and used to all kind of drudgery till they died; after which their skins were stripped and sold for what they were worth, and their bodies left to be devoured by dogs and birds of prey. But the common race of horses had not so good fortune, being kept by farmers and carriers, and other mean people, who put them to greater labor, and fed them worse. I described, as well as I could, our way of riding, the shape and use of a bridle, a saddle, a spur, and a whip, of harness and wheels. I added, that we fastened plates of a certain hard substance called iron at the bottom of their feet, to preserve their hoofs from being broken by the stony ways on which we often traveled.

My master, after some expressions of great indignation, wondered how we dared to venture upon a *Houyhnhnm's* back, for he was sure, that the meanest servant in his house would be able to shake off the strongest *Yahoo,* or by lying down, and rolling on his back, squeeze the brute to death. I answered, that our horses were trained up from three or four years old to the several uses we intended them for; that if any of them proved intolerably vicious, they were employed for carriages; that they were severely beaten while they were young for any mischievous tricks; that the males, designed for the common use of riding or draught, were generally castrated about two years after their birth, to take down their spirits, and make them more tame and gentle; that they were indeed sensible of rewards and punishments; but his Honor would please to consider, that they had not the least tincture of reason any more than the *Yahoos* in this country.

It put me to the pains of many circumlocutions to give my master a right idea of what I spoke; for their language doth not abound in variety of words, because their wants and passions are fewer than among us. But it is impossible to express his noble resentment at our savage treatment of the *Houyhnhnm* race, particularly after I had explained the manner and use of castrating horses among us, to hinder them from propagating their kind, and to render them more servile. He said, if it were possible there could be any country where *Yahoos* alone were endued with reason, they certainly must be the governing animal, because reason will in time always prevail against brutal strength. But, considering the frame of our bodies, and especially of mine, he thought no creature of equal bulk was so ill contrived, for employing that reason in the common offices of life; whereupon he desired to know whether those among whom I lived resembled me or the *Yahoos* of his country. I assured him, that I was as well shaped as most of my age; but the younger and the females were much more soft and tender, and the skins of the latter generally as white as milk. He said, I differed indeed from other *Yahoos,* being much more cleanly, and not altogether so deformed, but, in point of real advantage, he thought I differed for the worse. That my nails were of no use either to my fore or hinder feet; as to my forefeet, he could not properly call them by that name, for he never observed me to walk upon them; that they were too soft to bear the ground; that I generally went with them uncovered, neither was the covering I sometimes wore on them, of the same shape, or so strong as that on my feet behind. That I could not walk with any security, for if either of my hinder feet slipped, I must inevitably fall. He then began to find fault with other parts of my body, the flatness of my face, the prominence of my nose, my eyes placed directly in front, so that I could not look on either side without turning my head: that I was not able to feed myself, without lifting one of my forefeet to my mouth: and therefore nature had placed those joints to answer that necessity. He knew not what could be the use of those several clefts and divisions in my feet behind; these were too soft to bear the hardness and sharpness of stones without a covering made from the skin of some other brute; that my whole body wanted a fence against heat and cold, which I was forced to put on and off every day with tediousness and trouble. And lastly, that he observed every animal in this country naturally to abhor the *Yahoos,* whom the weaker avoided, and the stronger drove from them. So that supposing us to have the gift of reason, he could not see how it were possible to cure that natural antipathy which every creature discovered against us; nor consequently, how we could tame and render them serviceable. However, he would (as he said) debate the matter no farther, because he was more desirous to know my own story, the country where I was born, and the several actions and events of my life before I came hither.

I assured him, how extremely desirous I was that he should be satisfied in every point; but I doubted much, whether it would be possible for me to explain myself on several subjects whereof his Honor could have no conception, because I saw nothing in his country to which I could resemble them. That, however, I would do my best, and strive to express myself by similitudes, humbly desiring his assistance when I wanted proper words; which he was pleased to promise me.

I said, my birth was of honest parents in an island called England, which was remote from this country, as many days' journey as the strongest of his Honor's servants could travel in the annual course of the sun. That I was bred a surgeon, whose trade is to cure wounds and hurts in the body, got by accident or violence; that my country was governed by a female man, whom we called Queen. That I left it to get riches, whereby I might maintain myself and family when I should return. That, in my last voyage, I was commander of the ship, and had about fifty *Yahoos* under me, many of which died at sea, and I was forced to supply them by others picked out from several nations. That our ship was twice in danger of being sunk; the first time by a great storm, and the second, by striking against a rock. Here my master interposed, by asking me, how I could persuade strangers out of different countries to venture with me, after the losses I had sustained, and the hazards I had run. I said, they were fellows of desperate fortunes, forced to fly from the places of their birth, on account of their poverty or their crimes. Some were undone by lawsuits; others spent all they had in drinking, whoring, and gaming; others fled for treason; many for murder, theft, poisoning, robbery, perjury, forgery, coining false money; for committing rapes or sodomy; for flying from their colors, or deserting to the enemy; and most of them had broken prison. None of these durst return to their native countries for fear of being hanged, or of starving in a jail; and therefore were under the necessity of seeking a livelihood in other places.

During this discourse, my master was pleased often to interrupt me. I had made use of many circumlocutions in describing to him the nature of the several crimes for which most of our crew had been forced to fly their country. This labor took up several days' conversation, before he was able to comprehend me. He was wholly at a loss to know what could be the use or necessity of practicing those vices. To clear up which I endeavored to give some ideas of the desire of power and riches, of the terrible effects of lust, intemperance, malice, and envy. All this I was forced to define and describe by putting of cases, and making suppositions. After which, like one whose imagination was struck with something never seen or heard of before, he would lift up his eyes with amazement and indignation. Power, government, war, law, punishment, and a thousand other things had no terms, wherein that language could express them, which made the difficulty almost insuperable to give my master any conception of what I meant. But being of an excellent understanding, much improved by contemplation and converse, he at last arrived at a competent knowledge of what human nature in our parts of the world is capable to perform, and desired I would give him some particular account of that land which we call Europe, especially of my own country.

CHAPTER 5

The Author, at his master's commands, informs him of the state of England. *The causes of war among the princes of* Europe. *The Author begins to explain the* English *constitution.*

The reader may please to observe, that the following extract of many conversations I had with my master, contains a summary of the most material points, which were discoursed at several times for above two years; his Honor often desiring fuller satisfaction as I farther improved in the *Houyhnhnm* tongue. I laid before him, as well as I could, the whole state of Europe; I discoursed of trade and manufactures; of arts and sciences; and the answers I gave to all the questions he made, as they arose upon several subjects, were a fund of conversation not to be exhausted. But I shall here only set down the substance of what passed between us concerning my own country, reducing it into order as well as I can, without any regard to time or other circumstances, while I strictly adhere to truth. My only concern is, that I shall hardly be able to do justice to my master's arguments and expressions, which must needs suffer by my want of capacity, as well as by a translation into our barbarous English.

In obedience, therefore, to his Honor's commands, I related to him the Revolution under the Prince of Orange; the long war with France [10] en-

tered into by the said prince, and renewed by his successor, the present Queen, wherein the greatest powers of Christendom were engaged, and which still continued: I computed at his request, that about a million of *Yahoos* might have been killed in the whole progress of it; and perhaps a hundred or more cities taken, and five times as many ships burnt or sunk.

He asked me what were the usual causes or motives that made one country go to war with another. I answered they were innumerable; but I should only mention a few of the chief. Sometimes the ambition of princes, who never think they have land or people enough to govern; sometimes the corruption of ministers, who engage their master in a war in order to stifle or divert the clamor of the subjects against their evil administration. Difference in opinions [11] hath cost many millions of lives: for instance, whether flesh be bread, or bread be flesh; whether the juice of a certain berry be blood or wine; whether whistling be a vice or a virtue; whether it be better to kiss a post, or throw it into the fire; what is the best color for a coat, whether black, white, red, or gray; and whether it should be long or short, narrow or wide, dirty or clean; with many more. Neither are any wars so furious and bloody, or of so long continuance, as those occasioned by difference in opinion, especially if it be in things indifferent.

Sometimes the quarrel between two princes is to decide which of them shall dispossess a third of his dominions, where neither of them pretend to any right. Sometimes one prince quarreleth with another, for fear the other should quarrel with him. Sometimes a war is entered upon, because the enemy is too strong, and sometimes because he is too weak. Sometimes our neighbors want the things which we have, or have the things which we want; and we both fight, till they take ours or give us theirs. It is a very justifiable cause of war to invade a country after the people have been wasted by famine, destroyed by pestilence, or embroiled by factions among themselves. It is justifiable to enter into a war against our nearest ally, when one of his towns lies convenient for us, or a territory of land, that would render our dominions round and compact. If a prince sends forces into a nation, where the people are poor and ignorant, he may lawfully put half of them to death, and make slaves

---

10. war . . . France: from 1689–97 during the reign of William III, and from 1702–13 during the reign of Queen Anne.

11. Difference . . . opinions: referring to the controversies about transubstantiation, the use of music in churches, veneration of the crucifix, and ecclesiastical vestments.

of the rest, in order to civilize and reduce them from their barbarous way of living. It is a very kingly, honorable, and frequent practice, when one prince desires the assistance of another to secure him against an invasion, that the assistant, when he hath driven out the invader, should seize on the dominions himself, and kill, imprison, or banish the prince he came to relieve. Alliance by blood or marriage is a sufficient cause of war between princes; and the nearer the kindred is, the greater is their disposition to quarrel: poor nations are hungry, and rich nations are proud; and pride and hunger will ever be at variance. For these reasons, the trade of a soldier is held the most honorable of all others; because a soldier is a *Yahoo* hired to kill in cold blood as many of his own species, who have never offended him, as possibly he can.

There is likewise a kind of beggarly princes in Europe, not able to make war by themselves, who hire out their troops to richer nations, for so much a day to each man; of which they keep three-fourths to themselves, and it is the best part of their maintenance; such are those in many northern parts of Europe.

What you have told me (said my master), upon the subject of war, does indeed discover most admirably the effects of that reason you pretend to: however, it is happy that the shame is greater than the danger; and that nature hath left you utterly uncapable of doing much mischief.

For your mouths lying flat with your faces, you can hardly bite each other to any purpose, unless by consent. Then as to the claws upon your feet before and behind, they are so short and tender, that one of our *Yahoos* would drive a dozen of yours before him. And therefore in recounting the numbers of those who have been killed in battle, I cannot but think that you have *said the thing which is not.*

I could not forbear shaking my head, and smiling a little at his ignorance. And being no stranger to the art of war, I gave him a description of cannons, culverins, muskets, carabines, pistols, bullets, powder, swords, bayonets, sieges, retreats, attacks, undermines, countermines, bombardments, sea fights; ships sunk with a thousand men, twenty thousand killed on each side; dying groans, limbs flying in the air, smoke, noise, confusion, trampling to death under horses' feet; flight, pursuit, victory; fields strewed with carcasses left for food to dogs, and wolves, and birds of prey; plundering, stripping, ravishing, burning and destroying. And to set forth the valor of my own dear countrymen, I assured him, that I had seen them blow up a hundred enemies at once in a siege, and as many in a ship, and beheld the dead bodies drop down in pieces from the clouds, to the great diversion of all the spectators.

I was going on to more particulars, when my master commanded me silence. He said, whoever understood the nature of *Yahoos* might easily believe it possible for so vile an animal to be capable of every action I had named, if their strength and cunning equaled their malice. But as my discourse had increased his abhorrence of the whole species, so he found it gave him a disturbance in his mind, to which he was wholly a stranger before. He thought his ears being used to such abominable words, might by degrees admit them with less detestation. That although he hated the *Yahoos* of this country, yet he no more blamed them for their odious qualities, than he did a *gnnayh* (a bird of prey) for its cruelty, or a sharp stone for cutting his hoof. But when a creature pretending to reason could be capable of such enormities, he dreaded lest the corruption of that faculty might be worse than brutality itself. He seemed therefore confident, that instead of reason, we were only possessed of some quality fitted to increase our natural vices; as the reflection from a troubled stream returns the image of an ill-shapen body, not only larger, but more distorted.

He added, that he had heard too much upon the subject of war, both in this, and some former discourses. There was another point which a little perplexed him at present. I had said, that some of our crew left their country on account of being ruined by *Law;* that I had already explained the meaning of the word; but he was at a loss how it should come to pass, that the law which was intended for every man's preservation, should be any man's ruin. Therefore he desired to be farther satisfied what I meant by law, and the dispensers thereof, according to the present practice in my own country; because he thought nature and reason were sufficient guides for a reasonable animal, as we pretended to be, in showing us what we ought to do, and what to avoid.

I assured his Honor, that law was a science wherein I had not much conversed, further than by employing advocates, in vain, upon some injustices that had been done me: however, I would give him all the satisfaction I was able.

I said, there was a society of men among us,

bred up from their youth in the art of proving by words multiplied for the purpose, that white is black, and black is white, according as they are paid. To this society all the rest of the people are slaves. For example, if my neighbor hath a mind to my cow, he hires a lawyer to prove that he ought to have my cow from me. I must then hire another to defend my right, it being against all rules of law that any man should be allowed to speak for himself. Now in this case, I, who am the right owner, lie under two great disadvantages. First, my lawyer, being practiced almost from his cradle in defending falsehood, is quite out of his element when he would be an advocate for justice, which as an office unnatural, he always attempts with great awkwardness, if not with ill will. The second disadvantage is, that my lawyer must proceed with great caution, or else he will be reprimanded by the judges, and abhorred by his brethren, as one who would lessen the practice of the law. And therefore I have but two methods to preserve my cow. The first is, to gain over my adversary's lawyer with a double fee; who will then betray his client, by insinuating that he hath justice on his side. The second way is for my lawyer to make my cause appear as unjust as he can, by allowing the cow to belong to my adversary: and this, if it be skillfully done, will certainly bespeak the favor of the bench.

"Now, your Honor is to know, that these judges are persons appointed to decide all controversies of property, as well as for the trial of criminals, and picked out from the most dexterous lawyers, who are grown old or lazy, and having been biased all their lives against truth and equity, lie under such a fatal necessity of favoring fraud, perjury, and oppression, that I have known some of them to have refused a large bribe from the side where justice lay, rather than injure the faculty,[12] by doing any thing unbecoming their nature or their office.

"It is a maxim among these lawyers, that whatever hath been done before, may legally be done again: and therefore they take special care to record all the decisions formerly made against common justice, and the general reason of mankind. These, under the name of *precedents,* they produce as authorities, to justify the most iniquitous opinions; and the judges never fail of directing accordingly.

"In pleading, they studiously avoid entering into the merits of the cause; but are loud, violent, and tedious in dwelling upon all circumstances which are not to the purpose. For instance, in the case already mentioned: they never desire to know what claim or title my adversary hath to my cow; but whether the said cow were red or black; her horns long or short; whether the field I graze her in be round or square; whether she were milked at home or abroad; what diseases she is subject to, and the like; after which they consult precedents, adjourn the cause from time to time, and in ten, twenty, or thirty years, come to an issue.

"It is likewise to be observed, that this society hath a peculiar cant and jargon of their own, that no other mortal can understand, and wherein all their laws are written, which they take special care to multiply; whereby they have wholly confounded the very essence of truth and falsehood, of right and wrong; so that it will take thirty years to decide whether the field left me by my ancestors for six generations belong to me, or to a stranger three hundred miles off.

"In the trial of persons accused for crimes against the state, the method is much more short and commendable: the judge first sends to sound the disposition of those in power, after which he can easily hang or save the criminal, strictly preserving all the forms of law." [13]

Here my master interposing, said it was a pity, that creatures endowed with such prodigious abilities of mind as these lawyers, by the description I gave of them, must certainly be, were not rather encouraged to be instructors of others in wisdom and knowledge. In answer to which, I assured his Honor, that in all points out of their own trade, they were usually the most ignorant and stupid generation among us, the most despicable in common conversation, avowed enemies to all knowledge and learning, and equally disposed to pervert the general reason of mankind in every other subject of discourse, as in that of their own profession.

CHAPTER 6

A continuation of the state of England *under Queen Anne. The character of a first minister of state in the courts of* Europe.

---

12. **faculty:** profession.

13. **strictly . . . law:** Swift was particularly bitter against judges as a result of the attempt to convict the Drapier in the Irish Courts. The whole of this passage had been much altered by the publisher in the first edition, as he feared it would prejudice his case if legal action were taken against the book.

My master was yet wholly at a loss to understand what motives could incite this race of lawyers to perplex, disquiet, and weary themselves, engaging in a confederacy of injustice, merely for the sake of injuring their fellow animals; neither could he comprehend what I meant in saying they did it for hire. Whereupon I was at much pains to describe to him the use of money, the materials it was made of, and the value of the metals; that when a *Yahoo* had got a great store of this precious substance, he was able to purchase whatever he had a mind to; the finest clothing, the noblest houses, great tracts of land, the most costly meats and drinks, and have his choice of the most beautiful females. Therefore since money alone was able to perform all these feats, our *Yahoos* thought they could never have enough of it to spend or to save, as they found themselves inclined from their natural bent either to profusion or avarice. That the rich man enjoyed the fruit of the poor man's labor, and the latter were a thousand to one in proportion to the former. That the bulk of our people was forced to live miserably, by laboring every day for small wages to make a few live plentifully. I enlarged myself much on these and many other particulars to the same purpose; but his Honor was still to seek; [14] for he went upon a supposition that all animals had a title to their share in the productions of the earth, and especially those who presided over the rest. Therefore he desired I would let him know, what these costly meats were, and how any of us happened to want them. Whereupon I enumerated as many sorts as came into my head, with the various methods of dressing them, which could not be done without sending vessels by sea to every part of the world, as well for liquors to drink, as for sauces, and innumerable other conveniences. I assured him, that this whole globe of earth must be at least three times gone round, before one of our better female *Yahoos* could get her breakfast, or a cup to put it in. He said, that must needs be a miserable country which cannot furnish food for its own inhabitants. But what he chiefly wondered at, was how such vast tracts of ground as I described should be wholly without fresh water, and the people put to the necessity of sending over the sea for drink. I replied, that England (the dear place of my nativity) was computed to produce three times the quantity of food, more than its inhabitants are able to consume, as well as liquors extracted from

grain, or pressed out of the fruit of certain trees, which made excellent drink, and the same proportion in every other convenience of life. But, in order to feed the luxury and intemperance of the males, and the vanity of the females, we sent away the greatest part of our necessary things to other countries, from whence in return we brought the materials of diseases, folly, and vice, to spend among ourselves. Hence it follows of necessity, that vast numbers of our people are compelled to seek their livelihood by begging, robbing, stealing, cheating, pimping, forswearing, flattering, suborning, forging, gaming, lying, fawning, hectoring, voting, scribbling, stargazing, poisoning, whoring, canting, libeling, freethinking, and the like occupations: every one of which terms, I was at much pains to make him understand.

That wine was not imported among us from foreign countries, to supply the want of water or other drinks, but because it was a sort of liquid which made us merry, by putting us out of our senses; diverted all melancholy thoughts, begat wild extravagant imaginations in the brain, raised our hopes, and banished our fears, suspended every office of reason for a time, and deprived us of the use of our limbs, until we fell into a profound sleep; although it must be confessed, that we always awaked sick and dispirited, and that the use of this liquor filled us with diseases, which made our lives uncomfortable and short.

But beside all this, the bulk of our people supported themselves by furnishing the necessities or conveniences of life to the rich, and to each other. For instance, when I am at home and dressed as I ought to be, I carry on my body the workmanship of an hundred tradesmen; the building and furniture of my house employ as many more, and five times the number to adorn my wife.

I was going on to tell him of another sort of people, who get their livelihood by attending the sick, having upon some occasions informed his Honor that many of my crew had died of diseases. But here it was with the utmost difficulty, that I brought him to apprehend what I meant. He could easily conceive, that a *Houyhnhnm* grew weak and heavy a few days before his death, or by some accident might hurt a limb. But that nature, who worketh all things to perfection, should suffer any pains to breed in our bodies, he thought impossible, and desired to know the reason of so unaccountable an evil. I told him, we fed on a thousand things which operated contrary to each other; that we eat

14. **to seek**: at a loss.

when we were not hungry, and drank without the provocation of thirst; that we sat whole nights drinking strong liquors without eating a bit, which disposed us to sloth, inflamed our bodies, and precipitated or prevented digestion. That prostitute female *Yahoos* acquired a certain malady, which bred rottenness in the bones of those who fell into their embraces; that this and many other diseases were propagated from father to son, so that great numbers come into the world with complicated maladies upon them; that it would be endless to give him a catalogue of all diseases incident to human bodies; for they could not be fewer than five or six hundred, spread over every limb and joint; in short, every part, external and intestine, having diseases appropriated to each. To remedy which, there was a sort of people bred up among us, in the profession or pretense of curing the sick. And because I had some skill in the faculty, I would in gratitude to his Honor, let him know the whole mystery and method by which they proceed.

Their fundamental is, that all diseases arise from repletion, from whence they conclude, that a great evacuation of the body is necessary, either through the natural passage, or upwards at the mouth. Their next business is, from herbs, minerals, gums, oils, shells, salts, juices, seaweed, excrements, barks of trees, serpents, toads, frogs, spiders, dead men's flesh and bones, birds, beasts, and fishes, to form a composition for smell and taste the most abominable, nauseous, and detestable, they can possibly contrive, which the stomach immediately rejects with loathing; and this they call a vomit; or else from the same storehouse, with some other poisonous additions, they command us to take in at the orifice above or below (just as the physician then happens to be disposed) a medicine equally annoying and disgustful to the bowels; which relaxing the belly, drives down all before it, and this they call a purge, or a clyster. For nature (as the physicians allege) having intended the superior anterior orifice only for the intromission of solids and liquids, and the inferior posterior for ejection, these artists ingeniously considering that in all diseases nature is forced out of her seat, therefore to replace her in it, the body must be treated in a manner directly contrary, by interchanging the use of each orifice; forcing solids and liquids in at the anus, and making evacuations at the mouth.

But, besides real diseases, we are subject to many that are only imaginary, for which the physicians have invented imaginary cures; these have their several names, and so have the drugs that are proper for them, and with these our female *Yahoos* are always infested.

One great excellency in this tribe is their skill at prognostics, wherein they seldom fail; their predictions in real diseases, when they rise to any degree of malignity, generally portending death, which is always in their power, when recovery is not: and therefore, upon any unexpected signs of amendment, after they have pronounced their sentence, rather than be accused as false prophets, they know how to approve their sagacity to the world by a seasonable dose.

They are likewise of special use to husbands and wives, who are grown weary of their mates; to eldest sons, to great ministers of state, and often to princes.

I had formerly upon occasion discoursed with my master upon the nature of government in general, and particularly of our own excellent constitution, deservedly the wonder and envy of the whole world. But having here accidentally mentioned a minister of state, he commanded me some time after to inform him, what species of *Yahoo* I particularly meant by that appellation.

I told him, that a first or chief minister [15] of state, whom I intended to describe, was a creature wholly exempt from joy and grief, love and hatred, pity and anger; at least makes use of no other passions but a violent desire of wealth, power, and titles; that he applies his words to all uses, except to the indication of his mind; that he never tells a truth, but with an intent that you should take it for a lie; nor a lie, but with a design that you should take it for a truth; that those he speaks worst of behind their backs, are in the surest way to preferment; and whenever he begins to praise you to others or to yourself, you are from that day forlorn. The worst mark you can receive is a promise, especially when it is confirmed with an oath; after which every wise man retires, and gives over all hopes.

There are three methods by which a man may rise to be chief minister: the first is, by knowing how with prudence to dispose of a wife, a daughter, or a sister: the second, by betraying or undermining his predecessor: and the third is, by a furious zeal in public assemblies against the corruptions of the court. But a wise prince would rather choose to employ those who practice the last of

15. first . . . minister: This passage was also much modified when first printed.

these methods; because such zealots prove always the most obsequious and subservient to the will and passions of their master. That these ministers having all employments at their disposal, preserve themselves in power, by bribing the majority of a senate or great council; and at last, by an expedient called an Act of Indemnity [16] (whereof I described the nature to him) they secure themselves from after-reckonings, and retire from the public, laden with the spoils of the nation.

The palace of a chief minister is a seminary to breed up others in his own trade: the pages, lackeys, and porter, by imitating their master, become ministers of state in their several districts, and learn to excel in the three principal ingredients, of insolence, lying, and bribery. Accordingly, they have a subaltern court paid to them by persons of the best rank, and sometimes by the force of dexterity and impudence, arrive through several gradations to be successors to their lord.

He is usually governed by a decayed wench, or favorite footman, who are the tunnels through which all graces are conveyed, and may properly be called, in the last resort, the governors of the kingdom.

One day, my master, having heard me mention the nobility of my country, was pleased to make me a compliment which I could not pretend to deserve: that he was sure I must have been born of some noble family, because I far exceeded in shape, color, and cleanliness, all the *Yahoos* of his nation, although I seemed to fail in strength and agility, which must be imputed to my different way of living from those other brutes; and besides, I was not only endowed with the faculty of speech, but likewise with some rudiments of reason, to a degree, that with all his acquaintance I passed for a prodigy.

He made me observe, that among the *Houyhnhnms,* the white, the sorrel, and the iron-gray, were not so exactly shaped as the bay, the dapple-gray, and the black; nor born with equal talents of mind, or a capacity to improve them; and therefore continued always in the condition of servants, without ever aspiring to match out of their own race, which in that country would be reckoned monstrous and unnatural.

I made his Honor my most humble acknowledgments for the good opinion he was pleased to conceive of me; but assured him at the same time,

16. Act of Indemnity: granting exemption from the penalties arising from any unconstitutional or illegal proceeding.

that my birth was of the lower sort, having been born of plain honest parents, who were just able to give me a tolerable education; that nobility among us was altogether a different thing from the idea he had of it; that our young noblemen are bred from their childhood in idleness and luxury; that as soon as years will permit, they consume their vigor, and contract odious diseases among lewd females; and when their fortunes are almost ruined, they marry some woman of mean birth, disagreeable person, and unsound constitution, merely for the sake of money, whom they hate and despise. That the productions of such marriages are generally scrofulous, rickety, or deformed children; by which means the family seldom continues above three generations, unless the wife takes care to provide a healthy father among her neighbors or domestics, in order to improve and continue the breed. That a weak diseased body, a meager countenance, and sallow complexion, are the true marks of noble blood; and a healthy robust appearance is so disgraceful in a man of quality, that the world concludes his real father to have been a groom or a coachman. The imperfections of his mind run parallel with those of his body, being a composition of spleen, dullness, ignorance, caprice, sensuality, and pride.

Without the consent of this illustrious body, no law can be enacted, repealed, or altered; and these nobles have likewise the decision of all our possessions without appeal.

CHAPTER 7

The Author's great love of his native country. His master's observations upon the constitution and administration of England, as described by the Author, with parallel cases and comparisons. His master's observations upon human nature.

The reader may be disposed to wonder how I could prevail on myself to give so free a representation of my own species, among a race of mortals who were already too apt to conceive the vilest opinion of human kind, from that entire congruity betwixt me and their *Yahoos.* But I must freely confess, that the many virtues of those excellent quadrupeds placed in opposite view to human corruptions, had so far opened my eyes and enlarged my understanding, that I began to view the actions and passions of man in a very different light, and to think the honor of my own kind not worth managing;[17] which, besides, it was impossible for me to do before a person of so acute a judgment as my master, who daily convinced me of a thousand faults in myself, whereof I had not the least perception before, and which with us would never be numbered even among human infirmities. I had likewise learned from his example an utter detestation of all falsehood or disguise; and truth appeared so amiable to me, that I determined upon sacrificing everything to it.

Let me deal so candidly with the reader, as to confess, that there was yet a much stronger motive for the freedom I took in my representation of things. I had not been a year in this country, before I contracted such a love and veneration for the inhabitants, that I entered on a firm resolution never to return to human kind, but to pass the rest of my life among these admirable *Houyhnhnms* in the contemplation and practice of every virtue; where I could have no example or incitement to vice. But it was decreed by fortune, my perpetual enemy, that so great a felicity should not fall to my share. However, it is now some comfort to reflect, that in what I said of my countrymen, I *extenuated* their faults as much as I durst before so strict an examiner, and upon every article gave as *favorable* a turn as the matter would bear. For, indeed, who is there alive that will not be swayed by his bias and partiality to the place of his birth?

I have related the substance of several conversations I had with my master, during the greatest part of the time I had the honor to be in his service, but have indeed for brevity sake omitted much more than is here set down.

When I had answered all his questions, and his curiosity seemed to be fully satisfied, he sent for me one morning early, and commanding me to sit down at some distance (an honor which he had never before conferred upon me), he said, he had been very seriously considering my whole story, as far as it related both to myself and my country; that he looked upon us as a sort of animals to whose share, by what accident he could not conjecture, some small pittance of reason had fallen, whereof we made no other use than by its assistance to aggravate our natural corruptions, and to acquire new ones, which nature had not given us. That we disarmed ourselves of the few abilities she had bestowed, had been very successful in multiplying our original wants, and seemed to spend our whole

lives in vain endeavors to supply them by our own inventions. That as to myself, it was manifest I had neither the strength nor agility of a common *Yahoo;* that I walked infirmly on my hinder feet; had found out a contrivance to make my claws of no use or defense, and to remove the hair from my chin, which was intended as a shelter from the sun and the weather. Lastly, that I could neither run with speed, nor climb trees like my brethren (as he called them) the *Yahoos* in this country.

That our institutions of government and law were plainly owing to our gross defects in reason, and by consequence, in virtue; because reason alone is sufficient to govern a rational creature; which was therefore a character we had no pretense to challenge, even from the account I had given of my own people; although he manifestly perceived, that in order to favor them, I had concealed many particulars, and often *said the thing which was not.*

He was the more confirmed in this opinion, because he observed, that as I agreed in every feature of my body with other *Yahoos,* except where it was to my real disadvantage in point of strength, speed and activity, the shortness of my claws, and some other particulars where nature had no part; so from the representation I had given him of our lives, our manners, and our actions, he found as near a resemblance in the disposition of our minds. He said the *Yahoos* were known to hate one another more than they did any different species of animals; and the reason usually assigned was the odiousness of their own shapes, which all could see in the rest, but not in themselves. He had therefore begun to think it not unwise in us to cover our bodies, and by that invention conceal many of our deformities from each other, which would else be hardly supportable. But he now found he had been mistaken, and that the dissensions of those brutes in his country were owing to the same cause with ours, as I had described them. For if (said he) you throw among five *Yahoos* as much food as would be sufficient for fifty, they will, instead of eating peaceably, fall together by the ears, each single one impatient to *have all to itself;* and therefore a servant was usually employed to stand by while they were feeding abroad, and those kept at home were tied at a distance from each other. That if a cow died of age or accident, before a *Houyhnhnm* could secure it for his own *Yahoos,* those in the neighborhood would come in herds to seize it, and then would ensue such a battle as I had described, with terrible wounds made by their claws on both sides,

17. managing: treating with discretion.

although they seldom were able to kill one another, for want of such convenient instruments of death as we had invented. At other times the like battles have been fought between the *Yahoos* of several neighborhoods without any visible cause; those of one district watching all opportunities to surprise the next before they are prepared. But if they find their project hath miscarried, they return home, and, for want of enemies, engage in what I call a civil war among themselves.

That in some fields of his country, there are certain *shining stones* of several colors, whereof the *Yahoos* are violently fond, and when part of these stones are fixed in the earth, as it sometimes happeneth, they will dig with their claws for whole days to get them out, and carry them away, and hide them by heaps in their kennels; but still looking round with great caution, for fear their comrades should find out their treasure. My master said, he could never discover the reason of this unnatural appetite, or how these stones could be of any use to a *Yahoo;* but now he believed it might proceed from the same principle of avarice which I had ascribed to mankind: that he had once, by way of experiment, privately removed a heap of these stones from the place where one of his *Yahoos* had buried it: whereupon, the sordid animal missing his treasure, by his loud lamenting brought the whole herd to the place, there miserably howled, then fell to biting and tearing the rest; began to pine away, would neither eat, nor sleep, nor work, till he ordered a servant privately to convey the stones into the same hole, and hide them as before; which when his *Yahoo* had found, he presently recovered his spirits and good humor, but took care to remove them to a better hiding place, and hath ever since been a very serviceable brute.

My master farther assured me, which I also observed myself, that in the fields where these *shining stones* abound, the fiercest and most frequent battles are fought, occasioned by perpetual inroads of the neighboring *Yahoos.*

He said, it was common when two *Yahoos* discovered such a stone in a field, and were contending which of them should be the proprietor, a third would take the advantage, and carry it away from them both; which my master would needs contend to have some resemblance with our suits at law; wherein I thought it for our credit not to undeceive him; since the decision he mentioned was much more equitable than many decrees among us; because the plaintiff and defendant there

lost nothing beside the stone they contended for, whereas our courts of equity would never have dismissed the cause while either of them had anything left.

My master continuing his discourse, said, there was nothing that rendered the *Yahoos* more odious than their undistinguishing appetite to devour everything that came in their way, whether herbs, roots, berries, corrupted flesh of animals, or all mingled together: and it was peculiar in their temper, that they were fonder of what they could get by rapine or stealth at a greater distance, than much better food provided for them at home. If their prey held out, they would eat till they were ready to burst, after which nature had pointed out to them a certain root that gave them a general evacuation.

There was also another kind of root very juicy, but somewhat rare and difficult to be found, which the *Yahoos* sought for with much eagerness, and would suck it with great delight; it produced the same effects that wine hath upon us. It would make them sometimes hug, and sometimes tear one another; they would howl and grin, and chatter, and roll, and tumble, and then fall asleep in the mud.

I did indeed observe, that the *Yahoos* were the only animals in this country subject to any diseases; which, however, were much fewer than horses have among us, and contracted not by any ill treatment they meet with, but by the nastiness and greediness of that sordid brute. Neither has their language any more than a general appellation for those maladies, which is borrowed from the name of the beast, and called *Hnea-Yahoo,* or the *Yahoo's evil,* and the cure prescribed is a mixture of their own dung and urine forcibly put down the *Yahoo's* throat. This I have since often known to have been taken with success: and do here freely recommend it to my countrymen, for the public good, as an admirable specific against all diseases produced by repletion.

As to learning, government, arts, manufactures, and the like, my master confessed he could find little or no resemblance between the *Yahoos* of that country and those in ours. For he only meant to observe what parity there was in our natures. He had heard indeed some curious *Houyhnhnms* observe, that in most herds there was a sort of ruling *Yahoo* (as among us there is generally some leading or principal stag in a park), who was always more deformed in body, and mischievous in disposition, than any of the rest. That this leader had usually a favorite as like himself as he could get, whose employment was to lick his master's feet and posteriors, and drive the female *Yahoos* to his kennel; for which he was now and then rewarded with a piece of ass's flesh. This favorite is hated by the whole herd, and therefore to protect himself, keeps always near the person of his leader. He usually continues in office till a worse can be found; but the very moment he is discarded, his successor, at the head of all the *Yahoos* in that district, young and old, male and female, come in a body, and discharge their excrements upon him from head to foot. But how far this might be applicable to our courts and favorites, and ministers of state, my master said I could best determine.

I durst make no return to this malicious insinuation, which debased human understanding below the sagacity of a common hound, who has judgment enough to distinguish and follow the cry of the ablest dog in the pack, without being ever mistaken.

My master told me, there were some qualities remarkable in the *Yahoos,* which he had not observed me to mention, or at least very slightly, in the accounts I had given him of human kind. He said, those animals, like other brutes, had their females in common; but in this they differed, that the she-*Yahoo* would admit the male while she was pregnant; and that the hes would quarrel and fight with the females as fiercely as with each other. Both which practices were such degrees of infamous brutality, that no other sensitive creature ever arrived at.

Another thing he wondered at in the *Yahoos*, was their strange disposition to nastiness and dirt, whereas there appears to be a natural love of cleanliness in all other animals. As to the two former accusations, I was glad to let them pass without any reply, because I had not a word to offer upon them in defense of my species, which otherwise I certainly had done from my own inclinations. But I could have easily vindicated human kind from the imputation of singularity upon the last article, if there had been any swine in that country (as unluckily for me there were not), which although it may be a sweeter quadruped than a *Yahoo*, cannot I humbly conceive in justice pretend to more cleanliness; and so his Honor himself must have owned, if he had seen their filthy way of feeding, and their custom of wallowing and sleeping in the mud.

My master likewise mentioned another quality

which his servants had discovered in several *Yahoos,* and to him was wholly unaccountable. He said, a fancy would sometimes take a *Yahoo* to retire into a corner, to lie down and howl, and groan, and spurn away all that came near him, although he were young and fat, wanted neither food nor water; nor did the servants imagine what could possibly ail him. And the only remedy they found was to set him to hard work, after which he would infallibly come to himself. To this I was silent out of partiality to my own kind; yet here I could plainly discover the true seeds of spleen, which only seizeth on the lazy, the luxurious, and the rich; who, if they were forced to undergo the same regimen, I would undertake for the cure.

His Honor had further observed, that a female *Yahoo* would often stand behind a bank or a bush, to gaze on the young males passing by, and then appear, and hide, using many antic gestures and grimaces, at which time it was observed, that she had a most offensive smell; and when any of the males advanced, would slowly retire, looking often back, and with a counterfeit show of fear, run off into some convenient place where she knew the male would follow her.

At other times if a female stranger came among them, three or four of her own sex would get about her, and stare and chatter, and grin, and smell her all over; and then turn off with gestures that seemed to express contempt and disdain.

Perhaps my master might refine a little in these speculations, which he had drawn from what he observed himself, or had been told him by others; however, I could not reflect without some amazement, and much sorrow, that the rudiments of lewdness, coquetry, censure, and scandal, should have place by instinct in womankind.

I expected every moment, that my master would accuse the *Yahoos* of those unnatural appetites in both sexes, so common among us. But nature, it seems, hath not been so expert a schoolmistress; and these politer pleasures are entirely the productions of art and reason, on our side of the globe.

CHAPTER 8

The Author relates several particulars of the Yahoos. *The great virtues of the* Houyhnhnms. *The education and exercise of their youth. Their general assembly.*

As I ought to have understood human nature much better than I supposed it possible for my master to do, so it was easy to apply the character he gave of the *Yahoos* to myself and my countrymen; and I believed I could yet make farther discoveries from my own observation. I therefore often begged his Honor to let me go among the herds of *Yahoos* in the neighborhood, to which he always very graciously consented, being perfectly convinced that the hatred I bore those brutes would never suffer me to be corrupted by them; and his Honor ordered one of his servants, a strong sorrel nag, very honest and good-natured, to be my guard, without whose protection I durst not undertake such adventures. For I have already told the reader how much I was pestered by those odious animals upon my first arrival. And I afterwards failed very narrowly three or four times of falling into their clutches, when I happened to stray at any distance without my hanger. And I have reason to believe they had some imagination that I was of their own species, which I often assisted myself, by stripping up my sleeves, and showing my naked arms and breast in their sight, when my protector was with me. At which times they would approach as near as they durst, and imitate my actions after the manner of monkeys, but ever with great signs of hatred; as a tame jackdaw with cap and stockings is always persecuted by the wild ones, when he happens to be got among them.

They are prodigiously nimble from their infancy; however, I once caught a young male of three years old, and endeavored by all marks of tenderness to make it quiet; but the little imp fell a squalling, and scratching, and biting with such violence, that I was forced to let it go; and it was high time, for a whole troop of old ones came about us at the noise, but finding the cub was safe (for away it ran), and my sorrel nag being by, they durst not venture near us. I observed the young animal's flesh to smell very rank, and the stink was somewhat between a weasel and a fox, but much more disagreeable. I forgot another circumstance (and perhaps I might have the reader's pardon if it were wholly omitted), that while I held the odious vermin in my hands, it voided its filthy excrements of a yellow liquid substance, all over my clothes; but by good fortune there was a small brook hard by, where I washed myself as clean as I could; although I durst not come into my master's presence, until I were sufficiently aired.

By what I could discover, the *Yahoos* appear to be the most unteachable of all animals, their capacities never reaching higher than to draw or carry burdens. Yet I am of opinion, this defect ariseth chiefly from a perverse, restive disposition. For they are cunning, malicious, treacherous, and revengeful. They are strong and hardy, but of a cowardly spirit, and by consequence, insolent, abject, and cruel. It is observed, that the red-haired of both sexes are more libidinous and mischievous than the rest, whom yet they much exceed in strength and activity.

The *Houyhnhnms* keep the *Yahoos* for present use in huts not far from the house; but the rest are sent abroad to certain fields, where they dig up roots, eat several kinds of herbs, and search about for carrion, or sometimes catch weasels and *luhimuhs* (a sort of wild rat), which they greedily devour. Nature hath taught them to dig deep holes with their nails on the side of a rising ground, wherein they lie by themselves; only the kennels of the females are larger, sufficient to hold two or three cubs.

They swim from their infancy like frogs, and are able to continue long under water, where they often take fish, which the females carry home to their young. And upon this occasion, I hope the reader will pardon my relating an odd adventure.

Being one day abroad with my protector the sorrel nag, and the weather exceeding hot, I entreated him to let me bathe in a river that was near. He consented, and I immediately stripped myself stark naked, and went down softly into the stream. It happened that a young female *Yahoo,* standing behind a bank, saw the whole proceeding, and inflamed by desire, as the nag and I conjectured, came running with all speed, and leaped into the water, within five yards of the place where I bathed. I was never in my life so terribly frighted; the nag was grazing at some distance, not suspecting any harm. She embraced me after a most fulsome manner; I roared as loud as I could, and the nag came galloping towards me, whereupon she quitted her grasp, with the utmost reluctancy, and leaped upon the opposite bank, where she stood gazing and howling all the time I was putting on my clothes.

This was matter of diversion to my master and his family, as well as of mortification to myself. For now I could no longer deny that I was a real *Yahoo* in every limb and feature, since the females had a natural propensity to me, as one of their own species. Neither was the hair of this brute of a red color (which might have been some excuse for an appetite a little irregular), but black as a sloe, and her countenance did not make an appearance altogether so hideous as the rest of the kind; for, I think, she could not be above eleven years old.

Having already lived three years in this country, the reader I suppose will expect, that I should, like other travelers, give him some account of the manners and customs of its inhabitants, which it was indeed my principal study to learn.

As these noble *Houyhnhnms* are endowed by nature with a general disposition to all virtues, and have no conceptions or ideas of what is evil in a rational creature, so their grand maxim is, to cultivate reason, and to be wholly governed by it. Neither is reason among them a point problematical as with us, where men can argue with plausibility on both sides of a question; but strikes you with immediate conviction; as it must needs do where it is not mingled, obscured, or discolored by passion and interest. I remember it was with extreme difficulty that I could bring my master to understand the meaning of the word *opinion,* or how a point could be disputable; because reason taught us to affirm or deny only where we are certain; and beyond our knowledge we cannot do either. So that controversies, wranglings, disputes, and positiveness in false or dubious propositions, are evils unknown among the *Houyhnhnms.* In the like manner when I used to explain to him our several systems of natural philosophy, he would laugh that a creature pretending to reason, should value itself upon the knowledge of other people's conjectures, and in things, where that knowledge, if it were certain, could be of no use. Wherein he agreed entirely with the sentiments of Socrates, as Plato [18] delivers them; which I mention as the highest honor I can do that prince of philosophers. I have often since reflected what destruction such a doctrine would make in the libraries of Europe; and how many paths to fame would be then shut up in the learned world.

Friendship and benevolence are the two principal virtues among the *Houyhnhnms;* and these not confined to particular objects, but universal to the whole race. For a stranger from the remotest part is equally treated with the nearest neighbor, and wherever he goes, looks upon himself as at home. They preserve decency and civility in the highest degrees, but are altogether ignorant of ceremony. They have no fondness for their colts or foals, but the care they take in educating them proceeds entirely from the dictates of reason. And I observed my master to show the same affection to his neighbor's issue that he had for his own. They will have it that nature teaches them to love the whole species, and it is reason only that maketh a distinction of persons, where there is a superior degree of virtue.

When the matron *Houyhnhnms* have produced one of each sex, they no longer accompany with their consorts, except they lose one of their issue by some casualty, which very seldom happens; but in such a case they meet again, or when the like accident befalls a person whose wife is past bearing, some other couple bestows on him one of their own colts, and then go together a second time until the mother be pregnant. This caution is necessary to prevent the country from being overburthened with numbers. But the race of inferior *Houyhnhnms* bred up to be servants is not so strictly limited upon this article; these are allowed to produce three of each sex, to be domestics in the noble families.

In their marriages they are exactly careful to choose such colors as will not make any disagreeable mixture in the breed. Strength is chiefly valued in the male, and comeliness in the female; not upon the account of love, but to preserve the race from degenerating; for where a female happens to excel in strength, a consort is chosen with regard to comeliness. Courtship, love, presents, jointures, settlements, have no place in their thoughts; or terms whereby to express them in their language. The young couple meet and are joined, merely because it is the determination of their parents and friends: it is what they see done every day, and they look upon it as one of the necessary actions of a reasonable being. But the violation of marriage, or any other unchastity, was never heard of: and the married pair pass their lives with the same friendship, and mutual benevolence that they bear to all others of the same species, who come in their way; without jealousy, fondness, quarreling, or discontent.

In educating the youth of both sexes, their method is admirable, and highly deserves our imitation. These are not suffered to taste a grain of oats, except upon certain days, till eighteen years old; nor milk, but very rarely; and in summer they graze two hours in the morning, and as many in the evening, which their parents likewise observe; but the servants are not allowed above half that time, and a great part of their grass is brought home, which they eat at the most convenient hours, when they can be best spared from work.

18. **Plato:** in the fifth book of the *Republic,* where he makes a distinction between opinion or conjecture and real knowledge.

Temperance, industry, exercise, and cleanliness, are the lessons equally enjoined to the young ones of both sexes: and my master thought it monstrous in us to give the females a different kind of education from the males, except in some articles of domestic management; whereby as he truly observed, one-half of our natives were good for nothing but bringing children into the world: and to trust the care of their children to such useless animals, he said, was yet a greater instance of brutality.

But the *Houyhnhnms* train up their youth to strength, speed, and hardiness, by exercising them in running races up and down steep hills, and over hard stony grounds; and when they are all in a sweat, they are ordered to leap over head and ears into a pond or a river. Four times a year the youth of certain districts meet to show their proficiency in running and leaping, and other feats of strength or agility; where the victor is rewarded with a song made in his or her praise. On this festival the servants drive a herd of *Yahoos* into the field, laden with hay, and oats, and milk, for a repast to the *Houyhnhnms;* after which, these brutes are immediately driven back again, for fear of being noisome to the assembly.

Every fourth year, at the vernal equinox, there is a representative council of the whole nation, which meets in a plain about twenty miles from our house, and continues about five or six days. Here they inquire into the state and condition of the several districts; whether they abound or be deficient in hay or oats, or cows or *Yahoos.* And wherever there is any want (which is but seldom), it is immediately supplied by unanimous consent and contribution. Here likewise the regulation of children is settled: as for instance, if a *Houyhnhnm* hath two males, he changeth one of them with another who hath two females; and when a child hath been lost by any casualty, where the mother is past breeding, it is determined what family shall breed another to supply the loss.

CHAPTER 9

A grand debate at the general assembly of the Houyhnhnms, *and how it was determined. The learning of the* Houyhnhnms. *Their buildings. Their manner of burials. The defectiveness of their language.*

One of these grand assemblies was held in my time, about three months before my departure, whither my master went as the representative of our district. In this council was resumed their old debate, and indeed, the only debate that ever happened in their country; whereof my master after his return gave me a very particular account.

The question to be debated was, whether the *Yahoos* should be exterminated from the face of the earth. One of the members for the affirmative offered several arguments of great strength and weight, alleging, that as the *Yahoos* were the most filthy, noisome, and deformed animal which nature ever produced, so they were the most restive and indocible, mischievous and malicious: they would privately suck the teats of the *Houyhnhnms'* cows, kill and devour their cats, trample down their oats and grass, if they were not continually watched, and commit a thousand other extravagancies. He took notice of a general tradition, that *Yahoos* had not been always in their country; but, that many ages ago, two of these brutes appeared together upon a mountain; whether produced by the heat of the sun upon corrupted mud and slime, or from the ooze and froth of the sea, was never known. That these *Yahoos* engendered, and their brood in a short time grew so numerous as to overrun and infest the whole nation. That the *Houyhnhnms* to get rid of this evil, made a general hunting, and at last enclosed the whole herd; and destroying the older, every *Houyhnhnm* kept two young ones in a kennel, and brought them to such a degree of tameness, as an animal so savage by nature can be capable of acquiring; using them for draught and carriage. That there seemed to be much truth in this tradition, and that those creatures could not be *Ylnhniamshy* (or *aborigines* of the land), because of the violent hatred the *Houyhnhnms,* as well as all other animals, bore them; which although their evil disposition sufficiently deserved, could never have arrived at so high a degree, if they had been aborigines, or else they would have long since been rooted out. That the inhabitants taking a fancy to use the service of the *Yahoos,* had very imprudently neglected to cultivate the breed of asses, which were a comely animal, easily kept, more tame and orderly, without any offensive smell, strong enough for labor, although they yield to the other in agility of body; and if their braying be no agreeable sound, it is far preferable to the horrible howlings of the *Yahoos.*

Several others declared their sentiments to the same purpose, when my master proposed an expedient to the assembly, whereof he had indeed borrowed the hint from me. He approved of the tradition mentioned by the honorable member, who spoke before, and affirmed, that the two *Yahoos* said to be first seen among them, had been driven thither over the sea; that coming to land, and being forsaken by their companions, they retired to the mountains, and degenerating by degrees, became in process of time, much more savage than those of their own species in the country from whence these two originals came. The reason of his assertion was, that he had now in his possession a certain wonderful *Yahoo* (meaning myself), which most of them had heard of, and many of them had seen. He then related to them, how he first found me; that my body was all covered with an artificial composure of the skins and hairs of other animals; that I spoke in a language of my own, and had thoroughly learned theirs: that I had related to him the accidents which brought me thither: that when he saw me without my covering, I was an exact *Yahoo* in every part, only of a whiter color, less hairy, and with shorter claws. He added, how I had endeavored to persuade him, that in my own and other countries the *Yahoos* acted as the governing, rational animal, and held the *Houyhnhnms* in servitude: that he observed in me all the qualities of a *Yahoo,* only a little more civilized by some tincture of reason, which however was in a degree as far inferior to the *Houyhnhnm* race, as the *Yahoos* of their country were to me: that, among other things, I mentioned a custom we had of castrating *Houyhnhnms* when they were young, in order to render them tame; that the operation was easy and safe; that it was no shame to learn wisdom from brutes, as industry is taught by the ant, and building by the swallow. (For so I translate the word *lyhannh,* although it be a much larger fowl.) That this invention might be practiced upon the younger *Yahoos* here, which, besides rendering them tractable and fitter for use, would in an age put an end to the whole species without destroying life. That in the meantime the *Houyhnhnms* should be exhorted to cultivate the breed of asses, which, as they are in all respects more valuable brutes, so they have this advantage, to be fit for service at five years old, which the others are not till twelve.

This was all my master thought fit to tell me at that time, of what passed in the grand council. But he was pleased to conceal one particular, which related personally to myself, whereof I soon felt the unhappy effect, as the reader will know in its proper place, and from whence I date all the succeeding misfortunes of my life.

The *Houyhnhnms* have no letters, and consequently their knowledge is all traditional. But there happening few events of any moment among a people so well united, naturally disposed to every virtue, wholly governed by reason, and cut off from all commerce with other nations, the historical part is easily preserved without burthening their memories. I have already observed, that they are subject to no diseases, and therefore can have no need of physicians. However, they have excellent medicines composed of herbs, to cure accidental bruises and cuts in the pastern or frog of the foot by sharp stones, as well as other maims and hurts in the several parts of the body.

They calculate the year by the revolution of the sun and moon, but use no subdivision into weeks. They are well enough acquainted with the motions of those two luminaries, and understand the nature of eclipses; and this is the utmost progress of their astronomy.

In poetry they must be allowed to excel all other mortals; wherein the justness of their similes, and the minuteness, as well as exactness of their descriptions, are indeed inimitable. Their verses abound very much in both of these, and usually contain either some exalted notions of friendship and benevolence, or the praises of those who were victors in races, and other bodily exercises. Their buildings, although very rude and simple, are not inconvenient, but well contrived to defend them from all injuries of cold and heat. They have a kind of tree, which at forty years old loosens in the root, and falls with the first storm: it grows very straight, and being pointed like stakes with a sharp stone (for the *Houyhnhnms* know not the use of iron), they stick them erect in the ground about ten inches asunder, and then weave in oat-straw, or sometimes wattles betwixt them. The roof is made after the same manner, and so are the doors.

The *Houyhnhnms* use the hollow part between the pastern and the hoof of their forefeet, as we do our hands, and this with greater dexterity than I could at first imagine. I have seen a white mare of our family thread a needle (which I lent her on purpose) with that joint. They milk their cows, reap their oats, and do all the work which requires hands, in the same manner. They have a kind of hard flints, which by grinding against other stones, they form into instruments, that serve instead of wedges, axes, and hammers. With tools made of these flints, they likewise cut their hay, and reap their oats, which there groweth naturally in several fields: the *Yahoos* draw home the sheaves in carriages, and the servants tread them in certain covered huts, to get out the grain, which is kept in stores. They make a rude kind of earthen and wooden vessels, and bake the former in the sun.

If they can avoid casualties, they die only of old age, and are buried in the obscurest places that can be found, their friends and relations expressing neither joy nor grief at their departure; nor does the dying person discover the least regret that he is leaving the world, any more than if he were upon returning home from a visit to one of his neighbors. I remember my master having once made an appointment with a friend and his family to come to his house upon some affair of importance; on the day fixed, the mistress and her two children came very late; she made two excuses, first for her husband, who, as she said, happened that very morning to *Lhnuwnh.* The word is strongly expressive in their language, but not easily rendered into English; it signifies, *to retire to his first mother.* Her excuse for not coming sooner was, that her husband dying late in the morning, she was a good while consulting her servants about a convenient place where his body should be laid; and I observed she behaved herself at our house as cheerfully as the rest. She died about three months after.

They live generally to seventy or seventy-five years, very seldom to fourscore: some weeks before their death they feel a gradual decay, but without pain. During this time they are much visited by their friends, because they cannot go abroad with their usual ease and satisfaction. However, about ten days before their death, which they seldom fail in computing, they return the visits that have been made them by those who are nearest in the neighborhood, being carried in a convenient sledge drawn by *Yahoos;* which vehicle they use, not only upon this occasion, but when they grow old, upon long journeys, or when they are lamed by any accident. And therefore when the dying *Houyhnhnms* return those visits, they take a solemn leave of their friends, as if they were going to some remote part of the country, where they designed to pass the rest of their lives.

I know not whether it may be worth observing, that the *Houyhnhnms* have no word in their language to express any thing that is evil, except what they borrow from the deformities or ill qualities of the *Yahoos.* Thus they denote the folly of a servant, an omission of a child, a stone that cuts their feet, a continuance of foul or unseasonable weather, and the like, by adding to each the epithet of *Yahoo.* For instance, *Hhnm Yahoo, Whnaholm Yahoo, Ynlhmnawihlma Yahoo,* and an ill-contrived house *Ynholmhnmrohlnw Yahoo.*

I could with great pleasure enlarge farther upon the manners and virtues of this excellent people; but intending in a short time to publish a volume by itself expressly upon that subject, I refer the reader thither. And in the meantime, proceed to relate my own sad catastrophe.

CHAPTER 10

The Author's economy, and happy life among the Houyhnhnms. *His great improvement in virtue, by conversing with them. Their conversations. The Author has notice given him by his master that he must depart from the country. He falls into a swoon for grief, but submits. He contrives and finishes a canoe, by the help of a fellow-servant, and puts to sea at a venture.*

I had settled my little economy to my own heart's content. My master had ordered a room to be made for me after their manner, about six yards from the house; the sides and floors of which I plastered with clay, and covered with rush mats of my own contriving; I had beaten hemp, which there grows wild, and made of it a sort of ticking: this I filled with the feathers of several birds I had taken with springes made of *Yahoos'* hairs, and were excellent food. I had worked two chairs with my knife, the sorrel nag helping me in the grosser and more laborious part. When my clothes were worn to rags, I made myself others with the skins of rabbits, and of a certain beautiful animal about the same size, called *nnuhnoh,* the skin of which is covered with a fine down. Of these I likewise made very tolerable stockings. I soled my shoes with wood which I cut from a tree, and fitted to the upper leather, and when this was worn out, I supplied it with the skins of *Yahoos* dried in the sun. I often got honey out of hollow trees, which I mingled with water, or eat it with my bread. No man could more verify the truth of these two maxims, *That nature is very easily satisfied;* and *That necessity is the mother of invention.* I enjoyed perfect health of body, and tranquillity of mind; I did not feel the treachery or inconstancy of a friend, nor the injuries of a secret or open enemy. I had no occasion of bribing, flattering, or pimping, to procure the favor of any great man or of his minion.

I wanted no fence against fraud or oppression; here was neither physician to destroy my body, nor lawyer to ruin my fortune; no informer to watch my words and actions, or forge accusations against me for hire; here were no gibers, censurers, backbiters, pickpockets, highwaymen, housebreakers, attorneys, bawds, buffoons, gamesters, politicians, wits, splenetics, tedious talkers, controvertists, ravishers, murderers, robbers, virtuosos; no leaders or followers of party and faction; no encouragers to vice, by seducement or examples; no dungeon, axes, gibbets, whipping posts, or pillories; no cheating shopkeepers or mechanics; no pride, vanity, or affectation; no fops, bullies, drunkards, strolling whores, or poxes; no ranting, lewd, expensive wives; no stupid, proud pedants; no importunate, overbearing, quarrelsome, noisy, roaring, empty, conceited, swearing companions; no scoundrels, raised from the dust upon the merit of their vices, or nobility thrown into it on account of their virtues; no lords, fiddlers, judges or dancing masters.

I had the favor of being admitted to several *Houyhnhnms,* who came to visit or dine with my master; where his Honor graciously suffered me to wait in the room, and listen to their discourse. Both he and his company would often descend to ask me questions, and receive my answers. I had also sometimes the honor of attending my master in his visits to others. I never presumed to speak, except in answer to a question; and then I did it with inward regret, because it was a loss of so much time for improving myself: but I was infinitely delighted with the station of an humble auditor in such conversations, where nothing passed but what was useful, expressed in the fewest and most significant words; where (as I have already said) the greatest decency was observed, without the least degree of ceremony; where no person spoke without being pleased himself, and pleasing his companions; where there was no interruption, tediousness, heat, or difference of sentiments. They have a notion, that when people are met together, a short silence doth much improve conversation: this I found to be true; for during those little intermissions of talk, new ideas would arise in their minds, which very much enlivened the discourse. Their subjects are generally on friendship and benevolence, on order and economy; sometimes upon the visible operations of nature, or ancient traditions; upon the bounds and limits of virtue; upon the unerring rules of reason, or upon some determinations to be taken at the next great assembly; and often upon the various excellencies of poetry. I may add, without vanity, that my presence often gave them sufficient matter for discourse, because it afforded my master an occasion of letting his friends into the history of me and my country, upon which they were all pleased to descant in a manner not very advantageous to human kind; and for that reason I shall not repeat what they said: only I may be allowed to observe, that his Honor, to my great admiration, appeared to understand the nature of *Yahoos* much better than myself. He went through all our vices and follies, and discovered many which I had never mentioned to him, by only supposing what qualities a *Yahoo* of their country, with a small proportion of reason, might be capable of exerting; and concluded, with too much probability, how vile as well as miserable such a creature must be.

I freely confess, that all the little knowledge I have of any value, was acquired by the lectures I received from my master, and from hearing the discourses of him and his friends; to which I should be prouder to listen, than to dictate to the greatest and wisest assembly in Europe. I admired the strength, comeliness, and speed of the inhabitants; and such a constellation of virtues in such amiable persons produced in me the highest veneration. At first, indeed, I did not feel that natural awe which the *Yahoos* and all other animals bear towards them; but it grew upon me by degrees, much sooner than I imagined, and was mingled with a respectful love and gratitude, that they would condescend to distinguish me from the rest of my species.

When I thought of my family, my friends, my countrymen, or human race in general, I considered them as they really were, *Yahoos* in shape and disposition, perhaps a little more civilized, and qualified with the gift of speech, but making no other use of reason, than to improve and multiply those vices, whereof their brethren in this country had only the share that nature allotted them. When I happened to behold the reflection of my own form in a lake or fountain, I turned away my face in horror and detestation of myself, and could better endure the sight of a common *Yahoo,* than of my own person. By conversing with the *Houyhnhnms,* and looking upon them with delight, I fell to imitate their gait and gesture, which is now grown into a habit, and my friends often tell me in a blunt way, that *I trot like a horse;* which, however, I take for a great compliment. Neither shall I disown, that in speaking I am apt to fall into the voice and manner of the *Houyhnhnms,* and hear myself ridiculed on that account without the least mortification.

In the midst of all this happiness, and when I looked upon myself to be fully settled for life, my master sent for me one morning a little earlier than his usual hour. I observed by his countenance that he was in some perplexity, and at a loss how to begin what he had to speak. After a short silence, he told me, he did not know how I would take what he was going to say; that in the last general assembly, when the affair of the *Yahoos* was entered upon, the representatives had taken offense at his keeping a *Yahoo* (meaning myself) in his family more like a *Houyhnhnm* than a brute animal. That he was known frequently to converse with me, as if he could receive some advantage or pleasure in my company; that such a practice was not agreeable to reason or nature, or a thing ever heard of before among them. The assembly did therefore exhort him, either to employ me like the rest of my species, or command me to swim back to the place from whence I came. That the first of these expedients was utterly rejected by all the *Houyhnhnms* who had ever seen me at his house or their own: for they alleged, that because I had some rudiments of reason, added to the natural pravity of those animals, it was to be feared, I might be able to seduce them into the woody and mountainous parts of the country, and bring them in troops by night to destroy the *Houyhnhnms'* cattle, as being naturally of the ravenous kind, and averse from labor.

My master added, that he was daily pressed by the *Houyhnhnms* of the neighborhood to have the assembly's exhortation executed, which he could not put off much longer. He doubted it would be impossible for me to swim to another country, and therefore wished I would contrive some sort of vehicle resembling those I had described to him, that might carry me on the sea; in which work I should have the assistance of his own servants, as well as those of his neighbors. He concluded, that for his own part, he could have been content to keep me in his service as long as I lived; because he found I had cured myself of some bad habits and dispositions, by endeavoring, as far as my inferior nature was capable, to imitate the *Houyhnhnms.*

I should here observe to the reader, that a decree of the general assembly in this country is expressed by the word *hnhloayn,* which signifies an exhortation, as near as I can render it; for they have no conception how a rational creature can be compelled, but only advised, or exhorted; because no person can disobey reason, without giving up his claim to be a rational creature.

I was struck with the utmost grief and despair at my master's discourse; and being unable to support the agonies I was under, I fell into a swoon at his feet: when I came to myself, he told me, that he concluded I had been dead (for these people are subject to no such imbecilities of nature). I answered, in a faint voice, that death would have been too great an happiness; that although I could not blame the assembly's exhortation, or the urgency of his friends; yet, in my weak and corrupt judgment, I thought it might consist with reason to have been less rigorous. That I could not swim a league, and probably the nearest land to theirs might be distant above an hundred: that many materials, necessary for making a small vessel to carry me off, were wholly wanting in this country, which, however, I would attempt in obedience and gratitude to his Honor, although I concluded the thing to be impossible, and therefore looked on myself as already devoted to destruction. That the certain prospect of an unnatural death was the least of my evils: for, supposing I should escape with life by some strange adventure; how could I think with temper [19] of passing my days among *Yahoos,* and relapsing into my old corruptions, for want of examples to lead and keep me within the paths of virtue. That I knew too well upon what solid reasons all the determinations of the wise *Houyhnhnms* were founded, not to be shaken by arguments of mine, a miserable *Yahoo;* and therefore, after presenting him with my humble thanks for the offer of his servants' assistance in making a vessel, and desiring a reasonable time for so difficult a work, I told him I would endeavor to preserve a wretched being; and, if ever I returned to England, was not without hopes of being useful to my own species, by celebrating the praises of the renowned *Houyhnhnms,* and proposing their virtues to the imitation of mankind.

My master in a few words made me a very gracious reply, allowed me the space of two months to finish my boat; and ordered the sorrel nag, my fellow servant (for so at this distance I may presume to call him) to follow my instructions, because I

19. **temper:** calmness of mind.

told my master, that his help would be sufficient, and I knew he had a tenderness for me.

In his company my first business was to go to that part of the coast where my rebellious crew had ordered me to be set on shore. I got upon a height, and looking on every side into the sea, fancied I saw a small island, towards the northeast: I took out my pocket glass, and could then clearly distinguish it about five leagues off, as I computed; but it appeared to the sorrel nag to be only a blue cloud: for, as he had no conception of any country beside his own, so he could not be as expert in distinguishing remote objects at sea, as we who so much converse in that element.

After I had discovered this island, I considered no farther; but resolved it should, if possible, be the first place of my banishment, leaving the consequence to fortune.

I returned home, and consulting with the sorrel nag, we went into a copse at some distance, where I with my knife, and he with a sharp flint fastened very artificially,[20] after their manner, to a wooden handle, cut down several oak wattles about the thickness of a walking staff, and some larger pieces. But I shall not trouble the reader with a particular description of my own mechanics; let it suffice to say, that in six weeks' time, with the help of the sorrel nag, who performed the parts that required most labor, I finished a sort of Indian canoe, but much larger, covering it with the skins of Yahoos well stitched together, with hempen threads of my own making. My sail was likewise composed of the skins of the same animal; but I made use of the youngest I could get, the older being too tough and thick; and I likewise provided myself with four paddles. I laid in a stock of boiled flesh, of rabbits and fowls, and took with me two vessels, one filled with milk, and the other with water.

I tried my canoe in a large pond near my master's house, and then corrected in it what was amiss; stopping all the chinks with Yahoos' tallow, till I found it staunch, and able to bear me, and my freight. And when it was as complete as I could possibly make it, I had it drawn on a carriage very gently by Yahoos to the seaside, under the conduct of the sorrel nag, and another servant.

When all was ready, and the day came for my departure, I took leave of my master and lady, and the whole family, my eyes flowing with tears,

and my heart quite sunk with grief. But his Honor, out of curiosity, and, perhaps (if I may speak it without vanity) partly out of kindness, was determined to see me in my canoe, and got several of his neighboring friends to accompany him. I was forced to wait above an hour for the tide, and then observing the wind very fortunately bearing towards the island, to which I intended to steer my course, I took a second leave of my master: but as I was going to prostrate myself to kiss his hoof, he did me the honor to raise it gently to my mouth. I am not ignorant how much I have been censured for mentioning this last particular. For my detractors are pleased to think it improbable, that so illustrious a person should descend to give so great a mark of distinction to a creature so inferior as I. Neither have I forgot, how apt some travelers are to boast of extraordinary favors they have received. But if these censurers were better acquainted with the noble and courteous disposition of the Houyhnhnms, they would soon change their opinion.

I paid my respects to the rest of the Houyhnhnms in his Honor's company; then getting into my canoe, I pushed off from shore.

CHAPTER II

The Author's dangerous voyage. He arrives at New Holland, *hoping to settle there. Is wounded with an arrow by one of the natives. Is seized and carried by force into a* Portuguese *ship. The great civilities of the Captain. The Author arrives at* England.

I began this desperate voyage on February 15, 1714–15, at nine o'clock in the morning. The wind was very favorable; however, I made use at first only of my paddles; but considering I should soon be weary, and that the wind might probably chop about, I ventured to set up my little sail; and thus, with the help of the tide, I went at the rate of a league and a half an hour, as near as I could guess. My master and his friends continued on the shore, till I was almost out of sight; and I often heard the sorrel nag (who always loved me) crying out, *Hnuy illa nyha majah Yahoo,* Take care of thyself, gentle *Yahoo.*

My design was, if possible, to discover some small island uninhabited, yet sufficient by my labor to furnish me with necessaries of life, which I would have thought a greater happiness than to be first minister in the politest court of Europe; so horrible was the idea I conceived of returning to live in the

20. artificially: ingeniously.

society and under the government of *Yahoos.* For in such a solitude as I desired, I could at least enjoy my own thoughts, and reflect with delight on the virtues of those inimitable *Houyhnhnms,* without any opportunity of degenerating into the vices and corruptions of my own species.

The reader may remember what I related when my crew conspired against me, and confined me to my cabin. How I continued there several weeks, without knowing what course we took; and when I was put ashore in the longboat, how the sailors told me with oaths, whether true or false, that they knew not in what part of the world we were. However, I did then believe us to be about ten degrees southward of the Cape of Good Hope, or about forty-five degrees southern latitude, as I gathered from some general words I overheard among them, being I supposed to the southeast in their intended voyage to Madagascar. And although this were little better than conjecture, yet I resolved to steer my course eastward, hoping to reach the southwest coast of New Holland, and perhaps some such island as I desired, lying westward of it. The wind was full west, and by six in the evening I computed I had gone eastward at least eighteen leagues, when I spied a very small island about half a league off, which I soon reached. It was nothing but a rock with one creek, naturally arched by the force of tempests. Here I put in my canoe, and climbing up a part of the rock, I could plainly discover land to the east, extending from south to north. I lay all night in my canoe; and repeating my voyage early in the morning, I arrived in seven hours to the southeast point of New Holland.[21] This confirmed me in the opinion I have long entertained, that the maps and charts place this country at least three degrees more to the east than it really is; which thought I communicated many years ago to my worthy friend Mr. Herman Moll,[22] and gave him my reasons for it, although he hath rather chosen to follow other authors.

I saw no inhabitants in the place where I landed, and being unarmed, I was afraid of venturing far into the country. I found some shellfish on the shore, and eat them raw, not daring to kindle a fire, for fear of being discovered by the natives. I continued three days feeding on oysters and limpets,

to save my own provisions; and I fortunately found a brook of excellent water, which gave me great relief.

On the fourth day, venturing out early a little too far, I saw twenty or thirty natives upon a height, not above five hundred yards from me. They were stark naked, men, women, and children round a fire, as I could discover by the smoke. One of them spied me, and gave notice to the rest; five of them advanced towards me, leaving the women and children at the fire. I made what haste I could to the shore, and getting into my canoe, shoved off: the savages observing me retreat, ran after me; and before I could get far enough into the sea, discharged an arrow, which wounded me deeply on the inside of my left knee (I shall carry the mark to my grave). I apprehended the arrow might be poisoned, and paddling out of the reach of their darts (being a calm day), I made a shift to suck the wound, and dress it as well as I could.

I was at a loss what to do, for I durst not return to the same landing place, but stood to the north, and was forced to paddle; for the wind, though very gentle, was against me, blowing northwest. As I was looking about for a secure landing place, I saw a sail to the north-northeast, which appearing every minute more visible, I was in some doubt whether I should wait for them or no; but at last my detestation of the *Yahoo* race prevailed, and turning my canoe, I sailed and paddled together to the south, and got into the same creek from whence I set out in the morning, choosing rather to trust myself among these barbarians, than live with European *Yahoos.* I drew up my canoe as close as I could to the shore, and hid myself behind a stone by the little brook, which, as I have already said, was excellent water.

The ship came within half a league of this creek, and sent her longboat with vessels to take in fresh water (for the place it seems was very well known), but I did not observe it until the boat was almost on shore, and it was too late to seek another hiding place. The seamen at their landing observed my canoe, and rummaging it all over, easily conjectured that the owner could not be far off. Four of them well armed searched every cranny and lurking hole, until at last they found me flat on my face behind the stone. They gazed awhile in admiration at my strange uncouth dress; my coat made of skins, my wooden-soled shoes, and my furred stockings; from whence, however, they concluded I was not a native of the place, who all go

21. **New Holland:** The apparent confusion between the "southwest coast" and "southeast point" can be cleared up by reference to the very simple map Swift provided, in which the land of the Houyhnhnms is shown as a large island, west of the coast of Australia, which runs from the northwest to the southeast.
22. **Herman Moll:** a famous Dutch mapmaker, who settled in London in 1698.

naked. One of the seamen in Portuguese bid me rise, and asked who I was. I understood that language very well, and getting upon my feet, said, I was a poor *Yahoo,* banished from the *Houyhnhnms,* and desired they would please to let me depart. They admired to hear me answer them in their own tongue, and saw by my complexion I must be an European; but were at a loss to know what I meant by *Yahoos* and *Houyhnhnms,* and at the same time fell a laughing at my strange tone in speaking, which resembled the neighing of a horse. I trembled all the while betwixt fear and hatred. I again desired leave to depart, and was gently moving to my canoe; but they laid hold on me, desiring to know, what country I was of? whence I came? with many other questions. I told them, I was born in England, from whence I came about five years ago, and then their country and ours were at peace. I therefore hoped they would not treat me as an enemy, since I meant them no harm, but was a poor *Yahoo,* seeking some desolate place where to pass the remainder of his unfortunate life.

When they began to talk, I thought I never heard or saw anything so unnatural; for it appeared to me as monstrous as if a dog or a cow should speak in England, or a *Yahoo* in *Houyhnhnm-land.* The honest Portuguese were equally amazed at my strange dress, and the odd manner of delivering my words, which however they understood very well. They spoke to me with great humanity, and said they were sure their Captain would carry me *gratis* to Lisbon, from whence I might return to my own country; that two of the seamen would go back to the ship, to inform the Captain of what they had seen, and receive his orders; in the meantime, unless I would give my solemn oath not to fly, they would secure me by force. I thought it best to comply with their proposal. They were very curious to know my story, but I gave them very little satisfaction; and they all conjectured that my misfortunes had impaired my reason. In two hours the boat, which went loaden with vessels of water, returned with the Captain's commands to fetch me on board. I fell on my knees to preserve my liberty; but all was in vain, and the men having tied me with cords, heaved me into the boat, from whence I was taken into the ship, and from thence into the Captain's cabin.

His name was Pedro de Mendez; he was a very courteous and generous person; he entreated me to give some account of myself, and desired to know what I would eat or drink; said, I should be used as well as himself, and spoke so many obliging things, that I wondered to find such civilities from a *Yahoo.* However, I remained silent and sullen; I was ready to faint at the very smell of him and his men. At last I desired something to eat out of my own canoe; but he ordered me a chicken and some excellent wine, and then directed that I should be put to bed in a very clean cabin. I would not undress myself, but lay on the bedclothes, and in half an hour stole out, when I thought the crew was at dinner, and getting to the side of the ship was going to leap into the sea, and swim for my life, rather than continue among *Yahoos.* But one of the seamen prevented me, and having informed the Captain, I was chained to my cabin.

After dinner Don Pedro came to me, and desired to know my reason for so desperate an attempt; assured me he only meant to do me all the service he was able; and spoke so very movingly, that at last I descended to treat him like an animal which had some little portion of reason. I gave him a very short relation of my voyage; of the conspiracy against me by my own men; of the country where they set me on shore, and of my five years' residence there. All which he looked upon as if it were a dream or a vision; whereat I took great offense; for I had quite forgot the faculty of lying, so peculiar to *Yahoos* in all countries where they preside, and, consequently the disposition of suspecting truth in others of their own species. I asked him, whether it were the custom of his country to *say the thing that was not?* I assured him I had almost forgot what he meant by falsehood, and if I had lived a thousand years in *Houyhnhnm-land,* I should never have heard a lie from the meanest servant; that I was altogether indifferent whether he believed me or no; but however, in return for his favors, I would give so much allowance to the corruption of his nature, as to answer any objection he would please to make; and he might easily discover the truth.

The Captain, a wise man, after many endeavors to catch me tripping in some part of my story, at last began to have a better opinion of my veracity. But he added, that since I professed so inviolable an attachment to truth, I must give him my word of honor to bear him company in this voyage, without attempting anything against my life, or else he would continue me a prisoner until we arrived at Lisbon. I gave him the promise he required; but at the same time protested that I would suffer the greatest hardships rather than return to live among *Yahoos.*

Our voyage passed without any considerable accident. In gratitude to the Captain I sometimes sat with him at his earnest request, and strove to conceal my antipathy against human kind, although it often broke out, which he suffered to pass without observation. But the greatest part of the day, I confined myself to my cabin, to avoid seeing any of the crew. The Captain had often entreated me to strip myself of my savage dress, and offered to lend me the best suit of clothes he had. This I would not be prevailed on to accept, abhorring to cover myself with anything that had been on the back of a *Yahoo.* I only desired he would lend me two clean shirts, which having been washed since he wore them, I believed would not so much defile me. These I changed every second day, and washed them myself.

We arrived at Lisbon, Nov. 5, 1715. At our landing the Captain forced me to cover myself with his cloak, to prevent the rabble from crowding about me. I was conveyed to his own house, and at my earnest request, he led me up to the highest room backwards.[23] I conjured him to conceal from all persons what I had told him of the *Houyhnhnms,* because the least hint of such a story would not only draw numbers of people to see me, but probably put me in danger of being imprisoned, or burnt by the Inquisition. The Captain persuaded me to accept a suit of clothes newly made; but I would not suffer the tailor to take my measure; however, Don Pedro being almost my size, they fitted me well enough. He accoutered me with other necessaries all new, which I aired for twenty-four hours before I would use them.

The Captain had no wife, nor above three servants, none of which were suffered to attend at meals, and his whole deportment was so obliging, added to very good *human* understanding, that I really began to tolerate his company. He gained so far upon me, that I ventured to look out of the back window. By degrees I was brought into another room, from whence I peeped into the street, but drew my head back in a fright. In a week's time he seduced me down to the door. I found my terror gradually lessened, but my hatred and contempt seemed to increase. I was at last bold enough to walk the street in his company, but kept my nose well stopped with rue, or sometimes with tobacco.

23. backwards: at the rear of the house.

In ten days, Don Pedro, to whom I had given some account of my domestic affairs, put it upon me as a point of honor and conscience, that I ought to return to my native country, and live at home with my wife and children. He told me, there was an English ship in the port just ready to sail, and he would furnish me with all things necessary. It would be tedious to repeat his arguments, and my contradictions. He said it was altogether impossible to find such a solitary island as I had desired to live in; but I might command in my own house, and pass my time in a manner as recluse as I pleased.

I complied at last, finding I could not do better. I left Lisbon the 24th day of November, in an English merchantman, but who was the master I never inquired. Don Pedro accompanied me to the ship, and lent me twenty pounds. He took kind leave of me, and embraced me at parting, which I bore as well as I could. During this last voyage I had no commerce with the master or any of his men; but pretending I was sick, kept close in my cabin. On the 5th of December, 1715, we cast anchor in the Downs about nine in the morning, and at three in the afternoon I got safe to my house at Redriff.

My wife and family received me with great surprise and joy, because they concluded me certainly dead; but I must freely confess the sight of them filled me only with hatred, disgust, and contempt, and the more by reflecting on the near alliance I had to them. For, although since my unfortunate exile from the *Houyhnhnm* country, I had compelled myself to tolerate the sight of *Yahoos,* and to converse with Don Pedro de Mendez; yet my memory and imagination were perpetually filled with the virtues and ideas of those exalted *Houyhnhnms.* And when I began to consider, that by copulating with one of the *Yahoo* species I had become a parent of more, it struck me with the utmost shame, confusion, and horror.

As soon as I entered the house, my wife took me in her arms, and kissed me; at which, having not been used to the touch of that odious animal for so many years, I fell in a swoon for almost an hour. At the time I am writing it is five years [24] since my last return to England: during the first year, I could not endure my wife or children in my presence, the very smell of them was intolerable; much less could I suffer them to eat in the same room.

24. five years: i.e., the beginning of 1721. The first reference Swift makes to "writing a history of my Travels" is in a letter of April, 1721.

To this hour they dare not presume to touch my bread, or drink out of the same cup, neither was I ever able to let one of them take me by the hand. The first money I laid out was to buy two young stone-horses, which I keep in a good stable, and next to them the groom is my greatest favorite; for I feel my spirits revived by the smell he contracts in the stable. My horses understand me tolerably well; I converse with them at least four hours every day. They are strangers to bridle or saddle; they live in great amity with me, and friendship to each other.

CHAPTER 12

The Author's veracity. His design in publishing this work. His censure of those travelers who swerve from the truth. The Author clears himself from any sinister ends in writing. An objection answered. The method of planting colonies. His native country commended. The right of the Crown to those countries described by the Author is justified. The difficulty of conquering them. The Author takes his last leave of the reader; proposeth his manner of living for the future; gives good advice, and concludes.

Thus, gentle reader, I have given thee a faithful history of my travels for sixteen years and above seven months; wherein I have not been so studious of ornament as of truth. I could perhaps like others have astonished thee with strange improbable tales; but I rather chose to relate plain matter of fact in the simplest manner and style; because my principal design was to inform, and not to amuse thee.

It is easy for us who travel into remote countries, which are seldom visited by Englishmen or other Europeans, to form descriptions of wonderful animals both at sea and land. Whereas a traveler's chief aim should be to make men wiser and better, and to improve their minds by the bad as well as good example of what they deliver concerning foreign places.

I could heartily wish a law were enacted, that every traveler, before he were permitted to publish his voyages, should be obliged to make oath before the Lord High Chancellor that all he intended to print was absolutely true to the best of his knowledge; for then the world would no longer be deceived as it usually is, while some writers, to make their works pass the better upon the public, impose the grossest falsities on the unwary reader. I have perused several books of travels with great delight in my younger days; but having since gone over most parts of the globe, and been able to con-

tradict many fabulous accounts from my own observation, it hath given me a great disgust against this part of reading, and some indignation to see the credulity of mankind so impudently abused. Therefore, since my acquaintance were pleased to think my poor endeavors might not be unacceptable to my country, I imposed on myself as a maxim, never to be swerved from, that I would *strictly adhere to truth;* neither indeed can I be ever under the least temptation to vary from it, while I retain in my mind the lectures and example of my noble master, and the other illustrious *Houyhnhnms,* of whom I had so long the honor to be an humble hearer.

> *Nec si miserum Fortuna Sinonem*
> *Finxit, vanum etiam, mendacemque improba*
> *finget.*[25]

I know very well how little reputation is to be got by writings which require neither genius nor learning, nor indeed any other talent, except a good memory, or an exact journal. I know likewise, that writers of travels, like dictionary makers, are sunk into oblivion by the weight and bulk of those who come last, and therefore lie uppermost. And it is highly probable, that such travelers who shall hereafter visit the countries described in this work of mine, may, by detecting my errors (if there be any), and adding many new discoveries of their own, jostle me out of vogue, and stand in my place, making the world forget that I was ever an author. This indeed would be too great a mortification if I wrote for fame: but, as my sole intention was the PUBLIC GOOD, I cannot be altogether disappointed. For who can read of the virtues I have mentioned in the glorious *Houyhnhnms,* without being ashamed of his own vices, when he considers himself as the reasoning, governing animal of his country? I shall say nothing of those remote nations where *Yahoos* preside; amongst which the least corrupted are the *Brobdingnagians,* whose wise maxims in morality and government it would be our happiness to observe. But I forbear descanting further, and rather leave the judicious reader to his own remarks and applications.

I am not a little pleased that this work of mine can possibly meet with no censurers: for what objections can be made against a writer who relates only plain facts that happened in such distant countries, where we have not the least interest with

---

25. *Nec . . . finget:* "Though Fortune has made Sinon wretched, she shall not for all her malice make him a cheat and a liar."

respect either to trade or negotiations? I have carefully avoided every fault with which common writers of travels are often too justly charged. Besides, I meddle not the least with any party, but write without passion, prejudice, or ill will against any man or number of men whatsoever. I write for the noblest end, to inform and instruct mankind, over whom I may, without breach of modesty, pretend to some superiority, from the advantages I received by conversing so long among the most accomplished *Houyhnhnms.* I write without any view towards profit [26] or praise. I never suffer a word to pass that may look like reflection, or possibly give the least offense even to those who are most ready to take it. So that I hope I may with justice pronounce myself an author perfectly blameless, against whom the tribes of answerers, considerers, observers, reflecters, detecters, remarkers, will never be able to find matter for exercising their talents.

I confess, it was whispered to me, that I was bound in duty as a subject of England, to have given in a memorial to a secretary of state, at my first coming over; because, whatever lands are discovered by a subject, belong to the Crown. But I doubt whether our conquests in the countries I treat of, would be as easy as those of Ferdinando Cortes [27] over the naked Americans. The *Lilliputians* I think, are hardly worth the charge of a fleet and army to reduce them; and I question whether it might be prudent or safe to attempt the *Brobdingnagians;* or whether an English army would be much at their ease with the Flying Island [28] over their heads. The *Houyhnhnms,* indeed, appear not to be so well prepared for war, a science to which they are perfect strangers, and especially against missive weapons. However, supposing myself to be a minister of state, I could never give my advice for invading them. Their prudence, unanimity, unacquaintedness with fear, and their love of their country, would amply supply all defects in the military art. Imagine twenty thousand of them breaking into the midst of an European army, confounding the ranks, overturning the carriages, battering the warriors' faces into mummy by terrible yerks from their hinder hoofs; for they would well deserve the character given to Augustus: *Recalcitrat undique tutus.*[29] But instead of proposals for con-

26. **profit:** Swift sold the book for £200.   27. **Cortes:** who subdued the Mexicans with only a handful of Spanish troops.
28. **Flying Island:** one of the episodes of Book III, here omitted.
29. **Recalcitrat . . . tutus:** An odd way to bring in Horace's warning against approaching the Emperor Augustus at the wrong moment, when, like a restive horse, "he will kick himself clear on all sides" (*Satires,* II.i.20).

quering that magnanimous nation, I rather wish they were in a capacity or disposition to send a sufficient number of their inhabitants for civilizing Europe, by teaching us the first principles of honor, justice, truth, temperance, public spirit, fortitude, chastity, friendship, benevolence, and fidelity. The names of all which virtues are still retained among us in most languages and are to be met with in modern as well as ancient authors; which I am able to assert from my own small reading.

But I had another reason which made me less forward to enlarge his Majesty's dominions by my discoveries. To say the truth, I had conceived a few scruples with relation to the distributive justice of princes upon those occasions. For instance, a crew of pirates are driven by a storm they know not whither; at length a boy discovers land from the topmast; they go on shore to rob and plunder; they see an harmless people, are entertained with kindness, they give the country a new name, they take formal possession of it for the king, they set up a rotten plank or a stone for a memorial, they murder two or three dozen of the natives, bring away a couple more by force for a sample, return home, and get their pardon. Here commences a new dominion acquired with a title by *divine right.* Ships are sent with the first opportunity; the natives driven out or destroyed, their princes tortured to discover their gold; a free license given to all acts of inhumanity and lust; the earth reeking with the blood of its inhabitants: and this execrable crew of butchers employed in so pious an expedition, is a *modern colony* sent to convert and civilize an idolatrous and barbarous people.

But this description, I confess, doth by no means affect the British nation, who may be an example to the whole world for their wisdom, care, and justice in planting colonies; their liberal endowments for the advancement of religion and learning; their choice of devout and able pastors to propagate Christianity; their caution in stocking their provinces with people of sober lives and conversations from this the mother kingdom; their strict regard to the distribution of justice, in supplying the civil administration through all their colonies with officers of the greatest abilities, utter strangers to corruption; and to crown all, by sending the most vigilant and virtuous governors, who have no other views than the happiness of the people over whom they preside, and the honor of the King their master.

But, as those countries which I have described

do not appear to have a desire of being conquered, and enslaved, murdered or driven out by colonies; nor abound either in gold, silver, sugar, or tobacco; I did humbly conceive, they were by no means proper objects of our zeal, our valor, or our interest. However, if those whom it may concern think fit to be of another opinion, I am ready to depose, when I shall be lawfully called, that no European did ever visit these countries before me. I mean, if the inhabitants ought to be believed. . . .

But, as to the formality of taking possession in my Sovereign's name, it never came once into my thoughts; and if it had, yet as my affairs then stood, I should perhaps in point of prudence and self-preservation, have put it off to a better opportunity.

Having thus answered the *only* objection that can ever be raised against me as a traveler, I here take a final leave of my courteous readers, and return to enjoy my own speculations in my little garden at Redriff; to apply those excellent lessons of virtue which I learned among the *Houyhnhnms;* to instruct the *Yahoos* of my own family as far as I shall find them docible animals; to behold my figure often in a glass, and thus if possible habituate myself by time to tolerate the sight of a human creature: to lament the brutality of *Houyhnhnms* in my own country, but always treat their persons with respect, for the sake of my noble master, his family, his friends, and the whole *Houyhnhnm* race, whom these of ours have the honor to resemble in all their lineaments, however their intellectuals came to degenerate.

I began last week to permit my wife to sit at dinner with me, at the farthest end of a long table; and to answer (but with the utmost brevity) the few questions I asked her. Yet the smell of a *Yahoo* continuing very offensive, I always keep my nose well stopped with rue, lavender, or tobacco leaves. And although it be hard for a man late in life to remove old habits, I am not altogether out of hopes in some time to suffer a neighbor *Yahoo* in my company, without the apprehensions I am yet under of his teeth or his claws.

My reconcilement to the *Yahoo*-kind in general might not be so difficult, if they would be content with those vices and follies only which nature hath entitled them to. I am not in the least provoked at the sight of a lawyer, a pickpocket, a colonel, a fool, a lord, a gamester, a politician, a whoremonger, a physician, an evidence, a suborner, an attorney, a traitor, or the like; this is all according to the due course of things: but when I behold a lump of deformity, and diseases both in body and mind, smitten with *pride,*[30] it immediately breaks all the measures of my patience; neither shall I be ever able to comprehend how such an animal and such a vice could tally together. The wise and virtuous *Houyhnhnms,* who abound in all excellencies that can adorn a rational creature, have no name for this vice in their language, which hath no terms to express anything that is evil, except those whereby they describe the detestable qualities of their *Yahoos,* among which they were not able to distinguish this of pride, for want of thoroughly understanding human nature, as it showeth itself in other countries, where that animal presides. But I, who had more experience, could plainly observe some rudiments of it among the wild *Yahoos.*

But the *Houyhnhnms,* who live under the government of reason, are no more proud of the good qualities they possess, than I should be for not wanting a leg or an arm, which no man in his wits would boast of, although he must be miserable without them. I dwell the longer upon this subject from the desire I have to make the society of an English *Yahoo* by any means not insupportable; and therefore I here entreat those who have any tincture of this absurd vice, that they will not presume to appear in my sight.

Finis

30. *pride:* which the moralists represent as the chief error of mankind. Cf. Pope's *Essay on Man,* "In pride, in reasoning pride, our error lies," which the Church regarded as the deadliest of the seven deadly sins, and which was the cause of the fall of Satan, the great rebel against God.

GEOFFREY TILLOTSON, *Editor*

Alexander Pope

1688–1744

ALEXANDER POPE was born in time to catch a glimpse of another Londoner, the great poet Dryden, who died when Pope was twelve. He showed his precocity by greeting the sight in Latin, " Tantum Virgilium vidi," " I have seen the great Virgil." Pope was one of the poets who matured early. His parents must have been as anxious about him as they were proud — his obvious genius was accommodated, partly as a result of his hard studying, in so tiny and crippled a bodily shape that, later on, his friends would refer to his " little, tender and crazy carcase " and his enemies call him " ape " — " monkey " would have better fitted his size (he was less than five feet high), but " ape " cleverly drew on the first and last letters of his name. His father was a linen merchant and a Roman Catholic. At that time members of the Catholic Church were more or less persecuted in England and in consequence Alexander received little regular schooling. About 1700 the family moved out of the City to a small village near Windsor Forest, and later, just before his father's death in 1717, to Chiswick, which is now part of London. The year after, Pope and his mother (who did not die till 1733, at the age of 91) finally settled in a delightful villa on the beautiful banks of the Thames at Twickenham, where he spent much time and care on making a garden, and decorating its grotto with pretty stones.

While still in his teens he wrote distinguished poems, and soon became associated with the best writers of the time, first with Wycherley, Rowe, Gay, and Parnell, and later with Swift, Addison (whom he admired as a writer but disliked as a man), and Steele. With some of them he formed the Scriblerus Club, which informally drew up a program intended to encourage good writing by precept and example, and to discourage bad mainly by holding it up to ridicule — Pope's right to belong to such a group was abundantly clear from his having published the *Essay on Criticism* in 1711. By 1717 he had written more than enough splendid and often substantial poems to fill a weighty volume called *Works,* the companion volume having to wait until 1735.

Meanwhile he had translated the *Iliad* and the *Odyssey,* the sales of these handsome many-volumed editions being managed so profitably that by the time he reached his thirties he could live the sort of life he prized. His aim was elegance rather than display, an elegance that we can guess at from the writings, both in verse and prose, now that no traces are left of his villa and only a few of the garden. His happiness came mainly from his home life, and his men and women friends — he did not marry. With all the facts before us, however, we must conclude that some of his happiness came from getting into hot water. He was at the center of many quarrels, not all of which he himself picked. It was a quarrelsome age, and one of its favorite forms of poetry was satire. Pope is the greatest of our satirists in verse, as his friend Swift is the greatest in prose. Satire being in fashion, we must not take all the quarrels embodied in the poetry of the time as seriously as if the poets had gone to law. Satire is partly a game. For Pope there was an unusual satisfaction in writing it well — he defeated men who if the quarrel had been worked off physically could have killed him with a mere kick. Nor must we overrate the amount of the satire in his highly composite poetry. He pays as many compliments as insults, and amply shows his liking for the things he thinks good.

Not all his friends were literary men, and the course of his life was pegged out not only by the hundreds of books — new and reprinted, original and edited — he saw through the press but by the stages of his friendships with writers and also with distinguished, often noble, public men, to whose estates he liked to pay visits, and whom he entertained (not very lavishly) in his own villa. To the priest who was attending his deathbed in May 1744 he entrusted the last generalization he was to make, and it was partly about friendship: "There is nothing that is meritorious but virtue and friendship, and indeed friendship itself is only a part of virtue."

POPE AND HIS TIMES

Readers differ in what strikes them first when they are reading poetry — or prose for that matter. Some readers — and in the end they may be the best sort as readers of poetry — go first for the aesthetic content provided by word, music and image. Other readers go first for the intellectual content, for what could be given some sort of adequate representation in prose. But in the end even the first sort of reader must attend as closely as possible to the intellectual content.

The sense that Pope put into his poems is now the sense of two centuries ago. This means that when we are concerned with understanding what he says we are engaged in a historical inquiry, one aim of which is to remove the differences between a former age and our own. After the passage of the two centuries there is a great accumulation of oddness to allow for in what he said, for instance, about the people of his own time. So much to do with man is changed arbitrarily as generation succeeds generation. Much as man designs a new fashion in clothing every few years, he designs a new fashion in thinking and speech habits. But times differ in the way they regard the thinking of an earlier age. It would not occur to us to consult an earlier age as to what we should think. If our thinking is identical with that of an earlier age, as it often

is, the resemblance, if we are learned enough to note it, is taken as indicating that the past was sometimes sensible enough to think as we do. When we repeat an old thought we patronize the past as being, in this particular, modern, and we expect that we shall soon be thinking something different, and shedding this remaining trace of our musty forefathers. We have been introduced to the idea of development, which in the nineteenth century was seen to be the historical process. Most of the men of Pope's day — there were a few exceptions — could not be expected to foresee Darwin, who was to show conclusively that man and ape had a common ancestor, or Macaulay, who thought that the nineteenth century became more and more glorious as it progressed further and further from the past. The men of Pope's day had a strong feeling that they should see themselves as linked in some way to the past, but they did not quite know in what way. There was indeed a "battle of the books" (as it was called) in which one side was for linking the present to the historic past as its superior (Milton was greater than Homer), and the other for the reverse (Homer was greater than Milton). But whatever side was taken, men were deeply conscious of the historic past, and especially of the Roman past since it was less barbaric than the Greek and so represented the sort of civilization they themselves were aiming at. Pope was one of those who greatly favored the ancients, and especially the Romans. When he caught that glimpse of Dryden, he exclaimed that he had seen the great Virgil not the great Homer. Like some of his aristocratic friends, he tried to make his poetry resemble that of the Roman poets. No writer has praised a Greek poet better than Pope when he praised Homer, but his translation of Homer (a translation of Virgil was out of the question because Dryden had done one while Pope was a boy) made Homer as much as possible a Roman poet.

The result of all this is that unless we know the Romans and their literature, some coloring of Pope's meaning may be lost to us. Pope, however, did not overlook his first duty as an English poet — to write for Englishmen. Even when he mimicked the design of the epics of Homer and Virgil in shaping his *Rape of the Lock* and *Dunciad,* he made the result fully intelligible to England as a whole — the poem had not been long published before it was being read by servant girls. The moral of *The Rape of the Lock* is ". . . keep good Humour still whate'r we lose," which is an English moral — the Greeks and Romans did not honor good humor so much, any more, say, than the French do. When he "imitated" Horace, the poems he produced were good poems in their own right, and fully comprehensible to those ignorant of Horace.

The literature of Greece and Rome encouraged Pope to be a "moral poet," as Byron called him. Byron, who warmly admired Pope, was contrasting him with some of the poets of the early nineteenth century, who were apt to show more interest in rocks and stones and trees than in man. If Pope never thought of himself as a moral poet it was because for him all poets worth the name were that, and always had been. But the name Byron gave him was peculiarly appropriate because Pope was more thoroughly moral than the rest. One of his friends described even his early poems as "all over Morality." And in this he was encouraged by the ancients, and particularly Horace. Homer and Virgil were admired as great moralists, but their morals were largely embodied in their stories. In Horace, however, Pope found a poet who was moral more explicitly, and almost never narrative. Pope had no great love for narrative because he thought it was nearer to garrulity than speech; he preferred meaning that was more squarely addressed to the intellect. In other words, like Horace, he preferred thinking to the spinning of stories, a preference that is related to his love of "control." He liked to compose essays and epistles and epitaphs because these forms admit a more compact substance than the form of the story. He is a thoughtful poet, a poet prizing thoughts.

That his thoughts were his own goes without saying. He did, however, try to have thoughts such as might occur to anybody. His test for a sound thought was that it would come home to men's business and bosoms, to use the phrase of Bacon's he quotes in the preface to the *Essay on Man* — and "come home" was only another way of saying that it was there already. Pope wanted to express "what oft was thought" because such thoughts were, he believed, the best that man could come by. He distrusted the sort of thoughts that come to men only in certain unusual circumstances. And this had an effect on the way he designed his poems. They begin with thoughts. In the next century poets often began their poems with pictures. They described the scene out of which their thoughts arose. One of Matthew Arnold's poems for instance begins:

> In the deserted, moon-blanch'd street,
> How lonely rings the echo of my feet!
> Those windows, which I gaze at, frown,
> Silent and white, unopening down,
> Repellent as the world; — but see,
> A break between the housetops shows
> The moon! and, lost behind her, fading dim
> Into the dewy dark obscurity
> Down at the far horizon's rim,
> Doth a whole tract of heaven disclose!

At this point Arnold begins to think. He thinks about himself, and as it happens that leads him to think about mankind as a whole:

> For most men in a brazen prison live,
> Where, in the sun's hot eye,
> With heads bent o'er their toil, they languidly
> Their lives to some unmeaning taskwork give,
> Dreaming of nought beyond their prison-wall.

Sometimes Pope thinks about himself — as in *An Epistle to Dr. Arbuthnot*. And on that occasion he shows us the scene that prompted his thinking. It was a very different scene from Arnold's, but that is not the point. The point is that what is rare in Pope is frequent in Arnold. Pope liked to begin with a thought, and with a thought not about himself and the accidents of his own life, but about mankind. Arnold is interested first in himself, and sometimes not in mankind at all. For Pope the poet stood in the midst of his fellows.

I mentioned above that men change their speech habits as age succeeds age. Some of the speech habits of the poets of Pope's day differ strikingly from those of later times. All I can say here on this very big topic is that when Pope called sheep the "fleecy care" or birds the "winged tribe" he had perfectly good reasons for doing so, just as we have perfectly good reasons nowadays for not doing so. His use of those items of "poetic diction," as it came to be called, should be properly understood by modern readers or they will fail to understand exactly what Pope is saying. When he wrote about man, which he did for most of the time, he used diction that has remained our modern diction, and this because, despite all the changes, we still see men as Pope did — seeing Sir Plume, for instance, as ridiculous, and Atticus as a complexity of greatness and meanness. When Pope glanced away from man to write about external nature, he always wrote about it from the point of view of man. And the men of his time saw external nature differently from the way we see it, a change for which scientists are largely responsible. We cannot justly blame Pope for not seeing sheep and birds as we ourselves do. Instead we must see and understand him as a man of his own particular time, a man gifted to put his thoughts, whether about man or sheep, into glowing verse.

THE SORT OF POETRY POPE WROTE

It has been said that designers of decorations — wallpaper or fabrics — find that their patterns are based on either lines or dots. The line shoots or wanders away from where it starts, and the dot stays put — if it moves it is by revolving. It seems that the same sort of thing happens when men design pieces of literature, the results being describable as either wild like the line, or collected like the dot. Let us take an instance. This is how Milton in *Paradise Lost* describes Satan after his fall from heaven:

> his form had not yet lost
> All her original brightness, nor appeared
> Less than Archangel ruined, and the excess
> Of glory obscured: as when the sun new risen
> Looks through the horizontal misty air
> Shorn of his beams, or from behind the moon
> In dim eclipse disastrous twilight sheds
> On half the nations, and with fear of change
> Perplexes monarchs. Darkened so, yet shone
> Above them all the Archangel; but his face
> Deep scars of thunder had intrenched, and care
> Sat on his faded cheek, but under brows
> Of dauntless courage, and considerate pride
> Waiting revenge. Cruel his eye . . .
>
> (I.591–604)

Now look at Pope's description of one of the personages in *The Rape of the Lock*:

> Sir Plume, of amber snuffbox justly vain,
> And the nice conduct of a clouded cane
> With earnest eyes, and round unthinking face,
> He first the snuffbox opened, then the case . . .
>
> (IV.123–26)

As literature Milton's description of Satan and Pope's of Sir Plume may be considered of equal merit — it must have been as hard a task to create either picture, even though Milton, in describing Satan, had to gather his materials from among the things he had seen here and there during his life, while Pope had his already gathered for him (there was an actual person corresponding to Sir Plume, who was angry to find that Pope had, as it were, photographed him). Equally great as literature, Milton's description is more " wild " than " collected," and Pope's the reverse. To put it another way and to exaggerate in order to be clear, Milton's Satan exists like a tree in a field, Pope's Sir Plume like a set of dominoes in a box.

And yet for all his collectedness — his neatness, his conciseness, his dislike of the flamboyant and excited — Pope had a great deal of wildness in him. All great writers have. He confessed to a friend that he once had a plan of writing a " Persian fable," and that, if written, " It would have been a very wild thing." Of another projected poem, a fairy tale, he said the principle would have been " the more wild and exotic the better." From his other work we know that although very wild, they would also have been very much collected, as a cowboy controls the wildness of an unbroken horse.

> 'Tis more to guide, than spur the Muse's steed;
> Restrain his fury, than provoke his speed.
> (*Essay on Criticism*, ll. 84–85)

As a person, we recall, Pope collected his wildness. With much encouragement — even from his own writing! — he never laughed loudly. He would smile instead (and from what we know of him his smile would be tender as often as scornful or contemptuous). When we read his poetry — or his prose, for that matter — we should look for evidence of his wildness as well as for the perhaps more obvious evidence of his collectedness. Some great critics have failed to see it. Matthew Arnold called Pope the splendid high priest of an age of prose. His image is brilliant, and is also just in so far as one of Pope's qualities goes — the quality we find in such couplets, for instance, as

> Not with such majesty, such bold relief,
> The forms august, of king, or conquering chief,

E'er swelled on marble; as in verse have shined
(In polished verse) the manners and the mind.

(*Epistle to Augustus*, ll. 390–93)

But what becomes of Arnold's image when we
read the following couplets, from *Eloisa to
Abelard*:

Of all affliction taught a lover yet,
'Tis sure the hardest science to forget!
How shall I lose the sin, yet keep the sense,
And love th' offender, yet detest th' offense?
How the dear object from the crime remove,
Or how distinguish penitence from love?
Unequal task! a passion to resign,
For hearts so touched, so pierced, so lost as mine.
Ere such a soul regains its peaceful state,
How often must it love, how often hate!
How often hope, despair, resent, regret,
Conceal, disdain — do all things but forget.
But let Heaven seize it, all at once 'tis fired;
Not touched, but rapt; not wakened, but inspired!
Oh come! oh teach me Nature to subdue,
Renounce my love, my life, myself — and you.
Fill my fond heart with God alone, for he
Alone can rival, can succeed to thee.

(ll. 189–206)

To picture him as Arnold did is to ignore his
wildness. Samuel Johnson knew better. This is
how he praised Pope in his Life of him he included in his *Lives of the Poets:*

Of his intellectual character the constituent and
fundamental principle was Good Sense, a prompt
and intuitive perception of consonance and propriety. He saw immediately, of his own conceptions,
what was to be chosen, and what to be rejected;
and, in the works of others, what was to be
shunned, and what was to be copied.

But good sense alone is a sedate and quiescent
quality, which manages its possessions well, but
does not increase them; it collects few materials for
its own operations, and preserves safety, but never
gains supremacy. Pope had likewise genius; a mind
active, ambitious, and adventurous, always investigating, always aspiring; in its widest searches still
longing to go forward, in its highest flights still
wishing to be higher; always imagining something
greater than it knows, always endeavouring more
than it can do.

We may look first at the wildness in Pope's
meaning, in the intellectual content of his poetry.
He saw man as a wild thing. One of the lines

in his summary of man's nature (see below,
p. 422) runs:

Chaos of thought and passion, all confused.

His sense of man's wildness informs his work
completely because it is always about man, who
for men was "the proper study" — i.e., the
study that was appropriate for them, considering their powers. He is always drawing portraits
of men who are divided within themselves, almost chaotic with self-contradictions, though he
was always seeking to discover the clue to their
nature, and thought he had found it in what he
called the "ruling passion," i.e., the desire that
at a climax overbore everything else. One of his
greatest portraits is that of Atossa, who is a
whirl of feeling which falls into a pattern if
only that imposed by a passion for change:

But what are these to great Atossa's mind?
Scarce once herself, by turns all womankind!
Who, with herself, or others, from her birth
Finds all her life one warfare upon earth:
Shines, in exposing knaves, and painting fools,
Yet is, whate'er she hates and ridicules.
No thought advances, but her eddy brain
Whisks it about, and down it goes again.
Full sixty years the world has been her trade,
The wisest fool much time has ever made.
From loveless youth to unrespected age,
No passion gratified except her rage.
So much the fury still outran the wit,
The pleasure missed her, and the scandal hit.
Who breaks with her, provokes revenge from Hell,
But he's a bolder man who dares be well:
Her every turn with violence pursued,
Nor more a storm her hate than gratitude.
To that each passion turns, or soon or late;
Love, if it makes her yield, must make her hate:
Superiors? death! and equals? what a curse!
But an inferior not dependent? worse.
Offend her, and she knows not to forgive;
Oblige her, and she'll hate you while you live:
But die, and she'll adore you — Then the bust
And temple rise — then fall again to dust.
Last night, her lord was all that's good and great,
A knave this morning, and his will a cheat.
Strange! by the means defeated of the ends,
By Spirit robbed of power, by warmth of friends,
By wealth of followers! without one distress
Sick of herself through very selfishness!
Atossa, cursed with every granted prayer,
Childless with all her children, wants an heir.

To heirs unknown descends th' unguarded store
Or wanders, heaven-directed, to the poor.
(*Moral Essays*, ll. 115–150)

HIS USE OF THE COUPLET

The wildness in Pope's meaning will engage the reader constantly. But wildness also exists in his versification, though its presence there has not always been admitted. In the early nineteenth century, when poets were trying to write more in the manner of the seventeenth century than in that of the eighteenth, there was a greater admiration for such a couplet-writer as William Browne of Tavistock than for Pope. Browne, who was a thoroughly good poet, sometimes made the couplet as wild as Keats was to in his *Endymion*. Here are a few of Browne's from his *Britannia's Pastorals* (1613–16):

As I haue seene vpon a Bridall-day
Full many Maides clad in their best array,
In honour of the Bride come with their Flaskets
Fill'd full with flowres: others in wicker-baskets
Bring from the Marish Rushes, to o'er-spread
The ground, whereon to Church the Louers tread;
Whilst that the quaintest youth of all the Plaine
Vshers their way with many a piping straine:
So, as in ioy, at this faire Riuers birth,
Triton came vp a Channell with his mirth,
And call'd the neighb'ring Nymphes each in her
    turne
To poure their pretty Riuelets from their Vrne;
To waite vpon this new-deliuered Spring.
Some running through the Meadowes, with them
    bring
Cowslip and *Mynt:* and 'tis anothers lot
To light vpon some Gardeners curious knot,
Whence shee vpon her brest (loues sweet repose)
Doth bring the *Queene* of flowers, the *English
    Rose.*

Pope's couplets are constructed on a different pattern from these of Browne's. In every variety of verse the line is the unit. The reader should always pause, however briefly, at the end of a line, even if the syntax carries on without a break into the next. In Browne's verse, while the line is the unit, the grouping of the lines is wildly various. If we take the sentence as the unit of measurement, we shall find that the sentences vary within wide limits and sometimes conclude halfway along a line. This is true also of Pope's sentences as far as variety of length

goes, but when they are long their syntax is parceled out in units of two lines, and they never end in the middle of a line. For Pope as for all poets the line is the unit, but for him the units go steadily in pairs.

This pairing was sometimes felt to be too "collected" by the wild poets of the early nineteenth century (although not always — in "Lamia" Keats forsook Browne for Dryden as a model, which meant that he came much closer to Pope). Thinking of Pope, Keats spoke about metrists "swaying about upon a rocking horse." We have seen that Pope himself spoke of a real horse, and a fiery one, whose fury called for restraint. He also compared the procedure of the not very good poet Blackmore to a real horse, but to one that his trainer had controlled out of all equinity:

Friend Pope! be prudent, let your Muse take breath,
And never gallop Pegasus to death;
Lest stiff, and stately, void of fire, or force,
You limp, like Blackmore, on a Lord Mayor's horse.
(*The First Epistle of the First Book
of Horace Imitated*, ll. 13–16)

Pope's own versification is controlled, but the wildness is only just subdued. His horse is spirited as well as graceful.

The way to see Pope's couplets for what they are is first to find out what they mean. This is no easy task. When it is accomplished, however, we are doubly rewarded because we have both the meaning and the rhythm. The meter of verse underlies its rhythm — meter is what we might call the textbook account of how the accented and the unaccented syllables form a pattern. The meter of Pope's couplet is xa (where x stands for the unaccented, and a for the accented syllable) repeated ten times with a pause after the fifth — i.e., after the fifth accented syllable. But rhythm is meter when it has received life from the words. Very occasionally rhythm coincides with meter, in Pope's verse as in that of all other poets: for example,

By spirit robbed of power, by warmth of friends.

But mostly Pope's lines, like those of all poets, show the rhythm modifying the meter. And in Pope more than most poets modifying it very much because of the intensity of the thinking, which leads us when reading to multiply and deepen the accents. Here is an example from one of the poems quoted above, stresses being roughly suggested by typography, and pauses or slowness by dots, when they are not already provided for by punctuation:

Not with SUCH . . MAJesty, SUCH . . BOLD . . reLIEF,
The FORMS AUGUST . . of KING . . . or conquering CHIEF,
E'R SWELLED on MARble; as in VERSE have SHINED (IN POLished . . VERSE) and MANners and the MIND.

What has become of the rocking horse! Those who think Pope is a monotonous versifier do not understand what he is saying.

The example just given illustrates something else — that Pope relates his couplets with various degrees of closeness. In this example the pause at the end of the first is light because the sentence is pressing forward to its verb — " swelled." The sense usually pushes on past the breaks at the end of couplets to be completed only after several of them. And, as a further insurance against monotony, there is the constant changing of the tone of his voice — his tone is sometimes that of one making statements, sometimes that of one persuading or arguing, or threatening, or being kind or angry.

People now read Pope more devotedly, completely, and thoroughly than he has been read since his own times, and are therefore coming to see his greatness — his greatness not simply as a writer (that has always been allowed) but as a poet. Indeed if I were asked to name the greatest English poets I should name Chaucer, Shakespeare (who is mainly a dramatic poet), Milton, Pope and Wordsworth. I should find it painful to omit other names — particularly those of Spenser, Donne, Dryden, Keats, Tennyson and Hopkins — but for one reason or another would feel that they do not match up to the first five. Pope is intense, concentrated, complex, many-sided, classical (in the sense that almost every line he wrote strikes us as final and unimprovable), and all the other things I claim for him in my introduction to the *Epistle to Dr. Arbuthnot*. But it is not simply that. It is also that what he wrote amounts to so much in quantity. A great poet is a big poet as well as everything else. Because his excellence is uniform it does not greatly matter which poems figure in a selection. Any page of him shows most of his merits.

ESSAY ON CRITICISM

Nowadays a critic comments on literature both new and old, but in Pope's day he was mainly thought of as commenting only on new. The *Essay on Criticism* might therefore be called An Essay on Reviewing — to use a word that did not achieve its modern sense till a century later. Poets have always complained about the treatment they received from critics in their own day, so much so that Horace, the Roman poet, called them the " genus irritabile." Pope's poem is to be read as advice to reviewers, or, more generally, advice to those who read a work on its publication and comment on it. This explains why his commendation of his friend Walsh as the good critic dwells on his qualities of good nature and kindness. Let the critic be first of all a good man, free from envy and small-mindedness, encouragingly ready to see the merits in new work. No one asks kindness of a critic of past literature — the author is out of reach of kindness or unkindness. But it matters very much to a poet to have his poems treated unkindly while he is alive.

Much of the *Essay* being concerned with advice, how to criticize poetry well is also indirect advice on how to write poetry well. When critics, for instance, are advised not to fix on one aspect of a work to the exclusion of another — on words, say, to the exclusion of music — this is also advice to a poet. To address this double audience was an obvious advantage, and indeed there can be nowhere a more thorough discussion of the principles of good poetry and good criticism in the same short space. But the advice about the writing of poetry is part of the argument about criticism because Pope's plea for kindness is only on behalf of poets who are good poets. A bad poet cannot but expect to receive unkind treatment because he justly deserves it — he ought to be doing an honest job of work instead of aping his betters: he ought to be somebody's secretary or to be writing something practical, like a guidebook, or to be schoolmastering. And because Pope has taken the advice he gives — the poem itself exists to show that — his plea is to be respected.

Introduction. That 'tis as great a fault to judge ill, as to write ill, and a more dangerous one to the public. That a *true taste* is as rare to be found, as a *true genius*. That most men are born with some taste, but spoiled by false *education*. The multitude of *critics,* and causes of them. That we are to study our own *taste,* and know the *limits* of it. *Nature* the best guide of judgment. Improved by *art* and *rules,* which are but *methodized Nature. Rules* derived from the practice of the *ancient poets.* That therefore the *ancients* are necessary to be studied by a critic, particularly *Homer* and *Virgil.* Of *licenses,* and the use of them by the ancients. Reverence due to the *ancients,* and praise of them.

I

'Tis hard to say, if greater want of skill
Appear in writing or in judging ill;
But, of the two, less dangerous is th' offense
To tire our patience, than mislead our sense.°
Some few in that, but numbers err in this,
Ten censure wrong for one who writes amiss;
A fool might once himself alone expose,
Now one in verse makes many more in prose.
'Tis with our judgments as our watches, none
Go just-alike, yet each believes his own.   10
In poets as true genius is but rare,
True taste as seldom is the critic's share;
Both must alike from Heaven derive their light,
These born to judge, as well as those to write.
Let such teach others who themselves excel,
And censure freely who have written well.
Authors are partial to their wit,° 'tis true,
But are not critics to their judgment too?
    Yet if we look more closely, we shall find
Most have the seeds of judgment in their mind:
Nature affords at least a glimmering light;   21
The lines, though touched but faintly, are drawn
    right.
But as the slightest sketch, if justly traced,
Is by ill coloring but the more disgraced,
So by false learning is good sense defaced:
Some are bewildered in the maze of schools,°
And some made coxcombs° Nature meant but
    fools.
In search of wit these lose their common sense,
And then turn critics in their own defense:
Each burns alike, who can, or cannot write,   30
Or with a rival's, or an eunuch's spite.
All fools have still° an itching to deride,
And fain would be upon the laughing side.
If Maevius° scribble in Apollo's spite,
There are who judge still worse than he can write.
    Some have at first for wits, then poets passed,
Turned Critics next, and proved plain fools at last.
Some neither can for wits nor critics pass,
As heavy mules are neither horse nor ass.   39

Those half-learned witlings, numerous in our isle,
As half-formed insects on the banks of Nile;
Unfinished things, one knows not what to call,
Their generation's so equivocal:°
To tell° 'em, would a hundred tongues require,
Or one vain wit's, that might a hundred tire.
    But you who seek to give and merit fame,
And justly bear a critic's noble name,
Be sure yourself and your own reach to know,
How far your genius, taste, and learning go;
Launch not beyond your depth, but be discreet,   50
And mark that point where sense and dulness meet.
    Nature to all things fixed the limits fit,
And wisely curbed proud man's pretending° wit.
As on the land while here the ocean gains,
In other parts it leaves wide sandy plains;
Thus in the soul while memory° prevails,
The solid power of understanding fails;
Where beams of warm imagination play,
The memory's soft figures melt away.
One science° only will one genius fit;   60
So vast is art, so narrow human wit:
Not only bounded to peculiar° arts,
But oft in those confined to single parts.
Like kings we lose the conquests gained before,
By vain ambition still to make them more;
Each might his several province well command,
Would all but stoop to what they understand.
    First follow Nature, and your judgment frame
By her just standard, which is still the same:
Unerring Nature, still divinely bright,   70
One clear, unchanged, and universal light,
Life, force, and beauty must to all impart,
At once the source, and end, and test of art.
Art from that fund each just supply provides,
Works without show,° and without pomp presides:
In some fair body thus th' informing soul
With spirits feeds, with vigor fills the whole,
Each motion guides, and every nerve sustains;
Itself unseen, but in th' effects, remains.
Some, to whom Heaven in wit has been profuse,
Want as much more,° to turn it to its use;   81
For wit and judgment often are at strife,
Tho' meant each other's aid, like man and wife.
'Tis more to guide, than spur the Muse's steed;
Restrain his fury, than provoke his speed;
The wingèd courser, like a generous° horse,
Shows most true mettle° when you check his course.

ESSAY ON CRITICISM.   **4. sense:** judgment.   **17. wit:** The word "wit" had more meanings in Pope's time than it has now, and Pope made full use of them. At l. 28 the word has something like its modern sense (the capacity to make "a bright remark"); at l. 36 "wits" means "men of genius"; at l. 45 "wit" means "writer," at ll. 53 and 61 "intellect," and at l. 80 "genius." **26. schools:** schools of criticism.   **27. coxcombs:** pretenders to learning and taste.   **32. still:** always.   **34. Maevius:** a wretched poet, contemporary with Horace and Virgil.

41-43. As . . . equivocal: Insects were believed to be formed by the action of the sun on the slimy banks of the Nile, but because this was not known for certain, it was equivocal, doubtful.   **44. tell:** count.   **53. pretending:** aspiring.   **56. memory:** an aid to learning, hence learning itself.   **60. science:** object of knowledge, subject matter.   **62. peculiar:** particular.   **75. without show:** Horace had counseled that art should conceal its presence.   **81. more:** more intelligence.   **86. generous:** highbred.   **87. mettle:** "spirit; spriteliness; courage" (Johnson's Dictionary).

Those rules of old discovered, not devised,
Are Nature still, but Nature methodized;
Nature, like liberty, is but restrained   90
By the same laws which first herself ordained.
    Hear how learn'd Greece her useful rules indites,
When to repress, and when indulge our flights:
High on Parnassus' top her sons she showed,
And pointed out those arduous paths they trod;
Held from afar, aloft, th' immortal prize,
And urged the rest by equal steps to rise.
Just precepts thus from great examples given,
She drew from them what they derived from
        Heaven.
The generous critic fanned the poet's fire,   100
And taught the world with reason to admire.
Then Criticism the Muse's handmaid proved,
To dress her charms, and make her more beloved:
But following wits from that intention strayed,
Who could not win the mistress, wooed the maid;
Against the poets their own arms they turned,
Sure to hate most the men from whom they learned.
So modern 'pothecaries,° taught the art
By doctor's bills° to play the doctor's part,
Bold in the practice of mistaken rules,   110
Prescribe, apply, and call their masters fools.
Some on the leaves of ancient authors prey,
Nor time nor moths e'er spoiled so much as they.
Some dryly plain, without invention's aid,
Write dull receipts how poems may be made.
These leave the sense, their learning to display,
And those explain the meaning quite away.
    You then whose judgment the right course would
        steer,
Know well each ancient's proper° character;
His fable,° subject, scope in every page;   120
Religion, country, genius of his age:
Without all these at once before your eyes,
Cavil you may, but never criticize.
Be Homer's works your study and delight,
Read them by day, and meditate by night;
Thence form your judgment, thence your maxims
        bring,
And trace the Muses upward to their spring.°
Still with itself compared, his text peruse;
And let your comment be the Mantuan Muse.
    When first young Maro° in his boundless mind
A work t' outlast immortal Rome designed,   131
Perhaps he seemed above the critic's law,
And but from Nature's fountains scorned to draw:
But when t' examine every part he came,
Nature and Homer were, he found, the same.
Convinced, amazed, he checks the bold design;

And rules as strict his labored work confine,
As if the Stagirite° o'erlooked each line.
Learn hence for ancient rules a just esteem;
To copy Nature is to copy them.   140
    Some beauties yet no precepts can declare,°
For there's a happiness as well as care.
Music resembles poetry, in each
Are nameless graces which no methods teach,
And which a master hand alone can reach.
If, where the rules not far enough extend,
(Since rules were made but to promote their end)
Some lucky license answer to the full
Th' intent proposed, that license is a rule.
Thus Pegasus, a nearer way to take,   150
May boldly deviate from the common track:
Great wits sometimes may gloriously offend,
And rise to faults true critics dare not mend,
From vulgar bounds with brave disorder part,
And snatch a grace beyond the reach of art,
Which, without passing through the judgment,
        gains
The heart, and all its end at once attains.
In prospects, thus, some objects please our eyes,
Which out of Nature's common order rise,
The shapeless rock, or hanging precipice.   160
But though the ancients thus their rules invade,
(As kings dispense with laws themselves have
        made)
Moderns, beware! or° if you must offend
Against the precept, ne'er transgress its end;
Let it be seldom, and compelled by need;
And have, at least, their precedent to plead.
The critic else proceeds without remorse,
Seizes your fame, and puts his laws in force.
    I know there are, to whose presumptuous
        thoughts   169
Those freer beauties, even in them, seem faults.°
Some figures monstrous and misshaped appear,
Considered singly, or beheld too near,
Which, but proportioned to their light, or place,
Due distance reconciles to form and grace.
A prudent chief not always must display
His powers in equal ranks and fair array,
But with th' occasion and the place comply,
Conceal his force, nay seem sometimes to fly.
Those oft are stratagems which errors seem,

---

138. Stagirite: Aristotle, who was born at Stagira, a town in Thrace.   **141–53. Some . . . mend:** Cf. Dryden's preface to his translation of Du Fresnoy, where he praises Virgil for his luck with words: "These hits of Words a true *Poet* often finds, as I may say, without seeking: but he knows their Value when he finds them, and is infinitely pleas'd."   **163–80. or . . . dream:** that is, develop so intelligent an understanding of the ancient poems that you can confound the critics who find fault with yours by pointing to something in those poems that, though a fault when judged by rule-of-thumb criticism, is in fact a "glorious" fault, that is, no fault at all, but a new and precious creation.   **170. faults:** practices that deviate from the rules.

---

108. 'pothecaries: druggists.   **109. bills:** medical prescriptions.   **119. proper:** individual, distinctive.   **120. fable:** the matter he takes for his subject.   **127. spring:** Pierian spring; Hippocrene, the stream associated with the Pierides, the muses.   **129–30. Mantuan Muse . . . Maro:** Virgil.

Nor is it Homer nods,° but we that dream.   180
   Still green with bays° each ancient altar stands,
Above the reach of sacrilegious hands;
Secure from flames, from envy's fiercer rage,
Destructive war, and all-involving age.
See, from each clime the learn'd their incense bring!
Hear, in all tongues consenting paeans ring!
In praise so just let every voice be joined,
And fill the general chorus of mankind.°
Hail, bards triumphant! born in happier days;
Immortal heirs of universal praise!   190
Whose honors with increase of ages grow,
As streams roll down, enlarging as they flow;
Nations unborn your mighty names shall sound,
And worlds applaud that must not yet be found!
Oh may some spark of your celestial fire,
The last, the meanest of your sons inspire,
(That on weak wings, from far, pursues your
      flights;
Glows while he reads, but trembles as he writes)
To teach vain wits a science little known,   199
T' admire superior sense, and doubt their own!

II

Causes hindering a *true judgment.* 1. *Pride.* 2. *Imperfect learning.* 3. *Judging by parts,* and not by the whole. Critics in *wit, language, versification* only. 4. *Being too hard to please,* or *too apt to admire.* 5. *Partiality* — too much to a *sect* — to the *ancients* or *moderns.* 6. *Prejudice* or *prevention.* 7. *Singularity.* 8. *Inconstancy.* 9. *Party spirit.* 10. *Envy.* Against envy, and in praise of good nature. When severity is chiefly to be used by critics.

Of all the causes which conspire to blind
Man's erring judgment, and misguide the mind,
What the weak head with strongest bias rules,
Is pride, the never-failing vice of fools.
Whatever Nature has in worth denied,
She gives in large recruits° of needful pride;
For as in bodies, thus in souls, we find
What wants in blood and spirits, swelled with
      wind:
Pride, where wit fails, steps in to our defense,
And fills up all the mighty void of sense.   210
If once right reason drives that cloud away,
Truth breaks upon us with resistless day.
Trust not yourself; but your defects to know,
Make use of every friend — and every foe.
   A little learning is a dangerous thing;
Drink deep, or taste not the Pierian spring:°

There shallow draughts intoxicate the brain,
And drinking largely sobers us again.
Fired at first sight with what the Muse imparts,
In fearless youth we tempt° the heights of arts,
While from the bounded level of our mind,   221
Short views we take, nor see the lengths behind;
But more advanced, behold with strange surprise
New distant scenes of endless science° rise!
So pleased at first the towering Alps we try,
Mount o'er the vales, and seem to tread the sky,
Th' eternal snows appear already passed,
And the first clouds and mountains seem the last;
But, those attained, we tremble to survey
The growing labors of the lengthened way,   230
Th' increasing prospect tires our wandering eyes,
Hills peep o'er hills, and Alps on Alps arise!
   A perfect judge will read each work of wit
With the same spirit that its author writ:
Survey the whole, nor seek slight faults to find
Where Nature moves, and rapture warms the
      mind;
Nor lose, for that malignant dull delight,
The generous pleasure to be charmed with wit.
But in such lays as neither ebb, nor flow,
Correctly cold, and regularly low,   240
That shunning faults, one quiet tenor° keep;
We cannot blame indeed — but we may sleep.
In wit, as Nature, what affects our hearts
Is not th' exactness of peculiar parts;
'Tis not a lip, or eye, we beauty call,
But the joint force and full result of all.
Thus when we view some well-proportioned
      dome,°
(The world's just wonder, and even thine, O
      Rome!)
No single parts unequally surprise,
All comes united to th' admiring eyes;   250
No monstrous height, or breadth, or length appear;
The whole at once is bold, and regular.
   Whoever thinks a faultless piece to see,
Thinks what ne'er was, nor is, nor e'er shall be.
In every work regard the writer's end,
Since none can compass more than they intend;
And if the means be just, the conduct true,
Applause, in spite of trivial faults, is due.
As men of breeding, sometimes men of wit,
T' avoid great errors, must the less commit: 260
Neglect the rules each verbal critic lays,°
For not to know some trifles, is a praise.
Most critics, fond of some subservient art,
Still make the whole depend upon a part:
They talk of principles, but notions prize,
And all to one loved folly sacrifice.

---

180. Homer nods: referring to Horace's remark; i.e., even Homer occasionally errs.   **181. bays:** laurels.   **187–88. joined ... mankind:** a perfect rhyme in Pope's day.   **206. recruits:** supplies.   **216. Pierian spring:** Cf. l. 127n.

220. tempt: attempt.   **224. science:** intellectual knowledge.   **241. tenor:** continuity.   **247. dome:** (fine) dwelling, or cathedral.   **261. lays:** lays down.

Once on a time, La Mancha's knight,° they say,
A certain bard encountering on the way,
Discoursed in terms as just, with looks as sage,
As e'er could Dennis° of the Grecian stage;   270
Concluding all were desperate sots and fools,
Who durst depart from Aristotle's rules.
Our author, happy in a judge so nice,
Produced his play, and begged the knight's advice;
Made him observe the subject, and the plot,
The manners, passions,° unities;° what not?
All which, exact to rule, were brought about,
Were but a combat in the lists° left out.
"What! leave the combat out?" exclaims the
   knight;
Yes, or we must renounce the Stagirite.   280
"Not so, by Heaven" (he answers in a rage)
"Knights, squires, and steeds, must enter on the
   stage."
So vast a throng the stage can ne'er contain.
"Then build a new, or act it in a plain."
   Thus critics, of less judgment than caprice,
Curious° not knowing, not exact° but nice,°
Form short ideas; and offend in arts
(As most in manners) by a love to parts.
   Some to conceit° alone their taste confine,   289
And glittering thoughts struck out at every line;
Pleased with a work where nothing's just or fit;
One glaring chaos and wild heap of wit.
Poets like painters, thus, unskilled to trace
The naked nature and the living grace,
With gold and jewels cover every part,
And hide with ornaments their want of art.
True wit° is Nature to advantage dressed,
What oft was thought, but ne'er so well expressed;
Something, whose truth convinced at sight we find,
That gives us back the image of our mind.   300
As shades more sweetly recommend the light,
So modest plainness sets off sprightly wit.
For works may have more wit than does 'em good,
As bodies perish through excess of blood.
   Others for language all their care express,
And value books, as women men, for dress:
Their praise is still — the style is excellent:
The sense, they humbly take upon content.°
Words are like leaves; and where they most abound,
Much fruit of sense beneath is rarely found.   310

False eloquence, like the prismatic glass,
Its gaudy colors spreads on every place;
The face of Nature we no more survey,
All glares alike, without distinction gay:
But true expression, like th' unchanging sun,
Clears, and improves whate'er it shines upon,
It gilds all objects, but it alters none.
Expression is the dress° of thought, and still
Appears more decent,° as more suitable;
A vile conceit in pompous words expressed,   320
Is like a clown° in regal purple dressed:
For different styles with different subjects sort,
As several garbs with country, town, and court.
Some by old words to fame have made pretense,
Ancients in phrase, mere moderns in their sense;
Such labored nothings, in so strange a style,
Amaze th' unlearn'd, and make the learnèd smile.
Unlucky, as Fungoso in the play,°
These sparks with awkward vanity display
What the fine gentleman wore yesterday;   330
And but so mimic ancient wits at best,
As apes our grandsires, in their doublets dressed.
In words, as fashions, the same rule will hold;
Alike fantastic, if too new, or old:
Be not the first by whom the new are tried,
Nor yet the last to lay the old aside.
   But most by numbers° judge a poet's song;
And smooth or rough, with them is right or wrong:
In the bright Muse, though thousand charms con-
   spire,°
Her voice is all these tuneful fools admire;   340
Who haunt Parnassus but to please their ear,
Not mend their minds; as some to church repair,
Not for the doctrine, but the music there.
These equal syllables alone require,
Tho' oft the ear the open vowels tire;
While expletives their feeble aid do join;
And ten low words oft creep in one dull line;°
While they ring round the same unvaried chimes,
With sure returns of still expected rhymes.   349
Where'er you find "the cooling western breeze,"
In the next line, it "whispers thro' the trees":
If crystal streams "with pleasing murmurs creep,"
The reader's threatened (not in vain) with
   "sleep":
Then, at the last and only couplet fraught
With some unmeaning thing they call a thought,
A needless alexandrine ends the song,

267. La Mancha's knight: Don Quixote, in a spurious continuation of Cervantes' work. 270. Dennis: John Dennis, a critic, some thirty years older than Pope, who had a deep insight into the nature of the more emotional kinds of poetry and whose manners Pope thought too loud (see ll. 584–87 below). 276. passions: emotions. unities: It was believed that the Greek poets had integrated their plays by confining them to one story, one place, and one day (24 hours), and that Aristotle had recommended this practice. 278. lists: the field of ceremonial combat. 286. curious: finicky. exact: sound. nice: fastidious, hard to please. 289. conceit: extravagant metaphors and similes. 297. True wit: great literature. 308. content: trust.

318. dress: Pope accepts the old belief that dress, like the body, was the materialization of the inner self of the wearer. 319. decent: becoming, appropriate. 321. clown: rustic. 328. Fungoso ... play: a poor student in Jonson's Every Man out of his Humour, who followed fashion at a distance. 337. numbers: meter, sound. 339. conspire: unite. 345–47. Tho' ... line: These couplets, and several soon to follow, exemplify what they enunciate.

That, like a wounded snake, drags its slow length
  along.
Leave such to tune their own dull rhymes, and
  know
What's roundly smooth, or languishingly slow;
And praise the easy vigor of a line,   360
Where Denham's strength, and Waller's° sweetness
  join.
True ease in writing comes from art, not chance,
As those move easiest who have learned to dance.
'Tis not enough no harshness gives offense,
The sound must seem an echo to the sense:
Soft is the strain when Zephyr gently blows,
And the smooth stream in smoother numbers flows;
But when loud surges lash the sounding shore,
The hoarse, rough verse should like the torrent roar:
When Ajax° strives some rock's vast weight to
  throw,   370
The line too labors, and the words move slow;
Not so, when swift Camilla° scours the plain,
Flies o'er th' unbending corn, and skims along the
  main.
Hear how Timotheus'° varied lays surprise,
And bid alternate passions fall and rise!
While, at each change, the son of Libyan Jove
Now burns with glory, and then melts with love;
Now his fierce eyes with sparkling fury glow,
Now sighs steal out, and tears begin to flow: 379
Persians and Greeks like turns of Nature° found,
And the world's victor stood subdued by sound!
The power of music all our hearts allow,
And what Timotheus was, is Dryden now.
    Avoid extremes; and shun the fault of such,
Who still are pleased too little or too much.
At every trifle scorn to take offense,
That always shows great pride, or little sense;
Those heads, as stomachs, are not sure the best,
Which nauseate all, and nothing can digest.
Yet let not each gay turn° thy rapture move;   390
For fools admire, but men of sense approve:
As things seem large which we through mists
  descry,
Dulness is ever apt to magnify.
    Some foreign writers, some our own despise;
The ancients only, or the moderns prize.
Thus wit, like faith, by each man is applied
To one small sect, and all are damned beside.
Meanly they seek the blessing to confine,
And force that sun but on a part to shine,
Which not alone the southern wit sublimes,   400

But ripens spirits in cold northern climes;
Which from the first has shone on ages past,
Enlights the present, and shall warm the last;
Tho' each may feel increases and decays,
And see now clearer and now darker days.
Regard not then if wit be old or new,
But blame the false, and value still the true.
    Some ne'er advance a judgment of their own,
But catch the spreading notion of the town;
They reason and conclude by precedent,   410
And own stale nonsense which they ne'er invent.
Some judge of authors' names, not works, and then
Nor praise nor blame the writings, but the men.
Of all this servile herd, the worst is he
That in proud dulness joins with quality.°
A constant critic at the great man's board,
To fetch and carry nonsense for my lord.
What woeful stuff this madrigal would be,
In some starved hackney sonneteer, or me?
But let a lord once own the happy lines,   420
How the wit brightens! how the style refines!
Before his sacred name flies every fault,
And each exalted stanza teems with thought!
    The vulgar thus through imitation err;
As oft the learn'd by being singular;
So much they scorn the crowd, that if the throng
By chance go right, they purposely go wrong:
So schismatics° the plain believers quit,
And are but damned for having too much wit.
Some praise at morning what they blame at night;
But always think the last opinion right.   431
A Muse by these is like a mistress used,
This hour she's idolized, the next abused;
While their weak heads like towns unfortified,
Twixt sense and nonsense daily change their side.
Ask them the cause; they're wiser still, they say;
And still tomorrow's wiser than today.
We think our fathers fools, so wise we grow;
Our wiser sons, no doubt, will think us so.   439
Once school divines this zealous isle o'erspread;
Who knew most sentences,° was deepest read;
Faith, Gospel, all, seemed made to be disputed,
And none had sense enough to be confuted:
Scotists and Thomists,° now, in peace remain,
Amidst their kindred cobwebs in Duck Lane.°
If faith itself has different dresses worn,
What wonder modes in wit should take their turn?
Oft, leaving what is natural and fit,
The current folly proves° the ready wit;
And authors think their reputation safe,   450
Which lives as long as fools are pleased to laugh.

361. Denham ... Waller: these devoted seventeenth-century
poets were highly respected as the most gifted improvers of the
heroic couplet. **370. Ajax:** a particularly strong Greek hero in the
Iliad. **372. Camilla:** an Amazon in the *Aeneid*. **374. Timotheus:**
Alexander the Great's musician. **380. turns of Nature:** feelings.
390. turn: graceful phrase.

415. quality: people of rank. **428. schismatics:** sectarians in
religion. **441. sentences:** maxims. **444. Scotists and Thomists:** Followers of Duns Scotus and Thomas Aquinas formed two
schools of medieval philosophy. **445. Duck Lane:** in the City
of London, where old books were sold. **449. proves:** gives
occasion for the ready wit to prove itself.

Some valuing those of their own side, or mind,
Still make themselves the measure of mankind:
Fondly° we think we honor merit then,
When we but praise ourselves in other men.
Parties in wit attend on those of state,
And public faction doubles private hate.
Pride, malice, folly, against Dryden rose,
In various shapes of parsons, critics, beaux;   459
But sense survived, when merry jests were past;
For rising merit will buoy up at last.
Might he return, and bless once more our eyes,
New Blackmores and new Milbourns must arise:
Nay, should great Homer lift his awful head,
Zoilus° again would start up from the dead.
Envy will merit, as its shade, pursue;
But like a shadow, proves the substance true;
For envied wit, like Sol eclipsed, makes known
Th' opposing body's grossness, not its own.   469
When first that sun too powerful beams displays,
It draws up vapors which obscure its rays;
But even those clouds at last adorn its way,
Reflect new glories, and augment the day.

Be thou the first true merit to befriend;
His praise is lost, who stays till all commend.
Short is the date, alas, of modern rhymes,
And 'tis but just to let them live betimes.
No longer now that golden age appears,
When patriarch wits survived a thousand years:
Now length of fame (our second life) is lost,   480
And bare threescore is all even that can boast;
Our sons their fathers' failing language see,
And such as Chaucer is, shall Dryden be.
So when the faithful pencil has designed
Some bright idea of the master's mind,
Where a new world leaps out at his command,
And ready Nature waits upon his hand;
When the ripe colors soften and unite,
And sweetly melt into just shade and light;   489
When mellowing years their full perfection give,
And each bold figure just begins to live;
The treacherous colors the fair art betray,
And all the bright creation fades away!

Unhappy wit, like most mistaken things,°
Atones not for that envy which it brings.
In youth alone its empty praise we boast,
But soon the short-lived vanity is lost:
Like some fair flower the early spring supplies,
That gaily blooms, but even in blooming dies.
What is this wit, which must our cares employ?
The owner's wife, that other men enjoy;   501
Then most our trouble still when most admired,
And still the more we give, the more required;

Whose fame with pains we guard, but lose with
    ease,
Sure some to vex, but never all to please;
'Tis what the vicious fear, the virtuous shun,
By fools 'tis hated, and by knaves undone!

If wit so much from ignorance undergo,
Ah, let not learning too commence° its foe!
Of old, those met rewards who could excel,   510
And such were praised who but endeavored well:
Tho' triumphs were to generals only due,
Crowns were reserved to grace the soldiers too.
Now, they who reach Parnassus' lofty crown,
Employ their pains to spurn some others down;
And while self-love each jealous writer rules,
Contending wits become the sport of fools.
But still the worst with most regret commend,
For each ill author is as bad a friend.
To what base ends, and by what abject ways,   520
Are mortals urged through sacred lust of praise!
Ah ne'er so dire a thirst of glory boast,
Nor in the critic let the man be lost.
Good nature and good sense must ever join;
To err is human, to forgive, divine.

But if in noble minds some dregs remain
Not yet purged off, of spleen and sour disdain;
Discharge that rage on more provoking crimes,
Nor fear a dearth in these flagitious times.
No pardon vile obscenity should find,   530
Tho' wit and art conspire to move your mind;
But dulness with obscenity must prove
As shameful sure as impotence in love.
In the fat age of pleasure, wealth, and ease,
Sprung the rank weed, and thrived with large in-
    crease:
When love was all an easy monarch's° care;
Seldom at council, never in a war:
Jilts° ruled the state, and statesmen° farces writ;
Nay, wits had pensions, and young lords° had wit:
The Fair sat panting at a courtier's play,   540
And not a mask° went unimproved away:
The modest fan was lifted up no more,
And virgins smiled at what they blushed before.
The following license of a foreign reign°
Did all the dregs of bold Socinus° drain;
Then unbelieving priests reformed the nation,
And taught more pleasant methods of salvation;

509. **commence:** begin to be.   536. **easy monarch:** Charles II;
ease was a social grace much admired in his day, and in Pope's.
538. **Jilts:** a new term for harlots; an allusion to Charles's many
mistresses.   **statesmen:** the Duke of Buckinghamshire wrote
The Rehearsal, Sir Charles Sedley *The Mulberry Garden*, and Sir
George Etherege several lively plays.   539. **young lords:** the
most gifted were the Duke of Buckinghamshire, Lord Buckhurst
(later Earl of Dorset), and the Earl of Rochester.   541. **mask:**
gentlewomen often wore masks in public.   544. **foreign reign:**
that of William III, who hailed from the Low Countries. 545.
Socinus: Faustus Socinus (b. 1539) advocated various heresies,
including that denying divinity to Jesus.

454. **Fondly:** foolishly.   465. **Zoilus:** a critic who attacked Homer:
the dates of his life are uncertain but probably fell c. 350 B.C.
494. **mistaken things:** things on which people set a mistaken value.

Where Heaven's free subjects might their rights
   dispute,
Lest God himself should seem too absolute:
Pulpits their sacred satire learned to spare,   550
And Vice admired° to find a flatterer there!
Encouraged thus, wit's Titans° braved the skies,
And the press groaned with licensed blasphemies.
These monsters, critics! with your darts engage,
Here point your thunder, and exhaust your rage!
Yet shun their fault, who, scandalously nice,
Will needs mistake an author into vice;
All seems infected that th' infected spy,
As all looks yellow to the jaundiced eye.

III

Rules for the *conduct* of *manners* in a critic. 1. *Candor. Modesty. Good breeding. Sincerity,* and *freedom* of advice. 2. When one's counsel is to be restrained. Character of an *incorrigible poet.* And of an *impertinent critic.* Character of a *good critic.* The *history* of *criticism,* and characters of the best critics: *Aristotle. Horace. Dionysius. Petronius. Quintilian. Longinus.* Of the decay of criticism, and its revival. *Erasmus. Vida. Boileau. Lord Roscommon,* etc. Conclusion.

Learn then what morals critics ought to show,
For 'tis but half a judge's task, to know.   561
'Tis not enough, taste, judgment, learning, join;
In all you speak, let truth and candor shine:
That not alone what to your sense is due
All may allow; but seek your friendship too.
   Be silent always when you doubt your sense;
And speak, though sure, with seeming diffidence:
Some positive, persisting fops we know,
Who, if once wrong, will needs be always so;
But you, with pleasure own your errors past,   570
And make each day a critic on the last.
   'Tis not enough, your counsel still be true;
Blunt truths more mischief than nice falsehoods do;
Men must be taught as if you taught them not,
And things unknown proposed as things forgot.
Without good breeding, truth is disapproved;
That only makes superior sense beloved.
   Be niggards of advice on no pretense;°
For the worst avarice is that of sense.
With mean complacence ne'er betray your trust,°
Nor be so civil as to prove unjust.   581
Fear not the anger of the wise to raise;
Those best can bear reproof, who merit praise.
   'Twere well might critics still this freedom take,

But Appius° reddens at each word you speak,
And stares, tremendous, with a threatening eye,
Like some fierce tyrant in old tapestry.
Fear most to tax° an honorable° fool,
Whose right it is, uncensured, to be dull;
Such, without wit, are poets when they please,
As without learning they can take degrees.°   591
Leave dangerous truths to unsuccessful satires,
And flattery to fulsome dedicators,°
Whom, when they praise, the world believes no
   more,
Than when they promise to give scribbling o'er.
'Tis best sometimes your censure to restrain,
And charitably let the dull be vain:
Your silence there is better than your spite,
For who can rail so long as they can write?   599
Still humming on, their drowsy course they keep,
And lashed so long, like tops, are lashed asleep.°
False steps but help them to renew the race,
As, after stumbling, jades will mend their pace.
What crowds of these, impenitently bold,
In sounds and jingling syllables grown old,
Still run on° poets, in a raging vein,
Even to the dregs and squeezings of the brain,
Strain out the last dull droppings of their sense,
And rhyme with all the rage of impotence.
   Such shameless bards we have; and yet 'tis true,
There are as mad abandoned critics too.   611
The bookful blockhead, ignorantly read,
With loads of learnèd lumber in his head,
With his own tongue still edifies his ears,
And always listening to himself appears.
All books he reads, and all he reads assails,
From Dryden's Fables° down to Durfey's Tales.°
With him, most authors steal their works, or buy;
Garth did not write his own Dispensary.°
Name a new play, and he's the poet's friend,   620
Nay, showed his faults — but when would poets
   mend?
No place so sacred from such fops is barred,
Nor is Paul's church more safe than Paul's church-
   yard:°

---

551. **admired:** wondered, marveled.   552. **Titans:** grotesque giant sons of earth and heaven, who were hurled into Tartary for attempting to conquer heaven.   578. **on no pretense:** however good your reasons for being so.   580. **With . . . trust:** Do not betray your trust, your duty to give a just judgment, by being too polite, too humbly deferential.

585. **Appius:** Dennis, see above, l. 270n. He was the author of a tragedy *Appius and Virginia.* "Tremendous" was a favorite adjective of his.   588. **tax:** censure. **honorable:** the title (the Honorable) given to the children of certain ranks of the nobility.   591. **without . . . degrees:** Noblemen, and their sons, were allowed special privileges at the university.   592–93. **Satires . . . dedicators:** a perfect rhyme in Pope's day.   601. **asleep:** a top is said to sleep when it is moving at its greatest speed.   606. **run on:** continue writing as.   617. **Dryden's Fables:** stories from Chaucer and Boccaccio in modern English verse. **Durfey's Tales:** *Tales Tragical and Comical* (1704) by Thomas Durfey, a voluminous popular writer.   619. **Garth . . . Dispensary:** "A common slander at that time in prejudice of that deserving author" (Warburton). Garth, who became a friend of Pope, first published his mock-heroic *Dispensary* in 1699.   623. **Paul's churchyard:** that of St. Paul's, where booksellers had stalls.

Nay, fly to altars; there they'll talk you dead:
For fools rush in where angels fear to tread.
Distrustful sense with modest caution speaks,
It still looks home, and short excursions makes;
But rattling nonsense in full volleys breaks,
And never shocked,° and never turned aside,
Bursts out, resistless, with a thundering tide.   630

But where's the man, who counsel can bestow,
Still pleased to teach, and yet not proud to know?°
Unbiased, or by favor, or by spite;
Not dully prepossessed, nor blindly right;
Tho' learn'd, well-bred; and though well-bred,
        sincere;
Modestly bold, and humanly severe:
Who to a friend his faults can freely show,
And gladly praise the merit of a foe?
Blest with a taste exact, yet unconfined;
A knowledge both of books and human kind;   640
Generous converse;° a soul exempt from pride;
And love to praise, with reason on his side?

Such once were critics; such the happy few,
Athens and Rome in better ages knew.
The mighty Stagirite first left the shore,
Spread all his sails, and durst the deeps explore;
He steered securely, and discovered far,
Led by the light of the Maeonian Star.°
Poets, a race long unconfined, and free,
Still fond and proud of savage liberty,   650
Received his laws;° and stood convinced 'twas fit,
Who conquered Nature,° should preside o'er wit.

Horace still charms with graceful negligence,
And without method talks us into sense,
Will, like a friend, familiarly convey
The truest notions in the easiest way.
He, who supreme in judgment, as in wit,
Might boldly censure, as he boldly writ,
Yet judged with coolness, though he sung with fire;
His precepts teach but what his works inspire.   660
Our critics take a contrary extreme,
They judge with fury, but they write with fle'me:°
Nor suffers Horace more in wrong translations
By wits, than critics in as wrong quotations.

See Dionysius° Homer's thoughts refine,
And call new beauties forth from every line!

Fancy and art in gay Petronius° please,
The scholar's learning, with the courtier's ease.

In grave Quintilian's° copious work, we find
The justest rules, and clearest method joined: 670
Thus useful arms in magazines we place,
All ranged in order, and disposed with grace,
But less to please the eye, than arm the hand,
Still fit for use, and ready at command.

Thee, bold Longinus!° all the Nine inspire,
And bless their critic with a poet's fire.
An ardent judge, who zealous in his trust,
With warmth gives sentence, yet is always just;
Whose own example strengthens all his laws;
And is himself that great sublime he draws.   680

Thus long succeeding critics justly reigned,
License repressed, and useful laws ordained.
Learning and Rome alike in empire grew;
And arts still followed where her eagles flew;
From the same foes, at last, both felt their doom,
And the same age saw learning fall, and Rome.
With tyranny, then superstition joined,
As that the body, this enslaved the mind;
Much was believed, but little understood,
And to be dull was construed to be good;   690
A second deluge learning thus o'errun,
And the monks finished what the Goths begun.

At length Erasmus,° that great injured name,
(The glory° of the priesthood, and the shame!)°
Stemmed the wild torrent of a barbarous age,
And drove those holy Vandals° off the stage.

But see each Muse, in Leo's° golden days,
Starts from her trance, and trims her withered bays!
Rome's ancient Genius,° o'er its ruins spread,   699
Shakes off the dust, and rears his reverend head.
Then Sculpture and her sister arts revive;
Stones leaped to form, and rocks began to live;
With sweeter notes each rising temple rung;
A Raphael° painted, and a Vida° sung.
Immortal Vida: on whose honored brow
The poet's bays and critic's ivy° grow:
Cremona now shall ever boast thy name,
As next in place to Mantua,° next in fame!

629. shocked: stopped.   632. to know: of knowing.   641. converse: hold social intercourse.   648. Maeonian Star: Homer (Maeonia was thought to be his birthplace).   651. Received his laws: It had long been supposed that Aristotle's *Art of Poetry* contained strict rules for dramatic and other compositions.   652. conquered Nature: Aristotle investigated many aspects of the physical world.   662. fle'me: phlegm (clamminess) produced disease, and so came to mean dullness, apathy.   665. Dionysius: of Halicarnassus, a Greek critic of Horace's time.   667. Petronius: Petronius Arbiter acted as *arbiter elegantiae*, "umpire on questions of taste," in Nero's court.

669. Quintilian: Roman critic; his *Institutio Oratoria*, in twelve books, is extant and Pope knew it well.   675. Longinus: author of the fine *Treatise on the Sublime*, much valued in Pope's time.   693. Erasmus: the spirited humanist (1467–1536); his ironic *Praise of Folly* satirizes the abuses of learning, among other things.   694. glory: because he was a priest.   shame: because he attacked priests.   696. Vandals: Goths, Germanic barbarians.   697. Leo: Pope Leo X (1475–1521), a great patron of art and letters.   699. Genius: tutelary deity.   704. Raphael: (1483–1520) long considered the greatest of painters.   Vida: Italian poet.   706. ivy: commonly associated with Bacchus, and also with poets, ivy emblematized learning. Reserving the more normal laurel crowns for poets, Pope transfers the ivy crowns to critics.   707–08. Cremona . . . Mantua: the birthplaces of Vida and Virgil. Pope refers brilliantly to a famous line of Virgil's: "Mantua, alas! too near to the unfortunate Cremona" (*Eclogues*, ix. 28); Cremona had been parceled out to reward veteran soldiers.

But soon by impious arms from Latium° chased,
Their ancient bounds the banished Muses passed;
Thence arts o'er all the northern world advance,
But critic learning flourished most in France: 712
The rules, a nation born to serve, obeys;
And Boileau° still in right of Horace sways.
But we, brave Britons, foreign laws despised,
And kept unconquered, and uncivilized;
Fierce for the liberties of wit, and bold,
We still defied the Romans, as of old.
Yet some there were, among the sounder few
Of those who less presumed, and better knew,   720
Who durst assert the juster ancient cause,
And here restored wit's fundamental laws.
Such was the Muse, whose rules and practice tell,
" Nature's chief masterpiece is writing well."°
Such was Roscommon,° not more learn'd than
    good,
With manners generous as his noble blood;
To him the wit of Greece and Rome was known,
And every author's merit, but his own.
Such late was Walsh° — the Muse's judge and
    friend,
Who justly knew to blame or to commend;   730
To failings mild, but zealous for desert;
The clearest head, and the sincerest heart.
This humble praise, lamented shade! receive,
This praise at least a grateful Muse may give:
The Muse, whose early voice you taught to sing,
Prescribed her heights, and pruned° her tender
    wing,
(Her guide now lost) no more attempts to rise,
But in low numbers° short excursions tries:
Content, if hence th' unlearn'd their wants° may
    view,
The learn'd reflect on what before they knew: 740
Careless of censure, nor too fond of fame;
Still pleased to praise, yet not afraid to blame;
Averse alike to flatter, or offend;
Not free from faults, nor yet too vain to mend.

THE RAPE OF THE LOCK

The occasion of the poem is sufficiently indicated in
its dedicatory epistle, but we should not now be reading the poem if it only served to reconcile two families

---

709. **Latium**: Italy; Rome was sacked by the troops of the
Holy Roman Empire in 1527, and Pope suggests that learning
fled to other parts of Europe.   714. **Boileau**: Boileau-Despréaux
(1636–1711) wrote satires, epistles, *L'Art poétique*, and the
mock heroic *Lutrin*, all of them much admired in England.
724. **Nature's . . . well**: The line is quoted from the *Essay on
Poetry* (1682) by John Sheffield, Earl of Mulgrave and later
Duke of Buckinghamshire, a work of some deserved reputation
in its time.   725. **Roscommon**: Earl of Roscommon, Wentworth Dillon, who wrote *Essay on Translated Verse*.   729.
Walsh: William Walsh (1663–1708), friend of the young Pope
and his poetic mentor.   736. **pruned**: preened.   738. **low numbers**: humble verses.   739. **their wants**: what they lack.

---

belonging to the distant past. Nor should we be reading
it if it achieved no more than a brilliant mockery of
the form of the epic. Its success as a social emollient
and as a literary satire is not sufficient to make a poem
world-famous after two and a half centuries. It is still
read universally because, over and above everything
else, it is a good story that is firmly based on human
nature and well told. Lines and phrases from the poem
recur frequently in our later literature just because
what is at the heart of the poem is perennially repeating itself. That the poem is often recalled in the course
of Henry James's stories is pleasant proof that the
personages and the events of the poem exist timelessly.
If we do not know *Paradise Lost* and the epics of the
ancient world, our loss is great, for part of the interest
of the poem lies in its relation to epic poetry. But
Pope's little mock-epic calls first of all for knowledge
more worthwhile still — first-hand knowledge of what
is going on around us in our daily lives.

THE

RAPE of the LOCK

AN

HEROI-COMICAL [1]

P O E M

In Five Canto's

Nolueram, Belinda, tuos violare capillos,
Sed juvat hoc precibus me tribuisse tuis.
MARTIAL [2]

TO

Mrs.[3] ARABELLA FERMOR [4]

MADAM,
It will be in vain to deny that I have some regard for
this piece, since I dedicate it to you. Yet you may bear

RAPE OF THE LOCK.   1. **Heroi-comical**: mock-epic.   2. **Martial**:
Pope substitutes "Belinda" for Martial's "Polytime": the motto
may be translated: "I was loth, Belinda, to violate your locks;
but I am pleased to have granted that much to your prayers."
3. **Mrs**: the title of a lady whether married or single.   4. **Arabella
Fermor**: She was the daughter of Henry Fermor of Tusmore and
Somerton, Oxon., and of Ellen, second daughter and co-heir of
Sir George Browne of Wickhambreux, Kent, who is the Sir Plume
of the poem. The date of her birth is unknown, but probably fell
between 1688 and 1690. On March 25, 1693, we find her arriving
at the English Convent of Paris, where she stayed nine years,
absenting herself for considerable periods in order to "perfect her
French" in other houses. She returned to England in 1704, and
four years later began to be celebrated by the poets as a "beauty."
Late in 1714 or early in 1715 she married Francis Perkins of Ufton
Court, Berks. There were six children of the marriage. She died in
1738, two years after her husband. This dedication is written in
the manner of the polite correspondence of the time which modeled
itself on that of French writers of the seventeenth century, notable
among whom was Voiture. The letter that Belinda receives at
l. 118 belongs to an older fashion.

me witness, it was intended only to divert a few young ladies, who have good sense and good humor enough, to laugh not only at their sex's little unguarded follies, but at their own. But as it was communicated with the air of a secret, it soon found its way into the world. An imperfect copy having been offered to a bookseller, you had the good-nature [5] for my sake to consent to the publication of one more correct: this I was forced to before I had executed half my design, for the *machinery* was entirely wanting to complete it.

The *machinery*, Madam, is a term invented by the critics, to signify that part which the deities, angels, or demons are made to act in a poem: for the ancient poets are in one respect like many modern ladies; let an action be never so trivial in itself, they always make it appear of the utmost importance. These machines I determined to raise on a very new and odd foundation, the *Rosicrucian* doctrine [6] of spirits.

I know how disagreeable it is to make use of hard words before a lady; but 'tis so much the concern of a poet to have his works understood, and particularly by your sex, that you must give me leave to explain two or three difficult terms.

The *Rosicrucians* are a people I must bring you acquainted with. The best account I know of them is in a French book called *Le Comte de Gabalis*, which both in its title and size [7] is so like a *novel*, that many of the fair sex have read it for one by mistake. According to these gentlemen, the four elements are inhabited by spirits, which they call *sylphs, gnomes,*[8] *nymphs,* and *salamanders.* The *gnomes*, or demons of earth, delight in mischief; but the *sylphs*, whose habitation is in the air, are the best-conditioned creatures imaginable. For they say, any mortals may enjoy the most intimate familiarities with these gentle spirits, upon a condition very easy to all true *adepts,* an inviolate preservation of chastity.[9]

As to the following cantos, all the passages of them are as fabulous, as the vision at the beginning, or the transformation at the end; (except the loss of your hair, which I always mention with reverence). The human persons are as fictitious as the airy ones; and the character of *Belinda,*[10] as it is now managed, resembles you in nothing but in beauty.

If this poem had as many graces as there are in your person, or in your mind, yet I could never hope it

should pass through the world half so uncensured as you have done. But let its fortune be what it will, mine is happy enough, to have given me this occasion of assuring you that I am, with the truest esteem,

> *Madam,*
> *Your Most Obedient*
> *Humble Servant*
> A. POPE

CANTO I

What dire offense from amorous causes springs,°
What mighty contests rise from trivial things,
I sing — This verse to Caryll,° Muse! is due:
This, even Belinda may vouchsafe to view:
Slight is the subject, but not so the praise,
If she inspire, and he approve my lays.

Say what strange motive, goddess! could compel
A well-bred lord t' assault a gentle belle?
O say what stranger cause, yet unexplored,
Could make a gentle belle reject a lord?   10
In tasks so bold, can little men engage,
And in soft bosoms dwells such mighty rage?

Sol through white curtains° shot a timorous ray,
And oped those eyes that must eclipse the day:
Now lapdogs give themselves the rousing shake,
And sleepless lovers, just at twelve, awake:
Thrice rung the bell, the slipper knocked the
     ground,
And the pressed watch° returned a silver sound.
Belinda still her downy pillow pressed,
Her guardian Sylph prolonged the balmy rest: 20
'Twas he had summoned to her silent bed
The morning dream that hovered o'er her head;
A youth more glittering than a birthnight° beau,
(That even in slumber caused her cheek to glow)
Seemed to her ear his winning lips to lay,
And thus in whispers said, or seemed to say:

"Fairest of mortals, thou distinguished care
Of thousand bright inhabitants of air!
If e'er one vision touched thy infant thought,
Of all the nurse and all the priest have taught;   30
Of airy elves by moonlight shadows seen,
The silver token,° and the circled green,

---

5. **good sense . . . good humor . . . good-nature:** see Canto V, ll. 16, 30–31, below.   6. **Rosicrucian doctrine:** The Rosicrucians were a sect founded in Germany early in the seventeenth century.   7. **title and size:** *The Count de Soissons* and *The Count of Amboise* are two of the novels translated from the French and included in the series of "Modern Novels" (published by Richard Bentley) in which Ayres's translation of *Gabalis* appeared. The size of them all is duodecimo.   8. **gnomes:** In *Gabalis* these, like all the other spirits, are "good," but, living in the earth near to the Devil, they have been frightened into helping him to make "the Soul of a man become Mortal." Pope makes them mischievous by nature.   9. **chastity:** The renunciation of "all Carnal Commerce with Women" is, according to *Gabalis,* the first condition for men who wish to control the sylphs. Unless the sylphs could gain earthly lovers, they never achieved immortality.   10. **Belinda:** a fashionable name of the time. It was especially appropriate for one who was known to her friends as Belle Fermor.

Canto I.   1–12. **What . . . rage:** "The custom of beginning all *Poems* with a *Proposition* of the whole work, and an *Invocation* of some God for his assistance to go through with it, is . . . solemnly and religiously observed by all the ancient *Poets*" (a note of Cowley's for his epic *Davideis*).   3. **Caryll:** a generous Catholic friend of Pope's who owned land in Sussex. His concern to reconcile the families of the Fermors and Petres led to Pope's writing the poem.   13. **curtains:** those of the four-poster bed.   18. **pressed watch:** Striking a light was an inconvenience in the days before matches, and so there was a demand for "repeater" watches, England having the best manufacturers of them. The "repeating" as a response to pressure was a new device. When pressed by the finger a minute bell sounded the hour, and then 2, 4, and 6 for the quarter just passed.   23. **birthnight:** pertaining to celebrations at court on a royal birthday, when the courtiers' dresses were particularly splendid.   32. **silver token:** sixpence; to be left by fairies in the shoe of the maiden they favored.

Or virgins visited by angel powers,
With golden crowns and wreaths of heavenly flow-
ers;
Hear and believe! thy own importance know,
Nor bound thy narrow views to things below.
Some secret truths, from learnèd pride concealed,
To maids alone and children are revealed:
What though no credit doubting wits° may give?
The fair and innocent shall still believe.   40
Know, then, unnumbered spirits round thee fly,
The light militia of the lower sky:
These, though unseen, are ever on the wing,
Hang o'er the box,° and hover round the Ring.°
Think what an equipage thou hast in air,
And view with scorn two pages and a chair.°
As now your own, our beings were of old,
And once enclosed in woman's beauteous mold;
Thence, by a soft transition, we repair
From earthly vehicles to these of air,   50
Think not, when woman's transient breath is fled,
That all her vanities at once are dead;
Succeeding vanities she still regards,
And though she plays no more, o'erlooks the cards.
Her joy in gilded chariots, when alive,
And love of ombre,° after death survive.
For when the fair in all their pride expire,
To their first elements their souls retire:
The sprites of fiery termagants in flame
Mount up, and take a Salamander's° name.   60
Soft yielding minds to water glide away,
And sip, with Nymphs, their elemental tea.°
The graver prude sinks downward to a Gnome,
In search of mischief still on earth to roam.
The light coquettes in Sylphs aloft repair,
And sport and flutter in the fields of air.
      "Know further yet; whoever fair and chaste
Rejects mankind, is by some Sylph embraced:
For spirits, freed from mortal laws, with ease
Assume what sexes and what shapes they please.
What guards the purity of melting maids,   71
In courtly balls, and midnight masquerades,
Safe from the treacherous friend, the daring spark,°
The glance by day, the whisper in the dark,
When kind occasion prompts their warm desires,
When music softens, and when dancing fires?
'Tis but their Sylph, the wise celestials know,
Though honor is the word with men below.
      "Some nymphs there are, too conscious of their
face,

39. doubting wits: the skeptic was an increasingly familiar figure during the late seventeenth century and later.   44. box: theater box. Ring: a fashionable driving ground in Hyde Park. 46. chair: a sedan chair.   56. ombre: a fashionable game of the time, in which 40 cards only were dealt—the pack minus the 8's, 9's and 10's.   60. Salamander: a lizardlike animal supposed to live in fire.   61–62. away . . . tea: a perfect rhyme in Pope's day. In Pope's time tea was pronounced "tay."   73. spark: a contemptuous term for a showy man about town.

For life predestined to the Gnomes' embrace.   80
These swell their prospects and exalt their pride,
When offers are disdained, and love denied:
Then gay ideas crowd the vacant brain,
While peers, and dukes, and all their sweeping
train,
And garters, stars, and coronets° appear,
And in soft sounds, ' your Grace '° salutes their ear.
'Tis these that early taint the female soul,
Instruct the eyes of young coquettes to roll,
Teach infant cheeks a bidden blush° to know,
And little hearts to flutter at a beau.   90
      "Oft, when the world imagine women stray,
The Sylphs through mystic mazes guide their
way,
Thro' all the giddy circle they pursue,
And old impertinence expel by new.
What tender maid but must a victim fall
To one man's treat, but for another's ball?
When Florio speaks, what virgin could withstand,
If gentle Damon did not squeeze her hand?
With varying vanities, from every part,
They shift the moving toyshop of their heart;   100
Where wigs with wigs, with sword knots sword
knots strive,
Beaux banish beaux, and coaches coaches drive.°
This erring mortals levity may call;
Oh blind to truth! the Sylphs contrive it all.
      "Of these am I, who thy protection claim,
A watchful sprite, and Ariel is my name.
Late, as I ranged the crystal wilds of air,
In the clear mirror of thy ruling star
I saw, alas! some dread event impend,
Ere to the main this morning sun descend,   110
But heaven reveals not what, or how, or where:
Warned by the Sylph, oh pious maid, beware!
This to disclose is all thy guardian can:
Beware of all, but most beware of man! "
      He said; when Shock,° who thought she slept
too long,
Leaped up, and waked his mistress with his tongue.
'Twas then, Belinda, if report say true,
Thy eyes first opened on a billet-doux;
Wounds, charms, and ardors were no sooner read,
But all the vision vanished from thy head.   120
      And now, unveiled, the toilet stands displayed,
Each silver vase in mystic order laid.
First, robed in white, the nymph intent adores,
With head uncovered, the cosmetic powers.
A heavenly image in the glass appears,

85. garters . . . coronets: insignia of noble rank.   86. your Grace: a courtesy title given to a duke or a duchess.   89. bidden blush: rouged blush.   101–02. Where . . . drive: The versification and word order mimic Ovid's when describing heroic conflict.   115. Shock: the shock or shough, an Icelandic breed of dog fashionable as a lapdog.

To that she bends, to that her eyes she rears;
Th' inferior priestess, at her altar's side,
Trembling, begins the sacred rites of pride.
Unnumbered treasures ope at once, and here
The various offerings of the world appear;   130
From each she nicely culls with curious toil,
And decks the goddess with the glittering spoil.
This casket India's glowing gems unlocks,
And all Arabia breathes from yonder box.
The tortoise here and elephant unite,
Transformed to combs, the speckled, and the white.
Here files of pins extend their shining rows,
Puffs, powders, patches, Bibles,° billets-doux.
Now awful Beauty puts on all its arms;
The fair each moment rises in her charms,   140
Repairs her smiles, awakens every grace,
And calls forth all the wonders of her face;
Sees by degrees a purer blush arise,
And keener lightnings quicken in her eyes.
The busy Sylphs surround their darling care,
These set the head, and those divide the hair,
Some fold the sleeve, whilst others plait° the gown;
And Betty's° praised for labors not her own.

CANTO II

Not with more glories, in th' ethereal plain,
The sun first rises o'er the purpled main,
Than, issuing forth, the rival of his beams
Launched on the bosom of the silver Thames.
Fair nymphs, and well-dressed youths around her
        shone,
But every eye was fixed on her alone.
On her white breast a sparkling cross she wore,
Which Jews might kiss, and infidels adore.
Her lively looks a sprightly mind disclose,
Quick as her eyes, and as unfixed as those: 10
Favors to none, to all she smiles extends;
Oft she rejects, but never once offends.
Bright as the sun, her eyes the gazers strike,
And, like the sun, they shine on all alike.
Yet graceful ease, and sweetness void of pride,
Might hide her faults, if belles had faults to hide:
If to her share some female errors fall,
Look on her face, and you'll forget 'em all.
    This nymph, to the destruction of mankind,
Nourished two locks, which graceful hung behind
In equal curls, and well conspired to deck   21
With shining ringlets the smooth ivory neck.
Love in these labyrinths his slaves detains,
And mighty hearts are held in slender chains.
With hairy springes° we the birds betray

Slight lines of hair surprise the finny prey,
Fair tresses man's imperial race ensnare,
And beauty draws us with a single hair.
    Th' adventurous Baron the bright locks admired;
He saw, he wished, and to the prize aspired.   30
Resolved to win, he meditates the way,
By force to ravish, or by fraud betray;
For when success a lover's toil attends,
Few ask, if fraud or force attained his ends.
    For this, ere Phoebus rose, he had implored
Propitious heaven, and every power adored,
But chiefly Love — to Love an altar built,
Of twelve vast French romances, neatly gilt.
There lay three garters, half a pair of gloves;
And all the trophies of his former loves;   40
With tender billets-doux he lights the pyre,
And breathes three amorous sighs to raise the fire.
Then prostrate falls, and begs with ardent eyes
Soon to obtain, and long possess the prize:
The powers gave ear, and granted half his prayer,
The rest, the winds dispersed in empty air.
    But now secure° the painted vessel glides,
The sunbeams trembling on the floating tides:
While melting music steals upon the sky,
And softened sounds along the waters die;   50
Smooth flow the waves, the zephyrs gently play,
Belinda smiled, and all the world was gay.
All but the Sylph — with careful thoughts op-
        pressed,
Th' impending woe sat heavy on his breast.
He summons strait his denizens° of air;
The lucid squadrons round the sails repair:
Soft o'er the shrouds aërial whispers breathe,
That seemed but zephyrs to the train beneath.
Some to the sun their insect wings unfold,
Waft on the breeze, or sink in clouds of gold;   60
Transparent forms, too fine for mortal sight,
Their fluid bodies half dissolved in light.
Loose to the wind their airy garments flew,
Thin glittering textures of the filmy dew,
Dipped in the richest tincture of the skies,
Where light disports in ever-mingling dyes,
While every beam new transient colors flings,
Colors that change whene'er they wave their wings.
Amid the circle, on the gilded mast,
Superior by the head,° was Ariel placed;   70
His purple pinions opening to the sun,
He raised his azure wand, and thus begun.
    " Ye Sylphs and Sylphids,° to your chief give ear!
Fays, Fairies, Genii, Elves, and Daemons, hear!
Ye know the spheres and various tasks assigned
By laws eternal to th' aërial kind.
Some in the fields of purest aether play,

---

138. **Bibles:** Booksellers supplied Bibles in very small format for fashionable use.   147. **plait:** dispose in folds.   148. **Betty:** a generic term for a lady's maid.   **Canto II.**   25. **springes:** traps.

47. **secure:** free from care.   55. **denizens:** used in its proper sense of "naturalized aliens."   70. **Superior . . . head:** the hero of the epics was taller than his men.   73. **Sylphids:** female sylphs.

And bask and whiten in the blaze of day.
Some guide the course of wandering orbs on high,
Or roll the planets through the boundless sky.   80
Some less refined, beneath the moon's pale light
Pursue the stars that shoot athwart the night,
Or suck the mists in grosser air below,
Or dip their pinions in the painted bow,
Or brew fierce tempests on the wintry main,
Or o'er the glebe distill the kindly rain.
Others on earth o'er human race preside,
Watch all their ways, and all their actions guide:
Of these the chief the care of nations own,
And guard with arms divine the British throne.   90
    " Our humbler province is to tend the fair,
Not a less pleasing, though less glorious care;
To save the powder from too rude a gale,
Nor let th' imprisoned essences exhale;
To draw fresh colors from the vernal flowers;
To steal from rainbows e'er they drop in showers
A brighter wash;° to curl their waving hairs,
Assist their blushes, and inspire their airs;
Nay oft, in dreams, invention we bestow,
To change a flounce, or add a furbelow.   100
    " This day, black omens threat the brightest fair
That e'er deserved a watchful spirit's care;
Some dire disaster, or by force, or slight;°
But what, or where, the fates have wrapped in
    night.
Whether the nymph shall break Diana's law,°
Or some frail china jar receive a flaw,
Or stain her honor, or her new brocade;
Forget her prayers, or miss a masquerade;
Or lose her heart, or necklace, at a ball;
Or whether Heaven has doomed that Shock must
    fall.   110
Haste, then, ye spirits! to your charge repair:
The fluttering fan be Zephyretta's care;
The drops° to thee, Brillante, we consign;
And, Momentilla, let the watch be thine;
Do thou, Crispissa,° tend her favorite lock;
Ariel himself shall be the guard of Shock.
    " To fifty chosen Sylphs, of special note,
We trust th' important charge, the petticoat:
Oft have we known that sevenfold fence to fail,
Though stiff with hoops, and armed with ribs of
    whale.   120
Form a strong line about the silver bound,
And guard the wide circumference around.
    " Whatever spirit, careless of his charge,
His post neglects, or leaves the fair at large,
Shall feel sharp vengeance soon o'ertake his sins,
Be stopped in vials,° or transfixed with pins;

Or plunged in lakes of bitter washes lie,
Or wedged whole ages in a bodkin's eye:
Gums and pomatums° shall his flight restrain,
While clogged he beats his silken wings in vain;
Or alum styptics° with contracting power   131
Shrink his thin essence like a riveled° flower:
Or, as Ixion° fixed, the wretch shall feel
The giddy motion of the whirling mill,
In fumes of burning chocolate shall glow,
And tremble at the sea that froths below! "
    He spoke; the spirits from the sails descend;
Some, orb in orb, around the nymph extend;
Some thrid the mazy ringlets of her hair;
Some hang upon the pendants of her ear;   140
With beating hearts the dire event they wait,
Anxious, and trembling for the birth of fate.

CANTO III

Close by those meads, forever crowned with flowers,
Where Thames with pride surveys his rising towers,
There stands a structure of majestic frame,
Which from the neighboring Hampton° takes its
    name.
Here Britain's statesmen oft the fall foredoom
Of foreign tyrants, and of nymphs at home;
Here thou, great Anna! whom three realms obey,
Dost sometimes counsel take — and sometimes tea.
    Hither the heroes and the nymphs resort,
To taste awhile the pleasures of a court;   10
In various talk th' instructive hours they passed,
Who gave the ball, or paid the visit° last;
One speaks the glory of the British queen,
And one describes a charming Indian screen;
A third interprets motions, looks, and eyes;
At every word a reputation dies.
Snuff, or the fan, supply each pause of chat,
With singing, laughing, ogling, and all that.
    Meanwhile, declining from the noon of day,
The sun obliquely shoots his burning ray;   20
The hungry judges soon the sentence sign,
And wretches hang that jurymen may dine;
The merchant from th' Exchange returns in peace,
And the long labors of the toilet cease.
Belinda now, whom thirst of fame invites,
Burns to encounter two adventurous knights,
At ombre singly to decide their doom;
And swells her breast with conquests yet to come.
Straight the three bands prepare in arms to join,
Each band the number of the sacred nine.°   30

---

97. **wash:** a cosmetic lotion.   103. **slight:** sleight, trick.   105.
Diana's law: chastity.   113. **drops:** earrings.   115. **Crispissa:**
derived from the Latin *crispo*, I curl.   126. **vials:** phials, bottles.

129. **pomatums:** ointments.   131. **styptics:** astringents, which
stop bleeding.   132. **riveled:** shriveled.   133. **Ixion:** who, for
punishment, was tied to a perpetually turning wheel in Hades.
Canto III.   4. Hampton: Hampton Court was a royal residence,
which in Queen Anne's time was associated as much with wits as
with statesmen.   12. **visit:** a part of the daily routine of a fashionable lady.   30. **sacred nine:** the muses; Pope is suggesting that
the number of cards used in ombre has some significance.

Soon as she spreads her hand, th' aërial guard
Descend, and sit on each important card:
First Ariel perched upon a Matador,°
Then each, according to the rank they bore;
For Sylphs, yet mindful of their ancient race,
Are, as when women, wondrous fond of place.

Behold, four Kings in majesty revered,
With hoary whiskers° and a forky beard;
And four fair Queens whose hands sustain a flower,
Th' expressive emblem of their softer power;   40
Four Knaves in garbs succinct,° a trusty band,
Caps on their heads, and halberds° in their hand;
And particolored troops, a shining train,
Draw forth to combat on the velvet plain.

The skillful nymph reviews her force with care:
" Let Spades be trumps! " she said, and trumps they
     were.
Now move to war her sable Matadors,
In show like leaders of the swarthy Moors.
Spadillio° first, unconquerable lord!
Led off two captive trumps, and swept the board.
As many more Manillio° forced to yield,   51
And marched a victor from the verdant field.
Him Basto° followed, but his fate more hard
Gained but one trump and one plebeian card.
With his broad saber next, a chief in years,
The hoary Majesty of Spades appears,
Puts forth one manly leg, to sight revealed,
The rest, his many-colored robe concealed.
The rebel Knave, who dares his prince engage,
Proves the just victim of his royal rage.   60
Even mighty Pam,° that Kings and Queens o'er-
     threw
And mowed down armies in the fights of loo,
Sad chance of war! now destitute of aid,
Falls undistinguished by the victor Spade!

Thus far both armies to Belinda yield;
Now to the Baron fate inclines the field.
His warlike Amazon her host invades,
Th' imperial consort of the crown of Spades.
The Club's black tyrant first her victim died,
Spite of his haughty mien, and barbarous pride:
What boots the regal circle on his head,   71
His giant limbs, in state unwieldy spread;
That long behind he trails his pompous robe,
And, of all monarchs, only grasps the globe?
The Baron now his Diamonds pours apace;
Th' embroidered King who shows but half his
     face,

And his refulgent Queen, with powers combined,
Of broken troops an easy conquest find.
Clubs, Diamonds, Hearts, in wild disorder seen,
With throngs promiscuous strew the level green.
Thus when dispersed a routed army runs,   81
Of Asia's troops, and Afric's sable sons,
With like confusion different nations fly,
Of various habit, and of various dye,
The pierced battalions disunited fall,
In heaps on heaps; one fate o'erwhelms them all.

The Knave of Diamonds tries his wily arts,
And wins (oh shameful chance!) the Queen of
     Hearts.
At this, the blood the virgin's cheek forsook,
A livid paleness spreads o'er all her look;   90
She sees, and trembles at th' approaching ill,
Just in the jaws of ruin, and codille.°
And now (as oft in some distempered State)
On one nice trick depends the general fate.
An Ace of Hearts steps forth: The King unseen
Lurked in her hand, and mourned his captive
     Queen:
He springs to vengeance with an eager pace,
And falls like thunder on the prostrate Ace.
The nymph exulting fills with shouts the sky;
The walls, the woods, and long canals reply.   100

Oh thoughtless mortals! ever blind to fate,
Too soon dejected and too soon elate.
Sudden, these honors shall be snatched away,
And cursed forever this victorious day.

For lo! the board with cups and spoons is
     crowned,
The berries crackle, and the mill turns round;°
On shining altars of Japan° they raise
The silver lamp; the fiery spirits blaze:
From silver spouts the grateful liquors glide,
While China's earth receives the smoking tide:°
At once they gratify their scent and taste,   111
And frequent cups prolong the rich repast.
Straight hover round the fair her airy band;
Some, as she sipped, the fuming liquor fanned,
Some o'er her lap their careful plumes displayed,
Trembling, and conscious of the rich brocade.
Coffee (which makes the politician wise,
And see through all things with his half-shut eyes)
Sent up in vapors to the Baron's brain
New stratagems, the radiant lock to gain.   120
Ah cease, rash youth! desist ere 'tis too late,
Fear the just gods, and think of Scylla's fate!
Changed to a bird, and sent to flit in air,

---

33. Matador: The three cards of highest value in ombre are called
matadors. **38. whiskers:** moustache. **41. succinct:** girded up.
42. halberds: weapons combining spear and battle-ax. **49. Spa-
dillio,** the Ace of Spades. **51. Manillio:** the 2 of Spades which,
in ombre, is the card of highest value. **53. Basto:** the Ace of
Clubs, the third highest card. **61. Pam:** the Knave of Clubs,
which in the game of Loo, or Lu, took precedence even over the
Ace of trumps.

92. codille: If either of the opponents won more tricks than the
principal player, he was said to give the principal player *codille*.
106. berries . . . round: The coffee beans crackle when they are
roasted. **107. altars of Japan:** lacquered tables. **110. China's
. . . tide:** The coffee is being poured into the cup.

She dearly pays for Nisus' injured hair!°
  But when to mischief mortals bend their will,
How soon they find fit instruments of ill!
Just then, Clarissa drew with tempting grace
A two-edged weapon from her shining case:
So ladies in romance assist their knight,
Present the spear, and arm him for the fight.   130
He takes the gift with reverence, and extends
The little engine on his fingers' ends;
This just behind Belinda's neck he spread,
As o'er the fragrant steams she bends her head.
Swift to the lock a thousand sprites repair,
A thousand wings, by turns, blow back the hair;
And thrice they twitched the diamond in her ear;
Thrice she looked back, and thrice the foe drew
    near.
Just in that instant, anxious Ariel sought
The close recesses of the virgin's thought;   140
As on the nosegay in her breast reclined,
He watched th' ideas rising in her mind,
Sudden he viewed, in spite of all her art,
An earthly lover° lurking at her heart.
Amazed, confused, he found his power expired,
Resigned to fate, and with a sigh retired.
  The peer now spreads the glittering forfex° wide,
T'enclose the lock; now joins it, to divide.
Even then, before the fatal engine closed,
A wretched Sylph too fondly interposed;   150
Fate urged the shears, and cut the Sylph in twain,
(But airy substance soon unites again)°
The meeting points the sacred hair dissever
From the fair head, forever, and forever!
  Then flashed the living lightning from her eyes,
And screams of horror rend th' affrighted skies.
Not louder shrieks to pitying Heaven are cast,
When husbands, or when lapdogs breathe their
    last;
Or when rich china vessels fallen from high,
In glittering dust, and painted fragments lie!   160
  Let wreaths of triumph now my temples twine,
(The victor cried) the glorious prize is mine!
While fish in streams, or birds delight in air,
Or in a coach and six the British fair,
As long as Atalantis° shall be read,
Or the small pillow grace a lady's bed,
While visits shall be paid on solemn days,
When numerous wax-lights in bright order blaze,
While nymphs take treats, or assignations give,
So long my honor, name, and praise shall live!   170

What time would spare, from steel receives its
    date,°
And monuments, like men, submit to fate!
Steel could the labor of the gods destroy,
And strike to dust th' imperial towers of Troy;°
Steel could the works of mortal pride confound,
And hew triumphal arches to the ground.
What wonder then, fair nymph! thy hairs should
    feel,
The conquering force of unresisted steel?

CANTO IV

But anxious cares the pensive nymph oppressed,
And secret passions labored in her breast.
Not youthful kings in battle seized alive,
Not scornful virgins who their charms survive,
Not ardent lovers robbed of all their bliss,
Not ancient ladies when refused a kiss,
Not tyrants fierce that unrepenting die,
Not Cynthia when her manteau's° pinned awry,
E'er felt such rage, resentment, and despair,
As thou sad virgin! for thy ravished hair.   10
  For, that sad moment, when the Sylphs with-
    drew,
And Ariel weeping from Belinda flew,
Umbriel, a dusky, melancholy sprite
As ever sullied the fair face of light,
Down to the central earth, his proper scene,
Repaired to search the gloomy cave of Spleen.°
  Swift on his sooty pinions flits the Gnome,
And in a vapor° reached the dismal dome.
No cheerful breeze this sullen region knows,
The dreaded East is all the wind that blows.   20
Here in a grotto, sheltered close from air,
And screened in shades from day's detested glare,
She sighs forever on her pensive bed,
Pain at her side, and Megrim° at her head.
  Two handmaids wait the throne: alike in place,
But differing far in figure and in face.
Here stood Ill Nature like an ancient maid,
Her wrinkled form in black and white arrayed;
With store of prayers, for mornings, nights, and
    noons,
Her hand is filled; her bosom with lampoons.   30
  There Affectation, with a sickly mien,
Shows in her cheek the roses of eighteen,
Practiced to lisp, and hang the head aside,
Faints into airs, and languishes with pride;
On the rich quilt sinks with becoming woe,
Wrapped in a gown, for sickness, and for show.

122–24. Scylla's . . . hair: Scylla, daughter of Nisus, fell in love
with Minos, her father's enemy, and gave him a hair—on which
depended the safety of the kingdom—from her father's head.
Minos was horrified at her impiety. After his victory, Minos sailed
away. Scylla clung to his ship till beaten off by Nisus, who had
become a bird. She, after drowning, also became a bird. 144.
earthly lover: see dedicatory epistle. 147. forfex: Latin for scissors. 152. But . . . again: See *Paradise Lost*, VI. 327ff. 165.
Atalantis: a libelous novel by Mrs. Manley, 2 vols., 1709.

171. date: terminus. 173–74. labor . . . Troy: The walls of
Troy had been built by two gods. Canto IV. 8. manteau: a
loose upper garment. 16. Spleen: a new name for an old malady,
one that befell rich people, attacking their spleen. 18. vapor:
appropriately because the spleen was also called "the vapors."
24. Megrim: migraine.

The fair ones feel such maladies as these,
When each new nightdress gives a new disease.

A constant vapor o'er the palace flies;
Strange phantoms rising as the mists arise;   40
Dreadful, as hermit's dreams in haunted shades,
Or bright, as visions of expiring maids.
Now glaring fiends, and snakes on rolling spires,°
Pale specters, gaping tombs, and purple fires:
Now lakes of liquid gold, Elysian scenes,
And crystal domes, and angels in machines.

Unnumbered throngs on every side are seen,
Of bodies changed to various forms by Spleen.°
Here living teapots stand, one arm held out,
One bent; the handle this, and that the spout: 50
A pipkin° there, like Homer's tripod walks;
Here sighs a jar, and there a goose pie° talks;
Men prove with child, as powerful fancy works,
And maids turned bottles, call aloud for corks.

Safe passed the Gnome thro' this fantastic band,
A branch° of healing spleenwort in his hand.
Then thus addressed the power: "Hail, wayward
     queen!
Who rule the sex to fifty from fifteen:
Parent of vapors and of female wit,
Who give th' hysteric, or poetic fit,   60
On various tempers act by various ways,
Make some take physic, others scribble plays;
Who cause the proud their visits to delay,
And send the godly in a pet to pray.
A nymph there is, that all thy power disdains,
And thousands more in equal mirth maintains.
But oh! if e'er thy Gnome could spoil a grace,
Or raise a pimple on a beauteous face,
Like citron waters° matrons' cheeks inflame,
Or change complexions at a losing game;   70
If e'er with airy horns I planted heads,
Or rumpled petticoats, or tumbled beds,
Or caused suspicion when no soul was rude,
Or discomposed the headdress of a prude,
Or e'er to costive lap dog gave disease,
Which not the tears of brightest eyes could ease:
Hear me, and touch Belinda with chagrin;
That single act gives half the world the spleen."

The goddess with a discontented air   79
Seems to reject him, tho' she grants his prayer.
A wondrous bag with both her hands she binds,
Like that where once Ulysses held the winds;
There she collects the force of female lungs,
Sighs, sobs, and passions, and the war of tongues.

A vial next she fills with fainting fears,
Soft sorrows, melting griefs, and flowing tears.
The Gnome rejoicing bears her gifts away,
Spreads his black wings, and slowly mounts to day.

Sunk in Thalestris' arms the nymph he found,
Her eyes dejected and her hair unbound.   90
Full o'er their heads the swelling bag he rent,
And all the Furies issued at the vent.
Belinda burns with more than mortal ire,
And fierce Thalestris fans the rising fire.
" O wretched maid! " she spread her hands, and
     cried,
(While Hampton's echoes, "Wretched maid!" re-
     plied)
" Was it for this you took such constant care
The bodkin,° comb, and essence to prepare?
For this your locks in paper durance bound,
For this with torturing irons wreathed around?
For this with fillets strained your tender head,   101
And bravely bore the double loads of lead?
Gods! shall the ravisher display your hair,
While the fops envy, and the ladies stare!
Honor forbid! at whose unrivaled shrine
Ease, pleasure, virtue, all, our sex resign.
Methinks already I your tears survey,
Already hear the horrid things they say,
Already see you a degraded toast,
And all your honor in a whisper lost!   110
How shall I, then, your helpless fame defend?
'Twill then be infamy to seem your friend!
And shall this prize, th' inestimable prize,
Exposed thro' crystal to the gazing eyes,
And heightened by the diamond's circling rays,°
On that rapacious hand forever blaze?
Sooner shall grass in Hyde Park Circus grow,
And wits take lodgings in the sound of Bow;°
Sooner let earth, air, sea, to chaos fall,
Men, monkeys, lap dogs, parrots, perish all!"   120

She said; then raging to Sir Plume repairs,
And bids her beau demand the precious hairs:
(Sir Plume, of amber snuffbox justly vain,
And the nice conduct of a clouded cane)°
With earnest eyes, and round unthinking face,
He first the snuffbox opened, then the case,
And thus broke out — "My Lord, why, what the
     devil?
Zounds!° damn the lock! 'fore Gad, you must be
     civil!
Plague on't! 'tis past a jest — nay prithee, pox!

---

43. spires: spirals. **48–54. bodies . . . corks:** the medical books of the time testify to splenetic patients' suffering hallucinations such as these. **51. pipkin:** a small earthenware boiler. **52. goose pie:** *"Alludes to a real fact, a Lady of distinction imagin'd herself in this condition"* (Pope). **56. branch . . . hand:** Aeneas passed into Hades guarded by the golden bough he carried. Pope changes it to the herb that was supposed to be good for the spleen. **69. citron waters:** a brandy distilled from lemon rind.

98. bodkin: "an instrument to dress the hair" (Johnson's Dictionary). **114–15. Exposed . . . rays:** She thinks that the Baron will have some of the hair mounted in a ring. **118. Bow:** a locality in the City, which was now wholly occupied by merchants. **124. And . . . cane:** and the skilled management of a cane fashionably veined with dark color. **128. Zounds:** a corruption of "God's wounds."

Give her the hair " — he spoke, and rapped his
   box.   130
"It grieves me much" (replied the peer again)
"Who speaks so well should ever speak in vain.
But by this lock, this sacred lock I swear,
(Which never more shall join its parted hair;
Which never more its honors shall renew,
Clipped from the lovely head where late it grew)
That while my nostrils draw the vital air,
This hand, which won it, shall forever wear."
He spoke, and speaking, in proud triumph spread
The long-contended honors of her head.   140
  But Umbriel, hateful Gnome! forbears not so;
He breaks the vial whence the sorrows flow.
Then see! the nymph in beauteous grief appears,
Her eyes half languishing, half drowned in tears;
On her heaved bosom hung her drooping head,
Which, with a sigh, she raised; and thus she said.
  "Forever cursed be this detested day,
Which snatched my best, my favorite curl away!
Happy! ah ten times happy had I been,
If Hampton Court these eyes had never seen! 150
Yet am not I the first mistaken maid,
By love of courts to numerous ills betrayed.
Oh had I rather unadmired remained
In some lone isle, or distant northern land;
Where the gilt chariot never marks the way,
Where none learn ombre, none e'er taste bohea!°
There kept my charms concealed from mortal eye,
Like roses, that in deserts bloom and die.
What moved my mind with youthful lords to
   roam?
Oh had I stayed, and said my prayers at home!
'Twas this, the morning omens seemed to tell, 161
Thrice from my trembling hand the patch-box fell;
The tottering china shook without a wind,
Nay, Poll° sat mute, and Shock was most unkind!
A Sylph too warned me of the threats of fate,
In mystic visions, now believed too late!
See the poor remnants of these slighted hairs!
My hands shall rend what even thy rapine spares:
These, in two sable ringlets taught to break,
Once gave new beauties to the snowy neck; 170
The sister lock now sits uncouth, alone,
And in its fellow's fate foresees its own;
Uncurled it hangs, the fatal shears demands,
And tempts once more thy sacrilegious hands.
Oh hadst thou, cruel! been content to seize
Hairs less in sight, or any hairs but these!"

CANTO V

She said: the pitying audience melt in tears.
But Fate and Jove had stopped the Baron's ears.
In vain Thalestris with reproach assails,

156. bohea: a sort of tea.   164. Poll: the parrot.

For who can move when fair Belinda fails?
Not half so fixed the Trojan could remain,
While Anna begged and Dido raged in vain.°
Then grave Clarissa graceful waved her fan;
Silence ensued, and thus the nymph began.
  "Say why are beauties praised and honored
   most,°
The wise man's passion, and the vain man's toast?
Why decked with all that land and sea afford, 11
Why angels called, and angel-like adored?
Why round our coaches crowd the white-gloved
   beaux,
Why bows the side box from its inmost rows;
How vain are all these glories, all our pains,
Unless good sense preserve what beauty gains:
That men may say, when we the front box grace,°
'Behold the first in virtue as in face!'
Oh! if to dance all night, and dress all day,
Charmed the smallpox, or chased old age away;
Who would not scorn what housewife's cares pro-
   duce,   21
Or who would learn one earthly thing of use?
To patch, nay ogle, might become a saint,
Nor could it sure be such a sin to paint.
But since, alas! frail beauty must decay,
Curled or uncurled, since locks will turn to gray;
Since painted, or not painted, all shall fade,
And she who scorns a man, must die a maid;
What then remains but well our power to use,
And keep good humor still whate'er we lose? 30
And trust me, dear! good humor can prevail,
When airs, and flights, and screams, and scolding
   fail.
Beauties in vain their pretty eyes may roll;
Charms strike the sight, but merit wins the soul."
  So spoke the dame, but no applause ensued;
Belinda frowned, Thalestris called her prude.
"To arms, to arms!" the fierce virago cries,
And swift as lightning to the combat flies.
All side in parties, and begin th' attack;
Fans clap, silks rustle, and tough whalebones crack;
Heroes' and heroines' shouts confus'dly rise, 41
And bass and treble voices strike the skies.
No common weapons in their hands are found,
Like gods they fight, nor dread a mortal wound.
  So when bold Homer makes the gods engage,
And heavenly breasts with human passions rage;
'Gainst Pallas, Mars; Latona, Hermes arms;
And all Olympus rings with loud alarms:
Jove's thunder roars, Heaven trembles all around,

Canto V.   5–6. Not . . . vain: see *Aeneid*, IV.   9–34. Say . . .
soul: Pope introduced this speech in the edition of 1717, so as
"to open more clearly the moral of the poem." It is "a parody of
the speech of Sarpedon to Glaucus in [*Iliad*, XII]."   14–17. Why
. . . grace: The ladies preferred the front boxes (those facing the
stage) when at the theater, and the gentlemen the side boxes, the
citizens preferring the pit.

Blue Neptune storms, the bellowing deeps resound:
Earth shakes her nodding towers, the ground gives
    way,   51
And the pale ghosts start at the flash of day!
    Triumphant Umbriel on a sconce's° height
Clapped his glad wings, and sat to view the fight:
Propped on their bodkin spears, the sprites survey
The growing combat, or assist the fray.
    While thro' the press enraged Thalestris flies,
And scatters death around from both her eyes,
A beau and witling perished in the throng,
One died in metaphor, and one in song.   60
" O cruel nymph! a living death I bear,"
Cried Dapperwit, and sunk beside his chair.
A mournful glance Sir Fopling upwards cast,
" Those eyes are made so killing"° — was his last.
Thus on Maeander's° flowery margin lies
Th' expiring swan, and as he sings he dies.
    When bold Sir Plume had drawn Clarissa down,
Chloe stepped in, and killed him with a frown;
She smiled to see the doughty hero slain,
But, at her smile, the beau revived again.   70
    Now Jove suspends his golden scales in air,
Weighs the men's wits against the lady's hair;
The doubtful beam long nods from side to side;
At length the wits mount up, the hairs subside.
    See, fierce Belinda on the Baron flies,
With more than usual lightning in her eyes:
Nor feared the chief th' unequal fight to try,
Who sought no more than on his foe to die.
But this bold lord with manly strength endued,
She with one finger and a thumb subdued: 80
Just where the breath of life his nostrils drew,°
A charge of snuff the wily virgin threw;
The Gnomes direct, to every atom just,
The pungent grains of titillating dust.
Sudden with starting tears each eye o'erflows,
And the high dome re-echoes to his nose.
    "Now meet thy fate," incensed Belinda cried,
And drew a deadly bodkin from her side.
(The same, his ancient personage to deck,
Her great-great-grandsire wore about his neck, 90
In three seal rings; which after, melted down,
Formed a vast buckle for his widow's gown:
Her infant grandame's whistle next it grew,
The bells she jingled, and the whistle blew;
Then in a bodkin graced her mother's hairs,
Which long she wore, and now Belinda wears.)
    " Boast not my fall " (he cried) " insulting foe!
Thou by some other shalt be laid as low.
Nor think, to die dejects my lofty mind:

All that I dread is leaving you behind!   100
Rather than so, ah let me still survive,
And burn in Cupid's flames — but burn alive."
    " Restore the lock! " she cries; and all around
" Restore the lock! " the vaulted roofs rebound.
Not fierce Othello in so loud a strain
Roared for the handkerchief that caused his pain.
But see how oft ambitious aims are crossed,
And chiefs contend till all the prize is lost!
The lock, obtained with guilt, and kept with pain,
In every place is sought, but sought in vain: 110
With such a prize no mortal must be blessed,
So Heaven decrees! with Heaven who can contest?
    Some thought it mounted to the lunar sphere,
Since all things lost on earth are treasured there.°
There heroes' wits are kept in ponderous vases,
And beaux' in snuffboxes and tweezer cases.°
There broken vows and deathbed alms are found,
And lovers' hearts with ends of riband bound,
The courtier's promises, and sick man's prayers,
The smiles of harlots, and the tears of heirs,   120
Cages for gnats, and chains to yoke a flea,
Dried butterflies, and tomes of casuistry.
    But trust the Muse — she saw it upward rise,
Though marked by none but quick, poetic eyes:
(So Rome's great founder to the heavens withdrew,
To Proculus alone confessed in view)°
A sudden star, it shot thro' liquid air,
And drew behind a radiant trail of hair.
Not Berenice's° locks first rose so bright,
The heavens bespangling with disheveled light.
The Sylphs behold it kindling as it flies,   131
And pleased pursue its progress thro' the skies.
    This the beau monde shall from the Mall° survey,
And hail with music its propitious ray.
This the blest lover shall for Venus take,
And send up vows from Rosamonda's lake.°
This Partridge° soon shall view in cloudless skies,
When next he looks thro' Galileo's° eyes;
And hence th' egregious wizard shall foredoom
The fate of Louis,° and the fall of Rome.   140

114–22. Since . . . casuistry: Pope directs us to consult Ariosto's *Orlando Furioso*, where Orlando's lost wits are sought for on the moon. He modernizes Ariosto's instances of lost wits. 116. tweezer cases: neatly made receptacles for holding eyebrow pluckers, etc. 125–26. So . . . view: It was said that Romulus, who disappeared mysteriously, had been caught up into heaven. 129. Berenice: Jupiter was supposed to have made a constellation of her hair when it was stolen from the temple in which she hung it as a votive offering when her husband returned victorious from the wars. 133. Mall: a fashionable walk in St. James's Park. 136. Rosamonda's lake: an oblong pond in the same park. 137. Partridge: "John Partridge *was a ridiculous Star-gazer, who in his Almanacks every year, never fail'd to predict the downfall of the Pope, and the King of* France, *then at war with the* English" (Pope). 138. Galileo: His improvement of the telescope inaugurated a phase in the history of astronomy. 140. Louis: Louis XIV.

---

53. sconce: "a pensile candlestick" (Johnson's Dictionary), a curving candlestick holder attached to a plaque on the wall. 64. Those . . . killing: the song was from the opera *Camilla*. 65. Maeander: a celebrated river in Asia Minor from the windings of which we derive our verb. 81–86. Just . . . nose: The Baron's sneeze cancels his boast at IV. 133–38.

Then cease, bright nymph! to mourn thy ravished
    hair,
Which adds new glory to the shining sphere!
Not all the tresses that fair head can boast,
Shall draw such envy as the lock you lost.
For, after all the murders of your eye,
When, after millions slain, yourself shall die;
When those fair suns shall set, as set they must,
And all those tresses shall be laid in dust,
This lock, the Muse shall consecrate to fame,
And midst the stars inscribe Belinda's name.   150

ESSAY ON MAN

This famous poem is partly to be seen as a museum
piece: although the philosophical ideas expressed in the
poem sum up the thought of Pope's time (they were
not Pope's own ideas), that time is now 200 years away
from us — and our ideas of man and the universe
have had the benefit of the discoveries of Darwin,
Eddington, Freud, and Einstein. Many of the ideas of
the poem are now behind glass. But we all frequent
museums because they contain great works of art. The
Essay on Man is as beautiful as the Portland Vase.[1]

But though we do see the universe differently now
we do not see man so very differently from the way
Pope saw him. He is still the glory, jest, and riddle of
the world. And Pope is famous partly because he read
deep into that riddle — as well as into that glory.
Much of the poem — and this is true of all Pope's
poetry — is of permanent interest, as Chaucer's and
Shakespeare's poems are. One of the famous lines of
the poem contains the sentence " Whatever is, is right."
We may not believe with Pope that there is purpose in
the universe, and if not we shall not agree that it can
be said to be right. But no poet has seen more fully
and deeply what is contained in "whatever is," and
much of his vision of it is expressed in the *Essay on
Man* in language which, as we can say of that of *An
Epistle to Dr. Arbuthnot,* is classic.

Pope wrote the poem during 1730–32, partly inspired by conversations he had with his "guide,
philosopher and friend" Henry St. John, Lord Bolingbroke, to whom the poem is dedicated. It was published anonymously, epistle by epistle, during 1733–4.

EPISTLE I

ARGUMENT

Of the nature and state of man with respect to the
universe

Of *man* in the abstract. I. That we can judge only
with regard to our *own system*, being ignorant of the
relations of systems and things. II. That man is not to
be deemed *imperfect*, but a being suited to his *place*

[1] The Portland Vase is an ancient urn found in a sarcophagus near Rome, once owned by the Portland family and now
in the British Museum.

and *rank* in the creation, agreeable to the *general order*
of things, and conformable to *ends* and *relations* to
him unknown. III. That it is partly upon his *ignorance*
of *future* events, and partly upon the *hope* of a *future*
state, that all his happiness in the present depends.
IV. The *pride* of aiming at more knowledge, and
pretending to more perfection, the cause of man's error
and misery. The *impiety* of putting himself in the
place of *God,* and judging of the fitness or unfitness,
perfection or imperfection, justice or injustice of his
dispensations. V. The *absurdity* of conceiting himself
the *final cause* of the creation, or expecting that perfection in the *moral* world, which is not in the *natural.*
VI. The *unreasonableness* of his complaints against
Providence, while on the one hand he demands the
perfections of the angels, and on the other the bodily
qualifications of the brutes; though, to possess any of
the *sensitive faculties* in a higher degree, would render
him miserable. VII. That throughout the whole visible
world, an universal *order* and *gradation* in the sensual
and mental faculties is observed, which causes a *subordination* of creature to creature, and of all creatures
to man. The gradations of *sense, instinct, thought, reflection, reason;* that reason alone countervails all the
other faculties. VIII. How much further this *order* and
subordination of living creatures may extend, above
and below us; were any part of which broken, not that
part only, but the whole connected *creation* must be
destroyed. IX. The *extravagance, madness,* and *pride*
of such a desire. X. The consequence of all, the *absolute submission* due to Providence, both as to our
present and *future* state.

Awake, my St. John! leave all meaner things
To low ambition, and the pride of kings.
Let us (since life can little more supply
Than just to look about us and to die)
Expatiate free o'er all this scene of man;
A mighty maze! but not without a plan;
A wild, where weeds and flowers promiscuous
    shoot;
Or garden, tempting with forbidden fruit.
Together let us beat this ample field,
Try what the open, what the covert° yield;   10
The latent tracts, the giddy heights, explore
Of all who blindly creep,° or sightless soar;
Eye Nature's walks,° shoot folly as it flies,
And catch the manners living as they rise;
Laugh where we must, be candid° where we can;
But vindicate the ways of God to man.
    I. Say first, of God above, or man below,
What can we reason, but from what we know?

ESSAY ON MAN.   Epistle I.   9–10. beat . . . open . . . covert:
hunting terms; go backwards and forwards over the ground to see
what game are to be hunted in the open and in foliage that gives
them natural shelter.   12. all . . . creep: The blind creepers are
the low-minded and ignorant; the sightless soarers presumptuously
try to transcend the limits beyond which man cannot go.   13.
walks: "the region within which something moves" (*OED*).
15. candid: generous, kindly, indulgent.

Of man, what see we but his station here,
From which to reason, or to which refer?   20
Thro' worlds unnumbered tho' the God be known,
'Tis ours to trace him only in our own.
He,° who thro' vast immensity can pierce,
See worlds on worlds compose one universe,
Observe how system into system runs,
What other planets circle other suns,
What varied being peoples every star,
May tell why Heaven has made us as we are.
But of this frame the bearings, and the ties,
The strong connections, nice dependencies,   30
Gradations just, has thy° pervading soul
Looked thro'? or can a part contain the whole?

   Is the great chain,° that draws all to agree,
And drawn supports, upheld by God, or thee?

   II. Presumptuous man! the reason wouldst thou
     find,
Why formed so weak, so little, and so blind?
First, if thou canst, the harder reason guess,
Why formed no weaker, blinder, and no less?
Ask of thy mother earth, why oaks are made
Taller or stronger than the weeds they shade?   40
Or ask of yonder argent fields above,
Why Jove's° satellites° are less than Jove?

   Of systems possible, if 'tis confessed
That Wisdom Infinite must form the best,
Where all must full or not coherent be,°
And all that rises, rise in due degree;
Then, in the scale of reasoning life, 'tis plain,
There must be, somewhere, such a rank as man:
And all the question (wrangle e'er so long)
Is only this, if God has placed him wrong?   50

   Respecting man, whatever wrong we call,
May, must be right, as relative to all.
In human works, though labored on with pain,
A thousand movements scarce one purpose gain;
In God's, one single can its end produce;
Yet serves to second too some other use.
So man, who here seems principal alone,
Perhaps acts second to some sphere unknown,
Touches some wheel, or verges to some goal;
'Tis but a part we see, and not a whole.   60

   When the proud steed shall know why man re-
     strains
His fiery course, or drives him o'er the plains;
When the dull ox, why now he breaks the clod,
Is now a victim, and now Egypt's god:°

Then shall man's pride and dulness comprehend
His actions', passions', being's, use and end;
Why doing, suffering, checked, impelled; and why
This hour a slave, the next a deity.

   Then say not man's imperfect, Heaven in fault;
Say rather, man's as perfect as he ought: 70
His knowledge measured to his state and place;
His time a moment, and a point his space.
If to be perfect in a certain sphere,
What matter, soon or late, or here or there?
The blest today is as completely so,
As who began a thousand years ago.

   III. Heaven from all creatures hides the book of
     fate,
All but the page prescribed, their present state:
From brutes what men, from men what spirits
     know:
Or who could suffer being here below?   80
The lamb thy riot° dooms to bleed today,
Had he thy reason, would he skip and play?
Pleased to the last, he crops the flowery food,
And licks the hand just raised to shed his blood.
Oh blindness to the future! kindly given,
That each may fill the circle marked by Heaven:
Who sees with equal eye, as God of all,
A hero perish, or a sparrow fall,
Atoms or systems into ruin hurled,
And now a bubble burst, and now a world.   90

   Hope humbly then; with trembling pinions soar;
Wait the great teacher Death; and God adore.
What future bliss, he gives not thee to know,
But gives that hope to be thy blessing now.
Hope springs eternal in the human breast:
Man never is, but always to be blest:
The soul, uneasy and confined from home,°
Rests and expatiates in a life to come.

   Lo, the poor Indian! whose untutored mind
Sees God in clouds, or hears him in the wind;   100
His soul, proud science never taught to stray
Far as the solar walk,° or milky way;
Yet simple Nature to his hope has given,
Behind the cloud-topped hill, an humbler Heaven;
Some safer world in depth of woods embraced,
Some happier island in the watery waste,
Where slaves once more their native land behold,
No fiends torment, no Christians thirst for gold.
To be, contents his natural desire,
He asks no angel's wing, no seraph's fire;°   110
But thinks, admitted to that equal sky,
His faithful dog shall bear him company.

   IV. Go, wiser thou! and, in thy scale of sense,
Weigh thy opinion against Providence;

---

23. He: only such a fool as he.   **31. thy:** the reader as an
instance of mankind in all its limitations.   **33. chain:** It was
held that all created things were ordered as links in a chain
that reached up to God—angels being the highest links—and
down to the meanest.   **42. Jove's:** Jupiter's.   **satellites:** In
Latin a *satelles* is an attendant. Seventeenth-century astronomers
used the word, and its plural form (satéllités), to denote a smaller
star, or stars, attending a larger.   **45. Where . . . be:** Each
link in the chain must be present and complete or there will be
a gap.   **64. Egypt's god:** Apis, the sacred Memphian bull.

81. riot: wasteful living.   **97. from home:** away from heaven,
its original home.   **102. walk:** see above, l. 13n.   **110. seraph's
fire:** According to the supposed derivation of the word, a seraph
was traditionally thought of as fiery.

Call imperfection what thou fanciest such,
Say, here he° gives too little, there too much:
Destroy all creatures for thy sport or gust,
Yet cry, if man's unhappy, God's unjust;
If man alone engross not Heaven's high care,
Alone made perfect here, immortal there: 120
Snatch from his hand the balance and the rod,
Rejudge his justice, be the God of God.
    In pride, in reasoning pride, our error lies;
All quit their sphere, and rush into the skies.
Pride still is aiming at the blest abodes,
Men would be angels, angels would be gods.
Aspiring to be gods, if angels fell,
Aspiring to be angels, men rebel:
And who but wishes to invert the laws
Of order, sins against th' Eternal Cause.   130
    V. Ask for what end the heavenly bodies shine,
Earth for whose use? Pride answers, " 'Tis for
    mine:
For me kind Nature wakes her genial power,°
Suckles each herb, and spreads out every flower;
Annual for me, the grape, the rose renew
The juice nectareous, and the balmy dew;
For me, the mine a thousand treasures brings;
For me, health gushes from a thousand springs;
Seas roll to waft me, suns to light me rise;
My footstool earth, my canopy the skies."   140
    But errs not Nature from this gracious end,
From burning suns when livid deaths descend,
When earthquakes swallow, or when tempests
    sweep
Towns to one grave, whole nations to the deep?
" No " ('tis replied) " the first Almighty Cause°
Acts not by partial, but by general laws;
Th' exceptions few; some change since all began:
And what created perfect? " — Why then man?
If the great end be human happiness,
Then Nature deviates; and can man do less?   150
As much that end a constant course requires
Of showers and sunshine, as of man's desires;
As much eternal springs and cloudless skies,
As men forever temperate, calm, and wise.
If plagues or earthquakes break not Heaven's de-
    sign,
Why then a Borgia,° or a Catiline?°
Who knows but He, whose hand the lightning
    forms,
Who heaves old ocean, and who wings the storms,
Pours fierce ambition in a Caesar's mind,
Or turns young Ammon° loose to scourge man-
    kind?   160

From pride, from pride, our very reasoning springs;
Account for moral, as for natural things:
Why charge we Heaven in those, in these acquit?
In both, to reason right is to submit.
    Better for us, perhaps, it might appear,
Were there all harmony, all virtue here;
That never air or ocean felt the wind;
That never passion discomposed the mind.
But ALL subsists by elemental strife;
And passions are the elements of life.   170
The general order, since the whole began,
Is kept in Nature, and is kept in man.
    VI. What would this man? Now upward will he
    soar,
And little less than angel, would be more;
Now looking downwards, just as grieved appears
To want the strength of bulls, the fur of bears.
Made for his use all creatures if he call,
Say what their use, had he the powers of all?
Nature to these, without profusion, kind,
The proper organs, proper powers assigned;   180
Each seeming want compensated° of course,°
Here with degrees of swiftness, there of force;
All in exact proportion to the state;
Nothing to add, and nothing to abate.
Each beast, each insect, happy in its own:
Is Heaven unkind to man, and man alone?
Shall he alone, whom rational we call,
Be pleased with nothing, if not blessed with all?
    The bliss of man (could pride that blessing find)
Is not to act or think beyond mankind;   190
No powers of body or of soul to share,
But what his nature and his state can bear.
Why has not man a microscopic eye?
For this plain reason, man is not a fly.
Say what the use, were finer optics given,
T' inspect a mite, not comprehend the heaven?
Or touch, if tremblingly alive all o'er,
To smart and agonize at every pore?
Or quick effluvia° darting through the brain,
Die of a rose° in aromatic pain?   200
If nature thundered in his opening ears,
And stunned him with the music of the spheres,
How would he wish that Heaven had left him still
The whispering zephyr, and the purling rill?
Who finds not Providence all good and wise,
Alike in what it gives, and what it denies?
    VII. Far as creation's ample range extends,
The scale of sensual, mental powers ascends:
Mark how it mounts, to man's imperial race,
From the green myriads in the peopled grass: 210

---

116. he: God.   133. genial power: power of generation.   145.
first . . . Cause: God, as the creator.   156. Borgia: Cæsar
Borgia (1476–1507), son of Pope Alexander VI, notorious for
his career of crime and warfare.   Catiline: the dissolute Roman,
who plotted against the state.   160. Ammon: Alexander the
Great.

181. compensated: The contemporary pronunciation stressed the
second syllable.   of course: in the natural course of things.
199. effluvia: Epicurus held that smells reached the brain in a
stream of invisible particles.   200. Die . . . rose: "Die of a
wound" is instanced as an idiom in Johnson's "Plan for a
Dictionary."

What modes of sight betwixt each wide extreme,
The mole's dim curtain, and the lynx's beam:
Of smell, the headlong lioness° between,
And hound sagacious on the tainted green:
Of hearing, from the life that fills the flood,
To that which warbles thro' the vernal wood:
The spider's touch, how exquisitely fine!
Feels at each thread, and lives along the line:
In the nice bee, what sense so subtly true
From poisonous herbs extracts the healing dew?
How instinct varies in the groveling swine,   221
Compared, half-reasoning elephant,° with thine!
'Twixt that, and reason, what a nice barrier,°
Forever separate, yet forever near!
Remembrance and reflection how allied;
What thin partitions sense from thought divide:
And middle natures, how they long to join,
Yet never pass th' insuperable line!
Without this just gradation, could they be
Subjected, these to those, or all to thee?   230
The powers of all subdued by thee alone,
Is not thy reason all these powers in one?
     VIII. See, thro' this air, this ocean, and this earth,
All matter quick, and bursting into birth.
Above, how high progressive life may go!
Around, how wide! how deep extend below!
Vast chain of being! which from God began,
Natures ethereal, human, angel, man,
Beast, bird, fish, insect, what no eye can see,
No glass can reach; from Infinite to thee,   240
From thee to nothing. — On superior powers
Were we to press, inferior might on ours:
Or in the full creation leave a void,
Where, one step broken, the great scale's destroyed:
From Nature's chain whatever link you strike,
Tenth or ten thousandth, breaks the chain alike.
     And, if each system in gradation roll
Alike essential to th' amazing whole,
The least confusion but in one, not all
That system only, but the whole must fall.   250
Let earth unbalanced from her orbit fly,
Planets and suns run lawless thro' the sky;
Let ruling angels from their spheres be hurled,
Being on being wrecked, and world on world;
Heaven's whole foundations to their center nod,
And Nature tremble to the throne of God.
All this dread order break — for whom? for thee?
Vile worm! — Oh madness! pride! impiety!
     IX. What if the foot, ordained the dust to tread,
Or hand, to toil, aspired to be the head?   260
What if the head, the eye, or ear repined
To serve mere engines to the ruling mind?

Just as absurd for any part to claim
To be another, in this general frame:
Just as absurd, to mourn the tasks or pains,
The great directing Mind of All ordains.
     All are but parts of one stupendous whole,
Whose body Nature is, and God the soul;
That, changed thro' all, and yet in all the same;
Great in the earth, as in th' ethereal frame;   270
Warms in the sun, refreshes in the breeze,
Glows in the stars, and blossoms in the trees,
Lives thro' all life, extends thro' all extent,
Spreads undivided, operates unspent;
Breathes in our soul, informs our mortal part,
As full, as perfect, in a hair as heart;
As full, as perfect, in vile man that mourns,
As the rapt seraph that adores and burns:
To him no high, no low, no great, no small;
He fills, he bounds, connects, and equals° all.   280
     X. Cease then, nor order imperfection name:
Our proper bliss depends on what we blame.
Know thy own point: This kind, this due degree
Of blindness, weakness, Heaven bestows on thee.
Submit. — In this, or any other sphere,
Secure to be as blest as thou canst bear:
Safe in the hand of one disposing Power,
Or in the natal, or the mortal hour.
All Nature is but art, unknown to thee;
All chance, direction, which thou canst not see;
All discord, harmony not understood;   291
All partial evil, universal good:
And, spite of pride, in erring reason's spite,
One truth is clear, Whatever is, is right.

EPISTLE II

ARGUMENT

Of the nature and state of *man* with respect to *himself*,
as an individual

     I. *The* business of man not to pry into *God*, but to
study *himself*. His *middle nature*; his powers and frailties. The limits of his *capacity*. II. The two principles
of man, *self-love* and *reason*, both necessary. *Self-love*
the stronger, and why. Their end the same. III. The
passions and their use. The *predominant passion*, and
its force. Its necessity, in directing men to different
purposes. Its providential use, in fixing our principle,
and ascertaining our virtue. IV. *Virtue* and *vice* joined
in our *mixed nature*; the limits near, yet the things
separate and *evident*: What is the office of *reason*. V.
How odious *vice* in itself, and how we deceive ourselves into it. VI. That, however, the *ends of Providence* and *general good* are answered in our passions
and imperfections. How usefully these are distributed
to all *orders of men*. How useful they are to *society*.

---

213. lioness: the lion and lioness hunted "by the Ear, and not by
the Nostril" (Pope).   **222. elephant:** Of the elephant's "sagacity
. . . and even understanding many surprising relations are given"
(Johnson's Dictionary).   **223. barrier:** pronounced *bareer*.

280. equals: makes all equal.

And to the *individuals.* In every *state,* and every *age*
of life.

I. Know then thyself, presume not God to scan;
The proper study of mankind is man.
Placed on this isthmus of a middle state,
A being darkly wise, and rudely great:
With too much knowledge for the skeptic° side,
With too much weakness for the Stoic's pride,°
He hangs between; in doubt to act, or rest;
In doubt to deem himself a god, or beast;
In doubt his mind or body to prefer;
Born but to die, and reasoning but to err;   10
Alike in ignorance, his reason such,
Whether he thinks too little, or too much:
Chaos of thought and passion, all confused;
Still by himself abused, or disabused;
Created half to rise, and half to fall;
Great lord of all things, yet a prey to all;
Sole judge of truth, in endless error hurled:
The glory, jest, and riddle of the world!
     Go, wondrous creature! mount where science
          guides,
Go, measure earth, weigh air,° and state the tides°;
Instruct the planets in what orbs to run,   21
Correct old time,° and regulate the sun;
Go, soar with Plato to th' empyreal sphere,°
To the first good, first perfect, and first fair;
Or tread the mazy round his followers trod,
And quitting sense° call imitating God;
As Eastern priests in giddy circles run,
And turn their heads to imitate the sun.°
Go, teach Eternal Wisdom how to rule —
Then drop into thyself, and be a fool!   30
     Superior beings, when of late they saw
A mortal man unfold all Nature's law,
Admired such wisdom in an earthly shape,
And showed a Newton as we show an ape.
     Could he, whose rules the rapid comet bind,
Describe or fix one movement of his mind?

Who saw its fires here rise, and there descend,
Explain his own beginning, or his end?
Alas what wonder! man's superior part
Unchecked may rise, and climb from art to art;   40
But when his own great work is but begun,
What reason weaves, by passion is undone.
Trace science° then, with modesty thy guide;
First strip off all her equipage of pride;
Deduct what is but vanity, or dress,
Or learning's luxury, or idleness;
Or tricks to show the stretch of human brain,
Mere curious pleasure, or ingenious pain;
Expunge the whole, or lop th' excrescent parts
Of all our vices have created arts;   50
Then see how little the remaining sum,
Which served the past, and must the times to come!
     II. Two principles in human nature reign;
Self-love,° to urge, and reason, to restrain;
Nor this a good, nor that a bad we call,
Each works its end, to move or govern all:
And to their proper operation still,
Ascribe all good; to their improper, ill.
     Self-love, the spring of motion, acts the soul;
Reason's comparing balance rules the whole.   60
Man, but for that, no action could attend,
And but for this, were active to no end:
Fixed like a plant on his peculiar spot,
To draw nutrition, propagate, and rot;
Or, meteor-like, flame lawless thro' the void,
Destroying others, by himself destroyed.
     Most strength the moving principle requires;
Active its task, it prompts, impels, inspires.
Sedate and quiet the comparing lies,
Formed but to check, deliberate, and advise.   70
Self-love still stronger, as its objects nigh;
Reason's at distance, and in prospect lie:
That sees immediate good by present sense;
Reason, the future and the consequence.
Thicker than arguments, temptations throng,
At best more watchful this, but that more strong.
The action of the stronger to suspend,
Reason still use, to reason still attend.
Attention, habit and experience gains;
Each strengthens reason, and self-love restrains.   80
     Let subtle schoolmen teach these friends to fight,
More studious to divide than to unite;
And grace and virtue, sense and reason split,
With all the rash dexterity of wit.
Wits, just like fools, at war about a name,
Have full as oft no meaning, or the same.
Self-love and reason to one end aspire,
Pain their aversion, pleasure their desire;
But greedy That, its object would devour,

Epistle II. 5. skeptic: The Skeptic philosophers, like the Greek
Pyrrho and his followers, doubted man's ability to gain any
knowledge that was real. **6. Stoic's pride:** The Greek Stoics were
philosophers who practiced severe restraints on the will, and
sought to exempt the mind from participating in pleasure and
pain. **20. weigh air:** alluding to the experiments of scientists
like Torricelli and Boyle. **state the tides:** Newton and others had
sought to understand the operation of the tides. **22. Correct
. . . time:** referring to Newton's astronomical measurements of
time, and the discussions on the reform of the calendar prior to
its introduction in 1752. **23. empyreal sphere:** the outermost
sphere of the universe, where God was thought to abide and where
Plato may be supposed to have discovered his ideal types. **26. And
. . . sense:** some later followers of Plato who sought to achieve
a vision of the divine by shedding the bodily senses during induced
trances. **28. And . . . sun:** In a letter of September 13, 1719,
Pope mentioned "the Self-taught [Arabic] Philosopher [Hai Ebn
Yocktan]," who gave himself up to a devout exercise of making
his head giddy with various circumrotations, to imitate the
motions of the "celestial bodies." Pope puns in "turn their heads."

43. science: knowledge. **54. Self-love:** "each natural being
strives to keep going with its own particular go" (J. Laird, *Philosophical Incursion into English Literature,* 1946, p. 43).

This taste the honey, and not wound the flower:
Pleasure, or wrong or rightly understood,   91
Our greatest evil, or our greatest good.
   III. Modes of self-love the passions we may call:
'Tis real good, or seeming, moves them all:
But since not every good we can divide,
And reason bids us for our own provide;
Passions, tho' selfish, if their means be fair,
List° under reason, and deserve her care;
Those, that imparted,° court a nobler aim,
Exalt their kind, and take some virtue's name.   100
   In lazy apathy let Stoics boast
Their virtue fixed; 'tis fixed as in a frost;
Contracted all, retiring to the breast;
But strength of mind is exercise, not rest:
The rising tempest puts in act the soul,
Parts it may ravage, but preserves the whole.
On life's vast ocean diversely we sail,
Reason the card,° but passion is the gale;
Nor God alone in the still calm we find,   109
He mounts the storm, and walks upon the wind.
   Passions, like elements, though born to fight,
Yet, mixed and softened, in his work unite:
These 'tis enough to temper and employ;
But what composes man, can man destroy?
Suffice that reason keep to Nature's road,
Subject, compound them, follow her and God.
Love, Hope, and Joy, fair Pleasure's smiling train,
Hate, Fear, and Grief, the family of Pain,
These mixed with art, and to due bounds confined,
Make and maintain the balance of the mind:°   120
The lights and shades, whose well-accorded strife
Gives all the strength and color of our life.
   Pleasures are ever in our hands or eyes;
And when in act they cease, in prospect, rise:
Present to grasp, and future still to find,
The whole employ of body and mind.
All spread their charms, but charm not all alike;
On different senses different objects strike;
Hence different passions more or less inflame,
As strong or weak, the organs of the frame;   130
And hence one master passion in the breast,
Like Aaron's serpent,° swallows up the rest.
   As man, perhaps, the moment of his breath,
Receives the lurking principle of death;
The young disease, that must subdue at length,
Grows with his growth, and strengthens with his
      strength:
So, cast and mingled with his very frame,

The mind's disease, its ruling passion came;
Each vital humor which should feed the whole,
Soon flows to this, in body and in soul: 140
Whatever warms the heart, or fills the head,
As the mind opens, and its functions spread,
Imagination plies her dangerous art,
And pours it all upon the peccant part.
   Nature its mother, habit is its nurse;
Wit, spirit, faculties, but make it worse;
Reason itself but gives it edge and power;
As Heaven's blest beam turns vinegar more sour.
   We, wretched subjects, tho' to lawful sway,
In this weak queen some favorite still obey: 150
Ah! if she lend not arms, as well as rules,
What can she more than tell us we are fools?
Teach us to mourn our nature, not to mend,
A sharp accuser, but a helpless friend!
Or from a judge turn pleader, to persuade
The choice we make, or justify it made;
Proud of an easy conquest all along,
She but removes weak passions for the strong:
So, when small humors gather to a gout,
The doctor fancies he has driven them out.   160
   Yes, Nature's road must ever be preferred;
Reason is here no guide, but still a guard:
'Tis hers to rectify, not overthrow,
And treat this passion more as friend than foe:
A mightier Power the strong direction sends,
And several° men impels to several ends:
Like varying winds, by other passions tossed,
This drives them constant to a certain coast.
Let power or knowledge, gold or glory, please,
Or (oft more strong than all) the love of ease; 170
Thro' life 'tis followed, even at life's expense;
The merchant's toil, the sage's indolence,
The monk's humility, the hero's pride,
All, all alike, find reason on their side.
   Th' Eternal Art educing good from ill,°
Grafts on this passion our best principle:
'Tis thus the mercury of man is fixed,
Strong grows the virtue with his nature mixed;
The dross cements what else were too refined,
And in one interest body acts with mind.   180
   As fruits, ungrateful to the planter's care,
On savage stocks inserted, learn to bear;
The surest virtues thus from passions shoot,
Wild nature's vigor working at the root.
What crops of wit and honesty appear
From spleen, from obstinacy, hate, or fear!
See anger,° zeal and fortitude supply;
Even avarice, prudence; sloth, philosophy;

---

98. List: enlist.   99. Those ... imparted: the passions, when
reason is imparted to them.   108. card: "the circular piece of
stiff paper on which the 32 points are marked in the mariner's
compass" (OED).   120. balance ... mind: a key to Pope's
conception.   132. Aaron's serpent: Cf. Exod. 7: 10–12: "Aaron
cast down his rod ... and it became a serpent ... the magicians
of Egypt ... cast down every man his rod, and they became
serpents; but Aaron's rod swallowed up their rods."

166. several: different.   175–202. Th' ... knave: "[The] *providential Use* [of this Passion] in fixing our PRINCIPLE, and
ascertaining [confirming] our VIRTUE" (Pope).   187. anger:
"Generally accredited a useful passion when not in excess"
(Twickenham ed.).

Lust, thro' some certain strainers well refined,
Is gentle love, and charms all womankind;   190
Envy, to which th' ignoble mind's a slave,
Is emulation in the learn'd or brave;
Nor virtue, male or female, can we name,
But what will grow on pride, or grow on shame.

    Thus Nature gives us (let it check our pride)
The virtue nearest to our vice allied:
Reason the bias turns to good from ill,
And Nero reigns a Titus,° if he will.
The fiery soul abhorred in Catiline,°
In Decius° charms, in Curtius° is divine: 200
The same ambition can destroy or save,
And makes a patriot as it makes a knave.

    IV. This light and darkness in our chaos joined,
What shall divide? The God within the mind.

    Extremes in Nature equal ends produce,
In man they join to some mysterious use;
Tho' each by turns the other's bound invade,
As, in some well-wrought picture, light and shade,
And oft so mix, the difference is too nice
Where ends the virtue, or begins the vice.   210

    Fools! who from hence into the notion fall,
That vice or virtue there is none at all.
If white and black blend, soften, and unite
A thousand ways, is there no black or white?
Ask your own heart, and nothing is so plain;
'Tis to mistake them, costs the time and pain.

    V. Vice is a monster of so frightful mien,
As, to be hated, needs but to be seen;
Yet seen too oft, familiar with her face,
We first endure, then pity, then embrace.   220
But where th' extreme of vice, was ne'er agreed:
Ask where's the north? at York, 'tis on the Tweed;
In Scotland, at the Orcades; and there,
At Greenland, Zembla, or the Lord knows where.
No creature owns it in the first degree,
But thinks his neighbor farther gone than he;
Even those who dwell beneath its very zone,
Or never feel the rage, or never own;
What happier natures shrink at with affright,
The hard inhabitant contends is right.   230

    VI. Virtuous and vicious every man must be,
Few in th' extreme, but all in the degree;
The rogue and fool by fits is fair and wise;
And even the best, by fits, what they despise.
'Tis but by parts we follow good or ill;
For, vice or virtue, self directs it still;
Each individual seeks a several goal;
But Heaven's great view is one, and that the whole.

That counterworks each follow and caprice;
That disappoints th' effect of every vice;   240
That, happy frailties to all ranks applied;
Shame to the virgin, to the matron pride,
Fear to the statesman, rashness to the chief,
To kings presumption, and to crowds belief:
That, virtue's ends from vanity can raise,
Which seeks no interest, no reward but praise;
And build on wants, and on defects of mind,
The joy, the peace, the glory of mankind.

    Heaven forming each on other to depend,
A master, or a servant, or a friend,   250
Bids each on other for assistance call,
Till one man's weakness grows the strength of all.
Wants, frailties, passions, closer still ally
The common interest, or endear the tie.
To these we owe true friendship, love sincere,
Each home-felt joy that life inherits here;
Yet from the same we learn, in its decline,
Those joys, those loves, those interests to resign;
Taught half by reason, half by mere decay,
To welcome death, and calmly pass away.   260

    Whate'er the passion, knowledge, fame, or pelf,
Not one will change his neighbor with himself.
The learn'd is happy Nature to explore,
The fool is happy that he knows no more;
The rich is happy in the plenty given,
The poor contents him with the care of Heaven.
See the blind beggar dance, the cripple sing,
The sot a hero, lunatic a king;
The starving chemist° in his golden views
Supremely blest, the poet in his Muse.   270

    See some strange comfort every state attend,
And pride bestowed on all, a common friend;
See some fit passion every age supply,
Hope travels thro', nor quits us when we die.

    Behold the child, by Nature's kindly law,
Pleased with a rattle, tickled with a straw:
Some livelier plaything gives his youth delight,
A little louder, but as empty quite:
Scarfs,° garters, gold, amuse his riper stage,
And beads and prayer-books are the toys of age:
Pleased with this bauble still, as that before;   281
Till tired he sleeps, and life's poor play is o'er.

    Meanwhile Opinion gilds with varying rays
Those painted clouds that beautify our days;
Each want of happiness by hope supplied,
And each vacuity of sense by pride:
These build as fast as knowledge can destroy;
In Folly's cup still laughs the bubble, joy;
One prospect lost, another still we gain;
And not a vanity is given in vain;   290
Even mean self-love becomes, by force divine,

---

198. Titus: a cruel and profligate Roman, who, on becoming Emperor in A.D. 79, grew generous and peaceable. **199. Catiline:** see above, l. 156n; he died fighting fiercely. **200. Decius:** a Roman general who, dreaming before the battle of Vesuvius, 340 B.C., that on one side the General was doomed and on the other the army, rushed into the fight to ensure the victory of his men. **Curtius:** another Roman warrior.

269. chemist: The alchemists sought a method for changing base matter into gold. **279. Scarfs:** badges of office for soldiers or certain officials.

The scale to measure others' wants by thine.
See! and confess, one comfort still must rise,
'Tis this, Tho' man's a fool, yet God is wise.

EPISTLE III

ARGUMENT

Of the nature and state of *man* with respect to society

I. The whole universe one system of society. Nothing
made wholly for *itself,* nor yet wholly for *another.* The
happiness of *animals* mutual. II. *Reason* or *instinct* operate alike to the good of each individual. *Reason* or
instinct operate also to society, in all animals. III. How
far *society* carried by instinct. How much farther by
reason. IV. Of that which is called the *State of Nature.*
Reason instructed by instinct in the invention of *arts,*
and in the forms of *society.* V. Origin of political
societies. Origin of monarchy. Patriarchal government.
VI. Origin of true religion and government, from the
same principle, of love. Origin of superstition and
tyranny, from the same principle, of fear. The influence of self-love operating to the *social* and *public* good.
Restoration of true religion and government on their
first principle. Mixed government. Various forms of
each, and the true end of all.

Here then we rest: " The Universal Cause
Acts to one end, but acts by various laws."
In all the madness of superfluous health,
The trim of pride, the impudence of wealth,
Let this great truth be present night and day;
But most be present, if we preach or pray.
 I. Look round our world; behold the chain of
  love
Combining all below and all above.
See plastic Nature working to this end,
The single atoms each to other tend,   10
Attract, attracted to, the next in place
Formed and impelled its neighbor to embrace.
See matter next, with various life endued,
Press to one center still, the general good.
See dying vegetables life sustain,
See life dissolving vegetate again:
All forms that perish other forms supply,
(By turns we catch the vital breath, and die)
Like bubbles on the sea of matter born,
They rise, they break, and to that sea return.   20
Nothing is foreign: parts relate to whole;
One all-extending, all-preserving Soul
Connects each being, greatest with the least;
Made beast in aid of man, and man of beast;
All served, all serving: nothing stands alone;
The chain holds on, and where it ends, unknown.
 Has God, thou fool! worked solely for thy good,
Thy joy, thy pastime, thy attire, thy food?
Who for thy table feeds the wanton fawn,
For him as kindly spread the flowery lawn.   30

Is it for thee the lark ascends and sings?
Joy tunes his voice, joy elevates his wings.
Is it for thee the linnet pours his throat?
Loves of his own and raptures swell the note.
The bounding steed you pompously bestride,
Shares with his lord the pleasure and the pride.
Is thine alone the seed that strews the plain?
The birds of heaven shall vindicate their grain.
Thine the full harvest of the golden year?
Part pays, and justly, the deserving steer: 40
The hog, that plows not nor obeys thy call,
Lives on the labors of this lord of all.
 Know, Nature's children all divide her care;
The fur that warms a monarch, warmed a bear.
While man exclaims, " See all things for my use! "
" See man for mine! " replies a pampered goose:
And just as short of reason he must fall,
Who thinks all made for one, not one for all.
 Grant that the powerful still the weak control;
Be man the wit and tyrant of the whole: 50
Nature that tyrant checks; he only knows,
And helps, another creature's wants and woes.
Say, will the falcon, stooping from above,
Smit with her varying plumage, spare the dove?
Admires the jay the insect's gilded wings?
Or hears the hawk when Philomela° sings?
Man cares for all: to birds he gives his woods,
To beasts his pastures, and to fish his floods;
For some his interest prompts him to provide,
For more his pleasure, yet for more his pride: 60
All feed on one vain patron, and enjoy
Th' extensive blessing of his luxury.
That very life his learnèd hunger craves,
He saves from famine, from the savage° saves;
Nay, feasts the animal he dooms his feast,
And, till he ends the being, makes it blest;
Which sees no more the stroke, or feels the pain,
Than favored man by touch ethereal° slain.
The creature had his feast of life before;
Thou too must perish, when thy feast is o'er!   70
 To each unthinking being, Heaven a friend,
Gives not the useless knowledge of its end:
To man imparts it; but with such a view
As, while he dreads it, makes him hope it too:
The hour concealed, and so remote the fear,
Death still draws nearer, never seeming near.
Great standing miracle! that Heaven assigned
Its only thinking thing this turn of mind.
 II. Whether with reason, or with instinct blest,
Know, all enjoy that power which suits them best;
To bliss alike by that direction tend,   81

Epistle III. **56. Philomela:** the nightingale. **64. savage:** wild
beast. **68. touch ethereal:** "Several of the Ancients, and many
Orientals at this day, esteem'd those who were struck by Lightning as sacred Persons, and the particular Favourites of Heaven"
(Pope).

And find the means proportioned to their end.
Say, where full instinct is th' unerring guide,
What pope or council can they need beside?
Reason, however able, cool at best,
Cares not for service, or but serves when pressed,
Stays till we call, and then not often near;
But honest Instinct comes a volunteer,
Sure never to o'ershoot, but just to hit;
While still too wide or short is human wit;   90
Sure by quick Nature happiness to gain,
Which heavier reason labors at in vain,
This too serves always, reason never long;
One must go right, the other may go wrong.
See then the acting and comparing powers
One in their nature, which are two in ours;
And reason raise o'er instinct as you can,
In this 'tis God directs, in that 'tis man.
    Who taught the nations of the field and wood
To shun their poison, and to choose their food?
Prescient, the tides or tempests to withstand,   101
Build on the wave, or arch beneath the sand?
Who made the spider parallels design,
Sure as Demoivre,° without rule or line?
Who bid the stork, Columbus-like, explore
Heavens not his own, and worlds unknown before?
Who calls the council, states the certain day,
Who forms the phalanx, and who points the way?
    III. God in the nature of each being founds
Its proper bliss, and sets its proper bounds: 110
But as he framed a whole, the whole to bless,
On mutual wants built mutual happiness:
So from the first, eternal order ran,
And creature linked to creature, man to man.
Whate'er of life all-quickening aether keeps,
Or breathes thro' air, or shoots beneath the deeps,
Or pours profuse on earth, one nature feeds
The vital flame, and swells the genial seeds.
Not man alone, but all that roam the wood,
Or wing the sky, or roll along the flood,   120
Each loves itself, but not itself alone,
Each sex desires alike, till two are one.
Nor ends the pleasure with the fierce embrace;
They love themselves, a third time, in their race.
Thus beast and bird their common charge attend,
The mothers nurse it, and the sires defend;
The young dismissed to wander earth or air,
There stops the instinct, and there ends the care;
The link dissolves, each seeks a fresh embrace,
Another love succeeds, another race.   130
A longer care man's helpless kind demands;
That longer care contracts more lasting bands:
Reflection, reason, still the ties improve,
At once° extend the interest, and the love;

With choice we fix, with sympathy we burn;
Each virtue in each passion takes its turn;
And still new needs, new helps, new habits rise,
That graft benevolence on charities.
Still as one brood, and as another rose,
These natural love maintained, habitual those:
The last, scarce ripened into perfect man,   141
Saw helpless him from whom their life began:
Memory and forecast just returns engage,
That pointed back to youth, this on to age;
While pleasure, gratitude, and hope, combined,
Still spread the interest, and preserved the kind.
    IV. Nor think, in Nature's state they blindly
        trod;
The state of Nature was the reign of God:
Self-love and social at her birth began,
Union the bond of all things, and of man.   150
Pride then was not; nor arts, that pride to aid;
Man walked with beast, joint tenant of the shade;
The same his table, and the same his bed;
No murder clothed him, and no murder fed.
In the same temple, the resounding wood,
All vocal beings hymned their equal God:
The shrine with gore unstained, with gold un-
        dressed,
Unbribed, unbloody, stood the blameless priest:
Heaven's attribute was universal care,
And man's prerogative to rule, but spare.   160
Ah! how unlike the man of times to come!
Of half that live the butcher and the tomb;°
Who, foe to Nature, hears the general groan,
Murders their species, and betrays his own.
But just disease to luxury succeeds,
And every death its own avenger breeds;
The fury-passions from that blood began,
And turned on man a fiercer savage, man.
    See him from Nature rising slow to art!
To copy instinct then was reason's part;   170
Thus then to man the voice of Nature spake —
"Go, from the creatures thy instructions take:
Learn from the birds what food the thickets yield;
Learn from the beasts the physic of the field;
Thy arts of building from the bee receive;
Learn of the mole to plow, the worm to weave;
Learn of the little nautilus to sail,
Spread the thin oar, and catch the driving gale.
Here too all forms of social union find,
And hence let reason, late, instruct mankind: 180
Here subterranean works and cities see;
There towns aërial on the waving tree.
Learn each small people's genius, policies,
The ant's republic, and the realm of bees;
How those in common all their wealth bestow,

104. Demoivre: Abraham Demoivre (1667–1754), "an eminent Mathematician" (Pope).   134. At once: at one and the same time.

162. tomb: By eating animals' flesh man entombs it within his body.

And anarchy without confusion know;
And these forever, tho' a monarch reign,
Their separate cells and properties maintain.
Mark what unvaried laws preserve each state,
Laws wise as Nature, and as fixed as fate.   190
In vain thy reason finer webs shall draw,
Entangle justice in her net of law,
And right, too rigid, harden into wrong;
Still for the strong too weak, the weak too strong.
Yet go! and thus o'er all the creatures sway,
Thus let the wiser make the rest obey;
And, for those arts mere instinct could afford,
Be crowned as monarchs, or as gods adored."

    V. Great Nature spoke; observant men obeyed;
Cities were built, societies were made: 200
Here rose one little state; another near
Grew by like means, and joined, thro' love or fear.
Did here the trees with ruddier burdens bend,
And there the streams in purer rills descend?
What war could ravish, commerce could bestow,
And he returned a friend, who came a foe.
Converse and love mankind might strongly draw,
When love was liberty, and Nature law.
Thus states were formed; the name of king un-
    known,
Till common interest placed the sway in one.   210
'Twas virtue only (or in arts or arms,
Diffusing blessings, or averting harms)
The same which in a sire the sons obeyed,
A prince the father of a people made.

    VI. Till then, by Nature crowned, each patriarch
    sate,
King, priest, and parent of his growing state;
On him, their second Providence, they hung,
Their law his eye, their oracle his tongue.
He from the wondering furrow called the food,
Taught to command the fire, control the flood,   220
Draw forth the monsters of th' abyss profound,
Or fetch th' aërial eagle to the ground.
Till drooping, sickening, dying they began
Whom they revered as God to mourn as man:
Then, looking up from sire to sire, explored
One great first father, and that first adored.
Or plain tradition that this ALL begun,
Conveyed unbroken faith from sire to son;
The worker from the work distinct was known,
And simple reason never sought but one: 230
Ere wit oblique had broke that steady light,°
Man, like his Maker, saw that all was right;
To virtue, in the paths of pleasure, trod,
And owned a Father when he owned a God.
Love all the faith, and all th' allegiance then;
For Nature knew no right divine in men,
No ill could fear in God: and understood
A sovereign being but° a sovereign good.

True faith, true policy, united ran,
That was but love of God, and this of man.   240
    Who first taught souls enslaved, and realms un-
    done,
Th' enormous faith of many made for one;
That proud exception to all Nature's laws,
T' invert the world, and counterwork its Cause?
Force first made conquest, and that conquest, law;
Till Superstition taught the tyrant awe,
Then shared the tyranny, then lent it aid,
And gods of conquerors, slaves of subjects made:
She, midst the lightning's blaze, and thunder's
    sound,
When rocked the mountains, and when groaned
    the ground,   250
She taught the weak to bend, the proud to pray,
To Power unseen, and mightier far than they:
She, from the rending earth and bursting skies,
Saw gods descend, and fiends infernal rise:
Here fixed the dreadful, there the blest abodes;
Fear made her devils, and weak hope her gods;
Gods partial, changeful, passionate, unjust,
Whose attributes were rage, revenge, or lust;
Such as the souls of cowards might conceive,
And, formed like tyrants, tyrants would believe.
Zeal then, not charity, became the guide;   261
And hell was built on spite, and heaven on pride.
Then sacred seemed th' ethereal vault no more;
Altars grew marble then, and reeked with gore:
Then first the flamen° tasted living food;
Next his grim idol smeared with human blood;
With Heaven's own thunders shook the world be-
    low,
And played the god an engine on his foe.
    So drives self-love, thro' just and thro' unjust,
To one man's power, ambition, lucre, lust: 270
The same self-love, in all, becomes the cause
Of what restrains him, government and laws.
For, what one likes if others like as well,
What serves one will, when many wills rebel?
How shall he keep, what, sleeping or awake,
A weaker may surprise, a stronger take?
His safety must his liberty restrain:
All join to guard what each desires to gain.
Forced into virtue thus by self-defense,
Even kings learned justice and benevolence: 280
Self-love forsook the path it first pursued,
And found the private in the public good.
    'Twas then, the studious head or generous mind,
Follower of God or friend of humankind,
Poet or patriot, rose but to restore
The faith and moral, Nature gave before;
Relumed her ancient light, not kindled new;
If not God's image, yet his shadow drew:

---

231. light: light of reason.   **238. but:** meaning "could only be."   **265. flamen:** a priest appointed to serve a particular deity.

Taught power's due use to people and to kings,
Taught nor to slack, nor strain its tender strings,
The less, or greater, set so justly true,   291
That touching one must strike° the other too;
Till jarring interests of themselves create
Th' according music of a well-mixed state.
Such is the world's great harmony, that springs
From order, union, full consent of things:
Where small and great, where weak and mighty, made
To serve, not suffer, strengthen, not invade;
More powerful each as needful to the rest,
And, in proportion as it blesses, blest;   300
Draw to one point, and to one center bring
Beast, man, or angel, servant, lord, or king.
     For forms of government let fools contest;
Whate'er is best administered is best:
For modes of faith let graceless zealots fight;
His can't be wrong whose life is in the right:
In faith and hope the world will disagree,
But all mankind's concern is charity:
All must be false that thwart this one great end;
And all of God, that bless mankind or mend.   310
     Man, like the generous vine, supported lives;
The strength he gains is from th' embrace he gives.
On their own axis as the planets run,
Yet make at once their circle round the sun;
So two consistent motions act the soul;
And one regards itself, and one the whole.
     Thus God and Nature linked the general frame,
And bade self-love and social be the same.

EPISTLE IV

ARGUMENT

Of the nature and state of *man* with respect to happiness

I. False notions of happiness, philosophical and popular, answered. II. It is the end of all men, and attainable by all. God intends happiness to be *equal;* and to be so, it must be *social,* since all particular happiness depends on general, and since he governs by *general,* not *particular* laws. As it is necessary for *order,* and the peace and welfare of *society,* that *external goods* should be *unequal,* happiness is not made to consist in these. But, notwithstanding that inequality, the *balance* of happiness among *mankind* is kept even by Providence, by the two passions of *hope* and *fear.* III. What the happiness of *individuals* is, as far as is consistent with the constitution of this world; and that the *good man* has here the advantage. The error of imputing to *virtue* what are only the calamities of *Nature,* or of *fortune.* IV. The folly of expecting that God should alter his general laws in favor of particulars. V. That we are not judges who are good; but that, whoever they are,

they must be happiest. VI. That *external goods* are not the proper rewards, but often inconsistent with, or destructive of virtue. That even these can make no man happy without virtue: instanced in *riches; honors; nobility; greatness; fame; superior talents.* With pictures of human infelicity in men possessed of them all. VII. That *virtue only* constitutes a happiness, whose object is *universal,* and whose prospect *eternal.* That the *perfection* of *virtue* and *happiness* consists in a *conformity* to the *order* of *Providence* here, and a *resignation* to it here and hereafter.

Oh happiness! our being's end and aim!
Good, pleasure, ease, content! whate'er thy name:
That something still which prompts th' eternal sigh,
For which we bear to live, or dare to die,
Which still so near us, yet beyond us lies,
O'erlooked, seen double, by the fool, and wise.
Plant of celestial seed! if dropped below,
Say, in what mortal soil thou deignst to grow?
Fair opening to some court's propitious shine,
Or deep with diamonds in the flaming mine?   10
Twined with the wreaths Parnassian laurels yield,
Or reaped in iron harvests of the field?
Where grows? — where grows it not? If vain our toil,
We ought to blame the culture, not the soil:
Fixed to no spot is happiness sincere,°
'Tis nowhere to be found, or everywhere;
'Tis never to be bought, but always free,
And fled from monarchs, St. John! dwells with thee.
     I. Ask of the learn'd the way? The learn'd are blind;
This bids to serve, and that to shun mankind;   20
Some place the bliss in action, some in ease,
Those call it pleasure, and contentment these;
Some sunk to beasts, find pleasure end in pain;
Some swelled to gods, confess even virtue vain;
Or indolent, to each extreme they fall,
To trust in everything, or doubt of all.
     Who thus define it, say they more or less
Than this, that happiness is happiness?
     II. Take Nature's path, and mad Opinion's leave;
All states can reach it, and all heads conceive;   30
Obvious her goods, in no extreme they dwell;
There needs but thinking right, and meaning well;
And mourn our various portions as we please,
Equal is common sense, and common ease.
     Remember, man, " the Universal Cause
Acts not by partial, but by general laws ";
And makes what happiness we justly call
Subsist not in the good of one, but all.
There's not a blessing individuals find,

---

292. strike: to make a sound.

Epistle IV.   15. sincere: "pure, unmingled" (Johnson's Dictionary).

But some way leans and hearkens° to the kind: 40
No bandit fierce, no tyrant mad with pride,
No caverned hermit, rests self-satisfied:
Who most to shun or hate mankind pretend,
Seek an admirer, or would fix a friend:
Abstract what others feel, what others think,
All pleasures sicken, and all glories sink:
Each has his share; and who would more obtain,
Shall find, the pleasure pays not half the pain.

    Order is Heaven's first law; and this confessed,
Some are, and must be, greater than the rest,   50
More rich, more wise; but who infers from hence
That such are happier, shocks all common sense.
Heaven to mankind impartial we confess,
If all are equal in their happiness:
But mutual wants this happiness increase;
All Nature's difference keeps all Nature's peace.
Condition, circumstance is not the thing;
Bliss is the same in subject or in king,
In who obtain defense, or who defend,
In him who is, or him who finds a friend: 60
Heaven breathes thro' every member of the
    whole
One common blessing, as one common soul.
But fortune's gifts if each alike possessed,
And each were equal, must not all contest?
If then to all men happiness was meant,
God in externals could not place content.

    Fortune her gifts may variously dispose,
And these be happy called, unhappy those;
But Heaven's just balance equal will appear,
While those are placed in hope, and these in fear:
Not present good or ill, the joy or curse,   71
But future views of better, or of worse.

    Oh sons of earth! attempt ye still to rise,
By mountains piled on mountains, to the skies?
Heaven still with laughter the vain toil surveys,
And buries madmen in the heaps they raise.

    III. Know, all the good that individuals find,
Or God and Nature meant to mere mankind,
Reason's whole pleasure, all the joys of sense,
Lie in three words, health, peace, and competence.°
But health consists with temperance alone;   81
And peace, oh Virtue! peace is all thy own.
The good or bad the gifts of fortune gain;
But these less taste them, as they worse obtain.
Say, in pursuit of profit or delight,
Who risk the most, that take wrong means, or
    right?
Of Vice or Virtue, whether blest or curst,
Which meets contempt, or which compassion first?

Count all th' advantage prosperous Vice attains,
'Tis but what Virtue flies from and disdains: 90
And grant the bad what happiness they would,
One they must want, which is, to pass for good.

    Oh blind to truth, and God's whole scheme be-
    low,
Who fancy bliss to vice, to virtue woe!
Who sees and follows that great scheme the best,
Best knows the blessing, and will most be blest.
But fools the good alone unhappy call,
For ills or accidents that chance to all.
See Falkland° dies, the virtuous and the just!
See godlike Turenne° prostrate on the dust!   100
See Sidney° bleeds amid the martial strife!
Was this their virtue, or contempt of life?
Say, was it virtue, more tho' Heaven ne'er gave,
Lamented Digby!° sunk thee to the grave?
Tell me, if virtue made the son expire,
Why, full of days and honor, lives the sire?
Why drew Marseilles' good bishop purer breath,
When Nature sickened, and each gale was death?°
Or why so long (in life if long can be)
Lent Heaven a parent to the poor and me?°   110
    What makes all physical or moral ill?
There deviates Nature, and here wanders Will.
God sends not ill; if rightly understood,
Or partial ill is universal good,
Or change admits, or Nature lets it fall;
Short, and but rare, till man improved° it all.
We just as wisely might of Heaven complain
That righteous Abel was destroyed by Cain,
As that the virtuous son is ill at ease
When his lewd father gave the dire disease.   120
Think we, like some weak prince, th' Eternal
    Cause,
Prone for his favorites to reverse his laws?

    IV. Shall burning Etna, if a sage requires,
Forget to thunder, and recall her fires?°
On air or sea new motions be impressed,
Oh, blameless Bethel! to relieve thy breast?°
When the loose mountain trembles from on high,

---

40. **leans and hearkens:** a vivid phrase borrowed from Donne's "A Valediction: Forbidding Mourning"; Wakefield happily paraphrases "Man waits, as it were, all ear! for the approbation of another's feelings, before he can decide upon the reality of his own happiness from a present enjoyment." 80. **competence:** material necessities of life.

99. **Falkland:** Lucius Cary, second Viscount Falkland. At the request of Charles I he became Secretary of State in 1642. Opposed to violent and extremist policies, and despairing of his country's happiness after the outbreak of civil war, he successfully courted death at the Battle of Newbury, 1643. 100. **Turenne:** Marshal of France, killed in battle at Sassbach in Baden, 1675. 101. **Sidney:** Sir Philip, who was fatally wounded at Zutphen in 1586. 104. **Digby:** The Hon. Robert Digby, on whom Pope wrote an epitaph, had died in 1726. 107-08. **Why . . . death:** Belsunce, Bishop of Marseilles, ministered to the sick and dying during a plague of 1721 without succumbing to the disease. 109-10. **Or . . . me:** Pope's mother had died in 1733 at the age of 91. 116. **improved:** in an ironic sense. 123-24. **Shall . . . fires:** a reference to Empedocles, who, according to one version of the story, was killed by a volcanic eruption while seeking to investigate it. 125-26. **On . . . breast:** Hugh Bethel, a friend of Pope's, suffered from asthma, and the reference is probably to his discomfort during a voyage to Italy.

Shall gravitation cease, if you go by?
Or some old temple, nodding to its fall,   129
For Chartres'° head reserve the hanging wall?
    V. But still this world (so fitted for the knave)
Contents us not. A better shall we have?
A kingdom of the just then let it be:
But first consider how those just agree.
The good must merit God's peculiar care;
But who, but God, can tell us who they are?
One thinks on Calvin Heaven's own spirit fell;
Another deems him instrument of hell;
If Calvin feel Heaven's blessing, or its rod,
This cries there is, and that, there is no God.   140
What shocks one part will edify the rest,
Nor with one system can they all be blest.
The very best will variously incline,
And what rewards your virtue, punish mine.
Whatever is, is right. — This world, 'tis true,
Was made for Caesar — but for Titus° too:
And which more blest? who chained his country,
    say,
Or he whose virtue sighed to lose a day?
    " But sometimes Virtue starves, while Vice is
    fed."
What then? Is the reward of Virtue bread?   150
That, Vice may merit; 'tis the price of toil;
The knave deserves it, when he tills the soil,
The knave deserves it, when he tempts the main,
Where Folly fights for kings, or dives for gain.
The good man may be weak, be indolent;
Nor is his claim to plenty, but content.
But grant him riches, your demand is o'er?
    "No — shall the good want health, the good
    want power? "
Add health, and power, and every earthly thing,
" Why bounded power? why private? why no
    king?"   160
Nay, why external for internal given?
Why is not man a god, and earth a Heaven?
Who ask and reason thus, will scarce conceive
God gives enough, while he has more to give:
Immense the power, immense were the demand;
Say, at what part of Nature will they stand?
    VI. What nothing earthly gives, or can destroy,
The soul's calm sunshine, and the heartfelt joy,
Is Virtue's prize: A better would you fix?
Then give Humility a coach and six,   170
Justice a conqueror's sword, or Truth a gown,
Or Public Spirit its great cure, a crown.
Weak, foolish man! will Heaven reward us there
With the same trash mad mortals wish for here?
The boy and man an individual makes,

Yet sighst thou now for apples and for cakes?
Go, like the Indian, in another life
Expect thy dog, thy bottle, and thy wife:
As well as dream such trifles are assigned,
As toys and empires, for a godlike mind.   180
Rewards, that either would to Virtue bring
No joy, or be destructive of the thing:
How oft by these at sixty are undone
The virtues of a saint at twenty-one!
    To whom can riches give repute, or trust,
Content, or pleasure, but the good and just?
Judges and senates have been bought for gold,
Esteem and love were never to be sold.
Oh fool! to think God hates the worthy mind,
The lover and the love of humankind,   190
Whose life is healthful, and whose conscience clear,
Because he wants a thousand pounds a year.
    Honor and shame from no condition° rise;
Act well your part, there all the honor lies.
Fortune in men has some small difference made,
One flaunts in rags, one flutters in brocade;
The cobbler aproned, and the parson gowned,
The friar hooded, and the monarch crowned.
" What differ more " (you cry) " than crown and
    cowl? "
I'll tell you, friend! a wise man and a fool.   200
You'll find, if once the monarch acts the monk,
Or, cobbler-like, the parson will be drunk,
Worth makes the man, and want of it, the fellow;
The rest is all but leather or prunella.°
    Stuck o'er with titles and hung round with
    strings,°
That thou mayst be by kings, or whores of kings.
Boast the pure blood of an illustrious race,
In quiet flow from Lucrece° to Lucrece:
But by your fathers' worth if yours you rate,
Count me those only who were good and great.
Go! if your ancient, but ignoble blood   211
Has crept thro' scoundrels ever since the flood,
Go! and pretend your family is young;
Nor own, your fathers have been fools so long.
What can ennoble sots, or slaves, or cowards?
Alas! not all the blood of all the Howards.°
    Look next on greatness; say where greatness lies?
" Where, but among the heroes and the wise? "
Heroes are much the same, the point's agreed,
From Macedonia's madman° to the Swede;°   220
The whole strange purpose of their lives, to find

193. condition: rank.   204. leather or prunella: The cobbler's apron is of leather, the parson's gown of prunella (maroon serge).   205. strings: the ribbons of the Orders of Chivalry.   208. Lucrece: The Roman Lucretia, c. 500 B.C., after being raped by Sextus Tarquinius, secured a promise of vengeance from her husband and her father, and then stabbed herself.   216. Howards: The family of Howard ranks first among the English nobility.   220. Macedonia's madman: Alexander the Great. the Swede: Charles XII (1682-1718), an inveterate wager of wars.

130. Chartres: Francis Chartres, a notorious gambler and swindler of the day.   146. Titus: see above, II. 198n. Titus is said to have exclaimed, when he let a day go by without bestowing a present, "I have lost a day."

Or make, an enemy of all mankind!
Not one looks backward, onward still he goes,
Yet ne'er looks forward farther than his nose.
No less alike the politic and wise;
All sly slow things, with circumspective eyes:
Men in their loose unguarded hours they take,
Not that themselves are wise, but others weak.
But grant that those can conquer, these can cheat;
'Tis phrase absurd to call a villain great: 230
Who wickedly is wise, or madly brave,
Is but the more a fool, the more a knave.
Who noble ends by noble means obtains,
Or failing, smiles in exile or in chains,
Like good Aurelius° let him reign, or bleed
Like Socrates, that man is great indeed.

What's fame? a fancied life in others' breath,
A thing beyond us, even before our death.
Just what you hear, you have, and what's unknown
The same (my Lord) if Tully's,° or your own.
All that we feel of it begins and ends   241
In the small circle of our foes or friends;
To all beside as much an empty shade
An Eugene° living, as a Caesar dead;
Alike or when, or where, they shone, or shine,
Or on the Rubicon, or on the Rhine.
A wit's a feather, and a chief a rod;
An honest° man's the noblest work of God.
Fame but from death a villain's name can save,
As Justice tears his body from the grave;   250
When what t' oblivion better were resigned,
Is hung on high, to poison half mankind.
All fame is foreign, but of true desert;
Plays round the head, but comes not to the heart:
One self-approving hour whole years outweighs
Of stupid starers, and of loud huzzas;
And more true joy Marcellus° exiled feels,
Than Caesar with a senate at his heels.

In parts° superior what advantage lies?
Tell (for You° can) what is it to be wise?   260
'Tis but to know how little can be known;
To see all others' faults, and feel our own:
Condemned in business or in arts to drudge,
Without a second, or without a judge:
Truths would you teach, or save a sinking land?
All fear, none aid you, and few understand.
Painful pre-eminence! yourself to view
Above life's weakness, and its comforts too.

Bring then these blessings to a strict account;
Make fair deductions; see to what they mount:
How much of other each is sure to cost;   271
How each for other oft is wholly lost;
How inconsistent greater goods with these;
How sometimes life is risked, and always ease:
Think, and if still the things thy envy call,
Say, wouldst thou be the man to whom they fall?
To sigh for ribbons if thou art so silly,
Mark how they grace Lord Umbra,° or Sir Billy:°
Is yellow dirt° the passion of thy life?
Look but on Gripus, or on Gripus' wife: 280
If parts allure thee, think how Bacon shined,
The wisest, brightest, meanest of mankind:
Or ravished with the whistling of a name,
See Cromwell, damned to everlasting fame!
If all, united, thy ambition call,
From ancient story learn to scorn them all.
There, in the rich, the honored, famed, and great,
See the false scale of happiness complete!
In hearts of kings, or arms of queens who lay,
How happy! those to ruin, these betray.   290
Mark by what wretched steps their glory grows,
From dirt and seaweed as proud Venice rose;
In each how guilt and greatness equal ran,
And all that raised the hero, sunk the man:
Now Europe's laurels on their brows behold,
But stained with blood, or ill exchanged for gold:
Then see them broke with toils, or sunk in ease,
Or infamous for plundered provinces.
Oh wealth ill-fated! which no act of fame
E'er taught to shine, or sanctified from shame!   300
What greater bliss attends their close of life?
Some greedy minion, or imperious wife,
The trophied arches, storied halls invade
And haunt their slumbers in the pompous shade.
Alas! not dazzled with their noontide ray,
Compute the morn and evening to the day,
The whole amount of that enormous fame,
A tale, that blends their glory with their shame!

VII. Know then this truth (enough for man to
      know)
"Virtue alone is happiness below."   310
The only point where human bliss stands still,
And tastes the good without the fall to ill;
Where only Merit constant pay receives,
Is blest in what it takes, and what it gives;
The joy unequaled, if its end° it gain,
And if it lose, attended with no pain:
Without satiety, tho' e'er so blessed,
And but more relished as the more distressed:
The broadest mirth unfeeling Folly wears,

235. Aurelius: Marcus Aurelius (121–180), Roman Emperor and philosopher.   240. Tully: Cicero.   244. Eugene: Prince Eugene of Savoy (1663–1736), Commander of the armies of the Austrian Empire; he was joint victor with Marlborough at Blenheim and Malplaquet.   248. honest: virtuous, upright.   257. Marcellus: Marcus Marcellus sided with Pompey against Cæsar, and withdrew to Mytilene after the battle of Pharsalia, 48 B.C.   259. parts: intellectual talents.   260. You: The "you" at l. 128 above probably meant the reader. Here the word is given a capital, and means Bolingbroke.

278. Lord Umbra: a *shady* Lord. Sir Billy: allusion may be meant to Sir William Yonge, who had a reputation as a simpleton.   279. yellow dirt: gold.   315. end: eternal life.

Less pleasing far than Virtue's very tears: 320
Good, from each object, from each place acquired,
Forever exercised, yet never tired;
Never elated, while one man's oppressed;
Never dejected, while another's blessed;
And where no wants, no wishes can remain,
Since but to wish more virtue, is to gain.
  See the sole bliss Heaven could on all bestow!
Which who but feels can taste, but thinks can
    know:
Yet poor with fortune, and with learning blind,
The bad must miss; the good, untaught, will find;
Slave to no sect, who takes no private road,   331
But looks thro' Nature up to Nature's God;
Pursues that chain which links the immense de-
    sign,
Joins heaven and earth, and mortal and divine;
Sees, that no being any bliss can know,
But touches some above, and some below;
Learns, from this union of the rising whole,
The first, last purpose of the human soul;
And knows, where faith, law, morals, all began,
All end, in love of God, and love of man.   340
  For him alone, hope leads from goal to goal,
And opens still, and opens on his soul;
Till lengthened on to faith, and unconfined,
It pours the bliss that fills up all the mind.
He sees, why Nature plants in man alone
Hope of known bliss, and faith in bliss unknown:
(Nature, whose dictates to no other kind
Are given in vain, but what they seek they find)
Wise is her present; she connects in this
His greatest virtue with his greatest bliss;   350
At once his own bright prospect to be blest,
And strongest motive to assist the rest.
  Self-love thus pushed to social, to divine,
Gives thee to make thy neighbor's blessing thine.
Is this too little for the boundless heart?
Extend it, let thy enemies have part:
Grasp the whole worlds of reason, life, and sense,
In one close system of benevolence:
Happier as kinder, in whate'er degree,
And height of bliss but height of charity.   360
  God loves from whole to parts: but human soul
Must rise from individual to the whole.
Self-love but serves the virtuous mind to wake,
As the small pebble stirs the peaceful lake;
The center moved, a circle straight succeeds,
Another still, and still another spreads;
Friend, parent, neighbor, first it will embrace;
His country next; and next all human race;
Wide and more wide, th' o'erflowings of the mind
Take every creature in, of every kind;   370
Earth smiles around, with boundless bounty blest,
And Heaven beholds its image in his breast.
  Come then, my Friend! my Genius! come along;

Oh master of the poet, and the song!
And while the Muse now stoops, or now ascends,
To man's low passions, or their glorious ends,
Teach me, like thee, in various nature wise,
To fall with dignity, with temper° rise;
Formed by thy converse, happily to steer
From grave to gay, from lively to severe;   380
Correct with spirit, eloquent with ease,
Intent to reason, or polite to please.
Oh! while along the stream of time thy name
Expanded flies, and gathers all its fame,
Say, shall my little bark attendant sail,
Pursue the triumph, and partake the gale?
When statesmen, heroes, kings, in dust repose,
Whose sons shall blush their fathers were thy foes,
Shall then this verse to future age pretend
Thou wert my guide, philosopher, and friend?
That urged by thee, I turned the tuneful art   391
From sounds to things, from fancy to the heart;
For wit's false mirror held up Nature's light;
Showed erring pride, Whatever is, is right;
That Reason, Passion, answer one great aim;
That true Self-Love and Social are the same;
That Virtue only makes our bliss below;
And all our knowledge is, OURSELVES TO KNOW.

AN EPISTLE
TO DR. ARBUTHNOT

  This poem was designed to pay off some old scores
against writers Pope had quarreled with, but that is
only the dull part of the story. It would be fairer to
say that Pope felt the need to clarify and defend his
position as a writer and as a satirist. For this epistle
is one of the masterpieces of our literature. It is that
because its subject matter — even though partly commonplace or unpleasant — is recalled by a mind as
intense as it is magisterial, as quivering as it is serene,
as delicate as it is strong. And not only that, but by a
mind gifted with the power to achieve the sort of
utterance we call classic — utterance which, to put it
negatively, leaves nothing to be desired. Pope's expression here is like that achieved by Shakespeare in
Hamlet where every phrase hits a bull's eye, and usually by means of language used as nobody had used it
before. Illustration is invidious when the claim is for
something so widespread. Yet not all readers have seen
that the poem has this merit — for the simple reason
that a line like:

  Just hint a fault, and hesitate dislike

is so well known that its linguistic adventurousness is
overlooked. It was this poem that caused Charles Lamb
to ask, "Do you think I would not wish to have been
friends with such a man as this?" Lamb, who knew
that Pope had been charged with cruelty, was a man

378. temper: equanimity.

who thought it a privilege to associate with men of genius; he could glory in the beauty of the tiger even if part of the beauty lies in its teeth.

Pope was wise to address his poem to such a man as Arbuthnot, who was well respected, not only as an author himself, but as a medical doctor, who, as the poem recalls, had been "physician in ordinary" to Queen Anne. His kindly presence is implied in the poem, and he breaks in with remarks of his own, all of which help to lift the argument above the pettily personal. So does the use of the name Atticus (that of a Roman Knight, who was a friend of Cicero) instead of Addison. The inspiration for the character-sketch (ll. 193–214), which Pope had written earlier, came from his dislike of Addison the man — a dislike that he regretted because of his admiration for Addison the writer.

The poem was written during 1731–4, and published in 1735.

Shut, shut the door, good John!° fatigued, I said,
Tie up the knocker,° say I'm sick, I'm dead.
The Dog Star° rages! nay 'tis past a doubt,
All Bedlam,° or Parnassus, is let out:
Fire in each eye, and papers in each hand,
They rave, recite, and madden° round the land.
  What walls can guard me, or what shades can hide?
They pierce my thickets, thro' my grot° they glide;
By land, by water, they renew the charge;
They stop the chariot, and they board the barge.
No place is sacred, not the church is free;   11
Even Sunday shines no Sabbath day to me:
Then from the Mint° walks forth the man of rhyme,
Happy! to catch me just at dinner time.
  Is there a parson, much bemused in beer,
A maudlin poetess, a rhyming peer,
A clerk, foredoomed his father's soul to cross,
Who pens a stanza,° when he should engross?
Is there, who, locked from ink and paper, scrawls
With desperate charcoal round his darkened walls?
All fly to Twitnam, and in humble strain   21
Apply to me, to keep them mad or vain.
Arthur,° whose giddy son neglects the laws,
Imputes to me and my damned works the cause:
Poor Cornus° sees his frantic wife elope,
And curses wit, and poetry, and Pope.
  Friend to my life! (which did not you prolong,

The world had wanted many an idle song)
What drop or nostrum° can this plague remove?
Or which must end me, a fool's wrath or love?   30
A dire dilemma! either way I'm sped,°
If foes, they write, if friends, they read me dead.
Seized and tied down to judge, how wretched I!
Who can't be silent, and who will not lie:
To laugh, were want of goodness and of grace,
And to be grave, exceeds all power of face.
I sit with sad civility, I read
With honest anguish, and an aching head;
And drop at last, but in unwilling ears,
This saving counsel, "Keep your piece nine
    years."°   40
  "Nine years!" cries he, who high° in Drury
    Lane,°
Lulled by soft zephyrs thro' the broken pane,
Rhymes ere he wakes, and prints before Term°
    ends,
Obliged by hunger, and request of friends:
"The piece, you think, is incorrect? why, take it,
I'm all submission, what you'd have it, make it"
  Three things another's modest wishes bound,
My friendship, and a prologue,° and ten pound.
  Pitholeon° sends to me: "You know his Grace,
I want a patron; ask him for a place."   50
Pitholeon libeled me — "but here's a letter
Informs you, sir, 'twas when he knew no better.
Dare you refuse him? Curll° invites to dine,
He'll write a Journal,° or he'll turn divine."°
  Bless me! a packet. — "'Tis a stranger sues,
A virgin tragedy, an orphan Muse."
If I dislike it, "Furies, death and rage!"
If I approve, "Commend it to the stage."
There (thank my stars) my whole commission
    ends,
The players and I are, luckily, no friends.   60
Fired that the house reject him, "'Sdeath I'll print
    it,
And shame the fools — Your interest, sir, with
    Lintot."°
Lintot, dull rogue! will think your price too much:
"Not, sir, if you revise it, and retouch."
All my demurs but double his attacks;

EPISTLE TO DR. ARBUTHNOT. **1.** John: his servant. **2.** Tie ... knocker: The door knocker was muffled when sickness was in the house. **3.** Dog Star: Sirius; it was August (1734) when Pope put the poem into final shape, and the later summer was the time when poetry used to be rehearsed in Rome. **4.** Bedlam: a corruption of the name of a London lunatic asylum, St. Mary of Bethlehem. **6.** madden: a word Pope invented. **8.** grot: grotto. **13.** the Mint: a sanctuary for debtors in Southwark. **18.** stanza: It is therefore a love poem. **23.** Arthur: Arthur Moore, a politician, and his son James Moore Smythe, who used some of Pope's verses in a play. **25.** Cornus: Latin for horn; hence, a cuckold.

29. drop or nostrum: quack medicines. **31.** sped: dispatched, killed. **40.** Keep ... years: This was Horace's counsel to the poet too eager for fame. **40–41.** Note the transition, indeed the overlap, from paragraph to paragraph. **41.** high: in an attic. Drury Lane: then a disreputable neighborhood. **43.** Term: the legal terms, the periods preferred for publishing. **48.** a prologue: to a play; Dryden got as much as £6 for one. **49.** Pitholeon: "a foolish Poet at *Rhodes* ..." (Pope). **53.** Curll: Edmund Curl or Curll, a notorious publisher of private papers. **54.** Journal: periodical mixing "news and scandal" (Pope's note on *Dunciad*, II. 280). divine: Pope seems to have had the poet Leonard Welsted in mind here, who at this time was contemplating a religious work. **62.** Lintot: publisher of many of Pope's works.

At last he whispers, "Do; and we go snacks."°
Glad of a quarrel, straight I clap the door,
"Sir, let me see your works and you no more."°
'Tis sung, when Midas'° ears began to spring,
(Midas, a sacred person and a king)   70
His very minister who spied them first,
(Some say his queen) was forced to speak, or burst.
And is not mine, my friend, a sorer case,
When every coxcomb perks° them in my face?
    "Good friend, forbear! you deal in dangerous
        things.
I'd never name queens, ministers, or kings;
Keep close to ears,° and those let asses prick;
'Tis nothing" — Nothing? if they bite and kick?
Out with it, Dunciad! let the secret pass,
That secret to each fool, that he's an ass: 80
The truth once told (and wherefore should we lie?)
The queen of Midas slept, and so may I.
    You think this cruel? take it for a rule,
No creature smarts so little as a fool.
Let peals of laughter, Codrus!° round thee break,
Thou unconcerned canst hear the mighty crack:
Pit, box, and gallery in convulsions hurled,
Thou standst unshook amidst a bursting world.
Who shames a scribbler? break one cobweb thro',
He spins the slight, self-pleasing thread anew: 90
Destroy his fib or sophistry; in vain,
The creature's at his dirty work again,
Throned in the center of his thin designs,
Proud of a vast extent of flimsy lines!°
Whom have I hurt? has poet yet, or peer,
Lost the arched eyebrow, or Parnassian sneer?°
And has not Colley° still his lord, and whore?
His butchers Henley,° his Freemasons Moore?°
Does not one table Bavius° still admit?
Still to one bishop Philips° seem a wit?   100
Still Sappho° — "Hold! for God's sake — you'll
        offend,
No names — be calm — learn prudence of a friend:

I too could write, and I am twice as tall;°
But foes like these — " One flatterer's worse than
        all.
Of all mad creatures, if the learn'd are right,
It is the slaver kills, and not the bite.
A fool quite angry is quite innocent:
Alas! 'tis ten times worse when they repent.°
    One dedicates in high heroic prose,
And ridicules beyond a hundred foes: 110
One from all Grub Street° will my fame defend,
And, more abusive, calls himself my friend.
This prints my *Letters,* that expects a bribe,
And others roar aloud, "Subscribe,° subscribe."
    There are, who to my person pay their court:
I cough like Horace, and, tho' lean, am short,°
Ammon's great son° one shoulder had too high,
Such Ovid's nose,° and "Sir! you have an eye" —
Go on, obliging creatures, make me see
All that disgraced my betters, met in me.   120
Say for my comfort, languishing in bed,
"Just so immortal Maro° held his head":
And when I die, be sure you let me know
Great Homer died three thousand years ago.
    Why did I write? what sin to me unknown
Dipped me in ink, my parents', or my own?
As yet a child, nor yet a fool to fame,
I lisped in numbers, for the numbers came.
I left no calling for this idle trade,
No duty broke, no father disobeyed.   130
The Muse but served to ease some friend, not wife,
To help me thro' this long disease, my life,
To second, Arbuthnot! thy art and care,
And teach the being you preserved, to bear.
    But why then publish? Granville° the polite,
And knowing Walsh, would tell me I could write;
Well-natured Garth inflamed with early praise;
And Congreve loved, and Swift endured my lays;
The courtly Talbot, Somers, Sheffield read,
Even mitered Rochester would nod the head,   140
And St. John's self (great Dryden's friends° be-
        fore)
With open arms received one poet more.
Happy my studies, when by these approved!
Happier their author, when by these beloved!
From these the world will judge of men and books,
Not from the Burnets, Oldmixons, and Cookes.°

---

66. **go snacks:** divide profits; Dryden had used this colloquial
expression.   68. **Sir . . . more:** a line of powerful monosyllables,
with many stresses.   69. **Midas:** The King of Phrygia had his
ears turned into ass's ears after he had awarded Pan the prize in
his musical contest with Apollo.   74. **perks:** thrusts forward in
an impudent manner.   77. **Keep . . . ears:** Whisper your
satire, and into the ears of humble people.   85. **Codrus:** the
name, perhaps fictitious, of a poet ridiculed by Virgil and Juvenal.
93–94. **designs . . . lines:** words applicable also to poems.
96. **Parnassian sneer:** quoted from *Dunciad,* II. 5.   97. **Colley:**
Colley Cibber, actor, playwright, and Poet Laureate who was to
replace Theobald as hero of the revised *Dunciad* (1743).   98.
Henley: the popular preacher, who had delivered a "Butchers'
Lecture," a sermon for butchers, five years before. **Moore:**
James Moore Smythe, who was a prominent member of this
body.   99. **Bavius:** a minor poet who attacked Virgil and
Horace.   100. **Philips:** Ambrose Philips, Pope's old enemy, who
was now secretary to the Bishop of Armagh.   101. **Sappho:** Under
the name of the Greek poetess Pope repeatedly scored off Lady
Mary Wortley Montagu after their quarrel.

103. **twice as tall:** Pope was a dwarf.   108. **Alas . . . repent:**
Pope is probably referring to Aaron Hill or Thomas Cooke.
111. **Grub Street:** now Milton Street, then the home of literary
hacks.   114. **Subscribe:** Books were often published by subscription.   116. **I . . . short:** Horace had referred to his cough
and to his small plump body.   117. **Ammon's . . . son:** Alexander the Great.   118. **Ovid's nose:** Ovid's full name was
Ovidius Naso.   122. **Maro:** Virgil.   135–41. **Granville . . . St.
John:** a list of his early friends and patrons.   141. **friends:** in
apposition to "arms."   146. **Burnets . . . Cookes:** "Authors of
secret and scandalous History" (Pope).

Soft were my numbers; who could take offense
While pure description held the place of sense?
Like gentle Fanny's° was my flowery theme,
A painted mistress, or a purling stream.°   150
Yet then did Gildon° draw his venal quill;
I wished the man a dinner, and sat still.
Yet then did Dennis° rave in furious fret;
I never answered — I was not in debt.
If want provoked, or madness made them print,
I waged no war with Bedlam or the Mint.

Did some more sober critic come abroad;
If wrong, I smiled; if right, I kissed the rod.
Pains, reading, study, are their just pretense,
And all they want is spirit, taste, and sense.   160
Commas and points they set exactly right,
And 'twere a sin to rob them of their mite.
Yet ne'er one sprig of laurel graced these ribalds,
From slashing Bentley° down to piddling Tibalds:°
Each wight, who reads not, and but scans and
      spells,
Each word-catcher, that lives on syllables,
Even such small critics some regard may claim,
Preserved in Milton's or in Shakespeare's name.
Pretty! in amber to observe the forms   169
Of hairs, or straws, or dirt, or grubs, or worms!
The things, we know, are neither rich nor rare,
But wonder how the devil they got there.

Were others angry: I excused them too;
Well might they rage, I gave them but their due.
A man's true merit 'tis not hard to find;
But each man's secret standard in his mind,
That casting weight pride adds to emptiness,
This, who can gratify? for who can guess?
The bard° whom pilfered pastorals renown,
Who turns a Persian tale for half a crown,   180
Just writes to make his barrenness appear,
And strains, from hard-bound brains, eight lines a
      year;
He, who still wanting, tho' he lives on theft,
Steals much, spends little, yet has nothing left:
And he, who now to sense, now nonsense leaning,
Means not, but blunders round about a meaning:
And he, whose fustian's so sublimely bad,
It is not poetry, but prose run mad:
All these, my modest satire bade translate,
And owned that nine such poets made a Tate.°

How did they fume, and stamp, and roar, and
      chafe!   191
And swear, not Addison himself was safe.
   Peace to all such! but were there one whose
      fires
True genius kindles, and fair fame inspires;
Blest with each talent and each art to please,
And born to write, converse,° and live with ease:
Should such a man, too fond to rule° alone,
Bear, like the Turk, no brother near the throne,°
View him with scornful, yet with jealous eyes,
And hate for arts that caused himself to rise;   200
Damn with faint praise,° assent with civil leer,
And without sneering, teach the rest to sneer;
Willing to wound, and yet afraid to strike,°
Just hint a fault, and hesitate dislike;
Alike reserved to blame, or to commend,
A timorous foe, and a suspicious friend;
Dreading even fools, by flatterers besieged,
And so obliging, that he ne'er obliged;
Like Cato,° give his little senate laws,
And sit attentive to his own applause;   210
While wits and Templars° every sentence raise,
And wonder with a foolish face of praise —
Who but must laugh, if such a man there be?
Who would not weep, if Atticus were he?

   What tho' my name stood rubric on the walls,
Or plastered posts, with claps, in capitals?°
Or smoking forth, a hundred hawkers' load,
On wings of wind came flying all abroad?
I sought no homage from the race that write;
I kept, like Asian monarchs, from their sight: 220
Poems I heeded (now berhymed so long)
No more than thou, great George! a birthday song.
I ne'er with wits or witlings passed my days,
To spread about the itch of verse and praise;
Nor like a puppy daggled° through the town,
To fetch and carry singsong up and down;
Nor at rehearsals sweat, and mouthed, and cried,
With handkerchief and orange° at my side;
But sick of fops, and poetry, and prate,
To Bufo left the whole Castalian state.   230

149. Fanny: Pope's name for Hervey (see below, l. 305n.)
150. A . . . stream: The line, almost verbatim, from Addison, had
already been used by Pope for similar effect in his imitation of
Chaucer.   151. Gildon: He had attacked *The Rape of the Lock.*
153. Dennis: He also had attacked the same poem on its appearance in letters not printed till 1728.   164. Bentley: the only great
name that Pope attacks on intellectual grounds; though a master
of textual criticism when applied to ancient authors, Bentley had
made himself ridiculous by applying it to *Paradise Lost* as if it
were an ancient text.   Tibald: Lewis Theobald, the hero of the
Dunciad in its first shape.   179. The bard: Ambrose Philips.
190. Tate: With Brady, he had translated the Psalms into
humdrum meter.

196. converse: have social intercourse.   197. fond to rule: fond
of ruling.   198. Bear . . . throne: Cf. preface to Garth's *Claremont,*
1715: "Experience shows us every Day that there are Writers who
cannot bear a Brother shou'd succeed."   201. Damn . . . praise:
Cf. Aulus Gellius, *Noctes Atticae,* XIX. 3: "That it is more disgraceful to be praised coldly than to be accused bitterly."
Wycherley helped Pope with the phrasing of this famous line.
203. Willing . . . strike: Cf. *Essay on Criticism,* l. 742.   209.
Cato: A brilliant stroke, for Addison's famous play had taken him
for its hero, and Pope's famous Prologue for it had included the
line: "While *Cato* gives his little Senate laws."   211. Templars:
young barristers who occupied rooms in the Inner or Middle
Temple.   215-16. What . . . capitals: Booksellers advertised
their wares by pasting up title pages, like claps (placards):
Lintot's title pages often mixed red letters with the black.
225. daggled: traipsed.   228. orange: used as smelling salts
and disinfectant in the company of the unwashed.

Proud as Apollo on his forkèd hill,°
Sat full-blown Bufo,° puffed by every quill;
Fed with soft dedication all day long.
Horace and he went hand in hand in song.°
His library (where busts of poets dead
And a true Pindar stood without a head)
Received of wits an undistinguished race,
Who first his judgment asked, and then a place:
Much they extolled his pictures, much his seat,
And flattered every day, and some days eat: 240
Till grown more frugal in his riper days,
He paid some bards with port, and some with
　　praise;
To some a dry rehearsal was assigned,
And others (harder still) he paid in kind.
Dryden alone (what wonder?) came not nigh,
Dryden alone escaped this judging eye:
But still the Great have kindness in reserve,
He helped to bury whom he helped to starve.°
　　May some choice patron bless each gray goose
　　quill!
May every Bavius have his Bufo still!   250
So, when a statesman wants a day's defense,
Or envy holds a whole week's war with sense,
Or simple pride for flattery makes demands,
May dunce by dunce be whistled off my hands!
Blest be the Great! for those they take away,
And those they left me; for they left me Gay;
Left me to see neglected genius bloom,
Neglected die, and tell it on his tomb:
Of all thy blameless life the sole return
My verse, and Queensbury° weeping o'er thy urn!
　　Oh let me live my own! and die so too!   261
"To live and die is all I have to do"°:
Maintain a poet's dignity and ease,
And see what friends, and read what books I please:
Above a patron, tho' I condescend
Sometimes to call a minister my friend.
I was not born for courts or great affairs;
I pay my debts, believe, and say my prayers;
Can sleep without a poem in my head,
Nor know, if Dennis be alive or dead.   270
　　Why am I asked what next shall see the light?
Heavens! was I born for nothing but to write?
Has life no joys for me? or (to be grave)
Have I no friend to serve, no soul to save?

"I found him close with Swift"—"Indeed? no
　　doubt"
(Cries prating Balbus)° "something will come
　　out."
'Tis all in vain, deny it as I will.
"No, such a genius never can lie still";
And then for mine obligingly mistakes
The first Lampoon Sir Will,° or Bubo makes.
Poor guiltless I! and can I choose but smile,   281
When every coxcomb knows me by my *style?*
　　Curst be the verse, how well soe'er it flow,
That tends to make one worthy man my foe,
Give virtue scandal, innocence a fear,
Or from the soft-eyed virgin steal a tear!
But he who hurts a harmless neighbor's peace,
Insults fallen worth, or beauty in distress,
Who loves a lie, lame slander helps about,
Who writes a libel, or who copies out: 290
That fop, whose pride affects a patron's name,
Yet absent, wounds an author's honest fame:
Who can your merit selfishly approve,
And show the sense of it without the love;
Who has the vanity to call you friend,
Yet wants the honor, injured, to defend;°
Who tells whate'er you think, whate'er you say,
And, if he lie not, must at least betray:
Who to the *Dean,* and *silver bell* can swear,
And sees at Cannons what was never there;°   300
Who reads, but with a lust to misapply,
Make satire a lampoon, and fiction, lie.
A lash like mine no honest man shall dread,
But all such babbling blockheads in his stead.
　　Let Sporus° tremble—"What? that thing of
　　silk,
Sporus, that mere white curd of ass's milk?
Satire or sense, alas! can Sporus feel?
Who breaks a butterfly upon a wheel?"
　　Yet let me flap this bug with gilded wings,
This painted child of dirt, that stinks and stings;
Whose buzz the witty and the fair annoys,   311
Yet wit ne'er tastes, and beauty ne'er enjoys:
So well-bred spaniels civilly delight
In mumbling of the game they dare not bite.
Eternal smiles his emptiness betray,
As shallow streams run dimpling all the way.
Whether in florid impotence he speaks,
And, as the prompter breathes, the puppet squeaks;
Or at the ear of Eve, familiar toad,
Half froth, half venom, spits himself abroad,   320
In puns, or politics, or tales, or lies,
Or spite, or smut, or rhymes, or blasphemies.

---

231. forkèd hill: Parnassus.　**232. Bufo:** the Latin word for *toad;* appropriately used here (and by Mallet two years earlier) for a literary patron, since a prominent recent example happened to have the name Bubb Dodington.　**234. Horace . . . song:** Referring to Dodington's being given the place of Maecenas in a recent paraphrase from Ovid.　**248. He . . . starve:** "Mr. Dryden, after having liv'd in Exigencies, had a magnificent Funeral bestow'd upon him by the contributions of several Persons of Quality" (Pope).　**260. Queensbury:** Both Charles Douglas, third Duke of Queensbury, and his Duchess had befriended Gay.　**262. To . . . do:** Pope is virtually quoting Denham's "Of Prudence."

276. Balbus: a Roman lawyer.　**280. Sir Will:** Yonge.　**296. Yet . . . defend:** an instance of Pope's compression: "Yet wants the honour to defend you when you are injured."　**299–300.** This makes reference to details given in Pope's *Moral Essays IV.*　**305. Sporus:** Lord Hervey, who had recently attacked Pope; Pope regards him as an "effeminate courtier-poet."

His wit all seesaw, between *that* and *this,*
Now high, now low, now Master up, now Miss,
And he himself one vile antithesis.
Amphibious thing! that acting either part,
The trifling head, or the corrupted heart,
Fop at the toilet, flatterer at the board,
Now trips a lady, and now struts a lord.
Eve's tempter thus the rabbins° have expressed,
A cherub's face, a reptile all the rest;   331
Beauty that shocks you, parts that none will trust,
Wit that can creep, and pride that licks the dust.

   Not fortune's worshiper, nor fashion's fool,
Not lucre's madman, nor ambition's tool,
Not proud, nor servile, be one poet's praise
That, if he pleased, he pleased by manly ways:
That flattery, even to kings, he held a shame,
And thought a lie in verse or prose the same.
That not in fancy's maze he wandered long,   340
But stooped to truth and moralized his song:
That not for fame, but virtue's better end,
He stood the furious foe, the timid friend,
The damning critic, half-approving wit,
The coxcomb hit, or fearing to be hit;
Laughed at the loss of friends he never had,
The dull, the proud, the wicked, and the mad;
The distant threats of vengeance on his head,
The blow unfelt, the tear he never shed;
The tale revived, the lie so oft o'erthrown,   350
Th' imputed trash, and dulness not his own;
The morals blackened when the writings 'scape,
The libeled person, and the pictured shape;
Abuse, on all he loved, or loved him, spread,
A friend in exile, or a father, dead;
The whisper that to greatness still too near,
Perhaps, yet vibrates on his sovereign's ear —
Welcome for thee, fair Virtue! all the past:
For thee, fair Virtue! welcome even the *last!*

   " But why insult the poor, affront the great? "
A knave's a knave, to me, in every state: 361
Alike my scorn, if he succeed or fail,
Sporus at court, or Japhet° in a jail,
A hireling scribbler, or a hireling peer,
Knight of the Post° corrupt, or of the shire;
If on a pillary, or near a throne,
He gain his prince's ear, or lose his own.

   Yet soft by nature, more a dupe than wit,
Sappho can tell you how this man was bit:°
This dreaded satirist Dennis will confess   370
Foe to his pride, but friend to his distress:°
So humble, he has knocked at Tibbald's door,
Has drunk with Cibber, nay, has rhymed for
   Moore.
Full ten years slandered, did he once reply?

330. **rabbins:** rabbis. 363. **Japhet:** Japhet Crook, a forger.
365. **Knight . . . Post:** one who earned his living by giving false
evidence. 369. **bit:** deceived, "taken in." 371. **friend . . .
distress:** Pope had attempted to launch an edition of Dennis's
works by subscription in 1731.

Three thousand suns went down on Welsted's lie.°
To please a mistress one aspersed his life;
He lashed him not, but let her be his wife:
Let Budgell° charge low Grub Street on his quill,
And write whate'er he pleased, except his will;
Let the two Curlls° of town and court, abuse   380
His father, mother, body, soul, and Muse.
Yet why? that father held it for a rule,
It was a sin to call our neighbor fool:
That harmless mother thought no wife a whore:
Hear this, and spare his family, James Moore!
Unspotted names, and memorable long!
If there be force in virtue, or in song.

   Of gentle blood (part shed in honor's cause,
While yet in Britain honor had applause)
Each parent sprung — " What fortune, pray? " —
   Their own,   390
And better got, than Bestia's° from the throne.
Born to no pride, inheriting no strife,
Nor marrying discord° in a noble wife,
Stranger to civil and religious rage,
The good man walked innoxious thro' his age.
No courts he saw, no suits would ever try,
Nor dared an oath, nor hazarded a lie.
Unlearn'd, he knew no schoolman's subtle art,
No language, but the language of the heart.
By nature honest, by experience wise,   400
Healthy by temperance, and by exercise;
His life, tho' long, to sickness passed unknown,
His death was instant, and without a groan.
O grant me thus to live, and thus to die!
Who sprung from kings shall know less joy than I.

   O friend! may each domestic bliss be thine!
Be no unpleasing melancholy mine:
Me, let the tender office long engage,°
To rock the cradle of reposing age,
With lenient arts extend a mother's breath,   410
Make languor smile, and smooth the bed of death,
Explore° the thought, explain° the asking eye,
And keep a while one parent from the sky!
On cares like these if length of days attend,
May Heaven, to bless those days, preserve my
   friend,
Preserve him social, cheerful, and serene,
And just as rich as when he served a queen.
Whether that blessing be denied or given,
Thus far was right, the rest belongs to Heaven.

375. **Three . . . lie:** Cf. Ephesians IV. 26: "Let not the sun go
down upon your wrath." 378. **Budgell:** Apparently Eustace
Budgell, the author, forged the will of Dr. Matthew Tindal, by
which he inherited money to the detriment of the true heir.
380. **two Curlls.** Edmund Curll's name is used as a term of
abuse—the Curl of the town is Edmund, and of the court, Lord
Hervey. 391. **Bestia:** the name of a Roman consul who accepted bribes, and suggesting debauchery to an English ear.
393. **discord:** Pope is thinking of Discordia, a malevolent goddess
of the Greeks and Romans. 408. **Me . . . engage:** Pope's
mother had died two years before the poem was published:
Pope is using lines he had written in 1731. 412. **Explore:** find
by searching for. **explain:** make intelligible, interpret.

BERTRAND H. BRONSON, *Editor*

Samuel Johnson 1709–1784

& James Boswell

1740–1795

That a close personal attachment could be established between two men so different as Johnson and Boswell in character and experience would hardly have been predicted. Johnson's early impressions were of poverty and insecurity; Boswell's were of social position and established comfort. Johnson knew, long before he came of age, that success in life for him would depend mainly on his own personal effort and proof of merit. Boswell had reason to expect his way to be cleared by his father's distinction and the inheritance of an estate that had been in the family for generations. Johnson had an unprepossessing and craggy appearance, a reserved and defensive and odd bearing, which fenced him like a moat. Boswell had an outgoing good humor, an eager curiosity and readiness of sympathetic address that made him welcome in nearly any company, and invited friendship from all ages, types, and occupations. Johnson thought the world a place where much was to be endured and little to be enjoyed; Boswell thought it an inexhaustible banquet of varied delights, at which the chief call upon endurance was in keeping the appetite poignant and unjaded. Johnson saw suffering as normal; Boswell saw it as mostly avoidable, given a little judgment and moderate good luck. Johnson was a stern moralist, in precept and practice, and, if for-

giving to others, relentless toward himself. Boswell greatly admired moral strength but found it easier to be a man of pleasure. Johnson had a mind of extraordinary vigor, range, and logical resource, as well as a startling breadth of learning and an incomparably ready recollection. Boswell's mind was a weathercock so variable that he had to write down his impressions to convince himself of his own continuity. The staple of Boswell's journals, when they are — as is usual — concerned with his own progress, is the fascinated and indulgent register of his changes of feeling and attitude; Johnson's diaries, sparingly kept and reluctantly written, are full of self-accusation over supposed departures from a charted course or failures to make headway in it. When the two first met, Boswell was a twenty-two-year-old of no personal importance nor even (except in his own eyes) of much promise; Johnson was two and a half times his age, and famous as a poet (*The Vanity of Human Wishes*), moral essayist (The *Rambler*), biographer (*Life of Savage*), novelist (*Rasselas*), lexicographer, and personality. Yet, in spite of all this disparity, which could be illustrated without end, these men were in vital ways ideal counterparts, needing only to be brought into sympathetic contact in order to take up their complementary roles. How the event came about has been memorably recorded by Boswell in the first of the extracts that follow from his *Life of Johnson* (p. 452).

I

Johnson was born on September 18, 1709, a moment when the literary world now known as the Augustan Age was close to its zenith. The brilliant circle of Queen Anne " Wits " was just entering upon the years of its most character-istic and memorable expression. Johnson him-self would one day give a masterly summing up of the achievement of these writers, from the vantage point of one who, sympathetic but un-worshiping, had spent his mature working life in a London steeped in the familiar memory of their physical presence. But Johnson was not a native Londoner; he was born in the quiet ca-thedral town of Lichfield, a small country com-munity where manners and society changed but slowly and where one could tell whether one's neighbor took after a maternal grandparent or a father's cross-grained uncle. Johnson's roots were in the tangled and unstirred compost of this provincial society, and he never, in spite of his love of London, where he felt " the full tide of human existence," denied his anchorage in the place of his birth. The pull of the tide is best felt by one whose anchor does not drag.

Johnson's father, Michael, was a respectable member of the Lichfield community, but his business as bookseller, while it kept him in touch with people of education, seldom put him much above the level of bare subsistence. If his stock did not move rapidly from his shelves, there was the more time for his son to satisfy a desultory but omnivorous curiosity about a wider variety of books than would ordinarily be collected in a private library. Johnson had, besides, the benefit of a reasonably good school-ing in the Lichfield and Stourbridge grammar schools; and when he was by some temporary turn of good fortune enabled to enter Pembroke College, Oxford, he came there better prepared than most of his fellows to carry on the classical studies that then formed the main business of a university education. But regularity was by this time decidedly repugnant to him. He flouted the rules and neglected the college exercises; his studies were fitful and self-indulgent, and his amusements idle and troublesome to author-ity. *Mad, violent,* and *bitter* were the terms he later found to describe his conduct and state of mind at this time. " I was miserably poor, and I thought to fight my way by my literature and my wit; so I disregarded all power and all authority." In that era, if not in ours, a uni-versity student could go far along the road of inattention to work, and Johnson was not ex-pelled. But, whether from despondency or from a failure of funds, he left college at the Christ-mas holidays of his second year and returned home in a state of utmost dejection, entirely un-settled as to his future course. Two years later, and before he had found any regular occupa-tion, his father died, leaving him a meager por-tion of twenty pounds. Johnson meanwhile had been making, and continued to make, abortive efforts to get established as a schoolteacher and to secure literary work of one kind or another.

While he was still in this nadir of gloomy un-certainty, he married in the summer of 1735 a widow of forty-six with three children, aged ten, eighteen, and nineteen, and a fortune of seven or eight hundred pounds. He was twenty years her junior, nearly penniless, with no set-tled prospects, and in appearance (according to contemporary testimony) gaunt and rawboned to an unpleasant degree, his face scarred with scrofula that had also permanently affected his eyesight; he was given besides to convulsive twitches and oddities of gesture that made peo-ple stare. In spite of these formidable handicaps, Elizabeth Porter had had the inspired perspi-cacity to discern in him the " most sensible " man she had ever known; and for her, certainly, the risks were vastly greater than for him. It is not surprising that her older son, already eighteen, never forgave his mother for her folly. But at any rate, it is more than probable that by this supreme compliment of trust and belief in his human worth she saved Johnson from de-spair and even madness. In return, eighteen years after her death, he could confide to his private journal: " My grief for her departure is not abated; and I have less pleasure in any good that befalls me, because she does not partake it."

The years of Johnson's marriage were the most crucial years of his life. Until now, he had scarcely been able to force himself, such was his apathy and inertia, to complete the trans-lation of a travel book to which he was commit-ted, and which was already partly set up in print.

He had as yet never made a sustained effort to finish any considerable task. He and his wife were well aware of the universal disapproval of their marriage, among their acquaintances and friends; and Johnson could see that the burden of proving its rightness rested squarely on him. We know next to nothing about the character and personality of Mrs. Johnson. But it is certain that in one way and another, with her at his side, he was gradually enabled to loosen and throw off the fetters that had immobilized his will. His sense of obligation and responsibility, his personal pride, his dignity as a man, his ambition and hope, were kindled by the challenge of her presence, her faith in his powers, her affectionate respect and her justifiable need to have her judgment vindicated, to be made proud of her choice; and these elements together combined to forge in him a determined purpose not to fail. The springs of his creative life began to unlock. One by one, in the ensuing years of marriage, most of the works that were to give him his commanding position in his age appeared or were planned and projected. There is not a particle of evidence, nor anywhere a suggestion, that his wife ever tried to obstruct or deflect a single one of Johnson's more serious purposes, however laborious or time-consuming or careless of quick returns it might be. He once in all sincerity assured his cynical young friend Beauclerk that his marriage was a love match on both sides. Clearly, it also rested on a foundation of mutual respect and understanding. Save possibly from her husband, Elizabeth Johnson has never received her due for the part she played in Johnson's achievement.

The couple's first venture was to try to establish a boarding school, at Edial near Lichfield. They rented a large, solid brick house, and Mrs. Johnson put a good deal of money into furnishing and readying it for use. By the efforts of friends, a few pupils were enrolled from the neighborhood, including David Garrick, soon to·be famous, and his younger brother, but advertisement farther afield brought no result, and the total number of scholars never rose above eight. The school languished for about a year and expired.

It would be natural if the Johnsons began to grow restive under the coldly appraising eyes of their Lichfield neighbors, and to feel that less constant scrutiny would be a relief. Years later Johnson wrote that in a small country town " every human being is a spy." The couple commenced to think about the possibilities of London. Johnson had been working on a play, a classical tragedy, that he thought one of the London theater managers might be willing to produce; and in the spring of 1737 he and his pupil Garrick went up to see if they could gain a foothold and find a way of life in the city. Garrick was to study law, and Johnson would find work among the booksellers while he finished his play. Thanks largely to Edward Cave, the founder and proprietor of the *Gentleman's Magazine,* he did glimpse the possibility of a livelihood. Consequently, although the play made little progress, Johnson returned home in the summer with an optimistic report, and toward the end of the year the Johnsons packed up and moved to the decent obscurity of London.

For a long while the going was rocky indeed, but little by little Johnson began to establish himself, to get miscellaneous literary assignments with less of an effort than before, and to win time for more ambitious and independent performances. As early as the spring of 1739, his first important creative work, the poem *London,* brought him significant acclaim and went into four editions within a year. He was given the important and continuing job of writing up for the *Gentleman's Magazine* fictionalized reports — since factual reporting was then virtually illegal — of the parliamentary debates: really a major creative effort on the slenderest factual material, but read by the general public as a truthful record. The *Life of Richard Savage* (1744), the *Drury Lane Prologue* (1747), *Irene* (1749), *The Vanity of Human Wishes* (1749), the *Rambler* (1750-52), and the Dictionary (1755) followed in due course — the last, unhappily, appearing three years after his wife's death, to which he poignantly alluded in the immortal last sentence of his Preface. The *Idler* and *Rasselas* followed toward the end of the same decade (1758–59), while he was engaged on his great edition of Shakespeare. The *Shakespeare* finally appeared in 1765, but meanwhile three things of greatest moment had occurred to affect the course of Johnson's history. The first was the granting of a royal pension in the spring of 1762. The second was his meeting with Boswell, on May 16, 1763. The third was his acquaintance with the Henry Thrales, in 1764 or 1765, who were to make a second home for him during most of the last twenty years of his life, and to whom he was consequently indebted for much comfort and happiness. And we may add a fourth of equal consequence to us: the establishing of the Literary Club — that brilliant constellation of talents — in 1764.

The last two decades of Johnson's life were passed in a blaze of celebrity, but his conversation, rather than any biographical events or literary publications, was the chief agent of his increasing fame. Apart from some political pamphlets, written (albeit with much hard-headed good sense) on the negative side of historical progress, his most important work thereafter was the generalized digest of his trip to the Scottish Highlands and islands with Boswell, and his Prefaces to the poets, now called *Lives,* the ripe fruit of a life spent on letters and literary values and their place in the diapason of man's experience. These were published in 1779 and 1781. Three years later he died, on December 13, 1784.

II

The last quarter of Johnson's life was lived, we have noted, in the full glare of public attention, and also under the anatomizing lens of Boswell's probing curiosity.

The immediacy of Boswell's record introduces a danger not ordinarily to be reckoned with: the often noticeable disparity between Johnson's writing and Boswell's record of his talk. To put the matter abruptly, Johnson often talked for immediate victory, but he almost always wrote upon oath. There is a considered and formal finality about most of his writing that demands an answering sincerity in the reader. His talk, however, is always subject to correction by the spirit of the occasion that evoked it. He cannot, therefore, be quoted indifferently from the written or spoken record, as if both had an equal claim to be accepted as his conviction. For a hundred years, indeed, under the powerful influence of Macaulay's mischievous simplifications, readers were virtually persuaded to ignore Johnson's writing as mere hieroglyphics, and to look for the true Johnson in his conversation. There is enough truth in this position to make

it a most pernicious falsehood. Johnson's published writing is, in the main, the unrefracted image of his deepest nature, and should be taken at its face value. It is true that the man Johnson is to be found equally in his talk as in his writing, and that the revelation of character and personality which abides in contradiction and overstatement, in the impulsive expression of prejudice, or thrusting for advantage at the risk of inconsistency, is more evident in Boswell's reports than anywhere else. And of course this is a precious and revealing kind of truth. But, although we recognize, when we consult our own experience, that the conversation of ourselves and our acquaintances is always a distorted and imperfect representation of the truth that is in us — something that requires always to be corrected in the light of fuller knowledge — yet we are here liable to forget this obvious fact, because so full a record as Boswell's of actual conversation, so authentic and so vivid, is unique except in fiction and drama.

His record is neither of these, as we know; and reading it as history we are easily misled into granting it an authority and weight in particular utterances that the original participants would be quick to deny if they could. Boswell knew this, and continually does his best to provide the friendly correctives so necessary to a true reading. But again, a school of readers who despised him tried to trim away as much of Boswell as possible in order, as they thought, to do Johnson the service of letting him stand out clear. They were misguided; for Boswell is essential to the right interpretation of his subject. Furthermore, the better we know Boswell and the more we learn about what went into his book and how it took tangible form, the better chance we shall have of reading it with genuine comprehension.

III

Boswell in person is such a collection of assets and liabilities, of genius and imbecility, kindliness and malice, loyalty and betrayal, boundless vanity and abject humility, high spirits and bottomless depressions, lofty resolutions and headlong plunges, intellectual hunger and sensual debauchery, love of cloud castles and passion for factual truth, that his account is very difficult to cast up. He himself, indeed, found the prospect quite bewildering. " My life," he wrote to his friend Temple, " is one of the most romantic that I believe either you or I really know of; and yet I am a very sensible, good sort of man. What is the meaning of this? "

Boswell came of an ancient and very respectable Scottish family. He boasted that the blood of Robert the Bruce flowed in his veins. There is no reason to doubt his claim, but there might be some question whether he could carry it without spilling; the pride of it, he declared, " was his predominant passion." He was an eldest son, and heir to the estate of Auchinleck in Ayrshire. His father was a judge of the Court of Sessions, a strict and dour but humorous Presbyterian; and the regard in which he was generally held opened doors for Boswell and Johnson when they traveled in the Highlands. The father was steady and self-controlled, and found his son's mercurial temper more than he could usually bear. He was in such dread of some new folly that he bribed Boswell, upon the latter's coming of age, into signing himself into perpetual guardianship — a documentary club to bring Boswell to terms if he became too outrageous. But Lord Auchinleck was ready to be kind, even generously indulgent, if only the son would conform to his wishes — which he could never do — and live the sober, settled kind of life appropriate to a " laird." Boswell admired his father and really wished to please him, but inner compulsions were always overmastering his soberer purposes. Respect it as he might, his father's staid pattern of life was not for him; when he tried it, he sank into speechless gloom, from which he would break out into the wildest extravagance. He longed to be an army officer, for the typical peacetime reasons; but a commission required patronage as well as money; and after nearly a year of unsuccessful solicitation in London, he succumbed to his father's desire that he should go to Holland as Auchinleck himself had done, and study Roman law. After the exhilaration of London, where he had made friends with Johnson and many other notables, Utrecht bored him almost to distraction, but he tried hard to hold himself to a regular course, and for nearly a year was not altogether unsuccessful. Then, however, fortune favored him with his father's permission to depart under

most lucky auspices to Berlin — in company with Lord Keith, Earl Marischal of Scotland, friend of Frederick the Great, Voltaire, and Rousseau. He was thus fairly launched upon a career of celebrity chasing. Thereafter his orbit widened; he proceeded to Switzerland, where he " collected " the two notable *philosophes* just mentioned. Then he moved south into Italy, and added the reprobate, libertine, and popular hero, John Wilkes, to his belt; he had first met him in London a year previously. Next, he doubled over to present Rousseau's introduction to the Corsican patriot, Paoli, collecting the materials for his first important literary work, *The Journal of a Tour to Corsica; and Memoirs of Pascal Paoli,* published with *An Account of Corsica,* early in 1768.

In the Preface to this work, Boswell confessed to a hunger for literary fame. The book was at once translated into several foreign tongues, and in the third English edition he was able to announce that his desire had been gratified. He became at once a notable figure, and even succeeded in rousing his countrymen to quite a pitch of enthusiasm for the Corsicans and their heroic leader. After Corsica was ceded to France in the following year and Paoli escaped to England, Paoli's London residence became Boswell's headquarters in town, and the friendship between the two was never broken.

Meanwhile, Boswell had been admitted to the Scottish bar (July 29, 1766), and began a professional practice for which he found less and less time as the years went by. Until his death on May 19, 1795, it is singular, in a life so crammed (as we now realize) with trivial incident, how few important dates occurred, apart from those associated with Johnson. On November 25, 1769, he was married to his cousin, Margaret Montgomerie. In the summer of 1773 he made the extended tour through the north of Scotland with Johnson, of which his memorable record was published late in 1785. The great *Life* was published in May, 1791. There were his visits to London, to Oxford, to Ashbourne in Derbyshire to meet Johnson, and to Ireland. There were the births of his children, Veronica, Euphemia, Elizabeth, Alexander, and James. There was his father's death in 1782, and his own succession to the estate of Auchinleck; and the death of his wife, on June 4, 1789 — the last a calamity in the wake of which his own life rapidly deteriorated.

IV

Throughout all these years, however, Boswell was projecting new careers and adventures, pursuing celebrities new and old, vainly scheming to get into parliament, writing political pamphlets, throwing off articles for magazines and newspapers, and above all writing his diaries and journals. The last was felt as an absolute duty, possibly his supreme duty in life. It is hardly too much to say that his existence was one neverending correspondence course with himself. When he awoke in the morning, he jotted down instructions and admonitions for the day's proceedings. For example, on the day when, unknown to him, he was to meet Johnson for the first time, he wrote to himself before rising:

Send breeches mend by barber's boy. You are now on good plan. Breakfast neat today, toast, rolls, and butter, easily and not too laughable. Then Love's and get money, or first finish journal. Keep plan in mind and be earnest. Keep in this fine frame, and be directed by Temple. At night see Pringle. Go to Piazza and take some negus ere you go; or go cool and take letter and bid him [i.e., Pringle] settle all, but not too fast.

And when he retired at night, it was his custom to report — if possible — to himself in writing, in similar brief fashion, what the day had brought forth, and to tell himself what he thought of his conduct in it. As, for instance:

Received a letter from Mr. Johnson treating you with esteem and kindness; nobly elated by it, and resolved to maintain the dignity of yourself.
(Private Papers, VII.60)

Or, again,

You resolved to be yourself, to break free from slavery [to the current mistress]. What strength of mind you have had this winter, to go through so much business and at the same time have so violent a Passion! . . . You wavered and knew not how to determine. You saw yourself gone. . . . Was stunned, but resolved to be firm. To bed quite agitated.   (Private Papers, VII.114–115)

Or, once more,

You was in great vigor of genius, and in the library you dictated *Dorando*. You thought it excellent.
(Private Papers, VII.120 [4/15/1767])

These memoranda were full enough to prompt his memory and provide the basis for an informal regular journal, which he strove to keep up to date. This was written in the first, not as before, in the second, person; it was the completed report which he transmitted to himself — and, as it ultimately turned out, to posterity — of what on each day was done and said, seen and heard and felt, by him, or by others in his presence; and submitted for future examination and comparison with other scenes, past or to come. He could use it for enjoyment, or as source material for the books and essays he would write when time should serve, or as a private manual of instruction. " As a lady," he declared, " adjusts her dress before a mirror, a man adjusts his character by looking at his journal."

Boswell had tentatively begun such a record of his life by the time he was eighteen, and already foresaw what a treasury of experience it could prove to him if he could keep it up. In spite of his consuming egoism and *amour-propre,* he had deep within his nature a haunting sense of his own insufficiency, a desperate need for all the props and supports he could find — for particular advice and general wisdom, for the caveats of friends who knew his besetting weaknesses and for the encouraging example of stronger characters who stood firm against the temptations that he found irresistible. One of the valuable uses of his journals was in the amassing and hoarding of intellectual and spiritual stiffening against the devil and mischance. It was in significant part for his own immediate profit that he went to the trouble of preserving the wisdom and counsel that he extracted from his elders and betters.

The lack of sympathetic rapport between Boswell and his father is an important factor in the shaping of his life and accomplishment. Had Lord Auchinleck, like the father of Charles James Fox, been able to initiate his son into the ways of the world, constituting himself the cynical but sagacious mentor and companion of youth, it is likely that Johnson would have remained to Boswell no more than a celebrated name. This was a role the father was incapable of playing: from every point of view it was unthinkable. Never did a son stand in more constant need of sympathetic and understanding guidance; never was an adolescent more susceptible to influence; never was a boy less able to emulate a father's virtues. The two natures were mutually repellent. "I write to him with warmth," Boswell pathetically complains, "but my letters shock him." But Boswell had to pattern himself on others: he was formed to follow, not to lead. He spent much of his life in pursuit of notable personalities, but he was not a toady, not a sycophant. He had to find, outside, the strength that his own nature lacked. If his father could not accept him, a substitute must somewhere be found. In the long list of his friends and companions, the men of his own age are relatively unimportant. The clergyman, Temple, who was to him like a father-confessor, to whom especially he confided his sensual lapses ("Admonish me, but forgive me"), was the only contemporary who in the long run meant much in his life. His most valued friendships were with those of his father's generation. "I really," he once wrote in his journal, "feel myself happier in the company of those of whom I stand in awe than in any other company. [Such society] composes the uneasy tumult of my spirits, and gives me the pleasure of contemplating something at least comparatively great." This attitude of mind is very forcibly illustrated in his *Tour to Corsica,* in what he has to say about Paoli:

The contemplation of such a character really existing was of more service to me than all I had been able to draw from books, from conversation, or from the exertions of my own mind. . . . It was impossible for me . . . to have a little opinion of human nature in him. . . . I ventured to reason like a libertine, that I might be confirmed in virtuous principles by so illustrious a preceptor. . . . I took leave of Paoli with regret and agitation. . . . From having known intimately so exalted a character, my sentiments of human nature were raised, while, by a sort of contagion, I felt an honest ardor to distinguish myself, and be useful, as far as my situation and abilities would allow.

V

When Boswell came up to London in 1762, he came as fully determined to see Johnson as he was to visit St. Paul's or any other public monument. He was already familiar with his writings, and knew from the *Rambler* that here was a man from whom his own nature could draw the sustenance for which it hungered. He

had heard from their mutual friend Thomas Sheridan, and others, wonderful things of his talk, and he was impatient to experience such wisdom and wit. The wit would be an additional delight and give zest to the discourse, but it was the wisdom, and more especially the moral instruction, that Boswell most wanted.

Boswell's mode of existence from day to day, during the spring in which he first saw his polestar, has latterly become the notorious object of sniggering allusion, and it may at first seem paradoxical that so libidinous a puppy should be so keen for virtue. The paradox is superficial. These are opposite but equally valid demonstrations of Boswell's radical insecurity. In both directions he is trying, somewhat feverishly, to assure himself of his manhood, to become a force whose positive impact on his world will be beyond dispute. Either way he aggrandizes his stature in his own eyes. The testimony of the pulses is the easiest and most immediate kind of reassurance, and the level on which Boswell was willing to acquire it proves how desperate was his need to be reassured. But, again, he was bright enough to see that such a course in the long run did not tend to develop the sort of character to which the world paid tribute. He was a sensualist from weakness, not from principle: fundamentally he was religiously moral, and this was the side of his nature that Johnson was to love and nourish. Boswell wished above all things to acquire a character to win the respect of those whom he himself most admired. In Johnson he very soon discovered a talisman, from whose presence he could not but feel that moral strength emanated. After surviving the shock of their first meeting, which for less resilient — that is, more crystallized — natures than his would have been the last, Boswell continued to seek him out, and at the fourth meeting made explicit acknowledgment of his purpose:

Finding him in a placid humor, and wishing to avail myself of the opportunity which I fortunately had of consulting a sage, to hear whose wisdom, I conceived . . . men filled with a noble enthusiasm for intellectual improvement would gladly have resorted from distant lands, I opened my mind to him ingenuously, and gave him a little sketch of my life, to which he was pleased to listen with great attention. . . . Being at all times a curious examiner of the human mind, and pleased with an undisguised display of what had passed in it, he called to me with warmth, " Give me your hand; I have taken a liking to you." [And after their subsequent conversation, which Boswell reports:] " Sir, I am glad we have met. I hope we shall pass many evenings and mornings, too, together." We finished a couple of bottles of port, and sat till between one and two in the morning.

(Life, I.404, 410)

Not two months from that date, Johnson was traveling all the way to Harwich to see his new young friend off to Holland. Why? Among the motives leading to so benevolent a gesture, we may be sure that on Johnson's part there was, as well as a spontaneous response to good nature and to the flattery of youth's sincere deference to age, a recognition of Boswell's human need for strengthening and support, a sense that he himself had something to give that Boswell sorely lacked. Boswell interrupts his narrative of the interview quoted above to introduce a paragraph of more general comment:

I appeal to every impartial reader whether this faithful detail of his frankness, complacency, and kindness to a young man, a stranger and a Scotchman, does not refute the unjust opinion of the harshness of his general demeanor. His occasional reproofs of folly, impudence, or impiety, and even the sudden sallies of his constitutional irritability of temper, which have been preserved for the poignancy of their wit, have produced that opinion among those who have not considered that such instances . . . were, in fact, scattered through a long series of years: years, in which his time was chiefly spent in instructing and delighting mankind by his writings and conversation, in acts of piety to God, and good will to men.

VI

There is no reason to presume that Johnson was in the least mistaken in his general estimate of Boswell's worth. It has been variously suggested that their relation subsisted on a big-and-little-brother basis; that Johnson tolerated Boswell because he fed him unbounded adulation, and Johnson could browbeat and bully him without protest; that Johnson cherished the lesser man in order to ensure that his biography should be written with a proper stock of materials and with due recording of Johnson's conversational prowess; and that Johnson kept Boswell about for a priming device, to develop the situations and ask the questions that would set him off to most effect in company. The truth is that Johnson never developed any kind of dependency on Boswell, and that Boswell's dependency on Johnson was a valid tribute which did them both honor. Boswell was no " slave " and no " idolater," as Macaulay would have him. He came — whatever Macaulay might suppose — with the laudable desire to be improved, and he venerated his mentor and frequented his society — though by no means so assiduously as is generally supposed — because Johnson seldom disappointed his hopes of improvement. Johnson, for his part, took Boswell as he found him, enjoyed his good humor, was engaged by his busy curiosity, and was moved to reminiscence, to ripe reflection, to critical comment, to witty retort, by his flow of questions and observations. Johnson responded with instinctive sympathy to his filial need, and was glad, from the almost inexhaustible stores of his own knowledge of men, his wide learning, his profound and humane wisdom, to give and go on giving so long as he was asked. He would have been grateful to anyone who would sit with him and by converse keep the black dog outside. Boswell not only performed this service but gave him the additional satisfaction of knowing that he was doing active good. Soon after their acquaintance began, Boswell wrote to another friend, " The conversation of that great and good man has formed me to manly virtue, and kindled in my mind a generous ardor which I trust shall never be extinguished." And, however he might fail in performance, the flame never did go out. Perhaps no greater service can be rendered by one human being to another than the all but involuntary service here exemplified. It was the kind of benefit so memorably praised by Thoreau, " not a partial and transitory act, but a constant superfluity," which came from Johnson like warmth from the sun. Johnson's whole life and all that he wrote were, in Heaven's eye, in the service of moral purpose; but he was not a reformer: he did not think to cure the world's stomach-ache by warning it against eating green apples. The apple, he thought, had been eaten already, and there was little enough to be done about it but endure the pain with as little whining as possible.

VII

All the characteristic features of Boswell's genius at work with spontaneous and happy art upon congenial material are displayed in possibly the most famous and brilliant scene in the *Life,* the account of Johnson's first meeting with John Wilkes at the dinner of the brothers Dilly, in May, 1776. There was hardly a man of note in England whom Johnson more abominated than Wilkes. Wilkes was a notorious offender against the values Johnson most prized. He was a libertine in private life, a member of the Medmenham Abbey brotherhood, who turned the forms of religion into Rabelaisian license; and for his obscene verses on Woman he had been duly reprobated in the House of Lords. He was a rabble-rouser, who had done his utmost to weaken the King's authority by his cool and calculated ridicule and defiance of a House of Commons subservient to the Crown. The kind of liberty that was meant by those who cried "Wilkes and Liberty" was in Johnson's mind nothing more than license. And of such patriotism he declared that it was the last refuge of a scoundrel. He had directed his most pungent political tract, *The False Alarm,* specifically against Wilkes and his claim to be readmitted to parliament. "It will not be easily found," he had written, "why, among the innumerable wrongs of which a great part of mankind are hourly complaining, the whole care of the public should be transferred to Mr. Wilkes and the freeholders of Middlesex, who might all sink into nonexistence, without any other effect, than that there would be room made for a new rabble, and a new retailer of sedition and obscenity." Wilkes, besides, had fled the country for several years and had been outlawed for failure to reappear to answer the charges against him; had eventually surrendered and been sentenced to twelve months in jail. Persons rioting in his behalf had lost their lives.

Boswell, being familiar with the whole history of the violent and mutual hostility between Johnson and Wilkes, conceived, as he declares, an "irresistible wish" to bring them together. He opens his narrative with deliberation, conscious that it was "a very curious incident" and willing to take due credit for his part in it — which was in fact that of its only begetter. No one else would have dreamed of it, much less

tried to bring it to pass. "How to manage it," he admits, "was a nice and difficult matter." He first overcomes the objections of his host, Edward Dilly, to including Johnson when Wilkes is to be among the dinner guests; he does this by offering to take full responsibility. But to persuade Johnson even to enter a room with Wilkes will, he realizes, be a feat in itself. In a sentence that reveals in successive steps, and with ironic understatement, the complexity of his own attitude toward Johnson, he confides in the reader: "Notwithstanding the high veneration which I entertained for Dr. Johnson, I was sensible that he was sometimes a little actuated by the spirit of contradiction, and by means of that I hoped I should gain my point." With perfect knowledge and practiced skill he proceeds to draw out Leviathan with a hook, and the monster is unaware that he is caught. "I therefore," says Boswell, "while we were sitting quietly by ourselves at his house in an evening, took occasion to open my plan thus: 'Mr. Dilly, sir, sends his respectful compliments to you, and would be happy if you would do him the honor to dine with him on Wednesday next along with me, as I must soon go to Scotland.' JOHNSON: 'Sir, I am obliged to Mr. Dilly. I will wait upon him —' BOSWELL: 'Provided, sir, I suppose, that the company which he is to have, is agreeable to you.' JOHNSON: 'What do you mean, sir? What do you take me for? Do you think I am so ignorant of the world . . . that I am to prescribe to a gentleman what company he is to have at his table?'" There might be people very obnoxious at that table, hints Boswell, whipping the water into foam. "Well, sir, and what then?" Johnson exclaims, ". . . as if I could not meet any company whatever, occasionally." "Pray forgive me, sir," replies Boswell meekly, "I meant well. But you shall meet whoever comes, for me." "*Thus I secured him.*" The inimitable page that follows exhibits Boswell disposing with equal mastery of an unforeseen obstacle that arises on the very evening, half an hour before the dinner, from Johnson's forgetfully having ordered dinner at home with Mrs. Williams, Johnson's blind lodger. It is filled with vivid pictorial and dramatic detail: Boswell's consternation to find the Doctor covered with dust and "buffeting his books"; his vehement entreaties, first to Johnson, then to Mrs. Williams. "'Yes, sir,' said she, pretty peevishly, 'Dr. Johnson is to dine at home.' . . . She gradually softened to my solicitations . . . I flew back to him, still in dust . . . he roared, ' Frank, a clean shirt,' and was very soon dressed. When I had him fairly seated in a hackney coach with me, I exulted as much as a fortune hunter who has got an heiress into a post chaise with him to set out for Gretna Green " (p. 485). The sequel is in every respect worthy of this wonderful prologue, and must be read entire. The drama is superb, the persons display their essential selves, the conversation is witty, mischievously anecdotical, and classic. While Boswell keeps himself " snug and silent," watching what may ensue, Wilkes and Johnson join in good-natured fun at the expense of Boswell and the Scotch, and one of Johnson's best-known mots is elicited. (The dinner, we should recall, took place in the second year of our American Revolution.) " Amidst some patriotic groans . . ." writes Boswell, " somebody said, ' Poor old England is lost.' JOHNSON: ' Sir, it is not so much to be lamented that old England is lost, as that the Scotch have found it.' " There is nothing in the pages of the comic dramatists, and nothing in the greatest masters of the social novel, that surpasses this scene in conveying the sense of living and breathing reality. And it is all true; for a brief while, by virtue of Boswell's unparalleled talent, we are transported through time and space and rendered actually present in an eighteenth-century London dining-room, No. 22 the Poultry, Wednesday, May 15, 1776. Boswell's dual accomplishment on this occasion, as creative dramatist and ideal recorder, constitutes a double charge on our gratitude which we can never sufficiently acknowledge.

VIII

Boswell preserves and manages to convey with incomparable vividness the very habit of Johnson's conversation: its pursuit of underlying principles, its characteristic thrust toward the positions that command the area of debate, and its sinewy athletic challenge. We can see the man matching the play of ideas with a similar expenditure of physical force, using far more lung power than the occasion requires, and blowing out his breath in gusts after making a good point, like the picture of Boreas on an old map. This violence and muscularity is central

in Johnson's nature: he was not a temperate man. He could be rigidly abstemious, as Boswell tells us, but not moderate. Moderation lies in an equipoise between opposite tensions: it is the classical ideal of virtue, to be so perfectly balanced that one is effortlessly at rest. Johnson, on the contrary, needed always to be proving his strength; effort and living were for him synonymous terms. " To strive with difficulties and to conquer them," he once wrote, " is the highest human felicity; the next is, to strive, and deserve to conquer; but he whose life has passed without a contest, and who can boast neither success nor merit, can survey himself only as a useless filler of existence; and if he is content with his own character, must owe his satisfaction to insensibility." This conviction, radically Christian, but also felt in the blood, that life on earth is no place for rest, that we are here to fight for the good, permeates every aspect of Johnson's being. It is this that lends a dark and terrifying weight of guilt to his paradoxically inveterate habits of indolence and procrastination, causing him to load his private meditations with an urgency of self-condemnation that to some readers is merely ludicrous. In him, sloth contained more of disease than of vice; but by temperament and conviction he found himself incapable of distinguishing in his own case. His heart and his mind were united to the end in proclaiming, " I will be conquered: I will not capitulate." Knowing the fathomless subtlety of self-love, could one ever safely feel exonerated from blame? At what point was one freed from the moral imperative of " dogged " effort?

Certainly, Johnson was most essentially himself in combat with ideas. From his earliest years he displayed an unwillingness to take things on trust, to fall into step at command. What in the young is frequently called — and no doubt often is — sheer obstinacy, may develop in the mature man, given judgment, into strength of character, a habit of resistance to adventitious pressures. Young or old, Johnson was all his life temperamentally disposed to gainsay. In his youth, he told Boswell, he always chose the wrong side of a debate. And in later years, well knowing how interwoven are truth and falsehood, he would allow himself, in the heat of contest, to try how much of lesser or immediate truth could be found in the opposite camp. " A man," he once wrote, " heated in talk, and eager of victory, takes advantage of the mistakes or ignorance of his adversary, lays hold of concessions to which he knows he has no right, and urges proofs likely to prevail on his opponent, though he knows himself that they have no force." Once, hearing that a man with whom he had carried on a long argument had afterwards expressed elsewhere his thankfulness because Johnson had convinced him " that an opinion which he had embraced as a settled truth was no better than a vulgar error: ' Nay,' said Johnson, ' do not let him be thankful, for he was right, and I was wrong.'"

This negative habit was strikingly evident in a trick he had of commencing or summarizing a position with " No," before any of his hearers had signified an intention to contradict. " No, sir, he was irresistible." It was as if he were merely opening the door on a debate that had already been proceeding in the closed chamber of his own thoughts. And, indeed, conversation was for him but the audible part of a perpetual discussion, the ultimate goal of which was the discovery and defense of truth, not by guess, not by instinct, intuition, nor even by revelation (unless all else failed), but by rational means. Essentially, Johnson was dedicated to reclaiming as much as possible of human life from the rushlights and snares of irrationality and the " dangerous prevalence of imagination." In this incessant dialogue, he was, ideally, the devoted antagonist of falsehood and obfuscation. He feared the enemy, because he saw that the possibility of defeat was always imminent, from within or from without, whether from man's natural though corrupt love of the lie, as Bacon said, or from mere human liability to error. Therefore he entered every contest with a determination to win. At times, when he felt himself hard pressed, he was blustering and overbearing and willing to settle for the shadow, not the substance, of victory. Not to give ground in battle was essential. At the worst, to be exercising the mental faculties in a rational, discursive way was preferable to any sort of capitulation. On a wider ground, surrender in solitude to reverie, to uncontrolled imagination, to the "chasing of airy good," was abjectly to give away advantage. Therefore, the idling motor must always be thrown as soon as possible into gear. Johnson hated to be alone with his thoughts because the surrender to vacancy was then so much harder to resist. He dreaded the mild insanity of sleepless nights; they were a frightening reminder of how thin was the partition between the rational and irrational. So he clung to his companions far into the small hours, in the hope of wearying himself into slumber when retirement could no longer be postponed.

IX

The aggressive habit of his mind continued to the very end of his life. It is indicative that his last work, the *Lives of the Poets,* is his most unconstrained, most athletic and vigorous, most various and self-assured expression of his views on literature and the literary life. Not for nothing had he spent a great part of the last quarter-century in conversational debate, constantly exercising his intellectual muscle in that arena of impromptu challenge and defense against all comers. However it might be with the heavy body, there was evident no lethargy of the mind.

Nor was there any wavering or unsteadiness in his estimates of the great figures on whom he pronounces. It is very striking how he refuses to be seduced by his own enthusiasms or prejudices. Shakespeare, Dryden, and Pope were probably his best-loved authors. Yet, although he praises them all magnificently, his praise always discriminates: he tells where their special excellences lie, and, without abating any of the force of his admiration, turns his level judgment on their weaknesses, whether of character or of achievement, in order to reach a verdict that shall be dispassionate and just. His discussion of Shakespeare's and Dryden's faults of neglect or carelessness, and of Pope's affectation and self-deception in life as in letters, is a model for all hero-worshiping critics, showing the true height of praise that can offset shortcomings so considerable and so clearly discerned. And on the contrary, in the face of his antipathy to Milton the man and the republican, his noble, wholehearted tribute to Milton's towering grandeur is unshaded by the least hint of grudging reservation or disparagement. His judgment and his magnanimity are perfectly matched, and there is no trace of meanness anywhere, either in blame or praise. The critic himself is great, and without awe or false humility or pride salutes the greatness of the poet.

It has been customary to regard Johnson as the epitome of conservatism, as the last of the great Augustans, or rather, as a belated Augustan, the final bulwark to be borne down by the flood of the new Romanticism. Conservative he doubtless was, in politics, in religion, in literature, in precept, and, at least by intention, in practice. But we must be careful not to take his conservatism too simply, as a mere desire to preserve the *status quo,* a dislike of change. Principles apart, a temperament so dynamic as Johnson's could not be apathetic. His nature was passionate, and he held his principles passionately. "Everything about his character and manners," wrote Boswell, "was forcible and violent." When we call him conservative, we must think of a strenuous conservatism. But conservatism, of course, like any other attitude, becomes strenuous not while it is dominant and taken for granted but when it is confronting serious challenge. Johnson's age, however tamely some observers would picture it, was only superficially stable. The generally placid surface which we see from afar belies the truth that the actual state of affairs is just simmering to a boil. Everywhere accepted values were being undermined; the common core of agreement was dissolving. On the Continent the ferment of ideas was leading directly to the French Revolution. In England the Industrial Revolution had already begun, and the whole social pattern was being more and more rapidly altered by its impact. Around these great cycles of change were revolving many epicycles, religious, artistic, and literary. The forces at work were far too powerful to be successfully opposed; and, as always, the battle line was not clearly drawn on any wide front. Things gave way piecemeal, here and there, and bit by bit; and most of Johnson's generation display traits both new and old, both forward-looking and retrospective. The past itself becomes an avenue to the future: to cast an eye down its long vistas is to be lured away from the familiar present.

Johnson himself exhibits some of the complexities of his day. Anticlassical by temperament, he declared that there was always open an appeal from critical theory to nature, which in his case meant that he refused ultimately to be bound by any formal rule. For him there is only one final authority, and that is not literary, it is divine. Nevertheless, on a lower level he took his stand, by and large, in opposition to the powerfully disintegrating tendencies of his day. And since these tendencies have not even yet spent themselves, but bear us forward upon the same current, he seems perhaps to speak to us over a great distance. It requires of us some effort of will and sympathetic imagination to recover his critical position.

X

The basis of it, clearly, is religious. It rests squarely upon the radically democratic assumption, uncongenial to the prepossessions of our time, that we are all moral beings with a common stake in the working out on earth of our personal salvation.

Some truths, Johnson believed, are too important to be new. The most important truths have been known for a very long time. They require always to be restated. And because, as he says, of themselves "they raise no unaccustomed emotion in the mind," one of the paramount uses of literature is to restate them in fresh and varied ways, so that they may be vividly and meaningfully re-experienced. "Men more frequently require to be reminded than informed." The literary ideal, therefore, would be to convey the most important sentiments in the most effective manner to the widest possible audience. The pleasure of novelty, absent from the great and familiar verities, is restored to them by the felicity, or convincing power, with which they are presented — "what oft was thought, but ne'er so well expressed." It is this power for which Johnson especially admired Milton: his ability to give a different appearance to known truths, "with pregnancy and vigor of mind peculiar to himself. Whoever considers the few radical positions which the Scriptures afforded him will wonder by what energetic operation he expanded them to such extent and ramified them to so much variety."

The same ideal makes it natural to set a high value on generalization, the depersonalizing of experience, the distilling of particular instances into a statement comprehending the class as a whole. Johnson and his older contemporaries responded with a keen delight to "the grandeur of generality" — an emotion peculiarly antipathetic or, rather, all but unknown, to the modern sensibility. Yet, upon occasion, Johnson himself manages to combine generality with intensely personal statement, in an amalgam of which he alone had the secret, and which carries a lofty dignity about it that defies familiar approach, as if he were in intimate converse with the Spirit of History. The Preface to the Dictionary contains striking examples of such writing. Thus:

But these [i.e., his first ideal intentions] were the dreams of a poet doomed at last to wake a lexicographer. I soon found that it is too late to look for instruments, when the work calls for execution, and that whatever abilities I had brought to my task, with those I must finally perform it. To deliberate whenever I doubted, to inquire whenever I was ignorant, would have protracted the undertaking without end and, perhaps, without much improvement; for I did not find by my first experiments, that what I had not of my own was easily to be obtained; I saw that one inquiry only gave occasion to another, that book referred to book, that to search was not always to find, and to find was not always to be informed; and that thus to pursue perfection was, like the first inhabitants of Arcadia, to chase the sun, which, when they had reached the hill where he seemed to rest, was still beheld at the same distance from them.

I then contracted my design, determining to confide in myself, and no longer to solicit auxiliaries which produced more encumbrance than assistance; by this I obtained at least one advantage, that I set limits to my work, which would in time be ended, though not completed.

Characteristically, Johnson aimed at generalized statement in his writing, and approved, in his critical comment on the work of others, that which was inattentive to the disguises of local customs and manners, and particular instances. " Great thoughts," he declares, " are always general, and consist in positions not limited by exceptions, and in descriptions not descending to minuteness."

Johnson's ideal had already begun to be displaced in his own lifetime by a greater liking for the individual instance, picturesquely or vividly described; by an increasing distrust of the grand generalization, consequent upon the weakening of religious conviction and the fragmentation of agreement as to the purpose and destiny of man. Sensibility was increasingly cultivated as a virtue in and of itself; and the verbal celebration of fine feeling was audible between inarticulate sobs and floods of tears. Self-consciousness and egocentricity became more and more the order of the day, and feelings came to be prized rather for their claims to the distinction of rarity than for their purchase on another heart.

To an age prone to believe that salvation lies in the perfection of a " space ship," and that human perfectibility proceeds in a one-to-one ratio with the multiplication of " gadgets " that increase a man's accessibility to conflicting claims on his attention, Johnson offers a loud and tonic, " Why, no, sir! " If we will consent to listen to him, he will offer us, instead of panaceas applied from without, a variety of arguments and his personal example to convince us that we might profit by self-scrutiny. He will assure us that luck is not the measure of success, and that if success comes without being paid for in advance by unremitting effort, we shall either lose it, or be destroyed by it, or earn the right to keep it by paying off the debt. He will urge us to clear our minds of cant. He will warn us that we cannot ultimately evade the responsibility for our own acts and will enjoin us therefore to give the best that is in us. He will teach us that the cost of such a discharge of responsibility is nothing less than all we have, that the battle is incessant, and that our effort is of supreme importance. He will show us the sense of self-fulfillment and exhilaration that comes of acquitting oneself as best one can in the never-ending combat for the true and the good. " The certainty," he will tell us, " that life cannot be long, and the probability that it will be much shorter than nature allows, ought to awaken every man to the active prosecution of whatever he is desirous to perform. It is true that no diligence can ascertain success; death may intercept the swiftest career; but he who is cut off in the execution of an honest undertaking, has at least the honor of falling in his rank, and has fought the battle, though he missed the victory." Johnson, in a word, can add a cubit to our human stature, and make us proud that we belong to the same order of being.

JAMES BOSWELL

THE LIFE
OF SAMUEL JOHNSON

Not much about the *Life of Johnson* need be added here to what has been already said in the Introduction. After the success of the *Tour to the Hebrides* — really a segment of the *Life* — Boswell saw that he could not evade the longer task. He was irresolute, however, from the mere bulk of his collected materials, and was also distracted by his desire to get into politics and become a member of parliament. Supported by Edmond Malone, the friendly critic who had encouraged him in publishing the *Tour,* he set to work in the summer of 1786 to weave together in a connected narrative the biographical facts, the letters of Johnson, and the conversational episodes that originally formed portions of his own sprawling autobiographical record, but were now to find their proper places in a new configuration. As Geoffrey Scott, the brilliant editor of Boswell's journals, who died in 1929, has remarked, there was in the task so much of the mere drudgery of transcription, and so much of troublesome verification of historical fact, that the exhilaration of creative effort could play only a relatively small part in the act of composition. Boswell often sank under the burden of it. But he managed to keep faith with his responsibility and, at last, after nearly five years of toil, brought it to completion. During this period his wife died, but, although she had been a steadying influence, it is unlikely that with her conventional ideas of propriety, she could have given him in this work very much support or encouragement. The *Life* was published on May 16, 1791, and, in a little more than a year, the first edition had been sold off with a profit to Boswell of nearly the exact amount that Johnson received for the Dictionary. In celebration, he gave a little dinner to his bookseller, his friends, and children. He records: "I got into a pretty good state of joviality, though still dreary at bottom." The immediate satisfactions were relatively inconsiderable; his true rewards were posthumous.

from *May 16–August 6, 1763*

This is to me a memorable year, for in it I had the happiness to obtain the acquaintance of that extraordinary man whose memoirs I am now writing, an acquaintance which I shall ever esteem as one of the most fortunate circumstances in my life. Though then but two-and-twenty, I had for several years read his works with delight and instruction, and had the highest reverence for their author, which had grown up in my fancy into a kind of

mysterious veneration, by figuring to myself a state of solemn elevated abstraction, in which I supposed him to live in the immense metropolis of London. Mr. Gentleman, a native of Ireland, who passed some years in Scotland as a player, and as an instructor in the English language, a man whose talents and worth were depressed by misfortunes, had given me a representation of the figure and manner of "Dictionary Johnson," as he was then generally called; and during my first visit to London, which was for three months in 1760, Mr. Derrick the poet, who was Gentleman's friend and countryman, flattered me with hopes that he would introduce me to Johnson, an honor of which I was very ambitious. But he never found an opportunity, which made me doubt that he had promised to do what was not in his power; till Johnson some years afterwards told me, "Derrick, sir, might very well have introduced you. I had a kindness for Derrick, and am sorry he is dead."

In the summer of 1761 Mr. Thomas Sheridan [1] was at Edinburgh, and delivered lectures upon the English language and public speaking to large and respectable audiences. I was often in his company, and heard him frequently expatiate upon Johnson's extraordinary knowledge, talents, and virtues, repeat his pointed sayings, describe his particularities, and boast of his being his guest sometimes till two or three in the morning. At his house I hoped to have many opportunities of seeing the sage, as Mr. Sheridan obligingly assured me I should not be disappointed.

When I returned to London in the end of 1762, to my surprise and regret I found an irreconcilable difference had taken place between Johnson and Sheridan. A pension of two hundred pounds a year had been given to Sheridan. Johnson, who, as has been already mentioned, thought slightingly of Sheridan's art, upon hearing that he was also pensioned, exclaimed, "What! have they given *him* a pension? Then it is time for me to give up mine." Whether this proceeded from a momentary indig-

LIFE OF JOHNSON. **1. Sheridan:** son of a famous father, and father of a more famous son: the former was the close friend of Swift; the latter was the dramatist, Richard Brinsley Sheridan. Thomas was himself an actor and author, as well as a lecturer on elocution.

nation, as if it were an affront to his exalted merit that a player should be rewarded in the same manner with him, or was the sudden effect of a fit of peevishness, it was unluckily said, and, indeed, cannot be justified. Mr. Sheridan's pension was granted to him not as a player but as a sufferer in the cause of government, when he was manager of the Theatre Royal in Ireland, when parties ran high in 1753. And it must also be allowed that he was a man of literature, and had considerably improved the arts of reading and speaking with distinctness and propriety. . . .

Johnson complained that a man who disliked him repeated his sarcasm to Mr. Sheridan, without telling him what followed, which was, that after a pause he added, " However, I am glad that Mr. Sheridan has a pension, for he is a very good man." Sheridan could never forgive this hasty contemptuous expression. It rankled in his mind; and though I informed him of all that Johnson said, and that he would be very glad to meet him amicably, he positively declined repeated offers which I made, and once went off abruptly from a house where he and I were engaged to dine, because he was told that Dr. Johnson was to be there. I have no sympathetic feeling with such persevering resentment. It is painful when there is a breach between those who have lived together socially and cordially; and I wonder that there is not, in all such cases, a mutual wish that it should be healed. I could perceive that Mr. Sheridan was by no means satisfied with Johnson's acknowledging him to be a good man. That could not soothe his injured vanity. I could not but smile, at the same time that I was offended, to observe Sheridan, in the *Life of Swift* which he afterwards published, attempting, in the writhings of his resentment, to depreciate Johnson, by characterizing him as " A writer of gigantic fame in these days of little men "; that very Johnson whom he once so highly admired and venerated.

This rupture with Sheridan deprived Johnson of one of his most agreeable resources for amusement in his lonely evenings, for Sheridan's well-informed, animated, and bustling mind never suffered conversation to stagnate, and Mrs. Sheridan was a most agreeable companion to an intellectual man. She was sensible, ingenious, unassuming, yet communicative. I recollect, with satisfaction, many pleasing hours which I passed with her under the hospitable roof of her husband, who was to me a very kind friend. Her novel, entitled *Memoirs of Miss Sydney Biddulph,* contains an excellent moral, while it inculcates a future state of retribution; and what it teaches is impressed upon the mind by a series of as deep distress as can affect humanity, in the amiable and pious heroine who goes to her grave unrelieved, but resigned, and full of hope of " Heaven's mercy." Johnson paid her this high compliment upon it: " I know not, madam, that you have a right, upon moral principles, to make your readers suffer so much."

Mr. Thomas Davies the actor, who then kept a bookseller's shop in Russell Street, Covent Garden, told me that Johnson was very much his friend, and came frequently to his house, where he more than once invited me to meet him; but by some unlucky accident or other he was prevented from coming to us.

Mr. Thomas Davies was a man of good understanding and talents, with the advantage of a liberal education. Though somewhat pompous, he was an entertaining companion; and his literary performances have no inconsiderable share of merit. He was a friendly and very hospitable man. Both he and his wife (who has been celebrated for her beauty), though upon the stage for many years, maintained an uniform decency of character; and Johnson esteemed them, and lived in as easy an intimacy with them as with any family which he used to visit. Mr. Davies recollected several of Johnson's remarkable sayings, and was one of the best of the many imitators of his voice and manner, while relating them. He increased my impatience more and more to see the extraordinary man whose works I highly valued, and whose conversation was reported to be so peculiarly excellent.

At last, on Monday the 16th of May, when I was sitting in Mr. Davies's back parlor, after having drunk tea with him and Mrs. Davies, Johnson unexpectedly came into the shop; and Mr. Davies having perceived him through the glass door in the room in which we were sitting, advancing towards us, he announced his awful approach to me, somewhat in the manner of an actor in the part of Horatio, when he addresses Hamlet on the appearance of his father's ghost, " Look, my lord, it comes." I found that I had a very perfect idea of Johnson's figure, from the portrait of him painted by Sir Joshua Reynolds soon after he had published his Dictionary, in the attitude of sitting in his easy chair in deep meditation; which was the first picture his friend did for him, which Sir Joshua very kindly presented to me, and from which an engraving has been made for this work. Mr. Davies mentioned my name, and respectfully introduced me to him. I was much agitated, and recollecting his prejudice against the Scotch, of which I had heard much, I said to Davies, " Don't tell where I come from." " From Scotland," cried Davies, roguishly. " Mr. Johnson," said I, " I do indeed come from Scotland, but I cannot help it." I am willing to flatter myself that I meant this as light pleasantry to soothe and conciliate him, and not as an humiliating abasement at the expense of my country. But however that might be, this speech was somewhat unlucky; for with that quickness of wit for which he was so remarkable, he seized the expression " come from Scotland," which I used in the sense of being of that country; and, as if I had said that I had come away from it, or left it, retorted, " That, sir, I find, is what a very great many of your countrymen cannot help." This stroke stunned me a good deal; and when we had sat down, I felt myself not a little embarrassed, and apprehensive of what might come next. He then addressed himself to Davies: " What do you think of Garrick? He has refused me an order for the play for Miss Williams,[2] because he knows the house will be full, and that an order would be worth three shillings." Eager to take any opening to get into conversation with him, I ventured to say, " O, sir, I cannot think Mr. Garrick would grudge such a trifle to you." " Sir," said he, with a stern look, " I have known David Garrick longer than you have done: and I know no right you have to talk to me on the subject." Perhaps I deserved this check, for it was rather presumptuous in me, an entire stranger, to express any doubt of the justice of his animadversion upon his old acquaintance and pupil.[3] I now felt myself much mortified, and began to think that the hope which I had long indulged of obtaining his acquaintance was blasted.

And, in truth, had not my ardor been uncommonly strong, and my resolution uncommonly persevering, so rough a reception might have deterred me forever from making any further attempts. Fortunately, however, I remained upon the field not wholly discomfited, and was soon rewarded by hearing some of his conversation, of which I preserved the following short minute, without marking the questions and observations by which it was produced.

" People," he remarked, " may be taken in once, who imagine that an author is greater in private life than other men. Uncommon parts require uncommon opportunities for their exertion.

" In barbarous society, superiority of parts is of real consequence. Great strength or great wisdom is of much value to an individual. But in more polished times there are people to do everything for money; and then there are a number of other superiorities, such as those of birth and fortune, and rank, that dissipate men's attention, and leave no extraordinary share of respect for personal and intellectual superiority. This is wisely ordered by Providence, to preserve some equality among mankind."

" Sir, this book (*The Elements of Criticism*,[4] which he had taken up) is a pretty essay, and deserves to be held in some estimation, though much of it is chimerical."

Speaking of one who with more than ordinary boldness attacked public measures and the royal family, he said, " I think he is safe from the law, but he is an abusive scoundrel; and instead of applying to my Lord Chief Justice to punish him, I would send half a dozen footmen and have him well ducked."

" The notion of liberty amuses the people of England, and helps to keep off the *taedium vitae.* When a butcher tells you that *his heart bleeds for his country,* he has, in fact, no uneasy feeling."

" Sheridan will not succeed at Bath with his oratory. Ridicule has gone down before him, and, I doubt, Derrick is his enemy." [5]

" Derrick may do very well, as long as he can outrun his character, but the moment his character gets up with him, it is all over."

It is, however, but just to record, that some years afterwards, when I reminded him of this sarcasm,

---

2. **Miss Williams:** Anna Williams was a blind lady who lived mostly under Johnson's hospitable roof from 1752 until her death in 1783. She was a peevish inmate, but Johnson gave her credit for "universal curiosity and comprehensive knowledge." She had literary ambitions, and he helped her to publish *Miscellanies in Prose and Verse* in 1766. 3. "That this was a momentary sally against Garrick there can be no doubt; for at Johnson's desire he had, some years before, given a benefit night at his theater to this very person, by which she had got two hundred pounds. Johnson, indeed, upon all other occasions, when I was in his company, praised the very liberal charity of Garrick. I once mentioned to him, 'It is observed, sir, that you attack Garrick yourself, but will suffer nobody else to do it.' Johnson (smiling): 'Why, sir, that is true'" [Boswell].

4. *Elements of Criticism:* by Henry Home, Lord Kames (1762 and later dates). 5. "Mr. Sheridan was then reading lectures upon oratory at Bath, where Derrick was master of the ceremonies, or, as the phrase is, King" [B].

he said, "Well, but Derrick has now got a character that he need not run away from."

I was highly pleased with the extraordinary vigor of his conversation, and regretted that I was drawn away from it by an engagement at another place. I had, for a part of the evening, been left alone with him, and had ventured to make an observation now and then, which he received very civilly; so that I was satisfied that though there was a roughness in his manner, there was no ill nature in his disposition. Davies followed me to the door, and when I complained to him a little of the hard blows which the great man had given me, he kindly took upon him to console me by saying, "Don't be uneasy. I can see he likes you very well."

A few days afterwards I called on Davies, and asked him if he thought I might take the liberty of waiting on Mr. Johnson at his chambers in the Temple.[6] He said I certainly might, and that Mr. Johnson would take it as a compliment. So upon Tuesday the 24th of May, after having been enlivened by the witty sallies of Messrs. Thornton, Wilkes, Churchill, and Lloyd,[7] with whom I had passed the morning, I boldly repaired to Johnson. His chambers were on the first floor of No. 1, Inner Temple Lane, and I entered them with an impression given me by the Rev. Dr. Blair,[8] of Edinburgh, who had been introduced to him not long before, and described his having "found the Giant in his den," an expression which, when I came to be pretty well acquainted with Johnson, I repeated to him, and he was diverted at this picturesque account of himself. Dr. Blair had been presented to him by Dr. James Fordyce. At this time the controversy concerning the pieces published by Mr. James Macpherson, as translations of Ossian, was at its height. Johnson had all along denied their authenticity, and, what was still more provoking to their admirers, maintained that they had no merit. The subject having been introduced by Dr. Fordyce, Dr. Blair, relying on the internal evidence of their antiquity, asked Dr. Johnson whether he thought any man of a modern age could have written such poems? Johnson replied, "Yes, sir, many men, many women, and many children." Johnson, at this time, did not know that Dr. Blair had just published a dissertation, not only defending their authenticity, but seriously ranking them with the poems of Homer and Virgil; and when he was afterwards informed of this circumstance, he expressed some displeasure at Dr. Fordyce's having suggested the topic, and said, "I am not sorry that they got thus much for their pains. Sir, it was like leading one to talk of a book, when the author is concealed behind the door."

He received me very courteously, but it must be confessed that his apartment and furniture and morning dress were sufficiently uncouth. His brown suit of clothes looked very rusty; he had on a little old shriveled unpowdered wig, which was too small for his head; his shirt-neck and knees of his breeches were loose; his black worsted stockings ill drawn up; and he had a pair of unbuckled shoes by way of slippers. But all these slovenly particularities were forgotten the moment that he began to talk. Some gentlemen, whom I do not recollect, were sitting with him; and when they went away, I also rose; but he said to me, "Nay, don't go." "Sir," said I, "I am afraid that I intrude upon you. It is benevolent to allow me to sit and hear you." He seemed pleased with this compliment, which I sincerely paid him, and answered, "Sir, I am obliged to any man who visits me." I have preserved the following short minute of what passed this day.

"Madness frequently discovers itself merely by unnecessary deviation from the usual modes of the world. My poor friend Smart showed the disturbance of his mind by falling upon his knees and saying his prayers in the street, or in any other unusual place. Now although, rationally speaking, it is greater madness not to pray at all than to pray as Smart did, I am afraid there are so many who do not pray, that their understanding is not called in question."

Concerning this unfortunate poet, Christopher Smart, who was confined in a madhouse, he had, at another time, the following conversation with Dr. Burney.[9] BURNEY: "How does poor Smart do, sir; is he likely to recover?" JOHNSON: "It seems as if his mind had ceased to struggle with the disease; for he grows fat upon it." BURNEY: "Per-

---

6. **Temple:** one of the Law Societies, or "Inns of Court." There are four of these residential colleges, dating from medieval times: Lincoln's Inn, Gray's Inn, and the Inner and Middle Temple. They have the sole right of admitting to the English bar.   7. **Thornton . . . Lloyd:** Bonnell Thorton and Robert Lloyd were minor literary figures at this time. For the demagogue John Wilkes, see Intro., pp. 447–48. Wilkes was assisted by the satirist Charles Churchill in his attacks on the government in the antiministerial journal, the *North Briton,* for the forty-fifth number of which he was expelled from parliament.   8. **Dr. Blair:** Hugh Blair was the author of admired sermons and lectures on literary subjects.

9. **Dr. Burney:** Dr. Charles Burney was a well-known musician, historian of music, and father of the novelist, Fanny Burney.

haps, sir, that may be from want of exercise." JOHNSON: "No, sir; he has partly as much exercise as he used to have, for he digs in the garden. Indeed, before his confinement, he used for exercise to walk to the alehouse, but he was *carried* back again. I did not think he ought to be shut up. His infirmities were not noxious to society. He insisted on people praying with him; and I'd as lief pray with Kit Smart as anyone else. Another charge was, that he did not love clean linen; and I have no passion for it."

Johnson continued. "Mankind have a great aversion to intellectual labor, but even supposing knowledge to be easily attainable, more people would be content to be ignorant than would take even a little trouble to acquire it."

"The morality of an action depends on the motive from which we act. If I fling half a crown to a beggar with intention to break his head, and he picks it up and buys victuals with it, the physical effect is good; but, with respect to me, the action is very wrong. So, religious exercises, if not performed with an intention to please God, avail us nothing. As our Savior says of those who perform them from other motives, 'Verily they have their reward.'"

"The Christian religion has very strong evidences. It, indeed, appears in some degree strange to reason; but in history we have undoubted facts, against which, in reasoning *à priori,* we have more arguments than we have for them; but then, testimony has great weight, and casts the balance. I would recommend to every man whose faith is yet unsettled, Grotius — Dr. Pearson — and Dr. Clarke." [10]

Talking of Garrick, he said, "He is the first man in the world for sprightly conversation."

When I rose a second time, he again pressed me to stay, which I did.

He told me that he generally went abroad at four in the afternoon, and seldom came home till two in the morning. I took the liberty to ask if he did not think it wrong to live thus, and not make more use of his great talents. He owned it was a bad habit. On reviewing, at the distance of many years, my journal of this period, I wonder how, at my first visit, I ventured to talk to him so freely, and that he bore it with so much indulgence.

10. Grotius . . . Clarke: These were all famous seventeenth-century writers on divinity. Grotius was a great Dutch jurist as well.

Before we parted, he was so good as to promise to favor me with his company one evening at my lodgings; and, as I took my leave, shook me cordially by the hand. It is almost needless to add that I felt no little elation at having now so happily established an acquaintance of which I had been so long ambitious.

My readers will, I trust, excuse me for being thus minutely circumstantial, when it is considered that the acquaintance of Dr. Johnson was to me a most valuable acquisition, and laid the foundation of whatever instruction and entertainment they may receive from my collections concerning the great subject of the work which they are now perusing.

I did not visit him again till Monday, June 13, at which time I recollect no part of his conversation, except that when I told him I had been to see Johnson ride upon three horses, he said, "Such a man, sir, should be encouraged, for his performances show the extent of the human powers in one instance, and thus tend to raise our opinion of the faculties of man. He shows what may be attained by persevering application; so that every man may hope, that by giving as much application, although perhaps he may never ride three horses at a time, or dance upon a wire, yet he may be equally expert in whatever profession he has chosen to pursue."

He again shook me by the hand at parting, and asked me why I did not come oftener to him. Trusting that I was now in his good graces, I answered, that he had not given me much encouragement, and reminded him of the check I had received from him at our first interview. "Poh, poh!" said he, with a complacent smile, "never mind these things. Come to me as often as you can. I shall be glad to see you."

I had learned that his place of frequent resort was the Mitre Tavern in Fleet Street, where he loved to sit up late, and I begged I might be allowed to pass an evening with him there soon, which he promised I should. A few days afterwards I met him near Temple Bar, about one o'clock in the morning, and asked if he would then go to the Mitre. "Sir," said he, "it is too late; they won't let us in. But I'll go with you another night with all my heart."

A revolution of some importance in my plan of life had just taken place; for instead of procuring a commission in the foot guards, which was my own inclination, I had, in compliance with my father's wishes, agreed to study the law, and was soon to set out for Utrecht, to hear the lectures of an excellent civilian in that university, and then to proceed on my travels. Though very desirous of obtaining Dr. Johnson's advice and instructions on the mode of pursuing my studies, I was at this time so occupied, shall I call it? or so dissipated, by the amusements of London, that our next meeting was not till Saturday, June 25, when, happening to dine at Clifton's eating house, in Butcher Row, I was surprised to perceive Johnson come in and take his seat at another table. The mode of dining, or rather being fed, at such houses in London, is well known to many to be particularly unsocial, as there is no ordinary, or united company, but each person has his own mess, and is under no obligation to hold any intercourse with anyone. A liberal and full-minded man, however, who loves to talk, will break through this churlish and unsocial restraint. Johnson and an Irish gentleman got into a dispute concerning the cause of some part of mankind being black. "Why, sir," said Johnson, "it has been accounted for in three ways: either by supposing that they are the posterity of Ham, who was cursed; or that God at first created two kinds of men, one black and another white; or that by the heat of the sun the skin is scorched, and so acquires a sooty hue. This matter has been much canvassed among naturalists, but has never been brought to any certain issue." What the Irishman said is totally obliterated from my mind, but I remember that he became very warm and intemperate in his expressions, upon which Johnson rose, and quietly walked away. When he had retired, his antagonist took his revenge, as he thought, by saying, "He has a most ungainly figure, and an affectation of pomposity, unworthy of a man of genius."

Johnson had not observed that I was in the room. I followed him, however, and he agreed to meet me in the evening at the Mitre. I called on him, and we went thither at nine. We had a good supper, and port wine, of which he then sometimes drank a bottle. The orthodox High Church sound of the Mitre, the figure and manner of the celebrated Samuel Johnson, the extraordinary power and precision of his conversation, and the pride arising from finding myself admitted as his companion, produced a variety of sensations, and a pleasing elevation of mind beyond what I had ever before experienced. I find in my journal the

following minute of our conversation, which, though it will give but a very faint notion of what passed, is, in some degree, a valuable record; and it will be curious in this view, as showing how habitual to his mind were some opinions which appear in his works.

"Colley Cibber,[11] sir, was by no means a blockhead, but by arrogating to himself too much, he was in danger of losing that degree of estimation to which he was entitled. His friends gave out that he *intended* his birthday odes should be bad, but that was not the case, sir; for he kept them many months by him, and a few years before he died he showed me one of them, with great solicitude to render it as perfect as might be, and I made some corrections, to which he was not very willing to submit. I remember the following couplet in allusion to the king and himself:

> Perched on the eagle's soaring wing,
> The lowly linnet loves to sing.

Sir, he had heard something of the fabulous tale of the wren sitting upon the eagle's wing, and he had applied it to a linnet. Cibber's familiar style, however, was better than that which Whitehead[12] has assumed. *Grand* nonsense is insupportable. Whitehead is but a little man to inscribe verses to players."

I did not presume to controvert this censure, which was tinctured with his prejudice against players but I could not help thinking that a dramatic poet might with propriety pay a compliment to an eminent performer, as Whitehead has very happily done in his verses to Mr. Garrick.

"Sir, I do not think Gray a first-rate poet. He has not a bold imagination, nor much command of words. The obscurity in which he has involved himself will not persuade us that he is sublime. His 'Elegy in a Churchyard' has a happy selection of images, but I don't like what are called his great things. His Ode[13] which begins

> Ruin seize thee, ruthless King,
> Confusion on thy banners wait!

has been celebrated for its abruptness, and plunging into the subject all at once. But such arts as

11. **Cibber** (1671–1757): poet laureate, actor, and playwright, whose *Apology* for his life (1740) came in for much ridicule, and who was raised to the throne of Dulness in Pope's revised *Dunciad*. 12. **Whitehead:** William Whitehead also became poet laureate, and wrote plays and poems. 13. **Ode:** "The Bard," published in 1757.

these have no merit, unless when they are original. We admire them only once; and this abruptness has nothing new in it. We have had it often before. Nay, we have it in the old song of 'Johnny Armstrong';

Is there ever a man in all Scotland,
From the highest estate to the lowest degree, etc.

And then, sir,

Yes, there is a man in Westmoreland
And Johnny Armstrong they do him call.

There, now, you plunge at once into the subject. You have no previous narration to lead you to it. The two next lines in that Ode are, I think, very good:

Though fanned by conquest's crimson wing,
They mock the air with idle state."

Here let it be observed, that although his opinion of Gray's poetry was widely different from mine, and I believe from that of most men of taste, by whom it is with justice highly admired, there is certainly much absurdity in the clamor which has been raised, as if he had been culpably injurious to the merit of that bard, and had been actuated by envy. Alas! ye little short-sighted critics, could Johnson be envious of the talents of any of his contemporaries? That his opinion on this subject was what in private and in public he uniformly expressed, regardless of what others might think, we may wonder, and perhaps regret; but it is shallow and unjust to charge him with expressing what he did not think.

Finding him in a placid humor, and wishing to avail myself of the opportunity which I fortunately had of consulting a sage, to hear whose wisdom, I conceived, in the ardor of youthful imagination, that men filled with a noble enthusiasm for intellectual improvement would gladly have resorted from distant lands, I opened my mind to him ingenuously, and gave him a little sketch of my life, to which he was pleased to listen with great attention.

I acknowledged that, though educated very strictly in the principles of religion, I had for some time been misled into a certain degree of infidelity; but that I was come now to a better way of thinking, and was fully satisfied of the truth of the Christian revelation, though I was not clear as to every point considered to be orthodox. Being at all times a curious examiner of the

human mind, and pleased with an undisguised display of what had passed in it, he called to me with warmth, "Give me your hand; I have taken a liking to you." He then began to descant upon the force of testimony, and the little we could know of final causes; so that the objections of, why was it so? or why was it not so? ought not to disturb us; adding that he himself had at one period been guilty of a temporary neglect of religion, but that it was not the result of argument, but mere absence of thought.

After having given credit to reports of his bigotry, I was agreeably surprised when he expressed the following very liberal sentiment, which has the additional value of obviating an objection to our holy religion, founded upon the discordant tenets of Christians themselves: "For my part, sir, I think all Christians, whether Papists or Protestants, agree in the essential articles, and that their differences are trivial, and rather political than religious."

We talked of belief in ghosts. He said, "Sir, I make a distinction between what a man may experience by the mere strength of his imagination, and what imagination cannot possibly produce. Thus, suppose I should think that I saw a form, and heard a voice cry, 'Johnson, you are a very wicked fellow, and unless you repent you will certainly be punished'; my own unworthiness is so deeply impressed upon my mind, that I might *imagine* I thus saw and heard, and therefore I should not believe that an external communication had been made to me. But if a form should appear, and a voice should tell me that a particular man had died at a particular place, and a particular hour, a fact which I had no apprehension of, nor any means of knowing, and this fact, with all its circumstances, should afterwards be unquestionably proved, I should, in that case, be persuaded that I had supernatural intelligence imparted to me."

Here it is proper, once for all, to give a true and fair statement of Johnson's way of thinking upon the question, whether departed spirits are ever permitted to appear in this world, or in any way to operate upon human life. He has been ignorantly misrepresented as weakly credulous upon that subject; and, therefore, though I feel an inclination to disdain and treat with silent contempt so foolish a notion concerning my illustrious friend, yet as I find it has gained ground, it is necessary to refute it. The real fact then is, that Johnson had a very philosophical mind, and such a rational

respect for testimony, as to make him submit his
understanding to what was authentically proved,
though he could not comprehend why it was so.
Being thus disposed, he was willing to inquire into
the truth of any relation of supernatural agency, a
general belief of which has prevailed in all nations
and ages. But so far was he from being the dupe
of implicit faith, that he examined the matter with
a jealous attention, and no man was more ready
to refute its falsehood when he had discovered it.
Churchill, in his poem entitled "The Ghost,"
availed himself of the absurd credulity imputed
to Johnson, and drew a caricature of him under
the name of "Pomposo," representing him as one
of the believers of the story of a ghost in Cock
Lane, which, in the year 1762, had gained very
general credit in London. Many of my readers,
I am convinced, are to this hour under an impression that Johnson was thus foolishly deceived. It
will therefore surprise them a good deal when
they are informed upon undoubted authority that
Johnson was one of those by whom the imposture
was detected. The story had become so popular
that he thought it should be investigated; and in
this research he was assisted by the Rev. Dr.
Douglas, now Bishop of Salisbury, the great detector of impostures, who informs me that after the
gentlemen who went and examined into the evidence were satisfied of its falsity, Johnson wrote in
their presence an account of it, which was published in the newspapers and *Gentleman's Magazine,* and undeceived the world.

Our conversation proceeded. "Sir," said he, "I
am a friend to subordination, as most conducive
to the happiness of society. There is a reciprocal
pleasure in governing and being governed."

"Dr. Goldsmith is one of the first men we now
have as an author, and he is a very worthy man
too. He has been loose in his principles, but he is
coming right."

I mentioned Mallet's tragedy of *Elvira,* which
had been acted the preceding winter at Drury
Lane, and that the Hon. Andrew Erskine, Mr.
Dempster,[14] and myself, had joined in writing a
pamphlet, entitled *Critical Strictures,* against it.
That the mildness of Dempster's disposition had,
however, relented; and he had candidly said, "We

have hardly a right to abuse this tragedy; for bad
as it is, how vain should either of us be to write
one not near so good." JOHNSON: "Why no, sir;
this is not just reasoning. You *may* abuse a tragedy, though you cannot write one. You may scold
a carpenter who has made you a bad table, though
you cannot make a table. It is not your trade to
make tables."

When I talked to him of the paternal estate to
which I was heir, he said, "Sir, let me tell you,
that to be a Scotch landlord, where you have a
number of families dependent upon you, and attached to you, is, perhaps, as high a situation as
humanity can arrive at. A merchant upon the
'Change of London, with a hundred thousand
pounds, is nothing; an English duke, with an immense fortune, is nothing; he has no tenants who
consider themselves as under his patriarchal care,
and who will follow him to the field upon any
emergency."

His notion of the dignity of a Scotch landlord
had been formed upon what he had heard of the
Highland chiefs; for it is long since a Lowland
landlord has been so curtailed in his feudal authority, that he has little more influence over his tenants than an English landlord; and of late years
most of the Highland chiefs have destroyed, by
means too well known, the princely power which
they once enjoyed.

He proceeded: "Your going abroad, sir, and
breaking off idle habits, may be of great importance to you. I would go where there are courts
and learned men. There is a good deal of Spain
that has not been perambulated. I would have you
go thither. A man of inferior talents to yours may
furnish us with useful observations upon that country." His supposing me, at that period of life,
capable of writing an account of my travels that
would deserve to be read, elated me not a little.

I appeal to every impartial reader whether this
faithful detail of his frankness, complacency, and
kindness to a young man, a stranger and a Scotchman, does not refute the unjust opinion of the
harshness of his general demeanor. His occasional
reproofs of folly, impudence, or impiety, and even
the sudden sallies of his constitutional irritability
of temper, which have been preserved for the
poignancy of their wit, have produced that opinion
among those who have not considered that such
instances, though collected by Mrs. Piozzi into a

14. **Mallet . . . Dempster:** Erskine and Dempster were Edinburgh
cronies of Boswell's. David Mallet (Malloch) had alienated
himself from his fellow Scots by changing his name and attempting to blur his northern origin. He was a poet, playwright, and the
editor of Bolingbroke's works, which Johnson considered impious.

small volume,[15] and read over in a few hours, were, in fact, scattered through a long series of years: years, in which his time was chiefly spent in instructing and delighting mankind by his writings and conversation, in acts of piety to God, and goodwill to men.

I complained to him that I had not yet acquired much knowledge, and asked his advice as to my studies. He said, "Don't talk of study now. I will give you a plan; but it will require some time to consider of it." "It is very good in you," I replied, "to allow me to be with you thus. Had it been foretold to me some years ago that I should pass an evening with the author of the *Rambler,* how should I have exulted!" What I then expressed was sincerely from the heart. He was satisfied that it was, and cordially answered, "Sir, I am glad we have met. I hope we shall pass many evenings and mornings, too, together." We finished a couple of bottles of port, and sat till between one and two in the morning.

He wrote this year in the *Critical Review* the account of "Telemachus, a Mask," by the Rev. George Graham, of Eton College. The subject of this beautiful poem was particularly interesting to Johnson, who had much experience of "the conflict of opposite principles," which he describes as "The contention between pleasure and virtue, a struggle which will always be continued while the present system of nature shall subsist; nor can history or poetry exhibit more than pleasure triumphing over virtue, and virtue subjugating pleasure."

As Dr. Oliver Goldsmith will frequently appear in this narrative, I shall endeavor to make my readers in some degree acquainted with his singular character. He was a native of Ireland, and a contemporary with Mr. Burke, at Trinity College, Dublin, but did not then give much promise of future celebrity. He, however, observed to Mr. Malone, that "though he made no great figure in mathematics, which was a study in much repute there, he could turn an ode of Horace into English better than any of them." He afterwards studied physic at Edinburgh, and upon the Continent and, I have been informed, was enabled to pursue his travels on foot, partly by demanding at universities to enter the lists as a disputant, by which,

according to the custom of many of them, he was entitled to the premium of a crown, when luckily for him his challenge was not accepted; so that, as I once observed to Dr. Johnson, he *disputed* his passage through Europe. He then came to England, and was employed successively in the capacities of an usher to an academy, a corrector of the press, a reviewer, and a writer for a newspaper. He had sagacity enough to cultivate assiduously the acquaintance of Johnson, and his faculties were gradually enlarged by the contemplation of such a model. To me and many others it appeared that he studiously copied the manner of Johnson, though, indeed, upon a smaller scale.

At this time I think he had published nothing with his name, though it was pretty generally known that *one Dr. Goldsmith* was the author of *An Enquiry into the Present State of Polite Learning in Europe,* and of *The Citizen of the World,* a series of letters supposed to be written from London by a Chinese. No man had the art of displaying with more advantage as a writer, whatever literary acquisitions he made. "*Nihil quod tetigit non ornavit.*"[16] His mind resembled a fertile, but thin soil. There was a quick, but not a strong vegetation, of whatever chanced to be thrown upon it. No deep root could be struck. The oak of the forest did not grow there, but the elegant shrubbery and the fragrant parterre appeared in gay succession. It has been generally circulated and believed that he was a mere fool in conversation;[17] but, in truth, this has been greatly exaggerated. He had, no doubt, a more than common share of that hurry of ideas which we often find in his countrymen, and which sometimes produces a laughable confusion in expressing them. He was very much what the French call *un étourdi,*[18] and from vanity and an eager desire of being conspicu-

15. **Mrs. Piozzi . . . volume:** Mrs. Piozzi, earlier Hester Lynch Thrale, had been a rival of Boswell's for Johnson's affection, but after twenty years of intimate friendship had broken with him on the subject of her second marriage. Her *Anecdotes of the Late Samuel Johnson* (1786) had a great success, and are not so spiteful as Boswell implies.

16. "*Nihil . . . ornavit*": The Latin is part of the epitaph Johnson wrote on his friend for the memorial in Westminster Abbey: "He gave luster to every sort of writing he touched."
17. "In allusion to this, Mr. Horace Walpole, who admired his writings, said he was 'an inspired idiot'; and Garrick described him as one 'for shortness called Noll, / Who wrote like an angel, and talked like poor Poll.' Sir Joshua Reynolds mentioned to me that he frequently heard Goldsmith talk warmly of the pleasure of being liked, and observe how hard it would be if literary excellence should preclude a man from that satisfaction, which he perceived it often did, from the envy which attended it; and therefore Sir Joshua was convinced that he was intentionally more absurd, in order to lessen himself in social intercourse, trusting that his character would be sufficiently supported by his work. If it indeed was his intention to appear absurd in company, he was often very successful. But with due deference to Sir Joshua's ingenuity I think the conjecture too refined" [B].
18. *un étourdi:* "a giddy fellow."

ous wherever he was, he frequently talked carelessly without knowledge of the subject, or even without thought. His person was short, his countenance coarse and vulgar, his deportment that of a scholar awkwardly affecting the easy gentleman. Those who were in any way distinguished excited envy in him to so ridiculous an excess, that the instances of it are hardly credible. When accompanying two beautiful young ladies with their mother on a tour in France, he was seriously angry that more attention was paid to them than to him; and once at the exhibition of the *Fantoccini* in London, when those who sat next him observed with what dexterity a puppet was made to toss a pike, he could not bear that it should have such praise, and exclaimed with some warmth, " Pshaw! I can do it better myself." [19]

He, I am afraid, had no settled system of any sort, so that his conduct must not be strictly scrutinized; but his affections were social and generous, and when he had money he gave it away very liberally. His desire of imaginary consequence predominated over his attention to truth. When he began to rise into notice, he said he had a brother who was Dean of Durham,[20] a fiction so easily detected, that it is wonderful how he should have been so inconsiderate as to hazard it. He boasted to me at this time of the power of his pen in commanding money, which I believe was true in a certain degree, though in the instance he gave he was by no means correct. He told me that he had sold a novel for four hundred pounds. This was his *Vicar of Wakefield*. But Johnson informed me, that he had made the bargain for Goldsmith, and the price was sixty pounds. " And, sir," said he, " a sufficient price, too, when it was sold; for then the fame of Goldsmith had not been elevated, as it afterwards was, by his *Traveler,* and the bookseller had such faint hopes of profit by his bargain, that he kept the manuscript by him a long time, and did not publish it till after the *Traveler* had appeared. Then, to be sure, it was accidentally worth more money."

Mrs. Piozzi and Sir John Hawkins [21] have

strangely misstated the history of Goldsmith's situation and Johnson's friendly interference, when this novel was sold. I shall give it authentically from Johnson's own exact narration:

" I received one morning a message from poor Goldsmith that he was in great distress, and, as it was not in his power to come to me, begging that I would come to him as soon as possible. I sent him a guinea, and promised to come to him directly. I accordingly went as soon as I was dressed, and found that his landlady had arrested him for his rent, at which he was in a violent passion. I perceived that he had already changed my guinea, and had got a bottle of Madeira and a glass before him. I put the cork into the bottle, desired he would be calm, and began to talk to him of the means by which he might be extricated. He then told me that he had a novel ready for the press, which he produced to me. I looked into it, and saw its merit; told the landlady I should soon return, and having gone to a bookseller, sold it for sixty pounds. I brought Goldsmith the money, and he discharged his rent, not without rating his landlady in a high tone for having used him so ill."

My next meeting with Johnson was on Friday the 1st of July, when he and I and Dr. Goldsmith supped together at the Mitre. I was before this time pretty well acquainted with Goldsmith, who was one of the brightest ornaments of the Johnsonian school. Goldsmith's respectful attachment to Johnson was then at its height, for his own literary reputation had not yet distinguished him so much as to excite a vain desire of competition with his great master. He had increased my admiration of the goodness of Johnson's heart, by incidental remarks in the course of conversation, such as, when I mentioned Mr. Levet,[22] whom he entertained under his roof, " He is poor and honest, which is recommendation enough to Johnson "; and when I wondered that he was very kind to a man of whom I had heard a very bad character, " He is now become miserable, and that insures the protection of Johnson."

Goldsmith attempting this evening to maintain, I suppose from an affectation of paradox, " that knowledge was not desirable on its own account, for it often was a source of unhappiness." JOHNSON: " Why, sir, that knowledge may in some cases pro-

19. "He went home with Mr. Burke to supper; and broke his shin by attempting to exhibit to the company how much better he could jump over a stick than the puppets" [B]. 20. Dean of Durham: "I am willing to hope that there may have been some mistake as to this anecdote, though I had it from a dignitary of the Church. Dr Isaac Goldsmith, his near relation, was Dean of Cloyne, in 1747" [B]. 21. Hawkins: Sir John Hawkins, an old friend, had anticipated Boswell in writing Johnson's life: it appeared four times in 1787, Boswell was mentioned in it once, in a footnote.

22. Levet: Dr. Levet, without any proper medical schooling, was a practicing physician among the very poor. At his death, in 1782, Johnson celebrated his "single talent" in one of his finest poems.

duce unhappiness, I allow. But, upon the whole, knowledge, per se, is certainly an object which every man would wish to attain, although, perhaps, he may not take the trouble necessary for attaining it." . . .

Let me here apologize for the imperfect manner in which I am obliged to exhibit Johnson's conversation at this period. In the early part of my acquaintance with him, I was so wrapped in admiration of his extraordinary colloquial talents, and so little accustomed to his peculiar mode of expression, that I found it extremely difficult to recollect and record his conversation with its genuine vigor and vivacity. In progress of time, when my mind was, as it were, *strongly impregnated with the Johnsonian aether,* I could, with much more facility and exactness, carry in my memory and commit to paper the exuberant variety of his wisdom and wit.

At this time *Miss* Williams,[23] as she was then called, though she did not reside with him in the Temple under his roof, but had lodgings in Bolt Court, Fleet Street, had so much of his attention, that he every night drank tea with her before he went home, however late it might be, and she always sat up for him. This, it may be fairly conjectured, was not alone a proof of his regard for *her,* but of his own unwillingness to go into solitude, before that unseasonable hour at which he had habituated himself to expect the oblivion of repose. Dr. Goldsmith, being a privileged man, went with him this night, strutting away, and calling to me with an air of superiority, like that of an esoteric over an exoteric disciple of a sage of antiquity, "I go to Miss Williams." I confess, I then envied him this mighty privilege, of which he seemed so proud, but it was not long before I obtained the same mark of distinction. . . .

On Saturday, July 9, I found Johnson surrounded with a numerous levee, but have not preserved any part of his conversation. On the 14th we had another evening by ourselves at the Mitre. It happening to be a very rainy night, I made some commonplace observations on the relaxation of nerves and depression of spirits which such weather occasioned, adding, however, that it was good for the vegetable creation. Johnson, who, as we have already seen, denied that the temperature of the air had any influence on the human frame, answered,

with a smile of ridicule, "Why, yes, sir, it is good for vegetables, and for the animals who eat those vegetables, and for the animals who eat those animals." This observation of his aptly enough introduced a good supper; and I soon forgot, in Johnson's company, the influence of a moist atmosphere.

Feeling myself now quite at ease as his companion, though I had all possible reverence for him, I expressed a regret that I could not be so easy with my father, though he was not much older than Johnson, and certainly however respectable had not more learning and greater abilities to depress me. I asked him the reason of this. JOHNSON: "Why, sir, I am a man of the world. I live in the world, and I take, in some degree, the color of the world as it moves along. Your father is a judge in a remote part of the island, and all his notions are taken from the old world. Besides, sir, there must always be a struggle between a father and son, while one aims at power and the other at independence." I said, I was afraid my father would force me to be a lawyer. JOHNSON: "Sir, you need not be afraid of his forcing you to be a laborious practicing lawyer; that is not in his power. For as the proverb says, 'One man may lead a horse to the water, but twenty cannot make him drink.' He may be displeased that you are not what he wishes you to be, but that displeasure will not go far. If he insists only on your having as much law as is necessary for a man of property, and then endeavors to get you into parliament, he is quite in the right."

He enlarged very convincingly upon the excellence of rhyme over blank verse in English poetry. I mentioned to him that Dr. Adam Smith, in his lectures upon composition, when I studied under him in the College of Glasgow, had maintained the same opinion strenuously, and I repeated some of his arguments. JOHNSON: "Sir, I was once in company with Smith, and we did not take to each other; but had I known that he loved rhyme as much as you tell me he does, I should have *hugged* him."

Talking of those who denied the truth of Christianity, he said, "It is always easy to be on the negative side. If a man were now to deny that there is salt upon the table, you could not reduce him to an absurdity. Come, let us try this a little further. I deny that Canada is taken, and I can support my denial by pretty good arguments. The

23. For Miss Williams, see above, n. 2. She was eminently respectable, and no breath of scandal attached to her connection with Johnson.

French are a much more numerous people than we; and it is not likely that they would allow us to take it. 'But the ministry have assured us, in all the formality of the *Gazette,* that it is taken.' Very true. But the ministry have put us to an enormous expense by the war in America, and it is their interest to persuade us that we have got something for our money. 'But the fact is confirmed by thousands of men who were at the taking of it.' Ay, but these men have still more interest in deceiving us. They don't want that you should think the French have beat them, but that they have beat the French. Now suppose you should go over and find that it is really taken, that would only satisfy yourself; for when you come home, we will not believe you. We will say you have been bribed. Yet, sir, notwithstanding all these plausible objections, we have no doubt that Canada is really ours. Such is the weight of common testimony. How much stronger are the evidences of the Christian religion?"

"Idleness is a disease which must be combated, but I would not advise a rigid adherence to a particular plan of study. I myself have never persisted in any plan for two days together. A man ought to read just as inclination leads him; for what he reads as a task will do him little good. A young man should read five hours in a day, and so may acquire a great deal of knowledge."

To a man of vigorous intellect and ardent curiosity like his own, reading without a regular plan may be beneficial; though even such a man must submit to it, if he would attain a full understanding of any of the sciences.

To such a degree of unrestrained frankness had he now accustomed me, that in the course of this evening I talked of the numerous reflections which had been thrown out against him on account of his having accepted a pension from his present Majesty. "Why, sir," said he, with a hearty laugh, "it is a mighty foolish noise that they make.[24] I have accepted of a pension as a reward which has been thought due to my literary merit; and now that I have this pension, I am the same man in every respect that I have ever been; I retain the same principles. It is true, that I cannot now curse (smiling) the House of Hanover; nor would it be decent for me to drink King James's health in the wine that King George gives me money to

24. "When I mentioned the same idle clamor to him several years afterwards, he said, with a smile, 'I wish my pension were twice as large, that they might make twice as much noise'" [B].

pay for. But, sir, I think that the pleasure of cursing the House of Hanover, and drinking King James's health, are amply overbalanced by three hundred pounds a year."

There was here, most certainly, an affectation of more Jacobitism than he really had; and indeed an intention of admitting, for the moment, in a much greater extent than it really existed, the charge of disaffection imputed to him by the world, merely for the purpose of showing how dexterously he could repel an attack, even though he were placed in the most disadvantageous position; for I have heard him declare, that if holding up his right hand would have secured victory at Culloden to Prince Charles's army, he was not sure he would have held it up, so little confidence had he in the right claimed by the House of Stuart, and so fearful was he of the consequences of another revolution on the throne of Great Britain; and Mr. Topham Beauclerk assured me, he had heard him say this before he had his pension. At another time he said to Mr. Langton, "Nothing has ever offered, that has made it worth my while to consider the question fully." He, however, also said to the same gentleman, talking of King James II, "It was become impossible for him to reign any longer in this country." He no doubt had an early attachment to the House of Stuart, but his zeal had cooled as his reason strengthened. Indeed, I heard him once say that "after the death of a violent Whig, with whom he used to contend with great eagerness, he felt his Toryism much abated." I suppose he meant Mr. Walmsley.

Yet there is no doubt that at earlier periods he was wont often to exercise both his pleasantry and ingenuity in talking Jacobitism. My much respected friend, Dr. Douglas, now Bishop of Salisbury, has favored me with the following admirable instance from his Lordship's own recollection. One day when dining at old Mr. Langton's, where Miss Roberts, his niece, was one of the company, Johnson, with his usual complacent attention to the fair sex, took her by the hand and said, "My dear, I hope you are a Jacobite." Old Mr. Langton, who, though a high and steady Tory, was attached to the present royal family, seemed offended, and asked Johnson, with great warmth, what he could mean by putting such a question to his niece! "Why, sir," said Johnson, "I meant no offense to your niece, I meant her a great compliment. A Jacobite, sir, believes in the divine right of kings.

He that believes in the divine right of kings believes in a divinity. A Jacobite believes in the divine right of bishops. He that believes in the divine right of bishops believes in the divine authority of the Christian religion. Therefore, sir, a Jacobite is neither an atheist nor a deist. That cannot be said of a Whig; for *Whiggism is a negation of all principle.*"

He advised me, when abroad, to be as much as I could with the professors in the universities, and with the clergy; for from their conversation I might expect the best accounts of everything in whatever country I should be, with the additional advantage of keeping my learning alive.

It will be observed that, when giving me advice as to my travels, Dr. Johnson did not dwell upon cities and palaces and pictures and shows and Arcadian scenes. He was of Lord Essex's opinion, who advises his kinsman Roger Earl of Rutland, "rather to go an hundred miles to speak with one wise man, than five miles to see a fair town."

I described to him an impudent fellow [25] from Scotland, who affected to be a savage, and railed at all established systems. JOHNSON: "There is nothing surprising in this, sir. He wants to make himself conspicuous. He would tumble in a hogsty, as long as you looked at him and called to him to come out. But let him alone, never mind him, and he'll soon give it over."

I added that the same person maintained that there was no distinction between virtue and vice. JOHNSON: "Why, sir, if the fellow does not think as he speaks, he is lying; and I see not what honor he can propose to himself from having the character of a liar. But if he does really think that there is no distinction between virtue and vice, why, sir, when he leaves our houses let us count our spoons."

Sir David Dalrymple, now one of the judges of Scotland by the title of Lord Hailes, had contributed much to increase my high opinion of Johnson, on account of his writings, long before I attained to a personal acquaintance with him; I, in return, had informed Johnson of Sir David's eminent character for learning and religion; and Johnson was so much pleased, that at one of our evening meetings he gave him for his toast. I at this time kept up a very frequent correspondence with Sir David, and I read to Dr. Johnson tonight the following passage

from the letter which I had last received from him:

"It gives me pleasure to think that you have obtained the friendship of Mr. Samuel Johnson. He is one of the best moral writers which England has produced. At the same time, I envy you the free and undisguised converse with such a man. May I beg you to present my best respects to him, and to assure him of the veneration which I entertain for the author of the *Rambler* and of *Rasselas?* Let me recommend this last work to you; with the *Rambler* you certainly are acquainted. In *Rasselas* you will see a tender-hearted operator, who probes the wound only to heal it. Swift, on the contrary, mangles human nature. He cuts and slashes, as if he took pleasure in the operation, like the tyrant who said, '*Ita feri ut se sentiat emori.*'" [26] Johnson seemed to be much gratified by this just and well-turned compliment.

He recommended to me to keep a journal of my life, full and unreserved. He said it would be a very good exercise, and would yield me great satisfaction when the particulars were faded from my remembrance. I was uncommonly fortunate in having had a previous coincidence of opinion with him upon this subject, for I had kept such a journal for some time; and it was no small pleasure to me to have this to tell him, and to receive his approbation. He counseled me to keep it private, and said I might surely have a friend who would burn it in case of my death.[27] From this habit I have been enabled to give the world so many anecdotes, which would otherwise have been lost to posterity. I mentioned that I was afraid I put into my journal too many little incidents. JOHNSON: "There is nothing, sir, too little for so little a creature as man. It is by studying little things that we attain the great art of having as little misery and as much happiness as possible."

Next morning Mr. Dempster happened to call on me, and was so much struck even with the imperfect account which I gave him of Dr. Johnson's conversation, that to his honor be it recorded, when I complained that drinking port and sitting up late with him, affected my nerves for some time after,[28]

---

25. fellow: Boswell elsewhere identifies this man as James Macpherson, author of the poems attributed to Ossian. Macpherson claimed to have discovered the original Gaelic manuscript of a cycle of poems written by Ossian, a legendary Irish hero and bard.

26. 'Ita . . . emori': Suetonius quotes Caligula to this effect, in his *Lives of the Caesars*, Chapter 30: "Do it in such a way that he may feel the approach of death." **27.** With regard to his private records, this was Johnson's own intention and desire. Boswell's instincts were quite the opposite, and he did his best to preserve Johnson's diaries, as well as his own. The contrast epitomizes the difference between the neoclassic and modern attitudes. **28.** Reminding Johnson of such occasions many years later, Boswell received the reply, "Nay, sir, it was not the *wine* that made your head ache, but the *sense* that I put into it."

he said, "One had better be palsied at eighteen than not keep company with such a man."

On Tuesday, July 18, I found tall Sir Thomas Robinson sitting with Johnson. Sir Thomas said, that the King of Prussia valued himself upon three things: upon being a hero, a musician, and an author. JOHNSON: "Pretty well, sir, for one man. As to his being an author, I have not looked at his poetry; but his prose is poor stuff. He writes just as you might suppose Voltaire's footboy to do, who has been his amanuensis. He has such parts as the valet might have, and about as much of the coloring of the style as might be got by transcribing his works." When I was at Ferney, I repeated this to Voltaire, in order to reconcile him somewhat to Johnson, whom he, in affecting the English mode of expression, had previously characterized as "a superstitious dog," but after hearing such a criticism on Frederick the Great, with whom he was then on bad terms, he exclaimed, "An honest fellow!"

But I think the criticism much too severe; for the *Memoirs of the House of Brandenburg* are written as well as many works of that kind. His poetry, for the style of which he himself makes a frank apology, "*Jargonnant un français barbare*," [29] though fraught with pernicious ravings of infidelity, has, in many places, great animation, and in some a pathetic tenderness.

Upon this contemptuous animadversion on the King of Prussia, I observed to Johnson, "It would seem then, sir, that much less parts are necessary to make a king, than to make an author: for the King of Prussia is confessedly the greatest king now in Europe, yet you think he makes a very poor figure as an author."

Mr. Levet [30] this day showed me Dr. Johnson's library, which was contained in two garrets over his chambers, where Lintot, son of the celebrated bookseller of that name, had formerly his warehouse. I found a number of good books, but very dusty and in great confusion. The floor was strewed with manuscript leaves, in Johnson's own handwriting, which I beheld with a degree of veneration, supposing they perhaps might contain portions of the *Rambler,* or of *Rasselas.* I observed an apparatus for chemical experiments, of which Johnson was all his life very fond. The place seemed to be very favorable for retirement and meditation. Johnson told me, that he went up thither without mentioning it to his servant when he wanted to study secure from interruption, for he would not allow his servant to say he was not at home when he really was. "A servant's strict regard for truth," said he, "must be weakened by such a practice. A philosopher may know that it is merely a form of denial, but few servants are such nice distinguishers. If I accustom a servant to tell a lie for *me,* have I not reason to apprehend that he will tell many lies for *himself?*" I am, however, satisfied that every servant, of any degree of intelligence, understands saying his master is not at home, not at all as the affirmation of a fact, but as the customary words, intimating that his master wishes not to be seen; so that there can be no bad effect from it.

Mr. Temple, now vicar of St. Gluvias, Cornwall, who had been my intimate friend for many years, had at this time chambers in Farrar's buildings, at the bottom of Inner Temple Lane, which he kindly lent me upon my quitting my lodgings, he being to return to Trinity Hall, Cambridge. I found them particularly convenient for me, as they were so near Dr. Johnson's.

On Wednesday, July 20, Dr. Johnson, Mr. Dempster, and my uncle Dr. Boswell, who happened to be now in London, supped with me at these chambers. JOHNSON: "Pity is not natural to man. Children are always cruel. Savages are always cruel. Pity is acquired and improved by the cultivation of reason. We may have uneasy sensations for seeing a creature in distress, without pity; for we have not pity unless we wish to relieve them. When I am on my way to dine with a friend, and, finding it late, have bid the coachman make haste, if I happen to attend when he whips his horses, I may feel unpleasantly that the animals are put to pain, but I do not wish him to desist. No, sir, I wish him to drive on."

Mr. Alexander Donaldson, bookseller, of Edinburgh, had for some time opened a shop in London, and sold his cheap editions of the most popular English books, in defiance of the supposed common-law right of *literary property.* Johnson, though he concurred in the opinion which was afterwards sanctioned by a judgment of the House of Lords, that there was no such right, was at this time very angry that the booksellers of London, for whom he uniformly professed much regard, should suffer from an invasion of what they had ever con-

---

29. *"Jargonnant . . . barbare":* "Jabbering vile French." 30. Levet: Robert Levet was another "pensioner" of Johnson's household; see above, n. 22. He is said to have acquired his knowledge by serving as a waiter in a coffeehouse frequented by physicians, and listening to their conversation.

sidered to be secure; and he was loud and violent against Mr. Donaldson. " He is a fellow who takes advantage of the law to injure his brethren; for, notwithstanding that the statute secures only fourteen years of exclusive right, it has always been understood by the *trade* that he, who buys the copyright of a book from the author, obtains a perpetual property; and upon that belief, numberless bargains are made to transfer that property after the expiration of the statutory term. Now Donaldson, I say, takes advantage here, of people who have really an equitable title from usage; and if we consider how few of the books of which they buy the property succeed so well as to bring profit, we should be of opinion that the term of fourteen years is too short; it should be sixty years." DEMPSTER: " Donaldson, sir, is anxious for the encouragement of literature. He reduces the price of books, so that poor students may buy them." JOHNSON (laughing): " Well, sir, allowing that to be his motive, he is no better than Robin Hood, who robbed the rich in order to give to the poor."

It is remarkable that when the great question concerning literary property came to be ultimately tried before the supreme tribunal of this country, in consequence of the very spirited exertions of Mr. Donaldson, Dr. Johnson was zealous against a perpetuity, but he thought that the term of the exclusive right of authors should be considerably enlarged. He was then for granting a hundred years.

The conversation now turned upon Mr. David Hume's style. JOHNSON: " Why, sir, his style is not English; the structure of his sentences is French. Now the French structure and the English structure may, in the nature of things, be equally good. But if you allow that the English language is established, he is wrong. My name might originally have been Nicholson, as well as Johnson; but were you to call me Nicholson now, you would call me very absurdly."

Rousseau's treatise on the inequality of mankind [31] was at this time a fashionable topic. It gave rise to an observation by Mr. Dempster, that the advantages of fortune and rank were nothing to a wise man, who ought to value only merit. JOHNSON: " If man were a savage, living in the woods by himself, this might be true; but in civilized society we all depend upon each other, and our happiness is very much owing to the good opinion of mankind. Now, sir, in civilized society, external advantages make us more respected. A man with a good coat upon his back meets with a better reception than he who has a bad one. Sir, you may analyze this, and say what is there in it? But that will avail you nothing, for it is a part of a general system. Pound St. Paul's Church into atoms, and consider any single atom; it is, to be sure, good for nothing; but, put all these atoms together, and you have St. Paul's Church. So it is with human felicity, which is made up of many ingredients, each of which may be shown to be very insignificant. In civilized society, personal merit will not serve you so much as money will. Sir, you may make the experiment. Go into the street, and give one man a lecture on morality, and another a shilling, and see which will respect you most. If you wish only to support nature, Sir William Petty [32] fixes your allowance at three pounds a year, but, as times are much altered, let us call it six pounds. This sum will fill your belly, shelter you from the weather, and even get you a strong lasting coat, supposing it to be made of good bull's hide. Now, sir, all beyond this is artificial, and is desired in order to obtain a greater degree of respect from our fellow creatures. And, sir, if six hundred pounds a year procure a man more consequence and, of course, more happiness than six pounds a year, the same proportion will hold as to six thousand, and so on as far as opulence can be carried. Perhaps he who has a large fortune may not be so happy as he who has a small one; but that must proceed from other causes than from his having the large fortune; for, *caeteris paribus,*[33] he who is rich in a civilized society, must be happier than he who is poor, as riches, if properly used (and it is a man's own fault if they are not) must be productive of the highest advantages. Money, to be sure, of itself is of no use, for its only use is to part with it. Rousseau, and all those who deal in paradoxes, are led away by a childish desire of novelty. When I was a boy, I used always to choose the wrong side of a debate, because most ingenious things, that is to say, most new things, could be said upon it. Sir, there is nothing for which you may not muster up more plausible arguments, than those which are urged against wealth and other external advantages. Why, now, there is stealing; why should it be thought a

31. treatise . . . mankind: *Discours sur l'origine et les fondements de l'inégalité parmi les hommes* (1755).
32. Petty: an esteemed political economist of the previous century, author of *Political Arithmetick* (1690), and other treatises.
33. caeteris paribus: "supposing the rest equal."

rime? When we consider by what unjust methods property has been often acquired, and that what was unjustly got it must be unjust to keep, where is the harm in one man's taking the property of another from him? Besides, sir, when we consider the bad use that many people make of their property, and how much better use the thief may make of it, it may be defended as a very allowable practice. Yet, sir, the experience of mankind has discovered stealing to be so very bad a thing that they make no scruple to hang a man for it. When I was running about this town a very poor fellow, I was a great arguer for the advantages of poverty, but I was, at the same time, very sorry to be poor. Sir, all the arguments which are brought to represent poverty as no evil, show it to be evidently a great evil. You never find people laboring to convince you that you may live very happily upon a plentiful fortune. So you hear people talking how miserable a king must be, and yet they all wish to be in his place."

It was suggested that kings must be unhappy, because they are deprived of the greatest of all satisfactions, easy and unreserved society. JOHNSON: "That is an ill-founded notion. Being a king does not exclude a man from such society. Great kings have always been social. The King of Prussia, the only great king at present, is very social. Charles II, the last king of England who was a man of parts, was social; and our Henrys and Edwards were all social."

Mr. Dempster having endeavored to maintain that intrinsic merit *ought* to make the only distinction amongst mankind. JOHNSON: "Why, sir, mankind have found that this cannot be. How shall we determine the proportion of intrinsic merit? Were that to be the only distinction amongst mankind, we should soon quarrel about the degrees of it. Were all distinctions abolished, the strongest would not long acquiesce, but would endeavor to obtain a superiority by their bodily strength. But, sir, as subordination is very necessary for society, and contentions for superiority very dangerous, mankind, that is to say, all civilized nations, have settled it upon a plain invariable principle. A man is born to hereditary rank, or his being appointed to certain offices gives him a certain rank. Subordination tends greatly to human happiness. Were we all upon an equality, we should have no other enjoyment than mere animal pleasure."

I said, I considered distinction of rank to be of so much importance in civilized society, that if I were asked on the same day to dine with the first duke in England, and with the first man in Britain for genius, I should hesitate which to prefer. JOHNSON: "To be sure, sir, if you were to dine only once, and it were never to be known where you dined, you would choose rather to dine with the first man for genius; but to gain most respect, you should dine with the first duke in England. For nine people in ten that you meet with, would have a higher opinion of you for having dined with a duke; and the great genius himself would receive you better, because you had been with the great duke."

He took care to guard himself against any possible suspicion that his settled principles of reverence for rank and respect for wealth were at all owing to mean or interested motives, for he asserted his own independence as a literary man. "No man," said he, "who ever lived by literature, has lived more independently than I have done." He said he had taken longer time than he needed to have done in composing his Dictionary. He received our compliments upon that great work with complacency, and told us that the Academy *della Crusca* [34] could scarcely believe that it was done by one man.

Next morning I found him alone, and have preserved the following fragments of his conversation. Of a gentleman [35] who was mentioned, he said, "I have not met with any man for a long time who has given me such general displeasure. He is totally unfixed in his principles, and wants to puzzle other people." I said, his principles had been poisoned by a noted infidel writer, but that he was, nevertheless, a benevolent, good man. JOHNSON: "We can have no dependence upon that instinctive, that constitutional goodness which is not founded upon principle. I grant you that such a man may be a very amiable member of society. I can conceive him placed in such a situation that he is not much tempted to deviate from what is right; and as every man prefers virtue, when there is not some strong incitement to transgress its precepts, I can conceive him doing nothing wrong. But if such a man stood in need of money, I should not like to trust him; and I should certainly not trust him with young ladies, for *there* there is al-

34. *della Crusca:* the Florentine academy of learning, established to purify the Italian language, and responsible for an authoritative dictionary. 35. gentleman: probably Dempster. See above, n. 14.

ways temptation. Hume, and other skeptical innovators, are vain men, and will gratify themselves at any expense. Truth will not afford sufficient food to their vanity; so they have betaken themselves to error. Truth, sir, is a cow that will yield such people no more milk, and so they are gone to milk the bull. If I could have allowed myself to gratify my vanity at the expense of truth, what fame might I have acquired. Everything which Hume has advanced against Christianity had passed through my mind long before he wrote. Always remember this, that after a system is well settled upon positive evidence, a few partial objections ought not to shake it. The human mind is so limited, that it cannot take in all the parts of a subject, so that there may be objections raised against anything. There are objections against a *plenum,* and objections against a *vacuum;* yet one of them must certainly be true." [36]

I mentioned Hume's argument against the belief of miracles, that it is more probable that the witnesses to the truth of them are mistaken, or speak falsely, than that the miracles should be true. JOHNSON: "Why, sir, the great difficulty of proving miracles should make us very cautious in believing them. But let us consider: although God has made nature to operate by certain fixed laws, yet it is not unreasonable to think that he may suspend those laws, in order to establish a system highly advantageous to mankind. Now the Christtian religion is a most beneficial system, as it gives us light and certainty where we were before in darkness and doubt. The miracles which prove it are attested by men who had no interest in deceiving us, but who, on the contrary, were told that they should suffer persecution, and did actually lay down their lives in confirmation of the truth of the facts which they asserted. Indeed, for some centuries the heathens did not pretend to deny the miracles, but said they were performed by the aid of evil spirits. This is a circumstance of great weight. Then, sir, when we take the proofs derived from prophecies which have been so exactly fulfilled, we have most satisfactory evidence. Supposing a miracle possible, as to which, in my opinion, there can be no doubt, we have as strong evidence for the miracles in support of Christianity, as the nature of the thing admits."

At night, Mr. Johnson and I supped in a private

room at the Turk's Head Coffeehouse, in the Strand. " I encourage this house," said he, " for the mistress of it is a good civil woman, and has not much business."

" Sir, I love the acquaintance of young people, because, in the first place, I don't like to think myself growing old. In the next place, young acquaintances must last longest, if they do last; and then, sir, young men have more virtue than old men; they have more generous sentiments in every respect. I love the young dogs of this age: they have more wit and humor and knowledge of life than we had; but then the dogs are not so good scholars. Sir, in my early years I read very hard. It is a sad reflection, but a true one, that I knew almost as much at eighteen as I do now. My judgment, to be sure, was not so good; but I had all the facts. I remember very well, when I was at Oxford, an old gentleman said to me, ' Young man, ply your book diligently now, and acquire a stock of knowledge; for when years come upon you, you will find that poring upon books will be but an irksome task.' "

This account of his reading, given by himself in plain words, sufficiently confirms what I have already advanced upon the disputed question as to his application. It reconciles any seeming inconsistency in his way of talking upon it at different times; and shows that idleness and reading hard were with him relative terms, the import of which, as used by him, must be gathered from a comparison with what scholars of different degrees of ardor and assiduity have been known to do. And let it be remembered, that he was now talking spontaneously, and expressing his genuine sentiments, whereas at other times he might be induced, from his spirit of contradiction, or more properly from his love of argumentative contests, to speak lightly of his own application to study. It is pleasing to consider that the old gentleman's gloomy prophecy as to the irksomeness of books to men of an advanced age, which is too often fulfilled, was so far from being verified in Johnson, that his ardor for literature never failed, and his last writings had more ease and vivacity than any of his earlier productions.

He mentioned to me now, for the first time, that he had been distressed by melancholy, and for that reason had been obliged to fly from study and meditation, to the dissipating variety of life. Against melancholy he recommended constant oc-

36. There . . . true: i.e., either all space is occupied, or some of it is empty; but neither alternative is entirely acceptable.

cupation of mind, a great deal of exercise, moderation in eating and drinking, and especially to shun drinking at night. He said melancholy people were apt to fly to intemperance for relief, but that it sunk them much deeper in misery. He observed that laboring men who work hard, and live sparingly, are seldom or never troubled with low spirits.

He again insisted on the duty of maintaining subordination of rank. "Sir, I would no more deprive a nobleman of his respect, than of his money. I consider myself as acting a part in the great system of society, and I do to others as I would have them to do to me. I would behave to a nobleman as I should expect he would behave to me, were I a nobleman and he Sam. Johnson. Sir, there is one Mrs. Macaulay [37] in this town, a great republican. One day when I was at her house, I put on a very grave countenance, and said to her, 'Madam, I am now become a convert to your way of thinking. I am convinced that all mankind are upon an equal footing, and to give you an unquestionable proof, madam, that I am in earnest, here is a very sensible, civil, well-behaved fellow citizen, your footman; I desire that he may be allowed to sit down and dine with us.' I thus, sir, showed her the absurdity of the leveling doctrine. She has never liked me since. Sir, your levelers wish to level *down* as far as themselves; but they cannot bear leveling *up* to themselves. They would all have some people under them; why not then have some people above them?" I mentioned a certain author who disgusted me by his forwardness, and by showing no deference to noblemen into whose company he was admitted. JOHNSON: "Suppose a shoemaker should claim an equality with him, as he does with a lord; how he would stare. 'Why, sir, do you stare?' says the shoemaker. 'I do great service to society. 'Tis true, I am paid for doing it, but so are you, sir, and I am sorry to say it, paid better than I am, for doing something not so necessary. For mankind could do better without your books, than without my shoes.' Thus, sir, there would be a perpetual struggle for precedence, were there no fixed invariable rules for the distinction of rank, which creates no jealousy, as it is allowed to be accidental."

He said, Dr. Joseph Warton was a very agreeable man, and his *Essay on the Genius and Writings of Pope* a very pleasing book. I wondered that he delayed so long to give us the continuation of it.[38] JOHNSON: "Why, sir, I suppose he finds himself a little disappointed, in not having been able to persuade the world to be of his opinion as to Pope."

We have now been favored with the concluding volume, in which, to use a parliamentary expression, he has *explained,* so as not to appear quite so adverse to the opinion of the world, concerning Pope, as was at first thought; and we must all agree that his work is a most valuable accession to English literature.

A writer of deserved eminence being mentioned, Johnson said, "Why, sir, he is a man of good parts, but being originally poor, he has got a love of mean company and low jocularity, a very bad thing, sir. To laugh is good, and to talk is good. But you ought no more to think it enough if you laugh, than you are to think it enough if you talk. You may laugh in as many ways as you talk, and surely *every* way of talking that is practiced cannot be esteemed."

I spoke of Sir James Macdonald as a young man of most distinguished merit,[39] who united the highest reputation at Eton and Oxford, with the patriarchal spirit of a great Highland chieftain. I mentioned that Sir James had said to me, that he had never seen Mr. Johnson, but he had a great respect for him, though at the same time it was mixed with some degree of terror. JOHNSON: "Sir, if he were to be acquainted with me, it might lessen both."

The mention of this gentleman led us to talk of the Western Islands of Scotland, to visit which he expressed a wish that then appeared to me a very romantic fancy, which I little thought would be afterwards realized. He told me, that his father had put Martin's account [40] of those islands into his hands when he was very young, and that he was highly pleased with it; that he was particularly struck with the St. Kilda man's notion that the high church of Glasgow had been hollowed out of a rock, a circumstance to which old Mr. Johnson had directed his attention. He said, he would go to the Hebrides with me, when I returned from my travels, unless some very good companion

---

37. **Mrs. Macaulay:** Catherine Macaulay (1731–91), authoress on political subjects and education.

38. **continuation of it:** Part I was first published in 1756; Part II not until 1782.   39. **Macdonald . . . merit:** The hopes of all in this young Scot were terminated by his early death in Rome in 1766.   40. **account:** Martin Martin, *A Voyage to St. Kilda* (1698) and *A Description of the Western Islands of Scotland* (1703).

should offer when I was absent, which he did not think probable, adding, "There are few people whom I take so much to, as you." And when I talked of my leaving England, he said, with a very affectionate air, "My dear Boswell, I should be very unhappy at parting, did I think we were not to meet again." I cannot too often remind my readers, that, although such instances of his kindness are doubtless very flattering to me, yet I hope my recording them will be ascribed to a better motive than to vanity, for they afford unquestionable evidence of his tenderness and complacency, which some, while they were forced to acknowledge his great powers, have been so strenuous to deny.

He maintained that a boy at school was the happiest of human beings. I supported a different opinion, from which I have never yet varied, that a man is happier; and I enlarged upon the anxiety and sufferings which are endured at school. JOHNSON: "Ah! Sir, a boy's being flogged is not so severe as a man's having the hiss of the world against him. Men have a solicitude about fame; and the greater share they have of it, the more afraid they are of losing it." I silently asked myself, "Is it possible that the great Samuel Johnson really entertains any such apprehension, and is not confident that his exalted fame is established upon a foundation never to be shaken?"

He this evening drank a bumper to Sir David Dalrymple, "as a man of worth, a scholar, and a wit." "I have," said he, "never heard of him except from you; but let him know my opinion of him, for as he does not show himself much in the world, he should have the praise of the few who hear of him."

On Tuesday, July 26, I found Mr. Johnson alone. It was a very wet day, and I again complained of the disagreeable effects of such weather. JOHNSON: "Sir, this is all imagination, which physicians encourage; for man lives in air, as a fish lives in water, so that if the atmosphere press heavy from above, there is an equal resistance from below. To be sure, bad weather is hard upon people who are obliged to be abroad; and men cannot labor so well in the open air in bad weather, as in good, but, sir, a smith or a tailor, whose work is within doors, will surely do as much in rainy weather, as in fair. Some very delicate frames, indeed, may be affected by wet weather, but not common constitutions."

We talked of the education of children, and I asked him what he thought was best to teach them first. JOHNSON: "Sir, it is no matter what you teach them first, any more than what leg you shall put into your breeches first. Sir, you may stand disputing which is best to put in first, but in the meantime your breech is bare. Sir, while you are considering which of two things you should teach your child first, another boy has learned them both."

On Thursday, July 28, we again supped in private at the Turk's Head Coffeehouse. JOHNSON: "Swift has a higher reputation than he deserves. His excellence is strong sense; for his humor, though very well, is not remarkably good. I doubt whether the *Tale of a Tub* be his; for he never owned it, and it is much above his usual manner."

"Thomson,[41] I think, had as much of the poet about him as most writers. Everything appeared to him through the medium of his favorite pursuit. He could not have viewed those two candles burning but with a poetical eye."

"Has not ——[42] a great deal of wit, sir?" JOHNSON: "I do not think so, sir. He is, indeed, continually attempting wit, but he fails. And I have no more pleasure in hearing a man attempting wit and failing, than in seeing a man trying to leap over a ditch and tumbling into it."

He laughed heartily when I mentioned to him a saying of his concerning Mr. Thomas Sheridan, which Foote took a wicked pleasure to circulate. "Why, sir, Sherry is dull, naturally dull, but it must have taken him a great deal of pains to become what we now see him. Such an excess of stupidity, sir, is not in nature." "So," said he, "I allowed him all his own merit."

He now added, "Sheridan cannot bear me. I bring his declamation to a point. I ask him a plain question, 'What do you mean to teach?' Besides, sir, what influence can Mr. Sheridan have upon the language of this great country, by his narrow exertions? Sir, it is burning a farthing candle at Dover, to show light at Calais."

Talking of a young man[43] who was uneasy from thinking that he was very deficient in learning and knowledge, he said, "A man has no reason to complain who holds a middle place, and has many below him; and perhaps he has not six of his years above him; perhaps not one. Though he may not know anything perfectly, the general mass

---

41. **Thomson:** This is James Thomson (d. 1748), the author of *The Seasons* and *The Castle of Indolence*.   42. Edmund Burke is conjectured to have been the subject of this question.   43. **man:** probably Boswell himself.

of knowledge that he has acquired is considerable. Time will do for him all that is wanting."

The conversation then took a philosophical turn. JOHNSON: "Human experience, which is constantly contradicting theory, is the great test of truth. A system, built upon the discoveries of a great many minds, is always of more strength, than what is produced by the mere workings of any one mind, which, of itself, can do little. There is not so poor a book in the world that would not be a prodigious effort were it wrought out entirely by a single mind, without the aid of prior investigators. The French writers are superficial, because they are not scholars, and so proceed upon the mere power of their own minds; and we see how very little power they have."

"As to the Christian religion, sir, besides the strong evidence which we have for it, there is a balance in its favor from the number of great men who have been convinced of its truth, after a serious consideration of the question. Grotius was an acute man, a lawyer, a man accustomed to examine evidence, and he was convinced. Grotius was not a recluse, but a man of the world, who certainly had no bias to the side of religion. Sir Isaac Newton set out an infidel, and came to be a very firm believer."

He this evening again recommended to me to perambulate Spain. I said it would amuse him to get a letter from me dated at Salamanca. JOHNSON: "I love the University of Salamanca; for when the Spaniards were in doubt as to the lawfulness of their conquering America, the University of Salamanca gave it as their opinion that it was not lawful." He spoke this with great emotion, and with that generous warmth which dictated the lines in his *London,* against Spanish encroachment.

I expressed my opinion of my friend Derrick as but a poor writer. JOHNSON: "To be sure, sir, he is, but you are to consider that his being a literary man has got for him all that he has. It has made him King of Bath.[44] Sir, he has nothing to say for himself but that he is a writer. Had he not been a writer, he must have been sweeping the crossings in the streets, and asking halfpence from everybody that passed."

In justice, however, to the memory of Mr. Derrick, who was my first tutor in the ways of London, and showed me the town in all its variety of departments, both literary and sportive, the particulars of which Dr. Johnson advised me to put in writing, it is proper to mention what Johnson, at a subsequent period, said of him both as a writer and an editor: "Sir, I have often said, that if Derrick's letters had been written by one of a more established name, they would have been thought very pretty letters." And, "I sent Derrick to Dryden's relations to gather materials for his life; and I believe he got all that I myself should have got."

Poor Derrick! I remember him with kindness. . . .

Johnson said once to me, "Sir, I honor Derrick for his presence of mind. One night, when Floyd, another poor author, was wandering about the streets in the night, he found Derrick fast asleep upon a bulk;[45] upon being suddenly waked, Derrick started up, 'My dear Floyd, I am sorry to see you in this destitute state; will you go home with me to *my lodgings?*'"

I again begged his advice as to my method of study at Utrecht. "Come," said he, "let us make a day of it. Let us go down to Greenwich and dine, and talk of it there." The following Saturday was fixed for this excursion.

As we walked along the Strand tonight, arm in arm, a woman of the town accosted us, in the usual enticing manner. "No, no, my girl," said Johnson, "it won't do." He, however, did not treat her with harshness; and we talked of the wretched life of such women, and agreed that much more misery than happiness, upon the whole, is produced by illicit commerce between the sexes.

On Saturday, July 30, Dr. Johnson and I took a sculler at the Temple Stairs, and set out for Greenwich. I asked him if he really thought a knowledge of the Greek and Latin languages an essential requisite to a good education. JOHNSON: "Most certainly, sir; for those who know them have a very great advantage over those who do not. Nay, sir, it is wonderful what a difference learning makes upon people even in the common intercourse of life, which does not appear to be much connected with it." "And yet," said I, "people go through the world very well, and carry on the business of life to good advantage, without learning." JOHNSON: "Why, sir, that may be true in cases where learning cannot possibly be of any use; for instance, this boy rows us as well without learning,

---

44. King of Bath: master of ceremonies in the city of Bath, an office long held by Richard "Beau" Nash, who died in 1761.

45. bulk: a stall or projecting part of a building.

as if he could sing the song of Orpheus to the Argonauts, who were the first sailors." He then called to the boy, " What would you give, my lad, to know about the Argonauts? " " Sir," said the boy, " I would give what I have." Johnson was much pleased with his answer, and we gave him a double fare. Dr. Johnson then turning to me, " Sir," said he, " a desire of knowledge is the natural feeling of mankind; and every human being, whose mind is not debauched, will be willing to give all that he has, to get knowledge."

We landed at the Old Swan, and walked to Billingsgate, where we took oars and moved smoothly along the silver Thames. It was a very fine day. We were entertained with the immense number and variety of ships that were lying at anchor, and with the beautiful country on each side of the river.

I talked of preaching, and of the great success which those called Methodist have. JOHNSON: " Sir, it is owing to their expressing themselves in a plain and familiar manner, which is the only way to do good to the common people, and which clergymen of genius and learning ought to do from a principle of duty, when it is suited to their congregations; a practice, for which they will be praised by men of sense. To insist against drunkenness as a crime, because it debases reason, the noblest faculty of man, would be of no service to the common people, but to tell them that they may die in a fit of drunkenness, and show them how dreadful that would be, cannot fail to make a deep impression. Sir, when your Scotch clergy give up their homely manner, religion will soon decay in that country." Let this observation, as Johnson meant it, be ever remembered.

I was much pleased to find myself with Johnson at Greenwich, which he celebrates in his *London* as a favorite scene. I had the poem in my pocket, and read the lines aloud with enthusiasm:

On Thames's banks in silent thought we stood,
Where Greenwich smiles upon the silver flood:
Pleased with the seat which gave Eliza [46] birth,
We kneel, and kiss the consecrated earth.

He remarked that the structure of Greenwich hospital was too magnificent for a place of charity, and that its parts were too much detached, to make one great whole.

Buchanan,[47] he said, was a very fine poet; and observed that he was the first who complimented a lady, by ascribing to her the different perfections of the heathen goddesses, but that Johnston improved upon this, by making his lady, at the same time, free from their defects.

He dwelt upon Buchanan's elegant verses to Mary, Queen of Scots, *Nympha Caledoniae,* &c. and spoke with enthusiasm of the beauty of Latin verse. " All the modern languages," said he, " cannot furnish so melodious a line as

Formosam resonare doces Amarillida silvas.[48]

Afterwards he entered upon the business of the day, which was to give me his advice as to a course of study. And here I am to mention with much regret, that my record of what he said is miserably scanty. I recollect with admiration an animating blaze of eloquence, which roused every intellectual power in me to the highest pitch, but must have dazzled me so much that my memory could not preserve the substance of his discourse; for the note which I find of it is no more than this: " He ran over the grand scale of human knowledge; advised me to select some particular branch to excel in, but to acquire a little of every kind." The defect of my minutes will be fully supplied by a long letter upon the subject, which he favored me with, after I had been some time at Utrecht, and which my readers will have the pleasure to peruse in its proper place.

We walked in the evening in Greenwich Park. He asked me, I suppose, by way of trying my disposition, " Is not this very fine? " Having no exquisite relish of the beauties of nature, and being more delighted with " the busy hum of men," [49] I answered, " Yes, sir, but not equal to Fleet Street." JOHNSON: " You are right, sir."

I am aware that many of my readers may censure my want of taste. Let me, however, shelter myself under the authority of a very fashionable baronet [50] in the brilliant world, who, on his attention being

---

46. **Eliza:** Queen Elizabeth, of course, is meant. The royal palace of "Nonesuch" was pulled down by Charles II, and a marine hospital erected on the site.

47. **Buchanan:** George Buchanan (1506–82), a Scottish poet who wrote in Latin. So also did Arthur Johnston (1587–1641). 48. Virgil, *Eclogues,* I.5: "You teach the woods to echo lovely Amaryllis' name." 49. "the . . . men": See Milton's "L'Allegro," l. 118, p. 212, above. 50. **baronet:** "My friend Sir Michael Le Fleming. This gentleman, with all his experience of sprightly and elegant life, inherits, with the beautiful family domain, no inconsiderable share of that love of literature which distinguished his venerable grandfather, the bishop of Carlisle. He one day observed to me, of Dr. Johnson, in a felicity of phrase, 'There is a blunt dignity about him on every occasion' " [B].

called to the fragrance of a May evening in the country, observed, " This may be very well; but for my part, I prefer the smell of a flambeau at the playhouse."

We stayed so long at Greenwich, that our sail up the river, in our return to London, was by no means so pleasant as in the morning; for the night air was so cold that it made me shiver. I was the more sensible of it from having sat up all the night before recollecting and writing in my journal what I thought worthy of preservation, an exertion which, during the first part of my acquaintance with Johnson, I frequently made. I remember having sat up four nights in one week, without being much incommoded in the daytime.

Johnson, whose robust frame was not in the least affected by the cold, scolded me, as if my shivering had been a paltry effeminacy, saying, " Why do you shiver? " Sir William Scott, of the Commons,[51] told me that, when he complained of a headache in the post chaise, as they were traveling together to Scotland, Johnson treated him in the same manner: " At your age, sir, I had no headache." It is not easy to make allowance for sensations in others, which we ourselves have not at the time. We must all have experienced how very differently we are affected by the complaints of our neighbors, when we are well and when we are ill. In full health, we can scarcely believe that they suffer much, so faint is the image of pain upon our imagination; when softened by sickness, we readily sympathize with the sufferings of others.

We concluded the day at the Turk's Head Coffeehouse very socially. He was pleased to listen to a particular account which I gave him of my family, and of its hereditary estate, as to the extent and population of which he asked questions, and made calculations, recommending, at the same time, a liberal kindness to the tenantry, as people over whom the proprietor was placed by Providence. He took delight in hearing my description of the romantic seat of my ancestors. " I must be there, sir," said he, " and we will live in the old castle; and if there is not a room in it remaining, we will build one." I was highly flattered, but could scarcely indulge a hope that Auchinleck would indeed be honored by his presence, and celebrated by a description, as it afterwards was, in his *Journey to the Western Islands.*

51. **Commons:** that is, Doctors' Commons, whose members' practice of law was confined to the ecclesiastical courts and the Court of the Admiralty.

After we had again talked of my setting out for Holland, he said, " I must see thee out of England; I will accompany you to Harwich." I could not find words to express what I felt upon this unexpected and very great mark of his affectionate regard.

Next day, Sunday, July 31, I told him I had been that morning at a meeting of the people called Quakers, where I had heard a woman preach. JOHNSON: " Sir, a woman's preaching is like a dog's walking on his hinder legs. It is not done well; but you are surprised to find it done at all." . . .

On Wednesday, August 3, we had our last social evening at the Turk's Head Coffeehouse, before my setting out for foreign parts. I had the misfortune, before we parted, to irritate him unintentionally. I mentioned to him how common it was in the world to tell absurd stories of him, and to ascribe to him very strange sayings. JOHNSON: " What do they make me say, sir? " BOSWELL: " Why, sir, as an instance very strange indeed (laughing heartily as I spoke), David Hume told me, you said that you would stand before a battery of cannon to restore the Convocation[52] to its full powers." Little did I apprehend that he had actually said this, but I was soon convinced of my error; for, with a determined look, he thundered out, " And would I not, sir? Shall the Presbyterian *Kirk* of Scotland have its General Assembly, and the Church of England be denied its Convocation? " He was walking up and down the room while I told him the anecdote, but when he uttered this explosion of High Church zeal, he had come close to my chair, and his eyes flashed with indignation. I bowed to the storm, and diverted the force of it, by leading him to expatiate on the influence which religion derived from maintaining the Church with great external respectability.

I must not omit to mention that he this year wrote *The Life of Ascham,* and the dedication to the Earl of Shaftesbury, prefixed to the edition of that writer's[53] English works, published by Mr. Bennet.

On Friday, August 5, we set out early in the morning in the Harwich stagecoach. A fat elderly gentlewoman, and a young Dutchman, seemed the

52. **Convocation:** a formal gathering of clergy of the English Church, coincident with the meetings of parliament. Since 1717 it had been discontinued. 53. Besides writing the Life and the Dedication, there is reason to think that Johnson was the actual, though not the nominal, editor of this edition of Roger Ascham, and that he allowed Bennet the credit of it.

most inclined among us to conversation. At the inn where we dined, the gentlewoman said that she had done her best to educate her children, and, particularly, that she had never suffered them to be a moment idle. JOHNSON: "I wish, madam, you would educate me, too; for I have been an idle fellow all my life." "I am sure, sir," said she, "you have not been idle." JOHNSON: "Nay, madam, it is very true; and that gentleman there (pointing to me) has been idle. He was idle at Edinburgh. His father sent him to Glasgow, where he continued to be idle. He then came to London, where he has been very idle; and now he is going to Utrecht, where he will be as idle as ever." I asked him privately how he could expose me so. JOHNSON: "Poh, poh!" said he, "they knew nothing about you, and will think of it no more." In the afternoon the gentlewoman talked violently against the Roman Catholics, and of the horrors of the Inquisition. To the utter astonishment of all the passengers but myself, who knew that he could talk upon any side of a question, he defended the Inquisition, and maintained that "false doctrine should be checked on its first appearance; that the civil power should unite with the Church in punishing those who dared to attack the established religion, and that such only were punished by the Inquisition." He had in his pocket *Pomponius Mela de Situ Orbis*,[54] in which he read occasionally, and seemed very intent upon ancient geography. Though by no means niggardly, his attention to what was generally right was so minute, that having observed at one of the stages that I ostentatiously gave a shilling to the coachman, when the custom was for each passenger to give only sixpence, he took me aside and scolded me, saying that what I had done would make the coachman dissatisfied with all the rest of the passengers, who gave him no more than his due. This was a just reprimand; for in whatever way a man may indulge his generosity or his vanity in spending his money, for the sake of others he ought not to raise the price of any article for which there is a constant demand.

He talked of Mr. Blacklock's poetry, so far as it was descriptive of visible objects, and observed, that "as its author had the misfortune to be blind, we may be absolutely sure that such passages are combinations of what he has remembered of the works of other writers who could see. That foolish fellow, Spence,[55] has labored to explain philosophically how Blacklock may have done, by means of his own faculties, what it is impossible he should do. The solution, as I have given it, is plain. Suppose I know a man to be so lame that he is absolutely incapable to move himself, and I find him in a different room from that in which I left him; shall I puzzle myself with idle conjectures, that, perhaps, his nerves have by some unknown change all at once become effective? No, sir; it is clear how he got into a different room: he was *carried*."

Having stopped a night at Colchester, Johnson talked of that town with veneration, for having stood a siege for Charles I. The Dutchman alone now remained with us. He spoke English tolerably well; and thinking to recommend himself to us by expatiating on the superiority of the criminal jurisprudence of this country over that of Holland, he inveighed against the barbarity of putting an accused person to the torture, in order to force a confession. But Johnson was as ready for this as for the Inquisition. "Why, sir, you do not, I find, understand the law of your own country. The torture in Holland is considered as a favor to an accused person, for no man is put to the torture there, unless there is as much evidence against him as would amount to conviction in England. An accused person among you, therefore, has one chance more to escape punishment, than those who are tried among us."

At supper this night he talked of good eating with uncommon satisfaction. "Some people," said he, "have a foolish way of not minding, or pretending not to mind, what they eat. For my part, I mind my belly very studiously, and very carefully; for I look upon it, that he who does not mind his belly, will hardly mind anything else." He now appeared to me *Jean Bull philosophe*,[56] and he was, for the moment, not only serious, but vehement. Yet I have heard him, upon other occasions, talk with great contempt of people who were anxious to gratify their palates; and the 206th number of his *Rambler* is a masterly essay against gulosity.[57] His practice, indeed, I must acknowledge, may be considered as casting the balance of his different opinions upon this subject; for I never knew any man who relished good eating more than he did. When at table, he was totally absorbed in the busi-

---

54. *Pomponius . . . Orbis:* This work of Mela's was the first known geography of the ancient world to be written in Latin. Mela lived in the first century A.D.   55. **Spence:** Joseph Spence, *An Account of the Life, Character, and Poems of Mr. Blacklock* (1754).   56. *Jean . . . philosophe:* "John Bull turned philosopher."   57. **gulosity:** gluttony.

ness of the moment; his looks seemed riveted to his plate; nor would he, unless when in very high company, say one word, or even pay the least attention to what was said by others, till he had satisfied his appetite, which was so fierce, and indulged with such intenseness, that while in the act of eating, the veins of his forehead swelled, and generally a strong perspiration was visible. To those whose sensations were delicate, this could not but be disgusting; and it was doubtless not very suitable to the character of a philosopher, who should be distinguished by self-command. But it must be owned, that Johnson, though he could be rigidly *abstemious,* was not a *temperate* man either in eating or drinking. He could refrain, but he could not use moderately. He told me, that he had fasted two days without inconvenience, and that he had never been hungry but once. They who beheld with wonder how much he eat upon all occasions when his dinner was to his taste, could not easily conceive what he must have meant by hunger; and not only was he remarkable for the extraordinary quantity which he eat, but he was, or affected to be, a man of very nice discernment in the science of cookery. He used to descant critically on the dishes which had been at table where he had dined or supped, and to recollect very minutely what he had liked. I remember, when he was in Scotland, his praising " *Gordon's palates* " (a dish of palates [58] at the Hon. Alexander Gordon's) with a warmth of expression which might have done honor to more important subjects. " As for Maclaurin's imitation of a *made dish,* it was a wretched attempt. He about the same time was so much displeased with the performances of a nobleman's French cook, that he exclaimed with vehemence, " I'd throw such a rascal into the river "; and he then proceeded to alarm a lady at whose house he was to sup, by the following manifesto of his skill: " I, madam, who live at a variety of good tables, am a much better judge of cookery, than any person who has a very tolerable cook, but lives much at home, for his palate is gradually adapted to the taste of his cook; whereas, Madam, in trying by a wider range, I can more exquisitely judge." When invited to dine, even with an intimate friend, he was not pleased if something better than a plain dinner was not prepared for him. I have heard him say on such an occasion, " This was a good dinner enough, to be sure; but it was not a dinner to *ask* a man to." On the other hand,

58. palates: Cows' palates were formerly thought a delicacy.

he was wont to express, with great glee, his satisfaction when he had been entertained quite to his mind. One day when we had dined with his neighbor and landlord, in Bolt Court, Mr. Allen, the printer, whose old housekeeper had studied his taste in everything, he pronounced this eulogy: " Sir, we could not have had a better dinner, had there been a *synod of cooks.*"

While we were left by ourselves, after the Dutchman had gone to bed, Dr. Johnson talked of that studied behavior which many have recommended and practiced. He disapproved of it, and said, " I never considered whether I should be a grave man, or a merry man, but just let inclination, for the time, have its course."

He flattered me with some hopes that he would, in the course of the following summer, come over to Holland, and accompany me in a tour through the Netherlands.

I teased him with fanciful apprehensions of unhappiness. A moth having fluttered round the candle, and burned itself, he laid hold of this little incident to admonish me, saying, with a sly look and in a solemn but quiet tone, " That creature was its own tormentor, and I believe its name was Boswell."

Next day we got to Harwich, to dinner, and my passage in the packet boat to Helvoetsluys being secured and my baggage put on board, we dined at our inn by ourselves. I happened to say, it would be terrible if he should not find a speedy opportunity of returning to London, and be confined in so dull a place. JOHNSON: " Don't, sir, accustom yourself to use big words for little matters. It would *not* be *terrible,* though I *were* to be detained some time here." The practice of using words of disproportionate magnitude is, no doubt, too frequent everywhere, but, I think, most remarkable among the French, of which all who have traveled in France must have been struck with innumerable instances.

We went and looked at the church, and, having gone into it and walked up to the altar, Johnson, whose piety was constant and fervent, sent me to my knees, saying, " Now that you are going to leave your native country, recommend yourself to the protection of your Creator and Redeemer."

After we came out of the church, we stood talking for some time together of Bishop Berkeley's ingenious sophistry to prove the nonexistence of matter, and that everything in the universe is merely ideal. I observed, that though we are satisfied his doctrine is not true, it is impossible to refute it. I never shall forget the alacrity with which Johnson answered, striking his foot with mighty force against a large stone, till he rebounded from it, " I refute it *thus.*" This was a stout exemplification of the *first truths* of *Père Buffier,*[59] or the *original principles* of Reid and of Beattie, without admitting which, we can no more argue in metaphysics, than we can argue in mathematics without axioms. To me it is not conceivable how Berkeley can be answered by pure reasoning, but I know that the nice and difficult task was to have been undertaken by one of the most luminous minds[60] of the present age, had not politics "turned him from calm philosophy aside." What an admirable display of subtlety, united with brilliance, might his contending with Berkeley have afforded us! How must we, when we reflect on the loss of such an intellectual feast, regret that he should be characterized as the man,

Who born for the universe narrowed his mind,
And to party gave up what was meant for mankind?[61]

My revered friend walked down with me to the beach, where we embraced and parted with tenderness, and engaged to correspond by letters. I said, " I hope, sir, you will not forget me in my absence." JOHNSON: " Nay, sir, it is more likely you should forget me, than that I should forget you." As the vessel put out to sea, I kept my eyes upon him for a considerable time, while he remained rolling his majestic frame in his usual manner; and at last I perceived him walk back into the town, and he disappeared. . . .

from *October 16–26, 1769*

He honored me with his company at dinner on the 16th of October, at my lodgings in Old Bond Street, with Sir Joshua Reynolds, Mr. Garrick, Dr. Goldsmith, Mr. Murphy, Mr. Bickerstaffe,[62] and Mr. Thomas Davies. Garrick played round him with a fond vivacity, taking hold of the breasts of his coat, and, looking up in his face with a lively archness, complimented him on the good health which he seemed then to enjoy; while the sage, shaking his head, beheld him with a gentle complacency. One of the company not being come at the appointed hour, I proposed, as usual upon such occasions, to order dinner to be served, adding, " Ought six people to be kept waiting for one?" " Why, yes," answered Johnson, with a delicate humanity, " if the one will suffer more by your sitting down, than the six will do by waiting." Goldsmith, to divert the tedious minutes, strutted about, bragging of his dress, and I believe was seriously vain of it, for his mind was wonderfully prone to such impressions. " Come, come," said Garrick, " talk no more of that. You are, perhaps, the worst — eh, eh!"—Goldsmith was eagerly attempting to interrupt him, when Garrick went on, laughing ironically, " Nay, you will always *look* like a gentleman, but I am talking of being well or *ill dressed.*" " Well, let me tell you," said Goldsmith, " when my tailor brought home my bloom-colored coat, he said, ' Sir, I have a favor to beg of you. When anybody asks you who made your clothes, be pleased to mention John Filby, at the Harrow, in Water Lane.'" JOHNSON: " Why, sir, that was because he knew the strange color would attract crowds to gaze at it, and thus they might hear of him, and see how well he could make a coat even of so absurd a color."

After dinner our conversation first turned upon Pope. Johnson said his characters of men were admirably drawn, those of women not so well. He repeated to us, in his forcible, melodious manner, the concluding lines of the *Dunciad*. While he was talking loudly in praise of those lines, one of the company[63] ventured to say, " Too fine for such a poem — a poem on what?" JOHNSON (with a disdainful look): " Why, on *dunces*. It was worth while being a dunce then. Ah, sir, hadst *thou* lived in those days! It is not worth while being a dunce now, when there are no wits." Bickerstaffe observed, as a peculiar circumstance, that Pope's fame was higher when he was alive than it was then. Johnson said, his *Pastorals* were poor things, though the versification was fine. He told us, with high satisfaction, the anecdote of Pope's inquiring who was the author of his *London,* and saying, he will be soon *déterré.*[64] He observed, that in Dryden's

59. Père Buffier: The reference is to Claude Buffier (1661–1737), *Traité des vérités premières et de la source de nos jugements* ("Treatise on first truths and on the source of our judgments"). Thomas Reid was one of the leaders of the contemporary school of Scottish philosophers. James Beattie won more distinction as a poet and divine than as a philosopher. **60. minds:** Edmund Burke is meant. The phrase here is inexactly quoted from Pope's *Satires,* II.ii.5. **61.** From Goldsmith's spirited *Retaliation.* **62. Murphy, Bickerstaffe:** Arthur Murphy and Isaac Bickerstaffe were popular playwrights.

63. one . . . company: doubtless Boswell himself. **64. déterré:** "unearthed."

poetry there were passages drawn from a profundity which Pope could never reach. He repeated some fine lines on love, by the former (which I have now forgotten), and gave great applause to the character of Zimri.[65] Goldsmith said that Pope's character of Addison [66] showed a deep knowledge of the human heart. Johnson said that the description of the temple, in *The Mourning Bride*,[67] was the finest poetical passage he had ever read; he recollected none in Shakespeare equal to it. " But," said Garrick, all alarmed for " the God of his idolatry," " we know not the extent and variety of his powers. We are to suppose there are such passages in his works. Shakespeare must not suffer from the badness of our memories." Johnson, diverted by this enthusiastic jealousy, went on with great ardor: " No, sir; Congreve has *nature* " (smiling on the tragic eagerness of Garrick), but composing himself, he added, " Sir, this is not comparing Congreve on the whole with Shakespeare on the whole; but only maintaining that Congreve has one finer passage than any that can be found in Shakespeare. Sir, a man may have no more than ten guineas in the world, but he may have those ten guineas in one piece; and so may have a finer piece than a man who has ten thousand pounds; but then he has only one ten-guinea piece. What I mean is, that you can show me no passage where there is simply a description of material objects, without any intermixture of moral notions, which produces such an effect." Mr. Murphy mentioned Shakespeare's description of the night before the battle of Agincourt, but it was observed it had *men* in it. Mr. Davies suggested the speech of Juliet, in which she figures herself awaking in the tomb of her ancestors. Someone mentioned the description of Dover Cliff.[68] JOHNSON: " No, sir; it should be all precipice, all vacuum. The crows impede your fall. The diminished appearance of the boats, and other circumstances, are all very good description, but do not impress the mind at once with the horrible idea of immense height. The impression is divided; you pass on by computation, from one stage of the tremendous space to another. Had the girl in *The Mourning Bride* said she could not cast her shoe to the top of one of the pillars in the temple, it would not have aided the idea, but weakened it."

Talking of a barrister who had a bad utterance, someone (to rouse Johnson) wickedly said that he was unfortunate in not having been taught oratory by Sheridan. JOHNSON: " Nay, sir, if he had been taught by Sheridan, he would have cleared the room." GARRICK: " Sheridan has too much vanity to be a good man." We shall now see Johnson's mode of *defending* a man; taking him into his own hands, and discriminating. JOHNSON: " No, sir. There is, to be sure, in Sheridan, something to reprehend, and everything to laugh at; but, sir, he is not a bad man. No, sir, were mankind to be divided into good and bad, he would stand considerably within the ranks of good. And, sir, it must be allowed that Sheridan excels in plain declamation, though he can exhibit no character."

I should, perhaps, have suppressed this disquisition concerning a person of whose merit and worth I think with respect, had he not attacked Johnson so outrageously in his *Life of Swift,* and, at the same time, treated us his admirers as a set of pygmies. He who has provoked the lash of wit cannot complain that he smarts from it.

Mrs. Montagu,[69] a lady distinguished for having written an essay on Shakespeare, being mentioned, REYNOLDS: " I think that essay does her honor." JOHNSON: " Yes, sir, it does *her* honor, but it would do nobody else honor. I have, indeed, not read it all. But when I take up the end of a web, and find it pack thread, I do not expect, by looking further, to find embroidery. Sir, I will venture to say, there is not one sentence of true criticism in her book." GARRICK: " But, sir, surely it shows how much Voltaire has mistaken Shakespeare, which nobody else has done." JOHNSON: " Sir, nobody else has thought it worth while. And what merit is there in that? You may as well praise a schoolmaster for whipping a boy who has construed ill. No, sir, there is no real criticism in it: none showing the beauty of thought, as formed on the workings of the human heart."

The admirers of this essay may be offended at the slighting manner in which Johnson spoke of it; but let it be remembered, that he gave his honest opinion unbiased by any prejudice, or any proud jealousy of a woman intruding herself into the chair of criticism; for Sir Joshua Reynolds has told

---

65. **Zimri**: in Dryden's *Absalom and Achitophel*, a character standing for the Duke of Buckingham. 66. **Addison**: in *An Epistle to Dr. Arbuthnot*, ll. 193 ff. See p. 435, above. 67. **The . . . Bride**: by William Congreve, II.i. 68. **Dover Cliff**: See *King Lear*, IV.vi.17 ff.

69. **Mrs. Montagu**: Elizabeth Montagu, "Queen" of the Bluestockings, defended Shakespeare's reputation against the attacks of Voltaire.

me, that when the essay first came out, and it was not known who had written it, Johnson wondered how Sir Joshua could like it. At this time Sir Joshua himself had received no information concerning the author, except being assured by one of our most eminent literati that it was clear its author did not know the Greek tragedies in the original. One day at Sir Joshua's table, when it was related that Mrs. Montagu, in an excess of compliment to the author of a modern tragedy, had exclaimed, " I tremble for Shakespeare," Johnson said, " When Shakespeare has got —— for his rival, and Mrs. Montagu for his defender, he is in a poor state indeed."

Johnson proceeded: " The Scotchman [70] has taken the right method in his *Elements of Criticism*. I do not mean that he has taught us anything, but he has told us old things in a new way." MURPHY: " He seems to have read a great deal of French criticism, and wants to make it his own; as if he had been for years anatomizing the heart of man, and peeping into every cranny of it." GOLDSMITH: " It is easier to write that book than to read it." JOHNSON: " We have an example of true criticism in Burke's *Essay on the Sublime and Beautiful*,[71] and, if I recollect, there is also Du Bos; and Bouhours, who shows all beauty to depend on truth. There is no great merit in telling how many plays have ghosts in them, and how this ghost is better than that. You must show how terror is impressed on the human heart. In the description of night in *Macbeth*,[72] the beetle and the bat detract from the general idea of darkness, — inspissated [73] gloom."

Politics being mentioned, he said, " This petitioning is a new mode of distressing government, and a mighty easy one. I will undertake to get petitions either against quarter-guineas or half-guineas, with the help of a little hot wine. There must be no yielding to encourage this. The object is not important enough. We are not to blow up half a dozen palaces, because one cottage is burning."

The conversation then took another turn. JOHNSON: " It is amazing what ignorance of certain points one sometimes finds in men of eminence. A wit about town, who wrote Latin bawdy verses, asked me, how it happened that England and Scotland, which were once two kingdoms, were now

one: — and Sir Fletcher Norton [74] did not seem to know that there were such publications as the *Reviews.*"

" The ballad of Hardyknute [75] has no great merit, if it be really ancient. People talk of nature. But mere obvious nature may be exhibited with very little power of mind."

On Thursday, October 19, I passed the evening with him at his house. He advised me to complete a dictionary of words peculiar to Scotland, of which I showed him a specimen. " Sir," said he, " Ray has made a collection of North Country words. By collecting those of your country, you will do a useful thing towards the history of the language." He bade me also go on with collections which I was making upon the antiquities of Scotland. " Make a large book, a folio." BOSWELL: " But of what use will it be, sir?" JOHNSON: " Never mind the use; do it."

I complained that he had not mentioned Garrick in his Preface to Shakespeare, and asked him if he did not admire him. JOHNSON: " Yes, as ' a poor player, who frets and struts his hour upon the stage ' [76] — as a shadow." BOSWELL: " But has he not brought Shakespeare into notice?" JOHNSON: " Sir, to allow that, would be to lampoon the age. Many of Shakespeare's plays are the worse for being acted: Macbeth, for instance." BOSWELL: " What, sir, is nothing gained by decoration and action? Indeed, I do wish that you had mentioned Garrick." JOHNSON: " My dear sir, had I mentioned him, I must have mentioned many more: Mrs. Pritchard, Mrs. Cibber — nay, and Mr. Cibber, too; he too altered Shakespeare." BOSWELL: " You have read his apology,[77] sir?" JOHNSON: " Yes, it is very entertaining. But as for Cibber himself, taking from his conversation all that he ought not to have said, he was a poor creature. I remember when he brought me one of his odes to have my opinion of it, I could not bear such nonsense, and would not let him read it to the end; so little respect had I for *that great man!* (laughing). Yet I remember Richardson wondering that I could treat him with familiarity."

I mentioned to him that I had seen the execution of several convicts at Tyburn, two days before, and

---

70. **Scotchman:** Henry Home, Lord Kames. See n. 4, above. 71. **Burke's *Essay:*** first published 1757 and often thereafter. The two Frenchmen here mentioned were names of great influence in critical theory of the Neoclassical school.   72. ***Macbeth:*** III.ii.40 ff.   73. **inspissated:** thickened or condensed.

74. **Norton:** This man, who was often unfavorably noticed, was none the less Speaker of the House of Commons.   75. **Hardyknute:** "Hardyknute" was attributed to Elizabeth Halket, Lady Wardlaw. But many in Johnson's day believed it an ancient traditional ballad, and admired it the more for being old. Johnson thought ill of it in either case.   76. ***Macbeth,*** V.v.24-25.   77. **apology:** See n. 11, above.

that none of them seemed to be under any concern. JOHNSON: " Most of them, sir, have never thought at all." BOSWELL: " But is not the fear of death natural to man? " JOHNSON: " So much so, sir, that the whole of life is but keeping away the thoughts of it." He then, in a low and earnest tone, talked of his meditating upon the awful hour of his own dissolution, and in what manner he should conduct himself upon that occasion: " I know not," said he, " whether I should wish to have a friend by me, or have it all between God and myself."

Talking of our feeling for the distresses of others, JOHNSON: " Why, sir, there is much noise made about it, but it is greatly exaggerated. No, sir, we have a certain degree of feeling to prompt us to do good; more than that, Providence does not intend. It would be misery to no purpose." BOSWELL: " But suppose now, sir, that one of your intimate friends were apprehended for an offense for which he might be hanged." JOHNSON: " I should do what I could to bail him, and give him any other assistance; but if he were once fairly hanged, I should not suffer." BOSWELL: " Would you eat your dinner that day, sir? " JOHNSON: " Yes, sir; and eat it as if he were eating it with me. Why, there's Baretti,[78] who is to be tried for his life tomorrow; friends have risen up for him on every side; yet if he should be hanged, none of them will eat a slice of plum pudding the less. Sir, that sympathetic feeling goes a very little way in depressing the mind."

I told him that I had dined lately at Foote's, who showed me a letter which he had received from Tom Davies, telling him that he had not been able to sleep from the concern he felt on account of " This sad affair of Baretti," begging of him to try if he could suggest anything that might be of service; and, at the same time, recommending to him an industrious young man who kept a pickle shop. JOHNSON: " Ay, sir, here you have a specimen of human sympathy: a friend hanged, and a cucumber pickled. We know not whether Baretti or the pickle man has kept Davies from sleep; nor does he know himself. And as to his not sleeping, sir, Tom Davies is a very great man; Tom has been upon the stage and knows how to do those things: I have not been upon the stage, and cannot do those things." BOSWELL: " I have often blamed myself, sir, for not feeling for others as sensibly as

many say they do." JOHNSON: " Sir, don't be duped by them any more. You will find these very feeling people are not very ready to do you good. They *pay* you by *feeling.*"

BOSWELL: " Foote has a great deal of humor." JOHNSON: " Yes, sir." BOSWELL: " He has a singular talent of exhibiting character." JOHNSON: " Sir, it is not a talent; it is a vice; it is what others abstain from. It is not comedy, which exhibits the character of a species, as that of a miser gathered from many misers: it is a farce which exhibits individuals." BOSWELL: " Did not he think of exhibiting you, sir? " JOHNSON: " Sir, fear restrained him; he knew I would have broken his bones. I would have saved him the trouble of cutting off a leg; I would not have left him a leg to cut off." BOSWELL: " Pray, sir, is not Foote an infidel? " JOHNSON: " I do not know, sir, that the fellow is an infidel; but if he be an infidel, he is an infidel as a dog is an infidel; that is to say, he has never thought upon the subject." [79] BOSWELL: " I suppose, sir, he has thought superficially, and seized the first notions which occurred to his mind." JOHNSON: "Why, then, sir, still he is like a dog, that snatches the piece next him. Did you never observe that dogs have not the power of comparing? A dog will take a small bit of meat as readily as a large, when both are before him."

" Buchanan," he observed, " has fewer *centos* [80] than any modern Latin poet. He not only had great knowledge of the Latin language, but was a great poetical genius. Both the Scaligers praise him."

He again talked of the passage in Congreve with high commendation, and said, " Shakespeare never has six lines together without a fault. Perhaps you may find seven, but this does not refute my general

79. "When Mr. Foote was at Edinburgh, he thought fit to entertain a numerous Scotch company with a great deal of coarse jocularity, at the expense of Dr. Johnson, imagining it would be acceptable. I felt this as not civil to me; but sat very patiently till he had exhausted his merriment on that subject; and then observed, that surely Johnson must be allowed to have some sterling wit, and that I had heard him say a very good thing of Mr. Foote himself. 'Ah, my old friend Sam,' cried Foote, 'no man says better things: do let us have it.' Upon which I told the above story, which produced a very loud laugh from the company. But I never saw Foote so disconcerted. He looked grave and angry, and entered into a serious refutation of the justice of the remark. 'What, sir,' said he, 'talk thus of a man of liberal education — a man who for years was at the University of Oxford — a man who has added sixteen new characters to the English drama of his country!' " [B]. Samuel Foote (1720-77) was a not very respectable actor and dramatist whose chief skill lay in mimicking his contemporaries. He wrote many farces, based as a rule upon topics of the day. **80. centos:** scraps pieced together from older authors.

78. Giuseppe Baretti, an educated Italian who lived in terms of some intimacy with the London literary circle, and who had been engaged by the Thrales to tutor their children.

assertion. If I come to an orchard, and say there's no fruit here, and then comes a poring man, who finds two apples and three pears, and tells me, ' Sir, you are mistaken, I have found both apples and pears,' I should laugh at him; what would that be to the purpose? "

BOSWELL: " What do you think of Dr. Young's *Night Thoughts*,[81] sir? " JOHNSON: " Why, sir, there are very fine things in them." BOSWELL: " Is there not less religion in the nation now, sir, than there was formerly? " JOHNSON: " I don't know, sir, that there is." BOSWELL: " For instance, there used to be a chaplain in every great family, which we do not find now." JOHNSON: " Neither do you find any of the state servants which great families used formerly to have. There is a change of modes in the whole department of life." . . .

May 7, 1773

He did not give me full credit when I mentioned that I had carried on a short conversation by signs with some Esquimaux, who were then in London, particularly with one of them who was a priest. He thought I could not make them understand me. No man was more incredulous as to particular facts, which were at all extraordinary; and therefore no man was more scrupulously inquisitive, in order to discover the truth.

I dined with him this day at the house of my friends, Messrs. Edward and Charles Dilly, booksellers in the Poultry; there were present their elder brother Mr. Dilly of Bedfordshire, Dr. Goldsmith, Mr. Langton, Mr. Claxton, Rev. Dr. Mayo, a dissenting minister, the Rev. Mr. Toplady,[82] and my friend the Rev. Mr. Temple.

Hawkesworth's compilation of the voyages to the South Sea being mentioned, JOHNSON: " Sir, if you talk of it as a subject of commerce, it will be gainful; if as a book that is to increase human knowledge, I believe there will not be much of that. Hawkesworth can tell only what the voyagers have told him; and they have found very little, only one new animal, I think." BOSWELL: " But many insects, sir." JOHNSON: " Why, sir, as to insects, Ray reckons of British insects twenty thousand species. They might have stayed at home and discovered enough in that way."

Talking of birds, I mentioned Mr. Daines Barrington's [83] ingenious essay against the received notion of their migration. JOHNSON: " I think we have as good evidence for the migration of woodcocks as can be desired. We find they disappear at a certain time of the year, and appear again at a certain time of the year; and some of them, when weary in their flight, have been known to alight on the rigging of ships far out at sea." One of the company observed that there had been instances of some of them found in summer in Essex. JOHNSON: " Sir, that strengthens our argument. *Exceptio probat regulam*.[84] Some being found shows that, if all remained, many would be found. A few sick or lame ones may be found." GOLDSMITH: " There is a partial migration of the swallows; the stronger ones migrate, the others do not."

BOSWELL: " I am well assured that the people of Otaheite,[85] who have the bread tree, the fruit of which serves them for bread, laughed heartily when they were informed of the tedious process necessary with us to have bread — plowing, sowing, harrowing, reaping, threshing, grinding, baking." JOHNSON: " Why, sir, all ignorant savages will laugh when they are told of the advantages of the civilized life. Were you to tell men who live without houses how we pile brick upon brick, and rafter upon rafter, and that after a house is raised to a certain height, a man tumbles off a scaffold, and breaks his neck, [they] would laugh heartily at our folly in building; but it does not follow that men are better without houses. No, sir (holding up a slice of a good loaf), this is better than the bread tree."

He repeated an argument, which is to be found in his *Rambler,* against the notion that the brute creation is endowed with the faculty of reason: " Birds build by instinct; they never improve; they build their first nest as well as any one they ever build." [86] GOLDSMITH: " Yet we see if you take away a bird's nest with the eggs in it, she will make a slighter nest and lay again." JOHNSON: " Sir, that is because at first she has full time and makes her nest deliberately. In the case you mention she is pressed to lay, and must therefore make her nest quickly, and consequently it will be slight." GOLDSMITH: " The nidification [87] of birds is what is least

81. *Night Thoughts:* the best-known work of the poet and playwright, Edward Young. It was gradually enlarged to nine books in blank verse (1742–45) and was enormously popular for more than a century.   82. **Toplady:** the author of the favorite hymn, "Rock of Ages."

83. **Barrington:** amateur naturalist and correspondent of Gilbert White of Selborne, more than half of whose letters in *The Natural History of Selborne* are addressed to him.   84. *Exceptio . . . regulam:* "The exception proves the rule."   85. **Otaheite:** now called Tahiti.   86. *Rambler,* No. 41.   87. **nidification:** nestmaking.

known in natural history, though one of the most curious things in it."

I introduced the subject of toleration. JOHNSON: "Every society has a right to preserve public peace and order, and therefore has a good right to prohibit the propagation of opinions which have a dangerous tendency. To say the *magistrate* has this right, is using an inadequate word: it is the *society* for which the magistrate is agent. He may be morally or theologically wrong in restraining the propagation of opinions which he thinks dangerous, but he is politically right." MAYO: "I am of opinion, sir, that every man is entitled to liberty of conscience in religion, and that the magistrate cannot restrain that right." JOHNSON: "Sir, I agree with you. Every man has a right to liberty of conscience, and with that the magistrate cannot interfere. People confound liberty of thinking with liberty of talking, nay, with liberty of preaching. Every man has a physical right to think as he pleases, for it cannot be discovered how he thinks. He has not a moral right, for he ought to inform himself, and think justly. But, sir, no member of a society has a right to *teach* any doctrine contrary to what the society holds to be true. The magistrate, I say, may be wrong in what he thinks, but, while he thinks himself right, he may and ought to enforce what he thinks." MAYO: "Then, sir, we are to remain always in error, and truth never can prevail, and the magistrate was right in persecuting the first Christians." JOHNSON: "Sir, the only method by which religious truth can be established is by martyrdom. The magistrate has a right to enforce what he thinks, and he who is conscious of the truth has a right to suffer. I am afraid there is no other way of ascertaining the truth, but by persecution on the one hand and enduring it on the other." GOLDSMITH: "But how is a man to act, sir? Though firmly convinced of the truth of his doctrine, may he not think it wrong to expose himself to persecution? Has he a right to do so? Is it not, as it were, committing voluntary suicide?" JOHNSON: "Sir, as to voluntary suicide, as you call it, there are twenty thousand men in an army who will go without scruple to be shot at, and mount a breach for fivepence a day." GOLDSMITH: "But have they a moral right to do this?" JOHNSON: "Nay, sir, if you will not take the universal opinion of mankind, I have nothing to say. If mankind cannot defend their own way of thinking, I cannot defend it. Sir, if a man is in doubt whether it would be better for

him to expose himself to martyrdom or not, he should not do it. He must be convinced that he has a delegation from Heaven." GOLDSMITH: "I would consider whether there is the greater chance of good or evil upon the whole. If I see a man who has fallen into a well, I would wish to help him out, but if there is a greater probability that he shall pull me in, than that I shall pull him out, I would not attempt it. So were I to go to Turkey, I might wish to convert the grand Signor to the Christian faith; but when I considered that I should probably be put to death without effectuating my purpose in any degree, I should keep myself quiet." JOHNSON: "Sir, you must consider that we have perfect and imperfect obligations. Perfect obligations, which are generally not to do something, are clear and positive, as, ' thou shalt not kill.' But charity, for instance, is not definable by limits. It is a duty to give to the poor, but no man can say how much another should give to the poor, or when a man has given too little to save his soul. In the same manner, it is a duty to instruct the ignorant, and of consequence to convert infidels to Christianity, but no man in the common course of things is obliged to carry this to such a degree as to incur the danger of martyrdom, as no man is obliged to strip himself to the shirt in order to give charity. I have said that a man must be persuaded that he has a particular delegation from Heaven." GOLDSMITH: "How is this to be known? Our first reformers, who were burned for not believing bread and wine to be Christ — " JOHNSON (interrupting him): "Sir, they were not burned for not believing bread and wine to be Christ, but for insulting those who did believe it. And, sir, when the first reformers began, they did not intend to be martyred; as many of them ran away as could." BOSWELL: "But, sir, there was your countryman,[88] Elwal, who you told me challenged King George with his black guards, and his red guards." JOHNSON: "My countryman, Elwal, sir, should have been put in the stocks, a proper pulpit for him; and he'd have had a numerous audience. A man who preaches in the stocks will always have hearers enough." BOSWELL: "But Elwal thought himself in the right." JOHNSON: "We are not providing for mad people; there are places for them in the neighborhood" (meaning Moorfields). MAYO: "But, sir, is it not very hard that I should not be allowed to teach my children

---

88. countryman: Elwall came from the same *county* as Johnson.

what I really believe to be the truth? " JOHNSON: "Why, sir, you might contrive to teach your children *extra scandalum,* but, sir, the magistrate, if he knows it, has a right to restrain you. Suppose you teach your children to be thieves? " MAYO: "This is making a joke of the subject." JOHNSON: "Nay, sir, take it thus—that you teach them the community of goods, for which there are as many plausible arguments as for most erroneous doctrines. You teach them that all things at first were in common, and that no man had a right to anything but as he laid his hands upon it; and that this still is, or ought to be, the rule amongst mankind. Here, sir, you sap a great principle in society — property. And don't you think the magistrate would have a right to prevent you? Or suppose you should teach your children the notion of the Adamites, and they should run naked into the streets, would not the magistrate have a right to flog 'em into their doublets? " MAYO: "I think the magistrate has no right to interfere till there is some overt act." BOSWELL: "So, sir, though he sees an enemy to the state charging a blunderbuss, he is not to interfere till it is fired off? " MAYO: "He must be sure of its direction against the state." JOHNSON: "The magistrate is to judge of that. He has no right to restrain your thinking, because the evil centers in yourself. If a man were sitting at this table, and chopping off his fingers, the magistrate, as guardian of the community, has no authority to restrain him, however he might do it from kindness as a parent. Though, indeed, upon more consideration, I think he may, as it is probable that he who is chopping off his own fingers may soon proceed to chop off those of other people. If I think it right to steal Mr. Dilly's plate, I am a bad man, but he can say nothing to me. If I make an open declaration that I think so, he will keep me out of his house. If I put forth my hand, I shall be sent to Newgate. This is the gradation of thinking, preaching, and acting: if a man thinks erroneously, he may keep his thoughts to himself, and nobody will trouble him; if he preaches erroneous doctrine, society may expel him; if he acts in consequence of it, the law takes place, and he is hanged." MAYO: "But, sir, ought not Christians to have liberty of conscience? " JOHNSON: "I have already told you so, sir. You are coming back to where you were." BOSWELL: "Dr. Mayo is always taking a return post chaise, and going the stage over again. He has it at half price." JOHNSON: "Dr. Mayo, like other champions for un-

limited toleration, has got a set of words.[89] Sir, it is no matter, politically, whether the magistrate be right or wrong. Suppose a club were to be formed, to drink confusion to King George III, and a happy restoration to Charles III; this would be very bad with respect to the state, but every member of that club must either conform to its rules, or be turned out of it. Old Baxter, I remember, maintains that the magistrate should 'tolerate all things that are tolerable.' This is no good definition of toleration upon any principle, but it shows that he thought some things were not tolerable." TOPLADY: "Sir, you have untwisted this difficult subject with great dexterity."

During this argument, Goldsmith sat in restless agitation, from a wish to get in and *shine.* Finding himself excluded, he had taken his hat to go away but remained for some time with it in his hand, like a gamester who, at the close of a long night, lingers for a little while, to see if he can have a favorable opening to finish with success. Once when he was beginning to speak, he found himself overpowered by the loud voice of Johnson, who was at the opposite end of the table and did not perceive Goldsmith's attempt. Thus disappointed of his wish to obtain the attention of the company, Goldsmith in a passion threw down his hat, looking angrily at Johnson, and exclaimed in a bitter tone, *"Take it."* When Toplady was going to speak, Johnson uttered some sound, which led Goldsmith to think that he was beginning again, and taking the words from Toplady. Upon which, he seized this opportunity of venting his own envy and spleen, under the pretext of supporting another person: "Sir," said he to Johnson, "the gentleman has heard you patiently for an hour; pray allow us now to hear him." JOHNSON (sternly): "Sir, I was not interrupting the gentleman. I was only giving him a signal of my attention. Sir, you are impertinent." Goldsmith made no reply, but continued in the company for some time.

A gentleman present ventured to ask Dr. Johnson if there was not a material difference as to toleration of opinions which lead to action, and opinions merely speculative; for instance, would it be wrong in the magistrate to tolerate those who

89. "Dr. Mayo's calm temper and steady perseverance rendered him an admirable subject for the exercise of Dr. Johnson's powerful abilities. He never flinched, but after reiterated blows remained seemingly unmoved as at the first. The scintillations of Johnson's genius flashed every time he was struck, without his receiving any injury. Hence he obtained the epithet of 'The Literary Anvil' " [B].

preach against the doctrine of the Trinity? Johnson was highly offended and said, "I wonder, sir, how a gentleman of your piety can introduce this subject in a mixed company." He told me afterwards that the impropriety was that perhaps some of the company might have talked on the subject in such terms as would have shocked him, or he might have been forced to appear in their eyes a narrow-minded man. The gentleman, with submissive deference, said he had only hinted at the question from a desire to hear Dr. Johnson's opinion upon it. JOHNSON: "Why, then, sir, I think that permitting men to preach any opinion contrary to the doctrine of the established church tends, in a certain degree, to lessen the authority of the church, and, consequently, to lessen the influence of religion." "It may be considered," said the gentleman, "whether it would not be politic to tolerate in such a case." JOHNSON: "Sir, we have been talking of *right;* this is another question. *I* think it is *not* politic to tolerate in such a case."

Though he did not think it fit that so awful a subject should be introduced in a mixed company, and therefore at this time waived the theological question, yet his own orthodox belief in the sacred mystery of the Trinity is evinced beyond doubt by the following passage in his private devotions: " O Lord, hear my prayer, for Jesus Christ's sake, to whom with thee and the Holy Ghost, *three persons and one* God, be all honor and glory, world without end, Amen."

BOSWELL: "Pray, Mr. Dilly, how does Dr. Leland's *History of Ireland* sell? " JOHNSON (bursting forth with a generous indignation): "The Irish are in a most unnatural state, for we see there the minority prevailing over the majority. There is no instance, even in the ten persecutions, of such severity as that which the Protestants of Ireland have exercised against the Catholics. Did we tell them we have conquered them, it would be aboveboard; to punish them by confiscation and other penalties, as rebels, was monstrous injustice. King William was not their lawful sovereign; he had not been acknowledged by the parliament of Ireland, when they appeared in arms against him."

I here suggested something favorable of the Roman Catholics. TOPLADY: "Does not their invocation of saints suppose omnipresence in the saints? " JOHNSON: "No, sir, it supposes only pluripresence; and when spirits are divested of matter, it seems probable that they should see with more extent than when in an embodied state. There is, therefore, no approach to an invasion of any of the divine attributes, in the invocation of saints. But I think it is will-worship, and presumption. I see no command for it, and therefore think it is safer not to practice it."

He and Mr. Langton and I went together to the Club, where we found Mr. Burke, Mr. Garrick, and some other members, and amongst them our friend Goldsmith, who sat silently brooding over Johnson's reprimand to him after dinner. Johnson perceived this, and said aside to some of us, "I'll make Goldsmith forgive me," and then called to him in a loud voice, "Dr. Goldsmith — something passed today where you and I dined; I ask your pardon." Goldsmith answered placidly, "It must be much from you, sir, that I take ill." And so at once the difference was over, and they were on as easy terms as ever, and Goldsmith rattled away as usual.

In our way to the club tonight, when I regretted that Goldsmith would, upon every occasion, endeavor to shine, by which he often exposed himself, Mr. Langton observed that he was not like Addison, who was content with the fame of his writings and did not aim also at excellency in conversation, for which he found himself unfit; and that he said to a lady who complained of his having talked little in company, "Madam, I have but ninepence in ready money, but I can draw for a thousand pounds." I observed that Goldsmith had a great deal of gold in his cabinet but, not content with that, was always taking out his purse. JOHNSON: "Yes, sir, and that so often an empty purse! "

Goldsmith's incessant desire of being conspicuous in company was the occasion of his sometimes appearing to such disadvantage as one should hardly have supposed possible in a man of his genius. When his literary reputation had risen deservedly high, and his society was much courted, he became very jealous of the extraordinary attention which was everywhere paid to Johnson. One evening, in a circle of wits, he found fault with me for talking of Johnson as entitled to the honor of unquestionable superiority. "Sir," said he, "you are for making a monarchy of what should be a republic."

He was still more mortified, when talking in a company with fluent vivacity and, as he flattered himself, to the admiration of all who were present; a German who sat next him, and perceived Johnson rolling himself, as if about to speak, suddenly stopped him, saying, "Stay, stay—Toctor Shonson is going to say something." This was, no doubt, very provoking, especially to one so irritable as Goldsmith, who frequently mentioned it with strong expressions of indignation.

It may also be observed, that Goldsmith was sometimes content to be treated with an easy familiarity, but, upon occasions, would be consequential and important. An instance of this occurred in a small particular. Johnson had a way of contracting the names of his friends: as Beauclerk, Beau; Boswell, Bozzy; Langton, Lanky; Murphy, Mur; Sheridan, Sherry. I remember one day, when Tom Davies was telling that Dr. Johnson said, "We are all in labor for a name to *Goldy's* play," Goldsmith seemed displeased that such a liberty should be taken with his name, and said, "I have often desired him not to call me *Goldy.*" Tom was remarkably attentive to the most minute circumstance about Johnson. I recollect his telling me once, on my arrival in London, "Sir, our great friend has made an improvement on his appellation of old Mr. Sheridan. He calls him now *Sherry derry.*"

May, 1776

I am now to record a very curious incident in Dr. Johnson's life, which fell under my own observation; of which *pars magna fui,*[90] and which I am persuaded will, with the liberal-minded, be much to his credit.

My desire of being acquainted with celebrated men of every description had made me, much about the same time, obtain an introduction to Dr. Samuel Johnson and to John Wilkes, Esq. Two men more different could perhaps not be selected out of all mankind. They had even attacked one another with some asperity in their writings; yet I lived in habits of friendship with both. I could fully relish the excellence of each, for I have ever delighted in that intellectual chemistry, which can separate good qualities from evil in the same person.

Sir John Pringle,[91] "mine own friend and my father's friend," between whom and Dr. Johnson I in vain wished to establish an acquaintance, as I respected and lived in intimacy with both of them, observed to me once, very ingeniously, "It is not

in friendship as in mathematics, where two things, each equal to a third, are equal between themselves. You agree with Johnson as a middle quality, and you agree with me as a middle quality; but Johnson and I should not agree." Sir John was not sufficiently flexible, so I desisted, knowing, indeed, that the repulsion was equally strong on the part of Johnson, who, I know not from what cause, unless his being a Scotchman, had formed a very erroneous opinion of Sir John. But I conceived an irresistible wish, if possible, to bring Dr. Johnson and Mr. Wilkes together. How to manage it, was a nice and difficult matter.

My worthy booksellers and friends, Messrs. Dilly in the Poultry, at whose hospitable and well-covered table I have seen a greater number of literary men than at any other, except that of Sir Joshua Reynolds, had invited me to meet Mr. Wilkes and some more gentlemen, on Wednesday, May 15. "Pray," said I, "let us have Dr. Johnson." "What, with Mr. Wilkes? not for the world," said Mr. Edward Dilly. "Dr. Johnson would never forgive me." "Come," said I, "if you'll let me negotiate for you, I will be answerable that all shall go well." DILLY: "Nay, if you will take it upon you, I am sure I shall be very happy to see them both here."

Notwithstanding the high veneration which I entertained for Dr. Johnson, I was sensible that he was sometimes a little actuated by the spirit of contradiction, and by means of that I hoped I should gain my point. I was persuaded that if I had come upon him with a direct proposal, "Sir, will you dine in company with Jack Wilkes?" he would have flown into a passion, and would probably have answered, "Dine with Jack Wilkes, sir! I'd as soon dine with Jack Ketch."[92] I therefore, while we were sitting quietly by ourselves at his house in an evening, took occasion to open my plan thus: "Mr. Dilly, sir, sends his respectful compliments to you, and would be happy if you would do him the honor to dine with him on Wednesday next along with me, as I must soon go to Scotland." JOHNSON: "Sir, I am obliged to Mr. Dilly. I will wait upon him—" BOSWELL: "Provided, sir, I suppose, that the company which he is to have, is agreeable to you." JOHNSON: "What do you mean, sir? What do you take me for? Do you think I am so ignorant of the world, as to imagine that I am to prescribe to a gentleman what company he is

---

90. *pars . . . fui:* i.e., "for which I was mainly responsible."
91. *Pringle:* a friend, also, of Benjamin Franklin, and president of the Royal Society.

92. *Jack Ketch:* generic name for the official executioner. The original Jack Ketch labored in his vocation under Charles II.

to have at his table?" BOSWELL: "I beg your pardon, sir, for wishing to prevent you from meeting people whom you might not like. Perhaps he may have some of what he calls his patriotic friends with him." JOHNSON: "Well, sir, and what then? What care *I* for his *patriotic friends?* Poh!" BOSWELL: "I should not be surprised to find Jack Wilkes there." JOHNSON: "And if Jack Wilkes *should* be there, what is that to *me, sir?* My dear friend, let us have no more of this. I am sorry to be angry with you, but really it is treating me strangely to talk to me as if I could not meet any company whatever, occasionally." BOSWELL: "Pray forgive me, sir; I meant well. But you shall meet whoever comes, for me." Thus I secured him, and told Dilly that he would find him very well pleased to be one of his guests on the day appointed.

Upon the much expected Wednesday, I called on him about half an hour before dinner, as I often did when we were to dine out together, to see that he was ready in time, and to accompany him. I found him buffeting his books, as upon a former occasion, covered with dust, and making no preparation for going abroad. "How is this, sir?" said I. "Don't you recollect that you are to dine at Mr. Dilly's?" JOHNSON: "Sir, I did not think of going to Dilly's; it went out of my head. I have ordered dinner at home with Mrs. Williams." BOSWELL: "But, my dear sir, you know you were engaged to Mr. Dilly, and I told him so. He will expect you, and will be much disappointed if you don't come." JOHNSON: "You must talk to Mrs. Williams about this."

Here was a sad dilemma. I feared that what I was so confident I had secured would yet be frustrated. He had accustomed himself to show Mrs. Williams such a degree of humane attention, as frequently imposed some restraint upon him; and I knew that if she should be obstinate, he would not stir. I hastened downstairs to the blind lady's room, and told her I was in great uneasiness, for Dr. Johnson had engaged to me to dine this day at Mr. Dilly's, but that he had told me he had forgotten his engagement and had ordered dinner at home. "Yes, sir," said she, pretty peevishly, "Dr. Johnson is to dine at home." "Madam," said I, "his respect for you is such, that I know he will not leave you, unless you absolutely desire it. But as you have so much of his company, I hope you will be good enough to forgo it for a day, as Mr. Dilly is a very worthy man, has frequently had

agreeable parties at his house for Dr. Johnson, and will be vexed if the Doctor neglects him today. And then, madam, be pleased to consider my situation: I carried the message, and I assured Mr. Dilly that Dr. Johnson was to come, and no doubt he has made a dinner, and invited a company, and boasted of the honor he expected to have. I shall be quite disgraced if the Doctor is not there." She gradually softened to my solicitations, which were certainly as earnest as most entreaties to ladies upon any occasion, and was graciously pleased to empower me to tell Dr. Johnson "That all things considered, she thought he should certainly go." I flew back to him, still in dust, and careless of what should be the event, "indifferent in his choice to go or stay,"[93] but as soon as I had announced to him Mrs. Williams' consent, he roared, "Frank, a clean shirt," and was very soon dressed. When I had him fairly seated in a hackney coach with me, I exulted as much as a fortune hunter who has got an heiress into a post chaise with him to set out for Gretna Green.

When we entered Mr. Dilly's drawing room, he found himself in the midst of a company he did not know. I kept myself snug and silent, watching how he would conduct himself. I observed him whispering to Mr. Dilly, "Who is that gentleman, sir?" "Mr. Arthur Lee." JOHNSON: "Too, too, too" (under his breath), which was one of his habitual mutterings. Mr. Arthur Lee could not but be very obnoxious to Johnson, for he was not only a *patriot,* but an *American.* He was afterwards minister from the United States at the court of Madrid. "And who is the gentleman in lace?" "Mr. Wilkes, sir." This information confounded him still more; he had some difficulty to restrain himself and, taking up a book, sat down upon a window seat and read, or at least kept his eye upon it intently for some time, till he composed himself. His feelings, I dare say, were awkward enough. But he no doubt recollected his having rated me for supposing that he could be at all disconcerted by any company, and he, therefore, resolutely set himself to behave quite as an easy man of the world, who could adapt himself at once to the disposition and manners of those whom he might chance to meet.

The cheering sound of "Dinner is upon the table" dissolved his reverie, and we *all* sat down without any symptom of ill humor. There were

93. "indifferent ... stay": adapted from Addison's *Cato,* V.i.

present, beside Mr. Wilkes, and Mr. Arthur Lee, who was an old companion of mine when he studied physic at Edinburgh, Mr. (now Sir John) Miller, Dr. Lettsom, and Mr. Slater, the druggist. Mr. Wilkes placed himself next to Dr. Johnson, and behaved to him with so much attention and politeness that he gained upon him insensibly. No man eat more heartily than Johnson, or loved better what was nice and delicate. Mr. Wilkes was very assiduous in helping him to some fine veal. " Pray give me leave, sir — It is better here — A little of the brown — Some fat, sir — A little of the stuffing — Some gravy — Let me have the pleasure of giving you some butter — Allow me to recommend a squeeze of this orange — or the lemon, perhaps, may have more zest." " Sir, sir, I am obliged to you, sir," cried Johnson, bowing and turning his head to him with a look for some time of "'surly virtue " [94] but, in a short while, of complacency.

Foote being mentioned, Johnson said, " He is not a good mimic." One of the company added, " A merry Andrew, a buffoon." JOHNSON: " But he has wit, too, and is not deficient in ideas, or in fertility and variety of imagery, and not empty of reading; he has knowledge enough to fill up his part. One species of wit he has in an eminent degree, that of escape. You drive him into a corner with both hands, but he's gone, sir, when you think you have got him — like an animal that jumps over your head. Then he has a great range for his wit; he never lets truth stand between him and a jest, and he is sometimes mighty coarse. Garrick is under many restraints from which Foote is free." WILKES: " Garrick's wit is more like Lord Chesterfield's." JOHNSON: " The first time I was in company with Foote was at Fitzherbert's. Having no good opinion of the fellow, I was resolved not to be pleased; and it is very difficult to please a man against his will. I went on eating my dinner pretty sullenly, affecting not to mind him. But the dog was so very comical, that I was obliged to lay down my knife and fork, throw myself back upon my chair, and fairly laugh it out. No, sir, he was irresistible. He upon one occasion experienced, in an extraordinary degree, the efficacy of his powers of entertaining. Amongst the many and various modes which he tried of getting money, he became a partner with a small-beer brewer, and he was to have a share of the profits for procuring customers amongst his numerous acquaintance. Fitzherbert was one who

took his small beer, but it was so bad that the servants resolved not to drink it. They were at some loss how to notify their resolution, being afraid of offending their master, who they knew liked Foote much as a companion. At last they fixed upon a little black boy, who was rather a favorite, to be their deputy, and deliver their remonstrance; and having invested him with the whole authority of the kitchen, he was to inform Mr. Fitzherbert, in all their names, upon a certain day, that they would drink Foote's small beer no longer. On that day Foote happened to dine at Fitzherbert's, and this boy served at table; he was so delighted with Foote's stories and merriment and grimace that, when he went downstairs, he told them, ' This is the finest man I have ever seen. I will not deliver your message. I will drink his small beer.' "

Somebody observed that Garrick could not have done this. WILKES: " Garrick would have made the small beer still smaller. He is now leaving the stage, but he will play Scrub [95] all his life." I knew that Johnson would let nobody attack Garrick but himself, as Garrick once said to me, and I had heard him praise his liberality; so to bring out his commendation of his celebrated pupil, I said, loudly, " I have heard Garrick is liberal." JOHNSON: " Yes, sir, I know that Garrick has given away more money than any man in England that I am acquainted with, and that not from ostentatious views. Garrick was very poor when he began life, so when he came to have money, he probably was very unskillful in giving away, and saved when he should not. But Garrick began to be liberal as soon as he could; and I am of opinion, the reputation of avarice which he has had, has been very lucky for him, and prevented his having many enemies. You despise a man for avarice, but do not hate him. Garrick might have been much better attacked for living with more splendor than is suitable to a player; if they had had the wit to have assaulted him in that quarter, they might have galled him more. But they have kept clamoring about his avarice, which has rescued him from much obloquy and envy."

Talking of the great difficulty of obtaining authentic information for biography, Johnson told us, " When I was a young fellow, I wanted to write the life of Dryden, and in order to get materials, I applied to the only two persons then alive who

---

94. "surly virtue": "Johnson's *London, a Poem,* v.145" [B].   95. *Scrub:* a servant in Farquhar's *The Beaux' Stratagem,* III.iii.

had seen him; these were old Swinney,[96] and old Cibber. Swinney's information was no more than this, 'that at Will's Coffeehouse Dryden had a particular chair for himself, which was set by the fire in winter, and was then called his winter chair; and that it was carried out for him to the balcony in summer, and was then called his summer chair.' Cibber could tell no more but 'that he remembered him a decent old man, arbiter of critical disputes at Will's.' You are to consider that Cibber was then at a great distance from Dryden, had perhaps one leg only in the room, and durst not draw in the other." BOSWELL: "Yet Cibber was a man of observation?" JOHNSON: "I think not." BOSWELL: "You will allow his *Apology* to be well done." JOHNSON: "Very well done, to be sure, sir. That book is a striking proof of the justice of Pope's remark:

Each might his several province well command,
Would all but stoop to what they understand.[97]

BOSWELL: "And his plays are good." JOHNSON: "Yes, but that was his trade; *l'esprit du corps*; he had been all his life among players and playwriters. I wondered that he had so little to say in conversation, for he had kept the best company, and learned all that can be got by the ear. He abused Pindar to me, and then showed me an ode of his own, with an absurd couplet, making a linnet soar on an eagle's wing. I told him that when the ancients made a simile, they always made it like something real."

Mr. Wilkes remarked that "among all the bold flights of Shakespeare's imagination, the boldest was making Birnam Wood march to Dunsinane, creating a wood where there never was a shrub; a wood in Scotland! ha! ha! ha!" And he also observed that "the clannish slavery of the Highlands of Scotland was the single exception to Milton's remark of 'The mountain nymph, sweet Liberty,'[98] being worshipped in all hilly countries." "When I was at Inverary," said he, "on a visit to my old friend Archibald, Duke of Argyle, his dependents congratulated me on being such a favorite of his Grace. I said, 'It is then, gentlemen, truly lucky for me; for if I had displeased the Duke,

and he had wished it, there is not a Campbell among you but would have been ready to bring John Wilkes's head to him in a charger. It would have been only

Off with his head! so much for *Aylesbury*.

I was then member for Aylesbury."

Dr. Johnson and Mr. Wilkes talked of the contested passage in Horace's *Art of Poetry*, "*Difficile est proprie communia dicere.*"[99] Mr. Wilkes, according to my note, gave the interpretation thus: "It is difficult to speak with propriety of common things, as, if a poet had to speak of Queen Caroline drinking tea, he must endeavor to avoid the vulgarity of cups and saucers." But upon reading my note, he tells me that he meant to say that "the word *communia*, being a Roman law term, signifies here things *communis juris*, that is to say, what have never yet been treated by anybody, and this appears clearly from what followed:

— *Tuque*
Rectius Iliacum carmen deducis in actus
Quam si proferres ignota indictaque primus.[1]

You will easier make a tragedy out of the *Iliad* than on any subject not handled before." JOHNSON: "He means that it is difficult to appropriate to particular persons qualities which are common to all mankind, as Homer has done."

WILKES: "We have no city poet now; that is an office which has gone into disuse. The last was Elkanah Settle.[2] There is something in *names* which one cannot help feeling. Now *Elkanah Settle* sounds so *queer*, who can expect much from that name? We should have no hesitation to give it for John Dryden, in preference to Elkanah Settle, from the names only, without knowing their different merits. JOHNSON: "I suppose sir, Settle did as well for aldermen in his time as John Home could do now. Where did Beckford and Trecothick learn English?"[3]

Mr. Arthur Lee mentioned some Scotch who had taken possession of a barren part of America, and wondered why they should choose it. JOHNSON:

---

96. Swinney: "Owen McSwinney, who died in 1754, and bequeathed his fortune to Mrs. Woffington, the actress. He had been a Manager of Drury Lane Theater, and afterwards of the Queen's Theater in the Haymarket" (Malone). **97.** Pope, *Essay on Criticism*, I.66-67. See p. 400, above. **98.** 'The ... Liberty': "L'Allegro," l. 36. See p. 212, above.

99. "*Difficile . . . dicere*": *Ars Poetica*, ll. 128 ff. The meaning is still debated. **1.** The passage is thus translated by Fairclough (Loeb Library): "It is hard to treat in your own way what is common; and you are doing better in spinning into acts a song of Troy than if, for the first time, you were giving the world a theme unknown and unsung." **2.** Settle: a contemporary of Dryden's and the object of his satire, as Doeg in *Absalom and Achitophel*. **3. Where . . . English?**: London aldermen, neither remarkable for polished speech. Johnson implies that they learned English in the American colonies.

"Why, sir, all barrenness is comparative. The *Scotch* would not know it to be barren." BOSWELL: "Come, come, he is flattering the English. You have now been in Scotland, sir, and say if you did not see meat and drink enough there." JOHNSON: "Why, yes, sir, meat and drink enough to give the inhabitants sufficient strength to run away from home." All these quick and lively sallies were said sportively, quite in jest, and with a smile, which showed that he meant only wit. Upon this topic he and Mr. Wilkes could perfectly assimilate; here was a bond of union between them, and I was conscious that, as both of them had visited Caledonia, both were fully satisfied of the strange narrow ignorance of those who imagine that it is a land of famine. But they amused themselves with persevering in the old jokes. When I claimed a superiority for Scotland over England in one respect, that no man can be arrested there for a debt merely because another swears it against him, but there must first be the judgment of a court of law ascertaining its justice; and that a seizure of the person, before judgment is obtained, can take place only if his creditor should swear that he is about to fly from the country or, as it is technically expressed, is *in meditatione fugae.* WILKES: "That, I should think, may be safely sworn of all the Scotch nation." JOHNSON (to Mr. Wilkes): "You must know, sir, I lately took my friend Boswell, and showed him genuine civilized life in an English provincial town. I turned him loose at Lichfield, my native city, that he might see for once real civility, for you know he lives among savages in Scotland, and among rakes in London." WILKES: "Except when he is with grave, sober, decent people, like you and me." JOHNSON (smiling): "And we ashamed of him."

They were quite frank and easy. Johnson told the story of his asking Mrs. Macaulay [4] to allow her footman to sit down with them, to prove the ridiculousness of the arguments for the equality of mankind; and he said to me afterwards, with a nod of satisfaction, "You saw Mr. Wilkes acquiesced." Wilkes talked with all imaginable freedom of the ludicrous title given to the Attorney General, *Diabolus Regis,*[5] adding, "I have reason to know something about that officer, for I was prosecuted for a libel."[6] Johnson, who many peo-

ple would have supposed must have been furiously angry at hearing this talked of so lightly, said not a word. He was now, *indeed,* "a good-humored fellow."[7]

After dinner we had an accession of Mrs. Knowles, the Quaker lady, well known for her various talents, and of Mr. Alderman Lee. Amidst some patriotic groans, somebody (I think the alderman) said, "Poor old England is lost." JOHNSON: "Sir, it is not so much to be lamented that old England is lost, as that the Scotch have found it." WILKES: "Had Lord Bute governed Scotland only, I should not have taken the trouble to write his eulogy, and dedicate *Mortimer* to him."[8]

Mr. Wilkes held a candle to show a fine print of a beautiful female figure which hung in the room, and pointed out the elegant contour of the bosom with the finger of an arch connoisseur. He afterwards in a conversation with me waggishly insisted that all the time Johnson showed visible signs of a fervent admiration of the corresponding charms of the fair Quaker.

This record, though by no means so perfect as I could wish, will serve to give a notion of a very curious interview, which was not only pleasing at the time, but had the agreeable and benignant effect of reconciling any animosity, and sweetening any acidity which, in the various bustle of political contest, had been produced in the minds of two men, who, though widely different, had so many things in common — classical learning, modern literature, wit, and humor, and ready repartee — that it would have been much to be regretted if they had been forever at a distance from each other.

Mr. Burke gave me much credit for this successful *negotiation,* and pleasantly said, that "there was nothing equal to it in the whole history of the *Corps Diplomatique."*

I attended Dr. Johnson home, and had the satisfaction to hear him tell Mrs. Williams how much he had been pleased with Mr. Wilkes's company, and what an agreeable day he had passed.

---

4. Mrs. Macaulay: See n. 37, p. 469. 5. *Diabolus Regis:* i.e., the King's Devil, with a latent reference to *Advocatus Diaboli,* the Devil's Advocate. 6. libel: Wilkes is referring to the most notorious episode of his career, the protracted legal actions against

him, instigated by the Crown, consequent upon his forty-fifth number of the *North Briton.* See n. 7, p. 455. 7. good-humored fellow: When Johnson had once called himself so in a conversation with Boswell, the latter objected, saying that he was good-natured rather than good-humored. 8. This play, *The Fall of Mortimer,* was an old play republished in 1763 at Wilkes's instigation as a political weapon against the prime minister, Lord Bute, a Scot. There was an implied analogy between the relationship of Bute to George III (and his mother) and of Roger Mortimer to Edward III (and Queen Isabella, his mother).

I talked a good deal to him of the celebrated Margaret Caroline Rudd,[9] whom I had visited, induced by the fame of her talents, address, and irresistible power of fascination. To a lady who disapproved of my visiting her, he said on a former occasion, "Nay, madam, Boswell is in the right; I should have visited her myself, were it not that they have now a trick of putting everything into the newspapers." This evening he exclaimed, "I envy him his acquaintance with Mrs. Rudd."

I mentioned a scheme which I had of making a tour to the Isle of Man, and giving a full account of it, and that Mr. Burke had playfully suggested as a motto,

The proper study of mankind is Man.[10]

JOHNSON: "Sir, you will get more by the book than the jaunt will cost you; so you will have your diversion for nothing, and add to your reputation."

On the evening of the next day I took leave of him, being to set out for Scotland. I thanked him with great warmth for all his kindness. "Sir," said he, "you are very welcome. Nobody repays it with more."

How very false is the notion that has gone round the world of the rough and passionate and harsh manners of this great and good man. That he had occasional sallies of heat of temper, and that he was sometimes, perhaps, "too easily provoked" by absurdity and folly, and sometimes too desirous of triumph in colloquial contest, must be allowed. The quickness both of his perception and sensibility disposed him to sudden explosions of satire, to which his extraordinary readiness of wit was a strong and almost irresistible incitement. To adopt one of the finest images in Mr. Home's *Douglas,*

On each glance of thought
Decision followed, as the thunderbolt
Pursues the flash!

I admit that the beadle within him was often so eager to apply the lash that the judge had not time to consider the case with sufficient deliberation.

That he was occasionally remarkable for violence of temper may be granted, but let us ascertain the degree, and not let it be supposed that he was in a perpetual rage, and never without a club in his hand to knock down everyone who approached him. On the contrary, the truth is, that by much the greatest part of his time he was civil, obliging, nay, polite in the true sense of the word; so much so that many gentlemen who were long acquainted with him never received, or even heard a strong expression from him.

SAMUEL JOHNSON

LETTERS

Johnson's personal relations with his correspondents always determine the content and character of his letters. He is not one of those who cultivate the epistolary art for its own sake, or with a view to a posthumous collection. Nevertheless, his letters contain some of his most characteristic and even moving writing. The celebrated letter to Lord Chesterfield has brought him more credit than perhaps the circumstances of its composition entitle him to, although judged as one would judge a work of art it can never be too much admired. The known facts are that he made an insincere gesture (as he himself admitted to Boswell) by addressing his Proposals for the Dictionary to Lord Chesterfield; was accorded as much initial encouragement as a relatively unknown petitioner for financial support has a right to expect from a man often thus approached; was possibly treated rather like one of a number of patients in a doctor's waiting room, on some subsequent visit, and thereafter waited aloof and haughtily for the patron to exchange roles and seek him in turn; and finally chose to resent Chesterfield's not unfriendly, if too flippant, advance press notices in his behalf. If Chesterfield's two papers in the *World* were an indirect bid for a dedication, we may at least acknowledge that they were not a belated money bribe, and that Johnson had already as much as publicly signified his intention, seven years earlier, to dedicate the work to Chesterfield; and perhaps an uneasy consciousness that he would not be fulfilling a tacit commitment drove him into self-justification. All this does not derogate from the proud dignity of the letter, which was indubitably sincere and deeply felt.

The letter to Mrs. Montagu shows Johnson outdoing

9. **Margaret . . . Rudd:** Mrs. Rudd was tried for forgery, and acquitted, while her two companions, the brothers Perreau, were convicted and hanged. Boswell made himself very agreeable to her. 10. Pope, *Essay on Man,* II.2. See p. 422, above.

Chesterfield in courtliness, in a generous cause. The letter to Mrs. Boswell was written four years after Johnson had first offended that lady by holding her tapers upside down to make a brighter light, while the wax dripped onto her rugs. Her reservations about him were due not only to the Doctor's uncouthness but also to the fact that he encouraged her husband's passion for London, where, as she well knew, wasting time was but the most innocent of Boswell's self-indulgences. The letters to Mrs. Thrale, in their variety of mood, reveal some phases of a relationship which, after that with his wife, meant more to Johnson than any other. For twenty years he was treated like a member of the Thrale family; but when the letter of 1783 was written, Henry Thrale had died and Mrs. Thrale had signified her desire to marry an Italian musician, Gabriele Piozzi, a connection that Johnson joined with the rest of the world in disapproving. This caused an irreparable breach between the two friends.

The letter to Macpherson was a consequence of that author's efforts to cow Johnson into suppressing or retracting his expressions of disbelief in the antiquity of the poems of Ossian. Macpherson first tried to bring pressure through Johnson's publisher, to make him cancel a passage on Ossian in the *Journey to the Western Islands*. Next, he had the form of an apology brought to Johnson, which the latter was to publish. Thereafter, Macpherson seems to have threatened to administer a beating, and perhaps even challenged him to a duel. The story goes that after this exchange Johnson went abroad armed with a stout oak staff that had a head as big as a grapefruit.

I. To THE RIGHT HONORABLE THE EARL OF CHESTERFIELD

February 7, 1755.

My Lord:

I have been lately informed, by the proprietor of the *World*,[1] that two papers, in which my Dictionary is recommended to the public, were written by your lordship. To be so distinguished is an honor which, being very little accustomed to favors from the great, I know not well how to receive, or in what terms to acknowledge.

When, upon some slight encouragement, I first visited your lordship, I was overpowered, like the rest of mankind, by the enchantment of your address; and could not forbear to wish that I might boast myself *le vainqueur du vainqueur de la terre;*[2] — that I might obtain that regard for which I saw the world contending; but I found my attendance so little encouraged, that neither

pride nor modesty would suffer me to continue it. When I had once addressed your lordship in public, I had exhausted all the art of pleasing which a retired and uncourtly scholar can possess. I had done all that I could; and no man is well pleased to have his all neglected, be it ever so little.

Seven years, my Lord, have now passed, since I waited in your outward rooms, or was repulsed from your door, during which time I have been pushing on my work through difficulties of which it is useless to complain, and have brought it, at last, to the verge of publication, without one act of assistance, one word of encouragement, or one smile of favor. Such treatment I did not expect, for I never had a patron before.

The shepherd in Virgil grew at last acquainted with Love, and found him a native of the rocks.[3]

Is not a patron, my Lord, one who looks with unconcern on a man struggling for life in the water, and, when he has reached ground, encumbers him with help? The notice which you have been pleased to take of my labors, had it been early, had it been kind; but it has been delayed till I am indifferent, and cannot enjoy it; till I am solitary, and cannot impart it; till I am known, and do not want it. I hope it is no very cynical asperity not to confess obligations where no benefit has been received, or to be unwilling that the public should consider me as owing that to a patron, which Providence has enabled me to do for myself.

Having carried on my work thus far with so little obligation to any favorer of learning, I shall not be disappointed though I should conclude it, if less be possible, with less; for I have been long wakened from that dream of hope, in which I once boasted myself with so much exultation, my Lord,

your lordship's most humble,
most obedient servant,

Sam: Johnson.

II. To MRS. MONTAGU [4]

Gray's Inn, Dec. 17, 1759.

Madam:

Goodness so conspicuous as yours will be often solicited, and perhaps sometimes solicited by those who have little pretension to your favor. It is now

---

LETTERS. **1. *World:*** a paper in the tradition established by Addison and Steele. It ran between the years 1753 and 1756. Chesterfield's essays in this periodical were Nos. 100 and 101. **2. *le . . . terre:*** "the conqueror of the conqueror of the earth."

3. The . . . rocks: The reference is to *Eclogue,* I.43 ff. **4.** Elizabeth Montagu (1720–1800), a wealthy widow, authoress, and Queen of the Bluestockings. See *Life,* n. 69, p. 477.

my turn to introduce a petitioner, but such as I have reason to believe you will think worthy of your notice. Mrs. Ogle, who kept the music room in Soho Square, a woman who struggles with great industry for the support of eight children, hopes by a benefit concert to set herself free from a few debts, which she cannot otherwise discharge. She has, I know not why, so high an opinion of me as to believe that you will pay less regard to her application than to mine. You know, madam, I am sure you know, how hard it is to deny, and therefore would not wonder at my compliance, though I were to suppress a motive which you know not, the vanity of being supposed to be of any importance to Mrs. Montagu. But though I may be willing to see the world deceived for my advantage, I am not deceived myself, for I know that Mrs. Ogle will owe whatever favors she shall receive from the patronage which we humbly entreat on this occasion, much more to your compassion for honesty in distress, than to the request of,

> Madam,
>   Your most obedient and most humble
>   servant,
>   Sam: Johnson.

III. To JAMES MACPHERSON [5]

Mr. James Macpherson —

I received your foolish and impudent note. Whatever insult is offered me I will do my best to repel, and what I cannot do for myself, the law will do for me. I will not desist from detecting what I think a cheat, from any fear of the menaces of a ruffian.

You want me to retract. What shall I retract? I thought your book an imposture from the beginning. I think it upon yet surer reasons an imposture still. For this opinion I give the public my reasons which I here dare you to refute.

But however I may despise you, I reverence truth, and if you can prove the genuineness of the work I will confess it. Your rage I defy, your abilities since your Homer [6] are not so formidable, and what I have heard of your morals disposes me to

pay regard not to what you shall say, but to what you can prove.

You may print this if you will.

> Sam: Johnson.

Jan. 20, 1775

IV. To MRS. BOSWELL [7]

Madam:

Though I am well enough pleased with the taste of sweetmeats, very little of the pleasure which I received at the arrival of your jar of marmalade arose from eating it. I received it as a token of friendship, as a proof of reconciliation, things much sweeter than sweetmeats, and upon this consideration I return you, dear madam, my sincerest thanks. By having your kindness I think I have a double security for the continuance of Mr. Boswell's, which it is not to be expected that any man can long keep when the influence of a lady so highly and so justly valued operates against him. Mr. Boswell will tell you that I was always faithful to your interest, and always endeavored to exalt you in his estimation. You must now do the same for me. We must all help one another, and you must now consider me, as

> Dear madam, your most obliged,
>   and most humble servant,
>   Sam: Johnson.

July 22, 1777.

V. To MRS. THRALE
Ashbourne, October 6, 1777.

Dear Madam:

You are glad that I am absent; and I am glad that you are sick.[8] When you went away, what did you do with your aunt? I am glad she liked my Susy; I was always a Susy, when nobody else was a Susy. How have you managed at your new place? Could you all get lodgings in one house, and meat at one table? Let me hear the whole series of misery; for, as Dr. Young says, *I love horror.*[9]

7. Mrs. Boswell: see headnote, above.   **8. sick:** Johnson, after nearly fifteen years of intimacy, was virtually a member of the Thrale household. He was now visiting his lifelong friend, Dr. John Taylor, in Derbyshire. The Thrales were at the seaside, in Brighton. Mrs Thrale was expecting another child, and hoping for a son. Susy was a younger daughter toward whom Johnson was partial.   **9. I ... horror:** Edward Young's *The Revenge* (1721) opens on this note.

5. Macpherson: For Macpherson (1736–96), see headnote, above.   **6. Homer:** Macpherson published a prose translation of the *Iliad* in 1773.

Methinks you are now a great way off; and if I come, I have a great way to come to you; and then the sea is so cold, and the rooms are so dull; yet I do love to hear the sea roar and my mistress talk — For when she talks, ye gods! how she will talk.[10] I wish I were with you, but we are now near half the length of England asunder. It is frightful to think how much time must pass between writing this letter and receiving an answer, if any answer were necessary.

Taylor[11] is now going to have a ram; and then, after Aries and Taurus, we shall have Gemini. His oats are now in the wet; here is a deal of rain. Mr. Langdon bought, at Nottingham Fair, fifteen tun of cheese, which, at an ounce apiece, will suffice after dinner for four hundred and eighty thousand men. This is all the news that the place affords. I purpose soon to be at Lichfield, but know not just when, having been defeated of my first design. When I come to town, I am to be very busy about my *Lives*.[12] — Could not you do some of them for me?

I am glad Master huspelled you, and run you all on rucks,[13] and drove you about, and made you stir. Never be cross about it. Quiet and calmness you have enough of — a little hurry stirs life — and

Brushing o'er, adds motion to the pool.[14]

Now *pool* brings my master's excavations into my head. I wonder how I shall like them; I should like not to see them, till we all see them together. He will have no waterfall to roar like the Doctor's. I sat by it yesterday, and read Erasmus' *Militis Christiani Enchiridion*.[15] Have you got that book?

Make my compliments to dear Queeney.[16] I suppose she will dance at the Rooms, and your heart will go one knows not how.

I am, dearest, and dearest lady,
Your most humble servant,
Sam: Johnson.

10. For . . . talk: Johnson playfully called Henry Thrale his "Master" and Mrs. Thrale his "Mistress." He is here quoting Nathaniel Lee's *The Rival Queens*, I.i.375.   11. Taylor: Dr. Taylor spent much time and money on fine livestock. He owned a prize bull, and Johnson is amusing himself with astronomical analogies.   12. my *Lives*: He means, with the writing of his biographical prefaces later known as *Lives of the Poets*, published 1779–81.   13. huspelled . . . rucks: that is, "shook you up and jolted you into ruts (or ditches)."   14. Quoted from Dryden's *Cymon and Iphigenia*, l. 30.   15. *Militis . . . Enchiridion*: i.e., *The Christian Soldier's Handbook*.   16. Queeney: the Thrales' eldest daughter, just being introduced to society at Brighton and Bath.

VI. To MRS. THRALE

Bolt Court, Fleet Street,
June 19, 1783.

Dear Madam:

I am sitting down in no cheerful solitude to write a narrative which would once[17] have affected you with tenderness and sorrow, but which you will perhaps pass over now with the careless glance of frigid indifference. For this diminution of regard, however, I know not whether I ought to blame you, who may have reasons which I cannot know, and I do not blame myself, who have for a great part of human life done you what good I could, and have never done you evil.

I had been disordered in the usual way, and had been relieved by the usual methods, by opium and cathartics, but had rather lessened my dose of opium.

On Monday the 16th I sat for my picture, and walked a considerable way with little inconvenience. In the afternoon and evening I felt myself light and easy, and began to plan schemes of life. Thus I went to bed, and in a short time waked and sat up, as has been long my custom, when I felt a confusion and indistinctness in my head, which lasted, I suppose, about half a minute. I was alarmed, and prayed God that, however he might afflict my body, he would spare my understanding. This prayer, that I might try the integrity of my faculties, I made in Latin verse. The lines were not very good, but I knew them not to be very good; I made them easily, and concluded myself to be unimpaired in my faculties.

Soon after, I perceived that I had suffered a paralytic stroke, and that my speech was taken from me. I had no pain, and so little dejection in this dreadful state, that I wondered at my own apathy, and considered that perhaps death itself when it should come would excite less horror than seems now to attend it.

In order to rouse the vocal organs I took two drams. Wine has been celebrated for the production of eloquence. I put myself into violent motion, and I think repeated it; but all was vain. I then went to bed, and, strange as it may seem, I think, slept. When I saw light, it was time to contrive what I should do. Though God stopped my speech, he left me my hand. I enjoyed a mercy which was not

17. once: Henry Thrale had died, and a rift had opened between Mrs. Thrale and Johnson on account of her desire to remarry. See headnote, p. 490, above.

granted to my dear friend Lawrence,[18] who now perhaps overlooks me as I am writing, and rejoices that I have what he wanted. My first note was necessarily to my servant, who came in talking, and could not immediately comprehend why he should read what I put into his hands.

I then wrote a card to Mr. Allen,[19] that I might have a discreet friend at hand to act as occasion should require. In penning this note I had some difficulty: my hand, I knew not how nor why, made wrong letters. I then wrote to Dr. Taylor to come to me, and bring Dr. Heberden, and I sent to Dr. Brocklesby, who is my neighbor. My physicians are very friendly and very disinterested, and give me great hopes, but you may imagine my situation. I have so far recovered my vocal powers, as to repeat the Lord's Prayer with no very imperfect articulation. My memory, I hope, yet remains as it was, but such an attack produces solicitude for the safety of every faculty.

How this will be received by you I know not. I hope you will sympathize with me; but perhaps

My mistress gracious, mild, and good,
Cries, " Is he dumb? 'Tis time he should." [20]

But can this be possible? I hope it cannot. I hope that what, when I could speak, I spoke of you, and to you, will be in a sober and serious hour remembered by you; and surely it cannot be remembered but with some degree of kindness. I have loved you with virtuous affection; I have honored you with sincere esteem. Let not all our endearment be forgotten, but let me have in this great distress your pity and your prayers. You see I yet turn to you with my complaints as a settled and unalienable friend; do not, do not drive me from you, for I have not deserved either neglect or hatred.

To the girls, who do not write often, for Susy has written only once, and Miss Thrale owes me a letter, I earnestly recommend, as their guardian and friend, that they remember their Creator in the days of their youth.

I suppose you may wish to know how my disease is treated by the physicians. They put a blister upon my back, and two from my ear to my throat, one on a side. The blister on the back has done little, and those on the throat have not risen. I bullied

and bounced (it sticks to our last sand) [21] and compelled the apothecary to make his salve according to the Edinburgh Dispensatory, that it might adhere better. I have two on now of my own prescription. They likewise give me salt of hartshorn, which I take with no great confidence, but am satisfied that what can be done is done for me.

O God! give me comfort and confidence in Thee; forgive my sins; and if it be Thy good pleasure, relieve my diseases for Jesus Christ's sake. Amen.

I am almost ashamed of this querulous letter, but now it is written, let it go.

I am, Madam,
Your most humble servant,
Sam: Johnson.

The RAMBLER

The *Rambler* appeared on Tuesdays and Saturdays, from March 20, 1750, to March 14, 1752. Of the 208 numbers, Johnson wrote all but four. These periodical essays, following in the tradition of the *Spectator* papers, cover a considerable range of topics, literary and moral, and everywhere bear the seal of Johnson's somber and penetrating observation of human motivation and conduct. Their eloquence reflects the attention that the author at this time was devoting to the uses of words: he was midway in the compilation of the Dictionary, and probably nowhere else is his language so especially "Johnsonian" as in these essays.

No. 25. Tuesday, June 12, 1750

Possunt quia posse videntur.
(Virgil [*Aeneid*, V.231])

[For they can conquer who believe they can.]
(Dryden)

There are some vices and errors which, though often fatal to those in whom they are found, have yet, by the universal consent of mankind, been considered as entitled to some degree of respect, or have, at least, been exempted from contemptuous infamy, and condemned by the severest moralists with pity rather than detestation.

A constant and invariable example of this general partiality will be found in the different regard which has always been shown to rashness and cowardice, two vices, of which, though they may be conceived equally distant from the middle point

---

18. **Lawrence:** Johnson's physician for many years; he had just died. 19. **Mr. Allen:** Edmund Allen, printer, a friend and neighbor of Johnson's. 20. The quotation is adapted from Swift's "Verses on the Death of Dr. Swift," ll. 181–82.

21. **it . . . sand:** quoted from Pope, *Moral Essays*, I.225.

where true fortitude is placed, and may equally injure any public or private interest, yet the one is never mentioned without some kind of veneration, and the other always considered as a topic of unlimited and licentious censure, on which all the virulence of reproach may be lawfully exerted.

The same distinction is made, by the common suffrage, between profusion and avarice, and, perhaps, between many other opposite vices; and, as I have found reason to pay great regard to the voice of the people, in cases where knowledge has been forced upon them by experience, without long deductions or deep researches, I am inclined to believe that this distribution of respect is not without some agreement with the nature of things, and that in the faults which are thus invested with extraordinary privileges there are generally some latent principles of merit, some possibilities of future virtue, which may, by degrees, break from obstruction, and by time and opportunity be brought into act.

It may be laid down as an axiom, that it is more easy to take away superfluities than to supply defects, and, therefore, he that is culpable, because he has passed the middle point of virtue, is always accounted a fairer object of hope, than he who fails by falling short. The one has all that perfection requires, and more, but the excess may be easily retrenched; the other wants the qualities requisite to excellence, and who can tell how he shall obtain them? We are certain that the horse may be taught to keep pace with his fellows, whose fault is that he leaves them behind. We know that a few strokes of the axe will lop a cedar; but what arts of cultivation can elevate a shrub?

To walk with circumspection and steadiness in the right path, at an equal distance between the extremes of error, ought to be the constant endeavor of every reasonable being; nor can I think those teachers of moral wisdom much to be honored as benefactors to mankind, who are always enlarging upon the difficulty of our duties, and providing rather excuses for vice, than incentives to virtue.

But, since to most it will happen often, and to all sometimes, that there will be a deviation towards one side or the other, we ought always to employ our vigilance with most attention on that enemy from which there is greatest danger, and to stray, if we must stray, towards those parts from whence we may quickly and easily return.

Among other opposite qualities of the mind which may become dangerous, though in different degrees, I have often had occasion to consider the contrary effects of presumption and despondency; of heady confidence, which promises victory without contest, and heartless pusillanimity, which shrinks back from the thought of great undertakings, confounds difficulty with impossibility, and considers all advancement towards any new attainment as irreversibly prohibited.

Presumption will be easily corrected. Every experiment will teach caution, and miscarriages will hourly show that attempts are not always rewarded with success. The most precipitate ardor will in time be taught the necessity of methodical gradation and preparatory measures; and the most daring confidence be convinced that neither merit nor abilities can command events.

It is the advantage of vehemence and activity, that they are always hastening to their own reformation, because they incite us to try whether our expectations are well grounded, and therefore detect the deceits which they are apt to occasion. But timidity is a disease of the mind more obstinate and fatal; for a man once persuaded that any impediment is insuperable has given it, with respect to himself, that strength and weight which it had not before. He can scarcely strive with vigor and perseverance, when he has no hope of gaining the victory; and, since he never will try his strength, can never discover the unreasonableness of his fears.

There is often to be found in men devoted to literature a kind of intellectual cowardice, which whoever converses much among them may observe frequently to depress the alacrity of enterprise, and, by consequence, to retard the improvement of science. They have annexed to every species of knowledge some chimerical character of terror and inhibition, which they transmit, without much reflection, from one to another; they first fright themselves and then propagate the panic to their scholars and acquaintance. One study is inconsistent with a lively imagination, another with a solid judgment; one is improper in the early parts of life, another requires so much time that it is not to be attempted at an advanced age; one is dry and contracts the sentiments, another is diffuse and overburdens the memory; one is insufferable to taste and delicacy, and another wears out life in the study of words, and is useless to a wise man, who desires only the knowledge of things.

But of all the bugbears by which the *Infantes*

barbati,[1] boys both young and old, have been hitherto frighted from digressing into new tracts of learning, none has been more mischievously efficacious than an opinion that every kind of knowledge requires a peculiar genius, or mental constitution, framed for the reception of some ideas and the exclusion of others; and that to him whose genius is not adapted to the study which he prosecutes, all labor shall be vain and fruitless, vain as an endeavor to mingle oil and water or, in the language of chemistry, to amalgamate bodies of heterogeneous principles.

This opinion we may reasonably suspect to have been propagated, by vanity, beyond the truth. It is natural for those who have raised a reputation by any science, to exalt themselves as endowed by Heaven with peculiar powers, or marked out by an extraordinary designation for their profession; and to fright competitors away by representing the difficulties with which they must contend, and the necessity of qualities which are supposed to be not generally conferred, and which no man can know, but by experience, whether he enjoys.

To this discouragement it may be possibly answered that since a genius, whatever it be, is like fire in the flint, only to be produced by collision with a proper subject, it is the business of every man to try whether his faculties may not happily co-operate with his desires; and since they whose proficiency he admires knew their own force only by the event, he needs but engage in the same undertaking with equal spirit, and may reasonably hope for equal success.

There is another species of false intelligence, given by those who profess to show the way to the summit of knowledge, of equal tendency to depress the mind with false distrust of itself, and weaken it by needless solicitude and dejection. When a scholar whom they desire to animate consults them at his entrance on some new study, it is common to make flattering representations of its pleasantness and facility. Thus they generally attain one of two ends almost equally desirable: they either incite his industry by elevating his hopes, or produce a high opinion of their own abilities, since they are supposed to relate only what they have found, and to have proceeded with no less ease than they promise to their followers.

The student, inflamed by this encouragement, sets forward in the new path, and proceeds a few

RAMBLER. 1. *Infantes barbati:* "bearded children."

steps with great alacrity, but he soon finds asperities and intricacies of which he has not been forewarned, and, imagining that none ever were so entangled or fatigued before him, sinks suddenly into despair, and desists as from an expedition in which fate opposes him. Thus his terrors are multiplied by his hopes, and he is defeated without resistance, because he had no expectation of an enemy.

Of these treacherous instructors, the one destroys industry, by declaring that industry is vain, the other by representing it as needless; the one cuts away the root of hope, the other raises it only to be blasted. The one confines his pupil to the shore by telling him that his wreck is certain; the other sends him to sea without preparing him for tempests.

False hopes and false terrors are equally to be avoided. Every man who proposes to grow eminent by learning should carry in his mind at once the difficulty of excellence and the force of industry, and remember that fame is not conferred but as the recompense of labor, and that labor, vigorously continued, has not often failed of its reward.

No. 155. Tuesday, September 10, 1751

Steriles transmisimus annos,
Haec aevi mihi prima dies, haec limina vitae.
(Statius [*Thebaid*, I.362])

[Our barren years are past;
Be this of life the first, of sloth the last.]
(Elphinston)

No weakness of the human mind has more frequently incurred animadversion than the negligence with which men overlook their own faults, however flagrant, and the easiness with which they pardon them, however frequently repeated.

It seems generally believed that, as the eye cannot see itself, the mind has no faculties by which it can contemplate its own state, and that therefore we have not means of becoming acquainted with our real characters; an opinion which, like innumerable other postulates, an inquirer finds himself inclined to admit upon very little evidence, because it affords a ready solution of many difficulties. It will explain why the greatest abilities frequently fail to promote the happiness of those who possess them; why those who can distinguish with the utmost nicety the boundaries of vice and virtue, suffer them to be confounded in their own conduct; why the active and vigilant resign their affairs implicitly to the management of others; and why the cautious and fearful make hourly approaches towards ruin, without one sigh of solicitude or struggle for escape.

When a position teems thus with commodious consequences, who can without regret confess it to be false? Yet it is certain that declaimers have indulged a disposition to describe the dominion of the passions as extended beyond the limits that nature assigned. Self-love is often rather arrogant than blind; it does not hide our faults from ourselves, but persuades us that they escape the notice of others, and disposes us to resent censures lest we should confess them to be just. We are secretly conscious of defects and vices which we hope to conceal from the public eye, and please ourselves with innumerable impostures by which, in reality, nobody is deceived.

In proof of the dimness of our internal sight, or the general inability of man to determine rightly concerning his own character, it is common to urge the success of the most absurd and incredible flattery, and the resentment always raised by advice, however soft, benevolent, and reasonable. But flattery, if its operation be nearly examined, will be found to owe its acceptance not to our ignorance but knowledge of our failures, and to delight us rather as it consoles our wants than displays our possessions. He that shall solicit the favor of his patron by praising him for qualities which he can find in himself will be defeated by the more daring panegyrist who enriches him with adscititious [2] excellence. Just praise is only a debt, but flattery is a present. The acknowledgment of those virtues on which conscience congratulates us is a tribute that we can at any time exact with confidence, but the celebration of those which we only feign, or desire without any vigorous endeavors to attain them, is received as a confession of sovereignty over regions never conquered, as a favorable decision of disputable claims, and is more welcome as it is more gratuitous.

Advice is offensive, not because it lays us open to unexpected regret, or convicts us of any fault which had escaped our notice, but because it shows us that we are known to others as well as to ourselves; and the officious monitor is persecuted with hatred, not because his accusation is false, but because he assumes that superiority which we are not willing

2. **adscititious:** adopted from without.

to grant him, and has dared to detect what we desired to conceal.

For this reason advice is commonly ineffectual. If those who follow the call of their desires, without inquiry whither they are going, had deviated ignorantly from the paths of wisdom and were rushing upon dangers unforeseen, they would readily listen to information that recalls them from their errors, and catch the first alarm by which destruction or infamy is denounced. Few that wander in the wrong way mistake it for the right; they only find it more smooth and flowery, and indulge their own choice rather than approve it; therefore few are persuaded to quit it by admonition or reproof, since it impresses no new conviction, nor confers any powers of action or resistance. He that is gravely informed how soon profusion will annihilate his fortune hears with little advantage what he knew before, and catches at the next occasion of expense, because advice has no force to suppress his vanity. He that is told how certainly intemperance will hurry him to the grave runs with his usual speed to a new course of luxury, because his reason is not invigorated, nor his appetite weakened.

The mischief of flattery is, not that it persuades any man that he is what he is not, but that it suppresses the influence of honest ambition, by raising an opinion that honor may be gained without the toil of merit; and the benefit of advice arises commonly, not from any new light imparted to the mind, but from the discovery which it affords of the public suffrages. He that could withstand conscience is frighted at infamy, and shame prevails when reason was defeated.

As we all know our own faults, and know them commonly with many aggravations which human perspicacity cannot discover, there is, perhaps, no man, however hardened by impudence or dissipated by levity, sheltered by hypocrisy, or blasted by disgrace, who does not intend some time to review his conduct, and to regulate the remainder of his life by the laws of virtue. New temptations indeed attack him, new invitations are offered by pleasure and interest, and the hour of reformation is always delayed; every delay gives vice another opportunity of fortifying itself by habit; and the change of manners, though sincerely intended and rationally planned, is referred to the time when some craving passion shall be fully gratified, or some powerful allurement cease its importunity.

Thus procrastination is accumulated on procrastination, and one impediment succeeds another, till age shatters our resolution, or death intercepts the project of amendment. Such is often the end of salutary purposes, after they have long delighted the imagination, and appeased that disquiet which every mind feels from known misconduct, when the attention is not diverted by business or by pleasure.

Nothing surely can be more unworthy of a reasonable nature than to continue in a state so opposite to real happiness, as that all the peace of solitude and felicity of meditation must arise from resolutions of forsaking it. Yet the world will often afford examples of men who pass months and years in a continual war with their own convictions, and are daily dragged by habit or betrayed by passion into practices which they closed and opened their eyes with purposes to avoid, purposes which, though settled on conviction, the first impulse of momentary desire totally overthrows.

The influence of custom is indeed such that to conquer it will require the utmost efforts of fortitude and virtue, nor can I think any man more worthy of veneration and renown than those who have burst the shackles of habitual vice. This victory, however, has different degrees of glory, as of difficulty; it is more heroic as the objects of guilty gratification are more familiar, and the recurrence of solicitation more frequent. He that from experience of the folly of ambition resigns his offices may set himself free at once from temptation to squander his life in courts, because he cannot regain his former station. He who is enslaved by an amorous passion may quit his tyrant in disgust, and absence will without the help of reason overcome by degrees the desire of returning. But those appetites to which every place affords their proper object, and which require no preparatory measures or gradual advances, are more tenaciously adhesive; the wish is so near the enjoyment that compliance often precedes consideration, and before the powers of reason can be summoned the time for employing them is past.

Indolence is therefore one of the vices from which those whom it once infects are seldom reformed. Every other species of luxury operates upon some appetite that is quickly satiated, and requires some concurrence of art or accident which every place will not supply; but the desire of ease acts equally at all hours, and the longer it is indulged is the more increased. To do nothing is in every man's power; we can never want an opportunity of omitting duties. The lapse to indolence is soft and imperceptible, because it is only a mere cessation of activity; but the return to diligence is difficult, because it implies a change from rest to motion, from privation to reality.

> *Facilis descensus Averni:*
> *Noctes atque dies patet atri janua Ditis:*
> *Sed revocare gradum, superasque evadere ad auras,*
> *Hoc opus, hic labor est.*
>
> (Virgil [*Aeneid*, VI.126])
>
> [The gates of Hell are open night and day;
> Smooth the descent, and easy is the way:
> But to return, and view the cheerful skies;
> In this, the task and mighty labor lies.]
>
> (Dryden)

Of this vice, as of all others, every man who indulges it is conscious; we all know our own state, if we could be induced to consider it; and it might perhaps be useful to the conquest of all these ensnarers of the mind, if at certain stated days life was reviewed. Many things necessary are omitted because we vainly imagine that they may be always performed, and what cannot be done without pain will forever be delayed if the time of doing it be left unsettled. No corruption is great but by long negligence, which can scarcely prevail in a mind regularly and frequently awakened by periodical remorse. He that thus breaks his life into parts will find in himself a desire to distinguish every stage of his existence by some improvement, and delight himself with the approach of the day of recollection, as of the time which is to begin a new series of virtue and felicity.

The IDLER

The *Idler* ran in the *Universal Chronicle* from April 25, 1758, until April 5, 1760, appearing every Saturday. Johnson wrote 92 of the 104 numbers. The essays are shorter and lighter in tone than those of the earlier series, but the topics, on the whole, are similar in kind.

No. 60. Saturday, June 9, 1759

Criticism is a study by which men grow important and formidable at a very small expense. The power of invention has been conferred by nature upon few, and the labor of learning those sciences which may by mere labor be obtained is too great to be willingly endured; but every man can exert such judgment as he has upon the works of others; and he whom nature has made weak, and idleness keeps ignorant, may yet support his vanity by the name of a critic.

I hope it will give comfort to great numbers who are passing through the world in obscurity, when I inform them how easily distinction may be obtained. All the other powers of literature are coy and haughty; they must be long courted, and at last are not always gained; but Criticism is a goddess easy of access and forward of advance, who will meet the slow and encourage the timorous; the want of meaning she supplies with words, and the want of spirit she recompenses with malignity.

This profession has one recommendation peculiar to itself, that it gives vent to malignity without real mischief. No genius was ever blasted by the breath of critics. The poison which, if confined, would have burst the heart, fumes away in empty hisses, and malice is set at ease with very little danger to merit. The critic is the only man whose triumph is without another's pain, and whose greatness does not rise upon another's ruin.

To a study at once so easy and so reputable, so malicious and so harmless, it cannot be necessary to invite my readers by a long or labored exhortation; it is sufficient, since all would be critics if they could, to show by one eminent example that all can be critics if they will.

Dick Minim, after the common course of puerile studies, in which he was no great proficient, was put apprentice to a brewer, with whom he had lived two years, when his uncle died in the city, and left him a large fortune in the stocks. Dick had for six months before used the company of the lower players, of whom he had learned to scorn a trade, and being now at liberty to follow his genius, he resolved to be a man of wit and humor.[1] That he might be properly initiated in his new character, he frequented the coffeehouses near the theaters, where he listened very diligently, day after day, to those who talked of language and sentiments, and unities and catastrophes, till by slow degrees he began to think that he understood something of the stage, and hoped in time to talk himself.

But he did not trust so much to natural sagacity as wholly to neglect the help of books. When the theaters were shut, he retired to Richmond with a few select writers, whose opinions he impressed upon his memory by unwearied diligence, and

when he returned with other wits to the town, was able to tell, in very proper phrases, that the chief business of art is to copy nature; that a perfect writer is not to be expected, because genius decays as judgment increases; that the great art is the art of blotting; and that, according to the rule of Horace, every piece should be kept nine years.[2]

Of the great authors he now began to display the characters, laying down as an universal position that all had beauties and defects. His opinion was that Shakespeare, committing himself wholly to the impulse of nature, wanted that correctness which learning would have given him; and that Jonson, trusting to learning, did not sufficiently cast his eye on nature. He blamed the stanza of Spenser, and could not bear the hexameters of Sidney. Denham and Waller he held the first reformers of English numbers, and thought that if Waller could have obtained the strength of Denham, or Denham the sweetness of Waller, there had been nothing wanting to complete a Poet.[3] He often expressed his commiseration of Dryden's poverty, and his indignation at the age which suffered him to write for bread; he repeated with rapture the first lines of *All for Love*,[4] but wondered at the corruption of taste which could bear anything so unnatural as rhyming tragedies. In Otway he found uncommon powers of moving the passions, but was disgusted by his general negligence, and blamed him for making a conspirator his hero; and never concluded his disquisition without remarking how happily the sound of the clock is made to alarm the audience. Southerne [5] would have been his favorite, but that he mixes comic with tragic scenes, intercepts the natural course of the passions, and fills the mind with a wild confusion of mirth and melancholy. The versification of Rowe he thought too melodious for the stage, and too little varied in different passions. He made it the great fault of Congreve that all his persons were wits, and that he always wrote with more art than nature. He considered *Cato* [6] rather as a poem than a play, and allowed Addison to be the complete master of allegory and grave humor, but paid no great def-

2. every . . . years: *Ars Poetica*, l. 388.   3. Denham . . . Poet: Cf. Pope, *Essay on Criticism*, l. 361, p. 404, above.   4. Dryden's *All for Love*, based on Shakespeare's *Antony and Cleopatra*, abandons heroic couplets for blank verse.   5. Southerne: Although most of Thomas Southerne's plays are contemporary with Dryden's and Otway's, he lived almost to the midpoint of the next century. Nicholas Rowe, who died in 1718, is a more typical eighteenth-century figure.   6. Cato: Addison's *Cato* (1713) was a tragedy much admired by his contemporaries.

IDLER.   1. humor: temperament, caprice.

erence to him as a critic. He thought the chief merit of Prior was in his easy tales and lighter poems, though he allowed that his *Solomon* had many noble sentiments elegantly expressed. In Swift he discovered an inimitable vein of irony, and an easiness which all would hope and few would attain. Pope he was inclined to degrade from a poet to a versifier, and thought his numbers rather luscious than sweet. He often lamented the neglect of *Phaedra and Hippolytus,*[7] and wished to see the stage under better regulations.

These assertions passed commonly uncontradicted;[8] and if now and then an opponent started up, he was quickly repressed by the suffrages of the company, and Minim went away from every dispute with elation of heart and increase of confidence.

He now grew conscious of his abilities, and began to talk of the present state of dramatic poetry; wondered what was become of the comic genius which supplied our ancestors with wit and pleasantry, and why no writer could be found that durst now venture beyond a farce. He saw no reason for thinking that the vein of humor was exhausted, since we live in a country where liberty suffers every character to spread itself to its utmost bulk, and which therefore produces more originals than all the rest of the world together. Of tragedy he concluded business to be the soul, and yet often hinted that love predominates too much upon the modern stage.

He was now an acknowledged critic, and had his own seat in a coffeehouse, and headed a party in the pit. Minim has more vanity than ill-nature, and seldom desires to do much mischief; he will perhaps murmur a little in the ear of him that sits next him, but endeavors to influence the audience to favor by clapping when an actor exclaims *ye Gods,* or laments the misery of his country.

By degrees he was admitted to rehearsals, and many of his friends are of opinion that our present poets are indebted to him for their happiest thoughts: by his contrivance the bell was rung twice in *Barbarossa,* and by his persuasion the author of *Cleone*[9] concluded his play without a couplet; for what can be more absurd, said Minim, than that part of a play should be rhymed, and

part written in blank verse? and by what acquisition of faculties is the speaker who never could find rhymes before enabled to rhyme at the conclusion of an act?

He is the great investigator of hidden beauties, and is particularly delighted when he finds *the sound an echo to the sense.*[10] He has read all our poets with particular attention to this delicacy of versification, and wonders at the supineness with which their works have been hitherto perused, so that no man has found the sound of a drum in this distich:

> When Pulpit, drum ecclesiastic,
> Was beat with fist instead of a stick;[11]

and that the wonderful lines upon honor and a bubble have hitherto passed without notice:

> Honor is like the glassy bubble,
> Which costs philosophers such trouble;
> Where, one part cracked, the whole does fly,
> And wits are cracked to find out why.[12]

In these verses, says Minim, we have two striking accommodations of the sound to the sense. It is impossible to utter the [first] two lines emphatically without an act like that which they describe, *bubble* and *trouble* causing a momentary inflation of the cheeks by the retention of the breath, which is afterwards forcibly emitted, as in the practice of blowing bubbles. But the greatest excellence is in the third line, which is *cracked* in the middle to express a crack, and then shivers into monosyllables. Yet has this diamond lain neglected with common stones, and among the innumerable admirers of *Hudibras* the observation of this superlative passage has been reserved for the sagacity of Minim.

from the PREFACE TO
A DICTIONARY OF
THE ENGLISH LANGUAGE

How long Johnson had been thinking about the principles and method of his Dictionary before he drew up his Plan in 1747 is not known. Robert Dodsley, one of its publishers, was instrumental in its inception and in the decision to address the project to

---

7. Phaedra . . . Hippolytus: a play by Addison's friend, Edmund Smith, published in 1707. **8. uncontradicted:** The point is, of course, that Minim never ventures an opinion that transcends platitude. **9.** *Barbarossa* (1754) by Dr. John Brown; *Cleone* (1758) by Robert Dodsley.

10. the . . . sense: Pope, *Essay on Criticism,* l. 365, p. 404, above. **11.** Samuel Butler, *Hudibras,* I.i.11–12. **12.** *Hudibras.* II.ii.385–88.

Lord Chesterfield. The outline of procedure in the Plan was closely followed in the work itself, and, by and large, the Preface is a restatement of the Plan on a grander scale, and with the necessary change of tense. Johnson agreed on the sum of £1575 with the contracting publishers, and during the years of labor was advanced the whole sum in installments. He had the assistance of six copyists in transcribing, five of whom, as Boswell takes pains to point out, were Scots. The great work first appeared in two folio volumes, on April 15, 1755. Johnson had so clearly foreseen the requirements of his task that all subsequent dictionaries have proceeded along the same systematic lines. His held the field unrivaled for a hundred years.

It is the fate of those who toil at the lower employments of life to be rather driven by the fear of evil, than attracted by the prospect of good; to be exposed to censure, without hope of praise; to be disgraced by miscarriage, or punished for neglect, where success would have been without applause, and diligence without reward.

Among these unhappy mortals is the writer of dictionaries, whom mankind have considered, not as the pupil, but the slave of science, the pioneer [1] of literature, doomed only to remove rubbish and clear obstructions from the paths through which Learning and Genius press forward to conquest and glory, without bestowing a smile on the humble drudge that facilitates their progress. Every other author may aspire to praise; the lexicographer can only hope to escape reproach, and even this negative recompense has been yet granted to very few.

I have, notwithstanding this discouragement, attempted a dictionary of the English language, which, while it was employed in the cultivation of every species of literature, has itself been hitherto neglected; suffered to spread, under the direction of chance, into wild exuberance; resigned to the tyranny of time and fashion; and exposed to the corruptions of ignorance and caprices of innovation.

When I took the first survey of my undertaking, I found our speech copious without order, and energetic without rules: wherever I turned my view, there was perplexity to be disentangled and confusion to be regulated; choice was to be made out of boundless variety, without any established principle of selection; adulterations were to be detected, without a settled test of purity; and modes of expression to be rejected or received, without

PREFACE TO DICTIONARY. **1. pioneer:** in a military sense, one of a corps of engineers, whose job is to dig mines, "remove obstructions," and level the road for the main force that follows.

the suffrages of any writers of classical reputation or acknowledged authority.

Having therefore no assistance but from general grammar, I applied myself to the perusal of our writers; and, noting whatever might be of use to ascertain or illustrate any word or phrase, accumulated in time the materials of a dictionary, which, by degrees, I reduced to method, establishing to myself, in the progress of the work, such rules as experience and analogy suggested to me; experience, which practice and observation were continually increasing; and analogy, which, though in some words obscure, was evident in others.

In adjusting the ORTHOGRAPHY, which has been to this time unsettled and fortuitous, I found it necessary to distinguish those irregularities that are inherent in our tongue, and perhaps coeval with it, from others which the ignorance or negligence of later writers has produced. Every language has its anomalies, which, though inconvenient, and in themselves once unnecessary, must be tolerated among the imperfections of human things, and which require only to be registered, that they may not be increased, and ascertained, that they may not be confounded; but every language has likewise its improprieties and absurdities, which it is the duty of the lexicographer to correct or proscribe.

As language was at its beginning merely oral, all words of necessary or common use were spoken before they were written, and while they were unfixed by any visible signs, must have been spoken with great diversity, as we now observe those who cannot read catch sounds imperfectly, and utter them negligently. When this wild and barbarous jargon was first reduced to an alphabet, every penman endeavored to express, as he could, the sounds which he was accustomed to pronounce or to receive, and vitiated in writing such words as were already vitiated in speech. The powers of the letters, when they were applied to a new language, must have been vague and unsettled, and therefore different hands would exhibit the same sound by different combinations.

From this uncertain pronunciation arise in a great part the various dialects of the same country, which will always be observed to grow fewer, and less different, as books are multiplied; and from this arbitrary representation of sounds by letters proceeds that diversity of spelling observable in the Saxon remains, and I suppose in the first books of every nation, which perplexes or destroys analogy, and produces anomalous formations that, being once incorporated, can never be afterward dismissed or reformed.

Of this kind are the derivatives *length* from *long*, *strength* from *strong*, *darling* from *dear*, *breadth* from *broad*, from *dry*, *drought*, and from *high*, *height*, which Milton, in zeal for analogy, writes *highth; Quid te exempta juvat spinis de pluribus una;* [2] to change all would be too much, and to change one is nothing.

This uncertainty is most frequent in the vowels, which are so capriciously pronounced, and so differently modified, by accident or affectation, not only in every province, but in every mouth, that to them, as is well known to etymologists, little regard is to be shown in the deduction of one language from another.

Such defects are not errors in orthography, but spots of barbarity impressed so deep in the English language that criticism can never wash them away; these, therefore, must be permitted to remain untouched, but many words have likewise been altered by accident, or depraved by ignorance, as the pronunciation of the vulgar has been weakly followed; and some still continue to be variously written, as authors differ in their care or skill; of these it was proper to inquire the true orthography, which I have always considered as depending on their derivation, and have therefore referred them to their original languages. Thus I write *enchant, enchantment, enchanter,* after the French, and *incantation* after the Latin; thus *entire* is chosen rather than *intire,* because it passed to us not from the Latin *integer,* but from the French *entier.*

Of many words it is difficult to say whether they were immediately received from the Latin or the French, since at the time when we had dominions in France, we had Latin service in our churches. It is, however, my opinion, that the French generally supplied us, for we have few Latin words, among the terms of domestic use, which are not French; but many French which are very remote from Latin.

Even in words of which the derivation is apparent, I have been often obliged to sacrifice uniformity to custom; thus I write, in compliance with a numberless majority, *convey* and *inveigh, deceit* and *receipt, fancy* and *phantom;* sometimes the derivative varies from the primitive, as *explain* and *explanation, repeat,* and *repetition.* . . .

That part of my work on which I expect malignity most frequently to fasten is the EXPLANATION; in which I cannot hope to satisfy those who are perhaps not inclined to be pleased, since I have not always been able to satisfy myself. To interpret a language by itself is very difficult: many words cannot be explained by synonyms, because the idea signified by them has not more than one appellation; nor by paraphrase, because simple ideas cannot be described. When the nature of things is unknown, or the notion unsettled and indefinite, and various in various minds, the words by which such notions are conveyed, or such things denoted, will be ambiguous and perplexed. And such is the fate of hapless lexicography, that not only darkness, but light, impedes and distresses it; things may be not only too little, but too much known, to be happily illustrated. To explain, requires the use of terms less abstruse than that which is to be explained, and such terms cannot always be found; for as nothing can be proved but by supposing something intuitively known and evident without proof, so nothing can be defined but by the use of words too plain to admit a definition.

Other words there are, of which the sense is too subtle and evanescent to be fixed in a paraphrase; such are all those which are by the grammarians termed *expletives,* and, in dead languages, are suffered to pass for empty sounds, of no other use than to fill a verse, or to modulate a period, but which are easily perceived in living tongues to have power and emphasis, though it be sometimes such as no other form of expression can convey.

My labor has likewise been much increased by a class of verbs too frequent in the English language, of which the signification is so loose and general, the use so vague and indeterminate, and the senses detorted [3] so widely from the first idea, that it is hard to trace them through the maze of variation, to catch them on the brink of utter inanity, to circumscribe them by any limitations, or interpret them by any words of distinct and settled meaning; such are *bear, break, come, cast, fall, get, give, do, put, set, go, run, make, take, turn, throw.* If of these the whole power is not accurately delivered, it must be remembered that while our language is yet living, and variable by the caprice of everyone

---

2. *Quid . . . una:* "What good does it do you to pull out one thorn among so very many?" Horace, *Epistles*, II.ii.212.

3. **detorted:** perverted, "twisted away."

that speaks it, these words are hourly shifting their relations, and can no more be ascertained in a dictionary, than a grove, in the agitation of a storm, can be accurately delineated from its picture in the water.

The particles [4] are among all nations applied with so great latitude, that they are not easily reducible under any regular scheme of explication; this difficulty is not less, nor perhaps greater, in English than in other languages. I have labored them with diligence, I hope with success; such at least as can be expected in a task which no man, however learned or sagacious, has yet been able to perform.

Some words there are which I cannot explain, because I do not understand them. These might have been omitted very often with little inconvenience, but I would not so far indulge my vanity as to decline this confession; for when Tully owns himself ignorant whether *lessus,* in the twelve tables,[5] means a *funeral song* or *mourning garment;* [6] and Aristotle doubts whether οὐρεὺς in the *Iliad* signifies a *mule* or *muleteer,*[7] I may surely, without shame, leave some obscurities to happier industry, or future information.

The rigor of interpretative lexicography requires that *the explanation, and the word explained, should be always reciprocal;* this I have always endeavored but could not always attain. Words are seldom exactly synonymous; a new term was not introduced, but because the former was thought inadequate; names, therefore, have often many ideas, but few ideas have many names. It was then necessary to use the proximate word, for the deficiency of single terms can very seldom be supplied by circumlocution; nor is the inconvenience great of such mutilated interpretations, because the sense may easily be collected entire from the examples.

In every word of extensive use, it was requisite to mark the progress of its meaning, and show by what gradations of intermediate sense it has passed from its primitive to its remote and accidental signification; so that every foregoing explanation should tend to that which follows, and the series be regularly concatenated from the first notion to the last.

This is specious, but not always practicable; kindred senses may be so interwoven that the perplexity cannot be disentangled, nor any reason be assigned why one should be ranged before the other. When the radical idea branches out into parallel ramifications, how can a consecutive series be formed of senses in their nature collateral? The shades of meaning sometimes pass imperceptibly into each other, so that though on one side they apparently differ, yet it is impossible to mark the point of contact. Ideas of the same race, though not exactly alike, are sometimes so little different, that no words can express the dissimilitude, though the mind easily perceives it when they are exhibited together; and sometimes there is such a confusion of acceptations, that discernment is wearied, and distinction puzzled, and perseverance herself hurries to an end, by crowding together what she cannot separate.

These complaints of difficulty will, by those that have never considered words beyond their popular use, be thought only the jargon of a man willing to magnify his labors, and procure veneration to his studies by involution and obscurity. But every art is obscure to those that have not learned it; this uncertainty of terms, and commixture of ideas, is well known to those who have joined philosophy with grammar; and if I have not expressed them very clearly, it must be remembered that I am speaking of that which words are insufficient to explain.

The original sense of words is often driven out of use by their metaphorical acceptations, yet must be inserted for the sake of a regular origination. Thus I know not whether *ardor* is used for *material heat,* or whether *flagrant,* in English, ever signifies the same with *burning;* yet such are the primitive ideas of these words, which are therefore set first, though without examples, that the figurative senses may be commodiously deduced. . . .

Some of the examples have been taken from writers who were never mentioned as masters of elegance or models of style; but words must be sought where they are used, and in what pages, eminent for purity, can terms of manufacture or agriculture be found? Many quotations serve no other purpose than that of proving the bare existence of words, and are therefore selected with less scrupulousness than those which are to teach their structures and relations.

My purpose was to admit no testimony of living

---

4. **particles:** uninflected and subordinate elements of speech (e.g., preposition, conjunction, affix). 5. The "twelve tables" refer to the revered code of Roman law drawn up by the commission of Decemviri and published B.C. 451–50. 6. **Tully . . . garment:** Cicero, *Laws,* II.xxiii.59. 7. **Aristotle . . . muleteer:** Aristotle, *Poetics,* XXV.9.

authors, that I might not be misled by partiality, and that none of my contemporaries might have reason to complain; nor have I departed from this resolution, but when some performance of uncommon excellence excited my veneration, when my memory supplied me, from late books, with an example that was wanting, or when my heart, in the tenderness of friendship, solicited admission for a favorite name.

So far have I been from any care to grace my pages with modern decorations, that I have studiously endeavored to collect examples and authorities from the writers before the Restoration, whose works I regard as *the wells of English undefiled,*[8] as the pure sources of genuine diction. Our language, for almost a century, has, by the concurrence of many causes, been gradually departing from its original Teutonic character and deviating towards a Gallic structure and phraseology, from which it ought to be our endeavor to recall it, by making our ancient volumes the groundwork of style, admitting among the additions of later times only such as may supply real deficiencies, such as are readily adopted by the genius of our tongue, and incorporate easily with our native idioms.

But as every language has a time of rudeness antecedent to perfection, as well as of false refinement and declension, I have been cautious lest my zeal for antiquity might drive me into times too remote, and crowd my book with words now no longer understood. I have fixed Sidney's work for the boundary beyond which I make few excursions. From the authors which rose in the time of Elizabeth, a speech might be formed adequate to all the purposes of use and elegance. If the language of theology were extracted from Hooker and the translation of the Bible; the terms of natural knowledge from Bacon; the phrases of policy, war, and navigation from Raleigh; the dialect of poetry and fiction from Spenser and Sidney; and the diction of common life from Shakespeare, few ideas would be lost to mankind for want of English words in which they might be expressed.

It is not sufficient that a word is found, unless it be so combined as that its meaning is apparently determined by the tract and tenor of the sentence. Such passages I have therefore chosen, and when it happened that any author gave a definition of a term, or such an explanation as is equivalent to a definition, I have placed his authority as a supple-

8. *the . . . undefiled:* Spencer, *Faerie Queene,* IV.ii.33.

ment to my own, without regard to the chronological order that is otherwise observed.

Some words, indeed, stand unsupported by any authority, but they are commonly derivative nouns or adverbs formed from their primitives by regular and constant analogy, or names of things seldom occurring in books, or words of which I have reason to doubt the existence.

There is more danger of censure from the multiplicity than paucity of examples; authorities will sometimes seem to have been accumulated without necessity or use, and perhaps some will be found which might, without loss, have been omitted. But a work of this kind is not hastily to be charged with superfluities; those quotations which to careless or unskillful perusers appear only to repeat the same sense will often exhibit, to a more accurate examiner, diversities of signification or, at least, afford different shades of the same meaning. One will show the word applied to persons, another to things; one will express an ill, another a good, and a third a neutral sense; one will prove the expression genuine from an ancient author; another will show it elegant from a modern; a doubtful authority is corroborated by another of more credit; an ambiguous sentence is ascertained by a passage clear and determinate; the word, how often soever repeated, appears with new associates and in different combinations, and every quotation contributes something to the stability or enlargement of the language.

When words are used equivocally, I receive them in either sense; when they are metaphorical, I adopt them in their primitive acceptation.

I have sometimes, though rarely, yielded to the temptation of exhibiting a genealogy of sentiments, by showing how one author copied the thoughts and diction of another; such quotations are indeed little more than repetitions, which might justly be censured, did they not gratify the mind by affording a kind of intellectual history.

The various syntactical structures occurring in the examples have been carefully noted; the license or negligence with which many words have been hitherto used has made our style capricious and indeterminate; when the different combinations of the same word are exhibited together, the preference is readily given to propriety, and I have often endeavored to direct the choice.

Thus have I labored, by settling the orthography, displaying the analogy, regulating the structures, and ascertaining the signification of English words, to perform all the parts of a faithful lexicographer; but I have not always executed my own scheme, or satisfied my own expectations. The work, whatever proofs of diligence and attention it may exhibit, is yet capable of many improvements: the orthography which I recommend is still controvertible; the etymology which I adopt is uncertain, and perhaps frequently erroneous; the explanations are sometimes too much contracted, and sometimes too much diffused; the significations are distinguished rather with subtlety than skill; and the attention is harassed with unnecessary minuteness.

The examples are too often injudiciously truncated, and perhaps sometimes, I hope very rarely, alleged in a mistaken sense; for in making this collection I trusted more to memory than, in a state of disquiet and embarrassment, memory can contain, and purposed to supply at the review what was left incomplete in the first transcription.

Many terms appropriated to particular occupations, though necessary and significant, are undoubtedly omitted; and of the words most studiously considered and exemplified, many senses have escaped observation.

Yet these failures, however frequent, may admit extenuation and apology. To have attempted much is always laudable, even when the enterprise is above the strength that undertakes it. To rest below his own aim is incident to everyone whose fancy is active and whose views are comprehensive; nor is any man satisfied with himself because he has done much, but because he can conceive little. When first I engaged in this work, I resolved to leave neither words nor things unexamined, and pleased myself with a prospect of the hours which I should revel away in feasts of literature; with the obscure recesses of northern learning [9] which I should enter and ransack; the treasures with which I expected every search into those neglected mines to reward my labor; and the triumph with which I should display my acquisitions to mankind. When I had thus inquired into the original of words, I resolved to show likewise my attention to things; to pierce deep into every science, to inquire the nature of every substance of which I inserted the name, to limit every idea by a definition strictly logical, and exhibit every production of art or nature in an accurate description, that my book might

be in place of all other dictionaries whether appellative or technical. But these were the dreams of a poet doomed at last to wake a lexicographer. I soon found that it is too late to look for instruments when the work calls for execution, and that whatever abilities I had brought to my task, with those I must finally perform it. To deliberate whenever I doubted, to inquire whenever I was ignorant, would have protracted the undertaking without end and, perhaps, without much improvement; for I did not find by my first experiments, that what I had not of my own was easily to be obtained; I saw that one inquiry only gave occasion to another, that book referred to book, that to search was not always to find, and to find was not always to be informed; and that thus to pursue perfection was, like the first inhabitants of Arcadia, to chase the sun, which, when they had reached the hill where he seemed to rest, was still beheld at the same distance from them.

I then contracted my design, determining to confide in myself and no longer to solicit auxiliaries, which produced more encumbrance than assistance; by this I obtained at least one advantage, that I set limits to my work, which would in time be ended, though not completed. . . .

Of the event of this work, for which, having labored it with so much application, I cannot but have some degree of parental fondness, it is natural to form conjectures. Those who have been persuaded to think well of my design will require that it should fix our language, and put a stop to those alterations which time and chance have hitherto been suffered to make in it without opposition. With this consequence I will confess that I flattered myself for a while, but now begin to fear that I have indulged expectation which neither reason nor experience can justify. When we see men grow old and die at a certain time one after another, from century to century, we laugh at the elixir that promises to prolong life to a thousand years; and with equal justice may the lexicographer be derided, who, being able to produce no example of a nation that has preserved their words and phrases from mutability, shall imagine that his dictionary can embalm his language, and secure it from corruption and decay, that it is in his power to change sublunary nature, and clear the world at once from folly, vanity, and affectation.

With this hope, however, academies have been instituted, to guard the avenues of their languages,

9. **northern learning:** i.e., of northern Europe, as distinguished from Mediterranean, or classical, culture.

to retain fugitives, and repulse intruders; but their vigilance and activity have hitherto been vain; sounds are too volatile and subtle for legal restraints; to enchain syllables, and to lash the wind, are equally the undertakings of pride, unwilling to measure its desires by its strength. The French language has visibly changed under the inspection of the academy; [10] the style of Amelot's translation of Father Paul [11] is observed by *Le Courayer* to be *un peu passé;* and no Italian will maintain that the diction of any modern writer is not perceptibly different from that of *Boccace, Machiavel,* or *Caro.*[12]

Total and sudden transformations of a language seldom happen; conquests and migrations are now very rare; but there are other causes of change which, though slow in their operation and invisible in their progress, are perhaps as much superior to human resistance as the revolutions of the sky or intumescence of the tide. Commerce, however necessary, however lucrative, as it depraves the manners, corrupts the language; they that have frequent intercourse with strangers, to whom they endeavor to accommodate themselves, must in time learn a mingled dialect, like the jargon which serves the traffickers on the Mediterranean and Indian coasts. This will not always be confined to the exchange, the warehouse, or the port, but will be communicated by degrees to other ranks of the people, and be at last incorporated with the current speech.

There are likewise internal causes equally forcible. The language most likely to continue long without alteration would be that of a nation raised a little, and but a little, above barbarity, secluded from strangers, and totally employed in procuring the conveniences of life, either without books or, like some of the Mahometan countries, with very few; men thus busied and unlearned, having only such words as common use requires, would perhaps long continue to express the same notions by the same signs. But no such constancy can be expected in a people polished by arts, and classed by subordination, where one part of the community is sustained and accommodated by the labor of the other. Those who have much leisure to think will always

be enlarging the stock of ideas, and every increase of knowledge, whether real or fancied, will produce new words, or combinations of words. When the mind is unchained from necessity, it will range after convenience; when it is left at large in the fields of speculation, it will shift opinions; as any custom is disused, the words that expressed it must perish with it; as any opinion grows popular, it will innovate speech in the same proportion as it alters practice.

As by the cultivation of various sciences, a language is amplified, it will be more furnished with words deflected from original sense; the geometrician will talk of a courtier's zenith, or the eccentric virtue of a wild hero; and the physician, of sanguine expectations and phlegmatic delays. Copiousness of speech will give opportunities to capricious choice, by which some words will be preferred, and others degraded; vicissitudes of fashion will enforce the use of new, or extend the signification of known, terms. The tropes of poetry will make hourly encroachments, and the metaphorical will become the current sense; pronunciation will be varied by levity or ignorance, and the pen must at length comply with the tongue; illiterate writers will at one time or other, by public infatuation, rise into renown, who, not knowing the original import of words, will use them with colloquial licentiousness, confound distinction, and forget propriety. As politeness increases, some expressions will be considered as too gross and vulgar for the delicate, others as too formal and ceremonious for the gay and airy; new phrases are therefore adopted, which must, for the same reasons, be in time dismissed. Swift, in his petty treatise on the English language,[13] allows that new words must sometimes be introduced, but proposes that none should be suffered to become obsolete. But what makes a word obsolete, more than general agreement to forbear it? and how shall it be continued, when it conveys an offensive idea, or recalled again into the mouths of mankind, when it has once become unfamiliar by disuse and unpleasing by unfamiliarity?

There is another cause of alteration more prevalent than any other, which yet in the present state of the world cannot be obviated. A mixture of two languages will produce a third distinct from both, and they will always be mixed, where the

---

10. **academy:** the Académie Française, established in 1635 by Cardinal Richelieu to preside over the French literary world. 11. **Father Paul:** Paolo Sarpi, *History of the Council of Trent* (1619); translated from Italian into French by Amelot (1683); and by Courayer (1736), because Amelot's French was "a little out of date." 12. **Boccace . . . Caro:** Boccaccio died in 1375; Machiavelli died in 1527; Annibal Caro, a poet who translated the *Aeneid,* died about 1566.

13. **Swift . . . language:** *A Proposal for Correcting, Improving, and Ascertaining the English Tongue* (1712).

chief part of education, and the most conspicuous accomplishment, is skill in ancient or in foreign tongues. He that has long cultivated another language will find its words and combinations crowd upon his memory; and haste and negligence, refinement and affectation, will obtrude borrowed terms and exotic expressions.

The great pest of speech is frequency of translation. No book was ever turned from one language into another without imparting something of its native idiom. This is the most mischievous and comprehensive innovation; single words may enter by thousands, and the fabric of the tongue continue the same, but new phraseology changes much at once; it alters not the single stones of the building, but the order of the columns. If an academy should be established for the cultivation of our style, which I, who can never wish to see dependence multiplied, hope the spirit of English liberty will hinder or destroy, let them, instead of compiling grammars and dictionaries, endeavor, with all their influence, to stop the license of translators, whose idleness and ignorance, if it be suffered to proceed, will reduce us to babble a dialect of France.

If the changes that we fear be thus irresistible, what remains but to acquiesce with silence, as in the other insurmountable distresses of humanity? It remains that we retard what we cannot repel, that we palliate what we cannot cure. Life may be lengthened by care, though death cannot be ultimately defeated; tongues, like governments, have a natural tendency to degeneration; we have long preserved our constitution, let us make some struggles for our language.

In hope of giving longevity to that which its own nature forbids to be immortal, I have devoted this book, the labor of years, to the honor of my country, that we may no longer yield the palm of philology, without a contest, to the nations of the Continent. The chief glory of every people arises from its authors; whether I shall add anything by my own writings to the reputation of English literature must be left to time; much of my life has been lost under the pressures of disease, much has been trifled away, and much has always been spent in provision for the day that was passing over me; but I shall not think my employment useless or ignoble, if by my assistance foreign nations, and distant ages, gain access to the propagators of knowledge, and understand the teachers of truth;

if my labors afford light to the repositories of science, and add celebrity to *Bacon,* to *Hooker,* to *Milton,* and to *Boyle.*

When I am animated by this wish, I look with pleasure on my book, however defective, and deliver it to the world with the spirit of a man that has endeavored well. That it will immediately become popular I have not promised to myself: a few wild blunders, and risible absurdities, from which no work of such multiplicity was ever free, may for a time furnish folly with laughter, and harden ignorance in contempt; but useful diligence will at last prevail, and there never can be wanting some who distinguish desert; who will consider that no dictionary of a living tongue ever can be perfect, since while it is hastening to publication, some words are budding, and some falling away; that a whole life cannot be spent upon syntax and etymology, and that even a whole life would not be sufficient; that he, whose design includes whatever language can express, must often speak of what he does not understand; that a writer will sometimes be hurried by eagerness to the end, and sometimes faint with weariness under a task, which *Scaliger* compares [14] to the labors of the anvil and the mine; that what is obvious is not always known, and what is known is not always present; that sudden fits of inadvertency will surprise vigilance, slight avocations will seduce attention, and casual eclipses of the mind will darken learning; and that the writer shall often in vain trace his memory at the moment of need, for that which yesterday he knew with intuitive readiness, and which will come uncalled into his thoughts tomorrow.

In this work, when it shall be found that much is omitted, let it not be forgotten that much likewise is performed, and, though no book was ever spared out of tenderness to the author, and the world is little solicitous to know whence proceeded the faults of that which it condemns, yet it may gratify curiosity to inform it, that the *English Dictionary* was written with little assistance of the learned, and without any patronage of the great; not in the soft obscurities of retirement, or under the shelter of academic bowers, but amidst inconvenience and distraction, in sickness and in sorrow. It may repress the triumph of malignant criticism

14. *Scaliger* compares: J. C. Scaliger, *In Lexicorum Compilatores,* in his collected poems (ed. 1868, p. 38). He and his son, J. J. Scaliger, were two very famous Renaissance scholars.

to observe that, if our language is not here fully displayed, I have only failed in an attempt which no human powers have hitherto completed. If the lexicons of ancient tongues, now immutably fixed, and comprised in a few volumes, be yet, after the toil of successive ages, inadequate and delusive; if the aggregated knowledge, and co-operating diligence of the Italian academicians, did not secure them from the censure of Beni; [15] if the embodied critics of France, [16] when fifty years had been spent upon their work, were obliged to change its economy, and give their second edition another form, I may surely be contented without the praise of perfection, which, if I could obtain, in this gloom of solitude, what would it avail me? I have protracted my work till most of those whom I wished to please have sunk into the grave, and success and miscarriage are empty sounds; I therefore dismiss it with frigid tranquillity, having little to fear or hope from censure or from praise.

from the PREFACE TO SHAKESPEARE

Johnson had the intention to edit Shakespeare even before he undertook the Dictionary, and attached Proposals for a ten-volume duodecimo edition to his *Miscellaneous Observations on the Tragedy of Macbeth*, published in 1745. The Dictionary prevented his proceeding in this enterprise, but, when that was off his hands, he again issued Proposals in the late spring of 1756 for an edition to be completed before the end of 1757. He was dilatory in performance, however, and the work did not appear until 1765, before which time it was being charged that he had accepted subscriptions without intending to fulfill his obligation. The satirist Charles Churchill wrote:

He for subscribers baits his hook,
And takes their cash; but where's the book?
No matter where; wise fear, we know,
Forbids the robbing of a foe;
But what, to serve our private ends,
Forbids the cheating of our friends?

The taunt is credited with having stung Johnson into quickening his pace. In his *Life of Pope* he writes of such delays: "Perhaps no extensive and multifarious performance was ever effected within the term originally fixed in the undertaker's mind. He that runs against Time, has an antagonist not subject to casualties."

15. **Beni:** He complained that the Tuscan dialect had been made regulative and controlling.   16. **critics of France:** The French Academy had undertaken their dictionary in 1639; it was published in 1694.

By modern editorial standards, Johnson's collation of the early readings was negligent and far from exhaustive. What makes his edition memorable and still a potent element in our understanding of Shakespeare is the amount of lucid interpretation it contains of obscure passages other editors had either stumbled over or given up to conjectural emendation. Johnson deliberately denied himself the vanity of ingenious conjecture. His powerfully ratiocinative mind always made sense of a passage if any sense remained to be made. His notes, also, contain many penetrating observations of wider bearing than the immediate occasion requires — interpreting character, commenting on the mores of the Elizabethan age and on Shakespeare's practice, throwing out obiter dicta on a great variety of topics. They abound with illustrations of Johnson's critical views, pungent personality, and ripe wisdom. At the end of each play he customarily adds a "short stricture" on the play as a whole, but these are usually loose and casual, not balanced summaries.

The greatest of the component parts of this edition is the Preface — greatest of all prefaces to Shakespeare and by itself sufficient to establish Johnson among the first half-dozen English literary critics of all time. To the reader of today there may not at first, apart from its sturdily independent and unawed tone, seem to be anything very new or very striking in this preface. It contains no psychological subtleties; its defense of Shakespeare for disregarding the unities of time and place seems not very daring to a generation that has never known respect for them; its survey of Shakespeare's learning has been superseded by a multiplicity of special studies; its review of preceding editors, then recent but now familiar only to the specialist, cannot excite attention. But what Johnson said of Dryden and Addison may now be quoted in his own support: "A writer who obtains his full purpose loses himself in his own luster. Of an opinion which is no longer doubted, the evidence ceases to be examined. Of an art universally practiced, the first teacher is forgotten. Learning once made popular is no longer learning: it has the appearance of something which we have bestowed upon ourselves, as the dew appears to rise from the field which it refreshes." And again: "It is not uncommon for those who have grown wise by the labor of others to add a little of their own, and overlook their masters. Addison is now despised by some who perhaps would never have seen his defects, but by the lights which he afforded them."

Johnson's criticism in the Preface to Shakespeare is of this broad and general kind. It is remarkable in that its emphases still appear true and unexceptionable; that its critical positions almost all strike with immediate conviction; that its occasional prejudices always provoke us to examine our own; and that every idea is expressed with such eloquent sufficiency that we despair of saying it so well again, and turn away to other types, and another scale, of investigation.

One caveat may be offered in conclusion. It is easy to simplify Johnson's comparison of Shakespearean comedy and tragedy into a value-judgment favoring the comedies. But this he does not mean. He did not think that any comedy was *greater* than *Lear,* or *Hamlet,* or *Othello.* He *does* say that Shakespeare's natural disposition led him to comedy; that "in comedy he seems to repose, or luxuriate, as in a mode of thinking congenial to his nature."

That praises are without reason lavished on the dead, and that the honors due only to excellence are paid to antiquity, is a complaint likely to be always continued by those who, being able to add nothing to truth, hope for eminence from the heresies of paradox; or those who, being forced by disappointment upon consolatory expedients, are willing to hope from posterity what the present age refuses, and flatter themselves that the regard which is yet denied by envy will be at last bestowed by time.

Antiquity, like every other quality that attracts the notice of mankind, has undoubtedly votaries that reverence it, not from reason, but from prejudice. Some seem to admire indiscriminately whatever has been long preserved, without considering that time has sometimes co-operated with chance; all perhaps are more willing to honor past than present excellence; and the mind contemplates genius through the shades of age, as the eye surveys the sun through artificial opacity. The great contention of criticism is to find the faults of the moderns, and the beauties of the ancients. While an author is yet living we estimate his powers by his worst performance, and when he is dead we rate them by his best.

To works, however, of which the excellence is not absolute and definite, but gradual and comparative; to works not raised upon principles demonstrative and scientific, but appealing wholly to observation and experience, no other test can be applied than length of duration and continuance of esteem. What mankind have long possessed they have often examined and compared, and if they persist to value the possession, it is because frequent comparisons have confirmed opinion in its favor. As among the works of nature no man can properly call a river deep or a mountain high, without the knowledge of many mountains and many rivers; so in the productions of genius, nothing can be styled excellent till it has been compared with other works of the same kind. Demonstration immediately displays its power, and has nothing to hope or fear from the flux of years, but works tentative and experimental must be estimated by their proportion to the general and collective ability of man, as it is discovered in a long succession of endeavors. Of the first building that was raised, it might be with certainty determined that it was round or square, but whether it was spacious or lofty must have been referred to time. The Pythagorean scale of numbers was at once discovered to be perfect,[1] but the poems of Homer we yet know not to transcend the common limits of human intelligence, but by remarking, that nation after nation, and century after century, has been able to do little more than transpose his incidents, new-name his characters, and paraphrase his sentiments.

The reverence due to writings that have long subsisted arises therefore not from any credulous confidence in the superior wisdom of past ages, or gloomy persuasion of the degeneracy of mankind, but is the consequence of acknowledged and indubitable positions, that what has been longest known has been most considered, and what is most considered is best understood.

The poet of whose works I have undertaken the revision may now begin to assume the dignity of an ancient, and claim the privilege of established fame and prescriptive veneration. He has long outlived his century, the term commonly fixed as the test of literary merit. Whatever advantages he might once derive from personal allusions, local customs, or temporary opinions have for many years been lost; and every topic of merriment or motive of sorrow, which the modes of artificial life afforded him, now only obscure the scenes which they once illuminated. The effects of favor and competition are at an end; the tradition of his friendships and his enmities has perished; his works support no opinion with arguments, nor supply any faction with invectives; they can neither indulge vanity nor gratify malignity, but are read without any other reason than the desire of pleasure, and are therefore praised only as pleasure is obtained; yet, thus unassisted by interest or passion, they have passed through variations of taste and changes of manners and, as they devolved from one generation to another, have received new honors at every transmission.

But because human judgment, though it be grad-

PREFACE TO SHAKESPEARE. **1. The . . . perfect:** See Aristotle, *Metaphysics,* I.v. What Johnson means by the "scale" is not exactly clear. The multiplication table may be meant. Pythagoras attached mystical significance to odd and even numbers, and deduced all the principles of the cosmos from this balance or opposition.

ually gaining upon certainty, never becomes infallible, and approbation, though long continued, may yet be only the approbation of prejudice or fashion, it is proper to inquire by what peculiarities of excellence Shakespeare has gained and kept the favor of his countrymen.

Nothing can please many, and please long, but just representations of general nature. Particular manners can be known to few, and therefore few only can judge how nearly they are copied. The irregular combinations of fanciful invention may delight awhile, by that novelty of which the common satiety of life sends us all in quest; but the pleasures of sudden wonder are soon exhausted, and the mind can only repose on the stability of truth.

Shakespeare is, above all writers, at least above all modern writers, the poet of nature; the poet that holds up to his readers a faithful mirror of manners and of life. His characters are not modified by the customs of particular places, unpracticed by the rest of the world; by the peculiarities of studies or professions, which can operate but upon small numbers; or by the accidents of transient fashions or temporary opinions; they are the genuine progeny of common humanity, such as the world will always supply, and observation will always find. His persons act and speak by the influence of those general passions and principles by which all minds are agitated and the whole system of life is continued in motion. In the writings of other poets a character is too often an individual; in those of Shakespeare it is commonly a species.

It is from this wide extension of design that so much instruction is derived. It is this which fills the plays of Shakespeare with practical axioms and domestic wisdom. It was said of Euripides, that every verse was a precept;[2] and it may be said of Shakespeare, that from his works may be collected a system of civil and economical prudence. Yet his real power is not shown in the splendor of particular passages, but by the progress of his fable and the tenor of his dialogue; and he that tries to recommend him by select quotations will succeed like the pedant in Hierocles,[3] who, when he offered his house to sale, carried a brick in his pocket as a specimen.

It will not easily be imagined how much Shakespeare excels in accommodating his sentiments to real life, but by comparing him with other authors. It was observed of the ancient schools of declamation, that the more diligently they were frequented, the more was the student disqualified for the world, because he found nothing there which he should ever meet in any other place. The same remark may be applied to every stage but that of Shakespeare. The theater, when it is under any other direction, is peopled by such characters as were never seen, conversing in a language which was never heard, upon topics which will never arise in the commerce of mankind. But the dialogue of this author is often so evidently determined by the incident which produces it, and is pursued with so much ease and simplicity, that it seems scarcely to claim the merit of fiction, but to have been gleaned by diligent selection out of common conversation, and common occurrences.

Upon every other stage the universal agent is love, by whose power all good and evil is distributed, and every action quickened or retarded. To bring a lover, a lady, and a rival into the fable; to entangle them in contradictory obligations, perplex them with oppositions of interest, and harass them with violence of desires inconsistent with each other; to make them meet in rapture and part in agony; to fill their mouths with hyperbolical joy and outrageous sorrow; to distress them as nothing human ever was distressed; to deliver them as nothing human ever was delivered: is the business of a modern dramatist. For this probability is violated, life is misrepresented, and language is depraved. But love is only one of many passions, and, as it has no great influence upon the sum of life, it has little operation in the dramas of a poet, who caught his ideas from the living world, and exhibited only what he saw before him. He knew that any other passion, as it was regular or exorbitant, was a cause of happiness or calamity.

Characters thus ample and general were not easily discriminated and preserved, yet perhaps no poet ever kept his personages more distinct from each other. I will not say with Pope, that every speech may be assigned to the proper speaker,[4] because many speeches there are which have nothing characteristical; but, perhaps, though some may be equally adapted to every person, it will be difficult to find any that can be properly transferred from the present possessor to another claimant.

2. It . . . precept: by Cicero, *Familiar Epistles*, XVI.8. 3. Hierocles: *Commentary on the Golden Verses.*

4. Pope . . . speaker: Pope's Preface to Shakespeare, para. 4.

The choice is right, when there is reason for choice.

Other dramatists can only gain attention by hyperbolical or aggravated characters, by fabulous and unexampled excellence or depravity, as the writers of barbarous romances invigorated the reader by a giant and a dwarf; and he that should form his expectations of human affairs from the play, or from the tale, would be equally deceived. Shakespeare has no heroes; his scenes are occupied only by men who act and speak as the reader thinks that he should himself have spoken or acted on the same occasion. Even where the agency is supernatural the dialogue is level with life. Other writers disguise the most natural passions and most frequent incidents, so that he who contemplates them in the book will not know them in the world. Shakespeare approximates the remote, and familiarizes the wonderful; the event which he represents will not happen, but if it were possible, its effects would be probably such as he has assigned; and it may be said that he has not only shown human nature as it acts in real exigences, but as it would be found in trials to which it cannot be exposed.

This therefore is the praise of Shakespeare, that his drama is the mirror of life; that he who has mazed his imagination in following the phantoms which other writers raise up before him may here be cured of his delirious ecstasies, by reading human sentiments in human language, by scenes from which a hermit may estimate the transactions of the world, and a confessor predict the progress of the passions.

His adherence to general nature has exposed him to the censure of critics who form their judgments upon narrower principles. Dennis and Rymer think his Romans not sufficiently Roman; and Voltaire censures his kings as not completely royal. Dennis is offended, that Menenius, a senator of Rome, should play the buffoon;[5] and Voltaire perhaps thinks decency violated when the Danish usurper is represented as a drunkard.[6] But Shakespeare always makes nature predominate over accident, and, if he preserves the essential character, is not very careful of distinctions superinduced and adventitious. His story requires Romans or kings, but he thinks only on men. He knew that Rome, like every other city, had men of all dispositions,

and, wanting a buffoon, he went into the senate house for that which the senate house would certainly have afforded him. He was inclined to show an usurper and a murderer not only odious but despicable; he therefore added drunkenness to his other qualities, knowing that kings love wine like other men, and that wine exerts its natural power upon kings. These are the petty cavils of petty minds; a poet overlooks the casual distinction of country and condition, as a painter, satisfied with the figure, neglects the drapery.

The censure which he has incurred by mixing comic and tragic scenes, as it extends to all his works, deserves more consideration. Let the fact be the first stated, and then examined.

Shakespeare's plays are not in the rigorous and critical sense either tragedies or comedies, but compositions of a distinct kind, exhibiting the real state of sublunary nature, which partakes of good and evil, joy and sorrow, mingled with endless variety of proportion and innumerable modes of combination; and expressing the course of the world, in which the loss of one is the gain of another, in which, at the same time, the reveler is hasting to his wine, and the mourner burying his friend; in which the malignity of one is sometimes defeated by the frolic of another; and many mischiefs and many benefits are done and hindered without design.

Out of this chaos of mingled purposes and casualties, the ancient poets, according to the laws which custom had prescribed, selected some the crimes of men, and some their absurdities; some the momentous vicissitudes of life, and some the lighter occurences; some the terrors of distress, and some the gaieties of prosperity. Thus rose the two modes of imitation, known by the names of *tragedy* and *comedy,* compositions intended to promote different ends by contrary means, and considered as so little allied, that I do not recollect among the Greeks or Romans a single writer who attempted both.

Shakespeare has united the powers of exciting laughter and sorrow not only in one mind, but in one composition. Almost all his plays are divided between serious and ludicrous characters, and, in the successive evolutions of the design, sometimes produce seriousness and sorrow, and sometimes levity and laughter.

That this is a practice contrary to the rules of criticism will be readily allowed, but there is always

---

5. **buffoon:** John Dennis, *Essay on the Genius and Writings of Shakespeare* (1712), in Dennis's *Critical Works* (ed. Hooker, 1943), II.v. See Shakespeare's *Coriolanus*. 6. **drunkard:** Voltaire, *Du Théâtre Anglais, par Jérôme Carré* (1761).

an appeal open from criticism to nature. The end of writing is to instruct; the end of poetry is to instruct by pleasing. That the mingled drama may convey all the instruction of tragedy or comedy cannot be denied, because it includes both in its alternations of exhibition, and approaches nearer than either to the appearance of life, by showing how great machinations and slender designs may promote or obviate one another, and the high and the low cooperate in the general system by unavoidable concatenation.

It is objected that by this change of scenes the passions are interrupted in their progression, and that the principal event, being not advanced by a due gradation of preparatory incidents, wants at last the power to move, which constitutes the perfection of dramatic poetry. This reasoning is so specious that it is received as true even by those who in daily experience feel it to be false. The interchanges of mingled scenes seldom fail to produce the intended vicissitudes of passion. Fiction cannot move so much, but that the attention may be easily transferred; and though it must be allowed that pleasing melancholy be sometimes interrupted by unwelcome levity, yet let it be considered likewise, that melancholy is often not pleasing, and that the disturbance of one man may be the relief of another; that different auditors have different habitudes; and that, upon the whole, all pleasure consists in variety.

The players, who in their edition [7] divided our author's works into comedies, histories, and tragedies, seem not to have distinguished the three kinds by any very exact or definite ideas.

An action which ended happily to the principal persons, however serious or distressful through its intermediate incidents, in their opinion constituted a comedy. This idea of a comedy continued long amongst us, and plays were written which, by changing the catastrophe, were tragedies today and comedies tomorrow.

Tragedy was not in those times a poem of more general dignity or elevation than comedy; it required only a calamitous conclusion, with which the common criticism of that age was satisfied, whatever lighter pleasure it afforded in its progress.

History was a series of actions, with no other than chronological succession, independent of each other, and without any tendency to introduce or regulate the conclusion. It is not always very nicely distinguished from tragedy. There is not much nearer approach to unity of action in the tragedy of *Antony and Cleopatra* than in the history of *Richard the Second*. But a history might be continued through many plays; as it had no plan, it had no limits.

Through all these denominations of the drama, Shakespeare's mode of composition is the same; an interchange of seriousness and merriment, by which the mind is softened at one time, and exhilarated at another. But whatever be his purpose, whether to gladden or depress, or to conduct the story, without vehemence or emotion, through tracts of easy and familiar dialogue, he never fails to attain his purpose; as he commands us, we laugh or mourn, or sit silent with quiet expectation, in tranquillity without indifference.

When Shakespeare's plan is understood, most of the criticisms of Rymer [8] and Voltaire vanish away. The play of *Hamlet* is opened, without impropriety, by two sentinels; Iago bellows at Brabantio's window, without injury to the scheme of the play, though in terms which a modern audience would not easily endure; the character of Polonius is seasonable and useful; and the Gravediggers themselves may be heard with applause.

Shakespeare engaged in dramatic poetry with the world open before him; the rules of the ancients were yet known to few; the public judgment was unformed; he had no example of such fame as might force him upon imitation, nor critics of such authority as might restrain his extravagance. He therefore indulged his natural disposition, and his disposition, as Rymer has remarked, led him to comedy. In tragedy he often writes with great appearance of toil and study what is written at last with little felicity; but in his comic scenes he seems to produce without labor what no labor can improve. In tragedy he is always struggling after some occasion to be comic, but in comedy he seems to repose, or to luxuriate, as in a mode of thinking congenial to his nature. In his tragic scenes there is always something wanting, but his comedy often surpasses expectation or desire. His comedy pleases by the thoughts and the language, and his tragedy for the greater part by incident and action. His tragedy seems to be skill, his comedy to be instinct.

The force of his comic scenes has suffered little

---

7. **players . . . edition:** that is, John Heming and Henry Condell, members of Shakespeare's company and his first editors (1623).

8. See Thomas Rymer, *A Short View of Tragedy* (1693), Chapters 4 and 5.

diminution from the changes made by a century and a half, in manners or in words. As his personages act upon principles arising from genuine passion, very little modified by particular forms, their pleasures and vexations are communicable to all times and to all places; they are natural, and therefore durable; the adventitious peculiarities of personal habits are only superficial dyes, bright and pleasing for a little while, yet soon fading to a dim tinct, without any remains of former luster; but the discriminations of true passion are the colors of nature; they pervade the whole mass, and can only perish with the body that exhibits them. The accidental compositions of heterogeneous modes are dissolved by the chance which combined them, but the uniform simplicity of primitive qualities neither admits increase, nor suffers decay. The sand heaped by one flood is scattered by another, but the rock always continues in its place. The stream of time, which is continually washing the dissoluble fabrics of other poets, passes without injury by the adamant of Shakespeare.

If there be, what I believe there is, in every nation, a style which never becomes obsolete, a certain mode of phraseology so consonant and congenial to the analogy and principles of its respective language as to remain settled and unaltered, this style is probably to be sought in the common intercourse of life, among those who speak only to be understood, without ambition of elegance. The polite are always catching modish innovations, and the learned depart from established forms of speech, in hope of finding or making better; those who wish for distinction forsake the vulgar, when the vulgar is right; but there is a conversation above grossness and below refinement, where propriety resides, and where this poet seems to have gathered his comic dialogue. He is therefore more agreeable to the ears of the present age than any other author equally remote, and among his other excellences deserves to be studied as one of the original masters of our language.

These observations are to be considered not as unexceptionably constant, but as containing general and predominant truth. Shakespeare's familiar dialogue is affirmed to be smooth and clear, yet not wholly without ruggedness or difficulty, as a country may be eminently fruitful, though it has spots unfit for cultivation. His characters are praised as natural, though their sentiments are sometimes forced and their actions improbable; as the earth upon the whole is spherical, though its surface is varied with protuberances and cavities.

Shakespeare with his excellences has likewise faults, and faults sufficient to obscure and overwhelm any other merit. I shall show them in the proportion in which they appear to me, without envious malignity or superstitious veneration. No question can be more innocently discussed than a dead poet's pretensions to renown; and little regard is due to that bigotry which sets candor higher than truth.

His first defect is that to which may be imputed most of the evil in books or in men. He sacrifices virtue to convenience, and is so much more careful to please than to instruct, that he seems to write without any moral purpose. From his writings indeed a system of social duty may be selected, for he that thinks reasonably must think morally; but his precepts and axioms drop casually from him; he makes no just distribution of good or evil, nor is always careful to show in the virtuous a disapprobation of the wicked; he carries his persons indifferently through right and wrong, and at the close dismisses them without further care, and leaves their examples to operate by chance. This fault the barbarity of his age cannot extenuate, for it is always a writer's duty to make the world better, and justice is a virtue independent on time or place.

The plots are often so loosely formed, that a very slight consideration may improve them, and so carelessly pursued, that he seems not always fully to comprehend his own design. He omits opportunities of instructing or delighting which the train of his story seems to force upon him, and apparently rejects those exhibitions which would be more affecting, for the sake of those which are more easy.

It may be observed that in many of his plays the latter part is evidently neglected. When he found himself near the end of his work and in view of his reward, he shortened the labor, to snatch the profit. He therefore remits his efforts where he should most vigorously exert them, and his catastrophe is improbably produced or imperfectly represented.

He had no regard to distinction of time or place, but gives to one age or nation, without scruple, the customs, institutions, and opinions of another, at the expense not only of likelihood but of possibility. These faults Pope has endeavored, with more zeal than judgment, to transfer to his imagined interpolators. We need not wonder to find Hector quoting Aristotle, when we see the loves of Theseus and Hippolyta combined with the Gothic mythology of fairies. Shakespeare, indeed, was not the only violator of chronology, for in the same age Sidney, who wanted not the advantages of learning, has, in his *Arcadia,* confounded the pastoral with the feudal times, the days of innocence, quiet, and security with those of turbulence, violence, and adventure.

In his comic scenes he is seldom very successful, when he engages his characters in reciprocations of smartness and contest of sarcasm; their jests are commonly gross, and their pleasantry licentious; neither his gentlemen nor his ladies have much delicacy, nor are sufficiently distinguished from his clowns by any appearance of refined manners. Whether he represented the real conversation of his time is not easy to determine; the reign of Elizabeth is commonly supposed to have been a time of stateliness, formality, and reserve; yet perhaps the relaxations of that severity were not very elegant. There must, however, have been always some modes of gaiety preferable to others, and a writer ought to choose the best.

In tragedy his performance seems constantly to be worse, as his labor is more. The effusions of passion which exigence forces out are for the most part striking and energetic; but whenever he solicits his invention, or strains his faculties, the offspring of his throes is tumor, meanness, tediousness, and obscurity.

In narration he affects a disproportionate pomp of diction and a wearisome train of circumlocution, and tells the incident imperfectly in many words, which might have been more plainly delivered in few. Narration in dramatic poetry is naturally tedious, as it is unanimated and inactive and obstructs the progress of the action; it should therefore always be rapid, and enlivened by frequent interruption. Shakespeare found it an encumbrance, and instead of lightening it by brevity, endeavored to recommend it by dignity and splendor.

His declamations or set speeches are commonly cold and weak, for his power was the power of nature; when he endeavored, like other tragic writers, to catch opportunities of amplification, and instead of inquiring what the occasion demanded, to show how much his stores of knowledge could supply, he seldom escapes without the pity or resentment of his reader.

It is incident to him to be now and then entangled with an unwieldy sentiment which he cannot well express, and will not reject; he struggles with it awhile and, if it continues stubborn, comprises it in words such as occur, and leaves it to be disentangled and evolved by those who have more leisure to bestow upon it.

Not that always where the language is intricate the thought is subtle, or the image always great where the line is bulky; the equality of words to things is very often neglected, and trivial sentiments and vulgar ideas disappoint the attention to which they are recommended by sonorous epithets and swelling figures.

But the admirers of this great poet have most reason to complain when he approaches nearest to his highest excellence, and seems fully resolved to sink them in dejection, and mollify them with tender emotions by the fall of greatness, the danger of innocence, or the crosses of love. What he does best, he soon ceases to do. He is not long soft and pathetic without some idle conceit, or contemptible equivocation. He no sooner begins to move than he counteracts himself; and terror and pity, as they are rising in the mind, are checked and blasted by sudden frigidity.

A quibble is to Shakespeare what luminous vapors are to the traveler; he follows it at all adventures; it is sure to lead him out of his way, and sure to engulf him in the mire. It has some malignant power over his mind, and its fascinations are irresistible. Whatever be the dignity or profundity of his disquisition, whether he be enlarging knowledge or exalting affection, whether he be amusing attention with incidents, or enchaining it in suspense, let but a quibble spring up before him, and he leaves his work unfinished. A quibble is the golden apple for which he will always turn aside from his career, or stoop from his elevation. A quibble, poor and barren as it is, gave him such delight that he was content to purchase it by the sacrifice of reason, propriety, and truth. A quibble was to him the fatal Cleopatra for which he lost the world, and was content to lose it.

It will be thought strange that, in enumerating the defects of this writer, I have not yet mentioned his neglect of the unities, his violation of those laws which have been instituted and established by the joint authority of poets and of critics.

For his other deviations from the art of writing, I resign him to critical justice, without making any other demand in his favor, than that which must be indulged to all human excellence; that his virtues be rated with his failings. But, from the censure which this irregularity may bring upon him, I shall, with due reverence to that learning which I must oppose, adventure to try how I can defend him.

His histories, being neither tragedies nor comedies, are not subject to any of their laws; nothing more is necessary to all the praise which they expect than that the changes of action be so prepared as to be understood, that the incidents be various and affecting, and the characters consistent, natural, and distinct. No other unity is intended, and therefore none is to be sought.

In his other works he has well enough preserved the unity of action. He has not, indeed, an intrigue regularly perplexed and regularly unraveled; he does not endeavor to hide his design only to discover it, for this is seldom the order of real events, and Shakespeare is the poet of nature. But his plan has commonly what Aristotle requires, a beginning, a middle, and an end; one event is concatenated with another, and the conclusion follows by easy consequence. There are perhaps some incidents that might be spared, as in other poets there is much talk that only fills up time upon the stage; but the general system makes gradual advances, and the end of the play is the end of expectation.

To the unities of time and place he has shown no regard; and perhaps a nearer view of the principles on which they stand will diminish their value, and withdraw from them the veneration which, from the time of Corneille, they have very generally received, by discovering that they have given more trouble to the poet than pleasure to the auditor.

The necessity of observing the unities of time and place arises from the supposed necessity of making the drama credible. The critics hold it impossible that an action of months or years can be possibly believed to pass in three hours; or that the spectator can suppose himself to sit in the theater while ambassadors go and return between distant kings, while armies are levied and towns besieged, while an exile wanders and returns, or till he whom they saw courting his mistress, shall lament the untimely fall of his son. The mind revolts from evident falsehood, and fiction loses its force when it departs from the resemblance of reality.

From the narrow limitation of time necessarily arises the contraction of place. The spectator, who knows that he saw the first act at Alexandria, cannot suppose that he sees the next at Rome, at a distance to which not the dragons of Medea could, in so short a time, have transported him; he knows with certainty that he has not changed his place; and he knows that place cannot change itself; that what was a house cannot become a plain; that what was Thebes can never be Persepolis.

Such is the triumphant language with which a critic exults over the misery of an irregular poet, and exults commonly without resistance or reply. It is time therefore to tell him, by the authority of Shakespeare, that he assumes, as an unquestionable principle, a position which, while his breath is forming it into words, his understanding pronounces to be false. It is false, that any representation is mistaken for reality; that any dramatic fable in its materiality was ever credible or, for a single moment, was ever credited.

The objection arising from the impossibility of passing the first hour at Alexandria and the next at Rome supposes that, when the play opens the spectator really imagines himself at Alexandria, and believes that his walk to the theater has been a voyage to Egypt, and that he lives in the days of Antony and Cleopatra. Surely he that imagines this may imagine more. He that can take the stage at one time for the palace of the Ptolemies may take it in half an hour for the promontory of Actium. Delusion, if delusion be admitted, has no certain limitation; if the spectator can be once persuaded that his old acquaintance are Alexander and Caesar, that a room illuminated with candles is the plain of Pharsalia, or the bank of Granicus, he is in a state of elevation above the reach of reason or of truth, and from the heights of empyrean poetry may despise the circumscriptions of terrestrial nature. There is no reason why a mind thus wandering in ecstasy should count the clock, or why an hour should not be a century in that calenture of the brains that can make the stage a field.

The truth is that the spectators are always in their senses and know, from the first act to the last, that the stage is only a stage, and that the players are only players. They come to hear a certain number of lines recited with just gesture and elegant modulation. The lines relate to some action, and an action must be in some place; but the different actions that complete a story may be in places very remote from each other; and where is the absurdity of allowing that space to represent first Athens, and then Sicily, which was always known to be neither Sicily nor Athens but a modern theater?

By supposition, as place is introduced, time may be extended. The time required by the fable elapses for the most part between the acts; for, of so much of the action as is represented, the real and poetical duration is the same. If, in the first act, preparations for war against Mithridates are represented to be made in Rome, the event of the war may without absurdity be represented, in the catastrophe, as happening in Pontus; we know that there is neither war, nor preparation for war; we know that we are neither in Rome nor Pontus; that neither Mithridates nor Lucullus are before us. The drama exhibits successive imitations of successive actions; and why may not the second imitation represent an action that happened years after the first, if it be so connected with it that nothing but time can be supposed to intervene? Time is, of all modes of existence, most obsequious to the imagination; a lapse of years is as easily conceived as a passage of hours. In contemplation we easily contract the time of real actions, and therefore willingly permit it to be contracted when we only see their imitation.

It will be asked how the drama moves, if it is not credited. It is credited with all the credit due to a drama. It is credited, whenever it moves, as a just picture of a real original; as representing to the auditor what he would himself feel, if he were to do or suffer what is there feigned to be suffered or to be done. The reflection that strikes the heart is not that the evils before us are real evils, but that they are evils to which we ourselves may be exposed. If there be any fallacy, it is not that we fancy the players, but that we fancy ourselves, unhappy for a moment; but we rather lament the possibility than suppose the presence of misery, as a mother weeps over her babe when she remembers that death may take it from her. The delight of tragedy proceeds from our consciousness of fiction; if we thought murders and treasons real, they would please no more.

Imitations produce pain or pleasure not because they are mistaken for realities, but because they bring realities to mind. When the imagination is recreated by a painted landscape, the trees are not supposed capable to give us shade, or the fountains coolness; but we consider how we should be pleased with such fountains playing beside us, and such woods waving over us. We are agitated in reading the history of *Henry the Fifth,* yet no man takes his book for the field of Agincourt. A dramatic exhibition is a book recited with concomitants that increase or diminish its effect. Familiar comedy is often more powerful on the theater than in the page; imperial tragedy is always less. The humor of Petruchio may be heightened by grimace, but what voice or what gesture can hope to add dignity or force to the soliloquy of Cato? [9]

A play read affects the mind like a play acted. It is therefore evident that the action is not supposed to be real, and it follows that between the acts a longer or shorter time may be allowed to pass, and that no more account of space or duration is to be taken by the auditor of a drama than by the reader of a narrative, before whom may pass in an hour the life of a hero, or the revolutions of an empire.

Whether Shakespeare knew the unities and rejected them by design, or deviated from them by happy ignorance, it is, I think, impossible to decide and useless to inquire. We may reasonably suppose that, when he rose to notice, he did not want [10] the counsels and admonitions of scholars and critics, and that he at last deliberately persisted in a practice which he might have begun by chance. As nothing is essential to the fable but unity of action, and as the unities of time and place arise evidently from false assumptions and, by circumscribing the extent of the drama, lessen its variety, I cannot think it much to be lamented that they were not known by him, or not observed. Nor, if such another poet could arise, should I very vehemently reproach him, that his first act passed at Venice, and his next in Cyprus. Such violations of rules merely positive become the comprehensive genius of Shakespeare, and such censures are suitable to the minute and slender criticism of Voltaire:

Non usque adeo permiscuit imis
Longus summa dies, ut non, si voce Metelli
Serventur leges, malint a Caesare tolli.[11] . . .

As I practiced conjecture more, I learned to trust it less; and after I had printed a few plays, resolved to insert none of my own readings in the text.

9. soliloquy of Cato: Cato's soliloquy is the most famous passage in Addison's tragedy of *Cato,* V.i; in it Cato reasons on death, suicide, and immortality.   10. want: lack.   11. Lucan, *Pharsalia,* III.138-40, translated as follows by J. D. Duff: "The course of time has not wrought such confusion that the laws would not rather be trampled on by Caesar than saved by Metellus."

Upon this caution I now congratulate myself, for every day increases my doubt of my emendations.

Since I have confined my imagination to the margin, it must not be considered as very reprehensible if I have suffered it to play some freaks in its own dominion. There is no danger in conjecture, if it be proposed as conjecture; and while the text remains uninjured, those changes may be safely offered which are not considered even by him that offers them as necessary or safe.

If my readings are of little value, they have not been ostentatiously displayed or importunately obtruded. I could have written longer notes, for the art of writing notes is not of difficult attainment. The work is performed, first by railing at the stupidity, negligence, ignorance, and asinine tastelessness of the former editors, and showing, from all that goes before and all that follows, the inelegance and absurdity of the old reading; then by proposing something which to superficial readers would seem specious, but which the editor rejects with indignation; then by producing the true reading, with a long paraphrase, and concluding with loud acclamations on the discovery, and a sober wish for the advancement and prosperity of genuine criticism.

All this may be done, and perhaps done sometimes without impropriety. But I have always suspected that the reading is right which requires many words to prove it wrong; and the emendation wrong that cannot without so much labor appear to be right. The justness of a happy restoration strikes at once, and the moral precept may be well applied to criticism, *quod dubitas ne feceris.*[12]

To dread the shore which he sees spread with wrecks is natural to the sailor. I had before my eye so many critical adventures ended in miscarriage, that caution was forced upon me. I encountered in every page Wit struggling with its own sophistry, and Learning confused by the multiplicity of its views. I was forced to censure those whom I admired, and could not but reflect, while I was dispossessing their emendations, how soon the same fate might happen to my own, and how many of the readings which I have corrected may be by some other editor defended and established.

Critics I saw that others' names efface,
And fix their own, with labor, in the place;

Their own, like others, soon their place resigned,
Or disappeared, and left the first behind.[13]

(Pope)

That a conjectural critic should often be mistaken cannot be wonderful, either to others or himself, if it be considered that in his art there is no system, no principal and axiomatical truth that regulates subordinate positions. His chance of error is renewed at every attempt; an oblique view of the passage, a slight misapprehension of a phrase, a casual inattention to the parts connected, is sufficient to make him not only fail, but fail ridiculously; and when he succeeds best, he produces perhaps but one reading of many probable, and he that suggests another will always be able to dispute his claims.

It is an unhappy state, in which danger is hid under pleasure. The allurements of emendation are scarcely resistible. Conjecture has all the joy and all the pride of invention, and he that has once started a happy change is too much delighted to consider what objections may rise against it.

Yet conjectural criticism has been of great use in the learned world; nor is it my intention to depreciate a study that has exercised so many mighty minds, from the revival of learning to our own age, from the Bishop of Aleria[14] to English Bentley. The critics on ancient authors have, in the exercise of their sagacity, many assistances which the editor of Shakespeare is condemned to want. They are employed upon grammatical and settled languages, whose construction contributes so much to perspicuity that Homer has fewer passages unintelligible than Chaucer. The words have not only a known regimen, but invariable quantities, which direct and confine the choice. There are commonly more manuscripts than one; and they do not often conspire in the same mistakes. Yet Scaliger could confess to Salmasius how little satisfaction his emendations gave him: "*Illudunt nobis conjecturae nostrae, quarum nos pudet, posteaquam in meliores codices incidimus.*"[15] And Lipsius could complain that critics were making faults by trying to remove them: "*Ut olim vitiis, ita nunc remediis laboratur.*"[16] And indeed, where mere conjecture is to be

---

12. *quod . . . feceris:* i.e., "if you aren't sure yourself, refrain (from emendation)"; literally, "abstain from an action of which you doubt whether it be good or ill."

13. *The Temple of Fame,* ll. 37–40.   14. **Bishop of Aleria:** the librarian of Pope Sixtus IV: a great classical editor named Joannes Andreas (1417–80). Richard Bentley was one of the greatest of English classical scholars (1662–1742).   15. *Illudunt . . . incidimus:* "Our conjectures make us ridiculous and shame us when later we come across better manuscripts."   16. *Ut . . . laboratur:* "Whereas before we were

used, the emendations of Scaliger and Lipsius, notwithstanding their wonderful sagacity and erudition, are often vague and disputable, like mine or Theobald's.

Perhaps I may not be more censured for doing wrong than for doing little; for raising in the public expectations which at last I have not answered. The expectation of ignorance is indefinite, and that of knowledge is often tyrannical. It is hard to satisfy those who know not what to demand, or those who demand by design what they think impossible to be done. I have indeed disappointed no opinion more than my own; yet I have endeavored to perform my task with no slight solicitude. Not a single passage in the whole work has appeared to me corrupt, which I have not attempted to restore; or obscure, which I have not endeavored to illustrate. In many I have failed like others; and from many, after all my efforts, I have retreated, and confessed the repulse. I have not passed over, with affected superiority, what is equally difficult to the reader and to myself, but where I could not instruct him, have owned my ignorance. I might easily have accumulated a mass of seeming learning upon easy scenes, but it ought not to be imputed to negligence that, where nothing was necessary, nothing has been done, or that, where others have said enough, I have said no more.

Notes are often necessary, but they are necessary evils. Let him that is yet unacquainted with the powers of Shakespeare, and who desires to feel the highest pleasure that the drama can give, read every play from the first scene to the last, with utter negligence of all his commentators. When his fancy is once on the wing, let it not stoop at correction or explanation. When his attention is strongly engaged, let it disdain alike to turn aside to the name of Theobald and of Pope. Let him read on through brightness and obscurity, through integrity and corruption; let him preserve his comprehension of the dialogue and his interest in the fable. And when the pleasures of novelty have ceased, let him attempt exactness, and read the commentators.

Particular passages are cleared by notes, but the general effect of the work is weakened. The mind is refrigerated by interruption; the thoughts are diverted from the principal subject; the reader is weary, he suspects not why; and at last throws away the book, which he has too diligently studied.

Parts are not to be examined till the whole has been surveyed; there is a kind of intellectual remoteness necessary for the comprehension of any great work in its full design and its true proportions; a close approach shows the smaller niceties, but the beauty of the whole is discerned no longer.

It is not very grateful to consider how little the succession of editors has added to this author's power of pleasing. He was read, admired, studied, and imitated, while he was yet deformed with all the improprieties which ignorance and neglect could accumulate upon him; while the reading was yet not rectified, nor his allusions understood; yet then did Dryden pronounce " that Shakespeare was the man who, of all modern and perhaps ancient poets, had the largest and most comprehensive soul. All the images of nature were still present to him, and he drew them not laboriously, but luckily. When he describes anything, you more than see it, you feel it, too. Those who accuse him to have wanted learning, give him the greater commendation: he was naturally learned: he needed not the spectacles of books to read Nature; he looked inwards, and found her there. I cannot say he is everywhere alike; were he so, I should do him injury to compare him with the greatest of mankind. He is many times flat and insipid, his comic wit degenerating into clenches, his serious swelling into bombast. But he is always great, when some great occasion is presented to him: no man can say, he ever had a fit subject for his wit, and did not then raise himself as high above the rest of poets,

Quantum lenta solent inter viburna cupressi." [17]

It is to be lamented that such a writer should want a commentary, that his language should become obsolete or his sentiments obscure. But it is vain to carry wishes beyond the condition of human things; that which must happen to all has happened to Shakespeare, by accident and time; and more than has been suffered by any other writer since the use of types has been suffered by him through his own negligence of fame, or perhaps by that superiority of mind which despised its own performances, when it compared them with its powers, and judged those works unworthy to be preserved which the critics of following ages were to contend for the fame of restoring and explaining.

---

toiling over corruptions, now it is emendations that give us the trouble."   Justus Lipsius (1547–1606), a Flemish humanist, preceded Scaliger as professor at the University of Leyden.

17. *Quantum . . . cupressi:* Dryden, "An Essay of Dramatic Poesy." The Latin is from Virgil, *Eclogue,* I.25: "as cypresses tower above the bending osiers."

Among these candidates of inferior fame, I am now to stand the judgment of the public; and wish that I could confidently produce my commentary as equal to the encouragement which I have had the honor of receiving. Every work of this kind is by its nature deficient, and I should feel little solicitude about the sentence were it to be pronounced only by the skillful and the learned.

ON *HENRY IV*

None of Shakespeare's plays are more read than the first and second parts of *Henry the Fourth*. Perhaps no author has ever in two plays afforded so much delight. The great events are interesting, for the fate of kingdoms depends upon them; the slighter occurrences are diverting and, except one or two, sufficiently probable; the incidents are multiplied with wonderful fertility of invention, and the characters diversified with the utmost nicety of discernment, and the profoundest skill in the nature of man.

The prince, who is the hero both of the comic and tragic part, is a young man of great abilities and violent passions, whose sentiments are right, though his actions are wrong; whose virtues are obscured by negligence, and whose understanding is dissipated by levity. In his idle hours he is rather loose than wicked, and when the occasion forces out his latent qualities, he is great without effort, and brave without tumult. The trifler is roused into a hero, and the hero again reposes in the trifler. This character is great, original, and just.

Percy is a rugged soldier, choleric and quarrelsome, and has only the soldier's virtues, generosity and courage.

But Falstaff unimitated, unimitable Falstaff, how shall I describe thee? Thou compound of sense and vice; of sense which may be admired but not esteemed, of vice which may be despised, but hardly detested. Falstaff is a character loaded with faults, and with those faults which naturally produce contempt. He is a thief and a glutton, a coward and a boaster, always ready to cheat the weak and prey upon the poor; to terrify the timorous and insult the defenseless. At once obsequious and malignant, he satirizes in their absence those whom he lives by flattering. He is familiar with the prince only as an agent of vice, but of this familiarity he is so proud as not only to be supercilious and haughty with common men, but to think his interest of importance to the Duke of Lancaster. Yet the man thus corrupt, thus despicable, makes himself necessary to the prince that despises him, by the most pleasing of all qualities, perpetual gaiety, by an unfailing power of exciting laughter, which is the more freely indulged, as his wit is not of the splendid or ambitious kind, but consists in easy escapes and sallies of levity, which make sport but raise no envy. It must be observed that he is stained with no enormous or sanguinary crimes, so that his licentiousness is not so offensive but that it may be borne for his mirth.

The moral to be drawn from this representation is that no man is more dangerous than he that with a will to corrupt hath the power to please; and that neither wit nor honesty ought to think themselves safe with such a companion when they see Henry seduced by Falstaff.

ON POLONIUS

Polonius is a man bred in courts, exercised in business, stored with observation, confident of his knowledge, proud of his eloquence, and declining into dotage. His mode of oratory is truly represented as designed to ridicule the practice of those times, of prefaces that made no introduction, and of method that embarrassed rather than explained. This part of his character is accidental, the rest is natural. Such a man is positive and confident because he knows that his mind was once strong, and knows not that it is become weak. Such a man excels in general principles, but fails in the particular application. He is knowing in retrospect, and ignorant in foresight. While he depends upon his memory, and can draw from his repositories of knowledge, he utters weighty sentences and gives useful counsel; but as the mind in its enfeebled state cannot be kept long busy and intent, the old man is subject to sudden dereliction of his faculties; he loses the order of his ideas, and entangles himself in his own thoughts, till he recovers the leading principle, and falls again into his former train. This idea of dotage encroaching upon wisdom, will solve all the phenomena of the character of Polonius.

THE LIVES OF THE POETS

In the spring of 1777, Johnson was asked to supply concise biographical prefaces to a collective edition of the more considerable English poets. The idea was congenial, and he undertook it, apparently, without scrutinizing any list of authors. He neither decided the names to be included nor urged the dropping of any already chosen — except that four or five minor poets seem to have been added at his suggestion. Johnson labored at his task during four years, "dilatorily and hastily," as he described it: "unwilling to work and working with vigor and haste." Not all were published at the same time. The first four volumes, containing twenty-two prefaces (seventeen of them in volume iv), appeared in 1779. Six more volumes, with the remaining thirty prefaces, were published in 1781. In this series Cowley and Waller shared a volume, as did also Milton and Butler, while Dryden and Pope had each a volume to himself. The works of the poets were published separate from the prefaces, in fifty-six following volumes, and concluded with a two-volume index. The earliest poet included was Cowley; Collins and Gray were two of the latest.

The inequality of length among the prefaces had not been anticipated, and was due to the fact that on the most interesting or congenial figures Johnson was moved to write detailed biographies and a serial examination of the works. He kept to the original scale where he was not particularly engaged by his subject. The *Cowley,* the first considerable departure from the norm, is known to have been in the press by July, 1778. It is important today, not so much for its account of Cowley himself, as for the memorable discussion of wit and the Metaphysical school of poets, a name to which Johnson gave general currency, although he was not the first to use it. The essay on Milton is a magnificent tribute but was resented by Milton worshipers on its first appearance. It was written in six weeks, at the beginning of the year 1779.

The *Pope* was written last of all. It is the longest and (with the possible exception of the *Savage*), the finest, most subtly discriminating, of all the *Lives.* It is a tripartite essay, unfortunately too extensive for full inclusion here. The first part is a chronological account of Pope's life; the second, a character analysis rising out of, and transcending, the biographical evidence; 'and the last, a judicial review of the series of Pope's published writings. It is both a literary history and a psychological study. The complexity of Pope's nature and the greatness of his genius evoke the fullest exercise of Johnson's capacity for blending justice and mercy; for the impartial detection of motive, level judgment of conduct, and compassion for human weakness; and for magnanimous acknowledgment, with no self-protective reservations, of genuinely great achievement.

from MILTON

Milton has the reputation of having been in his youth eminently beautiful, so as to have been called the Lady of his college. His hair, which was of a light brown, parted at the foretop, and hung down upon his shoulders, according to the picture which he has given of Adam. He was, however, not of the heroic stature, but rather below the middle size, according to Mr. Richardson, who mentions him as having narrowly escaped from being "short and thick." [1] He was vigorous and active, and delighted in the exercise of the sword, in which he is related to have been eminently skillful. His weapon was, I believe, not the rapier, but the backsword, of which he recommends the use in his book on education.[2]

His eyes are said never to have been bright; but, if he was a dexterous fencer, they must have been once quick.

His domestic habits, so far as they are known, were those of a severe student. He drank little strong drink of any kind, and fed without excess in quantity, and in his earlier years without delicacy of choice. In his youth he studied late at night; but afterwards changed his hours, and rested in bed from nine to four in the summer, and five in winter. The course of his day was best known after he was blind. When he first rose he heard a chapter in the Hebrew Bible, and then studied till twelve; then took some exercise for an hour; then dined; then played on the organ and sung, or heard another sing; then studied to six; then entertained his visitors till eight; then supped and, after a pipe of tobacco and a glass of water, went to bed.

So is his life described; but this even tenor appears attainable only in colleges. He that lives in the world will sometimes have the succession of his practice broken and confused. Visitors, of whom Milton is represented to have had great numbers, will come and stay unseasonably; business, of which every man has some, must be done when others will do it.

When he did not care to rise early he had something read to him by his bedside; perhaps at this time his daughters were employed. He composed much in the morning and dictated in the day, sit-

LIFE OF MILTON. 1. "short . . . thick": Jonathan Richardson, *Explanatory Notes and Remarks on Paradise Lost* (1734), p. 2. 2. book on education: *Of Education: To Master Samuel Hartlib* (1644), final section.

ting obliquely in an elbow chair, with his leg thrown over the arm.

Fortune appears not to have had much of his care. In the civil wars he lent his personal estate to the parliament, but when, after the contest was decided, he solicited repayment, he met not only with neglect but " sharp rebuke "; and, having tired both himself and his friends, was given up to poverty and hopeless indignation, till he showed how able he was to do greater service. He was then made Latin secretary, with two hundred pounds a year, and had a thousand pounds for his *Defense of the People*. His widow, who after his death retired to Namptwich in Cheshire, and died about 1729, is said to have reported that he lost two thousand pounds by entrusting it to a scrivener; and that, in the general depredation upon the Church, he had grasped an estate of about sixty pounds a year belonging to Westminster Abbey, which, like other sharers of the plunder of rebellion, he was afterwards obliged to return. Two thousand pounds which he had placed in the Excise Office were also lost. There is yet no reason to believe that he was ever reduced to indigence; his wants being few were competently supplied. He sold his library before his death, and left his family fifteen hundred pounds; on which his widow laid hold, and only gave one hundred to each of his daughters.

His literature was unquestionably great. He read all the languages which are considered either as learned or polite: Hebrew, with its two dialects, Greek, Latin, Italian, French, and Spanish. In Latin his skill was such as places him in the first rank of writers and critics; and he appears to have cultivated Italian with uncommon diligence. The books in which his daughter, who used to read to him, represented him as most delighting, after Homer, which he could almost repeat, were Ovid's *Metamorphoses* and Euripides. His Euripides is, by Mr. Cradock's kindness, now in my hands; the margin is sometimes noted, but I have found nothing remarkable.

Of the English poets he set most value upon Spenser, Shakespeare, and Cowley. Spenser was apparently his favorite; Shakespeare he may easily be supposed to like, with every other skillful reader, but I should not have expected that Cowley, whose ideas of excellence were different from his own, would have had much of his approbation. His character of Dryden, who sometimes visited him,

was that he was a good rhymist, but no poet.

His theological opinions are said to have been first Calvinistical and afterwards, perhaps when he began to hate the Presbyterians, to have extended towards Arminianism. In the mixed questions of theology and government he never thinks that he can recede far enough from popery or prelacy, but what Baudius says of Erasmus seems applicable to him: " *magis habuit quod fugeret, quam quod sequeretur.* " [3] He had determined rather what to condemn than what to approve. He has not associated himself with any denomination of Protestants; we know rather what he was not, than what he was. He was not of the Church of Rome; he was not of the Church of England.

To be of no church is dangerous. Religion, of which the rewards are distant and which is animated only by faith and hope, will glide by degrees out of the mind unless it be invigorated and reimpressed by external ordinances, by stated calls to worship, and the salutary influence of example. Milton, who appears to have had full conviction of the truth of Christianity, and to have regarded the Holy Scriptures with the profoundest veneration, to have been untainted by any heretical peculiarity of opinion, and to have lived in a confirmed belief of the immediate and occasional agency of Providence, yet grew old without any visible worship. In the distribution of his hours, there was no hour of prayer, either solitary or with his household; omitting public prayers, he omitted all.

Of this omission the reason has been sought, upon a supposition which ought never to be made, that men live with their own approbation, and justify their conduct to themselves. Prayer certainly was not thought superfluous by him, who represents our first parents as praying acceptably in the state of innocence, and efficaciously after their fall. That he lived without prayer can hardly be affirmed; his studies and meditations were an habitual prayer. The neglect of it in his family was probably a fault for which he condemned himself, and which he intended to correct, but that death, as too often happens, intercepted his reformation.

His political notions were those of an acrimonious and surly republican, for which it is not known that he gave any better reason than that " a popular government was the most frugal; for the trappings

---

3. "*magis . . . sequeretur*": Dominic Baudius, *Epistolae*, II, letter 27. Johnson gives the sense of the Latin.

of a monarchy would set up an ordinary common-wealth." [4] It is surely very shallow policy that supposes money to be the chief good; and even this without considering that the support and expense of a court is for the most part only a particular kind of traffic, by which money is circulated without any national impoverishment.

Milton's republicanism was, I am afraid, founded in an envious hatred of greatness, and a sullen desire of independence; in petulance impatient of control, and pride disdainful of superiority. He hated monarchs in the state and prelates in the church; for he hated all whom he was required to obey. It is to be suspected that his predominant desire was to destroy rather than establish, and that he felt not so much the love of liberty as repugnance to authority.

It has been observed that they who most loudly clamor for liberty do not most liberally grant it. What we know of Milton's character in domestic relations is that he was severe and arbitrary. His family consisted of women; and there appears in his books something like a Turkish contempt of females, as subordinate and inferior beings. That his own daughters might not break the ranks, he suffered them to be depressed by a mean and penurious education. He thought woman made only for obedience, and man only for rebellion. . . .

One of the poems on which much praise has been bestowed is "Lycidas"; of which the diction is harsh, the rhymes uncertain, and the numbers unpleasing. What beauty there is, we must therefore seek in the sentiments and images. It is not to be considered as the effusion of real passion, for passion runs not after remote allusions and obscure opinions. Passion plucks no berries from the myrtle and ivy, nor calls upon Arethuse and Mincius, nor tells of "rough satyrs and fauns with cloven heel." Where there is leisure for fiction there is little grief.

In this poem there is no nature, for there is no truth; there is no art, for there is nothing new. Its form is that of a pastoral, easy, vulgar, and therefore disgusting; whatever images it can supply are long ago exhausted, and its inherent improbability always forces dissatisfaction on the mind. When Cowley tells of Hervey [5] that they studied together, it is easy to suppose how much he must miss the companion of his labors and the partner

of his discoveries; but what image of tenderness can be excited by these lines!

We drove afield, and both together heard
What time the grey-fly winds her sultry horn,
Battening our flocks with the fresh dews of night.

We know that they never drove afield, and that they had no flocks to batten; and though it be allowed that the representation may be allegorical, the true meaning is so uncertain and remote that it is never sought because it cannot be known when it is found.

Among the flocks and copses and flowers appear the heathen deities, Jove and Phoebus, Neptune and Aeolus, with a long train of mythological imagery, such as a college easily supplies. Nothing can less display knowledge or less exercise invention than to tell how a shepherd has lost his companion and must now feed his flocks alone, without any judge of his skill in piping; and how one god asks another god what is become of Lycidas, and how neither god can tell. He who thus grieves will excite no sympathy; he who thus praises will confer no honor.

This poem has yet a grosser fault. With these trifling fictions are mingled the most awful and sacred truths, such as ought never to be polluted with such irreverent combinations. The shepherd likewise is now a feeder of sheep, and afterwards an ecclesiastical pastor, a superintendent of a Christian flock. Such equivocations are always unskillful, but here they are indecent, and at least approach to impiety, of which, however, I believe the writer not to have been conscious.

Such is the power of reputation justly acquired that its blaze drives away the eye from nice examination. Surely no man could have fancied that he read "Lycidas" with pleasure had he not known its author.

Of the two pieces, "L'Allegro" and "Il Penseroso," I believe opinion is uniform; every man that reads them, reads them with pleasure. The author's design is not, what Theobald has remarked, merely to show how objects derived their colors from the mind, by representing the operation of the same things upon the gay and the melancholy temper, or upon the same man as he is differently disposed; but rather how, among the successive variety of appearances, every disposition of mind takes hold on those by which it may be gratified.

The *cheerful* man hears the lark in the morning; the *pensive* man hears the nightingale in the eve-

---

4. "a . . . commonwealth": quoted from John Toland's *Life of Milton* (1698), p. 139. 5. **Cowley . . . Hervey**: Abraham Cowley, "On the Death of Mr. William Hervey," in *Miscellanies* (1656).

ning. The *cheerful* man sees the cock strut, and hears the horn and hounds echo in the wood; then walks " not unseen " to observe the glory of the rising sun or listen to the singing milkmaid, and view the labors of the plowman and the mower; then casts his eyes about him over scenes of smiling plenty, and looks up to the distant tower, the residence of some fair inhabitant; thus he pursues rural gaiety through a day of labor or of play, and delights himself at night with the fanciful narratives of superstitious ignorance.

The *pensive* man at one time walks " unseen " to muse at midnight, and at another hears the sullen curfew. If the weather drives him home he sits in a room lighted only by " glowing embers "; or by a lonely lamp outwatches the North Star to discover the habitation of separate souls, and varies the shades of meditation by contemplating the magnificent or pathetic scenes of tragic and epic poetry. When the morning comes, a morning gloomy with rain and wind, he walks into the dark trackless woods, falls asleep by some murmuring water, and with melancholy enthusiasm expects some dream of prognostication or some music played by aerial performers.

Both Mirth and Melancholy are solitary, silent inhabitants of the breast that neither receive nor transmit communication; no mention is therefore made of a philosophical friend or a pleasant companion. The seriousness does not arise from any participation of calamity, nor the gaiety from the pleasures of the bottle.

The man of *cheerfulness* having exhausted the country tries what " towered cities " will afford, and mingles with scenes of splendor, gay assemblies, and nuptial festivities; but he mingles a mere spectator as, when the learned comedies of Jonson or the wild dramas of Shakespeare are exhibited, he attends the theater.

The *pensive* man never loses himself in crowds, but walks the cloister or frequents the cathedral. Milton probably had not yet forsaken the Church.

Both his characters delight in music; but he seems to think that cheerful notes would have obtained from Pluto a complete dismission of Eurydice, of whom solemn sounds only procured a conditional release.

For the old age of Cheerfulness he makes no provision, but Melancholy he conducts with great dignity to the close of life. His Cheerfulness is without levity, and his Pensiveness without asperity.

Through these two poems the images are properly selected and nicely distinguished, but the colors of the diction seem not sufficiently discriminated. I know not whether the characters are kept sufficiently apart. No mirth can, indeed, be found in his melancholy; but I am afraid that I always meet some melancholy in his mirth. They are two noble efforts of imagination. . . .

Those little pieces may be dispatched without much anxiety; a greater work calls for greater care. I am now to examine *Paradise Lost,* a poem which, considered with respect to design, may claim the first place, and with respect to performance the second, among the productions of the human mind.

By the general consent of critics the first praise of genius is due to the writer of an epic poem, as it requires an assemblage of all the powers which are singly sufficient for other compositions. Poetry is the art of uniting pleasure with truth, by calling imagination to the help of reason. Epic poetry undertakes to teach the most important truths by the most pleasing precepts, and therefore relates some great event in the most affecting manner. History must supply the writer with the rudiments of narration, which he must improve and exalt by a nobler art, must animate by dramatic energy, and diversify by retrospection and anticipation; morality must teach him the exact bounds and different shades of vice and virtue; from policy and the practice of life he has to learn the discriminations of character and the tendency of the passions, either single or combined; and physiology must supply him with illustrations and images. To put these materials to poetical use is required an imagination capable of painting nature and realizing fiction. Nor is he yet a poet till he has attained the whole extension of his language, distinguished all the delicacies of phrase and all the colors of words, and learned to adjust their different sounds to all the varieties of metrical modulation.

Bossu is of opinion that the poet's first work is to find a *moral,* which his fable is afterwards to illustrate and establish.[6] This seems to have been the process only of Milton: the moral of other poems is incidental and consequent; in Milton's only it is essential and intrinsic. His purpose was the most useful and the most arduous: " to vindicate the ways of God to man "; to show the reason-

6. **Bossu . . . establish:** Le Bossu, *Traité du Poème Épique,* I.7.

ableness of religion, and the necessity of obedience to the Divine Law.

To convey this moral there must be a *fable,* a narration artfully constructed so as to excite curiosity and surprise expectation. In this part of his work Milton must be confessed to have equaled every other poet. He has involved in his account of the fall of man the events which preceded, and those that were to follow it; he has interwoven the whole system of theology with such propriety that every part appears to be necessary, and scarcely any recital is wished shorter for the sake of quickening the progress of the main action.

The subject of an epic poem is naturally an event of great importance. That of Milton is not the destruction of a city, the conduct of a colony, or the foundation of an empire. His subject is the fate of worlds, the revolutions of heaven and of earth; rebellion against the Supreme King raised by the highest order of created beings; the overthrow of their host and the punishment of their crime; the creation of a new race of reasonable creatures; their original happiness and innocence, their forfeiture of immortality, and their restoration to hope and peace.

Great events can be hastened or retarded only by persons of elevated dignity. Before the greatness displayed in Milton's poem all other greatness shrinks away. The weakest of his agents are the highest and noblest of human beings, the original parents of mankind; with whose actions the elements consented; on whose rectitude or deviation of will depended the state of terrestrial nature and the condition of all the future inhabitants of the globe.

Of the other agents in the poem, the chief are such as it is irreverence to name on slight occasions. The rest were lower powers,

> of which the least could wield
> Those elements, and arm him with the force
> Of all their regions; [7]

powers which only the control of Omnipotence restrains from laying creation waste, and filling the vast expanse of space with ruin and confusion. To display the motives and actions of beings thus superior, so far as human reason can examine them or human imagination represent them, is the task which this mighty poet has undertaken and performed.

In the examination of epic poems much speculation is commonly employed upon the *characters.* The characters in the *Paradise Lost* which admit of examination are those of angels and of man; of angels good and evil, of man in his innocent and sinful state.

Among the angels the virtue of Raphael is mild and placid, of easy condescension and free communication; that of Michael is regal and lofty, and, as may seem, attentive to the dignity of his own nature. Abdiel and Gabriel appear occasionally, and act as every incident requires; the solitary fidelity of Abdiel is very amiably painted. [8]

Of the evil angels the characters are more diversified. To Satan, as Addison observes, such sentiments are given as suit " the most exalted and most depraved being." [9] Milton has been censured by Clarke for the impiety which sometimes breaks from Satan's mouth. For there are thoughts, as he justly remarks, which no observation of character can justify, because no good man would willingly permit them to pass, however transiently, through his own mind. [10] To make Satan speak as a rebel, without any such expressions as might taint the reader's imagination, was indeed one of the great difficulties in Milton's undertaking, and I cannot but think that he has extricated himself with great happiness. There is in Satan's speeches little that can give pain to a pious ear. The language of rebellion cannot be the same with that of obedience. The malignity of Satan foams in haughtiness and obstinacy; but his expressions are commonly general, and no otherwise offensive than as they are wicked.

The other chiefs of the celestial rebellion are very judiciously discriminated in the first and second books; and the ferocious character of Moloch appears, both in the battle and the council, with exact consistency.

To Adam and to Eve are given during their innocence such sentiments as innocence can generate and utter. Their love is pure benevolence and mutual veneration; their repasts are without luxury and their diligence without toil. Their addresses to their Maker have little more than the voice of admiration and gratitude. Fruition left them nothing to ask, and Innocence left them nothing to fear.

But with guilt enter distrust and discord, mutual

---

7. *Paradise Lost,* VI.221. Many of the following quotations from *Paradise Lost* may be found on pp. 224–72, above.

8. *Paradise Lost,* V.802 ff. 9. "the . . . being": *Spectator,* No. 303. 10. Clarke . . . mind: John Clarke, *Essay upon Study* (1731), p. 204.

accusation, and stubborn self-defense; they regard each other with alienated minds, and dread their Creator as the avenger of their transgression. At last they seek shelter in his mercy, soften to repentance, and melt in supplication. Both before and after the Fall the superiority of Adam is diligently sustained.

Of the *probable* and the *marvelous,* two parts of a vulgar epic poem which immerge the critic in deep consideration, the *Paradise Lost* requires little to be said. It contains the history of a miracle, of creation and redemption; it displays the power and the mercy of the Supreme Being; the probable therefore is marvelous, and the marvelous is probable. The substance of the narrative is truth; and, as truth allows no choice, it is, like necessity, superior to rule. To the accidental or adventitious parts, as to everything human, some slight exceptions may be made. But the main fabric is immovably supported.

It is justly remarked by Addison [11] that this poem has, by the nature of its subject, the advantage above all others, that it is universally and perpetually interesting. All mankind will, through all ages, bear the same relation to Adam and to Eve, and must partake of that good and evil which extend to themselves.

Of the *machinery,* so called from θεὸς ἀπὸ μηχανῆς,[12] by which is meant the occasional interposition of supernatural power, another fertile topic of critical remarks, here is no room to speak, because everything is done under the immediate and visible direction of Heaven; but the rule is so far observed that no part of the action could have been accomplished by any other means.

Of *episodes* I think there are only two, contained in Raphael's relation of the war in heaven and Michael's prophetic account of the changes to happen in this world.[13] Both are closely connected with the great action; one was necessary to Adam as a warning, the other as a consolation.

To the completeness or *integrity* of the design nothing can be objected; it has distinctly and clearly what Aristotle requires, a beginning, a middle, and an end. There is perhaps no poem of the same length from which so little can be taken without apparent mutilation. Here are no funeral games,

nor is there any long description of a shield.[14] The short digressions at the beginning of the third, seventh, and ninth books might doubtless be spared; but superfluities so beautiful who would take away? or who does not wish that the author of the *Iliad* had gratified succeeding ages with a little knowledge of himself? Perhaps no passages are more frequently or more attentively read than those extrinsic paragraphs; and, since the end of poetry is pleasure, that cannot be unpoetical with which all are pleased.

The questions, whether the action of the poem be strictly *one,* whether the poem can be properly termed *heroic,* and who is the hero, are raised by such readers as draw their principles of judgment rather from books than from reason. Milton, though he entitled *Paradise Lost* only a " poem," yet calls it himself " heroic song." [15] Dryden, petulantly and indecently, denies the heroism of Adam because he was overcome, but there is no reason why the hero should not be unfortunate except established practice, since success and virtue do not go necessarily together. Cato is the hero of Lucan, but Lucan's authority will not be suffered by Quintilian to decide.[16] However, if success be necessary, Adam's deceiver was at last crushed; Adam was restored to his Maker's favor, and therefore may securely resume his human rank.

After the scheme and fabric of the poem must be considered its component parts, the sentiments, and the diction.

The *sentiments,* as expressive of manners or appropriated to characters, are for the greater part unexceptionably just.

Splendid passages containing lessons of morality or precepts of prudence occur seldom. Such is the original formation of this poem that as it admits no human manners till the Fall, it can give little assistance to human conduct. Its end is to raise the thoughts above sublunary cares or pleasures. Yet the praise of that fortitude, with which Abdiel maintained his singularity of virtue against the scorn of multitudes, may be accommodated to all times; and Raphael's reproof of Adam's curiosity after the planetary motions, with the answer returned by Adam, may be confidently opposed to any rule of life which any poet has delivered.[17]

---

11. Addison: *Spectator,* No. 273. 12. θεὸς . . . μηχανῆς: Aristotle, *Poetics,* XV.10: *"Deus ex machina."* 13. Raphael's . . . world: *Paradise Lost,* V.577 ff., XI.334 ff.

14. funeral . . . shield: The references here are to Books XVIII and XXIII of the *Iliad.* 15. "heroic song": *Paradise Lost,* IX.25. 16. but . . . decide: i.e., Quintilian does not regard Lucan as beyond challenge. Of the *Pharsalia,* he declared it fitter to be studied by orators than by poets. 17. Raphael's . . . delivered: *Paradise Lost,* VIII.66 ff.

The thoughts which are occasionally called forth in the progress are such as could only be produced by an imagination in the highest degree fervid and active, to which materials were supplied by incessant study and unlimited curiosity. The heat of Milton's mind might be said to sublimate his learning, to throw off into his work the spirit of science, unmingled with its grosser parts.

He had considered creation in its whole extent, and his descriptions are therefore learned. He had accustomed his imagination to unrestrained indulgence, and his conceptions therefore were extensive. The characteristic quality of his poem is sublimity. He sometimes descends to the elegant, but his element is the great. He can occasionally invest himself with grace, but his natural port is gigantic loftiness. He can please when pleasure is required, but it is his peculiar power to astonish.

He seems to have been well acquainted with his own genius, and to know what it was that Nature had bestowed upon him more bountifully than upon others: the power of displaying the vast, illuminating the splendid, enforcing the awful, darkening the gloomy, and aggravating the dreadful; he therefore chose a subject on which too much could not be said, on which he might tire his fancy without the censure of extravagance.

The appearances of nature and the occurrences of life did not satiate his appetite of greatness. To paint things as they are requires a minute attention, and employs the memory rather than the fancy. Milton's delight was to sport in the wide regions of possibility; reality was a scene too narrow for his mind. He sent his faculties out upon discovery, into worlds where only imagination can travel, and delighted to form new modes of existence, and furnish sentiment and action to superior beings, to trace the counsels of hell, or accompany the choirs of heaven.

But he could not be always in other worlds; he must sometimes revisit earth, and tell of things visible and known. When he cannot raise wonder by the sublimity of his mind he gives delight by its fertility.

Whatever be his subject he never fails to fill the imagination. But his images and descriptions of the scenes or operations of Nature do not seem to be always copied from original form, nor to have the freshness, raciness, and energy of immediate observation. He saw Nature, as Dryden expresses it, "through the spectacles of books"; [18] and on most occasions calls learning to his assistance. The garden of Eden brings to his mind the vale of Enna, where Proserpine was gathering flowers. Satan makes his way through fighting elements, like Argo between the Cyanean rocks or Ulysses between the two *Sicilian* whirlpools, when he shunned Charybdis "on the larboard." The mythological allusions have been justly censured,[19] as not being always used with notice of their vanity; but they contribute variety to the narration, and produce an alternate exercise of the memory and the fancy.

His similes are less numerous and more various than those of his predecessors. But he does not confine himself within the limits of rigorous comparison; his great excellence is amplitude, and he expands the adventitious image beyond the dimensions which the occasion required. Thus, comparing the shield of Satan to the orb of the moon, he crowds the imagination with the discovery of the telescope and all the wonders which the telescope discovers.

Of his moral sentiments it is hardly praise to affirm that they excel those of all other poets; for this superiority he was indebted to his acquaintance with the sacred writings. The ancient epic poets, wanting the light of revelation, were very unskillful teachers of virtue; their principal characters may be great, but they are not amiable. The reader may rise from their works with a greater degree of active or passive fortitude, and sometimes of prudence; but he will be able to carry away few precepts of justice, and none of mercy.

From the Italian writers it appears that the advantages of even Christian knowledge may be possessed in vain. Ariosto's pravity is generally known; and, though the *Deliverance of Jerusalem* may be considered as a sacred subject, the poet [20] has been very sparing of moral instruction.

In Milton every line breathes sanctity of thought and purity of manners, except when the train of the narration requires the introduction of the rebellious spirits; and even they are compelled to acknowledge their subjection to God in such a manner as excites reverence and confirms piety.

Of human beings there are but two; but those

18. "through . . . books": *Essays* (ed. Ker), I.80, where Dryden says this is *not* true of Shakespeare.   19. censured: by Addison, *Spectator*, No. 297.   20. poet: Torquato Tasso (1544-95). Ariosto's "pravity" is exemplified by wild flights of imaginary adventure in a poem (the *Orlando Furioso*), grounded on the defense of Christendom against the Saracens.

two are the parents of mankind, venerable before their fall for dignity and innocence, and amiable after it for repentance and submission. In their first state their affection is tender without weakness, and their piety sublime without presumption. When they have sinned they show how discord begins in mutual frailty, and how it ought to cease in mutual forbearance; how confidence of the divine favor is forfeited by sin, and how hope of pardon may be obtained by penitence and prayer. A state of innocence we can only conceive, if indeed in our present misery it be possible to conceive it; but the sentiments and worship proper to a fallen and offending being we have all to learn, as we have all to practice.

The poet whatever be done is always great. Our progenitors in their first state conversed with angels; even when folly and sin had degraded them they had not in their humiliation "the port of mean suitors"; [21] and they rise again to reverential regard when we find that their prayers were heard.

As human passions did not enter the world before the Fall, there is in the *Paradise Lost,* little opportunity for the pathetic; but what little there is has not been lost. That passion which is peculiar to rational nature, the anguish arising from the consciousness of transgression and the horrors attending the sense of the divine displeasure, are very justly described and forcibly impressed. But the passions are moved only on one occasion; sublimity is the general and prevailing quality in this poem — sublimity variously modified, sometimes descriptive, sometimes argumentative.

The defects and faults of *Paradise Lost,* for faults and defects every work of man must have, it is the business of impartial criticism to discover. As in displaying the excellence of Milton I have not made long quotations, because of selecting beauties there had been no end, I shall in the same general manner mention that which seems to deserve censure; for what Englishman can take delight in transcribing passages which, if they lessen the reputation of Milton, diminish in some degree the honor of our country?

The generality of my scheme does not admit the frequent notice of verbal inaccuracies which Bentley,[22] perhaps better skilled in grammar than in

poetry, has often found, though he sometimes made them, and which he imputed to the obtrusions of a reviser whom the author's blindness obliged him to employ. A supposition rash and groundless, if he thought it true; and vile and pernicious if, as is said, he in private allowed it to be false.

The plan of *Paradise Lost* has this inconvenience, that it comprises neither human actions nor human manners. The man and woman who act and suffer are in a state which no other man or woman can ever know. The reader finds no transaction in which he can be engaged, beholds no condition in which he can by any effort of imagination place himself; he has, therefore, little natural curiosity or sympathy.

We all, indeed, feel the effects of Adam's disobedience; we all sin like Adam, and like him must all bewail our offenses; we have restless and insidious enemies in the fallen angels, and in the blessed spirits we have guardians and friends; in the redemption of mankind we hope to be included: in the description of heaven and hell we are surely interested, as we are all to reside hereafter either in the regions of horror or of bliss.

But these truths are too important to be new; they have been taught to our infancy; they have mingled with our solitary thoughts and familiar conversation, and are habitually interwoven with the whole texture of life. Being therefore not new they raise no unaccustomed emotion in the mind; what we knew before we cannot learn; what is not unexpected cannot surprise.

Of the ideas suggested by these awful scenes, from some we recede with reverence, except when stated hours require their association; and from others we shrink with horror, or admit them only as salutary inflictions, as counterpoises to our interests and passions. Such images rather obstruct the career of fancy than incite it.

Pleasure and terror are indeed the genuine sources of poetry; but poetical pleasure must be such as human imagination can at least conceive, and poetical terror such as human strength and fortitude may combat. The good and evil of eternity are too ponderous for the wings of wit; the mind sinks under them in passive helplessness, content with calm belief and humble adoration.

Known truths however may take a different appearance, and be conveyed to the mind by a new train of intermediate images. This Milton has undertaken, and performed with pregnancy and vigor

21. "the . . . suitors": *Paradise Lost,* XI.8.   22. Bentley: Richard Bentley, in the Preface to his edition of the poem (1732), suggests that Paradise was twice lost by the corruptions introduced by Milton's intermediary.

of mind peculiar to himself. Whoever considers the few radical positions which the Scriptures afforded him will wonder by what energetic operation he expanded them to such extent and ramified them to so much variety, restrained as he was by religious reverence from licentiousness of fiction.

Here is a full display of the united force of study and genius; of a great accumulation of materials, with judgment to digest and fancy to combine them; Milton was able to select from nature or from story, from ancient fable or from modern science, whatever could illustrate or adorn his thoughts. An accumulation of knowledge impregnated his mind, fermented by study and exalted by imagination.

It has been therefore said without an indecent hyperbole by one of his encomiasts, that in reading *Paradise Lost* we read a book of universal knowledge.

But original deficience cannot be supplied. The want of human interest is always felt. *Paradise Lost* is one of the books which the reader admires and lays down, and forgets to take up again. None ever wished it longer than it is. Its perusal is a duty rather than a pleasure. We read Milton for instruction, retire harassed and overburdened, and look elsewhere for recreation; we desert our master, and seek for companions.

Another inconvenience of Milton's design is that it requires the description of what cannot be described, the agency of spirits. He saw that immateriality supplied no images, and that he could not show angels acting but by instruments of action; he therefore invested them with form and matter. This being necessary was therefore defensible; and he should have secured the consistency of his system by keeping immateriality out of sight, and enticing his reader to drop it from his thoughts. But he has unhappily perplexed his poetry with his philosophy. His infernal and celestial powers are sometimes pure spirit and sometimes animated body. When Satan walks with his lance upon the "burning marl" he has a body; when in his passage between hell and the new world he is in danger of sinking in the vacuity and is supported by a gust of rising vapors he has a body; when he animates the toad he seems to be mere spirit that can penetrate matter at pleasure; when he "starts up in his own shape," he has at least a determined form; and when he is brought before Gabriel he has "a spear and a shield," which he had the

power of hiding in the toad, though the arms of the contending angels are evidently material.[23]

The vulgar inhabitants of Pandaemonium, being " incorporeal spirits," are " at large though without number " in a limited space, yet in the battle when they were overwhelmed by mountains their armor hurt them, " crushed in upon their substance, now grown gross by sinning." This likewise happened to the uncorrupted angels, who were overthrown " the sooner for their arms, for unarmed they might easily as spirits have evaded by contraction or remove." Even as spirits they are hardly spiritual, for " contraction " and " remove " are images of matter; but if they could have escaped without their armor, they might have escaped from it and left only the empty cover to be battered. Uriel, when he rides on a sunbeam, is material; Satan is material when he is afraid of the prowess of Adam.[24]

The confusion of spirit and matter which pervades the whole narration of the war of heaven fills it with incongruity; and the book in which it is related is, I believe, the favorite of children, and gradually neglected as knowledge is increased.

After the operation of immaterial agents which cannot be explained may be considered that of allegorical persons, which have no real existence. To exalt causes into agents, to invest abstract ideas with form, and animate them with activity has always been the right of poetry. But such airy beings are for the most part suffered only to do their natural office, and retire. Thus Fame tells a tale and Victory hovers over a general or perches on a standard, but Fame and Victory can do no more. To give them any real employment or ascribe to them any material agency is to make them allegorical no longer, but to shock the mind by ascribing effects to nonentity. In the *Prometheus* of Aeschylus we see Violence and Strength, and in the *Alcestis* of Euripides we see Death, brought upon the stage, all as active persons of the drama; but no precedents can justify absurdity.

Milton's allegory of Sin and Death is undoubtedly faulty. Sin is indeed the mother of Death, and may be allowed to be the portress of hell; but when they stop the journey of Satan, a journey described as real, and when Death offers him battle, the allegory is broken. That Sin and Death

23. See, for the allusions above, *Paradise Lost*, I.296; II.931; IV.800, 819, 990. 24. For the above, *Paradise Lost*, I.789; VI.651, 595 (in that order); IV.555, 590; IX.480 ff.

should have shown the way to hell might have been allowed; but they cannot facilitate the passage by building a bridge, because the difficulty of Satan's passage is described as real and sensible, and the bridge ought to be only figurative. The hell assigned to the rebellious spirits is described as not less local than the residence of man. It is placed in some distant part of space, separated from the regions of harmony and order by a chaotic waste and an unoccupied vacuity; but Sin and Death worked up a "mole of aggregated soil," cemented with asphaltus, a work too bulky for ideal architects.[25]

This unskillful allegory appears to me one of the greatest faults of the poem, and to this there was no temptation but the author's opinion of its beauty.

To the conduct of the narrative some objections may be made. Satan is with great expectation brought before Gabriel in paradise, and is suffered to go away unmolested. The creation of man is represented as the consequence of the vacuity left in heaven by the expulsion of the rebels; yet Satan mentions it as a report "rife in heaven" before his departure.[26]

To find sentiments for the state of innocence was very difficult; and something of anticipation perhaps is now and then discovered. Adam's discourse of dreams seems not to be the speculation of a new-created being. I know not whether his answer to the angel's reproof for curiosity does not want something of propriety; it is the speech of a man acquainted with many other men. Some philosophical notions, especially when the philosophy is false, might have been better omitted. The angel in a comparison speaks of "timorous deer," before deer were yet timorous, and before Adam could understand the comparison.[27]

Dryden remarks that Milton has some flats among his elevations.[28] This is only to say that all the parts are not equal. In every work one part must be for the sake of others; a palace must have passages, a poem must have transitions. It is no more to be required that wit should always be blazing than that the sun should always stand at noon. In a great work there is a vicissitude of

luminous and opaque parts, as there is in the world a succession of day and night. Milton, when he has expatiated in the sky, may be allowed sometimes to revisit earth; for what other author ever soared so high or sustained his flight so long?

Milton, being well versed in the Italian poets, appears to have borrowed often from them; and, as every man catches something from his companions, his desire of imitating Ariosto's levity has disgraced his work with the "Paradise of Fools," a fiction not in itself ill-imagined, but too ludicrous for its place.[29]

His play on words, in which he delights too often; his equivocations, which Bentley endeavors to defend by the example of the ancients; his unnecessary and ungraceful use of terms of art it is not necessary to mention, because they are easily remarked and generally censured, and at last bear so little proportion to the whole that they scarcely deserve the attention of a critic.

Such are the faults of that wonderful performance *Paradise Lost,* which he who can put in balance with its beauties must be considered not as nice but as dull, as less to be censured for want of candor than pitied for want of sensibility. . . .

"Rhyme," he says, and says truly, "is no necessary adjunct of true poetry."[30] But perhaps of poetry as a mental operation meter or music is no necessary adjunct; it is, however, by the music of meter that poetry has been discriminated in all languages, and in languages melodiously constructed with a due proportion of long and short syllables meter is sufficient. But one language cannot communicate its rules to another; where meter is scanty and imperfect some help is necessary. The music of the English heroic line strikes the ear so faintly that it is easily lost, unless all the syllables of every line co-operate together; this co-operation can be only obtained by the preservation of every verse unmingled with another as a distinct system of sounds, and this distinctness is obtained and preserved by the artifice of rhyme. The variety of pauses, so much boasted by the lovers of blank verse, changes the measures of an English poet to the periods of a declaimer; and there are only a few skillful and happy readers of Milton who enable their audience to perceive where the lines end

25. See *Paradise Lost,* II.648 ff.; X.283 ff.   26. See *Paradise Lost,* IV.874; VII.150; and I.650.   27. See *Paradise Lost,* V.100; VIII.179; and VI.857.   28. Dryden . . . elevations: Dryden, Preface to *Sylvae,* in *Essays* (ed. Ker), I.268.

29. *Paradise Lost,* III.444 ff.   30. "Rhyme . . . poetry": Preface to *Paradise Lost.*

or begin. " Blank verse," said an ingenious critic, " seems to be verse only to the eye." [31]

Poetry may subsist without rhyme, but English poetry will not often please; nor can rhyme ever be safely spared but where the subject is able to support itself. Blank verse makes some approach to that which is called the " lapidary style "; [32] has neither the easiness of prose nor the melody of numbers, and therefore tires by long continuance. Of the Italian writers without rhyme, whom Milton alleges as precedents, not one is popular; what reason could urge in its defense has been confuted by the ear.

But whatever be the advantage of rhyme I cannot prevail on myself to wish that Milton had been a rhymer, for I cannot wish his work to be other than it is; yet like other heroes he is to be admired rather than imitated. He that thinks himself capable of astonishing may write blank verse, but those that hope only to please must condescend to rhyme.

The highest praise of genius is original invention. Milton cannot be said to have contrived the structure of an epic poem, and therefore owes reverence to that vigor and amplitude of mind to which all generations must be indebted for the art of poetical narration, for the texture of the fable, the variation of incidents, the interposition of dialogue, and all the stratagems that surprise and enchain attention. But of all the borrowers from Homer, Milton is perhaps the least indebted. He was naturally a thinker for himself, confident of his own abilities and disdainful of help or hindrance; he did not refuse admission to the thoughts or images of his predecessors, but he did not seek them. From his contemporaries he neither courted nor received support; there is in his writings nothing by which the pride of other authors might be gratified or favor gained, no exchange of praise or solicitation of support. His great works were performed under discountenance and in blindness, but difficulties vanished at his touch; he was born for whatever is arduous; and his work is not the greatest of heroic poems, only because it is not the first.

from COWLEY

Wit, like all other things subject by their nature to the choice of man, has its changes and fashions, and at different times takes different forms. About the beginning of the seventeenth century appeared a race of writers that may be termed the Metaphysical poets, of whom in a criticism on the works of Cowley it is not improper to give some account.

The Metaphysical poets were men of learning, and to show their learning was their whole endeavor; but, unluckily resolving to show it in rhyme, instead of writing poetry they only wrote verses, and very often such verses as stood the trial of the finger better than of the ear; for the modulation was so imperfect that they were only found to be verses by counting the syllables.

If the father of criticism has rightly denominated poetry τέχνη μιμητικὴ, *an imitative art,*[1] these writers will without great wrong lose their right to the name of poets, for they cannot be said to have imitated anything: they neither copied nature nor life; neither painted the forms of matter nor represented the operations of intellect.

Those, however, who deny them to be poets allow them to be wits. Dryden confesses of himself and his contemporaries that they fall below Donne in wit, but maintains that they surpass him in poetry.[2]

If wit be well described by Pope as being " that which has been often thought, but was never before so well expressed," [3] they certainly never attained nor ever sought it, for they endeavored to be singular in their thoughts, and were careless of their diction. But Pope's account of wit is undoubtedly erroneous; he depresses it below its natural dignity, and reduces it from strength of thought to happiness of language.

If by a more noble and more adequate conception that be considered as wit which is at once natural and new, that which though not obvious is, upon its first production, acknowledged to be just; if it be that, which he that never found it, wonders how he missed; to wit of this kind the Metaphysical poets have seldom risen. Their thoughts are often new, but seldom natural; they are not obvious, but neither are they just; and the reader, far from wondering that he missed them, wonders more frequently by what perverseness of industry they were ever found.

But wit, abstracted from its effects upon the hearer, may be more rigorously and philosophically

---

31. "Blank . . . eye": William Locke; see Boswell's *Johnson* (ed. Hill-Powell), IV.43. 32. "lapidary style": i.e., the style of pompous inscription.

LIFE OF COWLEY. 1. *imitative art:* Aristotle, *Poetics,* I,V,VI, but without using the exact phrase. 2. Dryden . . . poetry: Dryden, *Essays* (ed. Ker), II.102. 3. "that . . . expressed": *Essay on Criticism,* ll. 297–98, p. 403, above.

considered as a kind of *discordia concors,* a combination of dissimilar images, or discovery of occult resemblances in things apparently unlike. Of wit, thus defined, they have more than enough. The most heterogeneous ideas are yoked by violence together; nature and art are ransacked for illustrations, comparisons, and allusions; their learning instructs, and their subtlety surprises; but the reader commonly thinks his improvement dearly bought, and, though he sometimes admires, is seldom pleased.

From this account of their compositions it will be readily inferred that they were not successful in representing or moving the affections. As they were wholly employed on something unexpected and surprising they had no regard to that uniformity of sentiment which enables us to conceive and to excite the pains and the pleasure of other minds: they never inquired what on any occasion they should have said or done, but wrote rather as beholders than partakers of human nature; as beings looking upon good and evil, impassive and at leisure; as Epicurean deities making remarks on the actions of men and the vicissitudes of life, without interest and without emotion. Their courtship was void of fondness, and their lamentation of sorrow. Their wish was only to say what they hoped had been never said before.

Nor was the sublime more within their reach than the pathetic; for they never attempted that comprehension and expanse of thought which at once fills the whole mind, and of which the first effect is sudden astonishment, and the second rational admiration. Sublimity is produced by aggregation, and littleness by dispersion. Great thoughts are always general, and consist in positions not limited by exceptions, and in descriptions not descending to minuteness. It is with great propriety that subtlety, which in its original import means exility [4] of particles, is taken in its metaphorical meaning for nicety of distinction. Those writers who lay on the watch for novelty could have little hope of greatness; for great things cannot have escaped former observation. Their attempts were always analytic: they broke every image into fragments, and could no more represent by their slender conceits and labored particularities the prospects of nature or the scenes of life, than he who dissects a sunbeam with a prism can exhibit the wide effulgence of a summer noon.

4. **exility:** thinness.

What they wanted, however, of the sublime they endeavored to supply by hyperbole; their amplification had no limits; they left not only reason but fancy behind them, and produced combinations of confused magnificence that not only could not be credited, but could not be imagined.

Yet great labor directed by great abilities is never wholly lost; if they frequently threw away their wit upon false conceits, they likewise sometimes struck out unexpected truth; if their conceits were far-fetched, they were often worth the carriage. To write on their plan it is at least necessary to read and think. No man could be born a Metaphysical poet, nor assume the dignity of a writer by descriptions copied from descriptions, by imitations borrowed from imitations, by traditional imagery and hereditary similes, by readiness of rhyme and volubility of syllables.

In perusing the works of this race of authors the mind is exercised either by recollection or inquiry; either something already learned is to be retrieved, or something new is to be examined. If their greatness seldom elevates, their acuteness often surprises; if the imagination is not always gratified, at least the powers of reflection and comparison are employed; and in the mass of materials, which ingenious absurdity has thrown together, genuine wit and useful knowledge may be sometimes found, buried perhaps in grossness of expression, but useful to those who know their value, and such as, when they are expanded to perspicuity and polished to elegance, may give luster to works which have more propriety though less copiousness of sentiment.

from POPE

The person of Pope is well known not to have been formed by the nicest model. He has, in his account of the "Little Club," [1] compared himself to a spider, and by another is described as protuberant behind and before. He is said to have been beautiful in his infancy, but he was of a constitution originally feeble and weak, and, as bodies of a tender frame are easily distorted, his deformity was probably in part the effect of his application. His stature was so low that, to bring him to a level with common tables, it was necessary to raise his

LIFE OF POPE. 1. "Little Club": This imaginary club is described in the *Guardian,* No. 92, a periodical, like the *Spectator,* which ran from March to October, 1713.

seat. But his face was not displeasing, and his eyes were animated and vivid.

By natural deformity or accidental distortion his vital functions were so much disordered that his life was a "long disease." [2] His most frequent assailant was the headache, which he used to relieve by inhaling the steam of coffee, which he very frequenty required.

Most of what can be told concerning his petty peculiarities was communicated by a female domestic of the Earl of Oxford, who knew him perhaps after the middle of life. He was then so weak as to stand in perpetual need of female attendance; extremely sensible of cold, so that he wore a kind of fur doublet under a shirt of very coarse warm linen with fine sleeves. When he rose he was invested in bodice made of stiff canvas, being scarce able to hold himself erect till they were laced, and he then put on a flannel waistcoat. One side was contracted. His legs were so slender that he enlarged their bulk with three pair of stockings, which were drawn on and off by the maid; for he was not able to dress or undress himself, and neither went to bed nor rose without help. His weakness made it very difficult for him to be clean.

His hair had fallen almost all away, and he used to dine sometimes with Lord Oxford, privately, in a velvet cap. His dress of ceremony was black, with a tie wig and a little sword.

The indulgence and accommodation which his sickness required had taught him all the unpleasing and unsocial qualities of a valetudinary man. He expected that everything should give way to his ease or humor, as a child whose parents will not hear her cry has an unresisted dominion in the nursery.

> C'est que l'enfant toujours est homme,
> C'est que l'homme est toujours enfant. [3]

When he wanted to sleep he "nodded in company," [4] and once slumbered at his own table while the Prince of Wales was talking of poetry.

The reputation which his friendship gave procured him many invitations, but he was a very troublesome inmate. He brought no servant, and had so many wants that a numerous attendance was scarcely able to supply them. Wherever he was

he left no room for another, because he exacted the attention and employed the activity of the whole family. His errands were so frequent and frivolous that the footmen in time avoided and neglected him, and the Earl of Oxford discharged some of the servants for their resolute refusal of his messages. The maids, when they had neglected their business, alleged that they had been employed by Mr. Pope. One of his constant demands was of coffee in the night, and to the woman that waited on him in his chamber he was very burdensome, but he was careful to recompense her want of sleep, and Lord Oxford's servant declared that in a house where her business was to answer his call she would not ask for wages.

He had another fault, easily incident to those who suffering much pain think themselves entitled to whatever pleasures they can snatch. He was too indulgent to his appetite: he loved meat highly seasoned and of strong taste, and, at the intervals of the table, amused himself with biscuits and dry conserves. If he sat down to a variety of dishes he would oppress his stomach with repletion, and though he seemed angry when a dram was offered him, did not forbear to drink it. His friends, who knew the avenues to his heart, pampered him with presents of luxury, which he did not suffer to stand neglected. The death of great men is not always proportioned to the luster of their lives. Hannibal, says Juvenal,[5] did not perish by a javelin or a sword; the slaughters of Cannae were revenged by a ring. The death of Pope was imputed by some of his friends to a silver saucepan, in which it was his delight to heat potted lampreys.

That he loved too well to eat is certain; but that his sensuality shortened his life will not be hastily concluded when it is remembered that a conformation so irregular lasted six and fifty years, notwithstanding such pertinacious diligence of study and meditation.

In all his intercourse with mankind he had great delight in artifice, and endeavored to attain all his purposes by indirect and unsuspected methods. "He hardly drank tea without a stratagem." [6] If at the house of his friends he wanted any accommodation he was not willing to ask for it in plain terms, but would mention it remotely as something convenient; though, when it was procured, he soon

---

2. "long disease": Pope's words in his *Epistle to Dr. Arbuthnot*, l. 131. Most of the following quotations from Pope may be found on pp. 432–37, above. 3. "The child is always the grown-up, the adult forever a child." 4. "nodded in company": Pope, *Imitations of Horace, Satires*, II.i.13.

5. Juvenal: *Satires*, X.163–66. Hannibal committed suicide, when a suppliant at the court of Bithynia, by taking poison which had been contained in a ring (B.C. 183). 6. "He . . . stratagem": Edward Young, *Satires*, VI.188.

made it appear for whose sake it had been recommended. Thus he teased Lord Orrery till he obtained a screen. He practiced his arts on such small occasions that Lady Bolingbroke used to say, in a French phrase, that " he played the politician about cabbages and turnips." His unjustifiable impression of *The Patriot King*,[7] as it can be imputed to no particular motive, must have proceeded from his general habit of secrecy and cunning: he caught an opportunity of a sly trick, and pleased himself with the thought of outwitting Bolingbroke.

In familiar or convivial conversation it does not appear that he excelled. He may be said to have resembled Dryden, as being not one that was distinguished by vivacity in company. It is remarkable that, so near his time, so much should be known of what he has written, and so little of what he has said; traditional memory retains no sallies of raillery nor sentences of observation, nothing either pointed or solid, either wise or merry. One apothegm only stands upon record. When an objection raised against his inscription for Shakespeare was defended by the authority of Patrick,[8] he replied — *horresco referens* — that " he would allow the publisher of a dictionary to know the meaning of a single word, but not of two words put together."

He was fretful and easily displeased, and allowed himself to be capriciously resentful. He would sometimes leave Lord Oxford silently, no one could tell why, and was to be courted back by more letters and messages than the footmen were willing to carry. The table was indeed infested by Lady Mary Wortley,[9] who was the friend of Lady Oxford and who, knowing his peevishness, could by no entreaties be restrained from contradicting him, till their disputes were sharpened to such asperity that one or the other quitted the house.

He sometimes condescended to be jocular with servants or inferiors, but by no merriment, either of others or his own, was he ever seen excited to laughter.

Of his domestic character frugality was a part eminently remarkable. Having determined not to be dependent he determined not to be in want, and therefore wisely and magnanimously rejected all temptations to expense unsuitable to his fortune. This general care must be universally approved, but it sometimes appeared in petty artifices of parsimony, such as the practice of writing his compositions on the back of letters, as may be seen in the remaining copy of the *Iliad*, by which perhaps in five years five shillings were saved; or in a niggardly reception of his friends and scantiness of entertainment, as when he had two guests in his house he would set at supper a single pint upon the table and, having himself taken two small glasses would retire and say, " Gentlemen, I leave you to your wine." Yet he tells his friends that " he has a heart for all, a house for all, and, whatever they may think, a fortune for all." [10]

He sometimes, however, made a splendid dinner, and is said to have wanted no part of the skill or elegance which such performances require. That this magnificence should be often displayed, that obstinate prudence with which he conducted his affairs would not permit; for his revenue, certain and casual, amounted only to about eight hundred pounds a year, of which, however, he declares himself able to assign one hundred to charity.

Of this fortune, which, as it arose from public approbation, was very honorably obtained, his imagination seems to have been too full; it would be hard to find a man so well entitled to notice by his wit, that ever delighted so much in talking of his money. In his Letters and in his Poems, his garden and his grotto, his quincunx and his vines, or some hints of his opulence, are always to be found. The great topic of his ridicule is poverty: the crimes with which he reproaches his antagonists are their debts, their habitation in the Mint,[11] and their want of a dinner. He seems to be of an opinion, not very uncommon in the world, that to want money is to want everything.

Next to the pleasure of contemplating his possessions seems to be that of enumerating the men of high rank with whom he was acquainted, and whose notice he loudly proclaims not to have been

7. His . . . King: Johnson described the incident earlier in his essay: Pope, intrusted with Lord Bolingbroke's MS for the purpose of getting a few copies of it printed, secretly ordered an edition of 1500 copies. These remained unknown to their author until after Pope's death. They were then delivered to him by the printer and promptly burned with indignation for Pope's perfidy. **8. Patrick:** Samuel Patrick was responsible for a Latin dictionary. Johnson "shudders" with mock horror "to bring up the anecdote," being himself a maker of a dictionary. The phrase is in *Aeneid,* II.204. **9. Wortley:** Lady Mary Wortley Montagu (d. 1762) was a brilliant letter writer and amateur poet with whom Pope, after a close attachment, had fallen out.

10. "he . . . all": Pope to Swift, March 23, 1736/37. **11. Mint:** a part of London infested by fugitives from the law, and the refuge of debtors in hiding.

obtained by any practices of meanness or servility, a boast which was never denied to be true, and to which very few poets have ever aspired. Pope never set genius to sale: he never flattered those whom he did not love, or praised those whom he did not esteem. Savage, however, remarked that he began a little to relax his dignity when he wrote a distich for " his Highness's dog." [12]

His admiration of the great seems to have increased in the advance of life. He passed over peers and statesmen to inscribe his *Iliad* to Congreve, with a magnanimity of which the praise had been complete, had his friend's virtue been equal to his wit. Why he was chosen for so great an honor it is not now possible to know; there is no trace in literary history of any particular intimacy between them. The name of Congreve appears in the Letters among those of his other friends, but without any observable distinction or consequence.

To his latter works, however, he took care to annex names dignified with titles, but was not very happy in his choice, for, except Lord Bathurst, none of his noble friends were such as that a good man would wish to have his intimacy with them known to posterity; he can derive little honor from the notice of Cobham, Burlington, or Bolingbroke.

Of his social qualities, if an estimate be made from his Letters, an opinion too favorable cannot easily be formed; they exhibit a perpetual and unclouded effulgence of general benevolence and particular fondness. There is nothing but liberality, gratitude, constancy, and tenderness. It has been so long said as to be commonly believed that the true characters of men may be found in their letters, and that he who writes to his friend lays his heart open before him. But the truth is that such were the simple friendships of the Golden Age, and are now the friendships only of children. Very few can boast of hearts which they dare lay open to themselves and of which, by whatever accident exposed, they do not shun a distinct and continued view; and certainly what we hide from ourselves we do not show to our friends. There is, indeed, no transaction which offers stronger temptations to fallacy and sophistication than epistolary intercourse. In the eagerness of conversation the first emotions of the mind often burst out before they are considered; in the tumult of business interest and passion have their genuine effect; but a friendly letter is a calm and deliberate performance in the cool of leisure, in the stillness of solitude, and surely no man sits down to depreciate by design his own character.

Friendship has no tendency to secure veracity, for by whom can a man so much wish to be thought better than he is as by him whose kindness he desires to gain or keep? Even in writing to the world there is less constraint: the author is not confronted with his reader, and takes his chance of approbation among the different dispositions of mankind; but a letter is addressed to a single mind of which the prejudices and partialities are known, and must therefore please, if not by favoring them, by forbearing to oppose them.

To charge those favorable representations which men give of their own minds, with the guilt of hypocritical falsehood, would show more severity than knowledge. The writer commonly believes himself. Almost every man's thoughts, while they are general, are right; and most hearts are pure while temptation is away. It is easy to awaken generous sentiments in privacy, to despise death when there is no danger, to glow with benevolence when there is nothing to be given. While such ideas are formed they are felt, and self-love does not suspect the gleam of virtue to be the meteor of fancy.

If the letters of Pope are considered merely as compositions, they seem to be premeditated and artificial. It is one thing to write because there is something which the mind wishes to discharge, and another to solicit the imagination because ceremony or vanity requires something to be written. Pope confesses his early letters to be vitiated with " affectation and ambition ";[13] to know whether he disentangled himself from these perverters of epistolary integrity his book and his life must be set in comparison.

One of his favorite topics is contempt of his own poetry. For this, if it had been real, he would deserve no commendation, and in this he was certainly not sincere; for his high value of himself was sufficiently observed, and of what could he be proud but of his poetry? He writes, he says, when " he has just nothing else to do," [14] yet Swift complains that he was never at leisure for conversation

---

12. "**his . . . dog**": Richard Savage, Johnson's friend and a poet himself, died in 1743. Johnson wrote and published his life in 1744; the account was afterwards included among the *Lives of the Poets*. Pope's verses on his Highness's dog at Kew are in all editions of his work.

13. "**affectation . . . ambition**": Pope's Preface to his Letters (1737). 14. "**he . . . do**": Swift, *Works* (ed. 1883), XVIII.138.

because he " had always some poetical scheme in his head." It was punctually required that his writing box should be set upon his bed before he rose; and Lord Oxford's domestic related that, in the dreadful winter of '40, she was called from her bed by him four times in one night to supply him with paper, lest he should lose a thought.

He pretends insensibility to censure and criticism, though it was observed by all who knew him that every pamphlet disturbed his quiet, and that his extreme irritability laid him open to perpetual vexation; but he wished to despise his critics, and therefore hoped that he did despise them.

As he happened to live in two reigns when the court paid little attention to poetry he nursed in his mind a foolish disesteem of kings, and proclaims that " he never sees courts." [15] Yet a little regard shown him by the Prince of Wales melted his obduracy, and he had not much to say when he was asked by his Royal Highness " how he could love a prince while he disliked kings." [16]

He very frequently professes contempt of the world, and represents himself as looking on mankind, sometimes with gay indifference, as on emmets [17] of a hillock below his serious attention, and sometimes with gloomy indignation, as on monsters more worthy of hatred than of pity. These were dispositions apparently counterfeited. How could he despise those whom he lived by pleasing, and on whose approbation his esteem of himself was superstructed? Why should he hate those to whose favor he owed his honor and his ease? Of things that terminate in human life the world is the proper judge: to despise its sentence, if it were possible, is not just; and if it were just is not possible. Pope was far enough from this unreasonable temper; he was sufficiently " a fool to Fame," [18] and his fault was that he pretended to neglect it. His levity and his sullenness were only in his letters; he passed through common life, sometimes vexed and sometimes pleased, with the natural emotions of common men.

His scorn of the great is repeated too often to be real; no man thinks much of that which he despises; and as falsehood is always in danger of inconsistency, he makes it his boast at another time that he lives among them.

It is evident that his own importance swells often in his mind. He is afraid of writing lest the clerks of the post office should know his secrets; he has many enemies; he considers himself as surrounded by universal jealousy; " after many deaths, and many dispersions, two or three of us," says he, " may still be brought together, not to plot, but to divert ourselves, and the world, too, if it pleases "; and they can live together, and " show what friends wits may be, in spite of all the fools in the world." [19] All this while it was likely that the clerks did not know his hand; he certainly had no more enemies than a public character like his inevitably excites, and with what degree of friendship the wits might live very few were so much fools as ever to inquire.

Some part of this pretended discontent he learned from Swift, and expresses it, I think, most frequently in his correspondence with him. Swift's resentment was unreasonable, but it was sincere; Pope's was the mere mimicry of his friend, a fictitious part which he began to play before it became him. When he was only twenty-five years old he related that " a glut of study and retirement had thrown him on the world," and that there was danger lest " a glut of the world should throw him back upon study and retirement." [20] To this Swift answered with great propriety that Pope had not yet either acted or suffered enough in the world to have become weary of it. And, indeed, it must be some very powerful reason that can drive back to solitude him who has once enjoyed the pleasures of society.

In the letters both of Swift and Pope there appears such narrowness of mind as makes them insensible of any excellence that has not some affinity with their own, and confines their esteem and approbation to so small a number, that whoever should form his opinion of the age from their representation would suppose them to have lived amidst ignorance and barbarity, unable to find among their contemporaries either virtue or intelligence, and persecuted by those that could not understand them.

When Pope murmurs at the world, when he professes contempt of fame, when he speaks of riches and poverty, of success and disappointment, with negligent indifference, he certainly does not express

15. "he . . . courts": Pope to Swift: Pope's *Works* (ed. Elwin and Courthope), VII.111, Jan., 1727/28.   16. "how . . . kings": O. Ruffhead, *Life of Pope* (1769), p. 535.   17. emmets: ants. 18. "a . . . Fame": Pope, *Epistle to Dr. Arbuthnot*, l. 127, p. 434, above.

19. "after . . . world": Pope to Swift, letters of Sept. 14, 1725, and March 23, 1736/37.   20. "a . . . retirement": *Works* (ed. Elwin and Courthope), VII.37, Aug., 1723.

his habitual and settled sentiments, but either willfully disguises his own character or, what is more likely, invests himself with temporary qualities, and sallies out in the colors of the present moment. His hopes and fears, his joys and sorrows, acted strongly upon his mind, and if he differed from others it was not by carelessness. He was irritable and resentful; his malignity to Philips,[21] whom he had first made ridiculous, and then hated for being angry, continued too long. Of his vain desire to make Bentley contemptible, I never heard any adequate reason. He was sometimes wanton in his attacks, and before Chandos, Lady Wortley, and Hill,[22] was mean in his retreat.

The virtues which seem to have had most of his affection were liberality and fidelity of friendship, in which it does not appear that he was other than he describes himself. His fortune did not suffer his charity to be splendid and conspicuous, but he assisted Dodsley[23] with a hundred pounds that he might open a shop; and of the subscription of forty pounds a year that he raised for Savage twenty were paid by himself. He was accused of loving money, but his love was eagerness to gain, not solicitude to keep it.

In the duties of friendship he was zealous and constant; his early maturity of mind commonly united him with men older than himself, and therefore, without attaining any considerable length of life, he saw many companions of his youth sink into the grave; but it does not appear that he lost a single friend by coldness or by injury: those who loved him once continued their kindness. His ungrateful mention of Allen[24] in his will was the effect of his adherence to one whom he had known much longer, and whom he naturally loved with greater fondness. His violation of the trust reposed in him by Bolingbroke[25] could have no motive

inconsistent with the warmest affection; he either thought the action so near to indifferent that he forgot it, or so laudable that he expected his friend to approve it.

It was reported, with such confidence as almost to enforce belief, that in the papers entrusted to his executors was found a defamatory *Life of Swift,* which he had prepared as an instrument of vengeance to be used, if any provocation should be ever given. About this I inquired of the Earl of Marchmont, who assured me that no such piece was among his remains.

The religion in which he lived and died was that of the Church of Rome, to which in his correspondence with Racine[26] he professes himself a sincere adherent. That he was not scrupulously pious in some part of his life is known by many idle and indecent applications of sentences taken from the Scriptures, a mode of merriment which a good man dreads for its profaneness, and a witty man disdains for its easiness and vulgarity. But to whatever levities he has been betrayed, it does not appear that his principles were ever corrupted, or that he ever lost his belief of revelation. The positions which he transmitted from Bolingbroke he seems not to have understood, and was pleased with an interpretation that made them orthodox.

A man of such exalted superiority and so little moderation would naturally have all his delinquencies observed and aggravated; those who could not deny that he was excellent would rejoice to find that he was not perfect.

Perhaps it may be imputed to the unwillingness with which the same man is allowed to possess many advantages that his learning has been depreciated. He certainly was in his early life a man of great literary curiosity, and when he wrote his *Essay on Criticism* had for his age a very wide acquaintance with books. When he entered into the living world it seems to have happened to him as to many others that he was less attentive to dead masters; he studied in the academy of Paracelsus,[27] and made the universe his favorite volume. He gathered his notions fresh from reality, not from the copies of authors, but the originals of nature. Yet there is no reason to believe that literature ever lost his esteem; he always professed to love reading,

21. **Philips:** Ambrose Philips (d. 1749), belittled by Pope for his *Pastorals* (1710).   22. **Chandos . . . Hill:** Pope is thought to have satirized the Duke of Chandos under the name of "Timon" in Epistle IV of *Moral Essays,* Lady Mary as "Sappho" in Epistle II, Aaron Hill as one of the divers in the Fleet Ditch contest (*Dunciad,* II.295). With these Pope tried to insinuate that he was unintentionally guilty of offense.   23. **Dodsley:** Robert Dodsley (1703-64), bookseller, publisher, poet, playwright, and editor. 24. **Allen:** Ralph Allen (1694-1764), a generous friend to needy authors and deserving causes; built Prior Park, near Bath, and made it a seat of hospitality. Pope became estranged from him, and in his will left Allen a sum represented to be the total amount of the benefits he had received. Johnson tells that it was £150, and adds that Allen gave it to the Bath Hospital, saying that Pope was always a bad accountant, and that ten times the sum would have been nearer the truth.   25. **Bolingbroke:** See n. 7, above.

26. **Racine:** i.e., Louis, son of the great dramatist J. B. Racine. He attacked Pope as impious, in *La Religion* (1742).   27. **Paracelsus** (1493-1541) wandered about the world, a learned adventurer, regarded with suspicion by established scholars. His academy was nowhere.

and Dobson,[28] who spent some time at his house translating his *Essay on Man,* when I asked him what learning he found him to possess, answered, "More than I expected." His frequent references to history, his allusions to various kinds of knowledge, and his images selected from art and nature, with his observations on the operations of the mind and the modes of life, show an intelligence perpetually on the wing, excursive, vigorous, and diligent, eager to pursue knowledge and attentive to retain it.

From this curiosity arose the desire of traveling, to which he alludes in his verses to Jervas,[29] and which, though he never found an opportunity to gratify it, did not leave him till his life declined.

Of his intellectual character the constituent and fundamental principle was good sense, a prompt and intuitive perception of consonance and propriety. He saw immediately, of his own conceptions, what was to be chosen and what to be rejected; and, in the works of others, what was to be shunned and what to be copied.

But good sense alone is a sedate and quiescent quality, which manages its possessions well but does not increase them; it collects few materials for its own operations, and preserves safety but never gains supremacy. Pope had likewise genius; a mind active, ambitious, and adventurous, always investigating, always aspiring; in its widest searches still longing to go forward, in its highest flights still wishing to be higher; always imagining something greater than it knows, always endeavoring more than it can do.

To assist these powers he is said to have had great strength and exactness of memory. That which he had heard or read was not easily lost; and he had before him not only what his own meditation suggested, but what he had found in other writers that might be accommodated to his present purpose.

These benefits of nature he improved by incessant and unwearied diligence; he had recourse to every source of intelligence, and lost no opportunity of information; he consulted the living as well as the dead; he read his compositions to his friends, and was never content with mediocrity when excellence could be attained. He considered poetry as the business of his life, and, however he might seem to lament his occupation, he followed it with constancy; to make verses was his first labor, and to mend them was his last.

From his attention to poetry he was never diverted. If conversation offered anything that could be improved he committed it to paper; if a thought, or perhaps an expression more happy than was common, rose to his mind, he was careful to write it; an independent distich was preserved for an opportunity of insertion, and some little fragments have been found containing lines, or parts of lines, to be wrought upon at some other time.

He was one of those few whose labor is their pleasure; he was never elevated to negligence, nor wearied to impatience; he never passed a fault unamended by indifference, nor quitted it by despair. He labored his works first to gain reputation, and afterwards to keep it.

Of composition there are different methods. Some employ at once memory and invention and, with little intermediate use of the pen, form and polish large masses by continued meditation, and write their productions only when, in their own opinion, they have completed them. It is related of Virgil that his custom was to pour out a great number of verses in the morning, and pass the day in retrenching exuberances and correcting inaccuracies. The method of Pope, as may be collected from his translation, was to write his first thoughts in his first words, and gradually to amplify, decorate, rectify, and refine them.

With such faculties and such dispositions he excelled every other writer in *poetical prudence;* he wrote in such a manner as might expose him to few hazards. He used almost always the same fabric of verse; and, indeed, by those few essays which he made of any other, he did not enlarge his reputation. Of this uniformity the certain consequence was readiness and dexterity. By perpetual practice language had in his mind a systematical arrangement; having always the same use for words, he had words so selected and combined as to be ready at his call. This increase of facility he confessed himself to have perceived in the progress of his translation.

But what was yet of more importance, his effusions were always voluntary, and his subjects chosen by himself. His independence secured him from drudging at a task, and laboring upon a barren topic; he never exchanged praise for money, nor opened a shop of condolence or congratulation. His poems, therefore, were scarce ever temporary. He

28. Dobson: William Dobson practiced the vanishing art of translation into Latin poetry; Prior's *Solomon* was so embalmed by him.   **29. Jervas:** Charles Jervas published a translation of *Don Quixote* in 1742.

suffered coronations and royal marriages to pass without a song, and derived no opportunities from recent events, nor any popularity from the accidental disposition of his readers. He was never reduced to the necessity of soliciting the sun to shine upon a birthday, of calling the Graces and Virtues to a wedding, or of saying what multitudes have said before him. When he could produce nothing new, he was at liberty to be silent.

His publications were for the same reason never hasty. He is said to have sent nothing to the press till it had lain two years under his inspection; it is at least certain that he ventured nothing without nice examination. He suffered the tumult of imagination to subside, and the novelties of invention to grow familiar. He knew that the mind is always enamored of its own productions, and did not trust his first fondness. He consulted his friends, and listened with great willingness to criticism; and, what was of more importance, he consulted himself, and let nothing pass against his own judgment.

He professed to have learned his poetry from Dryden, whom, whenever an opportunity was presented, he praised through his whole life with unvaried liberality; and perhaps his character may receive some illustration if he be compared with his master.

Integrity of understanding and nicety of discernment were not allotted in a less proportion to Dryden than to Pope. The rectitude of Dryden's mind was sufficiently shown by the dismission of his poetical prejudices, and the rejection of unnatural thoughts and rugged numbers. But Dryden never desired to apply all the judgment that he had. He wrote, and professed to write, merely for the people; and when he pleased others, he contented himself. He spent no time in struggles to rouse latent powers; he never attempted to make that better which was already good, nor often to mend what he must have known to be faulty. He wrote, as he tells us, with very little consideration; when occasion or necessity called upon him, he poured out what the present moment happened to supply, and, when once it had passed the press, ejected it from his mind; for when he had no pecuniary interest, he had no further solicitude.

Pope was not content to satisfy; he desired to excel, and therefore always endeavored to do his best; he did not court the candor, but dared the judgment, of his reader and, expecting no indulgence from others, he showed none to himself. He examined lines and words with minute and punctilious observation, and retouched every part with indefatigable diligence, till he had left nothing to be forgiven.

For this reason he kept his pieces very long in his hands, while he considered and reconsidered them. The only poems which can be supposed to have been written with such regard to the times as might hasten their publication were the two satires of "Thirty-Eight," of which Dodsley told me that they were brought to him by the author, that they might be fairly copied. "Almost every line," he said, "was then written twice over; I gave him a clean transcript, which he sent sometime afterwards to me for the press, with almost every line written twice over a second time."

His declaration that his care for his works ceased at their publication was not strictly true. His parental attention never abandoned them; what he found amiss in the first edition, he silently corrected in those that followed. He appears to have revised the *Iliad*, and freed it from some of its imperfections; and the *Essay on Criticism* received many improvements after its first appearance. It will seldom be found that he altered without adding clearness, elegance, or vigor. Pope had perhaps the judgment of Dryden; but Dryden certainly wanted the diligence of Pope.

In acquired knowledge the superiority must be allowed to Dryden, whose education was more scholastic, and who before he became an author had been allowed more time for study, with better means of information. His mind has a larger range, and he collects his images and illustrations from a more extensive circumference of science. Dryden knew more of man in his general nature, and Pope in his local manners. The notions of Dryden were formed by comprehensive speculation, and those of Pope by minute attention. There is more dignity in the knowledge of Dryden, and more certainty in that of Pope.

Poetry was not the sole praise of either, for both excelled likewise in prose; but Pope did not borrow his prose from his predecessor. The style of Dryden is capricious and varied, that of Pope is cautious and uniform; Dryden obeys the motions of his own mind, Pope constrains his mind to his own rules of composition. Dryden is sometimes vehement and rapid; Pope is always smooth, uniform, and gentle. Dryden's page is a natural field, rising into inequalities, and diversified by the varied exuberance of abundant vegetation; Pope's is a velvet lawn, shaven by the scythe, and leveled by the roller.

Of genius, that power which constitutes a poet, that quality without which judgment is cold and knowledge is inert, that energy which collects, combines, amplifies, and animates — the superiority must, with some hesitation, be allowed to Dryden. It is not to be inferred that of this poetical vigor Pope had only a little, because Dryden had more, for every other writer since Milton must give place to Pope; and even of Dryden it must be said that if he has brighter paragraphs, he has not better poems. Dryden's performances were always hasty, either excited by some external occasion or extorted by domestic necessity; he composed without consideration, and published without correction. What his mind could supply at call, or gather in one excursion, was all that he sought, and all that he gave. The dilatory caution of Pope enabled him to condense his sentiments, to multiply his images, and to accumulate all that study might produce or chance might supply. If the flights of Dryden therefore are higher, Pope continues longer on the wing. If of Dryden's fire the blaze is brighter, of Pope's the heat is more regular and constant. Dryden often surpasses expectation, and Pope never falls below it. Dryden is read with frequent astonishment, and Pope with perpetual delight.

This parallel will, I hope, when it is well considered, be found just; and if the reader should suspect me, as I suspect myself, of some partial fondness for the memory of Dryden, let him not too hastily condemn me; for meditation and inquiry may, perhaps, show him the reasonableness of my determination.

The works of Pope are now to be distinctly examined, not so much with attention to slight faults or petty beauties, as to the general character and effect of each performance. . . .

The design of *Windsor Forest* is evidently derived from *Cooper's Hill*,[30] with some attention to Waller's poem on *The Park;* but Pope cannot be denied to excel his masters in variety and elegance, and the art of interchanging description, narrative, and morality. The objection made by Dennis is the want of plan, of a regular subordination of parts terminating in the principal and original design.[31]

There is this want in most descriptive poems, because as the scenes, which they must exhibit successively, are all subsisting at the same time, the order in which they are shown must by necessity be arbitrary, and more is not to be expected from the last part than from the first. The attention, therefore, which cannot be detained by suspense, must be excited by diversity, such as his poem offers to its reader.

But the desire of diversity may be too much indulged; the parts of *Windsor Forest* which deserve least praise are those which were added to enliven the stillness of the scene, the appearance of Father Thames, and the transformation of Lodona. Addison had in his *Campaign* derided the " Rivers " that " rise from their oozy beds " to tell stories of heroes,[32] and it is therefore strange that Pope should adopt a fiction not only unnatural but lately censured. The story of Lodona [33] is told with sweetness, but a new metamorphosis is a ready and puerile expedient: nothing is easier than to tell how a flower was once a blooming virgin, or a rock an obdurate tyrant. . . .

The " Verses on the Unfortunate Lady " have drawn much attention by the illaudable singularity of treating suicide with respect, and they must be allowed to be written in some parts with vigorous animation, and in others with gentle tenderness; nor has Pope produced any poem in which the sense predominates more over the diction. But the tale is not skillfully told: it is not easy to discover the character of either the lady or her guardian. History relates that she was about to disparage herself by a marriage with an inferior; Pope praises her for the dignity of ambition, and yet condemns the uncle to detestation for his pride; the ambitious love of a niece may be opposed by the interest, malice, or envy of an uncle, but never by his pride. On such an occasion a poet may be allowed to be obscure, but inconsistency never can be right. . . .

One of his greatest though of his earliest works is the *Essay on Criticism,* which if he had written nothing else would have placed him among the first critics and the first poets, as it exhibits every mode of excellence that can embellish or dignify didactic composition: selection of matter, novelty of arrangement, justness of precept, splendor of illustration, and propriety of digression. I know not whether it be pleasing to consider that he pro-

30. *Cooper's Hill:* by Sir John Denham (1642). 31. The . . . design: Dennis, "Remarks on Pope's Homer," *Critical Works* (ed. Hooker), II.136.

32. stories of heroes: Addison, The Campaign, l. 470. 33. See *Windsor Forest*, ll. 171 ff.

duced this piece at twenty, and never afterwards excelled it; he that delights himself with observing that such powers may be so soon attained cannot but grieve to think that life was ever after at a stand.

To mention the particular beauties of the *Essay* would be unprofitably tedious, but I cannot forbear to observe that the comparison of a student's progress in the sciences with the journey of a traveler in the Alps [34] is perhaps the best that English poetry can show. A simile, to be perfect, must both illustrate and ennoble the subject; must show it to the understanding in a clearer view, and display it to the fancy with greater dignity; but either of these qualities may be sufficient to recommend it. In didactic poetry, of which the great purpose is instruction, a simile may be praised which illustrates, though it does not ennoble; in heroics, that may be admitted which ennobles, though it does not illustrate. That it may be complete it is required to exhibit, independently of its references, a pleasing image; for a simile is said to be a short episode. To this antiquity was so attentive that circumstances were sometimes added which, having no parallels, served only to fill the imagination, and produced what Perrault ludicrously called " comparisons with a long tail." [35] In their similes the greatest writers have sometimes failed: the ship race, compared with the chariot race, is neither illustrated nor aggrandized; [36] land and water make all the difference; when Apollo running after Daphne is likened to a greyhound chasing a hare,[37] there is nothing gained; the ideas of pursuit and flight are too plain to be made plainer, and a god and the daughter of a god are not represented much to their advantage by a hare and dog. The simile of the Alps has no useless parts, yet affords a striking picture by itself: it makes the foregoing position better understood, and enables it to take faster hold on the attention; it assists the apprehension, and elevates the fancy.

Let me likewise dwell a little on the celebrated paragraph,[38] in which it is directed that " the sound should seem an echo to the sense," a precept which Pope is allowed to have observed beyond any other English poet.

This notion of representative meter, and the desire of discovering frequent adaptations of the sound to the sense, have produced, in my opinion, many wild conceits and imaginary beauties. All that can furnish this representation are the sounds of the words considered singly, and the time in which they are pronounced. Every language has some words framed to exhibit the noises which they express, as *thump, rattle, growl, hiss*. These, however, are but few, and the poet cannot make them more, nor can they be of any use but when sound is to be mentioned. The time of pronunciation was in the dactylic measures of the learned languages capable of considerable variety; but that variety could be accommodated only to motion or duration, and different degrees of motion were perhaps expressed by verses rapid or slow, without much attention of the writer, when the image had full possession of his fancy; but our language having little flexibility, our verses can differ very little in their cadence. The fancied resemblances, I fear, arise sometimes merely from the ambiguity of words; there is supposed to be some relation between a *soft* line and a *soft* couch, or between *hard* syllables and *hard* fortune.

Motion, however, may be in some sort exemplified; and yet it may be suspected that even in such resemblances the mind often governs the ear, and the sounds are estimated by their meaning. One of the most successful attempts has been to describe the labor of Sisyphus:

With many a weary step, and many a groan,
Up a high hill he heaves a huge round stone;
The huge round stone, resulting with a bound,
Thunders impetuous down, and smokes along the
    ground.[39]

Who does not perceive the stone to move slowly upward, and roll violently back? But set the same numbers to another sense:

While many a merry tale, and many a song,
Cheered the rough road, we wished the rough road
    long.
The rough road then, returning in a round,
Mocked our impatient steps, for all was fairy
    ground.

We have now surely lost much of the delay, and much of the rapidity.

34. Alps: *Essay on Criticism*, ll. 219 ff., p. 402, above.   35. Perrault . . . tail: Charles Perrault (d. 1703), defender of the Moderns in the quarrel over their superiority or inferiority to the Ancients. Addison mentions his phrase in *Spectator*, No. 303. 36. ship . . . aggrandized: *Aeneid*, V.144–47.   37. Apollo . . . hare: Ovid, *Metamorphoses*, I.533 ff.   38. *Essay on Criticism*, ll. 337–83, pp. 403–04, above.

39. Pope, *Odyssey*, XI.735–38.

But to show how little the greatest master of numbers can fix the principles of representative harmony, it will be sufficient to remark that the poet, who tells us that

When Ajax strives some rock's vast weight to throw,
The line too labors, and the words move slow;
Not so when swift Camilla scours the plain,
Flies o'er th' unbending corn, and skims along the main,[40]

when he had enjoyed for about thirty years the praise of Camilla's lightness of foot, tried another experiment upon *sound* and *time,* and produced this memorable triplet:

Waller was smooth; but Dryden taught to join
The varying verse, the full resounding line,
The long majestic march, and energy divine.[41]

Here are the swiftness of the rapid race and the march of slow-paced majesty exhibited by the same poet in the same sequence of syllables, except that the exact prosodist will find the line of *swiftness* by one time longer than that of *tardiness.*

Beauties of this kind are commonly fancied, and when real are technical and nugatory, not to be rejected and not to be solicited.

To the praises which have been accumulated on *The Rape of the Lock* by readers of every class, from the critic to the waiting maid, it is difficult to make any addition. Of that which is universally allowed to be the most attractive of all ludicrous compositions, let it rather be now inquired from what sources the power of pleasing is derived.

Dr. Warburton, who excelled in critical perspicacity, has remarked that the preternatural agents are very happily adapted to the purposes of the poem.[42] The heathen deities can no longer gain attention: we should have turned away from a contest between Venus and Diana. The employment of allegorical persons always excites conviction of its own absurdity: they may produce effects, but cannot conduct actions; when the phantom is put in motion, it dissolves; thus Discord may raise a mutiny, but Discord cannot conduct a march nor besiege a town. Pope brought into view a new race of beings, with powers and passions proportionate to their operation. The sylphs and gnomes act at the toilet and the tea table, what more terrific and more powerful phantoms perform on the stormy ocean or the field of battle; they give their proper help, and do their proper mischief.

Pope is said by an objector not to have been the inventor of this petty nation, a charge which might with more justice have been brought against the author of the *Iliad,* who doubtless adopted the religious system of his country; for what is there but the names of his agents which Pope has not invented? Has he not assigned them characters and operations never heard of before? Has he not, at least, given them their first poetical existence? If this is not sufficient to denominate his work original, nothing original ever can be written.

In this work are exhibited in a very high degree the two most engaging powers of an author: new things are made familiar, and familiar things are made new. A race of aerial people never heard of before is presented to us in a manner so clear and easy that the reader seeks for no further information, but immediately mingles with his new acquaintance, adopts their interests, and attends their pursuits, loves a sylph and detests a gnome.

That familiar things are made new every paragraph will prove. The subject of the poem is an event below the common incidents of common life; nothing real is introduced that is not seen so often as to be no longer regarded, yet the whole detail of a female day is here brought before us invested with so much art of decoration that, though nothing is disguised, everything is striking, and we feel all the appetite of curiosity for that from which we have a thousand times turned fastidiously away.

The purpose of the poet is, as he tells us, to laugh at " the little unguarded follies of the female sex." It is therefore without justice that Dennis charges *The Rape of the Lock* with the want of a moral,[43] and for that reason sets it below *The Lutrin,* which exposes the pride and discord of the clergy. Perhaps neither Pope nor Boileau has made the world much better than he found it, but if they had both succeeded, it were easy to tell who would have deserved most from public gratitude. The freaks, and humors, and spleen, and vanity of women, as they embroil families in discord and fill houses with disquiet, do more to obstruct the happiness of life in a year than the ambition of the

40. *Essay on Criticism*, ll. 370–73, p. 404, above.   41. *Imitations of Horace,* Epistles II.i.267–69.   42. **poem:** William Warburton (d. 1779) was Pope's authorized editor. His comment occurs in his introductory remarks, 1751.

43. **Dennis . . . moral:** Dennis, *Critical Works* (ed. Hooker), II.330–31. Boileau's *Lutrin* (i.e., *The Lectern*) was translated by Nicholas Rowe in 1708, and by others about that date.

clergy in many centuries. It has been well observed that the misery of man proceeds not from any single crush of overwhelming evil, but from small vexations continually repeated.

It is remarked by Dennis likewise that the machinery is superfluous;[44] that by all the bustle of preternatural operation the main event is neither hastened nor retarded. To this charge an efficacious answer is not easily made. The sylphs cannot be said to help or to oppose, and it must be allowed to imply some want of art that their power has not been sufficiently intermingled with the action. Other parts may likewise be charged with want of connection; the game at *ombre* might be spared, but if the lady had lost her hair while she was intent upon her cards, it might have been inferred that those who are too fond of play will be in danger of neglecting more important interests. Those perhaps are faults, but what are such faults to so much excellence!

The Epistle of Eloïsa to Abelard is one of the most happy productions of human wit: the subject is so judiciously chosen that it would be difficult, in turning over the annals of the world, to find another which so many circumstances concur to recommend. We regularly interest ourselves most in the fortune of those who most deserve our notice. Abelard and Eloïsa were conspicuous in their days for eminence of merit. The heart naturally loves truth. The adventures and misfortunes of this illustrious pair are known from undisputed history. Their fate does not leave the mind in hopeless dejection, for they both found quiet and consolation in retirement and piety. So new and so affecting is their story that it supersedes invention, and imagination ranges at full liberty without straggling into scenes of fable.

The story thus skillfully adopted has been diligently improved. Pope has left nothing behind him which seems more the effect of studious perseverance and laborious revisal. Here is particularly observable the "curiosa felicitas," a fruitful soil, and careful cultivation. Here is no crudeness of sense, nor asperity of language.

The sources from which sentiments which have so much vigor and efficacy have been drawn are shown to be the mystic writers by the learned author of the *Essay on the Life and Writings of Pope*,[45] a book which teaches how the brow of criticism may be smoothed, and how she may be enabled, with all her severity, to attract and to delight.

The train of my disquisition has now conducted me to that poetical wonder, the translation of the *Iliad,* a performance which no age or nation can pretend to equal. To the Greeks translation was almost unknown; it was totally unknown to the inhabitants of Greece. They had no recourse to the barbarians for poetical beauties, but sought for everything in Homer, where, indeed, there is but little which they might not find.

The Italians have been very diligent translators, but I can hear of no version, unless perhaps Anguillara's *Ovid*[46] may be excepted, which is read with eagerness. The *Iliad*[47] of Salvini every reader may discover to be punctiliously exact; but it seems to be the work of a linguist skillfully pedantic, and his countrymen, the proper judges of its power to please, reject it with disgust.

Their predecessors the Romans have left some specimens of translation behind them, and that employment must have had some credit in which Tully and Germanicus engaged; but unless we suppose, what is perhaps true, that the plays of Terence were versions of Menander,[48] nothing translated seems ever to have risen to high reputation. The French, in the meridian hour of their learning, were very laudably industrious to enrich their own language with the wisdom of the ancients, but found themselves reduced, by whatever necessity, to turn the Greek and Roman poetry into prose. Whoever could read an author could translate him. From such rivals little can be feared.

The chief help of Pope in this arduous undertaking was drawn from the versions of Dryden. Virgil had borrowed much of his imagery from Homer, and part of the debt was now paid by his translator. Pope searched the pages of Dryden for happy combinations of heroic diction, but it will not be denied that he added much to what he found. He cultivated our language with so much diligence and art that he has left in his *Homer* a treasure of poetical elegances to posterity. His version may be said to have tuned the English tongue, for since its appearance no writer, however deficient in other powers, has wanted melody. Such a series of lines so elaborately corrected and so sweetly modulated took

44. Dennis . . . superfluous: *Critical Works*, II. 328.   45. author . . . *Pope*: Joseph Warton, *An Essay on the Genius and Writings of Pope* (1756–82).

46. Anguillara's *Ovid*: This translation, in ottava rima, was published in 1584.   47. *Iliad*: The date of Salvini's *Iliad* was 1723.   48. plays . . . Menander: It is now generally accepted that such is the fact.

possession of the public ear; the vulgar was enamored of the poem, and the learned wondered at the translation.

But in the most general applause discordant voices will always be heard. It has been objected by some, who wish to be numbered among the sons of learning, that Pope's version of Homer is not Homerical; that it exhibits no resemblance of the original and characteristic manner of the Father of Poetry, as it wants his awful simplicity, his artless grandeur, his unaffected majesty. This cannot be totally denied, but it must be remembered that *necessitas quod cogit defendit,* that may be lawfully done which cannot be forborne. Time and place will always enforce regard. In estimating this translation consideration must be had of the nature of our language, the form of our meter, and, above all, of the change which two thousand years have made in the modes of life and the habits of thought. Virgil wrote in a language of the same general fabric with that of Homer, in verses of the same measure, and in an age nearer to Homer's time by eighteen hundred years; yet he found even then the state of the world so much altered, and the demand for elegance so much increased, that mere nature would be endured no longer; and perhaps, in the multitude of borrowed passages, very few can be shown which he has not embellished.

There is a time when nations emerging from barbarity, and falling into regular subordination, gain leisure to grow wise, and feel the shame of ignorance and the craving pain of unsatisfied curiosity. To this hunger of the mind plain sense is grateful; that which fills the void removes uneasiness, and to be free from pain for a while is pleasure; but repletion generates fastidiousness, a saturated intellect soon becomes luxurious, and knowledge finds no willing reception till it is recommended by artificial diction. Thus it will be found in the progress of learning that in all nations the first writers are simple, and that every age improves in elegance. One refinement always makes way for another, and what was expedient to Virgil was necessary to Pope.

I suppose many readers of the English *Iliad,* when they have been touched with some unexpected beauty of the lighter kind, have tried to enjoy it in the original, where, alas! it was not to be found. Homer doubtless owes to his translator many Ovidian graces not exactly suitable to his character, but to have added can be no great crime if nothing be taken away. Elegance is surely to be desired if it be not gained at the expense of dignity. A hero would wish to be loved as well as to be reverenced.

To a thousand cavils one answer is sufficient; the purpose of a writer is to be read, and the criticism which would destroy the power of pleasing must be blown aside. Pope wrote for his own age and his own nation; he knew that it was necessary to color the images and point the sentiments of his author; he therefore made him graceful, but lost him some of his sublimity.

The copious notes with which the version is accompanied and by which it is recommended to many readers, though they were undoubtedly written to swell the volumes, ought not to pass without praise: commentaries which attract the reader by the pleasure of perusal have not often appeared; the notes of others are read to clear difficulties, those of Pope to vary entertainment.

It has, however, been objected with sufficient reason that there is in the commentary too much of unseasonable levity and affected gaiety; that too many appeals are made to the ladies, and the ease which is so carefully preserved is sometimes the ease of a trifler. Every art has its terms and every kind of instruction its proper style; the gravity of common critics may be tedious, but is less despicable than childish merriment.

Of the *Odyssey* nothing remains to be observed; the same general praise may be given to both translations, and a particular examination of either would require a large volume. The notes were written by Broome, who endeavored not unsuccessfully to imitate his master.

Of the *Dunciad* the hint is confessedly taken from Dryden's " Mac Flecknoe," but the plan is so enlarged and diversified as justly to claim the praise of an original, and affords perhaps the best specimen that has yet appeared of personal satire ludicrously pompous.

That the design was moral, whatever the author might tell either his readers or himself, I am not convinced. The first motive was the desire of revenging the contempt with which Theobald [49] had treated his *Shakespeare,* and regaining the honor which he had lost, by crushing his opponent. Theobald was not of bulk enough to fill a poem, and

49. Theobald: Lewis Theobald (pronounced Tibbald) attacked Pope's edition in *Shakespeare Restored, or, a Specimen of the Many Errors as Well Committed, as Unamended, by Mr. Pope, in His Late Edition of This Poet* (1726).

therefore it was necessary to find other enemies with other names, at whose expense he might divert the public.

In this design there was petulance and malignity enough, but I cannot think it very criminal. An author places himself uncalled before the tribunal of criticism, and solicits fame at the hazard of disgrace. Dullness or deformity are not culpable in themselves, but may be very justly reproached when they pretend to the honor of wit or the influence of beauty. If bad writers were to pass without reprehension, what should restrain them? *impune diem consumpserit ingens Telephus;* [50] and upon bad writers only will censure have much effect. The satire which brought Theobald and Moore [51] into contempt dropped impotent from Bentley, like the javelin of Priam. [52]

All truth is valuable, and satirical criticism may be considered as useful when it rectifies error and improves judgment: he that refines the public taste is a public benefactor.

The beauties of this poem are well known; its chief fault is the grossness of its images. Pope and Swift had an unnatural delight in ideas physically impure, such as every other tongue utters with unwillingness, and of which every ear shrinks from the mention.

But even this fault, offensive as it is, may be forgiven for the excellence of other passages, such as the formation and dissolution of Moore, the account of the Traveler, [53] the misfortune of the Florist, [54] and the crowded thoughts and stately numbers which dignify the concluding paragraph.

The alterations which have been made in the *Dunciad,* not always for the better, require that it should be published, as in the last collection, with all its variations.

The *Essay on Man* was a work of great labor and long consideration, but certainly not the happiest of Pope's performances. The subject is perhaps not very proper for poetry, and the poet was not sufficiently master of his subject; metaphysical morality was to him a new study; he was proud of his acquisitions and, supposing himself master of great secrets, was in haste to teach what he had not learned. Thus he tells us, in the first Epistle, that from the nature of the Supreme Being may be deduced an order of beings such as mankind, because Infinite Excellence can do only what is best. He finds out that these beings must be "somewhere," and that "all the question is whether man be in a wrong place." Surely if, according to the poet's Leibnitian reasoning, [55] we may infer that man ought to be only because he is, we may allow that his place is the right place, because he has it. Supreme Wisdom is not less infallible in disposing than in creating. But what is meant by "somewhere" and "place" and "wrong place" it had been vain to ask Pope, who probably had never asked himself.

Having exalted himself into the chair of wisdom he tells us much that every man knows, and much that he does not know himself; that we see but little, and that the order of the universe is beyond our comprehension, an opinion not very uncommon; and that there is a chain of subordinate beings "from infinite to nothing," of which himself and his readers are equally ignorant. But he gives us one comfort which, without his help, he supposes unattainable, in the position "that though we are fools, yet God is wise."

This *Essay* affords an egregious instance of the predominance of genius, the dazzling splendor of imagery, and the seductive powers of eloquence. Never were penury of knowledge and vulgarity of sentiment so happily disguised. The reader feels his mind full, though he learns nothing; and when he meets it in its new array no longer knows the talk of his mother and his nurse. When these wonder-working sounds sink into sense and the doctrine of the *Essay,* disrobed of its ornaments, is left to the powers of its naked excellence, what shall we discover? That we are, in comparison with our Creator, very weak and ignorant; that we do not uphold the chain of existence; and that we could not make one another with more skill than we are made. We may learn yet more: that the arts of human life were copied from the instinctive operations of other animals; that if the world be made for man, it may be said that man was made for geese. To these profound principles of natural knowledge are added some moral instructions equally new: that self-interest well un-

---

50. *impune . . . Telephus:* "Shall a vast *Telephus* take up the whole day without punishment? Juvenal, *Satires,* I.5.   51. Moore: James Moore Smythe, or "More," is ridiculed in *Dunciad,* II.35-46.   52. javelin of Priam: *Aeneid,* II.544. Priam's spear, hurled by the old man with feeble force, recoiled from his enemy Pyrrhus without doing any harm.   53. Traveler: *Dunciad,* IV.293-336.   54. Florist: *Dunciad,* IV.403-36.

55. Leibnitian reasoning: i.e., patterned after the thinking of Leibnitz (1646-1716), who argued a harmonious system in which spirit and matter were reconciled by God's supreme intention.

derstood will produce social concord; that men are mutual gainers by mutual benefits; that evil is sometimes balanced by good; that human advantages are unstable and fallacious, of uncertain duration and doubtful effect; that our true honor is not to have a great part, but to act it well; that virtue only is our own; and that happiness is always in our power.

Surely a man of no very comprehensive search may venture to say that he has heard all this before, but it was never till now recommended by such a blaze of embellishment or such sweetness of melody. The vigorous contraction of some thoughts, the luxuriant amplification of others, the incidental illustrations, and sometimes the dignity, sometimes the softness of the verses, enchain philosophy, suspend criticism, and oppress judgment by overpowering pleasure.

This is true of many paragraphs; yet if I had undertaken to exemplify Pope's felicity of composition before a rigid critic I should not select the *Essay on Man,* for it contains more lines unsuccessfully labored, more harshness of diction, more thoughts imperfectly expressed, more levity without elegance, and more heaviness without strength, than will easily be found in all his other works.

The "Characters of Men and Women" are the product of diligent speculation upon human life; much labor has been bestowed upon them, and Pope very seldom labored in vain. That his excellence may be properly estimated I recommend a comparison of his "Characters of Women" with Boileau's *Satire;* it will then be seen with how much more perspicacity female nature is investigated and female excellence selected; and he surely is no mean writer to whom Boileau shall be found inferior. The "Characters of Men," however, are written with more, if not with deeper, thought, and exhibit many passages exquisitely beautiful. "The Gem and the Flower" will not easily be equaled.[56] In the women's part are some defects: the character of Atossa is not so neatly finished as that of Clodio,[57] and some of the female characters may be found perhaps more frequently among men; what is said of Philomede[58] was true of Prior.

In the *Epistles to Lord Bathurst* and *Lord Burlington* Dr. Warburton has endeavored to find a train of thought which was never in the writer's head and, to support his hypothesis, has printed that first which was published last. In one the most valuable passage is perhaps the elogy on good sense,[59] and the other the end of the Duke of Buckingham.[60]

The *Epistle to Arbuthnot,* now arbitrarily called the *Prologue to the Satires,* is a performance consisting, as it seems, of many fragments wrought into one design, which by this union of scattered beauties contains more striking paragraphs than could probably have been brought together into an occasional work. As there is no stronger motive to exertion than self-defense, no part has more elegance, spirit, or dignity than the poet's vindication of his own character.[61] The meanest passage is the satire upon Sporus.[62] . . .

The *Imitations of Horace* seem to have been written as relaxations of his genius. This employment became his favorite by its facility; the plan was ready to his hand, and nothing was required but to accommodate as he could the sentiments of an old author to recent facts or familiar images; but what is easy is seldom excellent: such imitations cannot give pleasure to common readers. The man of learning may be sometimes surprised and delighted by an unexpected parallel, but the comparison requires knowledge of the original, which will likewise often detect strained applications. Between Roman images and English manners there will be an irreconcilable dissimilitude, and the work will be generally uncouth and parti-colored; neither original nor translated, neither ancient nor modern.

Pope had, in proportions very nicely adjusted to each other, all the qualities that constitute genius. He had invention, by which new trains of events are formed and new scenes of imagery displayed, as in *The Rape of the Lock,* and by which extrinsic and adventitious embellishments and illustrations are connected with a known subject, as in the *Essay on Criticism;* he had imagination, which strongly impresses on the writer's mind and enables him to convey to the reader the various forms of nature, incidents of life, and energies of passion, as in his *Eloïsa, Windsor Forest,* and the *Ethic Epistles;* he had judgment, which selects from life or nature what the present purpose requires and, by separat-

---

56. Gem . . . equaled: *Moral Essays,* I.141–48. 57. Atossa, Clodio: *Dunciad,* II.115 ff. and I.179 ff. (Wharton later substituted for "Clodio"). 58. Philomede: *Dunciad,* II.83 ff.

59. elogy . . . sense: *Dunciad,* IV.39 ff. 60. Buckingham: *Dunciad,* III.299 ff. 61. character: *Epistle to Dr. Arbuthnot,* ll. 334 ff., p. 437, above. 62. Sporus: *Epistle to Dr. Arbuthnot,* ll. 305 ff., p. 436, above.

ing the essence of things from its concomitants, often makes the representation more powerful than the reality; and he had colors of language always before him ready to decorate his matter with every grace of elegant expression, as when he accommodates his diction to the wonderful multiplicity of Homer's sentiments and descriptions.

Poetical expression includes sound as well as meaning. "Music," says Dryden, "is inarticulate poetry";[63] among the excellences of Pope, therefore, must be mentioned the melody of his meter. By perusing the works of Dryden he discovered the most perfect fabric of English verse, and habituated himself to that only which he found the best; in consequence of which restraint his poetry has been censured as too uniformly musical, and as glutting the ear with unvaried sweetness. I suspect this objection to be the cant of those who judge by principles rather than perception; and who would even themselves have less pleasure in his works if he had tried to relieve attention by studied discords, or affected to break his lines and vary his pauses.

But though he was thus careful of his versification he did not oppress his powers with superfluous rigor. He seems to have thought with Boileau that the practice of writing might be refined till the difficulty should overbalance the advantage. The construction of his language is not always strictly grammatical; with those rhymes which prescription had conjoined he contented himself, without regard to Swift's remonstrances,[64] though there was no striking consonance; nor was he very careful to vary his terminations or to refuse admission at a small distance to the same rhymes.

To Swift's edict for the exclusion of alexandrines and triplets he paid little regard; he admitted them, but, in the opinion of Fenton,[65] too rarely: he uses them more liberally in his translation than his poems.

He has a few double rhymes, and always, I think, unsuccessfully, except once in *The Rape of the Lock*.

Expletives he very early ejected from his verses; but he now and then admits an epithet rather commodious than important. Each of the six first lines of the *Iliad* might lose two syllables with very little diminution of the meaning; and sometimes, after

all his art and labor, one verse seems to be made for the sake of another. In his latter productions the diction is sometimes vitiated by French idioms, with which Bolingbroke had perhaps infected him.

I have been told that the couplet by which he declared his own ear to be most gratified was this:

Lo, where Maeotis sleeps, and hardly flows
The freezing Tanais thro' a waste of snows.[66]

But the reason of this preference I cannot discover.

It is remarked by Watts[67] that there is scarcely a happy combination of words or a phrase poetically elegant in the English language which Pope has not inserted into his version of Homer. How he obtained possession of so many beauties of speech it were desirable to know. That he gleaned from authors, obscure as well as eminent, what he thought brilliant or useful, and preserved it all in a regular collection, is not unlikely. When, in his last years, Hall's *Satires*[68] were shown him, he wished that he had seen them sooner.

New sentiments and new images others may produce, but to attempt any further improvement of versification will be dangerous. Art and diligence have now done their best, and what shall be added will be the effort of tedious toil and needless curiosity.

After all this it is surely superfluous to answer the question that has once been asked, whether Pope was a poet? otherwise than by asking in return, if Poet be not a poet, where is poetry to be found? To circumscribe poetry by a definition will only show the narrowness of the definer, though a definition which shall exclude Pope will not easily be made. Let us look round upon the present time, and back upon the past; let us inquire to whom the voice of mankind has decreed the wreath of poetry; let their productions be examined and their claims stated, and the pretensions of Pope will be no more disputed. Had he given the world only his version the name of poet must have been allowed him; if the writer of the *Iliad* were to class his successors he would assign a very high place to his translator, without requiring any other evidence of genius.

---

63. "Music . . . poetry": Preface to *Tyrannick Love* (1670).
64. remonstrances: Swift to Pope, June 28, 1715. See Boileau. *L'Art poétique*, I.64–68.   65. Fenton: Elijah Fenton was one of Pope's assistants in the translation of Homer.

66. *Dunciad*, III.87–88.   67. Watts: Isaac Watts, *The Improvement of the Mind* (1741), I.xx.36 "Few books," Johnson wrote in his *Life of Watts*, "have been perused by me with greater pleasure."   68. Hall's *Satires*: Joseph Hall, *Virgidemiarum* (1597–98). Hall's six books of satires treat of contemporary abuses and persons, with Juvenalian invective, and thus would have provided Pope with analogies.

GEORGE W. MEYER, *Editor*

William Wordsworth &

Samuel Taylor Coleridge

WORDSWORTH 1770–1850 COLERIDGE 1772–1834

Just south of the Solway Firth and the Scottish border, in the counties of Cumberland and Westmorland, lies the English Lake District, a hilly, glaciated area, some twenty miles across. On the northwestern edge of this region of almost incredible natural beauty William Wordsworth was born on April 7, 1770, in the village of Cockermouth, Cumberland. In the heart of these "dear native regions," with which most of his poetry is intimately associated, Wordsworth grew up and lived the greater part of his life.

William was the second in a family of four sons and one daughter born to John and Anne Cookson Wordsworth. The elder Wordsworth was an attorney who served as law agent to Sir James Lowther, later Lord Lonsdale, a tyrannical nobleman known appropriately as "the bad earl." Upon John Wordsworth fell the onerous duty of collecting rents from the Lowther tenants, among whom were acquaintances and neighbors. This circumstance and the fact that the Wordsworths occupied the largest house in town suggest that William and his brothers and sister lived somewhat apart from their Cockermouth contemporaries and were left much to their own resources for society and amusement. From these early years at Cocker-

mouth the poet's habits of solitude, self-dependence, and introspection, as well as his extraordinarily close attachment to his sister Dorothy (born December 25, 1771), probably originate.

We have his own word for it that Wordsworth was a difficult child:

I was of a stiff, moody, and violent temper; so much so that I remember going once into the attics of my grandfather's house at Penrith, upon some indignity having been put upon me, with an intention of destroying myself with one of the foils which I knew was kept there. I took the foil in hand, but my heart failed. Upon another occasion, while I was at my grandfather's house at Penrith, along with my eldest brother, Richard, we were whipping tops together in the large drawing room, on which the carpet was only laid down upon particular occasions. The walls were hung round with family pictures, and I said to my brother, " Dare you strike your whip through that old lady's petticoat? " He replied, " No, I won't." " Then," said I, " here goes "; and I struck my lash through her hooped petticoat, for which no doubt, though I have forgotten it, I was properly punished.

Wordsworth's childhood comportment filled his mother with mingled hope and despair. Prior to her death, shortly before his eighth birthday, she confided to a friend that " the only one of her five children about whose future life she was anxious, was William; and he, she said, would be remarkable either for good or for evil." Until several years after his graduation from college this issue remained in doubt.

From 1778 to 1787, when he entered St. John's College, Cambridge, Wordsworth attended Hawkshead Grammar School, an institution founded in 1585 by Edwin Sandys, Archbishop of York. In Wordsworth's day no school in England trained its students better in classics and in mathematics. Here on the shores of Esthwaite Water, hardly two miles from Lake Windermere, Wordsworth shared with his schoolmates the experiences described in the first two books of *The Prelude*. Here he developed the strength and skill that made him the "crack skater on Rydal Lake" and, even at the age of sixty, the equal of the youngest and hardiest mountain climber in the Lake District. Here also his abnormally acute senses awoke to "the mighty world of eye and ear" and began to store away for future imaginative use the materials of his poetry.

The pastoral freedom and excellent training at Hawkshead were not unmixed blessings for Wordsworth. At Cambridge he found himself a year ahead of most of his class and ill-prepared to meet the worldliness and indifference of the college faculty. Left much to his own devices, he indulged a natural adolescent tendency to indolence and, preferring pedestrian tours to study in the vacations, graduated without distinction. When he left Cambridge in January, 1791, he had little to recommend him but scattered translations — one of them obscene — from the poetry of Anacreon, Catullus, and Horace, and a long nostalgic series of octosyllabic couplets called "The Vale of Esthwaite."

For the next few years Wordsworth's behavior exasperated those who thought they knew what was best for him. His father had died in December, 1783, leaving a comfortable estate of £4,700, almost all of which was in the hands of Sir James Lowther, who refused to pay. By a brutal exhibition of feudal power in the English courts, Lowther kept the young Wordsworths from their inheritance until his death in 1802. Meanwhile the Wordsworth children were forced to depend upon guardian relatives, who were not pleased when William failed to equip himself at Cambridge for any profession by

which he might earn a living. In his freshman year he had considered becoming a lawyer, but he surrendered this idea when close study provoked headaches and a pain in his side. Later he thought he might emigrate to Barbados with his brother John, a sailor, and then it occurred to him that he might become a general in the army. After his graduation there seemed to Wordsworth and his guardians two possibilities for his future. He wanted to become tutor and companion to some hypothetical rich young man who wished to travel. They wanted him to return to Cambridge for postgraduate work in Oriental languages so that he might become a well-qualified minister in the Anglican Church. The prospect of "vegetating in a paltry curacy" Wordsworth found repulsive, and he persuaded his guardians to finance one more year of freedom from responsibility, this one to be spent in revolutionary France.

Ever since William the Conqueror triumphed at Hastings in 1066 there have been Englishmen who believe that France is the source and center of political and carnal vice. If they had not already shared this belief Wordsworth's guardians must have done so when their nephew returned to England, demonstrating conclusively that he was no longer fitted for the Church. To begin with, Wordsworth had seen enough of the revolution in Paris, Orléans, and Blois to convince him that French republicanism was "nothing out of nature's certain course." Michel Beaupuy, the French captain immortalized in the ninth book of *The Prelude*, had demonstrated to him that the revolutionary cause was the cause of the people, and Wordsworth returned home the champion of radical ideas that were anathema in respectable circles. As if this were not enough, Wordsworth had the effrontery to request still more financial aid so that he might transport to England and marry one Annette Vallon, a French girl several years senior who had borne him a daughter, Caroline, on December 15, 1792. The guardians refused and, fearing William's influence, denied him permission to see his sister.

In an attempt to raise money Wordsworth published *An Evening Walk* and *Descriptive Sketches*, poems which received favorable notice and caught the eye of young Coleridge but did not sell. When in February, 1793, England and France went to war, Wordsworth's sympathies lay with the French, and he faced the future without funds, family, or allegiance to his country. Almost desperate from disappointment and frustration, Wordsworth wrote *A Letter to the Bishop of Llandaff*,[1] which he had the prudence to suppress, and a poem, a watered-down version of which he published in 1842 under the title *Guilt and Sorrow*. Compounded of bitterness toward monarchical society and hopes for the republican future, these two works expressed the extreme radicalism from which Wordsworth, when he had survived the crisis described in the eleventh book of *The Prelude,* wisely retreated.

The rise and decline of Wordsworth's revolutionary ardor between 1793 and 1797 affords a striking parallel to the experience of young radicals in the 1930's and 1940's. Keenly aware of the economic and political injustice suffered by himself and by many of his fellow men, he naïvely assumed that any change must be for the better and grounded his faith in the new world to come on republican principles. He was certain that monarchy was decadent and must die, and for a brief interval he recommended violence to accelerate the destruction of priests and kings. The innate goodness of common humanity, nurtured by modern education, might then be counted upon to produce the millennium. But the course of republican change in France, unlike that in America, produced nothing of the sort. Instead it brought to power Maximilien Robespierre, father of the Terror. After Robespierre fell victim to the guillotine, the revived optimism of Wordsworth and other friends of the revolution turned to despair before the rise of a new dictator-tyrant, Napoleon Bonaparte, who, within a remarkably short time, threatened all of Europe with imperialistic war.

As the political and international horizon darkened, Wordsworth's personal fortunes improved as if by miracle. In 1795 he inherited £900 from a friend [2] and settled with Dorothy [3]

at Racedown, Dorsetshire, in a rent-free cottage owned by the Pinney family of Bristol. In September he met the other literary giant of the age, Samuel Taylor Coleridge.

Two years Wordsworth's junior (a fact he later refused to admit) Coleridge, born on October 21, 1772, was the ninth son and the fourteenth child of the Reverend John Coleridge, the absent-minded vicar of Ottery St. Mary, Devonshire. Favored by both parents as the child of their old age, Samuel incurred the resentment of his older brothers, with whom he could not compete physically. For compensation he turned to books (the *Arabian Nights* and other tales of wonder were his favorites) and created a world of imagination in which to live. He liked to read, for example, in the churchyard, where he would converse with gravestones while fancying himself one of the seven champions of Christendom as he struck down weeds with ruthless abandon. When he was eight, after a fight in which (not without provocation) he attempted to stab his brother Frank with a butcher knife, Coleridge ran away from home and slept all night in wet clothes at the edge of the river Otter. When he awoke he could not move his legs. Here began the rheumatic agonies that soon led Coleridge to opium and made his adult life a prolonged disaster.

Within a year of his father's death in 1781, Coleridge became a student at Christ's Hospital, an ancient charity school in London. Here he made a lifelong friend of Charles Lamb and distinguished himself for scholarship. His schoolboy precocity did not, however, stand up well at Jesus College, Cambridge, which he entered in February, 1791, just after Wordsworth's departure from the university. Coleridge began well enough; he wrote his brother George that he was studying mathematics three hours a day and reading and composing Greek verse " like a mad dog." But, alas, many pitfalls — sex, drink, gambling, drugs, and debt, not to mention all-night talk — were available to the undergraduate, then as now, and Coleridge promptly found them all. Owing close to £150, with nothing in his pockets but an Irish lottery ticket, he fled

---

[1] Richard Watson, the Bishop of Llandaff (Wales), though a native and a resident of the Lake District, had a reputation for political and religious liberalism. When he attacked French republicanism on January 25, 1793, four days after the execution of Louis XVI, Wordsworth was moved to reply.

[2] Raisley Calvert, the brother of a school friend of Wordsworth's, who died of tuberculosis in January, 1795. Wordsworth nursed him in his final illness.

[3] With them was Basil Montagu, the "Edward" of "To My Sister." Basil was the son of a widower friend to whom Wordsworth loaned most of the legacy received from Calvert. The elder

Montagu was primarily responsible for the temporary breach between Wordsworth and Coleridge in 1810. Young Basil, who was born in 1793, and who, as Wordsworth put it in 1798, "lies like a little devil," no doubt stimulated Wordsworth's interest in child psychology.

from Cambridge (December, 1793) in a panic of guilt and self-revulsion to enlist in the Fifteenth Light Dragoons under the alias of Silas Tomkyn Comberbacke (S. T. C.). From this preposterous situation (Coleridge could not curry a horse, much less ride one) he was rescued by his brothers who, by judicious application in the right places, secured his discharge on April 7, 1794. The grounds were " insanity."

His debts paid, Coleridge returned to Cambridge within four days, but he was never to graduate. A walking tour in June took him to Oxford where he met Robert Southey, another precocious youth with poetic aspirations. Their common interests in French republicanism and Godwin's *Political Justice* made them fast friends; for most of the next year they considered emigration to America and the establishment of a Utopian community to be called a pantisocracy. The plan of course failed; meanwhile Coleridge, reacting from unrequited love for one Mary Evans, became engaged to Sara Fricker, a sister of Southey's fiancée. At Southey's insistence, and out of a misguided sense of honor, Coleridge married Sara on October 4, 1795, about a month after his first meeting with William Wordsworth. By June, 1797, Wordsworth and Coleridge had discovered one another's genius, and in July the Wordsworths moved enthusiastically to Alfoxden, a large country house two miles from the Bristol Channel and three miles from Coleridge at Nether Stowey. Here Dorothy began the journals that both poets frequently drew upon for source material, and here began the daily intimacy and collaboration that within fourteen months enabled Wordsworth and Coleridge to produce the revolutionary collection of poems named *Lyrical Ballads.*

After 1798 Wordsworth's life was little more unusual — except for his poetry — than that of the average man working and raising a family in a rural community. In December, 1799, after spending the previous winter in Germany where they had gone with Coleridge, Wordsworth and his sister settled permanently in the vicinity of Grasmere in the Lake District. In 1802, after the Lonsdale debt had been paid — the joint share of William and Dorothy came to £3,825 — Wordsworth married his childhood friend, Mary Hutchinson. Between 1803 and 1810 they had five children, two of whom died in 1812.

In 1805 Wordsworth's favorite brother, John, went down with his ship near Weymouth. In 1813, thanks to the new Lord Lonsdale, Wordsworth became Distributor of Stamps for Westmorland, an office that required little work and paid between £400 and £600 a year. Meanwhile, as the numbers and prosperity of the family increased, the Wordsworths made a succession of moves to larger houses — from Dove Cottage to Allan Bank in 1808, to The Rectory in Grasmere in 1811, and finally to Rydal Mount, near Ambleside, in 1813. Here Wordsworth lived until his death on April 23, 1850.

The last decades of Wordsworth's life were years of increasing popularity and triumph. Throughout his great period, 1797–1814, he had withstood the denigrating criticism of conservative reviewers. Steadily, however, he had been creating a new taste and a new audience for poetry, and in the 1820's, aided greatly by Coleridge's praise in his *Biographia Literaria* (1817), Wordsworth came into his own. Edition after edition of his poems was called for, and Wordsworth suddenly found himself the center of a vast tourist traffic — twenty to thirty visitors, among them some of the world's most famous names, would call in a single day — that regarded Rydal as a national park, with Wordsworth the chief attraction. Dr. Thomas Arnold, the headmaster of Rugby, drawn as much by Wordsworth's fame as by the beauty of the region, spent vacations with his family at Fox How on the west bank of the Rothay, less than a mile from Rydal; between his son Matthew and the old poet developed one of the most important literary relationships in the nineteenth century. In 1839 Wordsworth was called to Oxford to receive the degree of Doctor of Civil Law. He was greeted with " thunders of applause, repeated over and over again . . . by undergraduates and Masters of Arts alike." In 1842 he resigned the office of Stamp Distributor, but was awarded £300 a year on the Civil List. When Robert Southey died in 1843, the young Queen Victoria conferred upon the venerable poet the highest literary honor at her disposal: Wordsworth was appointed poet laureate.

In his later years Wordsworth's poetic powers declined sharply, and he became a political conservative. There is, however, no sound basis for the view that he lost touch with life, became a turncoat reactionary, and could bring himself to speak only disparaging words of younger writers.

As for the younger writers, Wordsworth, like Dr. Johnson, made some estimates that were foolish but more that stand up well. He disliked Thomas Carlyle, whom he regarded as "sometimes insane" and "a pest to the English tongue."[1] To Wordsworth, Byron also was insane, perverse, and evil, full of power without feeling. Shelley he called the "greatest master of harmonious verse in our modern literature" but "too remote from the humanities," which he tries to "outsoar." Keats was a "youth of promise too great for the sorry company he keeps," and his verse, like that of Tennyson, was jeopardized by "overlusciousness." In 1845 Wordsworth declared Tennyson "decidedly the first of our living poets," and in 1846 — after the publication of "The Lost Leader"[2] — Wordsworth commented as follows upon Elizabeth Barrett's selection of Robert Browning for a husband: "Her choice is a very able man, and I trust that it will be a happy union, not doubting that they will speak more intelligibly to each other than (notwithstanding their abilities) they have yet done to the public."

The later life of Coleridge was less fortunate. After the great year of 1797–98 with the Wordsworths in Somersetshire when he wrote or began his finest poems — the "Ancient Mariner," "Christabel," and "Kubla Khan" — Coleridge's life becomes a tale of sadness almost unrelieved. On a visit to the north of England in 1799 he met and fell in love with Sara Hutchinson, whose sister Wordsworth married three years later. His move with his family in 1800 to Greta Hall, Keswick, within walking distance (for Coleridge) of the Wordsworths, gave no relief. By 1801 Coleridge was a confirmed opium addict; in 1802, in "Dejection: An Ode," he revealed the depths of his domestic misery, the hopelessness of his love for Sara Hutchinson, and the loss of his capacity for sustained creative work, which in his despair he considerably underrated. Having long hoped that a warmer climate might help his rheumatism and impatient to escape from his wife, Coleridge sailed in 1804 for Malta. On his return two years later (his sojourn abroad had not been uneventful; when Coleridge was in Rome, Napoleon ordered his arrest for what he regarded as certain slanders Coleridge had written about him earlier in the *Morning Post*) he was a physical and a mental wreck. Brandy had been added to opium in a vicious circle of hangover and depression, and Coleridge often woke screaming from pain and terror in the night. By 1808 he had begun his brilliant career as a lecturer on Shakespeare; he had also become jealous of Sara Hutchinson's friendship with Wordsworth, and he had separated from Mrs. Coleridge. From 1808 until 1810 he nevertheless lived with the Wordsworths, who had taken Allan Bank, a house large enough to accommodate not only their growing family but also Coleridge and his sons. For nine months of this period Coleridge, with Sara Hutchinson for amanuensis, produced at irregular intervals a periodical called the *Friend*. When Sara, in ill health, left to visit a brother in Wales, publication ceased, and Coleridge had lost over £200.

In October, 1810, Coleridge, obliged to go to London to find employment, traveled there from Grasmere in the carriage of Basil Montagu, Wordsworth's old friend (see p. 549, n. 3, above), in whose house he planned to live, at least temporarily. Before their departure Wordsworth, fearful of the plan, warned Montagu of what might be expected of Coleridge in a household (Montagu had recently married, for the third time). Coleridge and Montagu soon quarreled in London, and the latter, obviously in a temper ill befitting a lawyer, violated Wordsworth's well-intended confidence and told Coleridge that Wordsworth had called him a "rotten drunkard" and a "nuisance in his family." What was left of Coleridge was of course crushed. A reconciliation of sorts was in time effected, and Coleridge in 1828 toured the Rhineland with Wordsworth and his daughter, but the old love and understanding were forever gone.

Most of the remaining years of his life Coleridge spent in or around London in the households of John Morgan (an old Bristol acquaintance) and Dr. James Gillman of Highgate. These good people helped Coleridge in his not altogether futile struggle with opium, and,

---

[1] Carlyle, in turn, did not like Wordsworth, whom he described nevertheless as "a deep, earnest man, who had thought silently and painfully about many things . . . cold, hard, silent, practical . . . a man of immense head and great jaws like a crocodile's, cast in a mold designed for prodigious work."

[2] See headnote to "The Lost Leader," p. 845, below.

when circumstances are considered, Coleridge's performance in these years, especially from 1811 to 1817, seems prodigious. His Shakespeare lectures, 1811–12, were very successful; in 1813 the production at Drury Lane of his play *Remorse* (written in 1797 as *Osorio* and later revised) yielded about £400, more than all of his other literary efforts combined to that date; in 1815 he began collecting his poems (he was never able to finish "Christabel") and writing the preface that grew into the *Biographia Literaria* (1817). His lectures in 1818, again touching upon Shakespeare, represent his last significant venture directly concerned with poetry. In 1825 he published *Aids to Reflection,* an attempt at a Platonic idealization of Trinitarian Christianity, which he regarded as preliminary to a "Magnum Opus" that remained unfinished. Coleridge died on July 25, 1834, and was buried at Highgate, where he had lived since 1816. When Wordsworth in the presence of friends read the letter reporting the death of his old collaborator of the Quantock days, his voice faltered and broke; then Wordsworth declared Coleridge the "most *wonderful* man he had ever known."

II

Coleridge and Matthew Arnold, the best critics in nineteenth-century England, placed Wordsworth next to Shakespeare and Milton among modern English poets. There were two causes for Wordsworth's greatness: the historical and literary environment into which he was born, and his native genius, the origins and development of which he himself has described in *The Prelude.* The work of no other English writer since Shakespeare better exemplifies Arnold's theory that the creation of the literary masterwork requires a proper conjunction of the man and the moment.

In the age of Pope, poets dependent upon the patronage of the upper class limited themselves to subjects which would interest their conservative, aristocratic readers. Poet and reader alike, convinced that they enjoyed a civilization and a literature hardly capable of improvement, delighted in the polished reiteration of what they regarded as universal truths. Originality was discouraged, on the theory that if something had not already been said it probably was not worth

saying. External nature, the psychology of rustics, children, or the outcasts of society, as well as the private emotions and personal history of the poet himself, were considered to be eccentric, dull, and unrewarding subjects for poetry. The poet might touch upon such matters incidentally, in an effort to illuminate or make momentarily more enjoyable his universal truth, but in so doing he must never become emphatic or betray any enthusiasm for the indecorous subject in its own right. Above all, he must take care to write in a proper form, in the proper measure, and in proper language. The most respectable poetic forms were those tracing their lineage from classical antiquity: the epic, the epistle, the epitaph, the pastoral, the satire. The couplet in iambic pentameter was the preferred measure of expression. And the language was that used by gentle people in polite conversation. Words and phrases vulgarized by everyday use in trade, profession, work on the farm, or even ordinary domestic life, were to be avoided in a poem as in a drawing room. (Dr. Johnson, for example, objected to Shakespeare's use of "knife" and "blanket" in *Macbeth,* I.v.51–55.)

When Wordsworth and Coleridge began to write, there were chinks in the wall of the neoclassical tradition, but the wall had not yet been breached. In poetry James Thomson had achieved fame as an observer of natural appearances; Gray, Goldsmith, and Crabbe had permitted themselves to consider the lot of the poor; the Wartons, Edward Young, Collins, and Cowper had become increasingly emotional and subjective; Chatterton, in writing his medieval poetic forgeries, had used unclassical forms and meters. In prose Jean Jacques Rousseau had published his *Confessions,* and James Boswell, with shocking unrestraint, had told most of what he knew about the life and conversation of Dr. Johnson. Meanwhile, an economic revolution had raised the sentimental and humanitarian middle class to a position of wealth and power. This greatly increased the numbers of the reading public and helped to destroy the power of the aristocracy as arbiters of literary taste. Simultaneously, the forces of republicanism, founded on the idea that all men are essentially virtuous, had triumphed in America, and were ready to erupt across the Channel in monarchical France. All this was the inheritance of

Wordsworth and Coleridge, who became the literary embodiment of more than a century of liberating and progressive change.

With a single volume Wordsworth and Coleridge greatly extended the boundaries of poetry. The poems in *Lyrical Ballads* (1798) had little to do with aristocratic men of affairs, except perhaps to warn them that it was sinful to feel contempt for any living thing. This volume of "new" poetry opened with a tale of strange, almost hypnotic, effect told in ballad stanza by an aged sailor who had killed an albatross in southern seas and had suffered compulsive penitential pains ever since. It concluded with a majestic blank-verse meditation in which the speaker, Wordsworth himself, addressing his sister, described a landscape and explained how his memory of the scene had helped him through difficult times and led him to an understanding of his own mind and of its interrelationship with the world of external nature. Between these two poems — Coleridge's "The Rime of the Ancient Mariner" and Wordsworth's "Lines Composed a Few Miles above Tintern Abbey" — came twenty-one other pieces, eighteen of them by Wordsworth. There were poems about abandoned mothers, about convicts rotting in dungeons, about a poor man's instinctive sense of property, and about the victims of war and economic depression. There were poems on disprized love, on a mother's fear for her lost idiot son, on the true nature of the nightingale, and on the psychology of children. And there were poems — the "Ancient Mariner" was one of them — on the sin of pride and the advantages of a life of benevolence, on the limitations of book learning, and on what Wordsworth would later call "Nature's holy plan."

Such subjects were sufficiently unorthodox (some reviewers called them "low," "grotesque," and "childish") to startle many readers from the lethargy into which they had been lulled by the thematic monotony of most eighteenth-century verse. But even more arresting than the matter was the manner of *Lyrical Ballads*. The new subjects demanded a new style, and most of these poems were written in the plain, muscular English that ordinary men use in daily conversation. The studied artificiality of diction that had long been fashionable was rejected. A bird was a bird, not a "feathered chorister," a "wanderer of heaven," a member of the "plumy race," or a "tenant of the sky."[1] What was more, the young poets paid small attention to tradition in rhyme and meter. In the two-hundred-odd pages of *Lyrical Ballads* there were six poems in blank verse, one in Spenserian stanza, and many examples and adaptations of the ancient ballad stanza resurrected (to the scornful displeasure of Dr. Johnson) by Bishop Percy in his *Reliques of Ancient Poetry* (1765), but there was not a single specimen of the heroic couplet, hitherto the hallmark of major poetry in the eighteenth century.

The range and significance of *Lyrical Ballads* increased with the successive editions of 1800 (actually January, 1801) and 1802 (there was a reprinting of this edition in 1805). The 1800 edition, in two volumes, contained many new poems by Wordsworth, among them the "Lucy" poems, the "Matthew" group, and "Michael." In this edition, moreover, Wordsworth expanded the original "Advertisement" into the famous Preface, a document as revolutionary and influential in the history of criticism as *Lyrical Ballads* was in the history of poetry. Written in the summer of 1800 and expanded in 1802, this essay made clear that the poems in *Lyrical Ballads* were not the accidental produce of eccentric poetasters but the thoughtful creations of men learned in poetic theory and willing to defend their practice.

The subjects of these poems, Wordsworth explained, were taken from "humble and rustic life" because there "our elementary feelings coexist in a state of greater simplicity," and there "the passions of men are incorporated with the beautiful and permanent forms of nature." Since a poet, moreover, is a "man speaking to men" — not to the members of one social class, but to all men — the authors thought it proper to present their "incidents and situations from common life" in a "selection of language really used by men" — not rich men living in cities, but humble men living close to nature. Such men "hourly communicate with the best objects from which the best part of language is originally derived"; because they pay little attention to the

[1] Had Wordsworth and Coleridge found occasion to refer to what is usually found in any well-stocked barnyard, they would have called it by its given name, "manure," as Whitman soon did in "Song of Myself," even though it cost them the fine humor of Cowper's periphrasis in *The Task:* "The stable yields a stercoraceous heap,/Impregnated with quick-fermenting salts/And potent to resist the freezing blast."

demands of "social vanity," these men "convey their feelings and notions in simple and unelaborated expressions."[1] Then, as if to underline this deliberate departure from the impersonal and unemotional practice of the eighteenth century, Wordsworth announced that "All good poetry is the spontaneous overflow of powerful feelings."

Poems in Two Volumes (1807) revealed even more extensively than *Lyrical Ballads* Wordsworth's imaginative power and his originating and renovating genius in the shorter forms of English poetry. In these volumes were new poems destined to be ranked among the best in the language: "Resolution and Independence," "The Solitary Reaper," "Ode to Duty," the great "Ode"—later subtitled "Intimations of Immortality from Recollections of Early Childhood"—"Elegiac Stanzas," "Character of the Happy Warrior," and the familiar verses on the rainbow, the cuckoo, the daisy, and the daffodils. In addition to these, there were more than fifty sonnets.

Wordsworth's sonnets deserve a special word. In his note to "Nuns Fret Not at Their Convent's Narrow Room," Wordsworth tells us how he began to write sonnets:

One afternoon in 1801, my sister read to me the sonnets of Milton. I had long been well acquainted with them, but I was particularly struck on that occasion with the dignified simplicity and majestic harmony that runs through most of them—in character so totally different from the Italian, and still more so from Shakespeare's fine sonnets. I took fire . . . and produced three sonnets the same afternoon, the first I ever wrote except an irregular one at school.

Actually, Wordsworth had written several sonnets in his youth, and it was on May 21, 1802, not 1801, that he "took fire" from Dorothy's reading of Milton. Before this flame flickered out, only a few years before his death, Wordsworth wrote more than five hundred and thirty sonnets, most of them very good and many of them among the best ever written. Especially distinguished are those in which he rallied his countrymen against Napoleon and spoke with prophetic indignation against the materialistic

dry rot that was sapping England's strength from within. Characteristically, he took liberties with the form and greatly extended its range and variety; he used it to express himself on almost every conceivable subject except romantic love; like Milton, he often rejected the traditional Italianate break in thought at the end of the octave; and he experimented freely with the rhyme scheme of the sestet. In these ways Wordsworth restored to respectability, after a century and a half of almost total neglect, one of the noblest forms of lyrical utterance.

III

According to Matthew Arnold, "Wordsworth's poetry is great because of the extraordinary power with which Wordsworth feels the joy offered to us in nature, the joy offered to us in the simple primary affections and duties; and because of the extraordinary power with which . . . he shows us this joy, and renders it so as to make us share it." This is sound praise, but when Arnold wrote it he thought chiefly of Wordsworth's shorter poems and neglected the value of Wordsworth's "philosophic" poetry, particularly "Tintern Abbey," *The Prelude,* the "Intimations Ode," and *The Excursion.* In Arnold's opinion, these constituted a large part of the "poetical baggage" of which Wordsworth would have to be relieved if his reputation were to continue to prosper. Ironically, however, these were the poems that Wordsworth valued most, and they are the poems that have attracted most attention from twentieth-century critics, no doubt because they give us a clear and comprehensive expression of what we today so strikingly lack—an organic, unitary vision of man and nature, of the human mind, the earth, and the heavens, all activated by one spirit, all in harmonious relationship and dynamic interaction, inevitably progressing (though not without checks and interruptions) and increasingly characterized by "Beauty, a living presence of the earth."

Wordsworth was convinced that man can find happiness in this life, and he expressed this conviction both in his poetry and in his literary theory. In the Preface to *Lyrical Ballads* he announced that it was the duty of the poet—"who rejoices more than other men in the spirit of life that is in him"—not only to enjoy the air

---

[1] Although Coleridge had regarded the 1800 Preface as "half a child of my own brain," in 1802 he began to differ with some of Wordsworth's ideas, especially his ideas about the language of poetry (see the headnote to *Biographia Literaria* below).

he breathes but also to communicate his special awareness of the joy and dignity of living to his readers. Even when the subjects of poetry are distressing and painful, as they are, for example, in " To Toussaint L'Ouverture " or in *Paradise Lost* and *Samson Agonistes,* the poet must by his art contrive to make the total effect of the individual poem one of pleasure.

Wordsworth did not easily achieve the cheerful faith on which this view of the world and poetry was based, nor did he easily maintain it when it was achieved. He was not readily persuaded that " God's in his heaven — All's right with the world," or that " Whatever is, is right." Even so, it is reasonable to ask how Wordsworth came to believe that this " unintelligible " world affords us more pleasure than pain and that the ways of God are justifiable to men. Then, once having become convinced, how does any man — even a happy poet — keep his faith in the goodness of the universe when he is everywhere confronted with injustice, tyranny, and war, with the decay of physical and mental powers, with the disappointments and frustrations that accompany the years, with the loss of friends and children, and finally with the certain loss of life itself? Wordsworth faced these questions. They occurred to him as he experienced the two great crises of his imaginative life. The first of these was political in nature; it began in 1793, is reflected in " Tintern Abbey," and provided the climax for *The Prelude.* The second resulted from Wordsworth's disturbing consciousness of mutability and decay. It began in 1798 at Tintern Abbey, provided the impulse for the " Intimations Ode," reached a climax in Wordsworth's personal life in 1805, and yielded one of the main themes of *The Excursion.* Let us see how Wordsworth resolved these troublesome issues in his meditative poetry, especially in " Tintern Abbey " and the " Intimations Ode."

Not until 1797–98 did Wordsworth become thoroughly and thoughtfully convinced that the world and life were good. Because of his unusually happy childhood he had in an unthinking way *felt* this to be true in his earlier years. It was obscured, but only temporarily, by the events of 1793. In that year the pleasant order of Wordsworth's youthful imagination fell apart, and he found himself asking: How is it possible to accept life in a world where men and society are unjust?

Wordsworth's first answer was that acceptance is not possible; the world must be changed. Like the youthful Shelley and the radicals of our own 1930's, Wordsworth wished to destroy the apparent cause of evil, the existing government. But Robespierre and the Terror quickly taught him that violence breeds further violence and settles nothing. Meanwhile, he had been reading Dr. Edward Young's *The Complaint, or Night Thoughts* (1742), David Hartley's *Observations on Man, His Frame, His Duty, and His Expectations* (1749), and William Godwin's *Political Justice* (1793). All these works proclaimed the ability of the human mind to triumph over vicious passions, and two of them asserted that this triumph, with the ultimate promise of a moral and political utopia, was not only possible but inevitable. In the spring of 1794, when he was deep in these books and once more in the Lake District,[1] Wordsworth began to turn again to nature. At this time, more than a year before he met Coleridge and settled at Racedown with Dorothy, he discovered (and recorded in verses that he never published) the value of the

> Heart that vibrates evermore, awake
> To feeling for all forms that life can take,
> That wider still its sympathy extends
> And sees not any line where being ends;
> Sees sense, through Nature's rudest forms betrayed,
> Tremble obscure in fountain, rock, and shade,
> And while a secret power those forms endears
> Their social accent never vainly hears.

Implicit in these lines is the philosophy of nature Wordsworth expressed in his best poetry, as well as the moral with which Coleridge chose to conclude " The Rime of the Ancient Mariner ":

> He prayeth best, who loveth best
> All things both great and small;
> For the dear God who loveth us,
> He made and loveth all.

By 1797–98, then, love once again dominated Wordsworth's vision of the world. The feeling heart, sensitive and sympathetic to all nature, was the key to man's happiness, individual and social. Society could be improved and injustice

[1] Wordsworth was reunited with his sister at Halifax in the spring of 1794. From there they went to Windy Brow, a farmhouse owned by the Calverts, half a mile from Keswick. Here they were together for a fortnight in April.

banished not by sudden change in the form of government but by the gradual increase of happiness and virtue in the individuals who made up society. Wordsworth and Coleridge had agreed that their poetry should contribute to the reform of society by educating the reader in the virtues of benevolence and the manifold sources of joy available in nature.

When Wordsworth revisited the Wye, his confidence in the excellence of the world could never again be shaken by the painful awareness of "What man has made of man." He proclaimed this fact in "Tintern Abbey," the first of his great meditative poems. Therein, addressing his sister, he reveals that despite five unusually difficult years, during which he had known times of depression in "lonely rooms, and 'mid the din / Of towns and cities" where the "fretful stir / Unprofitable and the fever of the world" were too much with him — despite such years, his optimistic faith has been firmly re-established. "Therefore," he continues, in the most famous of his affirmatory passages,

> am I still
> A lover of the meadows and the woods,
> And mountains; and of all that we behold
> From this green earth; of all the mighty world
> Of eye, and ear — both what they half create,
> And what perceive; well pleased to recognize
> In nature and the language of the sense,
> The anchor of my purest thoughts, the nurse,
> The guide, the guardian of my heart, and soul
> Of all my moral being.

This, in very simple summary, is the central statement of the poem. But, skeptics will inquire, is the statement true? Is it possible that the memory and the revisiting of a landscape near Tintern Abbey could assure Wordsworth that life in an unjust and frenzied society is bearable? The answers to these questions are affirmative; they lie in the realm of poetic truth, where what ought to be counts for more than what is. In the poem the introductory description of the landscape is crucial. As Wordsworth sees it, this landscape is no ordinary bit of static rural scenery, but a symbol of the universe itself. The scene is peaceful, yet dynamic; serene, though in motion and alive. It is an image of the great world of nature, of which man — even man in cities — is a part. The memory of this image has often filled Wordsworth with the visionary power to "see into the

life of things," to look hopefully forward to the time, prophesied by Hartley and Godwin, when all men will participate in the peaceful harmony and joy toward which all nature tends.

Ironically, just as Wordsworth announced his ability to "see into the life of things" and thus answered to his own poetic satisfaction the question of social injustice, a second question, even more difficult, began to disturb him. As he gazed at the landscape, which he had first seen five years before, he made a startling discovery. He saw details that he could recall having seen in 1793, but which he had forgotten during the interval. These were the "gleams of half-extinguished thought," the "many recognitions dim and faint," that brought Wordsworth a moment of "sad perplexity" and caused him to wonder if the memories of this second visit would serve him as had the memories of the first. He was discovering that the memory is ever-changing and imperfect, and that the mind, of which memory is a part, is never from one moment to another the same. This prompted him to compare and contrast in the poem the three stages of his development from childhood to maturity and to notice, perhaps for the first time, that, although he had gained new and greater powers, something which he valued highly had been irretrievably lost. Wordsworth now faced the problem of mutability, decay, and death. After 1798, in his deepest meditations Wordsworth struggled with this problem, the second question that anyone who believes that nature leads us on "From joy to joy" must answer or give up his faith: How is it possible to accept life in a world where all men die? The "Intimations Ode" is Wordsworth's answer.

The "Intimations Ode" is Wordsworth's greatest short poem and one of the most complex utterances in English verse. Here we can only brush the surface of its meaning. In its first four stanzas Wordsworth tells us that, although he is still sensitive to beauty and capable of joy, he can no longer discover anywhere the "celestial" light or glory which as a child he saw everywhere in nature. At the end of stanza 4 he asks: "Where is it now, the glory and the dream?" The next four stanzas attempt to answer the question metaphorically. They suppose that the soul of the child has known a previous existence in Heaven. When the child arrives on earth the celestial radiance trails behind him, glorifying all that he perceives. But the business of the child on this temporal earth is growing up, and, almost imperceptibly as he grows, the celestial light is dimmed by the ordinary light of the natural sun. It is the child's nature to hasten the process of growth. This he does by joyfully mimicking the worldly activities of his elders. The sight of the child thus assisting " custom " to blunt his heavenly potentialities — especially the innocent capacity for joy that is his most priceless heritage — moves Wordsworth to despair in the melancholy closing lines of the eighth stanza. But the poet's recovery is immediate, and sustained to the end. Although the man can no longer see the celestial light, he remembers what he saw and how he felt. These recollections of early childhood he interprets as sufficient evidence for poetic faith in an ideal, immortal world lying behind and above this real one. Meanwhile, as in " Tintern Abbey," for his loss he has had " abundant recompense." The celestial light has been replaced by the light of experience in the " philosophic mind," the " hour / Of splendor in the grass" by the " soothing thoughts that spring / Out of human suffering." As the clouded sun sets at the end of the poet's day, the simplest natural object can provoke thoughts that lead to faith in immortality and are, therefore, " too deep for tears."

Whatever else the " Ode " may affirm, it says, as *The Prelude* says, that the origins of man's joy are fundamental, inevitable, and indestructible. In *The Prelude,* as we have seen, Wordsworth ascribed our love of nature to the love we receive in our mothers' arms. In the " Ode " he tells us metaphorically that our joy in the world comes " from God, who is our home." But this is not its only source. The supernaturalism in the " Ode " has a naturalistic parallel and equivalent in the love the child receives from his parents; in the fourth stanza the "babe leaps up on his mother's arm "; in the seventh the " six-years' darling of a pygmy size " is " Fretted by sallies of his mother's kisses, / With light upon him from his father's eyes "; and in the sixth the poor, tawdry, " homely nurse " of earth with " no unworthy aim " is motivated by " something of a mother's mind." The main point is that joy is born of love, and that it is natural for us to love. As Wordsworth saw it, so marvelously constructed is the human mind, so exquisitely fitted is it to the world in which it lives,

that once we experience love nothing can make this earth and this life permanently unattractive. This capacity for joy is the chief characteristic of the human mind, a miraculous compound of celestial and earthly elements. This is what Wordsworth reaffirmed in the ninth stanza of the " Ode," when he acclaimed those

> truths that wake,
> To perish never;
> Which neither listlessness, nor mad endeavor,
> Nor man nor boy,
> Nor all that is at enmity with joy,
> Can utterly abolish or destroy!

Wordsworth does not say, of course, that our joy and faith in life cannot be temporarily disturbed or shaken. He says that it cannot be " utterly " abolished or destroyed. A little less than a year after the completion of the " Ode " there occurred an event that helps to illustrate this point. On the night of February 5, 1805, John Wordsworth went down with his ship, the East Indiaman *Abergavenny,* off the Bill of Portland. A month after receiving word of this catastrophe, Wordsworth wrote to Sir George Beaumont and questioned the ways of God in terms that anticipate Thomas Hardy in his bleakest moments of late nineteenth-century pessimism. The " faith that looks through death " was shaken, and the " philosophic mind " temporarily paralyzed by an intolerable grief. In this time of urgent personal need Wordsworth turned from his new philosophy of immortality based on the psychology of childhood, and sought consolation from the older, more familiar arguments for eternal life contained in the *Night Thoughts* (VII.205–17) [1] of Dr. Edward Young.

For the time being Wordsworth's happiness was abolished and destroyed. But not " utterly." By May, 1805, in the sober optimism with which he concluded *The Prelude,* Wordsworth had reaffirmed his faith in the indestructibility of joy. Meanwhile, however, he had relearned an old lesson. In " Tintern Abbey " he had spoken of the " still sad music of humanity " and its power to " chasten and subdue." In the intervening years he had not forgotten this power, but he

---

[1] In this passage, which Wordsworth transcribed in his letter, Young asserted that a virtuous man must be immortal because it would be wasteful, unjust, and intolerable for him to be otherwise.

apparently believed that he had paid too little attention to it while he wrote at length in *The Prelude* of the virtually unassailable strength of his imagination rooted deeply in the " spots of time " (XII.208–25). He had perhaps been too well pleased with his own self-sufficiency, and too impatient, too unsympathetic with the plight of those men of stunted imagination who live forever in the " Inanimate cold world" of mechanical custom. The death of his brother reminded Wordsworth of his membership in the fraternity of suffering humanity. This renewed awareness of the brotherhood and of his neglected obligations to his fellow beings he announced in " Elegiac Stanzas, Suggested by a Picture of Peele Castle, in a Storm, Painted by Sir George Beaumont." After confessing, " A deep distress hath humanized my soul," Wordsworth bade solemn farewell to the "heart that lives alone, / Housed in a dream, at distance from the kind! "

Coleridge's reputation (the better part of it has grown steadily since his death) owes something to his association with the Wordsworths, and more to the irregularity of his personal behavior. With Byron and Shelley, Coleridge set a Romantic example for fantastic eccentricity that was more than emulated later in the century by others. Thanks, however, to the excellence of three poems and to the brilliance of his criticism, in both theory and practice, Coleridge's place high up among the masters of English literature is securely established.

The " Ancient Mariner," " Christabel," and " Kubla Khan " exhibit best the cardinal features of Coleridge's meteoric poetic genius.[1] " Enchantment," " witchery," " magic," and " miraculous " are words frequently and properly used in discussion of these poems because they succeed better than any other works of the period in creating for the reader the pure Romantic sense of wonder, the love of the strange, the remote, and the mysterious. They communicate Coleridge's delight in real and imaginary experience with a naïve freshness and enthusiastic vitality usually found only in the spontaneous verbal responses of children, to whom all things

are new. Children lack art and experience; in 1797–98 Coleridge possessed God's plenty of both.

Told in the ancient ballad stanza, ordinarily devoted to tales of heroism or unhappy love, the " Ancient Mariner " seems to be a simple story of minor crime, punishment, repentance, and forgiveness. The speaker, a graybeard bore, buttonholes a youthful wedding guest (he is " next of kin ") and causes him to miss the ceremony. The exterior semblance of the poem, like that of Wordsworth's child, belies its true immensity, however, and the mesmeric powers of the mariner's eye hold us for a second reading. As the motto appended to the poem in 1817 suggests, the tale is not of this earth alone: the mariner is the voice of an experience that transcends what man can learn in space and time; his audience represents unsophisticated innocence preoccupied with pleasures of the moment in a universe of whose full dimensions and population he is quite ignorant. The wedding guest is " a sadder and a wiser man " after listening to the mariner's archetypal narrative; he has missed the party, but he has learned vicariously what most men need a lifetime to discover — that life is a voyage of discovery that leads us all, by benevolent necessity, from innocence to sin and the cold isolation of Polar ice, to penitential sacrifice for all humanity, to grace and a return to good standing in the warm society of universal life.

Coleridge, in telling this story, set and maintained a breakneck narrative pace, radically extended the ballad stanza (once to nine lines), and distributed throughout the poem infinite riches of verbal melody, rhythm, and rhyme. Almost as much might be said of " Christabel " and " Kubla Khan," but these remained fragments. In the " Ancient Mariner " alone did Coleridge's " shaping spirit of imagination" work at full stretch. A " cormorant " reader, learned in metaphysics, all poetry, the literature of travel, science, religion, and Gothic romance, Coleridge, when he wrote this poem, unlocked the doors not only of his personal but of the race unconscious, and fused into unity the most disparate elements of his experience in nature and in books. This he did, incidentally, not by argument or logical exposition, both of which he thought left too little to the reader's imagination, but by suggestion, evocation, symbol, and

---

[1] Coleridge's other poems, "Dejection" excepted, are distinctly minor. The "Conversation Poems" (see headnote to "Frost at Midnight") deserve a word, however, for they anticipate the dramatic monologues of Robert Browning, and the introspective colloquial manner of much contemporary poetry.

association — the favorite methods and devices, since Edgar Allan Poe, of the most influential poets.

Coleridge's poetry nevertheless is limited in bulk and importance when compared with his criticism, which is voluminous and of the highest order of significance. When he began to lecture in 1808, a more than century-old controversy between French and British critics (some English critics took the neoclassic side) over Shakespeare's neglect of the unities of time, place, and action was still unsettled. The French, believing the unities indispensable for verisimilitude, argued that Shakespeare sang as does a bird, because he must; to them he was an untutored butcher-boy, ignorant of taste and art. Reacting against the French insistence upon literal stage delusion, Dr. Johnson went too far in the other direction (see "Preface to Shakespeare," pp. 507–18, above). Overstressing the rational potential of the audience, he claimed that its members are always aware of the unreality of stage action. Since, therefore, they can assume the truth of Othello's marriage to Desdemona in Venice, they can assume without strain Othello's murder of Desdemona in Cyprus.

Coleridge ended the controversy with his theories of organic unity and dramatic illusion. Observing that the Greeks needed the unities because of the chorus, and that Shakespeare had rejected both unities and chorus, Coleridge refused to accept Greek drama as a criterion for all drama. He saw the unities as artificial restrictions that would, if respected, inhibit modern dramatists and force their material mechanically into predetermined forms. Opposing the neoclassic view, he advanced the idea of organic unity — that a play, or any work of art, grows like a tree from the seed which is its origin; it must therefore be judged on its own merits as an individual unit which, ever developing from within, assumes a form and shape innate and proper to it and its species, but peculiarly its own. Well aware of the effectiveness of Shakespeare's plays (even in the garbled versions Garrick prospered with), Coleridge reasoned that

a successful dramatist — like a successful poet writing of the supernatural, as Coleridge had done in the "Ancient Mariner" and in "Christabel" — produces in the audience or the reader a "willing suspension of disbelief that constitutes poetic faith." Playwright or poet, in other words, so appeals to and engages the imagination of his audience that the latter voluntarily allows his rational powers to rest in abeyance as he encourages himself temporarily to believe that what he sees and hears or reads is real.

If his theory of dramatic illusion is Coleridge's most important contribution to dramatic criticism, his interpretation of Hamlet's character has been the most influential. Coleridge, like most people, admired Hamlet and found something of himself in him. With typical Romantic interest in the personality of the individual and neglect of the dramatic context in which alone the character exists, Coleridge, the noblest procrastinator of us all, believed that Hamlet failed because he thought too much. Most critics today reject or qualify this view; its tenacity is nowhere better revealed, however, than in the introductory line for Sir Laurence Olivier's movie *Hamlet* (1948): "This is the story of a man who could not make up his mind."

Wordsworth and Coleridge are inseparably linked as poets because of their epoch-making partnership in the composition of *Lyrical Ballads,* to which Coleridge added breadth and brilliance to Wordsworth's depth and solidity. But yet Coleridge's more permanent and pervasive importance is as a critic rather than as a poet. His definition of the imagination (see *Biographia Literaria,* XIII, p. 612, below), his description of the poet (see *ibid.,* XIV, p. 615, below), and his concept of organic as opposed to mechanical unity in works of art — these alone make him one of the greatest of modern literary theorists. When we have also his criticism of Shakespeare, fragmentary but vast and various, no one can question T. S. Eliot's judgment that Coleridge was the greatest of English critics.

WILLIAM WORDSWORTH

PREFACE

TO THE SECOND EDITION OF SEVERAL OF THE FORE-
GOING POEMS, PUBLISHED, WITH AN ADDITIONAL
VOLUME, UNDER THE TITLE OF

Lyrical Ballads

The first volume of these poems has already been submitted to general perusal. It was published as an experiment, which, I hoped, might be of some use to ascertain how far, by fitting to metrical arrangement a selection of the real language of men in a state of vivid sensation, that sort of pleasure and that quantity of pleasure may be imparted, which a poet may rationally endeavor to impart.

I had formed no very inaccurate estimate of the probable effect of those poems: I flattered myself that they who should be pleased with them would read them with more than common pleasure; and, on the other hand, I was well aware that by those who should dislike them they would be read with more than common dislike. The result has differed from my expectation in this only, that a greater number have been pleased than I ventured to hope I should please. . . .

The principal object, then, proposed in these poems, was to choose incidents and situations from common life, and to relate or describe them throughout, as far as was possible, in a selection of language really used by men, and, at the same time, to throw over them a certain coloring of imagination, whereby ordinary things should be presented to the mind in an unusual aspect; and further, and above all, to make these incidents and situations interesting by tracing in them, truly though not ostentatiously, the primary laws of our nature, chiefly, as far as regards the manner in which we associate ideas in a state of excitement. Humble and rustic life was generally chosen, because in that condition the essential passions of the heart find a better soil in which they can attain their maturity, are less under restraint, and speak a plainer and more emphatic language; because in that condition of life our elementary feelings coexist in a state of greater simplicity, and, consequently, may be more accurately contemplated, and more forcibly communicated; because the manners of rural life germinate from those elementary feelings, and, from the necessary character of rural occupations, are more easily comprehended, and are more durable; and, lastly, because in that condition the passions of men are incorporated with the beautiful and permanent forms of nature. The language, too, of these men has been adopted (purified indeed from what appear to be its real defects, from all lasting and rational causes of dislike or disgust), because such men hourly communicate with the best objects from which the best part of language is originally derived; and because, from their rank in society and the sameness and narrow circle of their intercourse, being less under the influence of social vanity, they convey their feelings and notions in simple and unelaborated expressions. Accordingly, such a language, arising out of repeated experience and regular feelings, is a more permanent, and a far more philosophical language, than that which is frequently substituted for it by poets, who think that they are conferring honor upon themselves and their art in proportion as they separate themselves from the sympathies of men, and indulge in arbitrary and capricious habits of expression, in order to furnish food for fickle tastes and fickle appetites of their own creation.[1] . . .

Not that I always began to write with a distinct purpose formally conceived, but habits of meditation have, I trust, so prompted and regulated my feelings, that my descriptions of such objects as strongly excite those feelings will be found to carry along with them a *purpose*. If this opinion be erroneous, I can have little right to the name of a poet. For all good poetry is the spontaneous overflow of powerful feelings; and though this be true, poems to which any value can be attached were never produced on any variety of subjects but by a man who, being possessed of more than usual organic sensibility, had also thought long and deeply. For our continued influxes of feeling are modified and directed by our thoughts, which are indeed the

PREFACE TO "LYRICAL BALLADS." 1. "It is worth while here to observe that the affecting parts of Chaucer are almost always expressed in language pure and universally intelligible even to this day" [Wordsworth's note].

representatives of all our past feelings; and as, by contemplating the relation of these general representatives to each other, we discover what is really important to men, so, by the repetition and continuance of this act, our feelings will be connected with important subjects, till at length, if we be originally possessed of much sensibility, such habits of mind will be produced that, by obeying blindly and mechanically the impulses of those habits, we shall describe objects, and utter sentiments, of such a nature, and in such connection with each other, that the understanding of the reader must necessarily be in some degree enlightened, and his affection strengthened and purified.

Having dwelt thus long on the subjects and aim of these poems, I shall request the reader's permission to apprise him of a few circumstances relating to their *style,* in order, among other reasons, that he may not censure me for not having performed what I never attempted. The reader will find that personifications of abstract ideas rarely occur in these volumes, and are utterly rejected as an ordinary device to elevate the style and raise it above prose. My purpose was to imitate, and, as far as is possible, to adopt the very language of men; and assuredly such personifications do not make any natural or regular part of that language. They are, indeed, a figure of speech occasionally prompted by passion, and I have made use of them as such; but have endeavored utterly to reject them as a mechanical device of style, or as a family language which writers in meter seem to lay claim to by prescription. I have wished to keep the reader in the company of flesh and blood, persuaded that by so doing I shall interest him. Others who pursue a different track will interest him likewise; I do not interfere with their claim, but wish to prefer a claim of my own. There will also be found in these volumes little of what is usually called poetic diction; as much pains has been taken to avoid it as is ordinarily taken to produce it; this has been done for the reason already alleged, to bring my language near to the language of men; and further, because the pleasure which I have proposed to myself to impart is of a kind very different from that which is supposed by many persons to be the proper object of poetry. Without being culpably particular, I do not know how to give my reader a more exact notion of the style in which it was my wish and intention to write, than by informing him that I have at all times endeavored to look steadily at my subject; consequently there is, I hope, in these poems

little falsehood of description, and my ideas are expressed in language fitted to their respective importance. Something must have been gained by this practice, as it is friendly to one property of all good poetry, namely, good sense; but it has necessarily cut me off from a large portion of phrases and figures of speech which from father to son have long been regarded as the common inheritance of poets. I have also thought it expedient to restrict myself still further, having abstained from the use of many expressions, in themselves proper and beautiful, but which have been foolishly repeated by bad poets, till such feelings of disgust are connected with them as it is scarcely possible by any art of association to overpower. . . .

Taking up the subject, then, upon general grounds, let me ask, what is meant by the word "poet"? What is a poet? To whom does he address himself? And what language is to be expected from him? He is a man speaking to men, a man, it is true, endowed with more lively sensibility, more enthusiasm and tenderness, who has a greater knowledge of human nature, and a more comprehensive soul, than are supposed to be common among mankind; a man pleased with his own passions and volitions, and who rejoices more than other men in the spirit of life that is in him, delighting to contemplate similar volitions and passions as manifested in the goings on of the universe, and habitually impelled to create them where he does not find them. To these qualities he has added a disposition to be affected more than any other men by absent things as if they were present; an ability of conjuring up in himself passions, which are indeed far from being the same as those produced by real events, yet (especially in those parts of the general sympathy which are pleasing and delightful) do more nearly resemble the passions produced by real events than anything which, from the motions of their own minds merely, other men are accustomed to feel in themselves — whence, and from practice, he has acquired a greater readiness and power in expressing what he thinks and feels, and especially those thoughts and feelings which, by his own choice, or from the structure of his own mind, arise in him without immediate external excitement.

But whatever portion of this faculty we may suppose even the greatest poet to possess, there cannot be a doubt that the language which it will suggest to him must often, in liveliness and truth, fall short of that which is uttered by men in real life under the actual pressure of those passions, certain shadows of which the poet thus produces, or feels to be produced, in himself.

However exalted a notion we would wish to cherish of the character of a poet, it is obvious that, while he describes and imitates passions, his employment is in some degree mechanical compared with the freedom and power of real and substantial action and suffering. So that it will be the wish of the poet to bring his feelings near to those of the persons whose feelings he describes, nay, for short spaces of time, perhaps, to let himself slip into an entire delusion, and even confound and identify his own feelings with theirs, modifying only the language which is thus suggested to him by a consideration that he describes for a particular purpose, that of giving pleasure. Here, then, he will apply the principle of selection which has been already insisted upon. He will depend upon this for removing what would otherwise be painful or disgusting in the passion; he will feel that there is no necessity to trick out or to elevate nature; and the more industriously he applies this principle the deeper will be his faith that no words which *his* fancy or imagination can suggest will be to be compared with those which are the emanations of reality and truth.

But it may be said by those who do not object to the general spirit of these remarks that, as it is impossible for the poet to produce upon all occasions language as exquisitely fitted for the passion as that which the real passion itself suggests, it is proper that he should consider himself as in the situation of a translator, who does not scruple to substitute excellences of another kind for those which are unattainable by him; and endeavors occasionally to surpass his original, in order to make some amends for the general inferiority to which he feels he must submit. But this would be to encourage idleness and unmanly despair. Further, it is the language of men who speak of what they do not understand; who talk of poetry, as of a matter of amusement and idle pleasure; who will converse with us as gravely about a *taste* for poetry, as they express it, as if it were a thing as indifferent as a taste for rope dancing, or Frontiniac or sherry.[2] Aristotle, I have been told, has said that poetry is the most philosophic of all writing;[3] it is so: its object is truth, not individual and local, but general and operative; not standing upon external testimony, but carried alive into the heart by passion; truth which is its own testimony, which gives competence and confidence to the tribunal to which it appeals, and receives them from the same tribunal. Poetry is the image of man and nature. The obstacles which stand in the way of the fidelity of the biographer and historian, and of their consequent utility, are incalculably greater than those which are to be encountered by the poet who comprehends the dignity of his art. The poet writes under one restriction only, namely, the necessity of giving immediate pleasure to a human being possessed of that information which may be expected from him, not as a lawyer, a physician, a mariner, an astronomer, or a natural philosopher, but as a man. Except this one restriction, there is no object standing between the poet and the image of things; between this, and the biographer and historian, there are a thousand. . . .

What has been thus far said applies to poetry in general, but especially to those parts of compositions where the poet speaks through the mouths of his characters; and upon this point it appears to authorize the conclusion that there are few persons of good sense who would not allow that the dramatic parts of composition are defective in proportion as they deviate from the real language of nature, and are colored by a diction of the poet's own, either peculiar to him as an individual poet or belonging simply to poets in general; to a body of men who, from the circumstance of their compositions being in meter, it is expected will employ a particular language.

It is not, then, in the dramatic parts of composition that we look for this distinction of language; but still it may be proper and necessary where the poet speaks to us in his own person and character. To this I answer by referring the reader to the description before given of a poet. Among the qualities there enumerated as principally conducing to form a poet, is implied nothing differing in kind from other man, but only in degree. The sum of what was said is, that the poet is chiefly distinguished from other men by a greater promptness to think and feel without immediate external excitement, and a greater power in expressing such thoughts and feelings as are produced in him in that manner. But these passions and thoughts and

2. **Frontiniac or sherry:** European wines, the first made in Frontignan, France; the other, originally, near Xeres (Jerez), Spain.
3. **Aristotle . . . writing:** Aristotle (B.C. 384–322) was one of the greatest of Greek philosophers. Wordsworth refers to the *Poetics*, IX.3, in which Aristotle asserts that poetry, because it expresses the universal rather than the particular, is more philosophical than history.

feelings are the general passions and thoughts and feelings of men. And with what are they connected? Undoubtedly with our moral sentiments and animal sensations, and with the causes which excite these; with the operations of the elements, and the appearances of the visible universe; with storm and sunshine, with the revolutions of the seasons, with cold and heat, with loss of friends and kindred, with injuries and resentments, gratitude and hope, with fear and sorrow. These, and the like, are the sensations and objects which the poet describes, as they are the sensations of other men and the objects which interest them. The poet thinks and feels in the spirit of human passions. How, then, can his language differ in any material degree from that of all other men who feel vividly and see clearly? It might be *proved* that it is impossible. But supposing that this were not the case, the poet might then be allowed to use a peculiar language when expressing his feelings for his own gratification, or that of men like himself. But poets do not write for poets alone, but for men. Unless, therefore, we are advocates for that admiration which subsists upon ignorance, and that pleasure which arises from hearing what we do not understand, the poet must descend from this supposed height; and, in order to excite rational sympathy, he must express himself as other men express themselves. To this it may be added, that while he is only selecting from the real language of men or, which amounts to the same thing, composing accurately in the spirit of such selection, he is treading upon safe ground, and we know what we are to expect from him. Our feelings are the same with respect to meter;[4] for, as it may be proper to remind the reader, the distinction of meter is regular and uniform, and not, like that which is produced by what is usually called "poetic diction," arbitrary, and subject to infinite caprices, upon which no calculation whatever can be made. In the one case, the reader is utterly at the mercy of the poet, respecting what imagery or diction he may choose to connect with the passion; whereas, in the other, the meter obeys certain laws, to which the poet and reader both willingly submit because they are certain, and because no interference is made by them with the passion but such as the concurring testimony of ages has shown to heighten and improve the pleasure which coexists with it. . . .

4. Here ends the description of the poet which Wordsworth added to the Preface in the edition of 1802.

I have said that poetry is the spontaneous overflow of powerful feelings; it takes its origin from emotion recollected in tranquillity; the emotion is contemplated till, by a species of reaction, the tranquillity gradually disappears, and an emotion, kindred to that which was before the subject of contemplation, is gradually produced, and does itself actually exist in the mind. In this mood successful composition generally begins, and in a mood similar to this it is carried on; but the emotion, of whatever kind, and in whatever degree, from various causes, is qualified by various pleasures, so that in describing any passions whatsoever, which are voluntarily described, the mind will, upon the whole, be in a state of enjoyment. If nature be thus cautious to preserve in a state of enjoyment a being so employed, the poet ought to profit by the lesson held forth to him, and ought especially to take care that, whatever passions he communicates to his reader, those passions, if his reader's mind be sound and vigorous, should always be accompanied with an overbalance of pleasure. Now the music of harmonious metrical language, the sense of difficulty overcome, and the blind association of pleasure which has been previously received from works of rhyme or meter of the same or similar construction, an indistinct perception perpetually renewed of language closely resembling that of real life, and yet, in the circumstance of meter, differing from it so widely — all these imperceptibly make up a complex feeling of delight, which is of the most important use in tempering the painful feeling always found intermingled with powerful descriptions of the deeper passions. This effect is always produced in pathetic and impassioned poetry; while, in lighter compositions, the ease and gracefulness with which the poet manages his numbers are themselves confessedly a principal source of the gratification of the reader. All that it is *necessary* to say, however, upon this subject, may be effected by affirming, what few persons will deny, that of two descriptions, either of passions, manners, or characters, each of them equally well executed, the one in prose and the other in verse, the verse will be read a hundred times where the prose is read once. . . .

Long as the reader has been detained, I hope he will permit me to caution him against a mode of false criticism which has been applied to poetry, in which the language closely resembles that of life and nature. Such verses have been triumphed over in parodies, of which Dr. Johnson's stanza is a fair specimen:

I put my hat upon my head
And walked into the Strand,[5]
And there I met another man
Whose hat was in his hand.

Immediately under these lines let us place one of the most justly admired stanzas of the " Babes in the Wood ":

These pretty babes with hand in hand
Went wandering up and down;
But never more they saw the man
Approaching from the town.

In both these stanzas the words, and the order of the words, in no respect differ from the most unimpassioned conversation. There are words in both, for example, " the Strand," and " the town," connected with none but the most familiar ideas; yet the one stanza we admit as admirable, and the other as a fair example of the superlatively contemptible. Whence arises this difference? Not from the meter, not from the language, not from the order of the words; but the *matter* expressed in Dr. Johnson's stanza is contemptible. The proper method of treating trivial and simple verses, to which Dr. Johnson's stanza would be a fair parallelism, is not to say, this is a bad kind of poetry, or, this is not poetry; but, this wants sense; it is neither interesting in itself, nor can *lead* to anything interesting; the images neither originate in that sane state of feeling which arises out of thought, nor can excite thought or feeling in the reader. This is the only sensible manner of dealing with such verses. Why trouble yourself about the species till you have previously decided upon the genus? Why take pains to prove that an ape is not a Newton, when it is self-evident that he is not a man?

One request I must make of my reader, which is, that in judging these poems he would decide by his own feelings genuinely, and not by reflection upon what will probably be the judgment of others. How common is it to hear a person say, I myself do not object to this style of composition, or this or that expression, but to such and such classes of people it will appear mean or ludicrous! This mode of criticism, so destructive of all sound unadulterated judgment, is almost universal; let the reader then abide, independently, by his own feelings, and, if he finds himself affected, let him not suffer such conjectures to interfere with his pleasure. . . .

From what has been said, and from a perusal of the poems, the reader will be able clearly to perceive the object which I had in view; he will determine how far it has been attained, and, what is a much more important question, whether it be worth attaining; and upon the decision of these two questions will rest my claim to the approbation of the public.

1800

THE REVERIE OF POOR SUSAN

" This arose out of my observation of the affecting music of these birds hanging in this way in the London streets during the freshness and stillness of the spring morning " [W].

At the corner of Wood Street, when daylight appears,°
Hangs a thrush that sings loud, it has sung for three years;
Poor Susan has passed by the spot, and has heard
In the silence of morning the song of the bird.

'Tis a note of enchantment; what ails her? She sees
A mountain ascending, a vision of trees;
Bright volumes of vapor through Lothbury glide,
And a river flows on through the vale of Cheapside.

Green pastures she views in the midst of the dale,
Down which she so often has tripped with her pail;   10
And a single small cottage, a nest like a dove's,
The one only dwelling on earth that she loves.

She looks, and her heart is in heaven; but they fade,
The mist and the river, the hill and the shade;
The stream will not flow, and the hill will not rise,
And the colors have all passed away from her eyes!

1797

✓ THE OLD CUMBERLAND BEGGAR

" Observed, and with great benefit to my own heart, when I was a child; written at Racedown and Alfoxden in my twenty-third year. The political economists were about that time beginning their war upon mendicity in all its forms, and by implication, if not directly, on almsgiving also. . . . The class of beggars, to which the old man here described belongs, will probably soon be extinct. It consisted of poor and, mostly, old and infirm persons, who confined themselves to a stated round in their neighborhood, and

---

5. the Strand: a principal business street in London.

REVERIE OF POOR SUSAN.   1–8. Wood Street, Lothbury, Cheapside: places in one of the busiest sections of London.

had certain fixed days on which, at different houses, they regularly received alms, sometimes in money, but mostly in provisions " [W].

I saw an aged beggar in my walk;
And he was seated, by the highway side,
On a low structure of rude masonry
Built at the foot of a huge hill, that they
Who lead their horses down the steep rough road
May thence remount at ease. The aged man
Had placed his staff across the broad smooth stone
That overlays the pile; and, from a bag
All white with flour, the dole of village dames,
He drew his scraps and fragments, one by one;
And scanned them with a fixed and serious look
Of idle computation. In the sun,   12
Upon the second step of that small pile,
Surrounded by those wild unpeopled hills,
He sat, and ate his food in solitude,
And ever, scattered from his palsied hand,
That, still attempting to prevent the waste,
Was baffled still, the crumbs in little showers
Fell on the ground; and the small mountain birds,
Not venturing yet to peck their destined meal,   20
Approached within the length of half his staff.

Him from my childhood have I known; and then
He was so old, he seems not older now;
He travels on, a solitary man,
So helpless in appearance, that for him
The sauntering horseman throws not with a slack
And careless hand his alms upon the ground,
But stops, that he may safely lodge the coin
Within the old man's hat; nor quits him so,
But still, when he has given his horse the rein,   30
Watches the aged beggar with a look
Sidelong, and half-reverted. She who tends
The tollgate, when in summer at her door
She turns her wheel, if on the road she sees
The aged beggar coming, quits her work,
And lifts the latch for him that he may pass.
The postboy, when his rattling wheels o'ertake
The aged beggar in the woody lane,
Shouts to him from behind; and if, thus warned,
The old man does not change his course, the boy
Turns with less noisy wheels to the roadside,   41
And passes gently by, without a curse
Upon his lips, or anger at his heart.

He travels on, a solitary man;
His age has no companion. On the ground
His eyes are turned, and, as he moves along
They move along the ground; and, evermore,
Instead of common and habitual sight
Of fields with rural works, of hill and dale,
And the blue sky, one little span of earth   50

Is all his prospect. Thus, from day to day,
Bow-bent, his eyes forever on the ground,
He plies his weary journey; seeing still,
And seldom knowing that he sees, some straw,
Some scattered leaf, or marks which, in one track,
The nails of cart or chariot wheel have left
Impressed on the white road — in the same line,
At distance still the same. Poor traveler!
His staff trails with him; scarcely do his feet
Disturb the summer dust; he is so still   60
In look and motion, that the cottage curs,
Ere he has passed the door, will turn away,
Weary of barking at him. Boys and girls,
The vacant and the busy, maids and youths,
And urchins newly breeched — all pass him by:
Him even the slow-paced wagon leaves behind.

But deem not this man useless. Statesmen! ye
Who are so restless in your wisdom, ye
Who have a broom still ready in your hands
To rid the world of nuisances; ye proud,   70
Heart-swol'n, while in your pride ye contemplate
Your talents, power, or wisdom, deem him not
A burthen of the earth! 'Tis Nature's law
That none, the meanest of created things,
Or forms created the most vile and brute,
The dullest or most noxious, should exist
Divorced from good — a spirit and pulse of good,
A life and soul, to every mode of being
Inseparably linked. Then be assured
That least of all can aught — that ever owned   80
The heaven-regarding eye and front sublime
Which man is born to — sink, howe'er depressed,
So low as to be scorned without a sin;
Without offense to God cast out of view;
Like the dry remnant of a garden flower
Whose seeds are shed, or as an implement
Worn out and worthless. While from door to door
This old man creeps, the villagers in him
Behold a record which together binds
Past deeds and offices of charity,   90
Else unremembered, and so keeps alive
The kindly mood in hearts which lapse of years,
And that half-wisdom half-experience gives,
Make slow to feel, and by sure steps resign
To selfishness and cold oblivious cares.
Among the farms and solitary huts,
Hamlets and thinly scattered villages,
Where'er the aged beggar takes his rounds,
The mild necessity of use compels
To acts of love; and habit does the work   100
Of reason; yet prepares that afterjoy
Which reason cherishes. And thus the soul,
By that sweet taste of pleasure unpursued,
Doth find herself insensibly disposed
To virtue and true goodness.

Some there are,
By their good works exalted, lofty minds
And meditative, authors of delight
And happiness, which to the end of time
Will live, and spread, and kindle; even such minds
In childhood, from this solitary being,   110
Or from like wanderer, haply have received
(A thing more precious far than all that books
Or the solicitudes of love can do!)
That first mild touch of sympathy and thought,
In which they found their kindred with a world
Where want and sorrow were. The easy man
Who sits at his own door, and, like the pear
That overhangs his head from the green wall,
Feeds in the sunshine; the robust and young,
The prosperous and unthinking, they who live
Sheltered, and flourish in a little grove   121
Of their own kindred; all behold in him
A silent monitor, which on their minds
Must needs impress a transitory thought
Of self-congratulation, to the heart
Of each recalling his peculiar boons,
His charters and exemptions; and, perchance,
Though he to no one give the fortitude
And circumspection needful to preserve
His present blessings, and to husband up   130
The respite of the season, he, at least,
And 'tis no vulgar service, makes them felt.

    Yet further. Many, I believe, there are
Who live a life of virtuous decency,
Men who can hear the Decalogue and feel
No self-reproach; who of the moral law
Established in the land where they abide
Are strict observers; and not negligent
In acts of love to those with whom they dwell,
Their kindred, and the children of their blood.
Praise be to such, and to their slumbers peace!   141
But of the poor man ask, the abject poor;
Go, and demand of him, if there be here
In this cold abstinence from evil deeds,
And these inevitable charities,
Wherewith to satisfy the human soul?
No — man is dear to man; the poorest poor
Long for some moments in a weary life
When they can know and feel that they have been,
Themselves, the fathers and the dealers-out   150
Of some small blessings; have been kind to such
As needed kindness, for this single cause,
That we have all of us one human heart.
Such pleasure is to one kind being known,
My neighbor, when with punctual care, each week
Duly as Friday comes, though pressed herself
By her own wants, she from her store of meal
Takes one unsparing handful for the scrip°

OLD CUMBERLAND BEGGAR.   158. scrip: a bag, wallet, or knap-
sack.

Of this old mendicant, and, from her door
Returning with exhilarated heart,   160
Sits by her fire, and builds her hope in Heaven.

    Then let him pass, a blessing on his head!
And while in that vast solitude to which
The tide of things has borne him, he appears
To breathe and live but for himself alone,
Unblamed, uninjured, let him bear about
The good which the benignant law of Heaven
Has hung around him, and, while life is his,
Still let him prompt the unlettered villagers
To tender offices and pensive thoughts.   170
    Then let him pass, a blessing on his head!
And, long as he can wander, let him breathe
The freshness of the valleys; let his blood
Struggle with frosty air and winter snows;
And let the chartered wind that sweeps the heath
Beat his gray locks against his withered face.
Reverence the hope whose vital anxiousness
Gives the last human interest to his heart.°
May never House, misnamed of Industry,°
Make him a captive! — for that pent-up din,   180
Those life-consuming sounds that clog the air,
Be his the natural silence of old age!
Let him be free of mountain solitudes;
And have around him, whether heard or not,
The pleasant melody of woodland birds.
Few are his pleasures; if his eyes have now
Been doomed so long to settle upon earth
That not without some effort they behold
The countenance of the horizontal sun,
Rising or setting, let the light at least   190
Find a free entrance to their languid orbs.
And let him, *where* and *when* he will, sit down
Beneath the trees, or on a grassy bank
Of highway side, and with the little birds
Share his chance-gathered meal; and, finally,
As in the eye of Nature he has lived,
So in the eye of Nature let him die!

                                          1797

WE ARE SEVEN

— A simple child,
That lightly draws its breath,
And feels its life in every limb,
What should it know of death?

I met a little cottage girl;
She was eight years old, she said;
Her hair was thick with many a curl
That clustered round her head.

179. House . . . Industry: a poorhouse.

She had a rustic, woodland air,
And she was wildly clad; 10
Her eyes were fair, and very fair;
Her beauty made me glad.

"Sisters and brothers, little maid,
How many may you be?"
"How many? Seven in all," she said,
And wondering looked at me.

"And where are they? I pray you tell."
She answered, "Seven are we;
And two of us at Conway dwell,
And two are gone to sea. 20

"Two of us in the churchyard lie,
My sister and my brother;
And, in the churchyard cottage, I
Dwell near them with my mother."

"You say that two at Conway dwell,
And two are gone to sea,
Yet ye are seven! I pray you tell,
Sweet maid, how this may be."

Then did the little maid reply,
"Seven boys and girls are we; 30
Two of us in the churchyard lie,
Beneath the churchyard tree."

"You run about, my little maid,
Your limbs they are alive;
If two are in the churchyard laid,
Then ye are only five."

"Their graves are green, they may be seen,"
The little maid replied,
"Twelve steps or more from my mother's door,
And they are side by side. 40

"My stockings there I often knit,
My kerchief there I hem;
And there upon the ground I sit,
And sing a song to them.

"And often after sunset, sir,
When it is light and fair,
I take my little porringer,°
And eat my supper there.

"The first that died was sister Jane;
In bed she moaning lay, 50
Till God released her of her pain;
And then she went away.

"So in the churchyard she was laid;
And, when the grass was dry,
Together round her grave we played,
My brother John and I.

"And when the ground was white with snow,
And I could run and slide,
My brother John was forced to go,
And he lies by her side." 60

"How many are you, then," said I,
"If they two are in Heaven?"
Quick was the little maid's reply,
"O Master! we are seven."

"But they are dead; those two are dead!
Their spirits are in Heaven!"
'Twas throwing words away; for still
The little maid would have her will,
And say, "Nay, we are seven!"

1798

EXPOSTULATION AND REPLY

"This poem is a favorite among the Quakers, as I
have learned on many occasions. It was composed in
front of the house at Alfoxden, in the spring of 1798"
[W].

"Why, William, on that old gray stone,
Thus for the length of half a day,
Why, William, sit you thus alone,
And dream your time away?

"Where are your books? — that light bequeathed
To beings else forlorn and blind!
Up! up! and drink the spirit breathed
From dead men to their kind.

"You look round on your Mother Earth,
As if she for no purpose bore you; 10
As if you were her first-born birth,
And none had lived before you!"

One morning thus, by Esthwaite Lake,°
When life was sweet, I knew not why,
To me my good friend Matthew° spake,
And thus I made reply:

"The eye — it cannot choose but see;
We cannot bid the ear be still;
Our bodies feel, where'er they be,
Against or with our will. 20

EXPOSTULATION AND REPLY. **13. Esthwaite Lake:** half a mile
from Hawkshead, where Wordsworth went to school. **15. Matthew:** probably William Taylor, headmaster of Hawkshead
School (1782–86) and Wordsworth's teacher. He is again referred
to in "The Tables Turned" and "The Two April Mornings," below.

WE ARE SEVEN. **47. porringer:** a deep dish for soup or porridge.

"Nor less I deem that there are powers
Which of themselves our minds impress;
That we can feed this mind of ours
In a wise passiveness.

"Think you, 'mid all this mighty sum
Of things forever speaking,
That nothing of itself will come,
But we must still be seeking?

"Then ask not wherefore, here, alone,
Conversing as I may,   30
I sit upon this old gray stone,
And dream my time away."

1798

THE TABLES TURNED

An Evening Scene on the Same Subject

Up! up! my friend,° and quit your books,
Or surely you'll grow double;
Up! up! my friend, and clear your looks;
Why all this toil and trouble?

The sun, above the mountain's head,
A freshening luster mellow
Through all the long green fields has spread,
His first sweet evening yellow.

Books! 'tis a dull and endless strife;
Come, hear the woodland linnet,   10
How sweet his music! on my life,
There's more of wisdom in it.

And hark! how blithe the throstle° sings!
He, too, is no mean preacher;
Come forth into the light of things,
Let Nature be your teacher.

She has a world of ready wealth,
Our minds and hearts to bless —
Spontaneous wisdom breathed by health,
Truth breathed by cheerfulness.   20

One impulse from a vernal wood
May teach you more of man,
Of moral evil and of good,
Than all the sages can.

Sweet is the lore which Nature brings;
Our meddling intellect
Misshapes the beauteous forms of things;
We murder to dissect.

THE TABLES TURNED. **1. friend:** Matthew. **13. throstle:** the song thrush.

Enough of Science and of Art;
Close up those barren leaves;   30
Come forth, and bring with you a heart
That watches and receives.

1798

LINES WRITTEN IN EARLY SPRING

"Actually composed while I was sitting by the side of the brook that runs down from the comb in which stands the village of Alford, through the grounds of Alfoxden" [W].

I heard a thousand blended notes,
While in a grove I sat reclined,
In that sweet mood when pleasant thoughts
Bring sad thoughts to the mind.

To her fair works did Nature link
The human soul that through me ran;
And much it grieved my heart to think
What man has made of man.

Through primrose tufts, in that green bower,
The periwinkle° trailed its wreaths;   10
And 'tis my faith that every flower
Enjoys the air it breathes.

The birds around me hopped and played,
Their thoughts I cannot measure;
But the least motion which they made
It seemed a thrill of pleasure.

The budding twigs spread out their fan,
To catch the breezy air;
And I must think, do all I can,
That there was pleasure there.   20

If this belief from heaven be sent,
If such be Nature's holy plan,°
Have I not reason to lament
What man has made of man?

1798

LINES

Composed a few miles above Tintern Abbey,° on revisiting the banks of the Wye during a tour, July 13, 1798

"No poem of mine was composed under circumstances more pleasant for me to remember than this. I

LINES WRITTEN IN EARLY SPRING. **10. periwinkle:** a trailing evergreen plant with small blue flowers, usually called myrtle in the United States. **21–22. If this . . . plan:** From 1798 until 1820 these lines read: "If I these thoughts may not prevent,/If such be of my creed the plan."
TINTERN ABBEY. Tintern Abbey is a picturesque ruin in Monmouthshire. Wordsworth saw it for the first time in the summer of 1793, when he was on his way to visit Robert Jones in Wales.

began it upon leaving Tintern, after crossing the Wye, and concluded it just as I was entering Bristol in the evening, after a ramble of four or five days, with my sister. Not a line of it was altered, and not any part of it written down till I reached Bristol " [W].

Five years have passed; five summers, with the
    length
Of five long winters! and again I hear
These waters, rolling from their mountain springs
With a soft inland murmur. Once again
Do I behold these steep and lofty cliffs,
That on a wild secluded scene impress
Thoughts of more deep seclusion; and connect
The landscape with the quiet of the sky.
The day is come when I again repose
Here, under this dark sycamore, and view   10
These plots of cottage ground, these orchard tufts,
Which at this season, with their unripe fruits,
Are clad in one green hue, and lose themselves
'Mid groves and copses. Once again I see
These hedgerows, hardly hedgerows, little lines
Of sportive wood run wild — these pastoral farms,
Green to the very door; and wreaths of smoke
Sent up, in silence, from among the trees!
With some uncertain notice, as might seem
Of vagrant dwellers in the houseless woods,   20
Or of some hermit's cave, where by his fire
The hermit sits alone.

               These beauteous forms,
Through a long absence, have not been to me
As is a landscape to a blind man's eye;
But oft, in lonely rooms, and 'mid the din
Of towns and cities, I have owed to them
In hours of weariness, sensations sweet,
Felt in the blood, and felt along the heart;
And passing even into my purer mind,
With tranquil restoration; feelings too   30
Of unremembered pleasure, such, perhaps,
As have no slight or trivial influence
On that best portion of a good man's life,
His little, nameless, unremembered acts
Of kindness and of love. Nor less, I trust,
To them I may have owed another gift,
Of aspect more sublime; that blessed mood,
In which the burthen of the mystery,
In which the heavy and the weary weight
Of all this unintelligible world,   40
Is lightened: that serene and blessed mood,
In which the affections gently lead us on,
Until, the breath of this corporeal frame
And even the motion of our human blood
Almost suspended, we are laid asleep
In body, and become a living soul,
While with an eye made quiet by the power
Of harmony, and the deep power of joy,
We see into the life of things.

                 If this
Be but a vain belief, yet, oh! how oft —   50
In darkness and amid the many shapes
Of joyless daylight; when the fretful stir
Unprofitable, and the fever of the world,
Have hung upon the beatings of my heart —
How oft, in spirit, have I turned to thee,
O sylvan Wye! thou wanderer through the woods,
How often has my spirit turned to thee!

    And now, with gleams of half-extinguished
        thought,
With many recognitions dim and faint,
And somewhat of a sad perplexity,   60
The picture of the mind revives again:
While here I stand, not only with the sense
Of present pleasure, but with pleasing thoughts
That in this moment there is life and food
For future years. And so I dare to hope,
Though changed, no doubt, from what I was when
    first
I came among these hills; when like a roe
I bounded o'er the mountains, by the sides
Of the deep rivers, and the lonely streams,
Wherever nature led — more like a man   70
Flying from something that he dreads, than one
Who sought the thing he loved. For nature then
(The coarser pleasures of my boyish days,
And their glad animal movements all gone by)
To me was all in all. I cannot paint
What then I was. The sounding cataract
Haunted me like a passion; the tall rock,
The mountain, and the deep and gloomy wood,
Their colors and their forms, were then to me
An appetite; a feeling and a love,   80
That had no need of a remoter charm,
By thought supplied, nor any interest
Unborrowed from the eye. That time is past,
And all its aching joys are now no more,
And all its dizzy raptures. Not for this
Faint° I, nor mourn nor murmur; other gifts
Have followed; for such loss, I would believe,
Abundant recompense. For I have learned
To look on nature, not as in the hour
Of thoughtless youth; but hearing oftentimes   90
The still, sad music of humanity,
Nor harsh nor grating, though of ample power
To chasten and subdue. And I have felt
A presence that disturbs me with the joy
Of elevated thoughts; a sense sublime
Of something far more deeply interfused,
Whose dwelling is the light of setting suns,
And the round ocean and the living air,
And the blue sky, and in the mind of man;
A motion and a spirit, that impels   100

86. **Faint:** lose spirit or courage.

All thinking things, all objects of all thought,
And rolls through all things. Therefore am I still
A lover of the meadows and the woods,
And mountains; and of all that we behold
From this green earth; of all the mighty world
Of eye, and ear — both what they half-create,
And what perceive;° well pleased to recognize
In nature and the language of the sense,
The anchor of my purest thoughts, the nurse,
The guide, the guardian of my heart, and soul 110
Of all my moral being.
                              Nor perchance,
If I were not thus taught, should I the more
Suffer my genial° spirits to decay;
For thou art with me here upon the banks
Of this fair river, thou my dearest friend,°
My dear, dear friend; and in thy voice I catch
The language of my former heart, and read
My former pleasures in the shooting lights
Of thy wild eyes. Oh! yet a little while
May I behold in thee what I was once, 120
My dear, dear sister! and this prayer I make,
Knowing that Nature never did betray
The heart that loved her; 'tis her privilege,
Through all the years of this our life, to lead
From joy to joy; for she can so inform
The mind that is within us, so impress
With quietness and beauty, and so feed

With lofty thoughts, that neither evil tongues,
Rash judgments, nor the sneers of selfish men,
Nor greetings where no kindness is, nor all 130
The dreary intercourse of daily life,
Shall e'er prevail against us, or disturb
Our cheerful faith, that all which we behold
Is full of blessings. Therefore let the moon
Shine on thee in thy solitary walk;
And let the misty mountain winds be free
To blow against thee: and, in after years,
When these wild ecstasies shall be matured
Into a sober pleasure; when thy mind
Shall be a mansion for all lovely forms, 140
Thy memory be as a dwelling place
For all sweet sounds and harmonies; oh! then,
If solitude, or fear, or pain, or grief,
Should be thy portion, with what healing thoughts
Of tender joy wilt thou remember me,
And these my exhortations! Nor, perchance —
If I should be where I no more can hear
Thy voice, nor catch from thy wild eyes these
    gleams
Of past existence — wilt thou then forget
That on the banks of this delightful stream 150
We stood together; and that I, so long
A worshiper of Nature, hither came
Unwearied in that service; rather say
With warmer love — oh! with far deeper zeal
Of holier love. Nor wilt thou then forget,
That after many wanderings, many years
Of absence, these steep woods and lofty cliffs,
And this green pastoral landscape, were to me
More dear, both for themselves and for thy sake!

1798

106–07. both . . . perceive: "This line has a close resemblance to an admirable line of Young, the exact expression of which I cannot recollect" [W]. The reference is to Edward Young's *The Complaint, or Night Thoughts on Life, Death, and Immortality* (1742–45), VI. 423–25. **113. genial:** cheerful, enlivening. **115. friend:** Dorothy Wordsworth.

THE PRELUDE

An Autobiographical Poem

In March, 1798, Wordsworth determined to write a three-part philosophical poem that would include an account of his own life. He intended to name the poem *The Recluse,* and he expected to finish it within a year and a half. Some time in the spring of 1798 he wrote out or improvised 107 lines of blank verse in which he announced his plans for the long poem in general and for the autobiographical portion in particular.

At Goslar, Germany, in the winter of 1798–99, Wordsworth began the autobiographical part of the long poem, and by the summer of 1799 he had written — except for the introductions — most of what are now Books I and II of *The Prelude.* Then, on October 12, 1799, he announced a change of plan. He had de-

cided to make the account of his life a separate poem which he would address to Samuel Taylor Coleridge. But he added almost nothing to it for four more years.

In the winter of 1803–04, stimulated by increasing family responsibilities, Coleridge's failing health, and a new and urgent sense of duty (he wrote the "Ode to Duty" at this time), Wordsworth resolved to get on with the autobiography. He wrote down for the first time the 269 lines that introduce *The Prelude,* and by the end of March, 1804, he had completed the first five books. Now he decided to extend the poem to include the history of his development down to 1797–98, the first year of his intimacy with Coleridge. Following this plan, Wordsworth completed the original version of

The Prelude, substantially as we have it today, in May, 1805.

In 1814 Wordsworth published *The Excursion,* Part II of *The Recluse.* In his 1814 Preface he referred to *The Prelude* as a "preparatory poem" to the larger work. Its relationship to *The Recluse,* he declared, was that of the "ante-chapel . . . to the body of a Gothic church." Unfortunately the main body of the church was left unfinished. Part III and all but Book I of Part I of *The Recluse* ("Home at Grasmere") Wordsworth never wrote. Between 1805 and 1839, however, he repeatedly revised *The Prelude.* Finally, on July 20, 1850, three months after his death, the poem was published. Only then did this, his most famous long poem, receive the title by which we know it. Wordsworth had always referred to it as "the poem to Coleridge" or "the poem on my own earlier life," but Mrs. Wordsworth, with an instinct for brevity in titles which her husband seldom shared, called it simply *The Prelude.* The following selections are from the 1850 text.

BOOK I

INTRODUCTION. CHILDHOOD AND SCHOOLTIME

Oh there is blessing in this gentle breeze,
A visitant that while it fans my cheek
Doth seem half-conscious of the joy it brings
From the green fields, and from yon azure sky.
Whate'er its mission, the soft breeze can come
To none more grateful than to me; escaped
From the vast city,° where I long had pined
A discontented sojourner, now free,
Free as a bird to settle where I will.
What dwelling shall receive me? in what vale   10
Shall be my harbor? underneath what grove
Shall I take up my home? and what clear stream
Shall with its murmur lull me into rest?
The earth is all before me. With a heart
Joyous, nor scared at its own liberty,
I look about; and should the chosen guide
Be nothing better than a wandering cloud,
I cannot miss my way. I breathe again!
Trances of thought and mountings of the mind
Come fast upon me; it is shaken off,   20
That burthen of my own unnatural self,
The heavy weight of many a weary day
Not mine, and such as were not made for me.
Long months of peace (if such bold word accord
With any promises of human life),
Long months of ease and undisturbed delight
Are mine in prospect; whither shall I turn.
By road or pathway, or through trackless field,
Up hill or down, or shall some floating thing
Upon the river point me out my course?   30

Dear Liberty! Yet what would it avail
But for a gift that consecrates the joy?
For I, methought, while the sweet breath of heaven
Was blowing on my body, felt within
A correspondent breeze, that gently moved
With quickening virtue, but is now become
A tempest, a redundant energy,
Vexing its own creation. Thanks to both,
And their congenial powers, that, while they join
In breaking up a long-continued frost,   40
Bring with them vernal promises, the hope
Of active days urged on by flying hours —
Days of sweet leisure, taxed with patient thought
Abstruse, nor wanting punctual service high,
Matins and vespers of harmonious verse!

Thus far, O friend!° did I, not used to make
A present joy the matter of a song,
Pour forth that day my soul in measured strains
That would not be forgotten, and are here
Recorded; to the open fields I told   50
A prophecy; poetic numbers came
Spontaneously to clothe in priestly robe
A renovated spirit singled out,
Such hope was mine, for holy services.
My own voice cheered me, and, far more, the mind's
Internal echo of the imperfect sound;
To both I listened, drawing from them both
A cheerful confidence in things to come.

Content and not unwilling now to give
A respite to this passion, I paced on   60
With brisk and eager steps; and came, at length,
To a green shady place, where down I sat
Beneath a tree, slackening my thoughts by choice
And settling into gentler happiness.
'Twas autumn, and a clear and placid day,
With warmth, as much as needed, from a sun
Two hours declined towards the west; a day
With silver clouds, and sunshine on the grass,
And in the sheltered and the sheltering grove
A perfect stillness. Many were the thoughts   70
Encouraged and dismissed, till choice was made
Of a known vale, whither my feet should turn,
Nor rest till they had reached the very door
Of the one cottage which methought I saw.
No picture of mere memory ever looked
So fair; and while upon the fancied scene
I gazed with growing love, a higher power
Than Fancy gave assurance of some work
Of glory there forthwith to be begun,
Perhaps too there performed. Thus long I
    mused,   80
Nor e'er lost sight of what I mused upon,

THE PRELUDE. **Book I:** 7. city: London, where Wordsworth lived from January to September, 1795.

46. friend: Throughout the poem the friend referred to, unless otherwise noted, is Samuel Taylor Coleridge.

Save when, amid the stately grove of oaks,
Now here, now there, an acorn, from its cup
Dislodged, through sere leaves rustled, or at once
To the bare earth dropped with a startling sound.
From that soft couch I rose not, till the sun
Had almost touched the horizon; casting then
A backward glance upon the curling cloud
Of city smoke, by distance ruralized;
Keen as a truant or a fugitive,   90
But as a pilgrim resolute, I took,
Even with the chance equipment of that hour,
The road that pointed toward the chosen vale.°
It was a splendid evening, and my soul
Once more made trial of her strength, nor lacked
Aeolian visitations;° but the harp
Was soon defrauded, and the banded host
Of harmony dispersed in straggling sounds,
And lastly utter silence! " Be it so;
Why think of anything but present good? "   100
So, like a homebound laborer, I pursued
My way beneath the mellowing sun, that shed
Mild influence; nor left in me one wish
Again to bend the Sabbath of that time
To a servile yoke. What need of many words?
A pleasant loitering journey, through three days
Continued, brought me to my hermitage.
I spare to tell of what ensued, the life
In common things — the endless store of things,
Rare, or at least so seeming, every day   110
Found all about me in one neighborhood —
The self-congratulation, and, from morn
To night, unbroken cheerfulness serene.
But speedily an earnest longing rose
To brace myself to some determined aim,
Reading or thinking; either to lay up
New stores, or rescue from decay the old
By timely interference; and therewith
Came hopes still higher, that with outward life
I might endue some airy fantasies   120
That had been floating loose about for years,
And to such beings temperately deal forth
The many feelings that oppressed my heart.
That hope hath been discouraged; welcome light
Dawns from the east, but dawns to disappear
And mock me with a sky that ripens not
Into a steady morning; if my mind,
Remembering the bold promise of the past,
Would gladly grapple with some noble theme,
Vain is her wish; where'er she turns she finds
Impediments from day to day renewed.   131

And now it would content me to yield up
Those lofty hopes awhile, for present gifts
Of humbler industry. But, oh, dear friend!
The poet, gentle creature as he is,
Hath, like the lover, his unruly times;
His fits when he is neither sick nor well,
Though no distress be near him but his own
Unmanageable thoughts; his mind, best pleased
While she as duteous as the mother dove,   140
Sits brooding, lives not always to that end,
But like the innocent bird, hath goadings on
That drive her as in trouble through the groves;
With me is now such passion, to be blamed
No otherwise than as it lasts too long.

When, as becomes a man who would prepare
For such an arduous work, I through myself
Make rigorous inquisition, the report
Is often cheering; for I neither seem
To lack that first great gift, the vital soul,   150
Nor general truths, which are themselves a sort
Of elements and agents, underpowers,
Subordinate helpers of the living mind;
Nor am I naked of external things,
Forms, images, nor numerous other aids
Of less regard, though won perhaps with toil
And needful to build up a poet's praise.
Time, place, and manners do I seek, and these
Are found in plenteous store, but nowhere such
As may be singled out with steady choice;   160
No little band of yet remembered names
Whom I, in perfect confidence, might hope
To summon back from lonesome banishment,
And make them dwellers in the hearts of men
Now living, or to live in future years.
Sometimes the ambitious power of choice, mistaking
Proud spring tide swellings for a regular sea,
Will settle on some British theme, some old
Romantic tale by Milton left unsung;
More often turning to some gentle place   170
Within the groves of chivalry, I pipe
To shepherd swains, or seated harp in hand,
Amid reposing knights by a riverside
Or fountain, listen to the grave reports
Of dire enchantments faced and overcome
By the strong mind, and tales of warlike feats,
Where spear encountered spear, and sword with
    sword
Fought, as if conscious of the blazonry
That the shield bore, so glorious was the strife;
Whence inspiration for a song that winds   180
Through ever-changing scenes of votive quest
Wrongs to redress, harmonious tribute paid
To patient courage and unblemished truth,
To firm devotion, zeal unquenchable,
And Christian meekness hallowing faithful loves.
Sometimes, more sternly moved, I would relate

89–93. city . . . vale: Wordsworth is describing the journey from Bristol, where he first met Coleridge, to Racedown, where he settled with his sister Dorothy in September, 1795. **96. Aeolian visitations:** impulses or thoughts that come and go with the wind, like the sounds made upon an Aeolian harp.

How vanquished Mithridates northward passed,°
And, hidden in the cloud of years, became
Odin, the father of a race by whom
Perished the Roman Empire; how the friends   190
And followers of Sertorius, out of Spain
Flying, found shelter in the Fortunate Isles,
And left their usages, their arts and laws,
To disappear by a slow gradual death,
To dwindle and to perish one by one,
Starved in those narrow bounds; but not the soul
Of Liberty, which fifteen hundred years
Survived, and, when the European came
With skill and power that might not be withstood,
Did, like a pestilence, maintain its hold   200
And wasted down by glorious death that race
Of natural heroes; or I would record
How, in tyrannic times, some high-souled man,
Unnamed among the chronicles of kings,
Suffered in silence for truth's sake; or tell,
How that one Frenchman,° through continued
     force
Of meditation on the inhuman deeds
Of those who conquered first the Indian Isles,
Went single in his ministry across
The ocean; not to comfort the oppressed,   210
But, like a thirsty wind, to roam about
Withering the oppressor: how Gustavus sought
Help at his need in Dalecarlia's mines:°
How Wallace° fought for Scotland; left the name
Of Wallace to be found, like a wild flower,
All over his dear country; left the deeds
Of Wallace, like a family of ghosts,
To people the steep rocks and river banks,
Her natural sanctuaries, with a local soul
Of independence and stern liberty.   220
Sometimes it suits me better to invent
A tale from my own heart, more near akin
To my own passions and habitual thoughts;

Some variegated story, in the main
Lofty, but the unsubstantial structure melts
Before the very sun that brightens it,
Mist into air dissolving! Then a wish,
My last and favorite aspiration, mounts
With yearning toward some philosophic song
Of truth that cherishes our daily life;   230
With meditations passionate from deep
Recesses in man's heart, immortal verse
Thoughtfully fitted to the Orphean lyre;
But from this awful burthen I full soon
Take refuge and beguile myself with trust
That mellower years will bring a riper mind
And clearer insight. Thus my days are passed
In contradiction; with no skill to part
Vague longing, haply bred by want of power,
From paramount impulse not to be withstood,   240
A timorous capacity, from prudence,
From circumspection, infinite delay.
Humility and modest awe, themselves
Betray me, serving often for a cloak
To a more subtle selfishness; that now
Locks every function up in blank reserve,
Now dupes me, trusting to an anxious eye
That with intrusive restlessness beats off
Simplicity and self-presented truth.
Ah! better far than this, to stray about   250
Voluptuously through fields and rural walks,
And ask no record of the hours, resigned
To vacant musing, unreproved neglect
Of all things, and deliberate holiday.
Far better never to have heard the name
Of zeal and just ambition, than to live
Baffled and plagued by a mind that every hour
Turns recreant to her task; takes heart again,
Then feels immediately some hollow thought
Hang like an interdict upon her hopes.   260
This is my lot; for either still I find
Some imperfection in the chosen theme,
Or see of absolute accomplishment
Much wanting, so much wanting, in myself,
That I recoil and droop, and seek repose
In listlessness from vain perplexity,
Unprofitably traveling toward the grave,
Like a false steward who hath much received
And renders nothing back.

           Was it for this
That one, the fairest of all rivers, loved   270
To blend his murmurs with my nurse's song,
And, from his alder shades and rocky falls,
And from his fords and shallows, sent a voice
That flowed along my dreams? For this, didst thou,
O Derwent!° winding among grassy holms
Where I was looking on, a babe in arms,

187–92. Mithridates, Odin, Sertorius, Fortunate Isles: Mithridates was king of Pontus, a country in northeast Asia Minor. After his defeat by Pompey in B.C. 66, he planned to march around the Black Sea, through what are now the Balkans, and attack Rome from the north. Wordsworth, working imaginatively out of Gibbon's *Decline and Fall of the Roman Empire*, Chapter X, here merges the history of Mithridates with the legend of Odin, a barbarian chieftain who supposedly led his tribe from the shores of Lake Maeotis (now the Sea of Azov) into Sweden, where they developed sufficient strength eventually to defeat the Roman oppressors. Sertorius was a Roman general who, aided by ships and men sent him by Mithridates, opposed the armies of the tyrannical Senatorial party for eight years until his assassination in B.C. 72. Wordsworth supposes that his followers sought refuge in the Fortunate Isles, probably the Canary Islands.
206. Frenchman: Dominique de Gourges, who went to Florida in 1567 and avenged a massacre of French Protestants by Spaniards.
212–13. Gustavus . . . mines: Gustavus I (1495–1560), liberator of Sweden from Denmark, evaded capture by disguising himself as a miner in Dalecarlia, a district in west central Sweden.
214. Wallace: Scottish patriot hero (1272–1305) in the wars against Edward I of England.

275. Derwent: a river that flows through Cockermouth close behind the house in which Wordsworth was born.

Make ceaseless music that composed my thoughts
To more than infant softness, giving me
Amid the fretful dwellings of mankind
A foretaste, a dim earnest, of the calm   280
That Nature breathes among the hills and groves.

   When he had left the mountains and received
On his smooth breast the shadow of those towers
That yet survive, a shattered monument
Of feudal sway,° the bright blue river passed
Along the margin of our terrace walk;
A tempting playmate whom we dearly loved.
Oh, many a time have I, a five-years' child,
In a small millrace severed from his stream,
Made one long bathing of a summer's day;   290
Basked in the sun, and plunged and basked again
Alternate, all a summer's day, or scoured
The sandy fields, leaping through flowery groves
Of yellow ragwort; or, when rock and hill,
The woods, and distant Skiddaw's° lofty height,
Were bronzed with deepest radiance, stood alone
Beneath the sky, as if I had been born
On Indian plains, and from my mother's hut
Had run abroad in wantonness, to sport
A naked savage, in the thundershower.   300

   Fair seedtime had my soul, and I grew up
Fostered alike by beauty and by fear:
Much favored in my birthplace, and no less
In that beloved vale° to which erelong
We were transplanted; there were we let loose
For sports of wider range. Ere I had told
Ten birthdays, when among the mountain slopes
Frost, and the breath of frosty wind, had snapped
The last autumnal crocus, 'twas my joy
With store of springes° o'er my shoulder hung   310
To range the open heights where woodcocks run
Along the smooth green turf. Through half the
   night,
Scudding away from snare to snare, I plied
That anxious visitation; moon and stars
Were shining o'er my head. I was alone,
And seemed to be a trouble to the peace
That dwelt among them. Sometimes it befell
In these night wanderings, that a strong desire
O'erpowered my better reason, and the bird
Which was the captive of another's toil   320
Became my prey; and when the deed was done
I heard among the solitary hills
Low breathings coming after me, and sounds

Of undistinguishable motion, steps
Almost as silent as the turf they trod.

   Nor less, when spring had warmed the cultured
   vale,
Moved we as plunderers where the mother bird
Had in high places built her lodge; though mean
Our object and inglorious, yet the end
Was not ignoble. Oh! when I have hung   330
Above the raven's nest, by knots of grass
And half-inch fissures in the slippery rock
But ill sustained, and almost (so it seemed)
Suspended by the blast that blew amain,
Shouldering the naked crag, oh, at that time
While on the perilous ridge I hung alone,
With what strange utterance did the loud dry
   wind
Blow through my ear! the sky seemed not a sky
Of earth — and with what motion moved the
   clouds!

   Dust as we are, the immortal spirit grows   340
Like harmony in music; there is a dark
Inscrutable workmanship that reconciles
Discordant elements, makes them cling together
In one society. How strange, that all
The terrors, pains, and early miseries,
Regrets, vexations, lassitudes interfused
Within my mind, should e'er have borne a part,
And that a needful part, in making up
The calm existence that is mine when I
Am worthy of myself! Praise to the end!   350
Thanks to the means which Nature deigned to
   employ;
Whether her fearless visitings, or those
That came with soft alarm, like hurtless light
Opening the peaceful clouds; or she would use
Severer interventions, ministry
More palpable, as best might suit her aim.

   One summer evening (led by her) I found
A little boat tied to a willow tree
Within a rocky cove, its usual home.
Straight I unloosed her chain, and stepping in   360
Pushed from the shore. It was an act of stealth
And troubled pleasure, nor without the voice
Of mountain echoes did my boat move on;
Leaving behind her still, on either side,
Small circles glittering idly in the moon,
Until they melted all into one track
Of sparkling light. But now, like one who rows,
Proud of his skill, to reach a chosen point
With an unswerving line, I fixed my view
Upon the summit of a craggy ridge,   370
The horizon's utmost boundary; far above
Was nothing but the stars and the gray sky.

283–85. towers . . . sway: Cockermouth Castle, a medieval ruin, easily seen from the Wordsworth terrace. **295. Skiddaw:** one of the tallest peaks (3054 feet) in the Lake District; about nine miles from Cockermouth. **304. vale:** Esthwaite, where Wordsworth entered school at Hawkshead in 1779. **310. springes:** snares for birds or small animals.

She was an elfin pinnace;° lustily
I dipped my oars into the silent lake,
And, as I rose upon the stroke, my boat
Went heaving through the water like a swan;
When, from behind that craggy steep till then
The horizon's bound, a huge peak, black and huge,
As if with voluntary power instinct,
Upreared its head. I struck and struck again, 380
And growing still in stature the grim shape
Towered up between me and the stars, and still,
For so it seemed, with purpose of its own
And measured motion like a living thing,
Strode after me. With trembling oars I turned,
And through the silent water stole my way
Back to the covert of the willow tree;
There in her mooring place I left my bark,
And through the meadow homeward went, in grave
And serious mood; but after I had seen   390
That spectacle, for many days, my brain
Worked with a dim and undetermined sense
Of unknown modes of being; o'er my thoughts
There hung a darkness, call it solitude
Or blank desertion. No familiar shapes
Remained, no pleasant images of trees,
Of sea or sky, no colors of green fields;
But huge and mighty forms, that do not live
Like living men,° moved slowly through the mind
By day, and were a trouble to my dreams.   400

Wisdom and Spirit of the universe!
Thou Soul that art the eternity of thought
That givest to forms and images a breath
And everlasting motion, not in vain
By day or starlight thus from my first dawn
Of childhood didst thou intertwine for me
The passions that build up our human soul;
Not with the mean and vulgar works of man,
But with high objects, with enduring things —
With life and nature — purifying thus   410
The elements of feeling and of thought,
And sanctifying, by such discipline,
Both pain and fear, until we recognize
A grandeur in the beatings of the heart.
Nor was this fellowship vouchsafed to me
With stinted kindness. In November days,
When vapors rolling down the valley made
A lonely scene more lonesome, among woods,
At noon and 'mid the calm of summer nights,
When, by the margin of the trembling lake,   420
Beneath the gloomy hills homeward I went
In solitude, such intercourse was mine;
Mine was it in the fields both day and night,
And by the waters, all the summer long.

And in the frosty season, when the sun
Was set, and visible for many a mile
The cottage windows blazed through twilight
     gloom,
I heeded not their summons; happy time
It was indeed for all of us — for me
It was a time of rapture! Clear and loud   430
The village clock tolled six — I wheeled about,
Proud and exulting like an untired horse
That cares not for his home. All shod with steel,
We hissed along the polished ice in games
Confederate, imitative of the chase
And woodland pleasures — the resounding horn,
The pack loud chiming, and the hunted hare.
So through the darkness and the cold we flew,
And not a voice was idle; with the din
Smitten, the precipices rang aloud;   440
The leafless trees and every icy crag
Tinkled like iron; while far distant hills
Into the tumult sent an alien sound
Of melancholy not unnoticed, while the stars
Eastward were sparkling clear, and in the west
The orange sky of evening died away.
Not seldom from the uproar I retired
Into a silent bay, or sportively
Glanced sideway, leaving the tumultuous throng,
To cut across the reflex of a star   450
That fled, and, flying still before me, gleamed
Upon the glassy plain; and oftentimes,
When we had given our bodies to the wind,
And all the shadowy banks on either side
Came sweeping through the darkness, spinning still
The rapid line of motion, then at once
Have I, reclining back upon my heels,
Stopped short; yet still the solitary cliffs
Wheeled by me — even as if the earth had rolled
With visible motion her diurnal round!   460
Behind me did they stretch in solemn train,
Feebler and feebler, and I stood and watched
Till all was tranquil as a dreamless sleep.

Ye Presences of Nature in the sky
And on the earth! Ye Visions of the hills!
And Souls of lonely places! can I think
A vulgar hope was yours when ye employed
Such ministry, when ye, through many a year
Haunting me thus among my boyish sports,
On caves and trees, upon the woods and hills,   470
Impressed, upon all forms, the characters
Of danger or desire; and thus did make
The surface of the universal earth,
With triumph and delight, with hope and fear,
Work like a sea?
                    Not uselessly employed,
Might I pursue this theme through every change
Of exercise and play, to which the year
Did summon us in his delightful round.

373. pinnace: a small boat, usually equipped with a sail.   398–
99. forms . . . men: The punctuation here is debatable; perhaps
the only comma should follow l. 398.

We were a noisy crew; the sun in heaven
Beheld not vales more beautiful than ours;   480
Nor saw a band in happiness and joy
Richer, or worthier of the ground they trod.
I could record with no reluctant voice
The woods of autumn, and their hazel bowers
With milk-white clusters hung; the rod and line,
True symbol of hope's foolishness, whose strong
And unreproved enchantment led us on
By rocks and pools shut out from every star,
All the green summer, to forlorn cascades
Among the windings hid of mountain brooks.   490
    Unfading recollections! at this hour
The heart is almost mine with which I felt,
From some hilltop on sunny afternoons,
The paper kite high among fleecy clouds
Pull at her rein like an impetuous courser;
Or, from the meadows sent on gusty days,
Beheld her breast the wind, then suddenly
Dashed headlong, and rejected by the storm.

Ye lowly cottages wherein we dwelt,°
A ministration of your own was yours;   500
Can I forget you, being as you were
So beautiful among the pleasant fields
In which ye stood? or can I here forget
The plain and seemly countenance with which
Ye dealt out your plain comforts? Yet had ye
Delights and exultations of your own.
Eager and never weary we pursued
Our home amusements by the warm peat fire
At evening, when with pencil, and smooth slate
In square divisions parceled out and all   510
With crosses and with ciphers scribbled o'er,
We schemed and puzzled, head opposed to head
In strife too humble to be named in verse:
Or round the naked table, snow-white deal,°
Cherry or maple, sat in close array,
And to the combat, loo or whist, led on°
A thick-ribbed army; not, as in the world,
Neglected and ungratefully thrown by
Even for the very service they had wrought,
But husbanded through many a long
    campaign.   520
Uncouth assemblage was it, where no few
Had changed their functions: some, plebeian cards
Which Fate, beyond the promise of their birth,
Had dignified, and called to represent
The persons of departed potentates.
Oh, with what echoes on the board they fell!
Ironic diamonds — clubs, hearts, diamonds, spades,

A congregation piteously akin!
Cheap matter offered they to boyish wit,
Those sooty knaves, precipitated down   530
With scoffs and taunts, like Vulcan out of heaven:°
The paramount ace, a moon in her eclipse,
Queens gleaming through their splendor's last
    decay,
And monarchs surly at the wrongs sustained
By royal visages. Meanwhile abroad
Incessant rain was falling, or the frost
Raged bitterly, with keen and silent tooth;
And, interrupting oft that eager game,
From under Esthwaite's splitting fields of ice
The pent-up air, struggling to free itself,   540
Gave out to meadow grounds and hills a loud
Protracted yelling, like the noise of wolves
Howling in troops along the Bothnic main.°

    Nor, sedulous as I have been to trace
How Nature by extrinsic passion first
Peopled the mind with forms sublime or fair,
And made me love them, may I here omit
How other pleasures have been mine, and joys
Of subtler origin; how I have felt,
Not seldom even in that tempestuous time,   550
Those hallowed and pure motions of the sense
Which seem, in their simplicity, to own
An intellectual charm; that calm delight
Which, if I err not, surely must belong
To those first-born affinities that fit
Our new existence to existing things,
And, in our dawn of being, constitute
The bond of union between life and joy.

    Yes, I remember when the changeful earth,
And twice five summers on my mind had
    stamped   560
The faces of the moving year, even then
I held unconscious intercourse with beauty
Old as creation, drinking in a pure
Organic pleasure from the silver wreaths
Of curling mist, or from the level plain
Of waters colored by impending clouds.

    The sands of Westmorland, the creeks and
    bays
Of Cumbria's° rocky limits, they can tell
How, when the Sea threw off his evening shade,
And to the shepherd's hut on distant hills   570
Sent welcome notice of the rising moon,
How I have stood, to fancies such as these

---

499. **cottages . . . dwelt:** Hawkshead students lived in the houses of the villagers. For nine years Wordsworth lived in the cottage of Anne Tyson, to whom he refers several times in *The Prelude.* 514. **deal:** pine or fir planks usually six feet long and at least seven inches wide.   516-35. **combat . . . visages:** an imitation of Pope, *The Rape of the Lock,* III.25-98, pp. 412-13, above.

531. **Vulcan . . . heaven:** Vulcan, otherwise known as Hephaestus or Mulciber, was the god of fire and blacksmith of Olympus. He was crippled when Zeus, his father, threw him from Olympus for interfering in a domestic quarrel. See *Paradise Lost,* I.738-46, p. 232, above.   543. **Bothnic main:** Gulf of Bothnia, between Finland and Sweden.   568. **Cumbria:** Cumberland.

A stranger, linking with the spectacle
No conscious memory of a kindred sight,
And bringing with me no peculiar sense
Of quietness or peace; yet have I stood,
Even while mine eye hath moved o'er many a
      league
Of shining water, gathering as it seemed,
Through every hairbreadth in that field of light,
New pleasure like a bee among the flowers.   580

      Thus oft amid those fits of vulgar joy
Which, through all seasons, on a child's pursuits
Are prompt attendants, 'mid that giddy bliss
Which, like a tempest, works along the blood
And is forgotten; even then I felt
Gleams like the flashing of a shield; the earth
And common face of Nature spake to me
Rememberable things; sometimes, 'tis true,
By chance collisions and quaint accidents
(Like those ill-sorted unions, work supposed
Of evil-minded fairies), yet not vain   591
Nor profitless, if haply they impressed
Collateral objects and appearances,
Albeit lifeless then, and doomed to sleep
Until maturer seasons called them forth
To impregnate and to elevate the mind.
   And if the vulgar joy by its own weight
Wearied itself out of the memory,
The scenes which were a witness of that joy
Remained in their substantial lineaments   600
Depicted on the brain, and to the eye
Were visible, a daily sight; and thus
By the impressive discipline of fear,
By pleasure and repeated happiness,
So frequently repeated, and by force
Of obscure feelings representative
Of things forgotten, these same scenes so bright,
So beautiful, so majestic in themselves,
Though yet the day was distant, did become
Habitually dear, and all their forms   610
And changeful colors by invisible links
Were fastened to the affections.

                    I began
My story early — not misled, I trust,
By an infirmity of love for days
Disowned by memory — ere the birth of spring
Planting my snowdrops among winter snows;
Nor will it seem to thee, O friend! so prompt
In sympathy, that I have lengthened out
With fond and feeble tongue a tedious tale.
Meanwhile, my hope has been, that I might
      fetch   620
Invigorating thoughts from former years;
Might fix the wavering balance of my mind,
And haply meet reproaches too, whose power

May spur me on, in manhood now mature
To honorable toil. Yet should these hopes
Prove vain, and thus should neither I be taught
To understand myself, nor thou to know
With better knowledge how the heart was framed
Of him thou lovest; need I dread from thee
Harsh judgments, if the song be loath to quit   630
Those recollected hours that have the charm
Of visionary things, those lovely forms
And sweet sensations that throw back our life,
And almost make remotest infancy
A visible scene, on which the sun is shining?

      One end at least hath been attained; my mind
Hath been revived, and if this genial mood
Desert me not, forthwith shall be brought down
Through later years the story of my life.
The road lies plain before me; 'tis a theme   640
Single and of determined bounds; and hence
I choose it rather at this time, than work
Of ampler or more varied argument,
Where I might be discomfited and lost;
And certain hopes are with me, that to thee
This labor will be welcome, honored friend!

from BOOK II

SCHOOLTIME (continued)

                    Blest the infant babe
(For with my best conjecture I would trace
Our being's earthly progress), blest the babe,
Nursed in his mother's arms, who sinks to sleep
Rocked on his mother's breast; who with his soul
Drinks in the feelings of his mother's eye!
For him, in one dear presence, there exists
A virtue which irradiates and exalts
Objects through widest intercourse of sense;   240
No outcast he, bewildered and depressed;
Along his infant veins are interfused
The gravitation and the filial bond
Of nature that connect him with the world.
Is there a flower, to which he points with hand
Too weak to gather it, already love
Drawn from love's purest earthly fount for him
Hath beautified that flower; already shades
Of pity cast from inward tenderness
Do fall around him upon aught that bears   250
Unsightly marks of violence or harm.
Emphatically such a being lives,
Frail creature as he is, helpless as frail,
An inmate of this active universe;
For, feeling has to him imparted power
That through the growing faculties of sense
Doth like an agent of the one great Mind
Create, creator and receiver both,

Working but in alliance with the works
Which it beholds. Such, verily, is the first   260
Poetic spirit of our human life,
By uniform control of after years,
In most, abated or suppressed; in some,
Through every change of growth and of decay,
Pre-eminent till death.

from BOOK XI

FRANCE (concluded)

O pleasant exercise of hope and joy!°
For mighty were the auxiliars which then stood
Upon our side, us who were strong in love!
Bliss was it in that dawn to be alive,
But to be young was very heaven! O times,
In which the meager, stale, forbidding ways   110
Of custom, law, and statute, took at once
The attraction of a country in romance!
When Reason seemed the most to assert her rights,
When most intent on making of herself
A prime enchantress — to assist the work,
Which then was going forward in her name!
Not favored spots alone, but the whole earth,
The beauty wore of promise — that which sets
(As at some moments might not be unfelt
Among the bowers of paradise itself)   120
The budding rose above the rose full-blown.
What temper at the prospect did not wake
To happiness unthought of? The inert
Were roused, and lively natures rapt away!
They who had fed their childhood upon dreams,
The playfellows of fancy, who had made
All powers of swiftness, subtlety, and strength
Their ministers, who in lordly wise had stirred
Among the grandest objects of the sense,
And dealt with whatsoever they found there   130
As if they had within some lurking right
To wield it; they, too, who of gentle mood
Had watched all gentle motions, and to these
Had fitted their own thoughts, schemers more mild,
And in the region of their peaceful selves —
Now was it that *both* found, the meek and lofty
Did both find, helpers to their hearts' desire,
And stuff at hand, plastic as they could wish,
Were called upon to exercise their skill,
Not in Utopia — subterranean fields —   140
Or some secreted island, Heaven knows where!
But in the very world, which is the world
Of all of us — the place where, in the end,
We find our happiness, or not at all! . . .

But now, become oppressors in their turn,
Frenchmen had changed a war of self-defense
For one of conquest, losing sight of all
Which they had struggled for; up mounted now,
Openly in the eye of earth and heaven,   210
The scale of liberty. I read her doom.
With anger vexed, with disappointment sore,
But not dismayed, nor taking to the shame
Of a false prophet. While resentment rose,
Striving to hide, what nought could heal, the
        wounds
Of mortified presumption, I adhered
More firmly to old tenets, and, to prove
Their temper, strained them more; and thus, in
        heat
Of contest, did opinions every day
Grow into consequence, till round my mind   220
They clung, as if they were its life, nay more,
The very being of the immortal soul. . . .

                So I fared,
Dragging all precepts, judgments, maxims, creeds,
Like culprits to the bar; calling the mind,
Suspiciously, to establish in plain day
Her titles and her honors; now believing,
Now disbelieving; endlessly perplexed
With impulse, motive, right and wrong, the ground
Of obligation, what the rule and whence   300
The sanction; till, demanding formal *proof,*
And seeking it in everything, I lost
All feeling of conviction, and, in fine,
Sick, wearied out with contrarieties,
Yielded up moral questions in despair. . . .

                Then it was —
Thanks to the bounteous Giver of all good! —
That the belovèd sister° in whose sight
Those days were passed, now speaking in a voice
Of sudden admonition — like a brook
That did but *cross* a lonely road, and now
Is seen, heard, felt, and caught at every turn,
Companion never lost through many a league —
Maintained for me a saving intercourse   341
With my true self; for, though bedimmed and
        changed
Much, as it seemed, I was no further changed
Than as a clouded, not a waning moon;
She whispered still that brightness would return;
She, in the midst of all, preserved me still
A poet, made me seek beneath that name,
And that alone, my office upon earth;
And, lastly, as hereafter will be shown,

Book XI: 105-44. O . . . all!: These lines were first published as
an independent poem in Coleridge's periodical *The Friend,* for
October 26, 1809.

335. sister: Dorothy Wordsworth, who joined her brother for
several weeks in the spring of 1794 at Windy Brow, half a mile
from Keswick, and lived with him permanently after the settlement at Racedown in September, 1795.

If willing audience fail not, Nature's self,   350
By all varieties of human love
Assisted, led me back through opening day
To those sweet counsels between head and heart
Whence grew that genuine knowledge, fraught
    with peace,
Which, through the later sinkings of this cause,
Hath still upheld me, and upholds me now. . . .

from BOOK XIII

IMAGINATION AND TASTE,
HOW IMPAIRED. AND RESTORED
(concluded)

From Nature doth emotion come, and moods
Of calmness equally are Nature's gift;
This is her glory; these two attributes
Are sister horns that constitute her strength.
Hence Genius, born to thrive by interchange
Of peace and excitation, finds in her
His best and purest friend; from her receives
That energy by which he seeks the truth,
From her that happy stillness of the mind
Which fits him to receive it when unsought.   10

Such benefit the humblest intellects
Partake of, each in their degree; 'tis mine
To speak, what I myself have known and felt;
Smooth task! for words find easy way, inspired
By gratitude, and confidence in truth.
Long time in search of knowledge did I range
The field of human life, in heart and mind
Benighted; but, the dawn beginning now
To reappear, 'twas proved that not in vain
I had been taught to reverence a power   20
That is the visible quality and shape
And image of right reason; that matures
Her processes by steadfast laws; gives birth
To no impatient or fallacious hopes,
No heat of passion or excessive zeal,
No vain conceits; provokes to no quick turns
Of self-applauding intellect; but trains
To meekness, and exalts by humble faith;
Holds up before the mind intoxicate
With present objects, and the busy dance   30
Of things that pass away, a temperate show
Of objects that endure; and by this course
Disposes her, when overfondly set
On throwing off incumbrances, to seek
In man, and in the frame of social life,
Whate'er there is desirable and good
Of kindred permanence, unchanged in form
And function, or, through strict vicissitude
Of life and death, revolving. Above all
Were re-established now those watchful thoughts

Which, seeing little worthy or sublime   41
In what the historian's pen so much delights
To blazon — power and energy detached
From moral purpose — early tutored me
To look with feelings of fraternal love
Upon the unassuming things that hold
A silent station in this beauteous world. . . .

Here, calling up to mind what then I saw,
A youthful traveler, and see daily now
In the familiar circuit of my home,
Here might I pause, and bend in reverence
To Nature, and the power of human minds,
To men as they are men within themselves.
How oft high service is performed within,
When all the external man is rude in show,
Not like a temple rich with pomp and gold,
But a mere mountain chapel, that protects   230
Its simple worshipers from sun and shower.
Of these, said I, shall be my song; of these,
If future years mature me for the task,
Will I record the praises, making verse
Deal boldly with substantial things; in truth
And sanctity of passion, speak of these,
That justice may be done, obeisance paid
Where it is due; thus haply shall I teach,
Inspire; through unadulterated ears
Pour rapture, tenderness, and hope, my theme   240
No other than the very heart of man,
As found among the best of those who live —
Not unexalted by religious faith,
Nor uninformed by books, good books, though
    few —
In Nature's presence; thence may I select
Sorrow, that is not sorrow, but delight;
And miserable love, that is not pain
To hear of, for the glory that redounds
Therefrom to human kind, and what we are. . . .

LUCY GRAY

or, Solitude

The following five poems, together with " I Traveled among Unknown Men," are known as the "Lucy" poems. Except for " I Traveled among Unknown Men," written in 1801, Wordsworth wrote these poems in Germany in the winter of 1798–99. The name Lucy appears in four of them, and all six resemble one another in sentiment and tone. The Lucy Gray who disappears from the bridge in the snowstorm, however, is obviously unrelated to the girls referred to in the other poems. We have no evidence that Wordsworth ever knew anyone named Lucy. Consequently there has been much speculation about Lucy's identity, just as there has been much speculation about Matthew Arnold's Marguerite. Was Lucy a real person? Was she Dorothy Wordsworth, or was she imaginary?

Probably we shall never know. Wordsworth first used the name in an unpublished fragment he wrote in the summer of 1798. Therein he seems to have been addressing his sister Dorothy. But Dorothy Wordsworth lived until 1855, and in all but one of the "Lucy" poems Lucy is dead. Perhaps Coleridge was close to the truth in April, 1799, when he wrote Thomas Poole: "Some months ago Wordsworth transmitted to me a most sublime epitaph ["A Slumber Did My Spirit Seal"]. Whether it had any reality I cannot say. Most probably, in some gloomier moment he had fancied the moment in which his sister might die."

Oft I had heard of Lucy Gray;
And, when I crossed the wild,
I chanced to see at break of day
The solitary child.

No mate, no comrade Lucy knew;
She dwelt on a wide moor,
— The sweetest thing that ever grew
Beside a human door!

You yet may spy the fawn at play,
The hare upon the green;   10
But the sweet face of Lucy Gray
Will nevermore be seen.

"Tonight will be a stormy night —
You to the town must go;
And take a lantern, child, to light
Your mother through the snow."

"That, Father! will I gladly do;
'Tis scarcely afternoon —
The minster clock° has just struck two,
And yonder is the moon!"   20

At this the father raised his hook,
And snapped a fagot band;°
He plied his work, and Lucy took
The lantern in her hand.

Not blither is the mountain roe;
With many a wanton stroke
Her feet disperse the powdery snow,
That rises up like smoke.

The storm came on before its time;
She wandered up and down;   30
And many a hill did Lucy climb,
But never reached the town.

The wretched parents all that night
Went shouting far and wide;
But there was neither sound nor sight
To serve them for a guide.

At daybreak on a hill they stood
That overlooked the moor;
And thence they saw the bridge of wood,
A furlong° from their door.   40

They wept — and, turning homeward, cried,
"In Heaven we all shall meet";
When in the snow the mother spied
The print of Lucy's feet.

Then downwards from the steep hill's edge
They tracked the footmarks small;
And through the broken hawthorn hedge,
And by the long stone wall;

And then an open field they crossed;
The marks were still the same;   50
They tracked them on, nor ever lost;
And to the bridge they came.

They followed from the snowy bank
Those footmarks, one by one,
Into the middle of the plank;
And further there were none!

— Yet some maintain that to this day
She is a living child;
That you may see sweet Lucy Gray
Upon the lonesome wild.   60

O'er rough and smooth she trips along,
And never looks behind;
And sings a solitary song
That whistles in the wind.

                                        1799

STRANGE FITS OF PASSION HAVE I KNOWN

Strange fits of passion have I known,
And I will dare to tell,
But in the lover's ear alone,
What once to me befell.

When she I loved looked every day
Fresh as a rose in June,
I to her cottage bent my way,
Beneath an evening moon.

Upon the moon I fixed my eye,
All over the wide lea;   10
With quickening pace my horse drew nigh
Those paths so dear to me.

LUCY GRAY. **19. minster clock:** church clock. **22. snapped . . . band:** broke the cord around a bundle of small branches to be used as fuel.

40. furlong: an eighth of a mile.

And now we reached the orchard plot;
And, as we climbed the hill,
The sinking moon to Lucy's cot
Came near, and nearer still.

In one of those sweet dreams I slept,
Kind Nature's gentlest boon!
And all the while my eyes I kept
On the descending moon.   20

My horse moved on; hoof after hoof
He raised, and never stopped;
When down behind the cottage roof
At once, the bright moon dropped.

What fond and wayward thoughts will slide
Into a lover's head!
" O mercy! " to myself I cried,
" If Lucy should be dead! "

                              1799

SHE DWELT AMONG THE UNTRODDEN WAYS

She dwelt among the untrodden ways
   Beside the springs of Dove,°
A maid whom there were none to praise
   And very few to love;

A violet by a mossy stone
   Half-hidden from the eye!
Fair as a star, when only one
   Is shining in the sky.

She lived unknown, and few could know
   When Lucy ceased to be;   10
But she is in her grave, and, oh,
   The difference to me!

                              1799

THREE YEARS SHE GREW IN SUN AND SHOWER

Three years she grew in sun and shower,
Then Nature said, "A lovelier flower
On earth was never sown;
This child I to myself will take;
She shall be mine, and I will make
A lady of my own.

SHE DWELT AMONG UNTRODDEN WAYS. **2. Dove:** a small stream
in central England, which takes its rise on the border of the
counties of Stafford and Derby.

" Myself will to my darling be
Both law and impulse; and with me
The girl, in rock and plain,
In earth and heaven, in glade and bower,   10
Shall feel an overseeing power
To kindle or restrain.

" She shall be sportive as the fawn
That wild with glee across the lawn,
Or up the mountain springs;
And hers shall be the breathing balm,
And hers the silence and the calm
Of mute insensate things.

" The floating clouds their state shall lend
To her; for her the willow bend;   20
Nor shall she fail to see
Even in the motions of the storm
Grace that shall mold the maiden's form
By silent sympathy.

" The stars of midnight shall be dear
To her; and she shall lean her ear
In many a secret place
Where rivulets dance their wayward round,
And beauty born of murmuring sound
Shall pass into her face.   30

" And vital feelings of delight
Shall rear her form to stately height,
Her virgin bosom swell;
Such thoughts to Lucy I will give
While she and I together live
Here in this happy dell."

Thus Nature spake — the work was done —
How soon my Lucy's race was run!
She died, and left to me
This heath, this calm, and quiet scene;   40
The memory of what has been,
And nevermore will be.

                              1799

A SLUMBER DID MY SPIRIT SEAL

A slumber did my spirit seal;
   I had no human fears;
She seemed a thing that could not feel
   The touch of earthly years

No motion has she now, no force;
   She neither hears nor sees;
Rolled round in earth's diurnal° course,
   With rocks, and stones, and trees.

                              1799

A SLUMBER. **7. diurnal:** daily.

I TRAVELED AMONG UNKNOWN MEN

" Written in Germany " [W].

I traveled among unknown men,
   In lands beyond the sea;
Nor, England! did I know till then
   What love I bore to thee.

'Tis past, that melancholy dream!
   Nor will I quit thy shore
A second time; for still I seem
   To love thee more and more.

Among thy mountains did I feel
   The joy of my desire;   10
And she I cherished turned her wheel
   Beside an English fire.

Thy mornings showed, thy nights concealed
   The bowers where Lucy played;
And thine too is the last green field
   That Lucy's eyes surveyed.

1801

MY HEART LEAPS UP WHEN I BEHOLD

My heart leaps up when I behold
   A rainbow in the sky;
So was it when my life began;
So is it now I am a man;
So be it when I shall grow old,
   Or let me die!
The child is father of the man;
And I could wish my days to be
Bound each to each by natural piety.

1802

RESOLUTION AND INDEPENDENCE

" Written at Town End, Grasmere. This old man I
met a few hundred yards from my cottage; and the
account of him is taken from his own mouth. I was
in the state of feeling described in the beginning of the
poem, while crossing over Barton Fell from Mr. Clark-
son's, at the foot of Ullswater, towards Askham. The
image of the hare I then observed on the ridge of the
Fell " [W].

1

There was a roaring in the wind all night;
The rain came heavily and fell in floods;

But now the sun is rising calm and bright;
The birds are singing in the distant woods;
Over his own sweet voice the stock dove broods;
The jay makes answer as the magpie chatters;
And all the air is filled with pleasant noise of
   waters.

2

All things that love the sun are out of doors;
The sky rejoices in the morning's birth;
The grass is bright with raindrops; on the moors
The hare is running races in her mirth;   11
And with her feet she from the plashy earth
Raises a mist, that, glittering in the sun,
Runs with her all the way, wherever she doth run.

3

I was a traveler then upon the moor,
I saw the hare that raced about with joy;
I heard the woods and distant waters roar,
Or heard them not, as happy as a boy;
The pleasant season did my heart employ;
My old remembrances went from me wholly;   20
And all the ways of men, so vain and melancholy.

4

But, as it sometimes chanceth, from the might
Of joy in minds that can no further go,
As high as we have mounted in delight
In our dejection do we sink as low;
To me that morning did it happen so;
And fears and fancies thick upon me came;
Dim sadness — and blind thoughts, I knew not,
   nor could name.

5

I heard the skylark warbling in the sky,
And I bethought me of the playful hare: 30
Even such a happy child of earth am I;
Even as these blissful creatures do I fare;
Far from the world I walk, and from all care;
But there may come another day to me —
Solitude, pain of heart, distress, and poverty.

6

My whole life I have lived in pleasant thought,
As if life's business were a summer mood;
As if all needful things would come unsought
To genial faith, still rich in genial good;
But how can he expect that others should   40
Build for him, sow for him, and at his call
Love him, who for himself will take no heed at
   all?

7

I thought of Chatterton,° the marvelous boy,
The sleepless soul that perished in his pride;
Of him° who walked in glory and in joy
Following his plow, along the mountainside:
By our own spirits are we deified;
We poets in our youth begin in gladness,
But thereof come in the end despondency and madness.

8

Now, whether it were by peculiar grace,   50
A leading from above, a something given,
Yet it befell, that, in this lonely place,
When I with these untoward thoughts had striven,
Beside a pool bare to the eye of Heaven
I saw a man before me unawares:
The oldest man he seemed that ever wore gray hairs.

9

As a huge stone is sometimes seen to lie°
Couched on the bald top of an eminence;
Wonder to all who do the same espy,
By what means it could thither come, and whence;
So that it seems a thing endued with sense;   61
Like a sea beast crawled forth, that on a shelf
Of rock or sand reposeth, there to sun itself;

10

Such seemed this man, not all alive nor dead,
Nor all asleep — in his extreme old age;
His body was bent double, feet and head
Coming together in life's pilgrimage;
As if some dire constraint of pain, or rage
Of sickness felt by him in times long past,
A more than human weight upon his frame had cast.   70

11

Himself he propped, limbs, body, and pale face,
Upon a long gray staff of shaven wood;
And, still as I drew near with gentle pace,
Upon the margin of that moorish flood
Motionless as a cloud the old man stood,
That heareth not the loud winds when they call
And moveth all together, if it move at all.

12

At length, himself unsettling, he the pond
Stirred with his staff, and fixedly did look
Upon the muddy water, which he conned,   80
As if he had been reading in a book;
And now a stranger's privilege I took,
And, drawing to his side, to him did say,
"This morning gives us promise of a glorious day."

13

A gentle answer did the old man make,
In courteous speech which forth he slowly drew;
And him with further words I tnus bespake,
"What occupation do you there pursue?
This is a lonesome place for one like you."
Ere he replied, a flash a mild surprise   90
Broke from the sable orbs of his yet vivid eyes,

14

His words came feebly, from a feeble chest,
But each in solemn order followed each,
With something of a lofty utterance dressed —
Choice word and measured phrase, above the reach
Of ordinary men; a stately speech;
Such as grave livers do in Scotland use,
Religious men, who give to God and man their dues.

15

He told, that to these waters he had come
To gather leeches,° being old and poor —   100
Employment hazardous and wearisome!
And he had many hardships to endure:
From pond to pond he roamed, from moor to moor;
Housing, with God's good help, by choice or chance,
And in this way he gained an honest maintenance.

16

The old man still stood talking by my side;
But now his voice to me was like a stream
Scarce heard; nor word from word could I divide;

RESOLUTION AND INDEPENDENCE. **43. Chatterton:** Thomas Chatterton (1752–70), a promising poet from Bristol who committed suicide at the age of seventeen by taking arsenic. **45. him:** Robert Burns (1759–96). **57–77. As . . . all:** "In these images, the conferring, the abstracting, and the modifying powers of the Imagination, immediately and mediately acting, are all brought into conjunction. The stone is endowed with something of the power of life to approximate it to the sea beast; and the sea beast stripped of some of its vital qualities to assimilate it to the stone; which intermediate image is thus treated for the purpose of bringing the original image, that of the stone, to a nearer resemblance to the figure and condition of the aged man, who is divested of so much of the indications of life and motion as to bring him to the point where the two objects unite and coalesce in just such comparison. After what has been said, the image of the cloud need not be commented upon" [W., Preface to the Edition of 1815]. **100. leeches:** aquatic, bloodsucking worms formerly much used for medical purposes.

And the whole body of the man did seem
Like one whom I had met with in a dream;   110
Or like a man from some far region sent,
To give me human strength, by apt admonishment.

17

My former thoughts returned: the fear that kills;
And hope that is unwilling to be fed;
Cold, pain, and labor, and all fleshly ills;
And mighty poets in their misery dead.
Perplexed, and longing to be comforted,
My question eagerly did I renew,
" How is it that you live, and what is it you do? "

18

He with a smile did then his words repeat;   120
And said, that, gathering leeches, far and wide
He traveled, stirring thus above his feet
The waters of the pools where they abide.
" Once I could meet with them on every side,
But they have dwindled long by slow decay;
Yet still I persevere, and find them where I may."

19

While he was talking thus, the lonely place,
The old man's shape, and speech — all troubled me;
In my mind's eye I seemed to see him pace
About the weary moors continually,   130
Wandering about alone and silently.
While I these thoughts within myself pursued,
He, having made a pause, the same discourse renewed.

20

And soon with this he other matter blended,
Cheerfully uttered, with demeanor kind,
But stately in the main; and when he ended,
I could have laughed myself to scorn to find
In that decrepit man so firm a mind.
" God," said I, " be my help and stay° secure;
I'll think of the leech gatherer on the lonely moor! "   140

1802

COMPOSED UPON WESTMINSTER BRIDGE

" Written on the roof of a coach, on my way to France " [W].

Earth has not anything to show more fair;
Dull would he be of soul who could pass by

139. stay: support.

A sight so touching in its majesty:
This city now doth, like a garment, wear
The beauty of the morning; silent, bare,
Ships, towers, domes, theaters, and temples lie
Open unto the fields, and to the sky;
All bright and glittering in the smokeless air.
Never did sun more beautifully steep
In his first splendor, valley, rock, or hill;   10
Ne'er saw I, never felt, a calm so deep!
The river glideth at his own sweet will;
Dear God! the very houses seem asleep;
And all that mighty heart is lying still!

1802

ON THE EXTINCTION OF THE VENETIAN REPUBLIC

Once did she hold the gorgeous east in fee;
And was the safeguard of the west;° the worth
Of Venice did not fall below her birth,
Venice, the eldest child of Liberty.°
She was a maiden city, bright and free;
No guile seduced, no force could violate;
And, when she took unto herself a mate,
She must espouse the everlasting sea.°
And what if she had seen those glories fade,
Those titles vanish, and that strength decay;   10
Yet shall some tribute of regret be paid
When her long life hath reached its final day:
Men are we, and must grieve when even the shade
Of that which once was great, is passed away.°

1802

TO TOUSSAINT L'OUVERTURE

Toussaint,° the most unhappy man of men!
Whether the whistling rustic tend his plow
Within thy hearing, or thy head be now

THE VENETIAN REPUBLIC. 1–2. Once . . . west: During the Middle Ages and the early Renaissance Venice was the leading commercial and naval power in the Mediterranean. 4. Venice . . . Liberty: Along with England and Switzerland, Venice symbolized for Wordsworth the incessant struggle of liberty against tyrannical power. 8. She . . . sea: In 1000 the Venetians defeated the Dalmatians in a naval battle. Thereafter each year on Ascension Day (the fortieth day after Easter) a ring was cast into the sea to signify the wedding of the Doge to the Adriatic, of which he was unmistakably master. See also Browning's "A Toccata of Galuppi's," ll. 5–6. 11–14. Yet . . . away: After a long and gradual decline in power Venice in 1797 fell to Napoleon, who divided her territory between France and Austria. TO TOUSSAINT L'OUVERTURE. 1. Toussaint: a Negro revolutionist (b. 1743) who declared the independence of Haiti from Napoleon and France in 1801. Defeated by the French, Toussaint was thrown into prison at Fort de Joux, near Besançon, France, where he died on April 27, 1803, soon after Wordsworth wrote this sonnet.

Pillowed in some deep dungeon's earless den —
O miserable chieftain! where and when
Wilt thou find patience? Yet die not; do thou
Wear rather in thy bonds a cheerful brow;
Though fallen thyself, never to rise again,
Live, and take comfort. Thou hast left behind
Powers that will work for thee: air, earth, and
    skies;   10
There's not a breathing of the common wind
That will forget thee; thou hast great allies;
Thy friends are exultations, agonies,
And love, and man's unconquerable mind.

1802

IT IS A BEAUTEOUS EVENING, CALM AND FREE

" This was composed on the beach near Calais, in the autumn of 1802 " [W].

It is a beauteous evening, calm and free;
The holy time is quiet as a nun
Breathless with adoration; the broad sun
Is sinking down in its tranquillity;
The gentleness of heaven broods o'er the sea.
Listen! the mighty Being is awake,
And doth with his eternal motion make
A sound like thunder — everlastingly.
Dear child! dear girl!° that walkest with me
    here,
If thou appear untouched by solemn thought,   10
Thy nature is not therefore less divine;
Thou liest in Abraham's bosom° all the year;
And worship'st at the temple's inner shrine,
God being with thee when we know it not.

1802

NEAR DOVER, SEPTEMBER, 1802

Inland, within a hollow vale, I stood,
And saw, while sea was calm and air was clear,
The coast of France — the coast of France how
    near!
Drawn almost into frightful neighborhood.
I shrunk; for verily the barrier flood
Was like a lake, or river bright and fair,
A span of waters; yet what power is there!
What mightiness for evil and for good!
Even so doth God protect us if we be

IT IS A BEAUTEOUS EVENING. **9. Dear . . . girl!:** Caroline Wordsworth, born December, 1792, the natural daughter of Wordsworth and Annette Vallon. **12. Abraham's bosom:** the name given by some theologians to a place nearer Heaven than earth where the departed souls of the blessed prepare for their final ascent to God (see Luke 16:19–31).

Virtuous and wise. Winds blow, and waters roll,
Strength to the brave, and power, and deity;   11
Yet in themselves are nothing! One decree
Spake laws to *them,* and said that by the soul
Only, the nations shall be great and free.

1802

IN LONDON, SEPTEMBER, 1802

" This was written immediately after my return from France to London, when I could not but be struck, as here described, with the vanity and parade of our own country, especially in great towns and cities, as contrasted with the quiet and, I may say, the desolation, that the Revolution had produced in France. This must be borne in mind, or else the reader may think that in this and the succeeding sonnets I have exaggerated the mischief engendered and fostered among us by undisturbed wealth. It would not be easy to conceive with what a depth of feeling I entered into the struggle carried on by the Spaniards for their deliverance from the usurped power of the French. Many times have I gone from Allan Bank in Grasmere Vale, where we were then residing, to the top of the Raise Gap, as it is called, so late as two o'clock in the morning, to meet the carrier bringing the newspaper from Keswick " [W].

O friend! I know not which way I must look
For comfort, being, as I am, oppressed,
To think that now our life is only dressed
For show; mean handiwork of craftsman,
    cook,
Or groom! We must run glittering like a
    brook
In the open sunshine, or we are unblessed;
The wealthiest man among us is the best;
No grandeur now in Nature or in book
Delights us. Rapine, avarice, expense,
This is idolatry, and these we adore;   10
Plain living and high thinking are no more;
The homely beauty of the good old cause
Is gone; our peace, our fearful innocence,
And pure religion breathing household laws.

1802

LONDON, 1802

Milton! thou shouldst be living at this hour;
England hath need of thee; she is a fen
Of stagnant waters: altar, sword, and pen,
Fireside, the heroic wealth of hall and bower,
Have forfeited their ancient English dower
Of inward happiness. We are selfish men;
Oh! raise us up, return to us again;
And give us manners, virtue, freedom, power.
Thy soul was like a star, and dwelt apart;

Thou hadst a voice whose sound was like the
   sea;
Pure as the naked heavens, majestic, free,   11
So didst thou travel on life's common way,
In cheerful godliness; and yet thy heart
The lowliest duties on herself did lay.

                   1802

IT IS NOT TO BE THOUGHT OF

It is not to be thought of that the flood
Of British freedom, which, to the open sea
Of the world's praise, from dark antiquity
Hath flowed, "with pomp of waters, unwith-
   stood,"°
Roused though it be full often to a mood
Which spurns the check of salutary bands,
That this most famous stream in bogs and sands
Should perish, and to evil and to good
Be lost forever. In our halls is hung
Armory of the invincible knights of old;   10
We must be free or die, who speak the tongue
That Shakespeare spake, the faith and morals hold
Which Milton held. In everything we are sprung
Of earth's first blood, have titles manifold.

                   1802

ENGLAND! THE TIME IS COME WHEN THOU SHOULDST WEAN

England! the time is come when thou shouldst
   wean
Thy heart from its emasculating food;
The truth should now be better understood;
Old things have been unsettled; we have seen
Fair seedtime, better harvest might have been
But for thy trespasses; and, at this day,
If for Greece, Egypt, India, Africa,
Aught good were destined, thou wouldst step be-
   tween.
England! all nations in this charge agree;
But worse, more ignorant in love and hate,   10
Far — far more abject, is thine enemy;
Therefore the wise pray for thee, though the freight
Of thy offenses be a heavy weight;
Oh grief that earth's best hopes rest all with thee!

                   1803

SHE WAS A PHANTOM OF DELIGHT°

She was a phantom of delight
When first she gleamed upon my sight,
A lovely apparition, sent
To be a moment's ornament;
Her eyes as stars of twilight fair;
Like twilight's, too, her dusky hair;
But all things else about her drawn
From Maytime and the cheerful dawn;
A dancing shape, an image gay,
To haunt, to startle, and waylay.   10

I saw her upon nearer view,
A spirit, yet a woman too!
Her household motions light and free,
And steps of virgin liberty;
A countenance in which did meet
Sweet records, promises as sweet;
A creature not too bright or good
For human nature's daily food;
For transient sorrows, simple wiles,
Praise, blame, love, kisses, tears, and smiles.   20

And now I see with eye serene
The very pulse of the machine;
A being breathing thoughtful breath,
A traveler between life and death;
The reason firm, the temperate will,
Endurance, foresight, strength, and skill;
A perfect woman, nobly planned,
To warn, to comfort, and command;
And yet a spirit still, and bright
With something of angelic light.   30

                   1804

I WANDERED LONELY AS A CLOUD°

I wandered lonely as a cloud
That floats on high o'er vales and hills,
When all at once I saw a crowd,
A host, of golden daffodils,
Beside the lake, beneath the trees,
Fluttering and dancing in the breeze.

SHE WAS A PHANTOM OF DELIGHT. Wordsworth acknowledged that
he wrote this poem about his wife, Mary Hutchinson Wordsworth.
I WANDERED LONELY. This poem was based on a personal experience first described by Dorothy Wordsworth in her *Journal* for
April 15, 1802: "The wind seized our breath. The lake was rough.
There was a boat by itself floating in the middle of the bay below
Water Millock. We rested again in the Water Millock Lane. The
hawthorns are black and green, the birches here and there greenish, but there is yet more of purple to be seen on the twigs. We
got over into a field to avoid some cows — people working. A few
primroses by the roadside — woodsorrel flower, the anemone,
scentless violets, strawberries, and that starry, yellow flower

IT IS NOT TO BE THOUGHT OF. 4. "with . . . unwithstood":
quoted from *Civil Wars*, I.7, by Samuel Daniel (1562–1619),
an Elizabethan poet and historian whom Wordsworth admired.

Continuous as the stars that shine
And twinkle on the milky way,
They stretched in never-ending line
Along the margin of a bay;   10
Ten thousand saw I at a glance,
Tossing their heads in sprightly dance.

The waves beside them danced, but they
Outdid the sparkling waves in glee;
A poet could not but be gay,
In such a jocund company;
I gazed — and gazed — but little thought
What wealth the show to me had brought:

For oft, when on my couch I lie
In vacant or in pensive mood,   20
They flash upon that inward eye
Which is the bliss of solitude;
And then my heart with pleasure fills,
And dances with the daffodils.

1804

THE SOLITARY REAPER

Behold her, single in the field,
Yon solitary Highland lass!
Reaping and singing by herself;
Stop here, or gently pass!
Alone she cuts and binds the grain,
And sings a melancholy strain;
O listen! for the vale profound
Is overflowing with the sound.

No nightingale did ever chant
More welcome notes to weary bands   10
Of travelers in some shady haunt,
Among Arabian sands;
A voice so thrilling ne'er was heard
In springtime from the cuckoo bird,

Breaking the silence of the seas
Among the farthest Hebrides.

Will no one tell me what she sings? —
Perhaps the plaintive numbers flow
For old, unhappy, far-off things,
And battles long ago;
Or is it some more humble lay,
Familiar matter of today?
Some natural sorrow, loss, or pain,
That has been, and may be again?

Whate'er the theme, the maiden sang
As if her song could have no ending;
I saw her singing at her work,
And o'er the sickle bending;
I listened, motionless and still;
And, as I mounted up the hill   30
The music in my heart I bore,
Long after it was heard no more.

1805

ODE

Intimations of Immortality from Recollections of Early Childhood

" This was composed during my residence at Town End, Grasmere. Two years at least passed between the writing of the four first stanzas and the remaining part. To the attentive and competent reader the whole sufficiently explains itself, but there may be no harm in adverting here to particular feelings or *experiences* of my own mind on which the structure of the poem partly rests. Nothing was more difficult for me in childhood than to admit the notion of death as a state applicable to my own being. I have said elsewhere

A simple child,
That lightly draws its breath,
And feels its life in every limb,
What should it know of death?

But it was not so much from feelings of animal vivacity that *my* difficulty came as from a sense of the indomitableness of the spirit within me. I used to brood over the stories of Enoch and Elijah, and almost to persuade myself that, whatever might become of others, I should be translated, in something of the same way, to Heaven. With a feeling congenial to this, I was often unable to think of external things as having external existence, and I communed with all that I saw as something not apart from, but inherent in, my own immaterial nature. Many times while going to school have I grasped at a wall or tree to recall myself from this abyss of idealism to the reality. At that time I was afraid of such processes. In later periods of life I have deplored, as we have all reason to do, a subjugation of an opposite character, and have rejoiced over the remembrances, as is expressed in the lines:

which Mrs. C. calls pile wort. When we were in the woods beyond Gowbarrow Park we saw a few daffodils close to the waterside. We fancied that the lake had floated the seeds ashore, and that the little colony had so sprung up. But as we went along there were more and yet more; and at last, under the boughs of the trees, we saw that there was a long belt of them along the shore, about the breadth of a country turnpike road. I never saw daffodils so beautiful. They grew among the mossy stones about and about them; some rested their heads upon these stones as on a pillow for weariness; and the rest tossed and reeled and danced, and seemed as if they verily laughed with the wind, that blew upon them over the lake, they looked so gay, ever glancing, ever changing. This wind blew directly over the lake to them. There was here and there a little knot, and a few stragglers a few yards higher up; but they were so few as not to disturb the simplicity, unity, and life of that one busy highway. We rested again and again. The bays were stormy, and we heard the waves at different distances, and in the middle of the water. Rain came on — we were wet when we reached Luff's. . . ."

> Obstinate questionings
> Of sense and outward things,
> Fallings from us, vanishings. . . .

To that dreamlike vividness and splendor which invest objects of sight in childhood, everyone, I believe, if he would look back, could bear testimony, and I need not dwell upon it here, but having in the poem regarded it as presumptive evidence of a prior state of existence, I think it right to protest against a conclusion, which has given pain to some good and pious persons, that I meant to inculcate such a belief. It is far too shadowy a notion to be recommended to faith, as more than an element in our instincts of immortality. But let us bear in mind that, though the idea is not advanced in revelation, there is nothing there to contradict it, and the fall of man presents an analogy in its favor. Accordingly, a pre-existent state has entered into the popular creeds of many nations, and, among all persons acquainted with classic literature, is known as an ingredient in Platonic philosophy. Archimedes said that he could move the world if he had a point whereon to rest his machine. Who has not felt the same aspirations as regards the world of his own mind? Having to wield some of its elements when I was impelled to write this poem on the "Immortality of the Soul," I took hold of the notion of pre-existence as having sufficient foundation in humanity for authorizing me to make for my purpose the best use of it I could as a poet" [W].

The child is father of the man;
And I could wish my days to be
Bound each to each by natural piety.

1

There was a time when meadow, grove, and
stream,
The earth, and every common sight,
To me did seem
Appareled in celestial light,
The glory and the freshness of a dream.
It is not now as it hath been of yore;
Turn wheresoe'er I may,
By night or day,
The things which I have seen I now can see no
more.

2

The rainbow comes and goes,   10
And lovely is the rose,
The moon doth with delight
Look round her when the heavens are bare;
Waters on a starry night
Are beautiful and fair;
The sunshine is a glorious birth;
But yet I know, where'er I go,
That there hath passed away a glory from the earth.

3

Now, while the birds thus sing a joyous song,
And while the young lambs bound   20
As to the tabor's sound,
To me alone there came a thought of grief,
A timely utterance gave that thought relief,
And I again am strong;
The cataracts blow their trumpets from the steep;
No more shall grief of mine the season wrong;
I hear the echoes through the mountains throng,
The winds come to me from the fields of sleep,
And all the earth is gay;
Land and sea   30
Give themselves up to jollity,
And with the heart of May
Doth every beast keep holiday;
Thou child of joy,
Shout round me, let me hear thy shouts, thou
happy
Shepherd boy!

4

Ye blessed creatures, I have heard the call
Ye to each other make; I see
The heavens laugh with you in your jubilee;
My heart is at your festival,   40
My head hath its coronal,
The fullness of your bliss, I feel — I feel it all.
Oh evil day! if I were sullen
While Earth herself is adorning,
This sweet May morning,
And the children are culling
On every side,
In a thousand valleys far and wide,
Fresh flowers; while the sun shines warm,
And the babe leaps up on his mother's arm: 50
I hear, I hear, with joy I hear!
— But there's a tree, of many, one,
A single field which I have looked upon,
Both of them speak of something that is gone;
The pansy at my feet
Doth the same tale repeat:
Whither is fled the visionary gleam?
Where is it now, the glory and the dream?

5

Our birth is but a sleep and a forgetting;
The soul that rises with us, our life's star,   60
Hath had elsewhere its setting,
And cometh from afar;
Not in entire forgetfulness,
And not in utter nakedness,

But trailing clouds of glory do we come
  From God, who is our home;
Heaven lies about us in our infancy!
Shades of the prison house begin to close
  Upon the growing boy,
But he beholds the light, and whence it flows,
  He sees it in his joy;   71
The youth, who daily farther from the east
  Must travel, still is Nature's priest,
  And by the vision splendid
  Is on his way attended;
At length the man perceives it die away,
And fade into the light of common day.

6

Earth fills her lap with pleasures of her own;
Yearnings she hath in her own natural kind,
And, even with something of a mother's mind,
  And no unworthy aim,   81
  The homely nurse doth all she can
To make her foster child, her inmate man,
  Forget the glories he hath known,
And that imperial palace whence he came.

7

Behold the child among his newborn blisses,
A six-years' darling of a pygmy size!
See, where 'mid work of his own hand he lies,
Fretted by sallies of his mother's kisses,
With light upon him from his father's eyes!   90
See, at his feet, some little plan or chart,
Some fragment from his dream of human life,
Shaped by himself with newly learnèd art;
  A wedding or a festival,
  A mourning or a funeral;
    And this hath now his heart,
    And unto this he frames his song;
    Then will he fit his tongue
To dialogues of business, love, or strife;
  But it will not be long   100
  Ere this be thrown aside,
  And with new joy and pride
The little actor cons another part,
Filling from time to time his " humorous stage "°
With all the persons, down to palsied age,
That life brings with her in her equipage;
    As if his whole vocation
    Were endless imitation.

8

Thou, whose exterior semblance doth belie
  Thy soul's immensity;   110

Thou best philosopher, who yet dost keep
Thy heritage, thou eye among the blind,
That, deaf and silent, read'st the eternal deep,
Haunted forever by the eternal mind —
    Mighty prophet! Seer blest!
    On whom those truths do rest,
Which we are toiling all our lives to find,
In darkness lost, the darkness of the grave;
Thou, over whom thy immortality
Broods like the day, a master o'er a slave,   120
A presence which is not to be put by;
Thou little child, yet glorious in the might°
Of heaven-born freedom on thy being's height,
Why with such earnest pains dost thou provoke
The years to bring the inevitable yoke,
Thus blindly with thy blessedness at strife?
Full soon thy soul shall have her earthly freight,
And custom lie upon thee with a weight,
Heavy as frost, and deep almost as life!

9

    O joy! that in our embers   130
    Is something that doth live,
    That nature yet remembers
    What was so fugitive!
The thought of our past years in me doth breed
Perpetual benediction: not indeed
For that which is most worthy to be blessed;
Delight and liberty, the simple creed
Of childhood, whether busy or at rest,
With new-fledged hope still fluttering in his breast:
    Not for these I raise   140
    The song of thanks and praise;
  But for those obstinate questionings
  Of sense and outward things,
  Fallings from us, vanishings;
  Blank misgivings of a creature
Moving about in worlds not realized,
High instincts before which our mortal nature
Did tremble like a guilty thing surprised;°
    But for those first affections,
    Those shadowy recollections,   150
  Which, be they what they may,
Are yet the fountain light of all our day,
Are yet a master light of all our seeing;
  Uphold us, cherish, and have power to make
Our noisy years seem moments in the being
Of the eternal silence; truths that wake,
    To perish never;

INTIMATIONS OF IMMORTALITY. **104.** "**humorous stage**": quoted from the dedicatory sonnet to Samuel Daniel's *Musophilus* (1599). **121–22. presence . . . might:** In the first published version of the poem these lines read: "To whom the grave/Is but a lonely bed without the sense or sight/Of day or the warm light,/A place of thought where we in waiting lie." The idea of lying awake in the grave, which Wordsworth thus expressed, proved "frightful" to Coleridge, and Wordsworth deleted these lines after 1815. **148. tremble . . . surprised:** an echo of Shakespeare's *Hamlet*, I.i.148–49, p. 100, above.

Which neither listlessness, nor mad endeavor,
   Nor man nor boy,
Nor all that is at enmity with joy,   160
Can utterly abolish or destroy!
   Hence in a season of calm weather
   Though inland far we be,
Our souls have sight of that immortal sea
   Which brought us hither,
   Can in a moment travel thither,
And see the children sport upon the shore,
And hear the mighty waters rolling evermore.

10

Then sing, ye birds, sing, sing a joyous song!
   And let the young lambs bound   170
   As to the tabor's sound!
We in thought will join your throng,
   Ye that pipe and ye that play,
   Ye that through your hearts today
   Feel the gladness of the May!
What though the radiance which was once so bright
Be now forever taken from my sight,
   Though nothing can bring back the hour
Of splendor in the grass, of glory in the flower;
   We will grieve not, rather find   180
   Strength in what remains behind;
   In the primal sympathy
   Which having been must ever be;
   In the soothing thoughts that spring
   Out of human suffering;
   In the faith that looks through death,
In years that bring the philosophic mind.

11

And O, ye fountains, meadows, hills, and groves,
Forebode not any severing of our loves!
Yet in my heart of hearts I feel your might;   190
I only have relinquished one delight
To live beneath your more habitual sway.
I love the brooks which down their channels fret,
Even more than when I tripped lightly as they;
The innocent brightness of a newborn day
   Is lovely yet;
The clouds that gather round the setting sun
Do take a sober coloring from an eye
That hath kept watch o'er man's mortality;
Another race hath been, and other palms are won.
Thanks to the human heart by which we live,   201
Thanks to its tenderness, its joys, and fears;
To me the meanest flower that blows can give
Thoughts that do often lie too deep for tears.

1802–04

"WITH HOW SAD STEPS, O MOON, THOU CLIMB'ST THE SKY"

"With how sad steps, O Moon, thou climb'st the
   sky,
How silently, and with how wan a face!"°
Where art thou? Thou so often seen on high
Running among the clouds a wood nymph's race!
Unhappy nuns, whose common breath's a sigh
Which they would stifle, move at such a pace!
The northern wind, to call thee to the chase,
Must blow tonight his bugle horn. Had I
The power of Merlin,° goddess! this should be:
And all the stars, fast as the clouds were riven,   10
Should sally forth, to keep thee company,
Hurrying and sparkling through the clear blue
   heaven.
But, Cynthia!° should to thee the palm be given,
Queen both for beauty and for majesty.

1804

NUNS FRET NOT AT THEIR CONVENT'S NARROW ROOM

Nuns fret not at their convent's narrow room;
And hermits are contented with their cells;
And students with their pensive citadels;
Maids at the wheel, the weaver at his loom,
Sit blithe and happy; bees that soar for bloom,
High as the highest peak of Furness Fells,°
Will murmur by the hour in foxglove bells.
In truth, the prison, into which we doom
Ourselves, no prison is; and hence for me,
In sundry moods, 'twas pastime to be bound   10
Within the sonnet's scanty plot of ground;
Pleased if some souls (for such there needs must
   be)
Who have felt the weight of too much liberty,
Should find brief solace there, as I have found.

1804

THE WORLD IS TOO MUCH WITH US; LATE AND SOON

The world is too much with us; late and soon,
Getting and spending, we lay waste our powers;
Little we see in Nature that is ours;
We have given our hearts away, a sordid boon!

"WITH HOW SAD STEPS". 1–2. With . . . face: These lines Words-
worth took from Sir Philip Sidney's *Astrophel and Stella*, Sonnet
XXI. 9. Merlin: magician famous in Arthurian romance. 13.
Cynthia: Artemis, or Diana, goddess of the moon. NUNS FRET
NOT. 6. Furness Fells: hills west of Lake Windermere. The
tallest peak is the Old Man of Coniston, 2633 feet high.

The sea that bares her bosom to the moon,
The winds that will be howling at all hours,
And are upgathered now like sleeping flowers;
For this, for everything, we are out of tune;
It moves us not. Great God! I'd rather be
A pagan suckled in a creed outworn,   10
So might I, standing on this pleasant lea,
Have glimpses that would make me less forlorn;
Have sight of Proteus rising from the sea;
Or hear old Triton° blow his wreathèd horn.

1804

THOUGHT OF A BRITON ON THE SUBJUGATION OF SWITZERLAND

Two voices° are there; one is of the sea,
One of the mountains; each a mighty voice;
In both from age to age thou didst rejoice;
They were thy chosen music, Liberty!
There came a tyrant,° and with holy glee
Thou fought'st against him, but hast vainly striven;
Thou from thy Alpine holds at length art driven,
Where not a torrent murmurs heard by thee.
Of one deep bliss thine ear hath been bereft:
Then cleave, O cleave to that which still is left;   10
For, high-souled maid, what sorrow would it be
That mountain floods should thunder as before,
And ocean bellow from his rocky shore,
And neither awful voice be heard by thee!

1806

SCORN NOT THE SONNET

Scorn not the sonnet; critic, you have frowned,
Mindless of its just honors; with this key
Shakespeare unlocked his heart; the melody
Of this small lute gave ease to Petrarch's wound;°
A thousand times this pipe did Tasso° sound;
With it Camoëns soothed an exile's grief;°
The sonnet glittered a gay myrtle leaf

THE WORLD IS TOO MUCH WITH US.   13-14. Proteus ... Triton: sons of Poseidon, or Neptune, god of the sea. Proteus tended his father's herd of seals, and could change shape at will. Triton was the herald of the seas, and used a conch shell for a trumpet. THOUGHT OF A BRITON.   1. Two voices: England and Switzerland.   5. tyrant: Napoleon, who invaded Switzerland in 1797 and completed her subjugation in 1802–03, while threatening England with invasion. SCORN NOT THE SONNET.   4. Petrarch's wound: Wordsworth refers to the sonnets written by the Italian poet (1304–74) to Laura after her death.   5. Tasso: Italian poet (1544–95), author of *Jerusalem Delivered*.   6. Camoens ... grief: Portuguese epic and lyric poet (1524–80) who, in exile at Goa, wrote laments for the death of Donna Caterina.   7–9. myrtle ... brow: Dante Alighieri (1265–1321), greatest of Italian poets and author of the *Divine Comedy*, loved Beatrice, who died in 1290 at the age of twenty-four. To her he addressed sonnets of love, symbolized by the myrtle, and of mourning, symbolized by the cypress.

Amid the cypress with which Dante crowned
His visionary brow:° a glowworm lamp,
It cheered mild Spenser, called from faeryland   10
To struggle through dark ways; and, when a damp
Fell round the path of Milton, in his hand
The thing became a trumpet; whence he blew
Soul-animating strains — alas, too few!

1827

LINES

"Composed at Grasmere, during a walk one evening, after a stormy day, the author having just read in a newspaper that the dissolution of Mr. Fox was hourly expected" [W].°

Loud is the vale! the voice is up
With which she speaks when storms are gone,
A mighty unison of streams!
Of all her voices, one!

Loud is the vale — this inland depth
In peace is roaring like the sea;
Yon star upon the mountaintop
Is listening quietly.

Sad was I, even to pain depressed,
Importunate and heavy load!   10
The Comforter hath found me here,
Upon this lonely road;

And many thousands now are sad —
Wait the fulfillment of their fear;
For he must die who is their stay,
Their glory disappear.

A power is passing from the earth
To breathless Nature's dark abyss;
But when the great and good depart
What is it more than this —   20

That man, who is from God sent forth,
Doth yet again to God return?
Such ebb and flow must ever be,
Then wherefore should we mourn?

1806

LINES.   Mr. Fox: Charles James Fox (b. 1749), William Pitt's successor as Minister of Foreign Affairs, died September 13, 1806. Once known as the "idol of the people," Fox had opposed British policy in the American and French revolutionary wars and had worked for the abolition of the slave trade, which was finally declared illegal in March, 1807.

SAMUEL TAYLOR COLERIDGE

THE RIME OF THE ANCIENT MARINER

IN SEVEN PARTS

Originally Coleridge and Wordsworth intended to write this poem in collaboration. Wordsworth's manner proved unsuited for the purpose, however, and after contributing half a dozen lines (particularly ll. 13–16 and 226–27) and suggesting the shooting of the albatross and the "reanimation of the dead bodies to work the ship," Wordsworth withdrew, and Coleridge proceeded alone. The details of the origin of the poem are contained in the opening paragraphs of Chapter XIV of Coleridge's *Biographia Literaria* (pp. 612–15, below), and in the Fenwick note (1843) to Wordsworth's "We Are Seven."

The effectiveness of the first (1798) version of the poem was reduced by Coleridge's overenthusiasm for archaic words and spellings, many of which he removed in subsequent editions. The Latin motto below was added in 1817, as was the marginal gloss, although the latter may have been written much earlier.

Facile credo, plures esse Naturas invisibiles quam visibiles in rerum universitate. Sed horum omnium familiam quis nobis enarrabit? et gradus et cognationes et discrimina et singulorum munera? Quid agunt? quae loca habitant? Harum rerum notitiam semper ambivit ingenium humanum, nunquam attigit. Juvat, interea, non diffiteor, quandoque in animo, tanquam in tabulà, majoris et melioris mundi imaginem contemplari: ne mens assuefacta hodiernae vitae minutiis se contrahat nimis, et tota subsidat in pusillas cogitationes. Sed veritati interea invigilandum est, modusque servandus, ut certa ab incertis, diem a nocte, distinguamus.[1]

[Thomas Burnet,[2] *Archaeologiae Philosophicae* (1692), p. 68]

THE RIME OF THE ANCIENT MARINER. **1.** *Facile . . . distinguamus:* "I find it easy to believe that there are more invisible than visible things in the universe. But who shall describe for us the families of all of them, their rank and relationships, the distinguishing features and singularities of each. What do they do? What places inhabit? The human mind has always circled about but never attained knowledge of these things. I do not doubt, however, that it is sometimes good to contemplate in the mind, as in a picture, the image of a greater and better world; otherwise the mind, accustomed to the minutiae of daily life, may contract too much and sink altogether to trivial thoughts. Meanwhile, however, we must be vigilant for truth and keep proportion, so that we may distinguish certainty from uncertainty, day from night." **2. Thomas Burnet:** Anglican divine (1635?–1715); a favorite author of Coleridge and Wordsworth (see p. 615, n. 12, below).

ARGUMENT

How a Ship having passed the Line was driven by storms to the cold Country towards the South Pole; and how from thence she made her course to the tropical Latitude of the Great Pacific Ocean; and of the strange things that befell; and in what manner the Ancient Mariner came back to his own Country.

PART I

An ancient Mariner meeteth three Gallants bidden to a wedding-feast, and detaineth one.

It is an ancient Mariner,
And he stoppeth one of three.
" By thy long gray beard and glittering eye,
Now wherefore stopp'st thou me?

The Bridegroom's doors are opened wide,
And I am next of kin;
The guests are met, the feast is set:
May'st hear the merry din."

He holds him with his skinny hand,
" There was a ship," quoth he.   10
" Hold off! unhand me, graybeard loon! "
Eftsoons° his hand dropt he.

The Wedding Guest is spell-bound by the eye of the old sea-faring man, and constrained to hear his tale.

He holds him with his glittering eye —
The Wedding Guest stood still,
And listens like a three years' child:
The Mariner hath his will.°

The Wedding Guest sat on a stone:
He cannot choose but hear;
And thus spake on that ancient man,
The bright-eyed Mariner.   20

" The ship was cheered, the harbor cleared,
Merrily did we drop
Below the kirk,° below the hill,
Below the lighthouse top.

12. Eftsoons: at once.   **13–16. He . . . will:** Wordsworth wrote this stanza.   **23. kirk:** church.

The Mariner tells how the ship sailed southward with a good wind and fair weather, till it reached the line.

The Sun came up upon the left,
Out of the sea came he!
And he shone bright, and on the right
Went down into the sea.

Higher and higher every day,
Till over the mast at noon —"   30
The Wedding Guest here beat his
      breast,
For he heard the loud bassoon.

The Wedding Guest heareth the bridal music; but the Mariner continueth his tale.

The bride hath paced into the hall,
Red as a rose is she;
Nodding their heads before her goes
The merry minstrelsy.°

The Wedding Guest he beat his breast,
Yet he cannot choose but hear;
And thus spake on that ancient man,
The bright-eyed Mariner.   40

The ship driven by a storm toward the south pole.

" And now the STORM-BLAST came, and
      he
Was tyrannous and strong:
He struck with his o'ertaking wings,
And chased us south along.

With sloping masts and dipping prow,
As who pursued with yell and blow
Still treads the shadow of his foe,
And forward bends his head,
The ship drove fast, loud roared the
      blast,
And southward aye we fled.   50

And now there came both mist and
      snow,
And it grew wondrous cold:
And ice, mast-high, came floating by,
As green as emerald.

The land of ice, and of fearful sounds where no living thing was to be seen.

And through the drifts the snowy
      clifts°
Did send a dismal sheen:
Nor shapes of men nor beasts we ken —
The ice was all between.

The ice was here, the ice was there,
The ice was all around: 60
It cracked and growled, and roared and
      howled,
Like noises in a swound!°

Till a great seabird, called the Albatross, came through the snow-fog, and was received with great joy and hospitality.

At length did cross an Albatross,
Thorough°the fog it came;
As if it had been a Christian soul,
We hailed it in God's name.

It ate the food it ne'er had eat,
And round and round it flew.
The ice did split with a thunder-fit;
The helmsman steered us through!   70

And lo! the Albatross proveth a bird of good omen, and followeth the ship as it returned northward through fog and floating ice.

And a good south wind sprung up be-
      hind;
The Albatross did follow,
And every day, for food or play,
Came to the mariners' hollo!

In mist or cloud, on mast or shroud,°
It perched for vespers° nine;
Whiles all the night, through fog-smoke
      white,
Glimmered the white Moon shine."

The ancient Mariner inhospitably killeth the pious bird of good omen.

" God save thee, ancient Mariner!
From the fiends, that plague thee
      thus! —   80
Why look'st thou so? " — With my
      crossbow
I shot the ALBATROSS.

PART II

The Sun now rose upon the right:°
Out of the sea came he,
Still hid in mist, and on the left
Went down into the sea.

And the good south wind still blew
      behind,
But no sweet bird did follow,
Nor any day for food or play
Came to the mariners' hollo!   90

His ship-mates cry out against the ancient Mariner, for kill'ng the bird of good luck.

And I had done a hellish thing,
And it would work 'em woe:
For all averred, I had killed the bird
That made the breeze to blow.
Ah wretch! said they, the bird to slay,
That made the breeze to blow!

But when the fog cleared off, they justify the same, and thus make them-

Nor dim nor red, like God's own head,
The glorious Sun uprist:
Then all averred, I had killed the bird
That brought the fog and mist.   100

---

36. minstrelsy: musicians.   **55. clifts:** cliffs.   **62. swound:**
swoon.

64. Thorough: through.   **75. shroud:** rope or line.   **76. vespers:**
evening religious services.   **83. The . . . right:** The ship, having
rounded the Horn, is now heading north into the Pacific.

selves accom-
plices in the
crime.

'Twas right, said they, such birds to
    slay,
That bring the fog and mist.

The fair
breeze con-
tinues; the
ship enters
the Pacific
Ocean, and
sails north-
ward, even
till it reaches
the Line.

The fair breeze blew, the white foam
    flew,
The furrow followed free;
We were the first that ever burst
Into that silent sea.

The ship
hath been
suddenly
becalmed.

Down dropt the breeze, the sails dropt
    down,
'Twas sad as sad could be;
And we did speak only to break
The silence of the sea!   110

All in a hot and copper sky,
The bloody Sun, at noon,
Right up above the mast did stand,
No bigger than the Moon.

Day after day, day after day,
We stuck, nor breath nor motion;
As idle as a painted ship
Upon a painted ocean.

And the
Albatross
begins to be
avenged.

Water, water, everywhere,
And all the boards did shrink;   120
Water, water, everywhere,
Nor any drop to drink.

The very deep did rot: O Christ!
That ever this should be!
Yea, slimy things did crawl with legs
Upon the slimy sea.

A Spirit had
followed
them; one of
the invisible
inhabitants of
this planet,
neither de-
parted souls
nor angels;
concerning
whom the
learned Jew,
Josephus, and
the Platonic
Constantino-
politan, Mi-
chael Psellus,
may be con-
sulted. They
are very nu-
merous, and
there is no
climate or
element with-
out one or
more.

About, about, in reel and rout
The death-fires° danced at night;
The water, like a witch's oils,
Burnt green, and blue and white.   130

And some in dreams assurèd were
Of the Spirit that plagued us so;
Nine fathom deep he had followed us
From the land of mist and snow.

And every tongue, through utter
    drought,
Was withered at the root;
We could not speak, no more than if
We had been choked with soot.

The ship-
mates, in
their sore
distress,
would fain
throw the
whole guilt
on the an-
cient Mar-
iner: in s'gn
whereof they
hang the dead
sea bird round
his neck.

Ah! wel-a-day! what evil looks
Had I from old and young!   140
Instead of the cross, the Albatross
About my neck was hung.

Part III

There passed a weary time. Each throat
Was parched, and glazed each eye.
A weary time! a weary time!
How glazed each weary eye,
When looking westward, I beheld
A something in the sky.

The ancient
Mariner be-
holdeth a sign
in the element
afar off.

At first it seemed a little speck,
And then it seemed a mist;   150
It moved and moved, and took at last
A certain shape, I wist.°

A speck, a mist, a shape, I wist!
And still it neared and neared:
As if it dodged a water sprite,
It plunged and tacked and veered.

At its nearer
approach, it
seemeth him
to be a ship;
and at a dear
ransom he
freeth his
speech from
the bonds of
thirst.

With throats unslaked, with black lips
    baked,
We could nor laugh nor wail;
Through utter drought all dumb we
    stood!
I bit my arm, I sucked the blood,   160
And cried, A sail! a sail!

With throats unslaked, with black lips
    baked,
Agape they heard me call:
Gramercy!° they for joy did grin,
And all at once their breath drew in,
As they were drinking all.

A flash of joy;

And horror
follows. For
can it be a
ship that
comes onward
without wind
or tide?

See! see! (I cried) she tacks no more!
Hither to work us weal;°
Without a breeze, without a tide,
She steadies with upright keel!   170

The western wave was all aflame.
The day was well nigh done!
Almost upon the western wave
Rested the broad bright Sun;
When that strange shape drove sud-
    denly
Betwixt us and the Sun.

---

128. **death-fires**: St. Elmo's fire, phosphorescent lights on a ship's
rigging, believed by sailors to be prophetic of disaster.

152. **wist**: knew. 164. **Gramercy**: great thanks. 168. **weal**:
good.

It seemeth
him but the
skeleton of
a ship.
And its ribs
are seen as
bars on the
face of the
setting Sun.

And straight the Sun was flecked with
   bars,
(Heaven's Mother send us grace!)
As if through a dungeon grate he
   peered
With broad and burning face.   180

Alas! (thought I, and my heart beat
   loud)
How fast she nears and nears!
Are those *her* sails that glance in the
   Sun,
Like restless gossameres?°

Are those *her* ribs through which the
   Sun

The Specter-
Woman and
her Death-
mate, and no
other on board
the skeleton
ship.

Did peer, as through a grate?
And is that Woman all her crew?
Is that a DEATH? and are there two?
Is DEATH that woman's mate?

Like vessel,
like crew!

Her lips were red, *her* looks were free,
Her locks were yellow as gold: 191
Her skin was as white as leprosy,
The Nightmare LIFE-IN-DEATH was
   she,
Who thicks man's blood with cold.

Death and
Life-in-Death
have diced for
the ship's
crew, and she
(the latter)
winneth the
ancient
Mariner.

The naked hulk alongside came,
And the twain were casting dice;
"The game is done! I've won! I've
   won!"
Quoth she, and whistles thrice.

No twilight
within the
courts of the
Sun.

The Sun's rim dips; the stars rush out:
At one stride comes the dark;   200
With far-heard whisper, o'er the sea,
Off shot the specter bark.

At the rising
of the Moon,

We listened and looked sideways up!
Fear at my heart, as at a cup,
My lifeblood seemed to sip!
The stars were dim, and thick the
   night,
The steersman's face by his lamp
   gleamed white;
From the sails the dew did drip —
Till clomb° above the eastern bar
The hornèd Moon, with one bright
   star   210
Within the nether tip.

One after
another,

One after one, by the star-dogged **Moon,**
Too quick for groan or sigh,
Each turned his face with a ghastly
   pang,
And cursed me with his eye.

His shipmates
drop down
dead.

Four times fifty living men,
(And I heard nor sigh nor groan)
With heavy thump, a lifeless lump,
They dropped down one by one.

But Life-in-
Death begins
her work on
the ancient
Mariner.

The souls did from their bodies fly —
They fled to bliss or woe!   221
And every soul, it passed me by,
Like the whizz of my crossbow!

PART IV

The Wedding
Guest feareth
that a Spirit
is talking to
him;

"I fear thee, ancient Mariner!
I fear thy skinny hand!
And thou art long, and lank, and
   brown,
As is the ribbed sea-sand.°

I fear thee and thy glittering eye,
And thy skinny hand, so brown." —

But the an-
cient Mariner
assureth him
of his bodily
life, and pro-
ceedeth to re-
late his hor-
rible penance.

Fear not, fear not, thou Wedding
   Guest!   230
This body dropt not down.

Alone, alone, all, all alone,
Alone on a wide wide sea!
And never a saint took pity on
My soul in agony.

He despiseth
the creatures
of the calm,

The many men, so beautiful!
And they all dead did lie:
And a thousand thousand slimy things
Lived on; and so did I.

And envieth
that *they*
should live,
and so many
lie dead.

I looked upon the rotting sea,   240
And drew my eyes away;
I looked upon the rotting deck,
And there the dead men lay.

I looked to heaven, and tried to pray;
But or ever a prayer had gusht,
A wicked whisper came, and made
My heart as dry as dust.

I closed my lids, and kept them close,
And the balls like pulses beat;
For the sky and the sea, and the sea
   and the sky   250
Lay like a load on my weary eye,
And the dead were at my feet.

---

184. gossameres: cobwebs floating in the air.   **209. clomb:**
climbed.

226–27. And . . . sea-sand: Wordsworth wrote these lines.

But the curse liveth for him in the eye of the dead men.

The cold sweat melted from their limbs,
Nor rot nor reek did they:
The look with which they looked on
    me
Had never passed away.

An orphan's curse would drag to hell
A spirit from on high;
But oh! more horrible than that

In his lone-liness and fix-edness he yearneth to-wards the journeying Moon, and the stars that still sojourn, yet still move on-ward; and ev-erywhere the blue sky be-longs to them, and is their ap-pointed rest, and their na-tive country and their own natural homes, which they enter unan-nounced, as lords that are certainly ex-pected and yet there is a silent joy at their arrival. By the light of the Moon he beholdeth God's crea-tures of the great calm.

Is the curse in a dead man's eye!   260
Seven days, seven nights, I saw that
    curse,
And yet I could not die.

The moving Moon went up the sky,
And nowhere did abide:
Softly she was going up,
And a star or two beside —

Her beams bemocked the sultry main,
Like April hoarfrost spread;
But where the ship's huge shadow
    lay,
The charmèd water burnt alway   270
A still and awful red.

Beyond the shadow of the ship,
I watched the water snakes:
They moved in tracks of shining white,
And when they reared, the elfish light
Fell off in hoary flakes.

Within the shadow of the ship
I watched their rich attire:
Blue, glossy green, and velvet black,
They coiled and swam; and every track
Was a flash of golden fire.   281

Their beauty and their happiness.

O happy living things! no tongue
Their beauty might declare:
A spring of love gushed from my heart,

He blesseth them in his heart.

And I blessed them unaware:
Sure my kind saint took pity on me,
And I blessed them unaware.

The spell begins to break.

The selfsame moment I could pray;
And from my neck so free
The Albatross fell off, and sank   290
Like lead into the sea.

PART V

Oh sleep! it is a gentle thing,
Beloved from pole to pole!
To Mary Queen the praise be given!
She sent the gentle sleep from Heaven,
That slid into my soul.

By grace of the holy Mother, the ancient Mar-iner is re-freshed with rain.

The silly° buckets on the deck,
That had so long remained,
I dreamt that they were filled with
    dew;
And when I awoke, it rained.   300

My lips were wet, my throat was cold,
My garments all were dank;
Sure I had drunken in my dreams,
And still my body drank.

I moved, and could not feel my limbs:
I was so light — almost
I thought that I had died in sleep,
And was a blessèd ghost.

He heareth sounds and seeth strange sights and commotions in the sky and the ele-ment.

And soon I heard a roaring wind:
It did not come anear;   310
But with its sound it shook the sails,
That were so thin and sere.

The upper air burst into life!
And a hundred fireflags sheen,
To and fro they were hurried about!
And to and fro, and in and out,
The wan stars danced between.°

And the coming wind did roar more
    loud,
And the sails did sigh like sedge;°
And the rain poured down from one
    black cloud;   320
The Moon was at its edge.

The thick black cloud was cleft, and
    still
The Moon was at its side:
Like waters shot from some high crag,
The lightning fell with never a jag,
A river steep and wide.

The loud wind never reached the ship,
Yet now the ship moved on!
Beneath the lightning and the Moon

The bodies of the ship's crew are in-spired and the ship moves on;

The dead men gave a groan.   330

They groaned, they stirred, they all up-
    rose,
Nor spake, nor moved their eyes;
It had been strange, even in a dream,
To have seen those dead men rise.

297. silly: because empty and useless.   313–17. The . . . between: Aurora Australis or Southern Lights.   319. sedge:
marsh grass.

The helmsman steered, the ship moved
    on;
Yet never a breeze upblew;
The mariners all 'gan work the ropes,
Where they were wont to do;
They raised their limbs like lifeless
    tools —
We were a ghastly crew.   340

The body of my brother's son
Stood by me, knee to knee:
The body and I pulled at one rope,
But he said nought to me.

But not by the souls of the men, nor by demons of earth or middle air, but by a blessed troop of angelic spirits, sent down by the invocation of the guardian saint.

" I fear thee, ancient Mariner! "
Be calm, thou Wedding Guest!
'Twas not those souls that fled in pain,
Which to their corses° came again,
But a troop of spirits blest:

For when it dawned — they dropped
    their arms,   350
And clustered round the mast;
Sweet sounds rose slowly through their
    mouths,
And from their bodies passed.

Around, around, flew each sweet sound,
Then darted to the Sun;
Slowly the sounds came back again,
Now mixed, now one by one.

Sometimes a-dropping from the sky
I heard the skylark sing;
Sometimes all little birds that are, 360
How they seemed to fill the sea and
    air
With their sweet jargoning!°

And now 'twas like all instruments,
Now like a lonely flute;
And now it is an angel's song,
That makes the heavens be mute.

It ceased; yet still the sails made on
A pleasant noise till noon,
A noise like of a hidden brook
In the leafy month of June,   370
That to the sleeping woods all night
Singeth a quiet tune.

Till noon we quietly sailed on,
Yet never a breeze did breathe:
Slowly and smoothly went the ship,
Moved onward from beneath.

The lonesome Spirit from the South Pole carries on the ship as far as the Line, in obedience to the angelic troop, but still requireth vengeance.

Under the keel nine fathom deep,
From the land of mist and snow,
The spirit slid; and it was he
That made the ship to go.   380
The sails at noon left off their tune,
And the ship stood still also.

The Sun, right up above the mast,
Had fixed her to the ocean:
But in a minute she 'gan stir,
With a short uneasy motion —
Backwards and forwards half her
    length
With a short uneasy motion.

Then like a pawing horse let go,
She made a sudden bound: 390
It flung the blood into my head,
And I fell down in a swound.

The Polar Spirit's fellow-demons, the invisible inhabitants of the element, take part in his wrong; and two of them relate, one to the other, that penance long and heavy for the ancient Mariner hath been accorded to the Polar Spirit, who returneth southward.

How long in that same fit I lay,
I have not to declare;°
But ere my living life returned,
I heard and in my soul discerned
Two voices in the air.

" Is it he? " quoth one, " Is this the
    man?
By him who died on cross,
With his cruel bow he laid full low
The harmless Albatross.   401

The spirit who bideth by himself
In the land of mist and snow,
He loved the bird that loved the man
Who shot him with his bow."

The other was a softer voice,
As soft as honeydew:
Quoth he, " The man hath penance
    done,
And penance more will do."

PART VI

FIRST VOICE

" But tell me, tell me! speak again,
Thy soft response renewing —   411
What makes that ship drive on so fast?
What is the ocean doing? "

SECOND VOICE

" Still as a slave before his lord,
The ocean hath no blast;
His great bright eye most silently
Up to the Moon is cast —

---

348. corses: corpses.   **362. jargoning:** singing.   **394. I . . . declare:** I cannot say.

If he may know which way to go;
For she guides him smooth or grim.
See, brother, see! how graciously   420
She looketh down on him."

FIRST VOICE

The Mariner
hath been
cast into a
trance; for
the angelic
power caus-
eth the vessel
to drive north-
ward faster
than human
life could
endure.

"But why drives on that ship so fast,
Without or wave or wind?"

SECOND VOICE

"The air is cut away before,
And closes from behind.

Fly, brother, fly! more high, more high!
Or we shall be belated:
For slow and slow that ship will go,
When the Mariner's trance is abated."

The super-
natural mo-
tion is re-
tarded; the
Mariner
awakes, and
his penance
begins anew.

I woke, and we were sailing on   430
As in a gentle weather:
'Twas night, calm night, the moon was
          high;
The dead men stood together.

All stood together on the deck,
For a charnel-dungeon° fitter:
All fixed on me their stony eyes,
That in the Moon did glitter.

The pang, the curse, with which they
          died,
Had never passed away:
I could not draw my eyes from theirs,
Nor turn them up to pray.   441

The curse is
finally expi-
ated.

And now this spell was snapt: once
          more
I viewed the ocean green,
And looked far forth, yet little saw
Of what had else been seen —

Like one, that on a lonesome road
Doth walk in fear and dread,
And having once turned round walks
          on,
And turns no more his head;
Because he knows a frightful fiend
Doth close behind him tread.   451

But soon there breathed a wind on me,
Nor sound nor motion made:
Its path was not upon the sea,
In ripple or in shade.

It raised my hair, it fanned my cheek
Like a meadow-gale of spring —
It mingled strangely with my fears,
Yet it felt like a welcoming.

Swiftly, swiftly flew the ship,   460
Yet she sailed softly too:
Sweetly, sweetly blew the breeze —
On me alone it blew.

And the an-
cient Mariner
beholdeth his
native coun-
try.

Oh! dream of joy! is this indeed
The lighthouse top I see?
Is this the hill? is this the kirk?
Is this mine own countree?

We drifted o'er the harbor-bar,
And I with sobs did pray —
O let me be awake, my God!   470
Or let me sleep alway.

The harbor-bay was clear as glass,
So smoothly it was strewn!
And on the bay the moonlight lay,
And the shadow of the Moon.

The rock shone bright, the kirk no less,
That stands above the rock:
The moonlight steeped in silentness
The steady weathercock.

And the bay was white with silent
          light,   480
Till rising from the same,
Full many shapes, that shadows were,
In crimson colors came.

The angelic
spirits leave
the dead
bodies,

And appear
in their own
forms of light.

A little distance from the prow
Those crimson shadows were:
I turned my eyes upon the deck —
Oh, Christ! what saw I there!

Each corse lay flat, lifeless and flat,
And, by the holy rood!°
A man all light, a seraph° man,   490
On every corse there stood.

This seraph band, each waved his
          hand:
It was a heavenly sight!
They stood as signals to the land,
Each one a lovely light;

This seraph band, each waved his hand,
No voice did they impart —
No voice; but oh! the silence sank
Like music on my heart.

---

435. charnel-dungeon: an underground prison, its occupants
abandoned to death and decay.

489. rood: cross.   **490. seraph:** luminiferous angel, higher in
rank than a cherub.

But soon I heard the dash of oars, 500
I heard the Pilot's cheer;
My head was turned perforce away
And I saw a boat appear.

The Pilot and the Pilot's boy,
I heard them coming fast:
Dear Lord in Heaven! it was a joy
The dead men could not blast.

I saw a third — I heard his voice:
It is the Hermit good!
He singeth loud his godly hymns   510
That he makes in the wood.
He'll shrieve° my soul, he'll wash away
The Albatross's blood.

PART VII

The Hermit of the Wood,

This Hermit good lives in that wood
Which slopes down to the sea.
How loudly his sweet voice he rears!
He loves to talk with mariners
That come from a far countree.

He kneels at morn, and noon, and
    eve —
He hath a cushion plump: 520
It is the moss that wholly hides
The rotted old oak stump.

The skiff boat neared: I heard them
    talk,
"Why, this is strange, I trow!
Where are those lights so many and
    fair,
That signal made but now?"

Approacheth the ship with wonder.

"Strange, by my faith!" the Hermit
    said —
"And they answered not our cheer!
The planks look warped! and see
    those sails,
How thin they are and sere!   530
I never saw aught like to them,
Unless perchance it were

Brown skeletons of leaves that lag
My forest-brook along;
When the ivy tod° is heavy with snow,
And the owlet whoops to the wolf be-
    low,
That eats the she-wolf's young."

"Dear Lord! it hath a fiendish look —
(The Pilot made reply)
I am afeared" — "Push on, push on!"
Said the Hermit cheerily.   541

The boat came closer to the ship,
But I nor spake nor stirred;
The boat came close beneath the ship,
And straight a sound was heard.

The ship suddenly sinketh.

Under the water it rumbled on,
Still louder and more dread:
It reached the ship, it split the bay;
The ship went down like lead.

The ancient Mariner is saved in the Pilot's boat.

Stunned by that loud and dreadful
    sound,   550
Which sky and ocean smote,
Like one that hath been seven days
    drowned
My body lay afloat;
But swift as dreams, myself I found
Within the Pilot's boat.

Upon the whirl, where sank the ship,
The boat spun round and round;
And all was still, save that the hill
Was telling of the sound.

I moved my lips — the Pilot shrieked
And fell down in a fit;   561
The holy Hermit raised his eyes,
And prayed where he did sit.

I took the oars: the Pilot's boy,
Who now doth crazy go,
Laughed loud and long, and all the
    while
His eyes went to and fro.
"Ha! ha!" quoth he, "full plain I
    see,
The Devil knows how to row."

And now, all in my own countree,
I stood on the firm land!   571
The Hermit stepped forth from the
    boat,
And scarcely he could stand.

The ancient Mariner earnestly entreateth the Hermit to shrieve him; and the penance of life falls on him.

"O shrieve me, shrieve me, holy man!"
The Hermit crossed° his brow.
"Say quick," quoth he, "I bid thee
    say —
What manner of man art thou?"

---

512. shrieve: shrive, listen to penitential confession.   **535. tod:**
bush.

575. crossed: made the sign of the cross.

Forthwith this frame of mine was
    wrenched
With a woful agony,
Which forced me to begin my tale;
And then it left me free.   581

And ever and anon throughout his future life an agony constraineth him to travel from land to land;

Since then, at an uncertain hour,
That agony returns:
And till my ghastly tale is told,
This heart within me burns.

I pass, like night, from land to land;
I have strange power of speech;
That moment that his face I see,
I know the man that must hear me:
To him my tale I teach.   590

What loud uproar bursts from that
    door!
The wedding guests are there:
But in the garden-bower the bride
And bridemaids singing are:
And hark the little vesper bell,
Which biddeth me to prayer!

O Wedding Guest! this soul hath been
Alone on a wide wide sea:
So lonely 'twas, that God himself
Scarce seemèd there to be.   600

O sweeter than the marriage feast,
'Tis sweeter far to me,
To walk together to the kirk
With a goodly company! —

To walk together to the kirk,
And all together pray,
While each to his great Father bends,
Old men, and babes, and loving friends
And youths and maidens gay!

And to teach, by his own example, love and reverence to all things that God made and loveth.

Farewell, farewell! but this I tell   610
To thee, thou Wedding Guest!
He prayeth well, who loveth well
Both man and bird and beast.

He prayeth best, who loveth best
All things both great and small;
For the dear God who loveth us,
He made and loveth all.

The Mariner, whose eye is bright,
Whose beard with age is hoar,   619
Is gone: and now the Wedding Guest
Turned from the bridegroom's door.

He went like one that hath been
    stunned,
And is of sense forlorn:°
A sadder and a wiser man,
He rose the morrow morn.

1797–98

CHRISTABEL

PREFACE

The first part of the following poem was written in the year 1797 at Stowey, in the county of Somerset. The second part, after my return from Germany, in the year 1800, at Keswick, Cumberland. It is probable that if the poem had been finished at either of the former periods, or if even the first and second part had been published in the year 1800, the impression of its originality would have been much greater than I dare at present expect. But for this I have only my own indolence to blame. The dates are mentioned for the exclusive purpose of precluding charges of plagiarism or servile imitation from myself. For there is amongst us a set of critics who seem to hold that every possible thought and image is traditional; who have no notion that there are such things as fountains in the world, small as well as great; and who would therefore charitably derive every rill they behold flowing from a perforation made in some other man's tank. I am confident, however, that as far as the present poem is concerned, the celebrated poets [1] whose writings I might be suspected of having imitated, either in particular passages, or in the tone and the spirit of the whole, would be among the first to vindicate me from the charge, and who, on any striking coincidence, would permit me to address them in this doggerel version of two monkish Latin hexameters.

    'Tis mine and it is likewise yours;
    But an if this will not do;
    Let it be mine, good friend! for I
    Am the poorer of the two.

I have only to add that the meter of Christabel is not, properly speaking, irregular, though it may seem so from its being founded on a new principle: namely, that of counting in each line the accents, not the syllables. Though the latter may vary from seven to twelve, yet in each line the accents will be found to be only four. Nevertheless, this occasional variation in number of syllables is not introduced wantonly, or for the mere ends of convenience, but in correspondence with some transition in the nature of the imagery or passion [STC].

623. forlorn: deprived. CHRISTABEL. **1. poets:** Scott and Byron.

Part I

'Tis the middle of night by the castle clock,
And the owls have awakened the crowing cock;
Tu — whit! —— Tu — whoo!
And hark, again! the crowing cock,
How drowsily it crew.

Sir Leoline, the Baron rich,
Hath a toothless mastiff bitch;
From her kennel beneath the rock
She maketh answer to the clock,
Four for the quarters, and twelve for the hour;   10
Ever and aye, by shine and shower,
Sixteen short howls, not over loud;
Some say, she sees my lady's shroud.

Is the night chilly and dark?
The night is chilly, but not dark.
The thin gray cloud is spread on high,
It covers but not hides the sky.
The moon is behind, and at the full
And yet she looks both small and dull.
The night is chill, the cloud is gray: 20
'Tis a month before the month of May,
And the spring comes slowly up this way.

The lovely lady, Christabel,
Whom her father loves so well,
What makes her in the wood so late,
A furlong from the castle gate?
She had dreams all yesternight
Of her own betrothèd knight;
And she in the midnight wood will pray
For the weal of her lover that's far away.   30

She stole along, she nothing spoke,
The sighs she heaved were soft and low,
And naught was green upon the oak
But moss and rarest mistletoe:
She kneels beneath the huge oak tree,
And in silence prayeth she.

The lady sprang up suddenly,
The lovely lady, Christabel!
It moaned as near, as near can be,
But what it is she cannot tell. —   40
On the other side it seems to be,
Of the huge, broad-breasted, old oak tree.

The night is chill; the forest bare;
Is it the wind that moaneth bleak?
There is not wind enough in the air
To move away the ringlet curl
From the lovely lady's cheek —
There is not wind enough to twirl

The one red leaf, the last of its clan,
That dances as often as dance it can,   50
Hanging so light, and hanging so high,
On the topmost twig that looks up at the sky.

Hush, beating heart of Christabel!
Jesu, Maria, shield her well!
She folded her arms beneath her cloak,
And stole to the other side of the oak.
    What sees she there?

There she sees a damsel bright,
Drest in a silken robe of white,
That shadowy in the moonlight shone: 60
The neck that made that white robe wan,
Her stately neck, and arms were bare;
Her blue-veined feet unsandeled were,
And wildly glittered here and there
The gems entangled in her hair.

I guess, 'twas frightful there to see
A lady so richly clad as she —
Beautiful exceedingly!

Mary mother, save me now!
(Said Christabel,) And who art thou?   70

The lady strange made answer meet,
And her voice was faint and sweet: —
Have pity on my sore distress,
I scarce can speak for weariness:
Stretch forth thy hand, and have no fear!
Said Christabel, How camest thou here?
And the lady, whose voice was faint and sweet,
Did thus pursue her answer meet: —

My sire is of a noble line,
And my name is Geraldine:
Five warriors seized me yestermorn,
Me, even me, a maid forlorn:
They choked my cries with force and fright,
And tied me on a palfrey white.
The palfrey was as fleet as wind,
And they rode furiously behind.
They spurred amain,° their steeds were white:
And once we crossed the shade of night.
As sure as Heaven shall rescue me,
I have no thought what men they be;   90
Nor do I know how long it is
(For I have lain entranced I wis)
Since one, the tallest of the five,
Took me from the palfrey's back,
A weary woman, scarce alive.
Some muttered words his comrades spoke:
He placed me underneath this oak;

87. amain: at full speed.

He swore they would return with haste;
Whither they went I cannot tell —
I thought I heard, some minutes past,   100
Sounds as of a castle bell.
Stretch forth thy hand (thus ended she),
And help a wretched maid to flee.

Then Christabel stretched forth her hand,
And comforted fair Geraldine:
O well, bright dame! may you command
The service of Sir Leoline;
And gladly our stout chivalry
Will he send forth and friends withal
To guide and guard you safe and free   110
Home to your noble father's hall.

She rose: and forth with steps they passed
That strove to be, and were not, fast.
Her gracious stars the lady blest,
And thus spake on sweet Christabel:
All our household are at rest,
The hall as silent as the cell;
Sir Leoline is weak in health,
And may not well awakened be,
But we will move as if in stealth,   120
And I beseech your courtesy,
This night, to share your couch with me.

They crossed the moat, and Christabel
Took the key that fitted well;
A little door she opened straight,
All in the middle of the gate;
The gate that was ironed within and without,
Where an army in battle array had marched out.
The lady sank, belike through pain,
And Christabel with might and main   130
Lifted her up, a weary weight,
Over the threshold of the gate:
Then the lady rose again,
And moved, as she were not in pain.

So free from danger, free from fear,
They crossed the court: right glad they were.
And Christabel devoutly cried
To the lady by her side,
Praise we the Virgin all divine
Who hath rescued thee from thy distress!   140

Alas, alas! said Geraldine,
I cannot speak for weariness.
So free from danger, free from fear,
They crossed the court: right glad they were.

Outside her kennel, the mastiff old
Lay fast asleep, in moonshine cold.
The mastiff old did not awake,
Yet she an angry moan did make!

And what can ail the mastiff bitch?
Never till now she uttered yell   150
Beneath the eye of Christabel.
Perhaps it is the owlet's scritch:°
For what can ail the mastiff bitch?

They passed the hall, that echoes still,
Pass as lightly as you will!
The brands were flat, the brands were dying,
Amid their own white ashes lying;
But when the lady passed, there came
A tongue of light, a fit of flame;
And Christabel saw the lady's eye,   160
And nothing else saw she thereby,
Save the boss of the shield of Sir Leoline tall,
Which hung in a murky old niche in the
     wall.
O softly tread, said Christabel,
My father seldom sleepeth well.

Sweet Christabel her feet doth bare,
And jealous of the listening air
They steal their way from stair to stair,
Now in glimmer, and now in gloom,
And now they pass the Baron's room,   170
As still as death, with stifled breath!
And now have reached her chamber door;
And now doth Geraldine press down
The rushes of the chamber floor.

The moon shines dim in the open air,
And not a moonbeam enters here.
But they without its light can see
The chamber carved so curiously,
Carved with figures strange and sweet,
All made out of the carver's brain,   180
For a lady's chamber meet:
The lamp with twofold silver chain
Is fastened to an angel's feet.

The silver lamp burns dead and dim;
But Christabel the lamp will trim.
She trimmed the lamp, and made it bright,
And left it swinging to and fro,
While Geraldine, in wretched plight,
Sank down upon the floor below.
O weary lady, Geraldine,   190
I pray you, drink this cordial wine!
It is a wine of virtuous powers;
My mother made it of wild flowers.

And will your mother pity me,
Who am a maiden most forlorn?
Christabel answered — Woe is me!
She died the hour that I was born.

152. scritch: screech.

I have heard the gray-haired friar tell
How on her deathbed she did say,
That she should hear the castle bell   200
Strike twelve upon my wedding day.
O mother dear! that thou wert here!
I would, said Geraldine, she were!

But soon with altered voice, said she —
"Off, wandering mother! Peak° and pine!
I have power to bid thee flee."
Alas! what ails poor Geraldine?
Why stares she with unsettled eye?
Can she the bodiless dead espy?
And why with hollow voice cries she,   210
"Off, woman, off! this hour is mine —
Though thou her guardian spirit be,
Off, woman, off! 'tis given to me."

Then Christabel knelt by the lady's side,
And raised to heaven her eyes so blue —
Alas! said she, this ghastly ride —
Dear lady! it hath wildered you!
The lady wiped her moist cold brow,
And faintly said, "'Tis over now!"

Again the wild-flower wine she drank: 220
Her fair large eyes 'gan glitter bright,
And from the floor whereon she sank,
The lofty lady stood upright:
She was most beautiful to see,
Like a lady of a far countree.

And thus the lofty lady spake —
"All they who live in the upper sky,
Do love you, holy Christabel!
And you love them, and for their sake
And for the good which me befell,   230
Even I in my degree will try,
Fair maiden, to requite you well.
But now unrobe yourself; for I
Must pray, ere yet in bed I lie."

Quoth Christabel, So let it be!
And as the lady bade, did she.
Her gentle limbs did she undress,
And lay down in her loveliness.
But through her brain of weal and woe
So many thoughts moved to and fro,   240
That vain it were her lids to close;
So halfway from the bed she rose,
And on her elbow did recline
To look at the lady Geraldine.

Beneath the lamp the lady bowed,
And slowly rolled her eyes around;

Then drawing in her breath aloud,
Like one that shuddered, she unbound
The cincture from beneath her breast:
Her silken robe, and inner vest,   250
Dropt to her feet, and full in view,
Behold! her bosom and half her side —
A sight to dream of, not to tell!
O shield her! shield sweet Christabel!

Yet Geraldine nor speaks nor stirs;
Ah! what a stricken look was hers!°
Deep from within she seems halfway
To lift some weight with sick assay,
And eyes the maid and seeks delay;
Then suddenly, as one defied,   260
Collects herself in scorn and pride,
And lay down by the Maiden's side! —
And in her arms the maid she took,
        Ah wel-a-day!
And with low voice and doleful look
These words did say:
"In the touch of this bosom there worketh a spell,
Which is lord of thy utterance, Christabel!
Thou knowest tonight, and wilt know tomorrow,
This mark of my shame, this seal of my sorrow;
        But vainly thou warrest,   271
            For this is alone in
        Thy power to declare,
            That in the dim forest
        Thou heard'st a low moaning,
And found'st a bright lady, surpassingly fair;
And didst bring her home with thee in love and
    in charity,
To shield her and shelter her from the damp air."

THE CONCLUSION TO PART I

It was a lovely sight to see
The lady Christabel, when she   280
Was praying at the old oak tree.
        Amid the jaggèd shadows
        Of mossy leafless boughs,
        Kneeling in the moonlight,
        To make her gentle vows;
Her slender palms together prest,
Heaving sometimes on her breast;
Her face resigned to bliss or bale —
Her face, oh call it fair not pale,
And both blue eyes more bright than clear,   290
Each about to have a tear.

With open eyes (ah woe is me!)
Asleep, and dreaming fearfully,
Fearfully dreaming, yet, I wis,
Dreaming that alone, which is —

---

205. Peak: grow thin.

256–61. Ah! . . . pride: these lines were added in 1828.

O sorrow and shame! Can this be she,
The lady, who knelt at the old oak tree?
And lo! the worker of these harms,
That holds the maiden in her arms,
Seems to slumber still and mild,   300
As a mother with her child.

A star hath set, a star hath risen,
O Geraldine! since arms of thine
Have been the lovely lady's prison.
O Geraldine! one hour was thine —
Thou'st had thy will! By tairn° and rill,
The night birds all that hour were still.
But now they are jubilant anew,
From cliff and tower, tu — whoo! tu — whoo!
Tu — whoo! tu — whoo! from wood and fell!° 310

And see! the lady Christabel
Gathers herself from out her trance;
Her limbs relax, her countenance
Grows sad and soft; the smooth thin lids
Close o'er her eyes; and tears she sheds —
Large tears that leave the lashes bright!
And oft the while she seems to smile
As infants at a sudden light!

Yea, she doth smile, and she doth weep,
Like a youthful hermitess,   320
Beauteous in a wilderness,
Who, praying always, prays in sleep.
And, if she move unquietly,
Perchance, 'tis but the blood so free
Comes back and tingles in her feet.
No doubt, she hath a vision sweet.
What if her guardian spirit 'twere,
What if she knew her mother near?
But this she knows, in joys and woes,
That saints will aid if men will call: 330
For the blue sky bends over all!

PART II

Each matin bell, the Baron saith,
Knells us back to a world of death.
These words Sir Leoline first said,
When he rose and found his lady dead:
These words Sir Leoline will say
Many a morn to his dying day!

And hence the custom and law began
That still at dawn the sacristan,°
Who duly pulls the heavy bell,   340
Five and forty beads° must tell
Between each stroke — a warning knell,

Which not a soul can choose but hear
From Bratha Head to Wyndermere.°

Saith Bracy the bard, So let it knell!
And let the drowsy sacristan
Still count as slowly as he can!
There is no lack of such, I ween,
As well fill up the space between.
In Langdale Pike° and Witch's Lair,   350
And Dungeon Ghyll° so foully rent,
With ropes of rock and bells of air
Three sinful sextons' ghosts are pent,
Who all give back, one after t'other,
The death-note to their living brother;
And oft too, by the knell offended,
Just as their one! two! three! is ended,
The devil mocks the doleful tale
With a merry peal from Borodale.

The air is still! through mist and cloud   360
That merry peal comes ringing loud;
And Geraldine shakes off her dread,
And rises lightly from the bed;
Puts on her silken vestments white,
And tricks her hair in lovely plight,°
And nothing doubting of her spell
Awakens the lady Christabel.
"Sleep you, sweet lady Christabel?
I trust that you have rested well."

And Christabel awoke and spied   370
The same who lay down by her side —
O rather say, the same whom she
Raised up beneath the old oak tree!
Nay, fairer yet! and yet more fair!
For she belike hath drunken deep
Of all the blessedness of sleep!
And while she spake, her looks, her air
Such gentle thankfulness declare,
That (so it seemed) her girded vests
Grew tight beneath her heaving breasts.   380
"Sure I have sinned!" said Christabel,
"Now heaven be praised if all be well!"
And in low faltering tones, yet sweet,
Did she the lofty lady greet
With such perplexity of mind
As dreams too lively leave behind.

So quickly she rose, and quickly arrayed
Her maiden limbs, and having prayed
That He, who on the cross did groan,
Might wash away her sins unknown,   390

306. tairn: small mountain lake. 310. fell: mountain. 339.
sacristan: sexton. 341. beads: prayers.

344–59. Bratha . . . Borodale: The places named in this passage
are in the Lake District. 350. Pike: peak. 351. Ghyll:
valley. 365. plight: plait, or condition.

She forthwith led fair Geraldine
To meet her sire, Sir Leoline.

The lovely maid and the lady tall
Are pacing both into the hall,
And pacing on through page and groom,
Enter the Baron's presence room.

The Baron rose, and while he prest
His gentle daughter to his breast,
With cheerful wonder in his eyes
The lady Geraldine espies,   400
And gave such welcome to the same,
As might beseem so bright a dame!

But when he heard the lady's tale,
And when she told her father's name,
Why waxed Sir Leoline so pale,
Murmuring o'er the name again,
Lord Roland de Vaux of Tryermaine?

Alas! they had been friends in youth;°
But whispering tongues can poison truth;
And constancy lives in realms above;   410
And life is thorny; and youth is vain;
And to be wroth with one we love
Doth work like madness in the brain.
And thus it chanced, as I divine,
With Roland and Sir Leoline.
Each spake words of high disdain
And insult to his heart's best brother:
They parted — ne'er to meet again!
But never either found another
To free the hollow heart from paining —   420
They stood aloof, the scars remaining,
Like cliffs which had been rent asunder;
A dreary sea now flows between; —
But neither heat, nor frost, nor thunder,
Shall wholly do away, I ween,
The marks of that which once hath been.

Sir Leoline, a moment's space,
Stood gazing on the damsel's face:
And the youthful Lord of Tryermaine
Came back upon his heart again.   430

O then the Baron forgot his age,
His noble heart swelled high with rage;
He swore by the wounds in Jesu's side
He would proclaim it far and wide,
With trump and solemn heraldry,
That they, who thus had wronged the dame,
Were base as spotted infamy!

408–26. Alas!... been: These lines appear to have been inspired by Coleridge's temporary estrangement from Robert
Southey.

" And if they dare deny the same,
My herald shall appoint a week,
And let the recreant traitors seek   440
My tourney court — that there and then
I may dislodge their reptile souls
From the bodies and forms of men! "
He spake: his eye in lightning rolls!
For the lady was ruthlessly seized; and he kenned
In the beautiful lady the child of his friend!

And now the tears were on his face,
And fondly in his arms he took
Fair Geraldine, who met the embrace,
Prolonging it with joyous look.   450
Which when she viewed, a vision fell
Upon the soul of Christabel,
The vision of fear, the touch and pain!
She shrunk and shuddered, and saw again —
(Ah, woe is me! Was it for thee,
Thou gentle maid! such sights to see?)

Again she saw that bosom old,
Again she felt that bosom cold,
And drew in her breath with a hissing sound:
Whereat the Knight turned wildly round,   460
And nothing saw, but his own sweet maid
With eyes upraised, as one that prayed.

The touch, the sight, had passed away,
And in its stead that vision blest,
Which comforted her after rest
While in the lady's arms she lay,
Had put a rapture in her breast,
And on her lips and o'er her eyes
Spread smiles like light!
                         With new surprise,
" What ails then my belovèd child? "   470
The Baron said — His daughter mild
Made answer, " All will yet be well! "
I ween, she had no power to tell
Aught else: so mighty was the spell.

Yet he, who saw this Geraldine,
Had deemed her sure a thing divine:
Such sorrow with such grace she blended,
As if she feared she had offended
Sweet Christabel, that gentle maid!
And with such lowly tones she prayed   480
She might be sent without delay
Home to her father's mansion.
                              " Nay!
" Nay, by my soul! " said Leoline.
" Ho! Bracy the bard, the charge be thine!
Go thou, with music sweet and loud,
And take two steeds with trappings proud,

And take the youth whom thou lov'st best
To bear thy harp, and learn thy song,
And clothe you both in solemn vest,
And over the mountains haste along,   490
Lest wandering folk, that are abroad,
Detain you on the valley road.

" And when he has crossed the Irthing flood,
My merry bard! he hastes, he hastes
Up Knorren Moor, through Halegarth Wood,
And reaches soon that castle good
Which stands and threatens Scotland's wastes.

" Bard Bracy! bard Bracy! your horses are fleet,
Ye must ride up the hall, your music so sweet,
More loud than your horses' echoing feet!   500
And loud and loud to Lord Roland call,
Thy daughter is safe in Langdale hall!
Thy beautiful daughter is safe and free —
Sir Leoline greets thee thus through me!
He bids thee come without delay
With all thy numerous array
And take thy lovely daughter home:
And he will meet thee on the way
With all his numerous array
White with their panting palfreys' foam: 510
And, by mine honor! I will say,
That I repent me of the day
When I spake words of fierce disdain
To Roland de Vaux of Tryermaine! —
— For since that evil hour hath flown,
Many a summer's sun hath shone;
Yet ne'er found I a friend again
Like Roland de Vaux of Tryermaine.

The lady fell, and clasped his knees,
Her face upraised, her eyes o'erflowing;   520
And Bracy replied, with faltering voice,
His gracious Hail on all bestowing! —
" Thy words, thou sire of Christabel,
Are sweeter than my harp can tell;
Yet might I gain a boon of thee,
This day my journey should not be,
So strange a dream hath come to me,
That I had vowed with music loud
To clear yon wood from thing unblest,
Warned by a vision in my rest!   530
For in my sleep I saw that dove,
That gentle bird, whom thou dost love,
And call'st by thy own daughter's name —
Sir Leoline! I saw the same
Fluttering, and uttering fearful moan,
Among the green herbs in the forest alone.
Which when I saw and when I heard,
I wondered what might ail the bird;

For nothing near it could I see,
Save the grass and green herbs underneath the old
    tree.   540
" And in my dream methought I went
To search out what might there be found;
And what the sweet bird's trouble meant,
That thus lay fluttering on the ground.
I went and peered, and could descry
No cause for her distressful cry;
But yet for her dear lady's sake
I stooped, methought, the dove to take,
When lo! I saw a bright green snake
Coiled around its wings and neck.   550
Green as the herbs on which it couched,
Close by the dove's its head it crouched;
And with the dove it heaves and stirs,
Swelling its neck as she swelled hers!
I woke; it was the midnight hour,
The clock was echoing in the tower;
But though my slumber was gone by,
This dream it would not pass away —
It seems to live upon my eye!
And thence I vowed this selfsame day   560
With music strong and saintly song
To wander through the forest bare,
Lest aught unholy loiter there."

Thus Bracy said: the Baron, the while,
Half listening heard him with a smile;
Then turned to Lady Geraldine,
His eyes made up of wonder and love;
And said in courtly accents fine,
" Sweet maid, Lord Roland's beauteous dove,
With arms more strong than harp or song,   570
Thy sire and I will crush the snake! "
He kissed her forehead as he spake,
And Geraldine in maiden wise
Casting down her large bright eyes,
With blushing cheek and courtesy fine
She turned her from Sir Leoline;
Softly gathering up her train,
That o'er her right arm fell again;
And folded her arms across her chest,
And couched her head upon her breast,   580
And looked askance at Christabel ——
Jesu, Maria, shield her well!

A snake's small eye blinks dull and shy;
And the lady's eyes they shrunk in her head,
Each shrunk up to a serpent's eye,
And with somewhat of malice, and more of
    dread,
At Christabel she looked askance! —
One moment — and the sight was fled!
But Christabel in dizzy trance
Stumbling on the unsteady ground   590

Shuddered aloud, with a hissing sound;
And Geraldine again turned round,
And like a thing that sought relief,
Full of wonder and full of grief,
She rolled her large bright eyes divine
Wildly on Sir Leoline.

The maid, alas! her thoughts are gone,
She nothing sees — no sight but one!
The maid, devoid of guile and sin,
I know not how, in fearful wise,   600
So deeply had she drunken in
That look, those shrunken serpent eyes,
That all her features were resigned
To this sole image in her mind:
And passively did imitate
That look of dull and treacherous hate!
And thus she stood, in dizzy trance,
Still picturing that look askance
With forced unconscious sympathy
Full before her father's view ——   610
As far as such a look could be
In eyes so innocent and blue!

And when the trance was o'er, the maid
Paused awhile, and inly prayed:
Then falling at the Baron's feet,
"By my mother's soul do I entreat
That thou this woman send away!"
She said: and more she could not say:
For what she knew she could not tell,
O'ermastered by the mighty spell.   620

Why is thy cheek so wan and wild,
Sir Leoline? Thy only child
Lies at thy feet, thy joy, thy pride,
So fair, so innocent, so mild;
The same, for whom thy lady died!
O by the pangs of her dear mother
Think thou no evil of thy child!
For her, and thee, and for no other,
She prayed the moment ere she died:
Prayed that the babe for whom she died,   630
Might prove her dear lord's joy and pride!
  That prayer her deadly pangs beguiled,
    Sir Leoline!
  And wouldst thou wrong thy only child,
    Her child and thine?

Within the Baron's heart and brain
If thoughts, like these, had any share,
They only swelled his rage and pain,
And did but work confusion there.
His heart was cleft with pain and rage,   640
His cheeks they quivered, his eyes were wild,
Dishonored thus in his old age;
Dishonored by his only child,

And all his hospitality
To the wronged daughter of his friend
By more than woman's jealousy
Brought thus to a disgraceful end —
He rolled his eye with stern regard
Upon the gentle minstrel bard,
And said in tones abrupt, austere —   650
"Why, Bracy! dost thou loiter here?
I bade thee hence!" The bard obeyed;
And turning from his own sweet maid,
The agèd knight, Sir Leoline,
Led forth the lady Geraldine!

The Conclusion to Part II

A little child, a limber elf,
Singing, dancing to itself,
A fairy thing with red round cheeks,
That always finds, and never seeks,
Makes such a vision to the sight   660
As fills a father's eyes with light;
And pleasures flow in so thick and fast
Upon his heart, that he at last
Must needs express his love's excess
With words of unmeant bitterness.
Perhaps 'tis pretty to force together
Thoughts so all unlike each other;
To mutter and mock a broken charm,
To dally with wrong that does no harm.
Perhaps 'tis tender too and pretty   670
At each wild word to feel within
A sweet recoil of love and pity.
And what, if in a world of sin
(O sorrow and shame should this be true!)
Such giddiness of heart and brain
Comes seldom save from rage and pain,
So talks as it's most used to do.

1797?–1801

FROST AT MIDNIGHT

This is one of Coleridge's "Conversation Poems." Invariably written in blank verse, these poems begin with the speaker, always Coleridge (he may or may not have an audience), in a mood of "wise passiveness": his mind is relaxed, almost quiescent, but his senses are exquisitely awake to the objects at hand, indoors or out. Gradually the involuntary activity of the senses rouses the mind from lethargy; an idea or emotion, usually the product of association and memory, comes into focus, and the poem gains in intensity and mounts to a crisis. Then in gentle decrescendo poem and speaker come full circle as they return to the random peacefulness of the beginning. Meanwhile, however, something of value has been added, and the reader turns from the poem a wiser, if not a sadder, man.

The frost performs its secret ministry,
Unhelped by any wind. The owlet's cry
Came loud — and hark, again! loud as before.
The inmates of my cottage, all at rest,
Have left me to that solitude, which suits
Abstruser musings: save that at my side
My cradled infant° slumbers peacefully.
'Tis calm indeed! so calm, that it disturbs
And vexes meditation with its strange
And extreme silentness. Sea, hill, and wood,　10
This populous village! Sea, and hill, and wood,
With all the numberless goings-on of life,
Inaudible as dreams! the thin blue flame
Lies on my low-burnt fire, and quivers not;
Only that film,° which fluttered on the grate,
Still flutters there, the sole unquiet thing.
Methinks, its motion in this hush of nature
Gives it dim sympathies with me who live,
Making it a companionable form,
Whose puny flaps and freaks the idling spirit　20
By its own moods interprets, everywhere
Echo or mirror seeking of itself,
And makes a toy of thought.

　　　　　　　　　　　But O! how oft,
How oft, at school,° with most believing mind,
Presageful, have I gazed upon the bars,
To watch that fluttering *stranger!* and as oft
With unclosed lids, already had I dreamt
Of my sweet birthplace, and the old church tower,
Whose bells, the poor man's only music, rang
From morn to evening, all the hot fair-day,　30
So sweetly, that they stirred and haunted me
With a wild pleasure, falling on mine ear
Most like articulate sounds of things to come!
So gazed I, till the soothing things, I dreamt,
Lulled me to sleep, and sleep prolonged my dreams!
And so I brooded all the following morn,
Awed by the stern preceptor's° face, mine eye
Fixed with mock study on my swimming book:
Save if the door half opened, and I snatched
A hasty glance, and still my heart leaped up,　40
For still I hoped to see the *stranger's* face,
Townsman, or aunt, or sister more beloved,
My playmate° when we both were clothed alike!

　Dear babe, that sleepest cradled by my side,
Whose gentle breathings, heard in this deep calm,
Fill up the interspersèd vacancies

And momentary pauses of the thought!
My babe so beautiful! it thrills my heart
With tender gladness, thus to look at thee,
And think that thou shalt learn far other lore,　50
And in far other scenes! For I was reared
In the great city, pent 'mid cloisters dim,
And saw nought lovely but the sky and stars.°
But *thou,* my babe! shalt wander like a breeze
By lakes and sandy shores, beneath the crags
Of ancient mountain, and beneath the clouds,
Which image in their bulk both lakes and shores
And mountain crags: so shalt thou see and hear
The lovely shapes and sounds intelligible
Of that eternal language, which thy God　60
Utters, who from eternity doth teach
Himself in all, and all things in himself.
Great universal Teacher! he shall mold
Thy spirit, and by giving make it ask.

　Therefore all seasons shall be sweet to thee,
Whether the summer clothe the general earth
With greenness, or the redbreast sit and sing
Betwixt the tufts of snow on the bare branch
Of mossy apple tree, while the nigh thatch
Smokes in the sun-thaw; whether the eave drops
　fall　70
Heard only in the trances of the blast,
Or if the secret ministry of frost
Shall hang them up in silent icicles,
Quietly shining to the quiet moon.

　　　　　　　　　　　　　　　1798

KUBLA KHAN

OR, A VISION IN A DREAM. A FRAGMENT.

　The following fragment is here published at the request of a poet of great and deserved celebrity,[1] and, as far as the author's own opinions are concerned, rather as a psychological curiosity than on the ground of any supposed *poetic* merits.

　In the summer of the year 1797, the author, then in ill health, had retired to a lonely farmhouse between Porlock and Linton, on the Exmoor confines of Somerset and Devonshire. In consequence of a slight indisposition, an anodyne had been prescribed, from the effects of which he fell asleep in his chair at the moment that he was reading the following sentence, or words of the same substance, in "Purchas's Pilgrimage": "Here the Khan Kubla commanded a palace to be built, and a stately garden thereunto. And thus ten miles of fertile ground were inclosed with a wall." The author continued for about three hours in a profound sleep, at least of the external senses, during which

FROST AT MIDNIGHT. **7. infant:** Hartley Coleridge. **15. film:** "In all parts of the kingdom these films are called *strangers* and supposed to portend the arrival of some absent friend" [C]. **24. school:** Christ's Hospital, London, **37. stern preceptor:** Boyer, master of Christ's Hospital; he once knocked Coleridge down and flogged him for saying that because he was an infidel he wished to become a cobbler instead of a clergyman. **43. playmate:** his sister Ann.

51–53. For . . . stars: Compare these lines with *The Prelude*, VIII.433-34 ("I did not pine like one in cities bred,/As was thy melancholy lot, dear friend"). KUBLA KHAN. **1. celebrity:** Byron.

time he has the most vivid confidence, that he could not have composed less than from two to three hundred lines; if that indeed can be called composition in which all the images rose up before him as *things,* with a parallel production of the correspondent expressions, without any sensation or consciousness of effort. On awaking he appeared to himself to have a distinct recollection of the whole, and taking his pen, ink, and paper, instantly and eagerly wrote down the lines that are here preserved. At this moment he was unfortunately called out by a person on business from Porlock and detained by him above an hour, and on his return to his room, found, to his no small surprise and mortification, that though he still retained some vague and dim recollection of the general purport of the vision, yet, with the exception of some eight or ten scattered lines and images, all the rest had passed away like the images on the surface of a stream into which a stone has been cast, but, alas! without the after restoration of the latter!

> Then all the charm
> Is broken — all that phantom world so fair
> Vanishes, and a thousand circlets spread,
> And each misshape[s] the other. Stay awhile,
> Poor youth! who scarcely dar'st lift up thine eyes —
> The stream will soon renew its smoothness, soon
> The visions will return! And lo, he stays,
> And soon the fragments dim of lovely forms
> Come trembling back, unite, and now once more
> The pool becomes a mirror.
> > ["The Picture, or the Lover's
> > Resolution," ll. 91–100]

Yet from the still surviving recollections in his mind, the author has frequently purposed to finish for himself what had been originally, as it were, given to him. Σαμερον αδιον ασω: [2] but the tomorrow is yet to come [STC].

In Xanadu did Kubla Khan°
A stately pleasure dome decree:
Where Alph, the sacred river, ran
Through caverns measureless to man
    Down to a sunless sea.
So twice five miles of fertile ground
With walls and towers were girdled round:
And there were gardens bright with sinuous rills,
Where blossomed many an incense-bearing tree;
And here were forests ancient as the hills,   10
Enfolding sunny spots of greenery.
But oh! that deep romantic chasm which slanted
Down the green hill athwart a cedarn cover!
A savage place! as holy and enchanted
As e'er beneath a waning moon was haunted

By woman wailing for her demon lover!
And from this chasm, with ceaseless turmoil seething,
As if this earth in fast thick pants were breathing,
A mighty fountain momently was forced:
Amid whose swift half-intermitted burst   20
Huge fragments vaulted like rebounding hail,
Or chaffy grain beneath the thresher's flail:
And 'mid these dancing rocks at once and ever
It flung up momently the sacred river.
Five miles meandering with a mazy motion
Through wood and dale the sacred river ran,
Then reached the caverns measureless to man,
And sank in tumult to a lifeless ocean:
And 'mid this tumult Kubla heard from far
Ancestral voices prophesying war!   30
    The shadow of the dome of pleasure
    Floated midway on the waves;
    Where was heard the mingled measure
    From the fountain and the caves.
It was a miracle of rare device,
A sunny pleasure dome with caves of ice!

A damsel with a dulcimer
In a vision once I saw:
It was an Abyssinian maid,
And on her dulcimer she played,   40
Singing of Mount Abora.
Could I revive within me
Her symphony and song,
To such a deep delight 'twould win me,
That with music loud and long,
I would build that dome in air,
That sunny dome! those caves of ice!
And all who heard should see them there,
And all should cry, Beware! Beware!
His flashing eyes, his floating hair!   50
Weave a circle round him thrice,°
And close your eyes with holy dread,
For he on honeydew hath fed,
And drunk the milk of Paradise.

                    1797?–1800

DEJECTION: AN ODE

WRITTEN APRIL 4, 1802

Coleridge wrote the first draft of this poem after hearing Dorothy Wordsworth read from her brother's most recently composed poems, "The Rainbow" and the opening stanzas of the "Intimations Ode" among them. Originally "Dejection" was a verse letter to Sara Hutchinson that ran to 338 lines in which Coleridge expatiated on his domestic misery and its sad

---

2. "I will sing you a sweeter song tomorrow" (Theocritus, *Idylls,* I.145).   1. Xanadu . . . Khan: Xanadu, named variously Xamdu, Xaindu, and Xandu by Samuel Purchas, was probably situated near what is now Peiping; it was the seat of Kublai Khan (1216–94), grandson of Genghis Khan and founder of the Mongol dynasty in China.

51. Weave . . . thrice: to exorcise or forestall any evil spirit which might possess him.

contrast with Wordsworth's happiness. During the summer Coleridge worked at the poem, reduced it to its present length and changed the name "Sara" first to "William" (Wordsworth), then to "Edmund," and finally to "Lady." When it first appeared, in the *Morning Post* of October 4, 1802 — Wordsworth's wedding day — "Dejection," the poem in which Coleridge announced the loss of his "shaping spirit of imagination," turned out paradoxically to be one of the best poems his imagination had ever shaped.

> Late, late yestreen I saw the new moon,
> With the old moon in her arms;
> And I fear, I fear, my master dear!
> We shall have a deadly storm.
> ["Ballad of Sir Patrick Spence"]

I

Well! If the bard was weather-wise, who made
  The grand old ballad of Sir Patrick Spence,
  This night, so tranquil now, will not go hence
Unroused by winds, that ply a busier trade
Than those which mold yon cloud in lazy flakes,
Or the dull sobbing draft, that moans and rakes
Upon the strings of this Eolian lute,°
  Which better far were mute.
  For lo! the new moon winter-bright!
  And overspread with phantom light,   10
  (With swimming phantom light o'erspread
  But rimmed and circled by a silver thread)
I see the old moon in her lap, foretelling
  The coming on of rain and squally blast.
And oh! that even now the gust were swelling,
  And the slant night shower driving loud and fast!
Those sounds which oft have raised me, whilst they awed,
  And sent my soul abroad,
Might now perhaps their wonted° impulse give,
Might startle this dull pain, and make it move and
  live!   20

II

A grief without a pang, void, dark, and drear,
A stifled, drowsy, unimpassioned grief,
Which finds no natural outlet, no relief,
  In word, or sigh, or tear —
O Lady!° in this wan and heartless mood,
To other thoughts by yonder throstle wooed,
  All this long eve, so balmy and serene,
Have I been gazing on the western sky,
  And its peculiar tint of yellow green:
And still I gaze — and with how blank an eye! 30

DEJECTION: AN ODE. **7. Eolian lute:** Eolian harp; named after Eolus, god of the winds, the harp was boxshaped with strings stretched across its open ends; a movement of air would cause the strings to vibrate and produce crude music. **19. wonted:** usual. **25. Lady:** Sara Hutchinson (see headnote).

And those thin clouds above, in flakes and bars,
That give away their motion to the stars;
Those stars, that glide behind them or between,
Now sparkling, now bedimmed, but always seen:
Yon crescent moon, as fixed as if it grew
In its own cloudless, starless lake of blue;
I see them all so excellently fair,
I see, not feel, how beautiful they are!

III

  My genial spirits fail;
  And what can these avail   40
To lift the smothering weight from off my breast?
  It were a vain endeavor,
  Though I should gaze forever
On that green light that lingers in the west:
I may not hope from outward forms to win
The passion and the life, whose fountains are
  within.

IV

O Lady! we receive but what we give,
And in our life alone does Nature live:
Ours is her wedding garment, ours her shroud!
  And would we aught behold, of higher worth,
Than that inanimate cold world allowed   51
To the poor loveless ever-anxious crowd,
  Ah! from the soul itself must issue forth
A light, a glory, a fair luminous cloud
  Enveloping the earth —
And from the soul itself must there be sent
  A sweet and potent voice, of its own birth,
Of all sweet sounds the life and element!

V

O pure of heart! thou need'st not ask of me
What this strong music in the soul may be!   60
What, and wherein it doth exist,
This light, this glory, this fair luminous mist,
This beautiful and beauty-making power.
  Joy, virtuous Lady! joy that ne'er was given,
Save to the pure, and in their purest hour,
Life, and life's effluence, cloud at once and shower,
Joy, Lady! is the spirit and the power,
Which wedding Nature to us gives in dower
  A new earth and new heaven,
Undreamt of by the sensual and the proud —   70
Joy is the sweet voice, joy the luminous cloud —
  We in ourselves rejoice!
And thence flows all that charms or ear or sight,
  All melodies the echoes of that voice,
All colors a suffusion from that light.

VI

There was a time when, though my path was
    rough,
This joy within me dallied with distress,
And all misfortunes were but as the stuff
    Whence fancy made me dreams of happiness:
For hope grew round me, like the twining vine, 80
And fruits, and foliage, not my own, seemed mine.
But now afflictions bow me down to earth:
Nor care I that they rob me of my mirth;
    But oh! each visitation
Suspends what nature gave me at my birth,
    My shaping spirit of imagination.
For not to think of what I needs must feel,
    But to be still and patient, all I can;
And haply by abstruse research to steal
    From my own nature all the natural man — 90
This was my sole resource, my only plan:
Till that which suits a part infects the whole,
And now is almost grown the habit of my soul.

VII

Hence, viper thoughts, that coil around my mind,
    Reality's dark dream!
I turn from you, and listen to the wind,
    Which long has raved unnoticed. What a scream
Of agony by torture lengthened out
That lute sent forth! Thou wind, that rav'st with-
    out,
    Bare crag, or mountain tairn,° or blasted
        tree,   100
Or pine grove whither woodman never clomb,
Or lonely house, long held the witches' home,
    Methinks were fitter instruments for thee,
Mad lutanist!° who in this month of showers,
Of dark-brown gardens, and of peeping flowers,
Mak'st devils' yule,° with worse than wintry song,
The blossoms, buds, and timorous leaves among.
    Thou actor, perfect in all tragic sounds!
Thou mighty poet, e'en to frenzy bold!
    What tell'st thou now about?   110
    'Tis of the rushing of an host in rout,
With groans, of trampled men, with smarting
    wounds —
At once they groan with pain, and shudder with
    the cold!
But hush! there is a pause of deepest silence!
    And all that noise, as of a rushing crowd,
With groans, and tremulous shudderings — all is
    over —
    It tells another tale, with sounds less deep and
        loud!

100. **tairn:** small mountain lake.   104. **Mad lutanist:** the wind.
106. **yule:** Christmas.

A tale of less affright,
And tempered with delight,
As Otway's° self had framed the tender lay, — 120
    'Tis of a little child
    Upon a lonesome wild,
Not far from home, but she hath lost her way:
And now moans low in bitter grief and fear,
And now screams loud, and hopes to make her
    mother hear.

VIII

'Tis midnight, but small thoughts have I of sleep:
Full seldom may my friend such vigils keep!
Visit her, gentle sleep! with wings of healing,
    And may this storm be but a mountain birth,
May all the stars hang bright above her dwelling,
    Silent as though they watched the sleeping earth!
    With light heart may she rise,   132
    Gay fancy, cheerful eyes,
Joy lift her spirit, joy attune her voice;
To her may all things live, from pole to pole,
Their life the eddying of her living soul!
    O simple spirit, guided from above,
Dear Lady! friend devoutest of my choice,
Thus mayest thou ever, evermore rejoice.

1802

from
BIOGRAPHIA LITERARIA

The *Biographia Literaria* found its origin in the summer of 1802 when Coleridge, having read Wordsworth's additions to the Preface to *Lyrical Ballads*
(third edition; see pp. 560–64, above), announced
in letters to friends his disagreement with some of
Wordsworth's theories and his intention to discuss
these differences in a " disquisition on the nature and
essence of poetry." Characteristically Coleridge did
nothing but talk about this project for the next thirteen years. Then, stimulated by Wordsworth's publication in March, 1815, of his collected poems, with a
new preface and supplementary essay, Coleridge determined to collect his poems and write a preface of his
own. This grew until, two years later and after incredible difficulties with his printers, Coleridge produced
his *Biographia Literaria,* in two volumes.

The title is a misnomer. Occasional autobiographical
details serve primarily to introduce and enliven discussions of Coleridge's views on philosophy, psychology, poetry, and contemporary book reviewers. In the
first volume Coleridge undertook to demonstrate that
the imagination and the fancy differed in kind, and

120. Otway: Thomas Otway (1652–85), English tragic dramatist,
noted for pathos. Originally the "tender lay" was "William's";
the "little child" (l. 121) is clearly Lucy Gray.

not, as Wordsworth had argued in 1815, merely in degree. But, after twelve chapters of labored preliminary exposition Coleridge wrote himself a letter, which he attributed to a friend, and, arguing that it would be unintelligible to the unprepared public mind, advised himself not to print the great "Chapter on the Imagination." The only part of this "Chapter" which he had in fact written was the brief and cryptic "conclusion" which appears below from Chapter XIII.

In the second volume Coleridge, working closely with the poetry of Shakespeare and Wordsworth, exhibits brilliantly the "symptoms" of poetic and imaginative power. Along the way, in chapters too lengthy for publication here, Coleridge defends the general purpose and direction of Wordsworth's theory and practice while expressing his dissent from the notion that the best language for poetry may be found among rustics, and from the argument that the language of poetry does not differ essentially from that of prose.

from CHAPTER XIII

The imagination, then, I consider either as primary, or secondary. The primary imagination I hold to be the living power and prime agent of all human perception, and as a repetition in the finite mind of the eternal act of creation in the infinite I AM. The secondary imagination I consider as an echo of the former, coexisting with the conscious will, yet still as identical with the primary in the *kind* of its agency, and differing only in *degree* and in the *mode* of its operation. It dissolves, diffuses, dissipates, in order to recreate; or where this process is rendered impossible, yet still at all events it struggles to idealize and to unify. It is essentially *vital*, even as all objects (*as* objects) are essentially fixed and dead.

Fancy, on the contrary, has no other counters to play with, but fixities and definites. The fancy is indeed no other than a mode of memory emancipated from the order of time and space; while it is blended with, and modified by that empirical phenomenon of the will, which we express by the word *choice*. But equally with the ordinary memory the fancy must receive all its materials ready made from the law of association.

CHAPTER XIV

Occasion of the Lyrical Ballads, and the objects originally proposed — Preface to the second edition — The ensuing controversy, its causes and acrimony — Philosophic definitions of a poem and poetry with scholia.

During the first year [1] that Mr. Wordsworth and I were neighbors, our conversations turned frequently on the two cardinal points of poetry, the power of exciting the sympathy of the reader by a faithful adherence to the truth of nature, and the power of giving the interest of novelty by the modifying colors of imagination. The sudden charm, which accidents of light and shade, which moonlight or sunset diffused over a known and familiar landscape, appeared to represent the practicability of combining both. These are the poetry of nature. The thought suggested itself (to which of us I do not recollect) that a series of poems might be composed of two sorts. In the one, the incidents and agents were to be, in part at least, supernatural; and the excellence aimed at was to consist in the interesting of the affections by the dramatic truth of such emotions as would naturally accompany such situations, supposing them real. And real in *this* sense they have been to every human being who, from whatever source of delusion, has at any time believed himself under supernatural agency. For the second class, subjects were to be chosen from ordinary life; the characters and incidents were to be such as will be found in every village and its vicinity where there is a meditative and feeling mind to seek after them or to notice them when they present themselves.

In this idea originated the plan of the *Lyrical Ballads* [2]; in which it was agreed that my endeavors should be directed to persons and characters supernatural, or at least romantic; yet so as to transfer from our inward nature a human interest and a semblance of truth sufficient to procure for these shadows of imagination that willing suspension of disbelief for the moment which constitutes poetic faith. Mr. Wordsworth, on the other hand, was to propose to himself as his object to give the charm of novelty to things of every day, and to excite a feeling analogous to the supernatural, by awakening the mind's attention from the lethargy of custom and directing it to the loveliness and the wonders of the world before us; an inexhaustible treasure, but for which, in consequence of the film of familiarity and selfish solicitude we have eyes, yet see not, ears that hear not, and hearts that neither feel nor understand. [3]

With this view I wrote "The Ancient Mariner," and was preparing among other poems, "The Dark

BIOGRAPHIA LITERARIA. 1. first year: 1797, at Alfoxden and Nether Stowey. 2. *Lyrical Ballads:* the first edition, 1798. 3. eyes ... understand: see Isa. 6:9–10.

Ladie," and the "Christabel," in which I should have more nearly realized my ideal than I had done in my first attempt. But Mr. Wordsworth's industry had proved so much more successful, and the number of his poems so much greater, that my compositions, instead of forming a balance, appeared rather an interpolation of heterogeneous matter. Mr. Wordsworth added two or three poems written in his own character, in the impassioned, lofty, and sustained diction, which is characteristic of his genius. In this form the *Lyrical Ballads* [4] were published; and were presented by him as an *experiment,* whether subjects, which from their nature rejected the usual ornaments and extracolloquial style of poems in general, might not be so managed in the language of ordinary life as to produce the pleasurable interest which it is the peculiar business of poetry to impart. To the second edition he added a preface of considerable length in which, notwithstanding some passages of apparently a contrary import, he was understood to contend for the extension of this style to poetry of all kinds, and to reject as vicious and indefensible all phrases and forms of style that were not included in what he (unfortunately, I think, adopting an equivocal expression) called the language of *real* life. From this preface, prefixed to poems in which it was impossible to deny the presence of original genius, however mistaken its direction might be deemed, arose the whole long-continued controversy.[5] For from the conjunction of perceived power with supposed heresy I explain the inveteracy and in some instances, I grieve to say, the acrimonious passions, with which the controversy has been conducted by the assailants.

Had Mr. Wordsworth's poems been the silly, the childish things, which they were for a long time described as being; had they been really distinguished from the compositions of other poets merely by meanness of language and inanity of thought; had they indeed contained nothing more than what is found in the parodies and pretended imitations of them; they must have sunk at once, a dead weight, into the slough of oblivion, and have dragged the preface along with them. But year after year increased the number of Mr. Wordsworth's admirers. They were found, too, not in the lower classes of the reading public, but chiefly among young men of strong sensibility and meditative minds; and their admiration (inflamed perhaps in some degree by opposition) was distinguished by its intensity, I might almost say, by its *religious* fervor. These facts, and the intellectual energy of the author, which was more or less consciously felt, where it was outwardly and even boisterously denied, meeting with sentiments of aversion to his opinions and of alarm at their consequences, produced an eddy of criticism which would of itself have borne up the poems by the violence, with which it whirled them round and round. With many parts of this preface, in the sense attributed to them, and which the words undoubtedly seem to authorize, I never concurred; but on the contrary objected to them as erroneous in principle, and as contradictory (in appearance at least) both to other parts of the same preface, and to the author's own practice in the greater number of the poems themselves. Mr. Wordsworth in his recent collection has, I find, degraded this prefatory disquisition to the end of his second volume, to be read or not at the reader's choice. But he has not, as far as I can discover, announced any change in his poetic creed. At all events, considering it as the source of a controversy, in which I have been honored more than I deserve by the frequent conjunction of my name with his, I think it expedient to declare once for all in what points I coincide with his opinions and in what points I altogether differ. But in order to render myself intelligible I must previously, in as few words as possible, explain my ideas, first, of a poem; and secondly, of poetry itself, in *kind,* and in *essence.*

The office of philosophical *disquisition* consists in just *distinction;* while it is the privilege of the philosopher to preserve himself constantly aware, that distinction is not division. In order to obtain adequate notions of any truth, we must intellectually separate its distinguishable parts; and this is the technical *process* of philosophy. But having so done, we must then restore them in our conceptions to the unity, in which they actually coexist; and this is the *result* of philosophy. A poem contains the same elements as a prose composition; the difference therefore must consist in a different combination of them, in consequence of a different object being proposed. According to the difference of the object will be the difference of the combination. It is possible, that the object may be merely to facilitate the recollection of any given facts or

4. *Lyrical Ballads:* the second edition, 1800 (actually publication was in January, 1801). 5. long-continued controversy: over Wordsworth's poetic theory and practice.

observations by artificial arrangement; and the composition will be a poem merely because it is distinguished from prose by meter or by rhyme, or by both conjointly. In this, the lowest sense, a man might attribute the name of a poem to the well-known enumeration of the days in the several months;

> Thirty days hath September,
> April, June, and November, &c.

and others of the same class and purpose. And as a particular pleasure is found in anticipating the recurrence of sounds and quantities, all compositions that have this charm superadded, whatever be their contents, *may* be entitled poems.

So much for the superficial *form*. A difference of object and contents supplies an additional ground of distinction. The immediate purpose may be the communication of truths; either of truth absolute and demonstrable, as in works of science; or of facts experienced and recorded, as in history. Pleasure, and that of the highest and most permanent kind, may *result* from the *attainment* of the end; but it is not itself the immediate end. In other works the communication of pleasure may be the immediate purpose; and though truth, either moral or intellectual, ought to be the *ultimate* end, yet this will distinguish the character of the author, not the class to which the work belongs. Blest indeed is that state of society in which the immediate purpose would be baffled by the perversion of the proper ultimate end; in which no charm of diction or imagery could exempt the Bathyllus even of an Anacreon,[6] or the Alexis of Virgil,[7] from disgust and aversion!

But the communication of pleasure may be the immediate object of a work not metrically composed; and that object may have been in a high degree attained, as in novels and romances. Would then the mere superaddition of meter, with or without rhyme, entitle *these* to the name of poems? The answer is, that nothing can permanently please which does not contain in itself the reason why it is so, and not otherwise. If meter be superadded, all other parts must be made consonant with it. They must be such as to justify the perpetual and distinct attention to each part which an exact cor-

respondent recurrence of accent and sound are calculated to excite. The final definition then, so deduced, may be thus worded. A poem is that species of composition which is opposed to works of science by proposing for its *immediate* object pleasure, not truth; and from all other species (having *this* object in common with it) it is discriminated by proposing to itself such delight from the *whole,* as is compatible with a distinct gratification from each component *part.*

Controversy is not seldom excited in consequence of the disputants attaching each a different meaning to the same word; and in few instances has this been more striking than in disputes concerning the present subject. If a man chooses to call every composition a poem which is rhyme, or measure, or both, I must leave his opinion uncontroverted. The distinction is at least competent to characterize the writer's intention. If it were subjoined that the whole is likewise entertaining or affecting as a tale, or as a series of interesting reflections, I of course admit this as another fit ingredient of a poem, and an additional merit. But if the definition sought for be that of a *legitimate* poem, I answer it must be one the parts of which mutually support and explain each other; all in their proportion harmonizing with and supporting the purpose and known influences of metrical arrangement. The philosophic critics of all ages coincide with the ultimate judgment of all countries in equally denying the praises of a just poem, on the one hand, to a series of striking lines or distichs,[8] each of which, absorbing the whole attention of the reader to itself, disjoins it from its context, and makes it a separate whole, instead of a harmonizing part; and on the other hand, to an unsustained composition from which the reader collects rapidly the general result, unattracted by the component parts. The reader should be carried forward, not merely or chiefly by the mechanical impulse of curiosity, or by a restless desire to arrive at the final solution; but by the pleasurable activity of mind excited by the attractions of the journey itself. Like the motion of a serpent, which the Egyptians made the emblem of intellectual power; or like the path of sound through the air; at every step he pauses and half recedes, and from the retrogressive movement collects the force which again carries him onward. "Praecipitandus est *liber* spiritus," [9] says Petronius

---

6. Bathyllus . . . Anacreon: Bathyllus was a beautiful boy celebrated in the odes of Anacreon, a Greek lyric poet (*ca.* 560–475 B.C.). 7. Alexis . . . Virgil: Alexis was a male slave loved by the shepherd Corydon (Virgil, *Eclogues,* II); Virgil (70–19 B.C.) was the author of the *Aeneid* and the most famous Roman poet.

8. distichs: pairs of lines, not necessarily couplets. 9. *"Praecipitandus . . . spiritus"*: "The free spirit is hurried onwards" (*Satyricon,* 118).

Arbiter [10] most happily. The epithet, *liber,* here balances the preceding verb; and it is not easy to conceive more meaning condensed in fewer words.

But if this should be admitted as a satisfactory character of a poem, we have still to seek for a definition of poetry. The writings of Plato, and Bishop Taylor,[11] and the *Theoria Sacra* [12] of Burnet, furnish undeniable proofs that poetry of the highest kind may exist without meter, and even without the contradistinguishing objects of a poem. The first chapter of Isaiah (indeed a very large portion of the whole book) is poetry in the most emphatic sense; yet it would be not less irrational than strange to assert, that pleasure, and not truth, was the immediate object of the prophet. In short, whatever *specific* import we attach to the word, poetry, there will be found involved in it, as a necessary consequence, that a poem of any length neither can be, or ought to be, all poetry. Yet if a harmonious whole is to be produced, the remaining parts must be preserved *in keeping* with the poetry; and this can be no otherwise effected than by such a studied selection and artificial arrangement as will partake of *one,* though not a *peculiar* property of poetry. And this again can be no other than the property of exciting a more continuous and equal attention than the language of prose aims at, whether colloquial or written.

My own conclusions on the nature of poetry, in the strictest use of the word, have been in part anticipated in the preceding disquisition on the fancy and imagination. What is poetry? is so nearly the same question with, what is a poet? that the answer to the one is involved in the solution of the other. For it is a distinction resulting from the poetic genius itself, which sustains and modifies the images, thoughts, and emotions of the poet's own mind.

The poet, described in *ideal* perfection, brings the whole soul of man into activity, with the subordination of its faculties to each other, according to their relative worth and dignity. He diffuses a tone and spirit of unity that blends, and (as it were) *fuses,* each into each, by that synthetic and magical power to which we have exclusively appropriated the name of imagination. This power, first put in action by the will and understanding, and retained under their irremissive, though gentle and unnoticed, control (*laxis effertur habenis* [13]) reveals itself in the balance or reconciliation of opposite or discordant qualities: of sameness with difference; of the general with the concrete; the idea with the image; the individual with the representative; the sense of novelty and freshness with old and familiar objects; a more than usual state of emotion with more than usual order; judgment ever awake and steady self-possession with enthusiasm and feeling profound or vehement; and while it blends and harmonizes the natural and the artificial, still subordinates art to nature; the manner to the matter; and our admiration of the poet to our sympathy with the poetry. " Doubtless," as Sir John Davies [14] observes of the soul (and his words may with slight alteration be applied, and even more appropriately, to the poetic imagination)

Doubtless this could not be, but that she turns
  Bodies to spirit by sublimation strange,
As fire converts to fire the things it burns,
  As we our food into our nature change.

From their gross matter she abstracts their forms,
  And draws a kind of quintessence from things;
Which to her proper nature she transforms,
  To bear them light on her celestial wings.

Thus does she, when from individual states
  She doth abstract the universal kinds;
Which then re-clothed in divers names and fates
  Steal access through our senses to our minds.

Finally, good sense is the body of poetic genius, fancy its drapery, motion its life, and imagination the soul that is everywhere and in each; and forms all into one graceful and intelligent whole.

SHAKESPEAREAN CRITICISM

Coleridge published no book under this title. On no other subject, however, did he talk and write so much or so well. When he died in 1834 he left behind in notes and marginalia tens of thousands of words devoted to England's greatest writer and his works. Jotted down in the course of Coleridge's lecture commitments from 1808 to 1818, these fragments were first collected and given a semblance of coherence by H. N. Coleridge, the poet's nephew, in *Literary Remains* (1836–39). In 1930 Professor Thomas Middleton Raysor, working from the manuscripts, and from short-

---

10. **Petronius Arbiter:** Roman satirist (A.D. ?–65) and director of amusement at the court of Nero.   11. **Bishop Taylor:** Jeremy Taylor (1613–67), an English divine whose sermons Coleridge much admired.   12. *Theoria Sacra: Telluris Theoria Sacra (The Sacred Theory of the Earth),* 1681–89, by Thomas Burnet, from whom Coleridge took the Latin motto for the "Ancient Mariner" (see p. 592, n. 1, above). Coleridge once contemplated rendering the *Sacred Theory* into English blank verse.

13. *laxis . . . habenis:* driven along with loose reins.   14. Sir John Davies: a minor English poet (1569–1626).

hand reports of the lectures not available to H. N. Coleridge, produced an expertly edited, definitive text from which the selections below are reprinted by permission of the Harvard University Press.

from HAMLET

. . . We will now pass to *Hamlet*, in order to obviate some of the general prejudices against the author, in reference to the character of the hero. Much has been objected to which ought to have been praised, and many beauties of the highest kind have been neglected because they are somewhat hidden.

The first question we should ask ourselves is — What did Shakespeare mean when he drew the character of Hamlet? He never wrote anything without design, and what was his design when he sat down to produce this tragedy? My belief is that he always regarded his story, before he began to write, much in the same light as a painter regards his canvas, before he begins to paint — as a mere vehicle for his thoughts — as the ground upon which he was to work. What then was the point to which Shakespeare directed himself in Hamlet? He intended to portray a person in whose view the external world and all its incidents and objects were comparatively dim and of no interest in themselves, and which began to interest only when they were reflected in the mirror of his mind. Hamlet beheld external things in the same way that a man of vivid imagination, who shuts his eyes, sees what has previously made an impression on his organs.

The poet places him in the most stimulating circumstances that a human being can be placed in. He is the heir apparent of a throne; his father dies suspiciously; his mother excludes her son from his throne by marrying his uncle. This is not enough; but the Ghost of the murdered father is introduced to assure the son that he was put to death by his own brother. What is the effect upon the son? — instant action and pursuit of revenge? No: endless reasoning and hesitating — constant urging and solicitation of the mind to act, and as constant an escape from action; ceaseless reproaches of himself for sloth and negligence, while the whole energy of his resolution evaporates in these reproaches. This, too, not from cowardice, for he is drawn as one of the bravest of his time — not from want of forethought or slowness of apprehension, for he sees through the very souls of all who surround

him, but merely from that aversion to action which prevails among such as have a world in themselves.

How admirable, too, is the judgment of the poet! Hamlet's own disordered fancy has not conjured up the spirit of his father; it has been seen by others: he is prepared by them to witness its reappearance, and when he does see it, Hamlet is not brought forward as having long brooded on the subject. The moment before the Ghost enters Hamlet speaks of other matters: he mentions the coldness of the night and observes that he has not heard the clock strike, adding, in reference to the custom of drinking, that it is

More honored in the breach than the observance.
[I.iv.16]

Owing to the tranquil state of his mind, he indulges in some moral reflections. Afterwards, the Ghost suddenly enters.

HOR. Look, my lord, it comes.
HAM. Angels and ministers of grace defend us!
[I.iv.38–39]

The same thing occurs in *Macbeth*: in the dagger-scene,[1] the moment before the hero sees it, he has his mind applied to some indifferent matters; " Go, tell thy mistress," &c. Thus in both cases the preternatural appearance has all the effect of abruptness, and the reader is totally divested of the notion that the figure is a vision of a highly wrought imagination.

Here Shakespeare adapts himself so admirably to the situation — in other words, so puts himself into it — that, though poetry, his language is the very language of nature. No terms associated with such feelings can occur to us so proper as those which he has employed, especially on the highest, the most august, and the most awful subjects that can interest a human being in this sentient world. That this is no mere fancy I can undertake to establish from hundreds, I might say thousands, of passages. No character he has drawn in the whole list of his plays could so well and fitly express himself as in the language Shakespeare has put into his mouth.

There is no indecision about Hamlet as far as his own sense of duty is concerned; he knows well what he ought to do, and over and over again he makes up his mind to do it. The moment the players, and the two spies set upon him, have with-

SHAKESPEAREAN CRITICISM: 1. dagger-scene: II.i.

drawn, of whom he takes leave with a line so expressive of his contempt,

Aye, so, God be wi' ye! — Now I am alone,
[II.ii.575]

he breaks out into a delirium of rage against himself for neglecting to perform the solemn duty he had undertaken, and contrasts the factitious and artificial display of feeling by the player with his own apparent indifference;

What's Hecuba to him or he to Hecuba,
That he should weep for her?
[II.ii.585–6]

Yet the player did weep for her, and was in an agony of grief at her sufferings, while Hamlet is unable to rouse himself to action in order that he may perform the command of his father, who had come from the grave to incite him to revenge: —

This is most brave,
That I, the son of a dear father murdered,
Prompted to my revenge by Heaven and Hell,
Must, like a whore, unpack my heart with words,
And fall a-cursing like a very drab,
A scullion.
[II.ii.611–16]

It is the same feeling, the same conviction of what is his duty, that makes Hamlet exclaim in a subsequent part of the tragedy:

How all occasions do inform against me
And spur my dull revenge! What is a man
If his chief good and market of his time
Be but to sleep and feed? A beast, no more.

. . . I do not know
Why yet I live to say "this thing's to do,"
Sith I have cause, and will, and strength, and means
To do't.
[IV.iv.32–35, 43–46]

Yet with all this strong conviction of duty, and with all this resolution arising out of strong conviction, nothing is done. This admirable and consistent character, deeply acquainted with his own feelings, painting them with such wonderful power and accuracy, and firmly persuaded that a moment ought not to be lost in executing the solemn charge committed to him, still yields to the same retiring from reality which is the result of having, what we express by the terms, a world within himself.

Such a mind as Hamlet's is near akin to madness. Dryden has somewhere said,

Great wit to madness nearly is allied,[2]

and he was right; for he means by "wit" that greatness of genius, which led Hamlet to a perfect knowledge of his own character, which, with all strength of motive, was so weak as to be unable to carry into act his own most obvious duty.

With all this he has a sense of imperfectness which becomes apparent when he is moralizing on the skull in the churchyard. Something is wanting to his completeness — something is deficient which remains to be supplied, and he is therefore described as attached to Ophelia. His madness is assumed, when he finds that witnesses have been placed behind the arras to listen to what passes, and when the heroine has been thrown in his way as a decoy.

Another objection has been taken by Dr. Johnson, and Shakespeare has been taxed very severely. I refer to the scene where Hamlet enters and finds his uncle praying, and refuses to take his life, excepting when he is in the height of his iniquity. To assail him at such a moment of confession and repentance, Hamlet declares,

Oh, this is hire and salary, not revenge.
[III.iii.79]

He therefore forbears and postpones his uncle's death until he can catch him in some act

That has no relish of salvation in't.
[III.iii.92]

This conduct, and this sentiment, Dr. Johnson has pronounced to be so atrocious and horrible as to be unfit to be put into the mouth of a human being. The fact, however, is that Dr. Johnson did not understand the character of Hamlet and censured accordingly: the determination to allow the guilty King to escape at such a moment is only part of the indecision and irresoluteness of the hero. Hamlet seizes hold of a pretext for not acting, when he might have acted so instantly and effectually: therefore, he again defers the revenge he was bound to seek and declares his determination to accomplish it at some time,

When he is drunk asleep, or in his rage,
Or in the incestuous pleasure of his bed.
[III.iii.89–90]

This, allow me to impress upon you most emphatically, was merely the excuse Hamlet made to

2. **Great . . . allied**: misquoted from *Absalom and Achitophel*, 163.

himself for not taking advantage of this particular and favorable moment for doing justice upon his guilty uncle at the urgent instance of the spirit of his father.

Dr. Johnson farther states that in the voyage to England Shakespeare merely follows the novel as he found it, as if the poet had no other reason for adhering to his original; but Shakespeare never followed a novel because he found such and such an incident in it, but because he saw that the story, as he read it, contributed to enforce or to explain some great truth inherent in human nature. He never could lack invention to alter or improve a popular narrative; but he did not wantonly vary from it when he knew that, as it was related, it would so well apply to his own great purpose. He saw at once how consistent it was with the character of Hamlet that, after still resolving, and still deferring, still determining to execute, and still postponing execution, he should finally, in the infirmity of his disposition, give himself up to his destiny and hopelessly place himself in the power and at the mercy of his enemies.

Even after the scene with Osric,[3] we see Hamlet

3. scene with Osric: V.ii.80–190.

still indulging in reflection, and hardly thinking of the task he has just undertaken: he is all dispatch and resolution as far as words and present intentions are concerned, but all hesitation and irresolution when called upon to carry his words and intentions into effect; so that, resolving to do everything, he does nothing. He is full of purpose but void of that quality of mind which accomplishes purpose.

Anything finer than this conception and working out of a great character is merely impossible. Shakespeare wished to impress upon us the truth that action is the chief end of existence — that no faculties of intellect, however brilliant, can be considered valuable, or indeed otherwise than as misfortunes, if they withdraw us from or render us repugnant to action, and lead us to think and think of doing until the time has elapsed when we can do anything effectually. In enforcing this moral truth, Shakespeare has shown the fulness and force of his powers: all that is amiable and excellent in nature is combined in Hamlet, with the exception of one quality. He is a man living in meditation, called upon to act by every motive human and divine, but the great object of his life is defeated by continually resolving to do, yet doing nothing but resolve.

George Gordon, Lord Byron

1788–1824

It is hardly possible to discuss Byron's poetry without telling the story of his life in some detail. His father was Captain Jack Byron, a nephew of the fifth Baron Byron, and a psychopathic spendthrift and sponger on women who had run through the fortunes of two heiresses. The first, a marchioness, he had acquired by divorce from her husband, and by her he had a daughter, Augusta Byron, later Augusta Leigh, the poet's half-sister. The second was a Scotswoman, Catherine Gordon of Gight, an explosive, unbalanced, ill-educated but affectionate woman whose only child was the poet. Byron was born in London on January 22, 1788, in great poverty and distress as his mother was returning from France to Scotland to get some relief from her rapacious spouse. He was handicapped at birth with a lameness that embittered his life (what was wrong, and which leg was affected, are still uncertain points), and he also had some glandular imbalance that forced him to a starvation diet in order to avoid grotesque corpulence. The mother brought up her boy in Aberdeen, where his religious training was naturally Presbyterian, giving many a later critic a somewhat dubious cliché about the "persisting Calvinism" in Byron's mind. When Byron was three his father died; when he was six his cousin, the heir to the Byron title, was killed, and when he was ten his great-uncle, who held the title, died and the poet became the sixth Lord Byron. The fact that Byron made so professional a job of being a lord is perhaps the result of his entering on that state when he was old enough to notice the difference his title made

in the attitude that society took toward him.

He was then educated at Harrow and at Trinity College, Cambridge. The most important of the friendships he formed there was with John Cam Hobhouse, in later life Lord Broughton, who founded a "Whig Club" at Cambridge, and whose influence had much to do with Byron's left-of-center political views. Byron's chief athletic interests were swimming and pistol-shooting, the latter a useful accomplishment in the days when gentlemen were expected to fight the odd duel, and he got around a regulation against keeping a dog at Cambridge by keeping a bear instead. What with his extravagance, his lack of discipline, and the liberties he took with his rank, he was anything but a model student. He announced more than once that he wished he had gone to Oxford instead, and the Cambridge authorities must often have wished so too. However, he acquired the usual gentleman's classical education, and while still an undergraduate he produced a slim volume of melodious if not very arresting lyrics. This volume was, after some vicissitudes, published in 1807 under the title given it by the publisher, *Hours of Idleness*. *Hours of Idleness* got roughly handled in the *Edinburgh Review,* and the result was Byron's first major satire, *English Bards and Scotch Reviewers* (1809). Although the motivation for this poem was revenge on the Edinburgh reviewer, Byron took the opportunity to satirize most of his poetic contemporaries, including Scott, Southey, Wordsworth and Coleridge.

Meanwhile Byron had been planning a variant

of the "Grand Tour" that it was fashionable for young well-to-do Englishmen to take. Instead of the usual journey to France and Italy, he decided to go first to Portugal and Spain, bypass Italy by way of Malta, and then travel in what were at that time Turkish dominions: Greece, Asia Minor, and the practically unknown Albania. He set out with Hobhouse on July 2, 1809, on the "Lisbon Packet." The Peninsular War was in progress, but life was made easy for people in Byron's social position, and one would never dream from his letters that this was the time and place of Goya's *Disasters of War*. The travelers passed through Malta, where a Mrs. Spencer Smith became the "Florence" of some of Byron's love poems, and on to Albania. Byron and his party were hospitably received by a local ruler, Ali Pasha, who found Byron as attractive as most people did, besides having political reasons for welcoming English visitors. Once, on suspicion that was no more than gossip, he had had fifteen women kidnapped and flung into the sea. Another woman narrowly escaped the same fate on a charge of infidelity: this incident was used by Byron as the basis for his tale *The Giaour,* and rumor maintained that Byron himself had been her lover. Next came Greece and Asia Minor, where Byron duplicated Leander's famous swim across the Hellespont, pondered over the sites of Marathon and Troy, and deplored the activities of Lord Elgin, who was engaged in hacking off the sculptures now called the Elgin Marbles from the ruined Parthenon and transporting them to England. Byron's satire on Lord Elgin's enterprise, "The Curse of Minerva" (i.e., Athene, the patron of Athens), was not published until 1815. Meanwhile he had begun to write a poem about his travels, *Childe Harold,* the first two cantos of the poem we now have.

On his return to England in July, 1811, he went back to Newstead, the estate of the Byrons, where he had established himself before he left, a rambling "Gothic" mansion he was later forced to sell. His mother died suddenly soon after his arrival, and the deaths of three close friends occurred about the same time. The relations between Byron and his mother had always been tense, especially after she had begun to see some of his father's extravagance reappearing in him, but they were fond enough of each other when they were not living together.

Byron now entered upon a phenomenally successful literary and social career. *Childe Harold,* as he said, made him famous overnight, and it was followed by a series of Oriental tales, *The Giaour, The Bride of Abydos, The Corsair,* and *Lara,* which appeared in 1813 and 1814. He wrote with great speed, completing the thousand-odd lines of *The Bride of Abydos* in four days, and he seldom revised. "I am like the tyger," he said: "If I miss my first Spring, I go growling back to my Jungle. There is no second. I can't correct; I can't, and I won't."

When Byron said in *Beppo:*

I've half a mind to tumble down to prose,
But verse is more in fashion — so here goes.

the last statement, incredible as it may seem now, was true when he wrote. Nobody would turn to poetry for stories nowadays, but in Byron's day there was a popular demand for verse tales that Byron did not create, though he did much to expand it. The melancholy misanthropy, so full of romantic *frisson,* the pirates and the harems, the exotic Orientalism, the easy and pleasant versification, swept London as they were later to sweep the Continent. As a celebrity Byron could hold his own even in the most absorbing period of the Napoleonic War. *The Corsair* sold 10,000 copies on the day of its publication by John Murray, and ran through seven editions in a month. Byron probably made more money from his poetry than any other English poet, though being a lord who derived his income from rents, he often gave his royalties away to friends. The first money he accepted on his own account was £700 for the copyright of *Lara.*

Apart from literature Byron had many other activities, both serious and scandalous. Before he had left England he had taken the seat in the House of Lords that his title gave him, and he now became active in Whig circles. His first speech was made in defence of the "frame-breakers," or workers who had destroyed some textile machines through fear of unemployment. He also supported a number of other liberal causes, including the relief of Catholics in Ireland. When Napoleon was banished to Elba, Byron wrote an ode on him in which he contrasted him unfavorably with Washington as a fighter for liberty. (There is an impressive musical setting of this ode, for orchestra and

Sprechgesang solo, by Arnold Schönberg.) But his hatred of the reactionary English government, especially Lord Castlereagh, was strong enough to give him a considerable admiration for Napoleon, even to the point of regretting the outcome of Waterloo: he had hoped, he said, to see Castlereagh's head on a pole. In fact his attitude to Napoleon always retained a good deal of self-identification.

Meanwhile Byron was carrying on some highly publicized affairs with several women of fashion. Lady Caroline Lamb, always something of an emotional exhibitionist, kept London, which on Byron's social level was still a small town, buzzing with gossip over her pursuit of Byron, her visits to him disguised, her tantrums, and her public scenes. Lady Oxford, whose children, in an erudite contemporary joke, were known as the Harleian Miscellany, was another mistress of his, and there were briefer encounters with others. Despite his crowded schedule, Byron began seriously to consider marriage, making a trusted confidante of Lady Melbourne, Caroline Lamb's mother-in-law, to whom he wrote many frank and unaffected letters. Given Byron's temperament, he could only marry some kind of *femme fatale;* and the only really fatal type of woman for him would be an earnest, humorless, rather inhibited female who would represent everything that was insular and respectable in English society. His choice fell on Annabella Milbanke, heiress to a title in her own right and niece of Lady Melbourne, and who otherwise reminds one a little of Mary Bennett in *Pride and Prejudice*. She was highly intelligent and had many interests, including mathematics (Byron called her the "Princess of Parallelograms," as in those days any woman with such an interest could expect to be teased about it), but her mind ran to rather vague maxims of general conduct, and to an interest in the moral reformation of other people which boded ill for marriage to an unreformed poet with an unusually concrete view of life.

The marriage lasted a year (January, 1815, to January, 1816) and then fell apart. A separation (they were never divorced) was agreed upon, and Lady Byron obtained custody of their daughter, Augusta Ada. Byron appears to have gone somewhat berserk in his matrimonial bonds, and his wife's doubts about his sanity were probably genuine. The situation was aggravated by financial difficulties and by the fact that gossip had begun to whisper about Byron and his half-sister Augusta. The combination of this exceptionally delicious scandal with the matrimonial one, along with his expression of some perverse pro-French political views, made things unpleasant for Byron, and although social disapproval was perhaps not as intense as he pretended or thought, he felt forced to leave England once more. He set out for the Continent on April 25, 1816, never to return to England.

He made his way to Geneva, where he met, by prearrangement, Shelley and his wife Mary Godwin, along with her stepsister, Claire (or Jane) Clairmont. The last named had visited Byron before his departure from England and had thrown herself, as biographers say, at his head, the result of this accurate if morally unguided missile being a daughter, Allegra, whom Byron eventually placed in an Italian convent to be brought up as a Roman Catholic, and who died there at the age of eight. The association with Shelley, one of Byron's few intellectual friends, is marked in the new poetry that Byron now began writing — the third canto of *Childe Harold; Manfred;* the two remarkable poems "Darkness" and "The Dream"; and the most poignant of his tales, "The Prisoner of Chillon." Shelley's reaction to Byron may be found in his poem "Julian and Maddalo," but for all the skepticism he ascribes to Byron, he was unable to convince him that Christianity was less reasonable than his own brand of Platonism.

In the fall of 1817 Byron went over the Alps and settled in Venice. His "Ode to Venice," *Beppo*, the opening of the fourth canto of *Childe Harold*, and two of his dramas, *Marino Faliero* and *The Two Foscari*, are some of the evidence for the fascination that this dreamlike World's Fair of a city had for him. At Venice he plunged into an extraordinary sexual debauch, but he also wrote some of his best poetry, including the fourth canto of *Childe Harold* and the beginning of his greatest work, *Don Juan*. In the spring of 1819 he met Teresa Guiccioli, the wife of an elderly Count, who was both attractive enough to hold Byron and astute enough to keep other women away from him. Byron moved into the Guiccioli household in Ravenna, and settled down with Teresa into what by Byronic standards was practically an old-fashioned marriage.

Ravenna saw the composition of *Sardanapalus* and *Cain,* as well as *The Vision of Judgment,* but his poetic energies were increasingly absorbed by *Don Juan.*

At that time the two great centers of classical civilization, Greece and Italy, were under foreign occupation: Greece was a Turkish dependency, and most of northern Italy was controlled by Austria. Byron and Shelley were passionate supporters of the efforts of Italian and Greek nationalists to get free of their foreign yokes. Teresa's family, the Gambas, were also Italian nationalists in sympathy, and hence were, as was Byron, closely watched and reported on by the Austrian police. The Gambas were forced to move from Ravenna to Pisa, and Byron followed them. At Pisa Byron rejoined the Shelleys, and here Shelley, on July 8, 1822, was drowned at sea and cremated on the shore. The cremation was carried out by Byron and their friend Edward Trelawny, an extraordinarily circumstantial liar who had reconstructed his past life along the general lines of a Byronic hero. Meanwhile Byron had broken with his publisher John Murray, and had formed an alliance through Shelley with Leigh Hunt, whom he brought to Pisa. The plan was to found a literary and left-wing political magazine, and this magazine, called *The Liberal,* printed a good deal of Byron's poetry, including *The Vision of Judgment,* in its four numbers. Hunt, however, was somewhat irresponsible (he is the original of Harold Skimpole in Dickens' *Bleak House*), and his absurd and even more Dickensian wife and their demonic children helped to keep relations strained.

Eventually the Gamba-Byron menage was forced to move on to Genoa, where Byron wrote some unimportant poems and finished what we have of *Don Juan* — sixteen cantos and a fragment of a seventeenth. Meanwhile a group of revolutionaries in Greece had been planning an insurrection against the Turkish authority, and knowing of Byron's sympathy with their cause, they offered him membership in their Committee. Byron had been meditating the possibility of going to Greece for some time, and on July 23, 1823, he left in the company of Trelawny and Pietro Gamba, Teresa's brother. He established connection at Missolonghi on January 5, 1824, with Prince Alexander Mavrocordato, the leader of the Western Greek revo-lutionaries, and put his money and his very real qualities of leadership at the service of the Greek cause. His health, which had been precarious for some time, broke down in a series of fevers, and he died at Missolonghi on April 19, 1824, three months after he had passed the thirty-sixth birthday which his valedictory poem records.

II

The main appeal of Byron's poetry is in the fact that it is Byron's. To read Byron's poetry is to hear all about Byron's marital difficulties, flirtations, love for Augusta, friendships, travels, and political and social views. And Byron is a consistently interesting person to hear about, this being why Byron, even at his worst of self-pity and egotism and blither and doggerel, is still so incredibly readable. He proves what many critics declare to be impossible, that a poem can make its primary impact as a historical and biographical document. The critical problem involved here is crucial to our understanding of not only Byron but literature as a whole. Even when Byron's poetry is not objectively very good, it is still important, because it is Byron's. But who was Byron to be so important? certainly not an exceptionally good or wise man. Byron is, strictly, neither a great poet nor a great man who wrote poetry, but something in between: a tremendous cultural force that was life and literature at once. How he came to be this is what we must try to explain as we review the four chief genres of his work: the lyrics, the tales (including *Childe Harold*), the dramas, and the later satires.

Byron's lyrical poetry affords a good exercise in critical catholicity, because it contains nothing that "modern" critics look for: no texture, no ambiguities, no intellectualized ironies, no intensity, no vividness of phrasing, the words and images being vague to the point of abstraction. The poetry seems to be a plain man's poetry, making poetic emotion out of the worn and blunted words of ordinary speech. Yet it is not written by a plain man: it is written, as Scott said, with the careless ease of a man of quality, and its most striking and obvious feature is its gentlemanly amateurism. It is, to be sure, in an amateur tradition, being a romantic, subjective, personal development of the kind of Courtly Love poetry that was written by Tudor and

Cavalier noblemen in earlier ages. Byron's frequent statements in prefaces that this would be his last work to trouble the public with, his offhand deprecating comments on his work, his refusal to revise, all give a studious impression of a writer who can take poetry or leave it alone. Byron held the view that lyrical poetry was an expression of passion, and that passion was essentially fitful, and he distrusted professional poets, who pretended to be able to summon passion at will and sustain it indefinitely. Poe was later to hold much the same view of poetry, but more consistently, for he drew the inference that a continuous long poem was impossible, whereas *Childe Harold* has the stretches of perfunctory, even slapdash writing that one would expect with such a theory.

In Byron's later lyrics, especially the *Hebrew Melodies* of 1815, where he was able to add some of his Oriental technicolor to the Old Testament, more positive qualities emerge, particularly in the rhythm. "The Destruction of Sennacherib" is a good reciter's piece (though not without its difficulties, as Tom Sawyer discovered), and anticipates some of the later experiments in verbal jazz by Poe and Swinburne. Some of the best of his poems bear the title "Stanzas for Music," and they have the flat conventional diction appropriate to poems that depend partly on another art for their sound:

One shade the more, one ray the less,
  Had half impaired the nameless grace
Which waves in every raven tress,
  Or softly lightens o'er her face;
Where thoughts serenely sweet express
  How pure, how dear their dwelling-place.

(If the reader would like a clue to the caressing rhythm of this stanza, he should read the iambic meters so as to give the stresses twice the length of the unstressed syllables. Then the lines will fall into four bars of three-four time, beginning on the third beat, and the rhythm of a nineteenth-century waltz will emerge.) We notice that while Byron's amateur predecessors wrote in a convention and Byron from personal experience, Byron was equally conventional, because his personal experience conformed to a literary pattern. Byron's life imitated literature: this is where his unique combination of the poetic and the personal begins.

Byron was naturally an extroverted person,

fond of company, of travel, of exploring new scenes, making new friends, falling in love with new women. Like Keats, in a much more direct way, he wanted a life of sensations rather than of thoughts. He was continually speculating about unknown sensations, such as how it would feel to have committed a murder, and he had the nervous dread of growing older that goes with the fear of slowing down in the rhythm of experience. His writing depends heavily on experience; he seldom describes any country that he has not seen, and for all his solitary role he shows, especially in *Don Juan,* a novelist's sense of established society.

It was an essential part of his strongly extroverted and empirical bent that he should not be a systematic thinker, nor much interested in people who were. He used his intelligence to make common-sense judgements on specific situations, and found himself unable to believe anything that he did not find confirmed in his own experience. In his numerous amours, for example, the absence of any sense of sin was as unanswerable a fact of his experience as the presence of it would have been to St. Augustine. He thought of sexual love as a product of reflex and mechanical habit, not of inner emotional drives. When he said: "I do not believe in the existence of what is called love," we are probably to take him quite literally. Nevertheless, his extroversion made him easily confused by efforts at self-analysis, and he flew into rages when he was accused of any lack of feeling. One reason why his marriage demoralized him so was that it forced such efforts on him.

Now if we look into Byron's tales and *Childe Harold* we usually find as the central character an inscrutable figure with hollow cheeks and blazing eyes, wrapped in a cloud of gloom, full of mysterious and undefined remorse, an outcast from society, a wanderer of the race of Cain. At times he suggests something demonic rather than human, a Miltonic Satan or fallen angel. This type of character is now known as the "Byronic hero," and wherever he has appeared since in literature there has been the influence, direct or indirect, of Byron. And if we ask how a witty, sociable, extroverted poet came to create such a character, we can see that it must have arisen as what psychologists call a projection of his inner self, that inner self that was so mysterious and inscrutable even to its owner.

Childe Harold and the other lowering heroes of Byron's tales not only popularized a conventional type of hero, but popularized Byron himself in that role. For Byron was a dark and melancholy-looking lord with a reputation for wickedness and free thought; he seemed to prefer the Continent to England, and took a detached view of middle-class and even Christian morality. He owned a gloomy Gothic castle and spent evenings with revelers in it; he was pale and thin with his ferocious dieting; he even had a lame foot. No wonder he said that strangers whom he met at dinner " looked as if his Satanic Majesty had been among them." The prince of darkness is a gentleman, and so was Byron.

Byron did not find the Byronic hero as enthralling as his public did, and he made several efforts to detach his own character from Childe Harold and his other heroes, with limited success. He says of Childe Harold that he wanted to make him an objective study of gloomy misanthropy, hence he deliberately cut humor out of the poem in order to preserve a unity of tone. But Byron's most distinctive talents did not have full scope in this part of his work.

Byron's tales are, on the whole, well-told and well-shaped stories. Perhaps he learned something from his own ridicule of Southey, who was also a popular writer of verse tales, sometimes of mammoth proportions. In any case he is well able to exploit the capacity of verse for dramatizing one or two central situations, leaving all the cumbersome apparatus of plot to be ignored or taken for granted. But he seemed unable to bring his various projections of his inner ghost to life: his heroes, like the characters of a detective story, are thin, bloodless, abstract, and popular. Nor could he seem to vary the tone, from romance to irony, from fantasy to humor, as Beckford does in *Vathek*. Byron was strongly attracted by Beckford, and is thinking of him at the very opening of *Childe Harold,* as Beckford had lived for two years in Portugal. When Byron writes:

Deep in yon cave Honorius long did dwell,
In hope to merit Heaven by making earth a Hell.

he obviously has in mind the demure remark in the opening of *Vathek:* " He did not think . . . that it was necessary to make a hell of this world to enjoy paradise in the next." But though

Byron is the wittiest of writers, the Byronic hero cannot manage much more than a gloomy smile.

The establishing of the Byronic hero was a major feat of characterization, but Byron had little power of characterization apart from this figure. Like many brilliant talkers, he had not much ear for the rhythms and nuances of other people's speech. Here again we find a close affinity between Byron's personality and the conventions of his art. For instance, in his life Byron seemed to have curiously little sense of women as human beings. Except for Lady Melbourne, he addressed himself to the female in them, took a hearty-male view of their intellectual interests, and concentrated on the ritual of love-making with the devotion of what an earlier age would have called a clerk of Venus. This impersonal and ritualistic approach to women is reflected in his tales and plays, where again it fits the conventions of Byronic romance. It is difficult for a heroine of strong character to make much headway against a gloomy misanthropic hero, and Byron's heroines, like the heroines of Gothic romance in general, are insipid prodigies of neurotic devotion.

In *English Bards and Scotch Reviewers* Byron spoke of Wordsworth as " that mild apostate from poetic rule." This poem is early, but Byron never altered his opinion of the Lake Poets as debasers of the currency of English poetry. His own poetic idol was Pope, whom he called " the moral poet of all civilization," and he thought of himself as continuing Pope's standards of clarity, craftsmanship and contact with real life against the introverted metaphysical mumblings of Coleridge and Wordsworth. Byron's early models were standard, even old-fashioned, later eighteenth-century models. *English Bards* is in the idiom of eighteenth-century satire, less of Pope than of Pope's successors, Churchill, Wolcot, and Gifford, and the first part of *Childe Harold,* with its pointless Spenserian stanza and its semi-facetious antique diction — fortunately soon dropped by Byron — is also an eighteenth-century stock pattern. Byron was friendly with Shelley, but owes little to him technically, and in his letters he expressed a vociferous dislike for the poetry of Keats (considerably toned down in the eleventh canto of *Don Juan*). His literary friends, Sheridan, Rogers, Gifford, were of the older generation, and even Tom Moore, his biographer and by far his closest friend among his poetic contemporaries, preserved, like so many Irish writers, something of the eighteenth-century manner.

It was also an eighteenth-century model that gave him the lead for the phase of poetry that began with *Beppo* in September, 1817, and exploited the possibilities of the eight-line (*ottava rima*) stanza used there and in *Don Juan* and *The Vision of Judgment*. Byron seems to have derived this stanza from a heroi-comical poem, " Whistlecraft," by John Hookham Frere, whom Byron had met in Spain, and which in its turn had owed something to the Italian romantic epics of the early Renaissance.

In the new flush of discovery, Byron wrote exultantly to his friend Douglas Kinnaird: " [*Don Juan*] is the sublime of *that there* sort of writing — it may be bawdy, but is it not good English? It may be profligate but is it not *life,* is it not *the thing?* Could any man have written it who has not lived in the world? " But even Byron was soon made aware that he was not as popular as he had been. The women who loved *The Corsair* hated *Don Juan,* for the reason that Byron gives with his usual conciseness on such subjects: " the wish of all women to exalt the *sentiment* of the passions, and to keep up the illusion which is their empire." Teresa, as soon as she understood anything of the poem, boycotted it, and forced Byron to promise not to go on with it, a promise he was able to evade only with great difficulty. His friend Harriet Wilson, significantly enough a courtesan who lived partly by blackmail, wrote him: " Dear *Adorable* Lord Byron, *don't* make a mere *coarse* old libertine of yourself."

Don Juan is traditionally the incautious amorist, the counterpart in love to Faust in knowledge, whose pursuit of women is so ruthless that he is eventually damned, as in the last scene of Mozart's opera *Don Giovanni.* Consequently he is a logical choice as a mask for Byron, but he is a mask that reveals the whole Byronic personality, instead of concealing the essence of it as Childe Harold does. The extroversion of Byron's temperament has full scope in *Don Juan.* There is hardly any characterization in the poem: even Don Juan never emerges clearly as a character. We see only what happens to him, and the other characters, even Haidée, float past as phantasmagoria of romance and adven-

ture. What one misses in the poem is the sense of engagement or participation. Everything happens to Don Juan, but he is never an active agent, and seems to take no responsibility for his life. He drifts from one thing to the next, appears to find one kind of experience as good as another, makes no judgments and no commitments. As a result the gloom and misanthropy, the secret past sins, the gnawing remorse of the earlier heroes is finally identified as a shoddier but more terrifying evil — boredom, the sense of the inner emptiness of life that is one of Byron's most powerfully compelling moods, and has haunted literature ever since, from the *ennui* of Baudelaire to the *Angst* and *nausée* of our own day.

The episodes of the poem are all stock Byronic scenes: Spain, the pirates of the Levant, the odalisques of Turkish harems, battlefields, and finally English high society. But there is as little plot as characterization: the poem exists for the sake of its author's comment. As Byron says:

This narrative is not meant for narration,
But a mere airy and fantastic basis,
To build up common things with common places.

Its wit is constantly if not continuously brilliant, and Byron's contempt of cant and prudery, his very real hatred of cruelty, his detached view of all social icons, whether conservative or popular, are well worth having. Not many poets give us as much common sense as Byron does. On the other hand the opposition to the poem made him increasingly self-conscious as he went on, and his technique of calculated bathos and his deliberate refusal to " grow metaphysical " — that is, pursue any idea beyond the stage of initial reaction — keep the poem too resolutely on one level. The larger imaginative vistas that we are promised (" a panoramic view of hell's in training ") do not materialize, and by the end of the sixteenth canto we have a sense of a rich but not inexhaustible vein rapidly thinning out. As *Don Juan* is not Don Juan's poem but Byron's poem, it could hardly have been ended, but only abandoned or cut short by its author's death. The Mozartian ending of the story Byron had already handled, in his own way, in *Manfred.*

Byron's religious views were certainly unusual in his day, but if we had to express them in a formula, it would be something like this: the best that we can imagine man doing is where our conception of God ought to start. Religions that foment cruelty and induce smugness, or ascribe cruelty and smugness to God, are superstitions. In *Heaven and Earth,* for example, the offstage deity who decrees the deluge at the end is clearly the moral inferior of every human creature he drowns. In *The Vision of Judgment* the sycophantic Southey is contrasted with John Wilkes, who fought King George hard all his life, but who, when encouraged to go on persecuting him after death, merely says:

> I don't like ripping up old stories, since
> His conduct was but natural in a prince.

This is a decent human attitude, consequently it must be the least we can expect from heaven, and so the poet takes leave of the poor old king "practising the hundredth Psalm."

III

Byron has probably had more influence outside England than any other English poet except Shakespeare. In English literature, though he is always classified with the Romantic poets, he is Romantic only because the Byronic hero is a Romantic figure: as we have seen, he has little technically in common with other English Romantics. But on the Continent Byron has been the arch-romantic of modern literature, and European nineteenth-century culture is as unthinkable without Byron as its history would be without Napoleon. From the painting of Delacroix to the music of Berlioz, from the poetry of Pushkin to the philosophy of Nietzsche, the spell of Byron is everywhere. Modern fiction would be miserably impoverished without the Byronic hero: Balzac, Stendhal, Dostoevsky, have all used him in crucial roles. In the more advanced political atmosphere of England, Byron was only a Whig intellectual, whereas in Greece and Italy he was a revolutionary fighter for freedom, a poetic Mazzini or Bolivar, though, like them, not a class leveler. As he said:

> I wish men to be free
> As much from mobs as kings — from you as me.

Among English readers the reputation of the Romantic and sentimental Byron has not kept pace with his reputation as a satirist, but it would be wrong to accept the assertion, so often made today, that Byron is of little importance apart from his satires and letters. An immense amount of imitation and use of Byron, conscious or unconscious, direct or indirect, has taken place in English literature, too, and nearly all of it is of the Romantic Byron. Melville (whose Ishmael is in the line of Cain), Conrad, Hemingway, A. E. Housman, Thomas Wolfe, D. H. Lawrence, W. H. Auden — these writers have little in common except that they all Byronize.

Byron's immediate influence in his own country, on the other hand, though certainly very great, was qualified in many ways, by queasiness about his morality, by a refusal to separate him from his posing heroes, by a feeling that he lacked the sterner virtues and wrote with too much pleasure and too few pains. The first canto of *Don Juan* centers on the nervous prudery of Donna Inez, who is, not surprisingly, modeled on Byron's wife. But Donna Inez was Britannia as well. The sands of the Regency aristocracy were running out, the tide of middle-class morality had already set in, and the age that we think of as Victorian, with its circulating libraries, its custom of reading aloud to large family circles, and its tendency not to be amused, at any rate by anything approaching the ribald, was on the way.

We have not yet shaken off our nineteenth-century inhibitions about Byron. A frequent twentieth-century jargon term for him is "immature," which endorses the Carlyle view that Byron is a poet to be outgrown. One thinks of Yeats's penetrating remark that we are never satisfied with the maturity of those whom we have admired in boyhood. Even those who have not admired Byron in boyhood have gone through a good deal of Byronism at that stage. There is certainly something youthful about the Byronic hero, and for some reason we feel more defensive about youth than about childhood, and more shamefaced about liking a poet who has captured a youthful imagination. If we replace "youthful" with the loaded term "adolescent" we can see how deeply ingrained this feeling is.

Among intellectuals the Southey type, who makes a few liberal gestures in youth to quiet his conscience and then plunges into a rapturous authoritarianism for the rest of his life, is much more common than the Byron type, who continues to be baffled by unanswered questions and simple anomalies, to make irresponsible jokes, to set his face against society, to respect the authority of his own mood — in short, to retain the rebellious or irreverent qualities of youth. Perhaps it is as dangerous to eliminate the adolescent in us as it is to eliminate the child. In any case the kind of poetic experience that Byronism represents should be obtained young, and in Byron. It may later be absorbed into more complex experiences, but to miss or renounce it is to impoverish whatever else we may attain.

WRITTEN AFTER SWIMMING FROM SESTOS TO ABYDOS

The story of Leander, the youth of Abydos who swam nightly across the Hellespont to Hero, priestess of Aphrodite at Sestos, and was drowned one stormy night, causing Hero's suicide, was the theme of an Alexandrian poem ascribed to the legendary pre-Homeric poet Musaeus. This poem in its turn was the basis of Christopher Marlowe's unfinished *Hero and Leander* (1598). Byron accomplished the swim (in the opposite direction) in an hour and ten minutes on May 3, 1810, and wrote this poem on May 9. His note reads in part: "On the 3rd of May, 1810 . . . Lieutenant Ekenhead . . . and the writer of these rhymes, swam from the European shore to the Asiatic. . . . The whole distance . . . was . . . upwards of four English miles, though the actual breadth is barely one. The rapidity of the current is such that no boat can row directly across. . . . The water was extremely cold, from the melting of the mountain snows. . . . The only thing that surprised me was that, as doubts had been entertained of the truth of Leander's story, no traveller had ever endeavoured to ascertain its practicability." In a letter to Henry Drury, Byron remarks: " . . . the immediate distance is not above a mile but the current renders it hazardous, so much so, that I doubt whether Leander's conjugal powers must not have been exhausted in his passage to Paradise." Byron also made his Don Juan a good swimmer:

He could, perhaps, have passed the Hellespont,
As once (a feat on which ourselves we prided)
Leander, Mr. Ekenhead, and I did.
[*Don Juan,* II.105]

I

If, in the month of dark December,
    Leander, who was nightly wont
(What maid will not the tale remember?)
    To cross thy stream, broad Hellespont!

II

If, when the wintry tempest roared,
    He sped to Hero, nothing loth,
And thus of old thy current poured,
    Fair Venus! how I pity both!

III

For *me,* degenerate modern wretch,
    Though in the genial month of May   10
My dripping limbs I faintly stretch,
    And think I've done a feat to-day.

IV

But since he crossed the rapid tide,
    According to the doubtful story,
To woo, — and — Lord knows what beside,
    And swam for Love, as I for Glory;

V

'Twere hard to say who fared the best:
    Sad mortals! thus the Gods still plague you!
He lost his labour, I my jest:
    For he was drowned, and I've the ague.   20

MAID OF ATHENS, ERE WE PART

Ζωή μου, σᾶς ἀγαπῶ.[1]

The Maid of Athens was a twelve-year-old girl named Theresa Macri, the youngest of three daughters of the widow of the English vice-consul, in whose house Byron stayed in Athens. That she had some claim to the title of maid seems clear from a later letter in which Byron speaks of bargaining with her mother, who at first "was mad enough to imagine I was going to marry the girl," and then, failing marriage, held out for 30,000 piastres. Theresa eventually married a Mr. Black, and died in the odor of Byronism. Byron's note on the refrain reads: "Romaic expression of tenderness: If I translate it, I shall affront the gentlemen, as it may seem that I supposed they could not; and if I do not, I may affront the ladies. For fear of any misconstruction on the part of the latter, I shall do so, begging pardon of the learned. It means, 'My life, I love you!' which sounds very prettily in all languages, and is as much in fashion in Greece at this day as, Juvenal tells us, the two first words were amongst the Roman ladies, whose erotic expressions were all Hellenised." The poem is dated Athens, 1810.

MAID OF ATHENS. 1. *Zoe mou sas agapo.*

I

Maid of Athens, ere we part,
Give, oh give me back my heart!
Or, since that has left my breast,
Keep it now, and take the rest!
Hear my vow before I go,
Ζωή μου, σᾶς ἀγαπῶ.

II

By those tresses unconfined,
Wooed by each Aegean wind;
By those lids whose jetty fringe
Kiss thy soft cheeks' blooming tinge;   10
By those wild eyes like the roe,
Ζωή μου, σᾶς ἀγαπῶ.

III

By that lip I long to taste;
By that zone-encircled waist;
By all the token-flowers that tell
What words can never speak so well;
By Love's alternate joy and woe,
Ζωή μου, σᾶς ἀγαπῶ.

IV

Maid of Athens! I am gone:
Think of me, sweet! when alone.   20
Though I fly to Istambol,
Athens holds my heart and soul:
Can I cease to love thee? No!
Ζωή μου, σᾶς ἀγαπῶ.

REMEMBER THEE! REMEMBER THEE!

Written in a fit of ill temper as a rejoinder to Lady Caroline Lamb, who, calling one morning and finding the poet out, wrote "Remember me!" in a copy of *Vathek* lying on his table.

I

Remember thee! remember thee!
    Till Lethe quench Life's burning stream
Remorse and Shame shall cling to thee,
    And haunt thee like a feverish dream!

II

Remember thee! Aye, doubt it not.
    Thy husband too shall think of thee:
By neither shalt thou be forgot,
    Thou *false* to him, thou *fiend* to me!

SHE WALKS IN BEAUTY

This and the following poem appeared in a volume called *Hebrew Melodies,* published in 1815 with the following advertisement: "The subsequent poems were written at the request of my friend, the Hon. Douglas Kinnaird, for a Selection of Hebrew Melodies, and have been published, with the music, arranged by Mr. Braham and Mr. Nathan." The poems are based on Biblical themes, and "She Walks in Beauty" has no place in the volume except that it was written about the same time. The inspiration is said to have been a beautiful woman, Lady Wilmot Horton, whom Byron had seen at a ball dressed in mourning with spangles on her dress. The poem is dated June 12, 1814.

I

She walks in Beauty, like the night
    Of cloudless climes and starry skies;
And all that's best of dark and bright
    Meet in her aspect and her eyes:
Thus mellowed to that tender light
    Which Heaven to gaudy day denies.

II

One shade the more, one ray the less,
    Had half impaired the nameless grace
Which waves in every raven tress,
    Or softly lightens o'er her face;   10
Where thoughts serenely sweet express,
    How pure, how dear their dwelling-place.

III

And on that cheek, and o'er that brow,
    So soft, so calm, yet eloquent,
The smiles that win, the tints that glow,
    But tell of days in goodness spent,
A mind at peace with all below,
    A heart whose love is innocent!

THE DESTRUCTION OF SENNACHERIB

This poem, one of the *Hebrew Melodies,* is dated Seaham, February 17, 1815. For the story told in the poem see II Kings 19.

I

The Assyrian came down like the wolf on the fold,
And his cohorts were gleaming in purple and gold;
And the sheen of their spears was like stars on the
        sea,
When the blue wave rolls nightly on deep Galilee.

II

Like the leaves of the forest when Summer is green,
That host with their banners at sunset were seen:

Like the leaves of the forest when Autumn hath
    blown,
That host on the morrow lay withered and strown.

III

For the angel of Death spread his wings on the blast,
And breathed in the face of the foe as he passed;
And the eyes of the sleepers waxed deadly and chill,
And their hearts but once heaved — and for ever
    grew still!   12

IV

And there lay the steed with his nostril all wide,
But through it there rolled not the breath of his
    pride;
And the foam of his gasping lay white on the turf,
And cold as the spray of the rock-beating surf.

V

And there lay the rider distorted and pale,
With the dew on his brow, and the rust on his
    mail:
And the tents were all silent — the banners alone —
The lances unlifted — the trumpet unblown.   20

VI

And the widows of Ashur° are loud in their wail,
And the idols are broke in the temple of Baal;
And the might of the Gentile, unsmote by the
    sword,
Hath melted like snow in the glance of the Lord!

STANZAS FOR MUSIC

Published in 1816, and usually ascribed to March 28
of that year, but the date and occasion are unknown.

I

There be none of Beauty's daughters
    With a magic like thee;
And like music on the waters
    Is thy sweet voice to me:
When, as if its sound were causing
The charmèd Ocean's pausing,
The waves lie still and gleaming,
And the lulled winds seem dreaming:

II

And the Midnight Moon is weaving
    Her bright chain o'er the deep;   10

THE DESTRUCTION OF SENNACHERIB. **21. Ashur:** Assyria.

Whose breast is gently heaving,
    As an infant's asleep:
So the spirit bows before thee,
To listen and adore thee;
With a full but soft emotion,
Like the swell of Summer's ocean.

SONNET ON CHILLON

This sonnet forms a prelude to Byron's tale *The
Prisoner of Chillon,* which commemorates the political and religious martyrdom of François Bonivard,
a sixteenth-century Genevese imprisoned for seven
years by the Duke of Savoy. Byron and Shelley
visited the Castle of Chillon, on Lake Geneva, on
June 26, 1816; Byron's poem was written soon after,
and the sonnet, which stresses the political rather than
the religious aspect of persecution, was appended later.

Eternal Spirit of the chainless Mind!
    Brightest in dungeons, Liberty! thou art,
    For there thy habitation is the heart —
The heart which love of thee alone can bind;
And when thy sons to fetters are consigned —
    To fetters, and the damp vault's dayless gloom,
    Their country conquers with their martyrdom,
And Freedom's fame finds wings on every wind.
Chillon! thy prison is a holy place,
    And thy sad floor an altar — for 'twas trod,   10
Until his very steps have left a trace
    Worn, as if thy cold pavement were a sod,
By Bonnivard! — May none those marks efface!
    For they appeal from tyranny to God.

DARKNESS

Written at Diodati, Switzerland, in July, 1816, during the sojourn with the Shelleys on Lake Geneva.
The somberness of the poem reflects the interest of the
group in reading and writing ghost stories, an interest
of which the most remarkable result was Mary Shelley's
Frankenstein.

I had a dream, which was not all a dream.
The bright sun was extinguished, and the stars
Did wander darkling in the eternal space,
Rayless, and pathless, and the icy Earth
Swung blind and blackening in the moonless air;
Morn came and went — and came, and brought no
    day,
And men forgot their passions in the dread
Of this their desolation; and all hearts
Were chilled into a selfish prayer for light:
And they did live by watchfires — and the thrones,
The palaces of crownèd kings — the huts,   11
The habitations of all things which dwell,
Were burnt for beacons; cities were consumed,
And men were gathered round their blazing homes

To look once more into each other's face;
Happy were those who dwelt within the eye
Of the volcanoes, and their mountain-torch:
A fearful hope was all the World contained;
Forests were set on fire — but hour by hour
They fell and faded — and the crackling trunks   20
Extinguished with a crash — and all was black.
The brows of men by the despairing light
Wore an unearthly aspect, as by fits
The flashes fell upon them; some lay down
And hid their eyes and wept; and some did rest
Their chins upon their clenchèd hands, and smiled;
And others hurried to and fro, and fed
Their funeral piles with fuel, and looked up
With mad disquietude on the dull sky,
The pall of a past World; and then again   30
With curses cast them down upon the dust,
And gnashed their teeth and howled: the wild birds shrieked,
And, terrified, did flutter on the ground
And flap their useless wings; the wildest brutes
Came tame and tremulous; and vipers crawled
And twined themselves among the multitude,
Hissing, but stingless — they were slain for food:
And War, which for a moment was no more,
Did glut himself again: — a meal was bought
With blood, and each sate sullenly apart   40
Gorging himself in gloom: no Love was left;
All earth was but one thought — and that was Death,
Immediate and inglorious; and the pang
Of famine fed upon all entrails — men
Died, and their bones were tombless as their flesh;
The meagre by the meagre were devoured,
Even dogs assailed their masters, all save one,
And he was faithful to a corse, and kept
The birds and beasts and famished men at bay,
Till hunger clung them, or the dropping dead   50
Lured their lank jaws; himself sought out no food,
But with a piteous and perpetual moan,
And a quick desolate cry, licking the hand
Which answered not with a caress — he died.
The crowd was famished by degrees; but two
Of an enormous city did survive,
And they were enemies: they met beside
The dying embers of an altar-place
Where had been heaped a mass of holy things
For an unholy usage; they raked up,   60
And shivering scraped with their cold skeleton hands
The feeble ashes, and their feeble breath
Blew for a little life, and made a flame
Which was a mockery; then they lifted up
Their eyes as it grew lighter, and beheld
Each other's aspects — saw, and shrieked, and died —
Even of their mutual hideousness they died,

Unknowing who he was upon whose brow
Famine had written Fiend. The World was void,
The populous and the powerful was a lump,   70
Seasonless, herbless, treeless, manless, lifeless —
A lump of death — a chaos of hard clay.
The rivers, lakes, and ocean all stood still,
And nothing stirred within their silent depths;
Ships sailorless lay rotting on the sea,
And their masts fell down piecemeal: as they dropped
They slept on the abyss without a surge —
The waves were dead; the tides were in their grave,
The Moon, their mistress, had expired before;
The winds were withered in the stagnant air,   80
And the clouds perished; Darkness had no need
Of aid from them — She was the Universe.

SO WE'LL GO NO MORE A-ROVING

In a letter to Thomas Moore dated Venice, February 28, 1817, Byron says: "The Carnival — that is, the latter part of it, and sitting up late o' nights, had knocked me up a little. . . . The mumming closed with a masked ball . . . where I went . . . and, though I did not dissipate much upon the whole, yet I find 'the sword wearing out the scabbard,' though I have but just turned the corner of twenty-nine." The poem below follows.

I

So we'll go no more a-roving
    So late into the night,
Though the heart be still as loving,
    And the moon be still as bright.

II

For the sword outwears its sheath,
    And the soul wears out the breast,
And the heart must pause to breathe,
    And Love itself have rest.

III

Though the night was made for loving,
    And the day returns too soon,   10
Yet we'll go no more a-roving
    By the light of the moon.

SONNET TO THE PRINCE REGENT

On the Repeal of
Lord Edward Fitzgerald's Forfeiture

Dated Bologna, August 12, 1819, and also known as "Sonnet to George the Fourth," which the Prince Regent became the next year. Lord Edward Fitzgerald was involved in the Irish uprising of 1798, was shot

when captured and died from the wound. A bill of
attainder was passed against him which was repealed
in 1819. Byron's interest in him was probably due to
Thomas Moore, who later wrote a life of Fitzgerald.

To be the father of the fatherless,
    To stretch the hand from the throne's height,
      and raise
His offspring, who expired in other days
To make thy sire's sway by a kingdom less, —
This is to be a monarch, and repress
    Envy into unutterable praise.
    Dismiss thy guard, and trust thee to such traits,
For who would lift a hand, except to bless?
    Were it not easy, sir, and is't not sweet
    To make thyself beloved? and to be   10
Omnipotent by mercy's means? for thus
    Thy sovereignty would grow but more complete:
A despot thou, and yet thy people free,
    And by the heart, not hand, enslaving us.

ON MY THIRTY-THIRD BIRTHDAY

Byron's thirty-third birthday was on January 22,
1821. On January 21 he wrote in his diary: "Tomorrow is my birthday — that is to say, at twelve o'
the clock, midnight, *i.e.,* in twelve minutes, I shall
have completed thirty and three years of age! — and
I go to my bed with a heaviness of heart at having
lived so long, and to so little purpose. . . . I don't
regret them [the years] so much for what I have done,
as for what I *might* have done." The quatrain below
follows.

    Through Life's dull road, so dim and dirty,
    I have dragged to three-and-thirty.
    What have these years left to me?
    Nothing — except thirty-three.

ON THIS DAY I COMPLETE MY THIRTY-SIXTH YEAR

Written at Missolonghi, Greece, on January 22, 1824,
and published in the *Morning Chronicle* on October
29, after the poet's death. Pietro Gamba tells how
Byron came out of his bedroom and said to his friends:
"You were complaining that I never write any poetry
now: — this is my birthday, and I have just finished
something, which, I think, is better than what I usually
write." It is not quite his last poem, but is still essentially his farewell to the world.

I

'Tis time this heart should be unmoved,
    Since others it hath ceased to move:
Yet, though I cannot be beloved,
      Still let me love!

II

My days are in the yellow leaf;
    The flowers and fruits of Love are gone;
The worm, the canker, and the grief
      Are mine alone!

III

The fire that on my bosom preys
    Is lone as some Volcanic isle;   10
No torch is kindled at its blaze —
      A funeral pile.

IV

The hope, the fear, the zealous care,
    The exalted portion of the pain
And power of love, I cannot share,
      But wear the chain.

V

But 'tis not *thus* — and 'tis not *here* —
    Such thoughts should shake my soul, nor
      now
Where Glory decks the hero's bier,
      Or binds his brow.   20

VI

The Sword, the Banner, and the Field,
    Glory and Greece, around me see!
The Spartan, borne upon his shield,
      Was not more free.

VII

Awake! (not Greece — she *is* awake!)
    Awake, my spirit! Think through *whom*
Thy life-blood tracks its parent lake,
      And then strike home!

VIII

Tread those reviving passions down,
    Unworthy manhood! — unto thee   30
Indifferent should the smile or frown
      Of Beauty be.

IX

If thou regret'st thy youth, *why live?*
    The land of honourable death
Is here: — up to the Field, and give
      Away thy breath!

X

Seek out — less often sought than found —
    A soldier's grave, for thee the best;
Then look around, and choose thy ground,
      And take thy Rest.   40

CHILDE HAROLD'S PILGRIMAGE

A Romaunt

Hobhouse records in his diary under October 31, 1809, that Byron had begun a new poem in Spenserian stanzas. This was at Janina in Epirus: the second canto was finished at Smyrna on March 28, 1810. After various changes the two cantos were published in 1812, after Byron's return to England, and instantly made him famous, the poem running through four editions between March and September. Byron's preface reads in part: " The following poem was written, for the most part, amidst the scenes which it attempts to describe. . . . The scenes attempted to be sketched are in Spain, Portugal, Epirus, Acarnania, and Greece. There, for the present, the poem stops: its reception will determine whether the author may venture to conduct his readers to the capital of the East. . . . A fictitious character is introduced for the sake of giving some connection to the piece. . . . It has been suggested to me by friends . . . that in this fictitious character, Childe [1] Harold, I may incur the suspicion of having intended some real personage: this I beg leave, once for all, to disclaim. . . ."

The hint that Byron intended to continue the poem was not picked up until after the collapse of his marriage and his second journey abroad. The third canto was written in Switzerland in May and June of 1816. It depicts Byron's journey from the Low Countries (the field of Waterloo) down the Rhine to Lake Leman and the Rhone, and contains appropriate reflections, mainly on the careers of Napoleon and Rousseau, and many personal comments on his wife, his daughter, and his own situation. The third canto was published in November of 1816.

The fourth canto was written, in its original form, in July, 1817, but considerably expanded before publication in the following April. Its scene is entirely Italian, beginning in Venice and passing through Ferrara and Florence to Rome, and it is accompanied by extensive historical notes, mainly by Hobhouse. In an epistolary dedication to Hobhouse, Byron speaks of the poem as " the longest, the most thoughtful and comprehensive of my compositions," and states that he had finally given up the effort to separate his own character from Childe Harold's, as a separation that no one paid any attention to anyway.

From Canto I we give some of the opening stanzas and the first lyric; also the lyric " To Inez," which is inserted between stanzas 84 and 85. This poem replaced the much more cheerful ballad, " The Girl of Cadiz," as more suitable to Harold's melancholy temperament. From the third canto are included the opening and some of the closing stanzas on Byron's daughter, and the famous Waterloo and Napoleon passages. From the fourth canto we give the " Bridge of Sighs " opening and the intensely personal conclusion.

from CANTO I

1

Oh, thou! in Hellas deemed of heavenly birth,
Muse! formed or fabled at the Minstrel's will!
Since shamed full oft by later lyres on earth,
Mine dares not call thee from thy sacred Hill:
Yet there I've wandered by thy vaunted rill;
Yes! sighed o'er Delphi's long deserted shrine,°
Where, save that feeble fountain, all is still;
Nor mote° my shell awake the weary Nine
To grace so plain a tale — this lowly lay of mine.

2

Whilome° in Albion's isle there dwelt a youth,   10
Who ne in Virtue's ways did take delight;
But spent his days in riot most uncouth,
And vexed with mirth the drowsy ear of Night.
Ah me! in sooth he was a shameless wight,
Sore given to revel, and ungodly glee;
Few earthly things found favour in his sight
Save concubines and carnal companie,
And flaunting wassailers° of high and low degree.

3

Childe Harold was he hight: — but whence his name
And lineage long, it suits me not to say;   20
Suffice it, that perchance they were of fame,
And had been glorious in another day:
But one sad losel° soils a name for ay,
However mighty in the olden time;
Nor all that heralds rake from coffined clay,
Nor florid prose, nor honied lies of rhyme,
Can blazon evil deeds, or consecrate a crime.

4

Childe Harold basked him in the Noontide sun,
Disporting there like any other fly;

Canto I: 6. Delphi's . . . shrine: "The little village of Castri stands partly on the site of Delphi. Along the path of the mountain, from Chrysso, are the remains of sepulchres hewn in and from the rock: —'One,' said the guide, 'of a king who broke his neck hunting.' His majesty had certainly chosen the fittest spot for such an achievement. A little above Castri is a cave, supposed the Pythian, of immense depth; the upper part of it is paved, and now a cowhouse" [part of Byron's note]. 8. mote: might. 10. Whilome: once upon a time. 18. flaunting wassailers: shameless drunkards. 23. losel: scoundrel.

CHILDE HAROLD'S PILGRIMAGE. 1. Childe: "It is almost superfluous to mention that the appellation 'Childe' . . . is used as more consonant with the old structure of versification which I have adopted" [from Byron's preface].

Nor deemed before his little day was done　　30
One blast might chill him into misery.
But long ere scarce a third of his passed by,
Worse than Adversity the Childe befell;
He felt the fulness of Satiety:
Then loathed he in his native land to dwell,
Which seemed to him more lone than Eremite's°
　　sad cell.

5

For he through Sin's long labyrinth had run,
Nor made atonement when he did amiss,
Had sighed to many though he loved but one,
And that loved one, alas! could ne'er be his.　　40
Ah, happy she! to 'scape from him whose kiss
Had been pollution unto aught so chaste;
Who soon had left her charms for vulgar bliss,
And spoiled her goodly lands to gild his waste,
Nor calm domestic peace had ever deigned to
　　taste. . . .

9

And none did love him! — though to hall and
　　bower
He gathered revellers from far and near,
He knew them flatterers of the festal hour,
The heartless Parasites of present cheer.
Yea! none did love him — not his lemans° dear —　50
But pomp and power alone are Woman's care,
And where these are light Eros finds a feere;°
Maidens, like moths, are ever caught by glare,
And Mammon wins his way where Seraphs might
　　despair.

10

Childe Harold had a mother — not forgot,
Though parting from that mother he did shun:
A sister whom he loved, but saw her not
Before his weary pilgrimage begun:
If friends he had, he bade adieu to none.
Yet deem not thence his breast a breast of steel:　60
Ye, who have known what 'tis to dote upon
A few dear objects, will in sadness feel
Such partings break the heart they fondly hope to
　　heal.

11

His house, his home, his heritage, his lands,
The laughing dames in whom he did delight,
Whose large blue eyes, fair locks, and snowy hands,
Might shake the Saintship of an Anchorite,
And long had fed his youthful appetite;

His goblets brimmed with every costly wine,
And all that mote to luxury invite,　　70
Without a sigh he left, to cross the brine,
And traverse Paynim° shores, and pass Earth's
　　central line.

12

The sails were filled, and fair the light winds blew,
As glad to waft him from his native home;
And fast the white rocks faded from his view,
And soon were lost in circumambient foam:
And then, it may be, of his wish to roam
Repented he, but in his bosom slept
The silent thought, nor from his lips did come
One word of wail, whilst others sate and wept,　80
And to the reckless gales unmanly moaning kept.

13

But when the Sun was sinking in the sea
He seized his harp, which he at times could string,
And strike, albeit with untaught melody,
When deemed he no strange ear was listening:
And now his fingers o'er it he did fling,
And tuned his farewell in the dim twilight;
While flew the vessel on her snowy wing,
And fleeting shores receded from his sight,
Thus to the elements he poured his last "Good
　　Night."　　90

CHILDE HAROLD'S GOOD NIGHT°

1

"Adieu, adieu! my native shore
　　Fades o'er the waters blue;
The night-winds sigh, the breakers roar,
　　And shrieks the wild sea-mew.
Yon Sun that sets upon the sea
　　We follow in his flight;
Farewell awhile to him and thee,
　　My native Land — Good Night!

2

"A few short hours and He will rise
　　To give the Morrow birth;　　10
And I shall hail the main and skies,
　　But not my mother Earth.
Deserted is my own good Hall,
　　Its hearth is desolate;
Wild weeds are gathering on the wall;
　　My Dog howls at the gate.

---

36. Eremite's: hermit's.　　**50. lemans:** mistresses.　　**52. feere:**
companion.

72. Paynim: pagan (or Mohammedan).　**Childe Harold's Good
Night:** In his preface Byron remarks that this poem was suggested
by "Lord Maxwell's Good Night," in the *Border Minstrelsy*,
edited by Sir Walter Scott.

3

"Come hither, hither, my little page!
　　Why dost thou weep and wail?
Or dost thou dread the billows' rage,
　　Or tremble at the gale?   20
But dash the tear-drop from thine eye;
　　Our ship is swift and strong:
Our fleetest falcon scarce can fly
　　More merrily along."

4

"Let winds be shrill, let waves roll high,
　　I fear not wave nor wind:
Yet marvel not, Sir Childe, that I
　　Am sorrowful in mind;
For I have from my father gone,
　　A mother whom I love,   30
And have no friends, save these alone,
　　But thee — and One above.

5

"My father blessed me fervently,
　　Yet did not much complain;
But sorely will my mother sigh
　　Till I come back again." —
"Enough, enough, my little lad!
　　Such tears become thine eye;
If I thy guileless bosom had,
　　Mine own would not be dry.   40

6

"Come hither, hither, my staunch yeoman,
　　Why dost thou look so pale?
Or dost thou dread a French foeman?
　　Or shiver at the gale?" —
"Deem'st thou I tremble for my life?
　　Sir Childe, I'm not so weak;
But thinking on an absent wife
　　Will blanch a faithful cheek.

7

"My spouse and boys dwell near thy hall,
　　Along the bordering Lake,   50
And when they on their father call,
　　What answer shall she make?" —
"Enough, enough, my yeoman good,
　　Thy grief let none gainsay;
But I, who am of lighter mood,
　　Will laugh to flee away.

8

"For who would trust the seeming sighs
　　Of wife or paramour?

Fresh feeres will dry the bright blue eyes
　　We late saw streaming o'er.   60
For pleasures past I do not grieve,
　　Nor perils gathering near;
My greatest grief is that I leave
　　No thing that claims a tear.

9

"And now I'm in the world alone,
　　Upon the wide, wide sea:
But why should I for others groan,
　　When none will sigh for me?
Perchance my Dog will whine in vain,
　　Till fed by stranger hands;   70
But long ere I come back again,
　　He'd tear me where he stands.

10

"With thee, my bark, I'll swiftly go
　　Athwart the foaming brine;
Nor care what land thou bear'st me to,
　　So not again to mine.
Welcome, welcome, ye dark-blue waves!
　　And when you fail my sight,
Welcome, ye deserts, and ye caves!
　　My native Land — Good Night!"   80

TO INEZ

1

Nay, smile not at my sullen brow;
　　Alas! I cannot smile again:
Yet Heaven avert that ever thou
　　Shouldst weep, and haply weep in vain.

2

And dost thou ask what secret woe
　　I bear, corroding Joy and Youth?
And wilt thou vainly seek to know
　　A pang, ev'n thou must fail to soothe?

3

It is not love, it is not hate,
　　Nor low Ambition's honours lost,   10
That bids me loathe my present state,
　　And fly from all I prized the most:

4

It is that weariness which springs
　　From all I meet, or hear, or see:
To me no pleasure Beauty brings;
　　Thine eyes have scarce a charm for me.

5

It is that settled, ceaseless gloom
   The fabled Hebrew Wanderer° bore;
That will not look beyond the tomb,
   But cannot hope for rest before.   20

6

What Exile from himself can flee?
   To zones though more and more remote,
Still, still pursues, where'er I be,
   The blight of Life — the Demon Thought.

7

Yet others rapt in pleasure seem,
   And taste of all that I forsake;
Oh! may they still of transport dream,
   And ne'er — at least like me — awake!

8

Through many a clime 'tis mine to go,
   With many a retrospection curst;   30
And all my solace is to know,
   Whate'er betides, I've known the worst.

9

What is that worst? Nay do not ask —
   In pity from the search forbear:
Smile on — nor venture to unmask
   Man's heart, and view the Hell that's there.

from CANTO III

1

Is thy face like thy mother's, my fair child!
ADA! sole daughter of my house and heart?
When last I saw thy young blue eyes they
   smiled,
And then we parted, — not as now we part,
But with a hope. —
           Awaking with a start,
The waters heave around me; and on high
The winds lift up their voices: I depart,
Whither I know not; but the hour's gone by,
When Albion's lessening shores could grieve or
   glad mine eye.

2

Once more upon the waters! yet once more!   10
And the waves bound beneath me as a steed
That knows his rider. Welcome to their roar!
Swift be their guidance, wheresoe'er it lead!

To Inez: 18. fabled Hebrew Wanderer: the Wandering Jew.

Though the strained mast should quiver as a reed,
And the rent canvass fluttering strew the gale,
Still must I on; for I am as a weed,
Flung from the rock, on Ocean's foam, to sail
Where'er the surge may sweep, the tempest's breath
   prevail.

3

In my youth's summer I did sing of One,
The wandering outlaw of his own dark mind;   20
Again I seize the theme, then but begun,
And bear it with me, as the rushing wind
Bears the cloud onwards: in that Tale I find
The furrows of long thought, and dried-up tears,
Which, ebbing, leave a sterile track behind,
O'er which all heavily the journeying years
Plod the last sands of life, — where not a flower
   appears.

4

Since my young days of passion — joy or pain —
Perchance my heart and harp have lost a string —
And both may jar: it may be that in vain   30
I would essay, as I have sung, to sing:
Yet, though a dreary strain, to this I cling;
So that it wean me from the weary dream
Of selfish grief or gladness — so it fling
Forgetfulness around me — it shall seem
To me, though to none else, a not ungrateful theme.

5

He, who grown agéd in this world of woe,
In deeds, not years, piercing the depths of life,
So that no wonder waits him — nor below
Can Love or Sorrow, Fame, Ambition, Strife,   40
Cut to his heart again with the keen knife
Of silent, sharp endurance — he can tell
Why Thought seeks refuge in lone caves, yet
   rife
With airy images, and shapes which dwell
Still unimpaired, though old, in the Soul's haunted
   cell.

6

'Tis to create, and in creating live
A being more intense, that we endow
With form our fancy, gaining as we give
The life we image, even as I do now —
What am I? Nothing: but not so art thou,   50
Soul of my thought! with whom I traverse earth,
Invisible but gazing, as I glow
Mixed with thy spirit, blended with thy birth,
And feeling still with thee in my crushed feelings'
   dearth.

7

Yet must I think less wildly: — I *have* thought
Too long and darkly, till my brain became,
In its own eddy boiling and o'erwrought,
A whirling gulf of phantasy and flame:
And thus, untaught in youth my heart to tame,
My springs of life were poisoned. 'Tis too late!   60
Yet am I changed; though still enough the same
In strength to bear what Time can not abate,
And feed on bitter fruits without accusing Fate.

8

Something too much of this: — but now 'tis past,
And the spell closes with its silent seal:
Long absent HAROLD re-appears at last —
He of the breast which fain no more would feel,
Wrung with the wounds which kill not, but ne'er
    heal;
Yet Time, who changes all, had altered him
In soul and aspect as in age: years steal   70
Fire from the mind as vigour from the limb;
And Life's enchanted cup but sparkles near the
    brim.

21

There was a sound of revelry by night,
And Belgium's Capital had gathered then
Her Beauty and her Chivalry — and bright
The lamps shone o'er fair women and brave men;
A thousand hearts beat happily; and when
Music arose with its voluptuous swell,
Soft eyes looked love to eyes which spake again,
And all went merry as a marriage bell;°   80
But hush! hark! a deep sound strikes like a rising
    knell!

22

Did ye not hear it? — No — 'twas but the Wind,
Or the car rattling o'er the stony street;
On with the dance! let joy be unconfined;
No sleep till morn, when Youth and Pleasure meet
To chase the glowing Hours with flying feet —
But hark! — that heavy sound breaks in once more,
As if the clouds its echo would repeat;
And nearer — clearer — deadlier than before!
Arm! Arm! it is — it is — the cannon's opening
    roar!

Canto III: 80. And . . . bell: "On the night previous to the action,
it is said that a ball was given at Brussels" [B].

23

Within a windowed niche of that high hall   91
Sate Brunswick's fated Chieftain;° he did hear
That sound the first amidst the festival,
And caught its tone with Death's prophetic ear;
And when they smiled because he deemed it near,
His heart more truly knew that peal too well
Which stretched his father on a bloody bier,
And roused the vengeance blood alone could quell;
He rushed into the field, and, foremost fighting,
    fell.

24

Ah! then and there was hurrying to and fro —   100
And gathering tears, and tremblings of distress,
And cheeks all pale, which but an hour ago
Blushed at the praise of their own loveliness —
And there were sudden partings, such as press
The life from out young hearts, and choking sighs
Which ne'er might be repeated; who could guess
If ever more should meet those mutual eyes,
Since upon night so sweet such awful morn could
    rise!

25

And there was mounting in hot haste — the steed,
The mustering squadron, and the clattering car, 110
Went pouring forward with impetuous speed,
And swiftly forming in the ranks of war —
And the deep thunder peal on peal afar;
And near, the beat of the alarming drum
Roused up the soldier ere the Morning Star;
While thronged the citizens with terror dumb,
Or whispering, with white lips — " The foe! They
    come! they come! "

26

And wild and high the " Cameron's Gathering "°
    rose!
The war-note of Lochiel,° which Albyn's° hills
Have heard, and heard, too, have her Saxon foes: —
How in the noon of night that pibroch thrills, 121
Savage and shrill! But with the breath which fills
Their mountain pipe, so fill the mountaineers
With the fierce native daring which instils
The stirring memory of a thousand years,
And Evan's — Donald's° — fame rings in each
    clansman's ears! . . .

92. Brunswick's . . . Chieftain: The Duke of Brunswick, nephew
of George III, was killed at the battle of Quatre Bras, two days
before Waterloo.   118. Cameron's Gathering: the clan song of
the Camerons.   119. Lochiel: the title of the chief of the clan
Cameron.   Albyn's: Albyn is the Gaelic name for Scotland.
126. Evan's—Donald's: "Sir Evan Cameron, and his descendant
Donald, the 'gentle Lochiel' of the 'forty-five' " [B]. Sir Evan
fought for James II; Donald for the Young Pretender in the 1745
rebellion.

36

There sunk the greatest, nor the worst of men,
Whose Spirit, antithetically mixed,
One moment of the mightiest, and again
On little objects with like firmness fixed;   130
Extreme in all things! hadst thou been betwixt,
Thy throne had still been thine, or never been;
For Daring made thy rise as fall: thou seek'st
Even now to re-assume the imperial mien,
And shake again the world, the Thunderer of the
    scene!

37

Conqueror and Captive of the Earth art thou!
She trembles at thee still, and thy wild name
Was ne'er more bruited in men's minds than
    now
That thou art nothing, save the jest of Fame,
Who wooed thee once, thy Vassal, and became 140
The flatterer of thy fierceness — till thou wert
A God unto thyself; nor less the same
To the astounded kingdoms all inert,
Who deemed thee for a time whate'er thou didst
    assert.

38

Oh, more or less than man — in high or low —
Battling with nations, flying from the field;
Now making monarchs' necks thy footstool, now
More than thy meanest soldier taught to yield;
An Empire thou couldst crush, command, rebuild,
But govern not thy pettiest passion, nor,   150
However deeply in men's spirits skilled,
Look through thine own, nor curb the lust of War,
Nor learn that tempted Fate will leave the loftiest
    Star.

39

Yet well thy soul hath brooked the turning tide
With that untaught innate philosophy,
Which, be it Wisdom, Coldness, or deep Pride,
Is gall and wormwood to an enemy.
When the whole host of hatred stood hard by,
To watch and mock thee shrinking, thou has
    smiled
With a sedate and all-enduring eye; —   160
When Fortune fled her spoiled and favourite child,
He stood unbowed beneath the ills upon him piled.

40

Sager than in thy fortunes; for in them
Ambition steeled thee on too far to show
That just habitual scorn, which could contemn
Men and their thoughts; 'twas wise to feel, not so
To wear it ever on thy lip and brow,

And spurn the instruments thou wert to use
Till they were turned unto thine overthrow:
'Tis but a worthless world to win or lose;   170
So hath it proved to thee, and all such lot who
    choose.

41

If, like a tower upon a headlong rock,
Thou hadst been made to stand or fall alone,
Such scorn of man had helped to brave the shock;
But men's thoughts were the steps which paved
    thy throne,
Their admiration thy best weapon shone;
The part of Philip's son° was thine — not then
(Unless aside thy Purple had been thrown)
Like stern Diogenes to mock at men:
For sceptred Cynics° Earth were far too wide a den.

42

But Quiet to quick bosoms is a Hell,   181
And *there* hath been thy bane; there is a fire
And motion of the Soul which will not dwell
In its own narrow being, but aspire
Beyond the fitting medium of desire;
And, but once kindled, quenchless evermore,
Preys upon high adventure, nor can tire
Of aught but rest; a fever at the core,
Fatal to him who bears, to all who ever bore.

113

I have not loved the World, nor the World me; 190
I have not flattered its rank breath, nor bowed
To its idolatries a patient knee,
Nor coined my cheek to smiles, — nor cried aloud
In worship of an echo: in the crowd
They could not deem me one of such — I stood
Among them, but not of them — in a shroud
Of thoughts which were not their thoughts, and
    still could,
Had I not filed° my mind, which thus itself
    subdued.

177. Philip's son: Alexander the Great.   **180. sceptred Cynics**:
"The great error of Napoleon, 'if we have writ our annals true,'
was a continued obtrusion on mankind of his want of all community of feeling for or with them; perhaps more offensive to
human vanity than the active cruelty of more trembling and
suspicious tyranny. Such were his speeches to public assemblies
as well as individuals; and the single expression which he is said
to have used on returning to Paris after the Russian winter had
destroyed his army, rubbing his hands over a fire, 'This is pleasanter than Moscow,' would probably alienate more favour from
his cause than the destruction and reverses which led to the
remark" [B].   **198. filed**: Byron refers to *Macbeth*, III.i.65.

114

I have not loved the World, nor the World me, —
But let us part fair foes; I do believe,   200
Though I have found them not, that there may be
Words which are things, — Hopes which will not
    deceive,
And Virtues which are merciful, nor weave
Snares for the failing: I would also deem
O'er others' griefs that some sincerely grieve —
That two, or one, are almost what they seem, —
That Goodness is no name — and Happiness no
    dream.

115

My daughter! with thy name this song begun!
My daughter! with thy name thus much shall
    end! —
I see thee not — I hear thee not — but none   210
Can be so wrapt in thee; Thou art the Friend
To whom the shadows of far years extend:
Albeit my brow thou never should'st behold,
My voice shall with thy future visions blend,
And reach into thy heart, — when mine is cold, —
A token and a tone, even from thy father's mould.

from CANTO IV

1

I stood in Venice, on the " Bridge of Sighs";
A Palace and a prison° on each hand:
I saw from out the wave her structures rise
As from the stroke of the Enchanter's wand:
A thousand Years their cloudy wings expand
Around me, and a dying Glory smiles
O'er the far times, when many a subject land
Looked to the wingéd Lion's° marble piles,
Where Venice sate in state, throned on her hundred
    isles!

2

She looks a sea Cybele,° fresh from Ocean,   10
Rising with her tiara of proud towers
At airy distance, with majestic motion,
A Ruler of the waters and their powers:
And such she was; — her daughters had their dow-
    ers

From spoils of nations, and the exhaustless East
Poured in her lap all gems in sparkling showers:
In purple was she robed, and of her feast
Monarchs partook, and deemed their dignity in-
    creased.

3

In Venice Tasso's echoes° are no more,
And silent rows the songless Gondolier;   20
Her palaces are crumbling to the shore,
And Music meets not always now the ear:
Those days are gone — but Beauty still is here.
States fall — Arts fade — but Nature doth not die,
Nor yet forget how Venice once was dear,
The pleasant place of all festivity,
The Revel of the earth — the Masque of Italy!

95

I speak not of men's creeds — they rest between
Man and his maker — but of things allowed,
Averred, and known, and daily, hourly seen —   30
The yoke that is upon us doubly bowed,
And the intent of Tyranny avowed,
The edict of Earth's rulers, who are grown
The apes of him who humbled once the proud,
And shook them from their slumbers on the throne;
Too glorious, were this all his mighty arm had done.

96

Can tyrants but by tyrants conquered be,
And Freedom find no Champion and no Child,
Such as Columbia saw arise when she
Sprung forth a Pallas,° armed and undefiled?   40
Or must such minds be nourished in the wild,
Deep in the unpruned forest, 'midst the roar
Of cataracts, where nursing Nature smiled
On infant Washington? Has Earth no more
Such seeds within her breast, or Europe no such
    shore?

97

But France got drunk with blood to vomit crime;
And fatal have her Saturnalia been
To Freedom's cause, in every age and clime;
Because the deadly days which we have seen,
And vile Ambition, that built up between   50
Man and his hopes an adamantine wall,
And the base pageant last upon the scene,
Are grown the pretext for the eternal thrall
Which nips Life's tree, and dooms man's worst —
    his second fall.

Canto IV: 2. Palace . . . prison: The Bridge of Sighs connects
the Doge's Palace with the San Marco prison.   8. Lion's: The
lion is the emblem of St. Mark, patron saint of Venice.   10.
Cybele: "Sabellicus, describing the appearance of Venice, has
made use of the above image, which would not be poetical were
it not true" [B]. Sabellicus was a fifteenth-century historian of
Venice. Cybele, the mother of the gods in some Roman cults,
was often represented as crowned with a tower.

19. Tasso's echoes: There used to be a custom of gondoliers' reciting stanzas of Tasso's sixteenth-century poem, Gerusalemme
Liberata (Jerusalem Delivered), which had practically disappeared
in Byron's day.   40. Sprung . . . Pallas: Pallas Athene was fabled
to have sprung full-grown from the forehead of Zeus.

98

Yet, Freedom! yet thy banner, torn but flying,
Streams like the thunder-storm *against* the wind!
Thy trumpet voice, though broken now and dying,
The loudest still the Tempest leaves behind;
Thy tree hath lost its blossoms, and the rind,
Chopped by the axe, looks rough and little worth,
But the sap lasts, — and still the seed we find   61
Sown deep, even in the bosom of the North;
So shall a better spring less bitter fruit bring forth.

133

It is not that I may not have incurred,
For my ancestral faults or mine, the wound
I bleed withal; and, had it been conferred
With a just weapon, it had flowed unbound;
But now my blood shall not sink in the ground —
To thee I do devote it — *Thou* shalt take
The vengeance, which shall yet be sought and
    found —   70
Which if *I* have not taken for the sake —
But let that pass — I sleep — but Thou shalt yet
    awake.

134

And if my voice break forth, 'tis not that now
I shrink from what is suffered: let him speak
Who hath beheld decline, upon my brow,
Or seen my mind's convulsion leave it weak;
But in this page a record will I seek.
Not in the air shall these my words disperse,
Though I be ashes; a far hour shall wreak
The deep prophetic fulness of this verse,   80
And pile on human heads the mountain of my
    curse!

135

That curse shall be Forgiveness. — Have I not —
Hear me, my mother Earth! behold it, Heaven! —
Have I not had to wrestle with my lot?
Have I not suffered things to be forgiven?
Have I not had my brain seared, my heart riven,
Hopes sapped, name blighted, Life's life lied away?
And only not to desperation driven,
Because not altogether of such clay
As rots into the souls of those whom I survey.   90

136

From mighty wrongs to petty perfidy
Have I not seen what human things could do?
From the loud roar of foaming calumny
To the small whisper of the as paltry few —
And subtler venom of the reptile crew,

The Janus glance° of whose significant eye,
Learning to lie with silence, would *seem* true —
And without utterance, save the shrug or sigh,
Deal round to happy fools its speechless obloquy.

137

But I have lived, and have not lived in vain: 100
My mind may lose its force, my blood its fire,
And my frame perish even in conquering pain;
But there is that within me which shall tire
Torture and Time, and breathe when I expire;
Something unearthly, which they deem not of,
Like the remembered tone of a mute lyre,
Shall on their softened spirits sink, and move
In hearts all rocky now the late remorse of Love.

177

Oh! that the Desert were my dwelling-place,
With one fair Spirit for my minister,   110
That I might all forget the human race,
And, hating no one, love but only her!
Ye elements! — in whose ennobling stir
I feel myself exalted — Can ye not
Accord me such a Being? Do I err
In deeming such inhabit many a spot?
Though with them to converse can rarely be our
    lot.

178

There is a pleasure in the pathless woods,
There is a rapture on the lonely shore,
There is society, where none intrudes,   120
By the deep Sea, and Music in its roar:
I love not Man the less, but Nature more,
From these our interviews, in which I steal
From all I may be, or have been before,
To mingle with the Universe, and feel
What I can ne'er express — yet can not all conceal.

179

Roll on, thou deep and dark blue Ocean — roll!
Ten thousand fleets sweep over thee in vain;
Man marks the earth with ruin — his control
Stops with the shore; — upon the watery plain   130
The wrecks are all thy deed, nor doth remain
A shadow of man's ravage, save his own,
When, for a moment, like a drop of rain,
He sinks into thy depths with bubbling groan —
Without a grave — unknelled, uncoffined, and un-
    known.

96. Janus glance: Janus, the god of doorways who gave his name
to January, was represented as double-faced.

184

And I have loved thee, Ocean! and my joy
Of youthful sports was on thy breast to be
Borne, like thy bubbles, onward: from a boy
I wantoned with thy breakers — they to me
Were a delight; and if the freshening sea   140
Made them a terror — 'twas a pleasing fear,
For I was as it were a Child of thee,
And trusted to thy billows far and near,
And laid my hand upon thy mane — as I do here.

185

My task is done — my song hath ceased — my
    theme
Has died into an echo; it is fit
The spell should break of this protracted dream.
The torch shall be extinguished which hath lit

My midnight lamp — and what is writ, is writ, —
Would it were worthier! but I am not now   150
That which I have been — and my visions flit
Less palpably before me — and the glow
Which in my Spirit dwelt is fluttering, faint, and
    low.

186

Farewell! a word that must be, and hath been —
A sound which makes us linger; — yet — farewell!
Ye! who have traced the Pilgrim to the scene
Which is his last — if in your memories dwell
A thought which once was his — if on ye swell
A single recollection — not in vain
He wore his sandal-shoon, and scallop-shell;   160
Farewell! with *him* alone may rest the pain,
If such there were — with *you,* the Moral of his
    Strain.

DON JUAN

The first hint that Byron was working on *Don Juan* is in a letter to John Murray, dated July 10, 1818, where he says that he has begun a "ludicrous" story in the style of *Beppo.* With his usual amazing facility he completed the first canto in September, accompanying it with a mock dedication to Southey, which contains one of his most violent assaults on that poet, along with some equally bitter reflections on "the intellectual eunuch Castlereagh." The professed reason for the attack on Southey was the malicious gossip that had been allegedly spread by Southey about the Shelley-Byron menage in Switzerland, or, as Byron said in a letter to Hobhouse, "On his return from Switzerland, two years ago, [Southey] said that Shelley and I 'had formed a League of Incest, and practised our precepts.'" The second canto was finished in January, 1819.

It is difficult for us to understand today how passionately sincere Byron's best friends, Kinnaird, Hobhouse, and John Murray, were in believing that *Don Juan* was a disgrace to Byron's reputation. They could not understand Byron's assertion that "it is the most moral of poems," nor the seriousness of his fight to maintain its integrity. "You shan't make *Canticles* of My Cantos," said Byron in response to pleas to bowdlerize the poem, and again: "You have so many 'divine' poems, is it nothing to have written a *Human* one?" Eventually Murray, with great hesitation, published the first two cantos on July 15, 1819 — anonymously, with only the printer's name on the title-page, and with the Southey "dedication" withdrawn.

Byron was chagrined by the unfavorable reaction, but went on with the poem, saying to Murray that "the outcry has not frightened but it has *hurt* me." Murray had paid Byron fifteen hundred guineas for the first two cantos (along with the "Ode on Venice"),

and twenty-five hundred for the next three along with three of Byron's plays. But his disapproval of the poem was so marked that Byron eventually gave the sixth, seventh and eighth cantos to John Hunt, Leigh Hunt's brother, which were published with a separate prose preface. Before the middle of 1823 he had finished sixteen cantos, and took the first fourteen stanzas of a seventeenth to Greece with him, hoping to be able to continue it there. But nothing was added to the poem in Greece, and the final fragment, left among his private papers, was not published until 1903.

After Don Juan's misadventure in the first canto, he was sent abroad, but his vessel was shipwrecked and the survivors suffered great hardships, only partly alleviated by eating first Juan's spaniel and then his tutor. Juan himself however refused to "dine with them on his pastor and his master." Juan was then cast up on a Greek island and tenderly nursed by Haidée, the lovely daughter of a Greek pirate named Lambro, described as "the mildest mannered man/ That ever scuttled ship or cut a throat." The latter returned unexpectedly, kidnapped Juan and sold him as a slave in Constantinople, while Haidée went mad with grief and died. Juan then became a slave in the harem of his mistress, a sultana who had fallen in love with him. After several adventures he escaped to the Russian army, then at war with Turkey, attracted favorable attention by his valor, and was sent to the court of Catherine II at St. Petersburg. The Empress then sent him on a diplomatic mission to England, and England is the scene of the poem from the tenth canto to the end. Byron says in the first canto that he plans a regular mock epic in the conventional epic number of twelve cantos, the last to be a satiric vision of "hell," which, as Byron explains elsewhere, could also be a symbol of marriage. This scheme soon broke down: Byron promised first fifty, then, in the poem itself, a hundred cantos. But, aside from a hint that he intended to make Don Juan become a Methodist for a while, we have little indication of how the poem was to proceed.

In such an embarrassment of riches it is hard to make anything but an arbitrary choice. The first canto, a superb piece of leisurely storytelling, is here given complete, along with the end of the third, with its famous lyric, its equally famous ridicule of the Lake poets, and the sudden changes of mood that are so characteristic of the poem.

CANTO I

1

I want a hero: an uncommon want,
   When every year and month sends forth a new
     one,
Till, after cloying the gazettes with cant,
   The age discovers he is not the true one:
Of such as these I should not care to vaunt,
   I'll therefore take our ancient friend Don Juan—
We all have seen him, in the pantomime,°
Sent to the devil somewhat ere his time.

2

Vernon, the butcher Cumberland, Wolfe, Hawke,
   Prince Ferdinand, Granby, Burgoyne, Keppel,
     Howe,°   10
Evil and good, have had their tithe of talk,
   And filled their sign-posts then, like Wellesley°
     now;
Each in their turn like Banquo's monarchs stalk,
   Followers of fame, " nine farrow "°of that sow:
France, too, had Buonaparté and Dumourier°
Recorded in the Moniteur and Courier.

3

Barnave, Brissot, Condorcet, Mirabeau,°
   Pétion, Clootz, Danton, Marat, La Fayette,
Were French, and famous people, as we know;
   And there were others, scarce forgotten yet,   20
Joubert, Hoche, Marceau, Lannes, Desaix, Moreau,
   With many of the military set,
Exceedingly remarkable at times,
But not at all adapted to my rhymes.

DON JUAN. **Canto I: 7. pantomime:** The story of Don Juan had been popular in English pantomime for over a century. **9–10. Vernon . . . Howe:** British eighteenth-century army commanders. The Duke of Cumberland (1721–65) was called "Butcher" because of his brutality to the defeated Jacobites after the rebellion of 1745. **12. Wellesley:** the Duke of Wellington. **14. "nine farrow":** See *Macbeth*, IV.i.65. **15. Dumourier:** or Dumouriez, a revolutionary turned royalist who lived on a pension in England. **17–21. Barnave . . . Moreau:** French Napoleonic and Revolutionary military leaders.

4

Nelson was once Britannia's god of war,
   And still should be so, but the tide is turned;
There's no more to be said of Trafalgar,
   'Tis with our hero quietly inurned;
Because the army's grown more popular,
   At which the naval people are concerned,   30
Besides, the prince is all for the land-service,
Forgetting Duncan, Nelson, Howe, and Jervis.°

5

Brave men were living before Agamemnon
   And since, exceeding valorous and sage,
A good deal like him too, though quite the same
     none;
   But then they shone not on the poet's page,
And so have been forgotten:—I condemn none,
   But can't find any in the present age
Fit for my poem (that is, for my new one);
So, as I said, I'll take my friend Don Juan.   40

6

Most epic poets plunge " in medias res "°
   (Horace makes this the heroic turnpike road),
And then your hero tells, whene'er you please,
   What went before—by way of episode,
While seated after dinner at his ease,
   Beside his mistress in some soft abode,
Palace, or garden, paradise, or cavern,
Which serves the happy couple for a tavern.

7

That is the usual method, but not mine—
   My way is to begin with the beginning;   50
The regularity of my design
   Forbids all wandering as the worst of sinning,
And therefore I shall open with a line
   (Although it cost me half an hour in spinning)
Narrating somewhat of Don Juan's father,
And also of his mother, if you'd rather.

8

In Seville was he born, a pleasant city,
   Famous for oranges and women—he
Who has not seen it will be much to pity,
   So says the proverb—and I quite agree;   60
Of all the Spanish towns is none more pretty,

32. Duncan . . . Jervis: British naval commanders. The Prince Regent's boasts about his military capacities were a common joke. He was never in any battle. **41. "in . . . res":** "in the midst of things." The practice of Homer and Virgil of beginning their epics at a well-advanced point in the action was noted in Horace's *Ars Poetica*.

Cadiz, perhaps — but that you soon may see: —
Don Juan's parents lived beside the river,
A noble stream, and called the Guadalquivir.

9

His father's name was Jóse — *Don,* of course,
    A true Hidalgo, free from every strain
Of Moor or Hebrew blood, he traced his source
    Through the most Gothic gentlemen of Spain;
A better cavalier ne'er mounted horse,
    Or, being mounted, e'er got down again,   70
Than Jóse, who begot our hero, who
Begot — but that's to come —— Well, to renew:

10

His mother was a learned lady, famed
    For every branch of every science known —
In every Christian language ever named,
    With virtues equalled by her wit alone:
She made the cleverest people quite ashamed,
    And even the good with inward envy groan,
Finding themselves so very much exceeded
In their own way by all the things that she did. 80

11

Her memory was a mine: she knew by heart
    All Calderon and greater part of Lopé,°
So that if any actor missed his part
    She could have served him for the prompter's
        copy;
For her Feinagle's° were an useless art,
    And he himself obliged to shut up shop — he
Could never make a memory so fine as
That which adorned the brain of Donna Inez.

12

Her favourite science was the mathematical,
    Her noblest virtue was her magnanimity;   90
Her wit (she sometimes tried at wit) was Attic all,
    Her serious sayings darkened to sublimity;
In short, in all things she was fairly what I call
    A prodigy — her morning dress was dimity,
Her evening silk, or, in the summer, muslin,
And other stuffs, with which I won't stay puzzling.

13

She knew the Latin — that is, "the Lord's prayer,"
    And Greek — the alphabet — I'm nearly sure;
She read some French romances here and there,

Although her mode of speaking was not pure;
For native Spanish she had no great care,   101
    At least her conversation was obscure;
Her thoughts were theorems, her words a problem,
As if she deemed that mystery would ennoble 'em.

14

She liked the English and the Hebrew tongue,
    And said there was analogy between 'em;
She proved it somehow out of sacred song,
    But I must leave the proofs to those who've seen
        'em,
But this I heard her say, and can't be wrong,
    And all may think which way their judgments
        lean 'em,   110
" 'Tis strange — the Hebrew noun which means
        ' I am,'°
The English always use to govern d—n."

15

Some women use their tongues — she *looked* a
        lecture,
    Each eye a sermon, and her brow a homily,
An all-in-all sufficient self-director,
    Like the lamented late Sir Samuel Romilly,°
The Law's expounder, and the State's corrector,
    Whose suicide was almost an anomaly —
One sad example more, that " All is vanity," —
(The jury brought their verdict in " Insanity.") 120

16

In short, she was a walking calculation,
    Miss Edgeworth's novels stepping from their cov-
        ers,
Or Mrs. Trimmer's books on education,
    Or " Coelebs' Wife " set out in quest of lovers,°
Morality's grim personification,
    In which not Envy's self a flaw discovers;
To others' share let " female errors fall,"
For she had not even one — the worst of all.

17

Oh! she was perfect past all parallel —
    Of any modern female saint's comparison;   130
So far above the cunning powers of hell,
    Her guardian angel had given up his garrison;

111. 'I am': i.e., God; see Exod. 3:14. 116. Romilly: Sir Samuel
Romilly was Lady Byron's legal adviser, and Byron called him
one of the "assassins" of his character. He committed suicide in
1818, a few days after his wife's death. This suicide is the subject
of a savage letter from Byron to his wife, dated November 18,
1818. 122-24. Miss . . . lovers: Maria Edgeworth (1767-1849),
Sarah Trimmer (1741-1810), and Hannah More (1745-1833) were
all purveyors of improving fiction for adolescent females. The last
named was the author of *Coelebs in Search of a Wife* (1809).

82. Calderon . . . Lopé: Calderon de la Barca (1600-81) and Lopé
de Vega (1562-1635) are the greatest dramatists of Spanish literature. 85. Feinagle's: Professor Gregor von Feinagle, who had
invented a mnemonic system, had lectured in London in 1811.

Even her minutest motions went as well
  As those of the best time-piece made by Har-
    rison:°
In virtues nothing earthly could surpass her,
Save thine " incomparable oil," Macassar!°

18

Perfect she was, but as perfection is
  Insipid in this naughty world of ours,
Where our first parents never learned to kiss
  Till they were exiled from their earlier bowers,
Where all was peace, and innocence, and bliss 141
  (I wonder how they got through the twelve
    hours),
Don Jóse, like a lineal son of Eve,
Went plucking various fruit without her leave.

19

He was a mortal of the careless kind,
  With no great love for learning, or the learn'd,
Who chose to go where'er he had a mind,
  And never dreamed his lady was concerned;
The world, as usual, wickedly inclined
  To see a kingdom or a house o'erturned, 150
Whispered he had a mistress, some said *two,*
But for domestic quarrels *one* will do.

20

Now Donna Inez had, with all her merit,
  A great opinion of her own good qualities;
Neglect, indeed, requires a saint to bear it,
  And such, indeed, she was in her moralities;
But then she had a devil of a spirit,
  And sometimes mixed up fancies with realities,
And let few opportunities escape
Of getting her liege lord into a scrape. 160

21

This was an easy matter with a man
  Oft in the wrong, and never on his guard;
And even the wisest, do the best they can,
  Have moments, hours, and days, so unprepared,
That you might " brain them with their lady's
    fan ";°
  And sometimes ladies hit exceeding hard,
And fans turn into falchions in fair hands,
And why and wherefore no one understands.

134. **Harrison:** John "Longitude" Harrison was a famous watch-
maker, and the inventor of watch compensation. 136. **Macassar:**
Macassar oil was used in hair dressing; its lethal effect on velvet-
covered furniture was the reason for the "antimacassar" protective covering. 165. "**brain . . . fan**": See *I Henry IV*, II.iii.25.

22

'Tis pity learned virgins ever wed
  With persons of no sort of education, 170
Or gentlemen, who, though well born and bred,
  Grow tired of scientific conversation;
I don't choose to say much upon this head,
  I'm a plain man, and in a single station,
But — Oh! ye lords of ladies intellectual,
Inform us truly, have they not hen-pecked you
  all?

23

Don Jóse and his lady quarrelled — *why,*
  Not any of the many could divine,
Though several thousand people chose to try,
  'Twas surely no concern of theirs nor mine;
I loathe that low vice — curiosity; 181
  But if there's anything in which I shine,
'Tis in arranging all my friends' affairs,
Not having, of my own, domestic cares.

24

And so I interfered, and with the best
  Intentions, but their treatment was not kind;
I think the foolish people were possessed,
  For neither of them could I ever find,
Although their porter afterwards confessed —
  But that's no matter, and the worst's behind, 190
For little Juan o'er me threw, down stairs,
A pail of housemaid's water unawares.

25

A little curly-headed, good-for-nothing,
  And mischief-making monkey from his birth;
His parents ne'er agreed except in doting
  Upon the most inquiet imp on earth;
Instead of quarrelling, had they been but both
  in
  Their senses, they'd have sent young master forth
To school, or had him soundly whipped at home,
To teach him manners for the time to come. 200

26

Don Jóse and the Donna Inez led
  For some time an unhappy sort of life,
Wishing each other, not divorced, but dead;
  They lived respectably as man and wife,
Their conduct was exceedingly well-bred,
  And gave no outward signs of inward strife,
Until at length the smothered fire broke out,
And put the business past all kind of doubt.

27

For Inez called some druggists and physicians,
  And tried to prove her loving lord was *mad,* 210
But as he had some lucid intermissions,
  She next decided he was only *bad;*
Yet when they asked her for her depositions,
  No sort of explanation could be had,
Save that her duty both to man and God
Required this conduct — which seemed very odd.

28

She kept a journal, where his faults were noted,
  And opened certain trunks of books and letters,
All which might, if occasion served, be quoted;
  And then she had all Seville for abettors, 220
Besides her good old grandmother (who doted);
  The hearers of her case became repeaters,
Then advocates, inquisitors, and judges,
Some for amusement, others for old grudges.

29

And then this best and meekest woman bore
  With such serenity her husband's woes,
Just as the Spartan ladies did of yore,
  Who saw their spouses killed, and nobly chose
Never to say a word about them more —
  Calmly she heard each calumny that rose, 230
And saw *his* agonies with such sublimity,
That all the world exclaimed, " What magnanim-
    ity!"

30

No doubt this patience, when the world is damning
    us,
  Is philosophic in our former friends;
'Tis also pleasant to be deemed magnanimous,
  The more so in obtaining our own ends;
And what the lawyers call a *" malus animus "*°
  Conduct like this by no means comprehends:
Revenge in person's certainly no virtue,
But then 'tis not *my* fault, if *others* hurt you. 240

31

And if our quarrels should rip up old stories,
  And help them with a lie or two additional,
I'm not to blame, as you well know — no more
    is
Any one else — they were become traditional;
Besides, their resurrection aids our glories
  By contrast, which is what we just were wishing
    all:
And science profits by this resurrection —
Dead scandals form good subjects for dissection.

237. "malus animus": malice aforethought.

32

Their friends had tried at reconciliation,
  Then their relations, who made matters worse,
('Twere hard to tell upon a like occasion 251
  To whom it may be best to have recourse —
I can't say much for friend or yet relation):
  The lawyers did their utmost for divorce,
But scarce a fee was paid on either side
Before, unluckily, Don Jóse died.

33

He died; and most unluckily, because,
  According to all hints I could collect
From counsel learned in those kinds of laws
  (Although their talk's obscure and circumspect),
His death contrived to spoil a charming cause; 261
  A thousand pities also with respect
To public feeling, which on this occasion
Was manifested in a great sensation.

34

But ah! he died; and buried with him lay
  The public feeling and the lawyer's fees:
His house was sold, his servants sent away,
  A Jew took one of his two mistresses,
A priest the other — at least so they say:
  I asked the doctors after his disease — 270
He died of the slow fever called the tertian,
And left his widow to her own aversion.

35

Yet Jóse was an honourable man,
  That I must say, who knew him very well;
Therefore his frailties I'll no further scan,
  Indeed there were not many more to tell:
And if his passions now and then outran
  Discretion, and were not so peaceable
As Numa's° (who was also named Pompilius),
He had been ill brought up, and was born bilious.

36

Whate'er might be his worthlessness or worth, 281
  Poor fellow! he had many things to wound him,
Let's own — since it can do no good on earth —
  It was a trying moment that which found him
Standing alone beside his desolate hearth,
  Where all his household gods lay shivered round
    him:
No choice was left his feelings or his pride,
Save death or Doctors' Commons° — so he died.

279. Numa's: Numa Pompilius, the second king of Rome, had a long and peaceful reign as the result of taking the advice of the nymph Egeria, who loved him.   288. Doctors' Commons: i.e., the divorce courts.

37

Dying intestate, Juan was sole heir
  To a chancery suit, and messuages° and lands,
Which, with a long minority and care,   291
  Promised to turn out well in proper hands:
Inez became sole guardian, which was fair,
  And answered but to nature's just demands;
An only son left with an only mother
Is brought up much more wisely than another.

38

Sagest of women, even of widows, she
  Resolved that Juan should be quite a paragon,
And worthy of the noblest pedigree:
  (His sire was of Castile, his dam from Aragon).
Then for accomplishments of chivalry,   301
  In case our lord the king should go to war again,
He learned the arts of riding, fencing, gunnery,
And how to scale a fortress — or a nunnery.

39

But that which Donna Inez most desired,
  And saw into herself each day before all
The learned tutors whom for him she hired,
  Was, that his breeding should be strictly moral:
Much into all his studies she inquired,
  And so they were submitted first to her, all,   310
Arts, sciences, no branch was made a mystery
To Juan's eyes, excepting natural history.

40

The languages, especially the dead,
  The sciences, and most of all the abstruse,
The arts, at least all such as could be said
  To be the most remote from common use,
In all these he was much and deeply read:
  But not a page of anything that's loose,
Or hints continuation of the species,   319
Was ever suffered, lest he should grow vicious.

41

His classic studies made a little puzzle,
  Because of filthy loves of gods and goddesses,
Who in the earlier ages raised a bustle,
  But never put on pantaloons or bodices;
His reverend tutors had at times a tussle,
  And for their Aeneids, Iliads, and Odysseys,
Were forced to make an odd sort of apology,
But Donna Inez dreaded the Mythology.

290. messuages: dwelling houses along with their outbuildings
and lands.

42

Ovid's a rake, as half his verses show him,
  Anacreon's morals are a still worse sample,   330
Catullus scarcely has a decent poem,
  I don't think Sappho's Ode a good example,
Although Longinus tells us there is no hymn
  Where the sublime soars forth on wings more
    ample;
But Virgil's songs are pure, except that horrid one
Beginning with "Formosum Pastor Corydon."

43

Lucretius' irreligion is too strong
  For early stomachs, to prove wholesome food;
I can't help thinking Juvenal was wrong,
  Although no doubt his real intent was good,   340
For speaking out so plainly in his song,
  So much indeed as to be downright rude;
And then what proper person can be partial
To all those nauseous epigrams of Martial?

44

Juan was taught from out the best edition,
  Expurgated by learned men, who place,
Judiciously, from out the schoolboy's vision,
  The grosser parts; but, fearful to deface
Too much their modest bard by this omission,
  And pitying sore his mutilated case,   350
They only add them all in an appendix,°
Which saves, in fact, the trouble of an index;

45

For there we have them all "at one fell swoop,"
  Instead of being scattered through the pages;
They stand forth marshalled in a handsome troop,
  To meet the ingenuous youth of future ages,
Till some less rigid editor shall stoop
  To call them back into their separate cages,
Instead of standing staring all together,
Like garden gods — and not so decent either.   360

46

The Missal too (it was the family Missal)
  Was ornamented in a sort of way
Which ancient mass-books often are, and this
    all
  Kinds of grotesques illumined; and how they,
Who saw those figures on the margin kiss all,
  Could turn their optics to the text and pray,
Is more than I know — But Don Juan's mother
Kept this herself, and gave her son another.

351. appendix: "Fact! There is, or was, such an edition, with all
the obnoxious epigrams of Martial placed by themselves at the
end" [B].

47

Sermons he read, and lectures he endured,
  And homilies and lives of all the saints;   370
To Jerome and to Chrysostom inured,
  He did not take such studies for restraints;
But how faith is acquired, and then insured,
  So well not one of the aforesaid paints
As Saint Augustine in his fine Confessions,
Which make the reader envy his transgressions.

48

This, too, was a sealed book to little Juan —
  I can't but say that his mamma was right,
If such an education was the true one.
  She scarcely trusted him from out her sight; 380
Her maids were old, and if she took a new one,
  You might be sure she was a perfect fright,
She did this during even her husband's life —
I recommend as much to every wife.

49

Young Juan waxed in godliness and grace;
  At six a charming child, and at eleven
With all the promise of as fine a face
  As e'er to man's maturer growth was given.
He studied steadily and grew apace,
  And seemed, at least, in the right road to heaven,
For half his days were passed at church, the other
Between his tutors, confessor, and mother.   392

50

At six, I said, he was a charming child,
  At twelve he was a fine, but quiet boy;
Although in infancy a little wild,
  They tamed him down amongst them: to destroy
His natural spirit not in vain they toiled,
  At least it seemed so; and his mother's joy
Was to declare how sage, and still, and steady,
Her young philosopher was grown already.   400

51

I had my doubts, perhaps, I have them still,
  But what I say is neither here nor there:
I knew his father well, and have some skill
  In character — but it would not be fair
From sire to son to augur good or ill:
  He and his wife were an ill sorted pair —
But scandal's my aversion — I protest
Against all evil speaking, even in jest.

52

For my part I say nothing — nothing — but
  This I will say — my reasons are my own — 410
That if I had an only son to put
  To school (as God be praised that I have none),
'Tis not with Donna Inez I would shut
  Him up to learn his catechism alone,
No — no — I'd send him out betimes to college,
For there it was I picked up my own knowl-
    edge.

53

For there one learns — 'tis not for me to boast,
  Though I acquired — but I pass over *that,*
As well as all the Greek I since have lost:
  I say that there's the place — but " *Verbum
    sat,*"°
I think I picked up too, as well as most,   421
  Knowledge of matters — but no matter *what* —
I never married — but, I think, I know
That sons should not be educated so.

54

Young Juan now was sixteen years of age,
  Tall, handsome, slender, but well knit: he seemed
Active, though not so sprightly, as a page;
  And everybody but his mother deemed
Him almost man; but she flew in a rage
  And bit her lips (for else she might have
    screamed)   430
If any said so, for to be precocious
Was in her eyes a thing the most atrocious.

55

Amongst her numerous acquaintances, all
  Selected for discretion and devotion,
There was the Donna Julia, whom to call
  Pretty were but to give a feeble notion
Of many charms in her as natural
  As sweetness to the flower, or salt to ocean,
Her zone to Venus, or his bow to Cupid,
(But this last simile is trite and stupid).   440

56

The darkness of her Oriental eye
  Accorded with her Moorish origin;
(Her blood was not all Spanish, by the by;
  In Spain, you know, this is a sort of sin).
When proud Granada fell, and, forced to fly,
  Boabdil° wept, of Donna Julia's kin

---

420. "*Verbum sat*": "A word [to the wise] is enough." **446. Boab-
dil:** the last Moorish King of Granada, in Southern Spain, finally
conquered by King Ferdinand in **1492.**

Some went to Africa, some stayed in Spain,
Her great great grandmamma chose to remain.

57

She married (I forget the pedigree)
    With an Hidalgo, who transmitted down   450
His blood less noble than such blood should be;
    At such alliances his sires would frown,
In that point so precise in each degree
    That they bred *in and in,* as might be shown,
Marrying their cousins — nay, their aunts, and
        nieces,
Which always spoils the breed, if it increases.

58

This heathenish cross restored the breed again,
    Ruined its blood, but much improved its flesh;
For from a root the ugliest in old Spain
    Sprung up a branch as beautiful as fresh;   460
The sons no more were short, the daughters plain:
    But there's a rumour which I fain would hush,
'Tis said that Donna Julia's grandmamma
Produced her Don more heirs at love than law.

59

However this might be, the race went on
    Improving still through every generation,
Until it centered in an only son,
    Who left an only daughter: my narration
May have suggested that this single one
    Could be but Julia (whom on this occasion   470
I shall have much to speak about), and she
Was married, charming, chaste, and twenty-three.

60

Her eye (I'm very fond of handsome eyes)
    Was large and dark, suppressing half its fire
Until she spoke, then through its soft disguise
    Flashed an expression more of pride than ire,
And love than either; and there would arise
    A something in them which was not desire,
But would have been, perhaps, but for the soul
Which struggled through and chastened down the
        whole.   480

61

Her glossy hair was clustered o'er a brow
    Bright with intelligence, and fair, and smooth;
Her eyebrow's shape was like the aërial bow,
    Her cheek all purple, with the beam of youth,
Mounting, at times, to a transparent glow,
    As if her veins ran lightning; she, in sooth,
Possessed an air and grace by no means common:
Her stature tall — I hate a dumpy woman.

62

Wedded she was some years, and to a man
    Of fifty, and such husbands are in plenty;   490
And yet, I think, instead of such a ONE
    'Twere better to have TWO of five-and-twenty,
Especially in countries near the sun:
    And now I think on't, " mi vien in mente,"°
Ladies even of the most uneasy virtue
Prefer a spouse whose age is short of thirty.

63

'Tis a sad thing, I cannot choose but say,
    And all the fault of that indecent sun,
Who cannot leave alone our helpless clay,
    But will keep baking, broiling, burning on,   500
That howsoever people fast and pray,
    The flesh is frail, and so the soul undone:
What men call gallantry, and gods adultery,
Is much more common where the climate's sultry.

64

Happy the nations of the moral North!
    Where all is virtue, and the winter season
Sends sin, without a rag on, shivering forth
    ('Twas snow° that brought St. Anthony to
        reason);
Where juries cast up what a wife is worth,
    By laying whate'er sum, in mulct, they please on
The lover, who must pay a handsome price,   511
Because it is a marketable vice.

65

Alfonso was the name of Julia's lord,
    A man well looking for his years, and who
Was neither much beloved nor yet abhorred:
    They lived together as most people do,
Suffering each other's foibles by accord,
    And not exactly either *one* or *two;*
Yet he was jealous, though he did not show it,
For jealousy dislikes the world to know it.   520

66

Julia was — yet I never could see why —
    With Donna Inez quite a favourite friend;
Between their tastes there was small sympathy,
    For not a line had Julia ever penned:
Some people whisper (but, no doubt, they lie,
    For malice still imputes some private end)
That Inez had, ere Don Alfonso's marriage,
Forgot with him her very prudent carriage;

494. "mi . . . mente": "It comes into my mind." 508. snow:
"For the particulars of St. Anthony's recipe for hot blood in cold
weather, see Mr. Alban Butler's *Lives of the Saints*" [B].

67

And that still keeping up the old connexion,
　Which time had lately rendered much more
　　chaste,　　　　　　　　　　　　　　　530
She took his lady also in affection,
　And certainly this course was much the best:
She flattered Julia with her sage protection,
　And complimented Don Alfonso's taste;
And if she could not (who can?) silence scandal,
At least she left it a more slender handle.

68

I can't tell whether Julia saw the affair
　With other people's eyes, or if her own
Discoveries made, but none could be aware　　539
　Of this, at least no symptom e'er was shown;
Perhaps she did not know, or did not care,
　Indifferent from the first, or callous grown:
I'm really puzzled what to think or say,
She kept her counsel in so close a way.

69

Juan she saw, and, as a pretty child,
　Caressed him often — such a thing might be
Quite innocently done, and harmless styled,
　When she had twenty years, and thirteen
　　he;
But I am not so sure I should have smiled
　When he was sixteen, Julia twenty-three;　　550
These few short years make wondrous alterations,
Particularly amongst sun-burnt nations.

70

Whate'er the cause might be, they had become
　Changed; for the dame grew distant, the youth
　　shy,
Their looks cast down, their greetings almost dumb,
　And much embarrassment in either eye;
There surely will be little doubt with some
　That Donna Julia knew the reason why,
But as for Juan, he had no more notion
Than he who never saw the sea of ocean.　　560

71

Yet Julia's very coldness still was kind,
　And tremulously gentle her small hand
Withdrew itself from his, but left behind
　A little pressure, thrilling, and so bland
And slight, so very slight, that to the mind
　'Twas but a doubt; but ne'er magician's wand
Wrought change with all Armida's° fairy art
Like what this light touch left on Juan's heart.

567. Armida's: the enchantress in Tasso's *Jerusalem Delivered*.

72

And if she met him, though she smiled no more,
　She looked a sadness sweeter than her smile, 570
As if her heart had deeper thoughts in store
　She must not own, but cherished more the while
For that compression in its burning core;
　Even innocence itself has many a wile,
And will not dare to trust itself with truth,
And love is taught hypocrisy from youth.

73

But passion most dissembles, yet betrays
　Even by its darkness; as the blackest sky
Foretells the heaviest tempest, it displays
　Its workings through the vainly guarded eye,
And in whatever aspect it arrays　　581
　Itself, 'tis still the same hypocrisy:
Coldness or anger, even disdain or hate,
Are masks it often wears, and still too late.

74

Then there were sighs, the deeper for suppression,
　And stolen glances, sweeter for the theft,
And burning blushes, though for no transgression,
　Tremblings when met, and restlessness when left;
All these are little preludes to possession,
　Of which young passion cannot be bereft,　　590
And merely tend to show how greatly love is
Embarrassed at first starting with a novice.

75

Poor Julia's heart was in an awkward state;
　She felt it going, and resolved to make
The noblest efforts for herself and mate,
　For honour's, pride's, religion's, virtue's sake,
Her resolutions were most truly great,
　And almost might have made a Tarquin° quake:
She prayed the Virgin Mary for her grace,
As being the best judge of a lady's case.　　600

76

She vowed she never would see Juan more,
　And next day paid a visit to his mother
And looked extremely at the opening door,
　Which, by the Virgin's grace, let in another;
Grateful she was, and yet a little sore —
　Again it opens, it can be no other,
'Tis surely Juan now — No! I'm afraid
That night the Virgin was no further prayed.

598. Tarquin: Tarquinius Superbus, the last king of Rome, was
expelled after his son Sextus made the famous assault on Lucretia
celebrated in Shakespeare's *Rape of Lucrece*.

77

She now determined that a virtuous woman   609
   Should rather face and overcome temptation,
That flight was base and dastardly, and no man
   Should ever give her heart the least sensation;
That is to say, a thought beyond the common
   Preference, that we must feel upon occasion,
For people who are pleasanter than others,
But then they only seem so many brothers.

78

And even if by chance — and who can tell?
   The devil's so very sly — she should discover
That all within was not so very well,
   And, if still free, that such or such a lover   620
Might please perhaps, a virtuous wife can quell
   Such thoughts, and be the better when they're
     over;
And if the man should ask, 'tis but denial:
I recommend young ladies to make trial.

79

And then there are such things as love divine,
   Bright and immaculate, unmixed and pure,
Such as the angels think so very fine,
   And matrons, who would be no less secure,
Platonic, perfect, " just such love as mine: "
   Thus Julia said — and thought so, to be sure;
And so I'd have her think, were I the man   631
On whom her reveries celestial ran.

80

Such love is innocent, and may exist
   Between young persons without any danger:
A hand may first, and then a lip be kist;
   For my part, to such doings I'm a stranger,
But *hear* these freedoms form the utmost list
   Of all o'er which such love may be a ranger:
If people go beyond, 'tis quite a crime,
But not my fault — I tell them all in time.   640

81

Love, then, but love within its proper limits
   Was Julia's innocent determination
In young Don Juan's favour, and to him its
   Exertion might be useful on occasion;
And, lighted at too pure a shrine to dim its
   Ethereal lustre, with what sweet persuasion
He might be taught, by love and her together —
I really don't know what, nor Julia either.

82

Fraught with this fine intention, and well fenced
   In mail of proof — her purity of soul,   650
She, for the future of her strength convinced,
   And that her honour was a rock, or mole,
Exceedingly sagely from that hour dispensed
   With any kind of troublesome control;
But whether Julia to the task was equal
Is that which must be mentioned in the sequel.

83

Her plan she deemed both innocent and feasible,
   And, surely, with a stripling of sixteen
Not scandal's fangs could fix on much that's seiz-
     able,
   Or if they did so, satisfied to mean   660
Nothing but what was good, her breast was peace-
     able:
   A quiet conscience makes one so serene!
Christians have burnt each other, quite persuaded
That all the Apostles would have done as they did.

84

And if in the mean time her husband died,
   But Heaven forbid that such a thought should
     cross
Her brain, though in a dream! (and then she
     sighed)
   Never could she survive that common loss;
But just suppose that moment should betide,
   I only say suppose it — *inter nos.*   670
(This should be *entre nous,* for Julia thought
In French, but then the rhyme would go for
     nought.)

85

I only say, suppose this supposition:
   Juan being then grown up to man's estate
Would fully suit a widow of condition,
   Even seven years hence it would not be too late;
And in the interim (to pursue this vision)
   The mischief, after all, could not be great,
For he would learn the rudiments of love,
I mean the seraph way of those above.   680

86

So much for Julia. Now we'll turn to Juan.
   Poor little fellow! he had no idea
Of his own case, and never hit the true one;
   In feelings quick as Ovid's Miss Medea,°
He puzzled over what he found a new one,

---

684. Ovid's ... Medea: See Ovid's *Metamorphoses*, VII, 9 ff.

But not as yet imagined it could be a
Thing quite in course, and not at all alarming,
Which, with a little patience, might grow charm-
ing.

87

Silent and pensive, idle, restless, slow,
   His home deserted for the lonely wood,   690
Tormented with a wound he could not know,
   His, like all deep grief, plunged in solitude:
I'm fond myself of solitude or so,
   But then, I beg it may be understood,
By solitude I mean a Sultan's, not
A hermit's, with a haram for a grot.

88

"Oh Love! in such a wilderness as this,
   Where transport and security entwine,
Here is the empire of thy perfect bliss,
   And here thou art a god indeed divine."°   700
The bard I quote from does not sing amiss,
   With the exception of the second line,
For that same twining "transport and security"
Are twisted to a phrase of some obscurity.

89

The poet meant, no doubt, and thus appeals
   To the good sense and senses of mankind,
The very thing which everybody feels,
   As all have found on trial, or may find,
That no one likes to be disturbed at meals
   Or love. — I won't say more about "entwined"
Or "transport," as we knew all that before,   711
But beg "Security" will bolt the door.

90

Young Juan wandered by the glassy brooks,
   Thinking unutterable things; he threw
Himself at length within the leafy nooks
   Where the wild branch of the cork forest grew;
There poets find materials for their books,
   And every now and then we read them through,
So that their plan and prosody are eligible,
Unless, like Wordsworth, they prove unintelligible.

91

He, Juan (and not Wordsworth), so pursued   721
   His self-communion with his own high soul,
Until his mighty heart, in its great mood,
   Had mitigated part, though not the whole

Of its disease; he did the best he could
   With things not very subject to control,
And turned, without perceiving his condition,
Like Coleridge, into a metaphysician.

92

He thought about himself, and the whole earth,
   Of man the wonderful, and of the stars,   730
And how the deuce they ever could have birth;
   And then he thought of earthquakes, and of
      wars,
How many miles the moon might have in girth,
   Of air-balloons, and of the many bars
To perfect knowledge of the boundless skies; —
And then he thought of Donna Julia's eyes.

93

In thoughts like these true wisdom may discern
   Longings sublime, and aspirations high,
Which some are born with, but the most part learn
   To plague themselves withal, they know not
      why:
'Twas strange that one so young should thus con-
     cern   741
   His brain about the action of the sky;
If *you* think 'twas philosophy that this did,
I can't help thinking puberty assisted.

94

He pored upon the leaves, and on the flowers,
   And heard a voice in all the winds; and then
He thought of wood-nymphs and immortal bowers,
   And how the goddesses came down to men:
He missed the pathway, he forgot the hours,
   And when he looked upon his watch again,   750
He found how much old Time had been a win-
     ner —
He also found that he had lost his dinner.

95

Sometimes he turned to gaze upon his book,
   Boscan, or Garcilasso;° — by the wind
Even as the page is rustled while we look,
   So by the poesy of his own mind
Over the mystic leaf his soul was shook,
   As if 'twere one whereon magicians bind
Their spells, and give them to the passing gale
According to some good old woman's tale.   760

96

Thus would he while his lonely hours away
   Dissatisfied, nor knowing what he wanted;

697–700. "Oh . . . divine": "Campbell's *Gertrude of Wyoming*— (I think)—the opening of Canto Second—but quote from memory" [B]. The passage occurs at the opening of the third part of Campbell's poem.

754. Boscan, or Garcilasso: Juan Boscan and Garcilaso de la Vega were Spanish poets of the early sixteenth century.

Nor glowing reverie, nor poet's lay,
  Could yield his spirit that for which it panted,
A bosom whereon he his head might lay,
  And hear the heart beat with the love it granted,
With —— several other things, which I forget,
Or which, at least, I need not mention yet.

97

Those lonely walks, and lengthening reveries,
  Could not escape the gentle Julia's eyes;   770
She saw that Juan was not at his ease;
  But that which chiefly may, and must surprise,
Is, that the Donna Inez did not tease
  Her only son with question or surmise;
Whether it was she did not see, or would not,
Or, like all very clever people, could not.

98

This may seem strange, but yet 'tis very common;
  For instance — gentlemen, whose ladies take
Leave to o'erstep the written rights of woman,
  And break the —— Which commandment is't
    they break?   780
(I have forgot the number, and think no man
  Should rashly quote, for fear of a mistake.)
I say, when these same gentlemen are jealous,
They make some blunder, which their ladies tell
    us.

99

A real husband always is suspicious,
  But still no less suspects in the wrong place,
Jealous of some one who had no such wishes,
  Or pandering blindly to his own disgrace,
By harbouring some dear friend extremely vicious;
  The last indeed's infallibly the case: 790
And when the spouse and friend are gone off
    wholly,
He wonders at their vice, and not his folly.

100

Thus parents also are at times short-sighted;
  Though watchful as the lynx, they ne'er dis-
    cover,
The while the wicked world beholds delighted,
  Young Hopeful's mistress, or Miss Fanny's lover,
Till some confounded escapade has blighted
  The plan of twenty years, and all is over;
And then the mother cries, the father swears,
And wonders why the devil he got heirs.   800

101

But Inez was so anxious, and so clear
  Of sight, that I must think, on this occasion,
She had some other motive much more near
  For leaving Juan to this new temptation,
But what that motive was, I shan't say here;
  Perhaps to finish Juan's education,
Perhaps to open Don Alfonso's eyes,
In case he thought his wife too great a prize.

102

It was upon a day, a summer's day; —
  Summer's indeed a very dangerous season,   810
And so is spring about the end of May;
  The sun, no doubt, is the prevailing reason;
But whatsoe'er the cause is, one may say,
  And stand convicted of more truth than treason,
That there are months which nature grows more
    merry in, —
March has its hares, and May must have its heroine.

103

'Twas on a summer's day — the sixth of June: —
  I like to be particular in dates,
Not only of the age, and year, but moon;   819
  They are a sort of post-house, where the Fates
Change horses, making history change its tune,
  Then spur away o'er empires and o'er states,
Leaving at last not much besides chronology,
Excepting the post-obits of theology.

104

'Twas on the sixth of June, about the hour
  Of half-past six — perhaps still nearer seven —
When Julia sate within as pretty a bower
  As e'er held houri in that heathenish heaven
Described by Mahomet, and Anacreon Moore,°
  To whom the lyre and laurels have been given,
With all the trophies of triumphant song —   831
He won them well, and may he wear them long!

105

She sate, but not alone; I know not well
  How this same interview had taken place,
And even if I knew, I should not tell —
  People should hold their tongues in any case;
No matter how or why the thing befell,
  But there were she and Juan, face to face —
When two such faces are so, 'twould be wise,
But very difficult, to shut their eyes.   840

829. **Anacreon Moore:** Byron's friend the poet Thomas Moore is
called Anacreon because he translated the odes of that Greek
lyrical poet in his youth.

106

How beautiful she looked! her conscious heart
   Glowed in her cheek, and yet she felt no wrong,
Oh Love! how perfect is thy mystic art,
   Strengthening the weak, and trampling on the
     strong!
How self-deceitful is the sagest part
   Of mortals whom thy lure hath led along! —
The precipice she stood on was immense,
So was her creed in her own innocence.

107

She thought of her own strength, and Juan's youth,
   And of the folly of all prudish fears,   850
Victorious virtue, and domestic truth,
   And then of Don Alfonso's fifty years:
I wish these last had not occurred, in sooth,
   Because that number rarely much endears,
And through all climes, the snowy and the sunny,
Sounds ill in love, whate'er it may in money.

108

When people say, "I've told you *fifty* times,"
   They mean to scold, and very often do;
When poets say, "I've written *fifty* rhymes,"
   They make you dread that they'll recite them too;
In gangs of *fifty*, thieves commit their crimes; 861
   At *fifty* love for love is rare, 'tis true,
But then, no doubt, it equally as true is,
A good deal may be bought for *fifty* Louis.

109

Julia had honour, virtue, truth, and love
   For Don Alfonso; and she inly swore,
By all the vows below to powers above,
   She never would disgrace the ring she wore,
Nor leave a wish which wisdom might reprove;
   And while she pondered this, besides much more,
One hand on Juan's carelessly was thrown,   871
Quite by mistake — she thought it was her own;

110

Unconsciously she leaned upon the other,
   Which played within the tangles of her hair;
And to contend with thoughts she could not
     smother
   She seemed, by the distraction of her air.
'Twas surely very wrong in Juan's mother
   To leave together this imprudent pair,
She who for many years had watched her son so —
I'm very certain *mine* would not have done so. 880

111

The hand which still held Juan's, by degrees
   Gently, but palpably confirmed its grasp,
As if it said, " Detain me, if you please; "
   Yet there's no doubt she only meant to clasp
His fingers with a pure Platonic squeeze;
   She would have shrunk as from a toad, or asp,
Had she imagined such a thing could rouse
A feeling dangerous to a prudent spouse.

112

I cannot know what Juan thought of this,
   But what he did, is much what you would do;
His young lip thanked it with a grateful kiss, 891
   And then, abashed at its own joy, withdrew
In deep despair, lest he had done amiss, —
   Love is so very timid when 'tis new:
She blushed, and frowned not, but she strove to
     speak,
And held her tongue, her voice was grown so weak.

113

The sun set, and up rose the yellow moon:
   The devil's in the moon for mischief; they
Who called her CHASTE, methinks, began too soon
   Their nomenclature; there is not a day,   900
The longest, not the twenty-first of June,
   Sees half the business in a wicked way,
On which three single hours of moonshine smile —
And then she looks so modest all the while.

114

There is a dangerous silence in that hour,
   A stillness, which leaves room for the full soul
To open all itself, without the power
   Of calling wholly back its self-control;
The silver light which, hallowing tree and tower,
   Sheds beauty and deep softness o'er the whole,
Breathes also to the heart, and o'er it throws 911
A loving languor, which is not repose.

115

And Julia sate with Juan, half embraced
   And half retiring from the glowing arm,
Which trembled like the bosom where 'twas placed;
   Yet still she must have thought there was no
     harm,
Or else 'twere easy to withdraw her waist;
   But then the situation had its charm,
And then —— God knows what next — I can't go
     on;
I'm almost sorry that I e'er begun.   920

116

Oh Plato! Plato! you have paved the way,
    With your confounded fantasies, to more
Immoral conduct by the fancied sway
    Your system feigns o'er the controlless core
Of human hearts, than all the long array
    Of poets and romancers: — You're a bore,
A charlatan, a coxcomb — and have been,
At best, no better than a go-between.

117

And Julia's voice was lost, except in sighs,
    Until too late for useful conversation;   930
The tears were gushing from her gentle eyes,
    I wish, indeed, they had not had occasion;
But who, alas! can love, and then be wise?
    Not that remorse did not oppose temptation;
A little still she strove, and much repented,
And whispering "I will ne'er consent" — con-
    sented.

118

'Tis said that Xerxes° offered a reward
    To those who could invent him a new pleasure;
Methinks the requisition's rather hard,
    And must have cost his majesty a treasure: 940
For my part, I'm a moderate-minded bard,
    Fond of a little love (which I call leisure);
I care not for new pleasures, as the old
Are quite enough for me, so they but hold.

119

Oh Pleasure! you're indeed a pleasant thing,
    Although one must be damned for you, no
        doubt:
I make a resolution every spring
    Of reformation, ere the year run out,
But somehow, this my vestal vow takes wing,
    Yet still, I trust, it may be kept throughout: 950
I'm very sorry, very much ashamed,
And mean, next winter, to be quite reclaimed.

120

Here my chaste Muse a liberty must take —
    Start not! still chaster reader — she'll be nice
        hence-
Forward, and there is no great cause to quake;
    This liberty is a poetic licence,
Which some irregularity may make
    In the design, and as I have a high sense
Of Aristotle and the Rules, 'tis fit
To beg his pardon when I err a bit.   960

937. Xerxes: the King of Persia who invaded Greece and was
defeated in the naval battle of Salamis. He is also the Ahasuerus
of the Biblical Book of Esther.

121

This licence is to hope the reader will
    Suppose from June the sixth (the fatal day
Without whose epoch my poetic skill
    For want of facts would all be thrown away),
But keeping Julia and Don Juan still
    In sight, that several months have passed; we'll
        say
'Twas in November, but I'm not so sure
About the day — the era's more obscure.

122

We'll talk of that anon. — 'Tis sweet to hear
    At midnight on the blue and moonlit deep   970
The song and oar of Adria's gondolier,
    By distance mellowed, o'er the waters sweep;
'Tis sweet to see the evening star appear;
    'Tis sweet to listen as the night-winds creep
From leaf to leaf; 'tis sweet to view on high
The rainbow, based on ocean, span the sky.

123

'Tis sweet to hear the watch-dog's honest bark
    Bay deep-mouthed welcome as we draw near
        home;
'Tis sweet to know there is an eye will mark
    Our coming, and look brighter when we come;
'Tis sweet to be awakened by the lark,   981
    Or lulled by falling waters; sweet the hum
Of bees, the voice of girls, the song of birds,
The lisp of children, and their earliest words.

124

Sweet is the vintage when the showering grapes
    In Bacchanal profusion reel to earth,
Purple and gushing; sweet are our escapes
    From civic revelry to rural mirth;
Sweet to the miser are his glittering heaps,
    Sweet to the father is his first-born's birth,   990
Sweet is revenge — especially to women,
Pillage to soldiers, prize-money to seamen.

125

Sweet is a legacy, and passing sweet
    The unexpected death of some old lady
Or gentleman of seventy years complete,
    Who've made "us youth" wait too — too long
        already
For an estate, or cash, or country seat,
    Still breaking, but with stamina so steady
That all the Israelites are fit to mob its   999
Next owner for their double-damned post-obits.°

1000. post-obits: loans to an heir falling due at the death of the
person whose property he inherits.

126

'Tis sweet to win, no matter how, one's laurels,
　By blood or ink; 'tis sweet to put an end
To strife; 'tis sometimes sweet to have our quarrels,
　Particularly with a tiresome friend:
Sweet is old wine in bottles, ale in barrels;
　Dear is the helpless creature we defend
Against the world; and dear the schoolboy spot
We ne'er forget, though there we are forgot.

127

But sweeter still than this, than these, than all,
　Is first and passionate love — it stands alone,
Like Adam's recollection of his fall;　　　　1011
　The tree of knowledge has been plucked — all's
　　known —
And life yields nothing further to recall
　Worthy of this ambrosial sin, so shown,
No doubt in fable, as the unforgiven
Fire which Prometheus filched for us from heaven.

128

Man's a strange animal, and makes strange use
　Of his own nature, and the various arts,
And likes particularly to produce
　Some new experiment to show his parts;　1020
This is the age of oddities let loose,
　Where different talents find their different marts;
You'd best begin with truth, and when you've lost
　your
Labour, there's a sure market for imposture.

129

What opposite discoveries we have seen!
　(Signs of true genius, and of empty pockets.)
One makes new noses, one a guillotine,
　One breaks your bones, one sets them in their
　　sockets;
But vaccination certainly has been
　A kind of antithesis to Congreve's rockets,° 1030
With which the Doctor° paid off an old pox,
By borrowing a new one from an ox.

130

Bread has been made (indifferent) from potatoes;
　And galvanism° has set some corpses grinning,
But has not answered like the apparatus
　Of the Humane Society's beginning,
By which men are unsuffocated gratis:

What wondrous new machines have late been
　　spinning!
I said the small pox has gone out of late;
Perhaps it may be followed by the great.°　1040

131

'Tis said the great came from America;
　Perhaps it may set out on its return, —
The population there so spreads, they say
　'Tis grown high time to thin it in its turn,
With war, or plague, or famine, any way,
　So that civilisation they may learn;
And which in ravage the more loathsome evil is —
Their real lues, or our pseudo-syphilis?

132

This is the patent age of new inventions
　For killing bodies, and for saving souls,　1050
All propagated with the best intentions;
　Sir Humphrey Davy's lantern,° by which coals
Are safely mined for in the mode he mentions,
　Tombuctoo travels, voyages° to the Poles,
Are ways to benefit mankind, as true,
Perhaps, as shooting them at Waterloo.

133

Man's a phenomenon, one knows not what,
　And wonderful beyond all wondrous measure;
'Tis pity, though, in this sublime world, that 1059
　Pleasure's a sin, and sometimes sin's a pleas-
　　ure;
Few mortals know what end they would be at,
　But whether glory, power, or love, or treasure,
The path is through perplexing ways, and when
The goal is gained, we die, you know — and
　then ——

134

What then? — I do not know, no more do you ——
　And so good night. — Return we to our story:
'Twas in November, when fine days are few,
　And the far mountains wax a little hoary,
And clap a white cape on their mantles blue;
　And the sea dashes round the promontory, 1070
And the loud breaker boils against the rock,
And sober suns must set at five o'clock.

1030. rockets: a new kind of artillery shell invented by Sir William
Congreve and used during the Napoleonic wars. 1031. Doctor:
i.e., Edward Jenner, the discoverer of vaccination. 1034. gal-
vanism: experiments on dead bodies with electricity were made
by Galvani's nephew in 1803.

1040. great: The "great pox," as distinct from smallpox, was
syphilis, or "lues" (l. 1048), said to have entered Europe for the
first time after the discovery of America. 1052. lantern: Sir
Humphrey Davy invented the safety lamp for miners in 1815.
1054. travels, voyages: Byron refers to recent books of travels
in Morocco and the Arctic Ocean.

135

'Twas, as the watchmen say, a cloudy night;
    No moon, no stars, the wind was low or loud
By gusts, and many a sparkling hearth was bright
    With the piled wood, round which the family
        crowd;
There's something cheerful in that sort of light,
    Even as a summer sky's without a cloud:
I'm fond of fire, and crickets, and all that,
A lobster salad, and champagne, and chat.   1080

136

'Twas midnight — Donna Julia was in bed,
    Sleeping, most probably — when at her door
Arose a clatter might awake the dead,
    If they had never been awoke before,
And that they have been so we all have read,
    And are to be so, at the least, once more; —
The door was fastened, but with voice and fist
First knocks were heard, then " Madam — Madam
        — hist!

137

" For God's sake, Madam — Madam — here's my
        master,
    With more than half the city at his back —   1090
Was ever heard of such a curst disaster!
    'Tis not my fault — I kept good watch — Alack!
Do pray undo the bolt a little faster —
    They're on the stair just now, and in a crack
Will all be here; perhaps he yet may fly —
Surely the window's not so very high! "

138

By this time Don Alfonso was arrived,
    With torches, friends, and servants in great num-
        ber;
The major part of them had long been wived,
    And therefore paused not to disturb the slumber
Of any wicked woman, who contrived   1101
    By stealth her husband's temples to encumber:
Examples of this kind are so contagious,
Were one not punished, all would be outrageous.

139

I can't tell how, or why, or what suspicion
    Could enter into Don Alfonso's head;
But for a cavalier of his condition
    It surely was exceedingly ill-bred,
Without a word of previous admonition,
    To hold a levée round his lady's bed,   1110
And summon lackeys, armed with fire and sword,
To prove himself the thing he most abhorred.

140

Poor Donna Julia! starting as from sleep
    (Mind — that I do not say — she had not slept),
Began at once to scream, and yawn, and weep;
    Her maid, Antonia, who was an adept,
Contrived to fling the bed-clothes in a heap,
    As if she had just now from out them crept;
I can't tell why she should take all this trouble
To prove her mistress had been sleeping double.

141

But Julia mistress, and Antonia maid,   1121
    Appeared like two poor harmless women, who
Of goblins, but still more of men afraid,
    Had thought one man might be deterred by two,
And therefore side by side were gently laid,
    Until the hours of absence should run through,
And truant husband should return, and say,
" My dear, I was the first who came away."

142

Now Julia found at length a voice, and cried,
    " In heaven's name, Don Alfonso, what d'ye
        mean?
Has madness seized you? would that I had died
    Ere such a monster's victim I had been!
What may this midnight violence betide,
    A sudden fit of drunkenness or spleen?
Dare you suspect me, whom the thought would
        kill?
Search, then, the room! " — Alfonso said, " I will."

143

He searched, they searched, and rummaged every-
        where,
    Closet and clothes-press, chest and window-
        seat,
And found much linen, lace, and several pair
    Of stockings, slippers, brushes, combs, complete,
With other articles of ladies fair,   1141
    To keep them beautiful, or leave them neat:
Arras they pricked and curtains with their swords,
And wounded several shutters, and some boards.

144

Under the bed they searched, and there they
        found —
    No matter what — it was not that they sought;
They opened the windows, gazing if the ground
    Had signs of footmarks, but the earth said
        naught;
And then they stared each other's faces round:

'Tis odd, not one of all these seekers thought,
And seems to me almost a sort of blunder,   1151
Of looking *in* the bed as well as under.

145

During this inquisition Julia's tongue
  Was not asleep — "Yes, search and search," she
    cried,
"Insult on insult heap, and wrong on wrong!
  It was for this that I became a bride!
For this in silence I have suffered long
  A husband like Alfonso at my side;
But now I'll bear no more, nor here remain,
If there be law or lawyers in all Spain.   1160

146

"Yes, Don Alfonso! husband now no more,
  If ever you indeed deserved the name,
Is't worthy of your years? — you have three-score —
  Fifty, or sixty, it is all the same —
Is't wise or fitting, causeless to explore
  For facts against a virtuous woman's fame?
Ungrateful, perjured, barbarous Don Alfonso,
How dare you think your lady would go on so?

147

"Is it for this I have disdained to hold
  The common privileges of my sex?   1170
That I have chosen a confessor so old
  And deaf, that any other it would vex,
And never once he has had cause to scold,
  But found my very innocence perplex
So much, he always doubted I was married —
How sorry you will be when I've miscarried!

148

"Was it for this that no Cortejo e'er
  I yet have chosen from out the youth of Seville?
Is it for this I scarce went anywhere,
  Except to bull-fights, mass, play, rout, and revel?
Is it for this, whate'er my suitors were,   1181
  I favoured none — nay, was almost uncivil?
Is it for this that General Count O'Reilly,
Who took Algiers,° declares I used him vilely?

149

"Did not the Italian Musico Cazzani
  Sing at my heart six months at least in vain?
Did not his countryman, Count Corniani,
  Call me the only virtuous wife in Spain?

1184. took Algiers: "Donna Julia here made a mistake. Count
O'Reilly did not take Algiers—but Algiers very nearly took him;
he and his army and fleet retreated with great loss, and not much
credit, from before that city, in the year 1775" [B].

Were there not also Russians, English, many?
  The Count Strongstroganoff I put in pain,   1190
And Lord Mount Coffeehouse, the Irish peer,
  Who killed himself for love (with wine) last year.

150

"Have I not had two bishops at my feet?
  The Duke of Ichar, and Don Fernan Nunez?
And is it thus a faithful wife you treat?
  I wonder in what quarter now the moon is:
I praise your vast forbearance not to beat
  Me also, since the time so opportune is —
Oh, valiant man! with sword drawn and cocked
    trigger,
Now, tell me, don't you cut a pretty figure?   1200

151

"Was it for this you took your sudden journey,
  Under pretence of business indispensable,
With that sublime of rascals your attorney,
  Whom I see standing there, and looking sensible
Of having played the fool? though both I spurn,
    he
Deserves the worst, his conduct's less defensible,
Because, no doubt, 'twas for his dirty fee,
And not from any love to you nor me.

152

"If he comes here to take a deposition,
  By all means let the gentleman proceed;   1210
You've made the apartment in a fit condition: —
  There's pen and ink for you, sir, when you
    need —
Let everything be noted with precision,
  I would not you for nothing should be feed —
But as my maid's undrest, pray turn your spies
    out."
"Oh!" sobbed Antonia, "I could tear their eyes
    out."

153

"There is the closet, there the toilet, there
  The antechamber — search them under, over;
There is the sofa, there the great arm-chair,
  The chimney — which would really hold a lover.
I wish to sleep, and beg you will take care   1221
  And make no further noise, till you discover
The secret cavern of this lurking treasure —
And when 'tis found, let me, too, have that pleasure.

154

"And now, Hidalgo! now that you have thrown
  Doubt upon me, confusion over all,
Pray have the courtesy to make it known
  Who is the man you search for? how d'ye call

Him? what's his lineage? let him but be shown —
　I hope he's young and handsome — is he tall?
Tell me — and be assured, that since you stain 1231
Mine honour thus; it shall not be in vain.

155

" At least, perhaps, he has not sixty years,
　At that age he would be too old for slaughter,
Or for so young a husband's jealous fears —
　(Antonia! let me have a glass of water.)
I am ashamed of having shed these tears,
　They are unworthy of my father's daughter;
My mother dreamed not in my natal hour,
That I should fall into a monster's power.　1240

156

" Perhaps 'tis of Antonia you are jealous,
　You saw that she was sleeping by my side,
When you broke in upon us with your fellows;
　Look where you please — we've nothing, sir, to
　　hide;
Only another time, I trust, you'll tell us,
　Or for the sake of decency abide
A moment at the door, that we may be
Drest to receive so much good company.

157

" And now, sir, I have done, and say no more;
　The little I have said may serve to show　1250
The guileless heart in silence may grieve o'er
　The wrongs to whose exposure it is slow: —
I leave you to your conscience as before,
　'Twill one day ask you, *why* you used me so?
God grant you feel not then the bitterest grief!
Antonia! where's my pocket-handkerchief? "

158

She ceased, and turned upon her pillow; pale
　She lay, her dark eyes flashing through their
　　tears,
Like skies that rain and lighten; as a veil,　1259
　Waved and o'ershading her wan cheek, appears
Her streaming hair; the black curls strive, but fail,
　To hide the glossy shoulder, which uprears
Its snow through all; — her soft lips lie apart,
And louder than her breathing beats her heart.

159

The Senhor Don Alfonso stood confused;
　Antonia bustled round the ransacked room,
And, turning up her nose, with looks abused
　Her master, and his myrmidons, of whom
Not one, except the attorney, was amused;

He, like Achates,° faithful to the tomb,　1270
So there were quarrels, cared not for the cause,
Knowing they must be settled by the laws.

160

With prying snub-nose, all small eyes, he stood.
　Following Antonia's motions here and there,
With much suspicion in his attitude;
　For reputations he had little care;
So that a suit or action were made good,
　Small pity had he for the young and fair,
And ne'er believed in negatives, till these
Were proved by competent false witnesses.　1280

161

But Don Alfonso stood with downcast looks,
　And, truth to say, he made a foolish figure;
When, after searching in five hundred nooks,
　And treating a young wife with so much rigour,
He gained no point, except some self-rebukes,
　Added to those his lady with such vigour
Had poured upon him for the last half-hour,
Quick, thick, and heavy — as a thunder-shower.

162

At first he tried to hammer an excuse,　　1289
　To which the sole reply was tears and sobs,
And indications of hysterics, whose
　Prologue is always certain throes, and throbs,
Gasps, and whatever else the owners choose:
　Alfonso saw his wife, and thought of Job's;
He saw, too, in perspective, her relations,
And then he tried to muster all his patience.

163

He stood in act to speak, or rather stammer,
　But sage Antonia cut him short before
The anvil of his speech received the hammer,
　With " Pray, sir, leave the room, and say no
　　more,　　　　　　　　　　　　　　1300
Or madam dies." — Alfonso mutter'd, " D—n her."
　But nothing else, the time of words was o'er;
He cast a rueful look or two, and did,
He knew not wherefore, that which he was bid.

164

With him retired his " *posse comitatus*,"°
　The attorney last, who lingered near the door
Reluctantly, still tarrying there as late as
　Antonia let him — not a little sore
At this most strange and unexplained " *hiatus*"

1270. **Achates:** the companion of Aeneas, whose fidelity has become proverbial.　1305. "*posse comitatus*": the full form of the modern word "posse."

In Don Alfonso's facts, which just now wore
An awkward look; as he revolved the case,   1311
The door was fastened in his legal face.

165

No sooner was it bolted, than — O shame!
Oh sin! Oh sorrow! and Oh womankind!
How can you do such things and keep your fame,
Unless this world, and t'other too, be blind?
Nothing so dear as an unfilched good name!
But to proceed — for there is more behind:
With much heartfelt reluctance be it said,   1319
Young Juan slipped, half-smothered, from the bed.

166

He had been hid — I don't pretend to say
How, nor can I indeed describe the where —
Young, slender, and packed easily, he lay,
No doubt, in little compass, round or square;
But pity him I neither must nor may
His suffocation by that pretty pair;
'Twere better, sure, to die so, than be shut
With maudlin Clarence in his Malmsey butt.°

167

And, secondly, I pity not, because
He had no business to commit a sin,   1330
Forbid by heavenly, fined by human laws,
At least 'twas rather early to begin;
But at sixteen the conscience rarely gnaws
So much as when we call our old debts in
At sixty years, and draw the accompts of evil,
And find a deuced balance with the devil.

168

Of his position I can give no notion;
'Tis written in the Hebrew Chronicle,°
How the physicians, leaving pill and potion,   1339
Prescribed, by way of blister, a young belle,
When old King David's blood grew dull in motion,
And that the medicine answered very well;
Perhaps 'twas in a different way applied,
For David lived, but Juan nearly died.

169

What's to be done? Alfonso will be back
The moment he has sent his fools away.
Antonia's skill was put upon the rack,
But no device could be brought into play —

1328. With . . . butt: referring to the legend that the Duke of
Clarence, brother of Edward IV and Richard III, was drowned in
a butt of his favorite wine; see Shakespeare's *Richard III,* I.iv.
1338. Hebrew Chronicle: See I Kings 1.

And how to parry the renewed attack?
    Besides, it wanted but few hours of day: 1350
Antonia puzzled; Julia did not speak,
But pressed her bloodless lip to Juan's cheek.

170

He turned his lip to hers, and with his hand
    Called back the tangles of her wandering hair;
Even then their love they could not all command,
    And half forgot their danger and despair:
Antonia's patience now was at a stand —
    "Come, come, 'tis no time now for fooling there,"
She whispered, in great wrath — "I must deposit
This pretty gentleman within the closet: 1360

171

"Pray, keep your nonsense for some luckier night —
    Who can have put my master in this mood?
What will become on't — I'm in such a fright,
    The devil's in the urchin, and no good —
Is this a time for giggling? this a plight?
    Why, don't you know that it may end in blood?
You'll lose your life, and I shall lose my place,
My mistress all, for the half-girlish face.

172

"Had it but been for a stout cavalier
    Of twenty-five or thirty — (come, make haste)
But for a child, what piece of work is here!   1371
    I really, madam, wonder at your taste —
(Come, sir, get in) — my master must be near:
    There, for the present, at the least, he's fast,
And if we can but till the morning keep
Our counsel — Juan, mind, you must not sleep."

173

Now, Don Alfonso entering, but alone,
    Closed the oration of the trusty maid:
She loitered, and he told her to be gone,
    An order somewhat sullenly obeyed;   1380
However, present remedy was none,
    And no great good seemed answered if she staid;
Regarding both with slow and sidelong view,
She snuffed the candle, curtsied, and withdrew.

174

Alfonso paused a minute — then begun
    Some strange excuses for his late proceeding;
He would not justify what he had done,
    To say the best, it was extreme ill-breeding;
But there were ample reasons for it, none
    Of which he specified in this his pleading: 1390
His speech was a fine sample, on the whole,
Of rhetoric, which the learned call *"rigmarole."*

175

Julia said nought; though all the while there rose
  A ready answer, which at once enables
A matron, who her husband's foible knows,
  By a few timely words to turn the tables,
Which, if it does not silence, still must pose, —
  Even if it should comprise a pack of fables;
'Tis to retort with firmness, and when he   1399
Suspects with *one,* do you reproach with *three.*

176

Julia, in fact, had tolerable grounds, —
  Alfonso's loves with Inez were well known;
But whether 'twas that one's own guilt confounds —
  But that can't be, as has been often shown,
A lady with apologies abounds; —
  It might be that her silence sprang alone
From delicacy to Don Juan's ear,
To whom she knew his mother's fame was dear.

177

There might be one more motive, which makes two,
  Alfonso ne'er to Juan had alluded, —   1410
Mentioned his jealousy, but never who
  Had been the happy lover, he concluded,
Concealed amongst his premises; 'tis true,
  His mind the more o'er this its mystery brooded
To speak of Inez now were, one may say,
Like throwing Juan in Alfonso's way.

178

A hint, in tender cases, is enough;
  Silence is best: besides there is a *tact* —
(That modern phrase appears to me sad stuff,
  But it will serve to keep my verse compact) —
Which keeps, when pushed by questions rather
    rough,   1421
  A lady always distant from the fact:
The charming creatures lie with such a grace,
There's nothing so becoming to the face.

179

They blush, and we believe them, at least I
  Have always done so; 'tis of no great use,
In any case, attempting a reply,
  For then their eloquence grows quite profuse;
And when at length they're out of breath, they
    sigh,
  And cast their languid eyes down, and let loose
A tear or two, and then we make it up;   1431
And then — and then — and then — sit down and
  sup.

180

Alfonso closed his speech, and begged her pardon,
  Which Julia half withheld, and then half granted,
And laid conditions, he thought very hard, on,
  Denying several little things he wanted:
He stood like Adam lingering near his garden,
  With useless penitence perplexed and haunted,
Beseeching she no further would refuse,
When, lo! he stumbled o'er a pair of shoes.   1440

181

A pair of shoes! — what then? not much, if they
  Are such as fit with ladies' feet, but these
(No one can tell how much I grieve to say)
  Were masculine; to see them, and to seize,
Was but a moment's act. — Ah! well-a-day!
  My teeth begin to chatter, my veins freeze —
Alfonso first examined well their fashion,
And then flew out into another passion.

182

He left the room for his relinquished sword,
  And Julia instant to the closet flew.   1450
" Fly, Juan, fly! for heaven's sake — not a word —
  The door is open — you may yet slip through
The passage you so often have explored —
  Here is the garden-key — Fly — fly — Adieu!
Haste — haste! I hear Alfonso's hurrying feet —
Day has not broke — there's no one in the street."

183

None can say that this was not good advice,
  The only mischief was, it came too late;
Of all experience 'tis the usual price,
  A sort of income-tax laid on by fate: 1460
Juan had reached the room-door in a trice,
  And might have done so by the garden-gate,
But met Alfonso in his dressing-gown,
Who threatened death — so Juan knocked him
  down.

184

Dire was the scuffle, and out went the light;
  Antonia cried out " Rape!" and Julia " Fire!"
But not a servant stirred to aid the fight.
  Alfonso, pommelled to his heart's desire,
Swore lustily he'd be revenged this night;   1469
  And Juan, too, blasphemed an octave higher;
His blood was up; though young, he was a Tar-
  tar,
And not at all disposed to prove a martyr.

185

Alfonso's sword had dropped ere he could draw it,
　And they continued battling hand to hand,
For Juan very luckily ne'er saw it;
　His temper not being under great command,
If at that moment he had chanced to claw it,
　Alfonso's days had not been in the land
Much longer. — Think of husbands', lovers' lives!
And how ye may be doubly widows — wives!

186

Alfonso grappled to detain the foe,　　　　1481
　And Juan throttled him to get away,
And blood ('twas from the nose) began to flow;
　At last, as they more faintly wrestling lay,
Juan contrived to give an awkward blow,
　And then his only garment quite gave way;
He fled, like Joseph, leaving it; but there,
I doubt, all likeness ends° between the pair.

187

Lights came at length, and men, and maids, who
　　found
　An awkward spectacle their eyes before;　　1490
Antonia in hysterics, Julia swooned,
　Alfonso leaning, breathless, by the door;
Some half-torn drapery scattered on the ground,
　Some blood, and several footsteps, but no more:
Juan the gate gained, turned the key about,
And liking not the inside, locked the out.

188

Here ends this canto. — Need I sing, or say,
　How Juan, naked, favoured by the night,
Who favours what she should not, found his way,
　And reached his home in an unseemly plight?
The pleasant scandal which arose next day,　　1501
　The nine days' wonder which was brought to
　　light,
And how Alfonso sued for a divorce,
Were in the English newspapers, of course.

189

If you would like to see the whole proceedings,
　The depositions and the cause at full,
The names of all the witnesses, the pleadings
　Of counsel to nonsuit, or to annul,
There's more than one edition, and the readings
　Are various, but they none of them are dull; 1510

The best is that in short-hand ta'en by Gurney,°
Who to Madrid on purpose made a journey.

190

But Donna Inez, to divert the train
　Of one of the most circulating scandals
That had for centuries been known in Spain,
　At least since the retirement of the Vandals,°
First vowed (and never had she vowed in vain)
　To Virgin Mary several pounds of candles;
And then, by the advice of some old ladies,　1519
She sent her son to be shipped off from Cadiz.

191

She had resolved that he should travel through
　All European climes, by land or sea,
To mend his former morals, and get new,
　Especially in France and Italy
(At least this is the thing most people do).
　Julia was sent into a convent: she
Grieved, but, perhaps, her feelings may be better
Shown in the following copy of her Letter: —

192

" They tell me 'tis decided you depart:
　'Tis wise — 'tis well, but not the less a pain;
I have no further claim on your young heart,　1531
　Mine is the victim, and would be again:
To love too much has been the only art
　I used; — I write in haste, and if a stain
Be on this sheet, 'tis not what it appears;
My eyeballs burn and throb, but have no tears.

193

" I loved, I love you, for this love have lost
　State, station, heaven, mankind's, my own esteem,
And yet cannot regret what it hath cost,
　So dear is still the memory of that dream;　1540
Yet, if I name my guilt, 'tis not to boast,
　None can deem harshlier of me than I deem:
I trace this scrawl because I cannot rest —
I've nothing to reproach or to request.

194

" Man's love is of man's life a thing apart,
　'Tis woman's whole existence; man may range
The court, camp, church, the vessel, and the mart;
　Sword, gown, gain, glory, offer in exchange
Pride, fame, ambition, to fill up his heart,

1488. all . . . ends: Joseph's resistance to the blandishments of
Potiphar's wife has made his name proverbial for chastity, as in
Fielding's *Joseph Andrews*; see Gen. 39.

1511. Gurney: William B. Gurney was a famous shorthand writer
and court reporter.　1516. Vandals: The Vandals invaded Spain
in the fifth century and gave their name to Andalusia.

And few there are whom these cannot estrange;
Men have all these resources, we but one,   1551
To love again, and be again undone.

195

" You will proceed in pleasure, and in pride,
   Beloved and loving many; all is o'er
For me on earth, except some years to hide
   My shame and sorrow deep in my heart's core:
These I could bear, but cannot cast aside
   The passion which still rages as before,—
And so farewell—forgive me, love me—No,
That word is idle now—but let it go.   1560

196

" My breast has been all weakness, is so yet;
   But still I think I can collect my mind;
My blood still rushes where my spirit's set,
   As roll the waves before the settled wind;
My heart is feminine, nor can forget—
   To all, except one image, madly blind;
So shakes the needle, and so stands the pole,
As vibrates my fond heart to my fixed soul.

197

" I have no more to say, but linger still,
   And dare not set my seal upon this sheet,   1570
And yet I may as well the task fulfil,
   My misery can scarce be more complete:
I had not lived till now, could sorrow kill;
   Death shuns the wretch who fain the blow would
      meet,
And I must even survive this last adieu,
And bear with life to love and pray for you! "

198

This note was written upon gilt-edged paper
   With a neat little crow-quill, slight and new;
Her small white hand could hardly reach the taper,
   It trembled as magnetic needles do,   1580
And yet she did not let one tear escape her;
   The seal a sun-flower; " *Elle vous suit partout*,"°
The motto, cut upon a white cornelian;
The wax was superfine, its hue vermilion.

199

This was Don Juan's earliest scrape; but whether
   I shall proceed with his adventures is
Dependent on the public altogether;
   We'll see, however, what they say to this,

Their favour in an author's cap's a feather,
   And no great mischief's done by their caprice;
And if their approbation we experience,   1591
Perhaps they'll have some more about a year hence.

200

My poem's epic, and is meant to be
   Divided in twelve books; each book containing,
With love, and war, a heavy gale at sea,
   A list of ships, and captains, and kings reigning,
New characters; the episodes are three:
   A panoramic view of hell's in training,
After the style of Virgil and of Homer,
So that my name of Epic's no misnomer.   1600

201

All these things will be specified in time,
   With strict regard to Aristotle's rules,
The *Vade Mecum*° of the true sublime,
   Which makes so many poets, and some fools:
Prose poets like blank-verse, I'm fond of rhyme,
   Good workmen never quarrel with their tools;
I've got new mythological machinery,
And very handsome supernatural scenery.

202

There's only one slight difference between
   Me and my epic brethren gone before,   1610
And here the advantage is my own, I ween
   (Not that I have not several merits more,
But this will more peculiarly be seen);
   They so embellish, that 'tis quite a bore
Their labyrinth of fables to thread through,
Whereas this story's actually true.

203

If any person doubt it, I appeal
   To history, tradition, and to facts,
To newspapers, whose truth all know and feel,
   To plays in five, and operas in three acts;   1620
All these confirm my statement a good deal,
   But that which more completely faith exacts
Is, that myself, and several now in Seville,
Saw Juan's last elopement with the devil.

204

If ever I should condescend to prose,
   I'll write poetical commandments, which
Shall supersede beyond all doubt all those
   That went before; in these I shall enrich
My text with many things that no one knows,

1582. "*Elle . . . partout*": "She follows you everywhere," an allusion to the sunflower's keeping its face toward the sun.

1603. *Vade Mecum:* handbook. "Aristotle's rules" were generally supposed to be rules for observing the unities of time, place, and action, none of which Byron observes.

And carry precept to the highest pitch: 1630
I'll call the work "Longinus o'er a Bottle,
Or, Every Poet his *own* Aristotle."°

205

Thou shalt believe in Milton, Dryden, Pope;
  Thou shalt not set up Wordsworth, Coleridge,
    Southey;
Because the first is crazed beyond all hope,
The second drunk, the third so quaint and
    mouthy:
With Crabbe it may be difficult to cope,
  And Campbell's Hippocrene is somewhat
    drouthy:
Thou shalt not steal from Samuel Rogers,° nor
Commit — flirtation with the muse of Moore.   1640

206

Thou shalt not covet Mr. Sotheby's° Muse,
  His Pegasus, nor anything that's his;
Thou shalt not bear false witness like "the
    Blues"° —
(There's one, at least, is very fond of this);
Thou shalt not write, in short, but what I choose:
  This is true criticism, and you may kiss —
Exactly as you please, or not, — the rod;
But if you don't, I'll lay it on, by G—d!

207

If any person should presume to assert
  This story is not moral, first, I pray,   1650
That they will not cry out before they're hurt,
  Then that they'll read it o'er again, and say
(But, doubtless, nobody will be so pert),
  That this is not a moral tale, though gay;
Besides, in Canto Twelfth, I mean to show
The very place where wicked people go.

208

If, after all, there should be some so blind
  To their own good this warning to despise,
Led by some tortuosity of mind,
  Not to believe my verse and their own eyes,   1660

And cry that they "the moral cannot find,"
  I tell him, if a clergyman, he lies;
Should captains the remark, or critics, make,
They also lie too — under a mistake.

209

The public approbation I expect,
  And beg they'll take my word about the moral,
Which I with their amusement will connect
  (So children cutting teeth receive a coral);
Meantime they'll doubtless please to recollect
  My epical pretensions to the laurel: 1670
For fear some prudish readers should grow skittish,
I've bribed my grandmother's review — the British.

210

I sent it in a letter to the Editor,
  Who thanked me duly by return of post —
I'm for a handsome article his creditor;
  Yet, if my gentle Muse he please to roast,
And break a promise after having made it her,
  Denying the receipt of what it cost,
And smear his page with gall instead of honey,
All I can say is — that he had the money.   1680

211

I think that with this holy new alliance
  I may ensure the public, and defy
All other magazines of art or science,
  Daily, or monthly or three monthly; I
Have not essayed to multiply their clients,
  Because they tell me 'twere in vain to try,
And that the Edinburgh Review and Quarterly
Treat a dissenting author very martyrly.

212

"*Non ego hoc ferrem calida juventâ
  Consule Planco*,"° Horace said, and so   1690
Say I; by which quotation there is meant a
  Hint that some six or seven good years ago
(Long ere I dreamt of dating from the Brenta°)
  I was most ready to return a blow,
And would not brook at all this sort of thing
In my hot youth — when George the Third was
    King.

213

But now at thirty years my hair is grey —
  (I wonder what it will be like at forty?
I thought of a peruke the other day —)

1631–32. "Longinus . . . Aristotle": Longinus' *On the Sublime* and Aristotle's *Poetics* were the two Classical authorities on literary criticism.   1637–39. Crabbe . . . Rogers: George Crabbe (1754–1832), author of *The Village*, Thomas Campbell (1777–1844), author of *The Pleasures of Hope* and *Gertrude of Wyoming* (quoted in st. 88, above), and Samuel Rogers (1763–1855), author of *The Pleasures of Memory*, were minor poets of the Romantic period. Rogers was a friend of Byron's, hence the difference of tone in the allusion. For "Hippocrene" see Keats, "Ode to a Nightingale," st. 2, p. 747, below.   1641. Sotheby: William Sotheby (1757–1833), best known as the translator of Homer and Virgil, had a substantial private income and was often a patron of other poets, hence the allusion in l. 1642.   1643. "the Blues": i.e., bluestockings, or pedantic women. The allusion in the next line is to Lady Byron.

1689–90. "*Non . . . Planco*": "I should not have borne this in the heat of my youth when Plancus was consul" (Horace, *Odes*, III.xiv).   1693. Brenta: a river near Venice. The line means "before I went abroad for the last time."

My heart is not much greener; and, in short, I
Have squandered my whole summer while 'twas
  May,   1701
And feel no more the spirit to retort; I
Have spent my life, both interest and principal,
And deem not, what I deemed, my soul invincible.

214

No more — no more — Oh! never more on me
 The freshness of the heart can fall like dew,
Which out of all the lovely things we see
 Extracts emotions beautiful and new;
Hived in our bosoms like the bag o' the bee.
 Think'st thou the honey with those objects grew?
Alas! 'twas not in them, but in thy power 1711
To double even the sweetness of a flower.

215

No more — no more — Oh! never more, my heart,
 Canst thou be my sole world, my universe!
Once all in all, but now a thing apart,
 Thou canst not be my blessing or my curse:
The illusion's gone for ever, and thou art
 Insensible, I trust, but none the worse,
And in thy stead I've got a deal of judgment,
Though heaven knows how it ever found a lodg-
 ment.   1720

216

My days of love are over; me no more
 The charms of maid, wife, and still less of
  widow,
Can make the fool of which they made before, —
 In short, I must not lead the life I did do;
The credulous hope of mutual minds is o'er,
 The copious use of claret is forbid too,
So for a good old-gentlemanly vice,
I think I must take up with avarice.

217

Ambition was my idol, which was broken
 Before the shrines of Sorrow, and of Pleasure;
And the two last have left me many a token 1731
 O'er which reflection may be made at leisure;
Now, like Friar Bacon's° brazen head, I've spoken,
 "Time is, Time was, Time's past: " — a chymic
  treasure
Is glittering youth, which I have spent betimes —
My heart in passion, and my head on rhymes.

1733. **Friar Bacon's:** The story of the legendary speaking brazen
head made by the medieval philosopher Roger Bacon is told in
Robert Greene's play, *Friar Bacon and Friar Bungay* (1594).

218

What is the end of fame? 'tis but to fill
 A certain portion of uncertain paper:
Some liken it to climbing up a hill,
 Whose summit, like all hills, is lost in vapour;
For this men write, speak, preach, and heroes kill,
 And bards burn what they call their "midnight
  taper,"   1742
To have, when the original is dust,
A name, a wretched picture, and worst bust.

219

What are the hopes of man? Old Egypt's King
 Cheops erected the first pyramid
And largest, thinking it was just the thing
 To keep his memory whole, and mummy hid:
But somebody or other rummaging,
 Burglariously broke his coffin's lid. 1750
Let not a monument give you or me hopes,
Since not a pinch of dust remains of Cheops.

220

But I, being fond of true philosophy,
 Say very often to myself, "Alas!
All things that have been born were born to die,
 And flesh (which Death mows down to hay) is
  grass;
You've passed your youth not so unpleasantly.
 And if you had it o'er again — 'twould pass —
So thank your stars that matters are no worse,
And read your Bible, sir, and mind your purse."

221

But for the present, gentle reader! and 1761
 Still gentler purchaser! the bard — that's I —
Must, with permission, shake you by the hand,
 And so your humble servant, and good-bye!
We meet again, if we should understand
 Each other; and if not, I shall not try
Your patience further than by this short sample —
'Twere well if others followed my example.

222

"Go, little book, from this my solitude!
 I cast thee on the waters — go thy ways! 1770
And if, as I believe, thy vein be good,
 The world will find thee after many days."
When Southey's read, and Wordsworth understood,
 I can't help putting in my claim to praise —
The four first rhymes are Southey's,° every line:
For God's sake, reader! take them not for mine!

1775. **Southey's:** The lines are from the last stanza of Southey's
"Epilogue to the Lay of the Laureate."

from CANTO III

78

And now they were diverted by their suite,
   Dwarfs, dancing-girls, black eunuchs, and a poet,
Which made their new establishment complete;
   The last was of great fame, and liked to show it;
His verses rarely wanted their due feet —
   And for this theme — he seldom sung below it,
He being paid to satirise or flatter,
As the psalm° says, "inditing a good matter."

79

He praised the present, and abused the past,
   Reversing the good custom of old days,   10
An Eastern anti-jacobin at last
   He turned, preferring pudding to *no* praise —
For some few years his lot had been o'ercast
   By his seeming independent in his lays,
But now he sung the Sultan and the Pacha
With truth like Southey, and with verse like Crashaw.°

80

He was a man who had seen many changes,
   And always changed as true as any needle;
His polar star being one which rather ranges,
   And not the fixed — he knew the way to wheedle:
So vile he 'scaped the doom which oft avenges; 21
   And being fluent (save indeed when fee'd ill),
He lied with such a fervour of intention —
There was no doubt he earned his laureate pension.

81

But he had genius, — when a turncoat has it,
   The "Vates irritabilis"° takes care
That without notice few full moons shall pass it;
   Even good men like to make the public stare: —
But to my subject — let me see — what was it? —
   Oh! — the third canto — and the pretty pair —
Their loves, and feasts, and house, and dress, and mode   31
Of living in their insular abode.

82

Their poet, a sad trimmer,° but no less
   In company a very pleasant fellow,
Had been the favourite of full many a mess
   Of men, and made them speeches when half mellow;

And though his meaning they could rarely guess,
   Yet still they deigned to hiccup or to bellow
The glorious meed of popular applause,
Of which the first ne'er knows the second cause. 40

83

But now being lifted into high society,
   And having picked up several odds and ends
Of free thoughts in his travels, for variety,
   He deemed, being in a lone isle, among friends,
That without any danger of a riot, he
   Might for long lying make himself amends;
And singing as he sung in his warm youth,
Agree to a short armistice with truth.

84

He had travelled 'mongst the Arabs, Turks, and Franks,
   And he knew the self-loves of the different nations;   50
And having lived with people of all ranks,
   Had something ready upon most occasions —
Which got him a few presents and some thanks.
   He varied with some skill his adulations;
To "do at Rome as Romans do," a piece
Of conduct was which he observed in Greece.

85

Thus, usually, when he was asked to sing,
   He gave the different nations something national;
'Twas all the same of him — "God save the king,"
   Or "*ça ira*,"° according to the fashion all: 60
His muse made increment of anything,
   From the high lyric down to the low rational:
If Pindar sang horse-races, what should hinder
Himself from being as pliable as Pindar?

86

In France, for instance, he would write a chanson;
   In England a six canto quarto tale;
In Spain he'd make a ballad or romance on
   The last war — much the same in Portugal;
In Germany, the Pegasus he'd prance on
   Would be old Goethe's — (see what says De Staël°);
In Italy he'd ape the "Trecentisti";°
In Greece, he'd sing some sort of hymn like this t'ye:

Canto III: 8. **psalm**: Ps. 45:1.   **16. Crashaw**: Richard Crashaw (1613–50), poet and Roman Catholic convert, whose "metaphysical" style of writing was out of fashion in Byron's day. **26. "Vates irritabilis"**: the irritable poet; see Coleridge, *Biographia Literaria*, II.   **33. trimmer**: time-serving compromiser.

60. "ça ira": a French Revolutionary song.   **70. De Staël**: Madame de Staël, whom Byron had met in England, said in her book *De L'Allemagne* (1810) that Goethe represented the entire literature of Germany.   **71. "Trecentisti"**: Italian poets of the fourteenth century: Dante, Petrarch, Boccaccio.

i

The isles of Greece, the isles of Greece!
  Where burning Sappho loved and sung,
Where grew the arts of war and peace,
  Where Delos° rose, and Phoebus sprung!
Eternal summer gilds them yet,
But all, except their sun, is set.

ii

The Scian and the Teian° muse,
  The hero's harp, the lover's lute,   80
Have found the fame your shores refuse:
  Their place of birth alone is mute
To sounds which echo further west
Than your sires' "Islands of the Blest."°

iii

The mountains look on Marathon —
  And Marathon looks on the sea;
And musing there an hour alone,
  I dreamed that Greece might still be free;
For standing on the Persians' grave,
I could not deem myself a slave.   90

iv

A king° sate on the rocky brow
  Which looks o'er sea-born Salamis;
And ships, by thousands, lay below,
  And men in nations; — all were his!
He counted them at break of day —
And when the sun set where were they?

v

And where are they? and where art thou,
  My country? On thy voiceless shore
The heroic lay is tuneless now —
  The heroic bosom beats no more!   100
And must thy lyre, so long divine,
Degenerate into hands like mine?

vi

'Tis something, in the dearth of fame,
  Though linked among a fettered race,
To feel at least a patriot's shame,
  Even as I sing, suffuse my face;

For what is left the poet here?
For Greeks a blush — for Greece a tear.

vii

Must *we* but weep o'er days more blest?
  Must *we* but blush? — Our fathers bled.   110
Earth! render back from out thy breast
  A remnant of our Spartan dead!
Of the three hundred grant but three,
To make a new Thermopylae!

viii

What, silent still? and silent all?
  Ah! no; — the voices of the dead
Sound like a distant torrent's fall,
  And answer, "Let one living head,
But one arise, — we come, we come!"
'Tis but the living who are dumb.   120

ix

In vain — in vain: strike other chords;
  Fill high the cup with Samian wine!
Leave battles to the Turkish hordes,
  And shed the blood of Scio's vine!
Hark! rising to the ignoble call —
How answers each bold Bacchanal!

x

You have the Pyrrhic° dance as yet;
  Where is the Pyrrhic phalanx gone?
Of two such lessons, why forget
  The nobler and the manlier one?   130
You have the letters Cadmus gave —
Think ye he meant them for a slave?

xi

Fill high the bowl with Samian wine!
  We will not think of themes like these!
It made Anacreon's song divine:
  He served — but served Polycrates° —
A tyrant; but our masters then
Were still, at least, our countrymen.

xii

The tyrant of the Chersonese°
  Was freedom's best and bravest friend;   140

---

76. **Delos:** the island in the Cyclades said to have been originally a floating island, and the place where Phoebus Apollo and his sister Artemis were born.   79. **Scian . . . Teian:** Scio and Teos were traditionally the birthplaces of Homer and Anacreon, respectively.   84. **"Islands . . . Blest":** "The *nesoi makaron* of the Greek poets were supposed to have been the Cape de Verd islands or the Canaries" [B].   91. **king:** Xerxes. See the note on Canto I, l. 937. He watched the battle of Salamis from a nearby mountain.

127. **Pyrrhic:** Pyrrhus, king of Epirus in the third century B.C. and winner of a "Pyrrhic victory" (i.e., one in which the victor's losses are great enough to amount to a defeat) over the Romans, fought with the Macedonian phalanx and is said to have invented a war dance.   136. **Polycrates:** a tyrant of Samos in the sixth century B.C.; Anacreon was one of his court poets.   139. **Chersonese:** a peninsula in Thrace, the modern Gallipoli. Miltiades, its ruler in the fifth century B.C., was the leader of the Greeks at Marathon.

That tyrant was Miltiades!
　Oh! that the present hour would lend
Another despot of the kind!
　Such chains as his were sure to bind.

xiii

Fill high the bowl with Samian wine!
　On Suli's rock, and Parga's° shore,
Exists the remnant of a line
　Such as the Doric° mothers bore;
And there, perhaps, some seed is sown,
The Heracleidan blood might own.　　　150

xiv

Trust not for freedom to the Franks°—
　They have a king who buys and sells;
In native swords, and native ranks,
　The only hope of courage dwells:
But Turkish force, and Latin fraud,
Would break your shield, however broad.

xv

Fill high the bowl with Samian wine!
　Our virgins dance beneath the shade—
I see their glorious black eyes shine;
　But gazing on each glowing maid,　　　160
My own the burning tear-drop laves,
To think such breasts must suckle slaves.

xvi

Place me on Sunium's° marbled steep,
　Where nothing, save the waves and I,
May hear our mutual murmurs sweep;
　There, swan-like, let me sing and die:
A land of slaves shall ne'er be mine—
Dash down yon cup of Samian wine!

87

Thus sung, or would, or could, or should have sung,
　The modern Greek, in tolerable verse;　　　170
If not like Orpheus quite, when Greece was young,
　Yet in these times he might have done much
　　　worse:
His strain displayed some feeling—right or wrong;
　And feeling, in a poet, is the source
Of others' feeling; but they are such liars,
And take all colours—like the hands of dyers.

88

But words are things, and a small drop of ink,
　Falling like dew, upon a thought, produces
That which makes thousands, perhaps millions,
　　　think;
　'Tis strange, the shortest letter which man uses
Instead of speech, may form a lasting link　　　181
　Of ages; to what straits old Time reduces
Frail man, when paper—even a rag like this,
Survives himself, his tomb, and all that's his!

89

And when his bones are dust, his grave a blank,
　His station, generation, even his nation,
Become a thing, or nothing, save to rank
　In chronological commemoration,
Some dull MS. oblivion long has sank,
　Or graven stone found in a barrack's station　190
In digging the foundation of a closet,
May turn his name up, as a rare deposit.

90

And glory long has made the sages smile;
　'Tis something, nothing, words, illusion, wind—
Depending more upon the historian's style
　Than on the name a person leaves behind:
Troy owes to Homer what whist owes to Hoyle:
　The present century was growing blind
To the great Marlborough's skill in giving knocks,
Until his late Life° by Archdeacon Coxe.　　　200

91

Milton's the prince of poets—so we say;
　A little heavy, but no less divine:
An independent being in his day—
　Learn'd, pious, temperate in love and wine;
But his life falling into Johnson's way,
　We're told this great high priest of all the Nine°
Was whipt at college—a harsh sire—odd spouse,
For the first Mrs. Milton left his house.°

92

All these are, *certes,* entertaining facts,
　Like Shakespeare's stealing deer, Lord Bacon's
　　　bribes;　　　210
Like Titus' youth, and Caesar's earliest acts;
　Like Burns (whom Doctor Currie well de-
　　　scribes);

---

146. Suli's . . . Parga's: towns in Albania.　148. Doric: The Dorian invasion of Greece after the Trojan War was called the "Return of the Heracleidae," because the Dorians claimed descent from Hercules.　151. Franks: Western Europeans.　163. Sunium's: the promontory at the southeastern tip of Attica.

200. late Life: *Memoirs of John, Duke of Marlborough,* by William Coxe, Archdeacon of Wilts, appeared in 1818–19.　206. Nine: i.e., the nine Muses.　208. For . . . house: "See Johnson's Life of Milton" [B], for which see pp. 519–29, above.　210–13. Like . . . pranks: For the Shakespeare legend see any annotated edition of the opening scene of *The Merry Wives of Windsor;*

Like Cromwell's pranks;° — but although truth
    exacts
  These amiable descriptions from the scribes,
As most essential to their hero's story,
They do not much contribute to his glory.

93

All are not moralists, like Southey, when°
  He prated to the world of " Pantisocrasy;"
Or Wordsworth unexcised, unhired, who then
  Seasoned his pedlar poems with democracy; 220
Or Coleridge, long before his flighty pen
  Let to the Morning Post its aristocracy;
When he and Southey, following the same path,
Espoused two partners (milliners of Bath).

94

Such names at present cut a convict figure,
  The very Botany Bay° in moral geography;
Their loyal treason, renegado rigour,
  Are good manure for their more bare biography,
Wordsworth's last quarto, by the way, is bigger
  Than any since the birthday of typography; 230
A drowsy frowzy poem, called the " Excursion,"°
Writ in a manner which is my aversion.

95

He there builds up a formidable dyke
  Between his own and others' intellect:
But Wordsworth's poem, and his followers, like
  Joanna Southcote's Shiloh,° and her sect,
Are things which in this century don't strike
  The public mind, — so few are the elect;
And the new births of both their stale virginities
Have proved but dropsies, taken for divinities. 240

Bacon was convicted by Parliament of taking bribes as Chancellor; Titus practised forgery in his youth; Caesar betrayed and crucified some pirates after making friends with them; the dissipation of Burns is described (and much exaggerated) in James Currie's life, published in 1800; Cromwell is said to have robbed orchards in his youth. **217-24. All . . . Bath:** "Pantisocracy": Coleridge and Southey had proposed to emigrate to America with ten other young men (and their wives) and establish a "pantisocracy" (equal government for all). Wordsworth was appointed Distributor of Stamps in Westmorland, a position in the excise, in 1813; the central figures of Wordsworth's *Peter Bell* and *The Excursion* are pedlars, hence "pedlar poems"; Coleridge began writing for the *Morning Post* in 1800 after giving up his earlier radical views; Southey and Coleridge married sisters, Edith and Sara Fricker, who were not milliners and came not from Bath but from Bristol. **226. Botany Bay:** penal settlement in Australia. **231. "Excursion":** Wordsworth's *The Excursion*, in nine books, was published in 1814. **236. Joanna . . . Shiloh:** Joanna Southcote, leader of a fanatical millennial sect, announced in 1814, at the age of sixty-four, that she was virginally pregnant with a new Messiah, whom she called "Shiloh." Her influence waned when her pregnancy turned out to be dropsy, of which she died.

96

But let me to my story: I must own,
  If I have any fault, it is digression,
Leaving my people to proceed alone,
  While I soliloquize beyond expression:
But these are my addresses from the throne,
  Which put off business to the ensuing session:
Forgetting each omission is a loss to
The world, not quite so great as Ariosto.°

97

I know that what our neighbours call " *longueurs,*"
  (We've not so good a *word,* but have the *thing,*
In that complete perfection which insures 251
  An epic from Bob Southey every Spring —)
Form not the true temptation which allures
  The reader; but 'twould not be hard to bring
Some fine examples of the *epopée,*
To prove its grand ingredient is *ennui.*

98

We learn from Horace,° " Homer sometimes
    sleeps ";
  We feel without him, Wordsworth sometimes
    wakes, —
To show with what complacency he creeps,
  With his dear " *Waggoners,*"° around his lakes.
He wishes for " a boat " to sail the deeps — 261
  Of ocean? — No, of air; and then he makes
Another outcry for " a little boat,"
And drivels seas to set it well afloat.

99

If he must fain sweep o'er the ethereal plain,
  And Pegasus runs restive in his " Waggon,"
Could he not beg the loan of Charles's Wain?°
  Or pray Medea for a single dragon?
Or if, too classic for his vulgar brain,
  He feared his neck to venture such a nag on,
And he must needs mount nearer to the moon, 271
Could not the blockhead ask for a balloon?

248. Arioste: the Italian poet (1474-1533) whose romantic epic, *Orlando Furioso,* is one of Byron's models. **257. Horace:** in the *Ars Poetica,* l. 359. **260. "Waggoners":** Wordsworth's *The Waggoner,* to which this refers, was published in 1819, just after *Peter Bell.* The first stanza of *Peter Bell* reads:

> There's something in a flying horse,
> There's something in a huge balloon;
> But through the clouds I'll never float
> Until I have a little Boat,
> Shaped like a crescent-moon.

267. Charles's Wain: the constellation usually called the Big Dipper. "Wain" means wagon.

100

"Pedlars," and "Boats," and "Waggons!" Oh! ye
    shades
  Of Pope and Dryden, are we come to this?
That trash of such sort not alone evades
  Contempt, but from the bathos' vast abyss
Floats scumlike uppermost, and these Jack Cades°
  Of sense and song above your graves may hiss —
The "little boatman" and his "Peter Bell"
Can sneer at him who drew "Achitophel"!°   280

101

T'our tale. — The feast was over, the slaves gone,
  The dwarfs and dancing girls had all retired;
The Arab lore and poet's song were done,
  And every sound of revelry expired;
The lady and her lover, left alone,
  The rosy flood of twilight's sky admired; —
Ave Maria!° o'er the earth and sea,
That heavenliest hour of Heaven is worthiest thee!

102

Ave Maria! blessed be the hour!
  The time, the clime, the spot, where I so oft 290
Have felt that moment in its fullest power
  Sink o'er the earth so beautiful and soft,
While swung the deep bell in the distant tower
  Or the faint dying day-hymn stole aloft,
And not a breath crept through the rosy air,
And yet the forest leaves seemed stirred with prayer.

103

Ave Maria! 'tis the hour of prayer!
  Ave Maria! 'tis the hour of love!
Ave Maria! may our spirits dare
  Look up to thine and to thy Son's above! 300
Ave Maria! oh that face so fair!
  Those downcast eyes beneath the Almighty
    dove —
What though 'tis but a pictured image? — strike —
That painting is no idol, — 'tis too like.

104

Some kinder casuits are pleased to say,
  In nameless print — that I have no devotion;
But set those persons down with me to pray,
  And you shall see who has the properest notion
Of getting into heaven the shortest way;
  My altars are the mountains and the ocean, 310
Earth, air, stars, — all that springs from the great
    Whole,
Who hath produced, and will receive the soul.

105

Sweet hour of twilight! — in the solitude
  Of the pine forest, and the silent shore
Which bounds Ravenna's immemorial wood,°
  Rooted where once the Adrian wave flowed o'er,
To where the last Caesarean fortress° stood,
  Evergreen forest — which Boccacio's lore°
And Dryden's lay made haunted ground to me,
How have I loved the twilight hour and thee! 320

106

The shrill cicalas, people of the pine,
  Making their summer lives one ceaseless song,
Were the sole echoes, save my steed's and mine,
  And vesper bell's that rose the boughs along;
The spectre huntsman of Onesti's line,
  His hell-dogs, and their chase, and the fair throng
Which learned from this example not to fly
From a true lover, — shadowed my mind's eye.

107

Oh, Hesperus!° thou bringest all good things —
  Home to the weary, to the hungry cheer, 330
To the young bird the parent's brooding wings,
  The welcome stall to the o'erlaboured steer;
Whate'er of peace about our hearthstone clings,
  Whate'er our household gods protect of dear,
Are gathered round us by thy look of rest;
Thou bring'st the child, too, to the mother's breast.

108

Soft hour! which wakes the wish and melts the
    heart
  Of those who sail the seas, on the first day
When they from their sweet friends are torn apart;
  Or fills with love the pilgrim on his way 340

---

277. Jack Cades: Jack Cade was the leader of a rebellion against
King Henry VI in 1450. See Shakespeare's *II Henry VI*. **280.**
"Achitophel": The author of the satire *Absalom and Achitophel*
was John Dryden, of whom Wordsworth had remarked in one of
his critical essays: "The verses of Dryden, once so highly celebrated, are forgotten" [quoted by Byron in a note]. **287. Ave**
Maria!: Hail, Mary; an invocation used in the vesper prayer,
hence symbolic of the close of the day.

315. wood: Ravenna, where Byron lived in 1820–21, was originally a port on the Adriatic, and is now five miles inland, separated from the sea by a pine forest. **317. fortress:** The old
fortified port of Augustus was demolished and turned into a
grove in the sixth century A.D. **318. Boccacio's lore:** one of
the tales in Boccaccio's *Decameron* was retold in Dryden's poem
Theodore and Honoria. The "Theodore" of Dryden is the
"Onesti" (l. 325) of Boccaccio. Byron's purpose in referring to
Dryden's poem is to show that there is more genuine feeling for
nature in Dryden than in Wordsworth. **329. Hesperus:** the
evening star. Byron is paraphrasing a fragment of Sappho.

As the far bell of vesper makes him start,
　　Seeming to weep the dying day's decay;
Is this a fancy which our reason scorns?
Ah! surely nothing dies but something mourns!

109

When Nero perished by the justest doom
　　Which ever the destroyer yet destroyed,
Amidst the road of liberated Rome,
　　Of nations freed, and the world overjoyed,
Some hands unseen strewed flowers upon his tomb:
　　Perhaps the weakness of a heart not void   350
Of feeling for some kindness done, when power
Had left the wretch an uncorrupted hour.

110

But I'm digressing; what on earth has Nero,
　　Or any such like sovereign buffoons,
To do with the transactions of my hero,

More than such madmen's fellow man — the
　　moon's?
Sure my invention must be down at zero,
　　And I grown one of many " wooden spoons "
Of verse (the name with which we Cantabs° please
To dub the last of honours in degrees).   360

111

I feel this tediousness will never do —
　　'Tis being *too* epic, and I must cut down
(In copying) this long canto into two;
　　They'll never find it out, unless I own
The fact, excepting some experienced few;
　　And then as an improvement 'twill be shown:
I'll prove that such the opinion of the critic is
From Aristotle° *passim.* — See Ποιητιϰῆς.

359. Cantabs: graduates of Cambridge.   **368. Aristotle:** Aristotle remarks in ch. xxiv of the *Poetics* that in epic "the beginning and the end must be capable of being brought within a single view" [Butcher trans.].

Percy Bysshe Shelley

1792–1822

"I am one whom men love not," Shelley wrote one day in a dejected mood. It was not true of his personal life, for he was exceptionally beloved by all his friends. But there was no public for his poetry; the critics derided it and the law condemned it. Almost to the present day he has suffered from popular misconceptions that have made him out either a softie or a villain. A weak, girlish portrait painted by a woman who knew it was a failure; the label "ineffectual angel" clamped on by a Victorian critic who had not studied his subject; a story-biography by a twentieth century Frenchman done for entertainment — these form one side of the picture. On the reverse we have the atheistic author of blasphemous poems, the immoral seducer of schoolgirls who drove his wife to suicide, practiced free love and preached subversive doctrines.

The two incompatible pictures are the extreme travesties of a central unity, since "a passion for reforming the world" was combined in Shelley with grace and tenderness beyond all common measure. A truer description of him was given by a fellow poet, Walter Savage Landor, who regretted that through ignorant prejudice he had never visited Shelley when both were living in Italy. He had come to appreciate how much he had missed:

Innocent and careless as a boy, he possessed all the delicate feelings of a gentleman, all the discrimination of a scholar, and united, in just degree, the ardor of the poet with the patience and forbearance of the philosopher. His generosity and charity went far beyond those of any man (I believe) at present in existence.[1]

This was the mature Shelley of his final phase. Though he did not live to be thirty, so much intense experience and so much thought were crowded into his short life that in five years he developed more than other men in fifty, and remarked once that if he should die tomorrow he had yet lived to be older than his father. By more ordinary reckoning the baronet, Sir Timothy, was to survive his unruly son by twenty-two years — his peaceful existence disturbed by eddies and reactions. Behind him stretched a dignified line of Sussex aristocrats traceable back to the fifteenth century; but although the poet's grandfather, Sir Bysshe Shelley, was a man of enterprise, oddity and humor, convention had settled solidly on Timothy, who slid smoothly through Oxford and the Grand Tour of Europe, besides winning a seat in Parliament through the safe assets of family connections and party influence. When his wife Elizabeth — a correct and cold-hearted lady — gave birth to their first son on August 4, 1792, this hard-headed country squire no doubt expected Percy Bysshe to follow in his tracks. And reasonably enough. As Santayana observes: "Few revolutionists would be such if they were heirs to a baronetcy." The boy was to be educated first at Syon House Academy, a respectable private school at Brentford, then at Eton and at Oxford, as befitted the son of a country squire.

[1] *Imaginary Conversations*, Vol. III, 1828.

Shelley, however, while learning Latin from the age of six and enjoying rural pranks on his father's estate, an only son surrounded by adoring sisters, found his own type and degree of education. Looking back on his boyhood — in "Hymn to Intellectual Beauty," V — he recalled how the fashionable Gothic tales of ghosts and haunted ruins (read in the school library) enthralled him until, puzzling deeply on the mystery of man's life and love and hatred, he awoke suddenly to a realizing sense of the Beauty there addressed. To that light, which "gives grace and truth to life's unquiet dream," he vowed to dedicate his own powers.

Already, then, Shelley had burst through the bounds of personal pleasures and comforts to fight all tyranny and slavery, whether practiced on nations or on individuals, and to attempt to lead men, so far as a single mind could do it, to a life of freedom, love, and apprehension of the beautiful. Poem after poem of his maturer years expresses the same striving. To name a few, it is the motivating power in *The Revolt of Islam,* the "Ode to Liberty," and *Hellas;* it is savage and denunciatory in "The Mask of Anarchy" and "Lines Written During the Castlereagh Administration"; it is transcendental in the great verse drama *Prometheus Unbound.* He was impatient of conventionalized creeds and cramping laws. Development, with Shelley, lay not in altering his basic ideas but in maturing the comprehension and expression of them through study and understanding, and in learning by hard experience that practical efforts were often a waste owing to lack of co-operation. In a community alien to his ideals his only hope of raising a firm edifice was to build it in words and images. These came, almost too readily, at his call.

Not surprisingly, at Eton the young Shelley looked on some of its customs as forms of tyranny. He had something better to do; his expanding mind had taken a decided turn to the scientific, and while he studied the "general principles of electricity" his experiments were so practical as to look like practical jokes. His interest in astronomy was to serve him well as a poet; many of his apparently airy fantasies, when examined closely, show an unusually clear grasp of the solar system and the stellar universe. At the same time, besides going ahead with Greek and Latin, he was scribbling a Gothic romance, *Zastrozzi,* replete with the horrors of its kind.

These activities, scientific, classical, and literary, were pursued with ever-growing zeal when at Michaelmas, 1810, Shelley went up to University College, Oxford. He had the luck of the wealthy in that Sir Timothy, thinking no harm could come of it, asked a friendly firm of printers to indulge his son's literary freaks. But Messrs. Slatter & Munday shook their heads over the bold opinions in a novel called *Leonora,* written jointly by Shelley and another odd fish of his year. Thomas Jefferson Hogg shared his friend's passion for the Greek philosophers and his hatred of the orthodox, though he was far from sharing Shelley's sensitivity. He claimed, too, a hand in Shelley's notorious pamphlet on *The Necessity of Atheism,* copies of which were burning in the booksellers' back kitchen twenty minutes after their first appearance in the shop. Shelley and Hogg exasperated the Master and Fellows by their pride and obstinacy when called up to be questioned. After only two terms at Oxford they were "publicly expelled from the College for contumacy in refusing to answer certain questions put to them."

The months that followed give us Shelley's least attractive period. His career was broken, his aim uncertain, his friend was a coarsening influence, and his inspired revolt was growing harsh and petulant. To banish uncertainty he tried hyperbole, and determined in this mood to enact the knight-errant by "rescuing" his sisters' discontented school-friend, Harriet Westbrook. They hurried to Edinburgh and were married in a fashion, despite Shelley's principles — as a conscientious revolutionary of the period he regarded the marriage bond as a degrading concession to false social conventions. For a while they moved about restlessly — as all moved who lived with Shelley — from town to town. Harriet welcomed her "tyrant" sister Eliza; Hogg tried to seduce the bride in Shelley's absence. All this was disillusioning to the idealist; but his enthusiasm mounted in politics and he set out for Dublin, armed with an "Address to the Irish People," pleading for charity to their ill-used Catholics. To this day the "Address" makes lively reading; the adventure ended in a resolve to labor for "an effect which will take place ages after I have mouldered in the dust." At the same time he was pressing acquaintanceship on the aging William Godwin, author of *Political*

Justice, whose radical ideas matched and influenced his own. Shelley had still to find his feet.

Yet he had been working on a long, philosophical, allegorical poem with the misleading title of *Queen Mab.* Highly and variously derivative, yet charged with the images and ideas of future work, this premature concoction — or news of it, since it was printed privately — got around, and branded the author at the very start of his mission. " There is no God! " he had written, and in his formidably learned notes used rational arguments to prove his case. What he upheld was the bleak doctrine of " Necessity," by which he meant, at this date, that a chain of undisplaceable causes and effects composed the universe. He was soon to progress to a conviction of man's own power over good and evil, but the symbolism of the later poems shrouded his meaning. The four monosyllables " There is no God " were thought to explain themselves.[1] From now onward he was handicapped with the social world which had, as ever, a keener ear for scandal than for poetry; so that when, in the following spring, the news went round that Shelley had left his wife and eloped with Godwin's daughter Mary his reputation as villain and blasphemer was complete.

His own friends — Hogg; Leigh Hunt, the encourager of all young poets; Thomas Love Peacock, the classical scholar and satiric novelist — knew that Shelley was in a turmoil of conflicting loyalties and indecisions. His poetry reflects it: in May of 1814 he was writing to Harriet,

> Thy look of love has power to calm
> The stormiest passion of my soul;

in the following month he was addressing Mary,

> We are not happy, sweet! our state
> Is strange and full of doubt and fear.

He has been laughed at by the worldly-wise for seriously proposing to the abandoned Harriet to come along to Switzerland where he had fled with his new love. Yet in a truly Shelleyan community such a solution might have worked. Already they had with them Mary's step-sister

Claire Clairmont, from whom there was to be almost no escape until Shelley's death. She was a thorn too in Mary's side. These two women, for all their love of Shelley, did not inhabit his ideal world. He came to know that, but tried for the most part to forget it. Shelley abhorred the limitation and exclusiveness of marriage; his Platonic search for Intellectual Beauty had its counterpart in human love. To worship of the beautiful there should be no boundaries; and in Shelley himself it was not only possible but natural to love many women, each for her own distinctiveness. This interdependence of idea and action makes it difficult to consider his writings apart from some attention to the outward pattern of his life.

Idealism and chivalry came up against spates of practical perplexities. Shelley wrote on, harried by financial troubles, by the predicament of Harriet and their children, by the pettifogging attacks of Mary's philosopher-father whose behavior was so much meaner than his principles. It was an escape, in 1816, to visit Lake Geneva, meet the self-exiled Byron, and indulge his passion for boating with his fellow poet. There was already a curious indifference about Shelley's hold on physical life. His desire for freedom had begun to include freedom from the body, which seemed to hamper and imprison his mental powers. When a tempest blew up on the lake one day, Byron and the boatmen sprang to the alert while Shelley sat motionless, declaring he was content to go to the bottom. Contemplating the high serenity of Mont Blanc he speculated:

> Has some unknown omnipotence unfurled
> The veil of life and death?
>
> [Mont Blanc, 53–54]

and he was later to describe life as a " dome of many-coloured glass " that *stained* the white radiance of eternity until death should shatter it.

From such happy companionship and transcendent musing Shelley was to return that autumn to the shock of Harriet's apparent suicide, and to the stunning legal decision by Lord Chancellor Eldon to deprive so unprincipled a rebel of the care of their children. It was a first-fruit of *Queen Mab,* and could only fan the poet's revolt against tyrannical law.

---

[1] This despite Shelley's note: "This negation must be understood solely to affect a creative Deity. The hypothesis of a pervading Spirit co-eternal with the universe remains unshaken."

I curse thee by a parent's outraged love,
By hopes long cherished and too lately lost,
By gentle feelings thou couldst never prove,
By griefs which thy stern nature never crossed,
["To the Lord Chancellor," V]

he wrote in the flood of his bitterness. But defeat and negation were not natural to Shelley without their converse of rebirth and hope. The following summer, on the Thames at Marlow, he wrote his twelve-canto poem *Laon and Cythna* which was again a plea for liberty and justice even in the face of the French Revolution's galling aftermath. To his timid publisher the poem looked both blasphemous and immoral, and Shelley was constrained to tone it down. It then appeared — and, like most of his publications, remained unsold — as *The Revolt of Islam.* It was his last big-scale work before he left with Mary, their two children (both destined to die shortly) and the inevitable Claire, for Italy.

Again they led a roving, restless, traveling existence. Shelley was frequently unwell, and while his intellect and creative mind raced forward, his body lagged, encumbering him so that he deplored the "heavy weight of hours" that chained and bowed a tameless spirit. Incessantly reading and thinking, broadening his intellect, he had now come to a maturity of imaginative power that was matched by an astonishing ability to manage human beings. He kept peace between Mary and Claire Clairmont, eased the strains of Claire and Byron over their joint offspring, by his salutary company rescued Byron from a condition bordering on degeneracy. He even fell in cheerfully with milord's inverted living habits; "I don't suppose this will kill me in a week or a fortnight," he commented in a letter to Peacock, "but I shall not try it longer."

A group known usually as the Pisan Circle revolved around Shelley in those years. Conspicuous among them was the adventurous Cornish seafarer E. J. Trelawny — a man with a glib tongue and a hearty egotism, except where Shelley was concerned. Thomas Medwin, a clever unscrupulous cousin from Sussex, hovered about the two poets seeking journalistic gossip. His best service was to introduce Edward and Jane Williams who fell most happily into the picture, the one as enthusiastic over yachts as Shelley, and more competent, the other a fair if not profound young lady who possessed, what

all the circle lacked, the gift of tranquilizing. Contrary to popular ideas, Shelley's was still the practical mind of the community. He might be heard of sitting in the ruined Baths of Caracalla to compose *Prometheus Unbound,* but he was also house-hunting for himself and Byron, ordering books and medicines from England, stretching inadequate finances, replying sternly to Godwin's insatiable demands for money — while in consideration for Mary he continued to send him sums beyond his means.

This was the prose of his Italian years. The poetry does not seem to have suffered from it. Shelley never expected his *Prometheus Unbound* to sell, but asked his publisher to "pet him and feed him with fine ink and good paper" believing it "the most perfect of my productions." He felt he had truly expressed, though not for popular understanding, the conviction that still moved him. Man was to overthrow evil and secure his liberation when he could not only "defy Power which seems omnipotent" but also "forgive wrongs darker than death or night," motivated by love even for his enemies. (The atheist was by this time close to Christianity, though he balked at the label.)

As his major poetic and philosophic utterance, he could afford to see *Prometheus* miss the common market. But *The Cenci,* a stage play in the Elizabethan manner built on a true Roman story, was a bid for immediate fame. He hoped to see it staged at Covent Garden with his favorite actress as the heroine. However, the managers shuddered at the theme of incest. It was Shelley's usual luck. Even a humorous political jest could not get by: *Swellfoot the Tyrant* gaily satirized George IV's indictment of Queen Caroline. Authority threatened prosecution, and the whole edition had to be suppressed.

The guardians of public morals would have been equally outraged by *Epipsychidion* in 1821, could they have pierced the obscurities in both poem and title. They would have found Shelley's most emphatic rejection of the narrowing principle of monogamy. No less than in *Prometheus,* he was urging the power and infinitude of love. That he was enchanted, on the personal side, by another imprisoned maiden, is less than half the story. While Emilia Viviani, the Italian girl in a convent, moved him to his utterance, he knew, or came to realize, her inadequacy as a symbol of that "light, and love, and immortality" beyond the mutations of human lives. The same spirit of Intellectual Beauty — "the Vision I had sought through grief and shame " — now penetrated him with its intensity. But Emily — though he exalted her as the shadow or incarnation of that love and truth — could never be "one with nature"; she was mortal and mutable like the rest of them. To Claire Clairmont he wrote critically, "Her moral nature is fine — but not above circumstances."

After that impassioned, frustrated urge for coalescence Shelley found a way to separate his worship of immortal beauty from his pleasure in the company of women. When Keats died in February, 1821, Shelley, knowing little of him personally, was the freer to generalize elegiacally on the untimely passing of a poetic soul. In *Adonais* mourning changed into triumph as he pictured the freed spirit flowing back to be "a portion of the Eternal, which must glow through time and change." Without fear of disillusion he could rejoice in the poet's merging into universal light and beauty and pervading love.

There was a freshening and partial relaxation of Shelley's own spirits in the spring of 1822. Captain Roberts was building a boat for him and Williams, and in expectation of the "perfect plaything for the summer" they looked for houses on the seacoast east of La Spezia, and found one only, "a white house with arches" that would take both families. Shelley delighted in the sweet serenity of Jane Williams, without feeling constrained to tear his soul apart. There is no more than a whisper of regret and loneliness in the gracious, dancing lines he addressed to her — "The Invitation," "The Recollection," "With a Guitar," and "In the Bay of Lerici." He was almost happy, though never at peace: a peace he valued more than life. Mortality sat ever more lightly on him. Should they not overturn the boat, he proposed to the unwilling Jane, and explore the unknown together? What life truly was, and for what, he was perhaps on the way to determining, by his own beliefs and standards, in the long poem, *The Triumph of Life,* that he was writing, mostly on the water. Trelawny records that Shelley, reflecting on "the System of the Universe," remarked to him, "I have no fears and some hopes. In our present gross material state our faculties are clouded — when Death removes our clay coverings the mys-tery will be solved."

A more practical project was afoot. Leigh Hunt, with wife and family, was on his way to Italy to launch a new periodical — the *Liberal* — with the editorial help of Shelley and Byron. Shelley sailed eagerly to Leghorn with Williams in the "perfect plaything" and spent a lively week with Hunt. When they set out on July 8 to return to Lerici a storm blew up and the schooner vanished. After days of fruitless search the remains of both were washed ashore near Viareggio. In Shelley's pocket was a copy of Keats' *Lamia* volume which seemed to have been hastily stuffed there. Trelawny, in whom was a touch of the dramatic, made a ceremony out of the quarantine law's requirement and, in the presence of Hunt and Byron, burned the bodies to ashes. *The Triumph of Life* remained an unfinished poem.

II

"I have re-read," wrote W. B. Yeats in 1900, "*Prometheus Unbound,* which I had hoped my fellow students would have studied as a sacred book, and it seems to me to have an even more certain place than I had thought, among the sacred books of the world." There have been many to whom it is natural to read Shelley at his best in this way, and as many to whom such respect seems outrageous. That is what sacred books are like.

As with other sacred books, *Prometheus Unbound* requires to be read and reread until separate lines and phrases come to reflect light and heat one upon another, and images that at first may seem meaningless, or mere decoration, or mechanical re-use of stock material begin to swing together like some incalculable cyclotron. "There is little enjoyment to be derived from his works," wrote F. S. Ellis, compiler of the *Shelley Lexicon,* "by those who read as they run; but they afford an ever-increasing and permanent treasure of delight to those who will be at the pains to study them." To use Shelley's own language, "transforming enlargements of the imagination" are offered: see *A Defence of Poetry* for explanations of this phrase. It may be added that such "enlargement" means not only increased power but a widened and heightened range of operations.

An attempt to summarize [1] the plot-structure of *Prometheus Unbound* shows that it hardly has one. Shelley knew better than to give his Mystery much overt action. The drama is in the moral transformations which his superhuman figures reflect and enact. Within sixty lines it is clear that Prometheus is deeply changed through his long ordeal: "aught evil wish Is dead within" (70–71). To measure this change he wishes to hear again the Curse he originally flung at his oppressor. But, though all remember, none who heard will repeat it; the dangers from Jupiter's vengeance are too evident. In the end the Phantasm of Jupiter himself gives the fierce and prophetic words utterance. Jupiter's response is immediate. More hideous Furies are directed to inflict new pangs. The last of these Furies, who speaks heartbroken philosophy, vanishes (634) at Prometheus' pitying reply. Jupiter has lost and his hour of doom is on its way. But so immense a change entails a time lag. In Act II, Asia and Panthea visit Demogorgon (see below) and Asia's question — "When shall the destined hour arrive? (II.iv.129) — is answered by action. Demogorgon ascends and (III.i) overthrows Jupiter. In the remaining scenes of Act III the transformation of the world is described. Act IV (added later) displays and celebrates the Renovation further and ends with a reminder from Demogorgon of how it has been achieved. In all this a central challenge to speculation is Demogorgon.

No one who reads much in Shelley can fail to notice how favorite a word "throne" is with him in his prose as in his verse. He uses it 146 times; Shakespeare, who might be supposed to have had more occasion, only 75 times: a proof of how radical was Shelley's concern with questions of government and control — in the state and in the individual. Demogorgon, indeed, is the unknown quantity in Shelley's Theory of Government or Power, a symbol for a speculative possibility that must, to many, seem overdaring.

"Necessity," indeed, has been the label under which Demogorgon has chiefly been discussed. It is a less informative label than it may seem: even Milton's fiends in Hell got nothing more than pastime from investigating it:

Fixed fate, free will, foreknowledge absolute,
And found no end, in wandering mazes lost.
[*Paradise Lost,* II.560–61 (see p. 239)]

Demogorgon himself speaks later on as though he would agree with Milton on this; and when Jupiter demands his name replies "Eternity" — not "Necessity." He adds, it is true, "Demand no direr name;" — the name, perhaps, that in Peacock's note the Arcadians held it impious to pronounce: not "Demogorgon," for Jupiter has used that twice, but the real name of the new incarnation.

The consultation or spell scene (II.iv) has received almost as many interpretations as there have been authorities, and this is no place in which to add another. I would only remark that its great theme — the Ultimate Authority, Principle of Principles — is not one upon which it seems proper to be vocally positive. Negatively, I doubt whether Asia is here receiving any course preparing her for her union with Prometheus as much as I doubt whether Demogorgon's Cave has anything to do with Plato's.[2] I do not see that she needs one; there is Panthea's last speech in Act I to consider: the aether of Asia's transforming presence has long been mingled with that of Prometheus.

At first the sisters see a "veiled form" upon the "ebon throne." When the veil falls it is as though a false hypothesis has been discarded and now it is a "mighty darkness" that the sisters see; the falling of the veil has increased the mystery. Those "rays of gloom" are not illumination but its inverse. The more Asia questions this source the less she learns. A moment comes when under Asia's pressure, Demogorgon's response grows suddenly violent:

ASIA. Who is the master of the slave?
DEMOGORGON.   If the abysm
    Could vomit forth its secrets. . . .

                                    [114–15]

It is as though Demogorgon were here using great self-control; almost as though any question or utterance on such themes were a sort of vomiting. There are things which can be thought and perhaps known but not said. As the Tao Tê Ching, LVI, has it:

He who speaks does not know;
He who knows does not speak.

---

[1] A useful detailed account will be found in A. M. D. Hughes, *Prometheus Unbound, etc.,* 1820 (2nd edition, 1957), pp. 184–89.

[2] See Neville Rogers, *Shelley at Work,* p. 156.

or, as Ludwig Wittgenstein put it:

Whereof one cannot speak, thereof one must be silent.[1]

Asia's insistence — which is the spell that brings forth the event — does, however, wring a denial and a declaration from Demogorgon. The denial is as to the utility here of talk about Fate or Necessity:

> For what would it avail . . .
>   What to bid speak
> Fate, Time, Occasion, Chance and Change?
>   [117–19]

They will have nothing to say upon this — which is beyond their realm, vast though that be. The declaration is:

>   To these
> All things are subject but eternal Love.
>   [119–20]

Asia's feminine style of agreement with this leads to her last demand and the arrival of the destiny.

Those who think Shelley lacking in humor or in dramatic invention may consider what is happening in Heaven through these very minutes during which Asia is releasing the Doom. Jupiter, who is far indeed from being only a symbol, is luxuriating in a superlative vaunt. He has everything, he fancies, to exult in: the congregated powers of heaven have at last really an occasion for indulgence, via nectar, in "the soul of joy."

> Rejoice! henceforth I am omnipotent.
>   [III.i.3]

That irrepressible nuisance, the soul of man, is to meet its match at last, for Jove and Thetis have begotten a strange wonder, Demogorgon:

> The dreadful might of ever-living limbs
>   [22]

now to clothe

>   that awful spirit unbeheld
>   [23]

will soon deal with the human being's "unextinguishable fire," "and trample out the spark." Turning to Thetis, whom he hails in the very images used by Panthea and the Voice in the

Air (which may be the voice of Prometheus, or the "familiar voice" of love — see II.v.41) he produces, ventriloquizing for her, a superb burlesque parody:

>   all my being

(she is supposed to cry)

> Like him whom the Numidian seps did thaw
> Into a dew with poison, is dissolved.
>   [39–41]

No nastier reptile[2] ever than this seps (sepsis, septic) is on record; and it is on this that Jove's inspiration swoops as "the thunder of the fiery wheels" is heard "griding the winds." And he lives his part, if any character did, until his most involuntary exit. The skill with which the possibility of any pity — except from Prometheus — is avoided is remarkable.

After this cosmic convulsion, so briefly executed, a pause is necessary. Shelley fills it with the most delicious passage in the drama. Apollo, who has been "held in heaven by wonder" (II.v.11) adds his eye-witness report and Asia's father, Jupiter's brother, Ocean, breathes his satisfaction. The close of this scene is poetry at its highest, a poetry of inexhaustible simplicity:

> [*A sound of waves is heard.*]
> OCEAN. It is the unpastured sea hungering for calm.
> Peace, monster; I come now. Farewell.
> APOLLO.   Farewell.
>   [III.ii.49–50]

III

The action of *Prometheus Unbound* has an elemental simplicity. The crisis comes as early as I.53 with the words "I pity thee"; the rest is outcome and description. After Jupiter's fall there remains only the spelling out of what has happened. One of the marvels of the play is the continued invention with which this is kept, on the whole, from flagging. This is the more astonishing because what might well have seemed at the start a disabling weakness of the design is so deftly handled. So long as Prometheus and the Oceanides remain symbols of "exultations,

---

[1] The closing sentence of *Tractatus Logico-Philosophicus.*

[2] See Lucan, *Pharsalia,* IX.763–88. A count of Shelley's uses of serpents shows the following proportion: as sympathetic 14; as odious 63. See "Reptile Lore in Shelley," Lloyd N. Jeffrey, *Keats-Shelley Journal,* VII.29. Yet H. N. Brailsford can write: "The snake is everywhere in his poems the incarnation of good."

agonies, and love, and man's unconquerable mind," all is well. But as soon as Prometheus starts to describe how they will contrive henceforward to kill time Shelley recognizes the danger. He reveals it in the phrase: " our unexhausted spirits " (III.iii.36). In fact, Prometheus and the sisters are near dwindling into nothing more than the poet's own ideal household.

The little company, however, are only by intermittent analogy human. They have, when prosperous, the inherent insipidity of immortals, and the more human their behavior the greater the danger. It is a proof of Shelley's tact that he makes them fade out almost as soon as they cease to be interesting. The moment of risk is in III.iii.26–36. Prometheus has just described the cave which is to be their " simple dwelling." No doubt it is more than it appears: a sanctum of the poetic consciousness where

> a fountain
> Leaps in the midst with an awakening sound.
> [13–14]

There they " will sit and talk." But the terrible words " ourselves unchanged " are uttered and the ennui of perfection hangs over them. What rescues them (40–63) is the arts. But in their concern with how, through the arts,

> . . . veil by veil, evil and error fall
> [62]

they have really become human again. We see why to Blake " Eternity is in love with the productions of time " is one of the " Proverbs of Hell."

Act IV of *Prometheus Unbound* is hard to speak of worthily. Edmund Blunden, however, can do so. After noting how it opens like a hunting horn, he says:

It must have been Shelley's opinion as he reconsidered the work that [the end of Act III] inclined too much towards a speech at a reformist's meeting to end such a lyric drama. The reformed world was certainly outlined there with a decisive mind: not with the extremist impossibility which is imputed to Shelley. . . . Feeling that the victory of Prometheus should not be concluded in that way, as if he had been writing a political poem and nothing more, Shelley presently caught the music which inspired the appropriate ending. It must be jubilant, aerial, adventurous — and the fourth act appears to

have been his equivalent of a ballet, springing from all he had enjoyed of spectacle, dance and music.
[*Shelley,* p. 220]

The new action, so far as there is one, is supplied by the courtship between Moon and Earth. The Spirit of the Earth has taken a hint offered by Asia (III.iv.86–90) who seems there to have been more than ordinarily prescient. Of this transcendent colloquy Blunden remarks:

It is the utmost assertion in all his writings of his creed of love, one and the same whether felt by man and woman or by whatever is, and while we hear with wonder the voices of his " lamps of heaven," and confess that they are the imaginary voices of nature, we know that human wooing has never been more beautifully remembered.
[p. 222]

The philosophic and prophetic character of his most exalted work makes it difficult: difficult sometimes to conceive the aim, difficult in any case to use the means with which he reaches toward that. And there is this additional difficulty. Shelley's *world* of thought has to an extreme degree the nature of a poem. The most certain things in it have the status of words in a poem, whose main virtue is that they represent and can convey something else, something quite different from any word — a meaning, or rather, an unending series or hierarchy of meanings, intricate and irregular. This is not to say that Shelley lived in a world of words; no man was more concerned with actuals throughout, or more live-hearted and immediate with people and with scenes; but it is the case that these actuals — living men and women, political situations, ideas — were to him, incessantly, as to few others, *symbols* or, in a strict sense, *images*. This visible, audible, tangible world — the world we can have our opinions of — is an image of the eternal. This, as F. M. Cornford remarks (*Plato's Cosmology,* p. 28) is " the cardinal doctrine of Platonism." Shelley is one of those who have been possessed by this doctrine. His " Hymn to Intellectual Beauty " gives a true account.

Accordingly, in his politics and his personal relations as in his poetry, he was concerned with people, things, and events as conveying, representing, symbolizing something forever beyond themselves and yet their essence. And what they might represent would often in turn represent, and so on and on. In his last and most elaborate use of the fountain-lighted cavern image (*The Triumph of Life,* 308–65)

>   the bright omnipresence
> Of morning through the orient cavern flowed,
> And the sun's image radiantly intense
>
> Burned on the waters of the well that glowed
> Like gold, and threaded all the forest's maze
> With winding paths of emerald fire; there stood
>
> Amid the sun, as he amid the blaze
> Of his own glory, on the vibrating
> Floor of the fountain, paved with flashing rays,
>
> A Shape all light.

This is both a dazzlingly exact depiction of what the eye could see by gazing into such reflections *and* a symbolic presentation of the awakening mind with every other word overcharged. For example, " winding paths." Cf. note to *PU,* I.742, p. 692, below.

This Shape, which is to undergo disguising transformations even in what is left of this un-finished poem, stood enclosed within " the bright omnipresence," within " the sun's image " and within the " flashing rays " of the reflection " in the waters " as " he [the sun] amid the blaze / Of his own glory." Is not this in analogy with the way in which a word, however illuminating, seems to enclose a meaning, and that again a further interpretation: or with the fashion in which a poem or work of art creates " a being within our being," " a world within a world "? That Shelley, in writing so, is aware of and deliberately using such parallels may be what he means in the Preface to *Prometheus Unbound* by " The imagery which I have employed will be found, in many instances, to have been drawn from the operations of the human mind "; a singularity he is willing to have imputed to his study of the Greek poets.

It may be hoped that these characteristics of Shelley's poetry will come to be more widely recognized. Meanwhile, the fact that a critic, however eminent, does not understand something, if a point at all, is a point against the critic, not against the poet. As with his peers, when we judge Shelley, it is not Shelley who is judged.

STANZAS — APRIL, 1814

Composed at Bracknell where Shelley had been the guest of Mrs. de Boinville and her daughter, Cornelia Turner. The poem may be read as an imaginary construction or as a record of experience.

Away! the moor is dark beneath the moon,
  Rapid clouds have drank the last pale beam of even:
Away! the gathering winds will call the darkness soon,
  And profoundest midnight shroud the serene lights of heaven.

Pause not! the time is past! Every voice cries, Away!
  Tempt not with one last tear thy friend's ungentle mood:
Thy lover's eye, so glazed and cold, dares not entreat thy stay:
  Duty and dereliction guide thee back to solitude.

Away, away! to thy sad and silent home;
  Pour bitter tears on its desolated hearth;   10
Watch the dim shades as like ghosts they go and come,
  And complicate strange webs of melancholy mirth.

The leaves of wasted autumn woods shall float around thine head:
  The blooms of dewy spring shall gleam beneath thy feet:
But thy soul or this world must fade in the frost that binds the dead,
  Ere midnight's frown and morning's smile, ere thou and peace may meet.

The cloud shadows of midnight possess their own repose,
  For the weary winds are silent, or the moon is in the deep:
Some respite to its turbulence unresting ocean knows;
  Whatever moves, or toils, or grieves, hath its appointed sleep.   20

Thou in the grave shalt rest — yet till the phantoms flee
  Which that house and heath and garden made dear to thee erewhile,
Thy remembrance, and repentance, and deep musings are not free
  From the music of two voices and the light of one sweet smile.

1814

HYMN TO INTELLECTUAL BEAUTY

Planned on the voyage (June, 1816) with Byron round Lake Geneva; written soon after.

I

The awful shadow of some unseen Power
　Floats though unseen among us, — visiting
　This various world with as inconstant wing
As summer winds that creep from flower to
　　flower, —
Like moonbeams that behind some piny mountain
　　shower,
　　It visits with inconstant glance
　　Each human heart and countenance;
Like hues and harmonies of evening, —
　　Like clouds in starlight widely spread, —
　　Like memory of music fled, —　　　　10
　　Like aught that for its grace may be
Dear, and yet dearer for its mystery.

II

Spirit of BEAUTY, that dost consecrate
　With thine own hues all thou dost shine upon
　Of human thought or form, — where art thou
　　gone?
Why dost thou pass away and leave our state,
This dim vast vale of tears, vacant and desolate?
　　Ask why the sunlight not for ever
　　Weaves rainbows o'er yon mountain-river,
Why aught should fail and fade that once is shown,
　　Why fear and dream and death and birth　21
　　Cast on the daylight of this earth
　　Such gloom, — why man has such a scope
For love and hate, despondency and hope?

III

No voice from some sublimer world hath ever
　To sage or poet these responses given —
　Therefore the names of Demon, Ghost, and
　　Heaven,
Remain the records of their vain endeavour,
Frail spells — whose uttered charm might not avail
　to sever,
　　From all we hear and all we see,　　　30
　　Doubt, chance, and mutability.
Thy light alone — like mist o'er mountains driven,
　Or music by the night-wind sent
　Through strings of some still instrument,
　Or moonlight on a midnight stream,
Gives grace and truth to life's unquiet dream.

IV

Love, Hope, and Self-esteem, like clouds depart
　And come, for some uncertain moments lent.
　Man were immortal, and omnipotent,

Didst thou, unknown and awful as thou art,　40
Keep with thy glorious train firm state within his
　heart.
　　Thou messenger of sympathies,
　　That wax and wane in lovers' eyes —
Thou — that to human thought art nourishment,
　Like darkness to a dying flame!
　Depart not as thy shadow came,
　Depart not — lest the grave should be,
Like life and fear, a dark reality.

V

While yet a boy I sought for ghosts, and sped
　Through many a listening chamber, cave and
　　ruin,
　　　　　　　　　　　　　　　　　　50
　And starlight wood, with fearful steps pursuing
Hopes of high talk with the departed dead.
I called on poisonous names with which our youth
　is fed;
　　I was not heard — I saw them not —
　　When musing deeply on the lot
Of life, at that sweet time when winds are woo-
　ing
　　All vital things that wake to bring
　　News of birds and blossoming, —
Sudden, thy shadow fell on me;
I shrieked, and clasped my hands in ecstasy!　60

VI

I vowed that I would dedicate my powers
　To thee and thine — have I not kept the vow?
　With beating heart and streaming eyes, even
　　now
I call the phantoms of a thousand hours
Each from his voiceless grave: they have in visioned
　bowers
　　Of studious zeal or love's delight
　　Outwatched with me the envious night —
They know that never joy illumed my brow
　Unlinked with hope that thou wouldst free
　This world from its dark slavery,　　　70
　That thou — O awful LOVELINESS,
Would'st give whate'er these words cannot express.

VII

The day becomes more solemn and serene
　When noon is past — there is a harmony
　In autumn, and a lustre in its sky,
Which through the summer is not heard or seen,
As if it could not be, as if it had not been!
　Thus let thy power, which like the truth
　Of nature on my passive youth
Descended, to my onward life supply　　　80

Its calm — to one who worships thee,
And every form containing thee,
  Whom, SPIRIT fair, thy spells did bind
To fear himself, and love all humankind.

1816

OZYMANDIAS

I met a traveller from an antique land
Who said: Two vast and trunkless legs of stone
Stand in the desert . . . Near them, on the sand,
Half sunk, a shattered visage lies, whose frown,
And wrinkled lip, and sneer of cold command,
Tell that its sculptor well those passions read
Which yet survive, stamped on these lifeless things,
The hand that mocked° them, and the heart that
    fed:°
And on the pedestal these words appear:
'My name is Ozymandias, king of kings: 10
Look on my works, ye Mighty, and despair!'
Nothing beside remains. Round the decay
Of that colossal wreck, boundless and bare
The lone and level sands stretch far away.

1817

ODE TO THE WEST WIND

" This poem was conceived and chiefly written in a
wood that skirts the Arno, near Florence, and on a
day when that tempestuous wind, whose temperature
is at once mild and animating, was collecting the
vapours which pour down the autumnal rains. They
began, as I foresaw, at sunset with a violent tempest
of hail and rain, attended by that magnificent thunder
and lightning peculiar to the Cisalpine regions.
" The phenomenon alluded to at the conclusion of
the third stanza is well known to naturalists. The vegetation at the bottom of the sea, of rivers, and of lakes,
sympathizes with that of the land in the change of
seasons, and is consequently influenced by the winds
which announce it " [S].
  In stanza III Shelley recalls an excursion made in
a small boat on December 8, 1818, to the Bay of Baiae,
at the northwestern end of the Bay of Naples, sheltered
by the promontory of Posilipo. To Peacock (December
22) he described how they observed at Baiae " the
ruins of its antique grandeur standing like rocks in
the transparent sea under our boat." Passing through
the cavern of the Cumaean Sibyl, they " came to a
calm and lovely basin of water, surrounded by dark
woody, hills, and profoundly solitary. Some vast ruins
of the Temple of Pluto stand on a lawny hill one side
of it, and are reflected in its windless mirror."
  The Being to whom this prayer is addressed is at

once the West Wind and that Power the Wind symbolizes. How this may be conceived must extend an inexhaustible invitation to speculation: Expiration, the
necessary prelude to Inspiration; the cyclic return of
the Destruction required for Preservation; the death
which is the condition for " a new birth " — in a
thought, a feeling, a culture; in a day, a year, an
epoch; in a cell, in an individual, in a society, in the
Universe. The poem is speaking of and for the poet,
but also of and for that which speaks through him.
And his words (as with a Hosea or an Isaiah) are an
" incantation " or spell or ritual bringing about that
which they utter.
  " Self-surrender, through which everything is lost,
and renewed, and identified with that power (the
wind), is here the essential moment expressed. We begin to be aware that the 'Wind' is spirit itself, or a
medium to its expression . . . Shelley explicitly calls
the West Wind 'spirit,' or 'Wild Spirit,' which is
'moving everywhere.' But this does not, or might not,
mean very much; and 'spirit' and 'wind' are terms
which possess an old common history. What matters is
that the actual and yet self-transcending cause of life
is real, and known, in the image of the West Wind "
(Leone Vivante, *English Poetry*, pp. 165–67).
  " The stanzaic form is a highly original invention
consisting of fourteen lines (three tercets and a couplet)
wrought out of the preliminary terza rima so that
while each moves along with the whole, each, in
itself, has the strength and compactness of a sonnet "
(Neville Rogers, *Shelley at Work*, p. 226). These five
stanzas are as intricately organized: in sense, image,
emotion, concept — passing from the woods to the
atmosphere to the seas, and then collecting what the
comparisons with " a dead leaf," " a swift cloud," " a
wave " can say of spiritual stress into a prayer that
such submission may become complete Possession (see
A Defence of Poetry, p. 721).

I

O wild West Wind, thou breath of Autumn's being,
Thou, from whose unseen presence the leaves dead
Are driven, like ghosts from an enchanter fleeing,

Yellow, and black, and pale, and hectic red,
Pestilence-stricken multitudes: O thou,
Who chariotest to their dark wintry bed

The wingèd seeds, where they lie cold and low,
Each like a corpse within its grave, until
Thine azure sister of the Spring shall blow

Her clarion o'er the dreaming earth, and fill   10
(Driving sweet buds like flocks to feed in air)
With living hues and odours plain and hill:
Wild Spirit, which art moving everywhere;
Destroyer and preserver;° hear, oh, hear!

OZYMANDIAS.   **6–8. those . . . fed:** The pride and cruelty depicted in the sculpture outlive the artist and his subject. **mocked:**
both imitated and derided.

ODE TO THE WEST WIND.   **14. Destroyer and preserver:** Apollo
was destroyer and healer, and, among the gods of India, Siva
and Vishnu.

II

Thou on whose stream, mid the steep sky's commo-
    tion,
Loose clouds like earth's decaying leaves are shed,
Shook from the tangled boughs° of Heaven and
    Ocean,

Angels of rain and lightning: there are spread
On the blue surface of thine aëry surge,
Like the bright hair uplifted from the head   20

Of some fierce Maenad, even from the dim verge
Of the horizon to the zenith's height,
The locks of the approaching storm.° Thou dirge

Of the dying year, to which this closing night
Will be the dome of a vast sepulchre,
Vaulted with all thy congregated might

Of vapours, from whose solid atmosphere
Black rain, and fire, and hail will burst: oh, hear!

III

Thou who didst waken from his summer dreams
The blue Mediterranean, where he lay,   30
Lulled by the coil of his crystàlline streams,

Beside a pumice isle in Baiae's bay,
And saw in sleep old palaces and towers
Quivering within the wave's intenser day,

All overgrown with azure moss° and flowers
So sweet, the sense faints picturing them! Thou
For whose path the Atlantic's level powers

Cleave themselves into chasms, while far below
The sea-blooms and the oozy woods which wear
The sapless foliage of the ocean, know   40

Thy voice, and suddenly grow gray with fear,
And tremble and despoil themselves: oh, hear!

IV

If I were a dead leaf thou mightest bear;
If I were a swift cloud to fly with thee;
A wave to pant beneath thy power, and share

The impulse of thy strength, only less free
Than thou, O uncontrollable!° If even
I were as in my boyhood, and could be

The comrade of thy wanderings over Heaven,
As then, when to outstrip thy skiey speed   50
Scarce seemed a vision; I would ne'er have striven

As thus with thee in prayer in my sore need.
Oh, lift me as a wave, a leaf, a cloud!
I fall upon the thorns of life! I bleed!

A heavy weight of hours has chained and bowed
One too like thee: tameless, and swift, and proud.

V

Make me thy lyre,° even as the forest is:
What if my leaves are falling like its own!
The tumult of thy mighty harmonies

Will take from both a deep, autumnal tone,   60
Sweet though in sadness. Be thou, Spirit fierce,
My spirit! Be thou me, impetuous one!

Drive my dead thoughts over the universe
Like withered leaves to quicken a new birth!
And, by the incantation of this verse,

Scatter, as from an unextinguished hearth
Ashes and sparks,° my words among mankind!
Be through my lips to unawakened° earth

The trumpet of a prophecy! O, Wind,
If Winter comes, can Spring be far behind?   70

1819

those delicate weeds that pave the bottom of the water." **47. O uncontrollable**: Cf. John 3:7–8, "Marvel not that I said unto thee, Ye must be born again. The wind bloweth where it listeth, and thou hearest the sound thereof, but canst not tell whence it cometh, and wither it goeth: so is every one that is born of the Spirit." **57. thy lyre**: "We live and move and think; but we are not the creators of our own origin and existence. We are not the arbiters of every motion of our own complicated nature; we are not the masters of our own imaginations and moods of mental being. There is a Power by which we are surrounded, like the atmosphere in which some motionless lyre is suspended, which visits with its breath our silent chords at will," Shelley, *Essay on Christianity*. See also *A Defence of Poetry*, p. 721, paragraph 2, below. **67. Ashes and sparks**: Cf. "It is brought to birth in the soul on a sudden, as light that is kindled by a leaping spark, and thereafter it nourishes itself," Plato, *Epistles*, VII. 341d. **68. un-awakened**: Cf. 29.

17. tangled boughs: waterspouts; waves swept up into the sky by whirlwinds. **20–23. Like . . . storm**: Hughes quotes from Shelley's *Critical Notices* of some Maenad figures on the pedestal of the Minerva in the Florence Gallery, "The tremendous spirit of superstition seems to have caught them in its whirlwinds and to bear them over the earth as the rapid volutions of a tempest have the ever-changing trunk of a waterspout, or as the torrent of a mountain river whirls the autumnal leaves resistlessly along in its full eddies. The hair, loose and flowing, seems caught in the tempest of their own tumultuous motion." The Maenads were devoted women who danced and sang in honor of Dionysus. **35. azure moss**: Shelley to Peacock, December 22, 1818, "The sea was so translucent that you could see the caverns clothed with glaucous sea-moss and the leaves and branches of

Prometheus Unbound

DRAMATIS PERSONAE

PROMETHEUS	APOLLO	HERCULES
DEMOGORGON	MERCURY	THE PHANTASM OF JUPITER
JUPITER	ASIA	THE SPIRIT OF THE EARTH
THE EARTH	PANTHEA ⎫ *Oceanides.*	THE SPIRIT OF THE MOON
OCEAN	IONE ⎭	SPIRITS OF THE HOURS
		SPIRITS, ECHOES, FAUNS, FURIES

Act I

SCENE. — *A Ravine of Icy Rocks in the Indian Caucasus.* PROMETHEUS *is discovered bound to the Precipice.* PANTHEA *and* IONE *are seated at his feet. Time, night. During the Scene, morning slowly breaks.*

PROMETHEUS. Monarch of Gods and Daemons,
   and all Spirits
But One,° who throng those bright and rolling
   worlds
Which Thou and I alone of living things
Behold with sleepless eyes! regard this Earth
Made multitudinous with thy slaves, whom thou
Requitest for knee-worship, prayer, and praise,
And toil, and hecatombs of broken hearts,
With fear and self-contempt and barren° hope.
Whilst me, who am thy foe, eyeless in hate,°
Hast thou made reign and triumph, to thy scorn,°
O'er mine own misery and thy vain revenge.   11
Three thousand years of sleep-unsheltered hours,
And moments aye divided by keen pangs
Till they seemed years, torture and solitude,
Scorn and despair, — these are mine empire: —
More glorious far than that which thou surveyest
From thine unenvied throne, O Mighty God!
Almighty,° had I deigned to share the shame
Of thine ill tyranny, and hung not here
Nailed to this wall of eagle-baffling mountain, 20
Black, wintry, dead, unmeasured; without herb,
Insect, or beast, or shape or sound of life.
Ah me! alas, pain, pain ever, for ever!

No change, no pause, no hope!° Yet I endure.
I ask the Earth, have not the mountains felt?
I ask yon Heaven, the all-beholding Sun,
Has it not seen? The Sea, in storm or calm,
Heaven's ever-changing Shadow,° spread below,
Have its deaf° waves not heard my agony?
Ah me! alas, pain, pain ever, for ever!   30
The crawling glaciers pierce me with the spears
Of their moon-freezing° crystals, the bright chains
Eat with their burning cold into my bones.
Heaven's wingèd hound, polluting from thy lips
His beak in poison not his own,° tears up
My heart; and shapeless sights come wandering by,
The ghastly people of the realm of dream,
Mocking me: and the Earthquake-fiends are
   charged
To wrench the rivets from my quivering wounds
When the rocks split and close again behind: 40
While from their loud abysses howling throng
The genii of the storm, urging the rage
Of whirlwind, and afflict me with keen hail.
And yet to me welcome is day and night,
Whether one breaks the hoar frost of the morn,
Or starry, dim, and slow, the other climbs
The leaden-coloured east; for then they lead
The wingless, crawling hours, one among whom
— As some dark Priest hales the reluctant victim
Shall drag thee, cruel King, to kiss the blood 50
From these pale feet, which then might trample thee
If they disdained not such a prostrate slave.
Disdain! Ah no! I pity thee. What ruin
Will hunt thee undefended through wide Heaven!
How will thy soul, cloven to its depth with terror,

Act I. 1–2. Monarch .... One: Jupiter rules tyrannically over all spirits but Prometheus, the mind of man, who has defied and cursed him. **8. barren:** without fruit. **9. eyeless in hate:** Jupiter is blinded by hate. **10. to ... scorn:** Jupiter scorns such a triumph and thereby is made a scorn himself. **18. Almighty:** If Prometheus had yielded, Jupiter's power would have been limitless.

24. no hope: Cf. 808, "Most vain all hope but love," and 701, 706. **28. Heaven's ... Shadow:** The Sea is often an image for the multitudes of mankind. **29. deaf:** even such uncaring ones. See *Triumph of Life*, 477, "For deaf as is a sea, which wrath makes hoary ...". **32. moon-freezing:** cold as if on the moon? **34–35. wingèd ... own:** the vulture, kissed by Jupiter as reward on his return. The phrase "heaven's wingèd hound" is from Aeschylus, *Prometheus Bound*, 1021–22. **53–57. I ... more:** the redeeming spring and release of the play.

Gape like a hell within! I speak in grief,
Not exultation, for I hate no more,°
As then ere misery made me wise. The curse
Once breathed on thee I would recall. Ye Moun-
　　tains,
Whose many-voicèd Echoes, through the mist　　60
Of cataracts, flung the thunder of that spell!
Ye icy Springs, stagnant with wrinkling frost,
Which vibrated to hear me, and then crept
Shuddering through India! Thou serenest Air,
Through which the Sun walks burning without
　　beams!°
And ye swift Whirlwinds, who on poisèd wings
Hung mute and moveless o'er yon hushed abyss,
As thunder, louder than your own, made rock
The orbèd world! If then my words had power,
Though I am changed so that aught evil wish　　70
Is dead within; although no memory be
Of what is hate, let them not lose it now!°
What was that curse? for ye all heard me speak.

FIRST VOICE [*from the Mountains*].

Thrice three hundred thousand years
　　O'er the Earthquake's couch we stood:
Oft, as men convulsed with fears,
　　We trembled in our multitude.

SECOND VOICE [*from the Springs*].

Thunderbolts had parched our water,
　　We had been stained with bitter blood,
And had run mute, 'mid shrieks of slaughter,
　　Thro' a city and a solitude.　　81

THIRD VOICE [*from the Air*].

I had clothed, since Earth uprose,
　　Its wastes in colours not their own,
And oft had my serene repose
　　Been cloven by many a rending groan.

FOURTH VOICE [*from the Whirlwinds*].

We had soared beneath these mountains
　　Unresting ages; nor had thunder,
Nor yon volcano's flaming fountains,
　　Nor any power above or under
Ever made us mute with wonder.　　90

FIRST VOICE

But never bowed our snowy crest
As at the voice of thine unrest.

SECOND VOICE

Never such a sound before
To the Indian waves we bore.
A pilot asleep on the howling sea
Leaped up from the deck in agony,
And heard, and cried, 'Ah, woe is me!'
And died as mad as the wild waves be.

THIRD VOICE

By such dread words from Earth to Heaven
My still realm was never riven:　　100
When its wound was closed, there stood
Darkness o'er the day° like blood.

FOURTH VOICE

And we shrank back: for dreams of ruin
To frozen caves our flight pursuing
Made us keep silence — thus — and thus —
Though silence is as hell to us.

THE EARTH. The tongueless Caverns of the craggy
　　hills
Cried, 'Misery!' then; the hollow Heaven replied,
'Misery!' And the Ocean's purple waves,
Climbing the land, howled to the lashing winds,
And the pale nations heard it, 'Misery!'　　III
PROMETHEUS. I heard a sound of voices: not the
　　voice
Which I gave forth. Mother, thy sons and thou
Scorn him, without whose all-enduring will
Beneath the fierce omnipotence of Jove,
Both they and thou had vanished,° like thin mist
Unrolled on the morning wind. Know ye not me,
The Titan?° He who made his agony
The barrier to your else all-conquering foe?
Oh, rock-embosomed lawns, and snow-fed streams,
Now seen athwart frore° vapours, deep below, 121
Through whose o'ershadowing woods I wandered
　　once
With Asia,° drinking life from her loved eyes;
Why scorns the spirit which informs ye, now
To commune with me? me alone, who checked,
As one who checks a fiend-drawn charioteer,
The falsehood and the force of him who reigns
Supreme, and with the groans of pining slaves

---

102. Darkness . . . day: Matt. 27:45, "Now from the sixth hour
there was darkness over all the land unto the ninth hour";
51, ". . . and the earth did quake; and the rocks were rent."
114–16. without . . . vanished: Only Prometheus had kept Jove
from destroying them.　　118. The Titan: Strictly speaking,
Prometheus is not a Titan; but the name is also given to divine
and semidivine beings descended from Titans.　　121. frore:
frosty.　　123. Asia: "Asia, one of the Oceanides, is the wife of
Prometheus—she was, according to other mythological interpretations, the same as Venus and Nature. When the benefactor
of mankind is liberated, Nature resumes the beauty of her prime,
and is united to her husband, the emblem of the human race, in
perfect and happy union," Mrs. Shelley's note. See III.iii,iv.

---

65. burning . . . beams: "Beyond the atmosphere the sun
would appear a rayless orb of fire in the midst of a black concave,"
Shelley's first note to *Queen Mab*. But see also *Paradise Lost*
I.594–96 (p. 231, above).　　69–72. If . . . now: Though he no
longer knows what hate is, let his former words have a power,
though a changed power.

Fills your dim glens and liquid wildernesses:°
Why answer ye not, still? Brethren!

THE EARTH.   They dare not.
PROMETHEUS. Who dares? for I would hear that
    curse again.   131
Ha, what an awful whisper rises up!
'Tis scarce like sound: it tingles through the frame
As lightning tingles, hovering ere it strike.
Speak, Spirit! from thine inorganic° voice
I only know that thou art moving near
And love. How cursed I him?

THE EARTH.   How canst thou hear
Who knowest not the language of the dead?°
PROMETHEUS. Thou art a living spirit; speak as
    they.
THE EARTH. I dare not speak like life, lest Heav-
    en's fell King
Should hear, and link me to some wheel of pain
More torturing than the one whereon I roll.   142
Subtle thou art and good, and though the Gods
Hear not this voice, yet thou art more than God,
Being wise and kind: earnestly hearken now.

PROMETHEUS. Obscurely through my brain, like
    shadows dim,
Sweep awful thoughts, rapid and thick. I feel
Faint, like one mingled in entwining love;
Yet 'tis not pleasure.

THE EARTH.   No, thou canst not hear:
Thou art immortal, and this tongue is known   150
Only to those who die.

PROMETHEUS.   And what art thou,°
O, melancholy Voice?

THE EARTH.   I am the Earth,
Thy mother; she within whose stony veins,°
To the last fibre of the loftiest tree
Whose thin leaves trembled in the frozen air,
Joy ran, as blood within a living frame,
When thou didst from her bosom, like a cloud
Of glory, arise, a spirit of keen joy!
And at thy voice her pining sons uplifted
Their prostrate brows from the polluting dust, 160
And our almighty Tyrant with fierce dread
Grew pale, until his thunder chained thee here.
Then, see those million worlds which burn and roll
Around us: their inhabitants beheld
My spherèd light wane in wide Heaven; the sea
Was lifted by strange tempest, and new fire
From earthquake-rifted mountains of bright snow
Shook its portentous hair beneath Heaven's frown;
Lightning and Inundation vexed the plains;

Blue thistles bloomed in cities; foodless toads   170
Within voluptuous chambers panting crawled:
When Plague had fallen on man, and beasts, and
    worm,
And Famine; and black blight on herb and tree;
And in the corn, and vines, and meadow-grass,
Teemed ineradicable poisonous weeds
Draining their growth, for my wan breast was dry
With grief; and the thin air, my breath was stained
With the contagion of a mother's hate
Breathed on her child's destroyer; ay, I heard
Thy curse, the which, if thou rememberest not, 180
Yet my innumerable seas and streams,
Mountains, and caves, and winds, and yon wide air,
And the inarticulate people of the dead,
Preserve, a treasured spell. We meditate
In secret joy and hope those dreadful words,
But dare not speak them.

PROMETHEUS.   Venerable mother!
All else who live and suffer take from thee
Some comfort; flowers, and fruits, and happy
    sounds,
And love, though fleeting; these may not be mine.
But mine own words, I pray, deny me not.   190

THE EARTH. They shall be told. Ere Babylon was
    dust,°
The Magus Zoroaster,° my dead child,
Met his own image walking in the garden.
That apparition, sole of men, he saw.
For know there are two worlds of life and death:
One that which thou beholdest; but the other
Is underneath the grave,° where do inhabit
The shadows of all forms that think and live
Till death unite them° and they part no more;
Dreams and the light imaginings of men,   200
And all that faith creates or love desires,
Terrible, strange, sublime and beauteous shapes.
There thou art, and dost hang, a writhing shade,
'Mid whirlwind-peopled mountains; all the gods
Are there, and all the powers of nameless worlds,
Vast, sceptred phantoms; heroes, men, and beasts;
And Demogorgon,° a tremendous gloom;
And he, the supreme Tyrant, on his throne
Of burning gold.° Son, one of these shall utter
The curse which all remember. Call at will   210
Thine own ghost, or the ghost of Jupiter,
Hades or Typhon,° or what mightier Gods

---

129. **liquid wildernesses:** the seas. Cf. III.ii.29–31.   135. **in-
organic:** the parts not making sense with one another.   138.
language . . . dead: There are three languages in this passage:
of the dead, of living mortals, and of immortals. Cf. III.iii.111.
151. **And . . . thou:** mortal? immortal?—or, possibly, who is
speaking now?   153. **stony veins:** The Earth and all upon her
were cold as stone before Prometheus came. Cf. III.iii.85–90.

191. **Ere . . . dust:** before the 6th century B.C.   192. **Zoroaster:** Zarathustra, the founder of the occult Magian religion.
Morally dualistic and puritanical, mystically ecstatic, the Zoro-
astrians believed in the eternal war of good and evil "powers."
Shelley perhaps had this story from Peacock.   197. **underneath
the grave:** In *Odyssey*, XI.601–14, Heracles is represented as
being a phantom in Hades *and* at the banquet among the immortal gods.   199. **unite them:** the shadows with the forms.
The passage seems to promise death even to immortals.   207.
Demogorgon: see Intro., p. 676, above.   209. **burning gold:**
Cf. 291.   212. **Hades or Typhon:** Pluto, god of the underworld;

From all-prolific Evil, since thy ruin
Have sprung, and trampled on my prostrate sons.
Ask, and they must reply: so the revenge
Of the Supreme may sweep through vacant shades,
As rainy wind through the abandoned gate
Of a fallen palace.
    PROMETHEUS.   Mother, let not aught
Of that which may be evil, pass again
My lips, or those of aught resembling me.   220
Phantasm of Jupiter, arise, appear!

IONE.

My wings are folded o'er mine ears:
    My wings are crossèd o'er mine eyes:
Yet through their silver shade appears,
    And through their lulling plumes arise,
A Shape, a throng of sounds;
    May it be no ill to thee
    O thou of many wounds!
Near whom, for our sweet sister's sake,
Ever thus we watch and wake.   230

PANTHEA.

The sound is of whirlwind underground,
    Earthquake, and fire, and mountains cloven;
The shape is awful like the sound,
    Clothed in dark purple, star-inwoven.
A sceptre of pale gold
    To stay° steps proud, o'er the slow cloud
    His veinèd hand doth hold.
Cruel he looks, but calm and strong,
Like one who does, not suffers wrong.

PHANTASM OF JUPITER. Why have the secret
    powers of this strange world   240
Driven me, a frail and empty phantom, hither
On direst storms? What unaccustomed sounds
Are hovering on my lips, unlike the voice
With which our pallid race hold ghastly talk
In darkness? And, proud sufferer, who art thou?
    PROMETHEUS. Tremendous Image, as thou art
    must be
He whom thou shadowest forth. I am his foe,
The Titan. Speak the words which I would hear,
Although no thought inform thine empty voice.
    THE EARTH. Listen! And though your echoes must
    be mute,   250
Gray mountains, and old woods, and haunted
    springs,
Prophetic caves,° and isle-surrounding streams,
Rejoice to hear what yet ye cannot speak.
    PHANTASM. A spirit° seizes me and speaks within:

It tears me as fire tears a thunder-cloud.
    PANTHEA. See, how he lifts his mighty looks, the
    Heaven
Darkens above.
    IONE.   He speaks! O shelter me!
    PROMETHEUS. I see the curse on gestures° proud
    and cold,
And looks of firm defiance, and calm hate,
And such despair as mocks itself with smiles,   260
Written as on a scroll: yet speak: Oh, speak!

PHANTASM.

Fiend, I defy thee! with a calm, fixed mind,
    All that thou canst inflict I bid thee do;
Foul Tyrant both of Gods and Human-kind,
    One only being shalt thou not subdue.
Rain then thy plagues upon me here,
Ghastly disease, and frenzying fear;
And let alternate frost and fire
Eat into me, and be thine ire
Lightning, and cutting hail, and legioned forms
Of furies, driving by upon the wounding storms.

Ay, do thy worst. Thou art omnipotent.   272
    O'er all things but thyself I gave thee pow-
    er,°
And my own will. Be thy swift mischiefs sent
    To blast mankind, from yon ethereal tower.
Let thy malignant spirit move
In darkness over those I love:
On me and mine I imprecate
The utmost torture of thy hate;
And thus devote to sleepless agony,   280
This undeclining head while thou must reign on
    high.

But thou, who art the God and Lord: O, thou,
    Who fillest° with thy soul this world of woe,
To whom all things of Earth and Heaven do
    bow
    In fear and worship: all-prevailing foe!
I curse thee! let a sufferer's curse
Clasp thee, his torturer, like remorse;
Till thin Infinity shall be
A robe of envenomed agony;
And thine Omnipotence a crown of pain,   290
To cling like burning gold round thy dissolving
    brain.

Heap on thy soul, by virtue of this Curse,
    Ill deeds, then be thou damned, beholding
    good;

Typhon, a hundred-headed monster, son of Earth; the embodiment of volcanoes and earthquakes, and of storms accompanying
volcanic disturbances.   **236. stay:** support.   **252. Prophetic
caves:** Cf. 658–63.   **254. A spirit:** the curse.

258. gestures: The Phantasm resembles Prometheus as he spoke
the curse.   **273. I . . . power:** Cf. II.iv.43-46.   **283. Who
fillest:** The source of evil is the soul of "Heaven's fell king."

Both° infinite as is the universe,
  And thou, and thy self-torturing solitude.
An awful image of calm power
Though now thou sittest, let the hour
Come, when thou must appear to be
That which thou art internally;
And after many a false and fruitless crime   300
Scorn track thy lagging° fall through boundless
  space and time.

PROMETHEUS. Were these my words, O Parent?
THE EARTH.   They were thine.
PROMETHEUS. It doth repent me: words are quick
  and vain;
Grief for awhile is blind, and so was mine.
I wish no living thing to suffer pain.

THE EARTH.

Misery, Oh misery to me,
That Jove at length should vanquish thee.
Wail, howl aloud, Land and Sea,
The Earth's rent heart shall answer ye.
Howl, Spirits of the living and the dead,   310
Your refuge, your defence lies fallen and van-
  quishèd.

FIRST ECHO.

Lies fallen and vanquishèd!

SECOND ECHO.

Fallen and vanquishèd!

IONE.

Fear not: 'tis but some passing spasm,
  The Titan is unvanquished still.
But see, where through the azure chasm
  Of yon forked and snowy hill
Trampling the slant winds on high
  With golden-sandalled feet, that glow
Under plumes of purple dye,   320
Like rose-ensanguined ivory,
  A Shape comes now,
Stretching on high from his right hand
A serpent-cinctured wand.°

PANTHEA. 'Tis Jove's world-wandering herald,
Mercury.

IONE.

And who are those with hydra° tresses
  And iron wings that climbed the wind,

Whom the frowning God represses
  Like vapours steaming up behind,
Clanging loud, an endless crowd —   330

PANTHEA.

These are Jove's tempest-walking hounds,
Whom he gluts with groans and blood,°
When charioted on sulphurous cloud
He bursts Heaven's bounds.

IONE.

Are they now led, from the thin dead
On new pangs to be fed?

PANTHEA.

The Titan looks as ever, firm, not proud.

FIRST FURY. Ha! I scent life!
SECOND FURY.   Let me but look into
  his eyes!
THIRD FURY. The hope of torturing him smells
  like a heap
Of corpses, to a death-bird after battle.   340
FIRST FURY. Darest thou delay, O Herald! take
  cheer, Hounds
Of Hell: what if the Son of Maia° soon
Should make us food and sport — who can please
  long
The Omnipotent?
  MERCURY.   Back to your towers of iron,
And gnash, beside the streams of fire, and wail
Your foodless teeth.° Geryon,° arise! and Gorgon,
Chimaera,° and thou Sphinx,° subtlest of fiends
Who ministered to Thebes Heaven's poisoned wine,
Unnatural love, and more unnatural° hate:
These shall perform your task.
  FIRST FURY.   Oh, mercy! mercy!
We die with our desire: drive us not back!   351
  MERCURY. Crouch then in silence.
                            Awful Suf-
  ferer!
To thee unwilling, most unwillingly
I come, by the great Father's will driven down,
To execute a doom of new revenge.
Alas! I pity thee, and hate myself

Hydra, a snake-headed monster.   **331–32. These ... blood:**
Cf. *Paradise Lost*, X.616, "See with what heat these dogs of Hell
advance/To waste and have havoc yonder World."   **342. Son of
Maia:** Mercury. Shelley translated the Homeric *Hymn to Mercury*, where the winged messenger's life and character are described.   **345–47. gnash ... teeth:** Gnash your teeth and
bewail that they are not to be fed.   Geryon: a three-bodied
giant killed by Hercules.   Chimaera: a fire-breathing monster.
Sphinx: a she-monster who murdered all Thebans unable to
guess her riddle. For solving it, Oedipus was given the kingdom
and Iocasta—his mother—as wife.   **349. Unnatural:** Here the
word applies both to Oedipus' marriage with his mother and to
the conflict between his sons.

294. Both: ill deeds and good.   **301. lagging:** long-delayed,
always falling behind in time.   **324. serpent-cinctured wand:**
the caduceus of Hermes (Mercury), which signified both health
and cunning. It was his official token of authority when he
guided souls to the other world.   **326. hydra:** snakelike, from

That I can do no more: aye from thy sight
Returning, for a season, Heaven seems Hell,
So thy worn form pursues me night and day,
Smiling reproach. Wise art thou, firm and good,
But vainly wouldst stand forth alone in strife   361
Against the Omnipotent; as yon clear lamps
That measure and divide the weary years
From which there is no refuge, long have taught
And long must teach. Even now thy Torturer arms
With the strange might of unimagined pains
The powers who scheme slow agonies in Hell,
And my commission is to lead them here,
Or what more subtle, foul, or savage fiends
People the abyss, and leave them to their task.   370
Be it not so! there is a secret known
To thee, and to none else of living things,
Which may transfer the sceptre of wide Heaven,
The fear of which perplexes the Supreme:
Clothe it° in words, and bid it clasp his throne
In intercession; bend thy soul in prayer,
And like a supplicant in some gorgeous fane,
Let the will kneel within thy haughty heart:
For benefits and meek submission tame
The fiercest and the mightiest.

     PROMETHEUS.   Evil minds   380
Change good to their own nature. I gave all
He has;° and in return he chains me here
Years, ages, night and day: whether the Sun
Split my parched skin, or in the moony night
The crystal-wingèd snow cling round my hair:
Whilst my belovèd race is trampled down
By his thought-executing ministers.°
Such is the tyrant's recompense: 'tis just:
He who is evil can receive no good;
And for a world bestowed, or a friend° lost,   390
He can feel hate, fear, shame; not gratitude:
He but requites me for his own misdeed.
Kindness to such is keen reproach, which breaks
With bitter stings the light sleep of Revenge.
Submission, thou dost know I cannot try:
For what submission but that fatal word,°
The death-seal of mankind's captivity,
Like the Sicilian's hair-suspended sword,°
Which trembles o'er his crown, would he accept,
Or could I yield? Which yet I will not yield.   400
Let others flatter Crime, where it sits throned
In brief Omnipotence: secure are they:
For Justice, when triumphant, will weep down
Pity, not punishment, on her own wrongs,

Too much avenged° by those who err. I wait,
Enduring thus, the retributive hour
Which since we spake is even nearer now.
But hark, the hell-hounds clamour: fear delay:
Behold! Heaven lowers° under thy Father's frown.
     MERCURY. Oh, that we might be spared: I to inflict
And thou to suffer! Once more answer me: 411
Thou knowest not the period° of Jove's power?
     PROMETHEUS. I know but this, that it must come.
     MERCURY.   Alas!
Thou canst not count thy years to come of pain?
     PROMETHEUS. They last while Jove must reign:
          nor more, nor less
Do I desire or fear.
     MERCURY.   Yet pause, and plunge
Into Eternity, where recorded time,
Even all that we imagine, age on age,
Seems but a point, and the reluctant mind
Flags wearily in its unending flight,   420
Till it sink, dizzy, blind, lost, shelterless;
Perchance it has not numbered the slow years
Which thou must spend in torture, unreprieved?
     PROMETHEUS. Perchance no thought can count
         them, yet they pass.
     MERCURY. If thou might'st dwell among the Gods
         the while
Lapped in voluptuous joy?
     PROMETHEUS.   I would not quit
This bleak ravine, these unrepentant pains.
     MERCURY. Alas! I wonder at, yet pity thee.
     PROMETHEUS. Pity the self-despising slaves of
         Heaven,
Not me, within whose mind sits peace serene,   430
As light in the sun, throned: how vain is talk!
Call up the fiends.
     IONE.   O, sister, look! White fire
Has cloven to the roots yon huge snow-loaded
     cedar;
How fearfully God's thunder howls behind!
     MERCURY. I must obey his words and thine: alas!
Most heavily remorse hangs at my heart!
     PANTHEA. See where the child° of Heaven, with
         wingèd feet,
Runs down the slanted sunlight of the dawn.
     IONE. Dear sister, close thy plumes over thine eyes
Lest thou behold and die: they come: they come
Blackening the birth of day with countless wings,
And hollow underneath, like death.   442
     FIRST FURY.   Prometheus!
     SECOND FURY. Immortal Titan!
     THIRD FURY.   Champion of
     Heaven's slaves!

---

375. it: the secret.   **381–82. I . . . has:** Cf. 273–74, and II.iv.43–44.   **387. thought-executing ministers:** carrying out Jove's thoughts. Cf. *King Lear*, III.ii.4, "You sulph'rous and thought-executing fires."   **390. friend:** Prometheus had been Jove's friend.   **396. that . . . word:** the secret.   **398. Like . . . sword:** Damocles, having extolled the felicity of his king, Dionysius of Sicily, for his wealth and power, was placed at a banquet under a naked sword suspended by a single horse-hair, to teach him what a tyrant's happiness is.

405. avenged: As virtue is its own reward, vice is its own punishment.   **409. lowers:** frowns, threatens.   **412. period:** end point; also, duration.   **437. child:** Mercury, whose departure marks the coming of day. Cf. *Paradise Lost*, IV.555–56 (p. 251, above).

PROMETHEUS. He whom some dreadful voice in-
   vokes is here,
Prometheus, the chained Titan. Horrible forms,
What and who are ye? Never yet there came
Phantasms so foul through monster-teeming Hell
From the all-miscreative brain of Jove;
Whilst I behold such execrable shapes,
Methinks I grow like what I contemplate,   450
And laugh and stare in loathsome sympathy.
   FIRST FURY. We are the ministers of pain, and
     fear,
And disappointment, and mistrust, and hate,
And clinging crime; and as lean dogs pursue
Through wood and lake some struck and sobbing
   fawn,
We track all things that weep, and bleed, and live,
When the great King betrays them to our will.
   PROMETHEUS. Oh! many fearful natures in one
     name,°
I know ye; and these lakes and echoes know
The darkness and the clangour of your wings. 460
But why more hideous than your loathèd selves
Gather ye up in legions from the deep?°
   SECOND FURY. We knew not that: Sisters, rejoice,
     rejoice!
   PROMETHEUS. Can aught exult in its deformity?
   SECOND FURY. The beauty of delight makes lovers
     glad,
Gazing on one another: so are we.
As from the rose which the pale priestess kneels
To gather for her festal crown of flowers
The aëreal crimson falls, flushing her cheek,
So from our victim's destined agony   470
The shade which is our form invests us round,
Else we are shapeless as our mother Night.
   PROMETHEUS. I laugh your power, and his who
     sent you here,
To lowest scorn. Pour forth the cup of pain.
   FIRST FURY. Thou thinkest we will rend thee bone
     from bone,
And nerve from nerve, working like fire within?
   PROMETHEUS. Pain is my element, as hate is thine;
Ye rend me now: I care not.
   SECOND FURY.   Dost imagine
We will but laugh into thy lidless° eyes?
   PROMETHEUS. I weigh not what ye do, but what
     ye suffer,   480
Being evil. Cruel was the power which called
You, or aught else so wretched, into light.
   THIRD FURY. Thou think'st we will live through
     thee, one by one,
Like animal life, and though we can obscure not
The soul which burns within, that we will dwell

Beside it, like a vain loud multitude
Vexing the self-content of wisest men:
That we will be dread thought beneath thy brain,
And foul desire round thine astonished heart,
And blood within thy labyrinthine veins   490
Crawling like agony?
   PROMETHEUS.   Why, ye are thus now;
Yet am I king over myself, and rule
The torturing and conflicting throngs within,
As Jove rules you when Hell grows mutinous.

CHORUS OF FURIES.

From the ends of the earth, from the ends of the
   earth,
Where the night has its grave and the morning
   its birth,
         Come, come, come!
Oh, ye who shake hills with the scream of your
   mirth,
When cities sink howling in ruin; and ye
Who with wingless footsteps trample the sea, 500
And close upon Shipwreck and Famine's track,
Sit chattering with joy on the foodless wreck;
         Come, come, come!
   Leave the bed, low, cold, and red,
   Strewed beneath a nation dead;
   Leave the hatred, as in ashes
     Fire is left for future burning:
   It will burst in bloodier flashes
     When ye stir it, soon returning:
   Leave the self-contempt implanted   510
   In young spirits, sense-enchanted,
     Misery's yet unkindled fuel:
   Leave Hell's secrets half unchanted
     To the maniac dreamer; cruel
   More than ye can be with hate
     Is he with fear.
         Come, come, come!
We are steaming up from Hell's wide gate
And we burthen the blast of the atmosphere,
But vainly we toil till ye come here.   520

IONE. Sister, I hear the thunder of new wings.
PANTHEA. These solid mountains quiver with the
   sound
Even as the tremulous air: their shadows make
The space within my plumes more black than night.

FIRST FURY.

   Your call was as a wingèd car
   Driven on whirlwinds fast and far;
   It rapt° us from red gulfs of war.

---

458. one name: Furies.   461–62. But ... deep?: Why are
they worse than ever known before?   479. lidless: eyes unable to close their lids to shut out this.

527. rapt: snatched away bodily, or carried away in spirit, from
earth, consciousness, or occupation.

SECOND FURY.

From wide cities, famine-wasted;

THIRD FURY.

Groans half heard, and blood untasted;

FOURTH FURY.

Kingly conclaves stern and cold,	530
Where blood with gold is bought and sold;

FIFTH FURY.

From the furnace, white and hot,
In which —

A FURY.

Speak not: whisper not:
I know all that ye would tell,
But to speak might break the spell
Which must bend the Invincible,
	The stern of thought;
He yet defies the deepest power of Hell.

A FURY.

Tear the veil!

ANOTHER FURY.

It is torn.

CHORUS.

	The pale stars of the morn
Shine on a misery, dire to be borne.°	540
Dost thou faint, mighty Titan? We laugh thee to
	scorn.
Dost thou boast the clear knowledge thou waken'dst
	for man?
Then was kindled within him a thirst which outran
Those perishing° waters; a thirst of fierce fever,
Hope, love, doubt, desire, which consume him for
	ever.
	One° came forth of gentle worth
	Smiling on the sanguine° earth;
	His words outlived him, like swift poison
		Withering up truth, peace, and pity.
	Look! where round the wide horizon	550
		Many a million-peopled city
	Vomits smoke in the bright air.

540. **dire . . . borne:** an echo of much English used in translation of Greek tragedy. 544. **perishing:** "clear knowledge" which can be said ironically to "clear dying?" 546. **One:** Jesus of Nazareth. In the subsequent passage instances of evil coming from good intentions and beginnings are cited: through the growth of Christianity, 546–66, 586–631; and through the French Revolution, 567–77, 648–54. 547. **sanguine:** hopeful, *and* bloodstained.

Hark that outcry of despair!
'Tis his mild and gentle ghost
	Wailing for the faith he kindled:
Look again, the flames almost
	To a glow-worm's lamp have dwindled:
The survivors round the embers
	Gather in dread.
		Joy, joy, joy!	560
Past ages crowd on thee, but each one remembers,
And the future is dark, and the present is spread
Like a pillow of thorns for thy slumberless head.

SEMICHORUS I.

Drops of bloody agony flow
From his white and quivering brow.
Grant a little respite now:
See a disenchanted nation°
Springs like day from desolation;
To Truth its state is dedicate,
And Freedom leads it forth, her mate;
A legioned band of linkèd brothers	571
Whom Love calls children —

SEMICHORUS II.

	'Tis another's:
See how kindred murder kin:
'Tis the vintage-time for death and sin:
Blood, like new wine, bubbles within:
	Till Despair smothers
The struggling world, which slaves and tyrants
	win.
	[*All the* FURIES *vanish, except one.*]
IONE. Hark, sister! what a low yet dreadful groan
Quite unsuppressed is tearing up the heart
Of the good Titan, as storms tear the deep,	580
And beasts hear the sea moan in inland caves.
Darest thou observe how the fiends torture him?
	PANTHEA. Alas! I looked forth twice, but will no
	more.
	IONE. What didst thou see?
	PANTHEA.	A woful sight: a
	youth°
With patient looks nailed to a crucifix.
	IONE. What next?
	PANTHEA.	The heaven around, the earth
	below
Was peopled with thick shapes of human death,
All horrible, and wrought by human hands,
And some appeared the work of human hearts,
For men were slowly killed by frowns and smiles:
And other sights too foul to speak and live	591
Were wandering by. Let us not tempt worse fear
By looking forth: those groans are grief enough.
	FURY. Behold an emblem: those who do endure

567. **disenchanted nation:** France. 584. **youth:** Jesus.

Deep wrongs for man, and scorn, and chains, but
  heap
Thousandfold torment on themselves and him.
  PROMETHEUS. Remit the anguish of that lighted
    stare;°
Close those wan lips; let that thorn-wounded brow
Stream not with blood; it mingles with thy tears!
Fix, fix those tortured orbs in peace and death, 600
So thy sick throes shake not that crucifix,
So those pale fingers play not with thy gore.
O, horrible! Thy name I will not speak,
It hath become a curse. I see, I see
The wise, the mild, the lofty, and the just,
Whom thy slaves hate for being like to thee,
Some hunted by foul lies from their heart's home,
An early-chosen, late-lamented home;
As hooded ounces° cling to the driven hind;
Some linked to corpses in unwholesome cells: 610
Some — Hear I not the multitude laugh loud? —
Impaled in lingering fire: and mighty realms
Float by my feet, like sea-uprooted isles,
Whose sons are kneaded down in common blood
By the red light of their own burning homes.
  FURY. Blood thou canst see, and fire; and canst
    hear groans;
Worse things, unheard, unseen, remain behind.
  PROMETHEUS. Worse?
  FURY.   In each human heart terror
    survives
The ravin it has gorged:° the loftiest fear
All that they would disdain to think were true:
Hypocrisy and custom make their minds   621
The fanes of many a worship, now outworn.
They dare not devise good for man's estate,
And yet they know not that they do not dare.
The good want° power, but to weep barren tears.
The powerful goodness want: worse need for them.
The wise want love; and those who love want
    wisdom;°
And all best things are thus confused to ill.
Many are strong and rich, and would be just,
But live among their suffering fellow-men   630
As if none felt: they know not° what they do.
  PROMETHEUS. Thy words are like a cloud of
    wingèd snakes;
And yet I pity those they torture not.
  FURY. Thou pitiest them? I speak no more!
                              [*Vanishes.*]
  PROMETHEUS.   Ah woe!
Ah woe! Alas! pain, pain ever, for ever!

I close my tearless eyes, but see more clear
Thy works within my woe-illumèd mind,
Thou subtle tyrant! Peace is in the grave.
The grave hides all things beautiful and good:
I am a God and cannot find it there,   640
Nor would I seek it: for, though dread revenge,
This is defeat, fierce king, not victory.
The sights with which thou torturest gird° my soul
With new endurance, till the hour arrives
When they shall be no types of things which are.
  PANTHEA. Alas! what sawest thou more?
  PROMETHEUS.   There are
    two woes:
To speak, and to behold; thou spare me one.
Names are there, Nature's sacred watchwords, they
Were borne aloft in bright emblazonry;
The nations thronged around, and cried aloud,
As with one voice, Truth, liberty, and love! 651
Suddenly fierce confusion fell from heaven
Among them: there was strife, deceit, and fear:
Tyrants rushed in, and did divide the spoil.
This was the shadow of the truth I saw.
  THE EARTH. I felt thy torture, son; with such
    mixed joy
As pain and virtue give. To cheer thy state
I bid ascend those subtle and fair spirits,
Whose homes° are the dim caves of human thought,
And who inhabit, as birds wing the wind,   660
Its world-surrounding aether:° they behold
Beyond that twilight realm, as in a glass,
The future: may they speak comfort to thee!
  PANTHEA. Look, sister, where a troop of spirits
    gather,
Like flocks of clouds in spring's delightful weather,
Thronging in the blue air!
  IONE.   And see! more come,
Like fountain-vapours when the winds are dumb,
That climb up the ravine in scattered lines.
And, hark! is it the music of the pines?
Is it the lake? Is it the waterfall?   670
  PANTHEA. 'Tis something sadder, sweeter far than
    all.

CHORUS OF SPIRITS.

From unremembered ages we
Gentle guides and guardians be
Of heaven-oppressed mortality;
And we breathe, and sicken not,
The atmosphere of human thought:
Be it dim, and dank, and gray,
Like a storm-extinguished day,

---

597. lighted stare: Jesus' gaze, penetrating to the meaning of
his torment.   **609. hooded ounces:** leopards used in hunting,
hooded as a means of control, suggesting the blindness of the
"foul lies."   **619. The . . . gorged:** the prey it has devoured.
625. want: lack.   **627. The . . . wisdom:** Cf. Lucifer's speech in
Byron's *Cain*, I, "Choose betwixt love and knowledge—since
there is/No other choice."   **631. they . . . not:** See Luke 23:34.

643. gird: armor.   **659. Whose homes:** Cf. 675–76.   **661.
aether:** "Light consists either of vibrations propagated through
a subtle medium (the aether), or of numerous minute particles
. . . ," Shelley's first note to *Queen Mab*.

Travelled o'er by dying gleams;
  Be it bright as all between   680
Cloudless skies and windless streams,
  Silent, liquid, and serene;
As the birds within the wind,
  As the fish within the wave,
As the thoughts of man's own mind
  Float through all above the grave;°
We make there our liquid lair,
Voyaging cloudlike and unpent°
Through the boundless element:
Thence we bear the prophecy   690
Which begins and ends in thee!

IONE. More yet come, one by one: the air around
  them
Looks radiant as the air around a star.

FIRST SPIRIT.

On a battle-trumpet's blast°
I fled hither, fast, fast, fast,
'Mid the darkness upward cast.
From the dust of creeds outworn,
From the tyrant's banner torn,
Gathering 'round me, onward borne,
There was mingled many a cry —   700
Freedom! Hope! Death! Victory!
Till they faded through the sky;
And one sound, above, around,
One sound beneath, around, above,
Was moving; 'twas the soul of Love;
'Twas the hope, the prophecy,
Which begins and ends in thee.°

SECOND SPIRIT.

A rainbow's arch stood on the sea,
Which rocked beneath, immovably;
And the triumphant storm did flee,   710
Like a conqueror, swift and proud,
Between, with many a captive cloud,
A shapeless, dark and rapid crowd,
Each by lightning riven in half:
I heard the thunder hoarsely laugh:
Mighty fleets were strewn like chaff
And spread beneath a hell of death
O'er the white waters. I alit
On a great ship lightning-split,
And speeded hither on the sigh   720
Of one who gave an enemy
His plank, then plunged aside to die.

THIRD SPIRIT.

I sate beside a sage's bed,
And the lamp was burning red°
Near the book where he had fed,
When a Dream with plumes of flame.
To his pillow hovering came,
And I knew it was the same
Which had kindled long ago
Pity, eloquence, and woe;   730
And the world awhile below
Wore the shade,° its lustre made.
It has borne me here as fleet
As Desire's lightning feet:
I must ride it back ere morrow,
Or the sage will wake in sorrow.

FOURTH SPIRIT.

On a poet's lips I slept
Dreaming like a love-adept
In the sound his breathing kept;
Nor seeks nor finds he mortal blisses, 740
But feeds on the aëreal kisses
Of shapes that haunt thought's wildernesses.°
He will watch from dawn to gloom
The lake-reflected sun° illume
The yellow bees in the ivy-bloom,
Nor heed nor see, what things they be;
But from these create he can
Forms more real than living man,
Nurslings of immortality!
One of these awakened me,   750
And I sped to succour thee.

IONE.

Behold'st thou not two shapes from the east
  and west
Come, as two doves to one belovèd nest,
Twin nurslings of the all-sustaining air
On swift still wings glide down the atmos-
  phere?
And, hark! their sweet, sad voices! 'tis de-
  spair
Mingled with love and then dissolved in sound.

685–86. As . . . grave: one of Shelley's characteristic spiraling, self-encompassing comparisons; these spirits voyage through the atmosphere of human thought as thoughts float through all who live. Cf. IV.81–82. **688. unpent:** unrestricted. **694 ff.:** The four spirits celebrate the victory of Love in different situations: heroic war, self-sacrifice, wise decision, creative imagining. **707. in thee:** in Prometheus.

724. red: fuel almost exhausted. **732. shade:** The world's illumination is as shadow to reality. **742. thought's wildernesses:** the not yet explored. "In the Greek Shakespeare, Sophocles, we find this image, 'Coming to many ways in the wanderings of careful thought'—a line of almost unfathomable depth of poetry; yet how simple are the images in which it is arrayed! . . . What a picture does this line suggest of the mind as a wilderness of intricate paths wide as the universe, which is here made its symbol; a world within a world which he who seeks some knowledge with respect to what he ought to do searches throughout . . . ," Shelley's notebook. See Neville Rogers, *Shelley at Work*, p. 15. **744. lake-reflected sun:** Cf. *Epipsychidion*, 88–90, "The sun-beams of those wells which ever leap/Under the lightnings of the soul—too deep/For the brief fathom-line of thought or sense."

PANTHEA. Canst thou speak, sister? all my words
  are drowned.
IONE. Their beauty gives me voice. See how they
  float
On their sustaining wings of skiey grain,°   760
Orange and azure deepening into gold:
Their soft smiles light the air like a star's fire.

CHORUS OF SPIRITS.

Hast thou beheld the form of Love?

FIFTH SPIRIT.

          As over wide dominions
I sped, like some swift cloud that wings the wide
  air's wildernesses,
That planet-crested shape swept by on lightning-
  braided pinions,
  Scattering the liquid joy of life from his am-
    brosial tresses:
His footsteps paved the world with light; but as I
  passed 'twas fading,
And hollow Ruin yawned behind: great sages
  bound in madness,
And headless patriots, and pale youths who per-
  ished, unupbraiding,
  Gleamed in the night. I wandered o'er, till thou,
    O King of sadness,   770
Turned by thy smile the worst I saw to recollected
  gladness.

SIXTH SPIRIT.

Ah, sister! Desolation° is a delicate thing:
  It walks not on the earth, it floats not on the air,
But treads with lulling footstep, and fans with
  silent wing
  The tender hopes which in their hearts the best
    and gentlest bear;
Who, soothed to false repose by the fanning plumes
  above
And the music-stirring motion of its soft and busy
  feet,
Dream visions of aëreal joy, and calls the monster,°
  Love,
And wake, and find the shadow Pain, as he°
  whom now we greet.

CHORUS.

  Though Ruin now Love's shadow be,   780
  Following him, destroyingly,

On Death's white and wingèd steed,°
  Which the fleetest cannot flee,
    Trampling down both flower and weed,
  Man and beast, and foul and fair,
  Like a tempest through the air;
  Thou shalt quell this horseman grim,
  Woundless though° in heart or limb.

PROMETHEUS. Spirits! how know ye this shall be?

CHORUS.

  In the atmosphere we breathe,   790
As buds grow red when the snow-storms flee,
  From Spring gathering up beneath,
Whose mild winds shake the elder brake,
And the wandering herdsmen know
That the white-thorn soon will blow:
  Wisdom, Justice, Love, and Peace,
  When they struggle to increase,
    Are to us as soft winds be
    To shepherd boys, the prophecy
    Which begins and ends in thee.   800

IONE. Where are the Spirits fled?
PANTHEA.   Only a sense
Remains of them, like the omnipotence
Of music, when the inspired voice and lute
Languish, ere yet the responses are mute,
Which through the deep and labyrinthine soul,
Like echoes through long caverns, wind and roll.
PROMETHEUS. How fair these airborn shapes! and
  yet I feel
Most vain all hope but love; and thou art far,
Asia! who, when my being overflowed,
Wert like a golden chalice to bright wine   810
Which else had sunk into the thirsty dust.
All things are still: alas! how heavily
This quiet morning weighs upon my heart;
Though I should dream I could even sleep with
  grief
If slumber were denied not. I would fain
Be what it is my destiny to be,
The saviour and the strength of suffering man,
Or sink into the original gulf° of things:
There is no agony, and no solace left;
Earth can console, Heaven can torment no more.°
PANTHEA. Hast thou forgotten one who watches
  thee   821
The cold dark night, and never sleeps but when
The shadow of thy spirit falls on her?°

---

760. On . . . grain: In *Paradise Lost*, V.284–85, the Seraph's wings shadowed his feet "from either heel with feathered mail,/ Sky-tinctured grain . . ."   **772 ff. Desolation . . . :** "For Homer says that the Goddess Calamity is delicate, and that her feet are tender. 'Her feet are soft', he says, 'for she treads not upon the ground but makes her path upon the heads of men,'" Shelley's translation of *Symposium*, 195d.   **778. the monster:** the false joy.   **779. he:** Prometheus, who likewise misjudged?

782. Death's . . . steed: Rev. 6:8, ". . . and behold a pale horse; and his name that sat on him was Death, and Hell followed with him . . ."   **788. Woundless though:** After the victory thou shalt be woundless.   **818. original gulf:** primordial Chaos.   **820. Earth . . . more:** Neither can Earth console nor Heaven torment now.   **823. The . . . her:** Cf. 732; II.i.31; III.iii.7.

PROMETHEUS. I said all hope was vain but love:
thou lovest.
PANTHEA. Deeply in truth; but the eastern star
looks white,
And Asia waits in that far Indian vale,
The scene of her sad exile; rugged once
And desolate and frozen, like this ravine;
But now invested with fair flowers and herbs,
And haunted by sweet airs and sounds, which flow
Among the woods and waters, from the aether° 831
Of her transforming presence, which would fade
If it were mingled not with thine. Farewell!°

[*End of the First Act*]

Act II

SCENE I. — *Morning. A lovely Vale in the
Indian Caucasus.* ASIA *alone.*

ASIA. From all the blasts of heaven thou° hast de-
scended:
Yes, like a spirit, like a thought, which makes
Unwonted tears throng to the horny° eyes,
And beatings haunt the desolated heart,
Which should have learnt repose: thou hast de-
scended
Cradled in tempests; thou dost wake, O Spring!
O child of many winds! As suddenly
Thou comest as the memory of a dream,
Which now is sad because it hath been sweet;
Like genius, or like joy which riseth up   10
As from the earth, clothing with golden clouds
The desert of our life.
This is the season, this the day, the hour;
At sunrise thou shouldst come, sweet sister mine,
Too long desired, too long delaying, come!
How like death-worms the wingless moments crawl!
The point of one white° star is quivering still
Deep in the orange light of widening morn
Beyond the purple mountains: through a chasm
Of wind-divided mist the darker lake   20
Reflects it: now it wanes: it gleams again
As the waves fade, and as the burning threads
Of woven cloud unravel in pale air:
'Tis lost! and through yon peaks of cloud-like snow
The roseate sunlight quivers: hear I not
The Aeolian music° of her sea-green plumes

Winnowing the crimson dawn?°
[PANTHEA *enters.*]
                              I feel, I see
Those eyes which burn through smiles that fade in
tears,
Like stars half quenched in mists of silver dew.
Belovèd and most beautiful, who wearest   30
The shadow of that soul° by which I live,
How late thou art! the spherèd sun had climbed
The sea; my heart was sick with hope, before
The printless° air felt thy belated plumes.
PANTHEA. Pardon, great Sister! but my wings were
faint
With the delight of a remembered dream,
As are the noontide plumes of summer winds
Satiate with sweet flowers.° I was wont to sleep
Peacefully, and awake refreshed and calm
Before the sacred Titan's fall, and thy   40
Unhappy love, had made, through use and pity,
Both love and woe familiar to my heart
As they had grown to thine: erewhile° I slept
Under the glaucous° caverns of old Ocean
Within dim bowers of green and purple moss,
Our young Ione's soft and milky arms
Locked then, as now, behind my dark, moist hair,
While my shut eyes and cheeks were pressed within
The folded depth of her life-breathing bosom:
But not as now, since I am made the wind   50
Which fails beneath the music that I bear
Of thy most wordless converse; since dissolved
Into the sense with which love talks, my rest
Was troubled and yet sweet; my waking hours
Too full of care and pain.
ASIA.   Lift up thine eyes,
And let me read thy dream.
PANTHEA.   As I have said
With our sea-sister at his feet I slept.
The mountain mists, condensing at our voice°
Under the moon, had spread their snowy flakes,
From the keen ice shielding our linkèd sleep.   60
Then two dreams came. One,° I remember not.
But in the other his pale wound-worn limbs
Fell from Prometheus, and the azure night
Grew radiant with the glory of that form
Which lives unchanged within, and his voice fell
Like music which makes giddy the dim brain,
Faint with intoxication of keen joy:
' Sister of her whose footsteps pave the world
With loveliness — more fair than aught but her,

---

831. aether: here, a life-giving atmosphere. 832–33: Of . . .
Farewell: Cf. "Love's Philosophy" (1819), "Nothing in the world
is single;/All things by a law divine/In one spirit meet and
mingle . . ."
    Act II, Sc. i. 1. thou: Spring. See I.829–34; Preface, paragraphs
3 and 4.   3. horny: dry, calloused, insensitive.   17. white:
See I.825.   26. Aeolian music: made by the winds sweeping
through the harp of Aeolus, god of the winds.

27. Winnowing . . . dawn: See *Paradise Lost*, V.268–70; the
winged Raphael, descending, "then with quick fan/Winnows the
buxom air."   31. that soul: Prometheus.   34. printless: used
as if the air were a ground to be walked on, or solid enough to
feel the imprint of a wing.   37–38. As . . . flowers: Cf. "To a
Skylark," 55.   43. erewhile: formerly.   44. glaucous: dull
grayish green or blue.   58. voice: command.   61. two . . .
One: See I.32.

Whose shadow thou art — lift thine eyes on me.'
I lifted them: the overpowering light   71
Of that immortal shape was shadowed o'er
By love; which, from his soft and flowing limbs,
And passion-parted lips, and keen, faint eyes,
Steamed forth like vaporous fire; an atmosphere
Which wrapped me in its all-dissolving power,
As the warm aether of the morning sun
Wraps ere it drinks some cloud of wandering dew.
I saw not, heard not, moved not, only felt
His presence flow and mingle through my blood
Till it° became his life, and his grew mine,   81
And I was thus absorbed, until it passed,
And like the vapours when the sun sinks down,
Gathering again in drops upon the pines,
And tremulous as they, in the deep night
My being was condensed; and as the rays°
Of thought were slowly gathered, I could hear
His voice, whose accents lingered ere they died
Like footsteps of weak melody: thy name
Among the many sounds alone I heard   90
Of what might be articulate; though still
I listened through the night when sound was none.
Ione wakened then, and said to me:
' Canst thou divine what troubles me to-night?
I always knew what I desired before,
Nor ever found delight to wish in vain.
But now I cannot tell thee what I seek;
I know not; something sweet, since it is sweet
Even to desire; it is thy sport, false sister;
Thou hast discovered some enchantment old,   100
Whose spells have stolen my spirit as I slept
And mingled it with thine: for when just now
We kissed, I felt within thy parted lips
The sweet air that sustained me, and the warmth
Of the life-blood, for loss of which I faint,
Quivered between our intertwining arms.'
I answered not, for the Eastern star grew pale,
But fled to thee.
          ASIA.   Thou speakest, but thy words
Are as the air: I feel them not: Oh, lift
Thine eyes, that I may read his written soul!   110
     PANTHEA. I lift them though they droóp beneath
          the load
Of that they would express: what canst thou see
But thine own fairest shadow imaged there?
     ASIA. Thine eyes are like the deep, blue, boundless
          heaven
Contracted to two circles underneath
Their long, fine lashes; dark, far, measureless,
Orb within orb, and line through line inwoven.
     PANTHEA. Why lookest thou as if a spirit passed?
     ASIA. There is a change: beyond their inmost
          depth

I see a shade, a shape: 'tis He, arrayed   120
In the soft light of his own smiles, which spread
Like radiance from the cloud-surrounded moon.
Prometheus, it is thine! depart not yet!
Say not those smiles that we shall meet again
Within that bright pavilion which their beams
Shall build o'er the waste world? The dream is told.
What shape is that between us? Its rude hair
Roughens the wind that lifts it, its regard
Is wild and quick, yet 'tis a thing of air,
For through its gray robe gleams the golden dew
Whose stars the noon has quenched not.   131
     DREAM.   Follow! Follow!
     PANTHEA. It is mine other dream.
     ASIA.   It disappears.
     PANTHEA. It passes now into my mind. Methought
As we sate here, the flower-infolding buds
Burst on yon lightning-blasted almond-tree,
When swift from the white Scythian° wilderness
A wind swept forth wrinkling the Earth with frost:
I looked, and all the blossoms were blown down;
But on each leaf was stamped, as the blue bells
Of Hyacinth° tell Apollo's written grief,   140
O, FOLLOW, FOLLOW!
     ASIA.   As you speak, your words
Fill, pause by pause, my own forgotten sleep
With shapes. Methought among these lawns to-
          gether
We wandered, underneath the young gray dawn,
And multitudes of dense white fleecy clouds
Were wandering in thick flocks along the moun-
          tains
Shepherded by the slow, unwilling wind;
And the white dew on the new-bladed grass,
Just piercing the dark earth, hung silently;
And there was more which I remember not: 150
But on the shadows of the morning clouds,
Athwart the purple mountain slope, was written
FOLLOW, O, FOLLOW! as they vanished by;
And on each herb, from which Heaven's dew had
          fallen,
The like was stamped, as with a withering fire;
A wind arose among the pines; it shook
The clinging music from their boughs, and then
Low, sweet, faint sounds, like the farewell of ghosts,
Were heard: O, FOLLOW, FOLLOW, FOLLOW ME!
And then I said: ' Panthea, look on me.'   160
But in the depth of those belovèd eyes
Still I saw, FOLLOW, FOLLOW!
     ECHO.   Follow, follow!
     PANTHEA. The crags, this clear spring morning,
          mock our voices

81-82. it: the ecstasy. Cf. Donne,"The Ecstasy," and Shakespeare, "The Phoenix and the Turtle."   86. the rays: Cf. III.iii.53.

136. Scythian: of an unbounded country stretching beyond the Black Sea, far into India.   140. Hyacinth: When inadvertently Apollo killed Hyacinthus, whom he loved, the youth was turned into a flower on whose leaves might be seen the Greek word expressing anguish, AI.

As they were spirit-tongued.
ASIA.   It is some being
Around the crags. What fine clear sounds! O, list!

ECHOES [*unseen*].

Echoes we: listen!
    We cannot stay:
As dew-stars glisten
    Then fade away —
        Child of Ocean!   170

ASIA. Hark! Spirits speak. The liquid responses
Of their aëreal tongues yet sound.
PANTHEA.   I hear.

ECHOES.

O, follow, follow,
    As our voice recedeth
Through the caverns hollow,
    Where the forest spreadeth;
    [*More distant*]
O, follow, follow!
    Through the caverns hollow,
As the song floats thou pursue,
Where the wild bee never flew,   180
Through the noontide darkness deep,
By the odour-breathing sleep
Of faint night flowers, and the waves
At the fountain-lighted° caves,
While our music, wild and sweet,
Mocks thy gently falling feet,
        Child of Ocean!

ASIA. Shall we pursue the sound? It grows more
    faint
And distant.
PANTHEA. List! the strain floats nearer now.

ECHOES.

In the world unknown   190
    Sleeps a voice unspoken;
By thy step alone
    Can its rest be broken;
        Child of Ocean!

ASIA. How the notes sink upon the ebbing wind!

ECHOES.

O, follow, follow!
    Through the caverns hollow,
As the song floats thou pursue,
By the woodland noontide dew;
By the forest, lakes, and fountains,   200
Through the many-folded mountains;

184. fountain-lighted: Cf. II.iii.26.

To the rents, and gulls, and chasms,
Where the Earth reposed from spasms,
On the day when He and thou
Parted, to commingle now;
        Child of Ocean!

ASIA. Come, sweet Panthea, link thy hand in
    mine,
And follow, ere the voices fade away.

SCENE II. — *A Forest, intermingled with
Rocks and Caverns.* ASIA *and* PANTHEA
*pass into it. Two young Fauns are sit-
ting on a Rock listening.*

SEMICHORUS I. OF SPIRITS.

The path through which that lovely twain
    Have passed, by cedar, pine, and yew,
    And each dark tree that ever grew,
    Is curtained out from Heaven's wide blue;
Nor sun, nor moon, nor wind, nor rain
        Can pierce its interwoven bowers,
    Nor aught, save where some cloud of dew,
Drifted along the earth-creeping breeze,
Between the trunks of the hoar trees,
    Hangs each a pearl in the pale flowers° 10
    Of the green laurel, blown anew;
And bends, and then fades silently,
One frail and fair anemone:
Or when some star of many a one
That climbs and wanders through steep night,
Has found the cleft through which alone
Beams fall from high those depths upon
Ere it is borne away, away,
By the swift Heavens that cannot stay,
It scatters drops of golden light,   20
Like lines of rain that ne'er unite:
And the gloom divine is all around,
And underneath is the mossy ground.

SEMICHORUS II.

There the voluptuous nightingales,
    Are awake through all the broad noonday.
When one with bliss or sadness fails,
        And through the windless ivy-boughs,
    Sick with sweet love, droops dying away
On its mate's music-panting bosom;
Another from the swinging blossom,   30
    Watching to catch the languid close
    Of the last strain, then lifts on high
The wings of the weak melody,

Sc. ii. 10. Hangs . . . flowers: Cf. *A Midsummer Night's
Dream*, II.i.15, "And hang a pearl in every cowslip's ear."

'Till some new strain of feeling bear
  The song, and all the woods are mute;
When there is heard through the dim air
The rush of wings, and rising there
  Like many a lake-surrounded flute,°
Sounds overflow the listener's brain
So sweet, that joy is almost pain.   40

SEMICHORUS I.

There those enchanted eddies play
  Of echoes, music-tongued, which draw,
  By Demogorgon's mighty law,
With melting rapture, or sweet awe,
All spirits on that secret way;
  As inland boats are driven to Ocean
Down streams made strong with mountain-
    thaw:°
    And first there comes a gentle sound
    To those in talk or slumber bound,
  And wakes the destined soft emotion, —
Attracts, impels them; those who saw°   51
  Say from the breathing earth behind
There steams a plume-uplifting wind
Which drives them on their path, while they
  Believe their own swift wings and feet
The sweet desires within obey:
And so they float upon their way,
Until, still sweet, but loud and strong,
  The storm of sound is driven along,
    Sucked up and hurrying: as they fleet   60
    Behind, its gathering billows meet
  And to the fatal mountain° bear
Like clouds amid the yielding air.

FIRST FAUN. Canst thou imagine where those
  spirits live
Which make such delicate music in the woods?
We haunt within the least frequented caves
And closest coverts, and we know these wilds,
Yet never meet them, though we hear them oft:
Where may they hide themselves?
SECOND FAUN.   'Tis hard to tell:
I have heard those more skilled in spirits say,   70
The bubbles, which the enchantment of the sun
Sucks from the pale faint water-flowers that pave
The oozy bottom of clear lakes and pools,
Are the pavilions where such dwell and float
Under the green and golden atmosphere
Which noontide kindles through the woven leaves;

And when these burst, and the thin fiery air,
The which they breathed within those lucent
  domes,
Ascends to flow like meteors through the night,
They ride on them, and rein their headlong speed,
And bow their burning crests, and glide in fire
Under the waters of the earth again.   82
  FIRST FAUN. If such live thus, have others other
    lives,
Under pink blossoms or within the bells
Of meadow flowers, or folded violets deep,
Or on their dying odours, when they die,
Or in the sunlight of the spherèd dew?
  SECOND FAUN. Ay, many more which we may
    well divine.
But, should we stay to speak, noontide would come,
And thwart° Silenus find his goats undrawn,°   90
And grudge to sing those wise and lovely songs
Of Fate, and Chance, and God, and Chaos old,
And Love, and the chained Titan's woful doom,
And how he shall be loosed, and make the earth
One brotherhood: delightful strains which cheer
Our solitary twilights, and which charm
To silence the unenvying nightingales.

SCENE III. — *A Pinnacle of Rock among
    Mountains.* ASIA *and* PANTHEA.

  PANTHEA. Hither the sound has borne us — to the
    realm
Of Demogorgon, and the mighty portal,
Like a volcano's meteor-breathing chasm,°
Whence the oracular vapour is hurled up
Which lonely men drink wandering in their youth,
And call truth, virtue, love, genius, or joy,
That maddening wine of life, whose dregs they
    drain
To deep intoxication; and uplift,
Like Maenads° who cry loud, Evoe!° Evoe!
The voice which is contagion° to the world.   10
  ASIA. Fit throne for such a Power! Magnificent!
How glorious art thou, Earth! And if thou be
The shadow of some spirit lovelier still,
Though evil stain its work, and it should be
Like its creation, weak yet beautiful,
I could fall down and worship that and thee.
Even now my heart adoreth: Wonderful!
Look, sister, ere the vapour dim thy brain:

---

38. **Like . . . flute:** Like reeds in a lake. Or the sweetness of a flute's sound borne across a lake.   **46–47. As . . . mountain-thaw:** This uses what is perhaps Shelley's supreme symbol. Cf. Asia's song ending II.   **51. those . . . saw:** seers who understood that Demogorgon's law moves men by necessity, yet allows them the sense of their own free will.   **62. fatal mountain:** the mountain toward which Panthea and Asia are moving, where they arrive at the opening of the next scene.

90. **And . . . undrawn:** See Virgil, *Eclogue,* VI. Two shepherds bind the drunken Silenus in a cave, and force him to sing. Silenus, a wood god, had the power of prophecy; he was chief of the Satyrs, and the teacher of Dionysus. Plato likened Socrates to him, in the *Symposium.*   **thwart:** stubborn, contradictious. **undrawn:** not milked.
    Sc. iii: 3. chasm: Cf. III.iii.125–28.   **9. Maenads:** See note to "Ode to the West Wind," p. 682, l. 23, above.   **Evoe:** the cry the Maenads shouted to their god.   **10. contagion:** destroying what "the world" most cares for.

Beneath is a wide plain of billowy mist,
As a lake, paving in the morning sky, 20
With azure waves which burst in silver light,
Some Indian vale. Behold it, rolling on
Under the curdling winds, and islanding
The peak whereon we stand, midway, around,
Encinctured by the dark and blooming forests,
Dim twilight-lawns, and stream-illumèd caves,
And wind-enchanted shapes of wandering mist;
And far on high the keen sky-cleaving mountains
From icy spires of sun-like radiance fling
The dawn, as lifted Ocean's dazzling spray, 30
From some Atlantic islet scattered up,
Spangles the wind with lamp-like water-drops.
The vale is girdled with their walls, a howl
Of cataracts from their thaw-cloven ravines,
Satiates the listening wind, continuous, vast,
Awful as silence. Hark! the rushing snow!
The sun-awakened avalanche! whose mass,
Thrice sifted by the storm, had gathered there
Flake after flake, in heaven-defying minds
As thought by thought is piled, till some great
    truth 40
Is loosened, and the nations echo round,
Shaken to their roots, as do the mountains now.
    PANTHEA. Look how the gusty sea of mist is break-
      ing
In crimson foam, even at our feet! it rises
As Ocean at the enchantment of the moon
Round foodless men wrecked on some oozy isle.
    ASIA. The fragments of the cloud are scattered up;
The wind that lifts them disentwines my hair;
Its billows now sweep o'er mine eyes; my brain
Grows dizzy; see'st thou shapes within the mist?
    PANTHEA. A countenance with beckoning smiles:
      there burns 51
An azure fire within its golden locks!
Another and another: hark! they speak!

SONG OF SPIRITS.

To the deep, to the deep,
    Down, down!
Through the shade of sleep,
Through the cloudy strife
Of Death and of Life;
Through the veil and the bar
Of things which seem and are 60
Even to the steps of the remotest throne,
    Down, down!

While the sound whirls around,
    Down, down!
As the fawn draws the hound,
As the lightning the vapour,
As a weak moth the taper;
Death, despair; love, sorrow;

Time both; to-day, to-morrow;°
As steel obeys the spirit of the stone, 70
    Down, down!

Through the gray, void abysm,
    Down, down!
Where the air is no prism,°
And the moon and stars are not,
And the cavern-crags wear not
The radiance of Heaven,
Nor the gloom to Earth given,
Where there is One pervading, One alone,
    Down, down! 80

In the depth of the deep,
    Down, down!
Like veiled lightning asleep,
Like the spark nursed in embers,
The last look Love remembers,
Like a diamond,° which shines
On the dark wealth of mines,
A spell is treasured but for thee° alone.
    Down, down!

We have bound thee, we guide thee; 90
    Down, down!
With the bright form beside thee;
Resist not the weakness,
Such strength is in meekness°
That the Eternal, the Immortal,
Must unloose through life's portal
The snake-like Doom coiled underneath° his
    throne
      By that alone.

SCENE IV. — *The Cave of* DEMOGORGON. ASIA
and PANTHEA.

    PANTHEA. What veilèd form sits on that ebon
      throne?
    ASIA. The veil has fallen.°

66–69. As . . . to-morrow: Vapor, taper, despair, and sorrow
attract lightning, the moth, death, and love; Time draws both
love and sorrow; today is pursued by tomorrow. **74. Where
. . . prism:** where space is totally empty, and according to the
Newtonian theory of light, does not transmit the light rays.
86. Like a diamond: Cf. Milton, *Comus,* 732–36, ". . . and the
unsought diamonds/Would so emblaze the forehead of the deep,/
And so bestud with stars, that they below/Would grow inured
to light, and come at last/To gaze upon the sun with shameless
brows." **88. thee:** Asia, who is accompanied by "the bright
form" of Panthea. **93–94. Resist . . . meekness:** Shelley has
a peculiar feeling for the word "weak." Cf. II.i.89; II.iii.15.
97. coiled underneath: Between his returns in the unending
cycle, Vishnu sleeps on the coils of the serpent.
    Sc. iv. 2. fallen: The falling of the veil leaves this Spirit as
inapprehensible as before.

PANTHEA.   I see a mighty darkness
Filling the seat of power, and rays of gloom
Dart round, as light from the meridian sun.
—Ungazed upon and shapeless; neither limb,
Nor form, nor outline; yet we feel it is
A living Spirit.
    DEMOGORGON. Ask what thou wouldst know.
    ASIA. What canst thou tell?
    DEMOGORGON.   All things thou dar'st demand.°
    ASIA. Who made the living world?
    DEMOGORGON.   God.
    ASIA.   Who made all
That it contains? thought, passion, reason, will,   10
Imagination?
    DEMOGORGON. God: Almighty God.
    ASIA. Who made that sense which, when the
      winds of Spring
In rarest visitation, or the voice
Of one belovèd heard in youth alone,
Fills the faint eyes with falling tears which dim
The radiant looks of unbewailing° flowers,
And leaves this peopled earth a solitude
When it returns no more?
    DEMOGORGON.   Merciful God.
    ASIA. And who made terror, madness, crime, re-
morse,
Which from the links of the great chain of things,
To every thought within the mind of man   21
Sway and drag heavily, and each one reels
Under the load towards the pit of death;
Abandoned hope, and love that turns to hate;
And self-contempt, bitterer to drink than blood;
Pain, whose unheeded and familiar speech
Is howling, and keen shrieks, day after day;
And Hell, or the sharp fear of Hell?°
    DEMOGORGON.   He reigns.
    ASIA. Utter his name: a world pining in pain
Asks but his name: curses shall drag him down.° 30
    DEMOGORGON. He reigns.
    ASIA.   I feel, I know it: who?°
    DEMOGORGON.   He reigns.
    ASIA. Who reigns? There was the Heaven and
      Earth at first,
And Light and Love; then Saturn, from whose
    throne
Time fell, an envious shadow: such the state
Of the earth's primal spirits beneath his sway,
As the calm joy of flowers and living leaves
Before the wind or sun has withered them
'And semivital worms; but he refused

The birthright of their being, knowledge, power,
The skill which wields the elements, the thought
Which pierces this dim universe like light,   41
Self-empire, and the majesty of love;
For thirst of which they fainted. Then Prometheus
Gave wisdom, which is strength, to Jupiter,
And with this law alone, 'Let man be free,'
Clothed him with the dominion of wide Heaven.
To know nor faith, nor love, nor law; to be
Omnipotent but friendless is to reign;°
And Jove now reigned; for on the race of man
First famine, and then toil, and then disease, 50
Strife, wounds, and ghastly death unseen before,
Fell; and the unseasonable seasons drove
With alternating shafts of frost and fire,
Their shelterless, pale tribes to mountain caves:
And in their desert hearts fierce wants he sent,
And mad disquietudes, and shadows idle
Of unreal good, which levied mutual war,
So ruining the lair wherein they raged.
Prometheus saw, and waked the legioned hopes°
Which sleep within folded Elysian flowers,   60
Nepenthe,° Moly,° Amaranth,° fadeless blooms,
That they might hide with thin and rainbow wings
The shape of Death; and Love he sent to bind
The disunited tendrils of that vine
Which bears the wine of life, the human heart;
And he tamed fire which, like some beast of prey,
Most terrible, but lovely, played beneath
The frown of man; and tortured° to his will
Iron and gold, the slaves and signs of power,
And gems and poisons, and all subtlest forms   70
Hidden beneath the mountains and the waves.
He gave man speech, and speech created thought,
Which is the measure of the universe;
And Science struck the thrones of earth and heaven,
Which shook, but fell not; and the harmonious
    mind
Poured itself forth in all-prophetic song;
And music lifted up the listening spirit
Until it walked, exempt from mortal care.
Godlike, o'er the clear billows of sweet sound;

47–48. To . . . reign: Cf. Lord Acton, "Power corrupts; absolute power tends to corrupt absolutely," and Shelley, *Queen Mab*, III.176–77, "Power like a desolating pestilence/Pollutes whate'er it touches." **59–70. Prometheus . . . poisons:** "The alleviations of his state Prometheus gave to man," 98–99, were not all good for him. **Nepenthe:** See Spenser, *Faerie Queene*, IV.iii.43, "Nepenthe is a drinck of sovrayne grace,/Devized by the gods for to asswage/Harts grief, and bitter gall away to chace . . .", and Milton, *Comus*, 675–77, "Not that Nepenthes which the wife of Thone/In Egypt gave to Jove-born Helena/Is of such power to stir up joy as this. . . ." See also "Triumph of Life," 358–59, "In her right hand she bore a crystal glass,/Mantling with bright Nepenthe." **Moly:** See *Comus*, 635–36, "And yet more med'cinal is it than that moly/That Hermes once to wise Ulysses gave." **Amaranth:** See *Paradise Lost*, III.353–55, "Immortal amarant, a flower which once/In Paradise, fast by the Tree of Life,/Began to bloom." **tortured:** twisted, bent, misused.

---

8. dar'st demand: "We are on that verge where words abandon us, and what wonder if we grow dizzy to look down the dark abyss of how little we know," Shelley's essay, *On Life*.   **16. unbewailing:** having a surety we do not have.   **24–28. Abandoned . . . Hell:** Who made all these?   **30. curses . . . down:** Asia (not Prometheus) is speaking. Cf. I.303–05.   **31. who?:** Asia is fulfilling the promise of the Echoes of II.i.190.

And human hands first mimicked and then
 mocked,°   80
With moulded limbs more lovely than its own,
The human form, till marble grew divine;
And mothers, gazing, drank the love men see
Reflected in their race, behold, and perish.°
He told the hidden power of herbs and springs,
And Disease drank and slept. Death grew like sleep.
He taught the implicated orbits woven
Of the wide-wandering stars;° and how the sun
Changes his lair, and by what secret spell
The pale moon is transformed, when her broad eye
Gazes not on the interlunar sea:°   91
He taught to rule, as life directs the limbs,
The tempest-wingèd chariots of the Ocean,
And the Celt knew the Indian.° Cities then
Were built, and through their snow-like columns
 flowed
The warm winds, and the azure aether shone,
And the blue sea and shadowy hills were seen.
Such, the alleviations of his state,
Prometheus gave to man, for which he hangs
Withering in destined pain: but who rains down
Evil, the immedicable° plague, which, while 101
Man looks on his creation like a God
And sees that it is glorious, drives him on,°
The wreck of his own will, the scorn of earth,°
The outcast, the abandoned, the alone?
Not Jove: while yet his frown shook Heaven, ay,
 when
His adversary from adamantine chains
Cursed him, he trembled like a slave. Declare
Who is his master? Is he too a slave?
 DEMOGORGON. All spirits are enslaved which serve
  things evil: 110
Thou knowest if Jupiter be such or no.
 ASIA. Whom calledst thou God?
 DEMOGORGON.   I spoke but as ye speak,
For Jove is the supreme of living things.
 ASIA. Who is the master of the slave?
 DEMOGORGON.   If the abysm
Could vomit forth its secrets. . . . But a voice

Is wanting, the deep truth is imageless;
For what would it avail to bid thee gaze
On the revolving world? What to bid speak
Fate, Time, Occasion, Chance, and Change? To
 these
All things are subject but eternal Love.° 120
 ASIA. So much I asked before, and my heart gave
The response thou hast given; and of such truths
Each to itself must be the oracle.
One more demand; and do thou answer me
As mine own soul would answer, did it know
That which I ask. Prometheus shall arise
Henceforth the sun of this rejoicing world:
When shall the destined hour arrive?
 DEMOGORGON.   Behold!°
 ASIA. The rocks are cloven, and through the pur-
 ple night
I see cars drawn by rainbow-wingèd steeds 130
Which trample the dim winds: in each there stands
A wild-eyed charioteer urging their flight.
Some look behind, as fiends pursued them there,
And yet I see no shapes but the keen stars:
Others, with burning eyes, lean forth, and drink
With eager lips the wind of their own speed,
As if the thing they loved fled on before,
And now, even now, they clasped it. Their bright
 locks
Stream like a comet's flashing hair: they all
Sweep onward.
 DEMOGORGON. These are the immortal Hours,
Of whom thou didst demand. One waits for thee.
 ASIA. A spirit with a dreadful countenance 142
Checks its dark chariot by the craggy gulf.
Unlike thy brethren, ghastly charioteer,
Who art thou? Whither wouldst thou bear me?
 Speak!
 SPIRIT. I am the shadow of a destiny
More dread than is my aspect: ere yon planet
Has set, the darkness° which ascends with me
Shall wrap in lasting night heaven's kingless throne.
 ASIA. What meanest thou?
 PANTHEA.   That terrible shadow floats
Up from its throne, as may the lurid smoke 151
Of earthquake-ruined cities o'er the sea.
Lo! it ascends the car; the coursers fly
Terrified: watch its path among the stars
Blackening the night!
 ASIA.   Thus I am answered: strange!
 PANTHEA. See, near the verge, another chariot
 stays;

---

80. mimicked . . . mocked: See *Ozymandias*, "the hand that mocked them." The sculptor improves on the human form by the loveliness of his enduring creations. **82–84. marble . . . perish:** Mothers-to-be were to look at statues in order to have beautiful offspring; men beholding such beauty die of love. **88. wide-wandering stars:** planets. **90–91. The . . . sea:** Between lunations, the bright face of the moon does not shine down upon the sea. Cf. *A Defence of Poetry*, p. 731, below, "it arrests the vanishing apparitions which haunt the interlunations of life." And see Milton, *Samson Agonistes*, 87–89 (p. 275, above). **92–94. He . . . Indian:** Prometheus taught man how to navigate sailing ships; the Briton could cross the sea and reach India. **101. immedicable:** incurable. **103. drives . . . on:** For Asia evil may have a function? Shelley had written much earlier of "the woe-fertilized world" (Rogers, 29). **104. The . . . earth:** Cf. Pope, *Essay on Man*, II, 18, "The glory, jest, and riddle of the world" (p. 422, above).

117–120. For . . . Love: Asia is answered; eternal Love alone is beyond mutability. See *Triumph of Life*, 475–76, "the wondrous story/How all things are transfigured except Love." **128. Behold!:** Demogorgon's answer is not in speech. Asia does not realize what is happening. Cf. 155. **148. the darkness:** Demogorgon, "that terrible shadow," 150, who is himself, it may be, the shadow of another.

An ivory shell inlaid with crimson fire,
Which comes and goes within its sculptured rim
Of delicate strange tracery; the young spirit
That guides it has the dove-like eyes of hope;   160
How its soft smiles attract the soul! as light
Lures wingèd insects through the lampless° air.

SPIRIT.

My coursers are fed with the lightning,
   They drink of the whirlwind's stream,
And when the red morning is bright'ning
   They bathe in the fresh sunbeam;
   They have strength for their swiftness I
      deem,
Then ascend with me, daughter of Ocean.

I desire: and their speed makes night kindle;
   I fear: they outstrip the Typhoon;   170
Ere the cloud piled on Atlas can dwindle
   We encircle the earth and the moon:
   We shall rest from long labours at noon:
Then ascend with me, daughter of Ocean.

SCENE V. — *The Car pauses within a Cloud
on the top of a snowy Mountain.* ASIA,
PANTHEA, *and the* SPIRIT OF THE HOUR.

SPIRIT.

On the brink of the night and the morning
   My coursers are wont to respire;
But the Earth has just whispered a warning
   That their flight must be swifter than fire:
They shall drink the hot speed of desire!

ASIA. Thou breathest on their nostrils, but my
   breath
Would give them swifter speed.
   SPIRIT.   Alas! it could not.
   PANTHEA. Oh Spirit! pause, and tell whence is the
   light
Which fills this cloud? the sun is yet unrisen.
   SPIRIT. The sun will rise not until noon. Apollo
Is held in heaven by wonder; and the light   11
Which fills this vapour, as the aëreal hue
Of fountain-gazing roses fills the water,
Flows from thy mighty sister.°
   PANTHEA.   Yes, I feel —
   ASIA. What is it with thee, sister? Thou art pale.
   PANTHEA. How thou art changed! I dare not look
   on thee;

I feel but see thee not.° I scarce endure
The radiance of thy beauty. Some good change
Is working in the elements, which suffer
Thy presence thus unveiled. The Nereids tell°   20
That on the day when the clear hyaline°
Was cloven at thine uprise, and thou didst stand
Within a veinèd shell, which floated on
Over the calm floor of the crystal sea,
Among the Aegean isles, and by the shores
Which bear thy name; love, like the atmosphere
Of the sun's fire filling the living world,
Burst from thee, and illumined earth and heaven
And the deep ocean and the sunless caves
And all that dwells within them; till grief cast   30
Eclipse upon the soul from which it came:
Such art thou now; nor is it I alone,
Thy sister, thy companion, thine own chosen one,
But the whole world which seeks thy sympathy.
Hearest thou not sounds i' the air which speak
   the love
Of all articulate beings? Feelest thou not
The inanimate winds enamoured of thee? List!
               [*Music.*]
   ASIA. Thy words are sweeter than aught else but
   his
Whose echoes they are: yet all love is sweet,
Given or returned. Common as light is love,   40
And its familiar voice wearies not ever.
Like the wide heaven, the all-sustaining air,
It makes the reptile equal to the God:
They who inspire it most are fortunate,
As I am now; but those who feel it most
Are happier still, after long sufferings,
As I shall soon become.°
   PANTHEA.   List! Spirits speak.

VOICE IN THE AIR [*singing*].

Life of Life! thy lips enkindle
   With their love the breath between them;
And thy smiles before they dwindle   50
   Make the cold air fire; then screen them
In those looks, where whoso gazes
Faints, entangled in their mazes.

Child of Light! thy limbs are burning
   Through the vest which seems to hide them;

---

162. lampless: "the desire of the moth for the star." A strange image for the smiles of hope. This, and the song which follows, may be thought to lapse from the height of the rest of this scene. But the song establishes this as the dawn hour.
   Sc. v. 10–14. The . . . sister: See Milton, "On the Morning of Christ's Nativity," 7, 79–84 (p. 209, above).

17. but . . . not: Cf. 64–65.   20–28. The . . . thee: See "Ode to the West Wind," 31. Asia now appears as the spirit of Love, or Intellectual Beauty, and is therefore identified with Aphrodite (Venus), who was said to be born of the sea foam. The Nereids, daughters of the Ocean king, tell of her rising from the sea, standing on a shell. This seems to be a description of Botticelli's picture "The Birth of Venus" in the Uffizi Gallery, Florence. Shelley, who took a keen interest in Italian painting, was in Florence during the fall of 1819.   hyaline: transparent, glassy, crystalline.   44–47. They . . . become: a study of the depth meanings of *fortunate* and *happy.*

As the radiant lines of morning
  Through the clouds ere they divide them;
And this atmosphere divinest
  Shrouds thee wheresoe'er thou shinest.

Fair are others; none beholds thee,   60
  But thy voice sounds low and tender
Like the fairest, for it folds thee
  From the sight, that liquid splendour,
And all feel,° yet see thee never,
  As I feel now, lost° for ever!

Lamp of Earth! where'er thou movest
  Its dim shapes are clad with brightness,
And the souls of whom thou lovest
  Walk upon the winds with lightness,
Till they fail, as I am failing,   70
Dizzy, lost, yet unbewailing!°

ASIA.

My soul is an enchanted boat,
  Which, like a sleeping swan, doth float
Upon the silver waves of thy sweet singing;
  And thine doth like an angel sit
  Beside a helm conducting it,
Whilst all the winds with melody are ringing.
  It seems to float ever, for ever,
  Upon that many-winding river,
Between mountains, woods, abysses,   80
  A paradise of wildernesses!°
Till, like one in slumber bound,
Borne to the ocean, I float down, around,
Into a sea profound, of ever-spreading sound:

Meanwhile thy spirit lifts its pinions
  In music's most serene dominions;
Catching the winds that fan that happy heaven.
  And we sail on, away, afar,
  Without a course, without a star,
But, by the instinct of sweet music driven;   90
  Till through Elysian garden islets
  By thee, most beautiful of pilots,
Where never mortal pinnace glided,
  The boat of my desire is guided:
Realms where the air we breathe is love,
Which in the winds and on the waves doth move,
Harmonizing this earth with what we feel above.

We° have passed Age's icy caves,°
  And Manhood's dark and tossing waves,
And Youth's smooth ocean,° smiling to betray:

Beyond the glassy gulfs° we flee   101
Of shadow-peopled° Infancy,
Through Death and Birth, to a diviner day;
  A paradise of vaulted bowers,
  Lit by downward-gazing flowers,
  And watery paths that wind between
  Wildernesses calm and green,
Peopled by shapes too bright to see,   108
And rest, having beheld;° somewhat like thee;
Which walk upon the sea,° and chant melodiously!

[End of the Second Act]

Act III

SCENE I. — *Heaven.* JUPITER *on his Throne;*
THETIS *and the other Deities assembled.*

JUPITER. Ye congregated powers of heaven, who
    share
The glory and the strength of him ye serve,
Rejoice! henceforth I am omnipotent.
All else had been subdued to me; alone
The soul of man, like unextinguished fire,
Yet burns towards heaven with fierce reproach, and
    doubt,
And lamentation, and reluctant prayer,
Hurling up insurrection,° which might make
Our antique empire insecure, though built
On eldest faith, and hell's coeval, fear;   10
And though my curses through the pendulous air,°
Like snow on herbless peaks, fall flake by flake,
And cling to it; though under my wrath's night
It climbs the crags of life, step after step,
Which wound it, as ice wounds unsandalled feet,
It yet remains supreme o'er misery,
Aspiring, unrepressed, yet soon to fall:
Even now have I begotten a strange wonder,
That fatal child, the terror of the earth,
Who waits but till the destined hour arrive,   20
Bearing from Demogorgon's vacant throne
The dreadful might of ever-living limbs
Which clothed that awful spirit unbeheld,
To redescend, and trample out the spark.°

64–65. **feel:** a more inclusive mode of knowing.   **lost:** a reversal
of the ordinary sense; Cf. Matt. 16:25, "whosoever will lose his
life for my sake shall find it."   **71. unbewailing:** Cf. II.iv.16.
81. wildernesses: the unexplored. Cf. I. 742.   **98–103:** By this
music Time is reversed.   **We:** Asia, "shadow of beauty unbeheld," is here speaking for regenerated Man.   **caves:** places
of thought.   **smooth ocean:** Cf. Gray, "The Bard," "Youth

on the prow and Pleasure at the helm."   **glassy gulfs:** invisible
intervals.   **shadow-peopled:** Cf. Wordsworth's "Intimations
of Immortality" Ode, 5, 59–67, (p. 589, above), "Heaven lies
about us in our infancy."   **109. And . . . beheld:** Cf. Milton,
"On Time," "Then long Eternity shall greet our bliss/With an
individual kiss,/And joy shall overtake us as a flood . . . Attired
with stars we shall for ever sit/Triumphing over Death, and
Chance, and thee, O Time."   **110. sea:** Cf. 74.
  Act III, Sc. i. 8. Hurling up insurrection: Cf. *Paradise Lost,*
I.669, "Hurling defiance toward the vault of Heaven" (p. 232,
above).   **11. pendulous air:** See *King Lear,* III.iv.66, "Now all
the plagues that in the pendulous air . . ."   **20–24. Who . . .
spark:** His and Thetis' "fatal child . . . mightier than either"
is to be the incarnation of Demogorgon.

Pour forth heaven's wine, Idaean Ganymede,
And let it fill the Daedal° cups like fire,
And from the flower-inwoven° soil divine
Ye all-triumphant harmonies arise,
As dew from earth under the twilight stars:
Drink! be the nectar circling through your veins
The soul of joy, ye ever-living Gods,   31
Till exultation burst in one wide voice
Like music from Elysian winds.
                              And thou
Ascend beside me, veilèd in the light
Of the desire which makes thee one with me,
Thetis, bright image of eternity!
When thou didst cry, 'Insufferable might!
God! Spare me! I sustain not the quick flames,
The penetrating presence; all my being,
Like him whom the Numidian seps° did thaw   40
Into a dew with poison, is dissolved,
Sinking through its foundations:' even then
Two mighty spirits, mingling, made a third
Mightier than either, which, unbodied now,
Between us floats, felt, although unbeheld,°
Waiting the incarnation, which ascends,
(Hear ye the thunder of the fiery wheels
Griding° the winds?) from Demogorgon's throne.
Victory! victory! Feel'st thou not, O world,
The earthquake of his chariot thundering up   50
Olympus?
[*The Car of the* HOUR *arrives.* DEMOGORGON *descends, and moves towards the Throne
of* JUPITER.]
            Awful shape, what art thou? Speak!
DEMOGORGON. Eternity.° Demand no direr name.
Descend, and follow me down the abyss.
I am thy child, as thou wert Saturn's child;
Mightier than thee: and we must dwell together
Henceforth in darkness. Lift thy lightnings not.
The tyranny of heaven none may retain,
Or reassume, or hold, succeeding thee:
Yet if thou wilt, as 'tis the destiny
Of trodden worms to writhe till they are dead,   60
Put forth thy might.
JUPITER.   Detested prodigy!

26. Daedal: skillful, inventive, variegated. In the manner of
Daedalus, the Greek artificer. A word favored by Shelley; see
"Ode to Liberty," "Hymn of Pan," "Mont Blanc," 86. **27.
flower-inwoven:** Cf. Milton, "On the Morning of Christ's Nativity," 20, 187–88 (p. 210, above). **40. seps:** a skink or
serpent lizard, from Greek *sepo*—rot; referring to the effect of
its bite. Hence, *sepsis:* putrefaction. Shelley is concerned with
every mode of radical transformation, in this instance one suitably
atrocious. **45. felt . . . unbeheld:** In his infatuate ignorance
Jupiter uses the very distinction being used (in II.v.17) at this
moment. This feeling can be as deceitful as other modes of
knowledge. **48. Griding:** cutting through with a strident or
grating sound; see *Paradise Lost,* VI.329–30, "The griding sword
with discontinuous wound/Passed through him." And *Faerie
Queene,* II.viii.36, "That through his thigh the mortall steele did
gryde." **52. Eternity:** Cf. 36, "no direr name." See Intro.,
p. 676, above.

Even thus beneath the deep Titanian prisons
I trample thee! thou lingerest?
                              Mercy! mercy!
No pity, no release, no respite! Oh,
That thou wouldst make mine enemy my judge,
Even where he hangs, seared by my long revenge,
On Caucasus! he would not doom me thus.
Gentle, and just, and dreadless, is he not
The monarch of the world? What then art thou?
No refuge! no appeal!
                    Sink with me then,   70
We two will sink on the wide waves of ruin,
Even as a vulture and a snake outspent
Drop, twisted in inextricable fight,
Into a shoreless sea.° Let hell unlock
Its mounded oceans of tempestuous fire,
And whelm on them into the bottomless void
This desolated world, and thee, and me,
The conqueror and the conquered, and the wreck
Of that for which they combated.
                              Ai! Ai!
The elements obey me not. I sink   80
Dizzily down, ever, for ever, down.
And, like a cloud, mine enemy above
Darkens my fall with victory! Ai, Ai!

SCENE II. — *The Mouth of a great River in
the Island Atlantis.* OCEAN *is discovered
reclining near the Shore;* APOLLO *stands
beside him.*

OCEAN. He fell, thou sayest, beneath his conqueror's frown?
APOLLO. Ay, when the strife was ended which
    made dim
The orb I rule, and shook the solid stars,
The terrors of his eye illumined heaven
With sanguine light, through the thick ragged
    skirts
Of the victorious darkness, as he fell:
Like the last glare of day's red agony,
Which, from a rent among the fiery clouds,
Burns far along the tempest-wrinkled deep.°
    OCEAN. He sunk to the abyss? To the dark void?
    APOLLO. An eagle so caught in some bursting
    cloud   11
On Caucasus, his thunder-baffled wings
Entangled in the whirlwind, and his eyes
Which gazed on the undazzling sun, now blinded
By the white lightning, while the ponderous hail
Beats on his struggling form, which sinks at length

72–74. Even . . . sea: an ancient image used repeatedly by
Shelley for an eternal opposition.

    Sc. ii. 9. Burns . . . deep: This line perhaps takes some of its
surpassing poetry from its place in the action of the play, but
goes far beyond explanation.

Prone, and the aëreal ice clings over it.
OCEAN. Henceforth the fields of heaven-reflecting
   sea
Which are my realm, will heave, unstained with
   blood,
Beneath the uplifting winds, like plains of corn 20
Swayed by the summer air; my streams will flow
Round many-peopled continents, and round
Fortunate isles; and from their glassy thrones
Blue Proteus and his humid nymphs shall mark
The shadow of fair ships, as mortals see
The floating bark of the light-laden moon
With that white star, its sightless° pilot's° crest,
Borne down the rapid sunset's ebbing sea;
Tracking their path no more by blood and groans,
And desolation, and the mingled voice   30
Of slavery and command; but by the light
Of wave-reflected flowers, and floating odours,
And music soft, and mild, free, gentle voices,
And sweetest music, such as spirits love.
   APOLLO. And I shall gaze not on the deeds which
   make
My mind obscure with sorrow, as eclipse
Darkens the sphere I guide; but list, I hear
The small, clear, silver lute of the young Spirit
That sits i' the morning star.
OCEAN.   Thou must away;
Thy steeds will pause at even, till when farewell:
The loud deep calls me home even now to feed it
With azure calm out of the emerald urns   42
Which stand for ever full beside my throne.
Behold the Nereids under the green sea,
Their wavering limbs borne on the wind-like
   stream,
Their white arms lifted o'er their streaming hair
With garlands pied and starry sea-flower crowns,
Hastening to grace their mighty sister's joy.
   [*A sound of waves is heard.*]
It is the unpastured sea hungering for calm.
Peace, monster; I come now. Farewell.   49
APOLLO.   Farewell.

SCENE III. — *Caucasus,* PROMETHEUS, HERCU-
LES, IONE, *the* EARTH, SPIRITS, ASIA, *and*
PANTHEA, *borne in the Car with the* SPIRIT
OF THE HOUR. HERCULES *unbinds* PROME-
THEUS, *who descends.*

HERCULES. Most glorious among Spirits, thus doth
   strength
To wisdom, courage, and long-suffering love,

And thee, who art the form they animate,
Minister like a slave.
   PROMETHEUS.   Thy gentle words
Are sweeter even than freedom long desired
And long delayed.
              Asia, thou light of life,
Shadow of beauty unbeheld: and ye,
Fair sister nymphs, who made long years of pain
Sweet to remember, through your love and care:
Henceforth we will not part. There is a cave,   10
All overgrown with trailing odorous plants,
Which curtain out the day with leaves and flowers,
And paved with veinèd emerald, and a fountain
Leaps in the midst with an awakening sound.
From its curved roof the mountain's frozen tears
Like snow, or silver, or long diamond spires,
Hang downward, raining forth a doubtful light:
And there is heard the ever-moving air,
Whispering without from tree to tree, and birds,
And bees; and all around are mossy seats,   20
And the rough walls are clothed with long soft
   grass;
A simple dwelling, which shall be our own;
Where we will sit and talk of time and change,
As the world ebbs and flows,° ourselves unchanged.
What can hide man from mutability?
And if ye sigh, then I will smile; and thou,
Ione, shalt chant fragments of sea-music,
Until I weep, when ye shall smile away
The tears she brought, which yet were sweet to
   shed.
We will entangle buds and flowers and beams   30
Which twinkle on the fountain's brim, and make
Strange combinations out of common things,
Like human babes in their brief innocence;
And we will search, with looks and words of love,
For hidden thoughts, each lovelier than the last,
Our unexhausted spirits; and like lutes
Touched by the skill of the enamoured wind,
Weave harmonies divine, yet ever new,
From difference sweet where discord cannot be;
And hither come, sped on the charmèd winds,   40
Which meet from all the points of heaven, as bees
From every flower aëreal Enna° feeds,
At their known island-homes in Himera,°
The echoes of the human world, which tell
Of the low voice of love, almost unheard,
And dove-eyed pity's murmured pain, and music,
Itself the echo° of the heart, and all
That tempers or improves man's life, now free;
And lovely apparitions, — dim at first,

---

27. **sightless:** invisible. **pilot:** The evening star seems to guide
the moon to the horizon.

Sc. iii. 24. **ebbs and flows:** Cf. *King Lear,* V.iii.17–19, "And
we'll wear out,/In a walled prison, packs and sects of great ones/
That ebb and flow by the moon."   **42–43. Enna:** a plain in Sicily.
Himera: a river in Sicily.   **47. echo:** Cf. *Twelfth Night,* II.iv.
21–22, "It gives a very echo to the seat/Where Love is throned."

Then radiant, as° the mind, arising bright   50
From the embrace of beauty (whence the forms
Of which these are the phantoms) casts on them
The gathered rays which are reality —
Shall visit us, the progeny immortal
Of Painting, Sculpture, and rapt Poesy,
And arts, though unimagined, yet to be.
The wandering voices and the shadows these
Of all that man becomes,° the mediators
Of that best worship, love, by him and us
Given and returned; swift shapes and sounds,
          which grow   60
More fair and soft as man grows wise and kind,
And, veil by veil, evil and error fall:
Such virtue has the cave and place around.
          [*Turning to the* SPIRIT OF THE HOUR]
For thee, fair Spirit, one toil remains. Ione,
Give her that curvèd shell, which Proteus old
Made Asia's nuptial boon, breathing within it
A voice to be accomplished, and which thou
Didst hide in grass under the hollow rock.
          IONE. Thou most desired Hour, more loved and
          lovely
Than all thy sisters, this is the mystic shell;   70
See the pale azure fading into silver
Lining it with a soft yet glowing light:
Looks it not like lulled music sleeping there?
          SPIRIT. It seems in truth the fairest shell of Ocean:
Its sound must be at once both sweet and strange.
          PROMETHEUS. Go, borne over the cities of man-
          kind
On whirlwind-footed coursers: once again
Outspeed the sun around the orbèd world;
And as thy chariot cleaves the kindling air,
Thou breathe into the many-folded shell,   80
Loosening its mighty music; it shall be
As thunder mingled with clear echoes: then
Return; and thou shalt dwell beside our cave.
And thou, O, Mother Earth! —
          THE EARTH.   I hear, I feel;
Thy lips are on me, and their touch runs down
Even to the adamantine central gloom
Along these marble nerves; 'tis life, 'tis joy,
And through my withered, old, and icy frame
The warmth of an immortal youth shoots down
Circling. Henceforth the many children fair   90
Folded in my sustaining arms; all plants,
And creeping forms, and insects rainbow-winged,
And birds, and beasts, and fish, and human shapes,
Which drew disease and pain from my wan bosom,
Draining the poison of despair, shall take
And interchange sweet nutriment; to me

50. as: in the measure that. So too in 61.   58. becomes: in
both senses—that which is fitting to man and that to which he
will change.

Shall they become like sister-antelopes
By one fair dam, snow-white and swift as wind,
Nursed among lilies near a brimming stream.
The dew-mists of my sunless sleep shall float   100
Under the stars like balm: night-folded flowers
Shall suck unwithering hues in their repose:
And men and beasts in happy dreams shall gather
Strength for the coming day, and all its joy:
And death shall be the last embrace of her
Who takes the life she gave, even as a mother
Folding her child, says, 'Leave me not again.'
          ASIA. Oh, mother! wherefore speak the name of
          death?
Cease they to love, and move, and breathe, and
          speak,
Who die?
          THE EARTH. It would avail not to reply: 110
Thou art immortal, and this tongue is known
But to the uncommunicating dead.
Death is the veil which those who live call life:
They sleep, and it is lifted: and meanwhile
In mild variety the seasons mild
With rainbow-skirted showers, and odorous winds,
And long blue meteors cleansing the dull night,
And the life-kindling shafts of the keen sun's
All-piercing bow, and the dew-mingled rain
Of the calm moonbeams, a soft influence mild,
Shall clothe the forests and the fields, ay, even   121
The crag-built deserts of the barren deep,
With ever-living leaves, and fruits, and flowers.
And thou! There is a cavern where my spirit
Was panted forth in anguish whilst thy pain
Made my heart mad, and those who did inhale it
Became mad too, and built a temple there,
And spoke, and were oracular, and lured
The erring nations round to mutual war,
And faithless faith, such as Jove kept with thee;
Which breath now rises, as amongst tall weeds   131
A violet's exhalation, and it fills
With a serener light and crimson air
Intense, yet soft, the rocks and woods around;
It feeds the quick growth of the serpent vine,
And the dark linkèd ivy tangling wild,
And budding, blown, or odour-faded blooms
Which star the winds with points of coloured light,
As they rain through them, and bright golden
          globes   139
Of fruit, suspended in their own green heaven,
And through their veinèd leaves and amber stems
The flowers whose purple and translucid bowls
Stand ever mantling with aëreal dew,
The drink of spirits: and it circles round,
Like the soft waving wings of noonday dreams,
Inspiring calm and happy thoughts, like mine,
Now thou art thus restored. This cave is thine.
Arise! Appear!

[*A* SPIRIT *rises in the likeness of a winged child.*]
This is my torch-bearer;
Who let his lamp out in old time with gazing
On eyes from which he kindled it° anew   150
With love, which is as fire, sweet daughter mine,
For such is that within thine own. Run, wayward,
And guide this company beyond the peak
Of Bacchic Nysa,° Maenad-haunted mountain,
And beyond Indus and its tribute rivers,
Trampling the torrent streams and glassy lakes
With feet unwet, unwearied, undelaying,
And up the green ravine, across the vale,°
Beside the windless and crystàlline pool,
Where ever lies, on unerasing waves,   160
The image of a temple, built above,
Distinct with column, arch, and architrave,
And palm-like capital, and over-wrought,
And populous with most living imagery,
Praxitelean shapes, whose marble smiles
Fill the hushed air with everlasting love.
It is deserted now, but once it bore
Thy name, Prometheus; there the emulous youths
Bore to thy honour through the divine gloom
The lamp which was thine emblem; even as those
Who bear the untransmitted° torch of hope   171
Into the grave, across the night of life,°
As thou hast borne it most triumphantly
To this far goal of Time. Depart, farewell.
Beside that temple is the destined cave.

SCENE IV. — *A Forest. In the Background a
Cave.* PROMETHEUS, ASIA, PANTHEA, IONE,
and the SPIRIT OF THE EARTH.

IONE. Sister, it is not earthly: how it glides
Under the leaves! how on its head there burns
A light, like a green star, whose emerald beams
Are twined with its fair hair! how, as it moves,
The splendour drops in flakes upon the grass!
Knowest thou it?
PANTHEA.   It is the delicate spirit
That guides the earth through heaven. From afar
The populous constellations call that light
The loveliest of the planets; and sometimes
It floats along the spray of the salt sea,   10
Or makes its chariot of a foggy cloud,
Or walks through fields or cities while men sleep,

Or o'er the mountain tops, or down the rivers,
Or through the green waste wilderness, as now,
Wondering at all it sees. Before Jove reigned
It loved our sister Asia, and it came
Each leisure hour to drink the liquid light
Out of her eyes, for which it said it thirsted
As one bit by a dipsas,° and with her
It made its childish confidence, and told her   20
All it had known or seen, for it saw much,
Yet idly reasoned what it saw; and called her —
For whence it sprung it knew not, nor do I —
Mother, dear mother.
THE SPIRIT OF THE EARTH [*running to* ASIA].
Mother, dearest mother;
May I then talk with thee as I was wont?
May I then hide my eyes in thy soft arms,
After thy looks have made them tired of joy?
May I then play beside thee the long noons,
When work is none in the bright silent air?
ASIA. I love thee, gentlest being, and henceforth
Can cherish thee unenvied: speak, I pray: 31
Thy simple talk once solaced, now delights.
SPIRIT OF THE EARTH. Mother, I am grown wiser,
          though a child
Cannot be wise like thee, within this day;
And happier too; happier and wiser both.
Thou knowest that toads, and snakes, and loathly
          worms,
And venomous and malicious beasts, and boughs
That bore ill berries in the woods, were ever
An hindrance to my walks o'er the green world:
And that, among the haunts of humankind,   40
Hard-featured men, or with proud, angry looks,
Or cold, staid gait, or false and hollow smiles,
Or the dull sneer of self-loved ignorance,
Or other such foul masks, with which ill thoughts
Hide that fair being whom we spirits call man;
And women too, ugliest of all things evil
(Though fair, even in a world where thou art fair,
When good and kind, free and sincere like thee),
When false or frowning, made me sick at heart
To pass them, though they slept, and I unseen,   50
Well, my path lately lay through a great city
Into the woody hills surrounding it:
A sentinel was sleeping at the gate:
When there was heard a sound, so loud, it shook
The towers amid the moonlight, yet more sweet
Than any voice but thine, sweetest of all;
A long, long sound, as it would never end:
And all the inhabitants leaped suddenly
Out of their rest, and gathered in the streets,
Looking in wonder up to Heaven, while yet   60
The music pealed along. I hid myself
Within a fountain in the public square,

---

150. kindled it: Cf. III.iv.116–19.   154. Nysa: the mountain
on which Dionysus was nursed by nymphs.   158. across the
vale: Many Indian readers of Shelley are convinced that this is
the vale of Kashmir and the "destined cave" the cavern of
Amarnath, sacred to Siva.   171. untransmitted: This hope no
one can receive from another.   172. night of life: Cf. III.iii.
113–14.

Sc. iv. 19. dipsas: a serpent whose bite caused intense thirst.

Where I lay like the reflex of the moon
Seen in a wave under green leaves; and soon
Those ugly human shapes and visages
Of which I spoke as having wrought me pain,
Passed floating through the air, and fading still
Into the winds that scattered them; and those
From whom they passed seemed mild and lovely
    forms
After some foul disguise had fallen, and all   70
Were somewhat changed, and after brief surprise
And greetings of delighted wonder, all
Went to their sleep again: and when the dawn
Came, wouldst thou think that toads, and snakes,
    and efts,
Could e'er be beautiful? yet so they were,
And that with little change of shape or hue:
All things had put their evil nature off:
I cannot tell my joy, when o'er a lake
Upon a drooping bough with nightshade twined,
I saw two azure halcyons clinging downward   80
And thinning one bright bunch of amber berries,°
With quick long beaks, and in the deep there lay
Those lovely forms imaged as in a sky;
So, with my thoughts full of these happy changes,
We meet again, the happiest change of all.
    ASIA. And never will we part, till thy chaste sister
Who guides the frozen and inconstant moon
Will look on thy more warm and equal light
Till her heart thaw like flakes of April snow
And love thee.
    SPIRIT OF THE EARTH. What; as Asia loves Pro-
    metheus?   90
    ASIA. Peace, wanton, thou art yet not old enough.
Think ye by gazing on each other's eyes
To multiply your lovely selves, and fill
With spherèd fires the interlunar air?°
    SPIRIT OF THE EARTH. Nay, mother, while my sister
    trims her lamp
'Tis hard I should go darkling.
    ASIA.   Listen; look!
    [The SPIRIT OF THE HOUR enters.]
    PROMETHEUS. We feel what thou hast heard and
    seen: yet speak.
    SPIRIT OF THE HOUR. Soon as the sound had ceased
    whose thunder filled
The abysses of the sky and the wide earth,
There was a change: the impalpable thin air   100
And the all-circling sunlight were transformed,
As if the sense of love dissolved in them
Had folded itself round the spherèd world.
My vision then grew clear, and I could see
Into the mysteries of the universe:
Dizzy as with delight I floated down,

Winnowing the lightsome air with languid plumes,
My coursers sought their birthplace in the sun,
Where they henceforth will live exempt from toil,
Pasturing flowers of vegetable fire;°   110
And where my moonlike car will stand within
A temple, gazed upon by Phidian forms°
Of thee, and Asia, and the Earth, and me,
And you fair nymphs looking the love we feel,—
In memory of the tidings it has borne,—
Beneath a dome fretted with graven flowers,
Poised on twelve columns of resplendent stone,
And open to the bright and liquid sky.
Yoked to it by an amphisbaenic snake°
The likeness of those wingèd steeds will mock 120
The flight from which they find repose. Alas,
Whither has wandered now my partial tongue
When all remains untold which ye would hear?
As I have said, I floated to the earth:
It was, as it is still, the pain of bliss
To move, to breathe, to be; I wandering went
Among the haunts and dwellings of mankind,
And first was disappointed not to see
Such mighty change as I had felt within
Expressed in outward things; but soon I looked,
And behold, thrones were kingless, and men walked
One with the other even as spirits do,   132
None fawned, none trampled; hate, disdain, or fear,
Self-love or self-contempt, on human brows
No more inscribed, as o'er the gate of hell,
' All hope abandon ye who enter here; '°
None frowned, none trembled, none with eager fear
Gazed on another's eye of cold command,
Until the subject of a tyrant's will
Became, worse fate, the abject° of his own,   140
Which spurred him, like an outspent horse, to
    death.
None wrought his lips in truth-entangling lines
Which smiled the lie his tongue disdained to speak;
None, with firm sneer, trod out in his own heart
The sparks of love and hope till there remained
Those bitter ashes, a soul self-consumed,
And the wretch crept a vampire among men,
Infecting all with his own hideous ill;
None talked that common, false, cold, hollow talk
Which makes the heart deny the yes it breathes,°
Yet question that unmeant hypocrisy   151
With such a self-mistrust as has no name.
And women, too, frank, beautiful, and kind

80-81. halcyons . . . berries: Kingfishers feed on the fruit of
the deadly nightshade which has ceased to be poisonous.   94.
interlunar air: Cf. II.iv.91.

110. vegetable fire: Cf. Paradise Lost, IV.218-20 (pp. 247-48,
above).   112. Phidian forms: figures wrought by the Greek
sculptor Phidias.   119. amphisbaenic snake: a fabulous serpent
with a head at each end, able to move both ways.   136. See
Dante, Inferno, III.9.   140. abject: a person of the meanest
condition, a menial. Cf. I.450-51.   150. the yes . . . breathes:
Cf. Blake, "If the Sun and Moon should doubt,/They'd immediately go out."

As the free heaven which rains fresh light and dew
On the wide earth, past; gentle radiant forms,
From custom's evil taint exempt and pure;
Speaking the wisdom once they could not think,
Looking emotions once they feared to feel,
And changed to all which once they dared not be,
Yet being now, made earth like heaven; nor pride,
Nor jealousy, nor envy, nor ill shame,   161
The bitterest of those drops of treasured gall,
Spoilt the sweet taste of the nepenthe, love.

Thrones, altars, judgement-seats, and prisons;
    wherein,
And beside which, by wretched men were borne
Sceptres, tiaras, swords, and chains, and tomes
Of reasoned wrong, glozed° on by ignorance,
Were like those monstrous and barbaric shapes,°
The ghost of a no-more-remembered fame,
Which, from their unworn obelisks, look forth 170
In triumph o'er the palaces and tombs
Of those who were their conquerors: mouldering
    round,
These imaged to the pride of kings and priests
A dark yet mighty faith, a power as wide
As is the world it wasted, and are now
But an astonishment; even so the tools
And emblems of its last captivity,
Amid the dwellings of the peopled earth,
Stand, not o'erthrown, but unregarded now.
And those foul shapes, abhorred by god and
    man, —   180
Which, under many a name and many a form
Strange, savage, ghastly, dark and execrable,
Were Jupiter, the tyrant of the world;
And which the nations, panic-stricken, served
With blood, and hearts broken by long hope, and
    love
Dragged to his altars soiled and garlandless,
And slain amid men's unreclaiming tears,
Flattering the thing they feared, which fear was
    hate,° —
Frown, mouldering fast, o'er their abandoned
    shrines:
The painted veil,° by those who were, called life,
Which mimicked, as with colours idly spread, 191
All men believed or hoped, is torn aside;
The loathsome mask has fallen, the man remains
Sceptreless, free, uncircumscribed, but man
Equal, unclassed, tribeless, and nationless,
Exempt from awe, worship, degree, the king
Over himself; just, gentle, wise: but man
Passionless? —— no, yet free from guilt or pain,

Which were, for his will made or suffered them,
Nor yet exempt, though ruling them like slaves,
From chance, and death, and mutability,   201
The clogs of that which else might oversoar
The loftiest star of unascended heaven,
Pinnacled dim in the intense inane.

[*End of the Third Act*]

Act IV

SCENE. — *A Part of the Forest near the Cave
of* PROMETHEUS. PANTHEA *and* IONE *are
sleeping: they awaken gradually during
the first Song.*

VOICE OF UNSEEN SPIRITS.

The pale stars are gone!
For the sun, their swift shepherd,
To their folds them compelling,
In the depths of the dawn,
Hastes, in meteor-eclipsing array, and they flee
Beyond his blue dwelling,
As fawns flee the leopard.
But where are ye?
[*A Train of dark Forms and Shadows passes by
confusedly, singing.*]

Here, oh, here:
We bear the bier   10
Of the Father of many a cancelled year.
Spectres we
Of the dead Hours be,
We bear Time to his tomb in eternity.

Strew, oh, strew
Hair, not yew!
Wet the dusty pall with tears, not dew!
Be the faded flowers
Of Death's bare bowers
Spread on the corpse of the King of Hours! 20

Haste, oh, haste!
As shades are chased,
Trembling, by day, from heaven's blue waste.
We melt away,
Like dissolving spray,
From the children of a diviner day,
With the lullaby
Of winds that die
On the bosom of their own harmony!

IONE.

What dark forms were they?   30

---

167. glozed: commented, also fawned.   168–76: Cf. "Ozymandias," p. 681, above.   180–88. foul . . . hate: e.g., Moloch
and other deities placated by human sacrifice.   190. painted
veil: Cf. III.iii.113; and "Sonnet," "Lift not the painted veil . . ."

PANTHEA.

The past Hours weak and gray,
With the spoil which their toil
    Raked together
From the conquest but One could foil.

IONE.

Have they passed?

PANTHEA.

                They have passed;
They outspeeded the blast,
While 'tis said, they are fled:

IONE.
Whither, oh, whither?

PANTHEA.

To the dark, to the past, to the dead.

VOICE OF UNSEEN SPIRITS.

Bright clouds float in heaven,   40
Dew-stars gleam on earth,
Waves assemble on ocean,
They are gathered and driven
By the storm of delight, by the panic of glee!
They shake with emotion,
They dance in their mirth.
    But where are ye?

The pine boughs are singing
Old songs with new gladness,
The billows and fountains   50
Fresh music are flinging,
Like the notes of a spirit from land and from
    sea;
The storms mock the mountains
With the thunder of gladness
    But where are ye?

IONE. What charioteers are these?
PANTHEA.   Where are their
    chariots?

SEMICHORUS OF HOURS.

The voice of the Spirits of Air and of Earth
    Have drawn back the figured curtain of sleep
Which covered our being and darkened our birth
    In the deep.

A VOICE.

In the deep?

SEMICHORUS II.

                Oh, below the deep.

SEMICHORUS I.

An hundred ages we had been kept   61
    Cradled in visions of hate and care,
And each one who waked as his brother slept,
    Found the truth —

SEMICHORUS II.

            Worse than his visions were!

SEMICHORUS I.

We have heard the lute of Hope in sleep;
    We have known the voice of Love in dreams;
We have felt the wand of Power, and leap —

SEMICHORUS II.

As the billows leap in the morning beams!

CHORUS.

Weave the dance on the floor of the breeze,
    Pierce with song heaven's silent light,   70
Enchant the day that too swiftly flees,
    To check its flight ere the cave of Night.

Once the hungry Hours were hounds
    Which chased the day like a bleeding deer,
And it limped and stumbled with many wounds
    Through the nightly dells of the desert year.

But now, oh weave the mystic measure
    Of music, and dance, and shapes of light,
Let the Hours, and the spirits of might and
        pleasure,
    Like the clouds and sunbeams, unite.

A VOICE.

                Unite! 80

PANTHEA. See, where the Spirits of the human
    mind
Wrapped in sweet sounds, as in bright veils, ap-
    proach.

CHORUS OF SPIRITS.

We join the throng
Of the dance and the song,
By the whirlwind of gladness borne along;
    As the flying-fish leap
    From the Indian deep,
And mix with the sea-birds, half asleep.

CHORUS OF HOURS.

Whence come ye, so wild and so fleet,
For sandals of lightning are on your feet,   90
And your wings are soft and swift as thought,
And your eyes are as love which is veilèd not?

CHORUS OF SPIRITS.

We come from the mind
Of human kind
Which was late so dusk, and obscene, and blind,
Now 'tis an ocean°
Of clear emotion,
A heaven of serene and mighty motion.

From that deep abyss
Of wonder and bliss,   100
Whose caverns are crystal palaces;
From those skiey towers
Where Thought's crowned powers
Sit watching your dance, ye happy Hours!

From the dim recesses
Of woven caresses,
Where lovers catch ye by your loose tresses
From the azure isles,
Where sweet Wisdom smiles,
Delaying your ships with her siren wiles.   110

From the temples high
Of Man's ear and eye,
Roofed over Sculpture and Poesy;
From the murmurings
Of the unsealed springs
Where Science bedews her Daedal wings.

Years after years,
Through blood, and tears,
And a thick hell of hatreds, and hopes, and fears;
We waded and flew,   120
And the islets were few
Where the bud-blighted flowers of happiness grew.

Our feet now, every palm,
Are sandalled with calm,
And the dew of our wings is a rain of balm;
And, beyond our eyes,
The human love lies
Which makes all it gazes on Paradise.

CHORUS OF SPIRITS AND HOURS.

Then weave the web of the mystic measure;
From the depths of the sky and the ends of the
     earth,   130
Come, swift Spirits of might and of pleasure,
Fill the dance and the music of mirth,
As the waves of a thousand streams rush by
To an ocean of splendour and harmony!

CHORUS OF SPIRITS.

Our spoil is won,
Our task is done,
We are free to dive, or soar, or run;
Beyond and around,
Or within the bound
Which clips the world with darkness round.   140

We'll pass the eyes
Of the starry skies
Into the hoar deep to colonize:°
Death, Chaos, and Night,
From the sound of our flight,
Shall flee, like mist from a tempest's might

And Earth, air, and Light,
And the Spirit of Might,
Which drives round the stars in their fiery flight;
And Love, Thought, and Breath,   150
The powers that quell Death,
Wherever we soar shall assemble beneath.

And our singing shall build
In the void's loose field
A world for the Spirit of Wisdom to wield;
We will take our plan
From the new world of man,
And our work shall be called the Promethean.

CHORUS OF HOURS.

Break the dance, and scatter the song;
Let some depart, and some remain.   160

SEMICHORUS I.

We, beyond heaven, are driven along:

SEMICHORUS II.

Us the enchantments of earth retain:

SEMICHORUS I.

Ceaseless, and rapid, and fierce, and free,
With the Spirits which build a new earth and sea,
And a heaven where yet heaven could never be.

SEMICHORUS II.

Solemn, and slow, and serene, and bright,
Leading the Day and outspeeding the Night,
With the powers of a world of perfect light.

SEMICHORUS I.

We whirl, singing loud, round the gathering sphere,
Till the trees, and the beasts, and the clouds appear
From its chaos made calm by love, not fear.   171

Act IV. 96–103. ocean . . . powers: Cf. "Ode to the West
Wind," III (p. 682, above).

141–43. We'll . . . colonize: a prophecy of space travel—"mur-
murings/Of the unsealed springs/Where Science bedews her

SEMICHORUS II.

We encircle the ocean and mountains of earth,
And the happy forms of its death and birth
Change to the music of our sweet mirth.

CHORUS OF HOURS AND SPIRITS.

Break the dance, and scatter the song,
  Let some depart, and some remain,
Wherever we fly we lead along
In leashes, like starbeams, soft yet strong,
    The clouds that are heavy with love's sweet rain.

PANTHEA. Ha! they are gone!
  IONE.   Yet feel you no de-
    light
From the past sweetness?   180
  PANTHEA.   As the bare green hill
When some soft cloud vanishes into rain,
Laughs with a thousand drops of sunny water
To the unpavilioned° sky!
  IONE.   Even whilst we speak
New notes arise. What is that awful° sound?
  PANTHEA. 'Tis the deep music of the rolling world
Kindling within the strings of the waved air
Aeolian modulations.
  IONE.   Listen too,
How every pause is filled with under-notes,
Clear, silver, icy, keen, awakening tones,   190
Which pierce the sense, and live within the soul,
As the sharp stars pierce winter's crystal air
And gaze upon themselves within the sea.°
  PANTHEA. But see where through two openings
    in the forest
Which hanging branches overcanopy,
And where two runnels of a rivulet,
Between the close moss violet-inwoven,
Have made their path of melody, like sisters
Who part with sighs that they may meet in smiles,
Turning their dear disunion° to an isle   200
Of lovely grief, a wood of sweet sad thoughts;
Two visions of strange radiance float upon
The ocean-like enchantment of strong sound,
Which flows intenser, keener, deeper yet
Under the ground and through the windless air.
  IONE. I see a chariot like that thinnest boat,
In which the Mother of the Months° is borne
By ebbing light into her western cave,
When she upsprings from interlunar dreams;°

O'er which is curved an orblike canopy°   210
Of gentle darkness, and the hills and woods,
Distinctly seen through that dusk aery veil,
Regard like° shapes in an enchanter's glass;
Its wheels° are solid clouds, azure and gold,
Such as the genii of the thunderstorm
Pile on the floor of the illumined sea
When the sun rushes under it; they roll
And move and grow as with an inward wind;
Within it sits a wingèd infant, white
Its countenance, like the whiteness of bright snow,
Its plumes are as feathers of sunny frost,   221
Its limbs gleam white, through the wind-flowing
    folds
Of its white robe, woof of ethereal pearl.
Its hair is white, the brightness of white light
Scattered in strings; yet its two eyes are heavens
Of liquid darkness, which the Deity
Within seems pouring, as a storm is poured
From jaggèd clouds, out of their arrowy lashes,
Tempering the cold and radiant air around,
With fire that is not brightness; in its hand   230
It sways a quivering moonbeam, from whose point
A guiding power directs the chariot's prow
Over its wheelèd clouds, which as they roll
Over the grass, and flowers, and waves, wake
    sounds,
Sweet as a singing rain of silver dew.
  PANTHEA. And from the other opening in the
    wood
Rushes, with loud and whirlwind harmony,
A sphere, which is as many thousand° spheres,
Solid as crystal, yet through all its mass
Flow, as through empty space, music and light:
Ten thousand orbs involving and involved,   241
Purple and azure, white, and green, and golden,
Sphere within sphere; and every space between
Peopled with unimaginable shapes,
Such as ghosts dream dwell in the lampless deep,
Yet each inter-transpicuous, and they whirl
Over each other with a thousand motions,
Upon a thousand sightless axles spinning,
And with the force of self-destroying° swiftness,
Intensely, slowly, solemnly roll on,   250
Kindling with mingled sounds, and many tones,
Intelligible words and music wild.
With mighty whirl the multitudinous orb
Grinds the bright brook into an azure mist
Of elemental subtlety, like light;
And the wild odour of the forest flowers,
The music of the living grass and air,
The emerald light of leaf-entangled beams

Daedal wings," 114-16.   **184. unpavilioned:** no longer roofed over.   **185. awful:** full of awe.   **190-93. awakening . . . sea:** Ione's description shadows forth the poet's aim—to bring powers within the soul to gaze upon themselves. Cf. Coleridge, *Biographia Literaria*, XII, "The postulate of philosophy . . . the heaven-descended KNOW THYSELF."   **200. dear disunion:** parallel to the past disunion of Moon and Earth.   **207. Mother . . . Months:** the moon.   **209. When . . . dreams:** Cf. II.iv.90-91.

210. orblike canopy: Cf. Coleridge, "Dejection: An Ode," 13, p. 610, above, "the old Moon in her lap."   **213. Regard like:** I see as.   **214. wheels:** Cf. Ezek. 10.   **238. many thousand:** the Earth's inconceivable complexity.   **249. self-destroying:** stability as the outcome of innumerable interdependent activities.

Round its intense yet self-conflicting speed,
Seem kneaded into one aëreal mass　　260
Which drowns the sense. Within the orb itself,
Pillowed upon its alabaster arms,
Like to a child o'erwearied with sweet toil,
On its own folded wings, and wavy hair,
The Spirit of the Earth is laid asleep,
And you can see its little lips are moving,
Amid the changing light of their own smiles,
Like one who talks of what he loves in dream.
　　IONE. 'Tis only mocking the orb's harmony.
　　PANTHEA. And from a star upon its forehead, shoot,　　270
Like swords of azure fire, or golden spears
With tyrant-quelling myrtle° overtwined,
Embleming heaven and earth united now,
Vast beams like spokes of some invisible wheel
Which whirl as the orb whirls, swifter than thought,
Filling the abyss with sun-like lightenings,
And perpendicular now, and now transverse,
Pierce the dark soil, and as they pierce and pass,
Make bare the secrets of the earth's deep heart;
Infinite mines of adamant and gold,　　280
Valueless stones, and unimagined gems,
And caverns on crystalline columns poised
With vegetable silver° overspread;
Wells of unfathomed fire, and water springs
Whence the great sea, even as a child is fed,
Whose vapours clothe earth's monarch mountain-
　　tops
With kingly, ermine snow. The beams flash on
And make appear the melancholy ruins
Of cancelled cycles; anchors, beaks of ships;
Planks turned to marble; quivers, helms, and spears,
And gorgon-headed targes,° and the wheels　　291
Of scythèd chariots,° and the emblazonry
Of trophies, standards, and armorial beasts,
Round which death laughed, sepulchred emblems
Of dead destruction, ruin within ruin!
The wrecks beside of many a city vast,
Whose population which the earth grew over
Was mortal, but not human; see, they lie,
Their monstrous works, and uncouth skeletons,
Their statues, homes and fanes; prodigious shapes
Huddled in gray annihilation, split,　　301
Jammed in the hard, black deep; and over these,
The anatomies of unknown wingèd things,
And fishes which were isles of living scale,
And serpents, bony chains, twisted around
The iron crags, or within heaps of dust
To which the tortuous strength of their last pangs
Had crushed the iron crags; and over these

The jaggèd alligator, and the might
Of earth-convulsing behemoth,° which once　　310
Were monarch beasts, and on the slimy shores,
And weed-overgrown continents of earth,
Increased and multiplied like summer worms
On an abandoned corpse, till the blue globe
Wrapped deluge round it like a cloak, and they
Yelled, gasped, and were abolished; or some
　　God
Whose throne was in a comet, passed, and cried,
'Be not!' And like my words they were no more.

THE EARTH.

The joy, the triumph, the delight, the madness!
The boundless, overflowing, bursting gladness,
The vaporous exultation not to be confined!　　321
Ha! ha! the animation of delight
Which wraps me, like an atmosphere of light,
And bears me as a cloud is borne by its own wind.

THE MOON.

Brother mine, calm wanderer,°
Happy globe of land and air,
Some Spirit is darted like a beam from thee,
　　Which penetrates my frozen frame,
　　And passes with the warmth of flame,
With love, and odour, and deep melody　　330
　　Through me, through me!

THE EARTH.

Ha! ha! the caverns of my hollow mountains,
My cloven fire-crags, sound-exulting fountains
Laugh with a vast and inextinguishable laughter.
　　The oceans, and the deserts, and the abysses,
　　And the deep air's unmeasured wildernesses,
Answer from all their clouds and billows, echoing
　　after.

They cry aloud as I do. Sceptred curse,°
Who all our green and azure universe
Threatenedst to muffle round with black destruc-
　　tion, sending　　340
A solid cloud to rain hot thunderstones,
And splinter and knead down my children's
　　bones,
All I bring forth, to one void mass battering and
　　blending, —

Until each crag-like tower, and storied column,
Palace, and obelisk, and temple solemn,
My imperial mountains crowned with cloud, and
　　snow, and fire;
　　My sea-like forests, every blade and blossom
　　Which finds a grave or cradle in my bosom,

---

272. **tyrant-quelling myrtle:** Cf. Milton, "Lycidas," 2 (p. 215, above).　283. **vegetable silver:** See III.iv.110, and note.　291. **targes:** shields with petrifying faces on them.　292. **scythèd chariots:** The ancient Britons used chariots having wheels mounted with sharp, sickle-shaped blades.

310. **behemoth:** See Job 40:15-24.　325. **wanderer:** The planets (from Greek *planetes*—wanderer) change their places relative to the fixed stars.　338. **Sceptred curse:** Jupiter.

Were stamped by thy strong hate into a lifeless
    mire:

How art thou sunk, withdrawn, covered, drunk
    up   350
By thirsty nothing, as the brackish cup
Drained by a desert-troop, a little drop for all;
    And from beneath, around, within, above,
    Filling thy void annihilation, love
Burst in like light on caves cloven by the thunder-
    ball.

THE MOON.

    The snow upon my lifeless mountains
    Is loosened into living fountains,
My solid oceans flow, and sing, and shine:
    A spirit from my heart bursts forth,
    It clothes with unexpected birth   360
My cold bare bosom: Oh! it must be thine
      On mine, on mine!

    Gazing on thee I feel, I know
    Green stalks burst forth, and bright flowers
    grow,
    And living shapes upon my bosom move:
    Music is in the sea and air,
    Wingèd clouds soar here and there,
Dark with the rain new buds are dreaming of:
    'Tis love, all love!

THE EARTH.

It interpenetrates my granite mass,   370
Through tangled roots and trodden clay doth
    pass
Into the utmost leaves and delicatest flowers;
    Upon the winds, among the clouds 'tis spread,
    It wakes a life in the forgotten dead,
They breathe a spirit up from their obscurest
    bowers.

And like a storm bursting its cloudy prison
    With thunder, and with whirlwind, has arisen
Out of the lampless caves of unimagined being:
    With earthquake shock and swiftness making
    shiver
    Thought's stagnant chaos, unremoved for ever,°
Till hate, and fear, and pain, light-vanquished
    shadows, fleeing,   381

Leave Man, who was a many-sided mirror,
    Which could distort to many a shape of error,
This true fair world of things, a sea reflecting love;
    Which over all his kind, as the sun's heaven
    Gliding o'er ocean, smooth, serene, and even,
Darting from starry depths radiance and life, doth
    move:

Leave Man, even as a leprous child is left,
    Who follows a sick beast to some warm cleft
Of rocks, through which the might of healing
    springs is poured;   390
    Then when it wanders home with rosy smile,
    Unconscious, and its mother fears awhile
It is a spirit, then, weeps on her child restored.

Man, oh, not men! a chain of linkèd thought,
    Of love and might to be divided not,
Compelling the elements with adamantine stress;
    As the sun rules, even with a tyrant's gaze,
    The unquiet republic of the maze
Of planets, struggling fierce towards heaven's free
    wilderness.

Man, one harmonious soul of many a soul,   400
    Whose nature is its own divine control,
Where all things flow to all, as rivers to the sea;
    Familiar acts are beautiful through love;
    Labour, and pain, and grief, in life's green grove
Sport like tame beasts, none knew how gentle they
    could be!

His will, with all mean passions, bad delights,
    And selfish cares, its trembling satellites,
A spirit ill to guide, but mighty to obey,
    Is as a tempest-wingèd ship, whose helm
    Love rules, through waves which dare not over-
    whelm,   410
Forcing life's wildest shores to own its sovereign
    sway.

All things confess his strength. Through the cold
    mass
    Of marble and of colour his dreams pass;
Bright threads whence mothers weave the robes
    their children wear;
    Language is a perpetual Orphic° song,
    Which rules with Daedal harmony a throng
Of thoughts and forms, which else senseless and
    shapeless were.

    The lightning is his slave; heaven's utmost deep
    Gives up her stars, and like a flock of sheep
They pass before his eye, are numbered, and roll
    on!
    The tempest is his steed, he strides the air;°   421
    And the abyss shouts from her depth laid bare,
Heaven, hast thou secrets? Man unveils me; I have
    none.

THE MOON.

    The shadow of white death has passed
    From my path in heaven at last,

---

380. unremoved for ever: never to be moved until hate, fear, and pain permit Man to be healed, as in 390. Cf. 404–05. 415. Orphic: As Orpheus with his music made trees and rocks follow him, so Language gives life, motion, and order. 421. strides

A clinging shroud of solid frost and sleep;
  And through my newly-woven bowers,
  Wander happy paramours,
Less mighty, but as mild as those who keep
    Thy vales more deep.   430

THE EARTH.

As the dissolving warmth of dawn may fold
A half unfrozen dew-globe, green, and gold,
And crystalline, till it becomes a wingèd mist,
And wanders up the vault of the blue day,
Outlives the noon, and on the sun's last ray
Hangs o'er the sea, a fleece of fire and amethyst.

THE MOON.

Thou art folded, thou art lying
In the light which is undying
Of thine own joy, and heaven's smile divine;
All suns and constellations shower   440
On thee a light, a life, a power
Which doth array thy sphere; thou pourest thine
  On mine, on mine!

THE EARTH.

I spin beneath my pyramid of night,°
Which points into the heavens dreaming de-
    light,
Murmuring victorious joy in my enchanted sleep;
  As a youth lulled in love-dreams faintly sigh-
      ing,
  Under the shadow of his beauty lying,
Which round his rest a watch of light and warmth
    doth keep.

THE MOON.

As in the soft and sweet eclipse,   450
When soul meets soul on lovers' lips,
High hearts are calm, and brightest eyes are dull;
  So when thy shadow falls on me,
  Then am I mute and still, by thee
Covered; of thy love, Orb most beautiful,
    Full, oh, too full!

Thou art speeding round the sun
Brightest world of many a one;
Green and azure sphere which shinest
With a light which is divinest   460
Among all the lamps of Heaven
To whom life and light is given;
I, thy crystal paramour
Borne beside thee by a power
Like the polar Paradise,°
Magnet-like of lovers' eyes;

I, a most enamoured maiden
Whose weak brain is overladen
With the pleasure of her love,
Maniac-like around thee move   470
Gazing, an insatiate bride,
On thy form from every side
Like a Maenad, round the cup
Which Agave° lifted up
In the weird Cadmaean forest.
Brother, wheresoe'er thou soarest
I must hurry, whirl and follow
Through the heavens wide and hollow,
Sheltered by the warm embrace
Of thy soul from hungry space,   480
Drinking from thy sense and sight
Beauty, majesty, and might,
As a lover or a chameleon
Grows like what it looks upon,
As a violet's gentle eye
Gazes on the azure sky
Until its hue grows like what it beholds,
  As a gray and watery mist
  Glows like solid amethyst
Athwart the western mountain it enfolds,   490
  When the sunset sleeps
    Upon its snow —

THE EARTH.

And the weak day weeps
  That it should be so.°
Oh, gentle Moon, the voice of thy delight
Falls on me like thy clear and tender light
Soothing the seaman, borne the summer night,
  Through isles for ever calm;
Oh, gentle Moon, thy crystal accents pierce
The caverns of my pride's deep universe,   500
Charming the tiger joy, whose tramplings fierce
  Made wounds which need thy balm.

PANTHEA. I rise as from a bath of sparkling water,
A bath of azure light, among dark rocks,
Out of the stream of sound.
  IONE.   Ah me! sweet sister,
The stream of sound has ebbed away from us,
And you pretend to rise out of its wave,
Because your words fall like the clear, soft dew
Shaken from a bathing wood-nymph's limbs and
    hair.
  PANTHEA. Peace! peace! A mighty Power, which
      is as darkness,   510
Is rising out of Earth, and from the sky
Is showered like night, and from within the air
Bursts, like eclipse which had been gathered up

---

the air: May the poet's other prophecies come true as fully.
444. pyramid of night: Cf. A. E. Housman, *Last Poems,* XXXVI,
"[Earth's] towering foolscap of eternal shade."   **465. polar
Paradise:** The moon keeps her face forever turned to the earth.

474. Agave: daughter of Cadmus, king of Thebes. In a frenzy,
she tore her son Pentheus to pieces for trying to prohibit the
women's Dionysiac festivals.   **493–94. weeps . . . so:** that it
is at an end. The dewfall.

Into the pores of sunlight: the bright visions,
Wherein the singing spirits rode and shone,
Gleam like pale meteors through a watery night.
   IONE. There is a sense of words upon mine ear.
   PANTHEA. An universal sound like words: Oh,
   list!

DEMOGORGON.

Thou, Earth, calm empire of a happy soul,
   Sphere of divinest shapes and harmonies,   520
Beautiful orb! gathering as thou dost roll
   The love which paves thy path along the skies:

THE EARTH.

I hear: I am as a drop of dew that dies.°

DEMOGORGON.

Thou, Moon, which gazest on the nightly Earth
   With wonder, as it gazes upon thee;
Whilst each to men, and beasts, and the swift birth
   Of birds, is beauty, love, calm, harmony:

THE MOON.

I hear: I am a leaf shaken by thee!

DEMOGORGON.

Ye Kings of suns and stars, Daemons and Gods,
   Aetherial Dominations,° who possess   530
Elysian, windless, fortunate abodes
   Beyond Heaven's constellated wilderness:

A VOICE FROM ABOVE.

Our great Republic hears, we are blest, and bless.

DEMOGORGON.

Ye happy Dead, whom beams of brightest verse
   Are clouds to hide, not colours to portray,
Whether your nature is that universe
   Which once ye saw and suffered —

A VOICE FROM BENEATH.

                   Or as they
Whom we have left, we change and pass away.

DEMOGORGON.

Ye elemental Genii, who have homes
   From man's high mind even to the central stone
Of sullen lead; from heaven's star-fretted domes
   To the dull weed some sea-worm battens on: 542

A CONFUSED VOICE.

We hear: thy words waken Oblivion.

DEMOGORGON.

Spirits, whose homes are flesh: ye beasts and birds,
   Ye worms, and fish; ye living leaves and buds;
Lightning and wind;, and ye untameable herds,
   Meteors and mists, which throng air's solitudes: —

A VOICE.

Thy voice to us is wind among still woods.

DEMOGORGON.

Man, who wert once a despot and a slave;
   A dupe and a deceiver; a decay;   550
A traveller from the cradle to the grave
   Through the dim night of this immortal day:

ALL.

Speak: thy strong words may never pass away.

DEMOGORGON.

This is the day, which down the void abysm
At the Earth-born's spell° yawns for Heaven's des-
   potism,
   And Conquest is dragged captive through the
   deep:
Love, from its awful throne of patient power
In the wise heart, from the last giddy hour
   Of dread endurance, from the slippery, steep,
And narrow verge of crag-like agony,° springs 560
And folds over the world its healing wings.

Gentleness, Virtue, Wisdom, and Endurance,
These are the seals of that most firm assurance
   Which bars the pit over Destruction's strength;
And if, with infirm hand, Eternity,
Mother of many acts and hours, should free
   The serpent that would clasp her with his length;°
These are the spells by which to reassume
An empire o'er the disentangled° doom.

To suffer woes which Hope thinks infinite;   570
To forgive wrongs darker than death or night;
   To defy Power, which seems omnipotent;
To love, and bear; to hope till Hope creates
From its own wreck the thing it contemplates;
   Neither to change, nor falter, nor repent;
This, like thy glory, Titan, is to be
Good, great and joyous, beautiful and free;
This is alone Life, Joy, Empire, and Victory.

1818–19

Cf. *Paradise Lost*, V.601, "Thrones, Dominations, Princedoms,
Virtues, Powers . . ." (p. 255, above).   **555. Earth-born's
spell:** Prometheus' spell. Cf. 568.   **560. crag-like agony:** The
image takes us back to the opening scene.   **567. The . . .
length:** Cf. II.iii.97.   **569. disentangled:** The disentangling is

523. dew . . . dies: so universal is the sound. Cf. 518, 431–36; and
the last line of Edwin Arnold's "The Light of Asia," "The Dewdrop slips into the shining Sea."   **530. Aetherial Dominations:**

THE CLOUD

I bring fresh showers for the thirsting flowers,
    From the seas and the streams;
I bear light shade for the leaves when laid
    In their noonday dreams.
From my wings are shaken the dews that waken
    The sweet buds every one,
When rocked to rest on their mother's breast,
    As she dances about the sun.
I wield the flail of the lashing hail,
    And whiten the green plains under,   10
And then again I dissolve it in rain,
    And laugh as I pass in thunder.

I sift the snow on the mountains below,
    And their great pines groan aghast;
And all the night 'tis my pillow white,
    While I sleep in the arms of the blast.
Sublime on the towers of my skiey bowers,
    Lightning my pilot sits;
In a cavern under is fettered the thunder,
    It struggles and howls at fits;°   20
Over earth and ocean, with gentle motion,
    This pilot is guiding me,
Lured by the love of the genii that move°
    In the depths of the purple sea;
Over the rills, and the crags, and the hills,
    Over the lakes and the plains,
Wherever he dream, under mountain or stream,
    The Spirit he loves remains;
And I all the while bask in Heaven's blue smile,
    Whilst he is dissolving in rains.   30

The sanguine Sunrise, with his meteor eyes,
    And his burning plumes outspread,
Leaps on the back of my sailing rack,
    When the morning star shines dead;
As on the jag of a mountain crag,
    Which an earthquake rocks and swings,
An eagle alit one moment may sit
    In the light of its golden wings.
And when Sunset may breathe, from the lit sea
    beneath,
    Its ardours of rest and of love,   40
And the crimson pall of eve may fall
    From the depth of Heaven above,
With wings folded I rest, on mine aëry nest,
    As still as a brooding dove.

That orbèd maiden with white fire laden,
    Whom mortals call the Moon,
Glides glimmering o'er my fleece-like floor,°
    By the midnight breezes strewn;

And wherever the beat of her unseen feet,
    Which only the angels hear,   50
May have broken the woof of my tent's thin roof,°
    The stars peep behind her and peer;
And I laugh to see them whirl and flee,
    Like a swarm of golden bees,
When I widen the rent in my wind-built tent,
    Till the calm rivers, lakes, and seas,
Like strips of the sky fallen through me on high,
    Are each paved with the moon and these.

I bind the Sun's throne with a burning zone,
    And the Moon's with a girdle of pearl;   60
The volcanoes are dim, and the stars reel and swim,
    When the whirlwinds my banner unfurl.
From cape to cape, with a bridge-like shape,
    Over a torrent sea,
Sunbeam-proof, I hang like a roof,—
    The mountains its columns be.
The triumphal arch through which I march
    With hurricane, fire, and snow,
When the Powers of the air are chained to my chair,
    Is the million-coloured bow;   70
The sphere-fire above its soft colours wove,
    While the moist Earth was laughing below.

I am the daughter of Earth and Water,
    And the nursling of the Sky;
I pass through the pores of the ocean and shores;
    I change, but I cannot die.
For after the rain when with never a stain
    The pavilion of Heaven is bare,
And the winds and sunbeams with their convex
    gleams
    Build up the blue dome of air,   80
I silently laugh at my own cenotaph,
    And out of the caverns of rain,
Like a child from the womb, like a ghost from the
    tomb,
    I arise and unbuild it again.

1820

TO A SKYLARK

Hail to thee, blithe Spirit!
    Bird thou never wert,°
That from Heaven, or near it,°
    Pourest thy full heart
In profuse strains of unpremeditated art.

51. roof: as seen from below.   TO A SKYLARK.   2. Bird . . .
wert: The blithe Spirit here addressed is even more the joy than
the bird it animates.   3. or near it: Cf. Browning, "Andrea
del Sarto," 98, "what's a heaven for?"

a prerequisite for regaining control.   THE CLOUD.   20. at fits:
intermittently?   23-30. Lured . . . rains: speculative electrical theory.   47. floor: as seen from above.

Higher still and higher
  From the earth thou springest
Like a cloud of fire;
  The blue deep thou wingest,
And singing still dost soar, and soaring ever singest.

In the golden lightning   11
  Of the sunken sun,
O'er which clouds are bright'ning,
  Thou dost float and run;
Like an unbodied joy° whose race is just begun.

The pale purple even
  Melts around thy flight;
Like a star of Heaven,
  In the broad daylight
Thou art unseen, but yet I hear thy shrill delight,

Keen as are the arrows   21
  Of that silver sphere,°
Whose intense lamp narrows
  In the white dawn clear
Until we hardly see — we feel° that it is there.

All the earth and air
  With thy voice is loud,
As, when night is bare,
  From one lonely cloud
The moon rains out her beams, and Heaven is over-
    flowed.   30

What thou art we know not;
  What is most like thee?
From rainbow clouds there flow not
  Drops so bright to see
As from thy presence showers a rain of melody.

Like a Poet hidden°
  In the light of thought,
Singing hymns unbidden,
  Till the world is wrought
To sympathy with hopes and fears it heeded not:

Like a high-born maiden   41
  In a palace-tower,
Soothing her love-laden
  Soul in secret hour
With music sweet as love, which overflows her
    bower:

Like a glow-worm golden
  In a dell of dew,

Scattering unbeholden
  Its aëreal hue
Among the flowers and grass, which screen it from
    the view!   50

Like a rose embowered
  In its own green leaves,
By warm winds deflowered,°
  Till the scent it gives
Makes faint with too much sweet those heavy-
    wingèd thieves:

Sound of vernal showers
  On the twinkling grass,
Rain-awakened flowers,
  All that ever was
Joyous, and clear, and fresh, thy music doth sur-
    pass:

Teach us, Sprite or Bird,   61
  What sweet thoughts are thine:
I have never heard
  Praise of love or wine
That panted forth a flood of rapture so divine.

Chorus Hymeneal,°
  Or triumphal chant,
Matched with thine would be all
  But an empty vaunt,
A thing wherein we feel there is some hidden want.

What objects are the fountains   71
  Of thy happy strain?
What fields, or waves, or mountains?
  What shapes of sky or plain?
What love of thine own kind? what ignorance of
    pain?

With thy clear keen joyance
  Languor cannot be:
Shadow of annoyance
  Never came near thee:
Thou lovest — but ne'er knew love's sad satiety. 80

Waking or asleep,°
  Thou of death must deem
Things more true and deep
  Than we mortals dream,
Or how could thy notes flow in such a crystal
    stream?

We look before and after,
  And pine for what is not:

---

15. **unbodied joy:** a joy escaped from the body. **22. that . . .
sphere:** the Morning Star, Phosphor, Lucifer, Light bringer.
25. feel: Cf. *PU*, II.v.17. **36. hidden:** a description of Shelley's
poetry at its highest.

53. **deflowered:** a metaphorical word here used literally. **66.
Hymeneal:** celebrating a marriage. **81. Waking or asleep:**
Cf. *PU*, III.iii.113–14.

Our sincerest laughter
  With some pain is fraught;
Our sweetest songs are those that tell of saddest
    thought.   90

Yet if we could scorn
  Hate, and pride, and fear;
If we were things born
  Not to shed a tear,
I know not how thy joy we ever should come near.

Better than all measures
  Of delightful sound,
Better than all treasures
  That in books are found,
Thy skill to poet were, thou scorner of the ground!

Teach me half the gladness   101
  That thy brain must know,
Such harmonious madness
  From my lips would flow
The world should listen then — as I am listening
  now.

                        1820

ODE TO LIBERTY

Yet, Freedom, yet, thy banner, torn but flying,
Streams like a thunder-storm against the wind.
         [Byron, *Childe Harold,* IV.98]

Unlike the "Ode to the West Wind," this Ode is in
the English "Pindaric" manner, and is correspondingly more elaborate in rhetoric, heavier in rhythm,
slower in pace. It draws not only on the political situation of its time, a period of popular uprisings in Spain,
Italy and Greece, but more deeply on its finest English precedent, Milton's *Areopagitica,* to which it refers
obliquely in line 75, as its "latest oracle." Even after
the Reformation, Shelley saw orthodox Christianity as
an oppression, effecting tyranny by superstition. This
attitude prevails from his earliest writings, despite his
"exceeding faith in the spirit of Christianity" (Leigh
Hunt). Shelley's notion of political liberty needs always
to be considered as an aspect of "intellectual beauty."
Thus, the two might be interchangeable in the following canceled passage of the "Ode to Liberty":

Within a cavern of man's trackless spirit
  Is throned an Image, so intensely fair
That the adventurous thoughts that wander near
  it
  Worship, and as they kneel, tremble and wear
The splendour of its presence, and the light
  Penetrates their dreamlike frame
Till they become charged with the strength of flame.

I

A glorious people vibrated again
  The lightning of the nations: Liberty

From heart to heart, from tower to tower, o'er
    Spain,
  Scattering contagious fire into the sky,
Gleamed. My soul spurned the chains of its dismay,
  And in the rapid plumes of song
  Clothed itself, sublime and strong,
(As a young eagle soars the morning clouds
    among,)
  Hovering in verse o'er its accustomed prey;
    Till from its station in the Heaven of fame   10
The Spirit's whirlwind rapt it, and the ray
  Of the remotest sphere of living flame
Which paves the void was from behind it flung,
  As foam from a ship's swiftness, when there came
  A voice out of the deep: I will record the same.

II

The Sun and the serenest Moon sprang forth:°
  The burning stars of the abyss were hurled
Into the depths of Heaven. The daedal earth,
  That island in the ocean of the world,
Hung in its cloud of all-sustaining air: 20
    But this divinest universe
    Was yet a chaos and a curse,
For thou° wert not: but, power from worst produc-
    ing worse,
  The spirit of the beasts was kindled there,
    And of the birds, and of the watery forms,
  And there was war among them, and despair
    Within them, raging without truce or terms:
The bosom of their violated nurse°
  Groaned, for beasts warred on beasts, and worms
    on worms,
  And men on men; each heart was as a hell of
    storms.   30

III

Man, the imperial shape, then multiplied
  His generations under the pavilion
Of the Sun's throne: palace and pyramid,°
  Temple and prison, to many a swarming million
Were, as to mountain-wolves their raggèd caves.
    This human living multitude
    Was savage, cunning, blind, and rude,
For thou wert not; but o'er the populous solitude,°
  Like one fierce cloud over a waste of waves,
    Hung Tyranny; beneath, sate deified   40
  The sister-pest,° congregator of slaves;
    Into the shadow of her pinions wide

ODE TO LIBERTY.   **16 ff.:** The voice is speaking.   **23. thou:**
Liberty.   **28. violated nurse:** the Earth.   **33–45. palace
. . . side:** The masters of "Palace and pyramid, temple and
prison" were as wolves to the "astonished herds of men."
populous solitude: the lonely crowd.   **sister-pest:** organized
religion; cf. 83.

Anarchs° and priests, who feed on gold and blood
   Till with the stain their inmost souls are dyed,
   Drove the astonished herds of men from every
     side.

IV

The nodding° promontories, and blue isles,
   And cloud-like mountains, and dividuous° waves
Of Greece, basked glorious in the open smiles
Of favouring Heaven: from their enchanted caves
Prophetic echoes flung dim melody.   50
      On the unapprehensive° wild
      The vine, the corn, the olive mild,
Grew savage yet, to human use unreconciled;
   And, like unfolded° flowers beneath the sea,
     Like the man's thought dark in the infant's
      brain,
   Like aught that is which wraps what is to be,
   Art's deathless dreams lay veiled by many a
     vein
Of Parian stone;° and, yet a speechless child,
   Verse murmured, and Philosophy did strain
   Her lidless° eyes for thee; when o'er the Aegean
     main   60

V

Athens arose: a city such as vision
   Builds from the purple crags and silver towers
Of battlemented cloud, as in derision°
Of kingliest masonry: the ocean-floors
Pave it; the evening sky pavilions° it;
      Its portals are inhabited
      By thunder-zonèd winds, each head
Within its cloudy wings with sun-fire garlanded,°—
   A divine work! Athens, diviner yet,°
     Gleamed with its crest of columns,° on the will
Of man, as on a mount of diamond, set;°   71
     For thou wert, and thine all-creative skill
Peopled, with forms that mock the eternal dead°
   In marble immortality, that hill
   Which was thine earliest throne and latest ora-
     cle.°

Anarchs: Tyranny knows no rule and therefore is anarchy.
46. nodding: their motion as watched from a small sailing
boat.   **47. dividuous:** separating. Cf. *Iliad*, XIV, "Too many
things lie between: shadowy mountains and sounding seas."
51. unapprehensive: unaware and unfearing.   **54. unfolded:**
perhaps a misprint for "enfolded"—not yet unfolded: cf. 56,
"wraps what is to be."   **58. Parian stone:** marble from Paros.
60. lidless: Philosophy can close its eyes to nothing.   **63. in
derision:** making the triumphs of royal builders seem petty.
65. pavilions: roofs.   **66–68. portals . . . garlanded:** within its
gates stand, as guardians, thunderbolt belted winds, their
heads lit "like the bright hair uplifted from the head of some
fierce Maenad."   **69. A . . . yet:** This visionary city is less
divine than Athens.   **70. crest of columns:** the Acropolis.
70–71. on . . . set: Cf. *Hellas*, 696–99, "But Greece and her
foundations are/Built below the tide of war,/Based on the
crystalline sea/Of thought and its eternity."   **73. mock
. . . dead:** imitate those who, though they are dead, are
eternal.   **74–75. hill . . . oracle:** the Areopagus from which

VI

Within the surface of Time's fleeting river
   Its wrinkled image lies, as then it lay
Immovably unquiet, and for ever
It trembles, but it cannot pass away!
The voices of thy bards and sages thunder   80
      With an earth-awakening blast
      Through the caverns of the past:
(Religion veils her eyes; Oppression shrinks
     aghast:)
   A wingèd sound of joy, and love, and wonder,
     Which soars where Expectation never flew,
   Rending the veil° of space and time asunder!
     One ocean feeds the clouds, and streams, and
      dew;
One Sun illumines Heaven; one Spirit vast
   With life and love makes chaos ever new,°   89
   As Athens doth the world with thy delight re-
     new.

.   .   .   .   .   .

The voice then relates the vicissitudes of Liberty in
Rome, in the dark ages, in Alfred's England, in Italy,
in Luther's Germany and Milton's England, in the
French Revolution, in Greece and Spain and Germany
again . . . and concludes:

.   .   .   .   .   .

XVIII

Come thou,° but lead out of the inmost cave
   Of man's deep spirit, as the morning-star
Beckons the Sun from the Eoan wave,°
     Wisdom. I hear the pennons of her car
Self-moving, like cloud chariated by flame;   260
      Comes she not, and come ye not,
      Rulers of eternal thought,°
To judge, with solemn truth, life's ill-apportioned
     lot?
   Blind Love, and equal Justice, and the Fame
     Of what has been, the Hope of what will be?
O Liberty! if such could be thy name°
     Wert thou disjoined from these, or they from
      thee:
If thine or theirs were treasures to be bought
   By blood or tears, have not the wise and free
   Wept tears, and blood like tears? — The solemn
     harmony   270

Milton named his *Areopagitica* (p. 218, above).   **86. Rending
the veil:** as Plato shows what is beyond the illusive flux.   **89.
makes . . . new:** Cf. "Destroyer and preserver", "Ode to the
West Wind," 14, p. 681, above.   **256. thou:** Liberty.   **258.
Eoan wave:** eastern, from Eos, the dawn.   **262. Rulers . . .
thought:** Love, Justice, Fame, Hope.   **266. if . . . name:**
Liberty, Love, Justice, must be inseparable.

XIX

Paused, and the Spirit of that mighty singing
  To its abyss was suddenly withdrawn;
Then, as a wild swan, when sublimely winging°
  Its path athwart the thunder-smoke of dawn,
Sinks headlong through the aëreal golden light
    On the heavy-sounding plain,
    When the bolt has pierced its brain;
As summer clouds dissolve, unburthened of their
    rain;
  As a far taper fades with fading night,
    As a brief insect dies with dying day,—   280
  My song, its pinions disarrayed of might,
    Drooped; o'er it closed the echoes far away
Of the great voice which did its flight sustain,
  As waves which lately paved his watery way
  Hiss round a drowner's head in their tempestu-
    ous play.

                                          1820

HYMN OF APOLLO

Pan has challenged Apollo

  Saying his Syrinx can give sweeter notes
  Than the stringèd instrument Apollo boasts.

Old Tmolus, God of the bare hill on which the contest
takes place, judges in Apollo's favour. Syrinx, pursued
by Pan, was transformed into the reed of which Pan-
pipes are made.

I

The sleepless Hours who watch me as I lie,
  Curtained with star-inwoven tapestries
From the broad moonlight of the sky,
  Fanning the busy dreams from my dim eyes,—
Waken me when their Mother, the gray Dawn,
Tells them that dreams and that the moon is gone.

II

Then I arise, and climbing Heaven's blue dome,
  I walk over the mountains and the waves,
Leaving my robe upon the ocean foam;
  My footsteps pave the clouds with fire; the caves
Are filled with my bright presence, and the air
Leaves the green Earth to my embraces bare.   12

III

The sunbeams are my shafts, with which I kill
  Deceit, that loves the night and fears the day;
All men who do or even imagine ill
  Fly me, and from the glory of my ray

273–82. Then . . . away: What the lines describe happens in
them till the last three take up again.

Good minds and open actions take new might,
Until diminished by the reign of Night.

IV

I feed the clouds, the rainbows and the flowers
  With their aethereal colours; the moon's globe 20
And the pure stars in their eternal bowers
  Are cinctured with my power as with a robe;
Whatever lamps on Earth or Heaven may shine
Are portions of one power, which is mine.

V

I stand at noon upon the peak of Heaven,
  Then with unwilling steps I wander down
Into the clouds of the Atlantic even;
  For grief that I depart they weep and frown:
What look is more delightful than the smile   29
With which I soothe them from the western isle?

VI

I am the eye with which the Universe
  Beholds itself and knows itself divine;
All harmony of instrument or verse,
  All prophecy, all medicine is mine,
All light of art or nature;—to my song
Victory and praise in its own right belong.

                                          1820

TO THE MOON

I

  Art thou pale for weariness
Of climbing heaven and gazing on the earth,
  Wandering companionless
Among the stars that have a different birth,—
And ever changing, like a joyless eye
That finds no object worth its constancy?

                                          1820

A DEFENCE OF POETRY

" The profoundest essay on the foundation of poetry
in English " (W. B. Yeats): Shelley's *Defence* has
been all this to many poets and students of poetry. We
may well wonder, therefore, how a critic as learned as
René Wellek can write, after quoting its final sentence:
" It must be obvious today that this kind of defence
of poetry defeats its own purpose." (*A History of
Modern Criticism*, Vol. II, p. 125.) In part the mistake
is as to this purpose and as to what Shelley is writing
about. Many things can be named " poetry " — from a
mass of reading matter upon which courses are given
and examinations held, up to the creative, imaginative

activities themselves. Shelley is writing about these last and what he has to say is again and again literally exact, as in that final sentence. If we understand his words aright, poets *are* "the unacknowledged legislators of the world." To affirm such things nobly enough protects and restores the connections of imagination with the reading matter, connections forever in danger from academic silt. It is these creative activities — not the printed pages nor the biographer's subjects — which are these "unacknowledged legislators." C. H. Baker has well pointed out how much the *Defence* and Shelley's highest poetry illume one another. It is itself at many points "high poetry," not to be hastily assessed. "All high poetry is infinite; it is as the first acorn, which contained all oaks potentially."

Another part of the mistake is in accepting a passing fashion in criticism as a secured result ("must be obvious today"). The *Defence* has helped and will continue to help creative minds "to serve the power which is seated on the throne of their own soul " — that soul " Whose nature is its own divine control" (*PU*, IV.401). Its prime theme is a perennial concern, though its historical illustrations may in places seem, to some professorial eyes, uninformed.

Shelley's immediate purpose was to answer, philosophically, *The Four Ages of Poetry,* a diverting attack on poetic endeavor as an anachronism, written by his friend Peacock, whose portrait-caricature of Shelley as Scythrop in *Nightmare Abbey* had so delighted the poet. The attack aroused in him, he writes to Peacock, " the greatest possible desire to break a lance with you, within the lists of a magazine, in honour of my mistress *Urania,"* though he dubs himself " the knight of the shield of shadow and the lance of gossamere." As first written, it contained many references and allusions to *The Four Ages* and to Peacock. These were cut out before publication, but echoes of Peacock's phrasing as well as of Plato's *Ion* and *Symposium* and of Sidney's *Apologie* are frequent. A few sentences from *The Four Ages* will show why it stirred Shelley so deeply: " While the historian and the philosopher are advancing in, and accelerating, the progress of knowledge, the poet is wallowing in the rubbish of departed ignorance, and raking up the ashes of dead savages to find gewgaws and rattles for the grown babies of the age. . . . A poet in our times is a semi-barbarian in a civilized community. . . . In whatever degree poetry is cultivated, it must necessarily be to the neglect of some branch of useful study: and it is a lamentable spectacle to see minds capable of better things, running to seed in the specious indolence of these empty aimless mockeries of intellectual exertion." It was to counter his friend's chuckling onslaught that Shelley wrote the *Defence.*

PART I

According to one mode of regarding those two classes of mental action, which are called reason and imagination, the former may be considered as mind contemplating the relations borne by one thought to another, however produced; and the latter, as mind acting upon those thoughts so as to colour them with its own light, and composing from them, as from elements, other thoughts, each containing within itself the principle of its own integrity.[1] The one [2] is the τὸ ποιεῖν, or the principle of synthesis, and has for its object those forms which are common to universal nature and existence itself; the other is the τὸ λογιζεὶν, or principle of analysis, and its action regards the relations of things, simply as relations; considering thoughts, not in their integral unity, but as the algebraical representations which conduct to certain general results. Reason is the enumeration of quantities already known; imagination is the perception of the value of those quantities, both separately and as a whole. Reason respects the differences, and imagination the similitudes of things. Reason is to the imagination as the instrument to the agent, as the body to the spirit, as the shadow to the substance.

Poetry, in a general sense, may be defined to be ' the expression of the imagination': and poetry is connate with the origin of man. Man is an instrument over which a series of external and internal impressions are driven, like the alternations of an ever-changing wind over an Aeolian lyre, which move it by their motion to ever-changing melody. But there is a principle within the human being, and perhaps within all sentient beings, which acts otherwise than in the lyre, and produces not melody alone, but harmony, by an internal adjustment of the sounds or motions thus excited to the impressions which excite them. It is as if the lyre could accommodate its chords to the motions of that which strikes them, in a determined proportion of sound; even as the musician can accommodate his voice to the sound of the lyre. A child at play by itself will express its delight by its voice and motions; and every inflexion of tone and every gesture will bear exact relation to a corresponding antitype in the pleasurable impressions which awakened it; it will be the reflected image of that impression; and as the lyre trembles and sounds after the wind has died away, so the child seeks, by prolonging in its

A DEFENCE OF POETRY. 1. each . . . integrity: Cf. "Nothing can permanently please which does not contain in itself the reason why it is so, and not otherwise." Coleridge, *Biographia Literaria*, XIV, p. 614, above. 2. one: imagination. Cf. Sidney, "The Greeks called him a Poet, which name hath, as the most excellent gone through other Languages. It commeth of this word *Poiein*, which is to make: wherein, I know not whether by lucke or wisedome, wee Englishmen have mette with the Greekes in calling him a maker."

voice and motions the duration of the effect, to prolong also a consciousness of the cause. In relation to the objects which delight a child, these expressions are, what poetry is to higher objects. The savage (for the savage is to ages what the child is to years) expresses the emotions produced in him by surrounding objects in a similar manner; and language and gesture, together with plastic or pictorial imitation, become the image of the combined effect of those objects, and of his apprehension of them. Man in society, with all his passions and his pleasures, next becomes the object of the passions and pleasures of man; an additional class of emotions produces an augmented treasure of expressions; and language, gesture, and the imitative arts, become at once the representation and the medium, the pencil and the picture, the chisel and the statue, the chord and the harmony. The social sympathies, or those laws from which, as from its elements, society results, begin to develop themselves from the moment that two human beings coexist; the future is contained within the present, as the plant within the seed; and equality, diversity, unity, contrast, mutual dependence, become the principles alone capable of affording the motives according to which the will of a social being is determined to action, inasmuch as he is social; and constitute pleasure in sensation, virtue in sentiment, beauty in art, truth in reasoning, and love in the intercourse of kind. Hence men, even in the infancy of society, observe a certain order in their words and actions, distinct from that of the objects and the impressions represented by them, all expression being subject to the laws of that from which it proceeds. But let us dismiss those more general considerations which might involve an inquiry into the principles of society itself, and restrict our view to the manner in which the imagination is expressed upon its forms.

In the youth of the world, men dance and sing and imitate natural objects, observing in these actions, as in all others, a certain rhythm or order. And, although all men observe a similar, they observe not the same order, in the motions of the dance, in the melody of the song, in the combinations of language, in the series of their imitations of natural objects. For there is a certain order or rhythm belonging to each of these classes of mimetic representation, from which the hearer and the spectator receive an intenser and purer pleasure than from any other: the sense of an approximation to this order has been called taste by modern writers.

Every man in the infancy of art observes an order which approximates more or less closely to that from which this highest delight results: but the diversity is not sufficiently marked, as that its gradations should be sensible, except in those instances where the predominance of this faculty of approximation to the beautiful (for so we may be permitted to name the relation between this highest pleasure and its cause) is very great. Those in whom it exists in excess are poets, in the most universal sense of the word; and the pleasure resulting from the manner in which they express the influence of society or nature upon their own minds, communicates itself to others, and gathers a sort of reduplication from that community. Their language is vitally metaphorical; that is, it marks the before unapprehended relations of things and perpetuates their apprehension, until the words which represent them become, through time, signs for portions or classes of thoughts [3] instead of pictures of integral thoughts; and then if no new poets should arise to create afresh the associations which have been thus disorganized, language will be dead to all the nobler purposes of human intercourse. These similitudes or relations are finely said by Lord Bacon to be ‘the same footsteps of nature impressed upon the various subjects of the world’; [4] and he considers the faculty which perceives them as the storehouse of axioms common to all knowledge. In the infancy of society every author is necessarily a poet, because language itself is poetry; and to be a poet is to apprehend the true and the beautiful, in a word, the good which exists in the relation, subsisting, first between existence and perception, and secondly between perception and expression. Every original language near to its source is in itself the chaos of a cyclic poem: the copiousness of lexicography and the distinctions of grammar are the works of a later age, and are merely the catalogue and the form of the creations of poetry.

But poets, or those who imagine and express this indestructible order, are not only the authors of language and of music, of the dance, and architecture, and statuary, and painting; they are the institutors of laws, and the founders of civil society, and the inventors of the arts of life, and the teachers, who draw into a certain propinquity with the beautiful and the true, that partial apprehension of the agencies of the invisible world which is called

3. **thoughts**: concepts merely, abstract notions.　4. ‘the . . . **world**’: *De Augment. Scient.*, i., lib. iii [Shelley’s note].

religion.[5] Hence all original religions are allegorical, or susceptible of allegory, and, like Janus,[6] have a double face of false and true. Poets, according to the circumstances of the age and nation in which they appeared, were called, in the earlier epochs of the world, legislators, or prophets: a poet essentially comprises and unites both these characters. For he not only beholds intensely the present as it is, and discovers those laws according to which present things ought to be ordered, but he beholds the future in the present, and his thoughts are the germs of the flower and the fruit of latest time. Not that I assert poets to be prophets in the gross sense of the word, or that they can foretell the form as surely as they foreknow the spirit of events: such is the pretence of superstition, which would make poetry an attribute of prophecy, rather than prophecy an attribute of poetry. A poet participates in the eternal, the infinite, and the one; as far as relates to his conceptions, time and place and number are not. The grammatical forms which express the moods of time, and the difference of persons, and the distinction of place, are convertible with respect to the highest poetry without injuring it as poetry; and the choruses of Aeschylus, and the book of *Job,* and Dante's *Paradise,* would afford, more than any other writings, examples of this fact, if the limits of this essay did not forbid citation. The creations of sculpture, painting, and music, are illustrations still more decisive.

Language, colour, form, and religious and civil habits of action, are all the instruments and materials of poetry; they may be called poetry by that figure of speech which considers the effect as a synonym of the cause.[7] But poetry in a more restricted sense expresses those arrangements of language, and especially metrical language, which are created by that imperial faculty, whose throne is curtained within the invisible nature of man. And this springs from the nature itself of language, which is a more direct representation of the actions and passions of our internal being, and is susceptible of more various and delicate combinations, than colour, form, or motion, and is more plastic and obedient to the control of that faculty of which it is the creation. For language is arbitrarily produced by the imagination, and has relation to thoughts alone; but all other materials, instruments, and conditions of art, have relations among each other, which limit and interpose between conception and expression. The former is as a mirror which reflects, the latter as a cloud which enfeebles, the light of which both are mediums of communication. Hence the fame of sculptors, painters, and musicians, although the intrinsic powers of the great masters of these arts may yield in no degree to that of those who have employed language as the hieroglyphic of their thoughts, has never equalled that of poets in the restricted sense of the term; as two performers of equal skill will produce unequal effects from a guitar and a harp. The fame of legislators and founders of religions, so long as their institutions last, alone seems to exceed that of poets in the restricted sense; but it can scarcely be a question, whether, if we deduct the celebrity which their flattery of the gross opinions of the vulgar usually conciliates, together with [8] that which belonged to them in their higher character of poets, any excess will remain.

We have thus circumscribed the word poetry within the limits of that art which is the most familiar and the most perfect expression of the faculty itself. It is necessary, however, to make the circle still narrower, and to determine the distinction between measured and unmeasured language; for the popular division into prose and verse is inadmissible in accurate philosophy.

Sounds as well as thoughts have relation both between each other and towards that which they represent, and a perception of the order of those relations has always been found connected with a perception of the order of the relations of thoughts. Hence the language of poets has ever affected a certain uniform and harmonious recurrence of sound, without which it were not poetry, and which is scarcely less indispensable to the communication of its influence, than the words themselves, without reference to that peculiar order. Hence the vanity of translation; it were as wise to cast a violet into a crucible that you might discover the formal principle of its colour and odour, as seek to transfuse from one language into another the creations of a poet. The plant must spring again from its seed, or it will bear no flower — and this is the burthen of the curse of Babel.

An observation of the regular mode of the re-

---

5. But . . . religion: all this by virtue of the definition following "and to be a poet" in the preceding paragraph. Shelley is here following Plato, "The exercise of every inventive art is poetry, and all such artists poets," *Symposium,* Shelley's translation.
6. Janus: a Roman god represented as looking before and behind.
7. effect . . . cause: being, by Shelley's definition, produced by poets.

8. together with: Shelley's point would have been clearer if he had written "from."

currence of harmony in the language of poetical minds, together with its relation to music, produced metre, or a certain system of traditional forms of harmony and language. Yet it is by no means essential that a poet should accommodate his language to this traditional form, so that the harmony, which is its spirit, be observed. The practice is indeed convenient and popular, and to be preferred, especially in such composition as includes much action: but every great poet must inevitably innovate upon the example of his predecessors in the exact structure of his peculiar versification. The distinction between poets and prose writers is a vulgar error. The distinction between philosophers and poets has been anticipated. Plato was essentially a poet — the truth and splendour of his imagery, and the melody of his language, are the most intense that it is possible to conceive. He rejected the measure of the epic, dramatic, and lyrical forms, because he sought to kindle a harmony in thoughts divested of shape and action, and he forbore to invent any regular plan of rhythm which would include, under determinate forms, the varied pauses of his style. Cicero sought to imitate the cadence of his periods, but with little success. Lord Bacon was a poet.[9] His language has a sweet and majestic rhythm, which satisfies the sense, no less than the almost superhuman wisdom of his philosophy satisfies the intellect; it is a strain which distends, and then bursts the circumference of the reader's mind, and pours itself forth together with it into the universal element with which it has perpetual sympathy. All the authors of revolutions in opinion are not only necessarily poets as they are inventors, nor even as their words unveil the permanent analogy of things by images which participate in the life of truth; but as their periods are harmonious and rhythmical, and contain in themselves the elements of verse; being the echo of the eternal music. Nor are those supreme poets, who have employed traditional forms of rhythm on account of the form and action of their subjects, less capable of perceiving and teaching the truth of things, than those who have omitted that form. Shakespeare, Dante, and Milton (to confine ourselves to modern writers) are philosophers of the very loftiest power.

A poem is the very image of life expressed in its eternal truth. There is this difference between a story and a poem, that a story is a catalogue of detached facts, which have no other connexion than time, place, circumstance, cause and effect; the other is the creation of actions according to the unchangeable forms of human nature, as existing in the mind of the Creator, which is itself the image of all other minds. The one is partial, and applies only to a definite period of time, and a certain combination of events which can never again recur; the other is universal, and contains within itself the germ of a relation to whatever motives or actions have place in the possible varieties of human nature. Time, which destroys the beauty and the use of the story of particular facts, stripped of the poetry which should invest them, augments that of poetry, and for ever develops new and wonderful applications of the eternal truth which it contains. Hence epitomes have been called the moths of just history; they eat out the poetry of it. A story of particular facts is as a mirror which obscures and distorts that which should be beautiful: poetry is a mirror which makes beautiful that which is distorted.

The parts of a composition may be poetical, without the composition as a whole being a poem. A single sentence may be considered as a whole, though it may be found in the midst of a series of unassimilated portions: a single word even may be a spark of inextinguishable thought. And thus all the great historians, Herodotus, Plutarch, Livy, were poets; and although the plan of these writers, especially that of Livy, restrained them from developing this faculty in its highest degree, they made copious and ample amends for their subjection, by filling all the interstices of their subjects with living images.

Having determined what is poetry, and who are poets, let us proceed to estimate its effects upon society.

Poetry is ever accompanied with pleasure: all spirits on which it falls open themselves to receive the wisdom which is mingled with its delight. In the infancy of the world, neither poets themselves nor their auditors are fully aware of the excellence of poetry: for it acts in a divine and unapprehended manner, beyond and above consciousness; and it is reserved for future generations to contemplate and measure the mighty cause and effect in all the strength and splendour of their union. Even in modern times, no living poet ever arrived at the fullness of his fame; the jury which sits in judgement upon a poet, belonging as he does to all time, must be composed of his peers: it must be impan-

---

9. **Lord . . . poet:** See the *Filum Labyrinthi*, and the *Essay on Death* particularly [S]. It may be added that it was Bacon who called epitomies the moths of history, in *The Advancement of Learning*, II.ii.5.

elled by Time from the selectest of the wise of many generations. A poet is a nightingale, who sits in darkness and sings to cheer its own solitude with sweet sounds; his auditors are as men entranced by the melody of an unseen musician, who feel that they are moved and softened, yet know not whence or why. The poems of Homer and his contemporaries were the delight of infant Greece; they were the elements of that social system which is the column upon which all succeeding civilization has reposed. Homer embodied the ideal perfection of his age in human character; nor can we doubt that those who read his verses were awakened to an ambition of becoming like to Achilles, Hector, and Ulysses: the truth and beauty of friendship, patriotism, and persevering devotion to an object, were unveiled to the depths in these immortal creations: the sentiments of the auditors must have been refined and enlarged by a sympathy with such great and lovely impersonations, until from admiring they imitated, and from imitation they identified themselves with the objects of their admiration. Nor let it be objected, that these characters are remote from moral perfection, and that they can by no means be considered as edifying patterns for general imitation. Every epoch, under names more or less specious, has deified its peculiar errors; Revenge is the naked idol of the worship of a semibarbarous age; and Self-deceit is the veiled image of unknown evil, before which luxury and satiety lie prostrate. But a poet considers the vices of his contemporaries as a temporary dress in which his creations must be arrayed, and which cover without concealing the eternal proportions of their beauty. An epic or dramatic personage is understood to wear them around his soul, as he may the ancient armour or the modern uniform around his body; whilst it is easy to conceive a dress more graceful than either. The beauty of the internal nature cannot be so far concealed by its accidental vesture, but that the spirit of its form shall communicate itself to the very disguise, and indicate the shape it hides from the manner in which it is worn. A majestic form and graceful motions will express themselves through the most barbarous and tasteless costume. Few poets of the highest class have chosen to exhibit the beauty of their conceptions in its naked truth and splendour; and it is doubtful whether the alloy of costume, habit, &c., be not necessary to temper this planetary music for mortal ears.

The whole objection, however, of the immorality

of poetry rests upon a misconception of the manner in which poetry acts to produce the moral improvement of man. Ethical science arranges the elements which poetry has created, and propounds schemes and proposes examples of civil and domestic life: nor is it for want of admirable doctrines that men hate, and despise, and censure, and deceive, and subjugate one another. But poetry acts in another and diviner manner. It awakens and enlarges the mind itself by rendering it the receptacle of a thousand unapprehended combinations of thought. Poetry lifts the veil from the hidden beauty of the world, and makes familiar objects be as if they were not familiar; it reproduces all that it represents, and the impersonations clothed in its Elysian light stand thenceforward in the minds of those who have once contemplated them as memorials of that gentle and exalted content [10] which extends itself over all thoughts and actions with which it coexists. The great secret of morals is love; or a going out of our own nature, and an identification of ourselves with the beautiful which exists in thought, action, or person, not our own. A man, to be greatly good, must imagine intensely and comprehensively; he must put himself in the place of another and of many others; the pains and pleasures of his species must become his own. The great instrument of moral good is the imagination; and poetry administers to the effect by acting upon the cause. Poetry enlarges the circumference of the imagination by replenishing it with thoughts of ever new delight, which have the power of attracting and assimilating to their own nature all other thoughts, and which form new intervals and interstices whose void for ever craves fresh food. Poetry strengthens the faculty which is the organ of the moral nature of man, in the same manner as exercise strengthens a limb. A poet therefore would do ill to embody his own conceptions of right and wrong, which are usually those of his place and time, in his poetical creations, which participate in neither. By this assumption of the inferior office of interpreting the effect, in which perhaps after all he might acquit himself but imperfectly, he would resign a glory in a participation in the cause. There is little danger that Homer, or any of the eternal poets, should have so far misunderstood themselves as to have abdicated this throne of their widest dominion. Those in whom the poetical faculty, though great, is less intense,

10. content: fulfillment.

as Euripides, Lucan, Tasso, Spenser, have frequently affected a moral aim, and the effect of their poetry is diminished in exact proportion to the degree in which they compel us to advert to this purpose.

Homer and the cyclic [11] poets were followed at a certain interval by the dramatic and lyrical poets of Athens, who flourished contemporaneously with all that is most perfect in the kindred expressions of the poetical faculty; architecture, painting, music, the dance, sculpture, philosophy, and, we may add, the forms of civil life. For although the scheme of Athenian society was deformed by many imperfections [12] which the poetry existing in chivalry and Christianity has erased from the habits and institutions of modern Europe; yet never at any other period has so much energy, beauty, and virtue, been developed; never was blind strength and stubborn form so disciplined and rendered subject to the will of man, or that will less repugnant to the dictates of the beautiful and the true, as during the century which preceded the death of Socrates. Of no other epoch in the history of our species have we records and fragments stamped so visibly with the image of the divinity in man. But it is poetry alone, in form, in action, or in language, which has rendered this epoch memorable above all others, and the storehouse of examples to everlasting time. For written poetry existed at that epoch simultaneously with the other arts, and it is an idle inquiry to demand which gave and which received the light, which all, as from a common focus, have scattered over the darkest periods of succeeding time. We know no more of cause and effect than a constant conjunction of events: poetry is ever found to coexist with whatever other arts contribute to the happiness and perfection of man. I appeal to what has already been established to distinguish between the cause and the effect.

It was at the period here adverted to, that the drama had its birth; and however a succeeding writer may have equalled or surpassed those few great specimens of the Athenian drama which have been preserved to us, it is indisputable that the art itself never was understood or practised according to the true philosophy of it, as at Athens. For the Athenians employed language, action, music, painting, the dance, and religious institutions, to produce a common effect in the representation of the highest idealisms of passion and of power; each division in the art was made perfect in its kind by artists of the most consummate skill, and was disciplined into a beautiful proportion and unity one towards the other. On the modern stage a few only of the elements capable of expressing the image of the poet's conception are employed at once. We have tragedy without music and dancing; and music and dancing without the highest impersonations of which they are the fit accompaniment, and both without religion and solemnity. Religious institution has indeed been usually banished from the stage. Our system of divesting the actor's face of a mask, on which the many expressions appropriated to his dramatic character might be moulded into one permanent and unchanging expression, is favourable only to a partial and inharmonious effect; it is fit for nothing but a monologue, where all the attention may be directed to some great master of ideal mimicry. The modern practice of blending comedy with tragedy, though liable to great abuse in point of practice, is undoubtedly an extension of the dramatic circle; but the comedy should be as in *King Lear,* universal, ideal, and sublime. It is perhaps the intervention of this principle which determines the balance in favour of *King Lear* against the *Oedipus Tyrannus* or the *Agamemnon,* or, if you will, the trilogies with which they are connected; unless the intense power of the choral poetry, especially that of the latter, should be considered as restoring the equilibrium. *King Lear,* if it can sustain this comparison, may be judged to be the most perfect specimen of the dramatic art existing in the world; in spite of the narrow conditions to which the poet was subjected by the ignorance of the philosophy of the drama which has prevailed in modern Europe. Calderon,[13] in his religious *Autos,* has attempted to fulfil some of the high conditions of dramatic representation neglected by Shakespeare; such as the establishing a relation between the drama and religion, and the accommodating them to music and dancing; but he omits the observation of conditions still more important, and more is lost than gained by the substitution of the rigidly-defined and ever-repeated idealisms of a distorted superstition for the living impersonations of the truth of human passion.

11. **Cyclic poets:** poets of the cycle or body of epic poetry of which the *Iliad* and *Odyssey* alone survive.   12. **imperfections:** notably, as Shelley elsewhere insists, slavery and the inferior status of women.

13. **Calderon:** Pedro Calderón de la Barca (1600–1681), Spanish poet and dramatist. The *Autos sacramentales* are allegorical plays, of which he is the master. Shelley translated scenes from his drama, *El Magico Prodigioso.*

But I digress. — The connexion of scenic exhibitions with the improvement or corruption of the manners of men, has been universally recognized: in other words, the presence or absence of poetry in its most perfect and universal form, has been found to be connected with good and evil in conduct or habit. The corruption which has been imputed to the drama as an effect, begins, when the poetry employed in its constitution ends: I appeal to the history of manners whether the periods of the growth of the one and the decline of the other have not corresponded with an exactness equal to any example of moral cause and effect.

The drama at Athens, or wheresoever else it may have approached to its perfection, ever co-existed with the moral and intellectual greatness of the age. The tragedies of the Athenian poets are as mirrors in which the spectator beholds himself, under a thin disguise of circumstance, stript of all but that ideal perfection and energy which every one feels to be the internal type of all that he loves, admires, and would become. The imagination is enlarged by a sympathy with pains and passions so mighty, that they distend in their conception the capacity of that by which they are conceived; the good affections are strengthened by pity, indignation, terror, and sorrow; and an exalted calm is prolonged from the satiety of this high exercise of them into the tumult of familiar life: [14] even crime is disarmed of half its horror and all its contagion by being represented as the fatal consequence of the unfathomable agencies of nature; error is thus divested of its wilfulness; men can no longer cherish it as the creation of their choice. In a drama of the highest order there is little food for censure or hatred; it teaches rather self-knowledge and self-respect. Neither the eye nor the mind can see itself, unless reflected upon that which it resembles. The drama, so long as it continues to express poetry, is as a prismatic and many-sided mirror, which collects the brightest rays [15] of human nature and divides and reproduces them from the simplicity of these elementary forms, and touches them with majesty and beauty, and multiplies all that it reflects, and endows it with the power of propagating its like wherever it may fall.

But in periods of the decay of social life, the drama sympathizes with that decay. Tragedy becomes a cold imitation of the form of the great masterpieces of antiquity, divested of all harmonious accompaniment of the kindred arts; and often the very form misunderstood, or a weak attempt to teach certain doctrines, which the writer considers as moral truths; and which are usually no more than specious flatteries of some gross vice or weakness, with which the author, in common with his auditors, is infected. Hence what has been called the classical and domestic drama. Addison's *Cato* is a specimen of the one; and would it were not superfluous to cite examples of the other! To such purposes poetry cannot be made subservient. Poetry is a sword of lightning, ever unsheathed, which consumes the scabbard that would contain it. And thus we observe that all dramatic writings of this nature are unimaginative in a singular degree; they affect sentiment and passion, which, divested of imagination, are other names for caprice and appetite. The period in our own history of the grossest degradation of the drama is the reign of Charles II, when all forms in which poetry had been accustomed to be expressed became hymns to the triumph of kingly power over liberty and virtue. Milton stood alone illuminating an age unworthy of him. At such periods the calculating principle pervades all the forms of dramatic exhibition, and poetry ceases to be expressed upon them. Comedy loses its ideal universality: wit succeeds to humour; we laugh from self complacency and triumph, instead of pleasure; malignity, sarcasm, and contempt, succeed to sympathetic merriment; we hardly laugh, but we smile. Obscenity, which is ever blasphemy against the divine beauty in life, becomes, from the very veil which it assumes, more active if less disgusting: it is a monster for which the corruption of society for ever brings forth new food, which it devours in secret.

The drama being that form under which a greater number of modes of expression of poetry are susceptible of being combined with any other, the connexion of poetry and social good is more observable in the drama than in whatever other form. And it is indisputable that the highest perfection of human society has ever corresponded with the highest dramatic excellence; and that the corruption or the extinction of the drama in a nation where it has once flourished, is a mark of a corruption of manners, and an extinction of the energies which sustain the soul of social life. But, as Machiavelli says of political institutions, that

---

14. **The imagination . . . life:** Shelley's comment on Aristotle's doctrine of the catharsis of tragedy: "effecting, through pity and terror, the purgation of such passions," *Poetics*, 6. Cf. the last line of Milton's *Samson Agonistes*: "And calm of mind, all passion spend" (p. 292, above). 15. **as . . . rays:** Cf. *PU*, III.iii.53.

life may be preserved and renewed, if men should arise capable of bringing back the drama to its principles. And this is true with respect to poetry in its most extended sense: all language, institution and form, require not only to be produced but to be sustained: the office and character of a poet participates in the divine nature as regards providence, no less than as regards creation.

. . . .

About seven pages of a historical sketch are here omitted as of less permanent interest.

. . . .

Dante and Milton were both deeply penetrated with the ancient religion of the civilised world; and its spirit exists in their poetry probably in the same proportion as its forms survived in the unreformed worship of modern Europe. The one preceded and the other followed the Reformation at almost equal intervals. Dante was the first religious reformer, and Luther surpassed him rather in the rudeness and acrimony, than in the boldness of his censures of papal usurpation. Dante was the first awakener of entranced Europe; he created a language, in itself music and persuasion, out of a chaos of inharmonious barbarisms. He was the congregator of those great spirits who presided over the resurrection of learning; the Lucifer of that starry flock which in the thirteenth century shone forth from republican Italy, as from a heaven, into the darkness of the benighted world. His very words are instinct with spirit; each is as a spark, a burning atom of inextinguishable thought; and many yet lie covered in the ashes of their birth, and pregnant with the lightning which has yet found no conductor. All high poetry is infinite; it is as the first acorn, which contained all oaks potentially. Veil after veil may be undrawn, and the inmost naked beauty of the meaning never exposed. A great poem is a fountain for ever overflowing with the waters of wisdom and delight; and after one person and one age has exhausted all its divine effluence which their peculiar relations enable them to share, another and yet another succeeds, and new relations are ever developed, the source of an unforeseen and an unconceived delight.

The age immediately succeeding to that of Dante, Petrarch, and Boccaccio, was characterised by a revival of painting, sculpture, and architecture. Chaucer caught the sacred inspiration, and the superstructure of English literature is based upon the materials of Italian invention.

But let us not be betrayed from a defence into a critical history of poetry and its influence on society. Be it enough to have pointed out the effects of poets, in the large and true sense of the word, upon their own and all succeeding times.

But poets have been challenged to resign the civic crown to reasoners and mechanists, on another plea. It is admitted that the exercise of the imagination is most delightful, but it is alleged that that of reason is more useful. Let us examine as the grounds of this distinction, what is here meant by utility. Pleasure or good, in a general sense, is that which the consciousness of a sensitive and intelligent being seeks, and in which, when found, it acquiesces. There are two kinds of pleasure, one durable, universal and permanent; the other transitory and particular. Utility may either express the means of producing the former or the latter. In the former sense, whatever strengthens and purifies the affections, enlarges the imagination, and adds spirit to sense, is useful. But a narrower meaning may be assigned to the word utility, confining it to express that which banishes the importunity of the wants of our animal nature, the surrounding men with security of life, the dispersing the grosser delusions of superstition, and the conciliating such a degree of mutual forbearance among men as may consist with the motives of personal advantage.

Undoubtedly the promoters of utility, in this limited sense, have their appointed office in society. They follow the footsteps of poets, and copy the sketches of their creations into the book of common life. They make space, and give time. Their exertions are of the highest value, so long as they confine their administration of the concerns of the inferior powers of our nature within the limits due to the superior ones. But whilst the sceptic destroys gross superstitions, let him spare to deface, as some of the French writers have defaced, the eternal truths charactered upon the imaginations of men. Whilst the mechanist abridges, and the political economist combines labour, let them beware that their speculations, for want of correspondence with those first principles which belong to the imagination, do not tend, as they have in modern England, to exasperate at once the extremes of luxury and want. They have exemplified the saying, ' To him that hath, more shall be given; and from him that hath not, the little that he hath shall be taken away.' [16] The rich have become richer, and the

16. 'To . . . away': See Mark 4:25.

poor have become poorer; and the vessel of the state is driven between the Scylla and Charybdis of anarchy and despotism. Such are the effects which must ever flow from an unmitigated exercise of the calculating faculty.

It is difficult to define pleasure in its highest sense; the definition involving a number of apparent paradoxes. For, from an inexplicable defect of harmony in the constitution of human nature, the pain of the inferior is frequently connected with the pleasures of the superior portions of our being. Sorrow, terror, anguish, despair itself, are often the chosen expressions of an approximation to the highest good. Our sympathy in tragic fiction depends on this principle; tragedy delights by affording a shadow of the pleasure which exists in pain. This is the source also of the melancholy which is inseparable from the sweetest melody. The pleasure that is in sorrow is sweeter than the pleasure of pleasure itself. And hence the saying, ' It is better to go to the house of mourning, than to the house of mirth.' [17] Not that this highest species of pleasure is necessarily linked with pain. The delight of love and friendship, the ecstasy of the admiration of nature, the joy of the perception and still more of the creation of poetry, is often wholly unalloyed.

The production and assurance of pleasure in this highest sense is true utility. Those who produce and preserve this pleasure are poets or poetical philosophers.

The exertions of Locke, Hume, Gibbon, Voltaire, Rousseau,[18] and their disciples, in favour of oppressed and deluded humanity, are entitled to the gratitude of mankind. Yet it is easy to calculate the degree of moral and intellectual improvement which the world would have exhibited, had they never lived. A little more nonsense would have been talked for a century or two; and perhaps a few more men, women, and children, burnt as heretics. We might not at this moment have been congratulating each other on the abolition of the Inquisition in Spain. But it exceeds all imagination to conceive what would have been the moral condition of the world if neither Dante, Petrarch, Boccaccio, Chaucer, Shakespeare, Calderon, Lord Bacon, nor Milton, had ever existed; if Raphael and Michael Angelo had never been born; if the Hebrew poetry had never been translated; if a revival of the study of Greek literature had never

taken place; if no monuments of ancient sculpture had been handed down to us; and if the poetry of the religion of the ancient world had been extinguished together with its belief. The human mind could never, except by the intervention of these excitements, have been awakened to the invention of the grosser sciences, and that application of analytical reasoning to the aberrations of society, which it is now attempted to exalt over the direct expression of the inventive and creative faculty itself.

We have more moral, political and historical wisdom, than we know how to reduce into practice; we have more scientific and economical knowledge than can be accommodated to the just distribution of the produce which it multiplies. The poetry in these systems of thought, is concealed by the accumulation of facts and calculating processes. There is no want of knowledge respecting what is wisest and best in morals, government, and political economy, or at least, what is wiser and better than what men now practise and endure. But we let ' I dare not wait upon I would, like the poor cat in the adage.' [19] We want the creative faculty to imagine that which we know; we want the generous impulse to act that which we imagine; we want the poetry of life: our calculations have outrun conception; we have eaten more than we can digest. The cultivation of those sciences which have enlarged the limits of the empire of man over the external world, has, for want of the poetical faculty, proportionally circumscribed those of the internal world; and man, having enslaved the elements, remains himself a slave. To what but a cultivation of the mechanical arts in a degree disproportioned to the presence of the creative faculty, which is the basis of all knowledge, is to be attributed the abuse of all invention for abridging and combining labour, to the exasperation of the inequality of mankind? From what other cause has it arisen that the discoveries which should have lightened, have added a weight to the curse imposed on Adam? Poetry, and the principle of Self, of which money is the visible incarnation, are the God and Mammon of the world.

The functions of the poetical faculty are two-fold; by one it creates new materials of knowledge and power and pleasure; by the other it engenders in the mind a desire to reproduce and arrange them according to a certain rhythm and order which

---

17. 'It . . . mirth': See Eccles. 7:2.   18. Rousseau: Although Rousseau has been thus classed, he was essentially a poet. The others, even Voltaire, were mere reasoners [S].

19. 'I . . . adage': *Macbeth*, I.vii.44.

may be called the beautiful and the good. The cultivation of poetry is never more to be desired than at periods when, from an excess of the selfish and calculating principle, the accumulation of the materials of external life exceed the quantity of the power of assimilating them to the internal laws of human nature. The body has then become too unwieldy for that which animates it.

Poetry is indeed something divine. It is at once the centre and circumference of knowledge; it is that which comprehends all science, and that to which all science must be referred. It is at the same time the root and blossom of all other systems of thought; it is that from which all spring, and that which adorns all; and that which, if blighted, denies the fruit and the seed, and withholds from the barren world the nourishment and the succession of the scions of the tree of life. It is the perfect and consummate surface and bloom of all things; it is as the odour and the colour of the rose to the texture of the elements which compose it, as the form and splendour of unfaded beauty to the secrets of anatomy and corruption. What were virtue, love, patriotism, friendship — what were the scenery of this beautiful universe which we inhabit; what were our consolations on this side of the grave — and what were our aspirations beyond it, if poetry did not ascend to bring light and fire from those eternal regions where the owl-winged faculty of calculation dare not ever soar? Poetry is not like reasoning, a power to be exerted according to the determination of the will. A man cannot say, ' I will compose poetry.' The greatest poet even cannot say it; for the mind in creation is as a fading coal, which some invisible influence, like an inconstant wind, awakens to transitory brightness; this power arises from within, like the colour of a flower which fades and changes as it is developed, and the conscious portions of our natures are unprophetic either of its approach or its departure. Could this influence be durable in its original purity and force, it is impossible to predict the greatness of the results; but when composition begins, inspiration is already on the decline, and the most glorious poetry that has ever been communicated to the world is probably a feeble shadow of the original conceptions of the poet. I appeal to the greatest poets of the present day, whether it is not an error to assert that the finest passages of poetry are produced by labour and study. The toil and the delay recommended by critics, can be justly interpreted to mean no more than a careful observa-

tion of the inspired moments, and an artificial connexion of the spaces between their suggestions by the intertexture of conventional expressions; a necessity only imposed by the limitedness of the poetical faculty itself; for Milton conceived the *Paradise Lost* as a whole before he executed it in portions. We have his own authority also for the muse having ' dictated ' to him the ' unpremeditated song.' [20] And let this be an answer to those who would allege the fifty-six various readings of the first line of the *Orlando Furioso*. Compositions so produced are to poetry what mosaic is to painting. This instinct and intuition of the poetical faculty is still more observable in the plastic and pictorial arts; a great statue or picture grows under the power of the artist as a child in the mother's womb; and the very mind which directs the hands in formation is incapable of accounting to itself for the origin, the gradations, or the media of the process.

Poetry is the record of the best and happiest moments of the happiest and best minds. We are aware of evanescent visitations of thought and feeling sometimes associated with place or person, sometimes regarding our own mind alone, and always arising unforeseen and departing unbidden, but elevating and delightful beyond all expression: so that even in the desire and regret they leave, there cannot but be pleasure, participating as it does in the nature of its object. It is as it were the interpenetration of a diviner nature [21] through our own; but its footsteps are like those of a wind over the sea, which the coming calm erases, and whose traces remain only, as on the wrinkled sand which paves it. These and corresponding conditions of being are experienced principally by those of the most delicate sensibility and the most enlarged imagination; and the state of mind produced by them is at war with every base desire. The enthusiasm of virtue, love, patriotism, and friendship, is essentially linked with such emotions; and whilst they last, self appears as what it is, an atom to a universe. Poets are not only subject to these experiences as spirits of the most refined organization, but they can colour all that they combine with the evanescent hues of this ethereal world; a word, a trait in the representation of a scene or a passion, will touch the enchanted chord, and reanimate, in

---

20. unpremeditated song: *Paradise Lost*, IX.21–24.   **21. diviner nature:** Cf. "A Poet is indeed a thing etherially light, winged, and sacred; nor can he compose any thing worth calling poetry until he becomes inspired, and, as it were, mad, or whilst any reason remains in him," Plato, *Ion*, Shelley's translation.

those who have ever experienced these emotions, the sleeping, the cold, the buried image of the past. Poetry thus makes immortal all that is best and most beautiful in the world; it arrests the vanishing apparitions which haunt the interlunations of life, and veiling them, or in language or in form, sends them forth among mankind, bearing sweet news of kindred joy to those with whom their sisters abide — abide, because there is no portal of expression from the caverns of the spirit which they inhabit into the universe of things. Poetry redeems from decay the visitations of the divinity in man.

Poetry turns all things to loveliness; it exalts the beauty of that which is most beautiful, and it adds beauty to that which is most deformed; it marries exultation and horror, grief and pleasure, eternity and change; it subdues to union under its light yoke, all irreconcilable things. It transmutes all that it touches, and every form moving within the radiance of its presence is changed by wondrous sympathy to an incarnation of the spirit which it breathes: its secret alchemy turns to potable gold the poisonous waters which flow from death through life; it strips the veil of familiarity from the world, and lays bare the naked and sleeping beauty, which is the spirit of its forms.

All things exist as they are perceived; at least in relation to the percipient. ' The mind is its own place, and of itself can make a heaven of hell, a hell of heaven.' [22] But poetry defeats the curse which binds us to be subjected to the accident of surrounding impressions. And whether it spreads its own figured curtain, or withdraws life's dark veil from before the scene of things, it equally creates for us a being within our being. It makes us the inhabitants of a world to which the familiar world is a chaos. It reproduces the common universe of which we are portions and percipients, and it purges from our inward sight the film of familiarity [23] which obscures from us the wonder of our being. It compels us to feel that which we perceive, and to imagine that which we know. It creates anew the universe, after it has been annihilated in our minds by the recurrence of impressions blunted by reiteration. It justifies the bold and true words

of Tasso: *Non merita nome di creatore, se non Iddio ed il Poeta.*[24]

A poet, as he is the author to others of the highest wisdom, pleasure, virtue and glory, so he ought personally to be the happiest, the best, the wisest, and the most illustrious of men. As to his glory, let time be challenged to declare whether the fame of any other institutor of human life be comparable to that of a poet. That he is the wisest, the happiest, and the best, inasmuch as he is a poet, is equally incontrovertible: the greatest poets have been men of the most spotless virtue, of the most consummate prudence, and, if we would look into the interior of their lives, the most fortunate of men: and the exceptions, as they regard those who possessed the poetic faculty in a high yet inferior degree, will be found on consideration to confine rather than destroy the rule. Let us for a moment stoop to the arbitration of popular breath, and usurping and uniting in our own persons the incompatible characters of accuser, witness, judge, and executioner, let us decide without trial, testimony, or form, that certain motives of those who are ' there sitting where we dare not soar,' [25] are reprehensible. Let us assume that Homer was a drunkard, that Virgil was a flatterer, that Horace was a coward, that Tasso was a madman, that Lord Bacon was a peculator, that Raphael was a libertine, that Spenser was a poet laureate. It is inconsistent with this division of our subject to cite living poets, but posterity has done ample justice to the great names now referred to. Their errors have been weighed and found to have been dust in the balance; if their sins ' were as scarlet, they are now white as snow ': [26] they have been washed in the blood of the mediator and redeemer, Time. Observe in what a ludicrous chaos the imputations of real or fictitious crime have been confused in the contemporary calumnies against poetry and poets; consider how little is, as it appears — or appears, as it is; look to your own motives, and judge not, lest ye be judged.

Poetry, as has been said, differs in this respect from logic, that it is not subject to the control of the active powers of the mind, and that its birth and recurrence have no necessary connexion with the consciousness or will. It is presumptuous to determine that these are the necessary conditions of all mental causation, when mental effects are ex-

---

22. 'The ... heaven': See *Paradise Lost*, I.254.   **23. film of familiarity:** Cf. "by awakening the mind's attention from the lethargy of custom and directing it to the loveliness and the wonders of the world before us; an inexhaustible treasure, but for which, in consequence of the film of familiarity and selfish solicitude we have eyes, yet see not, ears that hear not, and hearts that neither feel nor understand" (Coleridge, *Biographia Literaria*, XIV, p. 612, above).

24. *Non ... Poeta:* No one deserves the name of creator except God and the Poet.   **25.** 'there ... soar': See *Paradise Lost*, IV.829.   **26.** 'were ... snow': Isa. 1:18.

perienced unsusceptible of being referred to them. The frequent recurrence of the poetical power, it is obvious to suppose, may produce in the mind a habit of order and harmony correlative with its own nature and with its effects upon other minds. But in the intervals of inspiration, and they may be frequent without being durable, a poet becomes a man, and is abandoned to the sudden reflux of the influences under which others habitually live. But as he is more delicately organized than other men, and sensible to pain and pleasure, both his own and that of others, in a degree unknown to them, he will avoid the one and pursue the other with an ardour proportioned to this difference. And he renders himself obnoxious to calumny, when he neglects to observe the circumstances under which these objects of universal pursuit and flight have disguised themselves in one another's garments.

But there is nothing necessarily evil in this error, and thus cruelty, envy, revenge, avarice, and the passions purely evil, have never formed any portion of the popular imputations on the lives of poets.

I have thought it most favourable to the cause of truth to set down these remarks according to the order in which they were suggested to my mind, by a consideration of the subject itself, instead of observing the formality of a polemical reply; but if the view which they contain be just, they will be found to involve a refutation of the arguers against poetry, so far at least as regards the first division of the subject. I can readily conjecture what should have moved the gall of some learned and intelligent writers who quarrel with certain versifiers; I confess myself, like them, unwilling to be stunned by the Theseids [27] of the hoarse Codri [28] of the day. Bavius and Maevius [29] undoubtedly are, as they ever were, insufferable persons. But it belongs to a philosophical critic to distinguish rather than confound.

The first part of these remarks has related to poetry in its elements and principles; and it has been shown, as well as the narrow limits assigned them would permit, that what is called poetry, in a restricted sense, has a common source with all other forms of order and of beauty, according to which the materials of human life are susceptible of being arranged, and which is poetry in a universal sense.

The second part will have for its object an application of these principles to the present state of the cultivation of poetry, and a defence of the attempt to idealize the modern forms of manners and opinions, and compel them into a subordination to the imaginative and creative faculty. For the literature of England, an energetic development of which has ever preceded or accompanied a great and free development of the national will, has arisen as it were from a new birth. In spite of the low-thoughted envy which would undervalue contemporary merit, our own will be a memorable age in intellectual achievements, and we live among such philosophers and poets as surpass beyond comparison any who have appeared since the last national struggle for civil and religious liberty. The most unfailing herald, companion, and follower of the awakening of a great people to work a beneficial change in opinion or institution, is poetry. At such periods there is an accumulation of the power of communicating and receiving intense and impassioned conceptions respecting man and nature. The persons in whom this power resides may often, as far as regards many portions of their nature, have little apparent correspondence with that spirit of good of which they are the ministers. But even whilst they deny and abjure, they are yet compelled to serve, the power which is seated on the throne of their own soul. It is impossible to read the compositions of the most celebrated writers of the present day without being startled with the electric life which burns within their words. They measure the circumference and sound the depths of human nature with a comprehensive and all-penetrating spirit, and they are themselves perhaps the most sincerely astonished at its manifestations; for it is less their spirit than the spirit of the age. Poets are the hierophants of an unapprehended inspiration; the mirrors of the gigantic shadows which futurity casts upon the present; the words which express what they understand not; the trumpets which sing to battle, and feel not what they inspire; the influence which is moved not, but moves. Poets are the unacknowledged legislators of the world.

---

27. **Theseids**: inferior epics.   28. **Codri**: Codrus was satirized by Juvenal.   29. **Bavius and Maevius**: poetasters satirized by Virgil.

1821

WALTER J. BATE, *Editor*

John Keats

1795–1821

More than any other great poet, not only in English but in European literature, Keats is distinguished by his unusual promise. He is the classic example of the gifted poet who died young. Before his death at the age of twenty-five, he succeeded in writing verse that, in latent imaginative power and in mastery of phrase, ranks among the highest achievements in English poetry. Yet it is plain that his ability had only started to unfold. Far from being a mere youthful prodigy, he hardly began to write poetry until he was eighteen years old, and little of what he wrote before the age of twenty-two was of high value. In every way, his talent was clearly the sort that grows and improves with time and experience. Moreover, he possessed unusual sincerity and honesty. Such qualities are not only admirable in themselves; they also encourage an eager and open readiness of mind, a constant desire to improve. They prevent a poet from settling, with self-satisfaction or defensive pride, into one specialized manner. Keats's development after the age of twenty-two took massive and sure strides every few months. It is characteristic that, at the close of his brief career, we find him preparing virtually to discard the kinds of poetry with which he had been experimenting in favor of one that was very different and more demanding than any attained during the nineteenth century. Few English poets, therefore, have appealed to a greater variety of readers than Keats. For, besides the attraction of the high quality of the poetry he did write, there is a perennial fascination in speculating about the direction his talent would ultimately have taken. Finally, his rapid development provides us with a rare opportunity to discover what qualities and influences most stimulate and direct poetic genius.

LIFE OF KEATS

Keats was born in London at the end of October, 1795. The trials, anxieties, and loneliness of his brief life make a moving story. But his ability to prevent them from embittering and thwarting his character is even more moving to contemplate. When Keats was only eight years of age, his father, who kept a livery stable, was killed by a fall from a horse. Before he was fifteen his mother died of tuberculosis, leaving Keats the eldest of four orphans. By the time he was trying seriously to write poetry, his brother George left England and emigrated to America; and the same year (1818) his brother Tom died of tuberculosis, foreshadowing Keats's own death from tuberculosis three years later. Alone, bewildered, financially pressed, rendered still more anxious by an intense but unsatisfactory love affair, and with his poetry relatively unappreciated, he continued to hold before himself the ideals of sincerity, open-mindedness, and generosity. As a result, his outlook — as much as that of any other poet since Shakespeare — is characterized by a cheerful humor, an enthusiastic gusto, and an extraordinarily sympathetic and tolerant understanding of other people.

After the death of his parents, Keats, his two younger brothers, and a still younger sister were left in the hands of his maternal grandmother. Doubting her ability to look after them adequately, the grandmother, who was to die herself in another four years, appointed two businessmen as guardians to the four orphans, and placed in trust a substantial sum of money which, if Keats had received his share, would have freed him from want and possibly have lengthened his life. But the money had become tied up through unforeseen complications; there was a lawsuit that was to last almost twenty years; and the guardians proved to have been poorly selected. Keats, meanwhile, was attending a small school at Enfield, where he had become a close friend of Charles Cowden Clarke, the son of the headmaster. Clarke, eight years older, was struck by Keats's "high-mindedness, his utter unconsciousness of a mean motive, his placability, his generosity." Clarke, more than anyone else, awakened Keats's interest in literature. The two enthusiastically read and studied poetry together. When Keats came to Spenser's *Faerie Queene,* he went through it, said Clarke, "as a young horse would through a spring meadow — ramping." The magic of Spenser's phrasing opened a new door to him, and Keats responded with an excited imagination. In reading one line of *The Faerie Queene,* for example, he hoisted himself up, according to Clarke, "and looked burly and dominant, as he said, 'What an image that is — *sea-shouldering whales!*'" But the young Keats was to have less opportunity than he hoped for reading and helpful guidance. A year after his mother's death, his narrow and opinionated guardian, Richard Abbey, who felt that schooling beyond the elementary stage had little practical use, withdrew him from Enfield, and had him apprenticed to an apothecary-surgeon at Edmonton. Keats still made efforts, however, to walk over to the school at Enfield in order to visit Clarke and borrow books.

After four years of his apprenticeship (1811–15), Keats entered Guy's and St. Thomas's hospitals, London, as a medical student, remained there for almost a year, and received a certificate allowing him to practice. Keats, who was now twenty-one, had meanwhile tried to write some poetry; and the ambition to become a poet was taking a strong hold on his imagination. He hoped to become acquainted with some of the literary figures of the day, although he had no idea where to turn or how to discriminate among them. He read some of the poorer poets who were fashionable at the time, as well as some of the better ones. But at the back of his mind there was still a vivid sense of the great poets of England's past, especially Shakespeare; and it is these models rather than his contemporaries that were ultimately to nourish and develop his latent genius. Shortly before the close of his term of study at Guy's and St. Thomas's hospitals, Keats had met Leigh Hunt, well-known as a London literary figure, liberal in politics, a copious writer in both verse and prose, and editor of a magazine called the *Examiner.* Keats, who was attracted by Hunt's amiability and political liberalism, frequently visited him and his family at Hampstead, just outside London, and through Hunt met various men of literary interests, such as Charles Lamb, and Benjamin Robert Haydon, the painter. Touched by this attention, Keats wrote sonnets to Hunt and Haydon expressing his enthusiasm. Early in 1817 his first volume of *Poems* was published. It was Haydon who took Keats to see the Elgin marbles, a remarkable collection of sculpture and fragments, chiefly from the Parthenon at Athens. The sight of the collection increased Keats's interest in Greek art, and was to leave its effect on the calm and sculptural imagery of his later poetry, especially the great "Ode on a Grecian Urn."

In the spring of 1817, Keats went to the Isle of Wight and began his long poem *Endymion,* which he finished the following autumn. Both the small volume that preceded it and *Endymion* received little more than unfavorable notice. Political sentiment, at this time, frequently biased literary criticism; and, since Keats, when he was noticed at all, was regarded as a disciple of the radical Hunt, the unfavorable reviews in the Tory magazines were sharpened even further by political animosity. *Blackwood's* published a series of articles on "The Cockney School of Poetry," one of which (August, 1818) contained a heavy-handed attack on Keats, and sarcastically advised him to return to the apothecary business. The following month, the *Quarterly* ridiculed *Endymion.* The attacks were sufficiently venomous to encourage the rise of the sentimental legend, spread by Byron and Shelley, that Keats's early death was hastened by the hostile reception of his poems. But, however sensitive Keats was to the hostility of the reviews, he took it with manly courage. In fact, he was already becoming a severe and discriminating critic of his own work. During the previous winter (1817–18) he had been trying to write a more compact poetry, and to some extent had succeeded in *Isabella* (written early in 1818) and in shorter poems. Also, he had become interested in the theater, and had written for the *Champion* magazine on Edmund Kean, the Shakespearean actor. This sharpened his growing interest in the drama. The year 1818 also marks a sudden enlarging and maturing of his conception of the function of poetry — a conception in which poetry is of value only to the degree that it rises above the poet's own personality and is able to render the concrete world with objective truth and sympathetic warmth. Measured by this high standard, *Endymion,* he now realized, was "mawkish," and his mind, in writing it, had been "like a pack of scattered cards."

In the summer of 1818, Keats went on a walking tour through northern England, Scotland, and Ireland with his friend Charles Brown. A severe sore throat, the first sign of his fatal illness, forced him to conclude the trip early. Meanwhile, his brother George had already left for America. His other brother, Tom, was now gravely ill; and Keats nursed him until his death in December. Also, Keats had now met Fanny Brawne, the young daughter of a widow living at Hampstead. This moving, pathetic love affair, greatly intensified by his loneliness, seemed to bring Keats little except further anxiety and, after his illness became pronounced, an almost wild despair. His financial difficulties were growing. Yet, from the autumn of 1818 through the summer of the next year, Keats composed his greatest poetry: *Hyperion, The Eve of St. Agnes,* then the great odes, and, finally, during the summer of 1819, *Lamia* and a thorough revision of *Hyperion.* After the fall of 1819, Keats was able to do little except revise some of the poems that were to be published in his third and last volume (1820). He was soon suffering continual hemorrhages in the lungs, and, being assured by his physician that another English winter would kill him, he borrowed money and sailed in September, 1820, for Italy in the care of his friend, Joseph Severn. More even than the prolonged physical pain, the sense that everything in his life was now lost at last made him feel, he said, as though he had "coals of fire in my breast. It surprises me that the human heart is capable of containing and bearing so much misery." He died in Rome on February 23, 1821.

GENERAL CHARACTER OF KEATS'S POETRY

When we think of Keats's poetry, certain qualities at once stand out that distinguish it from the work of other poets. To begin with, his poetry is unusually concrete. The images and allusions are not abstract, as they often are in the verse of some of his contemporaries. For example, Shelley and even Wordsworth often *describe* an object, enumerating or suggesting its characteristics, whereas Keats actually *presents* the object. Thus Wordsworth begins one of his sonnets:

> It is a beauteous evening, calm and free;
> The holy time is quiet as a nun
> Breathless with adoration . . .

The evening is described successively as "beauteous," "calm," "free," and "quiet" — words which state the effect of the evening on the poet. The evening in Keats's "Ode to a Nightingale" is not "described." Specific, concrete objects are presented as they appear in the growing dark; and the general character of the evening and its effect on the poet are inferred from these by the reader:

> I cannot see what flowers are at my feet,
> Nor what soft incense hangs upon the boughs,
> But, in embalmèd darkness, guess each sweet
> Wherewith the seasonable month endows
> The grass, the thicket, and the fruit-tree wild . . .

Because of this strong and confident sense of concrete objects, Keats's poetry is sensuous. The reader's own senses are stimulated as if the object were physically present. Keats speaks, in the "Ode on Melancholy," of "the wealth of *globèd* peonies"; and one can virtually feel their roundness. Again, there is a vigorous, almost sculpturesque sense of outline and spatial depth about the great figures in *Hyperion,* as when Hyperion at night arose, "and on the stars / Lifted his *curvèd lids,* and kept them wide," or in Thea kneeling before the "frozen" despairing figure of Saturn:

One moon, with alteration slow, had shed
Her silver seasons four upon the night,
And still these two were postured motionless,
Like natural sculpture in cathedral cavern . . .

The physical firmness of Keats's imagery has intensity as well as depth and dimension. Thus he writes of the bitter Titan, Hyperion (Book I, ll. 186–89),

when he would *taste the spicy wreaths*
Of incense, breathed aloft from sacred hills,
Instead of *sweets, his ample palate took*
Savor of poisonous brass and metal sick . . .

The last example is typical in another way. For more than any other English poet, with the possible exception of Shakespeare, Keats exploits the physically direct senses of taste and touch in his imagery, as when the two interplay in the last stanza of the "Ode on Melancholy":

and *aching* Pleasure nigh,
Turning to Poison *while the bee-mouth sips* . . .
Though seen of none save him whose *strenuous tongue*
Can *burst* Joy's grape *against his palate fine;*
His soul shall *taste* the sadness of her might . . .

Keats's alert and immediate sensuousness is also made active and complete by his ability to focus more than one kind of sense impression into a single image. This would partly include the use of " synaesthesia," that is, the use of one sense impression to interpret or suggest another. Examples would be Keats's phrases, " the *touch* of *scent,*" "*fragrant* and enwreathèd *light,*" " embalmèd darkness," or " But here there is no *light,* / Save what from heaven is *with the breezes blown.*" Keats's brilliant use of synaesthetic imagery was to leave a pronounced effect on English and American poetry from the beginning of the Victorian era to the present day. But more uniquely characteristic of Keats is the use of one sense impression not to *replace* but to *supplement* others, and thus secure a richer, more massive completeness. In such instances, an appeal to several senses becomes actively unified into a single perception, sometimes through a direct listing, as " hushed, cool-rooted flowers, fragrant-eyed," but more often through indirect suggestion, as in the " draught of vintage," in the " Ode to a Nightingale," which is described as *" Tasting of . . . sunburnt* mirth "; or as when the senses of sight, touch, and odor are brought to bear in " fragrance soft and coolness to the eye," or " the small warm rain / Melts out the frozen incense from all flowers."

In addition to its firm, physical sensuousness, Keats's poetry, like that of Shakespeare, has a sympathetic depth, a penetrating and clairvoyant " in-feeling " that captures the inner vital character of the object. In *The Eve of St. Agnes,* for example, Madeline, retiring for the night, " unclasps her *warmèd* jewels." And the stained-glass casement is so suffused by the actively flowing moonlight that the multitude of soft colors interplay like " the tiger-moth's *deep-damasked* wings "; while in the midst is " a shielded scutcheon *blushed* with blood of queens and kings." Often, when joined with Keats's strong sense for tactile imagery, this sympathetic in-feeling can arouse a direct, organically felt participation: in *Endymion,* there are the active and nervous minnows " staying their wavy bodies 'gainst the stream "; in *The Eve of St. Agnes,* " The hare *limped trembling* through the frozen grass "; and, in the " Ode to a Nightingale," the sense of muscular pressure is felt in the description of the bird singing of summer " in *full-throated* ease." So, in his reading, Keats responded immediately to Spenser's " *sea-shouldering* whales " or to Shakespeare's description, in *Venus and Adonis,* of the delicate withdrawal of a snail: " He has left nothing," exclaimed Keats, " to say about nothing or anything: for look at snails . . ."; and he quotes

As the snail, whose *tender horns being hit,*
Shrinks back into its shelly cave *with pain*
And there all *smothered up* in shade doth sit, . . .

If a sparrow, he wrote in another letter, " comes before my window I take part in its existence and pick about the gravel."

We may describe the principal characteristic of Keats's poetry, therefore, as a firm and tenacious grasp of external objects — an ability to absorb himself in them to such a degree, and to render them with such completeness and such sympathetic insight, that the mind of the poet does not (as in so much other romantic poetry) stand as a veil between the reader and the object. Instead, the identity of the poet becomes transparent, the object itself emerging untrammeled and in its total individuality.

This characteristic of Keats exemplifies his own ideal of the poet as a chameleon who is himself "the most unpoetical of any thing in existence; because he has no identity — he is continually informing — and filling some other body." Keats was gradually coming to understand the nature and value of this sympathetic openness of the imagination, and wrote illuminating comments on it. This theoretical understanding greatly encouraged and guided his own instinctive potentiality to fulfill it. With most of the literary acquaintances he met through Leigh Hunt, the high-minded young Keats had had less in common than his generosity led him to assume. Meanwhile, however, he had been reading one of the greatest of English critics and journalists, William Hazlitt (1778–1830), and had come to admire him from a distance. This energetic, penetrating journalist, who saw so clearly the weaknesses of much of the literature of his own day, had evolved a conception of poetry which assumed that greatness of any sort — in art, in morality, in every act of life — consisted in the ability to lose oneself in something bigger. Shakespeare, above all, stood out for Hazlitt as the great example of a mind that could enter into the life and character that was outside him, instead of merely projecting his own *ego*. What appealed most to Keats in Hazlitt was his emphasis on sincerity, and with it a conception of poetry that lifted it beyond mere cleverness and fashion and viewed it as a vital form of awareness and understanding. Already, at twenty-two, he had felt disconcerted to find that so many literary men seemed less eagerly interested in the concrete reality without, and in attaining a large and vivid poetic sense of its meaning, than in asserting their own sense of importance, and in saying "things which make one *start,* without making one *feel.*" After attending a party in which they talked mainly of "fashionables," and, in everything they said and did, showed a self-conscious "mannerism," it struck him "what quality went to form a man of achievement, especially in Literature, and which Shakespeare possessed so enormously — I mean *Negative Capability*" (December 21, 1817); the capacity to shed one's egoistic sense of one's own identity through a vital and sincere interest in other things. He was learning, as Goethe said at a much more advanced age, that "a subjective nature has soon talked out his little internal material, and is at last ruined by mannerism," whereas the poet whose mind becomes a window to reality "is inexhaustible, and can be always new." This concept of the function of the poet was henceforth to affect Keats's life and thought in the most valuable way. It is this salutary and fruitful ideal, more than any other, that underlay and guided his sudden, remarkable development, and that offers the surest sign of his future growth.

The influence of Shakespeare, though ultimately greater than that of Milton, was more indirect and subterraneous: it was to color first Keats's *thinking* about poetry rather than his actual verse. When Keats was forced by ill health to cut short his walking tour in the summer of 1818, he returned to Hampstead intent on writing a poem of epic proportions, *Hyperion,* which was to be treated "in a more naked and Grecian Manner" than *Endymion;* and his imagination was now dominated by the greatest of English epics, Milton's *Paradise Lost.* *Hyperion* abounds with some of the more obvious Miltonic mannerisms. The adjective, for example, is often used in place of an adverb ("through all his bulk an agony / Crept *gradual*"). There are also the "Miltonic inversions" that Keats later decided were "unEnglish," such as putting the noun before the adjective ("palace bright," "hieroglyphics old"), or the verb before the subject ("Pale wox I"). In versification, also, Keats closely followed Milton's blank verse. But the influence of Milton far transcends the mere copying of stylistic devices, and pervades the entire conception of the poem.

Though there is every indication that a second major change was about to take place in Keats's approach to poetry — a transition quite as significant as that from his early verse to the great Miltonic fragment of *Hyperion* and the odes of May, 1819 — it is doubtful whether his Shakespearean relish for concrete life would have altered. It is more likely that it would have been supplemented and deepened by his belief that poetry must justify itself on broader grounds than he had previously assumed. Had this been the case, it is not improbable that he might even have fulfilled his "greatest ambition when I do feel ambitious" — to try within another six years or so to write "a few fine plays," and perhaps eventually accomplish "a revolution in modern dramatic writing." But after the final spurt of effort during the summer of 1819, Keats was able to write very little. From now until his death, there remain only the poignant letters to continue suggesting that his poetic gift was the greatest England has witnessed during the past two centuries and a half.

TO BYRON

Written in December, 1814, this sonnet is included in order to give one brief example of Keats's early verse at its lowest point. Conventional both in its sentimental plaintiveness and in its stock diction ("plaintive lute," "dying swan," and "pleasing woe"), it also illustrates the mannered laxity Keats caught from Leigh Hunt (for example, the adverb "beamily," l. 8). The sonnet, written when Keats was nineteen, is a clear indication of how far he was from being merely "precocious."

Byron! how sweetly sad thy melody!
  Attuning still the soul to tenderness,
  As if soft Pity, with unusual stress,
Had touched her plaintive lute, and thou, being by,
Hadst caught the tones, nor suffered them to die.
  O'ershadowing sorrow doth not make thee less
  Delightful: thou thy griefs dost dress
With a bright halo, shining beamily,
  As when a cloud the golden moon doth veil,
Its sides are tinged with a resplendent glow, 10
  And like fair veins in sable marble flow;
Still warble, dying swan! still tell the tale,
  The enchanting tale, the tale of pleasing woe.

TO ONE WHO HAS BEEN LONG

To one who has been long in city pent,
  'Tis very sweet to look into the fair
  And open face of heaven — to breathe a prayer
Full in the smile of the blue firmament.
Who is more happy, when, with heart's content,
  Fatigued he sinks into some pleasant lair
  Of wavy grass, and reads a debonair
And gentle tale of love and languishment?
Returning home at evening, with an ear
  Catching the notes of Philomel° — an eye 10

TO ONE WHO HAS BEEN LONG. **10. Philomel:** nightingale.

Watching the sailing cloudlet's bright career,
  He mourns that day so soon has glided by:
E'en like the passage of an angel's tear
  That falls through the clear ether silently.

June, 1816

ON FIRST LOOKING INTO CHAPMAN'S HOMER

This, the first of Keats's great sonnets, was composed (October, 1816) after his friend, Charles Cowden Clarke, introduced him to Homer in the translation of the Elizabethan poet, George Chapman.

Much have I traveled in the realms of gold,
  And many goodly states and kingdoms seen;
  Round many western islands have I been
Which bards in fealty to Apollo hold.
Oft of one wide expanse had I been told
  That deep-browed Homer ruled as his demesne;°
  Yet did I never breathe its pure serene
Till I heard Chapman speak out loud and bold:
Then felt I like some watcher of the skies
  When a new planet swims into his ken; 10
Or like stout Cortez° when with eagle eyes
  He stared at the Pacific — and all his men
Looked at each other with a wild surmise —
  Silent, upon a peak in Darien.

[handwritten: Comparing his discovery of Homer to discovery of something big like the Pacific Ocean.]

KEEN, FITFUL GUSTS

Keen, fitful gusts are whisp'ring here and there
  Among the bushes half leafless, and dry;
  The stars look very cold about the sky,
And I have many miles on foot to fare.
Yet feel I little of the cool bleak air,
  Or of the dead leaves rustling drearily,
  Or of those silver lamps that burn on high,
Or of the distance from home's pleasant lair:
For I am brimful of the friendliness
  That in a little cottage I have found; 10
Of fair-haired Milton's eloquent distress,°
  And all his love for gentle Lycid drowned;
Of lovely Laura° in her light green dress,
  And faithful Petrarch gloriously crowned.

Autumn, 1816

CHAPMAN'S HOMER. **6. demesne:** realm. **11. Cortez:** mistaken for Balboa. KEEN, FITFUL GUSTS. **11. Milton's . . . distress:** his elegy, "Lycidas," p. 215, above. **13. Laura:** the woman to whom Petrarch's sonnets were addressed.

TO HAYDON

Great spirits now on earth are sojourning;
  He of the cloud,° the cataract, the lake,
  Who on Helvellyn's° summit, wide awake,
Catches his freshness from Archangel's wing:
He of the rose,° the violet, the spring,
  The social smile, the chain for Freedom's sake:
And lo!° — whose stedfastness would never take
A meaner sound than Raphael's whispering.
And other spirits there are standing apart
  Upon the forehead of the age to come;   10
These, these will give the world another heart,
  And other pulses. Hear ye not the hum
Of mighty workings? ——
  Listen awhile ye nations, and be dumb.

                              November, 1816

ON THE GRASSHOPPER
AND CRICKET

The poetry of earth is never dead:
  When all the birds are faint with the hot sun,
  And hide in cooling trees, a voice will run
From hedge to hedge about the new-mown mead;
That is the Grasshopper's — he takes the lead
  In summer luxury — he has never done
  With his delights; for when tired out with fun
He rests at ease beneath some pleasant weed.
The poetry of earth is ceasing never:
  On a lone winter evening, when the frost   10
    Has wrought a silence, from the stove there
      shrills
The Cricket's song, in warmth increasing ever,
  And seems to one in drowsiness half lost,
    The Grasshopper's among some grassy hills.

                              December, 1816

ON SEEING THE ELGIN MARBLES
FOR THE FIRST TIME

My spirit is too weak; mortality
  Weighs heavily on me like unwilling sleep,
  And each imagined pinnacle and steep
Of godlike hardship tells me I must die
Like a sick eagle looking at the sky.
  Yet 'tis a gentle luxury to weep,
  That I have not the cloudy winds to keep
Fresh for the opening of the morning's eye.

Such dim-conceivèd glories of the brain
  Bring round the heart an indescribable feud;   10
So do these wonders a most dizzy pain,
  That mingles Grecian grandeur with the rude
Wasting of old Time — with a billowy main,
  A sun, a shadow of a magnitude.

                              March, 1817

ON SITTING DOWN TO READ
KING LEAR ONCE AGAIN

This and the sonnet "To Spenser" illustrate Keats's divided attitude at this time toward two kinds of poetry which he increasingly felt were impossible to reconcile. Compare his contrast of the "noble poet of romance" with the "miserable and mighty poet of the human Heart" in the letter of June 9, 1819, below.

O golden-tongued Romance with serene lute!
  Fair plumèd Syren! Queen of far away!
  Leave melodizing on this wintry day,
Shut up thine olden pages, and be mute:
Adieu! for once again the fierce dispute,
  Betwixt damnation and impassioned clay
  Must I burn through; once more humbly assay
The bitter-sweet of this Shakespearean fruit.
Chief Poet! and ye clouds of Albion,
  Begetters of our deep eternal theme,   10
When through the old oak forest I am gone,
  Let me not wander in a barren dream,
But when I am consumèd in the fire,
Give me new Phoenix° wings to fly at my desire.

                              January, 1818

WHEN I HAVE FEARS

This is Keats's first and probably most effective sonnet in the Shakespearean form.

When I have fears that I may cease to be
  Before my pen has gleaned my teeming brain,
Before high-pilèd books, in charact'ry,°
  Hold like rich garners the full-ripened grain;
When I behold, upon the night's starred face,
  Huge cloudy symbols of a high romance,
And think that I may never live to trace
  Their shadows, with the magic hand of chance;
And when I feel, fair creature of an hour,
  That I shall never look upon thee more,   10

TO HAYDON.   2. He . . . cloud: Wordsworth.   3. Helvellyn: a mountain in the Lake District in northern England.   5. He . . . rose: Leigh Hunt.   7. And lo: Haydon himself. See Intro., p. 734, above. Of the "great spirits," only Wordsworth somewhat survived Keats's increasing taste and knowledge.

"KING LEAR."   14. Phoenix: in Egyptian mythology, a bird able to rise in youthful vigor from its own ashes after being burned. WHEN I HAVE FEARS.   3. charact'ry: expressing character by signs and symbols.

Never have relish in the faery power
  Of unreflecting love! — then on the shore
Of the wide world I stand alone, and think
Till Love and Fame to nothingness do sink.

January, 1818

TO HOMER

Standing aloof in giant ignorance,
  Of thee I hear and of the Cyclades,°
As one who sits ashore and longs perchance
  To visit dolphin-coral in deep seas.
So thou wast blind! — but then the veil was rent;
  For Jove uncurtained Heaven to let thee live,
And Neptune made for thee a spumy tent,
  And Pan made sing for thee his forest-hive;
Aye, on the shores of darkness there is light,
  And precipices show untrodden green;   10
There is a budding morrow in midnight, —
  There is a triple sight in blindness keen;
Such seeing hadst thou, as it once befell
To Dian,° Queen of Earth, and Heaven, and Hell.

Spring, 1818

THE EVE OF ST. AGNES

Begun late in January, 1819, the first draft was completed a month later, though Keats continued making substantial changes in the wording. For the story, he drew on various sources, especially the episode of Biancofiore and Florio in Boccaccio's *Il Filocolo*. According to legend, maidens who performed the proper ceremony might be able on the Eve (January 21) of St. Agnes, the patron saint of virgins, to dream of the man they were destined to marry.

I

St. Agnes' Eve — Ah, bitter chill it was!
The owl, for all his feathers, was a-cold;
The hare limped trembling through the frozen grass,
And silent was the flock in woolly fold:
Numb were the Beadsman's° fingers, while he told
His rosary, and while his frosted breath,
Like pious incense from a censer old,
Seemed taking flight for heaven, without a death,
Past the sweet Virgin's picture, while his prayer he saith.

2

His prayer he saith, this patient, holy man;   10
Then takes his lamp, and riseth from his knees,
And back returneth, meager, barefoot, wan,
Along the chapel aisle by slow degrees:
The sculptured dead, on each side, seem to freeze,
Emprisoned in black, purgatorial rails:
Knights, ladies, praying in dumb orat'ries,°
He passeth by; and his weak spirit fails
To think how they may ache in icy hoods and mails.

3

Northward he turneth through a little door,
And scarce three steps, ere Music's golden tongue
Flattered to tears this aged man and poor;   21
But no — already had his deathbell rung:
The joys of all his life were said and sung:
His was harsh penance on St. Agnes' Eve:
Another way he went, and soon among
Rough ashes sat he for his soul's reprieve,
And all night kept awake, for sinners' sake to grieve.

4

That ancient Beadsman heard the prelude soft;
And so it chanced, for many a door was wide,
From hurry to and fro. Soon, up aloft,   30
The silver, snarling trumpets 'gan to chide:
The level chambers, ready with their pride,
Were glowing to receive a thousand guests:
The carvèd angels, ever eager-eyed,
Stared, where upon their heads the cornice rests,
With hair blown back, and wings put cross-wise on their breasts.

5

At length burst in the argent revelry,°
With plume, tiara, and all rich array,
Numerous as shadows haunting faerily
The brain, new stuffed, in youth, with triumphs gay   40
Of old romance. These let us wish away,
And turn, sole-thoughted, to one Lady there,
Whose heart had brooded, all that wintry day,
On love, and winged St. Agnes' saintly care,
As she had heard old dames full many times declare.

6

They told her how, upon St. Agnes' Eve,
Young virgins might have visions of delight,

TO HOMER. **2. Cyclades:** Greek isles in the Aegean Sea.
14. Dian: In later classical mythology, Diana was viewed as a goddess with three forms — Selene in the sky, Artemis on earth, and Hecate in the lower world. EVE OF ST. AGNES. **5. Beadsman:** one pensioned to pray for a benefactor.

16. orat'ries: small chapels for private devotion. **37. argent revelry:** revelers clad in silver.

And soft adorings from their loves receive
Upon the honeyed middle of the night,
If ceremonies due they did aright; 50
As, supperless to bed they must retire,
And couch supine their beauties, lily white;
Nor look behind, nor sideways, but require
Of Heaven with upward eyes for all that they
    desire.

7

Full of this whim was thoughtful Madeline:
The music, yearning like a god in pain,
She scarcely heard: her maiden eyes divine,
Fixed on the floor, saw many a sweeping train
Pass by — she heeded not at all: in vain
Came many a tiptoe, amorous cavalier, 60
And back retired; not cooled by high disdain,
But she saw not: her heart was otherwhere:
She sighed for Agnes' dreams, the sweetest of the
    year.

8

She danced along with vague, regardless eyes,
Anxious her lips, her breathing quick and short:
The hallowed hour was near at hand: she sighs
Amid the timbrels, and the thronged resort
Of whisperers in anger, or in sport;
'Mid looks of love, defiance, hate, and scorn,
Hoodwinked with faery fancy; all amort,° 70
Save to St. Agnes and her lambs unshorn,°
And all the bliss to be before to-morrow morn.

9

So, purposing each moment to retire,
She lingered still. Meantime, across the moors,
Had come young Porphyro, with heart on fire
For Madeline. Beside the portal doors,
Buttressed from moonlight, stands he, and implores
All saints to give him sight of Madeline,
But for one moment in the tedious hours,
That he might gaze and worship all unseen; 80
Perchance speak, kneel, touch, kiss — in sooth such
    things have been.

10

He ventures in: let no buzzed whisper tell:
All eyes be muffled, or a hundred swords
Will storm his heart, Love's fev'rous citadel:
For him, those chambers held barbarian hordes,

Hyena° foemen, and hot-blooded lords,
Whose very dogs would execrations howl
Against his lineage; not one breast affords
Him any mercy, in that mansion foul,
Save one old beldame,° weak in body and in soul.

11

Ah, happy chance! the aged creature came, 91
Shuffling along with ivory-headed wand,
To where he stood, hid from the torch's flame,
Behind a broad hall-pillar, far beyond
The sound of merriment and chorus bland:
He startled her; but soon she knew his face,
And grasped his fingers in her palsied hand,
Saying, "Mercy, Porphyro! hie thee from this
    place;
They are all here to-night, the whole blood-thirsty
    race!

12

"Get hence! get hence! there's dwarfish Hilde-
    brand; 100
He had a fever late, and in the fit
He cursèd thee and thine, both house and land:
Then there's that old Lord Maurice, not a whit
More tame for his gray hairs — Alas me! flit!
Flit like a ghost away." — "Ah, Gossip dear,
We're safe enough; here in this arm-chair sit,
And tell me how" — "Good Saints! not here,
    not here;
Follow me, child, or else these stones will be thy
    bier."

13

He followed through a lowly archèd way,
Brushing the cobwebs with his lofty plume, 110
And as she muttered "Well-a — well-a-day!"
He found him in a little moonlight room,
Pale, latticed, chill, and silent as a tomb.
"Now tell me where is Madeline," said he,
"O tell me, Angela, by the holy loom
Which none but secret sisterhood may see,
When they St. Agnes' wool are weaving piously."

14

"St. Agnes! Ah! it is St. Agnes' Eve —
Yet men will murder upon holy days:
Thou must hold water in a witch's sieve,° 120
And be liege-lord of all the Elves and Fays,°
To venture so: it fills me with amaze
To see thee, Porphyro! — St. Agnes' Eve!
God's help! my lady fair the conjuror° plays

---

70. amort: dead. **71. St. Agnes . . . unshorn:** On St. Agnes'
Day, when lambs were brought as an offering to the altar, the
wool was given to the nuns to be spun and woven (ll. 115-17).

86. Hyena: hyena-like. **90. beldame:** old woman. **120. witch's
sieve:** sieve made by witchcraft to hold water. **121. Fays:**
fairies. **124. conjuror:** magician; that is, by performing certain
rites, Madeline hopes to conjure up a true vision.

This very night: good angels her deceive!
But let me laugh awhile, I've mickle time to
    grieve."

15

Feebly she laugheth in the languid moon,
While Porphyro upon her face doth look,
Like puzzled urchin on an aged crone
Who keepeth closed a wondrous riddle-book,
As spectacled she sits in chimney nook.   131
But soon his eyes grew brilliant, when she told
His lady's purpose; and he scarce could brook
Tears, at the thought of those enchantments cold,
And Madeline asleep in lap of legends old.

16

Sudden a thought came like a full-blown rose,
Flushing his brow, and in his painèd heart
Made purple riot: then doth he propose
A stratagem, that makes the beldame start:
"A cruel man and impious thou art: 140
Sweet lady, let her pray, and sleep, and dream
Alone with her good angels, far apart
From wicked men like thee. Go, go!—I deem
Thou canst not surely be the same that thou didst
    seem."

17

"I will not harm her, by all saints I swear,"
Quoth Porphyro: "O may I ne'er find grace
When my weak voice shall whisper its last prayer,
If one of her soft ringlets I displace,
Or look with ruffian passion in her face:
Good Angela, believe me by these tears;   150
Or I will, even in a moment's space,
Awake, with horrid shout, my foemen's ears,
And beard them, though they be more fanged than
    wolves and bears."

18

"Ah! why wilt thou affright a feeble soul?
A poor, weak, palsy-stricken, churchyard thing,
Whose passing-bell° may ere the midnight toll;
Whose prayers for thee, each morn and evening,
Were never missed."—Thus plaining, doth she
    bring
A gentler speech from burning Porphyro;
So woeful, and of such deep sorrowing,   160
That Angela gives promise she will do
Whatever he shall wish, betide her weal or woe.

156. passing-bell: bell that announces death.

19

Which was, to lead him, in close secrecy,
Even to Madeline's chamber, and there hide
Him in a closet, of such privacy
That he might see her beauty unespied,
And win perhaps that night a peerless bride,
While legioned faeries paced the coverlet,
And pale enchantment held her sleepy-eyed.
Never on such a night have lovers met,   170
Since Merlin paid his Demon all the monstrous
    debt.°

20

"It shall be as thou wishest," said the Dame:
"All cates° and dainties shall be storèd there
Quickly on this feast-night: by the tambour
    frame°
Her own lute thou wilt see: no time to spare,
For I am slow and feeble, and scarce dare
On such a catering trust my dizzy head.
Wait here, my child, with patience; kneel in
    prayer
The while: Ah! thou must needs the lady wed,
Or may I never leave my grave among the dead."

21

So saying, she hobbled off with busy fear.   181
The lover's endless minutes slowly passed:
The dame returned, and whispered in his ear
To follow her; with aged eyes aghast
From fright of dim espial. Safe at last,
Through many a dusky gallery, they gain
The maiden's chamber, silken, hushed, and
    chaste;
Where Porphyro took covert, pleased amain.
His poor guide hurried back with agues in her
    brain.

22

Her falt'ring hand upon the balustrade,   190
Old Angela was feeling for the stair,
When Madeline, St. Agnes' charmèd maid,
Rose, like a missioned spirit, unaware:
With silver taper's light, and pious care,
She turned, and down the aged gossip led
To a safe level matting. Now prepare,
Young Porphyro, for gazing on that bed;
She comes, she comes again, like ring-dove frayed°
    and fled.

171. Merlin . . . debt: the magician Merlin, who owed his life
to a devil, and paid for it by committing evil deeds.   173. cates:
choice food.   174. tambour frame: drum-shaped embroidery
frame.   198. frayed: frightened.

23

Out went the taper as she hurried in;
Its little smoke, in pallid moonshine, died: 200
She closed the door, she panted, all akin
To spirits of the air, and visions wide:
No uttered syllable, or, woe betide!
But to her heart, her heart was voluble,
Paining with eloquence her balmy side;
As though a tongueless nightingale should swell
Her throat in vain, and die, heart-stifled, in her dell.

24

A casement high and triple-arched there was,
All garlanded with carven imag'ries   209
Of fruits, and flowers, and bunches of knot-grass,
And diamonded with panes of quaint device,
Innumerable of stains and splendid dyes,
As are the tiger-moth's deep-damasked wings;
And in the midst, 'mong thousand heraldries,
And twilight saints, and dim emblazonings,
A shielded scutcheon blushed with blood of queens
    and kings.

25

Full on this casement shone the wintry moon,
And threw warm gules° on Madeline's fair
    breast,
As down she knelt for heaven's grace and boon;
Rose-bloom fell on her hands, together pressed,
And on her silver cross soft amethyst,   221
And on her hair a glory, like a saint:
She seemed a splendid angel, newly dressed,
Save wings, for heaven:—Porphyro grew faint:
She knelt, so pure a thing, so free from mortal
    taint.

26

Anon his heart revives: her vespers done,
Of all its wreathèd pearls her hair she frees;
Unclasps her warmèd jewels one by one;
Loosens her fragrant bodice; by degrees
Her rich attire creeps rustling to her knees: 230
Half-hidden, like a mermaid in sea-weed,
Pensive awhile she dreams awake, and sees,
In fancy, fair St. Agnes in her bed,
But dares not look behind, or all the charm is fled.

27

Soon, trembling in her soft and chilly nest,
In sort of wakeful swoon, perplexed she lay,
Until the poppied warmth of sleep oppressed
Her soothèd limbs, and soul fatigued away;

Flown, like a thought, until the morrow-day;
Blissfully havened both from joy and pain;   240
Clasped like a missal where swart Paynims
    pray;°
Blinded alike from sunshine and from rain,
As though a rose should shut, and be a bud again.

28

Stol'n to this paradise, and so entranced,
Porphyro gazed upon her empty dress,
And listened to her breathing, if it chanced
To wake into a slumberous tenderness;
Which when he heard, that minute did he bless,
And breathed himself: then from the closet crept,
Noiseless as fear in a wide wilderness,   250
And over the hushed carpet, silent, stepped,
And 'tween the curtains peeped, where, lo!—how
    fast she slept.

29

Then by the bed-side, where the faded moon
Made a dim, silver twilight, soft he set
A table, and, half-anguished, threw thereon
A cloth of woven crimson, gold, and jet:—
O for some drowsy Morphean° amulet!
The boisterous, midnight, festive clarion,
The kettle-drum, and far-heard clarinet,   259
Affray his ears, though but in dying tone:—
The hall door shuts again, and all the noise is gone.

30

And still she slept an azure-lidded sleep,
In blanchèd linen, smooth, and lavendered,
While he from forth the closet brought a heap
Of candied apple, quince, and plum, and gourd;
With jellies soother than the creamy curd,
And lucent syrops, tinct with cinnamon;
Manna and dates, in argosy transferred
From Fez; and spicèd dainties, every one,
From silken Samarkand to cedared Lebanon.   270

31

These delicates he heaped with glowing hand
On golden dishes and in baskets bright
Of wreathèd silver: sumptuous they stand
In the retired quiet of the night,
Filling the chilly room with perfume light.—
"And now, my love, my seraph fair, awake!
Thou art my heaven, and I thine eremite:°

---

218. **gules:** the color red as used in heraldry; Keats is probably
thinking of its original meaning (a fur necklace dyed red).

241. **Clasped . . . pray:** clasped shut, as a prayer book (missal)
would be in a country of dark pagans (Paynims). 257. **Morphean:**
sleep-inducing (from Morpheus, the god of sleep.) 277. **eremite:**
hermit.

Open thine eyes, for meek St. Agnes' sake,
Or I shall drowse beside thee, so my soul doth
    ache."

32

Thus whispering, his warm, unnervèd arm 280
Sank in her pillow. Shaded was her dream
By the dusk curtains: — 'twas a midnight charm
Impossible to melt as icèd stream:
The lustrous salvers in the moonlight gleam;
Broad golden fringe upon the carpet lies:
It seemed he never, never could redeem
From such a stedfast spell his lady's eyes;
So mused awhile, entoiled in woofèd phantasies.

33

Awakening up, he took her hollow lute — 289
Tumultuous — and, in chords that tenderest be,
He played an ancient ditty, long since mute,
In Provence° called, "La belle dame sans
    mercy":°
Close to her ear touching the melody; —
Wherewith disturbed, she uttered a soft moan:
He ceased — she panted quick — and suddenly
Her blue affrayèd eyes wide open shone:
Upon his knees he sank, pale as smooth-sculptured
    stone.

34

Her eyes were open, but she still beheld,
Now wide awake, the vision of her sleep:
There was a painful change, that nigh expelled
The blisses of her dream so pure and deep 301
At which fair Madeline began to weep,
And moan forth witless words with many a sigh;
While still her gaze on Porphyro would keep;
Who knelt, with joinèd hands and piteous eye,
Fearing to move or speak, she looked so dream-
    ingly.

35

"Ah, Porphyro!" said she, "but even now
Thy voice was at sweet tremble in mine ear,
Made tuneable with every sweetest vow;
And those sad eyes were spiritual and clear: 310
How changed thou art! how pallid, chill, and
    drear!
Give me that voice again, my Porphyro,
Those looks immortal, those complainings dear!
Oh leave me not in this eternal woe,
For if thou diest, my Love, I know not where to
    go."

36

Beyond a mortal man impassioned far
At these voluptuous accents, he arose,
Ethereal, flushed, and like a throbbing star
Seen mid the sapphire heaven's deep repose;
Into her dream he melted, as the rose 320
Blended its odor with the violet —
Solution sweet: meantime the frost-wind blows
Like Love's alarum pattering the sharp sleet
Against the window-panes; St. Agnes' moon hath
    set.

37

'Tis dark: quick pattereth the flaw-blown° sleet:
"This is no dream, my bride, my Madeline!"
'Tis dark: the icèd gusts still rave and beat:
"No dream, alas! alas! and woe is mine!
Porphyro will leave me here to fade and pine. —
Cruel! what traitor could thee hither bring? 330
I curse not, for my heart is lost in thine,
Though thou forsakest a deceivèd thing;
A dove forlorn and lost with sick unprunèd wing."

38

"My Madeline! sweet dreamer! lovely bride!
Say, may I be for aye thy vassal blest?
Thy beauty's shield, heart-shaped and vermeil°
    dyed?
Ah, silver shrine, here will I take my rest
After so many hours of toil and quest,
A famished pilgrim — saved by miracle. 339
Though I have found, I will not rob thy nest
Saving of thy sweet self; if thou think'st well
To trust, fair Madeline, to no rude infidel.

39

"Hark! 'tis an elfin-storm from faery land,
Of haggard seeming, but a boon indeed:
Arise — arise! the morning is at hand; —
The bloated wassailers will never heed:
Let us away, my love, with happy speed;
There are no ears to hear, or eyes to see —
Drowned all in Rhenish° and the sleepy mead:
Awake! arise! my love, and fearless be, 350
For o'er the southern moors I have a home for
    thee."

40

She hurried at his words, beset with fears,
For there were sleeping dragons all around,
At glaring watch, perhaps, with ready spears —
Down the wide stairs a darkling way they
    found. —

---

292. Provence: district in southern France noted for its troubadours. **"La . . . mercy":** the fair lady without mercy."

325. flaw-blown: A flaw is a short, gusty storm. **336. vermeil:**
vermilion. **349. Rhenish:** wine from the Rhine district.

In all the house was heard no human sound.
A chain-drooped lamp was flickering by each
  door;
The arras,° rich with horseman, hawk, and
  hound,
Fluttered in the besieging wind's uproar;   359
And the long carpets rose along the gusty floor.

41

They glide, like phantoms, into the wide hall;
Like phantoms, to the iron porch, they glide;
Where lay the Porter, in uneasy sprawl,
With a huge empty flagon by his side:
The wakeful bloodhound rose, and shook his
  hide,
But his sagacious eye an inmate owns:
By one, and one, the bolts full easy slide: —
The chains lie silent on the footworn stones; —
The key turns, and the door upon its hinges groans.

42

And they are gone: aye, ages long ago   370
These lovers fled away into the storm.
That night the Baron dreamt of many a woe,
And all his warrior-guests, with shade and form
Of witch, and demon, and large coffin-worm,
Were long be-nightmared. Angela the old
Died palsy-twitched, with meager face deform;
The Beadsman, after thousands aves told,
For aye unsought-for slept among his ashes cold.

BRIGHT STAR

Bright star, would I were stedfast as thou art —
  Not in lone splendor hung aloft the night
And watching, with eternal lids apart,
  Like nature's patient, sleepless Eremite,
The moving waters at their priestlike task
  Of pure ablution round earth's human shores,
Or gazing on the new soft fallen mask
  Of snow upon the mountains and the moors —
No — yet still stedfast, still unchangeable,
  Pillowed upon my fair love's ripening breast,   10
To feel forever its soft fall and swell,
  Awake forever in a sweet unrest,
Still, still to hear her tender-taken breath,
And so live ever — or else swoon to death.

April, 1819

LA BELLE DAME SANS MERCI
(a ballad)

Keats took the title, "The Fair Lady Without Pity,"
from a medieval French poem by Alain Chartier, the

358. arras: tapestry.

translation of which was mistakenly assumed in
Keats's time to have been made by Chaucer.

O what can ail thee, Knight at arms,
  Alone and palely loitering?
The sedge has withered from the Lake
  And no birds sing!

1-12
An observer

O what can ail thee, Knight at arms,
  So haggard, and so woebegone?
The Squirrel's granary is full
  And the harvest's done.

I see a lily on thy brow
  With anguish moist and fever dew,   10
And on thy cheeks a fading rose
  Fast withereth too.

"I met a Lady in the Meads,
  Full beautiful, a faery's child
Her hair was long, her foot was light,
  And her eyes were wild.

"I made a Garland for her head,
  And bracelets too, and fragrant Zone
She looked at me as she did love
  And made sweet moan.   20

"I set her on my pacing steed
  And nothing else saw all day long
For sidelong would she bend and sing
  A faery's song.

"She found me roots of relish sweet
  And honey wild and manna dew
And sure in language strange she said
  I love thee true.

"She took me to her elfin grot
  And there she wept and sighed full sore,   30
And there I shut her wild wild eyes
  With kisses four.

"And there she lullèd me asleep
  And there I dreamed, Ah woe betide!
The latest dream I ever dreamt
  On the cold hill side.

"I saw pale Kings, and Princes too
  Pale warriors, death pale were they all;
They cried, La belle dame sans merci
  Thee hath in thrall.   40

"I saw their starved lips in the gloam
  With horrid warning gapèd wide,
And I awoke, and found me here
  On the cold hill's side.

" And this is why I sojourn here
  Alone and palely loitering;
Though the sedge is withered from the Lake
And no birds sing."

April, 1819

TO SLEEP

O soft embalmer of the still midnight,
  Shutting, with careful fingers and benign,
Our gloom-pleased eyes, embowered from the light,
  Enshaded in forgetfulness divine;
O soothest Sleep! if so it please thee, close
  In the midst of this thine hymn, my willing eyes,
Or wait the Amen, ere thy poppy throws
  Around my bed its lulling charities;
Then save me, or the passèd day will shine
Upon my pillow, breeding many woes;   10
  Save me from curious conscience, that still hoards
Its strength for darkness, burrowing like a mole;
  Turn the key deftly in the oilèd wards,
And seal the hushèd casket of my soul.

April, 1819

ODE TO PSYCHE

The " Ode to Psyche " is the first of the great odes that were written from the latter part of April through May, 1819, and it is thus Keats's first attempt to construct a new lyrical form that would lack the features he disliked in both the Petrarchan and Shakespearean sonnets. In the same letter as that in which he mentions his attempt to find a better sonnet form, he states, before copying out the " Ode to Psyche ": " The following poem . . . is the first and the only one with which I have taken even moderate pains. I have for the most part dash'd off my lines in a hurry. This I have done leisurely — I think it reads the more richly for it. . . ." In classical mythology, Psyche (the Greek word for " soul ") was a princess loved by Cupid, son of Venus. After difficulties with Venus, she was united with Cupid and given immortality.

O Goddess! hear these tuneless numbers, wrung
  By sweet enforcement and remembrance dear,
And pardon that thy secrets should be sung
  Even into thine own soft-conchèd° ear:
Surely I dreamt today, or did I see
  The wingèd Psyche with awakened eyes?
I wandered in a forest thoughtlessly,
  And, on the sudden, fainting with surprise,
Saw two fair creatures, couchèd side by side
  In deepest grass, beneath the whisp'ring roof 10
Of leaves and trembled blossoms, where there ran
  A brooklet, scarce espied:

ODE TO PSYCHE. 4. conchèd: formed like a shell.

'Mid hushed, cool-rooted flowers, fragrant-eyed,
  Blue, silver-white, and budded Tyrian,°
They lay calm-breathing on the bedded grass;
  Their arms embracèd, and their pinions too;
  Their lips touched not, but had not bade adieu,
As if disjoinèd by soft-handed slumber,
And ready still past kisses to outnumber
  At tender eye-dawn of aurorean° love: 20
    The wingèd boy I knew;
  But who wast thou, O happy, happy dove?
    His Psyche true!

O latest born° and loveliest vision far
  Of all Olympus' faded hierarchy!°
Fairer than Phoebe's sapphire-regioned star,°
  Or Vesper, amorous glow-worm of the sky;
Fairer than these, though temple thou hast none,
  Nor altar heaped with flowers;
Nor virgin-choir to make delicious moan   30
  Upon the midnight hours;
No voice, no lute, no pipe, no incense sweet
  From chain-swung censer teeming;
No shrine, no grove, no oracle, no heat
  Of pale-mouthed prophet dreaming!
O brightest! though too late° for antique vows,
  Too, too late for the fond believing lyre,
When holy were the haunted forest boughs,
  Holy the air, the water, and the fire;
Yet even in these days so far retired   40
  From happy pieties, thy lucent fans,°
  Fluttering among the faint Olympians,
I see, and sing, by my own eyes inspired.
So let me be thy choir, and make a moan
  Upon the midnight hours;
Thy voice, thy lute, thy pipe, thy incense sweet
  From swingèd censer teeming;
Thy shrine, thy grove, thy oracle, thy heat
  Of pale-mouthed prophet dreaming.

Yes, I will be thy priest, and build a fane   50
  In some untrodden region of my mind,
Where branchèd thoughts, new grown with pleasant pain,
  Instead of pines shall murmur in the wind:
Far, far around shall those dark-clustered trees
  Fledge the wild-ridgèd mountains steep by steep;
And there by zephyrs, streams, and birds, and bees,

14. Tyrian: "Tyrian purple," a dye used by the Greeks and Romans and made from shellfish. 20. aurorean: dawning (from Aurora, the Roman goddess of the dawn). 24. latest born: See l. 36n., below. 25. Olympus' . . . hierarchy: the hierarchy or collective group of classical deities. 26. Phoebe's . . . star: the moon, of which Diana (or Phoebe) was the goddess. 36. too late: regarded as a goddess too late (in Roman times) to have been officially worshiped in Greece. 41. fans: wings.

The moss-lain Dryads shall be lulled to sleep;
And in the midst of this wide quietness
A rosy sanctuary will I dress
With the wreathed trellis of a working brain,   60
  With buds, and bells, and stars without a name,
With all the gardener Fancy e'er could feign,
  Who breeding flowers, will never breed the same:
And there shall be for thee all soft delight
  That shadowy thought can win,
A bright torch, and a casement ope° at night,
  To let the warm Love in!

ODE TO A NIGHTINGALE

Composed in early May, 1819, this was probably
the first of Keats's great odes to be written in the set
ten-line stanza form that would combine, as he
thought, the virtues of both the Petrarchan and Shakespearean sonnets.

1

My heart aches, and a drowsy numbness pains
  My sense, as though of hemlock I had drunk,
Or emptied some dull opiate to the drains
  One minute past, and Lethe-wards° had sunk:
'Tis not through envy of thy happy lot,
  But being too happy in thine happiness—
    That thou, light-wingèd Dryad° of the trees,
      In some melodious plot
Of beechen green, and shadows numberless,
    Singest of summer in full-throated ease.   10

2

O, for a draught of vintage! that hath been
  Cooled a long age in the deep-delvèd earth,
Tasting of Flora° and the country green,
  Dance, and Provençal° song, and sunburnt mirth!
O for a beaker full of the warm South,
  Full of the true, the blushful Hippocrene,°
    With beaded bubbles winking at the brim,
      And purple-stainèd mouth;
That I might drink, and leave the world unseen,
    And with thee fade away into the forest dim:

3

Fade far away, dissolve, and quite forget   21
  What thou among the leaves hast never known,
The weariness, the fever, and the fret
  Here, where men sit and hear each other groan;
Where palsy shakes a few, sad, last gray hairs,
  Where youth grows pale, and specter-thin, and
      dies;°
    Where but to think is to be full of sorrow
      And leaden-eyed despairs,
Where Beauty cannot keep her lustrous eyes,
    Or new Love pine at them beyond to-morrow.

4

Away! away! for I will fly to thee,   31
  Not charioted by Bacchus and his pards,
But on the viewless wings of Poesy,°
  Though the dull brain perplexes and retards:
Already with thee! tender is the night,
  And haply the Queen-Moon is on her throne,
    Clustered around by all her starry Fays;°
      But here there is no light,
Save what from heaven is with the breezes blown
    Through verdurous glooms and winding mossy
      ways.   40

5

I cannot see what flowers are at my feet,
  Nor what soft incense hangs upon the boughs,
But, in embalmèd darkness, guess each sweet
  Wherewith the seasonable month endows°
The grass, the thicket, and the fruit-tree wild;
  White hawthorn, and the pastoral eglantine;
    Fast fading violets° covered up in leaves;
      And mid-May's eldest child,
The coming musk-rose,° full of dewy wine,°
    The murmurous haunt of flies on summer
      eves.°   50

66. **casement ope:** The image of open windows fascinated Keats.
Compare the "magic casements" in "Ode to a Nightingale"
(l. 69), or the mention of a "Window opening on Winander-
mere" in a letter to his brother (Oct. 14–31, 1818).   ODE TO A
NIGHTINGALE.   **4. Lethe:** the river in Hades, whose waters
brought forgetfulness.   **7. Dryad:** tree nymph.   **13. Flora:**
goddess of flowers.   **14. Provençal:** See *Eve of St. Agnes*,
l. 292n., above.   **16. Hippocrene:** a fountain, on Mt. Helicon,
the waters of which would inspire the poet who drank from it.

26. **youth . . . dies:** probably an allusion to Keats's brother,
Tom, who had died the preceding winter.   **32–33. Not . . .
Poesy:** not rescued from the ugliness of life by Bacchus, the
god of wine (whose chariot was often pictured as being drawn
by leopards), but by the poetic imagination.   **37. Fays:** fairies.
**44–50. seasonable . . . fading violets . . . musk-rose . . . wine
. . . summer eves:** The cluster of images here (as of others
throughout the ode) appears nostalgically in Keats's letters of
the spring of 1819, before the writing of the ode, and offers a
vivid example of the use of its materials by the poetic imagination.   For example, in a letter to his sister (April 17), he speaks
of securing some "seasonable" plants for her at a nursery, and
mentions desiring "claret-*wine cool* out of a cellar a mile *deep*,"
and a "strawberry bed to say your prayers to *Flora* in."   In a
letter to his brother (Feb. 14–May 3), he mentions drinking
claret, "cool and *feverless*," on "summer evenings," and concludes his letter, on May 3, by adding that "the *violets* are not
withered before the peeping of the first *rose*."

6

Darkling° I listen; and, for many a time
  I have been half in love with easeful Death,
Called him soft names in many a musèd rhyme,
  To take into the air my quiet breath;
Now more than ever seems it rich to die,
  To cease upon the midnight with no pain,
    While thou art pouring forth thy soul abroad
      In such an ecstasy!
Still wouldst thou sing, and I have ears in vain —
To thy high requiem become a sod.   60

7

Thou wast not born for death, immortal Bird!
  No hungry generations tread thee down;
The voice I hear this passing night was heard
  In ancient days by emperor and clown:
Perhaps the self-same song that found a path
  Through the sad heart of Ruth, when, sick for
      home,
    She stood in tears amid the alien corn;°
      The same that oft-times hath
Charmed magic casements, opening on the foam
  Of perilous seas, in faery lands forlorn.°   70

8

Forlorn! the very word is like a bell
  To toll me back from thee to my sole self!
Adieu! the fancy cannot cheat so well
  As she is famed to do, deceiving elf.
Adieu! adieu! thy plaintive anthem fades
  Past the near meadows, over the still stream,
    Up the hill-side; and now 'tis buried deep
      In the next valley-glades:
Was it a vision, or a waking dream?
  Fled is that music: — Do I wake or sleep? 80

ODE ON MELANCHOLY

The theme of the interconnection of melancholy and
joy is similar to that previously touched on in the
"Ode to a Nightingale" (ll. 1–6).

51. **Darkling:** in the dark.   66–67. **Through . . . corn:** See the
book of Ruth 2.   70. **forlorn:** now passed and lost. ODE ON
MELANCHOLY: A first stanza, later canceled, reads:

Though you should build a bark of dead men's bones,
  And rear a phantom gibbet for a mast,
Stitch creeds together for a sail, with groans
  To fill it out, blood-stained and aghast;
Although your rudder be a dragon's tail
  Long severed, yet still hard with agony,
    Your cordage large uprootings from the skull
Of bald Medusa, certes you would fail
  To find the Melancholy — whether she
    Dreameth in any isle of Lethe dull.   10

1

No, no, go not to Lethe,° neither twist
  Wolf's-bane,° tight-rooted, for its poisonous wine;
Nor suffer thy pale forehead to be kissed
  By nightshade, ruby grape of Proserpine;°
Make not your rosary of yew-berries,
  Nor let the beetle, nor the death-moth be
    Your mournful Psyche,° nor the downy owl
A partner in your sorrow's mysteries;
  For shade to shade will come too drowsily,
    And drown the wakeful anguish of the soul.°

2

But when the melancholy fit shall fall   11
  Sudden from heaven like a weeping cloud,
That fosters the droop-headed flowers all,
  And hides the green hill in an April shroud;
Then glut thy sorrow on a morning rose,
  Or on the rainbow of the salt sand-wave,
  Or on the wealth of globèd peonies;
Or if thy mistress some rich anger shows,
  Emprison her soft hand, and let her rave,   19
    And feed deep, deep upon her peerless eyes.

3

She° dwells with Beauty — Beauty that must die;
  And Joy, whose hand is ever at his lips
Bidding adieu; and aching Pleasure nigh,
  Turning to Poison° while the bee-mouth sips:
Aye, in the very temple of Delight
  Veiled Melancholy has her sovran shrine,
    Though seen of none save him whose strenu-
      ous tongue
Can burst Joy's grape against his palate fine;
His soul shall taste the sadness of her might,
  And be among her cloudy trophies hung.   30

May, 1819

1. **Lethe:** See "Ode to a Nightingale," l. 4n.   2. **Wolf's-bane:**
aconite, a yellow-flowered plant the roots of which contain poison.
4. **Proserpine:** bride of Pluto, ruler of the underworld. See
Fall of Hyperion, ll. 37–38, below.   6–7. **death-moth . . . Psyche:**
Psyche (the "soul") was symbolized by a butterfly. Hence, "Do
not take the death-moth instead of the butterfly as the symbol
of your soul."   9–10. **For . . . soul:** For the shades, or ghosts,
of melancholy and death will steal on you gradually; and
in that growing numbness you will lose the keen edge of perception with which the full meaning of melancholy, as it is inextricably bound up with joy, can be sensed and known.   21. **She:**
Melancholy, not the "mistress."   24. **Turning to Poison:** Two
months before the ode, Keats had written to his brother George
(March 19): "While we are laughing, the seed of some trouble is
put into the wide arable land of events — While we are laughing, it sprouts, it grows, and suddenly bears a *poison* fruit which
we must pluck."

ODE ON A GRECIAN URN

The theme and much of the imagery of this ode were suggested by the sight of the Elgin marbles and the Grecian urns in the British Museum. The last two lines of the poem are probably the most widely known lines of Keats. If they have also proved the most puzzling, it is probably because the statement " that is all / Ye know on earth, and all ye need to know " is usually regarded as Keats's own observation on the maxim, " Beauty is truth, truth beauty." Construed in this way, the last two lines seem merely a bald assertion rather than a convincing conclusion organically following from the body of the poem. In his interpretation of the ode (*The Finer Tone* [1953], pp. 58–62), Earl Wasserman persuasively argues that the statement " that is all / Ye know on earth . . ." applies, not merely to the maxim, " Beauty is truth," but also to the previous three lines (ll. 46–48). In other words, in a world of change and decay, all we can know is that the sort of insight the urn embodies is able to remain " a friend to man," reminding him that, at one level at least, " Beauty is truth." It can continue, as Mr. Wasserman says, to hold out to man " the promise that somewhere . . . songs are forever new, love is forever young, . . . beauty is truth. . . . The knowledge that in art this insight is forever available is the height of earthly wisdom; and it is all man needs to know, for it endows his earthly existence with a purpose and a meaning."

1

Thou still unravished bride of quietness,
  Thou foster-child of silence and slow time,
Sylvan° historian, who canst thus express
A flowery tale more sweetly than our rhyme:
What leaf-fringed legend haunts about thy shape
  Of deities or mortals, or of both,
    In Tempe° or the dales of Arcady?°
  What men or gods are these? What maidens loth?
What mad pursuit? What struggle to escape?
  What pipes and timbrels? What wild ecstasy?

2

Heard melodies are sweet, but those unheard   11
  Are sweeter; therefore, ye soft pipes, play on;
Not to the sensual ear,° but, more endeared,
  Pipe to the spirit ditties of no tone:
Fair youth, beneath the trees, thou canst not leave
  Thy song, nor ever can those trees be bare;
  Bold Lover, never, never canst thou kiss,
Though winning near the goal — yet, do not grieve;
  She cannot fade, though thou hast not thy bliss,
Forever wilt thou love, and she be fair!   20

3

Ah, happy, happy boughs! that cannot shed
  Your leaves, nor ever bid the Spring adieu;
And, happy melodist, unwearied,
  Forever piping songs forever new;
More happy love! more happy, happy love!
  Forever warm and still to be enjoyed,
    Forever panting, and forever young;
All breathing human passion far above,
  That leaves a heart high-sorrowful and cloyed,
    A burning forehead, and a parching tongue.

4

Who are these coming to the sacrifice?   31
  To what green altar, O mysterious priest,
Lead'st thou that heifer lowing at the skies,
  And all her silken flanks with garlands dressed?
What little town by river or sea shore,
  Or mountain-built with peaceful citadel,
    Is emptied of this folk, this pious morn?
And, little town, thy streets forevermore
  Will silent be; and not a soul to tell
    Why thou art desolate, can 'er return.   40

5

O Attic° shape! Fair attitude! with brede°
Of marble men and maidens overwrought,
With forest branches and the trodden weed;
  Thou, silent form, dost tease us out of thought
As doth eternity: Cold Pastoral!°
  When old age shall this generation waste,
    Thou shalt remain, in midst of other woe
Than ours, a friend to man, to whom thou say'st,
" Beauty is truth, truth beauty," — that is all   49
  Ye know on earth, and all ye need to know.°

May, 1819

THE FALL OF HYPERION

A Dream

Keats's revision of *Hyperion* was begun in August, 1819, while he was still at work on *Lamia*. He probably discontinued it by the end of September. The revision, especially the first canto, is a quite different poem from the former *Hyperion*. Much of the Miltonic style of the first version has evaporated; the blank verse of the revision is quieter, more relaxed, mellow, and idiomatic. What remains of the original story seems to have been destined for another purpose,

---

ODE ON A GRECIAN URN. 3. **Sylvan:** woodlike or rustic. 7. **Tempe:** a valley in Thessaly, Greece. **Arcady:** a hilly district, in southern Greece, noted as a center of pastoral life. 13. **sensual ear:** sensuous ear — the physical sense of hearing.

41. **Attic:** of Attica (Athens). **brede:** design. 45. **Cold Pastoral:** pastoral scene, coolly aloof from human bustle, and rendered fixed and immortal on the face of the urn. 46–50. **When . . . know:** See headnote above.

though the revision, like the original, is incomplete.
The new first canto carries further the condemnation
of the "dreaming" poet already implied in *Lamia*.

from CANTO I

Fanatics have their dreams, wherewith they weave
A paradise for a sect; the savage, too,
From forth the loftiest fashion of his sleep
Guesses at Heaven; pity these have not
Traced upon vellum or wild Indian leaf
The shadows of melodious utterance.
But bare of laurel they live, dream, and die;
For Poesy alone can tell her dreams —
With the fine spell of words alone can save
Imagination from the sable chain   10
And dumb enchantment — Who alive can say,
"Thou art no Poet — may'st not tell thy dreams"?
Since every man whose soul is not a clod
Hath visions, and would speak, if he had loved,
And been well nurtured in his mother tongue.
Whether the dream now purposed to rehearse
Be poet's or fanatic's will be known
When this warm scribe, my hand, is in the grave.

Methought I stood where trees of every clime,
Palm, myrtle, oak, and sycamore, and beech,   20
With plantane, and spice-blossoms, made a screen;
In neighborhood of fountains by the noise
Soft-showering in mine ears and by the touch
Of scent, not far from roses. Turning round
I saw an arbor with a drooping roof
Of trellis vines, and bells, and larger blooms,
Like floral censers, swinging light in air;
Before its wreathèd doorway, on a mound
Of moss, was spread a feast of summer fruits,
Which, nearer seen, seemed refuse of a meal   30
By angel tasted or our Mother Eve;
For empty shells were scattered on the grass,
And grape-stalks but half bare, and remnants more,
Sweet-smelling, whose pure kinds I could not know.
Still was more plenty than the fabled horn
Thrice emptied could pour forth, at banqueting
For Proserpine° returned to her own fields,
Where the white heifers low. And appetite,
More yearning than on earth I ever felt,
Growing within, I ate deliciously;   40
And, after not long, thirsted; for thereby
Stood a cool vessel of transparent juice,
Sipped by the wandered bee, the which I took,
And, pledging all the mortals of the world,
And all the dead whose names are in our lips,
Drank. That full draught is parent of my theme.

No Asian poppy nor elixir fine
Of the soon-fading, jealous Caliphat,°
No poison gendered in close monkish cell,
To thin the scarlet conclave of old men,°   50
Could so have rapt unwilling life away.
Among the fragrant husks and berries crushed
Upon the grass, I struggled hard against
The domineering potion, but in vain.
The cloudy swoon came on, and down I sunk,
Like a Silenus° on an antique vase.
How long I slumbered 'tis a chance to guess.
When sense of life returned, I started up
As if with wings, but the fair trees were gone,
The mossy mound and arbor were no more: 60
I looked around upon the carvèd sides
Of an old sanctuary with roof august,
Builded so high, it seemed that filmèd clouds
Might spread beneath, as o'er the stars of heaven.
So old the place was, I remembered none
The like upon the earth: what I had seen
Of grey cathedrals, buttressed walls, rent towers,
The superannuations of sunk realms,
Or Nature's rocks toiled hard in waves and winds,
Seemed but the faulture of decrepit things   70
To that eternal domèd monument.
Upon the marble at my feet there lay
Store of strange vessels, and large draperies,
Which needs had been of dyed asbestos wove,
Or in that place the moth could not corrupt,
So white the linen, so, in some, distinct
Ran imageries from a somber loom.
All in a mingled heap confused there lay
Robes, golden tongs, censer and chafing-dish,
Girdles, and chains, and holy jewelries.   80

Turning from these with awe, once more I raised
My eyes to fathom the space every way;
The embossèd roof, the silent massy range
Of columns north and south, ending in mist
Of nothing; then to eastward, where black gates
Were shut against the sunrise evermore.
Then to the west I looked, and saw far off
An image, huge of feature as a cloud,
At level of whose feet an altar slept,
To be approached on either side by steps   90
And marble balustrade, and patient travail
To count with toil the innumerable degrees.
Towards the altar sober-paced I went,
Repressing haste, as too unholy there;

---

48. soon-fading . . . Caliphat: The implication is that the caliphs
(descendants or successors of Mohammed — the title was often
assumed by the Turkish sultans) so frequently murdered each
other or were murdered by others that their reigns were short.
50. scarlet . . . men: secret meeting of cardinals. **56. Silenus:**
a woodland god, tutor and companion of Bacchus; usually por-
trayed as a drunken old man with a flat nose and pointed ears;
also applied as a term to a group of woodland gods, half man
and half goat.

FALL OF HYPERION. **Canto I: 37. Proserpine:** daughter of Ceres,
carried off to Hades by Pluto, but allowed to return once a year.

And, coming nearer, saw beside the shrine
One minist'ring; and there arose a flame.
When in mid-May the sickening east-wind
Shifts sudden to the south, the small warm rain
Melts out the frozen incense from all flowers,
And fills the air with so much pleasant health   100
That even the dying man forgets his shroud; —
Even so that lofty sacrificial fire,
Sending forth Maian° incense, spread around
Forgetfulness of everything but bliss,
And clouded all the altar with soft smoke;
From whose white fragrant curtains thus I heard
Language pronounced: "If thou canst not ascend
These steps, die on that marble where thou art.
Thy flesh, near cousin to the common dust,
Will parch for lack of nutriment — thy bones   110
Will wither in few years, and vanish so
That not the quickest eye could find a grain
Of what thou now art on that pavement cold.
The sands of thy short life are spent this hour,
And no hand in the universe can turn
Thy hourglass, if these gummèd leaves be burnt
Ere thou canst mount up these immortal steps."
I heard, I looked: two senses both at once,
So fine, so subtle, felt the tyranny
Of that fierce threat and the hard task proposed.
Prodigious seemed the toil; the leaves were yet   121
Burning, — when suddenly a palsied chill
Struck from the pavèd level up my limbs,
And was ascending quick to put cold grasp
Upon those streams that pulse beside the throat!
I shrieked, and the sharp anguish of my shriek
Stung my own ears — I strove hard to escape
The numbness, strove to gain the lowest step.
Slow, heavy, deadly was my pace: the cold
Grew stifling, suffocating, at the heart;   130
And when I clasped my hands I felt them not.
One minute before death, my icèd foot touched
The lowest stair; and, as it touched, life seemed
To pour in at the toes: I mounted up,
As once fair angels on a ladder flew
From the green turf to heaven. "Holy Power,"
Cried I, approaching near the hornèd shrine,
"What am I that should be so saved from death?
What am I that another death come not
To choke my utterance, sacrilegious, here?"   140
Then said the veilèd Shadow: "Thou hast felt
What 'tis to die and live again before
Thy fated hour; that thou hadst power to do so
Is thy own safety; thou hast dated on
Thy doom." "High Prophetess," said I, "purge
   off,
Benign, if so it please thee, my mind's film."
"None can usurp this height," returned that shade,

"But those to whom the miseries of the world
Are misery, and will not let them rest.
All else who find a haven in the world,   150
Where they may thoughtless sleep away their days,
If by a chance into this fane they come,
Rot on the pavement where thou rotted'st half."
"Are there not thousands in the world," said I,
Encouraged by the sooth voice of the shade,
"Who love their fellows even to the death;
Who feel the giant agony of the world;
And more, like slaves to poor humanity,
Labor for mortal good? I sure should see
Other men here, but I am here alone."   160
"Those whom thou spakest of are no visionaries,"
Rejoined that voice — "they are no dreamers weak;
They seek no wonder but the human face,
No music but a happy-noted voice —
They come not here, they have no thought to
   come —
And thou art here, for thou art less than they.
What benefit canst thou do, or all thy tribe,
To the great world? Thou art a dreaming thing,
A fever of thyself — think of the earth;
What bliss, even in hope, is there for thee?   170
What haven? every creature hath its home;
Every sole man hath days of joy and pain,
Whether his labors be sublime or low —
The pain alone, the joy alone, distinct:
Only the dreamer venoms all his days,
Bearing more woe than all his sins deserve.
Therefore, that happiness be somewhat shared,
Such things as thou art are admitted oft
Into like gardens thou didst pass erewhile,
And suffered in these temples: for that cause   180
Thou standest safe beneath this statue's knees."
"That I am favored for unworthiness,
By such propitious parley medicined
In sickness not ignoble, I rejoice,
Aye, and could weep for love of such award."
So answered I, continuing, "If it please,
Majestic Shadow, tell me: sure not all
Those melodies sung into the world's ear
Are useless: sure a poet is a sage;
A humanist, physician to all men.   190
That I am none I feel, as vultures feel
They are no birds when eagles are abroad.
What am I then: thou spakest of my tribe:
What tribe?" The tall shade veiled in drooping
   white
Then spake, so much more earnest, that the breath
Moved the thin linen folds that drooping hung
About a golden censer, from the hand
Pendent — "Art thou not of the dreamer tribe?
The poet and the dreamer are distinct,
Diverse, sheer opposite, antipodes.   200
The one pours out a balm upon the world,

---

103. **Maian**: in Greek mythology, Maia was the mother of
Hermes.

The other vexes it." Then shouted I
Spite of myself, and with a Pythia's° spleen,
"Apollo! faded! O far-flown Apollo!
Where is thy misty pestilence to creep
Into the dwellings, through the door crannies
Of all mock lyrists, large self-worshipers
And careless Hectorers° in proud bad verse?
Though I breathe death with them it will be life
To see them sprawl before me into graves.   210
Majestic Shadow, tell me where I am,
Whose altar this, for whom this incense curls;
What image this whose face I cannot see
For the broad marble knees; and who thou art,
Of accent feminine so courteous? "

Then the tall shade, in drooping linens veiled,
Spake out, so much more earnest, that her breath
Stirred the thin folds of gauze that drooping hung
About a golden censer, from her hand
Pendent; and by her voice I knew she shed   220
Long-treasured tears. " This temple, sad and lone,
Is all spared from the thunder of a war
Foughten long since by giant Hierarchy
Against rebellion: this old Image here,
Whose carvèd features wrinkled as he fell,
Is Saturn's; I, Moneta, left supreme,
Sole priestess of his desolation." —
I had no words to answer, for my tongue,
Useless, could find about its roofèd home
No syllable of a fit majesty   230
To make rejoinder to Moneta's mourn:
There was a silence, while the altar's blaze
Was fainting for sweet food. I looked thereon,
And on the pavèd floor, where nigh were piled
Faggots of cinnamon, and many heaps
Of other crispèd spicewood: then again
I looked upon the altar, and its horns
Whitened with ashes, and its lang'rous flame,
And then upon the offerings again;
And so by turns — till sad Moneta cried: 240
" The sacrifice is done, but not the less
Will I be kind to thee for thy good will.
My power, which to me is still a curse,
Shall be to thee a wonder; for the scenes
Still swooning vivid through my globèd brain,
With an electral° changing misery,
Thou shalt with these dull mortal eyes behold
Free from all pain, if wonder pain thee not."
As near as an immortal's spherèd words
Could to a mother's soften, were these last: 250
And yet I had a terror of her robes,
And chiefly of the veils, that from her brow
Hung pale, and curtained her in mysteries,

That made my heart too small to hold its blood.
This saw that Goddess, and with sacred hand
Parted the veils. Then saw I a wan face,
Not pined by human sorrows, but bright-blanched
By an immortal sickness which kills not;
It works a constant change, which happy death
Can put no end to; deathwards progressing   260
To no death was that visage; it had passed
The lily and the snow; and beyond these
I must not think now, though I saw that face.
But for her eyes I should have fled away.
They held me back with a benignant light,
Soft mitigated by divinest lids
Half closed, and visionless entire they seemed
Of all external things — they saw me not,
But, in blank splendor, beamed like the mild moon,
Who comforts those she sees not, who knows not
What eyes are upward cast. As I had found   271
A grain of gold upon a mountain's side,
And, twinged with avarice, strained out my eyes
To search its sullen entrails rich with ore,
So, at the view of sad Moneta's brow,
I ached to see what things the hollow brain
Behind enwombèd: what high tragedy
In the dark secret Chambers of her skull
Was acting, that could give so dread a stress
To her cold lips, and fill with such a light   280
Her planetary eyes, and touch her voice
With such a sorrow. . . .

THIS LIVING HAND

Probably written in 1819, these lines are commonly
supposed to have been addressed to Fanny Brawne.

This living hand, now warm and capable
Of earnest grasping, would, if it were cold
And in the icy silence of the tomb,
So haunt thy days and chill thy dreaming nights
That thou wouldst wish thine own heart dry of
    blood
So in my veins red life might stream again,
And thou be conscience-calmed — see here it is —
I hold it towards you.

TO AUTUMN

Written September 19, 1819. Three days later, Keats
wrote to his friend, J. H. Reynolds, from Winchester,
"How beautiful the season is now. How fine the air.
. . . I never liked stubble-fields so much as now —
Aye better than the chilly green of the spring. Somehow a stubble-field looks warm — in the same way
that some pictures look warm. This struck me so
much in my Sunday's walk that I composed upon it."

203. Pythia: priestess of the oracle at Delphi.   208. Hectorers:
bullying, browbeating writers; possibly an allusion to Byron.
246. electral: vital, vivid.

1

Season of mists and mellow fruitfulness,
  Close bosom-friend of the maturing sun;
Conspiring with him how to load and bless
  With fruit the vines that round the thatch-eaves
        run;
To bend with apples the mossed cottage-trees,
  And fill all fruit with ripeness to the core;
    To swell the gourd, and plump the hazel shells
  With a sweet kernel; to set budding more,
And still more, later flowers for the bees,
Until they think warm days will never cease,   10
    For Summer has o'er-brimmed their clammy
        cells.

2

Who hath not seen thee oft amid thy store?
  Sometimes whoever seeks abroad may find
Thee sitting careless on a granary floor,
  Thy hair soft-lifted by the winnowing wind;
Or on a half-reaped furrow sound asleep,
  Drowsed with the fume of poppies, while thy
        hook
    Spares the next swath and all its twinèd
        flowers:
And sometimes like a gleaner thou dost keep
  Steady thy laden head across a brook;   20
  Or by a cyder-press, with patient look,
    Thou watchest the last oozings hours by hours.

3

Where are the songs of Spring? Ay, where are
        they?
  Think not of them, thou hast thy music too, —
While barrèd clouds bloom the soft-dying day,
  And touch the stubble-plains with rosy hue;
Then in a wailful choir the small gnats mourn
  Among the river sallows,° borne aloft
    Or sinking as the light wind lives or dies;
And full-grown lambs loud bleat from hilly bourn;°
  Hedge-crickets sing; and now with treble soft
  The red-breast whistles from a garden-croft;°   32
    And gathering swallows twitter in the skies.

LETTERS

The letters of Keats are among the most appealing
in English literature. They touch upon both ideas and
ordinary daily experiences with insight, gusto, warmth,
and humor. Particularly valuable for interpreting what
was best in Keats, and sensing the direction in which
his unique promise lay, are his searching remarks on

TO AUTUMN. **28. sallows:** willows. **30. bourn:** region.
32. croft: a small, enclosed field.

---

poetry and the poetic character. Among them, as T. S.
Eliot has said, there is hardly one statement that "will
not be found to be true; and what is more, true for
greater and more mature poetry than anything that
Keats ever wrote."

The text of the letters is basically that of M. B.
Forman (Oxford, 1931, and later revised editions).
Capitalization has in general been changed to conform more closely with modern usage, but the original
spelling and punctuation have been retained.

I. To BENJAMIN BAILEY [1]

Saturday 22 Nov. 1817

My dear Bailey,
  I will get over the first part of this (*un*said) [2]
letter as soon as possible for it relates to the affair
of poor Crips — To a man of your nature such a
letter as Haydon's must have been extremely cutting — What occasions the greater part of the
world's quarrels? simply this, two minds meet and
do not understand each other time enough to prevent any shock or surprise at the conduct of either
party — As soon as I had known Haydon three
days I had got enough of his character not to have
been surprised at such a letter as he has hurt you
with. Nor when I knew it was it a principle with
me to drop his acquaintance although with you it
would have been an imperious feeling. I wish you
knew all that I think about Genius and the Heart
— and yet I think you are thoroughly acquainted
with my innermost breast in that respect, or you
could not have known me even thus long and still
hold me worthy to be your dear friend. In passing
however I must say of one thing that has pressed
upon me lately and encreased my humility and
capability of submission and that is this truth —
Men of Genius are great as certain ethereal chemi-
cals operating on the mass of neutral intellect —
but they have not any individuality, any determined character — I would call the top and head
of those who have a proper self Men of Power —
  But I am running my head into a subject which
I am certain I could not do justice to under five

---

1. Bailey was an undergraduate at Oxford, preparing to enter
the Church, when Keats first met him. Keats wrote Book III of
Endymion while visiting him at Oxford.   **2.** *un*said: Keats is
playing on the legal phrase "said letter"; the "said letter" would
be Haydon's to Bailey, the "unsaid "Keats's. Benjamin Robert
Haydon (1786–1846), the historical painter, had for a year
been friendly with Keats. See "To Haydon," l. 7n., above. The
background of the present incident is not clear. Cripps, a young
artist, had attracted Haydon's attention. Haydon implied he
would help to train Cripps, and then demanded an apprentice
fee which Keats tried to raise.

years study and 3 vols octavo — and moreover long to be talking about the Imagination — so my dear Bailey do not think of this unpleasant affair if possible — do not — I defy any harm to come of it — I defy. I'll shall write to Crips this week and request him to tell me all his goings on from time to time by letter wherever I may be — it will all go on well so don't because you have suddenly discover'd a coldness in Haydon suffer yourself to be teased. Do not my dear fellow. O I wish I was as certain of the end of all your troubles as that of your momentary start about the authenticity of the Imagination. I am certain of nothing but of the holiness of the Heart's affections and the truth of Imagination — What the Imagination seizes as Beauty must be Truth — whether it existed before or not — for I have the same idea of all our passions as of love they are all in their sublime, creative of essential Beauty. In a word, you may know my favorite speculation by my first book and the little song I sent in my last — which is a representation from the fancy of the probable mode of operating in these matters. The Imagination may be compared to Adam's dream [3] — he awoke and found it truth. I am the more zealous in this affair, because I have never yet been able to perceive how any thing can be known for truth by consequitive reasoning [4] — and yet it must be. Can it be that even the greatest philosopher ever arrived at his goal without putting aside numerous objections. However it may be, O for a life of sensations rather than of thoughts! It is "a Vision in the form of Youth" a shadow of reality to come — and this consideration has further convinced me for it has come as auxiliary to another favorite speculation of mine, that we shall enjoy ourselves here after by having what we called happiness on earth repeated in a finer tone and so repeated. And yet such a fate can only befall those who delight in sensation rather than hunger as you do after Truth. Adam's dream will do here and seems to be a conviction that Imagination and its empyreal reflection is the same as human life and its spiritual repetition. But as I was saying — the simple imaginative mind may have its rewards in the repetition of its own silent working coming continually on the spirit with a fine suddenness — to compare great things with small — have you never by being surprised with an old melody — in a delicious place — by a delicious

voice, felt over again your very speculations and surmises at the time it first operated on your soul — do you not remember forming to yourself the singer's face more beautiful than it was possible and yet with the elevation of the moment you did not think so — even then you were mounted on the wings of Imagination so high — that the prototype must be here after — that delicious face you will see. What a time! I am continually running away from the subject — sure this cannot be exactly the case with a complex mind — one that is imaginative and at the same time careful of its fruits — who would exist partly on sensation partly on thought — to whom it is necessary that years should bring the philosophic mind [5] — such an one I consider your's and therefore it is necessary to your eternal happiness that you not only drink this old wine of Heaven, which I shall call the redigestion of our most ethereal musings on earth; but also increase in knowledge and know all things. I am glad to hear you are in a fair way for Easter — you will soon get through your unpleasant reading and then! — but the world is full of troubles and I have not much reason to think myself pesterd with many — I think Jane or Marianne has a better opinion of me than I deserve — for really and truly I do not think my brothers illness connected with mine — you know more of the real cause than they do nor have I any chance of being rack'd as you have been — You perhaps at one time thought there was such a thing as worldly happiness to be arrived at, at certain periods of time marked out — you have of necessity from your disposition been thus led away — I scarcely remember counting upon my happiness — I look not for it if it be not in the present hour — nothing startles me beyond the moment. The setting sun will always set me to rights — or if a sparrow come before my window I take part in its existence and pick about the gravel. The first thing that strikes me on hearing a misfortune having befalled another is this. "Well it cannot be helped — he will have the pleasure of trying the resources of his spirit" — and I beg now my dear Bailey that hereafter should you observe any thing cold in me not to put it to the account of heartlessness but abstraction — for I assure you I sometimes feel not the influence of a passion or affection during a whole week — and so long this sometimes continues I begin to suspect myself and

3. **Adam's dream:** *Paradise Lost*, VIII. 460–90.   4. **consequitive reasoning:** abstract analysis, and consecutive, step-by-step logic.

5. **years . . . mind:** Keats is echoing Wordsworth, "Intimations of Immortality," l. 187, above.

the genuineness of my feelings at other times — thinking them a few barren tragedy-tears — My brother Tom is much improved — he is going to Devonshire — whither I shall follow him — at present I am just arrived at Dorking to change the scene — change the air and give me a spur to wind up my Poem, of which there are wanting 500 lines. I should have been here a day sooner but the Reynoldses persuaded me to stop in town to meet your friend Christie. There were Rice and Martin — we talked about ghosts. I will have some talk with Taylor and let you know — when please God I come down at Christmas. I will find that Examiner if possible. My best regards to Gleig. My brothers to you and Mrs Bentley's

> Your affectionate friend
> John Keats —

II. To GEORGE and THOMAS KEATS

Sunday 21 Dec. 1817

Hampstead Sunday

My dear Brothers,

I must crave your pardon for not having written ere this. . . .[6] I saw Kean[7] return to the public in 'Richard III.', and finely he did it, and, at the request of Reynolds, I went to criticize his Luke in Riches. The critique is in to-day's 'Champion', which I send you, with the Examiner, in which you will find very proper lamentation on the obsoletion of Christmas gambols and pastimes:[8] but it was mixed up with so much egotism of that driveling nature that pleasure is entirely lost. Hone, the publisher's trial, you must find very amusing; and, as Englishmen, very encouraging — his *Not Guilty* is a thing, which not to have been, would have dulled still more Liberty's emblazoning — Lord Ellenborough has been paid in his own coin — Wooler and Hone[9] have done us an essential service — I have had two very pleasant evenings with Dilke,[10] yesterday and to-day, and am at this moment just come from him, and feel in the humour to go on with this, began in the morning, and

from which he came to fetch me. I spent Friday evening with Wells,[11] and went next morning to see Death on the Pale Horse.[12] It is a wonderful picture, when West's age is considered; But there is nothing to be intense upon; no women one feels mad to kiss, no face swelling into reality — The excellence of every art is its intensity, capable of making all disagreeables evaporate, from their being in close relationship with Beauty and Truth.[13] Examine 'King Lear,' and you will find this exemplified throughout; but in this picture we have unpleasantness without any momentous depth of speculation excited, in which to bury its repulsiveness — The picture is larger than 'Christ rejected.'

I dined with Haydon the Sunday after you left, and had a very pleasant day, I dined too (for I have been out too much lately) with Horace Smith, and met his two brothers, with Hill and Kingston, and one Du Bois.[14] They only served to convince me, how superior humour is to wit in respect to enjoyment — These men say things which make one start, without making one feel; they are all alike; their manners are alike; they all know fashionables; they have a mannerism in their very eating and drinking, in their mere handling a decanter — They talked of Kean and his low company — Would I were with that company instead of yours, said I to myself! I know such like acquaintance will never do for me, and yet I am going to Reynolds on Wednesday. Brown and Dilke walked with me and back from the Christmas pantomime. I had not a dispute but a disquisition, with Dilke on various subjects; several things dove-tailed in my mind, and at once it struck me what quality went to form a Man of Achievement, especially in Literature, and which Shakespeare possessed so enormously — I mean *Negative Capability*,[15] that

---

6. A passage was here omitted in the only copy of the letter that has survived.   7. **Kean:** Edmund Kean (1787–1833), the noted tragic actor. Keats's review of his performance appeared in the *Champion*, Dec. 21, 1817.   8. **lamentation . . . pastimes:** The reference is to an essay of Leigh Hunt on this subject in the *Examiner*, Dec. 21 and 28, 1817.   9. **Wooler . . . Hone:** publishers. William Hone had been tried for libel.   10. **Dilke:** Charles Dilke (1789–1864), later known as an editor and scholar.

11. **Wells:** Charles Wells (1800–79), author of *Stories after Nature*. 12. **Death . . . Horse:** Benjamin West (1738–1820). His "Christ Rejected," referred to later in the paragraph, was criticized in the same terms by Hazlitt, whose critical opinions Keats closely followed.   13. **The . . . Truth:** If the imaginative grasp of an object is sufficiently intense, it takes so strong a hold of the mind that whatever qualities are irrelevant to its central character (the "disagreeables") evaporate. Its truth (or character) then "swells into reality" for us so vividly that the dynamic awareness of it is also "beautiful." In other words, reality taking form and meaning is "beauty" if it is vitally enough known and felt. Cf. "Ode on a Grecian Urn," ll. 49–50, see p. 749, above.   14. **Smith . . . Du Bois:** writers who contributed to magazines of the time. 15. We may interpret these difficult remarks, from here to the end of the paragraph, as follows: Our life is filled with change, uncertainties, mysteries; no one complete system of rigid categories will explain it fully. We can grasp and understand the elusive flux of life only by being imaginatively open-minded, sym-

is, when a man is capable of being in uncertainties, mysteries, doubts, without any irritable reaching after fact and reason — Coleridge, for instance, would let go by a fine isolated verisimilitude caught from the penetralium of mystery, from being incapable of remaining content with half-knowledge. This pursued through volumes would perhaps take us no further than this, that with a great poet the sense of Beauty overcomes every other consideration, or rather obliterates all consideration.

Shelley's poem [16] is out, and there are words about its being objected to as much as "Queen Mab" was. Poor Shelley, I think he has his quota of good qualities, in sooth la!! Write soon to your most sincere friend and affectionate brother

John.

III. *From* To JOHN HAMILTON REYNOLDS [17]

Tuesday 3 Feb. 1818

It may be said that we ought to read our contemporaries — that Wordsworth &c. should have their due from us. But, for the sake of a few fine imaginative or domestic passages, are we to be bullied into a certain philosophy engendered in the whims of an egotist — Every man has his speculations, but every man does not brood and peacock over them till he makes a false coinage and deceives himself.[18] Many a man can travel to the very bourne of Heaven, and yet want confidence to put down his half-seeing. Sancho will invent a journey heavenward as well as any body. We hate poetry that has a palpable design upon us — and if we do not agree, seems to put its hand in its breeches pocket. Poetry should be great and un-

obtrusive, a thing which enters into one's soul, and does not startle it or amaze it with itself, but with its subject. — How beautiful are the retired flowers! how would they lose their beauty were they to throng into the highway crying out, "admire me I am a violet! — dote upon me I am a primrose!" Modern poets differ from the Elizabethans in this. Each of the moderns like an Elector of Hanover governs his petty state, and knows how many straws are swept daily from the causeways in all his dominions and has a continual itching that all the housewives should have their coppers well scoured: the antients were emperors of vast provinces, they had only heard of the remote ones and scarcely cared to visit them. — I will cut all this — I will have no more of Wordsworth or Hunt in particular — Why should we be of the tribe of Manasseh, when we can wander with Esau? why should we kick against the pricks, when we can walk on roses? Why should we be owls, when we can be eagles? Why be teased with "nice eyed wagtails",[19] when we have in sight "the Cherub Contemplation"? [20] — Why with Wordsworth's "Matthew with a bough of wilding in his hand" [21] when we can have Jacques "under an oak &c."? [22] The secret of the bough of wilding will run through your head faster than I can write it — Old Matthew spoke to him some years ago on some nothing, and because he happens in an evening walk to imagine the figure of the old man — he must stamp it down in black and white, and it is henceforth sacred — I don't mean to deny Wordsworth's grandeur and Hunt's merit, but I mean to say we not be teazed with grandeur and merit when we can have them uncontaminated and unobtrusive. Let us have the old poets, and Robin Hood. Your letter and its sonnets gave me more pleasure than will the 4th Book of Childe Harold [23] and the whole of anybody's life and opinions. In return for your dish of filberts, I have gathered a few catkins,[24] I hope they'll look pretty.

IV. *From* To JOHN HAMILTON REYNOLDS

Sunday 3 May 1818

. . . I will return to Wordsworth — whether or no he has an extended vision or a circumscribed

---

pathetic, receptive — by extending every possible feeler that we may have potentially in us. But we can achieve this active awareness only by *negating* our own *egos*. We must not only rise above our own vanity and prejudices, but resist the temptation to make up our minds on everything, and to have always ready a neat answer. If we discard a momentary insight, for example, because we cannot fit it into a static category or systematic framework, we are selfishly asserting our own "identity." A great poet is less concerned with himself, and has his eyes on what is without. With him "the sense of Beauty"— the capacity to relish concrete reality in its full, if elusive, meaning — "overcomes every other consideration." In fact, it goes beyond and "obliterates" the act of "consideration"— of deliberating, analyzing, and piecing together experience in a logical structure. **16. Shelley's poem:** "Laon and Cyntha." **17.** Reynolds, a young clerk, slightly older than Keats, had been writing poetry for some years. **18.** Keats, in his contrast of Wordsworth with the Elizabethans, is following Hazlitt, for whom much of the poetry of the Romantic movement, especially that of Wordsworth, was subjective self-expression.

19. Leigh Hunt, *The Nymphs*, II.170. **20.** Milton, "Il Penseroso," l. 54. **21.** "The Two April Mornings," ll. 59-60. **22.** *As You Like It*, II.i.31. **23.** Byron's *Childe Harold*, which was to be published on April 28. **24. filberts . . . catkins:** Filberts are hazelnuts, catkins their blossom.

grandeur — whether he is an eagle in his nest, or on the wing — And to be more explicit and to show you how tall I stand by the giant, I will put down a simile of human life as far as I now perceive it; that is, to the point to which I say we both have arrived at — Well — I compare human life to a large mansion of many apartments, two of which I can only describe, the doors of the rest being as yet shut upon me. The first we step into we call the infant or thoughtless chamber, in which we remain as long as we do not think — We remain there a long while, and notwithstanding the doors of the second chamber remain wide open, showing a bright appearance, we care not to hasten to it; but are at length imperceptibly impelled by the awakening of this thinking principle within us — we no sooner get into the second chamber, which I shall call the chamber of maiden-thought, than we become intoxicated with the light and the atmosphere, we see nothing but pleasant wonders, and think of delaying there for ever in delight: However among the effects this breathing is father of is that tremendous one of sharpening one's vision into the heart and nature of man — of convincing one's nerves that the world is full of misery and heartbreak, pain, sickness and oppression — whereby this chamber of maiden thought becomes gradually darken'd and at the same time on all sides of it many doors are set open — but all dark — all leading to dark passages — We see not the ballance of good and devil. We are in a mist. *We* are now in that state — We feel the " burden of the mystery ", To this point was Wordsworth come, as far as I can conceive when he wrote ' Tintern Abbey ' and it seems to me that his Genius is explorative of those dark passages. Now if we live, and go on thinking, we too shall explore them — he is a Genius and superior to us, in so far as he can, more than we, make discoveries, and shed a light in them — Here I must think Wordsworth is deeper than Milton — though I think it has depended more upon the general and gregarious advance of intellect, than individual greatness of mind — From the Paradise Lost and the other works of Milton, I hope it is not too presuming, even between ourselves to say, that his philosophy, human and divine, may be tolerably understood by one not much advanced in years, In his time Englishmen were just emancipated from a great superstition — and men had got hold of certain points and resting places in reasoning which were too newly born to be doubted, and too much opposed by the mass of

Europe not to be thought etherial and authentically divine — who could gainsay his ideas on virtue, vice, and chastity in Comus, just at the time of the dismissal of cod-pieces and a hundred other disgraces? who would not rest satisfied with his hintings at good and evil in the Paradise Lost, when just free from the inquisition and burning in Smithfield? The Reformation produced such immediate and great benefits, that Protestantism was considered under the immediate eye of Heaven, and its own remaining dogmas and superstitions, then, as it were, regenerated, constituted those resting places and seeming sure points of reasoning — from that I have mentioned, Milton, whatever he may have thought in the sequel, appears to have been content with these by his writings — He did not think into the human heart, as Wordsworth has done — Yet Milton as a philosopher, had sure as great powers as Wordsworth — What is then to be inferr'd? O many things — It proves there is really a grand march of intellect —, It proves that a mighty providence subdues the mightiest minds to the service of the time being, whether it be in human knowledge or religion — I have often pitied a tutor who has to hear " Nom: Musa " [25] — so often dinn'd into his ears — I hope you may not have the same pain in this scribbling — I may have read these things before, but I never had even a thus dim perception of them; and moreover I like to say my lesson to one who will endure my tediousness for my own sake — After all there is certainly something real in the world — Moore's present to Hazlitt [26] is real — I like that Moore, and am glad I saw him at the theatre just before I left town. Tom has spit a leetle blood this afternoon, and that is rather a damper — but I know — the truth is there is something real in the world. Your third chamber of life shall be a lucky and a gentle one — stored with the wine of love — and the bread of friendship. When you see George if he should not have received a letter from me tell him he will find one at home most likely — tell Bailey I hope soon to see him — Remember me to all. The leaves have been out here, for mony a day — I have written to George for the first stanzas of my Isabel [27] — I shall have them soon and will copy the whole out for you.

Your affectionate friend
John Keats.

25. "Nom: Musa": the first lesson in Latin grammar: "Nominative: Musa," etc.   26. Probably a copy of one of Thomas Moore's books.   27. Isabel: Keats's poem, *Isabella*.

V. To MISS JEFFREY [28]

Wednesday 9 June 1819

Wentworth Place

My Dear young Lady,

I am exceedingly obliged by your two letters — Why I did not answer your first immediately was that I have had a little aversion to the south of Devon from the continual remembrance of my brother Tom. On that account I do not return to my old lodgings in Hampstead though the people of the house have become friends of mine — This however I could think nothing of, it can do no more than keep one's thoughts employed for a day or two. I like your description of Bradley [29] very much and I dare say shall be there in the course of the summer; it would be immediately but that a friend with ill health and to whom I am greatly attached call'd on me yesterday and proposed my spending a month with him at the back of the Isle of Wight. This is just the thing at present — the morrow will take care of itself — I do not like the name of Bishop's Teigntown — I hope the road from Teignmouth to Bradley does not lie that way — Your advice about the Indiaman is a very wise advice, because it just suits me, though you are a little in the wrong concerning its destroying the energies of mind: [30] on the contrary it would be the finest thing in the world to strengthen them — To be thrown among people who care not for you, with whom you have no sympathies forces the mind upon its own resources, and leaves it free to make its speculations of the differences of human character and to class them with the calmness of a botanist. An Indiaman is a little world. One of the great reasons that the English have produced the finest writers in the world is, that the English world has ill-treated them during their lives and foster'd them after their deaths. They have in general been trampled aside into the bye paths of life and seen the festerings of society. They have not been treated like the Raphaels of Italy. And where is the Englishman and poet who has given a magnificent entertainment at the christening of one of his hero's horses as Boyardo [31] did? He had a castle in the Appenine. He was a noble poet of romance; not a miserable and mighty poet of the human Heart. The middle age of Shakespeare was all clouded over; his days were not more happy than Hamlet's who is perhaps more like Shakespeare himself in his common every day life than any other of his characters — Ben Johnson was a common Soldier and in the Low Countries, in the face of two armies, fought a single combat with a French trooper and slew him — For all this I will not go on board an Indiaman, nor for example's sake run my head into dark alleys: I dare say my discipline is to come, and plenty of it too. I have been very idle lately, very averse to writing; both from the overpowering idea of our dead poets and from abatement of my love of fame. I hope I am a little more of a philosopher than I was, consequently a little less of a versifying pet-lamb. I have put no more in print or you should have had it. You will judge of my 1819 temper when I tell you that the thing I have most enjoyed this year has been writing an ode to Indolence. Why did you not make your long-haired sister put her great brown hard fist to paper and cross your letter? Tell her when you write again that I expect chequer-work — My friend Mr Brown is sitting opposite me employed in writing a life of *David*. He reads me passages as he writes them stuffing my infidel mouth as though I were a young rook — Infidel rooks do not provender with Elisha's ravens.[32] If he goes on as he has begun your new church had better not proceed, for parsons will be superseeded — and of course the clerks must follow. Give my love to your mother with the assurance that I can never forget her anxiety for my brother Tom. Believe also that I shall ever remember our leave-taking with *you*.

Ever sincerely yours
John Keats.

28. Miss Jeffrey: A member of a family friendly to Keats, at Teignmouth, Devon. It is uncertain to which of the daughters of the family the letter is addressed.   **29. Bradley:** in South Devon.   **30. Your . . . mind:** Keats had been speculating about the advisability of becoming a surgeon on an East India trade ship. In an earlier letter to Miss Jeffrey, he had mentioned this as a possibility.

31. Boyardo: Matteo Maria Boiardo (1434–94), an Italian poet who wrote chivalric romances based on the legends of Arthur and Charlemagne.   **32. Elisha's ravens:** Elijah, not Elisha, was fed by the ravens (I Kings 17:6).

Alfred, Lord Tennyson

1809–1892

Tennyson was born at Somersby in Lincolnshire on August 6, 1809, the birth year of Gladstone and Darwin and Lincoln and Poe; he was the third of eleven children, seven sons and four daughters. Like other lively and cultivated families of the pre-electronic era, and isolated as they were in the rectory of a rural parish, the young Tennysons made their own good times. Indoors there were the books of their father's library, from Shakespeare to Buffon, and writing, carving, clay-modeling, and such games as are mentioned in *In Memoriam,* LXXVIII; outdoors there were the Lincolnshire wolds and the life of birds and animals and, not far away, the North Sea. Mrs. Tennyson, evidently a robust mother, was a woman of simple piety; she lived to welcome the early *Idylls.* One moist and sulphurous element in the family was a Calvinistic aunt who could weep for hours in contemplation of the goodness of a God who had elected her while damning most of her friends, and who could impale the small boy with " Alfred, Alfred, when I look at you, I think of the words of Holy Scripture — 'Depart from me, ye cursed, into everlasting fire.'"

The father, the Reverend George Clayton Tennyson, was a sterner and more complex personality than his wife, and his moods determined the barometric pressures of the household. The elder son of a rich man, he had the normal expectations of inheritance; but he was displaced in favor of the younger son and forced into the church. Though he had no vocation, he was a zealous clergyman and was well liked in his parish; his brilliant talk was enjoyed in higher

circles. In his normal role as father he was also zealous. He himself educated his sons at home in Latin and Greek (Alfred had had only four or five years of formal schooling), and he encouraged the verse-writing of the three older boys, Frederick, Alfred, and Charles. On the other hand, Dr. Tennyson had his full share of the " black blood " of the Tennysons and brooded on his father's injustice and his own fate — while the favored younger brother enjoyed wealth and worldly prominence (later, like the " new-made lord " of *Maud,* he built himself a " gewgaw castle "). Dr. Tennyson's despondency drove him increasingly to alcoholic consolation and then to spells of insane violence. This story, which may well have contributed to " Locksley Hall " and *Maud,* was barely touched in the official *Memoir* of the poet (1897) and was first told fully in the biography (1949) by the poet's grandson, Sir Charles Tennyson. One can readily imagine how, for a sensitive young boy, even the happy periods of home life would be darkened by such an atmosphere, and why, when his father was in one of his spells, he more than once went out in the night and threw himself on a grave in the churchyard, praying for his own death.

Poems by Two Brothers was published by a provincial printer in the spring of 1827. In October Alfred and Charles went up to Trinity College, Cambridge, where Frederick already was. Tennyson, who had hardly been away from home before, did not much like the flat fen country or crowded communal life or the predominantly mathematical studies, which could be enjoyed by "None but dry-headed, calculat-ing, angular little gentlemen." In October, 1828, Arthur Hallam became a fellow student and in the course of the year the famous friendship began. Hallam, a year and a half Tennyson's junior, was the son of Henry Hallam, the his-torian, and had the literary and social sophistica-tion of Eton and London along with his own quick intelligence and charm; Tennyson's mind and frame were noble, his dress and manner rustic. Both were elected to a society of under-graduate intellectuals commonly known as the "Apostles," a group that included a number of young men destined for eminence. They were seriously concerned with religion, philosophy, and science, with social and political problems, and with literature; they were in advance of conventional opinion in admiring Wordsworth, Coleridge, Shelley, and Keats. Tennyson, who shrank from giving papers, occupied a sort of honorary niche on the strength of his poems. In June, 1829, his poem "Timbuctoo" won the university medal. In 1830 his first independent volume, *Poems, Chiefly Lyrical,* was published. In the summer of this year Tennyson and Hal-lam manifested their liberal sentiments by going to Spain with money from English sympathizers for Spanish rebels; the scenery of the Pyrenees left its impress on some of Tennyson's poems.

Early in 1831 Tennyson was called home from Cambridge by the illness of his father, who died in March, and he did not return to the uni-versity. Inheriting chiefly responsibilities, he lived with his mother and the family at Somersby. In July, 1832, he and Hallam made a tour on the Rhine. Another collection, *Poems,* dated 1833, appeared at the end of 1832 (it is cited under either date). This volume, which contained the first versions of a number of Ten-nyson's best-known early poems, had in the main a fair press; the notorious exception was a brutal article in the all-powerful *Quarterly Review* by John Wilson Croker, who hoped to do for the new poet what he had done for Keats. Tennyson, who was always morbidly sensitive to criticism, and who at this time, we may remember, was only twenty-three, was "al-most crushed," though Croker's savagery had the effect of provoking some defenses, including one — two years later — from John Stuart Mill. Tennyson published no more books until 1842; he spent this "ten years' silence" in revising

poems of 1832 and writing new ones. But hostile criticism — and harassing family problems — were not the only reasons for silence; there was also what may be called the one shattering event of his life, the sudden death of Arthur Hallam, at the age of twenty-two (September 15, 1833). During the next seventeen years Tennyson was sporadically composing the lyrics that became *In Memoriam.*

In 1837 the family moved from the familiar associations of Somersby to High Beech, Epping Forest, near London (an uprooting recorded in *In Memoriam,* c–cv), where they lived until 1840; other migrations cannot be chronicled here. Rural life was now varied by more frequent visits to London, where Tennyson became ac-quainted with Carlyle, Thackeray, Dickens, and many other writers. He kept up friendship with such old "Apostles" as James Spedding, and especially with another Cambridge friend, Ed-ward FitzGerald, the future translator of the *Rubáiyát.* In 1837–38 Tennyson had become en-gaged to Emily Sellwood, but his lack of both money and religious orthodoxy led to her father's breaking off the relation in 1840; these obstacles were not overcome until 1850.

Tennyson was, in face and figure, perhaps the most impressively bardlike of all English poets, tall, handsome, dark, a sort of gypsy Apollo. Sydney Dobell, the "Spasmodic" poet, when asked to describe him, said that, if he were pointed out to you as the man who had written the *Iliad,* you would answer "I can well believe it." For a more specific picture one may quote the much-quoted letter from Carlyle to Emerson (1844):

Alfred is one of the few British or Foreign Figures (a not increasing number I think!) who are and remain beautiful to me; — a true human soul, or some authentic approximation thereto, to whom your own soul can say, Brother! — However, I doubt he will not come; he often skips me, in these brief visits to Town; skips everybody indeed; being a man solitary and sad, as certain men are, dwelling in an element of gloom, — carrying a bit of Chaos about him, in short, which he is manufacturing into Cosmos! . . . He had his breeding at Cam-bridge, as if for the Law or Church; being master of a small annuity on his Father's decease, he preferred clubbing with his Mother and some Sisters, to live unpromoted and write Poems. In this way he lives still, now here, now there; the family always within reach of London, never in it;

he himself making rare and brief visits, lodging in some old comrade's rooms. I think he must be under forty, not much under it. One of the finest-looking men in the world. A great shock of rough dusty-dark hair; bright-laughing hazel eyes; massive aquiline face, most massive yet most delicate; of sallow-brown complexion, almost Indian-looking; clothes cynically loose, free-and-easy; — smokes infinite tobacco. His voice is musical metallic, — fit for loud laughter and piercing wail, and all that may lie between; speech and speculation free and plenteous: I do not meet, in these late decades, such company over a pipe! — We shall see what he will grow to.

As man and as poet, Tennyson embodied at least the normal quota of apparent contradictions. We may think of the tenderly devoted son who reminded his teary mother of her handkerchief with a "Dam your eyes, mother, dam your eyes!"; of the shy and slovenly young man from the country still present in the poet and prophet who received universal homage; of the friend of dukes and royalty who measured the airs of county families in the light of the starry spheres; of the mystic who clung to "the Reality of the Unseen" and the native of Lincolnshire who relished anecdotes of earthy reality; of the man whose "most passionate desire" was "to have a clearer and fuller vision of God" and whose notion of the height of luxury (Aldworth had some plumbing) was "to sit in a hot bath and read about little birds"; who knew the depths of melancholy and cherished the "glorious power" of humor in the greatest writers; who wrote (and was praised for) sentimental verses that embarrass us and who read aloud his poem on the pathological St. Simeon Stylites with gusts of laughter — but we need not pile up antitheses, however wholesome they were. And Tennyson's conversational phrases were not always in the exalted vein. He observed that the bland portrait of an elderly politician was "rather like a retired panther," and pronounced a source-hunting scholar "a louse upon the locks of literature"; thinking of nature's blind profusion and overpopulation, he shuddered at "the torrent of babies"; and one cannot forget his picture of the common English conception of God "as of an immeasurable clergyman."

The two volumes of collected poems, old and new, of 1842 established Tennyson, among the more literary, as the chief active poet of the time. But Tennyson and the family were having financial trouble that came to a head in 1843; he had invested their meager resources in a wood-carving enterprise that failed (a good deal was recovered in 1845 on the death of the manufacturer, whose life had been insured by the poet's brother-in-law, Edmund Lushington). One concrete and welcome proof of Tennyson's poetical standing was a pension of £200, secured by the efforts of Henry Hallam, Gladstone, Carlyle, and Richard Monckton Milnes (the last an old "Apostle," now an M.P. and noted host); the Prime Minister, Sir Robert Peel, gave in when Milnes persuaded him to read "Ulysses."

The Princess (1847) sold better than any previous book, but it disappointed Carlyle and FitzGerald and a number of critics; for most modern readers only the songs survive. In 1850 came In Memoriam, Tennyson's greatest work and probably the central poetic document of the Victorian age. The same year brought his long-delayed marriage to Emily Sellwood and his appointment as Poet Laureate in succession to Wordsworth. In 1853 the married pair settled at Farringford on the Isle of Wight, which remained their home for the rest of Tennyson's life; he was able, in 1868, to build a house, named Aldworth, in Sussex, which in the summer became a refuge from the tourists who swarmed over the Isle of Wight. Maud (1855) evoked, in the unhappy time of the Crimean War, a good deal of hostility. So too, among leading writers and other critical minds, did Idylls of the King, which were published from 1859 onward, but these poems greatly extended Tennyson's popular following in both England and America — and had some critical esteem as well. There is no need to chronicle the later years of multiplying books, editions, friends, and visitors, of growing prosperity and fame. In 1883 Gladstone persuaded the poet to accept a peerage, which provoked some unpleasant squibs in the press. Like Dickens and like no other English writer, Tennyson lived the last third of his life as a national or international institution — and the theatrical novelist enjoyed the Hollywood glare more than the poet. Tennyson died on October 6, 1892, at the age of eighty-three. The outward culmination of his immense success was his funeral; never had an English writer been borne to Westminster Abbey with such pomp and circumstance.

This biographical sketch has dwelt very disproportionately on Tennyson's earlier years of comparative loneliness, unhappiness, poverty, and modest critical repute (and some harsh abuse), the years in which he grew up and wrote many of his best and best-known poems, including *In Memoriam*. It has often been said that, because of moralistic critics, Mrs. Tennyson, and an equally conventional and worshipful public, a bold and original poet was eventually tamed into a purveyor of edifying lollipops. To pass by the supposed causes, one must dispute the supposed fact. In the first place, Tennyson could hardly escape altogether the taste that largely prevailed among both writers and readers when he was first publishing, and, like Dickens and many lesser authors, the early Tennyson had in him, along with much else, a streak of popular sentimentalism that yielded "O Darling Room," "Lady Clara Vere de Vere," "The May Queen," and "The Lord of Burleigh"; it was natural enough that, without any external influence, these should lead on to "Enoch Arden," the weaker *Idylls,* and other more or less regrettable things. Likewise, an early sonnet on Buonaparte as a madman who thought to quell English hearts of oak led on to some too simply patriotic and martial verses by the Laureate, though even these few pieces cannot be dismissed with a blanket condemnation; the "Ode on the Death of the Duke of Wellington" contained noble poetry as well as editorial eulogy, "The Charge of the Light Brigade" was effective journalism, and the vigorous "ballad of the fleet," "The Revenge," reproduced, quite properly, the Elizabethan man of action's feelings about Spain. (We might remember, too Tennyson's opinion of the English as "the most beastly self-satisfied nation in the world.") Most great authors, from Shakespeare down, have been betrayed by their own tincture of popular taste into some bad writing; if Tennyson, coming at a notoriously bad time, suffered in the usual way, he also did a great deal to raise the level of poetry and taste. And, in the second place, if like other men he grew more conservative with age, he could still write many great and original poems, such as the two "Northern Farmers," "Lucretius," "The Holy Grail," "The Last Tournament," "The Ancient Sage," and "Demeter and Persephone," not to mention the plays.

Any writer who achieves an enormous reputation in his own lifetime is assured of a reaction, for both legitimate and illegitimate reasons; recent cases, on a smaller scale than Tennyson's, are Shaw and T. S. Eliot. Younger writers must escape from a dominant mode, which may have been carried as far as it can go, and find new ways of expressing the ideas and feelings of their generations. During the Victorian age, in addition to the older Browning and Arnold, various groups and individuals, of whom some owed much to Tennyson and none could be untouched by his influence, naturally struck out on different lines — the " Spasmodics," the Pre-Raphaelites, Swinburne, Hardy, Meredith, Hopkins, and others. Then, as we have observed, reaction did not wait for Tennyson's death; throughout his career both the young innovator and the elderly popular oracle received a good deal of severe criticism as well as praise. And part of his popular fame was based on the appeal of his inferior or positively bad work, or on an uncritical clutching at his " message " of faith and hope. Finally, for late Victorian rebels and moderns reacting in the normal way against their predecessors, Tennyson was the most conspicuous scapegoat for all the supposedly Victorian shams and sins. It is now clear, if it was not long ago, that much of the general reaction against " Victorianism " was not only uninformed and uncritical but hypocritical, since we have, often in inverted or disguised forms, our full share of smugness, sentimentality, and the other " Victorian " vices.

The claims upon us of any bygone writer are of two kinds, and Tennyson's are strong in both ways. First, he is of prime historical importance as the most fully representative mirror and interpreter of his great age, an age of bewildering progress and bewildering anxiety. Secondly, when Tennyson's mediocre and bad writing has been stripped away, he still has, to quote Eliot, three qualities rarely found together except in the greatest poets: abundance, variety, and complete competence. We may survey Tennyson's long career and large output and try to illustrate these general criteria; and, though material, ideas, and attitudes cannot be separated from technique, a short sketch seems to require such a separation (and once in a while we may glance outside our restricted table of contents).

One astonishing item among Tennyson's abundant juvenilia is *The Devil and the Lady,* a play he wrote at fourteen and revised somewhat in the next year or two. This pseudo-Elizabethan frolic already shows its author's scientific and metaphysical concern: picturing the earth as a "petty clod" amid "suns and spheres and stars and belts and systems," he goes on to pose questions of Berkeleyan idealism. In the same period — in 1824 — on "a day when the whole world seemed to be darkened" for him — the boy went out and carved on a stone "Byron is dead"; Byron was the one great romantic poet who, in the first third of the century, made an impact that reached even the Somersby parsonage. Tennyson's share in *Poems by Two Brothers* (1827) was mostly thin, tinkling imitations of the lyrics of Byron and Moore; he had written far better things, but these were excluded from the book as unsuited to popular taste. Though academic prize poems are seldom memorable, "Timbuctoo" (1829), a revised version of a youthful piece, must be noticed because it embodies a conspicuous question — the effects of advancing civilization upon poetry. In "Timbuctoo" the poet, on a mountain above the strait of Gibraltar (the ancient Pillars of Hercules), is told by the Spirit of Fable that her fair city of myth and imagination and idealism will, under the pressure of science and technology, decay into "Low-built, mud-wall'd, barbarian settlements."

Poems, Chiefly Lyrical (1830) contained, along with the merely or mainly melodious, some poems that were to hold a place in the select canon of posterity. "Mariana" was Tennyson's first elaborate expression of the deeply felt theme of loneliness, his first elaborate interweaving of scene and mood. "The Poet" was a confident proclamation of the high prophetic power the romantic poets had claimed. "The Poet's Mind" asserted another tenet of the romantic creed and was a link between "Timbuctoo" and "The Hesperides"; it warned cold, skeptical reason away from the holy ground of imagination. And we must note the first disclosure of a central and enduring problem, the undermining of traditional religious faith, in the poem that bore the self-mocking title "Supposed Confessions of a Second-Rate Sensitive Mind Not in Unity with Itself"; the piece ended with a despairing cry significantly close to the refrain of "Mariana." "The Kraken" perhaps had no successors except that massive miniature of naked energy, "The Eagle."

This volume received a quite favorable welcome from a number of reviewers, including Leigh Hunt.

In the *Poems* of 1832 the Tennyson we know began to take shape clearly, even though we read the more famous pieces — "The Lady of Shalott," "Œnone," "The Palace of Art," and "The Lotos-Eaters" — in the much-revised versions that appeared in 1842. In these four poems, and in "The Hesperides," Tennyson was dealing with a problem that was evidently personal, a problem that had preoccupied Keats from "Sleep and Poetry" to *The Fall of Hyperion:* the artist's choice — which of course depends on his gifts as well as his will — between contemplative detachment from life and the acceptance of social and ethical responsibility, whether in action or in "public" poetry. (Modern words, in the continuing debate, are "involvement," "engagement," "commitment.") The young Tennyson, in spite of "The Poet" and the perhaps ambivalent "Palace of Art," seems to have been temperamentally inclined toward aesthetic detachment; but his revision, for 1842, of some poems of 1832 suggests a shift in the other direction. Along with critics' complaints, a partial change of heart may explain the unaccountable failure to reprint the unique and magical "Hesperides." In the original conclusion of "The Lady of Shalott" an unexpected jab at "The well-fed wits at Camelot" seems to set the secluded and now dead "artist" above and against an insensitive bourgeois world; the ending of 1842 invites the verdict, however sympathetic, that detachment from reality is fatal. Much more obvious evidence of Tennyson's getting into the stream of the contemporary and actual is the many new poems of 1842, poems written at various times in the preceding decade, such as "You Ask Me, Why," "Love Thou Thy Land," "Locksley Hall," and — by implication — "Morte d'Arthur," along with a number of tales and vignettes of English life which have a rather tepid attraction for modern readers. One must mention three poems that unhappily could not be included in these selections, the grimly bizarre "St. Simeon Stylites," the macabre ballad of "The Vision of Sin," and "The Two Voices." In this last, written after Hallam's death, the poet's faith in life and God struggles against the temptation of suicide upheld by nihilistic skepticism. These two voices of resolution and despair might be said to speak in the two great monologues, "Ulysses" and "Tithonus." Apropos of Tennyson's series of mythological poems, and the age's increasing demand that poetry should draw its material from modern life, a word may be added. Carlyle, though he was deeply stirred by "Ulysses," was apparently complaining of Tennyson's remote and antique themes when he described him as "sitting on a dung-heap among innumerable dead dogs." But all of Tennyson's fine mythological poems (except the last and weakest, "The Death of Œnone") were more or less intensely personal and modern in inspiration — and usually much better than his modern treatments of parallel themes. Much later, when he resolved to write "Demeter and Persephone," Tennyson indicated what had always been his way of approach: "when I write an antique like this I must put it into a frame — something modern about it. It is no use giving a mere *réchauffé* of old legends" (*Memoir*, II, 364). In this Tennyson was following the example of Keats and Shelley, who had revived classical myth as a vehicle for both private and public themes.

Modern scientific skepticism, even if it came partly from the "lying lips" of Sorrow, was a main source of tension and despair in *In Memoriam*, which was largely composed in the decade 1833–43. The sudden shock of Hallam's death brought together and greatly deepened all Tennyson's questionings of earlier years — in somewhat the same way as the death of a virtuous and promising young man had forced Milton to a questioning of God's providence and justice. But for Tennyson, two centuries later, the religious problem was immensely complicated by science and the general growth of rationalism. From boyhood to old age he kept in touch with science, especially astronomy, more closely perhaps than any other poet of the century, partly because of scientific curiosity but mainly because of the impact of scientific discovery and thought upon man's religious sense of his own being, of his place in nature, and his belief in survival after death. Even if law was the foundation, and the fetish, of nineteenth-century science — as it was, for instance, in that

very successful work of popularizing, *Vestiges of the Natural History of Creation* (1844), by Robert Chambers — there was cold comfort in cosmic and biological law that was utterly indifferent to man. Sir Charles Lyell's *Principles of Geology* (1830–33), which Tennyson read in 1837 if not earlier, stressed the immense tract of time required for natural processes, such as erosion, to work immense changes in land and sea, processes that went on in entire disregard of sentient life; both individuals and species appeared and disappeared, leaving only fossil records. Though *In Memoriam* was often acclaimed as a "reconciliation" of science and faith, modern readers may be more conscious of the poet's stark despair in "the night of fear," in the face of a blind, mechanical, meaningless universe in which man seems an insignificant and perhaps ephemeral accident. If we have grown used to living with such specters (or have been diverted by more immediate specters of universal destruction), they are still there; and no one has put the great questions more powerfully than Tennyson put them in sections LV–LVI.

Some modern writers and readers cling tenaciously to despair and look down their noses at anything that savors of affirmation. Tennyson, like most other Victorian writers, sought for something positive. His efforts toward affirmation in *In Memoriam* are of two kinds, and, for us, they are likely to seem of quite unequal validity. One was his "lesser faith" or hope in the general progress, the upward movement, of the race. Such a faith or hope had been current or intermittent for ages, and in the nineteenth century it had gained momentum and concreteness through the evolutionary doctrines of Lamarck and others and through the scientific and technological discoveries that were working radical changes in modes of life and thought. Tennyson's hope of progress, of the emergence of a higher type of man (exemplified by Hallam), could in expression be tinged with scientific language but was much more ethical than scientific — and was attended, or attenuated, by an increasingly dark view of his own age. Since many people vaguely associate *In Memoriam* with monkey business, we may remember that Tennyson was not concerned with Lamarckian or Darwinian mutation of species; the leading

English scientists before 1850 — or before (and often after) 1859 — upheld the successive creation of distinct species, along with the general concept of unity and analogy in the biological world.

Tennyson's central affirmation, which worked its way out of despair, was subjective, intuitive faith in love as the supreme experience and reality of life, a reality that implied a God of love and individual immortality. He had profound reverence for Christ but was not apparently an orthodox Christian. "There's a Something that watches over us; and our individuality endures," he said once; "that's my faith, and that's all my faith." Holding with passionate intensity to these minimal beliefs, Tennyson, without attempting to deny the grim facts of nature and history, took his stand on ground above both skeptical science and the traditional "argument from design" of rational religion. His answer, "I have felt" (*In Memoriam*, cxxiv), has been condemned by some readers in both skeptical and religious camps — though the former seldom quarrel with the equally intuitive negations of other writers, and the latter might find it difficult to prove the objectivity of their own faith. Tennyson had always had a mystical strain in him.

Idylls of the King (1859 ff.), which grew slowly in Tennyson's mind and became the fulfillment of a major ambition, were sniffed or snorted at in their own time by Carlyle, Browning, Swinburne, Meredith, Hopkins, and others, and they have been largely dismissed and ignored in ours; but, if some *Idylls* are weak and satiny romance or parable, some are powerful and moving pictures of an ideal society in decay, the waste land of a civilization without conscience and without love. These, rather than *Maud*, are the antiphonal voice to *In Memoriam*; the ape and the tiger have not died but triumphed, and the one far-off divine event can now be hardly even imagined. Though Tennyson had never had anything like Milton's early militant faith in a great reformation here and now, in his later years he may be said to have had some affinity with the disillusioned Milton who in *Paradise Lost* saw the great reformation only as the new heaven and new earth beyond the day of judgment. Tennyson's faith in progress — in the sense of regeneration, not of multiplying gadgets — had always been fixed on a dim and distant future (the far-off world, he said, often seemed nearer than the present) and was less of a belief than a hope and a dream.

To look over even a small selection from Tennyson is to be reminded also of the wide variety of style and tone that goes along with a wide variety of theme. Such major poets of our time as Yeats and Eliot and Frost — not to mention the host of good smaller poets — have a relatively limited range; we hear somewhat varied intonations of one always recognizable voice. But Tennyson is a ventriloquist, or a troupe of ventriloquists; to put the matter in another way, his poems are diverse objects made, as it were, by a whole corps of different craftsmen. We may think of the gulf between "The Hesperides" and the two "Northern Farmers," between "The Lady of Shalott" and "Ulysses," between "Tears, Idle Tears" and "Lucretius," between "Tithonus" and *Maud*, between *In Memoriam* and "The Holy Grail" — but there is no need of repeating a table of contents. In his art as well as in his thought and feeling Tennyson was inevitably the heir of the romantic poets, and criticism soon aligned him with Keats, but he was almost from the start an original master himself. Our space forbids any broad account of his varied qualities and we might concentrate chiefly on one, the studied refinement of phrase and rhythm which, in countless modulations, runs through much of his work.

Tennyson's poetic powers were no less precocious than long-lived; he was writing from the age of five up to eighty-three. We have already noticed, in the play he wrote at fourteen, the presence of astronomy and metaphysics, and here we may observe in the same play the minutely accurate, carefully composed scene-painting that bears the Tennysonian hallmark:

> Each hoar wave
> With crispèd undulation arching rose,
> Thence falling in white ridge with sinuous slope
> Dash'd headlong to the shore and spread along
> The sands its tender fringe of creamy spray.

And one must quote another phrase, not as characteristic Tennyson, but as something that might have been written yesterday, about a reed bed that may wave

> Its trembling shadows to the ambiguity
> Of moonlight.[1]

The virtues of sensibility and expression that Hallam praised in the volume of 1830, virtues more generally conspicuous in the volume of 1832, had their obverse side. The poet was very young — at the end of his life he said that he had been nearer thirty than twenty before he was anything of an artist; the substance of some early poems was thin or worse, luxuriance of imagination could be overluxuriant and descriptive details under uncertain control, and there were some stylistic mannerisms such as an excess of compound words. Although there was no excuse for Croker's violence, and not much for his blindness and deafness, he and some other critics in their flailing about hit on real as well as superficial faults. Tennyson, while suffering from reviewers as well as from his grief for Hallam, was attaining poetic maturity. In the process of selecting and rejecting early poems for the next edition, and of revising a number of those retained, he was wise enough to heed critical strictures and wise enough also to rely on his own increasingly disciplined taste. The story of early criticism and the poet's reactions, 1827–51, is expertly told in Edgar F. Shannon's *Tennyson and the Reviewers* (1952); a discerning complementary study is Joyce Green's "Tennyson's Development during the 'Ten Years' Silence' (1832–1842)," *Publications of the Modern Language Association*, LXVI (1951). Tennyson's rapid growth in power and depth as well as artistry is sufficiently illustrated by some of the new poems of 1842 that had been written in 1833, such as "St. Simeon Stylites" and "Ulysses," and "Morte d'Arthur," written in 1833–35.

What early unfavorable criticism called affectation was in Tennyson's mature work subdued, deepened, and enriched into the refinement and elaboration that came to be regarded as the dominant quality of his style. This view may be said to have become canonical with Walter Bagehot's critique of 1864, "Wordsworth, Tennyson, and Browning; or, Pure, Ornate, and Grotesque in English Poetry." But Tennysonian refinement was in the main a potent virtue and only on occasion a vice — and sometimes, most obviously in the "Northern Farmers" — it was far away. Of course if a reader can be imagined as coming to Tennyson from modern poetry, which does not carve "jewels five-words long" (the phrase is Tennyson's) and which has so largely cultivated the colloquial and casual in language and rhythm, nearly all of Tennyson may appear studiously composed and hence artificial; but such an impression would by no means constitute a valid condemnation. For one thing, modern colloquialism is quite as consciously artificial as any more formal style; like "natural acting" on the stage, it only gives the illusion of naturalness. For another, Tennyson was in accord with the immemorial tradition of European poetry which prescribed that the poet should wear his singing robes, not an open shirt and slacks. Everything depends upon what the theme and attitude require; and, since the house of poetry has many mansions, we could ill afford to lose the one dedicated to golden splendor — one to which Yeats and Eliot also have the key. At his frequent best, Tennyson's inlaid, beautifully contrived texture is akin to Virgil's; it has long been a commonplace that he is the most Virgilian of English poets. One half-humorous and inadequate reminder of what he learned from the classics is his saying that he knew the quantity of every English word except "scissors."

Great as Tennyson is in many modes, by instinct and endowment he is perhaps most of all a lyric poet, a poet of personal emotion. Many of his lyrics, both individual pieces and parts of larger works, could not be included here, but those we have — separate poems, a few of the songs from *The Princess*, about half of *In Memoriam*, the lyrics in *Maud* — are more than enough to place Tennyson easily first among the lyrists of the century. Within the lyrical range his fecundity, versatility, and felicity are astonishing. One of his deepest wells of inspiration — and not lyrical inspiration only — is what he called "the passion of the past," the indefinable regret and yearning (which in him had been especially strong in youth) for things in life that seem to have passed away for ever. Of this rich, somber, more or less universal feeling the most perfect expression is "Tears, Idle Tears," Ten-

---

[1] *The Devil and the Lady*, ed. Sir Charles Tennyson (1930), pp. 62, 6, and quoted by Sir Charles' kind permission.

nyson's masterpiece among the lyrics outside *In Memoriam* and, one might add, the most Virgilian of his lyrics. In *In Memoriam* the passion of the past naturally becomes remembrance of communion with Hallam, and ranges from the time when

> all the lavish hills would hum
> The murmur of a happy Pan

to the picture of the dark house in London where

> ghastly thro' the drizzling rain
> On the bald street breaks the blank day.

This last poem (section VII) naturally attracted Eliot's notice; the final line is at once a piece of modernity and, in its alliteration, monosyllables, and broken rhythm, a Tennysonian contrivance —completely and powerfully effective.

In Memoriam enshrines many themes and moods, and Tennyson's instinct served him well when it led him into "Short swallow-flights of song" rather than into a long philosophical poem. Some lyrics, naturally, are weak, and some have incidental flaws, but in the work as a whole the stylization of language and rhythm is marvellously right (one uses the adverb partly because the poems were written over so long a time). Even the best lyrics do not yield their full strength if read in isolation; each gains from its full context. And as the grave quatrains proceed in their undulating ebb and flow, variety is achieved within a general uniformity of style and movement that has a high ritualistic value. The intimately personal is raised to the universal and timeless. Since Tennyson had always been given to rendering states of mind through description of nature, we might note a few examples. In section XI, each of the five stanzas begins with "Calm," yet apparent rhetorical artifice becomes a kind of sublimation; the effect is of a man who can retain self-control only and barely by a ceremonial ordering of landscape and emotion. A later and happier mood, the sense of rebirth, is rendered through scene-painting in the single magnificent sentence that constitutes section LXXXVI. In section XCV, which many critics regard as the poetic pinnacle of *In Memoriam*, the mystical experience rises out of a homely everyday scene and then subsides into it again, though now objects are not just their familiar selves but have taken on a

symbolic life. A doctrinaire modernist might conceivably ask, "Why the 'white kine' instead of 'white cows'?" The not very difficult answer would cover many similar questions.

These sketchy remarks on some elements in Tennyson's thinking, feeling, and artistry do not go very far, and they pass by many important things, but perhaps they go far enough to suggest the nature of his many strong claims upon us. If I, a Victorian by birth, may testify from my own experience in a course on several Victorian poets, it is always inspiriting to find that many intelligent young students, who had acquired the condescending or hostile view of Tennyson, change their minds when they really read him. They discover that he is an interpreter not only of his own great and troubled age but in some respects of ours, and that he is, simply, one of the enduring poets who give enduring and very individual stimulus and satisfaction, that his artifice partakes of "the artifice of eternity."

MARIANA

"Mariana in the moated grange."
Measure for Measure

This poem of 1830, Tennyson's first notable treatment of isolation and the "death-wish," is more characteristic in its rendering of mood through scenic details, skillfully grouped, than in its blending of everyday realism with romantic and ominous mystery. There seems to be little Shakespearian suggestion beyond the name and echoes of the epigraph, adapted from *Measure for Measure*, III.i.277: "There at the moated grange resides this dejected Mariana."

> With blackest moss the flower-plots
>   Were thickly crusted, one and all;
> The rusted nails fell from the knots
>   That held the pear to the gable-wall.
> The broken sheds look'd sad and strange:
>   Unlifted was the clinking latch;
>   Weeded and worn the ancient thatch
> Upon the lonely moated grange.
>   She only said, "My life is dreary,
>   He cometh not," she said;
>   She said, "I am aweary, aweary,
>   I would that I were dead!"   10
>
> Her tears fell with the dews at even;
>   Her tears fell ere the dews were dried;
> She could not look on the sweet heaven,
>   Either at morn or eventide.

After the flitting of the bats,
  When thickest dark did trance° the sky,
  She drew her casement-curtain by,
And glanced athwart the glooming flats.   20
    She only said, " The night is dreary,
      He cometh not," she said;
    She said, " I am aweary, aweary,
      I would that I were dead! "

Upon the middle of the night,
  Waking she heard the night-fowl crow;
The cock sung out an hour ere light;
  From the dark fen the oxen's low
Came to her; without hope of change,
  In sleep she seem'd to walk forlorn,   30
Till cold winds woke the gray-eyed morn
About the lonely moated grange.
    She only said, " The day is dreary,
      He cometh not," she said;
    She said, " I am aweary, aweary,
      I would that I were dead! "

About a stone-cast from the wall
  A sluice with blacken'd waters slept,
And o'er it many, round and small,
  The cluster'd marish-mosses crept.   40
Hard by a poplar shook alway,
  All silver-green with gnarlèd bark:
For leagues no other tree did mark
  The level waste, the rounding gray.
    She only said, " My life is dreary,
      He cometh not," she said;
    She said, " I am aweary, aweary,
      I would that I were dead! "

And ever when the moon was low,
  And the shrill winds were up and away,   50
In the white curtain, to and fro,
  She saw the gusty shadow sway.
But when the moon was very low,
  And wild winds bound within their cell,
The shadow of the poplar fell
Upon her bed, across her brow.
    She only said, " The night is dreary,
      He cometh not," she said;
    She said, " I am aweary, aweary,
      I would that I were dead! "   60

All day within the dreamy house,
  The doors upon their hinges creak'd;
The blue fly sung in the pane; the mouse
  Behind the moldering wainscot shriek'd,
Or from the crevice peer'd about.
  Old faces glimmer'd thro' the doors,
  Old footsteps trod the upper floors,

Old voices called her from without.
    She only said, " My life is dreary,
      He cometh not," she said;   70
    She said, " I am aweary, aweary,
      I would that I were dead! "

The sparrow's chirrup on the roof,
  The slow clock ticking, and the sound
Which to the wooing wind aloof
  The poplar made, did all confound
Her sense; but most she loathed the hour
  When the thick-moted sunbeam lay
  Athwart the chambers, and the day
Was sloping toward his western bower.   80
    Then, said she, " I am very dreary,
      He will not come," she said;
    She wept, " I am aweary, aweary,
      Oh God, that I were dead! "

1830 [1]

THE HESPERIDES°

" Hesperus and his daughters three
That sing about the golden tree."
              Comus

   " The Hesperides " (1832), Tennyson's first elaborate treatment of myth, is much less familiar than it should be, since he never reprinted it (and came to regret not having done so). It is the most purely magical, and most elusive, poem he ever wrote. The difficulty, of a kind common in modern poetry but rare in Tennyson's age, is that there is next to nothing in the way of " prose statement," that the theme is developed wholly in images. Other early writings (Act I, Scene iii, of the youthful play, *The Devil and the Lady;* " Timbuctoo "; " The Poet's Mind "; " The Lady of Shalott ") suggest that " The Hesperides " celebrates the value of myth and the precious seclusion of the artistic imagination in the face of the encroachments of scientific progress and the world of action. G. R. Stange has a study of the poem in *Publications of the Modern Language Association,* LXVII (1952).
   The Hesperides were the nymphs who, with the aid of a dragon, guarded the golden apples that had been given to Hera when she wedded Zeus. They were placed, in different versions of the myth, on an Atlantic island or near Mount Atlas in northwest Africa; Tennyson's use of Hanno implies that he has the African scene in mind. Heracles, coming from the east, carried off the apples, but they were eventually restored. Tennyson might have seen the curious book by Edward Davies, *Celtic Researches* (1804), which says (p. 193): " Hercules had the task of procuring three yellow apples, from the garden of the Hesperides. These apples were metaphorical, and pointed at science, discipline, or mystery."

1. Dates at the end of poems indicate publication (left) and composition (right). THE HESPERIDES. **Epigraph.** Milton, *Comus,* 981–82.

MARIANA.   **18. trance:** entrance, put under a spell.

The North wind fall'n, in the new-starrèd night
Zidonian Hanno,° voyaging beyond
The hoary promontory of Soloë°
Past Thymiaterion,° in calmèd bays,
Between the southern and the western Horn,°
Heard neither warbling of the nightingale,
Nor melody o' the Libyan lotus flute
Blown seaward from the shore; but from a slope
That ran bloom-bright into the Atlantic blue,
Beneath a highland leaning down a weight   10
Of cliffs, and zoned below with cedar shade,
Came voices, like the voices in a dream,
Continuous, till he reached the outer sea.

SONG

I

The golden apple, the golden apple, the hallowed
    fruit,
Guard it well, guard it warily,
Singing airily,
Standing about the charmèd root.
Round about all is mute,
As the snow-field on the mountain-peaks,
As the sand-field at the mountain-foot.   20
Crocodiles° in briny creeks
Sleep and stir not: all is mute.
If ye sing not, if ye make false measure,
We shall lose eternal pleasure,
Worth eternal want of rest.
Laugh not loudly: watch the treasure
Of the wisdom of the west.
In a corner wisdom whispers. Five and three
(Let it not be preached abroad) make an awful
    mystery.
For the blossom unto threefold music bloweth; 30
Evermore it is born anew;
And the sap to threefold music floweth,
From the root
Drawn in the dark,
Up to the fruit,
Creeping under the fragrant bark,
Liquid gold, honeysweet, thro' and thro'.
Keen-eyed Sisters, singing airily,
Looking warily

Every way,   40
Guard the apple night and day,
Lest one from the East come and take it away.

II

Father Hesper, Father Hesper, watch, watch, ever
    and aye,
Looking under silver hair with a silver eye.
Father, twinkle not thy steadfast sight;
Kingdoms lapse, and climates change, and races
    die;
Honor comes with mystery;
Hoarded wisdom brings delight.
Number, tell them over and number
How many the mystic fruit-tree holds,   50
Lest the red-combed dragon slumber
Rolled together in purple folds.
Look to him, father, lest he wink, and the golden
    apple be stol'n away,
For his ancient heart is drunk with overwatchings
    night and day,
Round about the hallowed fruit-tree curled —
Sing away, sing aloud evermore in the wind, with-
    out stop,
Lest his scalèd eyelid drop,
For he is older than the world.
If he waken, we waken,
Rapidly leveling eager eyes.   60
If he sleep, we sleep,
Dropping the eyelid over the eyes.
If the golden apple be taken,
The world will be overwise.
Five links, a golden chain, are we,
Hesper, the dragon, and sisters three,
Bound about the golden tree.

III

Father Hesper, Father Hesper, watch, watch, night
    and day,
Lest the old wound of the world be healèd,
The glory unsealèd,   70
The golden apple stol'n away,
And the ancient secret revealèd.
Look from west to east along:
Father, old Himala° weakens, Caucasus° is bold
    and strong.
Wandering waters unto wandering waters call;
Let them clash together, foam and fall.
Out of watchings, out of wiles,
Comes the bliss of secret smiles.
All things are not told to all.
Half-round the mantling night is drawn,   80
Purple-fringèd with even and dawn.
Hesper° hateth Phosphor,° evening hateth morn.

2. **Hanno**: a Carthaginian navigator (Carthage was founded by Phoenicians from Sidon and Tyre); he wrote an account of his voyage (*c*. 490 B.C.) along the northwest coast of Africa. Tennyson presumably used *The Voyage of Hanno*, tr. T. Falconer (1797); Falconer has, with much else, remarks on the island of the Hesperides. 3. **Soloë**: "Soloeis, a promontory of Libya" (Falconer, p. 7); modern Cape Cantin in Morocco. 4. **Thymiaterion**: the name in Falconer's Greek text (Thymiaterium in his translation); modern Mehedia. 5. **southern . . . Horn**: so named in Falconer, pp. 11, 13; modern Sherbro Sound and Bissagos Bay. 21. **Crocodiles**: "another river . . . full of crocodiles and river horses" (Falconer, pp. 9–11).

74. **Himala**: the Himalayan mountains of India. **Caucasus**: the mountains between the Black and the Caspian Seas. 82. **Hesper**: the evening star. **Phosphor**: the morning star.

IV

Every flower and every fruit the redolent breath
Of this warm sea-wind ripeneth,
Arching the billow in his sleep;
But the land-wind wandereth,
Broken by the highland-steep,
Two streams upon the violet deep;
For the western sun and the western star,
And the low west-wind, breathing afar,   90
The end of day and beginning of night
Make the apple holy and bright;
Holy and bright, round and full, bright and blest,
Mellowed in a land of rest;
Watch it warily day and night;
All good things are in the west.
Till mid noon the cool east light
Is shut out by the round of the tall hillbrow;
But when the full-faced sunset yellowly
Stays on the flowering arch of the bough,   100
The luscious fruitage clustereth mellowly,
Golden-kerneled, golden-cored,
Sunset-ripened above on the tree.
The world is wasted with fire and sword,
But the apple of gold hangs over the sea.
Five links, a golden chain, are we,
Hesper, the dragon, and sisters three,
Daughters three,
Bound° about
All round about   110
The gnarlèd bole of the charmèd tree.
The golden apple, the golden apple, the hallowed
          fruit,
Guard it well, guard it warily,
Watch it warily,
Singing airily,
Standing about the charmèd root.

1832

THE LADY OF SHALOTT

Published in 1832; much revised, 1842. Tennyson's
"plot" is quite different, except in its denouement,
from Malory's story of the maid of Astolat (*Morte
d'Arthur,* XVIII.ix–xx), which he followed in his later
Idyll, "Lancelot and Elaine." Editors cite a brief Italian tale (in *The Italian Novelists,* tr. Thomas Roscoe
[1825], I, 45–46), which Tennyson may have read, but
this is only a condensed equivalent of Malory's chaps.
xix–xx and tells how "the lady of Scalot," dying for
love of Lancelot, was by her own wish floated down
to Camelot and how she was received there. The lyrical
tale, at once crisp and incantatory, clearly has allegorical overtones. Tennyson's summary — "The new-

born love for something, for some one in the wide
world from which she has been so long secluded, takes
her out of the region of shadows into that of realities "
(*Memoir,* I, 117) — would be somewhat altered in
focus by modern critics, who would link this poem
with his other early treatments of personal or artistic
isolation. Here the shock of reality is fatal to the
secluded artist.

PART I

On either side the river lie
Long fields of barley and of rye,
That clothe the wold and meet the sky;
And thro' the field the road runs by
          To many-tower'd Camelot;°
And up and down the people go,
Gazing where the lilies blow°
Round an island there below,
          The island of Shalott.

Willows whiten, aspens quiver,   10
Little breezes dusk and shiver
Thro' the wave that runs for ever
By the island in the river
          Flowing down to Camelot.
Four gray walls, and four gray towers,
Overlook a space of flowers,
And the silent isle imbowers
          The Lady of Shalott.

By the margin, willow-veil'd,
Slide the heavy barges trail'd   20
By slow horses; and unhail'd
The shallop flitteth silken-sail'd
          Skimming down to Camelot:
But who hath seen her wave her hand?
Or at the casement seen her stand?
Or is she known in all the land,
          The Lady of Shalott?

Only reapers, reaping early
In among the bearded barley,
Hear a song that echoes cheerly   30
From the river winding clearly,
          Down to tower'd Camelot;
And by the moon the reaper weary,
Piling sheaves in uplands airy,
Listening, whispers " 'Tis the fairy
          Lady of Shalott."

PART II

There she weaves by night and day
A magic web with colors gay.
She has heard a whisper say,

---

109. Bound: "Bound" in 1832 edition; "Round" in *Memoir,* I,
64, and *Works,* ed. Hallam, Lord Tennyson.

THE LADY OF SHALOTT.   **5. Camelot:** King Arthur's capital;
symbolically, the outer world in general.   **7. blow:** blossom.

A curse is on her if she stay   40
    To look down to Camelot.
She knows not what the curse may be,
And so she weaveth steadily,
And little other care hath she,
    The Lady of Shalott.

And moving thro' a mirror clear
That hangs before her all the year,
Shadows of the world appear.
There she sees the highway near
    Winding down to Camelot;   50
There the river eddy whirls,
And there the surly village-churls,
And the red cloaks of market girls,
    Pass onward from Shalott.

Sometimes a troop of damsels glad,
An abbot on an ambling pad,°
Sometimes a curly shepherd-lad,
Or long-hair'd page in crimson clad,
    Goes by to tower'd Camelot;
And sometimes thro' the mirror blue   60
The knights come riding two and two:
She hath no loyal knight and true,
    The Lady of Shalott.

But in her web she still delights
To weave the mirror's magic sights,
For often thro' the silent nights
A funeral, with plumes and lights
    And music, went to Camelot;
Or when the moon was overhead,
Came two young lovers lately wed: 70
"I am half sick of shadows," said
    The Lady of Shalott.

PART III

A bow-shot from her bower-eaves,
He rode between the barley-sheaves,
The sun came dazzling thro' the leaves,
And flamed upon the brazen greaves
    Of bold Sir Lancelot.
A red-cross knight for ever kneel'd
To a lady in his shield,
That sparkled on the yellow field,   80
    Beside remote Shalott.

The gemmy bridle glitter'd free,
Like to some branch of stars we see
Hung in the golden Galaxy.
The bridle bells rang merrily
    As he rode down to Camelot;
And from his blazon'd baldric slung
A mighty silver bugle hung,

56. pad: road horse.

And as he rode his armor rung,
    Beside remote Shalott.   90

All in the blue unclouded weather
Thick-jewel'd shone the saddle-leather,
The helmet and the helmet-feather
Burn'd like one burning flame together,
    As he rode down to Camelot;
As often thro' the purple night,
Below the starry clusters bright,
Some bearded meteor, trailing light,
    Moves over still Shalott.

His broad clear brow in sunlight glow'd;   100
On burnish'd hooves his war-horse trode;
From underneath his helmet flow'd
His coal-black curls as on he rode,
    As he rode down to Camelot.
From the bank and from the river
He flash'd into the crystal mirror,
"Tirra lirra," by the river
    Sang Sir Lancelot.

She left the web, she left the loom,
She made three paces thro' the room,   110
She saw the water-lily bloom,
She saw the helmet and the plume,
    She looked down to Camelot.
Out flew the web and floated wide;
The mirror crack'd from side to side;
"The curse is come upon me," cried
    The Lady of Shalott.

PART IV

In the stormy east-wind straining,
The pale yellow woods were waning,
The broad stream in his banks complaining,   120
Heavily the low sky raining
    Over tower'd Camelot;
Down she came and found a boat
Beneath a willow left afloat,
And round about the prow she wrote
    The Lady of Shalott.

And down the river's dim expanse
Like some bold seër in a trance,
Seeing all his own mischance —
With a glassy countenance   130
    Did she look to Camelot.
And at the closing of the day
She loosed the chain, and down she lay,
The broad stream bore her far away,
    The Lady of Shalott.

Lying, robed in snowy white
That loosely flew to left and right —

The leaves upon her falling light —
Thro' the noises of the night
    She floated down to Camelot;   140
And as the boat-head wound along
The willowy hills and fields among,
They heard her singing her last song,
    The Lady of Shalott.

Heard a carol, mournful, holy,
Chanted loudly, chanted lowly,
Till her blood was frozen slowly,
And her eyes were darken'd wholly,
    Turn'd to tower'd Camelot.
For ere she reach'd upon the tide   150
The first house by the water-side,
Singing in her song she died,
    The Lady of Shalott.

Under tower and balcony,
By garden-wall and gallery,
A gleaming shape she floated by,
Dead-pale between the houses high,
    Silent into Camelot.
Out upon the wharfs they came,
Knight and burgher, lord and dame,   160
And round the prow they read her name,
    The Lady of Shalott.

Who is this? and what is here?
And in the lighted palace near
Died the sound of royal cheer;
And they cross'd themselves for fear,
    All the knights at Camelot:
But Lancelot mused a little space;
He said, "She has a lovely face;
God in his mercy lend her grace,   170
    The Lady of Shalott."

    1832, 1842

ŒNONE

First published in 1832; much revised, 1842. The poem was begun in Spain, in the valley of Cauteretz, in 1830, and the scenery is more Spanish than Trojan. "Œnone" is an epyllion in the manner of Theocritus, a miniature epic or mythic tale closely interwoven with the natural setting; and the refrain is Theocritean. The main sources were presumably the epistles of Paris to Helen and of the deserted Œnone to Paris in Ovid's *Heroides.* The poem is related on one side to Tennyson's early and personal concern with loneliness and the desire for death — Œnone is a mythological Mariana. But in the central episode, the judgment of Paris, the poet shapes Pallas' traditional offer in terms of his own excellent political and social creed, and the poem

can hardly sustain the sermon imposed upon it; nor do we feel any ethical impact from Paris' choice of beauty over wisdom (cf. "The Palace of Art"). But the clear-cut scene-painting is in Tennyson's best vein; and the last paragraph, perhaps because of Virgilian and Aeschylean inspiration, rises above Theocritus to the epic or tragic level.

There lies a vale in Ida,° lovelier
Than all the valleys of Ionian hills.
The swimming vapor slopes athwart the glen,
Puts forth an arm, and creeps from pine to pine,
And loiters, slowly drawn. On either hand
The lawns and meadow-ledges midway down
Hang rich in flowers, and far below them roars
The long brook falling thro' the clov'n ravine
In cataract after cataract to the sea.
Behind the valley topmost Gargarus°   10
Stands up and takes the morning; but in front
The gorges, opening wide apart, reveal
Troas° and Ilion's column'd citadel,
The crown of Troas.
                Hither came at noon
Mournful Œnone, wandering forlorn
Of Paris, once her playmate on the hills.
Her cheek had lost the rose, and round her neck
Floated her hair or seem'd to float in rest.
She, leaning on a fragment twined with vine,
Sang to the stillness, till the mountain-shade   20
Sloped downward to her seat from the upper cliff.

  "O mother Ida, many-fountain'd Ida,
Dear mother Ida, harken ere I die.
For now the noonday quiet holds the hill;
The grasshopper is silent in the grass;
The lizard, with his shadow on the stone,
Rests like a shadow, and the winds are dead.
The purple flower droops, the golden bee
Is lily-cradled; I alone awake.
My eyes are full of tears, my heart of love,   30
My heart is breaking, and my eyes are dim,
And I am all aweary of my life.

  "O mother Ida, many-fountain'd Ida,
Dear mother Ida, harken ere I die.
Hear me, O earth, hear me, O hills, O caves
That house the cold crown'd snake! O mountain
    brooks,
I am the daughter of a River-God,
Hear me, for I will speak, and build up all
My sorrow with my song, as yonder walls
Rose slowly to a music slowly breathed,°   40

ŒNONE. **1. Ida:** a mountain range near Troy, in Ionia (northern Asia Minor); the epithet is Homeric. **10. Gargarus:** the highest peak of Ida. **13. Troas:** the city of Troy (Ilion) and the region around it. **39–40. as . . . breathed:** The walls of Troy were said to have been built by Apollo's music.

A cloud that gather'd shape; for it may be
That, while I speak of it, a little while
My heart may wander from its deeper woe.

"O mother Ida, many-fountain'd Ida,
Dear mother Ida, harken ere I die.
I waited underneath the dawning hills;
Aloft the mountain lawn was dewy-dark,
And dewy-dark aloft the mountain pine.
Beautiful Paris, evil-hearted Paris,
Leading a jet-black goat white-horn'd, white-
    hooved,   50
Came up from reedy Simois° all alone.

"O mother Ida, harken ere I die.
Far-off the torrent call'd me from the cleft;
Far up the solitary morning smote
The streaks of virgin snow. With down-dropt eyes
I sat alone; white-breasted like a star
Fronting the dawn he moved; a leopard skin
Droop'd from his shoulder, but his sunny hair
Cluster'd about his temples like a God's;
And his cheek brighten'd as the foam-bow° bright-
    ens   60
When the wind blows the foam, and all my heart
Went forth to embrace him coming ere he came.

"Dear mother Ida, harken ere I die.
He smiled, and opening out his milk-white palm
Disclosed a fruit of pure Hesperian gold,°
That smelt ambrosially, and while I look'd
And listen'd, the full-flowing river of speech
Came down upon my heart:
                              "'My own Œnone,
Beautiful-brow'd Œnone, my own soul,   69
Behold this fruit, whose gleaming rind ingrav'n
"For the most fair," would seem to award it thine,
As lovelier than whatever Oread haunt
The knolls of Ida, loveliest in all grace
Of movement, and the charm of married brows.'°

"Dear mother Ida, harken ere I die.
He prest the blossom of his lips to mine,
And added, 'This was cast upon the board,
When all the full-faced presence of the Gods
Ranged in the halls of Peleus;° whereupon
Rose feud, with question unto whom 't were due;
But light-foot Iris brought it yester-eve,   81
Delivering, that to me, by common voice
Elected umpire, Herè° comes to-day,
Pallas° and Aphrodite, claiming each

This meed of fairest. Thou, within the cave
Behind yon whispering tuft of oldest pine,
Mayst well behold them unbeheld, unheard
Hear all, and see thy Paris judge of Gods.'

"Dear mother Ida, harken ere I die.
It was the deep midnoon; one silvery cloud   90
Had lost his way between the piny sides
Of this long glen. Then to the bower they came,
Naked they came to that smooth-swarded bower,
And at their feet the crocus brake like fire,
Violet, amaracus,° and asphodel,
Lotos and lilies; and a wind arose,
And overhead the wandering ivy and vine,
This way and that, in many a wild festoon
Ran riot, garlanding the gnarlèd boughs
With bunch and berry and flower thro' and thro'.

"O mother Ida, harken ere I die.   101
On the tree-tops a crested peacock° lit,
And o'er him flow'd a golden cloud, and lean'd
Upon him, slowly dropping fragrant dew.
Then first I heard the voice of her to whom
Coming thro' heaven, like a light that grows
Larger and clearer, with one mind the Gods
Rise up for reverence. She to Paris made
Proffer of royal power, ample rule
Unquestion'd, overflowing revenue   110
Wherewith to embellish state, 'from many a vale°
And river-sunder'd champaign clothed with corn,°
Or labor'd mine undrainable of ore.
Honor,' she said, 'and homage, tax and toll,
From many an inland town and haven large,
Mast-throng'd beneath her shadowing citadel
In glassy bays among her tallest towers.'

"O mother Ida, harken ere I die.
Still she spake on and still she spake of power,
'Which in all action is the end of all;   120
Power fitted to the season; wisdom-bred
And throned of wisdom — from all neighbor
    crowns
Alliance and allegiance, till thy hand
Fail from the scepter-staff. Such boon from me,
From me, heaven's queen, Paris, to thee king-born,
A shepherd all thy life but yet king-born,
Should come most welcome, seeing men, in power
Only, are likest Gods, who have attain'd
Rest in a happy place and quiet seats
Above the thunder, with undying bliss   130
In knowledge of their own supremacy.'

51. **Simois:** a river. 60. **foam-bow:** rainbow. 65. **Hesperian gold:** See the headnote to "The Hesperides." 74. **married brows:** meeting eyebrows, an ancient mark of beauty. 79. The marriage of Peleus and Thetis (parents of Achilles) was attended by the gods. 83. **Herè:** wife of Zeus and queen of the gods (Juno). 84. **Pallas:** Athene, goddess of wisdom and war (Minerva).

95. **amaracus:** marjoram. 102. **peacock:** the bird of Here. 111–17. Evidently imitated from, and more studiously "composed" than, Milton's *Paradise Regained*, III.254–62. 112. **corn:** grain.

"Dear mother Ida, harken ere I die.
She ceased, and Paris held the costly fruit
Out at arm's-length, so much the thought of power
Flatter'd his spirit; but Pallas where she stood
Somewhat apart, her clear and barèd limbs
O'erthwarted with the brazen-headed spear
Upon her pearly shoulder leaning cold,
The while, above, her full and earnest eye
Over her snow-cold breast and angry cheek   140
Kept watch, waiting decision, made reply:

"'Self-reverence, self-knowledge, self-control,
These three alone lead life to sovereign power.
Yet not for power (power of herself
Would come uncall'd for) but to live by law,
Acting the law we live by without fear;
And, because right is right, to follow right
Were wisdom in the scorn of consequence.'

"Dear mother Ida, harken ere I die.
Again she said: 'I woo thee not with gifts.   150
Sequel of guerdon° could not alter me
To fairer, judge thou me by what I am,
So shalt thou find me fairest.
                                        Yet, indeed,
If gazing on divinity disrobed
Thy mortal eyes are frail to judge of fair,
Unbias'd by self-profit, O, rest thee sure
That I shall love thee well and cleave to thee,
So that my vigor, wedded to thy blood,
Shall strike within thy pulses, like a God's
To push thee forward thro' a life of shocks,   160
Dangers, and deeds, until endurance grow
Sinew'd with action, and the full-grown will,
Circled thro' all experiences, pure law,
Commeasure perfect freedom.'
                                        "Here she ceas'd,
And Paris ponder'd, and I cried, 'O Paris,
Give it to Pallas!' but he heard me not,
Or hearing would not hear me, woe is me!

"O mother Ida, many-fountain'd Ida,
Dear mother Ida, harken ere I die.
Idalian° Aphrodite beautiful,   170
Fresh as the foam, new-bathed in Paphian° wells,
With rosy slender fingers backward drew
From her warm brows and bosom her deep hair
Ambrosial, golden round her lucid throat
And shoulder; from the violets her light foot
Shone rosy-white, and o'er her rounded form

Between the shadows of the vine-bunches
Floated the glowing sunlights, as she moved.

"Dear mother Ida, harken ere I die.
She with a subtle smile in her mild eyes,   180
The herald of her triumph, drawing nigh
Half-whisper'd in his ear, 'I promise thee
The fairest and most loving wife in Greece.'
She spoke and laugh'd; I shut my sight for fear;
But when I look'd, Paris had raised his arm,
And I beheld great Herè's angry eyes,
As she withdrew into the golden cloud,
And I was left alone within the bower;
And from that time to this I am alone,
And I shall be alone until I die.   190

"Yet, mother Ida, harken ere I die.
Fairest — why fairest wife? am I not fair?
My love hath told me so a thousand times.
Methinks I must be fair, for yesterday,
When I past by, a wild and wanton pard,°
Eyed like the evening star, with playful tail
Crouch'd fawning in the weed. Most loving is she?
Ah me, my mountain shepherd, that my arms
Were wound about thee, and my hot lips prest
Close, close to thine in that quick-falling dew   200
Of fruitful kisses, thick as autumn rains
Flash in the pools of whirling Simois!

"O mother, hear me yet before I die.
They came, they cut away my tallest pines,°
My tall dark pines, that plumed the craggy ledge
High over the blue gorge, and all between
The snowy peak and snowwhite cataract
Foster'd the callow eaglet — from beneath
Whose thick mysterious boughs in the dark morn
The panther's roar came muffled, while I sat   210
Low in the valley. Never, never more
Shall lone Œnone see the morning mist
Sweep thro' them; never see them overlaid
With narrow moonlit slips of silver cloud,
Between the loud stream and the trembling stars.

"O mother, hear me yet before I die.
I wish that somewhere in the ruin'd folds,
Among the fragments tumbled from the glens,
Or the dry thickets, I could meet with her
The Abominable,° that uninvited came   220
Into the fair Peleïan banquet-hall,
And cast the golden fruit upon the board,
And bred this change; that I might speak my mind,
And tell her to her face how much I hate
Her presence, hated both of Gods and men.

"O mother, hear me yet before I die.
Hath he not sworn his love a thousand times,
In this green valley, under this green hill,
Even on this hand, and sitting on this stone?
Seal'd it with kisses? water'd it with tears? 230
O happy tears, and how unlike to these!
O happy heaven, how canst thou see my face?
O happy earth, how canst thou bear my weight?
O death, death, death, thou ever-floating cloud,
There are enough unhappy on this earth,
Pass by the happy souls, that love to live;
I pray thee, pass before my light of life,
And shadow all my soul, that I may die.
Thou weighest heavy on the heart within,
Weigh heavy on my eyelids; let me die. 240

"O mother, hear me yet before I die.
I will not die alone, for fiery thoughts
Do shape themselves within me, more and more,
Whereof I catch the issue, as I hear
Dead sounds at night come from the inmost hills,
Like footsteps upon wool. I dimly see
My far-off doubtful purpose,° as a mother
Conjectures of the features of her child
Ere it is born. Her child! — a shudder comes
Across me: never child be born of me, 250
Unblest, to vex me with his father's eyes!

"O mother, hear me yet before I die.
Hear me, O earth. I will not die alone,
Lest their shrill happy laughter come to me
Walking the cold and starless road of death
Uncomforted, leaving my ancient love°
With the Greek woman.° I will rise and go
Down into Troy, and ere the stars come forth
Talk with the wild Cassandra, for she says
A fire dances before her, and a sound 260
Rings ever in her ears of armèd men.°
What this may be I know not, but I know
That, wheresoe'er I am by night and day,
All earth and air seem only burning fire."

1832, 1842

✓ THE LOTOS-EATERS

Published in 1832; much revised, 1842. The prelude
of five Spenserian stanzas embodies recollections of
Spanish scenes from the visit of 1830 (cf. "Œnone").
Tennyson adapts the Homeric episode (*Odyssey*,

246–47. I . . . purpose: Œnone later refused to heal the
wounded Paris and, having let him die, killed herself (see
Tennyson's "The Death of Œnone"). 253–56. Hear . . . love:
An inspired echo of Dido's dream, *Aeneid*, IV.466–68. 257.
Greek woman: Helen. 259–61. Cassandra . . . men: a proph-
etess, daughter of King Priam and sister of Paris; cf. Aeschylus,
Agamemnon, 1256.

IX.82 ff.) to his recurrent theme of these years: man's,
or the artist's, acceptance or evasion of social responsibility. He also transforms the epic material and manner into his own most luxuriant lyrical vein. Escapist
languor is rendered with a verbal and rhythmical felicity that is both exquisite and enervated — and the
mood is not condemned, unless by general implication
or comparison with other poems, such as "Ulysses." In
the Choric Song alternate stanzas are given to pleasurable apathy and the pains of action at sea or at home,
and, to some degree, images are correspondingly given
a downward or upward movement.

"Courage!" he° said, and pointed toward the land,
"This mounting wave will roll us shoreward soon."
In the afternoon they came unto a land
In which it seemèd always afternoon.
All around the coast the languid air did swoon,
Breathing like one that hath a weary dream.
Full-faced above the valley stood the moon;
And, like a downward smoke, the slender stream
Along the cliff to fall and pause and fall did seem.

A land of streams! some, like a downward smoke,
Slow-dropping veils of thinnest lawn, did go; 11
And some thro' wavering lights and shadows broke,
Rolling a slumbrous sheet of foam below.
They saw the gleaming river seaward flow
From the inner land; far off, three mountain-tops,
Three silent pinnacles of aged snow,
Stood sunset-flush'd; and, dew'd with showery
  drops,
Up-clomb the shadowy pine above the woven copse.

The charmèd sunset linger'd low adown
In the red West; thro' mountain clefts the dale 20
Was seen far inland, and the yellow down
Border'd with palm, and many a winding vale
And meadow, set with slender galingale;
A land where all things always seem'd the same!
And round about the keel with faces pale,
Dark faces pale against that rosy flame,
The mild-eyed melancholy Lotos-eaters came.

Branches they bore of that enchanted stem,
Laden with flower and fruit, whereof they gave
To each, but whoso did receive of them 30
And taste, to him the gushing of the wave
Far far away did seem to mourn and rave
On alien shores; and if his fellow spake,
His voice was thin, as voices from the grave;
And deep-asleep he seem'd, yet all awake,
And music in his ears his beating heart did make.

They sat them down upon the yellow sand,
Between the sun and moon upon the shore;
And sweet it was to dream of Fatherland,

THE LOTOS-EATERS.   1. he: Odysseus.

Of child, and wife, and slave; but evermore   40
Most weary seem'd the sea, weary the oar,
Weary the wandering fields of barren foam.
Then some one said, "We will return no more;"
And all at once they sang, "Our island home°
Is far beyond the wave; we will no longer roam."

CHORIC SONG

I

There is sweet music here that softer falls
Than petals from blown° roses on the grass,
Or night-dews on still waters between walls
Of shadowy granite, in a gleaming pass;
Music that gentlier on the spirit lies,
Than tired eyelids upon tired eyes;
Music that brings sweet sleep down from the bliss-
    ful skies.
Here are cool mosses deep,
And thro' the moss the ivies creep,   9
And in the stream the long-leaved flowers weep,
And from the craggy ledge the poppy hangs in
    sleep.

II

Why are we weigh'd upon with heaviness,
And utterly consumed with sharp distress,
While all things else have rest from weariness?
All things have rest: why should we toil alone,
We only toil, who are the first of things,
And make perpetual moan,
Still from one sorrow to another thrown;
Nor ever fold our wings,
And cease from wanderings,   20
Nor steep our brows in slumber's holy balm;
Nor harken what the inner spirit sings,
"There is no joy but calm!"—
Why should we only toil, the roof and crown of
    things?

III

Lo! in the middle of the wood,
The folded leaf is woo'd from out the bud
With winds upon the branch, and there
Grows green and broad, and takes no care,
Sun-steep'd at noon, and in the moon
Nightly dew-fed; and turning yellow   30
Falls, and floats adown the air.
Lo! sweeten'd with the summer light,
The full-juiced apple, waxing over-mellow,
Drops in a silent autumn night.
All its allotted length of days
The flower ripens in its place,
Ripens and fades, and falls, and hath no toil,
Fast-rooted in the fruitful soil.

IV

Hateful is the dark-blue sky,
Vaulted o'er the dark-blue sea.   40
Death is the end of life; ah, why
Should life all labor be?
Let us alone. Time driveth onward fast,
And in a little while our lips are dumb.
Let us alone. What is it that will last?
All things are taken from us, and become
Portions and parcels of the dreadful past.
Let us alone. What pleasure can we have
To war with evil? Is there any peace
In ever climbing up the climbing wave?   50
All things have rest, and ripen toward the grave
In silence — ripen, fall, and cease:
Give us long rest or death, dark death, or dream-
    ful ease.

V

How sweet it were, hearing the downward stream,
With half-shut eyes ever to seem
Falling asleep in a half-dream!
To dream and dream, like yonder amber light,
Which will not leave the myrrh-bush on the height;
To hear each other's whisper'd speech;
Eating the Lotos day by day,   60
To watch the crisping° ripples on the beach,
And tender curving lines of creamy spray;
To lend our hearts and spirits wholly
To the influence of mild-minded melancholy;
To muse and brood and live again in memory,
With those old faces of our infancy
Heap'd over with a mound of grass,
Two handfuls of white dust, shut in an urn of
    brass!

VI

Dear is the memory of our wedded lives,°
And dear the last embraces of our wives   70
And their warm tears; but all hath suffer'd change;
For surely now our household hearths are cold,
Our sons inherit us, our looks are strange,
And we should come like ghosts to trouble joy.
Or else the island princes over-bold
Have eat° our substance, and the minstrel sings
Before them of the ten years' war in Troy,
And our great deeds, as half-forgotten things.
Is there confusion in the little isle?
Let what is broken so remain.   80
The Gods are hard to reconcile;
'Tis hard to settle order once again.
There is confusion worse than death,

---

44. island home: Ithaca, west of Greece.   Choric Song. 2.
blown: past maturity.

61. crisping: curling.   69–87. Stanza VI was added in 1842.
Though it is relatively Homeric in substance, line 79 seems to
glance at social and political unrest in England.   76. eat: the
past participle, in English usage; pronounced "et."

Trouble on trouble, pain on pain,
Long labor unto aged breath,
Sore tasks to hearts worn out by many wars
And eyes grown dim with gazing on the pilot-stars.

VII

But, propt on beds of amaranth° and moly,°
How sweet — while warm airs lull us, blowing
    lowly —
With half-dropt eyelid still,   90
Beneath a heaven dark and holy,
To watch the long bright river drawing slowly
His waters from the purple hill —
To hear the dewy echoes calling
From cave to cave thro' the thick-twinèd vine —
To watch the emerald-color'd water falling
Thro' many a woven acanthus-wreath divine!
Only to hear and see the far-off sparkling brine,
Only to hear were sweet, stretch'd out beneath the
    pine.

VIII

The Lotos blooms below the barren peak,   100
The Lotos blows by every winding creek;
All day the wind breathes low with mellower tone;
Thro' every hollow cave and alley lone
Round and round the spicy downs the yellow Lotos-
    dust is blown.
We have had enough of action, and of motion we,°
Roll'd to starboard, roll'd to larboard, when the
    surge was seething free,
Where the wallowing monster° spouted his foam-
    fountains in the sea.
Let us swear an oath, and keep it with an equal
    mind,
In the hollow Lotos-land to live and lie reclined
On the hills like Gods together, careless of man-
    kind.°
For they lie beside their nectar, and the bolts° are
    hurl'd   111
Far below them in the valleys, and the clouds are
    lightly curl'd
Round their golden houses, girdled with the gleam-
    ing world;
Where they smile in secret, looking over wasted
    lands,
Blight and famine, plague and earthquake, roaring
    deeps and fiery sands,

Clanging fights, and flaming towns, and sinking
    ships, and praying hands.
But they smile, they find a music centered in a
    doleful song
Steaming up, a lamentation and an ancient tale of
    wrong,
Like a tale of little meaning tho' the words are
    strong;
Chanted from an ill-used race of men that cleave
    the soil,   120
Sow the seed, and reap the harvest with enduring
    toil,
Storing yearly little dues of wheat, and wine and
    oil;
Till they perish and they suffer — some, 'tis whis-
    per'd — down in hell
Suffer endless anguish, others in Elysian° valleys
    dwell,
Resting weary limbs at last on beds of asphodel.°
Surely, surely, slumber is more sweet than toil, the
    shore
Than labor in the deep mid-ocean, wind and wave
    and oar;
O, rest ye, brother mariners, we will not wander
    more.

1832, 1842

ULYSSES

Written in October, 1833; published in 1842. Tennyson's first dramatic monologue on a classical theme is characteristic in its use of a universally familiar mythic figure and of an antique frame for modern and personal feelings, and in its elevated style. The Homeric Odysseus' motive (though he did sojourn with Circe and Calypso) was to get home to Ithaca and stay there. But the *Odyssey* itself (XI.100–37) foretold death at sea, a hint somewhat developed in later writings, and in Dante (*Inferno*, XXVI.90 ff.) he makes a fatal voyage into the unknown west in search of knowledge. While for Dante Ulysses is a type of pride (and deceitful counsel), for Tennyson, stricken by the death of Hallam (of which he received word on October 1, 1833), he represents the courageous facing of life — though resolution and fortitude are touched with weariness and despair. The poet's own comment, apropos of *In Memoriam*, was: "There is more about myself in 'Ulysses,' which was written under the sense of loss and all that had gone by, but that still life must be fought out to the end. It was more written with the feeling of his loss upon me than many poems in 'In Memoriam.'" (*Nineteenth Century*, XXXIII, 1893, p. 182; cf. *Memoir*, I, 196.) The poem is placed in its long tradition in W. B. Stanford's *The Ulysses Theme* (1954), pp. 202–04.

---

88. amaranth: a supposedly unfading flower. **moly:** the magical herb that protected Odysseus from Circe's spells, though here only a Homeric plant. **105–28.** Completely altered from the original and inferior ending—though the new ending, with its access of energy, is perhaps less in harmony with the tone of the whole. **107. monster:** whale. **110 ff.** The picture of the indifferent gods is developed from the Epicurean Lucretius (*De Rerum Natura*, II.646 ff., V.83 ff., VI.58 ff.). **111. bolts:** thunderbolts.

124. Elysian: Elysium was the Greek paradise for heroes.
125. asphodel: daffodils (in the Homeric Elysium).

It little profits that an idle king,
By this still hearth, among these barren crags,
Match'd with an aged wife, I mete and dole
Unequal laws unto a savage race,
That hoard, and sleep, and feed, and know not
    me.°
I cannot rest from travel; I will drink
Life to the lees. All times I have enjoy'd
Greatly, have suffer'd greatly, both with those
That loved me, and alone; on shore, and when
Thro' scudding drifts the rainy Hyades   10
Vext the dim sea. I am become a name;
For always roaming with a hungry heart
Much have I seen and known,—cities of men
And manners, climates, councils, governments,
Myself not least, but honor'd of them all,—
And drunk delight of battle with my peers,
Far on the ringing plains of windy Troy.
I am a part of all that I have met;
Yet all experience is an arch wherethro'
Gleams that untravel'd world whose margin fades
For ever and for ever when I move.   21
How dull it is to pause, to make an end,
To rust unburnish'd, not to shine in use!°
As tho' to breathe were life! Life piled on life
Were all too little, and of one to me
Little remains; but every hour is saved
From that eternal silence, something more,
A bringer of new things; and vile it were
For some three suns to store and hoard myself,
And this gray spirit yearning in desire   30
To follow knowledge like a sinking star,
Beyond the utmost bound of human thought.

    This is my son, mine own Telemachus,
To whom I leave the scepter and the isle,°—
Well-loved of me, discerning to fulfil
This labor, by slow prudence to make mild
A rugged people, and thro' soft degrees
Subdue them to the useful and the good.
Most blameless is he, centered in the sphere
Of common duties, decent not to fail   40
In offices of tenderness, and pay
Meet adoration to my household gods,
When I am gone. He works his work, I mine.

    There lies the port; the vessel puffs her sail;
There gloom the dark, broad seas. My mariners,°
Souls that have toil'd, and wrought, and thought
    with me,—
That ever with a frolic welcome took
The thunder and the sunshine, and opposed

Free hearts, free foreheads,—you and I are old;
Old age hath yet his honor and his toil.   50
Death closes all; but something ere the end,
Some work of noble note, may yet be done,
Not unbecoming men that strove with Gods.
The lights begin to twinkle from the rocks;
The long day wanes; the slow moon climbs;° the
    deep
Moans round with many voices. Come, my friends,
'Tis not too late to seek a newer world.
Push off, and sitting well in order smite
The sounding furrows; for my purpose holds
To sail beyond the sunset, and the baths   60
Of all the western stars, until I die.
It may be that the gulfs will wash us down;
It may be we shall touch the Happy Isles,°
And see the great Achilles,° whom we knew.
Tho' much is taken, much abides; and tho'
We are not now that strength which in old days
Moved earth and heaven, that which we are, we
    are,—
One equal temper of heroic hearts,
Made weak by time and fate, but strong in will
To strive, to seek, to find, and not to yield.   70

     1842   *1833*

TITHONUS

    The mortal Tithonus loved Eos, the goddess of dawn, who obtained for him from Zeus the gift of immortality but neglected to ask for eternal youth, so that he withered away into a repulsive subhuman creature ("Homeric Hymn to Aphrodite"). The theme of isolation and of death as an escape from the burden of living, which had haunted Tennyson from boyhood onward (cf. "Mariana," "Œnone"), is here greatly deepened by the loss of Hallam. This monologue is at the opposite pole from "Ulysses" (though even there the thought of death is not unwelcome), and is of perhaps still finer texture; and, not unnaturally, it has a more mythic quality. "Tithonus" was written apparently in 1833–34, revised in 1859, and published in 1860 (*Memoir*, I, 459; II, 9); the first version was printed and compared with the final one by M. J. Donahue, *Publications of the Modern Language Association*, LXIV (1949), 400 ff.

The woods decay, the woods decay and fall,
The vapors weep their burthen to the ground,
Man comes and tills the field and lies beneath,
And after many a summer dies the swan.
Me only cruel immortality

ULYSSES. **5.** Cf. *Hamlet*, IV.iv.35. **23.** Cf. *Hamlet*, IV.iv.39. **34–43.** In view of Tennyson's early and prolonged concern over contemplative detachment versus social responsibility, the latter might seem to be fulfilled by Telemachus, but in this poem the issue is rather between giving up and going on. **45** ff. In Homer, Odysseus had lost all his comrades by the time he reached Ithaca; in Dante, he sails westward from Circe's island, so that they are still with him. Tennyson obviously needs to have them.

54–55. The . . . climbs: Homeric voyages commonly begin in the evening; here the accent is on the evening of life. **63. Happy Isles:** Elysium. **64. Achilles:** Arthur Hallam?

Consumes; I wither slowly in thine arms,°
Here at the quiet limit of the world,
A white-hair'd shadow roaming like a dream
The ever-silent spaces of the East,
Far-folded mists, and gleaming halls of morn.   10

   Alas! for this gray shadow, once a man —
So glorious in his beauty and thy choice,
Who madest him thy chosen, that he seem'd
To his great heart none other than a God!
I ask'd thee, "Give me immortality."
Then didst thou grant mine asking with a smile,
Like wealthy men who care not how they give.
But thy strong Hours indignant work'd their wills,
And beat me down and marr'd and wasted me,
And tho' they could not end me, left me maim'd
To dwell in presence of immortal youth,   21
Immortal age beside immortal youth,
And all I was in ashes. Can thy love,
Thy beauty, make amends, tho' even now,
Close over us, the silver star,° thy guide,
Shines in those tremulous eyes that fill with tears
To hear me? Let me go; take back thy gift.
Why should a man desire in any way
To vary from the kindly° race of men,
Or pass beyond the goal of ordinance   30
Where all should pause, as is most meet for all?

   A soft air fans the cloud apart; there comes
A glimpse of that dark world where I was born.
Once more the old mysterious glimmer steals
From thy pure brows, and from thy shoulders pure,
And bosom beating with a heart renew'd.
Thy cheek begins to redden thro' the gloom,
Thy sweet eyes brighten slowly close to mine,
Ere yet they blind the stars, and the wild team
Which love thee, yearning for thy yoke, arise,   40
And shake the darkness from their loosen'd manes,
And beat the twilight into flakes of fire.

   Lo! ever thus thou growest beautiful
In silence, then before thine answer given
Departest, and thy tears are on my cheek.
   Why wilt thou ever scare me with thy tears,
And make me tremble lest a saying learnt,
In days far-off, on that dark earth, be true?
"The Gods themselves cannot recall their gifts."
   Ay me! ay me! with what another heart   50
In days far-off, and with what other eyes
I used to watch — if I be he that watch'd —
The lucid outline forming round thee; saw
The dim curls kindle into sunny rings;
Changed with thy mystic change, and felt my blood
Glow with the glow that slowly crimson'd all
Thy presence and thy portals, while I lay,
Mouth, forehead, eyelids, growing dewy-warm

With kisses balmier than half-opening buds
Of April, and could hear the lips that kiss'd   60
Whispering I knew not what of wild and sweet,
Like that strange song I heard Apollo sing,
While Ilion like a mist rose into towers.°

   Yet hold me not for ever in thine East;
How can my nature longer mix with thine?
Coldly thy rosy shadows bathe me, cold
Are all thy lights, and cold my wrinkled feet
Upon thy glimmering thresholds, when the steam
Floats up from those dim fields about the homes
Of happy men that have the power to die,   70
And grassy barrows of the happier dead.
Release me, and restore me to the ground.
Thou seest all things, thou wilt see my grave;
Thou wilt renew thy beauty morn by morn,
I earth in earth forget these empty courts,
And thee returning on thy silver wheels.

1860   *1833–34, 1859*

BREAK, BREAK, BREAK

This lyric was composed, Tennyson said, in a Lincolnshire lane at five in the morning between blossoming hedges (probably in the spring of 1834). His lifelong "passion of the past" (cf. "Tears, Idle Tears")
is here channeled into grief for Hallam's death — grief
to which nature and man, pursuing their normal course,
are indifferent. The meter is predominantly anapaes-
tic.

Break, break, break,
   On thy cold gray stones, O Sea!
And I would that my tongue could utter
   The thoughts that arise in me.

O, well for the fisherman's boy,
   That he shouts with his sister at play!
O, well for the sailor lad,
   That he sings in his boat on the bay!

And the stately ships go on
   To their haven under the hill;   10
But O for the touch of a vanish'd hand,
   And the sound of a voice that is still!

Break, break, break,
   At the foot of thy crags, O Sea!
But the tender grace of a day that is dead
   Will never come back to me.

1842   *1834?*

TITHONUS.   **6. thine arms:** the arms of Eos.   **25. silver star:**
Venus, the morning star.   **29. kindly:** following the course of
their nature.

62–63. Like . . . towers: Cf. "Œnone," above, II.39–40 and note.

LOCKSLEY HALL

Published in 1842. Writing to G. M. Hopkins in 1879, R. W. Dixon described "Locksley Hall" as an "ungentlemanly row," but such a representative of an earlier generation as Charles Kingsley said in 1850 that this poem had "most influence on the minds of the young men of our day" — an influence akin to that of the social verse of the 1930's, though doubtless more in accord with public opinion and faith in progress. Tennyson said that, while he was indebted to some Arabian poems translated by Sir William Jones, the narrative situation was imaginary (*Memoir*, I, 195); the attack of Mammonism may in part reflect the feud in the Tennyson family (see the Introduction). Some of the attitudes expressed are Tennyson's, though he is not to be identified with the speaker. It is odd that a poet who normally has the most sensitive metrical tact should have put a reflective monologue into galloping trochaics because English people liked that meter (*Memoir*, l.c.); at any rate the lines were highly quotable.

Comrades, leave me here a little, while as yet 'tis early morn;
Leave me here, and when you want me, sound upon the bugle-horn.

'Tis the place, and all around it, as of old, the curlews call,
Dreary gleams° about the moorland flying over Locksley Hall;

Locksley Hall, that in the distance overlooks the sandy tracts,
And the hollow ocean-ridges roaring into cataracts.

Many a night from yonder ivied casement, ere I went to rest,
Did I look on great Orion sloping slowly to the west.

Many a night I saw the Pleiads, rising thro' the mellow shade,
Glitter like a swarm of fireflies tangled in a silver braid.   10

Here about the beach I wander'd, nourishing a youth sublime
With the fairy tales of science, and the long result of time;

When the centuries behind me like a fruitful land reposed;
When I clung to all the present for the promise that it closed; °

When I dipt into the future far as human eye could see,
Saw the vision of the world and all the wonder that would be. —

In the spring a fuller crimson comes upon the robin's breast;°
In the spring the wanton lapwing gets himself another crest;

In the spring a livelier iris changes on the burnish'd dove;
In the spring a young man's fancy lightly turns to thoughts of love.   20

Then her cheek was pale and thinner than should be for one so young,
And her eyes on all my motions with a mute observance hung.

And I said, "My cousin Amy, speak, and speak the truth to me,
Trust me, cousin, all the current of my being sets to thee."

On her pallid cheek and forehead came a color and a light,
As I have seen the rosy red flushing in the northern night.

And she turn'd — her bosom shaken with a sudden storm of sighs —
All the spirit deeply dawning in the dark of hazel eyes —

Saying, "I have hid my feelings, fearing they should do me wrong;"
Saying, "Dost thou love me, cousin?" weeping, "I have loved thee long."   30

Love took up the glass of Time, and turn'd it in his glowing hands;
Every moment, lightly shaken, ran itself in golden sands.

Love took up the harp of Life, and smote on all the chords with might;
Smote the chord of Self, that, trembling, past in music out of sight.

Many a morning on the moorland did we hear the copses ring,
And her whisper throng'd my pulses with the fullness of the spring.

LOCKSLEY HALL.   **4. gleams:** of light.   **14. closed:** enclosed.

17. robin's breast: The English robin is a little garden bird with a vivid scarlet breast.

Many an evening by the waters did we watch the
    stately ships,
And our spirits rush'd together at the touching of
    the lips.

O my cousin, shallow-hearted! O my Amy, mine
    no more!
O the dreary, dreary moorland! O the barren, bar-
    ren shore!   40

Falser than all fancy fathoms, falser than all songs
    have sung,
Puppet to a father's threat, and servile to a shrew-
    ish tongue!

Is it well to wish thee happy? — having known me
    — to decline
On a range of lower feelings and a narrower heart
    than mine!

Yet it shall be; thou shalt lower to his level day by
    day,
What is fine within thee growing coarse to sym-
    pathize with clay.

As the husband is, the wife is; thou art mated with
    a clown,
And the grossness of his nature will have weight
    to drag thee down.

He will hold thee, when his passion shall have
    spent its novel force,
Something better than his dog, a little dearer than
    his horse.   50

What is this? his eyes are heavy; think not they
    are glazed with wine.
Go to him, it is thy duty; kiss him, take his hand
    in thine.

It may be my lord is weary, that his brain is over-
    wrought;
Soothe him with thy finer fancies, touch him with
    thy lighter thought.

He will answer to the purpose, easy things to under-
    stand —
Better thou wert dead before me, tho' I slew thee
    with my hand!

Better thou and I were lying, hidden from the
    heart's disgrace,
Roll'd in one another's arms, and silent in a last
    embrace.

Cursèd be the social wants that sin against the
    strength of youth!

Cursèd be the social lies that warp us from the
    living truth!   60

Cursèd be the sickly forms that err from honest
    Nature's rule!
Cursèd be the gold that gilds the straiten'd fore-
    head of the fool!

Well — 'tis well that I should bluster! — Hadst thou
    less unworthy proved —
Would to God — for I had loved thee more than
    ever wife was loved.

Am I mad, that I should cherish that which bears
    but bitter fruit?
I will pluck it from my bosom, tho' my heart be
    at the root.

Never, tho' my mortal summers to such length of
    years should come
As the many-winter'd crow that leads the clanging
    rookery home.

Where is comfort? in division of the records of the
    mind?
Can I part her from herself, and love her, as I knew
    her, kind?   70

I remember one that perish'd; sweetly did she speak
    and move;
Such a one do I remember, whom to look at was
    to love.

Can I think of her as dead, and love her for the
    love she bore?
No — she never loved me truly; love is love for
    evermore.

Comfort? comfort scorn'd of devils! this is truth
    the poet° sings,
That a sorrow's crown of sorrow is remembering
    happier things.

Drug thy memories, lest thou learn it, lest thy
    heart be put to proof,
In the dead unhappy night, and when the rain is
    on the roof.

Like a dog, he hunts in dreams, and thou art star-
    ing at the wall,
Where the dying night-lamp flickers, and the shad-
    ows rise and fall.   80

Then a hand shall pass before thee, pointing to his
    drunken sleep,

75. poet: Dante (*Inferno*, V.121-23).

To thy widow'd marriage-pillows, to the tears that
thou wilt weep.

Thou shalt hear the "Never, never," whisper'd by
the phantom years,
And a song from out the distance in the ringing
of thine ears;

And an eye shall vex thee, looking ancient kindness
on thy pain.
Turn thee, turn thee on thy pillow; get thee to thy
rest again.

Nay, but Nature brings thee solace; for a tender
voice will cry.
'Tis a purer life than thine, a lip to drain thy
trouble dry.

Baby lips will laugh me down; my latest rival
brings thee rest.
Baby fingers, waxen touches, press me from the
mother's breast.   90

O, the child too clothes the father with a dearness
not his due.
Half is thine and half is his; it will be worthy of
the two.

O, I see thee old and formal, fitted to thy petty
part,
With a little hoard of maxims preaching down a
daughter's heart.

"They were dangerous guides the feelings — she
herself was not exempt —
Truly, she herself had suffer'd" — Perish in thy
self-contempt!

Overlive it — lower yet — be happy! wherefore
should I care?
I myself must mix with action, lest I wither by
despair.

What is that which I should turn to, lighting upon
days like these?
Every door is barr'd with gold, and opens but to
golden keys.   100

Every gate is throng'd with suitors, all the markets
overflow.
I have but an angry fancy; what is that which I
should do?

I had been content to perish, falling on the foeman's
ground,
When the ranks are roll'd in vapor, and the winds
are laid with sound.

But the jingling of the guinea helps the hurt that
Honor feels,
And the nations do but murmur, snarling at each
other's heels.

Can I but relive in sadness? I will turn that earlier
page.
Hide me from my deep emotion, O thou wondrous
Mother-Age!

Make me feel the wild pulsation that I felt before
the strife,
When I heard my days before me, and the tumult
of my life;   110

Yearning for the large excitement that the coming
years would yield,
Eager-hearted as a boy when first he leaves his
father's field,

And at night along the dusky highway near and
nearer drawn,
Sees in heaven the light of London flaring like a
dreary dawn;

And his spirit leaps within him to be gone before
him then,
Underneath the light he looks at, in among the
throngs of men;

Men, my brothers, men the workers, ever reaping
something new;
That which they have done but earnest of the things
that they shall do.

For I dipt into the future, far as human eye could
see,
Saw the Vision of the world, and all the wonder
that would be;   120

Saw the heavens fill with commerce, argosies of
magic sails,
Pilots of the purple twilight, dropping down with
costly bales;

Heard the heavens fill with shouting, and there
rain'd a ghastly dew
From the nations' airy navies grappling in the
central blue;

Far along the world-wide whisper of the south-
wind rushing warm,
With the standards of the peoples plunging thro'
the thunderstorm;°

121-26. Saw . . . thunderstorm: These lines probably reflect contemporary interest in balloons, though they are, for us, grimly
prophetic.

Till the war-drum throbb'd no longer, and the
    battle-flags were furl'd
In the Parliament of man, the Federation of the
    world.

There the common sense of most shall hold a fret-
    ful realm in awe,
And the kindly earth shall slumber, lapt in uni-
    versal law.   130

So I triumph'd ere my passion sweeping thro' me
    left me dry,
Left me with the palsied heart, and left me with
    the jaundiced eye;

Eye, to which all order festers, all things here are
    out of joint.
Science moves, but slowly, slowly, creeping on from
    point to point;

Slowly comes a hungry people, as a lion, creeping
    nigher,
Glares at one that nods and winks behind a slowly-
    dying fire.°

Yet I doubt not thro' the ages one increasing pur-
    pose runs,
And the thoughts of men are widen'd with the
    process of the suns.

What is that to him that reaps not harvest of his
    youthful joys,
Tho' the deep heart of existence beat for ever like
    a boy's?   140

Knowledge comes, but wisdom lingers, and I linger
    on the shore,
And the individual withers, and the world is more
    and more.

Knowledge comes, but wisdom lingers, and he
    bears a laden breast,
Full of sad experience, moving toward the stillness
    of his rest.

Hark, my merry comrades call me, sounding on the
    bugle-horn,
They to whom my foolish passion were a target
    for their scorn.

Shall it not be scorn to me to harp on such a
    molder'd string?
I am shamed thro' all my nature to have loved
    so slight a thing.

Weakness to be wroth with weakness! woman's
    pleasure, woman's pain —
Nature made them blinder motions bounded in a
    shallower brain.   150

Woman is the lesser man, and all thy passions,
    match'd with mine,
Are as moonlight unto sunlight, and as water unto
    wine —

Here at least, where nature sickens, nothing. Ah,
    for some retreat
Deep in yonder shining Orient, where my life be-
    gan to beat,

Where in wild Mahratta-battle° fell my father evil-
    starr'd; —
I was left a trampled orphan, and a selfish uncle's
    ward.

Or to burst all links of habit — there to wander far
    away,
On from island unto island at the gateways of the
    day.

Larger constellations burning, mellow moons and
    happy skies,
Breadths of tropic shade and palms in cluster, knots
    of Paradise.   160

Never comes the trader, never floats an European
    flag,
Slides the bird o'er lustrous woodland, swings the
    trailer° from the crag;

Droops the heavy-blossom'd bower, hangs the
    heavy-fruited tree —
Summer isles of Eden lying in dark-purple spheres
    of sea.

There methinks would be enjoyment more than in
    this march of mind,
In the steamship, in the railway, in the thoughts
    that shake mankind.

There the passions cramp'd no longer shall have
    scope and breathing space;
I will take some savage woman, she shall rear my
    dusky race.

Iron-jointed, supple-sinew'd, they shall dive, and
    they shall run,
Catch the wild goat by the hair, and hurl their
    lances in the sun;   170

135-36. Slowly . . . fire: One English manifestation of political and social unrest was the Chartist movement, which reached its peak in 1842.

155. Mahratta-battle: The Mahrattas were a people of India who gave trouble to their British rulers. 162. trailer: vine.

Whistle back the parrot's call, and leap the rainbows of the brooks,
Not with blinded eyesight poring over miserable
   books —

Fool, again the dream, the fancy! but I *know* my
   words are wild,
But I count the gray barbarian lower than the
   Christian child.

I, to herd with narrow foreheads, vacant of our
   glorious gains,
Like a beast with lower pleasures, like a beast with
   lower pains!

Mated with a squalid savage — what to me were
   sun or clime?
I the heir of all the ages, in the foremost files of
   time —

I that rather held it better men should perish one
   by one,
Than that earth should stand at gaze like Joshua's
   moon in Ajalon!°   180

Not in vain the distance beacons. Forward, forward
   let us range,
Let the great world spin for ever down the ringing
   grooves° of change.

Thro' the shadow of the globe we sweep into the
   younger day;
Better fifty years of Europe than a cycle of Cathay.°

Mother-Age, — for mine I knew not, — help me as
   when life begun;
Rift the hills, and roll the waters, flash the lightnings, weigh the sun.

O, I see the crescent° promise of my spirit hath not
   set.
Ancient founts of inspiration well thro' all my fancy
   yet.

Howsoever these things be, a long farewell to
   Locksley Hall!
Now for me the woods may wither, now for me°
   the roof-tree fall.   190

Comes a vapor from the margin, blackening over
   heath and holt,

---

180. See Josh. 10:12.   **182.** When in 1830 Tennyson made his
first journey by train, he thought—in nocturnal darkness—that
the wheels ran in grooves (*Memoir*, I, 195).   **184. Cathay:**
an old name for China, here as a land of immemorial stagnation.
187. crescent: growing.   **190. for me:** so far as I am concerned.

Cramming all the blast before it, in its breast a
   thunderbolt.

Let it fall on Locksley Hall, with rain or hail, or
   fire or snow;
For the mighty wind arises, roaring seaward, and
   I go.

   1842   *1835–42*

TEARS, IDLE TEARS

The Princess, published in 1847 — the year of *Jane
Eyre* — was a serio-comic-romantic poem on the education and emancipation of women. The stern intellectual, Princess Ida, founds a college of like-minded
young women from which men are excluded, but she
eventually succumbs to love. While parts of the narrative have their interest, as a whole it cannot be said to
make strong claims upon the modern reader. But some
of the eleven interspersed lyrics, which reflect phases
of the story, are among Tennyson's finest. "Sweet and
Low" and "The Splendor Falls" (the latter inspired
by a boatman's echoing bugle on the lakes of Kil-
larney) were added in 1850. The richest of the group
in depth and verbal and rhythmical felicity is "Tears,
Idle Tears" — which is also that rare thing, a blank-
verse lyric. It expresses "the yearning that young people occasionally experience for that which seems to
have passed away from them for ever" (*Memoir*, II,
73).

Tears, idle tears, I know not what they mean,
Tears from the depth of some divine despair
Rise in the heart, and gather to the eyes,
In looking on the happy autumn-fields,
And thinking of the days that are no more.

Fresh as the first beam glittering on a sail,
That brings our friends up from the underworld,
Sad as the last which reddens over one
That sinks with all we love below the verge;
So sad, so fresh, the days that are no more.   10

Ah, sad and strange as in dark summer dawns
The earliest pipe of half-awaken'd birds
To dying ears, when unto dying eyes
The casement slowly grows a glimmering square;
So sad, so strange, the days that are no more.

Dear as remember'd kisses after death,
And sweet as those by hopeless fancy feign'd
On lips that are for others; deep as love,
Deep as first love, and wild with all regret;
O Death in Life, the days that are no more!   20

   1847

IN MEMORIAM A.H.H.

OBIIT MDCCCXXXIII

Something has been said of Arthur Hallam at several points in the Introduction. His friendship with Tennyson and his visits at Somersby led to his becoming engaged to Tennyson's sister Emily. After taking his degree in 1832, Hallam commenced the study of law in London. While traveling with his father he died in Vienna of apoplexy on September 15, 1833, at the age of twenty-two. His writings in verse and prose, which have been edited by T. H. Vail Motter (1943), are of some interest, notably his review of Tennyson's volume of 1830. Some of Hallam's distinguished contemporaries at Cambridge thought him the most brilliant of their set. Although their estimate may have been heightened by his early death, he clearly possessed a very quick, keen intellect, a breadth of literary and philosophical knowledge, fine integrity, and a charming blend of seriousness and gaiety. Still clearer is the depth of love and admiration he inspired in Tennyson. His death brought together and greatly intensified all the feelings that had long troubled the poet — loneliness and self-distrust, questionings about life and God and immortality, about the destiny of the individual and society in a world increasingly given over by scientific skepticism to blind and ruthless Nature.

Immediately after Hallam's death Tennyson began to seek relief in lyric utterance; the collection of lyrics, growing through seventeen years, was published in 1850. Written thus over a long period, and not for some time conceived of as a publishable whole, the poems have, in T. S. Eliot's phrase, "only the unity and continuity of a diary." (Although, as Eliot also says, "It is a diary of which we have to read every word," in an anthology lack of space admits of no appeal.) The long process of time naturally affected both Tennyson's private grief and the religious and philosophic questions it involved. Eleanor B. Mattes (*In Memoriam: The Way of a Soul* [1951]) has tried, so far as evidence and inference allow, to trace the currents of his feeling and thought, the impact of various books and ideas, and the dates of individual poems. The arrangement of poems does not, except in some small sequences, follow the order of composition, and has only the appearance of a chronological pattern. Four large divisions are established by the Christmastide sections (XXVIII, LXXVIII, CIV), which make the imagined time of the poem seem to be less than three years. In the standard general study, *A Commentary on Tennyson's In Memoriam* (3rd ed., 1910), A. C. Bradley sets up these divisions and their main themes in the following way (to give only a skeleton and leave out subdivisions):

Part I. I–XXVII: Absorption in grief.

Part II. XXVIII–LXXVII: Preoccupation with the question of individual survival after death and related problems.

Part III. LXXVIII–CIII: Section LXXVIII may be said to inaugurate the upward, affirmative movement of faith and hope. The question of immortality recedes, though

sections XC–XCV deal with possible communion between the living and the dead.

Part IV. CIV–CXXXI: A forward-looking conclusion based on the assurance of love as the soul of the world and of the dead man as the type of a nobler race to come.

Another division, which Tennyson's friend Sir James Knowles reported as the poet's own, has been upheld by M. J. Svaglic (*Journal of English and Germanic Philology* LXI, 1962, pp. 810–25): I–VIII, IX–XX, XXI–XXVII, XXVIII–XLIX, L–LVIII, LIX–LXXI, LXXII–XCVIII, XCIX–CIII, CIV–CXXXI.

Tennyson thought that he had invented the stanza (which he used in the previously published "You Ask Me, Why" and "Love Thou Thy Land"), but critics have pointed out examples in Sir Philip Sidney, Ben Jonson, and Lord Herbert.

Strong Son of God, immortal Love,°
  Whom we, that have not seen thy face,
  By faith, and faith alone, embrace,
Believing where we cannot prove;

Thine are these orbs of light and shade;°
  Thou madest Life in man and brute;
  Thou madest Death; and lo, thy foot
Is on the skull which thou hast made.

Thou wilt not leave us in the dust:
  Thou madest man, he knows not why,   10
  He thinks he was not made to die;
And thou hast made him: thou art just.

Thou seemest human and divine,
  The highest, holiest manhood, thou.
  Our wills are ours, we know not how;
Our wills are ours, to make them thine.

Our little systems° have their day;
  They have their day and cease to be;
  They are but broken° lights of thee,
And thou, O Lord, art more than they.   20

We have but faith: we cannot know,
  For knowledge is of things we see;
  And yet we trust it comes from thee,
A beam in darkness: let it grow.

IN MEMORIAM. **Prologue.** This section, written shortly before publication, should perhaps be read last—and even then appears as a more positively Christian affirmation than the work as a whole seems to warrant. **1. immortal Love:** Cf. I John 4.5; and George Herbert, "Immortal Love, author of this great frame . . . on that dust which thou hast made." **5. orbs . . . shade:** the sun, the earth, and the planets, and the cycle of light and darkness—and life and death. **17. systems:** of belief and thought. **19. broken:** refracted.

Let knowledge grow from more to more,
  But more of reverence in us dwell;
  That mind and soul, according well,
May make one music as before,°

But vaster. We are fools and slight;
  We mock thee when we do not fear:
  But help thy foolish ones to bear;
Help thy vain worlds to bear thy light.

Forgive what seem'd my sin in me,
  What seem'd my worth since I began;
  For merit lives from man to man,
And not from man, O Lord, to thee.

Forgive my grief for one removed,
  Thy creature, whom I found so fair.
  I trust he lives in thee, and there
I find him worthier to be loved.

Forgive these wild and wandering cries,
  Confusions of a wasted° youth;
  Forgive them where they fail in truth,
And in thy wisdom make me wise.

1849

I

I held it truth, with him° who sings
  To one clear harp in divers tones,
  That men may rise on stepping-stones
Of their dead selves to higher things.

But who shall so forecast the years
  And find in loss a gain to match?
  Or reach a hand thro' time to catch
The far-off interest° of tears?

Let Love clasp Grief lest both be drown'd,
  Let darkness keep her raven gloss.
  Ah, sweeter to be drunk with loss,
To dance with Death, to beat the ground,

Than that the victor Hours should scorn
  The long result of love, and boast,
  "Behold the man that loved and lost,
But all he was is overworn."

II

Old yew, which graspest at the stones
  That name the underlying dead,

Thy fibers net the dreamless head,
Thy roots are wrapt about the bones.°

The seasons bring the flower again,
  And bring the firstling to the flock;
  And in the dusk of thee the clock°
Beats out the little lives of men.   30

O, not for thee the glow, the bloom,
  Who changest not in any gale,   10
  Nor branding summer suns avail
To touch thy thousand years of gloom;

And gazing on thee, sullen tree,
  Sick for° thy stubborn hardihood,
  I seem to fail from out my blood
And grow incorporate into thee.   40

III°

O Sorrow, cruel fellowship,
  O Priestess in the vaults of Death,
  O sweet and bitter in a breath,
What whispers from thy lying lip?

"The stars," she whispers, "blindly run;
  A web is woven across the sky;
  From out waste places comes a cry,
And murmurs from the dying sun;

"And all the phantom, Nature, stands —
  With all the music in her tone,   10
  A hollow echo of my own, —
A hollow form with empty hands."

And shall I take a thing so blind,
  Embrace her as my natural good;
  Or crush her, like a vice of blood,
Upon the threshold of the mind?

V

I sometimes hold it half a sin
  To put in words the grief I feel;
  For words, like Nature, half reveal
And half conceal the Soul within.

But, for the unquiet heart and brain,
  A use in measured language lies;
  The sad mechanic exercise,
Like dull narcotics, numbing pain.

---

28. **as before:** as in the age of secure faith.   42. **wasted:** desolated.   **I.1. him:** Goethe.   8. **interest:** a commercial metaphor (cf. "loss" and "gain," 6).

II.1–4. Old . . . bones: Cf. Job 8:17.   7. **clock:** on the church tower.   14. **for:** with desire for.   **III.** The first statement of one major theme: the mechanistic view of a dying universe denies a providential order and leaves man an insignificant atom. The idea is made the deceptive utterance of Sorrow, but her voice is the poet's.

In words, like weeds,° I'll wrap me o'er,
   Like coarsest clothes against the cold;   10
   But that large grief which these enfold
Is given in outline and no more.

VII

Dark house, by which once more I stand
   Here in the long unlovely street,°
   Doors, where my heart was used to beat
So quickly, waiting for a hand,

A hand that can be clasp'd no more —
   Behold me, for I cannot sleep,
   And like a guilty thing I creep
At earliest morning to the door.

He is not here; but far away
   The noise of life begins again,   10
   And ghastly thro' the drizzling rain
On the bald street breaks the blank day.

X

I hear the noise about thy keel;°
   I hear the bell struck in the night;
   I see the cabin-window bright;
I see the sailor at the wheel.

Thou bring'st the sailor to his wife,
   And travel'd men from foreign lands;
   And letters unto trembling hands;
And, thy dark freight, a vanish'd life.

So bring him; we have idle dreams;
   This look of quiet flatters thus   10
   Our home-bred fancies. O, to us,
The fools of habit, sweeter seems

To rest beneath the clover sod,
   That takes the sunshine and the rains,
   Or where the kneeling hamlet drains
The chalice of the grapes of God;°

Than if with thee the roaring wells
   Should gulf him fathom-deep in brine,
   And hands so often clasp'd in mine,
Should toss with tangle° and with shells.   20

XI

Calm is the morn without a sound,
   Calm as to suit a calmer grief,

And only thro' the faded leaf
The chestnut pattering to the ground;

Calm and deep peace on this high wold,
   And on these dews that drench the furze,
   And all the silvery gossamers°
That twinkle into green and gold;

Calm and still light on yon great plain
   That sweeps with all its autumn bowers,   10
   And crowded farms and lessening towers,
To mingle with the bounding° main;

Calm and deep peace in this wide air,
   These leaves that redden to the fall,
   And in my heart, if calm at all,
If any calm, a calm despair;

Calm on the seas, and silver sleep,
   And waves that sway themselves in rest,
   And dead calm in that noble breast
Which heaves but with the heaving deep.   20

XV

To-night the winds begin to rise
   And roar from yonder dropping day;°
   The last red leaf is whirl'd away,
The rooks are blown about the skies;

The forest crack'd, the waters curl'd,
   The cattle huddled on the lea;
   And wildly dash'd on tower and tree
The sunbeam strikes along the world:

And but for fancies, which aver
   That all thy° motions gently pass   10
   Athwart a plane of molten glass,°
I scarce could brook the strain and stir

That makes the barren branches loud;
   And but for fear it is not so,
   The wild unrest that lives in woe
Would dote and pore on yonder cloud

That rises upward always higher,
   And onward drags a laboring breast,
   And topples round the dreary west,
A looming bastion fringed with fire.   20

XVI

What words are these have fall'n from me?
   Can calm despair and wild unrest°

V.9. weeds: clothes.   **VII.1–2. Dark . . . street:** The Hallam house in Wimpole Street, London.   **X.1–8. I . . . life:** The ship bringing Hallam's body to England.   **13–16. To . . . God:** An over-refined image of alternative places of burial—the churchyard or the chancel where villagers kneel for Holy Communion. **20. tangle:** seaweed.

XI.7. gossamers: cobwebs.   **12. bounding:** bordering, limiting.
XV.2. dropping day: the west.   **10. thy:** the ship's (cf. x.1–8).
11. plane . . . glass: a calm sea (cf. Job 37:18, Rev. 15:2).
XVI.2. calm . . . unrest: Cf. xi and xv.

Be tenants of a single breast,
Or Sorrow such a changeling be?

Or doth she only seem to take
    The touch of change in calm or storm,
    But knows no more of transient form
In her deep self, than some dead lake

That holds the shadow of a lark   10
    Hung in the shadow of a heaven?
    Or has the shock, so harshly given,
Confused me like the unhappy bark

That strikes by night a craggy shelf,
    And staggers blindly ere she sink?
    And stunn'd me from my power to think
And all my knowledge of myself;

And made me that delirious man
    Whose fancy fuses old and new,
    And flashes into false and true,
And mingles all without a plan?   20

XVIII

'Tis well; 'tis something; we may stand
    Where he in English earth is laid,°
    And from his ashes may be made
The violet of his native land.

'Tis little; but it looks in truth
    As if the quiet bones were blest
    Among familiar names to rest
And in the places of his youth.

Come then, pure hands, and bear the head
    That sleeps or wears the mask of sleep,   10
    And come, whatever loves to weep,
And hear the ritual of the dead.

Ah yet, even yet, if this might be,
    I, falling on his faithful heart,
    Would breathing thro' his lips impart
The life that almost dies in me;

That dies not, but endures with pain,
    And slowly forms the firmer mind,
    Treasuring the look it cannot find,
The words that are not heard again.   20

XIX°

The Danube to the Severn° gave
    The darken'd heart that beat no more;

They laid him by the pleasant shore,
    And in the hearing of the wave.

There twice a day the Severn fills;
    The salt sea-water passes by,
    And hushes half the babbling Wye,
And makes a silence in the hills.

The Wye is hush'd nor moved along,
    And hush'd my deepest grief of all,   10
    When fill'd with tears that cannot fall,
I brim with sorrow drowning song.

The tide flows down, the wave again
    Is vocal in its wooded walls;
    My deeper anguish also falls,
And I can speak a little then.

XXI°

I sing to him that rests below,
    And, since the grasses round me wave,
    I take the grasses of the grave,
And make them pipes° whereon to blow.

The traveler hears me now and then,
    And sometimes harshly will he speak:
    "This fellow would make weakness weak,
And melt the waxen hearts of men."

Another answers: "Let him be,
    He loves to make parade of pain,   10
    That with his piping he may gain
The praise that comes to constancy."

A third is wroth: "Is this an hour
    For private sorrow's barren song,
    When more and more the people throng
The chairs and thrones of civil power?°

"A time to sicken and to swoon,
    When Science reaches forth her arms
    To feel from world to world, and charms
Her secret from the latest moon?"°   20

Behold, ye speak an idle thing;
    Ye never knew the sacred dust.
    I do but sing because I must,
And pipe but as the linnets sing;

overlooks the Severn river where it flows into the Bristol Channel.
The tidal ebb and flow of the Severn and its tributary, the Wye,
are applied to the poet's utterance and silence.   **XXI.** Tennyson's old theme—here in new circumstances—of private versus
public poetry.   **4. pipes:** the musical pipes of the pastoral poet.
15-16. Cf. "Locksley Hall," 135-36.   **20. moon:** the planet
Neptune and its moon, discovered in 1846.

XVIII.2. Hallam was actually buried in Clevedon Church, not
in the churchyard.   **XIX.** Written at Tintern Abbey on the
Wye.   1. Danube . . . Severn. Hallam died in Vienna; Clevedon

And one is glad; her note is gay,
  For now her little ones have ranged;
  And one is sad; her note is changed,
Because her brood is stolen away.

XXII°

The path by which we twain did go,
  Which led by tracts that pleased us well,
  Thro' four sweet years° arose and fell,
From flower to flower, from snow to snow;

And we with singing cheer'd the way,
  And, crown'd with all the season lent,
  From April on to April went,
And glad at heart from May to May.

But where the path we walk'd began
  To slant the fifth autumnal slope,°   10
  As we descended following Hope,
There sat the Shadow° fear'd of man;

Who broke our fair companionship,
  And spread his mantle dark and cold,
  And wrapt thee formless in the fold,
And dull'd the murmur on thy lip,

And bore thee where I could not see
  Nor follow, tho' I walk in haste,
  And think that somewhere in the waste
The Shadow sits and waits for me.   20

XXIII

Now, sometimes in my sorrow shut,
  Or breaking into song by fits,
  Alone, alone, to where he sits,
The Shadow cloak'd from head to foot,

Who keeps the keys of all the creeds,
  I wander, often falling lame,
  And looking back to whence I came,
Or on to where the pathway leads;

And crying, How changed from where it ran
  Thro' lands where not a leaf was dumb,   10
  But all the lavish hills would hum
The murmur of a happy Pan;

When each by turns was guide to each,
  And Fancy light from Fancy caught,
  And Thought leapt out to wed with Thought
Ere Thought could wed itself with Speech;

And all we met was fair and good,
  And all was good that Time could bring,

And all the secret of the Spring
Moved in the chambers of the blood;   20

And many an old philosophy
  On Argive° heights divinely sang,
  And round us all the thicket rang
To many a flute of Arcady.°

XXIV

And was the day of my delight
  As pure and perfect as I say?
  The very source and fount of day
Is dash'd with wandering isles of night.°

If all was good and fair we met,
  This earth had been the Paradise
  It never look'd to human eyes
Since our first sun arose and set.

And is it that the haze of grief
  Makes former gladness loom so great?   10
  The lowness of the present state,
That sets the past in this relief?

Or that the past will always win
  A glory from its being far,
  And orb into the perfect star°
We saw not when we moved therein?

XXV

I know that this was Life,—the track
  Whereon with equal feet we fared;
  And then, as now, the day prepared
The daily burden for the back.

But this it was that made me move
  As light as carrier-birds in air;
  I loved the weight I had to bear,
Because it needed help of Love;

Nor could I weary, heart or limb,
  When mighty Love would cleave in twain   10
  The lading° of a single pain,
And part it, giving half to him.

XXVI

Still onward winds the dreary way;
  I with it, for I long to prove
  No lapse of moons can canker Love,
Whatever fickle tongues may say.

XXII. Sections XXII–XXV contrast the past and the present.
3. **four . . . years:** 1829–32.   10. September, 1833.   12. **Shadow:**
Death.

XXIII.22. Argive: Greek.   24. **Arcady:** Arcadia, a region of
Greece, has been in literary tradition an ideal pastoral world.
XXIV.3–4. The . . . night: Even the sun has spots.   15. As the
earth, viewed from outer space, would seem a perfect disk.
XXV.11. lading: burden.

And if that eye which watches guilt
   And goodness, and hath power to see
   Within the green the molder'd tree,
And towers fall'n as soon as built —

O, if indeed that eye foresee
   Or see — in Him is no before —   10
   In more of life true life no more
And Love the indifference to be,°

Then might I find, ere yet the morn
   Breaks hither over Indian seas,
   That Shadow° waiting with the keys,
To shroud me from my proper scorn.°

XXVII

I envy not in any moods
   The captive void of noble rage,
   The linnet born within the cage,
That never knew the summer woods;

I envy not the beast that takes
   His license in the field of time,°
   Unfetter'd by the sense of crime,
To whom a conscience never wakes;

Nor, what may count itself as blest,
   The heart that never plighted troth   10
   But stagnates in the weeds of sloth;
Nor any want-begotten° rest.

I hold it true, whate'er befall;
   I feel it, when I sorrow most;
   'Tis better to have loved and lost
Than never to have loved at all.

XXVIII°

The time draws near the birth of Christ.
   The moon is hid, the night is still;
   The Christmas bells from hill to hill
Answer each other in the mist.

Four voices of four hamlets round,°
   From far and near, on mead and moor,
   Swell out and fail, as if a door
Were shut between me and the sound;

Each voice four changes° on the wind,
   That now dilate, and now decrease,   10

Peace and goodwill, goodwill and peace,
Peace and goodwill, to all mankind.

This year° I slept and woke with pain,
   I almost wish'd no more to wake,
   And that my hold on life would break
Before I heard those bells again;

But they my troubled spirit rule,
   For they controll'd me when a boy;
   They bring me sorrow touch'd with joy,
The merry, merry bells of Yule.   20

XXX

With trembling fingers did we weave
   The holly round the Christmas hearth;
   A rainy cloud possess'd the earth,
And sadly fell our Christmas-eve.

At our old pastimes in the hall
   We gambol'd, making vain pretense
   Of gladness, with an awful sense
Of one mute Shadow° watching all.

We paused: the winds were in the beech;
   We heard them sweep the winter land;   10
   And in a circle hand-in-hand
Sat silent, looking each at each.

Then echo-like our voices rang;
   We sung, tho' every eye was dim,
   A merry song we sang with him
Last year; impetuously we sang.

We ceased; a gentler feeling crept
   Upon us: surely rest is meet.
   "They rest," we said, "their sleep is sweet,"
And silence follow'd, and we wept.   20

Our voices took a higher range;
   Once more we sang: "They do not die°
   Nor lose their mortal sympathy,
Nor change to us, altho' they change;

"Rapt from the fickle and the frail°
   With gather'd power, yet the same,
   Pierces the keen seraphic flame°
From orb to orb, from veil to veil."

Rise, happy morn, rise, holy morn,
   Draw forth the cheerful day from night: 30

O Father, touch the east, and light
The light that shone when Hope° was born.

XXXIV°

My own dim life should teach me this,
That life shall live for evermore,
Else earth is darkness at the core,
And dust and ashes all that is;

This round of green, this orb of flame,°
Fantastic beauty; such as lurks
In some wild poet, when he works
Without a conscience or an aim.

What then were God to such as I?
'Twere hardly worth my while to choose   10
Of things all mortal, or to use
A little patience ere I die;

'Twere best at once to sink to peace,
Like birds the charming serpent draws,
To drop head-foremost in the jaws
Of vacant darkness and to cease.

XXXV

Yet if some voice that man could trust
Should murmur from the narrow house,°
"The cheeks drop in, the body bows;
Man dies, nor is there hope in dust;"

Might I not say? "Yet even here,
But for one hour, O Love, I strive
To keep so sweet a thing alive."
But I should turn mine ears and hear

The moanings of the homeless sea,
The sound of streams that swift or slow   10
Draw down Æonian° hills, and sow
The dust of continents to be;

And Love would answer with a sigh,
"The sound of that forgetful shore°
Will change my sweetness more and more,
Half-dead to know that I shall die."

O me, what profits it to put
An idle case? If Death were seen

At first as Death, Love had not been,°
Or been in narrowest working shut,   20

Mere fellowship of sluggish moods,
Or in his coarsest Satyr-shape
Had bruised the herb and crush'd the grape,
And bask'd and batten'd in the woods.

XXXVI

Tho' truths in manhood darkly join,
Deep-seated in our mystic frame,°
We yield all blessing to the name
Of Him that made them current coin;

For Wisdom dealt with° mortal powers,
Where truth in closest words shall fail,°
When truth embodied in a tale
Shall enter in at lowly doors.

And so the Word° had breath, and wrought
With human hands the creed of creeds°   10
In loveliness of perfect deeds,
More strong than all poetic thought;

Which he may read that binds the sheaf,
Or builds the house, or digs the grave,
And those wild eyes that watch the wave
In roarings round the coral reef.

XXXIX°

Old warder of these buried bones,
And answering now my random stroke
With fruitful cloud and living smoke,°
Dark yew, that graspest at the stones

And dippest toward the dreamless head,
To thee too comes the golden hour
When flower is feeling after flower;
But Sorrow, — fixt upon the dead,

And darkening the dark graves of men, —
What whisper'd from her lying lips?   10
Thy gloom is kindled at the tips,°
And passes into gloom again.

32. **Hope:** Christ, as the agent of human immortality. **XXXIV.** Consciousness alone, without revelation, should compel belief in immortality, since without it the world and life would be meaningless. **5. This ... flame:** earth and sun. **XXXV.2. narrow house:** the grave. **11. Æonian:** lasting for aeons. Sir Charles Lyell's *Principles of Geology* (1830–33), which Tennyson read in 1837, emphasized the changes in the earth's surface caused by erosion and silt. **14. forgetful shore:** the mythological Lethe, river of oblivion; here, death as the end of consciousness.

18–19. **If ... been:** If man recognized death as extinction, love would not exist, or would be reduced to animal moods. Richard Ellmann describes Yeats's parallel argument in words that would fit Tennyson (*The Identity of Yeats*, 1954, p. 40). **XXXVI.1–2.** Though human consciousness in itself obscurely arrives at truths (here, immortality). **5. dealt with:** adapted itself to. **6. Where ... fail:** where formal philosophy fails. **9. the Word.** Tennyson (*Memoir*, I, 312) cited John 1, for "the Revelation of the Eternal Thought of the Universe." **10. creed of creeds:** the life of Christ. **XXXIX.** This section, written in 1868, glances back at II and III. **3. cloud ... smoke:** pollen. **11. tips:** flowers.

XLI

Thy spirit ere our fatal loss
  Did ever rise from high to higher,
  As mounts the heavenward altar-fire,
As flies the lighter thro' the gross.

But thou art turn'd to something strange,
  And I have lost the links that bound
  Thy changes; here upon the ground,
No more partaker of thy change.

Deep folly!° yet that this could be —
  That I could wing my will with might   10
  To leap the grades of life and light,
And flash at once, my friend, to thee!

For tho' my nature rarely yields
  To that vague fear implied in death,
  Nor shudders at the gulfs beneath,
The howlings from forgotten° fields;

Yet oft when sundown skirts the moor
  An inner trouble I behold,
  A spectral doubt which makes me cold,
That I shall be thy mate no more,   20

Tho' following with an upward mind
  The wonders that have come to thee,
  Thro' all the secular° to-be,
But evermore a life behind.

XLIII°

If Sleep and Death be truly one,
  And every spirit's folded bloom
  Thro' all its intervital° gloom
In some long trance should slumber on;

Unconscious of the sliding hour,
  Bare of the body, might it last,
  And silent traces of the past
Be all the color of the flower:

So then were nothing lost to man;
  So that still garden° of the souls   10
  In many a figured leaf enrolls
The total world° since life began;

And love will last as pure and whole
  As when he loved me here in Time,

And at the spiritual prime°
Rewaken with the dawning soul.

XLIV°

How fares it with the happy dead?
  For here the man is more and more;°
  But he forgets the days before
God shut the doorways of his head.°

The days have vanish'd, tone and tint,
  And yet perhaps the hoarding sense
  Gives out at times — he knows not whence —
A little flash, a mystic hint;°

And in the long harmonious years —
  If Death so taste Lethean springs —   10
  May some dim touch of earthly things
Surprise thee ranging with thy peers.

If such a dreamy touch should fall,
  O, turn thee round, resolve the doubt;
  My guardian angel will speak out
In that high place, and tell thee all.

XLV°

The baby new to earth and sky,
  What time his tender palm is prest
  Against the circle of the breast,
Has never thought that " this is I ";

But as he grows he gathers much,
  And learns the use of " I " and " me,"
  And finds " I am not what I see,
And other than the things I touch."

So rounds he to a separate mind
  From whence clear memory may begin,   10
  As thro' the frame that binds him in
His isolation grows defined.

This use may lie in blood and breath,
  Which else were fruitless of their due,
  Had man to learn himself anew
Beyond the second birth of death.

XLVI

We ranging down this lower track,°
  The path we came by, thorn and flower,
  Is shadow'd by the growing hour,°
Lest life should fail in looking back.

So be it: there° no shade can last
  In that deep dawn behind the tomb,
  But clear from marge to marge shall bloom
The eternal landscape of the past;

A lifelong tract of time reveal'd,
  The fruitful hours of still increase;   10
  Days order'd in a wealthy peace,
And those five years° its richest field.

O Love, thy province were not large,
  A bounded field, nor stretching far;°
  Look also, Love, a brooding star,
A rosy warmth from marge to marge.°

XLVII°

That each, who seems a separate whole,
  Should move his rounds, and fusing all
  The skirts of self again, should fall
Remerging in the general Soul,

Is faith as vague as all unsweet.
  Eternal form shall still divide
  The eternal soul from all beside;
And I shall know him when we meet;

And we shall sit at endless feast,
  Enjoying each the other's good.   10
  What vaster dream can hit the mood
Of Love on earth? He seeks at least

Upon the last and sharpest height,°
  Before the spirits fade away,
  Some landing-place, to clasp and say,
" Farewell! We lose ourselves in light."

XLVIII

If these brief lays, of Sorrow born,
  Were taken to be such as closed
  Grave doubts and answers here proposed,
Then these were such as men might scorn.

Her° care is not to part° and prove;
  She takes, when harsher moods remit,
  What slender shade of doubt may flit,
And makes it vassal unto love;

And hence, indeed, she sports with words,
  But better serves a wholesome law,   10
  And holds it sin and shame to draw
The deepest measure from the chords;

Nor dare she trust a larger lay,
  But rather loosens from the lip
  Short swallow-flights of song, that dip
Their wings in tears, and skim away.

L

Be near me when my light is low,
  When the blood creeps, and the nerves prick
  And tingle; and the heart is sick,
And all the wheels of being slow.

Be near me when the sensuous frame
  Is rack'd with pangs that conquer trust;
  And Time, a maniac scattering dust,
And Life, a Fury slinging flame.°

Be near me when my faith is dry,
  And men the flies of latter spring,   10
  That lay their eggs, and sting and sing
And weave their petty cells and die.

Be near me when I fade away,
  To point the term° of human strife,
  And on the low dark verge of life
The twilight of eternal day.

LIV

O, yet we trust that somehow good
  Will be the final goal of ill,
  To pangs of nature, sins of will,
Defects of doubt, and taints of blood;

That nothing walks with aimless feet;
  That not one life shall be destroy'd,
  Or cast as rubbish to the void,
When God hath made the pile complete;

That not a worm is cloven in vain;
  That not a moth with vain desire   10
  Is shrivel'd in a fruitless fire,
Or but subserves another's gain.

XLVI.1. **lower track:** earthly life.   **2–3.** Memory of the past is obscured as life proceeds.   **5. there:** in the next life.   **12. five years:** of friendship.   **13–14.** Love on earth.   **15–16.** Love enlarged in heaven.   **XLVII.** The poet rules out the idea, recurrent in religious thought, that the individual soul does not survive but is merged in the world-soul—though this is apparently admitted in 14-16 as an ultimate stage.   **13.** In the last of many existences (*Memoir*, I, 319).

XLVIII.5. **Her:** Sorrow's. **part:** sort out. **L.8. Fury . . . flame:** The Furies carried torches. **14. term:** limit.

Behold, we know not anything;
  I can but trust that good shall fall
  At last — far off — at last, to all,
And every winter change to spring.

So runs my dream; but what am I?
  An infant crying in the night;
  An infant crying for the light,
And with no language but a cry.   20

LV

The wish, that of the living whole
  No life may fail beyond the grave,
  Derives it not from what we have
The likest God within the soul?

Are God and Nature then at strife,
  That Nature lends such evil dreams?
  So careful of the type she seems,
So careless of the single life,°

That I, considering everywhere
  Her secret meaning in her deeds,
  And finding that of fifty seeds   10
She often brings but one to bear,°

I falter where I firmly trod,
  And falling with my weight of cares
  Upon the great world's altar-stairs
That slope thro' darkness up to God,

I stretch lame hands of faith, and grope,
  And gather dust and chaff, and call
  To what I feel is Lord of all,
And faintly trust the larger hope.°   20

LVI°

" So careful of the type? " but no.
  From scarpèd° cliff and quarried stone
  She° cries, " A thousand types are gone;
I care for nothing, all shall go.

" Thou makest thine appeal to me:
  I bring to life, I bring to death;
  The spirit does but mean the breath:
I know no more." And he, shall he,

Man, her last work, who seem'd so fair,
  Such splendid purpose in his eyes,   10
  Who roll'd the psalm to wintry skies,
Who built him fanes of fruitless prayer,

Who trusted God was love indeed
  And love Creation's final law —
  Tho' Nature, red in tooth and claw°
With ravine, shriek'd against his creed —

Who loved, who suffer'd countless ills,
  Who battled for the True, the Just,
  Be blown about the desert dust,
Or seal'd within the iron hills?°   20

No more? A monster then, a dream,
  A discord. Dragons of the prime,
  That tare each other in their slime,
Were mellow music match'd with him.

O life as futile, then, as frail!
  O for thy° voice to soothe and bless!
  What hope of answer, or redress?
Behind the veil, behind the veil.°

LVII

Peace; come away: the song of woe
  Is after all an earthly song.
  Peace; come away: we do him wrong
To sing so wildly: let us go.

Come; let us go: your cheeks are pale;
  But half my life I leave behind.
  Methinks my friend is richly shrined;
But I shall pass, my work will fail.

Yet in these ears, till hearing dies,
  One set slow bell will seem to toll   10
  The passing of the sweetest soul
That ever look'd with human eyes.

I hear it now, and o'er and o'er,
  Eternal greetings to the dead;
  And " Ave,° Ave, Ave," said,
" Adieu, adieu," for evermore.

LXX

I cannot see the features right,
  When on the gloom I strive to paint
  The face I know; the hues are faint
And mix with hollow masks of night;

LV.7–8. A belief in nature's concern for the species and indifference to the individual was current, e.g., from Buffon to Robert Chambers' *Vestiges* (1844); but see the note on LVI. **11–12.** The example is like one in Bishop Butler's *Analogy of Religion*, 1736 (Everyman ed., p. 80). **20. larger hope:** "that the whole human race would through, perhaps, ages of suffering, be at length purified and saved" (*Memoir*, I, 321–22). **LVI.** Lyell (see the note on XXXV.11) presented full evidence for the extinction of species as well as individuals. **2. scarpèd:** shorn away. **3. She:** Nature.

15. This, the most famous phrase in *In Memoriam*, crystallizes the idea of the ruthless struggle for survival that had been present in men's minds since antiquity. Cf. Erasmus Darwin (grandfather of Charles): "And one great Slaughter-house the warring world." **20.** Like other fossils. **26. thy:** Hallam's. **28. veil:** of death (see Eleanor B. Mattes, pp. 62–63). **LVII.15. Ave:** hail. Cf. "Frater Ave atque Vale."

Cloud-towers by ghostly masons wrought,
　A gulf that ever shuts and gapes,
　A hand that points, and pallèd° shapes
In shadowy thoroughfares of thought;

And crowds that stream from yawning doors,
　And shoals of pucker'd faces drive;　　　10
　Dark bulks that tumble half alive,
And lazy lengths on boundless shores;

Till all at once beyond the will
　I hear a wizard music roll,
　And thro' a lattice on the soul
Looks thy fair face and makes it still.°

LXXVIII°

Again at Christmas did we weave
　The holly round the Christmas hearth;
　The silent snow possess'd the earth,
And calmly fell our Christmas-eve.

The yule-clog° sparkled keen with frost,
　No wing of wind the region swept,
　But over all things brooding slept
The quiet sense of something lost.

As in the winters left behind,
　Again our ancient games had place,　　10
　The mimic picture's° breathing grace,
And dance and song and hoodman-blind.°

Who show'd a token of distress?
　No single tear, no mark of pain—
　O sorrow, then can sorrow wane?
O grief, can grief be changed to less?

O last regret, regret can die!
　No—mixt with all this mystic frame,
　Her deep relations are the same,
But with long use her tears are dry.　　20

LXXXII

I wage not any feud with Death
　For changes wrought on form and face;
　No lower life that earth's embrace
May breed with him can fright my faith.

Eternal process moving on,
　From state to state the spirit walks;°

And these° are but the shatter'd stalks,
Or ruin'd chrysalis of one.

Nor blame I Death, because he bare°
　The use of virtue out of earth;　　　10
　I know transplanted human worth
Will bloom to profit, otherwhere.

For this alone on Death I wreak
　The wrath that garners in my heart:
　He put our lives so far apart
We cannot hear each other speak.

LXXXVI°

Sweet after showers, ambrosial air,
　That rollest from the gorgeous gloom
　Of evening over brake and bloom
And meadow, slowly breathing bare

The round of space,° and rapt below
　Thro' all the dewy-tassel'd wood,
　And shadowing down the hornèd° flood
In ripples, fan my brows and blow

The fever from my cheek, and sigh
　The full new life that feeds thy breath　　10
　Throughout my frame, till Doubt and Death,
Ill brethren, let the fancy fly

From belt to belt of crimson° seas
　On leagues of odor streaming far,
　To where in yonder orient star
A hundred spirits whisper " Peace."

LXXXVII°

I past beside the reverend walls
　In which of old I wore the gown;
　I roved at random thro' the town,
And saw the tumult of the halls;

And heard once more in college fanes
　The storm their high-built organs make,
　And thunder-music, rolling, shake
The prophet blazon'd on the panes;

And caught once more the distant shout,
　The measured pulse of racing oars　　　10
　Among the willows; paced the shores
And many a bridge, and all about

The same gray flats again, and felt
　The same, but not the same; and last

LXX.7. **pallèd**: wrapped in palls.　**13–16.** As sleep comes on, he sees the face he could not picture when awake.　**LXXVIII.** The second Christmas (1834) inaugurates a more acceptant and cheerful mood than the first (xxx) had allowed.　**5. clog** (a dialect word): log.　**11. mimic picture**: tableau.　**12. hoodman-blind**: blindman's buff.　**LXXXII.6.** Cf. xxx.27–28 and xlvii.13.

7. these: See 2–3.　**9. bare:** bore away.　**LXXXVI.** The poet's sense of peace and rebirth, rendered in one exquisitely modulated sentence.　**4–5. slowly . . . space:** clearing the sky of clouds. **7. hornèd:** winding.　**13. crimson:** in successive sunsets. **LXXXVII.** A visit to Cambridge.

Up that long walk of limes I past
To see the rooms in which he dwelt.

Another name was on the door.
  I linger'd; all within was noise
  Of songs, and clapping hands, and boys
That crash'd the glass and beat the floor;   20

Where once we held debate, a band°
  Of youthful friends, on mind and art,
  And labor, and the changing mart,
And all the framework of the land;

When one would aim an arrow fair,
  But send it slackly from the string;
  And one would pierce an outer ring,
And one an inner, here and there;

And last the master-bowman, he,°
  Would cleave the mark. A willing ear   30
  We lent him. Who but hung to hear
The rapt oration flowing free

From point to point, with power and grace
  And music in the bounds of law,
  To those conclusions when we saw
The God within him light his face,

And seem to lift the form, and glow
  In azure orbits heavenly-wise;
  And over those ethereal eyes
The bar of Michael Angelo?°   40

LXXXIX°

Witch-elms that counterchange° the floor
  Of this flat lawn with dusk and bright;
  And thou, with all thy breadth and height
Of foliage, towering sycamore;

How often, hither wandering down,
  My Arthur found your shadows fair,
  And shook to all the liberal° air
The dust and din and steam of town!

He brought an eye for all he saw;
  He mixt in all our simple sports;   10
  They pleased him, fresh from brawling courts
And dusty purlieus of the law.

O joy to him in this retreat,
  Inmantled in ambrosial dark,
  To drink the cooler air, and mark
The landscape winking thro' the heat!

O sound to rout the brood of cares,
  The sweep of scythe in morning dew,
  The gust that round the garden flew,
And tumbled half the mellowing pears!   20

O bliss, when all in circle drawn
  About him, heart and ear were fed
  To hear him, as he lay and read
The Tuscan poets° on the lawn!

Or in the all-golden afternoon
  A guest, or happy sister, sung,
  Or here she brought the harp and flung
A ballad to the brightening moon.

Nor less it pleased in livelier moods,
  Beyond the bounding° hill to stray,   30
  And break the livelong summer day
With banquet in the distant woods;

Whereat we glanced from theme to theme,
  Discuss'd the books to love or hate,
  Or touch'd the changes of the state,
Or threaded some Socratic dream;

But if I praised the busy town,
  He loved to rail against it still,
  For " ground in yonder social mill
We rub each other's angles down,   40

" And merge," he said, " in form and gloss
  The picturesque of man and man."
  We talk'd: the stream beneath us ran,
The wine-flask lying couch'd in moss,

Or cool'd within the glooming wave;
  And last, returning from afar,
  Before the crimson-circled star
Had fall'n into her father's grave,°

And brushing ankle-deep in flowers,
  We heard behind the woodbine veil   50
  The milk that bubbled in the pail,
And buzzings of the honeyed hours.

XCV°

By night we linger'd on the lawn,°
  For underfoot the herb was dry;
  And genial warmth; and o'er the sky
The silvery haze of summer drawn;

24. **Tuscan poets:** Dante *et al.*   30. **bounding:** limiting.   **47-48.** Before the evening star (Venus) is lost in the setting sun. According to the nebular hypothesis, the planets originated from the sun.   **XCV.** This account of the poet's trancelike apprehension of the dead Hallam's presence, and of the divine order of the world, is commonly regarded as one of his supreme achievements.   1. **lawn:** at Somersby.

21. **band:** the "Apostles."   29. **he:** Hallam.   40. A ridge over the eyes, once remarked upon by Hallam himself (*Memoir*, I, 38). **LXXXIX.** Hallam's visits at Somersby.   1. **counterchange:** checker.   7. **liberal:** open, spacious.

And calm that let the tapers burn
  Unwavering: not a cricket chirr'd;
  The brook alone far-off was heard,
And on the board the fluttering urn.°

And bats went round in fragrant skies,
  And wheel'd or lit the filmy shapes°   10
  That haunt the dusk, with ermine capes
And woolly breasts and beaded eyes;

While now we sang old songs that peal'd
  From knoll to knoll, where, couch'd at ease,
  The white kine glimmer'd, and the trees
Laid their dark arms about the field.

But when those others, one by one,
  Withdrew themselves from me and night,
  And in the house light after light
Went out, and I was all alone,   20

A hunger seized my heart; I read
  Of that glad year° which once had been,
  In those fall'n leaves which kept their green,
The noble letters of the dead.

And strangely on the silence broke
  The silent-speaking words, and strange
  Was love's dumb cry defying change
To test his worth; and strangely spoke

The faith, the vigor, bold to dwell
  On doubts that drive the coward back,   30
  And keen thro' wordy snares to track
Suggestion to her inmost cell.

So word by word, and line by line,
  The dead man touch'd me from the past,
  And all at once it seem'd at last
The living soul° was flash'd on mine,

And mine in this was wound, and whirl'd
  About empyreal heights of thought,
  And came on that which is, and caught
The deep pulsations of the world,   40

Æonian° music measuring out
  The steps of Time — the shocks of Chance —
  The blows of Death. At length my trance
Was cancel'd, stricken thro' with doubt.

Vague words! but ah, how hard to frame
  In matter-molded forms of speech,

Or even for intellect to reach
Thro' memory that which I became;

Till now the doubtful dusk reveal'd
  The knolls once more where, couch'd at ease,   50
  The white kine glimmer'd, and the trees
Laid their dark arms about the field;

And suck'd from out the distant gloom
  A breeze began to tremble o'er
  The large leaves of the sycamore,
And fluctuate all the still perfume,

And gathering freshlier overhead
  Rock'd the full-foliaged elms, and swung
  The heavy-folded rose, and flung
The lilies to and fro, and said,   60

"The dawn, the dawn," and died away;
  And East and West, without a breath,
  Mixt their dim lights, like life and death,
To broaden into boundless day.

XCVI

You° say, but with no touch of scorn,
  Sweet-hearted, you, whose light-blue eyes
  Are tender over drowning flies,
You tell me, doubt is Devil-born.

I know not: one° indeed I knew
  In many a subtle question versed,
  Who touch'd a jarring lyre at first,
But ever strove to make it true;

Perplext in faith, but pure in deeds,
  At last he beat his music out.   10
  There lives more faith in honest doubt,
Believe me, than in half the creeds.

He fought his doubts and gather'd strength,
  He would not make his judgment blind,
  He faced the specters of the mind
And laid them; thus he came at length

To find a stronger faith his own,
  And Power was with him in the night,
  Which makes the darkness and the light,
And dwells not in the light alone,   20

But in the darkness and the cloud,
  As over Sinaï's peaks of old,°
  While Israel made their gods of gold,°
Altho' the trumpet blew so loud.

CIV°

The time draws near the birth of Christ;
  The moon is hid, the night is still;
  A single church below the hill
Is pealing, folded in the mist.

A single peal of bells below,
  That wakens at this hour of rest
  A single murmur in the breast,
That these are not the bells I know.

Like strangers' voices here they sound,
  In lands where not a memory strays,   10
  Nor landmark breathes of other days,
But all is new unhallow'd ground.

CV

To-night ungather'd let us leave
  This laurel, let this holly stand:
  We live within the stranger's land,
And strangely falls our Christmas-eve.

Our father's dust is left alone°
  And silent under other snows:
  There in due time the woodbine blows,°
The violet comes, but we are gone.

No more shall wayward grief abuse
  The genial hour with mask and mime;   10
  For change of place, like growth of time,
Has broke the bond of dying use.

Let cares that petty shadows cast,
  By which our lives are chiefly proved,°
  A little spare the night I loved,
And hold it solemn to the past.

But let no footstep beat the floor,
  Nor bowl of wassail mantle° warm;
  For who would keep an ancient form
Thro' which the spirit breathes no more?   20

Be neither song, nor game, nor feast;
  Nor harp be touch'd, nor flute be blown;
  No dance, no motion, save alone
What lightens in the lucid East

Of rising worlds° by yonder wood.
  Long sleeps the summer in the seed;
  Run out your measured arcs, and lead
The closing cycle rich in good.

CVI°

Ring out, wild bells, to the wild sky,
  The flying cloud, the frosty light:
  The year is dying in the night;
Ring out, wild bells, and let him die.

Ring out the old, ring in the new,
  Ring, happy bells, across the snow:
  The year is going, let him go;
Ring out the false, ring in the true.

Ring out the grief that saps the mind,
  For those that here we see no more;   10
  Ring out the feud of rich and poor,
Ring in redress to all mankind.

Ring out a slowly dying cause,
  And ancient forms of party strife;
  Ring in the nobler modes of life,
With sweeter manners, purer laws.

Ring out the want, the care, the sin,
  The faithless coldness of the times;
  Ring out, ring out my mournful rhymes,
But ring the fuller minstrel in.   20

Ring out false pride in place and blood,
  The civic slander and the spite;
  Ring in the love of truth and right,
Ring in the common love of good.

Ring out old shapes of foul disease;
  Ring out the narrowing lust of gold;
  Ring out the thousand wars of old,
Ring in the thousand years of peace.°

Ring in the valiant man and free,
  The larger heart, the kindlier hand;   30
  Ring out the darkness of the land,
Ring in the Christ that is to be.°

CXIV

Who loves not Knowledge? Who shall rail
  Against her beauty? May she mix
  With men and prosper! Who shall fix
Her pillars?° Let her work prevail.

But on her forehead sits a fire;
  She sets her forward countenance
  And leaps into the future chance,
Submitting all things to desire.

CIV-CV. The third Christmas of the poem, actually 1837, at the Tennysons' new home at High Beech, Epping Forest, north of London. CV.5. The poet's father was buried at Somersby in 1831. 7. blows: blossoms. 14. proved: tested. 18. mantle: froth. 25. worlds: stars.

CVI. New Year's Eve. 28. See Rev. 20. 32. The true spirit of Christlike goodness and love, free from bigotry and controversy (Memoir, I, 325-26). CXIV.3-4. Who . . . pillars? See Prov. 9:1, Job 38.

Half-grown as yet, a child, and vain —
  She cannot fight the fear of death.
  What is she, cut from love and faith,
But some wild Pallas from the brain°   10

Of demons? fiery-hot to burst
  All barriers in her onward race
  For power. Let her know her place;
She is the second, not the first.

A higher hand must make her mild,
  If all be not in vain, and guide
  Her footsteps, moving side by side
With Wisdom, like the younger child;   20

For she is earthly of the mind,
  But Wisdom heavenly of the soul.
  O friend, who camest to thy goal
So early, leaving me behind,

I would the great world grew like thee,
  Who grewest not alone in power
  And knowledge, but by year and hour
In reverence and in charity.

CXV

Now fades the last long streak of snow,
  Now burgeons every maze of quick°
  About the flowering squares,° and thick
By ashen roots the violets blow.°

Now rings the woodland loud and long,
  The distance takes a lovelier hue,
  And drown'd in yonder living blue
The lark becomes a sightless° song.

Now dance the lights on lawn and lea,
  The flocks are whiter down the vale,
  And milkier every milky sail   10
On winding stream or distant sea;

Where now the seamew pipes, or dives
  In yonder greening gleam,° and fly
  The happy birds, that change their sky
To build and brood, that live their lives

From land to land; and in my breast
  Spring wakens too, and my regret
  Becomes an April violet,
And buds and blossoms like the rest.   20

CXVIII°

Contemplate° all this work of Time,
  The giant laboring in his youth;
  Nor dream of human love and truth,
As dying Nature's° earth and lime;

But trust that those we call the dead
  Are breathers of an ampler day
  For ever nobler ends. They say,
The solid earth whereon we tread

In tracts of fluent heat began,°
  And grew to seeming-random forms,   10
  The seeming prey of cyclic storms,°
Till at the last arose the man;°

Who throve and branch'd from clime to clime,
  The herald of a higher race,°
  And of himself in higher place,°
If so he type° this work of time

Within himself, from more to more;
  Or, crown'd with attributes of woe
  Like glories, move his course, and show
That life is not as idle ore,   20

But iron dug from central gloom,
  And heated hot with burning fears,
  And dipt in baths of hissing tears,
And batter'd with the shocks of doom

To shape and use. Arise and fly
  The reeling Faun, the sensual feast;
  Move upward, working out the beast,
And let the ape and tiger die.

CXIX°

Doors, where my heart was used to beat
  So quickly, not as one that weeps
  I come once more; the city sleeps;
I smell the meadow in the street;

I hear a chirp of birds; I see
  Betwixt the black fronts long-withdrawn
  A light-blue lane of early dawn,
And think of early days and thee,

CXVIII. The analogy between cosmic and human evolution, between material and spiritual process. 1. Contemplate: accented on the second syllable. 4. Nature: here the flesh-and-bone body of man. 7–9. The nebular hypothesis concerning the origin of the solar system. 11. Apparently a reference to Cuvier's theory of cataclysmic change. 12–14. The general advance of man (not Darwinian mutation of species). 14. higher race: humanity of a higher type (cf. Epilogue 137–39). 15. higher place: life after death. 16. type: parallel, emulate. CXIX. Cf. VII.

12. Pallas Athene, goddess of wisdom, sprang full-armed from the brain of Zeus. CXV.2. maze of quick: hawthorn hedges. 3. squares: fields. 4. blow: blossom. 8. sightless: invisible. 14. gleam: the sea.

And bless thee, for thy lips are bland,
  And bright the friendship of thine eye;   10
  And in my thoughts with scarce a sigh
I take the pressure of thine hand.

CXX

I trust I have not wasted breath:
  I think we are not wholly brain,
  Magnetic mockeries;° not in vain,
Like Paul with beasts, I fought with Death;°

Not only cunning casts in clay:
  Let Science prove we are, and then
  What matters Science unto men,
At least to me? I would not stay.

Let him, the wiser man° who springs
  Hereafter, up from childhood shape   10
  His action like the greater ape,
But I was *born* to other things.

CXXI

Sad Hesper° o'er the buried sun
  And ready, thou, to die with him,
  Thou watchest all things ever dim
And dimmer, and a glory done.

The team is loosen'd from the wain,
  The boat is drawn upon the shore;
  Thou listenest to the closing door,
And life is darken'd in the brain.

Bright Phosphor,° fresher for the night,
  By thee the world's great work is heard   10
  Beginning, and the wakeful bird;
Behind thee comes the greater light.

The market boat is on the stream,
  And voices hail it from the brink;
  Thou hear'st the village hammer clink,
And see'st the moving of the team.

Sweet Hesper-Phosphor, double name
  For what is one, the first, the last,
  Thou, like my present and my past,
Thy place is changed; thou art the same.   20

CXXII

O, wast thou with me, dearest, then,°
  While I rose up against my doom,°

And yearn'd to burst the folded gloom,
  To bare the eternal heavens again,

To feel once more, in placid awe,
  The strong imagination roll
  A sphere of stars about my soul,
In all her motion one with law?

If thou wert with me, and the grave
  Divide us not, be with me now,   10
  And enter in at breast and brow,
Till all my blood, a fuller wave,

Be quicken'd with a livelier breath,
  And like an inconsiderate boy,
  As in the former flash of joy,
I slip° the thoughts of life and death;

And all the breeze of Fancy blows,
  And every dewdrop paints a bow,°
  The wizard lightnings deeply glow,
And every thought breaks out a rose.   20

CXXIII°

There rolls the deep where grew the tree.
  O earth, what changes hast thou seen!
  There where the long street roars hath been
The stillness of the central sea.

The hills are shadows, and they flow
  From form to form, and nothing stands;
  They melt like mist, the solid lands,
Like clouds they shape themselves and go.

But in my spirit will I dwell,
  And dream my dream, and hold it true;   10
  For tho' my lips may breathe adieu,
I cannot think the thing farewell.°

CXXIV°

That which we dare invoke to bless;
  Our dearest faith; our ghastliest doubt;
  He, They, One, All; within, without;
The Power in darkness whom we guess,° —

I found Him not in world or sun,
  Or eagle's wing, or insect's eye,°
  Nor thro' the questions men may try,
The petty cobwebs we have spun.

CXX.3. **Magnetic mockeries:** electric machines.   4. See I Cor.
15:32.   **9. wiser man:** an ironical reference to the scientist
who insists on man's merely animal nature and inheritance.
CXXI.1. **Hesper:** the evening star (symbol of the past).
9. Phosphor: the morning star (the present).   CXXII.1. **then:**
such moments as those described in LXXXVI and XCV.   **2.**
doom: grief for Hallam.

16. **slip:** escape.   18. **bow:** rainbow.   CXXIII. See the note
on XXXV.11.   9-12. Man is not part of the temporal flux.
CXXIV. A major assertion of the poet's intuitive faith.   1-4.
The God present in all faith and doubt and fear, however dimly
or variously conceived.   5-6. A rejection of the traditional
"argument from design," the rational proof of God's existence
derived from the order of nature.

If e'er when faith had fallen asleep,
  I heard a voice, "believe no more,"   10
  And heard an ever-breaking shore
That tumbled in the Godless deep,

A warmth within the breast would melt
  The freezing reason's colder part,°
  And like a man in wrath the heart
Stood up and answer'd, "I have felt."

No, like a child in doubt and fear:
  But that blind clamor° made me wise;
  Then was I as a child that cries,
But, crying, knows his father near;   20

And what I am beheld again
  What is,° and no man understands;
  And out of darkness came the hands
That reach thro' nature, molding men.°

CXXV

Whatever I have said or sung,
  Some bitter notes my harp would give,
  Yea, tho' there often seem'd to live
A contradiction on the tongue,

Yet Hope had never lost her youth,
  She did but look through dimmer eyes;
  Or Love but play'd with gracious lies,
Because he felt so fix'd in truth;

And if the song were full of care,
  He breathed the spirit of the song;   10
  And if the words were sweet and strong
He set his royal signet there;

Abiding with me till I sail
  To seek thee on the mystic deeps,
  And this electric force, that keeps
A thousand pulses dancing, fail.

CXXVI

Love is and was my lord and king,
  And in his presence I attend
  To hear the tidings of my friend,
Which every hour his couriers bring.

Love is and was my king and lord,
  And will be, tho' as yet I keep
  Within his court on earth, and sleep
Encompass'd by his faithful guard,

And hear at times a sentinel
  Who moves about from place to place,   10
  And whispers to the worlds of space,
In the deep night, that all is well.

CXXVII

And all is well, tho' faith and form
  Be sunder'd in the night of fear;
  Well roars the storm to those that hear
A deeper voice across the storm,°

Proclaiming social truth shall spread,
  And justice, even tho' thrice again
  The red fool-fury of the Seine
Should pile her barricades with dead.°

But ill for him that wears a crown,
  And him, the lazar, in his rags!   10
  They tremble, the sustaining crags;
The spires of ice are toppled down,

And molten up, and roar in flood;
  The fortress crashes from on high,
  The brute earth lightens to the sky,
And the great Æon° sinks in blood,

And compass'd by the fires of hell;
  While thou, dear spirit, happy star,
  O'erlook'st the tumult from afar,
And smilest, knowing all is well.   20

CXXVIII

The love that rose on stronger wings,
  Unpalsied when he met with Death,
  Is comrade of the lesser faith°
That sees the course of human things.

No doubt vast eddies in the flood
  Of onward time shall yet be made,
  And thronèd races may degrade;°
Yet, O ye mysteries of good,

Wild Hours that fly with Hope and Fear,
  If all your office had to do   10
  With old results that look like new —
If this were all your mission here,

To draw, to sheathe a useless sword,
  To fool the crowd with glorious lies,
  To cleave a creed in sects and cries,
To change the bearing of a word,

14. The cold rationalism that sees the world and man as a meaningless flux. **18. blind clamor:** of 10–12. **22. What is:** spiritual reality. **23–24.** Faith built on the inner consciousness can now partly admit what was rejected in 5–6 as inadequate, that God can work through nature.

CXXVII.1–4. All is well, not in the sense that life is smooth, but that love is the supreme power, as in CXXVI; "faith and form" seems to mean faith and its varying forms, and also enduring reality and social change. **7–8.** Apparently the French revolution of July, 1830. **16. Æon:** the modern age. **CXXVIII.3. lesser faith:** in social progress. **7. degrade:** degenerate.

To shift an arbitrary power,
  To cramp the student at his desk,
  To make old bareness picturesque
And tuft with grass a feudal tower,   20

Why, then my scorn might well descend
  On you and yours. I see in part
  That all, as in some piece of art,
Is toil coöperant to an end.°

CXXIX°

Dear friend, far off, my lost desire,
  So far, so near in woe and weal,
  O loved the most, when most I feel
There is a lower and a higher;

Known and unknown, human, divine;
  Sweet human hand and lips and eye;
  Dear heavenly friend that canst not die,
Mine, mine, for ever, ever mine;

Strange friend, past, present, and to be;
  Loved deeplier, darklier understood;
  Behold, I dream a dream of good,   10
And mingle all the world with thee.

CXXX

Thy voice is on the rolling air;
  I hear thee where the waters run;
  Thou standest in the rising sun,
And in the setting thou art fair.

What art thou then? I cannot guess;
  But tho' I seem in star and flower
  To feel thee some diffusive power,
I do not therefore love thee less.

My love involves the love before;
  My love is vaster passion now;   10
  Tho' mix'd with God and Nature thou,
I seem to love thee more and more.

Far off thou art, but ever nigh;
  I have thee still, and I rejoice;
  I prosper, circled with thy voice;
I shall not lose thee tho' I die.

CXXXI

O living will° that shalt endure
  When all that seems° shall suffer shock,
  Rise in the spiritual rock,°
Flow thro' our deeds and make them pure,

That we may lift from out of dust
  A voice as unto him that hears,
  A cry above the conquer'd years°
To one that with us works, and trust,

With faith that comes of self-control,
  The truths that never can be proved   10
  Until we close with all we loved,
And all we flow from, soul in soul.

EPILOGUE

O true and tried, so well and long,°
  Demand not thou a marriage lay;
  In that it is thy marriage day
Is music more than any song.

Nor have I felt so much of bliss
  Since first he told me that he° loved
  A daughter° of our house, nor proved
Since that dark day° a day like this;

Tho' I since then have number'd o'er
  Some thrice three years; they went and came,   10
  Remade the blood and changed the frame,
And yet is love not less, but more;

No longer caring to embalm
  In dying songs a dead regret,
  But like a statue solid-set,
And molded in colossal calm.

Regret is dead, but love is more
  Than in the summers that are flown,
  For I myself with these have grown
To something greater than before;   20

Which makes appear the songs I made
  As echoes out of weaker times,
  As half but idle brawling rhymes,
The sport of random sun and shade.

But where is she, the bridal flower,
  That must be made a wife ere noon?
  She enters, glowing like the moon
Of Eden on its bridal bower.

On me she bends her blissful eyes
  And then on thee;° they meet thy look   30

22–24. I . . . end: Cf. LIV.   CXXIX–CXXX. The poet can feel
Hallam in all the goodness and beauty of the world.   CXXXI.1.
living will: man's free will.   2. seems: merely seems.   3. rock:
Christ (I Cor. 10:4).

7. conquer'd years: the situation of I.13 is reversed.   Epilogue.
A celebration of the marriage of the poet's sister Cecilia and
Edmund Lushington, October 10, 1842. Tennyson spoke of
In Memoriam as a sort of *Divine Comedy*, beginning with death
and ending with marriage and the promise of a new life (*Memoir*,
I, 304; Bradley, pp. 237–38).   6. he: Hallam.   7. daughter:
Emily Tennyson.   8. dark day: of Hallam's death.   30. thee:
Lushington.

And brighten like the star that shook
Betwixt the palms of Paradise.°

O, when her life was yet in bud,
  He° too foretold the perfect rose.
  For thee she grew, for thee she grows
For ever, and as fair as good.

And thou art worthy, full of power;
  As gentle; liberal-minded, great,
  Consistent; wearing all that weight
Of learning lightly like a flower.°   40

But now set out: the noon is near,
  And I must give away the bride;
  She fears not, or with thee beside
And me behind her, will not fear.

For I that danced her on my knee,
  That watch'd her on her nurse's arm,
  That shielded all her life from harm,
At last must part with her to thee;

Now waiting to be made a wife,
  Her feet, my darling, on the dead;°   50
  Their pensive tablets° round her head,
And the most living words of life

Breathed in her ear. The ring is on,
  The " Wilt thou? " answer'd, and again
  The " Wilt thou? " ask'd, till out of twain
Her sweet " I will " has made you one.

Now sign your names, which shall be read,
  Mute symbols of a joyful morn,
  By village eyes as yet unborn.
The names are sign'd, and overhead   60

Begins the clash and clang that tells
  The joy to every wandering breeze;
  The blind wall rocks, and on the trees
The dead leaf trembles to the bells.

O happy hour, and happier hours
  Await them. Many a merry face
  Salutes them — maidens of the place,
That pelt us in the porch with flowers.

O happy hour, behold the bride
  With him to whom her hand I gave.   70
  They leave the porch, they pass the grave
That has to-day its sunny side.

To-day the grave is bright for me,
  For them the light of life increased,
  Who stay to share the morning feast,
Who rest to-night beside the sea.

Let all my genial spirits advance
  To meet and greet a whiter sun;
  My drooping memory will not shun
The foaming grape of eastern France.°   80

It circles round, and fancy plays,
  And hearts are warm'd and faces bloom,
  As drinking health to bride and groom
We wish them store of happy days.

Nor count me all to blame if I
  Conjecture of a stiller guest,°
  Perchance, perchance, among the rest,
And, tho' in silence, wishing joy.

But they must go, the time draws on,
  And those white-favor'd horses wait;   90
  They rise, but linger; it is late;
Farewell, we kiss, and they are gone.

A shade falls on us like the dark
  From little cloudlets on the grass,
  But sweeps away as out we pass
To range the woods, to roam the park,

Discussing how their courtship grew,
  And talk of others that are wed,
  And how she look'd, and what he said,
And back we come at fall of dew.   100

Again the feast, the speech, the glee,
  The shade of passing thought, the wealth
  Of words and wit, the double health,
The crowning cup, the three-times-three,

And last the dance; — till I retire.
  Dumb is that tower which spake so loud,
  And high in heaven the streaming cloud,
And on the downs a rising fire:

And rise, O moon, from yonder down,
  Till over down and over dale   110
  All night the shining vapor sail
And pass the silent-lighted town,

The white-faced halls, the glancing rills,
  And catch at every mountain head,
  And o'er the friths that branch and spread
Their sleeping silver thro' the hills;

31–32. The stars shook when Zeus nodded approval of the marriage of Peleus and Thetis (Catullus, LXIV.204–06). **34. He:** Hallam. **39–40.** Lushington was professor of Greek at Glasgow University. **50. on the dead:** on the tombs under the church floor. **51. tablets:** on the walls.

80. The . . . France: champagne. **86. guest:** Hallam.

And touch with shade the bridal doors,
  With tender gloom the roof, the wall;
  And breaking let the splendor fall
To spangle all the happy shores   120

By which they rest, and ocean sounds,
  And, star and system rolling past,
  A soul shall draw from out the vast
And strike his being into bounds,

And, moved thro' life of lower phase,°
  Result in man, be born and think,
  And act and love, a closer link
Betwixt us and the crowning race°

Of those that, eye to eye, shall look
  On knowledge; under whose command   130
  Is Earth and Earth's, and in their hand
Is Nature like an open book;

No longer half-akin to brute,
  For all we thought and loved and did,
  And hoped, and suffer'd, is but seed
Of what in them is flower and fruit;

Whereof the man that with me trod
  This planet was a noble type
  Appearing ere the times were ripe,
That friend of mine who lives in God,   140

That God, which ever lives and loves,
  One God, one law, one element,
  And one far-off divine event,°
To which the whole creation moves.

    1850   *1833–50*

MAUD

A Monodrama

Maud (1855) grew out of or around the lyric "O that 'twere possible," which was printed as an individual poem in 1837 and later, in much altered form, became section iv of Part II; the first draft of the lyric was written apparently in the autumn of 1833, after Hallam's death, and expressed the longing for reunion that animates parts of *In Memoriam. Maud* as a whole was written in 1854–55; some additions were made in 1856. The story may suggest Victorian melodramas, but it doubtless — like the situation in "Locksley Hall" — had a partial origin in the feud within the Tennyson clan which was referred to in the Introduction.

125. According to a current biological theory, the stages of life in the embryo paralleled the lower forms of animal life. **128–39.** See the note on CXVIII.12–14. **143–44. One . . . event:** See the note on LV.20.

(An early experience of Tennyson's, partly akin to that of his two heroes, is recounted in R. W. Rader, *Tennyson's Maud: The Biographical Genesis,* University of California, 1963.) Lonely and half-hysterical at the outset, the antiheroic hero assails the corruptions of business, the class barriers built on money, and so on. He has fallen below Maud's level because his father had been ruined by her father, his supposed friend. Though he wins her love, in spite of her hostile brother and the aristocratic suitor the brother favors, his happiness, his sense of a life reborn, is quickly blighted; the brother provokes a duel in which he is killed, Maud dies of the shock, and the hero, when he emerges from a period of madness, escapes from himself and his hollow world by going to war. The ending was condemned as jingoistic by a number of contemporary readers, who were living in the shadow of the Crimean War, but it may be thought dramatically consistent with the personality and experience of the hero; one of the "lost generation," he has, like some of Hemingway's heroes, alternated between violence and apathy, between self-centered complaint and selfless devotion, and he can now welcome the chance to enlist in a cause beyond himself.

Tennyson was very fond of *Maud,* his "little *Hamlet,*" and regularly read it to visitors. The work is a tour de force, in that "different phases of passion in one person take the place of different characters" (*Memoir,* I, 396). Such different phases of passion and the high-pitched tone of the poem suggest that Tennyson breathed some of the same air as the "Spasmodic" school of minor poets, who made some stir in the early 1850's. His technical virtuosity is amply apparent. And there are threads of symbolism, such as that of lilies and roses (the red color extends to blood and cannon fire). To some readers the poem as a whole may seem a mixture of the sour and the sentimental; but Tennyson's lyrical — and satirical — powers achieve some notable things, and, in a poet and a man who seems to have known little of romantic passion, "the new strong wine of love" inspires ecstasies that are surely not mere froth.

Part 1

i

1

I hate the dreadful hollow behind the little wood;
Its lips in the field above are dabbled with blood-red
  heath,
The red-ribb'd ledges drip with a silent horror of
  blood,
And Echo there, whatever is ask'd her, answers
  "Death."

2

For there in the ghastly pit long since a body was
  found,

His who had given me life — O father! O God!
    was it well? —
Mangled, and flatten'd, and crush'd, and dinted into
    the ground;
There yet lies the rock that fell with him when he
    fell.

3

Did he fling himself down? who knows? for a vast
    speculation had fail'd,
And ever he mutter'd and madden'd, and ever
    wann'd with despair,   10
And out he walk'd when the wind like a broken
    worldling wail'd,
And the flying gold of the ruin'd woodlands drove
    thro' the air.

4

I remember the time, for the roots of my hair were
    stirr'd
By a shuffled step, by a dead weight trail'd, by a
    whisper'd fright,
And my pulses closed their gates with a shock on
    my heart as I heard
The shrill-edged shriek of a mother divide the
    shuddering night.

5

Villainy somewhere! whose? One says, we are vil-
    lains all.
Not he; his honest fame should at least by me be
    maintained;
But that old man, now lord of the broad estate
    and the Hall,
Dropt off gorged from a scheme that had left us
    flaccid and drain'd.   20

6

Why do they prate of the blessings of peace? we
    have made them a curse,
Pickpockets, each hand lusting for all that is not
    its own;
And lust of gain, in the spirit of Cain, is it better
    or worse
Than the heart of the citizen hissing in war on his
    own hearthstone?

7

But these are the days of advance, the works of the
    men of mind,
When who but a fool would have faith in a trades-
    man's ware or his word?
Is it peace or war? Civil war, as I think, and that
    of a kind

The viler, as underhand, not openly bearing the
    sword.

8

Sooner or later I too may passively take the print
Of the golden age — why not? I have neither hope
    nor trust;   30
May make my heart as a millstone, set my face as
    a flint,
Cheat and be cheated, and die — who knows? we
    are ashes and dust.

9

Peace sitting under her olive, and slurring the days
    gone by,
When the poor are hovel'd and hustled together,
    each sex, like swine,
When only the ledger lives, and when only not all
    men lie;
Peace in her vineyard — yes! — but a company
    forges° the wine.

10

And the vitriol madness flushes up in the ruffian's
    head,
Till the filthy by-lane rings to the yell of the tram-
    pled wife,
And chalk and alum and plaster are sold to the
    poor for bread,
And the spirit of murder works in the very means
    of life,   40

11

And Sleep must lie down arm'd, for the villainous
    center-bits°
Grind on the wakeful ear in the hush of the moon-
    less nights,
While another° is cheating the sick of a few last
    gasps, as he sits
To pestle a poison'd poison behind his crimson
    lights.

12

When a Mammonite° mother kills her babe for a
    burial fee,
And Timour-Mammon° grins on a pile of chil-
    dren's bones,
Is it peace or war? better, war! loud war by land
    and by sea,
War with a thousand battles, and shaking a hun-
    dred thrones!

MAUD.   I.36. **forges:** adulterates.   **41. center-bits:** burglar's
drills.   **43. another:** a pharmacist.   **45. Mammonite:** devotee
of Mammon, money.   **46. Timour:** Tamerlane (Marlowe's
Tamburlaine), an example of ruthless conquest and slaughter,
in his modern commercial form, exploiting children in factories
and mines.

13

For I trust if an enemy's fleet came yonder round
    by the hill,
And the rushing battle-bolt sang from the three-
    decker out of the foam,   50
That the smooth-faced, snub-nosed rogue would
    leap from his counter and till,
And strike, if he could, were it but with his cheat-
    ing yardwand, home. —

14

What! am I raging alone as my father raged in his
    mood?
Must *I* too creep to the hollow and dash myself
    down and die
Rather than hold by the law that I made, never-
    more to brood
On a horror of shatter'd limbs and a wretched
    swindler's lie?

15

Would there be sorrow for *me*? there was *love* in
    the passionate shriek,
Love for the silent thing that had made false haste
    to the grave° —
Wrapt in a cloak, as I saw him, and thought he
    would rise and speak
And rave at the lie and the liar, ah God, as he used
    to rave.   60

16

I am sick of the Hall and the hill, I am sick of
    the moor and the main.
Why should I stay? can a sweeter chance ever come
    to me here?
O, having the nerves of motion as well as the
    nerves of pain,
Were it not wise if I fled from the place and the
    pit and the fear?

17

Workmen up at the Hall! — they are coming back
    from abroad;
The dark old place will be gilt by the touch of a
    millionaire.
I have heard, I know not whence, of the singular
    beauty of Maud;
I play'd with the girl when a child; she promised
    then to be fair.

18

Maud, with her venturous climbings and tumbles
    and childish escapes,

58. made . . . grave: committed suicide.

Maud, the delight of the village, the ringing joy
    of the Hall,   70
Maud, with her sweet purse-mouth when my father
    dangled the grapes,
Maud, the beloved of my mother, the moon-faced
    darling of all, —

19

What is she now? My dreams are bad. She may
    bring me a curse.
No, there is fatter game on the moor; she will let
    me alone.
Thanks; for the fiend best knows whether woman
    or man be the worse.
I will bury myself in myself, and the Devil may
    pipe to his own.

ii

Long have I sigh'd for a calm; God grant I may
    find it at last!
It will never be broken by Maud; she has neither
    savor nor salt.
But a cold and clear-cut face, as I found when her
    carriage past,
Perfectly beautiful; let it be granted her; where is
    the fault?   80
All that I saw — for her eyes were downcast, not
    to be seen —
Faultily faultless, icily regular, splendidly null,
Dead perfection, no more; nothing more, if it had
    not been
For a chance of travel, a paleness, an hour's defect
    of the rose,
Or an underlip, you may call it a little too ripe, too
    full,
Or the least little delicate aquiline curve in a sen-
    sitive nose,
From which I escaped heart-free, with the least
    little touch of spleen.

iii

Cold and clear-cut face, why come you so cruelly
    meek,
Breaking a slumber in which all spleenful folly was
    drown'd?
Pale with the golden beam of an eyelash dead on
    the cheek,   90
Passionless, pale, cold face, star-sweet on a gloom
    profound;
Womanlike, taking revenge too deep for a transient
    wrong
Done but in thought to your beauty, and ever as
    pale as before
Growing and fading and growing upon me with-
    out a sound,

Luminous, gemlike, ghostlike, deathlike, half the
    night long
Growing and fading and growing, till I could bear
    it no more,
But arose, and all by myself in my own dark gar-
    den ground,
Listening now to the tide in its broad-flung ship-
    wrecking roar,
Now to the scream of a madden'd beach dragg'd
    down by the wave,
Walk'd in a wintry wind by a ghastly glimmer, and
    found   100
The shining daffodil dead, and Orion low in his
    grave.°

iv

1

A million emeralds break from the ruby-budded
    lime
In the little grove where I sit — ah, wherefore
    cannot I be
Like things of the season gay, like the bountiful
    season bland,
When the far-off sail is blown by the breeze of a
    softer clime,
Half-lost in the liquid azure bloom of a crescent of
    sea,
The silent sapphire-spangled marriage ring of the
    land?

2

Below me, there, is the village, and looks how quiet
    and small!
And yet bubbles o'er like a city, with gossip, scan-
    dal, and spite;
And Jack on his ale-house bench has as many lies
    as a Czar;°   110
And here on the landward side, by a red rock,
    glimmers the Hall;
And up in the high Hall-garden I see her pass like
    a light;
But sorrow seize me if ever that light be my lead-
    ing star!

3

When have I bow'd to her father, the wrinkled
    head of the race?
I met her to-day with her brother, but not to her
    brother I bow'd;
I bow'd to his lady-sister as she rode by on the
    moor,
But the fire of a foolish pride flash'd over her beau-
    tiful face.

O child, you wrong your beauty, believe it, in being
    so proud;
Your father has wealth well-gotten, and I am name-
    less and poor.

4

I keep but a man and a maid, ever ready to slander
    and steal;   120
I know it, and smile a hard-set smile, like a stoic,
    or like
A wiser epicurean, and let the world have its way.
For nature is one with rapine, a harm no preacher
    can heal;
The Mayfly is torn by the swallow, the sparrow
    spear'd by the shrike,
And the whole little wood where I sit is a world of
    plunder and prey.

5

We are puppets, Man in his pride, and Beauty fair
    in her flower;
Do we move ourselves, or are moved by an unseen
    hand at a game
That pushes us off from the board, and others ever
    succeed?
Ah yet, we cannot be kind to each other here for
    an hour;
We whisper, and hint, and chuckle, and grin at a
    brother's shame;   130
However we brave it out, we men are a little
    breed.

6

A monstrous eft° was of old the lord and master of
    earth,
For him did his high sun flame, and his river bil-
    lowing ran,
And he felt himself in his force to be Nature's
    crowning race.
As nine months go to the shaping an infant ripe
    for his birth,
So many a million of ages have gone to the mak-
    ing of man:°
He now is first, but is he the last? is he not too
    base?

7

The man of science himself is fonder of glory, and
    vain,
An eye well-practised in nature, a spirit bounded
    and poor;
The passionate heart of the poet is whirl'd into
    folly and vice.   140

---

101. Orion . . . grave: The lowness of Orion marks the approach
of spring.   110. The first explicit reference to the Crimean
War of 1854–55.

132. eft: one of "the great old lizards of geology" (Tennyson).
135–36. As . . . man: See the note on *In Memoriam*, Epilogue,
125.

I would not marvel at either, but keep a temperate
brain;
For not to desire or admire,° if a man could learn
it, were more
Than to walk all day like the sultan of old in a
garden of spice.

8

For the drift of the Maker is dark, an Isis hid by
the veil.
Who knows the ways of the world, how God will
bring them about?
Our planet is one, the suns are many, the world
is wide.
Shall I weep if a Poland fall? shall I shriek if a
Hungary fail?
Or an infant civilization be ruled with rod or with
knout?
I have not made the world, and He that made it
will guide.

9

Be mine a philosopher's life in the quiet woodland
ways,   150
Where if I cannot be gay let a passionless peace be
my lot,
Far-off from the clamor of liars belied in the hubbub of lies;
From the long-neck'd geese of the world that are
ever hissing dispraise
Because their natures are little, and, whether he
heed it or not,
Where each man walks with his head in a cloud of
poisonous flies.

10

And most of all would I flee from the cruel madness of love,
The honey of poison-flowers and all the measureless
ill.
Ah, Maud, you milk-white fawn, you are all unmeet
for a wife.
Your mother is mute in her grave as her image in
marble above;
Your father is ever in London, you wander about
at your will;   160
You have but fed on the roses and lain in the lilies
of life.

v

1

A voice by the cedar tree
In the meadow under the Hall!
She is singing an air that is known to me,

A passionate ballad gallant and gay,
A martial song like a trumpet's call!
Singing alone in the morning of life,
In the happy morning of life and of May,
Singing of men that in battle array,
Ready in heart and ready in hand,   170
March with banner and bugle and fife
To the death, for their native land.

2

Maud with her exquisite face,
And wild voice pealing up to the sunny sky,
And feet like sunny gems on an English green,
Maud in the light of her youth and her grace,
Singing of Death, and of Honor that cannot die,
Till I well could weep for a time so sordid and
mean,
And myself so languid and base.

3

Silence, beautiful voice!   180
Be still, for you only trouble the mind
With a joy in which I cannot rejoice,
A glory I shall not find.
Still! I will hear you no more,
For your sweetness hardly leaves me a choice
But to move to the meadow and fall before
Her feet on the meadow grass, and adore,
Not her, who is neither courtly nor kind,
Not her, not her, but a voice.

vi

1

Morning arises stormy and pale,   190
No sun, but a wannish glare
In fold upon fold of hueless cloud;
And the budded peaks of the wood are bow'd,
Caught, and cuff'd by the gale:
I had fancied it would be fair.

2

Whom but Maud should I meet
Last night, when the sunset burn'd
On the blossom'd gable-ends
At the head of the village street,
Whom but Maud should I meet?   200
And she touch'd my hand with a smile so sweet,
She made me divine amends
For a courtesy° not return'd.

---

142. **admire:** wonder (Horace, *Epistles,* I.vi.1).   203. **courtesy:** bow (cf. I.114-19).

3

And thus a delicate spark
Of glowing and growing light
Thro' the livelong hours of the dark
Kept itself warm in the heart of my dreams,
Ready to burst in a color'd flame;
Till at last, when the morning came
In a cloud, it faded, and seems   210
But an ashen-gray delight.

4

What if with her sunny hair,
And smile as sunny as cold,
She meant to weave me a snare
Of some coquettish deceit,
Cleopatra-like as of old
To entangle me when we met,
To have her lion roll in a silken net
And fawn at a victor's feet.

5

Ah, what shall I be at fifty   220
Should Nature keep me alive,
If I find the world so bitter
When I am but twenty-five?
Yet, if she were not a cheat,
If Maud were all that she seem'd,
And her smile were all that I dream'd,
Then the world were not so bitter
But a smile could make it sweet.

6

What if, tho' her eye seem'd full
Of a kind intent to me,   230
What if that dandy-despot, he,
That jewel'd mass of millinery,
That oil'd and curl'd Assyrian bull°
Smelling of musk and of insolence,
Her brother, from whom I keep aloof,
Who wants the finer politic sense
To mask, tho' but in his own behoof,
With a glassy smile his brutal scorn —
What if he had told her yestermorn
How prettily for his own sweet sake   240
A face of tenderness might be feign'd,
And a moist mirage in desert eyes,
That so, when the rotten hustings shake
In another month to his brazen lies,
A wretched vote may be gain'd?

7

For a raven ever croaks, at my side,
Keep watch and ward, keep watch and ward,
Or thou wilt prove their tool.
Yea, too, myself from myself I guard,
For often a man's own angry pride   250
Is cap and bells° for a fool.

8

Perhaps the smile and tender tone
Came out of her pitying womanhood,
For am I not, am I not, here alone
So many a summer since she died,
My mother, who was so gentle and good?
Living alone in an empty house,
Here half-hid in the gleaming wood,
Where I hear the dead at midday moan,
And the shrieking rush of the wainscot mouse,   260
And my own sad name in corners cried,
When the shiver of dancing leaves is thrown
About its echoing chambers wide,
Till a morbid hate and horror have grown
Of a world in which I have hardly mixt,
And a morbid eating lichen fixt
On a heart half-turn'd to stone.

9

O heart of stone, are you flesh, and caught
By that you swore to withstand?
For what was it else within me wrought   270
But, I fear, the new strong wine of love,
That made my tongue so stammer and trip
When I saw the treasured splendor, her hand,
Come sliding out of her sacred glove,
And the sunlight broke from her lip?

10

I have play'd with her when a child;
She remembers it now we meet.
Ah, well, well, well, I *may* be beguiled
By some coquettish deceit.
Yet, if she were not a cheat,   280
If Maud were all that she seem'd,
And her smile had all that I dream'd,
Then the world were not so bitter
But a smile could make it sweet.

vii

1

Did I hear it half in a doze
    Long since, I know not where?
Did I dream it an hour ago,
    When asleep in this arm-chair?

---

233. curl'd ... bull: with hair curled like that of sculptured
Assyrian bulls.

251. cap and bells: insignia of a medieval court fool.

2

Men were drinking together,°
  Drinking and talking of me: 290
" Well, if it prove a girl, the boy
  Will have plenty; so let it be."

3

Is it an echo of something
  Read with a boy's delight,
Viziers nodding together
  In some Arabian night?

4

Strange, that I hear two men,
  Somewhere, talking of me:
" Well, if it prove a girl, my boy
  Will have plenty; so let it be."   300

viii

She came to the village church,
And sat by a pillar alone;
An angel watching an urn
Wept over her, carved in stone;
And once, but once, she lifted her eyes,
And suddenly, sweetly, strangely blush'd
To find they were met by my own;
And suddenly, sweetly, my heart beat stronger
And thicker, until I heard no longer
The snowy-banded,° dilettante,   310
Delicate-handed priest intone;
And thought, is it pride? and mused and sigh'd,
" No surely, now it cannot be pride."

ix

I was walking a mile,
More than a mile from the shore,
The sun look'd out with a smile
Betwixt the cloud and the moor;
And riding at set of day
Over the dark moor land,
Rapidly riding far away,   320
She waved to me with her hand.
There were two at her side,
Something flash'd in the sun,
Down by the hill I saw them ride,
In a moment they were gone;
Like a sudden spark
Struck vainly in the night,
Then returns the dark
With no more hope of light.

X

1

Sick, am I sick of a jealous dread?   330
Was not one of the two at her side
This new-made lord, whose splendor plucks
The slavish hat from the villager's head?
Whose old grandfather has lately died,
Gone to a blacker pit, for whom
Grimy nakedness dragging his trucks
And laying his trams in a poison'd gloom
Wrought, till he crept from a gutted mine
Master of half a servile shire,
And left his coal all turn'd into gold   340
To a grandson, first of his noble line,
Rich in the grace all women desire,
Strong in the power that all men adore,
And simper and set their voices lower,
And soften as if to a girl, and hold
Awe-stricken breaths at a work divine,
Seeing his gewgaw castle shine,
New as his title, built last year,
There amid perky larches and pine,
And over the sullen-purple moor —   350
Look at it — pricking a cockney ear.

2

What, has he found my jewel out?
For one of the two that rode at her side
Bound for the Hall, I am sure was he;
Bound for the Hall, and I think for a bride.
Blithe would her brother's acceptance be.
Maud could be gracious too, no doubt,
To a lord, a captain, a padded shape,
A bought commission, a waxen face,
A rabbit mouth that is ever agape —   360
Bought? what is it he cannot buy?
And therefore splenetic, personal, base,
A wounded thing with a rancorous cry,
At war with myself and a wretched race,
Sick, sick to the heart of life, am I.

3

Last week came one to the county town,
To preach our poor little army down,
And play the game of the despot kings,
Tho' the state has done it and thrice as well.
This broad-brimm'd hawker of holy things,   370
Whose ear is cramm'd with his cotton, and rings
Even in dreams to the chink of his pence,
This huckster put down war!° can he tell

289-300. Men . . . be: the two fathers, long ago, planning marriage for their children, cf. I.720-26. 310. snowy-banded: wearing the clerical white neckband, or stock, with two pendent strips.

370-73. This . . . war: The allusion to a Quaker pacifist and manufacturer was thought to be to John Bright, who opposed the Crimean War, but Tennyson said he did not know that Bright was a Quaker and that he had no individual in mind.

Whether war be a cause or a consequence?
Put down the passions that make earth hell!
Down with ambition, avarice, pride,
Jealousy, down! cut off from the mind
The bitter springs of anger and fear!
Down too, down at your own fireside,
With the evil tongue and the evil ear,   380
For each is at war with mankind!

4

I wish I could hear again
The chivalrous battle-song
That she warbled alone in her joy!
I might persuade myself then
She would not do herself this great wrong,
To take a wanton dissolute boy
For a man and leader of men.

5

Ah God, for a man with heart, head, hand,
Like some of the simple great ones gone   390
For ever and ever by,
One still strong man in a blatant land,
Whatever they call him — what care I? —
Aristocrat, democrat, autocrat — one
Who can rule and dare not lie!

6

And ah for a man to arise in me,
That the man I am may cease to be!

xi

1

O, let the solid ground
    Not fail beneath my feet
Before my life has found   400
    What some have found so sweet!
Then let come what come may,
What matter if I go mad,
I shall have had my day.

2

Let the sweet heavens endure,
    Not close and darken above me
Before I am quite quite sure
    That there is one to love me!
Then let come what come may
To a life that has been so sad,   410
I shall have had my day.

xii

1

Birds in the high Hall-garden
    When twilight was falling,
Maud, Maud, Maud, Maud,°
    They were crying and calling.

2

Where was Maud? in our wood;
    And I — who else? — was with her,
Gathering woodland lilies,
    Myriads blow° together.

3

Birds in our wood sang   420
    Ringing thro' the valleys,
Maud is here, here, here
    In among the lilies.°

4

I kiss'd her slender hand,
    She took the kiss sedately;
Maud is not seventeen,
    But she is tall and stately.

5

I to cry out on pride
    Who have won her favor!
O, Maud were sure of heaven   430
    If lowliness could save her!

6

I know the way she went
    Home with her maiden posy,
For her feet have touch'd the meadows
    And left the daisies rosy.°

7

Birds in the high Hall-garden
    Were crying and calling to her,
Where is Maud, Maud, Maud?
    One is come to woo her.

8

Look, a horse at the door,   440
    And little King Charley° snarling!

414. **Maud . . . Maud:** The repeated name is like the rook's
caw. **419. blow:** blossom. **420-23. Birds . . . lilies:** These
birds, unlike those of 412-15, are on the lovers' side (*Memoir*,
I, 379, 403). **435. rosy:** The daisies' heads were tilted and
showed their rosy underpetals. **441. King Charley:** The King
Charles is a small, silky breed of spaniel.

Go back, my lord, across the moor,
You are not her darling.

xiii

1

Scorn'd, to be scorn'd by one that I scorn,
Is that a matter to make me fret?
That a calamity hard to be borne?
Well, he may live to hate me yet.
Fool that I am to be vext with his pride!
I past him, I was crossing his lands;
He stood on the path a little aside;   450
His face, as I grant, in spite of spite,
Has a broad-blown comeliness, red and white,
And six feet two, as I think, he stands;
But his essences turn'd the live air sick,
And barbarous opulence jewel-thick
Sunn'd itself on his breast and his hands.

2

Who shall call me ungentle, unfair?
I long'd so heartily then and there
To give him the grasp of fellowship;
But while I past he was humming an air,   460
Stopt, and then with a riding-whip
Leisurely tapping a glossy boot,
And curving a contumelious lip,
Gorgonized me from head to foot
With a stony British stare.°

3

Why sits he here in his father's chair?
That old man never comes to his place;
Shall I believe him ashamed to be seen?
For only once, in the village street,
Last year, I caught a glimpse of his face,   470
A gray old wolf and a lean.
Scarcely, now, would I call him a cheat;
For then, perhaps, as a child of deceit,
She might by a true descent be untrue;
And Maud is as true as Maud is sweet,
Tho' I fancy her sweetness only due
To the sweeter blood by the other side;
Her mother has been a thing complete,
However she came to be so allied.
And fair without, faithful within,   480
Maud to him is nothing akin.
Some peculiar mystic grace
Made her only the child of her mother,
And heap'd the whole inherited sin

464–65. **Gorgonized . . . stare:** The Gorgon Medusa's head
turned beholders to stone.

On that huge scapegoat of the race,
All, all upon the brother.

4

Peace, angry spirit, and let him be!
Has not his sister smiled on me?

xiv

1

Maud has a garden of roses
And lilies fair on a lawn;   490
There she walks in her state
And tends upon bed and bower,
And thither I climb'd at dawn
And stood by her garden-gate.
A lion ramps at the top,
He is claspt by a passion-flower.

2

Maud's own little oak-room —
Which Maud, like a precious stone
Set in the heart of the carven gloom,
Lights with herself, when alone   500
She sits by her music and books
And her brother lingers late
With a roystering company — looks
Upon Maud's own garden-gate;
And I thought as I stood, if a hand, as white
As ocean-foam in the moon, were laid
On the hasp of the window, and my Delight
Had a sudden desire, like a glorious ghost, to glide,
Like a beam of the seventh heaven, down to my
    side,
There were but a step to be made.   510

3

The fancy flatter'd my mind,
And again seem'd overbold;
Now I thought that she cared for me,
Now I thought she was kind
Only because she was cold.

4

I heard no sound where I stood
But the rivulet on from the lawn
Running down to my own dark wood,
Or the voice of the long sea-wave as it swell'd
Now and then in the dim-gray dawn;   520
But I look'd, and round, all round the house I
    beheld
The death-white curtain drawn,
Felt a horror over me creep,
Prickle my skin and catch my breath,

Knew that the death-white curtain meant but sleep,
Yet I shudder'd and thought like a fool of the
   sleep of death.

xv

So dark a mind within me dwells,
   And I make myself such evil cheer,
That if *I* be dear to some one else,
   Then some one else may have much to fear;
But if *I* be dear to some one else,°   531
   Then I should be to myself more dear.
Shall I not take care of all that I think,
Yea, even of wretched meat and drink,
   If I be dear,
   If I be dear to some one else?

xvi

1

This lump of earth has left his estate
The lighter by the loss of his weight;
And so that he find what he went to seek,
And fulsome pleasure clog him, and drown   540
His heart in the gross mud-honey of town,
He may stay for a year who has gone for a week.
But this is the day when I must speak,
And I see my Oread coming down,
O, this is the day!
O beautiful creature, what am I
That I dare to look her way?
Think I may hold dominion sweet,
Lord of the pulse that is lord of her breast,
And dream of her beauty with tender dread,   550
From the delicate Arab arch° of her feet
To the grace that, bright and light as the crest
Of a peacock, sits on her shining head,
And she knows it not — O, if she knew it,
To know her beauty might half undo it!
I know it the one bright thing to save
My yet young life in the wilds of Time,
Perhaps from madness, perhaps from crime,
Perhaps from a selfish grave.

2

What, if she be fasten'd to this fool lord,   560
Dare I bid her abide by her word?
Should I love her so well if she
Had given her word to a thing so low?
Shall I love her as well if she
Can break her word were it even for me?
I trust that it is not so.

529-31. some one else: Maud.   551. Arab arch: high instep.

3

Catch not my breath, O clamorous heart,
Let not my tongue be a thrall to my eye,
For I must tell her before we part,
I must tell her, or die.   570

xvii

Go not, happy day,
   From the shining fields,
Go not, happy day,
   Till the maiden yields.
Rosy is the West,
   Rosy is the South,
Roses are her cheeks,
   And a rose her mouth.
When the happy Yes
   Falters from her lips,   580
Pass and blush the news
   Over glowing ships;
Over blowing seas,
   Over seas at rest,
Pass the happy news,
   Blush it thro' the West;
Till the red man dance
   By his red cedar-tree,
And the red man's babe
   Leap, beyond the sea.   590
Blush from West to East,
   Blush from East to West,
Till the West is East,
   Blush it thro' the West.
Rosy is the West,
   Rosy is the South,
Roses are her cheeks,
   And a rose her mouth.

xviii

1

I have led her home, my love, my only friend.
There is none like her, none.   600
And never yet so warmly ran my blood
And sweetly, on and on,
Calming itself to the long-wish'd-for end,
Full to the banks, close on the promised good.

2

None like her, none.
Just now the dry-tongued laurels' pattering talk
Seem'd her light foot along the garden walk,
And shook my heart to think she comes once more.
But even then I heard her close the door;
The gates of heaven are closed, and she is gone.

3

There is none like her, none,   611
Nor will be when our summers have deceased.
O, art thou sighing for Lebanon
In the long breeze that streams to thy delicious East,
Sighing for Lebanon,
Dark cedar,° tho' thy limbs have here increased,
Upon a pastoral slope as fair,
And looking to the South and fed
With honey'd rain and delicate air,
And haunted by the starry head   620
Of her whose gentle will has changed my fate,
And made my life a perfumed altar-flame;
And over whom thy darkness must have spread
With such delight as theirs of old, thy great
Forefathers of the thornless garden, there
Shadowing the snow-limb'd Eve from whom she
    came?

4

Here will I lie, while these long branches sway,
And you fair stars that crown a happy day
Go in and out as if at merry play,
Who am no more so all forlorn   630
As when it seem'd far better to be born
To labor and the mattock-harden'd hand
Than nursed at ease and brought to understand
A sad astrology, the boundless plan
That makes you tyrants in your iron skies,
Innumerable, pitiless, passionless eyes,
Cold fires, yet with power to burn and brand
His nothingness into man.

5

But now shine on, and what care I,
Who in this stormy gulf have found a pearl   640
The countercharm of space and hollow sky,
And do accept my madness, and would die
To save from some slight shame one simple girl? —

6

Would die, for sullen-seeming Death may give
More life to Love than is or ever was
In our low world, where yet 'tis sweet to live.
Let no one ask me how it came to pass;
It seems that I am happy, that to me
A livelier emerald twinkles in the grass,
A purer sapphire melts into the sea.   650

7

Not die, but live a life of truest breath,
And teach true life to fight with mortal wrongs.

O, why should Love, like men in drinking-songs,
Spice his fair banquet with the dust of death?
Make answer, Maud my bliss,
Maud made my Maud by that long loving kiss,
Life of my life, wilt thou not answer this?
" The dusky strand of Death inwoven here
With dear Love's tie, makes Love himself more
    dear."

8

Is that enchanted moan only the swell   660
Of the long waves that roll in yonder bay?
And hark the clock within, the silver knell
Of twelve sweet hours that past in bridal white,
And died to live, long as my pulses play;
But now by this my love has closed her sight
And given false death° her hand, and stolen away
To dreamful wastes where footless fancies dwell
Among the fragments of the golden day.
May nothing there her maiden grace affright!
Dear heart, I feel with thee the drowsy spell. 670
My bride to be, my evermore delight,
My own heart's heart, my ownest own, farewell;
It is but for a little space I go.
And ye meanwhile far over moor and fell
Beat to the noiseless music of the night!
Has our whole earth gone nearer to the glow
Of your soft splendors that you look so bright?
I have climb'd nearer out of lonely hell.
Beat, happy stars, timing with things below,
Beat with my heart more blest than heart can tell,
Blest, but for some dark undercurrent woe   681
That seems to draw — but it shall not be so;
Let all be well, be well.

xix

1

Her brother is coming back to-night,
Breaking up my dream of delight.

2

My dream? do I dream of bliss?
I have walk'd awake with Truth.
O, when did a morning shine
So rich in atonement as this
For my dark-dawning youth,   690
Darken'd watching a mother decline
And that dead man at her heart and mine;
For who was left to watch her but I?
Yet so did I let my freshness die.

613–16. O . . . cedar: Cf. the cedars of Lebanon, Song of Sol.
5:15, etc.

666. false death: sleep.

3

I trust that I did not talk
To gentle Maud in our walk —
For often in lonely wanderings
I have cursed him even to lifeless things —
But I trust that I did not talk,
Not touch on her father's sin.   700
I am sure I did but speak
Of my mother's faded cheek
When it slowly grew so thin
That I felt she was slowly dying
Vext with lawyers and harass'd with debt;
For how often I caught her with eyes all wet,
Shaking her head at her son and sighing
A world of trouble within!

4

And Maud, too, Maud was moved
To speak of the mother she loved   710
As one scarce less forlorn,
Dying abroad and it seems apart
From him who had ceased to share her heart,
And ever mourning over the feud,
The household Fury sprinkled with blood
By which our houses are torn.
How strange was what she said,
When only Maud and the brother
Hung over her dying bed —
That Maud's dark father and mine°   720
Had bound us one to the other,
Betrothed us over their wine,
On the day when Maud was born;
Seal'd her mine from her first sweet breath!
Mine, mine by a right, from birth till death!
Mine, mine — our fathers have sworn!

5

But the true blood spilt had in it a heat
To dissolve the precious seal on a bond,
That, if left uncancel'd, had been so sweet;
And none of us thought of a something beyond,
A desire that awoke in the heart of the child,   731
As it were a duty done to the tomb,
To be friends for her sake, to be reconciled;
And I was cursing them and my doom,
And letting a dangerous thought run wild
While often abroad in the fragrant gloom
Of foreign churches — I see her there,
Bright English lily, breathing a prayer
To be friends, to be reconciled!

6

But then what a flint is he!   740
Abroad, at Florence, at Rome,

720–26. Cf. I.289–300.

I find whenever she touch'd on me
This brother had laugh'd her down,
And at last, when each came home,
He had darken'd into a frown,
Chid her, and forbid her to speak
To me, her friend of the years before;
And this was what had redden'd her cheek
When I bow'd to her on the moor.

7

Yet Maud, altho' not blind   750
To the faults of his heart and mind,
I see she cannot but love him,
And says he is rough but kind,
And wishes me to approve him,
And tells me, when she lay
Sick once, with a fear of worse,
That he left his wine and horses and play,
Sat with her, read to her, night and day,
And tended her like a nurse.

8

Kind? but the death-bed desire   760
Spurn'd by this heir of the liar —
Rough but kind? yet I know
He has plotted against me in this,
That he plots against me still.
Kind to Maud? that were not amiss.
Well, rough but kind; why, let it be so,
For shall not Maud have her will?

9

For, Maud, so tender and true,
As long as my life endures
I feel I shall owe you a debt   770
That I never can hope to pay;
And if ever I should forget
That I owe this debt to you
And for your sweet sake to yours,
O, then, what then shall I say? —
If ever I *should* forget,
May God make me more wretched
Than ever I have been yet!

10

So now I have sworn to bury
All this dead body of hate,   780
I feel so free and so clear
By the loss of that dead weight,
That I should grow light-headed, I fear,
Fantastically merry,
But that her brother comes, like a blight
On my fresh hope, to the Hall to-night.

xx

1

Strange, that I felt so gay,
Strange, that *I* tried to-day
To beguile her melancholy;
The Sultan,° as we name him —   790
She did not wish to blame him —
But he vext her and perplext her
With his worldly talk and folly.
Was it gentle to reprove her
For stealing out of view
From a little lazy lover°
Who but claims her as his due?
Or for chilling his caresses
By the coldness of her manners,
Nay, the plainness of her dresses?   800
Now I know her but in two,
Nor can pronounce upon it
If one should ask me whether
The habit, hat, and feather,
Or the frock and gipsy bonnet
Be the neater and completer;
For nothing can be sweeter
Than maiden Maud in either.

2

But to-morrow, if we live,
Our ponderous squire will give   810
A grand political dinner
To half the squirelings near;
And Maud will wear her jewels,
And the bird of prey will hover,
And the titmouse hope to win her
With his chirrup at her ear.

3

A grand political dinner
To the men of many acres,
A gathering of the Tory,
A dinner and then a dance   820
For the maids and marriage-makers,
And every eye but mine will glance
At Maud in all her glory.

4

For I am not invited,
But, with the Sultan's pardon,
I am all as well delighted,
For I know her own rose-garden,
And mean to linger in it
Till the dancing will be over;

And then, O, then, come out to me   830
For a minute, but for a minute,
Come out to your own true lover,
That your true lover may see
Your glory also, and render
All homage to his own darling,
Queen Maud in all her splendor.

xxi

Rivulet crossing my ground,
And bringing me down from the Hall
This garden-rose that I found,
Forgetful of Maud and me,   840
And lost in trouble and moving round
Here at the head of a tinkling fall,
And trying to pass to the sea;
O rivulet, born at the Hall,
My Maud has sent it by thee —
If I read her sweet will right —
On a blushing mission to me,
Saying in odor and color, " Ah, be
Among the roses to-night."

xxii

1

Come into the garden, Maud,   850
For the black bat, night, has flown,
Come into the garden, Maud,
I am here at the gate alone;
And the woodbine spices are wafted abroad,
And the musk of the rose is blown.

2

For a breeze of morning moves,
And the planet of Love° is on high,
Beginning to faint in the light that she loves
On a bed of daffodil sky,
To faint in the light of the sun she loves,   860
To faint in his light, and to die.

3

All night have the roses heard
The flute, violin, bassoon;
All night has the casement jessamine stirr'd
To the dancers dancing in tune;
Till a silence fell with the waking bird,
And a hush with the setting moon.

4

I said to the lily, " There is but one,
With whom she has heart to be gay.

---

790. Sultan: Maud's brother.   **796. lover:** the "new-made
lord" of I.332 ff.

857. planet of Love: Venus.

When will the dancers leave her alone?   870
  She is weary of dance and play."
Now half to the setting moon are gone,
  And half to the rising day;
Low on the sand and loud on the stone
  The last wheel echoes away.

5

I said to the rose, " The brief night goes
  In babble and revel and wine.
O young lord-lover, what sighs are those,
  For one that will never be thine?
But mine, but mine," so I sware to the rose,   880
  " For ever and ever, mine."

6

And the soul of the rose went into my blood,
  As the music clash'd in the hall;
And long by the garden lake I stood,
  For I heard your rivulet fall
From the lake to the meadow and on to the wood,
  Our wood, that is dearer than all;

7

From the meadow your walks have left so sweet
  That whenever a March-wind sighs
He sets the jewel-print of your feet   890
  In violets blue as your eyes,
To the woody hollows in which we meet
  And the valleys of Paradise.

8

The slender acacia would not shake
  One long milk-bloom on the tree;
The white lake-blossom fell into the lake
  As the pimpernel dozed on the lea;
But the rose was awake all night for your sake,
  Knowing your promise to me;
The lilies and roses were all awake,   900
  They sigh'd for the dawn and thee.

9

Queen rose of the rosebud garden of girls,
  Come hither, the dances are done,
In gloss of satin and glimmer of pearls,
  Queen lily and rose in one;
Shine out, little head, sunning over with curls,
  To the flowers, and be their sun.

10

There has fallen a splendid tear
  From the passion-flower at the gate.
She is coming, my dove, my dear;   910
  She is coming, my life, my fate.

The red rose cries, " She is near, she is near; "
  And the white rose weeps, " She is late; "
The larkspur listens, " I hear, I hear; "
  And the lily whispers, " I wait."

11

She is coming, my own, my sweet;
  Were it ever so airy a tread,
My heart would hear her and beat,
  Were it earth in an earthy bed;
My dust would hear her and beat,   920
  Had I lain for a century dead,
Would start and tremble under her feet,
  And blossom in purple and red.

Part II

i

1

" The fault was mine, the fault was mine " —
Why am I sitting here so stunn'd and still,
Plucking the harmless wild-flower on the hill? —
It is this guilty hand! —
And there rises ever a passionate cry
From underneath in the darkening land —
What is it, that has been done?
O dawn of Eden bright over earth and sky,
The fires of hell brake out of thy rising sun,
The fires of hell and of hate;   10
For she, sweet soul, had hardly spoken a word,
When her brother ran in his rage to the gate,
He came with the babe-faced lord,
Heap'd on her terms of disgrace;
And while she wept, and I strove to be cool,
He fiercely gave me the lie,
Till I with as fierce an anger spoke,
And he struck me, madman, over the face,
Struck me before the languid fool,
Who was gaping and grinning by;   20
Struck for himself an evil stroke,
Wrought for his house an irredeemable woe.
For front to front in an hour we stood,
And a million horrible bellowing echoes broke
From the red-ribb'd hollow behind the wood,
And thunder'd up into heaven the Christless code
That must have life for a blow.
Ever and ever afresh they seem'd to grow.
Was it he lay there with a fading eye?
" The fault was mine," he whisper'd, " fly! "   30
Then glided out of the joyous wood
The ghastly Wraith of one that I know,
And there rang on a sudden a passionate cry,
A cry for a brother's blood;
It will ring in my heart and my ears, till I die, till
  I die.°

II.31–35. Then . . . die: a vision of Maud.

2

Is it gone? my pulses beat —
What was it? a lying trick of the brain?
Yet I thought I saw her stand,
A shadow there at my feet,
High over the shadowy land.   40
It is gone; and the heavens fall in a gentle rain,
When they should burst and drown with deluging
          storms
The feeble vassals of wine and anger and lust,
The little hearts that know not how to forgive.
Arise, my God, and strike, for we hold Thee just,
Strike dead the whole weak race of venomous
          worms,
That sting each other here in the dust;
We are not worthy to live.

ii

1

See what a lovely shell,°
Small and pure as a pearl,   50
Lying close to my foot,
Frail, but a work divine,
Made so fairly well
With delicate spire and whorl,
How exquisitely minute,
A miracle of design!

2

What is it? a learned man
Could give it a clumsy name.
Let him name it who can,
The beauty would be the same.   60

3

The tiny cell is forlorn,
Void of the little living will
That made it stir on the shore.
Did he stand at the diamond door
Of his house in a rainbow frill?
Did he push, when he was uncurl'd,
A golden foot or a fairy horn
Thro' his dim water-world?

4

Slight, to be crush'd with a tap
Of my finger-nail on the sand,   70
Small, but a work divine,
Frail, but of force to withstand,
Year upon year, the shock

Of cataract seas that snap
The three-decker's oaken spine
Athwart the ledges of rock,
Here on the Breton strand!°

5

Breton, not Briton; here
Like a shipwreck'd man on a coast
Of ancient fable and fear —   80
Plagued with a flitting to and fro,
A disease, a hard mechanic ghost
That never came from on high
Nor ever arose from below,
But only moves with the moving eye,
Flying along the land and the main —
Why should it look like Maud?
Am I to be overawed
By what I cannot but know
Is a juggle born of the brain?   90

6

Back from the Breton coast,
Sick of a nameless fear,
Back to the dark sea-line
Looking, thinking of all I have lost;
An old song vexes my ear,
But that of Lamech° is mine.

7

For years, a measureless ill,
For years, for ever, to part —
But she, she would love me still;
And as long, O God, as she   100
Have a grain of love for me,
So long, no doubt, no doubt,
Shall I nurse in my dark heart,
However weary, a spark of will
Not to be trampled out.

8

Strange, that the mind, when fraught
With a passion so intense
One would think that it well
Might drown all life in the eye, —
That it should, by being so overwrought,   110
Suddenly strike on a sharper sense
For a shell, or a flower, little things
Which else would have been past by!
And now I remember, I,
When he lay dying there,
I noticed one of his many rings —
For he had many, poor worm — and thought,
It is his mother's hair.

---

49 ff. The shell, surviving storms, perhaps symbolizes the hero's
"first and highest nature preserved amid the storms of passion"
(*Memoir*, I, 404).

77. Breton strand: Brittany, in France, whither the hero has
fled after the duel.   **96. Lamech:** See Gen. 4:23.

9

Who knows if he be dead?
Whether I need have fled?   120
Am I guilty of blood?
However this may be,
Comfort her, comfort her, all things good,
While I am over the sea!
Let me and my passionate love go by,
But speak to her all things holy and high,
Whatever happen to me!
Me and my harmful love go by;
But come to her waking, find her asleep,
Powers of the height, Powers of the deep, 130
And comfort her tho' I die!

iii

Courage, poor heart of stone!
I will not ask thee why
Thou canst not understand
That thou art left for ever alone;
Courage, poor stupid heart of stone! —
Or if I ask thee why,
Care not thou to reply:
She is but dead, and the time is at hand
When thou shalt more than die.   140

iv

1

O that 'twere possible°
After long grief and pain
To find the arms of my true love
Round me once again!

2

When I was wont to meet her
In the silent woody places
By the home that gave me birth,
We stood tranced in long embraces
Mixt with kisses sweeter, sweeter
Than anything on earth.   150

3

A shadow flits before me,
Not thou, but like to thee.
Ah, Christ, that it were possible
For one short hour to see
The souls we loved, that they might tell us
What and where they be!

4

It leads me forth at evening,
It lightly winds and steals

141–238. The germ of *Maud*. See the headnote.

In a cold white robe before me,
When all my spirit reels   160
At the shouts, the leagues of lights,
And the roaring of the wheels.

5

Half the night I waste in sighs,
Half in dreams I sorrow after
The delight of early skies;
In a wakeful doze I sorrow
For the hand, the lips, the eyes,
For the meeting of the morrow,
The delight of happy laughter,
The delight of low replies.   170

6

'Tis a morning pure and sweet,
And a dewy splendor falls
On the little flower that clings
To the turrets and the walls;
'Tis a morning pure and sweet,
And the light and shadow fleet.
She is walking in the meadow,
And the woodland echo rings;
In a moment we shall meet.
She is singing in the meadow,   180
And the rivulet at her feet
Ripples on in light and shadow
To the ballad that she sings.

7

Do I hear her sing as of old,
My bird with the shining head,
My own dove with the tender eye?
But there rings on a sudden a passionate cry,
There is some one dying or dead,
And a sullen thunder is roll'd;
For a tumult shakes the city,   190
And I wake, my dream is fled.
In the shuddering dawn, behold,
Without knowledge, without pity,
By the curtains of my bed
That abiding phantom cold!

8

Get thee hence, nor come again,
Mix not memory with doubt,
Pass, thou deathlike type of pain,
Pass and cease to move about!
'Tis the blot upon the brain   200
That *will* show itself without.

9

Then I rise, the eave-drops fall,
And the yellow vapors choke

The great city sounding wide;
The day comes, a dull red ball
Wrapt in drifts of lurid smoke
On the misty river-tide.

10

Thro' the hubbub of the market
I steal, a wasted frame;
It crosses here, it crosses there,   210
Thro' all that crowd confused and loud,
The shadow still the same;
And on my heavy eyelids
My anguish hangs like shame.

11

Alas for her that met me,
That heard me softly call,
Came glimmering thro' the laurels
At the quiet evenfall,
In the garden by the turrets
Of the old manorial hall!   220

12

Would the happy spirit descend
From the realms of light and song,
In the chamber or the street,
As she looks among the blest,
Should I fear to greet my friend
Or to say "Forgive the wrong,"
Or to ask her, "Take me, sweet,
To the regions of thy rest"?

13

But the broad light glares and beats,
And the shadow flits and fleets   230
And will not let me be;
And I loathe the squares and streets,
And the faces that one meets,
Hearts with no love for me.
Always I long to creep
Into some still cavern deep,
There to weep, and weep, and weep
My whole soul out to thee.

v

1

Dead, long dead,°
Long dead!   240
And my heart is a handful of dust,
And the wheels go over my head,
And my bones are shaken with pain,

239 ff. The hero goes through a period of insanity.

For into a shallow grave they are thrust,
Only a yard beneath the street,
And the hoofs of the horses beat, beat,
The hoofs of the horses beat,
Beat into my scalp and my brain,
With never an end to the stream of passing feet,
Driving, hurrying, marrying, burying,   250
Clamor and rumble, and ringing and clatter;
And here beneath it is all as bad,
For I thought the dead had peace, but it is not so.
To have no peace in the grave, is that not sad?
But up and down and to and fro,
Ever about me the dead men go;
And then to hear a dead man chatter
Is enough to drive one mad.

2

Wretchedest age, since Time began,°
They cannot even bury a man;   260
And tho' we paid our tithes in the days that are
    gone,
Not a bell was rung, not a prayer was read.
It is that which makes us loud in the world of the
    dead;
There is none that does his work, not one.
A touch of their office might have sufficed,
But the churchmen fain would kill their church,
As the churches have kill'd their Christ.

3

See, there is one of us sobbing,
No limit to his distress;
And another, a lord of all things, praying   270
To his own great self, as I guess;
And another, a statesman there, betraying
His party-secret, fool, to the press;
And yonder a vile physician, blabbing
The case of his patient — all for what?
To tickle the maggot born in an empty head,
And wheedle a world that loves him not,
For it is but a world of the dead.

4

Nothing but idiot gabble!
For the prophecy° given of old   280
And then not understood,
Has come to pass as foretold;
Not let any man think for the public good,
But babble, merely for babble.
For I never whisper'd a private affair
Within the hearing of cat or mouse,
No, not to myself in the closet alone,

259 ff. Imagining that he is dead, he feels the restlessness that, according to superstition, was felt by those buried without due rites.   280. prophecy: See Luke 12:2–3.

But I heard it shouted at once from the top of the
    house;
Everything came to be known.
Who told *him*° we were there? 290

5

Not that gray old wolf,° for he came not back
From the wilderness, full of wolves, where he used
    to lie;
He has gather'd the bones for his o'ergrown whelp
    to crack —
Crack them now for yourself, and howl, and die.

6

Prophet, curse me the blabbing lip,
And curse me the British vermin, the rat;
I know not whether he came in the Hanover ship,°
But I know that he lies and listens mute
In an ancient mansion's crannies and holes.
Arsenic, arsenic, sure, would do it, 300
Except that now we poison our babes, poor souls!
It is all used up for that.

7

Tell him now: she is standing here at my head;
Not beautiful now, not even kind;
He may take her now; for she never speaks her
    mind,
But is ever the one thing silent here.
She is not *of* us, as I divine;
She comes from another stiller world of the dead,
Stiller, not fairer than mine.

8

But I know where a garden grows, 310
Fairer than aught in the world beside,
All made up of the lily and rose
That blow by night, when the season is good,
To the sound of dancing music and flutes:
It is only flowers, they had no fruits,
And I almost fear they are not roses, but blood;
For the keeper° was one, so full of pride,
He linkt a dead man° there to a spectral bride;
For he, if he had not been a Sultan° of brutes,
Would he have that hole in his side? 320

9

But what will the old man° say?
He laid a cruel snare in a pit
To catch a friend of mine° one stormy day;
Yet now I could even weep to think of it;
For what will the old man say
When he comes to the second corpse° in the pit?

10

Friend, to be struck by the public foe,
Then to strike him and lay him low,
That were a public merit, far,
Whatever the Quaker° holds, from sin; 330
But the red life spilt for a private blow —
I swear to you, lawful and lawless war
Are scarcely even akin.

11

O me, why have they not buried me deep enough?
Is it kind to have made me a grave so rough,
Me, that was never a quiet sleeper?
Maybe still I am but half-dead;
Then I cannot be wholly dumb.
I will cry to the steps above my head
And somebody, surely, some kind heart will come
To bury me, bury me 341
Deeper, ever so little deeper.

Part III

1

My life has crept so long on a broken wing
Thro' cells of madness, haunts of horror and fear,
That I come to be grateful at last for a little thing.
My mood is changed, for it fell at a time of year
When the face of night is fair on the dewy downs,
And the shining daffodil dies, and the Charioteer°
And starry Gemini° hang like glorious crowns
Over Orion's grave low down in the west,
That like a silent lightning under the stars
She° seem'd to divide in a dream from a band of the
    blest, 10
And spoke of a hope for the world in the coming
    wars —
" And in that hope, dear soul, let trouble have rest,
Knowing I tarry for thee," and pointed to Mars
As he glow'd like a ruddy shield on the Lion's
    breast.°

---

290. *him:* Maud's brother. 291. wolf: Maud's father (cf.I.471). 297. The Norwegian rat appeared in England in the early eighteenth century; the phrase "Hanover rat" was applied by adherents of the Stuarts to followers of the early Hanoverian kings of England, who came to the throne in the person of George I, in 1714. 317. keeper: Maud's brother. 318. dead man: the hero. 319. Sultan: Cf. I.790.

321. old man: Maud's father. 323. friend of mine: the hero's father (see I.5 ff.). 326. second corpse: Maud's brother (the first was the hero's father). 330. Quaker: as opposed to fighting (cf. I.370). III.6. Charioteer: the constellation Auriga. 7. Gemini: the twin stars Castor and Pollux. 10. She: Maud. 13-14. The planet Mars and the constellation of the Lion (suggesting war and the symbolic British lion).

2

And it was but a dream, yet it yielded a dear delight
To have look'd, tho' but in a dream, upon eyes so fair,
That had been in a weary world my one thing bright;
And it was but a dream, yet it lighten'd my despair
When I thought that a war would arise in defense of the right,
That an iron tyranny° now should bend or cease,
The glory of manhood stand on his ancient height,
Nor Britain's one sole God be the millionaire.   22
No more shall commerce be all in all, and Peace
Pipe on her pastoral hillock a languid note,
And watch her harvest ripen, her herd increase,
Nor the cannon-bullet rust on a slothful shore,
And the cobweb woven across the cannon's throat
Shall shake its threaded tears in the wind no more.

3

And as months ran on and rumor of battle grew,
" It is time, it is time, O passionate heart," said I, —
For I cleaved to a cause that I felt to be pure and true, —   31
" It is time, O passionate heart and morbid eye,
That old hysterical mock-disease should die."
And I stood on a giant deck and mixt my breath
With a loyal people shouting a battle-cry,
Till I saw the dreary phantom° arise and fly
Far into the North, and battle, and seas of death.

4

Let it go or stay, so I wake to the higher aims
Of a land that has lost for a little her lust of gold,
And love of a peace that was full of wrongs and shames,   40
Horrible, hateful, monstrous, not to be told;
And hail once more to the banner of battle unroll'd!
Tho' many a light shall darken, and many shall weep
For those that are crush'd in the clash of jarring claims,
Yet God's just wrath shall be wreak'd on a giant liar,°
And many a darkness into the light shall leap,
And shine in the sudden making of splendid names,
And noble thought be freer under the sun,
And the heart of a people beat with one desire;
For the peace, that I deem'd no peace, is over and done,   50

And now by the side of the Black and the Baltic deep,°
And deathful-grinning mouths of the fortress, flames
The blood-red blossom of war with a heart of fire.

5

Let it flame or fade, and the war roll down like a wind,
We have proved we have hearts in a cause, we are noble still,
And myself have awaked, as it seems, to the better mind.
It is better to fight for the good than to rail at the ill;
I have felt with my native land, I am one with my kind,
I embrace the purpose of God, and the doom assign'd.

1855, 1856

NORTHERN FARMER

OLD STYLE

In this poem and the companion poem following, published in 1864 and 1869, respectively, there is much social history as well as humor and flavor. The new kind of farmer — who speaks less dialectal English than the old one — is self-seeking in his mercenary independence, in contrast with his predecessor, who had pride in his work and was loyal to the land and its owner. Each poem grew out of a saying Tennyson had heard: the germ of the first is lines 45 and 47, that of the second is lines 1–2 (*Memoir*, II, 9).

I

Wheer 'asta beän° saw° long and meä liggin'° 'ere aloän?
Noorse?° thourt nowt° o' a noorse; whoy, Doctor's abeän an' agoän;
Says that I moänt° 'a naw moor aäle, but I beänt a fool;
Git ma° my aäle, fur I beänt a-gawin' to breäk my rule.

II

Doctors, they knaws nowt, fur a° says what 's nawways true;
Naw soort o' koind o' use to saäy the things that a do.

---

20. tyranny: of the Czar.   **36. phantom:** Editors suggest the phantom of Maud (cf. II.iv), but would it be called "dreary"? It seems rather the "old hysterical mock-disease" of 33, just above.   **45. giant liar:** the Czar (cf. I.110).

51. The Crimean peninsula is in the Black Sea. NORTHERN FARMER (OLD STYLE).   **1. 'asta beän:** hast thou been.   **saw:** so. **liggin':** lying.   **2. noorse:** nurse.   **nowt:** nought.   **3. moänt 'a:** may not have.   **4. ma:** me.   **5. a:** he.

I've 'ed my point° o' aäle ivry noight sin' I beän
'ere.
An' I've 'ed my quart ivry market-noight for foorty
year.

III

Parson's a beän loikewoise, an' a sittin' 'ere o' my
bed.
"The Amoighty's a taäkin o' you° to 'issén,° my
friend," a said,   10
An' a towd° ma my sins, an's toithe° were due, an'
I gied it in hond;
I done moy duty boy° 'um, as I 'a done boy the
lond.

IV

Larn'd a ma' beä.° I reckons I 'annot sa mooch to
larn.
But a cast oop,° thot a did, 'bout Bessy Marris's
barne.°
Thaw° a knaws I hallus° voäted wi' Squoire an'
choorch an' staäte,
An' i' the woost o' toimes I wur niver agin the
raäte.°

V

An' I hallus coom'd to 's choorch afoor moy Sally
wur deäd,
An' 'eärd 'um a bummin' awaäy loike a buzzard-
clock° ower my 'eäd,
An' I niver knaw'd whot a meän'd but I thowt a
'ad summut° to saäy,
An' I thowt a said whot a owt° to 'a said, an I
coom'd awaäy.   20

VI

Bessy Marris's barne! tha knaws she laäid it to meä.
Mowt a beän,° mayhap, for she wur a bad un, sheä.
'Siver,° I kep 'um, I kep 'um, my lass, tha mun°
understond;
I done moy duty boy 'um, as I 'a done boy the
lond.

VII

But Parson a cooms an' a goäs, an 'a says it eäsy
an' freeä:
"The Amoighty's a taäkin o' you to 'issén, my
friend," says 'eä.

I weänt saäy men be loiars, thaw summun° said it
in 'aäste;
But 'e reäds woon sarmin° a weeäk, an' I 'a
stubb'd° Thurnaby waäste.

VIII

D' ya moind° the waäste, my lass? naw, naw, tha
was not born then;
Theer wur a boggle° in it, I often 'eärd 'um mysen;
Moäst loike a butter-bump,° fur I 'eärd 'um about
an' about,   31
But I stubb'd 'um oop wi' the lot, an' raäved an'
rembled° 'um out.

IX

Keäper's° it wur; fo' they fun° 'um theer a-laäid
of 'is faäce
Down i' the woild 'enemies° afoor I coom'd to the
plaäce.
Noäks or Thimbleby — toäner° 'ed shot 'um as
deäd as a naäil.
Noäks wur 'ang'd for it oop at 'soize° — but git ma
my aäle.

X

Dubbut° looök at the waäste; theer warn't not
feeäd° for a cow;
Nowt at all but bracken an' fuzz,° an' looök at it
now —
Warn't worth nowt a haäcre, an' now theer 's lots
o' feeäd,
Fourscoor° yows° upon it, an' some on it down i'
seeäd.°   40

XI

Nobbut° a bit on it 's left, an' I meän'd to 'a stubb'd
it at fall,
Done it ta-year° I meän'd, an' runn'd plow thruff°
it an' all,
If Godamoighty an' Parson 'ud nobbut° let ma
aloän, —
Meä, wi' haäte hoonderd haäcre o' Squoire's, an'
lond o' my oän.

XII

Do Godamoighty knaw what a's doing a-taäkin' o'
meä?

27. **summun:** someone (Ps. 116:11).   28. **woon sarmin:** one
sermon.   **stubb'd:** cleared.   29. **moind:** mind, remember.
30. **boggle:** bogy, ghost.   31. **butter-bump:** bittern.   32.
raäved an' rembled: tore up and threw away.   33. **Keäper's:**
the gamekeeper's.   **fun:** found.   34. **'enemies:** anemones.
35. **toäner:** one or other.   36. **'soize:** assizes.   37. **Dubbut:**
do but.   **feeäd:** feed.   38. **fuzz:** furze.   40. **fourscoor:** *ou*
as in *hour*.   **yows:** ewes.   **seeäd:** clover.   41. **Nobbut:**
nought but.   42. **ta-year:** this year.   **thruff:** through.   43.
'ud nobbut: would only.

---

7. **point:** pint.   10. **you:** *ou* as in *hour*.   **'issén:** himself.
11. **towd:** told.   **toithe:** tithe.   12. **boy:** by.   13. **Larn'd a
ma' beä:** learned he may be.   14. **a cast oop:** he brought up
against me.   **barne:** bairn.   15. **Thaw:** though.   **hallus:**
always.   16. **raäte:** poor-tax.   18. **buzzard-clock:** cockchafer.
19. **summut:** somewhat.   20. **owt:** ought.   22. **Mowt a beän:**
might have been.   23. **'Siver:** howsoever.   **mun:** must.

I beänt wonn as saws° 'ere a beän an' yonder a peä;
An' Squoire 'ull be sa mad an' all — a' dear, a' dear!
And I 'a managed for Squoire coom Michaelmas
    thutty year.

XIII

A mowt 'a taäen owd° Joänes, as 'ant° not a
    'ääpoth° o' sense,
Or a mowt 'a taäen young Robins — a niver
    mended a fence;   50
But Godamoighty a moost taäke meä an' taäke ma
    now,
Wi' aäf° the cows to cauve° an' Thurnaby hoälms°
    to plow!

XIV

Looök 'ow quoloty° smoiles when they seeäs ma a
    passin' boy,
Says to thessén,° naw doubt, "What a man a beä
    sewer-loy! "°
Fur they knaws what I beän to Squoire sin' fust° a
    coom'd to the 'All;
I done moy duty by Squoire an' I done moy duty
    boy hall.

XV

Squoire's i' Lunnon, an' summun I reckons 'ull 'a
    to wroite,
For whoä 's to howd° the lond ater° meä thot°
    muddles ma quoit;°
Sartin-sewer° I beä thot a weänt niver° give it to
    Joänes,
Naw, nor a moänt° to Robins — a niver rembles°
    the stoäns.   60

XVI

But summun 'ull come ater meä mayhap wi' 'is kit-
    tle o' steäm°
Huzzin' an' maäzin'° the blessed feälds wi' the
    divil's oän teäm.
Sin' I mun doy° I mun doy, thaw loife they says is
    sweet,
But sin' I mun doy I mun doy, for I couldn abeär
    to see it.

XVII

What atta° stannin' theer fur, an' doesn bring ma
    the aäle?
Doctor 's a 'toättler,° lass, an a 's hallus i' the owd
    taäle;°

---

46. wonn as saws: one that sows. 49. owd: old. 'ant: has
not. 'ääpoth: halfpenny-worth. 52. aäf: half. cauve:
calve. hoälms: holms, low land by a stream. 53. quoloty:
quality, the gentry. 54. thessén: themselves. sewer-loy:
surely. 55. sin fust: since first. 58. howd: hold. ater:
after. thot: that. quoit: quite. 59. Sartin-sewer: certain
sure. a weänt niver: he won't ever. 60. moänt: must not.
rembles: removes. 61. kittle o' steäm: steam thresher. 62.
Huzzin' an' maäzin': worrying and confusing. 63. doy: die.
65. atta: art thou. 66. 'toättler: teetotaler. taäle: tale.

I weänt breäk rules fur Doctor, a knaws naw moor
    nor a floy;°
Git ma my aäle, I tell tha, an' if I mun doy I mun
    doy.

1864

NORTHERN FARMER

NEW STYLE

I

Dosn't thou 'ear my 'erse's° legs, as they canters
    awaäy?
Proputty,° proputty, proputty — that's what I 'ears
    'em saäy.
Proputty, proputty, proputty — Sam, thou 's an ass
    for thy paäins;
Theer's moor sense i' one o' 'is legs, nor in all thy
    braäins.

II

Woä — theer 's a craw° to pluck wi' tha, Sam:
    yon's Parson's 'ouse —
Dosn't thou knaw that a man mun be eäther a man
    or a mouse?
Time to think on it then; for thou 'll be twenty to
    weeäk.°
Proputty, proputty — woä then, woä — let ma 'ear
    mysén° speäk.

III

Me an' thy muther, Sammy, 'as beän a-talkin' o'
    thee;
Thou 's beän talkin' to muther, an' she beän a-tellin'
    it me.   10
Thou 'll not marry for munny — thou 's sweet upo'
    Parson's lass —
Noä — thou 'll marry for luvv — an' we boäth on
    us thinks tha an ass.

IV

Seeä'd her to-daäy goä by — Saäint's-daäy — they
    was ringing the bells.
She 's a beauty, thou thinks — an' soä is scoors o'
    gells,°
Them as 'as munny an' all — wot 's a beauty? —
    the flower as blaws.
But proputty, proputty sticks, an' proputty, proputty
    graws.

V

Do'ant be stunt;° taäke time. I knaws what maäkes
    tha sa mad.

---

67. floy: fly. NORTHERN FARMER (NEW STYLE). 1. 'erse's:
horse's. 2. Proputty: property. 5. craw: crow. 7. to
weeäk: this week. 8. mysén: myself. 14. scoors o'gells:
scores of girls. 17. stunt: stubborn.

Warn't I craäzed fur the lasses mysén when I wur a
    lad?
But I knaw'd a Quaäker feller as often 'as towd° ma
    this:
"Doänt thou marry for munny, but goä wheer
    munny is!"   20

VI

An' I went wheer munny war; an' thy muther
    coom to 'and,
Wi' lots o' munny laaïd by, an' a nicetish bit o'
    land.
Maäybe she warn't a beauty — I niver giv it a
    thowt —
But warn't she as good to cuddle an' kiss as a lass
    as 'ant nowt?°

VII

Parson's lass 'ant nowt, an' she weant 'a° nowt
    when 'e 's deäd,
Mun be a guvness, lad, or summut, and addle° her
    breäd.
Why? fur 'e 's nobbut° a curate, an' weänt niver
    get hissén clear,°
An' 'e maäde the bed as 'e ligs° on afoor 'e coom'd
    to the shere.°

VIII

An' thin 'e coom'd to the parish wi' lots o' Varsity
    debt,
Stook to his taaïl they did, an' 'e 'ant got shut on°
    'em yet.   30
An' 'e ligs on 'is back i' the grip,° wi' noän to lend
    'im a shuvv,°
Woorse nor a far-welter'd yowe;° fur, Sammy, 'e
    married fur luvv.
Luvv? what's luvv? thou can luvv thy lass an' 'er
    munny too,
Maäkin' 'em goä togither, as they've good right to
    do.
Couldn I luvv thy muther by cause o' 'er munny
    laaïd by?
Naäy — fur I luvv'd 'er a vast sight moor fur it;
    reäson why.

X

Ay, an' thy muther says thou wants to marry the
    lass,
Cooms of a gentleman burn;° an' we boäth on us
    thinks tha an ass.

Woä then, proputty, wiltha?° — an ass as near as
    mays nowt° —
Woä then, wiltha? dangtha! — the bees is as fell as
    owt.°   40

XI

Breäk me a bit o' the esh° for his 'eäd, lad, out o'
    the fence!
Gentleman burn! what's gentleman burn? is it
    shillins an' pence?
Proputty, proputty's ivrything 'ere, an', Sammy, I'm
    blest
If it isn't the saäme oop yonder, fur them as 'as it's
    the best.

XII

Tis 'n them as 'as munny as breäks into 'ouses an'
    steäls,
Them as 'as coäts to their backs an' taäkes their
    regular meäls.
Noä, but it 's them as niver knaws wheer a meäl's
    to be 'ad.
Taäke my word for it, Sammy, the poor in a loomp
    is bad.

XIII

Them or thir feythers, tha sees, mun 'a beän° a
    laäzy lot,
Fur work mun 'a gone to the gittin' whiniver
    munny was got.   50
Feyther 'ad ammost° nowt; leästways 'is munny
    was 'id.
But e' tued an' moil'd° issén deäd, an' 'e died a
    good un, 'e did.

XIV

Looök thou theer wheer Wrigglesby beck° cooms
    out by the 'ill!
Feyther run oop° to the farm, an' I runs oop to the
    mill;
An' I 'll run oop to the brig,° an' that thou 'll live
    to see;
And if thou marries a good un I 'll leäve the land
    to thee.

XV

Thim 's my noätions, Sammy, wheerby I meäns to
    stick;
But if thou marries a bad un, I 'll leäve the land to
    Dick. —

---

19. towd: told.   **24.** 'ant nowt: has nothing.   **25.** weänt 'a: will
not have.   **26.** addle: earn.   **27.** nobbut: nothing but.
clear: of debt.   **28.** ligs: lies.   shere: shire.   **30.** shut on:
clear of.   **31.** grip: ditch.   shuvv: shove.   **32.** far-welter'd
yowe: ewe lying helpless on her back.   **38.** burn: born.

39. wiltha: wilt thou.   mays nowt: makes no difference.   **40.**
bees ... owt: flies are as fierce as anything.   **41.** esh: ash.
49. mun 'a beän: must have been.   **51.** ammost: almost.
52. tued an' moil'd: toiled and drudged.   **53.** beck: brook.
54. Feyther ... oop: father's land ran up.   **55.** brig: bridge.

Coom oop, proputty, proputty — that 's what I
   'ears 'im saäy —
Proputty, proputty, proputty — canter an' canter
   awaäy.   60

1869

"FRATER AVE ATQUE VALE"

During an Italian tour in 1880 Tennyson lingered on
Sirmione, a peninsula in the Lago di Garda where
Catullus (B.C. ?84–?54) had a cherished retreat. Tennyson had a special regard for the Roman lyrist, and
here he recalls, in a melodious pattern of *o*'s and *a*'s,
both a scene of happy associations and Catullus' lament
for his dead brother. Tennyson himself had lately lost
his favorite brother, Charles.

Row us out from Desenzano,° to your Sirmione
   row!
So they row'd, and there we landed — "O venusta
   Sirmio!"°
There to me thro' all the groves of olive in the
   summer glow,
There beneath the Roman ruin° where the purple
   flowers grow,
Came that "Ave atque Vale"° of the Poet's hope-
   less woe,
Tenderest of Roman poets nineteen hundred years
   ago,
"Frater Ave atque Vale" — as we wander'd to
   and fro
Gazing at the Lydian laughter° of the Garda Lake
   below
Sweet Catullus's all-but-island,° olive-silvery Sirmio!

1883   *1880*

TO VIRGIL

WRITTEN AT THE REQUEST OF THE MANTUANS FOR THE
NINETEENTH CENTENARY OF VIRGIL'S DEATH

Virgil was born near Mantua in 70 B.C. and died in
19 B.C. Mantua celebrated the nineteenth centenary of
his death in 1881; Tennyson's poem was published in
1882. This tribute from the most Virgilian of English
poets includes phrases that would fit much of his own

work. The rolling trochaic lines suggest something of
the sound of the Virgilian hexameter.

I

Roman Virgil, thou that singest° Ilion's lofty
   temples robed in fire,
Ilion° falling, Rome arising, wars, and filial faith,
   and Dido's pyre;

II

Landscape-lover, lord of language more than he°
   that sang the "Works and Days,"
All the chosen coin of fancy flashing out from many
   a golden phrase;

III

Thou that singest wheat and woodland, tilth and
   vineyard, hive and horse and herd;°
All the charm of all the Muses often flowering in a
   lonely word;

IV

Poet of the happy Tityrus piping underneath his
   beechen bowers;°
Poet of the poet-satyr whom the laughing shepherd
   bound with flowers;°

V

Chanter of the Pollio, glorying in the blissful years
   again to be,
Summers of the snakeless meadow, unlaborious
   earth and oarless sea;°   10

VI

Thou that seest Universal Nature moved by Universal Mind;
Thou majestic in thy sadness at the doubtful doom
   of human kind;°

VII

Light among the vanish'd ages; star that gildest
   yet this phantom shore;
Golden branch amid the shadows, kings and realms
   that pass to rise no more;°

"FRATER AVE ATQUE VALE." **1.** Desenzano: a town on Lake
Garda near Sirmione. **2.** O venusta [lovely] **Sirmio**: from
Catullus, XXXI.12. **4.** Roman ruin: traditionally said to be
the remains of Catullus' villa. **5.** Ave atque Vale: hail and
farewell (Catullus, CI.10). The Roman poet's woe was hopeless
because he could not look forward to reunion in an afterlife
(*Memoir*, II, 239). **8.** Lydian laughter: from Catullus, XXXI.
13. The ancient Etruscans of this region were said to be descended
from the Lydians of Asia Minor. **9.** all-but-island: peninsula
(Catullus, XXX.1).

TO VIRGIL. **1–2.** singest: in the *Aeneid*. **2.** Ilion: Troy.
3. he: the Greek poet Hesiod. **5.** Virgil's four *Georgics*.
7. *Eclogue* I. **8.** *Eclogue* VI. **9–10.** The fourth or "Messi-
anic" *Eclogue*, celebrating a new golden age of peace, in which
Virgil addresses his patron, the consul Asinius Pollio. **11–12.**
The *Aeneid*, especially VI. **14.** Virgil shines out of the past
like the golden bough that Aeneas carried into the underworld
(*Aeneid*, VI.208 ff.).

VIII

Now thy Forum roars no longer, fallen every purple
    Caesar's dome —
Tho' thine ocean-roll of rhythm sound for ever of
    Imperial Rome —

IX

Now the Rome of slaves hath perish'd, and the
    Rome of freemen holds her place,°
I, from out the Northern Island sunder'd once from
    all the human race,°

X

I salute thee, Mantovano,° I that loved thee since
    my day began,
Wielder of the stateliest measure ever molded by
    the lips of man.   20

1882

DEMETER AND PERSEPHONE

(IN ENNA)

This poem, the last of Tennyson's dramatic monologues based on classical myth, was written in May,
1887, and published in 1889; it is an astonishing production for a poet in his seventy-eighth year. Moreover,
though his initial or ostensible theme, suggested by his
son Hallam, was "Motherhood" (*Memoir*, II, 364) —
which might sound ominous — his treatment is more
"mythic" and "primitive" than most of the earlier
poems had been. Tennyson has not, to be sure, abandoned his old and fruitful habit of reinterpretation, and
the conclusion presents, in mythological terms, his
hope of progress, the "one far-off divine event, To
which the whole creation moves." Yet the speech of
Demeter (Ceres) to her daughter Persephone (Proserpine), now wife of the king of the underworld, while
it ends on the note of spring and rebirth and love,
creates a dominant effect of vague foreboding, of the
mysterious terrors that envelop life, of the menace of
sterility and death. As befits a poem concerned with
the visit to earth of the queen of Hades, much use is
made of images of light and darkness. Tennyson's
main source was apparently the "Homeric Hymn to
Demeter," which tells of the mother's long and agonized search for her daughter after Pluto had carried
her off. There are studies of the poem by G. R. Stange,
ELH, A Journal of English Literary History, XXI
(1954), and C. Dahl, *Victorian Studies*, I (1958).

Faint as a climate-changing bird that flies
All night across the darkness, and at dawn

Falls on the threshold of her native land,
And can no more, thou camest, O my child,
Led upward by the God of ghosts and dreams,°
Who laid thee at Eleusis,° dazed and dumb
With passing thro' at once from state to state,
Until I brought thee hither, that the day,
When here thy hands let fall the gather'd flower,°
Might break thro' clouded memories once again
On thy lost self. A sudden nightingale   11
Saw thee, and flash'd into a frolic of song
And welcome; and a gleam as of the moon,
When first she peers along the tremulous deep,
Fled wavering o'er thy face, and chased away
That shadow of a likeness to the king
Of shadows, thy dark mate. Persephone!
Queen of the dead no more — my child! Thine eyes
Again were human-godlike, and the Sun
Burst from a swimming fleece of winter gray,   20
And robed thee in his day from head to feet —
"Mother!" and I was folded in thine arms.

Child, those imperial, disimpassion'd eyes
Awed even me at first, thy mother — eyes
That oft had seen the serpent-wanded power°
Draw downward into Hades with his drift
Of flickering specters, lighted from below
By the red race of fiery Phlegethon;°
But when before have Gods or men beheld
The Life that had descended re-arise,   30
And lighted from above him by the Sun?
So mighty was the mother's childless cry,
A cry that rang thro' Hades, Earth, and Heaven!

So in this pleasant vale we stand again,
The field of Enna, now once more ablaze
With flowers that brighten as thy footstep falls,
All flowers — but for one black blur of earth
Left by that closing chasm, thro' which the car
Of dark Aïdoneus° rising rapt thee hence.
And here, my child, tho' folded in thine arms,   40
I feel the deathless heart of motherhood
Within me shudder, lest the naked glebe
Should yawn once more into the gulf, and thence
The shrilly whinnyings of the team of Hell,
Ascending, pierce the glad and songful air,
And all at once their arch'd necks, midnight-maned,
Jet upward thro' the midday blossom. No!
For, see, thy foot has touch'd it; all the space
Of blank earth-baldness clothes itself afresh,

---

17. With the liberation and unification of Italy in 1870, Rome
was freed from foreign and papal control.   18. An echo of
Eclogue I.66.   19. **Mantovano:** Mantuan.

DEMETER AND PERSEPHONE.   5. **God . . . dreams:** Hermes
(Mercury), who conducted the dead to Hades.   6. **Eleusis:**
a town in Attica which had a great temple to Demeter and was
the seat of the Eleusinian mysteries.   9. **Persephone,** gathering
flowers in the Sicilian vale of Enna, let them fall when she was
seized by Pluto.   25. **serpent-wanded power:** Hermes.   28.
Phlegethon: the river of fire in Hades.   39. **Aïdoneus:** Pluto,
who drove his chariot up through the earth to carry off
Persephone.

And breaks into the crocus-purple hour   50
That saw thee vanish.

              Child, when thou wert gone,
I envied human wives, and nested birds,
Yea, the cubb'd lioness; went in search of thee
Thro' many a palace, many a cot, and gave
Thy breast° to ailing infants in the night,
And set the mother waking in amaze
To find her sick one whole; and forth again
Among the wail of midnight winds, and cried,
" Where is my loved one? Wherefore do ye wail? "
And out from all the night an answer shrill'd,   60
" We know not, and we know not why we wail."
I climb'd on all the cliffs of all the seas,
And ask'd the waves that moan about the world,
" Where? do ye make your moaning for my
    child? "
And round from all the world the voices came,
" We know not, and we know not why we moan."
" Where? " and I stared from every eagle-peak,
I thridded° the black heart of all the woods,
I peer'd thro' tomb and cave, and in the storms
Of autumn swept across the city, and heard   70
The murmur of their temples chanting me,
Me, me, the desolate Mother! " Where? " — and
    turn'd,
And fled by many a waste, forlorn of man,
And grieved for man thro' all my grief for thee, —
The jungle rooted in his shatter'd hearth,
The serpent coil'd about his broken shaft,
The scorpion crawling over naked skulls; —
I saw the tiger in the ruin'd fane
Spring from his fallen God, but trace of thee
I saw not; and far on, and, following out   80
A league of labyrinthine darkness, came
On three gray heads° beneath a gleaming rift.
" Where? " and I heard one voice from all the
    three,
" We know not, for we spin the lives of men,
And not of Gods, and know not why we spin!
There is a Fate beyond us." Nothing knew.

    Last as the likeness of a dying man,
Without his knowledge, from him flits to warn
A far-off friendship that he comes no more,°
So he, the God of dreams, who heard my cry,   90
Drew from thyself the likeness of thyself
Without thy knowledge, and thy shadow past
Before me, crying, " The Bright one° in the high-
    est
Is brother of the Dark one° in the lowest,

And Bright and Dark have sworn that I, the child
Of thee, the great Earth-Mother, thee, the Power
That lifts her buried life from gloom to bloom,
Should be for ever and for evermore
The Bride of Darkness."

             So the Shadow wail'd.
Then I, Earth-Goddess, cursed the Gods of Heaven.
I would not mingle with their feasts; to me   101
Their nectar smack'd of hemlock on the lips,
Their rich ambrosia tasted aconite.
The man, that only lives and loves an hour,
Seem'd nobler than their hard Eternities.
My quick tears kill'd the flower, my ravings hush'd
The bird, and lost in utter grief I fail'd
To send my life thro' olive-yard and vine
And golden-grain, my gift to helpless man.
Rain-rotten died the wheat, the barley-spears   110
Were hollow-husk'd, the leaf fell, and the Sun,
Pale at my grief, drew down before his time
Sickening, and Ætna kept her winter snow.

    Then He,° the brother of this Darkness, He
Who still is highest, glancing from his height
On earth a fruitless fallow, when he miss'd
The wonted steam of sacrifice, the praise
And prayer of men, decreed that thou shouldst
    dwell
For nine white moons of each whole year with me,
Three dark ones in the shadow with thy King.   120

    Once more the reaper in the gleam of dawn
Will see me by the landmark far away,
Blessing his field, or seated in the dusk
Of even, by the lonely threshing-floor,
Rejoicing in the harvest and the grange.

    Yet I, Earth-Goddess, am but ill-content
With them who still are highest. Those gray heads,
What meant they by their " Fate beyond the Fates "
But younger kindlier Gods to bear us down,
As we bore down the Gods before us?° Gods,   130
To quench, not hurl the thunderbolt, to stay,
Not spread the plague, the famine; Gods indeed,
To send the noon into the night and break
The sunless halls of Hades into Heaven?
Till thy dark lord accept and love the Sun,
And all the Shadow die into the Light,
When thou shalt dwell the whole bright year with
    me,
And souls of men, who grew beyond their race,
And made themselves as Gods against the fear
Of Death and Hell; and thou that hast from men,
As Queen of Death, that worship which is Fear,
Henceforth, as having risen from out the dead, 142

---

55. Thy breast: Demeter's breast, which had nursed Persephone
in her infancy.   **68. thridded:** threaded.   **82. three ... heads:**
the Fates.   **87–89.** The idea may come from Lucretius,
De Rerum Natura, IV.34–37, 760–61.   **93. Bright one:** Zeus.
94. Dark one: Pluto.

114. He: Zeus.   **129–30.** Cf. Aeschylus, *Prometheus Bound*,
907 ff.; Keats, *Hyperion*, II.188 ff.

Shalt ever send thy life along with mine
From buried grain thro' springing blade, and bless
Their garner'd autumn also, reap with me,
Earth-Mother, in the harvest hymns of Earth
The worship which is Love, and see no more
The Stone, the Wheel,° the dimly-glimmering
    lawns
Of that Elysium, all the hatefui fires
Of torment, and the shadowy warrior glide   150
Along the silent field of Asphodel.°

1889   *1887*

CROSSING THE BAR

   The poem was written and published in 1889, in Tennyson's eighty-first year; he said that it came to him in a moment. A few days before his death he expressed the wish that it should be printed at the end of all editions of his poems (*Memoir,* II, 366–67). However one regards the poem, which has been both admired and detested, it may be thought that Tennyson faces death with a dignity and a sense of mystery that are somewhat lacking in Browning's equally characteristic "Prospice" and "Epilogue."

148. The . . . Wheel: traditional punishments in Hades: the stone forever rolled by Sisyphus, the wheel of Ixion. **150–51.** Cf. the ghost of Achilles, *Odyssey,* XI.538–39, and the note on "The Lotos-Eaters," 125.

Sunset and evening star,
   And one clear call for me!
And may there be no moaning of the bar,
   When I put out to sea,

But such a tide as moving seems asleep,
   Too full for sound and foam,
When that° which drew from out the boundless
   deep
Turns again home.

Twilight and evening bell,
   And after that the dark!   10
And may there be no sadness of farewell,
   When I embark;

For tho' from out our bourne of Time and Place
   The flood may bear me far,
I hope to see my Pilot face to face°
   When I have crost the bar.

1889   *1889*

CROSSING THE BAR.   **7–8. that:** the soul (cf. *In Memoriam*, Epilogue, 123–24). **15.** It has been objected that a pilot would be seen while navigating, and would be dropped when the ship left harbor. Tennyson's image is governed by the idea of the Pilot as "That Divine and Unseen Who is always guiding us" (*Memoir,* II, 367).

Robert Browning

1812–1889

The mental picture that most of us have of famous men in history is a static rather than a developing one. The usual image of Robert Browning in the popular mind is an apt illustration of this generality. The poet is most often remembered as he was at the height of his fame during the last two decades of his life, that is, from 1868 to 1889. This is to see him as a robust, hearty, elderly man, a great diner-out and visitor in fashionable homes, a constant attender at concerts and art exhibitions, honored by both of the great English universities, and also beloved and cared for by wealthy ladies, British as well as American. He was immensely successful, it seemed, in his public and his private life. Societies of earnest people, led by the London Browning Society, had sprung up in England and America to study the writings of the sage and prophet of the age. So busy was he, and so much a man of the social world, that the legend rose, abetted by his friend Henry James the American novelist, that the familiar man people saw was not the author of the rich body of poetry which everyone knew, but that Browning kept a "ghost" to write his verse.

Of course, there was nothing to the legend. Nor was this the Browning who had struggled hard, and for years desperately, from the beginning of his literary career in 1833 almost until he published *The Ring and the Book* in 1868–69, to make his voice as a poet heard by a deaf world. The British public had grossly and unfairly neglected him during his best days as a poet, and now honored and rewarded him, perhaps extravagantly. With his keen sense of irony,

the words of his fellow poet, Matthew Arnold, in a poem that was probably written as an answer to his own "Rabbi Ben Ezra," must have come home to him. In "Growing Old" Arnold remarks how bitter it is "To hear the world applaud the hollow ghost / Which blamed the living man." But few people who saw the stocky, bearded, brisk, and cheerful Browning of the 1870's and 1880's thought of him as "ghostly" in any sense. He was all too palpably there in the flesh.

Under the impact of the Industrial Revolution and the growth of empire, the London of the late nineteenth century was a very different place from what it was in Browning's youth. The suburb, Camberwell, where the poet was born on May 7, 1812, was across the Thames and south of the city. It is now a mass of brick buildings, alleys, and noisy streets. But when Browning was a boy, it was a green and pleasant place, and he remembered it all his life with nostalgia.

The Browning family was in modest circumstances. The poet's father, Robert Browning, Sr., was a clerk in the Bank of England on a small salary. In his youth he had been sent out to the family plantation in the West Indies, but when he revolted from the slavery and cruelty there and returned to England, his father, the first Robert Browning about whom we know much, found him a minor place in the Bank, which he held until his retirement in 1852. The poet's father was an amiable, mild, self-effacing person, more of a scholar than a man of business. In his youth he had hoped to be an artist, and all his life he drew sketches and illustrations to amuse his children and friends. His chief delight was in collecting odd and rare books, and much of his salary must have gone into that pleasure. In his library of 6000 volumes, made up of Greek, Latin, and recondite English books, the poet got most of his education.

Browning's mother, Sarah Anna Wiedemann, was of German and Scotch descent, and of a rigid and somewhat unimaginative mind and temperament. It was she who controlled the destinies of the family and made all decisions. Apart from her family her interest in life was almost wholly religious. She was an ardent member of the Congregational chapel, and in time brought all her family to worship there. Beyond that we know little of her, except that she had some gift in music, spent a good deal of time in her rose garden, and that her son and her daughter, Sarianna, who much resembled her, were passionately devoted to her all their lives. Her character and temperament influenced the poet far more than her husband's did.

Here, then, in Camberwell and later at New Cross, further to the southeast from London, young Browning was reared. He was a precocious schoolboy, and was often unruly and impatient. It is recorded that at his mother's chapel the preacher, George Clayton, publicly reproved " for restlessness and inattention Master Robert Browning." He rebelled from school, as he was later to rebel from London University, and was mainly taught by his father and a series of tutors and masters in Greek, Latin, French, music, and Italian. The odd learning for which he became famous was chiefly acquired at home by omnivorous reading. For his pleasure, he roamed the fields and woods nearby, rode horseback in the country lanes, or walked to the Dulwich Gallery to see its notable pictures. He grew up to be a passionate, brilliant, undisciplined boy with an inordinate estimate of his own powers, which were yet very great.

Such was the environment of this richly endowed young man. As he grew older his problem was how to break out of the physical and intellectual suburb into the great world of London, how to employ his extraordinary powers to become a significant and recognized person, how to escape from the constricting — and to him almost suffocating — ideas of the middle-class chapel-going and business world in which he found himself. His home was an oasis in a desert of materialism and smug provincialism. Early Victorian middle-class society had two main preoccupations — the daily task of making a living in an aggressive and expanding city, and the illiberal and narrow piety of the Dissenting chapel on Sunday. Very few of the young men of Camberwell and New Cross had the advantages of the great public schools like Arnold's Rugby, and even fewer went on to Oxford and Cambridge. For the most part, they were excluded by their poverty and by their limited abilities and imaginations from ever attaining a fuller and freer life. But for a young man of Browning's ambition, power, and taste, escape to the larger world was as necessary as breathing. For three quarters of his life he struggled in various ways to establish himself among his peers in this larger world — like his own *dramatis persona* Paracelsus he aspired and was defeated, aspired again and was baffled, and aspired again to achieve success at last.

One of the victories of Browning's adolescence was his triumph in persuading his family that he should become a poet. The Brownings' financial resources were limited, and the reasonable expectancy was that their son at manhood would enter some trade or profession by which he could support himself. Instead, until his marriage at thirty-four, his family supported him, and in addition paid for the publication of most of his poetry, which brought practically no financial return. He had to borrow money for his wedding journey to Italy, and then for many years he and his wife were mainly dependent upon her income. The world has reason to be grateful to him for this conduct, which at the time must have seemed extraordinarily selfish and stubborn.

When Browning was fourteen years old the first great avenue of escape into the intellectual world seemed to open before him. This was his discovery of Shelley, a poet little appreciated in 1826. From that poet's *Miscellaneous Poems* Browning went on to devour all of Shelley's works he could come by, including *Queen Mab,* and a new world was revealed to him. He became a disciple, and like his master a vegetarian in diet, an extreme liberal in politics, and an atheist in religion. For the better part of six years he preached Shelley, grinning with devilish delight when he upset the orthodox faith of a young lady of his affections or discomfited his friends. The young lady, Sarah Flower, soon recovered her faith sufficiently to write the famous hymn, " Nearer My God to Thee."

But there were strong and subtle forces working against Browning's rebellion. Of the pain that the wildness of the young man's opinions, especially his atheism, brought to his matter-of-fact and pious mother we have no record. But it must have been great. It is clear that Browning's intense affection for her gradually won him back from his atheism, and in his first poem *Pauline*, published in 1833, the young poet professes to believe in " God and truth " rather than Shelley. He disavows Shelley's doctrine as he was later in life to disavow Shelley himself. Mrs. Browning had won, not by the employment of reason, but by the tender ties of love, and her son's intellectual independence in religious inquiry was permanently impaired. He never managed to free himself entirely from the narrow and emotional bases of his mother's religion.

As he grew older, other avenues of possible escape opened before him. The chief one was literary. Shelley's religious opinions were repudiated, but his poetry and poetic method were still compelling. From 1833, when *Pauline* was published, until 1840, when *Sordello* appeared, Browning tried strenuously to make his voice heard in the literary world of London through the long " confessional " poem, recounting his deepest aspirations and defeats in the intensely personal manner of Shelley. But *Pauline* sold no copies and was hardly noticed by the reviewers, and survived only to shame its author. *Paracelsus* (1835) enjoyed a brief success and took Browning for a little while into the company of the great artistic and literary world of London. The society into which Browning came was brilliant: it included Macready, the greatest tragic actor of the day; John Forster, the influential literary critic; Wordsworth, who was in a few years to become poet laureate; and the painter Maclise, the friend of Dickens. At a dinner in 1836 Wordsworth himself proposed a toast to Browning and welcomed him to the company of the poets of England. But the colossal failure of *Sordello*, upon which he had spent seven years of hard labor, was a serious blow to Browning's reputation in literary London, and one from which he recovered only slowly.

In the meanwhile he made several attempts at writing drama for the stage; this lasted from 1837, when *Strafford* was produced, until his marriage in 1846. Upon this effort Browning broke his heart and his head, but his peculiar analytical talents were not suited to the acting stage, and none of his eight plays achieved success upon the boards. The plays are often full of magnificent poetry and superb analysis of character and motive, but are frequently lacking in external action and are recondite to the point of obscurity. In his attempts to become an accepted playwright Browning quarreled with Macready the tragedian and Forster the critic, and once again was baffled.

Though admired by a few and defended by his friends, Browning was at thirty-two a social figure in a limited circle, and a poet read by a small intellectual coterie. He was hardly prepared for the change in his way of life that was soon to come to him. In 1844 he went off to Italy to refresh his jaded spirit. Upon his return to England toward the end of the year, he found waiting for him two volumes of poems by Elizabeth Barrett. These poems, mainly lays, ballads, and romances, had been widely praised and had won for Miss Barrett the position of being, after Tennyson and Wordsworth, the foremost poet of the age. Browning read the poems with a rising excitement, and on January 10, 1845, wrote the lady: " I love your poems, dear Miss Barrett, and I love you too." But it was not until May of that year that Browning was permitted to call. He found Miss Barrett in her invalid's darkened room, a frail, small lady chained by weakness to her couch, her dark, heavy hair framing her sensitive and intelligent face. She saw few people beyond her family and wrote her poetry from her reading and her vivid imagination. She was then thirty-eight years old and had been an invalid for ten years. The passionate and jealous love which her father had for her was an even greater chain than her illness. The visits of Browning, or indeed of any man, were not welcomed by Mr. Barrett, and Browning had to come when Mr. Barrett was not at home. On Browning's side it was a case of love at first sight, or even before he had seen Miss Barrett. He proposed marriage after his first visit to her. Of course it was impossible, but his visits became more frequent, letters flew between them, and before a year was out an understanding had been reached. Miss Barrett began secretly to write her famous sonnet sequence, *Sonnets from the Portuguese.* Her health improved almost miraculously. Her father, perhaps sensing that he was losing control over his daughter's affections and actions, became more tyrannous than ever. And thus it came about that in September, 1846, Browning and Miss Barrett were married secretly and a week later fled to Italy.

The Browning who entered Miss Barrett's room in 1845 was assuredly not the confident, aggressive character we see in the modern play, *The Barretts of Wimpole Street.* Rather, while hopeful still that one day his genius would be recognized, he was humbled by his failure to obtain readers, and needed to have his confidence in himself restored by the admiration of a successful poet. In this, Miss Barrett succeeded and continued to succeed for a while after they were married and lived in Italy. But in those happy years of marriage it was Mrs. Browning that the visitors from America and England came to see. She was the poet and Browning only the husband — a man of talent, to be sure, extremely well informed about many things, a good man of business and entertaining company, a man one might rely upon. He could be seen in the streets of Florence with an old dog at his heels, poking into art shops or merely watching the bustling life of the city.

In 1850 Browning's long poem, "Christmas Eve and Easter Day," sold only 200 copies. This was disheartening, but after two years he resolved to try his fortune again. In the 1840's a few of his shorter poems, such as "The Bishop Orders His Tomb" and "My Last Duchess," had been well received; Walter Savage Landor, the revered veteran among the poets, had praised him; and he now resolved to try to make his voice heard with two volumes of short poems, dramatic monologues, and lyrics, dealing in part with art and music. The result is the two volumes of *Men and Women* (1855), one of the great achievements of English literature. But his great hopes were soon dashed when the reviewers found the poems obscure; John Ruskin, who by his great books on painting, architecture, and literature had become the arbiter of taste, disapproved; and the public showed little interest. It was a wounded and resentful Browning who returned from a visit to London to life in Italy. There he resumed his

place, overshadowed by his wife and allowed by that passionate and strong-minded lady to have little voice in the bringing up of their child. He was, rather, the stable element in the household, tempering as best he could the ardently held ideas of his wife upon public and private affairs. The Brownings were now financially in good condition through the immense sales of Mrs. Browning's *Aurora Leigh* (1856) and the beneficence of John Kenyon, a relative of Mrs. Browning's and a patron of poetry, who left them £11,000.

In 1861 Mrs. Browning died, and the grief-stricken husband and his thirteen-year-old son returned to London to make their home. There was much to be done. For the first time Browning had to assume in a real sense the role of parent and to make decisions. A home had to be established. An authoritative final edition of his wife's poetry had to be prepared. And yet, even in these dark hours of loneliness and grief, his own fortunes began to take a better turn. A selection of his poems prepared by friends enjoyed a considerable success in 1863, and his volume of new poems, *Dramatis Personae* (1864), achieved a second edition. News also came from America of the increasing popularity of his works. Greatly heartened, he resolved to produce a monumental work which would establish him once and forever among the great poets of England.

In 1864 he was fifty-two years old, and he had finally made an impression upon the public mind, mainly by his amazing short poems, lyrics, and dramatic monologues. But he wished to be remembered by an altogether greater achievement. He now aspired to write a poem of epic length in which he would employ all his peculiar techniques and talents — his mastery of the dramatic monologue in blank verse, his forte in reinterpreting fact, his defense of innocent and misunderstood virtue, his analysis of motive and character, the mobility and range of his expression. Above all he wished to give the public his reading of life in all its variety and scope. His great work was *The Ring and the Book,* a poem upon an obscure Roman murder case of the seventeenth century, in twelve dramatic monologues, amounting to more than 21,000 lines. It had taken four years of constant labor, and was published in four volumes in 1868–69.

The effect upon the reading public was impressive. Browning's reputation had been growing quietly at the universities among the younger men, and now his poem was hailed as "the greatest spiritual treasure since Shakespeare," and he was accepted almost everywhere as the peer of the laureate, Alfred Tennyson. Even though many readers objected to the nature of his subject, the inordinate length of the poem, and the poet's mannerisms, he was henceforth established by his contemporaries among the great poets of English literature. It was a somewhat superficial view of his reading of life that made an appeal to his fellow Victorians; it has remained for our own day to discover the full subtlety and depth of Browning's art.

In the two decades of life that remained to him he wrote an immense amount that added little to his fame, and his poetry grew more craggy and wayward as he allowed himself to indulge more and more in his peculiarities of style and subject. In his pride of accomplishment he bore prosperity less well than he had adversity. But the goal of a lifetime had been achieved; however imperfectly he was understood, the public was listening to his voice. Thus he had good reason to feel, in spite of life's ironies and disappointments — such as the failure of his son to achieve anything worthy of note — that for the valiant and enduring man old age was "the last of life, for which the first was made."

II

It has been said that in literature as in life sympathy often skips a generation. A reaction is especially likely to follow when a group of strong authors has captured the minds and imaginations of its generation almost completely. This was the case with the great figures of Victorian literature. During the first four decades of the twentieth century the critics, led by T. S. Eliot, were scornful of the Victorian poets, but now there are clear evidences of a reviving interest in them and a willingness once again to rank the greatest of them with their peers of older times in the main tradition of English literature. Browning has weathered the reaction, and now may be spoken of in the same breath with Chaucer, Spenser, Shakespeare, Donne, Milton, Dryden, Wordsworth, and Keats.

There had been, however, no very violent reaction on the part of the Victorian poets from their Romantic predecessors. There was, indeed, change, but also continuity. Tennyson carried on in the manner of Keats, and Arnold championed and followed Wordsworth. Browning, as we have seen, modeled his first long poems upon the practice of Shelley, and his plays, written early in his career, owe a great debt to the Shakespeare of the Romantic poets and critics, the Shakespeare of Coleridge, Lamb, Hazlitt, De Quincey, and Byron. This was the Shakespeare of the study rather than the writer of successful plays for the stage, the infallible Shakespeare whose management of the psychology of character and dramatic action was to be explained rather than questioned, the Shakespeare of the lofty and resounding blank verse.

Browning, like most great poets who deal with character and important moral issues, matured slowly, and the models provided for him by Shelley and Shakespeare were not the right ones for him. He had to work his way through the long, personal "confessional" poem of the Romantic tradition in *Pauline, Paracelsus,* and *Sordello* in order to find out what he could and could not do. From the process he learned a great deal about psychology, and he learned to watch and analyze his emotions and thoughts as they rose to the surface of his consciousness. In his career as a playwright also, he learned what he could not do, namely, endow and project a character in action on the stage with life and expression independent of its author. He was too much an analyst of motive to be a great playwright, but from his struggle to become one he learned such things as form, situation, order, and control. In the long partly autobiographical poems, and even more in the plays, there is a great deal of psychological action in the minds of the speakers, but Browning was not able to translate the feelings and thoughts of his characters into the external action and language required for success on the stage and for complete comprehension by readers. He made considerable progress in the swift dramatic episodes of *Pippa Passes* (1841). But only gradually did he find the right ground for himself, the soliloquy of a character — not himself — who, usually in a moment of crisis, speaks out his deepest thoughts and feelings, and is generally not conscious of how profoundly he is disclosing his true nature. This is, of course, the dramatic monologue.

In many aspects of poetry Browning was an innovator, but never more happily than in his development of the dramatic monologue. He can hardly be called the inventor of this form. Chaucer had used it, and so had Shakespeare in the monologues of *Hamlet*. And so had Tennyson, among Browning's contemporaries. But it was Browning who developed the dramatic monologue so completely, so subtly, and so penetratingly that he gave it new life and dimensions. It is most fitting that the form should be attached to his name. In it he has given English literature such great and memorable figures as the Duke in "My Last Duchess," the Bishop who orders his tomb, Lippi and Andrea, Pompilia, Caponsacchi, Guido, and the Pope, to name only a few from a great host. The dramatic monologue became a habit of Browning's thinking, and his natural mode of expression was at last to break the clear white light of his thought and feeling into its prismatic hues through the medium of many a borrowed ego.

The dramatic monologue is at its best when the poet employs all its elements: a speaker; his audience; interplay between them; dramatic occasion and present action; and, above all, revelation of character.

It must not be imagined that Browning arrived at perfection in the form at once and easily, or having reached that perfection was always able to sustain it. Many rival interests make claims against the pure delineation of personality that is the ideal of the monologue. For example, in "Porphyria's Lover" Browning is too much interested in the strange event, and the rhymed verse is not the best vehicle; in "My Last Duchess," which is nearly perfect, the character of the Duke looks like an afterthought, as if Browning's interest began with the plight of the young duchess, and the verse, though muted, is still rhymed. Even in "The Bishop Orders His Tomb," where blank verse is at last arrived at as the right verse form, the poet may be suspected of being more concerned with illustrating the corruption of Renaissance clergy than he is with the Bishop himself. The danger of caricature is not escaped in the speaker of the "Soliloquy of the Spanish Cloister" and in the Italian Person of Quality in "Up at a Villa." There is frequently, also, the intrusion of doctrine or

purpose — Browning's doctrine — into the utterances of his characters; his personality even in his full maturity is sometimes stronger than his art, and he is unable often to achieve that complete subjugation of his own person and opinions which so distinguishes Shakespeare. Yet when all is said, Browning is one of the great creators of character and types in our literature. His method of subtle analysis, penetrating even to the secret recesses of the heart, has had a palpable and lasting effect upon later English and American literature.

Closely connected with this achievement was another. Because he was the close observer and the conscientious recorder of life, Browning achieved an objectivity in his treatment of men and women which had not been characteristic of the Romantic poets, or of English poetry since the eighteenth century, with the exception of the Byron of "Beppo" and *Don Juan*. The predilection toward objectivity led Browning to be realistic in his description of life, in the characters he created, and in the language he employed — a language that sometimes shocked his fellow Victorians into thinking him vulgar. He dealt daringly with subjects that offended the proprieties of his time, and also with socially unapproved characters. He reintroduced new, racy, common words into the prevailing bardic utterances of the age of Tennyson. He put into verse such things as corsetstrings and bottles of ether and aching corns. It was sarcastically remarked that his finest lines were those from "Up at a Villa":

Bang-whang-whang goes the drum, *tootle-te-tootle*
   the fife;
No keeping one's haunches still; it's the greatest
   pleasure in life.

The pure and simple language of everyday life which Wordsworth had advocated in his Preface to the *Lyrical Ballads* (see pp. 560–64, above) and had sometimes employed was hardly what Wordsworth thought it was. Coleridge observed that Wordsworth had purified that language even when it was most simple, and Wordsworth himself found it inadequate to express the ideas of "Tintern Abbey" and the "Ode on Intimations of Immortality." Tennyson, following Wordsworth at a distance, had a natural richness and deliberateness in his use of language that led him inevitably to the grand style, and by the time he was deeply engaged upon his *Idylls of the King,* dealing with lofty subjects and noble personages, the formal, dignified language of the bard was fastened upon him and upon nineteenth-century poetry. Far from being vulgar, Browning's habit of familiar language is the very breath of life to modern verse, and he deserves the credit for liberating poetry from the crushing formality that had been fastened upon it.

His immense gusto for life and his determination to find out the deepest motives that moved men led him to pay close attention to the criminal and sensational event, and ultimately to base his masterpiece upon a sordid murder story. In the process of allowing each character to justify himself he created such a gallery of rogues as had not been seen in English literature since the days of the first Elizabeth — notable among them being the Duke of "My Last Duchess," the Bishop who orders his tomb, Sludge, Blougram, Guido Franceschini, Napoleon III, and the elderly man of *The Inn Album.* His practice, here too, broadened the range of modern poetry, and placed him in the line of Chaucer, Shakespeare, and the great novelists, such as Fielding and Dickens.

Using the same penetrating powers, but as if in contrast, Browning devoted a very large proportion of his poetry to the subject of love between men and women. Indeed, not since John Donne, a poet almost idolized by Browning, had the whole anatomy of love been so scrutinized. Donne taught Browning many things — the use of strong vivid language, the value of beginning a poem abruptly to arouse the reader's interest, and the delight in surprise and paradox. But chiefly, perhaps, Donne delighted Browning by his candid and fearless treatment of passion between men and women.

Browning's lovers are a varied lot: there is the lover of Porphyria with his mad logic; the insanely jealous woman of "The Laboratory"; the triumphantly successful and chivalric Count Gismond; and the dying but happy lover of "Confessions," who remembers

> How sad and bad and mad it was —
> But then, how it was sweet!

There are numbers of rejected lovers who behave with incredible nobility. Examples may be seen in "The Last Ride Together" and "Serenade at the Villa." There are lovers who let the good minute pass without acting upon it, such as the man and woman of "Youth and Art" and "The Statue and the Bust"; and there are others, like the speakers in "Cristina" and "Evelyn Hope," who, having failed in this existence, expect to catch up with their loves in some epoch future life.

Perhaps more interesting than these unsuccessful lovers are the subtle relationships between men and women in love. The situations here are often imagined as between husband and wife, and some of them are personal to Browning and Mrs. Browning rather than objective and "dramatic." The form of these poems also is more often lyrical than dramatic. Such is the record of the perfect fusion of souls in "By the Fireside":

> A moment after, and hands unseen
>   Were hanging the night around us fast;
> But we knew that a bar was broken between
>   Life and life; we were mixed at last
> In spite of the mortal screen.

But these moments are rare, and are recorded only when John Donne writes "The Ecstasy" or Browning this poem or "One Word More." There is a fainter recollection of a similar experience when he looks back in memory at the end of his life to "What came once when a woman leant / To feel for my brow where her kiss might fall."

More often by far the fusion of souls is not accomplished, as in "Two in the Campagna"; the good minute goes, and we are left with

> Infinite passion, and the pain
>   Of finite hearts that yearn.

These are but two aspects of Browning's treatment of the nature of love; elsewhere we find love eager and strenuous or satiated and dull, illicit or saintly, reminiscent and tender, rueful at lost opportunity, or triumphant over the ruins of time as it is in the small masterpiece, "Love among the Ruins." But everywhere it is a matter of grave moment and is seriously dealt with. It is not too much to say that his hopes for mankind were staked on the gospel of love between men and women.

In the twentieth century Browning has been praised most for his development of the dramatic monologue, his analysis of the passion of love, and for his refreshing diction. He has suffered most criticism where he attempted to erect a formal system of thought. In their troubled age the Victorians were hot for certainties in religious and philosophical matters and made their great poets assume the mantles of seers and sages. It was not enough to create beauty or depict men and women or illuminate the subtle complexities of secular life. The poet, if he aspired to be a nation's heritage, had to be the wise leader of the people, bearing a message from heaven. Both Tennyson and Browning were coerced by the climate of their times into offering answers to ultimate questions — the nature of God, the purpose of the universe and man's destiny in it, good and evil. The answers to these questions had to be given to a society which was shaken by momentous changes — the Industrial Revolution, the crumbling of the literal interpretation of the Scriptures under the impact of the Higher Criticism,[1] the advances in the sciences of astronomy and geology, and biological evolution. Both Tennyson and Browning gave answers that seemed satisfactory to many people in the Victorian period, but the solutions of these eternal problems made by one age seldom satisfy a later time.

This is especially true in Browning's case because he was not a philosopher and had little faith in man's intellect. After his brief youthful rebellion from his mother's religious beliefs when he was under the influence of Shelley, he fell back upon a profoundly felt intuition that love, divine and human, is the motive force of the world. The central fact of history, he felt, was that God so loved mankind that He sent his Son in the flesh to demonstrate that love. This theme is nobly treated in such poems as " Saul," " Cleon," and the Pope's soliloquy in *The Ring and the Book*. His faith, in this respect, was the orthodox Christian one, and can hardly be attacked. But upon it Browning erected a metaphysical system that argued that God's intelligence and strength were evident in the physical world around us. This superstructure to his cen-

tral faith, and his further " proofs " of immortality, were much more vulnerable to the attack of reason. As the years advanced Browning spent great resourcefulness and ingenuity in defending, with less and less success, the intellectualized system he had constructed, and he finally had to retreat into a nescience that almost admitted defeat and intellectual despair. He was at his best in his thought and melody when he forgot his formal message to his age and wrote meditatively of his deeper intuitions, as in " Abt Vogler," where he falls back upon the timeless idealism of man:

> On the earth the broken arcs; in the heaven,
>   a perfect round.

Darwin's conception of evolution came too late in Browning's life for him to grasp it. He thought he was " Darwinized," and was accustomed to point as proof to his " Caliban " and to passages in " Paracelsus " that he had written twenty-five years before *The Origin of Species* appeared in 1859. His conception of evolution was not, however, a scientific one, and he was adamant against any theory of the process of life which would exclude belief in a cause exterior to matter and acting upon it. Browning's conception was rather an extension of the older doctrines of progress and perfectibility which he had learned in his youth from Shelley. The decay of the doctrine of inevitable progress and the continuous advance of scientific knowledge have dated Browning's noble but patchwork philosophy. Later generations have found his position untenable.

Perhaps one of Browning's greatest assets as a poet is his cheerful and tonic view of life. His was not the hard-won and determined cheerfulness of Wordsworth, but rather the intuitive expression of a healthy, active, and courageous man. It is sometimes too strenuous and aggressive for a generation less certain of its part and of its future. We " greet the unseen with a cheer " far less heartily than he. But we can still appreciate and profit from his poetic exemplars of action, endurance, and courage, which have supported many men in the hour of need.

Another aspect of the poet's cheerfulness was his strong faith that " if virtue feeble were, Heaven itself would stoop to her," to use the words of another idealist. Early in his career Browning placed before him on his desk a pic-

---

[1] The Higher Criticism was a movement which started in Germany among scholars of the Bible and swept into England toward the middle of the nineteenth century. It challenged at many points the idea that the Bible was a literal transcription of the word of God, and tended to reduce the Old Testament merely to a literary document of the ancient Hebrews. It also challenged the authenticity of parts of the New Testament. George Eliot's translation of Strauss's *Leben Jesu* in 1846 introduced the movement to the public.

ture of Caravaggio's "Andromeda," "the perfect picture" as he called it, showing Andromeda being rescued from the sea beast by Perseus, and it became the lifelong symbol of his faith. He was sure that in the nick of time some god would come "in thunder from the stars" to rescue the imperiled maiden. The legend of Andromeda and its Christian cognate, the legend of St. George, appears in one form or another thirty times in *The Ring and the Book,* and how each speaker deals with the legend is a touchstone of his character. This chivalric idea not only informed a great many of Browning's poems, but it directed his life as well, as we may see in his elopement and marriage.

When Browning was at the peak of his powers, he elaborated twice in notable poems his conception of the function of art. Succinctly stated, the function of the artist was to interpret this earthly show of men and women under the eye of God, and with reference always to God. The creation of men and women was God's province; the poet's task was one of observation, interpretation, imitation in his faint degree, and then communication, both to God and man.

In 1851 Browning had been rereading Shelley and Shakespeare for the purpose of writing an introductory essay to a volume of Shelley's letters. The letters proved to be spurious, and the volume was withdrawn, but Shelley's notion that poets were "the unacknowledged legislators of mankind" combined with a sentence from *King Lear,* "We'll take upon 's the mystery of things / As if we were God's spies," to conjure up in Browning's mind an image of a poet. The result was the compact and sharply drawn monologue, "How It Strikes a Contemporary." The speaker, or "contemporary," is a sprucely dressed young man in the streets of Valladolid, and what "strikes" him is the figure of a poet (a good deal like Browning) who goes about observing everything, but never speaking, and who becomes the legend of the town. The heart of the matter is caught in these lines, spoken by the young man:

We merely kept a governor for form,
While this man walked about and took account
Of all thought, said and acted, then went
    home,

And wrote it fully to our Lord the King
Who has an itch to know things, he knows why,
And reads them in his bedroom of a night.

A more explicit statement of the function of the artist appears in "Fra Lippo Lippi," one of Browning's most successful dramatic monologues. Lippi, it will be remembered, with his irrepressible gaiety and his incorruptible innocence, has just escaped from the house of his patron because it is carnival time and he has not been able to resist the excitement of the streets. As the monologue begins he has been captured by the constables as a lawbreaker. Sitting upon the curb at the corner, he pours out the story of his life and his conception of his function as an artist. The world to him is no abstraction but the contemporary things and people he sees all about him. He has thrown over the traditional formalized art of the Church and instinctively reproduces as faithfully as he can the people and scenes around him. In so doing he teaches men to see, and he returns thanks and praise to God for the privilege of living.

However, you're my man, you've seen the world
— The beauty and the wonder and the power,
The shapes of things, their colors, lights and shades,
Changes, surprises — and God made it all!
— For what? Do you feel thankful, aye or no,
For this fair town's face, yonder river's line,
The mountain round it and the sky above,
Much more the figures of man, woman, child,
These are the frame to? What's it all about?
To be passed over, despised? or dwelt upon,
Wondered at? oh, this last of course! — you say.
But why not do as well as say — paint these
Just as they are, careless what comes of it?
God's works — paint any one, and count it crime
To let a truth slip. Don't object, "His works
Are here already; nature is complete:
Suppose you reproduce her — (which you can't)
There's no advantage! you must beat her, then."
For, don't you mark? we're made so that we love
First when we see them painted, things we have
    passed
Perhaps a hundred times nor cared to see;
And so they are better, painted — better to us,
Which is the same thing. Art was given for that;
God uses us to help each other so,
Lending our minds out. Have you noticed, now,
Your cullion's hanging face? A bit of chalk,
And trust me but you should, though! How much
    more,

If I drew higher things with the same truth!
That were to take the Prior's pulpit-place,
Interpret God to all of you! Oh, oh,
It makes me mad to see what men shall do
And we in our graves! This world's no blot for us,
Nor blank; it means intensely, and means good:
To find its meaning is my meat and drink.

Like Lippi, Browning has broken away from the formal and traditional ideas of the art of his time and prefers to depict the contemporary life around him in all its familiar realism. The artist cannot reproduce the scene he sees in all its beauty and completeness, but it is his peculiar gift to call our attention to things we have missed, to interpret them for us, and thus to communicate God's purpose and benevolence to us. Browning thought of himself as a pioneer in art, and foresaw a time when the artist would be free of restricting conventions. The artist's responsibility is primarily to God, and only secondarily to his fellow men and society.

These are some of the major strands in the warp and woof of Browning's poetry. He wrote with great insight upon timeless themes — life and duty, the personalities of men and women and their dilemmas and solutions. He appreciated and honored bold and noble character and action. He dealt in an intensely original manner with all kinds of human relationships, and endowed us with a poetry of great richness and variety. He left us a great store of delight, and taught us to see many familiar things that we had failed to notice. At his best, Browning deserved the generous praise which (putting Shakespeare out of the question) Landor accorded him in 1846:

Since Chaucer was alive and hale
No man has walked along our road with step
So active, so inquiring eye, and tongue
So varied in discourse.

III

It is becoming increasingly apparent to the critics of our own century that Browning was a far more skillful and conscious artist in poetry than his own age was inclined to think him. He was laughing at his critics when he made one of his characters say of a versifier:

That bard's a Browning, he neglects the form
But, ah, the sense, ye gods, the weighty sense!

It will be useful, therefore, to point out a few of Browning's special peculiarities in imagery, patterns of thought, meter, diction, and grammar — matters that come under the general heading of style.

The images that Browning uses in his poetry are innumerable and varied. We may cite a few of the most frequent and most characteristic. From the beginning of his career to the end the symbol for his central faith and hope is the Andromeda–St. George legend already commented upon; it so penetrates Browning's thought and feeling that it appears a hundred times in his poetry. The figure that is central to Browning's love poetry, the mortal screen that the lovers are always striving to break through, has also been mentioned above. Certain other characteristic images are always at hand. Whenever Mrs. Browning appears in his verse the figure is likely to be of the heavens — a star in "My Star," but more often the moon with its "Silent silver lights and darks undreamed of." Browning is also fond of contrasting light and dark, or heaven and hell, or heaven and the dim twilight of our earth, and these shades are used to apply to persons as well as situations. A favorite figure, akin to the spectrum of light to dark, expresses the Platonic notion of the imperfection of earth and the perfection of heaven in terms of the arc of the rainbow, broken and incomplete here, but perfect there.

Whenever Browning is writing heroic poetry, dramatic or personal, he is apt to imagine the act of heroism as a journey taken over rough land and with many difficulties, usually by a single and lonely person. There is generally, also, the atmosphere of a military exploit. In "The Lost Leader" the march is made by a company of faithful men. Childe Roland must endure alone the quest through the terrible country and the more terrifying psychological hazards until he comes to the dark tower and the tragic triumph that awaits him there. In "Prospice" the poet himself takes the imaginary journey up the steep pass of death, like his "peers / The heroes of old." In the Epilogue to his last volume of poems, *Asolando,* he looks back on his life and thinks of himself as one who "marched breast forward."

When we turn to Browning's meters we find that the prevailing impulse in him is to be free, to be natural and expressive, to be inventive in meeting the necessities of the moment. He found that the dramatic monologue fares best in blank verse, but there is no uniform pattern to his blank verse. It adapts itself to the speaker; its great characteristics are its variety and its resilience.

In his lyric measures Browning is equally inventive, and seems to fling down his verse as the opportunity occurs, often with what looks like amazingly good luck. It can flow softly and smoothly when he pleases, as he does in " In a Gondola " or in the running long lines of " A Toccata of Galuppi's," or in the alternating long and short lines of " Love among the Ruins,"

> Where the quiet-colored end of evening smiles
> Miles and miles. . . .

Or he can manage well the undulating harmonies of the long lines of " Saul " or the speculative melody of " Abt Vogler," as the improviser meditates over his music. But softness and sweetness are not usually Browning's aims. He likes on occasion to employ short abrupt measures, often scornful and informal, as in " Youth and Art ":

> Each life unfulfilled, you see;
>   It hangs still, patchy and scrappy:
> We have not sighed deep, laughed free,
>   Starved, feasted, despaired — been happy.

Sometimes the short line is used for point and command:

> Look not thou down but up!
> To uses of a cup . . .

Frequently, Browning's love of the grotesque invades his language and meter. This is to be seen in the playful tumbling lines of " The Pied Piper," with its haphazard rhymes, and also in " A Grammarian's Funeral," where the grotesque is used in the service of greatness, as the disciples of the scholar, defiant of the world's estimate of the man and fond of their master, climb up the mountain to the sepulcher.

> Let us begin and carry up this corpse,
>   Singing together.
> Leave we the common crofts, the vulgar thorpes
>   Each in its tether
> Sleeping safe on the bosom of the plain,
>   Cared-for till cock-crow . . .
> Look out if yonder be not day again
>   Rimming the rock-row!

Such comment by no means exhausts the endless variety of Browning's measures. In meter, as in most other things, he breaks away from all tradition, and is entirely original. He is especially fond of a five-line stanza, rhyming *ababa,* but that too undergoes many variations.

In creating his vast and varied body of poetry, Browning gradually hammered out a personal idiom. By nature strong-headed and intensely individualistic, he allowed himself considerable license with the language. His English was never that of the great public schools or the universities, and to his early contemporaries it appeared altogether eccentric. Frequently his mental force outranged his artistic powers, and he was obscure in his moral and emotional appeal because he could not manage his language. His problem, therefore, was to find a means of communication through poetry and still retain his individuality. Though he courted his oddities and was sometimes deliberately unusual, yet his primary aim was to achieve a natural broken speech. Browning was strong, but the English language was stronger. He was forced to compromise, and the compromise is an idiom that can be recognized instantly as Browning's. He writes characteristically a stiff and elliptical language, more expressive than beautiful. He is often colloquial, but equally often richly allusive from his recondite learning. He retains many learned and Latinate words, but moves toward the native English monosyllable which often makes his verse creak and grind with its knots of consonants:

> Irks care the crop-full bird? Frets doubt the
>   maw-crammed beast?

Often these discords are useful to his purpose. They show life and impulse and individuality, a congested expression struggling to break through. He may justly be called a " great though irregular master of English."

Browning's grammar, too, is his own, free and somewhat hit or miss. His sentences are frequently interrupted by long parentheses, but with patience the grammar will usually be seen to come right in the end. Often fettered by rhyme, he keeps plunging forward. He omits articles and relative pronouns. He likes to heap alliteration on his verse, as when Lippi describes himself as he appears in his own painting:

Mazed, motionless, and moon-struck . . .

One of his more superficial, but amusing, habits is to cut off the final consonants of prepositions and articles, as Calverly noted in his parody,

> I love to dock the smaller parts o' speech,
> As we curtail the already curtailed cur.

And this gives a staccato effect, one of speed.

All these eccentricities no doubt delayed his acceptance by the English public. But they do not ultimately obscure his strong imaginative and emotional appeal. He did not concede too much to his readers in subject or in manner. In his verse we find preserved his temperament with all its oddity and originality, its splendor and its color, and his passionate belief in the value of the individual. He was something new among the poets. "I like Browning," said Lockhart, Sir Walter Scott's son-in-law. "He's not the least like one of your damned literary men."

The order followed in this selection from Browning's poems is chronological. Grouped under the names of the volumes in which they first appeared — *Dramatic Lyrics, Dramatic Romances, Men and Women* — the poems appear here in the order Browning gave them on their first publication in book form. The one exception is "Porphyria's Lover," put first because it was written and printed several years before the other *Dramatic Lyrics* included here.

DRAMATIC LYRICS, 1842

PORPHYRIA'S LOVER

This poem was first printed as "Porphyria" in *The Monthly Repository* for January, 1836. In *Dramatic Lyrics* it was linked with a poem called "Johannes Agricola" under the title "Madhouse Cells." It was probably written in St. Petersburg, Russia, in March or April, 1834.

The rain set early in tonight,
  The sullen wind was soon awake,
It tore the elm-tops down for spite,
  And did its worst to vex the lake:
  I listened with heart fit to break.
When glided in Porphyria; straight
  She shut the cold out and the storm,
And kneeled and made the cheerless grate
  Blaze up, and all the cottage warm;
  Which done, she rose, and from her form   10
Withdrew the dripping cloak and shawl,

And laid her soiled gloves by, untied
Her hat and let the damp hair fall,
  And, last, she sat down by my side
  And called me. When no voice replied,
She put my arm about her waist,
  And made her smooth white shoulder bare,
And all her yellow hair displaced,
  And, stooping, made my cheek lie there,
  And spread, o'er all, her yellow hair,   20
Murmuring how she loved me — she
  Too weak, for all her heart's endeavor,
To set its struggling passion free
  From pride, and vainer ties dissever,
  And give herself to me for ever.
But passion sometimes would prevail,
  Nor could tonight's gay feast restrain
A sudden thought of one so pale
  For love of her, and all in vain:
  So, she was come through wind and rain.   30
Be sure I looked up at her eyes
  Happy and proud; at last I knew
Porphyria worshiped me; surprise
  Made my heart swell, and still it grew
  While I debated what to do.
That moment she was mine, mine, fair,
  Perfectly pure and good; I found
A thing to do, and all her hair
  In one long yellow string I wound
  Three times her little throat around,   40
And strangled her. No pain felt she;
  I am quite sure she felt no pain.
As a shut bud that holds a bee,
  I warily oped her lids; again
  Laughed the blue eyes without a stain.
And I untightened next the tress
  About her neck; her cheek once more
Blushed bright beneath my burning kiss:
  I propped her head up as before,
  Only, this time my shoulder bore   50
Her head, which droops upon it still;
  The smiling rosy little head,
So glad it has its utmost will,
  That all it scorned at once is fled,
  And I, its love, am gained instead!
Porphyria's love: she guessed not how
  Her darling one wish would be heard.
And thus we sit together now,
  And all night long we have not stirred,
  And yet God has not said a word!   60

MY LAST DUCHESS

Ferrara

The poem received its present title in the collected edition of 1849. A product of the poet's interest in Italian life and art, "My Last Duchess" is an early example of Browning's study of the Italian Renaissance, and also a milestone in his development of the dramatic monologue. It is probable that Browning had Alfonso II (1533–98), fifth Duke of Ferrara, as his model for the portrait of the duke of the poem.

That's my last Duchess painted on the wall,
Looking as if she were alive. I call
That piece a wonder, now; Frà Pandolf's° hands
Worked busily a day, and there she stands.
Will 't please you sit and look at her? I said
" Frà Pandolf " by design, for never read
Strangers like you that pictured countenance,
The depth and passion of its earnest glance,
But to myself they turned (since none puts by
The curtain I have drawn for you, but I)   10
And seemed as they would ask me, if they durst,
How such a glance came there; so, not the first
Are you to turn and ask thus. Sir,° 'twas not
Her husband's presence only, called that spot
Of joy into the Duchess' cheek; perhaps
Frà Pandolf chanced to say, " Her mantle laps
Over my lady's wrist too much," or, " Paint
Must never hope to reproduce the faint
Half-flush that dies along her throat." Such stuff
Was courtesy, she thought, and cause enough   20
For calling up that spot of joy. She had
A heart — how shall I say? — too soon made glad,
Too easily impressed; she liked whate'er
She looked on, and her looks went everywhere.
Sir, 'twas all one! My favor at her breast,
The dropping of the daylight in the west,
The bough of cherries some officious fool
Broke in the orchard for her, the white mule
She rode with round the terrace — all and each
Would draw from her alike the approving speech,
Or blush, at least. She thanked men — good! but
      thanked   31
Somehow — I know not how — as if she ranked
My gift of a nine-hundred-years-old name
With anybody's gift. Who'd stoop to blame
This sort of trifling? Even had you skill
In speech — (which I have not) — to make your
      will
Quite clear to such an one, and say, " Just this
Or that in you disgusts me; here you miss,
Or there exceed the mark " —and if she let
Herself be lessoned so, nor plainly set   40
Her wits to yours, forsooth, and made excuse,
— E'en then would be some stooping; and I choose
Never to stoop. Oh sir, she smiled, no doubt,

Whene'er I passed her; but who passed without
Much the same smile? This grew; I gave com-
      mands;
Then all smiles stopped together.° There she stands
As if alive. Will 't please you rise? We'll meet
The company below, then. I repeat,
The Count your master's known munificence
Is ample warrant that no just pretense   50
Of mine for dowry will be disallowed;
Though his fair daughter's self, as I avowed
At starting, is my object. Nay, we'll go
Together down, sir. Notice Neptune, though,
Taming a sea-horse, thought a rarity,
Which Claus° of Innsbruck cast in bronze for me!

INCIDENT OF THE FRENCH CAMP

This poem was probably written in December, 1841, when a second funeral of Napoleon was held in Paris. It is founded on oral legend. On April 23, 1809, Napoleon's army captured Ratisbon (Regensburg) from the Austrians. The city was stormed by Marshal Lannes (1769–1809), Duc de Montebello, who led the attackers in person. Lannes was fatally wounded a month later at the battle of Aspern.

You know, we French stormed Ratisbon:
      A mile or so away,
On a little mound, Napoleon
      Stood on our storming day;
With neck out-thrust, you fancy how,
      Legs wide, arms locked behind,
As if to balance the prone brow
      Oppressive with its mind.

Just as perhaps he mused, " My plans
      That soar, to earth may fall,   10
Let once my army-leader Lannes
      Waver at yonder wall " —
Out 'twixt the battery-smokes there flew
      A rider, bound on bound
Full-galloping; nor bridle drew
      Until he reached the mound.

Then off there flung in smiling joy,
      And held himself erect
By just his horse's mane, a boy;
      You hardly could suspect —   20
(So tight he kept his lips compressed,

45–46. I . . . together: Alfonso II had three wives, the first of whom was Lucrezia, daughter of Cosimo de' Medici, Duke of Florence. She was married at 14, and died at 17 — it was rumored of poison. When Browning was asked the meaning of these lines he said that "the commands were that she should be put to death, . . . or he might have had her shut up in a convent." 56. Claus: an imaginary artist.

MY LAST DUCHESS.   3. Frà Pandolf: an imaginary artist who was a friar.   13. Sir: the ambassador of Ferdinand II, Duke of Tyrol, with his capital at Innsbruck, with whom the Duke is negotiating for another wife—Ferdinand's sister.

Scarce any blood came through)
You looked twice ere you saw his breast
   Was all but shot in two.

"Well," cried he, "Emperor, by God's grace
   We've got you Ratisbon!
The Marshal's in the market-place,
   And you'll be there anon
To see your flag-bird° flap his vans°
   Where I, to heart's desire,   30
Perched him!" The chief's eye flashed; his plans
   Soared up again like fire.

The chief's eye flashed; but presently
   Softened itself, as sheathes
A film the mother-eagle's eye
   When her bruised eaglet breathes;
"You're wounded!" "Nay," the soldier's pride
   Touched to the quick, he said:
"I'm killed, Sire!" And his chief beside,
   Smiling the boy fell dead.   40

CRISTINA

In fancy a lover addresses Cristina, Queen of Spain
from 1829 to 1833 under Ferdinand VII, and Queen
Regent from 1833 to 1841. She was forced to abdicate
in 1841 when it was discovered that she had secretly
married an officer in the Army. The scandal of her
abdication was probably the occasion of the poem.
Cristina had a great reputation as a coquette and a
lover of pleasure.

"Cristina" has usually been taken to illustrate
Browning's interest in the "doctrine of elective affinities," which Goethe had promulgated in 1809 in his
novel *Wahlverwandschaften* (*Elective Affinities*). The
term is taken from chemistry and implies that, as in
physical substances, so in human beings there is a natural force which draws together certain persons of opposite sexes, instantaneously and almost irresistibly, no
matter what their different stations, circumstances, and
ages. It has been suggested, however, that Browning
means to depict the speaker as a rationalizing egoist
who is arguing with a skeptical friend.

She should never have looked at me
   If she meant I should not love her!
There are plenty . . . men, you call such,
   I suppose . . . she may discover
All her soul to, if she pleases,
   And yet leave much as she found them;
But I'm not so, and she knew it
   When she fixed me, glancing round them.

What? To fix me thus meant nothing?
   But I can't tell (there's my weakness)   10
What her look said! — no vile cant, sure,
   About "need to strew the bleakness
Of some lone shore with its pearl-seed
   That the sea feels" — no "strange yearning
That such souls have, most to lavish
   Where there's chance of least returning."°

Oh, we're sunk enough here, God knows!
   But not quite so sunk that moments,
Sure though seldom, are denied us,
   When the spirit's true endowments   20
Stand out plainly from its false ones,
   And apprise it if pursuing
Or the right way or the wrong way,
   To its triumph or undoing.

There are flashes struck from midnights,
   There are fire-flames noondays kindle,
Whereby piled-up honors perish,
   Whereby swollen ambitions dwindle,
While just this or that poor impulse,
   Which for once had play unstifled,   30
Seems the sole work of a lifetime,
   That away the rest have trifled.

Doubt you if, in some such moment,
   As she fixed me, she felt clearly,
Ages past the soul existed,
   Here an age 'tis resting merely,
And hence fleets again for ages,
   While the true end, sole and single,
It stops here for is, this love-way,
   With some other soul to mingle?   40

Else it loses what it lived for,
   And eternally must lose it;
Better ends may be in prospect,
   Deeper blisses (if you choose it),
But this life's end and this love-bliss
   Have been lost here. Doubt you whether
This she felt as, looking at me,
   Mine and her souls rushed together?

Oh, observe! Of course, next moment,
   The world's honors, in derision,   50
Trampled out the light for ever.
   Never fear but there's provision
Of the devil's to quench knowledge
   Lest we walk the earth in rapture!
— Making those who catch God's secret
   Just so much more prize their capture!

CRISTINA. **12-16. About . . . returning**: The speaker is sure that
Cristina's glance was not a condescending pity for him because
of his lower station in life. In the figure Browning uses here, the
speaker is the "lone shore" and Cristina's favor is the "pearl-
seed."

INCIDENT OF THE FRENCH CAMP.   **29. flag-bird**: Napoleon's emblem, the imperial eagle.   **vans**: webs of feathers.

Such am I: the secret's mine now!
  She has lost me, I have gained her;
Her soul's mine; and thus, grown perfect,
  I shall pass my life's remainder.   60
Life will just hold out the proving
  Both our powers, alone and blended;
And then, come the next life quickly!
  This world's use will have been ended.

DRAMATIC ROMANCES, 1845

THE LOST LEADER

Browning admitted that "The Lost Leader" was a "fancy portrait" of William Wordsworth, whose acceptance of a Civil List pension of £300 on October 15, 1842, and the laureateship on April 4, 1843, seemed like apostasy to the young poet devoted to the liberalism of Shelley, Byron, Hazlitt, and Leigh Hunt. The poem seems to have been written just before October 22, 1845, when Miss Barrett first saw it. In his later years Browning qualified his charges against Wordsworth but never entirely abandoned them.

Just for a handful of silver° he left us,
  Just for a riband° to stick in his coat —
Found the one gift of which fortune bereft us,
  Lost all the others she lets us devote;
They, with the gold to give, doled him out silver,
  So much was theirs who so little allowed;
How all our copper had gone for his service!
  Rags — were they purple, his heart had been proud!
We that had loved him so, followed him, honored him,
  Lived in his mild and magnificent eye,   10
Learned his great language, caught his clear accents,
  Made him our pattern to live and to die!
Shakespeare was of us, Milton was for us,
  Burns, Shelley were with us — they watch from their graves!
He alone breaks from the van and the freemen,
  — He alone sinks to the rear and the slaves!

We shall march prospering — not through his presence;
  Songs may inspirit us — not from his lyre;
Deeds will be done — while he boasts his quiescence,
  Still bidding crouch whom the rest bade aspire;
Blot out his name, then, record one lost soul more,
  One task more declined, one more footpath untrod,   22
One more devils' triumph and sorrow for angels,

One wrong more to man, one more insult to God!
Life's night begins; let him never come back to us!
  There would be doubt, hesitation, and pain,
Forced praise on our part — the glimmer of twilight,
  Never glad confident morning again!
Best fight on well, for we taught him — strike gallantly,
  Menace our heart ere we master his own;   30
Then let him receive the new knowledge and wait us,
  Pardoned in heaven, the first by the throne!

HOME-THOUGHTS, FROM ABROAD

This poem was probably written in England in the early spring of 1845, after Browning's return from Italy. Compare "De Gustibus —" p. 869, below.

Oh, to be in England
Now that April's there,
And whoever wakes in England
Sees, some morning, unaware,
That the lowest boughs and the brushwood sheaf
Round the elm-tree bole are in tiny leaf,
While the chaffinch sings on the orchard bough
In England — now!

And after April, when May follows,   9
And the whitethroat builds, and all the swallows!
Hark, where my blossomed pear-tree in the hedge
Leans to the field and scatters on the clover
Blossoms and dewdrops — at the bent spray's edge —
That's the wise thrush; he sings each song twice over,
Lest you should think he never could recapture
The first fine careless rapture!
And though the fields look rough with hoary dew,
All will be gay when noontide wakes anew
The buttercups, the little children's dower
— Far brighter than this gaudy melon-flower!   20

HOME-THOUGHTS, FROM THE SEA

The tradition that "Home-Thoughts, from the Sea" was written on Browning's first voyage to Italy in 1838 seems untenable. It is more likely that it was written in August, 1844, when Browning's ship, bound for Italy, lay off Cape St. Vincent, the southwestern point of Portugal. Here, on February 14, 1797, Nelson had received the surrender of the Spanish fleet.

Nobly, nobly Cape St. Vincent to the northwest died away;
Sunset ran, one glorious blood-red, reeking into Cadiz Bay;

THE LOST LEADER.   1. handful of silver: the pension referred to in the headnote.   2. riband: the laureateship.

Bluish 'mid the burning water, full in face Trafal-
    gar° lay;
In the dimmest northeast distance dawned Gibral-
    tar grand and gray;
"Here and here did England help me; how can I
    help England?" — say,
Whoso turns as I, this evening, turn to God to
    praise and pray,
While Jove's planet° rises yonder, silent over Africa.

MEETING AT NIGHT

In 1845 this poem and the poem which follows appeared under the title "Night and Morning." They
assumed their present titles in 1849. They were called
"new poems" by Miss Barrett when she first saw
them in October, 1845, and it is likely that they had
only recently been written. The landscapes suggest
Italy. Browning declared that both poems were written
from the point of view of the man.

The gray sea and the long black land;
And the yellow half-moon large and low;
And the startled little waves that leap
In fiery ringlets from their sleep,
As I gain the cove with pushing prow,
And quench its speed i' the slushy sand.

Then a mile of warm sea-scented beach;
Three fields to cross till a farm appears;
A tap at the pane, the quick sharp scratch
And blue spurt of a lighted match,   10
And a voice less loud, through its joys and fears,
Than the two hearts beating each to each!

PARTING AT MORNING

See the headnote for "Meeting at Night," above.
According to Browning, this second poem "is *his* confession of how fleeting is the belief (implied in the
first part) that such raptures are self-sufficient and enduring — as for the time they appear."

Round the cape of a sudden came the sea,
And the sun looked over the mountain's rim;
And straight was a path of gold for him,°
And the need of a world of men for me.

HOME-THOUGHTS, FROM THE SEA.   **3. Trafalgar:** a cape east of
Cadiz Bay. Here on Oct. 21, 1805, Nelson defeated the French
and Spanish fleets and was himself fatally wounded.   **7. Jove's
planet:** Jupiter, the evening star. PARTING AT MORNING.
3. him: the sun.

MEN AND WOMEN, 1855

LOVE AMONG THE RUINS

"Love among the Ruins" was written on January 1,
1852, in Paris. It reflects the immense rise of interest
in these years in archaeological exploration in Europe
and the Near East; the ancient city as Browning describes it resembles Herodotus' description of Babylon,
but owes some details to the Apocalypse of St. John,
and perhaps to I Chronicles 18 and 21. The city, however, seems to be a composite containing elements from
the descriptions of Tarquinia, Nineveh, Thebes, and
others as well. The modern scene may owe something
to the Italian Campagna, or to pictures of it.

Where the quiet-colored end of evening smiles
    Miles and miles
On the solitary pastures where our sheep
    Half-asleep
Tinkle homeward through the twilight, stray or
    stop
    As they crop —
Was the site once of a city great and gay,
    (So they say)
Of our country's very capital, its prince
    Ages since   10
Held his court in, gathered councils, wielding far
    Peace or war.

Now — the country does not even boast a tree
    As you see,
To distinguish slopes of verdure, certain rills
    From the hills
Intersect and give a name to (else they run
    Into one),
Where the domed and daring palace shot its
    spires
    Up like fires   20
O'er the hundred-gated circuit of a wall
    Bounding all,
Made of marble, men might march on nor be
    pressed,
    Twelve abreast.

And such plenty and perfection, see, of grass
    Never was!
Such a carpet as, this summer-time, o'erspreads
    And embeds
Every vestige of the city, guessed alone,
    Stock or stone —   30
Where a multitude of men breathed joy and woe
    Long ago;
Lust of glory pricked their hearts up, dread of
    shame
    Struck them tame;
And that glory and that shame alike, the gold
    Bought and sold.

Now — the single little turret that remains
    On the plains,
By the caper° overrooted, by the gourd
    Overscored,   40
While the patching houseleek's° head of blossom
    winks
    Through the chinks —
Marks the basement whence a tower in ancient
    time
    Sprang sublime,
And a burning ring, all round, the chariots traced
    As they raced,
And the monarch and his minions° and his dames
    Viewed the games.

And I know, while thus the quiet-colored eve
    Smiles to leave   50
To their folding, all our many-tinkling fleece
    In such peace,
And the slopes and rills in undistinguished gray
    Melt away —
That a girl with eager eyes and yellow hair
    Waits me there
In the turret whence the charioteers caught soul
    For the goal,
When the king looked, where she looks now,
    breathless, dumb
    Till I come.   60

But he looked upon the city, every side,
    Far and wide,
All the mountains topped with temples, all the
    glades'
    Colonnades,
All the causeys,° bridges, aqueducts — and then,
    All the men!
When I do come, she will speak not, she will stand,
    Either hand
On my shoulder, give her eyes the first embrace
    Of my face,   70
Ere we rush, ere we extinguish sight and speech
    Each on each.

In one year they sent a million fighters forth
    South and north,
And they built their gods a brazen pillar high
    As the sky,
Yet reserved a thousand chariots in full force —
    Gold, of course.
Oh heart! oh blood that freezes, blood that burns!
    Earth's returns   80
For whole centuries of folly, noise, and sin!

LOVE AMONG THE RUINS.   **39. caper:** a low, brambly bush.
41. houseleek: a small spreading plant.   **47. minions:** favorites,
lesser persons.   **65. causeys:** causeways, or raised roads over
low ground or swamps.

Shut them in,
With their triumphs and their glories and the rest!
    Love is best.

UP AT A VILLA — DOWN IN THE CITY

As Distinguished by an Italian Person of Quality

"Up at a Villa" was possibly written in September,
1850, when the Brownings occupied a villa on the
hills near Siena, or in the summer of 1853 at Bagni di
Lucca where conditions were similar to those in Siena.
It illustrates Browning's acute and humorous observation of Italian life.

Had I but plenty of money, money enough and to
    spare,
The house for me, no doubt, were a house in the
    city square;
Ah, such a life, such a life, as one leads at the win-
    dow there!

Something to see, by Bacchus,° something to hear,
    at least!
There, the whole day long, one's life is a perfect
    feast;
While up at a villa one lives, I maintain it, no more
    than a beast.

Well now, look at our villa! stuck like the horn of
    a bull
Just on a mountain-edge as bare as the creature's
    skull,
Save a mere shag of a bush with hardly a leaf to
    pull!
— I scratch my own, sometimes, to see if the hair's
    turned wool.   10

But the city, oh the city — the square with the
    houses! Why?
They are stone-faced, white as a curd, there's some-
    thing to take the eye!
Houses in four straight lines, not a single front
    awry;
You watch who crosses and gossips, who saunters,
    who hurries by;
Green blinds, as a matter of course, to draw when
    the sun gets high;
And the shops with fanciful signs which are painted
    properly.

What of a villa? Though winter be over in March
    by rights,
'Tis May perhaps ere the snow shall have withered
    well off the heights;

UP AT A VILLA.   **4. by Bacchus:** a mild Italian oath.

You've the brown plowed land before, where the
    oxen steam and wheeze,
And the hills oversmoked behind by the faint gray
    olive-trees.   20

Is it better in May, I ask you? You've summer all
    at once;
In a day he leaps complete with a few strong April
    suns.
'Mid the sharp short emerald wheat, scarce risen
    three fingers well,
The wild tulip, at end of its tube, blows out its
    great red bell
Like a thin clear bubble of blood, for the children
    to pick and sell.

Is it ever hot in the square? There's a fountain to
    spout and splash!
In the shade it sings and springs; in the shine such
    foam-bows flash
On the horses with curling fish-tails, that prance
    and paddle and pash
Round the lady atop in her conch° — fifty gazers do
    not abash,
Though all that she wears is some weeds round her
    waist in a sort of sash.   30

All the year long at the villa, nothing to see though
    you linger,
Except yon cypress that points like death's lean
    lifted forefinger.
Some think fireflies pretty, when they mix i' the
    corn and mingle,
Or thrid° the stinking hemp till the stalks of it seem
    a-tingle.
Late August or early September, the stunning cicala
    is shrill,
And the bees keep their tiresome whine round the
    resinous firs on the hill.
Enough of the seasons — I spare you the months of
    the fever and chill.

Ere you open your eyes in the city, the blessed
    church-bells begin;
No sooner the bells leave off than the diligence°
    rattles in;
You get the pick of the news, and it costs you never
    a pin.   40
By and by there's the traveling doctor gives pills,
    lets blood, draws teeth;
Or the Pulcinello-trumpet° breaks up the market
    beneath.

At the post office such a scene-picture° — the new
    play, piping hot!
And a notice how, only this morning, three liberal
    thieves° were shot.
Above it, behold the Archbishop's most fatherly of
    rebukes,
And beneath, with his crown and his lion, some
    little new law of the Duke's!
Or a sonnet° with flowery marge, to the Reverend
    Don So-and-so,
Who is Dante, Boccaccio, Petrarca, St. Jerome, and
    Cicero,
" And moreover " (the sonnet goes rhyming) " the
    skirts of St. Paul has reached,
Having preached us those six Lent-lectures more
    unctuous than ever he preached."   50
Noon strikes — here sweeps the procession! our
    Lady° borne smiling and smart
With a pink gauze gown all spangles, and seven
    swords stuck in her heart!
Bang-whang-whang goes the drum, *tootle-te-tootle*
    the fife;
No keeping one's haunches still; it's the greatest
    pleasure in life.

But bless you, it's dear — it's dear! fowls, wine, at
    double the rate.
They have clapped a new tax upon salt,° and what
    oil pays passing the gate
It's a horror to think of. And so, the villa for me,
    not the city!
Beggars can scarcely be choosers; but still — ah,
    the pity, the pity!
Look, two and two go the priests, then the monks
    with cowls and sandals,
And the penitents dressed in white shirts, a-holding
    the yellow candles;   60
One, he carries a flag up straight, and another a
    cross with handles,
And the Duke's guard brings up the rear, for the
    better prevention of scandals.

---

43. scene-picture: picture advertising the coming play. **44. liberal thieves:** men of the revolutionary party against Austria (which then controlled Italy), who practiced thievery on the side. **47. sonnet:** First written in Italy, the sonnet was used for all occasions, especially, as here, to compliment prominent persons. **51. our Lady:** the Virgin, here Our Lady of Sorrows. The seven swords represent her seven sorrows: (1) the prophecy that a sword should pierce her soul because of her Son; (2) her suffering in the flight into Egypt; (3) her grief when her Son was lost in Jerusalem before he was found in the Temple; (4) her pain when she saw Jesus bearing the cross; (5) her suffering when she saw the agony of Christ; (6) her pain when the side of her Son was pierced; and (7) her grief at the burial of Christ. **56. tax . . . salt:** Salt was a favorite commodity for taxation in Italy and other nations. All country produce was subject to tax as it entered the city.

29. conch: shell.   **34. thrid:** thread, fly through.   **39. diligence:** coach.   **42. Pulcinello-trumpet:** the trumpet used by strolling players to announce the arrival of Pulcinello, the buffoon of the puppet show.

Bang-whang-whang goes the drum, *tootle-te-tootle*
    the fife.
Oh, a day in the city square, there is no such pleas-
    ure in life!

FRA LIPPO LIPPI

Early in 1853 Browning was "writing—a first step
towards popularity for me—lyrics with more music
and painting than before, so as to get people to hear
and see. . . ." "Fra Lippo Lippi" was one of these.
In Florence and elsewhere, Browning saw many of
Lippi's pictures, especially "The Coronation of the
Virgin," which is described at the end of the poem. In
the story of the poem he mainly follows the colorful
account of Lippi's life in Vasari's *Delle Vite Pittori*
(1550), now available in English as *The Lives of the
Painters,* although for some details he used Baldinucci's
Account of the Artists, published in Italian at Florence
in 1767–74. Baldinucci emphasized more strongly than
Vasari the idea that Lippi was one of the first painters
to break with the stiff formal tradition of ecclesiastical
painting, to become a naturalistic and realistic artist,
and to introduce contemporary scenes and figures into
his work. In Lippi's view of the nature and function of
art Browning saw a parallel to his own conception of
the nature and function of poetry in the nineteenth
century in England, and he thought of himself as a
pioneer among his fellow poets as Lippi was among
the painters of his day. Also, like Lippi, Browning's
temperament was cheerful and energetic, and the sympathy with which he wrote this dramatic monologue
accounts for much of its success. Many of the opinions
expressed in the poem are more Browning's than
Lippi's.

    This poem illustrates well Browning's difference
from other Victorian poets. When in 1855 he was
called upon to read one of his new poems before Tennyson and D. G. Rossetti, he selected "Fra Lippo
Lippi." He could not have chosen a poem of his which
by its opinions on the nature of art, as well as by its
conversational blank verse and its colloquial language,
would challenge more effectively the formality and remoteness from reality of the poetry of that time.
Though Browning frequently used subjects from the
past, especially the Renaissance, he usually gave such
subjects a relevance to nineteenth-century England and
contemporary problems, and, as here, he employed
distinctly modern, colloquial language and familiar
manners. In his later poetry he more and more dealt
directly and frankly with the contemporary scene.

    Vasari's account of Lippi records that he was born
in 1412. At two years of age he became an orphan and
fell into the care of his father's sister, Mona Lapaccia.
When he was eight years old he was entered in the
Carmine monastery at Florence. There he filled his
schoolbooks with drawings, mainly caricatures. He
took holy orders, but soon left the monastery to follow
the career of a painter. He won the patronage of
Cosimo de' Medici, and on one occasion, when Cosimo

had him locked in the Medici Palace in order to force
him to finish a picture, he escaped by tying his bed-
clothes together and letting himself down into the
street. It is at this point that Browning's poem begins.
Lippi was a gay and cheerful person. After the time
which Browning represents in the poem, Lippi fell in
love with a nun and abducted her, and later had this
relationship recognized by the Church. He died in
1469.

I am poor brother Lippo, by your leave!
You need not clap your torches to my face.
Zooks,° what's to blame? you think you see a
    monk!
What, 'tis past midnight, and you go the rounds,
And here you catch me at an alley's end
Where sportive ladies leave their doors ajar?
The Carmine's my cloister; hunt it up,
Do—harry out, if you must show your zeal,
Whatever rat, there, haps on his wrong hole,
And nip each softling of a wee white mouse,   10
Weke, weke, that's crept to keep him company!
Aha, you know your betters! Then, you'll take
Your hand away that's fiddling on my throat,
And please to know me likewise. Who am I?
Why, one, sir, who is lodging with a friend
Three streets off—he's a certain . . . how d' ye
    call?
Master—a . . . Cosimo of the Medici,
I' the house that caps the corner. Boh! you were
    best!°
Remember and tell me, the day you're hanged,
How you affected such a gullet's gripe!   20
But you, sir,° it concerns you that your knaves
Pick up a manner nor discredit you;
Zooks, are we pilchards,° that they sweep the streets
And count fair prize what comes into their net?
He's Judas to a tittle, that man is!
Just such a face! Why, sir, you make amends.
Lord, I'm not angry! Bid your hangdogs go
Drink out this quarter-florin° to the health
Of the munificent House that harbors me
(And many more beside, lads! more beside!)   30
And all's come square again. I'd like his face—
His, elbowing on his comrade in the door
With the pike and lantern—for the slave that
    holds
John Baptist's° head a-dangle by the hair
With one hand ("Look you, now," as who should
    say)

And his weapon in the other, yet unwiped!
It's not your chance to have a bit of chalk,
A wood coal° or the like? or you should see!
Yes, I'm the painter, since you style me so.
What, brother Lippo's doings, up and down,   40
You know them and they take you?° like enough!
I saw the proper twinkle in your eye —
'Tell you, I liked your looks at very first.
Let's sit and set things straight now, hip to haunch.
Here's spring come, and the nights one makes up
    bands
To roam the town and sing out carnival,
And I've been three weeks shut within my mew,
A-painting for the great man, saints and saints
And saints again. I could not paint all night —
Ouf! I leaned out of window for fresh air.   50
There came a hurry of feet and little feet,
A sweep of lute strings, laughs, and whifts of
    song —
Flower o' the broom,°
Take away love, and our earth is a tomb!
Flower o' the quince,
I let Lisa go, and what good in life since?
Flower o' the thyme — and so on. Round they went.
Scarce had they turned the corner when a titter
Like the skipping of rabbits by moonlight — three
    slim shapes,
And a face that looked up . . . zooks, sir, flesh
    and blood,   60
That's all I'm made of! Into shreds it went,
Curtain and counterpane and coverlet,
All the bed furniture — a dozen knots,
There was a ladder! Down I let myself,
Hands and feet, scrambling somehow, and so
    dropped,
And after them. I came up with the fun
Hard by St. Laurence,° hail fellow, well met —
Flower o' the rose,
If I've been merry, what matter who knows?
And so as I was stealing back again   70
To get to bed and have a bit of sleep
Ere I rise up tomorrow and go work
On Jerome° knocking at his poor old breast
With his great round stone to subdue the flesh,
You snap me of the sudden. Ah, I see!
Though your eye twinkles still, you shake your
    head —
Mine's shaved — a monk, you say — the sting's in
    that!
If Master Cosimo announced himself,
Mum's the word naturally; but a monk!

Come, what am I a beast for? tell us, now!   80
I was a baby when my mother died°
And father died and left me in the street.
I starved there, God knows how, a year or two
On fig skins, melon pairings, rinds and shucks,
Refuse and rubbish. One fine frosty day,
My stomach being empty as your hat,
The wind doubled me up and down I went.
Old Aunt Lapaccia trussed me with one hand,
(Its fellow was a stinger as I knew)
And so along the wall, over the bridge,   90
By the straight cut to the convent. Six words there,
While I stood munching my first bread that month:
" So, boy, you're minded," quoth the good fat
    father,
Wiping his own mouth, 'twas refection time —
" To quit this very miserable world?
Will you renounce " . . . " the mouthful of
    bread? " thought I;
By no means! Brief, they made a monk of me;
I did renounce the world, its pride and greed,
Palace, farm, villa, shop, and banking house,
Trash, such as these poor devils of Medici   100
Have given their hearts to — all at eight years old.
Well, sir, I found in time, you may be sure,
'Twas not for nothing — the good bellyful,
The warm serge and the rope that goes all round,
And day-long blessèd idleness beside!
" Let's see what the urchin's fit for " — that came
    next.
Not overmuch their way, I must confess.
Such a to-do! They tried me with their books;
Lord, they'd have taught me Latin in pure waste!
Flower o' the clove,   110
All the Latin I construe is " amo," I love!
But, mind you, when a boy starves in the streets
Eight years together, as my fortune was,
Watching folk's faces to know who will fling
The bit of half-stripped grape bunch he desires,
And who will curse or kick him for his pains —
Which gentleman processional and fine,
Holding a candle to the Sacrament,
Will wink and let him lift a plate and catch
The droppings of the wax to sell again,   120
Or holla for the Eight° and have him whipped —
How say I? — nay, which dog bites, which lets drop
His bone from the heap of offal in the street —
Why, soul and sense of him grow sharp alike,
He learns the look of things, and none the less
For admonition from the hunger pinch.
I had a store of such remarks, be sure,
Which, after I found leisure, turned to use.
I drew men's faces on my copy books,   129

38. **wood coal:** charcoal.   41. **they . . . you:** engage your interest.   53. *Flower . . . broom:* The flower songs interspersed
in the narrative are called *stornelli* by the Italians. They are
usually three lines each.   67. **St. Laurence:** the Church of San
Lorenzo.   73. **Jerome:** Lippi painted a picture of St. Jerome
(340–420) for Cosimo.

81–135: See headnote, above.   121. **the Eight:** the magistrates
of Florence.

Scrawled them within the antiphonary's° marge,
Joined legs and arms to the long music notes,
Found eyes and nose and chin for A's and B's,
And made a string of pictures of the world
Betwixt the ins and outs of verb and noun,
On the wall, the bench, the door. The monks
    looked black.°
"Nay," quoth the Prior, "turn him out, d' ye say?
In no wise. Lose a crow and catch a lark.
What if at last we get our man of parts,
We Carmelites, like those Camaldolese°
And Preaching Friars,° to do our church up fine
And put the front on it that ought to be!"   141
And hereupon he bade me daub away.
Thank you! my head being crammed, the walls a
    blank,
Never was such prompt disemburdening.
First, every sort of monk, the black and white,
I drew them, fat and lean; then, folk at church,
From good old gossips waiting to confess
Their cribs° of barrel droppings, candle ends —
To the breathless fellow at the altar foot,
Fresh from his murder, safe and sitting there   150
With the little children round him in a row
Of admiration, half for his beard and half
For that white anger of his victim's son
Shaking a fist at him with one fierce arm,
Signing himself with the other because of Christ
(Whose sad face on the cross sees only this
After the passion of a thousand years)
Till some poor girl, her apron o'er her head,
(Which the intense eyes looked through) came at
    eve
On tiptoe, said a word, dropped in a loaf,   160
Her pair of earrings and a bunch of flowers
(The brute took growling), prayed, and so was
    gone.
I painted all, then cried, "'Tis ask and have;
Choose, for more's ready!" — laid the ladder flat,
And showed my covered bit of cloister wall.
The monks closed in a circle and praised loud
Till checked, taught what to see and not to see,
Being simple bodies — "That's the very man!
Look at the boy who stoops to pat the dog!
That woman's like the Prior's niece who comes   170
To care about his asthma; it's the life!"
But there my triumph's straw fire flared and
    funked;°
Their betters took their turn to see and say;
The Prior and the learned pulled a face
And stopped all that in no time. "How? what's
    here?

Quite from the mark of painting, bless us all!
Faces, arms, legs, and bodies like the true
As much as pea and pea! it's devil's game!
Your business is not to catch men with show,
With homage to the perishable clay,   180
But lift them over it, ignore it all,
Make them forget there's such a thing as flesh.
Your business is to paint the souls of men —
Man's soul, and it's a fire, smoke . . . no, it's
    not . . .
Its vapor done up like a newborn babe —
(In that shape when you die it leaves your mouth)
It's . . . well, what matters talking, it's the soul!
Gives us no more of body than shows soul!
Here's Giotto,° with his Saint a-praising God,   189
That sets us praising — why not stop with him?
Why put all thoughts of praise out of our head
With wonder at lines, colors, and what not?
Paint the soul, never mind the legs and arms!
Rub all out, try at it a second time.
Oh, that white smallish female with the breasts,
She's just my niece . . . Herodias,° I would say —
Who went and danced and got men's heads cut off!
Have it all out!" Now, is this sense, I ask?
A fine way to paint soul, by painting body
So ill, the eye can't stop there, must go further   200
And can't fare worse! Thus, yellow does for white
When what you put for yellow's simply black,
And any sort of meaning looks intense
When all beside itself means and looks naught.
Why can't a painter lift each foot in turn,
Left foot and right foot, go a double step,
Make his flesh liker and his soul more like,
Both in their order? Take the prettiest face,
The Prior's niece . . . patron saint — is it so pretty
You can't discover if it means hope, fear,   210
Sorrow or joy? won't beauty go with these?
Suppose I've made her eyes all right and blue,
Can't I take breath and try to add life's flash,
And then add soul and heighten them threefold?
Or say there's beauty with no soul at all —
(I never saw it — put the case the same —)
If you get simple beauty and naught else,
You get about the best thing God invents:
That's somewhat; and you'll find the soul you have
    missed,
Within yourself, when you return him thanks.   220
"Rub all out!" Well, well, there's my life, in short,
And so the thing has gone on ever since.
I'm grown a man no doubt, I've broken bounds;

---

130. **antiphonary:** the book of responses sung by the choirboys.
139. **Camaldolese:** a religious order with a monastery in Florence.
140. **Preaching Friars:** the Dominicans, another order.   148.
cribs: small thefts.   172. **funked:** turned to smoke.

189. **Giotto:** Giotto di Bondone (1276–1337), the most famous
of early Italian painters, also a sculptor and architect of renown.
Browning is here describing the monastic tradition in painting
against which Lippi revolts.   196. **Herodias:** the wife of Philip,
Herod's brother, and the mother of Salome. When John the
Baptist objected to Herod's marrying his brother's wife, Herodias
plotted the revenge which led to John's decapitation.

You should not take a fellow eight years old
And make him swear to never kiss the girls.
I'm my own master, paint now as I please —
Having a friend, you see, in the Corner-house!°
Lord, it's fast holding by the rings in front —
Those great rings serve more purposes than just
To plant a flag in, or tie up a horse!   230
And yet the old schooling sticks, the old grave eyes
Are peeping o'er my shoulder as I work,
The heads shake still — "It's art's decline, my son!
You're not of the true painters, great and old;
Brother Angelico's° the man, you'll find;
Brother Lorenzo stands his single peer;
Fag on at flesh, you'll never make the third!"·
Flower o' the pine,
You keep your mistr . . . manners, and I'll stick
    to mine!   239
I'm not the third, then; bless us, they must know!
Don't you think they're the likeliest to know,
They with their Latin? So, I swallow my rage,
Clench my teeth, suck my lips in tight, and paint
To please them — sometimes do and sometimes
    don't;
For, doing most, there's pretty sure to come
A turn, some warm eve finds me at my saints —
A laugh, a cry, the business of the world —
(Flower o' the peach,
Death for us all, and his own life for each!)   249
And my whole soul revolves, the cup runs over,
The world and life's too big to pass for a dream,
And I do these wild things in sheer despite,
And play the fooleries you catch me at,
In pure rage! The old mill horse, out at grass
After hard years, throws up his stiff heels so,
Although the miller does not preach to him
The only good of grass is to make chaff.
What would men have? Do they like grass or no —
May they or mayn't·they? all I want's the thing
Settled for ever one way. As it is,   260
You tell too many lies and hurt yourself;
You don't like what you only like too much,
You do like what, if given you at your word,
You find abundantly detestable.
For me, I think I speak as I was taught;
I always see the garden and God there
A-making man's wife; and, my lesson learned,
The value and significance of flesh,
I can't unlearn ten minutes afterwards.

You understand me; I'm a beast, I know.   270
But see, now — why, I see as certainly
As that the morning star's about to shine,
What will hap some day. We've a youngster here
Comes to our convent, studies what I do,
Slouches and stares and lets no atom drop.
His name is Guidi — he'll not mind the monks —
They call him Hulking Tom,° he lets them talk —
He picks my practice up — he'll paint apace,
I hope so — though I never live so long,
I know what's sure to follow. You be judge!   280
You speak no Latin more than I, belike;
However, you're my man, you've seen the world
— The beauty and the wonder and the power,
The shapes of things, their colors, lights and shades,
Changes, surprises — and God made it all!
— For what? Do you feel thankful, aye or no,
For this fair town's face, yonder river's line,
The mountain round it and the sky above,
Much more the figures of man, woman, child,
These are the frame to? What's it all about?   290
To be passed over, despised? or dwelt upon,
Wondered at? oh, this last of course! — you say.
But why not do as well as say — paint these
Just as they are, careless what comes of it?
God's works — paint any one, and count it crime
To let a truth slip. Don't object, "His works
Are here already; nature is complete:
Suppose you reproduce her — (which you can't)
There's no advantage! you must beat her, then."
For, don't you mark? we're made so that we love
First when we see them painted, things we have
    passed   301
Perhaps a hundred times nor cared to see;
And so they are better, painted — better to us,
Which is the same thing. Art was given for that;
God uses us to help each other so,
Lending our minds out. Have you noticed, now,
Your cullion's° hanging face? A bit of chalk,
And trust me but you should, though! How much
    more,
If I drew higher things with the same truth!
That were to take the Prior's pulpit-place,   310
Interpret God to all of you! Oh, oh,
It makes me mad to see what men shall do
And we in our graves! This world's no blot for us,
Nor blank; it means intensely, and means good:
To find its meaning is my meat and drink.
"Aye, but you don't so instigate to prayer!"
Strikes in the Prior; "when your meaning's plain
It does not say to folk — remember matins,

227. Corner-house: the palace in which Cosimo de' Medici lived, now known as the Palazzo Riccardi, at the corner of Via Cavour and Via Gori.   **235–36. Angelico, Lorenzo:** Fra Angelico, Giovanni da Fiesole (1387–1455), and Lorenzo Monaco (*c.* 1370–*c.* 1425) are cited as representatives of the traditional school of religious painters against which Lippi sets himself. Angelico is said to have knelt while painting; Lorenzo, the Monk, was of the Camaldolese order. Lippi hardly does justice to Angelico here.

273–77. youngster . . . Tom: Tomaso Guidi or Masaccio (1401–28). The best opinion now is that Masaccio who painted the famous Branacci frescoes was not Lippi's pupil but possibly his master. Like Lippi he was a realist.   **307. cullion:** low fellow.

Or, mind you fast next Friday!" Why, for this
What need of art at all? A skull and bones,   320
Two bits of stick nailed crosswise, or, what's best,
A bell to chime the hour with, does as well.
I painted a St. Laurence° six months since
At Prato,° splashed the fresco in fine style;
"How looks my painting, now the scaffold's
     down?"
I ask a brother. "Hugely," he returns —
"Already not one phiz° of your three slaves
Who turn the Deacon off his toasted side,
But's scratched and prodded to our heart's content,
The pious people have so eased their own   330
With coming to say prayers there in a rage;
We get on fast to see the bricks beneath.
Expect another job this time next year,
For pity and religion grow i' the crowd —
Your painting serves its purpose!" Hang the fools!

— That is — you'll not mistake an idle word
Spoke in a huff by a poor monk, God wot,
Tasting the air this spicy night which turns
The unaccustomed head like Chianti wine!°
Oh, the Church knows! don't misreport me, now!
It's natural a poor monk out of bounds   341
Should have his apt word to excuse himself;
And hearken how I plot to make amends.
I have bethought me: I shall paint a piece°
. . . There's for you! Give me six months, then go,
     see
Something in Sant' Ambrogio's! Bless the nuns!
They want a cast o' my office.° I shall paint
God in the midst, Madonna and her babe,
Ringed by a bowery, flowery angel brood,
Lilies and vestments and white faces, sweet   350
As puff on puff of grated orris root°
When ladies crowd to church at midsummer.
And then i' the front, of course a saint or two —
St. John,° because he saves the Florentines,
St. Ambrose, who puts down in black and white
The convent's friends and gives them a long day,
And Job, I must have him there past mistake,
The man of Uz (and Us without the z,
Painters who need his patience). Well, all these
Secured at their devotion, up shall come   360

Out of a corner when you least expect,
As one by a dark stair into a great light,
Music and talking, who but Lippo! I! —
Mazed, motionless, and moonstruck — I'm the man!
Back I shrink — what is this I see and hear?
I, caught up with my monk's things by mistake,
My old serge gown and rope that goes all round,
I, in this presence, this pure company!
Where's a hole, where's a corner for escape?
Then steps a sweet angelic slip of a thing   370
Forward, puts out a soft palm — "Not so fast!"
— Addresses the celestial presence, "nay —
He made you and devised you, after all,
Though he's none of you! Could St. John there
     draw —
His camel hair° make up a painting brush?
We come to brother Lippo for all that,
Iste perfecit opus!" So, all smile —
I shuffle sideways with my blushing face
Under the cover of a hundred wings   379
Thrown like a spread of kirtles° when you're gay
And play hot cockles,° all the doors being shut,
Till, wholly unexpected, in there pops
The hothead husband! Thus I scuttle off
To some safe bench behind, not letting go
The palm of her, the little lily thing
That spoke the good word for me in the nick,
Like the Prior's niece . . . St. Lucy, I would say.
And so all's saved for me, and for the church
A pretty picture gained. Go, six months hence!
Your hand, sir, and good-by; no lights, no
     lights!   390
The street's hushed, and I know my own way back,
Don't fear me! There's the gray beginning. Zooks!

BY THE FIRESIDE

In essence "By the Fireside" is autobiographical,
but not literally so. The meeting of souls described in
the poem actually occurred, but in Wimpole Street,
London, in 1845. In September, 1853, the Brownings
made an expedition to the ruined chapel beside the
mountain path to Prato Fiorito, the probable scene of
the poem, and the verses were written soon afterward
at Bagni di Lucca or in Florence by their fireside in
November. The poem is notable for its portrait of Mrs.
Browning (Leonor) and for its illustration of a favorite
doctrine of Browning's that the fate of men and women
is usually settled in a moment of decision to which all
past life leads. Contrast "Two in the Campagna," below, p. 873, and compare Shakespeare's "The Phoenix
and the Turtle" and Donne's "The Ecstasy."

323. St. Laurence: This saint was martyred in 258 by being roasted on a gridiron.   **324. Prato:** a town near Florence in whose church is some of Lippi's work.   **327. phiz:** face.   **339. Chianti wine:** a famous wine from a region south of Florence.   **344-77.** The picture which Lippi here plans to paint at St. Ambrose's Convent, so named for an early Father of the Church, is "The Coronation of the Virgin." It is now in the Accademia delle Velle Arti in Florence, where Browning saw it. The identi-fication of the figure near the words in the lower right-hand corner of the picture *"Iste perfecit opus"* ("This man made the work") as Lippi has been seriously challenged.   **347. cast . . . office:** a painting by me.   **351. orris root:** fragrant iris root, used as perfume.   **354. St. John:** the patron saint of Florence.

375. camel hair: "And John was clothed with camel's hair" (Mark 1: 6).   **380. kirtles:** gowns.   **381. hot cockles:** a form of blindman's buff; here, not so innocent as usual.

How well I know what I mean to do
   When the long dark autumn-evenings come;
And where, my soul, is thy pleasant hue?
   With the music of all thy voices, dumb
In life's November too!

I shall be found by the fire, suppose,
   O'er a great wise book as beseemeth age,
While the shutters flap as the cross-wind blows,
   And I turn the page, and I turn the page,
Not verse now, only prose!   10

Till the young ones whisper, finger on lip,
   "There he is at it, deep in Greek;
Now then, or never, out we slip
   To cut from the hazels by the creek
A mainmast for our ship!"

I shall be at it indeed, my friends!
   Greek puts already on either side
Such a branch-work forth as soon extends
   To a vista opening far and wide,
And I pass out where it ends.   20

The outside frame, like your hazel trees —
   But the inside archway widens fast,
And a rarer sort succeeds to these,
   And we slope to Italy at last
And youth, by green degrees.°

I follow wherever I am led,
   Knowing so well the leader's hand;
Oh woman-country, wooed not wed,
   Loved all the more by earth's male-lands,
Laid to their hearts instead!   30

Look at the ruined chapel again
   Halfway up in the Alpine gorge!
Is that a tower, I point you plain,
   Or is it a mill, or an iron-forge
Breaks solitude in vain?

A turn, and we stand in the heart of things;
   The woods are round us, heaped and dim;
From slab to slab how it slips and springs —
   The thread of water single and slim,
Through the ravage some torrent brings!   40

Does it feed the little lake below?
   That speck of white just on its marge
Is Pella;° see, in the evening-glow,
   How sharp the silver spearheads charge
When Alp meets heaven in snow!

On our other side is the straight-up rock;
   And a path is kept 'twixt the gorge and it
By boulder stones where lichens mock
   The marks on a moth, and small ferns fit
Their teeth to the polished block.   50

Oh the sense of the yellow mountain-flowers,
   And thorny balls, each three in one,
The chestnuts throw on our path in showers!
   For the drop of the woodland fruit's begun,
These early November hours,

That crimson the creeper's leaf across
   Like a splash of blood, intense, abrupt,
O'er a shield else gold from rim to boss,
   And lay it for show on the fairy-cupped
Elf-needled mat of moss,   60

By the rose-flesh mushrooms, undivulged
   Last evening — nay, in today's first dew
Yon sudden coral nipple bulged,
   Where a freaked fawn-colored flaky crew
Of toadstools peep indulged.

And yonder, at foot of the fronting ridge
   That takes the turn to a range beyond,
Is the chapel reached by the one-arched bridge
   Where the water is stopped in a stagnant
      pond
Danced over by the midge.   70

The chapel and bridge are of stone alike,
   Blackish gray and mostly wet;
Cut hemp-stalks steep in the narrow dike.
   See here again, how the lichens fret
And the roots of the ivy strike!

Poor little place, where its one priest comes
   On a festa-day, if he comes at all,
To the dozen folk from their scattered homes,
   Gathered within that precinct small
By the dozen ways one roams —   80

To drop from the charcoal-burners' huts,
   Or climb from the hemp-dressers' low shed,
Leave the grange° where the woodman stores his
      nuts,
   Or the wattled cote° where the fowlers spread
Their gear on the rock's bare juts.
It has some pretension too, this front,
   With its bit of fresco half-moon-wise
Set over the porch, Art's early wont.
   'Tis John in the Desert,° I surmise,
But has borne the weather's brunt —   90

BY THE FIRESIDE. **24–25.** These lines serve as a transition from
the interior scene described above to the mountain scene which
follows. **43. Pella:** This Italian town is considerably farther
north than Prato Fiorito, and has led some commentators to think
the scene an imaginary one.

83. grange: granary. **84. wattled cote:** a thatched shelter, made
of stakes interwoven with twigs or strips of wood. **89. John
. . . Desert:** St. John the Evangelist, who died in the desert. See
Browning's poem, "A Death in the Desert."

Not from the fault of the builder, though,
　For a penthouse properly projects
Where three carved beams make a certain show,
　Dating — good thought of our architect's —
'Five, six, nine, he lets you know.

And all day long a bird sings there,
　And a stray sheep drinks at the pond at times;
The place is silent and aware;
　It has had its scenes, its joys and crimes,
But that is its own affair.　　　　　　　100

My perfect wife, my Leonor,°
　Oh heart, my own, oh eyes, mine too,
Whom else could I dare look backward for,
　With whom beside should I dare pursue
The path gray heads abhor?

For it leads to a crag's sheer edge with them;
　Youth, flowery all the way, there stops —
Not they; age threatens and they contemn,
　Till they reach the gulf wherein youth drops,
One inch from life's safe hem!　　　　　110

With me, youth led . . . I will speak now,
　No longer watch you as you sit
Reading by firelight, that great brow
　And the spirit-small hand propping it,
Mutely, my heart knows how —

When, if I think but deep enough,
　You are wont to answer, prompt as rhyme;
And you, too, find without rebuff
　Response your soul seeks many a time
Piercing its fine flesh-stuff.　　　　　120

My own, confirm me! If I tread
　This path back, is it not in pride
To think how little I dreamed it led
　To an age so blest that, by its side,
Youth seems the waste instead?

My own, see where the years conduct!
　At first, 'twas something our two souls
Should mix as mists do; each is sucked
　In each now; on, the new stream rolls,
Whatever rocks obstruct.　　　　　　130

Think, when our one soul understands
　The great Word° which makes all things new,
When earth breaks up and heaven expands,
　How will the change strike me and you
In the house not made with hands?

Oh, I must feel your brain prompt mine,
　Your heart anticipate my heart,
You must be just before, in fine,
　See and make me see, for your part,
New depths of the divine!　　　　　　140

But who could have expected this
　When we two drew together first
Just for the obvious human bliss,
　To satisfy life's daily thirst
With a thing men seldom miss?

Come back with me to the first of all,
　Let us lean and love it over again,
Let us now forget and now recall,
　Break the rosary in a pearly rain,
And gather what we let fall!　　　　　150

What did I say? — that a small bird sings
　All day long, save when a brown pair
Of hawks from the wood float with wide wings
　Strained to a bell; 'gainst noonday glare
You count the streaks and rings.

But at afternoon or almost eve
　'Tis better; then the silence grows
To that degree, you half believe
　It must get rid of what it knows,
Its bosom does so heave.　　　　　　160

Hither we walked then, side by side,
　Arm in arm and cheek to cheek,
And still I questioned or replied,
　While my heart, convulsed to really speak
Lay choking in its pride.

Silent the crumbling bridge we cross,
　And pity and praise the chapel sweet,
And care about the fresco's loss,
　And wish for our souls a like retreat,
And wonder at the moss.　　　　　　170

Stoop and kneel on the settle° under,
　Look through the window's grated square:
Nothing to see! For fear of plunder,
　The cross is down and the altar bare,
As if thieves don't fear thunder.

We stoop and look in through the grate,
　See the little porch and rustic door,
Read duly the dead builder's date;
　Then cross the bridge that we crossed before,
Take the path again — but wait!　　　180

101. **Leonor:** a name for Mrs. Browning, adapted from Beethoven's opera, *Fidelio*, where Leonore is the devoted wife. **132. The . . . Word:** Rev. 21:1–7, "Behold, I make all things new."

171. **settle:** seat or ledge.

Oh moment, one and infinite!
    The water slips o'er stock and stone;
The west is tender, hardly bright;
    How gray at once is the evening grown —
One star, its chrysolite!°

We two stood there with never a third,
    But each by each, as each knew well;
The sights we saw and the sounds we heard,
    The lights and the shades made up a spell
Till the trouble grew and stirred.   190

Oh, the little more, and how much it is!
    And the little less, and what worlds away!
How a sound shall quicken content to bliss,
    Or a breath suspend the blood's best play,
And life be a proof of this!

Had she willed it, still had stood the screen
    So slight, so sure, 'twixt my love and her;
I could fix her face with a guard between,
    And find her soul as when friends confer,
Friends — lovers that might have been.   200

For my heart had a touch of the woodland-time,
    Wanting to sleep now over its best.
Shake the whole tree in the summer-prime,
    But bring to the last leaf no such test!
"Hold the last fast!" runs the rhyme.

For a chance to make your little much,
    To gain a lover and lose a friend,
Venture the tree and a myriad such,
    When nothing you mar but the year can mend;
But a last leaf — fear to touch!   210

Yet should it unfasten itself and fall
    Eddying down till it find your face
At some slight wind — best chance of all!
    Be your heart henceforth its dwelling-place
You trembled to forestall!

Worth how well, those dark gray eyes,
    That hair so dark and dear, how worth
That a man should strive and agonize,
    And taste a veriest hell on earth
For the hope of such a prize!   220

You might have turned and tried a man,
    Set him a space to weary and wear,
And prove which suited more your plan,
    His best of hope or his worst despair,
Yet end as he began.

But you spared me this, like the heart you are,
    And filled my empty heart at a word.

185. **chrysolite:** an olive-green stone, used as a gem.

If two lives join, there is oft a scar,
    They are one and one, with a shadowy third;
One near one is too far.   230

A moment after, and hands unseen
    Were hanging the night around us fast;
But we knew that a bar was broken between
    Life and life: we were mixed at last
In spite of the mortal screen.

The forests had done it; there they stood;
    We caught for a moment the powers at play;
They had mingled us so, for once and good,
    Their work was done — we might go or stay,
They relapsed to their ancient mood.   240

How the world is made for each of us!
    How all we perceive and know in it
Tends to some moment's product thus,
    When a soul declares itself — to wit,
By its fruit, the thing it does!

Be hate that fruit or love that fruit,
    It forwards the general deed of man,
And each of the Many helps to recruit
    The life of the race by a general plan;
Each living his own, to boot.   250

I am named and known by that moment's feat;
    There took my station and degree;
So grew my own small life complete,
    As nature obtained her best of me —
One born to love you, sweet!

And to watch you sink by the fireside now
    Back again, as you mutely sit
Musing by firelight, that great brow
    And the spirit-small hand propping it,
Yonder, my heart knows how!   260

So, earth has gained by one man the more,
    And the gain of earth must be heaven's gain too;
And the whole is well worth thinking o'er
    When autumn comes: which I mean to do
One day. as I said before.

MY STAR

"My Star" is traditionally interpreted as referring
to Mrs. Browning. The imagery fits that interpretation,
though later the poet more often used the moon to
symbolize his wife. When Browning made a selection
from his poems in 1872 he chose this one to be first in
the volume.

All that I know
  Of a certain star
Is, it can throw
  (Like the angled spar°)
Now a dart of red,
  Now a dart of blue;
Till my friends have said
  They would fain see, too,
My star that dartles the red and the blue!
Then it stops like a bird; like a flower, hangs
    furled;   10
  They must solace themselves with the Saturn°
    above it.
What matter to me if their star is a world?
  Mine has opened its soul to me; therefore I
    love it.

CHILDE ROLAND TO THE DARK TOWER CAME

(See Edgar's song in *Lear*.)

" Childe Roland to the Dark Tower Came " was
written, Browning tells us, on January 2, 1852, when
he had resolved to write a poem each day. On January 1 he wrote " Women and Roses," the record of a
vivid dream; on January 3 he wrote " Love among the
Ruins," containing much reminiscence.

In forcing himself to write, Browning drew upon
dream, nightmare, and reminiscence. His sources for
" Childe Roland " went much deeper into his subconscious than is indicated by his reference to Edgar's
line in *King Lear* (III.iv.187), his favorite play, which
he had recently been reading. He realized later that a
tower he had seen in the Carrara Mountains, a painting
he had seen in Paris, and the figure of a horse in a
tapestry in his drawing room in Florence had entered
into his conception. Even more fundamentally, fairy
tales vaguely remembered and a favorite book he had
almost memorized in his youth, Gerard de Lairesse's
The Art of Painting in All Its Branches (1778), supplied most of the details for his fantasy, especially
Lairesse's chapter " Of Things Deformed and Broken,
Falsely Called Painter-Like."

When he was asked late in life if he agreed with an
allegorical interpretation of the poem, Browning said,
" Oh, no, not at all. Understand I don't repudiate it,
either. I only mean I was conscious of no allegorical
intention in writing it." When a friend asked the
poet if the meaning of the poem could be expressed
in the phrase, " He that endureth to the end shall be
saved," he replied, " Yes, just about that." Browning,
writing in a dream, had employed one of the most
characteristic patterns of his poetry. In " Childe Roland " a journey is imagined, a march with military
overtones is made, as it is in " The Lost Leader,"

" How They Brought the Good News," " Prospice,"
the Epilogue to *Asolando,* and many other poems by
Browning. The goal is not so important as the manner
in which the journey is accomplished. In " Childe
Roland," as in " How They Brought the Good News,"
we do not know the outcome, but how Roland endures
the physical and psychological terrors which assail him
on his quest tells us the quality of his character. Compare T. S. Eliot's *Waste Land.* A "childe" was a
young esquire, a candidate for knighthood.

My first thought was, he lied in every word,
  That hoary cripple, with malicious eye
  Askance to watch the working of his lie
On mine, and mouth scarce able to afford
Suppression of the glee, that pursed and scored
  Its edge, at one more victim gained thereby.

What else should he be set for, with his staff?
  What, save to waylay with his lies, ensnare
  All travelers who might find him posted there,
And ask the road? I guessed what skull-like
    laugh   10
Would break, what crutch 'gin write my epitaph
  For pastime in the dusty thoroughfare,

If at his counsel I should turn aside
  Into that ominous tract which, all agree,
  Hides the Dark Tower. Yet acquiescingly
I did turn as he pointed; neither pride
Nor hope rekindling at the end descried,
  So much as gladness that some end might be.

For, what with my whole world-wide wandering,
  What with my search drawn out through years,
    my hope   20
  Dwindled into a ghost not fit to cope
With that obstreperous joy success would bring —
I hardly tried now to rebuke the spring
  My heart made, finding failure in its scope.

As when a sick man very near to death
  Seems dead indeed, and feels begin and end
  The tears, and takes the farewell of each friend,
And hears one bid the other go, draw breath
Freelier outside (" since all is o'er," he saith,
  " And the blow fallen no grieving can
    amend "),   30

While some discuss if near the other graves
  Be room enough for this, and when a day
  Suits best for carrying the corpse away,
With care about the banners, scarves, and staves:
And still the man hears all, and only craves
  He may not shame such tender love and stay.

Thus, I had so long suffered in this quest,
  Heard failure prophesied so oft, been writ

So many times among " The Band " — to wit,
   The knights who to the Dark Tower's search
      addressed   40
   Their steps — that just to fail as they, seemed best,
And all the doubt was now — should I be fit?

So, quiet as despair, I turned from him,
   That hateful cripple, out of his highway
   Into the path he pointed. All the day
Had been a dreary one at best, and dim
Was settling to its close, yet shot one grim
   Red leer to see the plain catch its estray.°

For mark! no sooner was I fairly found
   Pledged to the plain, after a pace or two,   50
   Than, pausing to throw backward a last view
O'er the safe road, 'twas gone; gray plain all round;
Nothing but plain to the horizon's bound.
   I might go on; naught else remained to do.

So, on I went. I think I never saw
   Such starved ignoble nature; nothing throve;
   For flowers — as well expect a cedar grove!
But cockle, spurge, according to their law
Might propagate their kind, with none to awe,
   You'd think; a burr had been a treasure-trove.

No! penury, inertness, and grimace,   61
   In some strange sort, were the land's portion.
   " See
Or shut your eyes," said Nature peevishly,
" It nothing skills; I cannot help my case;
'Tis the Last Judgment's fire must cure this place,
   Calcine° its clods and set my prisoners free."

If there pushed any ragged thistle-stalk
   Above its mates, the head was chopped; the
      bents°
   Were jealous else. What made those holes and
      rents
In the dock's harsh swarth leaves, bruised as to
      balk   70
All hope of greenness? 'tis a brute must walk
   Pashing their life out, with a brute's intents.

As for the grass, it grew as scant as hair
   In leprosy; thin dry blades pricked the mud
   Which underneath looked kneaded up with
      blood.
One stiff blind horse, his every bone a-stare,
Stood stupefied, however he came there;
   Thrust out past service from the devil's stud!

Alive? he might be dead for aught I know,
   With that red gaunt and colloped° neck
     a-strain,   80
And shut eyes underneath the rusty mane;
Seldom went such grotesqueness with such woe;
I never saw a brute I hated so;
   He must be wicked to deserve such pain.

I shut my eyes and turned them on my heart.
   As a man calls for wine before he fights,
   I asked one draught of earlier, happier sights,
Ere fitly I could hope to play my part.
Think first, fight afterwards — the soldier's art;
   One taste of the old time sets all to rights.   90

Not it! I fancied Cuthbert's reddening face
   Beneath its garniture of curly gold,
   Dear fellow, till I almost felt him fold
An arm in mine to fix me to the place,°
That way he used. Alas, one night's disgrace!
   Out went my heart's new fire and left it cold.

Giles then, the soul of honor — there he stands
   Frank as ten years ago when knighted first.
   What honest man should dare (he said) he
     durst.
Good — but the scene shifts — faugh! what hang-
     man hands   100
Pin to his breast a parchment? His own bands
   Read it. Poor traitor, spit upon and cursed!

Better this present than a past like that;
   Back therefore to my darkening path again!
   No sound, no sight as far as eye could strain.
Will the night send a howlet° or a bat?
I asked: when something on the dismal flat
   Came to arrest my thoughts and change their
     train.

A sudden little river crossed my path
   As unexpected as a serpent comes.   110
   No sluggish tide congenial to the glooms;
This, as it frothed by, might have been a bath
For the fiend's glowing hoof — to see the wrath
   Of its black eddy bespate° with flakes and
     spumes.

So petty yet so spiteful! All along,
   Low scrubby alders kneeled down over it;
   Drenched willows flung them headlong in a
     fit
Of mute despair, a suicidal throng;
The river which had done them all the wrong,
   Whate'er that was, rolled by, deterred no
     whit.   120

CHILDE ROLAND. **48. estray:** the victim who has strayed.
66. Calcine: to turn to powder by means of heat. **68. bents:**
coarse grasses.

80. colloped: ridged.   **94. fix . . . place:** strengthen my resolve.
106. howlet: owl.   **114. bespate:** spattered.

Which, while I forded — good saints, how I feared
  To set my foot upon a dead man's cheek,
  Each step, or feel the spear I thrust to seek
For hollows, tangled in his hair or beard!
  — It may have been a water-rat I speared,
  But, ugh! it sounded like a baby's shriek.

Glad was I when I reached the other bank.
  Now for a better country. Vain presage!
  Who were the strugglers, what war did they
    wage,
Whose savage trample thus could pad the
    dank   130
Soil to a plash? Toads in a poisoned tank,
  Or wild cats in a red-hot iron cage —

The fight must so have seemed in that fell cirque.°
  What penned them there, with all the plain to
    choose?
  No footprint leading to that horrid mews,
None out of it. Mad brewage set to work
  Their brains, no doubt, like galley-slaves the Turk
  Pits for his pastime, Christians against Jews.

And more than that — a furlong on — why, there!
  What bad use was that engine for, that
    wheel,   140
  Or brake,° not wheel — that harrow fit to reel
Men's bodies out like silk? with all the air
  Of Tophet's° tool, on earth left unaware,
  Or brought to sharpen its rusty teeth of steel.

Then came a bit of stubbed ground, once a wood,
  Next a marsh, it would seem, and now mere
    earth
Desperate and done with; (so a fool finds mirth,
Makes a thing and then mars it, till his mood
Changes and off he goes!) within a rood° —
  Bog, clay and rubble, sand and stark black
    dearth.   150

Now blotches rankling, colored gay and grim,
  Now patches where some leanness of the soil's
  Broke into moss or substances like boils;
Then came some palsied° oak, a cleft in him
  Like a distorted mouth that splits its rim
  Gaping at death, and dies while it recoils.

And just as far as ever from the end!
  Naught in the distance but the evening, naught
  To point my footstep further! At the thought,
A great black bird, Apollyon's° bosom friend, 160

Sailed past, nor beat his wide wing dragon-penned°
  That brushed my cap — perchance the guide I
    sought.

For, looking up, aware I somehow grew,
  'Spite of the dusk, the plain had given place
  All round to mountains — with such name to
    grace
Mere ugly heights and heaps now stolen in view.
How thus they had surprised me — solve it, you!
  How to get from them was no clearer case.

Yet half I seemed to recognize some trick
  Of mischief happened to me, God knows
    when —   170
  In a bad dream perhaps. Here ended, then,
Progress this way. When, in the very nick
Of giving up, one time more, came a click
  As when a trap shuts — you're inside the den!

Burningly it came on me all at once,
  This was the place! those two hills on the right,
  Crouched like two bulls locked horn in horn in
    fight;
While to the left, a tall scalped° mountain . . .
    Dunce,
Dotard, a-dozing at the very nonce,°
  After a life spent training for the sight!   180

What in the midst lay but the Tower itself?
  The round squat turret, blind as the fool's heart,
  Built of brown stone, without a counterpart
In the whole world. The tempest's mocking elf
Points to the shipman thus the unseen shelf
  He strikes on, only when the timbers start.

Not see? because of night perhaps? — why, day
  Came back again for that! before it left,
  The dying sunset kindled through a cleft;°
The hills, like giants at a hunting, lay,   190
Chin upon hand, to see the game at bay —
  " Now stab and end the creature — to the heft! "

Not hear? when noise was everywhere! it tolled
  Increasing like a bell. Names in my ears
  Of all the lost adventurers my peers —
How such a one was strong, and such was bold,
And such was fortunate, yet each of old
  Lost, lost! one moment knelled the woe of
    years.

There they stood, ranged along the hillsides, met
  To view the last of me, a living frame   200
  For one more picture! in a sheet of flame

---

133. cirque: circular arena. **141. brake:** a machine for separating fiber, such as flax or hemp. **143. Tophet:** Hell. **149. rood:** a rod, about 5½ yards. **154. palsied:** paralyzed, here struck by lightning. **160. Apollyon:** another name for the Devil.

161. dragon-penned: with pinions like a dragon. **178. scalped:** bare at the peak. **179. nonce:** moment. **189. cleft:** an opening in the hills.

I saw them and I knew them all. And yet
Dauntless the slug-horn° to my lips I set,
  And blew. "*Childe Roland to the Dark Tower
  came.*"

RESPECTABILITY

This poem was probably written in February, 1852,
when François Guizot (1787–1874), the statesman and
historian, delivered the *discours de reception* to Charles
Montalembert (1810–70) upon the latter's election to
the Académie Française, a branch of the Institut de
France. Convention compelled Guizot to receive
Montalembert, though there was enmity between the
two men. It has been suggested that Browning had in
mind as his unconventional lovers George Sand, the
novelist and radical, and Jules Sandeau, with whom
she lived after leaving her husband. The scene is Paris.

Dear, had the world in its caprice
  Deigned to proclaim, "I know you both,
  Have recognized your plighted troth,
Am sponsor for you; live in peace!" —
How many precious months and years
  Of youth had passed, that speed so fast,
  Before we found it out at last,
The world, and what it fears!

How much of priceless life were spent
  With men that every virtue decks,   10
  And women models of their sex,
Society's true ornament —
Ere we dared wander, nights like this,
  Through wind and rain, and watch the Seine,
  And feel the Boulevard break again
To warmth and light and bliss!

I know! the world proscribes not love;
  Allows my finger to caress
  Your lips' contour and downiness,
Provided it supply a glove.   20
The world's good word! — the Institute!
  Guizot receives Montalembert!
Eh? Down the court three lampions° flare;
Put forward your best foot!

HOW IT STRIKES
A CONTEMPORARY

This poem may have been written in Paris early in
1852. In considering the nature and function of poetry,
Browning had been reading Shelley and Shakespeare
as contrasting kinds of poets, subjective and dramatic.

(See the Introduction, p. 839.) Browning's own view
was expressed in his "Introductory Essay" to *Letters of Percy Bysshe Shelley* as follows: "The whole
poet's function [is that] of beholding with an understanding keenness the universe, nature, and man, in
their actual state of perfection in imperfection. . . ."
Browning was never in Valladolid, a town in north
central Spain, and the details of the poem are imaginary. For Browning's admiration of Shelley see
"Memorabilia," p. 861, below.

I only knew one poet in my life;
And this, or something like it, was his way.
  You saw go up and down Valladolid

A man of mark, to know next time you saw.
His very serviceable suit of black
Was courtly once and conscientious still,
And many might have worn it, though none did;
The cloak, that somewhat shone and showed the
  threads,
Had purpose, and the ruff, significance.
He walked and tapped the pavement with his cane,
Scenting the world, looking it full in face,   11
An old dog, bald and blindish, at his heels.
They turned up, now, the alley by the church,
That leads nowhither; now, they breathed them-
  selves
On the main promenade just at the wrong time;
You'd come upon his scrutinizing hat,
Making a peaked shade blacker than itself
Against the single window spared some house
Intact yet with its moldered Moorish work° —
Or else surprise the ferrel° of his stick   20
Trying the mortar's temper 'tween the chinks
Of some new shop a-building, French and fine.
He stood and watched the cobbler at his trade,
The man who slices lemons into drink,
The coffee roaster's brazier, and the boys
That volunteer to help him turn its winch.
He glanced o'er books on stalls with half an eye,
And flyleaf ballads° on the vendor's string,
And broad-edge bold-print posters by the wall.
He took such cognizance of men and things, 30
If any beat a horse, you felt he saw;
If any cursed a woman, he took note;
Yet stared at nobody — you stared at him,
And found, less to your pleasure than surprise,
He seemed to know you and expect as much.
So, next time that a neighbor's tongue was loosed,
It marked the shameful and notorious fact,
We had among us, not so much a spy,
As a recording chief-inquisitor,
The town's true master if the town but knew! 40

---

203. **slug-horn:** trumpet. Actually there is no such horn. Browning borrowed the word from Chatterton, who misunderstood the
word "slogan." RESPECTABILITY.   23. **lampions:** lamps. As
they come to the lighted court of the Institute, the woman
remarks ironically that they must appear at their best.

HOW IT STRIKES A CONTEMPORARY. 19. **Moorish work:** a survival
of the time when the Moors were masters of Spain. 20. **ferrel:**
the metal point. 28. **flyleaf ballads:** broadsides, ballads printed
on single sheets of paper.

We merely kept a governor for form,
While this man walked about and took account
Of all thought, said, and acted, then went home,
And wrote it fully to our Lord the King°
Who has an itch to know things, he knows why,
And reads them in his bedroom of a night.
Oh, you might smile! there wanted not a touch,
A tang of . . . well, it was not wholly ease
As back into your mind the man's look came.
Stricken in years a little — such a brow   50
His eyes had to live under! — clear as flint
On either side the formidable nose
Curved, cut, and colored like an eagle's claw.
Had he to do with A's surprising fate?
When altogether old B disappeared
And young C got his mistress — was't our friend,
His letter to the King, that did it all?
What paid the bloodless man for so much pains?
Our Lord the King has favorites manifold,
And shifts his ministry some once a month;   60
Our city gets new governors at whiles —
But never word or sign, that I could hear,
Notified to this man about the streets
The King's approval of those letters conned
The last thing duly at the dead of night.
Did the man love his office? Frowned our Lord,
Exhorting when none heard — "Beseech me not!
Too far above my people — beneath me!
I set the watch — how should the people know?
Forget them, keep me all the more in mind!"   70
Was some such understanding 'twixt the two?

I found no truth in one report at least —
That if you tracked him to his home, down lanes
Beyond the Jewry,° and as clean to pace,
You found he ate his supper in a room
Blazing with lights, four Titians° on the wall,
And twenty naked girls to change his plate!
Poor man, he lived another kind of life
In that new stuccoed third house by the bridge,
Fresh-painted, rather smart than otherwise!   80
The whole street might o'erlook him as he sat,
Leg crossing leg, one foot on the dog's back,
Playing a decent cribbage with his maid
(Jacynth, you're sure her name was) o'er the cheese
And fruit, three red halves of starved winter-pears,
Or treat of radishes in April. Nine,
Ten, struck the church clock, straight to bed went
    he.

My father, like the man of sense he was,
Would point him out to me a dozen times;
" 'St — 'St," he'd whisper, " the Corregidor!"°   90

I had been used to think that personage
Was one with lacquered breeches, lustrous belt,
And feathers like a forest in his hat,
Who blew a trumpet and proclaimed the news,
Announced the bullfights, gave each church its turn,
And memorized the miracle in vogue!
He had a great observance from us boys;
We were in error; that was not the man.

I'd like now, yet had haply been afraid,
To have just looked, when this man came to die,
And seen who lined the clean gay garret-sides   101
And stood about the neat low truckle-bed,
With the heavenly manner of relieving guard.
Here had been, mark, the general-in-chief,
Through a whole campaign of the world's life and
    death,
Doing the King's work all the dim day long,
In his old coat and up to knees in mud,
Smoked like a herring, dining on a crust —
And, now the day was won, relieved at once!
No further show or need for that old coat,   110
You are sure, for one thing! Bless us, all the while
How sprucely we are dressed out, you and I!°
A second, and the angels alter that.
Well, I could never write a verse — could you?
Let's to the Prado° and make the most of time.

MEMORABILIA

" Memorabilia " is a monument to Browning's early
adoration of Shelley, and is possibly a product of his
labors for the " Introductory Essay " that he wrote in
the fall of 1851 to accompany a collection of Shelley
letters which later proved to be spurious. According to
a friend, W. G. Kingsland, Browning was in the shop
of a London bookseller when a stranger entered and
began a conversation with the bookseller about Shelley,
remarking that he had seen and spoken to Shelley. The
stranger turned and broke into a laugh when he saw
Browning " staring at him with a blanched face."
Browning added to Kingsland, " I still remember vividly how strangely the presence of a man who had seen
and spoken with Shelley affected me." The title signifies " things worth remembering." See the headnote to
" How It Strikes a Contemporary," p. 860, above, and
the Introduction, p. 839.

Ah, did you once see Shelley plain,
    And did he stop and speak to you
And did you speak to him again?
    How strange it seems and new!

But you were living before that,
    And also you are living after;
And the memory I started at —
    My starting moves your laughter!

44. our . . . King: The king symbolizes God. In the first edition
all the pronouns referring to him were capitalized.   74. the
Jewry: the ghetto.   76. Titians: paintings by the great Italian,
Titian (1477–1575).   90. the Corregidor: the chief magistrate.

111-12. Bless . . . I!: This passage is an aside.   115. Prado: the
promenade where fashion and gaiety congregate.

I crossed a moor, with a name of its own
   And a certain use in the world no doubt,   10
Yet a handsbreadth of it shines alone
   'Mid the blank miles round about;

For there I picked up on the heather,
   And there I put inside my breast
A molted feather, an eagle-feather!
   Well, I forget the rest.

SAUL

The first nine sections of "Saul" were published as a fragment in the *Dramatic Romances* in 1845 at Miss Barrett's insistence; in 1855 ten new sections were added, with a few changes to accommodate the new matter. The first part of "Saul" was conceived in January, 1845, when Browning read Christopher Smart's great "Song to David." In his foreword to his "Ode to Musick on Saint Cecilia's Day" Smart said: "It would not be right to conclude without taking notice of a fine subject for an Ode on S. Cecilia's Day, . . . that is David's playing to King Saul when he was troubled with the evil spirit. He," continued Smart speaking of himself, "was much pleased with the hint [of the subject] at first, but at length was deterred from improving it by the greatness of the subject, and he thinks not without reason. The chusing [sic] of too high subjects has been the ruin of many a tolerable Genius." Browning's Biblical source is, of course, I Samuel 16:4–23. The first nine sections of "Saul" are written in the manner of Smart's poetry, as we shall see below.

In 1845, Browning was unable to bring the poem to a conclusion which satisfied him. In "Christmas Eve and Easter Day" (1850) he succeeded, with Mrs. Browning's help, in clarifying his religious ideas, and in 1852–53 he completed "Saul." The last ten sections of the poem are on a different philosophical and religious plane from the first nine. Sir Thomas Wyatt's *Seven Penitential Psalms,* a copy of which was in the Brownings' library in Florence, seems to have provided the framework for Browning's poem.

Christopher Smart, under whose spirit the first nine sections of the poem were written, devoted his whole genius to recording the good things of the earth in his poetry for the purpose of praising God. Browning adopts this manner and makes David praise the good things of the earth as arguments why King Saul should wish to live. David sings (sections 5 and 6) of the innocent happiness of nature, of the joys and comforts of the community of men and their ceremonies (7 and 9), and of the pride of the warrior all "brought to blaze on the head of one creature — King Saul!" At this point David has restored life to Saul. The medical aspect of the cure is complete.

But this is insufficient to move Saul to a zest for life. In the next nine sections Browning develops the theology which informs many of his poems, such as "Cleon," "Karshish," and "The Pope" in *The Ring and the Book,* to name only a few. David agrees with Saul (13) that the King is right in rejecting the mere comforts of earth as a reason for living. Even earthly fame (13 and 15) is not enough. Man needs a larger hope. God's power is evident in the universe and so is his wisdom (17). What is needed is overwhelming evidence of God's love for man. David, inspired suddenly to see that his own love for Saul is a microscopic representation of God's love for man, rises to prophetic vision at this point (18) and foretells the coming of Christ, sent to earth to assure us of God's love for man, and the immortality which is a consequence of that love. The end of the eighteenth section parallels the end of the ninth; the nineteenth section records the dazed ecstasy of David as he stumbles away from the healed King. The poem begins as David, keeping his flock in the fields again the next day, recollects his encounter with Saul.

I

Said Abner,° "At last thou art come! Ere I tell, ere
   thou speak,
Kiss my cheek, wish me well!" Then I wished it,
   and did kiss his cheek.
And he: "Since the King,° O my friend, for thy
   countenance sent,
Neither drunken nor eaten have we; nor until from
   his tent
Thou return with the joyful assurance the King
   liveth yet,
Shall our lip with the honey be bright, with the
   water be wet.
For out of the black mid-tent's silence, a space of
   three days,
Not a sound hath escaped to thy servants, of prayer
   nor of praise,
To betoken that Saul and the Spirit have ended
   their strife,
And that, faint in his triumph, the monarch sinks
   back upon life.   10

2

"Yet now my heart leaps, O beloved! God's child
   with his dew
On thy gracious gold hair, and those lilies still living
   and blue
Just broken to twine round thy harpstrings, as if no
   wild heat
Were now raging to torture the desert!"

3

Then I, as was meet,
Knelt down to the God of my fathers, and rose on
   my feet,
And ran o'er the sand burnt to powder. The tent
   was unlooped;

SAUL.   **1. Abner:** Saul's uncle and general of his army.   **3. the King:** Saul.

I pulled up the spear that obstructed, and under I
  stooped;
Hands and knees on the slippery grass-patch, all
  withered and gone,
That extends to the second enclosure, I groped my
  way on
Till I felt where the foldskirts fly open. Then once
  more I prayed,   20
And opened the foldskirts and entered, and was
  not afraid
But spoke, "Here is David, thy servant!" And no
  voice replied.
At the first I saw naught but the blackness; but
  soon I descried
A something more black than the blackness — the
  vast, the upright
Main prop which sustains the pavilion; and slow
  into sight
Grew a figure against it, gigantic and blackest of
  all.
Then a sunbeam, that burst through the tent-roof,
  showed Saul.

4

He stood as erect as that tent-prop, both arms
  stretched out wide
On the great cross-support in the center, that goes
  to each side;
He relaxed not a muscle, but hung there as, caught
  in his pangs   30
And waiting his change, the king-serpent° all
  heavily hangs,
Far away from his kind, in the pine, till deliverance
  come
With the springtime — so agonized Saul, drear and
  stark, blind and dumb.

5

Then I tuned my harp — took off the lilies we
  twine round its chords
Lest they snap 'neath the stress of the noontide —
  those sunbeams like swords!
And I first played the tune all our sheep know, as,
  one after one,
So docile they come to the pen-door till folding be
  done.
They are white and untorn by the bushes, for lo,
  they have fed
Where the long grasses stifle the water within the
  stream's bed;
And now one after one seeks its lodging, as star
  follows star   40
Into eve and the blue far above us — so blue and
  so far!

31. the king-serpent: perhaps the boa-constrictor, awaiting the
change of his skin in the spring.

6

— Then the tune for which quails on the cornland
  will each leave his mate
To fly after the player; then, what makes the crickets elate
Till for boldness they fight one another; and then,
  what has weight
To set the quick jerboa° a-musing outside his sand
  house —
There are none such as he for a wonder, half bird
  and half mouse!
God made all the creatures and gave them our love
  and our fear,
To give sign, we and they are his children, one
  family here.

7

Then I played the help-tune of our reapers, their
  wine-song, when hand
Grasps at hand, eye lights eye in good friendship,
  and great hearts expand   50
And grow one in the sense of this world's life. —
  And then, the last song
When the dead man is praised on his journey —
  "Bear, bear him along,
With his few faults shut up like dead flowerets!
  Are balm-seeds not here
To console us? The land has none left such as he
  on the bier.
Oh, would we might keep thee, my brother!" —
  And then, the glad chaunt
Of the marriage — first go the young maidens;
  next, she whom we vaunt
As the beauty, the pride of our dwelling. — And
  then, the great march°
Wherein man runs to man to assist him and but-
  tress an arch
Naught can break; who shall harm them, our
  friends? — Then, the chorus intoned
As the Levites° go up to the altar in glory en-
  throned.   60
But I stopped here; for here in the darkness Saul
  groaned.

8

And I paused, held my breath in such silence, and
  listened apart;
And the tent shook, for mighty Saul shuddered;
  and sparkles 'gan dart
From the jewels that woke in his turban, at once
  with a start,

45. jerboa: the leaping hare of the rodent family. It is called "half
bird" in the next line because of its speed and height in leaping.
57. the . . . march: of the battle.   60. Levites: priests, the sons
of Levi.

All its lordly male-sapphires,° and rubies coura-
    geous at heart.
So the head; but the body still moved not, still
    hung there erect.
And I bent once again to my playing, pursued it
    unchecked,
As I sang:

9

"Oh, our manhood's prime vigor! No spirit feels
    waste,
Not a muscle is stopped in its playing nor sinew un-
    braced.
Oh, the wild joys of living! the leaping from rock
    up to rock,   70
The strong rending of boughs from the fir-tree, the
    cool silver shock
Of the plunge in a pool's living water, the hunt of
    the bear,
And the sultriness showing the lion is couched in
    his lair.
And the meal, the rich dates yellowed over with
    gold dust divine,
And the locust-flesh steeped in the pitcher, the full
    draught of wine,
And the sleep in the dried river-channel where bul-
    rushes tell
That the water was wont to go warbling so softly
    and well.
How good is man's life, the mere living! how fit
    to employ
All the heart and the soul and the senses for ever in
    joy!
Hast thou loved the white locks of thy father,
    whose sword thou didst guard   80
When he trusted thee forth with the armies, for
    glorious reward?
Didst thou see the thin hands of thy mother, held
    up as men sung
The low song of the nearly departed, and hear her
    faint tongue
Joining in while it could to the witness, 'Let one
    more attest,
I have lived, seen God's hand through a lifetime,
    and all was for best'?
Then they sung through their tears in strong tri-
    umph, not much, but the rest.
And thy brothers, the help and the contest, the
    working whence grew
Such result as, from seething grape-bundles, the
    spirit strained true;
And the friends of thy boyhood — that boyhood of
    wonder and hope,

Present promise and wealth of the future beyond
    the eye's scope —   90
Till lo, thou art grown to a monarch; a people is
    thine;
And all gifts, which the world offers singly, on one
    head combine!
On one head, all the beauty and strength, love and
    rage (like the throe
That, a-work in the rock, helps its labor and lets
    the gold go)
High ambition and deeds which surpass it, fame
    crowning them — all
Brought to blaze on the head of one creature —
    King Saul!"°

10

And lo, with that leap of my spirit — heart, hand,
    harp and voice,
Each lifting Saul's name out of sorrow, each bid-
    ding rejoice
Saul's fame in the light it was made for — as when,
    dare I say,
The Lord's army, in rapture of service, strains
    through its array,   100
And upsoareth the cherubim-chariot — "Saul!"
    cried I, and stopped,
And waited the thing that should follow. Then
    Saul, who hung propped
By the tent's cross-support in the center, was struck
    by his name.
Have ye seen when spring's arrowy summons goes
    right to the aim,
And some mountain, the last to withstand her, that
    held (he alone,
While the vale laughed in freedom and flowers)
    on a broad bust of stone
A year's snow bound about for a breastplate —
    leaves grasp of the sheet?
Fold on fold all at once it crowds thunderously
    down to his feet,
And there fronts you, stark, black, but alive yet,
    your mountain of old,
With his rents, the successive bequeathings of ages
    untold —   110
Yea, each harm got in fighting your battles, each
    furrow and scar
Of his head thrust 'twixt you and the tempest — all
    hail, there they are!
— Now again to be softened with verdure, again
    hold the nest
Of the dove, tempt the goat and its young to the
    green on his crest
For their food in the ardors of summer. One long
    shudder thrilled

---

65. male-sapphires: brilliant blue gems, sometimes called star-
stones.

96. King Saul: Cf. l. 312.

All the tent till the very air tingled, then sank and
   was stilled
At the King's self left standing before me, released
   and aware.
What was gone, what remained? All to traverse
   'twixt hope and despair;
Death was past, life not come; so he waited. Awhile
   his right hand
Held the brow, helped the eyes left too vacant forth-
   with to remand   120
To their place what new objects should enter: 'twas
   Saul as before.
I looked up and dared gaze at those eyes, nor was
   hurt any more
Than by slow pallid sunsets in autumn, ye watch
   from the shore,
At their sad level gaze o'er the ocean — a sun's slow
   decline
Over hills which, resolved in stern silence, o'erlap
   and entwine
Base with base to knit strength more intensely; so,
   arm folded arm
O'er the chest whose slow heavings subsided.

11

What spell or what charm
(For, awhile there was trouble within me) what
   next should I urge
To sustain him where song had restored him? —
   Song filled to the verge
His cup with the wine of this life, pressing all that
   it yields   130
Of mere fruitage, the strength and the beauty; be-
   yond, on what fields,
Glean a vintage more potent and perfect to brighten
   the eye
And bring blood to the lip, and commend them the
   cup they put by?
He saith, " It is good"; still he drinks not; he lets
   me praise life,
Gives assent, yet would die for his own part.

12

Then fancies grew rife
Which had come long ago on the pasture, when
   round me the sheep
Fed in silence — above, the one eagle wheeled slow
   as in sleep;
And I lay in my hollow and mused on the world
   that might lie
'Neath his ken, though I saw but the strip 'twixt
   the hill and the sky;
And I laughed — " Since my days are ordained to
   be passed with my flocks,   140
Let me people at least, with my fancies, the plains
   and the rocks,

Dream the life I am never to mix with, and image
   the show
Of mankind as they live in those fashions I hardly
   shall know!
Schemes of life, its best rules and right uses, the
   courage that gains,
And the prudence that keeps what men strive for."
   And now these old trains
Of vague thought came again; I grew surer; so,
   once more the string
Of my harp made response to my spirit, as thus —

13

" Yea, my King,"
I began — " thou dost well in rejecting mere com-
   forts that spring
From the mere mortal life held in common by man
   and by brute:
In our flesh grows the branch of this life, in our
   soul it bears fruit.   150
Thou hast marked the slow rise of the tree — how
   its stem trembled first
Till it passed the kid's lip, the stag's antler; then
   safely outburst
The fan-branches all round; and thou mindest
   when these too, in turn
Broke a-bloom and the palm-tree seemed perfect;
   yet more was to learn,
E'en the good that comes in with the palm-fruit.
   Our dates shall we slight,
When their juice brings a cure for all sorrow? or
   care for the plight
Of the palm's self whose slow growth produced
   them? Not so! stem and branch
Shall decay, nor be known in their place, while the
   palm-wine shall stanch
Every wound of man's spirit in winter. I pour thee
   such wine.
Leave the flesh to the fate it was fit for! the spirit
   be thine!   160
By the spirit, when age shall o'ercome thee, thou
   still shalt enjoy
More indeed, than at first when inconscious,° the
   life of a boy.
Crush that life, and behold its wine running! Each
   deed thou hast done
Dies, revives, goes to work in the world; until e'en
   as the sun
Looking down on the earth, though clouds spoil
   him, though tempests efface,
Can find nothing his own deed produced not, must
   everywhere trace
The results of his past summer-prime — so, each
   ray of thy will,

162. inconscious: not conscious.

Every flash of thy passion and prowess, long over, shall thrill
Thy whole people, the countless, with ardor, till they too give forth
A like cheer to their sons, who in turn fill the south and the north   170
With the radiance thy deed was the germ of. Carouse in the past!
But the license of age has its limit; thou diest at last:
As the lion when age dims his eyeball, the rose at her height,
So with man — so his power and his beauty for ever take flight.
No! Again a long draught of my soul-wine!° Look forth o'er the years!
Thou hast done now with eyes for the actual;° begin with the seer's!
Is Saul dead? In the depth of the vale make his tomb — bid arise
A gray mountain of marble heaped four-square till, built to the skies,
Let it mark where the great First King slumbers: whose frame would ye know?
Up above see the rock's naked face, where the record shall go   180
In great characters cut by the scribe — Such was Saul, so he did;
With the sages directing the work, by the populace chid —
For not half, they'll affirm, is comprised there! Which fault to amend,
In the grove with his kind grows the cedar, whereon they shall spend
(See, in tablets 'tis level before them) their praise, and record
With the gold of the graver, Saul's story — the statesman's great word
Side by side with the poet's sweet comment. The river's a-wave
With smooth paper-reeds° grazing each other when prophet-winds rave:
So the pen gives unborn generations their due and their part
In thy being! Then, first of the mighty, thank God that thou art!"   190

14

And behold while I sang . . . but O Thou who didst grant me that day,
And before it not seldom hast granted thy help to essay,

Carry on and complete an adventure — my shield and my sword
In that act where my soul was thy servant, thy word was my word —
Still be with me, who then at the summit of human endeavor
And scaling the highest, man's thought could, gazed hopeless as ever
On the new stretch of heaven above me — till, mighty to save,
Just one lift of thy hand cleared that distance — God's throne from man's grave!
Let me tell out my tale to its ending — my voice to my heart
Which can scarce dare believe in what marvels last night I took part,   200
As this morning I gather the fragments, alone with my sheep,
And still fear lest the terrible glory evanish like sleep!
For I wake in the gray dewy covert, while Hebron° upheaves
The dawn struggling with night on his shoulder, and Kidron° retrieves
Slow the damage of yesterday's sunshine.

15

I say then — my song
While I sang thus, assuring the monarch, and ever more strong
Made a proffer of good to console him — he slowly resumed
His old motions and habitudes kingly. The right hand replumed
His black locks to their wonted composure, adjusted the swathes
Of his turban, and see — the huge sweat that his countenance bathes,   210
He wipes off with the robe; and he girds now his loins as of yore,
And feels slow for the armlets of price, with the clasp set before.
He is Saul, ye remember in glory — ere error° had bent
The broad brow from the daily communion; and still, though much spent
Be the life and the bearing that front you, the same, God did choose,
To receive what a man may waste, desecrate, never quite lose.°

---

175. **soul-wine:** insight into spiritual truth.   176. **actual:** that which exists to the senses.   188. **paper-reeds:** reeds from which papyrus was made.

203. **Hebron:** a mountain in Judea with the ancient city of Hebron upon it.   204. **Kidron:** a small stream near Jerusalem.   213. **error:** Saul had disobeyed God's command to exterminate all the Amalekites, and kept their king, Agag, and the best of their livestock. His disobedience caused God to decide that he should not remain king. See I Sam. 15.   216. **what . . . lose:** namely, his humanity, his likeness to God in spirit and mind.

So sank he along by the tent-prop till, stayed by the
    pile
Of his armor and war-cloak and garments, he
    leaned there awhile,
And sat out my singing — one arm round the tent-
    prop, to raise
His bent head, and the other hung slack — till I
    touched on the praise   220
I foresaw from all men in all time, to the man
    patient there;
And thus ended, the harp falling forward. Then
    first I was 'ware
That he sat, as I say, with my head just above his
    vast knees
Which were thrust out on each side around me,
    like oak-roots which please
To encircle a lamb when it slumbers. I looked up
    to know
If the best I could do had brought solace; he spoke
    not, but slow
Lifted up the hand slack at his side, till he laid it
    with care
Soft and grave, but in mild settled will, on my
    brow; through my hair
The large fingers were pushed, and he bent back
    my head, with kind power —
All my face back, intent to peruse it, as men do a
    flower.   230
Thus held he me there with his great eyes that
    scrutinized mine —
And oh, all my heart how it loved him! but where
    was the sign?
I yearned — "Could I help thee, my father, invent-
    ing a bliss,
I would add, to that life of the past, both the future
    and this;
I would give thee new life altogether, as good, ages
    hence,
As this moment — had love but the warrant, love's
    heart to dispense!"

16

Then the truth came upon me. No harp more — no
song more! outbroke —

17

"I have gone the whole round of creation; I saw
    and I spoke;
I, a work of God's hand for that purpose, received
    in my brain
And pronounced on the rest of his handwork — re-
    turned him again   240
His creation's approval or censure; I spoke as I
    saw:
I report, as a man may of God's work — all's love,
    yet all's law.

Now I lay down the judgeship he lent me. Each
    faculty tasked
To perceive him, has gained an abyss, where a dew-
    drop was asked.
Have I knowledge? confounded it shrivels at Wis-
    dom laid bare.
Have I forethought? how purblind, how blank, to
    the Infinite Care!
Do I task any faculty highest, to image success?
I but open my eyes — and perfection, no more and
    no less,
In the kind I imagined, full-fronts me, and God is
    seen God
In the star, in the stone, in the flesh, in the soul and
    the clod.   250
And thus looking within and around me, I ever re-
    new
(With that stoop of the soul which in bending up-
    raises it too)
The submission of man's nothing-perfect to God's
    all-complete,
As by each new obeisance in spirit, I climb to his
    feet.
Yet with all this abounding experience, this deity
    known,
I shall dare to discover some province, some gift of
    my own.
There's a faculty pleasant to exercise, hard to hood-
    wink,
I am fain to keep still in abeyance (I laugh as I
    think)
Lest, insisting to claim and parade in it, wot ye, I
    worst
E'en the Giver in one gift. — Behold, I could love
    if I durst!   260
But I sink the pretension as fearing a man may
    o'ertake
God's own speed in the one way of love; I abstain
    for love's sake.
— What, my soul? see thus far and no farther?
    when doors, great and small,
Nine-and-ninety flew ope at our touch, should the
    hundredth appall?
In the least things have faith, yet distrust in the
    greatest of all?
Do I find love so full in my nature, God's ultimate
    gift,
That I doubt his own love can compete with it?
    Here, the parts shift?
Here, the creature surpass the Creator — the end,
    what Began?
Would I fain in my impotent yearning do all for
    this man,
And dare doubt he alone shall not help him, who
    yet alone can?   270
Would it ever have entered my mind, the bare will,
    much less power,

To bestow on this Saul what I sang of, the marvelous dower
Of the life he was gifted and filled with? to make
such a soul,
Such a body, and then such an earth for insphering
the whole?
And doth it not enter my mind (as my warm tears
attest)
These good things being given, to go on, and give
one more, the best?
Aye, to save and redeem and restore him, maintain
at the height
This perfection — succeed with life's dayspring,
death's minute of night?
Interpose at the difficult minute, snatch Saul the
mistake,
Saul the failure, the ruin he seems now — and bid
him awake   280
From the dream, the probation, the prelude, to find
himself set
Clear and safe in new light and new life — a new
harmony yet
To be run, and continued, and ended — who
knows? — or endure!
The man taught enough, by life's dream, of the rest
to make sure;
By the pain-throb, triumphantly winning intensified bliss,
And the next world's reward and repose, by the
struggles in this.

18

" I believe it! 'Tis thou, God, that givest, 'tis I who
receive;
In the first is the last, in thy will is my power to
believe.
All's one gift; thou canst grant it moreover, as
prompt to my prayer
As I breathe out this breath, as I open these arms
to the air.   290
From thy will stream the worlds, life and nature,
thy dread Sabaoth;°
I will? — the mere atoms despise me! Why am I
not loath
To look that, even that in the face too? Why is it I
dare
Think but lightly of such impuissance? What stops
my despair?
This — 'tis not what man Does which exalts him,
but what man Would do!
See the King — I would help him but cannot, the
wishes fall through.
Could I wrestle to raise him from sorrow, grow
poor to enrich,

To fill up his life, starve my own out, I would —
knowing which,
I know that my service is perfect. Oh, speak through
me now!
Would I suffer for him that I love? So wouldst thou
— so wilt thou!   300
So shall crown thee the topmost, ineffablest, utter-
most crown —
And thy Love fill infinitude wholly, nor leave up
nor down
One spot for the creature to stand in! It is by no
breath,
Turn of eye, wave of hand, that salvation joins issue
with death!
As thy Love is discovered almighty, almighty be
proved
Thy power, that exists with and for it, of being
Beloved!
He who did most, shall bear most; the strongest
shall stand the most weak.
'Tis the weakness in strength, that I cry for! my
flesh, that I seek
In the Godhead! I seek and I find it. O Saul, it
shall be
A Face like my face that receives thee; a Man like
to me,   310
Thou shalt love and be loved by, for ever; a Hand
like this hand
Shall throw open the gates of new life to thee! See
the Christ stand! "

19

I know not too well how I found my way home in
the night.
There were witnesses, cohorts about me, to left and
to right,
Angels, powers, the unuttered, unseen, the alive, the
aware;
I repressed, I got through them as hardly, as strug-
glingly there,
As a runner beset by the populace famished for
news —
Life or death. The whole earth was awakened, hell
loosed with her crews;
And the stars of night beat with emotion, and
tingled and shot
Out in fire the strong pain of pent knowledge; but
I fainted not,   320
For the Hand still impelled me at once and sup-
ported, suppressed
All the tumult, and quenched it with quiet, and
holy behest,°
Till the rapture was shut in itself, and the earth
sank to rest.

---

291. Sabaoth: hosts or armies, here expressing God's omnipotence.

322. behest: command.

Anon at the dawn, all that trouble had withered
   from earth —
Not so much, but I saw it die out in the day's
   tender birth;
In the gathered intensity brought to the gray of the
   hills;
In the shuddering forests' held breath; in the sudden wind-thrills;
In the startled wild beasts that bore off, each with
   eye sidling still
Though averted with wonder and dread; in the
   birds stiff and chill
That rose heavily, as I approached them, made
   stupid with awe;   330
E'en the serpent that slid away silent — he felt the
   new law.°
The same stared in the white humid faces upturned
   by the flowers;
The same worked in the heart of the cedar and
   moved the vine-bowers;
And the little brooks witnessing murmured,
   persistent and low,
With their obstinate, all but hushed voices — " E'en
   so, it is so! "

"DE GUSTIBUS—"

Browning possibly wrote this poem at Bagni di
Lucca in 1849 when he was feeling a nostalgia for
England. The second part of the poem presents a scene
in southern Italy. Years later Browning wrote to a
friend, "Tell me all the news about Rome and
Naples. I am always thereabout in spirit." The title is
a reference to the Latin proverb, *De gustibus non est
disputandum,* "There is no arguing about tastes."

Your ghost will walk, you lover of trees,
   (If our loves remain)
     In an English lane,
By a cornfield-side a-flutter with poppies.
Hark, those two in the hazel coppice —
A boy and a girl, if the good fates please,
   Making love, say —
     The happier they!.
Draw yourself up from the light of the moon,
And let them pass, as they will too soon,   10
   With the beanflowers' boon,
   And the blackbird's tune,
   And May, and June!

What I love best in all the world
Is a castle, precipice-encurled,
In a gash of the wind-grieved Apennine.

331. **new law:** the conception, fundamental to all Browning's
religious thinking, that God is infinite in love, as proved by the
incarnation of Christ; that his love is equal to his power on the
one hand and his intelligence on the other.

Or look for me, old fellow of mine
(If I get my head from out the mouth
O' the grave, and loose my spirit's bands,
And come again to the land of lands) —   20
In a seaside house to the farther south,
Where the baked cicala dies of drouth,
And one sharp tree — 'tis a cypress — stands
By the many hundred years red-rusted,
Rough iron-spiked, ripe fruit-o'ercrusted,
My sentinel to guard the sands
To the water's edge. For, what expands
Before the house, but the great opaque
Blue breadth of sea without a break?
While, in the house, forever crumbles   30
Some fragment of the frescoed walls,
From blisters where a scorpion sprawls.
A girl barefooted brings, and tumbles
Down on the pavement, green-flesh melons,
And says there's news today — the king°
Was shot at, touched in the liver-wing,°
Goes with his Bourbon arm in a sling
— She hopes they have not caught the felons.
Italy, my Italy!
Queen Mary's saying serves for me —   40
   (When fortune's malice
     Lost her, Calais)°
Open my heart and you will see
Graved inside of it, "Italy."
Such lovers old are I and she;
So it always was, so shall ever be!

CLEON

After clarifying his religious beliefs in "Christmas
Eve and Easter Day" (1850) and "Saul," Browning,
it is clear from several poems written about this time,
became interested in speculating upon how Christianity
with its immense new hope struck the near contemporaries of its beginning. In the imaginary figure
of Cleon, who is supposed to be speaking about 50 A.D.,
Browning gives us a Greek poet, artist, musician, and
philosopher. He is a figure of the Greek decadence, and
though he has not the genius of the great Greeks in
any single art, he is nevertheless a complete epitome
of Greek culture, and argues from this fact that he represents a natural progress. He also possesses a Greek arrogance that impels him to question whether any good
can come from a region outside Greece. It is probable
that Matthew Arnold's "Empedocles on Etna" (1852)
suggested the subject to Browning. In the character of

"DE GUSTIBUS—" 35. **the king:** Ferdinand II, a Bourbon, Tyrant
of the Two Sicilies. He acquired the name "King Bomba," a term
of scorn conferred upon him in 1849, when with the help of the Austrians he crushed an uprising in his kingdom and bombarded his
chief cities. 36. **liver-wing:** right arm. 40-42. **Queen...Calais:**
Calais was lost to the English in 1558, when Mary Tudor was on
the throne. In her grief at the loss she said that at her death
"Calais" would be found written on her heart.

Empedocles Arnold had presented a figure of the Greek
decadence, a philosopher in the condition of despair
to which, Browning believed, Greek paganism in its
hopelessness would lead a profound mind. Empedocles
plunges into the crater. Cleon is a comparable figure.
The irony of the poem is that, as gifted as he is, he
is blinded by his arrogance from seeing that Christianity, here at his hand, offers everything that he yearns
for and everything that his reason tells him would perfect God's plan for the world. The quotation which
heads the poem is taken from Acts 17:28 and is a part
of the address of St. Paul to the Greeks from the
Areopagus in Athens. "Cleon" was probably written
in 1854.

"As certain also of your own poets have said" —

Cleon the poet (from the sprinkled isles,°
Lily on lily, that o'erlace the sea,
And laugh their pride when the light wave lisps,
　"Greece") —
To Protus in his Tyranny:° much health!

　They give thy letter to me, even now;
I read and seem as if I heard thee speak.
The master of thy galley still unlades
Gift after gift; they block my court at last
And pile themselves along its portico
Royal with sunset, like a thought of thee;　　10
And one white she-slave from the group dispersed
Of black and white slaves (like the checkerwork
Pavement, at once my nation's work and gift,
Now covered with this settle-down of doves),
One lyric woman, in her crocus vest
Woven of sea-wools,° with her two white hands
Commends to me the strainer and the cup
Thy lip hath bettered ere it blesses mine.

　Well-counseled, king, in thy munificence!
For so shall men remark, in such an act　　20
Of love for him whose song gives life its joy,
Thy recognition of the use of life;
Nor call thy spirit barely adequate
To help on life in straight ways, broad enough
For vulgar souls, by ruling and the rest.
Thou, in the daily building of thy tower —
Whether in fierce and sudden spasms of toil,
Or through dim lulls of unapparent growth,
Or when the general work 'mid good acclaim
Climbed with the eye to cheer the architect —　　30
Didst ne'er engage in work for mere work's sake —
Hadst ever in thy heart the luring hope
Of some eventual rest atop of it,
Whence, all the tumult of the building hushed,

Thou first of men mightst look out to the east;
The vulgar saw thy tower, thou sawest the sun.
For this, I promise on thy festival
To pour libation, looking o'er the sea,
Making this slave narrate thy fortunes, speak
Thy great words, and describe thy royal face —　40
Wishing thee wholly where Zeus lives the most,
Within the eventual element of calm.

　Thy letter's first requirement meets me here.
It is as thou hast heard: in one short life
I, Cleon, have effected all those things
Thou wonderingly dost enumerate.
That epos° on thy hundred plates of gold
Is mine — and also mine the little chant,
So sure to rise from every fishing-bark
When, lights at prow, the seamen haul their
　net.　　50
The image of the sun-god on the phare,°
Men turn from the sun's self to see, is mine;
The Poecile,° o'erstoried its whole length,
As thou didst hear, with painting, is mine too.
I know the true proportions of a man
And woman also, not observed before;
And I have written three books on the soul,
Proving absurd all written hitherto,
And putting us to ignorance again.
For music — why, I have combined the moods,°
Inventing one. In brief, all arts are mine;　　61
Thus much the people know and recognize,
Throughout our seventeen islands. Marvel not.
We of these latter days, with greater mind
Than our forerunners, since more composite,
Look not so great, beside their simple way,
To a judge who only sees one way at once,
One mind-point and no other at a time —
Compares the small part of a man of us
With some whole man of the heroic age,　　70
Great in his way — not ours, nor meant for ours.
And ours is greater, had we skill to know;
For, what we call this life of men on earth,
This sequence of the soul's achievements here
Being, as I find much reason to conceive,
Intended to be viewed eventually
As a great whole, not analyzed to parts,
But each part having reference to all —
How shall a certain part, pronounced complete,
Endure effacement by another part?　　80
Was the thing done? — then, what's to do again?
See, in the checkered pavement opposite,
Suppose the artist made a perfect rhomb,
And next a lozenge, then a trapezoid —

CLEON.　**1. sprinkled isles:** the Sporades, east of the Greek mainland.　**4. Tyranny:** used in its Greek sense; a tyrant was a ruler
having absolute power. No implication of oppression is intended.
16. sea-wools: fibers of sea plants.

47. epos: epic poem.　**51. sun . . . phare:** the statue of Apollo
on the lighthouse.　**53. Poecile:** the portico at Athens, covered
with paintings.　**60. moods:** The moods or modes in Greek music
were the equivalent of the scales in our music.

He did not overlay them, superimpose
The new upon the old and blot it out,
But laid them on a level in his work,
Making at last a picture; there it lies.
So, first the perfect separate forms were made,
The portions of mankind; and after, so,   90
Occurred the combination of the same.
For where had been a progress, otherwise?
Mankind, made up of all the single men —
In such a synthesis the labor ends.
Now mark me! those divine men of old time
Have reached, thou sayest well, each at one point
The outside verge that rounds our faculty;°
And where they reached, who can do more than
    reach?
It takes but little water just to touch
At some one point the inside of a sphere,   100
And, as we turn the sphere, touch all the rest
In due succession; but the finer air
Which not so palpably nor obviously,
Though no less universally, can touch
The whole circumference of that emptied sphere,
Fills it more fully than the water did;
Holds thrice the weight of water in itself
Resolved into a subtler element.
And yet the vulgar call the sphere first full
Up to the visible height — and after, void;   110
Not knowing air's more hidden properties.
And thus our soul, misknown, cries out to Zeus
To vindicate his purpose in our life;
Why stay we on the earth unless to grow?
Long since, I imaged, wrote the fiction out,
That he or other god descended here
And, once for all, showed simultaneously
What, in its nature, never can be shown,
Piecemeal or in succession — showed, I say,
The worth both absolute and relative   120
Of all his children from the birth of time,
His instruments for all appointed work.
I now go on to image — might we hear
The judgment which should give the due to each,
Show where the labor lay and where the ease,
And prove Zeus' self, the latent everywhere!°
This is a dream — but no dream, let us hope,
That years and days, the summers and the
    springs,
Follow each other with unwaning powers.
The grapes which dye thy wine are richer far,   130
Through culture, than the wild wealth of the rock;
The suave plum than the savage-tasted drupe;°
The pastured honeybee drops choicer sweet;

The flowers turn double, and the leaves turn
    flowers;
That young and tender crescent moon, thy slave,
Sleeping above her robe as buoyed by clouds,
Refines upon the women of my youth.
What, and the soul alone deteriorates?
I have not chanted verse like Homer, no —
Nor swept string like Terpander,° no — nor
    carved   140
And painted men like Phidias° and his friend;
I am not great as they are, point by point.
But I have entered into sympathy
With these four, running these into one soul,
Who, separate, ignored each other's art.
Say, is it nothing that I know them all?
The wild flower was the larger; I have dashed
Rose-blood upon its petals, pricked its cup's
Honey with wine, and driven its seed to fruit,
And show a better flower if not so large;   150
I stand myself. Refer this to the gods
Whose gift alone it is! which, shall I dare
(All pride apart) upon the absurd pretext
That such a gift by chance lay in my hand,
Discourse of lightly or depreciate?
It might have fallen to another's hand; what then?
I pass too surely; let at least truth stay!

And next, of what thou followest on to ask.
This being with me as I declare, O king,
My works, in all these varicolored kinds,   160
So done by me, accepted so by men —
Thou askest, if (my soul thus in men's hearts)
I must not be accounted to attain
The very crown and proper end of life?
Inquiring thence how, now life closeth up,
I face death with success in my right hand:
Whether I fear death less than dost thyself
The fortunate of men? "For" (writest thou)
"Thou leavest much behind, while I leave naught.
Thy life stays in the poems men shall sing,   170
The pictures men shall study; while my life,
Complete and whole now in its power and joy,
Dies altogether with my brain and arm,
Is lost indeed; since, what survives myself?
The brazen statue to o'erlook my grave,
Set on the promontory which I named.
And that — some supple courtier of my heir
Shall use its robed and sceptered arm, perhaps,
To fix the rope to, which best drags it down.
I go then; triumph thou, who dost not go!"   180

Nay, thou art worthy of hearing my whole mind.
Is this apparent, when thou turn'st to muse

---

97. outside . . . faculty: the apex of human ability.   126. latent
everywhere: Cleon is moving in his speculations toward the
Christian and pantheistic positions which Browning developed
often in his later poetry.   132. drupe: any fruit in which the pulp
encloses a stone, or seed; here a plum.

140. Terpander: a musician of the seventh century B.C., the founder of Greek classical music.   141. Phidias: Greek sculptor of the
fifth century B.C., who helped to decorate the Parthenon. His
friend was Pericles (490?–429 B.C.), the ruler who gave his name
to the great Athenian age.

Upon the scheme of earth and man in chief,
That admiration grows as knowledge grows?
That imperfection means perfection hid,
Reserved in part, to grace the aftertime?
If, in the morning of philosophy,
Ere aught had been recorded, nay perceived,
Thou, with the light now in thee, couldst have
    looked
On all earth's tenantry, from worm to bird,   190
Ere man, her last, appeared upon the stage —
Thou wouldst have seen them perfect, and deduced
The perfectness of others yet unseen.
Conceding which — had Zeus then questioned thee,
" Shall I go on a step, improve on this,
Do more for visible creatures than is done? "
Thou wouldst have answered, " Aye, by making
    each
Grow conscious in himself — by that alone.
All's perfect else; the shell sucks fast the rock,
The fish strikes through the sea, the snake both
    swims   200
And slides, forth range the beasts, the birds take
    flight,
Till life's mechanics can no further go —
And all this joy in natural life is put
Like fire from off thy finger into each,
So exquisitely perfect is the same.
But 'tis pure fire, and they mere matter are;
It has them, not they it; and so I choose
For man, thy last premeditated work
(If I might add a glory to the scheme)
That a third thing should stand apart from
    both,   210
A quality arise within his soul,
Which, intro-active, made to supervise
And feel the force it has, may view itself,
And so be happy." Man might live at first
The animal life; but is there nothing more?
In due time, let him critically learn
How he lives; and, the more he gets to know
Of his own life's adaptabilities,
The more joy-giving will his life become.
Thus man, who hath this quality, is best.   220

But thou, king, hadst more reasonably said:
" Let progress end at once — man make no step
Beyond the natural man, the better beast,
Using his senses, not the sense of sense."
In man there's failure, only since he left
The lower and inconscious forms of life.
We called it an advance, the rendering plain
Man's spirit might grow conscious of man's life,
And, by new lore so added to the old,
Take each step higher over the brute's head.   230
This grew the only life, the pleasure-house,
Watch-tower and treasure-fortress of the soul,
Which whole surrounding flats of natural life

Seemed only fit to yield subsistence to;
A tower that crowns a country. But alas,
The soul now climbs it just to perish there!
For thence we have discovered ('tis no dream —
We know this, which we had not else perceived)
That there's a world of capability
For joy, spread round about us, meant for us,   240
Inviting us; and still the soul craves all,
And still the flesh replies, " Take no jot more
Than ere thou clomb'st the tower to look abroad!
Nay, so much less as that fatigue has brought
Deduction to it." We struggle, fain to enlarge
Our bounded physical recipiency,
Increase our power, supply fresh oil to life,
Repair the waste of age and sickness; no,
It skills not! life's inadequate to joy,
As the soul sees joy, tempting life to take.   250
They praise a fountain in my garden here
Wherein a naiad sends the water-bow
Thin from her tube; she smiles to see it rise.
What if I told her, it is just a thread
From that great river which the hills shut up,
And mock her with my leave to take the same?
The artificer has given her one small tube
Past power to widen or exchange — what boots
To know she might spout oceans if she could?
She cannot lift beyond her first thin thread;   260
And so a man can use but a man's joy
While he sees God's. Is it for Zeus to boast,
" See, man, how happy I live, and despair —
That I may be still happier — for thy use! "
If this were so, we could not thank our lord,
As hearts beat on to doing; 'tis not so —
Malice it is not. Is it carelessness?
Still, no. If care — where is the sign? I ask,
And get no answer, and agree in sum,
O king, with thy profound discouragement,   270
Who seest the wider but to sigh the more.
Most progress is most failure; thou sayest well.

The last point now: thou dost except a case —
Holding joy not impossible to one
With artist-gifts — to such a man as I
Who leave behind me living works indeed;
For, such a poem, such a painting lives.
What? dost thou verily trip upon a word,
Confound the accurate view of what joy is
(Caught somewhat clearer by my eyes than thine)
With feeling joy? confound the knowing how   281
And showing how to live (my faculty)
With actually living? — Otherwise
Where is the artist's vantage o'er the king?
Because in my great epos I display
How divers men young, strong, fair, wise, can
    act —
Is this as though I acted? if I paint,
Carve the young Phoebus, am I therefore young?

Methinks I'm older that I bowed myself
The many years of pain that taught me art!   290
Indeed, to know is something, and to prove
How all this beauty might be enjoyed, is more;
But, knowing nought, to enjoy is something too.
Yon rower, with the molded muscles there,
Lowering the sail, is nearer it than I.
I can write love-odes; thy fair slave's an ode.
I get to sing of love, when grown too gray
For being beloved; she turns to that young man,
The muscles all a-ripple on his back.
I know the joy of kingship; well, thou art king!

"But," sayest thou (and I marvel, I repeat,   301
To find thee trip on such a mere word) "what
Thou writest, paintest, stays; that does not die;
Sappho° survives, because we sing her songs,
And Aeschylus,° because we read his plays!"
Why, if they live still, let them come and take
Thy slave in my despite, drink from thy cup,
Speak in my place. Thou diest while I survive?
Say rather that my fate is deadlier still,
In this, that every day my sense of joy   310
Grows more acute, my soul (intensified
By power and insight) more enlarged, more keen;
While every day my hairs fall more and more,
My hand shakes, and the heavy years increase —
The horror quickening still from year to year,
The consummation coming past escape,
When I shall know most, and yet least enjoy —
When all my works wherein I prove my worth,
Being present still to mock me in men's mouths,
Alive still, in the praise of such as thou,   320
I, I the feeling, thinking, acting man,
The man who loved his life so overmuch,
Sleep in my urn. It is so horrible,
I dare at times imagine to my need
Some future state revealed to us by Zeus,
Unlimited in capability
For joy, as this is in desire for joy
— To seek which, the joy-hunger forces us:
That, stung by straitness of our life, made strait
On purpose to make prized the life at large —   330
Freed by the throbbing impulse we call death,
We burst there as the worm into the fly,
Who, while a worm still, wants his wings. But no!
Zeus has not yet revealed it; and alas,
He must have done so, were it possible!

Live long and happy, and in that thought die:
Glad for what was! Farewell. And for the rest,
I cannot tell thy messenger aright
Where to deliver what he bears of thine

To one called Paulus;° we have heard his fame   340
Indeed, if Christus be not one with him —
I know not, nor am troubled much to know.
Thou canst not think a mere barbarian Jew,
As Paulus proves to be, one circumcised,
Hath access to a secret shut from us?
Thou wrongest our philosophy, O king,
In stooping to inquire of such an one,
As if his answer could impose at all!
He writeth, doth he? well, and he may write.
Oh, the Jew findeth scholars! certain slaves   350
Who touched on this same isle, preached him and
    Christ;
And (as I gathered from a bystander)
Their doctrine could be held by no sane man.

TWO IN THE CAMPAGNA

This poem was the product of explorations by the
Brownings in May, 1854, of the great open plain called
the Campagna which surrounds Rome. The Campagna,
with the ruins of the tombs of ancient Romans everywhere upon it, is appropriately known as "Rome's
ghost." The poem records a mood between lovers. Contrast it with "By the Fireside."

I wonder do you feel today
    As I have felt since, hand in hand,
We sat down on the grass, to stray
    In spirit better through the land,
This morn of Rome and May?

For me, I touched a thought, I know,
    Has tantalized me many times,
(Like turns of thread the spiders throw
    Mocking across our path) for rhymes
To catch at and let go.   10

Help me to hold it! First it left
    The yellowing fennel, run to seed
There, branching from the brickwork's cleft,
    Some old tomb's ruin; yonder weed
Took up the floating weft,

Where one small orange cup amassed
    Five beetles — blind and green they grope
Among the honey-meal; and last,
    Everywhere on the grassy slope
I traced it. Hold it fast!   20

The champaign with its endless fleece
    Of feathery grasses everywhere!
Silence and passion, joy and peace,
    An everlasting wash of air —
Rome's ghost since her decease.

---

304. **Sappho:** the great lyric poetess of Lesbos, born about 500 B.C.
305. **Aeschylus:** the earliest (525–456 B.C.) of the great writers of
tragedy.

340. **Paulus:** St. Paul of Tarsus, "the apostle to the Gentiles."
Paul began his "European mission" about the year 50 A.D. and
soon afterwards was in Athens.

Such life here, through such lengths of hours,
    Such miracles performed in play,
Such primal naked forms of flowers,
    Such letting nature have her way
While heaven looks from its towers!   30

How say you? Let us, O my dove,
    Let us be unashamed of soul,
As earth lies bare to heaven above!
    How is it under our control
To love or not to love?

I would that you were all to me,
    You that are just so much, no more.
Nor yours nor mine, nor slave nor free!
    Where does the fault lie? What the core
O' the wound, since wound must be?   40

I would I could adopt your will,
    See with your eyes, and set my heart
Beating by yours, and drink my fill
    At your soul's springs — your part my part
In life, for good and ill.

No. I yearn upward, touch you close,
    Then stand away. I kiss your cheek,
Catch your soul's warmth — I pluck the rose
    And love it more than tongue can speak —
Then the good minute goes.   50

Already how am I so far
    Out of that minute? Must I go
Still like the thistle ball, no bar,
    Onward, whenever light winds blow,
Fixed by no friendly star?

Just when I seemed about to learn!
    Where is the thread now? Off again!
The old trick! Only I discern —
    Infinite passion, and the pain
Of finite hearts that yearn.   60

DRAMATIS PERSONAE, 1864

ABT VOGLER

After He Has Been Extemporizing upon the Musical Instrument of His Invention

"Abt Vogler" was probably written in London soon after Mrs. Browning's death in 1861. Browning sought consolation in music, and the career of Abbé Georg Vogler (1749–1814) fitted the poet's need for a subject, for Vogler was at once a devout person and a notable extemporizer upon the organ. The musical instrument upon which he extemporized was a small portable organ of about 900 pipes, called an "orchestrion." Browning knew Vogler's system well, because John Relfe, Browning's music teacher and Musician in Ordinary to the king, had been a pupil of Vogler's at the same time as Weber and Meyerbeer. What we know of Vogler does not allow us to think him capable of the speculation which we find in the poem. He was inventive rather than meditative or profound. "Abt Vogler" should be compared to Browning's other poems on music. The thought of the poem is Browning's and may be called Christian-Platonic; that is, its idea that all things on earth are but faint and imperfect copies of perfect prototypes in Heaven is derived from Plato, and this notion is combined with the Christian conception that our lives on earth are merely periods of trial and struggle toward the perfection we shall find only in Heaven. This poem is near the peak of Browning's metaphysical verse.

Would that the structure brave, the manifold music
    I build,
    Bidding my organ obey, calling its keys to their
      work,
Claiming each slave of the sound, at a touch, as
    when Solomon° willed
    Armies of angels that soar, legions of demons
      that lurk,
Man, brute, reptile, fly — alien of end and of aim,
    Adverse, each from the other heaven-high, hell-
      deep removed —
Should rush into sight at once as he named the in-
    effable Name,
    And pile him a palace straight, to pleasure the
      princess he loved!

Would it might tarry like his, the beautiful build-
    ing of mine,
    This which my keys in a crowd pressed and im-
      portuned to raise!   10
Ah, one and all, how they helped, would dispart
    now and now combine,
    Zealous to hasten the work, heighten their master
      his praise!
And one would bury his brow with a blind plunge
    down to hell,
    Burrow awhile and build, broad on the roots of
      things,
Then up again swim into sight, having based me
    my palace well,
    Founded it, fearless of flame, flat on the nether
      springs.

And another would mount and march, like the ex-
    cellent minion° he was,

ABT VOGLER. 3. **Solomon:** Talmudic legend says that Solomon possessed a seal with the "ineffable Name" of God upon it, and by this seal he had power over supernatural beings. He spent thirteen years in building his palace. 17. **minion:** servant.

Aye, another and yet another, one crowd but
   with many a crest,
Raising my rampired walls of gold as transparent
   as glass,
   Eager to do and die, yield each his place to the
     rest;   20
For higher still and higher (as a runner tips with
   fire,
   When a great illumination surprises a festal
     night —
Outlining round and round Rome's dome from
   space to spire)°
   Up, the pinnacled glory reached, and the pride
     of my soul was in sight.

In sight? Not half! for it seemed, it was certain, to
   match man's birth,
   Nature in turn conceived, obeying an impulse
     as I;
And the emulous heaven yearned down, made
   effort to reach the earth,
   As the earth had done her best, in my passion,
     to scale the sky;
Novel splendors burst forth, grew familiar and
   dwelt with mine,
   Not a point nor peak but found and fixed its
     wandering star;   30
Meteor-moons, balls of blaze; and they did not pale
   nor pine,
   For earth had attained to heaven, there was no
     more near nor far.

Nay more; for there wanted not who walked in the
   glare and glow,
   Presences plain in the place; or, fresh from the
     Protoplast,°
Furnished for ages to come, when a kindlier wind
   should blow,
   Lured now to begin and live, in a house to their
     liking at last;
Or else the wonderful Dead who have passed
   through the body and gone,
   But were back once more to breathe in an old
     world worth their new;
What never had been, was now; what was, as it
   shall be anon;
   And what is — shall I say, matched both? for I
     was made perfect too.   40

All through my keys that gave their sounds to a
   wish of my soul,

All through my soul that praised as its wish
   flowed visibly forth,
All through music and me! For think, had I
   painted° the whole,
   Why, there it had stood, to see, nor the process
     so wonder-worth;
Had I written the same, made verse — still, effect
   proceeds from cause,
   Ye know why the forms are fair, ye hear how the
     tale is told;
It is all triumphant art, but art in obedience to laws,
   Painter and poet are proud in the artist-list en-
     rolled —

But here is the finger of God, a flash of the will
   that can,
   Existent behind all laws, that made them and,
     lo, they are!   50
And I know not if, save in this, such gift be al-
   lowed to man,
   That out of three sounds he frame, not a fourth
     sound, but a star.
Consider it well: each tone of our scale in itself is
   naught;
   It is everywhere in the world — loud, soft, and
     all is said;
Give it to me to use! I mix it with two in my
   thought;
   And, there! Ye have heard and seen: consider
     and bow the head!

Well, it is gone at last, the palace of music I reared;
   Gone! and the good tears start, the praises that
     come too slow;
For one is assured at first, one scarce can say that
   he feared,
   That he even gave it a thought, the gone thing
     was to go.   60
Never to be again! But many more of the kind
   As good, nay, better perchance; is this your com-
     fort to me?
To me, who must be saved because I cling with my
   mind
   To the same, same self, same love, same God;
     aye, what was, shall be.

Therefore to whom turn I but to thee, the ineffable
   Name?
   Builder and maker, thou, of houses not made
     with hands!°
What, have fear of change from thee who art ever
   the same?

21-23. For ... spire: The structure of Vogler's music rises in his imagination like the fire which ascends by streamers to illuminate the dome of St. Peter's to the cross on the top. Browning had witnessed such an event at Easter time in 1854 when he was in Rome. **34. Protoplast:** freshly created from the elemental stuff of life.

43. had I painted: Here Browning deals with a favorite idea: a comparison of the effects of the various arts. Music is usually judged the most affecting by Browning, but also the most transient in its effects. **66. houses ... hands:** See II Cor. 5:1.

Doubt that thy power can fill the heart that thy
   power expands?
There shall never be one lost good! What was, shall
   live as before;
   The evil is null, is nought, is silence implying
      sound;   70
What was good shall be good, with, for evil, so
   much good more;
   On the earth the broken arcs; in the heaven, a
      perfect round.

All we have willed or hoped or dreamed of good
   shall exist;
   Not its semblance, but itself; no beauty, nor good,
      nor power
Whose voice has gone forth, but each survives for
   the melodist
When eternity affirms the conception of an hour.
The high that proved too high, the heroic for earth
   too hard,
   The passion that left the ground to lose itself in
      the sky,
Are music sent up to God by the lover and the
   bard;
   Enough that he heard it once; we shall hear it
      by-and-by.   80

And what is our failure here but a triumph's evi-
   dence
   For the fullness of the days? Have we withered
      or agonized?
Why else was the pause prolonged but that singing
   might issue thence?
   Why rushed the discords in, but that harmony
      should be prized?
Sorrow is hard to bear, and doubt is slow to clear,
   Each sufferer says his say, his scheme of the weal
      and woe;
But God has a few of us whom he whispers in the
   ear;
   The rest may reason and welcome: 'tis we
      musicians know.

Well, it is earth with me; silence resumes her
   reign;
   I will be patient and proud, and soberly
      acquiesce.
Give me the keys. I feel for the common chord°
   again,   91
   Sliding by semitones till I sink to the minor
   — yes,
And I blunt it into a ninth, and I stand on alien
   ground,

91. **common chord**: the fundamental tone, a major or minor third,
and a perfect fifth. The C Major is the natural scale, without
sharps or flats, and is thus symbolic of the common level of ordinary life.

Surveying awhile the heights I rolled from into
   the deep;
Which, hark, I have dared and done, for my rest-
   ing-place is found,
   The C Major of this life; so, now I will try to
      sleep.

RABBI BEN EZRA

"Rabbi Ben Ezra" was possibly written in 1862.
Browning had known the work of Abraham Ibn Ezra
since 1854 and probably was familiar with the Jewish
philosopher's *Commentary on Isaiah*. The figure which
dominates the poem occurs in Isaiah 64:8: "But now,
O Lord, thou art our father; we are clay, and thou
our potter; and we all are the work of thy hand." The
image of the potter had been used extensively by Edward Fitzgerald in his *Rubáiyát of Omar Khayyám*
(1859), and that poem possibly was the spark that set
Browning off. Browning's poem may itself be answered
by Matthew Arnold's "Growing Old" (1867).
   Abraham Ibn Ezra (1092?–1167) was a Spanish rabbi
who in his middle years was driven by persecution
from Spain into a life of travel and scholarship. He was
a theologian, a philosopher, a linguist, and a scientist.
A strong believer in immortality, he found the second
half of his life much more productive and satisfactory
in every way than the first. The ideas in the poem are
Browning's, though in accord with what we know of
the rabbi's temperament.

Grow old along with me!
   The best is yet to be,
The last of life, for which the first was made;
   Our times are in His hand
   Who saith, "A whole I planned,
Youth shows but half; trust God; see all, nor be
   afraid!"

Not that, amassing flowers,
   Youth sighed, "Which rose make ours,
Which lily leave and then as best recall?"
   Not that, admiring stars,   10
   It yearned, "Nor Jove, nor Mars;
Mine be some figured° flame which blends, tran-
   scends them all!"

Not for such hopes and fears
   Annulling youth's brief years,
Do I remonstrate: folly wide the mark!
   Rather I prize the doubt
   Low kinds exist without,
Finished and finite clods, untroubled by a spark.

Poor vaunt of life indeed,
   Were man but formed to feed   20

RABBI BEN EZRA.   12. **figured**: imagined.

On joy, to solely seek and find and feast;
　　Such feasting ended, then
　　As sure an end to men;
Irks care the crop-full bird? Frets doubt the maw-
　　crammed beast?

　　Rejoice we are allied
　　To That which doth provide
And not partake, effect and not receive!
　　A spark disturbs our clod;
　　Nearer we hold of God
Who gives, than of his tribes that take, I must be-
　　lieve.　　　　　　　　　　　　　　　　　30

　　Then, welcome each rebuff
　　That turns earth's smoothness rough,
Each sting that bids nor sit nor stand but go!
　　Be our joys three-parts pain!
　　Strive, and hold cheap the strain;
Learn, nor account the pang; dare, never grudge
　　the throe!

　　For thence — a paradox
　　Which comforts while it mocks —
Shall life succeed in that it seems to fail;
　　What I aspired to be,　　　　　　　　40
　　And was not, comforts me;
A brute I might have been, but would not sink i'
　　the scale.

　　What is he but a brute
　　Whose flesh has soul to suit,
Whose spirit works lest arms and legs want play?
　　To man, propose this test —
　　Thy body at its best,
How far can that project thy soul on its lone way?

　　Yet gifts should prove their use;
　　I own the Past profuse　　　　　　　50
Of power each side, perfection every turn:
　　Eyes, ears took in their dole,
　　Brain treasured up the whole;
Should not the heart beat once, " How good to live
　　and learn "?

　　Not once beat, " Praise be Thine!
　　I see the whole design,
I, who saw power, see now Love perfect too;°
　　Perfect I call Thy plan;
　　Thanks that I was a man!
Maker, remake, complete — I trust what Thou shalt
　　do! "　　　　　　　　　　　　　　　　60

For pleasant is this flesh;
　　Our soul, in its rose-mesh
Pulled ever to the earth, still yearns for rest;
　　Would we some prize might hold
　　To match those manifold
Possessions of the brute — gain most, as we did
　　best!

　　Let us not always say,
　　" Spite of this flesh today
I strove, made head, gained ground upon the
　　whole! "
　　As the bird wings and sings,　　　　　70
　　Let us cry, " All good things
Are ours, nor soul helps flesh more, now, than flesh
　　helps soul! "

　　Therefore I summon age
　　To grant youth's heritage,°
Life's struggle having so far reached its term;°
　　Thence shall I pass, approved
　　A man, for aye removed
From the developed brute; a god though in the
　　germ.

　　And I shall thereupon
　　Take rest, ere I be gone　　　　　　80
Once more on my adventure° brave and new;
　　Fearless and unperplexed,
　　When I wage battle next,
What weapons to select, what armor to indue.°

　　Youth ended, I shall try
　　My gain or loss thereby;
Leave the fire ashes, what survives is gold;
　　And I shall weigh the same,
　　Give life its praise or blame;
Young, all lay in dispute; I shall know, being
　　old.　　　　　　　　　　　　　　　　90

　　For note, when evening shuts,
　　A certain moment cuts
The deed off, calls the glory from the gray;
　　A whisper from the west
　　Shoots — " Add this to the rest,
Take it and try its worth; here dies another
　　day."

　　So, still within this life,
　　Though lifted o'er its strife,
Let me discern, compare, pronounce at last,

56-57. I . . . too: God's power is equaled by his love. Compare
"Cleon," "Karshish," "Saul" and "The Pope."

74. youth's heritage: what youth should give us, a strong physical being, to be linked with the thoughtfulness of age.　75. term:
limit.　81. adventurer: life beyond the grave.　84. indue:
to put on.

" This rage was right i' the main,   100
   That acquiescence vain;
The Future I may face now I have proved° the
   Past."

   For more is not reserved
   To man, with soul just nerved
To act tomorrow what he learns today;
   Here, work enough to watch
   The Master work, and catch
Hints of the proper craft, tricks of the tool's true
   play.

   As it was better, youth
   Should strive, through acts uncouth,°   110
Toward making, than repose on aught found made;
   So, better, age, exempt
   From strife, should know, than tempt°
Further. Thou waitedst age: wait death nor be
   afraid!

   Enough now, if the Right
   And Good and Infinite
Be named here, as thou callest thy hand thine own,
   With knowledge absolute,
   Subject to no dispute
From fools that crowded youth, nor let thee feel
   alone.   120

   Be there, for once and all,
   Severed great minds from small,
Announced to each his station in the Past!
   Was I, the world arraigned,
   Where they, my soul disdained,
Right? Let age speak the truth and give us peace
   at last!

   Now, who shall arbitrate?
   Ten men love what I hate,
Shun what I follow, slight what I receive;
   Ten, who in ears and eyes   130
   Match me; we all surmise,
They this thing, and I that; whom shall my soul
   believe?

   Not on the vulgar mass
   Called " work " must sentence pass,
Things done, that took the eye and had the price;
   O'er which, from level stand,
   The low world laid its hand,
Found straightway to its mind, could value in a
   trice;

   But all the world's coarse thumb
   And finger failed to plumb,   140
So passed° in making up the main account;
   All instincts immature,
   All purposes unsure,
That weighed not as his work, yet swelled the man's
   amount;

   Thoughts hardly to be packed
   Into a narrow act,
Fancies that broke through language and escaped;
   All I could never be,
   All, men ignored in me,
This, I was worth to God, whose wheel the pitcher
   shaped.   150

   Ay, note that Potter's wheel,
   That metaphor! and feel
Why time spins fast, why passive lies our clay —
   Thou, to whom fools propound,
   When the wine makes its round,
" Since life fleets, all is change; the Past gone, seize
   today! "°

   Fool! All that is, at all,
   Lasts ever, past recall;
Earth changes, but thy soul and God stand sure;
   What entered into thee,   160
   That was, is, and shall be;
Time's wheel runs back or stops: Potter and clay
   endure.

   He fixed thee 'mid this dance
   Of plastic° circumstance,
This Present, thou, forsooth, would fain arrest;
   Machinery just meant
   To give thy soul its bent,
Try thee and turn thee forth, sufficiently impressed.

   What though the earlier grooves,
   Which ran the laughing loves   170
Around thy base, no longer pause and press?
   What though, about thy rim,
   Skull-things in order grim
Grow out, in graver mood, obey the sterner stress?

   Look not thou down but up!
   To uses of a cup,
The festal board, lamp's flash, and trumpet's peal,
   The new wine's foaming flow,
   The Master's lips aglow!
Thou, heaven's consummate cup, what need'st thou
   with earth's wheel?   180

---

102. proved: tried and judged. **110. uncouth:** awkward and unsure. **113. tempt:** experiment or attempt.

141. passed: neglected. **154-56. fools . . . today:** possibly addressed to the hedonistic philosophy *carpe diem* of Fitzgerald's *Rubáiyát*, sts. 82–90. **164. plastic:** molding, forming.

But I need, now as then,
Thee, God, who moldest men;
And since, not even while the whirl was worst,
Did I — to the wheel of life
With shapes and colors rife,
Bound dizzily — mistake my end, to slake Thy
thirst;

So, take and use Thy work;
Amend what flaws may lurk,
What strain o' the stuff, what warpings past the
aim!
My times be in Thy hand!   190
Perfect the cup as planned!
Let age approve of youth, and death complete the
same!

CONFESSIONS

This poem was probably written in Italy in 1859. It
was part of Browning's purpose to pluck romance from
familiar realism.

What is he buzzing in my ears?
  "Now that I come to die,
Do I view the world as a vale of tears?"
  Ah, reverend sir, not I!

What I viewed there once, what I view again
  Where the physic bottles stand
On the table's edge — is a suburb lane,
  With a wall to my bedside hand.

That lane sloped, much as the bottles do,
  From a house you could descry   10
O'er the garden wall; is the curtain blue
  Or green to a healthy eye?

To mine, it serves for the old June weather
  Blue above lane and wall;
And that farthest bottle labeled "Ether"
  Is the house o'ertopping all.

At a terrace, somewhere near the stopper,
  There watched for me, one June,
A girl; I know, sir, it's improper,
  My poor mind's out of tune.   20

Only, there was a way . . . you crept
  Close by the side, to dodge
Eyes in the house, two eyes except;
  They styled their house "The Lodge."

What right had a lounger up their lane?
  But, by creeping very close,
With the good wall's help — their eyes might strain
  And stretch themselves to Oes,°

CONFESSIONS. 28. Oes: that is, their eyes would be stretched
wide open, each like the letter O, in their efforts to see.

Yet never catch her and me together,
  As she left the attic, there,   30
By the rim of the bottle labeled "Ether,"
  And stole from stair to stair,

And stood by the rose-wreathed gate. Alas,
  We loved, sir — used to meet;
How sad and bad and mad it was —
  But then, how it was sweet!

MAY AND DEATH

First published in a literary annual, *The Keepsake,*
for 1857, this poem was revised when it was republished in 1864. It commemorates James (called Charles
in the poem) Silverthorne, Browning's cousin and
companion of his youth, who died in May, 1852. The
"wood" referred to in the poem is the Dulwich Wood,
and the plant of line 13 is the "spotted persicaria." Because its leaves are spotted with purple, the legend is
that it grew beneath the Cross and received its color
from the blood of Christ.

I wish that when you died last May,
  Charles, there had died along with you
Three parts of spring's delightful things;
  Aye, and, for me, the fourth part too.

A foolish thought, and worse, perhaps!
  There must be many a pair of friends
Who, arm in arm, deserve the warm
  Moon-births and the long evening-ends.

So, for their sake, be May still May!
  Let their new time, as mine of old,   10
Do all it did for me; I bid
  Sweet sights and sounds throng manifold.

Only, one little sight, one plant,
  Woods have in May, that starts up green
Save a sole streak which, so to speak,
  Is spring's blood, spilt its leaves between —

That, they might spare; a certain wood
  Might miss the plant; their loss were small;
But I — whene'er the leaf grows there,
  Its drop comes from my heart, that's all.   20

PROSPICE

This poem first appeared in the *Atlantic Monthly* for
June, 1864. It was probably written soon after the
death of Mrs. Browning on June 29, 1861. After his
wife's death Browning wrote in her testament the
words that Dante had written concerning Beatrice
(*Convito,* II.9): "Thus I believe, thus I affirm, thus I
am certain it is, that from this life I shall pass to an-

other, there, where that lady lives of whom my soul
was enamoured." As an expression of courage, compare " Prospice " with Tennyson's "Ulysses." The title
means " look forward."

Fear death? — to feel the fog in my throat,
    The mist in my face,
When the snows begin, and the blasts denote
    I am nearing the place,
The power of the night, the press of the storm,
    The post of the foe;
Where he stands, the Arch-Fear in a visible form,
    Yet the strong man must go;
For the journey is done and the summit attained,
    And the barriers fall,   10
Though a battle's to fight ere the guerdon be
        gained,
    The reward of it all.
I was ever a fighter, so — one fight more,
    The best and the last!
I would hate that death bandaged my eyes, and for-
        bore,
    And bade me creep past.
No! let me taste the whole of it, fare like my peers
    The heroes of old,
Bear the brunt, in a minute pay glad life's arrears
    Of pain, darkness, and cold.   20
For sudden the worst turns the best to the brave,
    The black minute's at end,
And the elements' rage, the fiend-voices that rave,
    Shall dwindle, shall blend,
Shall change, shall become first a peace out of pain,
    Then a light, then thy breast,
O thou soul of my soul! I shall clasp thee again,
    And with God be the rest!

YOUTH AND ART

This poem was probably written early in 1861. The
setting is the artistic group in Rome; the speaker and
the sculptor she addresses are imaginary English persons. The style of the poem is designed to express the
embittered ruefulness of the speaker at having lost the
opportunity afforded by love.

It once might have been, once only:
    We lodged in a street together,
You, a sparrow on the housetop lonely,
    I, a lone she-bird of his feather.

Your trade was with sticks and clay,
    You thumbed, thrust, patted and polished,
Then laughed, " They will see some day
    Smith made, and Gibson° demolished."

My business was song, song, song;
    I chirped, cheeped, trilled, and twittered,   10
" Kate Brown's on the boards ere long,
    And Grisi's° existence embittered! "

I earned no more by a warble
    Than you by a sketch in plaster;
You wanted a piece of marble,
    I needed a music master.

We studied hard in our styles,
    Chipped each at a crust like Hindoos,
For air, looked out on the tiles,
    For fun, watched each other's windows.   20

You lounged, like a boy of the south,
    Cap and blouse — nay, a bit of beard, too;
Or you got it, rubbing your mouth
    With fingers the clay adhered to.

And I — soon managed to find
    Weak points in the flower-fence facing,
Was forced to put up a blind
    And be safe in my corset lacing.

No harm! It was not my fault
    If you never turned your eye's tail up,   30
As I shook upon E *in alt,*°
    Or ran the chromatic scale up:

For spring bade the sparrows pair,
    And the boys and girls gave guesses,
And stalls in our street looked rare
    With bulrush and watercresses.

Why did not you pinch a flower
    In a pellet of clay and fling it?
Why did not I put a power
    Of thanks in a look, or sing it?   40

I did look, sharp as a lynx
    (And yet the memory rankles),
When models arrived, some minx
    Tripped upstairs, she and her ankles.

But I think I gave you as good!
    " That foreign fellow — who can know
How she pays, in a playful mood,
    For his tuning her that piano? "

Could you say so, and never say,
    " Suppose we join hands and fortunes,   50
And I fetch her from over the way,
    Her, piano, and long tunes and short tunes "?

YOUTH AND ART.   **8. Gibson:** John Gibson (1790–1866), regarded
as the foremost English sculptor of his day. He was a friend of
Browning's.

12. Grisi: Giulia Grisi (1811–69), the great Italian operatic
soprano.   **31. E *in alt:*** high E.

No, no; you would not be rash,
  Nor I rasher and something over;
You've to settle yet Gibson's hash,
  And Grisi yet lives in clover.

But you meet the Prince° at the Board,
  I'm queen myself at *bals-paré*,°
I've married a rich old lord,
  And you're dubbed knight and an R.A.° 60

Each life unfulfilled, you see;
  It hangs still, patchy and scrappy:
We have not sighed deep, laughed free,
  Starved, feasted, despaired — been happy.

And nobody calls you a dunce,
  And people suppose me clever;
This could but have happened once,
  And we missed it, lost it forever.

ASOLANDO, 1889

EPILOGUE

This poem concluded the *Asolando* volume. It bears the marks of being a final utterance and was probably written in the autumn of 1889. It has become famous as an expression of Browning's spirit and usually concludes all editions of his poetry. Compare it with "Prospice," above.

At the midnight in the silence of the sleep-time,
  When you set your fancies free,
Will they pass to where — by death, fools think,
    imprisoned —
Low he lies who once so loved you, whom you
    loved so,
           — Pity me?

Oh, to love so, be so loved, yet so mistaken!
  What had I on earth to do
With the slothful, with the mawkish, the unmanly?
Like the aimless, helpless, hopeless, did I drivel
          — Being — who? 10

One who never turned his back but marched breast
    forward,
  Never doubted clouds would break,
Never dreamed, though right were worsted, wrong
    would triumph,
Held we fall to rise, are baffled to fight better,
      Sleep to wake.

No, at noonday in the bustle of man's work-time
  Greet the unseen with a cheer!
Bid him forward, breast and back as either should
    be,
"Strive and thrive!" cry, "Speed — fight on, fare
    ever
      There as here!" 20

57. **Prince:** Albert, the Prince Consort, who was interested in the Royal Academy of Art. He died in 1861. 58. *bals-paré:* fancy-dress balls. 60. **R.A.:** member of the British Royal Academy of Arts.

George Bernard Shaw

1856–1950

At some point quite early in his life — none of his biographers mark the critical date — George Bernard Shaw discovered that life as most men live it is a joke, that men who take themselves and are taken by the world as sane, reasonable, capable, and efficient are in fact half-mad bumblers toying with a dangerous reality they do not even begin to understand. And the more certain these men seem, the more solemn and grave their language, the more stately their gestures, the firmer their grip on the helm of state, the more sure one may be, Shaw discovered, that they know nothing of what they are doing and, in fact, produce the exact opposite of the effects they intend.

One or two "Shavianisms" will suggest the nature of this perspective on life. Shaw once read in the newspaper that an escaped prisoner had been recaptured and in accordance with the established prison regulations loaded down with chains for six months. To the prison officials and the public at large this practice seemed eminently reasonable — it was the way things had always been done within their memory — but to Shaw it appeared both unjust and incredibly foolish. After all, he reasoned in an open letter to the authorities, the poor prisoner was being savagely mistreated to pay not for his own mistake but for that of his careless warders. No one can blame a prisoner for trying to escape — "The man was sentenced to be imprisoned, not to imprison himself" — but one can blame his warders who had all the odds on their side, "public money, bolts and bars, sentinels and rifles, walls and spikes."

Logically, Shaw concluded, the prisoner, who had succeeded magnificently, ought to be rewarded, while his guards, who had failed wretchedly, ought to be punished.

Shavian logic of this type is always irritating to its victims, and it could be savage on occasion. When in the 1920's the monkey-gland operation, invented by Dr. Voronoff, in which certain glands from apes are used to replace human glands, became popular, an eminent British scientist warned the public that the results would be dangerous since it would transfer to the humans involved those chief characteristics of the ape, cruelty and sensuality. Shaw's reply was swift and deadly. Writing in the name of a famous performing chimpanzee, he pointed out that no ape had ever ripped the glands from a man to graft them on an ape to extend his sexual life, that the apes had never had an Inquisition, that they had never invented fiendish tortures for one another or engaged in great wars using such devices as poison gas, and that no society was necessary for the protection of ape children as it was for human children. After a good deal more evidence of this kind, he concluded with the stinging admonition to man to "presume no further on this grotesque resemblance to us; [man] will remain what he is in spite of all Dr. Voronoff's efforts to make a respectable ape of him."

Ireland has produced a remarkable number of writers with this peculiar comic logic — Swift, Goldsmith, Wilde, Joyce, O'Casey — and it may well be that Shaw's perception about the nature of the human animal was given to him at birth in Dublin, July 26th, 1856. More likely he acquired it in his early years in a very strange house. His father was an unsuccessful merchant with a taste for drink and the trombone. His mother appears to have been a most charming woman, but without interest in running a household or in raising children. The one real concern in her life was singing, and her singing master, a man named Lee with a new theory for training the voice, soon became a lodger in the Shaw home. All day long the house was filled with singers practicing, and from listening to their music, Shaw later claimed, he derived his real education, and most particularly his sense of form. Although he had a governess and attended school, he apparently learned little there, and by the time his mother, disappointed by her husband's inability to make money or play the trombone well, moved off to London in 1872 with her two daughters, young Shaw was already at work as a clerk in the office of a land agent. Far from being a failure in trade, Shaw was a great success, and when the firm was left suddenly without a cashier, he filled in so effectively that the job was given to him permanently. Instead of being encouraged by this Shaw was dismayed. "Business, instead of expelling me as the worthless imposter I was, was fastening upon me with no intention of letting me go." He had made good in spite of himself, and terrified that the idiocy of the world, which couldn't tell a real cashier from a pretender, had trapped him, he threw up the job and fled in 1876 to London, where most Irish writers have gone for fame and fortune.

Once in London, Shaw moved in with his mother, who was already having a difficult time making ends meet. During the next ten years he held an occasional job, but on the whole his time was devoted to educating himself and becoming a writer. His days were largely spent in the reading room of the British Museum — where he was once found by a friend studying the score of *Don Giovanni* and reading *Das Kapital* at the same time — and here he read voraciously and wrote a steady five pages of fiction a day. These pages finally accumulated into four novels for which Shaw was unable to find a publisher until later years when he had become famous as a dramatist. At the same time that he was learning to write, he was making his first forays into politics. Marx was, he al-

ways said, a real revelation to him, not because he accepted Marxian economics but rather because of the insight Marx gave into the way in which power and money manifest themselves in social arrangements. Partly to train himself as an orator and partly to implement his views about the necessity for social and economic changes, Shaw made himself into a witty and effective orator, speaking anywhere and everywhere, including park corners, that he could find an audience. He became in time one of the most sought-after speakers of his day. After short periods of interest in several political groups, Shaw found in the Fabian Society the particular political ideology that suited him, and he remained a Fabian throughout his life — he was once referred to in Russia as "a good man fallen among Fabians." Fabianism was an idealistic variety of socialism, but the young intellectuals who made up the Society when Shaw joined, apparently believed in strong political action. And so on "Bloody Sunday," November 13, 1887, when the workers of London set off to march to Trafalgar Square to demonstrate their right to assemble and speak there, the Fabians, Shaw among them, marched along. On the way the police charged the procession, and in the midst of the scramble a man rushed up to Shaw and cried out to him: "Give us a lead. What are we to do?" Shaw, experiencing raw power for the first time, could only reply, "Nothing." The event showed Shaw both the physical weakness of the workers and the dangers of civil disorder, and from this time both he and the Fabians worked for social change through parliamentary means. Eventually they were successful, for the program of the English Labor Party was largely manufactured from the ideas of the Fabian intellectuals.

During these years of writing and politics, Shaw lived with his mother and off her small income. He didn't live very well — at one time he got along on sixpence a day — but he scarcely turned a hand to provide for himself. Far from being ashamed of this and trying to hide it, Shaw faced the facts openly and insisted that it was the duty of the artist to concern himself with his art, not with earning a living or cherishing his parents in their old age. And he was horribly frank about it: "I did not throw myself into the struggle for life: I threw my mother into it. I was not a staff to my father's old age:

I hung on to his coat tails." Had he failed as an artist we might regard such statements differently, but considering what came out of these ten years we can only laugh and half assent when Shaw says, "Callous as Comus to moral babble, I steadily wrote my five pages a day and made a man of myself (at my mother's expense) instead of a slave."

But in the late 1880's he began to use his talents remuneratively, first as a reviewer of paintings and books, and then as a music critic for a London paper. Under the name of Corno di Bassetto — an instrument producing exceedingly lugubrious sounds — Shaw wrote for several years some of the most honest and most impressive musical criticism of our time. It is still very much worth reading. It was during these years also that Shaw began his famous correspondence with the actress Ellen Terry, whom he did not see until after he had written her many love letters. But in 1898, after a breakdown of his health, he married an Irish heiress, Charlotte Payne-Townshend, with whom he lived childlessly ever after.

In the long run, Bernard Shaw managed his career with such remarkable canniness that his wildest departures from conventional behavior turned out to his own profit — he died a rich and famous man — but he remained always a determined reformer. In the 1890's it had become clear to him that public oratory, political pamphleteering, and newspaper reviewing were not going to bring about a better, more reasonable kind of world. So, in addition to these activities — which he never abandoned — Shaw began to write plays, hoping to drive home his points in the theater in terms of speech, character, and action.

Not all of Shaw's plays were produced when he wrote them. The early ones particularly were considered by many too scandalous in subject matter for public presentation, or too unusual and argumentative to attract a theater audience accustomed to unlikely melodramas and mindless farces. *Arms and the Man,* for example, nowadays considered uncontroversial and easy to understand, completely bewildered its first audience and the actors who played in it. But Shaw persisted, and by a combination of self-advertisement (which usually took the form of declaring himself to be greater than Shakespeare), badgering and flattering producers and

actors into staging his plays, and writing consistently better and better plays, he eventually became the foremost English dramatist of his time. What Shaw did was to make the English stage once again a place where serious ideas were discussed, where life and mind and vitality appeared once again in a theater which for over a hundred years had been given over almost entirely to claptrap. The magnitude of Shaw's accomplishment, which was no less than a theatrical revolution, is made more dramatic by consideration of this fact: of all the English plays written in the nineteenth century, only Oscar Wilde's *The Importance of Being Ernest* and some of Shaw's plays written in the 1890's will enter the permanent repertory of Western drama.

His principal plays with dates of publication are listed below:

Widower's Houses (1898)
Mrs. Warren's Profession (1898)
Arms and the Man (1898)
Candida (1898)
The Devil's Disciple (1900)
Caesar and Cleopatra (1900)
Man and Superman (1903)
Major Barbara (1907)
Androcles and the Lion (1913)
Pygmalion (1913)
Misalliance (1914)
Heartbreak House (1919)
Back to Methuselah (1921)
Saint Joan (1924)
The Apple Cart (1930)
In Good King Charles's Golden Days (1946)

II

What did Shaw write about? In part he dramatized the woolly-headedness, the bumbling, the stuffy self-satisfaction, and the pomposity of the British governing classes. In the guise of Bulgarian nobility, ancient savages of Briton, Roman officials, and contemporary soldiers, ministers, and businessmen, Shaw ridiculed the clumsy, awkward, conventional ways of thinking and doing which he believed perverted sense and justice in the world. In play after play he trotted these figures out to huff and puff in inflated clichés about what is good and decent and right, and then arranged fiendish traps for them that revealed how their unwillingness to think clearly caused them to bring about evil, indecency, and wrong. In his plays, conventional patriots and jingoes endanger their country, sternly moral parents and guardians force their daughters into truly immoral marriages based only on money and position, and salvationists bent on saving the soul of man destroy it.

Such a vision of human idiocy has turned many a man toward melancholy and pessimism, but not Shaw. In his plays as in his life, he found the human spectacle a comedy rather than a tragedy. He was able to laugh rather than cry because he believed that, however dreadful a muddle the world might be in, the forces working toward clarity, and sense, and justice were ultimately destined to win. Principally, he believed in the power of human reason to cut through sham and pretense and to bring events to a desired end. And so each of his plays contains, in addition to a plenitude of fools, one or more reasonable men — witty, clever, courageous, and utterly unconventional. These heroes are, like Shaw himself, above all vocal. Their voices — clear, direct, and pointedly rational — are the dominant sound in a Shavian play, rising above the confused hubbub of the fools in the background. Their wit, in the form of irony, is the instrument which exposes the fools and their beliefs for what they are and averts the ridiculous disaster they are constructing for themselves.

In Shaw's earliest plays, the victories which his rational heroes win over confusion and ignorance are immediate and completely satisfactory in themselves. He gradually became aware, however, that it was going to take rather longer than he had previously thought for good sense and mind to inherit the world. Forced by the events of history to take a longer view, he constructed a mythology of progress in which a power, which he labeled only the "Life Force," drives the world of men along toward an end which individual men cannot understand but must take on trust as good and worthwhile. The Life Force manifests itself principally in man's good sense, in his courage, and in his willingness to experiment and learn in great and small ways: when intelligent women determine to seek out intelligent fathers for their children, for example, or when nationalism replaces feudalism. But

chiefly, Shaw believed, the Life Force instrumented itself through the great rational saints, artists, and heroes of history. Supermen such as Saint Joan, Julius Caesar, Newton, and Napoleon were, in the Shavian view, no more than persons whose mental faculties were acute enough to penetrate conventional ways of thinking and to perceive the true order of reality and the great overwill of the world. These men have what Shaw termed the "Evolutionary Appetite," and this quality seemed to him as obvious a fact of life as physical appetite:

That there are forces at work which use individuals for purposes far transcending the purpose of keeping these individuals alive and prosperous and respectable and safe and happy in the middle station in life, which is all any good bourgeois can reasonably require, is established by the fact that men will, in the pursuit of knowledge and of social readjustments for which they will not be a penny the better, and are indeed often many pence the worse, face poverty, infamy, exile, imprisonment, dreadful hardship, and death. . . . There is no more mystery about this appetite for knowledge and power than about the appetite for food: both are known as facts only, the difference between them being that the appetite for food is necessary to the life of the hungry man and is therefore a personal appetite, whereas the other is an appetite for evolution, and therefore a superpersonal need.

Shaw believed himself to be one of the principal instruments of the Life Force — all his heroes, he modestly admitted, are imitations of himself — and both he and his dramatic heroes struggle for a good many aims that nowadays may seem merely cranky or outdated. Shaw was, for example, a vegetarian, an anti-vivisectionist, an opponent of vaccination, an advocate of comfortable clothing and phonetic spelling. (He left his considerable fortune for the purpose of the reform of English spelling.) His dramatic heroes argue for things that most people now take for granted: women's rights, wider distribution of income, sensibly arranged marriages, and more practical attitudes toward war, finance, and government. All of us would agree that these aims are sensible, or at least worthy of discussion, but they no longer seem startling. This does not invalidate those plays of Shaw's in which his heroes argue for such reforms, for it is not the presence of *particular* ideas in the plays that is crucial. In other words, the power of Shaw's drama does not lie in any *specific* program for reform it may offer; it lies instead in a certain quality of life which he dramatized superbly. We will continue to prize these plays because in them Shaw powerfully dramatized representatives of a continuing aspect of human nature: the cheerful, witty, ingenious and clever reasoner, filled with a sure hope for the future, resourceful in finding ways to ridicule and demolish nonsense, and magnificently capable of expressing his values in language and action. Men endowed with these qualities use ideas in the way other men use matches. But the dramatic focus is not on the many ideas they pick up, play with to make a point, and discard. The focus is rather on that marvelous idea-making faculty of mind; on the process, not the product.

III

This brings us directly to *Saint Joan*. Shaw wrote the play soon after a great war which in in all its senselessness and butchery threatened any optimistic belief in Progress or Creative Evolution. Trench warfare, barbed wire, poison gas, drum-fire barrages, the machine gun, and aerial bombardment seemed to suck down the hopes of Shaw and an entire generation of believers in the inevitable progress of mankind into the mud of Ypres and Verdun. But while the old cheerful optimism may never have returned to Shaw after World War I, his belief in the ultimate victory of sense did not die, and *Saint Joan* is the expression of his continuing though chastened hope.

Shaw's Joan comes to announce and die for two ideas new in the fifteenth century: Nationalism and Protestantism, and she comes to defeat two old ideas: feudalism and the concept of a universal authoritarian church. So complete has been the triumph of Joan's ideas that Shaw's twentieth-century audience can scarcely understand how anyone could have opposed them. And yet, as we read or watch *Saint Joan* we do so from a world as ripe for change as Joan's. Shaw has set a clever trap for us, for Joan's new ideas are by now our very old ideas. They are, in fact, the master concepts which created World War I and many of the subsequent disasters of the twentieth century. At the time when Joan focused and dramatized man's growing aware-

ness of himself as a member of a nation of people speaking the same language, Nationalism and Protestantism — the determination to decide one's relationship with God in the privacy of the individual soul — were useful and necessary ideas. They were expressions of the Life Force working step by step on its long way toward the perfect man and society. But what was new and useful in the fifteenth century, Shaw implies, may no longer work in the twentieth.

However, the mass of humankind is very conservative and once converted to a new idea holds onto it until it ceases to be new or useful and becomes instead dangerous. Much of the power of *Saint Joan* comes from the skill and understanding with which Shaw renders these conservative tendencies. There is, of course, the fool, who does things one way simply because that is the way they have always been done. The clerk Courcelles, for example, who cannot conceive why Joan should not be tortured: "It is the law. It is customary. It is always done." Then there is the English chaplain, de Stogumber, Colonel Blimp in medieval dress, who is already a confirmed Nationalist and Protestant in his actions, but who still mechanically speaks of himself as belonging to the old order. But the war had taught Shaw that the habit of mind that will not meet new situations with new ideas is more complex than mere folly — at once more noble and more wicked. And so he peoples his play with a wide variety of conservative defenders of the old order, ranging from the cynical Earl of Warwick, through the lethargic Dauphin, to the idealistic Bishop of Beauvais. Shaw permits himself only one sly and muted joke on these somber, frightening men who destroy Joan: even as they condemn her for her political radicalism and heresy, they themselves are unconsciously tinged with these new ideas. Much of the pleasure of *Saint Joan* comes from observing the skill with which Shaw portrays the combination of forces which oppose and destroy Joan; but in considering them it is well to remember that Shaw insisted that Joan had a fairer trial than most men get today. He is warning us that we are not dealing with villains from melodrama but with complicated human beings acting in a very human and frightening way.

And now to the hero. A miracle-working saint of the Catholic Church who has visions and hears angelic voices may seem a strange choice of hero for a rationalistic nineteenth-century liberal playwright. In part, no doubt, Shaw chose Joan because he loved to shock and surprise his audience, which was feeling very sentimental about a Joan who had recently been canonized to symbolize the power and suffering of France during the War. But all history was really grist for the Shavian mill. Wherever he looked he found the Life Force at work under many names and guises: Roman emperors, Christian martyrs, professors of phonetics, munitions makers, Catholic saints. All were for him the great geniuses, the supermen, of creative evolution. And as for miracles and visions that the world takes for supernatural events, Shaw deliberately makes them ordinary — hens beginning to lay eggs, or the wind shifting at an opportune time — to suggest that they are no more than the usual events of nature occurring at just the right time for the genius-saint, who is luckier as well as more clear-headed than most individuals. Chance favors them, and they are clever enough to make the most of good chance. Miracles accounted for, it would still seem that a rationalist would have to deny angelic voices and visions. Shaw allows Joan her supernatural experiences, but he makes her voices tell her only what her supreme common sense would tell her anyway. In other words, in Shaw's play Joan's supernatural guides are only the visual and aural projections of the crystal-clear mind and creative imagination of a genius.

In her abilities Joan resembles the heroes of Shaw's earlier plays, but just as World War I had forced him to look at conservatism and folly in a different light, it now caused him to reassess the price his heroes have to pay in order to validate their new ideas. In the earlier plays the supermen outwitted all the fools around them, reorganized their small worlds, and, in the fashion of comedy, lived happily ever after. Now, however, Shaw depicts a tragic world where the Life Force uses up its saints and prophets because new ideas can only be established by blood. Joan's death at the stake in Rouen was the only way in which ordinary men could be shocked deeply enough to cast off the old ways of thought and accept the new. Why this is so is in part a mystery and will remain so, but Shaw offers some understanding of the fact. Joan, like Socrates, Shaw once wrote, was an innocent who treated men whose understanding was not as clear as hers as fools. But she was playing unawares with dark and terrible forces which lie just below the seemingly reasonable, bright surface of the world. She had no comprehension of the " fury roused by the exposures of the stupidities of comparative dullards." She, again like Socrates, " had no suspicion of the extent " to which " her mental superiority had roused fear and hatred " against her " in the hearts of men toward whom she was conscious of nothing but good will and good service."

So Joan has to die to bring her new ideas to birth; and the realization that this must be so is tragic in the fullest sense. Despite this heavy knowledge, Shaw's optimism was not totally destroyed. Instead of leaving us before the flickering fires in the square at Rouen, he brings his Joan back on stage in the Epilogue, suffering and agony passed, to talk in her blunt country way and to laugh at the little men she has left behind, who still do not understand what miraculous happenings they have encountered. Shaw once said, " I have got the tragedian and I have got the clown in me, and the clown trips me up in the most dreadful way." But the ending of *Saint Joan,* where the irrepressible clown breaks through in Joan and Shaw, must leave us wondering whether the clown really tripped him up, or whether it is not the manifestation of his and the world's greatest power, an indomitable wit and a sense of humor which can survive everything and still find life both ludicrous and meaningful.

Saint Joan

Scene I

A fine spring morning on the river Meuse, between Lorraine and Champagne, in the year 1429 A.D., in the castle of Vaucouleurs.

Captain Robert de Baudricourt, a military squire, handsome and ·physically energetic, but with no will of his own, is disguising that defect in his usual fashion by storming terribly at his steward, a trodden worm, scanty of flesh, scanty of hair, who might be any age from 18 to 55, being the sort of man whom age cannot wither because he has never bloomed.

The two are in a sunny stone chamber on the first floor of the castle. At a plain strong oak table, seated in chair to match, the captain presents his left profile. The steward stands facing him at the other side of the table, if so deprecatory a stance as his can be called standing. The mullioned thirteenth-century window is open behind him. Near it in the corner is a turret with a narrow arched doorway leading to a winding stair which descends to the courtyard. There is a stout fourlegged stool under the table, and a wooden chest under the window.

ROBERT. No eggs! No eggs!! Thousand thunders, man, what do you mean by no eggs?

STEWARD. Sir: it is not my fault. It is the act of God.

ROBERT. Blasphemy. You tell me there are no eggs; and you blame your Maker for it.

STEWARD. Sir: what can I do? I cannot lay eggs.

ROBERT [*sarcastic*]. Ha! You jest about it.

STEWARD. No, sir, God knows. We all have to go without eggs just as you have, sir. The hens will not lay.

ROBERT. Indeed! [*Rising*]. Now listen to me, you.

STEWARD [*humbly*]. Yes, sir.

ROBERT. What am I?

STEWARD. What are you, sir?

ROBERT [*coming at him*]. Yes: what am I? Am I Robert, squire of Baudricourt and captain of this castle of Vaucouleurs; or am I a cowboy?

STEWARD. Oh, sir, you know you are a greater man here than the king himself.

ROBERT. Precisely. And now, do you know what you are?

STEWARD. I am nobody, sir, except that I have the honor to be your steward.

ROBERT [*driving him to the wall, adjective by adjective*]. You have not only the honor of being my steward, but the privilege of being the worst, most incompetent, drivelling snivelling jibbering jabbering idiot of a steward in France. [*He strides back to the table.*]

STEWARD [*cowering on the chest*]. Yes, sir: to a great man like you I must seem like that.

ROBERT [*turning*]. My fault, I suppose. Eh?

STEWARD [*coming to him deprecatingly*]. Oh, sir: you always give my most innocent words such a turn!

ROBERT. I will give your neck a turn if you dare tell me when I ask you how many eggs there are that you cannot lay any.

STEWARD [*protesting*]. Oh sir, oh sir —

ROBERT. No: not oh sir, oh sir, but no sir, no sir. My three Barbary hens and the black are the best layers in Champagne. And you come and tell me that there are no eggs! Who stole them? Tell me that, before I kick you out through the castle gate for a liar and a seller of my goods to thieves. The milk was short yesterday, too: do not forget that.

STEWARD [*desperate*]. I know, sir. I know only too well. There is no milk: there are no eggs: tomorrow there will be nothing.

ROBERT. Nothing! You will steal the lot: eh?

STEWARD. No, sir: nobody will steal anything. But there is a spell on us: we are bewitched.

ROBERT. That story is not good enough for me. Robert de Baudricourt burns witches and hangs thieves. Go. Bring me four dozen eggs and two gallons of milk here in this room before noon, or Heaven have mercy on your bones! I will teach you to make a fool of me. [*He resumes his seat with an air of finality.*]

STEWARD. Sir: I tell you there are no eggs. There will be none — not if you were to kill me for it — as long as The Maid is at the door.

ROBERT. The Maid! What maid? What are you talking about?

STEWARD. The girl from Lorraine, sir. From Domrémy.

ROBERT [*rising in fearful wrath*]. Thirty thousand thunders! Fifty thousand devils! Do you mean to say that that girl, who had the impudence to ask to see me two days ago, and whom I told you to send back to her father with my orders that he was to give her a good hiding, is here still?

STEWARD. I have told her to go, sir. She wont.

ROBERT. I did not tell you to tell her to go: I told you to throw her out. You have fifty men-at-arms and a dozen lumps of able-bodied servants to carry out my orders. Are they afraid of her?

STEWARD. She is so positive, sir.

ROBERT [seizing him by the scruff of the neck]. Positive! Now see here. I am going to throw you downstairs.

STEWARD. No, sir. Please.

ROBERT. Well, stop me by being positive. It's quite easy: any slut of a girl can do it.

STEWARD [hanging limp in his hands]. Sir, sir: you cannot get rid of her by throwing me out. [Robert has to let him drop. He squats on his knees on the floor, contemplating his master resignedly.] You see, sir, you are much more positive than I am. But so is she.

ROBERT. I am stronger than you are, you fool.

STEWARD. No, sir: it isnt that: it's your strong character, sir. She is weaker than we are: she is only a slip of a girl; but we cannot make her go.

ROBERT. You parcel of curs: you are afraid of her.

STEWARD [rising cautiously]. No sir: we are afraid of you; but she puts courage into us. She really doesnt seem to be afraid of anything. Perhaps you could frighten her, sir.

ROBERT [grimly]. Perhaps. Where is she now?

STEWARD. Down in the courtyard, sir, talking to the soldiers as usual. She is always talking to the soldiers except when she is praying.

ROBERT. Praying! Ha! You believe she prays, you idiot. I know the sort of girl that is always talking to soldiers. She shall talk to me a bit. [He goes to the window and shouts fiercely through it.] Hallo, you there!

A GIRL'S VOICE [bright, strong and rough]. Is it me, sir?

ROBERT. Yes, you.

THE VOICE. Be you captain?

ROBERT. Yes, damn your impudence, I be captain. Come up here. [To the soldiers in the yard] Shew her the way, you. And shove her along quick. [He leaves the window, and returns to his place at the table, where he sits magisterially.]

STEWARD [whispering]. She wants to go and be a soldier herself. She wants you to give her soldier's clothes. Armor, sir! And a sword! Actually! [He steals behind Robert.]

Joan appears in the turret doorway. She is an ablebodied country girl of 17 or 18, respectably dressed in red, with an uncommon face; eyes very wide apart and bulging as they often do in very imaginative people, a long well-shaped nose with wide nostrils, a short upper lip, resolute but full-lipped mouth, and handsome fighting chin. She comes eagerly to the table, delighted at having penetrated to Baudricourt's presence at last, and full of hope as to the results. His scowl does not check or frighten her in the least. Her voice is normally a hearty coaxing voice, very confident, very appealing, very hard to resist.

JOAN [bobbing a curtsey]. Good morning, captain squire. Captain: you are to give me a horse and armor and some soldiers, and send me to the Dauphin. Those are your orders from my Lord.

ROBERT [outraged]. Orders from your lord! And who the devil may your lord be? Go back to him, and tell him that I am neither duke nor peer at his orders: I am squire of Baudricourt; and I take no orders except from the king.

JOAN [reassuringly]. Yes, squire: that is all right. My Lord is the King of Heaven.

ROBERT. Why, the girl's mad. [To the steward] Why didnt you tell me so, you blockhead?

STEWARD. Sir: do not anger her: give her what she wants.

JOAN [impatient, but friendly]. They all say I am mad until I talk to them, squire. But you see that it is the will of God that you are to do what He has put into my mind.

ROBERT. It is the will of God that I shall send you back to your father with orders to put you under lock and key and thrash the madness out of you. What have you to say to that?

JOAN. You think you will, squire; but you will find it all coming quite different. You said you would not see me; but here I am.

STEWARD [appealing]. Yes, sir. You see, sir.

ROBERT. Hold your tongue, you.

STEWARD [abjectly]. Yes, sir.

ROBERT [to Joan, with a sour loss of confidence]. So you are presuming on my seeing you, are you?

JOAN [sweetly]. Yes, squire.

ROBERT [feeling that he has lost ground, brings down his two fists squarely on the table, and inflates his chest imposingly to cure the unwelcome and only too familiar sensation]. Now listen to me. I am going to assert myself.

JOAN [busily]. Please do, squire. The horse will cost sixteen francs. It is a good deal of money: but I can save it on the armor. I can find a soldier's armor that will fit me well enough: I am very hardy; and I do not need beautiful armor made to my measure like you wear. I shall not want many soldiers: the Dauphin will give me all I need to raise the siege of Orleans.

ROBERT [flabbergasted]. To raise the siege of Orleans!

JOAN. [simply]. Yes, squire: that is what God is sending me to do. Three men will be enough for you to send with me if they are good men and gentle to me. They have promised to come with me. Polly and Jack and —

ROBERT. Polly!! You impudent baggage, do you dare call squire Bertrand de Poulengey Polly to my face?

JOAN. His friends call him so, squire: I did not know he had any other name. Jack —

ROBERT. That is Monsieur John of Metz, I suppose?

JOAN. Yes, squire. Jack will come willingly: he is a very kind gentleman, and gives me money to give to the poor. I think John Godsave will come, and Dick the Archer, and their servants John of Honecourt and Julian. There will be no trouble for you, squire: I have arranged it all: you have only to give the order.

ROBERT [contemplating her in a stupor of amazement]. Well, I am damned!

JOAN [with unruffled sweetness]. No, squire: God is very merciful; and the blessed saints Catherine and Margaret, who speak to me every day [he gapes], will intercede for you. You will go to paradise; and your name will be remembered for ever as my first helper.

ROBERT [to the steward, still much bothered, but changing his tone as he pursues a new clue]. Is this true about Monsieur de Poulengey?

STEWARD [eagerly]. Yes, sir, and about Monsieur de Metz too. They both want to go with her.

ROBERT [thoughtful]. Mf! [He goes to the window, and shouts into the courtyard.] Hallo! You there: send Monsieur de Poulengey to me, will you? [He turns to Joan.] Get out; and wait in the yard.

JOAN [smiling brightly at him]. Right, squire. [She goes out.]

ROBERT [to the steward]. Go with her, you, you dithering imbecile. Stay within call; and keep your eye on her. I shall have her up here again.

STEWARD. Do so in God's name, sir. Think of those hens, the best layers in Champagne; and —

ROBERT. Think of my boot; and take your backside out of reach of it.

The steward retreats hastily and finds himself confronted in the doorway by Bertrand de Poulengey, a lymphatic French gentleman-at-arms, aged 36 or thereabout, employed in the department of the provost-marshal, dreamily absent-minded, seldom speaking unless spoken to, and then slow and obstinate in reply; altogether in contrast to the self-assertive, loud-mouthed, superficially energetic, fundamentally will-less Robert. The steward makes way for him, and vanishes.

Poulengey salutes, and stands awaiting orders.

ROBERT [genially]. It isnt service, Polly. A friendly talk. Sit down. [He hooks the stool from under the table with his instep.]

Poulengey, relaxing, comes into the room; places the stool between the table and the window: and sits down ruminatively. Robert, half sitting on the end of the table, begins the friendly talk.

ROBERT. Now listen to me, Polly. I must talk to you like a father.

Poulengey looks up at him gravely for a moment, but says nothing.

ROBERT. It's about this girl you are interested in. Now, I have seen her. I have talked to her. First, she's mad. That doesnt matter. Second, she's not a farm wench. She's a bourgeoise. That matters a good deal. I know her class exactly. Her father came here last year to represent his village in a lawsuit: he is one of their notables. A farmer. Not a gentleman farmer: he makes money by it, and lives by it. Still, not a laborer. Not a mechanic. He might have a cousin a lawyer, or in the Church. People of this sort may be of no account socially; but they can give a lot of bother to the authorities. That is to say, to me. Now no doubt it seems to you a very simple thing to take this girl away, humbugging her into the belief that you are taking her to the Dauphin. But if you get her into trouble, you may get me into no end of a mess, as I am her father's lord, and responsible for her protection. So friends or no friends, Polly, hands off her.

POULENGEY [with deliberate impressiveness]. I should as soon think of the Blessed Virgin herself in that way, as of this girl.

ROBERT [coming off the table]. But she says you and Jack and Dick have offered to go with her. What for? You are not going to tell me that you take her crazy notion of going to the Dauphin seriously, are you?

POULENGEY [slowly]. There is something about her. They are pretty foulmouthed and foulminded down there in the guardroom, some of them. But there hasnt been a word that has anything to do with her being a woman. They have stopped swearing before her. There is something. Something. It may be worth trying.

ROBERT. Oh, come, Polly! pull yourself together. Commonsense was never your strong point; but this is a little too much. [He retreats disgustedly.]

POULENGEY [unmoved]. What is the good of commonsense? If we had any commonsense we should join the Duke of Burgundy and the English king. They hold half the country, right down to the Loire. They have Paris. They have this castle: you know very well that we had to surrender it to the Duke of Bedford, and that you are only holding it on parole. The Dauphin is in Chinon, like a rat in a corner, except that he wont fight. We dont even know that he is the Dauphin: his mother says he isnt; and she ought to know. Think of that! the queen denying the legitimacy of her own son!

ROBERT. Well, she married her daughter to the English king. Can you blame the woman?

POULENGEY. I blame nobody. But thanks to her, the Dauphin is down and out; and we may as well face it. The English will take Orleans: the Bastard will not be able to stop them.

ROBERT. He beat the English the year before last at Montargis. I was with him.

POULENGEY. No matter: his men are cowed now; and he cant work miracles. And I tell you that nothing can save our side now but a miracle.

ROBERT. Miracles are all right, Polly. The only difficulty about them is that they dont happen nowadays.

POULENGEY. I used to think so. I am not so sure now. [Rising, and moving ruminatively towards the window]. At all events this is not a time to leave any stone unturned. There is something about the girl.

ROBERT. Oh! You think the girl can work miracles, do you?

POULENGEY. I think the girl herself is a bit of a miracle. Anyhow, she is the last card left in our hand. Better play her than throw up the game. [He wanders to the turret.]

ROBERT [wavering]. You really think that?

POULENGEY [turning]. Is there anything else left for us to think?

ROBERT [going to him]. Look here, Polly. If you were in my place would you let a girl like that do you out of sixteen francs for a horse?

POULENGEY. I will pay for the horse.

ROBERT. You will!

POULENGEY. Yes: I will back my opinion.

ROBERT. You will really gamble on a forlorn hope to the tune of sixteen francs?

POULENGEY. It is not a gamble.

ROBERT. What else is it?

POULENGEY. It is a certainty. Her words and her ardent faith in God have put fire into me.

ROBERT [giving him up]. Whew! You are as mad as she is.

POULENGEY [obstinately]. We want a few mad people now. See where the sane ones have landed us!

ROBERT [his irresoluteness now openly swamping his affected decisiveness]. I shall feel like a precious fool. Still, if you feel sure — ?

POULENGEY. I feel sure enough to take her to Chinon — unless you stop me.

ROBERT. This is not fair. You are putting the responsibility on me.

POULENGEY. It is on you whichever way you decide.

ROBERT. Yes: thats just it. Which way am I to decide? You dont see how awkward this is for me. [Snatching at a dilatory step with an unconscious hope that Joan will make up his mind for him]. Do you think I ought to have another talk to her?

POULENGEY [rising]. Yes. [He goes to the window and calls.] Joan!

JOAN'S VOICE. Will he let us go, Polly?

POULENGEY. Come up. Come in. [Turning to Robert] Shall I leave you with her?

ROBERT. No: stay here; and back me up.

Poulengey sits down on the chest. Robert goes back to his magisterial chair, but remains standing to inflate himself more imposingly. Joan comes in, full of good news.

JOAN. Jack will go halves for the horse.

ROBERT. Well!! [He sits, deflated.]

POULENGEY [gravely]. Sit down, Joan.

JOAN [checked a little, and looking to Robert]. May I?

ROBERT. Do what you are told.

Joan curtsies and sits down on the stool between them. Robert outfaces his perplexity with his most peremptory air.

ROBERT. What is your name?

JOAN [chattily]. They always call me Jenny in Lorraine. Here in France I am Joan. The soldiers call me The Maid.

ROBERT. What is your surname?

JOAN. Surname? What is that? My father sometimes calls himself d'Arc; but I know nothing about it. You met my father. He —

ROBERT. Yes, yes; I remember. You come from Domrémy in Lorraine, I think.

JOAN. Yes; but what does it matter? we all speak French.

ROBERT. Dont ask questions: answer them. How old are you?

JOAN. Seventeen: so they tell me. It might be nineteen. I dont remember.

ROBERT. What did you mean when you said that St Catherine and St Margaret talked to you every day?

JOAN. They do.

ROBERT. What are they like?

JOAN [suddenly obstinate]. I will tell you nothing about that: they have not given me leave.

ROBERT. But you actually see them; and they talk to you just as I am talking to you?

JOAN. No: it is quite different. I cannot tell you: you must not talk to me about my voices.

ROBERT. How do you mean? voices?

JOAN. I hear voices telling me what to do. They come from God.

ROBERT. They come from your imagination.

JOAN. Of course. That is how the messages of God come to us.

POULENGEY. Checkmate.

ROBERT. No fear! [To Joan] So God says you are to raise the siege of Orleans?

JOAN. And to crown the Dauphin in Rheims Cathedral.

ROBERT [*gasping*]. Crown the D — ! Gosh!

JOAN. And to make the English leave France.

ROBERT [*sarcastic*]. Anything else?

JOAN [*charming*]. Not just at present, thank you, squire.

ROBERT. I suppose you think raising a siege is as easy as chasing a cow out of a meadow. You think soldiering is anybody's job?

JOAN. I do not think it can be very difficult if God is on your side, and you are willing to put your life in His hand. But many soldiers are very simple.

ROBERT [*grimly*]. Simple! Did you ever see English soldiers fighting?

JOAN. They are only men. God made them just like us; but He gave them their own country and their own language; and it is not His will that they should come into our country and try to speak our language.

ROBERT. Who has been putting such nonsense into your head? Dont you know that soldiers are subject to their feudal lord, and that it is nothing to them or to you whether he is the duke of Burgundy or the king of England or the king of France? What has their language to do with it?

JOAN. I do not understand that a bit. We are all subject to the King of Heaven; and He gave us our countries and our languages, and meant us to keep to them. If it were not so it would be murder to kill an Englishman in battle; and you, squire, would be in great danger of hell fire. You must not think about your duty to your feudal lord, but about your duty to God.

POULENGEY. It's no use, Robert: she can choke you like that every time.

ROBERT. Can she, by Saint Dennis! We shall see. [*To Joan*] We are not talking about God: we are talking about practical affairs. I ask you again, girl, have you ever seen English soldiers fighting? Have you ever seen them plundering, burning, turning the countryside into a desert? Have you heard no tales of their Black Prince who was blacker than the devil himself, or of the English king's father?

JOAN. You must not be afraid, Robert —

ROBERT. Damn you, I am not afraid. And who gave you leave to call me Robert?

JOAN. You were called so in church in the name of our Lord. All the other names are your father's or your brother's or anybody's.

ROBERT. Tcha!

JOAN. Listen to me, squire. At Domrémy we had to fly to the next village to escape from the English soldiers. Three of them were left behind, wounded. I came to know these three poor goddams quite well. They had not half my strength.

ROBERT. Do you know why they are called goddams?

JOAN. No. Everyone calls them goddams.

ROBERT. It is because they are always calling on their God to condemn their souls to perdition. That is what goddam means in their language. How do you like it?

JOAN. God will be merciful to them; and they will act like His good children when they go back to the country He made for them, and made them for. I have heard the tales of the Black Prince. The moment he touched the soil of our country the devil entered into him, and made him a black fiend. But at home, in the place made for him by God, he was good. It is always so. If I went into England against the will of God to conquer England, and tried to live there and speak its language, the devil would enter into me; and when I was old I should shudder to remember the wickedness I did.

ROBERT. Perhaps. But the more devil you were the better you might fight. That is why the goddams will take Orleans. And you cannot stop them, nor ten thousand like you.

JOAN. One thousand like me can stop them. Ten like me can stop them with God on our side. [*She rises impetuously, and goes at him, unable to sit quiet any longer.*] You do not understand, squire. Our soldiers are always beaten because they are fighting only to save their skins; and the shortest way to save your skin is to run away. Our knights are thinking only of the money they will make in ransoms: it is not kill or be killed with them, but pay or be paid. But I will teach them all to fight that the will of God may be done in France; and then they will drive the poor goddams before them like sheep. You and Polly will live to see the day when there will not be an English soldier on the soil of France; and there will be but one king there: not the feudal English king, but God's French one.

ROBERT [*to Poulengey*]. This may be all rot, Polly; but the troops might swallow it, though nothing that we can say seems able to put any fight into them. Even the Dauphin might swallow it. And if she can put fight into him, she can put it into anybody.

POULENGEY. I can see no harm in trying. Can you? And there is something about the girl —

ROBERT [*turning to Joan*]. Now listen you to me; and [*desperately*] dont cut in before I have time to think.

JOAN [*plumping down on the stool again, like an obedient schoolgirl*]. Yes, squire.

ROBERT. Your orders are, that you are to go to Chinon under the escort of this gentleman and three of his friends.

JOAN [*radiant, clasping her hands*]. Oh, squire! Your head is all circled with light, like a saint's.

POULENGEY. How is she to get into the royal presence?

ROBERT [*who has looked up for his halo rather apprehensively*]. I dont know: how did she get into my presence? If the Dauphin can keep her out he is a better man than I take him for. [*Rising*]. I will send her to Chinon; and she can say I sent her. Then let come what may: I can do no more.

JOAN. And the dress? I may have a soldier's dress, maynt I, squire?

ROBERT. Have what you please. I wash my hands of it.

JOAN [*wildly excited by her success*]. Come, Polly. [*She dashes out.*]

ROBERT [*shaking Poulengey's hand*]. Goodbye, old man, I am taking a big chance. Few other men would have done it. But as you say, there is something about her.

POULENGEY. Yes: there is something about her. Goodbye. [*He goes out.*]

Robert, still very doubtful whether he has not been made a fool of by a crazy female, and a social inferior to boot, scratches his head and slowly comes back from the door.

The steward runs in with a basket.

STEWARD. Sir, sir —

ROBERT. What now?

STEWARD. The hens are laying like mad, sir. Five dozen eggs!

ROBERT [*stiffens convulsively: crosses himself: and forms with his pale lips the words*]. Christ in heaven! [*Aloud but breathless*]. She did come from God.

Scene II

Chinon, in Touraine. An end of the throne room in the castle, curtained off to make an antechamber. The Archbishop of Rheims, close on 50, a full-fed prelate with nothing of the ecclesiastic about him except his imposing bearing, and the Lord Chamberlain, Monseigneur de la Trémouille, a monstrous arrogant wineskin of a man, are waiting for the Dauphin. There is a door in the wall to the right of the two men. It is late in the afternoon on the 8th of March, 1429. The Archbishop stands with dignity whilst the Chamberlain, on his left, fumes about in the worst of tempers.

LA TRÉMOUILLE. What the devil does the Dauphin mean by keeping us waiting like this? I dont know how you have the patience to stand there like a stone idol.

THE ARCHBISHOP. You see, I am an archbishop; and an archbishop is a sort of idol. At any rate he has to learn to keep still and suffer fools patiently. Besides, my dear Lord Chamberlain, it is the Dauphin's royal privilege to keep you waiting, is it not?

LA TRÉMOUILLE. Dauphin be damned! saving your reverence. Do you know how much money he owes me?

THE ARCHBISHOP. Much more than he owes me, I have no doubt, because you are a much richer man. But I take it he owes you all you could afford to lend him. That is what he owes me.

LA TRÉMOUILLE. Twenty-seven thousand: that was his last haul. A cool twenty-seven thousand!

THE ARCHBISHOP. What becomes of it all? He never has a suit of clothes that I would throw to a curate.

LA TRÉMOUILLE. He dines on a chicken or a scrap of mutton. He borrows my last penny; and there is nothing to shew for it. [*A page appears in the doorway.*] At last!

THE PAGE. No, my lord: it is not His Majesty. Monsieur de Rais is approaching.

LA TRÉMOUILLE. Young Bluebeard! Why announce him?

THE PAGE. Captain La Hire is with him. Something has happened, I think.

Gilles de Rais, a young man of 25, very smart and self-possessed, and sporting the extravagance of a little curled beard dyed blue at a clean-shaven court, comes in. He is determined to make himself agreeable, but lacks natural joyousness, and is not really pleasant. In fact when he defies the Church some eleven years later he is accused of trying to extract pleasure from horrible cruelties, and hanged. So far, however, there is no shadow of the gallows on him. He advances gaily to the Archbishop. The page withdraws.

BLUEBEARD. Your faithful lamb, Archbishop. Good day, my lord. Do you know what has happened to La Hire?

LA TRÉMOUILLE. He has sworn himself into a fit, perhaps.

BLUEBEARD. No: just the opposite. Foul Mouthed Frank, the only man in Touraine who could beat him at swearing, was told by a soldier that he shouldnt use such language when he was at the point of death.

THE ARCHBISHOP. Nor at any other point. But was Foul Mouthed Frank on the point of death?

BLUEBEARD. Yes: he has just fallen into a well and been drowned. La Hire is frightened out of his wits.

Captain La Hire comes in: a war dog with no court manners and pronounced camp ones.

BLUEBEARD. I have just been telling the Chamberlain and the Archbishop. The Archbishop says you are a lost man.

LA HIRE. [*striding past Bluebeard, and planting himself between the Archbishop and La Trémouillee*]. This is nothing to joke about. It is worse than we thought. It was not a soldier, but an angel dressed as a soldier.

THE ARCHBISHOP
THE CHAMBERLAIN } [*exclaiming all together*]. An Angel!
BLUEBEARD

LA HIRE. Yes, an angel. She has made her way from Champagne with half a dozen men through the thick of everything: Burgundians, Goddams, deserters, robbers, and Lord knows who; and they never met a soul except the country folk. I know one of them: de Poulengey. He says she's an angel. If ever I utter an oath again may my soul be blasted to eternal damnation!

THE ARCHBISHOP. A very pious beginning, Captain.

Bluebeard and La Trémouille laugh at him. The page returns.

THE PAGE. His Majesty.

They stand perfunctorily at court attention. The Dauphin, aged 26, really King Charles the Seventh since the death of his father, but as yet uncrowned, comes in through the curtains with a paper in his hands. He is a poor creature physically; and the current fashion of shaving closely, and hiding every scrap of hair under the headcovering or headdress, both by women and men, makes the worst of his appearance. He has little narrow eyes, near together, a long pendulous nose that droops over his thick short upper lip, and the expression of a young dog accustomed to be kicked, yet incorrigible and irrepressible. But he is neither vulgar nor stupid; and he has a cheeky humor which enables him to hold his own in conversation. Just at present he is excited, like a child with a new toy. He comes to the Archbishop's left hand. Bluebeard and La Hire retire towards the curtains.

CHARLES. Oh, Archbishop, do you know what Robert de Baudricourt is sending me from Vaucouleurs?

THE ARCHBISHOP [*contemptuously*]. I am not interested in the newest toys.

CHARLES [*indignantly*]. It isnt a toy. [*Sulkily*]. However, I can get on very well without your interest.

THE ARCHBISHOP. Your Highness is taking offence very unnecessarily.

CHARLES. Thank you. You are always ready with a lecture, arnt you?

LA TRÉMOUILLE [*roughly*]. Enough grumbling. What have you got there?

CHARLES. What is that to you?

LA TRÉMOUILLE. It is my business to know what is passing between you and the garrison at Vau-

couleurs. [*He snatches the paper from the Dauphin's hand, and begins reading it with some difficulty, following the words with his finger and spelling them out syllable by syllable.*]

CHARLES [*mortified*]. You all think you can treat me as you please because I owe you money, and because I am no good at fighting. But I have the blood royal in my veins.

THE ARCHBISHOP. Even that has been questioned, your Highness. One hardly recognizes in you the grandson of Charles the Wise.

CHARLES. I want to hear no more of my grandfather. He was so wise that he used up the whole family stock of wisdom for five generations, and left me the poor fool I am, bullied and insulted by all of you.

THE ARCHBISHOP. Control yourself, sir. These outbursts of petulance are not seemly.

CHARLES. Another lecture! Thank you. What a pity it is that though you are an archbishop saints and angels dont come to see you!

THE ARCHBISHOP. What do you mean?

CHARLES. Aha! Ask that bully there [*pointing to La Trémouille*].

LA TRÉMOUILLE [*furious*]. Hold your tongue. Do you hear?

CHARLES. Oh, I hear. You neednt shout. The whole castle can hear. Why dont you go and shout at the English, and beat them for me?

LA TRÉMOUILLE [*raising his fist*]. You young —

CHARLES [*running behind the Archbishop*]. Dont you raise your hand to me. It's high treason.

LA HIRE. Steady, Duke! Steady!

THE ARCHBISHOP [*resolutely*]. Come, come! this will not do. My Lord Chamberlain: please! please! we must keep some sort of order. [*To the Dauphin*] And you, sir: if you cannot rule your kingdom, at least try to rule yourself.

CHARLES. Another lecture! Thank you.

LA TRÉMOUILLE [*handing over the paper to the Archbishop*]. Here: read the accursed thing for me. He has sent the blood boiling into my head: I cant distinguish the letters.

CHARLES [*coming back and peering round La Trémouille's left shoulder*]. I will read it for you if you like. I can read, you know.

LA TRÉMOUILLE [*with intense contempt, not at all stung by the taunt*]. Yes: reading is about all you are fit for: Can you make it out, Archbishop?

THE ARCHBISHOP. I should have expected more commonsense from De Baudricourt. He is sending some cracked country lass here —

CHARLES [*interrupting*]. No: he is sending a saint: an angel. And she is coming to me: to me, the king, and not to you, Archbishop, holy as you are. She knows the blood royal if you dont. [*He struts up to the curtains between Bluebeard and La Hire.*]

THE ARCHBISHOP. You cannot be allowed to see this crazy wench.

CHARLES [*turning*]. But I am the king; and I will.

LA TRÉMOUILLE [*brutally*]. Then she cannot be allowed to see you. Now!

CHARLES. I tell you I will. I am going to put my foot down —

BLUEBEARD [*laughing at him*]. Naughty! What would your wise grandfather say?

CHARLES. That just shews your ignorance, Bluebeard. My grandfather had a saint who used to float in the air when she was praying, and told him everything he wanted to know. My poor father had two saints, Marie de Maillé and the Gasque of Avignon. It is in our family; and I dont care what you say: I will have my saint too.

THE ARCHBISHOP. This creature is not a saint. She is not even a respectable woman. She does not wear women's clothes. She is dressed like a soldier, and rides round the country with soldiers. Do you suppose such a person can be admitted to your Highness's court?

LA HIRE. Stop. [*Going to the Archbishop*]. Did you say a girl in armor, like a soldier?

THE ARCHBISHOP. So De Baudricourt describes her.

LA HIRE. But by all the devils in hell — Oh, God forgive me, what am I saying? — by Our Lady and all the saints, this must be the angel that struck Foul Mouthed Frank dead for swearing.

CHARLES [*triumphant*]. You see! A miracle!

LA HIRE. She may strike the lot of us dead if we cross her. For Heaven's sake, Archbishop, be careful what you are doing.

THE ARCHBISHOP [*severely*]. Rubbish! Nobody has been struck dead. A drunken blackguard who has been rebuked a hundred times for swearing has fallen into a well, and been drowned. A mere coincidence.

LA HIRE. I do not know what a coincidence is. I do know that the man is dead, and that she told him he was going to die.

THE ARCHBISHOP. We are all going to die, Captain.

LA HIRE [*crossing himself*]. I hope not. [*He backs out of the conversation.*]

BLUEBEARD. We can easily find out whether she is an angel or not. Let us arrange when she comes that I shall be the Dauphin, and see whether she will find me out.

CHARLES. Yes: I agree to that. If she cannot find the blood royal I will have nothing to do with her.

THE ARCHBISHOP. It is for the Church to make saints: let De Baudricourt mind his own business, and not dare usurp the function of his priest. I say the girl shall not be admitted.

BLUEBEARD. But, Archbishop —

THE ARCHBISHOP [*sternly*]. I speak in the Church's name. [*To the Dauphin*] Do you dare say she shall?

CHARLES [*intimidated but sulky*]. Oh, if you make it an excommunication matter, I have nothing more to say, of course. But you havnt read the end of the letter. De Baudricourt says she will raise the siege of Orleans, and beat the English for us.

LA TRÉMOUILLE. Rot!

CHARLES. Well, will you save Orleans for us, with all your bullying?

LA TRÉMOUILLE [*savagely*]. Do not throw that in my face again: do you hear? I have done more fighting than you ever did or ever will. But I cannot be everywhere.

THE DAUPHIN. Well, thats something.

BLUEBEARD [*coming between the Archbishop and Charles*]. You have Jack Dunois at the head of your troops in Orleans: the brave Dunois, the handsome Dunois, the wonderful invincible Dunois, the darling of all the ladies, the beautiful bastard. Is it likely that the country lass can do what he cannot do?

CHARLES. Why doesnt he raise the siege, then?

LA HIRE. The wind is against him.

BLUEBEARD. How can the wind hurt him at Orleans? It is not on the Channel.

LA HIRE. It is on the river Loire; and the English hold the bridgehead. He must ship his men across the river and upstream, if he is to take them in the rear. Well, he cannot, because there is a devil of a wind blowing the other way. He is tired of paying the priests to pray for a west wind. What he needs is a miracle. You tell me that what the girl did to Foul Mouthed Frank was no miracle. No matter: it finished Frank. If she changes the wind for Dunois, that may not be a miracle either; but it may finish the English. What harm is there in trying?

THE ARCHBISHOP [*who has read the end of the letter and become more thoughtful*]. It is true that De Baudricourt seems extraordinarily impressed.

LA HIRE. De Baudricourt is a blazing ass; but he is a soldier; and if he thinks she can beat the English, all the rest of the army will think so too.

LA TRÉMOUILLE [*to the Archbishop, who is hesitating*]. Oh, let them have their way. Dunois' men will give up the town in spite of him if somebody does not put some fresh spunk into them.

THE ARCHBISHOP. The Church must examine the girl before anything decisive is done about her. However, since his Highness desires it, let her attend the Court.

LA HIRE. I will find her and tell her. [*He goes out.*]

CHARLES. Come with me, Bluebeard; and let us arrange so that she will not know who I am. You will pretend to be me. [*He goes out through the curtains.*]

BLUEBEARD. Pretend to be that thing! Holy Michael! [*He follows the Dauphin.*]

LA TRÉMOUILLE. I wonder will she pick him out!

THE ARCHBISHOP. Of course she will.

LA TRÉMOUILLE. Why? How is she to know?

THE ARCHBISHOP. She will know what everybody in Chinon knows: that the Dauphin is the meanest-looking and worst-dressed figure in the Court, and that the man with the blue beard is Gilles de Rais.

LA TRÉMOUILLE. I never thought of that.

THE ARCHBISHOP. You are not so accustomed to miracles as I am. It is part of my profession.

LA TRÉMOUILLE [*puzzled and a little scandalized*]. But that would not be a miracle at all.

THE ARCHBISHOP [*calmly*]. Why not?

LA TRÉMOUILLE. Well, come! what is a miracle?

THE ARCHBISHOP. A miracle, my friend, is an event which creates faith. That is the purpose and nature of miracles. They may seem very wonderful to the people who witness them, and very simple to those who perform them. That does not matter: if they confirm or create faith they are true miracles.

LA TRÉMOUILLE. Even when they are frauds, do you mean?

THE ARCHBISHOP. Frauds deceive. An event which creates faith does not deceive: therefore it is not a fraud, but a miracle.

LA TRÉMOUILLE [*scratching his neck in his perplexity*]. Well, I suppose as you are an archbishop you must be right. It seems a bit fishy to me. But I am no churchman, and dont understand these matters.

THE ARCHBISHOP. You are not a churchman; but you are a diplomatist and a soldier. Could you make our citizens pay war taxes, or our soldiers sacrifice their lives, if they knew what is really happening instead of what seems to them to be happening?

LA TRÉMOUILLE. No, by Saint Dennis: the fat would be in the fire before sundown.

THE ARCHBISHOP. Would it not be quite easy to tell them the truth?

LA TRÉMOUILLE. Man alive, they wouldnt believe it.

THE ARCHBISHOP. Just so. Well, the Church has to rule men for the good of their souls as you have to rule them for the good of their bodies. To do that, the Church must do as you do: nourish their faith by poetry.

LA TRÉMOUILLE. Poetry! I should call it humbug.

THE ARCHBISHOP. You would be wrong, my friend. Parables are not lies because they describe events that have never happened. Miracles are not frauds because they are often — I do not say always — very simple and innocent contrivances by which the priest fortifies the faith of his flock. When this girl picks out the Dauphin among his courtiers, it will not be a miracle for me, because I shall know how it has been done, and my faith will not be increased. But as for the others, if they feel the thrill of the supernatural, and forget their sinful clay in a sudden sense of the glory of God, it will be a miracle and a blessed one. And you will find that the girl herself will be more affected than anyone else. She will forget how she really picked him out. So, perhaps, will you.

LA TRÉMOUILLE. Well, I wish I were clever enough to know how much of you is God's archbishop and how much the most artful fox in Touraine. Come on, or we shall be late for the fun; and I want to see it, miracle or no miracle.

THE ARCHBISHOP [*detaining him a moment*]. Do not think that I am a lover of crooked ways. There is a new spirit rising in men: we are at the dawning of a wider epoch. If I were a simple monk, and had not to rule men, I should seek peace for my spirit with Aristotle and Pythagoras rather than with the saints and their miracles.

LA TRÉMOUILLE. And who the deuce was Pythagoras?

THE ARCHBISHOP. A sage who held that the earth is round, and that it moves round the sun.

LA TRÉMOUILLE. What an utter fool! Couldn't he use his eyes?

They go out together through the curtains, which are presently withdrawn, revealing the full depth of the throne room with the Court assembled. On the right are two Chairs of State on a dais. Bluebeard is standing theatrically on the dais, playing the king, and, like the courtiers, enjoying the joke rather obviously. There is a curtained arch in the wall behind the dais; but the main door, guarded by men-at-arms, is at the other side of the room; and a clear path across is kept and lined by the courtiers. Charles is in this path in the middle of the room. La Hire is on his right. The Archbishop, on his left, has taken his place by the dais: La Trémouille at the other side of it. The Duchess de la Trémouille, pretending to be the Queen, sits in the Consort's chair, with a group of ladies in waiting close by, behind the Archbishop.

The chatter of the courtiers makes such a noise that nobody notices the appearance of the page at the door.

THE PAGE. The Duke of — [*Nobody listens.*] The Duke of — [*The chatter continues. Indignant at his failure to command a hearing, he snatches the halberd of the nearest man-at-arms, and thumps the floor with it. The chatter ceases; and everybody looks at him in silence.*] Attention! [*He restores the halberd to the man-at-arms.*] The Duke of Vendôme presents Joan the Maid to his Majesty.

CHARLES [*putting his finger on his lip*]. Ssh! [*He hides behind the nearest courtier, peering out to see what happens.*]

BLUEBEARD [*majestically*]. Let her approach the throne.

Joan, dressed as a soldier, with her hair bobbed and hanging thickly round her face, is led in by a bashful and speechless nobleman, from whom she detaches herself to stop and look round eagerly for the Dauphin.

THE DUCHESS [*to the nearest lady in waiting*]. My dear! Her hair!

All the ladies explode in uncontrollable laughter.

BLUEBEARD [*trying not to laugh, and waving his hand in deprecation of their merriment*]. Ssh — ssh! Ladies! Ladies!!

JOAN [*not at all embarrassed*]. I wear it like this because I am a soldier. Where be Dauphin?

A titter runs through the Court as she walks to the dais.

BLUEBEARD [*condescendingly*]. You are in the presence of the Dauphin.

Joan looks at him sceptically for a moment, scanning him hard up and down to make sure. Dead silence, all watching her. Fun dawns in her face.

JOAN. Coom, Bluebeard! Thou canst not fool me. Where be Dauphin?

A roar of laughter breaks out as Gilles, with a gesture of surrender, joins in the laugh, and jumps down from the dais beside La Trémouille. Joan, also on the broad grin, turns back, searching along the row of courtiers, and presently makes a dive, and drags out Charles by the arm.

JOAN [*releasing him and bobbing him a little curtsey*]. Gentle little Dauphin, I am sent to you to drive the English away from Orleans and from France, and to crown you king in the cathedral at Rheims, where all true kings of France are crowned.

CHARLES [*triumphant, to the court*]. You see, all of you: she knew the blood royal. Who dare say now that I am not my father's son? [*To Joan*] But if you want me to be crowned at Rheims you must talk to the Archbishop, not to me. There he is! [*He is standing behind her.*]

JOAN [*turning quickly, overwhelmed with emotion*]. Oh, my lord! [*She falls on both knees before him, with bowed head, not daring to look up.*] My lord: I am only a poor country girl; and you are filled with the blessedness and glory of God

Himself; but you will touch me with your hands, and give me your blessing, wont you?

BLUEBEARD [*whispering to La Trémouille*]. The old fox blushes.

LA TRÉMOUILLE. Another miracle!

THE ARCHBISHOP [*touched, putting his hand on her head*]. Child: you are in love with religion.

JOAN [*startled: looking up at him*]. Am I? I never thought of that. Is there any harm in it?

THE ARCHBISHOP. There is no harm in it, my child. But there is danger.

JOAN [*rising, with a sunflush of reckless happiness irradiating her face*]. There is always danger, except in heaven. Oh, my lord, you have given me such strength, such courage. It must be a most wonderful thing to be Archbishop.

The Court smiles broadly: even titters a little.

THE ARCHBISHOP [*drawing himself up sensitively*]. Gentlemen: your levity is rebuked by this maid's faith. I am, God help me, all unworthy; but your mirth is a deadly sin.

Their faces fall. Dead silence.

BLUEBEARD. My lord: we were laughing at her, not at you.

THE ARCHBISHOP. What? Not at my unworthiness but at her faith! Gilles de Rais: this maid prophesied that the blasphemer should be drowned in his sin —

JOAN [*distressed*]. No!

THE ARCHBISHOP [*silencing her by a gesture*]. I prophesy now that you will be hanged in yours if you do not learn when to laugh and when to pray.

BLUEBEARD. My lord: I stand rebuked. I am sorry: I can say no more. But if you prophesy that I shall be hanged, I shall never be able to resist temptation, because I shall always be telling myself that I may as well be hanged for a sheep as a lamb.

The courtiers take heart at this. There is more tittering.

JOAN [*scandalized*]. You are an idle fellow, Bluebeard; and you have great impudence to answer the Archbishop.

LA HIRE [*with a huge chuckle*]. Well said, lass! Well said!

JOAN [*impatiently to the Archbishop*]. Oh, my lord, will you send all these silly folks away so that I may speak to the Dauphin alone?

LA HIRE [*goodhumoredly*]. I can take a hint. [*He salutes; turns on his heel; and goes out.*]

THE ARCHBISHOP. Come, gentlemen. The Maid comes with God's blessing, and must be obeyed.

The courtiers withdraw, some through the arch, others at the opposite side. The Archbishop marches across to the door, followed by the Duchess and La Trémouille. As the Archbishop passes Joan, she falls on her knees, and kisses the hem of his robe

fervently. He shakes his head in instinctive remon-
strance; gathers the robe from her; and goes out.
She is left kneeling directly in the Duchess's way.

THE DUCHESS [*coldly*]. Will you allow me to pass,
please?

JOAN [*hastily rising, and standing back*]. Beg
pardon, maam, I am sure.

The Duchess passes on. Joan stares after her;
then whispers to the Dauphin.

JOAN. Be that Queen?

CHARLES. No. She thinks she is.

JOAN [*again staring after the Duchess*]. Oo-oo-
ooh! [*Her awestruck amazement at the figure cut*
by the magnificently dressed lady is not wholly
complimentary.]

LA TRÉMOUILLE [*very surly*]. I'll trouble your
Highness not to gibe at my wife. [*He goes out.*
The others have already gone.]

JOAN [*to the Dauphin*]. Who be old Gruff-and-
Grum?

CHARLES. He is the Duke de la Trémouille.

JOAN. What be his job?

CHARLES. He pretends to command the army.
And whenever I find a friend I can care for, he
kills him.

JOAN. Why dost let him?

CHARLES [*petulantly moving to the throne side*
of the room to escape from her magnetic field].
How can I prevent him? He bullies me. They all
bully me.

JOAN. Art afraid?

CHARLES. Yes: I am afraid. It's no use preaching
to me about it. It's all very well for these big men
with their armor that is too heavy for me, and
their swords that I can hardly lift, and their muscle
and their shouting and their bad tempers. They
like fighting: most of them are making fools of
themselves all the time they are not fighting; but
I am quiet and sensible; and I dont want to kill
people: I only want to be left alone to enjoy myself in my own way. I never asked to be a king:
it was pushed on me. So if you are going to say
'Son of St. Louis: gird on the sword of your ancestors, and lead us to victory' you may spare your
breath to cool your porridge; for I cannot do it.
I am not built that way; and there is an end of it.

JOAN [*trenchant and masterful*]. Blethers! We
are all like that to begin with. I shall put courage
into thee.

CHARLES. But I dont want to have courage put
into me. I want to sleep in a comfortable bed, and
not live in continual terror of being killed or
wounded. Put courage into the others, and let
them have their bellyful of fighting; but let me
alone.

JOAN. It's no use, Charlie: thou must face what
God puts on thee. If thou fail to make thyself

king, thoult be a beggar: what else art fit for?
Come! Let me see thee sitting on the throne. I
have looked forward to that.

CHARLES. What is the good of sitting on the
throne when the other fellows give all the orders?
However! [*He sits enthroned, a piteous figure.*]
Here is the king for you! Look your fill at the poor
devil.

JOAN. Thourt not king yet, lad: thourt but
Dauphin. Be not led away by them around thee.
Dressing up dont fill empty noddle. I know the
people: the real people that make thy bread for
thee; and I tell thee they count no man king of
France until the holy oil has been poured on his
hair, and himself consecrated and crowned in
Rheims Cathedral. And thou needs new clothes,
Charlie. Why does not Queen look after thee
properly?

CHARLES. We're too poor. She wants all the
money we can spare to put on her own back. Besides, I like to see her beautifully dressed; and I
dont care what I wear myself. I should look ugly
anyhow.

JOAN. There is some good in thee, Charlie; but
it is not yet a king's good.

CHARLES. We shall see. I am not such a fool as I
look. I have my eyes open; and I can tell you that
one good treaty is worth ten good fights. These
fighting fellows lose all on the treaties that they
gain on the fights. If we can only have a treaty,
the English are sure to have the worst of it, because they are better at fighting than at thinking.

JOAN. If the English win, it is they that will
make the treaty: and then God help poor France!
Thou must fight, Charlie, whether thou will or
no. I will go first to hearten thee. We must take
our courage in both hands: aye, and pray for it
with both hands too.

CHARLES [*descending from his throne and again*
crossing the room to escape from her dominating
urgency]. Oh do stop talking about God and praying. I cant bear people who are always praying.
Isnt it bad enough to have to do it at the proper
times?

JOAN [*pitying him*]. Thou poor child, thou hast
never prayed in thy life. I must teach thee from
the beginning.

CHARLES. I am not a child: I am a grown man
and a father; and I will not be taught any more.

JOAN. Aye, you have a little son. He that will be
Louis the Eleventh when you die. Would you
not fight for him?

CHARLES. No: a horrid boy. He hates me. He
hates everybody, selfish little beast! I dont want to
be bothered with children. I dont want to be a
father; and I dont want to be a son: especially a son
of St Louis. I dont want to be any of these fine

things you all have your heads full of: I want to be just what I am. Why cant you mind your own business, and let me mind mine?

JOAN [*again contemptuous*]. Minding your own business is like minding your own body: it's the shortest way to make yourself sick. What is my business? Helping mother at home. What is thine? Petting lapdogs and sucking sugarsticks. I call that muck. I tell thee it is God's business we are here to do: not our own. I have a message to thee from God; and thou must listen to it, though thy heart break with the terror of it.

CHARLES. I dont want a message; but can you tell me any secrets? Can you do any cures? Can you turn lead into gold, or anything of that sort?

JOAN. I can turn thee into a king, in Rheims Cathedral; and that is a miracle that will take some doing, it seems.

CHARLES. If we go to Rheims, and have a coronation, Anne will want new dresses. We cant afford them. I am all right as I am.

JOAN. As you are! And what is that? Less than my father's poorest shepherd. Thourt not lawful owner of thy own land of France till thou be consecrated.

CHARLES. But I shall not be lawful owner of my own land anyhow. Will the consecration pay off my mortgages? I have pledged my last acre to the Archbishop and that fat bully. I owe money even to Bluebeard.

JOAN [*earnestly*]. Charlie: I come from the land, and have gotten my strength working on the land; and I tell thee that the land is thine to rule righteously and keep God's peace in, and not to pledge at the pawnshop as a drunken woman pledges her children's clothes. And I come from God to tell thee to kneel in the cathedral and solemnly give thy kingdom to Him for ever and ever, and become the greatest king in the world as His steward and His bailiff, His soldier and His servant. The very clay of France will become holy: her soldiers will be the soldiers of God: the rebel dukes will be rebels against God: the English will fall on their knees and beg thee let them return to their lawful homes in peace. Wilt be a poor little Judas, and betray me and Him that sent me?

CHARLES [*tempted at last*]. Oh, if I only dare!

JOAN. I shall dare, dare, and dare again, in God's name! Art for or against me?

CHARLES [*excited*]. I'll risk it, I warn you I shant be able to keep it up; but I'll risk it. You shall see. [*Running to the main door and shouting*]. Hallo! Come back, everybody. [*To Joan, as he runs back to the arch opposite*]. Mind you stand by and dont let me be bullied. [*Through the arch*]. Come along, will you: the whole Court. [*He sits down in the royal chair as they all hurry in to their former places, chattering and wondering.*] Now I'm in for it; but no matter: here goes! [*To the page*] Call for silence, you little beast, will you?

THE PAGE [*snatching a halberd as before and thumping with it repeatedly*]. Silence for His Majesty the King. The King speaks. [*Peremptorily*]. Will you be silent there? [*Silence*].

CHARLES [*rising*]. I have given the command of the army to The Maid. The Maid is to do as she likes with it. [*He descends from the dais.*]

General amazement. La Hire, delighted, slaps his steel thighpiece with his gauntlet.

LA TRÉMOUILLE [*turning threateningly towards Charles*]. What is this? *I* command the army.

Joan quickly puts her hand on Charles's shoulder as he instinctively recoils. Charles, with a grotesque effort culminating in an extravagant gesture, snaps his fingers in the Chamberlain's face.

JOAN. Thourt answered, old Gruff-and-Grum. [*Suddenly flashing out her sword as she divines that her moment has come*]. Who is for God and His Maid? Who is for Orleans with me?

LA HIRE [*carried away, drawing also*]. For God and His Maid! To Orleans!

ALL THE KNIGHTS [*following his lead with enthusiasm*]. To Orleans!

Joan, radiant, falls on her knees in thanksgiving to God. They all kneel, except the Archbishop, who gives his benediction with a sigh, and La Trémouille, who collapses, cursing.

Scene III

Orleans, April 29th, 1429. Dunois, aged 26, is pacing up and down a patch of ground on the south bank of the silver Loire, commanding a long view of the river in both directions. He has had his lance stuck up with a pennon, which streams in a strong east wind. His shield with its bend sinister lies beside it. He has his commander's baton in his hand. He is well built, carrying his armor easily. His broad brow and pointed chin give him an equilaterally triangular face, already marked by active service and responsibility, with the expression of a good-natured and capable man who has no affectations and no foolish illusions. His page is sitting on the ground, elbows on knees, cheeks on fists, idly watching the water. It is evening; and both man and boy are affected by the loveliness of the Loire.

DUNOIS [*halting for a moment to glance up at the streaming pennon and shake his head wearily before he resumes his pacing*]. West wind, west wind, west wind. Strumpet: steadfast when you should be wanton, wanton when you should be steadfast. West wind on the silver Loire: what rhymes to Loire? [*He looks again at the pennon, and shakes his fist at it.*] Change, curse you, change, English harlot of a wind, change. West, west, I tell you. [*With a growl he resumes his march in silence, but soon begins again.*] West wind, wanton wind, wilful wind, womanish wind, false wind from over the water, will you never blow again?

THE PAGE [*bounding to his feet*]. See! There! There she goes!

DUNOIS [*startled from his reverie: eagerly*]. Where? Who? The Maid?

THE PAGE. No: the kingfisher. Like blue lightning. She went into that bush.

DUNOIS [*furiously disappointed*]. Is that all? You infernal young idiot: I have a mind to pitch you into the river.

THE PAGE [*not afraid, knowing his man*]. It looked frightfully jolly, that flash of blue. Look! There goes the other!

DUNOIS [*running eagerly to the river brim*]. Where? Where?

THE PAGE [*pointing*]. Passing the reeds.

DUNOIS [*delighted*]. I see.

They follow the flight till the bird takes cover.

THE PAGE. You blew me up because you were not in time to see them yesterday.

DUNOIS. You knew I was expecting The Maid when you set up your yelping. I will give you something to yelp for next time.

THE PAGE. Arnt they lovely? I wish I could catch them.

DUNOIS. Let me catch you trying to trap them, and I will put you in the iron cage for a month to teach you what a cage feels like. You are an abominable boy.

THE PAGE [*laughs, and squats down as before*].

DUNOIS [*pacing*]. Blue bird, blue bird, since I am friend to thee, change thou the wind for me. No: it does not rhyme. He who has sinned for thee: thats better. No sense in it, though. [*He finds himself close to the page.*] You abominable boy! [*He turns away from him.*] Mary in the blue snood, kingfisher color: will you grudge me a west wind?

A SENTRY'S VOICE WESTWARD. Halt! Who goes there?

JOAN'S VOICE. The Maid.

DUNOIS. Let her pass. Hither, Maid! To me!

Joan, in splendid armor, rushes in in a blazing rage. The wind drops; and the pennon flaps idly down the lance; but Dunois is too much occupied with Joan to notice it.

JOAN [*bluntly*]. Be you Bastard of Orleans?

DUNOIS [*cool and stern, pointing to his shield*].

You see the bend sinister. Are you Joan the Maid?

JOAN. Sure.

DUNOIS. Where are your troops?

JOAN. Miles behind. They have cheated me. They have brought me to the wrong side of the river.

DUNOIS. I told them to.

JOAN. Why did you? The English are on the other side!

DUNOIS. The English are on both sides.

JOAN. But Orleans is on the other side. We must fight the English there. How can we cross the river?

DUNOIS [*grimly*]. There is a bridge.

JOAN. In God's name, then, let us cross the bridge, and fall on them.

DUNOIS. It seems simple; but it cannot be done.

JOAN. Who says so?

DUNOIS. I say so; and older and wiser heads than mine are of the same opinion.

JOAN [*roundly*]. Then your older and wiser heads are fatheads: they have made a fool of you; and now they want to make a fool of me too, bringing me to the wrong side of the river. Do you not know that I bring you better help than ever came to any general or any town?

DUNOIS [*smiling patiently*]. Your own?

JOAN. No: the help and counsel of the King of Heaven. Which is the way to the bridge?

DUNOIS. You are impatient, Maid.

JOAN. Is this a time for patience? Our enemy is at our gates; and here we stand doing nothing. Oh, why are you not fighting? Listen to me: I will deliver you from fear. I —

DUNOIS [*laughing heartily, and waving her off*]. No, no, my girl: if you delivered me from fear I should be a good knight for a story book, but a very bad commander of the army. Come! let me begin to make a soldier of you. [*He takes her to the water's edge.*] Do you see those two forts at this end of the bridge? the big ones?

JOAN. Yes. Are they ours or the goddams'?

DUNOIS. Be quiet, and listen to me. If I were in either of those forts with only ten men I could hold it against an army. The English have more than ten times ten goddams in those forts to hold them against us.

JOAN. They cannot hold them against God. God did not give them the land under those forts: they stole it from Him. He gave it to us. I will take those forts.

DUNOIS. Single-handed?

JOAN. Our men will take them. I will lead them.

DUNOIS. Not a man will follow you.

JOAN. I will not look back to see whether anyone is following me.

DUNOIS [*recognizing her mettle, and clapping her heartily on the shoulder*]. Good. You have the makings of a soldier in you. You are in love with war.

JOAN [*startled*]. Oh! And the Archbishop said I was in love with religion.

DUNOIS. I, God forgive me, am a little in love with war myself, the ugly devil! I am like a man with two wives. Do you want to be like a woman with two husbands?

JOAN [*matter-of-fact*]. I will never take a husband. A man in Toul took an action against me for breach of promise; but I never promised him. I am a soldier: I do not want to be thought of as a woman. I will not dress as a woman. I do not care for the things women care for. They dream of lovers, and of money. I dream of leading a charge, and of placing the big guns. You soldiers do not know how to use the big guns: you think you can win battles with a great noise and smoke.

DUNOIS [*with a shrug*]. True. Half the time the artillery is more trouble than it is worth.

JOAN. Aye, lad; but you cannot fight stone walls with horses: you must have guns, and much bigger guns too.

DUNOIS [*grinning at her familiarity, and echoing it*]. Aye, lass; but a good heart and a stout ladder will get over the stoniest wall.

JOAN. I will be first up the ladder when we reach the fort, Bastard. I dare you to follow me.

DUNOIS. You must not dare a staff officer, Joan: only company officers are allowed to indulge in displays of personal courage. Besides, you must know that I welcome you as a saint, not as a soldier. I have daredevils enough at my call, if they could help me.

JOAN. I am not a daredevil: I am a servant of God. My sword is sacred: I found it behind the altar in the church of St Catherine, where God hid it for me; and I may not strike a blow with it. My heart is full of courage, not of anger. I will lead; and your men will follow: that is all I can do. But I must do it: you shall not stop me.

DUNOIS. All in good time. Our men cannot take those forts by a sally across the bridge. They must come by water, and take the English in the rear on this side.

JOAN [*her military sense asserting itself*]. Then make rafts and put big guns on them; and let your men cross to us.

DUNOIS. The rafts are ready; and the men are embarked. But they must wait for God.

JOAN. What do you mean? God is waiting for them.

DUNOIS. Let Him send us a wind then. My boats are downstream: they cannot come up against both wind and current. We must wait until God changes the wind. Come: let me take you to the church.

JOAN. No. I love church; but the English will not yield to prayers: they understand nothing but hard knocks and slashes. I will not go to church until we have beaten them.

DUNOIS. You must: I have business for you there.

JOAN. What business?

DUNOIS. To pray for a west wind. I have prayed; and I have given two silver candlesticks; but my prayers are not answered. Yours may be: you are young and innocent.

JOAN. Oh yes: you are right. I will pray: I will tell St Catherine: she will make God give me a west wind. Quick: shew me the way to the church.

THE PAGE [*sneezes violently*]. At-cha!!!

JOAN. God bless you, child! Coom, Bastard.

They go out. The page rises to follow. He picks up the shield, and is taking the spear as well when he notices the pennon, which is now streaming eastward.

THE PAGE [*dropping the shield and calling excitedly after them*]. Seigneur! Seigneur! Mademoiselle!

DUNOIS [*running back*]. What is it? The kingfisher? [*He looks eagerly for it up the river.*]

JOAN [*joining them*]. Oh, a kingfisher! Where?

THE PAGE. No: the wind, the wind, the wind [*pointing to the pennon*]: that is what made me sneeze.

DUNOIS [*looking at the pennon*]. The wind has changed. [*He crosses himself.*] God has spoken. [*Kneeling and handing his baton to Joan*]. You command the king's army. I am your soldier.

THE PAGE [*looking down the river*]. The boats have put off. They are ripping upstream like anything.

DUNOIS [*rising*]. Now for the forts. You dared me to follow. Dare you lead?

JOAN [*bursting into tears and flinging her arms round Dunois, kissing him on both cheeks*]. Dunois, dear comrade in arms, help me. My eyes are blinded with tears. Set my foot on the ladder, and say 'Up, Joan.'

DUNOIS [*dragging her out*]. Never mind the tears: make for the flash of the guns.

JOAN [*in a blaze of courage*]. Ah!

DUNOIS [*dragging her along with him*]. For God and Saint Dennis!

THE PAGE [*shrilly*]. The Maid! The Maid! God and The Maid! Hurray-ay-ay! [*He snatches up the shield and lance, and capers out after them, mad with excitement.*]

Scene IV

A tent in the English camp. A bullnecked English chaplain of 50 is sitting on a stool at a table, hard at work writing. At the other side of the table an imposing nobleman, aged 46, is seated in a handsome chair turning over the leaves of an illuminated Book of Hours. The nobleman is enjoying himself: the chaplain is struggling with suppressed wrath. There is an unoccupied leather stool on the nobleman's left. The table is on his right.

THE NOBLEMAN. Now this is what I call workmanship. There is nothing on earth more exquisite than a bonny book, with well-placed columns of rich black writing in beautiful borders, and illuminated pictures cunningly inset. But nowadays, instead of looking at books, people read them. A book might as well be one of those orders for bacon and bran that you are scribbling.

THE CHAPLAIN. I must say, my lord, you take our situation very coolly. Very coolly indeed.

THE NOBLEMAN [*supercilious*]. What is the matter?

THE CHAPLAIN. The matter, my lord, is that we English have been defeated.

THE NOBLEMAN. That happens, you know. It is only in history books and ballads that the enemy is always defeated.

THE CHAPLAIN. But we are being defeated over and over again. First, Orleans —

THE NOBLEMAN [*poohpoohing*]. Oh, Orleans!

THE CHAPLAIN. I know what you are going to say, my lord: that was a clear case of witchcraft and sorcery. But we are still being defeated. Jargeau, Meung, Beaugency, just like Orleans. And now we have been butchered at Patay, and Sir John Talbot taken prisoner. [*He throws down his pen, almost in tears.*] I feel it, my lord: I feel it very deeply. I cannot bear to see my countrymen defeated by a parcel of foreigners.

THE NOBLEMAN. Oh! you are an Englishman, are you?

THE CHAPLAIN. Certainly not, my lord: I am a gentleman. Still, like your lordship, I was born in England; and it makes a difference.

THE NOBLEMAN. You are attached to the soil, eh?

THE CHAPLAIN. It pleases your lordship to be satirical at my expense: your greatness privileges you to be so with impunity. But your lordship knows very well that I am not attached to the soil in a vulgar manner, like a serf. Still, I have a feeling about it; [*with growing agitation*] and I am not ashamed of it; and [*rising wildly*] by God, if this goes on any longer I will fling my cassock to the devil, and take arms myself, and strangle the accursed witch with my own hands.

THE NOBLEMAN [*laughing at him goodnaturedly*]. So you shall, chaplain: so you shall, if we can do nothing better. But not yet, not quite yet.

The Chaplain resumes his seat very sulkily.

THE NOBLEMAN [*airily*]. I should not care very much about the witch — you see, I have made my pilgrimage to the Holy Land; and the Heavenly Powers, for their own credit, can hardly allow me to be worsted by a village sorceress — but the Bastard of Orleans is a harder nut to crack; and as he has been to the Holy Land too, honors are easy between us as far as that goes.

THE CHAPLAIN. He is only a Frenchman, my lord.

THE NOBLEMAN. A Frenchman! Where did you pick up that expression? Are these Burgundians and Bretons and Picards and Gascons beginning to call themselves Frenchmen, just as our fellows are beginning to call themselves Englishmen? They actually talk of France and England as their countries. Theirs, if you please! What is to become of me and you if that way of thinking comes into fashion?

THE CHAPLAIN. Why, my lord? Can it hurt us?

THE NOBLEMAN. Men cannot serve two masters. If this cant of serving their country once takes hold of them, goodbye to the authority of their feudal lords, and goodbye to the authority of the Church. That is, goodbye to you and me.

THE CHAPLAIN. I hope I am a faithful servant of the Church; and there are only six cousins between me and the barony of Stogumber, which was created by the Conqueror. But is that any reason why I should stand by and see Englishmen beaten by a French bastard and a witch from Lousy Champagne?

THE NOBLEMAN. Easy, man, easy: we shall burn the witch and beat the bastard all in good time. Indeed I am waiting at present for the Bishop of Beauvais, to arrange the burning with him. He has been turned out of his diocese by her faction.

THE CHAPLAIN. You have first to catch her, my lord.

THE NOBLEMAN. Or buy her. I will offer a king's ransom.

THE CHAPLAIN. A king's ransom! For that slut!

THE NOBLEMAN. One has to leave a margin. Some of Charles's people will sell her to the Burgundians; the Burgundians will sell her to us; and there will probably be three or four middlemen who will expect their little commissions.

THE CHAPLAIN. Monstrous. It is all those scoundrels of Jews: they get in every time money changes hands. I would not leave a Jew alive in Christendom if I had my way.

THE NOBLEMAN. Why not? The Jews generally give value. They make you pay; but they deliver the goods. In my experience the men who want something for nothing are invariably Christians.

A page appears.

THE PAGE. The Right Reverend the Bishop of Beauvais: Monseigneur Cauchon.

Cauchon, aged about 60, comes in. The page withdraws. The two Englishmen rise.

THE NOBLEMAN [*with effusive courtesy*]. My dear Bishop, how good of you to come! Allow me to introduce myself: Richard de Beauchamp, Earl of Warwick, at your service.

CAUCHON. Your lordship's fame is well known to me.

WARWICK. This reverend cleric is Master John de Stogumber.

THE CHAPLAIN [*glibly*]. John Bowyer Spenser Neville de Stogumber, at your service, my lord: Bachelor of Theology, and Keeper of the Private Seal to His Eminence the Cardinal of Winchester.

WARWICK [*to Cauchon*]. You call him the Cardinal of England, I believe. Our king's uncle.

CAUCHON. Messire John de Stogumber: I am always the very good friend of His Eminence. [*He extends his hand to the chaplain, who kisses his ring.*]

WARWICK. Do me the honor to be seated. [*He gives Cauchon his chair, placing it at the head of the table.*]

Cauchon accepts the place of honor with a grave inclination. Warwick fetches the leather stool carelessly, and sits in his former place. The chaplain goes back to his chair.

Though Warwick has taken second place in calculated deference to the Bishop, he assumes the lead in opening the proceedings as a matter of course. He is still cordial and expansive; but there is a new note in his voice which means that he is coming to business.

WARWICK. Well, my Lord Bishop, you find us in one of our unlucky moments. Charles is to be crowned at Rheims, practically by the young woman from Lorraine; and — I must not deceive you, nor flatter your hopes — we cannot prevent it. I suppose it will make a great difference to Charles's position.

CAUCHON. Undoubtedly. It is a masterstroke of The Maid's.

THE CHAPLAIN [*again agitated*]. We were not fairly beaten, my lord. No Englishman is ever fairly beaten.

Cauchon raises his eyebrow slightly, then quickly composes his face.

WARWICK. Our friend here takes the view that the young woman is a sorceress. It would, I presume, be the duty of your reverend lordship to denounce her to the Inquisition, and have her burnt for that offence.

CAUCHON. If she were captured in my diocese: yes.

WARWICK [*feeling that they are getting on capitally*]. Just so. Now I suppose there can be no reasonable doubt that she is a sorceress.

THE CHAPLAIN. Not the least. An arrant witch.

WARWICK [*gently reproving the interruption*]. We are asking for the Bishop's opinion, Messire John.

CAUCHON. We shall have to consider not merely our own opinions here, but the opinions — the prejudices, if you like — of a French court.

WARWICK [*correcting*]. A Catholic court, my lord.

CAUCHON. Catholic courts are composed of mortal men, like other courts, however sacred their function and inspiration may be. And if the men are Frenchmen, as the modern fashion calls them, I am afraid the bare fact that an English army has been defeated by a French one will not convince them that there is any sorcery in the matter.

THE CHAPLAIN. What! Not when the famous Sir Talbot himself has been defeated and actually taken prisoner by a drab from the ditches of Lorraine!

CAUCHON. Sir John Talbot, we all know, is a fierce and formidable soldier, Messire; but I have yet to learn that he is an able general. And though it pleases you to say that he has been defeated by this girl, some of us may be disposed to give a little of the credit to Dunois.

THE CHAPLAIN [*contemptuously*]. The Bastard of Orleans!

CAUCHON. Let me remind —

WARWICK [*interposing*]. I know what you are going to say, my lord. Dunois defeated me at Montargis.

CAUCHON [*bowing*]. I take that as evidence that the Seigneur Dunois is a very able commander indeed.

WARWICK. Your lordship is the flower of courtesy. I admit, on our side, that Talbot is a mere fighting animal, and that it probably served him right to be taken at Patay.

THE CHAPLAIN [*chafing*]. My lord: at Orleans this woman had her throat pierced by an English arrow, and was seen to cry like a child from the pain of it. It was a death wound; yet she fought all day; and when our men had repulsed all her attacks like true Englishmen, she walked alone to the wall of our fort with a white banner in her hand; and our men were paralyzed, and could neither shoot nor strike whilst the French fell on them and drove them on to the bridge, which immediately burst into flames and crumbled under them, letting them down into the river, where they were drowned in heaps. Was this your bastard's generalship? or were those flames the flames of hell, conjured up by witchcraft?

WARWICK. You will forgive Messire John's vehemence, my lord; but he has put our case. Dunois is a great captain, we admit; but why could he do nothing until the witch came?

CAUCHON. I do not say that there were no supernatural powers on her side. But the names on that white banner were not the names of Satan and Beelzebub, but the blessed names of our Lord and His holy mother. And your commander who was drowned — Clahz-da I think you call him —

WARWICK. Glasdale. Sir William Glasdale.

CAUCHON. Glass-dell, thank you. He was no saint; and many of our people think that he was drowned for his blasphemies against The Maid.

WARWICK [beginning to look very dubious]. Well, what are we to infer from all this, my lord? Has The Maid converted you?

CAUCHON. If she had, my lord, I should have known better than to have trusted myself here within your grasp.

WARWICK [blandly deprecating]. Oh! oh! My lord!

CAUCHON. If the devil is making use of this girl — and I believe he is —

WARWICK [reassured]. Ah! You hear, Messire John? I knew your lordship would not fail us. Pardon my interruption. Proceed.

CAUCHON. If it be so, the devil has longer views than you give him credit for.

WARWICK. Indeed? In what way? Listen to this, Messire John.

CAUCHON. If the devil wanted to damn a country girl, do you think so easy a task would cost him the winning of half a dozen battles? No, my lord: any trumpery imp could do that much if the girl could be damned at all. The Prince of Darkness does not condescend to such cheap drudgery. When he strikes, he strikes at the Catholic Church, whose realm is the whole spiritual world. When he damns, he damns the souls of the entire human race. Against that dreadful design The Church stands ever on guard. And it is as one of the instruments of that design that I see this girl. She is inspired, but diabolically inspired.

THE CHAPLAIN. I told you she was a witch.

CAUCHON [fiercely]. She is not a witch. She is a heretic.

THE CHAPLAIN. What difference does that make?

CAUCHON. You, a priest, ask me that! You English are strangely blunt in the mind. All these things that you call witchcraft are capable of a natural explanation. The woman's miracles would not impose on a rabbit: she does not claim them as miracles herself. What do her victories prove but that she has a better head on her shoulders than your swearing Glass-dells and mad bull Talbots, and that the courage of faith, even though it be a false faith, will always outstay the courage of wrath?

THE CHAPLAIN [hardly able to believe his ears]. Does your lordship compare Sir John Talbot, three times Governor of Ireland, to a mad bull?!!!

WARWICK. It would not be seemly for you to do so, Messire John, as you are still six removes from a barony. But as I am an earl, and Talbot is only a knight, I may make bold to accept the comparison. [To the Bishop] My lord: I wipe the slate as far as the witchcraft goes. None the less, we must burn the woman.

CAUCHON. I cannot burn her. The Church cannot take life. And my first duty is to seek this girl's salvation.

WARWICK. No doubt. But you do burn people occasionally.

CAUCHON. No. When The Church cuts off an obstinate heretic as a dead branch from the tree of life, the heretic is handed over to the secular arm. The Church has no part in what the secular arm may see fit to do.

WARWICK. Precisely. And I shall be the secular arm in this case. Well, my lord, hand over your dead branch; and I will see that the fire is ready for it. If you will answer for The Church's part, I will answer for the secular part.

CAUCHON [with smouldering anger]. I can answer for nothing. You great lords are too prone to treat The Church as a mere political convenience.

WARWICK [smiling and propitiatory]. Not in England, I assure you.

CAUCHON. In England more than anywhere else. No, my lord: the soul of this village girl is of equal value with yours or your king's before the throne of God; and my first duty is to save it. I will not suffer your lordship to smile at me as if I were repeating a meaningless form of words, and it were well understood between us that I should betray the girl to you. I am no mere political bishop: my faith is to me what your honor is to you; and if there be a loophole through which this baptized child of God can creep to her salvation, I shall guide her to it.

THE CHAPLAIN [rising in a fury]. You are a traitor.

CAUCHON [springing up]. You lie, priest. [Trembling with rage]. If you dare do what this woman has done — set your country above the holy Catholic Church — you shall go to the fire with her.

THE CHAPLAIN. My lord: I — I went too far. I — [He sits down with a submissive gesture.]

WARWICK [who has risen apprehensively]. My lord: I apologize to you for the word used by Messire John de Stogumber. It does not mean in England what it does in France. In your language traitor means betrayer: one who is perfidious, treacherous, unfaithful, disloyal. In our country it means simply one who is not wholly devoted to our English interests.

CAUCHON. I am sorry: I did not understand. [*He subsides into his chair with dignity.*]

WARWICK [*resuming his seat, much relieved*]. I must apologize on my own account if I have seemed to take the burning of this poor girl too lightly. When one has seen whole countrysides burnt over and over again as mere items in military routine, one has to grow a very thick skin. Otherwise one might go mad: at all events, I should. May I venture to assume that your lordship also, having to see so many heretics burned from time to time, is compelled to take — shall I say a professional view of what would otherwise be a very horrible incident?

CAUCHON. Yes: it is a painful duty: even, as you say, a horrible one. But in comparison with the horror of heresy it is less than nothing. I am not thinking of this girl's body, which will suffer for a few moments only, and which must in any event die in some more or less painful manner, but of her soul, which may suffer to all eternity.

WARWICK. Just so; and God grant that her soul may be saved! But the practical problem would seem to be how to save her soul without saving her body. For we must face it, my lord: if this cult of The Maid goes on, our cause is lost.

THE CHAPLAIN [*his voice broken like that of a man who has been crying*]. May I speak, my lord?

WARWICK. Really, Messire John, I had rather you did not, unless you can keep your temper.

THE CHAPLAIN. It is only this. I speak under correction; but The Maid is full of deceit: she pretends to be devout. Her prayers and confessions are endless. How can she be accused of heresy when she neglects no observance of a faithful daughter of The Church?

CAUCHON [*flaming up*]. A faithful daughter of The Church! The Pope himself at his proudest dare not presume as this woman presumes. She acts as if she herself were The Church. She brings the message of God to Charles; and The Church must stand aside. She will crown him in the cathedral of Rheims: she, not The Church! She sends letters to the king of England giving him God's command through her to return to his island on pain of God's vengeance, which she will execute. Let me tell you that the writing of such letters was the practice of the accursed Mahomet, the anti-Christ. Had she ever in all her utterances said one word of The Church? Never. It is always God and herself.

WARWICK. What can you expect? A beggar on horseback. Her head is turned.

CAUCHON. Who has turned it? The devil. And for a mighty purpose. He is spreading this heresy everywhere. The man Hus, burnt only thirteen years ago at Constance, infected all Bohemia with it. A man named WcLeef, himself an anointed priest, spread the pestilence in England; and to your shame you let him die in his bed. We have such people here in France too: I know the breed. It is cancerous: if it be not cut out, stamped out, burnt out, it will not stop until it has brought the whole body of human society into sin and corruption, into waste and ruin. By it an Arab camel driver drove Christ and His Church out of Jerusalem, and ravaged his way west like a wild beast until at last there stood only the Pyrenees and God's mercy between France and damnation. Yet what did the camel driver do at the beginning more than this shepherd girl is doing? He had his voices from the angel Gabriel: she has her voices from St Catherine and St Margaret and the Blessed Michael. He declared himself the messenger of God, and wrote in God's name to the kings of the earth. Her letters to them are going forth daily. It is not the Mother of God now to whom we must look for intercession, but to Joan the Maid. What will the world be like when The Church's accumulated wisdom and knowledge and experience, its councils of learned, venerable pious men, are thrust into the kennel by every ignorant laborer or dairymaid whom the devil can puff up with the monstrous self-conceit of being directly inspired from heaven? It will be a world of blood, of fury, of devastation, of each man striving for his own hand: in the end a world wrecked back into barbarism. For now you have only Mahomet and his dupes, and the Maid and her dupes; but what will it be when every girl thinks herself a Joan and every man a Mahomet? I shudder to the very marrow of my bones when I think of it. I have fought it all my life; and I will fight it to the end. Let all this woman's sins be forgiven her except only this sin; for it is the sin against the Holy Ghost; and if she does not recant in the dust before the world, and submit herself to the last inch of her soul to her Church, to the fire she shall go if she once falls into my hand.

WARWICK [*unimpressed*]. You feel strongly about it, naturally.

CAUCHON. Do not you?

WARWICK. I am a soldier, not a churchman. As a pilgrim I saw something of the Mahometans. They were not so ill-bred as I had been led to believe. In some respects their conduct compared favorably with ours.

CAUCHON [*displeased*]. I have noticed this before. Men go to the East to convert the infidels. And the infidels pervert them. The Crusader comes back more than half a Saracen. Not to mention that all Englishmen are born heretics.

THE CHAPLAIN. Englishmen heretics!!! [*Appealing to Warwick*]. My lord: must we endure this? His lordship is beside himself. How can what an Englishman believes be heresy? It is a contradiction in terms.

CAUCHON. I absolve you, Messire de Stogumber, on the ground of invincible ignorance. The thick air of your country does not breed theologians.

WARWICK. You would not say so if you heard us quarreling about religion, my lord! I am sorry you think I must be either a heretic or a blockhead because, as a travelled man, I know that the followers of Mahomet profess great respect for our Lord, and are more ready to forgive St Peter for being a fisherman than your lordship is to forgive Mahomet for being a camel driver. But at least we can proceed in this matter without bigotry.

CAUCHON. When men call the zeal of the Christian Church bigotry I know what to think.

WARWICK. They are only east and west views of the same thing.

CAUCHON [*bitterly ironical*]. Only east and west! Only!!

WARWICK. Oh, my Lord Bishop, I am not gainsaying you. You will carry The Church with you; but you have to carry the nobles also. To my mind there is a stronger case against The Maid than the one you have so forcibly put. Frankly, I am not afraid of this girl becoming another Mahomet, and superseding The Church by a great heresy. I think you exaggerate that risk. But have you noticed that in these letters of hers, she proposes to all the kings of Europe, as she has already pressed on Charles, a transaction which would wreck the whole social structure of Christendom?

CAUCHON. Wreck The Church. I tell you so.

WARWICK [*whose patience is wearing out*]. My lord: pray get The Church out of your head for a moment; and remember that there are temporal institutions in the world as well as spiritual ones. I and my peers represent the feudal aristocracy as you represent The Church. We are the temporal power. Well, do you not see how this girl's idea strikes at us?

CAUCHON. How does her idea strike at you, except as it strikes at all of us, through The Church?

WARWICK. Her idea is that the kings should give their realms to God, and then reign as God's bailiffs.

CAUCHON [*not interested*]. Quite sound theologically, my lord. But the king will hardly care, provided he reign. It is an abstract idea: a mere form of words.

WARWICK. By no means. It is a cunning device to supersede the aristocracy, and make the king sole and absolute autocrat. Instead of the king being merely the first among his peers, he becomes their master. That we cannot suffer: we call no man master. Nominally we hold our lands and dignities from the king, because there must be a keystone to the arch of human society; but we hold our lands in our own hands, and defend them with our own swords and those of our own tenants. Now by The Maid's doctrine the king will take our lands — our lands! — and make them a present to God; and God will then vest them wholly in the king.

CAUCHON. Need you fear that? You are the makers of kings after all. York or Lancaster in England, Lancaster or Valois in France: they reign according to your pleasure.

WARWICK. Yes; but only as long as the people follow their feudal lords, and know the king only as a traveling show, owning nothing but the highway that belongs to everybody. If the people's thoughts and hearts were turned to the king, and their lords became only the king's servants in their eyes, the king could break us across his knee one by one; and then what should we be but liveried courtiers in his halls?

CAUCHON. Still you need not fear, my lord. Some men are born kings; and some are born statesmen. The two are seldom the same. Where would the king find counsellors to plan and carry out such a policy for him?

WARWICK [*with a not too friendly smile*]. Perhaps in the Church, my lord.

Cauchon, with an equally sour smile, shrugs his shoulders, and does not contradict him.

WARWICK. Strike down the barons; and the cardinals will have it all their own way.

CAUCHON [*conciliatory, dropping his polemical tone*]. My lord: we shall not defeat The Maid if we strike against one another. I know well that there is a Will to Power in the world. I know that while it lasts there will be a struggle between the Emperor and the Pope, between the dukes and the political cardinals, between the barons and the kings. The devil divides us and governs. I see you are no friend to The Church: you are an earl first and last, as I am a churchman first and last. But can we not sink our differences in the face of a common enemy? I see now that what is in your mind is not that this girl has never once mentioned The Church, and thinks only of God and herself, but that she has never once mentioned the peerage, and thinks only of the king and herself.

WARWICK. Quite so. These two ideas of hers are the same idea at bottom. It goes deep, my lord. It is the protest of the individual soul against the interference of priest or peer between the private man and his God. I should call it Protestantism if I had to find a name for it.

CAUCHON [*looking hard at him*]. You understand it wonderfully well, my lord. Scratch an Englishman, and find a Protestant.

WARWICK [*playing the pink of courtesy*]. I think you are not entirely void of sympathy with The Maid's secular heresy, my lord. I leave you to find a name for it.

CAUCHON. You mistake me, my lord. I have no sympathy with her political presumptions. But as a priest I have gained a knowledge of the minds of the common people; and there you will find yet another most dangerous idea. I can express it only by such phrases as France for the French, England for the English, Italy for the Italians, Spain for the Spanish, and so forth. It is sometimes so narrow and bitter in country folk that it surprises me that this country girl can rise above the idea of her village for its villagers. But she can. She does. When she threatens to drive the English from the soil of France she is undoubtedly thinking of the whole extent of country in which French is spoken. To her the French-speaking people are what the Holy Scriptures describe as a nation. Call this side of her heresy Nationalism if you will: I can find you no better name for it. I can only tell you that it is essentially anti-Catholic and anti-Christian; for the Catholic Church knows only one realm, and that is the realm of Christ's kingdom. Divide that kingdom into nations, and you dethrone Christ. Dethrone Christ, and who will stand between our throats and the sword? The world will perish in a welter of war.

WARWICK. Well, if you will burn the Protestant, I will burn the Nationalist, though perhaps I shall not carry Messire John with me there. England for the English will appeal to him.

THE CHAPLAIN. Certainly England for the English goes without saying: it is the simple law of nature. But this woman denies to England her legitimate conquests, given her by God because of her peculiar fitness to rule over less civilized races for their own good. I do not understand what your lordships mean by Protestant and Nationalist: you are too learned and subtle for a poor clerk like myself. But I know as a matter of plain commonsense that the woman is a rebel; and that is enough for me. She rebels against Nature by wearing man's clothes, and fighting. She rebels against The Church by usurping the divine authority of the Pope. She rebels against God by her damnable league with Satan and his evil spirits against our army. And all these rebellions are only excuses for her great rebellion against England. That is not to be endured. Let her perish. Let her burn. Let her not infect the whole flock. It is expedient that one woman die for the people.

WARWICK [*rising*]. My lord: we seem to be agreed.

CAUCHON [*rising also, but in protest*]. I will not imperil my soul. I will uphold the justice of the Church. I will strive to the utmost for this woman's salvation.

WARWICK. I am sorry for the poor girl. I hate these severities. I will spare her if I can.

THE CHAPLAIN [*implacably*]. I would burn her with my own hands.

CAUCHON [*blessing him*]. Sancta simplicitas!

Scene V

The ambulatory in the cathedral of Rheims, near the door of the vestry. A pillar bears one of the stations of the cross. The organ is playing the people out of the nave after the coronation. Joan is kneeling in prayer before the station. She is beautifully dressed, but still in male attire. The organ ceases as Dunois, also splendidly arrayed, comes into the ambulatory from the vestry.

DUNOIS. Come, Joan! you have had enough praying. After that fit of crying you will catch a chill if you stay here any longer. It is all over: the cathedral is empty; and the streets are full. They are calling for The Maid. We have told them you are staying here alone to pray; but they want to see you again.

JOAN. No: let the king have all the glory.

DUNOIS. He only spoils the show, poor devil. No, Joan: you have crowned him; and you must go through with it.

JOAN [*shakes her head reluctantly*].

DUNOIS [*raising her*]. Come come! it will be over in a couple of hours. It's better than the bridge at Orleans: eh?

JOAN. Oh, dear Dunois, how I wish it were the bridge at Orleans again! We lived at that bridge.

DUNOIS. Yes, faith, and died too: some of us.

JOAN. Isnt it strange, Jack? I am such a coward: I am frightened beyond words before a battle; but it is so dull afterwards when there is no danger: oh, so dull! dull! dull!

DUNOIS. You must learn to be abstemious in war, just as you are in your food and drink, my little saint.

JOAN. Dear Jack: I think you like me as a soldier likes his comrade.

DUNOIS. You need it, poor innocent child of God. You have not many friends at court.

JOAN. Why do all these courtiers and knights and churchmen hate me? What have I done to them? I have asked nothing for myself except that my village shall not be taxed; for we cannot afford war taxes. I have brought them luck and victory: I have set them right when they were doing all sorts of stupid things: I have crowned Charles and made him a real king; and all the honors he is handing out have gone to them. Then why do they not love me?

DUNOIS [*rallying her*]. Sim-ple-ton! Do you expect stupid people to love you for shewing them up? Do blundering old military dug-outs love the successful young captains who supersede them? Do ambitious politicians love the climbers who take the front seats from them? Do archbishops enjoy being played off their own altars, even by saints? Why, I should be jealous of you myself if I were ambitious enough.

JOAN. You are the pick of the basket here, Jack: the only friend I have among all these nobles. I'll wager your mother was from the country. I will go back to the farm when I have taken Paris.

DUNOIS. I am not so sure that they will let you take Paris.

JOAN [*startled*]. What!

DUNOIS. I should have taken it myself before this if they had all been sound about it. Some of them would rather Paris took you, I think. So take care.

JOAN. Jack: the world is too wicked for me. If the goddams and the Burgundians do not make an end of me, the French will. Only for my voices I should lose all heart. That is why I had to steal away to pray here alone after the coronation. I'll tell you something, Jack. It is in the bells I hear my voices. Not to-day, when they all rang: that was nothing but jangling. But here in this corner, where the bells come down from heaven, and the echoes linger, or in the fields, where they come from a distance through the quiet of the countryside, my voices are in them. [*The cathedral clock chimes the quarter.*] Hark! [*She becomes rapt.*] Do you hear? 'Dear-child-of-God': just what you said. At the half-hour they will say 'Be-brave-go-on'. At the three-quarters they will say 'I-am-thy-Help'. But it is at the hour, when the great bell goes after 'God-will-save-France': it is then that St Margaret and St Catherine and sometimes even the blessed Michael will say things that I cannot tell beforehand. Then, oh then—

DUNOIS [*interrupting her kindly but not sympathetically*]. Then, Joan, we shall hear whatever we fancy in the booming of the bell. You make me uneasy when you talk about your voices: I should think you were a bit cracked if I hadnt noticed that you give me very sensible reasons for

what you do, though I hear you telling others you are only obeying Madame Saint Catherine.

JOAN [*crossly*]. Well, I have to find reasons for you, because you do not believe in my voices. But the voices come first; and I find the reasons after: whatever you may choose to believe.

DUNOIS. Are you angry, Joan?

JOAN. Yes. [*Smiling*]. No: not with you. I wish you were one of the village babies.

DUNOIS. Why?

JOAN. I could nurse you for awhile.

DUNOIS. You are a bit of a woman after all.

JOAN. No: not a bit: I am a soldier and nothing else. Soldiers always nurse children when they get a chance.

DUNOIS. That is true. [*He laughs.*]

King Charles, with Bluebeard on his left and La Hire on his right, comes from the vestry, where he has been disrobing. Joan shrinks away behind the pillar. Dunois is left between Charles and La Hire.

DUNOIS. Well, your Majesty is an anointed king at last. How do you like it?

CHARLES. I would not go through it again to be emperor of the sun and moon. The weight of those robes! I thought I should have dropped when they loaded that crown on to me. And the famous holy oil they talked so much about was rancid: phew! The Archbishop must be nearly dead: his robes must have weighed a ton: they are stripping him still in the vestry.

DUNOIS [*drily*]. Your Majesty should wear armor oftener. That would accustom you to heavy dressing.

CHARLES. Yes: the old jibe! Well, I am not going to wear armor: fighting is not my job. Where is The Maid?

JOAN [*coming forward between Charles and Bluebeard, and falling on her knee*]. Sire: I have made you king: my work is done. I am going back to my father's farm.

CHARLES [*surprised, but relieved*]. Oh, are you? Well, that will be very nice.

Joan rises, deeply discouraged.

CHARLES [*continuing heedlessly*]. A healthy life, you know.

DUNOIS. But a dull one.

BLUEBEARD. You will find the petticoats tripping you up after leaving them off for so long.

LA HIRE. You will miss the fighting. It's a bad habit, but a grand one, and the hardest of all to break yourself of.

CHARLES [*anxiously*]. Still, we dont want you to stay if you would really rather go home.

JOAN [*bitterly*]. I know well that none of you will be sorry to see me go. [*She turns her shoulder to Charles and walks past him to the more congenial neighborhood of Dunois and La Hire.*]

LA HIRE. Well, I shall be able to swear when I want to. But I shall miss you at times.

JOAN. La Hire: in spite of all your sins and swears we shall meet in heaven; for I love you as I love Pitou, my old sheep dog. Pitou could kill a wolf. You will kill the English wolves until they go back to their country and become good dogs of God, will you not?

LA HIRE. You and I together: yes.

JOAN. No: I shall last only a year from the beginning.

ALL THE OTHERS. What!

JOAN. I know it somehow.

DUNOIS. Nonsense!

JOAN. Jack: do you think you will be able to drive them out?

DUNOIS [*with quiet conviction*]. Yes: I shall drive them out. They beat us because we thought battles were tournaments and ransom markets. We played the fool while the goddams took war seriously. But I have learnt my lesson, and taken their measure. They have no roots here. I have beaten them before; and I shall beat them again.

JOAN. You will not be cruel to them, Jack?

DUNOIS. The goddams will not yield to tender handling. We did not begin it.

JOAN [*suddenly*]. Jack: before I go home, let us take Paris.

CHARLES [*terrified*]. Oh no no. We shall lose everything we have gained. Oh dont let us have any more fighting. We can make a very good treaty with the Duke of Burgundy.

JOAN. Treaty! [*She stamps with impatience.*]

CHARLES. Well, why not, now that I am crowned and anointed? Oh, that oil!

The Archbishop comes from the vestry, and joins the group between Charles and Bluebeard.

CHARLES. Archbishop: The Maid wants to start fighting again.

THE ARCHBISHOP. Have we ceased fighting, then? Are we at peace?

CHARLES. No: I suppose not; but let us be content with what we have done. Let us make a treaty. Our luck is too good to last; and now is our chance to stop before it turns.

JOAN. Luck! God has fought for us; and you call it luck! And you would stop while there are still Englishmen on this holy earth of dear France!

THE ARCHBISKOP [*sternly*]. Maid: the king addressed himself to me, not to you. You forget yourself. You very often forget yourself.

JOAN [*unabashed, and rather roughly*]. Then speak, you; and tell him that it is not God's will that he should take his hand from the plough.

THE ARCHBISHOP. If I am not so glib with the name of God as you are, it is because I interpret His will with the authority of the Church and of my sacred office. When you first came you respected it, and would not have dared to speak as you are now speaking. You came clothed with the virtue of humility; and because God blessed your enterprises accordingly, you have stained yourself with the sin of pride. The old Greek tragedy is rising among us. It is the chastisement of hubris.

CHARLES. Yes: she thinks she knows better than everyone else.

JOAN [*distressed, but naïvely incapable of seeing the effect she is producing*]. But I do know better than any of you seem to. And I am not proud: I never speak unless I know I am right.

BLUEBEARD ⎫ [*exclaiming* ⎧ Ha ha!
CHARLES ⎭ *together*]. ⎩ Just so.

THE ARCHBISHOP. How do you know you are right?

JOAN. I always know. My voices —

CHARLES. Oh, your voices, your voices. Why dont the voices come to me? I am king, not you.

JOAN. They do come to you; but you do not hear them. You have not sat in the field in the evening listening for them. When the angelus rings you cross yourself and have done with it; but if you prayed from your heart, and listened to the thrilling of the bells in the air after they stop ringing, you would hear the voices as well as I do. [*Turning brusquely from him*]. But what voices do you need to tell you what the blacksmith can tell you: that you must strike while the iron is hot? I tell you we must make a dash at Compiègne and relieve it as we relieved Orleans. Then Paris will open its gates; or if not, we will break through them. What is your crown worth without your capital?

LA HIRE. That is what I say too. We shall go through them like a red hot shot through a pound of butter. What do you say, Bastard?

DUNOIS. If our cannon balls were all as hot as your head, and we had enough of them, we should conquer the earth, no doubt. Pluck and impetuosity are good servants in war, but bad masters: they have delivered us into the hands of the English every time we have trusted to them. We never know when we are beaten: that is our great fault.

JOAN. You never know when you are victorious: that is a worse fault. I shall have to make you carry looking-glasses in battle to convince you that the English have not cut off all your noses. You would have been besieged in Orleans still, you and your councils of war, if I had not made you attack. You should always attack; and if you only hold on long enough the enemy will stop first. You dont know how to begin a battle; and you dont know how to use your cannons. And I do.

She squats down on the flags with crossed ankles, pouting.

DUNOIS. I know what you think of us, General Joan.

JOAN. Never mind that, Jack. Tell them what you think of me.

DUNOIS. I think that God was on your side; for I have not forgotten how the wind changed, and how our hearts changed when you came; and by my faith I shall never deny that it was in your sign that we conquered. But I tell you as a soldier that God is no man's daily drudge, and no maid's either. If you are worthy of it He will sometimes snatch you out of the jaws of death and set you on your feet again; but that is all: once on your feet you must fight with all your might and all your craft. For He has to be fair to your enemy too: dont forget that. Well, He set us on our feet through you at Orleans; and the glory of it has carried us through a few good battles here to the coronation. But if we presume on it further, and trust to God to do the work we should do ourselves, we shall be defeated; and serve us right!

JOAN. But —

DUNOIS. Sh! I have not finished. Do not think, any of you, that these victories of ours were won without generalship. King Charles: you have said no word in your proclamations of my part in this campaign; and I make no complaint of that; for the people will run after The Maid and her miracles and not after the Bastard's hard work finding troops for her and feeding them. But I know exactly how much God did for us through The Maid, and how much He left me to do by my own wits; and I tell you that your little hour of miracles is over, and that from this time on he who plays the war game best will win — if the luck is on his side.

JOAN. Ah! if, if, if, if! If ifs and ans were pots and pans there'd be no need of tinkers. [*Rising impetuously*]. I tell you, Bastard, your art of war is no use, because your knights are no good for real fighting. War is only a game to them, like tennis and all their other games: they make rules as to what is fair and what is not fair, and heap armor on themselves and on their poor horses to keep out the arrows; and when they fall they cant get up, and have to wait for their squires to come and lift them to arrange about the ransom with the man that has poked them off their horse. Cant you see that all the like of that is gone by and done with? What use is armor against gunpowder? And if it was, do you think men that are fighting for France and for God will stop to bargain about ransoms, as half your knights live by doing? No: they will fight to win; and they will give up their lives out of their own hand into the hand of God when they go into battle, as I do. Common folks understand this. They cannot afford armor and cannot pay ransoms; but they followed me half naked into the moat and up the ladder and over the wall. With them it is my life or thine, and God defend the right! You may shake your head, Jack; and Bluebeard may twirl his billygoat's beard and cock his nose at me; but remember the day your knights and captains refused to follow me to attack the English at Orleans! You locked the gates to keep me in; and it was the townsfolk and the common people that followed me, and forced the gate, and shewed you the way to fight in earnest.

BLUEBEARD [*offended*]. Not content with being Pope Joan, you must be Caesar and Alexander as well.

THE ARCHBISHOP. Pride will have a fall, Joan.

JOAN. Oh, never mind whether it is pride or not: is it true? is it commonsense?

LA HIRE. It is true. Half of us are afraid of having our handsome noses broken; and the other half are out for paying off their mortgages. Let her have her way, Dunois: she does not know everything; but she has got hold of the right end of the stick. Fighting is not what it was; and those who know least about it often make the best job of it.

DUNOIS. I know all that. I do not fight in the old way: I have learnt the lesson of Agincourt, of Poitiers and Crecy. I know how many lives any move of mine will cost; and if the move is worth the cost I make it and pay the cost. But Joan never counts the cost at all: she goes ahead and trusts to God: she thinks she has God in her pocket. Up to now she has had the numbers on her side; and she has won. But I know Joan; and I see that some day she will go ahead when she has only ten men to do the work of a hundred. And then she will find that God is on the side of the big battalions. She will be taken by the enemy. And the lucky man that makes the capture will receive sixteen thousand pounds from the Earl of Ouareek.

JOAN [*flattered*]. Sixteen thousand pounds! Eh, laddie, have they offered that for me? There cannot be so much money in the world.

DUNOIS. There is, in England. And now tell me, all of you, which of you will lift a finger to save Joan once the English have got her? I speak first, for the army. The day after she has been dragged from her horse by a goddam or a Burgundian, and he is not struck dead: the day after she is locked in a dungeon, and the bars and bolts do not fly open at the touch of St Peter's angel: the day when the enemy finds out that she is as vulnerable as I am and not a bit more invincible, she will not be worth the life of a single soldier to us; and I will not risk that life, much as I cherish her as a companion-in-arms.

JOAN. I dont blame you, Jack: you are right. I am not worth one soldier's life if God lets me be beaten; but France may think me worth my ransom after what God has done for her through me.

CHARLES. I tell you I have no money; and this coronation, which is all your fault, has cost me the last farthing I can borrow.

JOAN. The Church is richer than you. I put my trust in the Church.

THE ARCHBISHOP. Woman: they will drag you through the streets, and burn you as a witch.

JOAN [*running to him*]. Oh, my lord, do not say that. It is impossible. I a witch!

THE ARCHBISHOP. Peter Cauchon knows his business. The University of Paris has burnt a woman for saying that what you have done was well done, and according to God.

JOAN [*bewildered*]. But why? What sense is there in it? What I have done is according to God. They could not burn a woman for speaking the truth.

THE ARCHBISHOP. They did.

JOAN. But you know that she was speaking the truth. You would not let them burn me.

THE ARCHBISHOP. How could I prevent them?

JOAN. You would speak in the name of the Church. You are a great prince of the Church. I would go anywhere with your blessing to protect me.

THE ARCHBISHOP. I have no blessing for you while you are proud and disobedient.

JOAN. Oh, why will you go on saying things like that? I am not proud and disobedient. I am a poor girl, and so ignorant that I do not know A from B. How could I be proud? And how can you say that I am disobedient when I always obey my voices, because they come from God.

THE ARCHBISHOP. The voice of God on earth is the voice of the Church Militant; and all the voices that come to you are the echoes of your own wilfulness.

JOAN. It is not true.

THE ARCHBISHOP [*flushing angrily*]. You tell the Archbishop in his cathedral that he lies; and yet you say you are not proud and disobedient.

JOAN. I never said you lied. It was you that as good as said my voices lied. When have they ever lied? If you will not believe in them: even if they are only the echoes of my own commonsense, are they not always right? and are not your earthly counsels always wrong?

THE ARCHBISHOP [*indignantly*]. It is waste of time admonishing you.

CHARLES. It always comes back to the same thing. She is right; and everyone else is wrong.

THE ARCHBISHOP. Take this as your last warning. If you perish through setting your private judgment above the instructions of your spiritual directors, the Church disowns you, and leaves you to whatever fate your presumption may bring upon you. The Bastard has told you that if you persist in setting up your military conceit above the counsels of your commanders —

DUNOIS [*interposing*]. To put it quite exactly, if you attempt to relieve the garrison in Compiègne without the same superiority in numbers you had at Orleans —

THE ARCHBISHOP. The army will disown you, and will not rescue you. And His Majesty the King has told you that the throne has not the means of ransoming you.

CHARLES. Not a penny.

THE ARCHBISHOP. You stand alone: absolutely alone, trusting to your own conceit, your own ignorance, your own headstrong presumption, your own impiety in hiding all these sins under the cloak of a trust in God. When you pass through these doors into the sunlight, the crowd will cheer you. They will bring you their little children and their invalids to heal: they will kiss your hands and feet, and do what they can, poor simple souls, to turn your head, and madden you with the self-confidence that is leading you to your destruction. But you will be none the less alone: they cannot save you. We and we only can stand between you and the stake at which our enemies have burnt that wretched woman in Paris.

JOAN [*her eyes skyward*]. I have better friends and better counsel than yours.

THE ARCHBISHOP. I see that I am speaking in vain to a hardened heart. You reject our protection, and are determined to turn us all against you. In future, then, fend for yourself; and if you fail, God have mercy on your soul.

DUNOIS. That is the truth, Joan. Heed it.

JOAN. Where would you all have been now if I had heeded that sort of truth? There is no help, no counsel, in any of you. Yes: I am alone on earth: I have always been alone. My father told my brothers to drown me if I would not stay to mind his sheep while France was bleeding to death: France might perish if only our lambs were safe. I thought France would have friends at the court of the king of France; and I find only wolves fighting for pieces of her poor torn body. I thought God would have friends everywhere, because He is the friend of everyone; and in my innocence I believed that you who now cast me out would be like strong towers to keep harm from me. But I am wiser now; and nobody is any the worse for being wiser. Do not think you can frighten me by telling me that I am alone. France is alone; and God is alone; and what is my loneliness before the loneliness of my country and my God? I see now that the loneliness of God is His strength: what would He be if He listened to your jealous little counsels? Well, my loneliness shall be my strength too; it is better to be alone with God; His friendship will not fail me, nor His counsel, nor His love. In His strength I will dare, and dare, and dare, until I die. I will go out now to the common people, and let the love in their eyes comfort me for the hate in yours. You will all be glad to see me burnt; but if I go through the fire I shall go through it to their hearts for ever and ever. And so, God be with me!

She goes from them. They stare after her in glum silence for a moment. Then Gilles de Rais twirls his beard.

BLUEBEARD. You know, the woman is quite impossible. I dont dislike her, really; but what are you to do with such a character?

DUNOIS. As God is my judge, if she fell into the Loire I would jump in in full armor to fish her out. But if she plays the fool at Compiègne, and gets caught, I must leave her to her doom.

LA HIRE. Then you had better chain me up; for I could follow her to hell when the spirit rises in her like that.

THE ARCHBISHOP. She disturbs my judgment too: there is a dangerous power in her outbursts. But the pit is open at her feet; and for good or evil we cannot turn her from it.

CHARLES. If only she would keep quiet, or go home!

They follow her dispiritedly.

Scene VI

Rouen, 30th May 1431. A great stone hall in the castle, arranged for a trial-at-law, but not a trial-by-jury, the court being the Bishop's court with the Inquisition participating: hence there are two raised chairs side by side for the Bishop and the Inquisitor as judges. Rows of chairs radiating from them at an obtuse angle are for the canons, the doctors of law and theology, and the Dominican monks, who act as assessors. In the angle is a table for the scribes, with stools. There is also a heavy rough wooden stool for the prisoner. All these are at the inner end of the hall. The further end is open to the courtyard through a row of arches. The court is shielded from the weather by screens and curtains.

Looking down the great hall from the middle of the inner end, the judicial chairs and scribes' table are to the right. The prisoner's stool is to the left. There are arched doors right and left. It is a fine sunshiny May morning.

Warwick comes in through the arched doorway on the judges' side, followed by his page.

THE PAGE [*pertly*]. I suppose your lordship is aware that we have no business here. This is an ecclesiastical court; and we are only the secular arm.

WARWICK. I am aware of that fact. Will it please your impudence to find the Bishop of Beauvais for me, and give him a hint that he can have a word with me here before the trial, if he wishes?

THE PAGE [*going*]. Yes, my lord.

WARWICK. And mind you behave yourself. Do not address him as Pious Peter.

THE PAGE. No, my lord. I shall be kind to him, because, when The Maid is brought in, Pious Peter will have to pick a peck of pickled pepper.

Cauchon enters through the same door with a Dominican monk and a canon, the latter carrying a brief.

THE PAGE. The Right Reverend his lordship the Bishop of Beauvais. And two other reverend gentlemen.

WARWICK. Get out; and see that we are not interrupted.

THE PAGE. Right, my lord. [*He vanishes airily.*]

CAUCHON. I wish your lordship good-morrow.

WARWICK. Good-morrow to your lordship. Have I had the pleasure of meeting your friends before? I think not.

CAUCHON [*introducing the monk, who is on his right*]. This, my lord, is Brother John Lemaître, of the order of St Dominic. He is acting as deputy for the Chief Inquisitor into the evil of heresy in France. Brother John: the Earl of Warwick.

WARWICK. Your Reverence is most welcome. We have no Inquisitor in England, unfortunately; though we miss him greatly, especially on occasions like the present.

The Inquisitor smiles patiently, and bows. He is a mild elderly gentleman, but has evident reserves of authority and firmness.

CAUCHON [*introducing the Canon, who is on his left*]. This gentleman is Canon John D'Estivet, of the Chapter of Bayeux. He is acting as Promoter.

WARWICK. Promoter?

CAUCHON. Prosecutor, you would call him in civil law.

WARWICK. Ah! prosecutor. Quite, quite. I am very glad to make your acquaintance, Canon D'Estivet.

D'Estivet bows. [He is on the young side of middle age, well mannered, but vulpine beneath his veneer].

WARWICK. May I ask what stage the proceedings have reached? It is now more than nine months since The Maid was captured at Compiègne by the Burgundians. It is fully four months since I bought her from the Burgundians for a very handsome sum, solely that she might be brought to justice. It is very nearly three months since I delivered her up to you, my Lord Bishop, as a person suspected of heresy. May I suggest that you are taking a rather unconscionable time to make up your minds about a very plain case? Is this trial never going to end?

THE INQUISITOR [*smiling*]. It has not yet begun, my lord.

WARWICK. Not yet begun! Why, you have been at it eleven weeks!

CAUCHON. We have not been idle, my lord. We have held fifteen examinations of The Maid: six public and nine private.

THE INQUISITOR [*always patiently smiling*]. You see, my lord, I have been present at only two of these examinations. They were proceedings of the Bishop's court solely, and not of the Holy Office. I have only just decided to associate myself — that is, to associate the Holy Inquisition — with the Bishop's court. I did not at first think that this was a case of heresy at all. I regarded it as a political case, and The Maid as a prisoner of war. But having now been present at two of the examinations, I must admit that this seems to be one of the gravest cases of heresy within my experience. Therefore everything is now in order, and we proceed to trial this morning. [*He moves towards the judicial chairs.*]

CAUCHON. This moment, if your lordship's convenience allows.

WARWICK [*graciously*]. Well, that is good news, gentlemen. I will not attempt to conceal from you that our patience was becoming strained.

CAUCHON. So I gathered from the threats of your soldiers to drown those of our people who favor The Maid.

WARWICK. Dear me! At all events their intentions were friendly to you, my lord.

CAUCHON [*sternly*]. I hope not. I am determined that the woman shall have a fair hearing. The justice of the Church is not a mockery, my lord.

THE INQUISITOR [*returning*]. Never has there been a fairer examination within my experience, my lord. The Maid needs no lawyers to take her part: she will be tried by her most faithful friends, all ardently desirous to save her soul from perdition.

D'ESTIVET. Sir: I am the Promoter; and it has been my painful duty to present the case against the girl; but believe me, I would throw up my case today and hasten to her defence if I did not know that men far my superiors in learning and piety, in eloquence and persuasiveness, have been sent to reason with her, to explain to her the danger she is running, and the ease with which she may avoid it.

[*Suddenly bursting into forensic eloquence, to the disgust of Cauchon and the Inquisitor, who have listened to him so far with patronizing approval*]. Men have dared to say that we are acting from hate; but God is our witness that they lie. Have we tortured her? No. Have we ceased to exhort her; to implore her to have pity on herself; to come to the bosom of her Church as an erring but beloved child? Have we —

CAUCHON [*interrupting drily*]. Take care, Canon. All that you say is true; but if you make his lordship believe it I will not answer for your life, and hardly for my own.

WARWICK [*deprecating, but by no means denying*]. Oh, my lord, you are very hard on us poor English. But we certainly do not share your pious desire to save The Maid: in fact I tell you now plainly that her death is a political necessity which I regret but cannot help. If the Church lets her go —

CAUCHON [*with fierce and menacing pride*]. If the Church lets her go, woe to the man, were he the Emperor himself, who dares lay a finger on her! The Church is not subject to political necessity, my lord.

THE INQUISITOR [*interposing smoothly*]. You need have no anxiety about the result, my lord. You have an invincible ally in the matter: one who is far more determined than you that she shall burn.

WARWICK. And who is this very convenient partisan, may I ask?

THE INQUISITOR. The Maid herself. Unless you put a gag in her mouth you cannot prevent her from convicting herself ten times over every time she opens it.

D'ESTIVET. That is perfectly true, my lord. My hair bristles on my head when I hear so young a creature utter such blasphemies.

WARWICK. Well, by all means do your best for her if you are quite sure it will be of no avail. [*Looking hard at Cauchon*]. I should be sorry to have to act without the blessing of the Church.

CAUCHON [*with a mixture of cynical admiration and contempt*]. And yet they say Englishmen are hypocrites! You pay for your side, my lord, even at the peril of your soul. I cannot but admire such devotion; but I dare not go so far myself. I fear damnation.

WARWICK. If we feared anything we could never govern England, my lord. Shall I send your people in to you?

CAUCHON. Yes: it will be very good of your lordship to withdraw and allow the court to assemble.

Warwick turns on his heel, and goes out through the courtyard. Cauchon takes one of the judicial seats; and D'Estivet sits at the scribes' table, studying his brief.

CAUCHON [*casually, as he makes himself comfortable*]. What scoundrels these English nobles are!

THE INQUISITOR [*taking the other judicial chair on Cauchon's left*]. All secular power makes men scoundrels. They are not trained for the work; and they have not the Apostolic Succession. Our own nobles are just as bad.

The Bishop's assessors hurry into the hall, headed by Chaplain de Stogumber and Canon de Courcelles, a young priest of 30. The scribes sit at the table, leaving a chair vacant opposite D'Estivet. Some of the assessors take their seats: others stand chatting, waiting for the proceedings to begin formally. De Stogumber, aggrieved and obstinate, will not take his seat: neither will the Canon, who stands on his right.

CAUCHON. Good morning, Master de Stogumber. [*To the Inquisitor*] Chaplain to the Cardinal of England.

THE CHAPLAIN [*correcting him*]. Of Winchester, my lord. I have to make a protest, my lord.

CAUCHON. You make a great many.

THE CHAPLAIN. I am not without support, my lord. Here is Master de Courcelles, Canon of Paris, who associates himself with me in my protest.

CAUCHON. Well, what is the matter?

THE CHAPLAIN [*sulkily*]. Speak you, Master de Courcelles, since I do not seem to enjoy his lordship's confidence. [*He sits down in dudgeon next to Cauchon, on his right.*]

COURCELLES. My lord: we have been at great pains to draw up an indictment of The Maid on sixty-four counts. We are now told that they have been reduced, without consulting us.

THE INQUISITOR. Master de Courcelles: I am the culprit. I am overwhelmed with admiration for the zeal displayed in your sixty-four counts; but in accusing a heretic, as in other things, enough is enough. Also you must remember that all the members of the court are not so subtle and profound as you, and that some of your very great learning might appear to them to be very great nonsense. Therefore I have thought it well to have your sixty-four articles cut down to twelve—

COURCELLES [*thunderstruck*]. Twelve!!!

THE INQUISITOR. Twelve will, believe me, be quite enough for your purpose.

THE CHAPLAIN. But some of the most important points have been reduced almost to nothing. For instance, The Maid has actually declared that the blessed saints Margaret and Catherine, and the holy Archangel Michael, spoke to her in French. That is a vital point.

THE INQUISITOR. You think, doubtless, that they should have spoken in Latin?

CAUCHON. No: he thinks they should have spoken in English.

THE CHAPLAIN. Naturally, my lord.

THE INQUISITOR. Well, as we are all here agreed, I think, that these voices of The Maid are the voices of evil spirits tempting her to her damnation, it would not be very courteous to you, Master de Stogumber, or to the King of England, to assume that English is the devil's native language. So let it pass. The matter is not wholly omitted from the twelve articles. Pray take your places, gentlemen; and let us proceed to business.

All who have not taken their seats, do so.

THE CHAPLAIN. Well, I protest. That is all.

COURCELLES. I think it hard that all our work should go for nothing. It is only another example of the diabolical influence which this woman exercises over the court. [*He takes his chair, which is on the Chaplain's right.*]

CAUCHON. Do you suggest that I am under diabolical influence?

COURCELLES. I suggest nothing, my lord. But it seems to me that there is a conspiracy here to hush up the fact that The Maid stole the Bishop of Senlis's horse.

CAUCHON [*keeping his temper with difficulty*]. This is not a police court. Are we to waste our time on such rubbish?

COURCELLES [*rising, shocked*]. My lord: do you call the Bishop's horse rubbish?

THE INQUISITOR [*blandly*]. Master de Courcelles: The Maid alleges that she paid handsomely for the Bishop's horse, and that if he did not get the money the fault was not hers. As that may be true, the point is one on which The Maid may well be acquitted.

COURCELLES. Yes, if it were an ordinary horse. But the Bishop's horse! how can she be acquitted for that? [*He sits down again, bewildered and discouraged.*]

THE INQUISITOR. I submit to you, with great respect, that if we persist in trying The Maid on trumpery issues on which we may have to declare her innocent, she may escape us on the great main issue of heresy, on which she seems so far to insist on her own guilt. I will ask you, therefore, to say nothing, when The Maid is brought before us, of these stealings of horses, and dancings round fairy trees with the village children, and prayings at haunted wells, and a dozen other things which you were diligently inquiring into until my arrival. There is not a village girl in France against whom you could not prove such things: they all dance round haunted trees, and pray at magic wells. Some of them would steal the Pope's horse if they got the chance. Heresy, gentlemen, heresy is the charge we have to try. The detection and suppression of heresy is my peculiar business: I am here as an inquisitor, not as an ordinary magistrate. Stick to the heresy, gentlemen; and leave the other matters alone.

CAUCHON. I may say that we have sent to the girl's village to make inquiries about her, and there is practically nothing serious against her.

THE CHAPLAIN [*rising and clamoring together*]. Nothing serious, my lord —
COURCELLES [*rising and clamoring together*]. What! The fairy tree not —

CAUCHON [*out of patience*]. Be silent, gentlemen; or speak one at a time.

Courcelles collapses into his chair, intimidated.

THE CHAPLAIN [*sulkily resuming his seat*]. That is what The Maid said to us last Friday.

CAUCHON. I wish you had followed her counsel, sir. When I say nothing serious, I mean nothing that men of sufficiently large mind to conduct an inquiry like this would consider serious. I agree with my colleague the Inquisitor that it is on the count of heresy that we must proceed.

LADVENU [*a young but ascetically fine-drawn Dominican who is sitting next Courcelles, on his right*]. But is there any great harm in the girl's heresy? Is it not merely her simplicity? Many saints have said as much as Joan.

THE INQUISITOR [*dropping his blandness and speaking very gravely*]. Brother Martin: if you had seen what I have seen of heresy, you would not think it a light thing even in its most apparently harmless and even lovable and pious origins. Heresy begins with people who are to all appearance better than their neighbors. A gentle and pious girl, or a young man who has obeyed the command of our Lord by giving all his riches to the poor, and putting on the garb of poverty, the life of austerity, and the rule of humility and charity, may be the founder of a heresy that will wreck both Church and Empire if not ruthlessly stamped out in time. The records of the Holy Inquisition are full of histories we dare not give to the world, because they are beyond the belief of honest men and innocent women; yet they all began with saintly simpletons. I have seen this again and again. Mark what I say: the woman who quarrels with her clothes, and puts on the dress of a man, is like the man who throws off his fur gown and dresses like John the Baptist: they are followed, as surely as the night follows the day, by bands of wild women and men who refuse to wear any clothes at all. When maids will neither marry nor take regular vows, and men reject marriage and exalt their lusts into divine inspirations, then, as surely as the summer follows the spring, they begin with polygamy, and end by incest. Heresy at first seems innocent and even laudable; but it ends in such a monstrous horror of unnatural wickedness that the most tender-hearted among you, if you saw it at work as I have seen it, would clamor against the mercy of the Church in dealing with it. For two hundred years the Holy Office has striven with these diabolical madnesses; and it knows that they begin always by vain and ignorant persons setting up their own judgment against the Church, and taking it upon themselves to be the interpreters of God's will. You must not fall into the common error of mistaking these simpletons for liars and hypocrites. They believe honestly and sincerely that their diabolical inspiration is divine. Therefore you must be on your guard against your natural compassion. You are all, I hope, merciful men: how else could you have devoted your lives to the service of our gentle Savior? You are going to see before you a young girl, pious and chaste; for I must tell you, gentlemen, that the things said of her by our English friends are supported by no evidence, whilst there is abundant testimony that her excesses have been excesses of religion and charity and not of wordliness and wantonness. This girl is not one of those whose hard features are the sign of hard hearts, and whose brazen looks and lewd demeanor condemn them before they are accused. The devilish pride that has led her into her present peril has left no mark on her countenance. Strange as it may seem to you, it has even left no mark on her character outside those special matters in which she is proud; so that you will see a diabolical pride and a natural humility seated side by side in the self-same soul. Therefore be on your guard. God forbid that I should tell you to harden your hearts; for her punishment if we condemn her will be so cruel that we should forfeit our own hope of divine mercy were there one grain of malice against her in our hearts. But if you hate cruelty — and if any man here does not hate it I command him on his soul's salvation to quit this holy court — I say, if you hate cruelty, remember that nothing is so cruel in its consequences as the toleration of heresy. Remember also that no court of law can be so cruel as the common people are to those whom they suspect of heresy. The heretic in the hands of the Holy Office is safe from violence, is assured of a fair trial, and cannot suffer death, even when guilty, if repentance follows sin. Innumerable lives of heretics have been saved because the Holy Office has taken them out of the hands of the people, and because the people have yielded them up, knowing that the Holy Office would deal with them. Before the Holy Inquisition existed, and even now when its officers are not within reach, the unfortunate wretch suspected of heresy, perhaps quite ignorantly and unjustly, is stoned, torn in pieces, drowned, burned in his house with all his innocent children, without a trial, unshriven, unburied save as a dog is buried: all of them deeds hateful to God and most cruel to man. Gentlemen: I am compassionate by nature as well as by my profession; and though the work I have to do may seem cruel to those who do not know how much more cruel it would be to leave it undone, I would go to the stake myself sooner than do it if I did not know its righteousness, its necessity, its essential mercy. I ask you to address yourself to this trial in that conviction. Anger is a bad counsellor: cast out anger. Pity is sometimes worse: cast out pity. But do not cast out mercy. Remember only that justice comes first. Have you anything to say, my lord, before we proceed to trial?

CAUCHON. You have spoken for me, and spoken better than I could. I do not see how any sane man could disagree with a word that has fallen from you. But this I will add. The crude heresies of which you have told us are horrible; but their horror is like that of the black death: they rage for a while and then die out, because sound and sensible men will not under any incitement be reconciled to nakedness and incest and polygamy and the like. But we are confronted today throughout Europe with a heresy that is spreading among men not weak in mind nor diseased in brain: nay, the stronger the mind, the more obstinate the heretic. It is neither discredited by fantastic extremes nor corrupted by the common lusts of the flesh; but it, too, sets up the private judgment of the single erring mortal against the considered wisdom and experience of the Church. The mighty structure of Catholic Christendom will never be shaken by naked madmen or by the sins of Moab and Ammon. But it may be betrayed from within, and brought to barbarous ruin and desolation, by this arch heresy which the English Commander calls Protestantism.

THE ASSESSORS [*whispering*]. Protestantism! What was that? What does the Bishop mean? Is it a new heresy? The English Commander, he said. Did you ever hear of Protestantism? etc., etc.

CAUCHON [*continuing*]. And that reminds me. What provision has the Earl of Warwick made for the defence of the secular arm should The Maid prove obdurate, and the people be moved to pity her?

THE CHAPLAIN. Have no fear on that score, my lord. The noble earl has eight hundred men-at-arms at the gates. She will not slip through our English fingers even if the whole city be on her side.

CAUCHON [*revolted*]. Will you not add, God grant that she repent and purge her sin?

THE CHAPLAIN. That does not seem to me to be consistent; but of course I agree with your lordship.

CAUCHON [*giving him up with a shrug of contempt*]. The court sits.

THE INQUISITOR. Let the accused be brought in.

LADVENU [*calling*]. The accused. Let her be brought in.

Joan, chained by the ankles, is brought in through the arched door behind the prisoner's stool by a guard of English soldiers. With them is the Executioner and his assistants. They lead her to the prisoner's stool, and place themselves behind it after taking off her chain. She wears a page's black suit. Her long imprisonment and the strain of the examinations which have preceded the trial have left their mark on her; but her vitality still holds; she confronts the court unabashed, without a trace of the awe which their formal solemnity seems to require for the complete success of its impressiveness.

THE INQUISITOR [*kindly*]. Sit down, Joan. [*She sits on the prisoner's stool.*] You look very pale today. Are you not well?

JOAN. Thank you kindly: I am well enough. But the Bishop sent me some carp; and it made me ill.

CAUGHON. I am sorry. I told them to see that it was fresh.

JOAN. You meant to be good to me, I know; but it is a fish that does not agree with me. The English thought you were trying to poison me —

CAUCHON   }   [*together*].   } What!
THE CHAPLAIN }   } No, my lord.

JOAN [*continuing*]. They are determined that I shall be burnt as a witch; and they sent their doctor to cure me; but he was forbidden to bleed me because the silly people believe that a witch's witchery leaves her if she is bled; so he only called me filthy names. Why do you leave me in the hands of the English? I should be in the hands of the Church. And why must I be chained by the feet to a log of wood? Are you afraid I will fly away?

D'ESTIVET [*harshly*]. Woman: it is not for you to question the court: it is for us to question you.

COURCELLES. When you were left unchained, did you not try to escape by jumping from a tower sixty feet high? If you cannot fly like a witch, how is it that you are still alive?

JOAN. I suppose because the tower was not so high then. It has grown higher every day since you began asking me questions about it.

D'ESTIVET. Why did you jump from the tower?

JOAN. How do you know that I jumped?

D'ESTIVET. You were found lying in the moat. Why did you leave the tower?

JOAN. Why would anybody leave a prison if they could get out?

D'ESTIVET. You tried to escape?

JOAN. Of course I did; and not for the first time

either. If you leave the door of the cage open the bird will fly out.

D'ESTIVET [*rising*]. That is a confession of heresy. I call the attention of the court to it.

JOAN. Heresy, he calls it! Am I a heretic because I try to escape from prison?

D'ESTIVET. Assuredly, if you are in the hands of the Church, and you wilfully take yourself out of its hands, you are deserting the Church; and that is heresy.

JOAN. It is great nonsense. Nobody could be such a fool as to think that.

D'ESTIVET. You hear, my lord, how I am reviled in the execution of my duty by this woman. [*He sits down indignantly.*]

CAUCHON. I have warned you before, Joan, that you are doing yourself no good by these pert answers.

JOAN. But you will not talk sense to me. I am reasonable if you will be reasonable.

THE INQUISITOR [*interposing*]. This is not yet in order. You forget, Master Promoter, that the proceedings have not been formally opened. The time for questions is after she has sworn on the Gospels to tell us the whole truth.

JOAN. You say this to me every time. I have said again and again that I will tell you all that concerns this trial. But I cannot tell you the whole truth: God does not allow the whole truth to be told. You do not understand it when I tell it. It is an old saying that he who tells too much truth is sure to be hanged. I am weary of this argument: we have been over it nine times already. I have sworn as much as I will swear; and I will swear no more.

COURCELLES. My lord: she should be put to the torture.

THE INQUISITOR. You hear, Joan? That is what happens to the obdurate. Think before you answer. Has she been shewn the instruments?

THE EXECUTIONER. They are ready, my lord. She has seen them.

JOAN. If you tear me limb from limb until you separate my soul from my body you will get nothing out of me beyond what I have told you. What more is there to tell that you could understand? Besides, I cannot bear to be hurt; and if you hurt me I will say anything you like to stop the pain. But I will take it all back afterwards; so what is the use of it?

LADVENU. There is much in that. We should proceed mercifully.

COURCELLES. But the torture is customary.

THE INQUISITOR. It must not be applied wantonly. If the accused will confess voluntarily, then its use cannot be justified.

COURCELLES. But this is unusual and irregular. She refuses to take the oath.

LADVENU [*disgusted*]. Do you want to torture the girl for the mere pleasure of it?

COURCELLES [*bewildered*]. But it is not a pleasure. It is the law. It is customary. It is always done.

THE INQUISITOR. That is not so, Master, except when the inquiries are carried on by people who do not know their legal business.

COURCELLES. But the woman is a heretic. I assure you it is always done.

CAUCHON [*decisively*]. It will not be done today if it is not necessary. Let there be an end of this. I will not have it said that we proceeded on forced confessions. We have sent our best preachers and doctors to this woman to exhort and implore her to save her soul and body from the fire: we shall not now send the executioner to thrust her into it.

COURCELLES. Your lordship is merciful, of course. But it is a great responsibility to depart from the usual practice.

JOAN. Thou art a rare noodle, Master. Do what was done last time is thy rule, eh?

COURCELLES [*rising*]. Thou wanton: dost thou dare call me noodle?

THE INQUISITOR. Patience, Master, patience: I fear you will soon be only too terribly avenged.

COURCELLES [*mutters*]. Noodle indeed! [*He sits down, much discontented.*]

THE INQUISITOR. Meanwhile, let us not be moved by the rough side of a shepherd lass's tongue.

JOAN. Nay: I am no shepherd lass, though I have helped with the sheep like anyone else. I will do a lady's work in the house — spin or weave — against any woman in Rouen.

THE INQUISITOR. This is not a time for vanity, Joan. You stand in great peril.

JOAN. I know it: have I not been punished for my vanity? If I had not worn my cloth of gold surcoat in battle like a fool, that Burgundian soldier would never have pulled me backwards off my horse; and I should not have been here.

THE CHAPLAIN. If you are so clever at woman's work why do you not stay at home and do it?

JOAN. There are plenty of other women to do it; but there is nobody to do my work.

CAUCHON. Come! we are wasting time on trifles. Joan: I am going to put a most solemn question to you. Take care how you answer; for your life and salvation are at stake on it. Will you for all you have said and done, be it good or bad, accept the judgment of God's Church on earth? More especially as to the acts and words that are imputed to you in this trial by the Promoter here, will you submit your case to the inspired interpretation of the Church Militant?

JOAN. I am a faithful child of the Church. I will obey the Church —

CAUCHON [*hopefully leaning forward*]. You will?

JOAN. — provided it does not command anything impossible.

Cauchon sinks back in his chair with a heavy sigh. The Inquisitor purses his lips and frowns. Ladvenu shakes his head pitifully.

D'ESTIVET. She imputes to the Church the error and folly of commanding the impossible.

JOAN. If you command me to declare that all that I have done and said, and all the visions and revelations I have had, were not from God, then that is impossible: I will not declare it for anything in the world. What God made me do I will never go back on; and what He has commanded or shall command I will not fail to do in spite of any man alive. That is what I mean by impossible. And in case the Church should bid me do anything contrary to the command I have from God, I will not consent to it, no matter what it may be.

THE ASSESSORS [*shocked and indignant*]. Oh! The Church contrary to God! What do you say now? Flat heresy. This is beyond everything, etc., etc.

D'ESTIVET [*throwing down his brief*]. My lord: do you need anything more than this?

CAUCHON. Woman: you have said enough to burn ten heretics. Will you not be warned? Will you not understand?

THE INQUISITOR. If the Church Militant tells you that your revelations and visions are sent by the devil to tempt you to your damnation, will you not believe that the Church is wiser than you?

JOAN. I believe that God is wiser than I; and it is His commands that I will do. All the things that you call my crimes have come to me by the command of God. I say that I have done them by the order of God: it is impossible for me to say anything else. If any Churchman says the contrary I shall not mind him: I shall mind God alone, whose command I always follow.

LADVENU [*pleading with her urgently*]. You do not know what you are saying, child. Do you want to kill yourself? Listen. Do you not believe that you are subject to the Church of God on earth?

JOAN. Yes. When have I ever denied it?

LADVENU. Good. That means, does it not, that you are subject to our Lord the Pope, to the cardinals, the archbishops, and the bishops for whom his lordship stands here today?

JOAN. God must be served first.

D'ESTIVET. Then your voices command you not to submit yourself to the Church Militant?

JOAN. My voices do not tell me to disobey the Church; but God must be served first.

CAUCHON. And you, and not the Church, are to be the judge?

JOAN. What other judgment can I judge by but my own?

THE ASSESSORS [*scandalized*]. Oh! [*They cannot find words.*]

CAUCHON. Out of your own mouth you have condemned yourself. We have striven for your salvation to the verge of sinning ourselves: we have opened the door to you again and again; and you have shut it in our faces and in the face of God. Dare you pretend, after what you have said, that you are in a state of grace?

JOAN. If I am not, may God bring me to it: if I am, may God keep me in it!

LADVENU. That is a very good reply, my lord.

COURCELLES. Were you in a state of grace when you stole the Bishop's horse?

CAUCHON [*rising in a fury*]. Oh, devil take the Bishop's horse and you too! We are here to try a case of heresy; and no sooner do we come to the root of the matter than we are thrown back by idiots who understand nothing but horses. [*Trembling with rage, he forces himself to sit down.*]

THE INQUISITOR. Gentlemen, gentlemen: in clinging to these small issues you are The Maid's best advocates. I am not surprised that his lordship has lost patience with you. What does the Promoter say? Does he press these trumpery matters?

D'ESTIVET. I am bound by my office to press everything; but when the woman confesses a heresy that must bring upon her the doom of excommunication, of what consequence is it that she has been guilty also of offences which expose her to minor penances? I share the impatience of his lordship as to these minor charges. Only, with great respect, I must emphasize the gravity of two very horrible and blasphemous crimes which she does not deny. First, she has intercourse with evil spirits, and is therefore a sorceress. Second, she wears men's clothes, which is indecent, unnatural, and abominable; and in spite of our most earnest remonstrances and entreaties, she will not change them even to receive the sacrament.

JOAN. Is the blessed St Catherine an evil spirit? Is St Margaret? Is Michael the Archangel?

COURCELLES. How do you know that the spirit which appears to you is an archangel? Does he not appear to you as a naked man?

JOAN. Do you think God cannot afford clothes for him?

The assessors cannot help smiling, especially as the joke is against Courcelles.

LADVENU. Well answered, Joan.

THE INQUISITOR. It is, in effect, well answered. But no evil spirit would be so simple as to appear to a young girl in a guise that would scandalize her when he meant her to take him for a messenger from the Most High. Joan: the Church instructs you that these apparitions are demons seeking your soul's perdition. Do you accept the instruction of the Church?

JOAN. I accept the messenger of God. How could any faithful believer in the Church refuse him?

CAUCHON. Wretched woman: again I ask you, do you know what you are saying?

THE INQUISITOR. You wrestle in vain with the devil for her soul, my lord: she will not be saved. Now as to this matter of the man's dress. For the last time, will you put off that impudent attire, and dress as becomes your sex?

JOAN. I will not.

D'ESTIVET [*pouncing*]. The sin of disobedience, my lord.

JOAN [*distressed*]. But my voices tell me I must dress as a soldier.

LADVENU. Joan, Joan: does not that prove to you that the voices are the voices of evil spirits? Can you suggest to us one good reason why an angel of God should give you such shameless advice?

JOAN. Why, yes: what can be plainer commonsense? I was a soldier living among soldiers. I am a prisoner guarded by soldiers. If I were to dress as a woman they would think of me as a woman; and then what would become of me? If I dress as a soldier they think of me as a soldier, and I can live with them as I do at home with my brothers. That is why St Catherine tells me I must not dress as a woman until she gives me leave.

COURCELLES. When will she give you leave?

JOAN. When you take me out of the hands of the English soldiers. I have told you that I should be in the hands of the Church, and not left night and day with four soldiers of the Earl of Warwick. Do you want me to live with them in petticoats?

LADVENU. My lord: what she says is, God knows, very wrong and shocking; but there is a grain of worldly sense in it such as might impose on a simple village maiden.

JOAN. If we were as simple in the village as you are in your courts and palaces, there would soon be no wheat to make bread for you.

CAUCHON. That is the thanks you get for trying to save her, Brother Martin.

LADVENU. Joan: we are all trying to save you. His lordship is trying to save you. The Inquisitor could not be more just to you if you were his own daughter. But you are blinded by a terrible pride and self-sufficiency.

JOAN. Why do you say that? I have said nothing wrong. I cannot understand.

THE INQUISITOR. The blessed St Athanasius has laid it down in his creed that those who cannot understand are damned. It is not enough to be simple. It is not enough even to be what simple people call good. The simplicity of a darkened mind is no better than the simplicity of a beast.

JOAN. There is great wisdom in the simplicity of a beast, let me tell you; and sometimes great foolishness in the wisdom of scholars.

LADVENU. We know that, Joan: we are not so foolish as you think us. Try to resist the temptation to make pert replies to us. Do you see that man who stands behind you? [*He indicates the Executioner.*]

JOAN [*turning and looking at the man*]. Your torturer? But the Bishop said I was not to be tortured.

LADVENU. You are not to be tortured because you have confessed everything that is necessary to your condemnation. That man is not only the torturer: he is also the Executioner. Executioner: let The Maid hear your answers to my questions. Are you prepared for the burning of a heretic this day?

THE EXECUTIONER. Yes, Master.

LADVENU. Is the stake ready?

THE EXECUTIONER. It is. In the market-place. The English have built it too high for me to get near her and make the death easier. It will be a cruel death.

JOAN [*horrified*]. But you are not going to burn me now?

THE INQUISITOR. You realize it at last.

LADVENU. There are eight hundred English soldiers waiting to take you to the market-place the moment the sentence of excommunication has passed the lips of your judges. You are within a few short moments of that doom.

JOAN [*looking round desperately for rescue*]. Oh God!

LADVENU. Do not despair, Joan. The Church is merciful. You can save yourself.

JOAN [*hopefully*]. Yes: my voices promised me I should not be burnt. St Catherine bade me be bold.

CAUCHON. Woman: are you quite mad? Do you not see that your voices have deceived you?

JOAN. Oh no: that is impossible.

CAUCHON. Impossible! They have led you straight to your excommunication, and to the stake which is there waiting for you.

LADVENU [*pressing the point hard*]. Have they kept a single promise to you since you were taken at Compiègne? The devil has betrayed you. The Church holds out its arms to you.

JOAN [*despairing*]. Oh, it is true: it is true: my voices have deceived me. I have been mocked by devils: my faith is broken. I have dared and dared; but only a fool will walk into a fire: God, who gave me my commonsense, cannot will me to do that.

LADVENU. Now God be praised that He has saved

you at the eleventh hour! [*He hurries to the vacant seat at the scribes' table, and snatches a sheet of paper, on which he sets to work writing eagerly.*]

CAUCHON. Amen!

JOAN. What must I do?

CAUCHON. You must sign a solemn recantation of your heresy.

JOAN. Sign? That means to write my name. I cannot write.

CAUCHON. You have signed many letters before.

JOAN. Yes; but someone held my hand and guided the pen. I can make my mark.

THE CHAPLAIN [*who has been listening with growing alarm and indignation*]. My lord: do you mean that you are going to allow this woman to escape us?

THE INQUISITOR. The law must take its course, Master de Stogumber. And you know the law.

THE CHAPLAIN [*rising, purple with fury*]. I know that there is no faith in a Frenchman. [*Tumult, which he shouts down.*] I know what my lord the Cardinal of Winchester will say when he hears of this. I know what the Earl of Warwick will do when he learns that you intend to betray him. There are eight hundred men at the gate who will see that this abominable witch is burnt in spite of your teeth.

THE ASSESSORS [*meanwhile*]. What is this? What did he say? He accuses us of treachery! This is past bearing. No faith in a Frenchman! Did you hear that? This is an intolerable fellow. Who is he? Is this what English Churchmen are like? He must be mad or drunk, etc., etc.

THE INQUISITOR [*rising*]. Silence, pray! Gentlemen: pray silence! Master Chaplain: bethink you a moment of your holy office: of what you are, and where you are. I direct you to sit down.

THE CHAPLAIN [*folding his arms doggedly, his face working convulsively*]. I will NOT sit down.

CAUCHON. Master Inquisitor: this man has called me a traitor to my face before now.

THE CHAPLAIN. So you are a traitor. You are all traitors. You have been doing nothing but begging this damnable witch on your knees to recant all through this trial.

THE INQUISITOR [*placidly resuming his seat*]. If you will not sit, you must stand: that is all.

THE CHAPLAIN. I will NOT stand. [*He flings himself back into his chair.*]

LADVENU [*rising with the paper in his hand*]. My lord: here is the form of recantation for The Maid to sign.

CAUCHON. Read it to her.

JOAN. Do not trouble. I will sign it.

THE INQUISITOR. Woman: you must know what you are putting your hand to. Read it to her, Brother Martin. And let all be silent.

LADVENU [*reading quietly*]. 'I, Joan, commonly called The Maid, a miserable sinner, do confess that I have most grievously sinned in the following articles. I have pretended to have revelations from God and the angels and the blessed saints, and perversely rejected the Church's warnings that these were temptations by demons. I have blasphemed abominably by wearing an immodest dress, contrary to the Holy Scripture and the canons of the Church. Also I have clipped my hair in the style of a man, and, against all the duties which have made my sex especially acceptable in heaven, have taken up the sword, even to the shedding of human blood, inciting men to slay each other, invoking evil spirits to delude them, and stubbornly and most blasphemously imputing these sins to Almighty God. I confess to the sin of sedition, to the sin of idolatry, to the sin of disobedience, to the sin of pride, and to the sin of heresy. All of which sins I now renounce and abjure and depart from, humbly thanking you Doctors and Masters who have brought me back to the truth and into the grace of our Lord. And I will never return to my errors, but will remain in communion with our Holy Church and in obedience to our Holy Father the Pope of Rome. All this I swear by God Almighty and the Holy Gospels, in witness whereto I sign my name to this recantation.'

THE INQUISITOR. You understand this, Joan?

JOAN [*listless*]. It is plain enough, sir.

THE INQUISITOR. And it is true?

JOAN. It may be true. If it were not true, the fire would not be ready for me in the marketplace.

LADVENU [*taking up his pen and a book, and going to her quickly lest she should compromise herself again*]. Come, child: let me guide your hand. Take the pen. [*She does so; and they begin to write, using the book as a desk.*] J.E.H.A.N.E. So. Now make your mark by yourself.

JOAN [*makes her mark, and gives him back the pen, tormented by the rebellion of her soul against her mind and body*]. There!

LADVENU [*replacing the pen on the table, and handing the recantation to Cauchon with a reverence*]. Praise be to God, my brothers, the lamb has returned to the flock; and the shepherd rejoices in her more than in ninety and nine just persons. [*He returns to his seat.*]

THE INQUISITOR [*taking the paper from Cauchon*]. We declare thee by this act set free from the danger of excommunication in which thou stoodest. [*He throws the paper down to the table.*]

JOAN. I thank you.

THE INQUISITOR. But because thou has sinned most presumptuously against God and the Holy Church, and that thou mayest repent thy errors in solitary contemplation, and be shielded from all temptation to return to them, we, for the good of thy soul, and for a penance that may wipe out thy sins and bring thee finally unspotted to the throne of grace, do condemn thee to eat the bread of sorrow and drink the water of affliction to the end of thy earthly days in perpetual imprisonment.

JOAN [*rising in consternation and terrible anger*]. Perpetual imprisonment! Am I not then to be set free?

LADVENU [*mildly shocked*]. Set free, child, after such wickedness as yours! What are you dreaming of?

JOAN. Give me that writing. [*She rushes to the table; snatches up the paper; and tears it into fragments.*] Light your fire: do you think I dread it as much as the life of a rat in a hole? My voices were right.

LADVENU. Joan! Joan!

JOAN. Yes: they told me you were fools [*the word gives great offence*], and that I was not to listen to your fine words nor trust to your charity. You promised me my life; but you lied [*indignant exclamations*]. You think that life is nothing but not being stone dead. It is not the bread and water I fear: I can live on bread: when have I asked for more? It is no hardship to drink water if the water be clean. Bread has no sorrow for me, and water no affliction. But to shut me from the light of the sky and the sight of the fields and flowers; to chain my feet so that I can never again ride with the soldiers nor climb the hills: to make me breathe foul damp darkness, and keep from me everything that brings me back to the love of God when your wickedness and foolishness tempt me to hate Him: all this is worse than the furnace in the Bible that was heated seven times. I could do without my warhorse; I could drag about in a skirt; I could let the banners and the trumpets and the knights and soldiers pass me and leave me behind as they leave the other women, if only I could still hear the wind in the trees, the larks in the sunshine, the young lambs crying through the healthy frost, and the blessed blessed church bells that send my angel voices floating to me on the wind. But without these things I cannot live; and by your wanting to take them away from me, or from any human creature, I know that your counsel is of the devil, and that mine is of God.

THE ASSESSORS [*in great commotion*]. Blasphemy! blasphemy! She is possessed. She said our counsel was of the devil. And hers of God. Monstrous! The devil is in our midst, etc., etc.

D'ESTIVET [*shouting above the din*]. She is a relapsed heretic, obstinate, incorrigible, and altogether unworthy of the mercy we have shewn her. I call for her excommunication.

THE CHAPLAIN [*to the Executioner*]. Light your fire, man. To the stake with her.

The Executioner and his assistants hurry out through the courtyard.

LADVENU. You wicked girl: if your counsel were of God would He not deliver you?

JOAN. His ways are not your ways. He wills that I go through the fire to His bosom; for I am His child, and you are not fit that I should live among you. That is my last word to you.

The soldiers seize her.

CAUCHON [*rising*]. Not yet.

They wait. There is a dead silence. Cauchon turns to the Inquisitor with an inquiring look. The Inquisitor nods affirmatively. They rise solemnly, and intone the sentence antiphonally.

CAUCHON. We decree that thou art a relapsed heretic.

THE INQUISITOR. Cast out from the unity of the Church.

CAUCHON. Sundered from her body.

THE INQUISITOR. Infected with the leprosy of heresy.

CAUCHON. A member of Satan.

THE INQUISITOR. We declare that thou must be excommunicate.

CAUCHON. And now we do cast thee out, segregate thee, and abandon thee to the secular power.

THE INQUISITOR. Admonishing the same secular power that it moderate its judgment of thee in respect of death and division of the limbs. [*He resumes his seat.*]

CAUCHON. And if any true sign of penitence appear in thee, to permit our Brother Martin to administer to thee the sacrament of penance.

THE CHAPLAIN. Into the fire with the witch [*he rushes at her, and helps the soldiers to push her out*].

Joan is taken away through the courtyard. The assessors rise in disorder, and follow the soldiers, except Ladvenu, who has hidden his face in his hands.

CAUCHON [*rising again in the act of sitting down*]. No, no: this is irregular. The representative of the secular arm should be here to receive her from us.

THE INQUISITOR [*also on his feet again*]. That man is an incorrigible fool.

CAUCHON. Brother Martin: see that everything is done in order.

LADVENU. My place is at her side, my Lord. You must exercise your own authority. [*He hurries out.*]

CAUCHON. These English are impossible: they will thrust her straight into the fire. Look!

He points to the courtyard, in which the glow and flicker of fire can now be seen reddening the

May daylight. Only the Bishop and the Inquisitor are left in the court.

CAUCHON [*turning to go*]. We must stop that.

THE INQUISITOR [*calmly*]. Yes; but not too fast, my lord.

CAUCHON [*halting*]. But there is not a moment to lose.

THE INQUISITOR. We have proceeded in perfect order. If the English choose to put themselves in the wrong, it is not our business to put them in the right. A flaw in the procedure may be useful later on: one never knows. And the sooner it is over, the better for that poor girl.

CAUCHON [*relaxing*]. That is true. But I suppose we must see this dreadful thing through.

THE INQUISITOR. One gets used to it. Habit is everything. I am accustomed to the fire; it is soon over. But it is a terrible thing to see a young and innocent creature crushed between these mighty forces, the Church and the Law.

CAUCHON. You call her innocent!

THE INQUISITOR. Oh, quite innocent. What does she know of the Church and the Law? She did not understand a word we were saying. It is the ignorant who suffer. Come, or we shall be late for the end.

CAUCHON [*going with him*]. I shall not be sorry if we are: I am not so accustomed as you.

They are going out when Warwick comes in, meeting them.

WARWICK. Oh, I am intruding. I thought it was all over. [*He makes a feint of retiring.*]

CAUCHON. Do not go, my lord. It is all over.

THE INQUISITOR. The execution is not in our hands, my lord; but it is desirable that we should witness the end. So by your leave — [*He bows, and goes out through the courtyard.*]

CAUCHON. There is some doubt whether your people have observed the forms of law, my lord.

WARWICK. I am told that there is some doubt whether your authority runs in this city, my lord. It is not in your diocese. However, if you will answer for that I will answer for the rest.

CAUCHON. It is to God that we both must answer. Good morning, my lord.

WARWICK. My lord: good morning.

They look at one another for a moment with unconcealed hostility. Then Cauchon follows the Inquisitor out. Warwick looks round. Finding himself alone, he calls for attendance.

WARWICK. Hallo. Hallo: some attendance here! [*Silence.*] Hallo, there! [*Silence.*] Hallo! Brian, you young blackguard, where are you? [*Silence.*] Guard! [*Silence.*] They have all gone to see the burning: even that child.

The silence is broken by someone frantically howling and sobbing.

WARWICK. What in the devil's name — ?

The Chaplain staggers in from the courtyard like a demented creature, his face streaming with tears, making the piteous sounds that Warwick has heard. He stumbles to the prisoner's stool, and throws himself upon it with heartrending sobs.

WARWICK [*going to him and patting him on the shoulder*]. What is it, Master John? What is the matter?

THE CHAPLAIN [*clutching at his hand*]. My lord, my lord: for Christ's sake pray for my wretched guilty soul.

WARWICK [*soothing him*]. Yes, yes: of course I will. Calmly, gently —

THE CHAPLAIN [*blubbering miserably*]. I am not a bad man, my lord.

WARWICK. No, no: not at all.

THE CHAPLAIN. I meant no harm. I did not know what it would be like.

WARWICK [*hardening*]. Oh! You saw it, then?

THE CHAPLAIN. I did not know what I was doing. I am a hotheaded fool; and I shall be damned to all eternity for it.

WARWICK. Nonsense! Very distressing, no doubt; but it was not your doing.

THE CHAPLAIN [*lamentably*]. I let them do it. If I had known, I would have torn her from their hands. You dont know; you havn't seen: it is so easy to talk when you dont know. You madden yourself with words: you damn yourself because it feels grand to throw oil on the flaming hell of your own temper. But when it is brought home to you; when you see the thing you have done; when it is blinding your eyes, stifling your nostrils, tearing your heart, then — then — [*Falling on his knees*]. O God, take away this sight from me! O Christ, deliver me from this fire that is consuming me! She cried to Thee in the midst of it: Jesus! Jesus! Jesus! She is in Thy bosom; and I am in hell for evermore.

WARWICK [*summarily hauling him to his feet*]. Come come, man! you must pull yourself together. We shall have the whole town talking of this. [*He throws him not too gently into a chair at the table.*] If you have not the nerve to see these things, why do you not do as I do, and stay away?

THE CHAPLAIN [*bewildered and submissive*]. She asked for a cross. A soldier gave her two sticks tied together. Thank God he was an Englishman! I might have done it; but I did not: I am a coward, a mad dog, a fool. But he was an Englishman too.

WARWICK. The fool! they will burn him too if the priests get hold of him.

THE CHAPLAIN [*shaken with a convulsion*]. Some of the people laughed at her. They would have laughed at Christ. They were French people, my lord: I know they were French.

WARWICK. Hush! someone is coming. Control yourself.

Ladvenu comes back through the courtyard to Warwick's right hand, carrying a bishop's cross which he has taken from a church. He is very grave and composed.

WARWICK. I am informed that it is all over, Brother Martin.

LADVENU [*enigmatically*]. We do not know, my lord. It may have only just begun.

WARWICK. What does that mean, exactly?

LADVENU. I took this cross from the church for her that she might see it to the last: she had only two sticks that she put into her bosom. When the fire crept round us, and she saw that if I held the cross before her I should be burnt myself, she warned me to get down and save myself. My lord: a girl who could think of another's danger in such a moment was not inspired by the devil. When I had to snatch the cross from her sight, she looked up to heaven. And I do not believe that the heavens were empty. I firmly believe that her Saviour appeared to her then in His tenderest glory. She called to Him and died. This is not the end for her, but the beginning.

WARWICK. I am afraid it will have a bad effect on the people.

LADVENU. It had, my lord, on some of them. I heard laughter. Forgive me for saying that I hope and believe it was English laughter.

THE CHAPLAIN [*rising frantically*]. No: it was not. There was only one Englishman there that disgraced his country; and that was the mad dog, de Stogumber. [*He rushes wildly out, shrieking.*] Let them torture him. Let them burn him. I will go pray among her ashes. I am no better than Judas: I will hang myself.

WARWICK. Quick, Brother Martin: follow him: he will do himself some mischief. After him, quick.

Ladvenu hurries out, Warwick urging him. The Executioner comes in by the door behind the judges' chairs; and Warwick, returning, finds himself face to face with him.

WARWICK. Well, fellow: who are you?

THE EXECUTIONER [*with dignity*]. I am not addressed as fellow, my lord. I am the Master Executioner of Rouen: it is a highly skilled mystery. I am come to tell your lordship that your orders have been obeyed.

WARWICK. I crave your pardon, Master Executioner; and I will see that you lose nothing by having no relics to sell. I have your word, have I, that nothing remains, not a bone, not a nail, not a hair?

THE EXECUTIONER. Her heart would not burn, my lord; but everything that was left is at the bottom of the river. You have heard the last of her.

WARWICK [*with a wry smile, thinking of what Ladvenu said*]. The last of her? Hm! I wonder!

Epilogue

A restless fitfully windy night in June 1456, full of summer lightning after many days of heat. King Charles the Seventh of France, formerly Joan's Dauphin, now Charles the Victorious, aged 51, is in bed in one of his royal chateaux. The bed, raised on a dais of two steps, is towards the side of the room so as to avoid blocking a tall lancet window in the middle. Its canopy bears the royal arms in embroidery. Except for the canopy and the huge down pillows there is nothing to distinguish it from a broad settee with bed-clothes and a valance. Thus its occupant is in full view from the foot.

Charles is not asleep: he is reading in bed, or rather looking at the pictures in Fouquet's Boccaccio with his knees doubled up to make a reading-desk. Beside the bed on his left is a little table with a picture of the Virgin, lighted by candles of painted wax. The walls are hung from ceiling to floor with painted curtains which stir at times in the draughts. At first glance the prevailing yellow and red in these hanging pictures is somewhat flamelike when the folds breathe in the wind.

The door is on Charles's left, but in front of him close to the corner farthest from him. A large watchman's rattle, handsomely designed and gaily painted, is in the bed under his hand.

Charles turns a leaf. A distant clock strikes the half-hour softly. Charles shuts the book with a clap; throws it aside; snatches up the rattle; and whirls it energetically, making a deafening clatter. Ladvenu enters, 25 years older, strange and stark in bearing, and still carrying the cross from Rouen. Charles evidently does not expect him; for he springs out of bed on the farther side from the door.

CHARLES. Who are you? Where is my gentleman of the bedchamber? What do you want?

LADVENU [*solemnly*]. I bring you glad tidings of great joy. Rejoice, O king; for the taint is removed from your blood, and the stain from your crown. Justice, long delayed, is at last triumphant.

CHARLES. What are you talking about? Who are you?

LADVENU. I am Brother Martin.

CHARLES. And who, saving your reverence, may Brother Martin be?

LADVENU. I held this cross when The Maid perished in the fire. Twenty-five years have passed since then: nearly ten thousand days. And on every one of those days I have prayed to God to justify His daughter on earth as she is justified in heaven.

CHARLES [*reassured, sitting down on the foot of the bed*]. Oh, I remember now. I have heard of you. You have a bee in your bonnet about The Maid. Have you been at the inquiry?

LADVENU. I have given my testimony.

CHARLES. Is it over?

LADVENU. It is over.

CHARLES. Satisfactorily?

LADVENU. The ways of God are very strange.

CHARLES. How so?

LADVENU. At the trial which sent a saint to the stake as a heretic and a sorceress, the truth was told; the law was upheld; mercy was shewn beyond all custom; no wrong was done but the final and dreadful wrong of the lying sentence and the pitiless fire. At this inquiry from which I have just come, there was shameless perjury, courtly corruption, calumny of the dead who did their duty according to their lights, cowardly evasion of the issue, testimony made of idle tales that could not impose on a ploughboy. Yet out of this insult to justice, this defamation of the Church, this orgy of lying and foolishness, the truth is set in the noonday sun on the hilltop; the white robe of innocence is cleansed from the smirch of the burning faggots; the holy life is sanctified; the true heart that lived through the flame is consecrated; a great lie is silenced for ever; and a great wrong is set right before all men.

CHARLES. My friend: provided they can no longer say that I was crowned by a witch and a heretic, I shall not fuss about how the trick has been done. Joan would not have fussed about it if it came all right in the end: she was not that sort: I knew her. Is her rehabilitation complete? I made it pretty clear that there was to be no nonsense about it.

LADVENU. It is solemnly declared that her judges were full of corruption, cozenage, fraud, and malice. Four falsehoods.

CHARLES. Never mind the falsehoods: her judges are dead.

LADVENU. The sentence on her is broken, annulled, annihilated, set aside as non-existent, without value or effect.

CHARLES. Good. Nobody can challenge my consecration now, can they?

LADVENU. Not Charlemagne nor King David himself was more sacredly crowned.

CHARLES [*rising*]. Excellent. Think of what that means to me!

LADVENU. I think of what it means to her!

CHARLES. You cannot. None of us ever knew what anything meant to her. She was like nobody else; and she must take care of herself wherever she is; for *I* cannot take care of her; and neither can you, whatever you may think: you are not big enough. But I will tell you this about her. If you could bring her back to life, they would burn her again within six months, for all their present adoration of her. And you would hold up the cross, too, just the same. So [*crossing himself*] let her rest; and let you and I mind our own business, and not meddle with hers.

LADVENU. God forbid that I should have no share in her, nor she in me! [*He turns and strides out as he came, saying*] Henceforth my path will not lie through palaces, nor my conversation be with kings.

CHARLES [*following him towards the door, and shouting after him*]. Much good may it do you, holy man! [*He returns to the middle of the chamber, where he halts, and says quizzically to himself*] That was a funny chap. How did he get in? Where are my people? [*He goes impatiently to the bed, and swings the rattle. A rush of wind through the open door sets the walls swaying agitatedly. The candles go out. He calls in the darkness.*] Hallo! Someone come and shut the windows: everything is being blown all over the place. [*A flash of summer lightning shews up the lancet window. A figure is seen in silhouette against it.*] Who is there? Who is that? Help! Murder! [*Thunder. He jumps into bed, and hides under the clothes.*]

JOAN'S VOICE. Easy, Charlie, easy. What art making all that noise for? No one can hear thee. Thourt asleep. [*She is dimly seen in a pallid greenish light by the bedside.*]

CHARLES [*peeping out*]. Joan! Are you a ghost, Joan?

JOAN. Hardly even that, lad. Can a poor burnt-up lass have a ghost? I am but a dream that thourt dreaming. [*The light increases: they become plainly visible as he sits up.*] Thou looks older, lad.

CHARLES. I am older. Am I really asleep?

JOAN. Fallen asleep over thy silly book.

CHARLES. That's funny.

JOAN. Not so funny as that I am dead, is it?

CHARLES. Are you really dead?

JOAN. As dead as anybody ever is, laddie. I am out of the body.

CHARLES. Just fancy! Did it hurt much?

JOAN. Did what hurt much?

CHARLES. Being burnt.

JOAN. Oh, that! I cannot remember very well. I think it did at first; but then it all got mixed up; and I was not in my right mind until I was free of the body. But do not thou go handling fire and thinking it will not hurt thee. How hast been ever since?

CHARLES. Oh, not so bad. Do you know, I actually

lead my army out and win battles? Down into the moat up to my waist in mud and blood. Up the ladders with the stones and hot pitch raining down. Like you.

JOAN. No! Did I make a man of thee after all, Charlie?

CHARLES. I am Charles the Victorious now. I had to be brave because you were. Agnes put a little pluck into me too.

JOAN. Agnes! Who was Agnes?

CHARLES. Agnes Sorel. A woman I fell in love with. I dream of her often. I never dreamed of you before.

JOAN. Is she dead, like me?

CHARLES. Yes. But she was not like you. She was very beautiful.

JOAN [laughing heartily]. Ha ha! I was no beauty: I was always a rough one: a regular soldier. I might almost as well have been a man. Pity I wasnt: I should not have bothered you all so much then. But my head was in the skies; and the glory of God was upon me; and, man or woman, I should have bothered you as long as your noses were in the mud. Now tell me what has happened since you wise men knew no better than to make a heap of cinders of me?

CHARLES. Your mother and brothers have sued the courts to have your case tried over again. And the courts have declared that your judges were full of corruption and cozenage, fraud and malice.

JOAN. Not they. They were as honest a lot of poor fools as ever burned their betters.

CHARLES. The sentence on you is broken, annihilated, annulled: null, non-existent, without value or effect.

JOAN. I was burned, all the same. Can they unburn me?

CHARLES. If they could, they would think twice before they did it. But they have decreed that a beautiful cross be placed where the stake stood, for your perpetual memory and for your salvation.

JOAN. It is the memory and the salvation that sanctify the cross, not the cross that sanctifies the memory and the salvation. [She turns away, forgetting him.] I shall outlast that cross. I shall be remembered when men will have forgotten where Rouen stood.

CHARLES. There you go with your self-conceit, the same as ever! I think you might say a word of thanks to me for having had justice done at last.

CAUCHON [appearing at the window between them]. Liar!

CHARLES. Thank you.

JOAN. Why, if it isnt Peter Cauchon! How are you, Peter? What luck have you had since you burned me?

CAUCHON. None. I arraign the justice of Man. It is not the justice of God.

JOAN. Still dreaming of justice, Peter? See what justice came to with me! But what has happened to thee? Art dead or alive?

CAUCHON. Dead. Dishonored. They pursued me beyond the grave. They excommunicated my dead body: they dug it up and flung it into the common sewer.

JOAN. Your dead body did not feel the spade and the sewer as my live body felt the fire.

CAUCHON. But this thing that they have done against me hurts justice; destroys faith; saps the foundation of the Church. The solid earth sways like the treacherous sea beneath the feet of men and spirits alike when the innocent are slain in the name of law, and their wrongs are undone by slandering the pure of heart.

JOAN. Well, well, Peter, I hope men will be the better for remembering me; and they would not remember me so well if you had not burned me.

CAUCHON. They will be the worse for remembering me: they will see in me evil triumphing over good, falsehood over truth, cruelty over mercy, hell over heaven. Their courage will rise as they think of you, only to faint as they think of me. Yet God is my witness I was just: I was merciful: I was faithful to my light: I could do no other than I did.

CHARLES [scrambling out of the sheets and enthroning himself on the side of the bed]. Yes: it is always you good men that do the big mischiefs. Look at me! I am not Charles the Good, nor Charles the Wise, nor Charles the Bold. Joan's worshippers may even call me Charles the Coward because I did not pull her out of the fire. But I have done less harm than any of you. You people with your heads in the sky spend all your time trying to turn the world upside down; but I take the world as it is, and say that top-side-up is right-side-up; and I keep my nose pretty close to the ground. And I ask you, what king of France has done better, or been a better fellow in his little way?

JOAN. Art really king of France, Charlie? Be the English gone?

DUNOIS [coming through the tapestry on Joan's left, the candles relighting themselves at the same moment, and illuminating his armor and surcoat cheerfully]. I have kept my word: the English are gone.

JOAN. Praised be God! now is fair France a province in heaven. Tell me all about the fighting, Jack. Was it thou that led them? Wert thou God's captain to thy death?

DUNOIS. I am not dead. My body is very comfortably asleep in my bed at Chateaudun; but my spirit is called here by yours.

JOAN. And you fought them my way, Jack: eh? Not the old way, chaffering for ransoms; but The Maid's way: staking life against death, with the heart high and humble and void of malice, and nothing counting under God but France free and French. Was it my way, Jack?

DUNOIS. Faith, it was any way that would win. But the way that won was always your way. I give you best, lassie. I wrote a fine letter to set you right at the new trial. Perhaps I should never have let the priests burn you; but I was busy fighting; and it was the Church's business, not mine. There was no use in both of us being burned, was there?

CAUCHON. Ay! put the blame on the priests. But I, who am beyond praise and blame, tell you that the world is saved neither by its priests nor its soldiers, but by God and His Saints. The Church Militant sent this woman to the fire; but even as she burned, the flames whitened into the radiance of the Church Triumphant.

The clock strikes the third quarter. A rough male voice is heard trolling an improvised tune.

Rum tum trumpledum,
Bacon fat and rumpledum,
Old Saint mumpledum,
Pull his tail and stumpledum
O my Ma—ry Ann!

A ruffianly English soldier comes through the curtains and marches between Dunois and Joan.

DUNOIS. What villainous troubadour taught you that doggrel?

THE SOLDIER. No troubadour. We made it up ourselves as we marched. We were not gentlefolks and troubadours. Music straight out of the heart of the people, as you might say. Rum tum trumpledum, Bacon fat and rumpledum, Old Saint mumpledum, Pull his tail and stumpledum: that dont mean anything, you know; but it keeps you marching. Your servant, ladies and gentlemen. Who asked for a saint?

JOAN. Be you a saint?

THE SOLDIER. Yes, lady, straight from hell.

DUNOIS. A saint, and from hell!

THE SOLDIER. Yes, noble captain: I have a day off. Every year, you know. Thats my allowance for my one good action.

CAUCHON. Wretch! In all the years of your life did you do only one good action?

THE SOLDIER. I never thought about it: it came natural like. But they scored it up for me.

CHARLES. What was it?

THE SOLDIER. Why, the silliest thing you ever heard of. I —

JOAN [*interrupting him by strolling across to the bed, where she sits besides Charles*]. He tied two sticks together, and gave them to a poor lass that was going to be burned.

THE SOLDIER. Right. Who told you that?

JOAN. Never mind. Would you know her if you saw her again?

THE SOLDIER. Not I. There are so many girls! and they all expect you to remember them as if there was only one in the world. This one must have been a prime sort; for I have a day off every year for her; and so, until twelve o'clock punctually, I am a saint, at your service, noble lords and lovely ladies.

CHARLES. And after twelve?

THE SOLDIER. After twelve, back to the only place fit for the likes of me.

JOAN [*rising*]. Back there! You! that gave the lass the cross!

THE SOLDIER [*excusing his unsoldierly conduct*]. Well, she asked for it; and they were going to burn her. She had as good a right to a cross as they had; and they had dozens of them. It was her funeral, not theirs. Where was the harm in it?

JOAN. Man: I am not reproaching you. But I cannot bear to think of you in torment.

THE SOLDIER [*cheerfully*]. No great torment, lady. You see I was used to worse.

CHARLES. What! worse than hell?

THE SOLDIER. Fifteen years' service in the French wars. Hell was a treat after that.

Joan throws up her arms, and takes refuge from despair of humanity before the picture of the Virgin.

THE SOLDIER [*continuing*] — Suits me somehow. The day off was dull at first, like a wet Sunday. I don't mind it so much now. They tell me I can have as many as I like as soon as I want them.

CHARLES. What is hell like?

THE SOLDIER. You wont find it so bad, sir. Jolly. Like as if you were always drunk without the trouble and expense of drinking. Tip top company too: emperors and popes and kings and all sorts. They chip me about giving that young judy the cross; but I dont care: I stand up to them proper, and tell them that if she hadn't a better right to it than they, she'd be where they are. That dumfounds them, that does. All they can do is gnash their teeth, hell fashion; and I just laugh, and go off singing the old chanty: Rum tum trumple — Hullo! Who's that knocking at the door?

They listen. A long gentle knocking is heard.

CHARLES. Come in.

The door opens; and an old priest, white-haired, bent, with a silly but benevolent smile, comes in and trots over to Joan.

THE NEWCOMER. Excuse me, gentle lords and ladies. Do not let me disturb you. Only a poor old harmless English rector. Formerly chaplain to the cardinal: to my lord of Winchester. John de Stogumber, at your service. [*He looks at them inquiringly.*] Did you say anything? I am a little deaf, unfortunately. Also a little — well, not always in my right mind, perhaps; but still, it is a small village with a few simple people. I suffice: I suffice: they love me there; and I am able to do a little good. I am well connected, you see; and they indulge me.

JOAN. Poor old John! What brought thee to this state?

DE STOGUMBER. I tell my folks they must be very careful. I say to them, 'If you only saw what you think about you would think quite differently about it. It would give you a great shock. Oh, a great shock.' And they all say 'Yes, parson: we all know you are a kind man, and would not harm a fly.' That is a great comfort to me. For I am not cruel by nature, you know.

THE SOLDIER. Who said you were?

DE STOGUMBER. Well, you see, I did a very cruel thing once because I did not know what cruelty was like. I had not seen it, you know. That is the great thing: you must see it. And then you are redeemed and saved.

CAUCHON. Were not the sufferings of our Lord Christ enough for you?

DE STOGUMBER. No. Oh no: not at all. I had seen them in pictures, and read of them in books, and been greatly moved by them, as I thought. But it was no use: it was not our Lord that redeemed me, but a young woman whom I saw actually burned to death. It was dreadful: oh, most dreadful. But it saved me. I have been a different man ever since, though a little astray in my wits sometimes.

CAUCHON. Must then a Christ perish in torment in every age to save those that have no imagination?

JOAN. Well, if I saved all those he would have been cruel to if he had not been cruel to me, I was not burnt for nothing, was I?

DE STOGUMBER. Oh no; it was not you. My sight is bad: I cannot distinguish your features: but you are not she: oh no: she was burned to a cinder: dead and gone, dead and gone.

THE EXECUTIONER [*stepping from behind the bed curtains on Charles's right, the bed being between them*]. She is more alive than you, old man. Her heart would not burn; and it would not drown. I was a master at my craft: better than the master

of Paris, better than the master of Toulouse; but I could not kill The Maid. She is up and alive everywhere.

THE EARL OF WARWICK [*sallying from the bedcurtains on the other side, and coming to Joan's left hand*]. Madam: my congratulations on your rehabilitation. I feel that I owe you an apology.

JOAN. Oh, please dont mention it.

WARWICK [*pleasantly*]. The burning was purely political. There was no personal feeling against you, I assure you.

JOAN. I bear no malice, my lord.

WARWICK. Just so. Very kind of you to meet me in that way: a touch of true breeding. But I must insist on apologizing very amply. The truth is, these political necessities sometimes turn out to be political mistakes; and this one was a veritable howler; for your spirit conquered us, madam, in spite of our faggots. History will remember me for your sake, though the incidents of the connection were perhaps a little unfortunate.

JOAN. Ay, perhaps just a little, you funny man.

WARWICK. Still, when they make you a saint, you will owe your halo to me, just as this lucky monarch owes his crown to you.

JOAN [*turning from him*]. I shall owe nothing to any man: I owe everything to the spirit of God that was within me. But fancy me a saint! What would St. Catherine and St. Margaret say if the farm girl was cocked up beside them!

A clerical-looking gentleman in black frockcoat and trousers, and tall hat, in the fashion of the year 1920, suddenly appears before them in the corner on their right. They all stare at him. Then they burst into uncontrollable laughter.

THE GENTLEMAN. Why this mirth, gentlemen?

WARWICK. I congratulate you on having invented a most extraordinarily comic dress.

THE GENTLEMAN. I do not understand. You are all in fancy dress: I am properly dressed.

DUNOIS. All dress is fancy dress, is it not, except our natural skins?

THE GENTLEMAN. Pardon me: I am here on serious business, and cannot engage in frivolous discussions. [*He takes out a paper, and assumes a dry official manner.*] I am sent to announce to you that Joan of Arc, formerly known as The Maid, having been the subject of an inquiry instituted by the Bishop of Orleans.

JOAN [*interrupting*]. Ah! They remember me still in Orleans.

THE GENTLEMAN [*emphatically, to mark his indignation at the interruption*] — by the Bishop of Orleans into the claim of the said Joan of Arc to be canonized as a saint —

JOAN [*again interrupting*]. But I never made any such claim.

THE GENTLEMAN [as before] — the Church has examined the claim exhaustively in the usual course, and, having admitted the said Joan successively to the ranks of Venerable and Blessed, —

JOAN [chuckling]. Me venerable!

THE GENTLEMAN. — has finally declared her to have been endowed with heroic virtues and favored with private revelations, and calls the said Venerable and Blessed Joan to the communion of the Church Triumphant as Saint Joan.

JOAN [rapt]. Saint Joan!

THE GENTLEMAN. On every thirtieth day of May, being the anniversary of the death of the said most blessed daughter of God, there shall in every Catholic church to the end of time be celebrated a special office in commemoration of her; and it shall be lawful to dedicate a special chapel to her, and to place her image on its altar in every such church. And it shall be lawful and laudable for the faithful to kneel and address their prayers through her to the Mercy Seat.

JOAN. Oh no. It is for the saint to kneel. [She falls on her knees, still rapt.]

THE GENTLEMAN [putting up his paper, and retiring beside the Executioner]. In Basilica Vaticana, the sixteenth day of May, nineteen hundred and twenty.

DUNOIS [raising Joan]. Half an hour to burn you, dear Saint, and four centuries to find out the truth about you!

DE STOGUMBER. Sir: I was chaplain to the Cardinal of Winchester once. They always would call him the Cardinal of England. It would be a great comfort to me and to my master to see a fair statue to The Maid in Winchester Cathedral. Will they put one there, do you think?

THE GENTLEMAN. As the building is temporarily in the hands of the Anglican heresy, I cannot answer for that.

A vision of the statue in Winchester Cathedral is seen through the window.

DE STOGUMBER. Oh look! look! that is Winchester.

JOAN. Is that meant to be me? I was stiffer on my feet.

The vision fades.

THE GENTLEMAN. I have been requested by the temporal authorities of France to mention that the multiplication of public statutes to The Maid threatens to become an obstruction to traffic. I do so as a matter of courtesy to the said authorities, but must point out on behalf of the Church that The Maid's horse is no greater obstruction to traffic than any other horse.

JOAN. Eh! I am glad they have not forgotten my horse.

A vision of the statue before Rheims Cathedral appears.

JOAN. Is that funny little thing me too?

CHARLES. That is Rheims Cathedral where you had me crowned. It must be you.

JOAN. Who has broken my sword? My sword was never broken. It is the sword of France.

DUNOIS. Never mind. Swords can be mended. Your soul is unbroken; and you are the soul of France.

The vision fades. The Archbishop and the Inquisitor are now seen on the right and left of Cauchon.

JOAN. My sword shall conquer yet: the sword that never struck a blow. Though men destroyed my body, yet in my soul I have seen God.

CAUCHON [kneeling to her]. The girls in the field praise thee; for thou hast raised their eyes; and they see that there is nothing between them and heaven.

DUNOIS [kneeling to her]. The dying soldiers praise thee, because thou art a shield of glory between them and the judgment.

THE ARCHBISHOP [kneeling to her]. The princes of the Church praise thee, because thou hast redeemed the faith their worldlinesses have dragged through the mire.

WARWICK [kneeling to her]. The cunning counsellors praise thee, because thou hast cut the knots in which they have tied their own souls.

DE STOGUMBER [kneeling to her]. The foolish old men on their deathbeds praise thee, because their sins against thee are turned into blessings.

THE INQUISITOR [kneeling to her]. The judges in the blindness and bondage of the law praise thee, because thou hast vindicated the vision and the freedom of the living soul.

THE SOLDIER [kneeling to her]. The wicked out of hell praise thee, because thou hast shewn them that the fire that is not quenched is a holy fire.

THE EXECUTIONER [kneeling to her]. The tormentors and executioners praise thee, because thou hast shewn that their hands are guiltless of the death of the soul.

CHARLES [kneeling to her]. The unpretending praise thee, because thou hast taken upon thyself the heroic burdens that are too heavy for them.

JOAN. Woe unto me when all men praise me! I bid you remember that I am a saint, and that saints can work miracles. And now tell me: shall I rise from the dead, and come back to you a living woman?

A sudden darkness blots out the walls of the room as they all spring to their feet in consternation. Only the figures and the bed remain visible.

JOAN. What! Must I burn again? Are none of you ready to receive me?

CAUCHON. The heretic is always better dead. And

mortal eyes cannot distinguish the saint from the heretic. Spare them. [*He goes out as he came.*]

DUNOIS. Forgive us, Joan: we are not yet good enough for you. I shall go back to my bed. [*He also goes.*]

WARWICK. We sincerely regret our little mistake; but political necessities, though occasionally erroneous, are still imperative; so if you will be good enough to excuse me — [*He steals discreetly away.*]

THE ARCHBISHOP. Your return would not make me the man you once thought me. The utmost I can say is that though I dare not bless you, I hope I may one day enter into your blessedness. Meanwhile, however — [*He goes.*]

THE INQUISITOR. I who am of the dead, testified that day that you were innocent. But I do not see how The Inquisition could possibly be dispensed with under existing circumstances. Therefore — [*He goes.*]

DE STOGUMBER. Oh, do not come back: you must not come back. I must die in peace. Give us peace in our time, O Lord! [*He goes.*]

THE GENTLEMAN. The possibility of your resurrection was not contemplated in the recent proceedings for your canonization. I must return to Rome for fresh instructions. [*He bows formally, and withdraws.*]

THE EXECUTIONER. As a master in my profession I have to consider its interests. And, after all, my first duty is to my wife and children. I must have time to think over this. [*He goes.*]

CHARLES. Poor old Joan! They have all run away from you except this blackguard who has to go back to hell at twelve o'clock. And what can I do but follow Jack Dunois' example, and go back to bed too? [*He does so.*]

JOAN [*sadly*]. Goodnight, Charlie.

CHARLES [*mumbling in his pillows*]. Goo ni. [*He sleeps. The darkness envelops the bed.*]

JOAN [*to the soldier*]. And you, my one faithful? What comfort have you for Saint Joan?

THE SOLDIER. Well, what do they all amount to, these kings and captains and bishops and lawyers and such like? They just leave you in the ditch to bleed to death; and the next thing is, you meet them down there, for all the airs they give themselves. What I say is, you have as good a right to your notions as they have to theirs, and perhaps better. [*Settling himself for a lecture on the subject*]. You see, it's like this. If — [*The first stroke of midnight is heard softly from a distant bell.*] Excuse me: a pressing appointment — [*He goes on tiptoe.*]

The last remaining rays of light gather into a white radiance descending on Joan. The hour continues to strike.

JOAN. O God that madest this beautiful earth, when will it be ready to receive Thy saints? How long, O Lord, how long?

ALBERT J. GUERARD, *Editor*

Joseph Conrad

1857–1924

The twentieth-century novel has explored so many themes and has tried so many experiments that it is impossible to single out one writer as fully representative. Yet Joseph Conrad (publishing his first work in 1895, writing until his death in 1924, and very widely admired today) is surely the most important British figure to carry over from the nineteenth century to the twentieth. (Henry James [1843–1916] was a very great novelist and perhaps the first critic to think systematically and at length about the novel form. But he still seems, in spite of his belated British citizenship, more American than British.) James Joyce (1882–1941) and perhaps Virginia Woolf (1882–1941) were more experimental than Conrad. And there are doubtless many who prefer to Conrad's the work of D. H. Lawrence (1885–1930) and E. M. Forster (1879–) — the one very passionate in his view of life, the other very quiet and civilized. In the history of the novel the massive realistic novels of depressed and depressing lives of Arnold Bennett (1867–1931) are doubtless important. But all in all Conrad appears to offer the best introduction to the serious and innovating novel of our own time. And *Heart of Darkness,* though one of his shorter works, is fully representative of his dark preoccupations and restless genius and very rich art.

CONRAD'S LIFE

Joseph Conrad (Jósef Teodor Konrad Korzeniowski) was born in Russian-occupied Poland in 1857, the son of a Polish patriot and intellectual. He set foot on English soil for the first time when he was twenty, a young seaman knowing only a few words of the language. Yet eighteen years later, while still expecting to continue his career at sea, he published an intricate first novel, *Almayer's Folly.* There followed nearly thirty years of novel-writing. He died in Canterbury, England, in 1924, a few months after having declined a knighthood, having become more British than the British. Conrad's life consists of two desperate adventures successfully achieved. For one event is almost as astounding as the other: that the son of a Polish writer should become a master mariner in the British merchant marine; and that a sea captain should, at almost forty, become a novelist in a foreign language. A few years before this the journey to the Congo (on which *Heart of Darkness* is based) was the realization of a childhood dream. As a child in Poland Conrad had " put his finger on a spot in the very middle of the then white " (unexplored) heart of Africa on a map, and said he would someday go there.

Much of Conrad's later life and brooding temperament seems to be in response to the tragic events and gloomy atmospheres of his childhood. He had seen his father imprisoned for conspiracy against the Russians and had accompanied his parents in their exile to Vologda, in Russia, with its nine-and-a-half-month white winter. Both parents contracted tuberculosis. His mother died when he was seven; his father when he was eleven. In the years between these deaths, Conrad recalled, he lived in an atmosphere of " piety, resignation and silence."

The yearning of the sixteen-year-old boy to leave Poland, and to escape into another life, seems understandable enough, though it was much criticized by his friends. The departure from Poland at sixteen, for adventure in Marseilles and on the high seas; the definitive abandonment of the sea at forty-two (in fact his last berth was four years before this) — these are the two great " jumps " in a life which, Conrad insisted, had its continuity, fidelity, coherence. It is evident he always felt uneasy about the accusation that he had betrayed Poland, first by leaving her as a boy, finally by achieving fame as a writer in a foreign language. Perhaps he also felt uneasy because his own austere political conservatism seemed such a reversal of his father's liberalism.

The adventure begun when he left Poland at sixteen took him very far — possibly to gunrunning in the Caribbean and on the Mediterranean, and for a few days to South America; possibly to an affair with a woman who had been mistress of a " king "; possibly to a duel or attempted suicide; certainly to voyages in the Far East and some exposure to the atmosphere of Malayan intrigue; at least to hard-won, brief, and unspectacular success as an officer in the merchant marine. The word " possibly " must be used because Conrad himself has characteristically thrown a thick screen of words around the events of those earlier years. He tried — through *The Mirror of the Sea* and the novel *The Arrow of Gold,* and also through things said to friends — to convey a consistent story of what happened after he took up, still in his teens, with a group of romantic young Royalists in Marseilles. He would have us believe that he was one of the owners of a small ship named the *Tremolino* that smuggled messages and arms to Spain on behalf of Don Carlos, Pretender to the Spanish throne; that he had a brief affair with a onetime mistress of Don Carlos ("Rita de Laostola "); that he had been wounded near the heart in a duel with an American adventurer named J. M. K. Blunt, jealous of his success with Doña Rita. But the more scholars do research on these years, the darker their mystery becomes. It is at least possible, for instance, that the wound near his heart came not from a duel but from suicide attempted after gambling losses in Monte Carlo. We can only say that much possibly calculated ambiguity remains, almost a century after these events. This fact is itself of great interest in a novelist who so brilliantly dramatized concealment and evasion, and whose own temperamental evasiveness is reflected in the complicated structures of some of his novels. In *Heart of Darkness,* for instance, the narrator puts off almost intolerably our first direct meeting with Kurtz.

Conrad's later years are less ambiguous — his first sailing on a British ship in 1878, his voyage on the ill-fated *Palestine* (whose many misfortunes and ultimate sinking are dramatized in the short novel *Youth*); his first berth as officer on the clipper *Loch Etive,* his position as second mate on the *Narcissus,* his winning of a master's certificate, his voyages on the *Vidar* in the Malay Archipelago, his first and last wholly independent command (of the tiny *Otago*) in 1888, his temporary command of the steamer *Roi des Belges* on the Congo in 1890. There were other ships (nearly all sailing ships, not steamers) and other ports. But the first long-delayed and extremely difficult voyage on the barque *Otago* from Bangkok to Singapore, with a cholera- and dysentery-weakened crew, was the one that left its imprint on Conrad's work. The experience, as he reconstructed it in the imagination, became a crucial one of self-testing and of spiritual crisis. It also became associated, in his fiction, with two famous crimes at sea. This difficult voyage is reflected in certain pages of *Lord Jim* and of *Falk,* and above all in two fine short novels, *The Secret Sharer* and *The Shadow-Line.*

Like most human beings (but rather more than most) Joseph Conrad was a deeply divided man — divided between love of freedom and respect for authority; between sympathy for the outlaw, the rebel, the individualist and commitment to law and tradition; between dreaming and action; between a rich imaginative life and a severe distrust of the imagination. So too, of course, his life was more divided than most, between the years of wandering and adventure and, after 1894, his years as a married and sedentary writer who found the task of novel-writing nerve-wracking and monumentally difficult. Conrad came to know some of the most famous writers of his day, but his outward life in England was uneventful, and was much disturbed by sickness. At first he made very little money from his writing, though he won the respect of critics. Then in the last ten years, exhausted and now producing inferior books, he won both great renown and financial success. But the history of Conrad's life that matters, after 1895, is simply the history of his books.

CONRAD AND THE NOVEL

Writing his first great books just before the turn of the century, Conrad speaks to us with one of the first truly modern voices in the novel. He points the way to such recent masters as William Faulkner, William Styron, Malcolm Lowry, Lawrence Durrell and Graham Greene. The major nineteenth-century novelists, as we look back, fall into several distinct groups. One of these is composed of the enormously gifted, wildly abundant, often reckless creators of life — Scott, Dickens, Balzac, Tolstoy, Dostoevsky, Zola. Of these, all but Scott and Tolstoy displayed marked eccentricities of temperament and produced splendidly comic or grotesque distortions of reality. For many, this is their chief appeal today. Three highly personal, introspective novelists — Melville, Hawthorne, and Emily Brontë — might form another group, with their dark brooding pessimism and fierce intensities, and their innovating techniques. A third group, less in fashion today, would comprise the social realists who recorded as faithfully as possible the manners and morals of their time: Jane Austen, George Eliot, Anthony Trollope, Thackeray, William Dean Howells, Turgenev, Flaubert. Their methods were often realistic, painstaking, methodical; the author's temperamental bias and eccentricities were held in check. There are others more difficult to classify: Mark Twain, for instance. But none of these writers achieves Conrad's very particular blend of tragic seriousness and exciting narrative, of meditation and action, of public, even political subject and private dream. Conrad is one of the most personal of English novelists, and one of the first to think of the novel as a rigorous, challenging fine art.

Today it is common enough to see the novel as an art form, a form as demanding as poetry or painting or music. But this had not been true in the past. There had been good novelists of manly adventure, such as the Captain Marryat (*Mr. Midshipman Easy*) Conrad so much admired. And there had been at least Gustave Flaubert and Henry James to conceive of the novel as both a high art and a vehicle for subtle psychological insight. Stendhal early in the nineteenth century, Hardy and Robert Louis Stevenson near its end, combined dramatic (even melodramatic) plot and seriousness of theme. But Conrad moves further than anyone in this direction. He explores his glamorous settings and the exciting events of his stories through the medium of complex new novelistic techniques, with a deeply probing meditative interest in psychological and moral crisis, and with, for the English novel at least, an exceptional concern for form and style. He saw his work as engaged in a deeply personal communication with his readers, as appealing above all to their temperament, and as making this appeal through style. "And it is only through complete, unswerving devotion to the perfect blending of form and substance; it is only through an unremitting never-discouraged care for the shape and ring of sentences that an approach can be made to plasticity, to color; and the light of magic suggestiveness may be brought to play for an evanescent instant over the commonplace surface of words: of the old old words, worn thin, defaced by ages of careless usage."[1]

Some of Conrad's innovations in the novel may be subsumed under the highly flexible word *impressionism* — a word that has been applied, in fact, to a large number of very different novelists. Conradian impressionism implies a desire to convey to the reader not a logically ordered, chronological, straightforward, impersonal picture of life, but instead the shifting impressions life makes on a sensitive observer or narrator. Meeting someone for the first time, we may first of all be struck by an odd physical trait or trick of speech even before we have caught the stranger's name. And in the next hours or days, listening perhaps to rumors about him, we may leap to various conclusions (some of them false) long before we discover where this new friend was born, who his parents were, where he went to school, etc. Conrad (and his friend Ford Madox Ford) thus tried through fictional method to capture some of the fluid, often deceptive or misguided, always personal processes of responding to reality — to other

---

[1] From Conrad's Preface to *The Nigger of the "Narcissus."*

people, to one's self, to the events we observe. For the sake of this lifelike fluidity (and to escape the old artificial structuring of the novel) Conrad regularly dislocated chronology, teased the reader with long digressions, and conveyed much of what he had to say through the often fallible consciousness of a narrator. Sometimes he puzzles the reader with unexplained allusions and hazy information. For life, Conrad would say, is "like that" — puzzling, teasing, ambiguous. And, in real life, our attention very often focuses on some unimportant visual detail, while it shuns or ignores the obvious.

The changing responses of Marlow to Kurtz, in *Heart of Darkness*, and the way in which this short novel builds in the reader its impression of Kurtz and Marlow and Africa itself, offer a pure example of the impressionist method. Subtract the intimately personal responses of Marlow to what is happening, and you would have a totally different, far less interesting, story. A conventional novel might tell us rather obviously whether we should sympathize with Kurtz or condemn him utterly. But *Heart of Darkness* evokes instead, in Marlow and in the reader, a complex interplay of sympathy (which is a matter of emotional attachment, of identification) and judgment (which is an act of rational moral choice). This is one of the great enriching things we learn from nearly all of Conrad's novels: that life is not simple but complex in its demands and choices; that it is possible at the same time to sympathize with the outlaw and to condemn him; that we can feel disgust for a good man we morally approve of; further, that this same double pull of sympathy and judgment may exist with regard to the outlaw within, the insubordinate lover of freedom that exists secretly in one's self.

Conrad's first impressionist novels — *Almayer's Folly* (1895) and *An Outcast of the Islands* (1896) — were based on his Malayan voyages in 1887. They are stories of white men menaced or deteriorating as a result of involvement with native political intrigue. *Heart of Darkness* (1899), though based on Conrad's Congo experience of 1890, has a number of the same interests; the Bornean and the African jungles seem menacing in much the same way. A voyage on a sailing ship named the *Narcissus* (which Conrad chose to sail on because of her beauty) led to the short novel *The Nigger of the "Narcissus"* (1897). It is one of the greatest of all narratives of the sea, a loving testimony to a ship's and a crew's endurance under the stress of a terrible storm. But it is also a symbolic story of the human pilgrimage through life, and of the way egoism and cowardice in one man may bring out egoism and cowardice in a group. This is one of Conrad's particular strengths: that his stories take on symbolic overtones — take on, that is, larger meanings than the literal — while remaining unspoiled, enthralling records of real substantial life. The beautiful white female ship *Narcissus* is truly symbolic, yet no ship could be more solid and real. The same blend of real experience and symbolic enrichment, of outward physical adventure and inward psychological drama, is remarkably achieved in the long story *The Secret Sharer* (1910). The fugitive Leggatt who takes refuge on board the narrator-captain's ship is a real flesh and blood human being who has killed a rebellious member of his crew. But Leggatt is also the captain's double, someone with whom he must incorrigibly sympathize, a projection or embodiment of his own outlaw impulses and his own longing to go free. The lover of sea stories will also want to read *Typhoon* (1902) and *The Shadow-Line* (1917).

Lord Jim (1900) is the first of the great long impressionist novels, with Marlow once again both character and observer, actor and narrator. As he had felt a divided allegiance to Kurtz, so now he experiences a divided allegiance toward Jim, a younger man who has committed, though unintentionally, a crime. The novel dramatizes the very common human longing to be judged by intentions rather than by acts, and the equally common longing for a second chance. Many critics consider *Lord Jim* Conrad's greatest novel. Others prefer the long, wise, panoramic novel of South American politics, *Nostromo* (1904) — at once a remarkably vivid evocation of an imagined community and country, and a profound meditation on politics and history. As individual acts sometimes escape or transcend or fail to live up to our intentions, so too history may seem to be inconsecutive and absurd, a play of blind or blundering forces. Conrad wrote two more fine novels combining psychological and political interests. The exciting *The Secret Agent* (1907) deals with the moral squalor of revolutionists and counter-revolutionists, of anarchists and police alike, in the gloomy damp murk of late-nineteenth-century London. It is one of the first novels to treat seriously the world of spy and counterspy, and is thus a forerunner of Graham Greene's *The Confidential Agent* and Le Carré's *The Spy Who Came In from the Cold. Under Western Eyes* (1911) turns to the Russia of the Czars, and to the Geneva of the revolutionary exiles from Russia. Like *Lord Jim, Under Western Eyes* submits its protagonist to the most intense of psychological and moral conflicts, confronts him with the most difficult of "boundary choices." In this novel we see an interesting struggle between Conrad's intellectual distaste for the Russians (a distaste inevitable in a patriotic Pole of that time) and his novelistic sympathy for them. Conrad said he hated Dostoevsky, but in *Under Western Eyes* he wrote the most Dostoevskyan of English novels.

For many years Conrad struggled with sickness, nervous anxiety, debt. Like many other novelists, he first achieved popularity with a relatively inferior book. *Chance* (1912) is technically interesting, but distinctly less mature than *Lord Jim* or *Under Western Eyes. Victory* (1915), though also lacking some of the earlier Conradian richness and subtlety, is a highly readable novel of adventure and romance on a lonely island invaded by three particularly sadistic criminals. Conrad's last novels — *The Arrow of Gold* (1920), *The Rover* (1923), the long-delayed *The Rescue* (1919, begun 1895), the uncompleted *Suspense* (1925) — show many signs of physical fatigue and exhausted imagination. Yet even from these tired books there now and then shines forth an interesting conception, a vividly realized moment of life, a glowing resonant phrase. Like many older men, Conrad (who always talked with a thick accent) began to lose his touch with the idiom of his acquired language. But at his best, in earlier years, he was, of English novelists, one of the greatest masters of style.

Conrad's reputation, based solidly on the earlier novels, is today higher than it has ever been. He stands with the great subjective novelists who were also rich creators of a world — Dostoevsky and Faulkner, most notably — as an important moment in our modern consciousness. This is not to say that his work has no limitations. His is a man's world, and most of his

women are relatively uninteresting. Moreover he usually lacks a comic gift, though he has an ironic appreciation of the absurd, and though *The Secret Agent* is bitter sardonic comedy of a kind. He can overwrite: can fall into the lush grandiloquent verbiage he himself called "Conradese." Some of the adjectival vagueness of *Heart of Darkness* ("unspeakable," "intolerable," etc.) is necessary. But much of it could be dispensed with, and the story is certainly too long. Conrad's merits, however, far outweigh these limitations. He is unequaled as a writer of the sea and of life at sea and unequaled too as a writer of the jungle, giving symbolic meaning to jungle darkness and to wild tumescent growth. He is a novelist of profound psychological intuitions, dramatizing the eternal conflict between man's good intentions and his vagrant impulses, between the conscious will and the unconscious drive. He dramatized, before most psychologists discovered them, the processes of identification, and of unconscious or half-conscious sympathy. His world is nevertheless — for all its psychological bent — an intensely moral world, grounded on a respect for both society and the individual, and for the ancient virtues of fidelity and truth. There is scarcely a subject, scarcely an event that Conrad cannot, through the imagination, magnify and make more meaningful. But one of the strongest grounds for his appeal lies in something more elusive. This is that his novels, however public their themes or exotic their settings, speak to readers intimately. They seem to invade our lives. For this reason Conrad (who may seem difficult at first) will on a fifth or sixth reading of a story continue to communicate with us very personally. We become more and more attuned to his rich diction, his unusual syntax and his sinuous elaborate rhythms, which are among the loveliest in English prose.

"HEART OF DARKNESS"

Heart of Darkness (1899) is a major work of symbolist fiction — of fiction, that is, with larger and further meanings than appear on its surface or at a first reading. This quality of larger meaning, this power to suggest more than is actually said about human life, is found in a number of great narratives since earliest times. Recent critics, trying to account for the strong impact of *Heart of Darkness*, have referred to the Garden of Eden, to Dante's Inferno, to the Hades of Virgil, to the quest of the Holy Grail, to Jonah's sojourn in the belly of the whale, to the ideal of Buddhahood, and, more modernly, to the *id* (or savage unmoral life drive) described by the psychologist Freud. All of this is highly interesting and at least some of it is truly pertinent. But it ignores *Heart of Darkness*'s first and most obvious appeal. This is that it is a fine visual and atmospheric rendering of Conrad's own voyage up the Congo in 1890, when he too was in charge of a ship named the *Roi des Belges*, and went to Stanley Falls to pick up a company agent named not Kurtz but Georges Antoine Klein. We are dealing with a real ship on a real river, where on " silvery sandbanks hippos and alligators sunned themselves side by side." In this sentence we are very close to an essential Conrad. He remembers and records what he saw on the Congo, hippos and alligators among other things, but also he is trying for loveliness of rhythm and phrase, the loveliness achieved partly through alliteration: " On silvery sandbanks hippos and alligators sunned themselves side by side."

Conrad was concerned of course with the real historical fact and political horror of Belgian exploitation and enslavement of natives: " the vilest scramble for loot that ever disfigured the history of human conscience and geographical exploration." He wanted to get these things on the record. It might be natural to assume that Conrad with his brooding, pessimistic temperament had made the exploitation seem worse than it was. But there is much evidence that things were actually worse than Conrad painted them. Conrad kept a diary of his own march overland and he there speaks of a skeleton tied to a post, seen on July 29, 1890. But he does not use this macabre detail in his novelette. As for the reality, here is Richard Harding Davis, speaking of 1904, after fourteen more years of progress:

In the opinion of the State the soldiers, in killing game for food, wasted the State cartridges, and in consequence the soldiers, to show their officers that they did not expend the cartridges extravagantly on antelope and wild boar, for each empty cartridge brought in a human hand, the hand of a man, woman or child. These hands, drying in the sun, could be seen at the posts along the river. They

are no longer in evidence. Neither is the flower-bed of Lieutenant Dom, which was bordered with human skulls. A quaint conceit.

The man to blame for the atrocities, for each separate atrocity, is Leopold.

But here is Leopold himself, King of the colonizing Belgians, sounding very much like the pamphlet of Kurtz:

Our refined society attaches to human life (and with reason) a value unknown to barbarous communities. When our directing will is implanted among them its aim is to triumph over all obstacles, and results which would not be attained by lengthy speeches may follow philanthropic influence. But if, in view of this desirable spread of civilization, we count upon the means of action which confer upon us dominion and the sanction of right, it is not the less true that our ultimate end is a work of peace.[1]

So we must first read *Heart of Darkness* as a great rendering of one man's experience, and of a particular place and particular time: a moment (which extends almost to the present) in the history of imperialism. As then, so now men in search of power or security, and nations too, pretend that their real purposes are peace, progress, and freedom. And they end by deluding not only others but also themselves. This is the truth dramatized by Kurtz and his pamphlet — the seventeen pages of benevolent rhetoric, of self-intoxicating prose. Kurtz meant those glowing phrases when he wrote them. The more he wrote, the more he believed. He could make himself believe anything. But at last he cut through to a deeper sincerity when he scrawled the postscript: *"Exterminate all the brutes!"*

Africa then, and a moment in the history of modern imperialism, and a commentary on man's infinite power to deceive himself as well as others. Obviously one " subject " of *Heart of Darkness* is the man Kurtz — this trader in ivory who in the utter solitude of the Inner Station, away from white men and policemen and neighbors, begins to use " unsound methods." The onetime benevolent idealist gets ivory through terrorism, and decorates the stakes around his house with human heads. He has become one of the " devils " of the land, literally an evil divinity, worshipped in fit ceremonies.

[1] Both of these passages are cited in Robert Kimbrough's critical edition of *Heart of Darkness* (New York, 1963).

When Marlow arrives to rescue him, to take him back to civilization, he does not want to be rescued. It is interesting to note that when the journalist Henry Stanley's relief expedition found Emin Pasha, in 1889, he too did not want to be rescued. In *Heart of Darkness* as in his Malayan novels Conrad is concerned with the white man who traffics with natives, becomes a leader of natives, and is tempted to revert to barbarism.

Marlow refers to Kurtz as the "nightmare of my choice." This means that he takes Kurtz's side (even after he has discovered his criminality) against that of the flabby, demoralized, mean company employees of the Central Station. To explain this we may refer to another novel of Conrad's, *Under Western Eyes*. There a character remarks that there are those who burn and those who rot, and that it is sometimes preferable to burn than to rot. Kurtz is among those who burn. In his mad ambitions and intense desires, in his consciousness that there is such a thing as evil, such a thing as "the horror" (his dying words and last judgment on his own life), he belongs to the moral universe. The others, morally, are nothing. This is not to say that active crime is preferable to indifference and inertia, but that the story of a Kurtz can "matter" to other human beings, to us as readers, because it involves intense and genuine issues of good and evil. Conversely, the ordinary untempted socially useful man is likely, in fiction, to arouse very little interest.

In himself, Kurtz seems to represent two familiar conceptions of moral evil. The first is evil as savage, primitive energy, the evil of pure aggression and malevolent force, a sheer love of destruction. This is the Kurtz of the "unspeakable lusts" and the terrible unspecified desires. The second is the religious conception of evil as vacancy, as hollowness, as that moral emptiness which means a total absence of God. Kurtz is a "hollow man," lacking the inward moral force to resist his own barbaric impulses. We should further note — speaking now in psychological rather than moral terms — that Kurtz is immobilized. He cannot tear himself away from the Inner Station, and offers a striking image of physical and spiritual paralysis.

But if *Heart of Darkness* is about Africa, and Belgian exploitation, and Kurtz, it is also — quite as importantly, though a little less obviously —

about Marlow himself, the teller of the tale. It is he who appears, after all, on every page while Kurtz appears on only a few. Marlow is the narrator of the story but also its chief actor and it is chiefly his spiritual crisis we are watching. For Marlow's voyage to the Inner Station, his journey from Brussels and back to Brussels, his journey to and *through* the meeting with Kurtz, is also an introspective "voyage of the soul" — like Jonah's voyage, like Dante's, like the Ancient Mariner's, like Captain Ahab's in *Moby Dick*. Conrad said of his own journey in 1890: "Before the Congo I was a mere animal." The experience there had changed him into a more mature human being. And so for Marlow. The Inner Station, he tells us, is the "culminating point of my experience." He too goes back to Europe with his attitude toward life darkened, with an intensified pessimism . . . but also with a new maturity and a valuable self-knowledge.

The actual meeting with Kurtz is the climax, for Marlow, of what some anthropologists and critics call the *night journey*. In the night journey a physical adventure — to cut oneself off from familiar surroundings and companions in order to explore the unknown — may in reality dramatize or symbolize an introspective plunge, a journey into one's deepest self and most primitive recesses of being. The meeting with Kurtz suggests a culminating moment of introspection and spiritual crisis; and Marlow literally wrestles with the crazed and dying man as one might wrestle for the saving of his own soul. Marlow dimly recognizes in Kurtz a facet of himself, and a potentiality for barbarism. We may say — again to use the language of psychology and advertising — that Marlow identifies with Kurtz. Consider how closely Marlow connects Kurtz's dying with his own sickness: "And it is not my own extremity I remember best — a vision of grayness without form filled with physical pain, and a careless contempt for the evanescence of all things — even of this pain itself. No! It is his extremity I seem to have lived through." Given this close identification, it is tempting but unwise to try to pinpoint Kurtz's significance. At most we may suggest, very generally, that he is the risk-taker, the outlaw, the insubordinate lawless unsocial self. But he also represents the immobilization, the apathy and spiritual paralysis, that Conrad dreaded. Finally, whatever we say about Kurtz's significance, we must not for a moment forget his gaunt bony physical presence, must not forget that he is flesh-and-blood.

Most readers find *Heart of Darkness* — though overlong and at times excessively vague — a masterpiece of vivid impressionist rendering and a remarkable achievement of dark brooding atmosphere and sinister tone. *We are taken there* — both to the actual Congo and its savage darkness, and to Marlow's discovery that man's own dark potentialities are timeless and universal. The structure and method of the story carefully prepare the reader for this central meaning, and both imagery and incantatory style persuade him to accept it. On the Thames, on board this cruising yawl and among prosperous complacent men, Marlow suddenly remarks that "this also has been one of the dark places of the earth." And he talks about the very old times, about the Romans on the Thames who would have felt that utter savagery had closed around them. Evoking the loneliness, the solitude, and the temptations of the Romans, Marlow foreshadows the challenge of the Congo. He suggests that human nature is always the same, and that man is always imperiled when cut off from familiar surroundings and familiar restraints.

Heart of Darkness is full of such foreshadowings and connections; they prepare us to respond more fully to the later events. There is an insistence, for instance, on deathly immobilization in grass. The story flashes ahead very early to the death of one of Marlow's predecessors, Fresleven: "the grass growing through his ribs was tall enough to hide his bones." But grass also sprouts between the stones of Brussels, that city of a "whited sepulcher." Thus these images, and the ironic reference to Fresleven as a "supernatural being," prepare us not only for the story's concern with death but for the deification of Kurtz. It is significant that the critical struggle with Kurtz, after he has escaped from the ship, occurs on a trail through the grass.

These then are some of the ways *Heart of Darkness* achieves both unity and meaning: through the reiteration of key words (most of all the words *dark, darkness*), the repeated return to certain images or associations (such as *death–grass*), the sudden juxtaposition of vivid particulars and large abstractions. But the over-all movement of the narrative (its hesitations, its tendency to advance and withdraw, its evasiveness and love of digression) also reflects the nature of Marlow's experience — and, incidentally, of Conrad's temperament. Marlow wants us, of course, to live through his own sense of the experience as dreamlike. "It seems to me I am trying to tell you a dream — making a vain attempt, because no relation of a dream can convey the dream-sensation, the commingling of absurdity, surprise, and bewilderment in a tremor of struggling revolt." We feel, too, that Marlow simply cannot tell this story straightforwardly; that he must subject us to his own experience of repeated penetration and withdrawal. Again and again the story flashes ahead to reveal in a sudden clear light some event to be dramatized much later; and then at once returns to the present. We can think of the story as advancing and withdrawing as "in a succession of long dark waves borne by an incoming tide. The waves encroach on the shore fairly evenly, and presently a few more feet of sand have been won. But an occasional wave thrusts up unexpectedly, much farther than the others: even as far, say, as Kurtz and his Inner Station." [1] But when the time comes for an actual meeting with Kurtz, then the narrative is almost intolerably delayed. What is the intention of so much evasion and delay, so much teasing, unless it is to make the reader live through ambiguity? Perhaps also "to throw over him a brooding gloom, such a warm pall as those Two Fates in the home office might knit, back in the sepulchral city." [2]

Such seems the essential movement of *Heart of Darkness*: penetration and withdrawal. But we may also say that it traces a "large grand circle of awareness. It begins with the friends on the yacht under the dark above Gravesend and at last returns to them," [3] to the tranquil waterway that "leading to the uttermost ends of the earth flowed sombre under an overcast sky — seemed to lead into the heart of an immense darkness."

[1] Quoted from Albert J. Guerard, *Conrad the Novelist* (Harvard University Press, 1958).
[2] Ibid.
[3] Ibid.

Heart of Darkness

I

The *Nellie,* a cruising yawl, swung to her anchor without a flutter of the sails, and was at rest. The flood had made, the wind was nearly calm, and being bound down the river, the only thing for it was to come to and wait for the turn of the tide.

The sea-reach of the Thames stretched before us like the beginning of an interminable waterway. In the offing the sea and the sky were welded together without a joint, and in the luminous space the tanned sails of the barges drifting up with the tide seemed to stand still in red clusters of canvas sharply peaked, with gleams of varnished sprits. A haze rested on the low shores that ran out to sea in vanishing flatness. The air was dark above Gravesend, and farther back still seemed condensed into a mournful gloom, brooding motionless over the biggest, and the greatest, town on earth.

The Director of Companies was our captain and our host. We four affectionately watched his back as he stood in the bows looking to seaward. On the whole river there was nothing that looked half so nautical. He resembled a pilot, which to a seaman is trustworthiness personified. It was difficult to realise his work was not out there in the luminous estuary, but behind him, within the brooding gloom.

Between us there was, as I have already said somewhere, the bond of the sea. Besides holding our hearts together through long periods of separation, it had the effect of making us tolerant of each other's yarns — and even convictions. The Lawyer — the best of old fellows — had, because of his many years and many virtues, the only cushion on deck, and was lying on the only rug. The Accountant had brought out already a box of dominoes, and was toying architecturally with the bones. Marlow sat cross-legged right aft, leaning against the mizzenmast. He had sunken cheeks, a yellow complexion, a straight back, an ascetic aspect, and, with his arms dropped, the palms of hands outwards, resembled an idol. The Director, satisfied the anchor had good hold, made his way aft and sat down amongst us. We exchanged a few words lazily. Afterwards there was silence on board the yacht. For some reason or other we did not begin that game of dominoes. We felt meditative, and fit for nothing but placid staring. The day was ending in a serenity of still and exquisite brilliance. The water shone pacifically; the sky, without a speck, was a benign immensity of unstained light; the very mist on the Essex marshes was like a gauzy and radiant fabric, hung from the wooded rises inland, and draping the low shores in diaphanous folds. Only the gloom to the west, brooding over the upper reaches, became more sombre every minute, as if angered by the approach of the sun.

And at last, in its curved and imperceptible fall, the sun sank low, and from glowing white changed to a dull red without rays and without heat, as if about to go out suddenly, stricken to death by the touch of that gloom brooding over a crowd of men.

Forthwith a change came over the waters, and the serenity became less brilliant but more profound. The old river in its broad reach rested unruffled at the decline of day, after ages of good service done to the race that peopled its banks, spread out in the tranquil dignity of a waterway leading to the uttermost ends of the earth. We looked at the venerable stream not in the vivid flush of a short day that comes and departs for ever, but in the august light of abiding memories. And indeed nothing is easier for a man who has, as the phrase goes, " followed the sea " with reverence and affection, than to evoke the great spirit of the past upon the lower reaches of the Thames. The tidal current runs to and fro in its unceasing service, crowded with memories of men and ships it has borne to the rest of home or to the battles of the sea. It had known and served all the men of whom the nation is proud, from Sir Francis Drake to Sir John Franklin, knights all, titled and untitled — the great knights-errant of the sea. It had borne all the ships whose names are like jewels flashing in the night of time, from the *Golden Hind* returning with her round flanks full of treasure, to be visited by the Queen's Highness and thus pass out of the gigantic tale, to the *Erebus* and *Terror*, bound on other conquests — and that never returned. It had known the ships and the men. They had sailed from Deptford, from Greenwich, from Erith — the adventurers and the settlers; kings' ships and the ships of men on 'Change; captains, admirals, the dark "interlopers" of the Eastern trade, and the commissioned "generals" of East India fleets. Hunters for gold or pursuers of fame, they all had gone out on that stream, bearing the sword, and often the torch, messengers of the might within the land, bearers of a spark from the sacred fire. What greatness had not floated on the ebb of that river into the mystery of an unknown earth! . . . The dreams of men, the seed of commonwealths, the germs of empires.

The sun set; the dusk fell on the stream, and lights began to appear along the shore. The Chapman lighthouse, a three-legged thing erect on a mud-flat, shone strongly. Lights of ships moved in the fairway — a great stir of lights going up and going down. And farther west on the upper reaches the place of the monstrous town was still marked ominously on the sky, a brooding gloom in sunshine, a lurid glare under the stars.

"And this also," said Marlow suddenly, "has been one of the dark places of the earth."

He was the only man of us who still "followed the sea." The worst that could be said of him was that he did not represent his class. He was a seaman, but he was a wanderer too, while most seamen lead, if one may so express it, a sedentary life. Their minds are of the stay-at-home order, and their home is always with them — the ship; and so is their country — the sea. One ship is very much like another, and the sea is always the same. In the immutability of their surroundings the foreign shores, the foreign faces, the changing immensity of life, glide past, veiled not by a sense of mystery but by a slightly disdainful ignorance; for there is nothing mysterious to a seaman unless it be the sea itself, which is the mistress of his existence and as inscrutable as Destiny. For the rest, after his hours of work, a casual stroll or a casual spree on shore suffices to unfold for him the secret of a whole continent, and generally he finds the secret not worth knowing. The yarns of seamen have a direct simplicity, the whole meaning of which lies within the shell of a cracked nut. But Marlow was not typical (if his propensity to spin yarns be expected), and to him the meaning of an episode was not inside like a kernel but outside, enveloping the tale which brought it out only as a glow brings out a haze, in the likeness of one of these misty halos that sometimes are made visible by the spectral illumination of moonshine.

His remark did not seem at all surprising. It was just like Marlow. It was accepted in silence. No one took the trouble to grunt even; and presently he said, very slow:

"I was thinking of very old times, when the Romans first came here, nineteen hundred years ago — the other day. . . . Light came out of this river since — you say Knights? Yes; but it is like a running blaze on a plain, like a flash of lightning in the clouds. We live in the flicker — may it last as long as the old earth keeps rolling! But darkness was here yesterday. Imagine the feelings of a commander of a fine — what d'ye call 'em? — trireme in the Mediterranean, ordered suddenly to the north; run overland across the Gauls in a hurry; put in charge of one of these craft the legionaries — a wonderful lot of handy men they must have been too — used to build, apparently by the hundred, in a month or two, if we may believe what we read. Imagine him here — the very end of the world, a sea the colour of lead, a sky the colour of smoke, a kind of ship about as rigid as a concertina — and going up this river with stores, or orders, or what you like. Sandbanks, marshes, forests, savages — precious little to eat fit for a civilised man, nothing but Thames water to drink. No Falernian wine here, no going ashore. Here and there a military camp lost in a wilderness, like a needle in a bundle of hay — cold, fog, tempests, disease, exile, and death — death skulking in the air, in the water, in the bush. They must have been dying like flies here. Oh yes — he did it. Did it very well, too, no doubt, and without thinking much about it either, except afterwards to brag of what he had gone through in his time, perhaps. They were men enough to face the darkness. And perhaps he was cheered by keeping his eye on a chance of promotion to the fleet at Ravenna by and by, if he had good friends in Rome and survived the awful climate. Or think of a decent young citizen in a toga — perhaps too much dice, you know — coming out here in the train of some prefect, or tax-gatherer, or trader, even, to mend his fortunes. Land in a swamp, march through the woods, and in some inland post feel the savagery, the utter savagery, had closed round him — all that mysterious life of the wilderness that stirs in the forest, in the jungles, in the hearts of wild men. There's no initiation either into such mysteries. He has to live in the midst of the incomprehensible, which is also detestable. And it has a fascination, too, that goes to work upon him. The fascination of the abomination — you know. Imagine the growing regrets, the longing to escape, the powerless digust, the surrender, the hate."

He paused.

"Mind," he began again, lifting one arm from the elbow, the palm of the hand outwards, so that, with his legs folded before him, he had the pose of a Buddha preaching in European clothes and without a lotus-flower — "Mind, none of us would feel exactly like this. What saves us is efficiency — the devotion to efficiency. But these chaps were not much account, really. They were no colonists; their administration was merely a squeeze, and nothing more, I suspect. They were conquerors, and for that you want only brute force — nothing to boast of, when you have it, since your strength is just an accident arising from the weakness of others. They grabbed what they could get for the sake of what was to be got. It was just robbery with violence, aggravated murder on a great scale, and men going at it blind — as is very proper for those who tackle a darkness. The conquest of the earth, which mostly means the taking it away from those who have a different complexion or slightly flatter noses than ourselves, is not a pretty thing when you look into it too much. What redeems it is the idea only. An idea at the back of it; not a sentimental pretence but an idea; and an unselfish belief in the idea — something you can set up, and bow down before, and offer a sacrifice to. . . ."

He broke off. Flames glided in the river, small green flames, red flames, white flames, pursuing, overtaking, joining, crossing each other — then separating slowly or hastily. The traffic of the great city went on in the deepening night upon the sleepless river. We looked on, waiting patiently — there was nothing else to do till the end of the flood; but it was only after a long silence, when he said, in a hesitating voice, "I suppose you fellows remember I did once turn fresh-water sailor for a bit," that we knew we were fated, before the ebb began to run, to hear about one of Marlow's inconclusive experiences.

"I don't want to bother you much with what happened to me personally," be began, showing in this remark the weakness of many tellers of tales who seem so often unaware of what their audience would best like to hear; "yet to understand the effect of it on me you ought to know how I got out there, what I saw, how I went up that river to the

place where I first met the poor chap. It was the farthest point of navigation and the culminating point of my experience. It seemed somehow to throw a kind of light on everything about me — and into my thoughts. It was sombre enough too — and pitiful — not extraordinary in any way — not very clear either. No, not very clear. And yet it seemed to throw a kind of light.

"I had then, as you remember, just returned to London after a lot of Indian Ocean, Pacific, China Seas — a regular dose of the East — six years or so, and I was loafing about, hindering you fellows in your work and invading your homes, just as though I had got a heavenly mission to civilise you. It was very fine for a time, but after a bit I did get tired of resting. Then I began to look for a ship — I should think the hardest work on earth. But the ships wouldn't even look at me. And I got tired of that game too.

"Now when I was a little chap I had a passion for maps. I would look for hours at South America, or Africa, or Australia, and lose myself in all the glories of exploration. At that time there were many blank spaces on the earth, and when I saw one that looked particularly inviting on a map (but they all look that) I would put my finger on it and say, When I grow up I will go there. The North Pole was one of these places, I remember. Well, I haven't been there yet, and shall not try now. The glamour's off. Other places were scattered about the Equator, and in every sort of latitude all over the two hemispheres. I have been in some of them, and . . . well, we won't talk about that. But there was one yet — the biggest, the most blank, so to speak — that I had a hankering after.

"True, by this time it was not a blank space any more. It had got filled since my boyhood with rivers and lakes and names. It had ceased to be a blank space of delightful mystery — a white patch for a boy to dream gloriously over. It had become a place of darkness. But there was in it one river especially, a mighty big river, that you could see on the map, resembling an immense snake uncoiled, with its head in the sea, its body at rest curving afar over a vast country, and its tail lost in the depths of the land. And as I looked at the map of it in a shop-window, it fascinated me as a snake would a bird — a silly little bird. Then I remembered there was a big concern, a Company for trade on that river. Dash it all! I thought to myself, they can't trade without using some kind of craft on that lot of fresh water — steamboats! Why shouldn't I try to get charge of one? I went on along Fleet Street, but could not shake off the idea. The snake had charmed me.

"You understand it was a Continental concern, that Trading Society; but I have a lot of relations living on the Continent, because it's cheap and not so nasty as it looks, they say.

"I am sorry to own I began to worry them. This was already a fresh departure for me. I was not used to get things that way, you know. I always went my own road and on my own legs where I had a mind to go. I wouldn't have believed it of myself; but, then — you see — I felt somehow I must get there by hook or by crook. So I worried them. The men said, 'My dear fellow,' and did nothing. Then — would you believe it? — I tried the women. I, Charlie Marlow, set the women to work — to get a job. Heavens! Well, you see, the notion drove me. I had an aunt, a dear enthusiastic soul. She wrote: 'It will be delightful. I am ready to do anything, anything for you. It is a glorious idea. I know the wife of a very high personage in the Administration, and also a man who has lots of influence with,' etc. etc. She was determined to make no end of fuss to get me appointed skipper of a river steamboat, if such was my fancy.

"I got my appointment — of course; and I got it very quick. It appears the Company had received news that one of their captains had been killed in a scuffle with the natives. This was my chance, and it made me the more anxious to go. It was only months and months afterwards, when I made the attempt to recover what was left of the body, that I heard the original quarrel arose from a misunderstanding about some hens. Yes, two black hens. Fresleven — that was the fellow's name, a Dane — thought himself wronged somehow in the bargain, so he went ashore and started to hammer the chief of the village with a stick. Oh, it didn't surprise me in the least to hear this, and at the same time to be told that Fresleven was the gentlest, quietest creature that ever walked on two legs. No doubt he was; but he had been a couple of years already out there engaged in the noble cause, you know, and he probably felt the need at last of asserting his self-respect in some way. Therefore he whacked the old nigger mercilessly, while a big crowd of his people watched him, thunderstruck, till some man — I was told the chief's son — in desperation at hearing the old chap yell, made a tentative jab with a spear at the white man — and of course it went quite easy between the shoulder-blades. Then the whole population cleared into the forest, expecting all kinds of calamities to happen, while, on the other hand, the steamer Fresleven commanded left also in a bad panic, in charge of the engineer, I believe. Afterwards nobody seemed to trouble much about Fresleven's remains, till I got out and stepped into his shoes. I couldn't let it rest, though; but when an opportunity offered at last to meet my predecessor, the grass growing through his ribs was tall enough to hide his bones. They were all there. The supernatural being had not been touched after he fell. And the village was deserted, the huts gaped black, rotting, all askew within the fallen enclosures. A calamity had come to it, sure enough. The people had vanished. Mad terror had scattered them, men, women, and children, through the bush, and they had never returned. What became of the hens I don't know either. I should think the cause of progress got them, anyhow. However, through this glorious affair I got my appointment, before I had fairly begun to hope for it.

"I flew around like mad to get ready, and before forty-eight hours I was crossing the Channel to show myself to my employers, and sign the contract. In a very few hours I arrived in a city that always makes me think of a whited sepulchre. Prejudice no doubt. I had no difficulty in finding the Company's offices. It was the biggest thing in the town, and everybody I met was full of it. They were going to run an oversea empire, and make no end of coin by trade.

"A narrow and deserted street in deep shadow, high houses, innumerable windows with venetian blinds, a dead silence, grass sprouting between the stones, imposing carriage archways right and left, immense double doors standing ponderously ajar. I slipped through one of these cracks, went up a swept and ungarnished staircase, as arid as a desert, and opened the first door I came to. Two women, one fat and the other slim, sat on straw-bottomed chairs, knitting black wool. The slim one got up and walked straight at me — still knitting with downcast eyes — and only just as I began to think of getting out of her way, as you would for a somnambulist, stood still, and looked up. Her dress was as plain as an umbrella-cover, and she turned round without a word and preceded me into a waiting-room. I gave my name, and looked about. Deal table in the middle, plain chairs all round the walls, on one end a large shining map, marked with all the colours of a rainbow. There was a vast amount of red — good to see at any time, because one knows that some real work is done in there, a deuce of a lot of blue, a little green, smears of orange, and, on the East Coast, a purple patch, to show where the jolly pioneers of progress drink the jolly lager-beer. However, I wasn't going into any of these. I was going into the yellow. Dead in the centre. And the river was there — fascinating — deadly — like a snake. Ough! A door opened, a white-haired secretarial head, but wearing a compassionate expression, appeared, and a skinny forefinger beckoned me into the sanctuary. Its light was dim, and a heavy writing-desk squatted in the middle. From behind that structure came out an impression of pale plumpness in a frock-coat. The great man himself. He was five feet six, I should judge, and had his grip on the handle-end of ever so many millions. He shook hands, I fancy, murmured vaguely, was satisfied with my French. *Bon voyage.*

"In about forty-five seconds I found myself again in the waiting-room with the compassionate secretary, who, full of desolation and sympathy, made me sign some document. I believe I undertook amongst other things not to disclose any trade secrets. Well, I am not going to.

"I began to feel slightly uneasy. You know I am not used to such ceremonies, and there was something ominous in the atmosphere. It was just as though I had been let into some conspiracy — I don't know — something not quite right; and I was glad to get out. In the outer room the two women knitted black wool feverishly. People were arriving, and the younger one was walking back and forth introducing them. The old one sat on her chair. Her flat cloth slippers were propped up on a foot-warmer, and a cat reposed on her lap. She wore a starched white affair on her head, had a wart on one cheek, and silver-rimmed spectacles hung on the tip of her nose. She glanced at me above the glasses. The swift and indifferent placidity of that look troubled me. Two youths with foolish and cheery countenances were being piloted over, and she threw at them the same quick glance of unconcerned wisdom. She seemed to know all about them and about me too. An eerie feeling came over me. She seemed uncanny and fateful. Often far away there I thought of these two, guarding the door of Darkness, knitting black wool as for a warm pall, one introducing, introducing continuously to the unknown, the other scrutinising

the cheery and foolish faces with unconcerned old eyes. *Ave!* Old knitter of black wool. *Morituri te salutant.* Not many of those she looked at ever saw her again — not half, by a long way.

"There was yet a visit to the doctor. 'A simple formality,' assured me the secretary, with an air of taking an immense part in all my sorrows. Accordingly a young chap wearing his hat over the left eyebrow, some clerk I suppose — there must have been clerks in the business, though the house was as still as a house in a city of the dead — came from somewhere upstairs, and led me forth. He was shabby and careless, with ink-stains on the sleeves of his jacket, and his cravat was large and billowy, under a chin shaped like the toe of an old boot. It was a little too early for the doctor, so I proposed a drink, and thereupon he developed a vein of joviality. As we sat over our vermuths he glorified the Company's business, and by and by I expressed casually my surprise at him not going out there. He became very cool and collected all at once. 'I am not such a fool as I look, quoth Plato to his disciples,' he said sententiously, emptied his glass with great resolution, and we rose.

"The old doctor felt my pulse, evidently thinking of something else the while. 'Good, good for there,' he mumbled, and then with a certain eagerness asked me whether I would let him measure my head. Rather surprised, I said Yes, when he produced a thing like callipers and got the dimensions back and front and every way, taking notes carefully. He was an unshaven little man in a threadbare coat like a gaberdine, with his feet in slippers, and I thought him a harmless fool. 'I always ask leave, in the interests of science, to measure the crania of those going out there,' he said. 'And when they come back too?' I asked. 'Oh, I never see them,' he remarked; 'and, moreover, the changes take place inside, you know.' He smiled, as if at some quiet joke. 'So you are going out there. Famous. Interesting too.' He gave me a searching glance, and made another note. 'Ever any madness in your family?' he asked, in a matter-of-fact tone. I felt very annoyed. 'Is that question in the interests of science too?' 'It would be,' he said, without taking notice of my irritation, 'interesting for science to watch the mental changes of individuals, on the spot, but . . .' 'Are you an alienist?' I interrupted. 'Every doctor should be — a little,' answered that original imperturbably. 'I have a little theory which you Messieurs who go out there must help me to prove.

This is my share in the advantages my country shall reap from the possession of such a magnificent dependency. The mere wealth I leave to others. Pardon my questions, but you are the first Englishman coming under my observation . . .' I hastened to assure him I was not in the least typical. 'If I were,' said I, 'I wouldn't be talking like this with you.' 'What you say is rather profound, and probably erroneous,' he said, with a laugh. 'Avoid irritation more than exposure to the sun. Adieu. How do you English say, eh? Good-bye. Ah! Good-bye. Adieu. In the tropics one must before everything keep calm.' . . . He lifted a warning forefinger. . . . 'Du calme, du calme. Adieu.'

" One thing more remained to do — say good-bye to my excellent aunt. I found her triumphant. I had a cup of tea — the last decent cup of tea for many days — and in a room that most soothingly looked just as you would expect a lady's drawing-room to look, we had a long quiet chat by the fireside. In the course of these confidences it became quite plain to me I had been represented to the wife of the high dignitary, and goodness knows to how many more people besides, as an exceptional and gifted creature — a piece of good fortune for the Company — a man you don't get hold of every day. Good heavens! and I was going to take charge of a two-penny-halfpenny river-steamboat with a penny whistle attached! It appeared, however, I was also one of the Workers, with a capital — you know. Something like an emissary of light, something like a lower sort of apostle. There had been a lot of such rot let loose in print and talk just about that time, and the excellent woman, living right in the rush of all that humbug, got carried off her feet. She talked about 'weaning those ignorant millions from their horrid ways,' till, upon my word, she made me quite uncomfortable. I ventured to hint that the Company was run for profit.

" ' You forget, dear Charlie, that the labourer is worthy of his hire,' she said brightly. It's queer how out of touch with truth women are. They live in a world of their own, and there had never been anything like it, and never can be. It is too beautiful altogether, and if they were to set it up it would go to pieces before the first sunset. Some confounded fact we men have been living contentedly with ever since the day of creation would start up and knock the whole thing over.

" After this I got embraced, told to wear flannel, be sure to write often, and so on — and I left. In the street — I don't know why — a queer feeling came to me that I was an impostor. Odd thing that I, who used to clear out for any part of the world at twenty-four hours' notice, with less thought than most men give to the crossing of a street, had a moment — I won't say of hesitation, but of startled pause, before this commonplace affair. The best way I can explain it to you is by saying that, for a second or two, I felt as though, instead of going to the centre of a continent, I were about to set off for the centre of the earth.

" I left in a French steamer, and she called in every blamed port they have out there, for, as far as I could see, the sole purpose of landing soldiers and custom-house officers. I watched the coast. Watching a coast as it slips by the ship is like thinking about an enigma. There it is before you — smiling, frowning, inviting, grand, mean, insipid, or savage, and always mute with an air of whispering, Come and find out. This one was almost featureless, as if still in the making, with an aspect of monotonous grimness. The edge of a colossal jungle, so dark green as to be almost black, fringed with white surf, ran straight, like a ruled line, far, far away along a blue sea whose glitter was blurred by a creeping mist. The sun was fierce, the land seemed to glisten and drip with steam. Here and there greyish-whitish specks showed up clustered inside the white surf, with a flag flying above them perhaps — settlements some centuries old, and still no bigger than pin-heads on the untouched expanse of their background. We pounded along, stopped, landed soldiers; went on, landed custom-house clerks to levy toll in what looked like a God-forsaken wilderness, with a tin shed and a flag-pole lost in it; landed more soldiers — to take care of the custom-house clerks presumably. Some, I heard, got drowned in the surf; but whether they did or not, nobody seemed particularly to care. They were just flung out there, and on we went. Every day the coast looked the same, as though we had not moved; but we passed various places — trading places — with names like Gran' Bassam, Little Popo; names that seemed to belong to some sordid farce acted in front of a sinister back-cloth. The idleness of a passenger, my isolation amongst all these men with whom I had no point of contact, the oily and languid sea, the uniform sombreness of the coast, seemed to keep me away from the truth of things, within the toil of a mournful and senseless delusion. The voice of the surf heard now and then was a positive pleasure, like the speech of a brother. It was something natural, that had its reason, that had a meaning. Now and then a boat from the shore gave one a momentary contact with reality. It was paddled by black fellows. You could see from afar the white of their eyeballs glistening. They shouted, sang; their bodies streamed with perspiration; they had faces like grotesque masks — these chaps; but they had bone, muscle, a wild vitality, an intense energy of movement, that was as natural and true as the surf along their coast. They wanted no excuse for being there. They were a great comfort to look at. For a time I would feel I belonged still to a world of straightforward facts; but the feeling would not last long. Something would turn up to scare it away. Once, I remember, we came upon a man-of-war anchored off the coast. There wasn't even a shed there, and she was shelling the bush. It appears the French had one of their wars going on thereabouts. Her ensign dropped limp like a rag; the muzzles of the long six-inch guns stuck out all over the low hull; the greasy, slimy swell swung her up lazily and let her down, swaying her thin masts. In the empty immensity of earth, sky, and water, there she was, incomprehensible, firing into a continent. Pop, would go one of the six-inch guns; a small flame would dart and vanish, a little white smoke would disappear, a tiny projectile would give a feeble screech — and nothing happened. Nothing could happen. There was a touch of insanity in the proceeding, a sense of lugubrious drollery in the sight; and it was not dissipated by somebody on board assuring me earnestly there was a camp of natives — he called them enemies! — hidden out of sight somewhere.

"We gave her her letters (I heard the men in that lonely ship were dying of fever at the rate of three a day) and went on. We called at some more places with farcical names, where the merry dance of death and trade goes on in a still and earthy atmosphere as of an overheated catacomb; all along the formless coast bordered by dangerous surf, as if Nature herself had tried to ward off intruders; in and out of rivers, streams of death in life, whose banks were rotting into mud, whose waters, thickened into slime, invaded the contorted mangroves, that seemed to writhe at us in the extremity of an impotent despair. Nowhere did we stop long enough to get a particularised impression, but the general sense of vague and oppressive wonder grew upon me. It was like a weary pilgrimage amongst hints for nightmares.

"It was upward of thirty days before I saw the mouth of the big river. We anchored off the seat of the government. But my work would not begin till some two hundred miles farther on. So as soon as I could I made a start for a place thirty miles higher up.

"I had my passage on a little sea-going steamer. Her captain was a Swede, and knowing me for a seaman, invited me on the bridge. He was a young man, lean, fair, and morose, with lanky hair and a shuffling gait. As we left the miserable little wharf, he tossed his head contemptuously at the shore. 'Been living there?' he asked. I said, 'Yes.' 'Fine lot these government chaps — are they not?' he went on, speaking English with great precision and considerable bitterness. 'It is funny what some people will do for a few francs a month. I wonder what becomes of that kind when it goes up country?' I said to him I expected to see that soon. 'So-o-o!' he exclaimed. He shuffled athwart, keeping one eye ahead vigilantly. 'Don't be too sure,' he continued. 'The other day I took up a man who hanged himself on the road. He was a Swede, too.' 'Hanged himself! Why, in God's name?' I cried. He kept on looking out watchfully. 'Who knows? The sun too much for him, or the country perhaps.'

"At last we opened a reach. A rocky cliff appeared, mounds of turned-up earth by the shore, houses on a hill, others with iron roofs, amongst a waste of excavations, or hanging to the declivity. A continuous noise of the rapids above hovered over this scene of inhabited devastation. A lot of people, mostly black and naked, moved about like ants. A jetty projected into the river. A blinding sunlight drowned all this at times in a sudden recrudescence of glare. 'There's your Company's station,' said the Swede, pointing to three wooden barrack-like structures on the rocky slope. 'I will send your things up. Four boxes did you say? So. Farewell.'

"I came upon a boiler wallowing in the grass, then found a path leading up the hill. It turned aside for the boulders, and also for an undersized railway truck lying there on its back with its wheels in the air. One was off. The thing looked as dead as the carcass of some animal. I came upon more pieces of decaying machinery, a stack of rusty nails. To the left a clump of trees made a shady spot, where dark things seemed to stir feebly. I blinked, the path was steep. A horn tooted to the right, and I saw the black people run. A heavy and dull detonation shook the ground, a puff of smoke came out of the cliff, and that was all. No change appeared on the face of the rock. They were building a railway. The cliff was not in the way or anything; but this objectless blasting was all the work going on.

"A slight clinking behind me made me turn my head. Six black men advanced in a file, toiling up the path. They walked erect and slow, balancing small baskets full of earth on their heads, and the clink kept time with their footsteps. Black rags were wound round their loins, and the short ends behind waggled to and fro like tails. I could see every rib, the joints of their limbs were like knots in a rope; each had an iron collar on his neck, and all were connected together with a chain whose bights swung between them, rhythmically clinking. Another report from the cliff made me think suddenly of that ship of war I had seen firing into a continent. It was the same kind of ominous voice; but these men could by no stretch of imagination be called enemies. They were called criminals, and the outraged law, like the bursting shells, had come to them, an insoluble mystery from the sea. All their meagre breasts panted together, the violently dilated nostrils quivered, the eyes stared stonily uphill. They passed me within six inches, without a glance, with that complete, death-like indifference of unhappy savages. Behind this raw matter one of the reclaimed, the product of the new forces at work, strolled despondently, carrying a rifle by its middle. He had a uniform jacket with one button off, and seeing a white man on the path, hoisted his weapon to his shoulder with alacrity. This was simple prudence, white men being so much alike at a distance that he could not tell who I might be. He was speedily reassured, and with a large, white, rascally grin, and a glance at his charge, seemed to take me into partnership in his exalted trust. After all, I also was a part of the great cause of these high and just proceedings.

"Instead of going up, I turned and descended to the left. My idea was to let that chain-gang get out of sight before I climbed the hill. You know I am not particularly tender; I've had to strike and to fend off. I've had to resist and to attack sometimes — that's only one way of resisting — without counting the exact cost, according to the demands of such sort of life as I had blundered into. I've seen the devil of violence, and the devil of greed, and the devil of hot desire; but, by all the stars! these were strong, lusty, red-eyed devils, that swayed and drove men — men, I tell you. But as I stood on this hillside, I foresaw that in the blinding sunshine of that land I would become acquainted with a flabby, pretending, weak-eyed devil of a rapacious and pitiless folly. How insidious he could be, too, I was only to find out several months later and a thousand miles farther. For a moment I stood appalled, as though by a warning. Finally I descended the hill, obliquely, towards the trees I had seen.

"I avoided a vast artificial hole somebody had been digging on the slope, the purpose of which I found it impossible to divine. It wasn't a quarry or a sandpit, anyhow. It was just a hole. It might have been connected with the philanthropic desire of giving the criminals something to do. I don't know. Then I nearly fell into a very narrow ravine, almost no more than a scar in the hillside. I discovered that a lot of imported drainage-pipes for the settlement had been tumbled in there. There wasn't one that was not broken. It was a wanton smash-up. At last I got under the trees. My purpose was to stroll into the shade for a moment; but no sooner within than it seemed to me I had stepped into the gloomy circle of some Inferno. The rapids were near, and an uninterrupted, uniform, headlong, rushing noise filled the mournful stillness of the grove, where not a breath stirred, not a leaf moved, with a mysterious sound — as though the tearing pace of the launched earth had suddenly become audible.

"Black shapes crouched, lay, sat between the trees, leaning against the trunks, clinging to the earth, half coming out, half effaced within the dim light, in all the attitudes of pain, abandonment, and despair. Another mine on the cliff went off, followed by a slight shudder of the soil under my feet. The work was going on. The work! And this was the place where some of the helpers had withdrawn to die.

"They were dying slowly — it was very clear. They were not enemies, they were not criminals, they were nothing earthly now — nothing but black shadows of disease and starvation, lying confusedly in the greenish gloom. Brought from all the recesses of the coast in all the legality of time contracts, lost in uncongenial surroundings, fed on unfamiliar food, they sickened, became inefficient, and were then allowed to crawl away and rest. These moribund shapes were free as air — and nearly as thin. I began to distinguish the gleam of eyes under the trees. Then, glancing down, I saw a face near my hand. The black bones reclined at full length with one shoulder against the tree, and slowly the eyelids rose and the sunken eyes looked up at me, enormous and vacant, a kind of blind, white flicker in the depths of the orbs, which died out slowly. The man seemed young — almost a boy — but you know with them it's hard to tell. I found nothing else to do but to offer him one of my good Swede's ship's biscuits I had in my pocket. The fingers closed slowly on it and held — there was no other movement and no other glance. He had tied a bit of white worsted round his neck — Why? Where did he get it? Was it a badge — an ornament — a charm — a propitiatory act? Was there any idea at all connected with it? It looked startling round his black neck, this bit of white thread from beyond the seas.

"Near the same tree two more bundles of acute angles sat with their legs drawn up. One, with his chin propped on his knees, stared at nothing, in an intolerable and appalling manner: his brother phantom rested its forehead, as if overcome with a great weariness; and all about others were scattered in every pose of contorted collapse, as in some picture of a massacre or a pestilence. While I stood horror-struck, one of these creatures rose to his hands and knees, and went off on all-fours towards the river to drink. He lapped out of his hand, then sat up in the sunlight, crossing his shins in front of him, and after a time let his woolly head fall on his breastbone.

"I didn't want any more loitering in the shade, and I made haste towards the station. When near the buildings I met a white man, in such an unexpected elegance of get-up that in the first moment I took him for a sort of vision. I saw a high starched collar, white cuffs, a light alpaca jacket, snowy trousers, a clear necktie, and varnished boots. No hat. Hair parted, brushed, oiled, under a green-lined parasol held in a big white hand. He was amazing, and had a penholder behind his ear.

"I shook hands with this miracle, and I learned he was the Company's chief accountant, and that all the book-keeping was done at this station. He had come out for a moment, he said, 'to get a breath of fresh air.' The expression sounded wonderfully odd, with its suggestion of sedentary desk-life. I wouldn't have mentioned the fellow to you at all, only it was from his lips that I first heard the name of the man who is so indissolubly connected with the memories of that time. Moreover, I respected the fellow. Yes; I respected his collars, his vast cuffs, his brushed hair. His appearance was certainly that of a hairdresser's dummy; but in the great demoralisation of the land he kept up his appearance. That's backbone. His starched collars and got-up shirt-fronts were achievements of character. He had been out nearly three years; and, later, I could not help asking him how he managed to sport such linen. He had just the faintest blush, and said modestly, 'I've been teaching one of the native women about the station. It was difficult. She had a distaste for the work.' Thus this man had verily accomplished something. And he was devoted to his books, which were in apple-pie order.

"Everything else in the station was in a muddle, — heads, things, buildings. Strings of dusty niggers with splay feet arrived and departed; a stream of manufactured goods, rubbishy cottons, beads, and brass-wire set into the depths of darkness, and in return came a precious trickle of ivory.

"I had to wait in the station for ten days — an eternity. I lived in a hut in the yard, but to be out of the chaos I would sometimes get into the accountant's office. It was built of horizontal planks, and so badly put together that, as he bent over his high desk, he was barred from neck to heels with narrow strips of sunlight. There was no need to open the big shutter to see. It was hot there too; big flies buzzed fiendishly, and did not sting, but stabbed. I sat generally on the floor, while, of faultless appearance (and even slightly scented), perching on a high stool, he wrote, he wrote. Sometimes he stood up for exercise. When a truckle-bed with a sick man (some invalided agent from upcountry) was put in there, he exhibited a gentle annoyance. 'The groans of this sick person,' he said, 'distract my attention. And without that it is extremely difficult to guard against clerical errors in this climate.'

"One day he remarked, without lifting his head, 'In the interior you will no doubt meet Mr. Kurtz.' On my asking who Mr. Kurtz was, he said he was a first-class agent; and seeing my disappointment at this information, he added slowly, laying down his pen, 'He is a very remarkable person.' Further questions elicited from him that Mr. Kurtz was at present in charge of a trading-post, a very important one, in the true ivory-country, at 'the very bottom of there. Sends in as much ivory as all the others put together . . .' He began to write again. The sick man was too ill to groan. The flies buzzed in a great peace.

"Suddenly there was a growing murmur of voices and a great tramping of feet. A caravan had come in. A violent babble of uncouth sounds burst out on the other side of the planks. All the carriers were speaking together, and in the midst of the uproar the lamentable voice of the chief agent was heard 'giving it up' tearfully for the twentieth time that day. . . . He rose slowly. 'What a frightful row,' he said. He crossed the room gently to look at the sick man, and returning, said to me, 'He does not hear.' 'What! Dead?' I asked, startled. 'No, not yet,' he answered, with great composure. Then, alluding with a toss of the head to the tumult in the station-yard, 'When one has got to make correct entries, one comes to hate those savages — hate them to the death.' He remained thoughtful for a moment. 'When you see Mr. Kurtz,' he went on, 'tell him from me that everything here' — he glanced at the desk — 'is very satisfactory. I don't like to write to him — with those messengers of ours you never know who may get hold of your letter — at that Central Station.' He stared at me for a moment with his mild, bulging eyes. 'Oh, he will go far, very far,' he began again. 'He will be a somebody in the Administration before long. They, above — the Council in Europe, you know — mean him to be.'

"He turned to his work. The noise outside had ceased, and presently in going out I stopped at the door. In the steady buzz of flies the homeward-bound agent was lying flushed and insensible; the other, bent over his books, was making correct entries of perfectly correct transactions; and fifty feet below the doorstep I could see the still tree-tops of the grove of death.

"Next day I left that station at last, with a caravan of sixty men, for a two-hundred-mile tramp.

"No use telling you much about that. Paths, paths, everywhere; a stamped-in network of paths spreading over the empty land, through long grass, through burnt grass, through thickets, down and up chilly ravines, up and down stony hills ablaze with heat; and a solitude, a solitude, nobody, not a hut. The population had cleared out a long time ago. Well, if a lot of mysterious niggers armed with all kinds of fearful weapons suddenly took to travelling on the road between Deal and Gravesend, catching the yokels right and left to carry heavy loads for them, I fancy every farm and cottage thereabouts would get empty very soon. Only here the dwellings were gone too. Still, I passed through several abandoned villages. There's something pathetically childish in the ruins of grass walls. Day after day, with the stamp and shuffle of sixty pair of bare feet behind me, each pair under a 60-lb. load. Camp, cook, sleep, strike camp, march. Now and then a carrier dead in harness, at rest in the long grass near the path, with an empty water-gourd and his long staff lying by his side. A great silence around and above. Perhaps on some quiet night the tremor of far-off drums, sinking, swelling, a tremor vast, faint; a sound weird, appealing, suggestive, and wild — and perhaps with as pro-found a meaning as the sound of bells in a Chris-tian country. Once a white man in an unbuttoned uniform, camping on the path with an armed escort of lank Zanzibaris, very hospitable and festive — not to say drunk. Was looking after the upkeep of the road, he declared. Can't say I saw any road or any upkeep, unless the body of a middle-aged Negro, with a bullet-hole in the fore-head, upon which I absolutely stumbled three miles farther on, may be considered as a permanent improvement. I had a white companion too, not a bad chap, but rather too fleshy and with the exasperating habit of fainting on the hot hillsides, miles away from the least bit of shade and water. Annoying, you know, to hold your own coat like a parasol over a man's head while he is coming-to. I couldn't help asking him once what he meant by coming there at all. 'To make money, of course. What do you think?' he said scornfully. Then he got fever, and had to be carried in a hammock slung under a pole. As he weighed sixteen stone I had no end of rows with the carriers. They jibbed, ran away, sneaked off with their loads in the night — quite a mutiny. So, one evening, I made a speech in English with gestures, not one of which was lost to the sixty pairs of eyes before me, and the next morning I started the hammock off in front all right. An hour afterwards I came upon the whole concern wrecked in a bush — man, hammock, groans, blankets, horrors. The heavy pole has skinned his poor nose. He was very anxious for me to kill somebody, but there wasn't the shadow of a carrier near. I remembered the old doctor — 'It would be interesting for science to watch the mental changes of individuals, on the spot.' I felt I was becoming scientifically interest-ing. However, all that is to no purpose. On the fifteenth day I came in sight of the big river again, and hobbled into the Central Station. It was on a back water surrounded by scrub and forest, with a pretty border of smelly mud on one side, and on the three others enclosed by a crazy fence of rushes. A neglected gap was all the gate it had, and the first glance at the place was enough to let you see the flabby devil was running that show. White men with long staves in their hands appeared languidly from amongst the buildings, strolling up to take a look at me, and then retired out of sight somewhere. One of them, a stout, excitable chap with black moustaches, informed me with great volubility and many digressions, as soon as I told him who I was, that my steamer was at the bottom of the river. I was thunderstruck. What, how, why? Oh, it was 'all right.' The 'manager himself' was there. All quite correct. 'Everybody had behaved splendidly! splendidly!'—'You must,' he said in agitation, 'go and see the general manager at once. He is waiting!'

"I did not see the real significance of that wreck at once. I fancy I see it now, but I am not sure — not at all. Certainly the affair was too stupid — when I think of it — to be altogether natural. Still . . . But at the moment it presented itself simply as a confounded nuisance. The steamer was sunk. They had started two days before in a sudden hurry up the river with the manager on board, in charge of some volunteer skipper, and before they had been out three hours they tore the bottom out of her on stones, and she sank near the south bank. I asked myself what I was to do there, now my boat was lost. As a matter of fact, I had plenty to do in fishing my command out of the river. I had to set about it the very next day. That, and the repairs when I brought the pieces to the station, took some months.

"My first interview with the manager was curious. He did not ask me to sit down after my twenty-mile walk that morning. He was commonplace in complexion, in feature, in manners, and in voice. He was of middle size and of ordinary build. His eyes, of the usual blue, were perhaps remarkably cold, and he certainly could make his glance fall on one as trenchant and heavy as an axe. But even at these times the rest of his person seemed to disclaim the intention. Otherwise there was only an indefinable, faint expression of his lips, something stealthy — a smile — not a smile — I remember it, but I can't explain. It was unconscious, this smile was, though just after he had said something it got intensified for an instant.

It came at the end of his speeches like a seal applied on the words to make the meaning of the commonest phrase appear absolutely inscrutable. He was a common trader, from his youth up employed in these parts — nothing more. He was obeyed, yet he inspired neither love nor fear, nor even respect. He inspired uneasiness. That was it! Uneasiness. Not a definite mistrust — just uneasiness — nothing more. You have no idea how effective such a . . . a . . . faculty can be. He had no genius for organising, for initiative, or for order even. That was evident in such things as the deplorable state of the station. He had no learning, and no intelligence. His position had come to him — why? Perhaps because he was never ill . . . He had served three terms of three years out there . . . Because triumphant health in the general rout of constitutions is a kind of power in itself. When he went home on leave he rioted on a large scale — pompously. Jack ashore — with a difference — in externals only. This one could gather from his casual talk. He originated nothing, he could keep the routine going — that's all. But he was great. He was great by this little thing that it was impossible to tell what could control such a man. He never gave that secret away. Perhaps there was nothing within him. Such a suspicion made one pause — for out there there were no external checks. Once when various tropical diseases had laid low almost every 'agent' in the station, he was heard to say, 'Men who come out here should have no entrails.' He sealed the utterance with that smile of his, as though it had been a door opening into a darkness he had in his keeping. You fancied you had seen things — but the seal was on. When annoyed at meal-times by the constant quarrels of the white men about precedence, he ordered an immense round table to be made, for which a special house had to be built. This was the station's mess-room. Where he sat was the first place — the rest were nowhere. One felt this to be his unalterable conviction. He was neither civil nor uncivil. He was quiet. He allowed his 'boy' — an overfed young Negro from the coast — to treat the white men, under his very eyes, with provoking insolence.

"He began to speak as soon as he saw me. I had been very long on the road. He could not wait. Had to start without me. The up-river stations had to be relieved. There had been so many delays already that he did not know who was dead and who was alive, and how they got on — and so on, and so on. He paid no attention to my explanations, and, playing with a stick of sealing-wax, repeated several times that the situation was 'very grave, very grave.' There were rumours that a very important station was in jeopardy, and its chief, Mr. Kurtz, was ill. Hoped it was not true. Mr. Kurtz was . . . I felt weary and irritable. Hang Kurtz, I thought. I interrupted him by saying I had heard of Mr. Kurtz on the coast. 'Ah! So they talk of him down there,' he murmured to himself. Then he began again, assuring me Mr. Kurtz was the best agent he had, an exceptional man, of the greatest importance to the Company; therefore I could understand his anxiety. He was, he said, 'very, very uneasy.' Certainly he fidgeted on his chair a good deal, exclaimed, 'Ah, Mr. Kurtz!' broke the stick of sealing-wax and seemed dumbfounded by the accident. Next thing he wanted to know 'how long it would take to' . . . I interrupted him again. Being hungry, you know, and kept on my feet too, I was getting savage. 'How can I tell?' I said. 'I haven't even seen the wreck yet — some months, no doubt.' All this talk seemed to me so futile. 'Some months,' he said. 'Well, let us say three months before we can make a start. Yes. That ought to do the affair.' I flung out of his hut (he lived all alone in a clay hut with a sort of verandah) muttering to myself my opinion of him. He was a chattering idiot. Afterwards I took it back when it was borne in upon me startlingly with what extreme nicety he had estimated the time requisite for the 'affair.'

"I went to work the next day, turning, so to speak, my back on that station. In that way only it seemed to me I could keep my hold on the redeeming facts of life. Still, one must look about sometimes; and then I saw this station, these men strolling aimlessly about in the sunshine of the yard. I asked myself sometimes what it all meant. They wandered here and there with their absurd long staves in their hands, like a lot of faithless pilgrims bewitched inside a rotten fence. The word 'ivory' rang in the air, was whispered, was sighed. You would think they were praying to it. A taint of imbecile rapacity blew through it all, like a whiff from some corpse. By Jove! I've never seen anything so unreal in my life. And outside, the silent wilderness surrounding this cleared speck on the earth struck me as something great and invincible, like evil or truth, waiting patiently for the passing away of this fantastic invasion.

"Oh, these months! Well, never mind. Various things happened. One evening a grass shed full of calico, cotton prints, beads, and I don't know what else, burst into a blaze so suddenly that you would have thought the earth had opened to let an avenging fire consume all that trash. I was smoking my pipe quietly by my dismantled steamer, and saw them all cutting capers in the light, with their arms lifted high, when the stout man with moustaches came tearing down to the river, a tin pail in his hand, assured me that everybody was 'behaving splendidly, splendidly,' dipped about a quart of water and tore back again. I noticed there was a hole in the bottom of his pail.

"I strolled up. There was no hurry. You see the thing had gone off like a box of matches. It had been hopeless from the very first. The flame had leaped high, driven everybody back, lighted up everything — and collapsed. The shed was already a heap of embers glowing fiercely. A nigger was being beaten near by. They said he had caused the fire in some way; be that as it may, he was screeching most horribly. I saw him, later, for several days, sitting in a bit of shade looking very sick and trying to recover himself: afterwards he arose and went out — and the wilderness without a sound took him into its bosom again. As I approached the glow from the dark I found myself at the back of two men, talking. I heard the name of Kurtz pronounced, then the words, 'take advantage of this unfortunate accident.' One of the men was the manager. I wished him a good evening. 'Did you ever see anything like it — eh? it is incredible,' he said, and walked off. The other man remained. He was a first-class agent, young, gentlemanly, a bit reserved, with a forked little beard and a hooked nose. He was standoffish with the other agents, and they on their side said he was the manager's spy upon them. As to me, I had hardly ever spoken to him before. We got into talk, and by and by we strolled away from the hissing ruins. Then he asked me to his room, which was in the main building of the station. He struck a match, and I perceived that this young aristocrat had not only a silver-mounted dressing-case but also a whole candle all to himself. Just at that time the manager was the only man supposed to have any right to candles. Native mats covered the clay walls; a collection of spears, assegais, shields, knives, was hung up in trophies. The business entrusted to this fellow was the making of bricks — so I had been informed; but there wasn't a fragment of a brick anywhere in the station, and he had been there more than a year — waiting. It seems he could not make bricks without something. I don't know what — straw maybe. Anyway, it could not be found there, and as it was not likely to be sent from Europe, it did not appear clear to me what he was waiting for. An act of special creation perhaps. However, they were all waiting — all the sixteen or twenty pilgrims of them — for something; and upon my word it did not seem an uncongenial occupation, from the way they took it, though the only thing that ever came to them was disease — as far as I could see. They beguiled the time by backbiting and intriguing against each other in a foolish kind of way. There was an air of plotting about that station, but nothing came of it, of course. It was as unreal as everything else — as the philanthropic pretence of the whole concern, as their talk, as their government, as their show of work. The only real feeling was a desire to get appointed to a trading-post where ivory was to be had, so that they could earn percentages. They intrigued and slandered and hated each other only on that account — but as to effectually lifting a little finger — oh no. By heavens! there is something after all in the world allowing one man to steal a horse while another must not look at a halter. Steal a horse straight out. Very well. He has done it. Perhaps he can ride. But there is a way of looking at a halter that would provoke the most charitable of saints into a kick.

"I had no idea why he wanted to be sociable, but as we chatted in there it suddenly occurred to me the fellow was trying to get at something — in fact, pumping me. He alluded constantly to Europe, to the people I was supposed to know there — putting leading questions as to my acquaintances in the sepulchral city, and so on. His little eyes glittered like mica discs — with curiosity — though he tried to keep up a bit of superciliousness. At first I was astonished, but very soon I became awfully curious to see what he would find out from me. I couldn't possibly imagine what I had in me to make it worth his while. It was very pretty to see how he baffled himself, for in truth my body was full only of chills, and my head had nothing in it but that wretched steamboat business. It was evident he took me for a perfectly shameless prevaricator. At last he got angry, and, to conceal a movement of furious annoyance, he yawned. I rose. Then I noticed a small sketch in oils, on a panel, representing a woman, draped and blindfolded, carrying a lighted torch. The background was sombre — almost black. The movement of the woman was stately, and the effect of the torchlight on the face was sinister.

"It arrested me, and he stood by civilly, holding an empty half-pint champagne bottle (medical comforts) with the candle stuck in it. To my question he said Mr. Kurtz had painted this — in this very station more than a year ago — while waiting for means to go to his trading-post. 'Tell me, pray,' said I, 'who is this Mr. Kurtz?'

"'The chief of the Inner Station,' he answered in a short tone, looking away. 'Much obliged,' I said, laughing. 'And you are the brickmaker of the Central Station. Every one knows that.' He was silent for a while. 'He is a prodigy,' he said at last. 'He is an emissary of pity, and science, and progress, and devil knows what else. We want,' he began to declaim suddenly, 'for the guidance of the cause entrusted to us by Europe, so to speak, higher intelligence, wide sympathies, a singleness of purpose.' 'Who says that?' I asked. 'Lots of them,' he replied. 'Some even write that; and so *he* comes here, a special being, as you ought to know.' 'Why ought I to know?' I interrupted, really surprised. He paid no attention. 'Yes. To-day he is chief of the best station, next year he will be assistant-manager, two years more and . . . but I daresay you know what he will be in two years' time. You are of the new gang — the gang of virtue. The same people who sent him specially also recommended you. Oh, don't say no. I've my own eyes to trust.' Light dawned upon me. My dear aunt's influential acquaintances were producing an unexpected effect upon that young man. I nearly burst into a laugh. 'Do you read the Company's confidential correspondence?' I asked. He hadn't a word to say. It was great fun. 'When Mr. Kurtz,' I continued severely, 'is General Manager, you won't have the opportunity.'

"He blew the candle out suddenly, and we went outside. The moon had risen. Black figures strolled about listlessly, pouring water on the glow, whence proceeded a sound of hissing; steam ascended in the moonlight; the beaten nigger groaned somewhere. 'What a row the brute makes!' said the indefatigable man with the moustaches, appearing near us. 'Serve him right. Transgression — punishment — bang! Pitiless, pitiless. That's the only way. This will prevent all conflagrations for the future. I was just telling the manager . . .' He noticed my companion, and became crestfallen all at once. 'Not in bed yet,' he said, with a kind of servile heartiness; 'it's so natural. Ha! Danger —

agitation.' He vanished. I went on to the river-side, and the other followed me. I heard a scathing murmur at my ear, 'Heap of muffs — go to.' The pilgrims could be seen in knots gesticulating, dis-cussing. Several had still their staves in their hands. I verily believe they took these sticks to bed with them. Beyond the fence the forest stood up spec-trally in the moonlight, and through the dim stir, through the faint sounds of that lamentable court-yard, the silence of the land went home to one's very heart — its mystery, its greatness, the amazing reality of its concealed life. The hurt nigger moaned feebly somewhere near by, and then fetched a deep sigh that made me mend my pace away from there. I felt a hand introducing itself under my arm. 'My dear sir,' said the fellow, 'I don't want to be mis-understood, and especially by you, who will see Mr. Kurtz long before I can have that pleasure. I wouldn't like him to get a false idea of my dis-position. . . .

"I let him run on, this papier-mâché Mephi-stopheles, and it seemed to me that if I tried I could poke my forefinger through him, and would find nothing inside but a little loose dirt, maybe. He, don't you see, had been planning to be assistant-manager by and by under the present man, and I could see that the coming of that Kurtz had upset them both not a little. He talked precipitately, and I did not try to stop him. I had my shoulders against the wreck of my steamer, hauled up on the slope like a carcass of some big river animal. The smell of mud, of primeval mud, by Jove! was in my nostrils, the high stillness of primeval forest was before my eyes; there were shiny patches on the black creek. The moon had spread over everything a thin layer of silver — over the rank grass, over the mud, upon the wall of matted vegetation stand-ing higher than the wall of a temple, over the great river I could see through a sombre gap glit-tering, glittering, as it flowed broadly by without a murmur. All this was great, expectant, mute, while the man jabbered about himself. I wondered whether the stillness on the face of the immensity looking at us two were meant as an appeal or as a menace. What were we who had strayed in here? Could we handle that dumb thing, or would it handle us? I felt how big, how confoundedly big, was that thing that couldn't talk and perhaps was deaf as well. What was in there? I could see a little ivory coming out from there, and I had heard Mr. Kurtz was in there. I had heard enough about it too — God knows! Yet somehow it didn't bring any

image with it — no more than if I had been told an angel or a fiend was in there. I believed it in the same way one of you might believe there are in-habitants in the planet Mars. I knew once a Scotch sailmaker who was certain, dead sure, there were people in Mars. If you asked him for some idea how they looked and behaved, he would get shy and mutter something about 'walking on all-fours.' If you as much as smiled, he would — though a man of sixty — offer to fight you. I would not have gone so far as to fight for Kurtz, but I went for him near enough to a lie. You know I hate, detest, and can't bear a lie, not because I am straighter than the rest of us, but simply because it appals me. There is a taint of death, a flavour of mortality in lies — which is exactly what I hate and detest in the world — what I want to forget. It makes me miserable and sick, like biting something rotten would do. Temperament, I suppose. Well, I went near enough to it by letting the young fool there believe anything he liked to imagine as to my in-fluence in Europe. I became in an instant as much of a pretence as the rest of the bewitched pilgrims. This simply because I had a notion it somehow would be of help to that Kurtz whom at the time I did not see — you understand. He was just a word for me. I did not see the man in the name any more than you do. Do you see him? Do you see the story? Do you see anything? It seems to me I am trying to tell you a dream — making a vain attempt, because no relation of a dream can convey the dream-sensation, that commingling of absurd-ity, surprise, and bewilderment in a tremor of struggling revolt, that notion of being captured by the incredible which is of the very essence of dreams. . . ."

He was silent for a while.

". . . No, it is impossible; it is impossible to convey the life-sensation of any given epoch of one's existence — that which makes its truth, its meaning — its subtle and penetrating essence. It is impossible. We live, as we dream — alone. . . ."

He paused again as if reflecting, then added:

"Of course in this you fellows see more than I could then. You see me, whom you know. . . ."

It had become so pitch dark that we listeners could hardly see one another. For a long time al-ready he, sitting apart, had been no more to us than a voice. There was not a word from anybody. The others might have been asleep, but I was awake. I listened, I listened on the watch for the sentence, for the word, that would give me the clue to the faint uneasiness inspired by this narrative that seemed to shape itself without human lips in the heavy night-air of the river.

" . . . Yes — I let him run on," Marlow began again, " and think what he pleased about the powers that were behind me. I did! And there was nothing behind me! There was nothing but that wretched, old, mangled steamboat I was leaning against, while he talked fluently about ' the necessity for every man to get on.' ' And when one comes out here, you conceive, it is not to gaze at the moon.' Mr. Kurtz was a ' universal genius,' but even a genius would find it easier to work with ' adequate tools — intelligent men.' He did not make bricks — why, there was a physical impossibility in the way — as I was well aware; and if he did secretarial work for the manager, it was because ' no sensible man rejects wantonly the confidence of his superiors.' Did I see it? I saw it. What more did I want? What I really wanted was rivets, by heaven! Rivets. To get on with the work — to stop the hole. Rivets I wanted. There were cases of them down at the coast — cases — piled up — burst — split! You kicked a loose rivet at every second step in that station yard on the hillside. Rivets had rolled into the grove of death. You could fill your pockets with rivets for the trouble of stooping down — and there wasn't one rivet to be found where it was wanted. We had plates that would do, but nothing to fasten them with. And every week the messenger, a lone Negro, letter-bag on shoulder and staff in hand, left our station for the coast. And several times a week a coast caravan came in with trade goods — ghastly glazed calico that made you shudder only to look at it, glass beads value about a penny a quart, confounded spotted cotton handkerchiefs. And no rivets. Three carriers could have brought all that was wanted to set that steamboat afloat.

"He was becoming confidential now, but I fancy my unresponsive attitude must have exasperated him at last, for he judged it necessary to inform me he feared neither God nor devil, let alone any mere man. I said I could see that very well, but what I wanted was a certain quantity of rivets — and rivets were what really Mr. Kurtz wanted, if he had only known it. Now letters went to the coast every week. . . . ' My dear sir,' he cried, ' I write from dictation.' I demanded rivets. There was a way — for an intelligent man. He changed his manner; became very cold, and suddenly began to talk about a hippopotamus; wondered whether sleeping on board the steamer (I stuck to my salvage night and day) I wasn't disturbed. There was an old hippo that had the bad habit of getting out on the bank and roaming at night over the station grounds. The pilgrims used to turn out in a body and empty every rifle they could lay hands on at him. Some even had sat up o' nights for him. All this energy was wasted, though. ' That animal has a charmed life,' he said; ' but you can say this only of brutes in this country. No man — you apprehend me? — no man here bears a charmed life.' He stood there for a moment in the moonlight with his delicate hooked nose set a little askew, and his mica eyes glittering without a wink, then, with a curt Good-night, he strode off. I could see he was disturbed and considerably puzzled, which made me feel more hopeful than I had been for days. It was a great comfort to turn from that chap to my influential friend, the battered, twisted, ruined, tinpot steamboat. I clambered on board. She rang under my feet like an empty Huntley & Palmer biscuit-tin kicked along a gutter; she was nothing so solid in make, and rather less pretty in shape, but I had expended enough hard work on her to make me love her. No influential friend would have served me better. She had given me a chance to come out a bit — to find out what I could do. No, I don't like work. I had rather laze about and think of all the fine things that can be done. I don't like work — no man does — but I like what is in the work — the chance to find yourself. Your own reality — for yourself, not for others — what no other man can ever know. They can only see the mere show, and never can tell what it really means.

" I was not surprised to see somebody sitting aft, on the deck, with his legs dangling over the mud. You see I rather chummed with the few mechanics there were in that station, whom the other pilgrims naturally despised — on account of their imperfect manners, I suppose. This was the foreman — a boiler-maker by trade — a good worker. He was a lank, bony, yellow-faced man, with big intense eyes. His aspect was worried, and his head was as bald as the palm of my hand; but his hair in falling seemed to have stuck to his chin, and had prospered in the new locality, for his beard hung down to his waist. He was a widower with six young children (he had left them in charge of a sister of his to come out there), and the passion of his life was pigeon-flying. He was an enthusiast and a connoisseur. He would rave about pigeons. After work hours he used sometimes to come over from his hut for a talk about his children and his pigeons; at work, when he had to crawl in the mud under the bottom of the steamboat, he would tie up that beard of his in a kind of white serviette he brought for the purpose. It had loops to go over his ears. In the evening he could be seen squatted on the bank rinsing that wrapper in the creek with great care, then spreading it solemnly on a bush to dry.

"I slapped him on the back and shouted 'We shall have rivets!' He scrambled to his feet exclaiming 'No! Rivets!' as though he couldn't believe his ears. Then in a low voice, 'You . . . eh?' I don't know why we behaved like lunatics. I put my finger to the side of my nose and nodded mysteriously. 'Good for you!' he cried, snapped his fingers above his head, lifting one foot. I tried a jig. We capered on the iron deck. A frightful clatter came out of that hulk, and the virgin forest on the other bank of the creek sent it back in a thundering roll upon the sleeping station. It must have made some of the pilgrims sit up in their hovels. A dark figure obscured the lighted doorway of the manager's hut, vanished, then, a second or so after, the doorway itself vanished too. We stopped, and the silence driven away by the stamping of our feet flowed back again from the recesses of the land. The great wall of vegetation, an exuberant and entangled mass of trunks, branches, leaves, boughs, festoons, motionless in the moonlight, was like a rioting invasion of soundless life, a rolling wave of plants, piled up, crested, ready to topple over the creek, to sweep every little man of us out of his little existence. And it moved not. A deadened burst of mighty splashes and snorts reached us from afar, as though an ichthyosaurus had been taking a bath of glitter in the great river. 'After all,' said the boiler-maker in a reasonable tone, 'why shouldn't we get the rivets?' Why not, indeed! I did not know of any reason why we shouldn't. 'They'll come in three weeks,' I said confidently.

"But they didn't. Instead of rivets there came an invasion, an infliction, a visitation. It came in sections during the next three weeks, each section headed by a donkey carrying a white man in new clothes and tan shoes, bowing from that elevation right and left to the impressed pilgrims. A quarrelsome band of footsore sulky niggers trod on the heels of the donkey; a lot of tents, camp-stools, tin boxes, white cases, brown bales would be shot down in the courtyard, and the air of mystery would deepen a little over the muddle of the station. Five such instalments came, with their absurd air of disorderly flight with the loot of innumerable outfit shops and provision stores, that, one would think, they were lugging, after a raid, into the wilderness for equitable division. It was an inextricable mess of things decent in themselves but that human folly made look like the spoils of thieving.

"This devoted band called itself the Eldorado Exploring Expedition, and I believe they were sworn to secrecy. Their talk, however, was the talk of sordid buccaneers: it was reckless without hardihood, greedy without audacity, and cruel without courage; there was not an atom of foresight or of serious intention in the whole batch of them, and they did not seem aware these things are wanted for the work of the world. To tear treasure out of the bowels of the land was their desire, with no more moral purpose at the back of it than there is in burglars breaking into a safe. Who paid the expenses of the noble enterprise I don't know; but the uncle of our manager was leader of that lot.

"In exterior he resembled a butcher in a poor neighbourhood, and his eyes had a look of sleepy cunning. He carried his fat paunch with ostentation on his short legs, and during the time his gang infested the station spoke to no one but his nephew. You could see these two roaming about all day long with their heads close together in an everlasting confab.

"I had given up worrying myself about the rivets. One's capacity for that kind of folly is more limited than you would suppose. I said Hang!— and let things slide. I had plenty of time for meditation, and now and then I would give some thought to Kurtz. I wasn't very interested in him. No. Still, I was curious to see whether this man, who had come out equipped with moral ideas of some sort, would climb to the top after all, and how he would set about his work when there."

II

"One evening as I was lying flat on the deck of my steamboat, I heard voices approaching—and there were the nephew and the uncle strolling along the bank. I laid my head on my arm again, and had nearly lost myself in a doze, when somebody said in my ear, as it were: 'I am as harmless as a little child, but I don't like to be dictated to. Am I the manager—or am I not? I was ordered to send him there. It's incredible.' . . . I became aware that the two were standing on the shore alongside the forepart of the steamboat, just below my head. I did not move; it did not occur to me to move: I was sleepy. 'It *is* unpleasant,' grunted the uncle. 'He has asked the Administration to be sent there,' said the other, 'with the idea of showing what he could do; and I was instructed accordingly. Look at the influence that man must have. Is it not frightful?' They both agreed it was frightful, then made several bizarre remarks: 'Make rain and fine weather — one man — the Council — by the nose' — bits of absurd sentences that got the better of my drowsiness, so that I had pretty near the whole of my wits about me when the uncle said, 'The climate may do away with this difficulty for you. Is he alone there?' 'Yes,' answered the manager; 'he sent his assistant down the river with a note to me in these terms: "Clear this poor devil out of the country, and don't bother sending more of that sort. I had rather be alone than have the kind of men you can dispose of with me." It was more than a year ago. Can you imagine such impudence?' 'Anything since then?' asked the other hoarsely. 'Ivory,' jerked the nephew; 'lots of it — prime sort — lots — most annoying, from him.' 'And with that?' questioned the heavy rumble. 'Invoice,' was the reply fired out, so to speak. Then silence. They had been talking about Kurtz.

"I was broad awake by this time, but, lying perfectly at ease, remained still, having no inducement to change my position. 'How did that ivory come all this way?' growled the elder man, who seemed very vexed. The other explained that it had come with a fleet of canoes in charge of an English half-caste clerk Kurtz had with him; that Kurtz had apparently intended to return himself, the station being by that time bare of goods and stores, but after coming three hundred miles, had suddenly decided to go back, which he started to do alone in a small dugout with four paddlers, leaving the half-caste to continue down the river with the ivory. The two fellows there seemed astounded at anybody attempting such a thing. They were at a loss for an adequate motive. As for me, I seemed to see Kurtz for the first time. It was a distinct glimpse: the dugout, four paddling savages, and the lone white man turning his back suddenly on the headquarters, on relief, on thoughts of home — perhaps; setting his face towards the depths of the wilderness, towards his empty and desolate station. I did not know the motive. Perhaps he

was just simply a fine fellow who stuck to his work for its own sake. His name, you understand, had not been pronounced once. He was 'that man.' The half-caste, who, as far as I could see, had conducted a difficult trip with great prudence and pluck, was invariably alluded to as 'that scoundrel.' The 'scoundrel' had reported that the 'man' had been very ill — had recovered imperfectly. . . . The two below me moved away then a few paces, and strolled back and forth at some little distance. I heard: 'Military post — doctor — two hundred miles — quite alone now — unavoidable delays — nine months — no news — strange rumours.' They approached again, just as the manager was saying, 'No one, as far as I know, unless a species of wandering trader — a pestilential fellow, snapping ivory from the natives.' Who was it they were talking about now? I gathered in snatches that this was some man supposed to be in Kurtz's district, and of whom the manager did not approve. 'We will not be free from unfair competition till one of these fellows is hanged for an example,' he said. 'Certainly,' grunted the other; 'get him hanged! Why not? Anything — anything can be done in this country. That's what I say; nobody here, you understand, *here*, can endanger your position. And why? You stand the climate — you outlast them all. The danger is in Europe; but there before I left I took care to —' They moved off and whispered, then their voices rose again. 'The extraordinary series of delays is not my fault. I did my best.' The fat man sighed, 'Very sad.' 'And the pestiferous absurdity of his talk,' continued the other; 'he bothered me enough when he was here. "Each station should be like a beacon on the road towards better things, a centre for trade of course, but also for humanising, improving, instructing." Conceive you — that ass! And he wants to be manager! No, it's —' Here he got choked by excessive indignation, and I lifted my head the least bit. I was surprised to see how near they were — right under me. I could have spat upon their hats. They were looking on the ground, absorbed in thought. The manager was switching his leg with a slender twig: his sagacious relative lifted his head. 'You have been well since you came out this time?' he asked. The other gave a start. 'Who? I? Oh! Like a charm — like a charm. But the rest — oh, my goodness! All sick. They die so quick, too, that I haven't the time to send them out of the country — it's incredible!' 'H'm. Just so,' grunted the uncle. 'Ah! my boy, trust to this — I say, trust to this.' I saw him extend his short flipper of an arm for a gesture that took in the forest, the creek, the mud, the river — seemed to beckon with a dishonouring flourish before the sunlit face of the land a treacherous appeal to the lurking death, to the hidden evil, to the profound darkness of its heart. It was so startling that I leaped to my feet and looked back at the edge of the forest, as though I had expected an answer of some sort to that black display of confidence. You know the foolish notions that come to one sometimes. The high stillness confronted these two figures with its ominous patience, waiting for the passing away of a fantastic invasion.

"They swore aloud together — out of sheer fright, I believe — then, pretending not to know anything of my existence, turned back to the station. The sun was low; and leaning forward side by side, they seemed to be tugging painfully uphill their two ridiculous shadows of unequal length, that trailed behind them slowly over the tall grass without bending a single blade.

"In a few days the Eldorado Expedition went into the patient wilderness, that closed upon it as the sea closes over a diver. Long afterwards the news came that all the donkeys were dead. I know nothing as to the fate of the less valuable animals. They, no doubt, like the rest of us, found what they deserved. I did not inquire. I was then rather excited at the prospect of meeting Kurtz very soon. When I say very soon I mean it comparatively. It was just two months from the day we left the creek when we came to the bank below Kurtz's station.

"Going up that river was like travelling back to the earliest beginnings of the world, when vegetation rioted on the earth and the big trees were kings. An empty stream, a great silence, an impenetrable forest. The air was warm, thick, heavy, sluggish. There was no joy in the brilliance of sunshine. The long stretches of the waterway ran on, deserted, into the gloom of overshadowed distances. On silvery sandbanks hippos and alligators sunned themselves side by side. The broadening waters flowed through a mob of wooded islands; you lost your way on that river as you would in a desert, and butted all day long against shoals, trying to find the channel, till you thought yourself bewitched and cut off for ever from everything you had known once — somewhere — far away — in another existence perhaps. There were moments when one's past came back to one, as it will some-

times when you have not a moment to spare to yourself; but it came in the shape of an unrestful and noisy dream, remembered with wonder amongst the overwhelming realities of this strange world of plants, and water, and silence. And this stillness of life did not in the least resemble a peace. It was the stillness of an implacable force brooding over an inscrutable intention. It looked at you with a vengeful aspect. I got used to it afterwards; I did not see it any more; I had no time. I had to keep guessing at the channel; I had to discern, mostly by inspiration, the signs of hidden banks; I watched for sunken stones; I was learning to clap my teeth smartly before my heart flew out, when I shaved by a fluke some infernal sly old snag that would have ripped the life out of the tin-pot steamboat and drowned all the pilgrims; I had to keep a look-out for the signs of dead wood we could cut up in the night for next day's steaming. When you have to attend to things of that sort, to the mere incidents of the surface, the reality — the reality, I tell you — fades. The inner truth is hidden — luckily, luckily. But I felt it all the same; I felt often its mysterious stillness watching me at my monkey tricks, just as it watches you fellows performing on your respective tight-ropes for — what is it? half a crown a tumble — "

"Try to be civil, Marlow," growled a voice, and I knew there was at least one listener awake besides myself.

"I beg your pardon. I forgot the heartache which makes up the rest of the price. And indeed what does the price matter, if the trick be well done? You do your tricks very well. And I didn't do badly either, since I managed not to sink that steamboat on my first trip. It's a wonder to me yet. Imagine a blindfolded man set to drive a van over a bad road. I sweated and shivered over that business considerably, I can tell you. After all, for a seaman, to scrape the bottom of the thing that's supposed to float all the time under his care is the unpardonable sin. No one may know of it, but you never forget the thump — eh? A blow on the very heart. You remember it, you dream of it, you wake up at night and think of it — years after — and go hot and cold all over. I don't pretend to say that steamboat floated all the time. More than once she had to wade for a bit, with twenty cannibals splashing around and pushing. We had enlisted some of these chaps on the way for a crew. Fine fellows — cannibals — in their place. They were men one could work with, and I am grateful to them. And, after all, they did not eat each other before my face: they had brought along a provision of hippo-meat which went rotten, and made the mystery of the wilderness stink in my nostrils. Phoo! I can sniff it now. I had the manager on board and three or four pilgrims with their staves — all complete. Sometimes we came upon a station close by the bank, clinging to the skirts of the unknown, and the white men rushing out of a tumble-down hovel, with great gestures of joy and surprise and welcome, seemed very strange — had the appearance of being held there captive by a spell. The word 'ivory' would ring in the air for a while — and on we went again into the silence, along empty reaches, round the still bends, between the high walls of our winding way, reverberating in hollow claps the ponderous beat of the sternwheel. Trees, trees, millions of trees, massive, immense, running up high; and at their foot, hugging the bank against the stream, crept the little begrimed steamboat, like a sluggish beetle crawling on the floor of a lofty portico. It made you feel very small, very lost, and yet it was not altogether depressing, that feeling. After all, if you were small, the grimy beetle crawled on — which was just what you wanted it to do. Where the pilgrims imagined it crawled to I don't know. To some place where they expected to get something, I bet! For me it crawled towards Kurtz — exclusively; but when the steam-pipes started leaking we crawled very slow. The reaches opened before us and closed behind, as if the forest had stepped leisurely across the water to bar the way for our return. We penetrated deeper and deeper into the heart of darkness. It was very quiet there. At night sometimes the roll of drums behind the curtain of trees would run up the river and remain sustained faintly, as if hovering in the air high over our heads, till the first break of day. Whether it meant war, peace, or prayer we could not tell. The dawns were heralded by the descent of a chill stillness; the woodcutters slept, their fires burned low; the snapping of a twig would make you start. We were wanderers on a prehistoric earth, on an earth that wore the aspect of an unknown planet. We could have fancied ourselves the first of men taking possession of an accursed inheritance, to be subdued at the cost of profound anguish and of excessive toil. But suddenly, as we struggled round a bend, there would be a glimpse of rush walls, of peaked grass-roofs, a burst of yells, a whirl of black limbs, a mass of hands clapping, of feet stamping, of bodies swaying, of eyes rolling, under the droop of heavy and motionless foliage. The steamer toiled along slowly on the edge of a black and incomprehensible frenzy. The prehistoric man was cursing us, praying to us, welcoming us — who could tell? We were cut off from the comprehension of our surroundings; we glided past like phantoms, wondering and secretly appalled, as sane men would be before an enthusiastic outbreak in a madhouse. We could not understand because we were too far and could not remember, because we were travelling in the night of first ages, of those ages that are gone, leaving hardly a sign — and no memories.

" The earth seemed unearthly. We are accustomed to look upon the shackled form of a conquered monster, but there — there you could look at a thing monstrous and free. It was unearthly, and the men were — No, they were not inhuman. Well, you know, that was the worst of it — this suspicion of their not being inhuman. It would come slowly to one. They howled and leaped, and spun, and made horrid faces; but what thrilled you was just the thought of their humanity — like yours — the thought of your remote kinship with this wild and passionate uproar. Ugly. Yes, it was ugly enough; but if you were man enough you would admit to yourself that there was in you just the faintest trace of a response to the terrible frankness of that noise, a dim suspicion of there being a meaning in it which you — you so remote from the night of first ages — could comprehend. And why not? The mind of man is capable of anything — because everything is in it, all the past as well as all the future. What was there after all? Joy, fear, sorrow, devotion, valour, rage — who can tell? — but truth — truth stripped of its cloak of time. Let the fool gape and shudder — the man knows, and can look on without a wink. But he must at least be as much of a man as these on the shore. He must meet that truth with his own true stuff — with his own inborn strength. Principles? Principles won't do. Acquisitions, clothes, pretty rags — rags that would fly off at the first good shake. No; you want a deliberate belief. An appeal to me in this fiendish row — is there? Very well; I hear; I admit, but I have a voice too, and for good or evil mine is the speech that cannot be silenced. Of course, a fool, what with sheer fright and fine sentiments, is always safe. Who's that grunting? You wonder I didn't go ashore for a howl and a dance? Well, no — I didn't. Fine sentiments, you say? Fine sentiments be hanged! I had no time. I had to mess about with white-lead and strips of woollen blanket helping to put bandages on those leaky steam-pipes — I tell you. I had to watch the steering, and circumvent those snags, and get the tin-pot along by hook or by crook. There was surface-truth enough in these things to save a wiser man. And between whiles I had to look after the savage who was fireman. He was an improved specimen; he could fire up a vertical boiler. He was there below me, and, upon my word, to look at him was as edifying as seeing a dog in a parody of breeches and a feather hat, walking on his hind legs. A few months of training had done for that really fine chap. He squinted at the steam-gauge and at the water-gauge with an evident effort of intrepidity — and he had filed teeth too, the poor devil, and the wool of his pate shaved into queer patterns, and three ornamental scars on each of his cheeks. He ought to have been clapping his hands and stamping his feet on the bank, instead of which he was hard at work, a thrall to strange witchcraft, full of improving knowledge. He was useful because he had been instructed; and what he knew was this — that should the water in that transparent thing disappear, the evil spirit inside the boiler would get angry through the greatness of his thirst, and take a terrible vengeance. So he sweated and fired up and watched the glass fearfully (with an impromptu charm, made of rags, tied to his arm, and a piece of polished bone, as big as a watch, stuck flatways through his lower lip), while the wooded banks slipped past us slowly, the short noise was left behind, the interminable miles of silence — and we crept on, towards Kurtz. But the snags were thick, the water was treacherous and shallow, the boiler seemed indeed to have a sulky devil in it, and thus neither that fireman nor I had any time to peer into our creepy thoughts.

"Some fifty miles below the Inner Station we came upon a hut of reeds, an inclined and melancholy pole, with the unrecognisable tatters of what had been a flag of some sort flying from it, and a neatly stacked wood-pile. This was unexpected. We came to the bank, and on the stack of firewood found a flat piece of board with some faded pencil-writing on it. When deciphered it said: 'Wood for you. Hurry up. Approach cautiously.' There was a signature, but it was illegible — not Kurtz — a much longer word. Hurry up. Where? Up the river? 'Approach cautiously.' We had not done

so. But the warning could not have been meant for the place where it could be only found after approach. Something was wrong above. But what — and how much? That was the question. We commented adversely upon the imbecility of that telegraphic style. The bush around said nothing, and would not let us look very far, either. A torn curtain of red twill hung in the doorway of the hut, and flapped sadly in our faces. The dwelling was dismantled; but we could see a white man had lived there not very long ago. There remained a rude table — a plank on two posts; a heap of rubbish reposed in a dark corner, and by the door I picked up a book. It had lost its covers, and the pages had been thumbed into a state of extremely dirty softness; but the back had been lovingly stitched afresh with white cotton thread, which looked clean yet. It was an extraordinary find. Its title was, *An Inquiry into some Points of Seamanship*, by a man Towser, Towson — some such name — Master in His Majesty's Navy. The matter looked dreary reading enough, with illustrative diagrams and repulsive tables of figures, and the copy was sixty years old. I handled this amazing antiquity with the greatest possible tenderness, lest it should dissolve in my hands. Within, Towson or Towser was inquiring earnestly into the breaking strain of ships' chains and tackle, and other such matters. Not a very enthralling book; but at the first glance you could see there a singleness of intention, an honest concern for the right way of going to work, which made these humble pages, thought out so many years ago, luminous with another than a professional light. The simple old sailor, with his talk of chains and purchases, made me forget the jungle and the pilgrims in a delicious sensation of having come upon something unmistakably real. Such a book being there was wonderful enough; but still more astounding were the notes pencilled in the margin, and plainly referring to the text. I couldn't believe my eyes! They were in cipher! Yes, it looked like cipher. Fancy a man lugging with him a book of that description into this nowhere and studying it — and making notes — in cipher at that! It was an extravagant mystery.

"I had been dimly aware for some time of a worrying noise, and when I lifted my eyes I saw the wood-pile was gone, and the manager, aided by all the pilgrims, was shouting at me from the river-side. I slipped the book into my pocket. I assure you to leave off reading was like tearing myself away from the shelter of an old and solid friendship.

"I started the lame engine ahead. 'It must be this miserable trader — this intruder,' exclaimed the manager, looking back malevolently at the place we had left. 'He must be English,' I said. 'It will not save him from getting into trouble if he is not careful,' muttered the manager darkly. I observed with assumed innocence that no man was safe from trouble in this world.

"The current was more rapid now, the steamer seemed at her last gasp, the stern-wheel flopped languidly, and I caught myself listening on tiptoe for the next beat of the float, for in sober truth I expected the wretched thing to give up every moment. It was like watching the last flickers of a life. But still we crawled. Sometimes I would pick out a tree a little way ahead to measure our progress towards Kurtz by, but I lost it invariably before we got abreast. To keep the eyes so long on one thing was too much for human patience. The manager displayed a beautiful resignation. I fretted and fumed and took to arguing with myself whether or no I would talk openly with Kurtz; but before I could come to any conclusion it occurred to me that my speech or my silence, indeed any action of mine, would be a mere futility. What did it matter what any one knew or ignored? What did it matter who was manager? One gets sometimes such a flash of insight. The essentials of this affair lay deep under the surface, beyond my reach, and beyond my power of meddling.

"Towards the evening of the second day we judged ourselves about eight miles from Kurtz's station. I wanted to push on; but the manager looked grave, and told me the navigation up there was so dangerous that it would be advisable, the sun being very low already, to wait where we were till next morning. Moreover, he pointed out that if the warning to approach cautiously were to be followed, we must approach in daylight — not at dusk, or in the dark. This was sensible enough. Eight miles meant nearly three hours' steaming for us, and I could also see suspicious ripples at the upper end of the reach. Nevertheless, I was annoyed beyond expression at the delay, and most unreasonably too, since one night more could not matter much after so many months. As we had plenty of wood, and caution was the word, I brought up in the middle of the stream. The reach was narrow, straight, with high sides like a railway cutting. The dusk came gliding into it long before

the sun had set. The current ran smooth and swift, but a dumb immobility sat on the banks. The living trees, lashed together by the creepers and every living bush of the undergrowth, might have been changed into stone, even to the slenderest twig, to the lightest leaf. It was not sleep — it seemed unnatural, like a state of trance. Not the faintest sound of any kind could be heard. You looked on amazed, and began to suspect yourself of being deaf — then the night came suddenly, and struck you blind as well. About three in the morning some large fish leaped, and the loud splash made me jump as though a gun had been fired. When the sun rose there was a white fog, very warm and clammy, and more blinding than the night. It did not shift or drive; it was just there, standing all round you like something solid. At eight or nine, perhaps, it lifted as a shutter lifts. We had a glimpse of the towering multitude of trees, of the immense matted jungle, with the blazing little ball of the sun hanging over it — all perfectly still — and then the white shutter came down again, smoothly, as if sliding in greased grooves. I ordered the chain, which we had begun to heave in, to be paid out again. Before it stopped running with a muffled rattle, a cry, a very loud cry, as of infinite desolation, soared slowly in the opaque air. It ceased. A complaining clamour, modulated in savage discords, filled our ears. The sheer unexpectedness of it made my hair stir under my cap. I don't know how it struck the others: to me it seemed as though the mist itself had screamed, so suddenly, and apparently from all sides at once, did this tumultuous and mournful uproar arise. It culminated in a hurried outbreak of almost intolerably excessive shrieking, which stopped short, leaving us stiffened in a variety of silly attitudes, and obstinately listening to the nearly as appalling and excessive silence. 'Good God! What is the meaning — ?' stammered at my elbow one of the pilgrims — a little fat man, with sandy hair and red whiskers, who wore side-spring boots, and pink pyjamas tucked into his socks. Two others remained open-mouthed a whole minute, then dashed into the little cabin, to rush out incontinently and stand darting scared glances, with Winchesters at 'ready' in their hands. What we could see was just the steamer we were on, her outlines blurred as though she had been on the point of dissolving, and a misty strip of water, perhaps two feet broad, around her — and that was all. The rest of the world was nowhere, as far as our eyes and ears were concerned. Just nowhere. Gone, disappeared; swept off without leaving a whisper or a shadow behind.

"I went forward, and ordered the chain to be hauled in short, so as to be ready to trip the anchor and move the steamboat at once if necessary. 'Will they attack?' whispered an awed voice. 'We will all be butchered in this fog,' murmured another. The faces twitched with the strain, the hands trembled slightly, the eyes forgot to wink. It was very curious to see the contrast of expressions of the white men and of the black fellows of our crew, who were as much strangers to that part of the river as we, though their homes were only eight hundred miles away. The whites, of course greatly discomposed, had besides a curious look of being painfully shocked by such an outrageous row. The others had an alert, naturally interested expression; but their faces were essentially quiet, even those of the one or two who grinned as they hauled at the chain. Several exchanged short, grunting phrases, which seemed to settle the matter to their satisfaction. Their headman, a young, broad-chested black, severely draped in dark-blue fringed cloths, with fierce nostrils and his hair all done up artfully in oily ringlets, stood near me. 'Ah!' I said, just for good fellowship's sake. 'Catch 'im,' he snapped, with a bloodshot widening of his eyes and a flash of sharp teeth — 'catch 'im. Give 'im to us.' 'To you, eh?' I asked; 'what would you do with them?' 'Eat 'im!' he said curtly, and, leaning his elbow on the rail, looked out into the fog in a dignified and profoundly pensive attitude. I would no doubt have been properly horrified, had it not occurred to me that he and his chaps must be very hungry: that they must have been growing increasingly hungry for at least this month past. They had been engaged for six months (I don't think a single one of them had any clear idea of time, as we at the end of countless ages have. They still belonged to the beginnings of time — had no inherited experience to teach them, as it were), and of course, as long as there was a piece of paper written over in accordance with some farcical law or other made down the river, it didn't enter anybody's head to trouble how they would live. Certainly they had brought with them some rotten hippo-meat, which couldn't have lasted very long, anyway, even if the pilgrims hadn't, in the midst of a shocking hullabaloo, thrown a considerable quantity of it overboard. It looked like a high-handed proceeding; but it was really a case of legitimate self-defence. You can't breathe dead hippo waking, sleeping, and eating, and at the same time keep your precarious grip on existence. Besides that, they had given them every week three pieces of brass wire, each about nine inches long; and the theory was they were to buy their provisions with that currency in river-side villages. You can see how *that* worked. There were either no villages, or the people were hostile, or the director, who like the rest of us fed out of tins, with an occasional old he-goat thrown in, didn't want to stop the steamer for some more or less recondite reasons. So, unless they swallowed the wire itself, or made loops of it to snare the fishes with, I don't see what good their extravagant salary could be to them. I must say it was paid with a regularity worthy of a large and honourable trading company. For the rest, the only thing to eat — though it didn't look eatable in the least — I saw in their possession was a few lumps of some stuff like half-cooked dough, of a dirty lavender colour, they kept wrapped in leaves, and now and then swallowed a piece of, but so small that it seemed done more for the look of the thing than for any serious purpose of sustenance. Why in the name of all the gnawing devils of hunger they didn't go for us — they were thirty to five — and have a good tuck-in for once, amazes me now when I think of it. They were big powerful men, with not much capacity to weigh the consequences, with courage, with strength, even yet, though their skins were no longer glossy and their muscles no longer hard. And I saw that something restraining, one of those human secrets that baffle probability, had come into play there. I looked at them with a swift quickening of interest — not because it occurred to me I might be eaten by them before very long, though I own to you that just then I perceived — in a new light, as it were — how unwholesome the pilgrims looked, and I hoped, yes, I positively hoped, that my aspect was not so — what shall I say? — so — unappetising: a touch of fantastic vanity which fitted well with the dream-sensation that pervaded all my days at that time. Perhaps I had a little fever too. One can't live with one's finger everlastingly on one's pulse. I had often 'a little fever,' or a little touch of other things — the playful paw-strokes of the wilderness, the preliminary trifling before the more serious onslaught which came in due course. Yes; I looked at them as you would on any human being, with a curiosity of their impulses, motives, capacities, weaknesses, when brought to the test of an inexorable physical necessity. Restraint! What possible restraint? Was it superstition, disgust, patience, fear — or some kind of primitive honour? No fear can stand up to hunger, no patience can wear it out, disgust simply does not exist where hunger is; and as to superstition, beliefs, and what you may call principles, they are less than chaff in a breeze. Don't you know the devilry of lingering starvation, its exasperating torment, its black thoughts, its sombre and brooding ferocity? Well, I do. It takes a man all his inborn strength to fight hunger properly. It's really easier to face bereavement, dishonour, and the perdition of one's soul — than this kind of prolonged hunger. Sad, but true. And these chaps too had no earthly reason for any kind of scruple. Restraint! I would just as soon have expected restraint from a hyena prowling amongst the corpses of a battlefield. But there was the fact facing me — the fact dazzling, to be seen, like the foam on the depths of the sea, like a ripple on an unfathomable enigma, a mystery greater — when I thought of it — than the curious, inexplicable note of desperate grief in this savage clamour that had swept by us on the river-bank, behind the blind whiteness of the fog.

" Two pilgrims were quarrelling in hurried whispers as to which bank. 'Left.' 'No, no; how can you? Right, right, of course.' 'It is very serious,' said the manager's voice behind me; 'I would be desolated if anything should happen to Mr. Kurtz before we came up.' I looked at him, and had not the slightest doubt he was sincere. He was just the kind of man who would wish to preserve appearances. That was his restraint. But when he muttered something about going on at once, I did not even take the trouble to answer him. I knew, and he knew, that it was impossible. Were we to let go our hold of the bottom, we would be absolutely in the air — in space. We wouldn't be able to tell where we were going to — whether up or down stream, or across — till we fetched against one bank or the other — and then we wouldn't know at first which it was. Of course I made no move. I had no mind for a smash-up. You couldn't imagine a more deadly place for a shipwreck. Whether drowned at once or not, we were sure to perish speedily in one way or another. 'I authorise you to take all the risks,' he said, after a short silence. 'I refuse to take any,' I said shortly; which was just the answer he expected, though its tone might have surprised him. 'Well, I must defer to your judgment. You are captain,' he said, with marked civility. I turned my shoulder to him in sign of my appreciation, and looked into the fog. How long would it last? It was the most hopeless look-out. The approach to this Kurtz grubbing for ivory in the wretched bush was beset by as many dangers as though he had been an enchanted princess sleeping in a fabulous castle. 'Will they attack, do you think?' asked the manager, in a confidential tone.

" I did not think they would attack, for several obvious reasons. The thick fog was one. If they left the bank in their canoes they would get lost in it, as we would be if we attempted to move. Still, I had also judged the jungle of both banks quite impenetrable — and yet eyes were in it, eyes that had seen us. The river-side bushes were certainly very thick; but the undergrowth behind was evidently penetrable. However, during the short lift I had seen no canoes anywhere in the reach — certainly not abreast of the steamer. But what made the idea of attack inconceivable to me was the nature of the noise — of the cries we had heard. They had not the fierce character boding of immediate hostile intention. Unexpected, wild, and violent as they had been, they had given me an irresistible impression of sorrow. The glimpse of the steamboat had for some reason filled those savages with unrestrained grief. The danger, if any, I expounded, was from our proximity to a great human passion let loose. Even extreme grief may ultimately vent itself in violence — but more generally takes the form of apathy. . . .

" You should have seen the pilgrims stare! They had no heart to grin, or even to revile me; but I believe they thought me gone mad — with fright, maybe. I delivered a regular lecture. My dear boys, it was no good bothering. Keep a look-out? Well, you may guess I watched the fog for the signs of lifting as a cat watches a mouse; but for anything else our eyes were of no more use to us than if we had been buried miles deep in a heap of cotton-wool. It felt like it too — choking, warm, stifling. Besides, all I said, though it sounded extravagant, was absolutely true to fact. What we afterwards alluded to as an attack was really an attempt at repulse. The action was very far from being aggressive — it was not even defensive, in the usual sense: it was undertaken under the stress of desperation, and in its essence was purely protective.

" It developed itself, I should say, two hours after the fog lifted, and its commencement was at a spot, roughly speaking, about a mile and a half below Kurtz's station. We had just floundered and flopped round a bend, when I saw an islet, a mere grassy hummock of bright green, in the middle of the stream. It was the only thing of the kind; but as we opened the reach more, I perceived it was the head of a long sandbank, or rather of a chain of shallow patches stretching down the middle of the river. They were discoloured, just awash, and the whole lot was seen just under the water, exactly as a man's backbone is seen running down the middle of his back under the skin. Now, as far as I did see, I could go to the right or to the left of this. I didn't know either channel, of course. The banks looked pretty well alike, the depth appeared the same; but as I had been informed the station was on the west side, I naturally headed for the western passage.

"No sooner had we fairly entered it than I became aware it was much narrower than I had supposed. To the left of us there was the long uninterrupted shoal, and to the right a high steep bank heavily overgrown with bushes. Above the bush the trees stood in serried ranks. The twigs overhung the current thickly, and from distance to distance a large limb of some tree projected rigidly over the stream. It was then well on in the afternoon, the face of the forest was gloomy, and a broad strip of shadow had already fallen on the water. In this shadow we steamed up — very slowly, as you may imagine. I sheered her well inshore — the water being deepest near the bank, as the sounding-pole informed me.

"One of my hungry and forbearing friends was sounding in the bows just below me. This steamboat was exactly like a decked scow. On the deck there were two little teak-wood houses, with doors and windows. The boiler was in the fore-end, and the machinery right astern. Over the whole there was a light roof, supported on stanchions. The funnel projected through that roof, and in front of the funnel a small cabin built of light planks served for a pilot-house. It contained a couch, two camp-stools, a loaded Martini-Henry leaning in one corner, a tiny table, and the steering-wheel. It had a wide door in front and a broad shutter at each side. All these were always thrown open, of course. I spent my days perched up there on the extreme fore-end of that roof, before the door. At night I slept, or tried to, on the couch. An athletic black belonging to some coast tribe, and educated by my poor predecessor, was the helmsman. He sported a pair of brass earrings, wore a blue cloth wrapper from the waist to the ankles, and thought all the world of himself. He was the most unstable kind of fool I had ever seen. He steered with no end of a swagger while you were by; but if he lost sight of you, he became instantly the prey of an abject funk, and would let that cripple of a steamboat get the upper hand of him in a minute.

"I was looking down at the sounding-pole, and feeling much annoyed to see at each try a little more of it stick out of that river, when I saw my poleman give up the business suddenly, and stretch himself flat on the deck, without even taking the trouble to haul his pole in. He kept hold on it though, and it trailed in the water. At the same time the fireman, whom I could also see below me, sat down abruptly before his furnace and ducked his head. I was amazed. Then I had to look at the river mighty quick, because there was a snag in the fairway. Sticks, little sticks, were flying about — thick: they were whizzing before my nose, dropping below me, striking behind me against my pilot-house. All this time the river, the shore, the woods, were very quiet — perfectly quiet. I could only hear the heavy splashing thump of the stern-wheel and the patter of these things. We cleared the snag clumsily. Arrows, by Jove! We were being shot at! I stepped in quickly to close the shutter on the land-side. That fool-helmsman, his hands on the spokes, was lifting his knees high, stamping his feet, champing his mouth, like a reined-in horse. Confound him! And we were staggering within ten feet of the bank. I had to lean right out to swing the heavy shutter, and I saw a face amongst the leaves on the level with my own, looking at me very fierce and steady; and then suddenly, as though a veil had been removed from my eyes, I made out, deep in the tangled gloom, naked breasts, arms, legs, glaring eyes — the bush was swarming with human limbs in movement, glistening, of bronze colour. The twigs shook, swayed, and rustled, the arrows flew out of them, and then the shutter came to. 'Steer her straight,' I said to the helmsman. He held his head rigid, face forward; but his eyes rolled, he kept on lifting and setting down his feet gently, his mouth foamed a little. 'Keep quiet!' I said in a fury. I might just as well have ordered a tree not to sway in the wind. I darted out. Below me there was a great scuffle of feet on the iron deck; confused exclamations; a voice screamed, 'Can you turn back?' I caught sight of a V-shaped ripple on the water ahead. What? Another snag! A fusillade burst out under my feet. The pilgrims had opened with their Winchesters, and were simply squirting lead into that bush. A deuce of a lot of smoke came up and drove slowly forward. I swore at it. Now I couldn't see the ripple or the snag either. I stood in the doorway, peering, and the arrows came in swarms. They might have been poisoned, but they looked as though they wouldn't kill a cat. The bush began to howl. Our wood-cutters raised a warlike whoop; the report of a rifle just at my back deafened me. I glanced over my shoulder, and the pilot-house was yet full of noise and smoke when I made a dash at the wheel. The fool-nigger had dropped everything, to throw the shutter open and let off that Martini-Henry. He stood before the wide opening, glaring, and I yelled at him to come back, while I straightened the sudden twist out of that steamboat. There was no room to turn even if I had wanted to, the snag was somewhere very near ahead in that confounded smoke, there was no time to lose, so I just crowded her into the bank — right into the bank, where I knew the water was deep.

"We tore slowly along the overhanging bushes in a whirl of broken twigs and flying leaves. The fusillade below stopped short, as I had foreseen it would when the squirts got empty. I threw my head back to a glinting whizz that traversed the pilot-house, in at one shutter-hole and out at the other. Looking past that mad helmsman, who was shaking the empty rifle and yelling at the shore, I saw vague forms of men running bent double, leaping, gliding, distinct, incomplete, evanescent. Something big appeared in the air before the shutter, the rifle went overboard, and the man stepped back swiftly, looked at me over his shoulder in an extraordinary, profound, familiar manner, and fell upon my feet. The side of his head hit the wheel twice, and the end of what appeared a long cane clattered round and knocked over a little camp-stool. It looked as though after wrenching that thing from somebody ashore he had lost his balance in the effort. The thin smoke had blown away, we were clear of the snag, and looking ahead I could see that in another hundred yards or so I would be free to sheer off, away from the bank; but my feet felt so very warm and wet that I had to look down. The man had rolled on his back and stared straight up at me; both his hands clutched that cane. It was the shaft of a spear that, either thrown or lunged through the opening, had caught him in the side just below the ribs; the

blade had gone in out of sight, after making a frightful gash; my shoes were full; a pool of blood lay very still, gleaming dark-red under the wheel; his eyes shone with an amazing lustre. The fusillade burst out again. He looked at me anxiously, gripping the spear like something precious, with an air of being afraid I would try to take it away from him. I had to make an effort to free my eyes from his gaze and attend to the steering. With one hand I felt above my head for the line of the steam whistle, and jerked out screech after screech hurriedly. The tumult of angry and warlike yells was checked instantly, and then from the depths of the woods went out such a tremulous and prolonged wail of mournful fear and utter despair as may be imagined to follow the flight of the last hope from the earth. There was a great commotion in the bush; the shower of arrows stopped, a few dropping shots rang out sharply — then silence, in which the languid beat of the stern-wheel came plainly to my ears. I put the helm hard a-starboard at the moment when the pilgrim in pink pyjamas, very hot and agitated, appeared in the doorway. 'The manager sends me — ' he began in an official tone, and stopped short. 'Good God!' he said, glaring at the wounded man.

"We two whites stood over him, and his lustrous and inquiring glance enveloped us both. I declare it looked as though he would presently put to us some question in an understandable language; but he died without uttering a sound, without moving a limb, without twitching a muscle. Only in the very last moment, as though in response to some sign we could not see, to some whisper we could not hear, he frowned heavily, and that frown gave to his black death-mask an inconceivably sombre, brooding, and menacing expression. The lustre of inquiring glance faded swiftly into vacant glassiness. 'Can you steer?' I asked the agent eagerly. He looked very dubious; but I made a grab at his arm, and he understood at once I meant him to steer whether or no. To tell you the truth, I was morbidly anxious to change my shoes and socks. 'He is dead,' murmured the fellow, immensely impressed. 'No doubt about it,' said I, tugging like mad at the shoe-laces. 'And by the way, I suppose Mr. Kurtz is dead as well by this time.'

"For the moment that was the dominant thought. There was a sense of extreme disappointment, as though I had found out I had been striving after something altogether without a substance. I couldn't have been more disgusted if I had travelled all this way for the sole purpose of talking with Mr. Kurtz. Talking with . . . I flung one shoe overboard, and became aware that that was exactly what I had been looking forward to — a talk with Kurtz. I made the strange discovery that I had never imagined him as doing, you know, but as discoursing. I didn't say to myself, 'Now I will never see him,' or 'Now I will never shake him by the hand,' but, 'Now I will never hear him.' The man presented himself as a voice. Not of course that I did not connect him with some sort of action. Hadn't I been told in all the tones of jealousy and admiration that he had collected, bartered, swindled, or stolen more ivory than all the other agents together? That was not the point. The point was in his being a gifted creature, and that of all his gifts the one that stood out pre-eminently, that carried with it a sense of real presence, was his ability to talk, his words — the gift of expression, the bewildering, the illuminating, the most exalted and the most contemptible, the pulsating stream of light, or the deceitful flow from the heart of an impenetrable darkness.

"The other shoe went flying unto the devil-god of that river. I thought, By Jove! it's all over. We are too late; he has vanished — the gift has vanished, by means of some spear, arrow, or club. I will never hear that chap speak after all — and my sorrow had a startling extravagance of emotion, even such as I had noticed in the howling sorrow of these savages in the bush. I couldn't have felt more of lonely desolation somehow, had I been robbed of a belief or had missed my destiny in life. . . . Why do you sigh in this beastly way, somebody? Absurd? Well, absurd. Good Lord! mustn't a man ever — Here, give me some tobacco." . . .

There was a pause of profound stillness, then a match flared, and Marlow's lean face appeared, worn, hollow, with downward folds and dropped eyelids, with an aspect of concentrated attention; and as he took vigorous draws at his pipe, it seemed to retreat and advance out of the night in the regular flicker of the tiny flame. The match went out.

"Absurd!" he cried. "This is the worst of trying to tell . . . Here you all are, each moored with two good addresses, like a hulk with two anchors, a butcher round one corner, a policeman round another, excellent appetites, and temperature normal — you hear — normal from year's end to year's end. And you say, Absurd! Absurd be — ex-ploded! Absurd! My dear boys, what can you expect from a man who out of sheer nervousness had just flung overboard a pair of new shoes? Now I think of it, it is amazing I did not shed tears. I am, upon the whole, proud of my fortitude. I was cut to the quick at the idea of having lost the inestimable privilege of listening to the gifted Kurtz. Of course I was wrong. The privilege was waiting for me. Oh yes, I heard more than enough. And I was right, too. A voice. He was very little more than a voice. And I heard — him — it — this voice — other voices — all of them were so little more than voices — and the memory of that time itself lingers around me, impalpable, like a dying vibration of one immense jabber, silly, atrocious, sordid, savage, or simply mean, without any kind of sense. Voices, voices — even the girl herself — now — "

He was silent for a long time.

"I laid the ghost of his gifts at last with a lie," he began suddenly. "Girl! What? Did I mention a girl? Oh, she is out of it — completely. They — the women I mean — are out of it — should be out of it. We must help them to stay in that beautiful world of their own, lest ours gets worse. Oh, she had to be out of it. You should have heard the disinterred body of Mr. Kurtz saying, 'My Intended.' You would have perceived directly then how completely she was out of it. And the lofty frontal bone of Mr. Kurtz! They say the hair goes on growing sometimes, but this — ah — specimen was impressively bald. The wilderness had patted him on the head, and, behold, it was like a ball — an ivory ball; it had caressed him, and — lo! — he had withered; it had taken him, loved him, embraced him, got into his veins, consumed his flesh, and sealed his soul to its own by the inconceivable ceremonies of some devilish initiation. He was its spoiled and pampered favourite. Ivory? I should think so. Heaps of it, stacks of it. The old mud shanty was bursting with it. You would think there was not a single tusk left either above or below the ground in the whole country. 'Mostly fossil,' the manager had remarked disparagingly. It was no more fossil than I am; but they call it fossil when it is dug up. It appears these niggers do bury the tusks sometimes — but evidently they couldn't bury this parcel deep enough to save the gifted Mr. Kurtz from his fate. We filled the steamboat with it, and had to pile a lot on the deck. Thus he could see and enjoy as long as he could see, because the appreciation of this favour had remained with him to the last. You should have heard him say, 'My ivory.' Oh yes, I heard him. 'My Intended, my ivory, my station, my river, my —' everything belonged to him. It made me hold my breath in expectation of hearing the wilderness burst into a prodigious peal of laughter that would shake the fixed stars in their places. Everything belonged to him — but that was a trifle. The thing was to know what he belonged to, how many powers of darkness claimed him for their own. That was the reflection that made you creepy all over. It was impossible — it was not good for one either — trying to imagine. He had taken a high seat amongst the devils of the land — I mean literally. You can't understand. How could you? — with solid pavement under your feet, surrounded by kind neighbours ready to cheer you or to fall on you, stepping delicately between the butcher and the policeman, in the holy terror of scandal and gallows and lunatic asylums — how can you imagine what particular region of the first ages a man's untrammelled feet may take him into by the way of solitude — utter solitude without a policeman — by the way of silence — utter silence, where no warning voice of a kind neighbour can be heard whispering of public opinion? These little things make all the great difference. When they are gone you must fall back upon your own innate strength, upon your own capacity for faithfulness. Of course you may be too much of a fool to go wrong — too dull even to know you are being assaulted by the powers of darkness. I take it, no fool ever made a bargain for his soul with the devil: the fool is too much of a fool, or the devil too much of a devil — I don't know which. Or you may be such a thunderingly exalted creature as to be altogether deaf and blind to anything but heavenly sights and sounds. Then the earth for you is only a standing place — and whether to be like this is your loss or your gain I won't pretend to say. But most of us are neither one nor the other. The earth for us is a place to live in, where we must put up with sights, with sounds, with smells, too, by Jove! — breathe dead hippo, so to speak, and not be contaminated. And there, don't you see? your strength comes in, the faith in your ability for the digging of unostentatious holes to bury the stuff in — your power of devotion, not to yourself, but to an obscure, backbreaking business. And that's difficult enough. Mind, I am not trying to excuse or even explain — I am trying to account to myself for — for — Mr. Kurtz — for the shade of Mr. Kurtz. This initiated wraith

from the back of Nowhere honoured me with its amazing confidence before it vanished altogether. This was because it could speak English to me. The original Kurtz had been educated partly in England, and — as he was good enough to say himself — his sympathies were in the right place. His mother was half-English, his father was half-French. All Europe contributed to the making of Kurtz; and by and by I learned that, most appropriately, the International Society for the Suppression of Savage Customs had entrusted him with the making of a report, for its future guidance. And he had written it too. I've seen it. I've read it. It was eloquent, vibrating with eloquence, but too high-strung, I think. Seventeen pages of close writing he had found time for! But this must have been before his — let us say — nerves went wrong, and caused him to preside at certain midnight dances ending with unspeakable rites, which — as far as I reluctantly gathered from what I heard at various times — were offered up to him — do you understand? — to Mr. Kurtz himself. But it was a beautiful piece of writing. The opening paragraph, however, in the light of later information, strikes me now as ominous. He began with the argument that we whites, from the point of development we had arrived at, 'must necessarily appear to them [savages] in the nature of supernatural beings — we approach them with the might as of a deity,' and so on, and so on. 'By the simple exercise of our will we can exert a power for good practically unbounded,' etc. etc. From that point he soared and took me with him. The peroration was magnificent, though difficult to remember, you know. It gave me the notion of an exotic Immensity ruled by an august Benevolence. It made me tingle with enthusiasm. This was the unbounded power of eloquence — of words — of burning noble words. There were no practical hints to interrupt the magic current of phrases, unless a kind of note at the foot of the last page, scrawled evidently much later, in an unsteady hand, may be regarded as the exposition of a method. It was very simple, and at the end of that moving appeal to every altruistic sentiment it blazed at you, luminous and terrifying, like a flash of lightning in a serene sky: 'exterminate all the brutes!' The curious part was that he had apparently forgotten all about that valuable postscriptum, because, later on, when he in a sense came to himself, he repeatedly entreated me to take good care of 'my pamphlet' (he called it), as it was sure to have in the future a good influence upon his career. I had full information about all these things, and, besides, as it turned out, I was to have the care of his memory. I've done enough for it to give me the indisputable right to lay it, if I choose, for an everlasting rest in the dust-bin of progress, amongst all the sweepings and, figuratively speaking, all the dead cats of civilisation. But then, you see, I can't choose. He won't be forgotten. Whatever he was, he was not common. He had the power to charm or frighten rudimentary souls into an aggravated witch-dance in his honour; he could also fill the small souls of the pilgrims with bitter misgivings: he had one devoted friend at least, and he had conquered one soul in the world that was neither rudimentary nor tainted with self-seeking. No; I can't forget him, though I am not prepared to affirm the fellow was exactly worth the life we lost in getting to him. I missed my late helmsman awfully — I missed him even while his body was still lying in the pilot-house. Perhaps you will think it passing strange this regret for a savage who was no more account than a grain of sand in a black Sahara. Well, don't you see, he had done something, he had steered; for months I had him at my back — a help — an instrument. It was a kind of partnership. He steered for me — I had to look after him, I worried about his deficiencies, and thus a subtle bond had been created, of which I only became aware when it was suddenly broken. And the intimate profundity of that look he gave me when he received his hurt remains to this day in my memory — like a claim of distant kinship affirmed in a supreme moment.

"Poor fool! If he had only left that shutter alone. He had no restraint, no restraint — just like Kurtz — a tree swayed by the wind. As soon as I had put on a dry pair of slippers, I dragged him out, after first jerking the spear out of his side, which operation I confess I performed with my eyes shut tight. His heels leaped together over the little doorstep; his shoulders were pressed to my breast; I hugged him from behind desperately. Oh! he was heavy, heavy; heavier than any man on earth, I should imagine. Then without more ado I tipped him overboard. The current snatched him as though he had been a wisp of grass, and I saw the body roll over twice before I lost sight of it for ever. All the pilgrims and the manager were then congregated on the awning-deck about the pilot-house, chattering at each other like a flock of excited magpies, and there was a scandalised murmur at my heartless promptitude. What they wanted to

keep that body hanging about for I can't guess. Embalm it, maybe. But I had also heard another, and a very ominous, murmur on the deck below. My friends the wood cutters were likewise scandalised, and with a better show of reason — though I admit that the reason itself was quite inadmissible. Oh, quite! I had made up my mind that if my late helmsman was to be eaten, the fishes alone should have him. He had been a very second-rate helmsman while alive, but now he was dead he might have become a first-class temptation, and possibly cause some startling trouble. Besides, I was anxious to take the wheel, the man in pink pyjamas showing himself a hopeless duffer at the business.

"This I did directly the simple funeral was over. We were going half-speed, keeping right in the middle of the stream, and I listened to the talk about me. They had given up Kurtz, they had given up the station; Kurtz was dead, and the station had been burnt — and so on — and so on. The red haired pilgrim was beside himself with the thought that at least this poor Kurtz had been properly revenged. 'Say! We must have made a glorious slaughter of them in the bush. Eh? What do you think? Say?' He positively danced, the bloodthirsty little gingery beggar. And he had nearly fainted when he saw the wounded man! I could not help saying, 'You made a glorious lot of smoke, anyhow.' I had seen, from the way the tops of the bushes rustled and flew, that almost all the shots had gone too high. You can't hit anything unless you take aim and fire from the shoulder; but these chaps fired from the hip with their eyes shut. The retreat, I maintained — and I was right — was caused by the screeching of the steam-whistle. Upon this they forgot Kurtz, and began to howl at me with indignant protests.

"The manager stood by the wheel murmuring confidentially about the necessity of getting well away down the river before dark at all events, when I saw in the distance a clearing on the riverside and the outlines of some sort of building. 'What's this?' I asked. He clapped his hands in wonder. 'The station!' he cried. I edged in at once, still going half-speed.

"Through my glasses I saw the slope of a hill interspersed with rare trees and perfectly free from undergrowth. A long decaying building on the summit was half buried in the high grass; the large holes in the peaked roof gaped black from afar; the jungle and the woods made a background. There was no enclosure or fence of any kind; but there had been one apparently, for near the house half a dozen slim posts remained in a row, roughly trimmed, and with their upper ends ornamented with round carved balls. The rails, or whatever there had been between, had disappeared. Of course the forest surrounded all that. The river-bank was clear, and on the water side I saw a white man under a hat like a cart-wheel beckoning persistently with his whole arm. Examining the edge of the forest above and below, I was almost certain I could see movements — human forms gliding here and there. I steamed past prudently, then stopped the engines and let her drift down. The man on the shore began to shout, urging us to land. 'We have been attacked,' screamed the manager. 'I know — I know. It's all right,' yelled back the other, as cheerful as you please. 'Come along. It's all right. I am glad.'

"His aspect reminded me of something I had seen — something funny I had seen somewhere. As I manœuvred to get alongside, I was asking myself, 'What does this fellow look like?' Suddenly I got it. He looked like a harlequin. His clothes had been made of some stuff that was brown holland probably, but it was covered with patches all over, with bright patches, blue, red, and yellow — patches on the back, patches on the front, patches on elbows, on knees; coloured binding round his jacket, scarlet edging at the bottom of his trousers; and the sunshine made him look extremely gay and wonderfully neat withal, because you could see how beautifully all this patching had been done. A beardless, boyish face, very fair, no features to speak of, nose peeling, little blue eyes, smiles and frowns chasing each other over that open countenance like sunshine and shadow on a wind-swept plain. 'Look out, captain!' he cried; 'there's a snag lodged in here last night.' What! Another snag? I confess I swore shamefully. I had nearly holed my cripple, to finish off that charming trip. The harlequin on the bank turned his little pug nose up to me. 'You English?' he asked, all smiles. 'Are you?' I shouted from the wheel. The smiles vanished, and he shook his head as if sorry for my disappointment. Then he brightened up. 'Never mind!' he cried encouragingly. 'Are we in time?' I asked. 'He is up there,' he replied, with a toss of the head up the hill, and becoming gloomy all of a sudden. His face was like the autumn sky, overcast one moment and bright the next.

"When the manager, escorted by the pilgrims, all of them armed to the teeth, had gone to the house, this chap came on board. 'I say, I don't like this. These natives are in the bush,' I said. He assured me earnestly it was all right. 'They are simple people,' he added; 'well, I am glad you came. It took me all my time to keep them off.' 'But you said it was all right,' I cried. 'Oh, they meant no harm,' he said; and as I stared he corrected himself, 'Not exactly.' Then vivaciously, 'My faith, your pilot-house wants a clean up!' In the next breath he advised me to keep enough steam on the boiler to blow the whistle in case of any trouble. 'One good screech will do more for you than all your rifles. They are simple people,' he repeated. He rattled away at such a rate he quite overwhelmed me. He seemed to be trying to make up for lots of silence, and actually hinted, laughing, that such was the case. 'Don't you talk with Mr. Kurtz?' I said. 'You don't talk with that man — you listen to him,' he exclaimed with severe exaltation. 'But now — ' He waved his arm, and in the twinkling of an eye was in the uttermost depths of despondency. In a moment he came up again with a jump, possessed himself of both my hands, shook them continuously, while he gabbled: 'Brother sailor . . . honour . . . pleasure . . . delight . . . introduce myself . . . Russian . . . son of an arch-priest . . . Government of Tambov . . . What? Tobacco! English tobacco; the excellent English tobacco! Now, that's brotherly. Smoke? Where's a sailor that does not smoke?'

"The pipe soothed him, and gradually I made out he had run away from school, had gone to sea in a Russian ship; ran away again; served some time in English ships; was not reconciled with the arch-priest. He made a point of that. 'But when one is young one must see things, gather experience, ideas; enlarge the mind.' 'Here!' I interrupted. 'You can never tell! Here I met Mr. Kurtz,' he said, youthfully solemn and reproachful. I held my tongue after that. It appears he had persuaded a Dutch trading-house on the coast to fit him out with stores and goods, and had started for the interior with a light heart, and no more idea of what would happen to him than a baby. He had been wandering about that river for nearly two years alone, cut off from everybody and everything. 'I am not so young as I look. I am twenty-five,' he said. 'At first old Van Shuyten would tell me to go to the devil,' he narrated with keen enjoyment; 'but I stuck to him, and talked and talked, till at last he got afraid I would talk the hind-leg off his favourite dog, so he gave me some cheap things and a few guns, and told me he hoped he would never see my face again. Good old Dutchman, Van Shuyten. I sent him one small lot of ivory a year ago, so that he can't call me a little thief when I get back. I hope he got it. And for the rest I don't care. I had some wood stacked for you. That was my old house. Did you see?'

"I gave him Towson's book. He made as though he would kiss me, but restrained himself. 'The only book I had left, and I thought I had lost it,' he said, looking at it ecstatically. 'So many accidents happen to a man going about alone, you know. Canoes get upset sometimes — and sometimes you've got to clear out so quick when the people get angry.' He thumbed the pages. 'You made notes in Russian?' I asked. He nodded. 'I thought they were written in cipher,' I said. He laughed, then became serious. 'I had lots of trouble to keep these people off,' he said. 'Did they want to kill you?' I asked. 'Oh no!' he cried, and checked himself. 'Why did they attack us?' I pursued. He hesitated, then said shamefacedly, 'They don't want him to go.' 'Don't they?' I said curiously. He nodded a nod full of mystery and wisdom. 'I tell you,' he cried, 'this man has enlarged my mind.' He opened his arms wide, staring at me with his little blue eyes that were perfectly round."

III

"I looked at him, lost in astonishment. There he was before me, in motley, as though he had absconded from a troupe of mimes, enthusiastic, fabulous. His very existence was improbable, inexplicable, and altogether bewildering. He was an insoluble problem. It was inconceivable how he had existed, how he had succeeded in getting so far, how he had managed to remain — why he did not instantly disappear. 'I went a little farther,' he said, 'then still a little farther — till I had gone so far that I don't know how I'll ever get back. Never mind. Plenty time. I can manage. You take Kurtz away quick — quick — I tell you.' The glamour of youth enveloped his particoloured rags, his destitution, his loneliness, the essential desolation of his futile wanderings. For months — for years — his life hadn't been worth a day's purchase; and there he was gallantly, thoughtlessly alive, to all appearance indestructible solely by the virtue of his few years and of his unreflecting audacity. I was seduced into something like admiration — like envy. Glamour urged him on, glamour kept him

unscathed. He surely wanted nothing from the wilderness but space to breathe in and to push on through. His need was to exist, and to move onwards at the greatest possible risk, and with a maximum of privation. If the absolutely pure, uncalculating, unpractical spirit of adventure had ever ruled a human being, it ruled this be-patched youth. I almost envied him the possession of this modest and clear flame. It seemed to have consumed all thought of self so completely, that, even while he was talking to you, you forgot that it was he — the man before your eyes — who had gone through these things. I did not envy him his devotion to Kurtz, though. He had not meditated over it. It came to him, and he accepted it with a sort of eager fatalism. I must say that to me it appeared about the most dangerous thing in every way he had come upon so far.

"They had come together unavoidably, like two ships becalmed near each other, and lay rubbing sides at last. I suppose Kurtz wanted an audience, because on a certain occasion, when encamped in the forest, they had talked all night, or more probably Kurtz had talked. 'We talked of everything,' he said, quite transported at the recollection. 'I forgot there was such a thing as sleep. The night did not seem to last an hour. Everything! Everything! . . . Of love too.' 'Ah, he talked to you of love!' I said, much amused. 'It isn't what you think,' he cried, almost passionately. 'It was in general. He made me see things — things.'

"He threw his arms up. We were on deck at the time, and the head-man of my wood-cutters, lounging near by, turning upon him his heavy and glittering eyes. I looked around, and I don't know why, but I assure you that never, never before, did this land, this river, this jungle, the very arch of this blazing sky, appear to me so hopeless and so dark, so impenetrable to human thought, so pitiless to human weakness. 'And, ever since, you have been with him, of course?' I said.

"On the contrary. It appears their intercourse had been very much broken by various causes. He had, as he informed me proudly, managed to nurse Kurtz through two illnesses (he alluded to it as you would to some risky feat), but as a rule Kurtz wandered alone, far in the depths of the forest. 'Very often coming to this station, I had to wait days and days before he would turn up,' he said. 'Ah, it was worth waiting for! — sometimes.' 'What was he doing? exploring or what?' I asked. 'Oh yes, of course'; he had discovered lots of villages, a lake too — he did not know exactly in what direction; it was dangerous to inquire too much — but mostly his expeditions had been for ivory. 'But he had no goods to trade with by that time,' I objected. 'There's a good lot of cartridges left even yet,' he answered, looking away. 'To speak plainly, he raided the country,' I said. He nodded. 'Not alone, surely!' He muttered something about the villages round that lake. 'Kurtz got the tribe to follow him, did he?' I suggested. He fidgeted a little. 'They adored him,' he said. The tone of these words was so extraordinary that I looked at him searchingly. It was curious to see his mingled eagerness and reluctance to speak of Kurtz. The man filled his life, occupied his thoughts, swayed his emotions. 'What can you expect?' he burst out; 'he came to them with thunder and lightning, you know — and they had never seen anything like it — and very terrible. He could be very terrible. You can't judge Mr. Kurtz as you would an ordinary man. No, no, no! Now — just to give you an idea — I don't mind telling you, he wanted to shoot me too one day — but I don't judge him.' 'Shoot you!' I cried. 'What for?' 'Well, I had a small lot of ivory the chief of that village near my house gave me. You see I used to shoot game for them. Well, he wanted it, and wouldn't hear reason. He declared he would shoot me unless I gave him the ivory and then cleared out of the country, because he could do so, and had a fancy for it, and there was nothing on earth to prevent him killing whom he jolly well pleased. And it was true too. I gave him the ivory. What did I care! But I didn't clear out. No, no. I couldn't leave him. I had to be careful, of course, till we got friendly again for a time. He had his second illness then. Afterwards I had to keep out of the way; but I didn't mind. He was living for the most part in those villages on the lake. When he came down to the river, sometimes he would take to me, and sometimes it was better for me to be careful. This man suffered too much. He hated all this, and somehow he couldn't get away. When I had a chance I begged him to try and leave while there was time; I offered to go back with him. And he would say yes, and then he would remain; go off on another ivory hunt; disappear for weeks; forget himself amongst these people — forget himself — you know.' 'Why! he's mad,' I said. He protested indignantly. Mr. Kurtz couldn't be mad. If I had heard him talk, only two days ago, I wouldn't dare hint at such a thing. . . . I had taken up my binoculars while we talked, and

was looking at the shore, sweeping the limit of the forest at each side and at the back of the house. The consciousness of there being people in that bush, so silent, so quiet — as silent and quiet as the ruined house on the hill — made me uneasy. There was no sign on the face of nature of this amazing tale that was not so much told as suggested to me in desolate exclamations, completed by shrugs, in interrupted phrases, in hints ending in deep sighs. The woods were unmoved, like a mask — heavy, like the closed door of a prison — they looked with their air of hidden knowledge, of patient expectation, of unapproachable silence. The Russian was explaining to me that it was only lately that Mr. Kurtz had come down to the river, bringing along with him all the fighting men of that lake tribe. He had been absent for several months — getting himself adored, I suppose — and had come down unexpectedly, with the intention to all appearances of making a raid either across the river or down stream. Evidently the appetite for more ivory had got the better of the — what shall I say? — less material aspirations. However, he had got much worse suddenly. 'I heard he was lying helpless, and so I came up — took my chance,' said the Russian. 'Oh, he is bad, very bad.' I directed my glass to the house. There were no signs of life, but there was the ruined roof, the long mud wall peeping above the grass, with three little square window-holes, no two of the same size; all this brought within reach of my hand, as it were. And then I made a brusque movement, and one of the remaining posts of that vanished fence leaped up in the field of my glass. You remember I told you I had been struck at the distance by certain attempts at ornamentation, rather remarkable in the ruinous aspect of the place. Now I had suddenly a nearer view, and its first result was to make me throw my head back as if before a blow. Then I went carefully from post to post with my glass, and I saw my mistake. These round knobs were not ornamental but symbolic; they were expressive and puzzling, striking and disturbing — food for thought and also for the vultures if there had been any looking down from the sky; but at all events for such ants as were industrious enough to ascend the pole. They would have been even more impressive, those heads on the stakes, if their faces had not been turned to the house. Only one, the first I had made out, was facing my way. I was not so shocked as you may think. The start back I had given was really nothing but a movement of surprise. I had expected to see a knob of wood there, you know. I returned deliberately to the first I had seen — and there it was, black, dried, sunken, with closed eyelids — a head that seemed to sleep at the top of that pole, and, with the shrunken dry lips showing a narrow white line of the teeth, was smiling too, smiling continuously at some endless and jocose dream of that eternal slumber.

"I am not disclosing any trade secrets. In fact the manager said afterwards that Mr. Kurtz's methods had ruined the district. I have no opinion on that point, but I want you clearly to understand that there was nothing exactly profitable in these heads being there. They only showed that Mr. Kurtz lacked restraint in the gratification of his various lusts, that there was something wanting in him — some small matter which, when the pressing need arose, could not be found under his magnificent eloquence. Whether he knew of this deficiency himself I can't say. I think the knowledge came to him at last — only at the very last. But the wilderness had found him out early, and had taken on him a terrible vengeance for the fantastic invasion. I think it had whispered to him things about himself which he did not know, things of which he had no conception till he took counsel with this great solitude — and the whisper had proved irresistibly fascinating. It echoed loudly within him because he was hollow at the core. . . . I put down the glass, and the head that had appeared near enough to be spoken to seemed at once to have leaped away from me into inaccessible distance.

"The admirer of Mr. Kurtz was a bit crestfallen. In a hurried, indistinct voice he began to assure me he had not dared to take these — say, symbols — down. He was not afraid of the natives; they would not stir till Mr. Kurtz gave the word. His ascendancy was extraordinary. The camps of these people surrounded the place, and the chiefs came every day to see him. They would crawl . . . 'I don't want to know anything of the ceremonies used when approaching Mr. Kurtz,' I shouted. Curious, this feeling that came over me that such details would be more intolerable than those heads drying on the stakes under Mr. Kurtz's windows. After all, that was only a savage sight, while I seemed at one bound to have been transported into some lightless region of subtle horrors, where pure, uncomplicated savagery was a positive relief, being something that had a right to exist — obviously — in the sunshine. The young man looked at me with

surprise. I suppose it did not occur to him that Mr. Kurtz was no idol of mine. He forgot I hadn't heard any of these splendid monologues on, what was it? on love, justice, conduct of life — or what not. If it had come to crawling before Mr. Kurtz, he crawled as much as the veriest savage of them all. I had no idea of the conditions, he said: these heads were the heads of rebels. I shocked him excessively by laughing. Rebels! What would be the next definition I was to hear? There had been enemies, criminals, workers — and these were rebels. Those rebellious heads looked very subdued to me on their sticks. 'You don't know how such a life tries a man like Kurtz,' cried Kurtz's last disciple. 'Well, and you?' I said. 'I! I! I am a simple man. I have no great thoughts. I want nothing from anybody. How can you compare me to . . . ?' His feelings were too much for speech, and suddenly he broke down. 'I don't understand,' he groaned. 'I've been doing my best to keep him alive, and that's enough. I had no hand in all this. I have no abilities. There hasn't been a drop of medicine or a mouthful of invalid food for months here. He was shamefully abandoned. A man like this, with such ideas. Shamefully! Shamefully! I — I — haven't slept for the last ten nights. . . .'

"His voice lost itself in the calm of the evening. The long shadows of the forest had slipped down hill while we talked, had gone far beyond the ruined hovel, beyond the symbolic row of stakes. All this was in the gloom, while we down there were yet in the sunshine, and the stretch of the river abreast of the clearing glittered in a still and dazzling splendour, with a murky and overshadowed bend above and below. Not a living soul was seen on the shore. The bushes did not rustle.

"Suddenly round the corner of the house a group of men appeared, as though they had come up from the ground. They waded waist-deep in the grass, in a compact body, bearing an improvised stretcher in their midst. Instantly, in the emptiness of the landscape, a cry arose whose shrillness pierced the still air like a sharp arrow flying straight to the very heart of the land; and, as if by enchantment, streams of human beings — of naked human beings — with spears in their hands, with bows, with shields, with wild glances and savage movements, were poured into the clearing by the dark-faced and pensive forest. The bushes shook, the grass swayed for a time, and then everything stood still in attentive immobility.

"'Now, if he does not say the right thing to

them we are all done for,' said the Russian at my elbow. The knot of men with the stretcher had stopped too, half-way to the steamer, as if petrified. I saw the man on the stretcher sit up, lank and with an uplifted arm, above the shoulders of the bearers. 'Let us hope that the man who can talk so well of love in general will find some particular reason to spare us this time,' I said. I resented bitterly the absurd danger of our situation, as if to be at the mercy of that atrocious phantom had been a dishonouring necessity. I could not hear a sound, but through my glasses I saw the thin arm extended commandingly, the lower jaw moving, the eyes of that apparition shining darkly far in its bony head that nodded with grotesque jerks. Kurtz — Kurtz — that means 'short' in German — don't it? Well, the name was as true as everything else in his life — and death. He looked at least seven feet long. His covering had fallen off, and his body emerged from it pitiful and appalling as from a winding-sheet. I could see the cage of his ribs all astir, the bones of his arm waving. It was as though an animated image of death carved out of old ivory had been shaking its hand with menaces at a motionless crowd of men made of dark and glittering bronze. I saw him open his mouth wide — it gave him a weirdly voracious aspect, as though he had wanted to swallow all the air, all the earth, all the men before him. A deep voice reached me faintly. He must have been shouting. He fell back suddenly. The stretcher shook as the bearers staggered forward again, and almost at the same time I noticed that the crowd of savages was vanishing without any perceptible movement of retreat, as if the forest that had ejected these beings so suddenly had drawn them in again as the breath is drawn in a long aspiration.

"Some of the pilgrims behind the stretcher carried his arms — two shot-guns, a heavy rifle, and a light revolver-carbine — the thunderbolts of that pitiful Jupiter. The manager bent over him murmuring as he walked beside his head. They laid him down in one of the little cabins — just a room for a bedplace and a camp-stool or two, you know. We had brought his belated correspondence, and a lot of torn envelopes and open letters littered his bed. His hand roamed feebly amongst these papers. I was struck by the fire of his eyes and the composed languor of his expression. It was not so much the exhaustion of disease. He did not seem in pain. This shadow looked satiated and calm, as though for the moment it had had its fill of all the emotions.

"He rustled one of the letters, and looking straight in my face said, 'I am glad.' Somebody had been writing to him about me. These special recommendations were turning up again. The volume of tone he emitted without effort, almost without the trouble of moving his lips, amazed me. A voice! a voice! It was grave, profound, vibrating, while the man did not seem capable of a whisper. However, he had enough strength in him — factitious no doubt — to very nearly make an end of us, as you shall hear directly.

"The manager appeared silently in the doorway; I stepped out at once and he drew the curtain after me. The Russian, eyed curiously by the pilgrims, was staring at the shore. I followed the direction of his glance.

"Dark human shapes could be made out in the distance, flitting indistinctly against the gloomy border of the forest, and near the river two bronze figures, leaning on tall spears, stood in the sunlight under fantastic head-dresses of spotted skins, warlike and still in statuesque repose. And from right to left along the lighted shore moved a wild and gorgeous apparition of a woman.

"She walked with measured steps, draped in striped and fringed cloths, treading the earth proudly, with a slight jingle and flash of barbarous ornaments. She carried her head high; her hair was done in the shape of a helmet; she had brass leggings to the knee, brass wire gauntlets to the elbow, a crimson spot on her tawny cheek, innumerable necklaces of glass beads on her neck; bizarre things, charms, gifts of witch-men, that hung about her, glittered and trembled at every step. She must have had the value of several elephant tusks upon her. She was savage and superb, wild-eyed and magnificent; there was something ominous and stately in her deliberate progress. And in the hush that had fallen suddenly upon the whole sorrowful land, the immense wilderness, the colossal body of the fecund and mysterious life seemed to look at her, pensive, as though it had been looking at the image of its own tenebrous and passionate soul.

"She came abreast of the steamer, stood still, and faced us. Her long shadow fell to the water's edge. Her face had a tragic and fierce aspect of wild sorrow and of dumb pain mingled with the fear of some struggling, half-shaped resolve. She stood looking at us without a stir, and like the

wilderness itself, with an air of brooding over an inscrutable purpose. A whole minute passed, and
then she made a step forward. There was a low
jingle, a glint of yellow metal, a sway of fringed
draperies, and she stopped as if her heart had
failed her. The young fellow by my side growled.
The pilgrims murmured at my back. She looked
at us all as if her life had depended upon the unswerving steadiness of her glance. Suddenly she
opened her bared arms and threw them up rigid
above her head, as though in an uncontrollable
desire to touch the sky, and at the same time the
swift shadows darted out on the earth, swept
around on the river, gathering the steamer into a
shadowy embrace. A formidable silence hung over
the scene.

"She turned away slowly, walked on, following
the bank, and passed into the bushes to the left.
Once only her eyes gleamed back at us in the dusk
of the thickets before she disappeared.

"'If she had offered to come aboard I really
think I would have tried to shoot her,' said the man
of patches nervously. 'I had been risking my life
every day for the last fortnight to keep her out of
the house. She got in one day and kicked up a
row about those miserable rags I picked up in the
storeroom to mend my clothes with. I wasn't decent. At least it must have been that, for she talked
like a fury to Kurtz for an hour, pointing at me
now and then. I don't understand the dialect of
this tribe. Luckily for me, I fancy Kurtz felt too
ill that day to care, or there would have been mischief. I don't understand. . . . No — it's too much
for me. Ah, well, it's all over now.'

"At this moment I heard Kurtz's deep voice behind the curtain: 'Save me! — save the ivory, you
mean. Don't tell me. Save *me!* Why, I've had to
save you. You are interrupting my plans now. Sick!
Sick! Not so sick as you would like to believe.
Never mind. I'll carry my ideas out yet — I will
return. I'll show you what can be done. You with
your little peddling notions — you are interfering
with me. I will return. I . . .'

"The manager came out. He did me the honour
to take me under the arm and lead me aside. 'He
is very low, very low,' he said. He considered it
necessary to sigh, but neglected to be consistently
sorrowful. 'We have done all we could for him —
haven't we? But there is no disguising the fact, Mr.
Kurtz has done more harm than good to the Company. He did not see the time was not ripe for
vigorous action. Cautiously, cautiously — that's my

principle. We must be cautious yet. The district is
closed to us for a time. Deplorable! Upon the whole,
the trade will suffer. I don't deny there is a remarkable quantity of ivory — mostly fossil. We
must save it, at all events — but look how precarious the position is — and why? Because the
method is unsound.' 'Do you,' said I, looking at
the shore, 'call it "unsound method"?' 'Without
doubt,' he exclaimed hotly. 'Don't you?' . . . 'No
method at all,' I murmured after a while. 'Exactly,'
he exulted. 'I anticipated this. Shows a complete
want of judgment. It is my duty to point it out in
the proper quarter.' 'Oh,' said I, 'that fellow —
what's his name? — the brickmaker, will make a
readable report for you.' He appeared confounded
for a moment. It seemed to me I had never breathed
an atmosphere so vile, and I turned mentally to
Kurtz for relief — positively for relief. 'Nevertheless, I think Mr. Kurtz is a remarkable man,' I
said with emphasis. He started, dropped on me a
cold heavy glance, said very quietly, 'He *was*,' and
turned his back on me. My hour of favour was
over; I found myself lumped along with Kurtz as
a partisan of methods for which the time was not
ripe: I was unsound! Ah! but it was something to
have at least a choice of nightmares.

"I had turned to the wilderness really, not to
Mr. Kurtz, who, I was ready to admit, was as good
as buried. And for a moment it seemed to me as
if I also were buried in a vast grave full of unspeakable secrets. I felt an intolerable weight oppressing
my breast, the smell of the damp earth, the unseen
presence of victorious corruption, the darkness of
an impenetrable night. . . . The Russian tapped
me on the shoulder. I heard him mumbling and
stammering something about 'brother seaman —
couldn't conceal — knowledge of matters that
would affect Mr. Kurtz's reputation.' I waited. For
him evidently Mr. Kurtz was not in his grave; I
suspect that for him Mr. Kurtz was one of the
immortals. 'Well!' said I at last, 'speak out. As it
happens, I am Mr. Kurtz's friend — in a way.'

"He stated with a good deal of formality that
had we not been 'of the same profession,' he
would have kept the matter to himself without
regard to consequences. He suspected 'there was
an active ill-will towards him on the part of these
white men that —' 'You are right,' I said, remembering a certain conversation I had overheard.
'The manager thinks you ought to be hanged.' He
showed a concern at this intelligence which amused
me at first. 'I had better get out of the way quietly,'

he said earnestly. 'I can do no more for Kurtz now, and they would soon find some excuse. What's to stop them? There's a military post three hundred miles from here.' 'Well, upon my word,' said I, 'perhaps you had better go if you have any friends amongst the savages near by.' 'Plenty,' he said. 'They are simple people — and I want nothing, you know.' He stood biting his lip, then: 'I don't want any harm to happen to these whites here, but of course I was thinking of Mr. Kurtz's reputation — but you are a brother seaman and —' 'All right,' said I, after a time. 'Mr. Kurtz's reputation is safe with me.' I did not know how truly I spoke.

"He informed me, lowering his voice, that it was Kurtz who had ordered the attack to be made on the steamer. 'He hated sometimes the idea of being taken away — and then again . . . But I don't understand these matters. I am a simple man. He thought it would scare you away — that you would give it up, thinking him dead. I could not stop him. Oh, I had an awful time of it this last month.' 'Very well,' I said. 'He is all right now.' 'Ye-e-es,' he muttered, not very convinced apparently. 'Thanks,' said I; 'I shall keep my eyes open.' 'But quiet — eh?' he urged anxiously. 'It would be awful for his reputation if anybody here —' I promised a complete discretion with great gravity. 'I have a canoe and three black fellows waiting not very far. I am off. Could you give me a few Martini-Henry cartridges?' I could, and did, with proper secrecy. He helped himself, with a wink at me, to a handful of my tobacco. 'Between sailors — you know — good English tobacco.' At the door of the pilot-house he turned round — 'I say, haven't you a pair of shoes you could spare?' He raised one leg. 'Look.' The soles were tied with knotted strings sandal-wise under his bare feet. I rooted out an old pair, at which he looked with admiration before tucking it under his left arm. One of his pockets (bright red) was bulging with cartridges, from the other (dark blue) peeped 'Towson's Inquiry,' etc. etc. He seemed to think himself excellently well equipped for a renewed encounter with the wilderness. 'Ah! I'll never, never meet such a man again. You ought to have heard him recite poetry — his own too it was, he told me. Poetry!' He rolled his eyes at the recollection of these delights. 'Oh, he enlarged my mind!' 'Good-bye,' said I. He shook hands and vanished in the night. Sometimes I ask myself whether I had ever really seen him — whether it was possible to meet such a phenomenon! . . .

"When I woke up shortly after midnight his warning came to my mind with its hint of danger that seemed, in the starred darkness, real enough to make me get up for the purpose of having a look round. On the hill a big fire burned, illuminating fitfully a crooked corner of the station-house. One of the agents with a picket of a few of our blacks, armed for the purpose, was keeping guard over the ivory; but deep within the forest, red gleams that wavered, that seemed to sink and rise from the ground amongst confused columnar shapes of intense blackness, showed the exact position of the camp where Mr. Kurtz's adorers were keeping their uneasy vigil. The monotonous beating of a big drum filled the air with muffled shocks and a lingering vibration. A steady droning sound of many men chanting each to himself some weird incantation came out from the black, flat wall of the woods as the humming of bees comes out of a hive, and had a strange narcotic effect upon my half-awake senses. I believe I dozed off leaning over the rail, till an abrupt burst of yells, an overwhelming outbreak of a pent-up and mysterious frenzy, woke me up in a bewildered wonder. It was cut short all at once, and the low droning went on with an effect of audible and soothing silence. I glanced casually into the little cabin. A light was burning within, but Mr. Kurtz was not there.

"I think I would have raised an outcry if I had believed my eyes. But I didn't believe them at first — the thing seemed so impossible. The fact is I was completely unnerved by a sheer blank fright, pure abstract terror, unconnected with any distinct shape of physical danger. What made this emotion so overpowering was — how shall I define it? — the moral shock I received, as if something altogether monstrous, intolerable to thought and odious to the soul, had been thrust upon me unexpectedly. This lasted of course the merest fraction of a second, and then the usual sense of commonplace, deadly danger, the possibility of a sudden onslaught and massacre, or something of the kind, which I saw impending, was positively welcome and composing. It pacified me, in fact, so much, that I did not raise an alarm.

"There was an agent buttoned up inside an ulster and sleeping on a chair on deck within three feet of me. The yells had not awakened him; he snored very slightly; I left him to his slumbers and leaped ashore. I did not betray Mr. Kurtz — it was ordered I should never betray him — it was written

I should be loyal to the nightmare of my choice. I was anxious to deal with this shadow by myself alone — and to this day I don't know why I was so jealous of sharing with any one the peculiar blackness of that experience.

"As soon as I got on the bank I saw a trail — a broad trail through the grass. I remember the exultation with which I said to myself, 'He can't walk — he is crawling on all-fours — I've got him.' The grass was wet with dew. I strode rapidly with clenched fists. I fancy I had some vague notion of falling upon him and giving him a drubbing. I don't know. I had some imbecile thoughts. The knitting old woman with the cat obtruded herself upon my memory as a most improper person to be sitting at the other end of such an affair. I saw a row of pilgrims squirting lead in the air out of Winchesters held to the hip. I thought I would never get back to the steamer, and imagined myself living alone and unarmed in the woods to an advanced age. Such silly things — you know. And I remember I confounded the beat of the drum with the beating of my heart, and was pleased at its calm regularity.

"I kept to the track though — then stopped to listen. The night was very clear; a dark blue space, sparkling with dew and starlight, in which black things stood very still. I thought I could see a kind of motion ahead of me. I was strangely cocksure of everything that night. I actually left the track and ran in a wide semicircle (I verily believe chuckling to myself) so as to get in front of that stir, of that motion I had seen — if indeed I had seen anything. I was circumventing Kurtz as though it had been a boyish game.

"I came upon him, and, if he had not heard me coming, I would have fallen over him too, but he got up in time. He rose, unsteady, long, pale, indistinct, like a vapour exhaled by the earth, and swayed slightly, misty and silent before me; while at my back the fires loomed between the trees, and the murmur of many voices issued from the forest. I had cut him off cleverly; but when actually confronting him I seemed to come to my senses, I saw the danger in its right proportion. It was by no means over yet. Suppose he began to shout? Though he could hardly stand, there was still plenty of vigour in his voice. 'Go away — hide yourself,' he said, in that profound tone. It was very awful. I glanced back. We were within thirty yards of the nearest fire. A black figure stood up, strode on long black legs, waving long black arms, across the glow. It had horns — antelope horns, I think — on its head. Some sorcerer, some witch-man no doubt: it looked fiend-like enough. 'Do you know what you are doing?' I whispered. 'Perfectly,' he answered, raising his voice for that single word: it sounded to me far off and yet loud, like a hail through a speaking-trumpet. If he makes a row we are lost, I thought to myself. This clearly was not a case for fisticuffs, even apart from the very natural aversion I had to beat that Shadow — this wandering and tormented thing. 'You will be lost,' I said — 'utterly lost.' One gets sometimes such a flash of inspiration, you know. I did say the right thing, though indeed he could not have been more irretrievably lost than he was at this very moment, when the foundations of our intimacy were being laid — to endure — to endure — even to the end — even beyond.

"'I had immense plans,' he muttered irresolutely. 'Yes,' said I; 'but if you try to shout I'll smash your head with —' There was not a stick or a stone near. 'I will throttle you for good,' I corrected myself. 'I was on the threshold of great things,' he pleaded, in a voice of longing, with a wistfulness of tone that made my blood run cold. 'And now for this stupid scoundrel —' 'Your success in Europe is assured in any case,' I affirmed steadily. I did not want to have the throttling of him, you understand — and indeed it would have been very little use for any practical purpose. I tried to break the spell — the heavy, mute spell of the wilderness — that seemed to draw him to its pitiless breast by the awakening of forgotten and brutal instincts, by the memory of gratified and monstrous passions. This alone, I was convinced, had driven him out to the edge of the forest, to the bush, towards the gleam of fires, the throb of drums, the drone of weird incantations; this alone had beguiled his unlawful soul beyond the bounds of permitted aspirations. And, don't you see, the terror of the position was not in being knocked on the head — though I had a very lively sense of that danger too — but in this, that I had to deal with a being to whom I could not appeal in the name of anything high or low. I had, even like the niggers, to invoke him — himself — his own exalted and incredible degradation. There was nothing either above or below him, and I knew it. He had kicked himself loose of the earth. Confound the man! he had kicked the very earth to pieces. He was alone, and I before him did not know whether I stood on the ground or floated in the air. I've been telling you what we said — repeating the phrases we pronounced — but what's the good? They were common everyday words — the familiar, vague sounds exchanged on every waking day of life. But what of that? They had behind them, to my mind, the terrific suggestiveness of words heard in dreams, of phrases spoken in nightmares. Soul! If anybody had ever struggled with a soul, I am the man. And I wasn't arguing with a lunatic either. Believe me or not, his intelligence was perfectly clear — concentrated, it is true, upon himself with horrible intensity, yet clear; and therein was my only chance — barring, of course, the killing him there and then, which wasn't so good, on account of unavoidable noise. But his soul was mad. Being alone in the wilderness, it had looked within itself, and, by heavens! I tell you, it had gone mad. I had — for my sins, I suppose, to go through the ordeal of looking into it myself. No eloquence could have been so withering to one's belief in mankind as his final burst of sincerity. He struggled with himself too. I saw it — I heard it. I saw the inconceivable mystery of a soul that knew no restraint, no faith, and no fear, yet struggling blindly with itself. I kept my head pretty well; but when I had him at last stretched on the couch, I wiped my forehead, while my legs shook under me as though I had carried half a ton on my back down that hill. And yet I had only supported him, his bony arm clasped round my neck — and he was not much heavier than a child.

"When next day we left at noon, the crowd, of whose presence behind the curtain of trees I had been acutely conscious all the time, flowed out of the woods again, filled the clearing, covered the slope with a mass of naked, breathing, quivering, bronze bodies. I steamed up a bit, then swung down-stream, and two thousand eyes followed the evolutions of the splashing, thumping, fierce river-demon beating the water with its terrible tail and breathing black smoke into the air. In front of the first rank, along the river, three men, plastered with bright red earth from head to foot, strutted to and fro restlessly. When we came abreast again, they faced the river, stamped their feet, nodded their horned heads, swayed their scarlet bodies; they shook towards the fierce river-demon a bunch of black feathers, a mangy skin with a pendent tail — something that looked like a dried gourd; they shouted periodically together strings of amazing words that resembled no sounds of human language; and the deep murmurs of the crowd, in-

terrupted suddenly, were like the responses of some satanic litany.

"We had carried Kurtz into the pilot-house: there was more air there. Lying on the couch, he stared through the open shutter. There was an eddy in the mass of human bodies, and the woman with helmeted head and tawny cheeks rushed out to the very brink of the stream. She put out her hands, shouted something, and all that wild mob took up the shout in a roaring chorus of articulated, rapid, breathless utterance.

"'Do you understand this?' I asked.

"He kept on looking out past me with fiery, longing eyes, with a mingled expression of wistfulness and hate. He made no answer, but I saw a smile, a smile of indefinable meaning, appear on his colourless lips that a moment after twitched convulsively. 'Do I not?' he said slowly, gasping, as if the words had been torn out of him by a supernatural power.

"I pulled the string of the whistle, and I did this because I saw the pilgrims on deck getting out their rifles with an air of anticipating a jolly lark. At the sudden screech there was a movement of abject terror through that wedged mass of bodies. 'Don't! don't you frighten them away,' cried some one on deck disconsolately. I pulled the string time after time. They broke and ran, they leaped, they crouched, they swerved, they dodged the flying terror of the sound. The three red chaps had fallen flat, face down on the shore, as though they had been shot dead. Only the barbarous and superb woman did not so much as flinch, and stretched tragically her bare arms after us over the sombre and glittering river.

"And then that imbecile crowd down on the deck started their little fun, and I could see nothing more for smoke.

"The brown current ran swiftly out of the heart of darkness, bearing us down towards the sea with twice the speed of our upward progress; and Kurtz's life was running swiftly too, ebbing, ebbing out of his heart into the sea of inexorable time. The manager was very placid, he had no vital anxieties now, he took us both in with a comprehensive and satisfied glance: the 'affair' had come off as well as could be wished. I saw the time approaching when I would be left alone of the party of 'unsound method.' The pilgrims looked upon me with disfavour. I was, so to speak, numbered with the dead. It is strange how I accepted this unforeseen partnership, this choice of night-mares forced upon me in the tenebrous land invaded by these mean and greedy phantoms.

"Kurtz discoursed. A voice! a voice! It rang deep to the very last. It survived his strength to hide in the magnificent folds of eloquence the barren darkness of his heart. Oh, he struggled! he struggled! The wastes of his weary brain were haunted by shadowy images now — images of wealth and fame revolving obsequiously round his unextinguishable gift of noble and lofty expression. My Intended, my station, my career, my ideas — these were the subjects for the occasional utterances of elevated sentiments. The shade of the original Kurtz frequented the bedside of the hollow sham, whose fate it was to be buried presently in the mould of primeval earth. But both the diabolic love and the unearthly hate of the mysteries it had penetrated fought for the possession of that soul satiated with primitive emotions, avid of lying fame, of sham distinction, of all the appearances of success and power.

"Sometimes he was contemptibly childish. He desired to have kings meet him at railway stations on his return from some ghastly Nowhere, where he intended to accomplish great things. 'You show them you have in you something that is really profitable, and then there will be no limits to the recognition of your ability,' he would say. 'Of course you must take care of the motives — right motives — always.' The long reaches that were like one and the same reach, monotonous bends that were exactly alike, slipped past the steamer with their multitude of secular trees looking patiently after this grimy fragment of another world, the forerunner of change, of conquest, of trade, of massacres, of blessings. I looked ahead — piloting. 'Close the shutter,' said Kurtz suddenly one day; 'I can't bear to look at this.' I did so. There was a silence. 'Oh, but I will wring your heart yet!' he cried at the invisible wilderness.

"We broke down — as I had expected — and had to lie up for repairs at the head of an island. This delay was the first thing that shook Kurtz's confidence. One morning he gave me a packet of papers and a photograph — the lot tied together with a shoe-string. 'Keep this for me,' he said. 'This noxious fool' (meaning the manager) 'is capable of prying into my boxes when I am not looking.' In the afternoon I saw him. He was lying on his back with closed eyes, and I withdrew quietly, but I heard him mutter, 'Live rightly, die,

die . . .' I listened. There was nothing more. Was he rehearsing some speech in his sleep, or was it a fragment of a phrase from some newspaper article? He had been writing for the papers and meant to do so again, 'for the furthering of my ideas. It's a duty.'

"His was an impenetrable darkness. I looked at him as you peer down at a man who is lying at the bottom of a precipice where the sun never shines. But I had not much time to give him, because I was helping the engine-driver to take to pieces the leaky cylinders, to straighten a bent connecting-rod, and in other such matters. I lived in an infernal mess of rust, filings, nuts, bolts, spanners, hammers, ratchet-drills — things I abominate, because I don't get on with them. I tended the little forge we fortunately had aboard; I toiled wearily in a wretched scrap-heap — unless I had the shakes too bad to stand.

"One evening coming in with a candle I was startled to hear him say a little tremulously, 'I am lying here in the dark waiting for death.' The light was within a foot of his eyes. I forced myself to murmur, 'Oh, nonsense!' and stood over him as if transfixed.

"Anything approaching the change that came over his features I have never seen before, and hope never to see again. Oh, I wasn't touched. I was fascinated. It was as though a veil had been rent. I saw on that ivory face the expression of sombre pride, of ruthless power, of craven terror — of an intense and hopeless despair. Did he live his life again in every detail of desire, temptation, and surrender during that supreme moment of complete knowledge? He cried in a whisper at some image, at some vision — he cried out twice, a cry that was no more than a breath:

"'The horror! The horror!'

"I blew the candle out and left the cabin. The pilgrims were dining in the mess-room, and I took my place opposite the manager, who lifted his eyes to give me a questioning glance, which I successfully ignored. He leaned back, serene, with that peculiar smile of his sealing the unexpressed depths of his meanness. A continuous shower of small flies streamed upon the lamp, upon the cloth, upon our hands and faces. Suddenly the manager's boy put his insolent black head in the doorway, and said in a tone of scathing contempt:

"'Mistah Kurtz — he dead.'

"All the pilgrims rushed out to see. I remained, and went on with my dinner. I believe I was considered brutally callous. However, I did not eat much. There was a lamp in there — light, don't you know — and outside it was so beastly, beastly dark. I went no more near the remarkable man who had pronounced a judgment upon the adventures of his soul on this earth. The voice was gone. What else had been there? But I am of course aware that next day the pilgrims buried something in a muddy hole.

"And then they very nearly buried me.

"However, as you see, I did not go to join Kurtz there and then. I did not. I remained to dream the nightmare out to the end, and to show my loyalty to Kurtz once more. Destiny. My destiny! Droll thing life is — that mysterious arrangement of merciless logic for a futile purpose. The most you can hope from it is some knowledge of yourself — that comes too late — a crop of unextinguishable regrets. I have wrestled with death. It is the most unexciting contest you can imagine. It takes place in an impalpable greyness, with nothing underfoot, with nothing around, without spectators, without clamour, without glory, without the great desire of victory, without the great fear of defeat, in a sickly atmosphere of tepid scepticism, without much belief in your own right, and still less in that of your adversary. If such is the form of ultimate wisdom, then life is a greater riddle than some of us think it to be. I was within a hair's-breadth of the last opportunity for pronouncement, and I found with humiliation that probably I would have nothing to say. This is the reason why I affirm that Kurtz was a remarkable man. He had something to say. He said it. Since I had peeped over the edge myself, I understand better the meaning of his stare, that could not see the flame of the candle, but was wide enough to embrace the whole universe, piercing enough to penetrate all the hearts that beat in the darkness. He had summed up — he had judged. 'The horror!' He was a remarkable man. After all, this was the expression of some sort of belief; it had candour, it had conviction, it had a vibrating note of revolt in its whisper, it had the appalling face of a glimpsed truth — the strange commingling of desire and hate. And it is not my own extremity I remember best — a vision of greyness without form filled with physical pain, and a careless contempt for the evanescence of all things — even of this pain itself. No! It is his extremity that I seem to have lived through. True, he had made that last stride, he had stepped over the edge, while I

had been permitted to draw back my hesitating foot. And perhaps in this is the whole difference; perhaps all the wisdom, and all truth, and all sincerity, are just compressed into that inappreciable moment of time in which we step over the threshold of the invisible. Perhaps! I like to think my summing-up would not have been a word of careless contempt. Better his cry — much better. It was an affirmation, a moral victory paid for by innumerable defeats, by abominable terrors, by abominable satisfactions. But it was a victory! That is why I have remained loyal to Kurtz to the last, and even beyond, when a long time after I heard once more, not his own voice, but the echo of his magnificent eloquence thrown to me from a soul as translucently pure as a cliff of crystal.

"No, they did not bury me, though there is a period of time which I remember mistily, with a shuddering wonder, like a passage through some inconceivable world that had no hope in it and no desire. I found myself back in the sepulchral city resenting the sight of people hurrying through the streets to filch a little money from each other, to devour their infamous cookery, to gulp their unwholesome beer, to dream their insignificant and silly dreams. They trespassed upon my thoughts. They were intruders whose knowledge of life was to me an irritating pretence, because I felt so sure they could not possibly know the things I knew. Their bearing, which was simply the bearing of commonplace individuals going about their business in the assurance of perfect safety, was offensive to me like the outrageous flauntings of folly in the face of a danger it is unable to comprehend. I had no particular desire to enlighten them, but I had some difficulty in restraining myself from laughing in their faces, so full of stupid importance. I daresay I was not very well at that time. I tottered about the streets — there were various affairs to settle — grinning bitterly at perfectly respectable persons. I admit my behaviour was inexcusable, but then my temperature was seldom normal in these days. My dear aunt's endeavours to 'nurse up my strength' seemed altogether beside the mark. It was not my strength that wanted nursing, it was my imagination that wanted soothing. I kept the bundle of papers given me by Kurtz, not knowing exactly what to do with it. His mother had died lately, watched over, as I was told, by his Intended. A clean-shaved man, with an official manner and wearing gold-rimmed spectacles, called on me one day and made inquiries, at first circuitous, afterwards suavely pressing, about what he was pleased to denominate certain 'documents.' I was not surprised, because I had had two rows with the manager on the subject out there. I had refused to give up the smallest scrap out of that package, and I took the same attitude with the spectacled man. He became darkly menacing at last, and with much heat argued that the Company had the right to every bit of information about its 'territories.' And, said he, 'Mr. Kurtz's knowledge of unexplored regions must have been necessarily extensive and peculiar — owing to his great abilities and to the deplorable circumstances in which he had been placed: therefore —' I assured him Mr. Kurtz's knowledge, however extensive, did not bear upon the problems of commerce or administration. He invoked then the name of science. 'It would be an incalculable loss if,' etc. etc. I offered him the report on the 'Suppression of Savage Customs,' with the postscriptum torn off. He took it up eagerly, but ended by sniffing at it with an air of contempt. 'This is not what we had a right to expect,' he remarked. 'Expect nothing else,' I said. 'There are only private letters.' He withdrew upon some threat of legal proceedings, and I saw him no more; but another fellow, calling himself Kurtz's cousin, appeared two days later, and was anxious to hear all the details about his dear relative's last moments. Incidentally he gave me to understand that Kurtz had been essentially a great musician. 'There was the making of an immense success,' said the man, who was an organist, I believe, with lank grey hair flowing over a greasy coat-collar. I had no reason to doubt his statement; and to this day I am unable to say what was Kurtz's profession, whether he ever had any — which was the greatest of his talents. I had taken him for a painter who wrote for the papers, or else for a journalist who could paint — but even the cousin (who took snuff during the interview) could not tell me what he had been — exactly. He was a universal genius — on that point I agreed with the old chap, who thereupon blew his nose noisily into a large cotton handkerchief and withdrew in senile agitation, bearing off some family letters and memoranda without importance. Ultimately a journalist anxious to know something of the fate of his 'dear colleague' turned up. This visitor informed me Kurtz's proper sphere ought to have been politics 'on the popular side.' He had furry straight eyebrows, bristly hair cropped short, an eyeglass on a broad ribbon, and, becoming expansive, confessed his opinion that Kurtz really couldn't write a bit — 'but heavens! how that man could talk! He electrified large meetings. He had faith — don't you see? — he had the faith. He could get himself to believe anything — anything. He would have been a splendid leader of an extreme party.' 'What party?' I asked. 'Any party,' answered the other. 'He was an — an — extremist.' Did I not think so? I assented. Did I know, he asked, with a sudden flash of curiosity, 'what it was that had induced him to go out there?' 'Yes,' said I, and forthwith handed him the famous Report for publication, if he thought fit. He glanced through it hurriedly, mumbling all the time, judged 'it would do,' and took himself off with this plunder.

"Thus I was left at last with a slim packet of letters and the girl's portrait. She struck me as beautiful — I mean she had a beautiful expression. I know that the sunlight can be made to lie too, yet one felt that no manipulation of light and pose could have conveyed the delicate shade of truthfulness upon those features. She seemed ready to listen without mental reservation, without suspicion, without a thought for herself. I concluded I would go and give her back her portrait and those letters myself. Curiosity? Yes; and also some other feeling perhaps. All that had been Kurtz's had passed out of my hands: his soul, his body, his station, his plans, his ivory, his career. There remained only his memory and his Intended — and I wanted to give that up too to the past, in a way — to surrender personally all that remained of him with me to that oblivion which is the last word of our common fate. I don't defend myself. I had no clear perception of what it was I really wanted. Perhaps it was an impulse of unconscious loyalty, or the fulfilment of one of those ironic necessities that lurk in the fact of human existence. I don't know. I can't tell. But I went.

"I thought his memory was like the other memories of the dead that accumulate in every man's life — a vague impress on the brain of shadows that had fallen on it in their swift and final passage; but before the high and ponderous door, between the tall houses of a street as still and decorous as a well-kept alley in a cemetery, I had a vision of him on the stretcher, opening his mouth voraciously, as if to devour all the earth with all its mankind. He lived then before me; he lived as much as he had ever lived — a shadow insatiable of splendid appearances, of frightful realities; a shadow darker than the shadow of the night, and draped nobly in the folds of a gorgeous eloquence. The vision seemed to enter the house with me — the stretcher, the phantom-bearers, the wild crowd of obedient worshippers, the gloom of the forests, the glitter of the reach between the murky bends, the beat of the drum, regular and muffled like the beating of a heart — the heart of a conquering darkness. It was a moment of triumph for the wilderness, an invading and vengeful rush which, it seemed to me, I would have to keep back alone for the salvation of another soul. And the memory of what I had heard him say afar there, with the horned shapes stirring at my back, in the glow of fires, within the patient woods, those broken phrases came back to me, were heard again in their ominous and terrifying simplicity. I remembered his abject pleading, his abject threats, the colossal scale of his vile desires, the meanness, the torment, the tempestuous anguish of his soul. And later on I seemed to see his collected languid manner, when he said one day, ' This lot of ivory now is really mine. The Company did not pay for it. I collected it myself at a very great personal risk. I am afraid they will try to claim it as theirs though. H'm. It is a difficult case. What do you think I ought to do — resist? Eh? I want no more than justice.' . . . He wanted no more than justice — no more than justice. I rang the bell before a mahogany door on the first floor, and while I waited he seemed to stare at me out of the glassy panel — stare with that wide and immense stare, embracing, condemning, loathing all the universe. I seemed to hear the whispered cry, ' The horror! The horror! '

"The dusk was falling. I had to wait in a lofty drawing-room with three long windows from floor to ceiling that were like three luminous and be-draped columns. The bent gilt legs and backs of the furniture shone in distinct curves. The tall marble fireplace had a cold and monumental whiteness. A grand piano stood massively in a corner, with dark gleams on the flat surfaces like a sombre and polished sarcophagus. A high door opened — closed. I rose.

"She came forward, all in black, with a pale head, floating towards me in the dusk. She was in mourning. It was more than a year since his death, more than a year since the news came; she seemed as though she would remember and mourn for ever. She took both my hands in hers and murmured, ' I had heard you were coming.' I noticed she was not very young — I mean not girlish. She had a mature capacity for fidelity, for belief, for

suffering. The room seemed to have grown darker, as if all the sad light of the cloudy evening had taken refuge on her forehead. This fair hair, this pale visage, this pure brow, seemed surrounded by an ashy halo from which the dark eyes looked out at me. Their glance was guileless, profound, confident, and trustful. She carried her sorrowful head as though she were proud of that sorrow, as though she would say, I — I alone know how to mourn for him as he deserves. But while we were still shaking hands, such a look of awful desolation came upon her face that I perceived she was one of those creatures that are not the playthings of Time. For her he had died only yesterday. And, by Jove! the impression was so powerful that for me too he seemed to have died only yesterday — nay, this very minute. I saw her and him in the same instant of time — his death and her sorrow — I saw her sorrow in the very moment of his death. Do you understand? I saw them together — I heard them together. She had said, with a deep catch of the breath, ' I have survived '; while my strained ears seemed to hear distinctly, mingled with her tone of despairing regret, the summing-up whisper of his eternal condemnation. I asked myself what I was doing there, with a sensation of panic in my heart as though I had blundered into a place of cruel and absurd mysteries not fit for a human being to behold. She motioned me to a chair. We sat down. I laid the packet gently on the little table, and she put her hand over it. . . . ' You knew him well,' she murmured, after a moment of mourning silence.

" ' Intimacy grows quickly out there,' I said. ' I knew him as well as it is possible for one man to know another.'

" ' And you admired him,' she said. ' It was impossible to know him and not to admire him. Was it? '

" ' He was a remarkable man,' I said unsteadily. Then before the appealing fixity of her gaze, that seemed to watch for more words on my lips, I went on, ' It was impossible not to — '

" ' Love him,' she finished eagerly, silencing me into an appalled dumbness. ' How true! how true! But when you think that no one knew him so well as I! I had all his noble confidence. I knew him best.'

" ' You knew him best,' I repeated. And perhaps she did. But with every word spoken the room was growing darker, and only her forehead, smooth and white, remained illumined by the unextinguishable light of belief and love.

"'You were his friend,' she went on. 'His friend,' she repeated, a little louder. 'You must have been, if he had given you this, and sent you to me. I feel I can speak to you — and oh! I must speak. I want you — you who have heard his last words — to know I have been worthy of him. . . . It is not pride. . . . Yes! I am proud to know I understood him better than any one on earth — he told me so himself. And since his mother died I have had no one — no one — to — to —'

"I listened. The darkness deepened. I was not even sure whether he had given me the right bundle. I rather suspect he wanted me to take care of another batch of his papers which, after his death, I saw the manager examining under the lamp. And the girl talked, easing her pain in the certitude of my sympathy; she talked as thirsty men drink. I had heard that her engagement with Kurtz had been disapproved by her people. He wasn't rich enough or something. And indeed I don't know whether he had not been a pauper all his life. He had given me some reason to infer that it was his impatience of comparative poverty that drove him out there.

"'. . . Who was not his friend who had heard him speak once?' she was saying. 'He drew men towards him by what was best in them.' She looked at me with intensity. 'It is the gift of the great,' she went on, and the sound of her low voice seemed to have the accompaniment of all the other sounds, full of mystery, desolation, and sorrow, I had ever heard — the ripple of the river, the soughing of the trees swayed by the wind, the murmurs of the crowds, the faint ring of incomprehensible words cried from afar, the whisper of a voice speaking from beyond the threshold of an eternal darkness. 'But you have heard him! You know!' she cried.

"'Yes, I know,' I said with something like despair in my heart, but bowing my head before the faith that was in her, before that great and saving illusion that shone with an unearthly glow in the darkness, in the triumphant darkness from which I could not have defended her — from which I could not even defend myself.

"'What a loss to me — to us!' — she corrected herself with beautiful generosity; then added in a murmur, 'To the world.' By the last gleams of twilight I could see the glitter of her eyes, full of tears — of tears that would not fall.

"'I have been very happy — very fortunate — very proud,' she went on. 'Too fortunate. Too happy for a little while. And now I am unhappy for — for life.'

"She stood up; her fair hair seemed to catch all the remaining light in a glimmer of gold. I rose too.

"'And of all this,' she went on mournfully, 'of all his promise, and of all his greatness, of his generous mind, of his noble heart, nothing remains — nothing but a memory. You and I —'

"'We shall always remember him,' I said hastily.

"'No!' she cried. 'It is impossible that all this should be lost — that such a life should be sacrificed to leave nothing — but sorrow. You know what vast plans he had. I knew of them too — I could not perhaps understand — but others knew of them. Something must remain. His words, at least, have not died.'

"'His words will remain,' I said.

"'And his example,' she whispered to herself. 'Men looked up to him — his goodness shone in every act. His example —'

"'True,' I said; 'his example too. Yes, his example. I forgot that.'

"'But I do not. I cannot — I cannot believe — not yet. I cannot believe that I shall never see him again, that nobody will see him again, never, never, never.'

"She put out her arms as if after a retreating figure, stretching them black and with clasped pale hands across the fading and narrow sheen of the window. Never see him! I saw him clearly enough then. I shall see this eloquent phantom as long as I live, and I shall see her too, a tragic and familiar Shade, resembling in this gesture another one, tragic also, and bedecked with powerless charms, stretching bare brown arms over the glitter of the infernal stream, the stream of darkness. She said suddenly very low, 'He died as he lived.'

"'His end,' said I, with dull anger stirring in me, 'was in every way worthy of his life.'

"'And I was not with him,' she murmured. My anger subsided before a feeling of infinite pity.

"'Everything that could be done —' I mumbled.

"'Ah, but I believed in him more than any one on earth — more than his own mother, more than — himself. He needed me! Me! I would have treasured every sigh, every word, every sign, every glance.'

"I felt like a chill grip on my chest. 'Don't,' I said, in a muffled voice.

"'Forgive me. I — I — have mourned so long in silence — in silence. . . . You were with him — to the last? I think of his loneliness. Nobody near to understand him as I would have understood. Perhaps no one to hear. . . .'

" 'To the very end,' I said shakily. 'I heard his very last words. . . .' I stopped in a fright.

" 'Repeat them,' she murmured in a heart-broken tone. 'I want — I want — something — something — to — to live with.'

" I was on the point of crying at her, 'Don't you hear them?' The dusk was repeating them in a persistent whisper all around us, in a whisper that seemed to swell menacingly like the first whisper of a rising wind. 'The horror! The horror!'

" 'His last word — to live with,' she insisted. 'Don't you understand I loved him — I loved him — I loved him!'

" I pulled myself together and spoke slowly.

" 'The last word he pronounced was — your name.'

" I heard a light sigh and then my heart stood still, stopped dead short by an exulting and terrible cry, by the cry of inconceivable triumph and of unspeakable pain. 'I knew it — I was sure!' . . . She knew. She was sure. I heard her weeping; she had hidden her face in her hands. It seemed to me that the house would collapse before I could escape, that the heavens would fall upon my head. But nothing happened. The heavens do not fall for such a trifle. Would they have fallen, I wonder, if I had rendered Kurtz that justice which was his due? Hadn't he said he wanted only justice? But I couldn't. I could not tell her. It would have been too dark — too dark altogether. . . ."

Marlow ceased, and sat apart, indistinct and silent, in the pose of a meditating Buddha. Nobody moved for a time. "We have lost the first of the ebb," said the Director suddenly. I raised my head. The offing was barred by a black bank of clouds, and the tranquil waterway leading to the uttermost ends of the earth flowed sombre under an overcast sky — seemed to lead into the heart of an immense darkness.

REUBEN A. BROWER, *Editor*

William Butler Yeats

1865–1939

We value the poetry of Yeats, like other good poetry, because it fixes moments of experience in memorable image and distinctly heard rhythm, and so seems to make them timeless:

An aged man is but a paltry thing,
A tattered coat upon a stick, unless
Soul clap its hands and sing, and louder sing
For every tatter in its mortal dress. . . .

But we also feel in Yeats, for example in these lines from "Sailing to Byzantium," a distinctly "modern" quality; his art has an additional value for us because it belongs so definitely to our own time. Yeats's achievement matters especially to present-day readers because he wrote his way out of the nineteenth century, and because he helped the first generation of the twentieth to see and feel what their world was like. But his work was so entangled in the political and literary life of Ireland that the historical and biographical view is likely to swamp our reading of his poems. He was overly aware of the connection between his life and his art and almost too conscious of what he was doing; and, although we can see some kinds of meaning and value in Yeats only by setting his work in its biographical context, we had better begin by looking at the poetry itself. (An energetic and properly skeptical student will read no further until he has first read carefully five or six poems.) [1]

[1] "The Lake Isle of Innisfree," "To a Friend Whose Work Has Come to Nothing," "No Second Troy," "The Magi," "Sailing to Byzantium," "The Second Coming."

What does Yeats sound like, to a reader coming from Browning? To give a characteristically Irish answer, he sounds more like Tennyson, the poet he most "venerated" as a young man:

I will arise and go now, and go to Innisfree, . . .
And I shall have some peace there, for peace comes
    dropping slow,
Dropping from the veils of morning to where the
    cricket sings;
There midnight's all a glimmer, and noon a purple
    glow,
And evening full of the linnet's wings.
                    ("The Lake Isle of Innisfree")

We hear echoes of the earlier Tennyson who sings of the Lotos-Eaters coming "unto a land / In which it seemed always afternoon":

A land of streams! some, like a downward smoke,
Slow-dropping veils of thinnest lawn, did go . . .[2]
The longing to reach an other-world "isle" is definitely reminiscent of Shelley, another of Yeats's early admirations; and the lonely lake that appears here and in many of Yeats's poems recalls Keats's "La Belle Dame sans Merci," as in this rather bald imitation:

I wander by the edge
Of this desolate lake
Where wind cries in the sedge. . . .
        ("He Hears the Cry of the Sedge")

But here is a voice that we have never found in Keats:

Now all the truth is out,
Be secret and take defeat

[2] See p. 775.

From any brazen throat,
For how can you compete,
Being honour bred, with one
Who, were it proved he lies,
Were neither shamed in his own
Nor in his neighbours' eyes? . . .
("To a Friend Whose Work
Has Come to Nothing")

Where have we heard such rudeness of attack (to a friend!) and such bitter sympathy, in short lines heavily stressed and harshly rhymed? In Swift, in his addresses to friends and enemies. The spareness in use of images and the surprising power of any single one that is admitted are also Swiftian:

And strongly shoot a radiant Dart,
To shine through Life's declining Part.[1]

The title of Yeats's poem recalls the Augustan fondness for "occasional" poetry and social verse. The austere aristocratic tone is equally characteristic of Yeats, and it is very like him to find his poetic role in an eighteenth-century writer. (He in fact came to regard Swift and Burke as ideal writers and thinkers.)

But though Yeats plays many parts in his verse — that is a sign of his scope — there are poems which could have been written by no one else:

THE MAGI

Now as at all times I can see in the mind's eye,
In their stiff, painted clothes, the pale unsatisfied
    ones
Appear and disappear in the blue depth of the
    sky
With all their ancient faces like rain-beaten stones,
And all their helms of silver hovering side by side,
And all their eyes still fixed, hoping to find once
    more,
Being by Calvary's turbulence unsatisfied,
The uncontrollable mystery on the bestial floor.

Two features of this poem strike us at once: the completeness with which attention focuses on the Magi, and the wavering exaltation that gradually comes into the speaker's voice. What has happened to the familiar figures of the Three Kings, and what do they mean here? How does the speaker of this brief dramatic monologue address his audience?

[1] Swift, "Stella's Birth-Day, March 13, 1726/7," ll. 33-34, The lines quoted contain one of two striking images in a poem of eighty-eight lines, which is otherwise written in a plain conversational style.

We hear at first the voice of a man talking quietly to himself, but we soon feel that the " I " of this poem is a far from ordinary person. He *sees* the Magi "in the *mind's* eye," the "inward eye" of Wordsworth — his seeing is vision. Though he speaks with extraordinary collectedness, in one long, well-ordered sentence, his voice soars far away as the lines fall into gently balanced units:

Appear and disappear . . .
With all their ancient faces . . .
And all their helms . . .
And all their eyes . . .

The strongly accented lines are further lifted out of speech by their length: six stresses with heavy pauses seem very long to ears accustomed to blank verse.

But this foreignness of sound, the sense of lines going on and on, is very nice for a poem that takes us from here and now to a "sky-scape" of the mind where the Wise Men's quest is never-ending. In part the picture is expected and traditional — the aged seer-kings in rich garments and armor seen against the sky as they go toward Bethlehem. But there is an odd and recurrent emphasis in the way in which they are described. Their clothes are "stiff" and "painted," as if artificial and not fitted to their bodies; their faces, stony, "their eyes still fixed" in an immovable gaze. These hardly human and unsubstantial ("pale," "hovering") seekers are perpetually obsessed with the search for a "mystery." What they seek is in Christ, divinity revealed, the "mystery" that is "uncontrollable," in the sense of inconceivable, beyond man's grasp.

So far the poem seems simple enough, the Magi being taken as symbols of the unending search for the divine. But "uncontrollable" has another side, and in fact, most of the poem has "another side." "Bestial" recalls the stable of the Nativity, but with "uncontrollable" and "turbulence" it may also suggest that the divine birth was too human, linked with the primitive and subhuman. The Magi were "unsatisfied" with the Incarnation, with God made flesh; their dream was not fulfilled by a career that ended in the "turbulence" and bloodshed of Calvary. So "once more" they are "hoping to find" the Absolute uncontaminated by the human. In writing of "The Magi" and its companion piece, " The Dolls," Yeats spoke of ". . . how all thought among us is frozen into ' something other than human life.' "

We have had a vision, but a strange one, for we have been led to feel an unexpected irony in the quest of the Magi, an irony inherent in all seeking after dehumanized, abstract truth. Other disturbing implications enter — for example, that religious revelation is inseparable from primitive violence. But note that the " I " of the poem stands apart from the Magi; he accepts, perhaps welcomes, the connection of divine being with human suffering and violence. If we now reread the poem with an ear for his voice and rhythm, we can feel their perfect appropriateness. The prose control of meditative speech rightly checks the tendency to visionary song; it goes well, too, with the critical attitude toward the Magi, and fits the far from simple reverence of this rehandling of Christian myth.

The visions of Keats or Wordsworth were certainly not like this. But " The Magi " is a poem of 1913, not 1813, and the awareness it expresses is very much of its time. Here is a poet who has rebelled against the rationality and abstraction of nineteenth-century social and scientific thought, who has been attracted by the rediscovery of primitive elements in religion, perhaps by the new comparative study of myth. The lack of simple seriousness, the blend of irony and wonder, is another sign of a twentieth-century sensibility. It is also a sign of a revolution in Yeats's poetic personality and style. Fifteen or sixteen years before, he had written very differently of the Magi in a poem to the Rose (his symbol for Passion, Intellectual Beauty, and a number of things):

> Thy great leaves enfold
> The ancient beards, the helms of ruby and gold
> Of the crowned Magi; and the kings whose eyes
> Saw the Pierced Hands and Rood of elder rise
> In Druid vapour. . . .
>
> (" The Secret Rose ")

Whatever these rich and solemn lines may mean, they belong to a literary realm miles removed from Yeats's later poetry. To trace the journey by which the poet of " The Secret Rose " became the poet of " The Magi," we shall have to relate his growth to personal history and to history in the broad sense.

Yeats's development, from the late 1880's to his death in 1939, falls into four fairly distinct phases, each of which is characterized by a more or less dominant mode of poetry: (I) Solitary Pre-Raphaelite Song (1889–1904); (II) Poetry out of the Theater (1904–16); (III) Lyric Debate and Visionary Song (1916–29); and (IV) Poetry of Madness (1929–39). Before tracing the growth of the poet it will be useful to have in mind a brief outline of his life.

PERSONAL HISTORY

The first twenty years of Yeats's life, until he became a professional writer, might be called his " Sligo " period. He was born, June 13, 1865, in Dublin; but he was never a Dubliner at heart; his home by inheritance and imaginative sympathy was in Sligo, a county of western Ireland with barren mountains overlooking the sea and exquisite Lough Gill, the lake of " Innisfree." Both his father's and mother's family had long lived in various parts of the county; and his ancestors on both sides were, like Shaw's, Protestant Irish, in the main descendants from English immigrants to Ireland. His father, John Butler Yeats, the son and grandson of clergymen, had rejected the family faith and calling to become a painter. During Yeats's boyhood his parents moved back and forth from London to Dublin, setting up their household where J. B. Y. wanted to study or paint, or where he could afford to pay the rent. During the summers and sometimes for periods of a year or more, William and the other children went to stay with their mother at her parents' home in Sligo. Here " Willie," as his father called him, first discovered the Celtic dreamland of his early poems and stories; here he saw strange lights on the nearby mountains, heard ghostly rappings and strange buzzings, and filled his head with tales about Irish heroes and fairy folk.

Yeats's career as a man of letters began in a serious way with the family's return to London in 1887, where he published his first volume of verse, *The Wanderings of Oisin and Other Poems*, in 1889, and three years later, his second, *The Countess Kathleen and Various Legends and Lyrics* (which included " The Lake Isle of Innisfree "). As these books show, Yeats had now come under the influence of late followers of the Pre-Raphaelite Brotherhood, a movement in art and literature initiated in 1848 by the poet and painter, Dante Gabriel Rossetti. Rebelling against the Royal Academy with its worship of Raphael, the founding Brothers had called themselves "*Pre*-Raphaelites." Their ideal was vaguely medieval; at least their subjects in poetry and painting were religious or allegorically "spiritual." One allegiance seems common to the writers, from Rossetti to William Morris, who were affected by the movement — a belief in "the life of imagination," in an ideal dream world, which they sought in protest against the materialism of nineteenth-century England.

This notion of art as a voyage out of the crass material present was also driven into Yeats's thinking by all sorts of influences that he encountered in the 1880's and 1890's. In 1891, he had joined a number of other poets in forming the Rhymers Club. He later said that for him and his friends in the Club "perhaps the most powerful influence" after Rossetti was Walter Pater, the high priest of the aesthetic movement. Whatever Pater may have intended, he came to represent the aim of reducing life to moments of exquisite sensations, of cultivating "aesthetic states" utterly unlike other kinds of experience. His attitude seemed to be sanctioned also by the French Symbolists,[1] to whom Yeats and the Rhymers had been introduced by Arthur Symons, author of *The Symbolist Movement in Literature*. As they sat in the "candelight," says Yeats, ". . . it never seemed very difficult to murmur Villiers de L'Isle-Adam's words, 'As for living — our servants will do that for us.'" To these literary influences were added a number of bizarre but deadly serious interests in magic and theosophy, in societies devoted to occult knowledge such as "The Order of the Golden Dawn," and in the founding of a new religion for Ireland.

But while Yeats was living in this literary and religious wonderland he was also very much alive in another world, in the political and cultural activities of the Irish National movement. Yeats proved himself an efficient organizer of societies aimed to arouse interest in old and new Irish literature (1891–92); he worked hard as a propagandist for the Nationalists, and actually joined a revolutionary group, the Irish Repub-

lican Brotherhood (1896). His two lives had been oddly linked by his falling in love (1889) with Maud Gonne, a beautiful woman and an agitator against English rule of Ireland. While Yeats was trying to interest his beloved in secret cults, she drew him into noisy and even dangerous political demonstrations, such as those against Queen Victoria's Jubilee in 1897.

In 1896 he met Lady Augusta Gregory, a member of an old Anglo-Irish landholding family and an enthusiastic collector of local traditions and folklore. In part through her influence and in part because of Maud Gonne's repeated refusals to marry him, Yeats's political activities diminished, and his interests became more closely identified with the revival of Irish literature and art, the so-called "Irish Renaissance." Toward the end of the century he joined Lady Gregory in the founding of an Irish National Theatre, the society that organized the famous Abbey Players. For the next ten years Yeats put most of his time and energy into writing and producing plays, or into explaining and defending the policies of the Theatre. He wrote and published very little lyric poetry between *The Wind among the Reeds* (1899) and *The Green Helmet and Other Poems*, a volume which came out in 1910 and marks a turning point in Yeats's career.

About this time Yeats became an intimate associate of Ezra Pound, a young American poet who introduced him to the "modern" style in verse. He continued to write plays, but for an ideal rather than an actual theater, and from this time on he concentrated more fully on the business of being a poet; nearly all his best poetry was written during the last thirty years of his life. The rest of Yeats's personal history can be quickly outlined. In 1917 he married Miss Georgie Hyde-Lees and soon after began to rebuild as a country home Thoor Ballylee, part of an ancient castle near Lady Gregory's place, Coole Park. (The castle is the original of the "Tower" symbol in Yeats's later poems.) In 1922 he was appointed to the Senate of the newly founded Irish Free State, and in 1923 he won the Nobel prize for literature. But though Yeats's life in later years was more firmly focused on his art, after his marriage he entered on his most elaborate experiment in occult knowledge and religion, the studies and mysterious communications with spirits that led to

---

[1] Villiers de L'Isle-Adam (1838–89) was a French writer whose drama, *Axel*, was "a sacred book" to Yeats. The hero is the perfect type of the Symbolist dreamer-philosopher who withdraws from society to live the life of imagination.

his book of revelation, *A Vision* (first published in 1925).

The year 1929 marks the beginning of the last period of the poet's life. Because he had suffered a congestion of the lungs in the fall of 1927, he began the practice of spending his winters on the French or Italian Riviera. During the winter of 1928–29 he stayed at Rapallo, Italy, and early in 1929 he started writing an entirely new kind of lyric poem, the first of a series, "Words for Music Perhaps." The following summer was his last at Thoor Ballylee. In the remaining years Yeats continued to read and write as vigorously as ever, working on a new edition of *A Vision* (1937) and writing poems up to within a day or two of his death, on January 28, 1939, at Cap Martin, France. The variety of his life — which we have barely glimpsed — is matched by the variety of his several "careers" as a poet. As we shall see, Yeats showed a unique power of renewing and transforming his art during each of the phases that followed his first successes in poetry.

I. SOLITARY PRE-RAPHAELITE SONG
(1889–1904)

These early successes, exquisite lyrics such as "Innisfree" and "Who Goes with Fergus?" now seem rather minor, as they did to Yeats himself a few years after he had written them. The poet who interests us today and who stands among the first of our century is the one who rejected or reshaped many elements in his youthful poetic self. A composite portrait of the poet drawn from the early volumes (1889–99) would include some curious traits: he is a chanter of fairy songs that take us

> Up the airy mountain
> Down the rushy glen, . . .[1]

but he is also a melancholy singer who longs for an "isle in the water" and a weary lover who seeks consolation from "love's bitter mystery" in Celtic hero stories; finally, he is a worshiper of symbolic images such as the "Far-off, most secret, and inviolate Rose."

It is interesting to note that much of his early poetic character can be traced either to his

[1] William Allingham (1824–89), "The Fairies." Allingham was a popular Irish poet who had a considerable influence on Yeats's early work.

mother or his father. To his mother's family, the Middletons, Yeats owed his taste for mystery and for Celtic other-worlds. To his father his debt as a poet was enormous both early and late in his career. Throughout his life Yeats can be seen reacting against or fulfilling his father's ideals in art and poetry, and J. B. Y. in old age might have said that Willie had come round wonderfully to the standards he had imparted in their early reading of Shelley and Shakespeare. But as often happens, the young man was first influenced by elements in his inheritance that interested his father least. For the father too had something to do with the far-awayness, the mysterious loves and symbols of his son's early verse, features that remind us less of Old Ireland than of the Pre-Raphaelites. J. B. Y. had in fact begun his career as a Pre-Raphaelite and had introduced his son to the pictures and verse of Rossetti, but while the father rejected his masters in favor of the more realistic French painters, his son had continued to love the saints and mournful beauties of the older school.

But the wanness and weariness, the insistent loneliness of Yeats's early love poetry, is Pre-Raphaelitism as transmitted through the tired but elegant and erudite conversation of the Rhymers. It is hard to say how much the cloudy symbolism of these poems — particularly the "Rose" lyrics — owes to the Rhymers' passion for the French Symbolists. Certainly the theories of *symbolisme* gave support to Yeats's own belief that a poet's images disclose a reality beyond that known to the senses. But the belief can be traced equally well to many of his early literary and religious enthusiasms — to his love of Shelley and Blake, to his interest in magic, or to the secret wisdom of the Golden Dawn.

As Yeats's poetry grew more hazily symbolic, especially in the 1899 volume, *The Wind among the Reeds*, the typical speaker of his poems resembles more and more the conventional lover of nineteenth-century Romantic poetry. "Dream" and "dream-dimmed" are words often on his lips, and if he now talks less naïvely of longing for fairyland, he is always addressing a beloved who is hardly of this world or picturing their love as a state of passionate trance. The tone he adopts is terribly solemn; the high religious unction of "I will arise and go now" becomes the rule, and too much of the time this lover sounds like the worshiper of "The Secret Rose." Although Yeats probably intended to create a distinct "personal utterance" in these love poems, the over-all impression is one of monotony and inhuman somnolence.

II. POETRY OUT OF THE THEATER
(1904–16)

Yeats's progress from lonely song to lyric debate is connected with his discovery that he had been fighting a number of lost causes: Maud Gonne married another man, the Irish theatrical audience did not take kindly to being educated, a new religion was not born, and Yeats's enthusiasm for revolution waned when he saw "the little streets hurled upon the great." More important for the change in his style was his progress as a dramatist in making "characters talk to one another." We first surely detect speech breaking into song in a poem that probably reflects his difficulties in love, "The Folly of Being Comforted." With "No Second Troy," Yeats clearly has found a new voice as compared with that of the old "dream-dimmed" lover: "Why should I blame her that she filled my days / With misery . . . ?" He also begins to use a type of metaphor characteristic of his work from 1914 on. A modern feminist and city appear in the poem as another Helen in "no second Troy"; a familiar symbol from myth or history refers to a present-day situation while also expressing more intimate concerns, in this instance, the misery of a lover disillusioned with his beloved and his society.

The poet who had once thought that his aim of "personal utterance" was at odds with his father's insistence on "drama" had at length found a way of being both personal and dramatic. J. B. Y., he recalled, ". . . did not care even for a fine lyric passage unless he felt some actual man behind its elaboration of beauty, and he was always looking for the lineaments of some desirable, familiar life. . . . All must be an idealization of speech, and at some moment of passionate action or somnambulistic reverie." The latter sentence describes very aptly the two modes of expression dominant in Yeats's later poetry. In *Responsibilities* (1914), the contained violence of "To a Friend" stands beside "The

Magi," a poem that looks ahead to the union of both modes in lyrics focused on some great traditional symbol.

But before Yeats reached those successes he had first to make a conscious critical effort, which for him as for Keats meant also a personal and moral effort. In the period between 1912 and 1916 he set about quite deliberately to remake himself as a man and a poet, and in such a situation it is very like Yeats to seize on any source of power from the sublime to the ridiculous. He schools his inner life by the image of his "anti-self," the heroic man he would be, he rewrites his poems under the direction of Ezra Pound, a man twenty years younger than himself, and he consults a medium to talk with his attendant spirit. However comic the means, the end — the achievement of the poet — is admirable. It is not often that a poet or any man of fifty can learn from the young (an event very nearly as remarkable as communicating with another world). At the time when Yeats felt he was "drying up" and when he still had moments of longing for the fantasies of his youth,[1] he found a role in which he could positively embrace and balance both "dreams" and "responsibilities."

"The Fisherman" (1914) clearly announces Yeats's newly realized sense of himself and his audience. He will write no longer for actual Ireland, but for a man of heroic temper who will welcome poetry "cold / And passionate as the dawn." Here we see Yeats's myth-making power at its best: as the poem moves along, the "fisherman" very gradually takes on symbolic meaning; Yeats does not *make* his symbol, it makes itself. Although this man is "but a dream," he evokes a real past, the sterner Ireland of Swift and Burke. If Yeats is no longer a partisan, he is still responsive to national life. But now — and this is the important fact — he has discovered his relation to politics *as a poet*. In "Easter 1916" he honors a group of rebels, but in his own way, candidly acknowledging that they may have been wrong, that their hearts may have been "enchanted to a stone" by fanaticism, but also recognizing that in their action and death they have become beautiful. Yeats's balancing of loyalties in the poem is wonderfully matched by his interweaving of the

---

[1] See "Lines Written in Dejection," below.

old, dreamlike rhythms with a new hardness of speech.

III. LYRIC DEBATE AND VISIONARY SONG
(1916–29)

But Yeats attained a much subtler poise among his various selves in poetry written during the next few years, notably in the poems of *The Tower* (1928). He had at last seen how to reconcile action and reverie, speech and song, public and personal symbolism. Yeats did not "solve" anything in these poems; he succeeded rather in making poetry out of his irresolution: that is his peculiar inimitable feat. In "Sailing to Byzantium," "reverie" (in a special sense) seems the prime value, while in "Among School Children" there is an energetic balance between achievement and aiming at the unattainable. Though the two poems are so different, they disclose a similar progression, the mode of lyric debate that finally links the styles we have been tracing. So both begin with an old man talking in a matter-of-fact way ("That is no country for old men" and "I walk through the long schoolroom questioning"); each of the old men is keenly responsive to the sights and sounds of the real world, and each is ironically aware of the figure he cuts in an actual society; but they are at the same time excited by images of the soul's "magnificence" and of "heavenly glory." As they reflect, the debate between opposing desires and values becomes sharper, reaching a climax in a songlike prayer ("O sages," "O Presences"). In the strongly rhythmed lines of the close, images appear (the bird, the chestnut-tree) that symbolize a reconciliation between feelings aroused in the debate. Yeats has found his "form" — in the full athletic sense — just as Keats did in his odes. (The comparison is illuminating, because the kind of poetry first glimpsed in *Endymion* culminates in "Sailing to Byzantium" and because Keats can strike a note of assurance beyond the reach of Yeats and most poets of the past fifty years.)

But the attitudes Yeats dramatizes are not wholly opposed, at least not in the poems. The singer of Byzantium hears too well the "sensual music" he neglects. The old man of "Among School Children" knows that heavenly "Presences" like children "break hearts,"

and he happily asserts the value of what Yeats's father called "Personality," the harmonious expression of the whole man. Other poems in *The Tower* express a poise between Yeats's private and public loyalties, often in the form of an argument between the man who withdrew to his "tower" and the man who might have fought beside his countrymen. But in poems like "Sailing to Byzantium" Yeats succeeds more fully in connecting his opposing worlds because he takes as symbols figures or cities that have long had the kind of meaning he attaches to them. It makes all the difference that he now chooses to sail to Byzantium rather than to Innisfree. He "leans out," as his father would say, to larger, more public kinds of significance and is able to say a great deal more to readers aware of their place in history.

The way in which Yeats's symbols extend his range can be seen most clearly in "Two Songs from a Play." Both are visions in pure song; in both, speech rhythm almost disappears, though it still may be felt in the decorum and succinctness of the sentences:

> The Roman Empire stood appalled:
> It dropped the reins of peace and war
> When that fierce virgin and her Star
> Out of the fabulous darkness called.

But what has happened to debate? Yeats is again balancing different views of Christianity and of Greco-Roman civilization, but he no longer presents his choices through distinct voices and rhythms. Debate has been compressed into symbols or allusions with double, sometimes opposite, kinds of significance. So the "virgin" is at once Athena and Mary. The peace of Augustus which marked Christ's birth is both a moment of high civilization and the moment of a fatal relaxation of control, a dropping of "the reins of peace and war." Double meanings grow out of the very center of the poem. Its key metaphor is one of alternation, of a cyclical movement pervading history and all human activity.

But Yeats's historic symbols are not only backward-looking. Like those of T. S. Eliot and James Joyce they express a surprising sense of the present *in* the past, and they make us think of our moment in history, of modern crises, while talking about the turning point between pagan and Christian, or Babylonian and Greek, civilizations. " The Second Coming " is a nightmare vision of this " simultaneous " type:

And what rough beast, its hour come round at last,
Slouches towards Bethlehem to be born?

Bethlehem is now Berlin or Moscow or Rome, any city where a new cult of violence may be revealed. By playing on " slouches " Yeats says that a revelation is at hand but that revelations are mixed blessings. Earlier in the poem, by one of his cyclical images (" gyring "), he makes us feel both that the modern world is moving toward a crisis and that it is falling apart. Yeats has finally managed to turn " dream " into prophetic " history."

The form that Yeats achieved in the twenties, through which he balanced speech and song, the personal symbol and the historic, action and contemplation, remained with him during the rest of his career. Similar or identical symbols — Byzantium and Troy, gyres and towers, caves and tremendous statues — recur quite often and express the now familiar conflicts. But by the thirties there is some change in tone and intensity, perhaps a reflection of " the smiling public man " who had become a Senator in the Free State, a Nobel prize winner, and something of a national sage. Yeats now honors his early political and literary associates in verse that has the fine detachment and public decorum of Pope or Dr. Johnson. His " tower " is no longer the retreat of " Il Penseroso," [1] but the Anglo-Irish tradition, another country of the mind but one linked with actuality. " Vacillation," the poem that perhaps best sums up Yeats's career, is remarkable for the ripe good humor with which the poet puts behind him the old temptation to " find relief " in a life and art detached from ordinary humanity.

IV. POETRY OF MADNESS
(1929–39)

Tranquillity is hardly the keynote of the poems written during Yeats's fourth and last period. He appears in them as an old man, but as no sage, and even when descanting on the serenity that comes with his years, he surprises us: " Bodily decrepitude is wisdom." [2] The ugly

[1] See ll. 85–96 of " Il Penseroso," p. 214, above.
[2] See " After Long Silence," p. 1003, below.

facts are unblinkingly accepted; this old man, " mad as the mist and snow," has little in common with the prematurely aged singer of the 1890's who found consolation in other-world fantasies. Conventional religious and sexual experiences are seen through completely, and yet the rhythm of the later songs is oddly cheerful, the singer is terribly and happily hard-boiled. This return to ballad-like rhythms recalls Yeats's early imitations of Irish popular verse only to bring out a difference: the consoling " yet's," the tear in the beer of music-hall song, have vanished.

But there is a close relation between the singer of *Last Poems* (1936–39) and the poet-philosopher of *The Tower* period. One of the best of the late lyrics, " An Acre of Grass," is a kind of noble parody of poems written ten years earlier. The progression is still the familiar one, from quiet speech to prayer, from images of here and now to symbols of a life eagerly desired, but instead of asking for a life " out of nature " or for harmonious development, this poet rudely calls for " an old man's frenzy." His ideal Presences are not Plato and Homer, but Lear and Michelangelo, mad old men who also found victory in " seeing through." A similarly exultant note can be heard in " A Wild Old Wicked Man." There is the sexual heartiness of

" Because I am mad about women
I am mad about the hills,"

combined with bitter knowledge:

" All men live in suffering,
I know as few can know, . . ."

The first attitude apart from the second might be embarrassing, or at least of limited interest. Old age asserting youthful vigor is not a pleasant sight. But " a coarse old man " aware of his coarseness, who teaches his love that life is suffering, engages deeper and more complex feelings. Nevertheless, Yeats had his difficulties in managing the old men of his later poems, and, like his commentators, he often tries too hard to force the note of vitality and profundity in songs of " lust and rage." We find the richness that we miss in these songs in the symbolic, meditative poems of the familiar historical and personal sort: " The Gyres," " The Statues," " The Circus Animals' Desertion," " A Bronze Head." Yeats still moves in his mysterious way around the memory of a woman or a statue or a city, and as he talks and sings he unfolds and weighs antithetical views of character or history. Resolution becomes no easier; the poems almost fall apart as Yeats opens up his mind to every pull and counterpull.

The substance of Yeats's best poetry, early and late, matters to us because he expresses with dramatic truth and musical delight dreams and renunciations to which we attach value in our own private and public worlds. To have experienced the voyage into a city of the mind's creating, where we are both alone and in the company of the great minds of the past, or to have felt both the waste and the heroic quality of political action based on abstract principles, to have entertained at once the tranquillity and the madness of age—these are among the better things that poetry can do for us.

The poems of Yeats are reprinted from *The Collected Poems of W. B. Yeats,* The Macmillan Company, New York (1956). The dates printed below the poems at the *left* are those provided by Yeats himself as a part of the text in the *Collected Poems.* Some, if not all, of these dates are almost certainly *not* the dates of composition. Therefore, dates of composition, when they can be determined, have been printed below the poems at the *right.* These dates are based on information supplied by Yeats's biographers (Ellmann, Hone, Jeffares). Where a date has seemed no more than probable, an interrogation point follows the figure.

THE LAKE ISLE OF INNISFREE

This poem first appeared in the *National Observer,* December 13, 1890, and was reprinted in *The Countess Kathleen and Various Legends and Lyrics* (1892).

I will arise and go now, and go to Innisfree,°
And a small cabin build there, of clay and wattles
    made:
Nine bean-rows will I have there, a hive for the
    honeybee,
And live alone in the bee-loud glade.

And I shall have some peace there, for peace comes
    dropping slow,
Dropping from the veils of the morning to where
    the cricket sings;
There midnight's all a glimmer, and noon a purple
    glow,
And evening full of the linnet's wings.

I will arise and go now, for always night and day
I hear lake water lapping° with low sounds by the
    shore;   10
While I stand on the roadway, or on the pavements
    grey,
I hear it in the deep heart's core.
                          1890?

WHO GOES WITH FERGUS?

Who will go drive with Fergus° now,
And pierce the deep wood's woven shade,
And dance upon the level shore?
Young man, lift up your russet brow,
And lift your tender eyelids, maid,
And brood on hopes and fear no more.

And no more turn aside and brood
Upon love's bitter mystery;
For Fergus rules the brazen cars,
And rules the shadows of the wood,   10
And the white breast of the dim sea
And all dishevelled wandering stars.

THE FOLLY OF BEING COMFORTED

This poem was included in the volume *In the Seven Woods* (1903). The text printed here is that of *Later Poems,* by W. B. Yeats, The Macmillan Company, New York (1924).

One that is ever kind said yesterday:
"Your well-beloved's hair has threads of grey,
And little shadows come about her eyes;
Time can but make it easier to be wise

THE LAKE ISLE OF INNISFREE. **1. Innisfree:** "My father had read to me some passage out of *Walden,* and I planned to live some day in a cottage on a little island called Innisfree . . ." (*Autobiography,* p. 64). **10. I . . . lapping:** Cf. " 'I heard the water lapping on the crag,/And the long ripple washing in the reeds' " (Tennyson, *Morte d'Arthur,* ll. 116–17).

WHO GOES WITH FERGUS? **1. Fergus:** legendary king of Ulster, who gave up his throne to Conchobar and later went into exile. Cf. "I feast amid my people on the hill,/And pace the woods, and drive my chariot-wheels/In the white border of the murmuring sea;/And still I feel the crown upon my head" ("Fergus and the Druid," *Collected Poems,* pp. 32–33, ll. 17–20).

Though now it seem impossible, and so
Patience is all that you have need of."
                                        No,
I have not a crumb of comfort, not a grain,
Time can but make her beauty over again:
Because of that great nobleness of hers
The fire that stirs about her, when she stirs   10
Burns but more clearly. O she had not these ways,
When all the wild summer was in her gaze.
O heart! O heart! if she'd but turn her head,°
You'd know the folly of being comforted.

NO SECOND TROY

The opening lines refer to Maud Gonne and her
revolutionary activities. See Introduction, p. 986. The
heroic figure of the poem is not the actual woman,
but a "second" Helen of Troy. The Troy symbols recur in many of Yeats's poems and often express similar
parallels and contrasts between different civilizations.
See "Two Songs from a Play" and "Among School
Children," below. In this poem the contrast serves both
to ennoble and to satirize Ireland and Irish politics.
Compare the idiom and rhythm with those of poems
immediately preceding and following. "No Second
Troy" was first printed in *The Green Helmet and
Other Poems* (1910).

Why should I blame her that she filled my days
With misery, or that she would of late
Have taught to ignorant men most violent ways,
Or hurled the little streets upon the great,
Had they but courage equal to desire?
What could have made her peaceful with a mind
That nobleness made simple as a fire,
With beauty like a tightened bow, a kind
That is not natural in an age like this,
Being high and solitary and most stern?   10
Why, what could she have done, being what she is?
Was there another Troy for her to burn?

                                        1908?

TO A FRIEND WHOSE WORK
HAS COME TO NOTHING

"Lady Gregory in her *Life of Sir Hugh Lane* assumes that the poem which begins 'Now all the truth
is out,' was addressed to him. It was not; it was addressed to herself. — 1922" [Yeats's note]. The Corporation of Dublin had refused to provide a building
for a collection of French pictures offered to the city
by Sir Hugh Lane. This poem and the two that follow
were included in *Responsibilities* (1914).

FOLLY.   13. turn . . . head: Consider possible interpretations of
what the lover sees, and compare the similar balancing of attitudes in "No Second Troy," "Men Improve with the Years,"
and "After Long Silence," below.

Now all the truth is out,
Be secret and take defeat
From any brazen throat,
For how can you compete,
Being honour bred, with one
Who, were it proved he lies,
Were neither shamed in his own
Nor in his neighbours' eyes?
Bred to a harder thing
Than Triumph, turn away   10
And like a laughing string
Whereon mad fingers play
Amid a place of stone,
Be secret and exult,
Because of all things known
That is most difficult.

                                        1913

THE MAGI

For an interpretation of this poem, see Introduction,
p. 984, and the headnote to "The Dolls," below.

Now as at all times I can see in the mind's eye,
In their stiff, painted clothes, the pale unsatisfied
        ones
Appear and disappear in the blue depth of the sky
With all their ancient faces like rain-beaten
        stones,
And all their helms of silver hovering side by
        side,
And all their eyes still fixed, hoping to find once
        more,
Being by Calvary's turbulence° unsatisfied,
The uncontrollable mystery on the bestial floor.

                                        1913?

THE DOLLS

"The fable for this poem came into my head while
I was giving some lectures in Dublin. I had noticed
once again how all thought among us is frozen into
'something other than human life.' After I had made
the poem, I looked up one day into the blue of the
sky, and suddenly imagined, as if lost in the blue of
the sky, stiff figures in procession. I remembered that
they were the habitual image suggested by blue sky,
and looking for a second fable called them 'The Magi,'
complementary forms of those enraged dolls. — 1914"
[Y]. Compare this with: "Today a grotesque twopenny
doll was lying on the floor near the old woman. He
[the old man] picked it up and examined it as if comparing it with her. Then he held it up: 'Is it you is
after bringing that thing into the world,' he said,

THE MAGI.   7. Calvary's turbulence: Cf. "Galilean turbulence,"
in "Two Songs from a Play," l. 19n, p. 998, below. Cf. also
"The Second Coming," p. 996, below.

'woman of the house?'" (John Synge, *The Aran Islands*, p. 42)

A doll in the doll-maker's house
Looks at the cradle and bawls:
"That is an insult to us."
But the oldest of all the dolls,
Who had seen, being kept for show,
Generations of his sort,
Out-screams the whole shelf: "Although
There's not a man can report
Evil of this place,
The man and the woman bring   10
Hither, to our disgrace,
A noisy and filthy thing."
Hearing him groan and stretch
The doll-maker's wife is aware
Her husband has heard the wretch,
And crouched by the arm of his chair,
She murmurs into his ear,
Head upon shoulder leant:
"My dear, my dear, O dear,
It was an accident."   20

                            1912

THE WILD SWANS AT COOLE

Notice how the metaphorical significance of the "swans" grows quite naturally out of the setting and the narrative facts of the poem. Compare the "swan" symbol in "The Tower," III, ll. 19–24, below. "The Wild Swans" is a clear and harmonious piece of expression quite apart from any reference to particular places and persons. For a different type of biographical poem, see "Coole Park, 1929," below, which explains the importance of Coole to Yeats and his friends. "The Wild Swans at Coole" is the title poem of a volume published in 1917 (the Cuala Press edition), which also included the next three poems printed here.

The trees are in their autumn beauty,
The woodland paths are dry,
Under the October twilight the water
Mirrors a still sky;
Upon the brimming water among the stones
Are nine-and-fifty swans.

The nineteenth autumn° has come upon me
Since I first made my count;
I saw, before I had well finished,
All suddenly mount   10
And scatter wheeling in great broken rings
Upon their clamorous wings.

I have looked upon those brilliant creatures,
And now my heart is sore.°
All's changed since I, hearing at twilight,
The first time on this shore,
The bell-beat of their wings above my head,
Trod with a lighter tread.

Unwearied still, lover by lover,
They paddle in the cold   20
Companionable streams or climb the air;
Their hearts have not grown old;
Passion or conquest, wander where they will,
Attend upon them still.

But now they drift on the still water,
Mysterious, beautiful;
Among what rushes will they build,
By what lake's edge or pool
Delight men's eyes when I awake some day
To find they have flown away?   30

                            1916

MEN IMPROVE WITH THE YEARS

This lyric is focused on the symbolic image of the triton. Observe the many and varied connections between the image and other details of the poem, and how this interrelationship alters and enriches the meaning of the closing lines.

I am worn out with dreams;
A weather-worn, marble triton
Among the streams;
And all day long I look
Upon this lady's beauty
As though I had found in a book
A pictured beauty,
Pleased to have filled the eyes
Or the discerning ears,
Delighted to be but wise,   10
For men improve° with the years;
And yet, and yet,
Is this my dream, or the truth?
O would that we had met
When I had my burning youth!
But I grow old among dreams,
A weather-worn, marble triton
Among the streams.

                            1916

THE WILD SWANS. **7. nineteenth autumn:** 1916, the nineteenth year since Yeats first came to stay with Lady Gregory at Coole Park.

14. my ... sore: There is an oblique allusion in this and the next stanza to Yeats's continuing love for Maud Gonne, who had recently again refused to marry him. MEN IMPROVE. **11. improve:** The word takes on a different sense when it is related both to the lines that follow and to the "marble triton." The blend of opposing attitudes is characteristic. Cf. "The Folly of Being Comforted," above, and "After Long Silence," below.

LINES WRITTEN IN DEJECTION

Note the way in which Yeats now combines his earlier hypnotic rhythms with the movement of plain
speech. Compare this poem with "Men Improve with
the Years," above, and "Sailing to Byzantium," below.

When have I last looked on
The round green eyes and the long wavering bodies
Of the dark leopards of the moon?
All the wild witches, those most noble ladies,
For all their broom-sticks and their tears,
Their angry tears, are gone.
The holy centaurs° of the hills are vanished;
I have nothing but the embittered sun;
Banished heroic mother moon° and vanished,
And now that I have come to fifty years   10
I must endure the timid sun.

1915?

THE FISHERMAN

Here Yeats announces most clearly his intention of
creating a new audience and a new kind of poetry.
See Introduction, p. 988. The central image is a familiar one in Yeats: ". . . in boyhood when with rod and
fly, / Or the humbler worm, I climbed Ben Bulben's
back. . . ." ("The Tower," I, ll. 8–9, *Collected Poems*,
p. 192); "And I call to the mind's eye / . . . A man
climbing up to a place / The salt sea wind has swept
bare" ("At the Hawk's Well," ll. 4, 7–8, *Collected
Plays*, p. 208). The "man" is the hero Cuchulain.
The scorn expressed in this poem and the occasional
baldness of idiom and rhythm recall Swift. For further
connections between "fishermen," Swift, and the
Anglo-Irish tradition, see "The Tower," III, l. 2n., and
notes to "Blood and the Moon," I, II, below.

    Although I can see him still,
    The freckled man who goes

To a grey place on a hill
In grey Connemara° clothes
At dawn to cast his flies,
It's long since I began
To call up to the eyes
This wise and simple man.
All day I'd looked in the face
What I had hoped 'twould be   10
To write for my own race
And the reality;°
The living men that I hate,
The dead man° that I loved,
The craven man in his seat,
The insolent unreproved,
And no knave brought to book
Who has won a drunken cheer,   20
The witty man and his joke
Aimed at the commonest ear,
The clever man who cries
The catch-cries of the clown,
The beating down of the wise
And great Art beaten down.

Maybe a twelvemonth since
Suddenly I began,
In scorn of this audience,
Imagining a man,
And his sun-freckled face,
And grey Connemara cloth,   30
Climbing up to a place
Where stone is dark under froth,
And the down-turn of his wrist
When the flies drop in the stream;
A man who does not exist,
A man who is but a dream;
And cried, "Before I am old
I shall have written him one
Poem maybe as cold
And passionate as the dawn."   40

1914

EASTER 1916

    The occasion of this poem was an insurrection of ex-
treme Irish nationalists that took place on Easter Monday, 1916. The Easter Rising, as it was called, was repressed by the English; fifteen of the leaders, including

LINES WRITTEN IN DEJECTION. **7. centaurs:** creatures of Greek
myth, half man and half horse. The most famous of the centaurs,
Chiron, was a gifted musician and the teacher of Achilles,
Herakles, Jason, and other heroes; hence the centaur makes an
appropriate symbol for a young poet's dreams of an heroic
world. But the myth had for Yeats other meanings of a more
private sort: "I thought that all art should be a Centaur finding
in the popular lore its back and its strong legs" ("A World of
Fragments," *Autobiography*). Thus the poem also expresses
Yeats's regret for the decline of folklore and folk poetry.
9. heroic . . . moon: ". . . the simple unmysterious things living
as in a clear moonlight are of the nature of the sun, and the
vague, many-imaged things have in them the strength of the
moon. Did not the Egyptian carve it on emerald that all living
things have the sun for father and the moon for mother, and
has it not been said that a man of genius takes the most after
his mother?" ("Emotion of Multitude," Yeats's *Essays*.)
"Heroic" also suggests the moon as Artemis the fierce huntress;
"mother," Artemis in her Asiatic form as the mother goddess.
This image, like others in the poem, carries connotations of folk
culture, primitive religious power, and heroic nobility.

THE FISHERMAN. **4. Connemara:** a mountainous region in
County Galway, for Yeats an ideal Ireland where heroic manners
and the ancient art of the folk song still survived. Hence the
fisherman makes an appropriate symbol for the audience Yeats
would like to address. **12. the reality:** This and the following
lines contain more or less specific allusions to Yeats's experiences
in Irish literary circles, particularly in the theater. See Intro.,
p. 986. **14. The . . . man:** John Synge. Cf. "Coole Park, 1929,"
ll. 12–13, below, and "The Tragic Generation," *Autobiography*.

the four men named in the poem, were executed. Yeats, who had in general a dislike for revolutions, had originally not approved of the Rising, and his poem shows a far from simple attitude toward all followers of a patriotic "cause" (ll. 57–69). "Easter 1916" must not be read as a record of historical events or of Yeats's political opinions; it expresses a surprising imaginative transformation of fact. See Introduction, p. 988. First published in 1916, the poem was reprinted in *Michael Robartes and the Dancer* (1921), a volume that included "The Second Coming."

I have met them at close of day
Coming with vivid faces
From counter or desk among grey
Eighteenth-century houses.
I have passed with a nod of the head
Or polite meaningless words,
Or have lingered awhile and said
Polite meaningless words,
And thought before I had done
Of a mocking tale or a gibe   10
To please a companion
Around the fire at the club,
Being certain that they and I
But lived where motley is worn:
All changed, changed utterly:
A terrible beauty is born.

That woman's° days were spent
In ignorant good-will,
Her nights in argument
Until her voice grew shrill.   20
What voice more sweet than hers
When, young and beautiful,
She rode to harriers?
This man° had kept a school
And rode our wingèd horse;
This other° his helper and friend
Was coming into his force;
He might have won fame in the end,
So sensitive his nature seemed,
So daring and sweet his thought.   30
This other man° I had dreamed
A drunken, vainglorious lout.
He had done most bitter wrong
To some who are near my heart,
Yet I number him in the song;
He, too, has resigned his part

In the casual comedy;
He, too, has been changed in his turn,
Transformed utterly:
A terrible beauty is born.   40

Hearts with one purpose alone
Through summer and winter seem
Enchanted to a stone
To trouble the living stream.
The horse that comes from the road,
The rider, the birds that range
From cloud to tumbling cloud,
Minute by minute they change;
A shadow of cloud on the stream
Changes minute by minute;   50
A horse-hoof slides on the brim,
And a horse plashes within it;
The long-legged moor-hens dive,
And hens to moor-cocks call;
Minute by minute they live:
The stone's in the midst of all.

Too long a sacrifice
Can make a stone of the heart.
O when may it suffice?
That is Heaven's part, our part   60
To murmur name upon name,
As a mother names her child
When sleep at last has come
On limbs that had run wild.
What is it but nightfall?
No, no, not night but death;
Was it needless death after all?
For England may keep faith
For all that is done and said.
We know their dream; enough   70
To know they dreamed and are dead;
And what if excess of love
Bewildered them till they died?
I write it out in a verse—
MacDonagh and MacBride
And Connolly° and Pearse
Now and in time to be,
Wherever green is worn,
Are changed, changed utterly:
A terrible beauty is born.   80

September 25, 1916

THE SECOND COMING

The best introduction to the poem is Yeats's own comment, "A World of Fragments," in the *Autobiography*. This twentieth-century vision of a "second coming" recalls the familiar Christian prophecy, but

EASTER 1916. **17. That woman:** Countess Markiewicz (before her marriage, Constance Gore-Booth) took an active part in the Easter Rising and was sentenced to life imprisonment. In her youth she was famous for her beauty and ability as a rider (ll. 22–23). See "Eva Gore-Booth and Con Markiewicz," below. Cf. "A Political Prisoner," *Collected Poems*, pp. 181–82. **24. This man:** Patrick Pearse, leader in the Gaelic language movement, founder of a bilingual school, and a poet, commanded the forces of the rebels. **26. This other:** Thomas MacDonagh, a writer whose work Yeats had read and admired. **31. This . . . man:** Major John MacBride, the husband of Maud Gonne.

76. Connolly: James Connolly was Pearse's partner in leading the insurrection. In the late 90's Yeats and Maud Gonne had joined him in various anti-English demonstrations.

as elsewhere in Yeats Christ's birth has a double significance. The Nativity marked the beginning of Christian civilization, but also brought to an end the Greco-Roman cycle (*gyre*) that had lasted for "twenty centuries." According to this view, Christ's coming entailed a revival of the bloody violence of primitive religion, a revival expressed in the poem as an awakening of a sphinx-like creature (ll. 13–16). See "Two Songs from a Play," below; "The Magi," above; and Introduction, p. 990.

Turning and turning in the widening gyre°
The falcon cannot hear the falconer;
Things fall apart; the centre cannot hold;
Mere anarchy is loosed upon the world,
The blood-dimmed tide is loosed, and everywhere
The ceremony of innocence° is drowned;
The best lack all conviction, while the worst
Are full of passionate intensity.°

Surely some revelation is at hand;
Surely the Second Coming is at hand.   10
The Second Coming! Hardly are those words out
When a vast image out of *Spiritus Mundi*°
Troubles my sight: somewhere in sands of the
     desert
A shape with lion body and the head of a man,
A gaze blank and pitiless as the sun,
Is moving its slow thighs, while all about it
Reel shadows of the indignant desert birds.
The darkness drops again; but now I know
That twenty centuries of stony sleep
Were vexed to nightmare by a rocking cradle, 20
And what rough beast, its hour come round at last,
Slouches towards Bethlehem to be born?

                                        1919

SAILING TO BYZANTIUM

"Sailing to Byzantium" is the first poem in *The Tower* (1928), the volume that marks the culminating point in the development of Yeats's later style. The next four poems also appeared in the same volume. For further interpretation, see Introduction, p. 989.

THE SECOND COMING. **1. gyre:** refers to the phase of history now moving towards completion.   **4–8. anarchy ... intensity:** with allusion to revolutionary or reactionary mass movements, such as the Russian Revolution (note the date of poem) and fascism. **6. ceremony of innocence:** The connotations are Christian and aristocratic, "ceremony" suggesting both religious ritual and civilized behavior.   **12. Spiritus Mundi:** or *Anima Mundi*, in the belief of Yeats and of many mystics, the Spirit or Soul of the universe, with which all individual souls are connected; it is also the Great Memory, which is the repository of all individual memories from the past. Yeats sometimes refers to the *Anima Mundi* as "the subconscious": ". . . the general mind where that mind is scarcely separable from what we have begun to call 'the subconscious' . . ." ("Anima Mundi," *Essays*). It is accordingly the source from which the poet may draw images or symbols.

I

That is no country° for old men. The young
In one another's arms, birds in the trees
— Those dying generations — at their song,
The salmon-falls, the mackerel-crowded seas
Fish, flesh, or fowl, commend all summer long
Whatever is begotten, born, and dies.
Caught in that sensual music all neglect
Monuments of unageing intellect.

II

An aged man is but a paltry thing,
A tattered coat upon a stick, unless   10
Soul clap its hands and sing, and louder sing
For every tatter in its mortal dress,
Nor is there singing school but studying
Monuments of its own magnificence;
And therefore I have sailed the seas and come
To the holy city of Byzantium.

III

O sages standing in God's holy fire
As in the gold mosaic of a wall,°
Come from the holy fire, perne° in a gyre,°
And be the singing-masters of my soul.   20
Consume my heart away; sick with desire
And fastened to a dying animal
It knows not what it is; and gather me
Into the artifice of eternity.

IV

Once out of nature I shall never take
My bodily form from any natural thing,
But such a form as Grecian goldsmiths° make

SAILING TO BYZANTIUM. **1. That ... country:** Though the imagery of the stanza (*salmon-falls, mackerel-crowded seas*) suggests Ireland, the "country" of the poem is not to be located on a map. Similarly, though "Byzantium" refers to the capital of the Eastern Roman Empire and to "the holy city" of Greek Orthodox Christianity, the city of the poem is the ideal life of the soul expressed in sts. 2–4. The historic city was an apt symbol for Yeats's purpose, since it was famous for its holiness, for the somewhat rarefied and extremely subtle character of its intellectual life, and for its exquisite art.   **17–18. sages ... wall:** an allusion to the figures in mosaic on the walls of the Church of Hagia Sophia (meaning "Holy Wisdom"), the greatest of Byzantine architectural monuments. Byzantine art tended to be geometric and abstract; the human figure was rendered in a style far from naturalistic.   **19. Come ... gyre:** He begs the sage-saints to come down from the golden, fiery nimbus that surrounds them, and he sees them descend with a whirling (spool-like), spiral motion. **perne:** "When I was a child at Sligo I could see above my grandfather's trees a little column of smoke from 'the pern mill,' and was told that 'pern' was another name for the spool . . . on which the thread was wound" [Yeats's note to "Shepherd and Goatherd"].   **27. Grecian goldsmiths:** "I have read somewhere that in the Emperor's palace at Byzantium was a tree made of gold and silver, and artificial birds that sang" [Y].

Of hammered gold and gold enamelling
To keep a drowsy Emperor awake;
Or set upon a golden bough to sing   30
To lords and ladies of Byzantium
Of what is past, or passing, or to come.

1927   *1926*

THE TOWER

" The Tower," III, is the last poem of a sequence on themes similar to those of " Sailing to Byzantium," with which it should be carefully compared. The title refers to Thoor Ballylee, part of an ancient castle that Yeats had rebuilt as a country home, where he had lived off and on since 1919; but the more important meanings of " the tower " are symbolic. In " The Tower," II, it is associated with Ireland's heroic past and with memories of local tales that Yeats had retold in the *Celtic Twilight* and similar collections; more generally, like Byzantium, it stands for the aging poet-philosopher's ideal way of life: " It seems that I must bid the Muse go pack, / Choose Plato and Plotinus for a friend / Until imagination, ear and eye, / Can be content with argument and deal / In abstract things; . . ." (" The Tower," I, ll. 11–15, *Collected Poems*, p. 192). Compare with " Blood and the Moon," below. (See also " Yeats's Anti-Self," in the *Autobiography*.)

III

It is time that I wrote my will;
I choose upstanding men°
That climb the streams until
The fountain leap, and at dawn
Drop their cast at the side
Of dripping stone; I declare
They shall inherit my pride,
The pride of people that were
Bound neither to Cause° nor to State,
Neither to slaves that were spat on,   10
Nor to the tyrants that spat,
The people of Burke° and of Grattan°
That gave, though free to refuse —
Pride, like that of the morn,
When the headlong light is loose,
Or that of the fabulous horn,

Or that of the sudden shower
When all streams are dry,
Or that of the hour
When the swan must fix his eye   20
Upon a fading gleam,
Float out upon a long
Last reach of glittering stream
And there sing his last song.°
And I declare my faith:
I mock Plotinus' thought
And cry in Plato's teeth,
Death and life were not
Till man made up the whole,
Made lock, stock and barrel   30
Out of his bitter soul,
Aye, sun and moon and star, all,°
And further add to that
That, being dead, we rise,
Dream and so create
Translunar Paradise.°
I have prepared my peace
With learned Italian things
And the proud stones of Greece,
Poet's imaginings   40
And memories of love,
Memories of the words of women,
All those things whereof
Man makes a superhuman
Mirror-resembling° dream.

As at the loophole there
The daws chatter and scream,
And drop twigs layer upon layer.
When they have mounted up,
The mother bird will rest   50
On their hollow top,
And so warm her wild nest.°

I leave both faith and pride
To young upstanding men
Climbing the mountain-side,
That under bursting dawn
They may drop a fly;

THE TOWER. **2. upstanding men:** Cf. "The Fisherman," p. 994, above. Here the "fishermen" are regarded as inheritors of the Anglo-Irish tradition that Yeats admired increasingly in later years. See notes to "Blood and the Moon," below. **9. Cause:** referring to a religious "cause" or a political program. **12. Burke:** Edmund Burke (1729–97), British statesman, born in Dublin, who favored reconciliation with the American colonies (1775); later, a severe critic of the French Revolution. **Grattan:** Henry Grattan (1746–1820), a statesman who worked for an independent Irish parliament and for Catholic emancipation. To Yeats, he represents like Burke a moderate, aristocratic type of reformer, whose actions were "bound" neither by the Irish mob nor by the English "tyrants."

20–24. swan . . . song: an echo of "The Dying Swan," a poem by Yeats's friend, Sturge Moore. **26–32. I . . . all:** With a characteristic reversal of feeling, Yeats rejects the philosophers whom he had earlier chosen as his instructors ("The Tower," I.12). In a note to the poem dated 1928, he confessed that he had been mistaken about Plato's and Plotinus' thought and observed that the latter had written of the soul's power to create "all living things." (Plato also expressed similar beliefs; cf. *Laws*, X.896A.) **36. Translunar Paradise:** Cf. "the artifice of eternity" ("Sailing to Byzantium," l. 24, above), a phrase also implying that the poet-philosopher creates his own "heaven." **45. Mirror-resembling:** producing like a mirror a reflection of the world, but a reflection in which actuality is enlarged and idealized (*a superhuman . . . dream*). **46–52. As . . . nest:** a comparison to the ways in which the speaker has "prepared his peace."

Being of that metal made
Till it was broken by
This sedentary trade.°   60

Now shall I make my soul,
Compelling it to study
In a learned school°
Till the wreck of body,
Slow decay of blood,
Testy delirium
Or dull decrepitude,°
Or what worse evil come —
The death of friends, or death
Of every brilliant eye   70
That made a catch in the breath —
Seem but the clouds of the sky
When the horizon fades;
Or a bird's sleepy cry
Among the deepening shades.

1926   *1925*

TWO SONGS FROM A PLAY

The songs were written for Yeats's play, *The Resurrection* (1927). Both songs assume a cyclical view of history, which is expressed by the symbol of the Magnus Annus (the Great Year) of the ancients, an astronomical cycle of 2000 years or more, at the end of which the heavenly bodies reach the same positions in which they stood when first set in motion. The Magnus Annus is alluded to in Virgil's fourth *Eclogue,* a poem regarded in the Middle Ages as prophesying the birth of Christ, and which Yeats probably had in mind when writing his " Songs." In *A Vision* he gives a free translation of the opening lines of the fourth *Eclogue:* " ' . . . the latest age of the Cumaean song is at hand; the cycles in their vast array begin anew; Virgin Astraea comes, the reign of Saturn comes, and from the heights of Heaven a new generation of mankind descends ' " (*A Vision* [1938], pp. 243–44). On the " Songs," see Introduction, p. 989.

I

I saw a staring virgin stand
Where holy Dionysus° died,
And tear the heart out of his side,
And lay the heart upon her hand
And bear that beating heart away;°

And then did all the Muses sing
Of Magnus Annus at the spring,
As though God's death were but a play.°

Another Troy° must rise and set,
Another lineage feed the crow,   10
Another Argo's painted prow
Drive to a flashier bauble yet.
The Roman Empire stood appalled:
It dropped the reins of peace and war°
When that fierce virgin and her Star
Out of the fabulous darkness° called.

II

In pity for man's darkening thought
He walked that room and issued thence
In Galilean turbulence;°
The Babylonian starlight brought   20
A fabulous, formless darkness in;
Odour of blood when Christ was slain
Made all Platonic tolerance vain
And vain all Doric° discipline.

Everything that man esteems
Endures a moment or a day.
Love's pleasure drives his love away,
The painter's brush consumes his dreams;
The herald's cry, the soldier's tread
Exhaust his glory and his might: 30
Whatever flames upon the night
Man's own resinous° heart° has fed.

58–60. Being . . . trade: By becoming a poet he has lost the heroic quality of "the fisherman" (ll. 2–6).   61–63. Now . . . school: Cf. "singing school" ("Sailing to Byzantium," l. 13, p. 996, above).   67. dull decrepitude: Cf. "Bodily decrepitude is wisdom" ("After Long Silence," l. 7, p. 1003, below). TWO SONGS.   2. Dionysus: the god of wine, with whose cult Greek drama was closely associated.   3–5. tear . . . away: Athena, the virgin goddess, brought the heart of the dead Dionysus to Zeus.

6–8. Muses . . . play: Greek tragedies, depicting the death of heroes or demigods, were performed (*sung*) at spring festivals in honor of Dionysus. There is also an allusion to Easter. "Staring virgin" (l. 1) therefore may refer to both Athena and the Virgin Mary.   9. Another Troy: Rome. Cf. Virgil, *Eclogues,* IV.34–36: "When a second Tiphys will arise, and a second Argo to carry chosen heroes; there will also be a second war, and once again a great Achilles will be sent to Troy." Cf. also "The world's great age begins anew./The golden years return,/ . . . A loftier Argo cleaves the main,/Fraught with a later prize . . ." (Shelley, Chorus from *Hellas,* ll. 1060–61, 1072–73).   13–14. Roman . . . war: the peaceful reign of the emperor Augustus, 27 B.C.–A.D. 14.   16. fabulous darkness: Cf. "Babylonian starlight" (l. 20). Both phrases suggest the strange cults, such as Mithraism, that came to Rome from the East.   19. Galilean turbulence: By being born and by entering the world, Christ submitted to the violence of Calvary and brought not only the light of a new belief but the darkness of superstition and intolerance. The poem expresses the view that Christianity, like other Eastern cults, helped destroy the civilized order of the Greco-Roman world.   24. Doric: Spartan.   32. resinous: an allusion to the pine torches brandished by the women who worshiped Dionysus in nighttime rites. heart: The heart, as the Dionysiac element in man, is the source of both creation and destruction. The metaphors of the fourth stanza are expressive of the paradox that all achievement is self-destructive. They thus symbolize a cyclical movement similar to that of history. For an enlightening comment on this stanza, see "The Tragic Generation," *Autobiography.*

AMONG SCHOOL CHILDREN

The poem moves through the preparatory reflections and images of the earlier stanzas to the affirmations of the closing lines: "Labour is blossoming or dancing. . . ." The ideal of "labour" in which works of "beauty" or "wisdom" are created by harmonious activity of the whole man is central in Yeats's poetry and thought. See Introduction, p. 989.

I

I walk through the long schoolroom questioning;
A kind old nun in a white hood replies;
The children learn to cipher and to sing,
To study reading-books and history,
To cut and sew, be neat in everything
In the best modern way — the children's eyes
In momentary wonder stare upon
A sixty-year-old smiling public man.

2

I dream of a Ledaean° body, bent
Above a sinking fire, a tale that she   10
Told of a harsh reproof, or trivial event
That changed some childish day to tragedy —
Told, and it seemed that our two natures blent
Into a sphere from youthful sympathy,
Or else, to alter Plato's parable,°
Into the yolk and white of the one shell.°

3

And thinking of that fit of grief or rage
I look upon one child or t'other there
And wonder if she stood so at that age —
For even daughters of the swan can share   20
Something of every paddler's heritage —
And had that colour upon cheek or hair,
And thereupon my heart is driven wild:
She stands before me as a living child.

4

Her present image floats into the mind —
Did Quattrocento° finger fashion it
Hollow of cheek as though it drank the wind
And took a mess of shadows for its meat?

And I though never of Ledaean kind
Had pretty plumage once — enough of that,   30
Better to smile on all that smile, and show
There is a comfortable kind of old scarecrow.°

5

What youthful mother, a shape upon her lap
Honey of generation° had betrayed,°
And that must sleep, shriek, struggle to escape
As recollection or the drug decide,
Would think her son, did she but see that shape
With sixty or more winters on its head,
A compensation for the pang of his birth,
Or the uncertainty of his setting forth?   40

6

Plato thought nature but a spume that plays
Upon a ghostly paradigm of things;°
Solider Aristotle° played the taws
Upon the bottom of a king of kings;°
World-famous golden-thighed Pythagoras°
Fingered upon a fiddle-stick or strings
What a star sang and careless Muses heard:
Old clothes upon old sticks to scare a bird.°

AMONG SCHOOL CHILDREN. 9. **Ledaean:** like that of Helen of Troy, daughter of Leda. Cf. "No Second Troy," above. "Swan" and bird images recur in most of the following stanzas. 15. **Plato's parable:** as told in the *Symposium*, 189C-193D. According to the parable, human beings were once spherical in form; though subsequently divided in half, the one half longed to rejoin the other. 16. **shell:** like the "sphere," another metaphor of close relationship between two natures. The image also recalls the egg from which Helen of Troy was said to have been born. 26. **Quattrocento:** refers to fifteenth-century artists in Italy, more particularly to Botticelli (1444?-1510), who painted his madonnas and angels with lean and hollow cheeks.

32. **scarecrow:** Cf. "A tattered coat upon a stick" in "Sailing to Byzantium," l. 10, above. 33-34. **What . . . betrayed:** The syntax of the lines runs: "What youthful mother, with a shape upon her lap (i.e., her child) that honey of generation had betrayed . . ." 34. **Honey of generation:** Yeats took the phrase from *The Cave of the Nymphs* by Porphyry (A.D. 232/3-c. 305). He uses it in at least two different senses. He seems to mean first the "pleasure arising from generation," which the soul experiences in coming into life. The soul of the child is said to be "betrayed" by this pleasure, because in being born, it gives up the life it has enjoyed apart from the body. As it recalls that purer life, it "struggles to escape" (ll. 35, 36). Yeats also means by "honey of generation" a "drug" that destroys the memory of "prenatal freedom." If the drug works, the struggle ceases: the child's soul "struggles to escape / As recollection *or* the drug decide." The notion of the soul's "recollection" and "prenatal freedom" is Platonic. But in the context of the whole stanza, "honey of generation" may equally well refer to sexual desire or to the mother's desire to beget children. 41-42. **Plato . . . things:** Nature for Plato is mere appearance (*a spume*); reality lies in the spiritual (*ghostly*) form or scheme (*the paradigm*). 43. **Solider Aristotle:** In contrast to Plato, he insisted that form was immanent in matter; that is, he attributed a measure of reality to "solid" matter as well as to form. 43-44. **played . . . kings:** Aristotle was tutor to Alexander the Great. "The taws" are an instrument of discipline, used in Scottish and English schools, made of a leather strap divided at the end into narrow strips (*OED*). Aristotle "spanked" his royal pupil. 45. **golden-thighed Pythagoras:** The early Greek philosopher and religious teacher was regarded by his adoring disciples as a god with a "thigh of gold." The Pythagoreans combined various astronomical and musical discoveries in the doctrine of the "harmony of the spheres." Hence Yeats says that Pythagoras expressed musically "what a star sang." 48. **Old clothes . . . bird:** The line refers to the achievements of all three philosophers, to their "blear-eyed wisdom" (l. 60).

7

Both nuns and mothers worship images,°
But those the candles light are not as those   50
That animate a mother's reveries,
But keep a marble or a bronze repose.
And yet they too break hearts — O Presences
That passion, piety or affection knows,
And that all heavenly glory symbolise —
O self-born mockers° of man's enterprise;

8

Labour is blossoming or dancing where
The body is not bruised to pleasure soul,
Nor beauty born out of its own despair,
Nor blear-eyed wisdom out of midnight oil.   60
O chestnut-tree,° great-rooted blossomer,
Are you the leaf, the blossom or the bole?
O body swayed to music, O brightening glance,
How can we know the dancer from the dance?

                                                   1926

IN MEMORY OF EVA GORE-BOOTH AND CON MARKIEWICZ

Eva Gore-Booth was the younger sister of Constance
Markiewicz. (See "Easter 1916," l. 17n., above.) This
elegy expresses a judgment of the effect of political action on personality that recurs fairly often in Yeats's
later poems. It is anticipated in "Easter 1916," lines
57–58: "Too long a sacrifice / Can make a stone of
the heart." As in "Sailing to Byzantium," action seems
clearly inferior to contemplation. In other poems, such
as "Blood and the Moon" and "Vacillation," below,
Yeats very nearly reverses this evaluation. "Eva Gore-
Booth and Con Markiewicz" and the next six poems
were included in *The Winding Stair and Other Poems*
(1933).

I

The light of evening, Lissadell,°
Great windows open to the south,
Two girls in silk kimonos, both
Beautiful, one a gazelle.

49. **images:** both the statues of saints and the mother's idealized
images of her children. They are also "ikons" or symbols of
"heavenly glory," the "Presences" addressed in l. 53, which
resemble Plato's ideal forms of goodness and beauty.   56. **self-
born mockers:** Though the "Presences," the ideal concepts by
which human achievement is measured, are created by man,
they mock his efforts, since he can never realize them in fact.
61. **chestnut-tree:** an image of creation where beauty is inseparable from the life processes that produce it. The tree in blossom
symbolizes the "Unity of Being" that the whole poem celebrates.
Cf. ". . . blood, imagination, intellect, running together . . ."
("Personality and the Intellectual Essences," *Essays*). IN
MEMORY OF EVA GORE-BOOTH.   1. **Lissadell:** the "old Georgian
mansion" (l. 16) of the Gore-Booths, whom Yeats had visited
in 1894–95.

But a raving autumn shears
Blossom from the summer's wreath;
The older is condemned to death,
Pardoned, drags out lonely years
Conspiring among the ignorant.
I know not what the younger dreams —   10
Some vague Utopia — and she seems,
When withered old and skeleton-gaunt,
An image of such politics.
Many a time I think to seek
One or the other out and speak
Of that old Georgian mansion, mix
Pictures of the mind, recall
That table and the talk of youth,
Two girls in silk kimonos, both
Beautiful, one a gazelle.   20

II

Dear shadows, now you know it all,
All the folly of a fight
With a common wrong or right.
The innocent and the beautiful
Have no enemy but time;
Arise and bid me strike a match
And strike another till time catch;°
Should the conflagration climb,
Run till all the sages know.
We the great gazebo° built,   30
They convicted us of guilt;
Bid me strike a match and blow.

October, 1927

BLOOD AND THE MOON

In these two poems (from a sequence of four),
Yeats's "tower" becomes an emblem of the lively and
various Anglo-Irish culture of the eighteenth century,
which he compares with the present, "a time / Half
dead at the top" (I, ll. 11–12). The main significance
of "blood" — crude physical energy — is clear from
the opening lines of the first poem. The opposed symbol of "the moon" stands for wisdom, "the property

24–27. **The innocent . . . catch:** Innocence of spirit is lost in
time, in the activities of this world, but it may be recovered in
the state of mind known to "the sages," which is symbolized
by "fire." Cf. "sages standing in God's holy fire" ("Sailing to
Byzantium," l. 17, p. 996, above). In "Anima Mundi," *Essays*,
pp. 532–34, Yeats writes of "the Condition of Fire," the mood
of pure contemplative joy in which ". . . the images from *Anima
Mundi*, embodied there and drunk with that sweetness, would,
like a country drunkard who has thrown a wisp into his own
thatch, burn up time." He adds that he enters upon this mood
". . . the moment I cease to hate. I think the common condition
of our life is hatred."   30. **gazebo:** a garden house, or a tower
with windows, built especially for commanding a wide view; cf.
"great windows" (l. 2). "The great gazebo" suggests an absurd
and oversized structure and so symbolizes the grandiose political programs that the speaker and the sisters had "built" in
their youth.

of the dead, / A something incompatible with life"
(IV, ll. 49–50). See Introduction, p. 984, for "blood";
see also "The Second Coming" and "Two Songs
from a Play," above. The immediate occasion for the
poem was the assassination of Kevin O'Higgins, a minister of the Irish Free State and a friend of Yeats,
whom Yeats saw as an inheritor of the best Anglo-
Irish traditions.

Yeats also wrote elsewhere of the four chief figures
in eighteenth-century Anglo-Irish culture: "Born in
such community Berkeley with his belief in perception,
that abstract ideas are mere words, Swift with his love
of perfect nature, of the Houyhnhnms, his disbelief in
Newton's system and every sort of machine, Goldsmith and his delight in the particulars of common life
that shocked his contemporaries, Burke with his conviction that all states not grown slowly like a forest
tree are tyrannies, found in England an opposite that
stung their own thought into expression and made it
lucid" (Yeats, *Essays, 1931–1936*, p. 36).

I

Blessed be this place,
More blessed still this tower;
A bloody, arrogant power
Rose out of the race
Uttering, mastering° it,
Rose like these walls from these
Storm-beaten cottages —
In mockery I have set
A powerful emblem up,
And sing it rhyme upon rhyme   10
In mockery of a time
Half dead at the top.

II°

Alexandria's° was a beacon tower, and Babylon's°
An image of the moving heavens, a log-book of the
     sun's journey and the moon's;
And Shelley had his towers, thought's crowned
     powers° he called them once.

I declare this tower is my symbol; I declare
This winding, gyring, spiring treadmill of a stair is
     my ancestral stair;
That Goldsmith and the Dean, Berkeley and Burke
     have travelled there.

BLOOD AND THE MOON. I: 5. **Uttering, mastering:** The Anglo-
Irish gained the upper hand over the native race and in time created the culture through which it became articulate. Anglo-Irish
literature, for example, gave expression to the folk beliefs of
the native Irish. **II:** The unity of this section arises from the
"co-operation" among the allusive metaphors by which the four
men are characterized. Each metaphor (except perhaps that
used of Goldsmith) has links with the "blood-moon" themes.
13. Alexandria: the famous lighthouse on Pharos, an island in
the bay of Alexandria. **Babylon:** The temple towers of Babylon
were said to be "like heaven," because their structure was a
copy of the structure of the heavens. **15. Shelley . . . powers:**
Prometheus Unbound, IV, l. 103, above.

Swift° beating on his breast in sibylline frenzy blind
Because the heart in his blood-sodden breast had
     dragged him down into mankind,°   20
Goldsmith deliberately sipping at the honey-pot of
     his mind,°

And haughtier-headed° Burke that proved the State
     a tree,
That this unconquerable labyrinth of the birds, cen-
     tury after century,
Cast but dead leaves to mathematical equality;°

And God-appointed Berkeley that proved all things
     a dream,
That this pragmatical, preposterous pig of a world,
     its farrow that so solid seem,
Must vanish on the instant if the mind but change
     its theme;°

Saeva Indignatio° and the labourer's hire,°
The strength that gives our blood and state° magna-
     nimity of its own desire;
Everything that is not God consumed with intel-
     lectual fire.   30

THE NINETEENTH CENTURY
AND AFTER

An allusion to the English periodical of the same
title. In a letter, March 2, 1929, Yeats introduced this
poem with the remark, "I have come to find the
world's last great poetical period is over" (A. Norman
Jeffares, *W. B. Yeats, Man and Poet,* p. 254).

19. Swift: See Intro., pp. 984 and 988. "Sibylline frenzy blind"
refers to Swift's madness and to the lack of comprehension which
he met with in England and in Ireland. **20. Because . . . mankind:** For Swift's attitude toward the Yahoos, see *Gulliver's
Travels,* Book IV. **21. Goldsmith . . . mind:** The metaphor
hardly seems to express Goldsmith's "delight in the particulars
of common life." It suggests rather a dilettante, a man whose
thought was a savoring of ideas and sentiments. **22. haughtier-
headed:** without Goldsmith's sympathy for the lower classes, e.g.,
in "The Deserted Village." **22–24. State . . . equality:** For
Burke the state was a complex growth coming out of the past. He
maintained his organic view against supporters of the French
Revolution, who thought of the state as founded on *a priori*
(*mathematical*) principles of equality. Burke's "tree-State" gives
no "living" support to such theories, but does offer a home for
"birds," that is, for men, not for an abstract "political man."
25–27. Berkeley . . . theme: an eloquent expression of idealism,
though not an adequate account of Berkeley's philosophy. Yeats
characteristically reduces reality to dream and gives almost no
place to the observing mind of God, which in Berkeley's view
sustains the continuous existence of things. **28. Saeva In-
dignatio:** "savage indignation," a phrase from the Latin epitaph
that Swift wrote for himself. Cf. Yeats's translation, *Collected
Poems,* p. 241. **labourer's hire:** See l. 22n. **29. blood . . . state:**
"The glories of our blood and state / Are shadows, not substantial
things," from a song by the dramatist James Shirley (1596–1666),
who lived for a time in Ireland.

Though the great song° return no more
There's keen delight in what we have:
The rattle of pebbles on the shore
Under the receding wave.°

1929

COOLE PARK, 1929

Compare this poem with "The Wild Swans at
Coole," above, and with "Coole Park and Ballylee,
1931," *Collected Poems,* pp. 239–40. Also see Introduction, p. 986.

I meditate upon a swallow's flight,
Upon an aged woman° and her house,
A sycamore and lime-tree lost in night
Although that western cloud is luminous,
Great works constructed there in nature's spite
For scholars and for poets after us,
Thoughts long knitted into a single thought,
A dance-like glory that those walls begot.

There Hyde° before he had beaten into prose
That noble blade the Muses buckled on,   10
There one° that ruffled in a manly pose
For all his timid heart, there that slow man,
That meditative man, John Synge,° and those
Impetuous men, Shawe-Taylor° and Hugh Lane,
Found pride established in humility,
A scene well set and excellent company.

They came like swallows and like swallows went,
And yet a woman's powerful character
Could keep a swallow to its first intent;
And half a dozen in formation there,   20
That seemed to whirl upon a compass-point,
Found certainty upon the dreaming air,°

The intellectual sweetness of those lines
That cut through time or cross it withershins.°

Here, traveller, scholar, poet, take your stand
When all those rooms and passages are gone,
When nettles wave upon a shapeless mound
And saplings root among the broken stone,
And dedicate — eyes bent upon the ground,
Back turned upon the brightness of the sun   30
And all the sensuality of the shade° —
A moment's memory to that laurelled head.

VACILLATION

"Vacillation," VII, VIII, are the closing sections of
a poem that expresses one of Yeats's most characteristic states of mind, as he observed in reviewing his
own career: "The swordsman throughout repudiates
the saint, but not without vacillation. Is that perhaps
the sole theme — Usheen and Patrick 'So get you gone
Von Hügel though with blessings on your head'"?
(from a letter, June 30, 1932, quoted in Richard Ellman, *Yeats, The Man and the Masks,* p. 272).
"Usheen," or Oisin, *the swordsman,* is the legendary
poet-hero of Yeats's *The Wanderings of Oisin* (1889).
St. Patrick once argued at length with Oisin in an unsuccessful attempt to convert him to Christianity. (For
another expression of the conflict between Christianity
and the poet's art, see "The Tragic Generation," *Autobiography.*)

VII

The Soul. Seek out reality, leave things that seem.
The Heart. What, be a singer born and lack a
    theme?
The Soul. Isaiah's coal,° what more can man desire?
The Heart. Struck dumb in the simplicity of fire!°
The Soul. Look on that fire, salvation walks within.
The Heart. What theme had Homer but original
    sin?

THE NINETEENTH CENTURY. **1. great song:** the poetry of the
Romantics. Cf. "The world's great age begins anew" (Shelley,
Chorus from *Hellas,* l. 1060). Cf. "Two Songs from a Play,"
above. **3–4. rattle . . . wave:** Cf. ". . . you hear the grating roar/
Of pebbles which the waves draw back . . ." (Matthew Arnold,
"Dover Beach," ll. 9–10). COOLE PARK: **2. aged woman:** Lady
Gregory. **9. Hyde:** Douglas Hyde, folklorist and Gaelic poet,
played an important part in the revival of Irish literature. Yeats
writes of him as "the great poet who died in his youth," who later
"took for his model the newspaper upon his breakfast table"
(*Autobiography,* p. 188). **11. one:** Yeats. **13. Synge:** dramatist,
author of *The Playboy of the Western World.* See "The Tragic
Generation," *Autobiography.* **14. Shawe-Taylor:** John Shawe-
Taylor, a nephew of Lady Gregory, who had ". . . that instant
decision of the hawk, between the movement of whose wings and
the perception of whose eye no time passes capable of division"
(Yeats, *Essays,* p. 426). On his initiative a conference was held that
led to the Land Act of 1903, under the terms of which tenants
were enabled to purchase their lands from the owners. On Lane,
also a nephew of Lady Gregory, see "To a Friend Whose Work
Has Come to Nothing," above. **22. dreaming air:** perhaps the
trancelike peace favorable to imaginative creation.

23–24. lines . . . withershins: lines of activity in which men seem
to escape from time; they move into a state outside time (*cut
through it*), or they move counter to its flow and so arrest its
course (*cross it withershins*). On this opposition between time
and "the intellectual sweetness" of imaginative activity, see
"Eva Gore-Booth and Con Markiewicz," ll. 24–27, above.
30–31. Back . . . shade: Cf. "nature's spite" (l. 5); note the
imagery of light and shade in both the first and the last stanzas.
VACILLATION. **VII: 3. Isaiah's coal:** the live coal with which the
seraph touched Isaiah's "unclean lips" and "purged" him from
"sin" (Isa. 7:5–7). **4. Struck . . . fire!:** Unlike Isaiah, whom
the fire made more eloquent, the poet feels unable to sing of
"reality." As elsewhere in Yeats, "the condition of fire" symbolizes the state of pure contemplation, untouched by the
"complexities of mire or blood," in which reality is revealed to
poets and sages. See "Sailing to Byzantium," above, and
"Byzantium," *Collected Poems,* pp. 243–44.

VIII

Must we part, Von Hügel,° though much alike, for
we
Accept the miracles of the saints and honour sanc-
tity?
The body of Saint Teresa lies undecayed in tomb,
Bathed in miraculous oil, sweet odours from it
come,   10
Healing from its lettered slab. Those self-same
hands perchance
Eternalised the body of a modern saint that once
Had scooped out Pharaoh's mummy.° I — though
heart might find relief
Did I become a Christian man and choose for my
belief
What seems most welcome in the tomb — play a
predestined part.
Homer is my example and his unchristened heart.
The lion and the honeycomb,° what has Scripture
said?
So get you gone, Von Hügel, though with blessings
on your head.

1932

WORDS FOR MUSIC PERHAPS

XVII. AFTER LONG SILENCE

" After Long Silence " and the following poem are
from the cycle, " Words for Music Perhaps " (1929–
32), which includes the " Crazy Jane " poems. See Introduction, p. 987.

Speech after long silence; it is right,
All other lovers being estranged or dead,
Unfriendly lamplight hid under its shade,
The curtains drawn upon unfriendly night,
That we descant and yet again descant
Upon the supreme theme of Art and Song:
Bodily decrepitude is wisdom; young
We loved each other and were ignorant.°

1929

VIII: 7. **Von Hügel:** Roman Catholic philosopher, author of
*The Mystical Element of Religion as Studied in St. Catherine of
Genoa and her Friends* (1908). Here, Von Hügel has the role of
"a Christian man," corresponding to "The Soul" of "Vacillation,"
VII.   9–13. **Saint . . . mummy:** a reference to the Spanish Car-
melite nun and mystic writer, 1515–82. "Why should not the old
embalmers come back—as ghosts and bestow upon the saint all
the care once bestowed upon Rameses: why should I doubt the
tale that when St. Theresa's tomb was opened in the middle of
the nineteenth century the still undecayed lady dripped with fragrant oil?" (from a letter, January 3, 1932, quoted in A. Norman
Jeffares, *W. B. Yeats, Man and Poet*, p. 272).   17. **lion . . . honeycomb:** refers to Samson's discovery of honey "in the carcase of
the lion" and to his riddle: "Out of the eater came forth meat, and
out of the strong came forth sweetness" (Judg. 14:8–14).   AFTER
LONG SILENCE.   7–8. **Bodily . . . ignorant:** Cf. "The Folly of
Being Comforted," "Men Improve with the Years," and "Sailing
to Byzantium," above.

XVIII. MAD AS THE MIST AND SNOW

Bolt and bar the shutter,
For the foul winds blow:
Our minds are at their best this night,
And I seem to know
That everything outside us is
Mad as the mist and snow.

Horace there by Homer stands,
Plato stands below,
And here is Tully's° open page.
How many years ago   10
Were you and I unlettered lads
Mad as the mist and snow?

You ask what makes me sigh, old friend,
What makes me shudder so?
I shudder and I sigh to think
That even Cicero
And many-minded° Homer were
Mad as the mist and snow.

1929

AN ACRE OF GRASS

" An Acre of Grass " and the next two poems are
from *Last Poems* (1936–39). See Introduction, p. 990.

Picture and book remain,
An acre of green grass
For air and exercise,
Now strength of body goes;
Midnight, an old house
Where nothing stirs but a mouse.

My temptation is quiet.°
Here at life's end
Neither loose° imagination,
Nor the mill of the mind   10
Consuming its rag and bone,°
Can make the truth known.

MAD AS THE MIST AND SNOW.   9. **Tully:** Marcus Tullius Cicero,
Roman orator and philosophic writer.   17. **many-minded:** or
myriad-minded, an ancient epithet for Homer.   AN ACRE OF
GRASS.   7. **My . . . quiet:** Consider the very different meanings of this statement in relation to the preceding and the
following lines. The key to the poem lies in the contrast between
"quiet" and "frenzy" (l. 13).   9. **loose:** i.e., of an old man;
perhaps with a further reference to the uncontrolled fancies of
Yeats's earlier poems.   11. **rag and bone:** suggests the problems
that the aging mind goes over again and again, working like a
mill. The phrase also alludes to the refuse of past experiences,
all that is left the old man when the transforming power of imagination is gone. Cf. "the foul rag-and-bone shop of the heart"
("The Circus Animals' Desertion," *Collected Poems*, pp. 335–36).

Grant me an old man's frenzy,°
Myself must I remake
Till I am Timon° and Lear
Or that William Blake°
Who beat upon the wall
Till Truth obeyed his call;

A mind Michael Angelo knew
That can pierce the clouds,   20
Or inspired by frenzy
Shake the dead in their shrouds;°
Forgotten else by mankind,
An old man's eagle mind.

THE WILD OLD WICKED MAN

" The Wild Old Wicked Man " is one of many poems from Yeats's last period that are written in a style derived from Irish folk songs and ballads. He shows here his skill in using the bald idiom and plain rhythms of popular poetry to express states of mind that are serious and far from simple. Note, for example, that the poet-speaker is both a " young man " and a " wild old man," that he is a lover who has words and knowledge " that can pierce the heart." See Introduction, p. 990.

"Because I am mad about women
I am mad about the hills,"
Said that wild old wicked man
Who travels where God wills.
"Not to die on the straw at home,
Those hands to close these eyes,
That is all I ask, my dear,
From the old man in the skies.
            Daybreak and a candle-end.°

"Kind are all your words, my dear,   10
Do not the rest withhold.
Who can know the year, my dear,
When an old man's blood grows cold?
I have what no young man can have
Because he loves too much.

Words I have that can pierce the heart,
But what can he do but touch? "
            Daybreak and a candle-end.

Then said she to that wild old man,
His stout stick under his hand,   20
" Love to give or to withhold
Is not at my command.
I gave it all to an older man:
That old man in the skies.
Hands that are busy with His beads
Can never close those eyes."
            Daybreak and a candle-end.

" Go your ways, O go your ways,
I choose another mark,
Girls down on the seashore   30
Who understand the dark;
Bawdy talk for the fishermen;
A dance for the fisher-lads;
When dark hangs upon the water
They turn down their beds.
            Daybreak and a candle-end.

" A young man in the dark am I,
But a wild old man in the light,
That can make a cat laugh, or
Can touch by mother wit   40
Things hid in their marrow-bones
From time long passed away,
Hid from all those warty° lads
That by their bodies lay.
            Daybreak and a candle-end.

" All men live in suffering,
I know° as few can know,
Whether they take the upper road
Or stay content on the low,
Rower bent in his row-boat   50
Or weaver bent at his loom,
Horseman erect upon horseback
Or child hid in the womb.
            Daybreak and a candle-end.

" That some stream of lightning
From the old man in the skies
Can burn out that suffering
No right-taught man denies.
But a coarse old man am I,
I choose the second-best,   60
I forget it all awhile
Upon a woman's breast."°
            Daybreak and a candle-end.

13. frenzy: the passionate and energetic insight that is expressed and defined through the four symbolic "old men." 15. Timon: protagonist of Shakespeare's *Timon of Athens*, who in his mad hatred exulted in perceiving the unnaturalness of "the whole race of mankind" (*Timon of Athens*, IV.i.40). Cf. Lear's vision of "unaccommodated man" (*King Lear*, III.iv.105-14). 16. Blake: William Blake, the poet, who had mystical visions of divine "Truth." For Yeats, he was one of those near-madmen who ". . . discover symbolism to express the overflowing and bursting of the mind" (*A Vision*). 19-22. Michael Angelo . . . shrouds: Michelangelo's power of depicting the supernatural, especially in his Sistine Chapel fresco of *The Last Judgment* with its nightmarish scenes of the dead rising from their graves. THE WILD OLD WICKED MAN. 9. *Daybreak . . . candle-end:* As often in Yeats, the refrain has symbolic meaning when related to the rest of the poem.

43. warty: in Irish popular belief, a sign of sexual potency. 47. I know: Cf. "An old man's eagle mind" ("An Acre of Grass," l. 24, p. 1003, above). 55-62. For the opposition between Christian and pagan attitudes, compare "Vacillation," VIII, above.

A BRONZE HEAD

" A Bronze Head " is mainly focused on the opposition suggested by " human, superhuman " (l. 2), which is echoed later in " who can tell / Which of her forms has shown her substance right? " (ll. 10–11). The references to the statue of Maud Gonne in the Dublin Municipal Gallery and to the actual woman are of the most general sort.

Here at right of the entrance° this bronze head,
Human, superhuman, a bird's round eye,
Everything else° withered and mummy-dead.
What great tomb-haunter sweeps the distant sky
(Something may linger there though all else die;)
And finds there° nothing to make its terror less°
Hysterica passio° of its own emptiness?

No dark tomb-haunter once; her form all full
As though with magnanimity of light,
Yet a most gentle woman;° who can tell   10
Which of her forms has shown her substance°
    right?
Or maybe substance can be composite,
Profound McTaggart thought so, and in a breath
A mouthful held the extreme of life and death.°

But even at the starting-post, all sleek and new,
I saw the wildness in her and I thought
A vision of terror that it must live through
Had shattered her soul. Propinquity had brought
Imagination to that pitch where it casts out
All that is not itself: I had grown wild°   20
And wandered murmuring everywhere, " My child,
    my child! "

Or else I thought her supernatural;°
As though a sterner eye looked through her
    eye
On this foul world in its decline and fall;°
On gangling stocks grown great,° great stocks run
    dry,
Ancestral pearls all pitched into a sty,
Heroic reverie° mocked by clown and knave,
And wondered what was left for massacre° to
    save.

A BRONZE HEAD.   1. the entrance: of a tomb, or of a museum. 3. else: the rest of the body.   6. there: "the distant sky," the region beyond life known to the "tomb-haunter."   to ... less: "Less" may go with either "terror" or "Hysterica passio." If taken with "terror"—which is the more likely reading—the phrase means "to diminish its terror"; and then "Hysterica passio" stands in apposition with the whole idea expressed in l. 6. 7. Hysterica passio: hysteria, madness; cf. King Lear, II.ii. 240–41. "We all have something within ourselves to batter down and get our power from this fighting. I have never 'produced' a play in verse without showing the actors that the passion of the verse comes from the fact that the speakers are holding down violence or madness—'down Hysterica passio' (from a letter to Dorothy Wellesley, August 5 [1936], Letters on Poetry from W. B. Yeats to Dorothy Wellesley, p. 94).   10. a ... woman: "Her voice was ever soft,/Gentle, and low, an excellent thing in woman" (King Lear, V.iii.273–74).   11. substance: essence, that which determines the essential nature of a thing.   13–14. McTaggart ... death: John McT. E. McTaggart (1866–1925), philosopher, an atheist and convinced believer in immortality, who argued that "substance" is divisible, i.e., "composite." Yeats seems to say that the essential nature of man includes both extremes, "life" and "death," the "human" and the "superhuman."   18–20. Propinquity ... wild: Through association with his beloved he had become obsessed by the view of her that his imagination had created; he could see only a reflection of the "terror" that he himself attributed to her.   22. supernatural: Cf. "superhuman," l. 2, and note how the meaning of the word is qualified by the lines that follow. Cf. also ". . . beauty like a tightened bow, a kind/That is not natural in an age like this" ("No Second Troy," ll. 8–9, p. 992, above).   24. On ... fall: Cf. "Cleanse the foul body of th' infected world" (As You Like It, II.vii.60). Note also allusion to Edward Gibbon's History of the Decline and Fall of the Roman Empire.   25. gangling ... great: rise of lower and middle classes to power.   27. Heroic reverie: the passionate, trancelike exaltation of a tragic hero. The phrase describes both a type of character scorned by modern society and an ideal type of drama that the Irish audience had failed to appreciate. Cf. "The Fisherman," ll. 9–26, above, and "On Those That Hated The Playboy of the Western World, 1907," Collected Poems, p. 109.   28. massacre: the violence of "blood," which in Yeats's view is necessary for the birth of each new phase of civilization. Cf. "The Second Coming" and "Two Songs from a Play," p. 996 and p. 998, above.

T. S. Eliot

1888–1965

On June 21, 1917, *The Times Literary Supplement* of London gave a short review of a volume of poems entitled *Prufrock and Other Observations,* by T. S. Eliot. The author was an American, whose ancestors had come to Massachusetts from England in 1670. He was born in St. Louis in 1888 and had recently settled in London, where he worked as a clerk in the foreign department of Lloyds Bank in the City. The reviewer was far from enthusiastic.

Thirty-one years later, in 1948, Eliot was awarded the Nobel prize for literature, and in the same year, in honor of his sixtieth birthday, a Symposium of tributes to him was published in London. This contained contributions from forty-seven writers from more than a dozen different countries, and hailed the poet-critic-dramatist as perhaps the most powerful literary influence in the civilized world of today. It gave several glimpses of him in his early years; first as a quiet student at Harvard, where, however, he insisted on disciplining his natural shyness by going out to parties, and resisting his natural sedentary habits by taking boxing lessons and learning "how to swarm with passion up a rope." Then, on his removal to London in 1915 (after periods in Paris, Marburg, and Oxford) we see him recognized by a small circle of intellectuals as having genius, winning a reputation as a brilliant talker, though "with a studied primness of manner and speech," marked as somewhat of a dandy in his dress, and a lover of practical jokes.

In the London of 1915 the dictator of the *avant-garde* in literary taste was Ezra Pound.

Pound had come to England from the Midwest of America a few years before, full of revolutionary ideas about the reform of the language and content of poetry. Pound loved to "discover" young talent and to bring it to birth in the world of letters under his patronage. Though critics disagree violently about the value of Pound's own verse, he had a real enthusiasm for good writing, and he recognized Eliot's quality at once. He bullied Harriet Monroe into publishing "Prufrock" in her new magazine, *Poetry,* in June, 1915, and he introduced Eliot to Harriet Weaver, whose Egoist Press put out the first volume of his poems.

Once the early work had found publishers, Eliot needed no impresario. Slowly but steadily his reputation increased. In 1922 he founded the *Criterion,* the leading English literary review for many years, and a few years later he joined the publishing house of Faber and Gwyer (now Faber and Faber).

But the history of Eliot's mind and personality during the years since the 1920's is in his poems and essays rather than in the outward events of his life, and it is not too much to say that through them he has changed the current of taste and accomplishment of his age. If poets and critics have now ceased to value the Romantics and the Victorians as they were valued at the beginning of the century, and have exalted in their place the Elizabethans and Metaphysicals, Dante, and the French poets of the nineteenth century, Eliot more than anyone else is responsible.

He has pointed out that, when he began to

write in 1908, there were no poets in the recent past who were of any help to him as masters who could stir his own consciousness and teach him the use of his own voice. He had to go to writers of another age and to those in another language — to the English Jacobeans and to Baudelaire and the later French Symbolists. There he found models who seemed to him to be using the techniques of verse which could best communicate his own new vision.

First of all, they used the language of speech, and as Eliot says in "The Music of Poetry": "while poetry attempts to convey something beyond what can be conveyed in prose rhythms, it remains, all the same, one person talking to another. . . . Every revolution in poetry is apt to be, and sometimes announces itself as, a return to common speech. That is the revolution which Wordsworth announced in his prefaces, and he was right." Eliot as a young man, like Wordsworth, wanted to refresh and renew the poetic language by replacing the worn-out tradition of "poetic diction" with the natural rhythms of the spoken word of his own day. Along with this, he was fighting against what he calls in the essay on the Metaphysical poets "the dissociation of sensibility" (see p. 1050) and battling to create in its place a poetry founded on the use of what he calls in the "Hamlet" essay "the objective correlative" (see p. 1046). These two phrases of his coinage, he says later, "have had a success in the world astonishing to their author," and indeed they are rather ugly and clumsy critical terms. But they contain the core of his early theories of poetry, though they are both illustrations of positions held by the young poet where "his gratitude to those dead poets from whom he has learned, as well as his indifference to those whose aims have been alien to his own," have somewhat distorted his view of the poetry of the past.

What does he mean by "the dissociation of sensibility"? His argument in "The Metaphysical Poets" is that something "happened to the mind of England" between the time of Donne and the nineteenth century, whereby "thought" and "feeling," which before were united in poetic expression, became divorced. He says: "Tennyson and Browning are poets, and they think, but they do not feel their thought as immediately as the odor of a rose." Eliot's vocab-

ulary in this essay is a little confusing, but it is evident here that by "feeling" he means not "emotion" but "sensation." He sees the poets who have written since the seventeenth century as relying on explanation rather than on revelation in their use of language. Instead of evoking the idea directly through the sense image, he sees them as elaborating the intellectual and the sensuous as separate entities, and relating them by a process of wasteful diffusion. Eliot blames Milton and Dryden for this, and hits hard at the Victorians (though in later writings he modified several of these judgments). But the essay on the Metaphysicals is very valuable as an illumination of his own early practice, and gives the clue to the chief difficulty of his early poetry.

This difficulty rests mainly on the absence of logical connectives between the various sense images, and the reason for this is Eliot's early dislike of "thought" in poetry if it appears in the form of what he calls variously in the essay "meditation," "reflection," or "rumination." In contradiction to these terms he praises "a direct sensuous apprehension of thought, or a recreation of thought into feeling" and "the essential quality of transmuting ideas into sensations." In fact, Eliot is urging the abolition of abstract statements in poetry, and of all analysis and interpretation. This is not really the method of the Metaphysicals, who always express a strict logical content *as well as* the pattern of images. But Eliot's method is to make the association of sensuous imagery alone imply the intellectual content of the poem, without the intrusion of logical interpretation at all. He owns himself that though the method makes for great concentration and intensity, it does so sometimes at the cost of clarity, and there are few readers who would disagree with him. He declares in this essay that modern poetry *must* be difficult because of the complexity of modern civilization, but perhaps it is more this reliance on "feeling" or "sensation" to do all the work of the intellect, than the complexity of our civilization, that is at the root of Eliot's obscurity.

Just as in the essay on Metaphysical poets he argued that the only way of expressing "thought" should be by creating it into "feeling," so in the "Hamlet" essay he argues in the same way about "emotion." It too must be created in poetry through "sensory experience."

The only way of expressing emotion in the form of art is by finding an "objective correlative"; in other words, a set of objects, a situation, a chain of events which shall be the formula of that *particular* emotion; such that when the external facts, which must terminate in sensory experience, are given, the emotion is immediately evoked.

But this too seems an overstatement. The "Hamlet" essay ignores other elements in Shakespeare's use of language which create emotion besides "the skillful accumulations of imagined sensory impressions," and it is much more a description of Eliot's own early poetry than of Shakespeare's tragedies. We think at once of the series of vignettes embodying the plight of Prufrock; the accumulations of sensory impressions of which the Sweeney poems are constructed; of the sensations of drought created in the images of *The Waste Land* and of those of desiccated living in "The Hollow Men."

Eliot never wavered from his insistence that poetry is art, not "self-expression"; "not our feelings, but the pattern we make of our feelings is the center of value." But his art has always communicated "intense and personal experience." His poetry, indeed, in spite of all its obliquities, and the disguises and ventriloquisms that he adopts to "distance" his experience, forms a spiritual autobiography, which speaks to all sensitive readers of their own emotions and conflicts. It is true that the poet appears always as a strangely lonely figure. Other persons must have been involved in the intense and personal experiences, but no subjective human relationships emerge in the poems. We find nothing, for instance, of all that Yeats reveals in his poems of love and friendship. Yet in spite of Eliot's intense reserve, behind the mask of impersonality the drama is deeply human and individual, and its conflicts are those which are common in some degree to all. This is what made the younger generation of readers and writers respond so warmly to the early poetry, though their elders dismissed it as ugly and unintelligible.

What was this vision of the modern world which was projected with such vividness? The early poems have two backgrounds. The first is that of the poet's own social environment, the world of Prufrock, which has much in common with that of the novels of Henry James. The second is the background of the ugliness and squalor of the modern metropolis, the world of Sweeney and of many scenes in *The Waste Land*. Eliot has told us that the earliest literary inspiration behind this world, with its mixture of sordid realism and fantastic nightmare, came from the poetry of Baudelaire working on Eliot's own adolescent experiences in the city of St. Louis.

The figures that move about in these worlds, whether they are Brahmin or plebeian, suffer a common impoverishment of emotional vitality. They either live by the "formulated phrases" of an empty social convention and a decadent culture, or their lives are purely sordid and sensual. Some are vaguely conscious of isolation and rootlessness and insecurity, and the poet himself shares this spiritual coloring. He is a psychologically displaced person; he feels himself imprisoned in a disintegrating, alien, and often ugly society, which fills him with a sense of frustration and disgust. But it is a symptom of his predicament that, though he senses acutely the need to discover some escape from the prison of actuality, he shrinks from the necessary action toward achieving freedom and self-fulfillment. All he can do is to escape into his poetry, where he can objectify and dramatize the situation; where he can create in his own strange fragmentary images the moods of ironic and cynical repulsion and of unromantic disillusionment that mirror his condition.

In "The Love Song of J. Alfred Prufrock," written when Eliot was only twenty-three, all the characteristics of his early vision are already in being. The hero is an aging failure, caught in an interminable self-debate between the desire to live fully and the compulsion to conform to his social milieu. Eliot dramatizes brilliantly the double conflict between character and environment and between the warring elements within a single soul. He creates the sense of the emptiness, the barrenness, and the consequent frustration of a directionless and counterfeit culture, and the need for a vital purpose and order and wholeness of living. But "Prufrock" is a dramatic tragicomedy; the poet does not speak in his own person. Nor is there any definite and unified pattern of values set over against the aridity of the hero's environment and the disorder of his own spirit, though elements suggesting vitality and order are scattered in various images drawn from nature, history, and art. But in " Sweeney among the Nightingales," which appeared in Eliot's second volume of poems, in 1920, we find the embryo of the matter and the method which he was to enlarge and elaborate and deepen in *The Waste Land.* Here "the immense panorama of futility and anarchy which is contemporary history" is juxtaposed with the timeless values of myth and religion. "Sweeney" is an illustration of how intensity and concentration are gained at the expense of clarity, but its pictures and rhythms are most powerful and compelling. The realism is of the other end of the social scale from that of "Prufrock"; it is sordid and brutal, but the characters are equally rootless, sterile, and aimless. Eliot presents them under images of animals, of non-entity, of disorder. They have no vital relationship with the natural world, or with the spiritual world, or with each other. Opposed to them, by oblique suggestion, are the orders of Greek myth and tragedy and of the Christian story — all timeless patterns within which the temporal and physical worlds are given *meaning* in terms of moral law and spiritual significance.

But again these rival forces of the secular and the spiritual are not engaged in the poet's *own* consciousness any more than they are in "Prufrock." In *The Waste Land* (1922), however, the personal element is strongly felt, though it is overlaid with disguises. Indeed, one of the great difficulties of the poem is the sense of the struggle behind it to transmute personal and private experience into the universal and impersonal. Eliot's method is to evoke the emotional barrenness and the spiritual failure of communal and personal living in the civilization of the present, and to set it against reminders of the myths and faiths of the past, and the literature inspired by those faiths. This involves a labyrinth of allusions, and it is perhaps questionable whether a poem which has needed so much reference to outside sources unknown to the average reader, and such elaborate annotation and interpretation, " succeeds " poetically. The reader must at first spend more time sleuthing than enjoying the poetry. But as Eliot says: " We all have to choose whatever subject matter allows us the most powerful and most secret release; and that is a personal affair." The poem, moreover, in spite of its difficulty has established itself as the literary symbol of the social and psychic disintegration of our age. The agonies of the shadowy protagonist arise from his horror and disgust at the life he sees around him, and from his incapacity to surrender himself to the active and self-creative elements in his being. He is torn between the desire for rebirth and the desire to drift. And in " The Hollow Men " this latter mood has triumphed. In a condition of spiritual exhaustion the poet feels himself identified with those who give up the struggle and dwindle into colorless apathy and stagnation.

" The Hollow Men " was published in 1925, and during the next few years a profound change occurred in the nature of both Eliot's poetry and prose. He describes the direction of the change in the preface he wrote in 1928 for the second edition of *The Sacred Wood,* the collection of his early essays first published in 1920. He defined the central problem of these essays as that of " the integrity of poetry " — of poetry considered primarily as poetic art and not as anything else. He does not disown anything he had written in the book, but he has passed on, he says, to another problem, " that of the relation of poetry to the spiritual and social life of its time and of other times." The early essays deal mainly with revolutionary critical attitudes towards poetry and with the revaluation of poets neglected by the Victorians. They pay homage to the Jacobean dramatists and to the poets of the seventeenth century; they attack Milton, and they dismiss the popular nineteenth-century Romantics. Whether avowed or not, Eliot's target is often Matthew Arnold and the whole concept of poetry as " criticism of life." While these essays are often brilliant in themselves, and while they had an enormous influence on contemporary literary taste, they were, as we have seen, mainly useful to Eliot himself as clarifying his own ideas about the poetry *he* wished to write. It is significant that he wrote very little purely literary criticism after his own formative period.

Eliot had always been interested in the possibility of reviving poetic drama, and here too he proved himself a pioneer. He wrote an essay on " The Possibility of Poetic Drama " as early as 1920, though there he speaks of it as a " mirage." In 1933, however, we find him saying: " The ideal medium for poetry, to my mind, and the most direct means of social ' usefulness ' for poetry is the theater." Two years later *Murder in the Cathedral* was performed in Canterbury Cathedral. It was followed by *The Family Reunion* in 1939, and *The Cocktail Party* in 1949. Eliot's dramatic pattern is always the same. A single character, or a very small group, makes the choice of a way of life dedicated to ultimate values outside those of the temporal world. This way of life may lead to a martyr's death, but it is chosen " so that the Faith may be preserved alive."

All the poetry after " The Hollow Men " is written from within the Christian faith, but Eliot's religious poems have an atmosphere which is all their own. He has said that there is very little religious verse that reaches the highest level of poetry, and that he suspects that that is because of a " pious insincerity " in most of it. " People who write devotional verse are usually writing as they *want* to feel, rather than as they do feel." Eliot's religious poetry is never like this; indeed it is almost as much a poetry of doubt as of faith. " The Hollow Men " presents the despairing state in which the will, knowing that a choice *must* be made if any new spiritual vitality is to be kindled, is yet incapable of stirring itself to action. In the group of poems written during the next few years, the choice *has* been made, and all the later poetry creates a sense of gradual spiritual clarification, of process and progress in a new realm of being. But within that large framework there are many differing moods. This is what creates the deeply moving quality of " Ash Wednesday " (1930), and the so-called " Ariel " poems, which include the " Journey of the Magi " and " A Song for Simeon." These poems are completely different from any of the early work. The savage or satiric or despairing picture of the contemporary scene disappears altogether: the poems are all visionary dramatizations of the inner world. They alternate in moods of assurance and insecurity, of the pain of spiritual discipline and the gladness of submission, of the heaviness of doubt and conflict and the joyous sense of renewal. This sense of renewal pervades " Marina," the " Ariel " poem chosen for this volume. It is unlike any poem of its length by Eliot in that it is completely happy: it is as full of quiet ecstasy as " The Hollow Men " is full of anguished apathy. It tells of a moment of transcendence, when all that belongs to the death-haunted atmosphere of

doubt and failure fades into a new radiance of hope and the sense of grace, centered in the intangible, dreamlike and only half-comprehended figure of Marina. The world of the senses still exists in the strange beauty of the seascape and the figure, but it is absorbed into a new lighting where the worlds of nature and spirit melt into one another. And this union enfolds both the individual and the universe: it is " more distant than the stars and nearer than the eye."

" Marina " is an intensely personal poem under its thin dramatic disguise, and it brings the feeling of the presence of a new spiritual center in the life of the poet. In contrast, what is emphasized in the " Coriolan " poems, of which " Triumphal March " is the first, is the complete absence of any such center in the public living of the modern world. The poem shows a social and religious structure focused entirely on a figure representing material force and secular power, while " hidden " from all the organized mechanism of the " turning world " is the " still point " which it ignores. What the still point is, is not clarified in the poem, except insofar as it is something hidden within the worlds of physical nature and of time, which is yet distinct from both.

This central symbol of " the still point in the turning world," and the concept behind it, controls the whole pattern of Eliot's *Four Quartets*. The poems were written over the years 1935–42 and published in a single volume in 1943. They are four long poems of meditation which yet form a single unity, and it is clear from the over-all title that they have certain analogies with musical form. In content they gather up all Eliot's profoundest beliefs and insights about the life of the race and of the individual; about time, about history, about the use of the past in the present, and about the moments of illumination in which the human spirit transcends time and space and has apprehensions of a higher reality that is changeless.

For most of us such moments are "unattended," unexpected and not noted with attention; they come when we are distracted, drawn away from the purely temporal. They are flashes of ecstasy and illumination, like the shaft of sunlight and the winter lightning; they occur in memory, like the scent of the wild thyme; they are moments when the regular flow of life is interrupted and intensified, as with a waterfall in a stream. They come in our full identification with works of art. At any of these creative emotional moments, although we are still in time — for human life cannot exist anywhere except in "the turning world" — we are at the same moment in another "sphere of existence," that of spirit. Beyond such intense glimpses, the rest of the living of life must be in the *conscious* will to reach beyond the temporal, and to reconcile the pattern of daily living with the quality of the flashes of radiance by "prayer, observance, discipline, thought and action." And the ultimate symbol of the union of sense and spirit, of time and the timeless, is Incarnation. Eliot does not say *the* Incarnation, though as a Christian that is to him the central symbol of the whole concept. But all the varied moments when we reach the still point are incarnations; that is, they are revelations in a sense medium of a spiritual reality that transcends it.

In *Four Quartets* the range is far wider than in *The Waste Land;* it reaches from the prosaic level of colloquial discussion to the richest rhetoric and the most concentrated intensity. There is a great change too in the tones of the voice we hear speaking to us. The impersonal disguises have gone. The poet is openly "one person talking to another." The form of address is quite direct, "I," "we," "you"; and the speaker places himself among the rest of the suffering human race on its journey through time, and tells of the wisdom he has himself learnt, and of the help that it may be to others. This is Eliot's final view of the function of

poetry. The poet is first and foremost artist; his medium is language. "He has the privilege of contributing to the development and maintaining the quality, the capacity of the language to express wide range and subtle gradations of feeling and emotion." He must absorb the tradition of the past and explore all possibilities of extending its scope. But this is always intertwined with, and inseparable from, the human truth which is the material he must transmute into words. Eliot says that, when the poet is concentrating on the practical problems of his craft, he is no more concerned with the social consequences than is the scientist in his laboratory. But he adds: "without the context of the use to society neither the writer nor the scientist could have the conviction which sustains him." The task of the poet is always a dual one, that of the creation of language and of the revelation of life, and it is summed up by the "familiar compound ghost" of all the great poets, who appears in the last Quartet, "Little Gidding," and who tells his fellow poet:

our concern was speech, and speech impelled us
To purify the dialect of the tribe
And urge the mind to aftersight and foresight.

Whether Eliot will be numbered among the great poets only time can prove, but there is no question that he was the poet who performed both these two functions with most distinction in the first half of the twentieth century, and that his work, in both prose and verse, is central to any understanding of both the literature and the human problems of this era.

ALVIN B. KERNAN

A Note on MURDER IN THE CATHEDRAL

Murder in the Cathedral was written for the Canterbury festival in the summer of 1935 and produced in the Chapter House of the Cathedral, a few yards from the spot where Thomas Becket, Archbishop of Canterbury, was murdered seven and one-half centuries earlier. Since the audience of 1935 first saw the play in the cathedral where Becket defended his church

against the power of the sovereign, the meaning of his sacrifice was already established in this place. Simple representation of his struggle with the King and the state, his exile, his return, and at last his brutal murder by several drunken knights would have sufficed to evoke and celebrate once again the time-known Christian virtues of piety and self-sacrifice, and the continuing struggle between the spirit and the things of this world.

The historical details of Becket's life are referred to in Eliot's play: his humble beginnings, his rise to power as chancellor under Henry II, his political appointment as Archbishop of Canterbury, his subsequent surprising refusal to make the church merely an instrument of state, his exile in Italy and France, his truce with Henry, and then his renewed assertion on his return to Canterbury of the supremacy of God's laws and those of His church over the political needs of the secular state. But these and other historical facts are not the center of Eliot's play; instead, they come to seem of slight importance, almost intrusions on the main business going forward. That collection of vital statistics, the power struggles between church and state, king and baron, which we call History is made to seem nearly unreal by the deliberately "timeless" language Eliot uses to describe historical events. Take the following passage, for example:

SECOND PRIEST: What does the Archbishop do, and
  our Sovereign Lord the Pope
  With the stubborn King and the French King
  In ceaseless intrigue, combinations,
  In conference, meetings accepted; meetings refused,
  Meetings unended or endless
  At one place or another in France?
THIRD PRIEST: I see nothing quite conclusive in the
  art of temporal government,
  But violence, duplicity and frequent malversation.
  King rules or barons rule:
  The strong man strongly and the weak man
  by caprice.
  They have but one law, to seize the power
  and keep it,
  And the steadfast can manipulate the greed
  and lust of others,
  The feeble is devoured by his own.

Are these ceaseless intrigues and inconclusive combinations those of the power struggle in the twelfth century? or of the European democracies and dictatorships in the days of Hitler and Mussolini? or of the Cold War of the present? The language suggests all these possibilities, and more; and so implies that things do not really change in the world of power. Different men occupy the historical stage in different ages, but the game remains the same; since this is so, what seems important politically at any given moment comes to seem unreal and unimportant when viewed from eternity:

> We do not know very much of the future
> Except that from generation to generation
> The same things happen again and again.
> Men learn little from others' experience,
> But in the life of one man, never
> The same time returns.

History comes to represent in *Murder in the Cathedral* all the busy world of affairs, the statecraft of kings and great men, described by the Third Knight in his apology for the murder of Becket. But while the Knights, and the Tempters too, insist on the absolute importance of the historical world, Eliot shifts the focus of his play away from the hard events of rule and reign to the even harder spiritual events of "the life of one man," where "never the same time returns." Beneath the eddies of history, he opens up the spiritual crisis of Thomas Becket, not the Archbishop of the historical chronicles, but a unique, individual man with only one life and one soul to save or lose, and only one time to save or lose it in.

The drama centers not on Thomas's struggle with his king, but on his struggle with himself, with his pride "bred of sudden prosperity" and "confirmed by bitter adversity." When he first enters we see that he has already trained his will to accept death, but in the exchanges with the Tempters — morality-play figures representing his inner struggles — it becomes increasingly obvious that pride and the desire for power are still his motives. Though his language reveals this pride to us, Thomas is himself unaware of it until the Fourth Tempter appears unexpectedly and reveals that even the decision to accept martyrdom was not made out of humility but in an attempt to overpower the king from beyond the grave. Having perceived that,

> When king is dead, there's another king,
> And one more king is another reign;

having seen through the sham of earthly power, having understood that all the glitter of this world decays in time, Thomas has unconsciously resolved to find a more lasting power and glory:

Saint and Martyr rule from the tomb
Think, Thomas, think of enemies dismayed
Creeping in penance, frightened of a shade,
Think of the pilgrims standing in line.

This is the flaw in Becket's character, "to do the right thing for the wrong reason," and having found it, the Tempters combine to sing him a song of total despair, "man passes from unreality to unreality" until he comes at last to "wonder of his own greatness," which is now revealed as a grim joke.

But, having understood the joke, Thomas resists despair and finds somewhere within him the strength or grace to know what he has done and to submit his will totally to God's plan: "I shall no longer act or suffer, to the sword's end." His resignation is beautifully dramatized in the simple direct language of his Christmas sermon — a great contrast to his earlier tortured philosophizing about acting and suffering — in which he explains that peace on earth is never to be found in the historical scene but only in the hearts of men who have submitted themselves completely to God's mysterious order.

Thomas expresses his new-found peace most powerfully, but the flash of revelation after which his own pride and will are finally subdued is not dramatized. Such conversion, considering its nature, is perhaps "undramatic" and can never be adequately staged. The workings of the soul and mind of Becket, the saint, are beyond the range of ordinary men. Yet the experience he endures is an idealized — an heroic — form of an experience not uncommon to mankind. The choruses of the Old Women of Canterbury present this experience on a lower, more realistic level. During the course of the play their attitudes and feelings toward themselves and the world undergo constant change in response to the actions of Thomas, and the positions they take toward reality are roughly those Eliot had already defined in his earlier poetry. "Living and partly living," as they first appear, they resemble Prufrock and the Hollow Men — "We do not wish anything to happen." As the action quickens and the danger nears, they are frightened by the approaching crisis, which will require them to do and suffer, like such modern versions of themselves as Marie, or Lil, or the woman on the floor of the narrow canoe in *The Waste Land*. But where these earlier Eliot char-

acters saw their moment of greatness flicker, never asking the overwhelming question, the Old Women of Canterbury accept their fate, face the death of Thomas with all its terrifying implications for them of a world without God or goodness, and achieve at last an acceptance of their fearsome world. An acceptance based on a glimpse of meaning similar to that "infirm glory of the positive hour" that appears rarely in *The Waste Land* and a little more frequently in "Ash Wednesday" and *The Four Quartets*. It should be noted that Eliot has given this spiritual passage from death-in-life to total acceptance only to the saint and to the very poor. The middle classes, the Priests and the Knights of the play, are either lost in religious formalism — "My Lord, to vespers! You must not be absent from vespers" — or in a conventionality so massive that it blocks all sight of the terror and the peace that lie just below the surface of daily life — "It does go against the grain to kill an Archbishop, especially when you have been brought up in good church traditions."

Only the saint and those who are not insulated from the tedium, hopelessness, and brutality of life can know either the terror or the peace that are the subjects of Eliot's poems. And poetry is the only language that can carry these and other intense emotions. In a time when the theater was almost exclusively concerned with prose drama and realism, T. S. Eliot labored for a good part of his life to unite poetry and drama once again. He explains his reasons for believing that poetry is important to the theater in the following passage from his essay, "Poetry and Drama."

It is a function of all art to give us some perception of an order in life, by imposing an order upon it. . . . It seems to me that beyond the nameable, classifiable emotions and motives of our conscious life when directed toward action — the part of life which prose drama is wholly adequate to express — there is a fringe of indefinite extent, of feeling which we can only detect, so to speak, out of the corner of the eye and can never completely focus; of feeling of which we are only aware in a kind of temporary detachment from action. . . . This peculiar range of sensibility can be expressed by dramatic poetry, at its moments of greatest intensity. At such moments, we touch the border of those feelings which only music can express.

Eliot implies here that the full range and power of a poetic play, such as *Murder in the Cathedral,* exists in its poetry, which has two main functions. The first is to order experience. In *Murder in the Cathedral,* this means taking the events of Becket's life and giving them coherence or form, achieved by relating Becket's passage to martyrdom to other patterns of life. Most obviously, Eliot relates it, through the Chorus, to the experiences of ordinary life as it is lived by most men, who exist and hope and fear in the same way. But the poetry expands the sense of order by associating, through metaphor, Becket's life with the cycle of the year, passing from the bleakness of winter into the rebirth of spring. And beyond this, the poetry links, in various ways, the martyrdom of Becket with the archetypal martyrdom of Christ. The order thus achieved is of the kind that results when an object or event is no longer seen in isolation but as part of a much larger whole.

The second function of dramatic poetry, according to Eliot, is to create and define with as much precision as possible those feelings which, while an essential part of our being, are ordinarily impossible to name or talk about. An example from the play will make clear what Eliot meant. The Chorus is speaking:

I have smelt them, the death-bringers, senses are
    quickened
By subtle forebodings; I have heard

Fluting in the night-time, fluting and owls, have
    seen at noon
Scaly wings slanting over, huge and ridiculous.
    I have tasted
The savour of putrid flesh in the spoon. I have felt
The heaving of earth at nightfall, restless, absurd.
    I have heard
Laughter in the noises of beasts that make strange
    noises: jackal, jackass, jackdaw.

Literally, of course, the Chorus of Kentish women has seen, smelt, and heard none of these strange things; what they have given us is a string of metaphors designed to suggest an unlocalized uneasiness or fear existing out at the edges of consciousness, of a world where rot lies just below the surface of everything, where all that appears solid and fixed is faintly stirring, and where the existence of animals slyly suggests that human pretension to be something higher than beast is an absurdity. This is only the beginning of an adequate treatment of the " subtle forebodings " contained in this passage, but perhaps it is enough to suggest the kind of reading the play requires and to point out that its real life is contained in the poetically rendered emotional states that Becket and the Chorus pass through. In poetic drama of this quality, the full meaning of the play can be arrived at only by facing the poetry head on, not by ignoring it or tearing simple prose meanings from it.

THE LOVE SONG OF J. ALFRED PRUFROCK

First printed in *Poetry* June, 1915 (Chicago), but written several years earlier. The title is ironic. A love song is ordinarily addressed to an individual personality, but it seems probable that the " you " of the poem is either a part of Prufrock himself, or that he is addressing other " hollow men " who are in his own condition. That condition is suggested in the epigraph, which is from Dante's *Inferno,* Canto XXVII, lines 61–66. Dante asks one of the damned souls for its name, and it replies: " If I thought my answer were to one who could return to the world, I would not reply, but as none ever did return alive from this depth, without fear of infamy I answer thee." Prufrock also is in an inferno, and he can speak of his shame only because he thinks no one who hears his confession will condemn him for his cowardice. Eliot's use of the form of dramatic monologue should be compared with that of Browning. Eliot dispenses with all logical narrative sequence, and the situation is revealed by the different qualities of the sense images, by references to various historical figures, and by literary allusions. These form a pattern of contrasts between Prufrock's incapacity to act and the self-fulfillment of those who have lived by the instinct or principle of creative activity. The most pervasive contrast is with Marvell's poem " To His Coy Mistress." This extends not only to the opposition between Marvell's direct plea for the consummation of passion and Prufrock's own neurotic self-debate, but it hints in many subtle ways also at the contrast of the ideal of active self-fulfillment in general with that of the empty forms and frustrating trivialities of Prufrock's social environment.

---

*S'io credesse che mia risposta fosse
A persona che mai tornasse al mondo,
Questa fiamma staria senza piu scosse.
Ma perciocche giammai di questo fondo
Non torno vivo alcun, s'i'odo il vero,
Senza tema d'infamia ti rispondo.*

Let us go then, you and I,
When the evening is spread out against the sky
Like a patient etherised upon a table;
Let us go, through certain half-deserted streets,
The muttering retreats
Of restless nights in one-night cheap hotels
And sawdust restaurants with oyster-shells:
Streets that follow like a tedious argument
Of insidious intent
To lead you to an overwhelming question . . .   10
Oh, do not ask, "What is it?"
Let us go and make our visit.

In the room the women come and go
Talking of Michelangelo.
The yellow fog that rubs its back upon the window-
panes,
The yellow smoke that rubs its muzzle on the
window-panes
Licked its tongue into the corners of the evening,
Lingered upon the pools that stand in drains,
Let fall upon its back the soot that falls from chim-
neys,
Slipped by the terrace, made a sudden leap,   20
And seeing that it was a soft October night,
Curled once about the house, and fell asleep.

And indeed there will be time°
For the yellow smoke that slides along the street,
Rubbing its back upon the window-panes;
There will be time, there will be time
To prepare a face to meet the faces that you meet;
There will be time to murder and create,
And time for all the works and days° of hands
That lift and drop a question on your plate;   30
Time for you and time for me,
And time yet for a hundred indecisions,
And for a hundred visions and revisions,
Before the taking of a toast and tea.

In the room the women come and go
Talking of Michelangelo.

And indeed there will be time
To wonder, "Do I dare?" and, "Do I dare?"
Time to turn back and descend the stair,
With a bald spot in the middle of my hair —   40
[They will say: "How his hair is growing thin!"]
My morning coat, my collar mounting firmly to
the chin,

My necktie rich and modest, but asserted by a sim-
ple pin —
[They will say: "But how his arms and legs are
thin!"]
Do I dare
Disturb the universe?°
In a minute there is time
For decisions and revisions which a minute will
reverse.

For I have known them all already, known them
all: —   49
Have known the evenings, mornings, afternoons,
I have measured out my life with coffee spoons;
I know the voices dying with a dying fall°
Beneath the music from a farther room.
So how should I presume?

And I have known the eyes already, known them
all —
The eyes that fix you in a formulated phrase,
And when I am formulated, sprawling on a pin,
When I am pinned and wriggling on the wall,
Then how should I begin
To spit out all the butt-ends of my days and ways?
And how should I presume?   61

And I have known the arms already, known them
all —
Arms that are braceleted and white and bare
[But in the lamplight, downed with light brown
hair!]
Is it perfume from a dress
That makes me so digress?
Arms that lie along a table, or wrap about a shawl.
And should I then presume?
And how should I begin?

.   .   .   .

Shall I say, I have gone at dusk through narrow
streets   70
And watched the smoke that rises from the pipes
Of lonely men in shirt-sleeves, leaning out of windows? . . .

I should have been a pair of ragged claws
Scuttling across the floors of silent seas.

.   .   .   .

And the afternoon, the evening, sleeps so peace-
fully!
Smoothed by long fingers,
Asleep . . . tired . . . or it malingers,
Stretched on the floor, here beside you and me.
Should I, after tea and cakes and ices,   79

PRUFROCK. **23. there . . . time:** Cf. Marvell's "To His Coy
Mistress": "Had we but world enough and time. . . ." Marvell
argues throughout the poem that there *is* no time for "indecisions." **29. works . . . days:** the title of a poem by the Greek
poet Hesiod (*c.* 735 B.C.). It was addressed to his brother and
urged him to work hard at farming.

46. Disturb . . . universe: Cf. Marvell, who suggests that love
can make a new universe.   **52. a . . . fall:** Cf. the opening
speech of Duke Orsino in Shakespeare's *Twelfth Night.*

Have the strength to force the moment to its
    crisis?
But though I have wept and fasted, wept and
    prayed,
Though I have seen my head [grown slightly bald]
    brought in upon a platter,°
I am no prophet — and here's no great matter;
I have seen the moment of my greatness flicker,
And I have seen the eternal Footman° hold my
    coat, and snicker,
And in short, I was afraid.

And would it have been worth it, after all,
After the cups, the marmalade, the tea,
Among the porcelain, among some talk of you and
    me,
Would it have been worth while,   90
To have bitten off the matter with a smile,
To have squeezed the universe into a ball°
To roll it toward some overwhelming question,
To say: "I am Lazarus, come from the dead,
Come back to tell you all, I shall tell you all" —
If one, settling a pillow by her head,
    Should say: "That is not what I meant at all.
That is not it, at all."

And would it have been worth it, after all,
Would it have been worth while,   100
After the sunsets and the dooryards and the sprin-
    kled streets,
After the novels, after the teacups, after the skirts
    that trail along the floor —
And this, and so much more? —
It is impossible to say just what I mean!
But as if a magic lantern threw the nerves in pat-
    terns on a screen:
Would it have been worth while
If one, settling a pillow or throwing off a shawl,
And turning toward the window, should say:
    "That is not it at all,
    That is not what I mean, at all."   110

   .   .   .   .   .   .

No! I am not Prince Hamlet, nor was meant to be;
Am an attendant lord, one that will do
To swell a progress, start a scene or two,
Advise the prince; no doubt, an easy tool,
Deferential, glad to be of use,
Politic, cautious, and meticulous;
Full of high sentence, but a bit obtuse;

At times, indeed, almost ridiculous —
Almost, at times, the Fool.°

I grow old . . . I grow old . . .   120
I shall wear the bottoms of my trousers rolled.

Shall I part my hair behind? Do I dare to eat a
    peach?
I shall wear white flannel trousers, and walk upon
    the beach.
I have heard the mermaids singing, each to each.

I do not think that they will sing to me.
I have seen them riding seaward on the waves
Combing the white hair of the waves blown back
When the wind blows the water white and black.

We have lingered in the chambers of the sea
By sea-girls wreathed with seaweed red and brown
Till human voices wake us, and we drown.   131

SWEENEY
AMONG THE NIGHTINGALES

    The epigraph is from the *Agamemnon* of Aeschylus
and is the cry of Agamemnon as he is murdered by
Clytemnestra: "Alas, I am smitten deep with a mortal
blow." It is unlikely that any parallel is intended between this action and the scene in the poem. It is more
probable that Eliot is suggesting that the values represented in the worlds of Greek myth and tragedy have
been killed in the world of Sweeney. The nightingales
in the title suggest the myth of Philomela, used again
in *The Waste Land*. King Tereus raped his wife's sister, Philomela, and tore out her tongue so that she
should not tell. But the gods took pity on her and
changed her into a nightingale, an immortal voice in
the natural world, which lives on forever. Sweeney
and the other figures in the scene are deaf both to the
song and to the significance of the story behind it.

ὤμοι, πέπληλμαι καιρίαν πληγὴν ἔσω.

Apeneck Sweeney spreads his knees
Letting his arms hang down to laugh,
The zebra stripes along his jaw
Swelling to maculate giraffe.

The circles of the stormy moon
Slide westward toward the River Plate,°
Death and the Raven drift above
And Sweeney guards the hornèd gate.°

---

82. Though . . . platter: a reference to John the Baptist, beheaded
by **Herod** to please his wife Herodias. **85. the . . . Footman:**
Death. Even his final exit will be without dignity or respect.
92. squeezed . . . ball: Cf. Marvell: "Let us roll all our strength
and all/Our sweetness up into a ball,/And tear our pleasures
with rough strife/Through the iron gates of life"; Marvell has
"the strength to force the moment to its crisis" (l. 80). For
Prufrock this would break the death-in-life of his present existence and be like the return of Lazarus from the dead (John 11).

119. the Fool: There is no Fool in *Hamlet*, but Prufrock recognizes sadly that he corresponds to all the characters in the play
who are made use of by others, or are made the butt of their
ridicule. SWEENEY AMONG THE NIGHTINGALES. **6. River Plate:**
the estuary between Uruguay and Argentina. **8. the . . . gate:**
the gates of horn in Hades through which true dreams came to
the upper world.

Gloomy Orion and the Dog°
Are veiled; and hushed the shrunken seas; 10
The person in the Spanish cape
Tries to sit on Sweeney's knees

Slips and pulls the table cloth
Overturns a coffee-cup,
Reorganised upon the floor
She yawns and draws a stocking up;

The silent man in mocha brown
Sprawls at the window-sill and gapes;
The waiter brings in oranges
Bananas figs and hothouse grapes; 20

The silent vertebrate in brown
Contracts and concentrates, withdraws;
Rachel *née* Rabinovitch
Tears at the grapes with murderous paws;

She and the lady in the cape
Are suspect, thought to be in league;
Therefore the man with heavy eyes
Declines the gambit, shows fatigue,

Leaves the room and reappears
Outside the window, leaning in, 30
Branches of wistaria
Circumscribe a golden grin;

The host with someone indistinct
Converses at the door apart,
The nightingales are singing near
The Convent of the Sacred Heart,

And sang within the bloody wood°
When Agamemnon cried aloud,
And let their liquid siftings fall
To stain the stiff dishonoured shroud. 40

1918

9. **Orion . . . Dog**: the constellations.   37. **the . . . wood**: There
seems to be a telescoping of suggestions here. Agamemnon,
on his return from the Trojan War, was killed in a bath, not
a wood. The first chapter of Frazer's *The Golden Bough* tells the
story of the wood of Nemi, the scene of a bloody ritual in which
the old priest of the grove was killed by a younger one, who in his
turn became priest until he too was slain. Frazer regards this
ritual as bound up with that of the ancient fertility cults, which
linked the seasonal rhythms of winter and spring with the death
and resurrection of vegetation gods, particularly the wine god,
Dionysus. The origins of Greek drama have also been traced to
the festival of Dionysus, and the fertility cults expanded later
into the larger religious theme of death and resurrection. The
bloody wood, therefore, is appropriately linked here with the
nightingales' immortal song, the *Agamemnon*, and the Sacred
Heart.

THE HOLLOW MEN

The first epigraph to the poem is from Conrad's
Heart of Darkness (see above, p. 939). As Kurtz is
dying, Marlow describes how he lies "with a wide
and immense stare embracing, condemning, loathing
all the universe," and cries, "The horror! The horror!"
Marlow goes to dinner, and the manager's boy puts
his head in the doorway and says, "in a tone of scathing contempt — 'Mistah Kurtz — he dead.'" But Marlow, despite all the waste and degradation of Kurtz's
fate, is not contemptuous. He feels in Kurtz's cry "the
appalling face of glimpsed truth. . . . It was an affirmation, a moral victory paid for by innumerable defeats. . . . But it was a victory."

The second epigraph is an allusion to Guy Fawkes
Day in England, when children make straw effigies of
the "Guy" and collect pennies for fireworks. In the
plot to blow up the House of Commons in 1605, Guy
Fawkes had the job of firing the barrels of gunpowder
in the cellar. He was arrested before he could carry it
out, and executed. Both Mr. Kurtz and Guy Fawkes
are "lost violent souls," but they *chose* their fate, in
contrast to the hollow men who cannot exercise will
and choice. A remark from Eliot's essay on Baudelaire
illustrates his point: "So far as we are human, what
we do must be either evil or good; so far as we do evil
or good, we are human; and it is better, in a paradoxical way, to do evil than to do nothing; at least we exist." See Browning's "The Statue and the Bust" for a
similar attitude.

Mistah Kurtz — he dead.
A penny for the Old Guy

I

We are the hollow men
We are the stuffed men
Leaning together
Headpiece filled with straw. Alas!
Our dried voices, when
We whisper together
Are quiet and meaningless
As wind in dry grass
Or rats' feet over broken glass
In our dry cellar° 10

Shape without form, shade without colour,
Paralysed force, gesture without motion;

Those who have crossed
With direct eyes, to death's other Kingdom°
Remember us — if at all — not as lost
Violent souls, but only
As the hollow men
The stuffed men.

THE HOLLOW MEN. 10. **our . . . cellar**: in contrast to the living
Guy Fawkes in *his* cellar. 13–14. **Those . . . Kingdom**: those
who have crossed the river Acheron to hell. Cf. *Inferno*, III.

II

Eyes I dare not meet in dreams
In death's dream kingdom°   20
These do not appear:
There, the eyes are
Sunlight on a broken column
There, is a tree swinging
And voices are
In the wind's singing
More distant and more solemn
Than a fading star.

Let me be no nearer
In death's dream kingdom   30
Let me also wear
Such deliberate disguises
Rat's coat, crowskin, crossed staves
In a field
Behaving as the wind behaves
No nearer —

Not that final meeting
In the twilight kingdom°

III

This is the dead land
This is cactus land   40
Here the stone images
Are raised, here they receive
The supplication of a dead man's hand
Under the twinkle of a fading star.
Is it like this
In death's other kingdom
Waking alone
At the hour when we are
Trembling with tenderness
Lips that would kiss   50
Form prayers to broken stone.

IV

The eyes are not here
There are no eyes here
In this valley of dying stars
In this hollow valley
This broken jaw of our lost kingdoms

In this last of meeting places
We grope together

And avoid speech
Gathered on this beach of the tumid river° 60

Sightless, unless
The eyes reappear
As the perpetual star
Multifoliate rose°
Of death's twilight kingdom
The hope only
Of empty men.

V

Here we go round the prickly pear°
Prickly pear prickly pear
Here we go round the prickly pear   70
At five o'clock in the morning.

Between the idea
And the reality
Between the motion
And the act
Falls the Shadow
                    For Thine is the Kingdom

Between the conception
And the creation
Between the emotion   80
And the response
Falls the Shadow
                    Life is very long

Between the desire
And the spasm
Between the potency
And the existence
Between the essence
And the descent
Falls the Shadow   90
          For Thine is the Kingdom

For Thine is
Life is
For Thine is the

This is the way the world ends
This is the way the world ends
This is the way the world ends
Not with a bang but a whimper.

                              1925

60. tumid river: the river Acheron. See *Inferno*, III. Many details of the scene there are suggested in the poem. 63–64. perpetual . . . rose: Conducted by Beatrice, whose stern eyes turn to "eyes of light," Dante sees the Divine Essence "like a star in Heaven," while Paradise forms itself into the "multifoliate rose," whose petals are the souls of the blessed. See *Paradiso*, XXVIII.30. 68. *Here . . . pear:* The substitution of the prickly pear for the mulberry bush suggests the "cactus land" of l. 40. The going *round* indicates the lack of any *forward* movement, and perhaps the nursery-rhyme form hints at the childish world of illusion and make-believe which paralyzes the will and concludes in the "whimper" instead of the "bang" planned by the real Guy Fawkes.

20. death's . . . kingdom: This appears to be the condition of illusion and revery in which moral choice can be escaped; the condition in which Prufrock lived. 37–38. Not . . . kingdom: Taken together with the "eyes" of the first line of this section, this seems to refer to Dante's meeting with Beatrice in *Purgatorio*, XXX. Beatrice's eyes are stern, and she upbraids Dante with his failures and weaknesses. "The twilight kingdom," therefore, may refer to the active purgation from which the protagonist shrinks.

MARINA

The poem appeared first as No. 29 of the "Ariel" poems. These were a series of individual poems by various authors, published over a period of years by Faber and Faber, to which Eliot contributed five. The title is the name of the heroine of Shakespeare's play *Pericles*. Marina, the daughter of Pericles, was born at sea (hence her name) and was then thought to have been murdered by those in whose charge she was left. She was miraculously restored to her father when she was a grown woman. Pericles is the speaker. In contrast to the subject of the poem, which is the discovery of life where death had been accepted, the epigraph ironically recalls an opposite experience. It is from the play *Hercules Furens* of Seneca, at the moment when Hercules, having unknowingly killed his children in a fit of madness, returns to sanity, asks where he is, and realizes his loss. (See Introduction, p. 1011.)

Quis hic locus, quae regio, quae mundi plaga?

What seas what shores what grey rocks and what
    islands
What water lapping the bow
And scent of pine and the woodthrush singing
    through the fog
What images return
O my daughter.

Those who sharpen the tooth of the dog, meaning
Death
Those who glitter with the glory of the humming-
    bird, meaning
Death
Those who sit in the stye of contentment, mean-
    ing
Death   11
Those who suffer the ecstasy of the animals, mean-
    ing
Death
Are become unsubstantial, reduced by a wind,
A breath of pine, and the woodsong fog
By this grace dissolved in place

What is this face, less clear and clearer
The pulse in the arm, less strong and stronger° —
Given or lent? more distant than stars and nearer
    than the eye

Whispers and small laughter between leaves and
    hurrying feet°   20
Under sleep, where all the waters meet.

Bowsprit cracked with ice and paint cracked with
    heat.
I made this, I have forgotten
And remember.
The rigging weak and the canvas rotten
Between one June and another September.
Made this unknowing, half conscious, unknown,
    my own.
The garboard strake leaks, the seams need caulk-
    ing.°
This form, this face, this life
Living to live in a world of time beyond me; let
    me
Resign my life for this life, my speech for that un-
    spoken,   31
The awakened, lips parted, the hope, the new
    ships.

What seas what shores what granite islands to-
    wards my timbers
And woodthrush calling through the fog
My daughter.

1930

TRIUMPHAL MARCH

In the volume of *Collected Poems* this appears among "Unfinished Poems" as No. 1 under the general title "Coriolan." The second (and last) in the uncompleted series is "Difficulties of a Statesman." These poems differ from anything previously published by Eliot in that they have a direct political significance. Writing in the *Criterion* in the spring of 1929, he had declared: "We must prepare a state of mind towards something other than the facile alternatives of communist or fascist dictatorship." He saw fascistic nationalism as "a familiar conventional modern idea . . . the doctrine of success." The poem's setting is neither ancient Rome nor a modern city; it is a fusion of the two, suggesting the universality of the *idea* of a central figure with which the people identify both the nation and the Godhead. This is implicitly contrasted with a pattern of values having at its center the "still point" (see Introduction, p. 1011). The whole description of the Triumphal March should be contrasted with the entry of Christ into Jerusalem, riding upon an ass, with the multitudes on the way to the Temple crying: "Blessed be the King that cometh in the name of the Lord" (Mark 12, Luke 20).

Stone, bronze, stone, steel, stone, oakleaves, horses'
    heels
Over the paving.

MARINA. **17–18. What . . . stronger**: Cf. *Pericles*, V.i.154: "But are you flesh and blood? Have you a working pulse?" **20. Whispers . . . feet**: This seems to be a childhood memory, associated with a sense of ecstasy. It appears again in *Burnt Norton*, I, "for the leaves were full of children,/Hidden excitedly, containing laughter."

22–28. Bowsprit . . . caulking: At first glance this damaged and dilapidated ship seems out of keeping with the quality of the vision. But the importance seems to be in the "I made this." The presence of Marina is in some way connected with some half-understood constructive effort of the speaker, symbolized by the old ship. It has been the *means* of the revelation, and having served its purpose it can dissolve into the general sense of new life.

And the flags. And the trumpets. And so many
    eagles.
How many? Count them. And such a press of
    people.
We hardly knew ourselves that day, or knew the
    City.
This is the way to the temple, and we so many
    crowding the way.
So many waiting, how many waiting? what did it
    matter, on such a day?
Are they coming? No, not yet. You can see some
    eagles. And hear the trumpets.
Here they come. Is he coming?
The natural wakeful life of our Ego is a perceiv-
    ing.
We can wait with our stools and our sausages.   11
What comes first? Can you see? Tell us. It is

    5,800,000 rifles and carbines,
      102,000 machine guns,
       28,000 trench mortars,
       53,000 field and heavy guns,
I cannot tell how many projectiles, mines and fuses,
      13,000 aeroplanes,
      24,000 aeroplane engines,
      50,000 ammunition waggons,   20
now 55,000 army waggons,
      11,000 field kitchens,
       1,150 field bakeries.

What a time that took. Will it be he now? No,
Those are the golf club Captains, these the Scouts,
And now the *société gymnastique de Poissy*
And now come the Mayor and the Liverymen.
    Look
There he is now, look:
There is no interrogation in his eyes
Or in the hands, quiet over the horse's neck,   30
And the eyes watchful, waiting, perceiving, in-
    different.
O hidden under the dove's wing, hidden in the
    turtle's breast,
Under the palmtree at noon, under the running
    water
At the still point of the turning world. O hidden.

Now they go up to temple. Then the sacrifice.
Now come the virgins bearing urns, urns contain-
    ing
Dust
Dust
Dust of dust, and now
Stone, bronze, stone, steel, stone, oakleaves, horses'
    heels   40
Over the paving.

That is all we could see. But how many eagles!
    and how many trumpets!

(And Easter Day, we didn't get to the country,
So we took young Cyril to church. And they rang
    a bell
And he said right out loud, *crumpets.*°)
            Don't throw away that sausage,
It'll come in handy. He's artful. Please, will you
Give us a light?
Light
Light
*Et les soldats faisaient la haie? ILS LA FAI-
    SAIENT.*°   50

            1931

THE DRY SALVAGES

The title of each of the Quartets (" Burnt Norton,"
"East Coker," "The Dry Salvages," and "Little
Gidding") is the name of a place, associated in some
way with Eliot's own experience. His family went for
summer vacations to Cape Ann, and the atmosphere
and scenery of that coast entered deeply into his imaginative life. It is the background of "Marina," and in
Part I of "The Dry Salvages" it supplies the material
for what is perhaps Eliot's finest piece of sustained
descriptive imagery.

In each Quartet also, one of the elements (earth, air,
fire, water) dominates the imagery of the poem and
emphasizes the element in man's nature to which it is
an analogy. In "The Dry Salvages" the dominating
element is water. Human life appears first as the river
of racial consciousness alive in man's blood, and then
as the vast flux of the sea on which he is afloat. Part
III, as in the other Quartets, uses metaphors of traveling to suggest man's passage through time.

It will be noticed that this is the first poem (in this
selection) that is strongly and openly colored with
Christian terminology and reference.

For a discussion of the parallels with musical form
that Eliot uses throughout the Quartets, see *The Art
of T. S. Eliot* by Helen Gardner, Chapter 2, and also
Eliot's own remarks on this topic at the conclusion of
"The Music of Poetry" below.

(The Dry Salvages — presumably *les trois sau-
vages* — is a small group of rocks, with a beacon,
off the N.E. coast of Cape Ann, Massachusetts.
Salvages is pronounced to rhyme with *assuages.*
Groaner: a whistling buoy.)

I

I do not know much about gods; but I think that
    the river

TRIUMPHAL MARCH. **44-45. And . . .** *crumpets:* In the residential
districts of London, the sellers of muffins and crumpets used to
carry trays of them on their heads and ring a bell to advertise
their presence. The ignorant Cyril responds thus to the ringing
of the bell at Mass, at the elevation of the Host. **50.** *Et . . .
FAISAIENT:* "*Faire la haie*" is to form a military line, the
"hedge" being the bayonets of the ranks of soldiers. The suggestion here is presumably that the only light is that of the

Is a strong brown god — sullen, untamed and in-
tractable,
Patient to some degree, at first recognised as a
frontier;
Useful, untrustworthy, as a conveyor of commerce;
Then only a problem confronting the builder of
bridges.
The problem once solved, the brown god is almost
forgotten
By the dwellers in cities — ever, however, implac-
able,
Keeping his seasons and rages, destroyer, reminder
Of what men choose to forget. Unhonoured, un-
propitiated
By worshippers of the machine, but waiting, watch-
ing and waiting.   10
His rhythm was present in the nursery bedroom,
In the rank ailanthus of the April dooryard,
In the smell of grapes on the autumn table,
And the evening circle in the winter gaslight.

The river is within us, the sea is all about us;
The sea is the land's edge also, the granite
Into which it reaches, the beaches where it tosses
Its hints of earlier and other creation:
The starfish, the hermit crab, the whale's backbone;
The pools where it offers to our curiosity   20
The more delicate algae and the sea anemone.
It tosses up our losses, the torn seine,°
The shattered lobsterpot, the broken oar
And the gear of foreign dead men. The sea has
many voices,
Many gods and many voices.
                        The salt is on the
briar rose,
The fog is in the fir trees.
                        The sea howl
And the sea yelp, are different voices
Often together heard; the whine in the rigging,
The menace and caress of wave that breaks on
water,
The distant rote in the granite teeth,   30
And the wailing warning from the approaching
headland
Are all sea voices, and the heaving groaner
Rounded homewards, and the seagull:
And under the oppression of the silent fog
The tolling bell°
Measures time not our time, rung by the unhurried
Ground swell,° a time

Older than the time of chronometers, older
Than time counted by anxious worried women
Lying awake, calculating the future,   40
Trying to unweave, unwind, unravel
And piece together the past and the future,
Between midnight and dawn, when the past is all
deception,
The future futureless, before the morning watch°
When time stops and time is never ending;
And the ground swell, that is and was from the
beginning,
Clangs
The bell.

II

Where is there an end of it, the soundless wailing,
The silent withering of autumn flowers   50
Dropping their petals and remaining motionless;
Where is there an end to the drifting wreckage,
The prayer of the bone on the beach, the unpray-
able
Prayer at the calamitous annunciation?

There is no end, but addition: the trailing
Consequence of further days and hours,
While emotion takes to itself the emotionless
Years of living among the breakage
Of what was believed in as the most reliable —
And therefore the fittest for renunciation.   60

There is the final addition, the failing
Pride or resentment at failing powers,
The unattached devotion which might pass for de-
votionless,
In a drifting boat with a slow leakage,
The silent listening to the undeniable
Clamour of the bell of the last annunciation.

Where is the end of them, the fishermen sailing
Into the wind's tail, where the fog cowers?
We cannot think of a time that is oceanless
Or of an ocean not littered with wastage   70
Or of a future that is not liable
Like the past, to have no destination.

We have to think of them as forever bailing,
Setting and hauling, while the North East lowers
Over shallow banks unchanging and erosionless
Or drawing their money, drying sails at dockage;
Not as making a trip that will be unpayable
For a haul that will not bear examination.

gleaming steel; and the ranks of the army grow ever greater, just
as the letters are enlarged on the page. DRY SALVAGES. 22.
seine: a fishing net. 35. The . . . bell: not just the reminder of
death. It suggests also the Angelus, rung daily to commemorate
the Annunciation to the Virgin Mary of the birth of Christ, and
the bell at the consecration of the Host in the sacrament of the
Eucharist; both reminders of "time not our time." 37. Ground
swell: The clue to the meaning of this is the echo from the doxol-
ogy in l. 46: "as it was from the beginning, is now and ever shall
be": the ground swell is the presence of the permanence within the
flux, the Trinity. 44. before . . . watch: See Ps. 130:6: "My
soul fleeth unto the Lord, before the morning watch. I say, before
the morning watch."

There is no end of it, the voiceless wailing,
No end to the withering of withered flowers,   80
To the movement of pain that is painless and
    motionless,
To the drift of the sea and the drifting wreckage,
The bone's prayer to Death its God. Only the
    hardly, barely prayable
Prayer of the one Annunciation.°

It seems, as one becomes older,
That the past has another pattern, and ceases to be
    a mere sequence —
Or even development: the latter a partial fallacy,
Encouraged by superficial notions of evolution,
Which becomes, in the popular mind, a means of
    disowning the past.
The moments of happiness — not the sense of well-
    being,   90
Fruition, fulfilment, security or affection,
Or even a very good dinner, but the sudden illu-
    mination —
We had the experience but missed the meaning,
And approach to the meaning restores the experi-
    ence
In a different form, beyond any meaning
We can assign to happiness. I have said before
That the past experience revived in the meaning
Is not the experience of one life only
But of many generations — not forgetting
Something that is probably quite ineffable: 100
The backward look behind the assurance
Of recorded history, the backward half-look
Over the shoulder, towards the primitive terror.
Now, we come to discover that the moments of
    agony
(Whether, or not, due to misunderstanding,
Having hoped for the wrong things or dreaded the
    wrong things,
Is not in question) are likewise permanent
With such permanence as time has. We appreciate
    this better
In the agony of others, nearly experienced,
Involving ourselves, than in our own.   110
For our own past is covered by the currents of
    action,
But the torment of others remains an experience
Unqualified, unworn by subsequent attrition.
People change, and smile: but the agony abides.
Time the destroyer is time the preserver,
Like the river with its cargo of dead Negroes, cows
    and chicken coops,
The bitter apple and the bite in the apple.°

And the ragged rock° in the restless waters,
Waves wash over it, fogs conceal it;
On a halcyon day it is merely a monument,   120
In navigable weather it is always a seamark
To lay a course by: but in the sombre season
Or the sudden fury, is what it always was.

III

I sometimes wonder if that is what Krishna°
    meant —
Among other things — or one way of putting the
    same thing:
That the future is a faded song, a Royal Rose° or
    a lavender spray
Of wistful regret for those who are not yet here to
    regret,
Pressed between yellow leaves of a book that has
    never been opened.°
And the way up is the way down, the way forward
    is the way back.
You cannot face it steadily, but this thing is sure,
That time is no healer: the patient is no longer
    here.°   131
When the train starts, and the passengers are
    settled
To fruit, periodicals and business letters
(And those who saw them off have left the plat-
    form)
Their faces relax from grief into relief,
To the sleepy rhythm of a hundred hours.
Fare forward, travellers! not escaping from the past
Into different lives, or into any future;
You are not the same people who left that station
Or who will arrive at any terminus,   140
While the narrowing rails slide together behind
    you;
And on the deck of the drumming liner
Watching the furrow that widens behind you,
You shall not think "the past is finished"
Or "the future is before us."
At nightfall, in the rigging and the aerial,
Is a voice descanting (though not to the ear,
The murmuring shell of time, and not in any lan-
    guage)
"Fare forward, you who think that you are voy-
    aging;°
You are not those who saw the harbour   150
Receding, or those who will disembark.

84. Prayer . . . Annunciation: "Be it unto me according to thy word" (Luke 1:38). 115–17. Time . . . apple: Time preserves in our consciousness the memory of past agonies, carried along in our racial memory as the great flood on the Mississippi carried along its load of death. The symbol of man's death is the Fall.

118. the . . . rock: perhaps the Crucifixion; the agony which re-deemed man from time. 124. Krishna: the Hindu god and hero, worshiped as an incarnation of Vishnu, the preserver. See ll. 150–58n. 126. Royal Rose: a Jacobite song. 126–28. That . . . opened: The future is part of an endless sequence that repeats itself; all the future ever brings is regret for the past. 131. time . . . here: It is not time that heals; it is the sufferer who changes. 149. you . . . voyaging: any real development is never in time, it is in consciousness. It is there that we can "fare forward."

Here between the hither and the farther shore
While time is withdrawn, consider the future
And the past with an equal mind.
At the moment which is not of action or inaction
You can receive this: ' on whatever sphere of being
The mind of man may be intent
At the time of death '° — that is the one action
(And the time of death is every moment)
Which shall fructify in the lives of others: 160
And do not think of the fruit of action.
Fare forward.
                    O voyagers, O seamen,
You who come to port, and you whose bodies
Will suffer the trial and judgement of the sea,
Or whatever event, this is your real destination."
So Krishna, as when he admonished Arjuna
On the field of battle.°
                              Not fare well,
But fare forward, voyagers.

                              IV

Lady, whose shrine stands on the promontory,
Pray for all those who are in ships, those   170
Whose business has to do with fish, and
Those concerned with every lawful traffic
And those who conduct them.

Repeat a prayer also on behalf of
Women who have seen their sons or husbands
Setting forth, and not returning:
Figlia del tuo figlio,°
Queen of Heaven.

Also pray for those who were in ships, and   179
Ended their voyage on the sand,·in the sea's lips
Or in the dark throat which will not reject them
Or wherever cannot reach them the sound of the
          sea bell's
Perpetual angelus.

                              V

To communicate with Mars, converse with spirits,
To report the behaviour of the sea monster,

Describe the horoscope, haruspicate° or scry,°
Observe disease in signatures, evoke
Biography from the wrinkles of the palm
And tragedy from fingers; release omens
By sortilege, or tea leaves, riddle the inevitable
With playing cards, fiddle with pentagrams   191
Or barbituric acids, or dissect
The recurrent image into pre-conscious terrors —
To explore the womb, or tomb, or dreams; all these
          are usual
Pastimes and drugs, and features of the press:
And always will be, some of them especially
When there is distress of nations and perplexity
Whether on the shores of Asia, or in the Edgware
          Road.°
Men's curiosity searches past and future   199
And clings to that dimension. But to apprehend
The point of intersection of the timeless
With time, is an occupation for the saint —
No occupation either, but something given
And taken, in a lifetime's death in love,
Ardour and selflessness and self-surrender.
For most of us, there is only the unattended
Moment, the moment in and out of time,
The distraction fit, lost in a shaft of sunlight
The wild thyme unseen, or the winter lightning
Or the waterfall, or music heard so deeply   210
That it is not heard at all, but you are the music
While the music lasts. These are only hints and
          guesses,
Hints followed by guesses; and the rest
Is prayer, observance, discipline, thought and action.
The hint half guessed, the gift half understood, is
          Incarnation.
Here the impossible union
Of spheres of existence is actual,
Here the past and future
Are conquered, and reconciled,
Where action were otherwise movement   220
Of that which is only moved
And has in it no source of movement —
Driven by daemonic, chthonic°
Powers. And right action is freedom
From past and future also.
For most of us, this is the aim
Never here to be realised;
Who are only undefeated
Because we have gone on trying;
We, content at the last   230
If our temporal reversion nourish
(Not too far from the yew-tree)
The life of significant soil.

                              1941

156–58. 'on . . . death': quoted from the *Bhagavad-Gita* (the
Song of the Blessed), a sacred Hindu poem. 166–67. So
. . . battle: Arjuna hesitated to fight when some kinsmen
were in the opposing army. But Krishna, who was his charioteer,
urged that the way of salvation is in the performing of immediate
duties with complete detachment from personal interests. Such
action is the equal of the other "sphere of being," which is the
abstention from action, the life of contemplation. Eliot is saying,
therefore, that it is the quality of disinterested thought or action
in the present moment which is important. The time of death is
every moment, for no moment will come again. *This* moment is
our "real destination." 177. Figlia . . . figlio: "daughter of
thine own son"; the address of St. Bernard to the Virgin. *Paradiso*, XXXIII.

186. haruspicate: to practice divination. scry: descry. 198.
Edgware Road: a well-known London street. 223. chthonic:
relating to the earth spirits of the underworld.

Murder in the Cathedral

CHARACTERS

A CHORUS OF WOMEN OF CANTERBURY
THREE PRIESTS OF THE CATHEDRAL
A MESSENGER

ARCHBISHOP THOMAS BECKET
FOUR TEMPTERS
ATTENDANTS

Part I

The scene is the Archbishop's Hall, on December 2nd, 1170

CHORUS. Here let us stand, close by the cathedral.
    Here let us wait.
    Are we drawn by danger? Is it the knowledge
    of safety, that draws our feet
    Towards the cathedral? What danger can be
    For us, the poor, the poor women of Canterbury? What tribulation
    With which we are not already familiar?
    There is no danger
    For us, and there is no safety in the cathedral. Some presage of an act
    Which our eyes are compelled to witness, has forced our feet
    Towards the cathedral. We are forced to bear witness.

    Since golden October declined into sombre November
    And the apples were gathered and stored, and the land became brown sharp points of death in a waste of water and mud,
    The New Year waits, breathes, waits, whispers in darkness.
    While the labourer kicks off a muddy boot and stretches his hand to the fire,
    The New Year waits, destiny waits for the coming.
    Who has stretched out his hand to the fire and remembered the Saints at All Hallows,
    Remembered the martyrs and saints who wait? And who shall
    Stretch out his hand to the fire, and deny his master? Who shall be warm
    By the fire, and deny his master?

    Seven years and the summer is over,
    Seven years since the Archbishop left us,

    He who was always kind to his people.
    But it would not be well if he should return.
    King rules or barons rule;
    We have suffered various oppression,
    But mostly we are left to our own devices,
    And we are content if we are left alone.
    We try to keep our households in order;
    The merchant, shy and cautious, tries to compile a little fortune,
    And the labourer bends to his piece of earth, earth-colour, his own colour,
    Preferring to pass unobserved.
    Now I fear disturbance of the quiet seasons:
    Winter shall come bringing death from the sea,
    Ruinous spring shall beat at our doors,
    Root and shoot shall eat our eyes and our ears,
    Disastrous summer burn up the beds of our streams
    And the poor shall wait for another decaying October.
    Why should the summer bring consolation
    For autumn fires and winter fogs?
    What shall we do in the heat of summer
    But wait in barren orchards for another October?
    Some malady is coming upon us. We wait, we wait,
    And the saints and martyrs wait, for those who shall be martyrs and saints.
    Destiny waits in the hand of God, shaping the still unshapen:
    I have seen these things in a shaft of sunlight.
    Destiny waits in the hand of God, not in the hands of statesmen
    Who do, some well, some ill, planning and guessing,
    Having their aims which turn in their hands in the pattern of time.
    Come, happy December, who shall observe you, who shall preserve you?

Shall the Son of Man be born again in the
 litter of scorn?
For us, the poor, there is no action,
But only to wait and to witness.
[*Enter* PRIESTS.]
FIRST PRIEST. Seven years and the summer is over.
 Seven years since the Archbishop left us.
SECOND PRIEST. What does the Archbishop do, and
 our Sovereign Lord the Pope
With the stubborn King and the French King
In ceaseless intrigue, combinations,
In conference, meetings accepted, meetings re-
 fused,
Meetings unended or endless
At one place or another in France?
THIRD PRIEST. I see nothing quite conclusive in the
 art of temporal government,
But violence, duplicity and frequent malver-
 sation.
King rules or barons rule:
The strong man strongly and the weak man
 by caprice.
They have but one law, to seize the power
 and keep it,
And the steadfast can manipulate the greed
 and lust of others,
The feeble is devoured by his own.
FIRST PRIEST. Shall these things not end
Until the poor at the gate
Have forgotten their friend, their Father in
 God, have forgotten
That they had a friend?
[*Enter* MESSENGER.]
MESSENGER. Servants of God, and watchers of the
 temple,
I am here to inform you, without circumlo-
 cution:
The Archbishop is in England, and is close
 outside the city.
I was sent before in haste
To give you notice of his coming, as much
 as was possible,
That you may prepare to meet him.
FIRST PRIEST. What, is the exile ended, is our
 Lord Archbishop
Reunited with the King? What reconciliation
Of two proud men?
THIRD PRIEST.   What peace can be found
To grow between the hammer and the anvil?
SECOND PRIEST.   Tell us,
Are the old disputes at an end, is the wall of
 pride cast down
That divided them? Is it peace or war?
FIRST PRIEST.   Does he come
In full assurance, or only secure
In the power of Rome, the spiritual rule,

The assurance of right, and the love of the
 people?
MESSENGER. You are right to express a certain in-
 credulity.
He comes in pride and sorrow, affirming all
 his claims,
Assured, beyond doubt, of the devotion of
 the people,
Who receive him with scenes of frenzied en-
 thusiasm,
Lining the road and throwing down their
 capes.
Strewing the way with leaves and late flowers
 of the season.
The streets of the city will be packed to suf-
 focation,
And I think that his horse will be deprived
 of its tail,
A single hair of which becomes a precious
 relic.
He is at one with the Pope, and with the
 King of France,
Who indeed would have liked to detain him
 in his kingdom:
But as for our King, that is another matter.
FIRST PRIEST. But again, is it war or peace?
MESSENGER.   Peace, but not the kiss of peace.
A patched up affair, if you ask my opinion.
And if you ask me, I think the Lord Arch-
 bishop
Is not the man to cherish any illusions,
Or yet to diminish the least of his pretensions.
If you ask my opinion, I think that this peace
Is nothing like an end, or like a beginning.
It is common knowledge that when the Arch-
 bishop
Parted from the King, he said to the King,
My Lord, he said, I leave you as a man
Whom in this life I shall not see again.
I have this, I assure you, on the highest au-
 thority;
There are several opinions as to what he
 meant,
But no one considers it a happy prognostic.
                                            [*Exit.*]
FIRST PRIEST. I fear for the Archbishop, I fear for
 the Church,
I know that the pride bred of sudden pros-
 perity
Was but confirmed by bitter adversity.
I saw him as Chancellor, flattered by the King,
Liked or feared by courtiers, in their over-
 bearing fashion,
Despised and despising, always isolated,
Never one among them, always insecure;
His pride always feeding upon his own vir-
 tues,

Pride drawing sustenance from impartiality,
Pride drawing sustenance from generosity,
Loathing power given by temporal devolution,
Wishing subjection to God alone.
Had the King been greater, or had he been
  weaker
Things had perhaps been different for Thomas.

SECOND PRIEST. Yet our lord is returned. Our lord
  has come back to his own again.
We have had enough of waiting, from December to dismal December.
The Archbishop shall be at our head, dis-
  pelling dismay and doubt.
He will tell us what we are to do, he will
  give us our orders, instruct us.
Our Lord is at one with the Pope, and also
  the King of France.
We can lean on a rock, we can feel a firm
  foothold
Against the perpetual wash of tides of balance of forces of barons and landholders.
The rock of God is beneath our feet. Let us
  meet the Archbishop with cordial thanksgiving:
Our lord, our Archbishop returns. And when
  the Archbishop returns
Our doubts are dispelled. Let us therefore re-
  joice,
I say rejoice, and show a glad face for his
  welcome.
I am the Archbishop's man. Let us give the
  Archbishop welcome!

THIRD PRIEST. For good or ill, let the wheel turn.
The wheel has been still, these seven years,
  and no good.
For ill or good, let the wheel turn.
For who knows the end of good or evil?
Until the grinders cease
And the door shall be shut in the street,
And all the daughters of music shall be
  brought low.

CHORUS. Here is no continuing city, here is no
  abiding stay.
Ill the wind, ill the time, uncertain the profit,
  certain the danger.
O late late late, late is the time, late too late,
  and rotten the year;
Evil the wind, and bitter the sea, and grey
  the sky, grey grey grey.
O Thomas, return, Archbishop; return, return
  to France.
Return. Quickly. Quietly. Leave us to perish
  in quiet.
You come with applause, you come with rejoicing, but you come bringing death into
  Canterbury:

A doom on the house, a doom on yourself, a
  doom on the world.

We do not wish anything to happen.
Seven years we have lived quietly,
Succeeded in avoiding notice,
Living and partly living.
There have been oppression and luxury,
There have been poverty and licence,
There has been minor injustice.
Yet we have gone on living,
Living and partly living.
Sometimes the corn has failed us,
Sometimes the harvest is good,
One year is a year of rain,
Another a year of dryness,
One year the apples are abundant,
Another year the plums are lacking.
Yet we have gone on living,
Living and partly living.
We have kept the feasts, heard the masses,
We have brewed beer and cyder,
Gathered wood against the winter,
Talked at the corner of the fire,
Talked at the corners of streets,
Talked not always in whispers,
Living and partly living.
We have seen births, deaths and marriages,
We have had various scandals,
We have been afflicted with taxes,
We have had laughter and gossip,
Several girls have disappeared
Unaccountably, and some not able to.
We have all had our private terrors,
Our particular shadows, our secret fears.
But now a great fear is upon us, a fear not
  of one but of many,
A fear like birth and death, when we see
  birth and death alone
In a void apart. We
Are afraid in a fear which we cannot know,
  which we cannot face, which none under-
  stands,
And our hearts are torn from us, our brains
  unskinned like the layers of an onion, our
  selves are lost lost
In a final fear which none understands. O
  Thomas Archbishop,
O Thomas our Lord, leave us and leave us
  be, in our humble and tarnished frame of
  existence, leave us; do not ask us
To stand to the doom on the house, the
  doom on the Archbishop, the doom on the
  world.
Archbishop, secure and assured of your fate,
  unaffrayed among the shades, do you realise
  what you ask, do you realise what it means

To the small folk drawn into the pattern of fate, the small folk who live among small things,
The strain on the brain of the small folk who stand to the doom of the house, the doom of their lord, the doom of the world?
O Thomas, Archbishop, leave us, leave us, leave sullen Dover, and set sail for France. Thomas our Archbishop still our Archbishop even in France. Thomas Archbishop, set the white sail between the grey sky and the bitter sea, leave us, leave us for France.

SECOND PRIEST. What a way to talk at such a juncture!
You are foolish, immodest and babbling women.
Do you not know that the good Archbishop
Is likely to arrive at any moment?
The crowds in the streets will be cheering and cheering,
You go on croaking like frogs in the treetops:
But frogs at least can be cooked and eaten.
Whatever you are afraid of, in your craven apprehension,
Let me ask you at the least to put on pleasant faces,
And give a hearty welcome to our good Archbishop.
[*Enter* THOMAS.]

THOMAS. Peace. And let them be, in their exaltation.
They speak better than they know, and beyond your understanding.
They know and do not know, what it is to act or suffer.
They know and do not know, that action is suffering
And suffering is action. Neither does the agent suffer
Nor the patient act. But both are fixed
In an eternal action, an eternal patience
To which all must consent that it may be willed
And which all must suffer that they may will it,
That the pattern may subsist, for the pattern is the action
And the suffering, that the wheel may turn and still
Be forever still.

SECOND PRIEST. O my Lord, forgive me, I did not see you coming,
Engrossed by the chatter of these foolish women.
Forgive us, my Lord, you would have had a better welcome
If we had been sooner prepared for the event.

But your Lordship knows that seven years of waiting,
Seven years of prayer, seven years of emptiness,
Have better prepared our hearts for your coming,
Than seven days could make ready Canterbury.
However, I will have fires laid in all your rooms
To take the chill off our English December,
Your Lordship now being used to a better climate.
Your Lordship will find your rooms in order as you left them.

THOMAS. And will try to leave them in order as I find them.
I am more than grateful for all your kind attentions.
These are small matters. Little rest in Canterbury
With eager enemies restless about us.
Rebellious bishops, York, London, Salisbury,
Would have intercepted our letters,
Filled the coast with spies and sent to meet me
Some who hold me in bitterest hate.
By God's grace aware of their prevision
I sent my letters on another day,
Had fair crossing, found at Sandwich
Broc, Warenne, and the Sheriff of Kent,
Those who had sworn to have my head from me
Only John, the Dean of Salisbury,
Fearing for the King's name, warning against treason,
Made them hold their hands. So for the time
We are unmolested.

FIRST PRIEST.   But do they follow after?

THOMAS. For a little time the hungry hawk
Will only soar and hover, circling lower,
Waiting excuse, pretence, opportunity.
End will be simple, sudden, God-given.
Meanwhile the substance of our first act
Will be shadows, and the strife with shadows.
Heavier the interval than the consummation.
All things prepare the event. Watch.
[*Enter* FIRST TEMPTER.]

FIRST TEMPTER. You see, my Lord, I do not wait upon ceremony:
Here I have come, forgetting all acrimony,
Hoping that your present gravity
Will find excuse for my humble levity
Remembering all the good time past.
Your Lordship won't despise an old friend out of favour?
Old Tom, gay Tom, Becket of London,

Your Lordship won't forget that evening on
    the river
When the King, and you and I were all
    friends together?
Friendship should be more than biting Time
    can sever.
What, my Lord, now that you recover
Favour with the King, shall we say that sum-
    mer's over
Or that the good time cannot last?
Fluting in the meadows, viols in the hall,
Laughter and apple-blossom floating on the
    water,
Singing at nightfall, whispering in chambers,
Fires devouring the winter season,
Eating up the darkness, with wit and wine
    and wisdom!
Now that the King and you are in amity,
Clergy and laity may return to gaiety,
Mirth and sportfulness need not walk warily.

THOMAS. You talk of seasons that are past. I re-
    member
Not worth forgetting.

TEMPTER.   And of the new season.
Spring has come in winter. Snow in the
    branches
Shall float as sweet as blossoms. Ice along the
    ditches
Mirror the sunlight. Love in the orchard
Send the sap shooting. Mirth matches melan-
    choly.

THOMAS. We do not know very much of the future
Except that from generation to generation
The same things happen again and again.
Men learn little from others' experience.
But in the life of one man, never
The same time returns. Sever
The cord, shed the scale. Only
The fool, fixed in his folly, may think
He can turn the wheel on which he turns.

TEMPTER. My Lord, a nod is as good as a wink.
A man will often love what he spurns.
For the good times past, that are come again
I am your man.

THOMAS.   Not in this train
Look to your behaviour. You were safer
Think of penitence and follow your master.

TEMPTER. Not at this gait!
If you go so fast, others may go faster.
Your Lordship is too proud!
The safest beast is not the one that roars most
    loud,
This was not the way of the King our master!
You were not used to be so hard upon sinners
When they were your friends. Be easy, man!
The easy man lives to eat the best dinners.
Take a friend's advice. Leave well alone,

Or your goose may be cooked and eaten to the
    bone.

THOMAS. You come twenty years too late.

TEMPTER. Then I leave you to your fate.
I leave you to the pleasures of your higher
    vices,
Which will have to be paid for at higher prices.
Farewell, my Lord, I do not wait upon cere-
    mony,
I leave as I came, forgetting all acrimony,
Hoping that your present gravity
Will find excuse for my humble levity.
If you will remember me, my Lord, at your
    prayers,
I'll remember you at kissing-time below the
    stairs.

THOMAS. Leave-well-alone, the springtime fancy,
So one thought goes whistling down the wind.
The impossible is still temptation.
The impossible, the undesirable,
Voices under sleep, waking a dead world,
So that the mind may not be whole in the
    present.

[*Enter* SECOND TEMPTER.]

SECOND TEMPTER. Your Lordship has forgotten me,
    perhaps. I will remind you.
We met at Clarendon, at Northampton,
And last at Montmirail, in Maine. Now that
I have recalled them,
Let us but set these not too pleasant memories
In balance against other, earlier
And weightier ones: those of the Chancellor-
    ship.
See how the late ones rise! You, master of
    policy
Whom all acknowledged, should guide the
    state again.

THOMAS. Your meaning?

TEMPTER.   The Chancellorship that
    you resigned
When you were made Archbishop — that was
    a mistake
On your part — still may be regained. Think,
    my Lord,
Power obtained grows to glory,
Life lasting, a permanent possession.
A templed tomb, monument of marble.
Rule over men reckon no madness.

THOMAS. To the man of God what gladness?

TEMPTER.   Sadness
Only to those giving love to God alone.
Shall he who held the solid substance
Wander waking with deceitful shadows?
Power is present. Holiness hereafter.

THOMAS. Who then?

TEMPTER.   The Chancellor. King and
    Chancellor.

King commands. Chancellor richly rules.
This is a sentence not taught in the schools.
To set down the great, protect the poor,
Beneath the throne of God can man do more?
Disarm the ruffian, strengthen the laws,
Rule for the good of the better cause,
Dispensing justice make all even,
Is thrive on earth, and perhaps in heaven.

THOMAS. What means?

TEMPTER.   Real power
Is purchased at price of a certain submission.
Your spiritual power is earthly perdition.
Power is present, for him who will wield.

THOMAS. Who shall have it?

TEMPTER.   He who will come.

THOMAS. What shall be the month?

TEMPTER.   The last from
the first.

THOMAS. What shall we give for it?

TEMPTER.   Pretence of
priestly power.

THOMAS. Why should we give it?

TEMPTER.   For the power and
the glory.

THOMAS. No!

TEMPTER.   Yes! Or bravery will be broken,
Cabined in Canterbury, realmless ruler,
Self-bound servant of a powerless Pope,
The old stag, circled with hounds.

THOMAS. No!

TEMPTER.   Yes! men must manœuvre. Monarchs
also,
Waging war abroad, need fast friends at home.
Private policy is public profit;
Dignity still shall be dressed with decorum.

THOMAS. You forget the bishops
Whom I have laid under excommunication.

TEMPTER. Hungry hatred
Will not strive against intelligent self-interest.

THOMAS. You forget the barons. Who will not forget
Constant curbing of petty privilege.

TEMPTER. Against the barons
Is King's cause, churl's cause, Chancellor's
cause.

THOMAS. No! shall I, who keep the keys
Of heaven and hell, supreme alone in England,
Who bind and loose, with power from the
Pope,
Descend to desire a punier power?
Delegate to deal the doom of damnation,
To condemn kings, not serve among their
servants,
Is my open office. No! Go.

TEMPTER. Then I leave you to your fate.
Your sin soars sunward, covering kings' fal-
cons.

THOMAS. Temporal power, to build a good world,
To keep order, as the world knows order.
Those who put their faith in worldly order
Not controlled by the order of God,
In confident ignorance, but arrest disorder,
Make it fast, breed fatal disease,
Degrade what they exalt. Power with the
King —
I *was* the King, his arm, his better reason.
But what was once exaltation
Would now be only mean descent.
[*Enter* THIRD TEMPTER.]

THIRD TEMPTER. I am an unexpected visitor.

THOMAS.   I expected you.

TEMPTER. But not in this guise, or for my present
purpose.

THOMAS. No purpose brings surprise.

TEMPTER.   Well, my
Lord,
I am no trifler, and no politician.
To idle or intrigue at court
I have no skill. I am no courtier.
I know a horse, a dog, a wench;
I know how to hold my estates in order,
A country-keeping lord who minds his own
business.
It is we country lords who know the country
And we who know what the country needs.
It is our country. We care for the country.
We are the backbone of the nation.
We, not the plotting parasites
About the King. Excuse my bluntness:
I am a rough straightforward Englishman.

THOMAS. Proceed straight forward.

TEMPTER.   Purpose is plain.
Endurance of friendship does not depend
Upon ourselves, but upon circumstance.
But circumstance is not undetermined.
Unreal friendship may turn to real
But real friendship, once ended, cannot be
mended.
Sooner shall enmity turn to alliance.
The enmity that never knew friendship
Can sooner know accord.

THOMAS.   For a countryman
You wrap your meaning in as dark generality
As any courtier.

TEMPTER.   This is the simple fact!
You have no hope of reconciliation
With Henry the King. You look only
To blind assertion in isolation.
That is a mistake.

THOMAS.   O Henry, O my King!

TEMPTER.   Other
friends
May be found in the present situation.

King in England is not all-powerful;
King is in France, squabbling in Anjou;
Round him waiting hungry sons.
We are for England. We are in England.
You and I, my Lord, are Normans.
England is a land for Norman
Sovereignty. Let the Angevin
Destroy himself, fighting in Anjou.
He does not understand us, the English barons.
We are the people.

THOMAS. To what does this lead?

TEMPTER.   To a happy co-
alition
Of intelligent interests.

THOMAS.   But what have you —
If you do speak for barons —

TEMPTER.   For a powerful
party
Which has turned its eyes in your direction —
To gain from you, your Lordship asks.
For us, Church favour would be an advantage,
Blessing of Pope powerful protection
In the fight for liberty. You, my Lord,
In being with us, would fight a good stroke
At once, for England and for Rome,
Ending the tyrannous jurisdiction
Of king's court over bishop's court,
Of king's court over baron's court.

THOMAS. Which I helped to found.

TEMPTER.   Which you helped
to found.
But time past is time forgotten.
We expect the rise of a new constellation.

THOMAS. And if the Archbishop cannot trust the
King,
How can he trust those who work for King's
undoing?

TEMPTER. Kings will allow no power but their own;
Church and people have good cause against
the throne.

THOMAS. If the Archbishop cannot trust the Throne,
He has good cause to trust none but God alone.
I ruled once as Chancellor
And men like you were glad to wait at my
door.
Not only in the court, but in the field
And in the tilt-yard I made many yield.
Shall I who ruled like an eagle over doves
Now take the shape of a wolf among wolves?
Pursue your treacheries as you have done be-
fore:
No one shall say that I betrayed a king.

TEMPTER. Then, my Lord, I shall not wait at your
door.
And I well hope, before another spring
The King will show his regard for your loyalty.

THOMAS. To make, then break, this thought has
come before,
The desperate exercise of failing power.
Samson in Gaza did no more.
But if I break, I must break myself alone.
[*Enter* FOURTH TEMPTER.]

FOURTH TEMPTER. Well done, Thomas, your will is
hard to bend.
And with me beside you, you shall not lack a
friend.

THOMAS. Who are you? I expected
Three visitors, not four.

TEMPTER. Do not be surprised to receive one more.
Had I been expected, I had been here before.
I always precede expectation.

THOMAS.   Who are you?

TEMPTER. As you do not know me, I do not need a
name,
And, as you know me, that is why I come.
You know me, but have never seen my face.
To meet before was never time or place.

THOMAS. Say what you come to say.

TEMPTER.   It shall be said
at last.
Hooks have been baited with morsels of the
past.
Wantonness is weakness. As for the King,
His hardened hatred shall have no end.
You know truly, the King will never trust
Twice, the man who has been his friend.
Borrow use cautiously, employ
Your services as long as you have to lend.
You would wait for trap to snap
Having served your turn, broken and crushed.
As for barons, envy of lesser men
Is still more stubborn than king's anger.
Kings have public policy, barons private profit,
Jealousy raging possession of the fiend.
Barons are employable against each other;
Greater enemies must kings destroy.

THOMAS. What is your counsel?

TEMPTER.   Fare forward to
the end.
All other ways are closed to you
Except the way already chosen.
But what is pleasure, kingly rule,
Or rule of men beneath a king,
With craft in corners, stealthy stratagem,
To general grasp of spiritual power?
Man oppressed by sin, since Adam fell —
You hold the keys of heaven and hell.
Power to bind and loose: bind, Thomas, bind,
King and bishop under your heel.
King, emperor, bishop, baron, king:
Uncertain mastery of melting armies,
War, plague, and revolution,
New conspiracies, broken pacts;

To be master or servant within an hour,
This is the course of temporal power.
The Old King shall know it, when at last breath,
No sons, no empire, he bites broken teeth.
You hold the skein: wind, Thomas, wind
The thread of eternal life and death.
You hold this power, hold it.
THOMAS.   Supreme, in this land?
TEMPTER. Supreme, but for one.
THOMAS.   That I do not understand.
TEMPTER. It is not for me to tell you how this may be so;
    I am only here, Thomas, to tell you what you know.
THOMAS. How long shall this be?
TEMPTER. Save what you know already, ask nothing of me.
    But think, Thomas, think of glory after death.
    When king is dead, there's another king,
    And one more king is another reign.
    King is forgotten, when another shall come:
    Saint and Martyr rule from the tomb.
    Think, Thomas, think of enemies dismayed,
    Creeping in penance, frightened of a shade;
    Think of pilgrims, standing in line
    Before the glittering jewelled shrine,
    From generation to generation
    Bending the knee in supplication,
    Think of the miracles, by God's grace,
    And think of your enemies, in another place.
THOMAS. I have thought of these things.
TEMPTER.   That is why I tell you.
    Your thoughts have more power than kings to compel you.
    You have also thought, sometimes at your prayers,
    Sometimes hesitating at the angles of stairs,
    And between sleep and waking, early in the morning,
    When the bird cries, have thought of further scorning.
    That nothing lasts, but the wheel turns,
    The nest is rifled, and the bird mourns;
    That the shrine shall be pillaged, and the gold spent,
    The jewels gone for light ladies' ornament,
    The sanctuary broken, and its stores
    Swept into the laps of parasites and whores.
    When miracles cease, and the faithful desert you.
    And men shall only do their best to forget you.
    And later is worse, when men will not hate you
    Enough to defame or to execrate you,

But pondering the qualities that you lacked
Will only try to find the historical fact.
When men shall declare that there was no mystery
About this man who played a certain part in history.
THOMAS. But what is there to do? What is left to be done?
    Is there no enduring crown to be won?
TEMPTER. Yes, Thomas, yes; you have thought of that too.
    What can compare with glory of Saints
    Dwelling forever in presence of God?
    What earthly glory, of king or emperor,
    What earthly pride, that is not poverty
    Compared with richness of heavenly grandeur?
    Seek the way of martyrdom, make yourself the lowest
    On earth, to be high in heaven.
    And see far off below you, where the gulf is fixed,
    Your persecutors, in timeless torment,
    Parched passion, beyond expiation.
THOMAS.   No!
    Who are you, tempting with my own desires?
    Others have come, temporal tempters,
    With pleasure and power at palpable price.
    What do you offer? What do you ask?
TEMPTER. I offer what you desire. I ask
    What you have to give. Is it too much
    For such a vision of eternal grandeur?
THOMAS. Others offered real goods, worthless
    But real. You only offer
    Dreams to damnation.
TEMPTER.   You have often dreamt them.
THOMAS. Is there no way, in my soul's sickness,
    Does not lead to damnation in pride?
    I well know that these temptations
    Mean present vanity and future torment.
    Can sinful pride be driven out
    Only by more sinful? Can I neither act nor suffer
    Without perdition?
TEMPTER. You know and do not know, what it is to act or suffer.
    You know and do not know, that action is suffering,
    And suffering action. Neither does the agent suffer
    Nor the patient act. But both are fixed
    In an eternal action, an eternal patience
    To which all must consent that it may be willed
    And which all must suffer that they may will it,
    That the pattern may subsist, that the wheel may turn and still

Be forever still.

CHORUS. There is no rest in the house. There is no
 rest in the street.
I hear restless movement of feet. And the air
 is heavy and thick.
Thick and heavy the sky. And the earth presses
 up against our feet.
What is the sickly smell, the vapour? The dark
 green light from a cloud on a withered tree?
The earth is heaving to parturition of issue
 of hell. What is the sticky dew that forms
 on the back of my hand?

THE FOUR TEMPTERS. Man's life is a cheat and a dis-
 appointment;
All things are unreal,
Unreal or disappointing:
The Catherine wheel, the pantomime cat,
The prizes given at the children's party,
The prize awarded for the English Essay,
The scholar's degree, the statesman's decora-
 tion.
All things become less real, man passes
From unreality to unreality.
This man is obstinate, blind, intent
On self-destruction.
Passing from deception to deception,
From grandeur to grandeur to final illusion,
Lost in the wonder of his own greatness,
The enemy of society, enemy of himself.

THE THREE PRIESTS. O Thomas my Lord do not
 fight the intractable tide,
Do not sail the irresistible wind; in the storm,
Should we not wait for the sea to subside, in
 the night
Abide the coming of day, when the traveller
 may find his way,
The sailor lay course by the sun?

[CHORUS, PRIESTS and TEMPTERS *alternately*.]

C. Is it the owl that calls, or a signal between the
 trees?
P. Is the window-bar made fast, is the door under
 lock and bolt?
T. Is it rain that taps at the window, is it wind that
 pokes at the door?
C. Does the torch flame in the hall, the candle in
 the room?
P. Does the watchman walk by the wall?
T. Does the mastiff prowl by the gate?
C. Death has a hundred hands and walks by a
 thousand ways.
P. He may come in the sight of all, he may pass un-
 seen unheard.
T. Come whispering through the ear, or a sudden
 shock on the skull.
C. A man may walk with a lamp at night, and yet
 be downed in a ditch.
P. A man may climb the stair in the day, and slip
 on a broken step.

T. A man may sit at meat, and feel the cold in his
 groin.

CHORUS. We have not been happy, my Lord, we
 have not been too happy.
We are not ignorant women, we know what
 we must expect and not expect.
We know of oppression and torture,
We know of extortion and violence,
Destitution, disease,
The old without fire in winter,
The child without milk in summer,
Our labour taken away from us,
Our sins made heavier upon us.
We have seen the young man mutilated,
The torn girl trembling by the mill-stream.
And meanwhile we have gone on living,
Living and partly living,
Picking together the pieces,
Gathering faggots at nightfall,
Building a partial shelter,
For sleeping, and eating and drinking and
 laughter.

God gave us always some reason, some hope;
 but now a new terror has soiled us, which
 none can avert, none can avoid, flowing
 under our feet and over the sky;
Under doors and down chimneys, flowing in
 at the ear and the mouth and the eye.
God is leaving us, God is leaving us, more
 pang, more pain than birth or death.
Sweet and cloying through the dark air
Falls the stifling scent of despair;
The forms take shape in the dark air:
Puss-purr of leopard, footfall of padding bear,
Palm-pat of nodding ape, square hyaena wait-
 ing
For laughter, laughter, laughter. The Lords
 of Hell are here.
They curl round you, lie at your feet, swing
 and wing through the dark air.
O Thomas Archbishop, save us, save us, save
 yourself that we may be saved;
Destroy yourself and we are destroyed.

THOMAS. Now is my way clear, now is the meaning
 plain:
Temptation shall not come in this kind again.
The last temptation is the greatest treason:
To do the right deed for the wrong reason.
The natural vigour in the venial sin
Is the way in which our lives begin.
Thirty years ago, I searched all the ways
That lead to pleasure, advancement and praise.
Delight in sense, in learning and in thought,
Music and philosophy, curiosity,
The purple bullfinch in the lilac tree,
The tilt-yard skill, the strategy of chess,
Love in the garden, singing to the instrument,

Were all things equally desirable.
Ambition comes when early force is spent
And when we find no longer all things possible.
Ambition comes behind and unobservable.
Sin grows with doing good. When I imposed
  the King's law
In England, and waged war with him against
  Toulouse,
I beat the barons at their own game. I
Could then despise the men who thought me
  most contemptible,
The raw nobility, whose manners matched
  their fingernails.
While I ate out of the King's dish
To become servant of God was never my wish.
Servant of God has chance of greater sin
And sorrow, than the man who serves a king.
For those who serve the greater cause may
  make the cause serve them,
Still doing right: and striving with political
  men
May make that cause political, not by what
  they do
But by what they are. I know
What yet remains to show you of my history
Will seem to most of you at best futility,
Senseless self-slaughter of a lunatic,
Arrogant passion of a fanatic.
I know that history at all times draws
The strangest consequence from remotest
  cause.
But for every evil, every sacrilege,
Crime, wrong, oppression and the axe's edge,
Indifference, exploitation, you, and you,
And you, must all be punished. So must you.
I shall no longer act or suffer, to the sword's
  end.
Now my good Angel, whom God appoints
To be my guardian, hover over the swords'
  points.

Interlude

THE ARCHBISHOP *preaches in the Cathedral
on Christmas Morning, 1170*

'Glory to God in the highest, and on earth peace to
men of good will.' *The fourteenth verse of the second
chapter of the Gospel according to Saint Luke*. In the
Name of the Father, and of the Son, and of the Holy
Ghost. Amen.

Dear children of God, my sermon this Christmas
morning will be a very short one. I wish only that
you should meditate in your hearts the deep mean-

ing and mystery of our masses of Christmas Day.
For whenever Mass is said, we re-enact the Passion
and Death of Our Lord; and on this Christmas
Day we do this in celebration of His Birth. So that
at the same moment we rejoice in His coming for
the salvation of men, and offer again to God His
Body and Blood in sacrifice, oblation and satisfaction for the sins of the whole world. It was in this
same night that has just passed, that a multitude
of the heavenly host appeared before the shepherds
at Bethlehem, saying 'Glory to God in the highest,
and on earth peace to men of good will'; at this
same time of all the year that we celebrate at once
the Birth of Our Lord and His Passion and Death
upon the Cross. Beloved, as the World sees, this is
to behave in a strange fashion. For who in the
World will both mourn and rejoice at once and
for the same reason? For either joy will be over-
borne by mourning, or mourning will be cast out
by joy; so it is only in these our Christian mysteries
that we can rejoice and mourn at once for the same
reason. Now think for a moment about the meaning of this word 'peace.' Does it seem strange to
you that the angels should have announced Peace,
when ceaselessly the world has been stricken with
War and the fear of War? Does it seem to you
that the angelic voices were mistaken, and that
the promise was a disappointment and a cheat?

Reflect now, how Our Lord Himself spoke of
Peace. He said to His disciples, 'My peace I leave
with you, my peace I give unto you.' Did He mean
peace as we think of it: the kingdom of England
at peace with its neighbours, the barons at peace
with the King, the householder counting over his
peaceful gains, the swept hearth, his best wine for
a friend at the table, his wife singing to the children? Those men His disciples knew no such
things: they went forth to journey afar, to suffer
by land and sea, to know torture, imprisonment,
disappointment, to suffer death by martyrdom.
What then did He mean? If you ask that, remember then that He said also, 'Not as the world gives,
give I unto you.' So then, He gave to His disciples
peace, but not peace as the world gives.

Consider also one thing of which you have probably never thought. Not only do we at the feast of
Christmas celebrate at once Our Lord's Birth and
His Death: but on the next day we celebrate the
martyrdom of His first martyr, the blessed Stephen.
Is it an accident, do you think, that the day of the
first martyr follows immediately the day of the
Birth of Christ? By no means. Just as we rejoice
and mourn at once, in the Birth and in the Passion
of Our Lord; so also, in a smaller figure, we both
rejoice and mourn in the death of martyrs. We
mourn, for the sins of the world that has martyred
them; we rejoice, that another soul is numbered

among the Saints in Heaven, for the glory of God and for the salvation of men.

Beloved, we do not think of a martyr simply as a good Christian who has been killed because he is a Christian: for that would be solely to mourn. We do not think of him simply as a good Christian who has been elevated to the company of the Saints: for that would be simply to rejoice: and neither our mourning nor our rejoicing is as the world's is. A Christian martyrdom is never an accident, for Saints are not made by accident. Still less is a Christian martyrdom the effect of a man's will to become a Saint, as a man by willing and contriving may become a ruler of men. A martyrdom is always the design of God, for His love of men, to warn them and to lead them, to bring them back to His ways. It is never the design of man; for the true martyr is he who has become the instrument of God, who has lost his will in the will of God, and who no longer desires anything for him-self, not even the glory of being a martyr. So thus as on earth the Church mourns and rejoices at once, in a fashion that the world cannot understand; so in Heaven the Saints are most high, having made themselves most low, and are seen, not as we see them, but in the light of the Godhead from which they draw their being.

I have spoken to you to-day, dear children of God, of the martyrs of the past, asking you to remember especially our martyr of Canterbury, the blessed Archbishop Elphege; because it is fitting, on Christ's birth day, to remember what is that Peace which He brought; and because, dear children, I do not think I shall ever preach to you again; and because it is possible that in a short time you may have yet another martyr, and that one perhaps not the last. I would have you keep in your hearts these words that I say, and think of them at another time. In the Name of the Father, and of the Son, and of the Holy Ghost. Amen.

CHARACTERS

THREE PRIESTS
FOUR KNIGHTS

ARCHBISHOP THOMAS BECKET
CHORUS OF WOMEN OF CANTERBURY
ATTENDANTS

Part II

The first scene is in the Archbishop's Hall, the second scene is in the Cathedral, on December 29th, 1170

CHORUS. Does the bird sing in the South?
Only the sea-bird cries, driven inland by the storm.
What sign of the spring of the year?
Only the death of the old: not a stir, not a shoot, not a breath.
Do the days begin to lengthen?
Longer and darker the day, shorter and colder the night.
Still and stifling the air: but a wind is stored up in the East.
The starved crow sits in the field, attentive; and in the wood
The owl rehearses the hollow note of death.
What signs of a bitter spring?
The wind stored up in the East.
What, at the time of the birth of Our Lord, at Christmastide,
Is there not peace upon earth, goodwill among men?

The peace of this world is always uncertain, unless men keep the peace of God.
And war among men defiles this world, but death in the Lord renews it,
And the world must be cleaned in the winter, or we shall have only
A sour spring, a parched summer, an empty harvest.
Between Christmas and Easter what work shall be done?
The ploughman shall go out in March and turn the same earth
He has turned before, the bird shall sing the same song.
When the leaf is out on the tree, when the elder and may
Burst over the stream, and the air is clear and high,
And voices trill at windows, and children tumble in front of the door,
What work shall have been done, what wrong
Shall the bird's song cover, the green tree cover, what wrong
Shall the fresh earth cover? We wait, and the time is short
But waiting is long.
[*Enter the* FIRST PRIEST *with a banner of St. Stephen*

borne before him. The lines sung are in italics.]

FIRST PRIEST. Since Christmas a day: and the day of St. Stephen, First Martyr.

Princes moreover did sit, and did witness falsely against me.

A day that was always most dear to the Archbishop Thomas.

And he kneeled down and cried with a loud voice:

Lord, lay not this sin to their charge.

Princes moreover did sit.

[*Introit of St. Stephen is heard.*]

[*Enter the* SECOND PRIEST, *with a banner of St. John the Apostle borne before him.*]

SECOND PRIEST. Since St. Stephen a day: and the day of St. John the Apostle.

In the midst of the congregation he opened his mouth.

That which was from the beginning, which we have heard,

Which we have seen with our eyes, and our hands have handled

Of the word of life; that which we have seen and heard

Declare we unto you.

In the midst of the congregation.

[*Introit of St. John is heard.*]

[*Enter the* THIRD PRIEST, *with a banner of the Holy Innocents borne before him.*]

THIRD PRIEST. Since St. John the Apostle a day: and the day of the Holy Innocents.

Out of the mouth of very babes, O God.

As the voice of many waters, of thunder, of harps,

They sung as it were a new song.

The blood of thy saints have they shed like water,

And there was no man to bury them. Avenge, O Lord,

The blood of thy saints. In Rama, a voice heard, weeping.

Out of the mouth of very babes, O God!

[THE PRIESTS *stand together with the banners behind them.*]

FIRST PRIEST. Since the Holy Innocents a day: the fourth day from Christmas.

THE THREE PRIESTS. *Rejoice we all, keeping holy day.*

FIRST PRIEST. As for the people, so also for himself, he offereth for sins.

He lays down his life for the sheep.

THE THREE PRIESTS. *Rejoice we all, keeping holy day.*

FIRST PRIEST.   To-day?

SECOND PRIEST. To-day, what is to-day? For the day is half gone.

FIRST PRIEST. To-day, what is to-day? But another day, the dusk of the year.

SECOND PRIEST. To-day, what is to-day? Another night, and another dawn.

THIRD PRIEST. What day is the day that we know that we hope for or fear for?

Every day is the day we should fear from or hope from. One moment

Weighs like another. Only in retrospection, selection,

We say, that was the day. The critical moment

That is always now, and here. Even now, in sordid particulars

The eternal design may appear.

[*Enter the* FOUR KNIGHTS. *The banners disappear.*]

FIRST KNIGHT. Servants of the King.

FIRST PRIEST.   And known to us.

You are welcome. Have you ridden far?

FIRST KNIGHT. Not far to-day, but matters urgent

Have brought us from France. We rode hard,

Took ship yesterday, landed last night,

Having business with the Archbishop.

SECOND KNIGHT. Urgent business.

THIRD KNIGHT.   From the King.

SECOND KNIGHT. By the King's order.

FIRST KNIGHT.   Our men are outside.

FIRST PRIEST. You know the Archbishop's hospitality.

We are about to go to dinner.

The good Archbishop would be vexed

If we did not offer you entertainment

Before your business. Please dine with us.

Your men shall be looked after also.

Dinner before business. Do you like roast pork?

FIRST KNIGHT. Business before dinner. We will roast your pork

First, and dine upon it after.

SECOND KNIGHT. We must see the Archbishop.

THIRD KNIGHT.   Go,

tell the Archbishop

We have no need of his hospitality.

We will find our own dinner.

FIRST PRIEST [*to attendant*]. Go, tell His Lordship.

FOURTH KNIGHT. How much longer will you keep us waiting?

[*Enter* THOMAS.]

THOMAS [*to* PRIESTS]. However certain our expectation

The moment foreseen may be unexpected

When it arrives. It comes when we are

Engrossed with matters of other urgency.

On my table you will find

The papers in order, and the documents signed.

[*To* KNIGHTS.]

You are welcome, whatever your business may
    be.
You say, from the King?
FIRST KNIGHT.   Most surely from the
    King.
We must speak with you alone.
THOMAS [to PRIESTS].   Leave us then
    alone.
Now what is the matter?
FIRST KNIGHT.   This is the matter.
THE THREE KNIGHTS. You are the Archbishop in re-
    volt against the King; in rebellion to the
    King and the law of the land;
You are the Archbishop who was made by the
    King; whom he set in your place to carry
    out his command.
You are his servant, his tool, and his jack,
You wore his favours on your back,
You had your honours all from his hand;
    from him you had the power, the seal and
    the ring.
This is the man who was the tradesman's
    son: the backstairs brat who was born in
    Cheapside;
This is the creature that crawled upon the
    King; swollen with blood and swollen with
    pride.
Creeping out of the London dirt,
Crawling up like a louse on your shirt,
The man who cheated, swindled, lied; broke
    his oath and betrayed his King.
THOMAS. This is not true.
Both before and after I received the ring
I have been a loyal subject to the King.
Saving my order, I am at his command,
As his most faithful vassal in the land.
FIRST KNIGHT. Saving your order! let your order
    save you —
As I do not think it is like to do.
Saving your ambition is what you mean,
Saving your pride, envy and spleen.
SECOND KNIGHT. Saving your insolence and greed.
Won't you ask us to pray to God for you, in
    your need?
THIRD KNIGHT. Yes, we'll pray for you!
FIRST KNIGHT.   Yes, we'll
    pray for you!
THE THREE KNIGHTS. Yes, we'll pray that God may
    help you!
THOMAS. But, gentlemen, your business
Which you said so urgent, is it only
Scolding and blaspheming?
FIRST KNIGHT.   That was only
Our indignation, as loyal subjects.
THOMAS. Loyal? To whom?
FIRST KNIGHT.   To the King!
SECOND KNIGHT.   The King!

THIRD KNIGHT. The King!
THE THREE KNIGHTS.   God bless him!
THOMAS. Then let your new coat of loyalty be worn
Carefully, so it get not soiled or torn.
Have you something to say?
FIRST KNIGHT.   By the King's
    command.
Shall we say it now?
SECOND KNIGHT.   Without delay,
Before the old fox is off and away.
THOMAS.   What you
    have to say
By the King's command — if it be the King's
    command —
Should be said in public. If you make charges,
Then in public I will refute them.
FIRST KNIGHT.   No! here
    and now!
[They make to attack him, but the priests and
    attendants return and quietly interpose them-
    selves.]
THOMAS. Now and here!
FIRST KNIGHT. Of your earlier misdeeds I shall
    make no mention.
They are too well known. But after dissension
Had ended, in France, and you were endued
With your former privilege, how did you
    show your gratitude?
You had fled from England, not exiled
Or threatened, mind you; but in the hope
Of stirring up trouble in the French dominions.
You sowed strife aboard, you reviled
The King to the King of France, to the Pope,
Raising up against him false opinions.
SECOND KNIGHT. Yet the King, out of his charity,
And urged by your friends, offered clemency,
Made a pact of peace, and all dispute ended
Sent you back to your See as you demanded.
THIRD KNIGHT. And burying the memory of your
    transgressions
Restored your honours and your possessions.
All was granted for which you sued:
Yet how, I repeat, did you show your grat-
    itude?
FIRST KNIGHT. Suspending those who had crowned
    the young prince,
Denying the legality of his coronation.
SECOND KNIGHT. Binding with the chains of ana-
    thema.
THIRD KNIGHT. Using every means in your power to
    evince
The King's faithful servants, every one who
    transacts
His business in his absence, the business of the
    nation.
FIRST KNIGHT. These are the facts.
Say therefore if you will be content

To answer in the King's presence. Therefore
    were we sent.

THOMAS. Never was it my wish
    To uncrown the King's son, or to diminish
    His honour and power. Why should he wish
    To deprive my people of me and keep me
    from my own
    And bid me sit in Canterbury, alone?
    I would wish him three crowns rather than
    one,
    And as for the bishops, it is not my yoke
    That is laid upon them, or mine to revoke.
    Let them go to the Pope. It was he who con-
    demned them.

FIRST KNIGHT. Through you they were suspended.

SECOND KNIGHT.   By
    you be this amended.

THIRD KNIGHT. Absolve them.

FIRST KNIGHT.   Absolve them.

THOMAS.   I do not
    deny
    That this was done through me. But it is
    not I
    Who can loose whom the Pope has bound.
    Let them go to him, upon whom redounds
    Their contempt towards me, their contempt
    towards the Church shown.

FIRST KNIGHT. Be that as it may, here is the King's
    command:
    That you and your servants depart from this
    land.

THOMAS. If that *is* the King's command, I will be
    bold
    To say: seven years were my people without
    My presence; seven years of misery and pain.
    Seven years a mendicant on foreign charity
    I lingered abroad: seven years is no brevity.
    I shall not get those seven years back again.
    Never again, you must make no doubt,
    Shall the sea run between the shepherd and his
    fold.

FIRST KNIGHT. The King's justice, the King's maj-
    esty,
    You insult with gross indignity;
    Insolent madman, whom nothing deters
    From attaining his servants and ministers.

THOMAS. It is not I who insult the King,
    And there is higher than I or the King.
    It is not I, Becket from Cheapside,
    It is not against me, Becket, that you strive.
    It is not Becket who pronounces doom,
    But the Law of Christ's Church, the judge-
    ment of Rome.

FIRST KNIGHT. Priest, you have spoken in peril of
    your life.

SECOND KNIGHT. Priest, you have spoken in danger
    of the knife.

THIRD KNIGHT. Priest, you have spoken treachery
    and treason.

THE THREE KNIGHTS. Priest! traitor, confirmed in
    malfeasance.

THOMAS. I submit my cause to the judgement of
    Rome.
    But if you kill me, I shall rise from my tomb
    To submit my cause before God's throne.
    [*Exit.*]

FOURTH KNIGHT. Priest! monk! and servant! take,
    hold, detain,
    Restrain this man, in the King's name.

FIRST KNIGHT. Or answer with your bodies.

SECOND KNIGHT.   Enough
    of words.

THE FOUR KNIGHTS. We come for the King's justice,
    we come with swords. [*Exeunt.*]

CHORUS. I have smelt them, the death-bringers,
    senses are quickened
    By subtile forebodings; I have heard
    Fluting in the night-time, fluting and owls,
    have seen at noon
    Scaly wings slanting over, huge and ridiculous.
    I have tasted
    The savour of putrid flesh in the spoon. I
    have felt
    The heaving of earth at nightfall, restless, ab-
    surd. I have heard
    Laughter in the noises of beasts that make
    strange noises: jackal, jackass, jackdaw; the
    scurrying noise of mouse and jerboa; the
    laugh of the loon, the lunatic bird. I have
    seen
    Grey necks twisting, rat tails twining, in the
    thick light of dawn. I have eaten
    Smooth creatures still living, with the strong
    salt taste of living things under sea; I have
    tasted
    The living lobster, the crab, the oyster, the
    whelk and the prawn; and they live and
    spawn in my bowels, and my bowels dissolve
    in the light of dawn. I have smelt
    Death in the rose, death in the hollyhock,
    sweet pea, hyacinth, primrose and cowslip.
    I have seen
    Trunk and horn, tusk and hoof, in odd places;
    I have lain on the floor of the sea and breathed
    with the breathing of the sea-anemone,
    swallowed with ingurgitation of the sponge.
    I have lain in the soil and criticised the
    worm. In the air
    Flirted with the passage of the kite, I have
    plunged with the kite and cowered with
    the wren. I have felt
    The horn of the beetle, the scale of the viper,
    the mobile hard insensitive skin of the ele-

phant, the evasive flank of the fish. I have smelt

Corruption in the dish, incense in the latrine, the sewer in the incense, the smell of sweet soap in the wood path, a hellish sweet scent in the woodpath, while the ground heaved. I have seen

Rings of light coiling downwards, descending

To the horror of the ape. Have I not known, not known

What was coming to be? It was here, in the kitchen, in the passage,

In the mews in the barn in the byre in the market-place

In our veins our bowels our skulls as well

As well as in the plottings of potentates

As well as in the consultations of powers.

What is woven on the loom of fate

What is woven in the councils of princes

Is woven also in our veins, our brains,

Is woven like a pattern of living worms

In the guts of the women of Canterbury.

I have smelt them, the death-bringers; now is too late

For action, too soon for contrition.

Nothing is possible but the shamed swoon

Of those consenting to the last humiliation.

I have consented, Lord Archbishop, have consented.

Am torn away, subdued, violated,

United to the spiritual flesh of nature,

Mastered by the animal powers of spirit,

Dominated by the lust of self-demolition,

By the final utter uttermost death of spirit,

By the final ecstasy of waste and shame,

O Lord Archbishop, O Thomas Archbishop, forgive us, forgive us, pray for us that we may pray for you, out of our shame.

[Enter THOMAS.]

THOMAS. Peace, and be at peace with your thoughts and visions.

These things had to come to you and you to accept them.

This is your share of the eternal burden,

The perpetual glory. This is one moment,

But know that another

Shall pierce you with a sudden painful joy

When the figure of God's purpose is made complete.

You shall forget these things, toiling in the household,

You shall remember them, droning by the fire,

When age and forgetfulness sweeten memory

Only like a dream that has often been told

And often been changed in the telling. They will seem unreal.

Human kind cannot bear very much reality.

[Enter PRIESTS.]

PRIESTS [severally]. My Lord, you must not stop here. To the minster.

Through the cloister. No time to waste. They are coming back, armed. To the altar, to the altar.

THOMAS. All my life they have been coming, these feet. All my life

I have waited. Death will come only when I am worthy,

And if I am worthy, there is no danger.

I have therefore only to make perfect my will.

PRIESTS. My Lord, they are coming. They will break through presently.

You will be killed. Come to the altar.

Make haste, my Lord. Don't stop here talking. It is not right.

What shall become of us, my Lord, if you are killed; what shall become of us?

THOMAS. Peace! be quiet! remember where you are, and what is happening;

No life here is sought for but mine,

And I am not in danger: only near to death.

PRIESTS. My Lord, to vespers. You must not be absent from vespers. You must not be absent from the divine office. To vespers. Into the cathedral!

THOMAS. Go to vespers, remember me at your prayers.

They shall find the shepherd here; the flock shall be spared.

I have had a tremour of bliss, a wink of heaven, a whisper,

And I would no longer be denied; all things Proceed to a joyful consummation.

PRIESTS. Seize him! force him! drag him!

THOMAS. Keep your hands off!

PRIESTS. To vespers! Hurry.

[They drag him off. While the CHORUS speak, the scene is changed to the cathedral.]

CHORUS [While a Dies Iræ is sung in Latin by a choir in the distance].

Numb the hand and dry the eyelid,

Still the horror, but more horror

Than when tearing in the belly.

Still the horror, but more horror

Than when twisting in the fingers,

Than when splitting in the skull.

More than footfall in the passage,

More than shadow in the doorway,

More than fury in the hall.

The agents of hell disappear, the human, they shrink and dissolve

Into dust on the wind, forgotten, unmemo-
rable; only is here
The white flat face of Death, God's silent
servant,
And behind the face of Death the Judgement
And behind the Judgement the Void, more
horrid than active shapes of hell;
Emptiness, absence, separation from God;
The horror of the effortless journey, to the
empty land
Which is no land, only emptiness, absence,
the Void,
Where those who are men can no longer turn
the mind
To distraction, delusion, escape into dream,
pretence,
Where the soul is no longer deceived, for there
are no objects, no tones,
No colours, no forms to distract, to divert the
soul
From seeing itself, foully united forever,
nothing with nothing,
Not what we call death, but what beyond
death is not death,
We fear, we fear. Who shall then plead for me,
Who intercede for me, in my most need?

Dead upon the tree, my Saviour,
Let not be in vain Thy labour;
Help me, Lord, in my last fear.

Dust I am, to dust am bending,
From the final doom impending
Help me, Lord, for death is near.
[*In the cathedral.* THOMAS *and* PRIESTS.]
PRIESTS. Bar the door. Bar the door.
The door is barred.
We are safe. We are safe.
They dare not break in.
They cannot break in. They have not the force.
We are safe. We are safe.
THOMAS. Unbar the doors! throw open the doors!
I will not have the house of prayer, the church
of Christ,
The sanctuary, turned into a fortress.
The Church shall protect her own, in her own
way, not
As oak and stone; stone and oak decay,
Give no stay, but the Church shall endure.
The church shall be open, even to our enemies.
Open the door!
PRIEST. My Lord! these are not men, these come
not as men come, but
Like maddened beasts. They come not like
men, who
Respect the sanctuary, who kneel to the Body
of Christ,
But like beasts. You would bar the door

Against the lion, the leopard, the wolf or the
boar,
Why not more
Against beasts with the souls of damned men,
against men
Who would damn themselves to beasts. My
Lord! My Lord!
THOMAS. You think me reckless, desperate and mad.
You argue by results, as this world does,
To settle if an act be good or bad.
You defer to the fact. For every life and every
act
Consequence of good and evil can be shown.
And as in time results of many deeds are
blended
So good and evil in the end become con-
founded.
It is not in time that my death shall be known;
It is out of time that my decision is taken
If you call that decision
To which my whole being gives entire consent.
I give my life
To the Law of God above the Law of Man.
Unbar the door! unbar the door!
We are not here to triumph by fighting, by
stratagem, or by resistance,
Not to fight with beasts as men. We have
fought the beast
And have conquered. We have only to con-
quer
Now, by suffering. This is the easier victory.
Now is the triumph of the Cross, now
Open the door! I command it. OPEN THE DOOR!
[*The door is opened. The* KNIGHTS *enter,
slightly tipsy.*]
PRIESTS. This way, my Lord! Quick. Up the stair.
To the roof. To the crypt. Quick. Come.
Force him.
KNIGHTS. Where is Becket, the traitor to the King?
Where is Becket, the meddling priest?
Come down Daniel to the lions' den,
Come down Daniel for the mark of the
beast.

Are you washed in the blood of the Lamb?
Are you marked with the mark of the beast?
Come down Daniel to the lions' den,
Come down Daniel and join in the feast.

Where is Becket the Cheapside brat?
Where is Becket the faithless priest?
Come down Daniel to the lions' den,
Come down Daniel and join in the feast.

THOMAS. It is the just man who
Like a bold lion, should be without fear.
I am here.
No traitor to the King. I am a priest,

A Christian, saved by the blood of Christ,
Ready to suffer with my blood.
This is the sign of the Church always,
The sign of blood. Blood for blood.
His blood given to buy my life,
My blood given to pay for His death,
My death for His death.

FIRST KNIGHT. Absolve all those you have excommunicated.

SECOND KNIGHT. Resign the powers you have arrogated.

THIRD KNIGHT. Restore to the King the money you appropriated.

FIRST KNIGHT. Renew the obedience you have violated.

THOMAS. For my Lord I am now ready to die,
That His Church may have peace and liberty.
Do with me as you will, to your hurt and shame;
But none of my people, in God's name,
Whether layman or clerk, shall you touch.
This I forbid.

KNIGHTS. Traitor! traitor! traitor!

THOMAS. You, Reginald, three times traitor you:
Traitor to me as my temporal vassal,
Traitor to me as your spiritual lord,
Traitor to God in desecrating His Church.

FIRST KNIGHT. No faith do I owe to a renegade,
And what I owe shall now be paid.

THOMAS. Now to Almighty God, to the Blessed
Mary ever Virgin, to the blessed John the
Baptist, the holy apostles Peter and Paul, to
the blessed martyr Denys, and to all the Saints,
I commend my cause and that of the Church.
[*While the* KNIGHTS *kill him, we hear the*
CHORUS.]

CHORUS. Clear the air! clean the sky! wash the
wind! take stone from stone and wash them.
The land is foul, the water is foul, our beasts
and ourselves defiled with blood.
A rain of blood has blinded my eyes. Where
is England? Where is Kent? Where is Canterbury?
O far far far far in the past; and I wander in
a land of barren boughs: if I break them,
they bleed; I wander in a land of dry stones:
if I touch them they bleed.
How how can I ever return, to the soft quiet
seasons? Night stay with us, stop sun, hold
season, let the day not come, let the spring
not come.
Can I look again at the day and its common
things, and see them all smeared with blood,
through a curtain of falling blood?
We did not wish anything to happen.
We understood the private catastrophe,
The personal loss, the general misery,

Living and partly living;
The terror by night that ends in daily action,
The terror by day that ends in sleep;
But the talk in the market-place, the hand on
the broom,
The night-time heaping of the ashes,
The fuel laid on the fire at daybreak,
These acts marked a limit to our suffering.
Every horror had its definition,
Every sorrow had a kind of end:
In life there is not time to grieve long.
But this, this is out of life, this is out of time,
An instant eternity of evil and wrong.
We are soiled by a filth that we cannot clean,
united to supernatural vermin,
It is not we alone, it is not the house, it is not
the city that is defiled,
But the world that is wholly foul.
Clear the air! clean the sky! wash the wind!
take the stone from the stone, take the skin
from the arm, take the muscle from the
bone, and wash them. Wash the stone, wash
the bone, wash the brain, wash the soul,
wash them wash them!

[*The* KNIGHTS, *having completed the murder,
advance to the front of the stage and address the audience.*]

FIRST KNIGHT. We beg you to give us your attention for a few moments. We know that you
may be disposed to judge unfavourably of our
action. You are Englishmen, and therefore
you believe in fair play: and when you see
one man being set upon by four, then your
sympathies are all with the under dog. I respect such feelings, I share them. Nevertheless, I appeal to your sense of honor. You are
Englishmen, and therefore will not judge anybody without hearing both sides of the case.
That is in accordance with our long-established
principle of Trial by Jury. I am not myself
qualified to put our case to you. I am a man
of action and not of words. For that reason I
shall do no more than introduce the other
speakers, who, with their various abilities, and
different points of view, will be able to lay
before you the merits of this extremely complex problem. I shall call upon our eldest member to speak first, my neighbour in the country: Baron William de Traci.

THIRD KNIGHT. I am afraid I am not anything like
such an experienced speaker as my old friend
Reginald Fitz Urse would lead you to believe.
But there is one thing I should like to say, and
I might as well say it at once. It is this: in
what we have done, and whatever you may
think of it, we have been perfectly disinterested. [*The other* KNIGHTS: 'Hear! hear!']

We are not getting anything out of this. We have much more to lose than to gain. We are four plain Englishmen who put our country first. I dare say that we didn't make a very good impression when we came in just now. The fact is that we knew we had taken on a pretty stiff job; I'll only speak for myself, but I had drunk a good deal — I am not a drinking man ordinarily — to brace myself up for it. When you come to the point, it does go against the grain to kill an Archbishop, especially when you have been brought up in good Church traditions. So if we seemed a bit rowdy, you will understand why it was; and for my part I am awfully sorry about it. We realised this was our duty, but all the same we had to work ourselves up to it. And, as I said, *we* are not getting a penny out of this. We know perfectly well how things will turn out. King Henry — God bless him — will have to say, for reasons of state, that he never meant this to happen; and there is going to be an awful row; and at the best we shall have to spend the rest of our lives abroad. And even when reasonable people come to see that the Archbishop *had* to be put out of the way — and personally I had a tremendous admiration for him — you must have noticed what a good show he put up at the end — they won't give *us* any glory. No, we have done for ourselves, there's no mistake about that. So, as I said at the beginning, please give us at least the credit for being completely disinterested in this business. I think that is about all I have to say.

FIRST KNIGHT. I think we will all agree that William de Traci has spoken well and has made a very important point. The gist of his argument is this: that we have been completely disinterested. But our act itself needs more justification than that; and you must hear our other speakers. I shall next call upon Hugh de Morville, who has made a special study of statecraft and constitutional law. Sir Hugh de Morville.

SECOND KNIGHT. I should like first to recur to a point that was very well put by our leader, Reginald Fitz Urse: that you are Englishmen, and therefore your sympathies are always with the under dog. It is the English spirit of fair play. Now the worthy Archbishop, whose good qualities I very much admired, has throughout been presented as the under dog. But is this really the case? I am going to appeal not to your emotions but to your reason. You are hard-headed sensible people, as I can see, and not to be taken in by emotional clap-trap. I

therefore ask you to consider soberly: what were the Archbishop's aims? And what are King Henry's aims? In the answer to these questions lies the key to the problem.

The King's aim has been perfectly consistent. During the reign of the late Queen Matilda and the irruption of the unhappy usurper Stephen, the kingdom was very much divided. Our King saw that the one thing needful was to restore order: to curb the excessive powers of local government, which were usually exercised for selfish and often for seditious ends, and to reform the legal system. He therefore intended that Becket, who had proved himself an extremely able administrator — no one denies that — should unite the offices of Chancellor and Archbishop. Had Becket concurred with the King's wishes, we should have had an almost ideal State: a union of spiritual and temporal administration, under the central government. I knew Becket well, in various official relations; and I may say that I have never known a man so well qualified for the highest rank of the Civil Service. And what happened? The moment that Becket, at the King's instance, had been made Archbishop, he resigned the office of Chancellor, he became more priestly than the priests, he ostentatiously and offensively adopted an ascetic manner of life, he affirmed immediately that there was a higher order than that which our King, and he as the King's servant, had for so many years striven to establish; and that — God knows why — the two orders were incompatible.

You will agree with me that such interference by an Archbishop offends the instincts of a people like ours. So far, I know that I have your approval: I read it in your faces. It is only with the measures we have had to adopt, in order to set matters to rights, that you take issue. No one regrets the necessity for violence more than we do. Unhappily, there are times when violence is the only way in which social justice can be secured. At another time, you would condemn an Archbishop by vote of Parliament and execute him formally as a traitor, and no one would have to bear the burden of being called murderer. And at a later time still, even such temperate measures as these would become unnecessary. But, if you have now arrived at a just subordination of the pretensions of the Church to the welfare of the State, remember that it is we who took the first step. We have been instrumental in bringing about the state of affairs that you approve. We have served your interests; we merit your applause; and if there is any guilt whatever in the matter, you must share it with us.

FIRST KNIGHT. Morville has given us a great deal to think about. It seems to me that he has said almost the last word, for those who have been able to follow his very subtle reasoning. We have, however, one more speaker, who has I think another point of view to express. If there are any who are still unconvinced, I think that Richard Brito, coming as he does of a family distinguished for its loyalty to the Church, will be able to convince them. Richard Brito.

FOURTH KNIGHT. The speakers who have preceded me, to say nothing of our leader, Reginald Fitz Urse, have all spoken very much to the point. I have nothing to add along their particular lines of argument. What I have to say may be put in the form of a question: *Who killed the Archbishop?* As you have been eyewitnesses of this lamentable scene, you may feel some surprise at my putting it in this way. But consider the course of events. I am obliged, very briefly, to go over the ground traversed by the last speaker. While the late Archbishop was Chancellor, no one, under the King, did more to weld the country together, to give it the unity, the stability, order, tranquillity, and justice that it so badly needed. From the moment he became Archbishop, he completely reversed his policy; he showed himself to be utterly indifferent to the fate of the country, to be, in fact, a monster of egotism. This egotism grew upon him, until it became at last an undoubted mania. I have unimpeachable evidence to the effect that before he left France he clearly prophesied, in the presence of numerous witnesses, that he had not long to live, and that he would be killed in England. He used every means of provocation; from his conduct, step by step, there can be no inference except that he had determined upon a death by martyrdom. Even at the last, he could have given us reason: you have seen how he evaded our questions. And when he had deliberately exasperated us beyond human endurance, he could still have easily escaped; he could have kept himself from us long enough to allow our righteous anger to cool. That was just what he did not wish to happen; he insisted, while we were still inflamed with wrath, that the doors should be opened. Need I say more? I think, with these facts before you, you will unhesitatingly render a verdict of Suicide while of Unsound Mind. It is the only charitable verdict you can give, upon one who was, after all, a great man.

FIRST KNIGHT. Thank you, Brito, I think that there is no more to be said; and I suggest that you now disperse quietly to your homes. Please be careful not to loiter in groups at street corners, and do nothing that might provoke any public outbreak.

[*Exeunt* KNIGHTS.]

FIRST PRIEST. O father, father, gone from us, lost to us,
How shall we find you, from what far place
Do you look down on us? You now in Heaven,
Who shall now guide us, protect us, direct us?
After what journey through what further dread
Shall we recover your presence? When inherit
Your strength? The Church lies bereft,
Alone, desecrated, desolated, and the heathen shall build on the ruins,
Their world without God. I see it. I see it.

THIRD PRIEST. No. For the Church is stronger for this action,
Triumphant in adversity. It is fortified
By persecution: supreme, so long as men will die for it.
Go, weak sad men, lost erring souls, homeless in earth or heaven.
Go where the sunset reddens the last grey rock
Of Brittany, or the Gates of Hercules.
Go venture shipwreck on the sullen coasts
Where blackamoors make captive Christian men;
Go to the northern seas confined with ice
Where the dead breath makes numb the hand, makes dull the brain;
Find an oasis in the desert sun,
Go seek alliance with the heathen Saracen,
To share his filthy rites, and try to snatch
Forgetfulness in his libidinous courts,
Oblivion in the fountain by the date-tree;
Or sit and bite your nails in Aquitaine.
In the small circle of pain within the skull
You still shall tramp and tread one endless round
Of thought, to justify your action to yourselves,
Weaving a fiction which unravels as you weave,
Pacing forever in the hell of make-believe
Which never is belief: this is your fate on earth
And we must think no further of you.

FIRST PRIEST.   O my lord
The glory of whose new state is hidden from us,
Pray for us of your charity.

SECOND PRIEST.   Now in the sight of God

Conjoined with all the saints and martyrs gone before you,
Remember us.

THIRD PRIEST.   Let our thanks ascend
To God, who has given us another Saint in Canterbury.

CHORUS [*While a* Te Deum *is sung in Latin by a choir in the distance*].

We praise Thee, O God, for Thy glory displayed in all the creatures of the earth,
In the snow, in the rain, in the wind, in the storm; in all of Thy creatures, both the hunters and the hunted.
For all things exist only as seen by Thee, only as known by Thee, all things exist
Only in Thy light, and Thy glory is declared even in that which denies Thee; the darkness declares the glory of light.
Those who deny Thee could not deny, if Thou didst not exist; and their denial is never complete, for if it were so, they would not exist.
They affirm Thee in living; all things affirm Thee in living; the bird in the air, both the hawk and the finch; the beast on the earth, both the wolf and the lamb; the worm in the soil and the worm in the belly.
Therefore man, whom Thou hast made to be conscious of Thee, must consciously praise Thee, in thought and in word and in deed.
Even with the hand to the broom, the back bent in laying the fire, the knee bent in cleaning the hearth, we, the scrubbers and sweepers of Canterbury,
The back bent under toil, the knee bent under sin, the hands to the face under fear, the head bent under grief,
Even in us the voices of seasons, the snuffle of winter, the song of spring, the drone of summer, the voices of beasts and of birds, praise Thee.
We thank Thee for Thy mercies of blood, for Thy redemption by blood. For the blood of Thy martyrs and saints
Shall enrich the earth, shall create the holy places.
For wherever a saint has dwelt, wherever a martyr has given his blood for the blood of Christ,
There is holy ground, and the sanctity shall not depart from it
Though armies trample over it, though sightseers come with guide-books looking over it;
From where the western seas gnaw at the coast of Iona,
To the death in the desert, the prayer in forgotten places by the broken imperial column,
From such ground springs that which forever renews the earth
Though it is forever denied. Therefore, O God, we thank Thee
Who hast given such blessing to Canterbury.

Forgive us, O Lord, we acknowledge ourselves as type of the common man,
Of the men and women who shut the door and sit by the fire;
Who fear the blessing of God, the loneliness of the night of God, the surrender required, the deprivation inflicted;
Who fear the injustice of men less than the justice of God;
Who fear the hand at the window, the fire in the thatch, the fist in the tavern, the push into the canal,
Less than we fear the love of God.
We acknowledge our trespass, our weakness, our fault; we acknowledge
That the sin of the world is upon our heads; that the blood of the martyrs and the agony of the saints
Is upon our heads.
Lord, have mercy upon us.
Christ, have mercy upon us.
Lord, have mercy upon us.
Blessed Thomas, pray for us.

HAMLET

First entitled "Hamlet and his Problems"; a review of *The Problem of Hamlet* by J. M. Robertson. (See Introduction, pp. 1008–09.)

Few critics have even admitted that *Hamlet* the play is the primary problem, and Hamlet the character only secondary. And Hamlet the character has had an especial temptation for that most dangerous type of critic: the critic with a mind which is naturally of the creative order, but which through some weakness in creative power exercises itself in criticism instead. These minds often find in Hamlet a vicarious existence for their own artistic realization. Such a mind had Goethe, who made of Hamlet a Werther; and such had Coleridge,[1] who made of Hamlet a Coleridge; and probably neither of these men in writing about Hamlet remembered that his first business was to study a work of art. The kind of criticism that Goethe and Coleridge produced, in writing of Hamlet, is the most misleading kind possible. For they both possessed unquestionable critical insight, and both make their critical aberrations the more plausible by the substitution — of their own Hamlet for Shakespeare's — which their creative gift effects. We should be thankful that Walter Pater did not fix his attention on this play.

Two writers of our own time, Mr. J. M. Robertson and Professor Stoll of the University of Minnesota, have issued small books [2] which can be praised for moving in the other direction. Mr. Stoll performs a service in recalling to our attention the labors of the critics of the seventeenth and eighteenth centuries, observing that

they knew less about psychology than more recent Hamlet critics, but they were nearer in spirit to Shakespeare's art; and as they insisted on the importance of the effect of the whole rather than on the importance of the leading character, they were nearer, in their old-fashioned way, to the secret of dramatic art in general.

Qua work of art, the work of art cannot be interpreted; there is nothing to interpret; we can only criticize it according to standards, in comparison to other works of art; and for "interpretation" the chief task is the presentation of relevant historical facts which the reader is not assumed to know. Mr. Robertson points out, very pertinently, how critics have failed in their "interpretation" of *Hamlet* by ignoring what ought to be very obvious; that *Hamlet* is a stratification, that it represents the efforts of a series of men, each making what he could out of the work of his predecessors. The *Hamlet* of Shakespeare will appear to us very differently if, instead of treating the whole action of the play as due to Shakespeare's design, we perceive his *Hamlet* to be superposed upon much cruder material which persists even in the final form.

We know that there was an older play by Thomas Kyd, that extraordinary dramatic (if not poetic) genius who was in all probability the author of two plays so dissimilar as *The Spanish Tragedy* and *Arden of Feversham;* and what this play was like we can guess from three clues: from *The Spanish Tragedy* itself, from the tale of Belleforest upon which Kyd's *Hamlet* must have been based, and from a version acted in Germany in Shakespeare's lifetime which bears strong evidence of having been adapted from the earlier, not from the later, play. From these three sources it is clear that in the earlier play the motive was a revenge motive simply; that the action or delay is caused, as in *The Spanish Tragedy,* solely by the difficulty of assassinating a monarch surrounded by guards; and that the " madness " of Hamlet was feigned in order to escape suspicion, and successfully. In the final play of Shakespeare, on the other hand, there is a motive which is more important than that of revenge, and which explicitly " blunts " the latter; the delay in revenge is unexplained on grounds of necessity or expediency; and the effect of the " madness " is not to lull but to arouse the king's suspicion. The alteration is not complete enough, however, to be convincing. Furthermore, there are verbal parallels so close to *The Spanish Tragedy* as to leave no doubt that in places Shakespeare was merely *revising* the text of Kyd. And finally there are unexplained scenes — the Polonius-Laertes and the Polonius-Reynaldo scenes — for which there is little excuse; these scenes are not in the verse style of Kyd, and not beyond doubt in the style of Shakespeare. These Mr. Robertson believes to be scenes in the original play of Kyd reworked by a third hand, perhaps Chapman, before Shakespeare touched the play. And he concludes, with very strong show of reason, that the original play of Kyd was, like certain other revenge plays, in two parts of five acts each. The

HAMLET.   1. Cf. pp. 616–18, above.   2. Robertson's *The Problem of Hamlet* (1919) and Stoll's *Hamlet: An Historical and Comparative Study* (1919). Eliot's essay was a review of the former. Robertson suggests that perhaps some passages in *Hamlet* are not Shakespeare's original work.

upshot of Mr. Robertson's examination is, we believe, irrefragable: that Shakespeare's *Hamlet,* so far as it is Shakespeare's, is a play dealing with the effect of a mother's guilt upon her son, and that Shakespeare was unable to impose this motive successfully upon the "intractable" material of the old play.

Of the intractability there can be no doubt. So far from being Shakespeare's masterpiece, the play is most certainly an artistic failure. In several ways the play is puzzling, and disquieting as is none of the others. Of all the plays it is the longest and is possibly the one on which Shakespeare spent most pains; and yet he has left in it superfluous and inconsistent scenes which even hasty revision should have noticed. The versification is variable. Lines like

> Look, the morn, in russet mantle clad,
> Walks o'er the dew of yon high eastern hill.

are of the Shakespeare of *Romeo and Juliet.* The lines in Act V, Sc. ii,

> Sir, in my heart there was a kind of fighting
> That would not let me sleep . . .
> Up from my cabin,
> My sea-gown scarf'd about me, in the dark
> Grop'd I to find out them: had my desire;
> Finger'd their packet . . .

are of his quite mature style. Both workmanship and thought are in an unstable position. We are surely justified in attributing the play, with that other profoundly interesting play of "intractable" material and astonishing versification, *Measure for Measure,* to a period of crisis, after which follow the tragic successes which culminate in *Coriolanus. Coriolanus* may be not as "interesting" as *Hamlet,* but it is, with *Antony and Cleopatra,* Shakespeare's most assured artistic success. And probably more people have thought *Hamlet* a work of art because they found it interesting, than have found it interesting because it is a work of art. It is the "Mona Lisa" of literature.

The grounds of *Hamlet's* failure are not immediately obvious. Mr. Robertson is undoubtedly correct in concluding that the essential emotion of the play is the feeling of a son towards a guilty mother:

"[Hamlet's] tone is that of one who has suffered tortures on the score of his mother's degradation. . . . The guilt of a mother is an almost intolerable motive for drama, but it had to be maintained and emphasized to supply a psychological solution, or rather a hint of one."

This, however, is by no means the whole story. It is not merely the "guilt of a mother" that cannot be handled as Shakespeare handled the suspicion of Othello, the infatuation of Antony, or the pride of Coriolanus. The subject might conceivably have expanded into a tragedy like these, intelligible, self-complete, in the sunlight. *Hamlet,* like the sonnets, is full of some stuff that the writer could not drag to light, contemplate, or manipulate into art. And when we search for this feeling, we find it, as in the sonnets, very difficult to localize. You cannot point to it in the speeches; indeed, if you examine the two famous soliloquies you see the versification of Shakespeare, but a content which might be claimed by another, perhaps by the author of the *Revenge of Bussy d'Ambois,* Act V, Sc. i. [3] We find Shakespeare's Hamlet not in the action, not in any quotations that we might select, so much as in an unmistakable tone which is unmistakably not in the earlier play.

The only way of expressing emotion in the form of art is by finding an "objective correlative"; in other words, a set of objects, a situation, a chain of events which shall be the formula of that *particular* emotion; such that when the external facts, which must terminate in sensory experience, are given, the emotion is immediately evoked. If you examine any of Shakespeare's more successful tragedies, you will find this exact equivalence; you will find that the state of mind of Lady Macbeth walking in her sleep has been communicated to you by a skillful accumulation of imagined sensory impressions; the words of Macbeth on hearing of his wife's death strike us as if, given the sequence of events, these words were automatically released by the last event in the series. The artistic "inevitability" lies in this complete adequacy of the external to the emotion; and this is precisely what is deficient in *Hamlet.* Hamlet (the man) is dominated by an emotion which is inexpressible, because it is in *excess* of the facts as they appear. And the supposed identity of Hamlet with his author is genuine to this point: that Hamlet's bafflement at the absence of objective equivalent to his feelings is a prolongation of the bafflement of his creator in the face of his artistic problem. Hamlet is up against the difficulty that his disgust is occasioned by his mother, but that his mother is not an adequate equivalent for it; his disgust envelops and exceeds her. It is thus a feeling which he cannot understand; he cannot objectify it, and it therefore remains to poison life and

3. George Chapman (1559?–1634).

obstruct action. None of the possible actions can satisfy it; and nothing that Shakespeare can do with the plot can express Hamlet for him. And it must be noticed that the very nature of the *données* of the problem precludes objective equivalence. To have heightened the criminality of Gertrude would have been to provide the formula for a totally different emotion in Hamlet; it is just *because* her character is so negative and insignificant that she arouses in Hamlet the feeling which she is incapable of representing.

The "madness" of Hamlet lay to Shakespeare's hand; in the earlier play a simple ruse, and to the end, we may presume, understood as a ruse by the audience. For Shakespeare it is less than madness and more than feigned. The levity of Hamlet, his repetition of phrase, his puns, are not part of a deliberate plan of dissimulation, but a form of emotional relief. In the character Hamlet it is the buffoonery of an emotion which can find no outlet in action; in the dramatist it is the buffoonery of an emotion which he cannot express in art. The intense feeling, ecstatic or terrible, without an object or exceeding its object, is something which every person of sensibility has known; it is doubtless a subject of study for pathologists. It often occurs in adolescence: the ordinary person puts these feelings to sleep, or trims down his feelings to fit the business world; the artist keeps them alive by his ability to intensify the world to his emotions. The Hamlet of Laforgue [4] is an adolescent; the Hamlet of Shakespeare is not, he has not that explanation and excuse. We must simply admit that here Shakespeare tackled a problem which proved too much for him. Why he attempted it at all is an insoluble puzzle; under compulsion of what experience he attempted to express the inexpressibly horrible, we cannot ever know. We need a great many facts in his biography; and we should like to know whether, and when, and after or at the same time as what personal experience, he read Montaigne, II. xii, *Apologie de Raimond Sebond*. We should have, finally, to know something which is by hypothesis unknowable, for we assume it to be an experience which, in the manner indicated, exceeded the facts. We should have to understand things which Shakespeare did not understand himself.

1919

4. Jules Laforgue (1860–87), a French Symbolist poet who influenced Eliot strongly.

THE METAPHYSICAL POETS

By collecting these poems [1] from the work of a generation more often named than read, and more often read than profitably studied, Professor Grierson has rendered a service of some importance. Certainly the reader will meet with many poems already preserved in other anthologies, at the same time that he discovers poems such as those of Aurelian Townshend or Lord Herbert of Cherbury here included. But the function of such an anthology as this is neither that of Professor Saintsbury's admirable edition of Caroline poets nor that of the *Oxford Book of English Verse*. Mr. Grierson's book is in itself a piece of criticism and a provocation of criticism; and we think that he was right in including so many poems of Donne, elsewhere (though not in many editions) accessible, as documents in the case of "Metaphysical poetry." The phrase has long done duty as a term of abuse or as the label of a quaint and pleasant taste. The question is to what extent the so-called Metaphysicals formed a school (in our own time we should say a "movement"), and how far this so-called school or movement is a digression from the main current.

Not only is it extremely difficult to define Metaphysical poetry, but difficult to decide what poets practice it and in which of their verses. The poetry of Donne (to whom Marvell and Bishop King are sometimes nearer than any of the other authors) is late Elizabethan, its feeling often very close to that of Chapman. The "courtly" poetry is derivative from Jonson, who borrowed liberally from the Latin; it expires in the next century with the sentiment and witticism of Prior. There is finally the devotional verse of Herbert, Vaughan, and Crashaw (echoed long after by Christina Rossetti and Francis Thompson); Crashaw, sometimes more profound and less sectarian than the others, has a quality which returns through the Elizabethan period to the early Italians. It is difficult to find any precise use of metaphor, simile, or other conceit, which is common to all the poets and at the same time important enough as an element of style to isolate these poets as a group. Donne, and often Cowley, employ a device which is sometimes considered characteristically "Metaphysical"; the elaboration (contrasted with the condensation) of a figure of speech to the farthest stage to which in-

METAPHYSICAL POETS. 1. The essay first appeared in *The Times Literary Supplement* as a review of *Metaphysical Lyrics and Poems of the Seventeenth Century: Donne to Butler*, selected and edited by Herbert J. C. Grierson.

genuity can carry it. Thus Cowley develops the commonplace comparison of the world to a chess-board through long stanzas ("To Destiny"), and Donne, with more grace, in "A Valediction," the comparison of two lovers to a pair of compasses. But elsewhere we find, instead of the mere explication of the content of a comparison, a development by rapid association of thought which requires considerable agility on the part of the reader.

On a round ball
A workman that hath copies by, can lay
An Europe, Afrique, and an Asia,
And quickly make that, which was nothing, *All*,
    So doth each teare,
    Which thee doth weare,
A globe, yea, world by that impression grow,
Till thy tears mixt with mine doe overflow
This world, by waters sent from thee, my heaven
    dissolvèd so.[2]

Here we find at least two connections which are not implicit in the first figure, but are forced upon it by the poet: from the geographer's globe to the tear, and the tear to the deluge. On the other hand, some of Donne's most successful and characteristic effects are secured by brief words and sudden contrasts:

A bracelet of bright hair about the bone,[3]

where the most powerful effect is produced by the sudden contrast of associations of "bright hair" and of "bone." This telescoping of images and multiplied associations is characteristic of the phrase of some of the dramatists of the period which Donne knew: not to mention Shakespeare, it is frequent in Middleton, Webster, and Tourneur, and is one of the sources of the vitality of their language.

Johnson, who employed the term "Metaphysical poets," apparently having Donne, Cleveland, and Cowley chiefly in mind, remarks of them that "the most heterogeneous ideas are yoked by violence together." The force of this impeachment lies in the failure of the conjunction, the fact that often the ideas are yoked but not united; and if we are to judge of styles of poetry by their abuse, enough examples may be found in Cleveland to justify Johnson's condemnation. But a degree of heterogeneity of material compelled into unity by the operation of the poet's mind is omnipresent in poetry. We need not select for illustration such a line as:

Notre âme est un trois-mâts cherchant son Icarie; [4]

we may find it in some of the best lines of Johnson himself ("The Vanity of Human Wishes"):

His fate was destined to a barren strand,
A petty fortress, and a dubious hand;
He left a name at which the world grew pale,
To point a moral, or adorn a tale.

where the effect is due to a contrast of ideas, different in degree but the same in principle, as that which Johnson mildly reprehended. And in one of the finest poems of the age (a poem which could not have been written in any other age), the "Exequy" of Bishop King, the extended comparison is used with perfect success: the idea and the simile become one, in the passage in which the Bishop illustrates his impatience to see his dead wife, under the figure of a journey:

Stay for me there; I will not faile
To meet thee in that hollow Vale.
And think not much of my delay;
I am already on the way,
And follow thee with all the speed
Desire can make, or sorrows breed.
Each minute is a short degree,
And ev'ry houre a step toward· thee.
At night when I betake to rest,
Next morn I rise nearer my West
Of life, almost by eight houres sail,
Than when sleep breath'd his drowsy gale. . . .
But heark! My Pulse, like a soft Drum
Beats my approach, tells *Thee* I come;
And slow howere my marches be,
I shall at last sit down by *Thee*.

(In the last few lines there is that effect of terror which is several times attained by one of Bishop King's admirers, Edgar Poe.) Again, we may justly take these quatrains from Lord Herbert's Ode, stanzas which would, we think, be immediately pronounced to be of the Metaphysical school:

So when from hence we shall be gone,
    And be no more, nor you, nor I,
    As one another's mystery,
Each shall be both, yet both but one.

This said, in her up-lifted face.
    Her eyes, which did that beauty crown,
    Were like two starrs, that having faln down,
Look up again to find their place:

4. "Our soul is a three-master [ship] searching for her Icaria" (Charles Baudelaire [1821–67], "*Le Voyage*"). *Icarie* was the name of an imaginary Utopia created in a novel by Étienne Cabet in 1840.

2. John Donne, "A Valediction: Of Weeping," pp. 189–90 above.   3. "The Relique."

> While such a moveless silent peace
>   Did seize on their becalmed sense,
>   One would have thought some influence
> Their ravished spirits did possess.

There is nothing in these lines (with the possible exception of the stars, a simile not at once grasped, but lovely and justified) which fits Johnson's general observations on the Metaphysical poets in his essay on Cowley. A good deal resides in the richness of association which is at the same time borrowed from and given to the word " becalmed "; but the meaning is clear, the language simple and elegant. It is to be observed that the language of these poets is as a rule simple and pure; in the verse of George Herbert this simplicity is carried as far as it can go — a simplicity emulated without success by numerous modern poets. The *structure* of the sentences, on the other hand, is sometimes far from simple, but this is not a vice; it is a fidelity to thought and feeling. The effect, at its best, is far less artificial than that of an ode by Gray. And as this fidelity induces variety of thought and feeling, so it induces variety of music. We doubt whether, in the eighteenth century, could be found two poems in nominally the same meter, so dissimilar as Marvell's " Coy Mistress " and Crashaw's " Saint Teresa "; the one producing an effect of great speed by the use of short syllables, and the other an ecclesiastical solemnity by the use of long ones:

> Love, thou art absolute sole lord
>   Of life and death.

If so shrewd and sensitive (though so limited) a critic as Johnson failed to define Metaphysical poetry by its faults, it is worth while to inquire whether we may not have more success by adopting the opposite method: by assuming that the poets of the seventeenth century (up to the Revolution) were the direct and normal development of the precedent age; and, without prejudicing their case by the adjective " Metaphysical," consider whether their virtue was not something permanently valuable, which subsequently disappeared, but ought not to have disappeared, Johnson has hit, perhaps by accident, on one of their peculiarities, when he observes that " their attempts were always analytic "; he would not agree that, after the dissociation, they put the material together again in a new unity.

It is certain that the dramatic verse of the later Elizabethan and early Jacobean poets expresses a degree of development of sensibility which is not found in any of the prose, good as it often is. If we except Marlowe, a man of prodigious intelligence, these dramatists were directly or indirectly (it is at least a tenable theory) affected by Montaigne. Even if we except also Jonson and Chapman, these two were notably erudite, and were notably men who incorporated their erudition into their sensibility: their mode of feeling was directly and freshly altered by their reading and thought. In Chapman especially there is a direct sensuous apprehension of thought, or a recreation of thought into feeling, which is exactly what we find in Donne:

> in this one thing, all the discipline
> Of manners and of manhood is contained;
> A man to join himself with th' Universe
> In his main sway, and make in all things fit
> One with that All, and go on, round as it;
> Not plucking from the whole his wretched part,
> And into straits, or into nought revert,
> Wishing the complete Universe might be
> Subject to such a rag of it as he;
> But to consider great Necessity.[5]

We compare this with some modern passage:

> No, when the fight begins within himself,
> A man's worth something. God stoops o'er his head,
> Satan looks up between his feet — both tug —
> He's left, himself, i' the middle; the soul wakes
> And grows. Prolong that battle through his life![6]

It is perhaps somewhat less fair, though very tempting (as both poets are concerned with the perpetuation of love by offspring), to compare with the stanzas already quoted from Lord Herbert's Ode the following from Tennyson:

> One walked between his wife and child,
> With measured footfall firm and mild,
> And now and then he gravely smiled.
>   The prudent partner of his blood
>   Leaned on him, faithful, gentle, good,
>   Wearing the rose of womanhood.
> And in their double love secure,
> The little maiden walked demure,
> Pacing with downward eyelids pure.
>   These three made unity so sweet,
>   My frozen heart began to beat,
>   Remembering its ancient heat.[7]

The difference is not a simple difference of degree between poets. It is something which had happened to the mind of England between the time of Donne or Lord Herbert of Cherbury and the time

5. *The Revenge of Bussy d'Ambois*, IV.i.139–46.   6. Robert Browning, "Bishop Blougram's Apology."   7. Tennyson, "The Two Voices."

of Tennyson and Browning; it is the difference between the intellectual poet and the reflective poet. Tennyson and Browning are poets, and they think; but they do not feel their thought as immediately as the odor of a rose. A thought to Donne was an experience; it modified his sensibility. When a poet's mind is perfectly equipped for its work, it is constantly amalgamating disparate experience; the ordinary man's experience is chaotic, irregular, fragmentary. The latter falls in love, or reads Spinoza, and these two experiences have nothing to do with each other, or with the noise of the typewriter or the smell of cooking; in the mind of the poet these experiences are always forming new wholes.

We may express the difference by the following theory: The poets of the seventeenth century, the successors of the dramatists of the sixteenth, possessed a mechanism of sensibility which could devour any kind of experience. They are simple, artificial, difficult, or fantastic, as their predecessors were; no less nor more than Dante, Guido Cavalcanti, Guinizelli, or Cino.[8] In the seventeenth century a dissociation of sensibility set in, from which we have never recovered; and this dissociation, as is natural, was aggravated by the influence of the two most powerful poets of the century, Milton and Dryden. Each of these men performed certain poetic functions so magnificently well that the magnitude of the effect concealed the absence of others. The language went on and in some respects improved; the best verse of Collins, Gray, Johnson, and even Goldsmith satisfies some of our fastidious demands better than that of Donne or Marvell or King. But while the language became more refined, the feeling became more crude. The feeling, the sensibility, expressed in the "Country Churchyard" (to say nothing of Tennyson and Browning) is cruder than that in the "Coy Mistress."

The second effect of the influence of Milton and Dryden followed from the first, and was therefore slow in manifestation. The sentimental age began early in the eighteenth century, and continued. The poets revolted against the ratiocinative, the descriptive; they thought and felt by fits, unbalanced; they reflected. In one or two passages of Shelley's *Triumph of Life,* in the second *Hyperion,* there are traces of a struggle toward unification of sensibility. But Keats and Shelley died, and Tennyson and Browning ruminated.

After this brief exposition of a theory — too brief, perhaps, to carry conviction — we may ask, what would have been the fate of the "Metaphysical" had the current of poetry descended in a direct line from them, as it descended in a direct line to them? They would not, certainly, be classified as Metaphysical. The possible interests of a poet are unlimited; the more intelligent he is the better; the more intelligent he is the more likely that he will have interests: our only condition is that he turn them into poetry, and not merely meditate on them poetically. A philosophical theory which has entered into poetry is established, for its truth or falsity in one sense ceases to matter, and its truth in another sense is proved. The poets in question have, like other poets, various faults. But they were, at best, engaged in the task of trying to find the verbal equivalent for states of mind and feeling. And this means both that they are more mature, and that they wear better, than later poets of certainly not less literary ability.

It is not a permanent necessity that poets should be interested in philosophy, or in any other subject. We can only say that it appears likely that poets in our civilization, as it exists at present, must be *difficult.* Our civilization comprehends great variety and complexity, and this variety and complexity, playing upon a refined sensibility, must produce various and complex results. The poet must become more and more comprehensive, more allusive, more indirect, in order to force, to dislocate if necessary, language into his meaning. (A brilliant and extreme statement of this view, with which it is not requisite to associate oneself, is that of M. Jean Epstein, *La Poésie d'aujourd'hui.*) Hence we get something which looks very much like the conceit — we get, in fact, a method curiously similar to that of the "Metaphysical poets," similar also in its use of obscure words and of simple phrasing.

O géraniums diaphanes, guerroyeurs sortilèges,
Sacrilèges monomanes!
Emballages, dévergondages, douches! O pressoirs
Des vendanges des grands soirs!
Layettes aux abois,
Thyrses au fond des bois!
Transfusions, représailles,
Relevailles, compresses et l'éternelle potion,
Angélus! n'en pouvoir plus
De débâcles nuptiales! de débâcles nuptiales! [9]

8. These were all members of the thirteenth-century Tuscan school of lyric love poets.

9. Jules Laforgue, *Derniers vers X.* I am indebted for this translation to Professor Warren Ramsey (author of *Jules Laforgue and the Ironic Inheritance*). It is somewhat strange that Eliot sees a similarity between this poetry of disconnected substantives

The same poet could write also simply:

> *Elle est bien loin, elle pleure,*
> *Le grand vent se lamente aussi . . .*[10]

Jules Laforgue and Tristan Corbière,[11] in many of his poems, are nearer to the "school of Donne" than any modern English poet. But poets more classical than they have the same essential quality of transmuting ideas into sensations, of transforming an observation into a state of mind.

> *Pour l'enfant, amoureux de cartes et d'estampes,*
> *L'univers est égal à son vaste appétit.*
> *Ah, que le monde est grand à la clarté des lampes!*
> *Aux yeux du souvenir que le monde est petit!* [12]

In French literature the great master of the seventeenth century — Racine — and the great master of the nineteenth — Baudelaire — are in some ways more like each other than they are like any one else. The greatest two masters of diction are also the greatest two psychologists, the most curious explorers of the soul. It is interesting to speculate whether it is not a misfortune that two of the greatest masters of diction in our language, Milton and Dryden, triumph with a dazzling disregard of the soul. If we continued to produce Miltons and Drydens it might not so much matter, but as things are it is a pity that English poetry has remained so incomplete. Those who object to the "artificiality" of Milton or Dryden sometimes tell us to "look into our hearts and write." But that is not looking deep enough; Racine or Donne looked into a good deal more than the heart. One must look into the cerebral cortex, the nervous system, and the digestive tracts.

May we not conclude, then, that Donne, Crashaw, Vaughan, Herbert and Lord Herbert, Marvell, King, Cowley at his best, are in the direct current of English poetry, and that their faults should be reprimanded by this standard rather than coddled by antiquarian affection? They have been enough praised in terms which are implicit limitations because they are "Metaphysical" or "witty," "quaint" or "obscure," though at their best they have not these attributes more than other serious poets. On the other hand, we must not reject the criticism of Johnson (a dangerous person to disagree with) without having mastered it, without having assimilated the Johnsonian canons of taste. In reading the celebrated passage in his essay on Cowley we must remember that by wit he clearly means something more serious than we usually mean today; in his criticism of their versification we must remember in what a narrow discipline he was trained, but also how well trained; we must remember that Johnson tortures chiefly the chief offenders, Cowley and Cleveland. It would be a fruitful work, and one requiring a substantial book, to break up the classification of Johnson (for there has been none since) and exhibit these poets in all their difference of kind and of degree, from the massive music of Donne to the faint, pleasing tinkle of Aurelian Townshend — whose "Dialogue Between a Pilgrim and Time" is one of the few regrettable omissions from the excellent anthology of Professor Grierson.

1921

THE MUSIC OF POETRY

Eliot delivered the third W. P. Ker Memorial Lecture at the University of Glasgow, February 24, 1942. Printed by the Glasgow University Publications, August, 1942, and reprinted in *Partisan Review*, November–December, 1942.

I debated with myself for some time before electing, for this occasion, to talk about the subject the nature of which is vaguely indicated by my title. Circumstance and conscience conspire, in these times, to direct our attention to matters of a wider scope and perhaps of more general interest. It seems almost impertinent, even as a man of letters, to concern oneself with a purely literary subject: I find myself tempted to the opposite impertinence of talking about matters beyond my range. Even within my own field, there seem to be questions of greater urgency and relevance: the place of literature in culture, the place of culture itself in the society of the future, and all the educational problems implicit in the cultivation of letters. There are many problems of literature and the arts which lead towards political, sociological and religious

---

and the strictly controlled metaphysical "conceit":

Translucent geraniums, bellicose incantations,
Obsessed sacrileges!
Discarded wrappings, shamelessnesses, showers! O wine-presses
Of evening vintages!
O layettes at bay!
Thyrsis deep in the woods!
Transfusions, reprisals,
Churchings, compresses and the eternal medicine,
Angelus! O those intolerable
Disastrous marriages, O those ill-starred bridals!

10. "She is far away, she weeps; / the great wind grieves also" (*Derniers vers XI*, "*Sur une défunte*"). 11. Corbière: 1845–75. Another of the French Symbolist poets. 12. Baudelaire, "*Le Voyage*": "For the child, in love with maps and prints, / The universe matches his vast desires. / Ah, how big the world is, reading at night! / How small it is to the eyes of memory!"

speculation; and the question which is in every mind — the question of the condition of society after the war, of its limitations, necessities and possibilities, of its inevitable or of its desirable change — this insistent question might suggest, as a more suitable subject for a formal address on a distinguished foundation, some discussion of the place of literature in a changing world.

If I have resisted this temptation, it is for two reasons, the second of which supports the first. At a time when everyone is interested in the phenomena of change, and when any reflections on these phenomena, whether analytical or constructive, may command attention if only by stimulating controversy and eliciting contradictory opinion, there is a particular need to consider, now and then, problems which only seem unimportant, because they are no more important now than they always have been and always will be. The prime interest of a practitioner of verse like myself must be in the immediate future; not that we regard the future with either hope or fear, or are moved by either the aspiration or despair of excelling dead masters, but simply because our first concern is always the perennial question, what is to be done next? what direction is unexplored? what is there to be done immediately before us, which has not been done already, once and for all, as well as it can be done? When absorbed in these investigations, the poet is no more concerned with the social consequences than is the scientist in his laboratory — though without the context of the use to society, neither the writer nor the scientist could have the conviction which sustains him. This concern with the future requires a concern with the past also: for in order to know what there is to be done we need a pretty accurate knowledge of what has been done already; and this again leads to examination of those principles and conditions which hold good always, to distinguish them from those which only held good for one or another group of our predecessors.

If my subject is justifiable by its permanence, it is also the more fitting on a foundation designed to perpetuate the memory of W. P. Ker. I never met Ker: it is a cause of regret to me that I missed the one opportunity offered me, which came only a few weeks before his last journey to Switzerland. But I found myself asking the question: what would Ker prefer me to talk about, supposing that he could appraise my abilities and my limitations? Not a subject requiring a parade of learning, cer-

tainly; for he would be the first to detect, and the most qualified to denounce, such an imposture. I can think of no other great scholar who would have been more certain to perceive both the difference and the relation between his area and mine, and to condemn any trespass from one area to the other. He was a great scholar who was also a great humanist, who was always aware that the end of scholarship is understanding, and that the end of understanding poetry is enjoyment, and that this enjoyment is gusto disciplined by taste. He was remarkable, not only for the comprehensiveness and accuracy of his knowledge of medieval and modern European literature, a knowledge with a firm basis of Latin and Greek, but for his ability to enjoy the most diverse species of it, and for the intuition, fortified by a great memory, which enabled him to detect analogies or relationships which few other men, even as learned as he, would have noticed. Each compartment of his learning was at the disposal of every other: a line of modern verse could take him back to Iceland or Provence, or the rhythm of a popular Spanish ballad could evoke half a dozen modern comparisons. I recently read again the posthumous volume of lectures collected under the title of *Form and Style in Poetry* — mostly lecture notes, but Ker always wrote, and must have spoken, well. It is a book from which the poet, as much as the scholar and the general reader, can profit. I think it is worth while, before proceeding to conjectures of my own as to what we mean, or ought to mean, or can mean, when we say that a poem is musical or unmusical, to emphasize the difference between the approach of the scholar and that of the writer of verse.

The poet, when he talks or writes about poetry, has peculiar qualifications and peculiar limitations: if we allow for the latter we can better appreciate the former — a caution which I recommend to poets themselves as well as to the readers of what they say about poetry. I can never reread any of my own prose writings without acute embarrassment: I shirk the task, and consequently may not take account of all the assertions to which I have at one time or another committed myself; I may often repeat what I have said before, and I may equally well contradict myself. But I believe that the critical writings of poets, of which in the past there have been some very distinguished examples, owe a great deal of their interest to the fact that at the back of the poet's mind, if not as his ostensible purpose, he is always trying to defend the kind of poetry he is writing, or to formulate the kind that he wants to write. Especially when he is young, and actively engaged in battling for the kind of poetry which he practices, he sees the poetry of the past in relation to his own: and his gratitude to those dead poets from whom he has learned, as well as his indifference to those whose aims have been alien to his own, may be exaggerated. He is not so much a judge as an advocate. His knowledge even is likely to be partial: for his studies will have led him to concentrate on certain authors to the neglect of others. When he theorizes about poetic creation, he is likely to be generalizing one type of experience; when he ventures into aesthetics, he is likely to be less, rather than more competent than the philosopher; and he may do best merely to report, for the information of the philosopher, the data of his own introspection. What he writes about poetry, in short, must be assessed in relation to the poetry he writes. We must return to the scholar for ascertainment of facts, and to the more detached critic for impartial judgment. The critic, certainly, should be something of a scholar, and the scholar something of a critic. Ker, whose attention was devoted mainly to the literature of the past, and to problems of historical relationship, must be put in the category of scholars; but he had in a high degree the sense of value, the humane taste, the understanding of critical canons and the ability to apply them, without which the scholar's contribution can be only indirect.

There is another, more particular respect in which the scholar's and the practitioner's acquaintance with versification differs. Here, perhaps, I should be prudent to speak only of myself. I have never been able to retain the names of feet and meters, or to pay the proper respect to the accepted rules of scansion. At school, I enjoyed very much reciting Homer or Virgil — in my own fashion. Perhaps I had some instinctive suspicion that nobody really knew how Greek ought to be pronounced, or what interweaving of Greek and native rhythms the Roman ear might appreciate in Virgil; perhaps I had only an instinct of protective laziness. But certainly, when it came to applying rules of scansion to English verse, with its very different stresses and variable syllabic values, I wanted to know why one line was good and another bad; and this, scansion could not tell me. The only way to learn to manipulate any kind of English verse seemed to be by assimilation and imitation, by becoming so engrossed in the work of a particular poet that one could produce a recognizable derivative. This is not to say that I consider the analytical study of metric, of the abstract forms which sound so extraordinarily different when handled by different poets, to be an utter waste of time. It is only that a study of anatomy will not teach you how to make a hen lay eggs. I do not recommend any other way of beginning the study of Greek or Latin verse than with the aid of those rules of scansion which were established by grammarians after most of the poetry had been written: but if we could revive those languages sufficiently to be able to speak and hear them as the authors did, we could regard the rules with indifference. We have to learn a dead language by an artificial method, and we have to approach its versification by an artificial method, and our methods of teaching have to be applied to pupils most of whom have only a moderate gift for language. Even in approaching the poetry of our own language, we may find the classification of meters, of lines with different numbers of syllables and stresses in different places, useful at a preliminary stage, as a simplified map of a complicated territory: but it is only the study, not of poetry but of poems, that can train our ear. It is not from rules, or by cold-blooded imitation indeed, but by a deeper imitation that is achieved by analysis of style. When we imitated Shelley, it was not so much from a desire to write as he did, as from an invasion of the adolescent self by Shelley, which made Shelley's way, for the time, the only way in which to write.

The practice of English versification has, no doubt, been affected by awareness of the rules of prosody: it is a matter for the historical scholar to determine the influence of Latin upon those great innovators Wyatt and Surrey. The great grammarian Otto Jespersen has maintained that the structure of English grammar has been misunderstood in our attempts to make it conform to the categories of Latin — as in the supposed " subjunctive." In the history of versification, the question whether poets have misunderstood the rhythms of the language in imitating foreign models does not arise: we must accept the practices of great poets of the past, because they are practices upon which our ear has been trained and must be trained. I believe that a number of foreign influences have gone to enrich the range and variety of English verse. Some classical scholars hold the view — this is a matter beyond my competence — that the native measure of Latin poetry was accentual rather than syllabic, that it was overlaid by the influence of a very different language — Greek — and that it reverted to something approximating to its early form, in poems such as the *Pervigilium Veneris* [1] and the Christian hymns. If so, I cannot help suspecting that to the cultivated audience of the age of Virgil, part of the pleasure in the poetry arose from the presence in it of two metrical schemes in a kind of counterpoint: even though the audience may not necessarily have been able to analyze the experience. Similarly, it may be possible that the beauty of some English poetry is due to the presence of more than one metrical structure in it. Deliberate attempts to devise English meters on Latin models are usually very frigid. Among the most successful are a few exercises by Campion,[2] in his brief but too little read treatise on metrics; among the most eminent failures, in my opinion, are the experiments of Robert Bridges — I would give all his ingenious inventions for his earlier and more traditional lyrics. But when a poet has so thoroughly absorbed Latin poetry that its movement informs his verse without deliberate artifice — as with Milton and in some of Tennyson's poems — the result can be among the great triumphs of English versification.

What I think we have, in English poetry, is a kind of amalgam of systems of divers sources (though I do not like to use the word "system," for it has a suggestion of conscious invention rather than growth): an amalgam like the amalgam of races, and indeed partly due to racial origins. The rhythms of Anglo-Saxon, Celtic, Norman French, of Middle English and Scots, have all made their mark upon English poetry, together with the rhythms of Latin, and, at various periods, of French, Italian and Spanish. As with human beings in a composite race, different strains may be dominant in different individuals, even in members of the same family, so one or another element in the poetic compound may be more congenial to one or another poet or to one or another period. The kind of poetry we get is determined, from time to time, by the influence of one or another contemporary literature in a foreign language; or by circumstances which make one period of our own past more sympathetic than another; or by the prevailing emphases in education. But there is one law of nature more powerful than any of these varying currents, or influences from abroad or from the

past: the law that poetry must not stray too far from the ordinary everyday language which we use and hear. Whether poetry is accentual or syllabic, rhymed or rhymeless, formal or free, it cannot afford to lose its contact with the changing language of common intercourse.

It may appear strange, that when I profess to be talking about the "music" of poetry, I put such emphasis upon conversation. But I would remind you, first, that the music of poetry is not something which exists apart from the meaning. Otherwise, we could have poetry of great musical beauty which made no sense, and I have never come across such poetry. The apparent exceptions only show a difference of degree: there are poems in which we are moved by the music and take the sense for granted, just as there are poems in which we attend to the sense and are moved by the music without noticing it. Take an apparently extreme example — the non-sense verse of Edward Lear. His nonsense is not vacuity of sense: it is a parody of sense, and that is the sense of it. "The Jumblies" is a poem of adventure, and of nostalgia for the romance of foreign voyage and exploration; "The Yongy-Bongy-Bo" and "The Dong with a Luminous Nose" are poems of unrequited passion — "blues" in fact. We enjoy the music, which is of a higher order, and we enjoy the feeling of irresponsibility towards the sense. Or take a poem of another type, the "Blue Closet" of William Morris. It is a delightful poem, though I cannot explain what it means and I doubt whether the author could have explained it. It has an effect somewhat like that of a rune or charm, but runes and charms are very practical formulae designed to produce definite results, such as getting a cow out of a bog. But its obvious intention (and I think the author succeeds) is to produce the effect of a dream. It is not necessary, in order to enjoy the poem, to know what the dream means; but human beings have an unshakable belief that dreams mean something: they used to believe — and many still believe — that dreams disclose the secrets of the future; the orthodox modern faith is that they reveal the secrets — or at least the more horrid ones — of the past. It is a commonplace to observe that the meaning of a poem may wholly escape paraphrase. It is not quite so commonplace to observe that the meaning of a poem may be something larger than its author's conscious purpose, and something remote from its origins. One of the most obscure of modern poets was the French writer Stephane Mallarmé, of whom the French

MUSIC OF POETRY. 1. *Pervigilium Veneris*: anonymous Latin love poem, probably from the 2nd century A.D., l. 428n. 2. Campion: Thomas Campion (1567-1620), Elizabethan poet and musician.

sometimes say that his language is so peculiar that it can be understood only by foreigners. The late Roger Fry, and his friend Charles Mauron, published an English translation with notes to unriddle the meanings: when I learn that a difficult sonnet was inspired by seeing a painting on the ceiling reflected on the polished top of a table, or by seeing the light reflected from the foam on a glass of beer, I can only say that this may be a correct embryology, but it is not the meaning. If we are moved by a poem, it has meant something, perhaps something important, to us; if we are not moved, then it is, as poetry, meaningless. We can be deeply stirred by hearing the recitation of a poem in a language of which we understand no word; but if we are then told that the poem is gibberish and has no meaning, we shall consider that we have been deluded — this was no poem, it was merely an imitation of instrumental music. If, as we are aware, only a part of the meaning can be conveyed by paraphrase, that is because the poet is occupied with frontiers of consciousness beyond which words fail, though meanings still exist. A poem may appear to mean very different things to different readers, and all of these meanings may be different from what the author thought he meant. For instance, the author may have been writing some peculiar personal experience, which he saw quite unrelated to anything outside; yet for the reader the poem may become the expression of a general situation, as well as of some private experience of his own. The reader's interpretation may differ from the author's and be equally valid — it may even be better. There may be much more in a poem than the author was aware of. The different interpretations may all be partial formulations of one thing; the ambiguities may be due to the fact that the poem means more, not less, than ordinary speech can communicate.

So, while poetry attempts to convey something beyond what can be conveyed in prose rhythms, it remains, all the same, one person talking to another; and this is just as true if you sing it, for singing is another way of talking. The immediacy of poetry to conversation is not a matter on which we can lay down exact laws. Every revolution in poetry is apt to be, and sometimes to announce itself as, a return to common speech. That is the revolution which Wordsworth announced in his prefaces, and he was right: but the same revolution had been carried out a century before by Oldham, Waller, Denham and Dryden; and the same revolution was due again something over a century later. The followers of a revolution develop the new poetic idiom in one direction or another; they polish or perfect it; meanwhile the spoken language goes on changing, and the poetic idiom goes out of date. Perhaps we do not realize how natural the speech of Dryden must have sounded to the most sensitive of his contemporaries. No poetry, of course, is ever exactly the same speech that the poet talks and hears: but it has to be in such a relation to the speech of his time that the listener or reader can say " that is how I should talk if I could talk poetry." This is the reason why the best contemporary can give us a feeling of excitement and a sense of fulfillment different from any sentiment aroused by even very much greater poetry of a past age.

The music of poetry, then, must be a music latent in the common speech of its time. And that means also that it must be latent in the common speech of the poet's *place*. It would not be to my present purpose to inveigh against the ubiquity of standardized, or " B.B.C." English. If we all came to talk alike there would no longer be any point in our not writing alike: but until that time comes — and I hope it may be long postponed — it is the poet's business to use the speech which he finds about him, that with which he is most familiar. I shall always remember the impression of W. B. Yeats reading poetry aloud. To hear him read his own works was to be made to recognize how much the Irish way of speech is needed to bring out the beauties of Irish poetry: to hear Yeats reading William Blake was an experience of a different kind, more astonishing than satisfying. Of course, we do not want the poet merely to reproduce exactly the conversational idiom of himself, his family, his friends and his particular district: but what he finds there is the material out of which he must make his poetry. He must, like the sculptor, be faithful to the material in which he works; it is out of sounds that he has heard that he must make his melody and harmony.

It would be a mistake, however, to assume that all poetry ought to be melodious, or that melody is more than one of the components of the music of words. Some poetry is meant to be sung; most poetry, in modern times, is meant to be spoken — and there are many other things to be spoken of besides the murmur of innumerable bees or the moan of doves in immemorial elms.[3] Dissonance,

---

3. murmur . . . elms: See Tennyson's *The Princess*, VII.206–07.

even cacophony, has its place: just as, in a poem of any length, there must be transitions between passages of greater and less intensity, to give rhythm of fluctuating emotion essential to the musical structure of the whole; and the passages of less intensity will be, in relation to the level on which the total poem operates, prosaic — so that, in the sense implied by that context, it may be said that no poet can write a poem of amplitude unless he is a master of the prosaic.[4]

What matters, in short, is the whole poem: and if the whole poem need not be, and often should not be, wholly melodious, it follows that a poem is not made only out of " beautiful words." I doubt whether, from the point of view of *sound* alone, any word is more or less beautiful than another — within its own language, for the question whether some languages are not more beautiful than others is quite another question. The ugly words are the words not fitted for the company in which they find themselves; there are words which are ugly because of rawness or because of antiquation; there are words which are ugly because of foreignness or ill-breeding (e.g., *television*): but I do not believe that any word well-established in its own language is either beautiful or ugly. The music of a word is, so to speak, at a point of intersection: it arises from its relation first to the words immediately preceding and following it, and indefinitely to the rest of its context; and from another relation, that of its immediate meaning in that context to all the other meanings which it has had in other contexts, to its greater or less wealth of association. Not all words, obviously, are equally rich and well-connected: it is part of the business of the poet to dispose the richer among the poorer, at the right points, and we cannot afford to load a poem too heavily with the former — for it is only at certain moments that a word can be made to insinuate the whole history of a language and a civilization. This is an " allusiveness " which is not the fashion or eccentricity of a peculiar type of poetry; but an allusiveness which is in the nature of words, and which is equally the concern of every kind of poet. My purpose here is to insist that a " musical poem " is a poem which has a musical pattern of sound and a musical pattern of the secondary meanings of the words which compose it, and that these two patterns are indissoluble and one. And if you object that it is only the pure sound, apart from the sense, to which the adjective " musical " can be rightly applied, I can only reaffirm my previous assertion that the sound of a poem is as much an abstraction from the poem as is the sense.

The history of blank verse illustrates two interesting and related points: the dependence upon speech and the striking difference, in what is prosodically the same form, between dramatic blank verse and blank verse employed for epical, philosophical, meditative and idyllic purposes. The dependence of verse upon speech is much more direct in dramatic poetry than in any other. In most kinds of poetry, the necessity for its reminding us of contemporary speech is reduced by the latitude allowed for personal idiosyncrasy: a poem by Gerard Hopkins, for instance, may sound pretty remote from the way in which you and I express ourselves — or rather, from the way in which our fathers and grandfathers expressed themselves: but Hopkins does give the impression that his poetry has the necessary fidelity to his way of thinking and talking to himself. But in dramatic verse the poet is speaking in one character after another, through the medium of a company of actors trained by a producer, and of different actors and different producers at different times: his idiom must be comprehensive of all the voices, but present at a deeper level than is necessary when the poet speaks only for himself. Some of Shakespeare's later verse is very elaborate and peculiar: but it remains the language, not of one person, but of a world of persons. It is based upon the speech of three hundred years ago, yet when we hear it well rendered we can forget the distance of time — as is brought home to us most patently in one of those plays, of which *Hamlet* is the chief, which can fittingly be produced in modern dress. By the time of Otway [5] dramatic blank verse has become artificial and at best reminiscent; and when we get to the verse plays by nineteenth-century poets, of which the greatest is probably *The Cenci*,[6] it is difficult to preserve any illusion of reality. Nearly all the greater poets of the last century tried their hands at verse plays. These plays, which few people read more than once, are treated with respect as fine poetry; and their insipidity is usually attributed to the fact that the authors, though great poets, were

---

4. "This is the complementary doctrine to that of the 'touchstone' line of passage of Matthew Arnold: this test of the greatness of a poet is the way he writes his less intense, but structurally vital matter" [E].

5. Thomas Otway (1652–85). His *Venice Preserved* (1682) is sometimes spoken of as the last "Elizabethan" tragedy. 6. By Shelley, published 1819.

amateurs in the theater. But even if the poets had had greater natural gifts for the theater, or had toiled to acquire the craft, their plays would have been just as ineffective, unless their theatrical talent and experience had shown them the necessity for a different kind of versification. It is not primarily lack of plot, or lack of action and suspense, or imperfect realization of character, or lack of anything of what is called " theater," that makes these plays so lifeless: it is primarily that their rhythm of speech is something that we cannot associate with any human being except a poetry reciter.

Even under the powerful manipulation of Dryden dramatic blank verse shows a grave deterioration. There are splendid passages in *All for Love:* yet Dryden's characters talk more naturally at times in the heroic plays which he wrote in rhymed couplets, than they do in what would seem the more natural form of blank verse — though less naturally in English than the characters of Corneille and Racine in French. The causes for the rise and decline of any form of art are always complex, and we can always trace a number of contributory causes, while there seems to remain some deeper cause incapable of formulation: I should not care to advance any one reason why prose came to supersede verse in the theater. But I feel sure that one reason why blank verse cannot be employed now in the drama is that so much nondramatic poetry, and great nondramatic poetry, has been written in it in the last three hundred years. Our minds are saturated in these nondramatic works in what is formally the same kind of verse. If we can imagine, as a flight of fancy, Milton coming before Shakespeare, Shakespeare would have had to discover quite a different medium from that which he used and perfected. Milton handled blank verse in a way which no one has ever approached or ever will approach: and in so doing did more than anyone or anything else to make it impossible for the drama: though we may also believe that dramatic blank verse had exhausted its resources, and had no future in any event. Indeed, Milton almost made blank verse impossible for any purpose for a couple of generations. It was the precursors of Wordsworth — Thomson, Young, Cowper — who made the first efforts to rescue it from the degradation to which the eighteenth-century imitators of Milton had reduced it. There is much, and varied, fine blank verse in the nineteenth century: the nearest to colloquial speech is that of Browning — but, significantly, in his monologues rather than in his plays.

To make a generalization like this is not to imply any judgment of the relative stature of poets. It merely calls attention to the profound difference between dramatic and all other kinds of verse: a difference in the music, which is a difference in the relation to the current spoken language. It leads to my next point: which is that the task of the poet will differ, not only according to his personal constitution, but according to the period in which he finds himself. At some periods, the task is to explore the musical possibilities of an established convention of the relation of the idiom of verse to that of speech; at other periods, the task is to catch up with the changes in colloquial speech, which are fundamentally changes in thought and sensibility. This cyclical movement also has a very great influence upon our critical judgment. At a time like ours, when a refreshment of poetic diction similar to that brought about by Wordsworth has been called for (whether it has been satisfactorily accomplished or not) we are inclined, in our judgments upon the past, to exaggerate the importance of the innovators at the expense of the reputation of the developers: which might account for what will seem, surely, to a later age, our undue adulation of Donne and depreciation of Milton.

I have said enough, I think, to make clear that I do not believe that the task of the poet is primarily and always to effect a revolution in language. It would not be desirable, even if it were possible, to live in a state of perpetual revolution: the craving for continual novelty of diction and metric is as unwholesome as the obstinate adherence to the idiom of our grandfathers. There are times for exploration and times for the development of the territory acquired. The poet who did most for the English language is Shakespeare: and he carried out, in one short lifetime, the task of two poets. I have attempted to indicate his dual achievement elsewhere: I can only say here, briefly, that the development of Shakespeare's verse can be roughly divided into two periods. During the first, he was slowly adapting his form to colloquial speech: so that by the time he wrote *Antony and Cleopatra* he had devised a medium in which everything that any dramatic character might have to say, whether high or low, " poetical " or " prosiac," could be said with naturalness and beauty. Having got to this point, he began to elaborate. The first period — of the poet who began with *Venus and Adonis,* but who had already, in *Love's Labor's Lost,* begun to see what he had to do — is from artificiality to simplicity, from stiffness to sup pleness. The later plays move from simplicity towards elaboration. He is occupied with the other task of the poet — doing the work of two poets in one lifetime — that of experimenting to see how elaborate, how complicated, the music could be made without losing touch with colloquial speech altogether, and without his characters ceasing to be human beings. This is the poet of *Cymbeline, The Winter's Tale, Pericles,* and *The Tempest.* Of those whose exploration took them in this one direction only, Milton is the greatest master. We may think that Milton, in exploring the orchestral music of language, sometimes ceases to talk a social idiom at all; we may think that Wordsworth, in attempting to recover the social idiom, sometimes oversteps the mark and becomes pedestrian: but it is often true that only by going too far can we find out how far we can go; though one has to be a very great poet to justify such perilous adventures.

So far, I have spoken only of versification and not of poetic structure; and it is time for a reminder that the music of verse is not a line by line matter, but a question of the whole poem. Only with this in mind can we approach the vexed question of formal pattern and free verse. In the plays of Shakespeare a musical design can be discovered in particular scenes, and in his more perfect plays as wholes. It is a music of imagery as well as sound: Mr. Wilson Knight has shown in his examination of several of the plays, how much the use of recurrent imagery, and dominant imagery, throughout one play, has to do with the total effect. A play of Shakespeare is a very complex musical structure; the more easily grasped structure is that of forms such as the sonnet, the formal ode, the ballade, the villanelle, rondeau or sestina. It is sometimes assumed that modern poetry has done away with forms like these. I have seen signs of a return to them; and indeed I believe that the tendency to return to set, and even elaborate, patterns is permanent, as permanent as the need for a refrain or a chorus to a popular song. Some forms are more appropriate to some languages than to others, and all are more appropriate to some periods than to others. At one stage the stanza is a right and natural formalization of speech into pattern. But the stanza — and the more elaborate it is, the more rules to be observed in its proper execution, the more surely this happens — tends to become fixed to the idiom of the moment of its perfection. It quickly loses contact with the changing colloquial speech, being possessed by the mental outlook of a past genera-

tion; it becomes discredited when employed solely by those writers who, having no impulse to form within them, have recourse to pouring their liquid sentiment into a ready-made mold in which they vainly hope that it will set. In a perfect sonnet, what you admire is not so much the author's skill in adapting himself to the pattern as the skill and power with which he makes the pattern comply with what he has to say. Without this fitness, which is contingent upon period as well as individual genius, the rest is at best virtuosity: and where the musical element is the only element, that also vanishes. Elaborate forms return: but there have to be periods during which they are laid aside.

As for "free verse," I expressed my view twenty-five years ago by saying that no verse is free for the man who wants to do a good job. No one has better cause to know than I, that a great deal of bad prose has been written under the name of free verse: though whether its authors wrote bad prose or bad verse, or bad verse in one style or in another, seems to me a matter of indifference. But only a bad poet could welcome free verse as a liberation from form. It was a revolt against dead form, and a preparation for new form or for renewal of the old; it was an insistence upon the inner unity which is unique to every poem, against the outer unity which is typical. The poem comes before the form, in the sense that a form grows out of the attempt of somebody to say something; just as a system of prosody is only a formulation of the identities in the rhythms of a succession of poets influenced by each other.

Forms have to be broken and remade: but I believe that any language, so long as it remains the same language, imposes its laws and restrictions and permits its own license, dictates its own speech rhythms and sound patterns. And a language is always changing; its developments in vocabulary, in syntax, pronunciation and intonation — even, in the long run, its deterioration — must be accepted by the poet and made the best of. He in turn has the privilege of contributing to the development and maintaining the quality, the capacity of the language to express a wide range, and subtle gradation, of feeling and emotion; his task is both to respond to change and make it conscious, and to battle against degradation below the standards which he has learned from the past. The liberties that he may take are for the sake of order.

At what stage contemporary verse now finds itself, I must leave you to judge for yourselves. I suppose that it will be agreed that if the work of the last twenty years is worthy of being classified at all, it is as belonging to a period of search for a proper modern colloquial idiom. We have still a good way to go in the invention of a verse medium for the theater; a medium in which we shall be able to hear the speech of contemporary human beings, in which dramatic characters can express the purest poetry without highfalutin and in which they can convey the most commonplace message without absurdity. But when we reach a point at which the poetic idiom can be stabilized, then a period of musical elaboration can follow. I think that a poet may gain much from the study of music: how much technical knowledge of musical form is desirable I do not know, for I have not that technical knowledge myself. But I believe that the properties in which music concerns the poet most nearly, are the sense of rhythm and the sense of structure. I think that it might be possible for a poet to work too closely to musical analogies: the result might be an effect of artificiality; but I know that a poem, or a passage of a poem, may tend to realize itself first as a particular rhythm before it reaches expression in words, and that this rhythm may bring to birth the idea and the image; and I do not believe that this is an experience peculiar to myself. The use of recurrent themes is as natural to poetry as to music. There are possibilities for verse which bear some analogy to the development of a theme by different groups of instruments; there are possibilities of transitions in a poem comparable to the different movements of a symphony or a quartet; there are possibilities of contrapuntal arrangement of subject matter. It is in the concert room, rather than in the opera house, that the germ of a poem may be quickened. More than this I cannot say, but must leave the matter here to those who have had a musical education. But I would remind you again of the two tasks of poetry, the two directions in which language must at different times be worked: so that however far it may go in musical elaboration, we must expect a time to come when poetry will have again to be recalled to speech. The same problems arise, and always in new forms; and poetry has always before it, as F. S. Oliver said of politics, an "endless adventure."

A Note on Versification

I have never been able to retain the names of feet and meters, or to pay the proper respect to the accepted rules of scansion. . . . This is not to say that I consider the analytical study of metric, of the abstract forms which sound so extraordinarily different when handled by different poets, to be utter waste of time. It is only that a study of anatomy will not teach you how to make a hen lay eggs . . .
—T. S. ELIOT, "The Music of Poetry"

When we open a book of verse, we unconsciously prepare ourselves for a different kind of experience from what we get in a page of solid print. What is the basis of the difference? It is in the *sound pattern* of the language — poetry is distinguished from prose by its rhythms.

The study of versification is concerned with the ways in which the poet uses recurrent sound pattern to create formal verbal designs. In a full analysis of any poem, this is seen to be only a part of the total effect. Other topics inevitably intrude. For one thing, we can never discuss poetry without talking about its themes, its subject matter. And beyond the theme, the fact that subject and the structural form in which it realizes itself are inseparable leads to the discussion of the various forms of poetic expression: epic, drama, meditative, and lyric outlines. Then the discovery that the language of logical statement tends, in poetry, to give way to symbolic and metaphorical expression brings another large topic — perhaps the largest of all — since, as Yeats says: "It is not possible to separate an emotion or a spiritual state from the image that calls it up and gives it expression."

Since a poem is a unity, and language is the medium in which it is expressed, in practice none of these things — theme, structure, imagery — can be separated from the sound pattern through which alone we become aware of them. But a note on versification cannot go that far afield. It must limit itself to a short account of meters, rhymes, rhythms, and the word textures and values which combine to make the sound patterns. There is an infinite variety of these patterns, and different poets use the same pattern in widely different ways. They are all, however, differentiated from prose by their basis in *meter*. As we shall see later, meter is only a part of the larger subject of poetic rhythm, but since it is the part which can be stated factually, we will start with the facts.

METER

Meter means "measure." Verse is written in lines, which are measured according to the number and arrangement of accented and unaccented syllables within them. The unit of this measurement is the *foot*. English verse has borrowed the classical names for describing the number and order and character of the syllables which form "feet." Feet may be either disyllabic (formed of two syllables), or trisyllabic (formed of three syllables). They are named as follows:

Iamb: an unaccented syllable followed by an accented one:

The cúrfew tólls the knéll of párting dáy.

Trochee: an accented syllable followed by an unaccented one:

Téll me nót in móurnfŭl númbĕrs.

Spondee: two accented syllables together, as in the last two feet of the line,

The cumbrous elements — eárth, flóod, aír, fíre

Dactyl: an accented syllable followed by two unaccented ones:

Táke hĕr ŭp téndĕrlў

Anapest: Two unaccented syllables followed by an accented one:

Ĭ ăm mónarch ŏf áll Ĭ survéy

Although it is not difficult to find illustrations of all these types of feet, by far the most popular and all-pervasive movement of English verse is the iambic. It suits the nature of the language better than any other, and probably nine-tenths of English poetry uses that foot as its basic metrical unit.

The *line* of verse is composed of one or more feet. Again, the classical names are officially used: *monometer:* one foot; *dimeter:* two feet; *trimeter:* three feet; *tetrameter:* four feet (sometimes called octosyllabics); *pentameter:* five feet;

hexameter: six feet (also called alexandrines); *heptameter:* seven feet; *octameter:* eight feet.

Two measurements are therefore involved in meter: the *kind* of foot and the *number* of feet. These can be combined in any possible ways. " The curfew tolls the knell of parting day " is iambic pentameter; " Tell me not in mournful numbers " is trochaic tetrameter; " Take her up tenderly " is dactylic dimeter; and " I am monarch of all I survey," anapestic trimeter.

RHYME AND OTHER METRICAL DEVICES

Verse patterns may be either rhymed or unrhymed. Rhyme is an identity of sounds at the end of lines. This may be in the last syllable of the line (single or masculine rhyme),

> To hear the lark begin his *flight*,
> And singing startle the dull *night*,

or in the last two syllables (double or feminine rhyme),

> Then to come, in spite of *sorrow*,
> And at my window bid good-*morrow.*[1]

Dactylic verse requires a triple rhyme,

> Touch her not *scornfully.*
> Think of her *mournfully,*[2]

but in serious verse the rhyme is seldom more than double. Triple rhymes are found more often in comic or satiric verse — as in Byron's *Don Juan:*

> . . . Oh! ye lords of ladies intell*ectual*,
> Inform us truly, have they not hen*pecked you all?*[3]

or as in so many of the verses of Ogden Nash today.

The rhymes may be *internal*, within the line as well as at the end:

> Alas,
> We loved, sir — used to meet;
> How *sad* and *bad* and *mad* it was —
> But then, how it was sweet![4]

Or the rhymes may be *half-rhymes* or *slant rhymes*, where the sounds are similar, but not identical:

> Little Tommy *Tucker*
> Sang for his *supper.*
> What did he have?
> Brown bread and *butter.*

Modern poets are fond of using *assonance*, an identity of vowel sounds only, while the consonants are different. Louis MacNeice writes:

---

[1] Milton, "L'Allegro." See p. 212, above.
[2] Thomas Hood, "The Bridge of Sighs."
[3] See p. 643, above.
[4] Browning, "Confessions." See p. 879, above.

Not the twilight of the gods but a precise *dawn*
Of sallow and grey bricks, and the newsboys crying
    war.

An alternative to this is *consonance*, an identity of consonants while the vowels differ. The following example is from Wilfred Owen's " Strange Meeting ":

> It seemed that out of battle I *escaped*
> Down some profound dull tunnel, long since *scooped*
> Through granites which titanic wars had *groined.*
> Yet also there encumbered sleepers *groaned.*

RHYME SCHEMES

Lines of rhymed verse are usually grouped into patterns called rhyme schemes. These can vary from the single couplet to an elaborate arrangement such as Spenser's *Epithalamion*, which has a varying scheme of sixteen lines.

The *couplet* is any rhymed pattern of two lines, but its most popular forms are the iambic tetrameter, or octosyllabic (see the quotations from Milton's " L'Allegro " above) and the iambic pentameter. This latter form is usually called the *heroic couplet*, though that name was not used for it until late in the seventeenth century, when it was associated with the popular " heroic plays " of the time. More will be said about it later in the section on rhythm.

A three-rhymed pattern is called a *triplet* or *tercet*. The three lines may use one set of rhyming words, as in Tennyson's *The Eagle:*

> He clasps the crag with hooked hands;
> Close to the sun in lonely lands,
> Ring'd with the azure world, he stands,

or the rhymes may be linked from verse to verse. This form is called *terza rima*, and the rhymes run: *aba-bcb-cdc-ded* and so on. There are not many examples of it in English poetry. The finest is Shelley's " Ode to the West Wind ":

> O wild West Wind, thou breath of Autumn's being,
>   Thou, from whose unseen presence the leaves dead
> Are driven, like ghosts from an enchanter fleeing,
>
>   Yellow, and black, and pale, and hectic red,
> Pestilence-stricken multitudes! O thou
>   Who chariotest to their dark wintry bed
>
> The wingèd seeds, where they lie cold and low,
>   Each like a corpse within its grave, until
> Thine azure sister of the Spring shall blow
>
>   Her clarion o'er the dreaming earth . . .[5]

With the *quatrain* (any arrangement of four lines), we pass into patterns usually called

---

[5] See p. 681, above.

stanzas, and the variations of four-, five-, six-, seven-, and eight-line stanzas are too numerous to differentiate. But there are certain "named varieties": *rhyme royal*, first used in England by Chaucer, is a seven-line stanza in iambic pentameter, with the rhymes running *ababbcc*. It is the meter of Shakespeare's *Rape of Lucrece*.

> From the besieged Ardea all in post,
> Borne by the trustless wings of false desire,
> Lust-breathèd Tarquin leaves the Roman host,
> And to Collatium bears the lightless fire,
> Which, in pale embers hid, lurks to aspire,
>   And girdle with embracing flames the waist
>   Of Collatine's fair love, Lucrece the chaste.

Ottava rima was introduced from Italy in the sixteenth century. It is an eight-line stanza, also in iambic pentameter, rhyming *ababababcc*. It was Byron's favorite meter.

> The Angels all were singing out of tune,
>   And hoarse with having little else to do,
> Excepting to wind up the sun and moon,
>   Or curb a runaway young star or two,
> Or wild colt of a comet, which too soon
>   Broke out of bounds o'er the ethereal blue,
> Splitting some planet with its playful tail
> As boats are sometimes by a wanton whale.[1]

The Spenserian stanza has nine lines, eight in iambic pentameter, and the last an alexandrine, with the rhyme scheme *ababbcbcc*.

So passeth, in the passing of a day,
    Of mortall life the leafe, the bud, the flowre;
Ne more doth florish after first decay,
    That earst was sought to deck both bed and bowre
    Of many a lady, and many a Paramowre.
Gather therefore the Rose whilest yet is prime,
    For soone comes age that will her pride deflowre;
Gather the Rose of love whilest yet is time,
Whilest loving thou mayst lovèd be with equall crime.[2]

The *sonnet* is a complete poem of fourteen lines in iambic pentameter. There are many versions of the form, but the two general types are the Petrarchan and the Shakespearean. The *Petrarchan*, introduced from Italy in the sixteenth century, is divided into an octave, the first eight lines, usually playing on two rhymes, and a sestet, the last six lines, using either two or three rhymes. Wordsworth's sonnet on Westminster Bridge is a Petrarchan model.

> Earth has not anything to show more fair;
> Dull would he be of soul who could pass by
> A sight so touching in its majesty:
> This city now doth, like a garment, wear

> The beauty of the morning; silent, bare,
> Ships, towers, domes, theaters, and temples lie
> Open unto the fields, and to the sky;
> All bright and glittering in the smokeless air.
>
> Never did sun more beautifully steep
> In his first splendor, valley, rock, or hill;
> Ne'er saw I, never felt, a calm so deep!
> The river glideth at his own sweet will;
> Dear God! the very houses seem asleep;
> And all that mighty heart is lying still![3]

The *Shakespearean* sonnet form divides into three quatrains, each with its own two rhymes, and a final couplet with another rhyme.

> When in disgrace with fortune and men's eyes,
> I all alone beweep my outcast state,
> And trouble deaf heaven with my bootless cries,
> And look upon myself, and curse my fate,
>
> Wishing me like to one more rich in hope,
> Featured like him, like him with friends possessed,
> Desiring this man's art and that man's scope,
> With what I most enjoy contented least;
>
> Yet in these thoughts myself almost despising —
> Haply I think on thee: and then my state,
> Like to the lark at break of day arising
> From sullen earth, sings hymns at heaven's gate;
>
> For thy sweet love remembered such wealth brings
> That then I scorn to change my state with kings.[4]

UNRHYMED VERSE

Any stanzaic form may be written without rhymes, but the most popular unrhymed pattern is that of *blank verse*, the iambic pentameter not broken into formal units. Along with the couplet, this will be discussed more fully later in the section on rhythm.

Free verse dispenses with any regular metrical pattern, either of rhyme or accent. But as T. S. Eliot states in "*The Music of Poetry*," the term itself is a misnomer: "no verse is free for the man who wants to do a good job." And as he points out in an earlier essay, there is never any escape from meter in poetry; there is only mastery of it.

We may therefore formulate as follows: the ghost of some simple meter should lurk behind the arras in even the "freest" verse; to advance menacingly as we doze, and withdraw as we rouse. Or, freedom is only true freedom when it appears against a background of an artificial limitation.[5]

In these lines from *The Waste Land*, for instance, in spite of all the extra syllables, the uneven accents, and the differences in line length, the ghost of an iambic tetrameter lurks behind the arras.

----

[1] "The Vision of Judgment."
[2] *The Faerie Queene*, II.xii.75.
[3] See p. 584, above.
[4] Shakespeare, Sonnet XXIX.
[5] *The New Statesman*, March 3, 1917.

My friend, blood shaking my heart
The awful daring of a moment's surrender
Which an age of prudence can never retract
By this, and this only, we have existed
Which is not to be found in our obituaries
Or in memories draped by the beneficent spider
Or under seals broken by the lean solicitor
In our empty rooms. . . .[1]

OTHER VERBAL DEVICES

In all kinds of verse certain common devices are used to give variety to the metrical design. It will have been noted in the above examples of stanzaic and sonnet forms that in some lines the sense is enclosed in the single line, which is then called *end-stopped.* If the sense flows over into two, or several lines, they are then called *run-on.* A couplet where the sense is complete is a *closed couplet* (as in the lines from Pope below). If a sentence, or clause, ends in the middle of a line, the break which then occurs is called a *caesura,* and makes a pause in the reading of the line. In the Wordsworth sonnet quoted above, the first line is end-stopped; the second is run-on; and in the fifth there is a caesura. There is another caesura in the thirteenth, where the words "Dear God!" stand apart from the rest of the line and make a break in the sound pattern.

Other common sound effects are those of *alliteration,* the repetition of consonants; and *onomatopoeia,* the imitation of natural sounds in words. A succession of harsh, slow-moving syllables is called *cacophony;* and of light, harmonious ones, *euphony.* The following passage from Pope's *Essay on Criticism* gives illustrations of all these devices.

True ease in writing comes from art, not chance,
As those move easiest who have learned to dance.
'Tis not enough no harshness gives offense,
The sound must seem an echo to the sense:
Soft is the strain when Zephyr gently blows,
And the smooth stream in smoother numbers flows;
But when loud surges lash the sounding shore,
The hoarse, rough verse should like the torrent roar:
When Ajax strives some rock's vast weight to throw,
The line too labors, and the words move slow;
Not so, when swift Camilla scours the plain,
Flies o'er th' unbending corn, and skims along the
  main.[1]

  [1] See p. 404, above.

There is alliteration throughout the passage (which should be read aloud), and in the fifth and sixth lines, where the repetition of the "s" sound creates the softness and smoothness of wind and stream, it is combined with onomatopoeia. The lines on the torrent and on Ajax illustrate cacophony, and those on Camilla, euphony. In all, carefully and skillfully, Pope makes the sound of the words echo the actions described.

RHYTHM

When we have enumerated the kinds of feet and the number of feet in different lines, have named various rhyme schemes and listed verbal devices used by poets, we are not much nearer the realities of versification. We have given the mechanical framework, a set of rules and conventions which put verse apart from prose. But to attempt to reduce poetry to rules, to make the laws of versification into an authoritarian dictatorship to keep poets in order, would be quite useless. The rules do insist on the basic fact of *recurrent pattern.* They emphasize that it is the setting up of an expectation of certain returning sound effects that catches the ear and pleases it. The measurements of these sound effects is meter, but the *regular* metrical pattern is never more than a foundation, a norm from which to depart and return. It is part of a larger movement: the *rhythm.* Rhythm means *flow,* and flow is determined by considerations beyond those of the regular metrical schemes. The schemes create a formal outline, which sets a limit to the degree of variety the poet can practice, but his art is to exercise freedom within this self-imposed framework of necessity. Meter, therefore, is only one element in rhythm, and rhythm is both larger and deeper in significance than meter. Rhythms move in feeling more than in feet, and their effect may depend on irregularity as much as on regularity.

There is one unalterable rule in the study of versification: in the reading of poetry it is not the *regular* number and kind of syllables and feet which control the rhythm but the placing of the *particular* and *varied* accents or stresses or beats (these three words are interchangeable). The real direction and ordering of the rhythm comes from the poet's personal *voice,* which is heard speaking through the lines. Because the human ear is as individual in its range as any of the other senses, and the intonations it hears vary, different individuals may hear this voice differently. There are no precise rules of rhythm as there are of meter, and so no absolute laws of scansion (the placing of the stresses in reading). The poet's voice itself may have numberless different tones, but whatever tone it takes, it asserts that the regular metrical scheme it has chosen must obey the sense of what is being said, and be subordinated to the rhythmical movement required to express the thought and the feeling. To do this, the poet will vary the formal accentual pattern with reversals of the expected stress, with omissions or additions of syllables or feet, with surprises and even shocks. These are all deliberate and calculated: "It is not inspiration that exhausts one," says Yeats, "it is Art." Eliot too declares that "probably the larger part of the labor of the author is critical labor; the labor of sifting, combining, constructing, expunging, correcting, testing."

RHYTHMICAL VARIATIONS

Many variations of rhythmical stress can be heard by reading carefully any of the stanzas or the two sonnets quoted in the section on rhyme schemes. Although the basic sound pattern in each illustration is iambic pentameter, none keep to that regular beat, and it would be very dull if they did. But perhaps the differences can be heard more clearly if we listen to several "voices" using the same verse form, and note the various rhythmical possibilities that emerge.

Take blank verse. This is what it sounded like in *Gorboduc* (1561), the earliest play written in that meter:

The royal king and eke his sons are slain;
No ruler rests within the regal seat;
The heir, to whom the scepter 'longs, unknown; . . .
Lo, Britain's realm is left an open prey,
A present spoil for conquest to ensue.

It is clumsily regular. Its iambs, all end-stopped, plod along in regimented uniformity, and the result is a lifeless monotony.

Marlowe changed all that, and brought a new ease and flexibility to blank verse by varying the accents, by breaking the line with the caesura, by indicating dramatic pauses, and by allowing the sense to flow into a freer sentence structure.

Was this the face that launched a thousand ships,
And burnt the topless towers of Ilium? —
Sweet Helen, make me immortal with a kiss, —

Her lips suck forth my soul; see, where it flies!
Come, Helen, come, give me my soul again.
Here will I dwell, for heaven is in these lips,
And all is dross that is not Helena.[1]

Shakespeare's intonations are still nearer the speaking voice.

                    That it should come to this!
But two months dead! Nay, not so much, not two.
So excellent a King, that was, to this,
Hyperion to a satyr. So loving to my mother
That he might not beteem the winds of heaven
Visit her face too roughly. Heaven and earth!
Must I remember? Why, she would hang on him
As if increase of appetite had grown
By what it fed on. And yet within a month ——
Let me not think on 't —[2]

This is really dramatic blank verse: no single line is entirely regular, and the almost strangling fury and disgust come out in the broken, uneven rhythms and gasps of angry pain and nausea.

Milton's blank verse is not dramatic, but epic. It depends for its magnificence on sustained rhythmic nobility and sonorous sweep. But again, his finest effects are gained by playing the thought and feeling structure of his larger rhythms against the expected regular beat. Take his description of the fall of Satan:

            Him the Almighty Power
Hurled headlong flaming from the ethereal sky
With hideous ruin and combustion down
To bottomless perdition, there to dwell
In adamantine chains and penal fire,
Who durst defy the Omnipotent to arms.[3]

Here one line only, the fifth, keeps the regular metrical pattern. It supplies the conventional order against which the freedom and irregularity of the other lines are counterpointed. Their magnificent energy, indeed, is not only in the splendor of their diction, but in the movement which, in the sweep of a single sentence, creates the sense of Lucifer falling through space. The rush of the opening with its powerful beats carries through without pause to "perdition,"

---

[1] *Doctor Faustus*, XIII.91–97.
[2] *Hamlet*, I.ii.137–46. See p. 102, above.
[3] *Paradise Lost*, I.44–49. See p. 225, above.

and after this toppling descent, "there to dwell /
In adamantine chains and penal fire," checks
the rush into the feeling of the permanence of
Satan's doom.

In *Samson Agonistes* Milton allows himself
not only variations within the pentameter line,
but variations of line length itself to give
specific effects.

> O dark, dark, dark, amid the blaze of noon,
> Irrecoverably dark, total eclipse
> Without all hope of day![1]

Although the first line has ten syllables, it has
six stresses; the second has eleven syllables, but
only four beats; and the third, with only three
beats, stands as a complete line. The sound
goes underground, as it were, and the pause
which completes the line is filled with the echo
of "dark" and Samson's silent hopelessness.

If we turn to Browning from Milton, it is
difficult to realize that they are both using the
same meter:

> I am poor brother Lippo, by your leave!
> You need not clap your torches in my face.
> Zooks, what's to blame? you think you see a monk!
> What, 'tis past midnight, and you go the rounds,
> And here you catch me at an alley's end
> Where sportive ladies leave their doors ajar?
> The Carmine's my cloister; hunt it up,
> Do — [2]

Again we hear speech rhythms in individual
tones. The parentheses, the quick shifts and
breaks in thought, the questions, the ejacula-
tions, carry all the immediacy and spontaneity
of the natural voice. But the rhythms are facile
rather than subtle.

An equal variety of rhythmic flow and tone
can be heard in the heroic couplet. Marlowe
loads it with descriptive richness, but the end-
stopped lines tend towards monotony.

> Upon her head she wore a myrtle wreath,
> From whence her veil reached to the ground beneath.
> Her veil was artificial flowers and leaves,
> Whose workmanship both man and beast deceives.
> Many would praise the sweet smell as she passed,
> When 'twas the odor which her breath forth cast;
> And there for honey bees have sought in vain,
> And, beat from thence, have lighted there again.[3]

Donne was only nine years younger than Marlowe, but his heroic couplets certainly sound
very different.

> On a huge hill
> Cragged, and steep, Truth stands, and he that will
> Reach her, about must, and about must go;
> And what the hill's suddenness resists, win so;
> Yet strive so, that before age, death's twilight,
> Thy soul rest, for none can work in that night.[4]

Though this is in rhymed couplets, it has more
of the quality of Elizabethan blank verse than
of the nondramatic poetry of the period. The
pressure of the thinking mind bends the rhyme
out of regularity. In some lines it is emphasized
with heavy stress; in others ignored. The reader
must slow up to get the force of the ideas, must
identify himself, in an almost physical way,
with the breath pauses, with the image of
reaching and striving and resisting "the hill's
suddenness" by patient struggle. In the third
and fourth lines the slow, plodding effort
lengthens the lines by stresses on the last two
single words, and in the last line the Biblical
echo, "for the night cometh when no man can
work," brings home the deliberate *laboriousness*
which Donne is creating in the place of that easy
musical rhythm.

The rhythm of Donne's couplets moves slowly
with its burden of personal emotional meaning,
while that of Pope's has the brisk tone of the
man of the world conversing with his friends.
Instead of speaking in a sustained sentence of
several lines, he makes each couplet a unit in
itself, with its rhythm based on the symmetry
and neat opposition of its two halves. The
closed couplet is an artificial convention, but
within its framework of formal decorum Pope
packs it with pithy terseness.

> First slave to words, then vassal to a name,
> Then dupe to party; child and man the same;
> Bounded by Nature, narrowed still by art,
> A trifling head, and a contracted heart.[5]

In spite of its clipped trimness, this is full of
subtle sound variations and acute, witty precision. But Pope can inject real intensity of
feeling into couplets. In the Sporus portrait, he
introduces a dramatic element which enlarges
the rhythmical scope. One side of the conversation is in the negative tone of light contempt
taken by Dr. Arbuthnot, while Pope himself
sweeps that away in the positive, though controlled, vibrations of direct hatred.

---

[1] See p. 274, above.
[2] "Fra Lippo Lippi," ll. 1–8. See p. 849, above.
[3] *Hero and Leander*, I.17–22.

[4] Satire III, ll. 79–84.
[5] *Dunciad*, IV.501–05.

Let Sporus tremble — "What? that thing of silk,
Sporus, that mere white curd of ass's milk?
Satire or sense, alas! can Sporus feel?
Who breaks a butterfly upon a wheel?"
   Yet let me flap this bug with gilded wings,
This painted child of dirt, that stinks and stings;
Whose buzz the witty and the fair annoys,
Yet wit ne'er tastes, and beauty ne'er enjoys: . . .[1]

Browning used the couplet, as he used blank verse, to carry the tones of the ordinary speaking voice. The sense is never enclosed within the two lines; the rhymes are unaccented, and the meaning flows across them and ignores them.

                 Who'd stoop to blame
This sort of trifling? Even had you skill
In speech — (which I have not) — to make your will
Quite clear to such an one, and say, "Just this
Or that in you disgusts me; here you miss,
Or there exceed the mark" — [2]

SOUND AND SENSE

From these illustrations it is clear that though the interrelation of sound and sense is the foundation of rhythm, that interrelation is much more complex than Pope's lines on the subject, quoted earlier, suggest. It is not just a matter of actions being translated into imitative sounds, but of feeling and thought coming through the flow and quality of the language and the management of the sound pattern. There cannot be much feeling and thought if the metrical convention is too rigid or if the tone and pitch remain too long at one level. A poem may become monotonous, even if it is a monotony of pleasant sounds. For instance, the opening stanza of Meredith's "Love in the Valley" is very delightful.

Under yonder beech-tree single on the green-sward,
  Couched with her arms behind her golden head,
Knees and tresses folded to slip and ripple idly,
  Lies my young love sleeping in the shade.
Had I the heart to slide an arm beneath her,
  Press her parting lips as her waist I gather slow,
Waking in amazement she could not but embrace me:
  Then would she hold me and never let me go?

But when this is followed by twenty-five stanzas of the same rippling melody, the ear cloys, and the senses become blurred and comatose; the sound pattern is *too* sweet, *too* fluid, *too* flexible.

But versification may fail, of course, from a different kind of monotony, a prosiness where neither a regular beat nor a vital speech rhythm

asserts itself, and the verse becomes torpid Milton, great verbal artist though he is, can at times be rhythmically toneless. Some of the choruses in *Samson Agonistes*, for instance, are extraordinarily flat, all liveliness of movement stifled out of the verse.

Many are the sayings of the wise
In ancient and in modern books enrolled,
Extolling patience as the truest fortitude;
And to the bearing well of all calamities,
All chances incident to man's frail life,
Consolatories writ
With studied argument, and much persuasion
  sought, . . .[3]

Many rhythms are bad, however, not from monotony, but because of the choice of an unsuitable meter and diction for their subject matter — a clumsy adaptation of matter to medium. Cowper, for instance, ruined his "Verses Supposed to Be Written by Alexander Selkirk," by choosing to write them in the tripping anapest.

I am monarch of all I survey,
  My right there is none to dispute;
From the center all round to the sea,
  I am lord of the fowl and the brute.
Oh, Solitude! where are thy charms
  That sages have seen in thy face?
Better dwell in the midst of alarms,
  Than reign in this horrible place.

The sound pattern is better suited to comic opera than to expressing the horrors of shipwrecked isolation.

Wordsworth makes the same fatal choice of the anapest for "The Reverie of Poor Susan," for the sense of nostalgic longing in Susan's memories fails to communicate itself in that singsong meter.

Green pastures she views in the midst of the dale,
Down which she so often has tripped with her pail;
And a single small cottage, a nest like a dove's,
The one only dwelling on earth that she loves.[4]

Or again, when Sir Ronald Ross had finally proved how the female mosquito transfers the infection of malaria, he put his sense of thrilling triumph into a poem, one stanza of which runs:

I know this little thing
  A myriad men will save,
O Death, where is thy sting,
  Thy victory, O grave!

No one would deny the truth of the thought or the sincerity of the feeling, but they are *not*

[1] "Epistle to Dr. Arbuthnot," ll. 305–12. See p. 436, above.
[2] "My Last Duchess," ll. 34–39. See p. 843, above.
[3] See p. 280, above.
[4] See p. 564, above.

created in the words. To feel how a sense of triumph can be translated into rhythm, listen to Spenser in the *Epithalamion*.

Open the temple gates unto my love,
Open them wide that she may enter in,
And all the postes adorne as doth behove,
And all the pillours deck with girlands trim . . .
And let the roring Organs loudly play
The praises of the Lord in lively notes,
The whiles with hollow throates
The Choristers the joyous Antheme sing,
That al the woods may answere and their eccho ring.

But this is a simple joyous burst: to hear the mind working with concentrated force, keeping a complex stanza pattern and packing the lines with brain stuff as well as with emotional intensity, take the first stanza of Donne's "The Anniversary."

Áll kíngs, and áll their fávorites,

Áll glóry of hónors, beáuties, wíts,

The sún itsélf, which mákes tímes, as they páss,

Is élder by a yéar, nów, than it wás

When thóu and I fírst one anóther sáw:

All óther thíngs to their destrúction dráw,

Ónly óur lóve hath nó decáy;

This nó tomórrow háth, nor yésterday,

Rúnning it néver rúns from us awáy,

But trúly kéeps his fírst, lást, éverlásting dáy.[1]

The sixth line is a regular iambic, but until that is reached, the accents are wrenched to enforce a slowing up in the reading, so that all the weight of the temporal, and the passing, and the material, shall contrast with the light, sweeping movement of the triumph over time in the last half of the verse. After the summing up of the theme of mortality, "All other things to their destruction draw," the firm beats of "Only our love hath no decay," announce that triumph, and then the syllables move easily, with their four chiming rhymes, to end in the long, lingering, seven-beat exultation of eternal constancy.

The rhythmic creation of the totally opposing mood of empty despair is well illustrated in the opening lines of Eliot's "The Hollow Men."

We are the hollow men
We are the stuffed men
Leaning together

Headpiece filled with straw. Alas!
Our dried voices, when
We whisper together
Are quiet and meaningless
As wind in dry grass
Or rats' feet over broken glass
In our dry cellar

Shape without form, shade without colour,
Paralysed force, gesture without motion . . .[2]

The theme of the paragraph is the sense of banishment from human vitality, vitality either for good or for evil. That condition of meaningless neutrality is evoked in the unrhymed couplet at the end. It has no directed movement towards anything else, its language is as static and negative as its feeling, and the lifelessness of the hollow men is expressed in the very faint heartbeat of the rhythm in the introductory lines, with their halting uneven stresses. The "dried voices" are entirely without resonance or vigor; the words they whisper "lean together" with no interlocking harmony; and they are likened to the meaningless inhuman sounds of the wind in dry grass or "rats' feet over broken glass." The halting, harsh cacophony of vowels and consonants in that image carries something of the shattered fragments which is all "our dry cellar" contains.

As an example of a skillful *change* of mood within a single stanza take the first verse of Yeats's "Sailing to Byzantium."

That is no country for old men. The young
In one another's arms, birds in the trees
— Those dying generations — at their song,
The salmon-falls, the mackerel-crowded seas,
Fish, flesh, or fowl, commend all summer long
Whatever is begotten, born, and dies.
Caught in that sensual music all neglect
Monuments of unageing intellect.[3]

The poem is going to contrast the life of the body with that of the soul; the state of natural animal fertility with the inanimate creations of man's hands and minds; instinctive mortal joys with the immortal triumphs of art; transience with permanence. The contrasts are already pointed to in this stanza by the difference in the rhythm between the first six lines of the *ottava rima* and the last two.

The "country" is no place on the map; it is simply the world of nature and its delights. The abrupt opening sentence seems to dismiss it, but its beauty and sweetness come crowding in.

[1] See p. 188, above.   .

[2] See p. 1018, above.
[3] See p. 996, above.

The flow of the first phases, evoking the lovely summer world, is checked by the parenthesis, "those dying generations," the reminder of transience, but the "sensual music" asserts itself with the flowing, regular stress of "the salmon-falls, the mackerel-crowded seas," followed by the triple alliteration of "fish, flesh, or fowl." In the next line the ear expects "begotten, born" will lead to a parallel device, but instead, what might be called an alliterative disappointment comes. The finality of "and dies" reminds the reader again of the inevitable end of the natural cycle in which mortal music is "caught"; and the rhythm of that music is brought up short at the end of the seventh line in the hardening of the consonants in "neglect," followed by the three powerful heavily accented words which oppose the fleeting loveliness of bodies to the permanence of the immortal creations of mind and spirit.

WORD TEXTURE AND VALUE

From the analyses of these passages, it is very apparent that the matter of word texture and value cannot be separated from that of the sound pattern. Not only the changing rhythmic design from line to line, but the quality of the words themselves, their echoes from the past, their associations, their disposal and manipulation in a poem, all play their parts in the total effect of a poem.

Every age has a particular flavor in its use of poetic vocabulary. The history of poetic language is like that of the soil. However rich, poetic language is subject to erosion, and its fertility is constantly threatened by elements which destroy its vitality and impoverish its content. Time washes away its surface freshness and use exhausts its vigor until it becomes arid and sterile. The history of poetry is, in one sense, a cyclical history of the birth, maturing and decay of various traditions of poetic diction. Each is born in revolution, runs its course of development and elaboration, and degenerates into formalism and mechanical imitation.

It is usual to give the name "poetic diction" to a peculiarly artificial use of words which became popular in the eighteenth century, when a breeze was always a zephyr; a girl a nymph; fishes, birds, and sheep, the finny prey, the feathered choir, and the fleecy care; and rats, the whiskered vermin race. We cannot by any stretch of imagination, think of Donne calling a girl a nymph, or Wordsworth or Shelley calling birds the feathered choir, or of Eliot speaking of rats as the whiskered vermin race. But it was not the eighteenth century only which evolved a poetic diction; certain marked characteristics belong to each tradition. Before the enormous development of language which the Elizabethan and Jacobean dramatists illustrate, the early Elizabethan lyrists sang in a very simple vocabulary.

> Love in my bosom like a bee
>   Doth suck his sweet;
> Now with his wings he plays with me,
>   Now with his feet.
> Within mine eyes he makes his nest,
> His bed amidst my tender breast;
> And yet he robs me of my rest.
>   Ah, wanton, will ye? [1]

But that convention was much too easy for the complexity of thought and dramatic intensity which Donne and his followers demanded that the lyric should carry, so that in their era words became close-packed and concentrated in their condensation of emotional and intellectual meaning. At the opposite extreme from Donne, Milton changed the Elizabethan vocabulary into the Latinized eloquence of formal grandeur. But to the poets of the eighteenth century the language of both Donne or Milton was equally unsuitable. They needed a social literary medium which would communicate readily to an audience which prided itself on standards of clarity, elegance, and decorum in the use of language. That fashion in turn seemed false and artificial to Wordsworth, who demanded a return to the language of ordinary men. The later Romantics developed more particularly the sensuous suggestions of words, and loaded their poetry with them. That convention in turn weakened in the 1890's, and petered out into the ultrasensuous.

> I have forgot much, Cynara! Gone with the wind,
> Flung roses, roses, riotously with the throng,
> Dancing to put thy pale lost lilies out of mind. [2]

The modern generation has entirely discarded such florid gestures, and if they wish to express something of the same situation they do it in a deliberately "unpoetic" vocabulary.

> I have stuttered on my feet
> Clinched to the streamlined and butter smooth trulls
>   of the elite. [3]

[1] Thomas Lodge.
[2] Ernest Dowson.
[3] Louis MacNeice.

Apart from a "poetic diction" belonging in a general way to the language of every age, the problem of poetic diction in its simplest sense — the words — is at the foundation of every poem. Nature and training endow each poet with certain tendencies in his use of words. He will be thrifty like Housman or Hardy, or spendthrift like Marlowe or Swinburne; calm like Herbert or boisterous like Browning; graceful like Herrick or energetic like Hopkins. And in addition to his inherent bent, the whole conscious force of his artistry is towards the most exact equivalent he can attain between the words he uses and the effects he wishes to communicate. Hart Crane speaks for every poet: "Oh, it is hard! One must be drenched in words, literally soaked in them, to have the right ones form themselves into the proper patterns at the right moment."

Against the poet are ranged all the forces of custom and carelessness in the use of words. His readers have eyes blurred by the film of familiarity and ears muffled by common usage. Through his verbal pattern he must sharpen and intensify every significant sound, shade of meaning and association. He arranges his words so that they influence one another, like color values in painting, and work directly or obliquely on the emotions and senses in ways that *seem* inevitable.

> White in the moon the long road lies
> The moon stands blank above;
> White in the moon the long road lies
> That leads me from my love.

If Housman had written "that leads me *to* my love," the statement might have been factually true, but it would be poetically false. The feeling of the poem has already been created by the association of "white," "long," "blank" with the road and the moon; the forlornness and weariness and emptiness and chill are already there. The whole effect of a poem, indeed, can be ruined by a wrong word or rhyme. It is useless for Burns to prepare us for a beautiful lament with the opening,

> Ae fond kiss and then we sever!
> Ae fareweel, and then for ever!

if he starts the next stanza,

> I'll ne'er blame my partial fancy,
> Naething could resist my Nancy.

The mood is irrevocably shattered.

Poetry may work through the senses only, and appeal to eye, ear, touch, taste, and smell, as in this stanza of Ben Jonson:

> Have you seen but a bright flower grow
>   Before rude hands have touched it?
> Have you marked but the fall of the snow
>   Before the soil hath smutched it?
> Have you felt the wool of the beaver,
>   Or swan's down ever?
> Or have smelt o' the bud of the brier,
>   Or the nard in the fire?
> Or have tasted the bag of the bee?
> O so white, O so soft, O so sweet is she!

Or the words may generate so much activity in themselves that the reader feels almost muscularly involved in the response. As we have seen from an earlier example, Donne's verse in particular has this forceful energy.

> Batter my heart, three-personed God; for, you
> As yet but knock, breathe, shine, and seek to mend;
> That I may rise and stand, o'erthrow me, and bend
> Your force, to break, blow, burn, and make me new.[1]

Words can turn a moral platitude about the need for spiritual vitality in the face of bodily decay, into a vivid, concrete picture, as in the second stanza of "Sailing to Byzantium."

> An aged man is but a paltry thing,
> A tattered coat upon a stick, unless
> Soul clap its hands and sing, . . .[2]

Put in their full context, leading on from the first stanza, the words take on more than their surface meaning, for the picture of the scarecrow, the "thing," in its stiff and lifeless rigidity, contrasts with the flowing grace of "the young in one another's arms"; and the soul clapping its hands and singing is parallel to the birds at *their* song, "commending" the life of "whatever is begotten, born, and dies."

Eliot weaves a very complex and subtle pattern through association and verbal allusion. The home-coming of the typist in Part III of *The Waste Land* is a good illustration.

> At the violet hour, the evening hour that strives
> Homeward, and brings the sailor home from sea,
> The typist home at teatime, clears her breakfast, lights
> Her stove, and lays out food in tins.
> Out of the window perilously spread
> Her drying combinations touched by the sun's last
>   rays, . . .

The central lines describe the sordid and unappetizing quality of the typist's "home" and slovenly manner of living in the most prosaic

---

[1] See p. 192, above.
[2] See p. 996, above.

and direct words; but the picture they give is ironized and accentuated by framing it within other lines where allusive words recall memories of romantic scenes of evening, home-coming, and open windows. The "violet hour" suggests Sappho's lines to the evening star; "the sailor home from sea" echoes R. L. Stevenson's "Requiem"; while the conjunction of the window with the word "perilously" provokes a wry comparison with Keats's

> . . . magic casements, opening on the foam
> Of perilous seas, in faery lands forlorn.[1]

This juxtaposition of words calling up very different associations gives great compression of meaning by ironical contrast. Yeats gets a powerful effect of this sort in the final lines of "The Second Coming."

> And what rough beast, its hour come round at last,
> Slouches towards Bethlehem to be born?[2]

All the suggestions of Bethlehem to the Christian world — the simple shepherds, the stately Magi, the birth of the Prince of Peace — are brought into opposition with the words *rough beast* and *slouches*. The poem has established that Yeats sees a new historical cycle beginning in blood and violence, and the conclusion points to the birth of Christ as a similar era, doomed from the start to its present ending.

Even without all the weight and subtlety of suggestion which modern poets introduce, the mingling of different *qualities* of language has always made for effective musical pattern and added emotional richness. Shakespeare is the great master of the blending of the simple and the elaborate. The dying Hamlet addresses Horatio:

> If thou didst ever hold me in thy heart,
> Absent thee from felicity a while,
> And in this harsh world draw thy breath in pain
> To tell my story.[3]

Or Macbeth, returning from the murder of Duncan, cries:

> Will all great Neptune's ocean wash this blood
> Clean from my hand? No; this my hand will rather
> The multitudinous seas incarnadine
> Making the green one red.

In both these passages, the particular verbal texture of the short simple words interwoven with the dignity and resonance of latinizations

is peculiarly satisfying to the ear. The same thing happens in Wordsworth's "A Slumber Did My Spirit Seal":

> No motion has she now, no force;
> She neither hears nor sees;
> Rolled round in earth's diurnal course,
> With rocks, and stones, and trees.[4]

Both the agonizing thought of the inaction of the dead, and the majesty of the eternal measured movement of the earth's rotation, come through the contrast of the three short, almost monosyllabic, lines with the force of the lengthened third line of five beats and the one formal word in the whole poem — *diurnal*.

The precise use of *epithets* by poets is in sharp contrast to their usual careless usage in speech. Dorothy Wordsworth enters in her journal: "William tired himself seeking an epithet for the cuckoo," and Keats writes to Fanny Brawne, "I want a brighter word than bright, a fairer word than fair." Keat's own description of "the tiger-moth's deep-damasked wings,"[5] concentrates in *damasked* the suggestions of the shimmer of silk, the sheen of damascened metal, and the texture of a damask rose. Arnold's final line in "To Marguerite," "The unplumbed, salt, estranging sea," is haunting in its creation of the mystery, the bitterness, the loneliness of the human situation in the flux of life and time. Tennyson reveals a similar mood entirely in descriptive epithets.

> And ghastly thro' the drizzling rain
> On the bald street breaks the blank day.[6]

Another device is to blend the abstract and the concrete so that they set off one another: "proud pied April,"[7] "the lazy, leaden-stepping hours,"[8] "the same bright, patient stars."[9]

Another way to remind poetry readers of the patient search for words of the right music and meaning, the right interrelation and precision, is to study the revisions poets have made in their work. Milton's "airy tongues that syllable men's names,"[10] was first the rather vague "airy tongues that lure night wanderers"; Poe's famous lines

> the glory that was Greece
> And the grandeur that was Rome

1 See p. 748, above.
2 See p. 996, above.
3 See p. 146, above.

4 See p. 581, above.
5 *The Eve of St. Agnes.* See p. 743, above.
6 *In Memoriam,* VII. See p. 787, above.
7 Shakespeare, Sonnet XCVIII.
8 Milton, "On Time."
9 Keats, *Hyperion.*
10 Milton, *Comus.*

went through the stage of

> the beauty of fair Greece
> And the grandeur of old Rome.

The precise veracity of Keats's

> Not so much life as on a summer's day
> Robs not one light seed from the feathered grass [1]

might have remained

> Not so much life as on a summer's day
> Robs not at all the dandelion's fleece.

The great poet uses every value that he can wring from his medium; music, meaning, memory; simplicity and ornament; visual image and abstract idea; dramatic force, lyric intensity, sensuous suggestion. All these are distilled from the mass of language into the potent spirit of poetry. Or we can use Donne's image of molding metal on a forge, and say that the poet takes words to batter them, to break, blow, burn, and make them new; or that he has the power both to remint the old coinage of traditional expression and to issue new currency. But the best image of a poem is an organic one of growth. It arises and takes its own specific form out of the formless flux of life and language.

> Out of the sea of sound the life of music,
> Out of the slimy mud of words, out of the sleet and
>   hail of verbal imprecisions,
> Approximate thoughts and feelings, words that have
>   taken the place of thoughts and feelings,
> There spring the perfect order of speech, and the
>   beauty of incantation. [2]

[1] Keats, *Hyperion.*

[2] T. S. Eliot. *The Rock*, Chorus IX.

E. D.

Author-Title Index

Index of First Lines

B 7
C 8
D 9
E 0
F 1
G 2
H 3
I 4
J 5

RECIPROCALS OF BASIC FUNCTIONS

18. $\displaystyle\int \frac{1}{1 \pm \sin u}\, du = \tan u \mp \sec u + C$

19. $\displaystyle\int \frac{1}{1 \pm \cos u}\, du = -\cot u \pm \csc u + C$

20. $\displaystyle\int \frac{1}{1 \pm \tan u}\, du = \frac{1}{2}(u \pm \ln |\cos u \pm \sin u|) + C$

21. $\displaystyle\int \frac{1}{\sin u \cos u}\, du = \ln |\tan u| + C$

22. $\displaystyle\int \frac{1}{1 \pm \cot u}\, du = \frac{1}{2}(u \mp \ln |\sin u \pm \cos u|) + C$

23. $\displaystyle\int \frac{1}{1 \pm \sec u}\, du = u + \cot u \mp \csc u + C$

24. $\displaystyle\int \frac{1}{1 \pm \csc u}\, du = u - \tan u \pm \sec u + C$

25. $\displaystyle\int \frac{1}{1 \pm e^u}\, du = u - \ln(1 \pm e^u) + C$

POWERS OF TRIGONOMETRIC FUNCTIONS

26. $\displaystyle\int \sin^2 u\, du = \frac{1}{2}u - \frac{1}{4}\sin 2u + C$

27. $\displaystyle\int \cos^2 u\, du = \frac{1}{2}u + \frac{1}{4}\sin 2u + C$

28. $\displaystyle\int \tan^2 u\, du = \tan u - u + C$

29. $\displaystyle\int \sin^n u\, du = -\frac{1}{n}\sin^{n-1} u \cos u + \frac{n-1}{n}\int \sin^{n-2} u\, du$

30. $\displaystyle\int \cos^n u\, du = \frac{1}{n}\cos^{n-1} u \sin u + \frac{n-1}{n}\int \cos^{n-2} u\, du$

31. $\displaystyle\int \tan^n u\, du = \frac{1}{n-1}\tan^{n-1} u - \int \tan^{n-2} u\, du$

32. $\displaystyle\int \cot^2 u\, du = -\cot u - u + C$

33. $\displaystyle\int \sec^2 u\, du = \tan u + C$

34. $\displaystyle\int \csc^2 u\, du = -\cot u + C$

35. $\displaystyle\int \cot^n u\, du = -\frac{1}{n-1}\cot^{n-1} u - \int \cot^{n-2} u\, du$

36. $\displaystyle\int \sec^n u\, du = \frac{1}{n-1}\sec^{n-2} u \tan u + \frac{n-2}{n-1}\int \sec^{n-2} u\, du$

37. $\displaystyle\int \csc^n u\, du = -\frac{1}{n-1}\csc^{n-2} u \cot u + \frac{n-2}{n-1}\int \csc^{n-2} u\, du$

PRODUCTS OF TRIGONOMETRIC FUNCTIONS

38. $\displaystyle\int \sin mu \sin nu\, du = -\frac{\sin(m+n)u}{2(m+n)} + \frac{\sin(m-n)u}{2(m-n)} + C$

39. $\displaystyle\int \cos mu \cos nu\, du = \frac{\sin(m+n)u}{2(m+n)} + \frac{\sin(m-n)u}{2(m-n)} + C$

40. $\displaystyle\int \sin mu \cos nu\, du = -\frac{\cos(m+n)u}{2(m+n)} - \frac{\cos(m-n)u}{2(m-n)} + C$

41. $\displaystyle\int \sin^m u \cos^n u\, du = -\frac{\sin^{m-1} u \cos^{n+1} u}{m+n} + \frac{m-1}{m+n}\int \sin^{m-2} u \cos^n u\, du$

$$= \frac{\sin^{m+1} u \cos^{n-1} u}{m+n} + \frac{n-1}{m+n}\int \sin^m u \cos^{n-2} u\, du$$

PRODUCTS OF TRIGONOMETRIC AND EXPONENTIAL FUNCTIONS

42. $\displaystyle\int e^{au} \sin bu\, du = \frac{e^{au}}{a^2 + b^2}(a \sin bu - b \cos bu) + C$

43. $\displaystyle\int e^{au} \cos bu\, du = \frac{e^{au}}{a^2 + b^2}(a \cos bu + b \sin bu) + C$

POWERS OF u MULTIPLYING OR DIVIDING BASIC FUNCTIONS

44. $\displaystyle\int u \sin u\, du = \sin u - u \cos u + C$

45. $\displaystyle\int u \cos u\, du = \cos u + u \sin u + C$

46. $\displaystyle\int u^2 \sin u\, du = 2u \sin u + (2 - u^2) \cos u + C$

47. $\displaystyle\int u^2 \cos u\, du = 2u \cos u + (u^2 - 2) \sin u + C$

48. $\displaystyle\int u^n \sin u\, du = -u^n \cos u + n \int u^{n-1} \cos u\, du$

49. $\displaystyle\int u^n \cos u\, du = u^n \sin u - n \int u^{n-1} \sin u\, du$

50. $\displaystyle\int u^n \ln u\, du = \frac{u^{n+1}}{(n+1)^2}[(n+1)\ln u - 1] + C$

51. $\displaystyle\int u e^u\, du = e^u(u - 1) + C$

52. $\displaystyle\int u^n e^u\, du = u^n e^u - n \int u^{n-1} e^u\, du$

53. $\displaystyle\int u^n a^u\, du = \frac{u^n a^u}{\ln a} - \frac{n}{\ln a}\int u^{n-1} a^u\, du + C$

54. $\displaystyle\int \frac{e^u\, du}{u^n} = -\frac{e^u}{(n-1)u^{n-1}} + \frac{1}{n-1}\int \frac{e^u\, du}{u^{n-1}}$

55. $\displaystyle\int \frac{a^u\, du}{u^n} = -\frac{a^u}{(n-1)u^{n-1}} + \frac{\ln a}{n-1}\int \frac{a^u\, du}{u^{n-1}}$

56. $\displaystyle\int \frac{du}{u \ln u} = \ln |\ln u| + C$

POLYNOMIALS MULTIPLYING BASIC FUNCTIONS

57. $\displaystyle\int p(u)e^{au}\, du = \frac{1}{a}p(u)e^{au} - \frac{1}{a^2}p'(u)e^{au} + \frac{1}{a^3}p''(u)e^{au} - \cdots$ [signs alternate: $+ - + - \cdots$]

58. $\displaystyle\int p(u) \sin au\, du = -\frac{1}{a}p(u) \cos au + \frac{1}{a^2}p'(u) \sin au + \frac{1}{a^3}p''(u) \cos au - \cdots$ [signs alternate in pairs after first term: $+ + - - + + - - \cdots$]

59. $\displaystyle\int p(u) \cos au\, du = \frac{1}{a}p(u) \sin au + \frac{1}{a^2}p'(u) \cos au - \frac{1}{a^3}p''(u) \sin au - \cdots$ [signs alternate in pairs: $+ + - - + + - - \cdots$]

Calculus provides a way of viewing and analyzing the physical world. As with all mathematics courses, calculus involves equations and formulas. However, if you successfully learn to use all the formulas and solve all of the problems in the text but do not master the underlying *ideas*, you will have missed the most important part of calculus. If you master these ideas, you will have a widely applicable tool that goes far beyond textbook exercises.

Before starting your studies, you may find it helpful to leaf through this text to get a general feeling for its different parts:

- The opening page of each chapter gives you an overview of what that chapter is about, and the opening page of each section within a chapter gives you an overview of what that section is about. To help you locate specific information, sections are subdivided into topics that are marked with a box like this ■.

- Each section ends with a set of exercises. The answers to most odd-numbered exercises appear in the back of the book. If you find that your answer to an exercise does not match that in the back of the book, do not assume immediately that yours is incorrect—there may be more than one way to express the answer. For example, if your answer is $\sqrt{2}/2$ and the text answer is $1/\sqrt{2}$, then both are correct since your answer can be obtained by "rationalizing" the text answer. In general, if your answer does not match that in the text, then your best first step is to look for an algebraic manipulation or a trigonometric identity that might help you determine if the two answers are equivalent. If the answer is in the form of a decimal approximation, then your answer might differ from that in the text because of a difference in the number of decimal places used in the computations.

- The section exercises include regular exercises and four special categories: *Quick Check*, *Focus on Concepts*, *True/False*, and *Writing*.

  - The *Quick Check* exercises are intended to give you quick feedback on whether you understand the key ideas in the section; they involve relatively little computation, and have answers provided at the end of the exercise set.

  - The *Focus on Concepts* exercises, as their name suggests, key in on the main ideas in the section.

  - *True/False* exercises focus on key ideas in a different way. You must decide whether the statement is true in *all possible circumstances*, in which case you would declare it to be "true," or whether there are some circumstances in which it is not true, in which case you would declare it to be "false." In each such exercise you are asked to "Explain your answer." You might do this by noting a theorem in the text that shows the statement to be true or by finding a particular example in which the statement is not true.

  - *Writing* exercises are intended to test your ability to explain mathematical ideas in words rather than relying solely on numbers and symbols. All exercises requiring writing should be answered in complete, correctly punctuated logical sentences—not with fragmented phrases and formulas.

- Each chapter ends with two additional sets of exercises: *Chapter Review Exercises*, which, as the name suggests, is a select set of exercises that provide a review of the main concepts and techniques in the chapter, and *Making Connections*, in which exercises require you to draw on and combine various ideas developed throughout the chapter.

- Your instructor may choose to incorporate technology in your calculus course. Exercises whose solution involves the use of some kind of technology are tagged with icons to alert you and your instructor. Those exercises tagged with the icon ⌇ require graphing technology—either a graphing calculator or a computer program that can graph equations. Those exercises tagged with the icon [c] require a computer algebra system (CAS) such as *Mathematica*, *Maple*, or available on some graphing calculators.

- At the end of the text you will find a set of four appendices covering various topics such as a detailed review of trigonometry and graphing techniques using technology. Inside the front and back covers of the text you will find endpapers that contain useful formulas.

- The ideas in this text were created by real people with interesting personalities and backgrounds. Pictures and biographical sketches of many of these people appear throughout the book.

- Notes in the margin are intended to clarify or comment on important points in the text.

A Word of Encouragement

As you work your way through this text you will find some ideas that you understand immediately, some that you don't understand until you have read them several times, and others that you do not seem to understand, even after several readings. Do not become discouraged—some ideas are intrinsically difficult and take time to "percolate." You may well find that a hard idea becomes clear later when you least expect it.

Wiley Web Site for this Text

www.wiley.com/college/anton

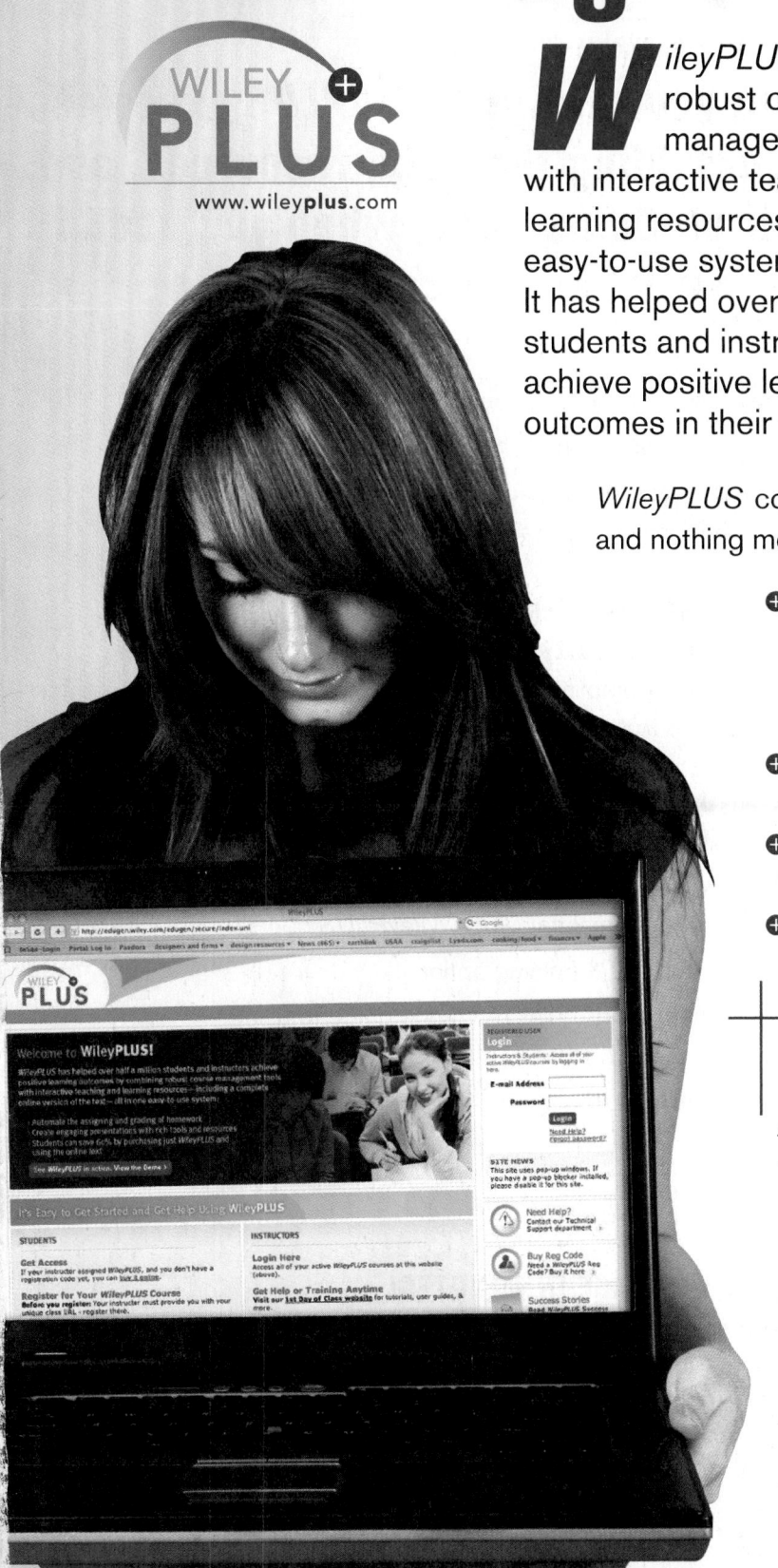

www.wileyplus.com

Wiley is committed to making your entire *WileyPLUS* experience productive & enjoyable by providing the help, resources, and personal support you & your students need, when you need it. It's all here: www.wileyplus.com −

TECHNICAL SUPPORT:

- ➕ A fully searchable knowledge base of FAQs and help documentation, available 24/7
- ➕ Live chat with a trained member of our support staff during business hours
- ➕ A form to fill out and submit online to ask any question and get a quick response
- ➕ **Instructor-only** phone line during business hours: 1.877.586.0192

FACULTY-LED TRAINING THROUGH THE WILEY FACULTY NETWORK:
Register online: www.wherefacultyconnect.com
Connect with your colleagues in a complimentary virtual seminar, with a personal mentor in your field, or at a live workshop to share best practices for teaching with technology.

1ST DAY OF CLASS...AND BEYOND!
Resources You & Your Students Need to Get Started & Use *WileyPLUS* from the first day forward.

- ➕ 2-Minute Tutorials on how to set up & maintain your *WileyPLUS* course
- ➕ User guides, links to technical support & training options
- ➕ *WileyPLUS for Dummies*: Instructors' quick reference guide to using *WileyPLUS*
- ➕ Student tutorials & instruction on how to register, buy, and use *WileyPLUS*

YOUR *WileyPLUS* ACCOUNT MANAGER:
Your personal *WileyPLUS* connection for any assistance you need!

SET UP YOUR *WileyPLUS* COURSE IN MINUTES!
Selected *WileyPLUS* courses with QuickStart contain pre-loaded assignments & presentations created by subject matter experts who are also experienced *WileyPLUS* users.

Interested? See and try WileyPLUS in action!
Details and Demo: www.wileyplus.com

9th
EDITION

CALCULUS

EARLY TRANSCENDENTALS

- **HOWARD ANTON** *Drexel University*
- **IRL BIVENS** *Davidson College*
- **STEPHEN DAVIS** *Davidson College*

with contributions by

Thomas Polaski *Winthrop University*

JOHN WILEY & SONS, INC.

WILEY

Publisher: Laurie Rosatone
Acquisitions Editor: David Dietz
Freelance Developmental Editor: Anne Scanlan-Rohrer
Marketing Manager: Jaclyn Elkins
Associate Editor: Michael Shroff/Will Art
Editorial Assistant: Pamela Lashbrook
Full Service Production Management: Carol Sawyer/The Perfect Proof
Senior Production Editor: Ken Santor
Senior Designer: Madelyn Lesure
Associate Photo Editor: Sheena Goldstein
Freelance Illustration: Karen Heyt
Cover Photo: © Eric Simonsen/Getty Images

This book was set in LaTeX by Techsetters, Inc., and printed and bound by R.R. Donnelley/Jefferson City. The cover was printed by R.R. Donnelley.

This book is printed on acid-free paper.

The paper in this book was manufactured by a mill whose forest management programs include sustained yield harvesting of its timberlands. Sustained yield harvesting principles ensure that the numbers of trees cut each year does not exceed the amount of new growth.

ISBN 978-0-470-18345-8

Printed in the United States of America

10 9 8 7 6 5 4 3 2 1

About HOWARD ANTON

Howard Anton wrote the original version of this text and was the author of the first six editions. He obtained his B.A. from Lehigh University, his M.A. from the University of Illinois, and his Ph.D. from the Polytechnic University of Brooklyn, all in mathematics. In the early 1960s he worked for Burroughs Corporation and Avco Corporation at Cape Canaveral, Florida, where he was involved with the manned space program. In 1968 he joined the Mathematics Department at Drexel University, where he taught full time until 1983. Since that time he has been an adjunct professor at Drexel and has devoted the majority of his time to textbook writing and activities for mathematical associations. Dr. Anton was president of the EPADEL Section of the Mathematical Association of America (MAA), served on the Board of Governors of that organization, and guided the creation of the Student Chapters of the MAA. He has published numerous research papers in functional analysis, approximation theory, and topology, as well as pedagogical papers. He is best known for his textbooks in mathematics, which are among the most widely used in the world. There are currently more than one hundred versions of his books, including translations into Spanish, Arabic, Portuguese, Italian, Indonesian, French, Japanese, Chinese, Hebrew, and German. For relaxation, Dr. Anton enjoys traveling and photography.

About IRL BIVENS

Irl C. Bivens, recipient of the George Polya Award and the Merten M. Hasse Prize for Expository Writing in Mathematics, received his A.B. from Pfeiffer College and his Ph.D. from the University of North Carolina at Chapel Hill, both in mathematics. Since 1982, he has taught at Davidson College, where he currently holds the position of professor of mathematics. A typical academic year sees him teaching courses in calculus, topology, and geometry. Dr. Bivens also enjoys mathematical history, and his annual History of Mathematics seminar is a perennial favorite with Davidson mathematics majors. He has published numerous articles on undergraduate mathematics, as well as research papers in his specialty, differential geometry. He has served on the editorial boards of the MAA Problem Book series and *The College Mathematics Journal* and is a reviewer for *Mathematical Reviews*. When he is not pursuing mathematics, Professor Bivens enjoys juggling, swimming, walking, and spending time with his son Robert.

About STEPHEN DAVIS

Stephen L. Davis received his B.A. from Lindenwood College and his Ph.D. from Rutgers University in mathematics. Having previously taught at Rutgers University and Ohio State University, Dr. Davis came to Davidson College in 1981, where he is currently a professor of mathematics. He regularly teaches calculus, linear algebra, abstract algebra, and computer science. A sabbatical in 1995–1996 took him to Swarthmore College as a visiting associate professor. Professor Davis has published numerous articles on calculus reform and testing, as well as research papers on finite group theory, his specialty. Professor Davis has held several offices in the Southeastern section of the MAA, including chair and secretary-treasurer. He is currently a faculty consultant for the Educational Testing Service Advanced Placement Calculus Test, a board member of the North Carolina Association of Advanced Placement Mathematics Teachers, and is actively involved in nurturing mathematically talented high school students through leadership in the Charlotte Mathematics Club. He was formerly North Carolina state director for the MAA. For relaxation, he plays basketball, juggles, and travels. Professor Davis and his wife Elisabeth have three children, Laura, Anne, and James, all former calculus students.

About THOMAS POLASKI, contributor to the ninth edition

Thomas W. Polaski received his B.S. from Furman University and his Ph.D. in mathematics from Duke University. He is currently a professor at Winthrop University, where he has taught since 1991. He was named Outstanding Junior Professor at Winthrop in 1996. He has published articles on mathematics pedagogy and stochastic processes and has authored a chapter in a forthcoming linear algebra textbook. Professor Polaski is a frequent presenter at mathematics meetings, giving talks on topics ranging from mathematical biology to mathematical models for baseball. He has been an MAA Visiting Lecturer and is a reviewer for *Mathematical Reviews*. Professor Polaski has been a reader for the Advanced Placement Calculus Tests for many years. In addition to calculus, he enjoys travel and hiking. Professor Polaski and his wife, LeDayne, have a daughter, Kate, and live in Charlotte, North Carolina.

To
my wife Pat and my children: Brian, David, and Lauren

In Memory of
my mother Shirley
my father Benjamin
my thesis advisor and inspiration, George Bachman
my benefactor in my time of need, Stephen Girard (1750–1831)
—HA

To
my son Robert
—IB

To
my wife Elisabeth
my children: Laura, Anne, and James
—SD

PREFACE

This ninth edition of *Calculus* maintains those aspects of previous editions that have led to the series' success—we continue to strive for student comprehension without sacrificing mathematical accuracy, and the exercise sets are carefully constructed to avoid unhappy surprises that can derail a calculus class. However, this edition also has many new features that we hope will attract new users and also motivate past users to take a fresh look at our work. We had two main goals for this edition:

- To make those adjustments to the order and content that would align the text more precisely with the most widely followed calculus outlines.
- To add new elements to the text that would provide a wider range of teaching and learning tools.

All of the changes were carefully reviewed by an advisory committee of outstanding teachers comprised of both users and nonusers of the previous edition. The charge of this committee was to ensure that all changes did not alter those aspects of the text that attracted users of the eighth edition and at the same time provide freshness to the new edition that would attract new users. Some of the more substantive changes are described below.

NEW FEATURES IN THIS EDITION

New Elements in the Exercises   We added new true/false exercises, new writing exercises, and new exercise types that were requested by reviewers of the eighth edition.

Making Connections   We added this new element to the end of each chapter. A Making Connections exercise synthesizes concepts drawn across multiple sections of its chapter rather than using ideas from a single section as is expected of a regular or review exercise.

Reorganization of Review Material   The precalculus review material that was in Chapter 1 of the eighth edition forms Chapter 0 of the ninth edition. The body of material in Chapter 1 of the eighth edition that is not generally regarded as precalculus review was moved to appropriate sections of the text in this edition. Thus, Chapter 0 focuses exclusively on those preliminary topics that students need to start the calculus course.

Parametric Equations Reorganized   In the eighth edition, parametric equations were introduced in the first chapter and picked up again later in the text. Many instructors asked that we return to the traditional organization, and we have done so; the material on parametric equations is now first introduced and then discussed in detail in Section 10.1 (*Parametric Curves*). However, to support those instructors who want to continue the eighth edition path of giving an early exposure to parametric curves, we have provided Web materials (Web Appendix I) as well as self-contained exercise sets on the topic in Section 6.4 (*Length of a Plane Curve*) and Section 6.5 (*Area of a Surface of Revolution*).

Also, Section 14.4 (*Surface Area; Parametric Surfaces*) has been reorganized so surfaces of the form $z = f(x, y)$ are discussed before surfaces defined parametrically.

Differential Equations Reorganized   We reordered and revised the chapter on differential equations so that instructors who cover only separable equations can do so without a forced diversion into general first-order equations and other unrelated topics. This chapter can be skipped entirely by those who do not cover differential equations at all in calculus.

New 2D Discussion of Centroids and Center of Gravity   In the eighth edition and earlier, centroids and center of gravity were covered only in three dimensions. In this edition we added a new section on that topic in Chapter 6 (*Applications of the Definite Integral*), so centroids and center of gravity can now be studied in two dimensions, as is common in many calculus courses.

Related Rates and Local Linearity Reorganized   The sections on related rates and local linearity were moved to follow the sections on implicit differentiation and loga-rithmic, exponential, and inverse trigonometric functions, thereby making a richer variety of techniques and functions available to study related rates and local linearity.

Rectilinear Motion Reorganized   The more technical aspects of rectilinear motion that were discussed in the introductory discussion of derivatives in the eighth edition have been deferred so as not to distract from the primary task of developing the notion of the derivative. This also provides a less fragmented development of rectilinear motion.

Other Reorganization   The section *Graphing Functions Using Calculators and Com-puter Algebra Systems*, which appeared in the text body of the eighth edition, is now a text appendix (Appendix A), and the sections *Mathematical Models* and *Second-Order Linear Homogeneous Differential Equations* are now posted on the Web site that supports the text.

OTHER FEATURES

Flexibility   This edition has a built-in flexibility that is designed to serve a broad spectrum of calculus philosophies—from traditional to "reform." Technology can be emphasized or not, and the order of many topics can be permuted freely to accommodate each instructor's specific needs.

Rigor   The challenge of writing a good calculus book is to strike the right balance between rigor and clarity. Our goal is to present precise mathematics to the fullest extent possible in an introductory treatment. Where clarity and rigor conflict, we choose clarity; however, we believe it to be important that the student understand the difference between a careful proof and an informal argument, so we have informed the reader when the arguments being presented are informal or motivational. Theory involving ϵ-δ arguments appears in a separate section so that it can be covered or not, as preferred by the instructor.

Rule of Four   The "rule of four" refers to presenting concepts from the verbal, algebraic, visual, and numerical points of view. In keeping with current pedagogical philosophy, we used this approach whenever appropriate.

Visualization   This edition makes extensive use of modern computer graphics to clarify concepts and to develop the student's ability to visualize mathematical objects, particularly those in 3-space. For those students who are working with graphing technology, there are many exercises that are designed to develop the student's ability to generate and analyze mathematical curves and surfaces.

Quick Check Exercises   Each exercise set begins with approximately five exercises (answers included) that are designed to provide students with an immediate assessment of whether they have mastered key ideas from the section. They require a minimum of computation and are answered by filling in the blanks.

Focus on Concepts Exercises   Each exercise set contains a clearly identified group of problems that focus on the main ideas of the section.

Technology Exercises   Most sections include exercises that are designed to be solved using either a graphing calculator or a computer algebra system such as *Mathematica*, *Maple*, or the open source program *Sage*. These exercises are marked with an icon for easy identification.

Applicability of Calculus   One of the primary goals of this text is to link calculus to the real world and the student's own experience. This theme is carried through in the examples and exercises.

Career Preparation   This text is written at a mathematical level that will prepare students for a wide variety of careers that require a sound mathematics background, including engineering, the various sciences, and business.

Trigonometry Review   Deficiencies in trigonometry plague many students, so we have included a substantial trigonometry review in Appendix B.

Appendix on Polynomial Equations   Because many calculus students are weak in solving polynomial equations, we have included an appendix (Appendix C) that reviews the Factor Theorem, the Remainder Theorem, and procedures for finding rational roots.

Principles of Integral Evaluation   The traditional Techniques of Integration is entitled "Principles of Integral Evaluation" to reflect its more modern approach to the material. The chapter emphasizes general methods and the role of technology rather than specific tricks for evaluating complicated or obscure integrals.

Historical Notes   The biographies and historical notes have been a hallmark of this text from its first edition and have been maintained. All of the biographical materials have been distilled from standard sources with the goal of capturing and bringing to life for the student the personalities of history's greatest mathematicians.

Margin Notes and Warnings   These appear in the margins throughout the text to clarify or expand on the text exposition or to alert the reader to some pitfall.

SUPPLEMENTS

SUPPLEMENTS FOR THE STUDENT

Print Supplements

The Student Solutions Manual (978-0470-37958-5) provides students with detailed solutions to odd-numbered exercises from the text. The structure of solutions in the manual matches those of worked examples in the textbook.

Student Companion Site

The Student Companion Site provides access to the following student supplements:

- Web Quizzes, which are short, fill-in-the-blank quizzes that are arranged by chapter and section.
- Additional textbook content, including answers to odd-numbered exercises and appendices.

WileyPLUS

WileyPLUS, Wiley's digital-learning environment, is loaded with all of the supplements above, and also features the following:

- The E-book, which is an exact version of the print text, but also features hyperlinks to questions, definitions, and supplements for quicker and easier support.
- The Student Study Guide provides concise summaries for quick review, checklists, common mistakes/pitfalls, and sample tests for each section and chapter of the text.
- The Graphing Calculator Manual helps students to get the most out of their graphing calculator and shows how they can apply the numerical and graphing functions of their calculators to their study of calculus.
- Guided Online (GO) Exercises prompt students to build solutions step by step. Rather than simply grading an exercise answer as wrong, GO problems show students precisely where they are making a mistake.
- Are You Ready? quizzes gauge student mastery of chapter concepts and techniques and provide feedback on areas that require further attention.
- Algebra and Trigonometry Refresher quizzes provide students with an opportunity to brush up on material necessary to master calculus, as well as to determine areas that require further review.

SUPPLEMENTS FOR THE INSTRUCTOR

Print Supplements

The Instructor's Solutions Manual (978-0470-37957-8) contains detailed solutions to all exercises in the text.

The Instructor's Manual (978-0470-37956-1) suggests time allocations and teaching plans for each section in the text. Most of the teaching plans contain a bulleted list of key points to emphasize. The discussion of each section concludes with a sample homework assignment.

The Test Bank (978-0470-40856-8) features nearly 7000 questions and answers for every section in the text.

Instructor Companion Site

The Instructor Companion Site provides detailed information on the textbook's features, contents, and coverage and provides access to the following instructor supplements:

- The Computerized Test Bank features nearly 7000 questions—mostly algorithmically generated—that allow for varied questions and numerical inputs.
- PowerPoint slides cover the major concepts and themes of each section in a chapter.
- Personal-Response System questions ("Clicker Questions") appear at the end of each PowerPoint presentation and provide an easy way to gauge classroom understanding.
- Additional textbook content, such as Calculus Horizons and Explorations, back-of-the-book appendices, and selected biographies.

WileyPLUS

WileyPLUS, Wiley's digital-learning environment, is loaded with all of the supplements above, and also features the following:

- Homework management tools, which easily allow you to assign and grade questions, as well as gauge student comprehension.
- QuickStart features predesigned reading and homework assignments. Use them as-is or customize them to fit the needs of your classroom.
- The E-book, which is an exact version of the print text but also features hyperlinks to questions, definitions, and supplements for quicker and easier support.
- Animated applets, which can be used in class to present and explore key ideas graphically and dynamically—especially useful for display of three-dimensional graphs in multivariable calculus.

ACKNOWLEDGMENTS

It has been our good fortune to have the advice and guidance of many talented people whose knowledge and skills have enhanced this book in many ways. For their valuable help we thank the following people.

Reviewers and Contributors to the Ninth Edition of Early Transcendentals Calculus

Frederick Adkins, *Indiana University of Pennsylvania*
Bill Allen, *Reedley College–Clovis Center*
Jerry Allison, *Black Hawk College*
Seth Armstrong, *Southern Utah University*
Przemyslaw Bogacki, *Old Dominion University*
Wayne P. Britt, *Louisiana State University*
Kristin Chatas, *Washtenaw Community College*
Michele Clement, *Louisiana State University*
Ray Collings, *Georgia Perimeter College*
David E. Dobbs, *University of Tennessee, Knoxville*
H. Edward Donley, *Indiana University of Pennsylvania*
Jim Edmondson, *Santa Barbara City College*
Michael Filaseta, *University of South Carolina*
Jose Flores, *University of South Dakota*
Mitch Francis, *Horace Mann*
Jerome Heaven, *Indiana Tech*
Patricia Henry, *Drexel University*
Danrun Huang, *St. Cloud State University*
Alvaro Islas, *University of Central Florida*
Bin Jiang, *Portland State University*
Ronald Jorgensen, *Milwaukee School of Engineering*
Raja Khoury, *Collin County Community College*

Carole King Krueger, *The University of Texas at Arlington*
Thomas Leness, *Florida International University*
Kathryn Lesh, *Union College*
Behailu Mammo, *Hofstra University*
John McCuan, *Georgia Tech*
Daryl McGinnis, *Columbus State Community College*
Michael Mears, *Manatee Community College*
John G. Michaels, *SUNY Brockport*
Jason Miner, *Santa Barbara City College*
Darrell Minor, *Columbus State Community College*
Kathleen Miranda, *SUNY Old Westbury*
Carla Monticelli, *Camden County College*
Bryan Mosher, *University of Minnesota*
Ferdinand O. Orock, *Hudson County Community College*
Altay Ozgener, *Manatee Community College*
Chuang Peng, *Morehouse College*
Joni B. Pirnot, *Manatee Community College*
Elise Price, *Tarrant County College*
Holly Puterbaugh, *University of Vermont*
Hah Suey Quan, *Golden West College*
Joseph W. Rody, *Arizona State University*
Constance Schober, *University of Central Florida*

Kurt Sebastian, *United States Coast Guard*
Paul Seeburger, *Monroe Community College*
Bradley Stetson, *Schoolcraft College*
Walter E. Stone, Jr., *North Shore Community College*
Eleanor Storey, *Front Range Community College, Westminster Campus*
Stefania Tracogna, *Arizona State University*
Francis J. Vasko, *Kutztown University*
Jim Voss, *Front Range Community College*
Anke Walz, *Kutztown Community College*
Xian Wu, *University of South Carolina*
Yvonne Yaz, *Milwaukee School of Engineering*
Richard A. Zang, *University of New Hampshire*

The following people read the ninth edition at various stages for mathematical and pedagogical accuracy and/or assisted with the critically important job of preparing answers to exercises:

Dean Hickerson, *University of California, Davis*
Ron Jorgensen, *Milwaukee School of Engineering*
Roger Lipsett
Georgia Mederer
David Ryeburn, *Simon Fraser University*
Neil Wigley

Reviewers and Contributors to the Ninth Edition of Late Transcendentals and Multivariable Calculus

David Bradley, *University of Maine*
Dean Burbank, *Gulf Coast Community College*
Jason Cantarella, *University of Georgia*
Yanzhao Cao, *Florida A&M University*
T.J. Duda, *Columbus State Community College*
Nancy Eschen, *Florida Community College, Jacksonville*
Reuben Farley, *Virginia Commonwealth University*
Zhuang-dan Guan, *University of California, Riverside*
Greg Henderson, *Hillsborough Community College*

Micah James, *University of Illinois*
Mohammad Kazemi, *University of North Carolina, Charlotte*
Przemo Kranz, *University of Mississippi*
Steffen Lempp, *University of Wisconsin, Madison*
Wen-Xiu Ma, *University of South Florida*
Vania Mascioni, *Ball State University*
David Price, *Tarrant County College*
Jan Rychtar, *University of North Carolina, Greensboro*
John T. Saccoman, *Seton Hall University*

Charlotte Simmons, *University of Central Oklahoma*
Don Soash, *Hillsborough Community College*
Bryan Stewart, *Tarrant County College*
Helene Tyler, *Manhattan College*
Pavlos Tzermias, *University of Tennessee, Knoxville*
Raja Varatharajah, *North Carolina A&T*
David Voss, *Western Illinois University*
Richard Watkins, *Tidewater Community College*
Xiao-Dong Zhang, *Florida Atlantic University*
Diane Zych, *Erie Community College*

Reviewers and Contributors to the Eighth Edition of Calculus

Gregory Adams, *Bucknell University*

Bill Allen, *Reedley College–Clovis Center*

Jerry Allison, *Black Hawk College*

Stella Ashford, *Southern University and A&M College*

Mary Lane Baggett, *University of Mississippi*

Christopher Barker, *San Joaquin Delta College*

Kbenesh Blayneh, *Florida A&M University*

David Bradley, *University of Maine*

Paul Britt, *Louisiana State University*

Judith Broadwin, *Jericho High School*

Andrew Bulleri, *Howard Community College*

Christopher Butler, *Case Western Reserve University*

Cheryl Cantwell, *Seminole Community College*

Judith Carter, *North Shore Community College*

Miriam Castroconde, *Irvine Valley College*

Neena Chopra, *The Pennsylvania State University*

Gaemus Collins, *University of California, San Diego*

Fielden Cox, *Centennial College*

Danielle Cross, *Northern Essex Community College*

Gary Crown, *Wichita State University*

Larry Cusick, *California State University–Fresno*

Stephan DeLong, *Tidewater Community College–Virginia Beach Campus*

Debbie A. Desrochers, *Napa Valley College*

Ryness Doherty, *Community College of Denver*

T.J. Duda, *Columbus State Community College*

Peter Embalabala, *Lincoln Land Community College*

Phillip Farmer, *Diablo Valley College*

Laurene Fausett, *Georgia Southern University*

Sally E. Fishbeck, *Rochester Institute of Technology*

Bob Grant, *Mesa Community College*

Richard Hall, *Cochise College*

Noal Harbertson, *California State University, Fresno*

Donald Hartig, *California Polytechnic State University*

Karl Havlak, *Angelo State University*

J. Derrick Head, *University of Minnesota–Morris*

Konrad Heuvers, *Michigan Technological University*

Tommie Ann Hill-Natter, *Prairie View A&M University*

Holly Hirst, *Appalachian State University*

Joe Howe, *St. Charles County Community College*

Shirley Huffman, *Southwest Missouri State University*

Gary S. Itzkowitz, *Rowan University*

John Johnson, *George Fox University*

Kenneth Kalmanson, *Montclair State University*

Grant Karamyan, *University of California, Los Angeles*

David Keller, *Kirkwood Community College*

Dan Kemp, *South Dakota State University*

Vesna Kilibarda, *Indiana University Northwest*

Cecilia Knoll, *Florida Institute of Technology*

Carole King Krueger, *The University of Texas at Arlington*

Holly A. Kresch, *Diablo Valley College*

John Kubicek, *Southwest Missouri State University*

Theodore Lai, *Hudson County Community College*

Richard Lane, *University of Montana*

Jeuel LaTorre, *Clemson University*

Marshall Leitman, *Case Western Reserve University*

Phoebe Lutz, *Delta College*

Ernest Manfred, *U.S. Coast Guard Academy*

James Martin, *Wake Technical Community College*

Vania Mascioni, *Ball State University*

Tamra Mason, *Albuquerque TVI Community College*

Thomas W. Mason, *Florida A&M University*

Roy Mathia, *The College of William and Mary*

John Michaels, *SUNY Brockport*

Darrell Minor, *Columbus State Community College*

Darren Narayan, *Rochester Institute of Technology*

Doug Nelson, *Central Oregon Community College*

Lawrence J. Newberry, *Glendale College*

Judith Palagallo, *The University of Akron*

Efton Park, *Texas Christian University*

Joanne Peeples, *El Paso Community College*

Gary L. Peterson, *James Madison University*

Lefkios Petevis, *Kirkwood Community College*

Thomas W. Polaski, *Winthrop University*

Richard Ponticelli, *North Shore Community College*

Holly Puterbaugh, *University of Vermont*

Douglas Quinney, *University of Keele*

B. David Redman, Jr., *Delta College*

William H. Richardson, *Wichita State University*

Lila F. Roberts, *Georgia Southern University*

Robert Rock, *Daniel Webster College*

John Saccoman, *Seton Hall University*

Avinash Sathaye, *University of Kentucky*

George W. Schultz, *St. Petersburg Junior College*

Paul Seeburger, *Monroe Community College*

Richard B. Shad, *Florida Community College–Jacksonville*

Mary Margaret Shoaf-Grubbs, *College of New Rochelle*

Charlotte Simmons, *University of Central Oklahoma*

Ann Sitomer, *Portland Community College*

Jeanne Smith, *Saddleback Community College*

Rajalakshmi Sriram, *Okaloosa-Walton Community College*

Mark Stevenson, *Oakland Community College*

Bryan Stewart, *Tarrant County College*

Bradley Stoll, *The Harker School*

Eleanor Storey, *Front Range Community College*

John A. Suvak, *Memorial University of Newfoundland*

Richard Swanson, *Montana State University*

Skip Thompson, *Radford University*

Helene Tyler, *Manhattan College*

Paramanathan Varatharajah, *North Carolina A&T State University*

David Voss, *Western Illinois University*

Jim Voss, *Front Range Community College*

Richard Watkins, *Tidewater Community College*

Bruce R. Wenner, *University of Missouri–Kansas City*

Jane West, *Trident Technical College*

Ted Wilcox, *Rochester Institute of Technology*

Janine Wittwer, *Williams College*

Diane Zych, *Erie Community College–North Campus*

The following people read the eighth edition at various stages for mathematical and pedagogical accuracy and/or assisted with the critically important job of preparing answers to exercises:

Elka Block, *Twin Prime Editorial*

Dean Hickerson, *University of California, Davis*

Thomas Polaski, *Winthrop University*

Frank Purcell, *Twin Prime Editorial*

David Ryeburn, *Simon Fraser University*

CONTENTS

THE ROOTS OF CALCULUS

Today's exciting applications of calculus have roots that can be traced to the work of the Greek mathematician Archimedes, but the actual discovery of the fundamental principles of calculus was made independently by Isaac Newton (English) and Gottfried Leibniz (German) in the late seventeenth century. The work of Newton and Leibniz was motivated by four major classes of scientific and mathematical problems of the time:

- Find the tangent line to a general curve at a given point.
- Find the area of a general region, the length of a general curve, and the volume of a general solid.
- Find the maximum or minimum value of a quantity—for example, the maximum and minimum distances of a planet from the Sun, or the maximum range attainable for a projectile by varying its angle of fire.
- Given a formula for the distance traveled by a body in any specified amount of time, find the velocity and acceleration of the body at any instant. Conversely, given a formula that specifies the acceleration of velocity at any instant, find the distance traveled by the body in a specified period of time.

Newton and Leibniz found a fundamental relationship between the problem of finding a tangent line to a curve and the problem of determining the area of a region. Their realization of this connection is considered to be the "discovery of calculus." Though Newton saw how these two problems are related ten years before Leibniz did, Leibniz published his work twenty years before Newton. This situation led to a stormy debate over who was the rightful discoverer of calculus. The debate engulfed Europe for half a century, with the scientists of the European continent supporting Leibniz and those from England supporting Newton. The conflict was extremely unfortunate because Newton's inferior notation badly hampered scientific development in England, and the Continent in turn lost the benefit of Newton's discoveries in astronomy and physics for nearly fifty years. In spite of it all, Newton and Leibniz were sincere admirers of each other's work.

ISAAC NEWTON (1642–1727)

Newton was born in the village of Woolsthorpe, England. His father died before he was born and his mother raised him on the family farm. As a youth he showed little evidence of his later brilliance, except for an unusual talent with mechanical devices—he apparently built a working water clock and a toy flour mill powered by a mouse. In 1661 he entered Trinity College in Cambridge with a deficiency in geometry. Fortunately, Newton caught the eye of Isaac Barrow, a gifted mathematician and teacher. Under Barrow's guidance Newton immersed himself in mathematics and science, but he graduated without any special distinction. Because the bubonic plague was spreading rapidly through London, Newton returned to his home in Woolsthorpe and stayed there during the years of 1665 and 1666. In those two momentous years the entire framework of modern science was miraculously created in Newton's mind. He discovered calculus, recognized the underlying principles of planetary motion and gravity, and determined that "white" sunlight was composed of all colors, red to violet. For whatever reasons he kept his discoveries to himself. In 1667 he returned to Cambridge to obtain his Master's degree and upon graduation became a teacher at Trinity. Then in 1669 Newton succeeded his teacher, Isaac Barrow, to the Lucasian chair of mathematics at Trinity, one of the most honored chairs of mathematics in the world.

Thereafter, brilliant discoveries flowed from Newton steadily. He formulated the law of gravitation and used it to explain the motion of the moon, the planets, and the tides; he formulated basic theories of light, thermodynamics, and hydrodynamics; and he devised and constructed the first modern reflecting telescope. Throughout his life Newton was hesitant to publish his major discoveries, revealing them only to a select circle of friends, perhaps because of a fear of criticism or controversy. In 1687, only after intense coaxing by the astronomer, Edmond Halley (disoverer of Halley's comet), did Newton publish his masterpiece, *Philosophiae Naturalis Principia Mathematica* (The Mathematical Principles of Natural Philosophy). This work is generally considered to be the most important and influential scientific book ever written. In it Newton explained the workings of the solar system and formulated the basic laws of motion, which to this day are fundamental in engineering and physics. However, not even the pleas of his friends could convince Newton to publish his discovery of calculus. Only after Leibniz published his results did Newton relent and publish his own work on calculus.

After twenty-five years as a professor, Newton suffered depression and a nervous breakdown. He gave up research in 1695 to accept a position as warden and later master of the London mint. During the twenty-five years that he worked at the mint, he did virtually no scientific or mathematical work. He was knighted in 1705 and on his death was buried in Westminster Abbey with all the honors his country could bestow. It is interesting to note that Newton was a learned theologian who viewed the primary value of his work to be its support of the existence of God. Throughout his life he worked passionately to date biblical events by relating them to astronomical phenomena. He was so consumed with this passion that he spent years searching the Book of Daniel for clues to the end of the world and the geography of hell.

Newton described his brilliant accomplishments as follows: "I seem to have been only like a boy playing on the seashore and diverting myself in now and then finding a smoother pebble or prettier shell than ordinary, whilst the great ocean of truth lay all undiscovered before me."

GOTTFRIED WILHELM LEIBNIZ (1646–1716)

This gifted genius was one of the last people to have mastered most major fields of knowledge—an impossible accomplishment in our own era of specialization. He was an expert in law, religion, philosophy, literature, politics, geology, metaphysics, alchemy, history, and mathematics.

Leibniz was born in Leipzig, Germany. His father, a professor of moral philosophy at the University of Leipzig, died when Leibniz was six years old. The precocious boy then gained access to his father's library and began reading voraciously on a wide range of subjects, a habit that he maintained throughout his life. At age fifteen he entered the University of Leipzig as a law student and by the age of twenty received a doctorate from the University of Altdorf. Subsequently, Leibniz followed a career in law and international politics, serving as counsel to kings and princes. During his numerous foreign missions, Leibniz came in contact with outstanding mathematicians and scientists who stimulated his interest in mathematics—most notably, the physicist Christian Huygens. In mathematics Leibniz was self-taught, learning the subject by reading papers and journals. As a result of this fragmented mathematical education, Leibniz often rediscovered the results of others, and this helped to fuel the debate over the discovery of calculus.

Leibniz never married. He was moderate in his habits, quick-tempered but easily appeased, and charitable in his judgment of other people's work. In spite of his great achievements, Leibniz never received the honors showered on Newton, and he spent his final years as a lonely embittered man. At his funeral there was one mourner, his secretary. An eyewitness stated, "He was buried more like a robber than what he really was—an ornament of his country."

© Arco Images/Alamy

0

BEFORE CALCULUS

The development of calculus in the seventeenth and eighteenth centuries was motivated by the need to understand physical phenomena such as the tides, the phases of the moon, the nature of light, and gravity.

One of the important themes in calculus is the analysis of relationships between physical or mathematical quantities. Such relationships can be described in terms of graphs, formulas, numerical data, or words. In this chapter we will develop the concept of a "function," which is the basic idea that underlies almost all mathematical and physical relationships, regardless of the form in which they are expressed. We will study properties of some of the most basic functions that occur in calculus, including polynomials, trigonometric functions, inverse trigonometric functions, exponential functions, and logarithmic functions.

FUNCTIONS

In this section we will define and develop the concept of a "function," which is the basic mathematical object that scientists and mathematicians use to describe relationships between variable quantities. Functions play a central role in calculus and its applications.

■ DEFINITION OF A FUNCTION

Many scientific laws and engineering principles describe how one quantity depends on another. This idea was formalized in 1673 by Gottfried Wilhelm Leibniz (see p. xx) who coined the term *function* to indicate the dependence of one quantity on another, as described in the following definition.

> **0.1.1** **DEFINITION** If a variable y depends on a variable x in such a way that each value of x determines exactly one value of y, then we say that ***y is a function of x***.

Four common methods for representing functions are:

- Numerically by tables
- Algebraically by formulas
- Geometrically by graphs
- Verbally

Table 0.1.1

INDIANAPOLIS 500
QUALIFYING SPEEDS

YEAR t	SPEED S (mi/h)
1989	223.885
1990	225.301
1991	224.113
1992	232.482
1993	223.967
1994	228.011
1995	231.604
1996	233.100
1997	218.263
1998	223.503
1999	225.179
2000	223.471
2001	226.037
2002	231.342
2003	231.725
2004	222.024
2005	227.598
2006	228.985

The method of representation often depends on how the function arises. For example:

- Table 0.1.1 shows the top qualifying speed S for the Indianapolis 500 auto race as a function of the year t. There is exactly one value of S for each value of t.

- Figure 0.1.1 is a graphical record of an earthquake recorded on a seismograph. The graph describes the deflection D of the seismograph needle as a function of the time T elapsed since the wave left the earthquake's epicenter. There is exactly one value of D for each value of T.

- Some of the most familiar functions arise from formulas; for example, the formula $C = 2\pi r$ expresses the circumference C of a circle as a function of its radius r. There is exactly one value of C for each value of r.

- Sometimes functions are described in words. For example, Isaac Newton's Law of Universal Gravitation is often stated as follows: The gravitational force of attraction between two bodies in the Universe is directly proportional to the product of their masses and inversely proportional to the square of the distance between them. This is the verbal description of the formula

$$F = G\frac{m_1 m_2}{r^2}$$

in which F is the force of attraction, m_1 and m_2 are the masses, r is the distance between them, and G is a constant. If the masses are constant, then the verbal description defines F as a function of r. There is exactly one value of F for each value of r.

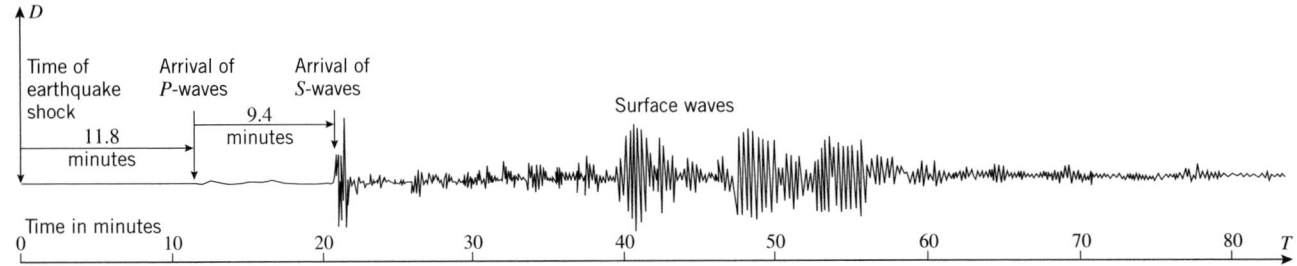

▲ Figure 0.1.1

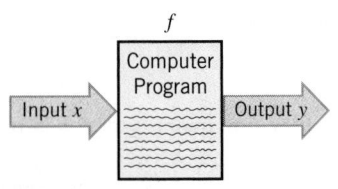

▲ Figure 0.1.2

In the mid-eighteenth century the Swiss mathematician Leonhard Euler (pronounced "oiler") conceived the idea of denoting functions by letters of the alphabet, thereby making it possible to refer to functions without stating specific formulas, graphs, or tables. To understand Euler's idea, think of a function as a computer program that takes an *input x*, operates on it in some way, and produces exactly one *output y*. The computer program is an object in its own right, so we can give it a name, say f. Thus, the function f (the computer program) associates a unique output y with each input x (Figure 0.1.2). This suggests the following definition.

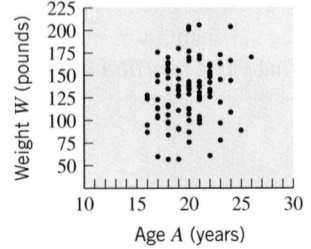

▲ Figure 0.1.3

0.1.2 DEFINITION A *function* f is a rule that associates a unique output with each input. If the input is denoted by x, then the output is denoted by $f(x)$ (read "f of x").

In this definition the term *unique* means "exactly one." Thus, a function cannot assign two different outputs to the same input. For example, Figure 0.1.3 shows a plot of weight versus age for a random sample of 100 college students. This plot does *not* describe W as a function of A because there are some values of A with more than one corresponding value of W. This is to be expected, since two people with the same age can have different weights.

■ INDEPENDENT AND DEPENDENT VARIABLES

For a given input x, the output of a function f is called the ***value*** of f at x or the ***image*** of x under f. Sometimes we will want to denote the output by a single letter, say y, and write

$$y = f(x)$$

This equation expresses y as a function of x; the variable x is called the ***independent variable*** (or ***argument***) of f, and the variable y is called the ***dependent variable*** of f. This terminology is intended to suggest that x is free to vary, but that once x has a specific value a corresponding value of y is determined. For now we will only consider functions in which the independent and dependent variables are real numbers, in which case we say that f is a ***real-valued function of a real variable***. Later, we will consider other kinds of functions.

Table 0.1.2

x	0	1	2	3
y	3	4	−1	6

▶ **Example 1**   Table 0.1.2 describes a functional relationship $y = f(x)$ for which

$f(0) = 3$ $\boxed{f \text{ associates } y = 3 \text{ with } x = 0.}$

$f(1) = 4$ $\boxed{f \text{ associates } y = 4 \text{ with } x = 1.}$

$f(2) = -1$ $\boxed{f \text{ associates } y = -1 \text{ with } x = 2.}$

$f(3) = 6$ $\boxed{f \text{ associates } y = 6 \text{ with } x = 3.}$ ◀

▶ **Example 2**   The equation

$$y = 3x^2 - 4x + 2$$

has the form $y = f(x)$ in which the function f is given by the formula

$$f(x) = 3x^2 - 4x + 2$$

Leonhard Euler (1707–1783) Euler was probably the most prolific mathematician who ever lived. It has been said that "Euler wrote mathematics as effortlessly as most men breathe." He was born in Basel, Switzerland, and was the son of a Protestant minister who had himself studied mathematics. Euler's genius developed early. He attended the University of Basel, where by age 16 he obtained both a Bachelor of Arts degree and a Master's degree in philosophy. While at Basel, Euler had the good fortune to be tutored one day a week in mathematics by a distinguished mathematician, Johann Bernoulli. At the urging of his father, Euler then began to study theology. The lure of mathematics was too great, however, and by age 18 Euler had begun to do mathematical research. Nevertheless, the influence of his father and his theological studies remained, and throughout his life Euler was a deeply religious, unaffected person. At various times Euler taught at St. Petersburg Academy of Sciences (in Russia), the University of Basel, and the Berlin Academy of Sciences. Euler's energy and capacity for work were virtually boundless. His collected works form more than 100 quarto-sized volumes and it is believed that much of his work has been lost. What is particularly astonishing is that Euler was blind for the last 17 years of his life, and this was one of his most productive periods! Euler's flawless memory was phenomenal. Early in his life he memorized the entire *Aeneid* by Virgil, and at age 70 he could not only recite the entire work but could also state the first and last sentence on each page of the book from which he memorized the work. His ability to solve problems in his head was beyond belief. He worked out in his head major problems of lunar motion that baffled Isaac Newton and once did a complicated calculation in his head to settle an argument between two students whose computations differed in the fiftieth decimal place.

Following the development of calculus by Leibniz and Newton, results in mathematics developed rapidly in a disorganized way. Euler's genius gave coherence to the mathematical landscape. He was the first mathematician to bring the full power of calculus to bear on problems from physics. He made major contributions to virtually every branch of mathematics as well as to the theory of optics, planetary motion, electricity, magnetism, and general mechanics.

For each input x, the corresponding output y is obtained by substituting x in this formula. For example,

$$f(0) = 3(0)^2 - 4(0) + 2 = 2$$
f associates $y = 2$ with $x = 0$.

$$f(-1.7) = 3(-1.7)^2 - 4(-1.7) + 2 = 17.47$$
f associates $y = 17.47$ with $x = -1.7$.

$$f(\sqrt{2}) = 3(\sqrt{2})^2 - 4\sqrt{2} + 2 = 8 - 4\sqrt{2}$$
f associates $y = 8 - 4\sqrt{2}$ with $x = \sqrt{2}$. ◄

■ GRAPHS OF FUNCTIONS

Figure 0.1.4 shows only portions of the graphs. Where appropriate, and unless indicated otherwise, it is understood that graphs shown in this text extend indefinitely beyond the boundaries of the displayed figure.

If f is a real-valued function of a real variable, then the **graph** of f in the xy-plane is defined to be the graph of the equation $y = f(x)$. For example, the graph of the function $f(x) = x$ is the graph of the equation $y = x$, shown in Figure 0.1.4. That figure also shows the graphs of some other basic functions that may already be familiar to you. In Appendix A we discuss techniques for graphing functions using graphing technology.

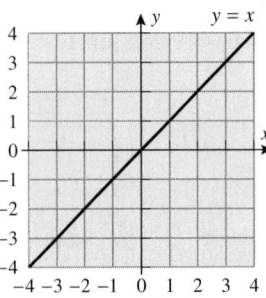
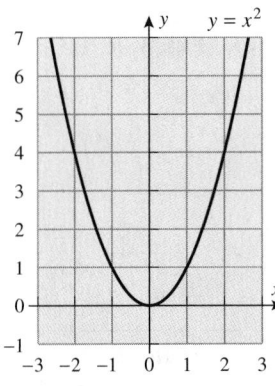
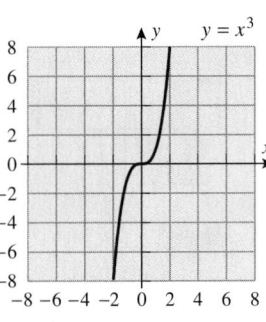

Since $\sqrt{x}$ is imaginary for negative values of x, there are no points on the graph of $y = \sqrt{x}$ in the region where $x < 0$.

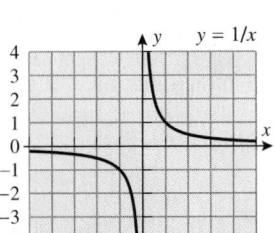
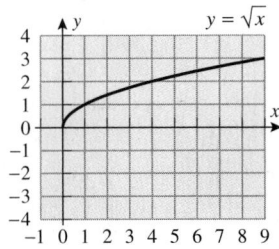
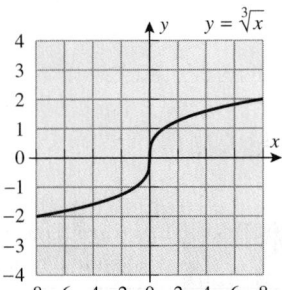

▲ Figure 0.1.4

Graphs can provide valuable visual information about a function. For example, since the graph of a function f in the xy-plane is the graph of the equation $y = f(x)$, the points on the graph of f are of the form $(x, f(x))$; that is, *the y-coordinate of a point on the graph of f is the value of f at the corresponding x-coordinate* (Figure 0.1.5). The values of x for which $f(x) = 0$ are the x-coordinates of the points where the graph of f intersects the x-axis (Figure 0.1.6). These values are called the **zeros** of f, the **roots** of $f(x) = 0$, or the **x-intercepts** of the graph of $y = f(x)$.

▲ **Figure 0.1.5**   The y-coordinate of a point on the graph of $y = f(x)$ is the value of f at the corresponding x-coordinate.

■ THE VERTICAL LINE TEST

Not every curve in the xy-plane is the graph of a function. For example, consider the curve in Figure 0.1.7, which is cut at two distinct points, (a, b) and (a, c), by a vertical line. This curve cannot be the graph of $y = f(x)$ for any function f; otherwise, we would have

$$f(a) = b \quad \text{and} \quad f(a) = c$$

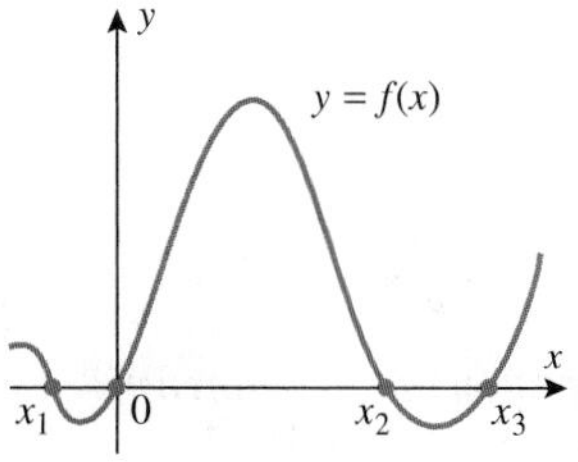

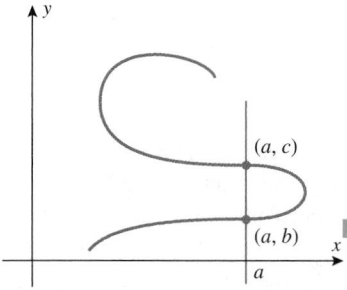

▲ **Figure 0.1.6** f has zeros at $x_1, 0, x_2$, and x_3.

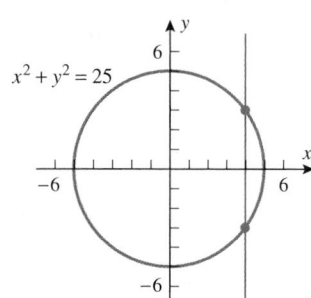

▲ **Figure 0.1.7** This curve cannot be the graph of a function.

Symbols such as $+x$ and $-x$ are deceptive, since it is tempting to conclude that $+x$ is positive and $-x$ is negative. However, this need not be so, since x itself can be positive or negative. For example, if x is negative, say $x = -3$, then $-x = 3$ is positive and $+x = -3$ is negative.

$x^2 + y^2 = 25$

▲ **Figure 0.1.8**

WARNING

To denote the negative square root you must write $-\sqrt{x}$. For example, the positive square root of 9 is $\sqrt{9} = 3$, whereas the negative square root of 9 is $-\sqrt{9} = -3$. (Do not make the mistake of writing $\sqrt{9} = \pm 3$.)

which is impossible, since f cannot assign two different values to a. Thus, there is no function f whose graph is the given curve. This illustrates the following general result, which we will call the *vertical line test*.

0.1.3 THE VERTICAL LINE TEST *A curve in the xy-plane is the graph of some function f if and only if no vertical line intersects the curve more than once.*

▶ **Example 3** The graph of the equation

$$x^2 + y^2 = 25$$

is a circle of radius 5 centered at the origin and hence there are vertical lines that cut the graph more than once (Figure 0.1.8). Thus this equation does not define y as a function of x. ◀

■ **THE ABSOLUTE VALUE FUNCTION**

Recall that the *absolute value* or *magnitude* of a real number x is defined by

$$|x| = \begin{cases} x, & x \geq 0 \\ -x, & x < 0 \end{cases}$$

The effect of taking the absolute value of a number is to strip away the minus sign if the number is negative and to leave the number unchanged if it is nonnegative. Thus,

$$|5| = 5, \quad \left|-\tfrac{4}{7}\right| = \tfrac{4}{7}, \quad |0| = 0$$

A more detailed discussion of the properties of absolute value is given in Web Appendix F. However, for convenience we provide the following summary of its algebraic properties.

0.1.4 PROPERTIES OF ABSOLUTE VALUE *If a and b are real numbers, then*

(a) $|-a| = |a|$ A number and its negative have the same absolute value.

(b) $|ab| = |a|\,|b|$ The absolute value of a product is the product of the absolute values.

(c) $|a/b| = |a|/|b|,\, b \neq 0$ The absolute value of a ratio is the ratio of the absolute values.

(d) $|a + b| \leq |a| + |b|$ The *triangle inequality*

The graph of the function $f(x) = |x|$ can be obtained by graphing the two parts of the equation

$$y = \begin{cases} x, & x \geq 0 \\ -x, & x < 0 \end{cases}$$

separately. Combining the two parts produces the V-shaped graph in Figure 0.1.9.

Absolute values have important relationships to square roots. To see why this is so, recall from algebra that every positive real number x has two square roots, one positive and one negative. By definition, the symbol $\sqrt{x}$ denotes the *positive* square root of x.

Care must be exercised in simplifying expressions of the form $\sqrt{x^2}$, since it is *not* always true that $\sqrt{x^2} = x$. This equation is correct if x is nonnegative, but it is false if x is negative. For example, if $x = -4$, then

$$\sqrt{x^2} = \sqrt{(-4)^2} = \sqrt{16} = 4 \neq x$$

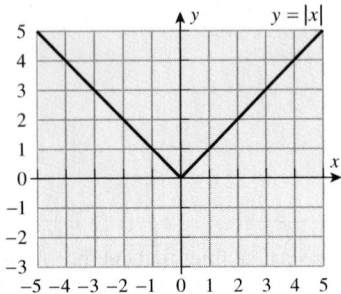

▲ Figure 0.1.9

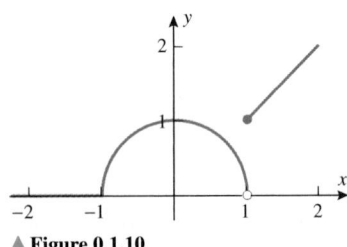

▲ Figure 0.1.10

A statement that is correct for all real values of x is

$$\sqrt{x^2} = |x| \qquad (1)$$

■ PIECEWISE-DEFINED FUNCTIONS

The absolute value function $f(x) = |x|$ is an example of a function that is defined **piecewise** in the sense that the formula for f changes, depending on the value of x.

▶ **Example 4**   Sketch the graph of the function defined piecewise by the formula

$$f(x) = \begin{cases} 0, & x \leq -1 \\ \sqrt{1 - x^2}, & -1 < x < 1 \\ x, & x \geq 1 \end{cases}$$

Solution.   The formula for f changes at the points $x = -1$ and $x = 1$. (We call these the **breakpoints** for the formula.) A good procedure for graphing functions defined piecewise is to graph the function separately over the open intervals determined by the breakpoints, and then graph f at the breakpoints themselves. For the function f in this example the graph is the horizontal ray $y = 0$ on the interval $(-\infty, -1]$, it is the semicircle $y = \sqrt{1 - x^2}$ on the interval $(-1, 1)$, and it is the ray $y = x$ on the interval $[1, +\infty)$. The formula for f specifies that the equation $y = 0$ applies at the breakpoint -1 [so $y = f(-1) = 0$], and it specifies that the equation $y = x$ applies at the breakpoint 1 [so $y = f(1) = 1$]. The graph of f is shown in Figure 0.1.10. ◀

REMARK | In Figure 0.1.10 the solid dot and open circle at the breakpoint $x = 1$ serve to emphasize that the point on the graph lies on the ray and not the semicircle. There is no ambiguity at the breakpoint $x = -1$ because the two parts of the graph join together continuously there.

© Brian Horisk/Alamy

The wind chill index measures the sensation of coldness that we feel from the combined effect of temperature and wind speed.

▶ **Example 5**   Increasing the speed at which air moves over a person's skin increases the rate of moisture evaporation and makes the person feel cooler. (This is why we fan ourselves in hot weather.) The **wind chill index** is the temperature at a wind speed of 4 mi/h that would produce the same sensation on exposed skin as the current temperature and wind speed combination. An empirical formula (i.e., a formula based on experimental data) for the wind chill index W at $32°$F for a wind speed of v mi/h is

$$W = \begin{cases} 32, & 0 \leq v \leq 3 \\ 55.628 - 22.07v^{0.16}, & 3 < v \end{cases}$$

A computer-generated graph of $W(v)$ is shown in Figure 0.1.11. ◀

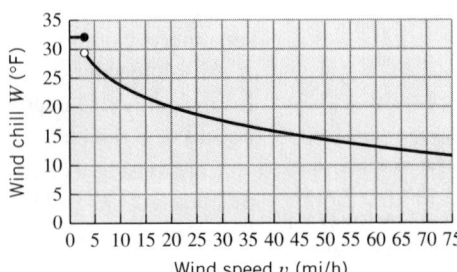

▶ **Figure 0.1.11** Wind chill versus wind speed at $32°$F

■ DOMAIN AND RANGE

If x and y are related by the equation $y = f(x)$, then the set of all allowable inputs (x-values) is called the **domain** of f, and the set of outputs (y-values) that result when x varies over the domain is called the **range** of f. For example, if f is the function defined by the table in Example 1, then the domain is the set $\{0, 1, 2, 3\}$ and the range is the set $\{-1, 3, 4, 6\}$.

Sometimes physical or geometric considerations impose restrictions on the allowable inputs of a function. For example, if y denotes the area of a square of side x, then these variables are related by the equation $y = x^2$. Although this equation produces a unique value of y for every real number x, the fact that lengths must be nonnegative imposes the requirement that $x \geq 0$.

One might argue that a physical square cannot have a side of length zero. However, it is often convenient mathematically to allow zero lengths, and we will do so throughout this text where appropriate.

When a function is defined by a mathematical formula, the formula itself may impose restrictions on the allowable inputs. For example, if $y = 1/x$, then $x = 0$ is not an allowable input since division by zero is undefined, and if $y = \sqrt{x}$, then negative values of x are not allowable inputs because they produce imaginary values for y and we have agreed to consider only real-valued functions of a real variable. In general, we make the following definition.

0.1.5 DEFINITION   If a real-valued function of a real variable is defined by a formula, and if no domain is stated explicitly, then it is to be understood that the domain consists of all real numbers for which the formula yields a real value. This is called the **natural domain** of the function.

The domain and range of a function f can be pictured by projecting the graph of $y = f(x)$ onto the coordinate axes as shown in Figure 0.1.12.

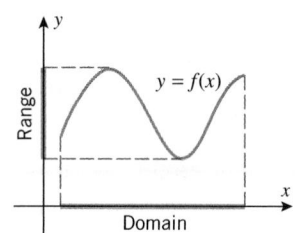

▲ **Figure 0.1.12**   The projection of $y = f(x)$ on the x-axis is the set of allowable x-values for f, and the projection on the y-axis is the set of corresponding y-values.

► **Example 6**   Find the natural domain of

(a) $f(x) = x^3$ (b) $f(x) = 1/[(x-1)(x-3)]$

(c) $f(x) = \tan x$ (d) $f(x) = \sqrt{x^2 - 5x + 6}$

Solution (a).   The function f has real values for all real x, so its natural domain is the interval $(-\infty, +\infty)$.

Solution (b).   The function f has real values for all real x, except $x = 1$ and $x = 3$, where divisions by zero occur. Thus, the natural domain is

$$\{x : x \neq 1 \text{ and } x \neq 3\} = (-\infty, 1) \cup (1, 3) \cup (3, +\infty)$$

Solution (c).   Since $f(x) = \tan x = \sin x / \cos x$, the function f has real values except where $\cos x = 0$, and this occurs when x is an odd integer multiple of $\pi/2$. Thus, the natural domain consists of all real numbers except

For a review of trigonometry see Appendix B.

$$x = \pm\frac{\pi}{2}, \pm\frac{3\pi}{2}, \pm\frac{5\pi}{2}, \dots$$

Solution (d).   The function f has real values, except when the expression inside the radical is negative. Thus the natural domain consists of all real numbers x such that

$$x^2 - 5x + 6 = (x-3)(x-2) \geq 0$$

This inequality is satisfied if $x \leq 2$ or $x \geq 3$ (verify), so the natural domain of f is

$$(-\infty, 2] \cup [3, +\infty) \quad ◄$$

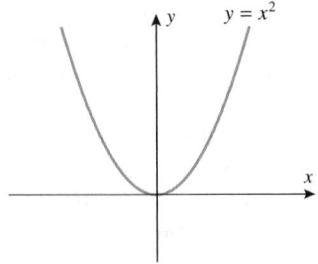

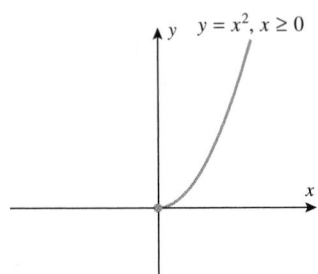

▲ **Figure 0.1.13**

In some cases we will state the domain explicitly when defining a function. For example, if $f(x) = x^2$ is the area of a square of side x, then we can write

$$f(x) = x^2, \quad x \geq 0$$

to indicate that we take the domain of f to be the set of nonnegative real numbers (Figure 0.1.13).

■ **THE EFFECT OF ALGEBRAIC OPERATIONS ON THE DOMAIN**

Algebraic expressions are frequently simplified by canceling common factors in the numerator and denominator. However, care must be exercised when simplifying formulas for functions in this way, since this process can alter the domain.

▶ **Example 7**   The natural domain of the function

$$f(x) = \frac{x^2 - 4}{x - 2} \tag{2}$$

consists of all real x except $x = 2$. However, if we factor the numerator and then cancel the common factor in the numerator and denominator, we obtain

$$f(x) = \frac{(x - 2)(x + 2)}{x - 2} = x + 2 \tag{3}$$

Since the right side of (3) has a value of $f(2) = 4$ and $f(2)$ was undefined in (2), the algebraic simplification has changed the function. Geometrically, the graph of (3) is the line in Figure 0.1.14a, whereas the graph of (2) is the same line but with a hole at $x = 2$, since the function is undefined there (Figure 0.1.14b). In short, the geometric effect of the algebraic cancellation is to eliminate the hole in the original graph. ◀

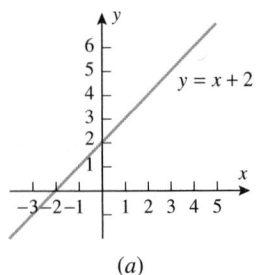

(a)

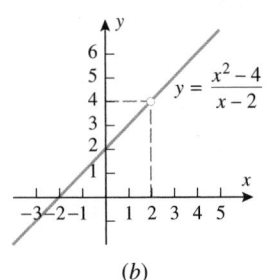

(b)

▲ **Figure 0.1.14**

Sometimes alterations to the domain of a function that result from algebraic simplification are irrelevant to the problem at hand and can be ignored. However, if the domain must be preserved, then one must impose the restrictions on the simplified function explicitly. For example, if we wanted to preserve the domain of the function in Example 7, then we would have to express the simplified form of the function as

$$f(x) = x + 2, \quad x \neq 2$$

▶ **Example 8**   Find the domain and range of

(a) $f(x) = 2 + \sqrt{x - 1}$ (b) $f(x) = (x + 1)/(x - 1)$

Solution (a).   Since no domain is stated explicitly, the domain of f is its natural domain, $[1, +\infty)$. As x varies over the interval $[1, +\infty)$, the value of $\sqrt{x - 1}$ varies over the interval $[0, +\infty)$, so the value of $f(x) = 2 + \sqrt{x - 1}$ varies over the interval $[2, +\infty)$, which is the range of f. The domain and range are highlighted in green on the x- and y-axes in Figure 0.1.15.

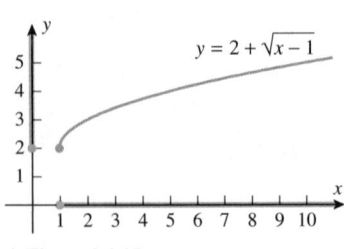

▲ **Figure 0.1.15**

Solution (b).   The given function f is defined for all real x, except $x = 1$, so the natural domain of f is

$$\{x : x \neq 1\} = (-\infty, 1) \cup (1, +\infty)$$

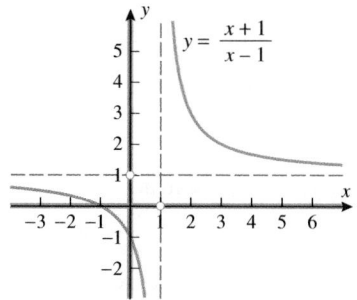

▲ Figure 0.1.16

To determine the range it will be convenient to introduce a dependent variable

$$y = \frac{x+1}{x-1} \tag{4}$$

Although the set of possible y-values is not immediately evident from this equation, the graph of (4), which is shown in Figure 0.1.16, suggests that the range of f consists of all y, except $y = 1$. To see that this is so, we solve (4) for x in terms of y:

$$(x-1)y = x+1$$
$$xy - y = x + 1$$
$$xy - x = y + 1$$
$$x(y-1) = y + 1$$
$$x = \frac{y+1}{y-1}$$

It is now evident from the right side of this equation that $y = 1$ is not in the range; otherwise we would have a division by zero. No other values of y are excluded by this equation, so the range of the function f is $\{y : y \neq 1\} = (-\infty, 1) \cup (1, +\infty)$, which agrees with the result obtained graphically. ◀

■ **DOMAIN AND RANGE IN APPLIED PROBLEMS**

In applications, physical considerations often impose restrictions on the domain and range of a function.

▶ **Example 9**   An open box is to be made from a 16-inch by 30-inch piece of cardboard by cutting out squares of equal size from the four corners and bending up the sides (Figure 0.1.17a).

(a) Let V be the volume of the box that results when the squares have sides of length x. Find a formula for V as a function of x.

(b) Find the domain of V.

(c) Use the graph of V given in Figure 0.1.17c to estimate the range of V.

(d) Describe in words what the graph tells you about the volume.

***Solution* (*a*).**   As shown in Figure 0.1.17b, the resulting box has dimensions $16 - 2x$ by $30 - 2x$ by x, so the volume $V(x)$ is given by

$$V(x) = (16 - 2x)(30 - 2x)x = 480x - 92x^2 + 4x^3$$

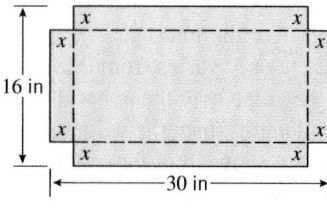

(a)

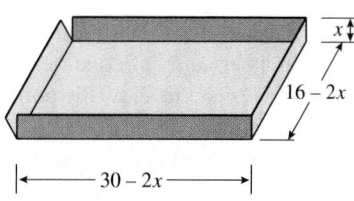

(b)

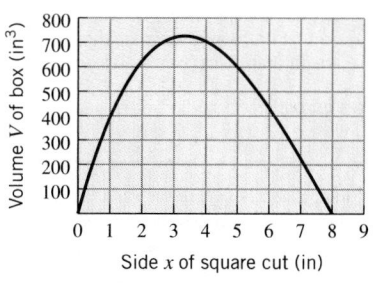

(c)

▲ Figure 0.1.17

Solution (b). The domain is the set of x-values and the range is the set of V-values. Because x is a length, it must be nonnegative, and because we cannot cut out squares whose sides are more than 8 in long (why?), the x-values in the domain must satisfy

$$0 \le x \le 8$$

Solution (c). From the graph of V versus x in Figure 0.1.17c we estimate that the V-values in the range satisfy

$$0 \le V \le 725$$

Note that this is an approximation. Later we will show how to find the range exactly.

Solution (d). The graph tells us that the box of maximum volume occurs for a value of x that is between 3 and 4 and that the maximum volume is approximately 725 in^3. The graph also shows that the volume decreases toward zero as x gets closer to 0 or 8, which should make sense to you intuitively. ◄

In applications involving time, formulas for functions are often expressed in terms of a variable t whose starting value is taken to be $t = 0$.

▶ **Example 10** At 8:05 A.M. a car is clocked at 100 ft/s by a radar detector that is positioned at the edge of a straight highway. Assuming that the car maintains a constant speed between 8:05 A.M. and 8:06 A.M., find a function $D(t)$ that expresses the distance traveled by the car during that time interval as a function of the time t.

Solution. It would be clumsy to use the actual clock time for the variable t, so let us agree to use the *elapsed* time in seconds, starting with $t = 0$ at 8:05 A.M. and ending with $t = 60$ at 8:06 A.M. At each instant, the distance traveled (in ft) is equal to the speed of the car (in ft/s) multiplied by the elapsed time (in s). Thus,

$$D(t) = 100t, \quad 0 \le t \le 60$$

The graph of D versus t is shown in Figure 0.1.18. ◄

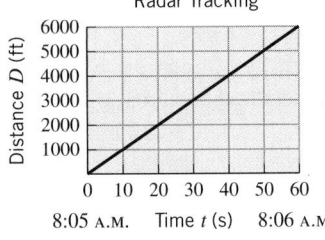

Radar Tracking

▲ **Figure 0.1.18**

■ ISSUES OF SCALE AND UNITS

In geometric problems where you want to preserve the "true" shape of a graph, you must use units of equal length on both axes. For example, if you graph a circle in a coordinate system in which 1 unit in the y-direction is smaller than 1 unit in the x-direction, then the circle will be squashed vertically into an elliptical shape (Figure 0.1.19).

However, sometimes it is inconvenient or impossible to display a graph using units of equal length. For example, consider the equation

$$y = x^2$$

If we want to show the portion of the graph over the interval $-3 \le x \le 3$, then there is no problem using units of equal length, since y only varies from 0 to 9 over that interval. However, if we want to show the portion of the graph over the interval $-10 \le x \le 10$, then there is a problem keeping the units equal in length, since the value of y varies between 0 and 100. In this case the only reasonable way to show all of the graph that occurs over the interval $-10 \le x \le 10$ is to compress the unit of length along the y-axis, as illustrated in Figure 0.1.20.

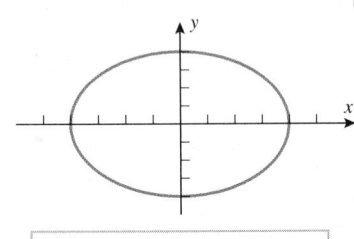

The circle is squashed because 1 unit on the y-axis has a smaller length than 1 unit on the x-axis.

▲ **Figure 0.1.19**

In applications where the variables on the two axes have unrelated units (say, centimeters on the y-axis and seconds on the x-axis), then nothing is gained by requiring the units to have equal lengths; choose the lengths to make the graph as clear as possible.

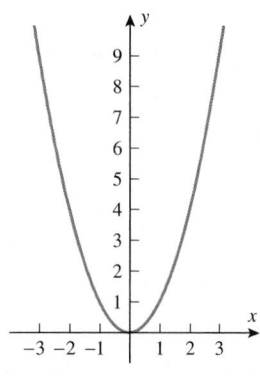 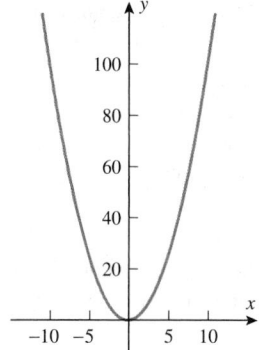

▶ **Figure 0.1.20**

✔ **QUICK CHECK EXERCISES 0.1**   (*See page 15 for answers.*)

1. Let $f(x) = \sqrt{x+1} + 4$.
   (a) The natural domain of f is _____.
   (b) $f(3) = $ _____
   (c) $f(t^2 - 1) = $ _____
   (d) $f(x) = 7$ if $x = $ _____
   (e) The range of f is _____.

2. Line segments in an xy-plane form "letters" as depicted.

   (a) If the y-axis is parallel to the letter I, which of the letters represent the graph of $y = f(x)$ for some function f?
   (b) If the y-axis is perpendicular to the letter I, which of the letters represent the graph of $y = f(x)$ for some function f?

3. The accompanying figure shows the complete graph of $y = f(x)$.
   (a) The domain of f is _____.
   (b) The range of f is _____.
   (c) $f(-3) = $ _____
   (d) $f\left(\frac{1}{2}\right) = $ _____
   (e) The solutions to $f(x) = -\frac{3}{2}$ are $x = $ _____ and $x = $ _____.

4. The accompanying table gives a 5-day forecast of high and low temperatures in degrees Fahrenheit (°F).
   (a) Suppose that x and y denote the respective high and low temperature predictions for each of the 5 days. Is y a function of x? If so, give the domain and range of this function.
   (b) Suppose that x and y denote the respective low and high temperature predictions for each of the 5 days. Is y a function of x? If so, give the domain and range of this function.

	MON	TUE	WED	THURS	FRI
HIGH	75	71	65	70	73
LOW	52	56	48	50	52

▲ **Table Ex-3**

5. Let l, w, and A denote the length, width, and area of a rectangle, respectively, and suppose that the width of the rectangle is half the length.
   (a) If l is expressed as a function of w, then $l = $ _____.
   (b) If A is expressed as a function of l, then $A = $ _____.
   (c) If w is expressed as a function of A, then $w = $ _____.

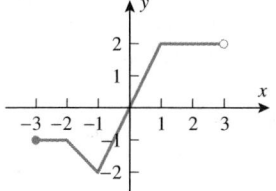

◀ **Figure Ex-3**

EXERCISE SET 0.1   ⊠ Graphing Utility

1. Use the accompanying graph to answer the following questions, making reasonable approximations where needed.
   (a) For what values of x is $y = 1$?
   (b) For what values of x is $y = 3$?
   (c) For what values of y is $x = 3$?
   (d) For what values of x is $y \leq 0$?
   (e) What are the maximum and minimum values of y and for what values of x do they occur?

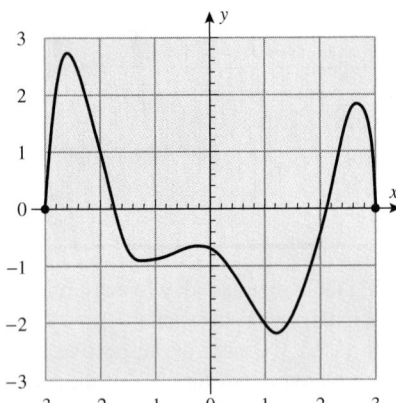

◀ **Figure Ex-1**

2. Use the accompanying table to answer the questions posed in Exercise 1.

x	-2	-1	0	2	3	4	5	6
y	5	1	-2	7	-1	1	0	9

▲ **Table Ex-2**

3. In each part of the accompanying figure, determine whether the graph defines y as a function of x.

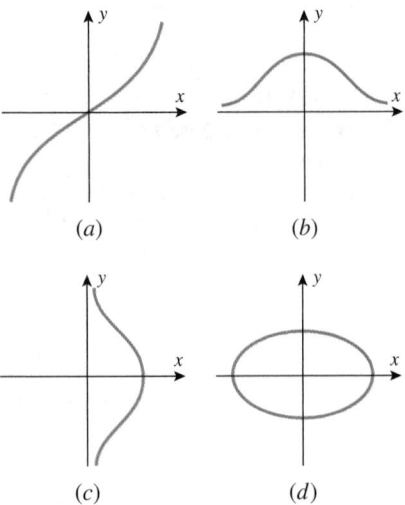

▲ **Figure Ex-3**

4. In each part, compare the natural domains of f and g.

   (a) $f(x) = \dfrac{x^2 + x}{x + 1}$; $g(x) = x$

   (b) $f(x) = \dfrac{x\sqrt{x} + \sqrt{x}}{x + 1}$; $g(x) = \sqrt{x}$

5. The accompanying graph shows the median income in U.S. households (adjusted for inflation) between 1990 and 2005. Use the graph to answer the following questions, making reasonable approximations where needed.
   (a) When was the median income at its maximum value, and what was the median income when that occurred?
   (b) When was the median income at its minimum value, and what was the median income when that occurred?
   (c) The median income was declining during the 2-year period between 2000 and 2002. Was it declining more rapidly during the first year or the second year of that period? Explain your reasoning.

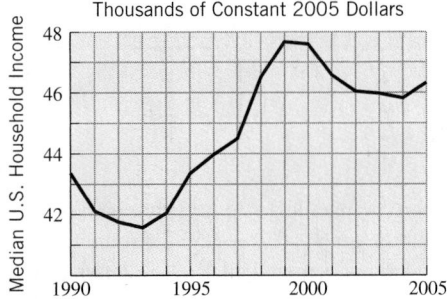

Median U.S. Household Income in Thousands of Constant 2005 Dollars

Source: U.S. Census Bureau, August 2006.

▲ **Figure Ex-5**

6. Use the median income graph in Exercise 5 to answer the following questions, making reasonable approximations where needed.
   (a) What was the average yearly growth of median income between 1993 and 1999?
   (b) The median income was increasing during the 6-year period between 1993 and 1999. Was it increasing more rapidly during the first 3 years or the last 3 years of that period? Explain your reasoning.
   (c) Consider the statement: "After years of decline, median income this year was finally higher than that of last year." In what years would this statement have been correct?

7. Find $f(0)$, $f(2)$, $f(-2)$, $f(3)$, $f(\sqrt{2}\,)$, and $f(3t)$.

(a) $f(x) = 3x^2 - 2$ (b) $f(x) = \begin{cases} \dfrac{1}{x}, & x > 3 \\ 2x, & x \le 3 \end{cases}$

8. Find $g(3)$, $g(-1)$, $g(\pi)$, $g(-1.1)$, and $g(t^2 - 1)$.

(a) $g(x) = \dfrac{x+1}{x-1}$ (b) $g(x) = \begin{cases} \sqrt{x+1}, & x \ge 1 \\ 3, & x < 1 \end{cases}$

9–10 Find the natural domain and determine the range of each function. If you have a graphing utility, use it to confirm that your result is consistent with the graph produced by your graphing utility. [*Note:* Set your graphing utility in radian mode when graphing trigonometric functions.] ■

9. (a) $f(x) = \dfrac{1}{x-3}$ (b) $F(x) = \dfrac{x}{|x|}$

(c) $g(x) = \sqrt{x^2 - 3}$ (d) $G(x) = \sqrt{x^2 - 2x + 5}$

(e) $h(x) = \dfrac{1}{1 - \sin x}$ (f) $H(x) = \sqrt{\dfrac{x^2 - 4}{x - 2}}$

10. (a) $f(x) = \sqrt{3 - x}$ (b) $F(x) = \sqrt{4 - x^2}$
(c) $g(x) = 3 + \sqrt{x}$ (d) $G(x) = x^3 + 2$
(e) $h(x) = 3 \sin x$ (f) $H(x) = (\sin \sqrt{x})^{-2}$

FOCUS ON CONCEPTS

11. (a) If you had a device that could record the Earth's population continuously, would you expect the graph of population versus time to be a continuous (unbroken) curve? Explain what might cause breaks in the curve.
   (b) Suppose that a hospital patient receives an injection of an antibiotic every 8 hours and that between injections the concentration C of the antibiotic in the bloodstream decreases as the antibiotic is absorbed by the tissues. What might the graph of C versus the elapsed time t look like?

12. (a) If you had a device that could record the temperature of a room continuously over a 24-hour period, would you expect the graph of temperature versus time to be a continuous (unbroken) curve? Explain your reasoning.
   (b) If you had a computer that could track the number of boxes of cereal on the shelf of a market continuously over a 1-week period, would you expect the graph of the number of boxes on the shelf versus time to be a continuous (unbroken) curve? Explain your reasoning.

13. A boat is bobbing up and down on some gentle waves. Suddenly it gets hit by a large wave and sinks. Sketch a rough graph of the height of the boat above the ocean floor as a function of time.

14. A cup of hot coffee sits on a table. You pour in some cool milk and let it sit for an hour. Sketch a rough graph of the temperature of the coffee as a function of time.

15–18 As seen in Example 3, the equation $x^2 + y^2 = 25$ does not define y as a function of x. Each graph in these exercises is a portion of the circle $x^2 + y^2 = 25$. In each case, determine whether the graph defines y as a function of x, and if so, give a formula for y in terms of x. ■

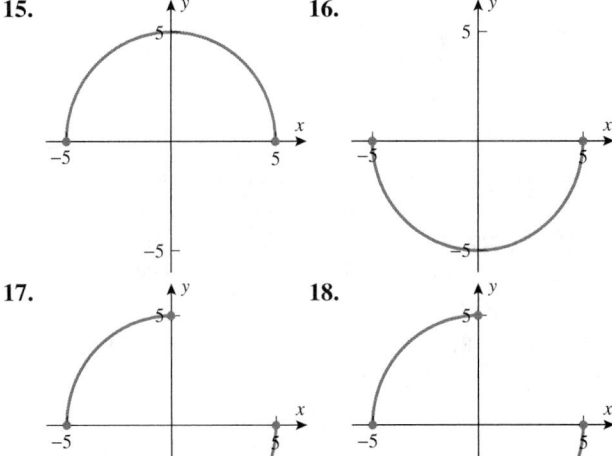

15.   16.

17.   18.

19–22 True–False Determine whether the statement is true or false. Explain your answer. ■

19. A curve that crosses the x-axis at two different points cannot be the graph of a function.

20. The natural domain of a real-valued function defined by a formula consists of all those real numbers for which the formula yields a real value.

21. The range of the absolute value function is all positive real numbers.

22. If $g(x) = 1/\sqrt{f(x)}$, then the domain of g consists of all those real numbers x for which $f(x) \ne 0$.

23. Use the equation $y = x^2 - 6x + 8$ to answer the following questions.
   (a) For what values of x is $y = 0$?
   (b) For what values of x is $y = -10$?
   (c) For what values of x is $y \ge 0$?
   (d) Does y have a minimum value? A maximum value? If so, find them.

24. Use the equation $y = 1 + \sqrt{x}$ to answer the following questions.
   (a) For what values of x is $y = 4$?
   (b) For what values of x is $y = 0$?
   (c) For what values of x is $y \ge 6$?   *(cont.)*

(d) Does y have a minimum value? A maximum value? If so, find them.

25. As shown in the accompanying figure, a pendulum of constant length L makes an angle θ with its vertical position. Express the height h as a function of the angle θ.

26. Express the length L of a chord of a circle with radius 10 cm as a function of the central angle θ (see the accompanying figure).

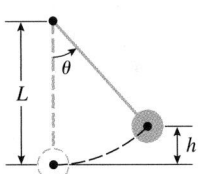

▲ **Figure Ex-25**

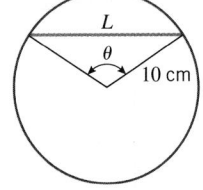

▲ **Figure Ex-26**

27–28 Express the function in piecewise form without using absolute values. [*Suggestion:* It may help to generate the graph of the function.] ■

27. (a) $f(x) = |x| + 3x + 1$ (b) $g(x) = |x| + |x - 1|$

28. (a) $f(x) = 3 + |2x - 5|$ (b) $g(x) = 3|x - 2| - |x + 1|$

29. As shown in the accompanying figure, an open box is to be constructed from a rectangular sheet of metal, 8 in by 15 in, by cutting out squares with sides of length x from each corner and bending up the sides.

(a) Express the volume V as a function of x.

(b) Find the domain of V.

(c) Plot the graph of the function V obtained in part (a) and estimate the range of this function.

(d) In words, describe how the volume V varies with x, and discuss how one might construct boxes of maximum volume.

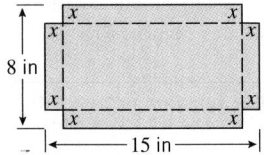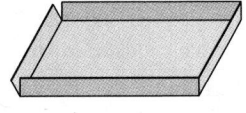

▲ **Figure Ex-29**

30. Repeat Exercise 29 assuming the box is constructed in the same fashion from a 6-inch-square sheet of metal.

31. A construction company has adjoined a 1000 ft² rectangular enclosure to its office building. Three sides of the enclosure are fenced in. The side of the building adjacent to the enclosure is 100 ft long and a portion of this side is used as the fourth side of the enclosure. Let x and y be the dimensions of the enclosure, where x is measured parallel to the building, and let L be the length of fencing required for those dimensions.

(a) Find a formula for L in terms of x and y.

(b) Find a formula that expresses L as a function of x alone.

(c) What is the domain of the function in part (b)?

(d) Plot the function in part (b) and estimate the dimensions of the enclosure that minimize the amount of fencing required.

32. As shown in the accompanying figure, a camera is mounted at a point 3000 ft from the base of a rocket launching pad. The rocket rises vertically when launched, and the camera's elevation angle is continually adjusted to follow the bottom of the rocket.

(a) Express the height x as a function of the elevation angle θ.

(b) Find the domain of the function in part (a).

(c) Plot the graph of the function in part (a) and use it to estimate the height of the rocket when the elevation angle is $\pi/4 \approx 0.7854$ radian. Compare this estimate to the exact height.

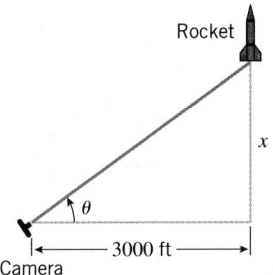

◀ **Figure Ex-32**

33. A soup company wants to manufacture a can in the shape of a right circular cylinder that will hold 500 cm³ of liquid. The material for the top and bottom costs 0.02 cent/cm², and the material for the sides costs 0.01 cent/cm².

(a) Estimate the radius r and the height h of the can that costs the least to manufacture. [*Suggestion:* Express the cost C in terms of r.]

(b) Suppose that the tops and bottoms of radius r are punched out from square sheets with sides of length $2r$ and the scraps are waste. If you allow for the cost of the waste, would you expect the can of least cost to be taller or shorter than the one in part (a)? Explain.

(c) Estimate the radius, height, and cost of the can in part (b), and determine whether your conjecture was correct.

34. The designer of a sports facility wants to put a quarter-mile (1320 ft) running track around a football field, oriented as in the accompanying figure on the next page. The football field is 360 ft long (including the end zones) and 160 ft wide. The track consists of two straightaways and two semicircles, with the straightaways extending at least the length of the football field.

(a) Show that it is possible to construct a quarter-mile track around the football field. [*Suggestion:* Find the shortest track that can be constructed around the field.]

(b) Let L be the length of a straightaway (in feet), and let x be the distance (in feet) between a sideline of the football field and a straightaway. Make a graph of L versus x. *(cont.)*

(c) Use the graph to estimate the value of x that produces the shortest straightaways, and then find this value of x exactly.

(d) Use the graph to estimate the length of the longest possible straightaways, and then find that length exactly.

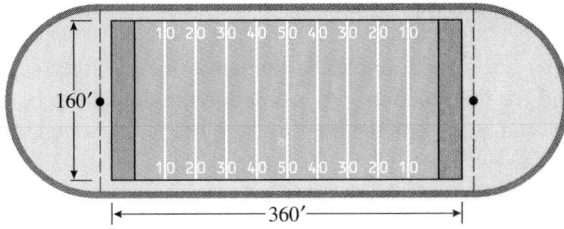

160′

360′

▲ **Figure Ex-34**

35–36 (i) Explain why the function f has one or more holes in its graph, and state the x-values at which those holes occur. (ii) Find a function g whose graph is identical to that of f, but without the holes. ■

35. $f(x) = \dfrac{(x+2)(x^2-1)}{(x+2)(x-1)}$ **36.** $f(x) = \dfrac{x^2+|x|}{|x|}$

37. In 2001 the National Weather Service introduced a new wind chill temperature (WCT) index. For a given outside temperature T and wind speed v, the wind chill temperature index is the equivalent temperature that exposed skin would feel with a wind speed of v mi/h. Based on a more accurate model of cooling due to wind, the new formula is

$$\text{WCT} = \begin{cases} T, & 0 \le v \le 3 \\ 35.74 + 0.6215T - 35.75v^{0.16} + 0.4275Tv^{0.16}, & 3 < v \end{cases}$$

where T is the temperature in °F, v is the wind speed in mi/h, and WCT is the equivalent temperature in °F. Find the WCT to the nearest degree if $T = 25\,°\text{F}$ and
(a) $v = 3$ mi/h   (b) $v = 15$ mi/h   (c) $v = 46$ mi/h.

Source: Adapted from UMAP Module 658, *Windchill*, W. Bosch and L. Cobb, COMAP, Arlington, MA.

38–40 Use the formula for the wind chill temperature index described in Exercise 37. ■

38. Find the air temperature to the nearest degree if the WCT is reported as $-60\,°\text{F}$ with a wind speed of 48 mi/h.

39. Find the air temperature to the nearest degree if the WCT is reported as $-10\,°\text{F}$ with a wind speed of 48 mi/h.

40. Find the wind speed to the nearest mile per hour if the WCT is reported as $5\,°\text{F}$ with an air temperature of $20\,°\text{F}$.

✔ **QUICK CHECK ANSWERS 0.1**

1. (a) $[-1, +\infty)$ (b) 6 (c) $|t|+4$ (d) 8 (e) $[4, +\infty)$ **2.** (a) M (b) I   **3.** (a) $[-3, 3)$ (b) $[-2, 2]$ (c) -1 (d) 1
(e) $-\frac{3}{4}$; $-\frac{3}{2}$ **4.** (a) yes; domain: $\{65, 70, 71, 73, 75\}$; range: $\{48, 50, 52, 56\}$ (b) no   **5.** (a) $l = 2w$ (b) $A = l^2/2$
(c) $w = \sqrt{A/2}$

0.2 NEW FUNCTIONS FROM OLD

Just as numbers can be added, subtracted, multiplied, and divided to produce other numbers, so functions can be added, subtracted, multiplied, and divided to produce other functions. In this section we will discuss these operations and some others that have no analogs in ordinary arithmetic.

■ **ARITHMETIC OPERATIONS ON FUNCTIONS**

Two functions, f and g, can be added, subtracted, multiplied, and divided in a natural way to form new functions $f + g$, $f - g$, fg, and f/g. For example, $f + g$ is defined by the formula

$$(f + g)(x) = f(x) + g(x) \tag{1}$$

which states that for each input the value of $f + g$ is obtained by adding the values of f and g. Equation (1) provides a formula for $f + g$ but does not say anything about the domain of $f + g$. However, for the right side of this equation to be defined, x must lie in the domains of both f and g, so we define the domain of $f + g$ to be the intersection of these two domains. More generally, we make the following definition.

> **0.2.1   DEFINITION**   Given functions f and g, we define
>
> $$(f + g)(x) = f(x) + g(x)$$
> $$(f - g)(x) = f(x) - g(x)$$
> $$(fg)(x) = f(x)g(x)$$
> $$(f/g)(x) = f(x)/g(x)$$
>
> For the functions $f + g$, $f - g$, and fg we define the domain to be the intersection of the domains of f and g, and for the function f/g we define the domain to be the intersection of the domains of f and g but with the points where $g(x) = 0$ excluded (to avoid division by zero).

If f is a constant function, that is, $f(x) = c$ for all x, then the product of f and g is cg, so multiplying a function by a constant is a special case of multiplying two functions.

▶ **Example 1**   Let

$$f(x) = 1 + \sqrt{x - 2} \quad \text{and} \quad g(x) = x - 3$$

Find the domains and formulas for the functions $f + g$, $f - g$, fg, f/g, and $7f$.

Solution.   First, we will find the formulas and then the domains. The formulas are

$$(f + g)(x) = f(x) + g(x) = (1 + \sqrt{x - 2}) + (x - 3) = x - 2 + \sqrt{x - 2} \quad (2)$$
$$(f - g)(x) = f(x) - g(x) = (1 + \sqrt{x - 2}) - (x - 3) = 4 - x + \sqrt{x - 2} \quad (3)$$
$$(fg)(x) = f(x)g(x) = (1 + \sqrt{x - 2})(x - 3) \quad (4)$$
$$(f/g)(x) = f(x)/g(x) = \frac{1 + \sqrt{x - 2}}{x - 3} \quad (5)$$
$$(7f)(x) = 7f(x) = 7 + 7\sqrt{x - 2} \quad (6)$$

The domains of f and g are $[2, +\infty)$ and $(-\infty, +\infty)$, respectively (their natural domains). Thus, it follows from Definition 0.2.1 that the domains of $f + g$, $f - g$, and fg are the intersection of these two domains, namely,

$$[2, +\infty) \cap (-\infty, +\infty) = [2, +\infty) \quad (7)$$

Moreover, since $g(x) = 0$ if $x = 3$, the domain of f/g is (7) with $x = 3$ removed, namely,

$$[2, 3) \cup (3, +\infty)$$

Finally, the domain of $7f$ is the same as the domain of f. ◀

We saw in the last example that the domains of the functions $f + g$, $f - g$, fg, and f/g were the natural domains resulting from the formulas obtained for these functions. The following example shows that this will not always be the case.

▶ **Example 2**   Show that if $f(x) = \sqrt{x}$, $g(x) = \sqrt{x}$, and $h(x) = x$, then the domain of fg is not the same as the natural domain of h.

Solution.   The natural domain of $h(x) = x$ is $(-\infty, +\infty)$. Note that

$$(fg)(x) = \sqrt{x}\sqrt{x} = x = h(x)$$

on the domain of fg. The domains of both f and g are $[0, +\infty)$, so the domain of fg is

$$[0, +\infty) \cap [0, +\infty) = [0, +\infty)$$

by Definition 0.2.1. Since the domains of fg and h are different, it would be misleading to write $(fg)(x) = x$ without including the restriction that this formula holds only for $x \geq 0$.

◄

■ COMPOSITION OF FUNCTIONS

We now consider an operation on functions, called *composition*, which has no direct analog in ordinary arithmetic. Informally stated, the operation of composition is performed by substituting some function for the independent variable of another function. For example, suppose that

$$f(x) = x^2 \quad \text{and} \quad g(x) = x + 1$$

If we substitute $g(x)$ for x in the formula for f, we obtain a new function

$$f(g(x)) = (g(x))^2 = (x + 1)^2$$

which we denote by $f \circ g$. Thus,

$$(f \circ g)(x) = f(g(x)) = (g(x))^2 = (x + 1)^2$$

In general, we make the following definition.

Although the domain of $f \circ g$ may seem complicated at first glance, it makes sense intuitively: To compute $f(g(x))$ one needs x in the domain of g to compute $g(x)$, and one needs $g(x)$ in the domain of f to compute $f(g(x))$.

0.2.2 DEFINITION Given functions f and g, the **composition** of f with g, denoted by $f \circ g$, is the function defined by

$$(f \circ g)(x) = f(g(x))$$

The domain of $f \circ g$ is defined to consist of all x in the domain of g for which $g(x)$ is in the domain of f.

▶ **Example 3** Let $f(x) = x^2 + 3$ and $g(x) = \sqrt{x}$. Find

(a) $(f \circ g)(x)$ (b) $(g \circ f)(x)$

Solution (a).   The formula for $f(g(x))$ is

$$f(g(x)) = [g(x)]^2 + 3 = (\sqrt{x})^2 + 3 = x + 3$$

Since the domain of g is $[0, +\infty)$ and the domain of f is $(-\infty, +\infty)$, the domain of $f \circ g$ consists of all x in $[0, +\infty)$ such that $g(x) = \sqrt{x}$ lies in $(-\infty, +\infty)$; thus, the domain of $f \circ g$ is $[0, +\infty)$. Therefore,

$$(f \circ g)(x) = x + 3, \quad x \geq 0$$

Solution (b).   The formula for $g(f(x))$ is

$$g(f(x)) = \sqrt{f(x)} = \sqrt{x^2 + 3}$$

Since the domain of f is $(-\infty, +\infty)$ and the domain of g is $[0, +\infty)$, the domain of $g \circ f$ consists of all x in $(-\infty, +\infty)$ such that $f(x) = x^2 + 3$ lies in $[0, +\infty)$. Thus, the domain of $g \circ f$ is $(-\infty, +\infty)$. Therefore,

$$(g \circ f)(x) = \sqrt{x^2 + 3}$$

Note that the functions $f \circ g$ and $g \circ f$ in Example 3 are not the same. Thus, the order in which functions are composed can (and usually will) make a difference in the end result.

There is no need to indicate that the domain is $(-\infty, +\infty)$, since this is the natural domain of $\sqrt{x^2 + 3}$. ◄

Compositions can also be defined for three or more functions; for example, $(f \circ g \circ h)(x)$ is computed as

$$(f \circ g \circ h)(x) = f(g(h(x)))$$

In other words, first find $h(x)$, then find $g(h(x))$, and then find $f(g(h(x)))$.

▶ **Example 4** Find $(f \circ g \circ h)(x)$ if

$$f(x) = \sqrt{x}, \quad g(x) = 1/x, \quad h(x) = x^3$$

Solution.

$$(f \circ g \circ h)(x) = f(g(h(x))) = f(g(x^3)) = f(1/x^3) = \sqrt{1/x^3} = 1/x^{3/2} \; ◀$$

▪ EXPRESSING A FUNCTION AS A COMPOSITION

Many problems in mathematics are solved by "decomposing" functions into compositions of simpler functions. For example, consider the function h given by

$$h(x) = (x+1)^2$$

To evaluate $h(x)$ for a given value of x, we would first compute $x+1$ and then square the result. These two operations are performed by the functions

$$g(x) = x+1 \quad \text{and} \quad f(x) = x^2$$

We can express h in terms of f and g by writing

$$h(x) = (x+1)^2 = [g(x)]^2 = f(g(x))$$

so we have succeeded in expressing h as the composition $h = f \circ g$.

The thought process in this example suggests a general procedure for decomposing a function h into a composition $h = f \circ g$:

- Think about how you would evaluate $h(x)$ for a specific value of x, trying to break the evaluation into two steps performed in succession.
- The first operation in the evaluation will determine a function g and the second a function f.
- The formula for h can then be written as $h(x) = f(g(x))$.

For descriptive purposes, we will refer to g as the "inside function" and f as the "outside function" in the expression $f(g(x))$. The inside function performs the first operation and the outside function performs the second.

▶ **Example 5** Express $\sin(x^3)$ as a composition of two functions.

Solution. To evaluate $\sin(x^3)$, we would first compute x^3 and then take the sine, so $g(x) = x^3$ is the inside function and $f(x) = \sin x$ the outside function. Therefore,

$$\sin(x^3) = f(g(x)) \qquad \boxed{g(x) = x^3 \text{ and } f(x) = \sin x} \; ◀$$

Table 0.2.1 gives some more examples of decomposing functions into compositions.

Table 0.2.1

COMPOSING FUNCTIONS

FUNCTION	$g(x)$ INSIDE	$f(x)$ OUTSIDE	COMPOSITION
$(x^2+1)^{10}$	x^2+1	x^{10}	$(x^2+1)^{10}=f(g(x))$
$\sin^3 x$	$\sin x$	x^3	$\sin^3 x=f(g(x))$
$\tan(x^5)$	x^5	$\tan x$	$\tan(x^5)=f(g(x))$
$\sqrt{4-3x}$	$4-3x$	$\sqrt{x}$	$\sqrt{4-3x}=f(g(x))$
$8+\sqrt{x}$	$\sqrt{x}$	$8+x$	$8+\sqrt{x}=f(g(x))$
$\dfrac{1}{x+1}$	$x+1$	$\dfrac{1}{x}$	$\dfrac{1}{x+1}=f(g(x))$

REMARK There is always more than one way to express a function as a composition. For example, here are two ways to express $(x^2+1)^{10}$ as a composition that differ from that in Table 0.2.1:

$$(x^2+1)^{10}=[(x^2+1)^2]^5=f(g(x)) \qquad \boxed{g(x)=(x^2+1)^2 \text{ and } f(x)=x^5}$$

$$(x^2+1)^{10}=[(x^2+1)^3]^{10/3}=f(g(x)) \qquad \boxed{g(x)=(x^2+1)^3 \text{ and } f(x)=x^{10/3}}$$

■ NEW FUNCTIONS FROM OLD

The remainder of this section will be devoted to considering the geometric effect of performing basic operations on functions. This will enable us to use known graphs of functions to visualize or sketch graphs of related functions. For example, Figure 0.2.1 shows the graphs of yearly new car sales $N(t)$ and used car sales $U(t)$ over a certain time period. Those graphs can be used to construct the graph of the total car sales

$$T(t)=N(t)+U(t)$$

by adding the values of $N(t)$ and $U(t)$ for each value of t. In general, the graph of $y=f(x)+g(x)$ can be constructed from the graphs of $y=f(x)$ and $y=g(x)$ by adding corresponding y-values for each x.

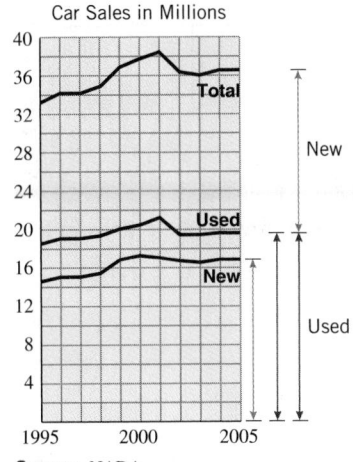

Car Sales in Millions

Source: NADA.

▲ **Figure 0.2.1**

▶ **Example 6** Referring to Figure 0.1.4 for the graphs of $y=\sqrt{x}$ and $y=1/x$, make a sketch that shows the general shape of the graph of $y=\sqrt{x}+1/x$ for $x\geq 0$.

Solution. To add the corresponding y-values of $y=\sqrt{x}$ and $y=1/x$ graphically, just imagine them to be "stacked" on top of one another. This yields the sketch in Figure 0.2.2. ◀

Use the technique in Example 6 to sketch the graph of the function

$$\sqrt{x}-\frac{1}{x}$$

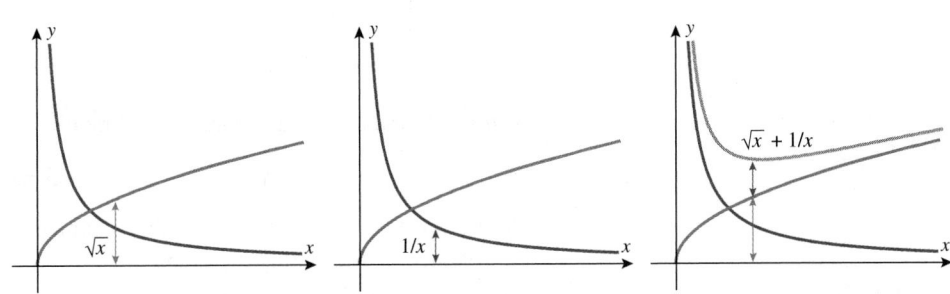

▶ **Figure 0.2.2**

Add the y-coordinates of $\sqrt{x}$ and $1/x$ to obtain the y-coordinate of $\sqrt{x}+1/x$.

■ **TRANSLATIONS**

Table 0.2.2 illustrates the geometric effect on the graph of $y = f(x)$ of adding or subtracting a *positive* constant c to f or to its independent variable x. For example, the first result in the table illustrates that adding a positive constant c to a function f adds c to each y-coordinate of its graph, thereby shifting the graph of f up by c units. Similarly, subtracting c from f shifts the graph down by c units. On the other hand, if a positive constant c is added to x, then the value of $y = f(x + c)$ at $x - c$ is $f(x)$; and since the point $x - c$ is c units to the left of x on the x-axis, the graph of $y = f(x + c)$ must be the graph of $y = f(x)$ shifted left by c units. Similarly, subtracting c from x shifts the graph of $y = f(x)$ right by c units.

Table 0.2.2

TRANSLATION PRINCIPLES

OPERATION ON $y = f(x)$	Add a positive constant c to $f(x)$	Subtract a positive constant c from $f(x)$	Add a positive constant c to x	Subtract a positive constant c from x
NEW EQUATION	$y = f(x) + c$	$y = f(x) - c$	$y = f(x + c)$	$y = f(x - c)$
GEOMETRIC EFFECT	Translates the graph of $y = f(x)$ up c units	Translates the graph of $y = f(x)$ down c units	Translates the graph of $y = f(x)$ left c units	Translates the graph of $y = f(x)$ right c units
EXAMPLE				

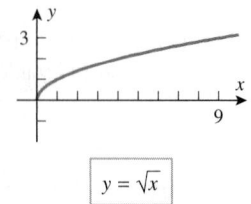

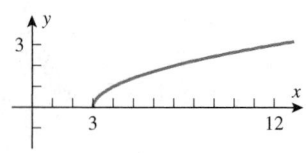

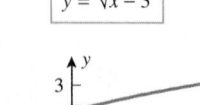

▲ **Figure 0.2.3**

Before proceeding to the next examples, it will be helpful to review the graphs in Figures 0.1.4 and 0.1.9.

▶ **Example 7** Sketch the graph of

$$\text{(a) } y = \sqrt{x - 3} \qquad \text{(b) } y = \sqrt{x + 3}$$

Solution. Using the translation principles given in Table 0.2.2, the graph of the equation $y = \sqrt{x - 3}$ can be obtained by translating the graph of $y = \sqrt{x}$ right 3 units. The graph of $y = \sqrt{x + 3}$ can be obtained by translating the graph of $y = \sqrt{x}$ left 3 units (Figure 0.2.3). ◀

▶ **Example 8** Sketch the graph of $y = x^2 - 4x + 5$.

Solution. Completing the square on the first two terms yields

$$y = (x^2 - 4x + 4) - 4 + 5 = (x - 2)^2 + 1$$

(see Web Appendix H for a review of this technique). In this form we see that the graph can be obtained by translating the graph of $y = x^2$ right 2 units because of the $x - 2$, and up 1 unit because of the $+1$ (Figure 0.2.4). ◀

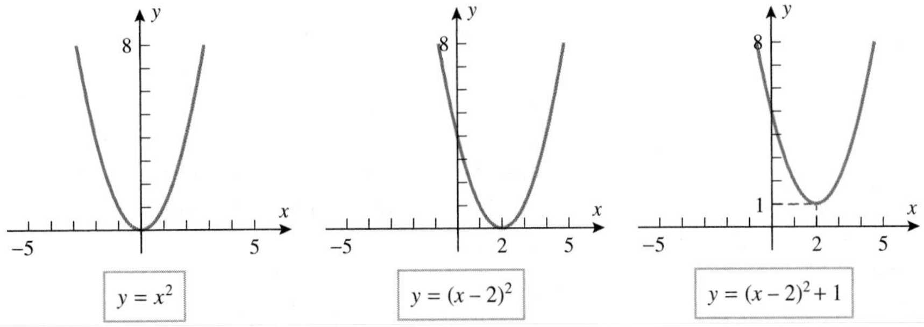

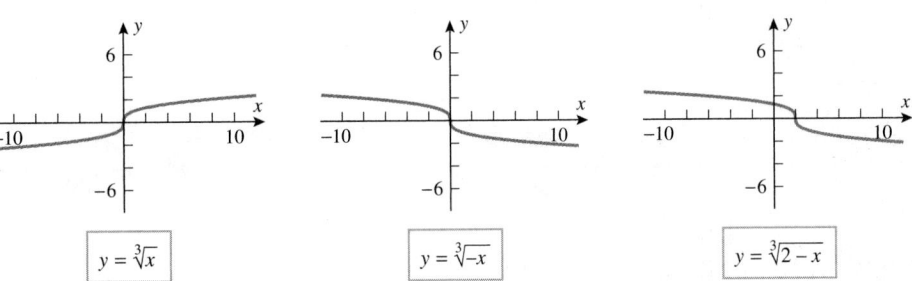

Figure 0.2.4

REFLECTIONS

The graph of $y = f(-x)$ is the reflection of the graph of $y = f(x)$ about the y-axis because the point (x, y) on the graph of $f(x)$ is replaced by $(-x, y)$. Similarly, the graph of $y = -f(x)$ is the reflection of the graph of $y = f(x)$ about the x-axis because the point (x, y) on the graph of $f(x)$ is replaced by $(x, -y)$ [the equation $y = -f(x)$ is equivalent to $-y = f(x)$]. This is summarized in Table 0.2.3.

Table 0.2.3
REFLECTION PRINCIPLES

OPERATION ON $y = f(x)$	Replace x by $-x$	Multiply $f(x)$ by -1
NEW EQUATION	$y = f(-x)$	$y = -f(x)$
GEOMETRIC EFFECT	Reflects the graph of $y = f(x)$ about the y-axis	Reflects the graph of $y = f(x)$ about the x-axis
EXAMPLE	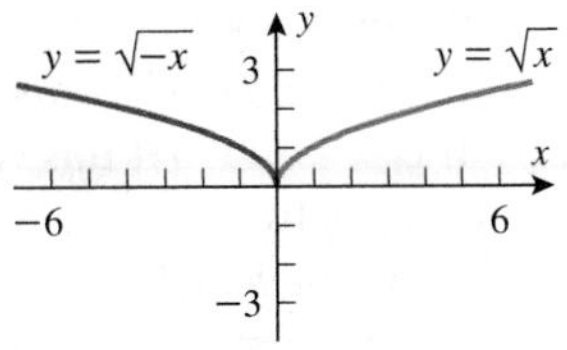	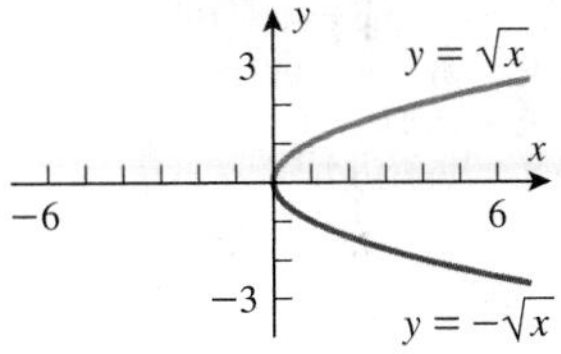

Example 9   Sketch the graph of $y = \sqrt[3]{2 - x}$.

Solution.   Using the translation and reflection principles in Tables 0.2.2 and 0.2.3, we can obtain the graph by a reflection followed by a translation as follows: First reflect the graph of $y = \sqrt[3]{x}$ about the y-axis to obtain the graph of $y = \sqrt[3]{-x}$, then translate this graph right 2 units to obtain the graph of the equation $y = \sqrt[3]{-(x - 2)} = \sqrt[3]{2 - x}$ (Figure 0.2.5). ◄

Figure 0.2.5

▶ **Example 10** Sketch the graph of $y = 4 - |x - 2|$.

Solution.   The graph can be obtained by a reflection and two translations: First translate the graph of $y = |x|$ right 2 units to obtain the graph of $y = |x - 2|$; then reflect this graph about the x-axis to obtain the graph of $y = -|x - 2|$; and then translate this graph up 4 units to obtain the graph of the equation $y = -|x - 2| + 4 = 4 - |x - 2|$ (Figure 0.2.6).

◀

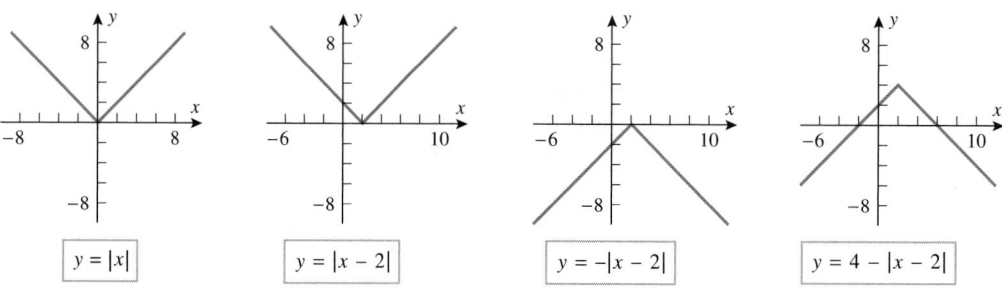

| $y = |x|$ | $y = |x - 2|$ | $y = -|x - 2|$ | $y = 4 - |x - 2|$ |

▲ **Figure 0.2.6**

■ STRETCHES AND COMPRESSIONS

Multiplying $f(x)$ by a *positive* constant c has the geometric effect of stretching the graph of $y = f(x)$ in the y-direction by a factor of c if $c > 1$ and compressing it in the y-direction by a factor of $1/c$ if $0 < c < 1$. For example, multiplying $f(x)$ by 2 doubles each y-coordinate, thereby stretching the graph vertically by a factor of 2, and multiplying by $\frac{1}{2}$ cuts each y-coordinate in half, thereby compressing the graph vertically by a factor of 2. Similarly, multiplying x by a *positive* constant c has the geometric effect of compressing the graph of $y = f(x)$ by a factor of c in the x-direction if $c > 1$ and stretching it by a factor of $1/c$ if $0 < c < 1$. [If this seems backwards to you, then think of it this way: The value of $2x$ changes twice as fast as x, so a point moving along the x-axis from the origin will only have to move half as far for $y = f(2x)$ to have the same value as $y = f(x)$, thereby creating a horizontal compression of the graph.] All of this is summarized in Table 0.2.4.

> Describe the geometric effect of multiplying a function f by a *negative* constant in terms of reflection and stretching or compressing. What is the geometric effect of multiplying the independent variable of a function f by a *negative* constant?

Table 0.2.4
STRETCHING AND COMPRESSING PRINCIPLES

OPERATION ON $y = f(x)$	Multiply $f(x)$ by c ($c > 1$)	Multiply $f(x)$ by c ($0 < c < 1$)	Multiply x by c ($c > 1$)	Multiply x by c ($0 < c < 1$)
NEW EQUATION	$y = cf(x)$	$y = cf(x)$	$y = f(cx)$	$y = f(cx)$
GEOMETRIC EFFECT	Stretches the graph of $y = f(x)$ vertically by a factor of c	Compresses the graph of $y = f(x)$ vertically by a factor of $1/c$	Compresses the graph of $y = f(x)$ horizontally by a factor of c	Stretches the graph of $y = f(x)$ horizontally by a factor of $1/c$
EXAMPLE	$y = 2\cos x$, $y = \cos x$	$y = \cos x$, $y = \frac{1}{2}\cos x$	$y = \cos x$, $y = \cos 2x$	$y = \cos \frac{1}{2}x$, $y = \cos x$

SYMMETRY

Figure 0.2.7 illustrates three types of symmetries: ***symmetry about the x-axis***, ***symmetry about the y-axis***, and ***symmetry about the origin***. As illustrated in the figure, a curve is symmetric about the x-axis if for each point (x, y) on the graph the point $(x, -y)$ is also on the graph, and it is symmetric about the y-axis if for each point (x, y) on the graph the point $(-x, y)$ is also on the graph. A curve is symmetric about the origin if for each point (x, y) on the graph, the point $(-x, -y)$ is also on the graph. (Equivalently, a graph is symmetric about the origin if rotating the graph $180°$ about the origin leaves it unchanged.) This suggests the following symmetry tests.

> Explain why the graph of a nonzero function cannot be symmetric about the x-axis.

(x, y)

$(x, -y)$

Symmetric about the x-axis

$(-x, y)$ ———— (x, y)

Symmetric about the y-axis

(x, y)

$(-x, -y)$

Symmetric about the origin

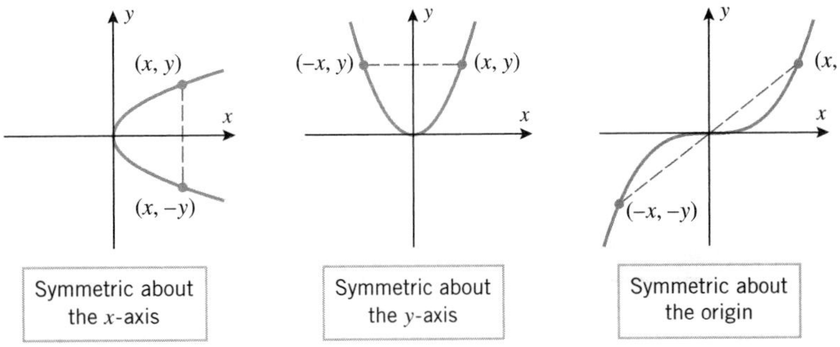

▶ **Figure 0.2.7**

0.2.3   THEOREM (*Symmetry Tests*)

(*a*) *A plane curve is symmetric about the y-axis if and only if replacing x by $-x$ in its equation produces an equivalent equation.*

(*b*) *A plane curve is symmetric about the x-axis if and only if replacing y by $-y$ in its equation produces an equivalent equation.*

(*c*) *A plane curve is symmetric about the origin if and only if replacing both x by $-x$ and y by $-y$ in its equation produces an equivalent equation.*

▶ **Example 11**   Use Theorem 0.2.3 to identify symmetries in the graph of $x = y^2$.

Solution.   Replacing y by $-y$ yields $x = (-y)^2$, which simplifies to the original equation $x = y^2$. Thus, the graph is symmetric about the x-axis. The graph is not symmetric about the y-axis because replacing x by $-x$ yields $-x = y^2$, which is not equivalent to the original equation $x = y^2$. Similarly, the graph is not symmetric about the origin because replacing x by $-x$ and y by $-y$ yields $-x = (-y)^2$, which simplifies to $-x = y^2$, and this is again not equivalent to the original equation. These results are consistent with the graph of $x = y^2$ shown in Figure 0.2.8. ◀

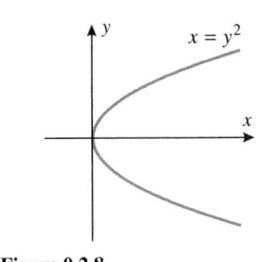

▲ **Figure 0.2.8**

EVEN AND ODD FUNCTIONS

A function f is said to be an ***even function*** if

$$f(-x) = f(x) \tag{8}$$

and is said to be an ***odd function*** if

$$f(-x) = -f(x) \tag{9}$$

Geometrically, the graphs of even functions are symmetric about the y-axis because replacing x by $-x$ in the equation $y = f(x)$ yields $y = f(-x)$, which is equivalent to the original equation $y = f(x)$ by (8) (see Figure 0.2.9). Similarly, it follows from (9) that graphs of odd functions are symmetric about the origin (see Figure 0.2.10). Some examples of even functions are x^2, x^4, x^6, and $\cos x$; and some examples of odd functions are x^3, x^5, x^7, and $\sin x$.

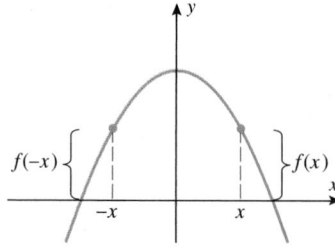

▲ **Figure 0.2.9** This is the graph of an even function since $f(-x) = f(x)$.

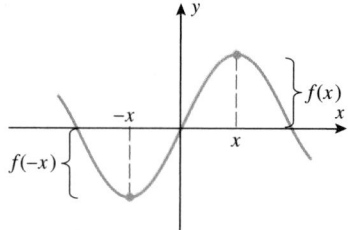

▲ **Figure 0.2.10** This is the graph of an odd function since $f(-x) = -f(x)$.

✔ QUICK CHECK EXERCISES 0.2 *(See page 27 for answers.)*

1. Let $f(x) = 3\sqrt{x} - 2$ and $g(x) = |x|$. In each part, give the formula for the function and state the corresponding domain.
(a) $f + g$: _____ Domain: _____
(b) $f - g$: _____ Domain: _____
(c) fg: _____ Domain: _____
(d) f/g: _____ Domain: _____

2. Let $f(x) = 2 - x^2$ and $g(x) = \sqrt{x}$. In each part, give the formula for the composition and state the corresponding domain.
(a) $f \circ g$: _____ Domain: _____
(b) $g \circ f$: _____ Domain: _____

3. The graph of $y = 1 + (x - 2)^2$ may be obtained by shifting the graph of $y = x^2$ _____ (left/right) by _____ unit(s) and then shifting this new graph _____ (up/down) by _____ unit(s).

4. Let
$$f(x) = \begin{cases} |x + 1|, & -2 \le x \le 0 \\ |x - 1|, & 0 < x \le 2 \end{cases}$$
(a) The letter of the alphabet that most resembles the graph of f is _____.
(b) Is f an even function?

EXERCISE SET 0.2  Graphing Utility

FOCUS ON CONCEPTS

1. The graph of a function f is shown in the accompanying figure. Sketch the graphs of the following equations.
(a) $y = f(x) - 1$ (b) $y = f(x - 1)$
(c) $y = \frac{1}{2}f(x)$ (d) $y = f\left(-\frac{1}{2}x\right)$

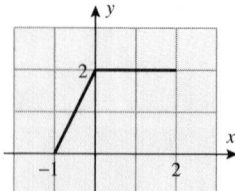

◀ **Figure Ex-1**

2. Use the graph in Exercise 1 to sketch the graphs of the following equations.
(a) $y = -f(-x)$ (b) $y = f(2 - x)$
(c) $y = 1 - f(2 - x)$ (d) $y = \frac{1}{2}f(2x)$

3. The graph of a function f is shown in the accompanying figure. Sketch the graphs of the following equations.
(a) $y = f(x + 1)$ (b) $y = f(2x)$
(c) $y = |f(x)|$ (d) $y = 1 - |f(x)|$

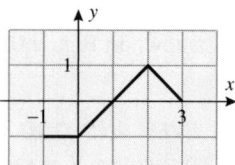

◀ **Figure Ex-3**

4. Use the graph in Exercise 3 to sketch the graph of the equation $y = f(|x|)$.

5–24 Sketch the graph of the equation by translating, reflecting, compressing, and stretching the graph of $y = x^2$, $y = \sqrt{x}$, $y = 1/x$, $y = |x|$, or $y = \sqrt[3]{x}$ appropriately. Then use a graphing utility to confirm that your sketch is correct. ∎

5. $y = -2(x+1)^2 - 3$

6. $y = \frac{1}{2}(x-3)^2 + 2$

7. $y = 1 + 2x - x^2$

8. $y = \frac{1}{2}(x^2 - 2x + 3)$

9. $y = 3 - \sqrt{x+1}$

10. $y = 1 + \sqrt{x-4}$

11. $y = \frac{1}{2}\sqrt{x} + 1$

12. $y = -\sqrt{3x}$

13. $y = \dfrac{1}{x-3}$

14. $y = \dfrac{1}{1-x}$

15. $y = 2 - \dfrac{1}{x+1}$

16. $y = \dfrac{x-1}{x}$

17. $y = |x+2| - 2$

18. $y = 1 - |x-3|$

19. $y = |2x-1| + 1$

20. $y = \sqrt{x^2 - 4x + 4}$

21. $y = 1 - 2\sqrt[3]{x}$

22. $y = \sqrt[3]{x-2} - 3$

23. $y = 2 + \sqrt[3]{x+1}$

24. $y + \sqrt[3]{x-2} = 0$

25. (a) Sketch the graph of $y = x + |x|$ by adding the corresponding y-coordinates on the graphs of $y = x$ and $y = |x|$.

   (b) Express the equation $y = x + |x|$ in piecewise form with no absolute values, and confirm that the graph you obtained in part (a) is consistent with this equation.

26. Sketch the graph of $y = x + (1/x)$ by adding corresponding y-coordinates on the graphs of $y = x$ and $y = 1/x$. Use a graphing utility to confirm that your sketch is correct.

27–28 Find formulas for $f + g$, $f - g$, fg, and f/g, and state the domains of the functions. ■

27. $f(x) = 2\sqrt{x-1}$, $g(x) = \sqrt{x-1}$

28. $f(x) = \dfrac{x}{1+x^2}$, $g(x) = \dfrac{1}{x}$

29. Let $f(x) = \sqrt{x}$ and $g(x) = x^3 + 1$. Find
   (a) $f(g(2))$
   (b) $g(f(4))$
   (c) $f(f(16))$
   (d) $g(g(0))$
   (e) $f(2+h)$
   (f) $g(3+h)$.

30. Let $g(x) = \sqrt{x}$. Find
   (a) $g(5s+2)$
   (b) $g(\sqrt{x}+2)$
   (c) $3g(5x)$
   (d) $\dfrac{1}{g(x)}$
   (e) $g(g(x))$
   (f) $(g(x))^2 - g(x^2)$
   (g) $g(1/\sqrt{x})$
   (h) $g((x-1)^2)$
   (i) $g(x+h)$.

31–34 Find formulas for $f \circ g$ and $g \circ f$, and state the domains of the compositions. ■

31. $f(x) = x^2$, $g(x) = \sqrt{1-x}$

32. $f(x) = \sqrt{x-3}$, $g(x) = \sqrt{x^2+3}$

33. $f(x) = \dfrac{1+x}{1-x}$, $g(x) = \dfrac{x}{1-x}$

34. $f(x) = \dfrac{x}{1+x^2}$, $g(x) = \dfrac{1}{x}$

35–40 Express f as a composition of two functions; that is, find g and h such that $f = g \circ h$. [*Note:* Each exercise has more than one solution.] ■

35. (a) $f(x) = \sqrt{x+2}$
   (b) $f(x) = |x^2 - 3x + 5|$

36. (a) $f(x) = x^2 + 1$
   (b) $f(x) = \dfrac{1}{x - 3}$

37. (a) $f(x) = \sin^2 x$
   (b) $f(x) = \dfrac{1}{5 + \cos x}$

38. (a) $f(x) = 3\sin(x^2)$
   (b) $f(x) = 3\sin^2 x + 4\sin x$

39. (a) $f(x) = (1 + \sin(x^2))^3$
   (b) $f(x) = \sqrt{1 - \sqrt[3]{x}}$

40. (a) $f(x) = \dfrac{1}{1 - x^2}$
   (b) $f(x) = |5 + 2x|$

41–44 True–False Determine whether the statement is true or false. Explain your answer. ■

41. The domain of $f + g$ is the intersection of the domains of f and g.

42. The domain of $f \circ g$ consists of all values of x in the domain of g for which $g(x) \neq 0$.

43. The graph of an even function is symmetric about the y-axis.

44. The graph of $y = f(x+2) + 3$ is obtained by translating the graph of $y = f(x)$ right 2 units and up 3 units.

FOCUS ON CONCEPTS

45. Use the data in the accompanying table to make a plot of $y = f(g(x))$.

x	-3	-2	-1	0	1	2	3
$f(x)$	-4	-3	-2	-1	0	1	2
$g(x)$	-1	0	1	2	3	-2	-3

▲ **Table Ex-45**

46. Find the domain of $g \circ f$ for the functions f and g in Exercise 45.

47. Sketch the graph of $y = f(g(x))$ for the functions graphed in the accompanying figure.

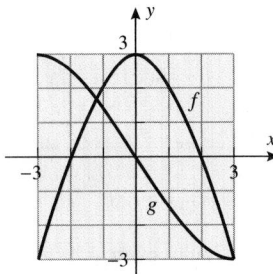

◀ **Figure Ex-47**

48. Sketch the graph of $y = g(f(x))$ for the functions graphed in Exercise 47.

49. Use the graphs of f and g in Exercise 47 to estimate the solutions of the equations $f(g(x)) = 0$ and $g(f(x)) = 0$.

50. Use the table given in Exercise 45 to solve the equations $f(g(x)) = 0$ and $g(f(x)) = 0$.

51–54 Find

$$\frac{f(x+h) - f(x)}{h} \quad \text{and} \quad \frac{f(w) - f(x)}{w - x}$$

Simplify as much as possible. ■

51. $f(x) = 3x^2 - 5$ **52.** $f(x) = x^2 + 6x$

53. $f(x) = 1/x$ **54.** $f(x) = 1/x^2$

55. Classify the functions whose values are given in the accompanying table as even, odd, or neither.

x	-3	-2	-1	0	1	2	3
$f(x)$	5	3	2	3	1	-3	5
$g(x)$	4	1	-2	0	2	-1	-4
$h(x)$	2	-5	8	-2	8	-5	2

▲ **Table Ex-55**

56. Complete the accompanying table so that the graph of $y = f(x)$ is symmetric about
(a) the y-axis   (b) the origin.

x	-3	-2	-1	0	1	2	3
$f(x)$	1		-1	0		-5	

▲ **Table Ex-56**

57. The accompanying figure shows a portion of a graph. Complete the graph so that the entire graph is symmetric about
(a) the x-axis   (b) the y-axis   (c) the origin.

58. The accompanying figure shows a portion of the graph of a function f. Complete the graph assuming that
(a) f is an even function   (b) f is an odd function.

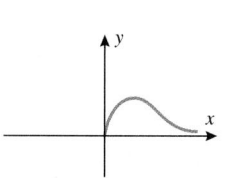

▲ **Figure Ex-57**

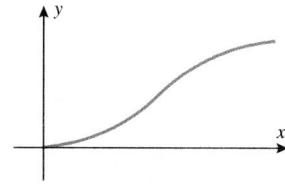

▲ **Figure Ex-58**

59. In each part, classify the function as even, odd, or neither.
(a) $f(x) = x^2$ (b) $f(x) = x^3$
(c) $f(x) = |x|$ (d) $f(x) = x + 1$
(e) $f(x) = \dfrac{x^5 - x}{1 + x^2}$ (f) $f(x) = 2$

60. Suppose that the function f has domain all real numbers. Determine whether each function can be classified as even or odd. Explain.
(a) $g(x) = \dfrac{f(x) + f(-x)}{2}$ (b) $h(x) = \dfrac{f(x) - f(-x)}{2}$

61. Suppose that the function f has domain all real numbers. Show that f can be written as the sum of an even function and an odd function. [*Hint:* See Exercise 60.]

62–63 Use Theorem 0.2.3 to determine whether the graph has symmetries about the x-axis, the y-axis, or the origin. ■

62. (a) $x = 5y^2 + 9$ (b) $x^2 - 2y^2 = 3$
(c) $xy = 5$

63. (a) $x^4 = 2y^3 + y$ (b) $y = \dfrac{x}{3 + x^2}$
(c) $y^2 = |x| - 5$

64–65 (i) Use a graphing utility to graph the equation in the first quadrant. [*Note:* To do this you will have to solve the equation for y in terms of x.] (ii) Use symmetry to make a hand-drawn sketch of the entire graph. (iii) Confirm your work by generating the graph of the equation in the remaining three quadrants. ■

64. $9x^2 + 4y^2 = 36$ **65.** $4x^2 + 16y^2 = 16$

66. The graph of the equation $x^{2/3} + y^{2/3} = 1$, which is shown in the accompanying figure, is called a ***four-cusped hypocycloid***.
(a) Use Theorem 0.2.3 to confirm that this graph is symmetric about the x-axis, the y-axis, and the origin.
(b) Find a function f whose graph in the first quadrant coincides with the four-cusped hypocycloid, and use a graphing utility to confirm your work.
(c) Repeat part (b) for the remaining three quadrants.

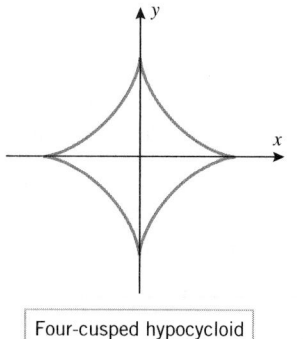

Four-cusped hypocycloid   ◀ **Figure Ex-66**

67. The equation $y = |f(x)|$ can be written as

$$y = \begin{cases} f(x), & f(x) \geq 0 \\ -f(x), & f(x) < 0 \end{cases}$$

which shows that the graph of $y = |f(x)|$ can be obtained from the graph of $y = f(x)$ by retaining the portion that lies on or above the x-axis and reflecting about the x-axis the portion that lies below the x-axis. Use this method to obtain the graph of $y = |2x - 3|$ from the graph of $y = 2x - 3$.

68–69 Use the method described in Exercise 67. ■

68. Sketch the graph of $y = |1 - x^2|$.

69. Sketch the graph of
   (a) $f(x) = |\cos x|$ (b) $f(x) = \cos x + |\cos x|$.

70. The *greatest integer function*, $\lfloor x \rfloor$, is defined to be the greatest integer that is less than or equal to x. For example, $\lfloor 2.7 \rfloor = 2$, $\lfloor -2.3 \rfloor = -3$, and $\lfloor 4 \rfloor = 4$. In each part, sketch the graph of $y = f(x)$.

   (a) $f(x) = \lfloor x \rfloor$ (b) $f(x) = \lfloor x^2 \rfloor$
   (c) $f(x) = \lfloor x \rfloor^2$ (d) $f(x) = \lfloor \sin x \rfloor$

71. Is it ever true that $f \circ g = g \circ f$ if f and g are nonconstant functions? If not, prove it; if so, give some examples for which it is true.

✔ **QUICK CHECK ANSWERS 0.2**

1. (a) $(f + g)(x) = 3\sqrt{x} - 2 + x$; $x \ge 0$ (b) $(f - g)(x) = 3\sqrt{x} - 2 - x$; $x \ge 0$ (c) $(fg)(x) = 3x^{3/2} - 2x$; $x \ge 0$
(d) $(f/g)(x) = \dfrac{3\sqrt{x} - 2}{x}$; $x > 0$ **2.** (a) $(f \circ g)(x) = 2 - x$; $x \ge 0$ (b) $(g \circ f)(x) = \sqrt{2 - x^2}$; $-\sqrt{2} \le x \le \sqrt{2}$
3. right; 2; up; 1   **4.** (a) W (b) yes

0.3 FAMILIES OF FUNCTIONS

Functions are often grouped into families according to the form of their defining formulas or other common characteristics. In this section we will discuss some of the most basic families of functions.

■ FAMILIES OF CURVES

The graph of a constant function $f(x) = c$ is the graph of the equation $y = c$, which is the horizontal line shown in Figure 0.3.1*a*. If we vary c, then we obtain a set or *family* of horizontal lines such as those in Figure 0.3.1*b*.

Constants that are varied to produce families of curves are called *parameters*. For example, recall that an equation of the form $y = mx + b$ represents a line of slope m and y-intercept b. If we keep b fixed and treat m as a parameter, then we obtain a family of lines whose members all have y-intercept b (Figure 0.3.2*a*), and if we keep m fixed and treat b as a parameter, we obtain a family of parallel lines whose members all have slope m (Figure 0.3.2*b*).

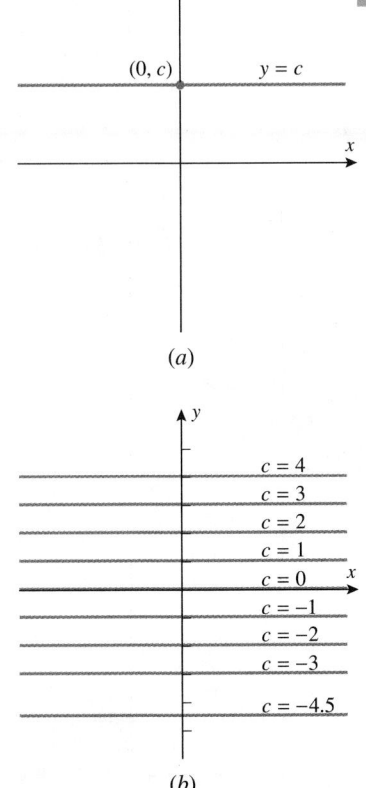

▲ Figure 0.3.1

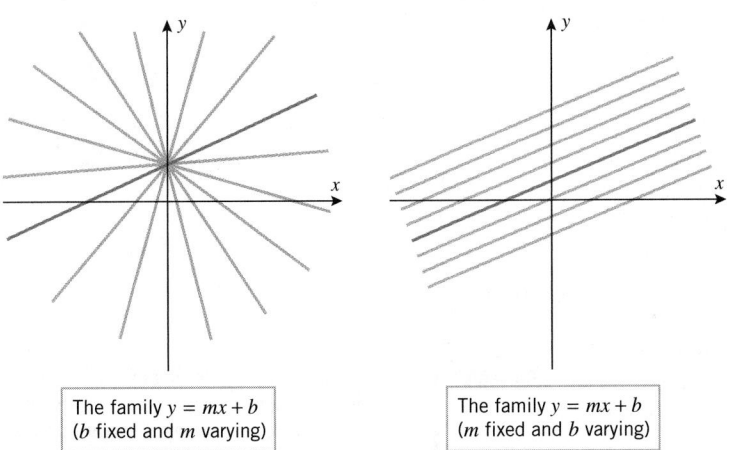

The family $y = mx + b$
(b fixed and m varying)

(*a*)

The family $y = mx + b$
(m fixed and b varying)

(*b*)

▶ Figure 0.3.2

◼ POWER FUNCTIONS; THE FAMILY $y = x^n$

A function of the form $f(x) = x^p$, where p is constant, is called a **_power function_**. For the moment, let us consider the case where p is a positive integer, say $p = n$. The graphs of the curves $y = x^n$ for $n = 1, 2, 3, 4$, and 5 are shown in Figure 0.3.3. The first graph is the line with slope 1 that passes through the origin, and the second is a parabola that opens up and has its vertex at the origin (see Web Appendix H).

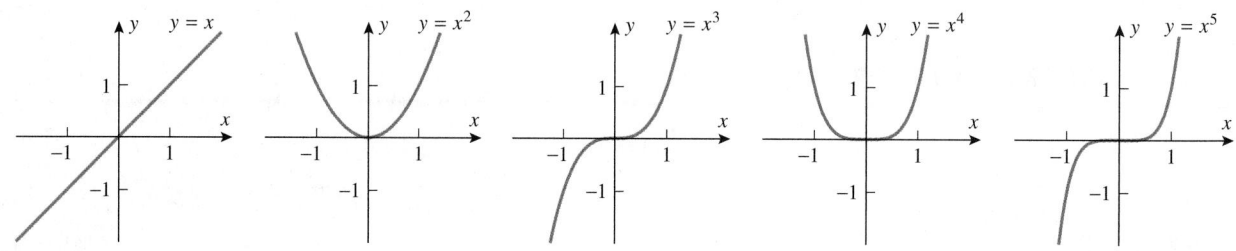

▲ **Figure 0.3.3**

For $n \geq 2$ the shape of the curve $y = x^n$ depends on whether n is even or odd (Figure 0.3.4):

- For even values of n, the functions $f(x) = x^n$ are even, so their graphs are symmetric about the y-axis. The graphs all have the general shape of the graph of $y = x^2$, and each graph passes through the points $(-1, 1)$, $(0, 0)$, and $(1, 1)$. As n increases, the graphs become flatter over the interval $-1 < x < 1$ and steeper over the intervals $x > 1$ and $x < -1$.

- For odd values of n, the functions $f(x) = x^n$ are odd, so their graphs are symmetric about the origin. The graphs all have the general shape of the curve $y = x^3$, and each graph passes through the points $(-1, -1)$, $(0, 0)$, and $(1, 1)$. As n increases, the graphs become flatter over the interval $-1 < x < 1$ and steeper over the intervals $x > 1$ and $x < -1$.

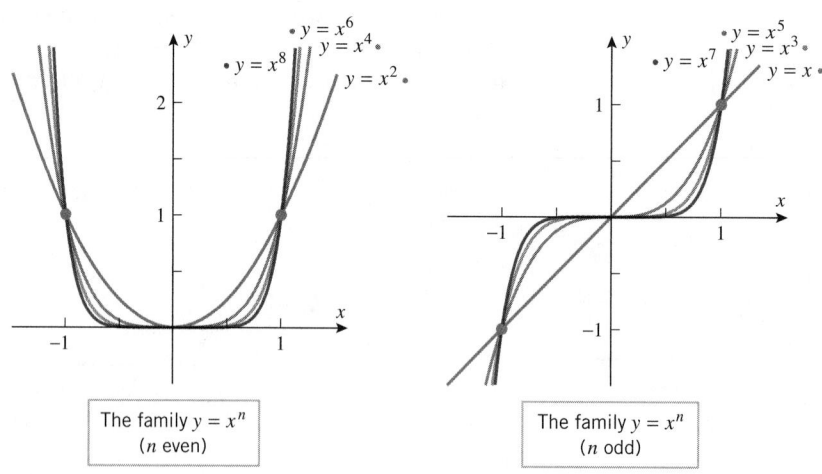

The family $y = x^n$
(n even)

The family $y = x^n$
(n odd)

▶ **Figure 0.3.4**

REMARK | The flattening and steepening effects can be understood by considering what happens when a number x is raised to higher and higher powers: If $-1 < x < 1$, then the absolute value of x^n _decreases_ as n increases, thereby causing the graphs to become flatter on this interval as n increases (try raising $\frac{1}{2}$ or $-\frac{1}{2}$ to higher and higher powers). On the other hand, if $x > 1$ or $x < -1$, then the absolute value of x^n _increases_ as n increases, thereby causing the graphs to become steeper on these intervals as n increases (try raising 2 or -2 to higher and higher powers).

■ THE FAMILY $y = x^{-n}$

If p is a negative integer, say $p = -n$, then the power functions $f(x) = x^p$ have the form $f(x) = x^{-n} = 1/x^n$. Figure 0.3.5 shows the graphs of $y = 1/x$ and $y = 1/x^2$. The graph of $y = 1/x$ is called an ***equilateral hyperbola*** (for reasons to be discussed later).

As illustrated in Figure 0.3.5, the shape of the curve $y = 1/x^n$ depends on whether n is even or odd:

- For even values of n, the functions $f(x) = 1/x^n$ are even, so their graphs are symmetric about the y-axis. The graphs all have the general shape of the curve $y = 1/x^2$, and each graph passes through the points $(-1, 1)$ and $(1, 1)$. As n increases, the graphs become steeper over the intervals $-1 < x < 0$ and $0 < x < 1$ and become flatter over the intervals $x > 1$ and $x < -1$.

- For odd values of n, the functions $f(x) = 1/x^n$ are odd, so their graphs are symmetric about the origin. The graphs all have the general shape of the curve $y = 1/x$, and each graph passes through the points $(1, -1)$ and $(-1, -1)$. As n increases, the graphs become steeper over the intervals $-1 < x < 0$ and $0 < x < 1$ and become flatter over the intervals $x > 1$ and $x < -1$.

- For both even and odd values of n the graph $y = 1/x^n$ has a break at the origin (called a ***discontinuity***), which occurs because division by zero is undefined.

By considering the value of $1/x^n$ for a fixed x as n increases, explain why the graphs become flatter or steeper as described here for increasing values of n.

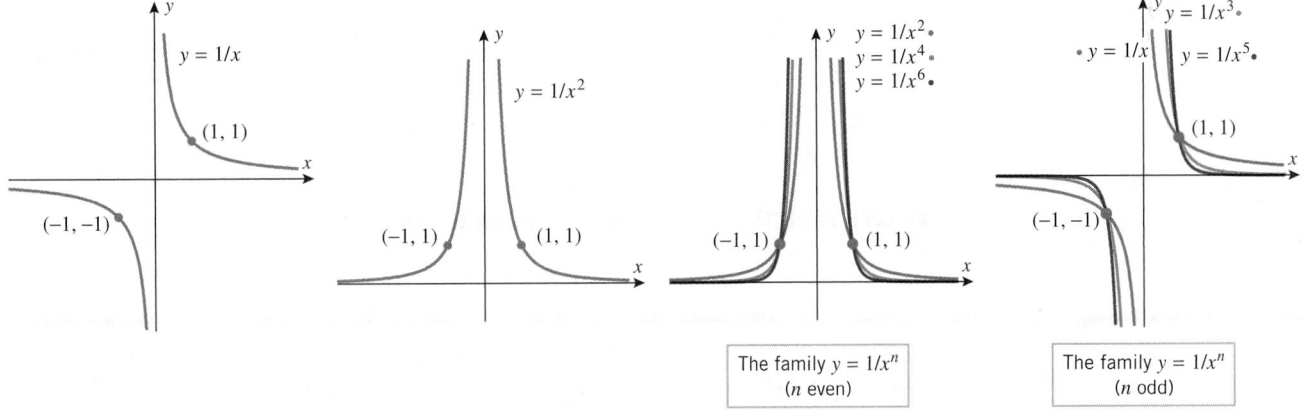

▲ **Figure 0.3.5**

■ INVERSE PROPORTIONS

Recall that a variable y is said to be ***inversely proportional to a variable x*** if there is a positive constant k, called the ***constant of proportionality***, such that

$$y = \frac{k}{x} \tag{1}$$

Since k is assumed to be positive, the graph of (1) has the same shape as $y = 1/x$ but is compressed or stretched in the y-direction. Also, it should be evident from (1) that doubling x multiplies y by $\frac{1}{2}$, tripling x multiplies y by $\frac{1}{3}$, and so forth.

Equation (1) can be expressed as $xy = k$, which tells us that the product of inversely proportional variables is a positive constant. This is a useful form for identifying inverse proportionality in experimental data.

Table 0.3.1

x	0.8	1	2.5	4	6.25	10
y	6.25	5	2	1.25	0.8	0.5

▶ **Example 1**   Table 0.3.1 shows some experimental data.

(a) Explain why the data suggest that y is inversely proportional to x.

(b) Express y as a function of x.

(c) Graph your function and the data together for $x > 0$.

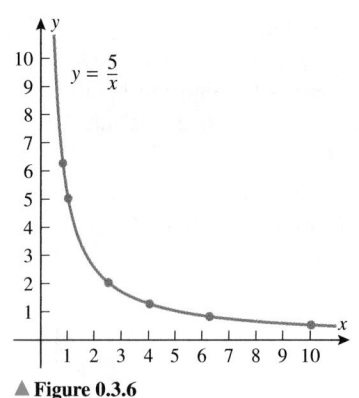

Solution.   For every data point we have $xy = 5$, so y is inversely proportional to x and $y = 5/x$. The graph of this equation with the data points is shown in Figure 0.3.6. ◄

Inverse proportions arise in various laws of physics. For example, *Boyle's law* in physics states that *if a fixed amount of an ideal gas is held at a constant temperature, then the product of the pressure P exerted by the gas and the volume V that it occupies is constant*; that is,

$$PV = k$$

This implies that the variables P and V are inversely proportional to one another. Figure 0.3.7 shows a typical graph of volume versus pressure under the conditions of Boyle's law. Note how doubling the pressure corresponds to halving the volume, as expected.

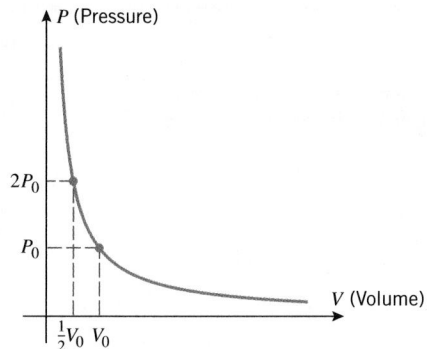

▲ **Figure 0.3.6**

▲ **Figure 0.3.7**   Doubling pressure corresponds to halving volume

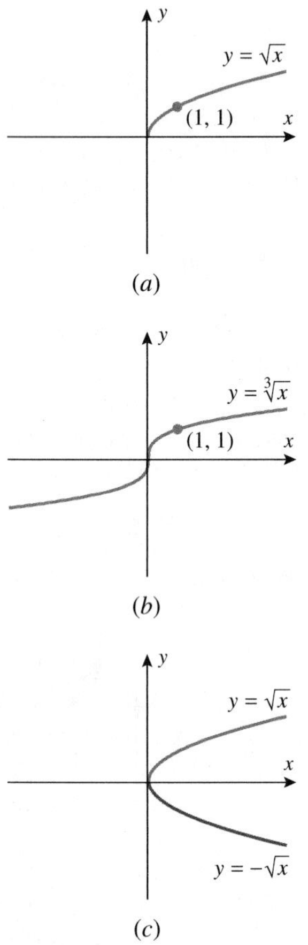

(a)

(b)

(c)

▲ **Figure 0.3.8**

■ POWER FUNCTIONS WITH NONINTEGER EXPONENTS

If $p = 1/n$, where n is a positive integer, then the power functions $f(x) = x^p$ have the form

$$f(x) = x^{1/n} = \sqrt[n]{x}$$

In particular, if $n = 2$, then $f(x) = \sqrt{x}$, and if $n = 3$, then $f(x) = \sqrt[3]{x}$. The graphs of these functions are shown in parts (a) and (b) of Figure 0.3.8.

Since every real number has a real cube root, the domain of the function $f(x) = \sqrt[3]{x}$ is $(-\infty, +\infty)$, and hence the graph of $y = \sqrt[3]{x}$ extends over the entire x-axis. In contrast, the graph of $y = \sqrt{x}$ extends only over the interval $[0, +\infty)$ because $\sqrt{x}$ is imaginary for negative x. As illustrated in Figure 0.3.8c, the graphs of $y = \sqrt{x}$ and $y = -\sqrt{x}$ form the upper and lower halves of the parabola $x = y^2$. In general, the graph of $y = \sqrt[n]{x}$ extends over the entire x-axis if n is odd, but extends only over the interval $[0, +\infty)$ if n is even.

Power functions can have other fractional exponents. Some examples are

$$f(x) = x^{2/3}, \quad f(x) = \sqrt[5]{x^3}, \quad f(x) = x^{-7/8} \tag{2}$$

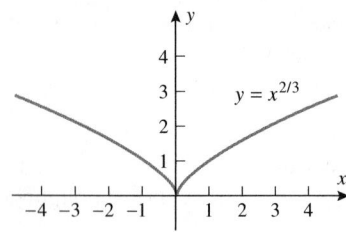

▲ **Figure 0.3.9**

The graph of $f(x) = x^{2/3}$ is shown in Figure 0.3.9. We will discuss expressions involving irrational exponents later.

TECHNOLOGY MASTERY

Graphing utililties sometimes omit portions of the graph of a function involving fractional exponents (or radicals). If $f(x) = x^{p/q}$, where p/q is a positive fraction in *lowest terms*, then you can circumvent this problem as follows:

- If p is even and q is odd, then graph $g(x) = |x|^{p/q}$ instead of $f(x)$.
- If p is odd and q is odd, then graph $g(x) = (|x|/x)|x|^{p/q}$ instead of $f(x)$.

Use a graphing utility to generate graphs of $f(x) = \sqrt[5]{x^3}$ and $f(x) = x^{-7/8}$ that show all of their significant features.

■ POLYNOMIALS

A *polynomial in x* is a function that is expressible as a sum of finitely many terms of the form cx^n, where c is a constant and n is a nonnegative integer. Some examples of polynomials are

$$2x + 1, \quad 3x^2 + 5x - \sqrt{2}, \quad x^3, \quad 4\,(= 4x^0), \quad 5x^7 - x^4 + 3$$

The function $(x^2 - 4)^3$ is also a polynomial because it can be expanded by the binomial formula (see the inside front cover) and expressed as a sum of terms of the form cx^n:

$$(x^2 - 4)^3 = (x^2)^3 - 3(x^2)^2(4) + 3(x^2)(4^2) - (4^3) = x^6 - 12x^4 + 48x^2 - 64 \quad (3)$$

A general polynomial can be written in either of the following forms, depending on whether one wants the powers of x in ascending or descending order:

$$c_0 + c_1 x + c_2 x^2 + \cdots + c_n x^n$$

$$c_n x^n + c_{n-1} x^{n-1} + \cdots + c_1 x + c_0$$

> A more detailed review of polynomials appears in Appendix C.

The constants $c_0, c_1, \ldots, c_n$ are called the *coefficients* of the polynomial. When a polynomial is expressed in one of these forms, the highest power of x that occurs with a nonzero coefficient is called the *degree* of the polynomial. Nonzero constant polynomials are considered to have degree 0, since we can write $c = cx^0$. Polynomials of degree 1, 2, 3, 4, and 5 are described as *linear*, *quadratic*, *cubic*, *quartic*, and *quintic*, respectively. For example,

> The constant 0 is a polynomial called the *zero polynomial*. In this text we will take the degree of the zero polynomial to be undefined. Other texts may use different conventions for the degree of the zero polynomial.

$$3 + 5x \qquad x^2 - 3x + 1 \qquad 2x^3 - 7$$

| Has degree 1 (linear) | Has degree 2 (quadratic) | Has degree 3 (cubic) |

$$8x^4 - 9x^3 + 5x - 3 \qquad \sqrt{3} + x^3 + x^5 \qquad (x^2 - 4)^3$$

| Has degree 4 (quartic) | Has degree 5 (quintic) | Has degree 6 [see (3)] |

The natural domain of a polynomial in x is $(-\infty, +\infty)$, since the only operations involved are multiplication and addition; the range depends on the particular polynomial. We already know that the graphs of polynomials of degree 0 and 1 are lines and that the graphs of polynomials of degree 2 are parabolas. Figure 0.3.10 shows the graphs of some typical polynomials of higher degree. Later, we will discuss polynomial graphs in detail, but for now it suffices to observe that graphs of polynomials are very well behaved in the sense that they have no discontinuities or sharp corners. As illustrated in Figure 0.3.10, the graphs of polynomials wander up and down for awhile in a roller-coaster fashion, but eventually that behavior stops and the graphs steadily rise or fall indefinitely as one travels along the curve in either the positive or negative direction. We will see later that the number of peaks and valleys is less than the degree of the polynomial.

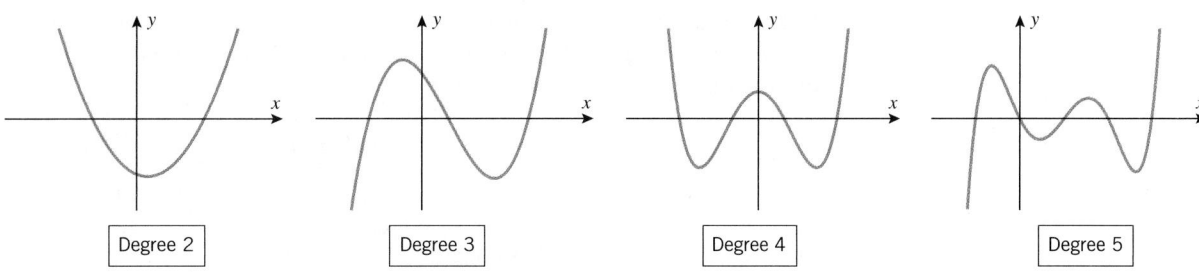

| Degree 2 | Degree 3 | Degree 4 | Degree 5 |

▲ **Figure 0.3.10**

■ RATIONAL FUNCTIONS

A function that can be expressed as a ratio of two polynomials is called a *rational function*. If $P(x)$ and $Q(x)$ are polynomials, then the domain of the rational function

$$f(x) = \frac{P(x)}{Q(x)}$$

consists of all values of x such that $Q(x) \neq 0$. For example, the domain of the rational function

$$f(x) = \frac{x^2 + 2x}{x^2 - 1}$$

consists of all values of x, except $x = 1$ and $x = -1$. Its graph is shown in Figure 0.3.11 along with the graphs of two other typical rational functions.

The graphs of rational functions with nonconstant denominators differ from the graphs of polynomials in some essential ways:

- Unlike polynomials whose graphs are continuous (unbroken) curves, the graphs of rational functions have discontinuities at the points where the denominator is zero.

- Unlike polynomials, rational functions may have numbers at which they are not defined. Near such points, many rational functions have graphs that closely approximate a vertical line, called a **vertical asymptote**. These are represented by the dashed vertical lines in Figure 0.3.11.

- Unlike the graphs of nonconstant polynomials, which eventually rise or fall indefinitely, the graphs of many rational functions eventually get closer and closer to some horizontal line, called a **horizontal asymptote**, as one traverses the curve in either the positive or negative direction. The horizontal asymptotes are represented by the dashed horizontal lines in the first two parts of Figure 0.3.11. In the third part of the figure the x-axis is a horizontal asymptote.

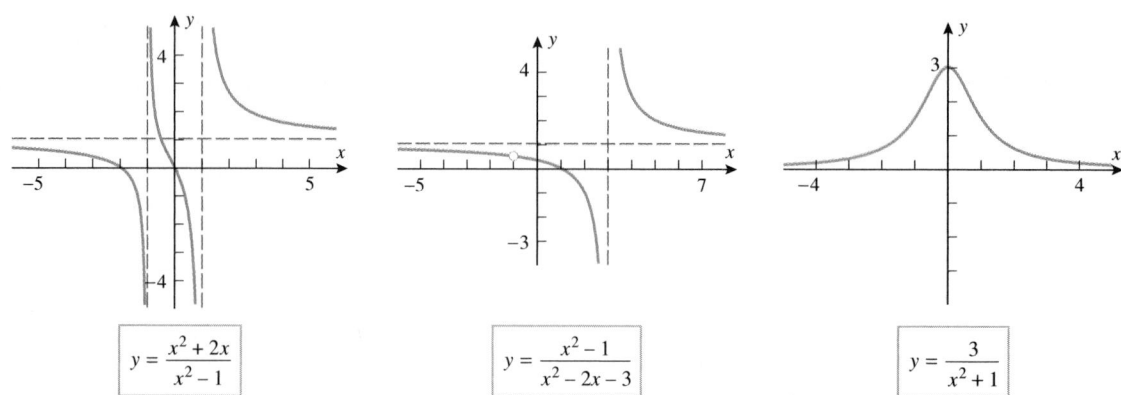

▲ **Figure 0.3.11**

ALGEBRAIC FUNCTIONS

Functions that can be constructed from polynomials by applying finitely many algebraic operations (addition, subtraction, multiplication, division, and root extraction) are called **algebraic functions**. Some examples are

$$f(x) = \sqrt{x^2 - 4}, \quad f(x) = 3\sqrt[3]{x}(2 + x), \quad f(x) = x^{2/3}(x + 2)^2$$

As illustrated in Figure 0.3.12, the graphs of algebraic functions vary widely, so it is difficult to make general statements about them. Later in this text we will develop general calculus methods for analyzing such functions.

THE FAMILIES $y = A \sin Bx$ AND $y = A \cos Bx$

Many important applications lead to trigonometric functions of the form

$$f(x) = A\sin(Bx - C) \quad \text{and} \quad g(x) = A\cos(Bx - C) \tag{4}$$

where A, B, and C are nonzero constants. The graphs of such functions can be obtained by stretching, compressing, translating, and reflecting the graphs of $y = \sin x$ and $y = \cos x$

In this text we will assume that the independent variable of a trigonometric function is in radians unless otherwise stated. A review of trigonometric functions can be found in Appendix B.

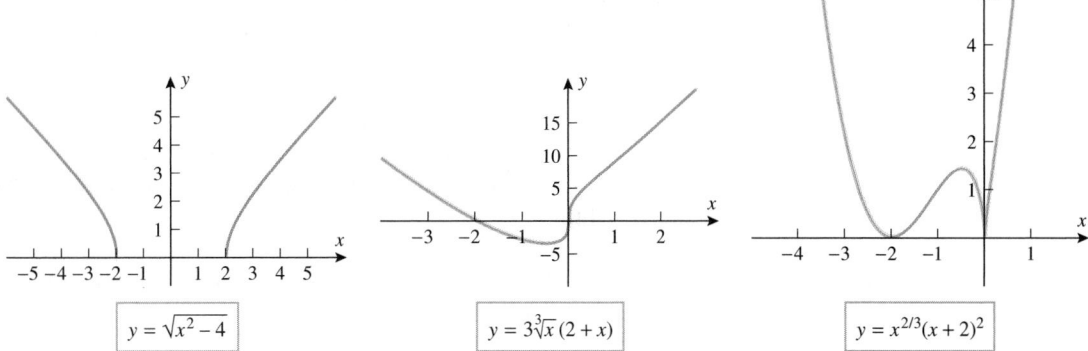

$$y = \sqrt{x^2 - 4}$$ $$y = 3\sqrt[3]{x}\,(2 + x)$$ $$y = x^{2/3}(x + 2)^2$$

▲ **Figure 0.3.12**

appropriately. To see why this is so, let us start with the case where $C = 0$ and consider how the graphs of the equations

$$y = A \sin Bx \quad \text{and} \quad y = A \cos Bx$$

relate to the graphs of $y = \sin x$ and $y = \cos x$. If A and B are positive, then the effect of the constant A is to stretch or compress the graphs of $y = \sin x$ and $y = \cos x$ vertically and the effect of the constant B is to compress or stretch the graphs of $\sin x$ and $\cos x$ horizontally. For example, the graph of $y = 2 \sin 4x$ can be obtained by stretching the graph of $y = \sin x$ vertically by a factor of 2 and compressing it horizontally by a factor of 4. (Recall from Section 0.2 that the multiplier of x *stretches* when it is less than 1 and *compresses* when it is greater than 1.) Thus, as shown in Figure 0.3.13, the graph of $y = 2 \sin 4x$ varies between -2 and 2, and repeats every $2\pi/4 = \pi/2$ units.

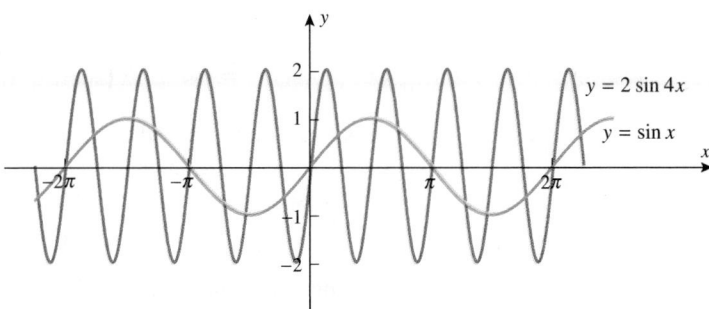

▶ **Figure 0.3.13**

In general, if A and B are positive numbers, then the graphs of

$$y = A \sin Bx \quad \text{and} \quad y = A \cos Bx$$

oscillate between $-A$ and A and repeat every $2\pi/B$ units, so we say that these functions have *amplitude* A and *period* $2\pi/B$. In addition, we define the *frequency* of these functions to be the reciprocal of the period, that is, the frequency is $B/2\pi$. If A or B is negative, then these constants cause reflections of the graphs about the axes as well as compressing or stretching them; and in this case the amplitude, period, and frequency are given by

$$\text{amplitude} = |A|, \quad \text{period} = \frac{2\pi}{|B|}, \quad \text{frequency} = \frac{|B|}{2\pi}$$

▶ **Example 2**   Make sketches of the following graphs that show the period and amplitude.

(a) $y = 3 \sin 2\pi x$ (b) $y = -3 \cos 0.5x$ (c) $y = 1 + \sin x$

Solution (a).   The equation is of the form $y = A \sin Bx$ with $A = 3$ and $B = 2\pi$, so the graph has the shape of a sine function, but it has an amplitude of $A = 3$ and a period of $2\pi/B = 2\pi/2\pi = 1$ (Figure 0.3.14*a*).

Solution (b).   The equation is of the form $y = A \cos Bx$ with $A = -3$ and $B = 0.5$, so the graph has the shape of a cosine curve that has been reflected about the x-axis (because $A = -3$ is negative), but with amplitude $|A| = 3$ and period $2\pi/B = 2\pi/0.5 = 4\pi$ (Figure 0.3.14*b*).

Solution (c).   The graph has the shape of a sine curve that has been translated up 1 unit (Figure 0.3.14*c*). ◄

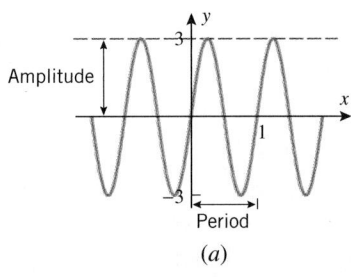

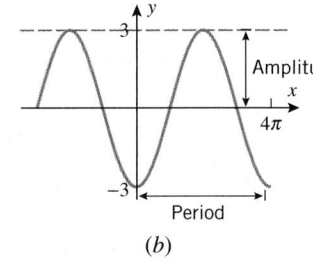

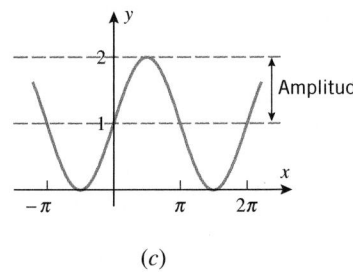

▲ **Figure 0.3.14**

■ **THE FAMILIES $y = A \sin(Bx - C)$ AND $y = A \cos(Bx - C)$**

To investigate the graphs of the more general families

$$y = A \sin(Bx - C) \quad \text{and} \quad y = A \cos(Bx - C)$$

it will be helpful to rewrite these equations as

$$y = A \sin\left[B\left(x - \frac{C}{B} \right) \right] \quad \text{and} \quad y = A \cos\left[B\left(x - \frac{C}{B} \right) \right]$$

In this form we see that the graphs of these equations can be obtained by translating the graphs of $y = A \sin Bx$ and $y = A \cos Bx$ to the left or right, depending on the sign of C/B. For example, if $C/B > 0$, then the graph of

$$y = A \sin[B(x - C/B)] = A \sin(Bx - C)$$

can be obtained by translating the graph of $y = A \sin Bx$ to the right by C/B units (Figure 0.3.15). If $C/B < 0$, the graph of $y = A \sin(Bx - C)$ is obtained by translating the graph of $y = A \sin Bx$ to the left by $|C/B|$ units.

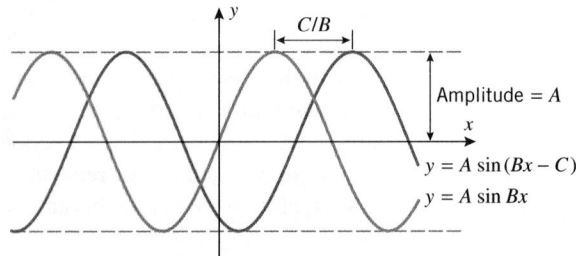

▶ **Figure 0.3.15**

▶ **Example 3**   Find the amplitude and period of

$$y = 3 \cos\left(2x + \frac{\pi}{2} \right)$$

and determine how the graph of $y = 3\cos 2x$ should be translated to produce the graph of this equation. Confirm your results by graphing the equation on a calculator or computer.

Solution. The equation can be rewritten as

$$y = 3\cos\left[2x - \left(-\frac{\pi}{2}\right)\right] = 3\cos\left[2\left(x - \left(-\frac{\pi}{4}\right)\right)\right]$$

which is of the form

$$y = A\cos\left[B\left(x - \frac{C}{B}\right)\right]$$

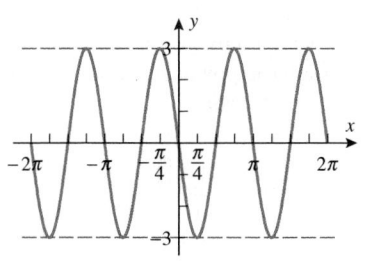

with $A = 3$, $B = 2$, and $C/B = -\pi/4$. It follows that the amplitude is $A = 3$, the period is $2\pi/B = \pi$, and the graph is obtained by translating the graph of $y = 3\cos 2x$ left by $|C/B| = \pi/4$ units (Figure 0.3.16). ◄

▲ **Figure 0.3.16**

✔ QUICK CHECK EXERCISES 0.3 (See page 38 for answers.)

1. Consider the family of functions $y = x^n$, where n is an integer. The graphs of $y = x^n$ are symmetric with respect to the y-axis if n is _____. These graphs are symmetric with respect to the origin if n is _____. The y-axis is a vertical asymptote for these graphs if n is _____.

2. What is the natural domain of a polynomial?

3. Consider the family of functions $y = x^{1/n}$, where n is a nonzero integer. Find the natural domain of these functions if n is
   (a) positive and even   (b) positive and odd
   (c) negative and even   (d) negative and odd.

4. Classify each equation as a polynomial, rational, algebraic, or not an algebraic function.
   (a) $y = \sqrt{x} + 2$ (b) $y = \sqrt{3}x^4 - x + 1$
   (c) $y = 5x^3 + \cos 4x$ (d) $y = \dfrac{x^2 + 5}{2x - 7}$
   (e) $y = 3x^2 + 4x^{-2}$

5. The graph of $y = A\sin Bx$ has amplitude _____ and is periodic with period _____.

EXERCISE SET 0.3   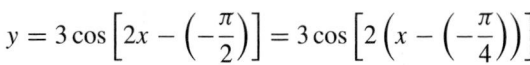 Graphing Utility

1. (a) Find an equation for the family of lines whose members have slope $m = 3$.
   (b) Find an equation for the member of the family that passes through $(-1, 3)$.
   (c) Sketch some members of the family, and label them with their equations. Include the line in part (b).

2. Find an equation for the family of lines whose members are perpendicular to those in Exercise 1.

3. (a) Find an equation for the family of lines with y-intercept $b = 2$.
   (b) Find an equation for the member of the family whose angle of inclination is $135°$.
   (c) Sketch some members of the family, and label them with their equations. Include the line in part (b).

4. Find an equation for
   (a) the family of lines that pass through the origin
   (b) the family of lines with x-intercept $a = 1$
   (c) the family of lines that pass through the point $(1, -2)$
   (d) the family of lines parallel to $2x + 4y = 1$.

5. Find an equation for the family of lines tangent to the circle with center at the origin and radius 3.

6. Find an equation for the family of lines that pass through the intersection of $5x - 3y + 11 = 0$ and $2x - 9y + 7 = 0$.

7. The U.S. Internal Revenue Service uses a 10-year linear depreciation schedule to determine the value of various business items. This means that an item is assumed to have a value of zero at the end of the tenth year and that at intermediate times the value is a linear function of the elapsed time. Sketch some typical depreciation lines, and explain the practical significance of the y-intercepts.

8. Find all lines through $(6, -1)$ for which the product of the x- and y-intercepts is 3.

FOCUS ON CONCEPTS

9–10 State a geometric property common to all lines in the family, and sketch five of the lines. ■

9. (a) The family $y = -x + b$
   (b) The family $y = mx - 1$
   (c) The family $y = m(x + 4) + 2$
   (d) The family $x - ky = 1$

10. (a) The family $y = b$
   (b) The family $Ax + 2y + 1 = 0$
   (c) The family $2x + By + 1 = 0$
   (d) The family $y - 1 = m(x + 1)$

11. In each part, match the equation with one of the accompanying graphs.
   (a) $y = \sqrt[5]{x}$ (b) $y = 2x^5$
   (c) $y = -1/x^8$ (d) $y = \sqrt{x^2 - 1}$
   (e) $y = \sqrt[4]{x - 2}$ (f) $y = -\sqrt[5]{x^2}$

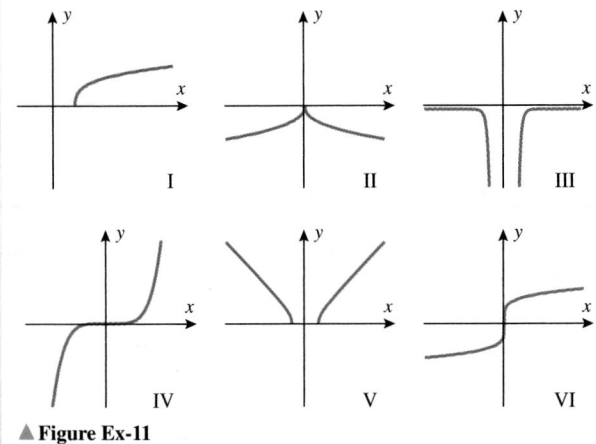

▲ **Figure Ex-11**

12. The accompanying table gives approximate values of three functions: one of the form kx^2, one of the form kx^{-3}, and one of the form $kx^{3/2}$. Identify which is which, and estimate k in each case.

x	0.25	0.37	2.1	4.0	5.8	6.2	7.9	9.3
$f(x)$	640	197	1.08	0.156	0.0513	0.0420	0.0203	0.0124
$g(x)$	0.0312	0.0684	2.20	8.00	16.8	19.2	31.2	43.2
$h(x)$	0.250	0.450	6.09	16.0	27.9	30.9	44.4	56.7

▲ **Table Ex-12**

13–14 Sketch the graph of the equation for $n = 1, 3,$ and 5 in one coordinate system and for $n = 2, 4,$ and 6 in another coordinate system. If you have a graphing utility, use it to check your work. ■

13. (a) $y = -x^n$ (b) $y = 2x^{-n}$ (c) $y = (x - 1)^{1/n}$

14. (a) $y = 2x^n$ (b) $y = -x^{-n}$
   (c) $y = -3(x + 2)^{1/n}$

15. (a) Sketch the graph of $y = ax^2$ for $a = \pm 1, \pm 2,$ and ± 3 in a single coordinate system.
   (b) Sketch the graph of $y = x^2 + b$ for $b = \pm 1, \pm 2,$ and ± 3 in a single coordinate system.
   (c) Sketch some typical members of the family of curves $y = ax^2 + b$.

16. (a) Sketch the graph of $y = a\sqrt{x}$ for $a = \pm 1, \pm 2,$ and ± 3 in a single coordinate system.

   (b) Sketch the graph of $y = \sqrt{x} + b$ for $b = \pm 1, \pm 2,$ and ± 3 in a single coordinate system.
   (c) Sketch some typical members of the family of curves $y = a\sqrt{x} + b$.

17–18 Sketch the graph of the equation by making appropriate transformations to the graph of a basic power function. If you have a graphing utility, use it to check your work. ■

17. (a) $y = 2(x + 1)^2$ (b) $y = -3(x - 2)^3$

   (c) $y = \dfrac{-3}{(x + 1)^2}$ (d) $y = \dfrac{1}{(x - 3)^5}$

18. (a) $y = 1 - \sqrt{x + 2}$ (b) $y = 1 - \sqrt[3]{x + 2}$

   (c) $y = \dfrac{5}{(1 - x)^3}$ (d) $y = \dfrac{2}{(4 + x)^4}$

19. Use the graph of $y = \sqrt{x}$ to help sketch the graph of $y = \sqrt{|x|}$.

20. Use the graph of $y = \sqrt[3]{x}$ to help sketch the graph of $y = \sqrt[3]{|x|}$.

21. As discussed in this section, Boyle's law states that at a constant temperature the pressure P exerted by a gas is related to the volume V by the equation $PV = k$.
   (a) Find the appropriate units for the constant k if pressure (which is force per unit area) is in newtons per square meter (N/m^2) and volume is in cubic meters (m^3).
   (b) Find k if the gas exerts a pressure of $20{,}000 \, N/m^2$ when the volume is 1 liter ($0.001 \, m^3$).
   (c) Make a table that shows the pressures for volumes of 0.25, 0.5, 1.0, 1.5, and 2.0 liters.
   (d) Make a graph of P versus V.

22. A manufacturer of cardboard drink containers wants to construct a closed rectangular container that has a square base and will hold $\frac{1}{10}$ liter ($100 \, cm^3$). Estimate the dimension of the container that will require the least amount of material for its manufacture.

23–24 A variable y is said to be ***inversely proportional to the square of a variable*** x if y is related to x by an equation of the form $y = k/x^2$, where k is a nonzero constant, called the ***constant of proportionality***. This terminology is used in these exercises. ■

23. According to ***Coulomb's law***, the force F of attraction between positive and negative point charges is inversely proportional to the square of the distance x between them.
   (a) Assuming that the force of attraction between two point charges is 0.0005 newton when the distance between them is 0.3 meter, find the constant of proportionality (with proper units).
   (b) Find the force of attraction between the point charges when they are 3 meters apart.
   (c) Make a graph of force versus distance for the two charges.   (cont.)

(d) What happens to the force as the particles get closer and closer together? What happens as they get farther and farther apart?

24. It follows from Newton's Law of Universal Gravitation that the weight W of an object (relative to the Earth) is inversely proportional to the square of the distance x between the object and the center of the Earth, that is, $W = C/x^2$.

(a) Assuming that a weather satellite weighs 2000 pounds on the surface of the Earth and that the Earth is a sphere of radius 4000 miles, find the constant C.

(b) Find the weight of the satellite when it is 1000 miles above the surface of the Earth.

(c) Make a graph of the satellite's weight versus its distance from the center of the Earth.

(d) Is there any distance from the center of the Earth at which the weight of the satellite is zero? Explain your reasoning.

25–28 True–False Determine whether the statement is true or false. Explain your answer. ■

25. Each curve in the family $y = 2x + b$ is parallel to the line $y = 2x$.

26. Each curve in the family $y = x^2 + bx + c$ is a translation of the graph of $y = x^2$.

27. If a curve passes through the point $(2, 6)$ and y is inversely proportional to x, then the constant of proportionality is 3.

28. Curves in the family $y = -5 \sin(A\pi x)$ have amplitude 5 and period $2/|A|$.

FOCUS ON CONCEPTS

29. In each part, match the equation with one of the accompanying graphs, and give the equations for the horizontal and vertical asymptotes.

(a) $y = \dfrac{x^2}{x^2 - x - 2}$ (b) $y = \dfrac{x - 1}{x^2 - x - 6}$

(c) $y = \dfrac{2x^4}{x^4 + 1}$ (d) $y = \dfrac{4}{(x + 2)^2}$

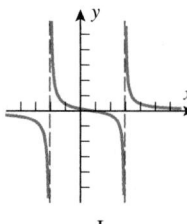
I

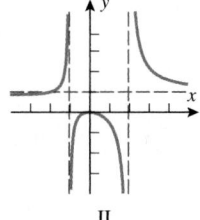
II

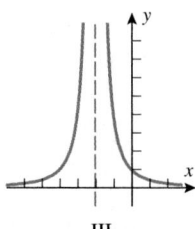
III

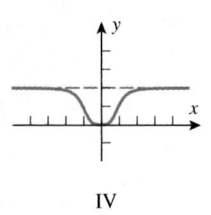
IV

▲ Figure Ex-29

30. Find an equation of the form $y = k/(x^2 + bx + c)$ whose graph is a reasonable match to that in the accompanying figure. If you have a graphing utility, use it to check your work.

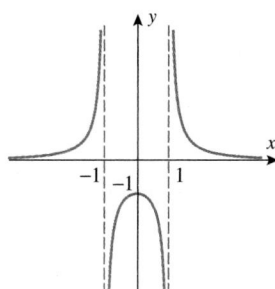

◀ Figure Ex-30

31–32 Find an equation of the form $y = D + A \sin Bx$ or $y = D + A \cos Bx$ for each graph. ■

31.

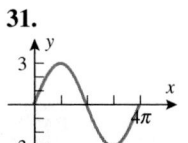
Not drawn to scale
(a)

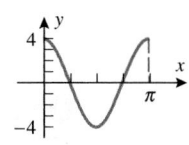
Not drawn to scale
(b)

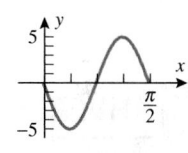
Not drawn to scale
(c)

▲ Figure Ex-31

32.

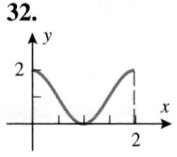
Not drawn to scale
(a)

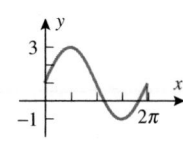
Not drawn to scale
(b)

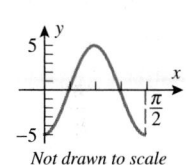
Not drawn to scale
(c)

▲ Figure Ex-32

33. In each part, find an equation for the graph that has the form $y = y_0 + A \sin(Bx - C)$.

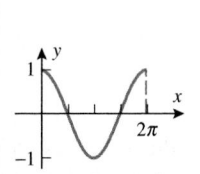
Not drawn to scale
(a)

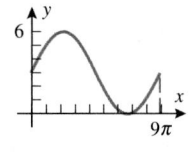
Not drawn to scale
(b)

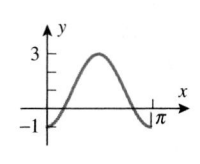
Not drawn to scale
(c)

▲ Figure Ex-33

34. In the United States, a standard electrical outlet supplies sinusoidal electrical current with a maximum voltage of $V = 120\sqrt{2}$ volts (V) at a frequency of 60 hertz (Hz). Write an equation that expresses V as a function of the time t, assuming that $V = 0$ if $t = 0$. [*Note:* 1 Hz = 1 cycle per second.]

35–36 Find the amplitude and period, and sketch at least two periods of the graph by hand. If you have a graphing utility, use it to check your work. ■

35. (a) $y = 3 \sin 4x$ (b) $y = -2 \cos \pi x$
(c) $y = 2 + \cos\left(\dfrac{x}{2}\right)$

36. (a) $y = -1 - 4 \sin 2x$ (b) $y = \frac{1}{2} \cos(3x - \pi)$
(c) $y = -4 \sin\left(\dfrac{x}{3} + 2\pi\right)$

37. Equations of the form
$$x = A_1 \sin \omega t + A_2 \cos \omega t$$

arise in the study of vibrations and other periodic motion. Express the equation
$$x = 5\sqrt{3} \sin 2\pi t + \tfrac{5}{2} \cos 2\pi t$$
in the form $x = A \sin(\omega t + \theta)$, and use a graphing utility to confirm that both equations have the same graph.

38. Determine the number of solutions of $x = 2 \sin x$, and use a graphing or calculating utility to estimate them.

✔ QUICK CHECK ANSWERS 0.3

1. even; odd; negative   **2.** $(-\infty, +\infty)$ **3.** (a) $[0, +\infty)$ (b) $(-\infty, +\infty)$ (c) $(0, +\infty)$ (d) $(-\infty, 0) \cup (0, +\infty)$ **4.** (a) algebraic (b) polynomial (c) not algebraic (d) rational (e) rational   **5.** $|A|$; $2\pi/|B|$

0.4 INVERSE FUNCTIONS; INVERSE TRIGONOMETRIC FUNCTIONS

*In everyday language the term "inversion" conveys the idea of a reversal. For example, in meteorology a temperature inversion is a reversal in the usual temperature properties of air layers, and in music a melodic inversion reverses an ascending interval to the corresponding descending interval. In mathematics the term **inverse** is used to describe functions that reverse one another in the sense that each undoes the effect of the other. In this section we discuss this fundamental mathematical idea. In particular, we introduce inverse trigonometric functions to address the problem of recovering an angle that could produce a given trigonometric function value.*

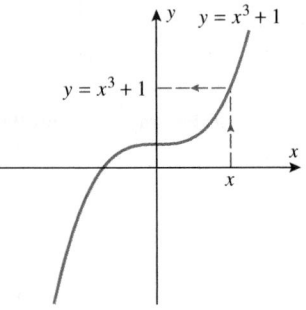

▲ **Figure 0.4.1**

■ INVERSE FUNCTIONS

The idea of solving an equation $y = f(x)$ for x as a function of y, say $x = g(y)$, is one of the most important ideas in mathematics. Sometimes, solving an equation is a simple process; for example, using basic algebra the equation
$$y = x^3 + 1 \qquad \boxed{y = f(x)}$$
can be solved for x as a function of y:
$$x = \sqrt[3]{y - 1} \qquad \boxed{x = g(y)}$$

The first equation is better for computing y if x is known, and the second is better for computing x if y is known (Figure 0.4.1).

Our primary interest in this section is to identify relationships that may exist between the functions f and g when an equation $y = f(x)$ is expressed as $x = g(y)$, or conversely. For example, consider the functions $f(x) = x^3 + 1$ and $g(y) = \sqrt[3]{y - 1}$ discussed above. When these functions are composed in either order, they cancel out the effect of one another in the sense that

$$g(f(x)) = \sqrt[3]{f(x) - 1} = \sqrt[3]{(x^3 + 1) - 1} = x$$
$$f(g(y)) = [g(y)]^3 + 1 = (\sqrt[3]{y - 1})^3 + 1 = y$$
(1)

Pairs of functions with these two properties are so important that there is special terminology for them.

0.4.1   DEFINITION   If the functions f and g satisfy the two conditions

$$g(f(x)) = x \text{ for every } x \text{ in the domain of } f$$
$$f(g(y)) = y \text{ for every } y \text{ in the domain of } g$$

then we say that **f is an inverse of g** and **g is an inverse of f** or that **f and g are inverse functions**.

WARNING

If f is a function, then the -1 in the symbol f^{-1} always denotes an inverse and *never* an exponent. That is,

$$f^{-1}(x) \ \ never \ means \ \ \frac{1}{f(x)}$$

It can be shown (Exercise 60) that if a function f has an inverse, then that inverse is unique. Thus, if a function f has an inverse, then we are entitled to talk about "the" inverse of f, in which case we denote it by the symbol f^{-1}.

▶ **Example 1**   The computations in (1) show that $g(y) = \sqrt[3]{y-1}$ is the inverse of $f(x) = x^3 + 1$. Thus, we can express g in inverse notation as

$$f^{-1}(y) = \sqrt[3]{y-1}$$

and we can express the equations in Definition 0.4.1 as

$$\begin{aligned} f^{-1}(f(x)) &= x \quad \text{for every } x \text{ in the domain of } f \\ f(f^{-1}(y)) &= y \quad \text{for every } y \text{ in the domain of } f^{-1} \end{aligned} \tag{2}$$

We will call these the *cancellation equations* for f and f^{-1}. ◀

■ CHANGING THE INDEPENDENT VARIABLE

The formulas in (2) use x as the independent variable for f and y as the independent variable for f^{-1}. Although it is often convenient to use different independent variables for f and f^{-1}, there will be occasions on which it is desirable to use the same independent variable for both. For example, if we want to graph the functions f and f^{-1} together in the same xy-coordinate system, then we would want to use x as the independent variable and y as the dependent variable for both functions. Thus, to graph the functions $f(x) = x^3 + 1$ and $f^{-1}(y) = \sqrt[3]{y-1}$ of Example 1 in the same xy-coordinate system, we would change the independent variable y to x, use y as the dependent variable for both functions, and graph the equations

$$y = x^3 + 1 \quad \text{and} \quad y = \sqrt[3]{x-1}$$

We will talk more about graphs of inverse functions later in this section, but for reference we give the following reformulation of the cancellation equations in (2) using x as the independent variable for both f and f^{-1}:

$$\begin{aligned} f^{-1}(f(x)) &= x \quad \text{for every } x \text{ in the domain of } f \\ f(f^{-1}(x)) &= x \quad \text{for every } x \text{ in the domain of } f^{-1} \end{aligned} \tag{3}$$

▶ **Example 2**   Confirm each of the following.

(a) The inverse of $f(x) = 2x$ is $f^{-1}(x) = \frac{1}{2}x$.

(b) The inverse of $f(x) = x^3$ is $f^{-1}(x) = x^{1/3}$.

The results in Example 2 should make sense to you intuitively, since the operations of multiplying by 2 and multiplying by $\frac{1}{2}$ in either order cancel the effect of one another, as do the operations of cubing and taking a cube root.

Solution (a).

$$f^{-1}(f(x)) = f^{-1}(2x) = \tfrac{1}{2}(2x) = x$$
$$f(f^{-1}(x)) = f\left(\tfrac{1}{2}x\right) = 2\left(\tfrac{1}{2}x\right) = x$$

Solution (b).
$$f^{-1}(f(x)) = f^{-1}(x^3) = \left(x^3\right)^{1/3} = x$$
$$f(f^{-1}(x)) = f(x^{1/3}) = \left(x^{1/3}\right)^3 = x \blacktriangleleft$$

> In general, if a function f has an inverse and $f(a) = b$, then the procedure in Example 3 shows that $a = f^{-1}(b)$; that is, f^{-1} maps each output of f back into the corresponding input (Figure 0.4.2).

▶ **Example 3**   Given that the function f has an inverse and that $f(3) = 5$, find $f^{-1}(5)$.

Solution.   Apply f^{-1} to both sides of the equation $f(3) = 5$ to obtain

$$f^{-1}(f(3)) = f^{-1}(5)$$

and now apply the first equation in (3) to conclude that $f^{-1}(5) = 3$. ◀

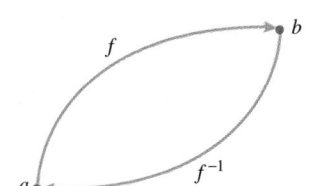

▲ **Figure 0.4.2** If f maps a to b, then f^{-1} maps b back to a.

DOMAIN AND RANGE OF INVERSE FUNCTIONS

The equations in (3) imply the following relationships between the domains and ranges of f and f^{-1}:

$$\begin{aligned} \text{domain of } f^{-1} &= \text{range of } f \\ \text{range of } f^{-1} &= \text{domain of } f \end{aligned} \tag{4}$$

One way to show that two sets are the same is to show that each is a subset of the other. Thus we can establish the first equality in (4) by showing that the domain of f^{-1} is a subset of the range of f and that the range of f is a subset of the domain of f^{-1}. We do this as follows: The first equation in (3) implies that f^{-1} is defined at $f(x)$ for all values of x in the domain of f, and this implies that the range of f is a subset of the domain of f^{-1}. Conversely, if x is in the domain of f^{-1}, then the second equation in (3) implies that x is in the range of f because it is the image of $f^{-1}(x)$. Thus, the domain of f^{-1} is a subset of the range of f. We leave the proof of the second equation in (4) as an exercise.

A METHOD FOR FINDING INVERSE FUNCTIONS

At the beginning of this section we observed that solving $y = f(x) = x^3 + 1$ for x as a function of y produces $x = f^{-1}(y) = \sqrt[3]{y - 1}$. The following theorem shows that this is not accidental.

> **0.4.2   THEOREM**   *If an equation $y = f(x)$ can be solved for x as a function of y, say $x = g(y)$, then f has an inverse and that inverse is $g(y) = f^{-1}(y)$.*

PROOF   Substituting $y = f(x)$ into $x = g(y)$ yields $x = g(f(x))$, which confirms the first equation in Definition 0.4.1, and substituting $x = g(y)$ into $y = f(x)$ yields $y = f(g(y))$, which confirms the second equation in Definition 0.4.1. ■

Theorem 0.4.2 provides us with the following procedure for finding the inverse of a function.

A Procedure for Finding the Inverse of a Function f

Step 1. Write down the equation $y = f(x)$.

Step 2. If possible, solve this equation for x as a function of y.

Step 3. The resulting equation will be $x = f^{-1}(y)$, which provides a formula for f^{-1} with y as the independent variable.

> An alternative way to obtain a formula for $f^{-1}(x)$ with x as the independent variable is to reverse the roles of x and y at the outset and solve the equation $x = f(y)$ for y as a function of x.

Step 4. If y is acceptable as the independent variable for the inverse function, then you are done, but if you want to have x as the independent variable, then you need to interchange x and y in the equation $x = f^{-1}(y)$ to obtain $y = f^{-1}(x)$.

▶ **Example 4**   Find a formula for the inverse of $f(x) = \sqrt{3x - 2}$ with x as the independent variable, and state the domain of f^{-1}.

Solution.   Following the procedure stated above, we first write

$$y = \sqrt{3x - 2}$$

Then we solve this equation for x as a function of y:

$$y^2 = 3x - 2$$
$$x = \tfrac{1}{3}(y^2 + 2)$$

which tells us that

$$f^{-1}(y) = \tfrac{1}{3}(y^2 + 2) \tag{5}$$

Since we want x to be the independent variable, we reverse x and y in (5) to produce the formula

$$f^{-1}(x) = \tfrac{1}{3}(x^2 + 2) \tag{6}$$

We know from (4) that the domain of f^{-1} is the range of f. In general, this need not be the same as the natural domain of the formula for f^{-1}. Indeed, in this example the natural domain of (6) is $(-\infty, +\infty)$, whereas the range of $f(x) = \sqrt{3x - 2}$ is $[0, +\infty)$. Thus, if we want to make the domain of f^{-1} clear, we must express it explicitly by rewriting (6) as

$$f^{-1}(x) = \tfrac{1}{3}(x^2 + 2), \quad x \geq 0 \; ◀$$

▧ EXISTENCE OF INVERSE FUNCTIONS

The procedure we gave above for finding the inverse of a function f was based on solving the equation $y = f(x)$ for x as a function of y. This procedure can fail for two reasons—the function f may not have an inverse, or it may have an inverse but the equation $y = f(x)$ cannot be solved explicitly for x as a function of y. Thus, it is important to establish conditions that ensure the existence of an inverse, even if it cannot be found explicitly.

If a function f has an inverse, then it must assign distinct outputs to distinct inputs. For example, the function $f(x) = x^2$ cannot have an inverse because it assigns the same value to $x = 2$ and $x = -2$, namely,

$$f(2) = f(-2) = 4$$

Thus, if $f(x) = x^2$ were to have an inverse, then the equation $f(2) = 4$ would imply that $f^{-1}(4) = 2$, and the equation $f(-2) = 4$ would imply that $f^{-1}(4) = -2$. But this is impossible because $f^{-1}(4)$ cannot have two different values. Another way to see that $f(x) = x^2$ has no inverse is to attempt to find the inverse by solving the equation $y = x^2$ for x as a function of y. We run into trouble immediately because the resulting equation $x = \pm\sqrt{y}$ does not express x as a *single* function of y.

A function that assigns distinct outputs to distinct inputs is said to be ***one-to-one*** or ***invertible***, so we know from the preceding discussion that if a function f has an inverse, then it must be one-to-one. The converse is also true, thereby establishing the following theorem.

0.4.3   THEOREM   *A function has an inverse if and only if it is one-to-one.*

Stated algebraically, a function f is one-to-one if and only if $f(x_1) \neq f(x_2)$ whenever $x_1 \neq x_2$; stated geometrically, a function f is one-to-one if and only if the graph of $y = f(x)$ is cut at most once by any horizontal line (Figure 0.4.3). The latter statement together with Theorem 0.4.3 provides the following geometric test for determining whether a function has an inverse.

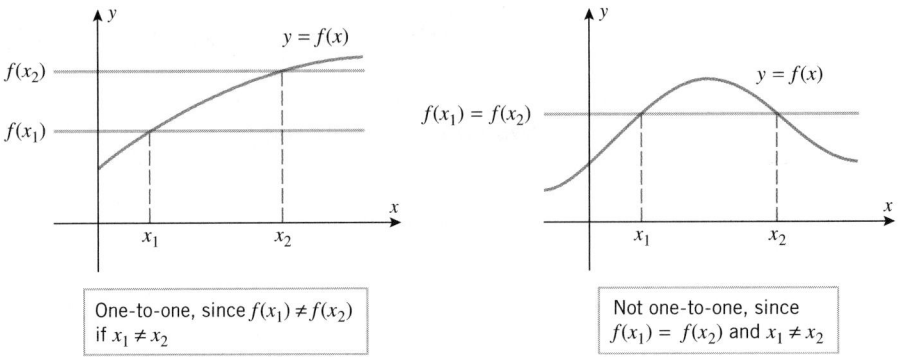

▶ **Figure 0.4.3**

> **0.4.4 THEOREM (*The Horizontal Line Test*)** *A function has an inverse function if and only if its graph is cut at most once by any horizontal line.*

▶ **Example 5** Use the horizontal line test to show that $f(x) = x^2$ has no inverse but that $f(x) = x^3$ does.

Solution. Figure 0.4.4 shows a horizontal line that cuts the graph of $y = x^2$ more than once, so $f(x) = x^2$ is not invertible. Figure 0.4.5 shows that the graph of $y = x^3$ is cut at most once by any horizontal line, so $f(x) = x^3$ is invertible. [Recall from Example 2 that the inverse of $f(x) = x^3$ is $f^{-1}(x) = x^{1/3}$.] ◀

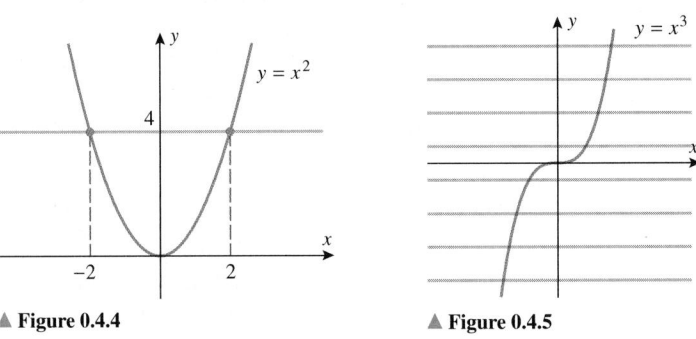

▲ **Figure 0.4.4**   ▲ **Figure 0.4.5**

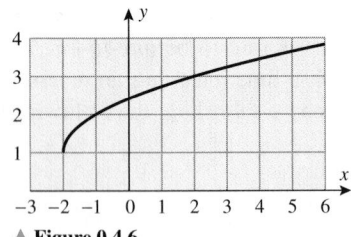

▲ **Figure 0.4.6**

The function $f(x) = x^3$ in Figure 0.4.5 is an example of an increasing function. Give an example of a decreasing function and compute its inverse.

▶ **Example 6** Explain why the function f that is graphed in Figure 0.4.6 has an inverse, and find $f^{-1}(3)$.

Solution. The function f has an inverse since its graph passes the horizontal line test. To evaluate $f^{-1}(3)$, we view $f^{-1}(3)$ as that number x for which $f(x) = 3$. From the graph we see that $f(2) = 3$, so $f^{-1}(3) = 2$. ◀

■ INCREASING OR DECREASING FUNCTIONS ARE INVERTIBLE

A function whose graph is always rising as it is traversed from left to right is said to be an ***increasing function***, and a function whose graph is always falling as it is traversed from left to right is said to be a ***decreasing function***. If x_1 and x_2 are points in the domain of a function f, then f is increasing if

$$f(x_1) < f(x_2) \quad \text{whenever } x_1 < x_2$$

and f is decreasing if

$$f(x_1) > f(x_2) \quad \text{whenever } x_1 < x_2$$

(Figure 0.4.7). It is evident geometrically that increasing and decreasing functions pass the horizontal line test and hence are invertible.

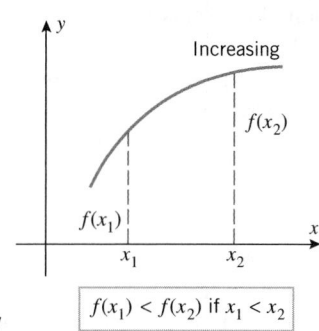

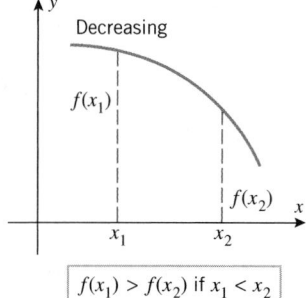

$$f(x_1) < f(x_2) \text{ if } x_1 < x_2 \qquad f(x_1) > f(x_2) \text{ if } x_1 < x_2$$

▶ **Figure 0.4.7**

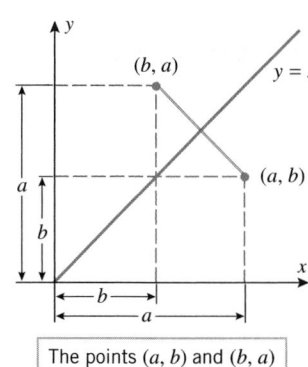

The points (a, b) and (b, a) are reflections about $y = x$.

▲ **Figure 0.4.8**

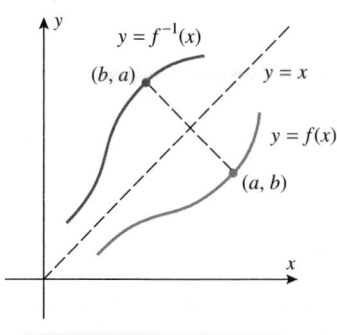

The graphs of f and f^{-1} are reflections about $y = x$.

▲ **Figure 0.4.9**

■ GRAPHS OF INVERSE FUNCTIONS

Our next objective is to explore the relationship between the graphs of f and f^{-1}. For this purpose, it will be desirable to use x as the independent variable for both functions so we can compare the graphs of $y = f(x)$ and $y = f^{-1}(x)$.

If (a, b) is a point on the graph $y = f(x)$, then $b = f(a)$. This is equivalent to the statement that $a = f^{-1}(b)$, which means that (b, a) is a point on the graph of $y = f^{-1}(x)$. In short, reversing the coordinates of a point on the graph of f produces a point on the graph of f^{-1}. Similarly, reversing the coordinates of a point on the graph of f^{-1} produces a point on the graph of f (verify). However, the geometric effect of reversing the coordinates of a point is to reflect that point about the line $y = x$ (Figure 0.4.8), and hence the graphs of $y = f(x)$ and $y = f^{-1}(x)$ are reflections of one another about this line (Figure 0.4.9). In summary, we have the following result.

0.4.5 **THEOREM** *If f has an inverse, then the graphs of $y = f(x)$ and $y = f^{-1}(x)$ are reflections of one another about the line $y = x$; that is, each graph is the mirror image of the other with respect to that line.*

▶ **Example 7** Figure 0.4.10 shows the graphs of the inverse functions discussed in Examples 2 and 4. ◀

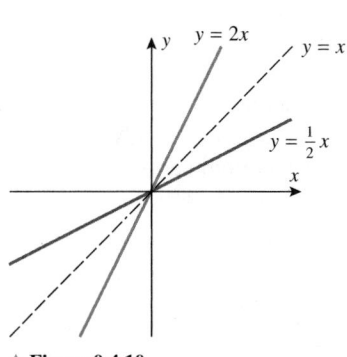

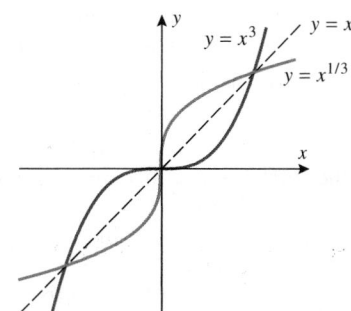

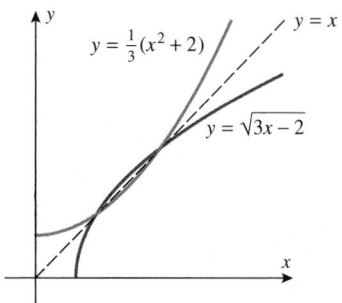

▲ **Figure 0.4.10**

RESTRICTING DOMAINS FOR INVERTIBILITY

If a function g is obtained from a function f by placing restrictions on the domain of f, then g is called a ***restriction*** of f. Thus, for example, the function

$$g(x) = x^3, \quad x \geq 0$$

is a restriction of the function $f(x) = x^3$. More precisely, it is called the restriction of x^3 to the interval $[0, +\infty)$.

Sometimes it is possible to create an invertible function from a function that is not invertible by restricting the domain appropriately. For example, we showed earlier that $f(x) = x^2$ is not invertible. However, consider the restricted functions

$$f_1(x) = x^2, \quad x \geq 0 \quad \text{and} \quad f_2(x) = x^2, \quad x \leq 0$$

the union of whose graphs is the complete graph of $f(x) = x^2$ (Figure 0.4.11). These restricted functions are each one-to-one (hence invertible), since their graphs pass the horizontal line test. As illustrated in Figure 0.4.12, their inverses are

$$f_1^{-1}(x) = \sqrt{x} \quad \text{and} \quad f_2^{-1}(x) = -\sqrt{x}$$

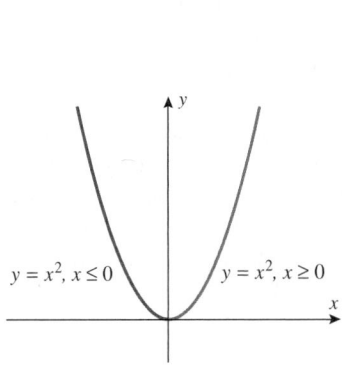

▲ Figure 0.4.11   ▲ Figure 0.4.12

INVERSE TRIGONOMETRIC FUNCTIONS

A common problem in trigonometry is to find an angle x using a known value of $\sin x$, $\cos x$, or some other trigonometric function. Recall that problems of this type involve the computation of "arc functions" such as $\arcsin x$, $\arccos x$, and so forth. We will conclude this section by studying these arc functions from the viewpoint of general inverse functions.

The six basic trigonometric functions do not have inverses because their graphs repeat periodically and hence do not pass the horizontal line test. To circumvent this problem we will restrict the domains of the trigonometric functions to produce one-to-one functions and then define the "inverse trigonometric functions" to be the inverses of these restricted functions. The top part of Figure 0.4.13 shows geometrically how these restrictions are made for $\sin x$, $\cos x$, $\tan x$, and $\sec x$, and the bottom part of the figure shows the graphs of the corresponding inverse functions

$$\sin^{-1} x, \quad \cos^{-1} x, \quad \tan^{-1} x, \quad \sec^{-1} x$$

(also denoted by $\arcsin x$, $\arccos x$, $\arctan x$, and $\arcsec x$). Inverses of $\cot x$ and $\csc x$ are of lesser importance and will be considered in the exercises.

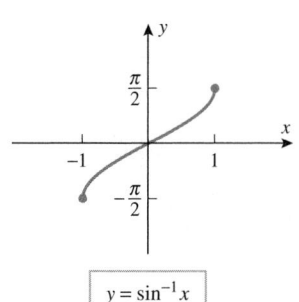

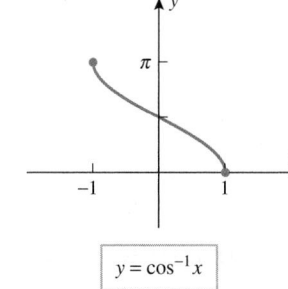

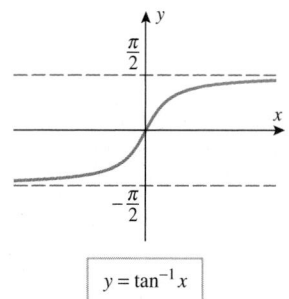

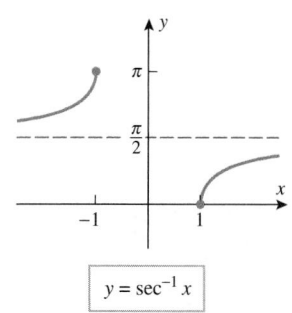

$$y = \sin x$$
$$-\frac{\pi}{2} \le x \le \frac{\pi}{2}$$

$$y = \cos x$$
$$0 \le x \le \pi$$

$$y = \tan x$$
$$-\frac{\pi}{2} < x < \frac{\pi}{2}$$

$$y = \sec x$$
$$0 \le x \le \pi, x \ne \frac{\pi}{2}$$

$$y = \sin^{-1} x$$

$$y = \cos^{-1} x$$

$$y = \tan^{-1} x$$

$$y = \sec^{-1} x$$

▲ **Figure 0.4.13**

If you have trouble visualizing the correspondence between the top and bottom parts of Figure 0.4.13, keep in mind that a reflection about $y = x$ converts vertical lines into horizontal lines, and vice versa; and it converts x-intercepts into y-intercepts, and vice versa.

The following formal definitions summarize the preceding discussion.

0.4.6   DEFINITION   The *inverse sine function*, denoted by $\sin^{-1}$, is defined to be the inverse of the restricted sine function

$$\sin x, \quad -\pi/2 \le x \le \pi/2$$

0.4.7   DEFINITION   The *inverse cosine function*, denoted by $\cos^{-1}$, is defined to be the inverse of the restricted cosine function

$$\cos x, \quad 0 \le x \le \pi$$

0.4.8   DEFINITION   The *inverse tangent function*, denoted by $\tan^{-1}$, is defined to be the inverse of the restricted tangent function

$$\tan x, \quad -\pi/2 < x < \pi/2$$

WARNING

The notations $\sin^{-1} x, \cos^{-1} x, \ldots$ are reserved exclusively for the inverse trigonometric functions and are not used for reciprocals of the trigonometric functions. If we want to express the reciprocal $1/\sin x$ using an exponent, we would write $(\sin x)^{-1}$ and *never* $\sin^{-1} x$.

0.4.9   DEFINITION*   The *inverse secant function*, denoted by $\sec^{-1}$, is defined to be the inverse of the restricted secant function

$$\sec x, \quad 0 \le x \le \pi \text{ with } x \ne \pi/2$$

---

*There is no universal agreement on the definition of $\sec^{-1} x$, and some mathematicians prefer to restrict the domain of $\sec x$ so that $0 \le x < \pi/2$ or $\pi \le x < 3\pi/2$, which was the definition used in some earlier editions of this text. Each definition has advantages and disadvantages, but we will use the current definition to conform with the conventions used by the CAS programs *Mathematica*, *Maple*, and *Sage*.

Table 0.4.1 summarizes the basic properties of the inverse trigonometric functions we have considered. You should confirm that the domains and ranges listed in this table are consistent with the graphs shown in Figure 0.4.13.

Table 0.4.1

PROPERTIES OF INVERSE TRIGONOMETRIC FUNCTIONS

FUNCTION	DOMAIN	RANGE	BASIC RELATIONSHIPS
$\sin^{-1}$	$[-1, 1]$	$[-\pi/2, \pi/2]$	$\sin^{-1}(\sin x) = x$ if $-\pi/2 \le x \le \pi/2$ $\sin(\sin^{-1} x) = x$ if $-1 \le x \le 1$
$\cos^{-1}$	$[-1, 1]$	$[0, \pi]$	$\cos^{-1}(\cos x) = x$ if $0 \le x \le \pi$ $\cos(\cos^{-1} x) = x$ if $-1 \le x \le 1$
$\tan^{-1}$	$(-\infty, +\infty)$	$(-\pi/2, \pi/2)$	$\tan^{-1}(\tan x) = x$ if $-\pi/2 < x < \pi/2$ $\tan(\tan^{-1} x) = x$ if $-\infty < x < +\infty$
$\sec^{-1}$	$(-\infty, -1] \cup [1, +\infty)$	$[0, \pi/2) \cup (\pi/2, \pi]$	$\sec^{-1}(\sec x) = x$ if $0 \le x \le \pi, x \ne \pi/2$ $\sec(\sec^{-1} x) = x$ if $|x| \ge 1$

■ EVALUATING INVERSE TRIGONOMETRIC FUNCTIONS

A common problem in trigonometry is to find an angle whose sine is known. For example, you might want to find an angle x in radian measure such that

$$\sin x = \tfrac{1}{2} \qquad (7)$$

and, more generally, for a given value of y in the interval $-1 \le y \le 1$ you might want to solve the equation

$$\sin x = y \qquad (8)$$

Because $\sin x$ repeats periodically, this equation has infinitely many solutions for x; however, if we solve this equation as

$$x = \sin^{-1} y$$

then we isolate the specific solution that lies in the interval $[-\pi/2, \pi/2]$, since this is the range of the inverse sine. For example, Figure 0.4.14 shows four solutions of Equation (7), namely, $-11\pi/6$, $-7\pi/6$, $\pi/6$, and $5\pi/6$. Of these, $\pi/6$ is the solution in the interval $[-\pi/2, \pi/2]$, so

$$\sin^{-1}\left(\tfrac{1}{2}\right) = \pi/6 \qquad (9)$$

In general, if we view $x = \sin^{-1} y$ as an angle in radian measure whose sine is y, then the restriction $-\pi/2 \le x \le \pi/2$ imposes the geometric requirement that the angle x in standard position terminate in either the first or fourth quadrant or on an axis adjacent to those quadrants.

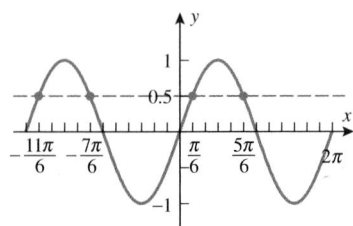

▲ **Figure 0.4.14**

TECHNOLOGY MASTERY

Refer to the documentation for your calculating utility to determine how to calculate inverse sines, inverse cosines, and inverse tangents; and then confirm Equation (9) numerically by showing that

$$\sin^{-1}(0.5) \approx 0.523598775598\ldots$$
$$\approx \pi/6$$

▶ **Example 8** Find exact values of

(a) $\sin^{-1}(1/\sqrt{2})$ (b) $\sin^{-1}(-1)$

by inspection, and confirm your results numerically using a calculating utility.

Solution (a). Because $\sin^{-1}(1/\sqrt{2}) > 0$, we can view $x = \sin^{-1}(1/\sqrt{2})$ as that angle in the first quadrant such that $\sin \theta = 1/\sqrt{2}$. Thus, $\sin^{-1}(1/\sqrt{2}) = \pi/4$. You can confirm this with your calculating utility by showing that $\sin^{-1}(1/\sqrt{2}) \approx 0.785 \approx \pi/4$.

If $x = \cos^{-1} y$ is viewed as an angle in radian measure whose cosine is y, in what possible quadrants can x lie? Answer the same question for

$$x = \tan^{-1} y \quad \text{and} \quad x = \sec^{-1} y$$

Solution (b). Because $\sin^{-1}(-1) < 0$, we can view $x = \sin^{-1}(-1)$ as an angle in the fourth quadrant (or an adjacent axis) such that $\sin x = -1$. Thus, $\sin^{-1}(-1) = -\pi/2$. You can confirm this with your calculating utility by showing that $\sin^{-1}(-1) \approx -1.57 \approx -\pi/2$. ◀

TECHNOLOGY MASTERY | Most calculators do not provide a direct method for calculating inverse secants. In such situations the identity

$$\sec^{-1} x = \cos^{-1}(1/x) \tag{10}$$

is useful (Exercise 48). Use this formula to show that

$$\sec^{-1}(2.25) \approx 1.11 \quad \text{and} \quad \sec^{-1}(-2.25) \approx 2.03$$

If you have a calculating utility (such as a CAS) that can find $\sec^{-1} x$ directly, use it to check these values.

■ IDENTITIES FOR INVERSE TRIGONOMETRIC FUNCTIONS

If we interpret $\sin^{-1} x$ as an angle in radian measure whose sine is x, and if that angle is *nonnegative*, then we can represent $\sin^{-1} x$ geometrically as an angle in a right triangle in which the hypotenuse has length 1 and the side opposite to the angle $\sin^{-1} x$ has length x (Figure 0.4.15a). Moreover, the unlabeled acute angle in Figure 0.4.15a is $\cos^{-1} x$, since the cosine of that angle is x, and the unlabeled side in that figure has length $\sqrt{1 - x^2}$ by the Theorem of Pythagoras (Figure 0.4.15b). This triangle motivates a number of useful identities involving inverse trigonometric functions that are valid for $-1 \leq x \leq 1$; for example,

$$\sin^{-1} x + \cos^{-1} x = \frac{\pi}{2} \tag{11}$$

$$\cos(\sin^{-1} x) = \sqrt{1 - x^2} \tag{12}$$

$$\sin(\cos^{-1} x) = \sqrt{1 - x^2} \tag{13}$$

$$\tan(\sin^{-1} x) = \frac{x}{\sqrt{1 - x^2}} \tag{14}$$

In a similar manner, $\tan^{-1} x$ and $\sec^{-1} x$ can be represented as angles in the right triangles shown in Figures 0.4.15c and 0.4.15d (verify). Those triangles reveal additional useful identities; for example,

$$\sec(\tan^{-1} x) = \sqrt{1 + x^2} \tag{15}$$

$$\sin(\sec^{-1} x) = \frac{\sqrt{x^2 - 1}}{x} \quad (x \geq 1) \tag{16}$$

There is little to be gained by memorizing these identities. What is important is the mastery of the *method* used to obtain them.

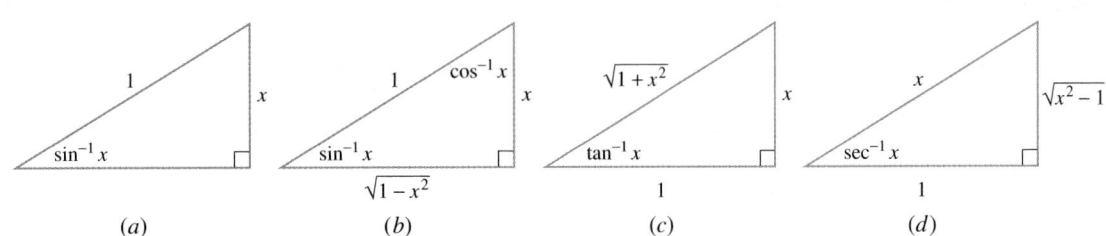

| (a) | (b) | (c) | (d) |

▲ **Figure 0.4.15**

REMARK | The triangle technique does not always produce the most general form of an identity. For example, in Exercise 59 we will ask you to derive the following extension of Formula (16) that is valid for $x \leq -1$ as well as $x \geq 1$:

$$\sin(\sec^{-1} x) = \frac{\sqrt{x^2 - 1}}{|x|} \quad (|x| \geq 1) \tag{17}$$

Referring to Figure 0.4.13, observe that the inverse sine and inverse tangent are odd functions; that is,

$$\sin^{-1}(-x) = -\sin^{-1}(x) \quad \text{and} \quad \tan^{-1}(-x) = -\tan^{-1}(x) \tag{18-19}$$

▶ **Example 9**   Figure 0.4.16 shows a computer-generated graph of $y = \sin^{-1}(\sin x)$. One might think that this graph should be the line $y = x$, since $\sin^{-1}(\sin x) = x$. Why isn't it?

Solution.   The relationship $\sin^{-1}(\sin x) = x$ is valid on the interval $-\pi/2 \le x \le \pi/2$, so we can say with certainty that the graphs of $y = \sin^{-1}(\sin x)$ and $y = x$ coincide on this interval (which is confirmed by Figure 0.4.16). However, outside of this interval the relationship $\sin^{-1}(\sin x) = x$ does not hold. For example, if the quantity x lies in the interval $\pi/2 \le x \le 3\pi/2$, then the quantity $x - \pi$ lies in the interval $-\pi/2 \le x \le \pi/2$, so

$$\sin^{-1}[\sin(x - \pi)] = x - \pi$$

Thus, by using the identity $\sin(x - \pi) = -\sin x$ and the fact that $\sin^{-1}$ is an odd function, we can express $\sin^{-1}(\sin x)$ as

$$\sin^{-1}(\sin x) = \sin^{-1}[-\sin(x - \pi)] = -\sin^{-1}[\sin(x - \pi)] = -(x - \pi)$$

This shows that on the interval $\pi/2 \le x \le 3\pi/2$ the graph of $y = \sin^{-1}(\sin x)$ coincides with the line $y = -(x - \pi)$, which has slope -1 and an x-intercept at $x = \pi$. This agrees with Figure 0.4.16. ◀

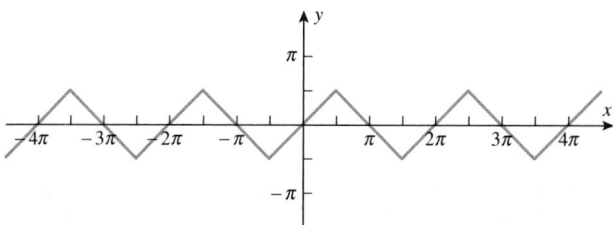

▶ **Figure 0.4.16**

![checkmark] **QUICK CHECK EXERCISES 0.4**   *(See page 52 for answers.)*

1. In each part, determine whether the function f is one-to-one.
   (a) $f(t)$ is the number of people in line at a movie theater at time t.
   (b) $f(x)$ is the measured high temperature (rounded to the nearest °F) in a city on the xth day of the year.
   (c) $f(v)$ is the weight of v cubic inches of lead.

2. A student enters a number on a calculator, doubles it, adds 8 to the result, divides the sum by 2, subtracts 3 from the quotient, and then cubes the difference. If the resulting number is x, then _____ was the student's original number.

3. If $(3, -2)$ is a point on the graph of an odd invertible function f, then _____ and _____ are points on the graph of f^{-1}.

4. In each part, determine the exact value without using a calculating utility.
   (a) $\sin^{-1}(-1) =$ _____
   (b) $\tan^{-1}(1) =$ _____
   (c) $\sin^{-1}\left(\tfrac{1}{2}\sqrt{3}\right) =$ _____
   (d) $\cos^{-1}\left(\tfrac{1}{2}\right) =$ _____
   (e) $\sec^{-1}(-2) =$ _____

5. In each part, determine the exact value without using a calculating utility.
   (a) $\sin^{-1}(\sin \pi/7) =$ _____
   (b) $\sin^{-1}(\sin 5\pi/7) =$ _____
   (c) $\tan^{-1}(\tan 13\pi/6) =$ _____
   (d) $\cos^{-1}(\cos 12\pi/7) =$ _____

EXERCISE SET 0.4   ![graph icon] Graphing Utility

1. In (a)–(d), determine whether f and g are inverse functions.
   (a) $f(x) = 4x$, $g(x) = \tfrac{1}{4}x$
   (b) $f(x) = 3x + 1$, $g(x) = 3x - 1$
   (c) $f(x) = \sqrt[3]{x - 2}$, $g(x) = x^3 + 2$
   (d) $f(x) = x^4$, $g(x) = \sqrt[4]{x}$

2. Check your answers to Exercise 1 with a graphing utility by determining whether the graphs of f and g are reflections of one another about the line $y = x$.

3. In each part, use the horizontal line test to determine whether the function f is one-to-one.
(a) $f(x) = 3x + 2$ (b) $f(x) = \sqrt{x - 1}$
(c) $f(x) = |x|$ (d) $f(x) = x^3$
(e) $f(x) = x^2 - 2x + 2$ (f) $f(x) = \sin x$

4. In each part, generate the graph of the function f with a graphing utility, and determine whether f is one-to-one.
(a) $f(x) = x^3 - 3x + 2$ (b) $f(x) = x^3 - 3x^2 + 3x - 1$

FOCUS ON CONCEPTS

5. In each part, determine whether the function f defined by the table is one-to-one.

(a)

x	1	2	3	4	5	6
$f(x)$	-2	-1	0	1	2	3

(b)

x	1	2	3	4	5	6
$f(x)$	4	-7	6	-3	1	4

6. A face of a broken clock lies in the xy-plane with the center of the clock at the origin and 3:00 in the direction of the positive x-axis. When the clock broke, the tip of the hour hand stopped on the graph of $y = f(x)$, where f is a function that satisfies $f(0) = 0$.
(a) Are there any times of the day that cannot appear in such a configuration? Explain.
(b) How does your answer to part (a) change if f must be an invertible function?
(c) How do your answers to parts (a) and (b) change if it was the tip of the minute hand that stopped on the graph of f?

7. (a) The accompanying figure shows the graph of a function f over its domain $-8 \le x \le 8$. Explain why f has an inverse, and use the graph to find $f^{-1}(2)$, $f^{-1}(-1)$, and $f^{-1}(0)$.
(b) Find the domain and range of f^{-1}.
(c) Sketch the graph of f^{-1}.

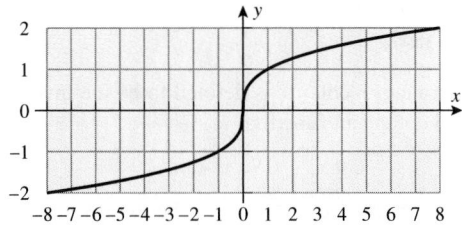

▲ **Figure Ex-7**

8. (a) Explain why the function f graphed in the accompanying figure has no inverse function on its domain $-3 \le x \le 4$.

(b) Subdivide the domain into three adjacent intervals on each of which the function f has an inverse.

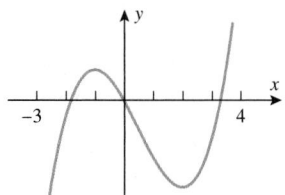

◀ **Figure Ex-8**

9–16 Find a formula for $f^{-1}(x)$. ■

9. $f(x) = 7x - 6$ **10.** $f(x) = \dfrac{x + 1}{x - 1}$

11. $f(x) = 3x^3 - 5$ **12.** $f(x) = \sqrt[5]{4x + 2}$

13. $f(x) = 3/x^2, \quad x < 0$ **14.** $f(x) = 5/(x^2 + 1), \quad x \ge 0$

15. $f(x) = \begin{cases} 5/2 - x, & x < 2 \\ 1/x, & x \ge 2 \end{cases}$

16. $f(x) = \begin{cases} 2x, & x \le 0 \\ x^2, & x > 0 \end{cases}$

17–20 Find a formula for $f^{-1}(x)$, and state the domain of the function f^{-1}. ■

17. $f(x) = (x + 2)^4, \quad x \ge 0$

18. $f(x) = \sqrt{x + 3}$ **19.** $f(x) = -\sqrt{3 - 2x}$

20. $f(x) = 3x^2 + 5x - 2, \quad x \ge 0$

21. Let $f(x) = ax^2 + bx + c, a > 0$. Find f^{-1} if the domain of f is restricted to
(a) $x \ge -b/(2a)$ (b) $x \le -b/(2a)$.

FOCUS ON CONCEPTS

22. The formula $F = \frac{9}{5}C + 32$, where $C \ge -273.15$ expresses the Fahrenheit temperature F as a function of the Celsius temperature C.
(a) Find a formula for the inverse function.
(b) In words, what does the inverse function tell you?
(c) Find the domain and range of the inverse function.

23. (a) One meter is about 6.214×10^{-4} miles. Find a formula $y = f(x)$ that expresses a length y in meters as a function of the same length x in miles.
(b) Find a formula for the inverse of f.
(c) Describe what the formula $x = f^{-1}(y)$ tells you in practical terms.

24. Let $f(x) = x^2, x > 1$, and $g(x) = \sqrt{x}$.
(a) Show that $f(g(x)) = x, x > 1$, and $g(f(x)) = x, x > 1$.
(b) Show that f and g are *not* inverses by showing that the graphs of $y = f(x)$ and $y = g(x)$ are not reflections of one another about $y = x$.
(c) Do parts (a) and (b) contradict one another? Explain.

25. (a) Show that $f(x) = (3 - x)/(1 - x)$ is its own inverse.
(b) What does the result in part (a) tell you about the graph of f?

26. Sketch the graph of a function that is one-to-one on $(-\infty, +\infty)$, yet not increasing on $(-\infty, +\infty)$ and not decreasing on $(-\infty, +\infty)$.

27. Let $f(x) = 2x^3 + 5x + 3$. Find x if $f^{-1}(x) = 1$.

28. Let $f(x) = \dfrac{x^3}{x^2 + 1}$. Find x if $f^{-1}(x) = 2$.

29. Prove that if $a^2 + bc \neq 0$, then the graph of

$$f(x) = \frac{ax + b}{cx - a}$$

is symmetric about the line $y = x$.

30. (a) Prove: If f and g are one-to-one, then so is the composition $f \circ g$.
(b) Prove: If f and g are one-to-one, then

$$(f \circ g)^{-1} = g^{-1} \circ f^{-1}$$

31–34 True–False Determine whether the statement is true or false. Explain your answer. ■

31. If f is an invertible function such that $f(2) = 2$, then $f^{-1}(2) = \frac{1}{2}$.

32. If f and g are inverse functions, then f and g have the same domain.

33. A one-to-one function is invertible.

34. The range of the inverse tangent function is the interval $-\pi/2 \leq y \leq \pi/2$.

35. Given that $\theta = \tan^{-1}\left(\frac{4}{3}\right)$, find the exact values of $\sin\theta$, $\cos\theta$, $\cot\theta$, $\sec\theta$, and $\csc\theta$.

36. Given that $\theta = \sec^{-1} 2.6$, find the exact values of $\sin\theta$, $\cos\theta$, $\tan\theta$, $\cot\theta$, and $\csc\theta$.

37. For which values of x is it true that
(a) $\cos^{-1}(\cos x) = x$ (b) $\cos(\cos^{-1} x) = x$
(c) $\tan^{-1}(\tan x) = x$ (d) $\tan(\tan^{-1} x) = x$?

38–39 Find the exact value of the given quantity. ■

38. $\sec\left[\sin^{-1}\left(-\frac{3}{4}\right)\right]$ **39.** $\sin\left[2\cos^{-1}\left(\frac{3}{5}\right)\right]$

40–41 Complete the identities using the triangle method (Figure 0.4.15). ■

40. (a) $\sin(\cos^{-1} x) = ?$ (b) $\tan(\cos^{-1} x) = ?$
(c) $\csc(\tan^{-1} x) = ?$ (d) $\sin(\tan^{-1} x) = ?$

41. (a) $\cos(\tan^{-1} x) = ?$ (b) $\tan(\cos^{-1} x) = ?$
(c) $\sin(\sec^{-1} x) = ?$ (d) $\cot(\sec^{-1} x) = ?$

42. (a) Use a calculating utility set to radian measure to make tables of values of $y = \sin^{-1} x$ and $y = \cos^{-1} x$ for $x = -1, -0.8, -0.6, \ldots, 0, 0.2, \ldots, 1$. Round your answers to two decimal places.

(b) Plot the points obtained in part (a), and use the points to sketch the graphs of $y = \sin^{-1} x$ and $y = \cos^{-1} x$. Confirm that your sketches agree with those in Figure 0.4.13.
(c) Use your graphing utility to graph $y = \sin^{-1} x$ and $y = \cos^{-1} x$; confirm that the graphs agree with those in Figure 0.4.13.

43. In each part, sketch the graph and check your work with a graphing utility.
(a) $y = \sin^{-1} 2x$ (b) $y = \tan^{-1} \frac{1}{2}x$

44. The *law of cosines* states that

$$c^2 = a^2 + b^2 - 2ab\cos\theta$$

where a, b, and c are the lengths of the sides of a triangle and θ is the angle formed by sides a and b. Find θ, to the nearest degree, for the triangle with $a = 2$, $b = 3$, and $c = 4$.

FOCUS ON CONCEPTS

45. (a) Use a calculating utility to evaluate the expressions $\sin^{-1}(\sin^{-1} 0.25)$ and $\sin^{-1}(\sin^{-1} 0.9)$, and explain what you think is happening in the second calculation.
(b) For what values of x in the interval $-1 \leq x \leq 1$ will your calculating utility produce a real value for the function $\sin^{-1}(\sin^{-1} x)$?

46. A soccer player kicks a ball with an initial speed of 14 m/s at an angle θ with the horizontal (see the accompanying figure). The ball lands 18 m down the field. If air resistance is neglected, then the ball will have a parabolic trajectory and the horizontal range R will be given by

$$R = \frac{v^2}{g}\sin 2\theta$$

where v is the initial speed of the ball and g is the acceleration due to gravity. Using $g = 9.8$ m/s^2, approximate two values of θ, to the nearest degree, at which the ball could have been kicked. Which angle results in the shorter time of flight? Why?

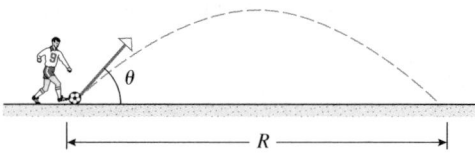

▲ **Figure Ex-46**

47–48 The function $\cot^{-1} x$ is defined to be the inverse of the restricted cotangent function

$$\cot x, \quad 0 < x < \pi$$

and the function $\csc^{-1} x$ is defined to be the inverse of the restricted cosecant function

$$\csc x, \quad -\pi/2 < x < \pi/2, \quad x \neq 0$$

Use these definitions in these and in all subsequent exercises that involve these functions. ■

47. (a) Sketch the graphs of $\cot^{-1} x$ and $\csc^{-1} x$.

(b) Find the domain and range of $\cot^{-1} x$ and $\csc^{-1} x$.

48. Show that

(a) $\cot^{-1} x = \begin{cases} \tan^{-1}(1/x), & \text{if } x > 0 \\ \pi + \tan^{-1}(1/x), & \text{if } x < 0 \end{cases}$

(b) $\sec^{-1} x = \cos^{-1} \dfrac{1}{x}$, if $|x| \geq 1$

(c) $\csc^{-1} x = \sin^{-1} \dfrac{1}{x}$, if $|x| \geq 1$.

49. Most scientific calculators have keys for the values of only $\sin^{-1} x$, $\cos^{-1} x$, and $\tan^{-1} x$. The formulas in Exercise 48 show how a calculator can be used to obtain values of $\cot^{-1} x$, $\sec^{-1} x$, and $\csc^{-1} x$ for positive values of x. Use these formulas and a calculator to find numerical values for each of the following inverse trigonometric functions. Express your answers in degrees, rounded to the nearest tenth of a degree.

(a) $\cot^{-1} 0.7$ (b) $\sec^{-1} 1.2$ (c) $\csc^{-1} 2.3$

50. An Earth-observing satellite has horizon sensors that can measure the angle θ shown in the accompanying figure. Let R be the radius of the Earth (assumed spherical) and h the distance between the satellite and the Earth's surface.

(a) Show that $\sin \theta = \dfrac{R}{R + h}$.

(b) Find θ, to the nearest degree, for a satellite that is 10,000 km from the Earth's surface (use $R = 6378$ km).

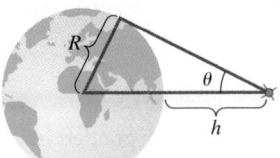

Earth   ◀ **Figure Ex-50**

51. The number of hours of daylight on a given day at a given point on the Earth's surface depends on the latitude λ of the point, the angle γ through which the Earth has moved in its orbital plane during the time period from the vernal equinox (March 21), and the angle of inclination ϕ of the Earth's axis of rotation measured from ecliptic north ($\phi \approx 23.45°$). The number of hours of daylight h can be approximated by the formula

$$h = \begin{cases} 24, & D \geq 1 \\ 12 + \frac{2}{15} \sin^{-1} D, & |D| < 1 \\ 0, & D \leq -1 \end{cases}$$

where

$$D = \frac{\sin \phi \sin \gamma \tan \lambda}{\sqrt{1 - \sin^2 \phi \sin^2 \gamma}}$$

and $\sin^{-1} D$ is in degree measure. Given that Fairbanks, Alaska, is located at a latitude of $\lambda = 65°$ N and also that $\gamma = 90°$ on June 20 and $\gamma = 270°$ on December 20, approximate

(a) the maximum number of daylight hours at Fairbanks to one decimal place

(b) the minimum number of daylight hours at Fairbanks to one decimal place.

Source: This problem was adapted from *TEAM, A Path to Applied Mathematics*, The Mathematical Association of America, Washington, D.C., 1985.

52. A camera is positioned x feet from the base of a missile launching pad (see the accompanying figure). If a missile of length a feet is launched vertically, show that when the base of the missile is b feet above the camera lens, the angle θ subtended at the lens by the missile is

$$\theta = \cot^{-1} \frac{x}{a + b} - \cot^{-1} \frac{x}{b}$$

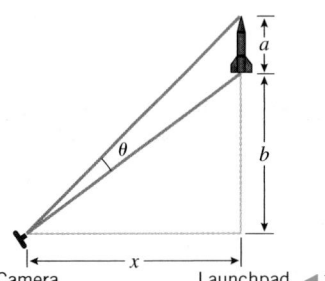

Camera   Launchpad   ◀ **Figure Ex-52**

53. An airplane is flying at a constant height of 3000 ft above water at a speed of 400 ft/s. The pilot is to release a survival package so that it lands in the water at a sighted point P. If air resistance is neglected, then the package will follow a parabolic trajectory whose equation relative to the coordinate system in the accompanying figure is

$$y = 3000 - \frac{g}{2v^2} x^2$$

where g is the acceleration due to gravity and v is the speed of the airplane. Using $g = 32$ ft/s², find the "line of sight" angle θ, to the nearest degree, that will result in the package hitting the target point.

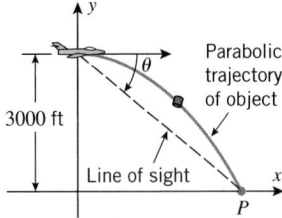

◀ **Figure Ex-53**

54. Prove:

(a) $\sin^{-1}(-x) = -\sin^{-1} x$

(b) $\tan^{-1}(-x) = -\tan^{-1} x$.

55. Prove:

(a) $\cos^{-1}(-x) = \pi - \cos^{-1} x$

(b) $\sec^{-1}(-x) = \pi - \sec^{-1} x$.

56. Prove:

(a) $\sin^{-1} x = \tan^{-1} \dfrac{x}{\sqrt{1 - x^2}}$ $(|x| < 1)$

(b) $\cos^{-1} x = \dfrac{\pi}{2} - \tan^{-1} \dfrac{x}{\sqrt{1 - x^2}}$ $(|x| < 1)$.

57. Prove:

$$\tan^{-1} x + \tan^{-1} y = \tan^{-1}\left(\frac{x+y}{1-xy}\right)$$

provided $-\pi/2 < \tan^{-1} x + \tan^{-1} y < \pi/2$. [*Hint:* Use an identity for $\tan(\alpha + \beta)$.]

58. Use the result in Exercise 57 to show that
 (a) $\tan^{-1}\frac{1}{2} + \tan^{-1}\frac{1}{3} = \pi/4$
 (b) $2\tan^{-1}\frac{1}{3} + \tan^{-1}\frac{1}{7} = \pi/4$.

59. Use identities (10) and (13) to obtain identity (17).

60. Prove: A one-to-one function f cannot have two different inverses.

✔ **QUICK CHECK ANSWERS 0.4**

---

1. (a) not one-to-one (b) not one-to-one (c) one-to-one **2.** $\sqrt[3]{x} - 1$ **3.** $(-2, 3)$; $(2, -3)$ **4.** (a) $-\pi/2$ (b) $\pi/4$ (c) $\pi/3$ (d) $\pi/3$ (e) $2\pi/3$ **5.** (a) $\pi/7$ (b) $2\pi/7$ (c) $\pi/6$ (d) $2\pi/7$

0.5 EXPONENTIAL AND LOGARITHMIC FUNCTIONS

When logarithms were introduced in the seventeenth century as a computational tool, they provided scientists of that period computing power that was previously unimaginable. Although computers and calculators have replaced logarithm tables for numerical calculations, the logarithmic functions have wide-ranging applications in mathematics and science. In this section we will review some properties of exponents and logarithms and then use our work on inverse functions to develop results about exponential and logarithmic functions.

■ IRRATIONAL EXPONENTS

Recall from algebra that if b is a nonzero real number, then nonzero *integer* powers of b are defined by

$$b^n = \underbrace{b \times b \times \cdots \times b}_{n \text{ factors}} \quad \text{and} \quad b^{-n} = \frac{1}{b^n}$$

and if $n = 0$, then $b^0 = 1$. Also, if p/q is a positive *rational* number expressed in lowest terms, then

$$b^{p/q} = \sqrt[q]{b^p} = (\sqrt[q]{b})^p \quad \text{and} \quad b^{-p/q} = \frac{1}{b^{p/q}}$$

If b is negative, then some fractional powers of b will have imaginary values—the quantity $(-2)^{1/2} = \sqrt{-2}$, for example. To avoid this complication, we will assume throughout this section that $b > 0$, even if it is not stated explicitly.

There are various methods for defining *irrational* powers such as

$$2^\pi, \quad 3^{\sqrt{2}}, \quad \pi^{-\sqrt{7}}$$

One approach is to define irrational powers of b via successive approximations using rational powers of b. For example, to define 2^π consider the decimal representation of π:

$$3.1415926\ldots$$

From this decimal we can form a sequence of rational numbers that gets closer and closer to π, namely,   3.1,   3.14,   3.141,   3.1415,   3.14159

and from these we can form a sequence of *rational* powers of 2:

$$2^{3.1}, \quad 2^{3.14}, \quad 2^{3.141}, \quad 2^{3.1415}, \quad 2^{3.14159}$$

Since the exponents of the terms in this sequence get successively closer to π, it seems plausible that the terms themselves will get successively closer to some number. It is that number that we *define* to be 2^π. This is illustrated in Table 0.5.1, which we generated using

Table 0.5.1

x	2^x
3	8.000000
3.1	8.574188
3.14	8.815241
3.141	8.821353
3.1415	8.824411
3.14159	8.824962
3.141592	8.824974
3.1415926	8.824977

a calculator. The table suggests that to four decimal places the value of 2^π is

$$2^\pi \approx 8.8250 \tag{1}$$

TECHNOLOGY MASTERY

Use a calculating utility to verify the results in Table 0.5.1, and then verify (1) by using the utility to compute 2^π directly.

With this notion for irrational powers, we remark without proof that the following familiar laws of exponents hold for all real values of p and q:

$$b^p b^q = b^{p+q}, \quad \frac{b^p}{b^q} = b^{p-q}, \quad \left(b^p\right)^q = b^{pq}$$

■ THE FAMILY OF EXPONENTIAL FUNCTIONS

A function of the form $f(x) = b^x$, where $b > 0$, is called an ***exponential function with base b***. Some examples are

$$f(x) = 2^x, \quad f(x) = \left(\tfrac{1}{2}\right)^x, \quad f(x) = \pi^x$$

Note that an exponential function has a constant base and variable exponent. Thus, functions such as $f(x) = x^2$ and $f(x) = x^\pi$ would *not* be classified as exponential functions, since they have a variable base and a constant exponent.

Figure 0.5.1 illustrates that the graph of $y = b^x$ has one of three general forms, depending on the value of b. The graph of $y = b^x$ has the following properties:

- The graph passes through $(0, 1)$ because $b^0 = 1$.
- If $b > 1$, the value of b^x increases as x increases. As you traverse the graph of $y = b^x$ from left to right, the values of b^x increase indefinitely. If you traverse the graph from right to left, the values of b^x decrease toward zero but never reach zero. Thus, the x-axis is a horizontal asymptote of the graph of b^x.
- If $0 < b < 1$, the value of b^x decreases as x increases. As you traverse the graph of $y = b^x$ from left to right, the values of b^x decrease toward zero but never reach zero. Thus, the x-axis is a horizontal asymptote of the graph of b^x. If you traverse the graph from right to left, the values of b^x increase indefinitely.
- If $b = 1$, then the value of b^x is constant.

Some typical members of the family of exponential functions are graphed in Figure 0.5.2. This figure illustrates that the graph of $y = (1/b)^x$ is the reflection of the graph of $y = b^x$ about the y-axis. This is because replacing x by $-x$ in the equation $y = b^x$ yields

$$y = b^{-x} = (1/b)^x$$

The figure also conveys that for $b > 1$, the larger the base b, the more rapidly the function $f(x) = b^x$ increases for $x > 0$.

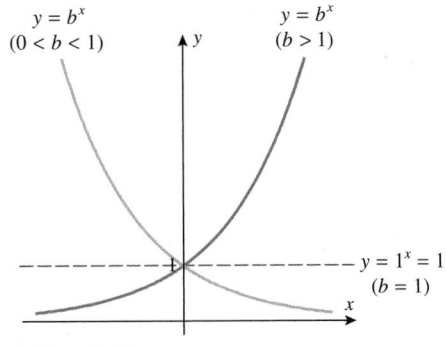

▲ **Figure 0.5.1**

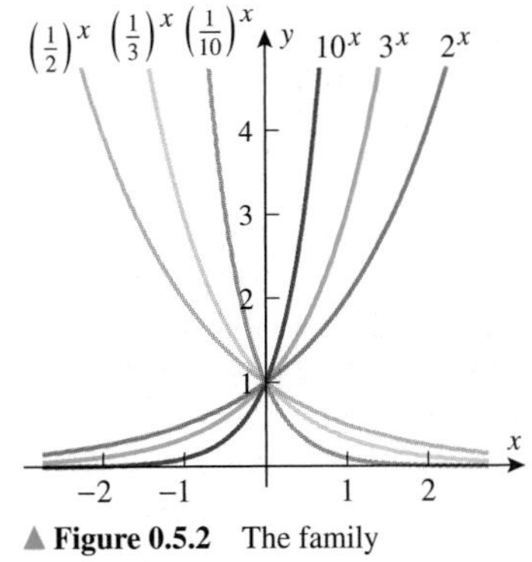

▲ **Figure 0.5.2**   The family
$y = b^x (b > 0)$

The domain and range of the exponential function $f(x) = b^x$ can also be found by examining Figure 0.5.1:

- If $b > 0$, then $f(x) = b^x$ is defined and has a real value for every real value of x, so the natural domain of every exponential function is $(-\infty, +\infty)$.

- If $b > 0$ and $b \neq 1$, then as noted earlier the graph of $y = b^x$ increases indefinitely as it is traversed in one direction and decreases toward zero but never reaches zero as it is traversed in the other direction. This implies that the range of $f(x) = b^x$ is $(0, +\infty)$.[*]

▶ **Example 1** Sketch the graph of the function $f(x) = 1 - 2^x$ and find its domain and range.

Solution. Start with a graph of $y = 2^x$. Reflect this graph across the x-axis to obtain the graph of $y = -2^x$, then translate that graph upward by 1 unit to obtain the graph of $y = 1 - 2^x$ (Figure 0.5.3). The dashed line in the third part of Figure 0.5.3 is a horizontal asymptote for the graph. You should be able to see from the graph that the domain of f is $(-\infty, +\infty)$ and the range is $(-\infty, 1)$. ◀

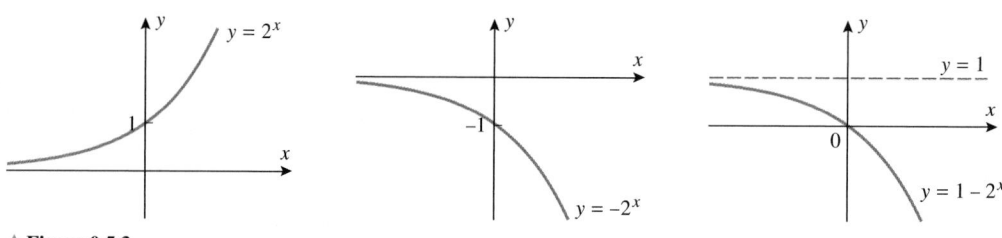

▲ **Figure 0.5.3**

■ THE NATURAL EXPONENTIAL FUNCTION

Among all possible bases for exponential functions there is one particular base that plays a special role in calculus. That base, denoted by the letter e, is a certain irrational number whose value to six decimal places is

$$e \approx 2.718282 \tag{2}$$

This base is important in calculus because, as we will prove later, $b = e$ is the only base for which the slope of the tangent line[**] to the curve $y = b^x$ at any point P on the curve is equal to the y-coordinate at P. Thus, for example, the tangent line to $y = e^x$ at $(0, 1)$ has slope 1 (Figure 0.5.4).

The function $f(x) = e^x$ is called the ***natural exponential function***. To simplify typography, the natural exponential function is sometimes written as $\exp(x)$, in which case the relationship $e^{x_1 + x_2} = e^{x_1} e^{x_2}$ would be expressed as

$$\exp(x_1 + x_2) = \exp(x_1) \exp(x_2)$$

The use of the letter e is in honor of the Swiss mathematician Leonhard Euler (biography on p. 3) who is credited with recognizing the mathematical importance of this constant.

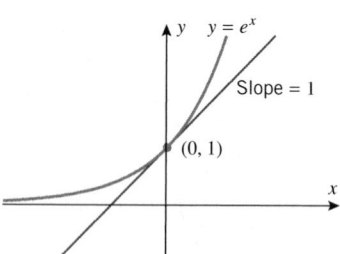

▲ **Figure 0.5.4** The tangent line to the graph of $y = e^x$ at $(0, 1)$ has slope 1.

---

[*]We are assuming without proof that the graph of $y = b^x$ is a curve without breaks, gaps, or holes.
[**]The precise definition of a tangent line will be discussed later. For now your intuition will suffice.

TECHNOLOGY MASTERY Your technology utility should have keys or commands for approximating e and for graphing the natural exponential function. Read your documentation on how to do this and use your utility to confirm (2) and to generate the graphs in Figures 0.5.2 and 0.5.4.

The constant e also arises in the context of the graph of the equation

$$y = \left(1 + \frac{1}{x}\right)^x \tag{3}$$

As shown in Figure 0.5.5, $y = e$ is a horizontal asymptote of this graph. As a result, the value of e can be approximated to any degree of accuracy by evaluating (3) for x sufficiently large in absolute value (Table 0.5.2).

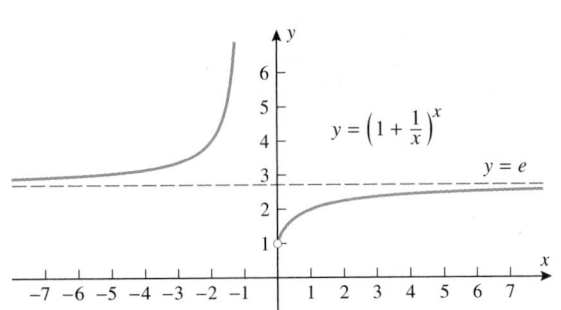

▲ Figure 0.5.5

Table 0.5.2

APPROXIMATIONS OF e BY $(1 + 1/x)^x$
FOR INCREASING VALUES OF x

x	$1 + \frac{1}{x}$	$\left(1 + \frac{1}{x}\right)^x$
1	2	≈ 2.000000
10	1.1	2.593742
100	1.01	2.704814
1000	1.001	2.716924
10,000	1.0001	2.718146
100,000	1.00001	2.718268
1,000,000	1.000001	2.718280

◼ LOGARITHMIC FUNCTIONS

Recall from algebra that a logarithm is an exponent. More precisely, if $b > 0$ and $b \neq 1$, then for a positive value of x the expression

$$\log_b x$$

(read "the logarithm to the base b of x") denotes that exponent to which b must be raised to produce x. Thus, for example,

$$\log_{10} 100 = 2, \quad \log_{10}(1/1000) = -3, \quad \log_2 16 = 4, \quad \log_b 1 = 0, \quad \log_b b = 1$$

$$\boxed{10^2 = 100} \qquad \boxed{10^{-3} = 1/1000} \qquad \boxed{2^4 = 16} \qquad \boxed{b^0 = 1} \qquad \boxed{b^1 = b}$$

Logarithms with base 10 are called *common logarithms* and are often written without explicit reference to the base. Thus, the symbol $\log x$ generally denotes $\log_{10} x$.

We call the function $f(x) = \log_b x$ the ***logarithmic function with base b***.

Logarithmic functions can also be viewed as inverses of exponential functions. To see why this is so, observe from Figure 0.5.1 that if $b > 0$ and $b \neq 1$, then the graph of $f(x) = b^x$ passes the horizontal line test, so b^x has an inverse. We can find a formula for this inverse with x as the independent variable by solving the equation

$$x = b^y$$

for y as a function of x. But this equation states that y is the logarithm to the base b of x, so it can be rewritten as

$$y = \log_b x$$

Thus, we have established the following result.

0.5.1 THEOREM   *If $b > 0$ and $b \neq 1$, then b^x and $\log_b x$ are inverse functions.*

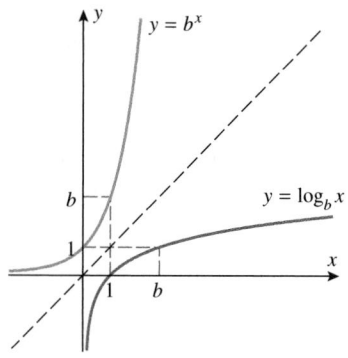

▲ **Figure 0.5.6**

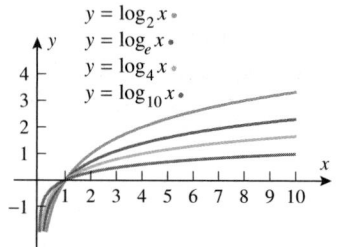

▲ **Figure 0.5.7** The family
$y = \log_b x \ (b > 1)$

TECHNOLOGY MASTERY

Use your graphing utility to generate
the graphs of $y = \ln x$ and $y = \log x$.

It follows from this theorem that the graphs of $y = b^x$ and $y = \log_b x$ are reflections of one another about the line $y = x$ (see Figure 0.5.6 for the case where $b > 1$). Figure 0.5.7 shows the graphs of $y = \log_b x$ for various values of b. Observe that they all pass through the point $(1, 0)$.

The most important logarithms in applications are those with base e. These are called *natural logarithms* because the function $\log_e x$ is the inverse of the natural exponential function e^x. It is standard to denote the natural logarithm of x by $\ln x$ (read "ell en of x"), rather than $\log_e x$. For example,

$$\ln 1 = 0, \quad \ln e = 1, \quad \ln 1/e = -1, \quad \ln(e^2) = 2$$

| Since $e^0 = 1$ | Since $e^1 = e$ | Since $e^{-1} = 1/e$ | Since $e^2 = e^2$ |

In general,

$$y = \ln x \quad \text{if and only if} \quad x = e^y$$

As shown in Table 0.5.3, the inverse relationship between b^x and $\log_b x$ produces a correspondence between some basic properties of those functions.

Table 0.5.3

CORRESPONDENCE BETWEEN PROPERTIES OF
LOGARITHMIC AND EXPONENTIAL FUNCTIONS

PROPERTY OF b^x	PROPERTY OF $\log_b x$
$b^0 = 1$	$\log_b 1 = 0$
$b^1 = b$	$\log_b b = 1$
Range is $(0, +\infty)$	Domain is $(0, +\infty)$
Domain is $(-\infty, +\infty)$	Range is $(-\infty, +\infty)$
x-axis is a horizontal asymptote	y-axis is a vertical asymptote

It also follows from the cancellation properties of inverse functions [see (3) in Section 0.4] that

$$\log_b(b^x) = x \quad \text{for all real values of } x$$
$$b^{\log_b x} = x \quad \text{for } x > 0 \tag{4}$$

In the special case where $b = e$, these equations become

$$\ln(e^x) = x \quad \text{for all real values of } x$$
$$e^{\ln x} = x \quad \text{for } x > 0 \tag{5}$$

In words, the functions b^x and $\log_b x$ cancel out the effect of one another when composed in either order; for example,

$$\log 10^x = x, \quad 10^{\log x} = x, \quad \ln e^x = x, \quad e^{\ln x} = x, \quad \ln e^5 = 5, \quad e^{\ln \pi} = \pi$$

■ **SOLVING EQUATIONS INVOLVING EXPONENTIALS AND LOGARITHMS**
You should be familiar with the following properties of logarithms from your earlier studies.

> **0.5.2 THEOREM (Algebraic Properties of Logarithms)** *If $b > 0, b \neq 1, a > 0, c > 0$, and r is any real number, then:*
>
> (a) $\log_b(ac) = \log_b a + \log_b c$ Product property
>
> (b) $\log_b(a/c) = \log_b a - \log_b c$ Quotient property
>
> (c) $\log_b(a^r) = r \log_b a$ Power property
>
> (d) $\log_b(1/c) = -\log_b c$ Reciprocal property

WARNING

Expressions of the form $\log_b(u + v)$ and $\log_b(u - v)$ have no useful simplifications. In particular,

$\log_b(u + v) \neq \log_b(u) + \log_b(v)$

$\log_b(u - v) \neq \log_b(u) - \log_b(v)$

These properties are often used to expand a single logarithm into sums, differences, and multiples of other logarithms and, conversely, to condense sums, differences, and multiples of logarithms into a single logarithm. For example,

$$\log \frac{xy^5}{\sqrt{z}} = \log xy^5 - \log \sqrt{z} = \log x + \log y^5 - \log z^{1/2} = \log x + 5 \log y - \tfrac{1}{2} \log z$$

$$5 \log 2 + \log 3 - \log 8 = \log 32 + \log 3 - \log 8 = \log \frac{32 \cdot 3}{8} = \log 12$$

$$\tfrac{1}{3} \ln x - \ln(x^2 - 1) + 2 \ln(x + 3) = \ln x^{1/3} - \ln(x^2 - 1) + \ln(x + 3)^2 = \ln \frac{\sqrt[3]{x}(x + 3)^2}{x^2 - 1}$$

An equation of the form $\log_b x = k$ can be solved for x by rewriting it in the exponential form $x = b^k$, and an equation of the form $b^x = k$ can be solved by rewriting it in the logarithm form $x = \log_b k$. Alternatively, the equation $b^x = k$ can be solved by taking *any* logarithm of both sides (but usually log or ln) and applying part (*c*) of Theorem 0.5.2. These ideas are illustrated in the following example.

▶ **Example 2**   Find x such that

$$\text{(a) } \log x = \sqrt{2} \qquad \text{(b) } \ln(x + 1) = 5 \qquad \text{(c) } 5^x = 7$$

Solution (a).   Converting the equation to exponential form yields

$$x = 10^{\sqrt{2}} \approx 25.95$$

Solution (b).   Converting the equation to exponential form yields

$$x + 1 = e^5 \quad \text{or} \quad x = e^5 - 1 \approx 147.41$$

Solution (c).   Converting the equation to logarithmic form yields

$$x = \log_5 7 \approx 1.21$$

Alternatively, taking the natural logarithm of both sides and using the power property of logarithms yields

$$x \ln 5 = \ln 7 \quad \text{or} \quad x = \frac{\ln 7}{\ln 5} \approx 1.21 \blacktriangleleft$$

Erik Simonsen/Getty Images
Power to satellites can be supplied by batteries, fuel cells, solar cells, or radio-isotope devices.

▶ **Example 3**   A satellite that requires 7 watts of power to operate at full capacity is equipped with a radioisotope power supply whose power output P in watts is given by the equation

$$P = 75e^{-t/125}$$

where t is the time in days that the supply is used. How long can the satellite operate at full capacity?

Solution.   The power P will fall to 7 watts when

$$7 = 75e^{-t/125}$$

The solution for t is as follows:

$$7/75 = e^{-t/125}$$

$$\ln(7/75) = \ln(e^{-t/125})$$

$$\ln(7/75) = -t/125$$

$$t = -125\ln(7/75) \approx 296.4$$

so the satellite can operate at full capacity for about 296 days. ◀

Here is a more complicated example.

▶ **Example 4**   Solve $\dfrac{e^x - e^{-x}}{2} = 1$ for x.

Solution.   Multiplying both sides of the given equation by 2 yields

$$e^x - e^{-x} = 2$$

or equivalently,

$$e^x - \frac{1}{e^x} = 2$$

Multiplying through by e^x yields

$$e^{2x} - 1 = 2e^x \quad \text{or} \quad e^{2x} - 2e^x - 1 = 0$$

This is really a quadratic equation in disguise, as can be seen by rewriting it in the form

$$\left(e^x\right)^2 - 2e^x - 1 = 0$$

and letting $u = e^x$ to obtain

$$u^2 - 2u - 1 = 0$$

Solving for u by the quadratic formula yields

$$u = \frac{2 \pm \sqrt{4+4}}{2} = \frac{2 \pm \sqrt{8}}{2} = 1 \pm \sqrt{2}$$

or, since $u = e^x$,

$$e^x = 1 \pm \sqrt{2}$$

But e^x cannot be negative, so we discard the negative value $1 - \sqrt{2}$; thus,

$$e^x = 1 + \sqrt{2}$$

$$\ln e^x = \ln(1 + \sqrt{2})$$

$$x = \ln(1 + \sqrt{2}) \approx 0.881 \quad ◀$$

■ CHANGE OF BASE FORMULA FOR LOGARITHMS

Scientific calculators generally have no keys for evaluating logarithms with bases other than 10 or e. However, this is not a serious deficiency because it is possible to express a logarithm with any base in terms of logarithms with any other base (see Exercise 42). For example, the following formula expresses a logarithm with base b in terms of natural logarithms:

$$\log_b x = \frac{\ln x}{\ln b} \tag{6}$$

We can derive this result by letting $y = \log_b x$, from which it follows that $b^y = x$. Taking the natural logarithm of both sides of this equation we obtain $y \ln b = \ln x$, from which (6) follows.

▶ **Example 5**   Use a calculating utility to evaluate $\log_2 5$ by expressing this logarithm in terms of natural logarithms.

Solution.   From (6) we obtain

$$\log_2 5 = \frac{\ln 5}{\ln 2} \approx 2.321928 \blacktriangleleft$$

■ LOGARITHMIC SCALES IN SCIENCE AND ENGINEERING

Logarithms are used in science and engineering to deal with quantities whose units vary over an excessively wide range of values. For example, the "loudness" of a sound can be measured by its ***intensity*** I (in watts per square meter), which is related to the energy transmitted by the sound wave—the greater the intensity, the greater the transmitted energy, and the louder the sound is perceived by the human ear. However, intensity units are unwieldy because they vary over an enormous range. For example, a sound at the threshold of human hearing has an intensity of about 10^{-12} W/m^2, a close whisper has an intensity that is about 100 times the hearing threshold, and a jet engine at 50 meters has an intensity that is about $10,000,000,000,000 = 10^{13}$ times the hearing threshold. To see how logarithms can be used to reduce this wide spread, observe that if

$$y = \log x$$

then increasing x by a *factor* of 10 *adds* 1 unit to y since

$$\log 10x = \log 10 + \log x = 1 + y$$

Table 0.5.4

β (dB)	I/I_0
0	$10^0 = 1$
10	$10^1 = 10$
20	$10^2 = 100$
30	$10^3 = 1000$
40	$10^4 = 10,000$
50	$10^5 = 100,000$
$\vdots$	$\vdots$
120	$10^{12} = 1,000,000,000,000$

Physicists and engineers take advantage of this property by measuring loudness in terms of the ***sound level*** β, which is defined by

$$\beta = 10 \log(I/I_0)$$

where $I_0 = 10^{-12}$ W/m^2 is a reference intensity close to the threshold of human hearing. The units of β are ***decibels*** (dB), named in honor of the telephone inventor Alexander Graham Bell. With this scale of measurement, *multiplying* the intensity I by a factor of 10 *adds* 10 dB to the sound level β (verify). This results in a more tractable scale than intensity for measuring sound loudness (Table 0.5.4). Some other familiar logarithmic scales are the ***Richter scale*** used to measure earthquake intensity and the **pH** *scale* used to measure acidity in chemistry, both of which are discussed in the exercises.

Regina Mitchell-Ryall, Tony Gray/NASA/Getty Images

The roar of a space shuttle near the launch pad would damage your hearing without ear protection.

▶ **Example 6**   A space shuttle taking off generates a sound level of 150 dB near the launch pad. A person exposed to this level of sound would experience severe physical injury. By comparison, a car horn at one meter has a sound level of 110 dB, near the threshold of pain for many people. What is the ratio of sound intensity of a space shuttle takeoff to that of a car horn?

Solution.   Let I_1 and β_1 ($= 150$ dB) denote the sound intensity and sound level of the space shuttle taking off, and let I_2 and β_2 ($= 110$ dB) denote the sound intensity and sound level of a car horn. Then

$$I_1/I_2 = (I_1/I_0)/(I_2/I_0)$$
$$\log(I_1/I_2) = \log(I_1/I_0) - \log(I_2/I_0)$$
$$10\log(I_1/I_2) = 10\log(I_1/I_0) - 10\log(I_2/I_0) = \beta_1 - \beta_2$$
$$10\log(I_1/I_2) = 150 - 100 = 40$$
$$\log(I_1/I_2) = 4$$

Thus, $I_1/I_2 = 10^4$, which tells us that the sound intensity of the space shuttle taking off is 10,000 times greater than a car horn! ◀

Table 0.5.5

x	e^x	$\ln x$
1	2.72	0.00
2	7.39	0.69
3	20.09	1.10
4	54.60	1.39
5	148.41	1.61
6	403.43	1.79
7	1096.63	1.95
8	2980.96	2.08
9	8103.08	2.20
10	22026.47	2.30
100	2.69×10^{43}	4.61
1000	1.97×10^{434}	6.91

■ **EXPONENTIAL AND LOGARITHMIC GROWTH**

The growth patterns of e^x and $\ln x$ illustrated in Table 0.5.5 are worth noting. Both functions increase as x increases, but they increase in dramatically different ways—the value of e^x increases extremely rapidly and that of $\ln x$ increases extremely slowly. For example, the value of e^x at $x = 10$ is over 22,000, but at $x = 1000$ the value of $\ln x$ has not even reached 7.

A function f is said to ***increase without bound*** as x increases if the values of $f(x)$ eventually exceed any specified positive number M (no matter how large) as x increases indefinitely. Table 0.5.5 strongly suggests that $f(x) = e^x$ increases without bound, which is consistent with the fact that the range of this function is $(0, +\infty)$. Indeed, if we choose any positive number M, then we will have $e^x = M$ when $x = \ln M$, and since the values of e^x increase as x increases, we will have

$$e^x > M \quad \text{if} \quad x > \ln M$$

(Figure 0.5.8). It is not clear from Table 0.5.5 whether $\ln x$ increases without bound as x increases because the values grow so slowly, but we know this to be so since the range of this function is $(-\infty, +\infty)$. To see this algebraically, let M be any positive number. We will have $\ln x = M$ when $x = e^M$, and since the values of $\ln x$ increase as x increases, we will have

$$\ln x > M \quad \text{if} \quad x > e^M$$

(Figure 0.5.9).

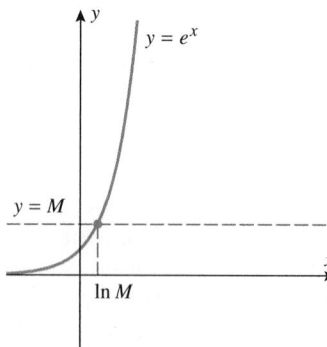

▲ **Figure 0.5.8**   The value of $y = e^x$ will exceed an arbitrary positive value of M when $x > \ln M$.

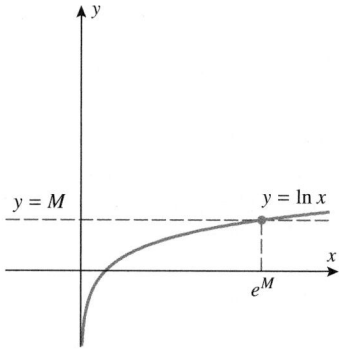

▲ **Figure 0.5.9**   The value of $y = \ln x$ will exceed an arbitrary positive value of M when $x > e^M$.

✔ **QUICK CHECK EXERCISES 0.5**   (*See page 63 for answers.*)

1. The function $y = \left(\frac{1}{2}\right)^x$ has domain _____ and range _____.

2. The function $y = \ln(1 - x)$ has domain _____ and range _____.

3. Express as a power of 4:
   (a) 1   (b) 2   (c) $\frac{1}{16}$ (d) $\sqrt{8}$ (e) 5.

4. Solve each equation for x.
   (a) $e^x = \frac{1}{2}$ (b) $10^{3x} = 1,000,000$
   (c) $7e^{3x} = 56$

5. Solve each equation for x.
   (a) $\ln x = 3$ (b) $\log(x - 1) = 2$
   (c) $2 \log x - \log(x + 1) = \log 4 - \log 3$

EXERCISE SET 0.5   ⊠ Graphing Utility

1–2 Simplify the expression without using a calculating utility. ⊠

1. (a) $-8^{2/3}$ (b) $(-8)^{2/3}$ (c) $8^{-2/3}$

2. (a) 2^{-4} (b) $4^{1.5}$ (c) $9^{-0.5}$

3–4 Use a calculating utility to approximate the expression. Round your answer to four decimal places. ⊠

3. (a) $2^{1.57}$ (b) $5^{-2.1}$

4. (a) $\sqrt[5]{24}$ (b) $\sqrt[8]{0.6}$

5–6 Find the exact value of the expression without using a calculating utility. ⊠

5. (a) $\log_2 16$ (b) $\log_2\left(\frac{1}{32}\right)$
   (c) $\log_4 4$ (d) $\log_9 3$

6. (a) $\log_{10}(0.001)$ (b) $\log_{10}(10^4)$
   (c) $\ln(e^3)$ (d) $\ln(\sqrt{e})$

7–8 Use a calculating utility to approximate the expression. Round your answer to four decimal places. ⊠

7. (a) $\log 23.2$ (b) $\ln 0.74$

8. (a) $\log 0.3$ (b) $\ln \pi$

9–10 Use the logarithm properties in Theorem 0.5.2 to rewrite the expression in terms of r, s, and t, where $r = \ln a$, $s = \ln b$, and $t = \ln c$. ⊠

9. (a) $\ln a^2 \sqrt{bc}$ (b) $\ln \dfrac{b}{a^3 c}$

10. (a) $\ln \dfrac{\sqrt[3]{c}}{ab}$ (b) $\ln \sqrt{\dfrac{ab^3}{c^2}}$

11–12 Expand the logarithm in terms of sums, differences, and multiples of simpler logarithms. ⊠

11. (a) $\log(10x\sqrt{x - 3})$ (b) $\ln \dfrac{x^2 \sin^3 x}{\sqrt{x^2 + 1}}$

12. (a) $\log \dfrac{\sqrt[3]{x + 2}}{\cos 5x}$ (b) $\ln \sqrt{\dfrac{x^2 + 1}{x^3 + 5}}$

13–15 Rewrite the expression as a single logarithm. ⊠

13. $4 \log 2 - \log 3 + \log 16$

14. $\frac{1}{2} \log x - 3 \log(\sin 2x) + 2$

15. $2 \ln(x + 1) + \frac{1}{3} \ln x - \ln(\cos x)$

16–23 Solve for x without using a calculating utility. ⊠

16. $\log_{10}(1 + x) = 3$ 17. $\log_{10}(\sqrt{x}) = -1$

18. $\ln(x^2) = 4$ 19. $\ln(1/x) = -2$

20. $\log_3(3^x) = 7$ 21. $\log_5(5^{2x}) = 8$

22. $\ln 4x - 3 \ln(x^2) = \ln 2$

23. $\ln(1/x) + \ln(2x^3) = \ln 3$

24–29 Solve for x without using a calculating utility. Use the natural logarithm anywhere that logarithms are needed. ⊠

24. $3^x = 2$ 25. $5^{-2x} = 3$

26. $3e^{-2x} = 5$ 27. $2e^{3x} = 7$

28. $e^x - 2xe^x = 0$ 29. $xe^{-x} + 2e^{-x} = 0$

30. Solve $e^{-2x} - 3e^{-x} = -2$ for x without using a calculating utility. [*Hint:* Rewrite the equation as a quadratic equation in $u = e^{-x}$.]

FOCUS ON CONCEPTS

31–34 In each part, identify the domain and range of the function, and then sketch the graph of the function without using a graphing utility. ⊠

31. (a) $f(x) = \left(\frac{1}{2}\right)^{x-1} - 1$ (b) $g(x) = \ln|x|$

32. (a) $f(x) = 1 + \ln(x - 2)$ (b) $g(x) = 3 + e^{x-2}$

33. (a) $f(x) = \ln(x^2)$ (b) $g(x) = e^{-x^2}$

34. (a) $f(x) = 1 - e^{-x+1}$ (b) $g(x) = 3 \ln \sqrt[3]{x - 1}$

35–38 True–False Determine whether the statement is true or false. Explain your answer. ⊠

35. The function $y = x^3$ is an exponential function.

36. The graph of the exponential function with base b passes through the point $(0, 1)$.

37. The natural logarithm function is the logarithmic function with base e.

38. The domain of a logarithmic function is the interval $x > 1$.

39. Use a calculating utility and the change of base formula (6) to find the values of $\log_2 7.35$ and $\log_5 0.6$, rounded to four decimal places.

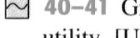 **40–41** Graph the functions on the same screen of a graphing utility. [Use the change of base formula (6), where needed.] ■

40. $\ln x$, e^x, $\log x$, 10^x

41. $\log_2 x$, $\ln x$, $\log_5 x$, $\log x$

42. (a) Derive the general change of base formula

$$\log_b x = \frac{\log_a x}{\log_a b}$$

(b) Use the result in part (a) to find the exact value of $(\log_2 81)(\log_3 32)$ without using a calculating utility.

FOCUS ON CONCEPTS

 43. (a) Is the curve in the accompanying figure the graph of an exponential function? Explain your reasoning.
(b) Find the equation of an exponential function that passes through the point $(4, 2)$.
(c) Find the equation of an exponential function that passes through the point $\left(2, \frac{1}{4}\right)$.
(d) Use a graphing utility to generate the graph of an exponential function that passes through the point $(2, 5)$.

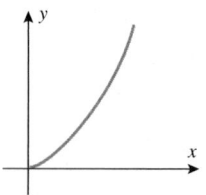

◀ **Figure Ex-43**

 44. (a) Make a conjecture about the general shape of the graph of $y = \log(\log x)$, and sketch the graph of this equation and $y = \log x$ in the same coordinate system.
(b) Check your work in part (a) with a graphing utility.

45. Find the fallacy in the following "proof" that $\frac{1}{8} > \frac{1}{4}$. Multiply both sides of the inequality $3 > 2$ by $\log \frac{1}{2}$ to get

$$3 \log \tfrac{1}{2} > 2 \log \tfrac{1}{2}$$
$$\log \left(\tfrac{1}{2}\right)^3 > \log \left(\tfrac{1}{2}\right)^2$$
$$\log \tfrac{1}{8} > \log \tfrac{1}{4}$$
$$\tfrac{1}{8} > \tfrac{1}{4}$$

46. Prove the four algebraic properties of logarithms in Theorem 0.5.2.

47. If equipment in the satellite of Example 3 requires 15 watts to operate correctly, what is the operational lifetime of the power supply?

48. The equation $Q = 12e^{-0.055t}$ gives the mass Q in grams of radioactive potassium-42 that will remain from some initial quantity after t hours of radioactive decay.
(a) How many grams were there initially?
(b) How many grams remain after 4 hours?
(c) How long will it take to reduce the amount of radioactive potassium-42 to half of the initial amount?

49. The acidity of a substance is measured by its pH value, which is defined by the formula

$$pH = -\log[H^+]$$

where the symbol $[H^+]$ denotes the concentration of hydrogen ions measured in moles per liter. Distilled water has a pH of 7; a substance is called *acidic* if it has pH < 7 and *basic* if it has pH > 7. Find the pH of each of the following substances and state whether it is acidic or basic.

	SUBSTANCE	$[H^+]$
(a)	Arterial blood	3.9×10^{-8} mol/L
(b)	Tomatoes	6.3×10^{-5} mol/L
(c)	Milk	4.0×10^{-7} mol/L
(d)	Coffee	1.2×10^{-6} mol/L

50. Use the definition of pH in Exercise 49 to find $[H^+]$ in a solution having a pH equal to
(a) 2.44   (b) 8.06.

51. The perceived loudness β of a sound in decibels (dB) is related to its intensity I in watts per square meter (W/m²) by the equation

$$\beta = 10 \log(I/I_0)$$

where $I_0 = 10^{-12}$ W/m². Damage to the average ear occurs at 90 dB or greater. Find the decibel level of each of the following sounds and state whether it will cause ear damage.

	SOUND	I
(a)	Jet aircraft (from 50 ft)	1.0×10^2 W/m²
(b)	Amplified rock music	1.0 W/m²
(c)	Garbage disposal	1.0×10^{-4} W/m²
(d)	TV (mid volume from 10 ft)	3.2×10^{-5} W/m²

52–54 Use the definition of the decibel level of a sound (see Exercise 51). ■

52. If one sound is three times as intense as another, how much greater is its decibel level?

53. According to one source, the noise inside a moving automobile is about 70 dB, whereas an electric blender generates 93 dB. Find the ratio of the intensity of the noise of the blender to that of the automobile.

54. Suppose that the intensity level of an echo is $\frac{2}{3}$ the intensity level of the original sound. If each echo results in another echo, how many echoes will be heard from a 120 dB sound given that the average human ear can hear a sound as low as 10 dB?

55. On the **Richter scale**, the magnitude M of an earthquake is related to the released energy E in joules (J) by the equation
$$\log E = 4.4 + 1.5M$$
(a) Find the energy E of the 1906 San Francisco earthquake that registered $M = 8.2$ on the Richter scale.

(b) If the released energy of one earthquake is 10 times that of another, how much greater is its magnitude on the Richter scale?

56. Suppose that the magnitudes of two earthquakes differ by 1 on the Richter scale. Find the ratio of the released energy of the larger earthquake to that of the smaller earthquake. [*Note:* See Exercise 55 for terminology.]

✔ QUICK CHECK ANSWERS 0.5

1. $(-\infty, +\infty)$; $(0, +\infty)$ **2.** $(-\infty, 1)$; $(-\infty, +\infty)$ **3.** (a) 4^0 (b) $4^{1/2}$ (c) 4^{-2} (d) $4^{3/4}$ (e) $4^{\log_4 5}$ **4.** (a) $\ln \frac{1}{2} = -\ln 2$ (b) 2
(c) $\ln 2$ **5.** (a) e^3 (b) 101 (c) 2

CHAPTER 0 REVIEW EXERCISES   ⌇ Graphing Utility

1. Sketch the graph of the function
$$f(x) = \begin{cases} -1, & x \le -5 \\ \sqrt{25 - x^2}, & -5 < x < 5 \\ x - 5, & x \ge 5 \end{cases}$$

2. Use the graphs of the functions f and g in the accompanying figure to solve the following problems.
(a) Find the values of $f(-2)$ and $g(3)$.
(b) For what values of x is $f(x) = g(x)$?
(c) For what values of x is $f(x) < 2$?
(d) What are the domain and range of f?
(e) What are the domain and range of g?
(f) Find the zeros of f and g.

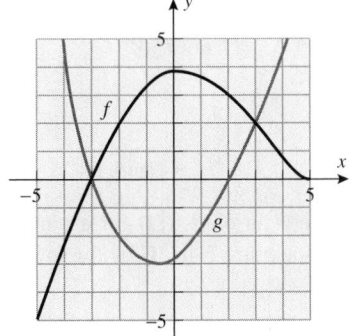

◀ **Figure Ex-2**

3. A glass filled with water that has a temperature of $40°$F is placed in a room in which the temperature is a constant $70°$F. Sketch a rough graph that reasonably describes the temperature of the water in the glass as a function of the elapsed time.

4. You want to paint the top of a circular table. Find a formula that expresses the amount of paint required as a function of the radius, and discuss all of the assumptions you have made in finding the formula.

5. A rectangular storage container with an open top and a square base has a volume of 8 cubic meters. Material for the base costs \$5 per square meter and material for the sides \$2 per square meter.
(a) Find a formula that expresses the total cost of materials as a function of the length of a side of the base.
(b) What is the domain of the cost function obtained in part (a)?

6. A ball of radius 3 inches is coated uniformly with plastic.
(a) Express the volume of the plastic as a function of its thickness.
(b) What is the domain of the volume function obtained in part (a)?

⌇ **7.** A box with a closed top is to be made from a 6 ft by 10 ft piece of cardboard by cutting out four squares of equal size (see the accompanying figure), folding along the dashed lines, and tucking the two extra flaps inside.
(a) Find a formula that expresses the volume of the box as a function of the length of the sides of the cut-out squares.
(b) Find an inequality that specifies the domain of the function in part (a).
(c) Use the graph of the volume function to estimate the dimensions of the box of largest volume.

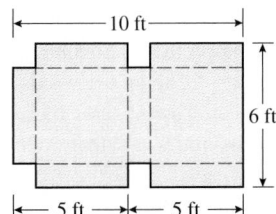

◀ **Figure Ex-7**

⌇ **8.** Let C denote the graph of $y = 1/x, x > 0$.
(a) Express the distance between the point $P(1, 0)$ and a point Q on C as a function of the x-coordinate of Q.
(b) What is the domain of the distance function obtained in part (a)?   *(cont.)*

(c) Use the graph of the distance function obtained in part (a) to estimate the point Q on C that is closest to the point P.

9. Sketch the graph of the equation $x^2 - 4y^2 = 0$.

10. Generate the graph of $f(x) = x^4 - 24x^3 - 25x^2$ in two different viewing windows, each of which illustrates a different property of f. Identify each viewing window and a characteristic of the graph of f that is illustrated well in the window.

11. Complete the following table.

x	−4	−3	−2	−1	0	1	2	3	4
$f(x)$	0	−1	2	1	3	−2	−3	4	−4
$g(x)$	3	2	1	−3	−1	−4	4	−2	0
$(f \circ g)(x)$									
$(g \circ f)(x)$									

▲ **Table Ex-11**

12. Let $f(x) = -x^2$ and $g(x) = 1/\sqrt{x}$. Find formulas for $f \circ g$ and $g \circ f$ and state the domain of each composition.

13. Given that $f(x) = x^2 + 1$ and $g(x) = 3x + 2$, find all values of x such that $f(g(x)) = g(f(x))$.

14. Let $f(x) = (2x - 1)/(x + 1)$ and $g(x) = 1/(x - 1)$.
(a) Find $f(g(x))$.
(b) Is the natural domain of the function $h(x) = (3 - x)/x$ the same as the domain of $f \circ g$? Explain.

15. Given that

$$f(x) = \frac{x}{x - 1}, \quad g(x) = \frac{1}{x}, \quad h(x) = x^2 - 1$$

find a formula for $f \circ g \circ h$ and state the domain of this composition.

16. Given that $f(x) = 2x + 1$ and $h(x) = 2x^2 + 4x + 1$, find a function g such that $f(g(x)) = h(x)$.

17. In each part, classify the function as even, odd, or neither.
(a) $x^2 \sin x$ (b) $\sin^2 x$ (c) $x + x^2$ (d) $\sin x \tan x$

18. (a) Write an equation for the graph that is obtained by reflecting the graph of $y = |x - 1|$ about the y-axis, then stretching that graph vertically by a factor of 2, then translating that graph down 3 units, and then reflecting that graph about the x-axis.
(b) Sketch the original graph and the final graph.

19. In each part, describe the family of curves.
(a) $(x - a)^2 + (y - a^2)^2 = 1$
(b) $y = a + (x - 2a)^2$

20. Find an equation for a parabola that passes through the points $(2, 0)$, $(8, 18)$, and $(-8, 18)$.

21. Suppose that the expected low temperature in Anchorage, Alaska (in °F), is modeled by the equation

$$T = 50 \sin \frac{2\pi}{365}(t - 101) + 25$$

where t is in days and $t = 0$ corresponds to January 1.
(a) Sketch the graph of T versus t for $0 \le t \le 365$.
(b) Use the model to predict when the coldest day of the year will occur.
(c) Based on this model, how many days during the year would you expect the temperature to be below 0°F?

22. The accompanying figure shows a model for the tide variation in an inlet to San Francisco Bay during a 24-hour period. Find an equation of the form $y = y_0 + y_1 \sin(at + b)$ for the model, assuming that $t = 0$ corresponds to midnight.

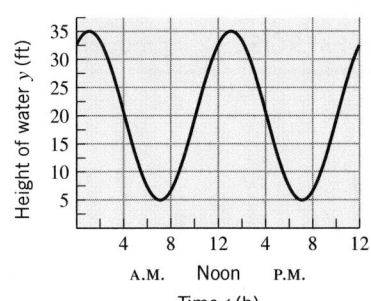

◀ **Figure Ex-22**

23. The accompanying figure shows the graphs of the equations $y = 1 + 2 \sin x$ and $y = 2 \sin(x/2) + 2 \cos(x/2)$ for $-2\pi \le x \le 2\pi$. Without the aid of a calculator, label each curve by its equation, and find the coordinates of the points A, B, C, and D. Explain your reasoning.

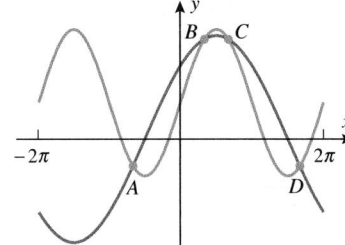

◀ **Figure Ex-23**

24. The electrical resistance R in ohms (Ω) for a pure metal wire is related to its temperature T in °C by the formula

$$R = R_0(1 + kT)$$

in which R_0 and k are positive constants.
(a) Make a hand-drawn sketch of the graph of R versus T, and explain the geometric significance of R_0 and k for your graph.
(b) In theory, the resistance R of a pure metal wire drops to zero when the temperature reaches absolute zero ($T = -273$°C). What information does this give you about k?
(c) A tungsten bulb filament has a resistance of 1.1 Ω at a temperature of 20°C. What information does this give you about R_0 for the filament?   (*cont.*)

(d) At what temperature will the tungsten filament have a resistance of 1.5 Ω?

25. (a) State conditions under which two functions, f and g, will be inverses, and give several examples of such functions.

(b) In words, what is the relationship between the graphs of $y = f(x)$ and $y = g(x)$ when f and g are inverse functions?

(c) What is the relationship between the domains and ranges of inverse functions f and g?

(d) What condition must be satisfied for a function f to have an inverse? Give some examples of functions that do not have inverses.

26. (a) State the restrictions on the domains of $\sin x$, $\cos x$, $\tan x$, and $\sec x$ that are imposed to make those functions one-to-one in the definitions of $\sin^{-1} x$, $\cos^{-1} x$, $\tan^{-1} x$, and $\sec^{-1} x$.

(b) Sketch the graphs of the restricted trigonometric functions in part (a) and their inverses.

27. In each part, find $f^{-1}(x)$ if the inverse exists.

(a) $f(x) = 8x^3 - 1$ (b) $f(x) = x^2 - 2x + 1$

(c) $f(x) = (e^x)^2 + 1$ (d) $f(x) = (x + 2)/(x - 1)$

(e) $f(x) = \sin\left(\dfrac{1 - 2x}{x}\right)$, $\dfrac{2}{4 + \pi} \le x \le \dfrac{2}{4 - \pi}$

(f) $f(x) = \dfrac{1}{1 + 3\tan^{-1} x}$

28. Let $f(x) = (ax + b)/(cx + d)$. What conditions on a, b, c, and d guarantee that f^{-1} exists? Find $f^{-1}(x)$.

29. In each part, find the exact numerical value of the given expression.

(a) $\cos[\cos^{-1}(4/5) + \sin^{-1}(5/13)]$

(b) $\sin[\sin^{-1}(4/5) + \cos^{-1}(5/13)]$

30. In each part, sketch the graph, and check your work with a graphing utility.

(a) $f(x) = 3\sin^{-1}(x/2)$

(b) $f(x) = \cos^{-1} x - \pi/2$

(c) $f(x) = 2\tan^{-1}(-3x)$

(d) $f(x) = \cos^{-1} x + \sin^{-1} x$

31. Suppose that the graph of $y = \log x$ is drawn with equal scales of 1 inch per unit in both the x- and y-directions. If a bug wants to walk along the graph until it reaches a height of 5 ft above the x-axis, how many miles to the right of the origin will it have to travel?

32. Suppose that the graph of $y = 10^x$ is drawn with equal scales of 1 inch per unit in both the x- and y-directions. If a bug wants to walk along the graph until it reaches a height of 100 mi above the x-axis, how many feet to the right of the origin will it have to travel?

33. Express the following function as a rational function of x:

$$3\ln\left(e^{2x}(e^x)^3\right) + 2\exp(\ln 1)$$

34. Suppose that $y = Ce^{kt}$, where C and k are constants, and let $Y = \ln y$. Show that the graph of Y versus t is a line, and state its slope and Y-intercept.

35. (a) Sketch the curves $y = \pm e^{-x/2}$ and $y = e^{-x/2}\sin 2x$ for $-\pi/2 \le x \le 3\pi/2$ in the same coordinate system, and check your work using a graphing utility.

(b) Find all x-intercepts of the curve $y = e^{-x/2}\sin 2x$ in the stated interval, and find the x-coordinates of all points where this curve intersects the curves $y = \pm e^{-x/2}$.

36. Suppose that a package of medical supplies is dropped from a helicopter straight down by parachute into a remote area. The velocity v (in feet per second) of the package t seconds after it is released is given by $v = 24.61(1 - e^{-1.3t})$.

(a) Graph v versus t.

(b) Show that the graph has a horizontal asymptote $v = c$.

(c) The constant c is called the **terminal velocity**. Explain what the terminal velocity means in practical terms.

(d) Can the package actually reach its terminal velocity? Explain.

(e) How long does it take for the package to reach 98% of its terminal velocity?

37. A breeding group of 20 bighorn sheep is released in a protected area in Colorado. It is expected that with careful management the number of sheep, N, after t years will be given by the formula

$$N = \frac{220}{1 + 10(0.83^t)}$$

and that the sheep population will be able to maintain itself without further supervision once the population reaches a size of 80.

(a) Graph N versus t.

(b) How many years must the state of Colorado maintain a program to care for the sheep?

(c) How many bighorn sheep can the environment in the protected area support? [*Hint:* Examine the graph of N versus t for large values of t.]

38. An oven is preheated and then remains at a constant temperature. A potato is placed in the oven to bake. Suppose that the temperature T (in °F) of the potato t minutes later is given by $T = 400 - 325(0.97^t)$. The potato will be considered done when its temperature is anywhere between 260°F and 280°F.

(a) During what interval of time would the potato be considered done?

(b) How long does it take for the difference between the potato and oven temperatures to be cut in half?

39. (a) Show that the graphs of $y = \ln x$ and $y = x^{0.2}$ intersect.

(b) Approximate the solution(s) of the equation $\ln x = x^{0.2}$ to three decimal places.

40. (a) Show that for $x > 0$ and $k \ne 0$ the equations

$$x^k = e^x \quad \text{and} \quad \frac{\ln x}{x} = \frac{1}{k}$$

have the same solutions.   *(cont.)*

(b) Use the graph of $y = (\ln x)/x$ to determine the values of k for which the equation $x^k = e^x$ has two distinct positive solutions.

(c) Estimate the positive solution(s) of $x^8 = e^x$.

41. Consider $f(x) = x^2 \tan x + \ln x, 0 < x < \pi/2$.

(a) Explain why f is one-to-one.

(b) Use a graphing utility to generate the graph of f. Then sketch the graphs of f and f^{-1} together. What are the asymptotes for each graph?

Joe McBride/Stone/Getty Images

1

LIMITS AND CONTINUITY

Air resistance prevents the velocity of a skydiver from increasing indefinitely. The velocity approaches a limit, called the "terminal velocity."

The development of calculus in the seventeenth century by Newton and Leibniz provided scientists with their first real understanding of what is meant by an "instantaneous rate of change" such as velocity and acceleration. Once the idea was understood conceptually, efficient computational methods followed, and science took a quantum leap forward. The fundamental building block on which rates of change rest is the concept of a "limit," an idea that is so important that all other calculus concepts are now based on it.

In this chapter we will develop the concept of a limit in stages, proceeding from an informal, intuitive notion to a precise mathematical definition. We will also develop theorems and procedures for calculating limits, and we will conclude the chapter by using the limits to study "continuous" curves.

1.1 LIMITS (AN INTUITIVE APPROACH)

The concept of a "limit" is the fundamental building block on which all calculus concepts are based. In this section we will study limits informally, with the goal of developing an intuitive feel for the basic ideas. In the next three sections we will focus on computational methods and precise definitions.

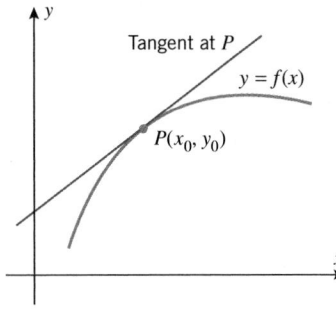

▲ **Figure 1.1.1**

Many of the ideas of calculus originated with the following two geometric problems:

THE TANGENT LINE PROBLEM Given a function f and a point $P(x_0, y_0)$ on its graph, find an equation of the line that is tangent to the graph at P (Figure 1.1.1).

THE AREA PROBLEM Given a function f, find the area between the graph of f and an interval $[a, b]$ on the x-axis (Figure 1.1.2).

Traditionally, that portion of calculus arising from the tangent line problem is called **differential calculus** and that arising from the area problem is called **integral calculus**. However, we will see later that the tangent line and area problems are so closely related that the distinction between differential and integral calculus is somewhat artificial.

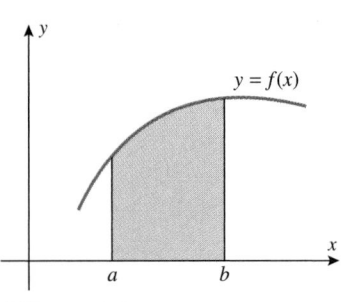

▲ **Figure 1.1.2**

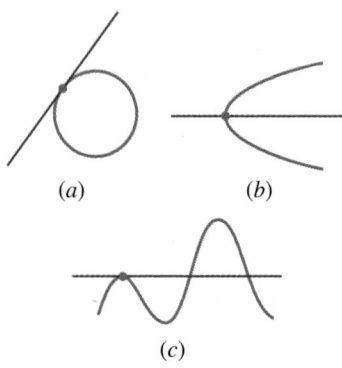

▲ **Figure 1.1.3**

■ TANGENT LINES AND LIMITS

In plane geometry, a line is called *tangent* to a circle if it meets the circle at precisely one point (Figure 1.1.3*a*). Although this definition is adequate for circles, it is not appropriate for more general curves. For example, in Figure 1.1.3*b*, the line meets the curve exactly once but is obviously not what we would regard to be a tangent line; and in Figure 1.1.3*c*, the line appears to be tangent to the curve, yet it intersects the curve more than once.

To obtain a definition of a tangent line that applies to curves other than circles, we must view tangent lines another way. For this purpose, suppose that we are interested in the tangent line at a point P on a curve in the xy-plane and that Q is any point that lies on the curve and is different from P. The line through P and Q is called a **secant line** for the curve at P. Intuition suggests that if we move the point Q along the curve toward P, then the secant line will rotate toward a *limiting position*. The line in this limiting position is what we will consider to be the **tangent line** at P (Figure 1.1.4*a*). As suggested by Figure 1.1.4*b*, this new concept of a tangent line coincides with the traditional concept when applied to circles.

▶ **Figure 1.1.4**

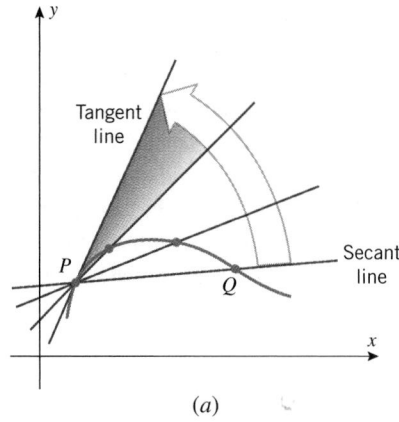

(*a*)

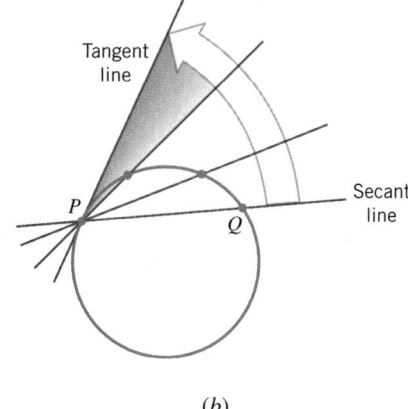

(*b*)

▶ **Example 1**   Find an equation for the tangent line to the parabola $y = x^2$ at the point $P(1, 1)$.

Solution.   If we can find the slope m_{tan} of the tangent line at P, then we can use the point P and the point-slope formula for a line (Web Appendix G) to write the equation of the tangent line as

$$y - 1 = m_{\text{tan}}(x - 1) \tag{1}$$

To find the slope m_{tan}, consider the secant line through P and a point $Q(x, x^2)$ on the parabola that is distinct from P. The slope m_{sec} of this secant line is

Why are we requiring that P and Q be distinct?

$$m_{\text{sec}} = \frac{x^2 - 1}{x - 1} \tag{2}$$

Figure 1.1.4*a* suggests that if we now let Q move along the parabola, getting closer and closer to P, then the limiting position of the secant line through P and Q will coincide with that of the tangent line at P. This in turn suggests that the value of m_{sec} will get closer and closer to the value of m_{tan} as P moves toward Q along the curve. However, to say that $Q(x, x^2)$ gets closer and closer to $P(1, 1)$ is algebraically equivalent to saying that x gets closer and closer to 1. Thus, the problem of finding m_{tan} reduces to finding the "limiting value" of m_{sec} in Formula (2) as x gets closer and closer to 1 (but with $x \neq 1$ to ensure that P and Q remain distinct).

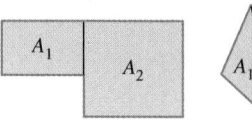

▲ Figure 1.1.5

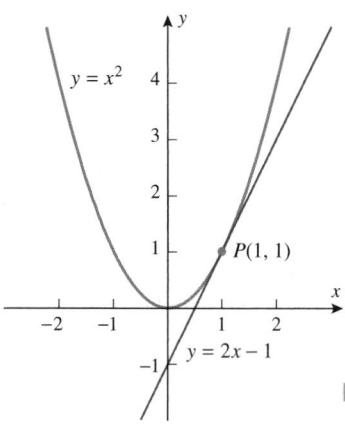

▲ Figure 1.1.6

We can rewrite (2) as

$$m_{\text{sec}} = \frac{x^2 - 1}{x - 1} = \frac{(x - 1)(x + 1)}{(x - 1)} = x + 1$$

where the cancellation of the factor $(x - 1)$ is allowed because $x \neq 1$. It is now evident that m_{sec} gets closer and closer to 2 as x gets closer and closer to 1. Thus, $m_{\text{tan}} = 2$ and (1) implies that the equation of the tangent line is

$$y - 1 = 2(x - 1) \quad \text{or equivalently} \quad y = 2x - 1$$

Figure 1.1.5 shows the graph of $y = x^2$ and this tangent line. ◄

■ AREAS AND LIMITS

Just as the general notion of a tangent line leads to the concept of *limit*, so does the general notion of area. For plane regions with straight-line boundaries, areas can often be calculated by subdividing the region into rectangles or triangles and adding the areas of the constituent parts (Figure 1.1.6). However, for regions with curved boundaries, such as that in Figure 1.1.7a, a more general approach is needed. One such approach is to begin by approximating the area of the region by inscribing a number of rectangles of equal width under the curve and adding the areas of these rectangles (Figure 1.1.7b). Intuition suggests that if we repeat that approximation process using more and more rectangles, then the rectangles will tend to fill in the gaps under the curve, and the approximations will get closer and closer to the exact area under the curve (Figure 1.1.7c). This suggests that we can define the area under the curve to be the limiting value of these approximations. This idea will be considered in detail later, but the point to note here is that once again the concept of a limit comes into play.

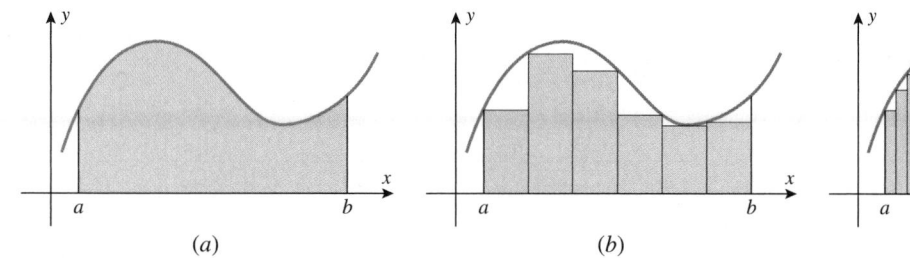

(a)   (b)   (c)

▲ Figure 1.1.7

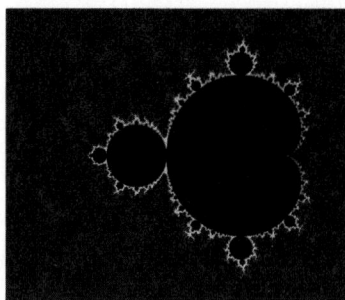

This figure shows a region called the **Mandelbrot Set**. *It illustrates how complicated a region in the plane can be and why the notion of area requires careful definition.*

■ DECIMALS AND LIMITS

Limits also arise in the familiar context of decimals. For example, the decimal expansion of the fraction $\frac{1}{3}$ is

$$\frac{1}{3} = 0.33333\ldots \tag{3}$$

in which the dots indicate that the digit 3 repeats indefinitely. Although you may not have thought about decimals in this way, we can write (3) as

$$\frac{1}{3} = 0.33333\ldots = 0.3 + 0.03 + 0.003 + 0.0003 + 0.00003 + \cdots \tag{4}$$

which is a sum with "infinitely many" terms. As we will discuss in more detail later, we interpret (4) to mean that the succession of finite sums

$$0.3, \quad 0.3 + 0.03, \quad 0.3 + 0.03 + 0.003, \quad 0.3 + 0.03 + 0.003 + 0.0003, \ldots$$

gets closer and closer to a limiting value of $\frac{1}{3}$ as more and more terms are included. Thus, limits even occur in the familiar context of decimal representations of real numbers.

■ LIMITS

Now that we have seen how limits arise in various ways, let us focus on the limit concept itself.

The most basic use of limits is to describe how a function behaves as the independent variable approaches a given value. For example, let us examine the behavior of the function

$$f(x) = x^2 - x + 1$$

for x-values closer and closer to 2. It is evident from the graph and table in Figure 1.1.8 that the values of $f(x)$ get closer and closer to 3 as values of x are selected closer and closer to 2 on either the left or the right side of 2. We describe this by saying that the "limit of $x^2 - x + 1$ is 3 as x approaches 2 from either side," and we write

$$\lim_{x \to 2} (x^2 - x + 1) = 3 \qquad (5)$$

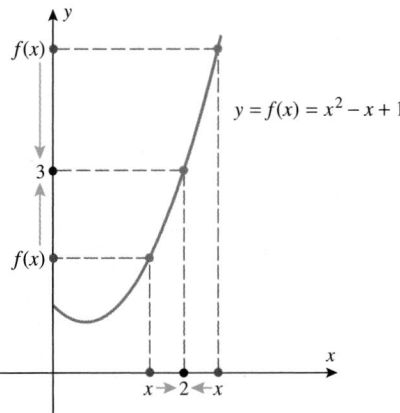

x	1.0	1.5	1.9	1.95	1.99	1.995	1.999	2	2.001	2.005	2.01	2.05	2.1	2.5	3.0
$f(x)$	1.000000	1.750000	2.710000	2.852500	2.970100	2.985025	2.997001		3.003001	3.015025	3.030100	3.152500	3.310000	4.750000	7.000000

Left side   Right side

▲ **Figure 1.1.8**

This leads us to the following general idea.

1.1.1   LIMITS (AN INFORMAL VIEW)   If the values of $f(x)$ can be made as close as we like to L by taking values of x sufficiently close to a (but not equal to a), then we write

$$\lim_{x \to a} f(x) = L \qquad (6)$$

which is read "the limit of $f(x)$ as x approaches a is L" or "$f(x)$ approaches L as x approaches a." The expression in (6) can also be written as

$$f(x) \to L \quad \text{as} \quad x \to a \qquad (7)$$

Since x is required to be different from a in (6), the value of f at a, or even whether f is defined at a, has no bearing on the limit L. The limit describes the behavior of f *close to* a but not *at* a.

▶ **Example 2** Use numerical evidence to make a conjecture about the value of

$$\lim_{x \to 1} \frac{x-1}{\sqrt{x}-1} \tag{8}$$

Solution. Although the function

$$f(x) = \frac{x-1}{\sqrt{x}-1} \tag{9}$$

TECHNOLOGY MASTERY

Use a graphing utility to generate the graph of the equation $y = f(x)$ for the function in (9). Find a window containing $x = 1$ in which all values of $f(x)$ are within 0.5 of $y = 2$ and one in which all values of $f(x)$ are within 0.1 of $y = 2$.

is undefined at $x = 1$, this has no bearing on the limit. Table 1.1.1 shows sample x-values approaching 1 from the left side and from the right side. In both cases the corresponding values of $f(x)$, calculated to six decimal places, appear to get closer and closer to 2, and hence we conjecture that

$$\lim_{x \to 1} \frac{x-1}{\sqrt{x}-1} = 2$$

This is consistent with the graph of f shown in Figure 1.1.9. In the next section we will show how to obtain this result algebraically. ◀

Table 1.1.1

x	0.99	0.999	0.9999	0.99999		1.00001	1.0001	1.001	1.01
$f(x)$	1.994987	1.999500	1.999950	1.999995		2.000005	2.000050	2.000500	2.004988

Left side →← Right side

▲ **Figure 1.1.9**

y

$y = f(x) = \dfrac{x-1}{\sqrt{x}-1}$

3

2

1

$x \to 1 \gets x$ 2 3 x

▶ **Example 3** Use numerical evidence to make a conjecture about the value of

$$\lim_{x \to 0} \frac{\sin x}{x} \tag{10}$$

Solution. With the help of a calculating utility set in radian mode, we obtain Table 1.1.2. The data in the table suggest that

$$\lim_{x \to 0} \frac{\sin x}{x} = 1 \tag{11}$$

The result is consistent with the graph of $f(x) = (\sin x)/x$ shown in Figure 1.1.10. Later in this chapter we will give a geometric argument to prove that our conjecture is correct. ◀

Use numerical evidence to determine whether the limit in (11) changes if x is measured in degrees.

Table 1.1.2

x (RADIANS)	$y = \dfrac{\sin x}{x}$
± 1.0	0.84147
± 0.9	0.87036
± 0.8	0.89670
± 0.7	0.92031
± 0.6	0.94107
± 0.5	0.95885
± 0.4	0.97355
± 0.3	0.98507
± 0.2	0.99335
± 0.1	0.99833
± 0.01	0.99998

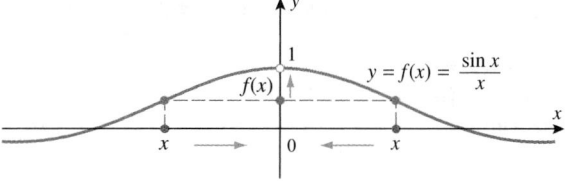

▶ **Figure 1.1.10**

As x approaches 0 from the left or right, $f(x)$ approaches 1.

■ SAMPLING PITFALLS

Numerical evidence can sometimes lead to incorrect conclusions about limits because of roundoff error or because the sample values chosen do not reveal the true limiting behavior. For example, one might *incorrectly* conclude from Table 1.1.3 that

$$\lim_{x \to 0} \sin\left(\frac{\pi}{x}\right) = 0$$

The fact that this is not correct is evidenced by the graph of f in Figure 1.1.11. The graph reveals that the values of f oscillate between -1 and 1 with increasing rapidity as $x \to 0$ and hence do not approach a limit. The data in the table deceived us because the x-values selected all happened to be x-intercepts for $f(x)$. This points out the need for having alternative methods for corroborating limits conjectured from numerical evidence.

Table 1.1.3

x	$\dfrac{\pi}{x}$	$f(x) = \sin\left(\dfrac{\pi}{x}\right)$
$x = \pm 1$	$\pm \pi$	$\sin(\pm\pi) = 0$
$x = \pm 0.1$	$\pm 10\pi$	$\sin(\pm 10\pi) = 0$
$x = \pm 0.01$	$\pm 100\pi$	$\sin(\pm 100\pi) = 0$
$x = \pm 0.001$	$\pm 1000\pi$	$\sin(\pm 1000\pi) = 0$
$x = \pm 0.0001$	$\pm 10{,}000\pi$	$\sin(\pm 10{,}000\pi) = 0$
$\vdots$	$\vdots$	$\vdots$

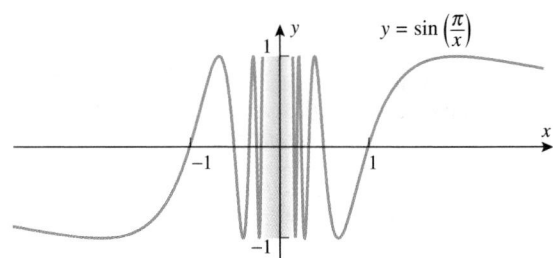

▲ **Figure 1.1.11**

■ **ONE-SIDED LIMITS**

The limit in (6) is called a ***two-sided limit*** because it requires the values of $f(x)$ to get closer and closer to L as values of x are taken from *either* side of $x = a$. However, some functions exhibit different behaviors on the two sides of an x-value a, in which case it is necessary to distinguish whether values of x near a are on the left side or on the right side of a for purposes of investigating limiting behavior. For example, consider the function

$$f(x) = \frac{|x|}{x} = \begin{cases} 1, & x > 0 \\ -1, & x < 0 \end{cases} \tag{12}$$

which is graphed in Figure 1.1.12. As x approaches 0 from the *right*, the values of $f(x)$ approach a limit of 1 [in fact, the values of $f(x)$ are exactly 1 for all such x], and similarly, as x approaches 0 from the *left*, the values of $f(x)$ approach a limit of -1. We denote these limits by writing

$$\lim_{x \to 0^+} \frac{|x|}{x} = 1 \quad \text{and} \quad \lim_{x \to 0^-} \frac{|x|}{x} = -1 \tag{13}$$

With this notation, the superscript "$+$" indicates a limit from the right and the superscript "$-$" indicates a limit from the left.

This leads to the general idea of a ***one-sided limit***.

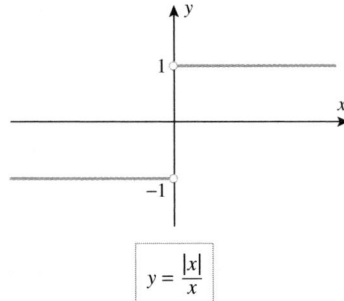

▲ **Figure 1.1.12**

As with two-sided limits, the one-sided limits in (14) and (15) can also be written as

$$f(x) \to L \quad \text{as} \quad x \to a^+$$

and

$$f(x) \to L \quad \text{as} \quad x \to a^-$$

respectively.

1.1.2   **ONE-SIDED LIMITS (AN INFORMAL VIEW)**   If the values of $f(x)$ can be made as close as we like to L by taking values of x sufficiently close to a (but greater than a), then we write

$$\lim_{x \to a^+} f(x) = L \tag{14}$$

and if the values of $f(x)$ can be made as close as we like to L by taking values of x sufficiently close to a (but less than a), then we write

$$\lim_{x \to a^-} f(x) = L \tag{15}$$

Expression (14) is read "the limit of $f(x)$ as x approaches a from the right is L" or "$f(x)$ approaches L as x approaches a from the right." Similarly, expression (15) is read "the limit of $f(x)$ as x approaches a from the left is L" or "$f(x)$ approaches L as x approaches a from the left."

■ **THE RELATIONSHIP BETWEEN ONE-SIDED LIMITS AND TWO-SIDED LIMITS**

In general, there is no guarantee that a function f will have a two-sided limit at a given point a; that is, the values of $f(x)$ may not get closer and closer to any *single* real number L as $x \to a$. In this case we say that

$$\lim_{x \to a} f(x) \quad \textit{does not exist}$$

Similarly, the values of $f(x)$ may not get closer and closer to a single real number L as $x \to a^+$ or as $x \to a^-$. In these cases we say that

$$\lim_{x \to a^+} f(x) \quad \textit{does not exist}$$

or that

$$\lim_{x \to a^-} f(x) \quad \textit{does not exist}$$

In order for the two-sided limit of a function $f(x)$ to exist at a point a, the values of $f(x)$ must approach some real number L as x approaches a, and this number must be the same regardless of whether x approaches a from the left or the right. This suggests the following result, which we state without formal proof.

1.1.3 **THE RELATIONSHIP BETWEEN ONE-SIDED AND TWO-SIDED LIMITS** The two-sided limit of a function $f(x)$ exists at a if and only if both of the one-sided limits exist at a and have the same value; that is,

$$\lim_{x \to a} f(x) = L \quad \text{if and only if} \quad \lim_{x \to a^-} f(x) = L = \lim_{x \to a^+} f(x)$$

▶ **Example 4** Explain why

$$\lim_{x \to 0} \frac{|x|}{x}$$

does not exist.

Solution. As x approaches 0, the values of $f(x) = |x|/x$ approach -1 from the left and approach 1 from the right [see (13)]. Thus, the one-sided limits at 0 are not the same. ◀

▶ **Example 5** For the functions in Figure 1.1.13, find the one-sided and two-sided limits at $x = a$ if they exist.

Solution. The functions in all three figures have the same one-sided limits as $x \to a$, since the functions are identical, except at $x = a$. These limits are

$$\lim_{x \to a^+} f(x) = 3 \quad \text{and} \quad \lim_{x \to a^-} f(x) = 1$$

In all three cases the two-sided limit does not exist as $x \to a$ because the one-sided limits are not equal. ◀

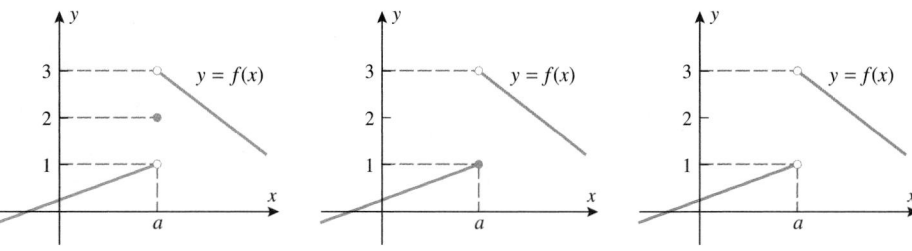

▶ **Figure 1.1.13**

▶ **Example 6** For the functions in Figure 1.1.14, find the one-sided and two-sided limits at $x = a$ if they exist.

Solution. As in the preceding example, the value of f at $x = a$ has no bearing on the limits as $x \to a$, so in all three cases we have

$$\lim_{x \to a^+} f(x) = 2 \quad \text{and} \quad \lim_{x \to a^-} f(x) = 2$$

Since the one-sided limits are equal, the two-sided limit exists and

$$\lim_{x \to a} f(x) = 2 \ \blacktriangleleft$$

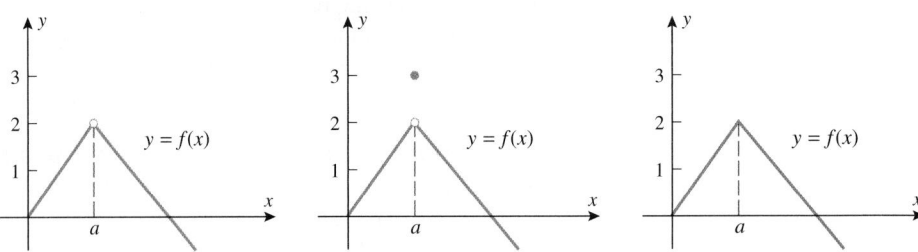

▲ **Figure 1.1.14**

■ INFINITE LIMITS

Sometimes one-sided or two-sided limits fail to exist because the values of the function increase or decrease without bound. For example, consider the behavior of $f(x) = 1/x$ for values of x near 0. It is evident from the table and graph in Figure 1.1.15 that as x-values are taken closer and closer to 0 from the right, the values of $f(x) = 1/x$ are positive and increase without bound; and as x-values are taken closer and closer to 0 from the left, the values of $f(x) = 1/x$ are negative and decrease without bound. We describe these limiting behaviors by writing

$$\lim_{x \to 0^+} \frac{1}{x} = +\infty \quad \text{and} \quad \lim_{x \to 0^-} \frac{1}{x} = -\infty$$

The symbols $+\infty$ and $-\infty$ here are *not* real numbers; they simply describe particular ways in which the limits fail to exist. Do not make the mistake of manipulating these symbols using rules of algebra. For example, it is *incorrect* to write $(+\infty) - (+\infty) = 0$.

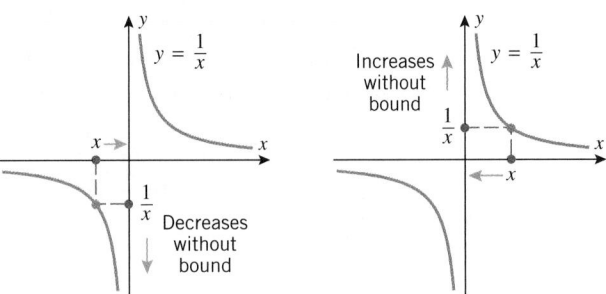

x	-1	-0.1	-0.01	-0.001	-0.0001	0	0.0001	0.001	0.01	0.1	1
$\dfrac{1}{x}$	-1	-10	-100	-1000	$-10,000$		10,000	1000	100	10	1

Left side ⟶   ⟵ Right side

▲ **Figure 1.1.15**

1.1.4 **INFINITE LIMITS (AN INFORMAL VIEW)** The expressions

$$\lim_{x \to a^-} f(x) = +\infty \quad \text{and} \quad \lim_{x \to a^+} f(x) = +\infty$$

denote that $f(x)$ increases without bound as x approaches a from the left and from the right, respectively. If both are true, then we write

$$\lim_{x \to a} f(x) = +\infty$$

Similarly, the expressions

$$\lim_{x \to a^-} f(x) = -\infty \quad \text{and} \quad \lim_{x \to a^+} f(x) = -\infty$$

denote that $f(x)$ decreases without bound as x approaches a from the left and from the right, respectively. If both are true, then we write

$$\lim_{x \to a} f(x) = -\infty$$

▶ **Example 7** For the functions in Figure 1.1.16, describe the limits at $x = a$ in appropriate limit notation.

Solution (a). In Figure 1.1.16a, the function increases without bound as x approaches a from the right and decreases without bound as x approaches a from the left. Thus,

$$\lim_{x \to a^+} \frac{1}{x - a} = +\infty \quad \text{and} \quad \lim_{x \to a^-} \frac{1}{x - a} = -\infty$$

Solution (b). In Figure 1.1.16b, the function increases without bound as x approaches a from both the left and right. Thus,

$$\lim_{x \to a} \frac{1}{(x - a)^2} = \lim_{x \to a^+} \frac{1}{(x - a)^2} = \lim_{x \to a^-} \frac{1}{(x - a)^2} = +\infty$$

Solution (c). In Figure 1.1.16c, the function decreases without bound as x approaches a from the right and increases without bound as x approaches a from the left. Thus,

$$\lim_{x \to a^+} \frac{-1}{x - a} = -\infty \quad \text{and} \quad \lim_{x \to a^-} \frac{-1}{x - a} = +\infty$$

Solution (d). In Figure 1.1.16d, the function decreases without bound as x approaches a from both the left and right. Thus,

$$\lim_{x \to a} \frac{-1}{(x - a)^2} = \lim_{x \to a^+} \frac{-1}{(x - a)^2} = \lim_{x \to a^-} \frac{-1}{(x - a)^2} = -\infty \quad ◀$$

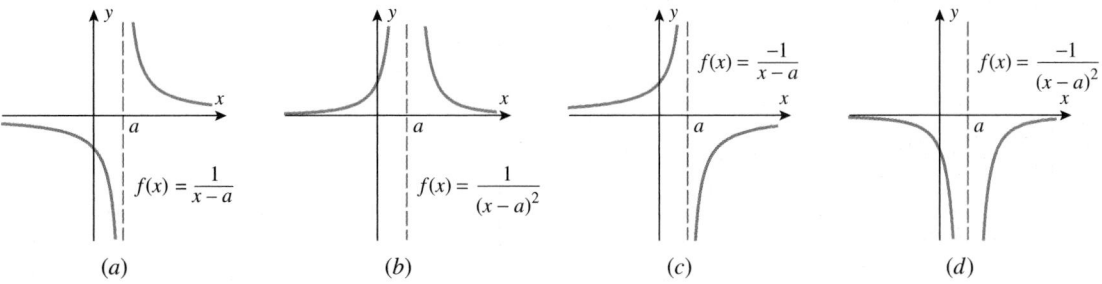

▲ **Figure 1.1.16**

■ VERTICAL ASYMPTOTES

Figure 1.1.17 illustrates geometrically what happens when any of the following situations occur:

$$\lim_{x \to a^-} f(x) = +\infty, \quad \lim_{x \to a^+} f(x) = +\infty, \quad \lim_{x \to a^-} f(x) = -\infty, \quad \lim_{x \to a^+} f(x) = -\infty$$

In each case the graph of $y = f(x)$ either rises or falls without bound, squeezing closer and closer to the vertical line $x = a$ as x approaches a from the side indicated in the limit. The line $x = a$ is called a ***vertical asymptote*** of the curve $y = f(x)$ (from the Greek word *asymptotos*, meaning "nonintersecting").

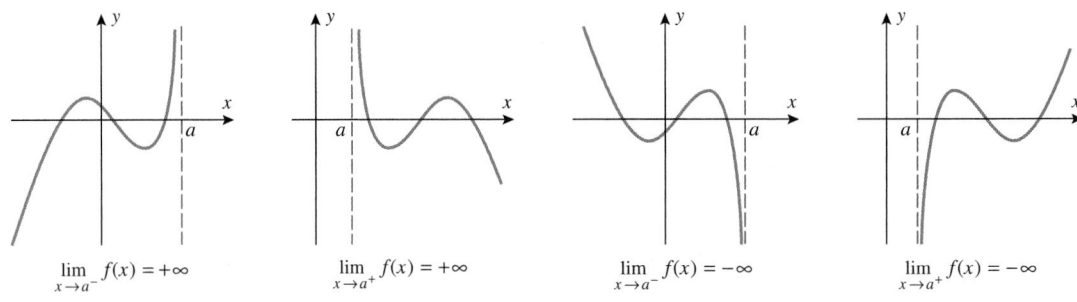

$$\lim_{x \to a^-} f(x) = +\infty \qquad \lim_{x \to a^+} f(x) = +\infty \qquad \lim_{x \to a^-} f(x) = -\infty \qquad \lim_{x \to a^+} f(x) = -\infty$$

▲ **Figure 1.1.17**

▶ **Example 8**   Referring to Figure 0.5.7 we see that the y-axis is a vertical asymptote for $y = \log_b x$ if $b > 1$ since

$$\lim_{x \to 0^+} \log_b x = -\infty$$

For the function in (16), find expressions for the left- and right-hand limits at each asymptote.

and referring to Figure 0.3.11 we see that $x = -1$ and $x = 1$ are vertical asymptotes of the graph of

$$f(x) = \frac{x^2 + 2x}{x^2 - 1} \qquad \blacktriangleleft \tag{16}$$

✔ **QUICK CHECK EXERCISES 1.1**   *(See page 80 for answers.)*

1. We write $\lim_{x \to a} f(x) = L$ provided the values of _____ can be made as close to _____ as desired, by taking values of _____ sufficiently close to _____ but not _____.

2. We write $\lim_{x \to a^-} f(x) = +\infty$ provided _____ increases without bound, as _____ approaches _____ from the left.

3. State what must be true about

$$\lim_{x \to a^-} f(x) \quad \text{and} \quad \lim_{x \to a^+} f(x)$$

in order for it to be the case that

$$\lim_{x \to a} f(x) = L$$

4. Use the accompanying graph of $y = f(x)$ $(-\infty < x < 3)$ to determine the limits.

    (a) $\lim_{x \to 0} f(x) =$ _____

    (b) $\lim_{x \to 2^-} f(x) =$ _____

    (c) $\lim_{x \to 2^+} f(x) =$ _____

    (d) $\lim_{x \to 3^-} f(x) =$ _____

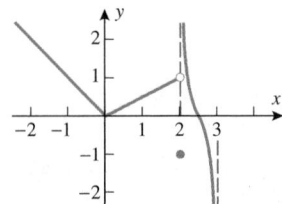

◀ **Figure Ex-4**

5. The slope of the secant line through $P(2, 4)$ and $Q(x, x^2)$ on the parabola $y = x^2$ is $m_{\text{sec}} = x + 2$. It follows that the slope of the tangent line to this parabola at the point P is _____.

EXERCISE SET 1.1   ⬚ Graphing Utility   [c] CAS

1–10 In these exercises, make reasonable assumptions about the graph of the indicated function outside of the region depicted. ■

1. For the function g graphed in the accompanying figure, find
(a) $\lim_{x \to 0^-} g(x)$ (b) $\lim_{x \to 0^+} g(x)$
(c) $\lim_{x \to 0} g(x)$ (d) $g(0)$.

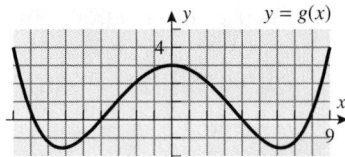
◀ **Figure Ex-1**

2. For the function G graphed in the accompanying figure, find
(a) $\lim_{x \to 0^-} G(x)$ (b) $\lim_{x \to 0^+} G(x)$
(c) $\lim_{x \to 0} G(x)$ (d) $G(0)$.

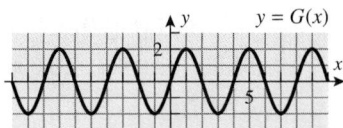
◀ **Figure Ex-2**

3. For the function f graphed in the accompanying figure, find
(a) $\lim_{x \to 3^-} f(x)$ (b) $\lim_{x \to 3^+} f(x)$
(c) $\lim_{x \to 3} f(x)$ (d) $f(3)$.

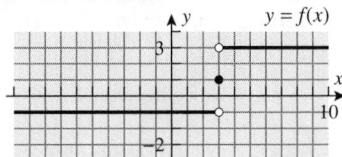
◀ **Figure Ex-3**

4. For the function f graphed in the accompanying figure, find
(a) $\lim_{x \to 2^-} f(x)$ (b) $\lim_{x \to 2^+} f(x)$
(c) $\lim_{x \to 2} f(x)$ (d) $f(2)$.

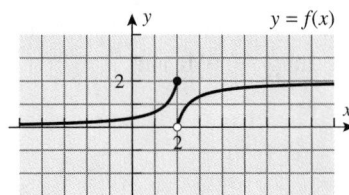
◀ **Figure Ex-4**

5. For the function F graphed in the accompanying figure, find
(a) $\lim_{x \to -2^-} F(x)$ (b) $\lim_{x \to -2^+} F(x)$
(c) $\lim_{x \to -2} F(x)$ (d) $F(-2)$.

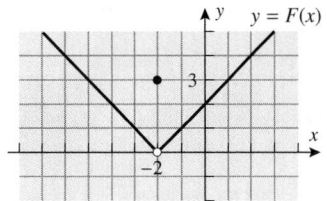
◀ **Figure Ex-5**

6. For the function G graphed in the accompanying figure, find
(a) $\lim_{x \to 0^-} G(x)$ (b) $\lim_{x \to 0^+} G(x)$
(c) $\lim_{x \to 0} G(x)$ (d) $G(0)$.

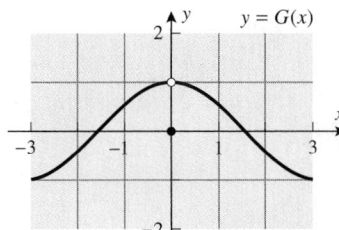
◀ **Figure Ex-6**

7. For the function f graphed in the accompanying figure, find
(a) $\lim_{x \to 3^-} f(x)$ (b) $\lim_{x \to 3^+} f(x)$
(c) $\lim_{x \to 3} f(x)$ (d) $f(3)$.

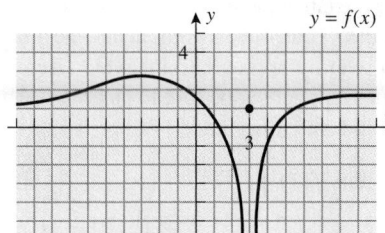
◀ **Figure Ex-7**

8. For the function ϕ graphed in the accompanying figure, find
(a) $\lim_{x \to 4^-} \phi(x)$ (b) $\lim_{x \to 4^+} \phi(x)$
(c) $\lim_{x \to 4} \phi(x)$ (d) $\phi(4)$.

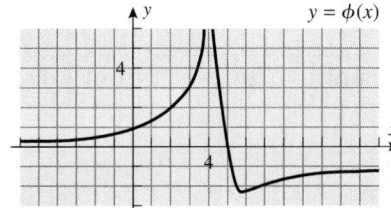
◀ **Figure Ex-8**

9. For the function f graphed in the accompanying figure on the next page, find
(a) $\lim_{x \to 0^-} f(x)$ (b) $\lim_{x \to 0^+} f(x)$
(c) $\lim_{x \to 0} f(x)$ (d) $f(0)$.

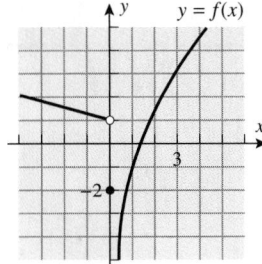

◀ **Figure Ex-9**

10. For the function g graphed in the accompanying figure, find

(a) $\lim\limits_{x \to 1^-} g(x)$ (b) $\lim\limits_{x \to 1^+} g(x)$

(c) $\lim\limits_{x \to 1} g(x)$ (d) $g(1)$.

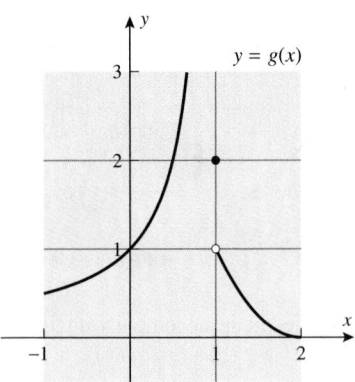

◀ **Figure Ex-10**

∼ **11–12** (i) Complete the table and make a guess about the limit indicated. (ii) Confirm your conclusions about the limit by graphing a function over an appropriate interval. [*Note:* For the inverse trigonometric function, be sure to put your calculating and graphing utilities in radian mode.] ▦

11. $f(x) = \dfrac{e^x - 1}{x}$; $\lim\limits_{x \to 0} f(x)$

x	-0.01	-0.001	-0.0001	0.0001	0.001	0.01
$f(x)$						

▲ **Table Ex-11**

12. $f(x) = \dfrac{\sin^{-1} 2x}{x}$; $\lim\limits_{x \to 0} f(x)$

x	-0.1	-0.01	-0.001	0.001	0.01	0.1
$f(x)$						

▲ **Table Ex-12**

[c] **13–16** (i) Make a guess at the limit (if it exists) by evaluating the function at the specified x-values. (ii) Confirm your conclusions about the limit by graphing the function over an appropriate interval. (iii) If you have a CAS, then use it to find the limit. [*Note:* For the trigonometric functions, be sure to put your calculating and graphing utilities in radian mode.] ▦

13. (a) $\lim\limits_{x \to 1} \dfrac{x - 1}{x^3 - 1}$; $x = 2, 1.5, 1.1, 1.01, 1.001, 0, 0.5, 0.9,$
                                 $0.99, 0.999$

(b) $\lim\limits_{x \to 1^+} \dfrac{x + 1}{x^3 - 1}$; $x = 2, 1.5, 1.1, 1.01, 1.001, 1.0001$

(c) $\lim\limits_{x \to 1^-} \dfrac{x + 1}{x^3 - 1}$; $x = 0, 0.5, 0.9, 0.99, 0.999, 0.9999$

14. (a) $\lim\limits_{x \to 0} \dfrac{\sqrt{x + 1} - 1}{x}$; $x = \pm 0.25, \pm 0.1, \pm 0.001,$
                                 ± 0.0001

(b) $\lim\limits_{x \to 0^+} \dfrac{\sqrt{x + 1} + 1}{x}$; $x = 0.25, 0.1, 0.001, 0.0001$

(c) $\lim\limits_{x \to 0^-} \dfrac{\sqrt{x + 1} + 1}{x}$; $x = -0.25, -0.1, -0.001,$
                                 -0.0001

15. (a) $\lim\limits_{x \to 0} \dfrac{\sin 3x}{x}$; $x = \pm 0.25, \pm 0.1, \pm 0.001, \pm 0.0001$

(b) $\lim\limits_{x \to -1} \dfrac{\cos x}{x + 1}$; $x = 0, -0.5, -0.9, -0.99, -0.999,$
                                 $-1.5, -1.1, -1.01, -1.001$

16. (a) $\lim\limits_{x \to -1} \dfrac{\tan(x + 1)}{x + 1}$; $x = 0, -0.5, -0.9, -0.99, -0.999,$
                                 $-1.5, -1.1, -1.01, -1.001$

(b) $\lim\limits_{x \to 0} \dfrac{\sin(5x)}{\sin(2x)}$; $x = \pm 0.25, \pm 0.1, \pm 0.001, \pm 0.0001$

17–20 True–False Determine whether the statement is true or false. Explain your answer. ▦

17. If $f(a) = L$, then $\lim_{x \to a} f(x) = L$.

18. If $\lim_{x \to a} f(x)$ exists, then so do $\lim_{x \to a^-} f(x)$ and $\lim_{x \to a^+} f(x)$.

19. If $\lim_{x \to a^-} f(x)$ and $\lim_{x \to a^+} f(x)$ exist, then so does $\lim_{x \to a} f(x)$.

20. If $\lim_{x \to a^+} f(x) = +\infty$, then $f(a)$ is undefined.

21–26 Sketch a possible graph for a function f with the specified properties. (Many different solutions are possible.) ▦

21. (i) the domain of f is $[-1, 1]$

(ii) $f(-1) = f(0) = f(1) = 0$

(iii) $\lim\limits_{x \to -1^+} f(x) = \lim\limits_{x \to 0} f(x) = \lim\limits_{x \to 1^-} f(x) = 1$

22. (i) the domain of f is $[-2, 1]$

(ii) $f(-2) = f(0) = f(1) = 0$

(iii) $\lim\limits_{x \to -2^+} f(x) = 2$, $\lim\limits_{x \to 0} f(x) = 0$, and $\lim_{x \to 1^-} f(x) = 1$

23. (i) the domain of f is $(-\infty, 0]$

(ii) $f(-2) = f(0) = 1$

(iii) $\lim\limits_{x \to -2} f(x) = +\infty$

24. (i) the domain of f is $(0, +\infty)$

(ii) $f(1) = 0$

(iii) the y-axis is a vertical asymptote for the graph of f

(iv) $f(x) < 0$ if $0 < x < 1$

25. (i) $f(-3) = f(0) = f(2) = 0$

(ii) $\lim\limits_{x \to -2^-} f(x) = +\infty$ and $\lim\limits_{x \to -2^+} f(x) = -\infty$

(iii) $\lim\limits_{x \to 1} f(x) = +\infty$

26. (i) $f(-1) = 0$, $f(0) = 1$, $f(1) = 0$

(ii) $\lim\limits_{x \to -1^-} f(x) = 0$ and $\lim\limits_{x \to -1^+} f(x) = +\infty$

(iii) $\lim\limits_{x \to 1^-} f(x) = 1$ and $\lim\limits_{x \to 1^+} f(x) = +\infty$

27–30 Modify the argument of Example 1 to find the equation of the tangent line to the specified graph at the point given. ■

27. the graph of $y = x^2$ at $(-1, 1)$

28. the graph of $y = x^2$ at $(0, 0)$

29. the graph of $y = x^4$ at $(1, 1)$

30. the graph of $y = x^4$ at $(-1, 1)$

FOCUS ON CONCEPTS

31. In the special theory of relativity the length l of a narrow rod moving longitudinally is a function $l = l(v)$ of the rod's speed v. The accompanying figure, in which c denotes the speed of light, displays some of the qualitative features of this function.

(a) What is the physical interpretation of l_0?

(b) What is $\lim\limits_{v \to c^-} l(v)$? What is the physical significance of this limit?

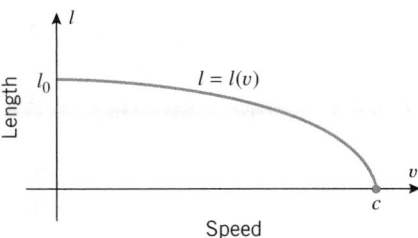

▲ **Figure Ex-31**

32. In the special theory of relativity the mass m of a moving object is a function $m = m(v)$ of the object's speed v. The accompanying figure, in which c denotes the speed of light, displays some of the qualitative features of this function.

(a) What is the physical interpretation of m_0?

(b) What is $\lim\limits_{v \to c^-} m(v)$? What is the physical significance of this limit?

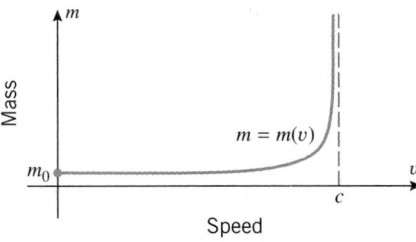

▲ **Figure Ex-32**

33. What do the graphs in Figure 0.5.4 imply about the value of
$$\lim_{x \to 0} \frac{e^x - 1}{x}$$
Explain your answer.

C **34.** Let
$$f(x) = \frac{x - \sin x}{x^3}$$

(a) Make a conjecture about the limit of f as $x \to 0^+$ by completing the table.

x	0.5	0.1	0.05	0.01
$f(x)$				

(b) Make another conjecture about the limit of f as $x \to 0^+$ by evaluating $f(x)$ at $x = 0.0001, 0.00001, 0.000001, 0.0000001, 0.00000001, 0.000000001$.

(c) The phenomenon exhibited in part (b) is called **catastrophic subtraction**. What do you think causes catastrophic subtraction? How does it put restrictions on the use of numerical evidence to make conjectures about limits?

(d) If you have a CAS, use it to show that the exact value of the limit is $\frac{1}{6}$.

35. Let
$$f(x) = \left(1 + x^2\right)^{1.1/x^2}$$

(a) Graph f in the window
$$[-1, 1] \times [2.5, 3.5]$$
and use the calculator's trace feature to make a conjecture about the limit of $f(x)$ as $x \to 0$.

(b) Graph f in the window
$$[-0.001, 0.001] \times [2.5, 3.5]$$
and use the calculator's trace feature to make a conjecture about the limit of $f(x)$ as $x \to 0$.

(c) Graph f in the window
$$[-0.000001, 0.000001] \times [2.5, 3.5]$$
and use the calculator's trace feature to make a conjecture about the limit of $f(x)$ as $x \to 0$.

(d) Later we will be able to show that
$$\lim_{x \to 0} \left(1 + x^2\right)^{1.1/x^2} \approx 3.00416602$$
What flaw do your graphs reveal about using numerical evidence (as revealed by the graphs you obtained) to make conjectures about limits?

36. Writing Two students are discussing the limit of $\sqrt{x}$ as x approaches 0. One student maintains that the limit is 0, while the other claims that the limit does not exist. Write a short paragraph that discusses the pros and cons of each student's position.

37. Writing Given a function f and a real number a, explain informally why
$$\lim_{x \to 0} f(x + a) = \lim_{x \to a} f(x)$$
(Here "equality" means that either both limits exist and are equal or that both limits fail to exist.)

1. $f(x)$; L; x; a **2.** $f(x)$; x; a **3.** Both one-sided limits must exist and equal L.   **4.** (a) 0 (b) 1 (c) $+\infty$ (d) $-\infty$ **5.** 4

1.2 COMPUTING LIMITS

In this section we will discuss techniques for computing limits of many functions. We base these results on the informal development of the limit concept discussed in the preceding section. A more formal derivation of these results is possible after Section 1.4.

■ **SOME BASIC LIMITS**

Our strategy for finding limits algebraically has two parts:

- First we will obtain the limits of some simple functions.
- Then we will develop a repertoire of theorems that will enable us to use the limits of those simple functions as building blocks for finding limits of more complicated functions.

We start with the following basic results, which are illustrated in Figure 1.2.1.

1.2.1 THEOREM *Let a and k be real numbers.*

(a) $\lim\limits_{x \to a} k = k$ (b) $\lim\limits_{x \to a} x = a$ (c) $\lim\limits_{x \to 0^-} \dfrac{1}{x} = -\infty$ (d) $\lim\limits_{x \to 0^+} \dfrac{1}{x} = +\infty$

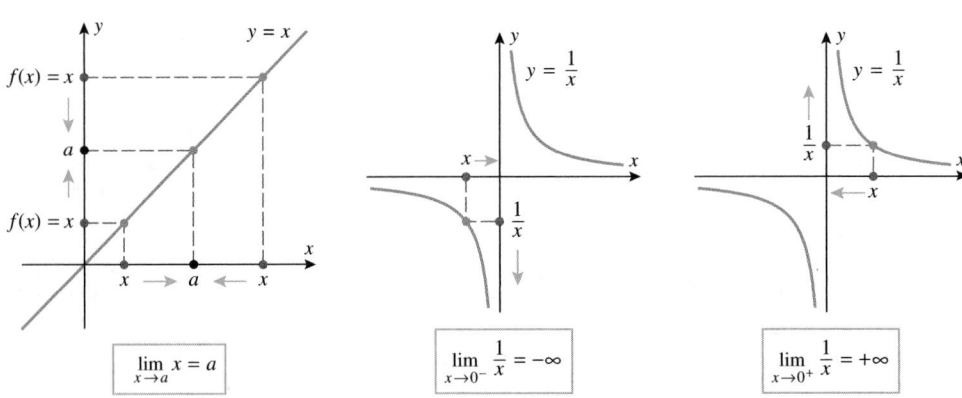

▲ **Figure 1.2.1**

The following examples explain these results further.

▶ **Example 1**   If $f(x) = k$ is a constant function, then the values of $f(x)$ remain fixed at k as x varies, which explains why $f(x) \to k$ as $x \to a$ for all values of a. For example,

$$\lim_{x \to -25} 3 = 3, \qquad \lim_{x \to 0} 3 = 3, \qquad \lim_{x \to \pi} 3 = 3 \;\blacktriangleleft$$

▶ **Example 2**   If $f(x) = x$, then as $x \to a$ it must also be true that $f(x) \to a$. For example,

$$\lim_{x \to 0} x = 0, \qquad \lim_{x \to -2} x = -2, \qquad \lim_{x \to \pi} x = \pi \;\blacktriangleleft$$

Do not confuse the algebraic size of a number with its closeness to zero. For positive numbers, the smaller the number the closer it is to zero, but for negative numbers, the larger the number the closer it is to zero. For example, -2 is larger than -4, but it is closer to zero.

▶ **Example 3**   You should know from your experience with fractions that for a fixed nonzero numerator, the closer the denominator is to zero, the larger the absolute value of the fraction. This fact and the data in Table 1.2.1 suggest why $1/x \to +\infty$ as $x \to 0^+$ and why $1/x \to -\infty$ as $x \to 0^-$. ◀

Table 1.2.1

	VALUES						CONCLUSION
x	-1	-0.1	-0.01	-0.001	-0.0001	$\cdots$	As $x \to 0^-$ the value of $1/x$
$1/x$	-1	-10	-100	-1000	$-10,000$	$\cdots$	decreases without bound.
x	1	0.1	0.01	0.001	0.0001	$\cdots$	As $x \to 0^+$ the value of $1/x$
$1/x$	1	10	100	1000	$10,000$	$\cdots$	increases without bound.

The following theorem, parts of which are proved in Appendix D, will be our basic tool for finding limits algebraically.

1.2.2   THEOREM   *Let a be a real number, and suppose that*

$$\lim_{x \to a} f(x) = L_1 \quad and \quad \lim_{x \to a} g(x) = L_2$$

That is, the limits exist and have values L_1 and L_2, respectively. Then:

(a) $\displaystyle \lim_{x \to a} [f(x) + g(x)] = \lim_{x \to a} f(x) + \lim_{x \to a} g(x) = L_1 + L_2$

(b) $\displaystyle \lim_{x \to a} [f(x) - g(x)] = \lim_{x \to a} f(x) - \lim_{x \to a} g(x) = L_1 - L_2$

(c) $\displaystyle \lim_{x \to a} [f(x)g(x)] = \left(\lim_{x \to a} f(x) \right)\left(\lim_{x \to a} g(x) \right) = L_1 L_2$

(d) $\displaystyle \lim_{x \to a} \frac{f(x)}{g(x)} = \frac{\displaystyle \lim_{x \to a} f(x)}{\displaystyle \lim_{x \to a} g(x)} = \frac{L_1}{L_2}, \quad provided\ L_2 \neq 0$

(e) $\displaystyle \lim_{x \to a} \sqrt[n]{f(x)} = \sqrt[n]{\lim_{x \to a} f(x)} = \sqrt[n]{L_1}, \quad provided\ L_1 > 0\ if\ n\ is\ even.$

Moreover, these statements are also true for the one-sided limits as $x \to a^-$ or as $x \to a^+$.

Theorem 1.2.2(e) remains valid for n even and $L_1 = 0$, provided $f(x)$ is nonnegative for x near a with $x \neq a$.

This theorem can be stated informally as follows:

(a) *The limit of a sum is the sum of the limits.*

(b) *The limit of a difference is the difference of the limits.*

(c) *The limit of a product is the product of the limits.*

(d) *The limit of a quotient is the quotient of the limits, provided the limit of the denominator is not zero.*

(e) *The limit of an nth root is the nth root of the limit.*

For the special case of part (c) in which $f(x) = k$ is a constant function, we have

$$\lim_{x \to a} (kg(x)) = \lim_{x \to a} k \cdot \lim_{x \to a} g(x) = k \lim_{x \to a} g(x) \qquad (1)$$

and similarly for one-sided limits. This result can be rephrased as follows:

> *A constant factor can be moved through a limit symbol.*

Although parts (*a*) and (*c*) of Theorem 1.2.2 are stated for two functions, the results hold for any finite number of functions. Moreover, the various parts of the theorem can be used in combination to reformulate expressions involving limits.

▶ **Example 4**

$$\lim_{x \to a}[f(x) - g(x) + 2h(x)] = \lim_{x \to a} f(x) - \lim_{x \to a} g(x) + 2 \lim_{x \to a} h(x)$$

$$\lim_{x \to a}[f(x)g(x)h(x)] = \left(\lim_{x \to a} f(x)\right)\left(\lim_{x \to a} g(x)\right)\left(\lim_{x \to a} h(x)\right)$$

$$\lim_{x \to a}[f(x)]^3 = \left(\lim_{x \to a} f(x)\right)^3 \qquad \boxed{\text{Take } g(x) = h(x) = f(x) \text{ in the last equation.}}$$

$$\lim_{x \to a}[f(x)]^n = \left(\lim_{x \to a} f(x)\right)^n \qquad \boxed{\begin{array}{l}\text{The extension of Theorem 1.2.2(c) in which}\\ \text{there are } n \text{ factors, each of which is } f(x)\end{array}}$$

$$\lim_{x \to a} x^n = \left(\lim_{x \to a} x\right)^n = a^n \qquad \boxed{\text{Apply the previous result with } f(x) = x.} \quad ◀$$

■ **LIMITS OF POLYNOMIALS AND RATIONAL FUNCTIONS AS $x \to a$**

▶ **Example 5**   Find $\lim_{x \to 5}(x^2 - 4x + 3)$.

Solution.

$$\lim_{x \to 5}(x^2 - 4x + 3) = \lim_{x \to 5} x^2 - \lim_{x \to 5} 4x + \lim_{x \to 5} 3 \qquad \boxed{\text{Theorem 1.2.2(a), (b)}}$$

$$= \lim_{x \to 5} x^2 - 4 \lim_{x \to 5} x + \lim_{x \to 5} 3 \qquad \boxed{\begin{array}{l}\text{A constant can be moved}\\ \text{through a limit symbol.}\end{array}}$$

$$= 5^2 - 4(5) + 3 \qquad \boxed{\text{The last part of Example 4}}$$

$$= 8 ◀$$

Observe that in Example 5 the limit of the polynomial $p(x) = x^2 - 4x + 3$ as $x \to 5$ turned out to be the same as $p(5)$. This is not an accident. The next result shows that, in general, the limit of a polynomial $p(x)$ as $x \to a$ is the same as the value of the polynomial at a. Knowing this fact allows us to reduce the computation of limits of polynomials to simply evaluating the polynomial at the appropriate point.

1.2.3   THEOREM   *For any polynomial*

$$p(x) = c_0 + c_1 x + \cdots + c_n x^n$$

and any real number a,

$$\lim_{x \to a} p(x) = c_0 + c_1 a + \cdots + c_n a^n = p(a)$$

PROOF

$$\lim_{x \to a} p(x) = \lim_{x \to a} \left(c_0 + c_1 x + \cdots + c_n x^n \right)$$

$$= \lim_{x \to a} c_0 + \lim_{x \to a} c_1 x + \cdots + \lim_{x \to a} c_n x^n$$

$$= \lim_{x \to a} c_0 + c_1 \lim_{x \to a} x + \cdots + c_n \lim_{x \to a} x^n$$

$$= c_0 + c_1 a + \cdots + c_n a^n = p(a) \quad \blacksquare$$

▶ **Example 6**   Find $\lim_{x \to 1} (x^7 - 2x^5 + 1)^{35}$.

Solution.   The function involved is a polynomial (why?), so the limit can be obtained by evaluating this polynomial at $x = 1$. This yields

$$\lim_{x \to 1} (x^7 - 2x^5 + 1)^{35} = 0 \quad \blacktriangleleft$$

Recall that a rational function is a ratio of two polynomials. The following example illustrates how Theorems 1.2.2(*d*) and 1.2.3 can sometimes be used in combination to compute limits of rational functions.

▶ **Example 7**   Find $\lim_{x \to 2} \dfrac{5x^3 + 4}{x - 3}$.

Solution.

$$\lim_{x \to 2} \frac{5x^3 + 4}{x - 3} = \frac{\displaystyle \lim_{x \to 2} (5x^3 + 4)}{\displaystyle \lim_{x \to 2} (x - 3)} \qquad \boxed{\text{Theorem 1.2.2}(d)}$$

$$= \frac{5 \cdot 2^3 + 4}{2 - 3} = -44 \qquad \boxed{\text{Theorem 1.2.3}} \quad \blacktriangleleft$$

The method used in the last example will not work for rational functions in which the limit of the denominator is zero because Theorem 1.2.2(*d*) is not applicable. There are two cases of this type to be considered—the case where the limit of the denominator is zero and the limit of the numerator is not, and the case where the limits of the numerator and denominator are both zero. If the limit of the denominator is zero but the limit of the numerator is not, then one can prove that the limit of the rational function does not exist and that one of the following situations occurs:

- The limit may be $-\infty$ from one side and $+\infty$ from the other.
- The limit may be $+\infty$.
- The limit may be $-\infty$.

Figure 1.2.2 illustrates these three possibilities graphically for rational functions of the form $1/(x - a)$, $1/(x - a)^2$, and $-1/(x - a)^2$.

▶ **Example 8**   Find

(a) $\displaystyle \lim_{x \to 4^+} \frac{2 - x}{(x - 4)(x + 2)}$ (b) $\displaystyle \lim_{x \to 4^-} \frac{2 - x}{(x - 4)(x + 2)}$ (c) $\displaystyle \lim_{x \to 4} \frac{2 - x}{(x - 4)(x + 2)}$

Solution.   In all three parts the limit of the numerator is -2, and the limit of the denominator is 0, so the limit of the ratio does not exist. To be more specific than this, we need

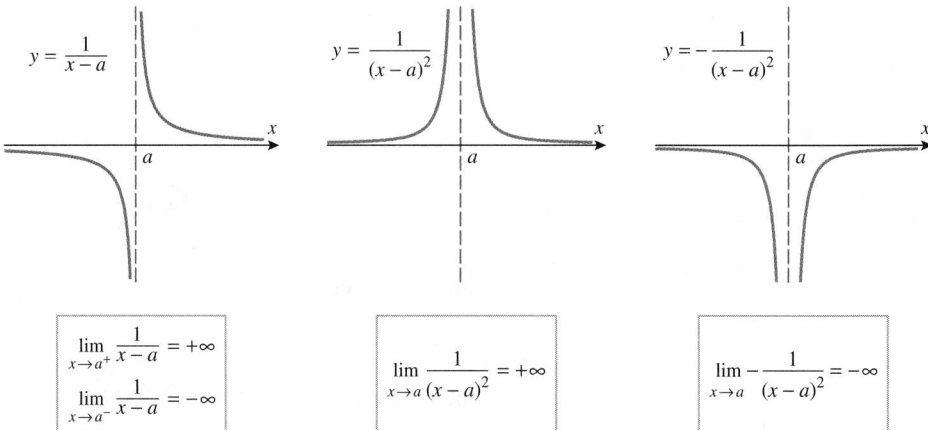

$$\lim_{x \to a^+} \frac{1}{x-a} = +\infty$$
$$\lim_{x \to a^-} \frac{1}{x-a} = -\infty$$

$$\lim_{x \to a} \frac{1}{(x-a)^2} = +\infty$$

$$\lim_{x \to a} -\frac{1}{(x-a)^2} = -\infty$$

▲ **Figure 1.2.2**

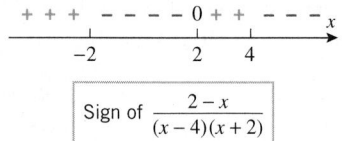

Sign of $\dfrac{2-x}{(x-4)(x+2)}$

▲ **Figure 1.2.3**

to analyze the sign of the ratio. The sign of the ratio, which is given in Figure 1.2.3, is determined by the signs of $2 - x$, $x - 4$, and $x + 2$. (The method of test points, discussed in Web Appendix E, provides a way of finding the sign of the ratio here.) It follows from this figure that as x approaches 4 from the right, the ratio is always negative; and as x approaches 4 from the left, the ratio is eventually positive. Thus,

$$\lim_{x \to 4^+} \frac{2-x}{(x-4)(x+2)} = -\infty \quad \text{and} \quad \lim_{x \to 4^-} \frac{2-x}{(x-4)(x+2)} = +\infty$$

Because the one-sided limits have opposite signs, all we can say about the two-sided limit is that it does not exist. ◄

In the case where $p(x)/q(x)$ is a rational function for which $p(a) = 0$ and $q(a) = 0$, the numerator and denominator must have one or more common factors of $x - a$. In this case the limit of $p(x)/q(x)$ as $x \to a$ can be found by canceling all common factors of $x - a$ and using one of the methods already considered to find the limit of the simplified function. Here is an example.

In Example 9(a), the simplified function $x - 3$ is defined at $x = 3$, but the original function is not. However, this has no effect on the limit as x *approaches* 3 since the two functions are identical if $x \neq 3$ (Exercise 50).

▶ **Example 9**   Find

(a) $\displaystyle\lim_{x \to 3} \frac{x^2 - 6x + 9}{x - 3}$ (b) $\displaystyle\lim_{x \to -4} \frac{2x + 8}{x^2 + x - 12}$ (c) $\displaystyle\lim_{x \to 5} \frac{x^2 - 3x - 10}{x^2 - 10x + 25}$

Solution (a).   The numerator and the denominator both have a zero at $x = 3$, so there is a common factor of $x - 3$. Then

$$\lim_{x \to 3} \frac{x^2 - 6x + 9}{x - 3} = \lim_{x \to 3} \frac{(x-3)^2}{x-3} = \lim_{x \to 3} (x - 3) = 0$$

Solution (b).   The numerator and the denominator both have a zero at $x = -4$, so there is a common factor of $x - (-4) = x + 4$. Then

$$\lim_{x \to -4} \frac{2x + 8}{x^2 + x - 12} = \lim_{x \to -4} \frac{2(x+4)}{(x+4)(x-3)} = \lim_{x \to -4} \frac{2}{x-3} = -\frac{2}{7}$$

Solution (c).   The numerator and the denominator both have a zero at $x = 5$, so there is a common factor of $x - 5$. Then

$$\lim_{x \to 5} \frac{x^2 - 3x - 10}{x^2 - 10x + 25} = \lim_{x \to 5} \frac{(x-5)(x+2)}{(x-5)(x-5)} = \lim_{x \to 5} \frac{x+2}{x-5}$$

However,

$$\lim_{x \to 5} (x+2) = 7 \neq 0 \quad \text{and} \quad \lim_{x \to 5} (x-5) = 0$$

so

$$\lim_{x \to 5} \frac{x^2 - 3x - 10}{x^2 - 10x + 25} = \lim_{x \to 5} \frac{x+2}{x-5}$$

does not exist. More precisely, the sign analysis in Figure 1.2.4 implies that

$$\lim_{x \to 5^+} \frac{x^2 - 3x - 10}{x^2 - 10x + 25} = \lim_{x \to 5^+} \frac{x+2}{x-5} = +\infty$$

and

$$\lim_{x \to 5^-} \frac{x^2 - 3x - 10}{x^2 - 10x + 25} = \lim_{x \to 5^-} \frac{x+2}{x-5} = -\infty \blacktriangleleft$$

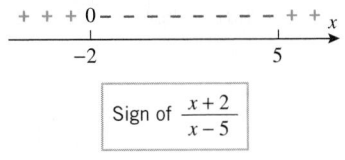

Sign of $\dfrac{x+2}{x-5}$

▲ **Figure 1.2.4**

Discuss the logical errors in the following statement: An indeterminate form of type 0/0 must have a limit of zero because zero divided by anything is zero.

A quotient $f(x)/g(x)$ in which the numerator and denominator both have a limit of zero as $x \to a$ is called an **indeterminate form of type 0/0.** The problem with such limits is that it is difficult to tell by inspection whether the limit exists, and, if so, its value. Informally stated, this is because there are two conflicting influences at work. The value of $f(x)/g(x)$ would tend to zero as $f(x)$ approached zero if $g(x)$ were to remain at some fixed nonzero value, whereas the value of this ratio would tend to increase or decrease without bound as $g(x)$ approached zero if $f(x)$ were to remain at some fixed nonzero value. But with both $f(x)$ and $g(x)$ approaching zero, the behavior of the ratio depends on precisely how these conflicting tendencies offset one another for the particular f and g.

Sometimes, limits of indeterminate forms of type 0/0 can be found by algebraic simplification, as in the last example, but frequently this will not work and other methods must be used. We will study such methods in later sections.

The following theorem summarizes our observations about limits of rational functions.

1.2.4 THEOREM *Let*

$$f(x) = \frac{p(x)}{q(x)}$$

be a rational function, and let a be any real number.

(a) *If $q(a) \neq 0$, then $\displaystyle\lim_{x \to a} f(x) = f(a)$.*

(b) *If $q(a) = 0$ but $p(a) \neq 0$, then $\displaystyle\lim_{x \to a} f(x)$ does not exist.*

■ **LIMITS INVOLVING RADICALS**

▶ **Example 10** Find $\displaystyle\lim_{x \to 1} \frac{x-1}{\sqrt{x}-1}$.

Solution. In Example 2 of Section 1.1 we used numerical evidence to conjecture that this limit is 2. Here we will confirm this algebraically. Since this limit is an indeterminate form of type 0/0, we will need to devise some strategy for making the limit (if it exists) evident. One such strategy is to rationalize the denominator of the function. This yields

$$\frac{x-1}{\sqrt{x}-1} = \frac{(x-1)(\sqrt{x}+1)}{(\sqrt{x}-1)(\sqrt{x}+1)} = \frac{(x-1)(\sqrt{x}+1)}{x-1} = \sqrt{x}+1 \quad (x \neq 1)$$

Therefore,

$$\lim_{x \to 1} \frac{x-1}{\sqrt{x}-1} = \lim_{x \to 1} (\sqrt{x}+1) = 2 \; \blacktriangleleft$$

Confirm the limit in Example 10 by factoring the numerator.

LIMITS OF PIECEWISE-DEFINED FUNCTIONS

For functions that are defined piecewise, a two-sided limit at a point where the formula changes is best obtained by first finding the one-sided limits at that point.

▶ **Example 11**   Let

$$f(x) = \begin{cases} 1/(x+2), & x < -2 \\ x^2 - 5, & -2 < x \le 3 \\ \sqrt{x+13}, & x > 3 \end{cases}$$

Find

(a) $\displaystyle\lim_{x \to -2} f(x)$ (b) $\displaystyle\lim_{x \to 0} f(x)$ (c) $\displaystyle\lim_{x \to 3} f(x)$

Solution (a).   We will determine the stated two-sided limit by first considering the corresponding one-sided limits. For each one-sided limit, we must use that part of the formula that is applicable on the interval over which x varies. For example, as x approaches -2 from the left, the applicable part of the formula is

$$f(x) = \frac{1}{x+2}$$

and as x approaches -2 from the right, the applicable part of the formula near -2 is

$$f(x) = x^2 - 5$$

Thus,

$$\lim_{x \to -2^-} f(x) = \lim_{x \to -2^-} \frac{1}{x+2} = -\infty$$

$$\lim_{x \to -2^+} f(x) = \lim_{x \to -2^+} (x^2 - 5) = (-2)^2 - 5 = -1$$

from which it follows that $\displaystyle\lim_{x \to -2} f(x)$ does not exist.

Solution (b).   The applicable part of the formula is $f(x) = x^2 - 5$ on both sides of 0, so there is no need to consider one-sided limits here. We see directly that

$$\lim_{x \to 0} f(x) = \lim_{x \to 0} (x^2 - 5) = 0^2 - 5 = -5$$

Solution (c).   Using the applicable parts of the formula for $f(x)$, we obtain

$$\lim_{x \to 3^-} f(x) = \lim_{x \to 3^-} (x^2 - 5) = 3^2 - 5 = 4$$

$$\lim_{x \to 3^+} f(x) = \lim_{x \to 3^+} \sqrt{x+13} = \sqrt{\lim_{x \to 3^+} (x+13)} = \sqrt{3+13} = 4$$

Since the one-sided limits are equal, we have

$$\lim_{x \to 3} f(x) = 4$$

We note that the limit calculations in parts (a), (b), and (c) are consistent with the graph of f shown in Figure 1.2.5. ◀

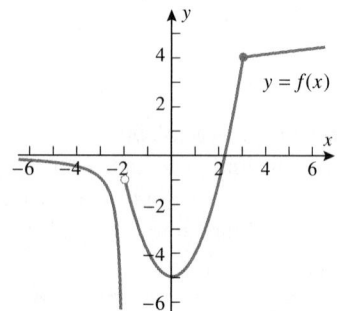

▲ **Figure 1.2.5**

✔ QUICK CHECK EXERCISES 1.2   (See page 88 for answers.)

1. In each part, find the limit by inspection.

(a) $\lim_{x \to 8} 7 =$ _____

(b) $\lim_{y \to 3^+} 12y =$ _____

(c) $\lim_{x \to 0^-} \dfrac{x}{|x|} =$ _____

(d) $\lim_{w \to 5} \dfrac{w}{|w|} =$ _____

(e) $\lim_{z \to 1^-} \dfrac{1}{1 - z} =$ _____

2. Given that $\lim_{x \to a} f(x) = 1$ and $\lim_{x \to a} g(x) = 2$, find the limits.

(a) $\lim_{x \to a} [3 f(x) + 2g(x)] =$ _____

(b) $\lim_{x \to a} \dfrac{2 f(x) + 1}{1 - f(x)g(x)} =$ _____

(c) $\lim_{x \to a} \dfrac{\sqrt{f(x) + 3}}{g(x)} =$ _____

3. Find the limits.

(a) $\lim_{x \to -1} (x^3 + x^2 + x)^{101} =$ _____

(b) $\lim_{x \to 2^-} \dfrac{(x - 1)(x - 2)}{x + 1} =$ _____

(c) $\lim_{x \to -1^+} \dfrac{(x - 1)(x - 2)}{x + 1} =$ _____

(d) $\lim_{x \to 4} \dfrac{x^2 - 16}{x - 4} =$ _____

4. Let
$$f(x) = \begin{cases} x + 1, & x \le 1 \\ x - 1, & x > 1 \end{cases}$$

Find the limits that exist.

(a) $\lim_{x \to 1^-} f(x) =$ _____

(b) $\lim_{x \to 1^+} f(x) =$ _____

(c) $\lim_{x \to 1} f(x) =$ _____

EXERCISE SET 1.2

1. Given that
$$\lim_{x \to a} f(x) = 2, \quad \lim_{x \to a} g(x) = -4, \quad \lim_{x \to a} h(x) = 0$$
find the limits.

(a) $\lim_{x \to a} [f(x) + 2g(x)]$

(b) $\lim_{x \to a} [h(x) - 3g(x) + 1]$

(c) $\lim_{x \to a} [f(x)g(x)]$

(d) $\lim_{x \to a} [g(x)]^2$

(e) $\lim_{x \to a} \sqrt[3]{6 + f(x)}$

(f) $\lim_{x \to a} \dfrac{2}{g(x)}$

2. Use the graphs of f and g in the accompanying figure to find the limits that exist. If the limit does not exist, explain why.

(a) $\lim_{x \to 2} [f(x) + g(x)]$

(b) $\lim_{x \to 0} [f(x) + g(x)]$

(c) $\lim_{x \to 0^+} [f(x) + g(x)]$

(d) $\lim_{x \to 0^-} [f(x) + g(x)]$

(e) $\lim_{x \to 2} \dfrac{f(x)}{1 + g(x)}$

(f) $\lim_{x \to 2} \dfrac{1 + g(x)}{f(x)}$

(g) $\lim_{x \to 0^+} \sqrt{f(x)}$

(h) $\lim_{x \to 0^-} \sqrt{f(x)}$

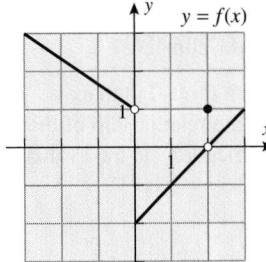

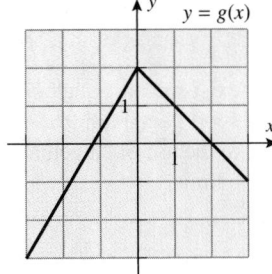

▲ **Figure Ex-2**

3–30 Find the limits. ■

3. $\lim_{x \to 2} x(x - 1)(x + 1)$

4. $\lim_{x \to 3} x^3 - 3x^2 + 9x$

5. $\lim_{x \to 3} \dfrac{x^2 - 2x}{x + 1}$

6. $\lim_{x \to 0} \dfrac{6x - 9}{x^3 - 12x + 3}$

7. $\lim_{x \to 1^+} \dfrac{x^4 - 1}{x - 1}$

8. $\lim_{t \to -2} \dfrac{t^3 + 8}{t + 2}$

9. $\lim_{x \to -1} \dfrac{x^2 + 6x + 5}{x^2 - 3x - 4}$

10. $\lim_{x \to 2} \dfrac{x^2 - 4x + 4}{x^2 + x - 6}$

11. $\lim_{x \to -1} \dfrac{2x^2 + x - 1}{x + 1}$

12. $\lim_{x \to 1} \dfrac{3x^2 - x - 2}{2x^2 + x - 3}$

13. $\lim_{t \to 2} \dfrac{t^3 + 3t^2 - 12t + 4}{t^3 - 4t}$

14. $\lim_{t \to 1} \dfrac{t^3 + t^2 - 5t + 3}{t^3 - 3t + 2}$

15. $\lim_{x \to 3^+} \dfrac{x}{x - 3}$

16. $\lim_{x \to 3^-} \dfrac{x}{x - 3}$

17. $\lim_{x \to 3} \dfrac{x}{x - 3}$

18. $\lim_{x \to 2^+} \dfrac{x}{x^2 - 4}$

19. $\lim_{x \to 2^-} \dfrac{x}{x^2 - 4}$

20. $\lim_{x \to 2} \dfrac{x}{x^2 - 4}$

21. $\lim_{y \to 6^+} \dfrac{y + 6}{y^2 - 36}$

22. $\lim_{y \to 6^-} \dfrac{y + 6}{y^2 - 36}$

23. $\lim_{y \to 6} \dfrac{y + 6}{y^2 - 36}$

24. $\lim_{x \to 4^+} \dfrac{3 - x}{x^2 - 2x - 8}$

25. $\lim_{x \to 4^-} \dfrac{3 - x}{x^2 - 2x - 8}$

26. $\lim_{x \to 4} \dfrac{3 - x}{x^2 - 2x - 8}$

27. $\lim_{x \to 2^+} \dfrac{1}{|2 - x|}$

28. $\lim_{x \to 3^-} \dfrac{1}{|x - 3|}$

29. $\lim_{x \to 9} \dfrac{x - 9}{\sqrt{x} - 3}$

30. $\lim_{y \to 4} \dfrac{4 - y}{2 - \sqrt{y}}$

31. Let
$$f(x) = \begin{cases} x - 1, & x \le 3 \\ 3x - 7, & x > 3 \end{cases}$$

(cont.)

Find

(a) $\lim\limits_{x \to 3^-} f(x)$ (b) $\lim\limits_{x \to 3^+} f(x)$ (c) $\lim\limits_{x \to 3} f(x)$.

32. Let

$$g(t) = \begin{cases} t - 2, & t < 0 \\ t^2, & 0 \le t \le 2 \\ 2t, & t > 2 \end{cases}$$

Find

(a) $\lim\limits_{t \to 0} g(t)$ (b) $\lim\limits_{t \to 1} g(t)$ (c) $\lim\limits_{t \to 2} g(t)$.

33–36 True–False Determine whether the statement is true or false. Explain your answer. ■

33. If $\lim_{x \to a} f(x)$ and $\lim_{x \to a} g(x)$ exist, then so does $\lim_{x \to a}[f(x) + g(x)]$.

34. If $\lim_{x \to a} g(x) = 0$ and $\lim_{x \to a} f(x)$ exists, then $\lim_{x \to a}[f(x)/g(x)]$ does not exist.

35. If $\lim_{x \to a} f(x)$ and $\lim_{x \to a} g(x)$ both exist and are equal, then $\lim_{x \to a}[f(x)/g(x)] = 1$.

36. If $f(x)$ is a rational function and $x = a$ is in the domain of f, then $\lim_{x \to a} f(x) = f(a)$.

37–38 First rationalize the numerator and then find the limit.

37. $\lim\limits_{x \to 0} \dfrac{\sqrt{x + 4} - 2}{x}$ **38.** $\lim\limits_{x \to 0} \dfrac{\sqrt{x^2 + 4} - 2}{x}$

39. Let

$$f(x) = \frac{x^3 - 1}{x - 1}$$

(a) Find $\lim_{x \to 1} f(x)$.

(b) Sketch the graph of $y = f(x)$.

40. Let

$$f(x) = \begin{cases} \dfrac{x^2 - 9}{x + 3}, & x \ne -3 \\ k, & x = -3 \end{cases}$$

(a) Find k so that $f(-3) = \lim_{x \to -3} f(x)$.

(b) With k assigned the value $\lim_{x \to -3} f(x)$, show that $f(x)$ can be expressed as a polynomial.

FOCUS ON CONCEPTS

41. (a) Explain why the following calculation is incorrect.

$$\lim_{x \to 0^+}\left(\frac{1}{x} - \frac{1}{x^2}\right) = \lim_{x \to 0^+}\frac{1}{x} - \lim_{x \to 0^+}\frac{1}{x^2}$$

$$= +\infty - (+\infty) = 0$$

(b) Show that $\lim\limits_{x \to 0^+}\left(\dfrac{1}{x} - \dfrac{1}{x^2}\right) = -\infty$.

42. (a) Explain why the following argument is incorrect.

$$\lim_{x \to 0}\left(\frac{1}{x} - \frac{2}{x^2 + 2x}\right) = \lim_{x \to 0}\frac{1}{x}\left(1 - \frac{2}{x + 2}\right)$$

$$= \infty \cdot 0 = 0$$

(b) Show that $\lim\limits_{x \to 0}\left(\dfrac{1}{x} - \dfrac{2}{x^2 + 2x}\right) = \dfrac{1}{2}$.

43. Find all values of a such that

$$\lim_{x \to 1}\left(\frac{1}{x - 1} - \frac{a}{x^2 - 1}\right)$$

exists and is finite.

44. (a) Explain informally why

$$\lim_{x \to 0^-}\left(\frac{1}{x} + \frac{1}{x^2}\right) = +\infty$$

(b) Verify the limit in part (a) algebraically.

45. Let $p(x)$ and $q(x)$ be polynomials, with $q(x_0) = 0$. Discuss the behavior of the graph of $y = p(x)/q(x)$ in the vicinity of $x = x_0$. Give examples to support your conclusions.

46. Suppose that f and g are two functions such that $\lim_{x \to a} f(x)$ exists but $\lim_{x \to a}[f(x) + g(x)]$ does not exist. Use Theorem 1.2.2. to prove that $\lim_{x \to a} g(x)$ does not exist.

47. Suppose that f and g are two functions such that both $\lim_{x \to a} f(x)$ and $\lim_{x \to a}[f(x) + g(x)]$ exist. Use Theorem 1.2.2 to prove that $\lim_{x \to a} g(x)$ exists.

48. Suppose that f and g are two functions such that

$$\lim_{x \to a} g(x) = 0 \quad \text{and} \quad \lim_{x \to a} \frac{f(x)}{g(x)}$$

exists. Use Theorem 1.2.2 to prove that $\lim_{x \to a} f(x) = 0$.

49. Writing According to Newton's Law of Universal Gravitation, the gravitational force of attraction between two masses is inversely proportional to the square of the distance between them. What results of this section are useful in describing the gravitational force of attraction between the masses as they get closer and closer together?

50. Writing Suppose that f and g are two functions that are equal except at a finite number of points and that a denotes a real number. Explain informally why both

$$\lim_{x \to a} f(x) \quad \text{and} \quad \lim_{x \to a} g(x)$$

exist and are equal, or why both limits fail to exist. Write a short paragraph that explains the relationship of this result to the use of "algebraic simplification" in the evaluation of a limit.

✔ QUICK CHECK ANSWERS 1.2

1. (a) 7 (b) 36 (c) −1 (d) 1 (e) $+\infty$ **2.** (a) 7 (b) −3 (c) 1   **3.** (a) −1 (b) 0 (c) $+\infty$ (d) 8
4. (a) 2 (b) 0 (c) does not exist

1.3 LIMITS AT INFINITY; END BEHAVIOR OF A FUNCTION

Up to now we have been concerned with limits that describe the behavior of a function $f(x)$ as x approaches some real number a. In this section we will be concerned with the behavior of $f(x)$ as x increases or decreases without bound.

■ LIMITS AT INFINITY AND HORIZONTAL ASYMPTOTES

If the values of a variable x increase without bound, then we write $x \to +\infty$, and if the values of x decrease without bound, then we write $x \to -\infty$. The behavior of a function $f(x)$ as x increases without bound or decreases without bound is sometimes called the **end behavior** of the function. For example,

$$\lim_{x \to -\infty} \frac{1}{x} = 0 \quad \text{and} \quad \lim_{x \to +\infty} \frac{1}{x} = 0 \tag{1–2}$$

are illustrated numerically in Table 1.3.1 and geometrically in Figure 1.3.1.

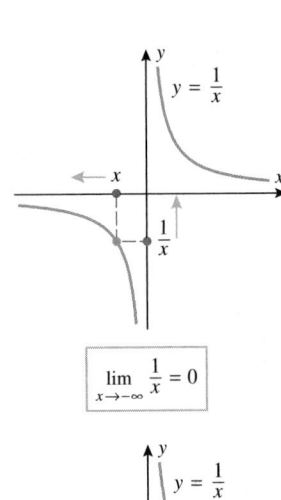

$$\lim_{x \to -\infty} \frac{1}{x} = 0$$

Table 1.3.1

	VALUES						CONCLUSION
x	−1	−10	−100	−1000	−10,000	$\cdots$	As $x \to -\infty$ the value of $1/x$
$1/x$	−1	−0.1	−0.01	−0.001	−0.0001	$\cdots$	increases toward zero.
x	1	10	100	1000	10,000	$\cdots$	As $x \to +\infty$ the value of $1/x$
$1/x$	1	0.1	0.01	0.001	0.0001	$\cdots$	decreases toward zero.

In general, we will use the following notation.

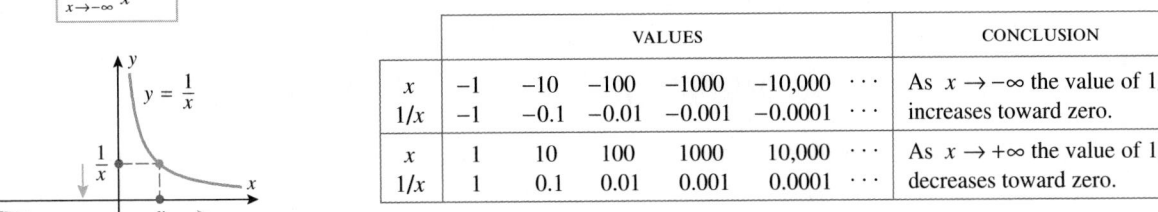

$$\lim_{x \to +\infty} \frac{1}{x} = 0$$

▲ **Figure 1.3.1**

1.3.1 LIMITS AT INFINITY (AN INFORMAL VIEW)   If the values of $f(x)$ eventually get as close as we like to a number L as x increases without bound, then we write

$$\lim_{x \to +\infty} f(x) = L \quad \text{or} \quad f(x) \to L \text{ as } x \to +\infty \tag{3}$$

Similarly, if the values of $f(x)$ eventually get as close as we like to a number L as x decreases without bound, then we write

$$\lim_{x \to -\infty} f(x) = L \quad \text{or} \quad f(x) \to L \text{ as } x \to -\infty \tag{4}$$

$$\lim_{x \to +\infty} f(x) = L$$

Figure 1.3.2 illustrates the end behavior of a function f when

$$\lim_{x \to +\infty} f(x) = L \quad \text{or} \quad \lim_{x \to -\infty} f(x) = L$$

In the first case the graph of f eventually comes as close as we like to the line $y = L$ as x increases without bound, and in the second case it eventually comes as close as we like to the line $y = L$ as x decreases without bound. If either limit holds, we call the line $y = L$ a **horizontal asymptote** for the graph of f.

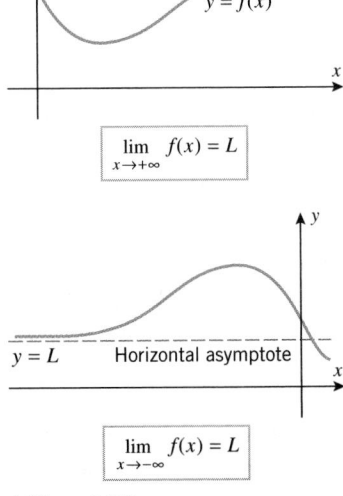

$$\lim_{x \to -\infty} f(x) = L$$

▲ **Figure 1.3.2**

▶ **Example 1**   It follows from (1) and (2) that $y = 0$ is a horizontal asymptote for the graph of $f(x) = 1/x$ in both the positive and negative directions. This is consistent with the graph of $y = 1/x$ shown in Figure 1.3.1. ◀

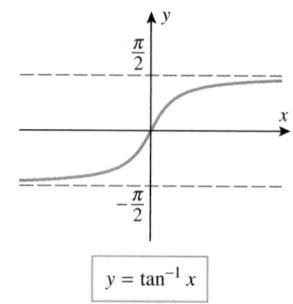

$$y = \tan^{-1} x$$

▲ **Figure 1.3.3**

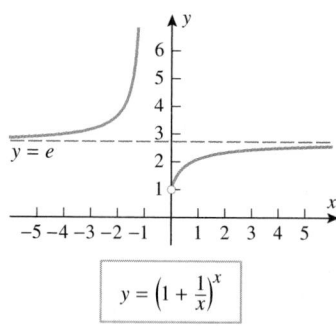

$$y = \left(1 + \frac{1}{x}\right)^x$$

▲ **Figure 1.3.4**

▶ **Example 2** Figure 1.3.3 is the graph of $f(x) = \tan^{-1} x$. As suggested by this graph,

$$\lim_{x \to +\infty} \tan^{-1} x = \frac{\pi}{2} \quad \text{and} \quad \lim_{x \to -\infty} \tan^{-1} x = -\frac{\pi}{2} \tag{5-6}$$

so the line $y = \pi/2$ is a horizontal asymptote for f in the positive direction and the line $y = -\pi/2$ is a horizontal asymptote in the negative direction. ◀

▶ **Example 3** Figure 1.3.4 is the graph of $f(x) = (1 + 1/x)^x$. As suggested by this graph,

$$\lim_{x \to +\infty} \left(1 + \frac{1}{x}\right)^x = e \quad \text{and} \quad \lim_{x \to -\infty} \left(1 + \frac{1}{x}\right)^x = e \tag{7-8}$$

so the line $y = e$ is a horizontal asymptote for f in both the positive and negative directions. ◀

■ **LIMIT LAWS FOR LIMITS AT INFINITY**

It can be shown that the limit laws in Theorem 1.2.2 carry over without change to limits at $+\infty$ and $-\infty$. Moreover, it follows by the same argument used in Section 1.2 that if n is a positive integer, then

$$\lim_{x \to +\infty} (f(x))^n = \left(\lim_{x \to +\infty} f(x)\right)^n \qquad \lim_{x \to -\infty} (f(x))^n = \left(\lim_{x \to -\infty} f(x)\right)^n \tag{9-10}$$

provided the indicated limit of $f(x)$ exists. It also follows that constants can be moved through the limit symbols for limits at infinity:

$$\lim_{x \to +\infty} kf(x) = k \lim_{x \to +\infty} f(x) \qquad \lim_{x \to -\infty} kf(x) = k \lim_{x \to -\infty} f(x) \tag{11-12}$$

provided the indicated limit of $f(x)$ exists.

Finally, if $f(x) = k$ is a constant function, then the values of f do not change as $x \to +\infty$ or as $x \to -\infty$, so

$$\lim_{x \to +\infty} k = k \qquad \lim_{x \to -\infty} k = k \tag{13-14}$$

▶ **Example 4**

(a) It follows from (1), (2), (9), and (10) that if n is a positive integer, then

$$\lim_{x \to +\infty} \frac{1}{x^n} = \left(\lim_{x \to +\infty} \frac{1}{x}\right)^n = 0 \quad \text{and} \quad \lim_{x \to -\infty} \frac{1}{x^n} = \left(\lim_{x \to -\infty} \frac{1}{x}\right)^n = 0$$

(b) It follows from (7) and the extension of Theorem 1.2.2(e) to the case $x \to +\infty$ that

$$\lim_{x \to +\infty} \left(1 + \frac{1}{2x}\right)^x = \lim_{x \to +\infty} \left[\left(1 + \frac{1}{2x}\right)^{2x}\right]^{1/2}$$

$$= \left[\lim_{x \to +\infty} \left(1 + \frac{1}{2x}\right)^{2x}\right]^{1/2} = e^{1/2} = \sqrt{e} \quad ◀$$

■ **INFINITE LIMITS AT INFINITY**

Limits at infinity, like limits at a real number a, can fail to exist for various reasons. One such possibility is that the values of $f(x)$ increase or decrease without bound as $x \to +\infty$ or as $x \to -\infty$. We will use the following notation to describe this situation.

1.3.2   INFINITE LIMITS AT INFINITY (AN INFORMAL VIEW)   If the values of $f(x)$ increase without bound as $x \to +\infty$ or as $x \to -\infty$, then we write

$$\lim_{x \to +\infty} f(x) = +\infty \quad \text{or} \quad \lim_{x \to -\infty} f(x) = +\infty$$

as appropriate; and if the values of $f(x)$ decrease without bound as $x \to +\infty$ or as $x \to -\infty$, then we write

$$\lim_{x \to +\infty} f(x) = -\infty \quad \text{or} \quad \lim_{x \to -\infty} f(x) = -\infty$$

as appropriate.

■ **LIMITS OF x^n AS $x \to \pm\infty$**

Figure 1.3.5 illustrates the end behavior of the polynomials x^n for $n = 1, 2, 3,$ and 4. These are special cases of the following general results:

$$\lim_{x \to +\infty} x^n = +\infty, \quad n = 1, 2, 3, \ldots \qquad \lim_{x \to -\infty} x^n = \begin{cases} -\infty, & n = 1, 3, 5, \ldots \\ +\infty, & n = 2, 4, 6, \ldots \end{cases} \qquad (15\text{–}16)$$

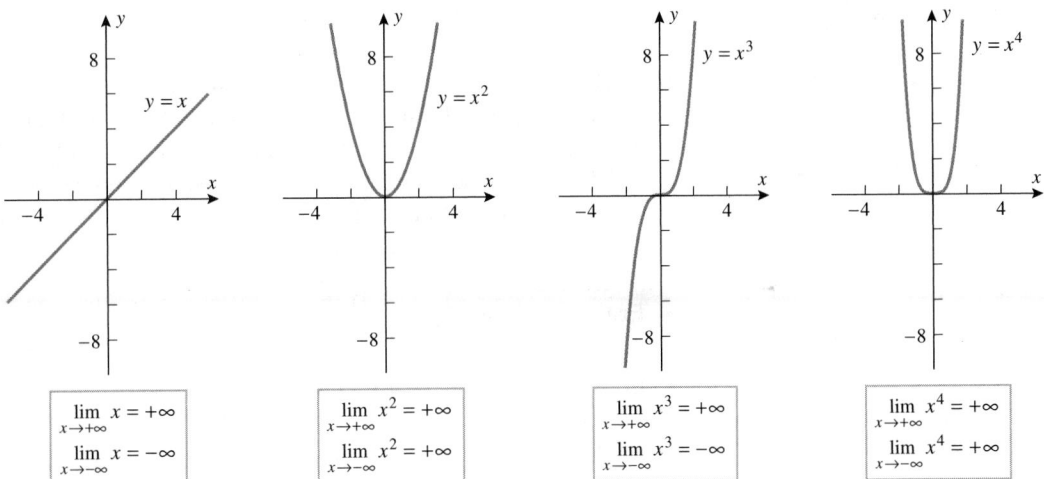

$$\lim_{x \to +\infty} x = +\infty$$
$$\lim_{x \to -\infty} x = -\infty$$

$$\lim_{x \to +\infty} x^2 = +\infty$$
$$\lim_{x \to -\infty} x^2 = +\infty$$

$$\lim_{x \to +\infty} x^3 = +\infty$$
$$\lim_{x \to -\infty} x^3 = -\infty$$

$$\lim_{x \to +\infty} x^4 = +\infty$$
$$\lim_{x \to -\infty} x^4 = +\infty$$

▲ **Figure 1.3.5**

Multiplying x^n by a positive real number does not affect limits (15) and (16), but multiplying by a negative real number reverses the sign.

▶ **Example 5**
$$\lim_{x \to +\infty} 2x^5 = +\infty, \qquad \lim_{x \to -\infty} 2x^5 = -\infty$$
$$\lim_{x \to +\infty} -7x^6 = -\infty, \qquad \lim_{x \to -\infty} -7x^6 = -\infty \ \blacktriangleleft$$

■ **LIMITS OF POLYNOMIALS AS $x \to \pm\infty$**

There is a useful principle about polynomials which, expressed informally, states:

The end behavior of a polynomial matches the end behavior of its highest degree term.

More precisely, if $c_n \neq 0$, then

$$\lim_{x \to -\infty} \left(c_0 + c_1 x + \cdots + c_n x^n \right) = \lim_{x \to -\infty} c_n x^n \tag{17}$$

$$\lim_{x \to +\infty} \left(c_0 + c_1 x + \cdots + c_n x^n \right) = \lim_{x \to +\infty} c_n x^n \tag{18}$$

We can motivate these results by factoring out the highest power of x from the polynomial and examining the limit of the factored expression. Thus,

$$c_0 + c_1 x + \cdots + c_n x^n = x^n \left(\frac{c_0}{x^n} + \frac{c_1}{x^{n-1}} + \cdots + c_n \right)$$

As $x \to -\infty$ or $x \to +\infty$, it follows from Example 4(a) that all of the terms with positive powers of x in the denominator approach 0, so (17) and (18) are certainly plausible.

▶ **Example 6**

$$\lim_{x \to -\infty} (7x^5 - 4x^3 + 2x - 9) = \lim_{x \to -\infty} 7x^5 = -\infty$$

$$\lim_{x \to -\infty} (-4x^8 + 17x^3 - 5x + 1) = \lim_{x \to -\infty} -4x^8 = -\infty \quad ◀$$

■ **LIMITS OF RATIONAL FUNCTIONS AS $x \to \pm\infty$**

One technique for determining the end behavior of a rational function is to divide each term in the numerator and denominator by the highest power of x that occurs in the denominator, after which the limiting behavior can be determined using results we have already established. Here are some examples.

▶ **Example 7** Find $\lim\limits_{x \to +\infty} \dfrac{3x + 5}{6x - 8}$.

Solution. Divide each term in the numerator and denominator by the highest power of x that occurs in the denominator, namely, $x^1 = x$. We obtain

$$\lim_{x \to +\infty} \frac{3x + 5}{6x - 8} = \lim_{x \to +\infty} \frac{3 + \dfrac{5}{x}}{6 - \dfrac{8}{x}} \qquad \boxed{\text{Divide each term by } x.}$$

$$= \frac{\lim\limits_{x \to +\infty} \left(3 + \dfrac{5}{x} \right)}{\lim\limits_{x \to +\infty} \left(6 - \dfrac{8}{x} \right)} \qquad \boxed{\begin{array}{l} \text{Limit of a quotient is the} \\ \text{quotient of the limits.} \end{array}}$$

$$= \frac{\lim\limits_{x \to +\infty} 3 + \lim\limits_{x \to +\infty} \dfrac{5}{x}}{\lim\limits_{x \to +\infty} 6 - \lim\limits_{x \to +\infty} \dfrac{8}{x}} \qquad \boxed{\begin{array}{l} \text{Limit of a sum is the} \\ \text{sum of the limits.} \end{array}}$$

$$= \frac{3 + 5 \lim\limits_{x \to +\infty} \dfrac{1}{x}}{6 - 8 \lim\limits_{x \to +\infty} \dfrac{1}{x}} = \frac{3 + 0}{6 + 0} = \frac{1}{2} \qquad \boxed{\begin{array}{l} \text{A constant can be moved through a} \\ \text{limit symbol; Formulas (2) and (13).} \end{array}} \quad ◀$$

▶ **Example 8** Find

$$\text{(a) } \lim_{x \to -\infty} \frac{4x^2 - x}{2x^3 - 5} \qquad \text{(b) } \lim_{x \to +\infty} \frac{5x^3 - 2x^2 + 1}{1 - 3x}$$

Solution (a). Divide each term in the numerator and denominator by the highest power of x that occurs in the denominator, namely, x^3. We obtain

$$\lim_{x \to -\infty} \frac{4x^2 - x}{2x^3 - 5} = \lim_{x \to -\infty} \frac{\dfrac{4}{x} - \dfrac{1}{x^2}}{2 - \dfrac{5}{x^3}} \qquad \boxed{\text{Divide each term by } x^3.}$$

$$= \frac{\lim\limits_{x \to -\infty} \left(\dfrac{4}{x} - \dfrac{1}{x^2} \right)}{\lim\limits_{x \to -\infty} \left(2 - \dfrac{5}{x^3} \right)} \qquad \boxed{\begin{array}{l}\text{Limit of a quotient is the}\\\text{quotient of the limits.}\end{array}}$$

$$= \frac{\lim\limits_{x \to -\infty} \dfrac{4}{x} - \lim\limits_{x \to -\infty} \dfrac{1}{x^2}}{\lim\limits_{x \to -\infty} 2 - \lim\limits_{x \to -\infty} \dfrac{5}{x^3}} \qquad \boxed{\begin{array}{l}\text{Limit of a difference is the}\\\text{difference of the limits.}\end{array}}$$

$$= \frac{4 \lim\limits_{x \to -\infty} \dfrac{1}{x} - \lim\limits_{x \to -\infty} \dfrac{1}{x^2}}{2 - 5 \lim\limits_{x \to -\infty} \dfrac{1}{x^3}} = \frac{0 - 0}{2 - 0} = 0 \qquad \boxed{\begin{array}{l}\text{A constant can be moved through}\\\text{a limit symbol; Formula (14) and}\\\text{Example 4.}\end{array}}$$

Solution (b). Divide each term in the numerator and denominator by the highest power of x that occurs in the denominator, namely, $x^1 = x$. We obtain

$$\lim_{x \to +\infty} \frac{5x^3 - 2x^2 + 1}{1 - 3x} = \lim_{x \to +\infty} \frac{5x^2 - 2x + \dfrac{1}{x}}{\dfrac{1}{x} - 3} \qquad (19)$$

In this case we cannot argue that the limit of the quotient is the quotient of the limits because the limit of the numerator does not exist. However, we have

$$\lim_{x \to +\infty} 5x^2 - 2x = +\infty, \qquad \lim_{x \to +\infty} \frac{1}{x} = 0, \qquad \lim_{x \to +\infty} \left(\frac{1}{x} - 3 \right) = -3$$

Thus, the numerator on the right side of (19) approaches $+\infty$ and the denominator has a finite *negative* limit. We conclude from this that the quotient approaches $-\infty$; that is,

$$\lim_{x \to +\infty} \frac{5x^3 - 2x^2 + 1}{1 - 3x} = \lim_{x \to +\infty} \frac{5x^2 - 2x + \dfrac{1}{x}}{\dfrac{1}{x} - 3} = -\infty \quad \blacktriangleleft$$

■ A QUICK METHOD FOR FINDING LIMITS OF RATIONAL FUNCTIONS AS $x \to +\infty$ OR $x \to -\infty$

Since the end behavior of a polynomial matches the end behavior of its highest degree term, one can reasonably conclude:

> *The end behavior of a rational function matches the end behavior of the quotient of the highest degree term in the numerator divided by the highest degree term in the denominator.*

▶ **Example 9**   Use the preceding observation to compute the limits in Examples 7 and 8.

Solution.

$$\lim_{x \to +\infty} \frac{3x + 5}{6x - 8} = \lim_{x \to +\infty} \frac{3x}{6x} = \lim_{x \to +\infty} \frac{1}{2} = \frac{1}{2}$$

$$\lim_{x \to -\infty} \frac{4x^2 - x}{2x^3 - 5} = \lim_{x \to -\infty} \frac{4x^2}{2x^3} = \lim_{x \to -\infty} \frac{2}{x} = 0$$

$$\lim_{x \to +\infty} \frac{5x^3 - 2x^2 + 1}{1 - 3x} = \lim_{x \to +\infty} \frac{5x^3}{(-3x)} = \lim_{x \to +\infty} \left(-\frac{5}{3}x^2\right) = -\infty \quad ◀$$

■ **LIMITS INVOLVING RADICALS**

▶ **Example 10**   Find

$$\text{(a)} \quad \lim_{x \to +\infty} \frac{\sqrt{x^2 + 2}}{3x - 6} \qquad \text{(b)} \quad \lim_{x \to -\infty} \frac{\sqrt{x^2 + 2}}{3x - 6}$$

In both parts it would be helpful to manipulate the function so that the powers of x are transformed to powers of $1/x$. This can be achieved in both cases by dividing the numerator and denominator by $|x|$ and using the fact that $\sqrt{x^2} = |x|$.

Solution (a).   As $x \to +\infty$, the values of x under consideration are positive, so we can replace $|x|$ by x where helpful. We obtain

$$\lim_{x \to +\infty} \frac{\sqrt{x^2 + 2}}{3x - 6} = \lim_{x \to +\infty} \frac{\dfrac{\sqrt{x^2 + 2}}{|x|}}{\dfrac{3x - 6}{|x|}} = \lim_{x \to +\infty} \frac{\dfrac{\sqrt{x^2 + 2}}{\sqrt{x^2}}}{\dfrac{3x - 6}{x}}$$

$$= \lim_{x \to +\infty} \frac{\sqrt{1 + \dfrac{2}{x^2}}}{3 - \dfrac{6}{x}} = \frac{\displaystyle\lim_{x \to +\infty} \sqrt{1 + \dfrac{2}{x^2}}}{\displaystyle\lim_{x \to +\infty}\left(3 - \dfrac{6}{x}\right)}$$

$$= \frac{\sqrt{\displaystyle\lim_{x \to +\infty}\left(1 + \dfrac{2}{x^2}\right)}}{\displaystyle\lim_{x \to +\infty}\left(3 - \dfrac{6}{x}\right)} = \frac{\sqrt{\left(\displaystyle\lim_{x \to +\infty} 1\right) + \left(2 \displaystyle\lim_{x \to +\infty}\dfrac{1}{x^2}\right)}}{\left(\displaystyle\lim_{x \to +\infty} 3\right) - \left(6 \displaystyle\lim_{x \to +\infty}\dfrac{1}{x}\right)}$$

$$= \frac{\sqrt{1 + (2 \cdot 0)}}{3 - (6 \cdot 0)} = \frac{1}{3}$$

It follows from Example 10 that the function

$$f(x) = \frac{\sqrt{x^2 + 2}}{3x - 6}$$

has an asymptote of $y = \frac{1}{3}$ in the positive direction and an asymptote of $y = -\frac{1}{3}$ in the negative direction. Confirm this using a graphing utility.

Solution (b).   As $x \to -\infty$, the values of x under consideration are negative, so we can replace $|x|$ by $-x$ where helpful. We obtain

$$\lim_{x \to -\infty} \frac{\sqrt{x^2 + 2}}{3x - 6} = \lim_{x \to -\infty} \frac{\dfrac{\sqrt{x^2 + 2}}{|x|}}{\dfrac{3x - 6}{|x|}} = \lim_{x \to -\infty} \frac{\dfrac{\sqrt{x^2 + 2}}{\sqrt{x^2}}}{\dfrac{3x - 6}{(-x)}}$$

$$= \lim_{x \to -\infty} \frac{\sqrt{1 + \dfrac{2}{x^2}}}{-3 + \dfrac{6}{x}} = -\frac{1}{3} \quad ◀$$

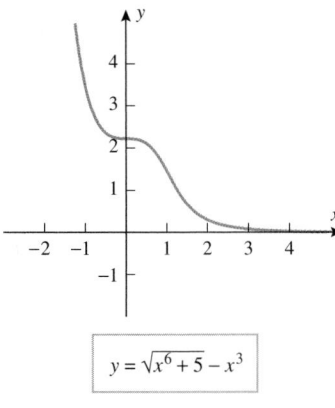

$$y = \sqrt{x^6 + 5} - x^3$$

(a)

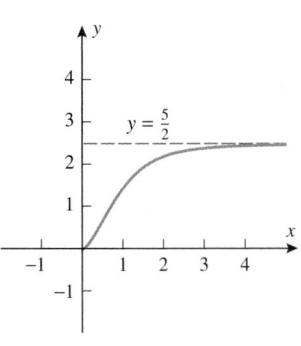

$$y = \sqrt{x^6 + 5x^3} - x^3, \ x \geq 0$$

(b)

▲ **Figure 1.3.6**

We noted in Section 1.1 that the standard rules of algebra do not apply to the symbols $+\infty$ and $-\infty$. Part (b) of Example 11 illustrates this. The terms $\sqrt{x^6 + 5x^3}$ and x^3 both approach $+\infty$ as $x \to +\infty$, but their difference does not approach 0.

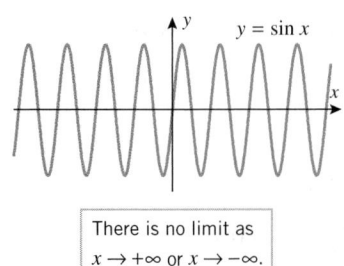

There is no limit as $x \to +\infty$ or $x \to -\infty$.

▲ **Figure 1.3.7**

▶ **Example 11** Find

$$\text{(a) } \lim_{x \to +\infty} (\sqrt{x^6 + 5} - x^3) \qquad \text{(b) } \lim_{x \to +\infty} (\sqrt{x^6 + 5x^3} - x^3)$$

Solution. Graphs of the functions $f(x) = \sqrt{x^6 + 5} - x^3$, and $g(x) = \sqrt{x^6 + 5x^3} - x^3$ for $x \geq 0$, are shown in Figure 1.3.6. From the graphs we might conjecture that the requested limits are 0 and $\frac{5}{2}$, respectively. To confirm this, we treat each function as a fraction with a denominator of 1 and rationalize the numerator.

$$\lim_{x \to +\infty} (\sqrt{x^6 + 5} - x^3) = \lim_{x \to +\infty} (\sqrt{x^6 + 5} - x^3) \left(\frac{\sqrt{x^6 + 5} + x^3}{\sqrt{x^6 + 5} + x^3} \right)$$

$$= \lim_{x \to +\infty} \frac{(x^6 + 5) - x^6}{\sqrt{x^6 + 5} + x^3} = \lim_{x \to +\infty} \frac{5}{\sqrt{x^6 + 5} + x^3}$$

$$= \lim_{x \to +\infty} \frac{\dfrac{5}{x^3}}{\sqrt{1 + \dfrac{5}{x^6}} + 1} \qquad \boxed{\sqrt{x^6} = x^3 \text{ for } x > 0}$$

$$= \frac{0}{\sqrt{1 + 0} + 1} = 0$$

$$\lim_{x \to +\infty} (\sqrt{x^6 + 5x^3} - x^3) = \lim_{x \to +\infty} (\sqrt{x^6 + 5x^3} - x^3) \left(\frac{\sqrt{x^6 + 5x^3} + x^3}{\sqrt{x^6 + 5x^3} + x^3} \right)$$

$$= \lim_{x \to +\infty} \frac{(x^6 + 5x^3) - x^6}{\sqrt{x^6 + 5x^3} + x^3} = \lim_{x \to +\infty} \frac{5x^3}{\sqrt{x^6 + 5x^3} + x^3}$$

$$= \lim_{x \to +\infty} \frac{5}{\sqrt{1 + \dfrac{5}{x^3}} + 1} \qquad \boxed{\sqrt{x^6} = x^3 \text{ for } x > 0}$$

$$= \frac{5}{\sqrt{1 + 0} + 1} = \frac{5}{2} \blacktriangleleft$$

▨ **END BEHAVIOR OF TRIGONOMETRIC, EXPONENTIAL, AND LOGARITHMIC FUNCTIONS**

Consider the function $f(x) = \sin x$ that is graphed in Figure 1.3.7. For this function the limits as $x \to +\infty$ and as $x \to -\infty$ fail to exist not because $f(x)$ increases or decreases without bound, but rather because the values vary between -1 and 1 without approaching some specific real number. In general, the trigonometric functions fail to have limits as $x \to +\infty$ and as $x \to -\infty$ because of periodicity. There is no specific notation to denote this kind of behavior.

In Section 0.5 we showed that the functions e^x and $\ln x$ both increase without bound as $x \to +\infty$ (Figures 0.5.8 and 0.5.9). Thus, in limit notation we have

$$\lim_{x \to +\infty} \ln x = +\infty \qquad \lim_{x \to +\infty} e^x = +\infty \qquad (20\text{–}21)$$

For reference, we also list the following limits, which are consistent with the graphs in Figure 1.3.8:

$$\lim_{x \to -\infty} e^x = 0 \qquad \lim_{x \to 0^+} \ln x = -\infty \qquad (22\text{–}23)$$

▲ **Figure 1.3.8**   ▲ **Figure 1.3.9**

Finally, the following limits can be deduced by noting that the graph of $y = e^{-x}$ is the reflection about the y-axis of the graph of $y = e^x$ (Figure 1.3.9).

$$\lim_{x \to +\infty} e^{-x} = 0 \qquad \lim_{x \to -\infty} e^{-x} = +\infty \qquad (24\text{--}25)$$

✔ **QUICK CHECK EXERCISES 1.3**   (*See page 100 for answers.*)

1. Find the limits.
   (a) $\displaystyle\lim_{x \to -\infty} (3 - x) = $ _____
   (b) $\displaystyle\lim_{x \to +\infty} \left(5 - \frac{1}{x}\right) = $ _____
   (c) $\displaystyle\lim_{x \to +\infty} \ln\left(\frac{1}{x}\right) = $ _____
   (d) $\displaystyle\lim_{x \to +\infty} \frac{1}{e^x} = $ _____

2. Find the limits that exist.
   (a) $\displaystyle\lim_{x \to -\infty} \frac{2x^2 + x}{4x^2 - 3} = $ _____
   (b) $\displaystyle\lim_{x \to +\infty} \frac{1}{2 + \sin x} = $ _____
   (c) $\displaystyle\lim_{x \to +\infty} \left(1 + \frac{1}{x}\right)^x = $ _____

3. Given that
   $$\lim_{x \to +\infty} f(x) = 2 \quad \text{and} \quad \lim_{x \to +\infty} g(x) = -3$$
   find the limits that exist.
   (a) $\displaystyle\lim_{x \to +\infty} [3f(x) - g(x)] = $ _____
   (b) $\displaystyle\lim_{x \to +\infty} \frac{f(x)}{g(x)} = $ _____
   (c) $\displaystyle\lim_{x \to +\infty} \frac{2f(x) + 3g(x)}{3f(x) + 2g(x)} = $ _____
   (d) $\displaystyle\lim_{x \to +\infty} \sqrt{10 - f(x)g(x)} = $ _____

4. Consider the graphs of $1/x$, $\sin x$, $\ln x$, e^x, and e^{-x}. Which of these graphs has a horizontal asymptote?

EXERCISE SET 1.3   〰 Graphing Utility

1–4 In these exercises, make reasonable assumptions about the end behavior of the indicated function. ▨

1. For the function g graphed in the accompanying figure, find
   (a) $\displaystyle\lim_{x \to -\infty} g(x)$ (b) $\displaystyle\lim_{x \to +\infty} g(x)$.

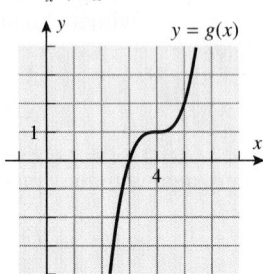

◀ **Figure Ex-1**

2. For the function ϕ graphed in the accompanying figure, find
   (a) $\displaystyle\lim_{x \to -\infty} \phi(x)$
   (b) $\displaystyle\lim_{x \to +\infty} \phi(x)$.

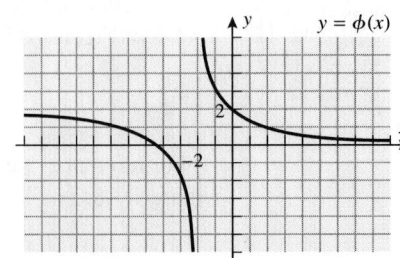

◀ **Figure Ex-2**

3. For the function ϕ graphed in the accompanying figure, find
(a) $\lim\limits_{x \to -\infty} \phi(x)$
(b) $\lim\limits_{x \to +\infty} \phi(x)$.

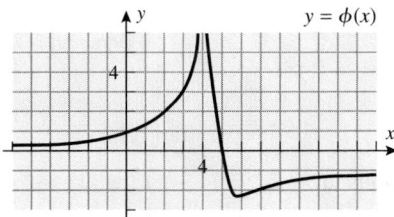

◄ **Figure Ex-3**

4. For the function G graphed in the accompanying figure, find
(a) $\lim\limits_{x \to -\infty} G(x)$
(b) $\lim\limits_{x \to +\infty} G(x)$.

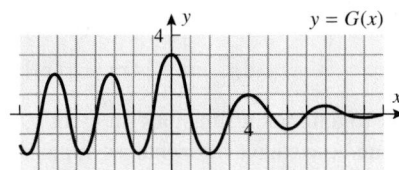

◄ **Figure Ex-4**

5. Given that
$$\lim\limits_{x \to +\infty} f(x) = 3, \quad \lim\limits_{x \to +\infty} g(x) = -5, \quad \lim\limits_{x \to +\infty} h(x) = 0$$
find the limits that exist. If the limit does not exist, explain why.
(a) $\lim\limits_{x \to +\infty} [f(x) + 3g(x)]$
(b) $\lim\limits_{x \to +\infty} [h(x) - 4g(x) + 1]$
(c) $\lim\limits_{x \to +\infty} [f(x)g(x)]$
(d) $\lim\limits_{x \to +\infty} [g(x)]^2$
(e) $\lim\limits_{x \to +\infty} \sqrt[3]{5 + f(x)}$
(f) $\lim\limits_{x \to +\infty} \dfrac{3}{g(x)}$
(g) $\lim\limits_{x \to +\infty} \dfrac{3h(x) + 4}{x^2}$
(h) $\lim\limits_{x \to +\infty} \dfrac{6f(x)}{5f(x) + 3g(x)}$

6. Given that
$$\lim\limits_{x \to -\infty} f(x) = 7 \quad \text{and} \quad \lim\limits_{x \to -\infty} g(x) = -6$$
find the limits that exist. If the limit does not exist, explain why.
(a) $\lim\limits_{x \to -\infty} [2f(x) - g(x)]$
(b) $\lim\limits_{x \to -\infty} [6f(x) + 7g(x)]$
(c) $\lim\limits_{x \to -\infty} [x^2 + g(x)]$
(d) $\lim\limits_{x \to -\infty} [x^2 g(x)]$
(e) $\lim\limits_{x \to -\infty} \sqrt[3]{f(x)g(x)}$
(f) $\lim\limits_{x \to -\infty} \dfrac{g(x)}{f(x)}$
(g) $\lim\limits_{x \to -\infty} \left[f(x) + \dfrac{g(x)}{x} \right]$
(h) $\lim\limits_{x \to -\infty} \dfrac{xf(x)}{(2x + 3)g(x)}$

7. (a) Complete the table and make a guess about the limit indicated.
$$f(x) = \tan^{-1}\left(\dfrac{1}{x}\right) \quad \lim\limits_{x \to 0^+} f(x)$$

x	0.1	0.01	0.001	0.0001	0.00001	0.000001
$f(x)$						

(b) Use Figure 1.3.3 to find the exact value of the limit in part (a).

8. Complete the table and make a guess about the limit indicated.
$$f(x) = x^{1/x} \quad \lim\limits_{x \to +\infty} f(x)$$

x	10	100	1000	10,000	100,000	1,000,000
$f(x)$						

9–40 Find the limits. ◾

9. $\lim\limits_{x \to +\infty} (1 + 2x - 3x^5)$

10. $\lim\limits_{x \to +\infty} (2x^3 - 100x + 5)$

11. $\lim\limits_{x \to +\infty} \sqrt{x}$

12. $\lim\limits_{x \to -\infty} \sqrt{5 - x}$

13. $\lim\limits_{x \to +\infty} \dfrac{3x + 1}{2x - 5}$

14. $\lim\limits_{x \to +\infty} \dfrac{5x^2 - 4x}{2x^2 + 3}$

15. $\lim\limits_{y \to -\infty} \dfrac{3}{y + 4}$

16. $\lim\limits_{x \to +\infty} \dfrac{1}{x - 12}$

17. $\lim\limits_{x \to -\infty} \dfrac{x - 2}{x^2 + 2x + 1}$

18. $\lim\limits_{x \to +\infty} \dfrac{5x^2 + 7}{3x^2 - x}$

19. $\lim\limits_{x \to +\infty} \dfrac{7 - 6x^5}{x + 3}$

20. $\lim\limits_{t \to -\infty} \dfrac{5 - 2t^3}{t^2 + 1}$

21. $\lim\limits_{t \to +\infty} \dfrac{6 - t^3}{7t^3 + 3}$

22. $\lim\limits_{x \to -\infty} \dfrac{x + 4x^3}{1 - x^2 + 7x^3}$

23. $\lim\limits_{x \to +\infty} \sqrt[3]{\dfrac{2 + 3x - 5x^2}{1 + 8x^2}}$

24. $\lim\limits_{s \to +\infty} \sqrt[3]{\dfrac{3s^7 - 4s^5}{2s^7 + 1}}$

25. $\lim\limits_{x \to -\infty} \dfrac{\sqrt{5x^2 - 2}}{x + 3}$

26. $\lim\limits_{x \to +\infty} \dfrac{\sqrt{5x^2 - 2}}{x + 3}$

27. $\lim\limits_{y \to -\infty} \dfrac{2 - y}{\sqrt{7 + 6y^2}}$

28. $\lim\limits_{y \to +\infty} \dfrac{2 - y}{\sqrt{7 + 6y^2}}$

29. $\lim\limits_{x \to -\infty} \dfrac{\sqrt{3x^4 + x}}{x^2 - 8}$

30. $\lim\limits_{x \to +\infty} \dfrac{\sqrt{3x^4 + x}}{x^2 - 8}$

31. $\lim\limits_{x \to +\infty} (\sqrt{x^2 + 3} - x)$

32. $\lim\limits_{x \to +\infty} (\sqrt{x^2 - 3x} - x)$

33. $\lim\limits_{x \to -\infty} \dfrac{1 - e^x}{1 + e^x}$

34. $\lim\limits_{x \to +\infty} \dfrac{1 - e^x}{1 + e^x}$

35. $\lim\limits_{x \to +\infty} \dfrac{e^x + e^{-x}}{e^x - e^{-x}}$

36. $\lim\limits_{x \to -\infty} \dfrac{e^x + e^{-x}}{e^x - e^{-x}}$

37. $\lim\limits_{x \to +\infty} \ln\left(\dfrac{2}{x^2}\right)$

38. $\lim\limits_{x \to 0^+} \ln\left(\dfrac{2}{x^2}\right)$

39. $\lim\limits_{x \to +\infty} \dfrac{(x + 1)^x}{x^x}$

40. $\lim\limits_{x \to +\infty} \left(1 + \dfrac{1}{x}\right)^{-x}$

41–44 True–False Determine whether the statement is true or false. Explain your answer. ◾

41. We have $\lim\limits_{x \to +\infty} \left(1 + \dfrac{1}{x}\right)^{2x} = (1 + 0)^{+\infty} = 1^{+\infty} = 1$.

42. If $y = L$ is a horizontal asymptote for the curve $y = f(x)$, then

$$\lim_{x \to -\infty} f(x) = L \quad \text{and} \quad \lim_{x \to +\infty} f(x) = L$$

43. If $y = L$ is a horizontal asymptote for the curve $y = f(x)$, then it is possible for the graph of f to intersect the line $y = L$ infinitely many times.

44. If a rational function $p(x)/q(x)$ has a horizontal asymptote, then the degree of $p(x)$ must equal the degree of $q(x)$.

FOCUS ON CONCEPTS

45. Assume that a particle is accelerated by a constant force. The two curves $v = n(t)$ and $v = e(t)$ in the accompanying figure provide velocity versus time curves for the particle as predicted by classical physics and by the special theory of relativity, respectively. The parameter c represents the speed of light. Using the language of limits, describe the differences in the long-term predictions of the two theories.

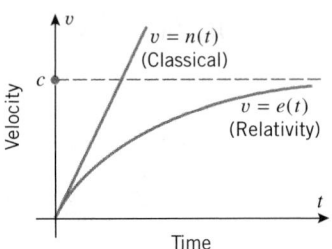

◀ **Figure Ex-45**

46. Let $T = f(t)$ denote the temperature of a baked potato t minutes after it has been removed from a hot oven. The accompanying figure shows the temperature versus time curve for the potato, where r is the temperature of the room.
   (a) What is the physical significance of $\lim_{t \to 0^+} f(t)$?
   (b) What is the physical significance of $\lim_{t \to +\infty} f(t)$?

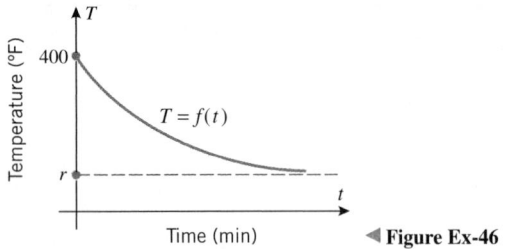

◀ **Figure Ex-46**

47. Let

$$f(x) = \begin{cases} 2x^2 + 5, & x < 0 \\ \dfrac{3 - 5x^3}{1 + 4x + x^3}, & x \geq 0 \end{cases}$$

Find
   (a) $\lim_{x \to -\infty} f(x)$
   (b) $\lim_{x \to +\infty} f(x)$.

48. Let

$$g(t) = \begin{cases} \dfrac{2 + 3t}{5t^2 + 6}, & t < 1{,}000{,}000 \\[2mm] \dfrac{\sqrt{36t^2 - 100}}{5 - t}, & t > 1{,}000{,}000 \end{cases}$$

Find
   (a) $\lim_{t \to -\infty} g(t)$
   (b) $\lim_{t \to +\infty} g(t)$.

49. Discuss the limits of $p(x) = (1 - x)^n$ as $x \to +\infty$ and $x \to -\infty$ for positive integer values of n.

50. In each part, find examples of polynomials $p(x)$ and $q(x)$ that satisfy the stated condition and such that $p(x) \to +\infty$ and $q(x) \to +\infty$ as $x \to +\infty$.
   (a) $\lim_{x \to +\infty} \dfrac{p(x)}{q(x)} = 1$
   (b) $\lim_{x \to +\infty} \dfrac{p(x)}{q(x)} = 0$
   (c) $\lim_{x \to +\infty} \dfrac{p(x)}{q(x)} = +\infty$
   (d) $\lim_{x \to +\infty} [p(x) - q(x)] = 3$

51. (a) Do any of the trigonometric functions $\sin x, \cos x, \tan x, \cot x, \sec x,$ and $\csc x$ have horizontal asymptotes?
   (b) Do any of the trigonometric functions have vertical asymptotes? Where?

52. Find

$$\lim_{x \to +\infty} \frac{c_0 + c_1 x + \cdots + c_n x^n}{d_0 + d_1 x + \cdots + d_m x^m}$$

where $c_n \neq 0$ and $d_m \neq 0$. [*Hint:* Your answer will depend on whether $m < n$, $m = n$, or $m > n$.]

FOCUS ON CONCEPTS

53–54 These exercises develop some versions of the *substitution principle*, a useful tool for the evaluation of limits.

53. (a) Explain why we can evaluate $\lim_{x \to +\infty} e^{x^2}$ by making the substitution $t = x^2$ and writing

$$\lim_{x \to +\infty} e^{x^2} = \lim_{t \to +\infty} e^t = +\infty$$

   (b) Suppose $g(x) \to +\infty$ as $x \to +\infty$. Given any function $f(x)$, explain why we can evaluate $\lim_{x \to +\infty} f[g(x)]$ by substituting $t = g(x)$ and writing

$$\lim_{x \to +\infty} f[g(x)] = \lim_{t \to +\infty} f(t)$$

   (Here, "equality" is interpreted to mean that either both limits exist and are equal or that both limits fail to exist.)
   (c) Why does the result in part (b) remain valid if $\lim_{x \to +\infty}$ is replaced everywhere by one of $\lim_{x \to -\infty}, \lim_{x \to c}, \lim_{x \to c^-}$, or $\lim_{x \to c^+}$?

54. (a) Explain why we can evaluate $\lim_{x \to +\infty} e^{-x^2}$ by making the substitution $t = -x^2$ and writing

$$\lim_{x \to +\infty} e^{-x^2} = \lim_{t \to -\infty} e^t = 0 \qquad \text{(cont.)}$$

(b) Suppose $g(x) \to -\infty$ as $x \to +\infty$. Given any function $f(x)$, explain why we can evaluate $\lim_{x \to +\infty} f[g(x)]$ by substituting $t = g(x)$ and writing

$$\lim_{x \to +\infty} f[g(x)] = \lim_{t \to -\infty} f(t)$$

(Here, "equality" is interpreted to mean that either both limits exist and are equal or that both limits fail to exist.)

(c) Why does the result in part (b) remain valid if $\lim_{x \to +\infty}$ is replaced everywhere by one of $\lim_{x \to -\infty}$, $\lim_{x \to c}$, $\lim_{x \to c^-}$, or $\lim_{x \to c^+}$?

55–62 Evaluate the limit using an appropriate substitution. ■

55. $\lim_{x \to 0^+} e^{1/x}$

56. $\lim_{x \to 0^-} e^{1/x}$

57. $\lim_{x \to 0^+} e^{\csc x}$

58. $\lim_{x \to 0^-} e^{\csc x}$

59. $\lim_{x \to +\infty} \dfrac{\ln 2x}{\ln 3x}$ [*Hint: $t = \ln x$*]

60. $\lim_{x \to +\infty} [\ln(x^2 - 1) - \ln(x + 1)]$ [*Hint: $t = x - 1$*]

61. $\lim_{x \to +\infty} \left(1 - \dfrac{1}{x}\right)^{-x}$ [*Hint: $t = -x$*]

62. $\lim_{x \to +\infty} \left(1 + \dfrac{2}{x}\right)^{x}$ [*Hint: $t = x/2$*]

63. Let $f(x) = b^x$, where $0 < b$. Use the substitution principle to verify the asymptotic behavior of f that is illustrated in Figure 0.5.1. [*Hint: $f(x) = b^x = (e^{\ln b})^x = e^{(\ln b)x}$*]

64. Prove that $\lim_{x \to 0} (1 + x)^{1/x} = e$ by completing parts (a) and (b).
(a) Use Equation (7) and the substitution $t = 1/x$ to prove that $\lim_{x \to 0^+} (1 + x)^{1/x} = e$.
(b) Use Equation (8) and the substitution $t = 1/x$ to prove that $\lim_{x \to 0^-} (1 + x)^{1/x} = e$.

65. Suppose that the speed v (in ft/s) of a skydiver t seconds after leaping from a plane is given by the equation $v = 190(1 - e^{-0.168t})$.
(a) Graph v versus t.
(b) By evaluating an appropriate limit, show that the graph of v versus t has a horizontal asymptote $v = c$ for an appropriate constant c.
(c) What is the physical significance of the constant c in part (b)?

66. The population p of the United States (in millions) in year t may be modeled by the function

$$p = \frac{50371.7}{151.3 + 181.626e^{-0.031636(t-1950)}}$$

(a) Based on this model, what was the U.S. population in 1950?
(b) Plot p versus t for the 200-year period from 1950 to 2150.

(c) By evaluating an appropriate limit, show that the graph of p versus t has a horizontal asymptote $p = c$ for an appropriate constant c.
(d) What is the significance of the constant c in part (b) for population predicted by this model?

67. (a) Compute the (approximate) values of the terms in the sequence

$$1.01^{101}, \ 1.001^{1001}, \ 1.0001^{10001}, \ 1.00001^{100001},$$
$$1.000001^{1000001}, \ 1.0000001^{10000001} \ldots$$

What number do these terms appear to be approaching?
(b) Use Equation (7) to verify your answer in part (a).
(c) Let $1 \le a \le 9$ denote a positive integer. What number is approached more and more closely by the terms in the following sequence?

$$1.01^{a0a}, \ 1.001^{a00a}, \ 1.0001^{a000a}, \ 1.00001^{a0000a},$$
$$1.000001^{a00000a}, \ 1.0000001^{a000000a} \ldots$$

(The powers are positive integers that begin and end with the digit a and have 0's in the remaining positions).

68. Let $f(x) = \left(1 + \dfrac{1}{x}\right)^x$.
(a) Prove the identity

$$f(-x) = \frac{x}{x - 1} \cdot f(x - 1)$$

(b) Use Equation (7) and the identity from part (a) to prove Equation (8).

69–73 The notion of an asymptote can be extended to include curves as well as lines. Specifically, we say that curves $y = f(x)$ and $y = g(x)$ are *asymptotic as $x \to +\infty$* provided

$$\lim_{x \to +\infty} [f(x) - g(x)] = 0$$

and are *asymptotic as $x \to -\infty$* provided

$$\lim_{x \to -\infty} [f(x) - g(x)] = 0$$

In these exercises, determine a simpler function $g(x)$ such that $y = f(x)$ is asymptotic to $y = g(x)$ as $x \to +\infty$ or $x \to -\infty$. Use a graphing utility to generate the graphs of $y = f(x)$ and $y = g(x)$ and identify all vertical asymptotes. ■

69. $f(x) = \dfrac{x^2 - 2}{x - 2}$ [*Hint: Divide $x - 2$ into $x^2 - 2$.*]

70. $f(x) = \dfrac{x^3 - x + 3}{x}$

71. $f(x) = \dfrac{-x^3 + 3x^2 + x - 1}{x - 3}$

72. $f(x) = \dfrac{x^5 - x^3 + 3}{x^2 - 1}$

73. $f(x) = \sin x + \dfrac{1}{x - 1}$

74. Writing In some models for learning a skill (e.g., juggling), it is assumed that the skill level for an individual increases with practice but cannot become arbitrarily high. How do concepts of this section apply to such a model?

75. Writing In some population models it is assumed that a given ecological system possesses a ***carrying capacity*** L. Populations greater than the carrying capacity tend to decline toward L, while populations less than the carrying capacity tend to increase toward L. Explain why these assumptions are reasonable, and discuss how the concepts of this section apply to such a model.

✔ **QUICK CHECK ANSWERS 1.3**

1. (a) $+\infty$ (b) 5 (c) $-\infty$ (d) 0 **2.** (a) $\frac{1}{2}$ (b) does not exist (c) e **3.** (a) 9 (b) $-\frac{2}{3}$ (c) does not exist (d) 4
4. $1/x$, e^x, and e^{-x} each has a horizontal asymptote.

1.4 LIMITS (DISCUSSED MORE RIGOROUSLY)

In the previous sections of this chapter we focused on the discovery of values of limits, either by sampling selected x-values or by applying limit theorems that were stated without proof. Our main goal in this section is to define the notion of a limit precisely, thereby making it possible to establish limits with certainty and to prove theorems about them. This will also provide us with a deeper understanding of some of the more subtle properties of functions.

■ **MOTIVATION FOR THE DEFINITION OF A TWO-SIDED LIMIT**

The statement $\lim_{x \to a} f(x) = L$ can be interpreted informally to mean that we can make the value of $f(x)$ as close as we like to the real number L by making the value of x sufficiently close to a. It is our goal to make the informal phrases "as close as we like to L" and "sufficiently close to a" mathematically precise.

To do this, consider the function f graphed in Figure 1.4.1a for which $f(x) \to L$ as $x \to a$. For visual simplicity we have drawn the graph of f to be increasing on an open interval containing a, and we have intentionally placed a hole in the graph at $x = a$ to emphasize that f need not be defined at $x = a$ to have a limit there.

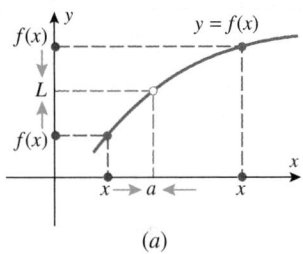 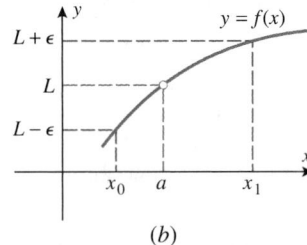 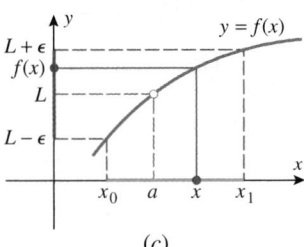

(a)   (b)   (c)

▲ **Figure 1.4.1**

Next, let us choose any positive number ϵ and ask how close x must be to a in order for the values of $f(x)$ to be within ϵ units of L. We can answer this geometrically by drawing horizontal lines from the points $L + \epsilon$ and $L - \epsilon$ on the y-axis until they meet the curve $y = f(x)$, and then drawing vertical lines from those points on the curve to the x-axis (Figure 1.4.1b). As indicated in the figure, let x_0 and x_1 be the points where those vertical lines intersect the x-axis.

Now imagine that x gets closer and closer to a (from either side). Eventually, x will lie inside the interval (x_0, x_1), which is marked in green in Figure 1.4.1c; and when this happens, the value of $f(x)$ will fall between $L - \epsilon$ and $L + \epsilon$, marked in red in the figure. Thus, we conclude:

> *If $f(x) \to L$ as $x \to a$, then for any positive number ϵ, we can find an open interval (x_0, x_1) on the x-axis that contains a and has the property that for each x in that interval (except possibly for $x = a$), the value of $f(x)$ is between $L - \epsilon$ and $L + \epsilon$.*

What is important about this result is that it holds no matter how small we make ϵ. However, making ϵ smaller and smaller forces $f(x)$ *closer and closer* to L—which is precisely the concept we were trying to capture mathematically.

Observe that in Figure 1.4.1 the interval (x_0, x_1) extends farther on the right side of a than on the left side. However, for many purposes it is preferable to have an interval that extends the same distance on both sides of a. For this purpose, let us choose any positive number δ that is smaller than both $x_1 - a$ and $a - x_0$, and consider the interval

$$(a - \delta, a + \delta)$$

This interval extends the same distance δ on both sides of a and lies inside of the interval (x_0, x_1) (Figure 1.4.2). Moreover, the condition

$$L - \epsilon < f(x) < L + \epsilon \qquad (1)$$

holds for every x in this interval (except possibly $x = a$), since this condition holds on the larger interval (x_0, x_1).

Since (1) can be expressed as

$$|f(x) - L| < \epsilon$$

and the condition that x lies in the interval $(a - \delta, a + \delta)$, but $x \neq a$, can be expressed as

$$0 < |x - a| < \delta$$

we are led to the following precise definition of a two-sided limit.

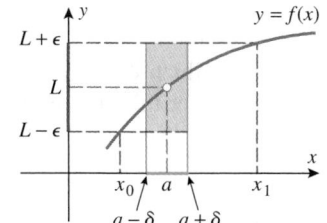

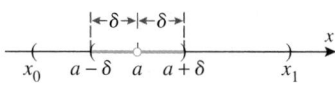

▲ **Figure 1.4.2**

The definitions of one-sided limits require minor adjustments to Definition 1.4.1. For example, for a limit from the right we need only assume that $f(x)$ is defined on an interval (a, b) extending to the right of a and that the ϵ condition is met for x in an interval $a < x < a + \delta$ extending to the right of a. A similar adjustment must be made for a limit from the left. (See Exercise 27.)

1.4.1 LIMIT DEFINITION Let $f(x)$ be defined for all x in some open interval containing the number a, with the possible exception that $f(x)$ need not be defined at a. We will write

$$\lim_{x \to a} f(x) = L$$

if given any number $\epsilon > 0$ we can find a number $\delta > 0$ such that

$$|f(x) - L| < \epsilon \quad \text{if} \quad 0 < |x - a| < \delta$$

This definition, which is attributed to the German mathematician Karl Weierstrass and is commonly called the "epsilon-delta" definition of a two-sided limit, makes the transition from an informal concept of a limit to a precise definition. Specifically, the informal phrase "as close as we like to L" is given quantitative meaning by our ability to choose the positive number ϵ arbitrarily, and the phrase "sufficiently close to a" is quantified by the positive number δ.

In the preceding sections we illustrated various numerical and graphical methods for *guessing* at limits. Now that we have a precise definition to work with, we can actually confirm the validity of those guesses with mathematical proof. Here is a typical example of such a proof.

▶ **Example 1**   Use Definition 1.4.1 to prove that $\lim\limits_{x \to 2} (3x - 5) = 1$.

Solution.   We must show that given any positive number ϵ, we can find a positive number δ such that

$$| \underbrace{(3x - 5)}_{f(x)} - \underbrace{1}_{L} | < \epsilon \quad \text{if} \quad 0 < |x - \underbrace{2}_{a}| < \delta \tag{2}$$

There are two things to do. First, we must *discover* a value of δ for which this statement holds, and then we must *prove* that the statement holds for that δ. For the discovery part we begin by simplifying (2) and writing it as

$$|3x - 6| < \epsilon \quad \text{if} \quad 0 < |x - 2| < \delta$$

Next we will rewrite this statement in a form that will facilitate the discovery of an appropriate δ:

$$3|x - 2| < \epsilon \quad \text{if} \quad 0 < |x - 2| < \delta$$
$$|x - 2| < \epsilon/3 \quad \text{if} \quad 0 < |x - 2| < \delta \tag{3}$$

It should be self-evident that this last statement holds if $\delta = \epsilon/3$, which completes the discovery portion of our work. Now we need to prove that (2) holds for this choice of δ. However, statement (2) is equivalent to (3), and (3) holds with $\delta = \epsilon/3$, so (2) also holds with $\delta = \epsilon/3$. This proves that $\lim\limits_{x \to 2} (3x - 5) = 1$. ◀

This example illustrates the general form of a limit proof: We *assume* that we are given a positive number ϵ, and we try to *prove* that we can find a positive number δ such that

$$|f(x) - L| < \epsilon \quad \text{if} \quad 0 < |x - a| < \delta \tag{4}$$

This is done by first discovering δ, and then proving that the discovered δ works. Since the argument has to be general enough to work for all positive values of ϵ, the quantity δ has to be expressed as a function of ϵ. In Example 1 we found the function $\delta = \epsilon/3$ by some simple algebra; however, most limit proofs require a little more algebraic and logical ingenuity. Thus, if you find our ensuing discussion of "ϵ-δ" proofs challenging, do not become discouraged; the concepts and techniques are intrinsically difficult. In fact, a precise understanding of limits evaded the finest mathematical minds for more than 150 years after the basic concepts of calculus were discovered.

Karl Weierstrass (1815–1897) Weierstrass, the son of a customs officer, was born in Ostenfelde, Germany. As a youth Weierstrass showed outstanding skills in languages and mathematics. However, at the urging of his dominant father, Weierstrass entered the law and commerce program at the University of Bonn. To the chagrin of his family, the rugged and congenial young man concentrated instead on fencing and beer drinking. Four years later he returned home without a degree. In 1839 Weierstrass entered the Academy of Münster to study for a career in secondary education, and he met and studied under an excellent mathematician named Christof Gudermann. Gudermann's ideas greatly influenced the work of Weierstrass. After receiving his teaching certificate, Weierstrass spent the next 15 years in secondary education teaching German, geography, and mathematics. In addition, he taught handwriting to small children. During this period much of Weierstrass's mathematical work was ignored because he was a secondary schoolteacher and not a college professor. Then, in 1854, he published a paper of major importance that created a sensation in the mathematics world and catapulted him to international fame overnight. He was immediately given an honorary Doctorate at the University of Königsberg and began a new career in college teaching at the University of Berlin in 1856. In 1859 the strain of his mathematical research caused a temporary nervous breakdown and led to spells of dizziness that plagued him for the rest of his life. Weierstrass was a brilliant teacher and his classes overflowed with multitudes of auditors. In spite of his fame, he never lost his early beer-drinking congeniality and was always in the company of students, both ordinary and brilliant. Weierstrass was acknowledged as the leading mathematical analyst in the world. He and his students opened the door to the modern school of mathematical analysis.

▶ **Example 2**   Prove that $\lim\limits_{x \to 0^+} \sqrt{x} = 0$.

Solution.   Note that the domain of $\sqrt{x}$ is $0 \le x$, so it is valid to discuss the limit as $x \to 0^+$. We must show that given $\epsilon > 0$, there exists a $\delta > 0$ such that

$$|\sqrt{x} - 0| < \epsilon \quad \text{if} \quad 0 < x - 0 < \delta$$

or more simply,

$$\sqrt{x} < \epsilon \quad \text{if} \quad 0 < x < \delta \tag{5}$$

But, by squaring both sides of the inequality $\sqrt{x} < \epsilon$, we can rewrite (5) as

$$x < \epsilon^2 \quad \text{if} \quad 0 < x < \delta \tag{6}$$

It should be self-evident that (6) is true if $\delta = \epsilon^2$; and since (6) is a reformulation of (5), we have shown that (5) holds with $\delta = \epsilon^2$. This proves that $\lim\limits_{x \to 0^+} \sqrt{x} = 0$. ◀

> In Example 2 the limit from the left and the two-sided limit do not exist at $x = 0$ because $\sqrt{x}$ is defined only for nonnegative values of x.

■ THE VALUE OF δ IS NOT UNIQUE

In preparation for our next example, we note that the value of δ in Definition 1.4.1 is not unique; once we have found a value of δ that fulfills the requirements of the definition, then any *smaller* positive number δ_1 will also fulfill those requirements. That is, if it is true that

$$|f(x) - L| < \epsilon \quad \text{if} \quad 0 < |x - a| < \delta$$

then it will also be true that

$$|f(x) - L| < \epsilon \quad \text{if} \quad 0 < |x - a| < \delta_1$$

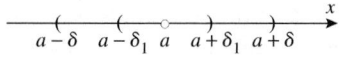

▲ **Figure 1.4.3**

This is because $\{x : 0 < |x - a| < \delta_1\}$ is a subset of $\{x : 0 < |x - a| < \delta\}$ (Figure 1.4.3), and hence if $|f(x) - L| < \epsilon$ is satisfied for all x in the larger set, then it will automatically be satisfied for all x in the subset. Thus, in Example 1, where we used $\delta = \epsilon/3$, we could have used any smaller value of δ such as $\delta = \epsilon/4$, $\delta = \epsilon/5$, or $\delta = \epsilon/6$.

▶ **Example 3**   Prove that $\lim\limits_{x \to 3} x^2 = 9$.

Solution.   We must show that given any positive number ϵ, we can find a positive number δ such that

$$|x^2 - 9| < \epsilon \quad \text{if} \quad 0 < |x - 3| < \delta \tag{7}$$

Because $|x - 3|$ occurs on the right side of this "if statement," it will be helpful to factor the left side to introduce a factor of $|x - 3|$. This yields the following alternative form of (7):

$$|x + 3||x - 3| < \epsilon \quad \text{if} \quad 0 < |x - 3| < \delta \tag{8}$$

> If you are wondering how we knew to make the restriction $\delta \le 1$, as opposed to $\delta \le 5$ or $\delta \le \frac{1}{2}$, for example, the answer is that 1 is merely a convenient choice—any restriction of the form $\delta \le c$ would work equally well.

We wish to bound the factor $|x + 3|$. If we knew, for example, that $\delta \le 1$, then we would have $-1 < x - 3 < 1$, so $5 < x + 3 < 7$, and consequently $|x + 3| < 7$. Thus, if $\delta \le 1$ and $0 < |x - 3| < \delta$, then

$$|x + 3||x - 3| < 7\delta$$

It follows that (8) will be satisfied for any positive δ such that $\delta \le 1$ and $7\delta < \epsilon$. We can achieve this by taking δ to be the minimum of the numbers 1 and $\epsilon/7$, which is sometimes written as $\delta = \min(1, \epsilon/7)$. This proves that $\lim\limits_{x \to 3} x^2 = 9$. ◀

■ LIMITS AS $x \to \pm\infty$

In Section 1.3 we discussed the limits

$$\lim_{x \to +\infty} f(x) = L \quad \text{and} \quad \lim_{x \to -\infty} f(x) = L$$

from an intuitive point of view. The first limit can be interpreted to mean that we can make the value of $f(x)$ as close as we like to L by taking x sufficiently large, and the second can be interpreted to mean that we can make the value of $f(x)$ as close as we like to L by taking x sufficiently far to the left of 0. These ideas are captured in the following definitions and are illustrated in Figure 1.4.4.

1.4.2 **DEFINITION** Let $f(x)$ be defined for all x in some infinite open interval extending in the positive x-direction. We will write

$$\lim_{x \to +\infty} f(x) = L$$

if given any number $\epsilon > 0$, there corresponds a positive number N such that

$$|f(x) - L| < \epsilon \quad \text{if} \quad x > N$$

1.4.3 **DEFINITION** Let $f(x)$ be defined for all x in some infinite open interval extending in the negative x-direction. We will write

$$\lim_{x \to -\infty} f(x) = L$$

if given any number $\epsilon > 0$, there corresponds a negative number N such that

$$|f(x) - L| < \epsilon \quad \text{if} \quad x < N$$

To see how these definitions relate to our informal concepts of these limits, suppose that $f(x) \to L$ as $x \to +\infty$, and for a given ϵ let N be the positive number described in Definition 1.4.2. If x is allowed to increase indefinitely, then eventually x will lie in the interval $(N, +\infty)$, which is marked in green in Figure 1.4.4a; when this happens, the value of $f(x)$ will fall between $L - \epsilon$ and $L + \epsilon$, marked in red in the figure. Since this is true for all positive values of ϵ (no matter how small), we can force the values of $f(x)$ as close as we like to L by making N sufficiently large. This agrees with our informal concept of this limit. Similarly, Figure 1.4.4b illustrates Definition 1.4.3.

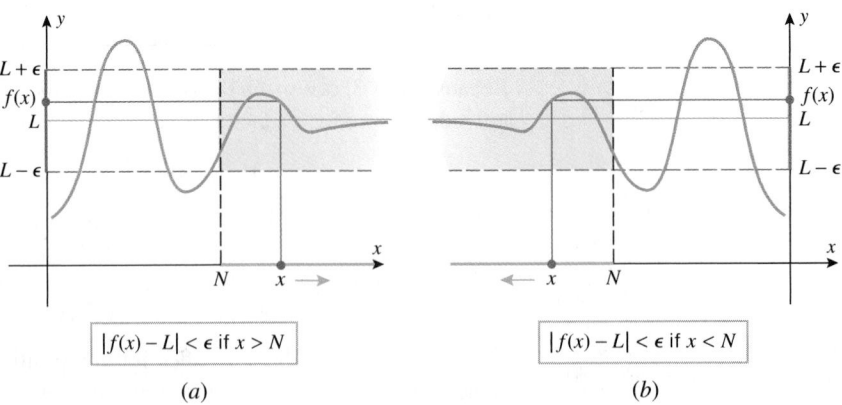

$$|f(x) - L| < \epsilon \text{ if } x > N$$

(a)

$$|f(x) - L| < \epsilon \text{ if } x < N$$

(b)

▲ **Figure 1.4.4**

▶ **Example 4** Prove that $\displaystyle\lim_{x \to +\infty} \frac{1}{x} = 0$.

Solution. Applying Definition 1.4.2 with $f(x) = 1/x$ and $L = 0$, we must show that given $\epsilon > 0$, we can find a number $N > 0$ such that

$$\left| \frac{1}{x} - 0 \right| < \epsilon \quad \text{if} \quad x > N \tag{9}$$

Because $x \to +\infty$ we can assume that $x > 0$. Thus, we can eliminate the absolute values in this statement and rewrite it as

$$\frac{1}{x} < \epsilon \quad \text{if} \quad x > N$$

or, on taking reciprocals,

$$x > \frac{1}{\epsilon} \quad \text{if} \quad x > N \tag{10}$$

It is self-evident that $N = 1/\epsilon$ satisfies this requirement, and since (10) and (9) are equivalent for $x > 0$, the proof is complete. ◄

■ INFINITE LIMITS

In Section 1.1 we discussed limits of the following type from an intuitive viewpoint:

$$\lim_{x \to a} f(x) = +\infty, \qquad \lim_{x \to a} f(x) = -\infty \tag{11}$$

$$\lim_{x \to a^+} f(x) = +\infty, \qquad \lim_{x \to a^+} f(x) = -\infty \tag{12}$$

$$\lim_{x \to a^-} f(x) = +\infty, \qquad \lim_{x \to a^-} f(x) = -\infty \tag{13}$$

Recall that each of these expressions describes a particular way in which the limit fails to exist. The $+\infty$ indicates that the limit fails to exist because $f(x)$ increases without bound, and the $-\infty$ indicates that the limit fails to exist because $f(x)$ decreases without bound. These ideas are captured more precisely in the following definitions and are illustrated in Figure 1.4.5.

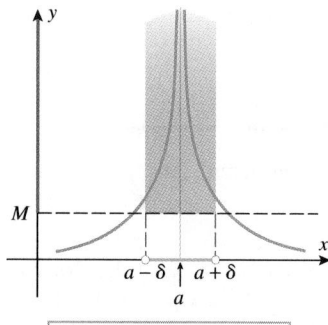

$f(x) > M$ if $0 < |x - a| < \delta$

(a)

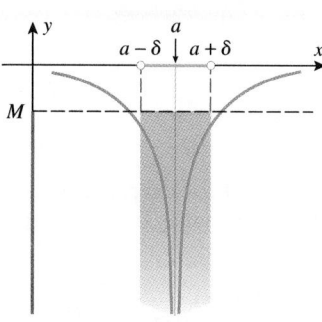

$f(x) < M$ if $0 < |x - a| < \delta$

(b)

▲ **Figure 1.4.5**

How would you define these limits?

$\lim_{x \to a^+} f(x) = +\infty \quad \lim_{x \to a^+} f(x) = -\infty$

$\lim_{x \to a^-} f(x) = +\infty \quad \lim_{x \to a^-} f(x) = -\infty$

$\lim_{x \to +\infty} f(x) = +\infty \quad \lim_{x \to +\infty} f(x) = -\infty$

$\lim_{x \to -\infty} f(x) = +\infty \quad \lim_{x \to -\infty} f(x) = -\infty$

1.4.4   DEFINITION   Let $f(x)$ be defined for all x in some open interval containing a, except that $f(x)$ need not be defined at a. We will write

$$\lim_{x \to a} f(x) = +\infty$$

if given any positive number M, we can find a number $\delta > 0$ such that $f(x)$ satisfies

$$f(x) > M \quad \text{if} \quad 0 < |x - a| < \delta$$

1.4.5   DEFINITION   Let $f(x)$ be defined for all x in some open interval containing a, except that $f(x)$ need not be defined at a. We will write

$$\lim_{x \to a} f(x) = -\infty$$

if given any negative number M, we can find a number $\delta > 0$ such that $f(x)$ satisfies

$$f(x) < M \quad \text{if} \quad 0 < |x - a| < \delta$$

To see how these definitions relate to our informal concepts of these limits, suppose that $f(x) \to +\infty$ as $x \to a$, and for a given M let δ be the corresponding positive number described in Definition 1.4.4. Next, imagine that x gets closer and closer to a (from either side). Eventually, x will lie in the interval $(a - \delta, a + \delta)$, which is marked in green in Figure 1.4.5a; when this happens the value of $f(x)$ will be greater than M, marked in red in the figure. Since this is true for any positive value of M (no matter how large), we can force the values of $f(x)$ to be as large as we like by making x sufficiently close to a. This agrees with our informal concept of this limit. Similarly, Figure 1.4.5b illustrates Definition 1.4.5.

▶ **Example 5**   Prove that $\lim\limits_{x \to 0} \dfrac{1}{x^2} = +\infty$.

Solution.   Applying Definition 1.4.4 with $f(x) = 1/x^2$ and $a = 0$, we must show that given a number $M > 0$, we can find a number $\delta > 0$ such that

$$\frac{1}{x^2} > M \quad \text{if} \quad 0 < |x - 0| < \delta \tag{14}$$

or, on taking reciprocals and simplifying,

$$x^2 < \frac{1}{M} \quad \text{if} \quad 0 < |x| < \delta \tag{15}$$

But $x^2 < 1/M$ if $|x| < 1/\sqrt{M}$, so that $\delta = 1/\sqrt{M}$ satisfies (15). Since (14) is equivalent to (15), the proof is complete. ◀

✔ **QUICK CHECK EXERCISES 1.4**   *(See page 109 for answers.)*

1. The definition of a two-sided limit states: $\lim\limits_{x \to a} f(x) = L$ if given any number _____ there is a number _____ such that $|f(x) - L| < \epsilon$ if _____.

2. Suppose that $f(x)$ is a function such that for any given $\epsilon > 0$, the condition $0 < |x - 1| < \epsilon/2$ guarantees that $|f(x) - 5| < \epsilon$. What limit results from this property?

3. Suppose that ϵ is any positive number. Find the largest value of δ such that $|5x - 10| < \epsilon$ if $0 < |x - 2| < \delta$.

4. The definition of limit at $+\infty$ states: $\lim\limits_{x \to +\infty} f(x) = L$ if given any number _____ there is a positive number _____ such that $|f(x) - L| < \epsilon$ if _____.

5. Find the smallest positive number N such that for each $x > N$, the value of $f(x) = 1/\sqrt{x}$ is within 0.01 of 0.

EXERCISE SET 1.4   ⬚ Graphing Utility

1. (a) Find the largest open interval, centered at the origin on the x-axis, such that for each x in the interval the value of the function $f(x) = x + 2$ is within 0.1 unit of the number $f(0) = 2$.
   (b) Find the largest open interval, centered at $x = 3$, such that for each x in the interval the value of the function $f(x) = 4x - 5$ is within 0.01 unit of the number $f(3) = 7$.
   (c) Find the largest open interval, centered at $x = 4$, such that for each x in the interval the value of the function $f(x) = x^2$ is within 0.001 unit of the number $f(4) = 16$.

2. In each part, find the largest open interval, centered at $x = 0$, such that for each x in the interval the value of $f(x) = 2x + 3$ is within ϵ units of the number $f(0) = 3$.
   (a) $\epsilon = 0.1$ (b) $\epsilon = 0.01$
   (c) $\epsilon = 0.0012$

3. (a) Find the values of x_0 and x_1 in the accompanying figure.
   (b) Find a positive number δ such that $|\sqrt{x} - 2| < 0.05$ if $0 < |x - 4| < \delta$.

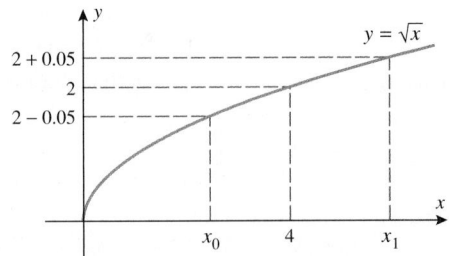

Not drawn to scale

▲ **Figure Ex-3**

4. (a) Find the values of x_0 and x_1 in the accompanying figure on the next page.
   (b) Find a positive number δ such that $|(1/x) - 1| < 0.1$ if $0 < |x - 1| < \delta$.

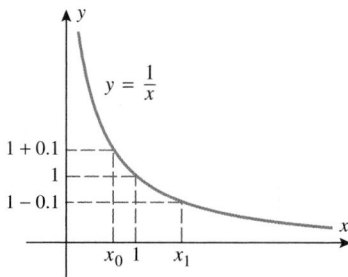

$y = \dfrac{1}{x}$

Not drawn to scale　◀ **Figure Ex-4**

5. Generate the graph of $f(x) = x^3 - 4x + 5$ with a graphing utility, and use the graph to find a number δ such that $|f(x) - 2| < 0.05$ if $0 < |x - 1| < \delta$. [*Hint:* Show that the inequality $|f(x) - 2| < 0.05$ can be rewritten as $1.95 < x^3 - 4x + 5 < 2.05$, and estimate the values of x for which $x^3 - 4x + 5 = 1.95$ and $x^3 - 4x + 5 = 2.05$.]

6. Use the method of Exercise 5 to find a number δ such that $|\sqrt{5x + 1} - 4| < 0.5$ if $0 < |x - 3| < \delta$.

7. Let $f(x) = x + \sqrt{x}$ with $L = \lim_{x \to 1} f(x)$ and let $\epsilon = 0.2$. Use a graphing utility and its trace feature to find a positive number δ such that $|f(x) - L| < \epsilon$ if $0 < |x - 1| < \delta$.

8. Let $f(x) = (\sin 2x)/x$ and use a graphing utility to conjecture the value of $L = \lim_{x \to 0} f(x)$. Then let $\epsilon = 0.1$ and use the graphing utility and its trace feature to find a positive number δ such that $|f(x) - L| < \epsilon$ if $0 < |x| < \delta$.

FOCUS ON CONCEPTS

9. What is wrong with the following "proof" that $\lim_{x \to 3} 2x = 6$? Suppose that $\epsilon = 1$ and $\delta = \frac{1}{2}$. Then if $|x - 3| < \frac{1}{2}$, we have

$$|2x - 6| = 2|x - 3| < 2\left(\tfrac{1}{2}\right) = 1 = \epsilon$$

Therefore, $\lim_{x \to 3} 2x = 6$.

10. What is wrong with the following "proof" that $\lim_{x \to 3} 2x = 6$? Given any $\delta > 0$, choose $\epsilon = 2\delta$. Then if $|x - 3| < \delta$, we have

$$|2x - 6| = 2|x - 3| < 2\delta = \epsilon$$

Therefore, $\lim_{x \to 3} 2x = 6$.

11. Recall from Example 1 that the creation of a limit proof involves two stages. The first is a *discovery* stage in which δ is found, and the second is the *proof* stage in which the discovered δ is shown to work. Fill in the blanks to give an explicit proof that the choice of $\delta = \epsilon/3$ in Example 1 works. Suppose that $\epsilon > 0$. Set $\delta = \epsilon/3$ and assume that $0 < |x - 2| < \delta$. Then

$$|(3x - 5) - 1| = |\text{_____}|$$
$$= 3 \cdot |\text{_____}| < 3 \cdot \text{_____} = \epsilon$$

12. Suppose that $f(x) = c$ is a constant function and that a is some fixed real number. Explain why *any* choice of $\delta > 0$ (e.g., $\delta = 1$) works to prove $\lim_{x \to a} f(x) = c$.

13–22 Use Definition 1.4.1 to prove that the limit is correct. ■

13. $\lim\limits_{x \to 2} 3 = 3$

14. $\lim\limits_{x \to 4} (x + 2) = 6$

15. $\lim\limits_{x \to 5} 3x = 15$

16. $\lim\limits_{x \to -1} (7x + 5) = -2$

17. $\lim\limits_{x \to 0} \dfrac{2x^2 + x}{x} = 1$

18. $\lim\limits_{x \to -3} \dfrac{x^2 - 9}{x + 3} = -6$

19. $\lim\limits_{x \to 1} f(x) = 3$, where $f(x) = \begin{cases} x + 2, & x \neq 1 \\ 10, & x = 1 \end{cases}$

20. $\lim\limits_{x \to 2} f(x) = 5$, where $f(x) = \begin{cases} 9 - 2x, & x \neq 2 \\ 49, & x = 2 \end{cases}$

21. $\lim\limits_{x \to 0} |x| = 0$

22. $\lim\limits_{x \to 2} f(x) = 5$, where $f(x) = \begin{cases} 9 - 2x, & x < 2 \\ 3x - 1, & x > 2 \end{cases}$

23–26 True–False Determine whether the statement is true or false. Explain your answer. ■

23. Suppose that $f(x) = mx + b, m \neq 0$. To prove that $\lim_{x \to a} f(x) = f(a)$, we can take $\delta = \epsilon/|m|$.

24. Suppose that $f(x) = mx + b, m \neq 0$. To prove that $\lim_{x \to a} f(x) = f(a)$, we can take $\delta = \epsilon/(2|m|)$.

25. For certain functions, the *same* δ will work for *all* $\epsilon > 0$ in a limit proof.

26. Suppose that $f(x) > 0$ for all x in the interval $(-1, 1)$. If $\lim_{x \to 0} f(x) = L$, then $L > 0$.

FOCUS ON CONCEPTS

27. Give rigorous definitions of $\lim_{x \to a^+} f(x) = L$ and $\lim_{x \to a^-} f(x) = L$.

28. Consider the statement that $\lim_{x \to a} |f(x) - L| = 0$.
    (a) Using Definition 1.4.1, write down precisely what this limit statement means.
    (b) Explain why your answer to part (a) shows that
    $$\lim_{x \to a} |f(x) - L| = 0 \quad \text{if and only if} \quad \lim_{x \to a} f(x) = L$$

29. (a) Show that
    $$|(3x^2 + 2x - 20) - 300| = |3x + 32| \cdot |x - 10|$$
    (b) Find an upper bound for $|3x + 32|$ if x satisfies $|x - 10| < 1$.
    (c) Fill in the blanks to complete a proof that
    $$\lim_{x \to 10} [3x^2 + 2x - 20] = 300$$
    Suppose that $\epsilon > 0$. Set $\delta = \min(1, \text{_____})$ and assume that $0 < |x - 10| < \delta$. Then
    $$\left|(3x^2 + 2x - 20) - 300\right| = |3x + 32| \cdot |x - 10|$$
    $$< \text{_____} \cdot |x - 10|$$
    $$< \text{_____} \cdot \text{_____}$$
    $$= \epsilon$$

30. (a) Show that
$$\left|\frac{28}{3x+1}-4\right|=\left|\frac{12}{3x+1}\right|\cdot|x-2|$$

(b) Is $|12/(3x+1)|$ bounded if $|x-2|<4$? If not, explain; if so, give a bound.

(c) Is $|12/(3x+1)|$ bounded if $|x-2|<1$? If not, explain; if so, give a bound.

(d) Fill in the blanks to complete a proof that
$$\lim_{x\to 2}\left[\frac{28}{3x+1}\right]=4$$

Suppose that $\epsilon>0$. Set $\delta=\min(1,\underline{\hspace{1cm}})$ and assume that $0<|x-2|<\delta$. Then
$$\left|\frac{28}{3x+1}-4\right|=\left|\frac{12}{3x+1}\right|\cdot|x-2|$$
$$<\underline{\hspace{1.5cm}}\cdot|x-2|$$
$$<\underline{\hspace{1cm}}\cdot\underline{\hspace{1cm}}$$
$$=\epsilon$$

31–36 Use Definition 1.4.1 to prove that the stated limit is correct. In each case, to show that $\lim_{x\to a}f(x)=L$, factor $|f(x)-L|$ in the form
$$|f(x)-L|=|\text{“something”}|\cdot|x-a|$$
and then bound the size of $|\text{“something”}|$ by putting restrictions on the size of δ. ■

31. $\lim_{x\to 1}2x^2=2$ [*Hint:* Assume $\delta\le 1$.]

32. $\lim_{x\to 3}(x^2+x)=12$ [*Hint:* Assume $\delta\le 1$.]

33. $\lim_{x\to -2}\dfrac{1}{x+1}=-1$ **34.** $\lim_{x\to 1/2}\dfrac{2x+3}{x}=8$

35. $\lim_{x\to 4}\sqrt{x}=2$ **36.** $\lim_{x\to 2}x^3=8$

37. Let
$$f(x)=\begin{cases}0,&\text{if }x\text{ is rational}\\ x,&\text{if }x\text{ is irrational}\end{cases}$$
Use Definition 1.4.1 to prove that $\lim_{x\to 0}f(x)=0$.

38. Let
$$f(x)=\begin{cases}0,&\text{if }x\text{ is rational}\\ 1,&\text{if }x\text{ is irrational}\end{cases}$$
Use Definition 1.4.1 to prove that $\lim_{x\to 0}f(x)$ does not exist. [*Hint:* Assume $\lim_{x\to 0}f(x)=L$ and apply Definition 1.4.1 with $\epsilon=\frac{1}{2}$ to conclude that $|1-L|<\frac{1}{2}$ and $|L|=|0-L|<\frac{1}{2}$. Then show $1\le|1-L|+|L|$ and derive a contradiction.]

39. (a) Find the values of x_1 and x_2 in the accompanying figure.

(b) Find a positive number N such that
$$\left|\frac{x^2}{1+x^2}-1\right|<\epsilon$$
for $x>N$.

(c) Find a negative number N such that
$$\left|\frac{x^2}{1+x^2}-1\right|<\epsilon$$
for $x<N$.

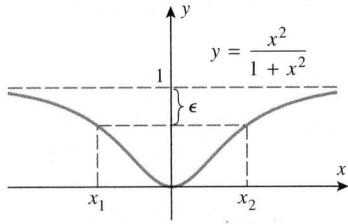

Not drawn to scale   ◀ **Figure Ex-39**

40. (a) Find the values of x_1 and x_2 in the accompanying figure.

(b) Find a positive number N such that
$$\left|\frac{1}{\sqrt[3]{x}}-0\right|=\left|\frac{1}{\sqrt[3]{x}}\right|<\epsilon$$
for $x>N$.

(c) Find a negative number N such that
$$\left|\frac{1}{\sqrt[3]{x}}-0\right|=\left|\frac{1}{\sqrt[3]{x}}\right|<\epsilon$$
for $x<N$.

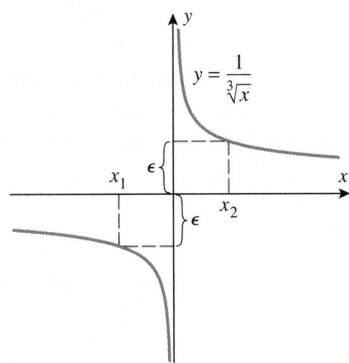

◀ **Figure Ex-40**

41–44 A positive number ϵ and the limit L of a function f at $+\infty$ are given. Find a positive number N such that $|f(x)-L|<\epsilon$ if $x>N$. ■

41. $\lim_{x\to +\infty}\dfrac{1}{x^2}=0;\ \epsilon=0.01$

42. $\lim_{x\to +\infty}\dfrac{1}{x+2}=0;\ \epsilon=0.005$

43. $\lim_{x\to +\infty}\dfrac{x}{x+1}=1;\ \epsilon=0.001$

44. $\lim_{x\to +\infty}\dfrac{4x-1}{2x+5}=2;\ \epsilon=0.1$

45–48 A positive number ϵ and the limit L of a function f at $-\infty$ are given. Find a negative number N such that $|f(x)-L|<\epsilon$ if $x<N$. ■

45. $\lim_{x\to -\infty}\dfrac{1}{x+2}=0;\ \epsilon=0.005$

46. $\lim_{x\to -\infty}\dfrac{1}{x^2}=0;\ \epsilon=0.01$

47. $\lim_{x\to -\infty}\dfrac{4x-1}{2x+5}=2;\ \epsilon=0.1$

48. $\lim\limits_{x \to -\infty} \dfrac{x}{x+1} = 1$; $\epsilon = 0.001$

49–54 Use Definition 1.4.2 or 1.4.3 to prove that the stated limit is correct. ■

49. $\lim\limits_{x \to +\infty} \dfrac{1}{x^2} = 0$

50. $\lim\limits_{x \to +\infty} \dfrac{1}{x+2} = 0$

51. $\lim\limits_{x \to -\infty} \dfrac{4x-1}{2x+5} = 2$

52. $\lim\limits_{x \to -\infty} \dfrac{x}{x+1} = 1$

53. $\lim\limits_{x \to +\infty} \dfrac{2\sqrt{x}}{\sqrt{x}-1} = 2$

54. $\lim\limits_{x \to -\infty} 2^x = 0$

55. (a) Find the largest open interval, centered at the origin on the x-axis, such that for each x in the interval, other than the center, the values of $f(x) = 1/x^2$ are greater than 100.
   (b) Find the largest open interval, centered at $x = 1$, such that for each x in the interval, other than the center, the values of the function $f(x) = 1/|x-1|$ are greater than 1000.
   (c) Find the largest open interval, centered at $x = 3$, such that for each x in the interval, other than the center, the values of the function $f(x) = -1/(x-3)^2$ are less than -1000.
   (d) Find the largest open interval, centered at the origin on the x-axis, such that for each x in the interval, other than the center, the values of $f(x) = -1/x^4$ are less than $-10{,}000$.

56. In each part, find the largest open interval centered at $x = 1$, such that for each x in the interval, other than the center, the value of $f(x) = 1/(x-1)^2$ is greater than M.
   (a) $M = 10$ (b) $M = 1000$ (c) $M = 100{,}000$

57–62 Use Definition 1.4.4 or 1.4.5 to prove that the stated limit is correct. ■

57. $\lim\limits_{x \to 3} \dfrac{1}{(x-3)^2} = +\infty$

58. $\lim\limits_{x \to 3} \dfrac{-1}{(x-3)^2} = -\infty$

59. $\lim\limits_{x \to 0} \dfrac{1}{|x|} = +\infty$

60. $\lim\limits_{x \to 1} \dfrac{1}{|x-1|} = +\infty$

61. $\lim\limits_{x \to 0} \left(-\dfrac{1}{x^4}\right) = -\infty$

62. $\lim\limits_{x \to 0} \dfrac{1}{x^4} = +\infty$

63–68 Use the definitions in Exercise 27 to prove that the stated one-sided limit is correct. ■

63. $\lim\limits_{x \to 2^+} (x+1) = 3$

64. $\lim\limits_{x \to 1^-} (3x+2) = 5$

65. $\lim\limits_{x \to 4^+} \sqrt{x-4} = 0$

66. $\lim\limits_{x \to 0^-} \sqrt{-x} = 0$

67. $\lim\limits_{x \to 2^+} f(x) = 2$, where $f(x) = \begin{cases} x, & x > 2 \\ 3x, & x \le 2 \end{cases}$

68. $\lim\limits_{x \to 2^-} f(x) = 6$, where $f(x) = \begin{cases} x, & x > 2 \\ 3x, & x \le 2 \end{cases}$

69–72 Write out the definition for the corresponding limit in the marginal note on page 105, and use your definition to prove that the stated limit is correct. ■

69. (a) $\lim\limits_{x \to 1^+} \dfrac{1}{1-x} = -\infty$ (b) $\lim\limits_{x \to 1^-} \dfrac{1}{1-x} = +\infty$

70. (a) $\lim\limits_{x \to 0^+} \dfrac{1}{x} = +\infty$ (b) $\lim\limits_{x \to 0^-} \dfrac{1}{x} = -\infty$

71. (a) $\lim\limits_{x \to +\infty} (x+1) = +\infty$ (b) $\lim\limits_{x \to -\infty} (x+1) = -\infty$

72. (a) $\lim\limits_{x \to +\infty} (x^2-3) = +\infty$ (b) $\lim\limits_{x \to -\infty} (x^3+5) = -\infty$

73. According to Ohm's law, when a voltage of V volts is applied across a resistor with a resistance of R ohms, a current of $I = V/R$ amperes flows through the resistor.
   (a) How much current flows if a voltage of 3.0 volts is applied across a resistance of 7.5 ohms?
   (b) If the resistance varies by ± 0.1 ohm, and the voltage remains constant at 3.0 volts, what is the resulting range of values for the current?
   (c) If temperature variations cause the resistance to vary by $\pm \delta$ from its value of 7.5 ohms, and the voltage remains constant at 3.0 volts, what is the resulting range of values for the current?
   (d) If the current is not allowed to vary by more than $\epsilon = \pm 0.001$ ampere at a voltage of 3.0 volts, what variation of $\pm \delta$ from the value of 7.5 ohms is allowable?
   (e) Certain alloys become **superconductors** as their temperature approaches absolute zero ($-273\,^\circ$C), meaning that their resistance approaches zero. If the voltage remains constant, what happens to the current in a superconductor as $R \to 0^+$?

74. Writing Compare informal Definition 1.1.1 with Definition 1.4.1.
   (a) What portions of Definition 1.4.1 correspond to the expression "values of $f(x)$ can be made as close as we like to L" in Definition 1.1.1? Explain.
   (b) What portions of Definition 1.4.1 correspond to the expression "taking values of x sufficiently close to a (but not equal to a)" in Definition 1.1.1? Explain.

75. Writing Compare informal Definition 1.3.1 with Definition 1.4.2.
   (a) What portions of Definition 1.4.2 correspond to the expression "values of $f(x)$ eventually get as close as we like to a number L" in Definition 1.3.1? Explain.
   (b) What portions of Definition 1.4.2 correspond to the expression "as x increases without bound" in Definition 1.3.1? Explain.

✔**QUICK CHECK ANSWERS 1.4**

1. $\epsilon > 0$; $\delta > 0$; $0 < |x-a| < \delta$ **2.** $\lim\limits_{x \to 1} f(x) = 5$ **3.** $\delta = \epsilon/5$ **4.** $\epsilon > 0$; N; $x > N$ **5.** $N = 10{,}000$

1.5 **CONTINUITY**

A thrown baseball cannot vanish at some point and reappear someplace else to continue its motion. Thus, we perceive the path of the ball as an unbroken curve. In this section, we translate "unbroken curve" into a precise mathematical formulation called continuity, and develop some fundamental properties of continuous curves.

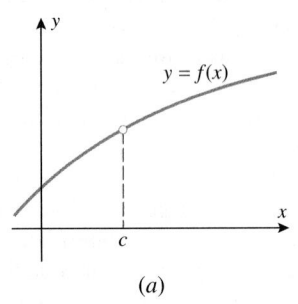

A baseball moves along a "continuous" trajectory after leaving the pitcher's hand.

■ **DEFINITION OF CONTINUITY**

Intuitively, the graph of a function can be described as a "continuous curve" if it has no breaks or holes. To make this idea more precise we need to understand what properties of a function can cause breaks or holes. Referring to Figure 1.5.1, we see that the graph of a function has a break or hole if any of the following conditions occur:

- The function f is undefined at c (Figure 1.5.1a).
- The limit of $f(x)$ does not exist as x approaches c (Figures 1.5.1b, 1.5.1c).
- The value of the function and the value of the limit at c are different (Figure 1.5.1d).

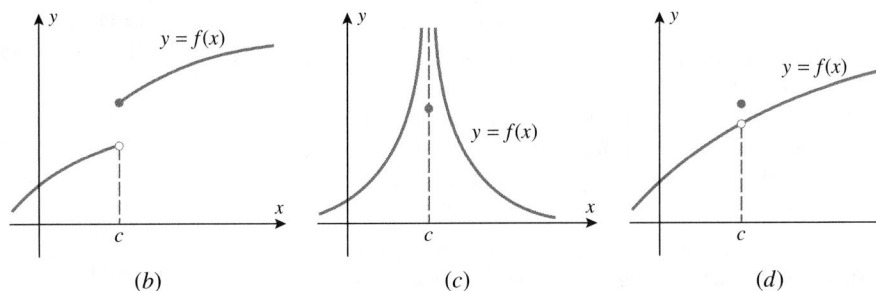

▲ **Figure 1.5.1**

This suggests the following definition.

The third condition in Definition 1.5.1 actually implies the first two, since it is tacitly understood in the statement

$$\lim_{x \to c} f(x) = f(c)$$

that the limit exists and the function is defined at c. Thus, when we want to establish continuity at c our usual procedure will be to verify the third condition only.

1.5.1   DEFINITION   A function f is said to be **continuous at $x = c$** provided the following conditions are satisfied:

1. $f(c)$ is defined.

2. $\lim_{x \to c} f(x)$ exists.

3. $\lim_{x \to c} f(x) = f(c)$.

If one or more of the conditions of this definition fails to hold, then we will say that f has a **discontinuity at $x = c$**. Each function drawn in Figure 1.5.1 illustrates a discontinuity at $x = c$. In Figure 1.5.1a, the function is not defined at c, violating the first condition of Definition 1.5.1. In Figure 1.5.1b, the one-sided limits of $f(x)$ as x approaches c both exist but are not equal. Thus, $\lim_{x \to c} f(x)$ does not exist, and this violates the second condition of Definition 1.5.1. We will say that a function like that in Figure 1.5.1b has a **jump discontinuity** at c. In Figure 1.5.1c, the one-sided limits of $f(x)$ as x approaches c are infinite. Thus, $\lim_{x \to c} f(x)$ does not exist, and this violates the second condition of Definition 1.5.1. We will say that a function like that in Figure 1.5.1c has an **infinite discontinuity** at c. In Figure 1.5.1d, the function is defined at c and $\lim_{x \to c} f(x)$ exists, but these two values are not equal, violating the third condition of Definition 1.5.1. We will say that a function like that in Figure 1.5.1*d* has a ***removable discontinuity*** at *c*. Exercises 33 and 34 help to explain why discontinuities of this type are given this name.

▶ **Example 1**   Determine whether the following functions are continuous at $x = 2$.

$$f(x) = \frac{x^2 - 4}{x - 2}, \qquad g(x) = \begin{cases} \dfrac{x^2 - 4}{x - 2}, & x \neq 2 \\ 3, & x = 2, \end{cases} \qquad h(x) = \begin{cases} \dfrac{x^2 - 4}{x - 2}, & x \neq 2 \\ 4, & x = 2 \end{cases}$$

Solution.   In each case we must determine whether the limit of the function as $x \to 2$ is the same as the value of the function at $x = 2$. In all three cases the functions are identical, except at $x = 2$, and hence all three have the same limit at $x = 2$, namely,

$$\lim_{x \to 2} f(x) = \lim_{x \to 2} g(x) = \lim_{x \to 2} h(x) = \lim_{x \to 2} \frac{x^2 - 4}{x - 2} = \lim_{x \to 2} (x + 2) = 4$$

The function f is undefined at $x = 2$, and hence is not continuous at $x = 2$ (Figure 1.5.2*a*). The function g is defined at $x = 2$, but its value there is $g(2) = 3$, which is not the same as the limit as x approaches 2; hence, g is also not continuous at $x = 2$ (Figure 1.5.2*b*). The value of the function h at $x = 2$ is $h(2) = 4$, which is the same as the limit as x approaches 2; hence, h is continuous at $x = 2$ (Figure 1.5.2*c*). (Note that the function h could have been written more simply as $h(x) = x + 2$, but we wrote it in piecewise form to emphasize its relationship to f and g.) ◀

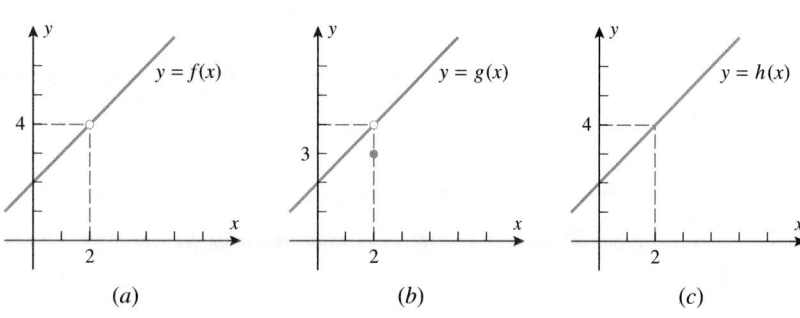

▲ **Figure 1.5.2**

A poor connection in a transmission cable can cause a discontinuity in the electrical signal it carries.

Chris Hondros/Getty Images

■ **CONTINUITY IN APPLICATIONS**

In applications, discontinuities often signal the occurrence of important physical events. For example, Figure 1.5.3*a* is a graph of voltage versus time for an underground cable that is accidentally cut by a work crew at time $t = t_0$ (the voltage drops to zero when the line is cut). Figure 1.5.3*b* shows the graph of inventory versus time for a company that restocks its warehouse to y_1 units when the inventory falls to y_0 units. The discontinuities occur at those times when restocking occurs.

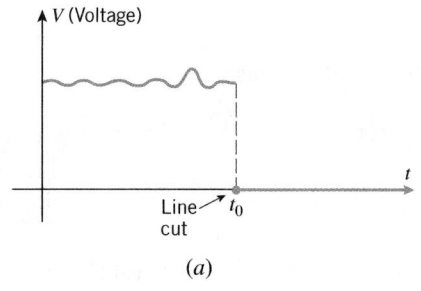

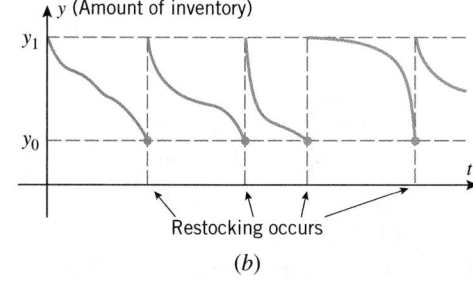

▲ **Figure 1.5.3**

CONTINUITY ON AN INTERVAL

If a function f is continuous at each number in an open interval (a, b), then we say that f is **continuous on (a, b)**. This definition applies to infinite open intervals of the form $(a, +\infty)$, $(-\infty, b)$, and $(-\infty, +\infty)$. In the case where f is continuous on $(-\infty, +\infty)$, we will say that f is **continuous everywhere**.

Because Definition 1.5.1 involves a two-sided limit, that definition does not generally apply at the endpoints of a closed interval $[a, b]$ or at the endpoint of an interval of the form $[a, b)$, $(a, b]$, $(-\infty, b]$, or $[a, +\infty)$. To remedy this problem, we will agree that a function is continuous at an endpoint of an interval if its value at the endpoint is equal to the appropriate one-sided limit at that endpoint. For example, the function graphed in Figure 1.5.4 is continuous at the right endpoint of the interval $[a, b]$ because

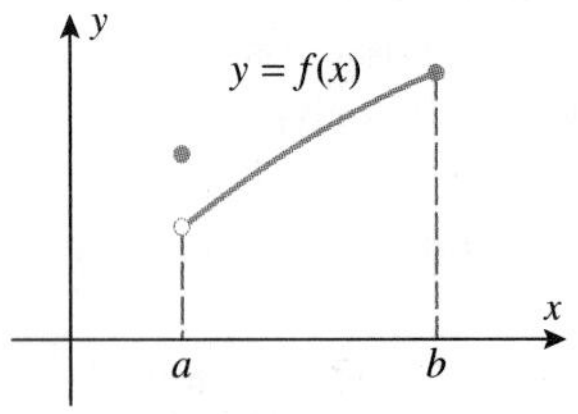

$$\lim_{x \to b^-} f(x) = f(b)$$

but it is not continuous at the left endpoint because

$$\lim_{x \to a^+} f(x) \neq f(a)$$

In general, we will say a function f is **continuous from the left** at c if

$$\lim_{x \to c^-} f(x) = f(c)$$

and is **continuous from the right** at c if

$$\lim_{x \to c^+} f(x) = f(c)$$

Using this terminology we define continuity on a closed interval as follows.

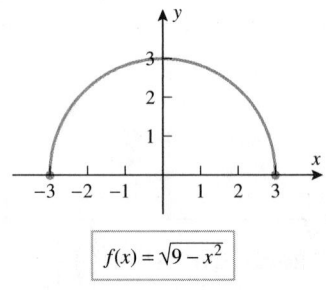

▲ Figure 1.5.4

> **1.5.2 DEFINITION** A function f is said to be **continuous on a closed interval $[a, b]$** if the following conditions are satisfied:
>
> **1.** f is continuous on (a, b).
>
> **2.** f is continuous from the right at a.
>
> **3.** f is continuous from the left at b.

Modify Definition 1.5.2 appropriately so that it applies to intervals of the form $[a, +\infty)$, $(-\infty, b]$, $(a, b]$, and $[a, b)$.

▶ **Example 2** What can you say about the continuity of the function $f(x) = \sqrt{9 - x^2}$?

Solution. Because the natural domain of this function is the closed interval $[-3, 3]$, we will need to investigate the continuity of f on the open interval $(-3, 3)$ and at the two endpoints. If c is any point in the interval $(-3, 3)$, then it follows from Theorem 1.2.2(e) that

$$\lim_{x \to c} f(x) = \lim_{x \to c} \sqrt{9 - x^2} = \sqrt{\lim_{x \to c} (9 - x^2)} = \sqrt{9 - c^2} = f(c)$$

which proves f is continuous at each point in the interval $(-3, 3)$. The function f is also continuous at the endpoints since

$$\lim_{x \to 3^-} f(x) = \lim_{x \to 3^-} \sqrt{9 - x^2} = \sqrt{\lim_{x \to 3^-} (9 - x^2)} = 0 = f(3)$$

$$\lim_{x \to -3^+} f(x) = \lim_{x \to -3^+} \sqrt{9 - x^2} = \sqrt{\lim_{x \to -3^+} (9 - x^2)} = 0 = f(-3)$$

$f(x) = \sqrt{9 - x^2}$

▲ Figure 1.5.5

Thus, f is continuous on the closed interval $[-3, 3]$ (Figure 1.5.5). ◄

■ **SOME PROPERTIES OF CONTINUOUS FUNCTIONS**

The following theorem, which is a consequence of Theorem 1.2.2, will enable us to reach conclusions about the continuity of functions that are obtained by adding, subtracting, multiplying, and dividing continuous functions.

1.5.3   THEOREM   *If the functions f and g are continuous at c, then*

(a) $f + g$ *is continuous at c.*

(b) $f - g$ *is continuous at c.*

(c) fg *is continuous at c.*

(d) f/g *is continuous at c if $g(c) \neq 0$ and has a discontinuity at c if $g(c) = 0$.*

We will prove part (d). The remaining proofs are similar and will be left to the exercises.

PROOF   First, consider the case where $g(c) = 0$. In this case $f(c)/g(c)$ is undefined, so the function f/g has a discontinuity at c.

Next, consider the case where $g(c) \neq 0$. To prove that f/g is continuous at c, we must show that

$$\lim_{x \to c} \frac{f(x)}{g(x)} = \frac{f(c)}{g(c)} \tag{1}$$

Since f and g are continuous at c,

$$\lim_{x \to c} f(x) = f(c) \quad \text{and} \quad \lim_{x \to c} g(x) = g(c)$$

Thus, by Theorem 1.2.2(d)

$$\lim_{x \to c} \frac{f(x)}{g(x)} = \frac{\lim_{x \to c} f(x)}{\lim_{x \to c} g(x)} = \frac{f(c)}{g(c)}$$

which proves (1).   ■

■ **CONTINUITY OF POLYNOMIALS AND RATIONAL FUNCTIONS**

The general procedure for showing that a function is continuous everywhere is to show that it is continuous at an *arbitrary* point. For example, we know from Theorem 1.2.3 that if $p(x)$ is a polynomial and a is *any* real number, then

$$\lim_{x \to a} p(x) = p(a)$$

This shows that polynomials are continuous everywhere. Moreover, since rational functions are ratios of polynomials, it follows from part (d) of Theorem 1.5.3 that rational functions are continuous at points other than the zeros of the denominator, and at these zeros they have discontinuities. Thus, we have the following result.

1.5.4   THEOREM

(a)   *A polynomial is continuous everywhere.*

(b)   *A rational function is continuous at every point where the denominator is nonzero, and has discontinuities at the points where the denominator is zero.*

TECHNOLOGY MASTERY

If you use a graphing utility to generate the graph of the equation in Example 3, there is a good chance you will see the discontinuity at $x = 2$ but not at $x = 3$. Try it, and explain what you think is happening.

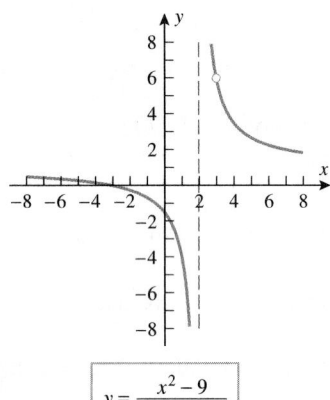

$$y = \frac{x^2 - 9}{x^2 - 5x + 6}$$

▲ **Figure 1.5.6**

▶ **Example 3** For what values of x is there a discontinuity in the graph of

$$y = \frac{x^2 - 9}{x^2 - 5x + 6}?$$

Solution. The function being graphed is a rational function, and hence is continuous at every number where the denominator is nonzero. Solving the equation

$$x^2 - 5x + 6 = 0$$

yields discontinuities at $x = 2$ and at $x = 3$ (Figure 1.5.6). ◀

▶ **Example 4** Show that $|x|$ is continuous everywhere (Figure 0.1.9).

Solution. We can write $|x|$ as

$$|x| = \begin{cases} x & \text{if } x > 0 \\ 0 & \text{if } x = 0 \\ -x & \text{if } x < 0 \end{cases}$$

so $|x|$ is the same as the polynomial x on the interval $(0, +\infty)$ and is the same as the polynomial $-x$ on the interval $(-\infty, 0)$. But polynomials are continuous everywhere, so $x = 0$ is the only possible discontinuity for $|x|$. Since $|0| = 0$, to prove the continuity at $x = 0$ we must show that

$$\lim_{x \to 0} |x| = 0 \qquad (2)$$

Because the piecewise formula for $|x|$ changes at 0, it will be helpful to consider the one-sided limits at 0 rather than the two-sided limit. We obtain

$$\lim_{x \to 0^+} |x| = \lim_{x \to 0^+} x = 0 \quad \text{and} \quad \lim_{x \to 0^-} |x| = \lim_{x \to 0^-} (-x) = 0$$

Thus, (2) holds and $|x|$ is continuous at $x = 0$. ◀

■ **CONTINUITY OF COMPOSITIONS**

The following theorem, whose proof is given in Appendix J, will be useful for calculating limits of compositions of functions.

In words, Theorem 1.5.5 states that a limit symbol can be moved through a function sign provided the limit of the expression inside the function sign exists and the function is continuous at this limit.

1.5.5 THEOREM *If* $\lim_{x \to c} g(x) = L$ *and if the function* f *is continuous at* L*, then* $\lim_{x \to c} f(g(x)) = f(L)$*. That is,*

$$\lim_{x \to c} f(g(x)) = f\left(\lim_{x \to c} g(x) \right)$$

This equality remains valid if $\lim_{x \to c}$ *is replaced everywhere by one of* $\lim_{x \to c^+}$*,* $\lim_{x \to c^-}$*,* $\lim_{x \to +\infty}$*, or* $\lim_{x \to -\infty}$*.*

In the special case of this theorem where $f(x) = |x|$, the fact that $|x|$ is continuous everywhere allows us to write

$$\lim_{x \to c} |g(x)| = \left| \lim_{x \to c} g(x) \right| \qquad (3)$$

provided $\lim_{x \to c} g(x)$ exists. Thus, for example,

$$\lim_{x \to 3} |5 - x^2| = \left| \lim_{x \to 3} (5 - x^2) \right| = |-4| = 4$$

The following theorem is concerned with the continuity of compositions of functions; the first part deals with continuity at a specific number and the second with continuity everywhere.

> **1.5.6 THEOREM**
>
> (a) *If the function g is continuous at c, and the function f is continuous at $g(c)$, then the composition $f \circ g$ is continuous at c.*
>
> (b) *If the function g is continuous everywhere and the function f is continuous everywhere, then the composition $f \circ g$ is continuous everywhere.*

PROOF We will prove part (a) only; the proof of part (b) can be obtained by applying part (a) at an arbitrary number c. To prove that $f \circ g$ is continuous at c, we must show that the value of $f \circ g$ and the value of its limit are the same at $x = c$. But this is so, since we can write

$$\lim_{x \to c} (f \circ g)(x) = \lim_{x \to c} f(g(x)) = f\left(\lim_{x \to c} g(x) \right) = f(g(c)) = (f \circ g)(c) \ \blacksquare$$

Theorem 1.5.5 g is continuous at c.

Can the absolute value of a function that is not continuous everywhere be continuous everywhere? Justify your answer.

We know from Example 4 that the function $|x|$ is continuous everywhere. Thus, if $g(x)$ is continuous at c, then by part (a) of Theorem 1.5.6, the function $|g(x)|$ must also be continuous at c; and, more generally, if $g(x)$ is continuous everywhere, then so is $|g(x)|$. Stated informally:

The absolute value of a continuous function is continuous.

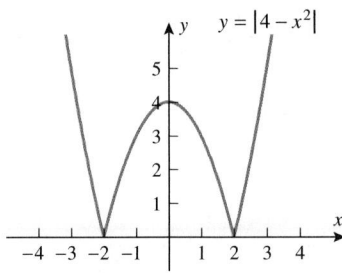

▲ **Figure 1.5.7**

For example, the polynomial $g(x) = 4 - x^2$ is continuous everywhere, so we can conclude that the function $|4 - x^2|$ is also continuous everywhere (Figure 1.5.7).

■ THE INTERMEDIATE-VALUE THEOREM

Figure 1.5.8 shows the graph of a function that is continuous on the closed interval $[a, b]$. The figure suggests that if we draw any horizontal line $y = k$, where k is between $f(a)$ and $f(b)$, then that line will cross the curve $y = f(x)$ at least once over the interval $[a, b]$. Stated in numerical terms, if f is continuous on $[a, b]$, then the function f must take on every value k between $f(a)$ and $f(b)$ at least once as x varies from a to b. For example, the polynomial $p(x) = x^5 - x + 3$ has a value of 3 at $x = 1$ and a value of 33 at $x = 2$. Thus, it follows from the continuity of p that the equation $x^5 - x + 3 = k$ has at least one solution in the interval $[1, 2]$ for every value of k between 3 and 33. This idea is stated more precisely in the following theorem.

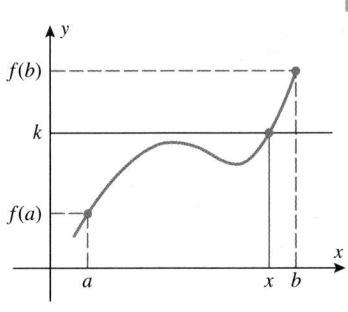

▲ **Figure 1.5.8**

> **1.5.7 THEOREM** (*Intermediate-Value Theorem*) *If f is continuous on a closed interval $[a, b]$ and k is any number between $f(a)$ and $f(b)$, inclusive, then there is at least one number x in the interval $[a, b]$ such that $f(x) = k$.*

Although this theorem is intuitively obvious, its proof depends on a mathematically precise development of the real number system, which is beyond the scope of this text.

■ APPROXIMATING ROOTS USING THE INTERMEDIATE-VALUE THEOREM

A variety of problems can be reduced to solving an equation $f(x) = 0$ for its roots. Sometimes it is possible to solve for the roots exactly using algebra, but often this is not possible and one must settle for decimal approximations of the roots. One procedure for approximating roots is based on the following consequence of the Intermediate-Value Theorem.

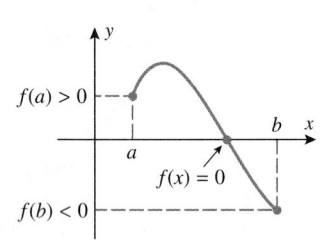

▲ **Figure 1.5.9**

> **1.5.8**   **THEOREM**   *If f is continuous on $[a, b]$, and if $f(a)$ and $f(b)$ are nonzero and have opposite signs, then there is at least one solution of the equation $f(x) = 0$ in the interval (a, b).*

This result, which is illustrated in Figure 1.5.9, can be proved as follows.

PROOF   Since $f(a)$ and $f(b)$ have opposite signs, 0 is between $f(a)$ and $f(b)$. Thus, by the Intermediate-Value Theorem there is at least one number x in the interval $[a, b]$ such that $f(x) = 0$. However, $f(a)$ and $f(b)$ are nonzero, so x must lie in the interval (a, b), which completes the proof. ■

Before we illustrate how this theorem can be used to approximate roots, it will be helpful to discuss some standard terminology for describing errors in approximations. If x is an approximation to a quantity x_0, then we call

$$\epsilon = |x - x_0|$$

the ***absolute error*** or (less precisely) the ***error*** in the approximation. The terminology in Table 1.5.1 is used to describe the size of such errors.

Table 1.5.1

ERROR	DESCRIPTION
$|x - x_0| \leq 0.1$	x approximates x_0 with an error of at most 0.1.
$|x - x_0| \leq 0.01$	x approximates x_0 with an error of at most 0.01.
$|x - x_0| \leq 0.001$	x approximates x_0 with an error of at most 0.001.
$|x - x_0| \leq 0.0001$	x approximates x_0 with an error of at most 0.0001.
$|x - x_0| \leq 0.5$	x approximates x_0 to the nearest integer.
$|x - x_0| \leq 0.05$	x approximates x_0 to 1 decimal place (i.e., to the nearest tenth).
$|x - x_0| \leq 0.005$	x approximates x_0 to 2 decimal places (i.e., to the nearest hundredth).
$|x - x_0| \leq 0.0005$	x approximates x_0 to 3 decimal places (i.e., to the nearest thousandth).

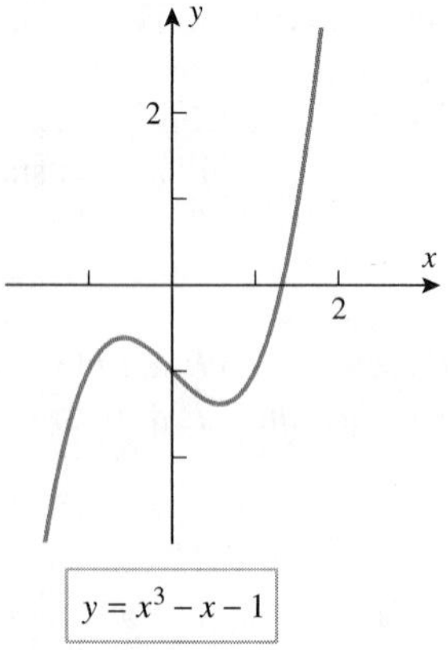

$y = x^3 - x - 1$

▲ **Figure 1.5.10**

▶ **Example 5**   The equation

$$x^3 - x - 1 = 0$$

cannot be solved algebraically very easily because the left side has no simple factors. However, if we graph $p(x) = x^3 - x - 1$ with a graphing utility (Figure 1.5.10), then we are led to conjecture that there is one real root and that this root lies inside the interval $[1, 2]$. The existence of a root in this interval is also confirmed by Theorem 1.5.8, since $p(1) = -1$ and $p(2) = 5$ have opposite signs. Approximate this root to two decimal-place accuracy.

Solution. Our objective is to approximate the unknown root x_0 with an error of at most 0.005. It follows that if we can find an interval of length 0.01 that contains the root, then the midpoint of that interval will approximate the root with an error of at most $\frac{1}{2}(0.01) = 0.005$, which will achieve the desired accuracy.

We know that the root x_0 lies in the interval $[1, 2]$. However, this interval has length 1, which is too large. We can pinpoint the location of the root more precisely by dividing the interval $[1, 2]$ into 10 equal parts and evaluating p at the points of subdivision using a calculating utility (Table 1.5.2). In this table $p(1.3)$ and $p(1.4)$ have opposite signs, so we know that the root lies in the interval $[1.3, 1.4]$. This interval has length 0.1, which is still too large, so we repeat the process by dividing the interval $[1.3, 1.4]$ into 10 parts and evaluating p at the points of subdivision; this yields Table 1.5.3, which tells us that the root is inside the interval $[1.32, 1.33]$ (Figure 1.5.11). Since this interval has length 0.01, its midpoint 1.325 will approximate the root with an error of at most 0.005. Thus, $x_0 \approx 1.325$ to two decimal-place accuracy. ◄

Table 1.5.2

x	1	1.1	1.2	1.3	1.4	1.5	1.6	1.7	1.8	1.9	2
$p(x)$	-1	-0.77	-0.47	-0.10	0.34	0.88	1.50	2.21	3.03	3.96	5

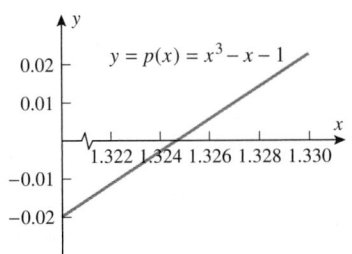

Table 1.5.3

x	1.3	1.31	1.32	1.33	1.34	1.35	1.36	1.37	1.38	1.39	1.4
$p(x)$	-0.103	-0.062	-0.020	0.023	0.066	0.110	0.155	0.201	0.248	0.296	0.344

▲ **Figure 1.5.11**

REMARK   To say that x approximates x_0 to n decimal places does *not* mean that the first n decimal places of x and x_0 will be the same when the numbers are rounded to n decimal places. For example, $x = 1.084$ approximates $x_0 = 1.087$ to two decimal places because $|x - x_0| = 0.003 \, (< 0.005)$. However, if we round these values to two decimal places, then we obtain $x \approx 1.08$ and $x_0 \approx 1.09$. Thus, if you approximate a number to n decimal places, then you should display that approximation to at least $n + 1$ decimal places to preserve the accuracy.

TECHNOLOGY MASTERY

Use a graphing or calculating utility to show that the root x_0 in Example 5 can be approximated as $x_0 \approx 1.3245$ to three decimal-place accuracy.

✔ QUICK CHECK EXERCISES 1.5   *(See page 120 for answers.)*

1. What three conditions are satisfied if f is continuous at $x = c$?

2. Suppose that f and g are continuous functions such that $f(2) = 1$ and $\lim\limits_{x \to 2} [f(x) + 4g(x)] = 13$. Find
   (a) $g(2)$
   (b) $\lim\limits_{x \to 2} g(x)$.

3. Suppose that f and g are continuous functions such that $\lim\limits_{x \to 3} g(x) = 5$ and $f(3) = -2$. Find $\lim\limits_{x \to 3} [f(x)/g(x)]$.

4. For what values of x, if any, is the function
$$f(x) = \frac{x^2 - 16}{x^2 - 5x + 4}$$
   discontinuous?

5. Suppose that a function f is continuous everywhere and that $f(-2) = 3$, $f(-1) = -1$, $f(0) = -4$, $f(1) = 1$, and $f(2) = 5$. Does the Intermediate-Value Theorem guarantee that f has a root on the following intervals?
   (a) $[-2, -1]$ (b) $[-1, 0]$ (c) $[-1, 1]$ (d) $[0, 2]$

EXERCISE SET 1.5  Graphing Utility

1–4 Let f be the function whose graph is shown. On which of the following intervals, if any, is f continuous?
(a) $[1, 3]$ (b) $(1, 3)$ (c) $[1, 2]$
(d) $(1, 2)$ (e) $[2, 3]$ (f) $(2, 3)$
For each interval on which f is not continuous, indicate which conditions for the continuity of f do not hold. ■

1. 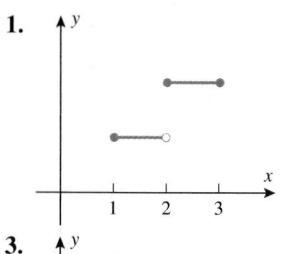   **2.**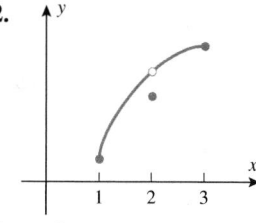

3. 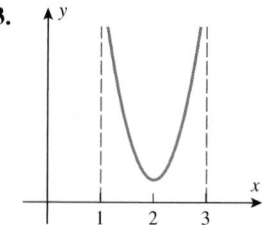   **4.**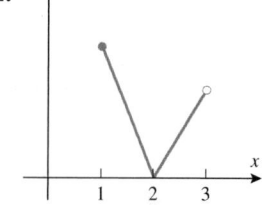

5. Consider the functions

$$f(x) = \begin{cases} 1, & x \neq 4 \\ -1, & x = 4 \end{cases} \quad \text{and} \quad g(x) = \begin{cases} 4x - 10, & x \neq 4 \\ -6, & x = 4 \end{cases}$$

In each part, is the given function continuous at $x = 4$?
(a) $f(x)$ (b) $g(x)$ (c) $-g(x)$ (d) $|f(x)|$
(e) $f(x)g(x)$ (f) $g(f(x))$ (g) $g(x) - 6f(x)$

6. Consider the functions

$$f(x) = \begin{cases} 1, & 0 \leq x \\ 0, & x < 0 \end{cases} \quad \text{and} \quad g(x) = \begin{cases} 0, & 0 \leq x \\ 1, & x < 0 \end{cases}$$

In each part, is the given function continuous at $x = 0$?
(a) $f(x)$ (b) $g(x)$ (c) $f(-x)$ (d) $|g(x)|$
(e) $f(x)g(x)$ (f) $g(f(x))$ (g) $f(x) + g(x)$

FOCUS ON CONCEPTS

7. In each part sketch the graph of a function f that satisfies the stated conditions.
(a) f is continuous everywhere except at $x = 3$, at which point it is continuous from the right.
(b) f has a two-sided limit at $x = 3$, but it is not continuous at $x = 3$.
(c) f is not continuous at $x = 3$, but if its value at $x = 3$ is changed from $f(3) = 1$ to $f(3) = 0$, it becomes continuous at $x = 3$.
(d) f is continuous on the interval $[0, 3)$ and is defined on the closed interval $[0, 3]$; but f is not continuous on the interval $[0, 3]$.

8. Assume that a function f is defined at $x = c$, and, with the aid of Definition 1.4.1, write down precisely what

condition (involving ϵ and δ) must be satisfied for f to be continuous at $x = c$. Explain why the condition $0 < |x - c| < \delta$ can be replaced by $|x - c| < \delta$.

9. A student parking lot at a university charges $2.00 for the first half hour (or any part) and $1.00 for each subsequent half hour (or any part) up to a daily maximum of $10.00.
(a) Sketch a graph of cost as a function of the time parked.
(b) Discuss the significance of the discontinuities in the graph to a student who parks there.

10. In each part determine whether the function is continuous or not, and explain your reasoning.
(a) The Earth's population as a function of time.
(b) Your exact height as a function of time.
(c) The cost of a taxi ride in your city as a function of the distance traveled.
(d) The volume of a melting ice cube as a function of time.

11–22 Find values of x, if any, at which f is not continuous. ■

11. $f(x) = 5x^4 - 3x + 7$ **12.** $f(x) = \sqrt[3]{x - 8}$

13. $f(x) = \dfrac{x + 2}{x^2 + 4}$ **14.** $f(x) = \dfrac{x + 2}{x^2 - 4}$

15. $f(x) = \dfrac{x}{2x^2 + x}$ **16.** $f(x) = \dfrac{2x + 1}{4x^2 + 4x + 5}$

17. $f(x) = \dfrac{3}{x} + \dfrac{x - 1}{x^2 - 1}$ **18.** $f(x) = \dfrac{5}{x} + \dfrac{2x}{x + 4}$

19. $f(x) = \dfrac{x^2 + 6x + 9}{|x| + 3}$ **20.** $f(x) = \left| 4 - \dfrac{8}{x^4 + x} \right|$

21. $f(x) = \begin{cases} 2x + 3, & x \leq 4 \\ 7 + \dfrac{16}{x}, & x > 4 \end{cases}$

22. $f(x) = \begin{cases} \dfrac{3}{x - 1}, & x \neq 1 \\ 3, & x = 1 \end{cases}$

23–28 True–False Determine whether the statement is true or false. Explain your answer. ■

23. If $f(x)$ is continuous at $x = c$, then so is $|f(x)|$.

24. If $|f(x)|$ is continuous at $x = c$, then so is $f(x)$.

25. If f and g are discontinuous at $x = c$, then so is $f + g$.

26. If f and g are discontinuous at $x = c$, then so is fg.

27. If $\sqrt{f(x)}$ is continuous at $x = c$, then so is $f(x)$.

28. If $f(x)$ is continuous at $x = c$, then so is $\sqrt{f(x)}$.

29–30 Find a value of the constant k, if possible, that will make the function continuous everywhere. ◼

29. (a) $f(x) = \begin{cases} 7x - 2, & x \le 1 \\ kx^2, & x > 1 \end{cases}$

 (b) $f(x) = \begin{cases} kx^2, & x \le 2 \\ 2x + k, & x > 2 \end{cases}$

30. (a) $f(x) = \begin{cases} 9 - x^2, & x \ge -3 \\ k/x^2, & x < -3 \end{cases}$

 (b) $f(x) = \begin{cases} 9 - x^2, & x \ge 0 \\ k/x^2, & x < 0 \end{cases}$

31. Find values of the constants k and m, if possible, that will make the function f continuous everywhere.

$$f(x) = \begin{cases} x^2 + 5, & x > 2 \\ m(x + 1) + k, & -1 < x \le 2 \\ 2x^3 + x + 7, & x \le -1 \end{cases}$$

32. On which of the following intervals is

$$f(x) = \frac{1}{\sqrt{x - 2}}$$

continuous?
 (a) $[2, +\infty)$ (b) $(-\infty, +\infty)$ (c) $(2, +\infty)$ (d) $[1, 2)$

33–36 A function f is said to have a ***removable discontinuity*** at $x = c$ if $\lim_{x \to c} f(x)$ exists but f is not continuous at $x = c$, either because f is not defined at c or because the definition for $f(c)$ differs from the value of the limit. This terminology will be needed in these exercises. ◼

33. (a) Sketch the graph of a function with a removable discontinuity at $x = c$ for which $f(c)$ is undefined.
 (b) Sketch the graph of a function with a removable discontinuity at $x = c$ for which $f(c)$ is defined.

34. (a) The terminology *removable discontinuity* is appropriate because a removable discontinuity of a function f at $x = c$ can be "removed" by redefining the value of f appropriately at $x = c$. What value for $f(c)$ removes the discontinuity?
 (b) Show that the following functions have removable discontinuities at $x = 1$, and sketch their graphs.

$$f(x) = \frac{x^2 - 1}{x - 1} \quad \text{and} \quad g(x) = \begin{cases} 1, & x > 1 \\ 0, & x = 1 \\ 1, & x < 1 \end{cases}$$

 (c) What values should be assigned to $f(1)$ and $g(1)$ to remove the discontinuities?

35–36 Find the values of x (if any) at which f is not continuous, and determine whether each such value is a removable discontinuity. ◼

35. (a) $f(x) = \dfrac{|x|}{x}$ (b) $f(x) = \dfrac{x^2 + 3x}{x + 3}$

 (c) $f(x) = \dfrac{x - 2}{|x| - 2}$

36. (a) $f(x) = \dfrac{x^2 - 4}{x^3 - 8}$ (b) $f(x) = \begin{cases} 2x - 3, & x \le 2 \\ x^2, & x > 2 \end{cases}$

 (c) $f(x) = \begin{cases} 3x^2 + 5, & x \ne 1 \\ 6, & x = 1 \end{cases}$

⋈ 37. (a) Use a graphing utility to generate the graph of the function $f(x) = (x + 3)/(2x^2 + 5x - 3)$, and then use the graph to make a conjecture about the number and locations of all discontinuities.
 (b) Check your conjecture by factoring the denominator.

⋈ 38. (a) Use a graphing utility to generate the graph of the function $f(x) = x/(x^3 - x + 2)$, and then use the graph to make a conjecture about the number and locations of all discontinuities.
 (b) Use the Intermediate-Value Theorem to approximate the locations of all discontinuities to two decimal places.

39. Prove that $f(x) = x^{3/5}$ is continuous everywhere, carefully justifying each step.

40. Prove that $f(x) = 1/\sqrt{x^4 + 7x^2 + 1}$ is continuous everywhere, carefully justifying each step.

41. Prove:
 (a) part (*a*) of Theorem 1.5.3
 (b) part (*b*) of Theorem 1.5.3
 (c) part (*c*) of Theorem 1.5.3.

42. Prove part (*b*) of Theorem 1.5.4.

43. (a) Use Theorem 1.5.5 to prove that if f is continuous at $x = c$, then $\lim_{h \to 0} f(c + h) = f(c)$.
 (b) Prove that if $\lim_{h \to 0} f(c + h) = f(c)$, then f is continuous at $x = c$. [*Hint:* What does this limit tell you about the continuity of $g(h) = f(c + h)$?]
 (c) Conclude from parts (a) and (b) that f is continuous at $x = c$ if and only if $\lim_{h \to 0} f(c + h) = f(c)$.

44. Prove: If f and g are continuous on $[a, b]$, and $f(a) > g(a)$, $f(b) < g(b)$, then there is at least one solution of the equation $f(x) = g(x)$ in (a, b). [*Hint:* Consider $f(x) - g(x)$.]

FOCUS ON CONCEPTS

45. Give an example of a function f that is defined on a closed interval, and whose values at the endpoints have opposite signs, but for which the equation $f(x) = 0$ has no solution in the interval.

46. Let f be the function whose graph is shown in Exercise 2. For each interval, determine (i) whether the hypothesis of the Intermediate-Value Theorem is satisfied, and (ii) whether the conclusion of the Intermediate-Value Theorem is satisfied.
 (a) $[1, 2]$ (b) $[2, 3]$ (c) $[1, 3]$

47. Show that the equation $x^3 + x^2 - 2x = 1$ has at least one solution in the interval $[-1, 1]$.

48. Prove: If $p(x)$ is a polynomial of odd degree, then the equation $p(x) = 0$ has at least one real solution.

49. The accompanying figure shows the graph of the equation $y = x^4 + x - 1$. Use the method of Example 5 to approximate the x-intercepts with an error of at most 0.05.

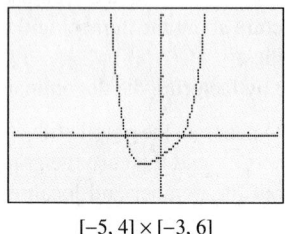

$[-5, 4] \times [-3, 6]$
xScl $= 1$, yScl $= 1$ ◀ **Figure Ex-49**

50. The accompanying figure shows the graph of the equation $y = 5 - x - x^4$. Use the method of Example 5 to approximate the roots of the equation $5 - x - x^4 = 0$ to two decimal-place accuracy.

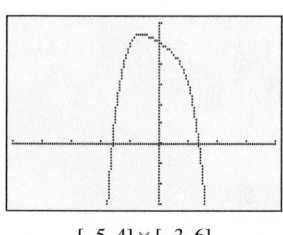

$[-5, 4] \times [-3, 6]$
xScl $= 1$, yScl $= 1$ ◀ **Figure Ex-50**

51. Use the fact that $\sqrt{5}$ is a solution of $x^2 - 5 = 0$ to approximate $\sqrt{5}$ with an error of at most 0.005.

52. A sprinter, who is timed with a stopwatch, runs a hundred yard dash in 10 s. The stopwatch is reset to 0, and the sprinter is timed jogging back to the starting block. Show that there is at least one point on the track at which the reading on the stopwatch during the sprint is the same as the reading during the return jog. [*Hint:* Use the result in Exercise 44.]

53. Prove that there exist points on opposite sides of the equator that are at the same temperature. [*Hint:* Consider the accompanying figure, which shows a view of the equator from a point above the North Pole. Assume that the temperature $T(\theta)$ is a continuous function of the angle θ, and consider the function $f(\theta) = T(\theta + \pi) - T(\theta)$.]

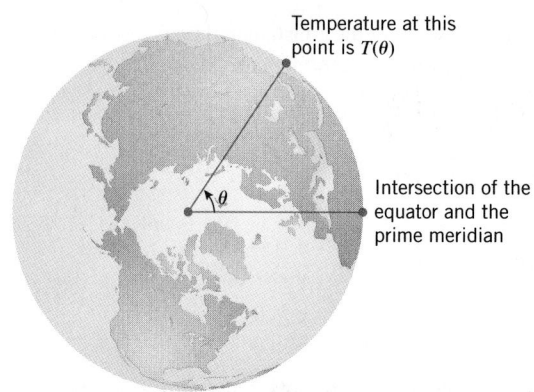

Temperature at this point is $T(\theta)$

Intersection of the equator and the prime meridian

▲ **Figure Ex-53**

54. Let R denote an elliptical region in the xy-plane, and define $f(z)$ to be the area within R that is on, or to the left of, the vertical line $x = z$. Prove that f is a continuous function of z. [*Hint:* Assume the ellipse is between the horizontal lines $y = a$ and $y = b$, $a < b$. Argue that $|f(z_1) - f(z_2)| \leq (b - a) \cdot |z_1 - z_2|$.]

55. Let R denote an elliptical region in the plane. For any line L, prove there is a line perpendicular to L that divides R in half by area. [*Hint:* Introduce coordinates so that L is the x-axis. Use the result in Exercise 54 and the Intermediate-Value Theorem.]

56. Suppose that f is continuous on the interval $[0, 1]$ and that $0 \leq f(x) \leq 1$ for all x in this interval.
 (a) Sketch the graph of $y = x$ together with a possible graph for f over the interval $[0, 1]$.
 (b) Use the Intermediate-Value Theorem to help prove that there is at least one number c in the interval $[0, 1]$ such that $f(c) = c$.

57. Writing It is often assumed that changing physical quantities such as the height of a falling object or the weight of a melting snowball, are continuous functions of time. Use specific examples to discuss the merits of this assumption.

58. Writing The Intermediate-Value Theorem (Theorem 1.5.7) is an example of what is known as an "existence theorem." In your own words, describe how to recognize an existence theorem, and discuss some of the ways in which an existence theorem can be useful.

✔ **QUICK CHECK ANSWERS 1.5**

1. $f(c)$ is defined; $\lim_{x \to c} f(x)$ exists; $\lim_{x \to c} f(x) = f(c)$ **2.** (a) 3 (b) 3 **3.** $-2/5$ **4.** $x = 1, 4$
5. (a) yes (b) no (c) yes (d) yes

CONTINUITY OF TRIGONOMETRIC, EXPONENTIAL, AND INVERSE FUNCTIONS

In this section we will discuss the continuity properties of trigonometric functions, exponential functions, and inverses of various continuous functions. We will also discuss some important limits involving such functions.

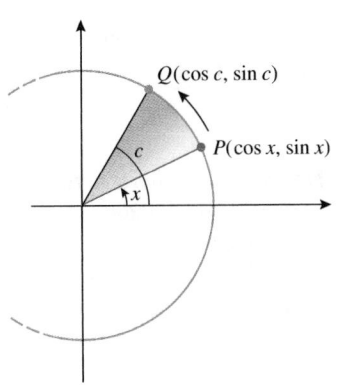

As x approaches c the point P approaches the point Q.

▲ **Figure 1.6.1**

Theorem 1.6.1 implies that the six basic trigonometric functions are continuous on their domains. In particular, $\sin x$ and $\cos x$ are continuous everywhere.

■ CONTINUITY OF TRIGONOMETRIC FUNCTIONS

Recall from trigonometry that the graphs of $\sin x$ and $\cos x$ are drawn as continuous curves. We will not formally prove that these functions are continuous, but we can motivate this fact by letting c be a fixed angle in radian measure and x a variable angle in radian measure. If, as illustrated in Figure 1.6.1, the angle x approaches the angle c, then the point $P(\cos x, \sin x)$ moves along the unit circle toward $Q(\cos c, \sin c)$, and the coordinates of P approach the corresponding coordinates of Q. This implies that

$$\lim_{x \to c} \sin x = \sin c \quad \text{and} \quad \lim_{x \to c} \cos x = \cos c \tag{1}$$

Thus, $\sin x$ and $\cos x$ are continuous at the arbitrary point c; that is, these functions are continuous everywhere.

The formulas in (1) can be used to find limits of the remaining trigonometric functions by expressing them in terms of $\sin x$ and $\cos x$; for example, if $\cos c \neq 0$, then

$$\lim_{x \to c} \tan x = \lim_{x \to c} \frac{\sin x}{\cos x} = \frac{\sin c}{\cos c} = \tan c$$

Thus, we are led to the following theorem.

1.6.1   THEOREM   *If c is any number in the natural domain of the stated trigonometric function, then*

$$\lim_{x \to c} \sin x = \sin c \qquad \lim_{x \to c} \cos x = \cos c \qquad \lim_{x \to c} \tan x = \tan c$$

$$\lim_{x \to c} \csc x = \csc c \qquad \lim_{x \to c} \sec x = \sec c \qquad \lim_{x \to c} \cot x = \cot c$$

▶ **Example 1**   Find the limit

$$\lim_{x \to 1} \cos\left(\frac{x^2 - 1}{x - 1}\right)$$

Solution.   Since the cosine function is continuous everywhere, it follows from Theorem 1.5.5 that

$$\lim_{x \to 1} \cos(g(x)) = \cos\left(\lim_{x \to 1} g(x)\right)$$

provided $\lim_{x \to 1} g(x)$ exists. Thus,

$$\lim_{x \to 1} \cos\left(\frac{x^2 - 1}{x - 1}\right) = \lim_{x \to 1} \cos(x + 1) = \cos\left(\lim_{x \to 1} (x + 1)\right) = \cos 2 \blacktriangleleft$$

■ CONTINUITY OF INVERSE FUNCTIONS

Since the graphs of a one-to-one function f and its inverse f^{-1} are reflections of one another about the line $y = x$, it is clear geometrically that if the graph of f has no breaks or holes in it, then neither does the graph of f^{-1}. This, and the fact that the range of f is the domain of f^{-1}, suggests the following result, which we state without formal proof.

To paraphrase Theorem 1.6.2, *the inverse of a continuous function is continuous.*

1.6.2 THEOREM *If f is a one-to-one function that is continuous at each point of its domain, then f^{-1} is continuous at each point of its domain; that is, f^{-1} is continuous at each point in the range of f.*

▶ **Example 2** Use Theorem 1.6.2 to prove that $\sin^{-1} x$ is continuous on the interval $[-1, 1]$.

Solution. Recall that $\sin^{-1} x$ is the inverse of the restricted sine function whose domain is the interval $[-\pi/2, \pi/2]$ and whose range is the interval $[-1, 1]$ (Definition 0.4.6 and Figure 0.4.13). Since $\sin x$ is continuous on the interval $[-\pi/2, \pi/2]$, Theorem 1.6.2 implies $\sin^{-1} x$ is continuous on the interval $[-1, 1]$. ◀

Arguments similar to the solution of Example 2 show that each of the inverse trigonometric functions defined in Section 0.4 is continuous at each point of its domain.

When we introduced the exponential function $f(x) = b^x$ in Section 0.5, we assumed that its graph is a curve without breaks, gaps, or holes; that is, we assumed that the graph of $y = b^x$ is a continuous curve. This assumption and Theorem 1.6.2 imply the following theorem, which we state without formal proof.

1.6.3 THEOREM *Let $b > 0$, $b \neq 1$.*

(a) *The function b^x is continuous on $(-\infty, +\infty)$.*

(b) *The function $\log_b x$ is continuous on $(0, +\infty)$.*

▶ **Example 3** Where is the function $f(x) = \dfrac{\tan^{-1} x + \ln x}{x^2 - 4}$ continuous?

Solution. The fraction will be continuous at all points where the numerator and denominator are both continuous and the denominator is nonzero. Since $\tan^{-1} x$ is continuous everywhere and $\ln x$ is continuous if $x > 0$, the numerator is continuous if $x > 0$. The denominator, being a polynomial, is continuous everywhere, so the fraction will be continuous at all points where $x > 0$ and the denominator is nonzero. Thus, f is continuous on the intervals $(0, 2)$ and $(2, +\infty)$. ◀

■ **OBTAINING LIMITS BY SQUEEZING**

In Section 1.1 we used numerical evidence to conjecture that

$$\lim_{x \to 0} \frac{\sin x}{x} = 1 \tag{2}$$

However, this limit is not easy to establish with certainty. The limit is an indeterminate form of type $0/0$, and there is no simple algebraic manipulation that one can perform to obtain the limit. Later in the text we will develop general methods for finding limits of indeterminate forms, but in this particular case we can use a technique called *squeezing*.

The method of squeezing is used to prove that $f(x) \to L$ as $x \to c$ by "trapping" or "squeezing" f between two functions, g and h, whose limits as $x \to c$ are known with *certainty* to be L. As illustrated in Figure 1.6.2, this forces f to have a limit of L as well. This is the idea behind the following theorem, which we state without proof.

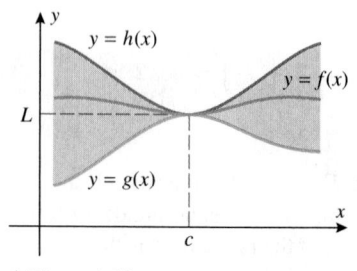

▲ **Figure 1.6.2**

1.6.4   THEOREM (*The Squeezing Theorem*)   *Let f, g, and h be functions satisfying*

$$g(x) \leq f(x) \leq h(x)$$

for all x in some open interval containing the number c, with the possible exception that the inequalities need not hold at c. If g and h have the same limit as x approaches c, say

$$\lim_{x \to c} g(x) = \lim_{x \to c} h(x) = L$$

then f also has this limit as x approaches c, that is,

$$\lim_{x \to c} f(x) = L$$

The Squeezing Theorem also holds for one-sided limits and limits at $+\infty$ and $-\infty$. How do you think the hypotheses would change in those cases?

To illustrate how the Squeezing Theorem works, we will prove the following results, which are illustrated in Figure 1.6.3.

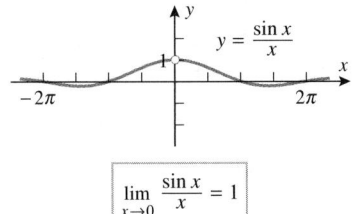

$$\lim_{x \to 0} \frac{\sin x}{x} = 1$$

1.6.5   THEOREM

(*a*) $$\lim_{x \to 0} \frac{\sin x}{x} = 1$$ (*b*) $$\lim_{x \to 0} \frac{1 - \cos x}{x} = 0$$

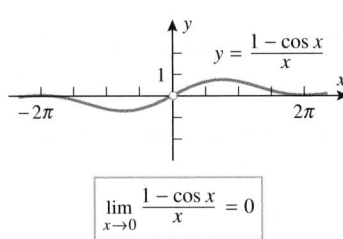

$$\lim_{x \to 0} \frac{1 - \cos x}{x} = 0$$

▲ **Figure 1.6.3**

PROOF (*a*)   In this proof we will interpret x as an angle in radian measure, and we will assume to start that $0 < x < \pi/2$. As illustrated in Figure 1.6.4, the area of a sector with central angle x and radius 1 lies between the areas of two triangles, one with area $\frac{1}{2} \tan x$ and the other with area $\frac{1}{2} \sin x$. Since the sector has area $\frac{1}{2}x$ (see marginal note), it follows that

$$\frac{1}{2} \tan x \geq \frac{1}{2}x \geq \frac{1}{2} \sin x$$

Multiplying through by $2/(\sin x)$ and using the fact that $\sin x > 0$ for $0 < x < \pi/2$, we obtain

$$\frac{1}{\cos x} \geq \frac{x}{\sin x} \geq 1$$

Next, taking reciprocals reverses the inequalities, so we obtain

$$\cos x \leq \frac{\sin x}{x} \leq 1 \tag{3}$$

which squeezes the function $(\sin x)/x$ between the functions $\cos x$ and 1. Although we derived these inequalities by assuming that $0 < x < \pi/2$, they also hold for $-\pi/2 < x < 0$ [since replacing x by $-x$ and using the identities $\sin(-x) = -\sin x$, and $\cos(-x) = \cos x$

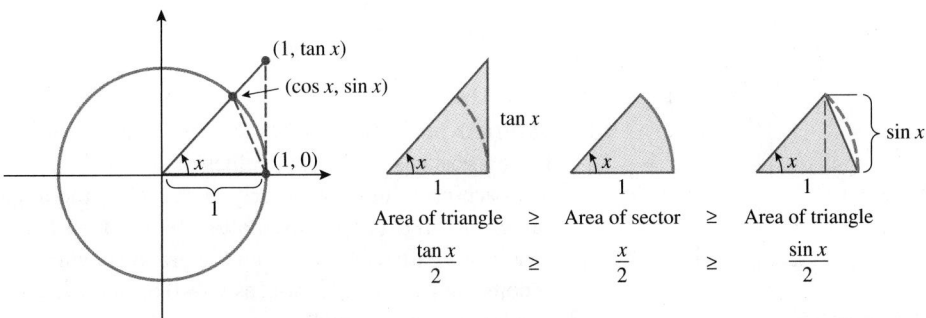

▶ **Figure 1.6.4**

Recall that the area A of a sector of radius r and central angle θ is

$$A = \frac{1}{2}r^2\theta$$

This can be derived from the relationship

$$\frac{A}{\pi r^2} = \frac{\theta}{2\pi}$$

which states that the area of the sector is to the area of the circle as the central angle of the sector is to the central angle of the circle.

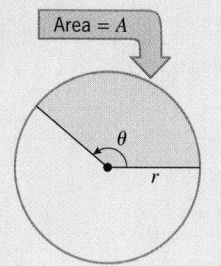

leaves (3) unchanged]. Finally, since

$$\lim_{x \to 0} \cos x = 1 \quad \text{and} \quad \lim_{x \to 0} 1 = 1$$

the Squeezing Theorem implies that

$$\lim_{x \to 0} \frac{\sin x}{x} = 1$$

PROOF (b)   For this proof we will use the limit in part (a), the continuity of the sine function, and the trigonometric identity $\sin^2 x = 1 - \cos^2 x$. We obtain

$$\lim_{x \to 0} \frac{1 - \cos x}{x} = \lim_{x \to 0} \left[\frac{1 - \cos x}{x} \cdot \frac{1 + \cos x}{1 + \cos x} \right] = \lim_{x \to 0} \frac{\sin^2 x}{(1 + \cos x)x}$$

$$= \left(\lim_{x \to 0} \frac{\sin x}{x} \right) \left(\lim_{x \to 0} \frac{\sin x}{1 + \cos x} \right) = (1)\left(\frac{0}{1 + 1} \right) = 0 \quad \blacksquare$$

▶ **Example 4**   Find

(a) $\displaystyle\lim_{x \to 0} \frac{\tan x}{x}$ (b) $\displaystyle\lim_{\theta \to 0} \frac{\sin 2\theta}{\theta}$ (c) $\displaystyle\lim_{x \to 0} \frac{\sin 3x}{\sin 5x}$

Solution (a).

$$\lim_{x \to 0} \frac{\tan x}{x} = \lim_{x \to 0} \left(\frac{\sin x}{x} \cdot \frac{1}{\cos x} \right) = \left(\lim_{x \to 0} \frac{\sin x}{x} \right) \left(\lim_{x \to 0} \frac{1}{\cos x} \right) = (1)(1) = 1$$

Solution (b).   The trick is to multiply and divide by 2, which will make the denominator the same as the argument of the sine function [just as in Theorem 1.6.5(a)]:

$$\lim_{\theta \to 0} \frac{\sin 2\theta}{\theta} = \lim_{\theta \to 0} 2 \cdot \frac{\sin 2\theta}{2\theta} = 2 \lim_{\theta \to 0} \frac{\sin 2\theta}{2\theta}$$

Now make the substitution $x = 2\theta$, and use the fact that $x \to 0$ as $\theta \to 0$. This yields

$$\lim_{\theta \to 0} \frac{\sin 2\theta}{\theta} = 2 \lim_{\theta \to 0} \frac{\sin 2\theta}{2\theta} = 2 \lim_{x \to 0} \frac{\sin x}{x} = 2(1) = 2$$

TECHNOLOGY MASTERY

Use a graphing utility to confirm the limits in Example 4, and if you have a CAS, use it to obtain the limits.

Solution (c).

$$\lim_{x \to 0} \frac{\sin 3x}{\sin 5x} = \lim_{x \to 0} \frac{\dfrac{\sin 3x}{x}}{\dfrac{\sin 5x}{x}} = \lim_{x \to 0} \frac{3 \cdot \dfrac{\sin 3x}{3x}}{5 \cdot \dfrac{\sin 5x}{5x}} = \frac{3 \cdot 1}{5 \cdot 1} = \frac{3}{5} \quad \blacktriangleleft$$

▶ **Example 5**   Discuss the limits

(a) $\displaystyle\lim_{x \to 0} \sin\left(\frac{1}{x} \right)$ (b) $\displaystyle\lim_{x \to 0} x \sin\left(\frac{1}{x} \right)$

Solution (a).   Let us view $1/x$ as an angle in radian measure. As $x \to 0^+$, the angle $1/x$ approaches $+\infty$, so the values of $\sin(1/x)$ keep oscillating between -1 and 1 without approaching a limit. Similarly, as $x \to 0^-$, the angle $1/x$ approaches $-\infty$, so again the values of $\sin(1/x)$ keep oscillating between -1 and 1 without approaching a limit. These conclusions are consistent with the graph shown in Figure 1.6.5. Note that the oscillations become more and more rapid as $x \to 0$ because $1/x$ increases (or decreases) more and more rapidly as x approaches 0.

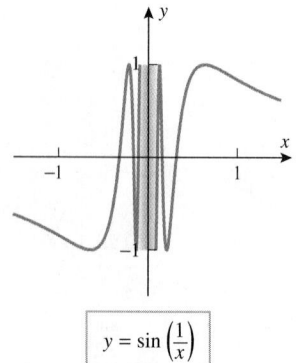

$y = \sin\left(\dfrac{1}{x}\right)$

▲ **Figure 1.6.5**

Solution (b). Since

$$-1 \le \sin\left(\frac{1}{x}\right) \le 1$$

it follows that if $x \ne 0$, then

$$-|x| \le x \sin\left(\frac{1}{x}\right) \le |x| \tag{4}$$

Since $|x| \to 0$ as $x \to 0$, the inequalities in (4) and the Squeezing Theorem imply that

$$\lim_{x \to 0} x \sin\left(\frac{1}{x}\right) = 0$$

This is consistent with the graph shown in Figure 1.6.6. ◄

Confirm (4) by considering the cases $x > 0$ and $x < 0$ separately.

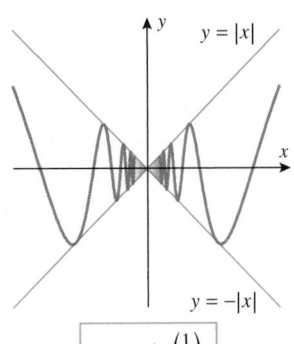

$y = x \sin\left(\frac{1}{x}\right)$

▲ **Figure 1.6.6**

REMARK | It follows from part (b) of this example that the function

$$f(x) = \begin{cases} x \sin(1/x), & x \ne 0 \\ 0, & x = 0 \end{cases}$$

is continuous at $x = 0$, since the value of the function and the value of the limit are the same at 0. This shows that the behavior of a function can be very complex in the vicinity of $x = c$, even though the function is continuous at c.

✔ QUICK CHECK EXERCISES 1.6   *(See page 128 for answers.)*

1. In each part, is the given function continuous on the interval $[0, \pi/2]$?
   (a) $\sin x$ (b) $\cos x$ (c) $\tan x$ (d) $\csc x$

2. Evaluate
   (a) $\displaystyle\lim_{x \to 0} \frac{\sin x}{x}$
   (b) $\displaystyle\lim_{x \to 0} \frac{1 - \cos x}{x}$.

3. Suppose a function f has the property that for all real numbers x
   $$3 - |x| \le f(x) \le 3 + |x|$$
   From this we can conclude that $f(x) \to$ _____ as $x \to$ _____.

4. In each part, give the largest interval on which the function is continuous.
   (a) e^x (b) $\ln x$ (c) $\sin^{-1} x$ (d) $\tan^{-1} x$

EXERCISE SET 1.6   ∿ Graphing Utility

1–8 Find the discontinuities, if any. ■

1. $f(x) = \sin(x^2 - 2)$

2. $f(x) = \cos\left(\dfrac{x}{x - \pi}\right)$

3. $f(x) = |\cot x|$

4. $f(x) = \sec x$

5. $f(x) = \csc x$

6. $f(x) = \dfrac{1}{1 + \sin^2 x}$

7. $f(x) = \dfrac{1}{1 - 2\sin x}$

8. $f(x) = \sqrt{2 + \tan^2 x}$

9–14 Determine where f is continuous. ■

9. $f(x) = \sin^{-1} 2x$

10. $f(x) = \cos^{-1}(\ln x)$

11. $f(x) = \dfrac{\ln(\tan^{-1} x)}{x^2 - 9}$

12. $f(x) = \exp\left(\dfrac{\sin x}{x}\right)$

13. $f(x) = \dfrac{\sin^{-1}(1/x)}{x}$

14. $f(x) = \ln|x| - 2\ln(x + 3)$

15–16 In each part, use Theorem 1.5.6(*b*) to show that the function is continuous everywhere. ■

15. (a) $\sin(x^3 + 7x + 1)$ (b) $|\sin x|$ $\cos^3(x + 1)$

16. (a) $|3 + \sin 2x|$ (b) $\sin(\sin x)$
(c) $\cos^5 x - 2\cos^3 x + 1$

17–42 Find the limits. ■

17. $\displaystyle\lim_{x \to +\infty} \cos\left(\frac{1}{x}\right)$

18. $\displaystyle\lim_{x \to +\infty} \sin\left(\frac{\pi x}{2 - 3x}\right)$

19. $\displaystyle\lim_{x \to +\infty} \sin^{-1}\left(\frac{x}{1 - 2x}\right)$

20. $\displaystyle\lim_{x \to +\infty} \ln\left(\frac{x + 1}{x}\right)$

21. $\displaystyle\lim_{x \to 0} e^{\sin x}$

22. $\displaystyle\lim_{x \to +\infty} \cos(2 \tan^{-1} x)$

23. $\displaystyle\lim_{\theta \to 0} \frac{\sin 3\theta}{\theta}$

24. $\displaystyle\lim_{h \to 0} \frac{\sin h}{2h}$

25. $\displaystyle\lim_{\theta \to 0^+} \frac{\sin \theta}{\theta^2}$

26. $\displaystyle\lim_{\theta \to 0} \frac{\sin^2 \theta}{\theta}$

27. $\displaystyle\lim_{x \to 0} \frac{\tan 7x}{\sin 3x}$

28. $\displaystyle\lim_{x \to 0} \frac{\sin 6x}{\sin 8x}$

29. $\displaystyle\lim_{x \to 0^+} \frac{\sin x}{5\sqrt{x}}$

30. $\displaystyle\lim_{x \to 0} \frac{\sin^2 x}{3x^2}$

31. $\displaystyle\lim_{x \to 0} \frac{\sin x^2}{x}$

32. $\displaystyle\lim_{h \to 0} \frac{\sin h}{1 - \cos h}$

33. $\displaystyle\lim_{t \to 0} \frac{t^2}{1 - \cos^2 t}$

34. $\displaystyle\lim_{x \to 0} \frac{x}{\cos\left(\frac{1}{2}\pi - x\right)}$

35. $\displaystyle\lim_{\theta \to 0} \frac{\theta^2}{1 - \cos \theta}$

36. $\displaystyle\lim_{h \to 0} \frac{1 - \cos 3h}{\cos^2 5h - 1}$

37. $\displaystyle\lim_{x \to 0^+} \sin\left(\frac{1}{x}\right)$

38. $\displaystyle\lim_{x \to 0} \frac{x^2 - 3\sin x}{x}$

39. $\displaystyle\lim_{x \to 0} \frac{2 - \cos 3x - \cos 4x}{x}$

40. $\displaystyle\lim_{x \to 0} \frac{\tan 3x^2 + \sin^2 5x}{x^2}$

41–42 (a) Complete the table and make a guess about the limit indicated. (b) Find the exact value of the limit. ■

41. $f(x) = \dfrac{\sin(x - 5)}{x^2 - 25}$; $\displaystyle\lim_{x \to 5} f(x)$

x	4	4.5	4.9	5.1	5.5	6
$f(x)$						

◀ **Table Ex-41**

42. $f(x) = \dfrac{\sin(x^2 + 3x + 2)}{x + 2}$; $\displaystyle\lim_{x \to -2} f(x)$

x	−2.1	−2.01	−2.001	−1.999	−1.99	−1.9
$f(x)$						

▲ **Table Ex-42**

43–46 True–False Determine whether the statement is true or false. Explain your answer. ■

43. Suppose that for all real numbers x, a function f satisfies

$$|f(x) + 5| \le |x + 1|$$

Then $\lim_{x \to -1} f(x) = -5$.

44. For $0 < x < \pi/2$, the graph of $y = \sin x$ lies below the graph of $y = x$ and above the graph of $y = x \cos x$.

45. If an invertible function f is continuous everywhere, then its inverse f^{-1} is also continuous everywhere.

46. Suppose that M is a positive number and that for all real numbers x, a function f satisfies

$$-M \le f(x) \le M$$

Then

$$\lim_{x \to 0} xf(x) = 0 \quad \text{and} \quad \lim_{x \to +\infty} \frac{f(x)}{x} = 0$$

FOCUS ON CONCEPTS

47. In an attempt to verify that $\lim_{x \to 0} (\sin x)/x = 1$, a student constructs the accompanying table.
(a) What mistake did the student make?
(b) What is the exact value of the limit illustrated by this table?

x	−0.01	−0.001	0.001	0.01
$\sin x/x$	0.017453	0.017453	0.017453	0.017453

▲ **Table Ex-47**

48. Consider $\lim_{x \to 0} (1 - \cos x)/x$, where x is in degrees. Why is it possible to evaluate this limit with little or no computation?

49. In the circle in the accompanying figure, a central angle of measure θ radians subtends a chord of length $c(\theta)$ and a circular arc of length $s(\theta)$. Based on your intuition, what would you conjecture is the value of $\lim_{\theta \to 0^+} c(\theta)/s(\theta)$? Verify your conjecture by computing the limit.

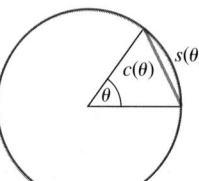

◀ **Figure Ex-49**

50. What is wrong with the following "proof" that $\lim_{x \to 0}[(\sin 2x)/x] = 1$? Since

$$\lim_{x \to 0}(\sin 2x - x) = \lim_{x \to 0} \sin 2x - \lim_{x \to 0} x = 0 - 0 = 0$$

if x is close to 0, then $\sin 2x - x \approx 0$ or, equivalently, $\sin 2x \approx x$. Dividing both sides of this approximate equality by x yields $(\sin 2x)/x \approx 1$. That is, $\lim_{x \to 0}[(\sin 2x)/x] = 1$.

51. Find a nonzero value for the constant k that makes

$$f(x) = \begin{cases} \dfrac{\tan kx}{x}, & x < 0 \\ 3x + 2k^2, & x \geq 0 \end{cases}$$

continuous at $x = 0$.

52. Is

$$f(x) = \begin{cases} \dfrac{\sin x}{|x|}, & x \neq 0 \\ 1, & x = 0 \end{cases}$$

continuous at $x = 0$? Explain.

53. In parts (a)–(c), find the limit by making the indicated substitution.

(a) $\lim\limits_{x \to +\infty} x \sin \dfrac{1}{x}$; $\quad t = \dfrac{1}{x}$

(b) $\lim\limits_{x \to -\infty} x \left(1 - \cos \dfrac{1}{x}\right)$; $\quad t = \dfrac{1}{x}$

(c) $\lim\limits_{x \to \pi} \dfrac{\pi - x}{\sin x}$; $\quad t = \pi - x$

54. Find $\lim\limits_{x \to 2} \dfrac{\cos(\pi/x)}{x - 2}$. $\left[\textit{Hint: Let } t = \dfrac{\pi}{2} - \dfrac{\pi}{x}.\right]$

55. Find $\lim\limits_{x \to 1} \dfrac{\sin(\pi x)}{x - 1}$. **56.** Find $\lim\limits_{x \to \pi/4} \dfrac{\tan x - 1}{x - \pi/4}$.

57. Find $\lim\limits_{x \to \pi/4} \dfrac{\cos x - \sin x}{x - \pi/4}$.

58. Suppose that f is an invertible function, $f(0) = 0$, f is continuous at 0, and $\lim_{x \to 0}(f(x)/x)$ exists. Given that $L = \lim_{x \to 0}(f(x)/x)$, show

$$\lim_{x \to 0} \dfrac{x}{f^{-1}(x)} = L$$

[*Hint:* Apply Theorem 1.5.5 to the composition $h \circ g$, where

$$h(x) = \begin{cases} f(x)/x, & x \neq 0 \\ L, & x = 0 \end{cases}$$

and $g(x) = f^{-1}(x)$.]

59–62 Apply the result of Exercise 58, if needed, to find the limits. ∎

59. $\lim\limits_{x \to 0} \dfrac{x}{\sin^{-1} x}$

60. $\lim\limits_{x \to 0} \dfrac{\tan^{-1} x}{x}$

61. $\lim\limits_{x \to 0} \dfrac{\sin^{-1} 5x}{x}$

62. $\lim\limits_{x \to 1} \dfrac{\sin^{-1}(x - 1)}{x^2 - 1}$

FOCUS ON CONCEPTS

63. In Example 5 we used the Squeezing Theorem to prove that

$$\lim_{x \to 0} x \sin \left(\dfrac{1}{x}\right) = 0$$

Why couldn't we have obtained the same result by writing

$$\lim_{x \to 0} x \sin \left(\dfrac{1}{x}\right) = \lim_{x \to 0} x \cdot \lim_{x \to 0} \sin \left(\dfrac{1}{x}\right)$$

$$= 0 \cdot \lim_{x \to 0} \sin \left(\dfrac{1}{x}\right) = 0?$$

64. Sketch the graphs of the curves $y = 1 - x^2$, $y = \cos x$, and $y = f(x)$, where f is a function that satisfies the inequalities

$$1 - x^2 \leq f(x) \leq \cos x$$

for all x in the interval $(-\pi/2, \pi/2)$. What can you say about the limit of $f(x)$ as $x \to 0$? Explain.

65. Sketch the graphs of the curves $y = 1/x$, $y = -1/x$, and $y = f(x)$, where f is a function that satisfies the inequalities

$$-\dfrac{1}{x} \leq f(x) \leq \dfrac{1}{x}$$

for all x in the interval $[1, +\infty)$. What can you say about the limit of $f(x)$ as $x \to +\infty$? Explain your reasoning.

66. Draw pictures analogous to Figure 1.6.2 that illustrate the Squeezing Theorem for limits of the forms $\lim_{x \to +\infty} f(x)$ and $\lim_{x \to -\infty} f(x)$.

67. (a) Use the Intermediate-Value Theorem to show that the equation $x = \cos x$ has at least one solution in the interval $[0, \pi/2]$.
(b) Show graphically that there is exactly one solution in the interval.
(c) Approximate the solution to three decimal places.

68. (a) Use the Intermediate-Value Theorem to show that the equation $x + \sin x = 1$ has at least one solution in the interval $[0, \pi/6]$.
(b) Show graphically that there is exactly one solution in the interval.
(c) Approximate the solution to three decimal places.

69. In the study of falling objects near the surface of the Earth, the *acceleration g due to gravity* is commonly taken to be a constant 9.8 m/s². However, the elliptical shape of the Earth and other factors cause variations in this value that depend on latitude. The following formula, known as the World Geodetic System 1984 (WGS 84) Ellipsoidal Gravity Formula, is used to predict the value of g at a latitude of ϕ degrees (either north or south of the equator):

$$g = 9.7803253359 \dfrac{1 + 0.0019318526461 \sin^2 \phi}{\sqrt{1 - 0.0066943799901 \sin^2 \phi}} \ \text{m/s}^2$$

(cont.)

(a) Use a graphing utility to graph the curve $y = g(\phi)$ for $0° \leq \phi \leq 90°$. What do the values of g at $\phi = 0°$ and at $\phi = 90°$ tell you about the WGS 84 ellipsoid model for the Earth?

(b) Show that $g = 9.8$ m/s^2 somewhere between latitudes of 38° and 39°.

70. Writing In your own words, explain the *practical value* of the Squeezing Theorem.

71. Writing A careful examination of the proof of Theorem 1.6.5 raises the issue of whether the proof might actually be a circular argument! Read the article "A Circular Argument" by Fred Richman in the March 1993 issue of *The College Mathematics Journal*, and write a short report on the author's principal points.

✔ QUICK CHECK ANSWERS 1.6

1. (a) yes (b) yes (c) yes (d) no   **2.** (a) 1 (b) 0   **3.** 3; 0   **4.** (a) $(-\infty, +\infty)$ (b) $(0, +\infty)$ (c) $[-1, 1]$ (d) $(-\infty, +\infty)$

CHAPTER 1 REVIEW EXERCISES   ⌇ Graphing Utility   [c] CAS

1. For the function f graphed in the accompanying figure, find the limit if it exists.

(a) $\lim\limits_{x \to 1} f(x)$ (b) $\lim\limits_{x \to 2} f(x)$ (c) $\lim\limits_{x \to 3} f(x)$

(d) $\lim\limits_{x \to 4} f(x)$ (e) $\lim\limits_{x \to +\infty} f(x)$ (f) $\lim\limits_{x \to -\infty} f(x)$

(g) $\lim\limits_{x \to 3^+} f(x)$ (h) $\lim\limits_{x \to 3^-} f(x)$ (i) $\lim\limits_{x \to 0} f(x)$

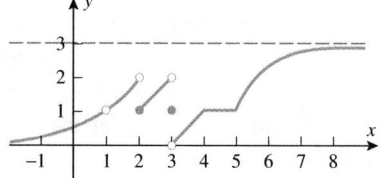

◀ **Figure Ex-1**

2. In each part, complete the table and make a conjecture about the value of the limit indicated. Confirm your conjecture by finding the limit analytically.

(a) $f(x) = \dfrac{x - 2}{x^2 - 4}$; $\lim\limits_{x \to 2^+} f(x)$

x	2.00001	2.0001	2.001	2.01	2.1	2.5
$f(x)$						

(b) $f(x) = \dfrac{\tan 4x}{x}$; $\lim\limits_{x \to 0} f(x)$

x	−0.01	−0.001	−0.0001	0.0001	0.001	0.01
$f(x)$						

⌇ **3.** (a) Approximate the value for the limit
$$\lim\limits_{x \to 0} \frac{3^x - 2^x}{x}$$
to three decimal places by constructing an appropriate table of values.

(b) Confirm your approximation using graphical evidence.

[c] **4.** Approximate
$$\lim\limits_{x \to 3} \frac{2^x - 8}{x - 3}$$
both by looking at a graph and by calculating values for some appropriate choices of x. Compare your answer with the value produced by a CAS.

5–10 Find the limits. ▪

5. $\lim\limits_{x \to -1} \dfrac{x^3 - x^2}{x - 1}$

6. $\lim\limits_{x \to 1} \dfrac{x^3 - x^2}{x - 1}$

7. $\lim\limits_{x \to -3} \dfrac{3x + 9}{x^2 + 4x + 3}$

8. $\lim\limits_{x \to 2^-} \dfrac{x + 2}{x - 2}$

9. $\lim\limits_{x \to +\infty} \dfrac{(2x - 1)^5}{(3x^2 + 2x - 7)(x^3 - 9x)}$

10. $\lim\limits_{x \to 0} \dfrac{\sqrt{x^2 + 4} - 2}{x^2}$

11. In each part, find the horizontal asymptotes, if any.

(a) $y = \dfrac{2x - 7}{x^2 - 4x}$

(b) $y = \dfrac{x^3 - x^2 + 10}{3x^2 - 4x}$

(c) $y = \dfrac{2x^2 - 6}{x^2 + 5x}$

12. In each part, find $\lim\limits_{x \to a} f(x)$, if it exists, where a is replaced by $0, 5^+, -5^-, -5, 5, -\infty$, and $+\infty$.

(a) $f(x) = \sqrt{5 - x}$

(b) $f(x) = \begin{cases} (x - 5)/|x - 5|, & x \neq 5 \\ 0, & x = 5 \end{cases}$

13–20 Find the limits. ▪

13. $\lim\limits_{x \to 0} \dfrac{\sin 3x}{\tan 3x}$

14. $\lim\limits_{x \to 0} \dfrac{x \sin x}{1 - \cos x}$

15. $\lim\limits_{x \to 0} \dfrac{3x - \sin(kx)}{x}$, $k \neq 0$

16. $\lim\limits_{\theta \to 0} \tan \left(\dfrac{1 - \cos \theta}{\theta} \right)$

17. $\lim\limits_{t \to \pi/2^+} e^{\tan t}$

18. $\lim\limits_{\theta \to 0^+} \ln(\sin 2\theta) - \ln(\tan \theta)$

19. $\lim\limits_{x \to +\infty} \left(1 + \dfrac{3}{x}\right)^{-x}$

20. $\lim\limits_{x \to +\infty} \left(1 + \dfrac{a}{x}\right)^{bx}$, $\quad a, b > 0$

21. If \$1000 is invested in an account that pays 7% interest compounded n times each year, then in 10 years there will be $1000(1 + 0.07/n)^{10n}$ dollars in the account. How much money will be in the account in 10 years if the interest is compounded quarterly ($n = 4$)? Monthly ($n = 12$)? Daily ($n = 365$)? Determine the amount of money that will be in the account in 10 years if the interest is compounded *continuously*, that is, as $n \to +\infty$.

22. (a) Write a paragraph or two that describes how the limit of a function can fail to exist at $x = a$, and accompany your description with some specific examples.

(b) Write a paragraph or two that describes how the limit of a function can fail to exist as $x \to +\infty$ or $x \to -\infty$, and accompany your description with some specific examples.

(c) Write a paragraph or two that describes how a function can fail to be continuous at $x = a$, and accompany your description with some specific examples.

23. (a) Find a formula for a rational function that has a vertical asymptote at $x = 1$ and a horizontal asymptote at $y = 2$.

(b) Check your work by using a graphing utility to graph the function.

24. Paraphrase the ϵ-δ definition for $\lim\limits_{x \to a} f(x) = L$ in terms of a graphing utility viewing window centered at the point (a, L).

25. Suppose that $f(x)$ is a function and that for any given $\epsilon > 0$, the condition $0 < |x - 2| < \frac{3}{4}\epsilon$ guarantees that $|f(x) - 5| < \epsilon$.

(a) What limit is described by this statement?

(b) Find a value of δ such that $0 < |x - 2| < \delta$ guarantees that $|8 f(x) - 40| < 0.048$.

26. The limit
$$\lim\limits_{x \to 0} \frac{\sin x}{x} = 1$$
ensures that there is a number δ such that
$$\left| \frac{\sin x}{x} - 1 \right| < 0.001$$
if $0 < |x| < \delta$. Estimate the largest such δ.

27. In each part, a positive number ϵ and the limit L of a function f at a are given. Find a number δ such that $|f(x) - L| < \epsilon$ if $0 < |x - a| < \delta$.

(a) $\lim\limits_{x \to 2} (4x - 7) = 1$; $\epsilon = 0.01$

(b) $\lim\limits_{x \to 3/2} \dfrac{4x^2 - 9}{2x - 3} = 6$; $\epsilon = 0.05$

(c) $\lim\limits_{x \to 4} x^2 = 16$; $\epsilon = 0.001$

28. Use Definition 1.4.1 to prove the stated limits are correct.

(a) $\lim\limits_{x \to 2} (4x - 7) = 1$

(b) $\lim\limits_{x \to 3/2} \dfrac{4x^2 - 9}{2x - 3} = 6$

29. Suppose that f is continuous at x_0 and that $f(x_0) > 0$. Give either an ϵ-δ proof or a convincing verbal argument to show that there must be an open interval containing x_0 on which $f(x) > 0$.

30. (a) Let
$$f(x) = \frac{\sin x - \sin 1}{x - 1}$$
Approximate $\lim\limits_{x \to 1} f(x)$ by graphing f and calculating values for some appropriate choices of x.

(b) Use the identity
$$\sin \alpha - \sin \beta = 2 \sin \frac{\alpha - \beta}{2} \cos \frac{\alpha + \beta}{2}$$
to find the exact value of $\lim\limits_{x \to 1} f(x)$.

31. Find values of x, if any, at which the given function is not continuous.

(a) $f(x) = \dfrac{x}{x^2 - 1}$

(b) $f(x) = |x^3 - 2x^2|$

(c) $f(x) = \dfrac{x + 3}{|x^2 + 3x|}$

32. Determine where f is continuous.

(a) $f(x) = \dfrac{x}{|x| - 3}$

(b) $f(x) = \cos^{-1}\left(\dfrac{1}{x}\right)$

(c) $f(x) = e^{\ln x}$

33. Suppose that
$$f(x) = \begin{cases} -x^4 + 3, & x \le 2 \\ x^2 + 9, & x > 2 \end{cases}$$
Is f continuous everywhere? Justify your conclusion.

34. One dictionary describes a continuous function as "one whose value at each point is closely approached by its values at neighboring points."

(a) How would you explain the meaning of the terms "neighboring points" and "closely approached" to a nonmathematician?

(b) Write a paragraph that explains why the dictionary definition is consistent with Definition 1.5.1.

35. Show that the conclusion of the Intermediate-Value Theorem may be false if f is not continuous on the interval $[a, b]$.

36. Suppose that f is continuous on the interval $[0, 1]$, that $f(0) = 2$, and that f has no zeros in the interval. Prove that $f(x) > 0$ for all x in $[0, 1]$.

37. Show that the equation $x^4 + 5x^3 + 5x - 1 = 0$ has at least two real solutions in the interval $[-6, 2]$.

CHAPTER 1 MAKING CONNECTIONS

In Section 1.1 we developed the notion of a tangent line to a graph at a given point by considering it as a limiting position of secant lines through that point (Figure 1.1.4a). In these exercises we will develop an analogous idea in which secant lines are replaced by "secant circles" and the tangent line is replaced by a "tangent circle" (called the *osculating circle*). We begin with the graph of $y = x^2$.

1. Recall that there is a unique circle through any three non-collinear points in the plane. For any positive real number x, consider the unique "secant circle" that passes through the fixed point $O(0, 0)$ and the variable points $Q(-x, x^2)$ and $P(x, x^2)$ (see the accompanying figure). Use plane geometry to explain why the center of this circle is the intersection of the y-axis and the perpendicular bisector of segment OP.

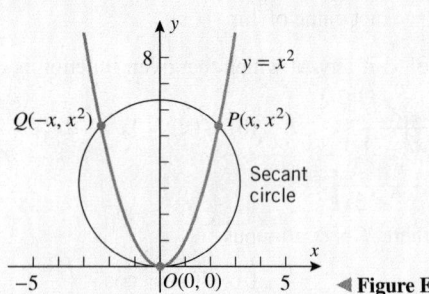

◀ **Figure Ex-1**

2. (a) Let $(0, C(x))$ denote the center of the circle in Exercise 1 and show that

$$C(x) = \tfrac{1}{2}x^2 + \tfrac{1}{2}$$

   (b) Show that as $x \to 0^+$, the secant circles approach a limiting position given by the circle that passes through the origin and is centered at $\left(0, \tfrac{1}{2}\right)$. As shown in the accom-

panying figure, this circle is the osculating circle to the graph of $y = x^2$ at the origin.

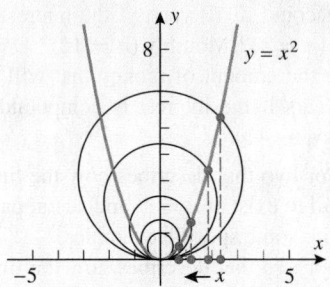

◀ **Figure Ex-2**

3. Show that if we replace the curve $y = x^2$ by the curve $y = f(x)$, where f is an even function, then the formula for $C(x)$ becomes

$$C(x) = \frac{1}{2}\left[f(0) + f(x) + \frac{x^2}{f(x) - f(0)}\right]$$

[Here we assume that $f(x) \neq f(0)$ for positive values of x close to 0.] If $\lim_{x \to 0^+} C(x) = L \neq f(0)$, then we define the osculating circle to the curve $y = f(x)$ at $(0, f(0))$ to be the unique circle through $(0, f(0))$ with center $(0, L)$. If $C(x)$ does not have a finite limit different from $f(0)$ as $x \to 0^+$, then we say that the curve has no osculating circle at $(0, f(0))$.

4. In each part, determine the osculating circle to the curve $y = f(x)$ at $(0, f(0))$, if it exists.
   (a) $f(x) = 4x^2$ (b) $f(x) = x^2 \cos x$
   (c) $f(x) = |x|$ (d) $f(x) = x \sin x$
   (e) $f(x) = \cos x$
   (f) $f(x) = x^2 g(x)$, where $g(x)$ is an even continuous function with $g(0) \neq 0$
   (g) $f(x) = x^4$

Photo by Kirby Lee/WireImage/Getty Images

2

THE DERIVATIVE

One of the crowning achievements of calculus is its ability to capture continuous motion mathematically, allowing that motion to be analyzed instant by instant.

Many real-world phenomena involve changing quantities—the speed of a rocket, the inflation of currency, the number of bacteria in a culture, the shock intensity of an earthquake, the voltage of an electrical signal, and so forth. In this chapter we will develop the concept of a "derivative," which is the mathematical tool for studying the rate at which one quantity changes relative to another. The study of rates of change is closely related to the geometric concept of a tangent line to a curve, so we will also be discussing the general definition of a tangent line and methods for finding its slope and equation.

2.1 TANGENT LINES AND RATES OF CHANGE

In this section we will discuss three ideas: tangent lines to curves, the velocity of an object moving along a line, and the rate at which one variable changes relative to another. Our goal is to show how these seemingly unrelated ideas are, in actuality, closely linked.

■ TANGENT LINES

In Example 1 of Section 1.1, we showed how the notion of a limit could be used to find an equation of a tangent line to a curve. At that stage in the text we did not have precise definitions of tangent lines and limits to work with, so the argument was intuitive and informal. However, now that limits have been defined precisely, we are in a position to give a mathematical definition of the tangent line to a curve $y = f(x)$ at a point $P(x_0, f(x_0))$ on the curve. As illustrated in Figure 2.1.1, consider a point $Q(x, f(x))$ on the curve that is distinct from P, and compute the slope m_{PQ} of the secant line through P and Q:

$$m_{PQ} = \frac{f(x) - f(x_0)}{x - x_0}$$

If we let x approach x_0, then the point Q will move along the curve and approach the point P. If the secant line through P and Q approaches a limiting position as $x \to x_0$, then we will regard that position to be the position of the tangent line at P. Stated another way, if the slope m_{PQ} of the secant line through P and Q approaches a limit as $x \to x_0$, then we regard that limit to be the slope $m_{\tan}$ of the tangent line at P. Thus, we make the following definition.

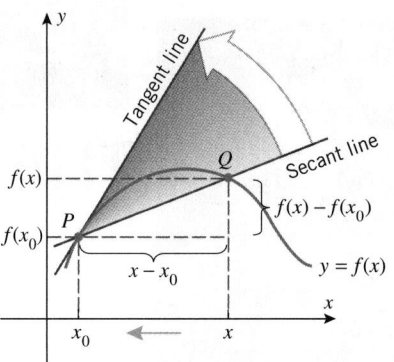

► **Figure 2.1.1**

2.1.1   DEFINITION   Suppose that x_0 is in the domain of the function f. The **tangent line** to the curve $y = f(x)$ at the point $P(x_0, f(x_0))$ is the line with equation

$$y - f(x_0) = m_{\tan}(x - x_0)$$

where

$$m_{\tan} = \lim_{x \to x_0} \frac{f(x) - f(x_0)}{x - x_0} \tag{1}$$

provided the limit exists. For simplicity, we will also call this the tangent line to $y = f(x)$ at x_0.

► **Example 1**   Use Definition 2.1.1 to find an equation for the tangent line to the parabola $y = x^2$ at the point $P(1, 1)$, and confirm the result agrees with that obtained in Example 1 of Section 1.1.

Solution.   Applying Formula (1) with $f(x) = x^2$ and $x_0 = 1$, we have

$$m_{\tan} = \lim_{x \to 1} \frac{f(x) - f(1)}{x - 1}$$

$$= \lim_{x \to 1} \frac{x^2 - 1}{x - 1}$$

$$= \lim_{x \to 1} \frac{(x - 1)(x + 1)}{x - 1} = \lim_{x \to 1}(x + 1) = 2$$

Thus, the tangent line to $y = x^2$ at $(1, 1)$ has equation

$$y - 1 = 2(x - 1) \quad \text{or equivalently} \quad y = 2x - 1$$

which agrees with Example 1 of Section 1.1. ◄

There is an alternative way of expressing Formula (1) that is commonly used. If we let h denote the difference

$$h = x - x_0$$

then the statement that $x \to x_0$ is equivalent to the statement $h \to 0$, so we can rewrite (1) in terms of x_0 and h as

$$m_{\tan} = \lim_{h \to 0} \frac{f(x_0 + h) - f(x_0)}{h} \tag{2}$$

Figure 2.1.2 shows how Formula (2) expresses the slope of the tangent line as a limit of slopes of secant lines.

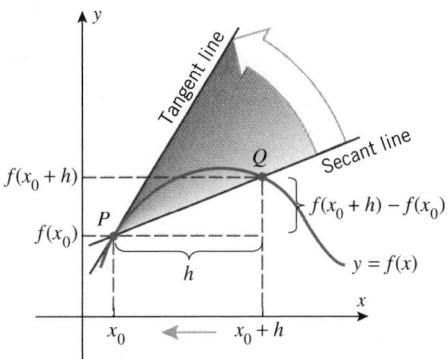

▶ **Figure 2.1.2**

▶ **Example 2**   Compute the slope in Example 1 using Formula (2).

Solution.   Applying Formula (2) with $f(x) = x^2$ and $x_0 = 1$, we obtain

$$m_{\tan} = \lim_{h \to 0} \frac{f(1 + h) - f(1)}{h}$$

$$= \lim_{h \to 0} \frac{(1 + h)^2 - 1^2}{h}$$

$$= \lim_{h \to 0} \frac{1 + 2h + h^2 - 1}{h} = \lim_{h \to 0} (2 + h) = 2$$

which agrees with the slope found in Example 1. ◀

> Formulas (1) and (2) for $m_{\tan}$ usually lead to indeterminate forms of type $0/0$, so you will generally need to perform algebraic simplifications or use other methods to determine limits of such indeterminate forms.

▶ **Example 3**   Find an equation for the tangent line to the curve $y = 2/x$ at the point $(2, 1)$ on this curve.

Solution.   First, we will find the slope of the tangent line by applying Formula (2) with $f(x) = 2/x$ and $x_0 = 2$. This yields

$$m_{\tan} = \lim_{h \to 0} \frac{f(2 + h) - f(2)}{h}$$

$$= \lim_{h \to 0} \frac{\dfrac{2}{2 + h} - 1}{h} = \lim_{h \to 0} \frac{\left(\dfrac{2 - (2 + h)}{2 + h}\right)}{h}$$

$$= \lim_{h \to 0} \frac{-h}{h(2 + h)} = -\left(\lim_{h \to 0} \frac{1}{2 + h}\right) = -\frac{1}{2}$$

Thus, an equation of the tangent line at $(2, 1)$ is

$$y - 1 = -\tfrac{1}{2}(x - 2) \quad \text{or equivalently} \quad y = -\tfrac{1}{2}x + 2$$

(see Figure 2.1.3). ◀

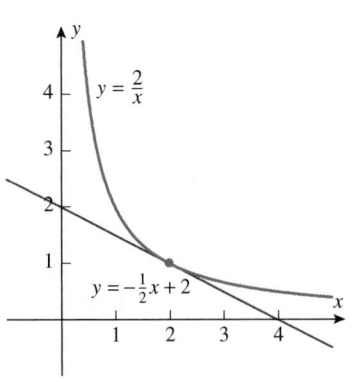

▲ **Figure 2.1.3**

▶ **Example 4** Find the slopes of the tangent lines to the curve $y = \sqrt{x}$ at $x_0 = 1$, $x_0 = 4$, and $x_0 = 9$.

Solution. We could compute each of these slopes separately, but it will be more efficient to find the slope for a general value of x_0 and then substitute the specific numerical values. Proceeding in this way we obtain

$$
\begin{aligned}
m_{\tan} &= \lim_{h \to 0} \frac{f(x_0 + h) - f(x_0)}{h} \\
&= \lim_{h \to 0} \frac{\sqrt{x_0 + h} - \sqrt{x_0}}{h} \\
&= \lim_{h \to 0} \frac{\sqrt{x_0 + h} - \sqrt{x_0}}{h} \cdot \frac{\sqrt{x_0 + h} + \sqrt{x_0}}{\sqrt{x_0 + h} + \sqrt{x_0}} \\
&= \lim_{h \to 0} \frac{x_0 + h - x_0}{h(\sqrt{x_0 + h} + \sqrt{x_0})} \\
&= \lim_{h \to 0} \frac{h}{h(\sqrt{x_0 + h} + \sqrt{x_0})} \\
&= \lim_{h \to 0} \frac{1}{\sqrt{x_0 + h} + \sqrt{x_0}} = \frac{1}{2\sqrt{x_0}}
\end{aligned}
$$

> Rationalize the numerator to help eliminate the indeterminate form of the limit.

The slopes at $x_0 = 1, 4$, and 9 can now be obtained by substituting these values into our general formula for $m_{\tan}$. Thus,

$$\text{slope at } x_0 = 1: \frac{1}{2\sqrt{1}} = \frac{1}{2}$$

$$\text{slope at } x_0 = 4: \frac{1}{2\sqrt{4}} = \frac{1}{4}$$

$$\text{slope at } x_0 = 9: \frac{1}{2\sqrt{9}} = \frac{1}{6}$$

(see Figure 2.1.4). ◀

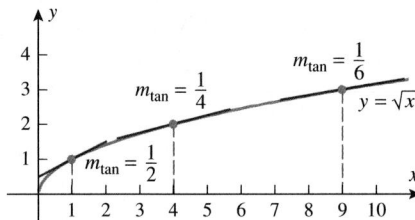

▶ **Figure 2.1.4**

■ VELOCITY

One of the important themes in calculus is the study of motion. To describe the motion of an object completely, one must specify its *speed* (how fast it is going) and the direction in which it is moving. The speed and the direction of motion together comprise what is called the *velocity* of the object. For example, knowing that the speed of an aircraft is 500 mi/h tells us how fast it is going, but not which way it is moving. In contrast, knowing that the velocity of the aircraft is 500 mi/h *due south* pins down the speed and the direction of motion.

Later, we will study the motion of objects that move along curves in two- or three-dimensional space, but for now we will only consider motion along a line; this is called *rectilinear motion*. Some examples are a piston moving up and down in a cylinder, a race

Carlos Santa Maria/iStockphoto
The velocity of an airplane describes its speed and direction.

car moving along a straight track, an object dropped from the top of a building and falling straight down, a ball thrown straight up and then falling down along the same line, and so forth.

For computational purposes, we will assume that a particle in rectilinear motion moves along a coordinate line, which we will call the *s*-axis. A graphical description of rectilinear motion along an *s*-axis can be obtained by making a plot of the *s*-coordinate of the particle versus the elapsed time *t* from starting time $t = 0$. This is called the ***position versus time curve*** for the particle. Figure 2.1.5 shows two typical position versus time curves. The first is for a car that starts at the origin and moves only in the positive direction of the *s*-axis. In this case *s* increases as *t* increases. The second is for a ball that is thrown straight up in the positive direction of an *s*-axis from some initial height s_0 and then falls straight down in the negative direction. In this case *s* increases as the ball moves up and decreases as it moves down.

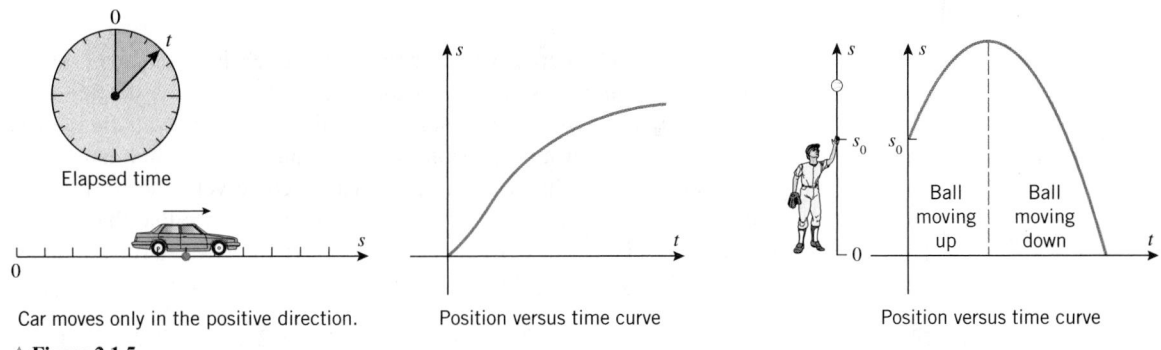

Car moves only in the positive direction.   Position versus time curve   Position versus time curve

▲ **Figure 2.1.5**

If a particle in rectilinear motion moves along an *s*-axis so that its position coordinate function of the elapsed time *t* is

$$s = f(t) \tag{3}$$

then f is called the ***position function of the particle***; the graph of (3) is the position versus time curve. The ***average velocity*** of the particle over a time interval $[t_0, t_0 + h]$, $h > 0$, is defined to be

$$v_{\text{ave}} = \frac{\text{change in position}}{\text{time elapsed}} = \frac{f(t_0 + h) - f(t_0)}{h} \tag{4}$$

Show that (4) is also correct for a time interval $[t_0 + h, t_0]$, $h < 0$.

▶ **Example 5** Suppose that $s = f(t) = 1 + 5t - 2t^2$ is the position function of a particle, where *s* is in meters and *t* is in seconds. Find the average velocities of the particle over the time intervals (a) [0, 2] and (b) [2, 3].

Solution (a). Applying (4) with $t_0 = 0$ and $h = 2$, we see that the average velocity is

$$v_{\text{ave}} = \frac{f(t_0 + h) - f(t_0)}{h} = \frac{f(2) - f(0)}{2} = \frac{3 - 1}{2} = \frac{2}{2} = 1 \text{ m/s}$$

The change in position

$$f(t_0 + h) - f(t_0)$$

is also called the ***displacement*** of the particle over the time interval between t_0 and $t_0 + h$.

Solution (b). Applying (4) with $t_0 = 2$ and $h = 1$, we see that the average velocity is

$$v_{\text{ave}} = \frac{f(t_0 + h) - f(t_0)}{h} = \frac{f(3) - f(2)}{1} = \frac{-2 - 3}{1} = \frac{-5}{1} = -5 \text{ m/s} ◀$$

For a particle in rectilinear motion, average velocity describes its behavior over an *interval* of time. We are interested in the particle's "instantaneous velocity," which describes

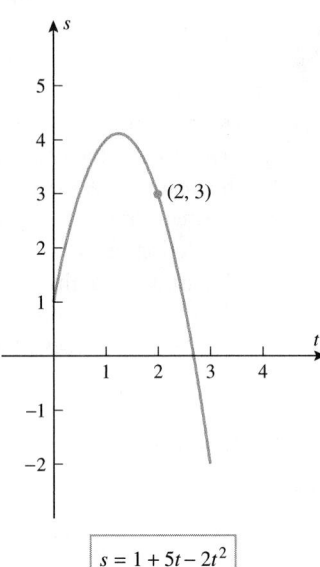

$$s = 1 + 5t - 2t^2$$

▲ **Figure 2.1.6**

Table 2.1.1

TIME INTERVAL	AVERAGE VELOCITY (m/s)
$2.0 \le t \le 3.0$	-5
$2.0 \le t \le 2.1$	-3.2
$2.0 \le t \le 2.01$	-3.02
$2.0 \le t \le 2.001$	-3.002
$2.0 \le t \le 2.0001$	-3.0002

Note the negative values for the velocities in Example 6. This is consistent with the fact that the object is moving in the negative direction along the s-axis.

Confirm the solution to Example 5(b) by computing the slope of an appropriate secant line.

its behavior at a specific *instant* in time. Formula (4) is not directly applicable for computing instantaneous velocity because the "time elapsed" at a specific instant is zero, so (4) is undefined. One way to circumvent this problem is to compute average velocities for small time intervals between $t = t_0$ and $t = t_0 + h$. These average velocities may be viewed as approximations to the "instantaneous velocity" of the particle at time t_0. If these average velocities have a limit as h approaches zero, then we can take that limit to be the *instantaneous velocity* of the particle at time t_0. Here is an example.

▶ **Example 6**   Consider the particle in Example 5, whose position function is

$$s = f(t) = 1 + 5t - 2t^2$$

The position of the particle at time $t = 2$ s is $s = 3$ m (Figure 2.1.6). Find the particle's instantaneous velocity at time $t = 2$ s.

Solution.   As a first approximation to the particle's instantaneous velocity at time $t = 2$ s, let us recall from Example 5(b) that the average velocity over the time interval from $t = 2$ to $t = 3$ is $v_{\text{ave}} = -5$ m/s. To improve on this initial approximation we will compute the average velocity over a succession of smaller and smaller time intervals. We leave it to you to verify the results in Table 2.1.1. The average velocities in this table appear to be approaching a limit of -3 m/s, providing strong evidence that the instantaneous velocity at time $t = 2$ s is -3 m/s. To confirm this analytically, we start by computing the object's average velocity over a general time interval between $t = 2$ and $t = 2 + h$ using Formula (4):

$$v_{\text{ave}} = \frac{f(2 + h) - f(2)}{h} = \frac{[1 + 5(2 + h) - 2(2 + h)^2] - 3}{h}$$

The object's instantaneous velocity at time $t = 2$ is calculated as a limit as $h \to 0$:

$$\text{instantaneous velocity} = \lim_{h \to 0} \frac{[1 + 5(2 + h) - 2(2 + h)^2] - 3}{h}$$

$$= \lim_{h \to 0} \frac{-2 + (10 + 5h) - (8 + 8h + 2h^2)}{h}$$

$$= \lim_{h \to 0} \frac{-3h - 2h^2}{h} = \lim_{h \to 0} (-3 - 2h) = -3$$

This confirms our numerical conjecture that the instantaneous velocity after 2 s is -3 m/s. ◀

Consider a particle in rectilinear motion with position function $s = f(t)$. Motivated by Example 6, we define the instantaneous velocity v_{inst} of the particle at time t_0 to be the limit as $h \to 0$ of its average velocities v_{ave} over time intervals between $t = t_0$ and $t = t_0 + h$. Thus, from (4) we obtain

$$v_{\text{inst}} = \lim_{h \to 0} \frac{f(t_0 + h) - f(t_0)}{h} \tag{5}$$

Geometrically, the average velocity v_{ave} between $t = t_0$ and $t = t_0 + h$ is the slope of the secant line through points $P(t_0, f(t_0))$ and $Q(t_0 + h, f(t_0 + h))$ on the position versus time curve, and the instantaneous velocity v_{inst} at time t_0 is the slope of the tangent line to the position versus time curve at the point $P(t_0, f(t_0))$ (Figure 2.1.7).

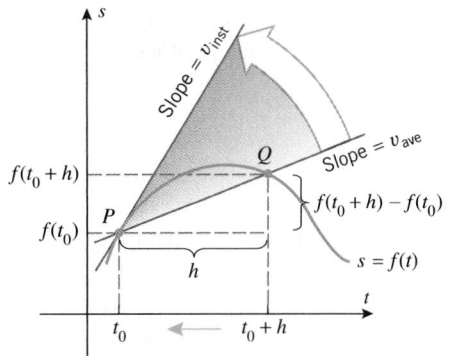

▶ **Figure 2.1.7**

■ SLOPES AND RATES OF CHANGE

Velocity can be viewed as *rate of change*—the rate of change of position with respect to time. Rates of change occur in other applications as well. For example:

- A microbiologist might be interested in the rate at which the number of bacteria in a colony changes with time.
- An engineer might be interested in the rate at which the length of a metal rod changes with temperature.
- An economist might be interested in the rate at which production cost changes with the quantity of a product that is manufactured.
- A medical researcher might be interested in the rate at which the radius of an artery changes with the concentration of alcohol in the bloodstream.

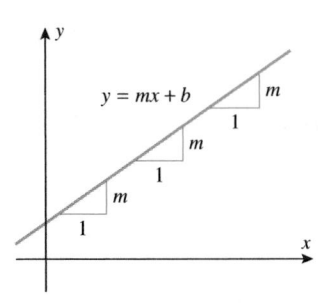

A 1-unit increase in x always produces an m-unit change in y.

▲ **Figure 2.1.8**

Our next objective is to define precisely what is meant by the "rate of change of y with respect to x" when y is a function of x. In the case where y is a linear function of x, say $y = mx + b$, the slope m is the natural measure of the rate of change of y with respect to x. As illustrated in Figure 2.1.8, each 1-unit increase in x anywhere along the line produces an m-unit change in y, so we see that y changes at a constant rate with respect to x along the line and that m measures this rate of change.

▶ **Example 7** Find the rate of change of y with respect to x if

$$\text{(a) } y = 2x - 1 \qquad \text{(b) } y = -5x + 1$$

Solution. In part (a) the rate of change of y with respect to x is $m = 2$, so each 1-unit increase in x produces a 2-unit increase in y. In part (b) the rate of change of y with respect to x is $m = -5$, so each 1-unit increase in x produces a 5-unit decrease in y. ◀

In applied problems, changing the units of measurement can change the slope of a line, so it is essential to include the units when calculating the slope and describing rates of change. The following example illustrates this.

▶ **Example 8** Suppose that a uniform rod of length 40 cm (= 0.4 m) is thermally insulated around the lateral surface and that the exposed ends of the rod are held at constant temperatures of 25°C and 5°C, respectively (Figure 2.1.9*a*). It is shown in physics that under appropriate conditions the graph of the temperature T versus the distance x from the left-hand end of the rod will be a straight line. Parts (*b*) and (*c*) of Figure 2.1.9 show two

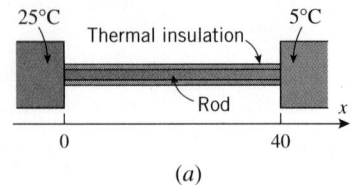

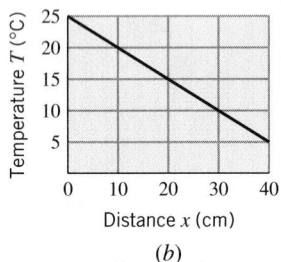

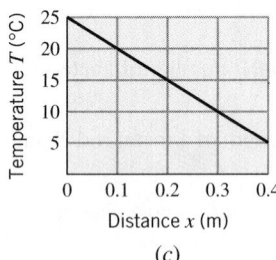

▲ **Figure 2.1.9**

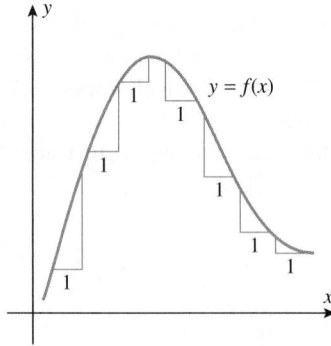

▲ **Figure 2.1.10**

such graphs: one in which x is measured in centimeters and one in which it is measured in meters. The slopes in the two cases are

$$m = \frac{5 - 25}{40 - 0} = \frac{-20}{40} = -0.5 \tag{6}$$

$$m = \frac{5 - 25}{0.4 - 0} = \frac{-20}{0.4} = -50 \tag{7}$$

The slope in (6) implies that the temperature *decreases* at a rate of $0.5°C$ per centimeter of distance from the left end of the rod, and the slope in (7) implies that the temperature decreases at a rate of $50°C$ per meter of distance from the left end of the rod. The two statements are equivalent physically, even though the slopes differ. ◄

Although the rate of change of y with respect to x is constant along a nonvertical line $y = mx + b$, this is not true for a general curve $y = f(x)$. For example, in Figure 2.1.10 the change in y that results from a 1-unit increase in x tends to have greater magnitude in regions where the curve rises or falls rapidly than in regions where it rises or falls slowly. As with velocity, we will distinguish between the average rate of change over an interval and the instantaneous rate of change at a specific point.

If $y = f(x)$, then we define the **average rate of change of y with respect to x over the interval $[x_0, x_1]$** to be

$$r_{\text{ave}} = \frac{f(x_1) - f(x_0)}{x_1 - x_0} \tag{8}$$

and we define the **instantaneous rate of change of y with respect to x at x_0** to be

$$r_{\text{inst}} = \lim_{x_1 \to x_0} \frac{f(x_1) - f(x_0)}{x_1 - x_0} \tag{9}$$

Geometrically, the average rate of change of y with respect to x over the interval $[x_0, x_1]$ is the slope of the secant line through the points $P(x_0, f(x_0))$ and $Q(x_1, f(x_1))$ (Figure 2.1.11), and the instantaneous rate of change of y with respect to x at x_0 is the slope of the tangent line at the point $P(x_0, f(x_0))$ (since it is the limit of the slopes of the secant lines through P).

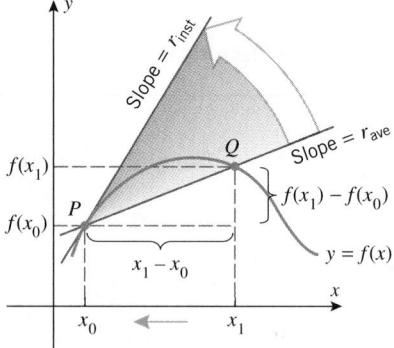

▶ **Figure 2.1.11**

If desired, we can let $h = x_1 - x_0$, and rewrite (8) and (9) as

$$r_{\text{ave}} = \frac{f(x_0 + h) - f(x_0)}{h} \tag{10}$$

$$r_{\text{inst}} = \lim_{h \to 0} \frac{f(x_0 + h) - f(x_0)}{h} \tag{11}$$

▶ **Example 9**   Let $y = x^2 + 1$.

(a) Find the average rate of change of y with respect to x over the interval $[3, 5]$.

(b) Find the instantaneous rate of change of y with respect to x when $x = -4$.

Solution (a).   We will apply Formula (8) with $f(x) = x^2 + 1$, $x_0 = 3$, and $x_1 = 5$. This yields

$$r_{ave} = \frac{f(x_1) - f(x_0)}{x_1 - x_0} = \frac{f(5) - f(3)}{5 - 3} = \frac{26 - 10}{2} = 8$$

Thus, y increases an average of 8 units per unit increase in x over the interval $[3, 5]$.

Solution (b).   We will apply Formula (9) with $f(x) = x^2 + 1$ and $x_0 = -4$. This yields

$$r_{inst} = \lim_{x_1 \to x_0} \frac{f(x_1) - f(x_0)}{x_1 - x_0} = \lim_{x_1 \to -4} \frac{f(x_1) - f(-4)}{x_1 - (-4)} = \lim_{x_1 \to -4} \frac{(x_1^2 + 1) - 17}{x_1 + 4}$$

$$= \lim_{x_1 \to -4} \frac{x_1^2 - 16}{x_1 + 4} = \lim_{x_1 \to -4} \frac{(x_1 + 4)(x_1 - 4)}{x_1 + 4} = \lim_{x_1 \to -4} (x_1 - 4) = -8$$

Thus, a small increase in x from $x = -4$ will produce approximately an 8-fold decrease in y. ◀

> Perform the calculations in Example 9 using Formulas (10) and (11).

■ RATES OF CHANGE IN APPLICATIONS

In applied problems, average and instantaneous rates of change must be accompanied by appropriate units. In general, the units for a rate of change of y with respect to x are obtained by "dividing" the units of y by the units of x and then simplifying according to the standard rules of algebra. Here are some examples:

- If y is in degrees Fahrenheit (°F) and x is in inches (in), then a rate of change of y with respect to x has units of degrees Fahrenheit per inch (°F/in).

- If y is in feet per second (ft/s) and x is in seconds (s), then a rate of change of y with respect to x has units of feet per second per second (ft/s/s), which would usually be written as ft/s².

- If y is in newton-meters (N·m) and x is in meters (m), then a rate of change of y with respect to x has units of newtons (N), since N·m/m = N.

- If y is in foot-pounds (ft·lb) and x is in hours (h), then a rate of change of y with respect to x has units of foot-pounds per hour (ft·lb/h).

▶ **Example 10**   The limiting factor in athletic endurance is cardiac output, that is, the volume of blood that the heart can pump per unit of time during an athletic competition. Figure 2.1.12 shows a stress-test graph of cardiac output V in liters (L) of blood versus workload W in kilogram-meters (kg·m) for 1 minute of weight lifting. This graph illustrates the known medical fact that cardiac output increases with the workload, but after reaching a peak value begins to decrease.

(a) Use the secant line shown in Figure 2.1.13a to estimate the average rate of change of cardiac output with respect to workload as the workload increases from 300 to 1200 kg·m.

(b) Use the line segment shown in Figure 2.1.13b to estimate the instantaneous rate of change of cardiac output with respect to workload at the point where the workload is 300 kg·m.

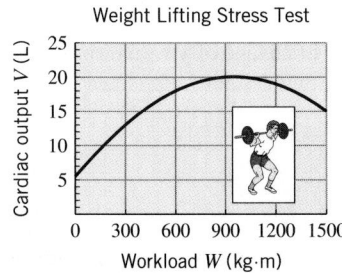

Weight Lifting Stress Test

Cardiac output V (L)

Workload W (kg·m)

▲ **Figure 2.1.12**

Solution (a).   Using the estimated points $(300, 13)$ and $(1200, 19)$ to find the slope of the secant line, we obtain

$$r_{\text{ave}} \approx \frac{19 - 13}{1200 - 300} \approx 0.0067 \frac{\text{L}}{\text{kg·m}}$$

This means that on average a 1-unit increase in workload produced a 0.0067 L increase in cardiac output over the interval.

Solution (b).   We estimate the slope of the cardiac output curve at $W = 300$ by sketching a line that appears to meet the curve at $W = 300$ with slope equal to that of the curve (Figure 2.1.13b). Estimating points $(0, 7)$ and $(900, 25)$ on this line, we obtain

$$r_{\text{inst}} \approx \frac{25 - 7}{900 - 0} = 0.02 \frac{\text{L}}{\text{kg·m}} \quad \blacktriangleleft$$

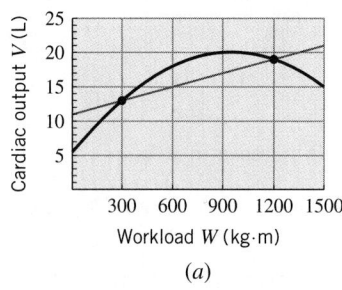

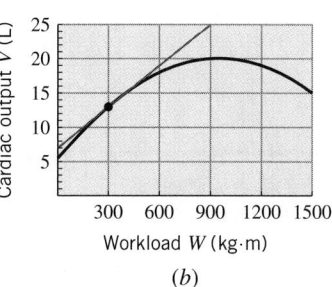

(a) $\qquad\qquad\qquad\qquad\qquad$ (b)

▶ **Figure 2.1.13**

✔ **QUICK CHECK EXERCISES 2.1**   *(See page 143 for answers.)*

1. The slope m_{tan} of the tangent line to the curve $y = f(x)$ at the point $P(x_0, f(x_0))$ is given by

$$m_{\text{tan}} = \lim_{x \to x_0} \underline{\qquad} = \lim_{h \to 0} \underline{\qquad}$$

2. The tangent line to the curve $y = (x - 1)^2$ at the point $(-1, 4)$ has equation $4x + y = 0$. Thus, the value of the limit

$$\lim_{x \to -1} \frac{x^2 - 2x - 3}{x + 1}$$

is $\underline{\qquad}$.

3. A particle is moving along an s-axis, where s is in feet. During the first 5 seconds of motion, the position of the particle is given by

$$s = 10 - (3 - t)^2, \quad 0 \le t \le 5$$

Use this position function to complete each part.

(a) Initially, the particle moves a distance of $\underline{\qquad}$ ft in the (positive/negative) $\underline{\qquad}$ direction; then it reverses direction, traveling a distance of $\underline{\qquad}$ ft during the remainder of the 5-second period.

(b) The average velocity of the particle over the 5-second period is $\underline{\qquad}$.

4. Let $s = f(t)$ be the equation of a position versus time curve for a particle in rectilinear motion, where s is in meters and t is in seconds. Assume that $s = -1$ when $t = 2$ and that the instantaneous velocity of the particle at this instant is 3 m/s. The equation of the tangent line to the position versus time curve at time $t = 2$ is $\underline{\qquad}$.

5. Suppose that $y = x^2 + x$.
(a) The average rate of change of y with respect to x over the interval $2 \le x \le 5$ is $\underline{\qquad}$.
(b) The instantaneous rate of change of y with respect to x at $x = 2$, r_{inst}, is given by the limit $\underline{\qquad}$.

EXERCISE SET 2.1

1. The accompanying figure on the next page shows the position versus time curve for an elevator that moves upward a distance of 60 m and then discharges its passengers.

(a) Estimate the instantaneous velocity of the elevator at $t = 10$ s.
(b) Sketch a velocity versus time curve for the motion of the elevator for $0 \le t \le 20$.

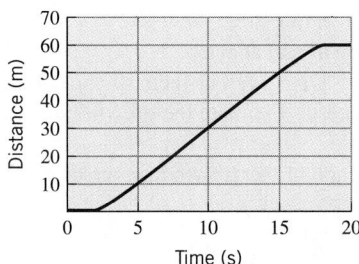

Distance (m) vs Time (s)

◀ **Figure Ex-1**

2. The accompanying figure shows the position versus time curve for an automobile over a period of time of 10 s. Use the line segments shown in the figure to estimate the instantaneous velocity of the automobile at time $t = 4$ s and again at time $t = 8$ s.

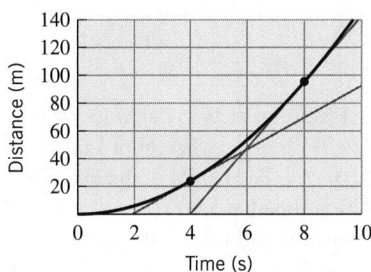

Distance (m) vs Time (s)

◀ **Figure Ex-2**

3. The accompanying figure shows the position versus time curve for a certain particle moving along a straight line. Estimate each of the following from the graph:
(a) the average velocity over the interval $0 \le t \le 3$
(b) the values of t at which the instantaneous velocity is zero
(c) the values of t at which the instantaneous velocity is either a maximum or a minimum
(d) the instantaneous velocity when $t = 3$ s.

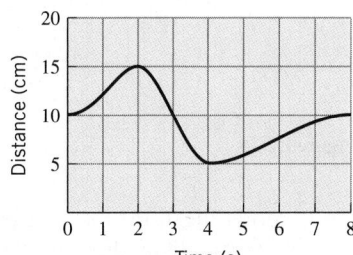

Distance (cm) vs Time (s)

◀ **Figure Ex-3**

4. The accompanying figure shows the position versus time curves of four different particles moving on a straight line. For each particle, determine whether its instantaneous velocity is increasing or decreasing with time.

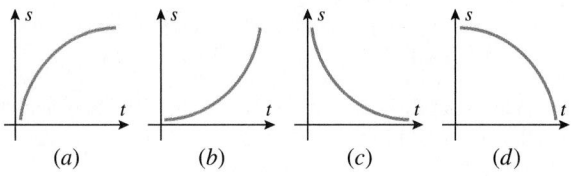

(a)   (b)   (c)   (d)

▲ **Figure Ex-4**

FOCUS ON CONCEPTS

5. If a particle moves at constant velocity, what can you say about its position versus time curve?

6. An automobile, initially at rest, begins to move along a straight track. The velocity increases steadily until suddenly the driver sees a concrete barrier in the road and applies the brakes sharply at time t_0. The car decelerates rapidly, but it is too late—the car crashes into the barrier at time t_1 and instantaneously comes to rest. Sketch a position versus time curve that might represent the motion of the car. Indicate how characteristics of your curve correspond to the events of this scenario.

7–10 For each exercise, sketch a curve and a line L satisfying the stated conditions. ▨

7. L is tangent to the curve and intersects the curve in at least two points.

8. L intersects the curve in exactly one point, but L is not tangent to the curve.

9. L is tangent to the curve at two different points.

10. L is tangent to the curve at two different points and intersects the curve at a third point.

11–14 A function $y = f(x)$ and values of x_0 and x_1 are given.
(a) Find the average rate of change of y with respect to x over the interval $[x_0, x_1]$.
(b) Find the instantaneous rate of change of y with respect to x at the specified value of x_0.
(c) Find the instantaneous rate of change of y with respect to x at an arbitrary value of x_0.
(d) The average rate of change in part (a) is the slope of a certain secant line, and the instantaneous rate of change in part (b) is the slope of a certain tangent line. Sketch the graph of $y = f(x)$ together with those two lines. ▨

11. $y = 2x^2$; $x_0 = 0$, $x_1 = 1$ **12.** $y = x^3$; $x_0 = 1$, $x_1 = 2$
13. $y = 1/x$; $x_0 = 2$, $x_1 = 3$ **14.** $y = 1/x^2$; $x_0 = 1$, $x_1 = 2$

15–18 A function $y = f(x)$ and an x-value x_0 are given.
(a) Find a formula for the slope of the tangent line to the graph of f at a general point $x = x_0$.
(b) Use the formula obtained in part (a) to find the slope of the tangent line for the given value of x_0. ▨

15. $f(x) = x^2 - 1$; $x_0 = -1$
16. $f(x) = x^2 + 3x + 2$; $x_0 = 2$
17. $f(x) = x + \sqrt{x}$; $x_0 = 1$
18. $f(x) = 1/\sqrt{x}$; $x_0 = 4$

19–22 True–False Determine whether the statement is true or false. Explain your answer. ▨

19. If $\lim\limits_{x \to 1} \dfrac{f(x) - f(1)}{x - 1} = 3$, then $\lim\limits_{h \to 0} \dfrac{f(1 + h) - f(1)}{h} = 3$.

20. A tangent line to a curve $y = f(x)$ is a particular kind of secant line to the curve.

21. The velocity of an object represents a change in the object's position.

22. A 50-foot horizontal metal beam is supported on either end by concrete pillars and a weight is placed on the middle of the beam. If $f(x)$ models how many inches the center of the beam sags when the weight measures x tons, then the units of the rate of change of $y = f(x)$ with respect to x are inches/ton.

23. Suppose that the outside temperature versus time curve over a 24-hour period is as shown in the accompanying figure.
   (a) Estimate the maximum temperature and the time at which it occurs.
   (b) The temperature rise is fairly linear from 8 A.M. to 2 P.M. Estimate the rate at which the temperature is increasing during this time period.
   (c) Estimate the time at which the temperature is decreasing most rapidly. Estimate the instantaneous rate of change of temperature with respect to time at this instant.

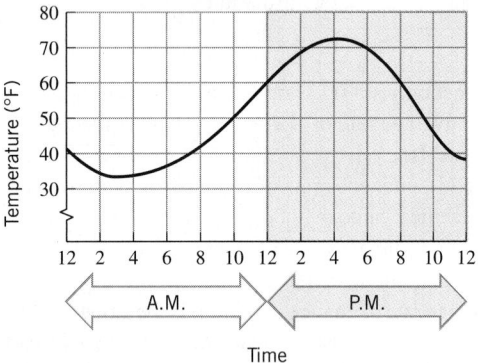

▲ **Figure Ex-23**

24. The accompanying figure shows the graph of the pressure p in atmospheres (atm) versus the volume V in liters (L) of 1 mole of an ideal gas at a constant temperature of 300 K (kelvins). Use the line segments shown in the figure to estimate the rate of change of pressure with respect to volume at the points where $V = 10$ L and $V = 25$ L.

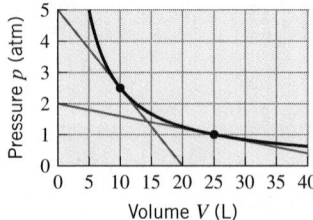

◄ **Figure Ex-24**

25. The accompanying figure shows the graph of the height h in centimeters versus the age t in years of an individual from birth to age 20.

(a) When is the growth rate greatest?
(b) Estimate the growth rate at age 5.
(c) At approximately what age between 10 and 20 is the growth rate greatest? Estimate the growth rate at this age.
(d) Draw a rough graph of the growth rate versus age.

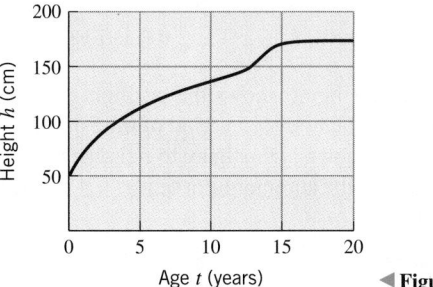

◄ **Figure Ex-25**

26. An object is released from rest (its initial velocity is zero) from the Empire State Building at a height of 1250 ft above street level (Figure Ex-26). The height of the object can be modeled by the position function $s = f(t) = 1250 - 16t^2$.
   (a) Verify that the object is still falling at $t = 5$ s.
   (b) Find the average velocity of the object over the time interval from $t = 5$ to $t = 6$ s.
   (c) Find the object's instantaneous velocity at time $t = 5$ s.

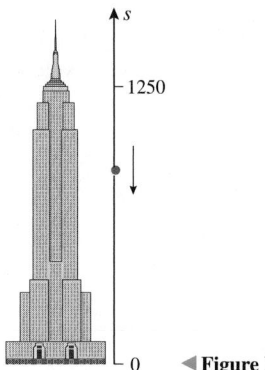

◄ **Figure Ex-26**

27. During the first 40 s of a rocket flight, the rocket is propelled straight up so that in t seconds it reaches a height of $s = 0.3t^3$ ft.
   (a) How high does the rocket travel in 40 s?
   (b) What is the average velocity of the rocket during the first 40 s?
   (c) What is the average velocity of the rocket during the first 1000 ft of its flight?
   (d) What is the instantaneous velocity of the rocket at the end of 40 s?

28. An automobile is driven down a straight highway such that after $0 \leq t \leq 12$ seconds it is $s = 4.5t^2$ feet from its initial position.

(cont.)

(a) Find the average velocity of the car over the interval [0, 12].

(b) Find the instantaneous velocity of the car at $t = 6$.

29. **Writing** Discuss how the tangent line to the graph of a function $y = f(x)$ at a point $P(x_0, f(x_0))$ is defined in terms of secant lines to the graph through point P.

30. **Writing** A particle is in rectilinear motion during the time interval $0 \le t \le 2$. Explain the connection between the instantaneous velocity of the particle at time $t = 1$ and the average velocities of the particle during portions of the interval $0 \le t \le 2$.

✔ **QUICK CHECK ANSWERS 2.1**

1. $\dfrac{f(x) - f(x_0)}{x - x_0}$; $\dfrac{f(x_0 + h) - f(x_0)}{h}$ 2. -4 3. (a) 9; positive; 4 (b) 1 ft/s   4. $s = 3t - 7$

5. (a) 8 (b) $\displaystyle\lim_{x \to 2} \dfrac{(x^2 + x) - 6}{x - 2}$ or $\displaystyle\lim_{h \to 0} \dfrac{[(2 + h)^2 + (2 + h)] - 6}{h}$.

2.2 THE DERIVATIVE FUNCTION

In this section we will discuss the concept of a "derivative," which is the primary mathematical tool that is used to calculate and study rates of change.

■ **DEFINITION OF THE DERIVATIVE FUNCTION**

In the last section we showed that if the limit

$$\lim_{h \to 0} \frac{f(x_0 + h) - f(x_0)}{h}$$

exists, then it can be interpreted either as the slope of the tangent line to the curve $y = f(x)$ at $x = x_0$ or as the instantaneous rate of change of y with respect to x at $x = x_0$ [see Formulas (2) and (11) of that section]. This limit is so important that it has a special notation:

$$f'(x_0) = \lim_{h \to 0} \frac{f(x_0 + h) - f(x_0)}{h} \tag{1}$$

You can think of f' (read "f prime") as a function whose input is x_0 and whose output is the number $f'(x_0)$ that represents either the slope of the tangent line to $y = f(x)$ at $x = x_0$ or the instantaneous rate of change of y with respect to x at $x = x_0$. To emphasize this function point of view, we will replace x_0 by x in (1) and make the following definition.

The expression
$$\frac{f(x + h) - f(x)}{h}$$
that appears in (2) is commonly called the *difference quotient*.

2.2.1 DEFINITION The function f' defined by the formula

$$f'(x) = \lim_{h \to 0} \frac{f(x + h) - f(x)}{h} \tag{2}$$

is called the *derivative of f with respect to x*. The domain of f' consists of all x in the domain of f for which the limit exists.

The term "derivative" is used because the function f' is *derived* from the function f by a limiting process.

▶ **Example 1** Find the derivative with respect to x of $f(x) = x^2$, and use it to find the equation of the tangent line to $y = x^2$ at $x = 2$.

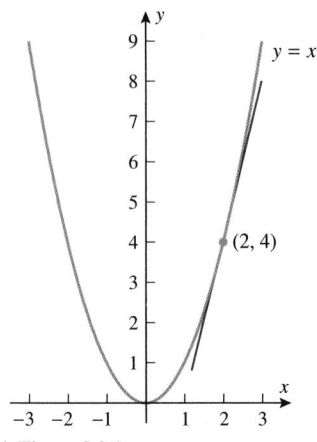

▲ **Figure 2.2.1**

Solution. It follows from (2) that

$$f'(x) = \lim_{h \to 0} \frac{f(x+h) - f(x)}{h} = \lim_{h \to 0} \frac{(x+h)^2 - x^2}{h}$$

$$= \lim_{h \to 0} \frac{x^2 + 2xh + h^2 - x^2}{h} = \lim_{h \to 0} \frac{2xh + h^2}{h}$$

$$= \lim_{h \to 0} (2x + h) = 2x$$

Thus, the slope of the tangent line to $y = x^2$ at $x = 2$ is $f'(2) = 4$. Since $y = 4$ if $x = 2$, the point-slope form of the tangent line is

$$y - 4 = 4(x - 2)$$

which we can rewrite in slope-intercept form as $y = 4x - 4$ (Figure 2.2.1). ◄

You can think of f' as a "slope-producing function" in the sense that the value of $f'(x)$ at $x = x_0$ is the slope of the tangent line to the graph of f at $x = x_0$. This aspect of the derivative is illustrated in Figure 2.2.2, which shows the graphs of $f(x) = x^2$ and its derivative $f'(x) = 2x$ (obtained in Example 1). The figure illustrates that the values of $f'(x) = 2x$ at $x = -2, 0,$ and 2 correspond to the slopes of the tangent lines to the graph of $f(x) = x^2$ at those values of x.

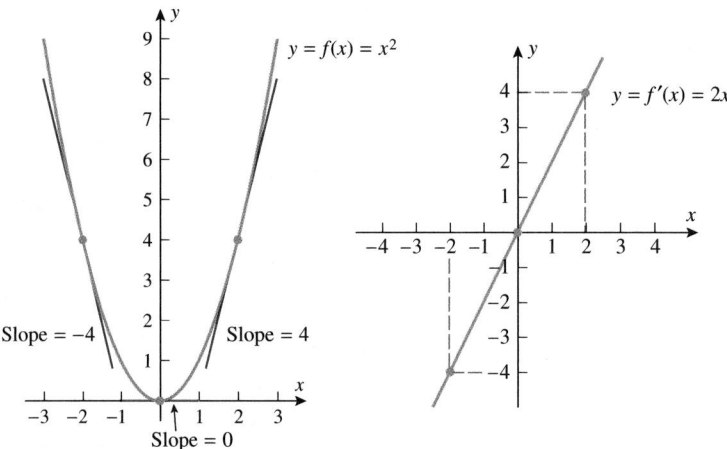

▶ **Figure 2.2.2**

In general, if $f'(x)$ is defined at $x = x_0$, then the point-slope form of the equation of the tangent line to the graph of $y = f(x)$ at $x = x_0$ may be found using the following steps.

Finding an Equation for the Tangent Line to $y = f(x)$ at $x = x_0$.

Step 1. Evaluate $f(x_0)$; the point of tangency is $(x_0, f(x_0))$.

Step 2. Find $f'(x)$ and evaluate $f'(x_0)$, which is the slope m of the line.

Step 3. Substitute the value of the slope m and the point $(x_0, f(x_0))$ into the point-slope form of the line

$$y - f(x_0) = f'(x_0)(x - x_0)$$

or, equivalently,

$$y = f(x_0) + f'(x_0)(x - x_0) \tag{3}$$

▶ **Example 2**

In Solution (a), the binomial formula is used to expand $(x + h)^3$. This formula may be found on the front endpaper.

(a) Find the derivative with respect to x of $f(x) = x^3 - x$.

(b) Graph f and f' together, and discuss the relationship between the two graphs.

Solution (a).

$$f'(x) = \lim_{h \to 0} \frac{f(x + h) - f(x)}{h}$$

$$= \lim_{h \to 0} \frac{[(x + h)^3 - (x + h)] - [x^3 - x]}{h}$$

$$= \lim_{h \to 0} \frac{[x^3 + 3x^2h + 3xh^2 + h^3 - x - h] - [x^3 - x]}{h}$$

$$= \lim_{h \to 0} \frac{3x^2h + 3xh^2 + h^3 - h}{h}$$

$$= \lim_{h \to 0} [3x^2 + 3xh + h^2 - 1] = 3x^2 - 1$$

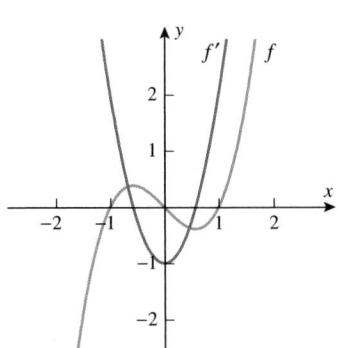

▲ **Figure 2.2.3**

Solution (b). Since $f'(x)$ can be interpreted as the slope of the tangent line to the graph of $y = f(x)$ at x, it follows that $f'(x)$ is positive where the tangent line has positive slope, is negative where the tangent line has negative slope, and is zero where the tangent line is horizontal. We leave it for you to verify that this is consistent with the graphs of $f(x) = x^3 - x$ and $f'(x) = 3x^2 - 1$ shown in Figure 2.2.3. ◀

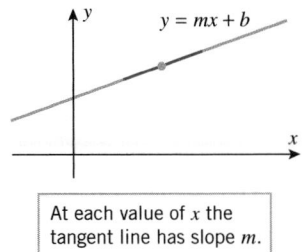

At each value of x the tangent line has slope m.

▲ **Figure 2.2.4**

▶ **Example 3** At each value of x, the tangent line to a line $y = mx + b$ coincides with the line itself (Figure 2.2.4), and hence all tangent lines have slope m. This suggests geometrically that if $f(x) = mx + b$, then $f'(x) = m$ for all x. This is confirmed by the following computations:

$$f'(x) = \lim_{h \to 0} \frac{f(x + h) - f(x)}{h}$$

$$= \lim_{h \to 0} \frac{[m(x + h) + b] - [mx + b]}{h}$$

$$= \lim_{h \to 0} \frac{mh}{h} = \lim_{h \to 0} m = m \quad ◀$$

The result in Example 3 is consistent with our earlier observation that the rate of change of y with respect to x along a line $y = mx + b$ is constant and that constant is m.

▶ **Example 4**

(a) Find the derivative with respect to x of $f(x) = \sqrt{x}$.

(b) Find the slope of the tangent line to $y = \sqrt{x}$ at $x = 9$.

(c) Find the limits of $f'(x)$ as $x \to 0^+$ and as $x \to +\infty$, and explain what those limits say about the graph of f.

Solution (a). Recall from Example 4 of Section 2.1 that the slope of the tangent line to $y = \sqrt{x}$ at $x = x_0$ is given by $m_{\text{tan}} = 1/(2\sqrt{x_0})$. Thus, $f'(x) = 1/(2\sqrt{x})$.

Solution (b). The slope of the tangent line at $x = 9$ is $f'(9)$. From part (a), this slope is $f'(9) = 1/(2\sqrt{9}) = \frac{1}{6}$.

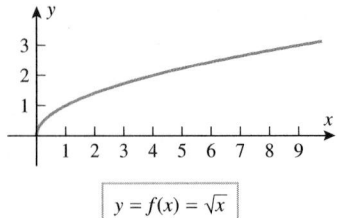

$$y = f(x) = \sqrt{x}$$

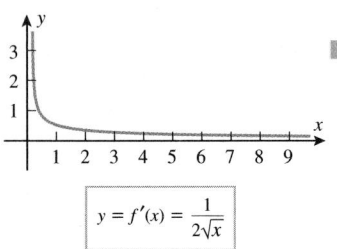

$$y = f'(x) = \frac{1}{2\sqrt{x}}$$

▲ **Figure 2.2.5**

***Solution* (c).** The graphs of $f(x) = \sqrt{x}$ and $f'(x) = 1/(2\sqrt{x})$ are shown in Figure 2.2.5. Observe that $f'(x) > 0$ if $x > 0$, which means that all tangent lines to the graph of $y = \sqrt{x}$ have positive slope at all points in this interval. Since

$$\lim_{x \to 0^+} \frac{1}{2\sqrt{x}} = +\infty \quad \text{and} \quad \lim_{x \to +\infty} \frac{1}{2\sqrt{x}} = 0$$

the graph of f becomes more and more vertical as $x \to 0^+$ and more and more horizontal as $x \to +\infty$. ◄

■ **COMPUTING INSTANTANEOUS VELOCITY**

It follows from Formula (5) of Section 2.1 (with t replacing t_0) that if $s = f(t)$ is the position function of a particle in rectilinear motion, then the instantaneous velocity at an arbitrary time t is given by

$$v_{\text{inst}} = \lim_{h \to 0} \frac{f(t + h) - f(t)}{h}$$

Since the right side of this equation is the derivative of the function f (with t rather than x as the independent variable), it follows that if $f(t)$ is the position function of a particle in rectilinear motion, then the function

$$v(t) = f'(t) = \lim_{h \to 0} \frac{f(t + h) - f(t)}{h} \qquad (4)$$

represents the instantaneous velocity of the particle at time t. Accordingly, we call (4) the ***instantaneous velocity function*** or, more simply, the ***velocity function*** of the particle.

▶ **Example 5** Recall the particle from Example 5 of Section 2.1 with position function $s = f(t) = 1 + 5t - 2t^2$. Here $f(t)$ is measured in meters and t is measured in seconds. Find the velocity function of the particle.

Solution. It follows from (4) that the velocity function is

$$v(t) = \lim_{h \to 0} \frac{f(t + h) - f(t)}{h} = \lim_{h \to 0} \frac{[1 + 5(t + h) - 2(t + h)^2] - [1 + 5t - 2t^2]}{h}$$

$$= \lim_{h \to 0} \frac{-2[t^2 + 2th + h^2 - t^2] + 5h}{h} = \lim_{h \to 0} \frac{-4th - 2h^2 + 5h}{h}$$

$$= \lim_{h \to 0} (-4t - 2h + 5) = 5 - 4t$$

where the units of velocity are meters per second. ◄

■ **DIFFERENTIABILITY**

It is possible that the limit that defines the derivative of a function f may not exist at certain points in the domain of f. At such points the derivative is undefined. To account for this possibility we make the following definition.

2.2.2 **DEFINITION** A function f is said to be ***differentiable at x_0*** if the limit

$$f'(x_0) = \lim_{h \to 0} \frac{f(x_0 + h) - f(x_0)}{h} \qquad (5)$$

exists. If f is differentiable at each point of the open interval (a, b), then we say that it is ***differentiable on (a, b)***, and similarly for open intervals of the form $(a, +\infty)$, $(-\infty, b)$, and $(-\infty, +\infty)$. In the last case we say that f is ***differentiable everywhere***.

Geometrically, a function f is differentiable at x_0 if the graph of f has a tangent line at x_0. Thus, f is not differentiable at any point x_0 where the secant lines from $P(x_0, f(x_0))$ to points $Q(x, f(x))$ distinct from P do not approach a unique *nonvertical* limiting position as $x \to x_0$. Figure 2.2.6 illustrates two common ways in which a function that is continuous at x_0 can fail to be differentiable at x_0. These can be described informally as

- corner points
- points of vertical tangency

At a corner point, the slopes of the secant lines have different limits from the left and from the right, and hence the *two-sided* limit that defines the derivative does not exist (Figure 2.2.7). At a point of vertical tangency the slopes of the secant lines approach $+\infty$ or $-\infty$ from the left and from the right (Figure 2.2.8), so again the limit that defines the derivative does not exist.

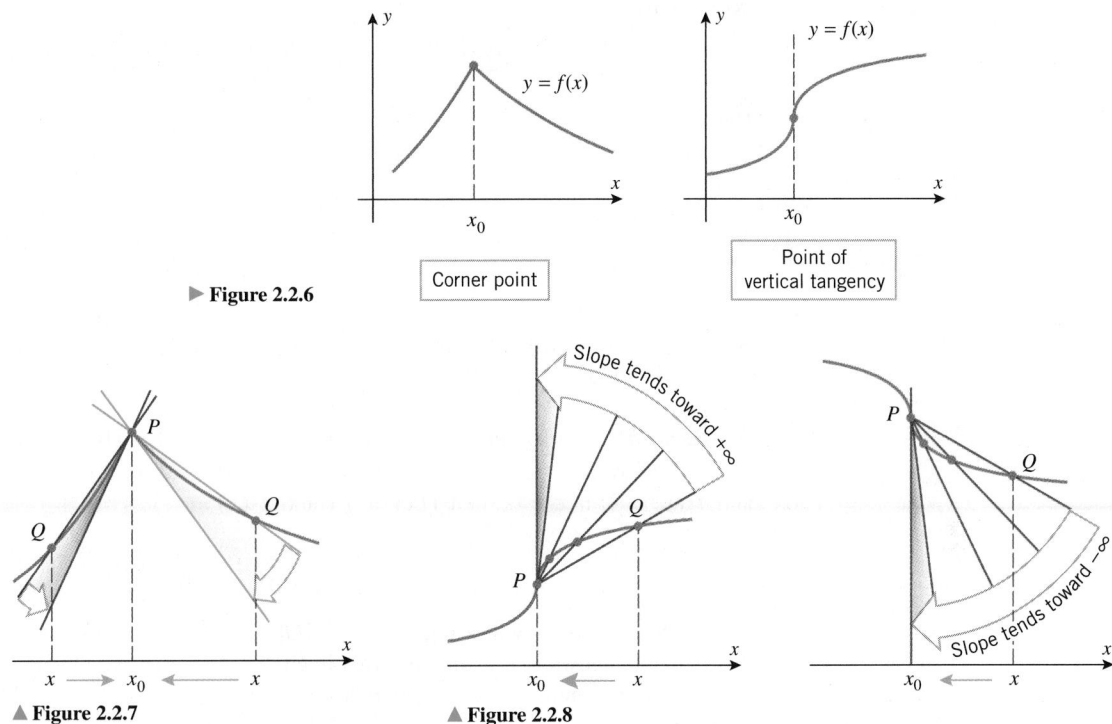

▶ **Figure 2.2.6**

Corner point

Point of vertical tangency

▲ **Figure 2.2.7**   ▲ **Figure 2.2.8**

There are other less obvious circumstances under which a function may fail to be differentiable. (See Exercise 49, for example.)

Differentiability at x_0 can also be described informally in terms of the behavior of the graph of f under increasingly stronger magnification at the point $P(x_0, f(x_0))$ (Figure 2.2.9). If f is differentiable at x_0, then under sufficiently strong magnification at P the

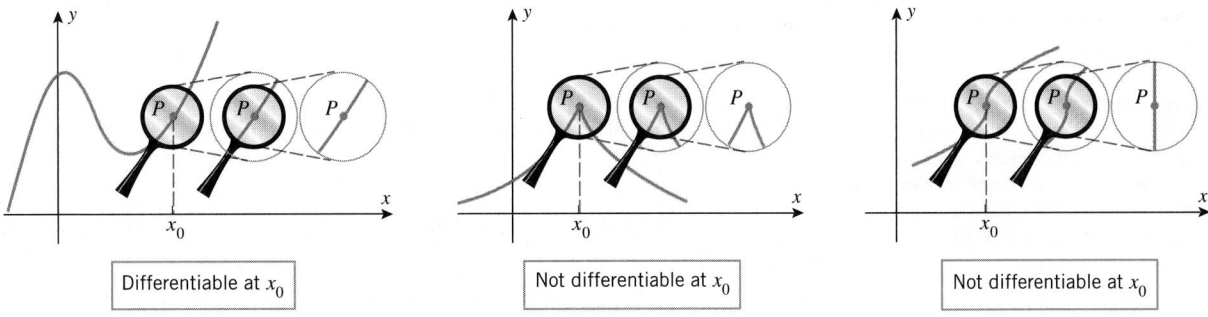

Differentiable at x_0 Not differentiable at x_0 Not differentiable at x_0

▲ **Figure 2.2.9**

graph looks like a nonvertical line (the tangent line); if a corner point occurs at x_0, then no matter how great the magnification at P the corner persists and the graph never looks like a nonvertical line; and if vertical tangency occurs at x_0, then the graph of f looks like a vertical line under sufficiently strong magnification at P.

$y = |x|$

▲ **Figure 2.2.10**

▶ **Example 6** The graph of $y = |x|$ in Figure 2.2.10 has a corner at $x = 0$, which implies that $f(x) = |x|$ is not differentiable at $x = 0$.

(a) Prove that $f(x) = |x|$ is not differentiable at $x = 0$ by showing that the limit in Definition 2.2.2 does not exist at $x = 0$.

(b) Find a formula for $f'(x)$.

Solution (a). From Formula (5) with $x_0 = 0$, the value of $f'(0)$, if it were to exist, would be given by

$$f'(0) = \lim_{h \to 0} \frac{f(0+h) - f(0)}{h} = \lim_{h \to 0} \frac{f(h) - f(0)}{h} = \lim_{h \to 0} \frac{|h| - |0|}{h} = \lim_{h \to 0} \frac{|h|}{h} \quad (6)$$

But

$$\frac{|h|}{h} = \begin{cases} 1, & h > 0 \\ -1, & h < 0 \end{cases}$$

so that

$$\lim_{h \to 0^-} \frac{|h|}{h} = -1 \quad \text{and} \quad \lim_{h \to 0^+} \frac{|h|}{h} = 1$$

Since these one-sided limits are not equal, the two-sided limit in (5) does not exist, and hence f is not differentiable at $x = 0$.

Solution (b). A formula for the derivative of $f(x) = |x|$ can be obtained by writing $|x|$ in piecewise form and treating the cases $x > 0$ and $x < 0$ separately. If $x > 0$, then $f(x) = x$ and $f'(x) = 1$; if $x < 0$, then $f(x) = -x$ and $f'(x) = -1$. Thus,

$$f'(x) = \begin{cases} 1, & x > 0 \\ -1, & x < 0 \end{cases}$$

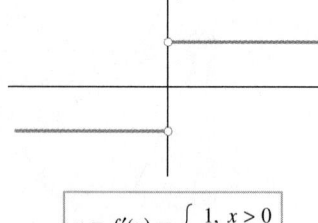

$y = f'(x) = \begin{cases} 1, x > 0 \\ -1, x < 0 \end{cases}$

▲ **Figure 2.2.11**

The graph of f' is shown in Figure 2.2.11. Observe that f' is not continuous at $x = 0$, so this example shows that a function that is continuous everywhere may have a derivative that fails to be continuous everywhere. ◀

THE RELATIONSHIP BETWEEN DIFFERENTIABILITY AND CONTINUITY

We already know that functions are not differentiable at corner points and points of vertical tangency. The next theorem shows that functions are not differentiable at points of discontinuity. We will do this by proving that if f is differentiable at a point, then it must be continuous at that point.

A theorem that says "If statement A is true, then statement B is true" is equivalent to the theorem that says "If statement B is not true, then statement A is not true." The two theorems are called *contrapositive forms* of one another. Thus, Theorem 2.2.3 can be rewritten in contrapositive form as "If a function f is not continuous at x_0, then f is not differentiable at x_0."

2.2.3 THEOREM *If a function f is differentiable at x_0, then f is continuous at x_0.*

PROOF We are given that f is differentiable at x_0, so it follows from (5) that $f'(x_0)$ exists and is given by

$$f'(x_0) = \lim_{h \to 0} \left[\frac{f(x_0 + h) - f(x_0)}{h} \right] \quad (7)$$

To show that f is continuous at x_0, we must show that $\lim_{x \to x_0} f(x) = f(x_0)$ or, equivalently,

$$\lim_{x \to x_0} [f(x) - f(x_0)] = 0$$

Expressing this in terms of the variable $h = x - x_0$, we must prove that

$$\lim_{h \to 0} [f(x_0 + h) - f(x_0)] = 0$$

However, this can be proved using (7) as follows:

$$\lim_{h \to 0} [f(x_0 + h) - f(x_0)] = \lim_{h \to 0} \left[\frac{f(x_0 + h) - f(x_0)}{h} \cdot h \right]$$

$$= \lim_{h \to 0} \left[\frac{f(x_0 + h) - f(x_0)}{h} \right] \cdot \lim_{h \to 0} h$$

$$= f'(x_0) \cdot 0 = 0 \quad \blacksquare$$

WARNING

The converse of Theorem 2.2.3 is false; that is, *a function may be continuous at a point but not differentiable at that point.* This occurs, for example, at corner points of continuous functions. For instance, $f(x) = |x|$ is continuous at $x = 0$ but not differentiable there (Example 6).

The relationship between continuity and differentiability was of great historical significance in the development of calculus. In the early nineteenth century mathematicians believed that if a continuous function had many points of nondifferentiability, these points, like the tips of a sawblade, would have to be separated from one another and joined by smooth curve segments (Figure 2.2.12). This misconception was corrected by a series of discoveries beginning in 1834. In that year a Bohemian priest, philosopher, and mathematician named Bernhard Bolzano discovered a procedure for constructing a continuous function that is not differentiable at any point. Later, in 1860, the great German mathematician Karl Weierstrass (biography on p. 102) produced the first formula for such a function. The graphs of such functions are impossible to draw; it is as if the corners are so numerous that any segment of the curve, when suitably enlarged, reveals more corners. The discovery of these functions was important in that it made mathematicians distrustful of their geometric intuition and more reliant on precise mathematical proof. Recently, such functions have started to play a fundamental role in the study of geometric objects called *fractals*. Fractals have revealed an order to natural phenomena that were previously dismissed as random and chaotic.

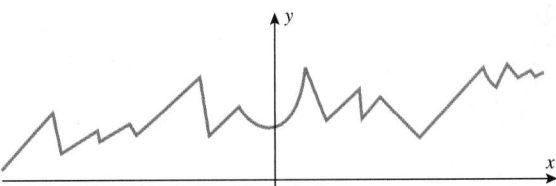

▶ **Figure 2.2.12**

Bernhard Bolzano (1781–1848) Bolzano, the son of an art dealer, was born in Prague, Bohemia (Czech Republic). He was educated at the University of Prague, and eventually won enough mathematical fame to be recommended for a mathematics chair there. However, Bolzano became an ordained Roman Catholic priest, and in 1805 he was appointed to a chair of Philosophy at the University of Prague. Bolzano was a man of great human compassion; he spoke out for educational reform, he voiced the right of individual conscience over government demands, and he lectured on the absurdity of war and militarism. His views so disenchanted Emperor Franz I of Austria that the emperor pressed the Archbishop of Prague to have Bolzano recant his statements. Bolzano refused and was then forced to retire in 1824 on a small pension. Bolzano's main contribution to mathematics was philosophical. His work helped convince mathematicians that sound mathematics must ultimately rest on rigorous proof rather than intuition. In addition to his work in mathematics, Bolzano investigated problems concerning space, force, and wave propagation.

■ DERIVATIVES AT THE ENDPOINTS OF AN INTERVAL

If a function f is defined on a closed interval $[a, b]$ but not outside that interval, then f' is not defined at the endpoints of the interval because derivatives are two-sided limits. To deal with this we define **left-hand derivatives** and **right-hand derivatives** by

$$f'_-(x) = \lim_{h \to 0^-} \frac{f(x+h) - f(x)}{h} \quad \text{and} \quad f'_+(x) = \lim_{h \to 0^+} \frac{f(x+h) - f(x)}{h}$$

respectively. These are called **one-sided derivatives**. Geometrically, $f'_-(x)$ is the limit of the slopes of the secant lines as x is approached from the left and $f'_+(x)$ is the limit of the slopes of the secant lines as x is approached from the right. For a closed interval $[a, b]$, we will understand the derivative at the left endpoint to be $f'_+(a)$ and at the right endpoint to be $f'_-(b)$ (Figure 2.2.13).

In general, we will say that f is **differentiable** on an interval of the form $[a, b]$, $[a, +\infty)$, $(-\infty, b]$, $[a, b)$, or $(a, b]$ if it is differentiable at all points inside the interval and the appropriate one-sided derivative exists at each included endpoint.

It can be proved that a function f is continuous from the left at those points where the left-hand derivative exists and is continuous from the right at those points where the right-hand derivative exists.

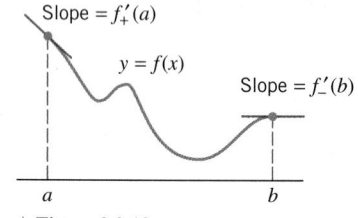

Slope $= f'_+(a)$

$y = f(x)$

Slope $= f'_-(b)$

▲ **Figure 2.2.13**

■ OTHER DERIVATIVE NOTATIONS

The process of finding a derivative is called **differentiation**. You can think of differentiation as an *operation* on functions that associates a function f' with a function f. When the independent variable is x, the differentiation operation is also commonly denoted by

$$f'(x) = \frac{d}{dx}[f(x)] \quad \text{or} \quad f'(x) = D_x[f(x)]$$

In the case where there is a dependent variable $y = f(x)$, the derivative is also commonly denoted by

$$f'(x) = y'(x) \quad \text{or} \quad f'(x) = \frac{dy}{dx}$$

With the above notations, the value of the derivative at a point x_0 can be expressed as

$$f'(x_0) = \frac{d}{dx}[f(x)]\Big|_{x=x_0}, \quad f'(x_0) = D_x[f(x)]\big|_{x=x_0}, \quad f'(x_0) = y'(x_0), \quad f'(x_0) = \frac{dy}{dx}\Big|_{x=x_0}$$

> Later, the symbols dy and dx will be given specific meanings. However, for the time being do not regard dy/dx as a ratio, but rather as a single symbol denoting the derivative.

If a variable w changes from some initial value w_0 to some final value w_1, then the final value minus the initial value is called an **increment** in w and is denoted by

$$\Delta w = w_1 - w_0 \tag{8}$$

Increments can be positive or negative, depending on whether the final value is larger or smaller than the initial value. The increment symbol in (8) should not be interpreted as a product; rather, Δw should be regarded as a single symbol representing the change in the value of w.

It is common to regard the variable h in the derivative formula

$$f'(x) = \lim_{h \to 0} \frac{f(x+h) - f(x)}{h} \tag{9}$$

as an increment Δx in x and write (9) as

$$f'(x) = \lim_{\Delta x \to 0} \frac{f(x + \Delta x) - f(x)}{\Delta x} \tag{10}$$

Moreover, if $y = f(x)$, then the numerator in (10) can be regarded as the increment

$$\Delta y = f(x + \Delta x) - f(x) \tag{11}$$

in which case

$$\frac{dy}{dx} = \lim_{\Delta x \to 0} \frac{\Delta y}{\Delta x} = \lim_{\Delta x \to 0} \frac{f(x + \Delta x) - f(x)}{\Delta x} \tag{12}$$

The geometric interpretations of Δx and Δy are shown in Figure 2.2.14.

Sometimes it is desirable to express derivatives in a form that does not use increments at all. For example, if we let $w = x + h$ in Formula (9), then $w \to x$ as $h \to 0$, so we can rewrite that formula as

$$f'(x) = \lim_{w \to x} \frac{f(w) - f(x)}{w - x} \tag{13}$$

(Compare Figures 2.2.14 and 2.2.15.)

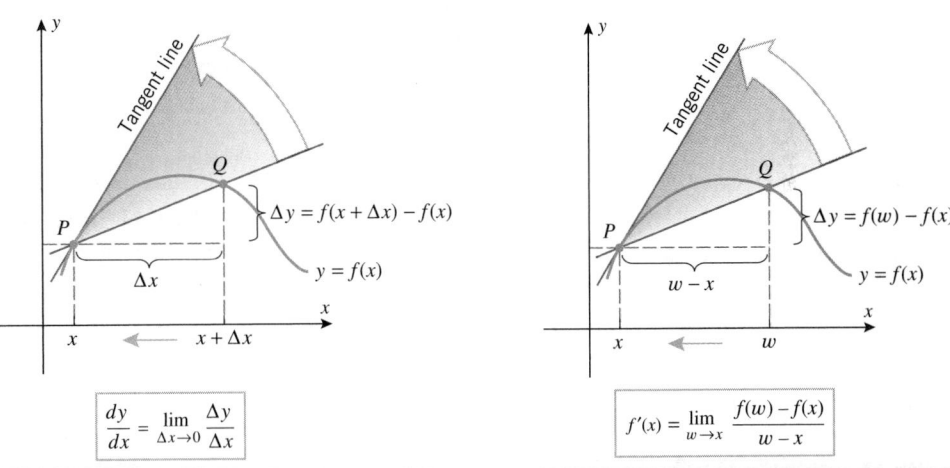

▲ **Figure 2.2.14**   ▲ **Figure 2.2.15**

When letters other than x and y are used for the independent and dependent variables, the derivative notations must be adjusted accordingly. Thus, for example, if $s = f(t)$ is the position function for a particle in rectilinear motion, then the velocity function $v(t)$ in (4) can be expressed as

$$v(t) = \frac{ds}{dt} = \lim_{\Delta t \to 0} \frac{\Delta s}{\Delta t} = \lim_{\Delta t \to 0} \frac{f(t + \Delta t) - f(t)}{\Delta t} \tag{14}$$

✔ **QUICK CHECK EXERCISES 2.2**   *(See page 155 for answers.)*

1. The function $f'(x)$ is defined by the formula

$$f'(x) = \lim_{h \to 0} \underline{\hspace{2cm}}$$

2. (a) The derivative of $f(x) = x^2$ is $f'(x) = $ _____.
   (b) The derivative of $f(x) = \sqrt{x}$ is $f'(x) = $ _____.

3. Suppose that the line $2x + 3y = 5$ is tangent to the graph of $y = f(x)$ at $x = 1$. The value of $f(1)$ is _____ and the value of $f'(1)$ is _____.

4. Which theorem guarantees us that if

$$\lim_{h \to 0} \frac{f(x_0 + h) - f(x_0)}{h}$$

exists, then $\lim_{x \to x_0} f(x) = f(x_0)$?

EXERCISE SET 2.2   ∿ Graphing Utility

1. Use the graph of $y = f(x)$ in the accompanying figure to estimate the value of $f'(1)$, $f'(3)$, $f'(5)$, and $f'(6)$.

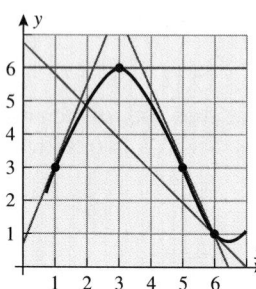

◀ **Figure Ex-1**

2. For the function graphed in the accompanying figure, arrange the numbers 0, $f'(-3)$, $f'(0)$, $f'(2)$, and $f'(4)$ in increasing order.

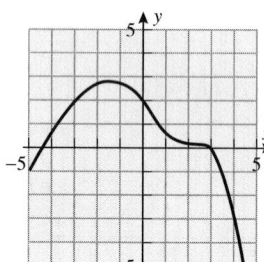

◀ **Figure Ex-2**

FOCUS ON CONCEPTS

3. (a) If you are given an equation for the tangent line at the point $(a, f(a))$ on a curve $y = f(x)$, how would you go about finding $f'(a)$?
   (b) Given that the tangent line to the graph of $y = f(x)$ at the point $(2, 5)$ has the equation $y = 3x - 1$, find $f'(2)$.
   (c) For the function $y = f(x)$ in part (b), what is the instantaneous rate of change of y with respect to x at $x = 2$?

4. Given that the tangent line to $y = f(x)$ at the point $(1, 2)$ passes through the point $(-1, -1)$, find $f'(1)$.

5. Sketch the graph of a function f for which $f(0) = -1$, $f'(0) = 0$, $f'(x) < 0$ if $x < 0$, and $f'(x) > 0$ if $x > 0$.

6. Sketch the graph of a function f for which $f(0) = 0$, $f'(0) = 0$, and $f'(x) > 0$ if $x < 0$ or $x > 0$.

7. Given that $f(3) = -1$ and $f'(3) = 5$, find an equation for the tangent line to the graph of $y = f(x)$ at $x = 3$.

8. Given that $f(-2) = 3$ and $f'(-2) = -4$, find an equation for the tangent line to the graph of $y = f(x)$ at $x = -2$.

9–14 Use Definition 2.2.1 to find $f'(x)$, and then find the tangent line to the graph of $y = f(x)$ at $x = a$. ▩

9. $f(x) = 2x^2$; $a = 1$

10. $f(x) = 1/x^2$; $a = -1$

11. $f(x) = x^3$; $a = 0$

12. $f(x) = 2x^3 + 1$; $a = -1$

13. $f(x) = \sqrt{x + 1}$; $a = 8$

14. $f(x) = \sqrt{2x + 1}$; $a = 4$

15–20 Use Formula (12) to find dy/dx. ▩

15. $y = \dfrac{1}{x}$

16. $y = \dfrac{1}{x + 1}$

17. $y = x^2 - x$

18. $y = x^4$

19. $y = \dfrac{1}{\sqrt{x}}$

20. $y = \dfrac{1}{\sqrt{x - 1}}$

21–22 Use Definition 2.2.1 (with appropriate change in notation) to obtain the derivative requested. ▩

21. Find $f'(t)$ if $f(t) = 4t^2 + t$.

22. Find dV/dr if $V = \frac{4}{3}\pi r^3$.

FOCUS ON CONCEPTS

23. Match the graphs of the functions shown in (a)–(f) with the graphs of their derivatives in (A)–(F).

(a)
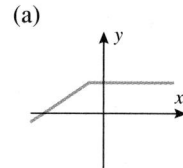

(b)
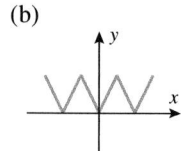

(c)
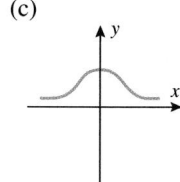

(d)
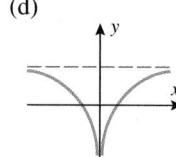

(e)
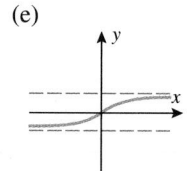

(f)
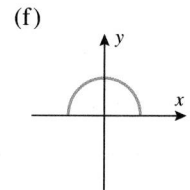

(A)
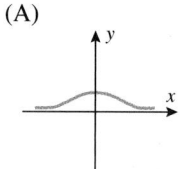

(B)
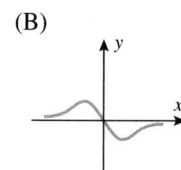

(C)
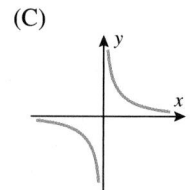

(D)
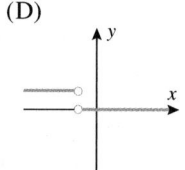

(E)
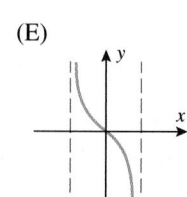

(F)
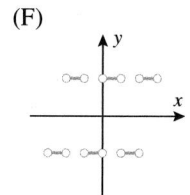

24. Let $f(x) = \sqrt{1 - x^2}$. Use a geometric argument to find $f'(\sqrt{2}/2)$.

25–26 Sketch the graph of the derivative of the function whose graph is shown. ■

25. (a)   (b)   (c)

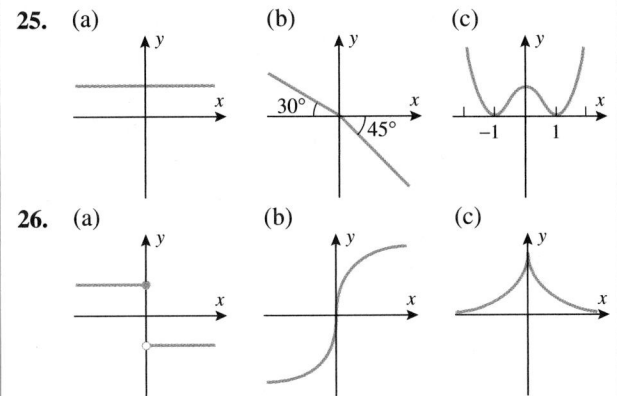

26. (a)   (b)   (c)

27–30 True–False Determine whether the statement is true or false. Explain your answer. ■

27. If a curve $y = f(x)$ has a horizontal tangent line at $x = a$, then $f'(a)$ is not defined.

28. If the tangent line to the graph of $y = f(x)$ at $x = -2$ has negative slope, then $f'(-2) < 0$.

29. If a function f is continuous at $x = 0$, then f is differentiable at $x = 0$.

30. If a function f is differentiable at $x = 0$, then f is continuous at $x = 0$.

31–32 The given limit represents $f'(a)$ for some function f and some number a. Find $f(x)$ and a in each case. ■

31. (a) $\displaystyle\lim_{\Delta x \to 0} \frac{\sqrt{1 + \Delta x} - 1}{\Delta x}$ (b) $\displaystyle\lim_{x_1 \to 3} \frac{x_1^2 - 9}{x_1 - 3}$

32. (a) $\displaystyle\lim_{h \to 0} \frac{\cos(\pi + h) + 1}{h}$ (b) $\displaystyle\lim_{x \to 1} \frac{x^7 - 1}{x - 1}$

33. Find $dy/dx|_{x=1}$, given that $y = 1 - x^2$.

34. Find $dy/dx|_{x=-2}$, given that $y = (x + 2)/x$.

35. Find an equation for the line that is tangent to the curve $y = x^3 - 2x + 1$ at the point $(0, 1)$, and use a graphing utility to graph the curve and its tangent line on the same screen.

36. Use a graphing utility to graph the following on the same screen: the curve $y = x^2/4$, the tangent line to this curve at $x = 1$, and the secant line joining the points $(0, 0)$ and $(2, 1)$ on this curve.

37. Let $f(x) = 2^x$. Estimate $f'(1)$ by
(a) using a graphing utility to zoom in at an appropriate point until the graph looks like a straight line, and then estimating the slope
(b) using a calculating utility to estimate the limit in Formula (13) by making a table of values for a succession of values of w approaching 1.

38. Let $f(x) = \sin x$. Estimate $f'(\pi/4)$ by
(a) using a graphing utility to zoom in at an appropriate point until the graph looks like a straight line, and then estimating the slope
(b) using a calculating utility to estimate the limit in Formula (13) by making a table of values for a succession of values of w approaching $\pi/4$.

39–40 The function f whose graph is shown below has values as given in the accompanying table.

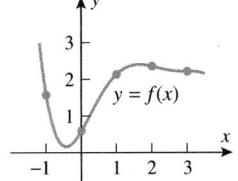

x	-1	0	1	2	3
$f(x)$	1.56	0.58	2.12	2.34	2.2

39. (a) Use data from the table to calculate the difference quotients
$$\frac{f(3) - f(1)}{3 - 1}, \quad \frac{f(2) - f(1)}{2 - 1}, \quad \frac{f(2) - f(0)}{2 - 0}$$
(b) Using the graph of $y = f(x)$, indicate which difference quotient in part (a) best approximates $f'(1)$ and which difference quotient gives the worst approximation to $f'(1)$.

40. Use data from the table to approximate the derivative values.
(a) $f'(0.5)$ (b) $f'(2.5)$

FOCUS ON CONCEPTS

41. Suppose that the cost of drilling x feet for an oil well is $C = f(x)$ dollars.
(a) What are the units of $f'(x)$?
(b) In practical terms, what does $f'(x)$ mean in this case?
(c) What can you say about the sign of $f'(x)$?
(d) Estimate the cost of drilling an additional foot, starting at a depth of 300 ft, given that $f'(300) = 1000$.

42. A paint manufacturing company estimates that it can sell $g = f(p)$ gallons of paint at a price of p dollars per gallon.
(a) What are the units of dg/dp?
(b) In practical terms, what does dg/dp mean in this case?
(c) What can you say about the sign of dg/dp?
(d) Given that $dg/dp|_{p=10} = -100$, what can you say about the effect of increasing the price from $10 per gallon to $11 per gallon?

43. It is a fact that when a flexible rope is wrapped around a rough cylinder, a small force of magnitude F_0 at one end can resist a large force of magnitude F at the other end. The size of F depends on the angle θ through which the rope is wrapped around the cylinder (see the accompanying figure). The figure shows the graph of F (in pounds) versus θ (in radians), where F is the magnitude of the force that can be resisted by a force with magnitude $F_0 = 10$ lb for a certain rope and cylinder.

(a) Estimate the values of F and $dF/d\theta$ when the angle $\theta = 10$ radians.

(b) It can be shown that the force F satisfies the equation $dF/d\theta = \mu F$, where the constant μ is called the *coefficient of friction*. Use the results in part (a) to estimate the value of μ.

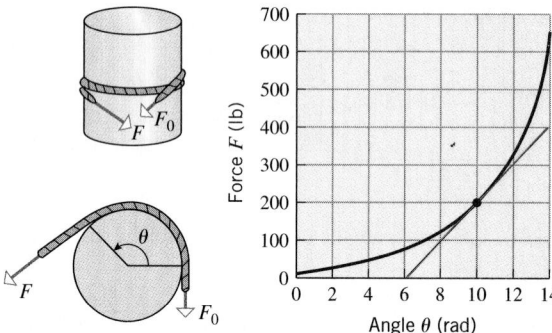

▲ **Figure Ex-43**

44. The accompanying figure shows the velocity versus time curve for a rocket in outer space where the only significant force on the rocket is from its engines. It can be shown that the mass $M(t)$ (in slugs) of the rocket at time t seconds satisfies the equation

$$M(t) = \frac{T}{dv/dt}$$

where T is the thrust (in lb) of the rocket's engines and v is the velocity (in ft/s) of the rocket. The thrust of the first stage of a *Saturn V* rocket is $T = 7{,}680{,}982$ lb. Use this value of T and the line segment in the figure to estimate the mass of the rocket at time $t = 100$.

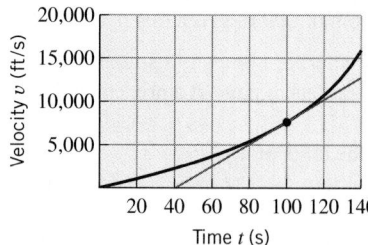

Time t (s)   ◀ **Figure Ex-44**

45. According to **Newton's Law of Cooling**, the rate of change of an object's temperature is proportional to the difference between the temperature of the object and that of the surrounding medium. The accompanying figure shows the graph of the temperature T (in degrees Fahrenheit) versus time t (in minutes) for a cup of coffee, initially with a temperature of 200°F, that is allowed to cool in a room with a constant temperature of 75°F.

(a) Estimate T and dT/dt when $t = 10$ min.

(b) Newton's Law of Cooling can be expressed as

$$\frac{dT}{dt} = k(T - T_0)$$

where k is the constant of proportionality and T_0 is the temperature (assumed constant) of the surrounding medium. Use the results in part (a) to estimate the value of k.

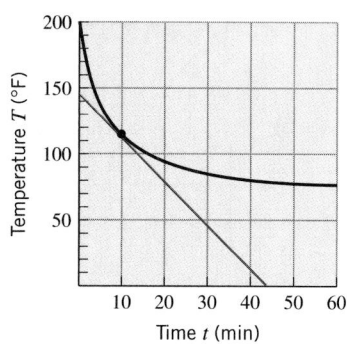

Time t (min)   ◀ **Figure Ex-45**

46. Show that $f(x)$ is continuous but not differentiable at the indicated point. Sketch the graph of f.

(a) $f(x) = \sqrt[3]{x}$, $x = 0$

(b) $f(x) = \sqrt[3]{(x-2)^2}$, $x = 2$

47. Show that

$$f(x) = \begin{cases} x^2 + 1, & x \le 1 \\ 2x, & x > 1 \end{cases}$$

is continuous and differentiable at $x = 1$. Sketch the graph of f.

48. Show that

$$f(x) = \begin{cases} x^2 + 2, & x \le 1 \\ x + 2, & x > 1 \end{cases}$$

is continuous but not differentiable at $x = 1$. Sketch the graph of f.

49. Show that

$$f(x) = \begin{cases} x \sin(1/x), & x \ne 0 \\ 0, & x = 0 \end{cases}$$

is continuous but not differentiable at $x = 0$. Sketch the graph of f near $x = 0$. (See Figure 1.6.6 and the remark following Example 5 in Section 1.6.)

50. Show that

$$f(x) = \begin{cases} x^2 \sin(1/x), & x \ne 0 \\ 0, & x = 0 \end{cases}$$

is continuous and differentiable at $x = 0$. Sketch the graph of f near $x = 0$.

FOCUS ON CONCEPTS

51. Suppose that a function f is differentiable at x_0 and that $f'(x_0) > 0$. Prove that there exists an open interval containing x_0 such that if x_1 and x_2 are any two points in this interval with $x_1 < x_0 < x_2$, then $f(x_1) < f(x_0) < f(x_2)$.

52. Suppose that a function f is differentiable at x_0 and define $g(x) = f(mx + b)$, where m and b are constants. Prove that if x_1 is a point at which $mx_1 + b = x_0$, then $g(x)$ is differentiable at x_1 and $g'(x_1) = mf'(x_0)$.

53. Suppose that a function f is differentiable at $x = 0$ with $f(0) = f'(0) = 0$, and let $y = mx$, $m \neq 0$, denote any line of nonzero slope through the origin.

(a) Prove that there exists an open interval containing 0 such that for all nonzero x in this interval $|f(x)| < \left|\frac{1}{2}mx\right|$. [*Hint:* Let $\epsilon = \frac{1}{2}|m|$ and apply Definition 1.4.1 to (5) with $x_0 = 0$.]

(b) Conclude from part (a) and the triangle inequality that there exists an open interval containing 0 such that $|f(x)| < |f(x) - mx|$ for all x in this interval.

(c) Explain why the result obtained in part (b) may be interpreted to mean that the tangent line to the graph

of f at the origin is the best *linear* approximation to f at that point.

54. Suppose that f is differentiable at x_0. Modify the argument of Exercise 53 to prove that the tangent line to the graph of f at the point $P(x_0, f(x_0))$ provides the best linear approximation to f at P. [*Hint:* Suppose that $y = f(x_0) + m(x - x_0)$ is any line through $P(x_0, f(x_0))$ with slope $m \neq f'(x_0)$. Apply Definition 1.4.1 to (5) with $x = x_0 + h$ and $\epsilon = \frac{1}{2}|f'(x_0) - m|$.]

55. Writing Write a paragraph that explains what it means for a function to be differentiable. Include examples of functions that are not differentiable as well as examples of functions that are differentiable.

56. Writing Explain the relationship between continuity and differentiability.

✔ **QUICK CHECK ANSWERS 2.2**

1. $\dfrac{f(x + h) - f(x)}{h}$ **2.** (a) $2x$ (b) $\dfrac{1}{2\sqrt{x}}$ **3.** 1; $-\frac{2}{3}$

4. Theorem 2.2.3: If f is differentiable at x_0, then f is continuous at x_0.

2.3 INTRODUCTION TO TECHNIQUES OF DIFFERENTIATION

In the last section we defined the derivative of a function f as a limit, and we used that limit to calculate a few simple derivatives. In this section we will develop some important theorems that will enable us to calculate derivatives more efficiently.

■ **DERIVATIVE OF A CONSTANT**

The simplest kind of function is a constant function $f(x) = c$. Since the graph of f is a horizontal line of slope 0, the tangent line to the graph of f has slope 0 for every x; and hence we can see geometrically that $f'(x) = 0$ (Figure 2.3.1). We can also see this algebraically since

$$f'(x) = \lim_{h \to 0} \frac{f(x + h) - f(x)}{h} = \lim_{h \to 0} \frac{c - c}{h} = \lim_{h \to 0} 0 = 0$$

Thus, we have established the following result.

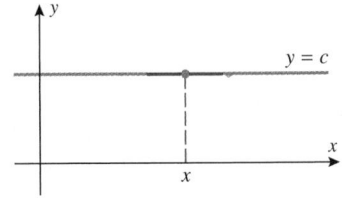

The tangent line to the graph of $f(x) = c$ has slope 0 for all x.

▲ **Figure 2.3.1**

2.3.1 THEOREM *The derivative of a constant function is 0; that is, if c is any real number, then*

$$\frac{d}{dx}[c] = 0 \tag{1}$$

▶ **Example 1**

$$\frac{d}{dx}[1] = 0, \quad \frac{d}{dx}[-3] = 0, \quad \frac{d}{dx}[\pi] = 0, \quad \frac{d}{dx}\left[-\sqrt{2}\right] = 0 \blacktriangleleft$$

■ DERIVATIVES OF POWER FUNCTIONS

The simplest power function is $f(x) = x$. Since the graph of f is a line of slope 1, it follows from Example 3 of Section 2.2 that $f'(x) = 1$ for all x (Figure 2.3.2). In other words,

$$\frac{d}{dx}[x] = 1 \tag{2}$$

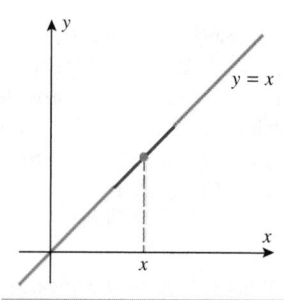

The tangent line to the graph of $f(x) = x$ has slope 1 for all x.

▲ **Figure 2.3.2**

Example 1 of Section 2.2 shows that the power function $f(x) = x^2$ has derivative $f'(x) = 2x$. From Example 2 in that section one can infer that the power function $f(x) = x^3$ has derivative $f'(x) = 3x^2$. That is,

$$\frac{d}{dx}[x^2] = 2x \quad \text{and} \quad \frac{d}{dx}[x^3] = 3x^2 \tag{3–4}$$

These results are special cases of the following more general result.

2.3.2   THEOREM (*The Power Rule*)   *If n is a positive integer, then*

$$\frac{d}{dx}[x^n] = nx^{n-1} \tag{5}$$

Verify that Formulas (2), (3), and (4) are the special cases of (5) in which $n = 1, 2,$ and 3.

The binomial formula can be found on the front endpaper of the text. Replacing y by h in this formula yields the identity used in the proof of Theorem 2.3.2.

PROOF   Let $f(x) = x^n$. Thus, from the definition of a derivative and the binomial formula for expanding the expression $(x + h)^n$, we obtain

$$\frac{d}{dx}[x^n] = f'(x) = \lim_{h \to 0} \frac{f(x + h) - f(x)}{h} = \lim_{h \to 0} \frac{(x + h)^n - x^n}{h}$$

$$= \lim_{h \to 0} \frac{\left[x^n + nx^{n-1}h + \frac{n(n-1)}{2!}x^{n-2}h^2 + \cdots + nxh^{n-1} + h^n\right] - x^n}{h}$$

$$= \lim_{h \to 0} \frac{nx^{n-1}h + \frac{n(n-1)}{2!}x^{n-2}h^2 + \cdots + nxh^{n-1} + h^n}{h}$$

$$= \lim_{h \to 0} \left[nx^{n-1} + \frac{n(n-1)}{2!}x^{n-2}h + \cdots + nxh^{n-2} + h^{n-1}\right]$$

$$= nx^{n-1} + 0 + \cdots + 0 + 0$$

$$= nx^{n-1} \quad ■$$

▶ **Example 2**

$$\frac{d}{dx}[x^4] = 4x^3, \quad \frac{d}{dx}[x^5] = 5x^4, \quad \frac{d}{dt}[t^{12}] = 12t^{11} \quad ◀$$

Although our proof of the power rule in Formula (5) applies only to *positive* integer powers of x, it is not difficult to show that the same formula holds for all integer powers of x (Exercise 82). Also, we saw in Example 4 of Section 2.2 that

$$\frac{d}{dx}[\sqrt{x}] = \frac{1}{2\sqrt{x}} \tag{6}$$

which can be expressed as

$$\frac{d}{dx}[x^{1/2}] = \frac{1}{2}x^{-1/2} = \frac{1}{2}x^{(1/2)-1}$$

Thus, Formula (5) is valid for $n = \frac{1}{2}$, as well. In fact, it can be shown that this formula holds for any real exponent. We state this more general result for our use now, although we won't be prepared to prove it until Chapter 3.

2.3.3 THEOREM (*Extended Power Rule*) *If r is any real number, then*

$$\frac{d}{dx}[x^r] = rx^{r-1} \tag{7}$$

In words, *to differentiate a power function, decrease the constant exponent by one and multiply the resulting power function by the original exponent.*

▶ **Example 3**

$$\frac{d}{dx}[x^\pi] = \pi x^{\pi-1}$$

$$\frac{d}{dx}\left[\frac{1}{x}\right] = \frac{d}{dx}[x^{-1}] = (-1)x^{-1-1} = -x^{-2} = -\frac{1}{x^2}$$

$$\frac{d}{dw}\left[\frac{1}{w^{100}}\right] = \frac{d}{dw}[w^{-100}] = -100w^{-101} = -\frac{100}{w^{101}}$$

$$\frac{d}{dx}[x^{4/5}] = \frac{4}{5}x^{(4/5)-1} = \frac{4}{5}x^{-1/5}$$

$$\frac{d}{dx}[\sqrt[3]{x}] = \frac{d}{dx}[x^{1/3}] = \frac{1}{3}x^{-2/3} = \frac{1}{3\sqrt[3]{x^2}} \ \blacktriangleleft$$

■ **DERIVATIVE OF A CONSTANT TIMES A FUNCTION**

Formula (8) can also be expressed in function notation as

$$(cf)' = cf'$$

2.3.4 THEOREM (*Constant Multiple Rule*) *If f is differentiable at x and c is any real number, then cf is also differentiable at x and*

$$\frac{d}{dx}[cf(x)] = c\frac{d}{dx}[f(x)] \tag{8}$$

PROOF

$$\frac{d}{dx}[cf(x)] = \lim_{h \to 0} \frac{cf(x+h) - cf(x)}{h}$$

$$= \lim_{h \to 0} c\left[\frac{f(x+h) - f(x)}{h}\right]$$

$$= c\lim_{h \to 0} \frac{f(x+h) - f(x)}{h} \qquad \boxed{\begin{array}{l}\text{A constant factor can be}\\ \text{moved through a limit sign.}\end{array}}$$

$$= c\frac{d}{dx}[f(x)] \ \blacksquare$$

In words, *a constant factor can be moved through a derivative sign.*

▶ **Example 4**

$$\frac{d}{dx}[4x^8] = 4\frac{d}{dx}[x^8] = 4[8x^7] = 32x^7$$

$$\frac{d}{dx}[-x^{12}] = (-1)\frac{d}{dx}[x^{12}] = -12x^{11}$$

$$\frac{d}{dx}\left[\frac{\pi}{x}\right] = \pi\frac{d}{dx}[x^{-1}] = \pi(-x^{-2}) = -\frac{\pi}{x^2} \quad ◀$$

■ **DERIVATIVES OF SUMS AND DIFFERENCES**

Formulas (9) and (10) can also be expressed as

$$(f + g)' = f' + g'$$
$$(f - g)' = f' - g'$$

2.3.5 **THEOREM** (***Sum and Difference Rules***) *If f and g are differentiable at x, then so are f + g and f − g and*

$$\frac{d}{dx}[f(x) + g(x)] = \frac{d}{dx}[f(x)] + \frac{d}{dx}[g(x)] \tag{9}$$

$$\frac{d}{dx}[f(x) - g(x)] = \frac{d}{dx}[f(x)] - \frac{d}{dx}[g(x)] \tag{10}$$

PROOF Formula (9) can be proved as follows:

$$\frac{d}{dx}[f(x) + g(x)] = \lim_{h \to 0} \frac{[f(x + h) + g(x + h)] - [f(x) + g(x)]}{h}$$

$$= \lim_{h \to 0} \frac{[f(x + h) - f(x)] + [g(x + h) - g(x)]}{h}$$

$$= \lim_{h \to 0} \frac{f(x + h) - f(x)}{h} + \lim_{h \to 0} \frac{g(x + h) - g(x)}{h} \qquad \boxed{\text{The limit of a sum is the sum of the limits.}}$$

$$= \frac{d}{dx}[f(x)] + \frac{d}{dx}[g(x)]$$

Formula (10) can be proved in a similar manner or, alternatively, by writing $f(x) - g(x)$ as $f(x) + (-1)g(x)$ and then applying Formulas (8) and (9). ■

In words, *the derivative of a sum equals the sum of the derivatives*, and *the derivative of a difference equals the difference of the derivatives.*

▶ **Example 5**

$$\frac{d}{dx}[2x^6 + x^{-9}] = \frac{d}{dx}[2x^6] + \frac{d}{dx}[x^{-9}] = 12x^5 + (-9)x^{-10} = 12x^5 - 9x^{-10}$$

$$\frac{d}{dx}\left[\frac{\sqrt{x} - 2x}{\sqrt{x}}\right] = \frac{d}{dx}[1 - 2\sqrt{x}]$$

$$= \frac{d}{dx}[1] - \frac{d}{dx}[2\sqrt{x}] = 0 - 2\left(\frac{1}{2\sqrt{x}}\right) = -\frac{1}{\sqrt{x}} \qquad \boxed{\text{See Formula (6).}} \quad ◀$$

Although Formulas (9) and (10) are stated for sums and differences of two functions, they can be extended to any finite number of functions. For example, by grouping and applying Formula (9) twice we obtain

$$(f + g + h)' = [(f + g) + h]' = (f + g)' + h' = f' + g' + h'$$

As illustrated in the following example, the constant multiple rule together with the extended versions of the sum and difference rules can be used to differentiate any polynomial.

▶ **Example 6** Find dy/dx if $y = 3x^8 - 2x^5 + 6x + 1$.

Solution.

$$\frac{dy}{dx} = \frac{d}{dx}[3x^8 - 2x^5 + 6x + 1]$$

$$= \frac{d}{dx}[3x^8] - \frac{d}{dx}[2x^5] + \frac{d}{dx}[6x] + \frac{d}{dx}[1]$$

$$= 24x^7 - 10x^4 + 6 \blacktriangleleft$$

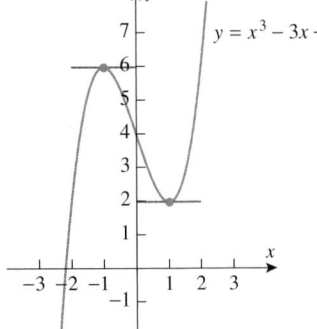

▲ **Figure 2.3.3**

▶ **Example 7** At what points, if any, does the graph of $y = x^3 - 3x + 4$ have a horizontal tangent line?

Solution. Horizontal tangent lines have slope zero, so we must find those values of x for which $y'(x) = 0$. Differentiating yields

$$y'(x) = \frac{d}{dx}[x^3 - 3x + 4] = 3x^2 - 3$$

Thus, horizontal tangent lines occur at those values of x for which $3x^2 - 3 = 0$, that is, if $x = -1$ or $x = 1$. The corresponding points on the curve $y = x^3 - 3x + 4$ are $(-1, 6)$ and $(1, 2)$ (see Figure 2.3.3). ◀

▶ **Example 8** Find the area of the triangle formed from the coordinate axes and the tangent line to the curve $y = 5x^{-1} - \frac{1}{5}x$ at the point $(5, 0)$.

Solution. Since the derivative of y with respect to x is

$$y'(x) = \frac{d}{dx}\left[5x^{-1} - \frac{1}{5}x\right] = \frac{d}{dx}[5x^{-1}] - \frac{d}{dx}\left[\frac{1}{5}x\right] = -5x^{-2} - \frac{1}{5}$$

the slope of the tangent line at the point $(5, 0)$ is $y'(5) = -\frac{2}{5}$. Thus, the equation of the tangent line at this point is

$$y - 0 = -\frac{2}{5}(x - 5) \quad \text{or equivalently} \quad y = -\frac{2}{5}x + 2$$

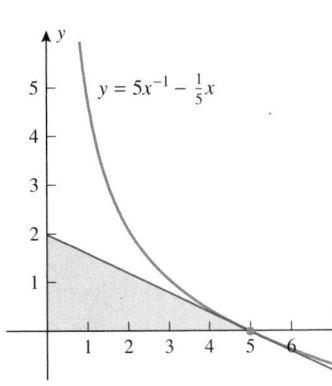

▲ **Figure 2.3.4**

Since the y-intercept of this line is 2, the right triangle formed from the coordinate axes and the tangent line has legs of length 5 and 2, so its area is $\frac{1}{2}(5)(2) = 5$ (Figure 2.3.4). ◀

■ HIGHER DERIVATIVES

The derivative f' of a function f is itself a function and hence may have a derivative of its own. If f' is differentiable, then its derivative is denoted by f'' and is called the *second derivative* of f. As long as we have differentiability, we can continue the process of differentiating to obtain third, fourth, fifth, and even higher derivatives of f. These successive derivatives are denoted by

$$f', \quad f'' = (f')', \quad f''' = (f'')', \quad f^{(4)} = (f''')', \quad f^{(5)} = (f^{(4)})', \ldots$$

If $y = f(x)$, then successive derivatives can also be denoted by

$$y', \quad y'', \quad y''', \quad y^{(4)}, \quad y^{(5)}, \ldots$$

Other common notations are

$$y' = \frac{dy}{dx} = \frac{d}{dx}[f(x)]$$

$$y'' = \frac{d^2 y}{dx^2} = \frac{d}{dx}\left[\frac{d}{dx}[f(x)]\right] = \frac{d^2}{dx^2}[f(x)]$$

$$y''' = \frac{d^3 y}{dx^3} = \frac{d}{dx}\left[\frac{d^2}{dx^2}[f(x)]\right] = \frac{d^3}{dx^3}[f(x)]$$

$$\vdots \qquad\qquad\qquad \vdots$$

These are called, in succession, the *first derivative*, the *second derivative*, the *third derivative*, and so forth. The number of times that f is differentiated is called the **order** of the derivative. A general nth order derivative can be denoted by

$$\frac{d^n y}{dx^n} = f^{(n)}(x) = \frac{d^n}{dx^n}[f(x)] \tag{11}$$

and the value of a general nth order derivative at a specific point $x = x_0$ can be denoted by

$$\left.\frac{d^n y}{dx^n}\right|_{x=x_0} = f^{(n)}(x_0) = \left.\frac{d^n}{dx^n}[f(x)]\right|_{x=x_0} \tag{12}$$

▶ **Example 9** If $f(x) = 3x^4 - 2x^3 + x^2 - 4x + 2$, then

$$f'(x) = 12x^3 - 6x^2 + 2x - 4$$
$$f''(x) = 36x^2 - 12x + 2$$
$$f'''(x) = 72x - 12$$
$$f^{(4)}(x) = 72$$
$$f^{(5)}(x) = 0$$
$$\vdots$$
$$f^{(n)}(x) = 0 \quad (n \geq 5) \blacktriangleleft$$

We will discuss the significance of second derivatives and those of higher order in later sections.

✔ **QUICK CHECK EXERCISES 2.3**   (*See page 163 for answers.*)

1. In each part, determine $f'(x)$.
   (a) $f(x) = \sqrt{6}$
   (b) $f(x) = \sqrt{6}x$
   (c) $f(x) = 6\sqrt{x}$
   (d) $f(x) = \sqrt{6x}$

2. In parts (a)–(d), determine $f'(x)$.
   (a) $f(x) = x^3 + 5$
   (b) $f(x) = x^2(x^3 + 5)$
   (c) $f(x) = \dfrac{x^3 + 5}{2}$
   (d) $f(x) = \dfrac{x^3 + 5}{x^2}$

3. The slope of the tangent line to the curve $y = x^2 + 4x + 7$ at $x = 1$ is _____.

4. If $f(x) = 3x^3 - 3x^2 + x + 1$, then $f''(x) =$ _____.

EXERCISE SET 2.3    Graphing Utility

1–8 Find dy/dx. ■

1. $y = 4x^7$

2. $y = -3x^{12}$

3. $y = 3x^8 + 2x + 1$

4. $y = \frac{1}{2}(x^4 + 7)$

5. $y = \pi^3$

6. $y = \sqrt{2}x + (1/\sqrt{2})$

7. $y = -\frac{1}{3}(x^7 + 2x - 9)$

8. $y = \dfrac{x^2 + 1}{5}$

9–16 Find $f'(x)$. ■

9. $f(x) = x^{-3} + \dfrac{1}{x^7}$

10. $f(x) = \sqrt{x} + \dfrac{1}{x}$

11. $f(x) = -3x^{-8} + 2\sqrt{x}$

12. $f(x) = 7x^{-6} - 5\sqrt{x}$

13. $f(x) = x^e + \dfrac{1}{x^{\sqrt{10}}}$

14. $f(x) = \sqrt[3]{\dfrac{8}{x}}$

15. $f(x) = ax^3 + bx^2 + cx + d$ (a, b, c, d constant)

16. $f(x) = \dfrac{1}{a}\left(x^2 + \dfrac{1}{b}x + c\right)$ (a, b, c constant)

17–18 Find $y'(1)$. ■

17. $y = 5x^2 - 3x + 1$

18. $y = \dfrac{x^{3/2} + 2}{x}$

19–20 Find dx/dt. ■

19. $x = t^2 - t$

20. $x = \dfrac{t^2 + 1}{3t}$

21–24 Find $dy/dx|_{x=1}$. ■

21. $y = 1 + x + x^2 + x^3 + x^4 + x^5$

22. $y = \dfrac{1 + x + x^2 + x^3 + x^4 + x^5 + x^6}{x^3}$

23. $y = (1 - x)(1 + x)(1 + x^2)(1 + x^4)$

24. $y = x^{24} + 2x^{12} + 3x^8 + 4x^6$

25–26 Approximate $f'(1)$ by considering the difference quotient
$$\frac{f(1 + h) - f(1)}{h}$$
for values of h near 0, and then find the exact value of $f'(1)$ by differentiating. ■

25. $f(x) = x^3 - 3x + 1$

26. $f(x) = \dfrac{1}{x^2}$

27–28 Use a graphing utility to estimate the value of $f'(1)$ by zooming in on the graph of f, and then compare your estimate to the exact value obtained by differentiating. ■

27. $f(x) = \dfrac{x^2 + 1}{x}$

28. $f(x) = \dfrac{x + 2x^{3/2}}{\sqrt{x}}$

29–32 Find the indicated derivative. ■

29. $\dfrac{d}{dt}[16t^2]$

30. $\dfrac{dC}{dr}$, where $C = 2\pi r$

31. $V'(r)$, where $V = \pi r^3$

32. $\dfrac{d}{d\alpha}[2\alpha^{-1} + \alpha]$

33–36 True–False Determine whether the statement is true or false. Explain your answer. ■

33. If f and g are differentiable at $x = 2$, then
$$\frac{d}{dx}[f(x) - 8g(x)]\Big|_{x=2} = f'(2) - 8g'(2)$$

34. If $f(x)$ is a cubic polynomial, then $f'(x)$ is a quadratic polynomial.

35. If $f'(2) = 5$, then
$$\frac{d}{dx}[4f(x) + x^3]\Big|_{x=2} = \frac{d}{dx}[4f(x) + 8]\Big|_{x=2} = 4f'(2) = 20$$

36. If $f(x) = x^2(x^4 - x)$, then
$$f''(x) = \frac{d}{dx}[x^2] \cdot \frac{d}{dx}[x^4 - x] = 2x(4x^3 - 1)$$

37. A spherical balloon is being inflated.
(a) Find a general formula for the instantaneous rate of change of the volume V with respect to the radius r, given that $V = \frac{4}{3}\pi r^3$.
(b) Find the rate of change of V with respect to r at the instant when the radius is $r = 5$.

38. Find $\dfrac{d}{d\lambda}\left[\dfrac{\lambda\lambda_0 + \lambda^6}{2 - \lambda_0}\right]$ (λ_0 is constant).

39. Find an equation of the tangent line to the graph of $y = f(x)$ at $x = -3$ if $f(-3) = 2$ and $f'(-3) = 5$.

40. Find an equation of the tangent line to the graph of $y = f(x)$ at $x = 2$ if $f(2) = -2$ and $f'(2) = -1$.

41–42 Find d^2y/dx^2. ■

41. (a) $y = 7x^3 - 5x^2 + x$ (b) $y = 12x^2 - 2x + 3$
(c) $y = \dfrac{x + 1}{x}$ (d) $y = (5x^2 - 3)(7x^3 + x)$

42. (a) $y = 4x^7 - 5x^3 + 2x$ (b) $y = 3x + 2$
(c) $y = \dfrac{3x - 2}{5x}$ (d) $y = (x^3 - 5)(2x + 3)$

43–44 Find y'''. ■

43. (a) $y = x^{-5} + x^5$ (b) $y = 1/x$
(c) $y = ax^3 + bx + c$ (a, b, c constant)

44. (a) $y = 5x^2 - 4x + 7$ (b) $y = 3x^{-2} + 4x^{-1} + x$
(c) $y = ax^4 + bx^2 + c$ (a, b, c constant)

45. Find
(a) $f'''(2)$, where $f(x) = 3x^2 - 2$
(b) $\dfrac{d^2y}{dx^2}\Big|_{x=1}$, where $y = 6x^5 - 4x^2$
(c) $\dfrac{d^4}{dx^4}[x^{-3}]\Big|_{x=1}$.

46. Find
(a) $y'''(0)$, where $y = 4x^4 + 2x^3 + 3$
(b) $\left.\dfrac{d^4 y}{dx^4}\right|_{x=1}$, where $y = \dfrac{6}{x^4}$.

47. Show that $y = x^3 + 3x + 1$ satisfies $y''' + xy'' - 2y' = 0$.

48. Show that if $x \ne 0$, then $y = 1/x$ satisfies the equation $x^3 y'' + x^2 y' - xy = 0$.

49–50 Use a graphing utility to make rough estimates of the locations of all horizontal tangent lines, and then find their exact locations by differentiating.

49. $y = \frac{1}{3}x^3 - \frac{3}{2}x^2 + 2x$ **50.** $y = \dfrac{x^2 + 9}{x}$

FOCUS ON CONCEPTS

51. Find a function $y = ax^2 + bx + c$ whose graph has an x-intercept of 1, a y-intercept of -2, and a tangent line with a slope of -1 at the y-intercept.

52. Find k if the curve $y = x^2 + k$ is tangent to the line $y = 2x$.

53. Find the x-coordinate of the point on the graph of $y = x^2$ where the tangent line is parallel to the secant line that cuts the curve at $x = -1$ and $x = 2$.

54. Find the x-coordinate of the point on the graph of $y = \sqrt{x}$ where the tangent line is parallel to the secant line that cuts the curve at $x = 1$ and $x = 4$.

55. Find the coordinates of all points on the graph of $y = 1 - x^2$ at which the tangent line passes through the point $(2, 0)$.

56. Show that any two tangent lines to the parabola $y = ax^2$, $a \ne 0$, intersect at a point that is on the vertical line halfway between the points of tangency.

---

57. Suppose that L is the tangent line at $x = x_0$ to the graph of the cubic equation $y = ax^3 + bx$. Find the x-coordinate of the point where L intersects the graph a second time.

58. Show that the segment of the tangent line to the graph of $y = 1/x$ that is cut off by the coordinate axes is bisected by the point of tangency.

59. Show that the triangle that is formed by any tangent line to the graph of $y = 1/x$, $x > 0$, and the coordinate axes has an area of 2 square units.

60. Find conditions on a, b, c, and d so that the graph of the polynomial $f(x) = ax^3 + bx^2 + cx + d$ has
(a) exactly two horizontal tangents
(b) exactly one horizontal tangent
(c) no horizontal tangents.

61. Newton's Law of Universal Gravitation states that the magnitude F of the force exerted by a point with mass M on a point with mass m is

$$F = \frac{GmM}{r^2}$$

where G is a constant and r is the distance between the bodies. Assuming that the points are moving, find a formula for the instantaneous rate of change of F with respect to r.

62. In the temperature range between $0°C$ and $700°C$ the resistance R [in ohms (Ω)] of a certain platinum resistance thermometer is given by

$$R = 10 + 0.04124T - 1.779 \times 10^{-5}T^2$$

where T is the temperature in degrees Celsius. Where in the interval from $0°C$ to $700°C$ is the resistance of the thermometer most sensitive and least sensitive to temperature changes? [*Hint:* Consider the size of dR/dT in the interval $0 \le T \le 700$.]

63–64 Use a graphing utility to make rough estimates of the intervals on which $f'(x) > 0$, and then find those intervals exactly by differentiating.

63. $f(x) = x - \dfrac{1}{x}$ **64.** $f(x) = x^3 - 3x$

65–68 You are asked in these exercises to determine whether a piecewise-defined function f is differentiable at a value $x = x_0$, where f is defined by different formulas on different sides of x_0. You may use without proof the following result, which is a consequence of the Mean-Value Theorem (discussed in Section 4.8). ***Theorem.** Let f be continuous at x_0 and suppose that $\lim_{x \to x_0} f'(x)$ exists. Then f is differentiable at x_0, and $f'(x_0) = \lim_{x \to x_0} f'(x)$.*

65. Show that

$$f(x) = \begin{cases} x^2 + x + 1, & x \le 1 \\ 3x, & x > 1 \end{cases}$$

is continuous at $x = 1$. Determine whether f is differentiable at $x = 1$. If so, find the value of the derivative there. Sketch the graph of f.

66. Let

$$f(x) = \begin{cases} x^2 - 16x, & x < 9 \\ \sqrt{x}, & x \ge 9 \end{cases}$$

Is f continuous at $x = 9$? Determine whether f is differentiable at $x = 9$. If so, find the value of the derivative there.

67. Let

$$f(x) = \begin{cases} x^2, & x \le 1 \\ \sqrt{x}, & x > 1 \end{cases}$$

Determine whether f is differentiable at $x = 1$. If so, find the value of the derivative there.

68. Let

$$f(x) = \begin{cases} x^3 + \frac{1}{16}, & x < \frac{1}{2} \\ \frac{3}{4}x^2, & x \ge \frac{1}{2} \end{cases}$$

Determine whether f is differentiable at $x = \frac{1}{2}$. If so, find the value of the derivative there.

69. Find all points where f fails to be differentiable. Justify your answer.
(a) $f(x) = |3x - 2|$ (b) $f(x) = |x^2 - 4|$

70. In each part, compute f', f'', f''', and then state the formula for $f^{(n)}$.

(a) $f(x) = 1/x$ (b) $f(x) = 1/x^2$

[*Hint:* The expression $(-1)^n$ has a value of 1 if n is even and -1 if n is odd. Use this expression in your answer.]

71. (a) Prove:
$$\frac{d^2}{dx^2}[cf(x)] = c\frac{d^2}{dx^2}[f(x)]$$
$$\frac{d^2}{dx^2}[f(x) + g(x)] = \frac{d^2}{dx^2}[f(x)] + \frac{d^2}{dx^2}[g(x)]$$
(b) Do the results in part (a) generalize to nth derivatives? Justify your answer.

72. Let $f(x) = x^8 - 2x + 3$; find
$$\lim_{w \to 2} \frac{f'(w) - f'(2)}{w - 2}$$

73. (a) Find $f^{(n)}(x)$ if $f(x) = x^n$, $n = 1, 2, 3, \ldots$.
(b) Find $f^{(n)}(x)$ if $f(x) = x^k$ and $n > k$, where k is a positive integer.
(c) Find $f^{(n)}(x)$ if
$$f(x) = a_0 + a_1 x + a_2 x^2 + \cdots + a_n x^n$$

74. (a) Prove: If $f''(x)$ exists for each x in (a, b), then both f and f' are continuous on (a, b).
(b) What can be said about the continuity of f and its derivatives if $f^{(n)}(x)$ exists for each x in (a, b)?

75. Let $f(x) = (mx + b)^n$, where m and b are constants and n is an integer. Use the result of Exercise 52 in Section 2.2 to prove that $f'(x) = nm(mx + b)^{n-1}$.

76–77 Verify the result of Exercise 75 for $f(x)$. ■

76. $f(x) = (2x + 3)^2$ **77.** $f(x) = (3x - 1)^3$

78–81 Use the result of Exercise 75 to compute the derivative of the given function $f(x)$. ■

78. $f(x) = \dfrac{1}{x - 1}$

79. $f(x) = \dfrac{3}{(2x + 1)^2}$

80. $f(x) = \dfrac{x}{x + 1}$

81. $f(x) = \dfrac{2x^2 + 4x + 3}{x^2 + 2x + 1}$

82. The purpose of this exercise is to extend the power rule (Theorem 2.3.2) to any integer exponent. Let $f(x) = x^n$, where n is any integer. If $n > 0$, then $f'(x) = nx^{n-1}$ by Theorem 2.3.2.
(a) Show that the conclusion of Theorem 2.3.2 holds in the case $n = 0$.
(b) Suppose that $n < 0$ and set $m = -n$ so that
$$f(x) = x^n = x^{-m} = \frac{1}{x^m}$$

Use Definition 2.2.1 and Theorem 2.3.2 to show that
$$\frac{d}{dx}\left[\frac{1}{x^m}\right] = -mx^{m-1} \cdot \frac{1}{x^{2m}}$$

and conclude that $f'(x) = nx^{n-1}$.

✔ **QUICK CHECK ANSWERS 2.3**

1. (a) 0 (b) $\sqrt{6}$ (c) $3/\sqrt{x}$ (d) $\sqrt{6}/(2\sqrt{x})$ **2.** (a) $3x^2$ (b) $5x^4 + 10x$ (c) $\frac{3}{2}x^2$ (d) $1 - 10x^{-3}$ **3.** 6   **4.** $18x - 6$

2.4 THE PRODUCT AND QUOTIENT RULES

In this section we will develop techniques for differentiating products and quotients of functions whose derivatives are known.

■ DERIVATIVE OF A PRODUCT

You might be tempted to conjecture that the derivative of a product of two functions is the product of their derivatives. However, a simple example will show this to be false. Consider the functions

$$f(x) = x \quad \text{and} \quad g(x) = x^2$$

The product of their derivatives is

$$f'(x)g'(x) = (1)(2x) = 2x$$

but their product is $h(x) = f(x)g(x) = x^3$, so the derivative of the product is

$$h'(x) = 3x^2$$

Thus, the derivative of the product is not equal to the product of the derivatives. The correct relationship, which is credited to Leibniz, is given by the following theorem.

Formula (1) can also be expressed as

$$(f \cdot g)' = f \cdot g' + g \cdot f'$$

2.4.1 **THEOREM** (*The Product Rule*)   *If f and g are differentiable at x, then so is the product f · g, and*

$$\frac{d}{dx}[f(x)g(x)] = f(x)\frac{d}{dx}[g(x)] + g(x)\frac{d}{dx}[f(x)] \tag{1}$$

PROOF   Whereas the proofs of the derivative rules in the last section were straightforward applications of the derivative definition, a key step in this proof involves adding and subtracting the quantity $f(x + h)g(x)$ to the numerator in the derivative definition. This yields

$$\frac{d}{dx}[f(x)g(x)] = \lim_{h \to 0} \frac{f(x + h) \cdot g(x + h) - f(x) \cdot g(x)}{h}$$

$$= \lim_{h \to 0} \frac{f(x + h)g(x + h) - f(x + h)g(x) + f(x + h)g(x) - f(x)g(x)}{h}$$

$$= \lim_{h \to 0} \left[f(x + h) \cdot \frac{g(x + h) - g(x)}{h} + g(x) \cdot \frac{f(x + h) - f(x)}{h} \right]$$

$$= \lim_{h \to 0} f(x + h) \cdot \lim_{h \to 0} \frac{g(x + h) - g(x)}{h} + \lim_{h \to 0} g(x) \cdot \lim_{h \to 0} \frac{f(x + h) - f(x)}{h}$$

$$= \left[\lim_{h \to 0} f(x + h) \right] \frac{d}{dx}[g(x)] + \left[\lim_{h \to 0} g(x) \right] \frac{d}{dx}[f(x)]$$

$$= f(x)\frac{d}{dx}[g(x)] + g(x)\frac{d}{dx}[f(x)]$$

[*Note:* In the last step $f(x + h) \to f(x)$ as $h \to 0$ because f is continuous at x by Theorem 2.2.3. Also, $g(x) \to g(x)$ as $h \to 0$ because $g(x)$ does not involve h and hence is treated as constant for the limit.] ∎

In words, *the derivative of a product of two functions is the first function times the derivative of the second plus the second function times the derivative of the first.*

▶ **Example 1**   Find dy/dx if $y = (4x^2 - 1)(7x^3 + x)$.

Solution.   There are two methods that can be used to find dy/dx. We can either use the product rule or we can multiply out the factors in y and then differentiate. We will give both methods.

Method 1. (*Using the Product Rule*)

$$\frac{dy}{dx} = \frac{d}{dx}[(4x^2 - 1)(7x^3 + x)]$$

$$= (4x^2 - 1)\frac{d}{dx}[7x^3 + x] + (7x^3 + x)\frac{d}{dx}[4x^2 - 1]$$

$$= (4x^2 - 1)(21x^2 + 1) + (7x^3 + x)(8x) = 140x^4 - 9x^2 - 1$$

Method 2. (*Multiplying First*)

$$y = (4x^2 - 1)(7x^3 + x) = 28x^5 - 3x^3 - x$$

Thus,

$$\frac{dy}{dx} = \frac{d}{dx}[28x^5 - 3x^3 - x] = 140x^4 - 9x^2 - 1$$

which agrees with the result obtained using the product rule. ◄

▶ **Example 2** Find ds/dt if $s = (1 + t)\sqrt{t}$.

Solution. Applying the product rule yields

$$\frac{ds}{dt} = \frac{d}{dt}[(1 + t)\sqrt{t}]$$

$$= (1 + t)\frac{d}{dt}[\sqrt{t}] + \sqrt{t}\frac{d}{dt}[1 + t]$$

$$= \frac{1 + t}{2\sqrt{t}} + \sqrt{t} = \frac{1 + 3t}{2\sqrt{t}} \quad ◄$$

■ DERIVATIVE OF A QUOTIENT

Just as the derivative of a product is not generally the product of the derivatives, so the derivative of a quotient is not generally the quotient of the derivatives. The correct relationship is given by the following theorem.

2.4.2 THEOREM (*The Quotient Rule*) *If f and g are both differentiable at x and if $g(x) \neq 0$, then f/g is differentiable at x and*

$$\frac{d}{dx}\left[\frac{f(x)}{g(x)}\right] = \frac{g(x)\dfrac{d}{dx}[f(x)] - f(x)\dfrac{d}{dx}[g(x)]}{[g(x)]^2} \tag{2}$$

Formula (2) can also be expressed as

$$\left(\frac{f}{g}\right)' = \frac{g \cdot f' - f \cdot g'}{g^2}$$

PROOF

$$\frac{d}{dx}\left[\frac{f(x)}{g(x)}\right] = \lim_{h \to 0} \frac{\dfrac{f(x + h)}{g(x + h)} - \dfrac{f(x)}{g(x)}}{h} = \lim_{h \to 0} \frac{f(x + h) \cdot g(x) - f(x) \cdot g(x + h)}{h \cdot g(x) \cdot g(x + h)}$$

Adding and subtracting $f(x) \cdot g(x)$ in the numerator yields

$$\frac{d}{dx}\left[\frac{f(x)}{g(x)}\right] = \lim_{h \to 0} \frac{f(x+h) \cdot g(x) - f(x) \cdot g(x) - f(x) \cdot g(x+h) + f(x) \cdot g(x)}{h \cdot g(x) \cdot g(x+h)}$$

$$= \lim_{h \to 0} \frac{\left[g(x) \cdot \dfrac{f(x+h) - f(x)}{h}\right] - \left[f(x) \cdot \dfrac{g(x+h) - g(x)}{h}\right]}{g(x) \cdot g(x+h)}$$

$$= \frac{\displaystyle\lim_{h \to 0} g(x) \cdot \lim_{h \to 0}\frac{f(x+h) - f(x)}{h} - \lim_{h \to 0} f(x) \cdot \lim_{h \to 0}\frac{g(x+h) - g(x)}{h}}{\displaystyle\lim_{h \to 0} g(x) \cdot \lim_{h \to 0} g(x+h)}$$

$$= \frac{\left[\displaystyle\lim_{h \to 0} g(x)\right] \cdot \dfrac{d}{dx}[f(x)] - \left[\displaystyle\lim_{h \to 0} f(x)\right] \cdot \dfrac{d}{dx}[g(x)]}{\displaystyle\lim_{h \to 0} g(x) \cdot \lim_{h \to 0} g(x+h)}$$

$$= \frac{g(x)\dfrac{d}{dx}[f(x)] - f(x)\dfrac{d}{dx}[g(x)]}{[g(x)]^2}$$

[See the note at the end of the proof of Theorem 2.4.1 for an explanation of the last step.]

∎

> In words, *the derivative of a quotient of two functions is the denominator times the derivative of the numerator minus the numerator times the derivative of the denominator, all divided by the denominator squared.*

Sometimes it is better to simplify a function first than to apply the quotient rule immediately. For example, it is easier to differentiate

$$f(x) = \frac{x^{3/2} + x}{\sqrt{x}}$$

by rewriting it as

$$f(x) = x + \sqrt{x}$$

as opposed to using the quotient rule.

▶ **Example 3**   Find $y'(x)$ for $y = \dfrac{x^3 + 2x^2 - 1}{x + 5}$.

Solution.   Applying the quotient rule yields

$$\frac{dy}{dx} = \frac{d}{dx}\left[\frac{x^3 + 2x^2 - 1}{x + 5}\right] = \frac{(x+5)\dfrac{d}{dx}[x^3 + 2x^2 - 1] - (x^3 + 2x^2 - 1)\dfrac{d}{dx}[x + 5]}{(x+5)^2}$$

$$= \frac{(x+5)(3x^2 + 4x) - (x^3 + 2x^2 - 1)(1)}{(x+5)^2}$$

$$= \frac{(3x^3 + 19x^2 + 20x) - (x^3 + 2x^2 - 1)}{(x+5)^2}$$

$$= \frac{2x^3 + 17x^2 + 20x + 1}{(x+5)^2} \quad ◀$$

▶ **Example 4**   Let $f(x) = \dfrac{x^2 - 1}{x^4 + 1}$.

(a) Graph $y = f(x)$, and use your graph to make rough estimates of the locations of all horizontal tangent lines.

(b) By differentiating, find the exact locations of the horizontal tangent lines.

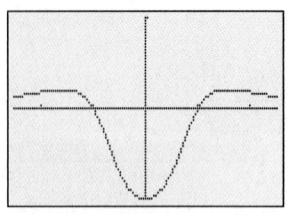

$[-2.5, 2.5] \times [-1, 1]$
xScl = 1, yScl = 1

$$y = \frac{x^2 - 1}{x^4 + 1}$$

▲ **Figure 2.4.1**

Solution (a).   In Figure 2.4.1 we have shown the graph of the equation $y = f(x)$ in the window $[-2.5, 2.5] \times [-1, 1]$. This graph suggests that horizontal tangent lines occur at $x = 0$, $x \approx 1.5$, and $x \approx -1.5$.

Solution (b). To find the exact locations of the horizontal tangent lines, we must find the points where $dy/dx = 0$. We start by finding dy/dx:

$$\frac{dy}{dx} = \frac{d}{dx}\left[\frac{x^2 - 1}{x^4 + 1}\right] = \frac{(x^4 + 1)\dfrac{d}{dx}[x^2 - 1] - (x^2 - 1)\dfrac{d}{dx}[x^4 + 1]}{(x^4 + 1)^2}$$

$$= \frac{(x^4 + 1)(2x) - (x^2 - 1)(4x^3)}{(x^4 + 1)^2} \quad \boxed{\begin{array}{l}\text{The differentiation is complete.}\\ \text{The rest is simplification.}\end{array}}$$

$$= \frac{-2x^5 + 4x^3 + 2x}{(x^4 + 1)^2} = -\frac{2x(x^4 - 2x^2 - 1)}{(x^4 + 1)^2}$$

Now we will set $dy/dx = 0$ and solve for x. We obtain

$$-\frac{2x(x^4 - 2x^2 - 1)}{(x^4 + 1)^2} = 0$$

The solutions of this equation are the values of x for which the numerator is 0, that is,

$$2x(x^4 - 2x^2 - 1) = 0$$

The first factor yields the solution $x = 0$. Other solutions can be found by solving the equation

$$x^4 - 2x^2 - 1 = 0$$

This can be treated as a quadratic equation in x^2 and solved by the quadratic formula. This yields

$$x^2 = \frac{2 \pm \sqrt{8}}{2} = 1 \pm \sqrt{2}$$

The minus sign yields imaginary values of x, which we ignore since they are not relevant to the problem. The plus sign yields the solutions

$$x = \pm\sqrt{1 + \sqrt{2}}$$

In summary, horizontal tangent lines occur at

$$x = 0, \quad x = \sqrt{1 + \sqrt{2}} \approx 1.55, \quad \text{and} \quad x = -\sqrt{1 + \sqrt{2}} \approx -1.55$$

which is consistent with the rough estimates that we obtained graphically in part (a). ◀

Derive the following rule for differentiating a reciprocal:

$$\left(\frac{1}{g}\right)' = -\frac{g'}{g^2}$$

Use it to find the derivative of

$$f(x) = \frac{1}{x^2 + 1}$$

■ **SUMMARY OF DIFFERENTIATION RULES**

The following table summarizes the differentiation rules that we have encountered thus far.

Table 2.4.1

RULES FOR DIFFERENTIATION

$\dfrac{d}{dx}[c] = 0$	$(f + g)' = f' + g'$	$(f \cdot g)' = f \cdot g' + g \cdot f'$	$\left(\dfrac{1}{g}\right)' = -\dfrac{g'}{g^2}$
$(cf)' = cf'$	$(f - g)' = f' - g'$	$\left(\dfrac{f}{g}\right)' = \dfrac{g \cdot f' - f \cdot g'}{g^2}$	$\dfrac{d}{dx}[x^r] = rx^{r-1}$

✔ **QUICK CHECK EXERCISES 2.4** *(See page 169 for answers.)*

1. (a) $\dfrac{d}{dx}[x^2 f(x)] = $ _____ (b) $\dfrac{d}{dx}\left[\dfrac{f(x)}{x^2 + 1}\right] = $ _____

   (c) $\dfrac{d}{dx}\left[\dfrac{x^2 + 1}{f(x)}\right] = $ _____

2. Find $F'(1)$ given that $f(1) = -1$, $f'(1) = 2$, $g(1) = 3$, and $g'(1) = -1$.
   (a) $F(x) = 2f(x) - 3g(x)$ (b) $F(x) = [f(x)]^2$
   (c) $F(x) = f(x)g(x)$ (d) $F(x) = f(x)/g(x)$

EXERCISE SET 2.4   ⌐∿⌐ Graphing Utility

1–4 Compute the derivative of the given function $f(x)$ by (a) multiplying and then differentiating and (b) using the product rule. Verify that (a) and (b) yield the same result. ▨

1. $f(x) = (x+1)(2x-1)$ **2.** $f(x) = (3x^2-1)(x^2+2)$

3. $f(x) = (x^2+1)(x^2-1)$

4. $f(x) = (x+1)(x^2-x+1)$

5–20 Find $f'(x)$. ▨

5. $f(x) = (3x^2+6)\left(2x-\frac{1}{4}\right)$

6. $f(x) = (2-x-3x^3)(7+x^5)$

7. $f(x) = (x^3+7x^2-8)(2x^{-3}+x^{-4})$

8. $f(x) = \left(\dfrac{1}{x}+\dfrac{1}{x^2}\right)(3x^3+27)$

9. $f(x) = (x-2)(x^2+2x+4)$

10. $f(x) = (x^2+x)(x^2-x)$

11. $f(x) = \dfrac{3x+4}{x^2+1}$ **12.** $f(x) = \dfrac{x-2}{x^4+x+1}$

13. $f(x) = \dfrac{x^2}{3x-4}$ **14.** $f(x) = \dfrac{2x^2+5}{3x-4}$

15. $f(x) = \dfrac{(2\sqrt{x}+1)(x-1)}{x+3}$

16. $f(x) = (2\sqrt{x}+1)\left(\dfrac{2-x}{x^2+3x}\right)$

17. $f(x) = (2x+1)\left(1+\dfrac{1}{x}\right)(x^{-3}+7)$

18. $f(x) = x^{-5}(x^2+2x)(4-3x)(2x^9+1)$

19. $f(x) = (x^7+2x-3)^3$ **20.** $f(x) = (x^2+1)^4$

21–22 Find $dy/dx|_{x=1}$. ▨

21. $y = \left(\dfrac{3x+2}{x}\right)(x^{-5}+1)$ **22.** $y = (2x^7-x^2)\left(\dfrac{x-1}{x+1}\right)$

⌐∿⌐ **23–24** Use a graphing utility to estimate the value of $f'(1)$ by zooming in on the graph of f, and then compare your estimate to the exact value obtained by differentiating. ▨

23. $f(x) = \dfrac{x}{x^2+1}$ **24.** $f(x) = \dfrac{x^2-1}{x^2+1}$

25. Find $g'(4)$ given that $f(4) = 3$ and $f'(4) = -5$.

(a) $g(x) = \sqrt{x}\,f(x)$ (b) $g(x) = \dfrac{f(x)}{x}$

26. Find $g'(3)$ given that $f(3) = -2$ and $f'(3) = 4$.

(a) $g(x) = 3x^2 - 5f(x)$ (b) $g(x) = \dfrac{2x+1}{f(x)}$

27. In parts (a)–(d), $F(x)$ is expressed in terms of $f(x)$ and $g(x)$. Find $F'(2)$ given that $f(2) = -1$, $f'(2) = 4$, $g(2) = 1$, and $g'(2) = -5$.

(a) $F(x) = 5f(x) + 2g(x)$ (b) $F(x) = f(x) - 3g(x)$
(c) $F(x) = f(x)g(x)$ (d) $F(x) = f(x)/g(x)$

28. Find $F'(\pi)$ given that $f(\pi) = 10$, $f'(\pi) = -1$, $g(\pi) = -3$, and $g'(\pi) = 2$.

(a) $F(x) = 6f(x) - 5g(x)$ (b) $F(x) = x(f(x) + g(x))$
(c) $F(x) = 2f(x)g(x)$ (d) $F(x) = \dfrac{f(x)}{4+g(x)}$

29–34 Find all values of x at which the tangent line to the given curve satisfies the stated property. ▨

29. $y = \dfrac{x^2-1}{x+2}$; horizontal   **30.** $y = \dfrac{x^2+1}{x-1}$; horizontal

31. $y = \dfrac{x^2+1}{x+1}$; parallel to the line $y = x$

32. $y = \dfrac{x+3}{x+2}$; perpendicular to the line $y = x$

33. $y = \dfrac{1}{x+4}$; passes through the origin

34. $y = \dfrac{2x+5}{x+2}$; y-intercept 2

FOCUS ON CONCEPTS

35. (a) What should it mean to say that two curves intersect at right angles?
   (b) Show that the curves $y = 1/x$ and $y = 1/(2-x)$ intersect at right angles.

36. Find all values of a such that the curves $y = a/(x-1)$ and $y = x^2 - 2x + 1$ intersect at right angles.

37. Find a general formula for $F''(x)$ if $F(x) = xf(x)$ and f and f' are differentiable at x.

38. Suppose that the function f is differentiable everywhere and $F(x) = xf(x)$.
   (a) Express $F'''(x)$ in terms of x and derivatives of f.
   (b) For $n \geq 2$, conjecture a formula for $F^{(n)}(x)$.

39. A manufacturer of athletic footwear finds that the sales of their ZipStride brand running shoes is a function $f(p)$ of the selling price p (in dollars) for a pair of shoes. Suppose that $f(120) = 9000$ pairs of shoes and $f'(120) = -60$ pairs of shoes per dollar. The revenue that the manufacturer will receive for selling $f(p)$ pairs of shoes at p dollars per pair is $R(p) = p \cdot f(p)$. Find $R'(120)$. What impact would a small increase in price have on the manufacturer's revenue?

40. Solve the problem in Exercise 39 under the assumption that $f(120) = 9000$ and $f'(120) = -80$.

41. Use the quotient rule (Theorem 2.4.2) to derive the formula for the derivative of $f(x) = x^{-n}$, where n is a positive integer.

✔ **QUICK CHECK ANSWERS 2.4**

1. (a) $x^2 f'(x) + 2x f(x)$ (b) $\dfrac{(x^2+1)f'(x) - 2xf(x)}{(x^2+1)^2}$ (c) $\dfrac{2xf(x) - (x^2+1)f'(x)}{[f(x)^2]}$ 2. (a) 7 (b) -4 (c) 7 (d) $\frac{5}{9}$

2.5 DERIVATIVES OF TRIGONOMETRIC FUNCTIONS

The main objective of this section is to obtain formulas for the derivatives of the six basic trigonometric functions. If needed, you will find a review of trigonometric functions in Appendix B.

We will assume in this section that the variable x in the trigonometric functions $\sin x$, $\cos x$, $\tan x$, $\cot x$, $\sec x$, and $\csc x$ is measured in radians. Also, we will need the limits in Theorem 1.6.5, but restated as follows using h rather than x as the variable:

$$\lim_{h \to 0} \frac{\sin h}{h} = 1 \quad \text{and} \quad \lim_{h \to 0} \frac{1 - \cos h}{h} = 0 \tag{1--2}$$

Let us start with the problem of differentiating $f(x) = \sin x$. Using the definition of the derivative we obtain

$$f'(x) = \lim_{h \to 0} \frac{f(x+h) - f(x)}{h}$$

$$= \lim_{h \to 0} \frac{\sin(x+h) - \sin x}{h}$$

$$= \lim_{h \to 0} \frac{\sin x \cos h + \cos x \sin h - \sin x}{h} \qquad \boxed{\text{By the addition formula for sine}}$$

$$= \lim_{h \to 0} \left[\sin x \left(\frac{\cos h - 1}{h} \right) + \cos x \left(\frac{\sin h}{h} \right) \right]$$

$$= \lim_{h \to 0} \left[\cos x \left(\frac{\sin h}{h} \right) - \sin x \left(\frac{1 - \cos h}{h} \right) \right] \qquad \boxed{\text{Algebraic reorganization}}$$

$$= \lim_{h \to 0} \cos x \cdot \lim_{h \to 0} \frac{\sin h}{h} - \lim_{h \to 0} \sin x \cdot \lim_{h \to 0} \frac{1 - \cos h}{h}$$

$$= \left(\lim_{h \to 0} \cos x \right)(1) - \left(\lim_{h \to 0} \sin x \right)(0) \qquad \boxed{\text{Formulas (1) and (2)}}$$

$$= \lim_{h \to 0} \cos x = \cos x \qquad \boxed{\begin{array}{l}\cos x \text{ does not involve the variable } h \text{ and hence} \\ \text{is treated as a constant in the limit computation.}\end{array}}$$

Thus, we have shown that

Formulas (1) and (2) and the derivation of Formulas (3) and (4) are only valid if h and x are in radians. See Exercise 49 for how Formulas (3) and (4) change when x is measured in degrees.

$$\frac{d}{dx}[\sin x] = \cos x \tag{3}$$

In the exercises we will ask you to use the same method to derive the following formula for the derivative of $\cos x$:

$$\frac{d}{dx}[\cos x] = -\sin x \tag{4}$$

▶ **Example 1**   Find dy/dx if $y = x \sin x$.

Solution.   Using Formula (3) and the product rule we obtain

$$\frac{dy}{dx} = \frac{d}{dx}[x \sin x]$$

$$= x \frac{d}{dx}[\sin x] + \sin x \frac{d}{dx}[x]$$

$$= x \cos x + \sin x \quad ◀$$

▶ **Example 2**   Find dy/dx if $y = \dfrac{\sin x}{1 + \cos x}$.

Solution.   Using the quotient rule together with Formulas (3) and (4) we obtain

$$\frac{dy}{dx} = \frac{(1 + \cos x) \cdot \dfrac{d}{dx}[\sin x] - \sin x \cdot \dfrac{d}{dx}[1 + \cos x]}{(1 + \cos x)^2}$$

$$= \frac{(1 + \cos x)(\cos x) - (\sin x)(-\sin x)}{(1 + \cos x)^2}$$

$$= \frac{\cos x + \cos^2 x + \sin^2 x}{(1 + \cos x)^2} = \frac{\cos x + 1}{(1 + \cos x)^2} = \frac{1}{1 + \cos x} \quad ◀$$

The derivatives of the remaining trigonometric functions are

Since Formulas (3) and (4) are valid only if x is in radians, the same is true for Formulas (5)–(8).

$$\frac{d}{dx}[\tan x] = \sec^2 x \qquad\qquad \frac{d}{dx}[\sec x] = \sec x \tan x \qquad (5\text{–}6)$$

$$\frac{d}{dx}[\cot x] = -\csc^2 x \qquad\qquad \frac{d}{dx}[\csc x] = -\csc x \cot x \qquad (7\text{–}8)$$

These can all be obtained using the definition of the derivative, but it is easier to use Formulas (3) and (4) and apply the quotient rule to the relationships

$$\tan x = \frac{\sin x}{\cos x}, \quad \cot x = \frac{\cos x}{\sin x}, \quad \sec x = \frac{1}{\cos x}, \quad \csc x = \frac{1}{\sin x}$$

For example,

$$\frac{d}{dx}[\tan x] = \frac{d}{dx}\left[\frac{\sin x}{\cos x}\right] = \frac{\cos x \cdot \dfrac{d}{dx}[\sin x] - \sin x \cdot \dfrac{d}{dx}[\cos x]}{\cos^2 x}$$

$$= \frac{\cos x \cdot \cos x - \sin x \cdot (-\sin x)}{\cos^2 x} = \frac{\cos^2 x + \sin^2 x}{\cos^2 x} = \frac{1}{\cos^2 x} = \sec^2 x$$

When finding the value of a derivative at a specific point $x = x_0$, it is important to substitute x_0 *after* the derivative is obtained. Thus, in Example 3 we made the substitution $x = \pi/4$ after f'' was calculated. What would have happened had we *incorrectly* substituted $x = \pi/4$ into $f'(x)$ before calculating f''?

▶ **Example 3**   Find $f''(\pi/4)$ if $f(x) = \sec x$.

$$f'(x) = \sec x \tan x$$

$$f''(x) = \sec x \cdot \frac{d}{dx}[\tan x] + \tan x \cdot \frac{d}{dx}[\sec x]$$

$$= \sec x \cdot \sec^2 x + \tan x \cdot \sec x \tan x$$

$$= \sec^3 x + \sec x \tan^2 x$$

Thus,

$$f''(\pi/4) = \sec^3(\pi/4) + \sec(\pi/4)\tan^2(\pi/4)$$
$$= (\sqrt{2})^3 + (\sqrt{2})(1)^2 = 3\sqrt{2} \blacktriangleleft$$

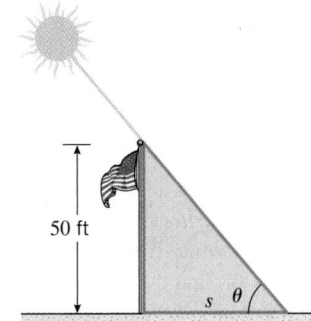

▲ **Figure 2.5.1**

50 ft

▶ **Example 4**   On a sunny day, a 50 ft flagpole casts a shadow that changes with the angle of elevation of the Sun. Let s be the length of the shadow and θ the angle of elevation of the Sun (Figure 2.5.1). Find the rate at which the length of the shadow is changing with respect to θ when $\theta = 45°$. Express your answer in units of feet/degree.

Solution.   The variables s and θ are related by $\tan\theta = 50/s$ or, equivalently,

$$s = 50\cot\theta \tag{9}$$

If θ is measured in radians, then Formula (7) is applicable, which yields

$$\frac{ds}{d\theta} = -50\csc^2\theta$$

which is the rate of change of shadow length with respect to the elevation angle θ in units of feet/radian. When $\theta = 45°$ (or equivalently $\theta = \pi/4$ radians), we obtain

$$\left.\frac{ds}{d\theta}\right|_{\theta=\pi/4} = -50\csc^2(\pi/4) = -100 \text{ feet/radian}$$

Converting radians (rad) to degrees (deg) yields

$$-100\,\frac{\text{ft}}{\text{rad}} \cdot \frac{\pi}{180}\,\frac{\text{rad}}{\text{deg}} = -\frac{5}{9}\pi\,\frac{\text{ft}}{\text{deg}} \approx -1.75 \text{ ft/deg}$$

Thus, when $\theta = 45°$, the shadow length is decreasing (because of the minus sign) at an approximate rate of 1.75 ft/deg increase in the angle of elevation. ◀

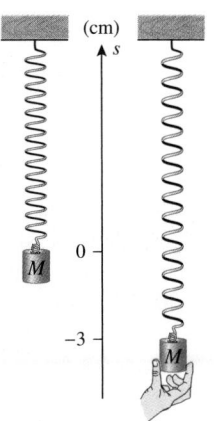

(cm)

s

0

−3

M

M

M

▲ **Figure 2.5.2**

▶ **Example 5**   As illustrated in Figure 2.5.2, suppose that a spring with an attached mass is stretched 3 cm beyond its rest position and released at time $t = 0$. Assuming that the position function of the top of the attached mass is

$$s = -3\cos t \tag{10}$$

where s is in centimeters and t is in seconds, find the velocity function and discuss the motion of the attached mass.

Solution.   The velocity function is

$$v = \frac{ds}{dt} = \frac{d}{dt}[-3\cos t] = 3\sin t$$

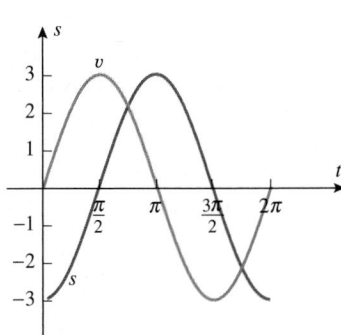

s

3

2

1

−1

−2

−3

v

s

$\frac{\pi}{2}$ π $\frac{3\pi}{2}$ 2π

t

▲ **Figure 2.5.3**

In Example 5, the top of the mass has its maximum speed when it passes through its rest position. Why? What is that maximum speed?

Figure 2.5.3 shows the graphs of the position and velocity functions. The position function tells us that the top of the mass oscillates between a low point of $s = -3$ and a high point of $s = 3$ with one complete oscillation occuring every 2π seconds [the period of (10)]. The top of the mass is moving up (the positive s-direction) when v is positive, is moving down when v is negative, and is at a high or low point when $v = 0$. Thus, for example, the top of the mass moves up from time $t = 0$ to time $t = \pi$, at which time it reaches the high point $s = 3$ and then moves down until time $t = 2\pi$, at which time it reaches the low point of $s = -3$. The motion then repeats periodically. ◀

✔**QUICK CHECK EXERCISES 2.5**   *(See page 174 for answers.)*

1. Find dy/dx.
  (a) $y = \sin x$ (b) $y = \cos x$
  (c) $y = \tan x$ (d) $y = \sec x$

2. Find $f'(x)$ and $f'(\pi/3)$ if $f(x) = \sin x \cos x$.

3. Use a derivative to evaluate each limit.
  (a) $\displaystyle\lim_{h \to 0} \frac{\sin\left(\frac{\pi}{2} + h\right) - 1}{h}$ (b) $\displaystyle\lim_{h \to 0} \frac{\csc(x + h) - \csc x}{h}$

EXERCISE SET 2.5   ∿ Graphing Utility

1–18 Find $f'(x)$. ■

1. $f(x) = 4\cos x + 2\sin x$ **2.** $f(x) = \dfrac{5}{x^2} + \sin x$

3. $f(x) = -4x^2 \cos x$ **4.** $f(x) = 2\sin^2 x$

5. $f(x) = \dfrac{5 - \cos x}{5 + \sin x}$ **6.** $f(x) = \dfrac{\sin x}{x^2 + \sin x}$

7. $f(x) = \sec x - \sqrt{2}\tan x$ **8.** $f(x) = (x^2 + 1)\sec x$

9. $f(x) = 4\csc x - \cot x$ **10.** $f(x) = \cos x - x\csc x$

11. $f(x) = \sec x \tan x$ **12.** $f(x) = \csc x \cot x$

13. $f(x) = \dfrac{\cot x}{1 + \csc x}$ **14.** $f(x) = \dfrac{\sec x}{1 + \tan x}$

15. $f(x) = \sin^2 x + \cos^2 x$ **16.** $f(x) = \sec^2 x - \tan^2 x$

17. $f(x) = \dfrac{\sin x \sec x}{1 + x\tan x}$ **18.** $f(x) = \dfrac{(x^2 + 1)\cot x}{3 - \cos x \csc x}$

19–24 Find d^2y/dx^2. ■

19. $y = x\cos x$ **20.** $y = \csc x$

21. $y = x\sin x - 3\cos x$ **22.** $y = x^2 \cos x + 4\sin x$

23. $y = \sin x \cos x$ **24.** $y = \tan x$

25. Find the equation of the line tangent to the graph of $\tan x$ at
  (a) $x = 0$ (b) $x = \pi/4$ (c) $x = -\pi/4$.

26. Find the equation of the line tangent to the graph of $\sin x$ at
  (a) $x = 0$ (b) $x = \pi$ (c) $x = \pi/4$.

27. (a) Show that $y = x\sin x$ is a solution to $y'' + y = 2\cos x$.
  (b) Show that $y = x\sin x$ is a solution of the equation $y^{(4)} + y'' = -2\cos x$.

28. (a) Show that $y = \cos x$ and $y = \sin x$ are solutions of the equation $y'' + y = 0$.
  (b) Show that $y = A\sin x + B\cos x$ is a solution of the equation $y'' + y = 0$ for all constants A and B.

29. Find all values in the interval $[-2\pi, 2\pi]$ at which the graph of f has a horizontal tangent line.
  (a) $f(x) = \sin x$ (b) $f(x) = x + \cos x$
  (c) $f(x) = \tan x$ (d) $f(x) = \sec x$

∿ **30.** (a) Use a graphing utility to make rough estimates of the values in the interval $[0, 2\pi]$ at which the graph of $y = \sin x \cos x$ has a horizontal tangent line.
  (b) Find the exact locations of the points where the graph has a horizontal tangent line.

31. A 10 ft ladder leans against a wall at an angle θ with the horizontal, as shown in the accompanying figure. The top of the ladder is x feet above the ground. If the bottom of the ladder is pushed toward the wall, find the rate at which x changes with respect to θ when $\theta = 60°$. Express the answer in units of feet/degree.

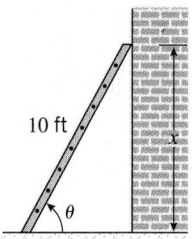

10 ft θ

◀ **Figure Ex-31**

32. An airplane is flying on a horizontal path at a height of 3800 ft, as shown in the accompanying figure. At what rate is the distance s between the airplane and the fixed point P changing with respect to θ when $\theta = 30°$? Express the answer in units of feet/degree.

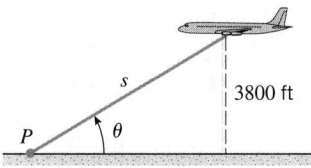

s 3800 ft

P θ

◀ **Figure Ex-32**

33. A searchlight is trained on the side of a tall building. As the light rotates, the spot it illuminates moves up and down the side of the building. That is, the distance D between ground level and the illuminated spot on the side of the building is a function of the angle θ formed by the light beam and the horizontal (see the accompanying figure). If the searchlight is located 50 m from the building, find the rate at which D is changing with respect to θ when $\theta = 45°$. Express your answer in units of meters/degree.

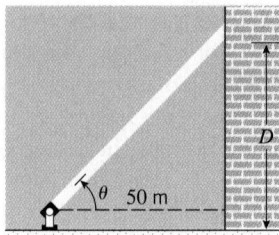

θ 50 m D

◀ **Figure Ex-33**

34. An Earth-observing satellite can see only a portion of the Earth's surface. The satellite has horizon sensors that can detect the angle θ shown in the accompanying figure. Let r be the radius of the Earth (assumed spherical) and h the distance of the satellite from the Earth's surface.

(a) Show that $h = r(\csc \theta - 1)$.

(b) Using $r = 6378$ km, find the rate at which h is changing with respect to θ when $\theta = 30°$. Express the answer in units of kilometers/degree.

Source: Adapted from *Space Mathematics*, NASA, 1985.

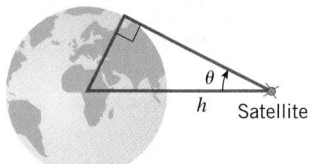

Earth   ◀ **Figure Ex-34**

35–38 True–False Determine whether the statement is true or false. Explain your answer. ■

35. If $g(x) = f(x) \sin x$, then $g'(x) = f'(x) \cos x$.

36. If $g(x) = f(x) \sin x$, then $g'(0) = f(0)$.

37. If $f(x) \cos x = \sin x$, then $f'(x) = \sec^2 x$.

38. Suppose that $g(x) = f(x) \sec x$, where $f(0) = 8$ and $f'(0) = -2$. Then

$$g'(0) = \lim_{h \to 0} \frac{f(h) \sec h - f(0)}{h} = \lim_{h \to 0} \frac{8(\sec h - 1)}{h}$$

$$= 8 \cdot \frac{d}{dx}[\sec x]\bigg|_{x=0} = 8 \sec 0 \tan 0 = 0$$

39–40 Make a conjecture about the derivative by calculating the first few derivatives and observing the resulting pattern. ■

39. $\dfrac{d^{87}}{dx^{87}}[\sin x]$ **40.** $\dfrac{d^{100}}{dx^{100}}[\cos x]$

41. Let $f(x) = \cos x$. Find all positive integers n for which $f^{(n)}(x) = \sin x$.

42. Let $f(x) = \sin x$. Find all positive integers n for which $f^{(n)}(x) = \sin x$.

FOCUS ON CONCEPTS

43. In each part, determine where f is differentiable.

(a) $f(x) = \sin x$ (b) $f(x) = \cos x$

(c) $f(x) = \tan x$ (d) $f(x) = \cot x$

(e) $f(x) = \sec x$ (f) $f(x) = \csc x$

(g) $f(x) = \dfrac{1}{1 + \cos x}$ (h) $f(x) = \dfrac{1}{\sin x \cos x}$

(i) $f(x) = \dfrac{\cos x}{2 - \sin x}$

44. (a) Derive Formula (4) using the definition of a derivative.

(b) Use Formulas (3) and (4) to obtain (7).

(c) Use Formula (4) to obtain (6).

(d) Use Formula (3) to obtain (8).

45. Use Formula (1), the alternative form for the definition of derivative given in Formula (13) of Section 2.2, that is,

$$f'(x) = \lim_{w \to x} \frac{f(w) - f(x)}{w - x}$$

and the difference identity

$$\sin \alpha - \sin \beta = 2 \sin \left(\frac{\alpha - \beta}{2} \right) \cos \left(\frac{\alpha + \beta}{2} \right)$$

to show that $\dfrac{d}{dx}[\sin x] = \cos x$.

46. Follow the directions of Exercise 45 using the difference identity

$$\cos \alpha - \cos \beta = -2 \sin \left(\frac{\alpha - \beta}{2} \right) \sin \left(\frac{\alpha + \beta}{2} \right)$$

to show that $\dfrac{d}{dx}[\cos x] = -\sin x$.

47. (a) Show that $\lim\limits_{h \to 0} \dfrac{\tan h}{h} = 1$.

(b) Use the result in part (a) to help derive the formula for the derivative of $\tan x$ directly from the definition of a derivative.

48. Without using any trigonometric identities, find

$$\lim_{x \to 0} \frac{\tan(x + y) - \tan y}{x}$$

[*Hint:* Relate the given limit to the definition of the derivative of an appropriate function of y.]

49. The derivative formulas for $\sin x$, $\cos x$, $\tan x$, $\cot x$, $\sec x$, and $\csc x$ were obtained under the assumption that x is measured in radians. If x is measured in degrees, then

$$\lim_{x \to 0} \frac{\sin x}{x} = \frac{\pi}{180}$$

(See Exercise 49 of Section 1.6). Use this result to prove that if x is measured in degrees, then

(a) $\dfrac{d}{dx}[\sin x] = \dfrac{\pi}{180} \cos x$

(b) $\dfrac{d}{dx}[\cos x] = -\dfrac{\pi}{180} \sin x$.

50. **Writing** Suppose that f is a function that is differentiable everywhere. Explain the relationship, if any, between the periodicity of f and that of f'. That is, if f is periodic, must f' also be periodic? If f' is periodic, must f also be periodic?

✔ **QUICK CHECK ANSWERS 2.5**

1. (a) $\cos x$ (b) $-\sin x$ (c) $\sec^2 x$ (d) $\sec x \tan x$ **2.** $f'(x) = \cos^2 x - \sin^2 x$, $f'(\pi/3) = -\frac{1}{2}$

3. (a) $\dfrac{d}{dx}[\sin x]\Big|_{x=\pi/2} = 0$ (b) $\dfrac{d}{dx}[\csc x] = -\csc x \cot x$

2.6 THE CHAIN RULE

In this section we will derive a formula that expresses the derivative of a composition $f \circ g$ in terms of the derivatives of f and g. This formula will enable us to differentiate complicated functions using known derivatives of simpler functions.

■ DERIVATIVES OF COMPOSITIONS

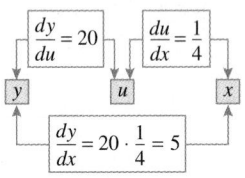

Mike Brinson/Getty Images

The cost of a car trip is a combination of fuel efficiency and the cost of gasoline.

Suppose you are traveling to school in your car, which gets 20 miles per gallon of gasoline. The number of miles you can travel in your car without refueling is a function of the number of gallons of gas you have in the gas tank. In symbols, if y is the number of miles you can travel and u is the number of gallons of gas you have initially, then y is a function of u, or $y = f(u)$. As you continue your travels, you note that your local service station is selling gasoline for \$4 per gallon. The number of gallons of gas you have initially is a function of the amount of money you spend for that gas. If x is the number of dollars you spend on gas, then $u = g(x)$. Now 20 miles per gallon is the rate at which your mileage changes with respect to the amount of gasoline you use, so

$$f'(u) = \frac{dy}{du} = 20 \text{ miles per gallon}$$

Similarly, since gasoline costs \$4 per gallon, each dollar you spend will give you 1/4 of a gallon of gas, and

$$g'(x) = \frac{du}{dx} = \frac{1}{4} \text{ gallons per dollar}$$

Notice that the number of miles you can travel is also a function of the number of dollars you spend on gasoline. This fact is expressible as the composition of functions

$$y = f(u) = f(g(x))$$

You might be interested in how many miles you can travel per dollar, which is dy/dx. Intuition suggests that rates of change multiply in this case (see Figure 2.6.1), so

$$\frac{dy}{dx} = \frac{dy}{du} \cdot \frac{du}{dx} = \frac{20 \text{ miles}}{1 \text{ gallon}} \cdot \frac{1 \text{ gallons}}{4 \text{ dollars}} = \frac{20 \text{ miles}}{4 \text{ dollars}} = 5 \text{ miles per dollar}$$

The following theorem, the proof of which is given in Appendix J, formalizes the preceding ideas.

$$\frac{dy}{du} = 20 \quad \frac{du}{dx} = \frac{1}{4}$$

y u x

$$\frac{dy}{dx} = 20 \cdot \frac{1}{4} = 5$$

Rates of change multiply:

$$\frac{dy}{dx} = \frac{dy}{du} \cdot \frac{du}{dx}$$

▲ **Figure 2.6.1**

The name "chain rule" is appropriate because the desired derivative is obtained by a two-link "chain" of simpler derivatives.

2.6.1   THEOREM (*The Chain Rule*)   *If g is differentiable at x and f is differentiable at $g(x)$, then the composition $f \circ g$ is differentiable at x. Moreover, if*

$$y = f(g(x)) \quad and \quad u = g(x)$$

then $y = f(u)$ and

$$\frac{dy}{dx} = \frac{dy}{du} \cdot \frac{du}{dx} \tag{1}$$

Formula (1) is easy to remember because the left side is exactly what results if we "cancel" the du's on the right side. This "canceling" device provides a good way of deducing the correct form of the chain rule when different variables are used. For example, if w is a function of x and x is a function of t, then the chain rule takes the form

$$\frac{dw}{dt} = \frac{dw}{dx} \cdot \frac{dx}{dt}$$

▶ **Example 1**   Find dy/dx if $y = \cos(x^3)$.

Solution.   Let $u = x^3$ and express y as $y = \cos u$. Applying Formula (1) yields

$$\frac{dy}{dx} = \frac{dy}{du} \cdot \frac{du}{dx}$$

$$= \frac{d}{du}[\cos u] \cdot \frac{d}{dx}[x^3]$$

$$= (-\sin u) \cdot (3x^2)$$

$$= (-\sin(x^3)) \cdot (3x^2) = -3x^2 \sin(x^3) ◀$$

▶ **Example 2**   Find dw/dt if $w = \tan x$ and $x = 4t^3 + t$.

Solution.   In this case the chain rule computations take the form

$$\frac{dw}{dt} = \frac{dw}{dx} \cdot \frac{dx}{dt}$$

$$= \frac{d}{dx}[\tan x] \cdot \frac{d}{dt}[4t^3 + t]$$

$$= (\sec^2 x) \cdot (12t^2 + 1)$$

$$= [\sec^2(4t^3 + t)] \cdot (12t^2 + 1) = (12t^2 + 1)\sec^2(4t^3 + t) ◀$$

▮ AN ALTERNATIVE VERSION OF THE CHAIN RULE

Formula (1) for the chain rule can be unwieldy in some problems because it involves so many variables. As you become more comfortable with the chain rule, you may want to dispense with writing out the dependent variables by expressing (1) in the form

Confirm that (2) is an alternative version of (1) by letting $y = f(g(x))$ and $u = g(x)$.

$$\frac{d}{dx}[f(g(x))] = (f \circ g)'(x) = f'(g(x))g'(x) \tag{2}$$

A convenient way to remember this formula is to call f the "outside function" and g the "inside function" in the composition $f(g(x))$ and then express (2) in words as:

The derivative of $f(g(x))$ is the derivative of the outside function evaluated at the inside function times the derivative of the inside function.

$$\frac{d}{dx}[f(g(x))] = \underbrace{f'(g(x))}_{} \cdot \underbrace{g'(x)}_{}$$

Derivative of the outside function evaluated at the inside function

Derivative of the inside function

▶ **Example 3** (*Example 1 revisited*)   Find $h'(x)$ if $h(x) = \cos(x^3)$.

Solution.   We can think of h as a composition $f(g(x))$ in which $g(x) = x^3$ is the inside function and $f(x) = \cos x$ is the outside function. Thus, Formula (2) yields

$$h'(x) = \underbrace{f'(g(x))}_{\substack{\text{Derivative of the outside} \\ \text{function evaluated at the} \\ \text{inside function}}} \cdot \underbrace{g'(x)}_{\substack{\text{Derivative of the} \\ \text{inside function}}}$$

$$= f'(x^3) \cdot 3x^2$$

$$= -\sin(x^3) \cdot 3x^2 = -3x^2 \sin(x^3)$$

which agrees with the result obtained in Example 1.   ◀

▶ **Example 4**

$$\frac{d}{dx}[\tan^2 x] = \frac{d}{dx}[(\tan x)^2] = \underbrace{(2 \tan x)}_{\substack{\text{Derivative of the outside} \\ \text{function evaluated at the} \\ \text{inside function}}} \cdot \underbrace{(\sec^2 x)}_{\substack{\text{Derivative of the} \\ \text{inside function}}} = 2 \tan x \sec^2 x$$

$$\frac{d}{dx}[\sqrt{x^2 + 1}] = \underbrace{\frac{1}{2\sqrt{x^2 + 1}}}_{\substack{\text{Derivative of the outside} \\ \text{function evaluated at the} \\ \text{inside function}}} \cdot \underbrace{2x}_{\substack{\text{Derivative of the} \\ \text{inside function}}} = \frac{x}{\sqrt{x^2 + 1}}$$

See Formula (6) of Section 2.3.   ◀

■ GENERALIZED DERIVATIVE FORMULAS

There is a useful third variation of the chain rule that strikes a middle ground between Formulas (1) and (2). If we let $u = g(x)$ in (2), then we can rewrite that formula as

$$\frac{d}{dx}[f(u)] = f'(u)\frac{du}{dx} \tag{3}$$

This result, called the ***generalized derivative formula*** for f, provides a way of using the derivative of $f(x)$ to produce the derivative of $f(u)$, where u is a function of x. Table 2.6.1 gives some examples of this formula.

Table 2.6.1
GENERALIZED DERIVATIVE FORMULAS

$$\frac{d}{dx}[u^r] = ru^{r-1}\frac{du}{dx}$$

$$\frac{d}{dx}[\sin u] = \cos u\,\frac{du}{dx} \qquad\qquad \frac{d}{dx}[\cos u] = -\sin u\,\frac{du}{dx}$$

$$\frac{d}{dx}[\tan u] = \sec^2 u\,\frac{du}{dx} \qquad\qquad \frac{d}{dx}[\cot u] = -\csc^2 u\,\frac{du}{dx}$$

$$\frac{d}{dx}[\sec u] = \sec u \tan u\,\frac{du}{dx} \qquad\qquad \frac{d}{dx}[\csc u] = -\csc u \cot u\,\frac{du}{dx}$$

▶ **Example 5** Find

(a) $\dfrac{d}{dx}[\sin(2x)]$ (b) $\dfrac{d}{dx}[\tan(x^2+1)]$ (c) $\dfrac{d}{dx}\left[\sqrt{x^3+\csc x}\right]$

(d) $\dfrac{d}{dx}[x^2-x+2]^{3/4}$ (e) $\dfrac{d}{dx}\left[(1+x^5\cot x)^{-8}\right]$

Solution (a).   Taking $u=2x$ in the generalized derivative formula for $\sin u$ yields

$$\frac{d}{dx}[\sin(2x)]=\frac{d}{dx}[\sin u]=\cos u\frac{du}{dx}=\cos 2x\cdot\frac{d}{dx}[2x]=\cos 2x\cdot 2=2\cos 2x$$

Solution (b).   Taking $u=x^2+1$ in the generalized derivative formula for $\tan u$ yields

$$\frac{d}{dx}[\tan(x^2+1)]=\frac{d}{dx}[\tan u]=\sec^2 u\frac{du}{dx}$$

$$=\sec^2(x^2+1)\cdot\frac{d}{dx}[x^2+1]=\sec^2(x^2+1)\cdot 2x$$

$$=2x\sec^2(x^2+1)$$

Solution (c).   Taking $u=x^3+\csc x$ in the generalized derivative formula for $\sqrt{u}$ yields

$$\frac{d}{dx}\left[\sqrt{x^3+\csc x}\right]=\frac{d}{dx}[\sqrt{u}]=\frac{1}{2\sqrt{u}}\frac{du}{dx}=\frac{1}{2\sqrt{x^3+\csc x}}\cdot\frac{d}{dx}[x^3+\csc x]$$

$$=\frac{1}{2\sqrt{x^3+\csc x}}\cdot(3x^2-\csc x\cot x)=\frac{3x^2-\csc x\cot x}{2\sqrt{x^3+\csc x}}$$

Solution (d).   Taking $u=x^2-x+2$ in the generalized derivative formula for $u^{3/4}$ yields

$$\frac{d}{dx}[x^2-x+2]^{3/4}=\frac{d}{dx}[u^{3/4}]=\frac{3}{4}u^{-1/4}\frac{du}{dx}$$

$$=\frac{3}{4}(x^2-x+2)^{-1/4}\cdot\frac{d}{dx}[x^2-x+2]$$

$$=\frac{3}{4}(x^2-x+2)^{-1/4}(2x-1)$$

Solution (e).   Taking $u=1+x^5\cot x$ in the generalized derivative formula for u^{-8} yields

$$\frac{d}{dx}\left[(1+x^5\cot x)^{-8}\right]=\frac{d}{dx}[u^{-8}]=-8u^{-9}\frac{du}{dx}$$

$$=-8(1+x^5\cot x)^{-9}\cdot\frac{d}{dx}[1+x^5\cot x]$$

$$=-8(1+x^5\cot x)^{-9}\cdot\left[x^5(-\csc^2 x)+5x^4\cot x\right]$$

$$=(8x^5\csc^2 x-40x^4\cot x)(1+x^5\cot x)^{-9}\quad◀$$

Sometimes you will have to make adjustments in notation or apply the chain rule more than once to calculate a derivative.

▶ **Example 6** Find

(a) $\dfrac{d}{dx}\left[\sin(\sqrt{1+\cos x}\,)\right]$ (b) $\dfrac{d\mu}{dt}$ if $\mu=\sec\sqrt{\omega t}$ (ω constant)

Solution (a). Taking $u = \sqrt{1 + \cos x}$ in the generalized derivative formula for $\sin u$ yields

$$\frac{d}{dx}\left[\sin(\sqrt{1 + \cos x}\,)\right] = \frac{d}{dx}[\sin u] = \cos u\,\frac{du}{dx}$$

$$= \cos(\sqrt{1 + \cos x}\,) \cdot \frac{d}{dx}\left[\sqrt{1 + \cos x}\,\right]$$

$$= \cos(\sqrt{1 + \cos x}\,) \cdot \frac{-\sin x}{2\sqrt{1 + \cos x}}$$

> We used the generalized derivative formula for $\sqrt{u}$ with $u = 1 + \cos x$.

$$= -\frac{\sin x \cos(\sqrt{1 + \cos x}\,)}{2\sqrt{1 + \cos x}}$$

Solution (b).

$$\frac{d\mu}{dt} = \frac{d}{dt}[\sec\sqrt{\omega t}\,] = \sec\sqrt{\omega t}\,\tan\sqrt{\omega t}\,\frac{d}{dt}[\sqrt{\omega t}\,]$$

> We used the generalized derivative formula for $\sec u$ with $u = \sqrt{\omega t}$.

$$= \sec\sqrt{\omega t}\,\tan\sqrt{\omega t}\,\frac{\omega}{2\sqrt{\omega t}}$$

> We used the generalized derivative formula for $\sqrt{u}$ with $u = \omega t$. ◄

▧ DIFFERENTIATING USING COMPUTER ALGEBRA SYSTEMS

Even with the chain rule and other differentiation rules, some derivative computations can be tedious to perform. For complicated derivatives, engineers and scientists often use computer algebra systems such as *Mathematica*, *Maple*, or *Sage*. For example, although we have all the mathematical tools to compute

TECHNOLOGY MASTERY

If you have a CAS, use it to perform the differentiation in (4).

$$\frac{d}{dx}\left[\frac{(x^2 + 1)^{10}\sin^3(\sqrt{x}\,)}{\sqrt{1 + \csc x}}\right] \tag{4}$$

by hand, the computation is sufficiently involved that it may be more efficient (and less error-prone) to use a computer algebra system.

✔ QUICK CHECK EXERCISES 2.6   *(See page 181 for answers.)*

1. The chain rule states that the derivative of the composition of two functions is the derivative of the _____ function evaluated at the _____ function times the derivative of the _____ function.

2. If y is a differentiable function of u, and u is a differentiable function of x, then

$$\frac{dy}{dx} = \underline{\qquad} \cdot \underline{\qquad}$$

3. Find dy/dx.
   (a) $y = (x^2 + 5)^{10}$ (b) $y = \sqrt{1 + 6x}$

4. Find dy/dx.
   (a) $y = \sin(3x + 2)$ (b) $y = (x^2\tan x)^4$

5. Suppose that $f(2) = 3$, $f'(2) = 4$, $g(3) = 6$, and $g'(3) = -5$. Evaluate
   (a) $h'(2)$, where $h(x) = g(f(x))$
   (b) $k'(3)$, where $k(x) = f\left(\frac{1}{3}g(x)\right)$.

EXERCISE SET 2.6   ⬜ Graphing Utility   ⃞c CAS

1. Given that
$$f'(0) = 2, g(0) = 0 \quad \text{and} \quad g'(0) = 3$$
find $(f \circ g)'(0)$.

2. Given that
$$f'(9) = 5, g(2) = 9 \quad \text{and} \quad g'(2) = -3$$
find $(f \circ g)'(2)$.

3. Let $f(x) = x^5$ and $g(x) = 2x - 3$.
   (a) Find $(f \circ g)(x)$ and $(f \circ g)'(x)$.
   (b) Find $(g \circ f)(x)$ and $(g \circ f)'(x)$.

4. Let $f(x) = 5\sqrt{x}$ and $g(x) = 4 + \cos x$.
   (a) Find $(f \circ g)(x)$ and $(f \circ g)'(x)$.
   (b) Find $(g \circ f)(x)$ and $(g \circ f)'(x)$.

FOCUS ON CONCEPTS

5. Given the following table of values, find the indicated derivatives in parts (a) and (b).

x	$f(x)$	$f'(x)$	$g(x)$	$g'(x)$
3	5	−2	5	7
5	3	−1	12	4

  (a) $F'(3)$, where $F(x) = f(g(x))$
  (b) $G'(3)$, where $G(x) = g(f(x))$

6. Given the following table of values, find the indicated derivatives in parts (a) and (b).

x	$f(x)$	$f'(x)$	$g(x)$	$g'(x)$
−1	2	3	2	−3
2	0	4	1	−5

  (a) $F'(-1)$, where $F(x) = f(g(x))$
  (b) $G'(-1)$, where $G(x) = g(f(x))$

7–26 Find $f'(x)$. ■

7. $f(x) = (x^3 + 2x)^{37}$
8. $f(x) = (3x^2 + 2x - 1)^6$

9. $f(x) = \left(x^3 - \dfrac{7}{x}\right)^{-2}$
10. $f(x) = \dfrac{1}{(x^5 - x + 1)^9}$

11. $f(x) = \dfrac{4}{(3x^2 - 2x + 1)^3}$
12. $f(x) = \sqrt{x^3 - 2x + 5}$

13. $f(x) = \sqrt{4 + \sqrt{3x}}$
14. $f(x) = \sqrt[4]{x} \;\; (= \sqrt{\sqrt{x}})$

15. $f(x) = \sin\left(\dfrac{1}{x^2}\right)$
16. $f(x) = \tan\sqrt{x}$

17. $f(x) = 4\cos^5 x$
18. $f(x) = 4x + 5\sin^4 x$

19. $f(x) = \cos^2(3\sqrt{x})$
20. $f(x) = \tan^4(x^3)$

21. $f(x) = 2\sec^2(x^7)$
22. $f(x) = \cos^3\left(\dfrac{x}{x+1}\right)$

23. $f(x) = \sqrt{\cos(5x)}$
24. $f(x) = \sqrt{3x - \sin^2(4x)}$

25. $f(x) = [x + \csc(x^3 + 3)]^{-3}$

26. $f(x) = [x^4 - \sec(4x^2 - 2)]^{-4}$

27–40 Find dy/dx. ■

27. $y = x^3 \sin^2(5x)$
28. $y = \sqrt{x}\tan^3(\sqrt{x})$

29. $y = x^5 \sec(1/x)$
30. $y = \dfrac{\sin x}{\sec(3x+1)}$

31. $y = \cos(\cos x)$
32. $y = \sin(\tan 3x)$

33. $y = \cos^3(\sin 2x)$
34. $y = \dfrac{1 + \csc(x^2)}{1 - \cot(x^2)}$

35. $y = (5x + 8)^7 \left(1 - \sqrt{x}\right)^6$
36. $y = (x^2 + x)^5 \sin^8 x$

37. $y = \left(\dfrac{x-5}{2x+1}\right)^3$
38. $y = \left(\dfrac{1+x^2}{1-x^2}\right)^{17}$

39. $y = \dfrac{(2x+3)^3}{(4x^2 - 1)^8}$
40. $y = [1 + \sin^3(x^5)]^{12}$

C **41–42** Use a CAS to find dy/dx. ■

41. $y = [x\sin 2x + \tan^4(x^7)]^5$

42. $y = \tan^4\left(2 + \dfrac{(7-x)\sqrt{3x^2 + 5}}{x^3 + \sin x}\right)$

43–50 Find an equation for the tangent line to the graph at the specified value of x. ■

43. $y = x\cos 3x$, $x = \pi$

44. $y = \sin(1 + x^3)$, $x = -3$

45. $y = \sec^3\left(\dfrac{\pi}{2} - x\right)$, $x = -\dfrac{\pi}{2}$

46. $y = \left(x - \dfrac{1}{x}\right)^3$, $x = 2$ **47.** $y = \tan(4x^2)$, $x = \sqrt{\pi}$

48. $y = 3\cot^4 x$, $x = \dfrac{\pi}{4}$ **49.** $y = x^2\sqrt{5 - x^2}$, $x = 1$

50. $y = \dfrac{x}{\sqrt{1 - x^2}}$, $x = 0$

51–54 Find d^2y/dx^2. ■

51. $y = x\cos(5x) - \sin^2 x$ **52.** $y = \sin(3x^2)$

53. $y = \dfrac{1+x}{1-x}$ **54.** $y = x\tan\left(\dfrac{1}{x}\right)$

55–58 Find the indicated derivative. ■

55. $y = \cot^3(\pi - \theta)$; find $\dfrac{dy}{d\theta}$.

56. $\lambda = \left(\dfrac{au + b}{cu + d}\right)^6$; find $\dfrac{d\lambda}{du}$ $(a, b, c, d$ constants$)$.

57. $\dfrac{d}{d\omega}[a\cos^2 \pi\omega + b\sin^2 \pi\omega]$ $(a, b$ constants$)$

58. $x = \csc^2\left(\dfrac{\pi}{3} - y\right)$; find $\dfrac{dx}{dy}$.

≈ 59. (a) Use a graphing utility to obtain the graph of the function $f(x) = x\sqrt{4 - x^2}$.
   (b) Use the graph in part (a) to make a rough sketch of the graph of f'.
   (c) Find $f'(x)$, and then check your work in part (b) by using the graphing utility to obtain the graph of f'.
   (d) Find the equation of the tangent line to the graph of f at $x = 1$, and graph f and the tangent line together.

≈ 60. (a) Use a graphing utility to obtain the graph of the function $f(x) = \sin x^2 \cos x$ over the interval $[-\pi/2, \pi/2]$.
   (b) Use the graph in part (a) to make a rough sketch of the graph of f' over the interval.
   (c) Find $f'(x)$, and then check your work in part (b) by using the graphing utility to obtain the graph of f' over the interval.
   (d) Find the equation of the tangent line to the graph of f at $x = 1$, and graph f and the tangent line together over the interval.

61–64 True–False Determine whether the statement is true or false. Explain your answer. ■

61. If $y = f(x)$, then $\dfrac{d}{dx}[\sqrt{y}] = \sqrt{f'(x)}$.

62. If $y = f(u)$ and $u = g(x)$, then $dy/dx = f'(x) \cdot g'(x)$.

63. If $y = \cos[g(x)]$, then $dy/dx = -\sin[g'(x)]$.

64. If $y = \sin^3(3x^3)$, then $dy/dx = 27x^2 \sin^2(3x^3) \cos(3x^3)$.

65. If an object suspended from a spring is displaced vertically from its equilibrium position by a small amount and released, and if the air resistance and the mass of the spring are ignored, then the resulting oscillation of the object is called **simple harmonic motion**. Under appropriate conditions the displacement y from equilibrium in terms of time t is given by

$$y = A \cos \omega t$$

where A is the initial displacement at time $t = 0$, and ω is a constant that depends on the mass of the object and the stiffness of the spring (see the accompanying figure). The constant $|A|$ is called the **amplitude** of the motion and ω the **angular frequency**.

(a) Show that
$$\frac{d^2y}{dt^2} = -\omega^2 y$$

(b) The **period** T is the time required to make one complete oscillation. Show that $T = 2\pi/\omega$.

(c) The **frequency** f of the vibration is the number of oscillations per unit time. Find f in terms of the period T.

(d) Find the amplitude, period, and frequency of an object that is executing simple harmonic motion given by $y = 0.6 \cos 15t$, where t is in seconds and y is in centimeters.

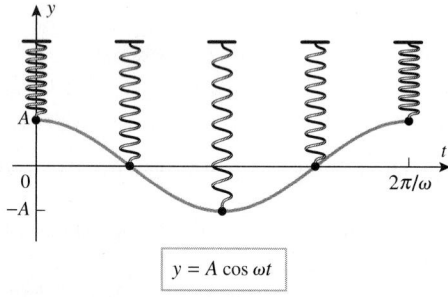

▲ **Figure Ex-65**

66. Find the value of the constant A so that $y = A \sin 3t$ satisfies the equation
$$\frac{d^2y}{dt^2} + 2y = 4 \sin 3t$$

FOCUS ON CONCEPTS

67. Use the graph of the function f in the accompanying figure to evaluate
$$\frac{d}{dx}\left[\sqrt{x + f(x)}\right]\Bigg|_{x=-1}$$

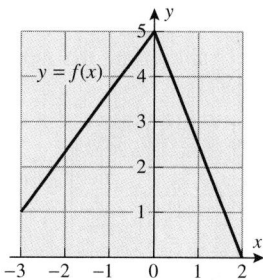

◀ **Figure Ex-67**

68. Using the function f in Exercise 67, evaluate
$$\frac{d}{dx}[f(2 \sin x)]\Bigg|_{x=\pi/6}$$

69. The accompanying figure shows the graph of atmospheric pressure p (lb/in^2) versus the altitude h (mi) above sea level.

(a) From the graph and the tangent line at $h = 2$ shown on the graph, estimate the values of p and dp/dh at an altitude of 2 mi.

(b) If the altitude of a space vehicle is increasing at the rate of 0.3 mi/s at the instant when it is 2 mi above sea level, how fast is the pressure changing with time at this instant?

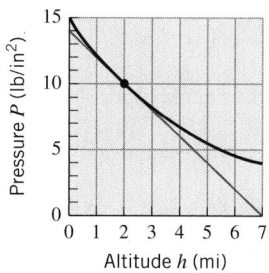

◀ **Figure Ex-69**

70. The force F (in pounds) acting at an angle θ with the horizontal that is needed to drag a crate weighing W pounds along a horizontal surface at a constant velocity is given by

$$F = \frac{\mu W}{\cos \theta + \mu \sin \theta}$$

where μ is a constant called the **coefficient of sliding friction** between the crate and the surface (see the accompanying figure). Suppose that the crate weighs 150 lb and that $\mu = 0.3$.

(a) Find $dF/d\theta$ when $\theta = 30°$. Express the answer in units of pounds/degree.

(b) Find dF/dt when $\theta = 30°$ if θ is decreasing at the rate of 0.5°/s at this instant.

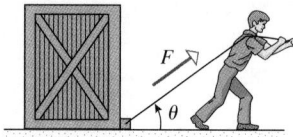

◀ **Figure Ex-70**

71. Recall that
$$\frac{d}{dx}(|x|) = \begin{cases} 1, & x > 0 \\ -1, & x < 0 \end{cases}$$
Use this result and the chain rule to find
$$\frac{d}{dx}(|\sin x|)$$
for nonzero x in the interval $(-\pi, \pi)$.

72. Use the derivative formula for $\sin x$ and the identity
$$\cos x = \sin\left(\frac{\pi}{2} - x\right)$$
to obtain the derivative formula for $\cos x$.

73. Let
$$f(x) = \begin{cases} x\sin\dfrac{1}{x}, & x \neq 0 \\ 0, & x = 0 \end{cases}$$
(a) Show that f is continuous at $x = 0$.
(b) Use Definition 2.2.1 to show that $f'(0)$ does not exist.
(c) Find $f'(x)$ for $x \neq 0$.
(d) Determine whether $\lim\limits_{x \to 0} f'(x)$ exists.

74. Let
$$f(x) = \begin{cases} x^2\sin\dfrac{1}{x}, & x \neq 0 \\ 0, & x = 0 \end{cases}$$
(a) Show that f is continuous at $x = 0$.
(b) Use Definition 2.2.1 to find $f'(0)$.
(c) Find $f'(x)$ for $x \neq 0$.
(d) Show that f' is not continuous at $x = 0$.

75. Given the following table of values, find the indicated derivatives in parts (a) and (b).

x	$f(x)$	$f'(x)$
2	1	7
8	5	−3

(a) $g'(2)$, where $g(x) = [f(x)]^3$
(b) $h'(2)$, where $h(x) = f(x^3)$

76. Given that $f'(x) = \sqrt{3x + 4}$ and $g(x) = x^2 - 1$, find $F'(x)$ if $F(x) = f(g(x))$.

77. Given that $f'(x) = \dfrac{x}{x^2 + 1}$ and $g(x) = \sqrt{3x - 1}$, find $F'(x)$ if $F(x) = f(g(x))$.

78. Find $f'(x^2)$ if $\dfrac{d}{dx}[f(x^2)] = x^2$.

79. Find $\dfrac{d}{dx}[f(x)]$ if $\dfrac{d}{dx}[f(3x)] = 6x$.

80. Recall that a function f is *even* if $f(-x) = f(x)$ and *odd* if $f(-x) = -f(x)$, for all x in the domain of f. Assuming that f is differentiable, prove:
(a) f' is odd if f is even
(b) f' is even if f is odd.

81. Draw some pictures to illustrate the results in Exercise 80, and write a paragraph that gives an informal explanation of why the results are true.

82. Let $y = f_1(u)$, $u = f_2(v)$, $v = f_3(w)$, and $w = f_4(x)$. Express dy/dx in terms of dy/du, dw/dx, du/dv, and dv/dw.

83. Find a formula for
$$\frac{d}{dx}[f(g(h(x)))]$$

84. **Writing** The "co" in "cosine" comes from "complementary," since the cosine of an angle is the sine of the complementary angle, and vice versa:
$$\cos x = \sin\left(\frac{\pi}{2} - x\right) \quad \text{and} \quad \sin x = \cos\left(\frac{\pi}{2} - x\right)$$
Suppose that we define a function g to be a *cofunction* of a function f if
$$g(x) = f\left(\frac{\pi}{2} - x\right) \quad \text{for all } x$$
Thus, cosine and sine are cofunctions of each other, as are cotangent and tangent, and also cosecant and secant. If g is the cofunction of f, state a formula that relates g' and the cofunction of f'. Discuss how this relationship is exhibited by the derivatives of the cosine, cotangent, and cosecant functions.

✔ **QUICK CHECK ANSWERS 2.6**

1. outside; inside; inside   2. $\dfrac{dy}{du} \cdot \dfrac{du}{dx}$ 3. (a) $10(x^2 + 5)^9 \cdot 2x = 20x(x^2 + 5)^9$ (b) $\dfrac{1}{2\sqrt{1 + 6x}} \cdot 6 = \dfrac{3}{\sqrt{1 + 6x}}$

4. (a) $3\cos(3x + 2)$ (b) $4(x^2\tan x)^3(2x\tan x + x^2\sec^2 x)$ 5. (a) $g'(f(2))f'(2) = -20$ (b) $f'\left(\dfrac{1}{3}g(3)\right) \cdot \dfrac{1}{3}g'(3) = -\dfrac{20}{3}$

CHAPTER 2 REVIEW EXERCISES   ⬜ Graphing Utility   🄲 CAS

1. Explain the difference between average and instantaneous rates of change, and discuss how they are calculated.

2. In parts (a)–(d), use the function $y = \frac{1}{2}x^2$.

(a) Find the average rate of change of y with respect to x over the interval $[3, 4]$.
(b) Find the instantaneous rate of change of y with respect to x at $x = 3$.

(cont.)

(c) Find the instantaneous rate of change of y with respect to x at a general x-value.

(d) Sketch the graph of $y = \frac{1}{2}x^2$ together with the secant line whose slope is given by the result in part (a), and indicate graphically the slope of the tangent line that corresponds to the result in part (b).

3. Complete each part for the function $f(x) = x^2 + 1$.
   (a) Find the slope of the tangent line to the graph of f at a general x-value.
   (b) Find the slope of the tangent line to the graph of f at $x = 2$.

4. A car is traveling on a straight road that is 120 mi long. For the first 100 mi the car travels at an average velocity of 50 mi/h. Show that no matter how fast the car travels for the final 20 mi it cannot bring the average velocity up to 60 mi/h for the entire trip.

5. At time $t = 0$ a car moves into the passing lane to pass a slow-moving truck. The average velocity of the car from $t = 1$ to $t = 1 + h$ is

$$v_{\text{ave}} = \frac{3(h+1)^{2.5} + 580h - 3}{10h}$$

Estimate the instantaneous velocity of the car at $t = 1$, where time is in seconds and distance is in feet.

6. A skydiver jumps from an airplane. Suppose that the distance she falls during the first t seconds before her parachute opens is $s(t) = 976((0.835)^t - 1) + 176t$, where s is in feet. Graph s versus t for $0 \le t \le 20$, and use your graph to estimate the instantaneous velocity at $t = 15$.

7. A particle moves on a line away from its initial position so that after t hours it is $s = 3t^2 + t$ miles from its initial position.
   (a) Find the average velocity of the particle over the interval $[1, 3]$.
   (b) Find the instantaneous velocity at $t = 1$.

8. State the definition of a derivative, and give two interpretations of it.

9. Use the definition of a derivative to find dy/dx, and check your answer by calculating the derivative using appropriate derivative formulas.
   (a) $y = \sqrt{9 - 4x}$ (b) $y = \dfrac{x}{x+1}$

10. Suppose that $f(x) = \begin{cases} x^2 - 1, & x \le 1 \\ k(x-1), & x > 1. \end{cases}$
   For what values of k is f
   (a) continuous?   (b) differentiable?

11. The accompanying figure shows the graph of $y = f'(x)$ for an unspecified function f.
   (a) For what values of x does the curve $y = f(x)$ have a horizontal tangent line?
   (b) Over what intervals does the curve $y = f(x)$ have tangent lines with positive slope?

(c) Over what intervals does the curve $y = f(x)$ have tangent lines with negative slope?

(d) Given that $g(x) = f(x) \sin x$, find $g''(0)$.

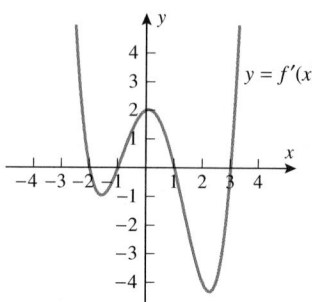

◀ **Figure Ex-11**

12. Sketch the graph of a function f for which $f(0) = 1$, $f'(0) = 0$, $f'(x) > 0$ if $x < 0$, and $f'(x) < 0$ if $x > 0$.

13. According to the U.S. Bureau of the Census, the estimated and projected midyear world population, N, in billions for the years 1950, 1975, 2000, 2025, and 2050 was 2.555, 4.088, 6.080, 7.841, and 9.104, respectively. Although the increase in population is not a continuous function of the time t, we can apply the ideas in this section if we are willing to approximate the graph of N versus t by a continuous curve, as shown in the accompanying figure.
   (a) Use the tangent line at $t = 2000$ shown in the figure to approximate the value of dN/dt there. Interpret your result as a rate of change.
   (b) The instantaneous **growth rate** is defined as

$$\frac{dN/dt}{N}$$

Use your answer to part (a) to approximate the instantaneous growth rate at the start of the year 2000. Express the result as a percentage and include the proper units.

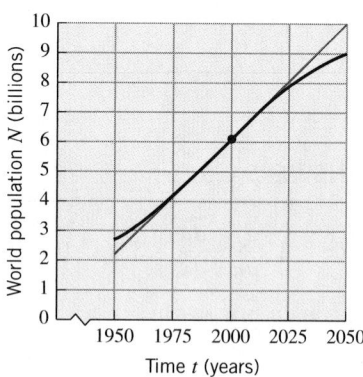

◀ **Figure Ex-13**

14. Use a graphing utility to graph the function

$$f(x) = |x^4 - x - 1| - x$$

and estimate the values of x where the derivative of this function does not exist.

c **15–18** (a) Use a CAS to find $f'(x)$ via Definition 2.2.1; (b) check the result by finding the derivative by hand; (c) use the CAS to find $f''(x)$. ▪

15. $f(x) = x^2 \sin x$

16. $f(x) = \sqrt{x} + \cos^2 x$

17. $f(x) = \dfrac{2x^2 - x + 5}{3x + 2}$

18. $f(x) = \dfrac{\tan x}{1 + x^2}$

19. The amount of water in a tank t minutes after it has started to drain is given by $W = 100(t - 15)^2$ gal.
   (a) At what rate is the water running out at the end of 5 min?
   (b) What is the average rate at which the water flows out during the first 5 min?

20. Use the formula $V = l^3$ for the volume of a cube of side l to find
   (a) the average rate at which the volume of a cube changes with l as l increases from $l = 2$ to $l = 4$
   (b) the instantaneous rate at which the volume of a cube changes with l when $l = 5$.

∿ **21–22** Zoom in on the graph of f on an interval containing $x = x_0$ until the graph looks like a straight line. Estimate the slope of this line and then check your answer by finding the exact value of $f'(x_0)$. ▪

21. (a) $f(x) = x^2 - 1$, $x_0 = 1.8$
   (b) $f(x) = \dfrac{x^2}{x - 2}$, $x_0 = 3.5$

22. (a) $f(x) = x^3 - x^2 + 1$, $x_0 = 2.3$
   (b) $f(x) = \dfrac{x}{x^2 + 1}$, $x_0 = -0.5$

23. Suppose that a function f is differentiable at $x = 1$ and
$$\lim_{h \to 0} \frac{f(1 + h)}{h} = 5$$
Find $f(1)$ and $f'(1)$.

24. Suppose that a function f is differentiable at $x = 2$ and
$$\lim_{x \to 2} \frac{x^3 f(x) - 24}{x - 2} = 28$$
Find $f(2)$ and $f'(2)$.

25. Find the equations of all lines through the origin that are tangent to the curve $y = x^3 - 9x^2 - 16x$.

26. Find all values of x for which the tangent line to the curve $y = 2x^3 - x^2$ is perpendicular to the line $x + 4y = 10$.

27. Let $f(x) = x^2$. Show that for any distinct values of a and b, the slope of the tangent line to $y = f(x)$ at $x = \frac{1}{2}(a + b)$ is equal to the slope of the secant line through the points (a, a^2) and (b, b^2). Draw a picture to illustrate this result.

28. In each part, evaluate the expression given that $f(1) = 1$, $g(1) = -2$, $f'(1) = 3$, and $g'(1) = -1$.
   (a) $\dfrac{d}{dx}[f(x)g(x)]\Big|_{x=1}$
   (b) $\dfrac{d}{dx}\left[\dfrac{f(x)}{g(x)}\right]\Big|_{x=1}$
   (c) $\dfrac{d}{dx}\left[\sqrt{f(x)}\right]\Big|_{x=1}$
   (d) $\dfrac{d}{dx}[f(1)g'(1)]$

29–32 Find $f'(x)$. ▪

29. (a) $f(x) = x^8 - 3\sqrt{x} + 5x^{-3}$
   (b) $f(x) = (2x + 1)^{101}(5x^2 - 7)$

30. (a) $f(x) = \sin x + 2\cos^3 x$
   (b) $f(x) = (1 + \sec x)(x^2 - \tan x)$

31. (a) $f(x) = \sqrt{3x + 1}(x - 1)^2$
   (b) $f(x) = \left(\dfrac{3x + 1}{x^2}\right)^3$

32. (a) $f(x) = \cot\left(\dfrac{\csc 2x}{x^3 + 5}\right)$
   (b) $f(x) = \dfrac{1}{2x + \sin^3 x}$

33–34 Find the values of x at which the curve $y = f(x)$ has a horizontal tangent line. ▪

33. $f(x) = (2x + 7)^6(x - 2)^5$
34. $f(x) = \dfrac{(x - 3)^4}{x^2 + 2x}$

35. Find all lines that are simultaneously tangent to the graph of $y = x^2 + 1$ and to the graph of $y = -x^2 - 1$.

36. (a) Let n denote an even positive integer. Generalize the result of Exercise 35 by finding all lines that are simultaneously tangent to the graph of $y = x^n + n - 1$ and to the graph of $y = -x^n - n + 1$.
   (b) Let n denote an odd positive integer. Are there any lines that are simultaneously tangent to the graph of $y = x^n + n - 1$ and to the graph of $y = -x^n - n + 1$? Explain.

37. Find all values of x for which the line that is tangent to $y = 3x - \tan x$ is parallel to the line $y - x = 2$.

∿ **38.** Approximate the values of x at which the tangent line to the graph of $y = x^3 - \sin x$ is horizontal.

39. Suppose that $f(x) = M \sin x + N \cos x$ for some constants M and N. If $f(\pi/4) = 3$ and $f'(\pi/4) = 1$, find an equation for the tangent line to $y = f(x)$ at $x = 3\pi/4$.

40. Suppose that $f(x) = M \tan x + N \sec x$ for some constants M and N. If $f(\pi/4) = 2$ and $f'(\pi/4) = 0$, find an equation for the tangent line to $y = f(x)$ at $x = 0$.

41. Suppose that $f'(x) = 2x \cdot f(x)$ and $f(2) = 5$.
   (a) Find $g'(\pi/3)$ if $g(x) = f(\sec x)$.
   (b) Find $h'(2)$ if $h(x) = [f(x)/(x - 1)]^4$.

CHAPTER 2 MAKING CONNECTIONS

1. Suppose that f is a function with the properties (i) f is differentiable everywhere, (ii) $f(x + y) = f(x)f(y)$ for all values of x and y, (iii) $f(0) \neq 0$, and (iv) $f'(0) = 1$.
   (a) Show that $f(0) = 1$. [*Hint:* Consider $f(0 + 0)$.]
   (b) Show that $f(x) > 0$ for all values of x. [*Hint:* First show that $f(x) \neq 0$ for any x by considering $f(x - x)$.]
   (c) Use the definition of derivative (Definition 2.2.1) to show that $f'(x) = f(x)$ for all values of x.

2. Suppose that f and g are functions each of which has the properties (i)–(iv) in Exercise 1.
   (a) Show that $y = f(2x)$ satisfies the equation $y' = 2y$ in two ways: using property (ii), and by directly applying the chain rule (Theorem 2.6.1).
   (b) If k is any constant, show that $y = f(kx)$ satisfies the equation $y' = ky$.
   (c) Find a value of k such that $y = f(x)g(x)$ satisfies the equation $y' = ky$.
   (d) If $h = f/g$, find $h'(x)$. Make a conjecture about the relationship between f and g.

3. (a) Apply the product rule (Theorem 2.4.1) twice to show that if f, g, and h are differentiable functions, then $f \cdot g \cdot h$ is differentiable and
   $$(f \cdot g \cdot h)' = f' \cdot g \cdot h + f \cdot g' \cdot h + f \cdot g \cdot h'$$
   (b) Suppose that f, g, h, and k are differentiable functions. Derive a formula for $(f \cdot g \cdot h \cdot k)'$.

(c) Based on the result in part (a), make a conjecture about a formula differentiating a product of n functions. Prove your formula using induction.

4. (a) Apply the quotient rule (Theorem 2.4.2) twice to show that if f, g, and h are differentiable functions, then $(f/g)/h$ is differentiable where it is defined and
   $$[(f/g)/h]' = \frac{f' \cdot g \cdot h - f \cdot g' \cdot h - f \cdot g \cdot h'}{g^2 h^2}$$
   (b) Derive the derivative formula of part (a) by first simplifying $(f/g)/h$ and then applying the quotient and product rules.
   (c) Apply the quotient rule (Theorem 2.4.2) twice to derive a formula for $[f/(g/h)]'$.
   (d) Derive the derivative formula of part (c) by first simplifying $f/(g/h)$ and then applying the quotient and product rules.

5. Assume that $h(x) = f(x)/g(x)$ is differentiable. Derive the quotient rule formula for $h'(x)$ (Theorem 2.4.2) in two ways:
   (a) Write $h(x) = f(x) \cdot [g(x)]^{-1}$ and use the product and chain rules (Theorems 2.4.1 and 2.6.1) to differentiate h.
   (b) Write $f(x) = h(x) \cdot g(x)$ and use the product rule to derive a formula for $h'(x)$.

 **EXPANDING THE CALCULUS HORIZON**

To learn how derivatives can be used in the field of robotics, see the module entitled **Robotics** at:

www.wiley.com/college/anton

3

TOPICS IN DIFFERENTIATION

Craig Lovell/Corbis Images

The growth and decline of animal populations and natural resources can be modeled using basic functions studied in calculus.

We begin this chapter by extending the process of differentiation to functions that are either difficult or impossible to differentiate directly. We will discuss a combination of direct and indirect methods of differentiation that will allow us to develop a number of new derivative formulas that include the derivatives of logarithmic, exponential, and inverse trigonometric functions. Later in the chapter, we will consider some applications of the derivative. These will include ways in which different rates of change can be related as well as the use of linear functions to approximate nonlinear functions. Finally, we will discuss L'Hôpital's rule, a powerful tool for evaluating limits.

3.1 IMPLICIT DIFFERENTIATION

Up to now we have been concerned with differentiating functions that are given by equations of the form $y = f(x)$. In this section we will consider methods for differentiating functions for which it is inconvenient or impossible to express them in this form.

■ FUNCTIONS DEFINED EXPLICITLY AND IMPLICITLY

An equation of the form $y = f(x)$ is said to define y *explicitly* as a function of x because the variable y appears alone on one side of the equation and does not appear at all on the other side. However, sometimes functions are defined by equations in which y is not alone on one side; for example, the equation

$$yx + y + 1 = x \tag{1}$$

is not of the form $y = f(x)$, but it still defines y as a function of x since it can be rewritten as

$$y = \frac{x-1}{x+1}$$

Thus, we say that (1) defines y *implicitly* as a function of x, the function being

$$f(x) = \frac{x-1}{x+1}$$

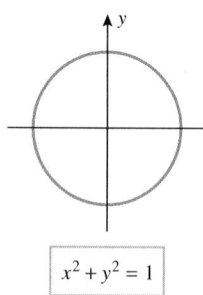

$$x^2 + y^2 = 1$$

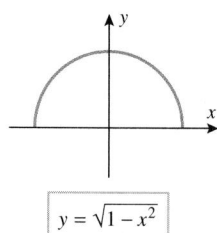

$$y = \sqrt{1 - x^2}$$

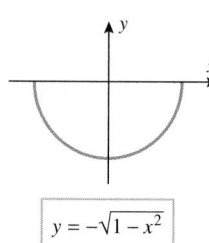

$$y = -\sqrt{1 - x^2}$$

▲ **Figure 3.1.1**

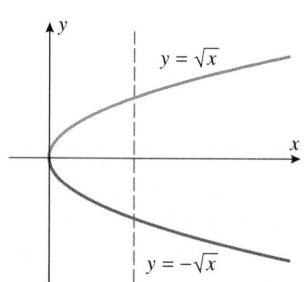

▲ **Figure 3.1.2** The graph of $x = y^2$ does not pass the vertical line test, but the graphs of $y = \sqrt{x}$ and $y = -\sqrt{x}$ do.

An equation in x and y can implicitly define more than one function of x. This can occur when the graph of the equation fails the vertical line test, so it is not the graph of a function of x. For example, if we solve the equation of the circle

$$x^2 + y^2 = 1 \tag{2}$$

for y in terms of x, we obtain $y = \pm\sqrt{1 - x^2}$, so we have found two functions that are defined implicitly by (2), namely,

$$f_1(x) = \sqrt{1 - x^2} \quad \text{and} \quad f_2(x) = -\sqrt{1 - x^2} \tag{3}$$

The graphs of these functions are the upper and lower semicircles of the circle $x^2 + y^2 = 1$ (Figure 3.1.1). This leads us to the following definition.

3.1.1 DEFINITION We will say that a given equation in x and y defines the function f *implicitly* if the graph of $y = f(x)$ coincides with a portion of the graph of the equation.

▶ **Example 1** The graph of $x = y^2$ is not the graph of a function of x, since it does not pass the vertical line test (Figure 3.1.2). However, if we solve this equation for y in terms of x, we obtain the equations $y = \sqrt{x}$ and $y = -\sqrt{x}$, whose graphs pass the vertical line test and are portions of the graph of $x = y^2$ (Figure 3.1.2). Thus, the equation $x = y^2$ implicitly defines the functions

$$f_1(x) = \sqrt{x} \quad \text{and} \quad f_2(x) = -\sqrt{x} \blacktriangleleft$$

Although it was a trivial matter in the last example to solve the equation $x = y^2$ for y in terms of x, it is difficult or impossible to do this for some equations. For example, the equation

$$x^3 + y^3 = 3xy \tag{4}$$

can be solved for y in terms of x, but the resulting formulas are too complicated to be practical. Other equations, such as $\sin(xy) = y$, cannot be solved for y by any elementary method. Thus, even though an equation may define one or more functions of x, it may not be possible or practical to find explicit formulas for those functions.

Fortunately, CAS programs, such as *Mathematica* and *Maple*, have "implicit plotting" capabilities that can graph equations such as (4). The graph of this equation, which is called the *Folium of Descartes*, is shown in Figure 3.1.3a. Parts (b) and (c) of the figure show the graphs (in blue) of two functions that are defined implicitly by (4).

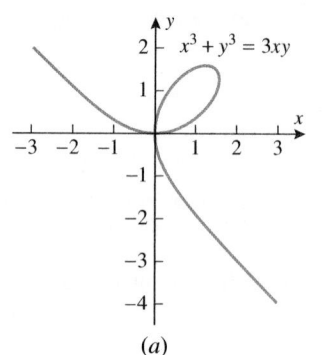

(a)

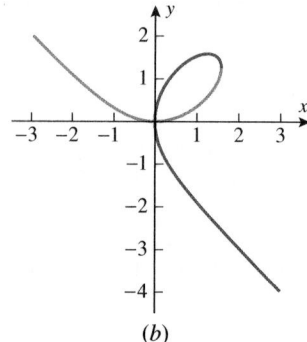

(b)

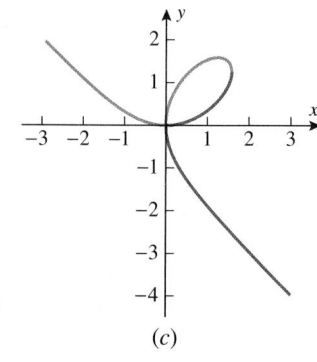

(c)

▲ **Figure 3.1.3**

■ **IMPLICIT DIFFERENTIATION**

In general, it is not necessary to solve an equation for y in terms of x in order to differentiate the functions defined implicitly by the equation. To illustrate this, let us consider the simple equation

$$xy = 1 \tag{5}$$

One way to find dy/dx is to rewrite this equation as

$$y = \frac{1}{x} \tag{6}$$

from which it follows that

$$\frac{dy}{dx} = -\frac{1}{x^2} \tag{7}$$

Another way to obtain this derivative is to differentiate both sides of (5) *before* solving for y in terms of x, treating y as a (temporarily unspecified) differentiable function of x. With this approach we obtain

$$\frac{d}{dx}[xy] = \frac{d}{dx}[1]$$

$$x\frac{d}{dx}[y] + y\frac{d}{dx}[x] = 0$$

$$x\frac{dy}{dx} + y = 0$$

$$\frac{dy}{dx} = -\frac{y}{x}$$

If we now substitute (6) into the last expression, we obtain

$$\frac{dy}{dx} = -\frac{1}{x^2}$$

which agrees with Equation (7). This method of obtaining derivatives is called ***implicit differentiation***.

▶ **Example 2**   Use implicit differentiation to find dy/dx if $5y^2 + \sin y = x^2$.

$$\frac{d}{dx}[5y^2 + \sin y] = \frac{d}{dx}[x^2]$$

$$5\frac{d}{dx}[y^2] + \frac{d}{dx}[\sin y] = 2x$$

$$5\left(2y\frac{dy}{dx}\right) + (\cos y)\frac{dy}{dx} = 2x \qquad \boxed{\text{The chain rule was used here because } y \text{ is a function of } x.}$$

$$10y\frac{dy}{dx} + (\cos y)\frac{dy}{dx} = 2x$$

René Descartes (1596–1650) Descartes, a French aristocrat, was the son of a government official. He graduated from the University of Poitiers with a law degree at age 20. After a brief probe into the pleasures of Paris he became a military engineer, first for the Dutch Prince of Nassau and then for the German Duke of Bavaria. It was during his service as a soldier that Descartes began to pursue mathematics seriously and develop his analytic geometry. After the wars, he returned to Paris where he stalked the city as an eccentric, wearing a sword in his belt and a plumed hat. He lived in leisure, seldom arose before 11 A.M., and dabbled in the study of human physiology, philosophy, glaciers, meteors, and rainbows. He eventually moved to Holland, where he published his *Discourse on the Method*, and finally to Sweden where he died while serving as tutor to Queen Christina. Descartes is regarded as a genius of the first magnitude. In addition to major contributions in mathematics and philosophy he is considered, along with William Harvey, to be a founder of modern physiology.

Solving for dy/dx we obtain

$$\frac{dy}{dx} = \frac{2x}{10y + \cos y} \tag{8}$$

Note that this formula involves both x and y. In order to obtain a formula for dy/dx that involves x alone, we would have to solve the original equation for y in terms of x and then substitute in (8). However, it is impossible to do this, so we are forced to leave the formula for dy/dx in terms of x and y. ◄

▶ **Example 3**   Use implicit differentiation to find d^2y/dx^2 if $4x^2 - 2y^2 = 9$.

Solution.   Differentiating both sides of $4x^2 - 2y^2 = 9$ with respect to x yields

$$8x - 4y\frac{dy}{dx} = 0$$

from which we obtain

$$\frac{dy}{dx} = \frac{2x}{y} \tag{9}$$

Differentiating both sides of (9) yields

$$\frac{d^2y}{dx^2} = \frac{(y)(2) - (2x)(dy/dx)}{y^2} \tag{10}$$

Substituting (9) into (10) and simplifying using the original equation, we obtain

$$\frac{d^2y}{dx^2} = \frac{2y - 2x(2x/y)}{y^2} = \frac{2y^2 - 4x^2}{y^3} = -\frac{9}{y^3} \quad ◄$$

In Examples 2 and 3, the resulting formulas for dy/dx involved both x and y. Although it is usually more desirable to have the formula for dy/dx expressed in terms of x alone, having the formula in terms of x and y is not an impediment to finding slopes and equations of tangent lines provided the x- and y-coordinates of the point of tangency are known. This is illustrated in the following example.

▶ **Example 4**   Find the slopes of the tangent lines to the curve $y^2 - x + 1 = 0$ at the points $(2, -1)$ and $(2, 1)$.

Solution.   We could proceed by solving the equation for y in terms of x, and then evaluating the derivative of $y = \sqrt{x - 1}$ at $(2, 1)$ and the derivative of $y = -\sqrt{x - 1}$ at $(2, -1)$ (Figure 3.1.4). However, implicit differentiation is more efficient since it can be used for the slopes of *both* tangent lines. Differentiating implicitly yields

$$\frac{d}{dx}[y^2 - x + 1] = \frac{d}{dx}[0]$$

$$\frac{d}{dx}[y^2] - \frac{d}{dx}[x] + \frac{d}{dx}[1] = \frac{d}{dx}[0]$$

$$2y\frac{dy}{dx} - 1 = 0$$

$$\frac{dy}{dx} = \frac{1}{2y}$$

At $(2, -1)$ we have $y = -1$, and at $(2, 1)$ we have $y = 1$, so the slopes of the tangent lines to the curve at those points are

$$\left.\frac{dy}{dx}\right|_{\substack{x=2 \\ y=-1}} = -\frac{1}{2} \quad \text{and} \quad \left.\frac{dy}{dx}\right|_{\substack{x=2 \\ y=1}} = \frac{1}{2} \quad ◄$$

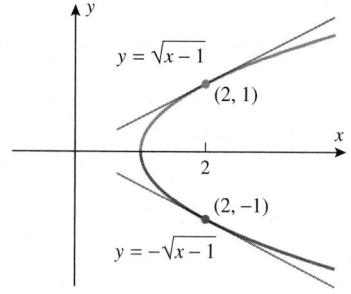

$y = \sqrt{x - 1}$

$(2, 1)$

$(2, -1)$

$y = -\sqrt{x - 1}$

▲ **Figure 3.1.4**

▶ **Example 5**

(a) Use implicit differentiation to find dy/dx for the Folium of Descartes $x^3 + y^3 = 3xy$.

(b) Find an equation for the tangent line to the Folium of Descartes at the point $\left(\frac{3}{2}, \frac{3}{2}\right)$.

(c) At what point(s) in the first quadrant is the tangent line to the Folium of Descartes horizontal?

Solution (a).   Differentiating implicitly yields

$$\frac{d}{dx}[x^3 + y^3] = \frac{d}{dx}[3xy]$$

$$3x^2 + 3y^2\frac{dy}{dx} = 3x\frac{dy}{dx} + 3y$$

$$x^2 + y^2\frac{dy}{dx} = x\frac{dy}{dx} + y$$

$$(y^2 - x)\frac{dy}{dx} = y - x^2$$

$$\frac{dy}{dx} = \frac{y - x^2}{y^2 - x} \tag{11}$$

Formula (11) cannot be evaluated at $(0, 0)$ and hence provides no information about the nature of the Folium of Descartes at the origin. Based on the graphs in Figure 3.1.3, what can you say about the differentiability of the implicitly defined functions graphed in blue in parts (b) and (c) of the figure?

Solution (b).   At the point $\left(\frac{3}{2}, \frac{3}{2}\right)$, we have $x = \frac{3}{2}$ and $y = \frac{3}{2}$, so from (11) the slope m_{tan} of the tangent line at this point is

$$m_{\text{tan}} = \frac{dy}{dx}\bigg|_{\substack{x=3/2 \\ y=3/2}} = \frac{(3/2) - (3/2)^2}{(3/2)^2 - (3/2)} = -1$$

Thus, the equation of the tangent line at the point $\left(\frac{3}{2}, \frac{3}{2}\right)$ is

$$y - \tfrac{3}{2} = -1\left(x - \tfrac{3}{2}\right) \quad\text{or}\quad x + y = 3$$

which is consistent with Figure 3.1.5.

Solution (c).   The tangent line is horizontal at the points where $dy/dx = 0$, and from (11) this occurs only where $y - x^2 = 0$ or

$$y = x^2 \tag{12}$$

Substituting this expression for y in the equation $x^3 + y^3 = 3xy$ for the curve yields

$$x^3 + (x^2)^3 = 3x^3$$
$$x^6 - 2x^3 = 0$$
$$x^3(x^3 - 2) = 0$$

whose solutions are $x = 0$ and $x = 2^{1/3}$. From (12), the solutions $x = 0$ and $x = 2^{1/3}$ yield the points $(0, 0)$ and $(2^{1/3}, 2^{2/3})$, respectively. Of these two, only $(2^{1/3}, 2^{2/3})$ is in the first quadrant. Substituting $x = 2^{1/3}$, $y = 2^{2/3}$ into (11) yields

$$\frac{dy}{dx}\bigg|_{\substack{x=2^{1/3} \\ y=2^{2/3}}} = \frac{0}{2^{4/3} - 2^{2/3}} = 0$$

We conclude that $(2^{1/3}, 2^{2/3}) \approx (1.26, 1.59)$ is the only point on the Folium of Descartes in the first quadrant at which the tangent line is horizontal (Figure 3.1.6). ◀

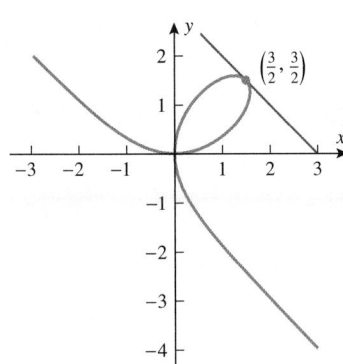

▲ **Figure 3.1.5**

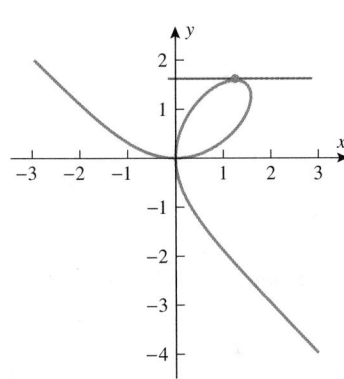

▲ **Figure 3.1.6**

■ **DIFFERENTIABILITY OF FUNCTIONS DEFINED IMPLICITLY**

When differentiating implicitly, it is assumed that y represents a differentiable function of x. If this is not so, then the resulting calculations may be nonsense. For example, if we differentiate the equation

$$x^2 + y^2 + 1 = 0 \tag{13}$$

we obtain

$$2x + 2y\frac{dy}{dx} = 0 \quad \text{or} \quad \frac{dy}{dx} = -\frac{x}{y}$$

However, this derivative is meaningless because there are no real values of x and y that satisfy (13) (why?); and hence (13) does not define any real functions implicitly.

The nonsensical conclusion of these computations conveys the importance of knowing whether an equation in x and y that is to be differentiated implicitly actually defines some differentiable function of x implicitly. Unfortunately, this can be a difficult problem, so we will leave the discussion of such matters for more advanced courses in analysis.

✔ **QUICK CHECK EXERCISES 3.1**   (*See page 192 for answers.*)

1. The equation $xy + 2y = 1$ defines implicitly the function $y =$ _____.

2. Use implicit differentiation to find dy/dx for $x^2 - y^3 = xy$.

3. The slope of the tangent line to the graph of $x + y + xy = 3$ at $(1, 1)$ is _____.

4. Use implicit differentiation to find d^2y/dx^2 for $\sin y = x$.

EXERCISE SET 3.1   c CAS

1–2

(a) Find dy/dx by differentiating implicitly.

(b) Solve the equation for y as a function of x, and find dy/dx from that equation.

(c) Confirm that the two results are consistent by expressing the derivative in part (a) as a function of x alone. ■

1. $x + xy - 2x^3 = 2$ 2. $\sqrt{y} - \sin x = 2$

3–12 Find dy/dx by implicit differentiation. ■

3. $x^2 + y^2 = 100$ 4. $x^3 + y^3 = 3xy^2$

5. $x^2y + 3xy^3 - x = 3$ 6. $x^3y^2 - 5x^2y + x = 1$

7. $\dfrac{1}{\sqrt{x}} + \dfrac{1}{\sqrt{y}} = 1$ 8. $x^2 = \dfrac{x + y}{x - y}$

9. $\sin(x^2y^2) = x$ 10. $\cos(xy^2) = y$

11. $\tan^3(xy^2 + y) = x$ 12. $\dfrac{xy^3}{1 + \sec y} = 1 + y^4$

13–18 Find d^2y/dx^2 by implicit differentiation. ■

13. $2x^2 - 3y^2 = 4$ 14. $x^3 + y^3 = 1$

15. $x^3y^3 - 4 = 0$ 16. $xy + y^2 = 2$

17. $y + \sin y = x$ 18. $x \cos y = y$

19–20 Find the slope of the tangent line to the curve at the given points in two ways: first by solving for y in terms of x and differentiating and then by implicit differentiation. ■

19. $x^2 + y^2 = 1$; $(1/2, \sqrt{3}/2), (1/2, -\sqrt{3}/2)$

20. $y^2 - x + 1 = 0$; $(10, 3), (10, -3)$

21–24 True–False Determine whether the statement is true or false. Explain your answer. ■

21. If an equation in x and y defines a function $y = f(x)$ implicitly, then the graph of the equation and the graph of f are identical.

22. The function

$$f(x) = \begin{cases} \sqrt{1 - x^2}, & 0 < x \leq 1 \\ -\sqrt{1 - x^2}, & -1 \leq x \leq 0 \end{cases}$$

is defined implicitly by the equation $x^2 + y^2 = 1$.

23. The function $|x|$ is not defined implicitly by the equation $(x + y)(x - y) = 0$.

24. If y is defined implicitly as a function of x by the equation $x^2 + y^2 = 1$, then $dy/dx = -x/y$.

25–28 Use implicit differentiation to find the slope of the tangent line to the curve at the specified point, and check that your answer is consistent with the accompanying graph on the next page. ■

25. $x^4 + y^4 = 16$; $(1, \sqrt[4]{15})$ [*Lamé's special quartic*]

26. $y^3 + yx^2 + x^2 - 3y^2 = 0$; $(0, 3)$ [*trisectrix*]

27. $2(x^2 + y^2)^2 = 25(x^2 - y^2)$; $(3, 1)$ [*lemniscate*]

28. $x^{2/3} + y^{2/3} = 4$; $(-1, 3\sqrt{3})$ [*four-cusped hypocycloid*]

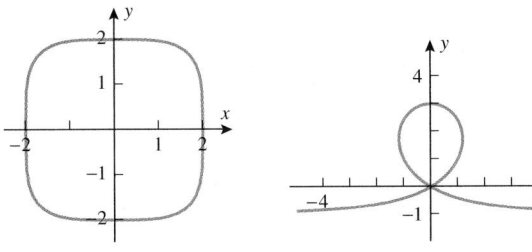

▲ **Figure Ex-25**   ▲ **Figure Ex-26**

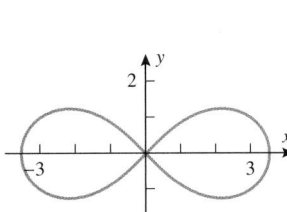 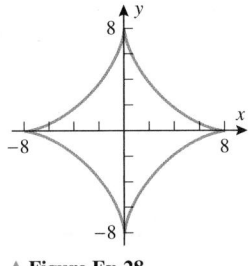

▲ **Figure Ex-27**   ▲ **Figure Ex-28**

33–34 These exercises deal with the rotated ellipse C whose equation is $x^2 - xy + y^2 = 4$. ▨

33. Show that the line $y = x$ intersects C at two points P and Q and that the tangent lines to C at P and Q are parallel.

34. Prove that if $P(a, b)$ is a point on C, then so is $Q(-a, -b)$ and that the tangent lines to C through P and through Q are parallel.

35. Find the values of a and b for the curve $x^2 y + a y^2 = b$ if the point $(1, 1)$ is on its graph and the tangent line at $(1, 1)$ has the equation $4x + 3y = 7$.

36. At what point(s) is the tangent line to the curve $y^3 = 2x^2$ perpendicular to the line $x + 2y - 2 = 0$?

37–38 Two curves are said to be *orthogonal* if their tangent lines are perpendicular at each point of intersection, and two families of curves are said to be *orthogonal trajectories* of one another if each member of one family is orthogonal to each member of the other family. This terminology is used in these exercises. ▨

37. The accompanying figure shows some typical members of the families of circles $x^2 + (y - c)^2 = c^2$ (black curves) and $(x - k)^2 + y^2 = k^2$ (gray curves). Show that these families are orthogonal trajectories of one another. [*Hint:* For the tangent lines to be perpendicular at a point of intersection, the slopes of those tangent lines must be negative reciprocals of one another.]

38. The accompanying figure shows some typical members of the families of hyperbolas $xy = c$ (black curves) and $x^2 - y^2 = k$ (gray curves), where $c \neq 0$ and $k \neq 0$. Use the hint in Exercise 37 to show that these families are orthogonal trajectories of one another.

FOCUS ON CONCEPTS

29. In the accompanying figure, it appears that the ellipse $x^2 + xy + y^2 = 3$ has horizontal tangent lines at the points of intersection of the ellipse and the line $y = -2x$. Use implicit differentiation to explain why this is the case.

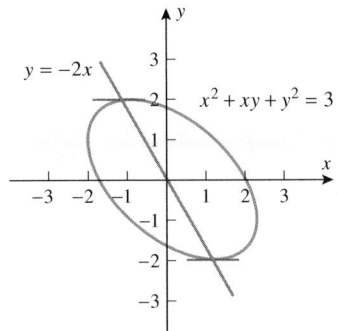

◀ **Figure Ex-29**

30. (a) A student claims that the ellipse $x^2 - xy + y^2 = 1$ has a horizontal tangent line at the point $(1, 1)$. Without doing any computations, explain why the student's claim must be incorrect.

(b) Find all points on the ellipse $x^2 - xy + y^2 = 1$ at which the tangent line is horizontal.

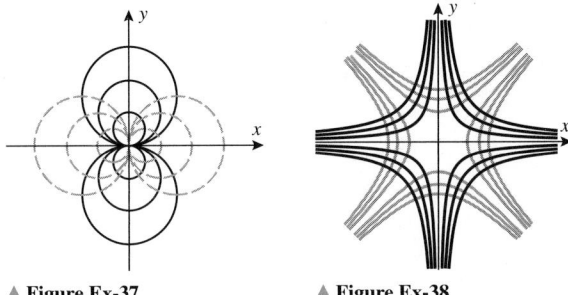

▲ **Figure Ex-37**   ▲ **Figure Ex-38**

[c] **39.** (a) Use the implicit plotting capability of a CAS to graph the curve C whose equation is $x^3 - 2xy + y^3 = 0$.

(b) Use the graph in part (a) to estimate the x-coordinates of a point in the first quadrant that is on C and at which the tangent line to C is parallel to the x-axis.

(c) Find the exact value of the x-coordinate in part (b).

[c] **40.** (a) Use the implicit plotting capability of a CAS to graph the curve C whose equation is $x^3 - 2xy + y^3 = 0$.

(b) Use the graph to guess the coordinates of a point in the first quadrant that is on C and at which the tangent line to C is parallel to the line $y = -x$. *(cont.)*

[c] **31.** (a) Use the implicit plotting capability of a CAS to graph the equation $y^4 + y^2 = x(x - 1)$.

(b) Use implicit differentiation to help explain why the graph in part (a) has no horizontal tangent lines.

(c) Solve the equation $y^4 + y^2 = x(x - 1)$ for x in terms of y and explain why the graph in part (a) consists of two parabolas.

32. Use implicit differentiation to find all points on the graph of $y^4 + y^2 = x(x - 1)$ at which the tangent line is vertical.

(c) Use implicit differentiation to verify your conjecture in part (b).

41. Prove that for every nonzero rational number r, the tangent line to the graph of $x^r + y^r = 2$ at the point $(1, 1)$ has slope -1.

42. Find equations for two lines through the origin that are tangent to the ellipse $2x^2 - 4x + y^2 + 1 = 0$.

43. Writing Write a paragraph that compares the concept of an *explicit* definition of a function with that of an *implicit* definition of a function.

44. Writing A student asks: "Suppose implicit differentiation yields an undefined expression at a point. Does this mean that dy/dx is undefined at that point?" Using the equation $x^2 - 2xy + y^2 = 0$ as a basis for your discussion, write a paragraph that answers the student's question.

✔ QUICK CHECK ANSWERS 3.1

1. $\dfrac{1}{x+2}$ **2.** $\dfrac{dy}{dx} = \dfrac{2x - y}{x + 3y^2}$ **3.** -1 **4.** $\dfrac{d^2y}{dx^2} = \sec^2 y \tan y$

3.2 DERIVATIVES OF LOGARITHMIC FUNCTIONS

In this section we will obtain derivative formulas for logarithmic functions, and we will explain why the natural logarithm function is preferred over logarithms with other bases in calculus.

■ DERIVATIVES OF LOGARITHMIC FUNCTIONS

We will establish that $f(x) = \ln x$ is differentiable for $x > 0$ by applying the derivative definition to $f(x)$. To evaluate the resulting limit, we will need the fact that $\ln x$ is continuous for $x > 0$ (Theorem 1.6.3), and we will need the limit

$$\lim_{v \to 0} (1 + v)^{1/v} = e \tag{1}$$

This limit can be obtained from limits (7) and (8) of Section 1.3 by making the substitution $v = 1/x$ and using the fact that $v \to 0^+$ as $x \to +\infty$ and $v \to 0^-$ as $x \to -\infty$. This produces two equal one-sided limits that together imply (1) (see Exercise 64 of Section 1.3).

$$\frac{d}{dx}[\ln x] = \lim_{h \to 0} \frac{\ln(x + h) - \ln x}{h}$$

$$= \lim_{h \to 0} \frac{1}{h} \ln\left(\frac{x + h}{x}\right) \qquad \boxed{\begin{array}{l}\text{The quotient property of} \\ \text{logarithms in Theorem 0.5.2}\end{array}}$$

$$= \lim_{h \to 0} \frac{1}{h} \ln\left(1 + \frac{h}{x}\right)$$

$$= \lim_{v \to 0} \frac{1}{vx} \ln(1 + v) \qquad \boxed{\begin{array}{l}\text{Let } v = h/x \text{ and note that} \\ v \to 0 \text{ if and only if } h \to 0.\end{array}}$$

$$= \frac{1}{x} \lim_{v \to 0} \frac{1}{v} \ln(1 + v) \qquad \boxed{\begin{array}{l}x \text{ is fixed in this limit computation, so } 1/x \\ \text{can be moved through the limit sign.}\end{array}}$$

$$= \frac{1}{x} \lim_{v \to 0} \ln(1 + v)^{1/v} \qquad \boxed{\begin{array}{l}\text{The power property of} \\ \text{logarithms in Theorem 0.5.2}\end{array}}$$

$$= \frac{1}{x} \ln\left[\lim_{v \to 0} (1 + v)^{1/v}\right] \qquad \boxed{\begin{array}{l}\ln x \text{ is continuous on } (0, +\infty) \text{ so we can} \\ \text{move the limit through the function symbol.}\end{array}}$$

$$= \frac{1}{x} \ln e$$

$$= \frac{1}{x} \qquad \boxed{\text{Since } \ln e = 1}$$

Thus,

$$\frac{d}{dx}[\ln x] = \frac{1}{x}, \quad x > 0 \tag{2}$$

A derivative formula for the general logarithmic function $\log_b x$ can be obtained from (2) by using Formula (6) of Section 0.5 to write

$$\frac{d}{dx}[\log_b x] = \frac{d}{dx}\left[\frac{\ln x}{\ln b}\right] = \frac{1}{\ln b}\frac{d}{dx}[\ln x]$$

It follows from this that

$$\frac{d}{dx}[\log_b x] = \frac{1}{x \ln b}, \quad x > 0 \tag{3}$$

Note that, among all possible bases, the base $b = e$ produces the simplest formula for the derivative of $\log_b x$. This is one of the reasons why the natural logarithm function is preferred over other logarithms in calculus.

▶ **Example 1**

(a) Figure 3.2.1 shows the graph of $y = \ln x$ and its tangent lines at the points $x = \frac{1}{2}, 1, 3$, and 5. Find the slopes of those tangent lines.

(b) Does the graph of $y = \ln x$ have any horizontal tangent lines? Use the derivative of $\ln x$ to justify your answer.

Solution (a). From (2), the slopes of the tangent lines at the points $x = \frac{1}{2}, 1, 3$, and 5 are $1/x = 2, 1, \frac{1}{3}$, and $\frac{1}{5}$, respectively, which is consistent with Figure 3.2.1.

Solution (b). It does not appear from the graph of $y = \ln x$ that there are any horizontal tangent lines. This is confirmed by the fact that $dy/dx = 1/x$ is not equal to zero for any real value of x. ◀

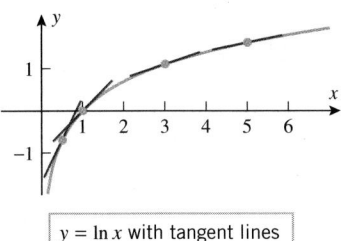

$y = \ln x$ with tangent lines

▲ **Figure 3.2.1**

If u is a differentiable function of x, and if $u(x) > 0$, then applying the chain rule to (2) and (3) produces the following generalized derivative formulas:

$$\frac{d}{dx}[\ln u] = \frac{1}{u} \cdot \frac{du}{dx} \quad \text{and} \quad \frac{d}{dx}[\log_b u] = \frac{1}{u \ln b} \cdot \frac{du}{dx} \tag{4–5}$$

▶ **Example 2** Find $\dfrac{d}{dx}[\ln(x^2 + 1)]$.

Solution. Using (4) with $u = x^2 + 1$ we obtain

$$\frac{d}{dx}[\ln(x^2 + 1)] = \frac{1}{x^2 + 1} \cdot \frac{d}{dx}[x^2 + 1] = \frac{1}{x^2 + 1} \cdot 2x = \frac{2x}{x^2 + 1} \quad ◀$$

When possible, the properties of logarithms in Theorem 0.5.2 should be used to convert products, quotients, and exponents into sums, differences, and constant multiples *before* differentiating a function involving logarithms.

▶ **Example 3**

$$\frac{d}{dx}\left[\ln\left(\frac{x^2 \sin x}{\sqrt{1+x}}\right)\right] = \frac{d}{dx}\left[2\ln x + \ln(\sin x) - \frac{1}{2}\ln(1+x)\right]$$

$$= \frac{2}{x} + \frac{\cos x}{\sin x} - \frac{1}{2(1+x)}$$

$$= \frac{2}{x} + \cot x - \frac{1}{2+2x} \quad ◀$$

Figure 3.2.2 shows the graph of $f(x) = \ln|x|$. This function is important because it "extends" the domain of the natural logarithm function in the sense that the values of $\ln|x|$ and $\ln x$ are the same for $x > 0$, but $\ln|x|$ is defined for all nonzero values of x, and $\ln x$ is only defined for positive values of x.

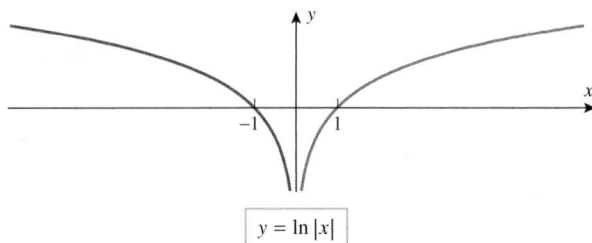

$y = \ln|x|$

▶ **Figure 3.2.2**

The derivative of $\ln|x|$ for $x \neq 0$ can be obtained by considering the cases $x > 0$ and $x < 0$ separately:

Case $x > 0$. In this case $|x| = x$, so

$$\frac{d}{dx}[\ln|x|] = \frac{d}{dx}[\ln x] = \frac{1}{x}$$

Case $x < 0$. In this case $|x| = -x$, so it follows from (4) that

$$\frac{d}{dx}[\ln|x|] = \frac{d}{dx}[\ln(-x)] = \frac{1}{(-x)} \cdot \frac{d}{dx}[-x] = \frac{1}{x}$$

Since the same formula results in both cases, we have shown that

$$\frac{d}{dx}[\ln|x|] = \frac{1}{x} \quad \text{if } x \neq 0 \tag{6}$$

▶ **Example 4**   From (6) and the chain rule,

$$\frac{d}{dx}[\ln|\sin x|] = \frac{1}{\sin x} \cdot \frac{d}{dx}[\sin x] = \frac{\cos x}{\sin x} = \cot x \quad ◀$$

■ LOGARITHMIC DIFFERENTIATION

We now consider a technique called *logarithmic differentiation* that is useful for differentiating functions that are composed of products, quotients, and powers.

▶ **Example 5**   The derivative of

$$y = \frac{x^2 \sqrt[3]{7x - 14}}{(1 + x^2)^4} \tag{7}$$

is messy to calculate directly. However, if we first take the natural logarithm of both sides and then use its properties, we can write

$$\ln y = 2\ln x + \tfrac{1}{3}\ln(7x - 14) - 4\ln(1 + x^2)$$

Differentiating both sides with respect to x yields

$$\frac{1}{y}\frac{dy}{dx} = \frac{2}{x} + \frac{7/3}{7x - 14} - \frac{8x}{1 + x^2}$$

Thus, on solving for dy/dx and using (7) we obtain

$$\frac{dy}{dx} = \frac{x^2 \sqrt[3]{7x - 14}}{(1 + x^2)^4}\left[\frac{2}{x} + \frac{1}{3x - 6} - \frac{8x}{1 + x^2}\right] \blacktriangleleft$$

REMARK | Since $\ln y$ is only defined for $y > 0$, the computations in Example 5 are only valid for $x > 2$ (verify). However, because the derivative of $\ln y$ is the same as the derivative of $\ln|y|$, and because $\ln|y|$ is defined for $y < 0$ as well as $y > 0$, it follows that the formula obtained for dy/dx is valid for $x < 2$ as well as $x > 2$. In general, whenever a derivative dy/dx is obtained by logarithmic differentiation, the resulting derivative formula will be valid for all values of x for which $y \neq 0$. It may be valid at those points as well, but it is not guaranteed.

■ DERIVATIVES OF REAL POWERS OF x

We know from Theorem 2.3.2 and Exercise 82 in Section 2.3, that the differentiation formula

$$\frac{d}{dx}[x^r] = rx^{r-1} \tag{8}$$

holds for constant integer values of r. We will now use logarithmic differentiation to show that this formula holds if r is *any* real number (rational or irrational). In our computations we will assume that x^r is a differentiable function and that the familiar laws of exponents hold for real exponents.

In the next section we will discuss differentiating functions that have exponents which are not constant.

Let $y = x^r$, where r is a real number. The derivative dy/dx can be obtained by logarithmic differentiation as follows:

$$\ln|y| = \ln|x^r| = r\ln|x|$$

$$\frac{d}{dx}[\ln|y|] = \frac{d}{dx}[r\ln|x|]$$

$$\frac{1}{y}\frac{dy}{dx} = \frac{r}{x}$$

$$\frac{dy}{dx} = \frac{r}{x}y = \frac{r}{x}x^r = rx^{r-1}$$

✔ QUICK CHECK EXERCISES 3.2   *(See page 196 for answers.)*

1. The equation of the tangent line to the graph of $y = \ln x$ at $x = e^2$ is _____.

2. Find dy/dx.
   (a) $y = \ln 3x$ (b) $y = \ln\sqrt{x}$
   (c) $y = \log(1/|x|)$

3. Use logarithmic differentiation to find the derivative of

$$f(x) = \frac{\sqrt{x + 1}}{\sqrt[3]{x - 1}}$$

4. $\displaystyle\lim_{h \to 0}\frac{\ln(1 + h)}{h} =$ _____

EXERCISE SET 3.2

1–26 Find dy/dx. ■

1. $y = \ln 5x$

2. $y = \ln\dfrac{x}{3}$

3. $y = \ln|1 + x|$

4. $y = \ln(2 + \sqrt{x})$

5. $y = \ln|x^2 - 1|$

6. $y = \ln|x^3 - 7x^2 - 3|$

7. $y = \ln\left(\dfrac{x}{1 + x^2}\right)$

8. $y = \ln\left|\dfrac{1 + x}{1 - x}\right|$

9. $y = \ln x^2$

10. $y = (\ln x)^3$

11. $y = \sqrt{\ln x}$

12. $y = \ln\sqrt{x}$

13. $y = x\ln x$

14. $y = x^3\ln x$

15. $y = x^2\log_2(3 - 2x)$

16. $y = x[\log_2(x^2 - 2x)]^3$

17. $y = \dfrac{x^2}{1 + \log x}$

18. $y = \dfrac{\log x}{1 + \log x}$

19. $y = \ln(\ln x)$　　　　**20.** $y = \ln(\ln(\ln x))$

21. $y = \ln(\tan x)$　　　**22.** $y = \ln(\cos x)$

23. $y = \cos(\ln x)$　　　**24.** $y = \sin^2(\ln x)$

25. $y = \log(\sin^2 x)$　　**26.** $y = \log(1 - \sin^2 x)$

27–30 Use the method of Example 3 to help perform the indicated differentiation. ■

27. $\dfrac{d}{dx}[\ln((x-1)^3(x^2+1)^4)]$

28. $\dfrac{d}{dx}[\ln((\cos^2 x)\sqrt{1+x^4})]$

29. $\dfrac{d}{dx}\left[\ln \dfrac{\cos x}{\sqrt{4-3x^2}}\right]$　　**30.** $\dfrac{d}{dx}\left[\ln \sqrt{\dfrac{x-1}{x+1}}\right]$

31–34 True–False Determine whether the statement is true or false. Explain your answer. ■

31. The slope of the tangent line to the graph of $y = \ln x$ at $x = a$ approaches infinity as $a \to 0^+$.

32. If $\lim_{x \to +\infty} f'(x) = 0$, then the graph of $y = f(x)$ has a horizontal asymptote.

33. The derivative of $\ln |x|$ is an odd function.

34. We have

$$\frac{d}{dx}((\ln x)^2) = \frac{d}{dx}(2(\ln x)) = \frac{2}{x}$$

35–38 Find dy/dx using logarithmic differentiation. ■

35. $y = x\sqrt[3]{1+x^2}$　　　**36.** $y = \sqrt[5]{\dfrac{x-1}{x+1}}$

37. $y = \dfrac{(x^2-8)^{1/3}\sqrt{x^3+1}}{x^6 - 7x + 5}$　**38.** $y = \dfrac{\sin x \cos x \tan^3 x}{\sqrt{x}}$

39. Find
(a) $\dfrac{d}{dx}[\log_x e]$　　　(b) $\dfrac{d}{dx}[\log_x 2]$.

40. Find
(a) $\dfrac{d}{dx}[\log_{(1/x)} e]$　　(b) $\dfrac{d}{dx}[\log_{(\ln x)} e]$.

41–44 Find the equation of the tangent line to the graph of $y = f(x)$ at $x = x_0$. ■

41. $f(x) = \ln x;\ x_0 = e^{-1}$　　**42.** $f(x) = \log x;\ x_0 = 10$

43. $f(x) = \ln(-x);\ x_0 = -e$　　**44.** $f(x) = \ln |x|;\ x_0 = -2$

FOCUS ON CONCEPTS

45. (a) Find the equation of a line through the origin that is tangent to the graph of $y = \ln x$.
(b) Explain why the y-intercept of a tangent line to the curve $y = \ln x$ must be 1 unit less than the y-coordinate of the point of tangency.

46. Use logarithmic differentiation to verify the product and quotient rules. Explain what properties of $\ln x$ are important for this verification.

47. Find a formula for the area $A(w)$ of the triangle bounded by the tangent line to the graph of $y = \ln x$ at $P(w, \ln w)$, the horizontal line through P, and the y-axis.

48. Find a formula for the area $A(w)$ of the triangle bounded by the tangent line to the graph of $y = \ln x^2$ at $P(w, \ln w^2)$, the horizontal line through P, and the y-axis.

49. Verify that $y = \ln(x + e)$ satisfies $dy/dx = e^{-y}$, with $y = 1$ when $x = 0$.

50. Verify that $y = -\ln(e^2 - x)$ satisfies $dy/dx = e^y$, with $y = -2$ when $x = 0$.

51. Find a function f such that $y = f(x)$ satisfies $dy/dx = e^{-y}$, with $y = 0$ when $x = 0$.

52. Find a function f such that $y = f(x)$ satisfies $dy/dx = e^y$, with $y = -\ln 2$ when $x = 0$.

53–55 Find the limit by interpreting the expression as an appropriate derivative. ■

53. (a) $\displaystyle\lim_{x \to 0} \frac{\ln(1+3x)}{x}$　(b) $\displaystyle\lim_{x \to 0} \frac{\ln(1-5x)}{x}$

54. (a) $\displaystyle\lim_{\Delta x \to 0} \frac{\ln(e^2 + \Delta x) - 2}{\Delta x}$　(b) $\displaystyle\lim_{w \to 1} \frac{\ln w}{w - 1}$

55. (a) $\displaystyle\lim_{x \to 0} \frac{\ln(\cos x)}{x}$　(b) $\displaystyle\lim_{h \to 0} \frac{(1+h)^{\sqrt{2}} - 1}{h}$

56. Modify the derivation of Equation (2) to give another proof of Equation (3).

57. Writing Review the derivation of the formula

$$\frac{d}{dx}[\ln x] = \frac{1}{x}$$

and then write a paragraph that discusses all the ingredients (theorems, limit properties, etc.) that are needed for this derivation.

58. Writing Write a paragraph that explains how logarithmic differentiation can replace a difficult differentiation computation with a simpler computation.

✔**QUICK CHECK ANSWERS 3.2**

1. $y = \dfrac{x}{e^2} + 1$　**2.** (a) $\dfrac{dy}{dx} = \dfrac{1}{x}$ (b) $\dfrac{dy}{dx} = \dfrac{1}{2x}$ (c) $\dfrac{dy}{dx} = -\dfrac{1}{x \ln 10}$　**3.** $\dfrac{\sqrt{x+1}}{\sqrt[3]{x-1}}\left[\dfrac{1}{2(x+1)} - \dfrac{1}{3(x-1)}\right]$　**4.** 1

3.3 DERIVATIVES OF EXPONENTIAL AND INVERSE TRIGONOMETRIC FUNCTIONS

In this section we will show how the derivative of a one-to-one function can be used to obtain the derivative of its inverse function. This will provide the tools we need to obtain derivative formulas for exponential functions from the derivative formulas for logarithmic functions and to obtain derivative formulas for inverse trigonometric functions from the derivative formulas for trigonometric functions.

See Section 0.4 for a review of one-to-one functions and inverse functions.

Our first goal in this section is to obtain a formula relating the derivative of the inverse function f^{-1} to the derivative of the function f.

▶ **Example 1**   Suppose that f is a one-to-one differentiable function such that $f(2) = 1$ and $f'(2) = \frac{3}{4}$. Then the tangent line to $y = f(x)$ at the point $(2, 1)$ has equation

$$y - 1 = \tfrac{3}{4}(x - 2)$$

The tangent line to $y = f^{-1}(x)$ at the point $(1, 2)$ is the reflection about the line $y = x$ of the tangent line to $y = f(x)$ at the point $(2, 1)$ (Figure 3.3.1), and its equation can be obtained by interchanging x and y:

$$x - 1 = \tfrac{3}{4}(y - 2) \quad \text{or} \quad y - 2 = \tfrac{4}{3}(x - 1)$$

Notice that the slope of the tangent line to $y = f^{-1}(x)$ at $x = 1$ is the reciprocal of the slope of the tangent line to $y = f(x)$ at $x = 2$. That is,

$$(f^{-1})'(1) = \frac{1}{f'(2)} = \frac{4}{3} \quad ◀ \tag{1}$$

Since $2 = f^{-1}(1)$ for the function f in Example 1, it follows that $f'(2) = f'(f^{-1}(1))$. Thus, Formula (1) can also be expressed as

$$(f^{-1})'(1) = \frac{1}{f'(f^{-1}(1))}$$

In general, if f is a differentiable and one-to-one function, then

$$(f^{-1})'(x) = \frac{1}{f'(f^{-1}(x))} \tag{2}$$

provided $f'(f^{-1}(x)) \neq 0$.

Formula (2) can be confirmed using implicit differentiation. The equation $y = f^{-1}(x)$ is equivalent to $x = f(y)$. Differentiating with respect to x we obtain

$$1 = \frac{d}{dx}[x] = \frac{d}{dx}[f(y)] = f'(y) \cdot \frac{dy}{dx}$$

so that

$$\frac{dy}{dx} = \frac{1}{f'(y)} = \frac{1}{f'(f^{-1}(x))}$$

Also from $x = f(y)$ we have $dx/dy = f'(y)$, which gives the following alternative version of Formula (2):

$$\frac{dy}{dx} = \frac{1}{dx/dy} \tag{3}$$

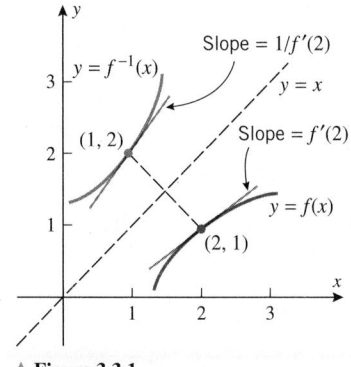

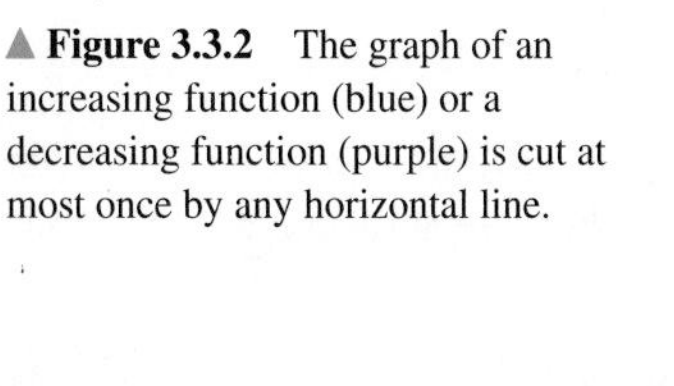

▲ **Figure 3.3.1**

▲ **Figure 3.3.2**   The graph of an increasing function (blue) or a decreasing function (purple) is cut at most once by any horizontal line.

▪ INCREASING OR DECREASING FUNCTIONS ARE ONE-TO-ONE

If the graph of a function f is always increasing or always decreasing over the domain of f, then a horizontal line will cut the graph of f in at most one point (Figure 3.3.2), so f

must have an inverse function (see Section 0.4). We will prove in the next chapter that f is increasing on any interval on which $f'(x) > 0$ (since the graph has positive slope) and that f is decreasing on any interval on which $f'(x) < 0$ (since the graph has negative slope). These intuitive observations, together with Formula (2), suggest the following theorem, which we state without formal proof.

3.3.1   THEOREM *Suppose that the domain of a function f is an open interval on which $f'(x) > 0$ or on which $f'(x) < 0$. Then f is one-to-one, $f^{-1}(x)$ is differentiable at all values of x in the range of f, and the derivative of $f^{-1}(x)$ is given by Formula (2).*

▶ **Example 2** Consider the function $f(x) = x^5 + x + 1$.

(a) Show that f is one-to-one on the interval $(-\infty, +\infty)$.

(b) Find a formula for the derivative of f^{-1}.

(c) Compute $(f^{-1})'(1)$.

> In general, once it is established that f^{-1} is differentiable, one has the option of calculating the derivative of f^{-1} using Formula (2) or (3), or by differentiating implicitly, as in Example 2.

Solution (a). Since

$$f'(x) = 5x^4 + 1 > 0$$

for all real values of x, it follows from Theorem 3.3.1 that f is one-to-one on the interval $(-\infty, +\infty)$.

Solution (b). Let $y = f^{-1}(x)$. Differentiating $x = f(y) = y^5 + y + 1$ implicitly with respect to x yields

$$\frac{d}{dx}[x] = \frac{d}{dx}[y^5 + y + 1]$$

$$1 = (5y^4 + 1)\frac{dy}{dx}$$

$$\frac{dy}{dx} = \frac{1}{5y^4 + 1} \tag{4}$$

We cannot solve $x = y^5 + y + 1$ for y in terms of x, so we leave the expression for dy/dx in Equation (4) in terms of y.

Solution (c). From Equation (4),

$$(f^{-1})'(1) = \left.\frac{dy}{dx}\right|_{x=1} = \left.\frac{1}{5y^4 + 1}\right|_{x=1}$$

Thus, we need to know the value of $y = f^{-1}(x)$ at $x = 1$, which we can obtain by solving the equation $f(y) = 1$ for y. This equation is $y^5 + y + 1 = 1$, which, by inspection, is satisfied by $y = 0$. Thus,

$$(f^{-1})'(1) = \left.\frac{1}{5y^4 + 1}\right|_{y=0} = 1 \blacktriangleleft$$

■ **DERIVATIVES OF EXPONENTIAL FUNCTIONS**

Our next objective is to show that the general exponential function b^x ($b > 0, b \neq 1$) is differentiable everywhere and to find its derivative. To do this, we will use the fact that

b^x is the inverse of the function $f(x) = \log_b x$. We will assume that $b > 1$. With this assumption we have $\ln b > 0$, so

$$f'(x) = \frac{d}{dx}[\log_b x] = \frac{1}{x \ln b} > 0 \quad \text{for all } x \text{ in the interval } (0, +\infty)$$

It now follows from Theorem 3.3.1 that $f^{-1}(x) = b^x$ is differentiable for all x in the range of $f(x) = \log_b x$. But we know from Table 0.5.3 that the range of $\log_b x$ is $(-\infty, +\infty)$, so we have established that b^x is differentiable everywhere.

To obtain a derivative formula for b^x we rewrite $y = b^x$ as

$$x = \log_b y$$

and differentiate implicitly using Formula (5) of Section 3.2 to obtain

$$1 = \frac{1}{y \ln b} \cdot \frac{dy}{dx}$$

Solving for dy/dx and replacing y by b^x we have

$$\frac{dy}{dx} = y \ln b = b^x \ln b$$

Thus, we have shown that

How does the derivation of Formula (5) change if $0 < b < 1$?

$$\frac{d}{dx}[b^x] = b^x \ln b \tag{5}$$

In the special case where $b = e$ we have $\ln e = 1$, so that (5) becomes

$$\frac{d}{dx}[e^x] = e^x \tag{6}$$

In Section 0.5 we stated that $b = e$ is the only base for which the slope of the tangent line to the curve $y = b^x$ at any point P on the curve is the y-coordinate at P (see page 54). Verify this statement.

Moreover, if u is a differentiable function of x, then it follows from (5) and (6) that

$$\frac{d}{dx}[b^u] = b^u \ln b \cdot \frac{du}{dx} \quad \text{and} \quad \frac{d}{dx}[e^u] = e^u \cdot \frac{du}{dx} \tag{7-8}$$

It is important to distinguish between differentiating an exponential function b^x (variable exponent and constant base) and a power function x^b (variable base and constant exponent). For example, compare the derivative

$$\frac{d}{dx}[x^2] = 2x$$

to the derivative of 2^x in Example 3.

▶ **Example 3** The following computations use Formulas (7) and (8).

$$\frac{d}{dx}[2^x] = 2^x \ln 2$$

$$\frac{d}{dx}[e^{-2x}] = e^{-2x} \cdot \frac{d}{dx}[-2x] = -2e^{-2x}$$

$$\frac{d}{dx}[e^{x^3}] = e^{x^3} \cdot \frac{d}{dx}[x^3] = 3x^2 e^{x^3}$$

$$\frac{d}{dx}[e^{\cos x}] = e^{\cos x} \cdot \frac{d}{dx}[\cos x] = -(\sin x)e^{\cos x} \quad ◀$$

Functions of the form $f(x) = u^v$ in which u and v are *nonconstant* functions of x are neither exponential functions nor power functions. Functions of this form can be differentiated using logarithmic differentiation.

▶ **Example 4** Use logarithmic differentiation to find $\dfrac{d}{dx}[(x^2 + 1)^{\sin x}]$.

Solution. Setting $y = (x^2 + 1)^{\sin x}$ we have

$$\ln y = \ln[(x^2 + 1)^{\sin x}] = (\sin x) \ln(x^2 + 1)$$

Differentiating both sides with respect to x yields

$$\frac{1}{y}\frac{dy}{dx} = \frac{d}{dx}[(\sin x)\ln(x^2+1)]$$

$$= (\sin x)\frac{1}{x^2+1}(2x) + (\cos x)\ln(x^2+1)$$

Thus,

$$\frac{dy}{dx} = y\left[\frac{2x\sin x}{x^2+1} + (\cos x)\ln(x^2+1)\right]$$

$$= (x^2+1)^{\sin x}\left[\frac{2x\sin x}{x^2+1} + (\cos x)\ln(x^2+1)\right] \blacktriangleleft$$

▓ DERIVATIVES OF THE INVERSE TRIGONOMETRIC FUNCTIONS

To obtain formulas for the derivatives of the inverse trigonometric functions, we will need to use some of the identities given in Formulas (11) to (17) of Section 0.4. Rather than memorize those identities, we recommend that you review the "triangle technique" that we used to obtain them.

To begin, consider the function $\sin^{-1} x$. If we let $f(x) = \sin x \ (-\pi/2 \le x \le \pi/2)$, then it follows from Formula (2) that $f^{-1}(x) = \sin^{-1} x$ will be differentiable at any point x where $\cos(\sin^{-1} x) \ne 0$. This is equivalent to the condition

$$\sin^{-1} x \ne -\frac{\pi}{2} \quad \text{and} \quad \sin^{-1} x \ne \frac{\pi}{2}$$

so it follows that $\sin^{-1} x$ is differentiable on the interval $(-1, 1)$.

A derivative formula for $\sin^{-1} x$ on $(-1, 1)$ can be obtained by using Formula (2) or (3) or by differentiating implicitly. We will use the latter method. Rewriting the equation $y = \sin^{-1} x$ as $x = \sin y$ and differentiating implicitly with respect to x, we obtain

$$\frac{d}{dx}[x] = \frac{d}{dx}[\sin y]$$

$$1 = \cos y \cdot \frac{dy}{dx}$$

$$\frac{dy}{dx} = \frac{1}{\cos y} = \frac{1}{\cos(\sin^{-1} x)}$$

> Observe that $\sin^{-1} x$ is only differentiable on the interval $(-1, 1)$, even though its domain is $[-1, 1]$. This is because the graph of $y = \sin x$ has horizontal tangent lines at the points $(\pi/2, 1)$ and $(-\pi/2, -1)$, so the graph of $y = \sin^{-1} x$ has vertical tangent lines at $x = \pm 1$.

At this point we have succeeded in obtaining the derivative; however, this derivative formula can be simplified using the identity indicated in Figure 3.3.3. This yields

$$\frac{dy}{dx} = \frac{1}{\sqrt{1-x^2}}$$

Thus, we have shown that

$$\frac{d}{dx}[\sin^{-1} x] = \frac{1}{\sqrt{1-x^2}} \qquad (-1 < x < 1)$$

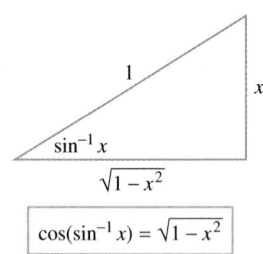

$$\cos(\sin^{-1} x) = \sqrt{1-x^2}$$

▲ **Figure 3.3.3**

More generally, if u is a differentiable function of x, then the chain rule produces the following generalized version of this formula:

$$\frac{d}{dx}[\sin^{-1} u] = \frac{1}{\sqrt{1-u^2}}\frac{du}{dx} \qquad (-1 < u < 1)$$

The method used to derive this formula can be used to obtain generalized derivative formulas for the remaining inverse trigonometric functions. The following is a complete list of these formulas, each of which is valid on the natural domain of the function that multiplies du/dx.

$$\frac{d}{dx}[\sin^{-1} u] = \frac{1}{\sqrt{1-u^2}}\frac{du}{dx} \qquad \frac{d}{dx}[\cos^{-1} u] = -\frac{1}{\sqrt{1-u^2}}\frac{du}{dx} \qquad (9\text{--}10)$$

$$\frac{d}{dx}[\tan^{-1} u] = \frac{1}{1+u^2}\frac{du}{dx} \qquad \frac{d}{dx}[\cot^{-1} u] = -\frac{1}{1+u^2}\frac{du}{dx} \qquad (11\text{--}12)$$

The appearance of $|u|$ in (13) and (14) will be explained in Exercise 58.

$$\frac{d}{dx}[\sec^{-1} u] = \frac{1}{|u|\sqrt{u^2-1}}\frac{du}{dx} \qquad \frac{d}{dx}[\csc^{-1} u] = -\frac{1}{|u|\sqrt{u^2-1}}\frac{du}{dx} \qquad (13\text{--}14)$$

▶ **Example 5** Find dy/dx if

(a) $y = \sin^{-1}(x^3)$ (b) $y = \sec^{-1}(e^x)$

Solution (a). From (9)

$$\frac{dy}{dx} = \frac{1}{\sqrt{1-(x^3)^2}}(3x^2) = \frac{3x^2}{\sqrt{1-x^6}}$$

Solution (b). From (13)

$$\frac{dy}{dx} = \frac{1}{e^x\sqrt{(e^x)^2-1}}(e^x) = \frac{1}{\sqrt{e^{2x}-1}} \quad ◀$$

✔ **QUICK CHECK EXERCISES 3.3**   (See page 203 for answers.)

1. Suppose that a one-to-one function f has tangent line $y = 5x + 3$ at the point $(1, 8)$. Evaluate $(f^{-1})'(8)$.

2. In each case, from the given derivative, determine whether the function f is invertible.
   (a) $f'(x) = x^2 + 1$ (b) $f'(x) = x^2 - 1$
   (c) $f'(x) = \sin x$ (d) $f'(x) = \dfrac{\pi}{2} + \tan^{-1} x$

3. Evaluate the derivative.
   (a) $\dfrac{d}{dx}[e^x]$ (b) $\dfrac{d}{dx}[7^x]$
   (c) $\dfrac{d}{dx}[\cos(e^x + 1)]$ (d) $\dfrac{d}{dx}[e^{3x-2}]$

4. Let $f(x) = e^{x^3+x}$. Use $f'(x)$ to verify that f is one-to-one.

EXERCISE SET 3.3   ⌗ Graphing Utility

FOCUS ON CONCEPTS

1. Let $f(x) = x^5 + x^3 + x$.
   (a) Show that f is one-to-one and confirm that $f(1) = 3$.
   (b) Find $(f^{-1})'(3)$.

2. Let $f(x) = x^3 + 2e^x$.
   (a) Show that f is one-to-one and confirm that $f(0) = 2$.
   (b) Find $(f^{-1})'(2)$.

3–4 Find $(f^{-1})'(x)$ using Formula (2), and check your answer by differentiating f^{-1} directly. ▧

3. $f(x) = 2/(x+3)$ 4. $f(x) = \ln(2x+1)$

5–6 Determine whether the function f is one-to-one by examining the sign of $f'(x)$. ▧

5. (a) $f(x) = x^2 + 8x + 1$
   (b) $f(x) = 2x^5 + x^3 + 3x + 2$
   (c) $f(x) = 2x + \sin x$
   (d) $f(x) = \left(\frac{1}{2}\right)^x$

6. (a) $f(x) = x^3 + 3x^2 - 8$
   (b) $f(x) = x^5 + 8x^3 + 2x - 1$
   (c) $f(x) = \dfrac{x}{x+1}$
   (d) $f(x) = \log_b x, \quad 0 < b < 1$

7–10 Find the derivative of f^{-1} by using Formula (3), and check your result by differentiating implicitly. ■

7. $f(x) = 5x^3 + x - 7$ **8.** $f(x) = 1/x^2, \quad x > 0$

9. $f(x) = 2x^5 + x^3 + 1$

10. $f(x) = 5x - \sin 2x, \quad -\dfrac{\pi}{4} < x < \dfrac{\pi}{4}$

FOCUS ON CONCEPTS

11. Figure 0.4.8 is a "proof by picture" that the reflection of a point $P(a, b)$ about the line $y = x$ is the point $Q(b, a)$. Establish this result rigorously by completing each part.
   (a) Prove that if P is not on the line $y = x$, then P and Q are distinct, and the line $\overleftrightarrow{PQ}$ is perpendicular to the line $y = x$.
   (b) Prove that if P is not on the line $y = x$, the midpoint of segment PQ is on the line $y = x$.
   (c) Carefully explain what it means geometrically to reflect P about the line $y = x$.
   (d) Use the results of parts (a)–(c) to prove that Q is the reflection of P about the line $y = x$.

12. Prove that the reflection about the line $y = x$ of a line with slope m, $m \neq 0$, is a line with slope $1/m$. [*Hint:* Apply the result of the previous exercise to a pair of points on the line of slope m and to a corresponding pair of points on the reflection of this line about the line $y = x$.]

13. Suppose that f and g are increasing functions. Determine which of the functions $f(x) + g(x)$, $f(x)g(x)$, and $f(g(x))$ must also be increasing.

14. Suppose that f and g are one-to-one functions. Determine which of the functions $f(x) + g(x)$, $f(x)g(x)$, and $f(g(x))$ must also be one-to-one.

15–26 Find dy/dx. ■

15. $y = e^{7x}$ **16.** $y = e^{-5x^2}$

17. $y = x^3 e^x$ **18.** $y = e^{1/x}$

19. $y = \dfrac{e^x - e^{-x}}{e^x + e^{-x}}$ **20.** $y = \sin(e^x)$

21. $y = e^{x \tan x}$ **22.** $y = \dfrac{e^x}{\ln x}$

23. $y = e^{(x - e^{3x})}$ **24.** $y = \exp(\sqrt{1 + 5x^3})$

25. $y = \ln(1 - xe^{-x})$ **26.** $y = \ln(\cos e^x)$

27–30 Find $f'(x)$ by Formula (7) and then by logarithmic differentiation. ■

27. $f(x) = 2^x$ **28.** $f(x) = 3^{-x}$

29. $f(x) = \pi^{\sin x}$ **30.** $f(x) = \pi^{x \tan x}$

31–35 Find dy/dx using the method of logarithmic differentiation. ■

31. $y = (x^3 - 2x)^{\ln x}$ **32.** $y = x^{\sin x}$

33. $y = (\ln x)^{\tan x}$ **34.** $y = (x^2 + 3)^{\ln x}$

35. $y = (\ln x)^{\ln x}$

36. (a) Explain why Formula (5) cannot be used to find $(d/dx)[x^x]$.
   (b) Find this derivative by logarithmic differentiation.

37–52 Find dy/dx. ■

37. $y = \sin^{-1}(3x)$ **38.** $y = \cos^{-1}\left(\dfrac{x+1}{2}\right)$

39. $y = \sin^{-1}(1/x)$ **40.** $y = \cos^{-1}(\cos x)$

41. $y = \tan^{-1}(x^3)$ **42.** $y = \sec^{-1}(x^5)$

43. $y = (\tan x)^{-1}$ **44.** $y = \dfrac{1}{\tan^{-1} x}$

45. $y = e^x \sec^{-1} x$ **46.** $y = \ln(\cos^{-1} x)$

47. $y = \sin^{-1} x + \cos^{-1} x$ **48.** $y = x^2(\sin^{-1} x)^3$

49. $y = \sec^{-1} x + \csc^{-1} x$ **50.** $y = \csc^{-1}(e^x)$

51. $y = \cot^{-1}(\sqrt{x})$ **52.** $y = \sqrt{\cot^{-1} x}$

53–56 True–False Determine whether the statement is true or false. Explain your answer. ■

53. If a function $y = f(x)$ satisfies $dy/dx = y$, then $y = e^x$.

54. If $y = f(x)$ is a function such that dy/dx is a rational function, then $f(x)$ is also a rational function.

55. $\dfrac{d}{dx}(\log_b |x|) = \dfrac{1}{x \ln b}$

56. We can conclude from the derivatives of $\sin^{-1} x$ and $\cos^{-1} x$ that $\sin^{-1} x + \cos^{-1} x$ is constant.

57. (a) Use Formula (2) to prove that
$$\frac{d}{dx}[\cot^{-1} x]\Big|_{x=0} = -1$$
   (b) Use part (a) above, part (a) of Exercise 48 in Section 0.4, and the chain rule to show that
$$\frac{d}{dx}[\cot^{-1} x] = -\frac{1}{1 + x^2}$$
   for $-\infty < x < +\infty$.
   (c) Conclude from part (b) that
$$\frac{d}{dx}[\cot^{-1} u] = -\frac{1}{1 + u^2}\frac{du}{dx}$$
   for $-\infty < u < +\infty$.

58. (a) Use part (c) of Exercise 48 in Section 0.4 and the chain rule to show that
$$\frac{d}{dx}[\csc^{-1} x] = -\frac{1}{|x|\sqrt{x^2 - 1}}$$
   for $1 < |x|$.
   (b) Conclude from part (a) that
$$\frac{d}{dx}[\csc^{-1} u] = -\frac{1}{|u|\sqrt{u^2 - 1}}\frac{du}{dx}$$
   for $1 < |u|$.

(cont.)

(c) Use Equation (11) in Section 0.4 and parts (b) and (c) of Exercise 48 in that section to show that if $|x| \geq 1$ then, $\sec^{-1} x + \csc^{-1} x = \pi/2$. Conclude from part (a) that

$$\frac{d}{dx}[\sec^{-1} x] = \frac{1}{|x|\sqrt{x^2 - 1}}$$

(d) Conclude from part (c) that

$$\frac{d}{dx}[\sec^{-1} u] = \frac{1}{|u|\sqrt{x^2 - 1}}\frac{du}{dx}$$

59–60 Find dy/dx by implicit differentiation. ■

59. $x^3 + x\tan^{-1} y = e^y$ **60.** $\sin^{-1}(xy) = \cos^{-1}(x - y)$

61. (a) Show that $f(x) = x^3 - 3x^2 + 2x$ is not one-to-one on $(-\infty, +\infty)$.
(b) Find the largest value of k such that f is one-to-one on the interval $(-k, k)$.

62. (a) Show that the function $f(x) = x^4 - 2x^3$ is not one-to-one on $(-\infty, +\infty)$.
(b) Find the smallest value of k such that f is one-to-one on the interval $[k, +\infty)$.

63. Let $f(x) = x^4 + x^3 + 1, 0 \leq x \leq 2$.
(a) Show that f is one-to-one.
(b) Let $g(x) = f^{-1}(x)$ and define $F(x) = f(2g(x))$. Find an equation for the tangent line to $y = F(x)$ at $x = 3$.

64. Let $f(x) = \dfrac{\exp(4 - x^2)}{x}, x > 0$.
(a) Show that f is one-to-one.
(b) Let $g(x) = f^{-1}(x)$ and define $F(x) = f([g(x)]^2)$. Find $F'\left(\frac{1}{2}\right)$.

65. Show that for any constants A and k, the function $y = Ae^{kt}$ satisfies the equation $dy/dt = ky$.

66. Show that for any constants A and B, the function

$$y = Ae^{2x} + Be^{-4x}$$

satisfies the equation

$$y'' + 2y' - 8y = 0$$

67. Show that
(a) $y = xe^{-x}$ satisfies the equation $xy' = (1 - x)y$
(b) $y = xe^{-x^2/2}$ satisfies the equation $xy' = (1 - x^2)y$.

68. Show that the rate of change of $y = 100e^{-0.2x}$ with respect to x is proportional to y.

69. Show that

$$y = \frac{60}{5 + 7e^{-t}} \quad \text{satisfies} \quad \frac{dy}{dt} = r\left(1 - \frac{y}{K}\right)y$$

for some constants r and K, and determine the values of these constants.

70. Suppose that the population of oxygen-dependent bacteria in a pond is modeled by the equation

$$P(t) = \frac{60}{5 + 7e^{-t}}$$

where $P(t)$ is the population (in billions) t days after an initial observation at time $t = 0$.
(a) Use a graphing utility to graph the function $P(t)$.
(b) In words, explain what happens to the population over time. Check your conclusion by finding $\lim_{t \to +\infty} P(t)$.
(c) In words, what happens to the *rate* of population growth over time? Check your conclusion by graphing $P'(t)$.

71–76 Find the limit by interpreting the expression as an appropriate derivative. ■

71. $\displaystyle\lim_{x \to 0} \frac{e^{3x} - 1}{x}$ **72.** $\displaystyle\lim_{x \to 0} \frac{\exp(x^2) - 1}{x}$

73. $\displaystyle\lim_{h \to 0} \frac{10^h - 1}{h}$ **74.** $\displaystyle\lim_{h \to 0} \frac{\tan^{-1}(1 + h) - \pi/4}{h}$

75. $\displaystyle\lim_{\Delta x \to 0} \frac{9\left[\sin^{-1}\left(\frac{\sqrt{3}}{2} + \Delta x\right)\right]^2 - \pi^2}{\Delta x}$

76. $\displaystyle\lim_{w \to 2} \frac{3\sec^{-1} w - \pi}{w - 2}$

77. **Writing** Let G denote the graph of an invertible function f and consider G as a fixed set of points in the plane. Suppose we relabel the coordinate axes so that the x-axis becomes the y-axis and vice versa. Carefully explain why now the same set of points G becomes the graph of f^{-1} (with the coordinate axes in a nonstandard position). Use this result to explain Formula (2).

78. **Writing** Suppose that f has an inverse function. Carefully explain the connection between Formula (2) and implicit differentiation of the equation $x = f(y)$.

✔ **QUICK CHECK ANSWERS 3.3**

1. $\frac{1}{5}$ **2.** (a) yes (b) no (c) no (d) yes   **3.** (a) e^x (b) $7^x \ln 7$ (c) $-e^x \sin(e^x + 1)$ (d) $3e^{3x-2}$
4. $f'(x) = e^{x^3 + x} \cdot (3x^2 + 1) > 0$ for all x

3.4 RELATED RATES

In this section we will study related rates problems. In such problems one tries to find the rate at which some quantity is changing by relating the quantity to other quantities whose rates of change are known.

■ **DIFFERENTIATING EQUATIONS TO RELATE RATES**

Figure 3.4.1 shows a liquid draining through a conical filter. As the liquid drains, its volume V, height h, and radius r are functions of the elapsed time t, and at each instant these variables are related by the equation

$$V = \frac{\pi}{3}r^2 h$$

If we were interested in finding the rate of change of the volume V with respect to the time t, we could begin by differentiating both sides of this equation with respect to t to obtain

$$\frac{dV}{dt} = \frac{\pi}{3}\left[r^2\frac{dh}{dt} + h\left(2r\frac{dr}{dt}\right)\right] = \frac{\pi}{3}\left(r^2\frac{dh}{dt} + 2rh\frac{dr}{dt}\right)$$

Thus, to find dV/dt at a specific time t from this equation we would need to have values for r, h, dh/dt, and dr/dt at that time. This is called a ***related rates problem*** because the goal is to find an unknown rate of change by *relating* it to other variables whose values and whose rates of change at time t are known or can be found in some way. Let us begin with a simple example.

▶ **Figure 3.4.1**

▶ **Example 1**   Suppose that x and y are differentiable functions of t and are related by the equation $y = x^3$. Find dy/dt at time $t = 1$ if $x = 2$ and $dx/dt = 4$ at time $t = 1$.

Solution.   Using the chain rule to differentiate both sides of the equation $y = x^3$ with respect to t yields

$$\frac{dy}{dt} = \frac{d}{dt}[x^3] = 3x^2\frac{dx}{dt}$$

Thus, the value of dy/dt at time $t = 1$ is

$$\left.\frac{dy}{dt}\right|_{t=1} = 3(2)^2 \left.\frac{dx}{dt}\right|_{t=1} = 12 \cdot 4 = 48 \quad ◀$$

Arni Katz/Phototake

Oil spill from a ruptured tanker.

▶ **Example 2**   Assume that oil spilled from a ruptured tanker spreads in a circular pattern whose radius increases at a constant rate of 2 ft/s. How fast is the area of the spill increasing when the radius of the spill is 60 ft?

Solution.   Let

$$t = \text{number of seconds elapsed from the time of the spill}$$
$$r = \text{radius of the spill in feet after } t \text{ seconds}$$
$$A = \text{area of the spill in square feet after } t \text{ seconds}$$

(Figure 3.4.2). We know the rate at which the radius is increasing, and we want to find the rate at which the area is increasing at the instant when $r = 60$; that is, we want to find

$$\frac{dA}{dt}\bigg|_{r=60} \quad \text{given that} \quad \frac{dr}{dt} = 2 \text{ ft/s}$$

This suggests that we look for an equation relating A and r that we can differentiate with respect to t to produce a relationship between dA/dt and dr/dt. But A is the area of a circle of radius r, so

$$A = \pi r^2 \tag{1}$$

Differentiating both sides of (1) with respect to t yields

$$\frac{dA}{dt} = 2\pi r \frac{dr}{dt} \tag{2}$$

Thus, when $r = 60$ the area of the spill is increasing at the rate of

$$\frac{dA}{dt}\bigg|_{r=60} = 2\pi(60)(2) = 240\pi \text{ ft}^2/\text{s} \approx 754 \text{ ft}^2/\text{s} \quad ◀$$

With some minor variations, the method used in Example 2 can be used to solve a variety of related rates problems. We can break the method down into five steps.

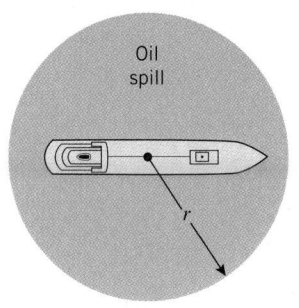

▲ **Figure 3.4.2**

WARNING

We have italicized the word "After" in Step 5 because it is a common error to substitute numerical values before performing the differentiation. For instance, in Example 2 had we substituted the known value of $r = 60$ in (1) before differentiating, we would have obtained $dA/dt = 0$, which is obviously incorrect.

A Strategy for Solving Related Rates Problems

Step 1. Assign letters to all quantities that vary with time and any others that seem relevant to the problem. Give a definition for each letter.

Step 2. Identify the rates of change that are known and the rate of change that is to be found. Interpret each rate as a derivative.

Step 3. Find an equation that relates the variables whose rates of change were identified in Step 2. To do this, it will often be helpful to draw an appropriately labeled figure that illustrates the relationship.

Step 4. Differentiate both sides of the equation obtained in Step 3 with respect to time to produce a relationship between the known rates of change and the unknown rate of change.

Step 5. *After* completing Step 4, substitute all known values for the rates of change and the variables, and then solve for the unknown rate of change.

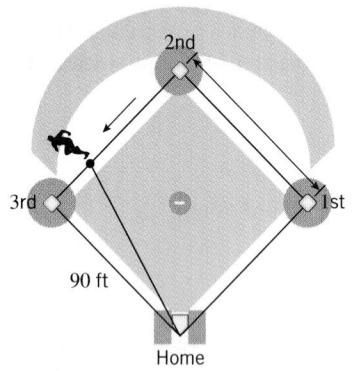

▲ **Figure 3.4.3**

The quantity

$$\frac{dx}{dt}\bigg|_{x=20}$$

is negative because x is decreasing with respect to t.

▶ **Example 3** A baseball diamond is a square whose sides are 90 ft long (Figure 3.4.3). Suppose that a player running from second base to third base has a speed of 30 ft/s at the instant when he is 20 ft from third base. At what rate is the player's distance from home plate changing at that instant?

Solution. We are given a constant speed with which the player is approaching third base, and we want to find the rate of change of the distance between the player and home plate at a particular instant. Thus, let

$$t = \text{number of seconds since the player left second base}$$
$$x = \text{distance in feet from the player to third base}$$
$$y = \text{distance in feet from the player to home plate}$$

(Figure 3.4.4). Thus, we want to find

$$\frac{dy}{dt}\bigg|_{x=20} \quad \text{given that} \quad \frac{dx}{dt}\bigg|_{x=20} = -30 \text{ ft/s}$$

As suggested by Figure 3.4.4, an equation relating the variables x and y can be obtained using the Theorem of Pythagoras:

$$x^2 + 90^2 = y^2 \tag{3}$$

Differentiating both sides of this equation with respect to t yields

$$2x\frac{dx}{dt} = 2y\frac{dy}{dt}$$

from which we obtain

$$\frac{dy}{dt} = \frac{x}{y}\frac{dx}{dt} \tag{4}$$

When $x = 20$, it follows from (3) that

$$y = \sqrt{20^2 + 90^2} = \sqrt{8500} = 10\sqrt{85}$$

so that (4) yields

$$\frac{dy}{dt}\bigg|_{x=20} = \frac{20}{10\sqrt{85}}(-30) = -\frac{60}{\sqrt{85}} \approx -6.51 \text{ ft/s}$$

The negative sign in the answer tells us that y is decreasing, which makes sense physically from Figure 3.4.4. ◀

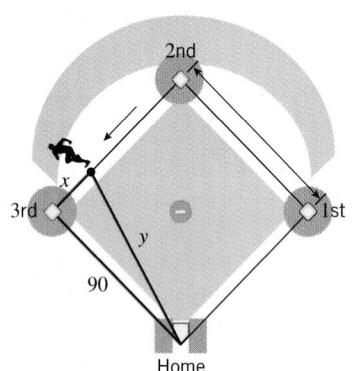

▲ **Figure 3.4.4**

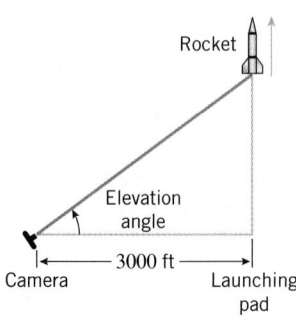

▲ **Figure 3.4.5**

▶ **Example 4** In Figure 3.4.5 we have shown a camera mounted at a point 3000 ft from the base of a rocket launching pad. If the rocket is rising vertically at 880 ft/s when it is 4000 ft above the launching pad, how fast must the camera elevation angle change at that instant to keep the camera aimed at the rocket?

Solution. Let

$$t = \text{number of seconds elapsed from the time of launch}$$
$$\phi = \text{camera elevation angle in radians after } t \text{ seconds}$$
$$h = \text{height of the rocket in feet after } t \text{ seconds}$$

(Figure 3.4.6). At each instant the rate at which the camera elevation angle must change

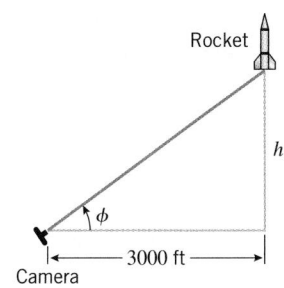

Figure 3.4.6

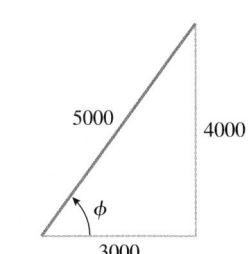

Figure 3.4.7

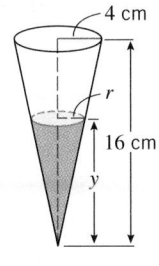

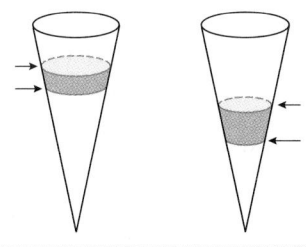

The same volume has drained, but the change in height is greater near the bottom than near the top.

Figure 3.4.9

is $d\phi/dt$, and the rate at which the rocket is rising is dh/dt. We want to find

$$\frac{d\phi}{dt}\bigg|_{h=4000} \quad \text{given that} \quad \frac{dh}{dt}\bigg|_{h=4000} = 880 \text{ ft/s}$$

From Figure 3.4.6 we see that

$$\tan\phi = \frac{h}{3000} \tag{5}$$

Differentiating both sides of (5) with respect to t yields

$$(\sec^2\phi)\frac{d\phi}{dt} = \frac{1}{3000}\frac{dh}{dt} \tag{6}$$

When $h = 4000$, it follows that

$$(\sec\phi)\big|_{h=4000} = \frac{5000}{3000} = \frac{5}{3}$$

(see Figure 3.4.7), so that from (6)

$$\left(\frac{5}{3}\right)^2 \frac{d\phi}{dt}\bigg|_{h=4000} = \frac{1}{3000} \cdot 880 = \frac{22}{75}$$

$$\frac{d\phi}{dt}\bigg|_{h=4000} = \frac{22}{75} \cdot \frac{9}{25} = \frac{66}{625} \approx 0.11 \text{ rad/s} \approx 6.05 \text{ deg/s} \blacktriangleleft$$

▶ **Example 5** Suppose that liquid is to be cleared of sediment by allowing it to drain through a conical filter that is 16 cm high and has a radius of 4 cm at the top (Figure 3.4.8). Suppose also that the liquid is forced out of the cone at a constant rate of 2 cm³/min.

(a) Do you think that the depth of the liquid will decrease at a constant rate? Give a verbal argument that justifies your conclusion.

(b) Find a formula that expresses the rate at which the depth of the liquid is changing in terms of the depth, and use that formula to determine whether your conclusion in part (a) is correct.

(c) At what rate is the depth of the liquid changing at the instant when the liquid in the cone is 8 cm deep?

Solution (a). For the volume of liquid to decrease by a *fixed amount*, it requires a greater decrease in depth when the cone is close to empty than when it is almost full (Figure 3.4.9). This suggests that for the volume to decrease at a constant rate, the depth must decrease at an increasing rate.

Solution (b). Let

$$t = \text{time elapsed from the initial observation (min)}$$
$$V = \text{volume of liquid in the cone at time } t \text{ (cm}^3)$$
$$y = \text{depth of the liquid in the cone at time } t \text{ (cm)}$$
$$r = \text{radius of the liquid surface at time } t \text{ (cm)}$$

(Figure 3.4.8). At each instant the rate at which the volume of liquid is changing is dV/dt, and the rate at which the depth is changing is dy/dt. We want to express dy/dt in terms of y given that dV/dt has a constant value of $dV/dt = -2$. (We must use a minus sign here because V *decreases* as t increases.)

From the formula for the volume of a cone, the volume V, the radius r, and the depth y are related by

$$V = \tfrac{1}{3}\pi r^2 y \tag{7}$$

If we differentiate both sides of (7) with respect to t, the right side will involve the quantity dr/dt. Since we have no direct information about dr/dt, it is desirable to eliminate r from (7) before differentiating. This can be done using similar triangles. From Figure 3.4.8 we see that

$$\frac{r}{y} = \frac{4}{16} \quad \text{or} \quad r = \frac{1}{4}y$$

Substituting this expression in (7) gives

$$V = \frac{\pi}{48}y^3 \tag{8}$$

Differentiating both sides of (8) with respect to t we obtain

$$\frac{dV}{dt} = \frac{\pi}{48}\left(3y^2 \frac{dy}{dt}\right)$$

or

$$\frac{dy}{dt} = \frac{16}{\pi y^2}\frac{dV}{dt} = \frac{16}{\pi y^2}(-2) = -\frac{32}{\pi y^2} \tag{9}$$

which expresses dy/dt in terms of y. The minus sign tells us that y is decreasing with time, and

$$\left|\frac{dy}{dt}\right| = \frac{32}{\pi y^2}$$

tells us how fast y is decreasing. From this formula we see that $|dy/dt|$ increases as y decreases, which confirms our conjecture in part (a) that the depth of the liquid decreases more quickly as the liquid drains through the filter.

Solution (c). The rate at which the depth is changing when the depth is 8 cm can be obtained from (9) with $y = 8$:

$$\left.\frac{dy}{dt}\right|_{y=8} = -\frac{32}{\pi(8^2)} = -\frac{1}{2\pi} \approx -0.16 \text{ cm/min} \blacktriangleleft$$

✔ **QUICK CHECK EXERCISES 3.4**   *(See page 211 for answers.)*

---

1. If $A = x^2$ and $\dfrac{dx}{dt} = 3$, find $\left.\dfrac{dA}{dt}\right|_{x=10}$.

2. If $A = x^2$ and $\dfrac{dA}{dt} = 3$, find $\left.\dfrac{dx}{dt}\right|_{x=10}$.

3. A 10-foot ladder stands on a horizontal floor and leans against a vertical wall. Use x to denote the distance along the floor from the wall to the foot of the ladder, and use y to denote the distance along the wall from the floor to the top of the ladder. If the foot of the ladder is dragged away from the wall, find an equation that relates rates of change of x and y with respect to time.

4. Suppose that a block of ice in the shape of a right circular cylinder melts so that it retains its cylindrical shape. Find an equation that relates the rates of change of the volume (V), height (h), and radius (r) of the block of ice.

EXERCISE SET 3.4

1–4 Both x and y denote functions of t that are related by the given equation. Use this equation and the given derivative information to find the specified derivative. ■

1. Equation: $y = 3x + 5$.
   (a) Given that $dx/dt = 2$, find dy/dt when $x = 1$.
   (b) Given that $dy/dt = -1$, find dx/dt when $x = 0$.

2. Equation: $x + 4y = 3$.
   (a) Given that $dx/dt = 1$, find dy/dt when $x = 2$.
   (b) Given that $dy/dt = 4$, find dx/dt when $x = 3$.

3. Equation: $4x^2 + 9y^2 = 1$.
   (a) Given that $dx/dt = 3$, find dy/dt when
      $(x, y) = \left(\frac{1}{2\sqrt{2}}, \frac{1}{3\sqrt{2}}\right)$.   *(cont.)*

(b) Given that $dy/dt = 8$, find dx/dt when $(x, y) = \left(\frac{1}{3}, -\frac{\sqrt{5}}{9}\right)$.

4. Equation: $x^2 + y^2 = 2x + 4y$.
   (a) Given that $dx/dt = -5$, find dy/dt when $(x, y) = (3, 1)$.
   (b) Given that $dy/dt = 6$, find dx/dt when $(x, y) = (1 + \sqrt{2}, 2 + \sqrt{3})$.

FOCUS ON CONCEPTS

5. Let A be the area of a square whose sides have length x, and assume that x varies with the time t.
   (a) Draw a picture of the square with the labels A and x placed appropriately.
   (b) Write an equation that relates A and x.
   (c) Use the equation in part (b) to find an equation that relates dA/dt and dx/dt.
   (d) At a certain instant the sides are 3 ft long and increasing at a rate of 2 ft/min. How fast is the area increasing at that instant?

6. In parts (a)–(d), let A be the area of a circle of radius r, and assume that r increases with the time t.
   (a) Draw a picture of the circle with the labels A and r placed appropriately.
   (b) Write an equation that relates A and r.
   (c) Use the equation in part (b) to find an equation that relates dA/dt and dr/dt.
   (d) At a certain instant the radius is 5 cm and increasing at the rate of 2 cm/s. How fast is the area increasing at that instant?

7. Let V be the volume of a cylinder having height h and radius r, and assume that h and r vary with time.
   (a) How are dV/dt, dh/dt, and dr/dt related?
   (b) At a certain instant, the height is 6 in and increasing at 1 in/s, while the radius is 10 in and decreasing at 1 in/s. How fast is the volume changing at that instant? Is the volume increasing or decreasing at that instant?

8. Let l be the length of a diagonal of a rectangle whose sides have lengths x and y, and assume that x and y vary with time.
   (a) How are dl/dt, dx/dt, and dy/dt related?
   (b) If x increases at a constant rate of $\frac{1}{2}$ ft/s and y decreases at a constant rate of $\frac{1}{4}$ ft/s, how fast is the size of the diagonal changing when $x = 3$ ft and $y = 4$ ft? Is the diagonal increasing or decreasing at that instant?

9. Let θ (in radians) be an acute angle in a right triangle, and let x and y, respectively, be the lengths of the sides adjacent to and opposite θ. Suppose also that x and y vary with time.
   (a) How are $d\theta/dt$, dx/dt, and dy/dt related?
   (b) At a certain instant, $x = 2$ units and is increasing at 1 unit/s, while $y = 2$ units and is decreasing at $\frac{1}{4}$ unit/s. How fast is θ changing at that instant? Is θ increasing or decreasing at that instant?

10. Suppose that $z = x^3 y^2$, where both x and y are changing with time. At a certain instant when $x = 1$ and $y = 2$, x is decreasing at the rate of 2 units/s, and y is increasing at the rate of 3 units/s. How fast is z changing at this instant? Is z increasing or decreasing?

11. The minute hand of a certain clock is 4 in long. Starting from the moment when the hand is pointing straight up, how fast is the area of the sector that is swept out by the hand increasing at any instant during the next revolution of the hand?

12. A stone dropped into a still pond sends out a circular ripple whose radius increases at a constant rate of 3 ft/s. How rapidly is the area enclosed by the ripple increasing at the end of 10 s?

13. Oil spilled from a ruptured tanker spreads in a circle whose area increases at a constant rate of 6 mi²/h. How fast is the radius of the spill increasing when the area is 9 mi²?

14. A spherical balloon is inflated so that its volume is increasing at the rate of 3 ft³/min. How fast is the diameter of the balloon increasing when the radius is 1 ft?

15. A spherical balloon is to be deflated so that its radius decreases at a constant rate of 15 cm/min. At what rate must air be removed when the radius is 9 cm?

16. A 17 ft ladder is leaning against a wall. If the bottom of the ladder is pulled along the ground away from the wall at a constant rate of 5 ft/s, how fast will the top of the ladder be moving down the wall when it is 8 ft above the ground?

17. A 13 ft ladder is leaning against a wall. If the top of the ladder slips down the wall at a rate of 2 ft/s, how fast will the foot be moving away from the wall when the top is 5 ft above the ground?

18. A 10 ft plank is leaning against a wall. If at a certain instant the bottom of the plank is 2 ft from the wall and is being pushed toward the wall at the rate of 6 in/s, how fast is the acute angle that the plank makes with the ground increasing?

19. A softball diamond is a square whose sides are 60 ft long. Suppose that a player running from first to second base has a speed of 25 ft/s at the instant when she is 10 ft from second base. At what rate is the player's distance from home plate changing at that instant?

20. A rocket, rising vertically, is tracked by a radar station that is on the ground 5 mi from the launchpad. How fast is the rocket rising when it is 4 mi high and its distance from the radar station is increasing at a rate of 2000 mi/h?

21. For the camera and rocket shown in Figure 3.4.5, at what rate is the camera-to-rocket distance changing when the rocket is 4000 ft up and rising vertically at 880 ft/s?

22. For the camera and rocket shown in Figure 3.4.5, at what rate is the rocket rising when the elevation angle is $\pi/4$ radians and increasing at a rate of 0.2 rad/s?

23. A satellite is in an elliptical orbit around the Earth. Its distance r (in miles) from the center of the Earth is given by

$$r = \frac{4995}{1 + 0.12 \cos \theta}$$

where θ is the angle measured from the point on the orbit nearest the Earth's surface (see the accompanying figure).

(a) Find the altitude of the satellite at **perigee** (the point nearest the surface of the Earth) and at **apogee** (the point farthest from the surface of the Earth). Use 3960 mi as the radius of the Earth.

(b) At the instant when θ is $120°$, the angle θ is increasing at the rate of $2.7°/\text{min}$. Find the altitude of the satellite and the rate at which the altitude is changing at this instant. Express the rate in units of mi/min.

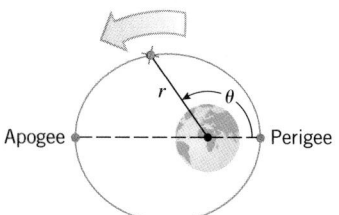

◀ **Figure Ex-23**

24. An aircraft is flying horizontally at a constant height of 4000 ft above a fixed observation point (see the accompanying figure). At a certain instant the angle of elevation θ is $30°$ and decreasing, and the speed of the aircraft is 300 mi/h.

(a) How fast is θ decreasing at this instant? Express the result in units of deg/s.

(b) How fast is the distance between the aircraft and the observation point changing at this instant? Express the result in units of ft/s. Use 1 mi = 5280 ft.

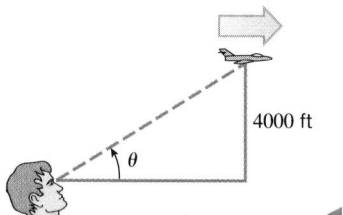

4000 ft

θ

◀ **Figure Ex-24**

25. A conical water tank with vertex down has a radius of 10 ft at the top and is 24 ft high. If water flows into the tank at a rate of 20 ft³/min, how fast is the depth of the water increasing when the water is 16 ft deep?

26. Grain pouring from a chute at the rate of 8 ft³/min forms a conical pile whose height is always twice its radius. How fast is the height of the pile increasing at the instant when the pile is 6 ft high?

27. Sand pouring from a chute forms a conical pile whose height is always equal to the diameter. If the height increases at a constant rate of 5 ft/min, at what rate is sand pouring from the chute when the pile is 10 ft high?

28. Wheat is poured through a chute at the rate of 10 ft³/min and falls in a conical pile whose bottom radius is always half the altitude. How fast will the circumference of the base be increasing when the pile is 8 ft high?

29. An aircraft is climbing at a $30°$ angle to the horizontal. How fast is the aircraft gaining altitude if its speed is 500 mi/h?

30. A boat is pulled into a dock by means of a rope attached to a pulley on the dock (see the accompanying figure). The rope is attached to the bow of the boat at a point 10 ft below the pulley. If the rope is pulled through the pulley at a rate of 20 ft/min, at what rate will the boat be approaching the dock when 125 ft of rope is out?

Pulley

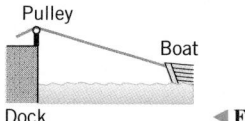

Boat

Dock   ◀ **Figure Ex-30**

31. For the boat in Exercise 30, how fast must the rope be pulled if we want the boat to approach the dock at a rate of 12 ft/min at the instant when 125 ft of rope is out?

32. A man 6 ft tall is walking at the rate of 3 ft/s toward a streetlight 18 ft high (see the accompanying figure).

(a) At what rate is his shadow length changing?

(b) How fast is the tip of his shadow moving?

◀ **Figure Ex-32**

33. A beacon that makes one revolution every 10 s is located on a ship anchored 4 kilometers from a straight shoreline. How fast is the beam moving along the shoreline when it makes an angle of $45°$ with the shore?

34. An aircraft is flying at a constant altitude with a constant speed of 600 mi/h. An antiaircraft missile is fired on a straight line perpendicular to the flight path of the aircraft so that it will hit the aircraft at a point P (see the accompanying figure). At the instant the aircraft is 2 mi from the impact point P the missile is 4 mi from P and flying at 1200 mi/h. At that instant, how rapidly is the distance between missile and aircraft decreasing?

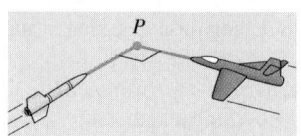

◀ **Figure Ex-34**

35. Solve Exercise 34 under the assumption that the angle between the flight paths is 120° instead of the assumption that the paths are perpendicular. [*Hint:* Use the law of cosines.]

36. A police helicopter is flying due north at 100 mi/h and at a constant altitude of $\frac{1}{2}$ mi. Below, a car is traveling west on a highway at 75 mi/h. At the moment the helicopter crosses over the highway the car is 2 mi east of the helicopter.
(a) How fast is the distance between the car and helicopter changing at the moment the helicopter crosses the highway?
(b) Is the distance between the car and helicopter increasing or decreasing at that moment?

37. A particle is moving along the curve whose equation is
$$\frac{xy^3}{1+y^2} = \frac{8}{5}$$
Assume that the x-coordinate is increasing at the rate of 6 units/s when the particle is at the point $(1, 2)$.
(a) At what rate is the y-coordinate of the point changing at that instant?
(b) Is the particle rising or falling at that instant?

38. A point P is moving along the curve whose equation is $y = \sqrt{x^3 + 17}$. When P is at $(2, 5)$, y is increasing at the rate of 2 units/s. How fast is x changing?

39. A point P is moving along the line whose equation is $y = 2x$. How fast is the distance between P and the point $(3, 0)$ changing at the instant when P is at $(3, 6)$ if x is decreasing at the rate of 2 units/s at that instant?

40. A point P is moving along the curve whose equation is $y = \sqrt{x}$. Suppose that x is increasing at the rate of 4 units/s when $x = 3$.
(a) How fast is the distance between P and the point $(2, 0)$ changing at this instant?
(b) How fast is the angle of inclination of the line segment from P to $(2, 0)$ changing at this instant?

41. A particle is moving along the curve $y = x/(x^2 + 1)$. Find all values of x at which the rate of change of x with respect to time is three times that of y. [Assume that dx/dt is never zero.]

42. A particle is moving along the curve $16x^2 + 9y^2 = 144$. Find all points (x, y) at which the rates of change of x and y with respect to time are equal. [Assume that dx/dt and dy/dt are never both zero at the same point.]

43. The *thin lens equation* in physics is
$$\frac{1}{s} + \frac{1}{S} = \frac{1}{f}$$
where s is the object distance from the lens, S is the image distance from the lens, and f is the focal length of the lens. Suppose that a certain lens has a focal length of 6 cm and that an object is moving toward the lens at the rate of 2 cm/s. How fast is the image distance changing at the instant when the object is 10 cm from the lens? Is the image moving away from the lens or toward the lens?

44. Water is stored in a cone-shaped reservoir (vertex down). Assuming the water evaporates at a rate proportional to the surface area exposed to the air, show that the depth of the water will decrease at a constant rate that does not depend on the dimensions of the reservoir.

45. A meteor enters the Earth's atmosphere and burns up at a rate that, at each instant, is proportional to its surface area. Assuming that the meteor is always spherical, show that the radius decreases at a constant rate.

46. On a certain clock the minute hand is 4 in long and the hour hand is 3 in long. How fast is the distance between the tips of the hands changing at 9 o'clock?

47. Coffee is poured at a uniform rate of 20 cm³/s into a cup whose inside is shaped like a truncated cone (see the accompanying figure). If the upper and lower radii of the cup are 4 cm and 2 cm and the height of the cup is 6 cm, how fast will the coffee level be rising when the coffee is halfway up? [*Hint:* Extend the cup downward to form a cone.]

◀ **Figure Ex-47**

✔ **QUICK CHECK ANSWERS 3.4**

1. 60 **2.** $\dfrac{3}{20}$ **3.** $x\dfrac{dx}{dt} + y\dfrac{dy}{dt} = 0$ **4.** $\dfrac{dV}{dt} = 2\pi rh\dfrac{dr}{dt} + \pi r^2\dfrac{dh}{dt}$

3.5 LOCAL LINEAR APPROXIMATION; DIFFERENTIALS

In this section we will show how derivatives can be used to approximate nonlinear functions by linear functions. Also, up to now we have been interpreting dy/dx as a single entity representing the derivative. In this section we will define the quantities dx and dy themselves, thereby allowing us to interpret dy/dx as an actual ratio.

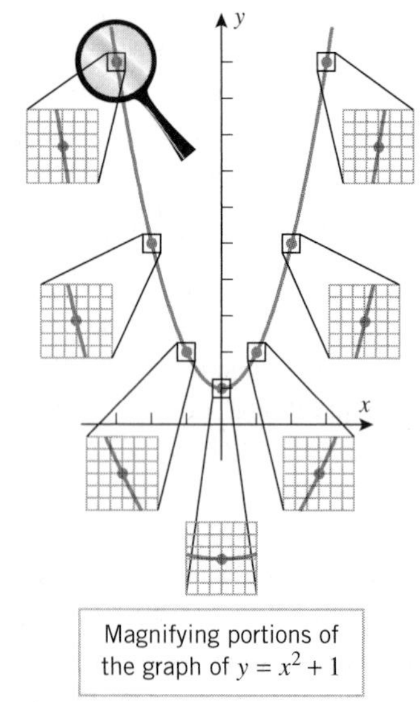

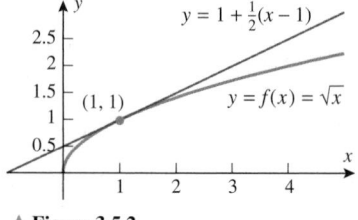

Magnifying portions of
the graph of $y = x^2 + 1$

▲ **Figure 3.5.1**

Recall from Section 2.2 that if a function f is differentiable at x_0, then a sufficiently magnified portion of the graph of f centered at the point $P(x_0, f(x_0))$ takes on the appearance of a straight line segment. Figure 3.5.1 illustrates this at several points on the graph of $y = x^2 + 1$. For this reason, a function that is differentiable at x_0 is sometimes said to be *locally linear* at x_0.

The line that best approximates the graph of f in the vicinity of $P(x_0, f(x_0))$ is the tangent line to the graph of f at x_0, given by the equation

$$y = f(x_0) + f'(x_0)(x - x_0)$$

[see Formula (3) of Section 2.2]. Thus, for values of x near x_0 we can approximate values of $f(x)$ by

$$f(x) \approx f(x_0) + f'(x_0)(x - x_0) \tag{1}$$

This is called the *local linear approximation* of f at x_0. This formula can also be expressed in terms of the increment $\Delta x = x - x_0$ as

$$f(x_0 + \Delta x) \approx f(x_0) + f'(x_0)\Delta x \tag{2}$$

▶ **Example 1**

(a) Find the local linear approximation of $f(x) = \sqrt{x}$ at $x_0 = 1$.

(b) Use the local linear approximation obtained in part (a) to approximate $\sqrt{1.1}$, and compare your approximation to the result produced directly by a calculating utility.

Solution (a). Since $f'(x) = 1/(2\sqrt{x})$, it follows from (1) that the local linear approximation of $\sqrt{x}$ at a point x_0 is

$$\sqrt{x} \approx \sqrt{x_0} + \frac{1}{2\sqrt{x_0}}(x - x_0)$$

Thus, the local linear approximation at $x_0 = 1$ is

$$\sqrt{x} \approx 1 + \tfrac{1}{2}(x - 1) \tag{3}$$

The graphs of $y = \sqrt{x}$ and the local linear approximation $y = 1 + \tfrac{1}{2}(x - 1)$ are shown in Figure 3.5.2.

Solution (b). Applying (3) with $x = 1.1$ yields

$$\sqrt{1.1} \approx 1 + \tfrac{1}{2}(1.1 - 1) = 1.05$$

Since the tangent line $y = 1 + \tfrac{1}{2}(x - 1)$ in Figure 3.5.2 lies above the graph of $f(x) = \sqrt{x}$, we would expect this approximation to be slightly too large. This expectation is confirmed by the calculator approximation $\sqrt{1.1} \approx 1.04881$. ◀

$y = 1 + \tfrac{1}{2}(x - 1)$

$(1, 1)$

$y = f(x) = \sqrt{x}$

▲ **Figure 3.5.2**

Examples 1 and 2 illustrate important ideas and are not meant to suggest that you should use local linear approximations for computations that your calculating utility can perform. The main application of local linear approximation is in modeling problems where it is useful to replace complicated functions by simpler ones.

▶ **Example 2**

(a) Find the local linear approximation of $f(x) = \sin x$ at $x_0 = 0$.

(b) Use the local linear approximation obtained in part (a) to approximate $\sin 2°$, and compare your approximation to the result produced directly by your calculating device.

Solution (a). Since $f'(x) = \cos x$, it follows from (1) that the local linear approximation of $\sin x$ at a point x_0 is
$$\sin x \approx \sin x_0 + (\cos x_0)(x - x_0)$$

Thus, the local linear approximation at $x_0 = 0$ is
$$\sin x \approx \sin 0 + (\cos 0)(x - 0)$$

which simplifies to
$$\sin x \approx x \tag{4}$$

Solution (b). The variable x in (4) is in radian measure, so we must first convert $2°$ to radians before we can apply this approximation. Since
$$2° = 2\left(\frac{\pi}{180}\right) = \frac{\pi}{90} \approx 0.0349066 \text{ radian}$$

it follows from (4) that $\sin 2° \approx 0.0349066$. Comparing the two graphs in Figure 3.5.3, we would expect this approximation to be slightly larger than the exact value. The calculator approximation $\sin 2° \approx 0.0348995$ shows that this is indeed the case. ◀

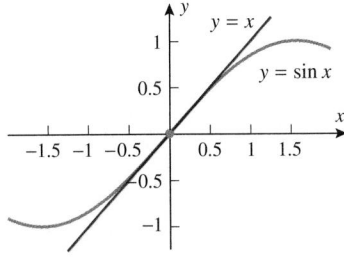

▲ **Figure 3.5.3**

ERROR IN LOCAL LINEAR APPROXIMATIONS

As a general rule, the accuracy of the local linear approximation to $f(x)$ at x_0 will deteriorate as x gets progressively farther from x_0. To illustrate this for the approximation $\sin x \approx x$ in Example 2, let us graph the function
$$E(x) = |\sin x - x|$$

which is the absolute value of the error in the approximation (Figure 3.5.4).

In Figure 3.5.4, the graph shows how the absolute error in the local linear approximation of $\sin x$ increases as x moves progressively farther from 0 in either the positive or negative direction. The graph also tells us that for values of x between the two vertical lines, the absolute error does not exceed 0.01. Thus, for example, we could use the local linear approximation $\sin x \approx x$ for all values of x in the interval $-0.35 < x < 0.35$ (radians) with confidence that the approximation is within ± 0.01 of the exact value.

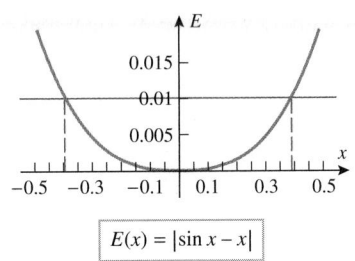

$E(x) = |\sin x - x|$

▲ **Figure 3.5.4**

DIFFERENTIALS

Newton and Leibniz each used a different notation when they published their discoveries of calculus, thereby creating a notational divide between Britain and the European continent that lasted for more than 50 years. The **Leibniz notation** dy/dx eventually prevailed because it suggests correct formulas in a natural way, the chain rule
$$\frac{dy}{dx} = \frac{dy}{du} \cdot \frac{du}{dx}$$

being a good example.

Up to now we have interpreted dy/dx as a single entity representing the derivative of y with respect to x; the symbols "dy" and "dx," which are called **differentials**, have had no meanings attached to them. Our next goal is to define these symbols in such a way that dy/dx can be treated as an actual ratio. To do this, assume that f is differentiable at a point x, *define* dx to be an independent variable that can have any real value, and *define* dy by the formula
$$dy = f'(x)\, dx \tag{5}$$

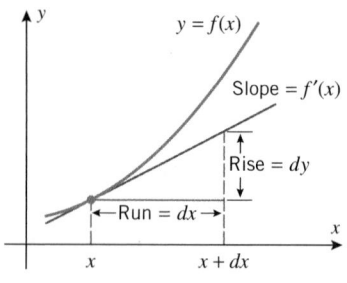

▲ **Figure 3.5.5**

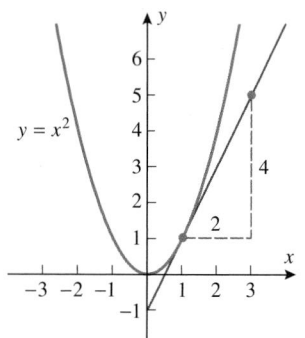

▲ **Figure 3.5.6**

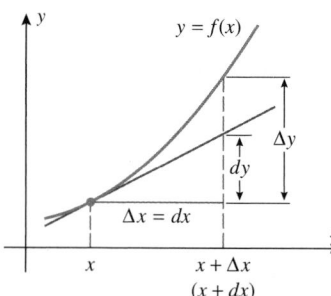

▲ **Figure 3.5.7**

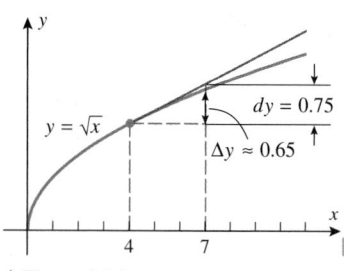

▲ **Figure 3.5.8**

If $dx \neq 0$, then we can divide both sides of (5) by dx to obtain

$$\frac{dy}{dx} = f'(x) \qquad (6)$$

Thus, we have achieved our goal of defining dy and dx so their ratio is $f'(x)$. Formula (5) is said to express (6) in **differential form**.

To interpret (5) geometrically, note that $f'(x)$ is the slope of the tangent line to the graph of f at x. The differentials dy and dx can be viewed as a corresponding rise and run of this tangent line (Figure 3.5.5).

▶ **Example 3** Express the derivative with respect to x of $y = x^2$ in differential form, and discuss the relationship between dy and dx at $x = 1$.

Solution. The derivative of y with respect to x is $dy/dx = 2x$, which can be expressed in differential form as

$$dy = 2x\, dx$$

When $x = 1$ this becomes

$$dy = 2\, dx$$

This tells us that if we travel along the tangent line to the curve $y = x^2$ at $x = 1$, then a change of dx units in x produces a change of $2\, dx$ units in y. Thus, for example, a run of $dx = 2$ units produces a rise of $dy = 4$ units along the tangent line (Figure 3.5.6). ◀

It is important to understand the distinction between the increment Δy and the differential dy. To see the difference, let us assign the independent variables dx and Δx the same value, so $dx = \Delta x$. Then Δy represents the change in y that occurs when we start at x and travel *along the curve* $y = f(x)$ until we have moved $\Delta x\ (= dx)$ units in the x-direction, while dy represents the change in y that occurs if we start at x and travel *along the tangent line* until we have moved $dx\ (= \Delta x)$ units in the x-direction (Figure 3.5.7).

▶ **Example 4** Let $y = \sqrt{x}$. Find dy and Δy at $x = 4$ with $dx = \Delta x = 3$. Then make a sketch of $y = \sqrt{x}$, showing dy and Δy in the picture.

Solution. With $f(x) = \sqrt{x}$ we obtain

$$\Delta y = f(x + \Delta x) - f(x) = \sqrt{x + \Delta x} - \sqrt{x} = \sqrt{7} - \sqrt{4} \approx 0.65$$

If $y = \sqrt{x}$, then

$$\frac{dy}{dx} = \frac{1}{2\sqrt{x}}, \quad \text{so} \quad dy = \frac{1}{2\sqrt{x}}\, dx = \frac{1}{2\sqrt{4}}(3) = \frac{3}{4} = 0.75$$

Figure 3.5.8 shows the curve $y = \sqrt{x}$ together with dy and Δy. ◀

■ **LOCAL LINEAR APPROXIMATION FROM THE DIFFERENTIAL POINT OF VIEW**

Although Δy and dy are generally different, the differential dy will nonetheless be a good approximation of Δy provided $dx = \Delta x$ is close to 0. To see this, recall from Section 2.2 that

$$f'(x) = \lim_{\Delta x \to 0} \frac{\Delta y}{\Delta x}$$

It follows that if Δx is close to 0, then we will have $f'(x) \approx \Delta y / \Delta x$ or, equivalently,

$$\Delta y \approx f'(x) \Delta x$$

If we agree to let $dx = \Delta x$, then we can rewrite this as

$$\Delta y \approx f'(x)\, dx = dy \qquad (7)$$

In words, this states that for values of dx near zero the differential dy closely approximates the increment Δy (Figure 3.5.7). But this is to be expected since the graph of the tangent line at x is the local linear approximation of the graph of f.

■ ERROR PROPAGATION

In real-world applications, small errors in measured quantities will invariably occur. These measurement errors are of importance in scientific research—all scientific measurements come with measurement errors included. For example, your height might be measured as 170 ± 0.5 cm, meaning that your exact height lies somewhere between 169.5 and 170.5 cm. Researchers often must use these inexactly measured quantities to compute other quantities, thereby *propagating* the errors from the measured quantitites to the computed quantities. This phenomenon is called ***error propagation***. Researchers must be able to estimate errors in the computed quantities. Our goal is to show how to estimate these errors using local linear approximation and differentials. For this purpose, suppose

x_0 is the exact value of the quantity being measured
$y_0 = f(x_0)$ is the exact value of the quantity being computed
x is the measured value of x_0
$y = f(x)$ is the computed value of y

We define $dx\,(=\Delta x) = x - x_0$ to be the ***measurement error*** of x
$\Delta y = f(x) - f(x_0)$ to be the ***propagated error*** of y

It follows from (7) with x_0 replacing x that the propagated error Δy can be approximated by

$$\Delta y \approx dy = f'(x_0)\,dx \qquad (8)$$

Unfortunately, there is a practical difficulty in applying this formula since the value of x_0 is unknown. (Keep in mind that only the measured value x is known to the researcher.) This being the case, it is standard practice in research to use the measured value x in place of x_0 in (8) and use the approximation

$$\Delta y \approx dy = f'(x)\,dx \qquad (9)$$

for the propagated error.

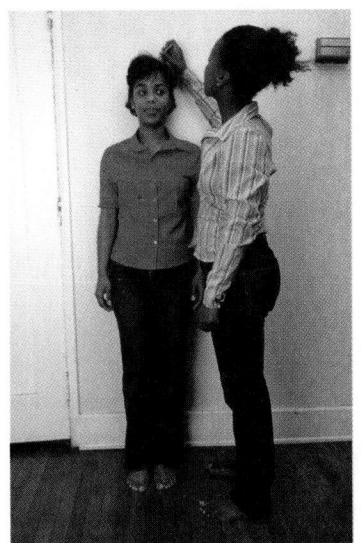

© Michael Newman/PhotoEdit

Real-world measurements inevitably have small errors.

Note that measurement error is positive if the measured value is greater than the exact value and is negative if it is less than the exact value. The sign of the propagated error conveys similar information.

Explain why an error estimate of at most $\pm\frac{1}{32}$ inch is reasonable for a ruler that is calibrated in sixteenths of an inch.

▶ **Example 5**   Suppose that the side of a square is measured with a ruler to be 10 inches with a measurement error of at most $\pm\frac{1}{32}$ in. Estimate the error in the computed area of the square.

Solution.   Let x denote the exact length of a side and y the exact area so that $y = x^2$. It follows from (9) with $f(x) = x^2$ that if dx is the measurement error, then the propagated error Δy can be approximated as

$$\Delta y \approx dy = 2x\,dx$$

Substituting the measured value $x = 10$ into this equation yields

$$dy = 20\,dx \qquad (10)$$

But to say that the measurement error is at most $\pm\frac{1}{32}$ means that

$$-\frac{1}{32} \le dx \le \frac{1}{32}$$

Multiplying these inequalities through by 20 and applying (10) yields

$$20\left(-\tfrac{1}{32}\right) \le dy \le 20\left(\tfrac{1}{32}\right) \quad \text{or equivalently} \quad -\tfrac{5}{8} \le dy \le \tfrac{5}{8}$$

Thus, the propagated error in the area is estimated to be within $\pm\frac{5}{8}$ in^2. ◀

If the true value of a quantity is q and a measurement or calculation produces an error Δq, then $\Delta q / q$ is called the ***relative error*** in the measurement or calculation; when expressed as a percentage, $\Delta q / q$ is called the ***percentage error***. As a practical matter, the true value q is usually unknown, so that the measured or calculated value of q is used instead; and the relative error is approximated by dq/q.

▶ **Example 6** The radius of a sphere is measured with a percentage error within $\pm 0.04\%$. Estimate the percentage error in the calculated volume of the sphere.

Solution. The volume V of a sphere is $V = \frac{4}{3}\pi r^3$, so

$$\frac{dV}{dr} = 4\pi r^2$$

from which it follows that $dV = 4\pi r^2\, dr$. Thus, the relative error in V is approximately

$$\frac{dV}{V} = \frac{4\pi r^2\, dr}{\frac{4}{3}\pi r^3} = 3\frac{dr}{r} \tag{11}$$

> Formula (11) tells us that, as a rule of thumb, the percentage error in the computed volume of a sphere is approximately 3 times the percentage error in the measured value of its radius. As a rule of thumb, how is the percentage error in the computed area of a square related to the percentage error in the measured value of a side?

We are given that the relative error in the measured value of r is $\pm 0.04\%$, which means that

$$-0.0004 \le \frac{dr}{r} \le 0.0004$$

Multiplying these inequalities through by 3 and applying (11) yields

$$3(-0.0004) \le \frac{dV}{V} \le 3(0.0004) \quad \text{or equivalently} \quad -0.0012 \le \frac{dV}{V} \le 0.0012$$

Thus, we estimate the percentage error in the calculated value of V to be within $\pm 0.12\%$.

◀

▮ MORE NOTATION; DIFFERENTIAL FORMULAS

The symbol df is another common notation for the differential of a function $y = f(x)$. For example, if $f(x) = \sin x$, then we can write $df = \cos x\, dx$. We can also view the symbol "d" as an *operator* that acts on a function to produce the corresponding differential. For example, $d[x^2] = 2x\, dx$, $d[\sin x] = \cos x\, dx$, and so on. All of the general rules of differentiation then have corresponding differential versions:

DERIVATIVE FORMULA	DIFFERENTIAL FORMULA
$\dfrac{d}{dx}[c] = 0$	$d[c] = 0$
$\dfrac{d}{dx}[cf] = c\dfrac{df}{dx}$	$d[cf] = c\, df$
$\dfrac{d}{dx}[f+g] = \dfrac{df}{dx} + \dfrac{dg}{dx}$	$d[f+g] = df + dg$
$\dfrac{d}{dx}[fg] = f\dfrac{dg}{dx} + g\dfrac{df}{dx}$	$d[fg] = f\, dg + g\, df$
$\dfrac{d}{dx}\left[\dfrac{f}{g}\right] = \dfrac{g\dfrac{df}{dx} - f\dfrac{dg}{dx}}{g^2}$	$d\left[\dfrac{f}{g}\right] = \dfrac{g\, df - f\, dg}{g^2}$

For example,

$$
\begin{aligned}
d[x^2 \sin x] &= (x^2 \cos x + 2x \sin x)\, dx \\
&= x^2(\cos x\, dx) + (2x\, dx)\sin x \\
&= x^2 d[\sin x] + (\sin x)\, d[x^2]
\end{aligned}
$$

illustrates the differential version of the product rule.

✔ **QUICK CHECK EXERCISES 3.5**   *(See page 219 for answers.)*

1. The local linear approximation of f at x_0 uses the _____ line to the graph of $y = f(x)$ at $x = x_0$ to approximate values of _____ for values of x near _____.

2. Find an equation for the local linear approximation to $y = 5 - x^2$ at $x_0 = 2$.

3. Let $y = 5 - x^2$. Find dy and Δy at $x = 2$ with $dx = \Delta x = 0.1$.

4. The intensity of light from a light source is a function $I = f(x)$ of the distance x from the light source. Suppose that a small gemstone is measured to be 10 m from a light source, $f(10) = 0.2 \text{ W/m}^2$, and $f'(10) = -0.04 \text{ W/m}^3$. If the distance $x = 10$ m was obtained with a measurement error within ± 0.05 m, estimate the percentage error in the calculated intensity of the light on the gemstone.

EXERCISE SET 3.5   ▱ Graphing Utility

1. (a) Use Formula (1) to obtain the local linear approximation of x^3 at $x_0 = 1$.
   (b) Use Formula (2) to rewrite the approximation obtained in part (a) in terms of Δx.
   (c) Use the result obtained in part (a) to approximate $(1.02)^3$, and confirm that the formula obtained in part (b) produces the same result.

2. (a) Use Formula (1) to obtain the local linear approximation of $1/x$ at $x_0 = 2$.
   (b) Use Formula (2) to rewrite the approximation obtained in part (a) in terms of Δx.
   (c) Use the result obtained in part (a) to approximate $1/2.05$, and confirm that the formula obtained in part (b) produces the same result.

FOCUS ON CONCEPTS

3. (a) Find the local linear approximation of the function $f(x) = \sqrt{1 + x}$ at $x_0 = 0$, and use it to approximate $\sqrt{0.9}$ and $\sqrt{1.1}$.
   (b) Graph f and its tangent line at x_0 together, and use the graphs to illustrate the relationship between the exact values and the approximations of $\sqrt{0.9}$ and $\sqrt{1.1}$.

4. A student claims that whenever a local linear approximation is used to approximate the square root of a number, the approximation is too large.
   (a) Write a few sentences that make the student's claim precise, and justify this claim geometrically.
   (b) Verify the student's claim algebraically using approximation (1).

5–10 Confirm that the stated formula is the local linear approximation at $x_0 = 0$. ▨

5. $(1 + x)^{15} \approx 1 + 15x$

6. $\dfrac{1}{\sqrt{1 - x}} \approx 1 + \dfrac{1}{2}x$

7. $\tan x \approx x$

8. $\dfrac{1}{1 + x} \approx 1 - x$

9. $e^x \approx 1 + x$

10. $\ln(1 + x) \approx x$

11–16 Confirm that the stated formula is the local linear approximation of f at $x_0 = 1$, where $\Delta x = x - 1$. ▨

11. $f(x) = x^4$; $(1 + \Delta x)^4 \approx 1 + 4\Delta x$

12. $f(x) = \sqrt{x}$; $\sqrt{1 + \Delta x} \approx 1 + \dfrac{1}{2}\Delta x$

13. $f(x) = \dfrac{1}{2 + x}$; $\dfrac{1}{3 + \Delta x} \approx \dfrac{1}{3} - \dfrac{1}{9}\Delta x$

14. $f(x) = (4 + x)^3$; $(5 + \Delta x)^3 \approx 125 + 75\Delta x$

15. $\tan^{-1} x$; $\tan^{-1}(1 + \Delta x) \approx \dfrac{\pi}{4} + \dfrac{1}{2}\Delta x$

16. $\sin^{-1}\left(\dfrac{x}{2}\right)$; $\sin^{-1}\left(\dfrac{1}{2} + \dfrac{1}{2}\Delta x\right) \approx \dfrac{\pi}{6} + \dfrac{1}{\sqrt{3}}\Delta x$

▱ **17–20** Confirm that the formula is the local linear approximation at $x_0 = 0$, and use a graphing utility to estimate an interval of x-values on which the error is at most ± 0.1. ▨

17. $\sqrt{x + 3} \approx \sqrt{3} + \dfrac{1}{2\sqrt{3}}x$

18. $\dfrac{1}{\sqrt{9 - x}} \approx \dfrac{1}{3} + \dfrac{1}{54}x$

19. $\tan 2x \approx 2x$

20. $\dfrac{1}{(1 + 2x)^5} \approx 1 - 10x$

21. (a) Use the local linear approximation of $\sin x$ at $x_0 = 0$ obtained in Example 2 to approximate $\sin 1°$, and compare the approximation to the result produced directly by your calculating device.
   (b) How would you choose x_0 to approximate $\sin 44°$?
   (c) Approximate $\sin 44°$; compare the approximation to the result produced directly by your calculating device.

22. (a) Use the local linear approximation of $\tan x$ at $x_0 = 0$ to approximate $\tan 2°$, and compare the approximation to the result produced directly by your calculating device.
   (b) How would you choose x_0 to approximate $\tan 61°$?
   (c) Approximate $\tan 61°$; compare the approximation to the result produced directly by your calculating device.

23–31 Use an appropriate local linear approximation to estimate the value of the given quantity. ▨

23. $(3.02)^4$

24. $(1.97)^3$

25. $\sqrt{65}$

26. $\sqrt{24}$ **27.** $\sqrt{80.9}$ **28.** $\sqrt{36.03}$

29. $\sin 0.1$ **30.** $\tan 0.2$ **31.** $\cos 31°$

32. $\ln(1.01)$ **33.** $\tan^{-1}(0.99)$

FOCUS ON CONCEPTS

34. The approximation $(1 + x)^k \approx 1 + kx$ is commonly used by engineers for quick calculations.
  (a) Derive this result, and use it to make a rough estimate of $(1.001)^{37}$.
  (b) Compare your estimate to that produced directly by your calculating device.
  (c) If k is a positive integer, how is the approximation $(1 + x)^k \approx 1 + kx$ related to the expansion of $(1 + x)^k$ using the binomial theorem?

35. Use the approximation $(1 + x)^k \approx 1 + kx$, along with some mental arithmetic to show that $\sqrt[3]{8.24} \approx 2.02$ and $4.08^{3/2} \approx 8.24$.

36. Referring to the accompanying figure, suppose that the angle of elevation of the top of the building, as measured from a point 500 ft from its base, is found to be $\theta = 6°$. Use an appropriate local linear approximation, along with some mental arithmetic to show that the building is about 52 ft high.

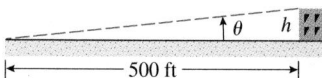

|← 500 ft →| ◀ **Figure Ex-36**

37. (a) Let $y = x^2$. Find dy and Δy at $x = 2$ with $dx = \Delta x = 1$.
  (b) Sketch the graph of $y = x^2$, showing dy and Δy in the picture.

38. (a) Let $y = x^3$. Find dy and Δy at $x = 1$ with $dx = \Delta x = 1$.
  (b) Sketch the graph of $y = x^3$, showing dy and Δy in the picture.

39–42 Find formulas for dy and Δy. ■

39. $y = x^3$ **40.** $y = 8x - 4$

41. $y = x^2 - 2x + 1$ **42.** $y = \sin x$

43–46 Find the differential dy. ■

43. (a) $y = 4x^3 - 7x^2$ (b) $y = x \cos x$

44. (a) $y = 1/x$ (b) $y = 5 \tan x$

45. (a) $y = x\sqrt{1 - x}$ (b) $y = (1 + x)^{-17}$

46. (a) $y = \dfrac{1}{x^3 - 1}$ (b) $y = \dfrac{1 - x^3}{2 - x}$

47–50 True–False Determine whether the statement is true or false. Explain your answer. ■

47. A differential dy is defined to be a very small change in y.

48. The error in approximation (2) is the same as the error in approximation (7).

49. A local linear approximation to a function can never be identically equal to the function.

50. A local linear approximation to a nonconstant function can never be constant.

51–54 Use the differential dy to approximate Δy when x changes as indicated. ■

51. $y = \sqrt{3x - 2}$; from $x = 2$ to $x = 2.03$

52. $y = \sqrt{x^2 + 8}$; from $x = 1$ to $x = 0.97$

53. $y = \dfrac{x}{x^2 + 1}$; from $x = 2$ to $x = 1.96$

54. $y = x\sqrt{8x + 1}$; from $x = 3$ to $x = 3.05$

55. The side of a square is measured to be 10 ft, with a possible error of ± 0.1 ft.
  (a) Use differentials to estimate the error in the calculated area.
  (b) Estimate the percentage errors in the side and the area.

56. The side of a cube is measured to be 25 cm, with a possible error of ± 1 cm.
  (a) Use differentials to estimate the error in the calculated volume.
  (b) Estimate the percentage errors in the side and volume.

57. The hypotenuse of a right triangle is known to be 10 in exactly, and one of the acute angles is measured to be $30°$, with a possible error of $\pm 1°$.
  (a) Use differentials to estimate the errors in the sides opposite and adjacent to the measured angle.
  (b) Estimate the percentage errors in the sides.

58. One side of a right triangle is known to be 25 cm exactly. The angle opposite to this side is measured to be $60°$, with a possible error of $\pm 0.5°$.
  (a) Use differentials to estimate the errors in the adjacent side and the hypotenuse.
  (b) Estimate the percentage errors in the adjacent side and hypotenuse.

59. The electrical resistance R of a certain wire is given by $R = k/r^2$, where k is a constant and r is the radius of the wire. Assuming that the radius r has a possible error of $\pm 5\%$, use differentials to estimate the percentage error in R. (Assume k is exact.)

60. A 12-foot ladder leaning against a wall makes an angle θ with the floor. If the top of the ladder is h feet up the wall, express h in terms of θ and then use dh to estimate the change in h if θ changes from $60°$ to $59°$.

61. The area of a right triangle with a hypotenuse of H is calculated using the formula $A = \frac{1}{4}H^2 \sin 2\theta$, where θ is one of the acute angles. Use differentials to approximate the error in calculating A if $H = 4$ cm (exactly) and θ is measured to be $30°$, with a possible error of $\pm 15'$.

62. The side of a square is measured with a possible percentage error of ±1%. Use differentials to estimate the percentage error in the area.

63. The side of a cube is measured with a possible percentage error of ±2%. Use differentials to estimate the percentage error in the volume.

64. The volume of a sphere is to be computed from a measured value of its radius. Estimate the maximum permissible percentage error in the measurement if the percentage error in the volume must be kept within ±3%. ($V = \frac{4}{3}\pi r^3$ is the volume of a sphere of radius r.)

65. The area of a circle is to be computed from a measured value of its diameter. Estimate the maximum permissible percentage error in the measurement if the percentage error in the area must be kept within ±1%.

66. A steel cube with 1-inch sides is coated with 0.01 inch of copper. Use differentials to estimate the volume of copper in the coating. [*Hint:* Let ΔV be the change in the volume of the cube.]

67. A metal rod 15 cm long and 5 cm in diameter is to be covered (except for the ends) with insulation that is 0.1 cm thick. Use differentials to estimate the volume of insulation. [*Hint:* Let ΔV be the change in volume of the rod.]

68. The time required for one complete oscillation of a pendulum is called its *period*. If L is the length of the pendulum and the oscillation is small, then the period is given by $P = 2\pi\sqrt{L/g}$, where g is the constant acceleration due to gravity. Use differentials to show that the percentage error in P is approximately half the percentage error in L.

69. If the temperature T of a metal rod of length L is changed by an amount ΔT, then the length will change by the amount $\Delta L = \alpha L \Delta T$, where α is called the ***coefficient of linear expansion***. For moderate changes in temperature α is taken as constant.
  (a) Suppose that a rod 40 cm long at 20°C is found to be 40.006 cm long when the temperature is raised to 30°C. Find α.
  (b) If an aluminum pole is 180 cm long at 15°C, how long is the pole if the temperature is raised to 40°C? [Take $\alpha = 2.3 \times 10^{-5}/°C$.]

70. If the temperature T of a solid or liquid of volume V is changed by an amount ΔT, then the volume will change by the amount $\Delta V = \beta V \Delta T$, where β is called the ***coefficient of volume expansion***. For moderate changes in temperature β is taken as constant. Suppose that a tank truck loads 4000 gallons of ethyl alcohol at a temperature of 35°C and delivers its load sometime later at a temperature of 15°C. Using $\beta = 7.5 \times 10^{-4}/°C$ for ethyl alcohol, find the number of gallons delivered.

71. **Writing** Explain why the local linear approximation of a function value is equivalent to the use of a differential to approximate a change in the function.

72. **Writing** The local linear approximation

$$\sin x \approx x$$

is known as the *small angle approximation* and has both practical and theoretical applications. Do some research on some of these applications, and write a short report on the results of your investigations.

✔ QUICK CHECK ANSWERS 3.5

---

1. tangent; $f(x)$; x_0 **2.** $y = 1 + (-4)(x - 2)$ or $y = -4x + 9$ **3.** $dy = -0.4$, $\Delta y = -0.41$ **4.** within ±1%

3.6 L'HÔPITAL'S RULE; INDETERMINATE FORMS

In this section we will discuss a general method for using derivatives to find limits. This method will enable us to establish limits with certainty that earlier in the text we were only able to conjecture using numerical or graphical evidence. The method that we will discuss in this section is an extremely powerful tool that is used internally by many computer programs to calculate limits of various types.

■ INDETERMINATE FORMS OF TYPE 0/0

Recall that a limit of the form

$$\lim_{x \to a} \frac{f(x)}{g(x)} \tag{1}$$

in which $f(x) \to 0$ and $g(x) \to 0$ as $x \to a$ is called an ***indeterminate form of type 0/0***. Some examples encountered earlier in the text are

$$\lim_{x \to 1} \frac{x^2 - 1}{x - 1} = 2, \quad \lim_{x \to 0} \frac{\sin x}{x} = 1, \quad \lim_{x \to 0} \frac{1 - \cos x}{x} = 0$$

The first limit was obtained algebraically by factoring the numerator and canceling the common factor of $x - 1$, and the second two limits were obtained using geometric methods. However, there are many indeterminate forms for which neither algebraic nor geometric methods will produce the limit, so we need to develop a more general method.

To motivate such a method, suppose that (1) is an indeterminate form of type $0/0$ in which f' and g' are continuous at $x = a$ and $g'(a) \neq 0$. Since f and g can be closely approximated by their local linear approximations near a, it is reasonable to expect that

$$\lim_{x \to a} \frac{f(x)}{g(x)} = \lim_{x \to a} \frac{f(a) + f'(a)(x - a)}{g(a) + g'(a)(x - a)} \tag{2}$$

Since we are assuming that f' and g' are continuous at $x = a$, we have

$$\lim_{x \to a} f'(x) = f'(a) \quad \text{and} \quad \lim_{x \to a} g'(x) = g'(a)$$

and since the differentiability of f and g at $x = a$ implies the continuity of f and g at $x = a$, we have

$$f(a) = \lim_{x \to a} f(x) = 0 \quad \text{and} \quad g(a) = \lim_{x \to a} g(x) = 0$$

Thus, we can rewrite (2) as

$$\lim_{x \to a} \frac{f(x)}{g(x)} = \lim_{x \to a} \frac{f'(a)(x - a)}{g'(a)(x - a)} = \lim_{x \to a} \frac{f'(a)}{g'(a)} = \lim_{x \to a} \frac{f'(x)}{g'(x)} \tag{3}$$

This result, called **L'Hôpital's rule**, converts the given indeterminate form into a limit involving derivatives that is often easier to evaluate.

Although we motivated (3) by assuming that f and g have continuous derivatives at $x = a$ and that $g'(a) \neq 0$, the result is true under less stringent conditions and is also valid for one-sided limits and limits at $+\infty$ and $-\infty$. The proof of the following precise statement of L'Hôpital's rule is omitted.

3.6.1   THEOREM (*L'Hôpital's Rule for Form 0/0*)   *Suppose that f and g are differentiable functions on an open interval containing $x = a$, except possibly at $x = a$, and that*

$$\lim_{x \to a} f(x) = 0 \quad \text{and} \quad \lim_{x \to a} g(x) = 0$$

If $\lim_{x \to a} [f'(x)/g'(x)]$ exists, or if this limit is $+\infty$ or $-\infty$, then

$$\lim_{x \to a} \frac{f(x)}{g(x)} = \lim_{x \to a} \frac{f'(x)}{g'(x)}$$

Moreover, this statement is also true in the case of a limit as $x \to a^-$, $x \to a^+$, $x \to -\infty$, or as $x \to +\infty$.

WARNING

Note that in L'Hôpital's rule the numerator and denominator are differentiated individually. This is *not* the same as differentiating $f(x)/g(x)$.

In the examples that follow we will apply L'Hôpital's rule using the following three-step process:

Applying L'Hôpital's Rule

Step 1. Check that the limit of $f(x)/g(x)$ is an indeterminate form of type $0/0$.

Step 2. Differentiate f and g separately.

Step 3. Find the limit of $f'(x)/g'(x)$. If this limit is finite, $+\infty$, or $-\infty$, then it is equal to the limit of $f(x)/g(x)$.

▶ **Example 1** Find the limit

$$\lim_{x \to 2} \frac{x^2 - 4}{x - 2}$$

using L'Hôpital's rule, and check the result by factoring.

Solution. The numerator and denominator have a limit of 0, so the limit is an indeterminate form of type $0/0$. Applying L'Hôpital's rule yields

$$\lim_{x \to 2} \frac{x^2 - 4}{x - 2} = \lim_{x \to 2} \frac{\dfrac{d}{dx}[x^2 - 4]}{\dfrac{d}{dx}[x - 2]} = \lim_{x \to 2} \frac{2x}{1} = 4$$

This agrees with the computation

$$\lim_{x \to 2} \frac{x^2 - 4}{x - 2} = \lim_{x \to 2} \frac{(x - 2)(x + 2)}{x - 2} = \lim_{x \to 2} (x + 2) = 4 \;\blacktriangleleft$$

The limit in Example 1 can be interpreted as the limit form of a certain derivative. Use that derivative to evaluate the limit.

▶ **Example 2** In each part confirm that the limit is an indeterminate form of type $0/0$, and evaluate it using L'Hôpital's rule.

(a) $\displaystyle\lim_{x \to 0} \frac{\sin 2x}{x}$ (b) $\displaystyle\lim_{x \to \pi/2} \frac{1 - \sin x}{\cos x}$ (c) $\displaystyle\lim_{x \to 0} \frac{e^x - 1}{x^3}$

(d) $\displaystyle\lim_{x \to 0^-} \frac{\tan x}{x^2}$ (e) $\displaystyle\lim_{x \to 0} \frac{1 - \cos x}{x^2}$ (f) $\displaystyle\lim_{x \to +\infty} \frac{x^{-4/3}}{\sin(1/x)}$

Solution (a). The numerator and denominator have a limit of 0, so the limit is an indeterminate form of type $0/0$. Applying L'Hôpital's rule yields

$$\lim_{x \to 0} \frac{\sin 2x}{x} = \lim_{x \to 0} \frac{\dfrac{d}{dx}[\sin 2x]}{\dfrac{d}{dx}[x]} = \lim_{x \to 0} \frac{2 \cos 2x}{1} = 2$$

WARNING

Applying L'Hôpital's rule to limits that are not indeterminate forms can produce incorrect results. For example, the computation

$$\lim_{x \to 0} \frac{x + 6}{x + 2} = \lim_{x \to 0} \frac{\dfrac{d}{dx}[x + 6]}{\dfrac{d}{dx}[x + 2]}$$

$$= \lim_{x \to 0} \frac{1}{1} = 1$$

is *not valid*, since the limit is not an indeterminate form. The correct result is

$$\lim_{x \to 0} \frac{x + 6}{x + 2} = \frac{0 + 6}{0 + 2} = 3$$

Observe that this result agrees with that obtained by substitution in Example 4(b) of Section 1.6.

Solution (b). The numerator and denominator have a limit of 0, so the limit is an indeterminate form of type $0/0$. Applying L'Hôpital's rule yields

$$\lim_{x \to \pi/2} \frac{1 - \sin x}{\cos x} = \lim_{x \to \pi/2} \frac{\dfrac{d}{dx}[1 - \sin x]}{\dfrac{d}{dx}[\cos x]} = \lim_{x \to \pi/2} \frac{-\cos x}{-\sin x} = \frac{0}{-1} = 0$$

Guillaume François Antoine de L'Hôpital (1661–1704) French mathematician. L'Hôpital, born to parents of the French high nobility, held the title of Marquis de Sainte-Mesme Comte d'Autrement. He showed mathematical talent quite early and at age 15 solved a difficult problem about cycloids posed by Pascal. As a young man he served briefly as a cavalry officer, but resigned because of nearsightedness. In his own time he gained fame as the author of the first textbook ever published on differential calculus, *L'Analyse des* *Infiniment Petits pour l'Intelligence des Lignes Courbes* (1696). L'Hôpital's rule appeared for the first time in that book. Actually, L'Hôpital's rule and most of the material in the calculus text were due to John Bernoulli, who was L'Hôpital's teacher. L'Hôpital dropped his plans for a book on integral calculus when Leibniz informed him that he intended to write such a text. L'Hôpital was apparently generous and personable, and his many contacts with major mathematicians provided the vehicle for disseminating major discoveries in calculus throughout Europe.

Solution (c). The numerator and denominator have a limit of 0, so the limit is an indeterminate form of type 0/0. Applying L'Hôpital's rule yields

$$\lim_{x \to 0} \frac{e^x - 1}{x^3} = \lim_{x \to 0} \frac{\dfrac{d}{dx}[e^x - 1]}{\dfrac{d}{dx}[x^3]} = \lim_{x \to 0} \frac{e^x}{3x^2} = +\infty$$

Solution (d). The numerator and denominator have a limit of 0, so the limit is an indeterminate form of type 0/0. Applying L'Hôpital's rule yields

$$\lim_{x \to 0^-} \frac{\tan x}{x^2} = \lim_{x \to 0^-} \frac{\sec^2 x}{2x} = -\infty$$

Solution (e). The numerator and denominator have a limit of 0, so the limit is an indeterminate form of type 0/0. Applying L'Hôpital's rule yields

$$\lim_{x \to 0} \frac{1 - \cos x}{x^2} = \lim_{x \to 0} \frac{\sin x}{2x}$$

Since the new limit is another indeterminate form of type 0/0, we apply L'Hôpital's rule again:

$$\lim_{x \to 0} \frac{1 - \cos x}{x^2} = \lim_{x \to 0} \frac{\sin x}{2x} = \lim_{x \to 0} \frac{\cos x}{2} = \frac{1}{2}$$

Solution (f). The numerator and denominator have a limit of 0, so the limit is an indeterminate form of type 0/0. Applying L'Hôpital's rule yields

$$\lim_{x \to +\infty} \frac{x^{-4/3}}{\sin(1/x)} = \lim_{x \to +\infty} \frac{-\frac{4}{3}x^{-7/3}}{(-1/x^2)\cos(1/x)} = \lim_{x \to +\infty} \frac{\frac{4}{3}x^{-1/3}}{\cos(1/x)} = \frac{0}{1} = 0 \blacktriangleleft$$

■ **INDETERMINATE FORMS OF TYPE ∞/∞**

When we want to indicate that the limit (or a one-sided limit) of a function is $+\infty$ or $-\infty$ without being specific about the sign, we will say that the limit is ∞. For example,

$$\lim_{x \to a^+} f(x) = \infty \quad \text{means} \quad \lim_{x \to a^+} f(x) = +\infty \quad \text{or} \quad \lim_{x \to a^+} f(x) = -\infty$$

$$\lim_{x \to +\infty} f(x) = \infty \quad \text{means} \quad \lim_{x \to +\infty} f(x) = +\infty \quad \text{or} \quad \lim_{x \to +\infty} f(x) = -\infty$$

$$\lim_{x \to a} f(x) = \infty \quad \text{means} \quad \lim_{x \to a^+} f(x) = \pm\infty \quad \text{and} \quad \lim_{x \to a^-} f(x) = \pm\infty$$

The limit of a ratio, $f(x)/g(x)$, in which the numerator has limit ∞ and the denominator has limit ∞ is called an **indeterminate form of type ∞/∞**. The following version of L'Hôpital's rule, which we state without proof, can often be used to evaluate limits of this type.

3.6.2 THEOREM (L'Hôpital's Rule for Form ∞/∞) *Suppose that f and g are differentiable functions on an open interval containing x = a, except possibly at x = a, and that*

$$\lim_{x \to a} f(x) = \infty \quad \text{and} \quad \lim_{x \to a} g(x) = \infty$$

If $\lim_{x \to a}[f'(x)/g'(x)]$ exists, or if this limit is $+\infty$ or $-\infty$, then

$$\lim_{x \to a} \frac{f(x)}{g(x)} = \lim_{x \to a} \frac{f'(x)}{g'(x)}$$

Moreover, this statement is also true in the case of a limit as $x \to a^-$, $x \to a^+$, $x \to -\infty$, or as $x \to +\infty$.

▶ **Example 3** In each part confirm that the limit is an indeterminate form of type ∞/∞ and apply L'Hôpital's rule.

$$\text{(a)} \lim_{x \to +\infty} \frac{x}{e^x} \qquad \text{(b)} \lim_{x \to 0^+} \frac{\ln x}{\csc x}$$

Solution (a). The numerator and denominator both have a limit of $+\infty$, so we have an indeterminate form of type ∞/∞. Applying L'Hôpital's rule yields

$$\lim_{x \to +\infty} \frac{x}{e^x} = \lim_{x \to +\infty} \frac{1}{e^x} = 0$$

Solution (b). The numerator has a limit of $-\infty$ and the denominator has a limit of $+\infty$, so we have an indeterminate form of type ∞/∞. Applying L'Hôpital's rule yields

$$\lim_{x \to 0^+} \frac{\ln x}{\csc x} = \lim_{x \to 0^+} \frac{1/x}{-\csc x \cot x} \tag{4}$$

This last limit is again an indeterminate form of type ∞/∞. Moreover, any additional applications of L'Hôpital's rule will yield powers of $1/x$ in the numerator and expressions involving $\csc x$ and $\cot x$ in the denominator; thus, repeated application of L'Hôpital's rule simply produces new indeterminate forms. We must try something else. The last limit in (4) can be rewritten as

$$\lim_{x \to 0^+} \left(-\frac{\sin x}{x} \tan x \right) = -\lim_{x \to 0^+} \frac{\sin x}{x} \cdot \lim_{x \to 0^+} \tan x = -(1)(0) = 0$$

Thus,

$$\lim_{x \to 0^+} \frac{\ln x}{\csc x} = 0 \blacktriangleleft$$

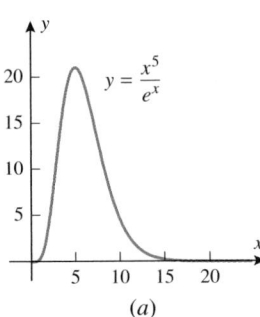

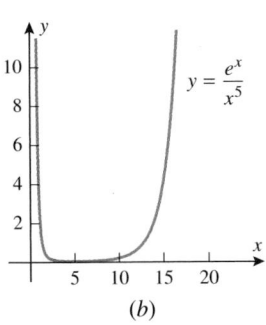

▲ **Figure 3.6.1**

■ ANALYZING THE GROWTH OF EXPONENTIAL FUNCTIONS USING L'HÔPITAL'S RULE

If n is any positive integer, then $x^n \to +\infty$ as $x \to +\infty$. Such integer powers of x are sometimes used as "measuring sticks" to describe how rapidly other functions grow. For example, we know that $e^x \to +\infty$ as $x \to +\infty$ and that the growth of e^x is very rapid (Table 0.5.5); however, the growth of x^n is also rapid when n is a high power, so it is reasonable to ask whether high powers of x grow more or less rapidly than e^x. One way to investigate this is to examine the behavior of the ratio x^n/e^x as $x \to +\infty$. For example, Figure 3.6.1a shows the graph of $y = x^5/e^x$. This graph suggests that $x^5/e^x \to 0$ as $x \to +\infty$, and this implies that the growth of the function e^x is sufficiently rapid that its values eventually overtake those of x^5 and force the ratio toward zero. Stated informally, "e^x eventually grows more rapidly than x^5." The same conclusion could have been reached by putting e^x on top and examining the behavior of e^x/x^5 as $x \to +\infty$ (Figure 3.6.1b). In this case the values of e^x eventually overtake those of x^5 and force the ratio toward $+\infty$. More generally, we can use L'Hôpital's rule to show that e^x *eventually grows more rapidly than any positive integer power of x*, that is,

$$\lim_{x \to +\infty} \frac{x^n}{e^x} = 0 \quad \text{and} \quad \lim_{x \to +\infty} \frac{e^x}{x^n} = +\infty \tag{5–6}$$

Both limits are indeterminate forms of type ∞/∞ that can be evaluated using L'Hôpital's rule. For example, to establish (5), we will need to apply L'Hôpital's rule n times. For this purpose, observe that successive differentiations of x^n reduce the exponent by 1 each time, thus producing a constant for the nth derivative. For example, the successive derivatives of x^3 are $3x^2, 6x$, and 6. In general, the nth derivative of x^n is $n(n-1)(n-2)\cdots 1 = n!$ (verify).[*] Thus, applying L'Hôpital's rule n times to (5) yields

$$\lim_{x \to +\infty} \frac{x^n}{e^x} = \lim_{x \to +\infty} \frac{n!}{e^x} = 0$$

Limit (6) can be established similarly.

▨ INDETERMINATE FORMS OF TYPE $0 \cdot \infty$

Thus far we have discussed indeterminate forms of type $0/0$ and ∞/∞. However, these are not the only possibilities; in general, the limit of an expression that has one of the forms

$$\frac{f(x)}{g(x)}, \quad f(x) \cdot g(x), \quad f(x)^{g(x)}, \quad f(x) - g(x), \quad f(x) + g(x)$$

is called an *indeterminate form* if the limits of $f(x)$ and $g(x)$ individually exert conflicting influences on the limit of the entire expression. For example, the limit

$$\lim_{x \to 0^+} x \ln x$$

is an *indeterminate form of type $0 \cdot \infty$* because the limit of the first factor is 0, the limit of the second factor is $-\infty$, and these two limits exert conflicting influences on the product. On the other hand, the limit

$$\lim_{x \to +\infty} [\sqrt{x}(1 - x^2)]$$

is not an indeterminate form because the first factor has a limit of $+\infty$, the second factor has a limit of $-\infty$, and these influences work together to produce a limit of $-\infty$ for the product.

Indeterminate forms of type $0 \cdot \infty$ can sometimes be evaluated by rewriting the product as a ratio, and then applying L'Hôpital's rule for indeterminate forms of type $0/0$ or ∞/∞.

WARNING

It is tempting to argue that an indeterminate form of type $0 \cdot \infty$ has value 0 since "zero times anything is zero." However, this is fallacious since $0 \cdot \infty$ is not a product of numbers, but rather a statement about limits. For example, here are two indeterminate forms of type $0 \cdot \infty$ whose limits are *not* zero:

$$\lim_{x \to 0} \left(x \cdot \frac{1}{x} \right) = \lim_{x \to 0} 1 = 1$$

$$\lim_{x \to 0^+} \left(\sqrt{x} \cdot \frac{1}{x} \right) = \lim_{x \to 0^+} \left(\frac{1}{\sqrt{x}} \right)$$

$$= +\infty$$

▶ **Example 4** Evaluate

    (a) $\displaystyle\lim_{x \to 0^+} x \ln x$ (b) $\displaystyle\lim_{x \to \pi/4} (1 - \tan x) \sec 2x$

Solution (a). The factor x has a limit of 0 and the factor $\ln x$ has a limit of $-\infty$, so the stated problem is an indeterminate form of type $0 \cdot \infty$. There are two possible approaches: we can rewrite the limit as

$$\lim_{x \to 0^+} \frac{\ln x}{1/x} \quad \text{or} \quad \lim_{x \to 0^+} \frac{x}{1/\ln x}$$

the first being an indeterminate form of type ∞/∞ and the second an indeterminate form of type $0/0$. However, the first form is the preferred initial choice because the derivative of $1/x$ is less complicated than the derivative of $1/\ln x$. That choice yields

$$\lim_{x \to 0^+} x \ln x = \lim_{x \to 0^+} \frac{\ln x}{1/x} = \lim_{x \to 0^+} \frac{1/x}{-1/x^2} = \lim_{x \to 0^+} (-x) = 0$$

Solution (b). The stated problem is an indeterminate form of type $0 \cdot \infty$. We will convert it to an indeterminate form of type $0/0$:

$$\lim_{x \to \pi/4} (1 - \tan x) \sec 2x = \lim_{x \to \pi/4} \frac{1 - \tan x}{1/\sec 2x} = \lim_{x \to \pi/4} \frac{1 - \tan x}{\cos 2x}$$

$$= \lim_{x \to \pi/4} \frac{-\sec^2 x}{-2 \sin 2x} = \frac{-2}{-2} = 1 \quad ◄$$

---

[*]Recall that for $n \geq 1$ the expression $n!$, read ***n-factorial***, denotes the product of the first n positive integers.

■ INDETERMINATE FORMS OF TYPE $\infty - \infty$

A limit problem that leads to one of the expressions

$$(+\infty) - (+\infty), \quad (-\infty) - (-\infty),$$
$$(+\infty) + (-\infty), \quad (-\infty) + (+\infty)$$

is called an ***indeterminate form of type*** $\infty - \infty$. Such limits are indeterminate because the two terms exert conflicting influences on the expression: one pushes it in the positive direction and the other pushes it in the negative direction. However, limit problems that lead to one of the expressions

$$(+\infty) + (+\infty), \quad (+\infty) - (-\infty),$$
$$(-\infty) + (-\infty), \quad (-\infty) - (+\infty)$$

are not indeterminate, since the two terms work together (those on the top produce a limit of $+\infty$ and those on the bottom produce a limit of $-\infty$).

Indeterminate forms of type $\infty - \infty$ can sometimes be evaluated by combining the terms and manipulating the result to produce an indeterminate form of type $0/0$ or ∞/∞.

▶ **Example 5**   Evaluate $\displaystyle\lim_{x \to 0^+} \left(\frac{1}{x} - \frac{1}{\sin x} \right)$.

Solution.   Both terms have a limit of $+\infty$, so the stated problem is an indeterminate form of type $\infty - \infty$. Combining the two terms yields

$$\lim_{x \to 0^+} \left(\frac{1}{x} - \frac{1}{\sin x} \right) = \lim_{x \to 0^+} \frac{\sin x - x}{x \sin x}$$

which is an indeterminate form of type $0/0$. Applying L'Hôpital's rule twice yields

$$\lim_{x \to 0^+} \frac{\sin x - x}{x \sin x} = \lim_{x \to 0^+} \frac{\cos x - 1}{\sin x + x \cos x}$$

$$= \lim_{x \to 0^+} \frac{-\sin x}{\cos x + \cos x - x \sin x} = \frac{0}{2} = 0 \blacktriangleleft$$

■ INDETERMINATE FORMS OF TYPE 0^0, ∞^0, 1^∞

Limits of the form

$$\lim f(x)^{g(x)}$$

can give rise to ***indeterminate forms of the types*** 0^0, ∞^0, ***and*** 1^∞. (The interpretations of these symbols should be clear.) For example, the limit

$$\lim_{x \to 0^+} (1 + x)^{1/x}$$

whose value we know to be e [see Formula (1) of Section 3.2] is an indeterminate form of type 1^∞. It is indeterminate because the expressions $1 + x$ and $1/x$ exert two conflicting influences: the first approaches 1, which drives the expression toward 1, and the second approaches $+\infty$, which drives the expression toward $+\infty$.

Indeterminate forms of types 0^0, ∞^0, and 1^∞ can sometimes be evaluated by first introducing a dependent variable

$$y = f(x)^{g(x)}$$

and then computing the limit of $\ln y$. Since

$$\ln y = \ln[f(x)^{g(x)}] = g(x) \cdot \ln[f(x)]$$

the limit of $\ln y$ will be an indeterminate form of type $0 \cdot \infty$ (verify), which can be evaluated by methods we have already studied. Once the limit of $\ln y$ is known, it is a straightforward matter to determine the limit of $y = f(x)^{g(x)}$, as we will illustrate in the next example.

▶ **Example 6** Find $\lim\limits_{x \to 0}(1 + \sin x)^{1/x}$.

Solution. As discussed above, we begin by introducing a dependent variable

$$y = (1 + \sin x)^{1/x}$$

and taking the natural logarithm of both sides:

$$\ln y = \ln(1 + \sin x)^{1/x} = \frac{1}{x}\ln(1 + \sin x) = \frac{\ln(1 + \sin x)}{x}$$

Thus,

$$\lim_{x \to 0}\ln y = \lim_{x \to 0}\frac{\ln(1 + \sin x)}{x}$$

which is an indeterminate form of type $0/0$, so by L'Hôpital's rule

$$\lim_{x \to 0}\ln y = \lim_{x \to 0}\frac{\ln(1 + \sin x)}{x} = \lim_{x \to 0}\frac{(\cos x)/(1 + \sin x)}{1} = 1$$

Since we have shown that $\ln y \to 1$ as $x \to 0$, the continuity of the exponential function implies that $e^{\ln y} \to e^1$ as $x \to 0$, and this implies that $y \to e$ as $x \to 0$. Thus,

$$\lim_{x \to 0}(1 + \sin x)^{1/x} = e \quad ◀$$

✔ **QUICK CHECK EXERCISES 3.6**   *(See page 228 for answers.)*

1. In each part, does L'Hôpital's rule apply to the given limit?
   (a) $\lim\limits_{x \to 1}\dfrac{2x - 2}{x^3 + x - 2}$
   (b) $\lim\limits_{x \to 0}\dfrac{\cos x}{x}$
   (c) $\lim\limits_{x \to 0}\dfrac{e^{2x} - 1}{\tan x}$

2. Evaluate each of the limits in Quick Check Exercise 1.

3. Using L'Hôpital's rule, $\lim\limits_{x \to +\infty}\dfrac{e^x}{500x^2} = $ _____.

EXERCISE SET 3.6   ∿ Graphing Utility   [C] CAS

1–2 Evaluate the given limit without using L'Hôpital's rule, and then check that your answer is correct using L'Hôpital's rule. ▨

1. (a) $\lim\limits_{x \to 2}\dfrac{x^2 - 4}{x^2 + 2x - 8}$
   (b) $\lim\limits_{x \to +\infty}\dfrac{2x - 5}{3x + 7}$

2. (a) $\lim\limits_{x \to 0}\dfrac{\sin x}{\tan x}$
   (b) $\lim\limits_{x \to 1}\dfrac{x^2 - 1}{x^3 - 1}$

3–6 True–False Determine whether the statement is true or false. Explain your answer. ▨

3. L'Hôpital's rule does not apply to $\lim\limits_{x \to -\infty}\dfrac{\ln x}{x}$.

4. For any polynomial $p(x)$, $\lim\limits_{x \to +\infty}\dfrac{p(x)}{e^x} = 0$.

5. If n is chosen sufficiently large, then $\lim\limits_{x \to +\infty}\dfrac{(\ln x)^n}{x} = +\infty$.

6. $\lim\limits_{x \to 0^+}(\sin x)^{1/x} = 0$

7–45 Find the limits. ▨

7. $\lim\limits_{x \to 0}\dfrac{e^x - 1}{\sin x}$

8. $\lim\limits_{x \to 0}\dfrac{\sin 2x}{\sin 5x}$

9. $\lim\limits_{\theta \to 0}\dfrac{\tan \theta}{\theta}$

10. $\lim\limits_{t \to 0}\dfrac{te^t}{1 - e^t}$

11. $\lim\limits_{x \to \pi^+}\dfrac{\sin x}{x - \pi}$

12. $\lim\limits_{x \to 0^+}\dfrac{\sin x}{x^2}$

13. $\lim\limits_{x \to +\infty}\dfrac{\ln x}{x}$

14. $\lim\limits_{x \to +\infty}\dfrac{e^{3x}}{x^2}$

15. $\lim\limits_{x \to 0^+}\dfrac{\cot x}{\ln x}$

16. $\lim\limits_{x \to 0^+}\dfrac{1 - \ln x}{e^{1/x}}$

17. $\lim\limits_{x \to +\infty}\dfrac{x^{100}}{e^x}$

18. $\lim\limits_{x \to 0^+}\dfrac{\ln(\sin x)}{\ln(\tan x)}$

19. $\lim\limits_{x \to 0}\dfrac{\sin^{-1} 2x}{x}$

20. $\lim\limits_{x \to 0}\dfrac{x - \tan^{-1} x}{x^3}$

21. $\lim\limits_{x \to +\infty} xe^{-x}$

22. $\lim\limits_{x \to \pi^-}(x - \pi)\tan \tfrac{1}{2}x$

23. $\lim\limits_{x \to +\infty} x \sin\dfrac{\pi}{x}$

24. $\lim\limits_{x \to 0^+}\tan x \ln x$

25. $\lim\limits_{x \to \pi/2^-}\sec 3x \cos 5x$

26. $\lim\limits_{x \to \pi}(x - \pi)\cot x$

27. $\lim\limits_{x \to +\infty}(1 - 3/x)^x$

28. $\lim\limits_{x \to 0}(1 + 2x)^{-3/x}$

29. $\lim\limits_{x \to 0} (e^x + x)^{1/x}$

30. $\lim\limits_{x \to +\infty} (1 + a/x)^{bx}$

31. $\lim\limits_{x \to 1} (2 - x)^{\tan[(\pi/2)x]}$

32. $\lim\limits_{x \to +\infty} [\cos(2/x)]^{x^2}$

33. $\lim\limits_{x \to 0} (\csc x - 1/x)$

34. $\lim\limits_{x \to 0} \left(\dfrac{1}{x^2} - \dfrac{\cos 3x}{x^2} \right)$

35. $\lim\limits_{x \to +\infty} (\sqrt{x^2 + x} - x)$

36. $\lim\limits_{x \to 0} \left(\dfrac{1}{x} - \dfrac{1}{e^x - 1} \right)$

37. $\lim\limits_{x \to +\infty} [x - \ln(x^2 + 1)]$

38. $\lim\limits_{x \to +\infty} [\ln x - \ln(1 + x)]$

39. $\lim\limits_{x \to 0^+} x^{\sin x}$

40. $\lim\limits_{x \to 0^+} (e^{2x} - 1)^x$

41. $\lim\limits_{x \to 0^+} \left[-\dfrac{1}{\ln x} \right]^x$

42. $\lim\limits_{x \to +\infty} x^{1/x}$

43. $\lim\limits_{x \to +\infty} (\ln x)^{1/x}$

44. $\lim\limits_{x \to 0^+} (-\ln x)^x$

45. $\lim\limits_{x \to \pi/2^-} (\tan x)^{(\pi/2) - x}$

46. Show that for any positive integer n

(a) $\lim\limits_{x \to +\infty} \dfrac{\ln x}{x^n} = 0$ (b) $\lim\limits_{x \to +\infty} \dfrac{x^n}{\ln x} = +\infty.$

FOCUS ON CONCEPTS

47. (a) Find the error in the following calculation:

$$\lim\limits_{x \to 1} \frac{x^3 - x^2 + x - 1}{x^3 - x^2} = \lim\limits_{x \to 1} \frac{3x^2 - 2x + 1}{3x^2 - 2x}$$

$$= \lim\limits_{x \to 1} \frac{6x - 2}{6x - 2} = 1$$

(b) Find the correct limit.

48. (a) Find the error in the following calculation:

$$\lim\limits_{x \to 2} \frac{e^{3x^2 - 12x + 12}}{x^4 - 16} = \lim\limits_{x \to 2} \frac{(6x - 12)e^{3x^2 - 12x + 12}}{4x^3} = 0$$

(b) Find the correct limit.

49–52 Make a conjecture about the limit by graphing the function involved with a graphing utility; then check your conjecture using L'Hôpital's rule. ■

49. $\lim\limits_{x \to +\infty} \dfrac{\ln(\ln x)}{\sqrt{x}}$

50. $\lim\limits_{x \to 0^+} x^x$

51. $\lim\limits_{x \to 0^+} (\sin x)^{3/\ln x}$

52. $\lim\limits_{x \to (\pi/2)^-} \dfrac{4 \tan x}{1 + \sec x}$

53–56 Make a conjecture about the equations of horizontal asymptotes, if any, by graphing the equation with a graphing utility; then check your answer using L'Hôpital's rule. ■

53. $y = \ln x - e^x$

54. $y = x - \ln(1 + 2e^x)$

55. $y = (\ln x)^{1/x}$

56. $y = \left(\dfrac{x + 1}{x + 2} \right)^x$

57. Limits of the type

$$0/\infty, \quad \infty/0, \quad 0^\infty, \quad \infty \cdot \infty, \quad +\infty + (+\infty),$$
$$+\infty - (-\infty), \quad -\infty + (-\infty), \quad -\infty - (+\infty)$$

are *not* indeterminate forms. Find the following limits by inspection.

(a) $\lim\limits_{x \to 0^+} \dfrac{x}{\ln x}$

(b) $\lim\limits_{x \to +\infty} \dfrac{x^3}{e^{-x}}$

(c) $\lim\limits_{x \to (\pi/2)^-} (\cos x)^{\tan x}$

(d) $\lim\limits_{x \to 0^+} (\ln x) \cot x$

(e) $\lim\limits_{x \to 0^+} \left(\dfrac{1}{x} - \ln x \right)$

(f) $\lim\limits_{x \to -\infty} (x + x^3)$

58. There is a myth that circulates among beginning calculus students which states that all indeterminate forms of types 0^0, ∞^0, and 1^∞ have value 1 because "anything to the zero power is 1" and "1 to any power is 1." The fallacy is that 0^0, ∞^0, and 1^∞ are not powers of numbers, but rather descriptions of limits. The following examples, which were suggested by Prof. Jack Staib of Drexel University, show that such indeterminate forms can have any positive real value:

(a) $\lim\limits_{x \to 0^+} [x^{(\ln a)/(1 + \ln x)}] = a$ (form 0^0)

(b) $\lim\limits_{x \to +\infty} [x^{(\ln a)/(1 + \ln x)}] = a$ (form ∞^0)

(c) $\lim\limits_{x \to 0} [(x + 1)^{(\ln a)/x}] = a$ (form 1^∞).

Verify these results.

59–62 Verify that L'Hôpital's rule is of no help in finding the limit; then find the limit, if it exists, by some other method. ■

59. $\lim\limits_{x \to +\infty} \dfrac{x + \sin 2x}{x}$

60. $\lim\limits_{x \to +\infty} \dfrac{2x - \sin x}{3x + \sin x}$

61. $\lim\limits_{x \to +\infty} \dfrac{x(2 + \sin 2x)}{x + 1}$

62. $\lim\limits_{x \to +\infty} \dfrac{x(2 + \sin x)}{x^2 + 1}$

63. The accompanying schematic diagram represents an electrical circuit consisting of an electromotive force that produces a voltage V, a resistor with resistance R, and an inductor with inductance L. It is shown in electrical circuit theory that if the voltage is first applied at time $t = 0$, then the current I flowing through the circuit at time t is given by

$$I = \frac{V}{R}(1 - e^{-Rt/L})$$

What is the effect on the current at a fixed time t if the resistance approaches 0 (i.e., $R \to 0^+$)?

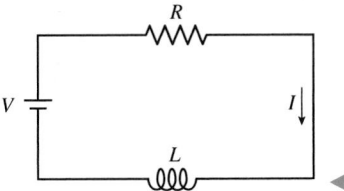

◀ **Figure Ex-63**

64. (a) Show that $\lim\limits_{x \to \pi/2} (\pi/2 - x) \tan x = 1.$

(b) Show that

$$\lim\limits_{x \to \pi/2} \left(\frac{1}{\pi/2 - x} - \tan x \right) = 0$$

(c) It follows from part (b) that the approximation

$$\tan x \approx \frac{1}{\pi/2 - x}$$

should be good for values of x near $\pi/2$. Use a calculator to find $\tan x$ and $1/(\pi/2 - x)$ for $x = 1.57$; compare the results.

C 65. (a) Use a CAS to show that if k is a positive constant, then

$$\lim_{x \to +\infty} x(k^{1/x} - 1) = \ln k$$

(b) Confirm this result using L'Hôpital's rule. [*Hint:* Express the limit in terms of $t = 1/x$.]

(c) If n is a positive integer, then it follows from part (a) with $x = n$ that the approximation

$$n(\sqrt[n]{k} - 1) \approx \ln k$$

should be good when n is large. Use this result and the square root key on a calculator to approximate the values of $\ln 0.3$ and $\ln 2$ with $n = 1024$, then compare the values obtained with values of the logarithms generated directly from the calculator. [*Hint:* The nth roots for which n is a power of 2 can be obtained as successive square roots.]

66. Find all values of k and l such that

$$\lim_{x \to 0} \frac{k + \cos lx}{x^2} = -4$$

FOCUS ON CONCEPTS

67. Let $f(x) = x^2 \sin(1/x)$.

(a) Are the limits $\lim_{x \to 0^+} f(x)$ and $\lim_{x \to 0^-} f(x)$ indeterminate forms?

(b) Use a graphing utility to generate the graph of f, and use the graph to make conjectures about the limits in part (a).

(c) Use the Squeezing Theorem (1.6.4) to confirm that your conjectures in part (b) are correct.

68. (a) Explain why L'Hôpital's rule does not apply to the problem

$$\lim_{x \to 0} \frac{x^2 \sin(1/x)}{\sin x}$$

(b) Find the limit.

69. Find $\lim_{x \to 0^+} \dfrac{x \sin(1/x)}{\sin x}$ if it exists.

70. Suppose that functions f and g are differentiable at $x = a$ and that $f(a) = g(a) = 0$. If $g'(a) \neq 0$, show that

$$\lim_{x \to a} \frac{f(x)}{g(x)} = \frac{f'(a)}{g'(a)}$$

without using L'Hôpital's rule. [*Hint:* Divide the numerator and denominator of $f(x)/g(x)$ by $x - a$ and use the definitions for $f'(a)$ and $g'(a)$.]

71. Writing Were we to use L'Hôpital's rule to evaluate either

$$\lim_{x \to 0} \frac{\sin x}{x} \quad \text{or} \quad \lim_{x \to +\infty} \left(1 + \frac{1}{x}\right)^x$$

we could be accused of circular reasoning. Explain why.

72. Writing Exercise 58 shows that the indeterminate forms 0^0 and ∞^0 can assume any positive real value. However, it is often the case that these indeterminate forms have value 1. Read the article "Indeterminate Forms of Exponential Type" by John Baxley and Elmer Hayashi in the June–July 1978 issue of *The American Mathematical Monthly*, and write a short report on why this is the case.

✔ QUICK CHECK ANSWERS 3.6

1. (a) yes (b) no (c) yes   **2.** (a) $\frac{1}{2}$ (b) does not exist (c) 2   **3.** $+\infty$

CHAPTER 3 REVIEW EXERCISES   ⌁ Graphing Utility

1–2 (a) Find dy/dx by differentiating implicitly. (b) Solve the equation for y as a function of x, and find dy/dx from that equation. (c) Confirm that the two results are consistent by expressing the derivative in part (a) as a function of x alone. ■

1. $x^3 + xy - 2x = 1$ **2.** $xy = x - y$

3–6 Find dy/dx by implicit differentiation. ■

3. $\dfrac{1}{y} + \dfrac{1}{x} = 1$ **4.** $x^3 - y^3 = 6xy$

5. $\sec(xy) = y$ **6.** $x^2 = \dfrac{\cot y}{1 + \csc y}$

7–8 Find d^2y/dx^2 by implicit differentiation. ■

7. $3x^2 - 4y^2 = 7$ **8.** $2xy - y^2 = 3$

9. Use implicit differentiation to find the slope of the tangent line to the curve $y = x \tan(\pi y/2)$, $x > 0$, $y > 0$ (*the quadratrix of Hippias*) at the point $\left(\frac{1}{2}, \frac{1}{2}\right)$.

10. At what point(s) is the tangent line to the curve $y^2 = 2x^3$ perpendicular to the line $4x - 3y + 1 = 0$?

11. Prove that if P and Q are two distinct points on the rotated ellipse $x^2 + xy + y^2 = 4$ such that P, Q, and the origin are collinear, then the tangent lines to the ellipse at P and Q are parallel.

12. Find the coordinates of the point in the first quadrant at which the tangent line to the curve $x^3 - xy + y^3 = 0$ is parallel to the x-axis.

13. Find the coordinates of the point in the first quadrant at which the tangent line to the curve $x^3 - xy + y^3 = 0$ is parallel to the y-axis.

14. Use implicit differentiation to show that the equation of the tangent line to the curve $y^2 = kx$ at (x_0, y_0) is

$$y_0 y = \tfrac{1}{2}k(x + x_0)$$

15–16 Find dy/dx by first using algebraic properties of the natural logarithm function. ■

15. $y = \ln\left(\dfrac{(x+1)(x+2)^2}{(x+3)^3(x+4)^4}\right)$ **16.** $y = \ln\left(\dfrac{\sqrt{x}\sqrt[3]{x+1}}{\sin x \sec x}\right)$

17–34 Find dy/dx. ■

17. $y = \ln 2x$

18. $y = (\ln x)^2$

19. $y = \sqrt[3]{\ln x + 1}$

20. $y = \ln(\sqrt[3]{x+1})$

21. $y = \log(\ln x)$

22. $y = \dfrac{1 + \log x}{1 - \log x}$

23. $y = \ln(x^{3/2}\sqrt{1+x^4})$

24. $y = \ln\left(\dfrac{\sqrt{x}\cos x}{1 + x^2}\right)$

25. $y = e^{\ln(x^2+1)}$

26. $y = \ln\left(\dfrac{1 + e^x + e^{2x}}{1 - e^{3x}}\right)$

27. $y = 2xe^{\sqrt{x}}$

28. $y = \dfrac{a}{1 + be^{-x}}$

29. $y = \dfrac{1}{\pi}\tan^{-1} 2x$

30. $y = 2^{\sin^{-1} x}$

31. $y = x^{(e^x)}$

32. $y = (1 + x)^{1/x}$

33. $y = \sec^{-1}(2x + 1)$

34. $y = \sqrt{\cos^{-1} x^2}$

35–36 Find dy/dx using logarithmic differentiation. ■

35. $y = \dfrac{x^3}{\sqrt{x^2+1}}$ **36.** $y = \sqrt[3]{\dfrac{x^2 - 1}{x^2 + 1}}$

37. (a) Make a conjecture about the shape of the graph of $y = \tfrac{1}{2}x - \ln x$, and draw a rough sketch.
   (b) Check your conjecture by graphing the equation over the interval $0 < x < 5$ with a graphing utility.
   (c) Show that the slopes of the tangent lines to the curve at $x = 1$ and $x = e$ have opposite signs.
   (d) What does part (c) imply about the existence of a horizontal tangent line to the curve? Explain.
   (e) Find the exact x-coordinates of all horizontal tangent lines to the curve.

38. Recall from Section 0.5 that the loudness β of a sound in decibels (dB) is given by $\beta = 10\log(I/I_0)$, where I is the intensity of the sound in watts per square meter (W/m^2) and I_0 is a constant that is approximately the intensity of a sound at the threshold of human hearing. Find the rate of change of β with respect to I at the point where
   (a) $I/I_0 = 10$ (b) $I/I_0 = 100$ (c) $I/I_0 = 1000$.

39. A particle is moving along the curve $y = x\ln x$. Find all values of x at which the rate of change of y with respect to time is three times that of x. [Assume that dx/dt is never zero.]

40. Find the equation of the tangent line to the graph of $y = \ln(5 - x^2)$ at $x = 2$.

41. Find the value of b so that the line $y = x$ is tangent to the graph of $y = \log_b x$. Confirm your result by graphing both $y = x$ and $y = \log_b x$ in the same coordinate system.

42. In each part, find the value of k for which the graphs of $y = f(x)$ and $y = \ln x$ share a common tangent line at their point of intersection. Confirm your result by graphing $y = f(x)$ and $y = \ln x$ in the same coordinate system.
   (a) $f(x) = \sqrt{x} + k$ (b) $f(x) = k\sqrt{x}$

43. If f and g are inverse functions and f is differentiable on its domain, must g be differentiable on its domain? Give a reasonable informal argument to support your answer.

44. In each part, find $(f^{-1})'(x)$ using Formula (2) of Section 3.3, and check your answer by differentiating f^{-1} directly.
   (a) $f(x) = 3/(x + 1)$ (b) $f(x) = \sqrt{e^x}$

45. Find a point on the graph of $y = e^{3x}$ at which the tangent line passes through the origin.

46. Show that the rate of change of $y = 5000e^{1.07x}$ is proportional to y.

47. Show that the rate of change of $y = 3^{2x}5^{7x}$ is proportional to y.

48. The equilibrium constant k of a balanced chemical reaction changes with the absolute temperature T according to the law

$$k = k_0 \exp\left(-\frac{q(T - T_0)}{2T_0 T}\right)$$

where k_0, q, and T_0 are constants. Find the rate of change of k with respect to T.

49. Show that the function $y = e^{ax}\sin bx$ satisfies

$$y'' - 2ay' + (a^2 + b^2)y = 0$$

for any real constants a and b.

50. Show that the function $y = \tan^{-1} x$ satisfies

$$y'' = -2\sin y \cos^3 y$$

51. Suppose that the population of deer on an island is modeled by the equation

$$P(t) = \frac{95}{5 - 4e^{-t/4}}$$

where $P(t)$ is the number of deer t weeks after an initial observation at time $t = 0$.
   (a) Use a graphing utility to graph the function $P(t)$.
   (b) In words, explain what happens to the population over time. Check your conclusion by finding $\lim_{t \to +\infty} P(t)$.
   (c) In words, what happens to the *rate* of population growth over time? Check your conclusion by graphing $P'(t)$.

52. In each part, find each limit by interpreting the expression as an appropriate derivative.
   (a) $\lim\limits_{h \to 0} \dfrac{(1 + h)^\pi - 1}{h}$ (b) $\lim\limits_{x \to e} \dfrac{1 - \ln x}{(x - e)\ln x}$

53. Suppose that $\lim f(x) = \pm\infty$ and $\lim g(x) = \pm\infty$. In each of the four possible cases, state whether $\lim[f(x) - g(x)]$ is an indeterminate form, and give a reasonable informal argument to support your answer.

54. (a) Under what conditions will a limit of the form

$$\lim_{x \to a} [f(x)/g(x)]$$

be an indeterminate form?

(b) If $\lim_{x \to a} g(x) = 0$, must $\lim_{x \to a}[f(x)/g(x)]$ be an indeterminate form? Give some examples to support your answer.

55–58 Evaluate the given limit. ■

55. $\displaystyle\lim_{x \to +\infty} (e^x - x^2)$

56. $\displaystyle\lim_{x \to 1} \sqrt{\frac{\ln x}{x^4 - 1}}$

57. $\displaystyle\lim_{x \to 0} \frac{x^2 e^x}{\sin^2 3x}$

58. $\displaystyle\lim_{x \to 0} \frac{a^x - 1}{x}, \quad a > 0$

59. An oil slick on a lake is surrounded by a floating circular containment boom. As the boom is pulled in, the circular containment area shrinks. If the boom is pulled in at the rate of 5 m/min, at what rate is the containment area shrinking when the containment area has a diameter of 100 m?

60. The hypotenuse of a right triangle is growing at a constant rate of a centimeters per second and one leg is decreasing t at a constant rate of b centimeters per second. How fast is the acute angle between the hypotenuse and the other leg changing at the instant when both legs are 1 cm?

61. In each part, use the given information to find Δx, Δy, and dy.
(a) $y = 1/(x - 1)$; x decreases from 2 to 1.5.
(b) $y = \tan x$; x increases from $-\pi/4$ to 0.
(c) $y = \sqrt{25 - x^2}$; x increases from 0 to 3.

62. Use an appropriate local linear approximation to estimate the value of $\cot 46°$, and compare your answer to the value obtained with a calculating device.

63. The base of the Great Pyramid at Giza is a square that is 230 m on each side.
(a) As illustrated in the accompanying figure, suppose that an archaeologist standing at the center of a side measures the angle of elevation of the apex to be $\phi = 51°$ with an error of $\pm 0.5°$. What can the archaeologist reasonably say about the height of the pyramid?
(b) Use differentials to estimate the allowable error in the elevation angle that will ensure that the error in calculating the height is at most ± 5 m.

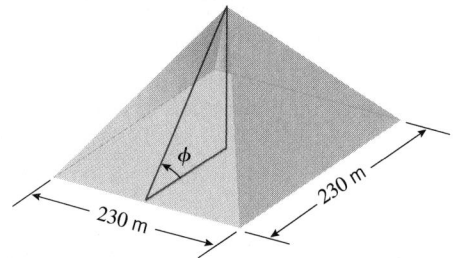

▲ **Figure Ex-63**

CHAPTER 3 MAKING CONNECTIONS

In these exercises we explore an application of exponential functions to radioactive decay, and we consider another approach to computing the derivative of the natural exponential function.

1. Consider a simple model of radioactive decay. We assume that given any quantity of a radioactive element, the fraction of the quantity that decays over a period of time will be a constant that depends on only the particular element and the length of the time period. We choose a time parameter $-\infty < t < +\infty$ and let $A = A(t)$ denote the amount of the element remaining at time t. We also choose units of measure such that the initial amount of the element is $A(0) = 1$, and we let $b = A(1)$ denote the amount at time $t = 1$. Prove that the function $A(t)$ has the following properties.

(a) $A(-t) = \dfrac{1}{A(t)}$ [*Hint:* For $t > 0$, you can interpret $A(t)$ as the fraction of any given amount that remains after a time period of length t.]

(b) $A(s + t) = A(s) \cdot A(t)$ [*Hint:* First consider positive s and t. For the other cases use the property in part (a).]

(c) If n is any nonzero integer, then

$$A\left(\frac{1}{n}\right) = (A(1))^{1/n} = b^{1/n}$$

(d) If m and n are integers with $n \neq 0$, then

$$A\left(\frac{m}{n}\right) = (A(1))^{m/n} = b^{m/n}$$

(e) Assuming that $A(t)$ is a continuous function of t, then $A(t) = b^t$. [*Hint:* Prove that if two continuous functions agree on the set of rational numbers, then they are equal.]

(f) If we replace the assumption that $A(0) = 1$ by the condition $A(0) = A_0$, prove that $A = A_0 b^t$.

2. Refer to Figure 1.3.4.

(a) Make the substitution $h = 1/x$ and conclude that

$$(1 + h)^{1/h} < e < (1 - h)^{-1/h} \quad \text{for } h > 0$$

and

$$(1 - h)^{-1/h} < e < (1 + h)^{1/h} \quad \text{for } h < 0$$

(b) Use the inequalities in part (a) and the Squeezing Theorem to prove that

$$\lim_{h \to 0} \frac{e^h - 1}{h} = 1$$

(c) Explain why the limit in part (b) confirms Figure 0.5.4.

(d) Use the limit in part (b) to prove that

$$\frac{d}{dx}(e^x) = e^x$$

Stone/Getty Images

4

THE DERIVATIVE IN GRAPHING AND APPLICATIONS

Derivatives can help to find the most cost-effective location for an offshore oil-drilling rig.

In this chapter we will study various applications of the derivative. For example, we will use methods of calculus to analyze functions and their graphs. In the process, we will show how calculus and graphing utilities, working together, can provide most of the important information about the behavior of functions. Another important application of the derivative will be in the solution of optimization problems. For example, if time is the main consideration in a problem, we might be interested in finding the quickest way to perform a task, and if cost is the main consideration, we might be interested in finding the least expensive way to perform a task. Mathematically, optimization problems can be reduced to finding the largest or smallest value of a function on some interval, and determining where the largest or smallest value occurs. Using the derivative, we will develop the mathematical tools necessary for solving such problems. We will also use the derivative to study the motion of a particle moving along a line, and we will show how the derivative can help us to approximate solutions of equations.

4.1 ANALYSIS OF FUNCTIONS I: INCREASE, DECREASE, AND CONCAVITY

Although graphing utilities are useful for determining the general shape of a graph, many problems require more precision than graphing utilities are capable of producing. The purpose of this section is to develop mathematical tools that can be used to determine the exact shape of a graph and the precise locations of its key features.

▦ INCREASING AND DECREASING FUNCTIONS

The terms *increasing*, *decreasing*, and *constant* are used to describe the behavior of a function as we travel left to right along its graph. For example, the function graphed in Figure 4.1.1 can be described as increasing to the left of $x = 0$, decreasing from $x = 0$ to $x = 2$, increasing from $x = 2$ to $x = 4$, and constant to the right of $x = 4$.

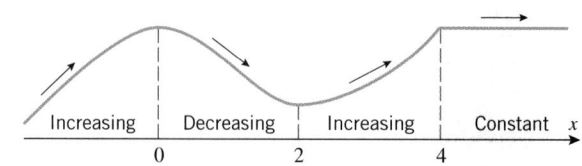

▶ **Figure 4.1.1**

The following definition, which is illustrated in Figure 4.1.2, expresses these intuitive ideas precisely.

The definitions of "increasing," "decreasing," and "constant" describe the behavior of a function on an *interval* and not at a point. In particular, it is not inconsistent to say that the function in Figure 4.1.1 is decreasing on the interval [0, 2] and increasing on the interval [2, 4].

4.1.1   DEFINITION   Let f be defined on an interval, and let x_1 and x_2 denote points in that interval.

(a) f is *increasing* on the interval if $f(x_1) < f(x_2)$ whenever $x_1 < x_2$.

(b) f is *decreasing* on the interval if $f(x_1) > f(x_2)$ whenever $x_1 < x_2$.

(c) f is *constant* on the interval if $f(x_1) = f(x_2)$ for all points x_1 and x_2.

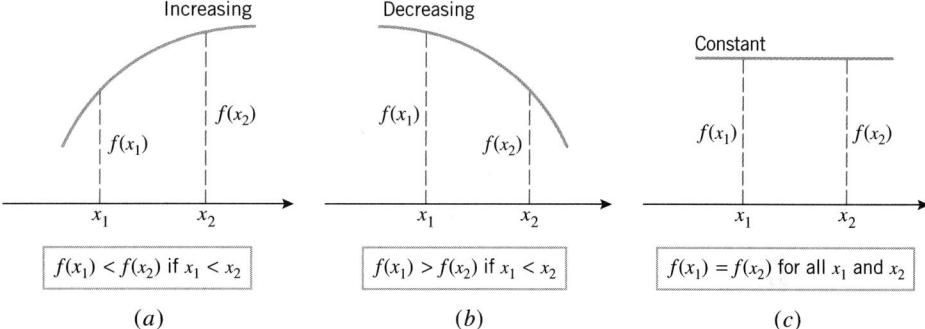

▶ **Figure 4.1.2**

(a) (b) (c)

Figure 4.1.3 suggests that a differentiable function f is increasing on any interval where each tangent line to its graph has positive slope, is decreasing on any interval where each tangent line to its graph has negative slope, and is constant on any interval where each tangent line to its graph has zero slope. This intuitive observation suggests the following important theorem that will be proved in Section 4.8.

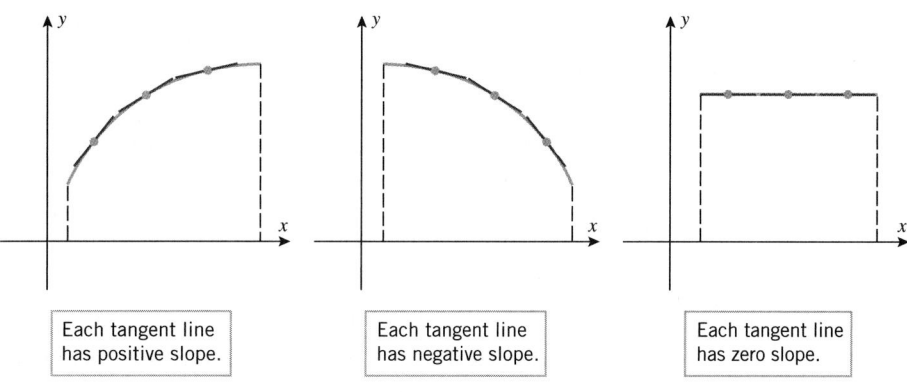

▶ **Figure 4.1.3**

Observe that the derivative conditions in Theorem 4.1.2 are only required to hold *inside* the interval [a, b], even though the conclusions apply to the entire interval.

4.1.2   THEOREM   *Let f be a function that is continuous on a closed interval $[a, b]$ and differentiable on the open interval (a, b).*

(a)   *If $f'(x) > 0$ for every value of x in (a, b), then f is increasing on $[a, b]$.*

(b)   *If $f'(x) < 0$ for every value of x in (a, b), then f is decreasing on $[a, b]$.*

(c)   *If $f'(x) = 0$ for every value of x in (a, b), then f is constant on $[a, b]$.*

Although stated for closed intervals, Theorem 4.1.2 is applicable on any interval on which f is continuous. For example, if f is continuous on $[a, +\infty)$ and $f'(x) > 0$ on $(a, +\infty)$, then f is increasing on $[a, +\infty)$; and if f is continuous on $(-\infty, +\infty)$ and $f'(x) < 0$ on $(-\infty, +\infty)$, then f is decreasing on $(-\infty, +\infty)$.

▶ **Example 1**   Find the intervals on which $f(x) = x^2 - 4x + 3$ is increasing and the intervals on which it is decreasing.

Solution.   The graph of f in Figure 4.1.4 suggests that f is decreasing for $x \leq 2$ and increasing for $x \geq 2$. To confirm this, we analyze the sign of f'. The derivative of f is

$$f'(x) = 2x - 4 = 2(x - 2)$$

It follows that

$$f'(x) < 0 \quad \text{if} \quad x < 2$$
$$f'(x) > 0 \quad \text{if} \quad 2 < x$$

Since f is continuous everywhere, it follows from the comment after Theorem 4.1.2 that

$$f \text{ is decreasing on } (-\infty, 2]$$
$$f \text{ is increasing on } [2, +\infty)$$

These conclusions are consistent with the graph of f in Figure 4.1.4. ◀

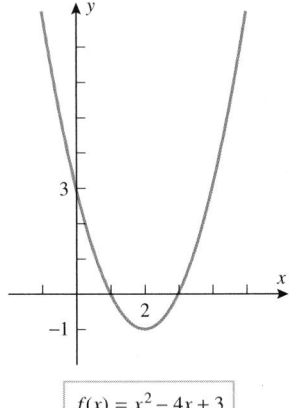

$f(x) = x^2 - 4x + 3$

▶ **Figure 4.1.4**

▶ **Example 2**   Find the intervals on which $f(x) = x^3$ is increasing and the intervals on which it is decreasing.

Solution.   The graph of f in Figure 4.1.5 suggests that f is increasing over the entire x-axis. To confirm this, we differentiate f to obtain $f'(x) = 3x^2$. Thus,

$$f'(x) > 0 \quad \text{if} \quad x < 0$$
$$f'(x) > 0 \quad \text{if} \quad 0 < x$$

Since f is continuous everywhere,

$$f \text{ is increasing on } (-\infty, 0]$$
$$f \text{ is increasing on } [0, +\infty)$$

Since f is increasing on the adjacent intervals $(-\infty, 0]$ and $[0, +\infty)$, it follows that f is increasing on their union $(-\infty, +\infty)$ (see Exercise 59). ◀

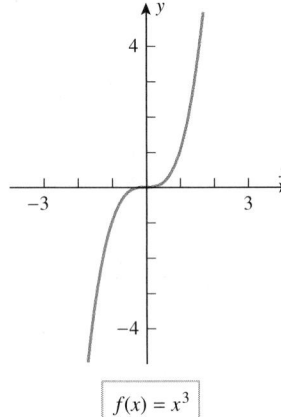

$f(x) = x^3$

▶ **Figure 4.1.5**

▶ **Example 3**

(a) Use the graph of $f(x) = 3x^4 + 4x^3 - 12x^2 + 2$ in Figure 4.1.6 to make a conjecture about the intervals on which f is increasing or decreasing.

(b) Use Theorem 4.1.2 to determine whether your conjecture is correct.

Solution (a).   The graph suggests that the function f is decreasing if $x \leq -2$, increasing if $-2 \leq x \leq 0$, decreasing if $0 \leq x \leq 1$, and increasing if $x \geq 1$.

Solution (b).   Differentiating f we obtain

$$f'(x) = 12x^3 + 12x^2 - 24x = 12x(x^2 + x - 2) = 12x(x + 2)(x - 1)$$

The sign analysis of f' in Table 4.1.1 can be obtained using the method of test points discussed in Web Appendix E. The conclusions in Table 4.1.1 confirm the conjecture in part (a). ◀

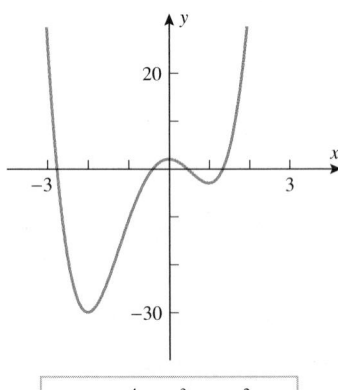

$f(x) = 3x^4 + 4x^3 - 12x^2 + 2$

▶ **Figure 4.1.6**

Table 4.1.1

INTERVAL	$(12x)(x+2)(x-1)$	$f'(x)$	CONCLUSION
$x < -2$	$(-)(-)(-)$	$-$	f is decreasing on $(-\infty, -2]$
$-2 < x < 0$	$(-)(+)(-)$	$+$	f is increasing on $[-2, 0]$
$0 < x < 1$	$(+)(+)(-)$	$-$	f is decreasing on $[0, 1]$
$1 < x$	$(+)(+)(+)$	$+$	f is increasing on $[1, +\infty)$

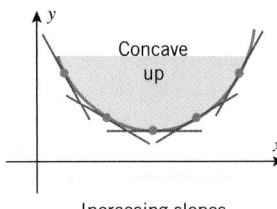

■ CONCAVITY

Although the sign of the derivative of f reveals where the graph of f is increasing or decreasing, it does not reveal the direction of *curvature*. For example, the graph is increasing on both sides of the point in Figure 4.1.7, but on the left side it has an upward curvature ("holds water") and on the right side it has a downward curvature ("spills water"). On intervals where the graph of f has upward curvature we say that f is *concave up*, and on intervals where the graph has downward curvature we say that f is *concave down*.

Figure 4.1.8 suggests two ways to characterize the concavity of a differentiable function f on an open interval:

- f is concave up on an open interval if its tangent lines have increasing slopes on that interval and is concave down if they have decreasing slopes.
- f is concave up on an open interval if its graph lies above its tangent lines on that interval and is concave down if it lies below its tangent lines.

Our formal definition for "concave up" and "concave down" corresponds to the first of these characterizations.

▶ **Figure 4.1.7**

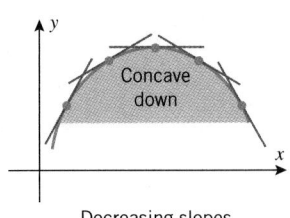

▶ **Figure 4.1.8**

> **4.1.3 DEFINITION**   If f is differentiable on an open interval, then f is said to be *concave up* on the open interval if f' is increasing on that interval, and f is said to be *concave down* on the open interval if f' is decreasing on that interval.

Since the slopes of the tangent lines to the graph of a differentiable function f are the values of its derivative f', it follows from Theorem 4.1.2 (applied to f' rather than f) that f' will be increasing on intervals where f'' is positive and that f' will be decreasing on intervals where f'' is negative. Thus, we have the following theorem.

> **4.1.4 THEOREM**   *Let f be twice differentiable on an open interval.*
>
> (a) *If $f''(x) > 0$ for every value of x in the open interval, then f is concave up on that interval.*
>
> (b) *If $f''(x) < 0$ for every value of x in the open interval, then f is concave down on that interval.*

▶ **Example 4**   Figure 4.1.4 suggests that the function $f(x) = x^2 - 4x + 3$ is concave up on the interval $(-\infty, +\infty)$. This is consistent with Theorem 4.1.4, since $f'(x) = 2x - 4$ and $f''(x) = 2$, so

$$f''(x) > 0 \quad \text{on the interval } (-\infty, +\infty)$$

Also, Figure 4.1.5 suggests that $f(x) = x^3$ is concave down on the interval $(-\infty, 0)$ and concave up on the interval $(0, +\infty)$. This agrees with Theorem 4.1.4, since $f'(x) = 3x^2$ and $f''(x) = 6x$, so

$$f''(x) < 0 \quad \text{if } x < 0 \quad \text{and} \quad f''(x) > 0 \quad \text{if } x > 0 \blacktriangleleft$$

■ INFLECTION POINTS

We see from Example 4 and Figure 4.1.5 that the graph of $f(x) = x^3$ changes from concave down to concave up at $x = 0$. Points where a curve changes from concave up to concave down or vice versa are of special interest, so there is some terminology associated with them.

> **4.1.5**   **DEFINITION**   If f is continuous on an open interval containing a value x_0, and if f changes the direction of its concavity at the point $(x_0, f(x_0))$, then we say that f has an ***inflection point at x_0***, and we call the point $(x_0, f(x_0))$ on the graph of f an ***inflection point*** of f (Figure 4.1.9).

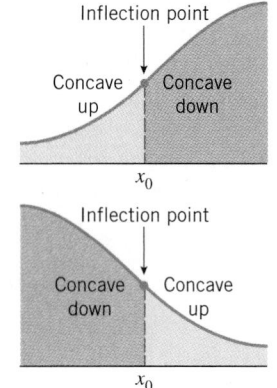

▶ **Figure 4.1.9**

▶ **Example 5**   Figure 4.1.10 shows the graph of the function $f(x) = x^3 - 3x^2 + 1$. Use the first and second derivatives of f to determine the intervals on which f is increasing, decreasing, concave up, and concave down. Locate all inflection points and confirm that your conclusions are consistent with the graph.

Solution.   Calculating the first two derivatives of f we obtain

$$f'(x) = 3x^2 - 6x = 3x(x - 2)$$

$$f''(x) = 6x - 6 = 6(x - 1)$$

The sign analysis of these derivatives is shown in the following tables:

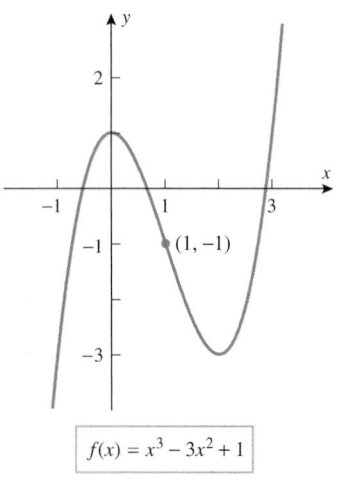

$f(x) = x^3 - 3x^2 + 1$

▶ **Figure 4.1.10**

INTERVAL	$(3x)(x-2)$	$f'(x)$	CONCLUSION
$x < 0$	$(-)(-)$	$+$	f is increasing on $(-\infty, 0]$
$0 < x < 2$	$(+)(-)$	$-$	f is decreasing on $[0, 2]$
$x > 2$	$(+)(+)$	$+$	f is increasing on $[2, +\infty)$

INTERVAL	$6(x-1)$	$f''(x)$	CONCLUSION
$x < 1$	$(-)$	$-$	f is concave down on $(-\infty, 1)$
$x > 1$	$(+)$	$+$	f is concave up on $(1, +\infty)$

The second table shows that there is an inflection point at $x = 1$, since f changes from concave down to concave up at that point. The inflection point is $(1, f(1)) = (1, -1)$. All of these conclusions are consistent with the graph of f. ◀

One can correctly guess from Figure 4.1.10 that the function $f(x) = x^3 - 3x^2 + 1$ has an inflection point at $x = 1$ without actually computing derivatives. However, sometimes changes in concavity are so subtle that calculus is essential to confirm their existence and identify their location. Here is an example.

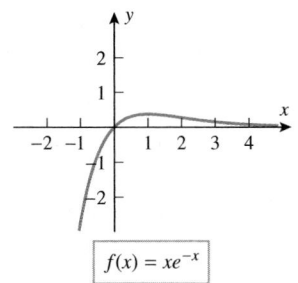

Figure 4.1.11

▶ **Example 6** Figure 4.1.11 suggests that the function $f(x) = xe^{-x}$ has an inflection point but its exact location is not evident from the graph in this figure. Use the first and second derivatives of f to determine the intervals on which f is increasing, decreasing, concave up, and concave down. Locate all inflection points.

Solution. Calculating the first two derivatives of f we obtain (verify)

$$f'(x) = (1 - x)e^{-x}$$
$$f''(x) = (x - 2)e^{-x}$$

Keeping in mind that e^{-x} is positive for all x, the sign analysis of these derivatives is easily determined:

INTERVAL	$(1-x)(e^{-x})$	$f'(x)$	CONCLUSION
$x < 1$	$(+)(+)$	$+$	f is increasing on $(-\infty, 1]$
$x > 1$	$(-)(+)$	$-$	f is decreasing on $[1, +\infty)$

INTERVAL	$(x-2)(e^{-x})$	$f''(x)$	CONCLUSION
$x < 2$	$(-)(+)$	$-$	f is concave down on $(-\infty, 2)$
$x > 2$	$(+)(+)$	$+$	f is concave up on $(2, +\infty)$

The second table shows that there is an inflection point at $x = 2$, since f changes from concave down to concave up at that point. All of these conclusions are consistent with the graph of f. ◀

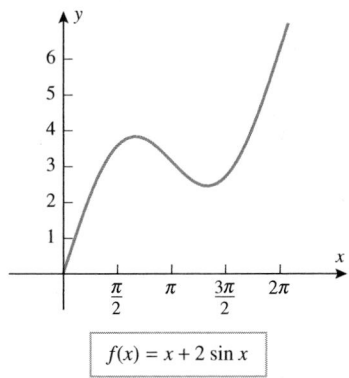

Figure 4.1.12

▶ **Example 7** Figure 4.1.12 shows the graph of the function $f(x) = x + 2\sin x$ over the interval $[0, 2\pi]$. Use the first and second derivatives of f to determine where f is increasing, decreasing, concave up, and concave down. Locate all inflection points and confirm that your conclusions are consistent with the graph.

Solution. Calculating the first two derivatives of f we obtain

$$f'(x) = 1 + 2\cos x$$
$$f''(x) = -2\sin x$$

Since f' is a continuous function, it changes sign on the interval $(0, 2\pi)$ only at points where $f'(x) = 0$ (why?). These values are solutions of the equation

$$1 + 2\cos x = 0 \quad \text{or equivalently} \quad \cos x = -\tfrac{1}{2}$$

There are two solutions of this equation in the interval $(0, 2\pi)$, namely, $x = 2\pi/3$ and $x = 4\pi/3$ (verify). Similarly, f'' is a continuous function, so its sign changes in the interval $(0, 2\pi)$ will occur only at values of x for which $f''(x) = 0$. These values are solutions of the equation

$$-2\sin x = 0$$

There is one solution of this equation in the interval $(0, 2\pi)$, namely, $x = \pi$. With the help of these "sign transition points" we obtain the sign analysis shown in the following tables:

INTERVAL	$f'(x) = 1 + 2\cos x$	CONCLUSION
$0 < x < 2\pi/3$	$+$	f is increasing on $[0, 2\pi/3]$
$2\pi/3 < x < 4\pi/3$	$-$	f is decreasing on $[2\pi/3, 4\pi/3]$
$4\pi/3 < x < 2\pi$	$+$	f is increasing on $[4\pi/3, 2\pi]$

INTERVAL	$f''(x) = -2\sin x$	CONCLUSION
$0 < x < \pi$	$-$	f is concave down on $(0, \pi)$
$\pi < x < 2\pi$	$+$	f is concave up on $(\pi, 2\pi)$

The second table shows that there is an inflection point at $x = \pi$, since f changes from concave down to concave up at that point. All of these conclusions are consistent with the graph of f. ◄

In the preceding examples the inflection points of f occurred wherever $f''(x) = 0$. However, this is not always the case. Here is a specific example.

> ► **Example 8** Find the inflection points, if any, of $f(x) = x^4$.

Solution. Calculating the first two derivatives of f we obtain

$$f'(x) = 4x^3$$

$$f''(x) = 12x^2$$

Since $f''(x)$ is positive for $x < 0$ and for $x > 0$, the function f is concave up on the interval $(-\infty, 0)$ and on the interval $(0, +\infty)$. Thus, there is no change in concavity and hence no inflection point at $x = 0$, even though $f''(0) = 0$ (Figure 4.1.13). ◄

We will see later that if a function f has an inflection point at $x = x_0$ and $f''(x_0)$ exists, then $f''(x_0) = 0$. Also, we will see in Section 4.3 that an inflection point may also occur where $f''(x)$ is not defined.

The signs in the two tables of Example 7 can be obtained either using the method of test points or using the unit circle definition of the sine and cosine functions.

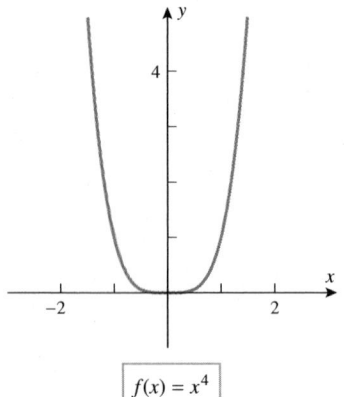

$f(x) = x^4$

▶ **Figure 4.1.13**

Give an argument to show that the function $f(x) = x^4$ graphed in Figure 4.1.13 is concave up on the interval $(-\infty, +\infty)$.

■ **INFLECTION POINTS IN APPLICATIONS**

Inflection points of a function f are those points on the graph of $y = f(x)$ where the slopes of the tangent lines change from increasing to decreasing or vice versa (Figure 4.1.14). Since the slope of the tangent line at a point on the graph of $y = f(x)$ can be interpreted as the rate of change of y with respect to x at that point, we can interpret inflection points in the following way:

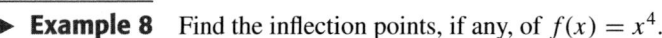

Inflection points mark the places on the curve $y = f(x)$ where the rate of change of y with respect to x changes from increasing to decreasing, or vice versa.

This is a subtle idea, since we are dealing with a change in a rate of change. It can help with your understanding of this idea to realize that inflection points may have interpretations in more familiar contexts. For example, consider the statement "Oil prices rose sharply during the first half of the year but have since begun to level off." If the price of oil is plotted as a function of time of year, this statement suggests the existence of an inflection point

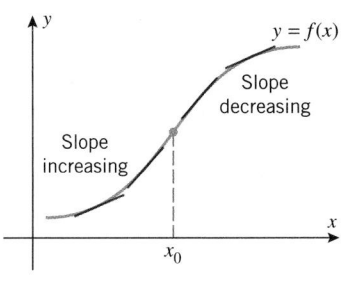

on the graph near the end of June. (Why?) To give a more visual example, consider the flask shown in Figure 4.1.15. Suppose that water is added to the flask so that the volume increases at a constant rate with respect to the time t, and let us examine the rate at which the water level y rises with respect to t. Initially, the level y will rise at a slow rate because of the wide base. However, as the diameter of the flask narrows, the rate at which the level y rises will increase until the level is at the narrow point in the neck. From that point on the rate at which the level rises will decrease as the diameter gets wider and wider. Thus, the narrow point in the neck is the point at which the rate of change of y with respect to t changes from increasing to decreasing.

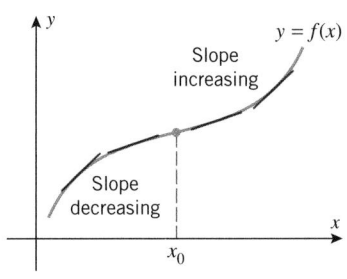

▶ **Figure 4.1.14**

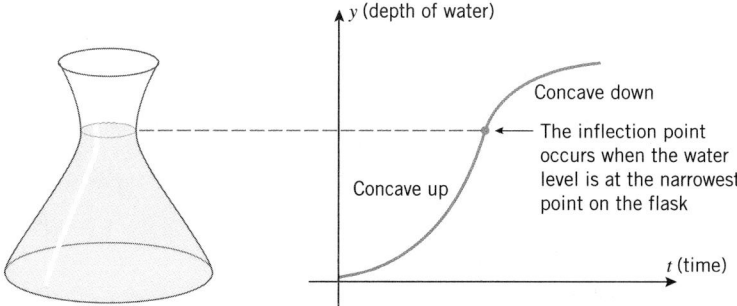

▶ **Figure 4.1.15**

▊ LOGISTIC CURVES

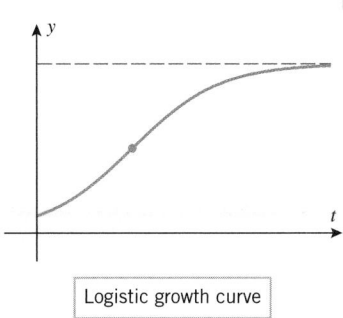

Logistic growth curve

▲ **Figure 4.1.16**

When a population grows in an environment in which space or food is limited, the graph of population versus time is typically an S-shaped curve of the form shown in Figure 4.1.16. The scenario described by this curve is a population that grows slowly at first and then more and more rapidly as the number of individuals producing offspring increases. However, at a certain point in time (where the inflection point occurs) the environmental factors begin to show their effect, and the growth rate begins a steady decline. Over an extended period of time the population approaches a limiting value that represents the upper limit on the number of individuals that the available space or food can sustain. Population growth curves of this type are called *logistic growth curves*.

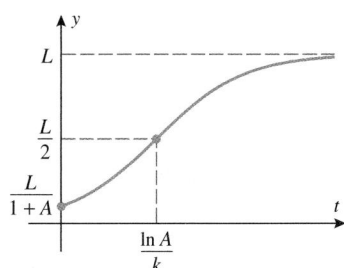

▲ **Figure 4.1.17**

▶ **Example 9**   We will see in a later chapter that logistic growth curves arise from equations of the form

$$y = \frac{L}{1 + Ae^{-kt}} \tag{1}$$

where y is the population at time t ($t \geq 0$) and A, k, and L are positive constants. Show that Figure 4.1.17 correctly describes the graph of this equation when $A > 1$.

Solution.   It follows from (1) that at time $t = 0$ the value of y is

$$y = \frac{L}{1 + A}$$

and it follows from (1) and the fact that $0 < e^{-kt} \leq 1$ for $t \geq 0$ that

$$\frac{L}{1 + A} \leq y < L \tag{2}$$

(verify). This is consistent with the graph in Figure 4.1.17. The horizontal asymptote at $y = L$ is confirmed by the limit

$$\lim_{t \to +\infty} y = \lim_{t \to +\infty} \frac{L}{1 + Ae^{-kt}} = \frac{L}{1 + 0} = L \tag{3}$$

Physically, Formulas (2) and (3) tell us that L is an upper limit on the population and that the population approaches this limit over time. Again, this is consistent with the graph in Figure 4.1.17.

To investigate intervals of increase and decrease, concavity, and inflection points, we need the first and second derivatives of y with respect to t. By multiplying both sides of Equation (1) by $e^{kt}(1 + Ae^{-kt})$, we can rewrite (1) as

$$ye^{kt} + Ay = Le^{kt}$$

Using implicit differentiation, we can derive that

$$\frac{dy}{dt} = \frac{k}{L}y(L - y) \tag{4}$$

$$\frac{d^2y}{dt^2} = \frac{k^2}{L^2}y(L - y)(L - 2y) \tag{5}$$

(Exercise 70). Since $k > 0$, $y > 0$, and $L - y > 0$, it follows from (4) that $dy/dt > 0$ for all t. Thus, y is always increasing, which is consistent with Figure 4.1.17.

Since $y > 0$ and $L - y > 0$, it follows from (5) that

$$\frac{d^2y}{dt^2} > 0 \quad \text{if} \quad L - 2y > 0$$

$$\frac{d^2y}{dt^2} < 0 \quad \text{if} \quad L - 2y < 0$$

Thus, the graph of y versus t is concave up if $y < L/2$, concave down if $y > L/2$, and has an inflection point where $y = L/2$, all of which is consistent with Figure 4.1.17.

Finally, we leave it for you to solve the equation

$$\frac{L}{2} = \frac{L}{1 + Ae^{-kt}}$$

for t to show that the inflection point occurs at

$$t = \frac{1}{k}\ln A = \frac{\ln A}{k} \quad \blacktriangleleft \tag{6}$$

✔ QUICK CHECK EXERCISES 4.1   (See page 244 for answers.)

1. (a) A function f is increasing on (a, b) if _____ whenever $a < x_1 < x_2 < b$.
   (b) A function f is decreasing on (a, b) if _____ whenever $a < x_1 < x_2 < b$.
   (c) A function f is concave up on (a, b) if f' is _____ on (a, b).
   (d) If $f''(a)$ exists and f has an inflection point at $x = a$, then $f''(a)$ _____.

2. Let $f(x) = 0.1(x^3 - 3x^2 - 9x)$. Then

   $$f'(x) = 0.1(3x^2 - 6x - 9) = 0.3(x + 1)(x - 3)$$

   $$f''(x) = 0.6(x - 1)$$

   (a) Solutions to $f'(x) = 0$ are $x =$ _____.
   (b) The function f is increasing on the interval(s) _____.

(c) The function f is concave down on the interval(s) _____.
(d) _____ is an inflection point on the graph of f.

3. Suppose that $f(x)$ has derivative $f'(x) = (x - 4)^2 e^{-x/2}$. Then $f''(x) = -\frac{1}{2}(x - 4)(x - 8)e^{-x/2}$.
   (a) The function f is increasing on the interval(s) _____.
   (b) The function f is concave up on the interval(s) _____.
   (c) The function f is concave down on the interval(s) _____.

4. Consider the statement "The rise in the cost of living slowed during the first half of the year." If we graph the cost of living versus time for the first half of the year, how does the graph reflect this statement?

EXERCISE SET 4.1   Graphing Utility   [c] CAS

1. In each part, sketch the graph of a function f with the stated properties, and discuss the signs of f' and f''.
   (a) The function f is concave up and increasing on the interval $(-\infty, +\infty)$.
   (b) The function f is concave down and increasing on the interval $(-\infty, +\infty)$.
   (c) The function f is concave up and decreasing on the interval $(-\infty, +\infty)$.
   (d) The function f is concave down and decreasing on the interval $(-\infty, +\infty)$.

2. In each part, sketch the graph of a function f with the stated properties.
   (a) f is increasing on $(-\infty, +\infty)$, has an inflection point at the origin, and is concave up on $(0, +\infty)$.
   (b) f is increasing on $(-\infty, +\infty)$, has an inflection point at the origin, and is concave down on $(0, +\infty)$.
   (c) f is decreasing on $(-\infty, +\infty)$, has an inflection point at the origin, and is concave up on $(0, +\infty)$.
   (d) f is decreasing on $(-\infty, +\infty)$, has an inflection point at the origin, and is concave down on $(0, +\infty)$.

3. Use the graph of the equation $y = f(x)$ in the accompanying figure to find the signs of dy/dx and d^2y/dx^2 at the points A, B, and C.

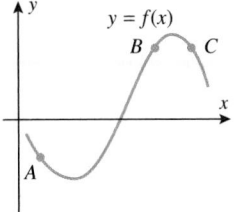

◀ **Figure Ex-3**

4. Use the graph of the equation $y = f'(x)$ in the accompanying figure to find the signs of dy/dx and d^2y/dx^2 at the points A, B, and C.

5. Use the graph of $y = f''(x)$ in the accompanying figure to determine the x-coordinates of all inflection points of f. Explain your reasoning.

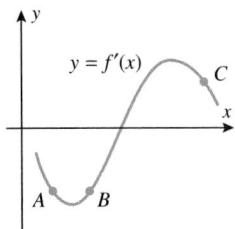

▲ **Figure Ex-4**

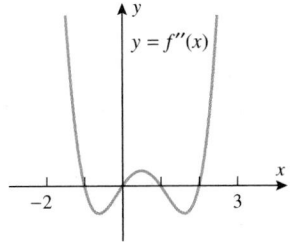

▲ **Figure Ex-5**

6. Use the graph of $y = f'(x)$ in the accompanying figure to replace the question mark with $<$, $=$, or $>$, as appropriate. Explain your reasoning.
   (a) $f(0)$? $f(1)$ (b) $f(1)$? $f(2)$ (c) $f'(0)$? 0
   (d) $f'(1)$? 0   (e) $f''(0)$? 0   (f) $f''(2)$? 0

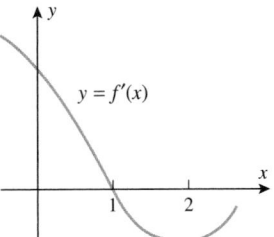

◀ **Figure Ex-6**

7. In each part, use the graph of $y = f(x)$ in the accompanying figure to find the requested information.
   (a) Find the intervals on which f is increasing.
   (b) Find the intervals on which f is decreasing.
   (c) Find the open intervals on which f is concave up.
   (d) Find the open intervals on which f is concave down.
   (e) Find all values of x at which f has an inflection point.

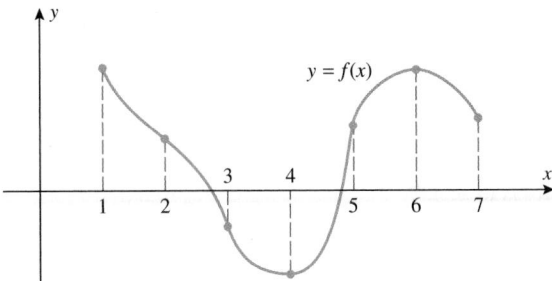

▲ **Figure Ex-7**

8. Use the graph in Exercise 7 to make a table that shows the signs of f' and f'' over the intervals $(1, 2)$, $(2, 3)$, $(3, 4)$, $(4, 5)$, $(5, 6)$, and $(6, 7)$.

9–10 A sign chart is presented for the first and second derivatives of a function f. Assuming that f is continuous everywhere, find: (a) the intervals on which f is increasing, (b) the intervals on which f is decreasing, (c) the open intervals on which f is concave up, (d) the open intervals on which f is concave down, and (e) the x-coordinates of all inflection points. ▨

9.

INTERVAL	SIGN OF $f'(x)$	SIGN OF $f''(x)$
$x < 1$	$-$	$+$
$1 < x < 2$	$+$	$+$
$2 < x < 3$	$+$	$-$
$3 < x < 4$	$-$	$-$
$4 < x$	$-$	$+$

10.

INTERVAL	SIGN OF $f'(x)$	SIGN OF $f''(x)$
$x < 1$	$+$	$+$
$1 < x < 3$	$+$	$-$
$3 < x$	$+$	$+$

11–14 True–False Assume that f is differentiable everywhere. Determine whether the statement is true or false. Explain your answer. ■

11. If f is decreasing on $[0, 2]$, then $f(0) > f(1) > f(2)$.

12. If $f'(1) > 0$, then f is increasing on $[0, 2]$.

13. If f is increasing on $[0, 2]$, then $f'(1) > 0$.

14. If f' is increasing on $[0, 1]$ and f' is decreasing on $[1, 2]$, then f has an inflection point at $x = 1$.

15–32 Find: (a) the intervals on which f is increasing, (b) the intervals on which f is decreasing, (c) the open intervals on which f is concave up, (d) the open intervals on which f is concave down, and (e) the x-coordinates of all inflection points. ■

15. $f(x) = x^2 - 3x + 8$ **16.** $f(x) = 5 - 4x - x^2$

17. $f(x) = (2x + 1)^3$ **18.** $f(x) = 5 + 12x - x^3$

19. $f(x) = 3x^4 - 4x^3$ **20.** $f(x) = x^4 - 5x^3 + 9x^2$

21. $f(x) = \dfrac{x - 2}{(x^2 - x + 1)^2}$ **22.** $f(x) = \dfrac{x}{x^2 + 2}$

23. $f(x) = \sqrt[3]{x^2 + x + 1}$ **24.** $f(x) = x^{4/3} - x^{1/3}$

25. $f(x) = (x^{2/3} - 1)^2$ **26.** $f(x) = x^{2/3} - x$

27. $f(x) = e^{-x^2/2}$ **28.** $f(x) = xe^{x^2}$

29. $f(x) = \ln \sqrt{x^2 + 4}$ **30.** $f(x) = x^3 \ln x$

31. $f(x) = \tan^{-1}(x^2 - 1)$ **32.** $f(x) = \sin^{-1} x^{2/3}$

33–38 Analyze the trigonometric function f over the specified interval, stating where f is increasing, decreasing, concave up, and concave down, and stating the x-coordinates of all inflection points. Confirm that your results are consistent with the graph of f generated with a graphing utility. ■

33. $f(x) = \sin x - \cos x$; $[-\pi, \pi]$

34. $f(x) = \sec x \tan x$; $(-\pi/2, \pi/2)$

35. $f(x) = 1 - \tan(x/2)$; $(-\pi, \pi)$

36. $f(x) = 2x + \cot x$; $(0, \pi)$

37. $f(x) = (\sin x + \cos x)^2$; $[-\pi, \pi]$

38. $f(x) = \sin^2 2x$; $[0, \pi]$

FOCUS ON CONCEPTS

39. In parts (a)–(c), sketch a continuous curve $y = f(x)$ with the stated properties.
(a) $f(2) = 4$, $f'(2) = 0$, $f''(x) > 0$ for all x
(b) $f(2) = 4$, $f'(2) = 0$, $f''(x) < 0$ for $x < 2$, $f''(x) > 0$ for $x > 2$

(c) $f(2) = 4$, $f''(x) < 0$ for $x \neq 2$ and $\lim_{x \to 2^+} f'(x) = +\infty$, $\lim_{x \to 2^-} f'(x) = -\infty$

40. In each part sketch a continuous curve $y = f(x)$ with the stated properties.
(a) $f(2) = 4$, $f'(2) = 0$, $f''(x) < 0$ for all x
(b) $f(2) = 4$, $f'(2) = 0$, $f''(x) > 0$ for $x < 2$, $f''(x) < 0$ for $x > 2$
(c) $f(2) = 4$, $f''(x) > 0$ for $x \neq 2$ and $\lim_{x \to 2^+} f'(x) = -\infty$, $\lim_{x \to 2^-} f'(x) = +\infty$

41–46 If f is increasing on an interval $[0, b)$, then it follows from Definition 4.1.1 that $f(0) < f(x)$ for each x in the interval $(0, b)$. Use this result in these exercises. ■

41. Show that $\sqrt[3]{1 + x} < 1 + \frac{1}{3}x$ if $x > 0$, and confirm the inequality with a graphing utility. [*Hint:* Show that the function $f(x) = 1 + \frac{1}{3}x - \sqrt[3]{1 + x}$ is increasing on $[0, +\infty)$.]

42. Show that $x < \tan x$ if $0 < x < \pi/2$, and confirm the inequality with a graphing utility. [*Hint:* Show that the function $f(x) = \tan x - x$ is increasing on $[0, \pi/2)$.]

43. Use a graphing utility to make a conjecture about the relative sizes of x and $\sin x$ for $x \geq 0$, and prove your conjecture.

44. Use a graphing utility to make a conjecture about the relative sizes of $1 - x^2/2$ and $\cos x$ for $x \geq 0$, and prove your conjecture. [*Hint:* Use the result of Exercise 43.]

45. (a) Show that $\ln(x + 1) \leq x$ if $x \geq 0$.
(b) Show that $\ln(x + 1) \geq x - \frac{1}{2}x^2$ if $x \geq 0$.
(c) Confirm the inequalities in parts (a) and (b) with a graphing utility.

46. (a) Show that $e^x \geq 1 + x$ if $x \geq 0$.
(b) Show that $e^x \geq 1 + x + \frac{1}{2}x^2$ if $x \geq 0$.
(c) Confirm the inequalities in parts (a) and (b) with a graphing utility.

47–48 Use a graphing utility to generate the graphs of f' and f'' over the stated interval; then use those graphs to estimate the x-coordinates of the inflection points of f, the intervals on which f is concave up or down, and the intervals on which f is increasing or decreasing. Check your estimates by graphing f. ■

47. $f(x) = x^4 - 24x^2 + 12x$, $-5 \leq x \leq 5$

48. $f(x) = \dfrac{1}{1 + x^2}$, $-5 \leq x \leq 5$

49–50 Use a CAS to find f'' and to approximate the x-coordinates of the inflection points to six decimal places. Confirm that your answer is consistent with the graph of f. ■

49. $f(x) = \dfrac{10x - 3}{3x^2 - 5x + 8}$ **50.** $f(x) = \dfrac{x^3 - 8x + 7}{\sqrt{x^2 + 1}}$

51. Use Definition 4.1.1 to prove that $f(x) = x^2$ is increasing on $[0, +\infty)$.

52. Use Definition 4.1.1 to prove that $f(x) = 1/x$ is decreasing on $(0, +\infty)$.

53–54 Determine whether the statements are true or false. If a statement is false, find functions for which the statement fails to hold. ■

53. (a) If f and g are increasing on an interval, then so is $f + g$.
 (b) If f and g are increasing on an interval, then so is $f \cdot g$.

54. (a) If f and g are concave up on an interval, then so is $f + g$.
 (b) If f and g are concave up on an interval, then so is $f \cdot g$.

55. In each part, find functions f and g that are increasing on $(-\infty, +\infty)$ and for which $f - g$ has the stated property.
 (a) $f - g$ is decreasing on $(-\infty, +\infty)$.
 (b) $f - g$ is constant on $(-\infty, +\infty)$.
 (c) $f - g$ is increasing on $(-\infty, +\infty)$.

56. In each part, find functions f and g that are positive and increasing on $(-\infty, +\infty)$ and for which f/g has the stated property.
 (a) f/g is decreasing on $(-\infty, +\infty)$.
 (b) f/g is constant on $(-\infty, +\infty)$.
 (c) f/g is increasing on $(-\infty, +\infty)$.

57. (a) Prove that a general cubic polynomial

$$f(x) = ax^3 + bx^2 + cx + d \quad (a \neq 0)$$

 has exactly one inflection point.
 (b) Prove that if a cubic polynomial has three x-intercepts, then the inflection point occurs at the average value of the intercepts.
 (c) Use the result in part (b) to find the inflection point of the cubic polynomial $f(x) = x^3 - 3x^2 + 2x$, and check your result by using f'' to determine where f is concave up and concave down.

58. From Exercise 57, the polynomial $f(x) = x^3 + bx^2 + 1$ has one inflection point. Use a graphing utility to reach a conclusion about the effect of the constant b on the location of the inflection point. Use f'' to explain what you have observed graphically.

59. Use Definition 4.1.1 to prove:
 (a) If f is increasing on the intervals $(a, c]$ and $[c, b)$, then f is increasing on (a, b).
 (b) If f is decreasing on the intervals $(a, c]$ and $[c, b)$, then f is decreasing on (a, b).

60. Use part (a) of Exercise 59 to show that $f(x) = x + \sin x$ is increasing on the interval $(-\infty, +\infty)$.

61. Use part (b) of Exercise 59 to show that $f(x) = \cos x - x$ is decreasing on the interval $(-\infty, +\infty)$.

62. Let $y = 1/(1 + x^2)$. Find the values of x for which y is increasing most rapidly or decreasing most rapidly.

63–66 Suppose that water is flowing at a constant rate into the container shown. Make a rough sketch of the graph of the water level y versus the time t. Make sure that your sketch conveys where the graph is concave up and concave down, and label the y-coordinates of the inflection points. ■

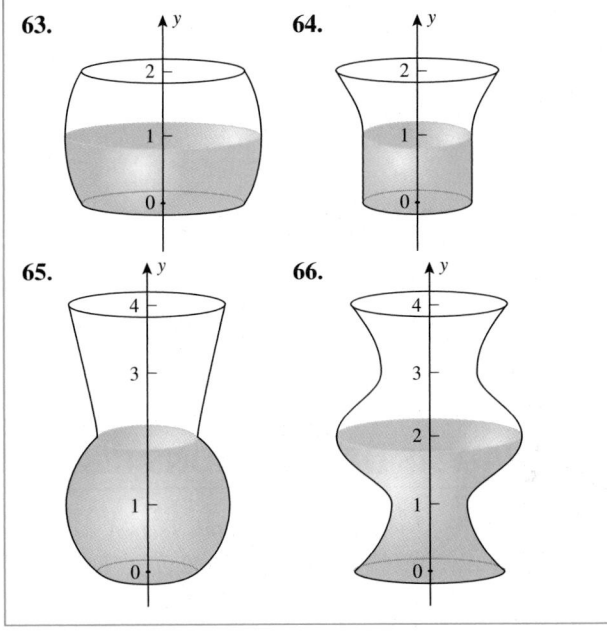

67. Suppose that a population y grows according to the logistic model given by Formula (1).
 (a) At what rate is y increasing at time $t = 0$?
 (b) In words, describe how the rate of growth of y varies with time.
 (c) At what time is the population growing most rapidly?

68. Suppose that the number of individuals at time t in a certain wildlife population is given by

$$N(t) = \frac{340}{1 + 9(0.77)^t}, \quad t \geq 0$$

 where t is in years. Use a graphing utility to estimate the time at which the size of the population is increasing most rapidly.

69. Suppose that the spread of a flu virus on a college campus is modeled by the function

$$y(t) = \frac{1000}{1 + 999e^{-0.9t}}$$

 where $y(t)$ is the number of infected students at time t (in days, starting with $t = 0$). Use a graphing utility to estimate the day on which the virus is spreading most rapidly.

70. The logistic growth model given in Formula (1) is equivalent to

$$ye^{kt} + Ay = Le^{kt}$$

 where y is the population at time t ($t \geq 0$) and A, k, and L

are positive constants. Use implicit differentiation to verify that

$$\frac{dy}{dt} = \frac{k}{L}y(L - y)$$

$$\frac{d^2y}{dt^2} = \frac{k^2}{L^2}y(L - y)(L - 2y)$$

71. Assuming that A, k, and L are positive constants, verify that the graph of $y = L/(1 + Ae^{-kt})$ has an inflection point at $\left(\frac{1}{k}\ln A, \frac{1}{2}L\right)$.

72. **Writing** An approaching storm causes the air temperature to fall. Make a statement that indicates there is an inflection point in the graph of temperature versus time. Explain how the existence of an inflection point follows from your statement.

73. **Writing** Explain what the sign analyses of $f'(x)$ and $f''(x)$ tell us about the graph of $y = f(x)$.

✔ **QUICK CHECK ANSWERS 4.1**

1. (a) $f(x_1) < f(x_2)$ (b) $f(x_1) > f(x_2)$ (c) increasing (d) $= 0$ **2.** (a) $-1, 3$ (b) $(-\infty, -1]$ and $[3, +\infty)$ (c) $(-\infty, 1)$
(d) $(1, -1.1)$ **3.** (a) $(-\infty, +\infty)$ (b) $(4, 8)$ (c) $(-\infty, 4), (8, +\infty)$ **4.** The graph is increasing and concave down.

4.2 ANALYSIS OF FUNCTIONS II: RELATIVE EXTREMA; GRAPHING POLYNOMIALS

In this section we will develop methods for finding the high and low points on the graph of a function and we will discuss procedures for analyzing the graphs of polynomials.

■ RELATIVE MAXIMA AND MINIMA

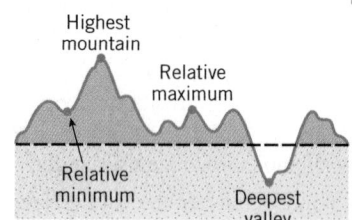
▲ Figure 4.2.1

If we imagine the graph of a function f to be a two-dimensional mountain range with hills and valleys, then the tops of the hills are called "relative maxima," and the bottoms of the valleys are called "relative minima" (Figure 4.2.1). The relative maxima are the high points in their *immediate vicinity*, and the relative minima are the low points. A relative maximum need not be the highest point in the entire mountain range, and a relative minimum need not be the lowest point—they are just high and low points *relative* to the nearby terrain. These ideas are captured in the following definition.

> **4.2.1 DEFINITION** A function f is said to have a ***relative maximum*** at x_0 if there is an open interval containing x_0 on which $f(x_0)$ is the largest value, that is, $f(x_0) \geq f(x)$ for all x in the interval. Similarly, f is said to have a ***relative minimum*** at x_0 if there is an open interval containing x_0 on which $f(x_0)$ is the smallest value, that is, $f(x_0) \leq f(x)$ for all x in the interval. If f has either a relative maximum or a relative minimum at x_0, then f is said to have a ***relative extremum*** at x_0.

▶ **Example 1** We can see from Figure 4.2.2 that:

- $f(x) = x^2$ has a relative minimum at $x = 0$ but no relative maxima.
- $f(x) = x^3$ has no relative extrema.
- $f(x) = x^3 - 3x + 3$ has a relative maximum at $x = -1$ and a relative minimum at $x = 1$.
- $f(x) = \frac{1}{2}x^4 - \frac{4}{3}x^3 - x^2 + 4x + 1$ has relative minima at $x = -1$ and $x = 2$ and a relative maximum at $x = 1$.

- $f(x) = \cos x$ has relative maxima at all even multiples of π and relative minima at all odd multiples of π. ◄

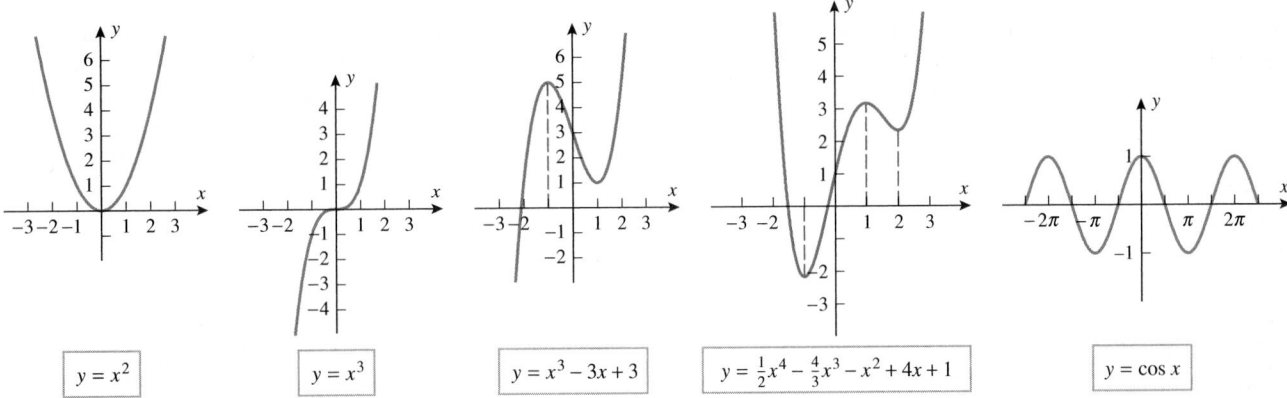

$$y = x^2$$ $$y = x^3$$ $$y = x^3 - 3x + 3$$ $$y = \tfrac{1}{2}x^4 - \tfrac{4}{3}x^3 - x^2 + 4x + 1$$ $$y = \cos x$$

▲ **Figure 4.2.2**

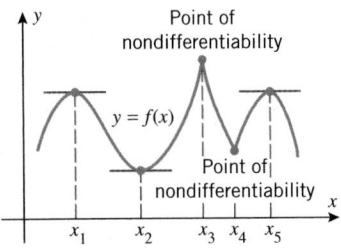

▲ **Figure 4.2.3** The points x_1, x_2, x_3, x_4, and x_5 are critical points. Of these, x_1, x_2, and x_5 are stationary points.

The relative extrema for the five functions in Example 1 occur at points where the graphs of the functions have horizontal tangent lines. Figure 4.2.3 illustrates that a relative extremum can also occur at a point where a function is not differentiable. In general, we define a *critical point* for a function f to be a point in the domain of f at which either the graph of f has a horizontal tangent line or f is not differentiable. To distinguish between the two types of critical points we call x a *stationary point* of f if $f'(x) = 0$. The following theorem, which is proved in Appendix J, states that the critical points for a function form a complete set of candidates for relative extrema on the interior of the domain of the function.

> **4.2.2   THEOREM**   *Suppose that f is a function defined on an open interval containing the point x_0. If f has a relative extremum at $x = x_0$, then $x = x_0$ is a critical point of f; that is, either $f'(x_0) = 0$ or f is not differentiable at x_0.*

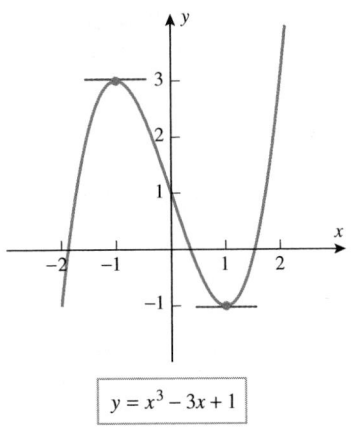

$$y = x^3 - 3x + 1$$

▲ **Figure 4.2.4**

What is the maximum number of critical points that a polynomial of degree n can have? Why?

► **Example 2**   Find all critical points of $f(x) = x^3 - 3x + 1$.

Solution.   The function f, being a polynomial, is differentiable everywhere, so its critical points are all stationary points. To find these points we must solve the equation $f'(x) = 0$. Since

$$f'(x) = 3x^2 - 3 = 3(x + 1)(x - 1)$$

we conclude that the critical points occur at $x = -1$ and $x = 1$. This is consistent with the graph of f in Figure 4.2.4. ◄

► **Example 3**   Find all critical points of $f(x) = 3x^{5/3} - 15x^{2/3}$.

Solution.   The function f is continuous everywhere and its derivative is

$$f'(x) = 5x^{2/3} - 10x^{-1/3} = 5x^{-1/3}(x - 2) = \frac{5(x - 2)}{x^{1/3}}$$

We see from this that $f'(x) = 0$ if $x = 2$ and $f'(x)$ is undefined if $x = 0$. Thus $x = 0$ and $x = 2$ are critical points and $x = 2$ is a stationary point. This is consistent with the graph of f shown in Figure 4.2.5. ◄

TECHNOLOGY MASTERY | Your graphing utility may have trouble producing portions of the graph in Figure 4.2.5 because of the fractional exponents. If this is the case for you, graph the function

$$y = 3(|x|/x)|x|^{5/3} - 15|x|^{2/3}$$

which is equivalent to $f(x)$ for $x \neq 0$. Appendix A explores the method suggested here in more detail.

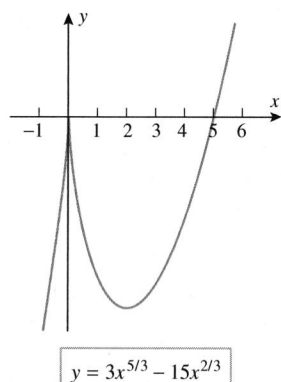

$$y = 3x^{5/3} - 15x^{2/3}$$

▲ **Figure 4.2.5**

■ FIRST DERIVATIVE TEST

Theorem 4.2.2 asserts that the relative extrema must occur at critical points, but it does *not* say that a relative extremum occurs at *every* critical point. For example, for the eight critical points in Figure 4.2.6, relative extrema occur at each x_0 in the top row but not at any x_0 in the bottom row. Moreover, at the critical points in the first row the derivatives have opposite signs on the two sides of x_0, whereas at the critical points in the second row the signs of the derivatives are the same on both sides. This suggests:

> *A function f has a relative extremum at those critical points where f' changes sign.*

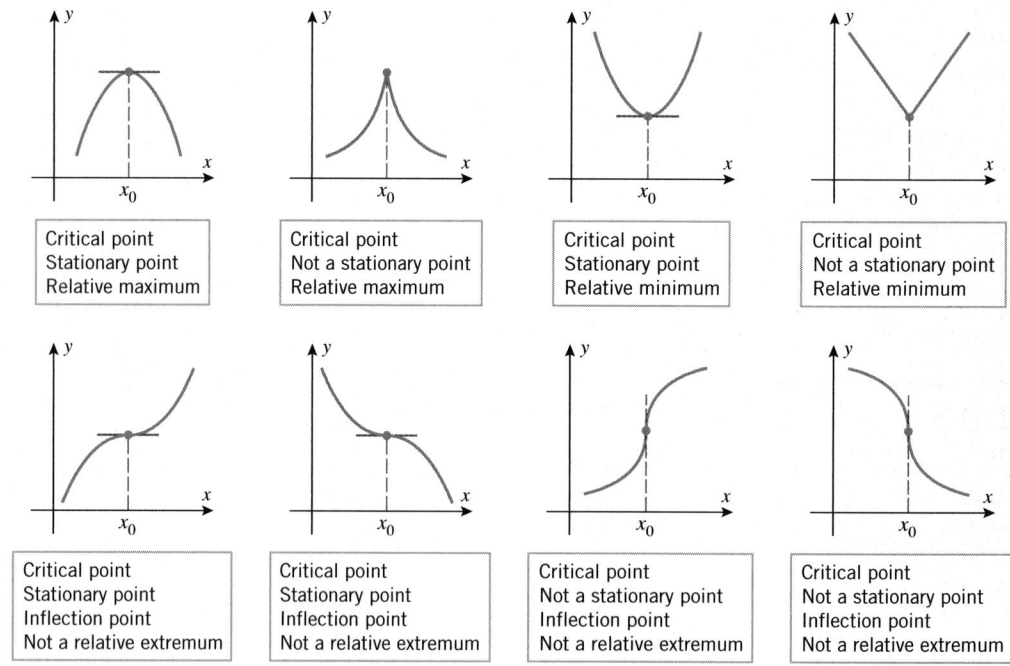

▲ **Figure 4.2.6**

We can actually take this a step further. At the two relative maxima in Figure 4.2.6 the derivative is positive on the left side and negative on the right side, and at the two relative minima the derivative is negative on the left side and positive on the right side. All of this is summarized more precisely in the following theorem.

4.2.3 THEOREM (*First Derivative Test*) *Suppose that* f *is continuous at a critical point* x_0.

(a) *If* $f'(x) > 0$ *on an open interval extending left from* x_0 *and* $f'(x) < 0$ *on an open interval extending right from* x_0, *then* f *has a relative maximum at* x_0.

(b) *If* $f'(x) < 0$ *on an open interval extending left from* x_0 *and* $f'(x) > 0$ *on an open interval extending right from* x_0, *then* f *has a relative minimum at* x_0.

(c) *If* $f'(x)$ *has the same sign on an open interval extending left from* x_0 *as it does on an open interval extending right from* x_0, *then* f *does not have a relative extremum at* x_0.

Informally stated, parts (*a*) and (*b*) of Theorem 4.2.3 tell us that for a continuous function, relative maxima occur at critical points where the derivative changes from $+$ to $-$ and relative minima where it changes from $-$ to $+$.

Use the first derivative test to confirm the behavior at x_0 of each graph in Figure 4.2.6.

PROOF We will prove part (*a*) and leave parts (*b*) and (*c*) as exercises. We are assuming that $f'(x) > 0$ on the interval (a, x_0) and that $f'(x) < 0$ on the interval (x_0, b), and we want to show that

$$f(x_0) \geq f(x)$$

for all x in the interval (a, b). However, the two hypotheses, together with Theorem 4.1.2 and its associated marginal note imply that f is increasing on the interval $(a, x_0]$ and decreasing on the interval $[x_0, b)$. Thus, $f(x_0) \geq f(x)$ for all x in (a, b) with equality only at x_0. ∎

▶ **Example 4** We showed in Example 3 that the function $f(x) = 3x^{5/3} - 15x^{2/3}$ has critical points at $x = 0$ and $x = 2$. Figure 4.2.5 suggests that f has a relative maximum at $x = 0$ and a relative minimum at $x = 2$. Confirm this using the first derivative test.

Solution. We showed in Example 3 that

$$f'(x) = \frac{5(x - 2)}{x^{1/3}}$$

A sign analysis of this derivative is shown in Table 4.2.1. The sign of f' changes from $+$ to $-$ at $x = 0$, so there is a relative maximum at that point. The sign changes from $-$ to $+$ at $x = 2$, so there is a relative minimum at that point. ◀

Table 4.2.1

INTERVAL	$5(x-2)/x^{1/3}$	$f'(x)$
$x < 0$	$(-)/(-)$	$+$
$0 < x < 2$	$(-)/(+)$	$-$
$x > 2$	$(+)/(+)$	$+$

SECOND DERIVATIVE TEST

There is another test for relative extrema that is based on the following geometric observation: A function f has a relative maximum at a stationary point if the graph of f is concave down on an open interval containing that point, and it has a relative minimum if it is concave up (Figure 4.2.7).

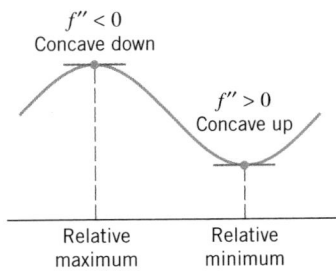

$f'' < 0$
Concave down

$f'' > 0$
Concave up

Relative maximum Relative minimum

▲ **Figure 4.2.7**

4.2.4 THEOREM (*Second Derivative Test*) *Suppose that* f *is twice differentiable at the point* x_0.

(a) *If* $f'(x_0) = 0$ *and* $f''(x_0) > 0$, *then* f *has a relative minimum at* x_0.

(b) *If* $f'(x_0) = 0$ *and* $f''(x_0) < 0$, *then* f *has a relative maximum at* x_0.

(c) *If* $f'(x_0) = 0$ *and* $f''(x_0) = 0$, *then the test is inconclusive; that is,* f *may have a relative maximum, a relative minimum, or neither at* x_0.

The second derivative test is often easier to apply than the first derivative test. However, the first derivative test can be used at any critical point of a continuous function, while the second derivative test applies only at stationary points where the second derivative exists.

We will prove parts (a) and (c) and leave part (b) as an exercise.

PROOF (a) We are given that $f'(x_0) = 0$ and $f''(x_0) > 0$, and we want to show that f has a relative minimum at x_0. Expressing $f''(x_0)$ as a limit and using the two given conditions we obtain

$$f''(x_0) = \lim_{x \to x_0} \frac{f'(x) - f'(x_0)}{x - x_0} = \lim_{x \to x_0} \frac{f'(x)}{x - x_0} > 0$$

This implies that for x sufficiently close to but different from x_0 we have

$$\frac{f'(x)}{x - x_0} > 0 \qquad (1)$$

Thus, there is an open interval extending left from x_0 and an open interval extending right from x_0 on which (1) holds. On the open interval extending left the denominator in (1) is negative, so $f'(x) < 0$, and on the open interval extending right the denominator is positive, so $f'(x) > 0$. It now follows from part (b) of the first derivative test (Theorem 4.2.3) that f has a relative minimum at x_0.

PROOF (c) To prove this part of the theorem we need only provide functions for which $f'(x_0) = 0$ and $f''(x_0) = 0$ at some point x_0, but with one having a relative minimum at x_0, one having a relative maximum at x_0, and one having neither at x_0. We leave it as an exercise for you to show that three such functions are $f(x) = x^4$ (relative minimum at $x = 0$), $f(x) = -x^4$ (relative maximum at $x = 0$), and $f(x) = x^3$ (neither a relative maximum nor a relative minimum at x_0). ∎

▶ **Example 5**   Find the relative extrema of $f(x) = 3x^5 - 5x^3$.

Solution.   We have

$$f'(x) = 15x^4 - 15x^2 = 15x^2(x^2 - 1) = 15x^2(x + 1)(x - 1)$$
$$f''(x) = 60x^3 - 30x = 30x(2x^2 - 1)$$

Solving $f'(x) = 0$ yields the stationary points $x = 0$, $x = -1$, and $x = 1$. As shown in the following table, we can conclude from the second derivative test that f has a relative maximum at $x = -1$ and a relative minimum at $x = 1$.

STATIONARY POINT	$30x(2x^2 - 1)$	$f''(x)$	SECOND DERIVATIVE TEST
$x = -1$	-30	$-$	f has a relative maximum
$x = 0$	0	0	Inconclusive
$x = 1$	30	$+$	f has a relative minimum

The test is inconclusive at $x = 0$, so we will try the first derivative test at that point. A sign analysis of f' is given in the following table:

INTERVAL	$15x^2(x + 1)(x - 1)$	$f'(x)$
$-1 < x < 0$	$(+)(+)(-)$	$-$
$0 < x < 1$	$(+)(+)(-)$	$-$

Since there is no sign change in f' at $x = 0$, there is neither a relative maximum nor a relative minimum at that point. All of this is consistent with the graph of f shown in Figure 4.2.8. ◀

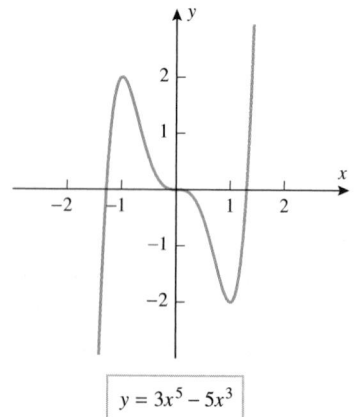

$y = 3x^5 - 5x^3$

▲ **Figure 4.2.8**

■ GEOMETRIC IMPLICATIONS OF MULTIPLICITY

Our final goal in this section is to outline a general procedure that can be used to analyze and graph polynomials. To do so, it will be helpful to understand how the graph of a polynomial behaves in the vicinity of its roots. For example, it would be nice to know what property of the polynomial in Example 5 produced the inflection point and horizontal tangent at the root $x = 0$.

Recall that a root $x = r$ of a polynomial $p(x)$ has ***multiplicity m*** if $(x - r)^m$ divides $p(x)$ but $(x - r)^{m+1}$ does not. A root of multiplicity 1 is called a ***simple root***. Figure 4.2.9 and the following theorem show that the behavior of a polynomial in the vicinity of a real root is determined by the multiplicity of that root (we omit the proof).

4.2.5   THE GEOMETRIC IMPLICATIONS OF MULTIPLICITY   *Suppose that $p(x)$ is a polynomial with a root of multiplicity m at $x = r$.*

(a)   *If m is even, then the graph of $y = p(x)$ is tangent to the x-axis at $x = r$, does not cross the x-axis there, and does not have an inflection point there.*

(b)   *If m is odd and greater than 1, then the graph is tangent to the x-axis at $x = r$, crosses the x-axis there, and also has an inflection point there.*

(c)   *If $m = 1$ (so that the root is simple), then the graph is not tangent to the x-axis at $x = r$, crosses the x-axis there, and may or may not have an inflection point there.*

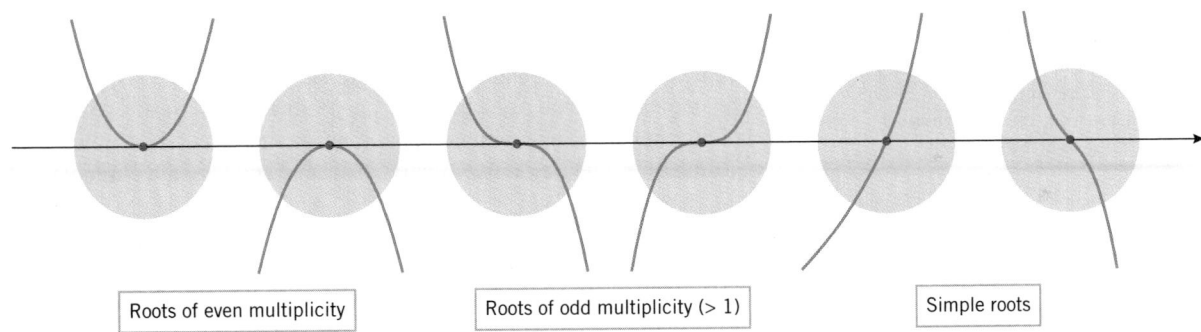

Roots of even multiplicity   Roots of odd multiplicity (> 1)   Simple roots

▲ **Figure 4.2.9**

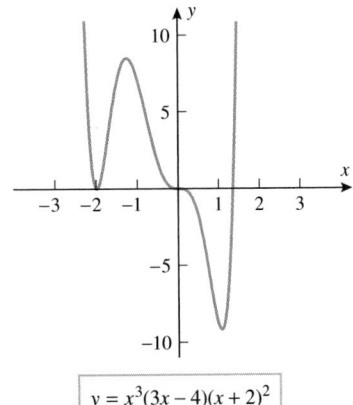

$$y = x^3(3x - 4)(x + 2)^2$$

▲ **Figure 4.2.10**

► **Example 6**   Make a conjecture about the behavior of the graph of

$$y = x^3(3x - 4)(x + 2)^2$$

in the vicinity of its x-intercepts, and test your conjecture by generating the graph.

Solution.   The x-intercepts occur at $x = 0$, $x = \frac{4}{3}$, and $x = -2$. The root $x = 0$ has multiplicity 3, which is odd, so at that point the graph should be tangent to the x-axis, cross the x-axis, and have an inflection point there. The root $x = -2$ has multiplicity 2, which is even, so the graph should be tangent to but not cross the x-axis there. The root $x = \frac{4}{3}$ is simple, so at that point the curve should cross the x-axis without being tangent to it. All of this is consistent with the graph in Figure 4.2.10. ◄

ANALYSIS OF POLYNOMIALS

Historically, the term "curve sketching" meant using calculus to help draw the graph of a function by hand—the graph was the goal. Since graphs can now be produced with great precision using calculators and computers, the purpose of curve sketching has changed. Today, we typically start with a graph produced by a calculator or computer, then use curve sketching to identify important features of the graph that the calculator or computer might have missed. Thus, the goal of curve sketching is no longer the graph itself, but rather the information it reveals about the function.

Polynomials are among the simplest functions to graph and analyze. Their significant features are symmetry, intercepts, relative extrema, inflection points, and the behavior as $x \to +\infty$ and as $x \to -\infty$. Figure 4.2.11 shows the graphs of four polynomials in x. The graphs in Figure 4.2.11 have properties that are common to all polynomials:

- The natural domain of a polynomial is $(-\infty, +\infty)$.

- Polynomials are continuous everywhere.

- Polynomials are differentiable everywhere, so their graphs have no corners or vertical tangent lines.

- The graph of a nonconstant polynomial eventually increases or decreases without bound as $x \to +\infty$ and as $x \to -\infty$. This is because the limit of a nonconstant polynomial as $x \to +\infty$ or as $x \to -\infty$ is $\pm\infty$, depending on the sign of the term of highest degree and whether the polynomial has even or odd degree [see Formulas (17) and (18) of Section 1.3 and the related discussion].

- The graph of a polynomial of degree n (> 2) has at most n x-intercepts, at most $n - 1$ relative extrema, and at most $n - 2$ inflection points. This is because the x-intercepts, relative extrema, and inflection points of a polynomial $p(x)$ are among the real solutions of the equations $p(x) = 0$, $p'(x) = 0$, and $p''(x) = 0$, and the polynomials in these equations have degree n, $n - 1$, and $n - 2$, respectively. Thus, for example, the graph of a quadratic polynomial has at most two x-intercepts, one relative extremum, and no inflection points; and the graph of a cubic polynomial has at most three x-intercepts, two relative extrema, and one inflection point.

> For each of the graphs in Figure 4.2.11, count the number of x-intercepts, relative extrema, and inflection points, and confirm that your count is consistent with the degree of the polynomial.

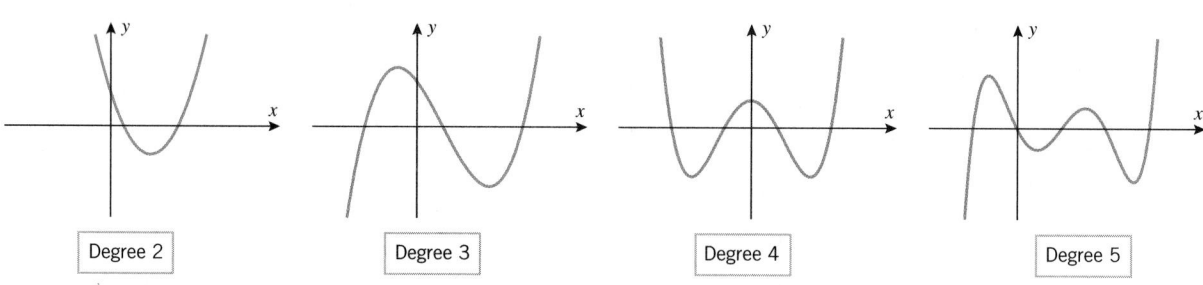

| Degree 2 | Degree 3 | Degree 4 | Degree 5 |

▲ **Figure 4.2.11**

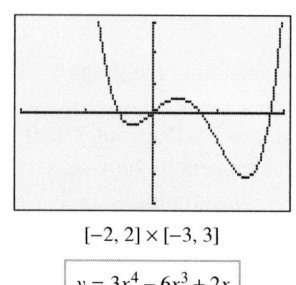

$[-2, 2] \times [-3, 3]$

$y = 3x^4 - 6x^3 + 2x$

▲ **Figure 4.2.12**

▶ **Example 7**   Figure 4.2.12 shows the graph of

$$y = 3x^4 - 6x^3 + 2x$$

produced on a graphing calculator. Confirm that the graph is not missing any significant features.

Solution.   We can be confident that the graph shows all significant features of the polynomial because the polynomial has degree 4 and we can account for four roots, three relative extrema, and two inflection points. Moreover, the graph suggests the correct behavior as

$x \to +\infty$ and as $x \to -\infty$, since

$$\lim_{x \to +\infty} (3x^4 - 6x^3 + 2x) = \lim_{x \to +\infty} 3x^4 = +\infty$$

$$\lim_{x \to -\infty} (3x^4 - 6x^3 + 2x) = \lim_{x \to -\infty} 3x^4 = +\infty \blacktriangleleft$$

▶ **Example 8**   Sketch the graph of the equation

$$y = x^3 - 3x + 2$$

and identify the locations of the intercepts, relative extrema, and inflection points.

Solution.   The following analysis will produce the information needed to sketch the graph:

A review of polynomial factoring is given in Appendix C.

- *x-intercepts:* Factoring the polynomial yields

$$x^3 - 3x + 2 = (x + 2)(x - 1)^2$$

which tells us that the x-intercepts are $x = -2$ and $x = 1$.

- *y-intercept:* Setting $x = 0$ yields $y = 2$.

- *End behavior:* We have

$$\lim_{x \to +\infty} (x^3 - 3x + 2) = \lim_{x \to +\infty} x^3 = +\infty$$

$$\lim_{x \to -\infty} (x^3 - 3x + 2) = \lim_{x \to -\infty} x^3 = -\infty$$

so the graph increases without bound as $x \to +\infty$ and decreases without bound as $x \to -\infty$.

- *Derivatives:*

$$\frac{dy}{dx} = 3x^2 - 3 = 3(x - 1)(x + 1)$$

$$\frac{d^2y}{dx^2} = 6x$$

- *Increase, decrease, relative extrema, inflection points:* Figure 4.2.13 gives a sign analysis of the first and second derivatives and indicates its geometric significance. There are stationary points at $x = -1$ and $x = 1$. Since the sign of dy/dx changes from $+$ to $-$ at $x = -1$, there is a relative maximum there, and since it changes from $-$ to $+$ at $x = 1$, there is a relative minimum there. The sign of d^2y/dx^2 changes from $-$ to $+$ at $x = 0$, so there is an inflection point there.

- *Final sketch:* Figure 4.2.14 shows the final sketch with the coordinates of the intercepts, relative extrema, and inflection point labeled. ◀

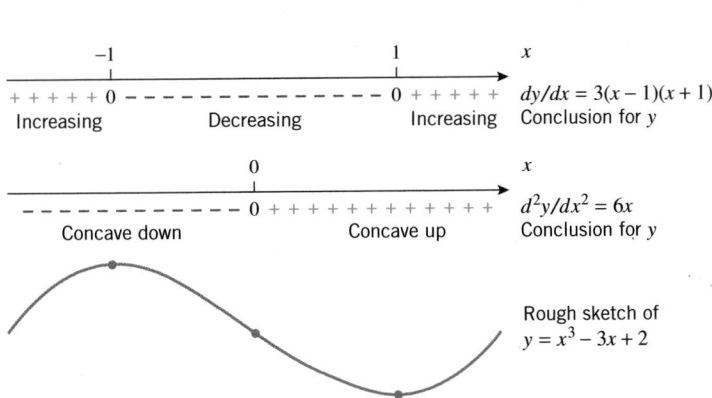

▲ **Figure 4.2.13**

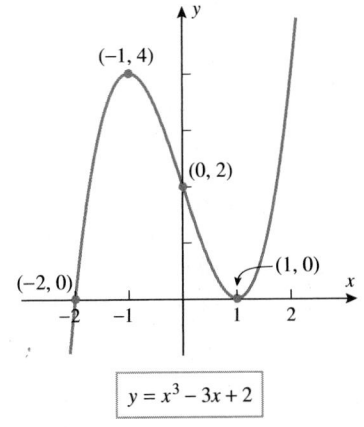

▲ **Figure 4.2.14**

✔ **QUICK CHECK EXERCISES 4.2**   *(See page 254 for answers.)*

1. A function f has a relative maximum at x_0 if there is an open interval containing x_0 on which $f(x)$ is _____ $f(x_0)$ for every x in the interval.

2. Suppose that f is defined everywhere and $x = 2, 3, 5, 7$ are critical points for f. If $f'(x)$ is positive on the intervals $(-\infty, 2)$ and $(5, 7)$, and if $f'(x)$ is negative on the intervals $(2, 3)$, $(3, 5)$, and $(7, +\infty)$, then f has relative maxima at $x =$ _____ and f has relative minima at $x =$ _____.

3. Suppose that f is defined everywhere and $x = -2$ and $x = 1$ are critical points for f. If $f''(x) = 2x + 1$, then f has a relative _____ at $x = -2$ and f has a relative _____ at $x = 1$.

4. Let $f(x) = (x^2 - 4)^2$. Then $f'(x) = 4x(x^2 - 4)$ and $f''(x) = 4(3x^2 - 4)$. Identify the locations of the (a) relative maxima, (b) relative minima, and (c) inflection points on the graph of f.

EXERCISE SET 4.2    Graphing Utility   [c] CAS

1. In each part, sketch the graph of a continuous function f with the stated properties.
   (a) f is concave up on the interval $(-\infty, +\infty)$ and has exactly one relative extremum.
   (b) f is concave up on the interval $(-\infty, +\infty)$ and has no relative extrema.
   (c) The function f has exactly two relative extrema on the interval $(-\infty, +\infty)$, and $f(x) \to +\infty$ as $x \to +\infty$.
   (d) The function f has exactly two relative extrema on the interval $(-\infty, +\infty)$, and $f(x) \to -\infty$ as $x \to +\infty$.

2. In each part, sketch the graph of a continuous function f with the stated properties.
   (a) f has exactly one relative extremum on $(-\infty, +\infty)$, and $f(x) \to 0$ as $x \to +\infty$ and as $x \to -\infty$.
   (b) f has exactly two relative extrema on $(-\infty, +\infty)$, and $f(x) \to 0$ as $x \to +\infty$ and as $x \to -\infty$.
   (c) f has exactly one inflection point and one relative extremum on $(-\infty, +\infty)$.
   (d) f has infinitely many relative extrema, and $f(x) \to 0$ as $x \to +\infty$ and as $x \to -\infty$.

3. (a) Use both the first and second derivative tests to show that $f(x) = 3x^2 - 6x + 1$ has a relative minimum at $x = 1$.
   (b) Use both the first and second derivative tests to show that $f(x) = x^3 - 3x + 3$ has a relative minimum at $x = 1$ and a relative maximum at $x = -1$.

4. (a) Use both the first and second derivative tests to show that $f(x) = \sin^2 x$ has a relative minimum at $x = 0$.
   (b) Use both the first and second derivative tests to show that $g(x) = \tan^2 x$ has a relative minimum at $x = 0$.
   (c) Give an informal verbal argument to explain without calculus why the functions in parts (a) and (b) have relative minima at $x = 0$.

5. (a) Show that both of the functions $f(x) = (x - 1)^4$ and $g(x) = x^3 - 3x^2 + 3x - 2$ have stationary points at $x = 1$.
   (b) What does the second derivative test tell you about the nature of these stationary points?

   (c) What does the first derivative test tell you about the nature of these stationary points?

6. (a) Show that $f(x) = 1 - x^5$ and $g(x) = 3x^4 - 8x^3$ both have stationary points at $x = 0$.
   (b) What does the second derivative test tell you about the nature of these stationary points?
   (c) What does the first derivative test tell you about the nature of these stationary points?

7–14 Locate the critical points and identify which critical points are stationary points. ■

7. $f(x) = 4x^4 - 16x^2 + 17$ 8. $f(x) = 3x^4 + 12x$

9. $f(x) = \dfrac{x + 1}{x^2 + 3}$ 10. $f(x) = \dfrac{x^2}{x^3 + 8}$

11. $f(x) = \sqrt[3]{x^2 - 25}$ 12. $f(x) = x^2(x - 1)^{2/3}$

13. $f(x) = |\sin x|$ 14. $f(x) = \sin |x|$

15–18 True–False Assume that f is continuous everywhere. Determine whether the statement is true or false. Explain your answer. ■

15. If f has a relative maximum at $x = 1$, then $f(1) \geq f(2)$.

16. If f has a relative maximum at $x = 1$, then $x = 1$ is a critical point for f.

17. If $f''(x) > 0$, then f has a relative minimum at $x = 1$.

18. If $p(x)$ is a polynomial such that $p'(x)$ has a simple root at $x = 1$, then p has a relative extremum at $x = 1$.

19–20 The graph of a function $f(x)$ is given. Sketch graphs of $y = f'(x)$ and $y = f''(x)$. ■

19.

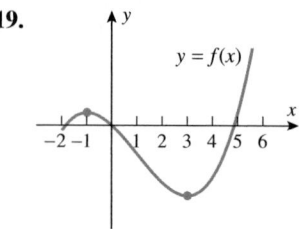

20.

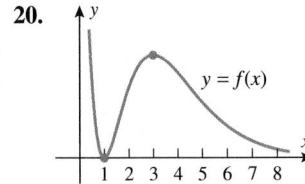

21–24 Use the graph of f' shown in the figure to estimate all values of x at which f has (a) relative minima, (b) relative maxima, and (c) inflection points. (d) Draw a rough sketch of the graph of a function f with the given derivative. ■

21. **22.**

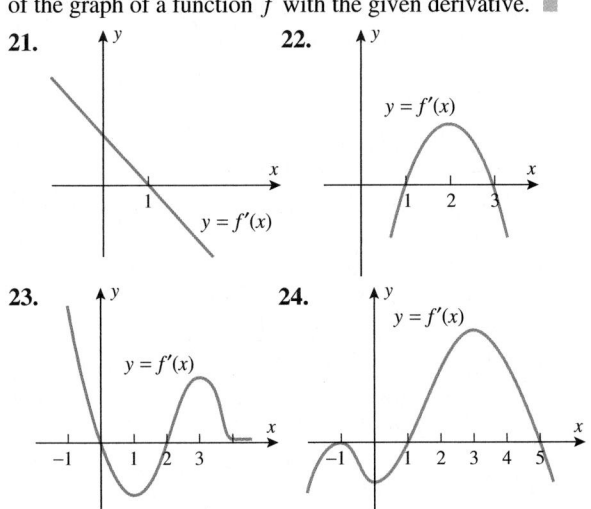

23. **24.**

25–32 Use the given derivative to find all critical points of f, and at each critical point determine whether a relative maximum, relative minimum, or neither occurs. Assume in each case that f is continuous everywhere. ■

25. $f'(x) = x^2(x^3 - 5)$ **26.** $f'(x) = 4x^3 - 9x$

27. $f'(x) = \dfrac{2 - 3x}{\sqrt[3]{x + 2}}$ **28.** $f'(x) = \dfrac{x^2 - 7}{\sqrt[3]{x^2 + 4}}$

29. $f'(x) = xe^{1 - x^2}$ **30.** $f'(x) = x^4(e^x - 3)$

31. $f'(x) = \ln\left(\dfrac{2}{1 + x^2}\right)$ **32.** $f'(x) = e^{2x} - 5e^x + 6$

33–36 Find the relative extrema using both first and second derivative tests. ■

33. $f(x) = 1 + 8x - 3x^2$ **34.** $f(x) = x^4 - 12x^3$

35. $f(x) = \sin 2x$, $0 < x < \pi$ **36.** $f(x) = (x - 3)e^x$

37–50 Use any method to find the relative extrema of the function f. ■

37. $f(x) = x^4 - 4x^3 + 4x^2$ **38.** $f(x) = x(x - 4)^3$

39. $f(x) = x^3(x + 1)^2$ **40.** $f(x) = x^2(x + 1)^3$

41. $f(x) = 2x + 3x^{2/3}$ **42.** $f(x) = 2x + 3x^{1/3}$

43. $f(x) = \dfrac{x + 3}{x - 2}$ **44.** $f(x) = \dfrac{x^2}{x^4 + 16}$

45. $f(x) = \ln(2 + x^2)$ **46.** $f(x) = \ln|2 + x^3|$

47. $f(x) = e^{2x} - e^x$ **48.** $f(x) = (xe^x)^2$

49. $f(x) = |3x - x^2|$ **50.** $f(x) = |1 + \sqrt[3]{x}|$

51–60 Give a graph of the polynomial and label the coordinates of the intercepts, stationary points, and inflection points. Check your work with a graphing utility. ■

51. $p(x) = x^2 - 3x - 4$ **52.** $p(x) = 1 + 8x - x^2$

53. $p(x) = 2x^3 - 3x^2 - 36x + 5$

54. $p(x) = 2 - x + 2x^2 - x^3$

55. $p(x) = (x + 1)^2(2x - x^2)$

56. $p(x) = x^4 - 6x^2 + 5$

57. $p(x) = x^4 - 2x^3 + 2x - 1$ **58.** $p(x) = 4x^3 - 9x^4$

59. $p(x) = x(x^2 - 1)^2$ **60.** $p(x) = x(x^2 - 1)^3$

61. In each part: (i) Make a conjecture about the behavior of the graph in the vicinity of its x-intercepts. (ii) Make a rough sketch of the graph based on your conjecture and the limits of the polynomial as $x \to +\infty$ and as $x \to -\infty$. (iii) Compare your sketch to the graph generated with a graphing utility.
(a) $y = x(x - 1)(x + 1)$ (b) $y = x^2(x - 1)^2(x + 1)^2$
(c) $y = x^2(x - 1)^2(x + 1)^3$ (d) $y = x(x - 1)^5(x + 1)^4$

62. Sketch the graph of $y = (x - a)^m(x - b)^n$ for the stated values of m and n, assuming that $a < b$ (six graphs in total).
(a) $m = 1$, $n = 1, 2, 3$ (b) $m = 2$, $n = 2, 3$
(c) $m = 3$, $n = 3$

63–66 Find the relative extrema in the interval $0 < x < 2\pi$, and confirm that your results are consistent with the graph of f generated with a graphing utility. ■

63. $f(x) = |\sin 2x|$ **64.** $f(x) = \sqrt{3}x + 2\sin x$

65. $f(x) = \cos^2 x$ **66.** $f(x) = \dfrac{\sin x}{2 - \cos x}$

67–70 Use a graphing utility to make a conjecture about the relative extrema of f, and then check your conjecture using either the first or second derivative test. ■

67. $f(x) = x \ln x$ **68.** $f(x) = \dfrac{2}{e^x + e^{-x}}$

69. $f(x) = x^2 e^{-2x}$ **70.** $f(x) = 10 \ln x - x$

71–72 Use a graphing utility to generate the graphs of f' and f'' over the stated interval, and then use those graphs to estimate the x-coordinates of the relative extrema of f. Check that your estimates are consistent with the graph of f. ■

71. $f(x) = x^4 - 24x^2 + 12x$, $-5 \le x \le 5$

72. $f(x) = \sin \frac{1}{2}x \cos x$, $-\pi/2 \le x \le \pi/2$

73–76 Use a CAS to graph f' and f'', and then use those graphs to estimate the x-coordinates of the relative extrema of f. Check that your estimates are consistent with the graph of f. ■

73. $f(x) = \dfrac{10x^3 - 3}{3x^2 - 5x + 8}$ **74.** $f(x) = \dfrac{\tan^{-1}(x^2 - x)}{x^2 + 4}$

75. $f(x) = \sqrt{x^4 + \cos^2 x}$ **76.** $f(x) = x^2(e^{2x} - e^x)$

77. In each part, find k so that f has a relative extremum at the point where $x = 3$.

(a) $f(x) = x^2 + \dfrac{k}{x}$ (b) $f(x) = \dfrac{x}{x^2 + k}$

78. (a) Use a CAS to graph the function
$$f(x) = \frac{x^4 + 1}{x^2 + 1}$$
and use the graph to estimate the x-coordinates of the relative extrema.

(b) Find the exact x-coordinates by using the CAS to solve the equation $f'(x) = 0$.

79. Functions similar to
$$f(x) = \frac{1}{\sqrt{2\pi}} e^{-x^2/2}$$
arise in a wide variety of statistical problems.

(a) Use the first derivative test to show that f has a relative maximum at $x = 0$, and confirm this by using a graphing utility to graph f.

(b) Sketch the graph of
$$f(x) = \frac{1}{\sqrt{2\pi}} e^{-(x-\mu)^2/2}$$
where μ is a constant, and label the coordinates of the relative extrema.

80. Functions of the form
$$f(x) = \frac{x^n e^{-x}}{n!}, \quad x > 0$$
where n is a positive integer, arise in the statistical study of traffic flow.

(a) Use a graphing utility to generate the graph of f for $n = 2, 3, 4$, and 5, and make a conjecture about the number and locations of the relative extrema of f.

(b) Confirm your conjecture using the first derivative test.

81. Let h and g have relative maxima at x_0. Prove or disprove:

(a) $h + g$ has a relative maximum at x_0

(b) $h - g$ has a relative maximum at x_0.

82. Sketch some curves that show that the three parts of the first derivative test (Theorem 4.2.3) can be false without the assumption that f is continuous at x_0.

83. Writing Discuss the relative advantages or disadvantages of using the first derivative test versus using the second derivative test to classify candidates for relative extrema on the interior of the domain of a function. Include specific examples to illustrate your points.

84. Writing If $p(x)$ is a polynomial, discuss the usefulness of knowing zeros for p, p', and p'' when determining information about the graph of p.

✔ **QUICK CHECK ANSWERS 4.2**

1. less than or equal to   **2.** $2, 7; 5$ **3.** maximum; minimum   **4.** (a) $(0, 16)$ (b) $(-2, 0)$ and $(2, 0)$
(c) $(-2/\sqrt{3}, 64/9)$ and $(2/\sqrt{3}, 64/9)$

4.3 ANALYSIS OF FUNCTIONS III: RATIONAL FUNCTIONS, CUSPS, AND VERTICAL TANGENTS

In this section we will discuss procedures for graphing rational functions and other kinds of curves. We will also discuss the interplay between calculus and technology in curve sketching.

■ PROPERTIES OF GRAPHS

In many problems, the properties of interest in the graph of a function are:

- symmetries
- x-intercepts
- relative extrema
- intervals of increase and decrease
- asymptotes

- periodicity
- y-intercepts
- concavity
- inflection points
- behavior as $x \to +\infty$ or as $x \to -\infty$

Some of these properties may not be relevant in certain cases; for example, asymptotes are characteristic of rational functions but not of polynomials, and periodicity is characteristic of trigonometric functions but not of polynomial or rational functions. Thus, when analyzing the graph of a function f, it helps to know something about the general properties of the family to which it belongs.

In a given problem you will usually have a definite objective for your analysis of a graph. For example, you may be interested in showing all of the important characteristics of the function, you may only be interested in the behavior of the graph as $x \to +\infty$ or as $x \to -\infty$, or you may be interested in some specific feature such as a particular inflection point. Thus, your objectives in the problem will dictate those characteristics on which you want to focus.

■ GRAPHING RATIONAL FUNCTIONS

Recall that a rational function is a function of the form $f(x) = P(x)/Q(x)$ in which $P(x)$ and $Q(x)$ are polynomials. Graphs of rational functions are more complicated than those of polynomials because of the possibility of asymptotes and discontinuities (see Figure 0.3.11, for example). If $P(x)$ and $Q(x)$ have no common factors, then the information obtained in the following steps will usually be sufficient to obtain an accurate sketch of the graph of a rational function.

> *Graphing a Rational Function $f(x) = P(x)/Q(x)$ if $P(x)$ and $Q(x)$ have no Common Factors*
>
> **Step 1. (symmetries).** Determine whether there is symmetry about the y-axis or the origin.
>
> **Step 2. (x- and y-intercepts).** Find the x- and y-intercepts.
>
> **Step 3. (vertical asymptotes).** Find the values of x for which $Q(x) = 0$. The graph has a vertical asymptote at each such value.
>
> **Step 4. (sign of $f(x)$).** The only places where $f(x)$ can change sign are at the x-intercepts or vertical asymptotes. Mark the points on the x-axis at which these occur and calculate a sample value of $f(x)$ in each of the open intervals determined by these points. This will tell you whether $f(x)$ is positive or negative over that interval.
>
> **Step 5. (end behavior).** Determine the end behavior of the graph by computing the limits of $f(x)$ as $x \to +\infty$ and as $x \to -\infty$. If either limit has a finite value L, then the line $y = L$ is a horizontal asymptote.
>
> **Step 6. (derivatives).** Find $f'(x)$ and $f''(x)$.
>
> **Step 7. (conclusions and graph).** Analyze the sign changes of $f'(x)$ and $f''(x)$ to determine the intervals where $f(x)$ is increasing, decreasing, concave up, and concave down. Determine the locations of all stationary points, relative extrema, and inflection points. Use the sign analysis of $f(x)$ to determine the behavior of the graph in the vicinity of the vertical asymptotes. Sketch a graph of f that exhibits these conclusions.

▶ **Example 1** Sketch a graph of the equation

$$y = \frac{2x^2 - 8}{x^2 - 16}$$

and identify the locations of the intercepts, relative extrema, inflection points, and asymptotes.

Solution. The numerator and denominator have no common factors, so we will use the procedure just outlined.

- *Symmetries:* Replacing x by $-x$ does not change the equation, so the graph is symmetric about the y-axis.

- x- and y-intercepts: Setting $y = 0$ yields the x-intercepts $x = -2$ and $x = 2$. Setting $x = 0$ yields the y-intercept $y = \frac{1}{2}$.

- *Vertical asymptotes:* We observed above that the numerator and denominator of y have no common factors, so the graph has vertical asymptotes at the points where the denominator of y is zero, namely, at $x = -4$ and $x = 4$.

- *Sign of y:* The set of points where x-intercepts or vertical asymptotes occur is $\{-4, -2, 2, 4\}$. These points divide the x-axis into the open intervals

$$(-\infty, -4), \quad (-4, -2), \quad (-2, 2), \quad (2, 4), \quad (4, +\infty)$$

We can find the sign of y on each interval by choosing an arbitrary test point in the interval and evaluating $y = f(x)$ at the test point (Table 4.3.1). This analysis is summarized on the first line of Figure 4.3.1a.

Table 4.3.1

SIGN ANALYSIS OF $y = \dfrac{2x^2 - 8}{x^2 - 16}$

INTERVAL	TEST POINT	VALUE OF y	SIGN OF y
$(-\infty, -4)$	-5	$14/3$	$+$
$(-4, -2)$	-3	$-10/7$	$-$
$(-2, 2)$	0	$1/2$	$+$
$(2, 4)$	3	$-10/7$	$-$
$(4, +\infty)$	5	$14/3$	$+$

- *End behavior:* The limits

$$\lim_{x \to +\infty} \frac{2x^2 - 8}{x^2 - 16} = \lim_{x \to +\infty} \frac{2 - (8/x^2)}{1 - (16/x^2)} = 2$$

$$\lim_{x \to -\infty} \frac{2x^2 - 8}{x^2 - 16} = \lim_{x \to -\infty} \frac{2 - (8/x^2)}{1 - (16/x^2)} = 2$$

yield the horizontal asymptote $y = 2$.

- *Derivatives:*

$$\frac{dy}{dx} = \frac{(x^2 - 16)(4x) - (2x^2 - 8)(2x)}{(x^2 - 16)^2} = -\frac{48x}{(x^2 - 16)^2}$$

$$\frac{d^2y}{dx^2} = \frac{48(16 + 3x^2)}{(x^2 - 16)^3} \quad \text{(verify)}$$

Conclusions and graph:

- The sign analysis of y in Figure 4.3.1a reveals the behavior of the graph in the vicinity of the vertical asymptotes: The graph increases without bound as $x \to -4^-$ and decreases without bound as $x \to -4^+$; and the graph decreases without bound as $x \to 4^-$ and increases without bound as $x \to 4^+$ (Figure 4.3.1b).

- The sign analysis of dy/dx in Figure 4.3.1a shows that the graph is increasing to the left of $x = 0$ and is decreasing to the right of $x = 0$. Thus, there is a relative maximum at the stationary point $x = 0$. There are no relative minima.

- The sign analysis of d^2y/dx^2 in Figure 4.3.1a shows that the graph is concave up to the left of $x = -4$, is concave down between $x = -4$ and $x = 4$, and is concave up to the right of $x = 4$. There are no inflection points.

The graph is shown in Figure 4.3.1c. ◄

The procedure we stated for graphing a rational function $P(x)/Q(x)$ applies only if the polynomials $P(x)$ and $Q(x)$ have no common factors. How would you find the graph if those polynomials have common factors?

▶ **Example 2**   Sketch a graph of

$$y = \frac{x^2 - 1}{x^3}$$

and identify the locations of all asymptotes, intercepts, relative extrema, and inflection points.

Solution.   The numerator and denominator have no common factors, so we will use the procedure outlined previously.

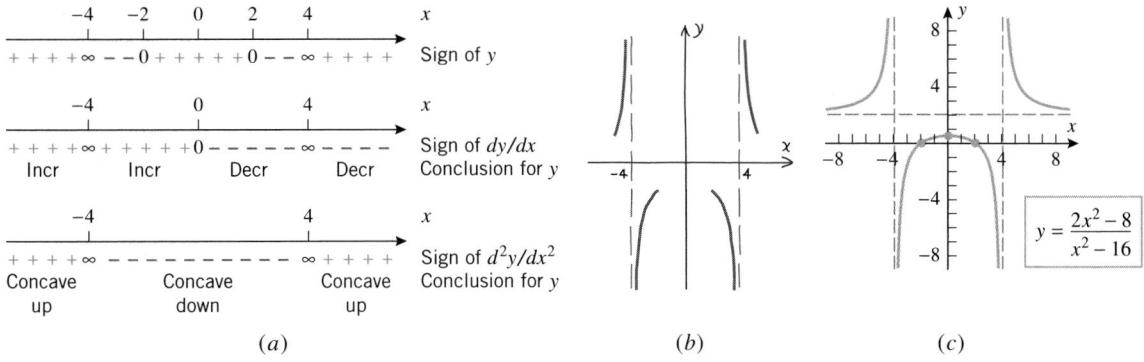

△ **Figure 4.3.1**

Table 4.3.2

SIGN ANALYSIS OF $y = \dfrac{x^2 - 1}{x^3}$

INTERVAL	TEST POINT	VALUE OF y	SIGN OF y
$(-\infty, -1)$	-2	$-\dfrac{3}{8}$	$-$
$(-1, 0)$	$-\dfrac{1}{2}$	6	$+$
$(0, 1)$	$\dfrac{1}{2}$	-6	$-$
$(1, +\infty)$	2	$\dfrac{3}{8}$	$+$

- *Symmetries:* Replacing x by $-x$ and y by $-y$ yields an equation that simplifies to the original equation, so the graph is symmetric about the origin.

- *x- and y-intercepts:* Setting $y = 0$ yields the x-intercepts $x = -1$ and $x = 1$. Setting $x = 0$ leads to a division by zero, so there is no y-intercept.

- *Vertical asymptotes:* Setting $x^3 = 0$ yields the solution $x = 0$. This is not a root of $x^2 - 1$, so $x = 0$ is a vertical asymptote.

- *Sign of y:* The set of points where x-intercepts or vertical asymptotes occur is $\{-1, 0, 1\}$. These points divide the x-axis into the open intervals

$$(-\infty, -1), \quad (-1, 0), \quad (0, 1), \quad (1, +\infty)$$

Table 4.3.2 uses the method of test points to produce the sign of y on each of these intervals.

- *End behavior:* The limits

$$\lim_{x \to +\infty} \frac{x^2 - 1}{x^3} = \lim_{x \to +\infty} \left(\frac{1}{x} - \frac{1}{x^3} \right) = 0$$

$$\lim_{x \to -\infty} \frac{x^2 - 1}{x^3} = \lim_{x \to -\infty} \left(\frac{1}{x} - \frac{1}{x^3} \right) = 0$$

yield the horizontal asymptote $y = 0$.

- *Derivatives:*

$$\frac{dy}{dx} = \frac{x^3(2x) - (x^2 - 1)(3x^2)}{(x^3)^2} = \frac{3 - x^2}{x^4} = \frac{(\sqrt{3} + x)(\sqrt{3} - x)}{x^4}$$

$$\frac{d^2y}{dx^2} = \frac{x^4(-2x) - (3 - x^2)(4x^3)}{(x^4)^2} = \frac{2(x^2 - 6)}{x^5} = \frac{2(x - \sqrt{6})(x + \sqrt{6})}{x^5}$$

Conclusions and graph:

- The sign analysis of y in Figure 4.3.2a reveals the behavior of the graph in the vicinity of the vertical asymptote $x = 0$: The graph increases without bound as $x \to 0^-$ and decreases without bound as $x \to 0^+$ (Figure 4.3.2b).

- The sign analysis of dy/dx in Figure 4.3.2a shows that there is a relative minimum at $x = -\sqrt{3}$ and a relative maximum at $x = \sqrt{3}$.

- The sign analysis of d^2y/dx^2 in Figure 4.3.2a shows that the graph changes concavity at the vertical asymptote $x = 0$ and that there are inflection points at $x = -\sqrt{6}$ and $x = \sqrt{6}$.

The graph is shown in Figure 4.3.2c. To produce a slightly more accurate sketch, we used a graphing utility to help plot the relative extrema and inflection points. You should confirm that the approximate coordinates of the inflection points are $(-2.45, -0.34)$ and $(2.45, 0.34)$ and that the approximate coordinates of the relative minimum and relative maximum are $(-1.73, -0.38)$ and $(1.73, 0.38)$, respectively. ◀

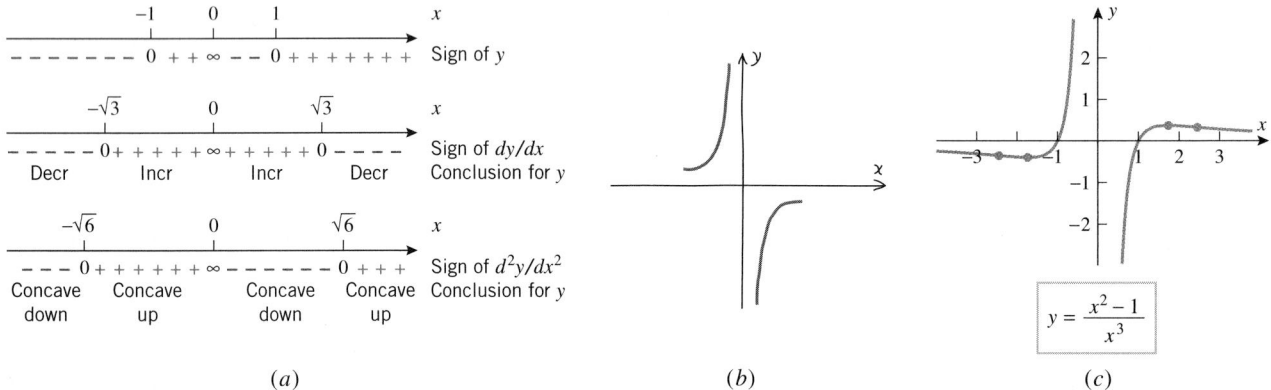

▲ Figure 4.3.2

RATIONAL FUNCTIONS WITH OBLIQUE OR CURVILINEAR ASYMPTOTES

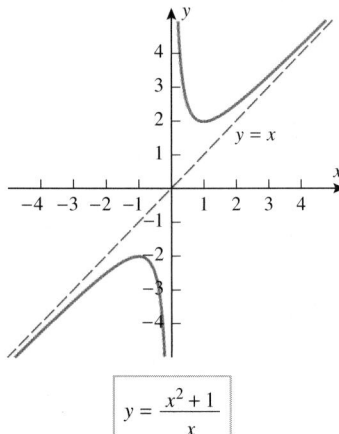

▲ Figure 4.3.3

In the rational functions of Examples 1 and 2, the degree of the numerator did not exceed the degree of the denominator, and the asymptotes were either vertical or horizontal. If the numerator of a rational function has greater degree than the denominator, then other kinds of "asymptotes" are possible. For example, consider the rational functions

$$f(x) = \frac{x^2 + 1}{x} \quad \text{and} \quad g(x) = \frac{x^3 - x^2 - 8}{x - 1} \tag{1}$$

By division we can rewrite these as

$$f(x) = x + \frac{1}{x} \quad \text{and} \quad g(x) = x^2 - \frac{8}{x - 1}$$

Since the second terms both approach 0 as $x \to +\infty$ or as $x \to -\infty$, it follows that

$$(f(x) - x) \to 0 \quad \text{as } x \to +\infty \text{ or as } x \to -\infty$$
$$(g(x) - x^2) \to 0 \quad \text{as } x \to +\infty \text{ or as } x \to -\infty$$

Geometrically, this means that the graph of $y = f(x)$ eventually gets closer and closer to the line $y = x$ as $x \to +\infty$ or as $x \to -\infty$. The line $y = x$ is called an **oblique** or **slant asymptote** of f. Similarly, the graph of $y = g(x)$ eventually gets closer and closer to the parabola $y = x^2$ as $x \to +\infty$ or as $x \to -\infty$. The parabola is called a **curvilinear asymptote** of g. The graphs of the functions in (1) are shown in Figures 4.3.3 and 4.3.4.

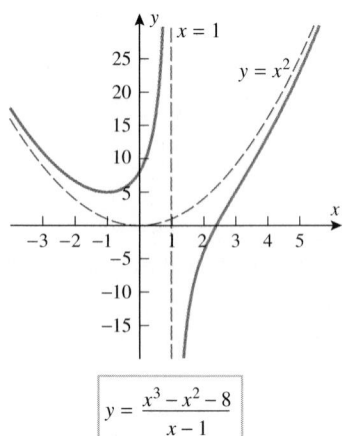

▲ Figure 4.3.4

In general, if $f(x) = P(x)/Q(x)$ is a rational function, then we can find quotient and remainder polynomials $q(x)$ and $r(x)$ such that

$$f(x) = q(x) + \frac{r(x)}{Q(x)}$$

and the degree of $r(x)$ is less than the degree of $Q(x)$. Then $r(x)/Q(x) \to 0$ as $x \to +\infty$ and as $x \to -\infty$, so $y = q(x)$ is an asymptote of f. This asymptote will be an oblique line if the degree of $P(x)$ is one greater than the degree of $Q(x)$, and it will be curvilinear if the degree of $P(x)$ exceeds that of $Q(x)$ by two or more. Problems involving these kinds of asymptotes are given in the exercises (Exercises 17 and 18).

■ **GRAPHS WITH VERTICAL TANGENTS AND CUSPS**

Figure 4.3.5 shows four curve elements that are commonly found in graphs of functions that involve radicals or fractional exponents. In all four cases, the function is not differentiable at x_0 because the secant line through $(x_0, f(x_0))$ and $(x, f(x))$ approaches a vertical position as x approaches x_0 from either side. Thus, in each case, the curve has a vertical tangent line at $(x_0, f(x_0))$. In parts (a) and (b) of the figure, there is an inflection point at x_0 because there is a change in concavity at that point. In parts (c) and (d), where $f'(x)$ approaches $+\infty$ from one side of x_0 and $-\infty$ from the other side, we say that the graph has a **cusp** at x_0.

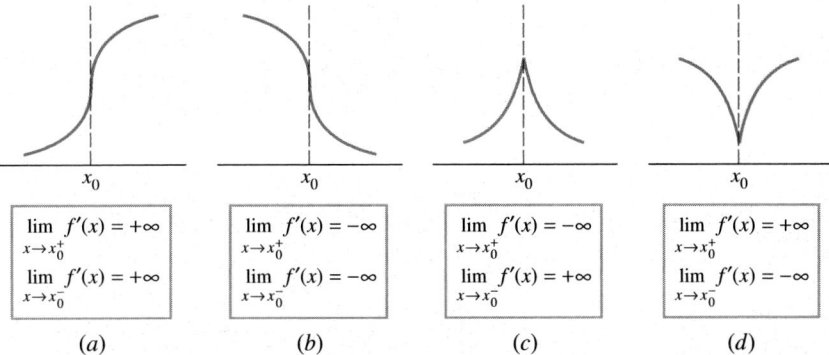

▶ **Figure 4.3.5**

(a) $\quad$ (b) $\quad$ (c) $\quad$ (d)

The steps that are used to sketch the graph of a rational function can serve as guidelines for sketching graphs of other types of functions. This is illustrated in Examples 3, 4, and 5.

▶ **Example 3** Sketch the graph of $y = (x - 4)^{2/3}$.

- *Symmetries:* There are no symmetries about the coordinate axes or the origin (verify). However, the graph of $y = (x - 4)^{2/3}$ is symmetric about the line $x = 4$ since it is a translation (4 units to the right) of the graph of $y = x^{2/3}$, which is symmetric about the y-axis.

- *x- and y-intercepts:* Setting $y = 0$ yields the x-intercept $x = 4$. Setting $x = 0$ yields the y-intercept $y = \sqrt[3]{16} \approx 2.5$.

- *Vertical asymptotes:* None, since $f(x) = (x - 4)^{2/3}$ is continuous everywhere.

- *End behavior:* The graph has no horizontal asymptotes since

$$\lim_{x \to +\infty} (x - 4)^{2/3} = +\infty \quad \text{and} \quad \lim_{x \to -\infty} (x - 4)^{2/3} = +\infty$$

- *Derivatives:*

$$\frac{dy}{dx} = f'(x) = \frac{2}{3}(x - 4)^{-1/3} = \frac{2}{3(x - 4)^{1/3}}$$

$$\frac{d^2y}{dx^2} = f''(x) = -\frac{2}{9}(x - 4)^{-4/3} = -\frac{2}{9(x - 4)^{4/3}}$$

- *Vertical tangent lines:* There is a vertical tangent line and cusp at $x = 4$ of the type in Figure 4.3.5d since $f(x) = (x - 4)^{2/3}$ is continuous at $x = 4$ and

$$\lim_{x \to 4^+} f'(x) = \lim_{x \to 4^+} \frac{2}{3(x - 4)^{1/3}} = +\infty$$

$$\lim_{x \to 4^-} f'(x) = \lim_{x \to 4^-} \frac{2}{3(x - 4)^{1/3}} = -\infty$$

Conclusions and graph:

- The function $f(x) = (x - 4)^{2/3} = ((x - 4)^{1/3})^2$ is nonnegative for all x. There is a zero for f at $x = 4$.

- There is a critical point at $x = 4$ since f is not differentiable there. We saw above that a cusp occurs at this point. The sign analysis of dy/dx in Figure 4.3.6a and the first derivative test show that there is a relative minimum at this cusp since $f'(x) < 0$ if $x < 4$ and $f'(x) > 0$ if $x > 4$.

- The sign analysis of d^2y/dx^2 in Figure 4.3.6a shows that the graph is concave down on both sides of the cusp.

The graph is shown in Figure 4.3.6b. ◄

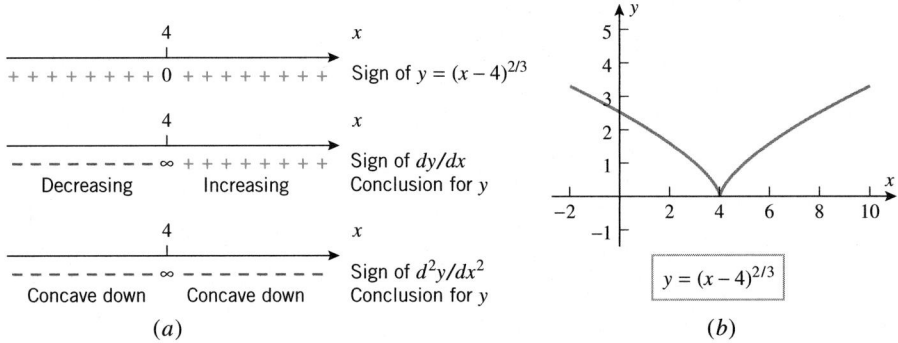

▶ **Figure 4.3.6**   (a)   (b)

▶ **Example 4**   Sketch the graph of $y = 6x^{1/3} + 3x^{4/3}$.

Solution.   It will help in our analysis to write

$$f(x) = 6x^{1/3} + 3x^{4/3} = 3x^{1/3}(2 + x)$$

- *Symmetries:* There are no symmetries about the coordinate axes or the origin (verify).

- *x- and y-intercepts:* Setting $y = 3x^{1/3}(2 + x) = 0$ yields the x-intercepts $x = 0$ and $x = -2$. Setting $x = 0$ yields the y-intercept $y = 0$.

- *Vertical asymptotes:* None, since $f(x) = 6x^{1/3} + 3x^{4/3}$ is continuous everywhere.

- *End behavior:* The graph has no horizontal asymptotes since

$$\lim_{x \to +\infty} (6x^{1/3} + 3x^{4/3}) = \lim_{x \to +\infty} 3x^{1/3}(2 + x) = +\infty$$

$$\lim_{x \to -\infty} (6x^{1/3} + 3x^{4/3}) = \lim_{x \to -\infty} 3x^{1/3}(2 + x) = +\infty$$

- *Derivatives:*

$$\frac{dy}{dx} = f'(x) = 2x^{-2/3} + 4x^{1/3} = 2x^{-2/3}(1 + 2x) = \frac{2(2x + 1)}{x^{2/3}}$$

$$\frac{d^2y}{dx^2} = f''(x) = -\frac{4}{3}x^{-5/3} + \frac{4}{3}x^{-2/3} = \frac{4}{3}x^{-5/3}(-1 + x) = \frac{4(x - 1)}{3x^{5/3}}$$

- *Vertical tangent lines:* There is a vertical tangent line at $x = 0$ since f is continuous there and

$$\lim_{x \to 0^+} f'(x) = \lim_{x \to 0^+} \frac{2(2x + 1)}{x^{2/3}} = +\infty$$

$$\lim_{x \to 0^-} f'(x) = \lim_{x \to 0^-} \frac{2(2x + 1)}{x^{2/3}} = +\infty$$

This and the change in concavity at $x = 0$ mean that $(0, 0)$ is an inflection point of the type in Figure 4.3.5a.

Conclusions and graph:

- From the sign analysis of y in Figure 4.3.7a, the graph is below the x-axis between the x-intercepts $x = -2$ and $x = 0$ and is above the x-axis if $x < -2$ or $x > 0$.

- From the formula for dy/dx we see that there is a stationary point at $x = -\frac{1}{2}$ and a critical point at $x = 0$ at which f is not differentiable. We saw above that a vertical tangent line and inflection point are at that critical point.

- The sign analysis of dy/dx in Figure 4.3.7a and the first derivative test show that there is a relative minimum at the stationary point at $x = -\frac{1}{2}$ (verify).

- The sign analysis of d^2y/dx^2 in Figure 4.3.7a shows that in addition to the inflection point at the vertical tangent there is an inflection point at $x = 1$ at which the graph changes from concave down to concave up.

The graph is shown in Figure 4.3.7b. ◄

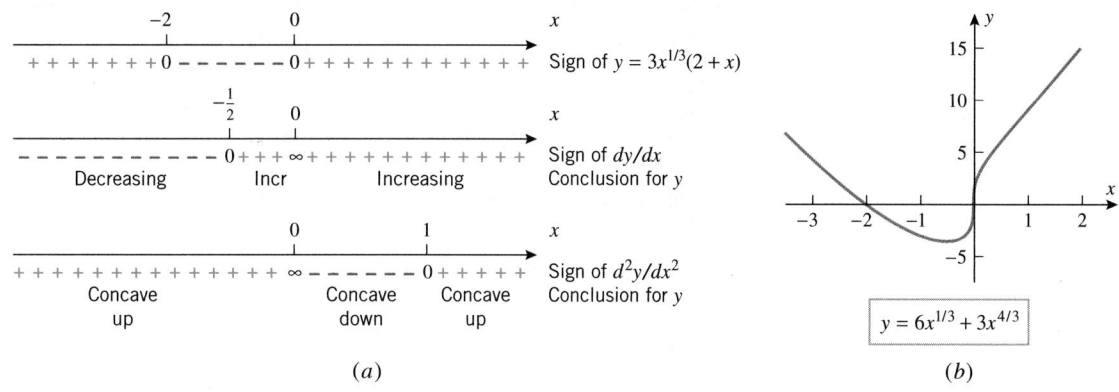

▲ **Figure 4.3.7**

GRAPHING OTHER KINDS OF FUNCTIONS

We have discussed methods for graphing polynomials, rational functions, and functions with cusps and vertical tangent lines. The same calculus tools that we used to analyze these functions can also be used to analyze and graph trigonometric functions, logarithmic and exponential functions, and an endless variety of other kinds of functions.

▶ **Example 5** Sketch the graph of $y = e^{-x^2/2}$ and identify the locations of all relative extrema and inflection points.

Solution.

- *Symmetries:* Replacing x by $-x$ does not change the equation, so the graph is symmetric about the y-axis.

- *x- and y-intercepts:* Setting $y = 0$ leads to the equation $e^{-x^2/2} = 0$, which has no solutions since all powers of e have positive values. Thus, there are no x-intercepts. Setting $x = 0$ yields the y-intercept $y = 1$.

- *Vertical asymptotes:* There are no vertical asymptotes since $e^{-x^2/2}$ is continuous on $(-\infty, +\infty)$.

- *End behavior:* The x-axis ($y = 0$) is a horizontal asymptote since

$$\lim_{x \to -\infty} e^{-x^2/2} = \lim_{x \to +\infty} e^{-x^2/2} = 0$$

- *Derivatives:*

$$\frac{dy}{dx} = e^{-x^2/2}\frac{d}{dx}\left[-\frac{x^2}{2}\right] = -xe^{-x^2/2}$$

$$\frac{d^2y}{dx^2} = -x\frac{d}{dx}[e^{-x^2/2}] + e^{-x^2/2}\frac{d}{dx}[-x]$$

$$= x^2 e^{-x^2/2} - e^{-x^2/2} = (x^2 - 1)e^{-x^2/2}$$

Conclusions and graph:

- The sign analysis of y in Figure 4.3.8*a* is based on the fact that $e^{-x^2/2} > 0$ for all x. This shows that the graph is always above the x-axis.

- The sign analysis of dy/dx in Figure 4.3.8*a* is based on the fact that $dy/dx = -xe^{-x^2/2}$ has the same sign as $-x$. This analysis and the first derivative test show that there is a stationary point at $x = 0$ at which there is a relative maximum. The value of y at the relative maximum is $y = e^0 = 1$.

- The sign analysis of d^2y/dx^2 in Figure 4.3.8*a* is based on the fact that $d^2y/dx^2 = (x^2 - 1)e^{-x^2/2}$ has the same sign as $x^2 - 1$. This analysis shows that there are inflection points at $x = -1$ and $x = 1$. The graph changes from concave up to concave down at $x = -1$ and from concave down to concave up at $x = 1$. The coordinates of the inflection points are $(-1, e^{-1/2}) \approx (-1, 0.61)$ and $(1, e^{-1/2}) \approx (1, 0.61)$.

The graph is shown in Figure 4.3.8*b*. ◄

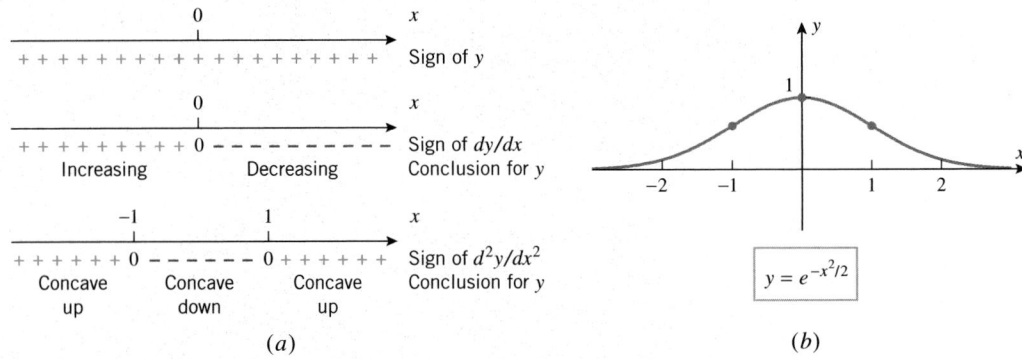

▲ **Figure 4.3.8**

■ GRAPHING USING CALCULUS AND TECHNOLOGY TOGETHER

Thus far in this chapter we have used calculus to produce graphs of functions; the graph was the end result. Now we will work in the reverse direction by *starting* with a graph produced by a graphing utility. Our goal will be to use the tools of calculus to determine the exact locations of relative extrema, inflection points, and other features suggested by that graph and to determine whether the graph may be missing some important features that we would like to see.

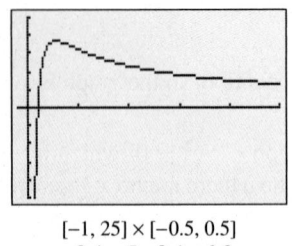

$[-1, 25] \times [-0.5, 0.5]$
$x\text{Scl} = 5, y\text{Scl} = 0.2$

$$y = \frac{\ln x}{x}$$

▲ **Figure 4.3.9**

▶ **Example 6**   Use a graphing utility to generate the graph of $f(x) = (\ln x)/x$, and discuss what it tells you about relative extrema, inflection points, asymptotes, and end behavior. Use calculus to find the locations of all key features of the graph.

Solution.   Figure 4.3.9 shows a graph of f produced by a graphing utility. The graph suggests that there is an x-intercept near $x = 1$, a relative maximum somewhere between

$x = 0$ and $x = 5$, an inflection point near $x = 5$, a vertical asymptote at $x = 0$, and possibly a horizontal asymptote $y = 0$. For a more precise analysis of this information we need to consider the derivatives

$$f'(x) = \frac{x\left(\dfrac{1}{x}\right) - (\ln x)(1)}{x^2} = \frac{1 - \ln x}{x^2}$$

$$f''(x) = \frac{x^2\left(-\dfrac{1}{x}\right) - (1 - \ln x)(2x)}{x^4} = \frac{2x \ln x - 3x}{x^4} = \frac{2 \ln x - 3}{x^3}$$

- *Relative extrema:* Solving $f'(x) = 0$ yields the stationary point $x = e$ (verify). Since

$$f''(e) = \frac{2 - 3}{e^3} = -\frac{1}{e^3} < 0$$

there is a relative maximum at $x = e \approx 2.7$ by the second derivative test.

- *Inflection points:* Since $f(x) = (\ln x)/x$ is only defined for positive values of x, the second derivative $f''(x)$ has the same sign as $2 \ln x - 3$. We leave it for you to use the inequalities $(2 \ln x - 3) < 0$ and $(2 \ln x - 3) > 0$ to show that $f''(x) < 0$ if $x < e^{3/2}$ and $f''(x) > 0$ if $x > e^{3/2}$. Thus, there is an inflection point at $x = e^{3/2} \approx 4.5$.

- *Asymptotes:* Applying L'Hôpital's rule we have

$$\lim_{x \to +\infty} \frac{\ln x}{x} = \lim_{x \to +\infty} \frac{(1/x)}{1} = \lim_{x \to +\infty} \frac{1}{x} = 0$$

so that $y = 0$ is a horizontal asymptote. Also, there is a vertical asymptote at $x = 0$ since

$$\lim_{x \to 0^+} \frac{\ln x}{x} = -\infty$$

(why?).

- *Intercepts:* Setting $f(x) = 0$ yields $(\ln x)/x = 0$. The only real solution of this equation is $x = 1$, so there is an x-intercept at this point. ◄

✔ QUICK CHECK EXERCISES 4.3   (See page 266 for answers.)

1. Let $f(x) = \dfrac{3(x + 1)(x - 3)}{(x + 2)(x - 4)}$. Given that

$$f'(x) = \frac{-30(x - 1)}{(x + 2)^2(x - 4)^2}, \qquad f''(x) = \frac{90(x^2 - 2x + 4)}{(x + 2)^3(x - 4)^3}$$

determine the following properties of the graph of f.
- (a) The x- and y-intercepts are _____.
- (b) The vertical asymptotes are _____.
- (c) The horizontal asymptote is _____.
- (d) The graph is above the x-axis on the intervals _____.
- (e) The graph is increasing on the intervals _____.
- (f) The graph is concave up on the intervals _____.
- (g) The relative maximum point on the graph is _____.

2. Let $f(x) = \dfrac{x^2 - 4}{x^{8/3}}$. Given that

$$f'(x) = \frac{-2(x^2 - 16)}{3x^{11/3}}, \qquad f''(x) = \frac{2(5x^2 - 176)}{9x^{14/3}}$$

determine the following properties of the graph of f.

- (a) The x-intercepts are _____.
- (b) The vertical asymptote is _____.
- (c) The horizontal asymptote is _____.
- (d) The graph is above the x-axis on the intervals _____.
- (e) The graph is increasing on the intervals _____.
- (f) The graph is concave up on the intervals _____.
- (g) Inflection points occur at $x = $ _____.

3. Let $f(x) = (x - 2)^2 e^{x/2}$. Given that

$$f'(x) = \tfrac{1}{2}(x^2 - 4)e^{x/2}, \qquad f''(x) = \tfrac{1}{4}(x^2 + 4x - 4)e^{x/2}$$

determine the following properties of the graph of f.
- (a) The horizontal asymptote is _____.
- (b) The graph is above the x-axis on the intervals _____.
- (c) The graph is increasing on the intervals _____.
- (d) The graph is concave up on the intervals _____.
- (e) The relative minimum point on the graph is _____.
- (f) The relative maximum point on the graph is _____.
- (g) Inflection points occur at $x = $ _____.

EXERCISE SET 4.3   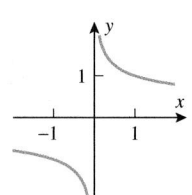 Graphing Utility

~ **1–14** Give a graph of the rational function and label the co-ordinates of the stationary points and inflection points. Show the horizontal and vertical asymptotes and label them with their equations. Label point(s), if any, where the graph crosses a horizontal asymptote. Check your work with a graphing utility.

1. $\dfrac{2x - 6}{4 - x}$

2. $\dfrac{8}{x^2 - 4}$

3. $\dfrac{x}{x^2 - 4}$

4. $\dfrac{x^2}{x^2 - 4}$

5. $\dfrac{x^2}{x^2 + 4}$

6. $\dfrac{(x^2 - 1)^2}{x^4 + 1}$

7. $\dfrac{x^3 + 1}{x^3 - 1}$

8. $2 - \dfrac{1}{3x^2 + x^3}$

9. $\dfrac{4}{x^2} - \dfrac{2}{x} + 3$

10. $\dfrac{3(x + 1)^2}{(x - 1)^2}$

11. $\dfrac{(3x + 1)^2}{(x - 1)^2}$

12. $3 + \dfrac{x + 1}{(x - 1)^4}$

13. $\dfrac{x^2 + x}{1 - x^2}$

14. $\dfrac{x^2}{1 - x^3}$

~ **15–16** In each part, make a rough sketch of the graph using asymptotes and appropriate limits but no derivatives. Compare your graph to that generated with a graphing utility.

15. (a) $y = \dfrac{3x^2 - 8}{x^2 - 4}$

(b) $y = \dfrac{x^2 + 2x}{x^2 - 1}$

16. (a) $y = \dfrac{2x - x^2}{x^2 + x - 2}$

(b) $y = \dfrac{x^2}{x^2 - x - 2}$

17. Show that $y = x + 3$ is an oblique asymptote of the graph of $f(x) = x^2/(x - 3)$. Sketch the graph of $y = f(x)$ showing this asymptotic behavior.

18. Show that $y = 3 - x^2$ is a curvilinear asymptote of the graph of $f(x) = (2 + 3x - x^3)/x$. Sketch the graph of $y = f(x)$ showing this asymptotic behavior.

~ **19–24** Sketch a graph of the rational function and label the co-ordinates of the stationary points and inflection points. Show the horizontal, vertical, oblique, and curvilinear asymptotes and label them with their equations. Label point(s), if any, where the graph crosses an asymptote. Check your work with a graphing utility.

19. $x^2 - \dfrac{1}{x}$

20. $\dfrac{x^2 - 2}{x}$

21. $\dfrac{(x - 2)^3}{x^2}$

22. $x - \dfrac{1}{x} - \dfrac{1}{x^2}$

23. $\dfrac{x^3 - 4x - 8}{x + 2}$

24. $\dfrac{x^5}{x^2 + 1}$

FOCUS ON CONCEPTS

25. In each part, match the function with graphs I–VI.

(a) $x^{1/3}$ (b) $x^{1/4}$ (c) $x^{1/5}$
(d) $x^{2/5}$ (e) $x^{4/3}$ (f) $x^{-1/3}$

I
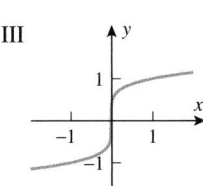

II
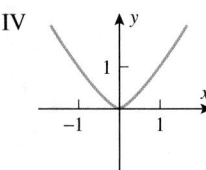

III
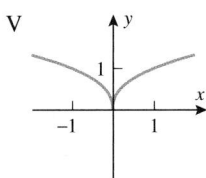

IV
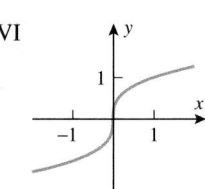

V

VI

▲ **Figure Ex-25**

26. Sketch the general shape of the graph of $y = x^{1/n}$, and then explain in words what happens to the shape of the graph as n increases if
(a) n is a positive even integer
(b) n is a positive odd integer.

27–30 True–False Determine whether the statement is true or false. Explain your answer.

27. Suppose that $f(x) = P(x)/Q(x)$, where P and Q are polynomials with no common factors. If $y = 5$ is a horizontal asymptote for the graph of f, then P and Q have the same degree.

28. If the graph of f has a vertical asymptote at $x = 1$, then f cannot be continuous at $x = 1$.

29. If the graph of f' has a vertical asymptote at $x = 1$, then f cannot be continuous at $x = 1$.

30. If the graph of f has a cusp at $x = 1$, then f cannot have an inflection point at $x = 1$.

~ **31–38** Give a graph of the function and identify the locations of all critical points and inflection points. Check your work with a graphing utility.

31. $\sqrt{4x^2 - 1}$

32. $\sqrt[3]{x^2 - 4}$

33. $2x + 3x^{2/3}$

34. $2x^2 - 3x^{4/3}$

35. $4x^{1/3} - x^{4/3}$

36. $5x^{2/3} + x^{5/3}$

37. $\dfrac{8 + x}{2 + \sqrt[3]{x}}$

38. $\dfrac{8(\sqrt{x} - 1)}{x}$

39–44 Give a graph of the function and identify the locations of all relative extrema and inflection points. Check your work with a graphing utility. ■

39. $x + \sin x$ **40.** $x - \tan x$

41. $\sqrt{3}\cos x + \sin x$ **42.** $\sin x + \cos x$

43. $\sin^2 x - \cos x, \quad -\pi \le x \le 3\pi$

44. $\sqrt{\tan x}, \quad 0 \le x < \pi/2$

 45–54 Using L'Hôpital's rule (Section 3.6) one can verify that

$$\lim_{x \to +\infty} \frac{e^x}{x} = +\infty, \quad \lim_{x \to +\infty} \frac{x}{e^x} = 0, \quad \lim_{x \to -\infty} xe^x = 0$$

In these exercises: (a) Use these results, as necessary, to find the limits of $f(x)$ as $x \to +\infty$ and as $x \to -\infty$. (b) Sketch a graph of $f(x)$ and identify all relative extrema, inflection points, and asymptotes (as appropriate). Check your work with a graphing utility. ■

45. $f(x) = xe^x$ **46.** $f(x) = xe^{-x}$

47. $f(x) = x^2 e^{-2x}$ **48.** $f(x) = x^2 e^{2x}$

49. $f(x) = x^2 e^{-x^2}$ **50.** $f(x) = e^{-1/x^2}$

51. $f(x) = \dfrac{e^x}{1-x}$ **52.** $f(x) = x^{2/3} e^x$

53. $f(x) = x^2 e^{1-x}$ **54.** $f(x) = x^3 e^{x-1}$

55–60 Using L'Hôpital's rule (Section 3.6) one can verify that

$$\lim_{x \to +\infty} \frac{\ln x}{x^r} = 0, \quad \lim_{x \to +\infty} \frac{x^r}{\ln x} = +\infty, \quad \lim_{x \to 0^+} x^r \ln x = 0$$

for any positive real number r. In these exercises: (a) Use these results, as necessary, to find the limits of $f(x)$ as $x \to +\infty$ and as $x \to 0^+$. (b) Sketch a graph of $f(x)$ and identify all relative extrema, inflection points, and asymptotes (as appropriate). Check your work with a graphing utility. ■

55. $f(x) = x \ln x$ **56.** $f(x) = x^2 \ln x$

57. $f(x) = x^2 \ln(2x)$ **58.** $f(x) = \ln(x^2 + 1)$

59. $f(x) = x^{2/3} \ln x$ **60.** $f(x) = x^{-1/3} \ln x$

FOCUS ON CONCEPTS

61. Consider the family of curves $y = xe^{-bx}$ $(b > 0)$.
 (a) Use a graphing utility to generate some members of this family.
 (b) Discuss the effect of varying b on the shape of the graph, and discuss the locations of the relative extrema and inflection points.

62. Consider the family of curves $y = e^{-bx^2}$ $(b > 0)$.
 (a) Use a graphing utility to generate some members of this family.
 (b) Discuss the effect of varying b on the shape of the graph, and discuss the locations of the relative extrema and inflection points.

63. (a) Determine whether the following limits exist, and if so, find them:
$$\lim_{x \to +\infty} e^x \cos x, \quad \lim_{x \to -\infty} e^x \cos x$$

(b) Sketch the graphs of the equations $y = e^x$, $y = -e^x$, and $y = e^x \cos x$ in the same coordinate system, and label any points of intersection.
(c) Use a graphing utility to generate some members of the family $y = e^{ax} \cos bx$ $(a > 0$ and $b > 0)$, and discuss the effect of varying a and b on the shape of the curve.

64. Consider the family of curves $y = x^n e^{-x^2/n}$, where n is a positive integer.
(a) Use a graphing utility to generate some members of this family.
(b) Discuss the effect of varying n on the shape of the graph, and discuss the locations of the relative extrema and inflection points.

65. The accompanying figure shows the graph of the *derivative* of a function h that is defined and continuous on the interval $(-\infty, +\infty)$. Assume that the graph of h' has a vertical asymptote at $x = 3$ and that
$$h'(x) \to 0^+ \text{ as } x \to -\infty$$
$$h'(x) \to -\infty \text{ as } x \to +\infty$$
(a) What are the critical points for $h(x)$?
(b) Identify the intervals on which $h(x)$ is increasing.
(c) Identify the x-coordinates of relative extrema for $h(x)$ and classify each as a relative maximum or relative minimum.
(d) Estimate the x-coordinates of inflection points for $h(x)$.

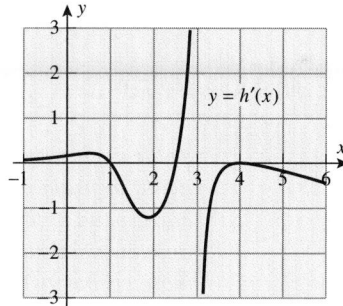

◀ **Figure Ex-65**

66. Let $f(x) = (1 - 2x)h(x)$, where $h(x)$ is as given in Exercise 65. Suppose that $x = 5$ is a critical point for $f(x)$.
(a) Estimate $h(5)$.
(b) Use the second derivative test to determine whether $f(x)$ has a relative maximum or a relative minimum at $x = 5$.

67. A rectangular plot of land is to be fenced off so that the area enclosed will be 400 ft². Let L be the length of fencing needed and x the length of one side of the rectangle. Show that $L = 2x + 800/x$ for $x > 0$, and sketch the graph of L versus x for $x > 0$.

68. A box with a square base and open top is to be made from sheet metal so that its volume is 500 in³. Let S be the area of the surface of the box and x the length of a side of the square base. Show that $S = x^2 + 2000/x$ for $x > 0$, and sketch the graph of S versus x for $x > 0$.

69. The accompanying figure shows a computer-generated graph of the polynomial $y = 0.1x^5(x - 1)$ using a viewing window of $[-2, 2.5] \times [-1, 5]$. Show that the choice of the vertical scale caused the computer to miss important features of the graph. Find the features that were missed and make your own sketch of the graph that shows the missing features.

70. The accompanying figure shows a computer-generated graph of the polynomial $y = 0.1x^5(x + 1)^2$ using a viewing window of $[-2, 1.5] \times [-0.2, 0.2]$. Show that the choice of the vertical scale caused the computer to miss important features of the graph. Find the features that were missed and make your own sketch of the graph that shows the missing features.

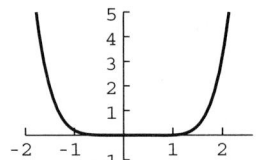

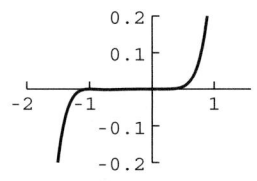

Generated by Mathematica 　　　*Generated by Mathematica*

▲ **Figure Ex-69** 　　　▲ **Figure Ex-70**

71. **Writing** Suppose that $x = x_0$ is a point at which a function f is continuous but not differentiable and that $f'(x)$ approaches different finite limits as x approaches x_0 from either side. Invent your own term to describe the graph of f at such a point and discuss the appropriateness of your term.

72. **Writing** Suppose that the graph of a function f is obtained using a graphing utility. Discuss the information that calculus techniques can provide about f to add to what can already be inferred about f from the graph as shown on your utility's display.

✔ **QUICK CHECK ANSWERS 4.3**

---

1. (a) $(-1, 0), (3, 0), \left(0, \frac{9}{8}\right)$ (b) $x = -2$ and $x = 4$ (c) $y = 3$ (d) $(-\infty, -2), (-1, 3),$ and $(4, +\infty)$ (e) $(-\infty, -2)$ and $(-2, 1]$
(f) $(-\infty, -2)$ and $(4, +\infty)$ (g) $\left(1, \frac{4}{3}\right)$ **2.** (a) $(-2, 0), (2, 0)$ (b) $x = 0$ (c) $y = 0$ (d) $(-\infty, -2)$ and $(2, +\infty)$
(e) $(-\infty, -4]$ and $(0, 4]$ (f) $(-\infty, -4\sqrt{11/5})$ and $(4\sqrt{11/5}, +\infty)$ (g) $\pm 4\sqrt{11/5} \approx \pm 5.93$ **3.** (a) $y = 0$ (as $x \to -\infty$)
(b) $(-\infty, 2)$ and $(2, +\infty)$ (c) $(-\infty, -2]$ and $[2, +\infty)$ (d) $(-\infty, -2 - 2\sqrt{2})$ and $(-2 + 2\sqrt{2}, +\infty)$ (e) $(2, 0)$
(f) $(-2, 16e^{-1}) \approx (-2, 5.89)$ (g) $-2 \pm 2\sqrt{2}$

4.4 ABSOLUTE MAXIMA AND MINIMA

At the beginning of Section 4.2 we observed that if the graph of a function f is viewed as a two-dimensional mountain range (Figure 4.2.1), then the relative maxima and minima correspond to the tops of the hills and the bottoms of the valleys; that is, they are the high and low points in their immediate vicinity. In this section we will be concerned with the more encompassing problem of finding the highest and lowest points over the entire mountain range, that is, we will be looking for the top of the highest hill and the bottom of the deepest valley. In mathematical terms, we will be looking for the largest and smallest values of a function over an interval.

■ **ABSOLUTE EXTREMA**

We will begin with some terminology for describing the largest and smallest values of a function on an interval.

4.4.1 DEFINITION Consider an interval in the domain of a function f and a point x_0 in that interval. We say that f has an **absolute maximum** at x_0 if $f(x) \leq f(x_0)$ for all x in the interval, and we say that f has an **absolute minimum** at x_0 if $f(x_0) \leq f(x)$ for all x in the interval. We say that f has an **absolute extremum** at x_0 if it has either an absolute maximum or an absolute minimum at that point.

If f has an absolute maximum at the point x_0 on an interval, then $f(x_0)$ is the largest value of f on the interval, and if f has an absolute minimum at x_0, then $f(x_0)$ is the smallest value of f on the interval. In general, there is no guarantee that a function will actually have an absolute maximum or minimum on a given interval (Figure 4.4.1).

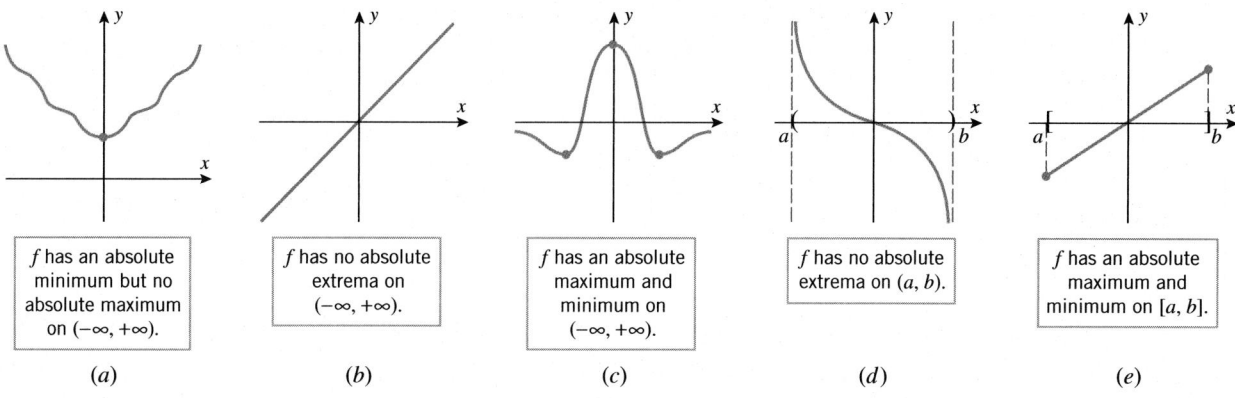

f has an absolute minimum but no absolute maximum on $(-\infty, +\infty)$.	f has no absolute extrema on $(-\infty, +\infty)$.	f has an absolute maximum and minimum on $(-\infty, +\infty)$.	f has no absolute extrema on (a, b).	f has an absolute maximum and minimum on $[a, b]$.
(a)	(b)	(c)	(d)	(e)

▲ **Figure 4.4.1**

◼ THE EXTREME VALUE THEOREM

Parts (a)–(d) of Figure 4.4.1 show that a continuous function may or may not have absolute maxima or minima on an infinite interval or on a finite open interval. However, the following theorem shows that a continuous function must have both an absolute maximum and an absolute minimum on every *finite closed* interval [see part (e) of Figure 4.4.1].

> The hypotheses in the Extreme-Value Theorem are essential. That is, if either the interval is not closed or f is not continuous on the interval, then f need not have absolute extrema on the interval (Exercises 4–6).

4.4.2 **THEOREM** (*Extreme-Value Theorem*) *If a function f is continuous on a finite closed interval $[a, b]$, then f has both an absolute maximum and an absolute minimum on $[a, b]$.*

REMARK | Although the proof of this theorem is too difficult to include here, you should be able to convince yourself of its validity with a little experimentation—try graphing various continuous functions over the interval $[0, 1]$, and convince yourself that there is no way to avoid having a highest and lowest point on a graph. As a physical analogy, if you imagine the graph to be a roller-coaster track starting at $x = 0$ and ending at $x = 1$, the roller coaster will have to pass through a highest point and a lowest point during the trip.

The Extreme-Value Theorem is an example of what mathematicians call an ***existence theorem***. Such theorems state conditions under which certain objects exist, in this case absolute extrema. However, knowing that an object exists and finding it are two separate things. We will now address methods for determining the locations of absolute extrema under the conditions of the Extreme-Value Theorem.

If f is continuous on the finite closed interval $[a, b]$, then the absolute extrema of f occur either at the endpoints of the interval or inside on the open interval (a, b). If the absolute extrema happen to fall inside, then the following theorem tells us that they must occur at critical points of f.

> Theorem 4.4.3 is also valid on infinite open intervals, that is, intervals of the form $(-\infty, +\infty)$, $(a, +\infty)$, and $(-\infty, b)$.

4.4.3 **THEOREM** *If f has an absolute extremum on an open interval (a, b), then it must occur at a critical point of f.*

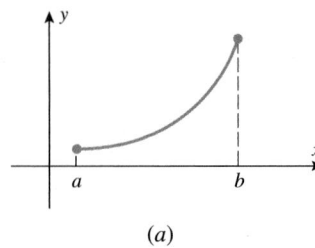

(a)

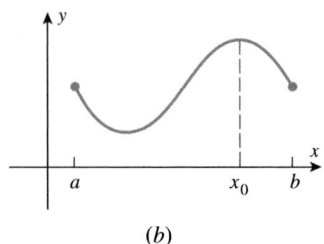

(b)

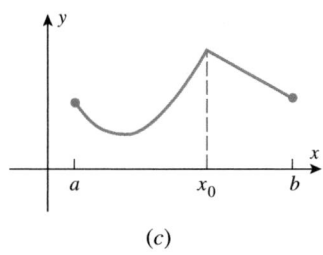

(c)

▲ **Figure 4.4.2** In part (a) the absolute maximum occurs at an endpoint of $[a, b]$, in part (b) it occurs at a stationary point in (a, b), and in part (c) it occurs at a critical point in (a, b) where f is not differentiable.

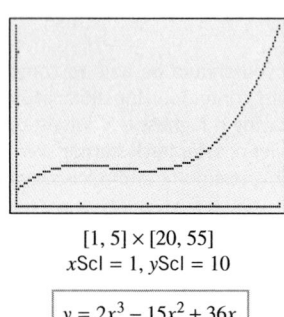

$[1, 5] \times [20, 55]$
xScl = 1, yScl = 10

$y = 2x^3 - 15x^2 + 36x$

▲ **Figure 4.4.3**

Table 4.4.1

x	-1	0	$\frac{1}{8}$	1
$f(x)$	9	0	$-\frac{9}{8}$	3

PROOF If f has an absolute maximum on (a, b) at x_0, then $f(x_0)$ is also a relative maximum for f; for if $f(x_0)$ is the largest value of f on all (a, b), then $f(x_0)$ is certainly the largest value for f in the immediate vicinity of x_0. Thus, x_0 is a critical point of f by Theorem 4.2.2. The proof for absolute minima is similar. ■

It follows from this theorem that if f is continuous on the finite closed interval $[a, b]$, then the absolute extrema occur either at the endpoints of the interval or at critical points inside the interval (Figure 4.4.2). Thus, we can use the following procedure to find the absolute extrema of a continuous function on a finite closed interval $[a, b]$.

A Procedure for Finding the Absolute Extrema of a Continuous Function f on a Finite Closed Interval [a, b]

Step 1. Find the critical points of f in (a, b).

Step 2. Evaluate f at all the critical points and at the endpoints a and b.

Step 3. The largest of the values in Step 2 is the absolute maximum value of f on $[a, b]$ and the smallest value is the absolute minimum.

▶ **Example 1** Find the absolute maximum and minimum values of the function $f(x) = 2x^3 - 15x^2 + 36x$ on the interval $[1, 5]$, and determine where these values occur.

Solution. Since f is continuous and differentiable everywhere, the absolute extrema must occur either at endpoints of the interval or at solutions to the equation $f'(x) = 0$ in the open interval $(1, 5)$. The equation $f'(x) = 0$ can be written as

$$6x^2 - 30x + 36 = 6(x^2 - 5x + 6) = 6(x - 2)(x - 3) = 0$$

Thus, there are stationary points at $x = 2$ and at $x = 3$. Evaluating f at the endpoints, at $x = 2$, and at $x = 3$ yields

$$f(1) = 2(1)^3 - 15(1)^2 + 36(1) = 23$$
$$f(2) = 2(2)^3 - 15(2)^2 + 36(2) = 28$$
$$f(3) = 2(3)^3 - 15(3)^2 + 36(3) = 27$$
$$f(5) = 2(5)^3 - 15(5)^2 + 36(5) = 55$$

from which we conclude that the absolute minimum of f on $[1, 5]$ is 23, occurring at $x = 1$, and the absolute maximum of f on $[1, 5]$ is 55, occurring at $x = 5$. This is consistent with the graph of f in Figure 4.4.3. ◀

▶ **Example 2** Find the absolute extrema of $f(x) = 6x^{4/3} - 3x^{1/3}$ on the interval $[-1, 1]$, and determine where these values occur.

Solution. Note that f is continuous everywhere and therefore the Extreme-Value Theorem guarantees that f has a maximum and a minimum value in the interval $[-1, 1]$. Differentiating, we obtain

$$f'(x) = 8x^{1/3} - x^{-2/3} = x^{-2/3}(8x - 1) = \frac{8x - 1}{x^{2/3}}$$

Thus, $f'(x) = 0$ at $x = \frac{1}{8}$, and $f'(x)$ is undefined at $x = 0$. Evaluating f at these critical points and endpoints yields Table 4.4.1, from which we conclude that an absolute minimum value of $-\frac{9}{8}$ occurs at $x = \frac{1}{8}$, and an absolute maximum value of 9 occurs at $x = -1$. ◀

■ **ABSOLUTE EXTREMA ON INFINITE INTERVALS**

We observed earlier that a continuous function may or may not have absolute extrema on an infinite interval (see Figure 4.4.1). However, certain conclusions about the existence of absolute extrema of a continuous function f on $(-\infty, +\infty)$ can be drawn from the behavior of $f(x)$ as $x \to -\infty$ and as $x \to +\infty$ (Table 4.4.2).

Table 4.4.2
ABSOLUTE EXTREMA ON INFINITE INTERVALS

LIMITS	$\lim\limits_{x \to -\infty} f(x) = +\infty$ $\lim\limits_{x \to +\infty} f(x) = +\infty$	$\lim\limits_{x \to -\infty} f(x) = -\infty$ $\lim\limits_{x \to +\infty} f(x) = -\infty$	$\lim\limits_{x \to -\infty} f(x) = -\infty$ $\lim\limits_{x \to +\infty} f(x) = +\infty$	$\lim\limits_{x \to -\infty} f(x) = +\infty$ $\lim\limits_{x \to +\infty} f(x) = -\infty$
CONCLUSION IF f **IS CONTINUOUS EVERYWHERE**	f has an absolute minimum but no absolute maximum on $(-\infty, +\infty)$.	f has an absolute maximum but no absolute minimum on $(-\infty, +\infty)$.	f has neither an absolute maximum nor an absolute minimum on $(-\infty, +\infty)$.	f has neither an absolute maximum nor an absolute minimum on $(-\infty, +\infty)$.
GRAPH				

▶ **Example 3** What can you say about the existence of absolute extrema on $(-\infty, +\infty)$ for polynomials?

Solution. If $p(x)$ is a polynomial of odd degree, then

$$\lim_{x \to +\infty} p(x) \quad \text{and} \quad \lim_{x \to -\infty} p(x) \tag{1}$$

have opposite signs (one is $+\infty$ and the other is $-\infty$), so there are no absolute extrema. On the other hand, if $p(x)$ has even degree, then the limits in (1) have the same sign (both $+\infty$ or both $-\infty$). If the leading coefficient is positive, then both limits are $+\infty$, and there is an absolute minimum but no absolute maximum; if the leading coefficient is negative, then both limits are $-\infty$, and there is an absolute maximum but no absolute minimum. ◀

▶ **Example 4** Determine by inspection whether $p(x) = 3x^4 + 4x^3$ has any absolute extrema. If so, find them and state where they occur.

Solution. Since $p(x)$ has even degree and the leading coefficient is positive, $p(x) \to +\infty$ as $x \to \pm\infty$. Thus, there is an absolute minimum but no absolute maximum. From Theorem 4.4.3 [applied to the interval $(-\infty, +\infty)$], the absolute minimum must occur at a critical point of p. Since p is differentiable everywhere, we can find all critical points by solving the equation $p'(x) = 0$. This equation is

$$12x^3 + 12x^2 = 12x^2(x + 1) = 0$$

from which we conclude that the critical points are $x = 0$ and $x = -1$. Evaluating p at these critical points yields

$$p(0) = 0 \quad \text{and} \quad p(-1) = -1$$

Therefore, p has an absolute minimum of -1 at $x = -1$ (Figure 4.4.4). ◀

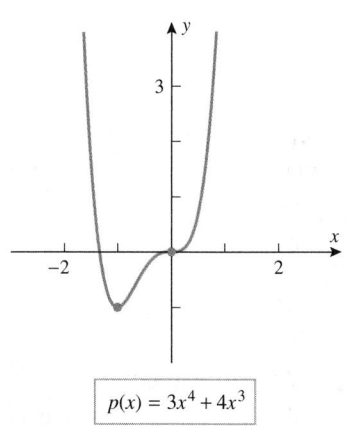

$p(x) = 3x^4 + 4x^3$

▲ **Figure 4.4.4**

■ **ABSOLUTE EXTREMA ON OPEN INTERVALS**

We know that a continuous function may or may not have absolute extrema on an open interval. However, certain conclusions about the existence of absolute extrema of a continuous function f on a finite open interval (a, b) can be drawn from the behavior of $f(x)$ as $x \to a^+$ and as $x \to b^-$ (Table 4.4.3). Similar conclusions can be drawn for intervals of the form $(-\infty, b)$ or $(a, +\infty)$.

Table 4.4.3
ABSOLUTE EXTREMA ON OPEN INTERVALS

LIMITS	$\lim\limits_{x \to a^+} f(x) = +\infty$ $\lim\limits_{x \to b^-} f(x) = +\infty$	$\lim\limits_{x \to a^+} f(x) = -\infty$ $\lim\limits_{x \to b^-} f(x) = -\infty$	$\lim\limits_{x \to a^+} f(x) = -\infty$ $\lim\limits_{x \to b^-} f(x) = +\infty$	$\lim\limits_{x \to a^+} f(x) = +\infty$ $\lim\limits_{x \to b^-} f(x) = -\infty$
CONCLUSION IF f **IS CONTINUOUS ON** (a, b)	f has an absolute minimum but no absolute maximum on (a, b).	f has an absolute maximum but no absolute minimum on (a, b).	f has neither an absolute maximum nor an absolute minimum on (a, b).	f has neither an absolute maximum nor an absolute minimum on (a, b).
GRAPH				

▶ **Example 5** Determine whether the function

$$f(x) = \frac{1}{x^2 - x}$$

has any absolute extrema on the interval $(0, 1)$. If so, find them and state where they occur.

Solution. Since f is continuous on the interval $(0, 1)$ and

$$\lim_{x \to 0^+} f(x) = \lim_{x \to 0^+} \frac{1}{x^2 - x} = \lim_{x \to 0^+} \frac{1}{x(x - 1)} = -\infty$$

$$\lim_{x \to 1^-} f(x) = \lim_{x \to 1^-} \frac{1}{x^2 - x} = \lim_{x \to 1^-} \frac{1}{x(x - 1)} = -\infty$$

the function f has an absolute maximum but no absolute minimum on the interval $(0, 1)$. By Theorem 4.4.3 the absolute maximum must occur at a critical point of f in the interval $(0, 1)$. We have

$$f'(x) = -\frac{2x - 1}{\left(x^2 - x\right)^2}$$

so the only solution of the equation $f'(x) = 0$ is $x = \frac{1}{2}$. Although f is not differentiable at $x = 0$ or at $x = 1$, these values are doubly disqualified since they are neither in the domain of f nor in the interval $(0, 1)$. Thus, the absolute maximum occurs at $x = \frac{1}{2}$, and this absolute maximum is

$$f\left(\tfrac{1}{2}\right) = \frac{1}{\left(\tfrac{1}{2}\right)^2 - \tfrac{1}{2}} = -4$$

(Figure 4.4.5). ◀

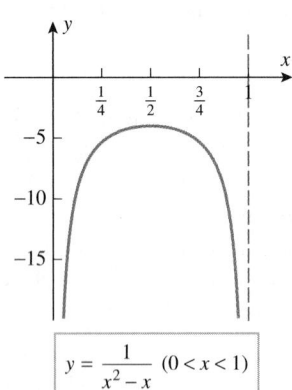

$$y = \frac{1}{x^2 - x} \quad (0 < x < 1)$$

▲ **Figure 4.4.5**

■ **ABSOLUTE EXTREMA OF FUNCTIONS WITH ONE RELATIVE EXTREMUM**

If a continuous function has only one relative extremum on a finite or infinite interval, then that relative extremum must of necessity also be an absolute extremum. To understand why

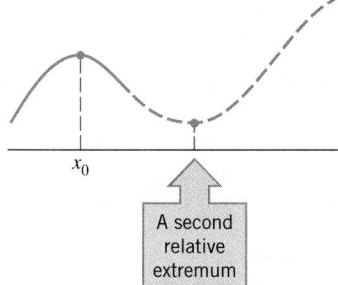

x_0

A second relative extremum

▲ **Figure 4.4.6**

this is so, suppose that f has a relative maximum at x_0 in an interval, and there are no other relative extrema of f on the interval. If $f(x_0)$ is *not* the absolute maximum of f on the interval, then the graph of f has to make an upward turn somewhere on the interval to rise above $f(x_0)$. However, this cannot happen because in the process of making an upward turn it would produce a second relative extremum (Figure 4.4.6). Thus, $f(x_0)$ must be the absolute maximum as well as a relative maximum. This idea is captured in the following theorem, which we state without proof.

4.4.4 THEOREM *Suppose that f is continuous and has exactly one relative extremum on an interval, say at x_0.*

(a) If f has a relative minimum at x_0, then $f(x_0)$ is the absolute minimum of f on the interval.

(b) If f has a relative maximum at x_0, then $f(x_0)$ is the absolute maximum of f the interval.

This theorem is often helpful in situations where other methods are difficult or tedious to apply.

▶ **Example 6** Find the absolute extrema, if any, of the function $f(x) = e^{(x^3 - 3x^2)}$ on the interval $(0, +\infty)$.

Solution. We have

$$\lim_{x \to +\infty} f(x) = +\infty$$

(verify), so f does not have an absolute maximum on the interval $(0, +\infty)$. However, the continuity of f together with the fact that

$$\lim_{x \to 0^+} f(x) = e^0 = 1$$

is finite allow for the possibility that f has an absolute minimum on $(0, +\infty)$. If so, it would have to occur at a critical point of f, so we consider

$$f'(x) = e^{(x^3 - 3x^2)}(3x^2 - 6x) = 3x(x - 2)e^{(x^3 - 3x^2)}$$

Since $e^{(x^3 - 3x^2)} > 0$ for all values of x, we see that $x = 0$ and $x = 2$ are the only critical points of f. Of these, only $x = 2$ is in the interval $(0, +\infty)$, so this is the point at which an absolute minimum could occur. To see whether an absolute minimum actually does occur at this point, we can apply part *(a)* of Theorem 4.4.4. Since

$$f''(x) = e^{(x^3 - 3x^2)}(3x^2 - 6x)^2 + e^{(x^3 - 3x^2)}(6x - 6)$$

$$= [(3x^2 - 6x)^2 + (6x - 6)]e^{(x^3 - 3x^2)}$$

we have

$$f''(2) = (0 + 6)e^{-4} = 6e^{-4} > 0$$

so a relative minimum occurs at $x = 2$ by the second derivative test. Thus, $f(x)$ has an absolute minimum at $x = 2$, and this absolute minimum is $f(2) = e^{-4} \approx 0.0183$ (Figure 4.4.7). ◀

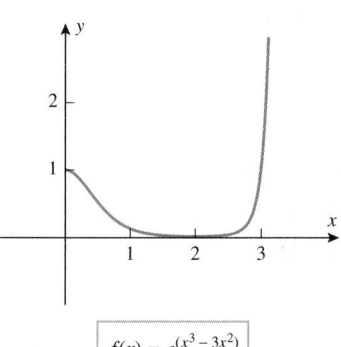

$f(x) = e^{(x^3 - 3x^2)}$

▲ **Figure 4.4.7**

Does the function in Example 6 have an absolute minimum on the interval $(-\infty, +\infty)$?

✔ QUICK CHECK EXERCISES 4.4   *(See page 274 for answers.)*

1. Use the accompanying graph to find the x-coordinates of the relative extrema and absolute extrema of f on $[0, 6]$.

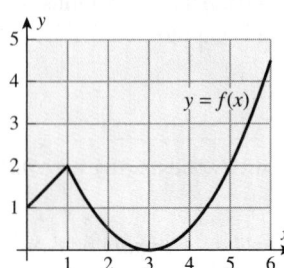
◀ **Figure Ex-1**

2. Suppose that a function f is continuous on $[-4, 4]$ and has critical points at $x = -3, 0, 2$. Use the accompanying table to determine the absolute maximum and absolute minimum values, if any, for f on the indicated intervals.
   (a) $[1, 4]$ (b) $[-2, 2]$ (c) $[-4, 4]$ (d) $(-4, 4)$

x	-4	-3	-2	-1	0	1	2	3	4
$f(x)$	2224	-1333	0	1603	2096	2293	2400	2717	6064

3. Let $f(x) = x^3 - 3x^2 - 9x + 25$. Use the derivative $f'(x) = 3(x + 1)(x - 3)$ to determine the absolute maximum and absolute minimum values, if any, for f on each of the given intervals.
   (a) $[0, 4]$ (b) $[-2, 4]$ (c) $[-4, 2]$
   (d) $[-5, 10]$ (e) $(-5, 4)$

EXERCISE SET 4.4   ⬚ Graphing Utility   [C] CAS

FOCUS ON CONCEPTS

1–2 Use the graph to find x-coordinates of the relative extrema and absolute extrema of f on $[0, 7]$. ▦

1.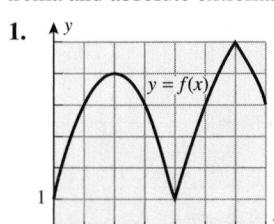

2.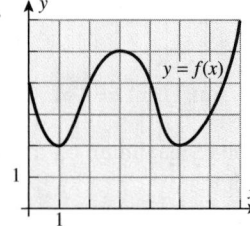

3. In each part, sketch the graph of a continuous function f with the stated properties on the interval $[0, 10]$.
   (a) f has an absolute minimum at $x = 0$ and an absolute maximum at $x = 10$.
   (b) f has an absolute minimum at $x = 2$ and an absolute maximum at $x = 7$.
   (c) f has relative minima at $x = 1$ and $x = 8$, has relative maxima at $x = 3$ and $x = 7$, has an absolute minimum at $x = 5$, and has an absolute maximum at $x = 10$.

4. In each part, sketch the graph of a continuous function f with the stated properties on the interval $(-\infty, +\infty)$.
   (a) f has no relative extrema or absolute extrema.
   (b) f has an absolute minimum at $x = 0$ but no absolute maximum.
   (c) f has an absolute maximum at $x = -5$ and an absolute minimum at $x = 5$.

5. Let
$$f(x) = \begin{cases} \dfrac{1}{1-x}, & 0 \le x < 1 \\ 0, & x = 1 \end{cases}$$
Explain why f has a minimum value but no maximum value on the closed interval $[0, 1]$.

6. Let
$$f(x) = \begin{cases} x, & 0 < x < 1 \\ \frac{1}{2}, & x = 0, 1 \end{cases}$$
Explain why f has neither a minimum value nor a maximum value on the closed interval $[0, 1]$.

7–16 Find the absolute maximum and minimum values of f on the given closed interval, and state where those values occur. ▦

7. $f(x) = 4x^2 - 12x + 10$; $[1, 2]$

8. $f(x) = 8x - x^2$; $[0, 6]$

9. $f(x) = (x - 2)^3$; $[1, 4]$

10. $f(x) = 2x^3 + 3x^2 - 12x$; $[-3, 2]$

11. $f(x) = \dfrac{3x}{\sqrt{4x^2 + 1}}$; $[-1, 1]$

12. $f(x) = (x^2 + x)^{2/3}$; $[-2, 3]$

13. $f(x) = x - 2\sin x$; $[-\pi/4, \pi/2]$

14. $f(x) = \sin x - \cos x$; $[0, \pi]$

15. $f(x) = 1 + |9 - x^2|$; $[-5, 1]$

16. $f(x) = |6 - 4x|$; $[-3, 3]$

17–20 True–False Determine whether the statement is true or false. Explain your answer. ▦

17. If a function f is continuous on $[a, b]$, then f has an absolute maximum on $[a, b]$.

18. If a function f is continuous on (a, b), then f has an absolute minimum on (a, b).

19. If a function f has an absolute minimum on (a, b), then there is a critical point of f in (a, b).

20. If a function f is continuous on $[a, b]$ and f has no relative extreme values in (a, b), then the absolute maximum value of f exists and occurs either at $x = a$ or at $x = b$.

21–28 Find the absolute maximum and minimum values of f, if any, on the given interval, and state where those values occur. ■

21. $f(x) = x^2 - x - 2$; $(-\infty, +\infty)$

22. $f(x) = 3 - 4x - 2x^2$; $(-\infty, +\infty)$

23. $f(x) = 4x^3 - 3x^4$; $(-\infty, +\infty)$

24. $f(x) = x^4 + 4x$; $(-\infty, +\infty)$

25. $f(x) = 2x^3 - 6x + 2$; $(-\infty, +\infty)$

26. $f(x) = x^3 - 9x + 1$; $(-\infty, +\infty)$

27. $f(x) = \dfrac{x^2 + 1}{x + 1}$; $(-5, -1)$

28. $f(x) = \dfrac{x - 2}{x + 1}$; $(-1, 5]$

29–42 Use a graphing utility to estimate the absolute maximum and minimum values of f, if any, on the stated interval, and then use calculus methods to find the exact values. ■

29. $f(x) = (x^2 - 2x)^2$; $(-\infty, +\infty)$

30. $f(x) = (x - 1)^2(x + 2)^2$; $(-\infty, +\infty)$

31. $f(x) = x^{2/3}(20 - x)$; $[-1, 20]$

32. $f(x) = \dfrac{x}{x^2 + 2}$; $[-1, 4]$

33. $f(x) = 1 + \dfrac{1}{x}$; $(0, +\infty)$

34. $f(x) = \dfrac{2x^2 - 3x + 3}{x^2 - 2x + 2}$; $[1, +\infty)$

35. $f(x) = \dfrac{2 - \cos x}{\sin x}$; $[\pi/4, 3\pi/4]$

36. $f(x) = \sin^2 x + \cos x$; $[-\pi, \pi]$

37. $f(x) = x^3 e^{-2x}$; $[1, 4]$

38. $f(x) = \dfrac{\ln(2x)}{x}$; $[1, e]$

39. $f(x) = 5\ln(x^2 + 1) - 3x$; $[0, 4]$

40. $f(x) = (x^2 - 1)e^x$; $[-2, 2]$

41. $f(x) = \sin(\cos x)$; $[0, 2\pi]$

42. $f(x) = \cos(\sin x)$; $[0, \pi]$

43. Find the absolute maximum and minimum values of
$$f(x) = \begin{cases} 4x - 2, & x < 1 \\ (x - 2)(x - 3), & x \geq 1 \end{cases}$$
on $\left[\frac{1}{2}, \frac{7}{2}\right]$.

44. Let $f(x) = x^2 + px + q$. Find the values of p and q such that $f(1) = 3$ is an extreme value of f on $[0, 2]$. Is this value a maximum or minimum?

45–46 If f is a periodic function, then the locations of all absolute extrema on the interval $(-\infty, +\infty)$ can be obtained by finding the locations of the absolute extrema for one period and using the periodicity to locate the rest. Use this idea in these exercises to find the absolute maximum and minimum values of the function, and state the x-values at which they occur. ■

45. $f(x) = 2\cos x + \cos 2x$ **46.** $f(x) = 3\cos\dfrac{x}{3} + 2\cos\dfrac{x}{2}$

47–48 One way of proving that $f(x) \leq g(x)$ for all x in a given interval is to show that $0 \leq g(x) - f(x)$ for all x in the interval; and one way of proving the latter inequality is to show that the absolute minimum value of $g(x) - f(x)$ on the interval is nonnegative. Use this idea to prove the inequalities in these exercises. ■

47. Prove that $\sin x \leq x$ for all x in the interval $[0, 2\pi]$.

48. Prove that $\cos x \geq 1 - (x^2/2)$ for all x in the interval $[0, 2\pi]$.

49. What is the smallest possible slope for a tangent to the graph of the equation $y = x^3 - 3x^2 + 5x$?

50. (a) Show that $f(x) = \sec x + \csc x$ has a minimum value but no maximum value on the interval $(0, \pi/2)$.
  (b) Find the minimum value in part (a).

c **51.** Show that the absolute minimum value of
$$f(x) = x^2 + \dfrac{x^2}{(8 - x)^2}, \quad x > 8$$
occurs at $x = 10$ by using a CAS to find $f'(x)$ and to solve the equation $f'(x) = 0$.

52. The concentration $C(t)$ of a drug in the bloodstream t hours after it has been injected is commonly modeled by an equation of the form
$$C(t) = \dfrac{K(e^{-bt} - e^{-at})}{a - b}$$
where $K > 0$ and $a > b > 0$.
  (a) At what time does the maximum concentration occur?
  (b) Let $K = 1$ for simplicity, and use a graphing utility to check your result in part (a) by graphing $C(t)$ for various values of a and b.

53. Suppose that the equations of motion of a paper airplane during the first 12 seconds of flight are
$$x = t - 2\sin t, \quad y = 2 - 2\cos t \quad (0 \leq t \leq 12)$$
What are the highest and lowest points in the trajectory, and when is the airplane at those points?

54. The accompanying figure shows the path of a fly whose equations of motion are
$$x = \dfrac{\cos t}{2 + \sin t}, \quad y = 3 + \sin(2t) - 2\sin^2 t \quad (0 \leq t \leq 2\pi)$$
  (a) How high and low does it fly?
  (b) How far left and right of the origin does it fly?

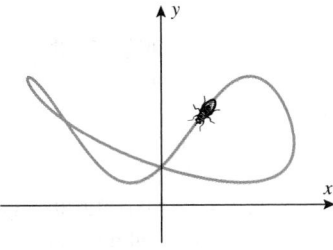

◀ **Figure Ex-54**

55. Let $f(x) = ax^2 + bx + c$, where $a > 0$. Prove that $f(x) \geq 0$ for all x if and only if $b^2 - 4ac \leq 0$. [*Hint:* Find the minimum of $f(x)$.]

56. Prove Theorem 4.4.3 in the case where the extreme value is a minimum.

57. *Writing* Suppose that f is continuous and positive-valued everywhere and that the x-axis is an asymptote for the graph of f, both as $x \to -\infty$ and as $x \to +\infty$. Explain why f cannot have an absolute minimum but may have a relative minimum.

58. *Writing* Explain the difference between a relative maximum and an absolute maximum. Sketch a graph that illustrates a function with a relative maximum that is not an absolute maximum, and sketch another graph illustrating an absolute maximum that is not a relative maximum. Explain how these graphs satisfy the given conditions.

✔ **QUICK CHECK ANSWERS 4.4**

1. There is a relative minimum at $x = 3$, a relative maximum at $x = 1$, an absolute minimum at $x = 3$, and an absolute maximum at $x = 6$.   **2.** (a) max, 6064; min, 2293 (b) max, 2400; min, 0 (c) max, 6064; min, -1333 (d) no max; min, -1333
3. (a) max, $f(0) = 25$; min, $f(3) = -2$ (b) max, $f(-1) = 30$; min, $f(3) = -2$ (c) max, $f(-1) = 30$; min, $f(-4) = -51$
(d) max, $f(10) = 635$; min, $f(-5) = -130$ (e) max, $f(-1) = 30$; no min

4.5 APPLIED MAXIMUM AND MIMIMUM PROBLEMS

In this section we will show how the methods discussed in the last section can be used to solve various applied optimization problems.

■ **CLASSIFICATION OF OPTIMIZATION PROBLEMS**
The applied optimization problems that we will consider in this section fall into the following two categories:

- Problems that reduce to maximizing or minimizing a continuous function over a finite closed interval.

- Problems that reduce to maximizing or minimizing a continuous function over an infinite interval or a finite interval that is not closed.

For problems of the first type the Extreme-Value Theorem (4.4.2) guarantees that the problem has a solution, and we know that the solution can be obtained by examining the values of the function at the critical points and at the endpoints. However, for problems of the second type there may or may not be a solution. If the function is continuous and has exactly one relative extremum of the appropriate type on the interval, then Theorem 4.4.4 guarantees the existence of a solution and provides a method for finding it. In cases where this theorem is not applicable some ingenuity may be required to solve the problem.

■ **PROBLEMS INVOLVING FINITE CLOSED INTERVALS**
In his *On a Method for the Evaluation of Maxima and Minima*, the seventeenth century French mathematician Pierre de Fermat solved an optimization problem very similar to the one posed in our first example. Fermat's work on such optimization problems prompted the French mathematician Laplace to proclaim Fermat the "true inventor of the differential calculus." Although this honor must still reside with Newton and Leibniz, it is the case that Fermat developed procedures that anticipated parts of differential calculus.

▶ **Example 1**   A garden is to be laid out in a rectangular area and protected by a chicken wire fence. What is the largest possible area of the garden if only 100 running feet of chicken wire is available for the fence?

Solution.   Let

$$x = \text{length of the rectangle (ft)}$$
$$y = \text{width of the rectangle (ft)}$$
$$A = \text{area of the rectangle (ft}^2)$$

Then

$$A = xy \tag{1}$$

Since the perimeter of the rectangle is 100 ft, the variables x and y are related by the equation

$$2x + 2y = 100 \quad \text{or} \quad y = 50 - x \tag{2}$$

(See Figure 4.5.1.) Substituting (2) in (1) yields

$$A = x(50 - x) = 50x - x^2 \tag{3}$$

Because x represents a length, it cannot be negative, and because the two sides of length x cannot have a combined length exceeding the total perimeter of 100 ft, the variable x must satisfy

$$0 \le x \le 50 \tag{4}$$

Thus, we have reduced the problem to that of finding the value (or values) of x in [0, 50], for which A is maximum. Since A is a polynomial in x, it is continuous on [0, 50], and so the maximum must occur at an endpoint of this interval or at a critical point.

From (3) we obtain

$$\frac{dA}{dx} = 50 - 2x$$

Setting $dA/dx = 0$ we obtain

$$50 - 2x = 0$$

▲ Figure 4.5.1

Perimeter
$2x + 2y = 100$

Pierre de Fermat (1601–1665) Fermat, the son of a successful French leather merchant, was a lawyer who practiced mathematics as a hobby. He received a Bachelor of Civil Laws degree from the University of Orleans in 1631 and subsequently held various government positions, including a post as councillor to the Toulouse parliament. Although he was apparently financially successful, confidential documents of that time suggest that his performance in office and as a lawyer was poor, perhaps because he devoted so much time to mathematics. Throughout his life, Fermat fought all efforts to have his mathematical results published. He had the unfortunate habit of scribbling his work in the margins of books and often sent his results to friends without keeping copies for himself. As a result, he never received credit for many major achievements until his name was raised from obscurity in the mid-nineteenth century. It is now known that Fermat, simultaneously and independently of Descartes, developed analytic geometry. Unfortunately, Descartes and Fermat argued bitterly over various problems so that there was never any real cooperation between these two great geniuses.

Fermat solved many fundamental calculus problems. He obtained the first procedure for differentiating polynomials, and solved many important maximization, minimization, area, and tangent problems. His work served to inspire Isaac Newton. Fermat is best known for his work in number theory, the study of properties of and relationships between whole numbers. He was the first

mathematician to make substantial contributions to this field after the ancient Greek mathematician Diophantus. Unfortunately, none of Fermat's contemporaries appreciated his work in this area, a fact that eventually pushed Fermat into isolation and obscurity in later life. In addition to his work in calculus and number theory, Fermat was one of the founders of probability theory and made major contributions to the theory of optics. Outside mathematics, Fermat was a classical scholar of some note, was fluent in French, Italian, Spanish, Latin, and Greek, and he composed a considerable amount of Latin poetry.

One of the great mysteries of mathematics is shrouded in Fermat's work in number theory. In the margin of a book by Diophantus, Fermat scribbled that for integer values of n greater than 2, the equation $x^n + y^n = z^n$ has no nonzero integer solutions for x, y, and z. He stated, "I have discovered a truly marvelous proof of this, which however the margin is not large enough to contain." This result, which became known as "Fermat's last theorem," appeared to be true, but its proof evaded the greatest mathematical geniuses for 300 years until Professor Andrew Wiles of Princeton University presented a proof in June 1993 in a dramatic series of three lectures that drew international media attention (see *New York Times*, June 27, 1993). As it turned out, that proof had a serious gap that Wiles and Richard Taylor fixed and published in 1995. A prize of 100,000 German marks was offered in 1908 for the solution, but it is worthless today because of inflation.

Table 4.5.1

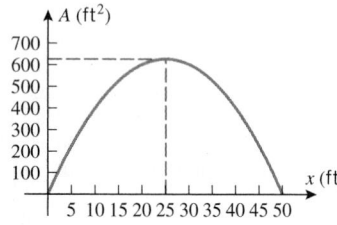

x	0	25	50
A	0	625	0

A (ft^2)

Figure 4.5.2

In Example 1 we included $x = 0$ and $x = 50$ as possible values of x, even though these correspond to rectangles with two sides of length zero. If we view this as a purely mathematical problem, then there is nothing wrong with this. However, if we view this as an applied problem in which the rectangle will be formed from physical material, then it would make sense to exclude these values.

or $x = 25$. Thus, the maximum occurs at one of the values

$$x = 0, \quad x = 25, \quad x = 50$$

Substituting these values in (3) yields Table 4.5.1, which tells us that the maximum area of 625 ft^2 occurs at $x = 25$, which is consistent with the graph of (3) in Figure 4.5.2. From (2) the corresponding value of y is 25, so the rectangle of perimeter 100 ft with greatest area is a square with sides of length 25 ft. ◄

Example 1 illustrates the following five-step procedure that can be used for solving many applied maximum and minimum problems.

A Procedure for Solving Applied Maximum and Minimum Problems

Step 1. Draw an appropriate figure and label the quantities relevant to the problem.

Step 2. Find a formula for the quantity to be maximized or minimized.

Step 3. Using the conditions stated in the problem to eliminate variables, express the quantity to be maximized or minimized as a function of one variable.

Step 4. Find the interval of possible values for this variable from the physical restrictions in the problem.

Step 5. If applicable, use the techniques of the preceding section to obtain the maximum or minimum.

▶ **Example 2**   An open box is to be made from a 16-inch by 30-inch piece of cardboard by cutting out squares of equal size from the four corners and bending up the sides (Figure 4.5.3). What size should the squares be to obtain a box with the largest volume?

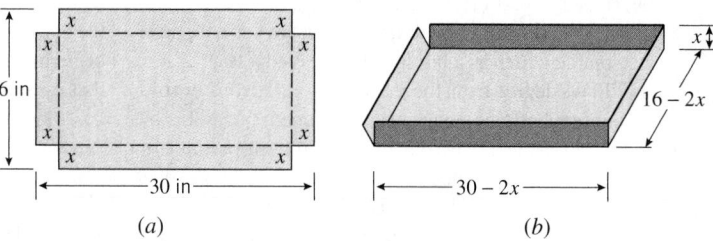

▶ **Figure 4.5.3**   (*a*)   (*b*)

Solution.   For emphasis, we explicitly list the steps of the five-step problem-solving procedure given above as an outline for the solution of this problem. (In later examples we will follow these guidelines without listing the steps.)

- *Step 1:* Figure 4.5.3*a* illustrates the cardboard piece with squares removed from its corners. Let

  $x = $ length (in inches) of the sides of the squares to be cut out

  $V = $ volume (in cubic inches) of the resulting box

- *Step 2:* Because we are removing a square of side x from each corner, the resulting box will have dimensions $16 - 2x$ by $30 - 2x$ by x (Figure 4.5.3*b*). Since the volume of a box is the product of its dimensions, we have

  $$V = (16 - 2x)(30 - 2x)x = 480x - 92x^2 + 4x^3 \tag{5}$$

- *Step 3:* Note that our volume expression is already in terms of the single variable x.
- *Step 4:* The variable x in (5) is subject to certain restrictions. Because x represents a length, it cannot be negative, and because the width of the cardboard is 16 inches, we cannot cut out squares whose sides are more than 8 inches long. Thus, the variable x in (5) must satisfy

$$0 \le x \le 8$$

and hence we have reduced our problem to finding the value (or values) of x in the interval $[0, 8]$ for which (5) is a maximum.

- *Step 5:* From (5) we obtain

$$\frac{dV}{dx} = 480 - 184x + 12x^2 = 4(120 - 46x + 3x^2)$$
$$= 4(x - 12)(3x - 10)$$

Setting $dV/dx = 0$ yields

$$x = \tfrac{10}{3} \quad \text{and} \quad x = 12$$

Since $x = 12$ falls outside the interval $[0, 8]$, the maximum value of V occurs either at the critical point $x = \frac{10}{3}$ or at the endpoints $x = 0$, $x = 8$. Substituting these values into (5) yields Table 4.5.2, which tells us that the greatest possible volume $V = \frac{19,600}{27}$ in³ ≈ 726 in³ occurs when we cut out squares whose sides have length $\frac{10}{3}$ inches. This is consistent with the graph of (5) shown in Figure 4.5.4. ◄

Table 4.5.2

x	0	$\frac{10}{3}$	8
V	0	$\frac{19,600}{27} \approx 726$	0

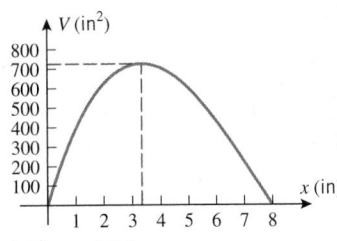

▲ **Figure 4.5.4**

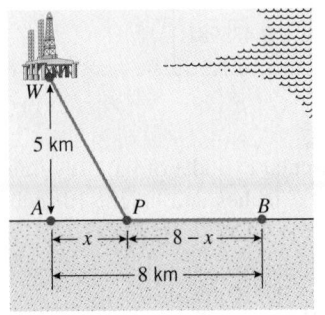

▲ **Figure 4.5.5**

▶ **Example 3**   Figure 4.5.5 shows an offshore oil well located at a point W that is 5 km from the closest point A on a straight shoreline. Oil is to be piped from W to a shore point B that is 8 km from A by piping it on a straight line under water from W to some shore point P between A and B and then on to B via pipe along the shoreline. If the cost of laying pipe is \$1,000,000/km under water and \$500,000/km over land, where should the point P be located to minimize the cost of laying the pipe?

Solution.   Let

$$x = \text{distance (in kilometers) between } A \text{ and } P$$
$$c = \text{cost (in millions of dollars) for the entire pipeline}$$

From Figure 4.5.5 the length of pipe under water is the distance between W and P. By the Theorem of Pythagoras that length is

$$\sqrt{x^2 + 25} \tag{6}$$

Also from Figure 4.5.5, the length of pipe over land is the distance between P and B, which is

$$8 - x \tag{7}$$

From (6) and (7) it follows that the total cost c (in millions of dollars) for the pipeline is

$$c = 1(\sqrt{x^2 + 25}) + \tfrac{1}{2}(8 - x) = \sqrt{x^2 + 25} + \tfrac{1}{2}(8 - x) \tag{8}$$

Because the distance between A and B is 8 km, the distance x between A and P must satisfy

$$0 \le x \le 8$$

We have thus reduced our problem to finding the value (or values) of x in the interval $[0, 8]$ for which c is a minimum. Since c is a continuous function of x on the closed interval $[0, 8]$, we can use the methods developed in the preceding section to find the minimum.

From (8) we obtain

$$\frac{dc}{dx} = \frac{x}{\sqrt{x^2 + 25}} - \frac{1}{2}$$

Setting $dc/dx = 0$ and solving for x yields

$$\frac{x}{\sqrt{x^2 + 25}} = \frac{1}{2} \tag{9}$$

$$x^2 = \frac{1}{4}(x^2 + 25)$$

$$x = \pm\frac{5}{\sqrt{3}}$$

TECHNOLOGY MASTERY

If you have a CAS, use it to check all of the computations in Example 3. Specifically, differentiate c with respect to x, solve the equation $dc/dx = 0$, and perform all of the numerical calculations.

The number $-5/\sqrt{3}$ is not a solution of (9) and must be discarded, leaving $x = 5/\sqrt{3}$ as the only critical point. Since this point lies in the interval $[0, 8]$, the minimum must occur at one of the values

$$x = 0, \quad x = 5/\sqrt{3}, \quad x = 8$$

Substituting these values into (8) yields Table 4.5.3, which tells us that the least possible cost of the pipeline (to the nearest dollar) is $c = \$8,330,127$, and this occurs when the point P is located at a distance of $5/\sqrt{3} \approx 2.89$ km from A. ◄

Table 4.5.3

x	0	$\frac{5}{\sqrt{3}}$	8
c	9	$\frac{10}{\sqrt{3}} + \left(4 - \frac{5}{2\sqrt{3}}\right) \approx 8.330127$	$\sqrt{89} \approx 9.433981$

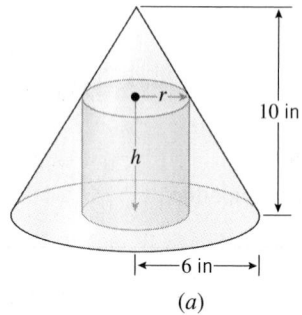

(a)

(b)

▲ **Figure 4.5.6**

► **Example 4** Find the radius and height of the right circular cylinder of largest volume that can be inscribed in a right circular cone with radius 6 inches and height 10 inches (Figure 4.5.6a).

Solution. Let
$r =$ radius (in inches) of the cylinder
$h =$ height (in inches) of the cylinder
$V =$ volume (in cubic inches) of the cylinder

The formula for the volume of the inscribed cylinder is

$$V = \pi r^2 h \tag{10}$$

To eliminate one of the variables in (10) we need a relationship between r and h. Using similar triangles (Figure 4.5.6b) we obtain

$$\frac{10 - h}{r} = \frac{10}{6} \quad \text{or} \quad h = 10 - \frac{5}{3}r \tag{11}$$

Substituting (11) into (10) we obtain

$$V = \pi r^2 \left(10 - \frac{5}{3}r\right) = 10\pi r^2 - \frac{5}{3}\pi r^3 \tag{12}$$

which expresses V in terms of r alone. Because r represents a radius, it cannot be negative, and because the radius of the inscribed cylinder cannot exceed the radius of the cone, the variable r must satisfy

$$0 \leq r \leq 6$$

Thus, we have reduced the problem to that of finding the value (or values) of r in $[0, 6]$ for which (12) is a maximum. Since V is a continuous function of r on $[0, 6]$, the methods developed in the preceding section apply.

From (12) we obtain

$$\frac{dV}{dr} = 20\pi r - 5\pi r^2 = 5\pi r(4 - r)$$

Setting $dV/dr = 0$ gives

$$5\pi r(4 - r) = 0$$

so $r = 0$ and $r = 4$ are critical points. Since these lie in the interval $[0, 6]$, the maximum must occur at one of the values

$$r = 0, \quad r = 4, \quad r = 6$$

Table 4.5.4

r	0	4	6
V	0	$\frac{160}{3}\pi$	0

Substituting these values into (12) yields Table 4.5.4, which tells us that the maximum volume $V = \frac{160}{3}\pi \approx 168$ in^3 occurs when the inscribed cylinder has radius 4 in. When $r = 4$ it follows from (11) that $h = \frac{10}{3}$. Thus, the inscribed cylinder of largest volume has radius $r = 4$ in and height $h = \frac{10}{3}$ in. ◄

■ PROBLEMS INVOLVING INTERVALS THAT ARE NOT BOTH FINITE AND CLOSED

► **Example 5**   A closed cylindrical can is to hold 1 liter (1000 cm^3) of liquid. How should we choose the height and radius to minimize the amount of material needed to manufacture the can?

Solution.   Let

$$h = \text{height (in cm) of the can}$$
$$r = \text{radius (in cm) of the can}$$
$$S = \text{surface area (in cm}^2\text{) of the can}$$

Assuming there is no waste or overlap, the amount of material needed for manufacture will be the same as the surface area of the can. Since the can consists of two circular disks of radius r and a rectangular sheet with dimensions h by $2\pi r$ (Figure 4.5.7), the surface area will be

$$S = 2\pi r^2 + 2\pi rh \tag{13}$$

Since S depends on two variables, r and h, we will look for some condition in the problem that will allow us to express one of these variables in terms of the other. For this purpose,

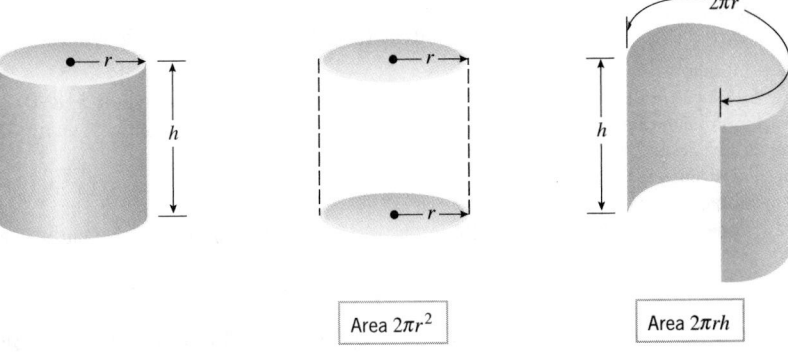

Area $2\pi r^2$ Area $2\pi rh$

▲ **Figure 4.5.7**

observe that the volume of the can is 1000 cm³, so it follows from the formula $V = \pi r^2 h$ for the volume of a cylinder that

$$1000 = \pi r^2 h \quad \text{or} \quad h = \frac{1000}{\pi r^2} \tag{14-15}$$

Substituting (15) in (13) yields

$$S = 2\pi r^2 + \frac{2000}{r} \tag{16}$$

Thus, we have reduced the problem to finding a value of r in the interval $(0, +\infty)$ for which S is minimum. Since S is a continuous function of r on the interval $(0, +\infty)$ and

$$\lim_{r \to 0^+} \left(2\pi r^2 + \frac{2000}{r} \right) = +\infty \quad \text{and} \quad \lim_{r \to +\infty} \left(2\pi r^2 + \frac{2000}{r} \right) = +\infty$$

the analysis in Table 4.4.3 implies that S does have a minimum on the interval $(0, +\infty)$. Since this minimum must occur at a critical point, we calculate

$$\frac{dS}{dr} = 4\pi r - \frac{2000}{r^2} \tag{17}$$

Setting $dS/dr = 0$ gives

$$r = \frac{10}{\sqrt[3]{2\pi}} \approx 5.4 \tag{18}$$

Since (18) is the only critical point in the interval $(0, +\infty)$, this value of r yields the minimum value of S. From (15) the value of h corresponding to this r is

$$h = \frac{1000}{\pi(10/\sqrt[3]{2\pi})^2} = \frac{20}{\sqrt[3]{2\pi}} = 2r$$

It is not an accident here that the minimum occurs when the height of the can is equal to the diameter of its base (Exercise 29).

Second Solution. The conclusion that a minimum occurs at the value of r in (18) can be deduced from Theorem 4.4.4 and the second derivative test by noting that

$$\frac{d^2 S}{dr^2} = 4\pi + \frac{4000}{r^3}$$

is positive if $r > 0$ and hence is positive if $r = 10/\sqrt[3]{2\pi}$. This implies that a relative minimum, and therefore a minimum, occurs at the critical point $r = 10/\sqrt[3]{2\pi}$.

Third Solution. An alternative justification that the critical point $r = 10/\sqrt[3]{2\pi}$ corresponds to a minimum for S is to view the graph of S versus r (Figure 4.5.8). ◄

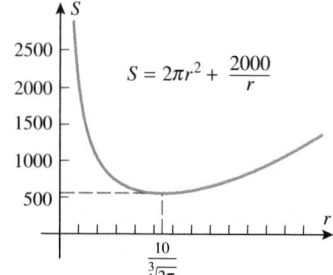

▲ **Figure 4.5.8**

In Example 5, the surface area S has no absolute maximum, since S increases without bound as the radius r approaches 0 (Figure 4.5.8). Thus, had we asked for the dimensions of the can requiring the *maximum* amount of material for its manufacture, there would have been no solution to the problem. Optimization problems with no solution are sometimes called *ill posed*.

▶ **Example 6** Find a point on the curve $y = x^2$ that is closest to the point $(18, 0)$.

Solution. The distance L between $(18, 0)$ and an arbitrary point (x, y) on the curve $y = x^2$ (Figure 4.5.9) is given by

$$L = \sqrt{(x - 18)^2 + (y - 0)^2}$$

Since (x, y) lies on the curve, x and y satisfy $y = x^2$; thus,

$$L = \sqrt{(x - 18)^2 + x^4} \tag{19}$$

Because there are no restrictions on x, the problem reduces to finding a value of x in $(-\infty, +\infty)$ for which (19) is a minimum. The distance L and the square of the distance L^2

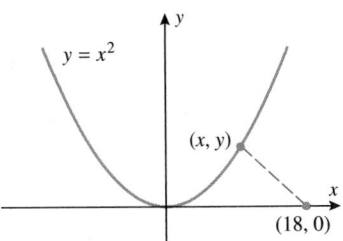

$y = x^2$

(x, y)

$(18, 0)$

▲ Figure 4.5.9

are minimized at the same value (see Exercise 66). Thus, the minimum value of L in (19) and the minimum value of

$$S = L^2 = (x - 18)^2 + x^4 \tag{20}$$

occur at the same x-value.

From (20),

$$\frac{dS}{dx} = 2(x - 18) + 4x^3 = 4x^3 + 2x - 36 \tag{21}$$

so the critical points satisfy $4x^3 + 2x - 36 = 0$ or, equivalently,

$$2x^3 + x - 18 = 0 \tag{22}$$

To solve for x we will begin by checking the divisors of -18 to see whether the polynomial on the left side has any integer roots (see Appendix C). These divisors are $\pm 1, \pm 2, \pm 3, \pm 6$, ± 9, and ± 18. A check of these values shows that $x = 2$ is a root, so $x - 2$ is a factor of the polynomial. After dividing the polynomial by this factor we can rewrite (22) as

$$(x - 2)(2x^2 + 4x + 9) = 0$$

Thus, the remaining solutions of (22) satisfy the quadratic equation

$$2x^2 + 4x + 9 = 0$$

But this equation has no real solutions (using the quadratic formula), so $x = 2$ is the only critical point of S. To determine the nature of this critical point we will use the second derivative test. From (21),

$$\frac{d^2 S}{dx^2} = 12x^2 + 2, \quad \text{so} \quad \left. \frac{d^2 S}{dx^2} \right|_{x=2} = 50 > 0$$

which shows that a relative minimum occurs at $x = 2$. Since $x = 2$ yields the only relative extremum for L, it follows from Theorem 4.4.4 that an absolute minimum value of L also occurs at $x = 2$. Thus, the point on the curve $y = x^2$ closest to $(18, 0)$ is

$$(x, y) = (x, x^2) = (2, 4) \blacktriangleleft$$

■ **AN APPLICATION TO ECONOMICS**

Three functions of importance to an economist or a manufacturer are

$C(x) = $ total cost of producing x units of a product during some time period

$R(x) = $ total revenue from selling x units of the product during the time period

$P(x) = $ total profit obtained by selling x units of the product during the time period

These are called, respectively, the *cost function*, *revenue function*, and *profit function*. If all units produced are sold, then these are related by

$$P(x) = R(x) - C(x) \tag{23}$$

[profit] = [revenue] – [cost]

The total cost $C(x)$ of producing x units can be expressed as a sum

$$C(x) = a + M(x) \tag{24}$$

where a is a constant, called *overhead*, and $M(x)$ is a function representing *manufacturing cost*. The overhead, which includes such fixed costs as rent and insurance, does not depend on x; it must be paid even if nothing is produced. On the other hand, the manufacturing cost $M(x)$, which includes such items as cost of materials and labor, depends on the number of items manufactured. It is shown in economics that with suitable simplifying assumptions, $M(x)$ can be expressed in the form

$$M(x) = bx + cx^2$$

where b and c are constants. Substituting this in (24) yields

$$C(x) = a + bx + cx^2 \qquad (25)$$

If a manufacturing firm can sell all the items it produces for p dollars apiece, then its total revenue $R(x)$ (in dollars) will be

$$R(x) = px \qquad (26)$$

and its total profit $P(x)$ (in dollars) will be

$$P(x) = [\text{total revenue}] - [\text{total cost}] = R(x) - C(x) = px - C(x)$$

Thus, if the cost function is given by (25),

$$P(x) = px - (a + bx + cx^2) \qquad (27)$$

Depending on such factors as number of employees, amount of machinery available, economic conditions, and competition, there will be some upper limit l on the number of items a manufacturer is capable of producing and selling. Thus, during a fixed time period the variable x in (27) will satisfy

$$0 \le x \le l$$

By determining the value or values of x in $[0, l]$ that maximize (27), the firm can determine how many units of its product must be manufactured and sold to yield the greatest profit. This is illustrated in the following numerical example.

▶ **Example 7**   A liquid form of antibiotic manufactured by a pharmaceutical firm is sold in bulk at a price of $200 per unit. If the total production cost (in dollars) for x units is

$$C(x) = 500,000 + 80x + 0.003x^2$$

and if the production capacity of the firm is at most 30,000 units in a specified time, how many units of antibiotic must be manufactured and sold in that time to maximize the profit?

Solution.   Since the total revenue for selling x units is $R(x) = 200x$, the profit $P(x)$ on x units will be

$$P(x) = R(x) - C(x) = 200x - (500,000 + 80x + 0.003x^2) \qquad (28)$$

Jim Karageorge/Getty Images

A pharmaceutical firm's profit is a function of the number of units produced.

Since the production capacity is at most 30,000 units, x must lie in the interval $[0, 30,000]$. From (28)

$$\frac{dP}{dx} = 200 - (80 + 0.006x) = 120 - 0.006x$$

Setting $dP/dx = 0$ gives

$$120 - 0.006x = 0 \quad \text{or} \quad x = 20,000$$

Since this critical point lies in the interval $[0, 30,000]$, the maximum profit must occur at one of the values

$$x = 0, \quad x = 20,000, \quad \text{or} \quad x = 30,000$$

Substituting these values in (28) yields Table 4.5.5, which tells us that the maximum profit $P = \$700,000$ occurs when $x = 20,000$ units are manufactured and sold in the specified time. ◀

Table 4.5.5

x	0	20,000	30,000
$P(x)$	−500,000	700,000	400,000

■ MARGINAL ANALYSIS

Economists call $P'(x)$, $R'(x)$, and $C'(x)$ the **marginal profit**, **marginal revenue**, and **marginal cost**, respectively; and they interpret these quantities as the *additional* profit, revenue, and cost that result from producing and selling one additional unit of the product when the production and sales levels are at x units. These interpretations follow from the local linear approximations of the profit, revenue, and cost functions. For example, it follows from Formula (2) of Section 3.5 that when the production and sales levels are at x units the local linear approximation of the profit function is

$$P(x + \Delta x) \approx P(x) + P'(x)\Delta x$$

Thus, if $\Delta x = 1$ (one additional unit produced and sold), this formula implies

$$P(x + 1) \approx P(x) + P'(x)$$

and hence the *additional* profit that results from producing and selling one additional unit can be approximated as

$$P(x + 1) - P(x) \approx P'(x)$$

Similarly, $R(x + 1) - R(x) \approx R'(x)$ and $C(x + 1) - C(x) \approx C'(x)$.

■ A BASIC PRINCIPLE OF ECONOMICS

It follows from (23) that $P'(x) = 0$ has the same solution as $C'(x) = R'(x)$, and this implies that the maximum profit must occur at a point where the marginal revenue is equal to the marginal cost; that is:

If profit is maximum, then the cost of manufacturing and selling an additional unit of a product is approximately equal to the revenue generated by the additional unit.

In Example 7, the maximum profit occurs when $x = 20{,}000$ units. Note that

$$C(20{,}001) - C(20{,}000) = \$200.003 \quad \text{and} \quad R(20{,}001) - R(20{,}000) = \$200$$

which is consistent with this basic economic principle.

✔ QUICK CHECK EXERCISES 4.5   (See page 288 for answers.)

1. A positive number x and its reciprocal are added together. The smallest possible value of this sum is obtained by minimizing $f(x) = $ _____ for x in the interval _____.

2. Two nonnegative numbers, x and y, have a sum equal to 10. The largest possible product of the two numbers is obtained by maximizing $f(x) = $ _____ for x in the interval _____.

3. A rectangle in the xy-plane has one corner at the origin, an adjacent corner at the point $(x, 0)$, and a third corner at a point on the line segment from $(0, 4)$ to $(3, 0)$. The largest possible area of the rectangle is obtained by maximizing $A(x) = $ _____ for x in the interval _____.

4. An open box is to be made from a 20-inch by 32-inch piece of cardboard by cutting out x-inch by x-inch squares from the four corners and bending up the sides. The largest possible volume of the box is obtained by maximizing $V(x) = $ _____ for x in the interval _____.

EXERCISE SET 4.5

1. Find a number in the closed interval $\left[\frac{1}{2}, \frac{3}{2}\right]$ such that the sum of the number and its reciprocal is
   (a) as small as possible
   (b) as large as possible.

2. How should two nonnegative numbers be chosen so that their sum is 1 and the sum of their squares is
   (a) as large as possible
   (b) as small as possible?

3. A rectangular field is to be bounded by a fence on three sides and by a straight stream on the fourth side. Find the dimensions of the field with maximum area that can be enclosed using 1000 ft of fence.

4. The boundary of a field is a right triangle with a straight stream along its hypotenuse and with fences along its other two sides. Find the dimensions of the field with maximum area that can be enclosed using 1000 ft of fence.

5. A rectangular plot of land is to be fenced in using two kinds of fencing. Two opposite sides will use heavy-duty fencing selling for $3 a foot, while the remaining two sides will use standard fencing selling for $2 a foot. What are the dimensions of the rectangular plot of greatest area that can be fenced in at a cost of $6000?

6. A rectangle is to be inscribed in a right triangle having sides of length 6 in, 8 in, and 10 in. Find the dimensions of the rectangle with greatest area assuming the rectangle is positioned as in Figure Ex-6.

7. Solve the problem in Exercise 6 assuming the rectangle is positioned as in Figure Ex-7.

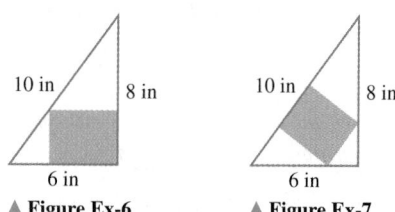

▲ Figure Ex-6   ▲ Figure Ex-7

8. A rectangle has its two lower corners on the x-axis and its two upper corners on the curve $y = 16 - x^2$. For all such rectangles, what are the dimensions of the one with largest area?

9. Find the dimensions of the rectangle with maximum area that can be inscribed in a circle of radius 10.

10. Find the point P in the first quadrant on the curve $y = x^{-2}$ such that a rectangle with sides on the coordinate axes and a vertex at P has the smallest possible perimeter.

11. A rectangular area of 3200 ft^2 is to be fenced off. Two opposite sides will use fencing costing $1 per foot and the remaining sides will use fencing costing $2 per foot. Find the dimensions of the rectangle of least cost.

12. Show that among all rectangles with perimeter p, the square has the maximum area.

13. Show that among all rectangles with area A, the square has the minimum perimeter.

14. A wire of length 12 in can be bent into a circle, bent into a square, or cut into two pieces to make both a circle and a square. How much wire should be used for the circle if the total area enclosed by the figure(s) is to be
    (a) a maximum   (b) a minimum?

15. A rectangle R in the plane has corners at $(\pm 8, \pm 12)$, and a 100 by 100 square S is positioned in the plane so that its

sides are parallel to the coordinate axes and the lower left corner of S is on the line $y = -3x$. What is the largest possible area of a region in the plane that is contained in both R and S?

16. Solve the problem in Exercise 15 if S is a 16 by 16 square.

17. Solve the problem in Exercise 15 if S is positioned with its lower left corner on the line $y = -6x$.

18. A rectangular page is to contain 42 square inches of printable area. The margins at the top and bottom of the page are each 1 inch, one side margin is 1 inch, and the other side margin is 2 inches. What should the dimensions of the page be so that the least amount of paper is used?

19. A box with a square base is taller than it is wide. In order to send the box through the U.S. mail, the height of the box and the perimeter of the base can sum to no more than 108 in. What is the maximum volume for such a box?

20. A box with a square base is wider than it is tall. In order to send the box through the U.S. mail, the width of the box and the perimeter of one of the (nonsquare) sides of the box can sum to no more than 108 in. What is the maximum volume for such a box?

21. An open box is to be made from a 3 ft by 8 ft rectangular piece of sheet metal by cutting out squares of equal size from the four corners and bending up the sides. Find the maximum volume that the box can have.

22. A closed rectangular container with a square base is to have a volume of 2250 in^3. The material for the top and bottom of the container will cost $2 per in^2, and the material for the sides will cost $3 per in^2. Find the dimensions of the container of least cost.

23. A closed rectangular container with a square base is to have a volume of 2000 cm^3. It costs twice as much per square centimeter for the top and bottom as it does for the sides. Find the dimensions of the container of least cost.

24. A container with square base, vertical sides, and open top is to be made from 1000 ft^2 of material. Find the dimensions of the container with greatest volume.

25. A rectangular container with two square sides and an open top is to have a volume of V cubic units. Find the dimensions of the container with minimum surface area.

26. A church window consisting of a rectangle topped by a semicircle is to have a perimeter p. Find the radius of the semicircle if the area of the window is to be maximum.

27. Find the dimensions of the right circular cylinder of largest volume that can be inscribed in a sphere of radius R.

28. Find the dimensions of the right circular cylinder of greatest surface area that can be inscribed in a sphere of radius R.

29. A closed, cylindrical can is to have a volume of V cubic units. Show that the can of minimum surface area is achieved when the height is equal to the diameter of the base.

30. A closed cylindrical can is to have a surface area of S square units. Show that the can of maximum volume is achieved when the height is equal to the diameter of the base.

31. A cylindrical can, open at the top, is to hold 500 cm^3 of liquid. Find the height and radius that minimize the amount of material needed to manufacture the can.

32. A soup can in the shape of a right circular cylinder of radius r and height h is to have a prescribed volume V. The top and bottom are cut from squares as shown in Figure Ex-32. If the shaded corners are wasted, but there is no other waste, find the ratio r/h for the can requiring the least material (including waste).

33. A box-shaped wire frame consists of two identical wire squares whose vertices are connected by four straight wires of equal length (Figure Ex-33). If the frame is to be made from a wire of length L, what should the dimensions be to obtain a box of greatest volume?

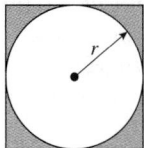
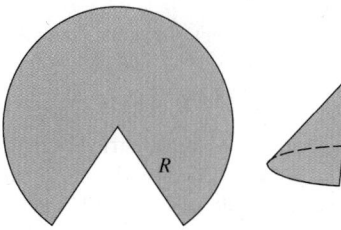

▲ **Figure Ex-32**   ▲ **Figure Ex-33**

34. Suppose that the sum of the surface areas of a sphere and a cube is a constant.
   (a) Show that the sum of their volumes is smallest when the diameter of the sphere is equal to the length of an edge of the cube.
   (b) When will the sum of their volumes be greatest?

35. Find the height and radius of the cone of slant height L whose volume is as large as possible.

36. A cone is made from a circular sheet of radius R by cutting out a sector and gluing the cut edges of the remaining piece together (Figure Ex-36). What is the maximum volume attainable for the cone?

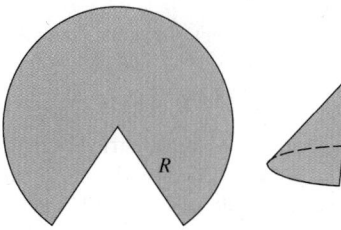

▲ **Figure Ex-36**

37. A cone-shaped paper drinking cup is to hold 100 cm^3 of water. Find the height and radius of the cup that will require the least amount of paper.

38. Find the dimensions of the isosceles triangle of least area that can be circumscribed about a circle of radius R.

39. Find the height and radius of the right circular cone with least volume that can be circumscribed about a sphere of radius R.

40. A commercial cattle ranch currently allows 20 steers per acre of grazing land; on the average its steers weigh 2000 lb at market. Estimates by the Agriculture Department indicate that the average market weight per steer will be reduced by 50 lb for each additional steer added per acre of grazing land. How many steers per acre should be allowed in order for the ranch to get the largest possible total market weight for its cattle?

41. A company mines low-grade nickel ore. If the company mines x tons of ore, it can sell the ore for $p = 225 - 0.25x$ dollars per ton. Find the revenue and marginal revenue functions. At what level of production would the company obtain the maximum revenue?

42. A fertilizer producer finds that it can sell its product at a price of $p = 300 - 0.1x$ dollars per unit when it produces x units of fertilizer. The total production cost (in dollars) for x units is

$$C(x) = 15{,}000 + 125x + 0.025x^2$$

If the production capacity of the firm is at most 1000 units of fertilizer in a specified time, how many units must be manufactured and sold in that time to maximize the profit?

43. (a) A chemical manufacturer sells sulfuric acid in bulk at a price of $100 per unit. If the daily total production cost in dollars for x units is

$$C(x) = 100{,}000 + 50x + 0.0025x^2$$

and if the daily production capacity is at most 7000 units, how many units of sulfuric acid must be manufactured and sold daily to maximize the profit?
   (b) Would it benefit the manufacturer to expand the daily production capacity?
   (c) Use marginal analysis to approximate the effect on profit if daily production could be increased from 7000 to 7001 units.

44. A firm determines that x units of its product can be sold daily at p dollars per unit, where

$$x = 1000 - p$$

The cost of producing x units per day is

$$C(x) = 3000 + 20x$$

   (a) Find the revenue function $R(x)$.
   (b) Find the profit function $P(x)$.
   (c) Assuming that the production capacity is at most 500 units per day, determine how many units the company must produce and sell each day to maximize the profit.
   (d) Find the maximum profit.
   (e) What price per unit must be charged to obtain the maximum profit?

45. In a certain chemical manufacturing process, the daily weight y of defective chemical output depends on the total weight x of all output according to the empirical formula

$$y = 0.01x + 0.00003x^2$$

where x and y are in pounds. If the profit is $100 per pound of nondefective chemical produced and the loss is $20 per pound of defective chemical produced, how many pounds of chemical should be produced daily to maximize the total daily profit?

46. An independent truck driver charges a client $15 for each hour of driving, plus the cost of fuel. At highway speeds of v miles per hour, the trucker's rig gets $10 - 0.07v$ miles per gallon of diesel fuel. If diesel fuel costs $2.50 per gallon, what speed v will minimize the cost to the client?

47. A trapezoid is inscribed in a semicircle of radius 2 so that one side is along the diameter (Figure Ex-47). Find the maximum possible area for the trapezoid. [*Hint:* Express the area of the trapezoid in terms of θ.]

48. A drainage channel is to be made so that its cross section is a trapezoid with equally sloping sides (Figure Ex-48). If the sides and bottom all have a length of 5 ft, how should the angle θ ($0 \le \theta \le \pi/2$) be chosen to yield the greatest cross-sectional area of the channel?

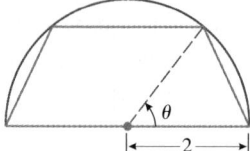

▲ **Figure Ex-47**   ▲ **Figure Ex-48**

49. A lamp is suspended above the center of a round table of radius r. How high above the table should the lamp be placed to achieve maximum illumination at the edge of the table? [Assume that the illumination I is directly proportional to the cosine of the angle of incidence ϕ of the light rays and inversely proportional to the square of the distance l from the light source (Figure Ex-49).]

50. A plank is used to reach over a fence 8 ft high to support a wall that is 1 ft behind the fence (Figure Ex-50). What is the length of the shortest plank that can be used? [*Hint:* Express the length of the plank in terms of the angle θ shown in the figure.]

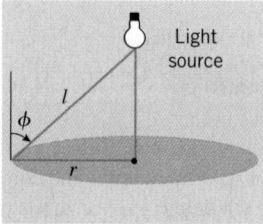
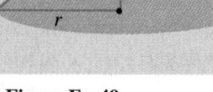

▲ **Figure Ex-49**   ▲ **Figure Ex-50**

51. Find the coordinates of the point P on the curve

$$y = \frac{1}{x^2} \quad (x > 0)$$

where the segment of the tangent line at P that is cut off by the coordinate axes has its shortest length.

52. Find the x-coordinate of the point P on the parabola

$$y = 1 - x^2 \quad (0 < x \le 1)$$

where the triangle that is enclosed by the tangent line at P and the coordinate axes has the smallest area.

53. Where on the curve $y = (1 + x^2)^{-1}$ does the tangent line have the greatest slope?

54. Suppose that the number of bacteria in a culture at time t is given by $N = 5000(25 + te^{-t/20})$.
  (a) Find the largest and smallest number of bacteria in the culture during the time interval $0 \le t \le 100$.
  (b) At what time during the time interval in part (a) is the number of bacteria decreasing most rapidly?

55. The shoreline of Circle Lake is a circle with diameter 2 mi. Nancy's training routine begins at point E on the eastern shore of the lake. She jogs along the north shore to a point P and then swims the straight line distance, if any, from P to point W diametrically opposite E (Figure Ex-55). Nancy swims at a rate of 2 mi/h and jogs at 8 mi/h. How far should Nancy jog in order to complete her training routine in
  (a) the least amount of time
  (b) the greatest amount of time?

56. A man is floating in a rowboat 1 mile from the (straight) shoreline of a large lake. A town is located on the shoreline 1 mile from the point on the shoreline closest to the man. As suggested in Figure Ex-56, he intends to row in a straight line to some point P on the shoreline and then walk the remaining distance to the town. To what point should he row in order to reach his destination in the least time if
  (a) he can walk 5 mi/h and row 3 mi/h
  (b) he can walk 5 mi/h and row 4 mi/h?

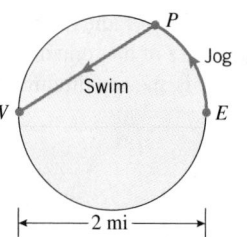
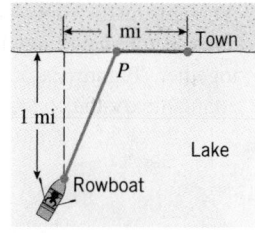

▲ **Figure Ex-55**   ▲ **Figure Ex-56**

57. A pipe of negligible diameter is to be carried horizontally around a corner from a hallway 8 ft wide into a hallway 4 ft wide (Figure Ex-57 on the next page). What is the maximum length that the pipe can have?

  Source: An interesting discussion of this problem in the case where the diameter of the pipe is not neglected is given by Norman Miller in the *American Mathematical Monthly*, Vol. 56, 1949, pp. 177–179.

58. A concrete barrier whose cross section is an isosceles triangle runs parallel to a wall. The height of the barrier is 3 ft, the width of the base of a cross section is 8 ft, and the barrier is positioned on level ground with its base 1 ft from the wall. A straight, stiff metal rod of negligible diameter has one end on the ground, the other end against the wall, and touches the top of the barrier (Figure Ex-58). What is the minimum length the rod can have?

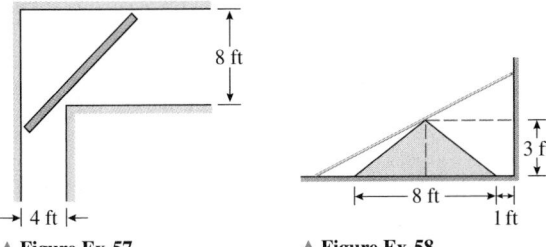

▲ **Figure Ex-57**   ▲ **Figure Ex-58**

59. Suppose that the intensity of a point light source is directly proportional to the strength of the source and inversely proportional to the square of the distance from the source. Two point light sources with strengths of S and $8S$ are separated by a distance of 90 cm. Where on the line segment between the two sources is the total intensity a minimum?

60. Given points $A(2, 1)$ and $B(5, 4)$, find the point P in the interval $[2, 5]$ on the x-axis that maximizes angle APB.

61. The lower edge of a painting, 10 ft in height, is 2 ft above an observer's eye level. Assuming that the best view is obtained when the angle subtended at the observer's eye by the painting is maximum, how far from the wall should the observer stand?

FOCUS ON CONCEPTS

62. *Fermat's principle* (biography on p. 275) in optics states that light traveling from one point to another follows that path for which the total travel time is minimum. In a uniform medium, the paths of "minimum time" and "shortest distance" turn out to be the same, so that light, if unobstructed, travels along a straight line. Assume that we have a light source, a flat mirror, and an observer in a uniform medium. If a light ray leaves the source, bounces off the mirror, and travels on to the observer, then its path will consist of two line segments, as shown in Figure Ex-62. According to Fermat's principle, the path will be such that the total travel time t is minimum or, since the medium is uniform, the path will be such that the total distance traveled from A to P to B is as small as possible. Assuming the minimum occurs when $dt/dx = 0$, show that the light ray will strike the mirror at the point P where the "angle of incidence" θ_1 equals the "angle of reflection" θ_2.

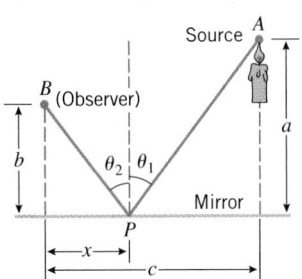

◀ **Figure Ex-62**

63. Fermat's principle (Exercise 62) also explains why light rays traveling between air and water undergo bending (refraction). Imagine that we have two uniform media (such as air and water) and a light ray traveling from a source A in one medium to an observer B in the other medium (Figure Ex-63). It is known that light travels at a constant speed in a uniform medium, but more slowly in a dense medium (such as water) than in a thin medium (such as air). Consequently, the path of shortest time from A to B is not necessarily a straight line, but rather some broken line path A to P to B allowing the light to take greatest advantage of its higher speed through the thin medium. *Snell's law of refraction* (biography on p. 288) states that the path of the light ray will be such that

$$\frac{\sin \theta_1}{v_1} = \frac{\sin \theta_2}{v_2}$$

where v_1 is the speed of light in the first medium, v_2 is the speed of light in the second medium, and θ_1 and θ_2 are the angles shown in Figure Ex-63. Show that this follows from the assumption that the path of minimum time occurs when $dt/dx = 0$.

64. A farmer wants to walk at a constant rate from her barn to a straight river, fill her pail, and carry it to her house in the least time.

(a) Explain how this problem relates to Fermat's principle and the light-reflection problem in Exercise 62.

(b) Use the result of Exercise 62 to describe geometrically the best path for the farmer to take.

(c) Use part (b) to determine where the farmer should fill her pail if her house and barn are located as in Figure Ex-64.

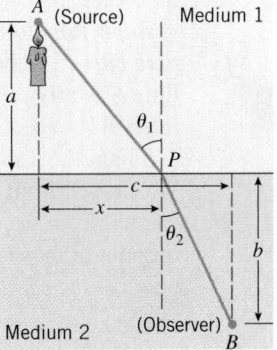

▲ **Figure Ex-63**   ▲ **Figure Ex-64**

65. If an unknown physical quantity x is measured n times, the measurements $x_1, x_2, \ldots, x_n$ often vary because of uncontrollable factors such as temperature, atmospheric pressure, and so forth. Thus, a scientist is often faced with the problem of using n different observed measurements to obtain an estimate $\bar{x}$ of an unknown quantity x. One method for making such an estimate is based on the *least squares principle*, which states that the estimate $\bar{x}$

should be chosen to minimize

$$s = (x_1 - \bar{x})^2 + (x_2 - \bar{x})^2 + \cdots + (x_n - \bar{x})^2$$

which is the sum of the squares of the deviations between the estimate $\bar{x}$ and the measured values. Show that the estimate resulting from the least squares principle is

$$\bar{x} = \frac{1}{n}(x_1 + x_2 + \cdots + x_n)$$

that is, $\bar{x}$ is the arithmetic average of the observed values.

66. Prove: If $f(x) \geq 0$ on an interval and if $f(x)$ has a maximum value on that interval at x_0, then $\sqrt{f(x)}$ also has a maximum value at x_0. Similarly for minimum values. [*Hint:* Use the fact that $\sqrt{x}$ is an increasing function on the interval $[0, +\infty)$.]

67. Writing Discuss the importance of finding intervals of possible values imposed by physical restrictions on variables in an applied maximum or minimum problem.

✔ QUICK CHECK ANSWERS 4.5

1. $x + \dfrac{1}{x}$; $(0, +\infty)$ **2.** $x(10 - x)$; $[0, 10]$ **3.** $x\left(-\frac{4}{3}x + 4\right) = -\frac{4}{3}x^2 + 4x$; $[0, 3]$
4. $x(20 - 2x)(32 - 2x) = 4x^3 - 104x^2 + 640x$; $[0, 10]$

4.6 RECTILINEAR MOTION

In this section we will continue the study of rectilinear motion that we began in Section 2.1. We will define the notion of "acceleration" mathematically, and we will show how the tools of calculus developed earlier in this chapter can be used to analyze rectilinear motion in more depth.

■ REVIEW OF TERMINOLOGY

Recall from Section 2.1 that a particle that can move in either direction along a coordinate line is said to be in ***rectilinear motion***. The line might be an x-axis, a y-axis, or a coordinate line inclined at some angle. In general discussions we will designate the coordinate line as the s-axis. We will assume that units are chosen for measuring distance and time and that we begin observing the motion of the particle at time $t = 0$. As the particle moves along the s-axis, its coordinate s will be some function of time, say $s = s(t)$. We call $s(t)$ the ***position function*** of the particle,[*] and we call the graph of s versus t the ***position versus time curve***. If the coordinate of a particle at time t_1 is $s(t_1)$ and the coordinate at a later time t_2 is $s(t_2)$, then $s(t_2) - s(t_1)$ is called the ***displacement*** of the particle over the time interval $[t_1, t_2]$. The displacement describes the change in position of the particle.

Figure 4.6.1 shows a typical position versus time curve for a particle in rectilinear motion. We can tell from that graph that the coordinate of the particle at time $t = 0$ is s_0, and we can tell from the sign of s when the particle is on the negative or the positive side of the origin as it moves along the coordinate line.

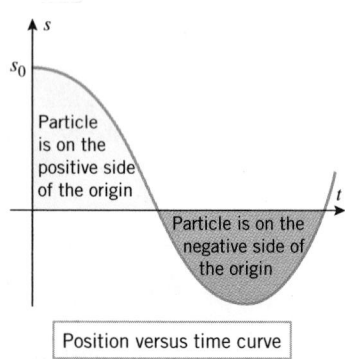

Particle is on the positive side of the origin

Particle is on the negative side of the origin

Position versus time curve

▲ **Figure 4.6.1**

[*]In writing $s = s(t)$, rather than the more familiar $s = f(t)$, we are using the letter s both as the dependent variable and the name of the function. This is common practice in engineering and physics.

Willebrord van Roijen Snell (1591–1626) Dutch mathematician. Snell, who succeeded his father to the post of Professor of Mathematics at the University of Leiden in 1613, is most famous for the result of light refraction that bears his name. Although this phenomenon was studied as far back as the ancient Greek astronomer Ptolemy, until Snell's work the relationship was incorrectly thought to be $\theta_1/v_1 = \theta_2/v_2$. Snell's law was published by Descartes in 1638 without giving proper credit to Snell. Snell also discovered a method for determining distances by triangulation that founded the modern technique of mapmaking.

▶ **Example 1** Figure 4.6.2*a* shows the position versus time curve for a particle moving along an *s*-axis. In words, describe how the position of the particle changes with time.

Solution. The particle is at $s = -3$ at time $t = 0$. It moves in the positive direction until time $t = 4$, since s is increasing. At time $t = 4$ the particle is at position $s = 3$. At that time it turns around and travels in the negative direction until time $t = 7$, since s is decreasing. At time $t = 7$ the particle is at position $s = -1$, and it remains stationary thereafter, since s is constant for $t > 7$. This is illustrated schematically in Figure 4.6.2*b*. ◀

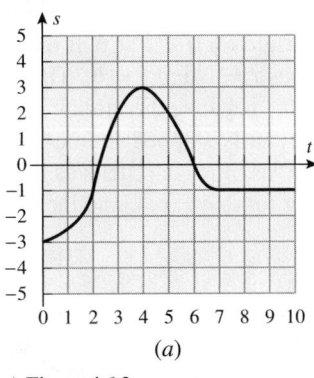

(*a*)

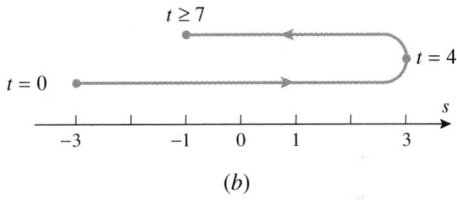

(*b*)

▲ **Figure 4.6.2**

■ VELOCITY AND SPEED

We should more properly call $v(t)$ the ***instantaneous velocity function*** to distinguish instantaneous velocity from average velocity. However, we will follow the standard practice of referring to it as the "velocity function," leaving it understood that it describes instantaneous velocity.

Recall from Formula (5) of Section 2.1 and Formula (4) of Section 2.2 that the instantaneous velocity of a particle in rectilinear motion is the derivative of the position function. Thus, if a particle in rectilinear motion has position function $s(t)$, then we define its ***velocity function*** $v(t)$ to be

$$v(t) = s'(t) = \frac{ds}{dt} \tag{1}$$

The sign of the velocity tells which way the particle is moving—a positive value for $v(t)$ means that s is increasing with time, so the particle is moving in the positive direction, and a negative value for $v(t)$ means that s is decreasing with time, so the particle is moving in the negative direction. If $v(t) = 0$, then the particle has momentarily stopped.

For a particle in rectilinear motion it is important to distinguish between its ***velocity***, which describes how fast and in what direction the particle is moving, and its ***speed***, which describes only how fast the particle is moving. We make this distinction by defining speed to be the absolute value of velocity. Thus a particle with a velocity of 2 m/s has a speed of 2 m/s and is moving in the positive direction, while a particle with a velocity of -2 m/s also has a speed of 2 m/s but is moving in the negative direction.

Since the instantaneous speed of a particle is the absolute value of its instantaneous velocity, we define its ***speed function*** to be

$$|v(t)| = |s'(t)| = \left| \frac{ds}{dt} \right| \tag{2}$$

The speed function, which is always nonnegative, tells us how fast the particle is moving but not its direction of motion.

▶ **Example 2** Let $s(t) = t^3 - 6t^2$ be the position function of a particle moving along an *s*-axis, where s is in meters and t is in seconds. Find the velocity and speed functions, and show the graphs of position, velocity, and speed versus time.

Solution. From (1) and (2), the velocity and speed functions are given by

$$v(t) = \frac{ds}{dt} = 3t^2 - 12t \quad \text{and} \quad |v(t)| = |3t^2 - 12t|$$

The graphs of position, velocity, and speed versus time are shown in Figure 4.6.3. Observe that velocity and speed both have units of meters per second (m/s), since s is in meters (m) and time is in seconds (s). ◄

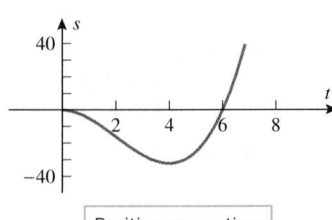

Position versus time

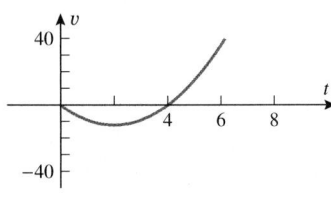

Velocity versus time

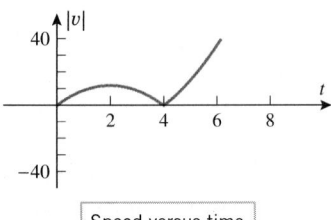

Speed versus time

▲ **Figure 4.6.3**

The graphs in Figure 4.6.3 provide a wealth of visual information about the motion of the particle. For example, the position versus time curve tells us that the particle is on the negative side of the origin for $0 < t < 6$, is on the positive side of the origin for $t > 6$, and is at the origin at times $t = 0$ and $t = 6$. The velocity versus time curve tells us that the particle is moving in the negative direction if $0 < t < 4$, is moving in the positive direction if $t > 4$, and is momentarily stopped at times $t = 0$ and $t = 4$ (the velocity is zero at those times). The speed versus time curve tells us that the speed of the particle is increasing for $0 < t < 2$, decreasing for $2 < t < 4$, and increasing again for $t > 4$.

ACCELERATION

In rectilinear motion, the rate at which the instantaneous velocity of a particle changes with time is called its ***instantaneous acceleration***. Thus, if a particle in rectilinear motion has velocity function $v(t)$, then we define its ***acceleration function*** to be

$$a(t) = v'(t) = \frac{dv}{dt} \tag{3}$$

Alternatively, we can use the fact that $v(t) = s'(t)$ to express the acceleration function in terms of the position function as

$$a(t) = s''(t) = \frac{d^2s}{dt^2} \tag{4}$$

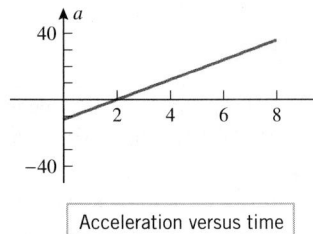

Acceleration versus time

▲ **Figure 4.6.4**

► **Example 3** Let $s(t) = t^3 - 6t^2$ be the position function of a particle moving along an s-axis, where s is in meters and t is in seconds. Find the acceleration function $a(t)$, and show the graph of acceleration versus time.

Solution. From Example 2, the velocity function of the particle is $v(t) = 3t^2 - 12t$, so the acceleration function is

$$a(t) = \frac{dv}{dt} = 6t - 12$$

and the acceleration versus time curve is the line shown in Figure 4.6.4. Note that in this example the acceleration has units of m/s², since v is in meters per second (m/s) and time is in seconds (s). ◄

SPEEDING UP AND SLOWING DOWN

We will say that a particle in rectilinear motion is ***speeding up*** when its speed is increasing and is ***slowing down*** when its speed is decreasing. In everyday language an object that is speeding up is said to be "accelerating" and an object that is slowing down is said to be "decelerating"; thus, one might expect that a particle in rectilinear motion will be speeding up when its acceleration is positive and slowing down when it is negative. Although this is true for a particle moving in the positive direction, it is *not* true for a particle moving in the negative direction—a particle with negative velocity is speeding up when its acceleration is negative and slowing down when its acceleration is positive. This is because a positive acceleration implies an increasing velocity, and increasing a negative velocity decreases its absolute value; similarly, a negative acceleration implies a decreasing velocity, and decreasing a negative velocity increases its absolute value.

The preceding informal discussion can be summarized as follows (Exercise 41):

If $a(t) = 0$ over a certain time interval, what does this tell you about the motion of the particle during that time?

INTERPRETING THE SIGN OF ACCELERATION   *A particle in rectilinear motion is speeding up when its velocity and acceleration have the same sign and slowing down when they have opposite signs.*

▶ **Example 4**   In Examples 2 and 3 we found the velocity versus time curve and the acceleration versus time curve for a particle with position function $s(t) = t^3 - 6t^2$. Use those curves to determine when the particle is speeding up and slowing down, and confirm that your results are consistent with the speed versus time curve obtained in Example 2.

Solution.   Over the time interval $0 < t < 2$ the velocity and acceleration are negative, so the particle is speeding up. This is consistent with the speed versus time curve, since the speed is increasing over this time interval. Over the time interval $2 < t < 4$ the velocity is negative and the acceleration is positive, so the particle is slowing down. This is also consistent with the speed versus time curve, since the speed is decreasing over this time interval. Finally, on the time interval $t > 4$ the velocity and acceleration are positive, so the particle is speeding up, which again is consistent with the speed versus time curve. ◀

■ **ANALYZING THE POSITION VERSUS TIME CURVE**

The position versus time curve contains all of the significant information about the position and velocity of a particle in rectilinear motion:

- If $s(t) > 0$, the particle is on the positive side of the s-axis.
- If $s(t) < 0$, the particle is on the negative side of the s-axis.
- The slope of the curve at any time is equal to the instantaneous velocity at that time.
- Where the curve has positive slope, the velocity is positive and the particle is moving in the positive direction.
- Where the curve has negative slope, the velocity is negative and the particle is moving in the negative direction.
- Where the slope of the curve is zero, the velocity is zero, and the particle is momentarily stopped.

Information about the acceleration of a particle in rectilinear motion can also be deduced from the position versus time curve by examining its concavity. For example, we know that the position versus time curve will be concave up on intervals where $s''(t) > 0$ and will be concave down on intervals where $s''(t) < 0$. But we know from (4) that $s''(t)$ is the acceleration, so that on intervals where the position versus time curve is concave up the particle has a positive acceleration, and on intervals where it is concave down the particle has a negative acceleration.

Table 4.6.1 summarizes our observations about the position versus time curve.

Table 4.6.1
ANALYSIS OF PARTICLE MOTION

POSITION VERSUS TIME CURVE	CHARACTERISTICS OF THE CURVE AT $t = t_0$	BEHAVIOR OF THE PARTICLE AT TIME $t = t_0$
	• $s(t_0) > 0$ • Curve has positive slope. • Curve is concave down.	• Particle is on the positive side of the origin. • Particle is moving in the positive direction. • Velocity is decreasing. • Particle is slowing down.
	• $s(t_0) > 0$ • Curve has negative slope. • Curve is concave down.	• Particle is on the positive side of the origin. • Particle is moving in the negative direction. • Velocity is decreasing. • Particle is speeding up.
	• $s(t_0) < 0$ • Curve has negative slope. • Curve is concave up.	• Particle is on the negative side of the origin. • Particle is moving in the negative direction. • Velocity is increasing. • Particle is slowing down.
	• $s(t_0) > 0$ • Curve has zero slope. • Curve is concave down.	• Particle is on the positive side of the origin. • Particle is momentarily stopped. • Velocity is decreasing.

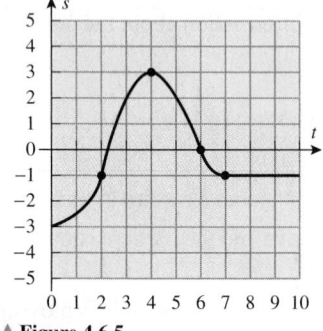

▲ **Figure 4.6.5**

▶ **Example 5** Use the position versus time curve in Figure 4.6.5 to determine when the particle in Example 1 is speeding up and slowing down.

Solution. From $t = 0$ to $t = 2$, the acceleration and velocity are positive, so the particle is speeding up. From $t = 2$ to $t = 4$, the acceleration is negative and the velocity is positive, so the particle is slowing down. At $t = 4$, the velocity is zero, so the particle has momentarily stopped. From $t = 4$ to $t = 6$, the acceleration is negative and the velocity is negative, so the particle is speeding up. From $t = 6$ to $t = 7$, the acceleration is positive and the velocity is negative, so the particle is slowing down. Thereafter, the velocity is zero, so the particle has stopped. ◄

▶ **Example 6** Suppose that the position function of a particle moving on a coordinate line is given by $s(t) = 2t^3 - 21t^2 + 60t + 3$. Analyze the motion of the particle for $t \geq 0$.

Solution. The velocity and acceleration functions are

$$v(t) = s'(t) = 6t^2 - 42t + 60 = 6(t - 2)(t - 5)$$
$$a(t) = v'(t) = 12t - 42 = 12\left(t - \tfrac{7}{2}\right)$$

• *Direction of motion:* The sign analysis of the velocity function in Figure 4.6.6 shows that the particle is moving in the positive direction over the time interval $0 \leq t < 2$, stops momentarily at time $t = 2$, moves in the negative direction over the time interval $2 < t < 5$, stops momentarily at time $t = 5$, and then moves in the positive direction thereafter.

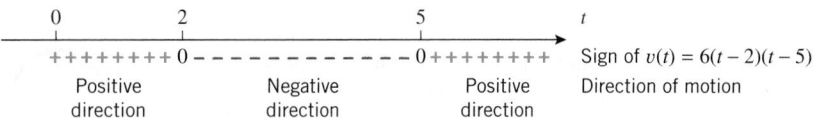

▲ **Figure 4.6.6**

- *Change in speed:* A comparison of the signs of the velocity and acceleration functions is shown in Figure 4.6.7. Since the particle is speeding up when the signs are the same and is slowing down when they are opposite, we see that the particle is slowing down over the time interval $0 \le t < 2$ and stops momentarily at time $t = 2$. It is then speeding up over the time interval $2 < t < \frac{7}{2}$. At time $t = \frac{7}{2}$ the instantaneous acceleration is zero, so the particle is neither speeding up nor slowing down. It is then slowing down over the time interval $\frac{7}{2} < t < 5$ and stops momentarily at time $t = 5$. Thereafter, it is speeding up.

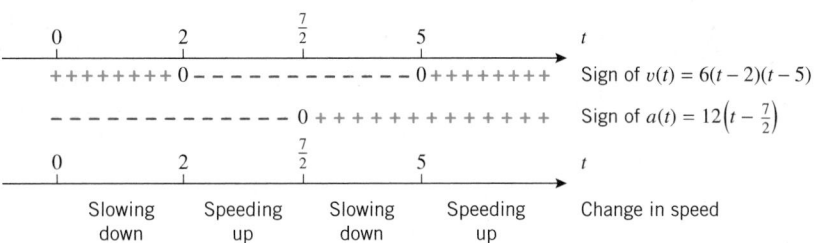

▲ **Figure 4.6.7**

Conclusions: The diagram in Figure 4.6.8 summarizes the above information schematically. The curved line is descriptive only; the actual path is back and forth on the coordinate line. The coordinates of the particle at times $t = 0, t = 2, t = \frac{7}{2}$, and $t = 5$ were computed from $s(t)$. Segments in red indicate that the particle is speeding up and segments in blue indicate that it is slowing down. ◄

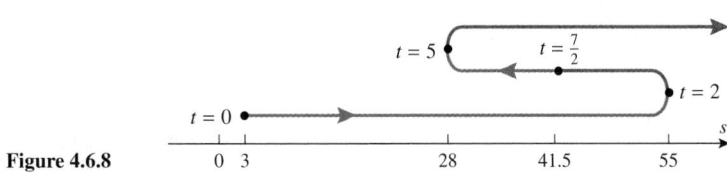

▶ **Figure 4.6.8**

✔ QUICK CHECK EXERCISES 4.6   (See page 296 for answers.)

1. For a particle in rectilinear motion, the velocity and position functions $v(t)$ and $s(t)$ are related by the equation _____, and the acceleration and velocity functions $a(t)$ and $v(t)$ are related by the equation _____.

2. Suppose that a particle moving along the s-axis has position function $s(t) = 7t - 2t^2$. At time $t = 3$, the particle's position is _____, its velocity is _____, its speed is _____, and its acceleration is _____.

3. A particle in rectilinear motion is speeding up if the signs of its velocity and acceleration are _____, and it is slowing down if these signs are _____.

4. Suppose that a particle moving along the s-axis has position function $s(t) = t^4 - 24t^2$ over the time interval $t \ge 0$. The particle slows down over the time interval(s) _____.

EXERCISE SET 4.6   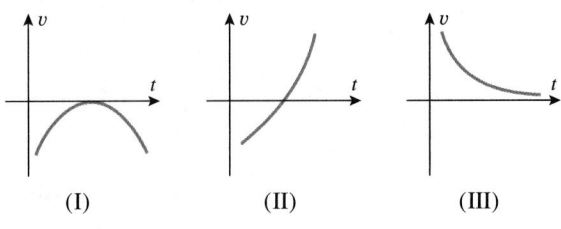 Graphing Utility

FOCUS ON CONCEPTS

1. The graphs of three position functions are shown in the accompanying figure. In each case determine the signs of the velocity and acceleration, and then determine whether the particle is speeding up or slowing down.

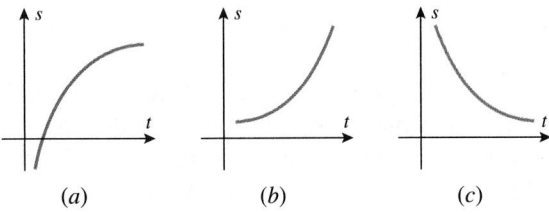

(a)   (b)   (c)

▲ **Figure Ex-1**

2. The graphs of three velocity functions are shown in the accompanying figure. In each case determine the sign of the acceleration, and then determine whether the particle is speeding up or slowing down.

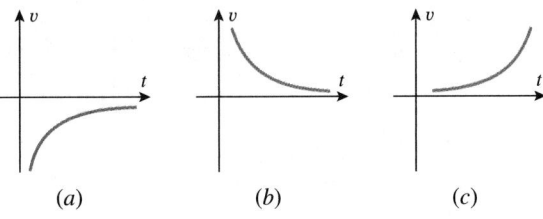

(a)   (b)   (c)

▲ **Figure Ex-2**

3. The graph of the position function of a particle moving on a horizontal line is shown in the accompanying figure.
   (a) Is the particle moving left or right at time t_0?
   (b) Is the acceleration positive or negative at time t_0?
   (c) Is the particle speeding up or slowing down at time t_0?
   (d) Is the particle speeding up or slowing down at time t_1?

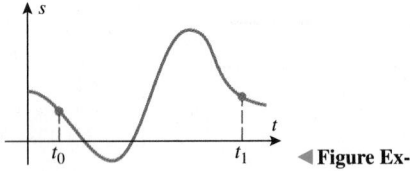

◀ **Figure Ex-3**

4. For the graphs in the accompanying figure, match the position functions (a)–(c) with their corresponding velocity functions (I)–(III).

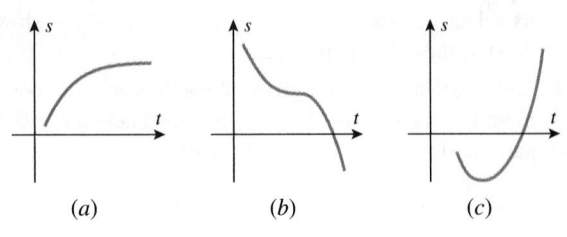

(a)   (b)   (c)

5. Sketch a reasonable graph of s versus t for a mouse that is trapped in a narrow corridor (an s-axis with the positive direction to the right) and scurries back and forth as follows. It runs right with a constant speed of 1.2 m/s for a while, then gradually slows down to 0.6 m/s, then quickly speeds up to 2.0 m/s, then gradually slows to a stop but immediately reverses direction and quickly speeds up to 1.2 m/s.

6. The accompanying figure shows the position versus time curve for an ant that moves along a narrow vertical pipe, where t is measured in seconds and the s-axis is along the pipe with the positive direction up.
   (a) When, if ever, is the ant above the origin?
   (b) When, if ever, does the ant have velocity zero?
   (c) When, if ever, is the ant moving down the pipe?

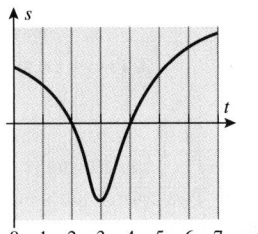

0 1 2 3 4 5 6 7   ◀ **Figure Ex-6**

7. The accompanying figure shows the graph of velocity versus time for a particle moving along a coordinate line. Make a rough sketch of the graphs of speed versus time and acceleration versus time.

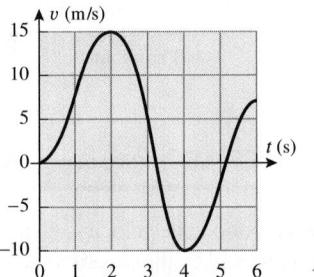

◀ **Figure Ex-7**

8. The accompanying figure (on the next page) shows the position versus time graph for an elevator that ascends 40 m from one stop to the next.
   (a) Estimate the velocity when the elevator is halfway up to the top.   *(cont.)*

(b) Sketch rough graphs of the velocity versus time curve and the acceleration versus time curve.

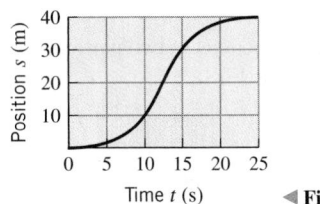

Time t (s) ◀ **Figure Ex-8**

9–12 True–False Determine whether the statement is true or false. Explain your answer. ■

9. A particle is speeding up when its position versus time graph is increasing.

10. Velocity is the derivative of position with respect to time.

11. Acceleration is the absolute value of velocity.

12. If the position versus time curve is increasing and concave down, then the particle is slowing down.

13. The accompanying figure shows the velocity versus time graph for a test run on a Pontiac Grand Prix GTP. Using this graph, estimate
(a) the acceleration at 60 mi/h (in ft/s^2)
(b) the time at which the maximum acceleration occurs.
Source: Data from *Car and Driver Magazine*, July 2003.

14. The accompanying figure shows the velocity versus time graph for a test run on a Chevrolet Malibu. Using this graph, estimate
(a) the acceleration at 60 mi/h (in ft/s^2)
(b) the time at which the maximum acceleration occurs.
Source: Data from *Car and Driver Magazine*, November 2003.

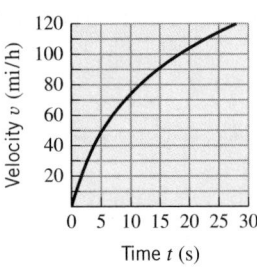

▲ **Figure Ex-13**

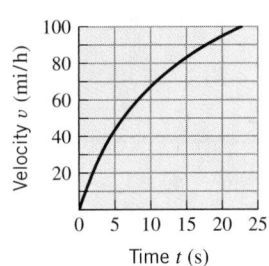

▲ **Figure Ex-14**

15–16 The function $s(t)$ describes the position of a particle moving along a coordinate line, where s is in meters and t is in seconds.
(a) Make a table showing the position, velocity, and acceleration to two decimal places at times $t = 1, 2, 3, 4, 5$.
(b) At each of the times in part (a), determine whether the particle is stopped; if it is not, state its direction of motion.
(c) At each of the times in part (a), determine whether the particle is speeding up, slowing down, or neither. ■

15. $s(t) = \sin \dfrac{\pi t}{4}$ **16.** $s(t) = t^4 e^{-t}, \quad t \geq 0$

17–22 The function $s(t)$ describes the position of a particle moving along a coordinate line, where s is in feet and t is in seconds.
(a) Find the velocity and acceleration functions.
(b) Find the position, velocity, speed, and acceleration at time $t = 1$.
(c) At what times is the particle stopped?
(d) When is the particle speeding up? Slowing down?
(e) Find the total distance traveled by the particle from time $t = 0$ to time $t = 5$. ■

17. $s(t) = t^3 - 3t^2, \quad t \geq 0$

18. $s(t) = t^4 - 4t^2 + 4, \quad t \geq 0$

19. $s(t) = 9 - 9\cos(\pi t/3), \quad 0 \leq t \leq 5$

20. $s(t) = \dfrac{t}{t^2 + 4}, \quad t \geq 0$

21. $s(t) = (t^2 + 8)e^{-t/3}, \quad t \geq 0$

22. $s(t) = \frac{1}{4}t^2 - \ln(t + 1), \quad t \geq 0$

23. Let $s(t) = t/(t^2 + 5)$ be the position function of a particle moving along a coordinate line, where s is in meters and t is in seconds. Use a graphing utility to generate the graphs of $s(t)$, $v(t)$, and $a(t)$ for $t \geq 0$, and use those graphs where needed.
(a) Use the appropriate graph to make a rough estimate of the time at which the particle first reverses the direction of its motion; and then find the time exactly.
(b) Find the exact position of the particle when it first reverses the direction of its motion.
(c) Use the appropriate graphs to make a rough estimate of the time intervals on which the particle is speeding up and on which it is slowing down; and then find those time intervals exactly.

24. Let $s(t) = t/e^t$ be the position function of a particle moving along a coordinate line, where s is in meters and t is in seconds. Use a graphing utility to generate the graphs of $s(t)$, $v(t)$, and $a(t)$ for $t \geq 0$, and use those graphs where needed.
(a) Use the appropriate graph to make a rough estimate of the time at which the particle first reverses the direction of its motion; and then find the time exactly.
(b) Find the exact position of the particle when it first reverses the direction of its motion.
(c) Use the appropriate graphs to make a rough estimate of the time intervals on which the particle is speeding up and on which it is slowing down; and then find those time intervals exactly.

25–32 A position function of a particle moving along a coordinate line is given. Use the method of Example 6 to analyze the motion of the particle for $t \geq 0$, and give a schematic picture of the motion (as in Figure 4.6.8). ■

25. $s = -4t + 3$ **26.** $s = 5t^2 - 20t$

27. $s = t^3 - 9t^2 + 24t$ **28.** $s = t^3 - 6t^2 + 9t + 1$

29. $s = 16te^{-(t^2/8)}$

30. $s = t + \dfrac{25}{t+2}$

31. $s = \begin{cases} \cos t, & 0 \le t < 2\pi \\ 1, & t \ge 2\pi \end{cases}$

32. $s = \begin{cases} 2t(t-2)^2, & 0 \le t < 3 \\ 13 - 7(t-4)^2, & t \ge 3 \end{cases}$

33. Let $s(t) = 5t^2 - 22t$ be the position function of a particle moving along a coordinate line, where s is in feet and t is in seconds.
  (a) Find the maximum speed of the particle during the time interval $1 \le t \le 3$.
  (b) When, during the time interval $1 \le t \le 3$, is the particle farthest from the origin? What is its position at that instant?

34. Let $s = 100/(t^2 + 12)$ be the position function of a particle moving along a coordinate line, where s is in feet and t is in seconds. Find the maximum speed of the particle for $t \ge 0$, and find the direction of motion of the particle when it has its maximum speed.

35–36 A position function of a particle moving along a coordinate line is provided. (a) Evaluate s and v when $a = 0$. (b) Evaluate s and a when $v = 0$. ■

35. $s = \ln(3t^2 - 12t + 13)$ **36.** $s = t^3 - 6t^2 + 1$

37. Let $s = \sqrt{2t^2 + 1}$ be the position function of a particle moving along a coordinate line.
  (a) Use a graphing utility to generate the graph of v versus t, and make a conjecture about the velocity of the particle as $t \to +\infty$.
  (b) Check your conjecture by finding $\lim\limits_{t \to +\infty} v$.

38. (a) Use the chain rule to show that for a particle in rectilinear motion $a = v(dv/ds)$.

(b) Let $s = \sqrt{3t + 7}, t \ge 0$. Find a formula for v in terms of s and use the equation in part (a) to find the acceleration when $s = 5$.

39. Suppose that the position functions of two particles, P_1 and P_2, in motion along the same line are
$$s_1 = \tfrac{1}{2}t^2 - t + 3 \quad \text{and} \quad s_2 = -\tfrac{1}{4}t^2 + t + 1$$
respectively, for $t \ge 0$.
  (a) Prove that P_1 and P_2 do not collide.
  (b) How close do P_1 and P_2 get to each other?
  (c) During what intervals of time are they moving in opposite directions?

40. Let $s_A = 15t^2 + 10t + 20$ and $s_B = 5t^2 + 40t, t \ge 0$, be the position functions of cars A and B that are moving along parallel straight lanes of a highway.
  (a) How far is car A ahead of car B when $t = 0$?
  (b) At what instants of time are the cars next to each other?
  (c) At what instant of time do they have the same velocity? Which car is ahead at this instant?

41. Prove that a particle is speeding up if the velocity and acceleration have the same sign, and slowing down if they have opposite signs. [*Hint:* Let $r(t) = |v(t)|$ and find $r'(t)$ using the chain rule.]

42. Writing A speedometer on a bicycle calculates the bicycle's speed by measuring the time per rotation for one of the bicycle's wheels. Explain how this measurement can be used to calculate an average velocity for the bicycle, and discuss how well it approximates the instantaneous velocity for the bicycle.

43. Writing A toy rocket is launched into the air and falls to the ground after its fuel runs out. Describe the rocket's acceleration and when the rocket is speeding up or slowing down during its flight. Accompany your description with a sketch of a graph of the rocket's acceleration versus time.

✔**QUICK CHECK ANSWERS 4.6**

1. $v(t) = s'(t);\ a(t) = v'(t)$ **2.** 3; -5; 5; -4 **3.** the same; opposite   **4.** $2 < t < 2\sqrt{3}$

4.7 NEWTON'S METHOD

In Section 1.5 we showed how to approximate the roots of an equation $f(x) = 0$ using the Intermediate-Value Theorem. In this section we will study a technique, called "Newton's Method," that is usually more efficient than that method. Newton's Method is the technique used by many commercial and scientific computer programs for finding roots.

■ **NEWTON'S METHOD**

In beginning algebra one learns that the solution of a first-degree equation $ax + b = 0$ is given by the formula $x = -b/a$, and the solutions of a second-degree equation

$$ax^2 + bx + c = 0$$

are given by the quadratic formula. Formulas also exist for the solutions of all third- and fourth-degree equations, although they are too complicated to be of practical use. In 1826 it was shown by the Norwegian mathematician Niels Henrik Abel that it is impossible to construct a similar formula for the solutions of a *general* fifth-degree equation or higher. Thus, for a *specific* fifth-degree polynomial equation such as

$$x^5 - 9x^4 + 2x^3 - 5x^2 + 17x - 8 = 0$$

it may be difficult or impossible to find exact values for all of the solutions. Similar difficulties occur for nonpolynomial equations such as

$$x - \cos x = 0$$

For such equations the solutions are generally approximated in some way, often by the method we will now discuss.

Suppose that we are trying to find a root r of the equation $f(x) = 0$, and suppose that by some method we are able to obtain an initial rough estimate, x_1, of r, say by generating the graph of $y = f(x)$ with a graphing utility and examining the x-intercept. If $f(x_1) = 0$, then $r = x_1$. If $f(x_1) \neq 0$, then we consider an easier problem, that of finding a root to a linear equation. The best linear approximation to $y = f(x)$ near $x = x_1$ is given by the tangent line to the graph of f at x_1, so it might be reasonable to expect that the x-intercept to this tangent line provides an improved approximation to r. Call this intercept x_2 (Figure 4.7.1). We can now treat x_2 in the same way we did x_1. If $f(x_2) = 0$, then $r = x_2$. If $f(x_2) \neq 0$, then construct the tangent line to the graph of f at x_2, and take x_3 to be the x-intercept of this tangent line. Continuing in this way we can generate a succession of values $x_1, x_2, x_3, x_4, \ldots$ that will usually approach r. This procedure for approximating r is called *Newton's Method*.

To implement Newton's Method analytically, we must derive a formula that will tell us how to calculate each improved approximation from the preceding approximation. For this purpose, we note that the point-slope form of the tangent line to $y = f(x)$ at the initial

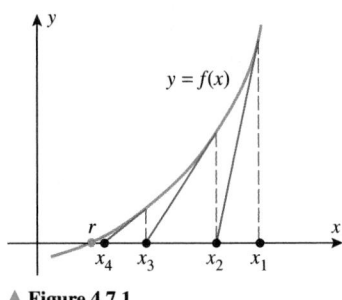

▲ **Figure 4.7.1**

Niels Henrik Abel (1802–1829) Norwegian mathematician. Abel was the son of a poor Lutheran minister and a remarkably beautiful mother from whom he inherited strikingly good looks. In his brief life of 26 years Abel lived in virtual poverty and suffered a succession of adversities, yet he managed to prove major results that altered the mathematical landscape forever. At the age of thirteen he was sent away from home to a school whose better days had long passed. By a stroke of luck the school had just hired a teacher named Bernt Michael Holmboe, who quickly discovered that Abel had extraordinary mathematical ability. Together, they studied the calculus texts of Euler and works of Newton and the later French mathematicians. By the time he graduated, Abel was familar with most of the great mathematical literature. In 1820 his father died, leaving the family in dire financial straits. Abel was able to enter the University of Christiania in Oslo only because he was granted a free room and several professors supported him directly from their salaries. The University had no advanced courses in mathematics, so Abel took a preliminary degree in 1822 and then continued to study mathematics on his own. In 1824 he published at his own expense the proof that it is impossible to solve the general fifth-degree polynomial equation algebraically. With the hope that this landmark paper would lead to his recognition and acceptance by the European mathematical community, Abel sent the paper to the great German mathematician Gauss, who casually declared it to be a "monstrosity" and tossed it aside. However, in 1826 Abel's paper on the fifth-degree equation and other work was published in the first issue of a new journal, founded by his friend, Leopold Crelle. In the summer of 1826 he completed a landmark work on transcendental functions, which he submitted to the French Academy of Sciences. He hoped to establish himself as a major mathematician, for many young mathematicians had gained quick distinction by having their work accepted by the Academy. However, Abel waited in vain because the paper was either ignored or misplaced by one of the referees, and it did not surface again until two years after his death. That paper was later described by one major mathematician as "...the most important mathematical discovery that has been made in our century...." After submitting his paper, Abel returned to Norway, ill with tuberculosis and in heavy debt. While eking out a meager living as a tutor, he continued to produce great work and his fame spread. Soon great efforts were being made to secure a suitable mathematical position for him. Fearing that his great work had been lost by the Academy, he mailed a proof of the main results to Crelle in January of 1829. In April he suffered a violent hemorrhage and died. Two days later Crelle wrote to inform him that an appointment had been secured for him in Berlin and his days of poverty were over! Abel's great paper was finally published by the Academy twelve years after his death.

approximation x_1 is

$$y - f(x_1) = f'(x_1)(x - x_1) \tag{1}$$

If $f'(x_1) \neq 0$, then this line is not parallel to the x-axis and consequently it crosses the x-axis at some point $(x_2, 0)$. Substituting the coordinates of this point in (1) yields

$$-f(x_1) = f'(x_1)(x_2 - x_1)$$

Solving for x_2 we obtain

$$x_2 = x_1 - \frac{f(x_1)}{f'(x_1)} \tag{2}$$

The next approximation can be obtained more easily. If we view x_2 as the starting approximation and x_3 the new approximation, we can simply apply (2) with x_2 in place of x_1 and x_3 in place of x_2. This yields

$$x_3 = x_2 - \frac{f(x_2)}{f'(x_2)} \tag{3}$$

provided $f'(x_2) \neq 0$. In general, if x_n is the nth approximation, then it is evident from the pattern in (2) and (3) that the improved approximation x_{n+1} is given by

> ### Newton's Method
>
> $$x_{n+1} = x_n - \frac{f(x_n)}{f'(x_n)}, \quad n = 1, 2, 3, \ldots$$
> $\tag{4}$

▶ **Example 1** Use Newton's Method to approximate the real solutions of

$$x^3 - x - 1 = 0$$

Solution. Let $f(x) = x^3 - x - 1$, so $f'(x) = 3x^2 - 1$ and (4) becomes

$$x_{n+1} = x_n - \frac{x_n^3 - x_n - 1}{3x_n^2 - 1} \tag{5}$$

From the graph of f in Figure 4.7.2, we see that the given equation has only one real solution. This solution lies between 1 and 2 because $f(1) = -1 < 0$ and $f(2) = 5 > 0$. We will use $x_1 = 1.5$ as our first approximation ($x_1 = 1$ or $x_1 = 2$ would also be reasonable choices).

Letting $n = 1$ in (5) and substituting $x_1 = 1.5$ yields

$$x_2 = 1.5 - \frac{(1.5)^3 - 1.5 - 1}{3(1.5)^2 - 1} \approx 1.34782609 \tag{6}$$

(We used a calculator that displays nine digits.) Next, we let $n = 2$ in (5) and substitute x_2 to obtain

$$x_3 = x_2 - \frac{x_2^3 - x_2 - 1}{3x_2^2 - 1} \approx 1.32520040 \tag{7}$$

If we continue this process until two identical approximations are generated in succession, we obtain

$$x_1 = 1.5$$
$$x_2 \approx 1.34782609$$
$$x_3 \approx 1.32520040$$
$$x_4 \approx 1.32471817$$
$$x_5 \approx 1.32471796$$
$$x_6 \approx 1.32471796$$

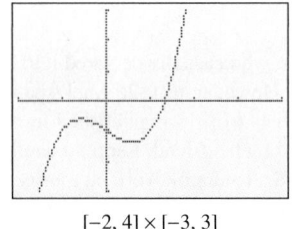

$[-2, 4] \times [-3, 3]$
xScl $= 1$, yScl $= 1$

$y = x^3 - x - 1$

▲ **Figure 4.7.2**

TECHNOLOGY MASTERY

Many calculators and computer programs calculate internally with more digits than they display. Where possible, you should use stored calculated values rather than values displayed from earlier calculations. Thus, in Example 1 the value of x_2 used in (7) should be the stored value, not the value in (6).

At this stage there is no need to continue further because we have reached the display accuracy limit of our calculator, and all subsequent approximations that the calculator generates will likely be the same. Thus, the solution is approximately $x \approx 1.32471796$. ◄

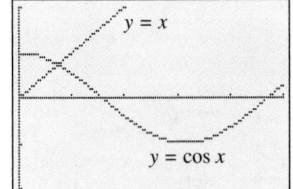

$[0, 5] \times [-2, 2]$
$x\mathrm{Scl} = 1, y\mathrm{Scl} = 1$

▲ **Figure 4.7.3**

► **Example 2**   It is evident from Figure 4.7.3 that if x is in radians, then the equation

$$\cos x = x$$

has a solution between 0 and 1. Use Newton's Method to approximate it.

Solution.   Rewrite the equation as

$$x - \cos x = 0$$

and apply (4) with $f(x) = x - \cos x$. Since $f'(x) = 1 + \sin x$, (4) becomes

$$x_{n+1} = x_n - \frac{x_n - \cos x_n}{1 + \sin x_n} \tag{8}$$

From Figure 4.7.3, the solution seems closer to $x = 1$ than $x = 0$, so we will use $x_1 = 1$ (radian) as our initial approximation. Letting $n = 1$ in (8) and substituting $x_1 = 1$ yields

$$x_2 = 1 - \frac{1 - \cos 1}{1 + \sin 1} \approx 0.750363868$$

Next, letting $n = 2$ in (8) and substituting this value of x_2 yields

$$x_3 = x_2 - \frac{x_2 - \cos x_2}{1 + \sin x_2} \approx 0.739112891$$

If we continue this process until two identical approximations are generated in succession, we obtain

$$x_1 = 1$$
$$x_2 \approx 0.750363868$$
$$x_3 \approx 0.739112891$$
$$x_4 \approx 0.739085133$$
$$x_5 \approx 0.739085133$$

Thus, to the accuracy limit of our calculator, the solution of the equation $\cos x = x$ is $x \approx 0.739085133$. ◄

■ SOME DIFFICULTIES WITH NEWTON'S METHOD

When Newton's Method works, the approximations usually converge toward the solution with dramatic speed. However, there are situations in which the method fails. For example, if $f'(x_n) = 0$ for some n, then (4) involves a division by zero, making it impossible to generate x_{n+1}. However, this is to be expected because the tangent line to $y = f(x)$ is parallel to the x-axis where $f'(x_n) = 0$, and hence this tangent line does not cross the x-axis to generate the next approximation (Figure 4.7.4).

Newton's Method can fail for other reasons as well; sometimes it may overlook the root you are trying to find and converge to a different root, and sometimes it may fail to converge altogether. For example, consider the equation

$$x^{1/3} = 0$$

which has $x = 0$ as its only solution, and try to approximate this solution by Newton's Method with a starting value of $x_0 = 1$. Letting $f(x) = x^{1/3}$, Formula (4) becomes

$$x_{n+1} = x_n - \frac{(x_n)^{1/3}}{\frac{1}{3}(x_n)^{-2/3}} = x_n - 3x_n = -2x_n$$

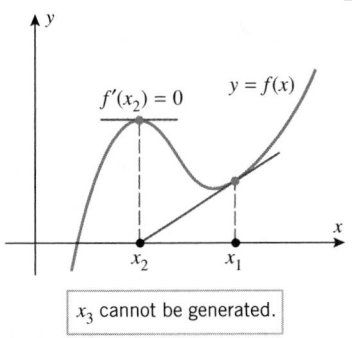

x_3 cannot be generated.

▲ **Figure 4.7.4**

Beginning with $x_1 = 1$, the successive values generated by this formula are

$$x_1 = 1, \quad x_2 = -2, \quad x_3 = 4, \quad x_4 = -8, \ldots$$

which obviously do not converge to $x = 0$. Figure 4.7.5 illustrates what is happening geometrically in this situation.

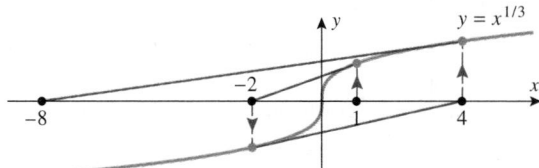

▶ **Figure 4.7.5**

To learn more about the conditions under which Newton's Method converges and for a discussion of error questions, you should consult a book on numerical analysis. For a more in-depth discussion of Newton's Method and its relationship to contemporary studies of chaos and fractals, you may want to read the article, "Newton's Method and Fractal Patterns," by Philip Straffin, which appears in *Applications of Calculus*, MAA Notes, Vol. 3, No. 29, 1993, published by the Mathematical Association of America.

✔**QUICK CHECK EXERCISES 4.7**   *(See page 302 for answers.)*

1. Use the accompanying graph to estimate x_2 and x_3 if Newton's Method is applied to the equation $y = f(x)$ with $x_1 = 8$.

2. Suppose that $f(1) = 2$ and $f'(1) = 4$. If Newton's Method is applied to $y = f(x)$ with $x_1 = 1$, then $x_2 =$ _____.

3. Suppose we are given that $f(0) = 3$ and that $x_2 = 3$ when Newton's Method is applied to $y = f(x)$ with $x_1 = 0$. Then $f'(0) =$ _____.

4. If Newton's Method is applied to $y = e^x - 1$ with $x_1 = \ln 2$, then $x_2 =$ _____.

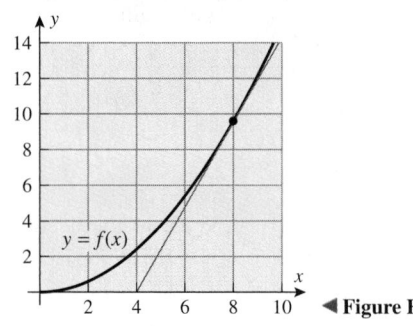

◀ **Figure Ex-1**

EXERCISE SET 4.7   ～ Graphing Utility

In this exercise set, express your answers with as many decimal digits as your calculating utility can display, but use the procedure in the Technology Mastery on p. 298. ■

1. Approximate $\sqrt{2}$ by applying Newton's Method to the equation $x^2 - 2 = 0$.

2. Approximate $\sqrt{5}$ by applying Newton's Method to the equation $x^2 - 5 = 0$.

3. Approximate $\sqrt[3]{6}$ by applying Newton's Method to the equation $x^3 - 6 = 0$.

4. To what equation would you apply Newton's Method to approximate the nth root of a?

5–8 The given equation has one real solution. Approximate it by Newton's Method. ■

5. $x^3 - 2x - 2 = 0$ 6. $x^3 + x - 1 = 0$

7. $x^5 + x^4 - 5 = 0$ 8. $x^5 - 3x + 3 = 0$

～ **9–14** Use a graphing utility to determine how many solutions the equation has, and then use Newton's Method to approximate the solution that satisfies the stated condition. ■

9. $x^4 + x^2 - 4 = 0; \ x < 0$

10. $x^5 - 5x^3 - 2 = 0; \ x > 0$

11. $2\cos x = x; \ x > 0$ 12. $\sin x = x^2; \ x > 0$

13. $x - \tan x = 0$; $\pi/2 < x < 3\pi/2$

14. $1 + e^x \sin x = 0$; $\pi/2 < x < 3\pi/2$

15–20 Use a graphing utility to determine the number of times the curves intersect; and then apply Newton's Method, where needed, to approximate the x-coordinates of all intersections. ■

15. $y = x^3$ and $y = 1 - x$

16. $y = \sin x$ and $y = x^3 - 2x^2 + 1$

17. $y = x^2$ and $y = \sqrt{2x + 1}$

18. $y = \frac{1}{8}x^3 - 1$ and $y = \cos x - 2$

19. $y = 1$ and $y = e^x \sin x$; $0 < x < \pi$

20. $y = e^{-x}$ and $y = \ln x$

21–24 True–False Determine whether the statement is true or false. Explain your answer. ■

21. Newton's Method uses the tangent line to $y = f(x)$ at $x = x_n$ to compute x_{n+1}.

22. Newton's Method is a process to find exact solutions to $f(x) = 0$.

23. If $f(x) = 0$ has a root, then Newton's Method starting at $x = x_1$ will approximate the root nearest x_1.

24. Newton's Method can be used to appoximate a point of intersection of two curves.

25. The *mechanic's rule* for approximating square roots states that $\sqrt{a} \approx x_{n+1}$, where

$$x_{n+1} = \frac{1}{2}\left(x_n + \frac{a}{x_n}\right), \quad n = 1, 2, 3, \ldots$$

and x_1 is any positive approximation to $\sqrt{a}$.
(a) Apply Newton's Method to

$$f(x) = x^2 - a$$

to derive the mechanic's rule.
(b) Use the mechanic's rule to approximate $\sqrt{10}$.

26. Many calculators compute reciprocals using the approximation $1/a \approx x_{n+1}$, where

$$x_{n+1} = x_n(2 - ax_n), \quad n = 1, 2, 3, \ldots$$

and x_1 is an initial approximation to $1/a$. This formula makes it possible to perform divisions using multiplications and subtractions, which is a faster procedure than dividing directly.
(a) Apply Newton's Method to

$$f(x) = \frac{1}{x} - a$$

to derive this approximation.
(b) Use the formula to approximate $\frac{1}{17}$.

27. Use Newton's Method to approximate the absolute minimum of $f(x) = \frac{1}{4}x^4 + x^2 - 5x$.

28. Use Newton's Method to approximate the absolute maximum of $f(x) = x \sin x$ on the interval $[0, \pi]$.

29. For the function

$$f(x) = \frac{e^{-x}}{1 + x^2}$$

use Newton's Method to approximate the x-coordinates of the inflection points to two decimal places.

30. Use Newton's Method to approximate the absolute maximum of $f(x) = (1 - 2x) \tan^{-1} x$.

31. Use Newton's Method to approximate the coordinates of the point on the parabola $y = x^2$ that is closest to the point $(1, 0)$.

32. Use Newton's Method to approximate the dimensions of the rectangle of largest area that can be inscribed under the curve $y = \cos x$ for $0 \le x \le \pi/2$ (Figure Ex-32).

33. (a) Show that on a circle of radius r, the central angle θ that subtends an arc whose length is 1.5 times the length L of its chord satisfies the equation $\theta = 3 \sin(\theta/2)$ (Figure Ex-33).
(b) Use Newton's Method to approximate θ.

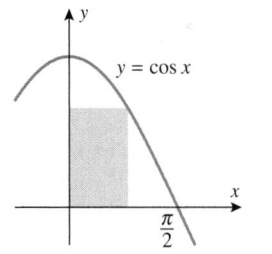

▲ **Figure Ex-32**   ▲ **Figure Ex-33**

34. A *segment* of a circle is the region enclosed by an arc and its chord (Figure Ex-34). If r is the radius of the circle and θ the angle subtended at the center of the circle, then it can be shown that the area A of the segment is $A = \frac{1}{2}r^2(\theta - \sin \theta)$, where θ is in radians. Find the value of θ for which the area of the segment is one-fourth the area of the circle. Give θ to the nearest degree.

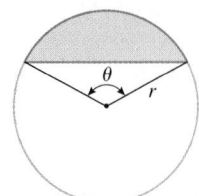

◀ **Figure Ex-34**

35–36 Use Newton's Method to approximate all real values of y satisfying the given equation for the indicated value of x. ■

35. $xy^4 + x^3y = 1$; $x = 1$ **36.** $xy - \cos\left(\frac{1}{2}xy\right) = 0$; $x = 2$

37. An *annuity* is a sequence of equal payments that are paid or received at regular time intervals. For example, you may want to deposit equal amounts at the end of each year into an interest-bearing account for the purpose of accumulating a lump sum at some future time. If, at the end of each year, interest of $i \times 100\%$ on the account balance for that year is added to the account, then the account is said to pay $i \times 100\%$ interest, *compounded annually*. It can be shown that if payments of Q dollars are deposited at the end of each year into an account that pays $i \times 100\%$ compounded annually, then at the time when the nth payment and the accrued interest for the past year are deposited, the amount $S(n)$ in the account is given by the formula

$$S(n) = \frac{Q}{i}[(1+i)^n - 1]$$

Suppose that you can invest \$5000 in an interest-bearing account at the end of each year, and your objective is to have \$250,000 on the 25th payment. Approximately what annual compound interest rate must the account pay for you to achieve your goal? [*Hint:* Show that the interest rate i satisfies the equation $50i = (1+i)^{25} - 1$, and solve it using Newton's Method.]

FOCUS ON CONCEPTS

38. (a) Use a graphing utility to generate the graph of

$$f(x) = \frac{x}{x^2 + 1}$$

  and use it to explain what happens if you apply Newton's Method with a starting value of $x_1 = 2$. Check your conclusion by computing $x_2, x_3, x_4,$ and x_5.

  (b) Use the graph generated in part (a) to explain what happens if you apply Newton's Method with a start-

ing value of $x_1 = 0.5$. Check your conclusion by computing $x_2, x_3, x_4,$ and x_5.

39. (a) Apply Newton's Method to $f(x) = x^2 + 1$ with a starting value of $x_1 = 0.5$, and determine if the values of $x_2, \ldots, x_{10}$ appear to converge.

  (b) Explain what is happening.

40. In each part, explain what happens if you apply Newton's Method to a function f when the given condition is satisfied for some value of n.

  (a) $f(x_n) = 0$ (b) $x_{n+1} = x_n$

  (c) $x_{n+2} = x_n \neq x_{n+1}$

41. **Writing** Compare Newton's Method and the Intermediate-Value Theorem (1.5.7; see Example 5 in Section 1.5) as methods to locate solutions to $f(x) = 0$.

42. **Writing** Newton's Method uses a local linear approximation to $y = f(x)$ at $x = x_n$ to find an "improved" approximation x_{n+1} to a zero of f. Your friend proposes a process that uses a local quadratic approximation to $y = f(x)$ at $x = x_n$ (that is, matching values for the function and its first two derivatives) to obtain x_{n+1}. Discuss the pros and cons of this proposal. Support your statements with some examples.

✔ **QUICK CHECK ANSWERS 4.7**

1. $x_2 \approx 4, x_3 \approx 2$ **2.** $\frac{1}{2}$ **3.** -1 **4.** $\ln 2 - \frac{1}{2} \approx 0.193147$

4.8 ROLLE'S THEOREM; MEAN-VALUE THEOREM

In this section we will discuss a result called the Mean-Value Theorem. This theorem has so many important consequences that it is regarded as one of the major principles in calculus.

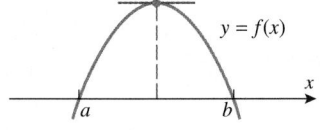

▲ **Figure 4.8.1**

■ **ROLLE'S THEOREM**

We will begin with a special case of the Mean-Value Theorem, called Rolle's Theorem, in honor of the mathematician Michel Rolle. This theorem states the geometrically obvious fact that if the graph of a differentiable function intersects the x-axis at two places, a and b, then somewhere between a and b there must be at least one place where the tangent line is horizontal (Figure 4.8.1). The precise statement of the theorem is as follows.

4.8.1   THEOREM (*Rolle's Theorem*)   *Let f be continuous on the closed interval $[a, b]$ and differentiable on the open interval (a, b). If*

$$f(a) = 0 \quad and \quad f(b) = 0$$

then there is at least one point c in the interval (a, b) such that $f'(c) = 0$.

PROOF   We will divide the proof into three cases: the case where $f(x) = 0$ for all x in (a, b), the case where $f(x) > 0$ at some point in (a, b), and the case where $f(x) < 0$ at some point in (a, b).

CASE 1   If $f(x) = 0$ for all x in (a, b), then $f'(c) = 0$ at every point c in (a, b) because f is a constant function on that interval.

CASE 2   Assume that $f(x) > 0$ at some point in (a, b). Since f is continuous on $[a, b]$, it follows from the Extreme-Value Theorem (4.4.2) that f has an absolute maximum on $[a, b]$. The absolute maximum value cannot occur at an endpoint of $[a, b]$ because we have assumed that $f(a) = f(b) = 0$, and that $f(x) > 0$ at some point in (a, b). Thus, the absolute maximum must occur at some point c in (a, b). It follows from Theorem 4.4.3 that c is a critical point of f, and since f is differentiable on (a, b), this critical point must be a stationary point; that is, $f'(c) = 0$.

CASE 3   Assume that $f(x) < 0$ at some point in (a, b). The proof of this case is similar to Case 2 and will be omitted. ■

▶ **Example 1**   Find the two x-intercepts of the function $f(x) = x^2 - 5x + 4$ and confirm that $f'(c) = 0$ at some point c between those intercepts.

Solution.   The function f can be factored as

$$x^2 - 5x + 4 = (x - 1)(x - 4)$$

so the x-intercepts are $x = 1$ and $x = 4$. Since the polynomial f is continuous and differentiable everywhere, the hypotheses of Rolle's Theorem are satisfied on the interval $[1, 4]$. Thus, we are guaranteed the existence of at least one point c in the interval $(1, 4)$ such that $f'(c) = 0$. Differentiating f yields

$$f'(x) = 2x - 5$$

Solving the equation $f'(x) = 0$ yields $x = \frac{5}{2}$, so $c = \frac{5}{2}$ is a point in the interval $(1, 4)$ at which $f'(c) = 0$ (Figure 4.8.2). ◀

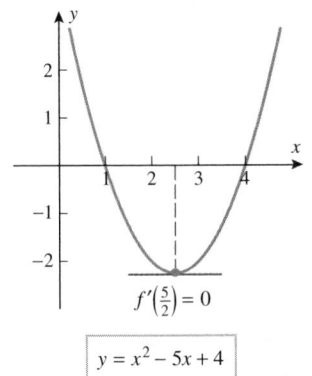

▲ **Figure 4.8.2**

▶ **Example 2**   The differentiability requirement in Rolle's Theorem is critical. If f fails to be differentiable at even one place in the interval (a, b), then the conclusion of the

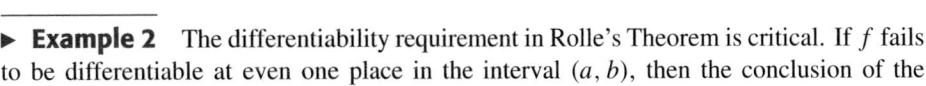

Michel Rolle (1652–1719) French mathematician. Rolle, the son of a shopkeeper, received only an elementary education. He married early and as a young man struggled hard to support his family on the meager wages of a transcriber for notaries and attorneys. In spite of his financial problems and minimal education, Rolle studied algebra and Diophantine analysis (a branch of number theory) on his own. Rolle's fortune changed dramatically in 1682 when he published an elegant solution of a difficult, unsolved problem in Diophantine analysis. The public recognition of his achievement led to a patronage under minister Louvois, a job as an elementary mathematics teacher, and eventually to a short-term administrative post in the Ministry of War. In 1685 he joined the Académie des Sciences in a low-level position for which he received no regular salary until 1699. He stayed at the Académie until he died of apoplexy in 1719.

While Rolle's forte was always Diophantine analysis, his most important work was a book on the algebra of equations, called *Traité d'algèbre*, published in 1690. In that book Rolle firmly established the notation $\sqrt[n]{a}$ [earlier written as $\sqrt{(n)\ a}$] for the nth root of a, and proved a polynomial version of the theorem that today bears his name. (Rolle's Theorem was named by Giusto Bellavitis in 1846.) Ironically, Rolle was one of the most vocal early antagonists of calculus. He strove intently to demonstrate that it gave erroneous results and was based on unsound reasoning. He quarreled so vigorously on the subject that the Académie des Sciences was forced to intervene on several occasions. Among his several achievements, Rolle helped advance the currently accepted size order for negative numbers. Descartes, for example, viewed -2 as smaller than -5. Rolle preceded most of his contemporaries by adopting the current convention in 1691.

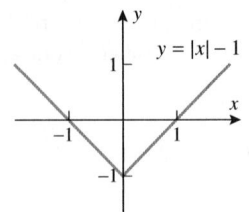

▲ Figure 4.8.3

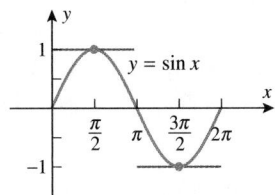

▲ Figure 4.8.4

In Examples 1 and 3 we were able to find exact values of c because the equation $f'(x) = 0$ was easy to solve. However, in the applications of Rolle's Theorem it is usually the *existence of* c that is important and not its actual value.

theorem may not hold. For example, the function $f(x) = |x| - 1$ graphed in Figure 4.8.3 has roots at $x = -1$ and $x = 1$, yet there is no horizontal tangent to the graph of f over the interval $(-1, 1)$. ◄

► **Example 3**   If f satisfies the conditions of Rolle's Theorem on $[a, b]$, then the theorem guarantees the existence of *at least* one point c in (a, b) at which $f'(c) = 0$. There may, however, be more than one such c. For example, the function $f(x) = \sin x$ is continuous and differentiable everywhere, so the hypotheses of Rolle's Theorem are satisfied on the interval $[0, 2\pi]$ whose endpoints are roots of f. As indicated in Figure 4.8.4, there are two points in the interval $[0, 2\pi]$ at which the graph of f has a horizontal tangent, $c_1 = \pi/2$ and $c_2 = 3\pi/2$. ◄

■ **THE MEAN-VALUE THEOREM**

Rolle's Theorem is a special case of a more general result, called the **Mean-Value Theorem**. Geometrically, this theorem states that between any two points $A(a, f(a))$ and $B(b, f(b))$ on the graph of a differentiable function f, there is at least one place where the tangent line to the graph is parallel to the secant line joining A and B (Figure 4.8.5).

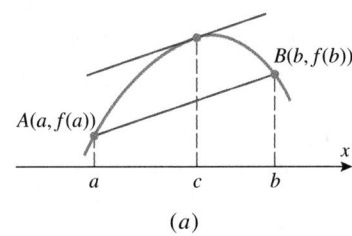

       (*a*)   (*b*)

▲ Figure 4.8.5

Note that the slope of the secant line joining $A(a, f(a))$ and $B(b, f(b))$ is

$$\frac{f(b) - f(a)}{b - a}$$

and that the slope of the tangent line at c in Figure 4.8.5a is $f'(c)$. Similarly, in Figure 4.8.5b the slopes of the tangent lines at c_1 and c_2 are $f'(c_1)$ and $f'(c_2)$, respectively. Since nonvertical parallel lines have the same slope, the Mean-Value Theorem can be stated precisely as follows.

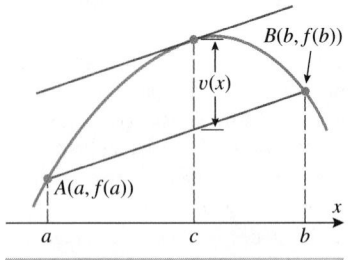

The tangent line is parallel to the secant line where the vertical distance $v(x)$ between the secant line and the graph of f is maximum.

▲ Figure 4.8.6

4.8.2   THEOREM (*Mean-Value Theorem*)   *Let f be continuous on the closed interval* $[a, b]$ *and differentiable on the open interval* (a, b). *Then there is at least one point c in* (a, b) *such that*

$$f'(c) = \frac{f(b) - f(a)}{b - a} \tag{1}$$

MOTIVATION FOR THE PROOF OF THEOREM 4.8.2   Figure 4.8.6 suggests that (1) will hold (i.e., the tangent line will be parallel to the secant line) at a point c where the vertical distance between the curve and the secant line is maximum. Thus, to prove the Mean-Value Theorem it is natural to begin by looking for a formula for the vertical distance $v(x)$ between the curve $y = f(x)$ and the secant line joining $(a, f(a))$ and $(b, f(b))$.

PROOF OF THEOREM 4.8.2   Since the two-point form of the equation of the secant line joining $(a, f(a))$ and $(b, f(b))$ is

$$y - f(a) = \frac{f(b) - f(a)}{b - a}(x - a)$$

or, equivalently,

$$y = \frac{f(b) - f(a)}{b - a}(x - a) + f(a)$$

the difference $v(x)$ between the height of the graph of f and the height of the secant line is

$$v(x) = f(x) - \left[\frac{f(b) - f(a)}{b - a}(x - a) + f(a)\right] \tag{2}$$

Since $f(x)$ is continuous on $[a, b]$ and differentiable on (a, b), so is $v(x)$. Moreover,

$$v(a) = 0 \quad \text{and} \quad v(b) = 0$$

so that $v(x)$ satisfies the hypotheses of Rolle's Theorem on the interval $[a, b]$. Thus, there is a point c in (a, b) such that $v'(c) = 0$. But from Equation (2)

$$v'(x) = f'(x) - \frac{f(b) - f(a)}{b - a}$$

so

$$v'(c) = f'(c) - \frac{f(b) - f(a)}{b - a}$$

Since $v'(c) = 0$, we have

$$f'(c) = \frac{f(b) - f(a)}{b - a} \quad \blacksquare$$

▶ **Example 4**   Show that the function $f(x) = \frac{1}{4}x^3 + 1$ satisfies the hypotheses of the Mean-Value Theorem over the interval $[0, 2]$, and find all values of c in the interval $(0, 2)$ at which the tangent line to the graph of f is parallel to the secant line joining the points $(0, f(0))$ and $(2, f(2))$.

Solution.   The function f is continuous and differentiable everywhere because it is a polynomial. In particular, f is continuous on $[0, 2]$ and differentiable on $(0, 2)$, so the hypotheses of the Mean-Value Theorem are satisfied with $a = 0$ and $b = 2$. But

$$f(a) = f(0) = 1, \quad f(b) = f(2) = 3$$

$$f'(x) = \frac{3x^2}{4}, \quad f'(c) = \frac{3c^2}{4}$$

so in this case Equation (1) becomes

$$\frac{3c^2}{4} = \frac{3 - 1}{2 - 0} \quad \text{or} \quad 3c^2 = 4$$

which has the two solutions $c = \pm 2/\sqrt{3} \approx \pm 1.15$. However, only the positive solution lies in the interval $(0, 2)$; this value of c is consistent with Figure 4.8.7. ◀

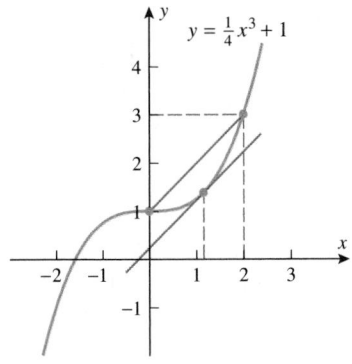

▲ **Figure 4.8.7**

▇ VELOCITY INTERPRETATION OF THE MEAN-VALUE THEOREM

There is a nice interpretation of the Mean-Value Theorem in the situation where $x = f(t)$ is the position versus time curve for a car moving along a straight road. In this case, the right side of (1) is the average velocity of the car over the time interval from $a \leq t \leq b$, and the left side is the instantaneous velocity at time $t = c$. Thus, the Mean-Value Theorem implies that at least once during the time interval the instantaneous velocity must equal the average velocity. This agrees with our real-world experience—if the average velocity for a trip is 40 mi/h, then sometime during the trip the speedometer has to read 40 mi/h.

▶ **Example 5**   You are driving on a straight highway on which the speed limit is 55 mi/h. At 8:05 A.M. a police car clocks your velocity at 50 mi/h and at 8:10 A.M. a second police car posted 5 mi down the road clocks your velocity at 55 mi/h. Explain why the police have a right to charge you with a speeding violation.

Solution.   You traveled 5 mi in 5 min $\left(= \frac{1}{12} \text{ h}\right)$, so your average velocity was 60 mi/h. Therefore, the Mean-Value Theorem guarantees the police that your instantaneous velocity was 60 mi/h at least once over the 5 mi section of highway. ◀

■ CONSEQUENCES OF THE MEAN-VALUE THEOREM

We stated at the beginning of this section that the Mean-Value Theorem is the starting point for many important results in calculus. As an example of this, we will use it to prove Theorem 4.1.2, which was one of our fundamental tools for analyzing graphs of functions.

4.1.2   THEOREM (*Revisited*)   *Let f be a function that is continuous on a closed interval $[a, b]$ and differentiable on the open interval (a, b).*

(a)   *If $f'(x) > 0$ for every value of x in (a, b), then f is increasing on $[a, b]$.*

(b)   *If $f'(x) < 0$ for every value of x in (a, b), then f is decreasing on $[a, b]$.*

(c)   *If $f'(x) = 0$ for every value of x in (a, b), then f is constant on $[a, b]$.*

PROOF (a)   Suppose that x_1 and x_2 are points in $[a, b]$ such that $x_1 < x_2$. We must show that $f(x_1) < f(x_2)$. Because the hypotheses of the Mean-Value Theorem are satisfied on the entire interval $[a, b]$, they are satisfied on the subinterval $[x_1, x_2]$. Thus, there is some point c in the open interval (x_1, x_2) such that

$$f'(c) = \frac{f(x_2) - f(x_1)}{x_2 - x_1}$$

or, equivalently,

$$f(x_2) - f(x_1) = f'(c)(x_2 - x_1) \tag{3}$$

Since c is in the open interval (x_1, x_2), it follows that $a < c < b$; thus, $f'(c) > 0$. However, $x_2 - x_1 > 0$ since we assumed that $x_1 < x_2$. It follows from (3) that $f(x_2) - f(x_1) > 0$ or, equivalently, $f(x_1) < f(x_2)$, which is what we were to prove. The proofs of parts (b) and (c) are similar and are left as exercises. ■

■ THE CONSTANT DIFFERENCE THEOREM

We know from our earliest study of derivatives that the derivative of a constant is zero. Part (c) of Theorem 4.1.2 is the converse of that result; that is, a function whose derivative is zero on an interval must be constant on that interval. If we apply this to the difference of two functions, we obtain the following useful theorem.

4.8.3   THEOREM (*Constant Difference Theorem*)   *If f and g are differentiable on an interval, and if $f'(x) = g'(x)$ for all x in that interval, then $f - g$ is constant on the interval; that is, there is a constant k such that $f(x) - g(x) = k$ or, equivalently,*

$$f(x) = g(x) + k$$

for all x in the interval.

PROOF Let x_1 and x_2 be any points in the interval such that $x_1 < x_2$. Since the functions f and g are differentiable on the interval, they are continuous on the interval. Since $[x_1, x_2]$ is a subinterval, it follows that f and g are continuous on $[x_1, x_2]$ and differentiable on (x_1, x_2). Moreover, it follows from the basic properties of derivatives and continuity that the same is true of the function

$$F(x) = f(x) - g(x)$$

Since

$$F'(x) = f'(x) - g'(x) = 0$$

it follows from part (c) of Theorem 4.1.2 that $F(x) = f(x) - g(x)$ is constant on the interval $[x_1, x_2]$. This means that $f(x) - g(x)$ has the same value at any two points x_1 and x_2 in the interval, and this implies that $f - g$ is constant on the interval. ∎

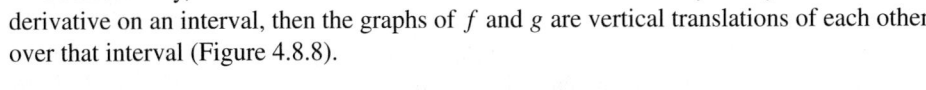

Geometrically, the Constant Difference Theorem tells us that if f and g have the same derivative on an interval, then the graphs of f and g are vertical translations of each other over that interval (Figure 4.8.8).

If $f'(x) = g'(x)$ on an interval, then the graphs of f and g are vertical translations of each other.

▲ **Figure 4.8.8**

▶ **Example 6** Part (c) of Theorem 4.1.2 is sometimes useful for establishing identities. For example, although we do not need calculus to prove the identity

$$\sin^{-1} x + \cos^{-1} x = \frac{\pi}{2} \qquad (-1 \le x \le 1) \tag{4}$$

it can be done by letting $f(x) = \sin^{-1} x + \cos^{-1} x$. It follows from Formulas (9) and (10) of Section 3.3 that

$$f'(x) = \frac{d}{dx}[\sin^{-1} x] + \frac{d}{dx}[\cos^{-1} x] = \frac{1}{\sqrt{1 - x^2}} - \frac{1}{\sqrt{1 - x^2}} = 0$$

so $f(x) = \sin^{-1} x + \cos^{-1} x$ is constant on the interval $[-1, 1]$. We can find this constant by evaluating f at any convenient point in this interval. For example, using $x = 0$ we obtain

$$f(0) = \sin^{-1} 0 + \cos^{-1} 0 = 0 + \frac{\pi}{2} = \frac{\pi}{2}$$

which proves (4). ◀

✔ **QUICK CHECK EXERCISES 4.8**   (See page 310 for answers.)

1. Let $f(x) = x^2 - x$.
   (a) An interval on which f satisfies the hypotheses of Rolle's Theorem is _____.
   (b) Find all values of c that satisfy the conclusion of Rolle's Theorem for the function f on the interval in part (a).

2. Use the accompanying graph of f to find an interval $[a, b]$ on which Rolle's Theorem applies, and find all values of c in that interval that satisfy the conclusion of the theorem.

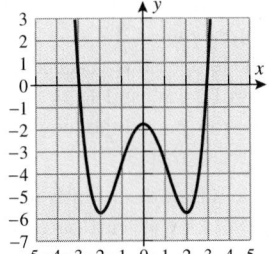

◀ **Figure Ex-2**

3. Let $f(x) = x^2 - x$.
   (a) Find a point b such that the slope of the secant line through $(0, 0)$ and $(b, f(b))$ is 1.
   (b) Find all values of c that satisfy the conclusion of the Mean-Value Theorem for the function f on the interval $[0, b]$, where b is the point found in part (a).

4. Use the graph of f in the accompanying figure to estimate all values of c that satisfy the conclusion of the Mean-Value Theorem on the interval
   (a) $[0, 8]$ (b) $[0, 4]$.

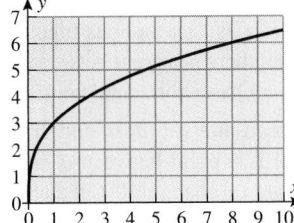

◀ **Figure Ex-4**

5. Find a function f such that the graph of f contains the point $(1, 5)$ and such that for every value of x_0 the tangent line to the graph of f at x_0 is parallel to the tangent line to the graph of $y = x^2$ at x_0.

EXERCISE SET 4.8   ∿ Graphing Utility

1–4 Verify that the hypotheses of Rolle's Theorem are satisfied on the given interval, and find all values of c in that interval that satisfy the conclusion of the theorem. ■

1. $f(x) = x^2 - 8x + 15$; $[3, 5]$
2. $f(x) = x^3 - 3x^2 + 2x$; $[0, 2]$
3. $f(x) = \cos x$; $[\pi/2, 3\pi/2]$
4. $f(x) = \ln(4 + 2x - x^2)$; $[-1, 3]$

5–8 Verify that the hypotheses of the Mean-Value Theorem are satisfied on the given interval, and find all values of c in that interval that satisfy the conclusion of the theorem. ■

5. $f(x) = x^2 - x$; $[-3, 5]$
6. $f(x) = x^3 + x - 4$; $[-1, 2]$
7. $f(x) = \sqrt{x + 1}$; $[0, 3]$
8. $f(x) = x - \dfrac{1}{x}$; $[3, 4]$

∿ 9. (a) Find an interval $[a, b]$ on which
$$f(x) = x^4 + x^3 - x^2 + x - 2$$
satisfies the hypotheses of Rolle's Theorem.
 (b) Generate the graph of $f'(x)$, and use it to make rough estimates of all values of c in the interval obtained in part (a) that satisfy the conclusion of Rolle's Theorem.
 (c) Use Newton's Method to improve on the rough estimates obtained in part (b).

∿ 10. Let $f(x) = x^3 - 4x$.
 (a) Find the equation of the secant line through the points $(-2, f(-2))$ and $(1, f(1))$.
 (b) Show that there is only one point c in the interval $(-2, 1)$ that satisfies the conclusion of the Mean-Value Theorem for the secant line in part (a).
 (c) Find the equation of the tangent line to the graph of f at the point $(c, f(c))$.
 (d) Use a graphing utility to generate the secant line in part (a) and the tangent line in part (c) in the same coordinate system, and confirm visually that the two lines seem parallel.

11–14 True–False Determine whether the statement is true or false. Explain your answer. ■

11. Rolle's Theorem says that if f is a continuous function on $[a, b]$ and $f(a) = f(b)$, then there is a point between a and b at which the curve $y = f(x)$ has a horizontal tangent line.

12. If f is continuous on a closed interval $[a, b]$ and differentiable on (a, b), then there is a point between a and b at which the instantaneous rate of change of f matches the average rate of change of f over $[a, b]$.

13. The Constant Difference Theorem says that if two functions have derivatives that differ by a constant on an interval, then the functions are equal on the interval.

14. One application of the Mean-Value Theorem is to prove that a function with positive derivative on an interval must be increasing on that interval.

FOCUS ON CONCEPTS

15. Let $f(x) = \tan x$.
 (a) Show that there is no point c in the interval $(0, \pi)$ such that $f'(c) = 0$, even though $f(0) = f(\pi) = 0$.
 (b) Explain why the result in part (a) does not contradict Rolle's Theorem.

16. Let $f(x) = x^{2/3}$, $a = -1$, and $b = 8$.
 (a) Show that there is no point c in (a, b) such that
$$f'(c) = \frac{f(b) - f(a)}{b - a}$$
 (b) Explain why the result in part (a) does not contradict the Mean-Value Theorem.

17. (a) Show that if f is differentiable on $(-\infty, +\infty)$, and if $y = f(x)$ and $y = f'(x)$ are graphed in the same coordinate system, then between any two x-intercepts of f there is at least one x-intercept of f'.
 (b) Give some examples that illustrate this.

18. Review Formulas (8) and (9) in Section 2.1 and use the Mean-Value Theorem to show that if f is differentiable on $(-\infty, +\infty)$, then for any interval $[x_0, x_1]$ there is at least one point in (x_0, x_1) where the instantaneous rate of change of y with respect to x is equal to the average rate of change over the interval.

19–21 Use the result of Exercise 18 in these exercises. ■

19. An automobile travels 4 mi along a straight road in 5 min. Show that the speedometer reads exactly 48 mi/h at least once during the trip.

20. At 11 A.M. on a certain morning the outside temperature was 76°F. At 11 P.M. that evening it had dropped to 52°F.
 (a) Show that at some instant during this period the temperature was decreasing at the rate of 2°F/h.
 (b) Suppose that you know the temperature reached a high of 88°F sometime between 11 A.M. and 11 P.M. Show that at some instant during this period the temperature was decreasing at a rate greater than 3°F/h.

21. Suppose that two runners in a 100 m dash finish in a tie. Show that they had the same velocity at least once during the race.

22. Use the fact that

$$\frac{d}{dx}[x\ln(2-x)] = \ln(2-x) - \frac{x}{2-x}$$

to show that the equation $x = (2-x)\ln(2-x)$ has at least one solution in the interval $(0, 1)$.

23. (a) Use the Constant Difference Theorem (4.8.3) to show that if $f'(x) = g'(x)$ for all x in the interval $(-\infty, +\infty)$, and if f and g have the same value at some point x_0, then $f(x) = g(x)$ for all x in $(-\infty, +\infty)$.

   (b) Use the result in part (a) to confirm the trigonometric identity $\sin^2 x + \cos^2 x = 1$.

24. (a) Use the Constant Difference Theorem (4.8.3) to show that if $f'(x) = g'(x)$ for all x in $(-\infty, +\infty)$, and if $f(x_0) - g(x_0) = c$ at some point x_0, then

$$f(x) - g(x) = c$$

   for all x in $(-\infty, +\infty)$.

   (b) Use the result in part (a) to show that the function

$$h(x) = (x-1)^3 - (x^2+3)(x-3)$$

   is constant for all x in $(-\infty, +\infty)$, and find the constant.

   (c) Check the result in part (b) by multiplying out and simplifying the formula for $h(x)$.

25. Let $g(x) = xe^x - e^x$. Find $f(x)$ so that $f'(x) = g'(x)$ and $f(1) = 2$.

26. Let $g(x) = \tan^{-1} x$. Find $f(x)$ so that $f'(x) = g'(x)$ and $f(1) = 2$.

FOCUS ON CONCEPTS

27. (a) Use the Mean-Value Theorem to show that if f is differentiable on an interval, and if $|f'(x)| \leq M$ for all values of x in the interval, then

$$|f(x) - f(y)| \leq M|x - y|$$

   for all values of x and y in the interval.

   (b) Use the result in part (a) to show that

$$|\sin x - \sin y| \leq |x - y|$$

   for all real values of x and y.

28. (a) Use the Mean-Value Theorem to show that if f is differentiable on an open interval, and if $|f'(x)| \geq M$ for all values of x in the interval, then

$$|f(x) - f(y)| \geq M|x - y|$$

   for all values of x and y in the interval.

   (b) Use the result in part (a) to show that

$$|\tan x - \tan y| \geq |x - y|$$

   for all values of x and y in the interval $(-\pi/2, \pi/2)$.

   (c) Use the result in part (b) to show that

$$|\tan x + \tan y| \geq |x + y|$$

   for all values of x and y in the interval $(-\pi/2, \pi/2)$.

29. (a) Use the Mean-Value Theorem to show that

$$\sqrt{y} - \sqrt{x} < \frac{y - x}{2\sqrt{x}}$$

   if $0 < x < y$.

   (b) Use the result in part (a) to show that if $0 < x < y$, then $\sqrt{xy} < \frac{1}{2}(x + y)$.

30. Show that if f is differentiable on an open interval and $f'(x) \neq 0$ on the interval, the equation $f(x) = 0$ can have at most one real root in the interval.

31. Use the result in Exercise 30 to show the following:

   (a) The equation $x^3 + 4x - 1 = 0$ has exactly one real root.

   (b) If $b^2 - 3ac < 0$ and if $a \neq 0$, then the equation

$$ax^3 + bx^2 + cx + d = 0$$

   has exactly one real root.

32. Use the inequality $\sqrt{3} < 1.8$ to prove that

$$1.7 < \sqrt{3} < 1.75$$

   [*Hint:* Let $f(x) = \sqrt{x}, a = 3$, and $b = 4$ in the Mean-Value Theorem.]

33. Use the Mean-Value Theorem to prove that

$$\frac{x}{1+x^2} < \tan^{-1} x < x \quad (x > 0)$$

34. (a) Show that if f and g are functions for which

$$f'(x) = g(x) \quad \text{and} \quad g'(x) = f(x)$$

   for all x, then $f^2(x) - g^2(x)$ is a constant.

   (b) Show that the function $f(x) = \frac{1}{2}(e^x + e^{-x})$ and the function $g(x) = \frac{1}{2}(e^x - e^{-x})$ have this property.

35. (a) Show that if f and g are functions for which

$$f'(x) = g(x) \quad \text{and} \quad g'(x) = -f(x)$$

   for all x, then $f^2(x) + g^2(x)$ is a constant.

   (b) Give an example of functions f and g with this property.

FOCUS ON CONCEPTS

36. Let f and g be continuous on $[a, b]$ and differentiable on (a, b). Prove: If $f(a) = g(a)$ and $f(b) = g(b)$, then there is a point c in (a, b) such that $f'(c) = g'(c)$.

37. Illustrate the result in Exercise 36 by drawing an appropriate picture.

38. (a) Prove that if $f''(x) > 0$ for all x in (a, b), then $f'(x) = 0$ at most once in (a, b).

   (b) Give a geometric interpretation of the result in (a).

---

39. (a) Prove part (*b*) of Theorem 4.1.2.

   (b) Prove part (*c*) of Theorem 4.1.2.

40. Use the Mean-Value Theorem to prove the following result: Let f be continuous at x_0 and suppose that $\lim_{x \to x_0} f'(x)$ exists. Then f is differentiable at x_0, and

$$f'(x_0) = \lim_{x \to x_0} f'(x)$$

   [*Hint:* The derivative $f'(x_0)$ is given by

$$f'(x_0) = \lim_{x \to x_0} \frac{f(x) - f(x_0)}{x - x_0}$$

   provided this limit exists.]

41. Let
$$f(x) = \begin{cases} 3x^2, & x \leq 1 \\ ax + b, & x > 1 \end{cases}$$
Find the values of a and b so that f will be differentiable at $x = 1$.

42. (a) Let
$$f(x) = \begin{cases} x^2, & x \leq 0 \\ x^2 + 1, & x > 0 \end{cases}$$
Show that
$$\lim_{x \to 0^-} f'(x) = \lim_{x \to 0^+} f'(x)$$
but that $f'(0)$ does not exist.
   (b) Let
$$f(x) = \begin{cases} x^2, & x \leq 0 \\ x^3, & x > 0 \end{cases}$$
Show that $f'(0)$ exists but $f''(0)$ does not.

43. Use the Mean-Value Theorem to prove the following result: The graph of a function f has a point of vertical tangency at $(x_0, f(x_0))$ if f is continuous at x_0 and $f'(x)$ approaches either $+\infty$ or $-\infty$ as $x \to x_0^+$ and as $x \to x_0^-$.

44. **Writing** Suppose that $p(x)$ is a nonconstant polynomial with zeros at $x = a$ and $x = b$. Explain how both the Extreme-Value Theorem (4.4.2) and Rolle's Theorem can be used to show that p has a critical point between a and b.

45. **Writing** Find and describe a physical situation that illustrates the Mean-Value Theorem.

✔ QUICK CHECK ANSWERS 4.8

1. (a) $[0, 1]$ (b) $c = \frac{1}{2}$ **2.** $[-3, 3]$; $c = -2, 0, 2$ **3.** (a) $b = 2$ (b) $c = 1$ **4.** (a) 1.5 (b) 0.8   **5.** $f(x) = x^2 + 4$

CHAPTER 4 REVIEW EXERCISES    Graphing Utility   CAS

1. (a) If $x_1 < x_2$, what relationship must hold between $f(x_1)$ and $f(x_2)$ if f is increasing on an interval containing x_1 and x_2? Decreasing? Constant?
   (b) What condition on f' ensures that f is increasing on an interval $[a, b]$? Decreasing? Constant?

2. (a) What condition on f' ensures that f is concave up on an open interval? Concave down?
   (b) What condition on f'' ensures that f is concave up on an open interval? Concave down?
   (c) In words, what is an inflection point of f?

3–10 Find: (a) the intervals on which f is increasing, (b) the intervals on which f is decreasing, (c) the open intervals on which f is concave up, (d) the open intervals on which f is concave down, and (e) the x-coordinates of all inflection points. ■

3. $f(x) = x^2 - 5x + 6$

4. $f(x) = x^4 - 8x^2 + 16$

5. $f(x) = \dfrac{x^2}{x^2 + 2}$

6. $f(x) = \sqrt[3]{x + 2}$

7. $f(x) = x^{1/3}(x + 4)$

8. $f(x) = x^{4/3} - x^{1/3}$

9. $f(x) = 1/e^{x^2}$

10. $f(x) = \tan^{-1} x^2$

11–14 Analyze the trigonometric function f over the specified interval, stating where f is increasing, decreasing, concave up, and concave down, and stating the x-coordinates of all inflection points. Confirm that your results are consistent with the graph of f generated with a graphing utility. ■

11. $f(x) = \cos x$; $[0, 2\pi]$

12. $f(x) = \tan x$; $(-\pi/2, \pi/2)$

13. $f(x) = \sin x \cos x$; $[0, \pi]$

14. $f(x) = \cos^2 x - 2 \sin x$; $[0, 2\pi]$

15. In each part, sketch a continuous curve $y = f(x)$ with the stated properties.
   (a) $f(2) = 4$, $f'(2) = 1$, $f''(x) < 0$ for $x < 2$, $f''(x) > 0$ for $x > 2$
   (b) $f(2) = 4$, $f''(x) > 0$ for $x < 2$, $f''(x) < 0$ for $x > 2$, $\lim\limits_{x \to 2^-} f'(x) = +\infty$, $\lim\limits_{x \to 2^+} f'(x) = +\infty$
   (c) $f(2) = 4$, $f''(x) < 0$ for $x \neq 2$, $\lim\limits_{x \to 2^-} f'(x) = 1$, $\lim\limits_{x \to 2^+} f'(x) = -1$

16. In parts (a)–(d), the graph of a polynomial with degree at most 6 is given. Find equations for polynomials that produce graphs with these shapes, and check your answers with a graphing utility.

(a)
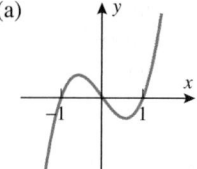

(b)
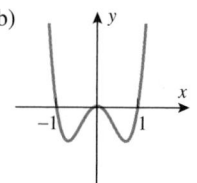

(c)
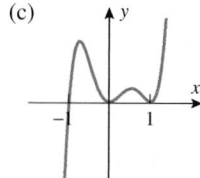

(d)
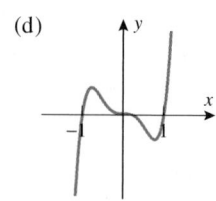

17. For a general quadratic polynomial

$$f(x) = ax^2 + bx + c \quad (a \neq 0)$$

find conditions on a, b, and c to ensure that f is always increasing or always decreasing on $[0, +\infty)$.

18. For the general cubic polynomial

$$f(x) = ax^3 + bx^2 + cx + d \quad (a \neq 0)$$

find conditions on a, b, c, and d to ensure that f is always increasing or always decreasing on $(-\infty, +\infty)$.

19. Use a graphing utility to estimate the value of x at which

$$f(x) = \frac{2^x}{1 + 2^{x+1}}$$

is increasing most rapidly.

20. Prove that for any positive constants a and k, the graph of

$$y = \frac{a^x}{1 + a^{x+k}}$$

has an inflection point at $x = -k$.

21. (a) Where on the graph of $y = f(x)$ would you expect y to be increasing or decreasing most rapidly with respect to x?
    (b) In words, what is a relative extremum?
    (c) State a procedure for determining where the relative extrema of f occur.

22. Determine whether the statement is true or false. If it is false, give an example for which the statement fails.
    (a) If f has a relative maximum at x_0, then $f(x_0)$ is the largest value that $f(x)$ can have.
    (b) If the largest value for f on the interval (a, b) is at x_0, then f has a relative maximum at x_0.
    (c) A function f has a relative extremum at each of its critical points.

23. (a) According to the first derivative test, what conditions ensure that f has a relative maximum at x_0? A relative minimum?
    (b) According to the second derivative test, what conditions ensure that f has a relative maximum at x_0? A relative minimum?

24–26 Locate the critical points and identify which critical points correspond to stationary points. ■

24. (a) $f(x) = x^3 + 3x^2 - 9x + 1$
    (b) $f(x) = x^4 - 6x^2 - 3$

25. (a) $f(x) = \dfrac{x}{x^2 + 2}$ (b) $f(x) = \dfrac{x^2 - 3}{x^2 + 1}$

26. (a) $f(x) = x^{1/3}(x - 4)$ (b) $f(x) = x^{4/3} - 6x^{1/3}$

27. In each part, find all critical points, and use the first derivative test to classify them as relative maxima, relative minima, or neither.
    (a) $f(x) = x^{1/3}(x - 7)^2$
    (b) $f(x) = 2\sin x - \cos 2x, \quad 0 \leq x \leq 2\pi$
    (c) $f(x) = 3x - (x - 1)^{3/2}$

28. In each part, find all critical points, and use the second derivative test (where possible) to classify them as relative maxima, relative minima, or neither.
    (a) $f(x) = x^{-1/2} + \frac{1}{9}x^{1/2}$
    (b) $f(x) = x^2 + 8/x$
    (c) $f(x) = \sin^2 x - \cos x, \quad 0 \leq x \leq 2\pi$

29–36 Give a graph of the function f, and identify the limits as $x \to \pm\infty$, as well as locations of all relative extrema, inflection points, and asymptotes (as appropriate). ■

29. $f(x) = x^4 - 3x^3 + 3x^2 + 1$

30. $f(x) = x^5 - 4x^4 + 4x^3$

31. $f(x) = \tan(x^2 + 1)$ 32. $f(x) = x - \cos x$

33. $f(x) = \dfrac{x^2}{x^2 + 2x + 5}$ 34. $f(x) = \dfrac{25 - 9x^2}{x^3}$

35. $f(x) = \begin{cases} \frac{1}{2}x^2, & x \leq 0 \\ -x^2, & x > 0 \end{cases}$

36. $f(x) = (1 + x)^{2/3}(3 - x)^{1/3}$

37–44 Use any method to find the relative extrema of the function f. ■

37. $f(x) = x^3 + 5x - 2$ 38. $f(x) = x^4 - 2x^2 + 7$

39. $f(x) = x^{4/5}$ 40. $f(x) = 2x + x^{2/3}$

41. $f(x) = \dfrac{x^2}{x^2 + 1}$ 42. $f(x) = \dfrac{x}{x + 2}$

43. $f(x) = \ln(1 + x^2)$ 44. $f(x) = x^2 e^x$

45–46 When using a graphing utility, important features of a graph may be missed if the viewing window is not chosen appropriately. This is illustrated in Exercises 45 and 46. ■

45. (a) Generate the graph of $f(x) = \frac{1}{3}x^3 - \frac{1}{400}x$ over the interval $[-5, 5]$, and make a conjecture about the locations and nature of all critical points.
    (b) Find the exact locations of all the critical points, and classify them as relative maxima, relative minima, or neither.
    (c) Confirm the results in part (b) by graphing f over an appropriate interval.

46. (a) Generate the graph of

$$f(x) = \frac{1}{5}x^5 - \frac{7}{8}x^4 + \frac{1}{3}x^3 + \frac{7}{2}x^2 - 6x$$

over the interval $[-5, 5]$, and make a conjecture about the locations and nature of all critical points.
    (b) Find the exact locations of all the critical points, and classify them as relative maxima, relative minima, or neither.
    (c) Confirm the results in part (b) by graphing portions of f over appropriate intervals. [*Note:* It will not be possible to find a single window in which all of the critical points are discernible.]

47. (a) Use a graphing utility to generate the graphs of $y = x$ and $y = (x^3 - 8)/(x^2 + 1)$ together over the interval $[-5, 5]$, and make a conjecture about the relationship between the two graphs.

(b) Confirm your conjecture in part (a).

48. Use implicit differentiation to show that a function defined implicitly by $\sin x + \cos y = 2y$ has a critical point whenever $\cos x = 0$. Then use either the first or second derivative test to classify these critical points as relative maxima or minima.

49. Let

$$f(x) = \frac{2x^3 + x^2 - 15x + 7}{(2x - 1)(3x^2 + x - 1)}$$

Graph $y = f(x)$, and find the equations of all horizontal and vertical asymptotes. Explain why there is no vertical asymptote at $x = \frac{1}{2}$, even though the denominator of f is zero at that point.

c **50.** Let

$$f(x) = \frac{x^5 - x^4 - 3x^3 + 2x + 4}{x^7 - 2x^6 - 3x^5 + 6x^4 + 4x - 8}$$

(a) Use a CAS to factor the numerator and denominator of f, and use the results to determine the locations of all vertical asymptotes.

(b) Confirm that your answer is consistent with the graph of f.

51. (a) What inequality must $f(x)$ satisfy for the function f to have an absolute maximum on an interval I at x_0?

(b) What inequality must $f(x)$ satisfy for f to have an absolute minimum on an interval I at x_0?

(c) What is the difference between an absolute extremum and a relative extremum?

52. According to the Extreme-Value Theorem, what conditions on a function f and a given interval guarantee that f will have both an absolute maximum and an absolute minimum on the interval?

53. In each part, determine whether the statement is true or false, and justify your answer.

(a) If f is differentiable on the open interval (a, b), and if f has an absolute extremum on that interval, then it must occur at a stationary point of f.

(b) If f is continuous on the open interval (a, b), and if f has an absolute extremum on that interval, then it must occur at a stationary point of f.

54–56 In each part, find the absolute minimum m and the absolute maximum M of f on the given interval (if they exist), and state where the absolute extrema occur. ■

54. (a) $f(x) = 1/x$; $[-2, -1]$

(b) $f(x) = x^3 - x^4$; $[-1, \frac{3}{2}]$

(c) $f(x) = x - \tan x$; $[-\pi/4, \pi/4]$

(d) $f(x) = -|x^2 - 2x|$; $[1, 3]$

55. (a) $f(x) = x^2 - 3x - 1$; $(-\infty, +\infty)$

(b) $f(x) = x^3 - 3x - 2$; $(-\infty, +\infty)$

(c) $f(x) = e^x/x^2$; $(0, +\infty)$

(d) $f(x) = x^x$; $(0, +\infty)$

56. (a) $f(x) = 2x^5 - 5x^4 + 7$; $(-1, 3)$

(b) $f(x) = (3 - x)/(2 - x)$; $(0, 2)$

(c) $f(x) = 2x/(x^2 + 3)$; $(0, 2]$

(d) $f(x) = x^2(x - 2)^{1/3}$; $(0, 3]$

57. In each part, use a graphing utility to estimate the absolute maximum and minimum values of f, if any, on the stated interval, and then use calculus methods to find the exact values.

(a) $f(x) = (x^2 - 1)^2$; $(-\infty, +\infty)$

(b) $f(x) = x/(x^2 + 1)$; $[0, +\infty)$

(c) $f(x) = 2 \sec x - \tan x$; $[0, \pi/4]$

(d) $f(x) = x/2 + \ln(x^2 + 1)$; $[-4, 0]$

58. Prove that $x \leq \sin^{-1} x$ for all x in $[0, 1]$.

c **59.** Let

$$f(x) = \frac{x^3 + 2}{x^4 + 1}$$

(a) Generate the graph of $y = f(x)$, and use the graph to make rough estimates of the coordinates of the absolute extrema.

(b) Use a CAS to solve the equation $f'(x) = 0$ and then use it to make more accurate approximations of the coordinates in part (a).

60. A church window consists of a blue semicircular section surmounting a clear rectangular section as shown in the accompanying figure. The blue glass lets through half as much light per unit area as the clear glass. Find the radius r of the window that admits the most light if the perimeter of the entire window is to be P feet.

61. Find the dimensions of the rectangle of maximum area that can be inscribed inside the ellipse $(x/4)^2 + (y/3)^2 = 1$ (see the accompanying figure).

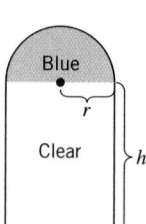

▲ Figure Ex-60

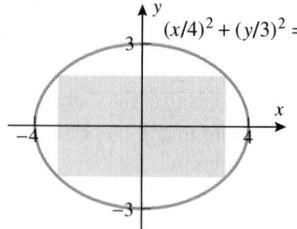

▲ Figure Ex-61

c **62.** As shown in the accompanying figure on the next page, suppose that a boat enters the river at the point $(1, 0)$ and maintains a heading toward the origin. As a result of the strong current, the boat follows the path

$$y = \frac{x^{10/3} - 1}{2x^{2/3}}$$

where x and y are in miles.

(a) Graph the path taken by the boat.

(b) Can the boat reach the origin? If not, discuss its fate and find how close it comes to the origin.

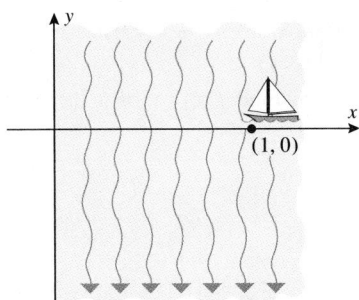

◀ **Figure Ex-62**

63. A sheet of cardboard 12 in square is used to make an open box by cutting squares of equal size from the four corners and folding up the sides. What size squares should be cut to obtain a box with largest possible volume?

64. Is it true or false that a particle in rectilinear motion is speeding up when its velocity is increasing and slowing down when its velocity is decreasing? Justify your answer.

65. (a) Can an object in rectilinear motion reverse direction if its acceleration is constant? Justify your answer using a velocity versus time curve.
  (b) Can an object in rectilinear motion have increasing speed and decreasing acceleration? Justify your answer using a velocity versus time curve.

66. Suppose that the position function of a particle in rectilinear motion is given by the formula $s(t) = t/(2t^2 + 8)$ for $t \geq 0$.
  (a) Use a graphing utility to generate the position, velocity, and acceleration versus time curves.
  (b) Use the appropriate graph to make a rough estimate of the time when the particle reverses direction, and then find that time exactly.
  (c) Find the position, velocity, and acceleration at the instant when the particle reverses direction.
  (d) Use the appropriate graphs to make rough estimates of the time intervals on which the particle is speeding up and the time intervals on which it is slowing down, and then find those time intervals exactly.
  (e) When does the particle have its maximum and minimum velocities?

67. For parts (a)–(f), suppose that the position function of a particle in rectilinear motion is given by the formula

$$s(t) = \frac{t^2 + 1}{t^4 + 1}, \quad t \geq 0$$

  (a) Use a CAS to find simplified formulas for the velocity function $v(t)$ and the acceleration function $a(t)$.
  (b) Graph the position, velocity, and acceleration versus time curves.
  (c) Use the appropriate graph to make a rough estimate of the time at which the particle is farthest from the origin and its distance from the origin at that time.
  (d) Use the appropriate graph to make a rough estimate of the time interval during which the particle is moving in the positive direction.

  (e) Use the appropriate graphs to make rough estimates of the time intervals during which the particle is speeding up and the time intervals during which it is slowing down.
  (f) Use the appropriate graph to make a rough estimate of the maximum speed of the particle and the time at which the maximum speed occurs.

68. Draw an appropriate picture, and describe the basic idea of Newton's Method without using any formulas.

69. Use Newton's Method to approximate all three solutions of $x^3 - 4x + 1 = 0$.

70. Use Newton's Method to approximate the smallest positive solution of $\sin x + \cos x = 0$.

71. Use a graphing utility to determine the number of times the curve $y = x^3$ intersects the curve $y = (x/2) - 1$. Then apply Newton's Method to approximate the x-coordinates of all intersections.

72. According to *Kepler's law*, the planets in our solar system move in elliptical orbits around the Sun. If a planet's closest approach to the Sun occurs at time $t = 0$, then the distance r from the center of the planet to the center of the Sun at some later time t can be determined from the equation

$$r = a(1 - e \cos \phi)$$

where a is the average distance between centers, e is a positive constant that measures the "flatness" of the elliptical orbit, and ϕ is the solution of *Kepler's equation*

$$\frac{2\pi t}{T} = \phi - e \sin \phi$$

in which T is the time it takes for one complete orbit of the planet. Estimate the distance from the Earth to the Sun when $t = 90$ days. [First find ϕ from Kepler's equation, and then use this value of ϕ to find the distance. Use $a = 150 \times 10^6$ km, $e = 0.0167$, and $T = 365$ days.]

73. Using the formulas in Exercise 72, find the distance from the planet Mars to the Sun when $t = 1$ year. For Mars use $a = 228 \times 10^6$ km, $e = 0.0934$, and $T = 1.88$ years.

74. Suppose that f is continuous on the closed interval $[a, b]$ and differentiable on the open interval (a, b), and suppose that $f(a) = f(b)$. Is it true or false that f must have at least one stationary point in (a, b)? Justify your answer.

75. In each part, determine whether all of the hypotheses of Rolle's Theorem are satisfied on the stated interval. If not, state which hypotheses fail; if so, find all values of c guaranteed in the conclusion of the theorem.
  (a) $f(x) = \sqrt{4 - x^2}$ on $[-2, 2]$
  (b) $f(x) = x^{2/3} - 1$ on $[-1, 1]$
  (c) $f(x) = \sin(x^2)$ on $[0, \sqrt{\pi}]$

76. In each part, determine whether all of the hypotheses of the Mean-Value Theorem are satisfied on the stated interval. If not, state which hypotheses fail; if so, find all values of c guaranteed in the conclusion of the theorem.
  (a) $f(x) = |x - 1|$ on $[-2, 2]$ *(cont.)*

(b) $f(x) = \dfrac{x+1}{x-1}$ on [2, 3]

(c) $f(x) = \begin{cases} 3 - x^2 & \text{if } x \le 1 \\ 2/x & \text{if } x > 1 \end{cases}$ on [0, 2]

77. Use the fact that

$$\frac{d}{dx}(x^6 - 2x^2 + x) = 6x^5 - 4x + 1$$

to show that the equation $6x^5 - 4x + 1 = 0$ has at least one solution in the interval (0, 1).

78. Let $g(x) = x^3 - 4x + 6$. Find $f(x)$ so that $f'(x) = g'(x)$ and $f(1) = 2$.

CHAPTER 4 MAKING CONNECTIONS

1. Suppose that $g(x)$ is a function that is defined and differentiable for all real numbers x and that $g(x)$ has the following properties:

(i) $g(0) = 2$ and $g'(0) = -\frac{2}{3}$.

(ii) $g(4) = 3$ and $g'(4) = 3$.

(iii) $g(x)$ is concave up for $x < 4$ and concave down for $x > 4$.

(iv) $g(x) \ge -10$ for all x.

Use these properties to answer the following questions.

(a) How many zeros does g have?

(b) How many zeros does g' have?

(c) Exactly one of the following limits is possible:

$$\lim_{x \to +\infty} g'(x) = -5, \quad \lim_{x \to +\infty} g'(x) = 0, \quad \lim_{x \to +\infty} g'(x) = 5$$

Identify which of these results is possible and draw a rough sketch of the graph of such a function $g(x)$. Explain why the other two results are impossible.

2. The two graphs in the accompanying figure depict a function $r(x)$ and its derivative $r'(x)$.

(a) Approximate the coordinates of each inflection point on the graph of $y = r(x)$.

(b) Suppose that $f(x)$ is a function that is continuous everywhere and whose *derivative* satisfies

$$f'(x) = (x^2 - 4) \cdot r(x)$$

What are the critical points for $f(x)$? At each critical point, identify whether $f(x)$ has a (relative) maximum, minimum, or neither a maximum or minimum. Approximate $f''(1)$.

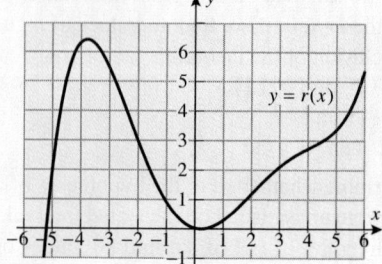

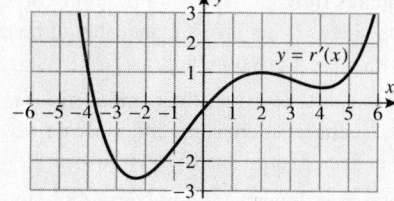

◀ **Figure Ex-2**

3. With the function $r(x)$ as provided in Exercise 2, let $g(x)$ be a function that is continuous everywhere such that $g'(x) = x - r(x)$. For which values of x does $g(x)$ have an inflection point?

4. Suppose that f is a function whose derivative is continuous everywhere. Assume that there exists a real number c such that when Newton's Method is applied to f, the inequality

$$|x_n - c| < \frac{1}{n}$$

is satisfied for all values of $n = 1, 2, 3, \ldots$.

(a) Explain why

$$|x_{n+1} - x_n| < \frac{2}{n}$$

for all values of $n = 1, 2, 3, \ldots$.

(b) Show that there exists a positive constant M such that

$$|f(x_n)| \le M |x_{n+1} - x_n| < \frac{2M}{n}$$

for all values of $n = 1, 2, 3, \ldots$.

(c) Prove that if $f(c) \ne 0$, then there exists a positive integer N such that

$$\frac{|f(c)|}{2} < |f(x_n)|$$

if $n > N$. [*Hint:* Argue that $f(x) \to f(c)$ as $x \to c$ and then apply Definition 1.4.1 with $\epsilon = \frac{1}{2}|f(c)|$.]

(d) What can you conclude from parts (b) and (c)?

5. What are the important elements in the argument suggested by Exercise 4? Can you extend this argument to a wider collection of functions?

6. A bug crawling on a linoleum floor along the edge of a plush carpet encounters an irregularity in the form of a 2 in by 3 in rectangular section of carpet that juts out into the linoleum as illustrated in Figure Ex-6a on the next page.

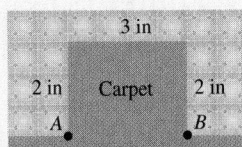

◀ **Figure Ex-6a**

The bug crawls at 0.7 in/s on the linoleum, but only at 0.3 in/s through the carpet, and its goal is to travel from point A to point B. Four possible routes from A to B are as follows: (i) crawl on linoleum along the edge of the carpet; (ii) crawl through the carpet to a point on the wider side of the rectangle, and finish the journey on linoleum along the edge of the carpet; (iii) crawl through the carpet to a point on the shorter side of the rectangle, and finish the journey on linoleum along the edge of the carpet; or (iv) crawl through the carpet directly to point B. (See Figure Ex-6b.)

(a) Calculate the times it would take the bug to crawl from A to B via routes (i) and (iv).

(b) Suppose the bug follows route (ii) and use x to represent the total distance the bug crawls on linoleum. Identify the appropriate interval for x in this case, and determine the shortest time for the bug to complete the journey using route (ii).

(c) Suppose the bug follows route (iii) and again use x to represent the total distance the bug crawls on linoleum. Identify the appropriate interval for x in this case, and determine the shortest time for the bug to complete the journey using route (iii).

(d) Which of routes (i), (ii), (iii), or (iv) is quickest? What is the shortest time for the bug to complete the journey?

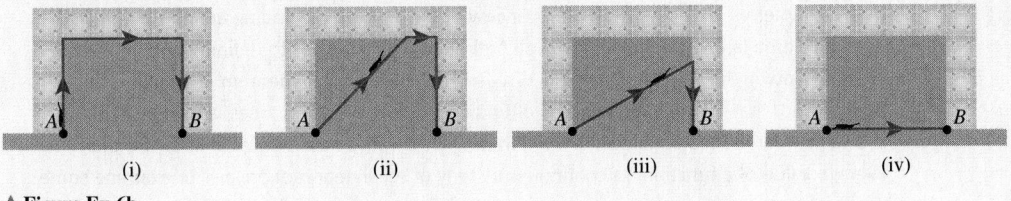

▲ **Figure Ex-6b**

Jon Ferrey/Allsport/Getty Images

5

INTEGRATION

If a dragster moves with varying velocity over a certain time interval, it is possible to find the distance it travels during that time interval using techniques of calculus.

In this chapter we will begin with an overview of the problem of finding areas—we will discuss what the term "area" means, and we will outline two approaches to defining and calculating areas. Following this overview, we will discuss the Fundamental Theorem of Calculus, which is the theorem that relates the problems of finding tangent lines and areas, and we will discuss techniques for calculating areas. We will then use the ideas in this chapter to define the average value of a function, to continue our study of rectilinear motion, and to examine some consequences of the chain rule in integral calculus. We conclude the chapter by studying functions defined by integrals, with a focus on the natural logarithm function.

5.1 AN OVERVIEW OF THE AREA PROBLEM

In this introductory section we will consider the problem of calculating areas of plane regions with curvilinear boundaries. All of the results in this section will be reexamined in more detail later in this chapter. Our purpose here is simply to introduce and motivate the fundamental concepts.

■ THE AREA PROBLEM

Formulas for the areas of polygons, such as squares, rectangles, triangles, and trapezoids, were well known in many early civilizations. However, the problem of finding formulas for regions with curved boundaries (a circle being the simplest example) caused difficulties for early mathematicians.

The first real progress in dealing with the general area problem was made by the Greek mathematician Archimedes, who obtained areas of regions bounded by circular arcs, parabolas, spirals, and various other curves using an ingenious procedure that was later called the *method of exhaustion*. The method, when applied to a circle, consists of inscribing a succession of regular polygons in the circle and allowing the number of sides to increase indefinitely (Figure 5.1.1). As the number of sides increases, the polygons tend to "exhaust" the region inside the circle, and the areas of the polygons become better and better approximations of the exact area of the circle.

To see how this works numerically, let $A(n)$ denote the area of a regular n-sided polygon inscribed in a circle of radius 1. Table 5.1.1 shows the values of $A(n)$ for various choices of n. Note that for large values of n the area $A(n)$ appears to be close to π (square units),

Table 5.1.1

n	$A(n)$
100	3.13952597647
200	3.14107590781
300	3.14136298250
400	3.14146346236
500	3.14150997084
1000	3.14157198278
2000	3.14158748588
3000	3.14159035683
4000	3.14159136166
5000	3.14159182676
10,000	3.14159244688

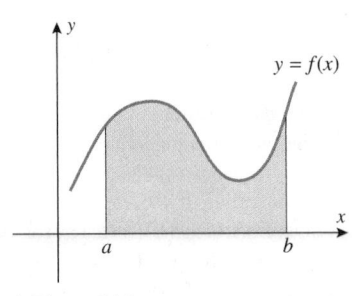

▲ Figure 5.1.1

as one would expect. This suggests that for a circle of radius 1, the method of exhaustion is equivalent to an equation of the form

$$\lim_{n \to \infty} A(n) = \pi$$

Since Greek mathematicians were suspicious of the concept of "infinity," they avoided its use in mathematical arguments. As a result, computation of area using the method of exhaustion was a very cumbersome procedure. It remained for Newton and Leibniz to obtain a general method for finding areas that explicitly used the notion of a limit. We will discuss their method in the context of the following problem.

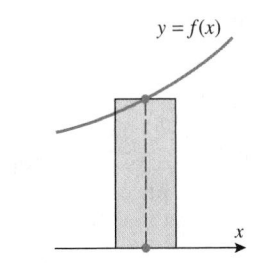

▲ Figure 5.1.2

> **5.1.1 THE AREA PROBLEM** Given a function f that is continuous and nonnegative on an interval $[a, b]$, find the area between the graph of f and the interval $[a, b]$ on the x-axis (Figure 5.1.2).

■ THE RECTANGLE METHOD FOR FINDING AREAS

One approach to the area problem is to use Archimedes' method of exhaustion in the following way:

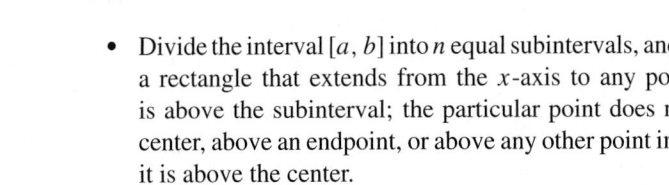

▲ Figure 5.1.3

- Divide the interval $[a, b]$ into n equal subintervals, and over each subinterval construct a rectangle that extends from the x-axis to any point on the curve $y = f(x)$ that is above the subinterval; the particular point does not matter—it can be above the center, above an endpoint, or above any other point in the subinterval. In Figure 5.1.3 it is above the center.

- For each n, the total area of the rectangles can be viewed as an *approximation* to the exact area under the curve over the interval $[a, b]$. Moreover, it is evident intuitively that as n increases these approximations will get better and better and will approach the exact area as a limit (Figure 5.1.4). That is, if A denotes the exact area under the curve and A_n denotes the approximation to A using n rectangles, then

$$A = \lim_{n \to +\infty} A_n$$

We will call this the *rectangle method* for computing A.

Logically speaking, we cannot really talk about computing areas without a precise mathematical definition of the term "area." Later in this chapter we will give such a definition, but for now we will treat the concept intuitively.

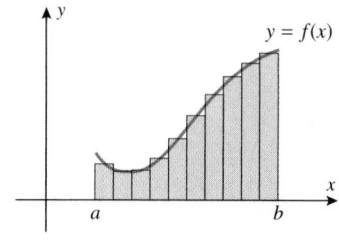
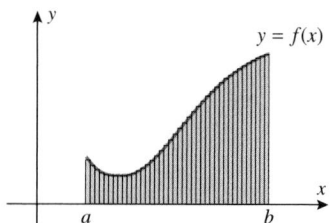

▲ **Figure 5.1.4**

To illustrate this idea, we will use the rectangle method to approximate the area under the curve $y = x^2$ over the interval $[0, 1]$ (Figure 5.1.5). We will begin by dividing the interval $[0, 1]$ into n equal subintervals, from which it follows that each subinterval has length $1/n$; the endpoints of the subintervals occur at

$$0, \ \frac{1}{n}, \ \frac{2}{n}, \ \frac{3}{n}, \ldots, \ \frac{n-1}{n}, \ 1$$

Archimedes (287 B.C.–212 B.C.) Greek mathematician and scientist. Born in Syracuse, Sicily, Archimedes was the son of the astronomer Pheidias and possibly related to Heiron II, king of Syracuse. Most of the facts about his life come from the Roman biographer, Plutarch, who inserted a few tantalizing pages about him in the massive biography of the Roman soldier, Marcellus. In the words of one writer, "the account of Archimedes is slipped like a tissue-thin shaving of ham in a bull-choking sandwich."

Archimedes ranks with Newton and Gauss as one of the three greatest mathematicians who ever lived, and he is certainly the greatest mathematician of antiquity. His mathematical work is so modern in spirit and technique that it is barely distinguishable from that of a seventeenth-century mathematician, yet it was all done without benefit of algebra or a convenient number system. Among his mathematical achievements, Archimedes developed a general method (exhaustion) for finding areas and volumes, and he used the method to find areas bounded by parabolas and spirals and to find volumes of cylinders, paraboloids, and segments of spheres. He gave a procedure for approximating π and bounded its value between $3\frac{10}{71}$ and $3\frac{1}{7}$. In spite of the limitations of the Greek numbering system, he devised methods for finding square roots and invented a method based on the Greek myriad (10,000) for representing numbers as large as 1 followed by 80 million billion zeros.

Of all his mathematical work, Archimedes was most proud of his discovery of a method for finding the volume of a sphere—he showed that the volume of a sphere is two-thirds the volume of the smallest cylinder that can contain it. At his request, the figure of a sphere and cylinder was engraved on his tombstone.

In addition to mathematics, Archimedes worked extensively in mechanics and hydrostatics. Nearly every schoolchild knows Archimedes as the absent-minded scientist who, on realizing that a floating object displaces its weight of liquid, leaped from his bath and ran naked through the streets of Syracuse shouting, "Eureka, Eureka!"—(meaning, "I have found it!"). Archimedes actually cre-

ated the discipline of hydrostatics and used it to find equilibrium positions for various floating bodies. He laid down the fundamental postulates of mechanics, discovered the laws of levers, and calculated centers of gravity for various flat surfaces and solids. In the excitement of discovering the mathematical laws of the lever, he is said to have declared, "Give me a place to stand and I will move the earth."

Although Archimedes was apparently more interested in pure mathematics than its applications, he was an engineering genius. During the second Punic war, when Syracuse was attacked by the Roman fleet under the command of Marcellus, it was reported by Plutarch that Archimedes' military inventions held the fleet at bay for three years. He invented super catapults that showered the Romans with rocks weighing a quarter ton or more, and fearsome mechanical devices with iron "beaks and claws" that reached over the city walls, grasped the ships, and spun them against the rocks. After the first repulse, Marcellus called Archimedes a "geometrical Briareus (a hundred-armed mythological monster) who uses our ships like cups to ladle water from the sea."

Eventually the Roman army was victorious and contrary to Marcellus' specific orders the 75-year-old Archimedes was killed by a Roman soldier. According to one report of the incident, the soldier cast a shadow across the sand in which Archimedes was working on a mathematical problem. When the annoyed Archimedes yelled, "Don't disturb my circles," the soldier flew into a rage and cut the old man down.

Although there is no known likeness or statue of this great man, nine works of Archimedes have survived to the present day. Especially important is his treatise, *The Method of Mechanical Theorems*, which was part of a palimpsest found in Constantinople in 1906. In this treatise Archimedes explains how he made some of his discoveries, using reasoning that anticipated ideas of the integral calculus. Thought to be lost, the Archimedes palimpsest later resurfaced in 1998, when it was purchased by an anonymous private collector for two million dollars.

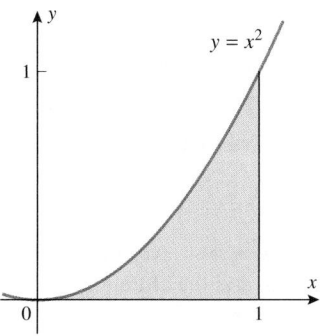

▲ **Figure 5.1.5**

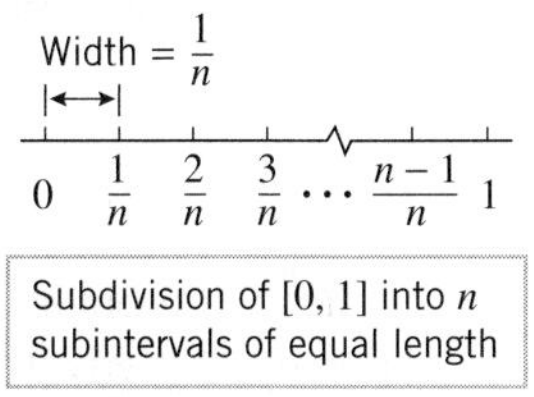

Width $= \frac{1}{n}$

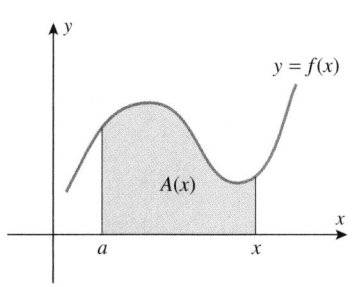

Subdivision of $[0, 1]$ into n subintervals of equal length

▲ **Figure 5.1.6**

TECHNOLOGY MASTERY

Use a calculating utility to compute the value of A_{10} in Table 5.1.2. Some calculating utilities have special commands for computing sums such as that in (1) for any specified value of n. If your utility has this feature, use it to compute A_{100} as well.

(Figure 5.1.6). We want to construct a rectangle over each of these subintervals whose height is the value of the function $f(x) = x^2$ at some point in the subinterval. To be specific, let us use the right endpoints, in which case the heights of our rectangles will be

$$\left(\frac{1}{n}\right)^2, \ \left(\frac{2}{n}\right)^2, \ \left(\frac{3}{n}\right)^2, \dots, \ 1^2$$

and since each rectangle has a base of width $1/n$, the total area A_n of the n rectangles will be

$$A_n = \left[\left(\frac{1}{n}\right)^2 + \left(\frac{2}{n}\right)^2 + \left(\frac{3}{n}\right)^2 + \cdots + 1^2\right]\left(\frac{1}{n}\right) \tag{1}$$

For example, if $n = 4$, then the total area of the four approximating rectangles would be

$$A_4 = \left[\left(\tfrac{1}{4}\right)^2 + \left(\tfrac{2}{4}\right)^2 + \left(\tfrac{3}{4}\right)^2 + 1^2\right]\left(\tfrac{1}{4}\right) = \tfrac{15}{32} = 0.46875$$

Table 5.1.2 shows the result of evaluating (1) on a computer for some increasingly large values of n. These computations suggest that the exact area is close to $\frac{1}{3}$. Later in this chapter we will prove that this area is exactly $\frac{1}{3}$ by showing that

$$\lim_{n \to \infty} A_n = \tfrac{1}{3}$$

Table 5.1.2

n	4	10	100	1000	10,000	100,000
A_n	0.468750	0.385000	0.338350	0.333834	0.333383	0.333338

■ **THE ANTIDERIVATIVE METHOD FOR FINDING AREAS**

Although the rectangle method is appealing intuitively, the limits that result can only be evaluated in certain cases. For this reason, progress on the area problem remained at a rudimentary level until the latter part of the seventeenth century when Isaac Newton and Gottfried Leibniz independently discovered a fundamental relationship between areas and derivatives. Briefly stated, they showed that if f is a nonnegative continuous function on the interval $[a, b]$, and if $A(x)$ denotes the area under the graph of f over the interval $[a, x]$, where x is any point in the interval $[a, b]$ (Figure 5.1.7), then

$$A'(x) = f(x) \tag{2}$$

The following example confirms Formula (2) in some cases where a formula for $A(x)$ can be found using elementary geometry.

▲ **Figure 5.1.7**

▶ **Example 1**   For each of the functions f, find the area $A(x)$ between the graph of f and the interval $[a, x] = [-1, x]$, and find the derivative $A'(x)$ of this area function.

(a) $f(x) = 2$ (b) $f(x) = x + 1$ (c) $f(x) = 2x + 3$

Solution (a).   From Figure 5.1.8a we see that

$$A(x) = 2(x - (-1)) = 2(x + 1) = 2x + 2$$

is the area of a rectangle of height 2 and base $x + 1$. For this area function,

$$A'(x) = 2 = f(x)$$

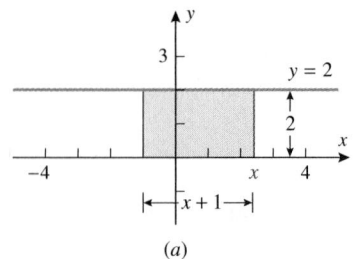

(a)

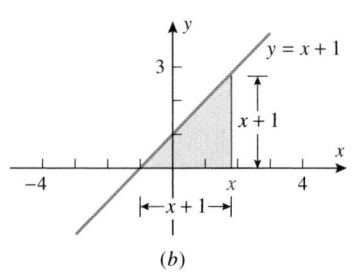

(b)

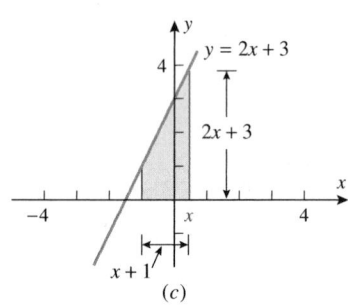

(c)

▲ **Figure 5.1.8**

How does the solution to Example 2 change if the interval $[0, 1]$ is replaced by the interval $[-1, 1]$?

Solution (b).   From Figure 5.1.8*b* we see that

$$A(x) = \frac{1}{2}(x + 1)(x + 1) = \frac{x^2}{2} + x + \frac{1}{2}$$

is the area of an isosceles right triangle with base and height equal to $x + 1$. For this area function,

$$A'(x) = x + 1 = f(x)$$

Solution (c).   Recall that the formula for the area of a trapezoid is $A = \frac{1}{2}(b + b')h$, where b and b' denote the lengths of the parallel sides of the trapezoid, and the altitude h denotes the distance between the parallel sides. From Figure 5.1.8*c* we see that

$$A(x) = \frac{1}{2}((2x + 3) + 1)(x - (-1)) = x^2 + 3x + 2$$

is the area of a trapezoid with parallel sides of lengths 1 and $2x + 3$ and with altitude $x - (-1) = x + 1$. For this area function,

$$A'(x) = 2x + 3 = f(x) \blacktriangleleft$$

Formula (2) is important because it relates the area function A and the region-bounding function f. Although a formula for $A(x)$ may be difficult to obtain directly, its derivative, $f(x)$, is given. If a formula for $A(x)$ can be recovered from the given formula for $A'(x)$, then the area under the graph of f over the interval $[a, b]$ can be obtained by computing $A(b)$.

The process of finding a function from its derivative is called ***antidifferentiation***, and a procedure for finding areas via antidifferentiation is called the ***antiderivative method***. To illustrate this method, let us revisit the problem of finding the area in Figure 5.1.5.

▶ **Example 2**   Use the antiderivative method to find the area under the graph of $y = x^2$ over the interval $[0, 1]$.

Solution.   Let x be any point in the interval $[0, 1]$, and let $A(x)$ denote the area under the graph of $f(x) = x^2$ over the interval $[0, x]$. It follows from (2) that

$$A'(x) = x^2 \tag{3}$$

To find $A(x)$ we must look for a function whose derivative is x^2. By guessing, we see that one such function is $\frac{1}{3}x^3$, so by Theorem 4.8.3

$$A(x) = \frac{1}{3}x^3 + C \tag{4}$$

for some real constant C. We can determine the specific value for C by considering the case where $x = 0$. In this case (4) implies that

$$A(0) = C \tag{5}$$

But if $x = 0$, then the interval $[0, x]$ reduces to a single point. If we agree that the area above a single point should be taken as zero, then $A(0) = 0$ and (5) implies that $C = 0$. Thus, it follows from (4) that

$$A(x) = \frac{1}{3}x^3$$

is the area function we are seeking. This implies that the area under the graph of $y = x^2$ over the interval $[0, 1]$ is

$$A(1) = \frac{1}{3}(1^3) = \frac{1}{3}$$

This is consistent with the result that we previously obtained numerically. ◀

As Example 2 illustrates, antidifferentiation is a process in which one tries to "undo" a differentiation. One of the objectives in this chapter is to develop efficient antidifferentiation procedures.

■ THE RECTANGLE METHOD AND THE ANTIDERIVATIVE METHOD COMPARED

The rectangle method and the antiderivative method provide two very different approaches to the area problem, each of which is important. The antiderivative method is usually the more efficient way to *compute* areas, but it is the rectangle method that is used to formally *define* the notion of area, thereby allowing us to prove mathematical results about areas. The underlying idea of the rectangle approach is also important because it can be adapted readily to such diverse problems as finding the volume of a solid, the length of a curve, the mass of an object, and the work done in pumping water out of a tank, to name a few.

✔ QUICK CHECK EXERCISES 5.1   *(See page 322 for answers.)*

1. Let R denote the region below the graph of $f(x) = \sqrt{1 - x^2}$ and above the interval $[-1, 1]$.
   (a) Use a geometric argument to find the area of R.
   (b) What estimate results if the area of R is approximated by the total area within the rectangles of the accompanying figure?

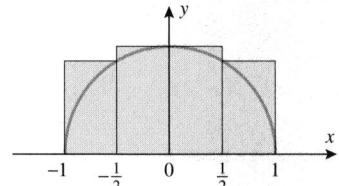

◀ **Figure Ex-1**

2. Suppose that when the area A between the graph of a function $y = f(x)$ and an interval $[a, b]$ is approximated by the areas of n rectangles, the total area of the rectangles is $A_n = 2 + (2/n)$, $n = 1, 2, \ldots$. Then, $A = $ _____.

3. The area under the graph of $y = x^2$ over the interval $[0, 3]$ is _____.

4. Find a formula for the area $A(x)$ between the graph of the function $f(x) = x$ and the interval $[0, x]$, and verify that $A'(x) = f(x)$.

5. The area under the graph of $y = f(x)$ over the interval $[0, x]$ is $A(x) = x + e^x - 1$. It follows that $f(x) = $ _____.

EXERCISE SET 5.1

1–12 Estimate the area between the graph of the function f and the interval $[a, b]$. Use an approximation scheme with n rectangles similar to our treatment of $f(x) = x^2$ in this section. If your calculating utility will perform automatic summations, estimate the specified area using $n = 10, 50$, and 100 rectangles. Otherwise, estimate this area using $n = 2, 5$, and 10 rectangles. ■

1. $f(x) = \sqrt{x}$; $[a, b] = [0, 1]$

2. $f(x) = \dfrac{1}{x + 1}$; $[a, b] = [0, 1]$

3. $f(x) = \sin x$; $[a, b] = [0, \pi]$

4. $f(x) = \cos x$; $[a, b] = [0, \pi/2]$

5. $f(x) = \dfrac{1}{x}$; $[a, b] = [1, 2]$

6. $f(x) = \cos x$; $[a, b] = [-\pi/2, \pi/2]$

7. $f(x) = \sqrt{1 - x^2}$; $[a, b] = [0, 1]$

8. $f(x) = \sqrt{1 - x^2}$; $[a, b] = [-1, 1]$

9. $f(x) = e^x$; $[a, b] = [-1, 1]$

10. $f(x) = \ln x$; $[a, b] = [1, 2]$

11. $f(x) = \sin^{-1} x$; $[a, b] = [0, 1]$

12. $f(x) = \tan^{-1} x$; $[a, b] = [0, 1]$

13–18 Graph each function over the specified interval. Then use simple area formulas from geometry to find the area function $A(x)$ that gives the area between the graph of the specified function f and the interval $[a, x]$. Confirm that $A'(x) = f(x)$ in every case. ■

13. $f(x) = 3$; $[a, x] = [1, x]$

14. $f(x) = 5$; $[a, x] = [2, x]$

15. $f(x) = 2x + 2$; $[a, x] = [0, x]$

16. $f(x) = 3x - 3$; $[a, x] = [1, x]$

17. $f(x) = 2x + 2$; $[a, x] = [1, x]$

18. $f(x) = 3x - 3$; $[a, x] = [2, x]$

19–22 True–False Determine whether the statement is true or false. Explain your answer. ■

19. If $A(n)$ denotes the area of a regular n-sided polygon inscribed in a circle of radius 2, then $\lim_{n \to +\infty} A(n) = 2\pi$.

20. If the area under the curve $y = x^2$ over an interval is approximated by the total area of a collection of rectangles, the approximation will be too large.

21. If $A(x)$ is the area under the graph of a nonnegative continuous function f over an interval $[a, x]$, then $A'(x) = f(x)$.

22. If $A(x)$ is the area under the graph of a nonnegative continuous function f over an interval $[a, x]$, then $A(x)$ will be a continuous function.

26. Let A denote the area between the graph of $f(x) = 1/x$ and the interval $[1, 2]$, and let B denote the area between the graph of f and the interval $\left[\frac{1}{2}, 1\right]$. Explain geometrically why $A = B$.

FOCUS ON CONCEPTS

23. Explain how to use the formula for $A(x)$ found in the solution to Example 2 to determine the area between the graph of $y = x^2$ and the interval $[3, 6]$.

24. Repeat Exercise 23 for the interval $[-3, 9]$.

25. Let A denote the area between the graph of $f(x) = \sqrt{x}$ and the interval $[0, 1]$, and let B denote the area between the graph of $f(x) = x^2$ and the interval $[0, 1]$. Explain geometrically why $A + B = 1$.

27–28 The area $A(x)$ under the graph of f and over the interval $[a, x]$ is given. Find the function f and the value of a. ▨

27. $A(x) = x^2 - 4$ **28.** $A(x) = x^2 - x$

29. Writing Compare and contrast the rectangle method and the antiderivative method.

30. Writing Suppose that f is a nonnegative continuous function on an interval $[a, b]$ and that $g(x) = f(x) + C$, where C is a positive constant. What will be the area of the region *between* the graphs of f and g?

✔**QUICK CHECK ANSWERS 5.1**

1. (a) $\dfrac{\pi}{2}$ (b) $1 + \dfrac{\sqrt{3}}{2}$ **2.** 2   **3.** 9   **4.** $A(x) = \dfrac{x^2}{2}$; $A'(x) = \dfrac{2x}{2} = x = f(x)$ **5.** $e^x + 1$

5.2 THE INDEFINITE INTEGRAL

In the last section we saw how antidifferentiation could be used to find exact areas. In this section we will develop some fundamental results about antidifferentiation.

▨ **ANTIDERIVATIVES**

5.2.1 DEFINITION   A function F is called an *antiderivative* of a function f on a given open interval if $F'(x) = f(x)$ for all x in the interval.

For example, the function $F(x) = \frac{1}{3}x^3$ is an antiderivative of $f(x) = x^2$ on the interval $(-\infty, +\infty)$ because for each x in this interval

$$F'(x) = \frac{d}{dx}\left[\frac{1}{3}x^3\right] = x^2 = f(x)$$

However, $F(x) = \frac{1}{3}x^3$ is not the only antiderivative of f on this interval. If we add any constant C to $\frac{1}{3}x^3$, then the function $G(x) = \frac{1}{3}x^3 + C$ is also an antiderivative of f on $(-\infty, +\infty)$, since

$$G'(x) = \frac{d}{dx}\left[\frac{1}{3}x^3 + C\right] = x^2 + 0 = f(x)$$

In general, once any single antiderivative is known, other antiderivatives can be obtained by adding constants to the known antiderivative. Thus,

$$\tfrac{1}{3}x^3, \quad \tfrac{1}{3}x^3 + 2, \quad \tfrac{1}{3}x^3 - 5, \quad \tfrac{1}{3}x^3 + \sqrt{2}$$

are all antiderivatives of $f(x) = x^2$.

It is reasonable to ask if there are antiderivatives of a function f that cannot be obtained by adding some constant to a known antiderivative F. The answer is *no*—once a single antiderivative of f on an open interval is known, all other antiderivatives on that interval are obtainable by adding constants to the known antiderivative. This is so because Theorem 4.8.3 tells us that if two functions have the same derivative on an open interval, then the functions differ by a constant on the interval. The following theorem summarizes these observations.

5.2.2 THEOREM *If $F(x)$ is any antiderivative of $f(x)$ on an open interval, then for any constant C the function $F(x) + C$ is also an antiderivative on that interval. Moreover, each antiderivative of $f(x)$ on the interval can be expressed in the form $F(x) + C$ by choosing the constant C appropriately.*

■ **THE INDEFINITE INTEGRAL**

The process of finding antiderivatives is called ***antidifferentiation*** or ***integration***. Thus, if

$$\frac{d}{dx}[F(x)] = f(x) \tag{1}$$

then ***integrating*** (or ***antidifferentiating***) the function $f(x)$ produces an antiderivative of the form $F(x) + C$. To emphasize this process, Equation (1) is recast using ***integral notation***,

$$\int f(x)\,dx = F(x) + C \tag{2}$$

where C is understood to represent an arbitrary constant. It is important to note that (1) and (2) are just different notations to express the same fact. For example,

$$\int x^2\,dx = \tfrac{1}{3}x^3 + C \quad \text{is equivalent to} \quad \frac{d}{dx}\left[\tfrac{1}{3}x^3\right] = x^2$$

Note that if we differentiate an antiderivative of $f(x)$, we obtain $f(x)$ back again. Thus,

$$\frac{d}{dx}\left[\int f(x)\,dx\right] = f(x) \tag{3}$$

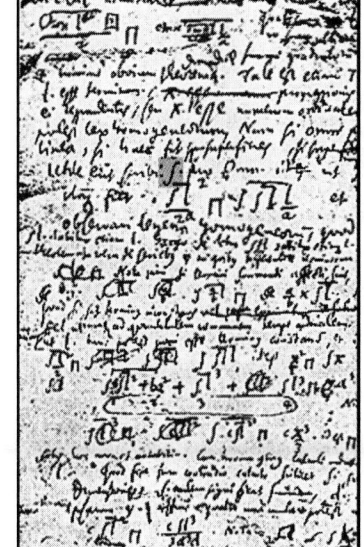

Reproduced from C. I. Gerhardt's "Briefwechsel von G. W. Leibniz mit Mathematikern (1899)."

Extract from the manuscript of Leibniz dated October 29, 1675 in which the integral sign first appeared (see yellow highlight).

The expression $\int f(x)\,dx$ is called an ***indefinite integral***. The adjective "indefinite" emphasizes that the result of antidifferentiation is a "generic" function, described only up to a constant term. The "elongated s" that appears on the left side of (2) is called an ***integral sign***,[*] the function $f(x)$ is called the ***integrand***, and the constant C is called the ***constant of integration***. Equation (2) should be read as:

The integral of $f(x)$ with respect to x is equal to $F(x)$ plus a constant.

The differential symbol, dx, in the differentiation and antidifferentiation operations

$$\frac{d}{dx}[\ \ ] \quad \text{and} \quad \int [\ \ ]\,dx$$

---

[*]This notation was devised by Leibniz. In his early papers Leibniz used the notation "omn." (an abbreviation for the Latin word "omnes") to denote integration. Then on October 29, 1675 he wrote, "It will be useful to write $\int$ for omn., thus $\int l$ for omn. $l\ldots$." Two or three weeks later he refined the notation further and wrote $\int[\ \ ]\,dx$ rather than $\int$ alone. This notation is so useful and so powerful that its development by Leibniz must be regarded as a major milestone in the history of mathematics and science.

serves to identify the independent variable. If an independent variable other than x is used, say t, then the notation must be adjusted appropriately. Thus,

$$\frac{d}{dt}[F(t)] = f(t) \quad \text{and} \quad \int f(t)\,dt = F(t) + C$$

are equivalent statements. Here are some examples of derivative formulas and their equivalent integration formulas:

DERIVATIVE FORMULA	EQUIVALENT INTEGRATION FORMULA
$\dfrac{d}{dx}[x^3] = 3x^2$	$\displaystyle\int 3x^2\,dx = x^3 + C$
$\dfrac{d}{dx}[\sqrt{x}] = \dfrac{1}{2\sqrt{x}}$	$\displaystyle\int \dfrac{1}{2\sqrt{x}}\,dx = \sqrt{x} + C$
$\dfrac{d}{dt}[\tan t] = \sec^2 t$	$\displaystyle\int \sec^2 t\,dt = \tan t + C$
$\dfrac{d}{du}[u^{3/2}] = \dfrac{3}{2}u^{1/2}$	$\displaystyle\int \dfrac{3}{2}u^{1/2}\,du = u^{3/2} + C$

For simplicity, the dx is sometimes absorbed into the integrand. For example,

$$\int 1\,dx \quad \text{can be written as} \quad \int dx$$

$$\int \frac{1}{x^2}\,dx \quad \text{can be written as} \quad \int \frac{dx}{x^2}$$

■ INTEGRATION FORMULAS

Integration is essentially educated guesswork—given the derivative f of a function F, one tries to guess what the function F is. However, many basic integration formulas can be obtained directly from their companion differentiation formulas. Some of the most important are given in Table 5.2.1.

Table 5.2.1
INTEGRATION FORMULAS

DIFFERENTIATION FORMULA	INTEGRATION FORMULA	DIFFERENTIATION FORMULA	INTEGRATION FORMULA
1. $\dfrac{d}{dx}[x] = 1$	$\displaystyle\int dx = x + C$	8. $\dfrac{d}{dx}[-\csc x] = \csc x \cot x$	$\displaystyle\int \csc x \cot x\,dx = -\csc x + C$
2. $\dfrac{d}{dx}\left[\dfrac{x^{r+1}}{r+1}\right] = x^r \ (r \neq -1)$	$\displaystyle\int x^r\,dx = \dfrac{x^{r+1}}{r+1} + C \ (r \neq -1)$	9. $\dfrac{d}{dx}[e^x] = e^x$	$\displaystyle\int e^x\,dx = e^x + C$
3. $\dfrac{d}{dx}[\sin x] = \cos x$	$\displaystyle\int \cos x\,dx = \sin x + C$	10. $\dfrac{d}{dx}\left[\dfrac{b^x}{\ln b}\right] = b^x \ (0 < b, b \neq 1)$	$\displaystyle\int b^x\,dx = \dfrac{b^x}{\ln b} + C \ (0 < b, b \neq 1)$
4. $\dfrac{d}{dx}[-\cos x] = \sin x$	$\displaystyle\int \sin x\,dx = -\cos x + C$	11. $\dfrac{d}{dx}[\ln|x|] = \dfrac{1}{x}$	$\displaystyle\int \dfrac{1}{x}\,dx = \ln|x| + C$
5. $\dfrac{d}{dx}[\tan x] = \sec^2 x$	$\displaystyle\int \sec^2 x\,dx = \tan x + C$	12. $\dfrac{d}{dx}[\tan^{-1} x] = \dfrac{1}{1+x^2}$	$\displaystyle\int \dfrac{1}{1+x^2}\,dx = \tan^{-1} x + C$
6. $\dfrac{d}{dx}[-\cot x] = \csc^2 x$	$\displaystyle\int \csc^2 x\,dx = -\cot x + C$	13. $\dfrac{d}{dx}[\sin^{-1} x] = \dfrac{1}{\sqrt{1-x^2}}$	$\displaystyle\int \dfrac{1}{\sqrt{1-x^2}}\,dx = \sin^{-1} x + C$
7. $\dfrac{d}{dx}[\sec x] = \sec x \tan x$	$\displaystyle\int \sec x \tan x\,dx = \sec x + C$	14. $\dfrac{d}{dx}[\sec^{-1}|x|] = \dfrac{1}{x\sqrt{x^2-1}}$	$\displaystyle\int \dfrac{1}{x\sqrt{x^2-1}}\,dx = \sec^{-1}|x| + C$

See Exercise 72 for a justification of Formula 14 in Table 5.2.1.

▶ **Example 1** The second integration formula in Table 5.2.1 will be easier to remember if you express it in words:

To integrate a power of x (other than −1), add 1 to the exponent and divide by the new exponent.

Although Formula 2 in Table 5.2.1 is not applicable to integrating x^{-1}, this function can be integrated by rewriting the integral in Formula 11 as

$$\int \frac{1}{x}\,dx = \int x^{-1}\,dx = \ln|x| + C$$

Here are some examples:

$$\int x^2\,dx = \frac{x^3}{3} + C \qquad \boxed{r = 2}$$

$$\int x^3\,dx = \frac{x^4}{4} + C \qquad \boxed{r = 3}$$

$$\int \frac{1}{x^5}\,dx = \int x^{-5}\,dx = \frac{x^{-5+1}}{-5+1} + C = -\frac{1}{4x^4} + C \qquad \boxed{r = -5}$$

$$\int \sqrt{x}\,dx = \int x^{\frac{1}{2}}\,dx = \frac{x^{\frac{1}{2}+1}}{\frac{1}{2}+1} + C = \tfrac{2}{3}x^{\frac{3}{2}} + C = \tfrac{2}{3}(\sqrt{x})^3 + C \qquad \boxed{r = \tfrac{1}{2}} ◀$$

■ **PROPERTIES OF THE INDEFINITE INTEGRAL**

Our first properties of antiderivatives follow directly from the simple constant factor, sum, and difference rules for derivatives.

> **5.2.3 THEOREM** *Suppose that $F(x)$ and $G(x)$ are antiderivatives of $f(x)$ and $g(x)$, respectively, and that c is a constant. Then:*
>
> (a) *A constant factor can be moved through an integral sign; that is,*
> $$\int cf(x)\,dx = cF(x) + C$$
>
> (b) *An antiderivative of a sum is the sum of the antiderivatives; that is,*
> $$\int [f(x) + g(x)]\,dx = F(x) + G(x) + C$$
>
> (c) *An antiderivative of a difference is the difference of the antiderivatives; that is,*
> $$\int [f(x) - g(x)]\,dx = F(x) - G(x) + C$$

PROOF In general, to establish the validity of an equation of the form

$$\int h(x)\,dx = H(x) + C$$

one must show that

$$\frac{d}{dx}[H(x)] = h(x)$$

We are given that $F(x)$ and $G(x)$ are antiderivatives of $f(x)$ and $g(x)$, respectively, so we know that

$$\frac{d}{dx}[F(x)] = f(x) \quad \text{and} \quad \frac{d}{dx}[G(x)] = g(x)$$

Thus,

$$\frac{d}{dx}[cF(x)] = c\frac{d}{dx}[F(x)] = cf(x)$$

$$\frac{d}{dx}[F(x) + G(x)] = \frac{d}{dx}[F(x)] + \frac{d}{dx}[G(x)] = f(x) + g(x)$$

$$\frac{d}{dx}[F(x) - G(x)] = \frac{d}{dx}[F(x)] - \frac{d}{dx}[G(x)] = f(x) - g(x)$$

which proves the three statements of the theorem. ■

The statements in Theorem 5.2.3 can be summarized by the following formulas:

$$\int cf(x)\,dx = c\int f(x)\,dx \tag{4}$$

$$\int [f(x) + g(x)]\,dx = \int f(x)\,dx + \int g(x)\,dx \tag{5}$$

$$\int [f(x) - g(x)]\,dx = \int f(x)\,dx - \int g(x)\,dx \tag{6}$$

However, these equations must be applied carefully to avoid errors and unnecessary complexities arising from the constants of integration. For example, if you use (4) to integrate $2x$ by writing

$$\int 2x\,dx = 2\int x\,dx = 2\left(\frac{x^2}{2} + C\right) = x^2 + 2C$$

then you will have an unnecessarily complicated form of the arbitrary constant. This kind of problem can be avoided by inserting the constant of integration in the final result rather than in intermediate calculations. Exercises 65 and 66 explore how careless application of these formulas can lead to errors.

▶ **Example 2** Evaluate

$$\text{(a)} \int 4\cos x\,dx \qquad \text{(b)} \int (x + x^2)\,dx$$

Solution (a). Since $F(x) = \sin x$ is an antiderivative for $f(x) = \cos x$ (Table 5.2.1), we obtain

$$\int 4\cos x\,dx = 4\int \cos x\,dx = 4\sin x + C$$
$$\boxed{(4)}$$

Solution (b). From Table 5.2.1 we obtain

$$\int (x + x^2)\,dx = \int x\,dx + \int x^2\,dx = \frac{x^2}{2} + \frac{x^3}{3} + C \ \blacktriangleleft$$
$$\boxed{(5)}$$

Parts (b) and (c) of Theorem 5.2.3 can be extended to more than two functions, which in combination with part (a) results in the following general formula:

$$\int [c_1 f_1(x) + c_2 f_2(x) + \cdots + c_n f_n(x)]\,dx$$
$$= c_1 \int f_1(x)\,dx + c_2 \int f_2(x)\,dx + \cdots + c_n \int f_n(x)\,dx \tag{7}$$

▶ **Example 3**

$$\int (3x^6 - 2x^2 + 7x + 1)\, dx = 3\int x^6\, dx - 2\int x^2\, dx + 7\int x\, dx + \int 1\, dx$$

$$= \frac{3x^7}{7} - \frac{2x^3}{3} + \frac{7x^2}{2} + x + C \blacktriangleleft$$

Sometimes it is useful to rewrite an integrand in a different form before performing the integration. This is illustrated in the following example.

▶ **Example 4** Evaluate

(a) $\displaystyle\int \frac{\cos x}{\sin^2 x}\, dx$ (b) $\displaystyle\int \frac{t^2 - 2t^4}{t^4}\, dt$ (c) $\displaystyle\int \frac{x^2}{x^2 + 1}\, dx$

Solution (*a*).

$$\int \frac{\cos x}{\sin^2 x}\, dx = \int \frac{1}{\sin x}\frac{\cos x}{\sin x}\, dx = \int \csc x \cot x\, dx = -\csc x + C$$

> Formula 8 in Table 5.2.1

Solution (*b*).

$$\int \frac{t^2 - 2t^4}{t^4}\, dt = \int \left(\frac{1}{t^2} - 2\right) dt = \int (t^{-2} - 2)\, dt$$

$$= \frac{t^{-1}}{-1} - 2t + C = -\frac{1}{t} - 2t + C$$

Solution (*c*). By adding and subtracting 1 from the numerator of the integrand, we can rewrite the integral in a form in which Formulas 1 and 12 of Table 5.2.1 can be applied:

$$\int \frac{x^2}{x^2 + 1}\, dx = \int \left(\frac{x^2 + 1}{x^2 + 1} - \frac{1}{x^2 + 1}\right) dx$$

$$= \int \left(1 - \frac{1}{x^2 + 1}\right) dx = x - \tan^{-1} x + C \blacktriangleleft$$

Perform the integration in part (c) by first performing a long division on the integrand.

■ **INTEGRAL CURVES**

Graphs of antiderivatives of a function f are called *integral curves* of f. We know from Theorem 5.2.2 that if $y = F(x)$ is any integral curve of $f(x)$, then all other integral curves are vertical translations of this curve, since they have equations of the form $y = F(x) + C$. For example, $y = \frac{1}{3}x^3$ is one integral curve for $f(x) = x^2$, so all the other integral curves have equations of the form $y = \frac{1}{3}x^3 + C$; conversely, the graph of any equation of this form is an integral curve (Figure 5.2.1).

In many problems one is interested in finding a function whose derivative satisfies specified conditions. The following example illustrates a geometric problem of this type.

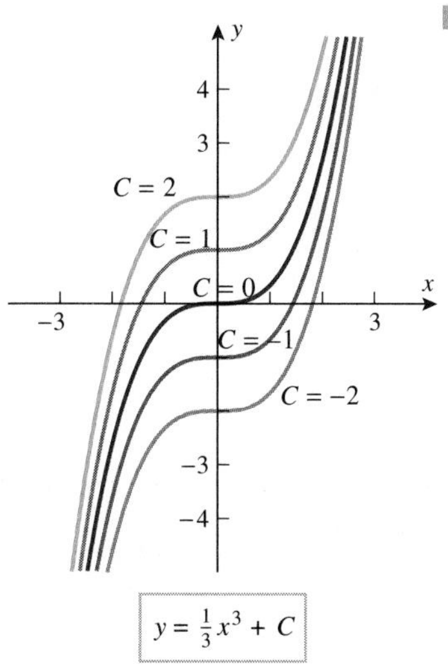

▶ **Example 5** Suppose that a curve $y = f(x)$ in the xy-plane has the property that at each point (x, y) on the curve, the tangent line has slope x^2. Find an equation for the curve given that it passes through the point $(2, 1)$.

Solution. Since the slope of the line tangent to $y = f(x)$ is dy/dx, we have $dy/dx = x^2$, and

$$y = \int x^2\, dx = \frac{1}{3}x^3 + C$$

$y = \frac{1}{3}x^3 + C$

▲ **Figure 5.2.1**

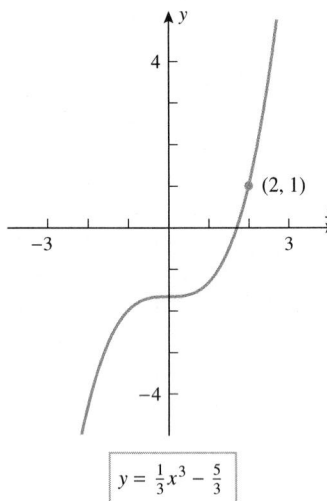

$$y = \frac{1}{3}x^3 - \frac{5}{3}$$

▲ **Figure 5.2.2**

Since the curve passes through $(2, 1)$, a specific value for C can be found by using the fact that $y = 1$ if $x = 2$. Substituting these values in the above equation yields

$$1 = \tfrac{1}{3}(2^3) + C \quad \text{or} \quad C = -\tfrac{5}{3}$$

so an equation of the curve is

$$y = \tfrac{1}{3}x^3 - \tfrac{5}{3}$$

(Figure 5.2.2). ◀

■ INTEGRATION FROM THE VIEWPOINT OF DIFFERENTIAL EQUATIONS

We will now consider another way of looking at integration that will be useful in our later work. Suppose that $f(x)$ is a known function and we are interested in finding a function $F(x)$ such that $y = F(x)$ satisfies the equation

$$\frac{dy}{dx} = f(x) \tag{8}$$

The solutions of this equation are the antiderivatives of $f(x)$, and we know that these can be obtained by integrating $f(x)$. For example, the solutions of the equation

$$\frac{dy}{dx} = x^2 \tag{9}$$

are

$$y = \int x^2 \, dx = \frac{x^3}{3} + C$$

Equation (8) is called a ***differential equation*** because it involves a derivative of an unknown function. Differential equations are different from the kinds of equations we have encountered so far in that the unknown is a *function* and not a *number* as in an equation such as $x^2 + 5x - 6 = 0$.

Sometimes we will not be interested in finding all of the solutions of (8), but rather we will want only the solution whose graph passes through a specified point (x_0, y_0). For example, in Example 5 we solved (9) for the integral curve that passed through the point $(2, 1)$.

For simplicity, it is common in the study of differential equations to denote a solution of $dy/dx = f(x)$ as $y(x)$ rather than $F(x)$, as earlier. With this notation, the problem of finding a function $y(x)$ whose derivative is $f(x)$ and whose graph passes through the point (x_0, y_0) is expressed as

$$\frac{dy}{dx} = f(x), \quad y(x_0) = y_0 \tag{10}$$

This is called an ***initial-value problem***, and the requirement that $y(x_0) = y_0$ is called the ***initial condition*** for the problem.

▶ **Example 6**   Solve the initial-value problem

$$\frac{dy}{dx} = \cos x, \quad y(0) = 1$$

Solution.   The solution of the differential equation is

$$y = \int \cos x \, dx = \sin x + C \tag{11}$$

The initial condition $y(0) = 1$ implies that $y = 1$ if $x = 0$; substituting these values in (11) yields

$$1 = \sin(0) + C \quad \text{or} \quad C = 1$$

Thus, the solution of the initial-value problem is $y = \sin x + 1$. ◀

■ **SLOPE FIELDS**

If we interpret dy/dx as the slope of a tangent line, then at a point (x, y) on an integral curve of the equation $dy/dx = f(x)$, the slope of the tangent line is $f(x)$. What is interesting about this is that the slopes of the tangent lines to the integral curves can be obtained without actually solving the differential equation. For example, if

$$\frac{dy}{dx} = \sqrt{x^2 + 1}$$

then we know without solving the equation that at the point where $x = 1$ the tangent line to an integral curve has slope $\sqrt{1^2 + 1} = \sqrt{2}$; and more generally, at a point where $x = a$, the tangent line to an integral curve has slope $\sqrt{a^2 + 1}$.

A geometric description of the integral curves of a differential equation $dy/dx = f(x)$ can be obtained by choosing a rectangular grid of points in the xy-plane, calculating the slopes of the tangent lines to the integral curves at the gridpoints, and drawing small portions of the tangent lines through those points. The resulting picture, which is called a *slope field* or *direction field* for the equation, shows the "direction" of the integral curves at the gridpoints. With sufficiently many gridpoints it is often possible to visualize the integral curves themselves; for example, Figure 5.2.3a shows a slope field for the differential equation $dy/dx = x^2$, and Figure 5.2.3b shows that same field with the integral curves imposed on it—the more gridpoints that are used, the more completely the slope field reveals the shape of the integral curves. However, the amount of computation can be considerable, so computers are usually used when slope fields with many gridpoints are needed.

Slope fields will be studied in more detail later in the text.

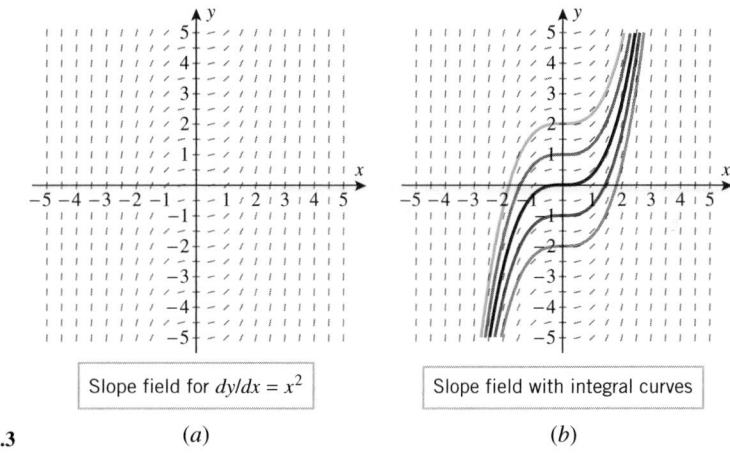

Slope field for $dy/dx = x^2$ Slope field with integral curves

▶ **Figure 5.2.3**   (a)   (b)

✔ **QUICK CHECK EXERCISES 5.2**   (*See page 332 for answers.*)

1. A function F is an antiderivative of a function f on an interval if _____ for all x in the interval.

2. Write an equivalent integration formula for each given derivative formula.

   (a) $\dfrac{d}{dx}[\sqrt{x}] = \dfrac{1}{2\sqrt{x}}$ (b) $\dfrac{d}{dx}[e^{4x}] = 4e^{4x}$

3. Evaluate the integrals.

   (a) $\displaystyle\int [x^3 + x + 5]\,dx$ (b) $\displaystyle\int [\sec^2 x - \csc x \cot x]\,dx$

4. The graph of $y = x^2 + x$ is an integral curve for the func-

tion $f(x) = $ _____. If G is a function whose graph is also an integral curve for f, and if $G(1) = 5$, then $G(x) = $ _____.

5. A slope field for the differential equation

   $$\frac{dy}{dx} = \frac{2x}{x^2 - 4}$$

   has a line segment with slope _____ through the point $(0, 5)$ and has a line segment with slope _____ through the point $(-4, 1)$.

EXERCISE SET 5.2   ◩ Graphing Utility   [C] CAS

1. In each part, confirm that the formula is correct, and state a corresponding integration formula.

   (a) $\dfrac{d}{dx}[\sqrt{1+x^2}] = \dfrac{x}{\sqrt{1+x^2}}$

   (b) $\dfrac{d}{dx}[xe^x] = (x+1)e^x$

2. In each part, confirm that the stated formula is correct by differentiating.

   (a) $\displaystyle\int x \sin x \, dx = \sin x - x \cos x + C$

   (b) $\displaystyle\int \dfrac{dx}{(1-x^2)^{3/2}} = \dfrac{x}{\sqrt{1-x^2}} + C$

FOCUS ON CONCEPTS

3. What is a *constant of integration*? Why does an answer to an integration problem involve a constant of integration?

4. What is an *integral curve* of a function f? How are two integral curves of a function f related?

5–8 Find the derivative and state a corresponding integration formula. ◾

5. $\dfrac{d}{dx}[\sqrt{x^3+5}]$

6. $\dfrac{d}{dx}\left[\dfrac{x}{x^2+3}\right]$

7. $\dfrac{d}{dx}[\sin(2\sqrt{x})]$

8. $\dfrac{d}{dx}[\sin x - x \cos x]$

9–10 Evaluate the integral by rewriting the integrand appropriately, if required, and applying the power rule (Formula 2 in Table 5.2.1). ◾

9. (a) $\displaystyle\int x^8 \, dx$ (b) $\displaystyle\int x^{5/7} \, dx$ (c) $\displaystyle\int x^3 \sqrt{x} \, dx$

10. (a) $\displaystyle\int \sqrt[3]{x^2} \, dx$ (b) $\displaystyle\int \dfrac{1}{x^6} \, dx$ (c) $\displaystyle\int x^{-7/8} \, dx$

11–14 Evaluate each integral by applying Theorem 5.2.3 and Formula 2 in Table 5.2.1 appropriately. ◾

11. $\displaystyle\int \left[5x + \dfrac{2}{3x^5}\right] dx$

12. $\displaystyle\int \left[x^{-1/2} - 3x^{7/5} + \tfrac{1}{9}\right] dx$

13. $\displaystyle\int [x^{-3} - 3x^{1/4} + 8x^2] \, dx$

14. $\displaystyle\int \left[\dfrac{10}{y^{3/4}} - \sqrt[3]{y} + \dfrac{4}{\sqrt{y}}\right] dy$

15–34 Evaluate the integral and check your answer by differentiating. ◾

15. $\displaystyle\int x(1+x^3) \, dx$

16. $\displaystyle\int (2+y^2)^2 \, dy$

17. $\displaystyle\int x^{1/3}(2-x)^2 \, dx$

18. $\displaystyle\int (1+x^2)(2-x) \, dx$

19. $\displaystyle\int \dfrac{x^5 + 2x^2 - 1}{x^4} \, dx$

20. $\displaystyle\int \dfrac{1 - 2t^3}{t^3} \, dt$

21. $\displaystyle\int \left[\dfrac{2}{x} + 3e^x\right] dx$

22. $\displaystyle\int \left[\dfrac{1}{2t} - \sqrt{2}e^t\right] dt$

23. $\displaystyle\int [3\sin x - 2\sec^2 x] \, dx$

24. $\displaystyle\int [\csc^2 t - \sec t \tan t] \, dt$

25. $\displaystyle\int \sec x(\sec x + \tan x) \, dx$

26. $\displaystyle\int \csc x(\sin x + \cot x) \, dx$

27. $\displaystyle\int \dfrac{\sec\theta}{\cos\theta} \, d\theta$

28. $\displaystyle\int \dfrac{dy}{\csc y}$

29. $\displaystyle\int \dfrac{\sin x}{\cos^2 x} \, dx$

30. $\displaystyle\int \left[\phi + \dfrac{2}{\sin^2\phi}\right] d\phi$

31. $\displaystyle\int [1 + \sin^2\theta \csc\theta] \, d\theta$

32. $\displaystyle\int \dfrac{\sec x + \cos x}{2\cos x} \, dx$

33. $\displaystyle\int \left[\dfrac{1}{2\sqrt{1-x^2}} - \dfrac{3}{1+x^2}\right] dx$

34. $\displaystyle\int \left[\dfrac{4}{x\sqrt{x^2-1}} + \dfrac{1+x+x^3}{1+x^2}\right] dx$

35. Evaluate the integral

   $$\int \dfrac{1}{1+\sin x} \, dx$$

   by multiplying the numerator and denominator by an appropriate expression.

36. Use the double-angle formula $\cos 2x = 2\cos^2 x - 1$ to evaluate the integral

   $$\int \dfrac{1}{1+\cos 2x} \, dx$$

37–40 True–False Determine whether the statement is true or false. Explain your answer. ◾

37. If $F(x)$ is an antiderivative of $f(x)$, then

   $$\int f(x) \, dx = F(x) + C$$

38. If C denotes a constant of integration, the two formulas

   $$\int \cos x \, dx = \sin x + C$$

   $$\int \cos x \, dx = (\sin x + \pi) + C$$

   are both correct equations.

39. The function $f(x) = e^{-x} + 1$ is a solution to the initial-value problem

   $$\dfrac{dy}{dx} = -\dfrac{1}{e^x}, \quad y(0) = 1$$

40. Every integral curve of the slope field

   $$\dfrac{dy}{dx} = \dfrac{1}{\sqrt{x^2+1}}$$

   is the graph of an increasing function of x.

41. Use a graphing utility to generate some representative integral curves of the function $f(x) = 5x^4 - \sec^2 x$ over the interval $(-\pi/2, \pi/2)$.

42. Use a graphing utility to generate some representative integral curves of the function $f(x) = (x - 1)/x$ over the interval $(0, 5)$.

43–46 Solve the initial-value problems. ■

43. (a) $\dfrac{dy}{dx} = \sqrt[3]{x}, \ y(1) = 2$

(b) $\dfrac{dy}{dt} = \sin t + 1, \ y\left(\dfrac{\pi}{3}\right) = \dfrac{1}{2}$

(c) $\dfrac{dy}{dx} = \dfrac{x + 1}{\sqrt{x}}, \ y(1) = 0$

44. (a) $\dfrac{dy}{dx} = \dfrac{1}{(2x)^3}, \ y(1) = 0$

(b) $\dfrac{dy}{dt} = \sec^2 t - \sin t, \ y\left(\dfrac{\pi}{4}\right) = 1$

(c) $\dfrac{dy}{dx} = x^2 \sqrt{x^3}, \ y(0) = 0$

45. (a) $\dfrac{dy}{dx} = 4e^x, \ y(0) = 1$ (b) $\dfrac{dy}{dt} = \dfrac{1}{t}, \ y(-1) = 5$

46. (a) $\dfrac{dy}{dt} = \dfrac{3}{\sqrt{1 - t^2}}, \ y\left(\dfrac{\sqrt{3}}{2}\right) = 0$

(b) $\dfrac{dy}{dx} = \dfrac{x^2 - 1}{x^2 + 1}, \ y(1) = \dfrac{\pi}{2}$

47–50 A particle moves along an s-axis with position function $s = s(t)$ and velocity function $v(t) = s'(t)$. Use the given information to find $s(t)$. ■

47. $v(t) = 32t; \ s(0) = 20$ **48.** $v(t) = \cos t; \ s(0) = 2$

49. $v(t) = 3\sqrt{t}; \ s(4) = 1$ **50.** $v(t) = 3e^t; \ s(1) = 0$

51. Find the general form of a function whose second derivative is $\sqrt{x}$. [*Hint:* Solve the equation $f''(x) = \sqrt{x}$ for $f(x)$ by integrating both sides twice.]

52. Find a function f such that $f''(x) = x + \cos x$ and such that $f(0) = 1$ and $f'(0) = 2$. [*Hint:* Integrate both sides of the equation twice.]

53–57 Find an equation of the curve that satisfies the given conditions. ■

53. At each point (x, y) on the curve the slope is $2x + 1$; the curve passes through the point $(-3, 0)$.

54. At each point (x, y) on the curve the slope is $(x + 1)^2$; the curve passes through the point $(-2, 8)$.

55. At each point (x, y) on the curve the slope is $- \sin x$; the curve passes through the point $(0, 2)$.

56. At each point (x, y) on the curve the slope equals the square of the distance between the point and the y-axis; the point $(-1, 2)$ is on the curve.

57. At each point (x, y) on the curve, y satisfies the condition $d^2y/dx^2 = 6x$; the line $y = 5 - 3x$ is tangent to the curve at the point where $x = 1$.

58. In each part, use a CAS to solve the initial-value problem.

(a) $\dfrac{dy}{dx} = x^2 \cos 3x, \ y(\pi/2) = -1$

(b) $\dfrac{dy}{dx} = \dfrac{x^3}{(4 + x^2)^{3/2}}, \ y(0) = -2$

59. (a) Use a graphing utility to generate a slope field for the differential equation $dy/dx = x$ in the region $-5 \le x \le 5$ and $-5 \le y \le 5$.

(b) Graph some representative integral curves of the function $f(x) = x$.

(c) Find an equation for the integral curve that passes through the point $(2, 1)$.

60. (a) Use a graphing utility to generate a slope field for the differential equation $dy/dx = e^x/2$ in the region $-1 \le x \le 4$ and $-1 \le y \le 4$.

(b) Graph some representative integral curves of the function $f(x) = e^x/2$.

(c) Find an equation for the integral curve that passes through the point $(0, 1)$.

61–64 The given slope field figure corresponds to one of the differential equations below. Identify the differential equation that matches the figure, and sketch solution curves through the highlighted points.

(a) $\dfrac{dy}{dx} = 2$ (b) $\dfrac{dy}{dx} = -x$

(c) $\dfrac{dy}{dx} = x^2 - 4$ (d) $\dfrac{dy}{dx} = e^{x/3}$ ■

61.   **62.**

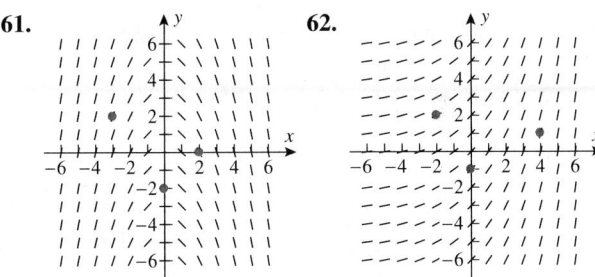

63.   **64.**

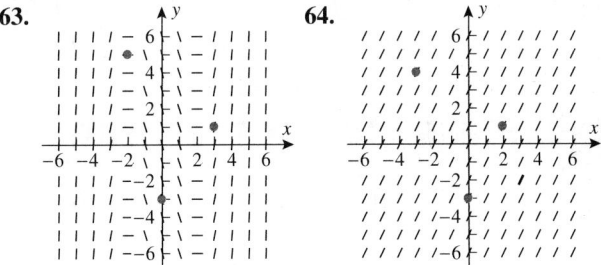

FOCUS ON CONCEPTS

65. Critique the following "proof" that an arbitrary constant must be zero:

$$C = \int 0 \, dx = \int 0 \cdot 0 \, dx = 0 \int 0 \, dx = 0$$

66. Critique the following "proof" that an arbitrary constant must be zero:

$$0 = \left(\int x \, dx \right) - \left(\int x \, dx \right)$$

$$= \int (x - x) \, dx = \int 0 \, dx = C$$

67. (a) Show that

$$F(x) = \tan^{-1} x \quad \text{and} \quad G(x) = -\tan^{-1}(1/x)$$

differ by a constant on the interval $(0, +\infty)$ by showing that they are antiderivatives of the same function.

(b) Find the constant C such that $F(x) - G(x) = C$ by evaluating the functions $F(x)$ and $G(x)$ at a particular value of x.

(c) Check your answer to part (b) by using trigonometric identities.

68. Let F and G be the functions defined by

$$F(x) = \frac{x^2 + 3x}{x} \quad \text{and} \quad G(x) = \begin{cases} x + 3, & x > 0 \\ x, & x < 0 \end{cases}$$

(a) Show that F and G have the same derivative.

(b) Show that $G(x) \neq F(x) + C$ for any constant C.

(c) Do parts (a) and (b) contradict Theorem 5.2.2? Explain.

69–70 Use a trigonometric identity to evaluate the integral. ■

69. $\displaystyle\int \tan^2 x \, dx$ **70.** $\displaystyle\int \cot^2 x \, dx$

71. Use the identities $\cos 2\theta = 1 - 2\sin^2 \theta = 2\cos^2 \theta - 1$ to help evaluate the integrals

(a) $\displaystyle\int \sin^2(x/2) \, dx$ (b) $\displaystyle\int \cos^2(x/2) \, dx$

72. Recall that

$$\frac{d}{dx}[\sec^{-1} x] = \frac{1}{|x|\sqrt{x^2 - 1}}$$

Use this to verify Formula 14 in Table 5.2.1.

73. The speed of sound in air at $0°C$ (or 273 K on the Kelvin scale) is 1087 ft/s, but the speed v increases as the temperature T rises. Experimentation has shown that the rate of change of v with respect to T is

$$\frac{dv}{dT} = \frac{1087}{2\sqrt{273}} T^{-1/2}$$

where v is in feet per second and T is in kelvins (K). Find a formula that expresses v as a function of T.

74. Suppose that a uniform metal rod 50 cm long is insulated laterally, and the temperatures at the exposed ends are maintained at $25°C$ and $85°C$, respectively. Assume that an x-axis is chosen as in the accompanying figure and that the temperature $T(x)$ satisfies the equation

$$\frac{d^2 T}{dx^2} = 0$$

Find $T(x)$ for $0 \leq x \leq 50$.

◀ **Figure Ex-74**

75. Writing What is an *initial-value problem*? Describe the sequence of steps for solving an initial-value problem.

76. Writing What is a *slope field*? How are slope fields and integral curves related?

✔ **QUICK CHECK ANSWERS 5.2**

1. $F'(x) = f(x)$ **2.** (a) $\displaystyle\int \frac{1}{2\sqrt{x}} \, dx = \sqrt{x} + C$ (b) $\displaystyle\int 4e^{4x} \, dx = e^{4x} + C$

3. (a) $\frac{1}{4}x^4 + \frac{1}{2}x^2 + 5x + C$ (b) $\tan x + \csc x + C$ **4.** $2x + 1;\ x^2 + x + 3$ **5.** $0;\ -\frac{2}{3}$

5.3 INTEGRATION BY SUBSTITUTION

*In this section we will study a technique, called **substitution**, that can often be used to transform complicated integration problems into simpler ones.*

■ ***u*-SUBSTITUTION**

The method of substitution can be motivated by examining the chain rule from the viewpoint of antidifferentiation. For this purpose, suppose that F is an antiderivative of f and that g is a differentiable function. The chain rule implies that the derivative of $F(g(x))$ can be expressed as

$$\frac{d}{dx}[F(g(x))] = F'(g(x))g'(x)$$

which we can write in integral form as

$$\int F'(g(x))g'(x)\,dx = F(g(x)) + C \tag{1}$$

or since F is an antiderivative of f,

$$\int f(g(x))g'(x)\,dx = F(g(x)) + C \tag{2}$$

For our purposes it will be useful to let $u = g(x)$ and to write $du/dx = g'(x)$ in the differential form $du = g'(x)\,dx$. With this notation (2) can be expressed as

$$\int f(u)\,du = F(u) + C \tag{3}$$

The process of evaluating an integral of form (2) by converting it into form (3) with the substitution

$$u = g(x) \quad \text{and} \quad du = g'(x)\,dx$$

is called the **method of u-substitution**. Here our emphasis is *not* on the interpretation of the expression $du = g'(x)\,dx$. Rather, the differential notation serves primarily as a useful "bookkeeping" device for the method of u-substitution. The following example illustrates how the method works.

▶ **Example 1**   Evaluate $\int (x^2 + 1)^{50} \cdot 2x\,dx$.

Solution.   If we let $u = x^2 + 1$, then $du/dx = 2x$, which implies that $du = 2x\,dx$. Thus, the given integral can be written as

$$\int (x^2 + 1)^{50} \cdot 2x\,dx = \int u^{50}\,du = \frac{u^{51}}{51} + C = \frac{(x^2 + 1)^{51}}{51} + C \;\blacktriangleleft$$

It is important to realize that in the method of u-substitution you have control over the choice of u, but once you make that choice you have no control over the resulting expression for du. Thus, in the last example we *chose* $u = x^2 + 1$ but $du = 2x\,dx$ was *computed*. Fortunately, our choice of u, combined with the computed du, worked out perfectly to produce an integral involving u that was easy to evaluate. However, in general, the method of u-substitution will fail if the chosen u and the computed du cannot be used to produce an integrand in which no expressions involving x remain, or if you cannot evaluate the resulting integral. Thus, for example, the substitution $u = x^2$, $du = 2x\,dx$ will not work for the integral

$$\int 2x \sin x^4\,dx$$

because this substitution results in the integral

$$\int \sin u^2\,du$$

which still cannot be evaluated in terms of familiar functions.

In general, there are no hard and fast rules for choosing u, and in some problems no choice of u will work. In such cases other methods need to be used, some of which will be discussed later. Making appropriate choices for u will come with experience, but you may find the following guidelines, combined with a mastery of the basic integrals in Table 5.2.1, helpful.

Guidelines for u-Substitution

Step 1. Look for some composition $f(g(x))$ within the integrand for which the substitution

$$u = g(x), \quad du = g'(x)\,dx$$

produces an integral that is expressed entirely in terms of u and its differential du. This may or may not be possible.

Step 2. If you are successful in Step 1, then try to evaluate the resulting integral in terms of u. Again, this may or may not be possible.

Step 3. If you are successful in Step 2, then replace u by $g(x)$ to express your final answer in terms of x.

■ **EASY TO RECOGNIZE SUBSTITUTIONS**

The easiest substitutions occur when the integrand is the derivative of a known function, except for a constant added to or subtracted from the independent variable.

▶ **Example 2**

$$\int \sin(x+9)\,dx = \int \sin u\,du = -\cos u + C = -\cos(x+9) + C$$

$$u = x + 9$$
$$du = 1 \cdot dx = dx$$

$$\int (x-8)^{23}\,dx = \int u^{23}\,du = \frac{u^{24}}{24} + C = \frac{(x-8)^{24}}{24} + C \blacktriangleleft$$

$$u = x - 8$$
$$du = 1 \cdot dx = dx$$

Another easy u-substitution occurs when the integrand is the derivative of a known function, except for a constant that multiplies or divides the independent variable. The following example illustrates two ways to evaluate such integrals.

▶ **Example 3** Evaluate $\int \cos 5x\,dx$.

Solution.

$$\int \cos 5x\,dx = \int (\cos u) \cdot \frac{1}{5}\,du = \frac{1}{5}\int \cos u\,du = \frac{1}{5}\sin u + C = \frac{1}{5}\sin 5x + C$$

$$u = 5x$$
$$du = 5\,dx \text{ or } dx = \tfrac{1}{5}\,du$$

Alternative Solution. There is a variation of the preceding method that some people prefer. The substitution $u = 5x$ requires $du = 5\,dx$. If there were a factor of 5 in the integrand, then we could group the 5 and dx together to form the du required by the substitution. Since there is no factor of 5, we will insert one and compensate by putting a factor of $\frac{1}{5}$ in front of the integral. The computations are as follows:

$$\int \cos 5x\,dx = \frac{1}{5}\int \cos 5x \cdot 5\,dx = \frac{1}{5}\int \cos u\,du = \frac{1}{5}\sin u + C = \frac{1}{5}\sin 5x + C \blacktriangleleft$$

$$u = 5x$$
$$du = 5\,dx$$

More generally, if the integrand is a composition of the form $f(ax + b)$, where $f(x)$ is an easy to integrate function, then the substitution $u = ax + b$, $du = a\,dx$ will work.

▶ Example 4

$$\int \frac{dx}{\left(\frac{1}{3}x - 8\right)^5} = \int \frac{3\,du}{u^5} = 3\int u^{-5}\,du = -\frac{3}{4}u^{-4} + C = -\frac{3}{4}\left(\frac{1}{3}x - 8\right)^{-4} + C \blacktriangleleft$$

$$u = \tfrac{1}{3}x - 8$$
$$du = \tfrac{1}{3}\,dx \text{ or } dx = 3\,du$$

▶ Example 5 Evaluate $\displaystyle\int \frac{dx}{1 + 3x^2}$.

Solution. Substituting

$$u = \sqrt{3}x, \quad du = \sqrt{3}\,dx$$

yields

$$\int \frac{dx}{1 + 3x^2} = \frac{1}{\sqrt{3}}\int \frac{du}{1 + u^2} = \frac{1}{\sqrt{3}}\tan^{-1} u + C = \frac{1}{\sqrt{3}}\tan^{-1}(\sqrt{3}x) + C \blacktriangleleft$$

With the help of Theorem 5.2.3, a complicated integral can sometimes be computed by expressing it as a sum of simpler integrals.

▶ Example 6

$$\int \left(\frac{1}{x} + \sec^2 \pi x\right) dx = \int \frac{dx}{x} + \int \sec^2 \pi x \, dx$$

$$= \ln|x| + \int \sec^2 \pi x \, dx$$

$$= \ln|x| + \frac{1}{\pi}\int \sec^2 u \, du$$

$$u = \pi x$$
$$du = \pi\,dx \text{ or } dx = \frac{1}{\pi}\,du$$

$$= \ln|x| + \frac{1}{\pi}\tan u + C = \ln|x| + \frac{1}{\pi}\tan \pi x + C \blacktriangleleft$$

The next four examples illustrate a substitution $u = g(x)$ where $g(x)$ is a nonlinear function.

▶ Example 7 Evaluate $\displaystyle\int \sin^2 x \cos x \, dx$.

Solution. If we let $u = \sin x$, then

$$\frac{du}{dx} = \cos x, \quad \text{so} \quad du = \cos x \, dx$$

Thus,

$$\int \sin^2 x \cos x \, dx = \int u^2 \, du = \frac{u^3}{3} + C = \frac{\sin^3 x}{3} + C \blacktriangleleft$$

▶ **Example 8**   Evaluate $\displaystyle\int \frac{e^{\sqrt{x}}}{\sqrt{x}}\,dx$.

Solution.   If we let $u = \sqrt{x}$, then

$$\frac{du}{dx} = \frac{1}{2\sqrt{x}}, \quad \text{so} \quad du = \frac{1}{2\sqrt{x}}\,dx \quad \text{or} \quad 2\,du = \frac{1}{\sqrt{x}}\,dx$$

Thus,

$$\int \frac{e^{\sqrt{x}}}{\sqrt{x}}\,dx = \int 2e^u\,du = 2\int e^u\,du = 2e^u + C = 2e^{\sqrt{x}} + C \;\blacktriangleleft$$

▶ **Example 9**   Evaluate $\displaystyle\int t^4\sqrt[3]{3 - 5t^5}\,dt$.

Solution.

$$\int t^4\sqrt[3]{3 - 5t^5}\,dt = -\frac{1}{25}\int \sqrt[3]{u}\,du = -\frac{1}{25}\int u^{1/3}\,du$$

$$\boxed{\begin{array}{l} u = 3 - 5t^5 \\ du = -25t^4\,dt \text{ or } -\frac{1}{25}\,du = t^4\,dt \end{array}}$$

$$= -\frac{1}{25}\frac{u^{4/3}}{4/3} + C = -\frac{3}{100}\left(3 - 5t^5\right)^{4/3} + C \;\blacktriangleleft$$

▶ **Example 10**   Evaluate $\displaystyle\int \frac{e^x}{\sqrt{1 - e^{2x}}}\,dx$.

Solution.   Substituting

$$u = e^x, \quad du = e^x\,dx$$

yields

$$\int \frac{e^x}{\sqrt{1 - e^{2x}}}\,dx = \int \frac{du}{\sqrt{1 - u^2}} = \sin^{-1}u + C = \sin^{-1}(e^x) + C \;\blacktriangleleft$$

■ **LESS APPARENT SUBSTITUTIONS**

The method of substitution is relatively straightforward, provided the integrand contains an easily recognized composition $f(g(x))$ and the remainder of the integrand is a constant multiple of $g'(x)$. If this is not the case, the method may still apply but may require more computation.

▶ **Example 11**   Evaluate $\displaystyle\int x^2\sqrt{x - 1}\,dx$.

Solution.   The composition $\sqrt{x - 1}$ suggests the substitution

$$u = x - 1 \quad \text{so that} \quad du = dx \tag{4}$$

From the first equality in (4)

$$x^2 = (u + 1)^2 = u^2 + 2u + 1$$

so that

$$\int x^2\sqrt{x - 1}\,dx = \int (u^2 + 2u + 1)\sqrt{u}\,du = \int (u^{5/2} + 2u^{3/2} + u^{1/2})\,du$$

$$= \tfrac{2}{7}u^{7/2} + \tfrac{4}{5}u^{5/2} + \tfrac{2}{3}u^{3/2} + C$$

$$= \tfrac{2}{7}(x - 1)^{7/2} + \tfrac{4}{5}(x - 1)^{5/2} + \tfrac{2}{3}(x - 1)^{3/2} + C \;\blacktriangleleft$$

▶ **Example 12** Evaluate $\displaystyle\int \cos^3 x \, dx$.

Solution. The only compositions in the integrand that suggest themselves are

$$\cos^3 x = (\cos x)^3 \quad \text{and} \quad \cos^2 x = (\cos x)^2$$

However, neither the substitution $u = \cos x$ nor the substitution $u = \cos^2 x$ work (verify). In this case, an appropriate substitution is not suggested by the composition contained in the integrand. On the other hand, note from Equation (2) that the derivative $g'(x)$ appears as a factor in the integrand. This suggests that we write

$$\int \cos^3 x \, dx = \int \cos^2 x \cos x \, dx$$

and solve the equation $du = \cos x \, dx$ for $u = \sin x$. Since $\sin^2 x + \cos^2 x = 1$, we then have

$$\int \cos^3 x \, dx = \int \cos^2 x \cos x \, dx = \int (1 - \sin^2 x) \cos x \, dx = \int (1 - u^2) \, du$$

$$= u - \frac{u^3}{3} + C = \sin x - \frac{1}{3}\sin^3 x + C \; \blacktriangleleft$$

▶ **Example 13** Evaluate $\displaystyle\int \frac{dx}{a^2 + x^2} \, dx$, where $a \neq 0$ is a constant.

Solution. Some simple algebra and an appropriate u-substitution will allow us to use Formula 12 in Table 5.2.1.

$$\int \frac{dx}{a^2 + x^2} = \int \frac{a(dx/a)}{a^2(1 + (x/a)^2)} = \frac{1}{a}\int \frac{dx/a}{1 + (x/a)^2} \qquad \boxed{\begin{array}{l} u = x/a \\ du = dx/a \end{array}}$$

$$= \frac{1}{a}\int \frac{du}{1 + u^2} = \frac{1}{a}\tan^{-1} u + C = \frac{1}{a}\tan^{-1}\frac{x}{a} + C \; \blacktriangleleft$$

The method of Example 13 leads to the following generalizations of Formulas 12, 13, and 14 in Table 5.2.1 for $a > 0$:

$$\int \frac{du}{a^2 + u^2} = \frac{1}{a}\tan^{-1}\frac{u}{a} + C \tag{5}$$

$$\int \frac{du}{\sqrt{a^2 - u^2}} = \sin^{-1}\frac{u}{a} + C \tag{6}$$

$$\int \frac{du}{u\sqrt{u^2 - a^2}} = \frac{1}{a}\sec^{-1}\left|\frac{u}{a}\right| + C \tag{7}$$

▶ **Example 14** Evaluate $\displaystyle\int \frac{dx}{\sqrt{2 - x^2}}$.

Solution. Applying (6) with $u = x$ and $a = \sqrt{2}$ yields

$$\int \frac{dx}{\sqrt{2 - x^2}} = \sin^{-1}\frac{x}{\sqrt{2}} + C \; \blacktriangleleft$$

INTEGRATION USING COMPUTER ALGEBRA SYSTEMS

The advent of computer algebra systems has made it possible to evaluate many kinds of integrals that would be laborious to evaluate by hand. For example, a handheld calculator evaluated the integral

$$\int \frac{5x^2}{(1+x)^{1/3}} \, dx = \frac{3(x+1)^{2/3}(5x^2 - 6x + 9)}{8} + C$$

in about a second. The computer algebra system *Mathematica*, running on a personal computer, required even less time to evaluate this same integral. However, just as one would not want to rely on a calculator to compute $2 + 2$, so one would not want to use a CAS to integrate a simple function such as $f(x) = x^2$. Thus, even if you have a CAS, you will want to develop a reasonable level of competence in evaluating basic integrals. Moreover, the mathematical techniques that we will introduce for evaluating basic integrals are precisely the techniques that computer algebra systems use to evaluate more complicated integrals.

✔ QUICK CHECK EXERCISES 5.3   (*See page 340 for answers.*)

1. Indicate the u-substitution.

   (a) $\displaystyle\int 3x^2(1+x^3)^{25}\,dx = \int u^{25}\,du$ if $u = $ _____ and $du = $ _____.

   (b) $\displaystyle\int 2x \sin x^2\,dx = \int \sin u\,du$ if $u = $ _____ and $du = $ _____.

   (c) $\displaystyle\int \frac{18x}{1+9x^2}\,dx = \int \frac{1}{u}\,du$ if $u = $ _____ and $du = $ _____.

   (d) $\displaystyle\int \frac{3}{1+9x^2}\,dx = \int \frac{1}{1+u^2}\,du$ if $u = $ _____ and $du = $ _____.

2. Supply the missing integrand corresponding to the indicated u-substitution.

   (a) $\displaystyle\int 5(5x-3)^{-1/3}\,dx = \int$ _____ du; $u = 5x - 3$

   (b) $\displaystyle\int (3 - \tan x) \sec^2 x\,dx = \int$ _____ du; $u = 3 - \tan x$

   (c) $\displaystyle\int \frac{\sqrt[3]{8+\sqrt{x}}}{\sqrt{x}}\,dx = \int$ _____ du; $u = 8 + \sqrt{x}$

   (d) $\displaystyle\int e^{3x}\,dx = \int$ _____ du; $u = 3x$

EXERCISE SET 5.3   〜 Graphing Utility   [C] CAS

1–12 Evaluate the integrals using the indicated substitutions.

1. (a) $\displaystyle\int 2x(x^2+1)^{23}\,dx$; $u = x^2 + 1$

   (b) $\displaystyle\int \cos^3 x \sin x\,dx$; $u = \cos x$

2. (a) $\displaystyle\int \frac{1}{\sqrt{x}} \sin \sqrt{x}\,dx$; $u = \sqrt{x}$

   (b) $\displaystyle\int \frac{3x\,dx}{\sqrt{4x^2+5}}$; $u = 4x^2 + 5$

3. (a) $\displaystyle\int \sec^2(4x+1)\,dx$; $u = 4x + 1$

   (b) $\displaystyle\int y\sqrt{1+2y^2}\,dy$; $u = 1 + 2y^2$

4. (a) $\displaystyle\int \sqrt{\sin \pi\theta} \cos \pi\theta\,d\theta$; $u = \sin \pi\theta$

   (b) $\displaystyle\int (2x+7)(x^2+7x+3)^{4/5}\,dx$; $u = x^2 + 7x + 3$

5. (a) $\displaystyle\int \cot x \csc^2 x\,dx$; $u = \cot x$

   (b) $\displaystyle\int (1 + \sin t)^9 \cos t\,dt$; $u = 1 + \sin t$

6. (a) $\displaystyle\int \cos 2x\,dx$; $u = 2x$ (b) $\displaystyle\int x \sec^2 x^2\,dx$; $u = x^2$

7. (a) $\displaystyle\int x^2\sqrt{1+x}\,dx$; $u = 1 + x$

   (b) $\displaystyle\int [\csc(\sin x)]^2 \cos x\,dx$; $u = \sin x$

8. (a) $\displaystyle\int \sin(x - \pi)\,dx$; $u = x - \pi$

   (b) $\displaystyle\int \frac{5x^4}{(x^5+1)^2}\,dx$; $u = x^5 + 1$

9. (a) $\displaystyle\int \frac{dx}{x \ln x}$; $u = \ln x$

   (b) $\displaystyle\int e^{-5x}\,dx$; $u = -5x$

10. (a) $\int \dfrac{\sin 3\theta}{1 + \cos 3\theta}\,d\theta$; $u = 1 + \cos 3\theta$

(b) $\int \dfrac{e^x}{1 + e^x}\,dx$; $u = 1 + e^x$

11. (a) $\int \dfrac{x^2\,dx}{1 + x^6}$; $u = x^3$

(b) $\int \dfrac{dx}{x\sqrt{1 - (\ln x)^2}}$; $u = \ln x$

12. (a) $\int \dfrac{dx}{x\sqrt{9x^2 - 1}}$; $u = 3x$

(b) $\int \dfrac{dx}{\sqrt{x}(1 + x)}$; $u = \sqrt{x}$

FOCUS ON CONCEPTS

13. Explain the connection between the chain rule for differentiation and the method of u-substitution for integration.

14. Explain how the substitution $u = ax + b$ helps to perform an integration in which the integrand is $f(ax + b)$, where $f(x)$ is an easy to integrate function.

15–56 Evaluate the integrals using appropriate substitutions.

15. $\int (4x - 3)^9\,dx$

16. $\int x^3\sqrt{5 + x^4}\,dx$

17. $\int \sin 7x\,dx$

18. $\int \cos \dfrac{x}{3}\,dx$

19. $\int \sec 4x \tan 4x\,dx$

20. $\int \sec^2 5x\,dx$

21. $\int e^{2x}\,dx$

22. $\int \dfrac{dx}{2x}$

23. $\int \dfrac{dx}{\sqrt{1 - 4x^2}}$

24. $\int \dfrac{dx}{1 + 16x^2}$

25. $\int t\sqrt{7t^2 + 12}\,dt$

26. $\int \dfrac{x}{\sqrt{4 - 5x^2}}\,dx$

27. $\int \dfrac{6}{(1 - 2x)^3}\,dx$

28. $\int \dfrac{x^2 + 1}{\sqrt{x^3 + 3x}}\,dx$

29. $\int \dfrac{x^3}{(5x^4 + 2)^3}\,dx$

30. $\int \dfrac{\sin(1/x)}{3x^2}\,dx$

31. $\int e^{\sin x} \cos x\,dx$

32. $\int x^3 e^{x^4}\,dx$

33. $\int x^2 e^{-2x^3}\,dx$

34. $\int \dfrac{e^x + e^{-x}}{e^x - e^{-x}}\,dx$

35. $\int \dfrac{e^x}{1 + e^{2x}}\,dx$

36. $\int \dfrac{t}{t^4 + 1}\,dt$

37. $\int \dfrac{\sin(5/x)}{x^2}\,dx$

38. $\int \dfrac{\sec^2(\sqrt{x})}{\sqrt{x}}\,dx$

39. $\int \cos^4 3t \sin 3t\,dt$

40. $\int \cos 2t \sin^5 2t\,dt$

41. $\int x \sec^2(x^2)\,dx$

42. $\int \dfrac{\cos 4\theta}{(1 + 2\sin 4\theta)^4}\,d\theta$

43. $\int \cos 4\theta \sqrt{2 - \sin 4\theta}\,d\theta$

44. $\int \tan^3 5x \sec^2 5x\,dx$

45. $\int \dfrac{\sec^2 x\,dx}{\sqrt{1 - \tan^2 x}}$

46. $\int \dfrac{\sin \theta}{\cos^2 \theta + 1}\,d\theta$

47. $\int \sec^3 2x \tan 2x\,dx$

48. $\int [\sin(\sin \theta)] \cos \theta\,d\theta$

49. $\int \dfrac{dx}{e^x}$

50. $\int \sqrt{e^x}\,dx$

51. $\int \dfrac{dx}{\sqrt{x}\,e^{(2\sqrt{x})}}$

52. $\int \dfrac{e^{\sqrt{2y+1}}}{\sqrt{2y + 1}}\,dy$

53. $\int \dfrac{y}{\sqrt{2y + 1}}\,dy$

54. $\int x\sqrt{4 - x}\,dx$

55. $\int \sin^3 2\theta\,d\theta$

56. $\int \sec^4 3\theta\,d\theta$ [*Hint:* Apply a trigonometric identity.]

57–60 Evaluate each integral by first modifying the form of the integrand and then making an appropriate substitution, if needed.

57. $\int \dfrac{t + 1}{t}\,dt$

58. $\int e^{2\ln x}\,dx$

59. $\int [\ln(e^x) + \ln(e^{-x})]\,dx$

60. $\int \cot x\,dx$

61–62 Evaluate the integrals with the aid of Formulas (5), (6), and (7).

61. (a) $\int \dfrac{dx}{\sqrt{9 - x^2}}$ **(b)** $\int \dfrac{dx}{5 + x^2}$ **(c)** $\int \dfrac{dx}{x\sqrt{x^2 - \pi}}$

62. (a) $\int \dfrac{e^x}{4 + e^{2x}}\,dx$ **(b)** $\int \dfrac{dx}{\sqrt{9 - 4x^2}}$ **(c)** $\int \dfrac{dy}{y\sqrt{5y^2 - 3}}$

63–65 Evaluate the integrals assuming that n is a positive integer and $b \neq 0$.

63. $\int (a + bx)^n\,dx$

64. $\int \sqrt[n]{a + bx}\,dx$

65. $\int \sin^n(a + bx) \cos(a + bx)\,dx$

66. Use a CAS to check the answers you obtained in Exercises 63–65. If the answer produced by the CAS does not match yours, show that the two answers are equivalent. [*Suggestion: Mathematica* users may find it helpful to apply the Simplify command to the answer.]

FOCUS ON CONCEPTS

67. (a) Evaluate the integral $\int \sin x \cos x\,dx$ by two methods: first by letting $u = \sin x$, and then by letting $u = \cos x$.

(b) Explain why the two apparently different answers obtained in part (a) are really equivalent.

68. (a) Evaluate the integral $\int (5x - 1)^2\,dx$ by two methods: first square and integrate, then let $u = 5x - 1$.

(b) Explain why the two apparently different answers obtained in part (a) are really equivalent.

69–72 Solve the initial-value problems. ■

69. $\dfrac{dy}{dx} = \sqrt{5x + 1},\ y(3) = -2$

70. $\dfrac{dy}{dx} = 2 + \sin 3x,\ y(\pi/3) = 0$

71. $\dfrac{dy}{dt} = -e^{2t},\ y(0) = 6$

72. $\dfrac{dy}{dt} = \dfrac{1}{25 + 9t^2},\ y\left(-\dfrac{5}{3}\right) = \dfrac{\pi}{30}$

73. (a) Evaluate $\int [x/\sqrt{x^2 + 1}]\,dx$.

(b) Use a graphing utility to generate some typical integral curves of $f(x) = x/\sqrt{x^2 + 1}$ over the interval $(-5, 5)$.

74. (a) Evaluate $\int [x/(x^2 + 1)]\,dx$.

(b) Use a graphing utility to generate some typical integral curves of $f(x) = x/(x^2 + 1)$ over the interval $(-5, 5)$.

75. Find a function f such that the slope of the tangent line at a point (x, y) on the curve $y = f(x)$ is $\sqrt{3x + 1}$ and the curve passes through the point $(0, 1)$.

76. A population of minnows in a lake is estimated to be 100,000 at the beginning of the year 2005. Suppose that t years after the beginning of 2005 the rate of growth of the population $p(t)$ (in thousands) is given by $p'(t) = (3 + 0.12t)^{3/2}$. Estimate the projected population at the beginning of the year 2010.

77. Derive integration Formula (6).

78. Derive integration Formula (7).

79. Writing If you want to evaluate an integral by u-substitution, how do you decide what part of the integrand to choose for u?

80. Writing The evaluation of an integral can sometimes result in apparently different answers (Exercises 67 and 68). Explain why this occurs and give an example. How might you show that two apparently different answers are actually equivalent?

✓ **QUICK CHECK ANSWERS 5.3**

1. (a) $1 + x^3$; $3x^2\,dx$ (b) x^2; $2x\,dx$ (c) $1 + 9x^2$; $18x\,dx$ (d) $3x$; $3\,dx$ **2.** (a) $u^{-1/3}$ (b) $-u$ (c) $2\sqrt[3]{u}$ (d) $\frac{1}{3}e^u$

5.4 THE DEFINITION OF AREA AS A LIMIT; SIGMA NOTATION

Our main goal in this section is to use the rectangle method to give a precise mathematical definition of the "area under a curve."

■ **SIGMA NOTATION**

To simplify our computations, we will begin by discussing a useful notation for expressing lengthy sums in a compact form. This notation is called *sigma notation* or *summation notation* because it uses the uppercase Greek letter Σ (sigma) to denote various kinds of sums. To illustrate how this notation works, consider the sum

$$1^2 + 2^2 + 3^2 + 4^2 + 5^2$$

in which each term is of the form k^2, where k is one of the integers from 1 to 5. In sigma notation this sum can be written as

$$\sum_{k=1}^{5} k^2$$

which is read "the summation of k^2, where k runs from 1 to 5." The notation tells us to form the sum of the terms that result when we substitute successive integers for k in the expression k^2, starting with $k = 1$ and ending with $k = 5$.

More generally, if $f(k)$ is a function of k, and if m and n are integers such that $m \le n$, then

$$\sum_{k=m}^{n} f(k) \tag{1}$$

denotes the sum of the terms that result when we substitute successive integers for k, starting with $k = m$ and ending with $k = n$ (Figure 5.4.1).

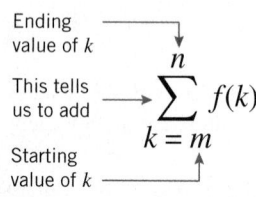

Ending value of k

This tells us to add $\displaystyle\sum_{k=m}^{n} f(k)$

Starting value of k

▲ **Figure 5.4.1**

▶ **Example 1**

$$\sum_{k=4}^{8} k^3 = 4^3 + 5^3 + 6^3 + 7^3 + 8^3$$

$$\sum_{k=1}^{5} 2k = 2\cdot 1 + 2\cdot 2 + 2\cdot 3 + 2\cdot 4 + 2\cdot 5 = 2 + 4 + 6 + 8 + 10$$

$$\sum_{k=0}^{5} (2k + 1) = 1 + 3 + 5 + 7 + 9 + 11$$

$$\sum_{k=0}^{5} (-1)^k (2k + 1) = 1 - 3 + 5 - 7 + 9 - 11$$

$$\sum_{k=-3}^{1} k^3 = (-3)^3 + (-2)^3 + (-1)^3 + 0^3 + 1^3 = -27 - 8 - 1 + 0 + 1$$

$$\sum_{k=1}^{3} k \sin\left(\frac{k\pi}{5}\right) = \sin\frac{\pi}{5} + 2\sin\frac{2\pi}{5} + 3\sin\frac{3\pi}{5} \quad \blacktriangleleft$$

The numbers m and n in (1) are called, respectively, the *lower* and *upper limits of summation*; and the letter k is called the *index of summation*. It is not essential to use k as the index of summation; any letter not reserved for another purpose will do. For example,

$$\sum_{i=1}^{6} \frac{1}{i}, \quad \sum_{j=1}^{6} \frac{1}{j}, \quad \text{and} \quad \sum_{n=1}^{6} \frac{1}{n}$$

all denote the sum

$$1 + \frac{1}{2} + \frac{1}{3} + \frac{1}{4} + \frac{1}{5} + \frac{1}{6}$$

If the upper and lower limits of summation are the same, then the "sum" in (1) reduces to a single term. For example,

$$\sum_{k=2}^{2} k^3 = 2^3 \quad \text{and} \quad \sum_{i=1}^{1} \frac{1}{i+2} = \frac{1}{1+2} = \frac{1}{3}$$

In the sums

$$\sum_{i=1}^{5} 2 \quad \text{and} \quad \sum_{j=0}^{2} x^3$$

the expression to the right of the Σ sign does not involve the index of summation. In such cases, we take all the terms in the sum to be the same, with one term for each allowable value of the summation index. Thus,

$$\sum_{i=1}^{5} 2 = 2 + 2 + 2 + 2 + 2 \quad \text{and} \quad \sum_{j=0}^{2} x^3 = x^3 + x^3 + x^3$$

■ **CHANGING THE LIMITS OF SUMMATION**

A sum can be written in more than one way using sigma notation with different limits of summation and correspondingly different summands. For example,

$$\sum_{i=1}^{5} 2i = 2 + 4 + 6 + 8 + 10 = \sum_{j=0}^{4} (2j + 2) = \sum_{k=3}^{7} (2k - 4)$$

On occasion we will want to change the sigma notation for a given sum to a sigma notation with different limits of summation.

■ **PROPERTIES OF SUMS**

When stating general properties of sums it is often convenient to use a subscripted letter such as a_k in place of the function notation $f(k)$. For example,

$$\sum_{k=1}^{5} a_k = a_1 + a_2 + a_3 + a_4 + a_5 = \sum_{j=1}^{5} a_j = \sum_{k=-1}^{3} a_{k+2}$$

$$\sum_{k=1}^{n} a_k = a_1 + a_2 + \cdots + a_n = \sum_{j=1}^{n} a_j = \sum_{k=-1}^{n-2} a_{k+2}$$

Our first properties provide some basic rules for manipulating sums.

5.4.1 THEOREM

(a) $\displaystyle\sum_{k=1}^{n} ca_k = c\sum_{k=1}^{n} a_k$ (*if c does not depend on k*)

(b) $\displaystyle\sum_{k=1}^{n}(a_k + b_k) = \sum_{k=1}^{n} a_k + \sum_{k=1}^{n} b_k$

(c) $\displaystyle\sum_{k=1}^{n}(a_k - b_k) = \sum_{k=1}^{n} a_k - \sum_{k=1}^{n} b_k$

We will prove parts (a) and (b) and leave part (c) as an exercise.

PROOF (a)

$$\sum_{k=1}^{n} ca_k = ca_1 + ca_2 + \cdots + ca_n = c(a_1 + a_2 + \cdots + a_n) = c\sum_{k=1}^{n} a_k$$

PROOF (b)

$$\sum_{k=1}^{n}(a_k + b_k) = (a_1 + b_1) + (a_2 + b_2) + \cdots + (a_n + b_n)$$

$$= (a_1 + a_2 + \cdots + a_n) + (b_1 + b_2 + \cdots + b_n) = \sum_{k=1}^{n} a_k + \sum_{k=1}^{n} b_k \quad ∎$$

Restating Theorem 5.4.1 in words:

(a) *A constant factor can be moved through a sigma sign.*

(b) *Sigma distributes across sums.*

(c) *Sigma distributes across differences.*

■ **SUMMATION FORMULAS**

The following theorem lists some useful formulas for sums of powers of integers. The derivations of these formulas are given in Appendix D.

5.4.2 THEOREM

(a) $\displaystyle\sum_{k=1}^{n} k = 1 + 2 + \cdots + n = \frac{n(n+1)}{2}$

(b) $\displaystyle\sum_{k=1}^{n} k^2 = 1^2 + 2^2 + \cdots + n^2 = \frac{n(n+1)(2n+1)}{6}$

(c) $\displaystyle\sum_{k=1}^{n} k^3 = 1^3 + 2^3 + \cdots + n^3 = \left[\frac{n(n+1)}{2}\right]^2$

▶ **Example 2** Evaluate $\displaystyle\sum_{k=1}^{30} k(k+1)$.

Solution.

$$\sum_{k=1}^{30} k(k+1) = \sum_{k=1}^{30} (k^2 + k) = \sum_{k=1}^{30} k^2 + \sum_{k=1}^{30} k$$

$$= \frac{30(31)(61)}{6} + \frac{30(31)}{2} = 9920 \qquad \boxed{\text{Theorem 5.4.2}(a),\,(b)} \ \blacktriangleleft$$

In formulas such as

$$\sum_{k=1}^{n} k = \frac{n(n+1)}{2} \quad \text{or} \quad 1 + 2 + \cdots + n = \frac{n(n+1)}{2}$$

the left side of the equality is said to express the sum in **open form** and the right side is said to express it in **closed form**. The open form indicates the summands and the closed form is an explicit formula for the sum.

▶ **Example 3** Express $\displaystyle\sum_{k=1}^{n} (3+k)^2$ in closed form.

Solution.

$$\sum_{k=1}^{n} (3+k)^2 = 4^2 + 5^2 + \cdots + (3+n)^2$$

$$= [1^2 + 2^2 + 3^3 + 4^2 + 5^2 + \cdots + (3+n)^2] - [1^2 + 2^2 + 3^2]$$

$$= \left(\sum_{k=1}^{3+n} k^2\right) - 14$$

$$= \frac{(3+n)(4+n)(7+2n)}{6} - 14 = \frac{1}{6}(73n + 21n^2 + 2n^3) \ \blacktriangleleft$$

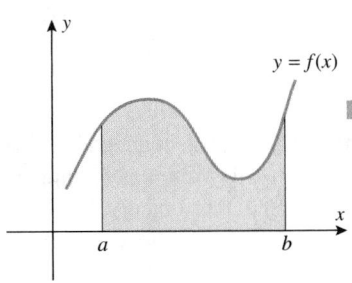

▲ **Figure 5.4.2**

■ **A DEFINITION OF AREA**

We now turn to the problem of giving a precise definition of what is meant by the "area under a curve." Specifically, suppose that the function f is continuous and nonnegative on the interval $[a, b]$, and let R denote the region bounded below by the x-axis, bounded on the sides by the vertical lines $x = a$ and $x = b$, and bounded above by the curve $y = f(x)$ (Figure 5.4.2). Using the rectangle method of Section 5.1, we can motivate a definition for the area of R as follows:

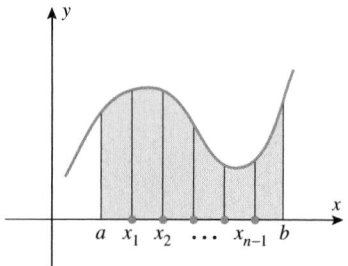

▲ Figure 5.4.3

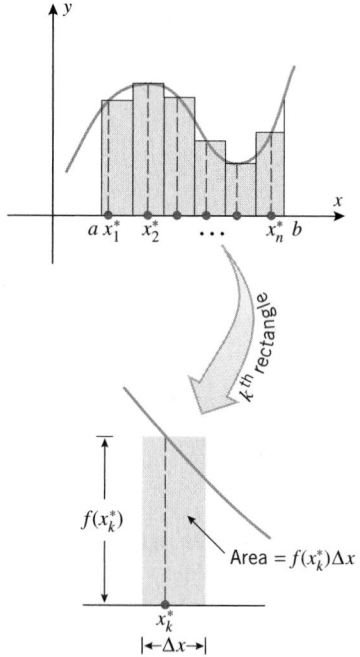

▲ Figure 5.4.4

- Divide the interval $[a, b]$ into n equal subintervals by inserting $n - 1$ equally spaced points between a and b, and denote those points by

$$x_1, x_2, \ldots, x_{n-1}$$

(Figure 5.4.3). Each of these subintervals has width $(b - a)/n$, which is customarily denoted by

$$\Delta x = \frac{b - a}{n}$$

- Over each subinterval construct a rectangle whose height is the value of f at an arbitrarily selected point in the subinterval. Thus, if

$$x_1^*, x_2^*, \ldots, x_n^*$$

denote the points selected in the subintervals, then the rectangles will have heights $f(x_1^*), f(x_2^*), \ldots, f(x_n^*)$ and areas

$$f(x_1^*)\Delta x, \quad f(x_2^*)\Delta x, \ldots, \quad f(x_n^*)\Delta x$$

(Figure 5.4.4).

- The union of the rectangles forms a region R_n whose area can be regarded as an approximation to the area A of the region R; that is,

$$A = \text{area}(R) \approx \text{area}(R_n) = f(x_1^*)\Delta x + f(x_2^*)\Delta x + \cdots + f(x_n^*)\Delta x$$

(Figure 5.4.5). This can be expressed more compactly in sigma notation as

$$A \approx \sum_{k=1}^{n} f(x_k^*)\Delta x$$

- Repeat the process using more and more subdivisions, and define the area of R to be the "limit" of the areas of the approximating regions R_n as n increases without bound. That is, we define the area A as

$$A = \lim_{n \to +\infty} \sum_{k=1}^{n} f(x_k^*)\Delta x$$

In summary, we make the following definition.

The limit in (2) is interpreted to mean that given any number $\epsilon > 0$ the inequality

$$\left| A - \sum_{k=1}^{n} f(x_k^*)\Delta x \right| < \epsilon$$

holds when n is sufficiently large, no matter how the points x_k^* are selected.

5.4.3 DEFINITION (Area Under a Curve) If the function f is continuous on $[a, b]$ and if $f(x) \geq 0$ for all x in $[a, b]$, then the **area** A under the curve $y = f(x)$ over the interval $[a, b]$ is defined by

$$A = \lim_{n \to +\infty} \sum_{k=1}^{n} f(x_k^*)\Delta x \tag{2}$$

REMARK There is a difference in interpretation between $\lim_{n \to +\infty}$ and $\lim_{x \to +\infty}$, where n represents a positive integer and x represents a real number. Later we will study limits of the type $\lim_{n \to +\infty}$ in detail, but for now suffice it to say that the computational techniques we have used for limits of type $\lim_{x \to +\infty}$ will also work for $\lim_{n \to +\infty}$.

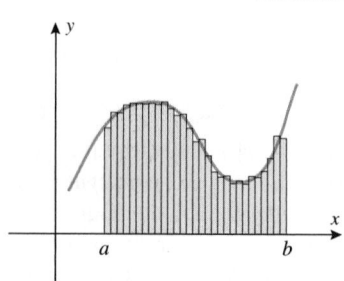

▲ Figure 5.4.5   area(R_n) ≈ area(R)

The values of $x_1^*, x_2^*, \ldots, x_n^*$ in (2) can be chosen arbitrarily, so it is conceivable that different choices of these values might produce different values of A. Were this to happen, then Definition 5.4.3 would not be an acceptable definition of area. Fortunately, this does not happen; it is proved in advanced courses that if f is continuous (as we have assumed), then the same value of A results no matter how the x_k^* are chosen. In practice they are chosen in some systematic fashion, some common choices being

- the left endpoint of each subinterval
- the right endpoint of each subinterval
- the midpoint of each subinterval

To be more specific, suppose that the interval $[a, b]$ is divided into n equal parts of length $\Delta x = (b - a)/n$ by the points $x_1, x_2, \ldots, x_{n-1}$, and let $x_0 = a$ and $x_n = b$ (Figure 5.4.6). Then,

$$x_k = a + k\Delta x \quad \text{for } k = 0, 1, 2, \ldots, n$$

Thus, the left endpoint, right endpoint, and midpoint choices for $x_1^*, x_2^*, \ldots, x_n^*$ are given by

$$x_k^* = x_{k-1} = a + (k - 1)\Delta x \qquad \boxed{\text{Left endpoint}} \tag{3}$$

$$x_k^* = x_k = a + k\Delta x \qquad \boxed{\text{Right endpoint}} \tag{4}$$

$$x_k^* = \tfrac{1}{2}(x_{k-1} + x_k) = a + \left(k - \tfrac{1}{2}\right)\Delta x \qquad \boxed{\text{Midpoint}} \tag{5}$$

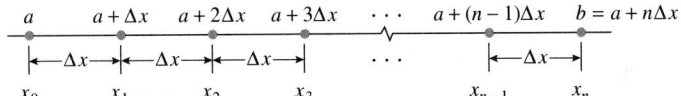

▶ **Figure 5.4.6**

When applicable, the antiderivative method will be the method of choice for finding exact areas. However, the following examples will help to reinforce the ideas that we have just discussed.

▶ **Example 4**   Use Definition 5.4.3 with x_k^* as the right endpoint of each subinterval to find the area between the graph of $f(x) = x^2$ and the interval $[0, 1]$.

Solution.   The length of each subinterval is

$$\Delta x = \frac{b - a}{n} = \frac{1 - 0}{n} = \frac{1}{n}$$

so it follows from (4) that

$$x_k^* = a + k\Delta x = \frac{k}{n}$$

Thus,

$$\sum_{k=1}^{n} f(x_k^*)\Delta x = \sum_{k=1}^{n} (x_k^*)^2 \Delta x = \sum_{k=1}^{n} \left(\frac{k}{n}\right)^2 \frac{1}{n} = \frac{1}{n^3} \sum_{k=1}^{n} k^2$$

$$= \frac{1}{n^3}\left[\frac{n(n + 1)(2n + 1)}{6}\right] \qquad \boxed{\text{Part (b) of Theorem 5.4.2}}$$

$$= \frac{1}{6}\left(\frac{n}{n} \cdot \frac{n + 1}{n} \cdot \frac{2n + 1}{n}\right) = \frac{1}{6}\left(1 + \frac{1}{n}\right)\left(2 + \frac{1}{n}\right)$$

from which it follows that

$$A = \lim_{n \to +\infty} \sum_{k=1}^{n} f(x_k^*)\Delta x = \lim_{n \to +\infty}\left[\frac{1}{6}\left(1 + \frac{1}{n}\right)\left(2 + \frac{1}{n}\right)\right] = \frac{1}{3}$$

Observe that this is consistent with the results in Table 5.1.2 and the related discussion in Section 5.1. ◄

In the solution to Example 4 we made use of one of the "closed form" summation formulas from Theorem 5.4.2. The next result collects some consequences of Theorem 5.4.2 that can facilitate computations of area using Definition 5.4.3.

What pattern is revealed by parts (b)–(d) of Theorem 5.4.4? Does part (a) also fit this pattern? What would you conjecture to be the value of

$$\lim_{n \to +\infty} \frac{1}{n^m} \sum_{k=1}^{n} k^{m-1}$$

5.4.4 THEOREM

(a) $\displaystyle \lim_{n \to +\infty} \frac{1}{n} \sum_{k=1}^{n} 1 = 1$ (b) $\displaystyle \lim_{n \to +\infty} \frac{1}{n^2} \sum_{k=1}^{n} k = \frac{1}{2}$

(c) $\displaystyle \lim_{n \to +\infty} \frac{1}{n^3} \sum_{k=1}^{n} k^2 = \frac{1}{3}$ (d) $\displaystyle \lim_{n \to +\infty} \frac{1}{n^4} \sum_{k=1}^{n} k^3 = \frac{1}{4}$

The proof of Theorem 5.4.4 is left as an exercise for the reader.

▶ **Example 5**   Use Definition 5.4.3 with x_k^* as the midpoint of each subinterval to find the area under the parabola $y = f(x) = 9 - x^2$ and over the interval $[0, 3]$.

Solution.   Each subinterval has length

$$\Delta x = \frac{b - a}{n} = \frac{3 - 0}{n} = \frac{3}{n}$$

so it follows from (5) that

$$x_k^* = a + \left(k - \frac{1}{2}\right) \Delta x = \left(k - \frac{1}{2}\right)\left(\frac{3}{n}\right)$$

Thus,

$$f(x_k^*)\Delta x = [9 - (x_k^*)^2]\Delta x = \left[9 - \left(k - \frac{1}{2}\right)^2 \left(\frac{3}{n}\right)^2\right]\left(\frac{3}{n}\right)$$

$$= \left[9 - \left(k^2 - k + \frac{1}{4}\right)\left(\frac{9}{n^2}\right)\right]\left(\frac{3}{n}\right)$$

$$= \frac{27}{n} - \frac{27}{n^3}k^2 + \frac{27}{n^3}k - \frac{27}{4n^3}$$

from which it follows that

$$A = \lim_{n \to +\infty} \sum_{k=1}^{n} f(x_k^*)\Delta x$$

$$= \lim_{n \to +\infty} \sum_{k=1}^{n} \left(\frac{27}{n} - \frac{27}{n^3}k^2 + \frac{27}{n^3}k - \frac{27}{4n^3}\right)$$

$$= \lim_{n \to +\infty} 27\left[\frac{1}{n}\sum_{k=1}^{n}1 - \frac{1}{n^3}\sum_{k=1}^{n}k^2 + \frac{1}{n}\left(\frac{1}{n^2}\sum_{k=1}^{n}k\right) - \frac{1}{4n^2}\left(\frac{1}{n}\sum_{k=1}^{n}1\right)\right]$$

$$= 27\left[1 - \frac{1}{3} + 0 \cdot \frac{1}{2} - 0 \cdot 1\right] = 18 \quad \boxed{\text{Theorem 5.4.4}} \quad ◄$$

■ NUMERICAL APPROXIMATIONS OF AREA

The antiderivative method discussed in Section 5.1 (and to be studied in more detail later) is an appropriate tool for finding the exact area under a curve when an antiderivative of the integrand can be found. However, if an antiderivative cannot be found, then we must resort to *approximating* the area. Definition 5.4.3 provides a way of doing this. It follows from this definition that if n is large, then

$$\sum_{k=1}^{n} f(x_k^*)\Delta x = \Delta x \sum_{k=1}^{n} f(x_k^*) = \Delta x[f(x_1^*) + f(x_2^*) + \cdots + f(x_n^*)] \qquad (6)$$

will be a good approximation to the area A. If one of Formulas (3), (4), or (5) is used to choose the x_k^* in (6), then the result is called the **left endpoint approximation**, the **right endpoint approximation**, or the **midpoint approximation**, respectively (Figure 5.4.7).

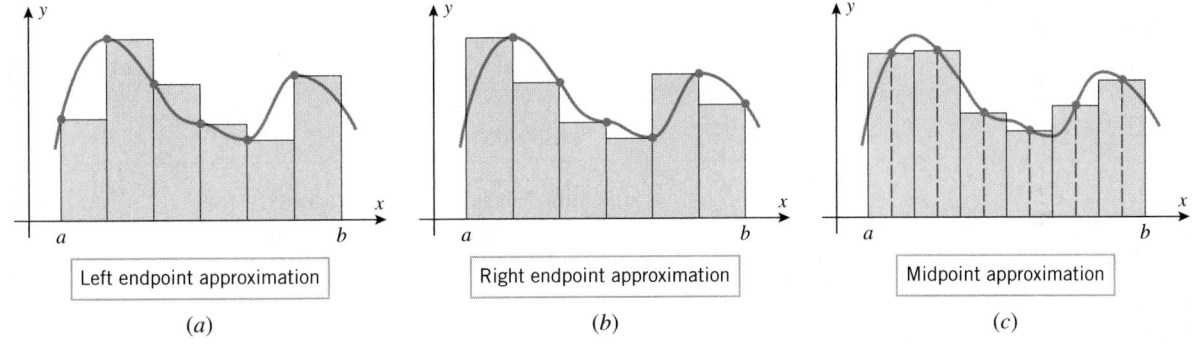

| Left endpoint approximation | Right endpoint approximation | Midpoint approximation |
| (*a*) | (*b*) | (*c*) |

▲ **Figure 5.4.7**

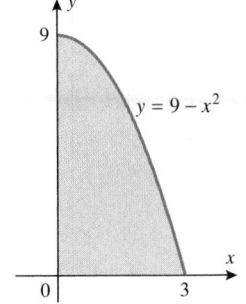

▲ **Figure 5.4.8**

▶ **Example 6**   Find the left endpoint, right endpoint, and midpoint approximations of the area under the curve $y = 9 - x^2$ over the interval $[0, 3]$ with $n = 10, n = 20$, and $n = 50$ (Figure 5.4.8). Compare the accuracies of these three methods.

Solution.   Details of the computations for the case $n = 10$ are shown to six decimal places in Table 5.4.1 and the results of all the computations are given in Table 5.4.2. We showed in Example 5 that the exact area is 18 (i.e., 18 square units), so in this case the midpoint approximation is more accurate than the endpoint approximations. This is also evident geometrically from Figure 5.4.9. You can also see from the figure that in this case the left endpoint approximation overestimates the area and the right endpoint approximation underestimates it. Later in the text we will investigate the error that results when an area is approximated by the midpoint rule. ◀

■ NET SIGNED AREA

In Definition 5.4.3 we assumed that f is continuous and nonnegative on the interval $[a, b]$. If f is continuous and attains both positive and negative values on $[a, b]$, then the limit

$$\lim_{n \to +\infty} \sum_{k=1}^{n} f(x_k^*)\Delta x \qquad (7)$$

no longer represents the area between the curve $y = f(x)$ and the interval $[a, b]$ on the x-axis; rather, it represents a difference of areas—the area of the region that is above the interval $[a, b]$ and below the curve $y = f(x)$ minus the area of the region that is below the interval $[a, b]$ and above the curve $y = f(x)$. We call this the **net signed area**

Table 5.4.1

$n = 10, \Delta x = (b-a)/n = (3-0)/10 = 0.3$

k	LEFT ENDPOINT APPROXIMATION		RIGHT ENDPOINT APPROXIMATION		MIDPOINT APPROXIMATION	
	x_k^*	$9 - (x_k^*)^2$	x_k^*	$9 - (x_k^*)^2$	x_k^*	$9 - (x_k^*)^2$
1	0.0	9.000000	0.3	8.910000	0.15	8.977500
2	0.3	8.910000	0.6	8.640000	0.45	8.797500
3	0.6	8.640000	0.9	8.190000	0.75	8.437500
4	0.9	8.190000	1.2	7.560000	1.05	7.897500
5	1.2	7.560000	1.5	6.750000	1.35	7.177500
6	1.5	6.750000	1.8	5.760000	1.65	6.277500
7	1.8	5.760000	2.1	4.590000	1.95	5.197500
8	2.1	4.590000	2.4	3.240000	2.25	3.937500
9	2.4	3.240000	2.7	1.710000	2.55	2.497500
10	2.7	1.710000	3.0	0.000000	2.85	0.877500
		64.350000		55.350000		60.075000

$\Delta x \sum_{k=1}^{n} f(x_k^*)$	(0.3)(64.350000) $= 19.305000$	(0.3)(55.350000) $= 16.605000$	(0.3)(60.075000) $= 18.022500$

Table 5.4.2

n	LEFT ENDPOINT APPROXIMATION	RIGHT ENDPOINT APPROXIMATION	MIDPOINT APPROXIMATION
10	19.305000	16.605000	18.022500
20	18.663750	17.313750	18.005625
50	18.268200	17.728200	18.000900

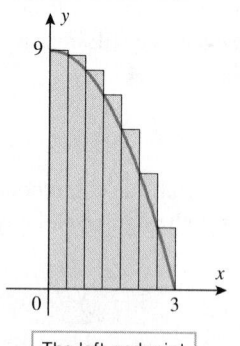
The left endpoint approximation overestimates the area.

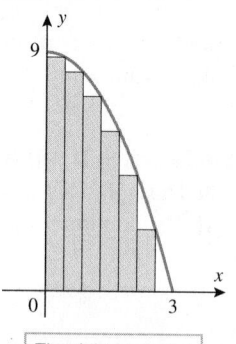
The right endpoint approximation underestimates the area.

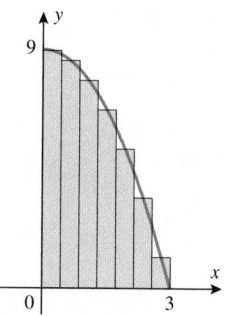
The midpoint approximation is better than the endpoint approximations.

▲ Figure 5.4.9

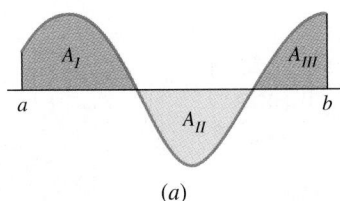

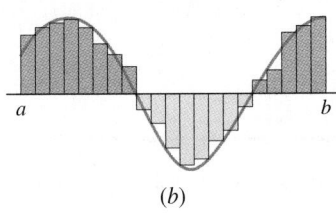

▲ **Figure 5.4.10**

between the graph of $y = f(x)$ and the interval $[a, b]$. For example, in Figure 5.4.10a, the net signed area between the curve $y = f(x)$ and the interval $[a, b]$ is

$$(A_I + A_{III}) - A_{II} = \left[\text{area above } [a, b]\right] - \left[\text{area below } [a, b]\right]$$

To explain why the limit in (7) represents this net signed area, let us subdivide the interval $[a, b]$ in Figure 5.4.10a into n equal subintervals and examine the terms in the sum

$$\sum_{k=1}^{n} f(x_k^*)\Delta x \tag{8}$$

If $f(x_k^*)$ is positive, then the product $f(x_k^*)\Delta x$ represents the area of the rectangle with height $f(x_k^*)$ and base Δx (the pink rectangles in Figure 5.4.10b). However, if $f(x_k^*)$ is negative, then the product $f(x_k^*)\Delta x$ is the *negative* of the area of the rectangle with height $|f(x_k^*)|$ and base Δx (the green rectangles in Figure 5.4.10b). Thus, (8) represents the total area of the pink rectangles minus the total area of the green rectangles. As n increases, the pink rectangles fill out the regions with areas A_I and A_{III} and the green rectangles fill out the region with area A_{II}, which explains why the limit in (7) represents the signed area between $y = f(x)$ and the interval $[a, b]$. We formalize this in the following definition.

As with Definition 5.4.3, it can be proved that the limit in (9) always exists and that the same value of A results no matter how the points in the subintervals are chosen.

5.4.5 DEFINITION (*Net Signed Area*) If the function f is continuous on $[a, b]$, then the **net signed area** A between $y = f(x)$ and the interval $[a, b]$ is defined by

$$A = \lim_{n \to +\infty} \sum_{k=1}^{n} f(x_k^*)\Delta x \tag{9}$$

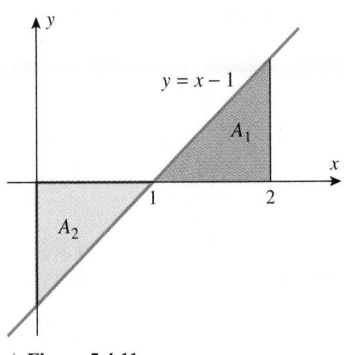

▲ **Figure 5.4.11**

Figure 5.4.11 shows the graph of $f(x) = x - 1$ over the interval $[0, 2]$. It is geometrically evident that the areas A_1 and A_2 in that figure are equal, so we expect the net signed area between the graph of f and the interval $[0, 2]$ to be zero.

▶ **Example 7** Confirm that the net signed area between the graph of $f(x) = x - 1$ and the interval $[0, 2]$ is zero by using Definition 5.4.5 with x_k^* chosen to be the left endpoint of each subinterval.

Solution. Each subinterval has length

$$\Delta x = \frac{b - a}{n} = \frac{2 - 0}{n} = \frac{2}{n}$$

so it follows from (3) that

$$x_k^* = a + (k - 1)\Delta x = (k - 1)\left(\frac{2}{n}\right)$$

Thus,

$$\sum_{k=1}^{n} f(x_k^*)\Delta x = \sum_{k=1}^{n}(x_k^* - 1)\Delta x = \sum_{k=1}^{n}\left[(k - 1)\left(\frac{2}{n}\right) - 1\right]\left(\frac{2}{n}\right)$$

$$= \sum_{k=1}^{n}\left[\left(\frac{4}{n^2}\right)k - \frac{4}{n^2} - \frac{2}{n}\right]$$

from which it follows that

$$A = \lim_{n \to +\infty} \sum_{k=1}^{n} f(x_k^*)\Delta x = \lim_{n \to +\infty} \left[4\left(\frac{1}{n^2}\sum_{k=1}^{n}k\right) - \frac{4}{n}\left(\frac{1}{n}\sum_{k=1}^{n}1\right) - 2\left(\frac{1}{n}\sum_{k=1}^{n}1\right) \right]$$

$$= 4\left(\frac{1}{2}\right) - 0 \cdot 1 - 2 \cdot 1 = 0 \qquad \boxed{\text{Theorem 5.4.4}}$$

This confirms that the net signed area is zero. ◄

✔ **QUICK CHECK EXERCISES 5.4**   (*See page 352 for answers.*)

1. (a) Write the sum in two ways:

$$\frac{1}{2} + \frac{1}{4} + \frac{1}{6} + \frac{1}{8} = \sum_{k=1}^{4} \underline{\hspace{1cm}} = \sum_{j=0}^{3} \underline{\hspace{1cm}}$$

   (b) Express the sum $10 + 10^2 + 10^3 + 10^4 + 10^5$ using sigma notation.

2. Express the sums in closed form.

   (a) $\displaystyle\sum_{k=1}^{n} k$ (b) $\displaystyle\sum_{k=1}^{n}(6k+1)$ (c) $\displaystyle\sum_{k=1}^{n} k^2$

3. Divide the interval $[1, 3]$ into $n = 4$ subintervals of equal length.

   (a) Each subinterval has width _____.

   (b) The left endpoints of the subintervals are _____.
   (c) The midpoints of the subintervals are _____.
   (d) The right endpoints of the subintervals are _____.

4. Find the left endpoint approximation for the area between the curve $y = x^2$ and the interval $[1, 3]$ using $n = 4$ equal subdivisions of the interval.

5. The right endpoint approximation for the net signed area between $y = f(x)$ and an interval $[a, b]$ is given by

$$\sum_{k=1}^{n} \frac{6k+1}{n^2}$$

   Find the exact value of this net signed area.

EXERCISE SET 5.4 $\boxed{c}$ CAS

1. Evaluate.

   (a) $\displaystyle\sum_{k=1}^{3} k^3$ (b) $\displaystyle\sum_{j=2}^{6}(3j-1)$ (c) $\displaystyle\sum_{i=-4}^{1}(i^2 - i)$

   (d) $\displaystyle\sum_{n=0}^{5} 1$ (e) $\displaystyle\sum_{k=0}^{4}(-2)^k$ (f) $\displaystyle\sum_{n=1}^{6}\sin n\pi$

2. Evaluate.

   (a) $\displaystyle\sum_{k=1}^{4} k\sin\frac{k\pi}{2}$ (b) $\displaystyle\sum_{j=0}^{5}(-1)^j$ (c) $\displaystyle\sum_{i=7}^{20}\pi^2$

   (d) $\displaystyle\sum_{m=3}^{5} 2^{m+1}$ (e) $\displaystyle\sum_{n=1}^{6}\sqrt{n}$ (f) $\displaystyle\sum_{k=0}^{10}\cos k\pi$

3–8 Write each expression in sigma notation but do not evaluate. ■

3. $1 + 2 + 3 + \cdots + 10$

4. $3 \cdot 1 + 3 \cdot 2 + 3 \cdot 3 + \cdots + 3 \cdot 20$

5. $2 + 4 + 6 + 8 + \cdots + 20$ 6. $1 + 3 + 5 + 7 + \cdots + 15$

7. $1 - 3 + 5 - 7 + 9 - 11$ 8. $1 - \frac{1}{2} + \frac{1}{3} - \frac{1}{4} + \frac{1}{5}$

9. (a) Express the sum of the even integers from 2 to 100 in sigma notation.
   (b) Express the sum of the odd integers from 1 to 99 in sigma notation.

10. Express in sigma notation.
    (a) $a_1 - a_2 + a_3 - a_4 + a_5$
    (b) $-b_0 + b_1 - b_2 + b_3 - b_4 + b_5$
    (c) $a_0 + a_1 x + a_2 x^2 + \cdots + a_n x^n$
    (d) $a^5 + a^4 b + a^3 b^2 + a^2 b^3 + ab^4 + b^5$

11–16 Use Theorem 5.4.2 to evaluate the sums. Check your answers using the summation feature of a calculating utility. ■

11. $\displaystyle\sum_{k=1}^{100} k$ 12. $\displaystyle\sum_{k=1}^{100}(7k+1)$ 13. $\displaystyle\sum_{k=1}^{20} k^2$

14. $\displaystyle\sum_{k=4}^{20} k^2$ 15. $\displaystyle\sum_{k=1}^{30} k(k-2)(k+2)$

16. $\displaystyle\sum_{k=1}^{6}(k - k^3)$

17–20 Express the sums in closed form. ■

17. $\displaystyle\sum_{k=1}^{n}\frac{3k}{n}$ 18. $\displaystyle\sum_{k=1}^{n-1}\frac{k^2}{n}$ 19. $\displaystyle\sum_{k=1}^{n-1}\frac{k^3}{n^2}$

20. $\displaystyle\sum_{k=1}^{n}\left(\frac{5}{n} - \frac{2k}{n}\right)$

21–24 True–False Determine whether the statement is true or false. Explain your answer. ■

21. For all positive integers n
$$1^3 + 2^3 + \cdots + n^3 = (1 + 2 + \cdots + n)^2$$

22. The midpoint approximation is the average of the left endpoint approximation and the right endpoint approximation.

23. Every right endpoint approximation for the area under the graph of $y = x^2$ over an interval $[a, b]$ will be an overestimate.

24. For any continuous function f, the area between the graph of f and an interval $[a, b]$ (on which f is defined) is equal to the absolute value of the net signed area between the graph of f and the interval $[a, b]$.

FOCUS ON CONCEPTS

25. (a) Write the first three and final two summands in the sum
$$\sum_{k=1}^{n} \left(2 + k \cdot \frac{3}{n}\right)^4 \frac{3}{n}$$
Explain why this sum gives the right endpoint approximation for the area under the curve $y = x^4$ over the interval $[2, 5]$.
   (b) Show that a change in the index range of the sum in part (a) can produce the left endpoint approximation for the area under the curve $y = x^4$ over the interval $[2, 5]$.

26. For a function f that is continuous on $[a, b]$, Definition 5.4.5 says that the net signed area A between $y = f(x)$ and the interval $[a, b]$ is
$$A = \lim_{n \to +\infty} \sum_{k=1}^{n} f(x_k^*) \Delta x$$
Give geometric interpretations for the symbols n, x_k^*, and Δx. Explain how to interpret the limit in this definition.

27–30 Divide the specified interval into $n = 4$ subintervals of equal length and then compute
$$\sum_{k=1}^{4} f(x_k^*) \Delta x$$
with x_k^* as (a) the left endpoint of each subinterval, (b) the midpoint of each subinterval, and (c) the right endpoint of each subinterval. Illustrate each part with a graph of f that includes the rectangles whose areas are represented in the sum. ■

27. $f(x) = 3x + 1$; $[2, 6]$ 28. $f(x) = 1/x$; $[1, 9]$

29. $f(x) = \cos x$; $[0, \pi]$ 30. $f(x) = 2x - x^2$; $[-1, 3]$

C **31–34** Use a calculating utility with summation capabilities or a CAS to obtain an approximate value for the area between the curve $y = f(x)$ and the specified interval with $n = 10$, 20, and 50 subintervals using the (a) left endpoint, (b) midpoint, and (c) right endpoint approximations. ■

31. $f(x) = 1/x$; $[1, 2]$ 32. $f(x) = 1/x^2$; $[1, 3]$

33. $f(x) = \sqrt{x}$; $[0, 4]$ 34. $f(x) = \sin x$; $[0, \pi/2]$

35–40 Use Definition 5.4.3 with x_k^* as the *right* endpoint of each subinterval to find the area under the curve $y = f(x)$ over the specified interval. ■

35. $f(x) = x/2$; $[1, 4]$ 36. $f(x) = 5 - x$; $[0, 5]$

37. $f(x) = 9 - x^2$; $[0, 3]$ 38. $f(x) = 4 - \frac{1}{4}x^2$; $[0, 3]$

39. $f(x) = x^3$; $[2, 6]$ 40. $f(x) = 1 - x^3$; $[-3, -1]$

41–44 Use Definition 5.4.3 with x_k^* as the *left* endpoint of each subinterval to find the area under the curve $y = f(x)$ over the specified interval. ■

41. $f(x) = x/2$; $[1, 4]$ 42. $f(x) = 5 - x$; $[0, 5]$

43. $f(x) = 9 - x^2$; $[0, 3]$ 44. $f(x) = 4 - \frac{1}{4}x^2$; $[0, 3]$

45–48 Use Definition 5.4.3 with x_k^* as the *midpoint* of each subinterval to find the area under the curve $y = f(x)$ over the specified interval. ■

45. $f(x) = 2x$; $[0, 4]$ 46. $f(x) = 6 - x$; $[1, 5]$

47. $f(x) = x^2$; $[0, 1]$ 48. $f(x) = x^2$; $[-1, 1]$

49–52 Use Definition 5.4.5 with x_k^* as the *right* endpoint of each subinterval to find the net signed area between the curve $y = f(x)$ and the specified interval. ■

49. $f(x) = x$; $[-1, 1]$. Verify your answer with a simple geometric argument.

50. $f(x) = x$; $[-1, 2]$. Verify your answer with a simple geometric argument.

51. $f(x) = x^2 - 1$; $[0, 2]$ 52. $f(x) = x^3$; $[-1, 1]$

53. (a) Show that the area under the graph of $y = x^3$ and over the interval $[0, b]$ is $b^4/4$.
   (b) Find a formula for the area under $y = x^3$ over the interval $[a, b]$, where $a \geq 0$.

54. Find the area between the graph of $y = \sqrt{x}$ and the interval $[0, 1]$. [*Hint:* Use the result of Exercise 25 of Section 5.1.]

55. An artist wants to create a rough triangular design using uniform square tiles glued edge to edge. She places n tiles in a row to form the base of the triangle and then makes each successive row two tiles shorter than the preceding row. Find a formula for the number of tiles used in the design. [*Hint:* Your answer will depend on whether n is even or odd.]

56. An artist wants to create a sculpture by gluing together uniform spheres. She creates a rough rectangular base that has 50 spheres along one edge and 30 spheres along the other. She then creates successive layers by gluing spheres in the grooves of the preceding layer. How many spheres will there be in the sculpture?

57–60 Consider the sum

$$\sum_{k=1}^{4}[(k+1)^3 - k^3] = [5^3 - 4^3] + [4^3 - 3^3]$$
$$+ [3^3 - 2^3] + [2^3 - 1^3]$$
$$= 5^3 - 1^3 = 124$$

For convenience, the terms are listed in reverse order. Note how cancellation allows the entire sum to collapse like a telescope. A sum is said to *telescope* when part of each term cancels part of an adjacent term, leaving only portions of the first and last terms uncanceled. Evaluate the telescoping sums in these exercises.

57. $\displaystyle\sum_{k=5}^{17}(3^k - 3^{k-1})$

58. $\displaystyle\sum_{k=1}^{50}\left(\frac{1}{k} - \frac{1}{k+1}\right)$

59. $\displaystyle\sum_{k=2}^{20}\left(\frac{1}{k^2} - \frac{1}{(k-1)^2}\right)$

60. $\displaystyle\sum_{k=1}^{100}(2^{k+1} - 2^k)$

61. (a) Show that

$$\frac{1}{1\cdot 3} + \frac{1}{3\cdot 5} + \cdots + \frac{1}{(2n-1)(2n+1)} = \frac{n}{2n+1}$$

$$\left[Hint: \frac{1}{(2n-1)(2n+1)} = \frac{1}{2}\left(\frac{1}{2n-1} - \frac{1}{2n+1}\right)\right]$$

(b) Use the result in part (a) to find

$$\lim_{n\to+\infty}\sum_{k=1}^{n}\frac{1}{(2k-1)(2k+1)}$$

62. (a) Show that

$$\frac{1}{1\cdot 2} + \frac{1}{2\cdot 3} + \frac{1}{3\cdot 4} + \cdots + \frac{1}{n(n+1)} = \frac{n}{n+1}$$

$$\left[Hint: \frac{1}{n(n+1)} = \frac{1}{n} - \frac{1}{n+1}\right]$$

(b) Use the result in part (a) to find

$$\lim_{n\to+\infty}\sum_{k=1}^{n}\frac{1}{k(k+1)}$$

63. Let $\bar{x}$ denote the arithmetic average of the n numbers $x_1, x_2, \ldots, x_n$. Use Theorem 5.4.1 to prove that

$$\sum_{i=1}^{n}(x_i - \bar{x}) = 0$$

64. Let

$$S = \sum_{k=0}^{n}ar^k$$

Show that $S - rS = a - ar^{n+1}$ and hence that

$$\sum_{k=0}^{n}ar^k = \frac{a - ar^{n+1}}{1 - r} \quad (r \neq 1)$$

(A sum of this form is called a *geometric sum*.)

65. By writing out the sums, determine whether the following are valid identities.

(a) $\displaystyle\int\left[\sum_{i=1}^{n}f_i(x)\right]dx = \sum_{i=1}^{n}\left[\int f_i(x)\,dx\right]$

(b) $\displaystyle\frac{d}{dx}\left[\sum_{i=1}^{n}f_i(x)\right] = \sum_{i=1}^{n}\left[\frac{d}{dx}[f_i(x)]\right]$

66. Which of the following are valid identities?

(a) $\displaystyle\sum_{i=1}^{n}a_i b_i = \sum_{i=1}^{n}a_i \sum_{i=1}^{n}b_i$ (b) $\displaystyle\sum_{i=1}^{n}a_i^2 = \left(\sum_{i=1}^{n}a_i\right)^2$

(c) $\displaystyle\sum_{i=1}^{n}\frac{a_i}{b_i} = \frac{\displaystyle\sum_{i=1}^{n}a_i}{\displaystyle\sum_{i=1}^{n}b_i}$ (d) $\displaystyle\sum_{i=1}^{n}a_i = \sum_{j=0}^{n-1}a_{j+1}$

67. Prove part (c) of Theorem 5.4.1.

68. Prove Theorem 5.4.4.

69. **Writing** What is *net signed area*? How does this concept expand our application of the rectangle method?

70. **Writing** Based on Example 6, one might conjecture that the midpoint approximation always provides a better approximation than either endpoint approximation. Discuss the merits of this conjecture.

✔**QUICK CHECK ANSWERS 5.4**

1. (a) $\dfrac{1}{2k}$; $\dfrac{1}{2(j+1)}$ (b) $\displaystyle\sum_{k=1}^{5}10^k$ **2.** (a) $\dfrac{n(n+1)}{2}$ (b) $3n(n+1) + n$ (c) $\dfrac{n(n+1)(2n+1)}{6}$ **3.** (a) 0.5 (b) 1, 1.5, 2, 2.5

(c) 1.25, 1.75, 2.25, 2.75 (d) 1.5, 2, 2.5, 3 **4.** 6.75 **5.** $\displaystyle\lim_{n\to+\infty}\dfrac{3n^2 + 4n}{n^2} = 3$

5.5 THE DEFINITE INTEGRAL

In this section we will introduce the concept of a "definite integral," which will link the concept of area to other important concepts such as length, volume, density, probability, and work.

■ **RIEMANN SUMS AND THE DEFINITE INTEGRAL**

In our definition of net signed area (Definition 5.4.5), we assumed that for each positive number n, the interval $[a, b]$ was subdivided into n subintervals of equal length to create bases for the approximating rectangles. For some functions it may be more convenient to use rectangles with different widths (see Making Connections Exercises 2 and 3); however, if we are to "exhaust" an area with rectangles of different widths, then it is important that successive subdivisions be constructed in such a way that the widths of all the rectangles approach zero as n increases (Figure 5.5.1). Thus, we must preclude the kind of situation that occurs in Figure 5.5.2 in which the right half of the interval is never subdivided. If this kind of subdivision were allowed, the error in the approximation would not approach zero as n increased.

A **partition** of the interval $[a, b]$ is a collection of points

$$a = x_0 < x_1 < x_2 < \cdots < x_{n-1} < x_n = b$$

that divides $[a, b]$ into n subintervals of lengths

$$\Delta x_1 = x_1 - x_0, \quad \Delta x_2 = x_2 - x_1, \quad \Delta x_3 = x_3 - x_2, \ldots, \quad \Delta x_n = x_n - x_{n-1}$$

The partition is said to be **regular** provided the subintervals all have the same length

$$\Delta x_k = \Delta x = \frac{b - a}{n}$$

For a regular partition, the widths of the approximating rectangles approach zero as n is made large. Since this need not be the case for a general partition, we need some way to measure the "size" of these widths. One approach is to let max Δx_k denote the largest of the subinterval widths. The magnitude max Δx_k is called the **mesh size** of the partition. For example, Figure 5.5.3 shows a partition of the interval $[0, 6]$ into four subintervals with a mesh size of 2.

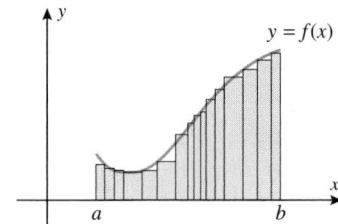

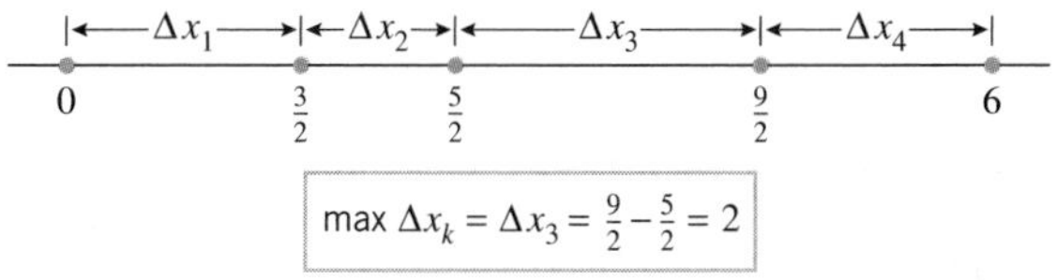

▲ **Figure 5.5.1**

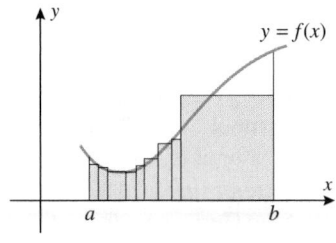

▲ **Figure 5.5.2**

$|\!\leftarrow\!\!-\!\!\Delta x_1\!\!-\!\!\rightarrow\!|\!\leftarrow\!\Delta x_2\!\rightarrow\!|\!\leftarrow\!\!-\!\!-\!\!\Delta x_3\!\!-\!\!-\!\!\rightarrow\!|\!\leftarrow\!\!-\!\!\Delta x_4\!\!-\!\!\rightarrow\!|$

$$0 \qquad \frac{3}{2} \qquad \frac{5}{2} \qquad \frac{9}{2} \qquad 6$$

$$\boxed{\max \Delta x_k = \Delta x_3 = \frac{9}{2} - \frac{5}{2} = 2}$$

▶ **Figure 5.5.3**

If we are to generalize Definition 5.4.5 so that it allows for unequal subinterval widths, we must replace the constant length Δx by the variable length Δx_k. When this is done the sum

$$\sum_{k=1}^{n} f(x_k^*)\Delta x \quad \text{is replaced by} \quad \sum_{k=1}^{n} f(x_k^*)\Delta x_k$$

We also need to replace the expression $n \to +\infty$ by an expression that guarantees us that the lengths of all subintervals approach zero. We will use the expression max $\Delta x_k \to 0$ for this purpose. Based on our intuitive concept of area, we would then expect the net signed area A between the graph of f and the interval $[a, b]$ to satisfy the equation

$$A = \lim_{\max \Delta x_k \to 0} \sum_{k=1}^{n} f(x_k^*)\Delta x_k$$

Some writers use the symbol $\|\Delta\|$ rather than max Δx_k for the mesh size of the partition, in which case max $\Delta x_k \to 0$ would be replaced by $\|\Delta\| \to 0$.

(We will see in a moment that this is the case.) The limit that appears in this expression is one of the fundamental concepts of integral calculus and forms the basis for the following definition.

5.5.1   **DEFINITION**   A function f is said to be *integrable* on a finite closed interval $[a, b]$ if the limit

$$\lim_{\max \Delta x_k \to 0} \sum_{k=1}^{n} f(x_k^*) \Delta x_k$$

exists and does not depend on the choice of partitions or on the choice of the points x_k^* in the subintervals. When this is the case we denote the limit by the symbol

$$\int_a^b f(x)\, dx = \lim_{\max \Delta x_k \to 0} \sum_{k=1}^{n} f(x_k^*) \Delta x_k$$

which is called the *definite integral* of f from a to b. The numbers a and b are called the *lower limit of integration* and the *upper limit of integration*, respectively, and $f(x)$ is called the *integrand*.

The notation used for the definite integral deserves some comment. Historically, the expression "$f(x)\, dx$" was interpreted to be the "infinitesimal area" of a rectangle with height $f(x)$ and "infinitesimal" width dx. By "summing" these infinitesimal areas, the entire area under the curve was obtained. The integral symbol "$\int$" is an "elongated s" that was used to indicate this summation. For us, the integral symbol "$\int$" and the symbol "dx" can serve as reminders that the definite integral is actually a limit of a *summation* as $\Delta x_k \to 0$. The sum that appears in Definition 5.5.1 is called a *Riemann sum*, and the definite integral is sometimes called the *Riemann integral* in honor of the German mathematician Bernhard Riemann who formulated many of the basic concepts of integral calculus. (The reason for the similarity in notation between the definite integral and the indefinite integral will become clear in the next section, where we will establish a link between the two types of "integration.")

Georg Friedrich Bernhard Riemann (1826–1866) German mathematician. Bernhard Riemann, as he is commonly known, was the son of a Protestant minister. He received his elementary education from his father and showed brilliance in arithmetic at an early age. In 1846 he enrolled at Göttingen University to study theology and philology, but he soon transferred to mathematics. He studied physics under W. E. Weber and mathematics under Carl Friedrich Gauss, whom some people consider to be the greatest mathematician who ever lived. In 1851 Riemann received his Ph.D. under Gauss, after which he remained at Göttingen to teach. In 1862, one month after his marriage, Riemann suffered an attack of pleurisy, and for the remainder of his life was an extremely sick man. He finally succumbed to tuberculosis in 1866 at age 39.

An interesting story surrounds Riemann's work in geometry. For his introductory lecture prior to becoming an associate professor, Riemann submitted three possible topics to Gauss. Gauss surprised Riemann by choosing the topic Riemann liked the least, the foundations of geometry. The lecture was like a scene from a movie. The old and failing Gauss, a giant in his day, watching intently as his brilliant and youthful protégé skillfully pieced together portions of the old man's own work into a complete and beautiful system. Gauss is said to have gasped with delight as the lecture neared its end, and on the way home he marveled at his student's brilliance. Gauss died shortly thereafter. The results presented by Riemann that day eventually evolved into a fundamental tool that Einstein used some 50 years later to develop relativity theory.

In addition to his work in geometry, Riemann made major contributions to the theory of complex functions and mathematical physics. The notion of the definite integral, as it is presented in most basic calculus courses, is due to him. Riemann's early death was a great loss to mathematics, for his mathematical work was brilliant and of fundamental importance.

The limit that appears in Definition 5.5.1 is somewhat different from the kinds of limits discussed in Chapter 1. Loosely phrased, the expression

$$\lim_{\max \Delta x_k \to 0} \sum_{k=1}^{n} f(x_k^*) \Delta x_k = L$$

is intended to convey the idea that we can force the Riemann sums to be as close as we please to L, regardless of how the values of x_k^* are chosen, by making the mesh size of the partition sufficiently small. While it is possible to give a more formal definition of this limit, we will simply rely on intuitive arguments when applying Definition 5.5.1.

Although a function need not be continuous on an interval to be integrable on that interval (Exercise 42), we will be interested primarily in definite integrals of continuous functions. The following theorem, which we will state without proof, says that if a function is continuous on a finite closed interval, then it is integrable on that interval, and its definite integral is the net signed area between the graph of the function and the interval.

5.5.2   THEOREM   *If a function f is continuous on an interval $[a, b]$, then f is integrable on $[a, b]$, and the net signed area A between the graph of f and the interval $[a, b]$ is*

$$A = \int_a^b f(x)\, dx \tag{1}$$

REMARK   Formula (1) follows from the integrability of f, since the integrability allows us to use any partitions to evaluate the integral. In particular, if we use *regular* partitions of $[a, b]$, then

$$\Delta x_k = \Delta x = \frac{b - a}{n}$$

for all values of k. This implies that $\max \Delta x_k = (b - a)/n$, from which it follows that $\max \Delta x_k \to 0$ if and only if $n \to +\infty$. Thus,

$$\int_a^b f(x)\, dx = \lim_{\max \Delta x_k \to 0} \sum_{k=1}^{n} f(x_k^*) \Delta x_k = \lim_{n \to +\infty} \sum_{k=1}^{n} f(x_k^*) \Delta x = A$$

In the simplest cases, definite integrals of continuous functions can be calculated using formulas from plane geometry to compute signed areas.

▶ **Example 1**   Sketch the region whose area is represented by the definite integral, and evaluate the integral using an appropriate formula from geometry.

(a) $\displaystyle\int_1^4 2\, dx$ (b) $\displaystyle\int_{-1}^2 (x + 2)\, dx$ (c) $\displaystyle\int_0^1 \sqrt{1 - x^2}\, dx$

In Example 1, it is understood that the units of area are the squared units of length, even though we have not stated the units of length explicitly.

Solution (a).   The graph of the integrand is the horizontal line $y = 2$, so the region is a rectangle of height 2 extending over the interval from 1 to 4 (Figure 5.5.4a). Thus,

$$\int_1^4 2\, dx = (\text{area of rectangle}) = 2(3) = 6$$

Solution (b).   The graph of the integrand is the line $y = x + 2$, so the region is a trapezoid whose base extends from $x = -1$ to $x = 2$ (Figure 5.5.4b). Thus,

$$\int_{-1}^2 (x + 2)\, dx = (\text{area of trapezoid}) = \frac{1}{2}(1 + 4)(3) = \frac{15}{2}$$

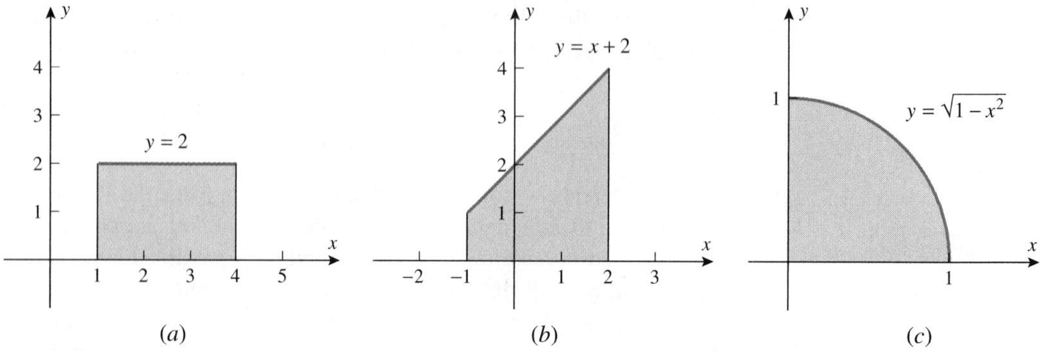

▲ **Figure 5.5.4**

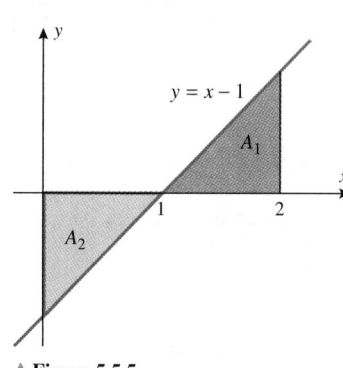

▲ **Figure 5.5.5**

Solution (c).   The graph of $y = \sqrt{1 - x^2}$ is the upper semicircle of radius 1, centered at the origin, so the region is the right quarter-circle extending from $x = 0$ to $x = 1$ (Figure 5.5.4c). Thus,

$$\int_0^1 \sqrt{1 - x^2}\, dx = (\text{area of quarter-circle}) = \frac{1}{4}\pi(1^2) = \frac{\pi}{4} \blacktriangleleft$$

▶ **Example 2**   Evaluate

$$\text{(a)} \int_0^2 (x - 1)\, dx \qquad \text{(b)} \int_0^1 (x - 1)\, dx$$

Solution.   The graph of $y = x - 1$ is shown in Figure 5.5.5, and we leave it for you to verify that the shaded triangular regions both have area $\frac{1}{2}$. Over the interval $[0, 2]$ the net signed area is $A_1 - A_2 = \frac{1}{2} - \frac{1}{2} = 0$, and over the interval $[0, 1]$ the net signed area is $-A_2 = -\frac{1}{2}$. Thus,

$$\int_0^2 (x - 1)\, dx = 0 \quad \text{and} \quad \int_0^1 (x - 1)\, dx = -\frac{1}{2}$$

(Recall that in Example 7 of Section 5.4, we used Definition 5.4.5 to show that the net signed area between the graph of $y = x - 1$ and the interval $[0, 2]$ is zero.) ◀

■ **PROPERTIES OF THE DEFINITE INTEGRAL**

It is assumed in Definition 5.5.1 that $[a, b]$ is a finite closed interval with $a < b$, and hence the upper limit of integration in the definite integral is greater than the lower limit of integration. However, it will be convenient to extend this definition to allow for cases in which the upper and lower limits of integration are equal or the lower limit of integration is greater than the upper limit of integration. For this purpose we make the following special definitions.

5.5.3   **DEFINITION**

(a)   If a is in the domain of f, we define

$$\int_a^a f(x)\, dx = 0$$

(b)   If f is integrable on $[a, b]$, then we define

$$\int_b^a f(x)\, dx = -\int_a^b f(x)\, dx$$

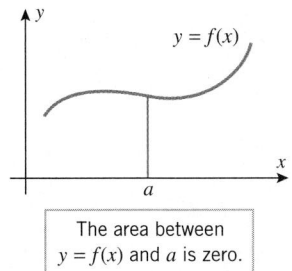

The area between
$y = f(x)$ and a is zero.

▲ **Figure 5.5.6**

Part (a) of this definition is consistent with the intuitive idea that the area between a point on the x-axis and a curve $y = f(x)$ should be zero (Figure 5.5.6). Part (b) of the definition is simply a useful convention; it states that interchanging the limits of integration reverses the sign of the integral.

▶ **Example 3**

(a) $\displaystyle\int_{1}^{1} x^2 \, dx = 0$

(b) $\displaystyle\int_{1}^{0} \sqrt{1 - x^2} \, dx = -\int_{0}^{1} \sqrt{1 - x^2} \, dx = -\frac{\pi}{4}$ ◀

Example 1(c)

Because definite integrals are defined as limits, they inherit many of the properties of limits. For example, we know that constants can be moved through limit signs and that the limit of a sum or difference is the sum or difference of the limits. Thus, you should not be surprised by the following theorem, which we state without formal proof.

5.5.4   THEOREM   *If f and g are integrable on $[a, b]$ and if c is a constant, then cf, $f + g$, and $f - g$ are integrable on $[a, b]$ and*

(a) $\displaystyle\int_{a}^{b} cf(x) \, dx = c \int_{a}^{b} f(x) \, dx$

(b) $\displaystyle\int_{a}^{b} [f(x) + g(x)] \, dx = \int_{a}^{b} f(x) \, dx + \int_{a}^{b} g(x) \, dx$

(c) $\displaystyle\int_{a}^{b} [f(x) - g(x)] \, dx = \int_{a}^{b} f(x) \, dx - \int_{a}^{b} g(x) \, dx$

Part (*b*) of this theorem can be extended to more than two functions. More precisely,

$$\int_{a}^{b} [f_1(x) + f_2(x) + \cdots + f_n(x)] \, dx$$
$$= \int_{a}^{b} f_1(x) \, dx + \int_{a}^{b} f_2(x) \, dx + \cdots + \int_{a}^{b} f_n(x) \, dx$$

Some properties of definite integrals can be motivated by interpreting the integral as an area. For example, if f is continuous and nonnegative on the interval $[a, b]$, and if c is a point between a and b, then the area under $y = f(x)$ over the interval $[a, b]$ can be split into two parts and expressed as the area under the graph from a to c plus the area under the graph from c to b (Figure 5.5.7), that is,

$$\int_{a}^{b} f(x) \, dx = \int_{a}^{c} f(x) \, dx + \int_{c}^{b} f(x) \, dx$$

This is a special case of the following theorem about definite integrals, which we state without proof.

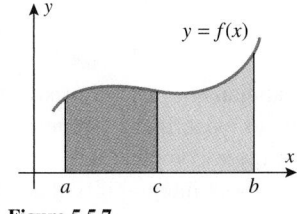

▲ **Figure 5.5.7**

5.5.5 **THEOREM** *If f is integrable on a closed interval containing the three points a, b, and c, then*

$$\int_a^b f(x)\,dx = \int_a^c f(x)\,dx + \int_c^b f(x)\,dx$$

no matter how the points are ordered.

The following theorem, which we state without formal proof, can also be motivated by interpreting definite integrals as areas.

5.5.6 **THEOREM**

(a) *If f is integrable on $[a, b]$ and $f(x) \geq 0$ for all x in $[a, b]$, then*

$$\int_a^b f(x)\,dx \geq 0$$

(b) *If f and g are integrable on $[a, b]$ and $f(x) \geq g(x)$ for all x in $[a, b]$, then*

$$\int_a^b f(x)\,dx \geq \int_a^b g(x)\,dx$$

Part (*b*) of Theorem 5.5.6 states that the direction (sometimes called the *sense*) of the inequality $f(x) \geq g(x)$ is unchanged if one integrates both sides. Moreover, if $b > a$, then both parts of the theorem remain true if $\geq$ is replaced by $\leq$, $>$, or $<$ throughout.

Net signed area ≥ 0

▲ **Figure 5.5.8**

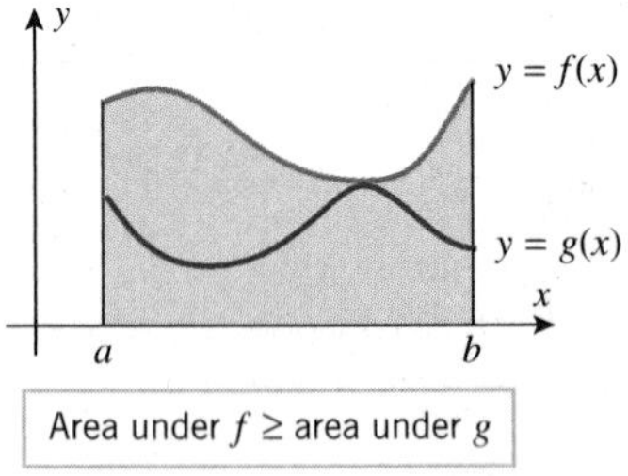

Area under $f \geq$ area under g

▲ **Figure 5.5.9**

Geometrically, part (*a*) of this theorem states the obvious fact that if f is nonnegative on $[a, b]$, then the net signed area between the graph of f and the interval $[a, b]$ is also nonnegative (Figure 5.5.8). Part (*b*) has its simplest interpretation when f and g are nonnegative on $[a, b]$, in which case the theorem states that if the graph of f does not go below the graph of g, then the area under the graph of f is at least as large as the area under the graph of g (Figure 5.5.9).

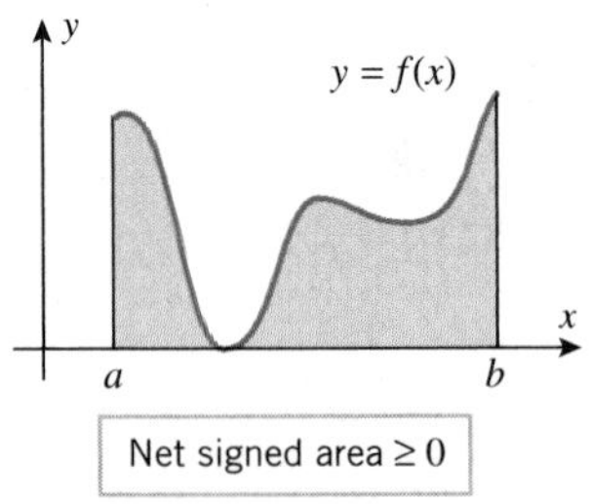

▶ **Example 4** Evaluate

$$\int_0^1 (5 - 3\sqrt{1 - x^2})\,dx$$

Solution. From parts (*a*) and (*c*) of Theorem 5.5.4 we can write

$$\int_0^1 (5 - 3\sqrt{1 - x^2})\,dx = \int_0^1 5\,dx - \int_0^1 3\sqrt{1 - x^2}\,dx = \int_0^1 5\,dx - 3\int_0^1 \sqrt{1 - x^2}\,dx$$

The first integral in this difference can be interpreted as the area of a rectangle of height 5 and base 1, so its value is 5, and from Example 1 the value of the second integral is $\pi/4$. Thus,

$$\int_0^1 (5 - 3\sqrt{1 - x^2})\,dx = 5 - 3\left(\frac{\pi}{4}\right) = 5 - \frac{3\pi}{4} \quad ◀$$

■ **DISCONTINUITIES AND INTEGRABILITY**

In the late nineteenth and early twentieth centuries, mathematicians began to investigate conditions under which the limit that defines an integral fails to exist, that is, conditions under which a function fails to be integrable. The matter is quite complex and beyond the scope of this text. However, there are a few basic results about integrability that are important to know; we begin with a definition.

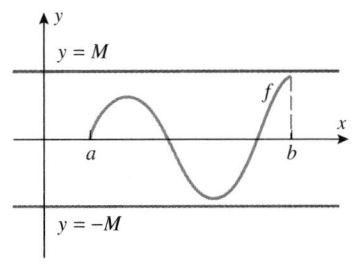

f is bounded on [a, b].

▲ **Figure 5.5.10**

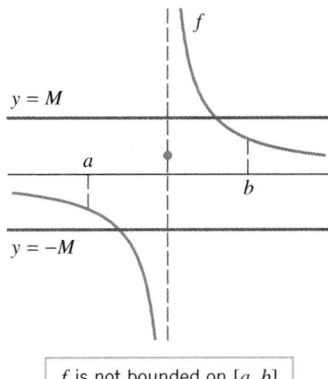

f is not bounded on [a, b].

▲ **Figure 5.5.11**

5.5.7   DEFINITION   A function f that is defined on an interval is said to be **bounded** on the interval if there is a positive number M such that

$$-M \leq f(x) \leq M$$

for all x in the interval. Geometrically, this means that the graph of f over the interval lies between the lines $y = -M$ and $y = M$.

For example, a continuous function f is bounded on *every* finite closed interval because the Extreme-Value Theorem (4.4.2) implies that f has an absolute maximum and an absolute minimum on the interval; hence, its graph will lie between the lines $y = -M$ and $y = M$, provided we make M large enough (Figure 5.5.10). In contrast, a function that has a vertical asymptote inside of an interval is not bounded on that interval because its graph over the interval cannot be made to lie between the lines $y = -M$ and $y = M$, no matter how large we make the value of M (Figure 5.5.11).

The following theorem, which we state without proof, provides some facts about integrability for functions with discontinuities. In the exercises we have included some problems that are concerned with this theorem (Exercises 42, 43, and 44).

5.5.8   THEOREM   *Let f be a function that is defined on the finite closed interval $[a, b]$.*

(a)   If f has finitely many discontinuities in $[a, b]$ but is bounded on $[a, b]$, then f is integrable on $[a, b]$.

(b)   If f is not bounded on $[a, b]$, then f is not integrable on $[a, b]$.

✔ **QUICK CHECK EXERCISES 5.5**   *(See page 362 for answers.)*

1. In each part, use the partition of $[2, 7]$ in the accompanying figure.

▲ **Figure Ex-1**

   (a) What is n, the number of subintervals in this partition?
   (b) $x_0 =$ _____; $x_1 =$ _____; $x_2 =$ _____;
       $x_3 =$ _____; $x_4 =$ _____
   (c) $\Delta x_1 =$ _____; $\Delta x_2 =$ _____; $\Delta x_3 =$ _____;
       $\Delta x_4 =$ _____
   (d) The mesh of this partition is _____.

2. Let $f(x) = 2x - 8$. Use the partition of $[2, 7]$ in Quick Check Exercise 1 and the choices $x_1^* = 2$, $x_2^* = 4$, $x_3^* = 5$, and $x_4^* = 7$ to evaluate the Riemann sum

$$\sum_{k=1}^{4} f(x_k^*)\Delta x_k$$

3. Use the accompanying figure to evaluate

$$\int_2^7 (2x - 8)\, dx$$

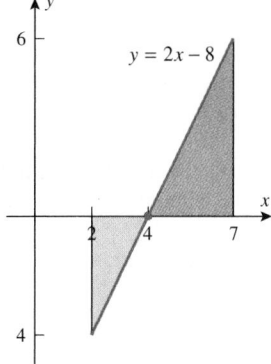

◀ **Figure Ex-3**

4. Suppose that $g(x)$ is a function for which

$$\int_{-2}^{1} g(x)\, dx = 5 \quad \text{and} \quad \int_{1}^{2} g(x)\, dx = -2$$

Use this information to evaluate the definite integrals.

   (a) $\displaystyle\int_{1}^{2} 5g(x)\, dx$ (b) $\displaystyle\int_{-2}^{2} g(x)\, dx$

   (c) $\displaystyle\int_{1}^{1} [g(x)]^2\, dx$ (d) $\displaystyle\int_{2}^{-2} 4g(x)\, dx$

EXERCISE SET 5.5

1–4 Find the value of

(a) $\displaystyle\sum_{k=1}^{n} f(x_k^*)\,\Delta x_k$ (b) $\max \Delta x_k$. ▨

1. $f(x) = x + 1$; $a = 0, b = 4$; $n = 3$;

$\Delta x_1 = 1, \Delta x_2 = 1, \Delta x_3 = 2$;

$x_1^* = \frac{1}{3}, x_2^* = \frac{3}{2}, x_3^* = 3$

2. $f(x) = \cos x$; $a = 0, b = 2\pi$; $n = 4$;

$\Delta x_1 = \pi/2, \Delta x_2 = 3\pi/4, \Delta x_3 = \pi/2, \Delta x_4 = \pi/4$;

$x_1^* = \pi/4, x_2^* = \pi, x_3^* = 3\pi/2, x_4^* = 7\pi/4$

3. $f(x) = 4 - x^2$; $a = -3, b = 4$; $n = 4$;

$\Delta x_1 = 1, \Delta x_2 = 2, \Delta x_3 = 1, \Delta x_4 = 3$;

$x_1^* = -\frac{5}{2}, x_2^* = -1, x_3^* = \frac{1}{4}, x_4^* = 3$

4. $f(x) = x^3$; $a = -3, b = 3$; $n = 4$;

$\Delta x_1 = 2, \Delta x_2 = 1, \Delta x_3 = 1, \Delta x_4 = 2$;

$x_1^* = -2, x_2^* = 0, x_3^* = 0, x_4^* = 2$

5–8 Use the given values of a and b to express the following limits as integrals. (Do not evaluate the integrals.) ▨

5. $\displaystyle\lim_{\max \Delta x_k \to 0} \sum_{k=1}^{n} (x_k^*)^2 \Delta x_k$; $a = -1, b = 2$

6. $\displaystyle\lim_{\max \Delta x_k \to 0} \sum_{k=1}^{n} (x_k^*)^3 \Delta x_k$; $a = 1, b = 2$

7. $\displaystyle\lim_{\max \Delta x_k \to 0} \sum_{k=1}^{n} 4x_k^*(1 - 3x_k^*)\Delta x_k$; $a = -3, b = 3$

8. $\displaystyle\lim_{\max \Delta x_k \to 0} \sum_{k=1}^{n} (\sin^2 x_k^*)\Delta x_k$; $a = 0, b = \pi/2$

9–10 Use Definition 5.5.1 to express the integrals as limits of Riemann sums. (Do not evaluate the integrals.) ▨

9. (a) $\displaystyle\int_{1}^{2} 2x\,dx$ (b) $\displaystyle\int_{0}^{1} \frac{x}{x+1}\,dx$

10. (a) $\displaystyle\int_{1}^{2} \sqrt{x}\,dx$ (b) $\displaystyle\int_{-\pi/2}^{\pi/2} (1 + \cos x)\,dx$

FOCUS ON CONCEPTS

11. Explain informally why Theorem 5.5.4(a) follows from Definition 5.5.1.

12. Explain informally why Theorem 5.5.6(a) follows from Definition 5.5.1.

13–16 Sketch the region whose signed area is represented by the definite integral, and evaluate the integral using an appropriate formula from geometry, where needed. ▨

13. (a) $\displaystyle\int_{0}^{3} x\,dx$ (b) $\displaystyle\int_{-2}^{-1} x\,dx$

(c) $\displaystyle\int_{-1}^{4} x\,dx$ (d) $\displaystyle\int_{-5}^{5} x\,dx$

14. (a) $\displaystyle\int_{0}^{2} \left(1 - \tfrac{1}{2}x\right) dx$ (b) $\displaystyle\int_{-1}^{1} \left(1 - \tfrac{1}{2}x\right) dx$

(c) $\displaystyle\int_{2}^{3} \left(1 - \tfrac{1}{2}x\right) dx$ (d) $\displaystyle\int_{0}^{3} \left(1 - \tfrac{1}{2}x\right) dx$

15. (a) $\displaystyle\int_{0}^{5} 2\,dx$ (b) $\displaystyle\int_{0}^{\pi} \cos x\,dx$

(c) $\displaystyle\int_{-1}^{2} |2x - 3|\,dx$ (d) $\displaystyle\int_{-1}^{1} \sqrt{1 - x^2}\,dx$

16. (a) $\displaystyle\int_{-10}^{-5} 6\,dx$ (b) $\displaystyle\int_{-\pi/3}^{\pi/3} \sin x\,dx$

(c) $\displaystyle\int_{0}^{3} |x - 2|\,dx$ (d) $\displaystyle\int_{0}^{2} \sqrt{4 - x^2}\,dx$

17. In each part, evaluate the integral, given that

$$f(x) = \begin{cases} |x - 2|, & x \geq 0 \\ x + 2, & x < 0 \end{cases}$$

(a) $\displaystyle\int_{-2}^{0} f(x)\,dx$ (b) $\displaystyle\int_{-2}^{2} f(x)\,dx$

(c) $\displaystyle\int_{0}^{6} f(x)\,dx$ (d) $\displaystyle\int_{-4}^{6} f(x)\,dx$

18. In each part, evaluate the integral, given that

$$f(x) = \begin{cases} 2x, & x \leq 1 \\ 2, & x > 1 \end{cases}$$

(a) $\displaystyle\int_{0}^{1} f(x)\,dx$ (b) $\displaystyle\int_{-1}^{1} f(x)\,dx$

(c) $\displaystyle\int_{1}^{10} f(x)\,dx$ (d) $\displaystyle\int_{1/2}^{5} f(x)\,dx$

FOCUS ON CONCEPTS

19–20 Use the areas shown in the figure to find

(a) $\displaystyle\int_{a}^{b} f(x)\,dx$ (b) $\displaystyle\int_{b}^{c} f(x)\,dx$

(c) $\displaystyle\int_{a}^{c} f(x)\,dx$ (d) $\displaystyle\int_{a}^{d} f(x)\,dx$. ▨

19.

20.

21. Find $\int_{-1}^{2}[f(x)+2g(x)]\,dx$ if

$$\int_{-1}^{2}f(x)\,dx=5\quad\text{and}\quad\int_{-1}^{2}g(x)\,dx=-3$$

22. Find $\int_{1}^{4}[3f(x)-g(x)]\,dx$ if

$$\int_{1}^{4}f(x)\,dx=2\quad\text{and}\quad\int_{1}^{4}g(x)\,dx=10$$

23. Find $\int_{1}^{5}f(x)\,dx$ if

$$\int_{0}^{1}f(x)\,dx=-2\quad\text{and}\quad\int_{0}^{5}f(x)\,dx=1$$

24. Find $\int_{3}^{-2}f(x)\,dx$ if

$$\int_{-2}^{1}f(x)\,dx=2\quad\text{and}\quad\int_{1}^{3}f(x)\,dx=-6$$

25–28 Use Theorem 5.5.4 and appropriate formulas from geometry to evaluate the integrals. ■

25. $\int_{-1}^{3}(4-5x)\,dx$ **26.** $\int_{-2}^{2}(1-3|x|)\,dx$

27. $\int_{0}^{1}(x+2\sqrt{1-x^2})\,dx$ **28.** $\int_{-3}^{0}(2+\sqrt{9-x^2})\,dx$

29–32 True–False Determine whether the statement is true or false. Explain your answer. ■

29. If $f(x)$ is integrable on $[a,b]$, then $f(x)$ is continuous on $[a,b]$.

30. It is the case that

$$0<\int_{-1}^{1}\frac{\cos x}{\sqrt{1+x^2}}\,dx$$

31. If the integral of $f(x)$ over the interval $[a,b]$ is negative, then $f(x)\le0$ for $a\le x\le b$.

32. The function

$$f(x)=\begin{cases}0,&x\le0\\x^2,&x>0\end{cases}$$

is integrable over every closed interval $[a,b]$.

33–34 Use Theorem 5.5.6 to determine whether the value of the integral is positive or negative. ■

33. (a) $\int_{2}^{3}\frac{\sqrt{x}}{1-x}\,dx$ (b) $\int_{0}^{4}\frac{x^2}{3-\cos x}\,dx$

34. (a) $\int_{-3}^{-1}\frac{x^4}{\sqrt{3-x}}\,dx$ (b) $\int_{-2}^{2}\frac{x^3-9}{|x|+1}\,dx$

35. Prove that if f is continuous and if $m\le f(x)\le M$ on $[a,b]$, then

$$m(b-a)\le\int_{a}^{b}f(x)\,dx\le M(b-a)$$

36. Find the maximum and minimum values of $\sqrt{x^3+2}$ for $0\le x\le3$. Use these values, and the inequalities in Exercise 35, to find bounds on the value of the integral

$$\int_{0}^{3}\sqrt{x^3+2}\,dx$$

37–38 Evaluate the integrals by completing the square and applying appropriate formulas from geometry. ■

37. $\int_{0}^{10}\sqrt{10x-x^2}\,dx$ **38.** $\int_{0}^{3}\sqrt{6x-x^2}\,dx$

39–40 Evaluate the limit by expressing it as a definite integral over the interval $[a,b]$ and applying appropriate formulas from geometry. ■

39. $\lim\limits_{\max\Delta x_k\to0}\sum\limits_{k=1}^{n}(3x_k^*+1)\Delta x_k;\;a=0,b=1$

40. $\lim\limits_{\max\Delta x_k\to0}\sum\limits_{k=1}^{n}\sqrt{4-(x_k^*)^2}\,\Delta x_k;\;a=-2,b=2$

FOCUS ON CONCEPTS

41. Let $f(x)=C$ be a constant function.
(a) Use a formula from geometry to show that

$$\int_{a}^{b}f(x)\,dx=C(b-a)$$

(b) Show that any Riemann sum for $f(x)$ over $[a,b]$ evaluates to $C(b-a)$. Use Definition 5.5.1 to show that

$$\int_{a}^{b}f(x)\,dx=C(b-a)$$

42. Define a function f on $[0,1]$ by

$$f(x)=\begin{cases}1,&0<x\le1\\0,&x=0\end{cases}$$

Use Definition 5.5.1 to show that

$$\int_{0}^{1}f(x)\,dx=1$$

43. It can be shown that every interval contains both rational and irrational numbers. Accepting this to be so, do you believe that the function

$$f(x)=\begin{cases}1&\text{if }x\text{ is rational}\\0&\text{if }x\text{ is irrational}\end{cases}$$

is integrable on a closed interval $[a,b]$? Explain your reasoning.

44. Define the function f by

$$f(x) = \begin{cases} \dfrac{1}{x}, & x \neq 0 \\ 0, & x = 0 \end{cases}$$

It follows from Theorem 5.5.8(b) that f is not integrable on the interval $[0, 1]$. Prove this to be the case by applying Definition 5.5.1. [*Hint:* Argue that no matter how small the mesh size is for a partition of $[0, 1]$, there will always be a choice of x_1^* that will make the Riemann sum in Definition 5.5.1 as large as we like.]

45. In each part, use Theorems 5.5.2 and 5.5.8 to determine whether the function f is integrable on the interval $[-1, 1]$.

(a) $f(x) = \cos x$

(b) $f(x) = \begin{cases} x/|x|, & x \neq 0 \\ 0, & x = 0 \end{cases}$

(c) $f(x) = \begin{cases} 1/x^2, & x \neq 0 \\ 0, & x = 0 \end{cases}$

(d) $f(x) = \begin{cases} \sin 1/x, & x \neq 0 \\ 0, & x = 0 \end{cases}$

46. Writing Write a short paragraph that discusses the similarities and differences between indefinite integrals and definite integrals.

47. Writing Write a paragraph that explains informally what it means for a function to be "integrable."

✔ **QUICK CHECK ANSWERS 5.5**

1. (a) $n = 4$ (b) $2, 3, 4.5, 6.5, 7$ (c) $1, 1.5, 2, 0.5$ (d) 2 **2.** 3 **3.** 5 **4.** (a) -10 (b) 3 (c) 0 (d) -12

5.6 THE FUNDAMENTAL THEOREM OF CALCULUS

In this section we will establish two basic relationships between definite and indefinite integrals that together constitute a result called the "Fundamental Theorem of Calculus." One part of this theorem will relate the rectangle and antiderivative methods for calculating areas, and the second part will provide a powerful method for evaluating definite integrals using antiderivatives.

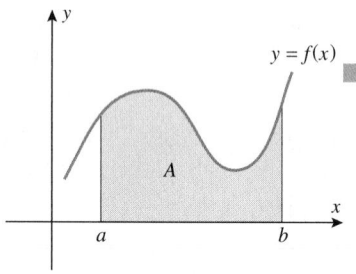

▲ **Figure 5.6.1**

■ **THE FUNDAMENTAL THEOREM OF CALCULUS**

As in earlier sections, let us begin by assuming that f is nonnegative and continuous on an interval $[a, b]$, in which case the area A under the graph of f over the interval $[a, b]$ is represented by the definite integral

$$A = \int_a^b f(x)\, dx \tag{1}$$

(Figure 5.6.1).

Recall that our discussion of the antiderivative method in Section 5.1 suggested that if $A(x)$ is the area under the graph of f from a to x (Figure 5.6.2), then

- $A'(x) = f(x)$
- $A(a) = 0$ The area under the curve from a to a is the area above the single point a, and hence is zero.
- $A(b) = A$ The area under the curve from a to b is A.

The formula $A'(x) = f(x)$ states that $A(x)$ is an antiderivative of $f(x)$, which implies that every other antiderivative of $f(x)$ on $[a, b]$ can be obtained by adding a constant to $A(x)$. Accordingly, let

$$F(x) = A(x) + C$$

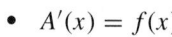

▲ **Figure 5.6.2**

be any antiderivative of $f(x)$, and consider what happens when we subtract $F(a)$ from $F(b)$:

$$F(b) - F(a) = [A(b) + C] - [A(a) + C] = A(b) - A(a) = A - 0 = A$$

Hence (1) can be expressed as

$$\int_a^b f(x)\,dx = F(b) - F(a)$$

In words, this equation states:

> *The definite integral can be evaluated by finding any antiderivative of the integrand and then subtracting the value of this antiderivative at the lower limit of integration from its value at the upper limit of integration.*

Although our evidence for this result assumed that f is nonnegative on $[a, b]$, this assumption is not essential.

5.6.1 **THEOREM** (*The Fundamental Theorem of Calculus, Part 1*) *If f is continuous on $[a, b]$ and F is any antiderivative of f on $[a, b]$, then*

$$\int_a^b f(x)\,dx = F(b) - F(a) \qquad (2)$$

PROOF Let $x_1, x_2, \ldots, x_{n-1}$ be any points in $[a, b]$ such that

$$a < x_1 < x_2 < \cdots < x_{n-1} < b$$

These values divide $[a, b]$ into n subintervals

$$[a, x_1], [x_1, x_2], \ldots, [x_{n-1}, b] \qquad (3)$$

whose lengths, as usual, we denote by

$$\Delta x_1, \Delta x_2, \ldots, \Delta x_n$$

(see Figure 5.6.3). By hypothesis, $F'(x) = f(x)$ for all x in $[a, b]$, so F satisfies the hypotheses of the Mean-Value Theorem (4.8.2) on each subinterval in (3). Hence, we can find points $x_1^*, x_2^*, \ldots, x_n^*$ in the respective subintervals in (3) such that

$$F(x_1) - F(a) = F'(x_1^*)(x_1 - a) = f(x_1^*)\Delta x_1$$
$$F(x_2) - F(x_1) = F'(x_2^*)(x_2 - x_1) = f(x_2^*)\Delta x_2$$
$$F(x_3) - F(x_2) = F'(x_3^*)(x_3 - x_2) = f(x_3^*)\Delta x_3$$
$$\vdots$$
$$F(b) - F(x_{n-1}) = F'(x_n^*)(b - x_{n-1}) = f(x_n^*)\Delta x_n$$

Adding the preceding equations yields

$$F(b) - F(a) = \sum_{k=1}^{n} f(x_k^*)\Delta x_k \qquad (4)$$

Let us now increase n in such a way that max $\Delta x_k \to 0$. Since f is assumed to be continuous, the right side of (4) approaches $\int_a^b f(x)\,dx$ by Theorem 5.5.2 and Definition 5.5.1. However,

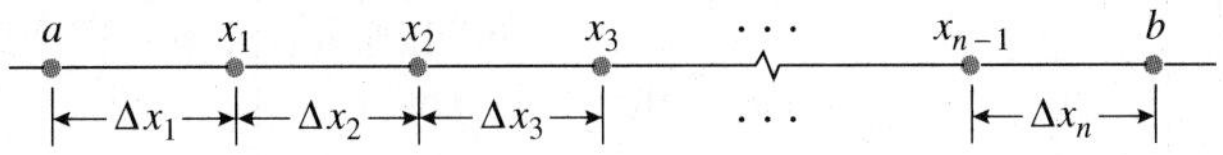

▶ **Figure 5.6.3**

the left side of (4) is independent of n; that is, the left side of (4) remains constant as n increases. Thus,

$$F(b) - F(a) = \lim_{\max \Delta x_k \to 0} \sum_{k=1}^{n} f(x_k^*) \Delta x_k = \int_a^b f(x)\,dx \quad \blacksquare$$

It is standard to denote the difference $F(b) - F(a)$ as

$$F(x)\Big]_a^b = F(b) - F(a) \quad \text{or} \quad \left[F(x)\right]_a^b = F(b) - F(a)$$

For example, using the first of these notations we can express (2) as

$$\int_a^b f(x)\,dx = F(x)\Big]_a^b \tag{5}$$

We will sometimes write

$$F(x)\Big]_{x=a}^b = F(b) - F(a)$$

when it is important to emphasize that a and b are values for the variable x.

▶ **Example 1**   Evaluate $\displaystyle\int_1^2 x\,dx$.

The integral in Example 1 represents the area of a certain trapezoid. Sketch the trapezoid, and find its area using geometry.

Solution.   The function $F(x) = \frac{1}{2}x^2$ is an antiderivative of $f(x) = x$; thus, from (2)

$$\int_1^2 x\,dx = \frac{1}{2}x^2\Big]_1^2 = \frac{1}{2}(2)^2 - \frac{1}{2}(1)^2 = 2 - \frac{1}{2} = \frac{3}{2} \quad \blacktriangleleft$$

▶ **Example 2**   In Example 5 of Section 5.4 we used the definition of area to show that the area under the graph of $y = 9 - x^2$ over the interval $[0, 3]$ is 18 (square units). We can now solve that problem much more easily using the Fundamental Theorem of Calculus:

$$A = \int_0^3 (9 - x^2)\,dx = \left[9x - \frac{x^3}{3}\right]_0^3 = \left(27 - \frac{27}{3}\right) - 0 = 18 \quad \blacktriangleleft$$

▶ **Example 3**

(a) Find the area under the curve $y = \cos x$ over the interval $[0, \pi/2]$ (Figure 5.6.4).

(b) Make a conjecture about the value of the integral

$$\int_0^\pi \cos x\,dx$$

and confirm your conjecture using the Fundamental Theorem of Calculus.

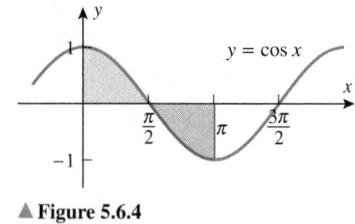

▲ Figure 5.6.4

Solution (a).   Since $\cos x \geq 0$ over the interval $[0, \pi/2]$, the area A under the curve is

$$A = \int_0^{\pi/2} \cos x\,dx = \sin x\Big]_0^{\pi/2} = \sin\frac{\pi}{2} - \sin 0 = 1$$

Solution (b).   The given integral can be interpreted as the signed area between the graph of $y = \cos x$ and the interval $[0, \pi]$. The graph in Figure 5.6.4 suggests that over the interval $[0, \pi]$ the portion of area above the x-axis is the same as the portion of area below the x-axis, so we conjecture that the signed area is zero; this implies that the value of the integral is zero. This is confirmed by the computations

$$\int_0^\pi \cos x \, dx = \sin x \Big]_0^\pi = \sin \pi - \sin 0 = 0 \quad \blacktriangleleft$$

■ THE RELATIONSHIP BETWEEN DEFINITE AND INDEFINITE INTEGRALS

Observe that in the preceding examples we did not include a constant of integration in the antiderivatives. In general, when applying the Fundamental Theorem of Calculus there is no need to include a constant of integration because it will drop out anyway. To see that this is so, let F be any antiderivative of the integrand on $[a, b]$, and let C be any constant; then

$$\int_a^b f(x) \, dx = \big[F(x) + C\big]_a^b = [F(b) + C] - [F(a) + C] = F(b) - F(a)$$

Thus, for purposes of evaluating a definite integral we can omit the constant of integration in

$$\int_a^b f(x) \, dx = \big[F(x) + C\big]_a^b$$

and express (5) as

$$\int_a^b f(x) \, dx = \int f(x) \, dx \,\Big]_a^b \tag{6}$$

which relates the definite and indefinite integrals.

▶ **Example 4**

$$\int_1^9 \sqrt{x} \, dx = \int x^{1/2} \, dx \,\Big]_1^9 = \frac{2}{3} x^{3/2} \,\Big]_1^9 = \frac{2}{3}(27 - 1) = \frac{52}{3} \quad \blacktriangleleft$$

▶ **Example 5**   Table 5.2.1 will be helpful for the following computations.

$$\int_4^9 x^2 \sqrt{x} \, dx = \int_4^9 x^{5/2} \, dx = \frac{2}{7} x^{7/2} \,\Big]_4^9 = \frac{2}{7}(2187 - 128) = \frac{4118}{7} = 588\frac{2}{7}$$

$$\int_0^{\pi/2} \frac{\sin x}{5} \, dx = -\frac{1}{5} \cos x \,\Big]_0^{\pi/2} = -\frac{1}{5}\left[\cos\left(\frac{\pi}{2}\right) - \cos 0\right] = -\frac{1}{5}[0 - 1] = \frac{1}{5}$$

$$\int_0^{\pi/3} \sec^2 x \, dx = \tan x \,\Big]_0^{\pi/3} = \tan\left(\frac{\pi}{3}\right) - \tan 0 = \sqrt{3} - 0 = \sqrt{3}$$

$$\int_0^{\ln 3} 5e^x \, dx = 5e^x \,\Big]_0^{\ln 3} = 5[e^{\ln 3} - e^0] = 5[3 - 1] = 10$$

$$\int_{-e}^{-1} \frac{1}{x} \, dx = \ln|x| \,\Big]_{-e}^{-1} = \ln|-1| - \ln|-e| = 0 - 1 = -1$$

TECHNOLOGY MASTERY

If you have a CAS, read the documentation on evaluating definite integrals and then check the results in Example 5.

$$\int_{-1/2}^{1/2} \frac{1}{\sqrt{1 - x^2}} \, dx = \sin^{-1} x \,\Big]_{-1/2}^{1/2} = \sin^{-1}\left(\frac{1}{2}\right) - \sin^{-1}\left(-\frac{1}{2}\right) = \frac{\pi}{6} - \left(-\frac{\pi}{6}\right) = \frac{\pi}{3} \quad \blacktriangleleft$$

WARNING The requirements in the Fundamental Theorem of Calculus that f be continuous on $[a, b]$ and that F be an antiderivative for f over the entire interval $[a, b]$ are important to keep in mind. Disregarding these assumptions will likely lead to incorrect results. For example, the function $f(x) = 1/x^2$ fails on two counts to be continuous at $x = 0$: $f(x)$ is not defined at $x = 0$ and $\lim_{x \to 0} f(x)$ does not exist. Thus, the Fundamental Theorem of Calculus should not be used to integrate f on any interval that contains $x = 0$. However, if we ignore this and mistakenly apply Formula (2) over the interval $[-1, 1]$, we might *incorrectly* compute $\int_{-1}^{1}(1/x^2)\,dx$ by evaluating an antiderivative, $-1/x$, at the endpoints, arriving at the answer

$$-\frac{1}{x}\Bigg]_{-1}^{1} = -[1 - (-1)] = -2$$

But $f(x) = 1/x^2$ is a nonnegative function, so clearly a negative value for the definite integral is impossible.

The Fundamental Theorem of Calculus can be applied without modification to definite integrals in which the lower limit of integration is greater than or equal to the upper limit of integration.

▶ **Example 6**

$$\int_{1}^{1} x^2\,dx = \frac{x^3}{3}\Bigg]_{1}^{1} = \frac{1}{3} - \frac{1}{3} = 0$$

$$\int_{4}^{0} x\,dx = \frac{x^2}{2}\Bigg]_{4}^{0} = \frac{0}{2} - \frac{16}{2} = -8$$

The latter result is consistent with the result that would be obtained by first reversing the limits of integration in accordance with Definition 5.5.3(b):

$$\int_{4}^{0} x\,dx = -\int_{0}^{4} x\,dx = -\frac{x^2}{2}\Bigg]_{0}^{4} = -\left[\frac{16}{2} - \frac{0}{2}\right] = -8 \quad ◀$$

To integrate a continuous function that is defined piecewise on an interval $[a, b]$, split this interval into subintervals at the breakpoints of the function, and integrate separately over each subinterval in accordance with Theorem 5.5.5.

▶ **Example 7** Evaluate $\int_{0}^{3} f(x)\,dx$ if

$$f(x) = \begin{cases} x^2, & x < 2 \\ 3x - 2, & x \geq 2 \end{cases}$$

Solution. See Figure 5.6.5. From Theorem 5.5.5 we can integrate from 0 to 2 and from 2 to 3 separately and add the results. This yields

$$\int_{0}^{3} f(x)\,dx = \int_{0}^{2} f(x)\,dx + \int_{2}^{3} f(x)\,dx = \int_{0}^{2} x^2\,dx + \int_{2}^{3} (3x - 2)\,dx$$

$$= \frac{x^3}{3}\Bigg]_{0}^{2} + \left[\frac{3x^2}{2} - 2x\right]_{2}^{3} = \left(\frac{8}{3} - 0\right) + \left(\frac{15}{2} - 2\right) = \frac{49}{6} \quad ◀$$

If f is a continuous function on the interval $[a, b]$, then we define the **total area** between the curve $y = f(x)$ and the interval $[a, b]$ to be

$$\text{total area} = \int_{a}^{b} |f(x)|\,dx \tag{7}$$

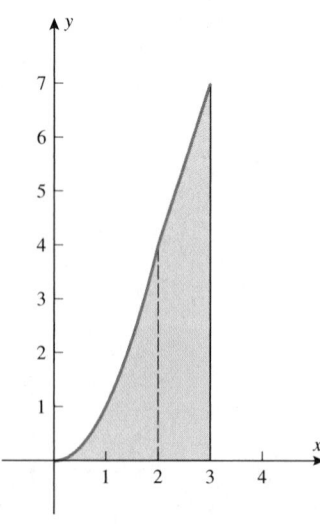

▲ **Figure 5.6.5**

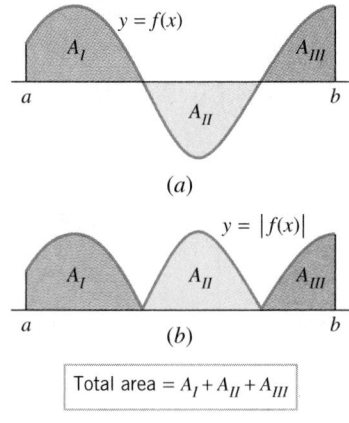

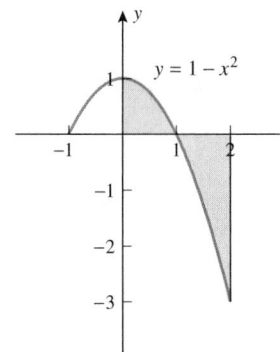

Total area = $A_I + A_{II} + A_{III}$

▲ **Figure 5.6.6**

▲ **Figure 5.6.7**

(Figure 5.6.6). To compute total area using Formula (7), begin by dividing the interval of integration into subintervals on which $f(x)$ does not change sign. On the subintervals for which $0 \leq f(x)$ replace $|f(x)|$ by $f(x)$, and on the subintervals for which $f(x) \leq 0$ replace $|f(x)|$ by $-f(x)$. Adding the resulting integrals then yields the total area.

▶ **Example 8** Find the total area between the curve $y = 1 - x^2$ and the x-axis over the interval $[0, 2]$ (Figure 5.6.7).

Solution. The area A is given by

$$A = \int_0^2 |1 - x^2|\, dx = \int_0^1 (1 - x^2)\, dx + \int_1^2 -(1 - x^2)\, dx$$

$$= \left[x - \frac{x^3}{3} \right]_0^1 - \left[x - \frac{x^3}{3} \right]_1^2$$

$$= \frac{2}{3} - \left(-\frac{4}{3} \right) = 2 \quad ◀$$

■ **DUMMY VARIABLES**

To evaluate a definite integral using the Fundamental Theorem of Calculus, one needs to be able to find an antiderivative of the integrand; thus, it is important to know what kinds of functions have antiderivatives. It is our next objective to show that all continuous functions have antiderivatives, but to do this we will need some preliminary results.

Formula (6) shows that there is a close relationship between the integrals

$$\int_a^b f(x)\, dx \quad \text{and} \quad \int f(x)\, dx$$

However, the definite and indefinite integrals differ in some important ways. For one thing, the two integrals are different kinds of objects—the definite integral is a *number* (the net signed area between the graph of $y = f(x)$ and the interval $[a, b]$), whereas the indefinite integral is a *function*, or more accurately a family of functions [the antiderivatives of $f(x)$]. However, the two types of integrals also differ in the role played by the variable of integration. In an indefinite integral, the variable of integration is "passed through" to the antiderivative in the sense that integrating a function of x produces a function of x, integrating a function of t produces a function of t, and so forth. For example,

$$\int x^2\, dx = \frac{x^3}{3} + C \quad \text{and} \quad \int t^2\, dt = \frac{t^3}{3} + C$$

In contrast, the variable of integration in a definite integral is not passed through to the end result, since the end result is a number. Thus, integrating a function of x over an interval and integrating the same function of t over the same interval of integration produce the same value for the integral. For example,

$$\int_1^3 x^2\, dx = \frac{x^3}{3}\Big]_{x=1}^3 = \frac{27}{3} - \frac{1}{3} = \frac{26}{3} \quad \text{and} \quad \int_1^3 t^2\, dt = \frac{t^3}{3}\Big]_{t=1}^3 = \frac{27}{3} - \frac{1}{3} = \frac{26}{3}$$

However, this latter result should not be surprising, since the area under the graph of the curve $y = f(x)$ over an interval $[a, b]$ on the x-axis is the same as the area under the graph of the curve $y = f(t)$ over the interval $[a, b]$ on the t-axis (Figure 5.6.8).

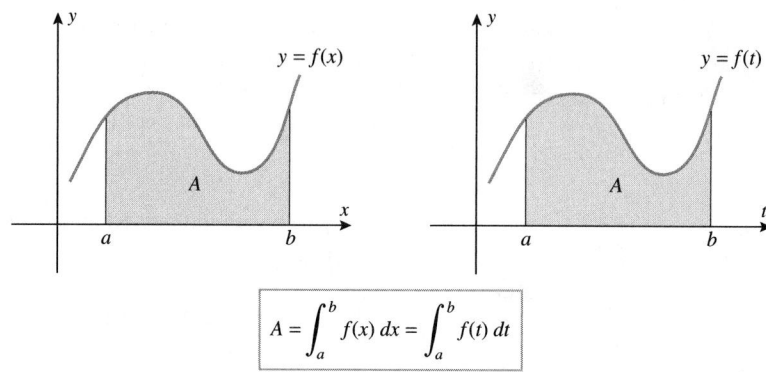

▶ **Figure 5.6.8**

$$A = \int_a^b f(x)\, dx = \int_a^b f(t)\, dt$$

Because the variable of integration in a definite integral plays no role in the end result, it is often referred to as a ***dummy variable***. In summary:

Whenever you find it convenient to change the letter used for the variable of integration in a definite integral, you can do so without changing the value of the integral.

■ THE MEAN-VALUE THEOREM FOR INTEGRALS

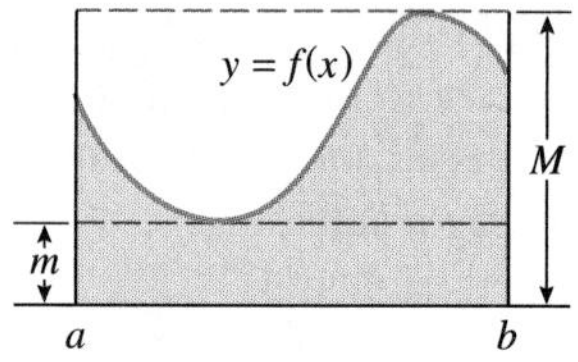

To reach our goal of showing that continuous functions have antiderivatives, we will need to develop a basic property of definite integrals, known as the *Mean-Value Theorem for Integrals*. In Section 5.8 we will interpret this theorem using the concept of the "average value" of a continuous function over an interval. Here we will need it as a tool for developing other results.

Let f be a continuous nonnegative function on $[a, b]$, and let m and M be the minimum and maximum values of $f(x)$ on this interval. Consider the rectangles of heights m and M over the interval $[a, b]$ (Figure 5.6.9). It is clear geometrically from this figure that the area

$$A = \int_a^b f(x)\, dx$$

under $y = f(x)$ is at least as large as the area of the rectangle of height m and no larger than the area of the rectangle of height M. It seems reasonable, therefore, that there is a rectangle over the interval $[a, b]$ of some appropriate height $f(x^*)$ between m and M whose area is precisely A; that is,

$$\int_a^b f(x)\, dx = f(x^*)(b - a)$$

(Figure 5.6.10). This is a special case of the following result.

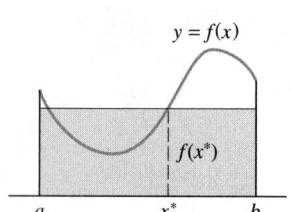

▲ **Figure 5.6.9**

$y = f(x)$

$y = f(x)$

$f(x^*)$

$a \qquad x^* \qquad b$

The area of the shaded rectangle is equal to the area of the shaded region in Figure 5.6.9.

▲ **Figure 5.6.10**

5.6.2 THEOREM (*The Mean-Value Theorem for Integrals*) *If f is continuous on a closed interval $[a, b]$, then there is at least one point x^* in $[a, b]$ such that*

$$\int_a^b f(x)\, dx = f(x^*)(b - a) \tag{8}$$

PROOF By the Extreme-Value Theorem (4.4.2), f assumes a maximum value M and a minimum value m on $[a, b]$. Thus, for all x in $[a, b]$,

$$m \leq f(x) \leq M$$

and from Theorem 5.5.6(b)

$$\int_a^b m \, dx \le \int_a^b f(x) \, dx \le \int_a^b M \, dx$$

or

$$m(b-a) \le \int_a^b f(x) \, dx \le M(b-a) \tag{9}$$

or

$$m \le \frac{1}{b-a} \int_a^b f(x) \, dx \le M$$

This implies that

$$\frac{1}{b-a} \int_a^b f(x) \, dx \tag{10}$$

is a number between m and M, and since $f(x)$ assumes the values m and M on $[a, b]$, it follows from the Intermediate-Value Theorem (1.5.7) that $f(x)$ must assume the value (10) at some x^* in $[a, b]$; that is,

$$\frac{1}{b-a} \int_a^b f(x) \, dx = f(x^*) \quad \text{or} \quad \int_a^b f(x) \, dx = f(x^*)(b-a) \quad \blacksquare$$

▶ **Example 9**   Since $f(x) = x^2$ is continuous on the interval $[1, 4]$, the Mean-Value Theorem for Integrals guarantees that there is a point x^* in $[1, 4]$ such that

$$\int_1^4 x^2 \, dx = f(x^*)(4 - 1) = (x^*)^2 (4 - 1) = 3(x^*)^2$$

But

$$\int_1^4 x^2 \, dx = \frac{x^3}{3} \Bigg]_1^4 = 21$$

so that

$$3(x^*)^2 = 21 \quad \text{or} \quad (x^*)^2 = 7 \quad \text{or} \quad x^* = \pm\sqrt{7}$$

Thus, $x^* = \sqrt{7} \approx 2.65$ is the point in the interval $[1, 4]$ whose existence is guaranteed by the Mean-Value Theorem for Integrals. ◀

■ **PART 2 OF THE FUNDAMENTAL THEOREM OF CALCULUS**

In Section 5.1 we suggested that if f is continuous and nonnegative on $[a, b]$, and if $A(x)$ is the area under the graph of $y = f(x)$ over the interval $[a, x]$ (Figure 5.6.2), then $A'(x) = f(x)$. But $A(x)$ can be expressed as the definite integral

$$A(x) = \int_a^x f(t) \, dt$$

(where we have used t rather than x as the variable of integration to avoid confusion with the x that appears as the upper limit of integration). Thus, the relationship $A'(x) = f(x)$ can be expressed as

$$\frac{d}{dx} \left[\int_a^x f(t) \, dt \right] = f(x)$$

This is a special case of the following more general result, which applies even if f has negative values.

5.6.3 **THEOREM** (*The Fundamental Theorem of Calculus, Part 2*) *If f is continuous on an interval, then f has an antiderivative on that interval. In particular, if a is any point in the interval, then the function F defined by*

$$F(x) = \int_a^x f(t)\, dt$$

is an antiderivative of f; that is, $F'(x) = f(x)$ for each x in the interval, or in an alternative notation

$$\frac{d}{dx}\left[\int_a^x f(t)\, dt\right] = f(x) \tag{11}$$

PROOF We will show first that $F(x)$ is defined at each x in the interval. If $x > a$ and x is in the interval, then Theorem 5.5.2 applied to the interval $[a, x]$ and the continuity of f ensure that $F(x)$ is defined; and if x is in the interval and $x \leq a$, then Definition 5.5.3 combined with Theorem 5.5.2 ensures that $F(x)$ is defined. Thus, $F(x)$ is defined for all x in the interval.

Next we will show that $F'(x) = f(x)$ for each x in the interval. If x is not an endpoint, then it follows from the definition of a derivative that

$$F'(x) = \lim_{h \to 0} \frac{F(x+h) - F(x)}{h}$$

$$= \lim_{h \to 0} \frac{1}{h}\left[\int_a^{x+h} f(t)\, dt - \int_a^x f(t)\, dt\right]$$

$$= \lim_{h \to 0} \frac{1}{h}\left[\int_a^{x+h} f(t)\, dt + \int_x^a f(t)\, dt\right]$$

$$= \lim_{h \to 0} \frac{1}{h}\int_x^{x+h} f(t)\, dt \qquad \boxed{\text{Theorem 5.5.5}} \tag{12}$$

Applying the Mean-Value Theorem for Integrals (5.6.2) to the integral in (12) we obtain

$$\frac{1}{h}\int_x^{x+h} f(t)\, dt = \frac{1}{h}[f(t^*) \cdot h] = f(t^*) \tag{13}$$

where t^* is some number between x and $x + h$. Because t^* is trapped between x and $x + h$, it follows that $t^* \to x$ as $h \to 0$. Thus, the continuity of f at x implies that $f(t^*) \to f(x)$ as $h \to 0$. Therefore, it follows from (12) and (13) that

$$F'(x) = \lim_{h \to 0}\left(\frac{1}{h}\int_x^{x+h} f(t)\, dt\right) = \lim_{h \to 0} f(t^*) = f(x)$$

If x is an endpoint of the interval, then the two-sided limits in the proof must be replaced by the appropriate one-sided limits, but otherwise the arguments are identical. ■

In words, Formula (11) states:

If a definite integral has a variable upper limit of integration, a constant lower limit of integration, and a continuous integrand, then the derivative of the integral with respect to its upper limit is equal to the integrand evaluated at the upper limit.

▶ **Example 10** Find

$$\frac{d}{dx}\left[\int_1^x t^3\, dt\right]$$

by applying Part 2 of the Fundamental Theorem of Calculus, and then confirm the result by performing the integration and then differentiating.

Solution. The integrand is a continuous function, so from (11)

$$\frac{d}{dx}\left[\int_1^x t^3 \, dt\right] = x^3$$

Alternatively, evaluating the integral and then differentiating yields

$$\int_1^x t^3 \, dt = \frac{t^4}{4}\bigg]_{t=1}^x = \frac{x^4}{4} - \frac{1}{4}, \quad \frac{d}{dx}\left[\frac{x^4}{4} - \frac{1}{4}\right] = x^3$$

so the two methods for differentiating the integral agree. ◄

▶ **Example 11** Since

$$f(x) = \frac{\sin x}{x}$$

is continuous on any interval that does not contain the origin, it follows from (11) that on the interval $(0, +\infty)$ we have

$$\frac{d}{dx}\left[\int_1^x \frac{\sin t}{t} \, dt\right] = \frac{\sin x}{x}$$

Unlike the preceding example, there is no way to evaluate the integral in terms of familiar functions, so Formula (11) provides the only simple method for finding the derivative. ◄

■ DIFFERENTIATION AND INTEGRATION ARE INVERSE PROCESSES

The two parts of the Fundamental Theorem of Calculus, when taken together, tell us that differentiation and integration are inverse processes in the sense that each undoes the effect of the other. To see why this is so, note that Part 1 of the Fundamental Theorem of Calculus (5.6.1) implies that

$$\int_a^x f'(t) \, dt = f(x) - f(a)$$

which tells us that if the value of $f(a)$ is known, then the function f can be recovered from its derivative f' by integrating. Conversely, Part 2 of the Fundamental Theorem of Calculus (5.6.3) states that

$$\frac{d}{dx}\left[\int_a^x f(t) \, dt\right] = f(x)$$

which tells us that the function f can be recovered from its integral by differentiating. Thus, differentiation and integration can be viewed as inverse processes.

It is common to treat parts 1 and 2 of the Fundamental Theorem of Calculus as a single theorem and refer to it simply as the *Fundamental Theorem of Calculus*. This theorem ranks as one of the greatest discoveries in the history of science, and its formulation by Newton and Leibniz is generally regarded to be the "discovery of calculus."

■ INTEGRATING RATES OF CHANGE

The Fundamental Theorem of Calculus

$$\int_a^b f(x) \, dx = F(b) - F(a) \tag{14}$$

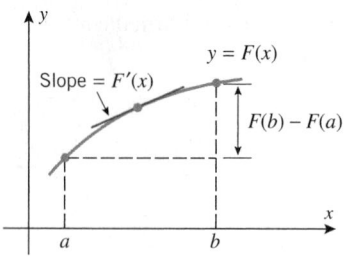

Integrating the slope of $y = F(x)$ over the interval $[a, b]$ produces the change $F(b) - F(a)$ in the value of $F(x)$.

▲ **Figure 5.6.11**

has a useful interpretation that can be seen by rewriting it in a slightly different form. Since F is an antiderivative of f on the interval $[a, b]$, we can use the relationship $F'(x) = f(x)$ to rewrite (14) as

$$\int_a^b F'(x)\,dx = F(b) - F(a) \tag{15}$$

In this formula we can view $F'(x)$ as the rate of change of $F(x)$ with respect to x, and we can view $F(b) - F(a)$ as the *change* in the value of $F(x)$ as x increases from a to b (Figure 5.6.11). Thus, we have the following useful principle.

5.6.4 INTEGRATING A RATE OF CHANGE Integrating the rate of change of $F(x)$ with respect to x over an interval $[a, b]$ produces the change in the value of $F(x)$ that occurs as x increases from a to b.

Here are some examples of this idea:

- If $s(t)$ is the position of a particle in rectilinear motion, then $s'(t)$ is the instantaneous velocity of the particle at time t, and

$$\int_{t_1}^{t_2} s'(t)\,dt = s(t_2) - s(t_1)$$

is the displacement (or the change in the position) of the particle between the times t_1 and t_2.

- If $P(t)$ is a population (e.g., plants, animals, or people) at time t, then $P'(t)$ is the rate at which the population is changing at time t, and

$$\int_{t_1}^{t_2} P'(t)\,dt = P(t_2) - P(t_1)$$

is the change in the population between times t_1 and t_2.

- If $A(t)$ is the area of an oil spill at time t, then $A'(t)$ is the rate at which the area of the spill is changing at time t, and

$$\int_{t_1}^{t_2} A'(t)\,dt = A(t_2) - A(t_1)$$

is the change in the area of the spill between times t_1 and t_2.

- If $P'(x)$ is the marginal profit that results from producing and selling x units of a product (see Section 4.5), then

$$\int_{x_1}^{x_2} P'(x)\,dx = P(x_2) - P(x_1)$$

is the change in the profit that results when the production level increases from x_1 units to x_2 units.

Mitchell Funk/Getty Images
Mathematical analysis plays an important role in understanding human population growth.

✔ **QUICK CHECK EXERCISES 5.6**   (*See page 376 for answers.*)

1. (a) If $F(x)$ is an antiderivative for $f(x)$, then

$$\int_a^b f(x)\,dx = \underline{\hspace{1cm}}$$

(b) $\displaystyle\int_a^b F'(x)\,dx = \underline{\hspace{1cm}}$

(c) $\displaystyle\frac{d}{dx}\left[\int_a^x f(t)\,dt\right] = \underline{\hspace{1cm}}$

2. (a) $\displaystyle\int_0^2 (3x^2 - 2x)\,dx = $ _____

(b) $\displaystyle\int_{-\pi}^{\pi} \cos x\,dx = $ _____

(c) $\displaystyle\int_0^{\frac{1}{2}\ln 5} e^x\,dx = $ _____

(d) $\displaystyle\int_{-1/2}^{1/2} \frac{1}{\sqrt{1-x^2}}\,dx = $ _____

3. For the function $f(x) = 3x^2 - 2x$ and an interval $[a, b]$, the point x^* guaranteed by the Mean-Value Theorem for Integrals is $x^* = \frac{2}{3}$. It follows that

$$\int_a^b (3x^2 - 2x)\,dx = \underline{\hspace{2cm}}$$

4. The area of an oil spill is increasing at a rate of $25t$ ft^2/s t seconds after the spill. Between times $t = 2$ and $t = 4$ the area of the spill increases by _____ ft^2.

EXERCISE SET 5.6   ⌁ Graphing Utility   ⓒ CAS

1. In each part, use a definite integral to find the area of the region, and check your answer using an appropriate formula from geometry.

(a)   (b)   (c)

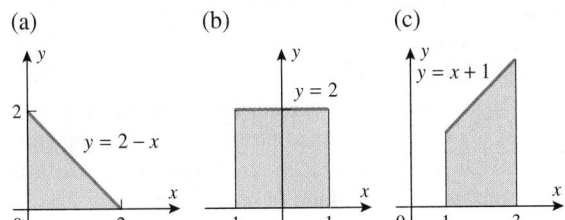

2. In each part, use a definite integral to find the area under the curve $y = f(x)$ over the stated interval, and check your answer using an appropriate formula from geometry.
(a) $f(x) = x$; $[0, 5]$
(b) $f(x) = 5$; $[3, 9]$
(c) $f(x) = x + 3$; $[-1, 2]$

3. In each part, sketch the analogue of Figure 5.6.10 for the specified region. [Let $y = f(x)$ denote the upper boundary of the region. If x^* is unique, label both it and $f(x^*)$ on your sketch. Otherwise, label $f(x^*)$ on your sketch, and determine all values of x^* that satisfy Equation (8).]
(a) The region in part (a) of Exercise 1.
(b) The region in part (b) of Exercise 1.
(c) The region in part (c) of Exercise 1.

4. In each part, sketch the analogue of Figure 5.6.10 for the function and interval specified. [If x^* is unique, label both it and $f(x^*)$ on your sketch. Otherwise, label $f(x^*)$ on your sketch, and determine all values of x^* that satisfy Equation (8).]
(a) The function and interval in part (a) of Exercise 2.
(b) The function and interval in part (b) of Exercise 2.
(c) The function and interval in part (c) of Exercise 2.

5–10 Find the area under the curve $y = f(x)$ over the stated interval. ◼

5. $f(x) = x^3$; $[2, 3]$ **6.** $f(x) = x^4$; $[-1, 1]$
7. $f(x) = 3\sqrt{x}$; $[1, 4]$ **8.** $f(x) = x^{-2/3}$; $[1, 27]$
9. $f(x) = e^{2x}$; $[0, \ln 2]$ **10.** $f(x) = \dfrac{1}{x}$; $[1, 5]$

11–12 Find all values of x^* in the stated interval that satisfy Equation (8) in the Mean-Value Theorem for Integrals (5.6.2), and explain what these numbers represent. ◼

11. (a) $f(x) = \sqrt{x}$; $[0, 3]$
     (b) $f(x) = x^2 + x$; $[-12, 0]$

12. (a) $f(x) = \sin x$; $[-\pi, \pi]$ (b) $f(x) = 1/x^2$; $[1, 3]$

13–30 Evaluate the integrals using Part 1 of the Fundamental Theorem of Calculus. ◼

13. $\displaystyle\int_{-2}^{1} (x^2 - 6x + 12)\,dx$ **14.** $\displaystyle\int_{-1}^{2} 4x(1 - x^2)\,dx$

15. $\displaystyle\int_1^4 \frac{4}{x^2}\,dx$ **16.** $\displaystyle\int_1^2 \frac{1}{x^6}\,dx$

17. $\displaystyle\int_4^9 2x\sqrt{x}\,dx$ **18.** $\displaystyle\int_1^4 \frac{1}{x\sqrt{x}}\,dx$

19. $\displaystyle\int_{-\pi/2}^{\pi/2} \sin\theta\,d\theta$ **20.** $\displaystyle\int_0^{\pi/4} \sec^2\theta\,d\theta$

21. $\displaystyle\int_{-\pi/4}^{\pi/4} \cos x\,dx$ **22.** $\displaystyle\int_0^{\pi/3} (2x - \sec x\tan x)\,dx$

23. $\displaystyle\int_{\ln 2}^{3} 5e^x\,dx$ **24.** $\displaystyle\int_{1/2}^{1} \frac{1}{2x}\,dx$

25. $\displaystyle\int_0^{1/\sqrt{2}} \frac{dx}{\sqrt{1 - x^2}}$ **26.** $\displaystyle\int_{-1}^{1} \frac{dx}{1 + x^2}$

27. $\displaystyle\int_{\sqrt{2}}^{2} \frac{dx}{x\sqrt{x^2 - 1}}$ **28.** $\displaystyle\int_{-\sqrt{2}}^{-2/\sqrt{3}} \frac{dx}{x\sqrt{x^2 - 1}}$

29. $\displaystyle\int_1^4 \left(\frac{1}{\sqrt{t}} - 3\sqrt{t}\right) dt$ **30.** $\displaystyle\int_{\pi/6}^{\pi/2} \left(x + \frac{2}{\sin^2 x}\right) dx$

31–34 Use Theorem 5.5.5 to evaluate the given integrals. ◼

31. (a) $\displaystyle\int_{-1}^{1} |2x - 1|\,dx$ (b) $\displaystyle\int_0^{3\pi/4} |\cos x|\,dx$

32. (a) $\displaystyle\int_{-1}^{2} \sqrt{2 + |x|}\,dx$ (b) $\displaystyle\int_0^{\pi/2} \left|\tfrac{1}{2} - \cos x\right| dx$

33. (a) $\displaystyle\int_{-1}^{1} |e^x - 1|\, dx$ (b) $\displaystyle\int_{1}^{4} \frac{|2-x|}{x}\, dx$

34. (a) $\displaystyle\int_{-3}^{3} \left| x^2 - 1 - \frac{15}{x^2+1} \right|\, dx$

(b) $\displaystyle\int_{0}^{\sqrt{3}/2} \left| \frac{1}{\sqrt{1-x^2}} - \sqrt{2} \right|\, dx$

35–36 A function $f(x)$ is defined piecewise on an interval. In these exercises: (a) Use Theorem 5.5.5 to find the integral of $f(x)$ over the interval. (b) Find an antiderivative of $f(x)$ on the interval. (c) Use parts (a) and (b) to verify Part 1 of the Fundamental Theorem of Calculus. ▪

35. $f(x) = \begin{cases} x, & 0 \le x \le 1 \\ x^2, & 1 < x \le 2 \end{cases}$

36. $f(x) = \begin{cases} \sqrt{x}, & 0 \le x < 1 \\ 1/x^2, & 1 \le x \le 4 \end{cases}$

37–40 True–False Determine whether the statement is true or false. Explain your answer. ▪

37. There does not exist a differentiable function $F(x)$ such that $F'(x) = |x|$.

38. If $f(x)$ is continuous on the interval $[a, b]$, and if the definite integral of $f(x)$ over this interval has value 0, then the equation $f(x) = 0$ has at least one solution in the interval $[a, b]$.

39. If $F(x)$ is an antiderivative of $f(x)$ and $G(x)$ is an antiderivative of $g(x)$, then

$$\int_a^b f(x)\, dx = \int_a^b g(x)\, dx$$

if and only if

$$G(a) + F(b) = F(a) + G(b)$$

40. If $f(x)$ is continuous everywhere and

$$F(x) = \int_0^x f(t)\, dt$$

then the equation $F(x) = 0$ has at least one solution.

41–44 Use a calculating utility to find the midpoint approximation of the integral using $n = 20$ subintervals, and then find the exact value of the integral using Part 1 of the Fundamental Theorem of Calculus. ▪

41. $\displaystyle\int_{1}^{3} \frac{1}{x^2}\, dx$ **42.** $\displaystyle\int_{0}^{\pi/2} \sin x\, dx$

43. $\displaystyle\int_{-1}^{1} \sec^2 x\, dx$ **44.** $\displaystyle\int_{1}^{3} \frac{1}{x}\, dx$

45–48 Sketch the region described and find its area. ▪

45. The region under the curve $y = x^2 + 1$ and over the interval $[0, 3]$.

46. The region below the curve $y = x - x^2$ and above the x-axis.

47. The region under the curve $y = 3\sin x$ and over the interval $[0, 2\pi/3]$.

48. The region below the interval $[-2, -1]$ and above the curve $y = x^3$.

49–52 Sketch the curve and find the total area between the curve and the given interval on the x-axis. ▪

49. $y = x^2 - x$; $[0, 2]$ **50.** $y = \sin x$; $[0, 3\pi/2]$

51. $y = e^x - 1$; $[-1, 1]$ **52.** $y = \dfrac{x^2 - 1}{x^2}$; $\left[\frac{1}{2}, 2\right]$

53. A student wants to find the area enclosed by the graphs of $y = 1/\sqrt{1 - x^2}$, $y = 0$, $x = 0$, and $x = 0.8$.
(a) Show that the exact area is $\sin^{-1} 0.8$.
(b) The student uses a calculator to approximate the result in part (a) to two decimal places and obtains an incorrect answer of 53.13. What was the student's error? Find the correct approximation.

FOCUS ON CONCEPTS

54. Explain why the Fundamental Theorem of Calculus may be applied without modification to definite integrals in which the lower limit of integration is greater than or equal to the upper limit of integration.

55. (a) If $h'(t)$ is the rate of change of a child's height measured in inches per year, what does the integral $\int_0^{10} h'(t)\, dt$ represent, and what are its units?
(b) If $r'(t)$ is the rate of change of the radius of a spherical balloon measured in centimeters per second, what does the integral $\int_1^2 r'(t)\, dt$ represent, and what are its units?
(c) If $H(t)$ is the rate of change of the speed of sound with respect to temperature measured in ft/s per °F, what does the integral $\int_{32}^{100} H(t)\, dt$ represent, and what are its units?
(d) If $v(t)$ is the velocity of a particle in rectilinear motion, measured in cm/h, what does the integral $\int_{t_1}^{t_2} v(t)\, dt$ represent, and what are its units?

56. (a) Use a graphing utility to generate the graph of

$$f(x) = \frac{1}{100}(x+2)(x+1)(x-3)(x-5)$$

and use the graph to make a conjecture about the sign of the integral

$$\int_{-2}^{5} f(x)\, dx$$

(b) Check your conjecture by evaluating the integral.

57. Define $F(x)$ by

$$F(x) = \int_1^x (3t^2 - 3)\, dt$$

(a) Use Part 2 of the Fundamental Theorem of Calculus to find $F'(x)$.
(b) Check the result in part (a) by first integrating and then differentiating.

58. Define $F(x)$ by

$$F(x) = \int_{\pi/4}^{x} \cos 2t \, dt$$

(a) Use Part 2 of the Fundamental Theorem of Calculus to find $F'(x)$.

(b) Check the result in part (a) by first integrating and then differentiating.

59–62 Use Part 2 of the Fundamental Theorem of Calculus to find the derivatives. ■

59. (a) $\dfrac{d}{dx} \int_{1}^{x} \sin(t^2) \, dt$ (b) $\dfrac{d}{dx} \int_{0}^{x} e^{\sqrt{t}} \, dt$

60. (a) $\dfrac{d}{dx} \int_{0}^{x} \dfrac{dt}{1+\sqrt{t}}$ (b) $\dfrac{d}{dx} \int_{1}^{x} \ln t \, dt$

61. $\dfrac{d}{dx} \int_{x}^{0} t \sec t \, dt$ [*Hint:* Use Definition 5.5.3(b).]

62. $\dfrac{d}{du} \int_{0}^{u} |x| \, dx$

63. Let $F(x) = \int_{4}^{x} \sqrt{t^2 + 9} \, dt$. Find

(a) $F(4)$ (b) $F'(4)$ (c) $F''(4)$.

64. Let $F(x) = \int_{\sqrt{3}}^{x} \tan^{-1} t \, dt$. Find

(a) $F(\sqrt{3})$ (b) $F'(\sqrt{3})$ (c) $F''(\sqrt{3})$.

65. Let $F(x) = \int_{0}^{x} \dfrac{t-3}{t^2+7} \, dt$ for $-\infty < x < +\infty$.

(a) Find the value of x where F attains its minimum value.

(b) Find intervals over which F is only increasing or only decreasing.

(c) Find open intervals over which F is only concave up or only concave down.

C **66.** Use the plotting and numerical integration commands of a CAS to generate the graph of the function F in Exercise 65 over the interval $-20 \le x \le 20$, and confirm that the graph is consistent with the results obtained in that exercise.

67. (a) Over what open interval does the formula

$$F(x) = \int_{1}^{x} \dfrac{dt}{t}$$

represent an antiderivative of $f(x) = 1/x$?

(b) Find a point where the graph of F crosses the x-axis.

68. (a) Over what open interval does the formula

$$F(x) = \int_{1}^{x} \dfrac{1}{t^2 - 9} \, dt$$

represent an antiderivative of

$$f(x) = \dfrac{1}{x^2 - 9}?$$

(b) Find a point where the graph of F crosses the x-axis.

69. (a) Suppose that a reservoir supplies water to an industrial park at a constant rate of $r = 4$ gallons per minute (gal/min) between 8:30 A.M. and 9:00 A.M. How much water does the reservoir supply during that time period?

(b) Suppose that one of the industrial plants increases its water consumption between 9:00 A.M. and 10:00 A.M. and that the rate at which the reservoir supplies water increases linearly, as shown in the accompanying figure. How much water does the reservoir supply during that 1-hour time period?

(c) Suppose that from 10:00 A.M. to 12 noon the rate at which the reservoir supplies water is given by the formula $r(t) = 10 + \sqrt{t}$ gal/min, where t is the time (in minutes) since 10:00 A.M. How much water does the reservoir supply during that 2-hour time period?

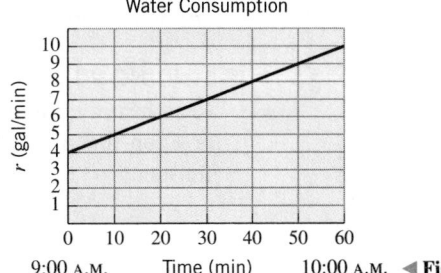

Water Consumption

9:00 A.M.   Time (min)   10:00 A.M.   ◄ **Figure Ex-69**

70. A traffic engineer monitors the rate at which cars enter the main highway during the afternoon rush hour. From her data she estimates that between 4:30 P.M. and 5:30 P.M. the rate $R(t)$ at which cars enter the highway is given by the formula $R(t) = 100(1 - 0.0001t^2)$ cars per minute, where t is the time (in minutes) since 4:30 P.M.

(a) When does the peak traffic flow into the highway occur?

(b) Estimate the number of cars that enter the highway during the rush hour.

71–72 Evaluate each limit by interpreting it as a Riemann sum in which the given interval is divided into n subintervals of equal width. ■

71. $\displaystyle \lim_{n \to +\infty} \sum_{k=1}^{n} \dfrac{\pi}{4n} \sec^2 \left(\dfrac{\pi k}{4n} \right)$; $\left[0, \dfrac{\pi}{4} \right]$

72. $\displaystyle \lim_{n \to +\infty} \sum_{k=1}^{n} \dfrac{n}{n^2 + k^2}$; $[0, 1]$

73. Prove the Mean-Value Theorem for Integrals (Theorem 5.6.2) by applying the Mean-Value Theorem (4.8.2) to an antiderivative F for f.

74. Writing Write a short paragraph that describes the various ways in which integration and differentiation may be viewed as inverse processes. (Be sure to discuss both definite and indefinite integrals.)

75. Writing Let f denote a function that is continuous on an interval $[a, b]$, and let x^* denote the point guaranteed by the Mean-Value Theorem for Integrals. Explain geometrically why $f(x^*)$ may be interpreted as a "mean" or average value of $f(x)$ over $[a, b]$. (In Section 5.8 we will discuss the concept of "average value" in more detail.)

1. (a) $F(b) - F(a)$ (b) $F(b) - F(a)$ (c) $f(x)$ 2. (a) 4 (b) 0 (c) $\sqrt{5} - 1$ (d) $\pi/3$ 3. 0   4. 150 ft^2

5.7 RECTILINEAR MOTION REVISITED USING INTEGRATION

In Section 4.6 we used the derivative to define the notions of instantaneous velocity and acceleration for a particle in rectilinear motion. In this section we will resume the study of such motion using the tools of integration.

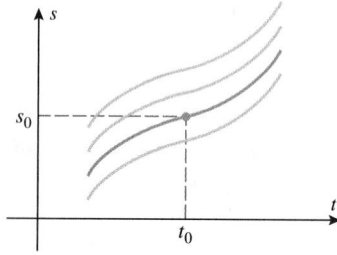

There is a unique position function such that $s(t_0) = s_0$.

▲ **Figure 5.7.1**

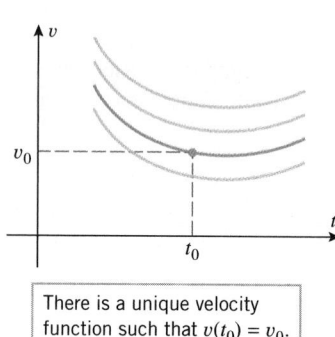

There is a unique velocity function such that $v(t_0) = v_0$.

▲ **Figure 5.7.2**

■ FINDING POSITION AND VELOCITY BY INTEGRATION

Recall from Formulas (1) and (3) of Section 4.6 that if a particle in rectilinear motion has position function $s(t)$, then its instantaneous velocity and acceleration are given by the formulas

$$v(t) = s'(t) \quad \text{and} \quad a(t) = v'(t)$$

It follows from these formulas that $s(t)$ is an antiderivative of $v(t)$ and $v(t)$ is an antiderivative of $a(t)$; that is,

$$s(t) = \int v(t)\, dt \qquad \text{and} \qquad v(t) = \int a(t)\, dt \qquad (1\text{–}2)$$

By Formula (1), if we know the velocity function $v(t)$ of a particle in rectilinear motion, then by integrating $v(t)$ we can produce a family of position functions with that velocity function. If, in addition, we know the position s_0 of the particle at any time t_0, then we have sufficient information to find the constant of integration and determine a unique position function (Figure 5.7.1). Similarly, if we know the acceleration function $a(t)$ of the particle, then by integrating $a(t)$ we can produce a family of velocity functions with that acceleration function. If, in addition, we know the velocity v_0 of the particle at any time t_0, then we have sufficient information to find the constant of integration and determine a unique velocity function (Figure 5.7.2).

▶ **Example 1**   Suppose that a particle moves with velocity $v(t) = \cos \pi t$ along a coordinate line. Assuming that the particle has coordinate $s = 4$ at time $t = 0$, find its position function.

Solution.   The position function is

$$s(t) = \int v(t)\, dt = \int \cos \pi t \, dt = \frac{1}{\pi} \sin \pi t + C$$

Since $s = 4$ when $t = 0$, it follows that

$$4 = s(0) = \frac{1}{\pi} \sin 0 + C = C$$

Thus,

$$s(t) = \frac{1}{\pi} \sin \pi t + 4 \quad ◀$$

■ COMPUTING DISPLACEMENT AND DISTANCE TRAVELED BY INTEGRATION

Recall that the displacement over a time interval of a particle in rectilinear motion is its final coordinate minus its initial coordinate. Thus, if the position function of the particle is $s(t)$, then its displacement (or change in position) over the time interval $[t_0, t_1]$ is $s(t_1) - s(t_0)$. This can be written in integral form as

$$\left[\begin{array}{c} \text{displacement} \\ \text{over the time} \\ \text{interval } [t_0, t_1] \end{array}\right] = \int_{t_0}^{t_1} v(t)\, dt = \int_{t_0}^{t_1} s'(t)\, dt = s(t_1) - s(t_0) \qquad (3)$$

Recall that Formula (3) is a special case of the formula

$$\int_a^b F'(x)\, dx = F(b) - F(a)$$

for integrating a rate of change.

In contrast, to find the distance traveled by the particle over the time interval $[t_0, t_1]$ (distance traveled in the positive direction plus the distance traveled in the negative direction), we must integrate the absolute value of the velocity function; that is,

$$\left[\begin{array}{c} \text{distance traveled} \\ \text{during time} \\ \text{interval } [t_0, t_1] \end{array}\right] = \int_{t_0}^{t_1} |v(t)|\, dt \qquad (4)$$

Since the absolute value of velocity is speed, Formulas (3) and (4) can be summarized informally as follows:

Integrating velocity over a time interval produces displacement, and integrating speed over a time interval produces distance traveled.

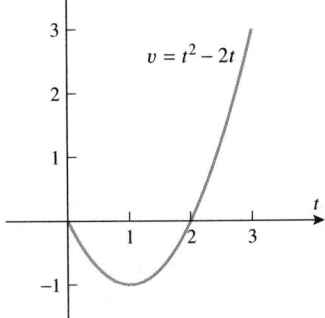

▲ **Figure 5.7.3**

▶ **Example 2** Suppose that a particle moves on a coordinate line so that its velocity at time t is $v(t) = t^2 - 2t$ m/s (Figure 5.7.3).

(a) Find the displacement of the particle during the time interval $0 \le t \le 3$.

(b) Find the distance traveled by the particle during the time interval $0 \le t \le 3$.

Solution (a). From (3) the displacement is

$$\int_0^3 v(t)\, dt = \int_0^3 (t^2 - 2t)\, dt = \left[\frac{t^3}{3} - t^2\right]_0^3 = 0$$

Thus, the particle is at the same position at time $t = 3$ as at $t = 0$.

Solution (b). The velocity can be written as $v(t) = t^2 - 2t = t(t - 2)$, from which we see that $v(t) \le 0$ for $0 \le t \le 2$ and $v(t) \ge 0$ for $2 \le t \le 3$. Thus, it follows from (4) that the distance traveled is

$$\int_0^3 |v(t)|\, dt = \int_0^2 -v(t)\, dt + \int_2^3 v(t)\, dt$$

$$= \int_0^2 -(t^2 - 2t)\, dt + \int_2^3 (t^2 - 2t)\, dt$$

$$= -\left[\frac{t^3}{3} - t^2\right]_0^2 + \left[\frac{t^3}{3} - t^2\right]_2^3 = \frac{4}{3} + \frac{4}{3} = \frac{8}{3} \text{ m} \quad ◀$$

In physical problems it is important to associate correct units with definite integrals. In general, the units for

$$\int_a^b f(x)\, dx$$

are units of $f(x)$ times units of x, since the integral is the limit of Riemann sums, each of whose terms has these units. For example, if $v(t)$ is in meters per second (m/s) and t is in seconds (s), then

$$\int_a^b v(t)\, dt$$

is in meters since

$$(\text{m/s}) \times \text{s} = \text{m}$$

■ **ANALYZING THE VELOCITY VERSUS TIME CURVE**

In Section 4.6 we showed how to use the position versus time curve to obtain information about the behavior of a particle in rectilinear motion (Table 4.6.1). Similarly, there is valuable information that can be obtained from the velocity versus time curve. For example, the integral in (3) can be interpreted geometrically as the *net signed area* between the graph of $v(t)$ and the interval $[t_0, t_1]$, and the integral in (4) can be interpreted as the *total area* between the graph of $v(t)$ and the interval $[t_0, t_1]$. Thus we have the following result.

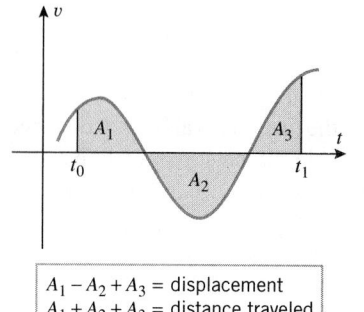

$A_1 - A_2 + A_3$ = displacement
$A_1 + A_2 + A_3$ = distance traveled

▲ **Figure 5.7.4**

> **5.7.1**   FINDING DISPLACEMENT AND DISTANCE TRAVELED FROM THE VELOCITY
> VERSUS TIME CURVE   For a particle in rectilinear motion, the net signed area between
> the velocity versus time curve and the interval $[t_0, t_1]$ on the t-axis represents the dis-
> placement of the particle over that time interval, and the total area between the velocity
> versus time curve and the interval $[t_0, t_1]$ on the t-axis represents the distance traveled
> by the particle over that time interval (Figure 5.7.4).

▶ **Example 3**   Figure 5.7.5 shows three velocity versus time curves for a particle in rectilinear motion along a horizontal line with the positive direction to the right. In each case find the displacement and the distance traveled over the time interval $0 \le t \le 4$, and explain what that information tells you about the motion of the particle.

Solution (a).   In part (*a*) of the figure the area and the net signed area over the interval are both 2. Thus, at the end of the time period the particle is 2 units to the right of its starting point and has traveled a distance of 2 units.

Solution (b).   In part (*b*) of the figure the net signed area is -2, and the total area is 2. Thus, at the end of the time period the particle is 2 units to the left of its starting point and has traveled a distance of 2 units.

Solution (c).   In part (*c*) of the figure the net signed area is 0, and the total area is 2. Thus, at the end of the time period the particle is back at its starting point and has traveled a distance of 2 units. More specifically, it traveled 1 unit to the right over the time interval $0 \le t \le 1$ and then 1 unit to the left over the time interval $1 \le t \le 2$ (why?). ◀

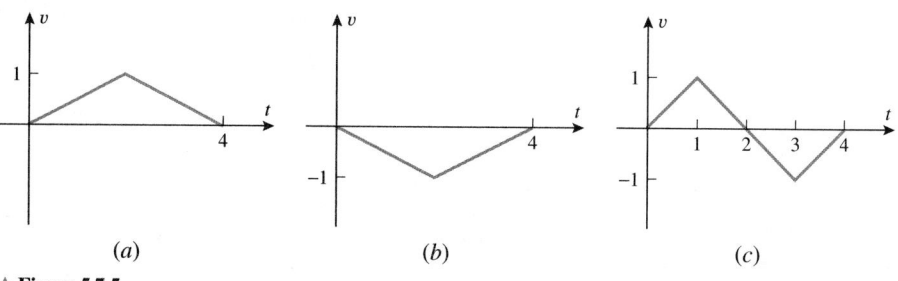

(a)   (b)   (c)

▲ **Figure 5.7.5**

▮ CONSTANT ACCELERATION

One of the most important cases of rectilinear motion occurs when a particle has *constant acceleration*. We will show that if a particle moves with constant acceleration along an s-axis, and if the position and velocity of the particle are known at some point in time, say when $t = 0$, then it is possible to derive formulas for the position $s(t)$ and the velocity $v(t)$ at any time t. To see how this can be done, suppose that the particle has constant acceleration

$$a(t) = a \qquad (5)$$

and

$$s = s_0 \quad \text{when} \quad t = 0 \qquad (6)$$
$$v = v_0 \quad \text{when} \quad t = 0 \qquad (7)$$

where s_0 and v_0 are known. We call (6) and (7) the *initial conditions*.

With (5) as a starting point, we can integrate $a(t)$ to obtain $v(t)$, and we can integrate $v(t)$ to obtain $s(t)$, using an initial condition in each case to determine the constant of integration. The computations are as follows:

$$v(t) = \int a(t)\, dt = \int a\, dt = at + C_1 \tag{8}$$

To determine the constant of integration C_1 we apply initial condition (7) to this equation to obtain

$$v_0 = v(0) = a \cdot 0 + C_1 = C_1$$

Substituting this in (8) and putting the constant term first yields

$$v(t) = v_0 + at$$

Since v_0 is constant, it follows that

$$s(t) = \int v(t)\, dt = \int (v_0 + at)\, dt = v_0 t + \tfrac{1}{2}at^2 + C_2 \tag{9}$$

To determine the constant C_2 we apply initial condition (6) to this equation to obtain

$$s_0 = s(0) = v_0 \cdot 0 + \tfrac{1}{2}a \cdot 0 + C_2 = C_2$$

Substituting this in (9) and putting the constant term first yields

$$s(t) = s_0 + v_0 t + \tfrac{1}{2}at^2$$

In summary, we have the following result.

5.7.2 CONSTANT ACCELERATION If a particle moves with constant acceleration a along an s-axis, and if the position and velocity at time $t = 0$ are s_0 and v_0, respectively, then the position and velocity functions of the particle are

$$s(t) = s_0 + v_0 t + \tfrac{1}{2}at^2 \tag{10}$$

$$v(t) = v_0 + at \tag{11}$$

How can you tell from the graph of the velocity versus time curve whether a particle moving along a line has constant acceleration?

▶ **Example 4**   Suppose that an intergalactic spacecraft uses a sail and the "solar wind" to produce a constant acceleration of 0.032 m/s^2. Assuming that the spacecraft has a velocity of 10,000 m/s when the sail is first raised, how far will the spacecraft travel in 1 hour, and what will its velocity be at the end of this hour?

Solution.   In this problem the choice of a coordinate axis is at our discretion, so we will choose it to make the computations as simple as possible. Accordingly, let us introduce an s-axis whose positive direction is in the direction of motion, and let us take the origin to coincide with the position of the spacecraft at the time $t = 0$ when the sail is raised. Thus, Formulas (10) and (11) apply with

$$s_0 = s(0) = 0, \quad v_0 = v(0) = 10{,}000, \quad \text{and} \quad a = 0.032$$

Since 1 hour corresponds to $t = 3600$ s, it follows from (10) that in 1 hour the spacecraft travels a distance of

$$s(3600) = 10{,}000(3600) + \tfrac{1}{2}(0.032)(3600)^2 \approx 36{,}200{,}000 \text{ m}$$

and it follows from (11) that after 1 hour its velocity is

$$v(3600) = 10{,}000 + (0.032)(3600) \approx 10{,}100 \text{ m/s} \blacktriangleleft$$

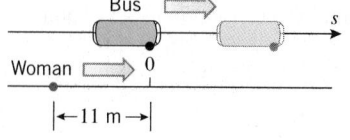

▲ **Figure 5.7.6**

▶ **Example 5**   A bus has stopped to pick up riders, and a woman is running at a constant velocity of 5 m/s to catch it. When she is 11 m behind the front door the bus pulls away with a constant acceleration of 1 m/s². From that point in time, how long will it take for the woman to reach the front door of the bus if she keeps running with a velocity of 5 m/s?

Solution.   As shown in Figure 5.7.6, choose the s-axis so that the bus and the woman are moving in the positive direction, and the front door of the bus is at the origin at the time $t = 0$ when the bus begins to pull away. To catch the bus at some later time t, the woman will have to cover a distance $s_w(t)$ that is equal to 11 m plus the distance $s_b(t)$ traveled by the bus; that is, the woman will catch the bus when

$$s_w(t) = s_b(t) + 11 \tag{12}$$

Since the woman has a constant velocity of 5 m/s, the distance she travels in t seconds is $s_w(t) = 5t$. Thus, (12) can be written as

$$s_b(t) = 5t - 11 \tag{13}$$

Since the bus has a constant acceleration of $a = 1$ m/s², and since $s_0 = v_0 = 0$ at time $t = 0$ (why?), it follows from (10) that

$$s_b(t) = \tfrac{1}{2}t^2$$

Substituting this equation into (13) and reorganizing the terms yields the quadratic equation

$$\tfrac{1}{2}t^2 - 5t + 11 = 0 \quad \text{or} \quad t^2 - 10t + 22 = 0$$

Solving this equation for t using the quadratic formula yields two solutions:

$$t = 5 - \sqrt{3} \approx 3.3 \quad \text{and} \quad t = 5 + \sqrt{3} \approx 6.7$$

(verify). Thus, the woman can reach the door at two different times, $t = 3.3$ s and $t = 6.7$ s. The reason that there are two solutions can be explained as follows: When the woman first reaches the door, she is running faster than the bus and can run past it if the driver does not see her. However, as the bus speeds up, it eventually catches up to her, and she has another chance to flag it down. ◀

■ FREE-FALL MODEL

Motion that occurs when an object near the Earth is imparted some initial velocity (up or down) and thereafter moves along a vertical line is called *free-fall motion*. In modeling free-fall motion we assume that the only force acting on the object is the Earth's gravity and that the object stays sufficiently close to the Earth that the gravitational force is constant. In particular, air resistance and the gravitational pull of other celestial bodies are neglected.

In our model we will ignore the physical size of the object by treating it as a particle, and we will assume that it moves along an s-axis whose origin is at the surface of the Earth and whose positive direction is up. With this convention, the s-coordinate of the particle is the height of the particle above the surface of the Earth (Figure 5.7.7).

It is a fact of physics that a particle with free-fall motion has constant acceleration. The magnitude of this constant, denoted by the letter g, is called the *acceleration due to gravity* and is approximately 9.8 m/s² or 32 ft/s², depending on whether distance is measured in meters or feet.*

Recall that a particle is speeding up when its velocity and acceleration have the same sign and is slowing down when they have opposite signs. Thus, because we have chosen

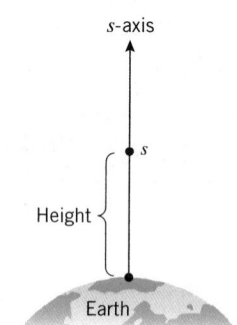

▲ **Figure 5.7.7**

---

*Strictly speaking, the constant g varies with the latitude and the distance from the Earth's center. However, for motion at a fixed latitude and near the surface of the Earth, the assumption of a constant g is satisfactory for many applications.

the positive direction to be up, it follows that the acceleration $a(t)$ of a particle in free fall is negative for all values of t. To see that this is so, observe that an upward-moving particle (positive velocity) is slowing down, so its acceleration must be negative; and a downward-moving particle (negative velocity) is speeding up, so its acceleration must also be negative. Thus, we conclude that

$$a(t) = -g \tag{14}$$

It now follows from this and Formulas (10) and (11) that the position and velocity functions for a particle in free-fall motion are

$$s(t) = s_0 + v_0 t - \tfrac{1}{2}gt^2 \tag{15}$$

$$v(t) = v_0 - gt \tag{16}$$

How would Formulas (14), (15), and (16) change if we choose the direction of the positive s-axis to be down?

Corbis.Bettmann
Nolan Ryan's rookie baseball card.

▶ **Example 6**   Nolan Ryan, a member of the Baseball Hall of Fame and one of the fastest baseball pitchers of all time, was able to throw a baseball 150 ft/s (over 102 mi/h). During his career, he had the opportunity to pitch in the Houston Astrodome, home to the Houston Astros Baseball Team from 1965 to 1999. The Astrodome was an indoor stadium with a ceiling 208 ft high. Could Nolan Ryan have hit the ceiling of the Astrodome if he were capable of giving a baseball an upward velocity of 100 ft/s from a height of 7 ft?

Solution.   Since distance is in feet, we take $g = 32$ ft/s^2. Initially, we have $s_0 = 7$ ft and $v_0 = 100$ ft/s, so from (15) and (16) we have

$$s(t) = 7 + 100t - 16t^2$$
$$v(t) = 100 - 32t$$

The ball will rise until $v(t) = 0$, that is, until $100 - 32t = 0$. Solving this equation we see that the ball is at its maximum height at time $t = \tfrac{25}{8}$. To find the height of the ball at this instant we substitute this value of t into the position function to obtain

$$s\left(\tfrac{25}{8}\right) = 7 + 100\left(\tfrac{25}{8}\right) - 16\left(\tfrac{25}{8}\right)^2 = 163.25 \text{ ft}$$

which is roughly 45 ft short of hitting the ceiling. ◀

In Example 6 the ball is moving up when the velocity is positive and is moving down when the velocity is negative, so it makes sense physically that the velocity is zero when the ball reaches its peak.

▶ **Example 7**   A penny is released from rest near the top of the Empire State Building at a point that is 1250 ft above the ground (Figure 5.7.8). Assuming that the free-fall model applies, how long does it take for the penny to hit the ground, and what is its speed at the time of impact?

Solution.   Since distance is in feet, we take $g = 32$ ft/s^2. Initially, we have $s_0 = 1250$ and $v_0 = 0$, so from (15)

$$s(t) = 1250 - 16t^2 \tag{17}$$

Impact occurs when $s(t) = 0$. Solving this equation for t, we obtain

$$1250 - 16t^2 = 0$$
$$t^2 = \frac{1250}{16} = \frac{625}{8}$$
$$t = \pm\frac{25}{\sqrt{8}} \approx \pm 8.8 \text{ s}$$

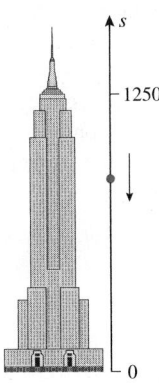

▲ **Figure 5.7.8**

Since $t \geq 0$, we can discard the negative solution and conclude that it takes $25/\sqrt{8} \approx 8.8$ s for the penny to hit the ground. To obtain the velocity at the time of impact, we substitute $t = 25/\sqrt{8}$, $v_0 = 0$, and $g = 32$ in (16) to obtain

$$v\left(\frac{25}{\sqrt{8}}\right) = 0 - 32\left(\frac{25}{\sqrt{8}}\right) = -200\sqrt{2} \approx -282.8 \text{ ft/s}$$

Thus, the speed at the time of impact is

$$\left|v\left(\frac{25}{\sqrt{8}}\right)\right| = 200\sqrt{2} \approx 282.8 \text{ ft/s}$$

which is more than 192 mi/h. ◄

✔ QUICK CHECK EXERCISES 5.7 (See page 385 for answers.)

1. Suppose that a particle is moving along an s-axis with velocity $v(t) = 2t + 1$. If at time $t = 0$ the particle is at position $s = 2$, the position function of the particle is $s(t) =$ _____.

2. Let $v(t)$ denote the velocity function of a particle that is moving along an s-axis with constant acceleration $a = -2$. If $v(1) = 4$, then $v(t) =$ _____.

3. Let $v(t)$ denote the velocity function of a particle in rectilinear motion. Suppose that $v(0) = -1$, $v(3) = 2$, and the

velocity versus time curve is a straight line. The displacement of the particle between times $t = 0$ and $t = 3$ is _____, and the distance traveled by the particle over this period of time is _____.

4. Based on the free-fall model, from what height must a coin be dropped so that it strikes the ground with speed 48 ft/s?

EXERCISE SET 5.7 ∿ Graphing Utility [C] CAS

FOCUS ON CONCEPTS

1. In each part, the velocity versus time curve is given for a particle moving along a line. Use the curve to find the displacement and the distance traveled by the particle over the time interval $0 \le t \le 3$.

(a)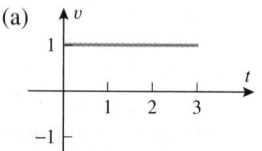

(b)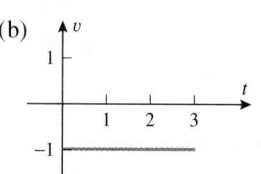

(c)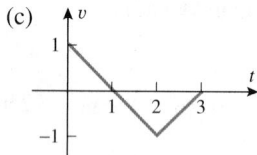

(d)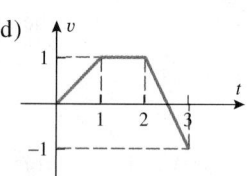

2. Sketch a velocity versus time curve for a particle that travels a distance of 5 units along a coordinate line during the time interval $0 \le t \le 10$ and has a displacement of 0 units.

3. The accompanying figure shows the acceleration versus time curve for a particle moving along a coordinate line. If the initial velocity of the particle is 20 m/s, estimate
(a) the velocity at time $t = 4$ s
(b) the velocity at time $t = 6$ s.

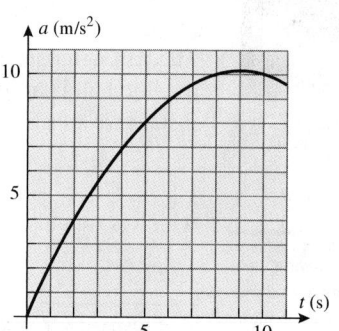

◄ **Figure Ex-3**

4. The accompanying figure shows the velocity versus time curve over the time interval $1 \le t \le 5$ for a particle moving along a horizontal coordinate line.
(a) What can you say about the sign of the acceleration over the time interval?
(b) When is the particle speeding up? Slowing down?
(c) What can you say about the location of the particle at time $t = 5$ relative to its location at time $t = 1$? Explain your reasoning.

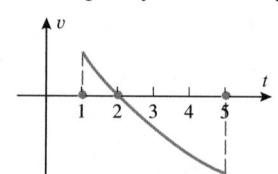

◄ **Figure Ex-4**

5–8 A particle moves along an s-axis. Use the given information to find the position function of the particle. ▩

5. (a) $v(t) = 3t^2 - 2t$; $s(0) = 1$
   (b) $a(t) = 3 \sin 3t$; $v(0) = 3$; $s(0) = 3$

6. (a) $v(t) = 1 + \sin t$; $s(0) = -3$
   (b) $a(t) = t^2 - 3t + 1$; $v(0) = 0$; $s(0) = 0$

7. (a) $v(t) = 3t + 1$; $s(2) = 4$
   (b) $a(t) = t^{-2}$; $v(1) = 0$; $s(1) = 2$

8. (a) $v(t) = t^{2/3}$; $s(8) = 0$
   (b) $a(t) = \sqrt{t}$; $v(4) = 1$; $s(4) = -5$

9–12 A particle moves with a velocity of $v(t)$ m/s along an s-axis. Find the displacement and the distance traveled by the particle during the given time interval. ▩

9. (a) $v(t) = \sin t$; $0 \le t \le \pi/2$
   (b) $v(t) = \cos t$; $\pi/2 \le t \le 2\pi$

10. (a) $v(t) = 3t - 2$; $0 \le t \le 2$
    (b) $v(t) = |1 - 2t|$; $0 \le t \le 2$

11. (a) $v(t) = t^3 - 3t^2 + 2t$; $0 \le t \le 3$
    (b) $v(t) = \sqrt{t} - 2$; $0 \le t \le 3$

12. (a) $v(t) = t - \sqrt{t}$; $0 \le t \le 4$
    (b) $v(t) = \dfrac{1}{\sqrt{t+1}}$; $0 \le t \le 3$

13–16 A particle moves with acceleration $a(t)$ m/s^2 along an s-axis and has velocity v_0 m/s at time $t = 0$. Find the displacement and the distance traveled by the particle during the given time interval. ▩

13. $a(t) = 3$; $v_0 = -1$; $0 \le t \le 2$

14. $a(t) = t - 2$; $v_0 = 0$; $1 \le t \le 5$

15. $a(t) = 1/\sqrt{3t + 1}$; $v_0 = \frac{4}{3}$; $1 \le t \le 5$

16. $a(t) = \sin t$; $v_0 = 1$; $\pi/4 \le t \le \pi/2$

17. In each part, use the given information to find the position, velocity, speed, and acceleration at time $t = 1$.
    (a) $v = \sin \frac{1}{2}\pi t$; $s = 0$ when $t = 0$
    (b) $a = -3t$; $s = 1$ and $v = 0$ when $t = 0$

18. In each part, use the given information to find the position, velocity, speed, and acceleration at time $t = 1$.
    (a) $v = \cos \frac{1}{3}\pi t$; $s = 0$ when $t = \frac{3}{2}$
    (b) $a = 4e^{2t-2}$; $s = 1/e^2$ and $v = (2/e^2) - 3$ when $t = 0$

19. Suppose that a particle moves along a line so that its velocity v at time t is given by

$$v(t) = \begin{cases} 5t, & 0 \le t < 1 \\ 6\sqrt{t} - \dfrac{1}{t}, & 1 \le t \end{cases}$$

where t is in seconds and v is in centimeters per second (cm/s). Estimate the time(s) at which the particle is 4 cm from its starting position.

20. Suppose that a particle moves along a line so that its velocity v at time t is given by

$$v(t) = \frac{3}{t^2 + 1} - 0.5t, \quad t \ge 0$$

where t is in seconds and v is in centimeters per second (cm/s). Estimate the time(s) at which the particle is 2 cm from its starting position.

21. Suppose that the velocity function of a particle moving along an s-axis is $v(t) = 20t^2 - 110t + 120$ ft/s and that the particle is at the origin at time $t = 0$. Use a graphing utility to generate the graphs of $s(t)$, $v(t)$, and $a(t)$ for the first 6 s of motion.

22. Suppose that the acceleration function of a particle moving along an s-axis is $a(t) = 4t - 30$ m/s^2 and that the position and velocity at time $t = 0$ are $s_0 = -5$ m and $v_0 = 3$ m/s. Use a graphing utility to generate the graphs of $s(t)$, $v(t)$, and $a(t)$ for the first 25 s of motion.

23–26 True–False Determine whether the statement is true or false. Explain your answer. Each question refers to a particle in rectilinear motion. ▩

23. If the particle has constant acceleration, the velocity versus time graph will be a straight line.

24. If the particle has constant nonzero acceleration, its position versus time curve will be a parabola.

25. If the total area between the velocity versus time curve and a time interval $[a, b]$ is positive, then the displacement of the particle over this time interval will be nonzero.

26. If $D(t)$ denotes the distance traveled by the particle over the time interval $[0, t]$, then $D(t)$ is an antiderivative for the speed of the particle.

[C] **27–30** For the given velocity function $v(t)$:
(a) Generate the velocity versus time curve, and use it to make a conjecture about the sign of the displacement over the given time interval.
(b) Use a CAS to find the displacement. ▩

27. $v(t) = 0.5 - t \sin t$; $0 \le t \le 5$

28. $v(t) = 0.5 - t \cos \pi t$; $0 \le t \le 1$

29. $v(t) = 0.5 - te^{-t}$; $0 \le t \le 5$

30. $v(t) = t \ln(t + 0.1)$; $0 \le t \le 1$

31. Suppose that at time $t = 0$ a particle is at the origin of an x-axis and has a velocity of $v_0 = 25$ cm/s. For the first 4 s thereafter it has no acceleration, and then it is acted on by a retarding force that produces a constant negative acceleration of $a = -10$ cm/s^2.
    (a) Sketch the acceleration versus time curve over the interval $0 \le t \le 12$.
    (b) Sketch the velocity versus time curve over the time interval $0 \le t \le 12$.
    (c) Find the x-coordinate of the particle at times $t = 8$ s and $t = 12$ s. *(cont.)*

(d) What is the maximum x-coordinate of the particle over the time interval $0 \leq t \leq 12$?

32–36 In these exercises assume that the object is moving with constant acceleration in the positive direction of a coordinate line, and apply Formulas (10) and (11) as appropriate. In some of these problems you will need the fact that 88 ft/s = 60 mi/h. ■

32. A car traveling 60 mi/h along a straight road decelerates at a constant rate of 11 ft/s^2.
    (a) How long will it take until the speed is 45 mi/h?
    (b) How far will the car travel before coming to a stop?

33. Spotting a police car, you hit the brakes on your new Porsche to reduce your speed from 90 mi/h to 60 mi/h at a constant rate over a distance of 200 ft.
    (a) Find the acceleration in ft/s^2.
    (b) How long does it take for you to reduce your speed to 55 mi/h?
    (c) At the acceleration obtained in part (a), how long would it take for you to bring your Porsche to a complete stop from 90 mi/h?

34. A particle moving along a straight line is accelerating at a constant rate of 5 m/s^2. Find the initial velocity if the particle moves 60 m in the first 4 s.

35. A car that has stopped at a toll booth leaves the booth with a constant acceleration of 4 ft/s^2. At the time the car leaves the booth it is 2500 ft behind a truck traveling with a constant velocity of 50 ft/s. How long will it take for the car to catch the truck, and how far will the car be from the toll booth at that time?

36. In the final sprint of a rowing race the challenger is rowing at a constant speed of 12 m/s. At the point where the leader is 100 m from the finish line and the challenger is 15 m behind, the leader is rowing at 8 m/s but starts accelerating at a constant 0.5 m/s^2. Who wins?

37–46 Assume that a free-fall model applies. Solve these exercises by applying Formulas (15) and (16). In these exercises take $g = 32$ ft/s^2 or $g = 9.8$ m/s^2, depending on the units. ■

37. A projectile is launched vertically upward from ground level with an initial velocity of 112 ft/s.
    (a) Find the velocity at $t = 3$ s and $t = 5$ s.
    (b) How high will the projectile rise?
    (c) Find the speed of the projectile when it hits the ground.

38. A projectile fired downward from a height of 112 ft reaches the ground in 2 s. What is its initial velocity?

39. A projectile is fired vertically upward from ground level with an initial velocity of 16 ft/s.
    (a) How long will it take for the projectile to hit the ground?
    (b) How long will the projectile be moving upward?

40. In 1939, Joe Sprinz of the San Francisco Seals Baseball Club attempted to catch a ball dropped from a blimp at a height of 800 ft (for the purpose of breaking the record for catching a ball dropped from the greatest height set the preceding year by members of the Cleveland Indians).
    (a) How long does it take for a ball to drop 800 ft?
    (b) What is the velocity of a ball in miles per hour after an 800 ft drop (88 ft/s = 60 mi/h)?
    [*Note:* As a practical matter, it is unrealistic to ignore wind resistance in this problem; however, even with the slowing effect of wind resistance, the impact of the ball slammed Sprinz's glove hand into his face, fractured his upper jaw in 12 places, broke five teeth, and knocked him unconscious. He dropped the ball!]

41. A projectile is launched upward from ground level with an initial speed of 60 m/s.
    (a) How long does it take for the projectile to reach its highest point?
    (b) How high does the projectile go?
    (c) How long does it take for the projectile to drop back to the ground from its highest point?
    (d) What is the speed of the projectile when it hits the ground?

42. (a) Use the results in Exercise 41 to make a conjecture about the relationship between the initial and final speeds of a projectile that is launched upward from ground level and returns to ground level.
    (b) Prove your conjecture.

43. A projectile is fired vertically upward with an initial velocity of 49 m/s from a tower 150 m high.
    (a) How long will it take for the projectile to reach its maximum height?
    (b) What is the maximum height?
    (c) How long will it take for the projectile to pass its starting point on the way down?
    (d) What is the velocity when it passes the starting point on the way down?
    (e) How long will it take for the projectile to hit the ground?
    (f) What will be its speed at impact?

44. A man drops a stone from a bridge. What is the height of the bridge if
    (a) the stone hits the water 4 s later
    (b) the sound of the splash reaches the man 4 s later? [Take 1080 ft/s as the speed of sound.]

45. In Example 6, how fast would Nolan Ryan have to throw a ball upward from a height of 7 ft in order to hit the ceiling of the Astrodome?

46. A rock thrown downward with an unknown initial velocity from a height of 1000 ft reaches the ground in 5 s. Find the velocity of the rock when it hits the ground.

47. **Writing** Make a list of important features of a velocity versus time curve, and interpret each feature in terms of the motion.

48. **Writing** Use Riemann sums to argue informally that integrating speed over a time interval produces the distance traveled.

5.8 AVERAGE VALUE OF A FUNCTION AND ITS APPLICATIONS

In this section we will define the notion of the "average value" of a function, and we will give various applications of this idea.

■ AVERAGE VELOCITY REVISITED

Let $s = s(t)$ denote the position function of a particle in rectilinear motion. In Section 2.1 we defined the average velocity v_{ave} of the particle over the time interval $[t_0, t_1]$ to be

$$v_{\text{ave}} = \frac{s(t_1) - s(t_0)}{t_1 - t_0}$$

Let $v(t) = s'(t)$ denote the velocity function of the particle. We saw in Section 5.7 that integrating $s'(t)$ over a time interval gives the displacement of the particle over that interval. Thus,

$$\int_{t_0}^{t_1} v(t)\, dt = \int_{t_0}^{t_1} s'(t)\, dt = s(t_1) - s(t_0)$$

It follows that

$$v_{\text{ave}} = \frac{s(t_1) - s(t_0)}{t_1 - t_0} = \frac{1}{t_1 - t_0} \int_{t_0}^{t_1} v(t)\, dt \tag{1}$$

▶ **Example 1**   Suppose that a particle moves along a coordinate line so that its velocity at time t is $v(t) = 2 + \cos t$. Find the average velocity of the particle during the time interval $0 \le t \le \pi$.

Solution.   From (1) the average velocity is

$$\frac{1}{\pi - 0} \int_0^\pi (2 + \cos t)\, dt = \frac{1}{\pi} \left[2t + \sin t \right]_0^\pi = \frac{1}{\pi}(2\pi) = 2 \quad ◄$$

We will see that Formula (1) is a special case of a formula for what we will call the *average value* of a continuous function over a given interval.

■ AVERAGE VALUE OF A CONTINUOUS FUNCTION

In scientific work, numerical information is often summarized by an *average value* or *mean value* of the observed data. There are various kinds of averages, but the most common is the **arithmetic mean** or **arithmetic average**, which is formed by adding the data and dividing by the number of data points. Thus, the arithmetic average $\bar{a}$ of n numbers $a_1, a_2, \ldots, a_n$ is

$$\bar{a} = \frac{1}{n}(a_1 + a_2 + \cdots + a_n) = \frac{1}{n} \sum_{k=1}^{n} a_k$$

In the case where the a_k's are values of a function f, say,

$$a_1 = f(x_1), a_2 = f(x_2), \ldots, a_n = f(x_n)$$

then the arithmetic average $\bar{a}$ of these function values is

$$\bar{a} = \frac{1}{n} \sum_{k=1}^{n} f(x_k)$$

We will now show how to extend this concept so that we can compute not only the arithmetic average of finitely many function values but an average of *all* values of $f(x)$ as x varies over a closed interval $[a, b]$. For this purpose recall the Mean-Value Theorem for Integrals (5.6.2), which states that if f is continuous on the interval $[a, b]$, then there is at least one point x^* in this interval such that

$$\int_a^b f(x)\, dx = f(x^*)(b - a)$$

The quantity

$$f(x^*) = \frac{1}{b - a} \int_a^b f(x)\, dx$$

will be our candidate for the average value of f over the interval $[a, b]$. To explain what motivates this, divide the interval $[a, b]$ into n subintervals of equal length

$$\Delta x = \frac{b - a}{n} \tag{2}$$

and choose arbitrary points $x_1^*, x_2^*, \ldots, x_n^*$ in successive subintervals. Then the arithmetic average of the values $f(x_1^*), f(x_2^*), \ldots, f(x_n^*)$ is

$$\text{ave} = \frac{1}{n}[f(x_1^*) + f(x_2^*) + \cdots + f(x_n^*)]$$

or from (2)

$$\text{ave} = \frac{1}{b - a}[f(x_1^*)\Delta x + f(x_2^*)\Delta x + \cdots + f(x_n^*)\Delta x] = \frac{1}{b - a}\sum_{k=1}^{n} f(x_k^*)\Delta x$$

Taking the limit as $n \to +\infty$ yields

$$\lim_{n \to +\infty} \frac{1}{b - a}\sum_{k=1}^{n} f(x_k^*)\Delta x = \frac{1}{b - a}\int_a^b f(x)\, dx$$

Since this equation describes what happens when we compute the average of "more and more" values of $f(x)$, we are led to the following definition.

Note that the Mean-Value Theorem for Integrals, when expressed in form (3), ensures that there is always at least one point x^* in $[a, b]$ at which the value of f is equal to the average value of f over the interval.

5.8.1   DEFINITION   If f is continuous on $[a, b]$, then the ***average value*** (or ***mean value***) of f on $[a, b]$ is defined to be

$$f_{\text{ave}} = \frac{1}{b - a}\int_a^b f(x)\, dx \tag{3}$$

REMARK   When f is nonnegative on $[a, b]$, the quantity f_{ave} has a simple geometric interpretation, which can be seen by writing (3) as

$$f_{\text{ave}} \cdot (b - a) = \int_a^b f(x)\, dx$$

The left side of this equation is the area of a rectangle with a height of f_{ave} and base of length $b - a$, and the right side is the area under $y = f(x)$ over $[a, b]$. Thus, f_{ave} is the height of a rectangle constructed over the interval $[a, b]$, whose area is the same as the area under the graph of f over that interval (Figure 5.8.1).

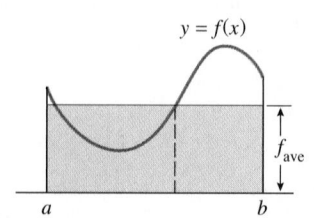

▲ **Figure 5.8.1**

▶ **Example 2**   Find the average value of the function $f(x) = \sqrt{x}$ over the interval $[1, 4]$, and find all points in the interval at which the value of f is the same as the average.

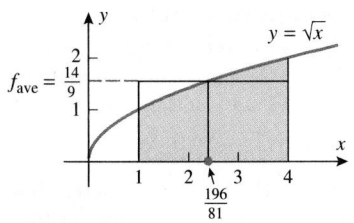

▲ Figure 5.8.2

Solution.

$$f_{ave} = \frac{1}{b-a} \int_a^b f(x)\,dx = \frac{1}{4-1} \int_1^4 \sqrt{x}\,dx = \frac{1}{3}\left[\frac{2x^{3/2}}{3}\right]_1^4$$

$$= \frac{1}{3}\left[\frac{16}{3} - \frac{2}{3}\right] = \frac{14}{9} \approx 1.6$$

The x-values at which $f(x) = \sqrt{x}$ is the same as this average satisfy $\sqrt{x} = 14/9$, from which we obtain $x = 196/81 \approx 2.4$ (Figure 5.8.2). ◄

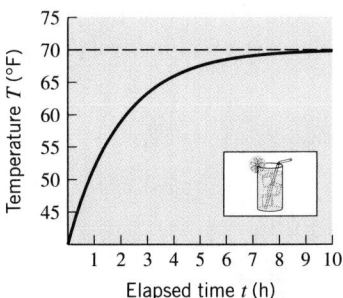

▲ Figure 5.8.3

In Example 3, the temperature T of the lemonade rises from an initial temperature of $40°\,$F toward the room temperature of $70°\,$F. Explain why the formula

$$T = 70 - 30e^{-0.5t}$$

is a good model for this situation.

▶ **Example 3**   A glass of lemonade with a temperature of $40°\,$F is left to sit in a room whose temperature is a constant $70°\,$F. Using a principle of physics called **Newton's Law of Cooling**, one can show that if the temperature of the lemonade reaches $52°\,$F in 1 hour, then the temperature T of the lemonade as a function of the elapsed time t is modeled by the equation

$$T = 70 - 30e^{-0.5t}$$

where T is in degrees Fahrenheit and t is in hours. The graph of this equation, shown in Figure 5.8.3, conforms to our everyday experience that the temperature of the lemonade gradually approaches the temperature of the room. Find the average temperature T_{ave} of the lemonade over the first 5 hours.

Solution.   From Definition 5.8.1 the average value of T over the time interval $[0, 5]$ is

$$T_{ave} = \frac{1}{5} \int_0^5 (70 - 30e^{-0.5t})\,dt \tag{4}$$

To evaluate the definite integral, we first find the indefinite integral

$$\int (70 - 30e^{-0.5t})\,dt$$

by making the substitution

$$u = -0.5t \quad \text{so that} \quad du = -0.5\,dt \quad (\text{or } dt = -2\,du)$$

Thus,

$$\int (70 - 30e^{-0.5t})\,dt = \int (70 - 30e^u)(-2)\,du = -2(70u - 30e^u) + C$$

$$= -2[70(-0.5t) - 30e^{-0.5t}] + C = 70t + 60e^{-0.5t} + C$$

and (4) can be expressed as

$$T_{ave} = \frac{1}{5}\left[70t + 60e^{-0.5t}\right]_0^5 = \frac{1}{5}\left[\left(350 + 60e^{-2.5}\right) - 60\right]$$

$$= 58 + 12e^{-2.5} \approx 59°\text{F} \blacktriangleleft$$

■ **AVERAGE VALUE AND AVERAGE VELOCITY**

We now have two ways to calculate the average velocity of a particle in rectilinear motion, since

$$\frac{s(t_1) - s(t_0)}{t_1 - t_0} = \frac{1}{t_1 - t_0} \int_{t_0}^{t_1} v(t)\,dt \tag{5}$$

and both of these expressions are equal to the average velocity. The left side of (5) gives the average rate of change of s over $[t_0, t_1]$, while the right side gives the average value of

$v = s'$ over the interval $[t_0, t_1]$. That is, *the average velocity of the particle over the time interval $[t_0, t_1]$ is the same as the average value of the velocity function over that interval.*

Since velocity functions are generally continuous, it follows from the marginal note associated with Definition 5.8.1 that a particle's average velocity over a time interval matches the particle's velocity at some time in the interval.

▶ **Example 4**   Show that if a body released from rest (initial velocity zero) is in free fall, then its average velocity over a time interval $[0, T]$ during its fall is its velocity at time $t = T/2$.

Solution.   It follows from Formula (16) of Section 5.7 with $v_0 = 0$ that the velocity function of the body is $v(t) = -gt$. Thus, its average velocity over a time interval $[0, T]$ is

$$v_{ave} = \frac{1}{T - 0} \int_0^T v(t)\, dt$$

$$= \frac{1}{T} \int_0^T -gt\, dt$$

$$= -\frac{g}{T} \left[\frac{1}{2} t^2 \right]_0^T = -g \cdot \frac{T}{2} = v\left(\frac{T}{2} \right) \blacktriangleleft$$

The result of Example 4 can be generalized to show that the average velocity of a particle with constant acceleration during a time interval $[a, b]$ is the velocity at time $t = (a + b)/2$. (See Exercise 18.)

✔**QUICK CHECK EXERCISES 5.8**   *(See page 390 for answers.)*

1. The arithmetic average of n numbers, $a_1, a_2, \ldots, a_n$ is _____.

2. If f is continuous on $[a, b]$, then the average value of f on $[a, b]$ is _____.

3. If f is continuous on $[a, b]$, then the Mean-Value Theorem for Integrals guarantees that for at least one point x^* in $[a, b]$ _____ equals the average value of f on $[a, b]$.

4. The average value of $f(x) = 4x^3$ on $[1, 3]$ is _____.

EXERCISE SET 5.8   Ⓒ CAS

1. (a) Find f_{ave} of $f(x) = 2x$ over $[0, 4]$.
   (b) Find a point x^* in $[0, 4]$ such that $f(x^*) = f_{ave}$.
   (c) Sketch a graph of $f(x) = 2x$ over $[0, 4]$, and construct a rectangle over the interval whose area is the same as the area under the graph of f over the interval.

2. (a) Find f_{ave} of $f(x) = x^2$ over $[0, 2]$.
   (b) Find a point x^* in $[0, 2]$ such that $f(x^*) = f_{ave}$.
   (c) Sketch a graph of $f(x) = x^2$ over $[0, 2]$, and construct a rectangle over the interval whose area is the same as the area under the graph of f over the interval.

3–12 Find the average value of the function over the given interval. ■

3. $f(x) = 3x$; $[1, 3]$

4. $f(x) = \sqrt[3]{x}$; $[-1, 8]$

5. $f(x) = \sin x$; $[0, \pi]$

6. $f(x) = \sec x \tan x$; $[0, \pi/3]$

7. $f(x) = 1/x$; $[1, e]$

8. $f(x) = e^x$; $[-1, \ln 5]$

9. $f(x) = \dfrac{1}{1 + x^2}$; $[1, \sqrt{3}]$

10. $f(x) = \dfrac{1}{\sqrt{1 - x^2}}$; $\left[-\frac{1}{2}, 0\right]$

11. $f(x) = e^{-2x}$; $[0, 4]$

12. $f(x) = \sec^2 x$; $[-\pi/4, \pi/4]$

FOCUS ON CONCEPTS

13. Let $f(x) = 3x^2$.
    (a) Find the arithmetic average of the values $f(0.4)$, $f(0.8)$, $f(1.2)$, $f(1.6)$, and $f(2.0)$.
    (b) Find the arithmetic average of the values $f(0.1)$, $f(0.2)$, $f(0.3), \ldots, f(2.0)$.
    (c) Find the average value of f on $[0, 2]$.
    (d) Explain why the answer to part (c) is less than the answers to parts (a) and (b).

14. In parts (a)–(d), let $f(x) = 1 + (1/x)$.
    (a) Find the arithmetic average of the values $f\left(\frac{6}{5}\right)$, $f\left(\frac{7}{5}\right)$, $f\left(\frac{8}{5}\right)$, $f\left(\frac{9}{5}\right)$, and $f(2)$.
    (b) Find the arithmetic average of the values $f(1.1)$, $f(1.2)$, $f(1.3), \ldots, f(2)$. *(cont.)*

(c) Find the average value of f on $[1, 2]$.

(d) Explain why the answer to part (c) is greater than the answers to parts (a) and (b).

15. In each part, the velocity versus time curve is given for a particle moving along a line. Use the curve to find the average velocity of the particle over the time interval $0 \le t \le 3$.

(a)   (b)

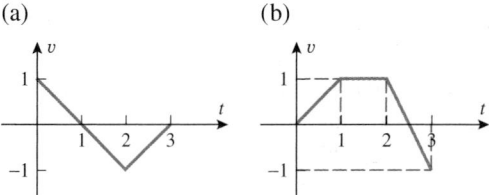

16. Suppose that a particle moving along a line starts from rest and has an average velocity of 2 ft/s over the time interval $0 \le t \le 5$. Sketch a velocity versus time curve for the particle assuming that the particle is also at rest at time $t = 5$. Explain how your curve satisfies the required properties.

17. Suppose that f is a linear function. Using the graph of f, explain why the average value of f on $[a, b]$ is

$$f\left(\frac{a+b}{2}\right)$$

18. Suppose that a particle moves along a coordinate line with constant acceleration. Show that the average velocity of the particle during a time interval $[a, b]$ matches the velocity of the particle at the midpoint of the interval.

19–22 True–False Determine whether the statement is true or false. Explain your answer. (Assume that f and g denote continuous functions on an interval $[a, b]$ and that f_{ave} and g_{ave} denote the respective average values of f and g on $[a, b]$.) ■

19. If $g_{\text{ave}} < f_{\text{ave}}$, then $g(x) \le f(x)$ on $[a, b]$.

20. The average value of a constant multiple of f is the same multiple of f_{ave}; that is, if c is any constant,

$$(c \cdot f)_{\text{ave}} = c \cdot f_{\text{ave}}$$

21. The average of the sum of two functions on an interval is the sum of the average values of the two functions on the interval; that is,

$$(f + g)_{\text{ave}} = f_{\text{ave}} + g_{\text{ave}}$$

22. The average of the product of two functions on an interval is the product of the average values of the two functions on the interval; that is

$$(f \cdot g)_{\text{ave}} = f_{\text{ave}} \cdot g_{\text{ave}}$$

23. (a) Suppose that the velocity function of a particle moving along a coordinate line is $v(t) = 3t^3 + 2$. Find the average velocity of the particle over the time interval $1 \le t \le 4$ by integrating.

(b) Suppose that the position function of a particle moving along a coordinate line is $s(t) = 6t^2 + t$. Find the average velocity of the particle over the time interval $1 \le t \le 4$ algebraically.

24. (a) Suppose that the acceleration function of a particle moving along a coordinate line is $a(t) = t + 1$. Find the average acceleration of the particle over the time interval $0 \le t \le 5$ by integrating.

(b) Suppose that the velocity function of a particle moving along a coordinate line is $v(t) = \cos t$. Find the average acceleration of the particle over the time interval $0 \le t \le \pi/4$ algebraically.

25. Water is run at a constant rate of 1 ft³/min to fill a cylindrical tank of radius 3 ft and height 5 ft. Assuming that the tank is initially empty, make a conjecture about the average weight of the water in the tank over the time period required to fill it, and then check your conjecture by integrating. [Take the weight density of water to be 62.4 lb/ft³.]

26. (a) The temperature of a 10 m long metal bar is 15°C at one end and 30°C at the other end. Assuming that the temperature increases linearly from the cooler end to the hotter end, what is the average temperature of the bar?

(b) Explain why there must be a point on the bar where the temperature is the same as the average, and find it.

27. A traffic engineer monitors the rate at which cars enter the main highway during the afternoon rush hour. From her data she estimates that between 4:30 P.M. and 5:30 P.M. the rate $R(t)$ at which cars enter the highway is given by the formula $R(t) = 100(1 - 0.0001t^2)$ cars per minute, where t is the time (in minutes) since 4:30 P.M. Find the average rate, in cars per minute, at which cars enter the highway during the first half-hour of rush hour.

28. Suppose that the value of a yacht in dollars after t years of use is $V(t) = 275,000e^{-0.17t}$. What is the average value of the yacht over its first 10 years of use?

29. A large juice glass containing 60 ml of orange juice is replenished by a server. The accompanying figure shows the rate at which orange juice is poured into the glass in milliliters per second (ml/s). Show that the average rate of change of the volume of juice in the glass during these 5 s is equal to the average value of the rate of flow of juice into the glass.

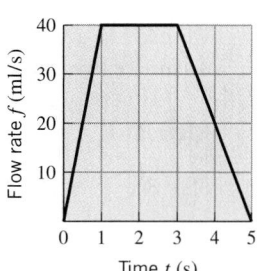

Time t (s)   ◀ **Figure Ex-29**

c **30.** The function J_0 defined by

$$J_0(x) = \frac{1}{\pi} \int_0^\pi \cos(x \sin t) \, dt$$

is called the **Bessel function of order zero**.
(a) Find a function f and an interval $[a, b]$ for which $J_0(1)$ is the average value of f over $[a, b]$.
(b) Estimate $J_0(1)$.
(c) Use a CAS to graph the equation $y = J_0(x)$ over the interval $0 \le x \le 8$.
(d) Estimate the smallest positive zero of J_0.

31. Find a positive value of k such that the average value of $f(x) = \sqrt{3x}$ over the interval $[0, k]$ is 6.

32. Suppose that a tumor grows at the rate of $r(t) = kt$ grams per week for some positive constant k, where t is the num-ber of weeks since the tumor appeared. When, during the second 26 weeks of growth, is the mass of the tumor the same as its average mass during that period?

33. **Writing** Consider the following statement: *The average value of the rate of change of a function over an interval is equal to the average rate of change of the function over that interval.* Write a short paragraph that explains why this statement may be interpreted as a rewording of Part 1 of the Fundamental Theorem of Calculus.

34. **Writing** If an automobile gets an average of 25 miles per gallon of gasoline, then it is also the case that on average the automobile expends 1/25 gallon of gasoline per mile. In-terpret this statement using the concept of the average value of a function over an interval.

✔ **QUICK CHECK ANSWERS 5.8**

1. $\dfrac{1}{n} \sum_{k=1}^{n} a_k$ **2.** $\dfrac{1}{b-a} \int_a^b f(x) \, dx$ **3.** $f(x^*)$ **4.** 40

5.9 EVALUATING DEFINITE INTEGRALS BY SUBSTITUTION

In this section we will discuss two methods for evaluating definite integrals in which a substitution is required.

■ **TWO METHODS FOR MAKING SUBSTITUTIONS IN DEFINITE INTEGRALS**

Recall from Section 5.3 that indefinite integrals of the form

$$\int f(g(x)) g'(x) \, dx$$

can sometimes be evaluated by making the u-substitution

$$u = g(x), \quad du = g'(x) \, dx \tag{1}$$

which converts the integral to the form

$$\int f(u) \, du$$

To apply this method to a definite integral of the form

$$\int_a^b f(g(x)) g'(x) \, dx$$

we need to account for the effect that the substitution has on the x-limits of integration. There are two ways of doing this.

Method 1.

First evaluate the indefinite integral

$$\int f(g(x)) g'(x) \, dx$$

by substitution, and then use the relationship

$$\int_a^b f(g(x))g'(x)\,dx = \left[\int f(g(x))g'(x)\,dx\right]_a^b$$

to evaluate the definite integral. This procedure does not require any modification of the x-limits of integration.

Method 2.

Make the substitution (1) directly in the definite integral, and then use the relationship $u = g(x)$ to replace the x-limits, $x = a$ and $x = b$, by corresponding u-limits, $u = g(a)$ and $u = g(b)$. This produces a new definite integral

$$\int_{g(a)}^{g(b)} f(u)\,du$$

that is expressed entirely in terms of u.

▶ **Example 1**   Use the two methods above to evaluate $\displaystyle\int_0^2 x(x^2 + 1)^3\,dx$.

Solution by Method 1.   If we let

$$u = x^2 + 1 \quad \text{so that} \quad du = 2x\,dx \tag{2}$$

then we obtain

$$\int x(x^2 + 1)^3\,dx = \frac{1}{2}\int u^3\,du = \frac{u^4}{8} + C = \frac{(x^2 + 1)^4}{8} + C$$

Thus,

$$\int_0^2 x(x^2 + 1)^3\,dx = \left[\int x(x^2 + 1)^3\,dx\right]_{x=0}^2$$

$$= \frac{(x^2 + 1)^4}{8}\Bigg]_{x=0}^2 = \frac{625}{8} - \frac{1}{8} = 78$$

Solution by Method 2.   If we make the substitution $u = x^2 + 1$ in (2), then

$$\text{if} \quad x = 0, \quad u = 1$$
$$\text{if} \quad x = 2, \quad u = 5$$

Thus,

$$\int_0^2 x(x^2 + 1)^3\,dx = \frac{1}{2}\int_1^5 u^3\,du$$

$$= \frac{u^4}{8}\Bigg]_{u=1}^5 = \frac{625}{8} - \frac{1}{8} = 78$$

which agrees with the result obtained by Method 1. ◀

The following theorem states precise conditions under which Method 2 can be used.

5.9.1   THEOREM   *If g' is continuous on $[a, b]$ and f is continuous on an interval containing the values of $g(x)$ for $a \le x \le b$, then*

$$\int_a^b f(g(x))g'(x)\,dx = \int_{g(a)}^{g(b)} f(u)\,du$$

PROOF   Since f is continuous on an interval containing the values of $g(x)$ for $a \leq x \leq b$, it follows that f has an antiderivative F on that interval. If we let $u = g(x)$, then the chain rule implies that

$$\frac{d}{dx}F(g(x)) = \frac{d}{dx}F(u) = \frac{dF}{du}\frac{du}{dx} = f(u)\frac{du}{dx} = f(g(x))g'(x)$$

for each x in $[a, b]$. Thus, $F(g(x))$ is an antiderivative of $f(g(x))g'(x)$ on $[a, b]$. Therefore, by Part 1 of the Fundamental Theorem of Calculus (5.6.1)

$$\int_a^b f(g(x))g'(x)\,dx = F(g(x))\Big]_a^b = F(g(b)) - F(g(a)) = \int_{g(a)}^{g(b)} f(u)\,du \quad \blacksquare$$

The choice of methods for evaluating definite integrals by substitution is generally a matter of taste, but in the following examples we will use the second method, since the idea is new.

▶ **Example 2**   Evaluate

$$\text{(a)} \int_0^{\pi/8} \sin^5 2x \cos 2x\,dx \qquad \text{(b)} \int_2^5 (2x - 5)(x - 3)^9\,dx$$

Solution (a).   Let

$$u = \sin 2x \quad \text{so that} \quad du = 2\cos 2x\,dx \quad \left(\text{or } \tfrac{1}{2}\,du = \cos 2x\,dx\right)$$

With this substitution,

$$\text{if} \quad x = 0, \quad u = \sin(0) = 0$$
$$\text{if} \quad x = \pi/8, \quad u = \sin(\pi/4) = 1/\sqrt{2}$$

so

$$\int_0^{\pi/8} \sin^5 2x \cos 2x\,dx = \frac{1}{2}\int_0^{1/\sqrt{2}} u^5\,du$$

$$= \frac{1}{2}\cdot\frac{u^6}{6}\Big]_{u=0}^{1/\sqrt{2}} = \frac{1}{2}\left[\frac{1}{6(\sqrt{2})^6} - 0\right] = \frac{1}{96}$$

Solution (b).   Let

$$u = x - 3 \quad \text{so that} \quad du = dx$$

This leaves a factor of $2x - 5$ unresolved in the integrand. However,

$$x = u + 3, \quad \text{so} \quad 2x - 5 = 2(u + 3) - 5 = 2u + 1$$

With this substitution,

$$\text{if} \quad x = 2, \quad u = 2 - 3 = -1$$
$$\text{if} \quad x = 5, \quad u = 5 - 3 = 2$$

so

$$\int_2^5 (2x - 5)(x - 3)^9\,dx = \int_{-1}^2 (2u + 1)u^9\,du = \int_{-1}^2 (2u^{10} + u^9)\,du$$

$$= \left[\frac{2u^{11}}{11} + \frac{u^{10}}{10}\right]_{u=-1}^2 = \left(\frac{2^{12}}{11} + \frac{2^{10}}{10}\right) - \left(-\frac{2}{11} + \frac{1}{10}\right)$$

$$= \frac{52{,}233}{110} \approx 474.8 \quad \blacktriangleleft$$

▶ **Example 3**   Evaluate

$$\text{(a) } \int_0^{3/4} \frac{dx}{1-x} \qquad \text{(b) } \int_0^{\ln 3} e^x (1 + e^x)^{1/2} \, dx$$

Solution (a).   Let

$$u = 1 - x \quad \text{so that} \quad du = -dx$$

With this substitution,

$$\text{if} \quad x = 0, \quad u = 1$$
$$\text{if} \quad x = \tfrac{3}{4}, \quad u = \tfrac{1}{4}$$

Thus,

$$\int_0^{3/4} \frac{dx}{1-x} = -\int_1^{1/4} \frac{du}{u}$$

$$= -\ln |u| \Big]_{u=1}^{1/4} = -\left[\ln \left(\frac{1}{4}\right) - \ln(1) \right] = \ln 4$$

Solution (b).   Make the u-substitution

$$u = 1 + e^x, \quad du = e^x \, dx$$

and change the x-limits of integration ($x = 0, x = \ln 3$) to the u-limits

$$u = 1 + e^0 = 2, \quad u = 1 + e^{\ln 3} = 1 + 3 = 4$$

This yields

The u-substitution in Example 3(a) produces an integral in which the upper u-limit is smaller than the lower u-limit. Use Definition 5.5.3(b) to convert this integral to one whose lower limit is smaller than the upper limit and verify that it produces an integral with the same value as that in the example.

$$\int_0^{\ln 3} e^x (1 + e^x)^{1/2} \, dx = \int_2^4 u^{1/2} \, du$$

$$= \frac{2}{3} u^{3/2} \Big]_{u=2}^4 = \frac{2}{3}[4^{3/2} - 2^{3/2}] = \frac{16 - 4\sqrt{2}}{3} \quad ◀$$

✔ **QUICK CHECK EXERCISES 5.9**   (*See page 396 for answers.*)

1. Assume that g' is continuous on $[a, b]$ and that f is continuous on an interval containing the values of $g(x)$ for $a \le x \le b$. If F is an antiderivative for f, then

$$\int_a^b f(g(x))g'(x) \, dx = \underline{\hspace{1cm}}$$

2. In each part, use the substitution to replace the given integral with an integral involving the variable u. (Do not evaluate the integral.)

(a) $\int_0^2 3x^2 (1 + x^3)^3 \, dx; \ u = 1 + x^3$

(b) $\int_0^2 \frac{x}{\sqrt{5 - x^2}} \, dx; \ u = 5 - x^2$

(c) $\int_0^1 \frac{e^{\sqrt{x}}}{\sqrt{x}} \, dx; \ u = \sqrt{x}$

3. Evaluate the integral by making an appropriate substitution.

(a) $\int_{-\pi}^0 \sin(3x - \pi) \, dx = \underline{\hspace{1cm}}$

(b) $\int_2^3 \frac{x}{x^2 - 2} \, dx = \underline{\hspace{1cm}}$

(c) $\int_0^{\pi/2} \sqrt[3]{\sin x} \cos x \, dx = \underline{\hspace{1cm}}$

EXERCISE SET 5.9 ⬜ Graphing Utility ⬜C⬜ CAS

1–4 Express the integral in terms of the variable u, but do not evaluate it. ▪

1. (a) $\displaystyle\int_1^3 (2x-1)^3\,dx;\ u=2x-1$

(b) $\displaystyle\int_0^4 3x\sqrt{25-x^2}\,dx;\ u=25-x^2$

(c) $\displaystyle\int_{-1/2}^{1/2} \cos(\pi\theta)\,d\theta;\ u=\pi\theta$

(d) $\displaystyle\int_0^1 (x+2)(x+1)^5\,dx;\ u=x+1$

2. (a) $\displaystyle\int_{-1}^4 (5-2x)^8\,dx;\ u=5-2x$

(b) $\displaystyle\int_{-\pi/3}^{2\pi/3} \frac{\sin x}{\sqrt{2+\cos x}}\,dx;\ u=2+\cos x$

(c) $\displaystyle\int_0^{\pi/4} \tan^2 x\,\sec^2 x\,dx;\ u=\tan x$

(d) $\displaystyle\int_0^1 x^3\sqrt{x^2+3}\,dx;\ u=x^2+3$

3. (a) $\displaystyle\int_0^1 e^{2x-1}\,dx;\ u=2x-1$

(b) $\displaystyle\int_e^{e^2} \frac{\ln x}{x}\,dx;\ u=\ln x$

4. (a) $\displaystyle\int_1^{\sqrt 3} \frac{\sqrt{\tan^{-1}x}}{1+x^2}\,dx;\ u=\tan^{-1}x$

(b) $\displaystyle\int_1^{\sqrt e} \frac{dx}{x\sqrt{1-(\ln x)^2}};\ u=\ln x$

5–18 Evaluate the definite integral two ways: first by a u-substitution in the definite integral and then by a u-substitution in the corresponding indefinite integral. ▪

5. $\displaystyle\int_0^1 (2x+1)^3\,dx$

6. $\displaystyle\int_1^2 (4x-2)^3\,dx$

7. $\displaystyle\int_0^1 (2x-1)^3\,dx$

8. $\displaystyle\int_1^2 (4-3x)^8\,dx$

9. $\displaystyle\int_0^8 x\sqrt{1+x}\,dx$

10. $\displaystyle\int_{-3}^0 x\sqrt{1-x}\,dx$

11. $\displaystyle\int_0^{\pi/2} 4\sin(x/2)\,dx$

12. $\displaystyle\int_0^{\pi/6} 2\cos 3x\,dx$

13. $\displaystyle\int_{-2}^{-1} \frac{x}{(x^2+2)^3}\,dx$

14. $\displaystyle\int_{1-\pi}^{1+\pi} \sec^2\left(\tfrac14 x - \tfrac14\right)dx$

15. $\displaystyle\int_{-\ln 3}^{\ln 3} \frac{e^x}{e^x+4}\,dx$

16. $\displaystyle\int_0^{\ln 5} e^x(3-4e^x)\,dx$

17. $\displaystyle\int_1^3 \frac{dx}{\sqrt{x}\,(x+1)}$

18. $\displaystyle\int_{\ln 2}^{\ln(2/\sqrt3)} \frac{e^{-x}\,dx}{\sqrt{1-e^{-2x}}}$

19–22 Evaluate the definite integral by expressing it in terms of u and evaluating the resulting integral using a formula from geometry. ▪

19. $\displaystyle\int_{-5/3}^{5/3} \sqrt{25-9x^2}\,dx;\ u=3x$

20. $\displaystyle\int_0^2 x\sqrt{16-x^4}\,dx;\ u=x^2$

21. $\displaystyle\int_{\pi/3}^{\pi/2} \sin\theta\sqrt{1-4\cos^2\theta}\,d\theta;\ u=2\cos\theta$

22. $\displaystyle\int_{e^{-3}}^{e^3} \frac{\sqrt{9-(\ln x)^2}}{x}\,dx;\ u=\ln x$

23. A particle moves with a velocity of $v(t)=\sin\pi t$ m/s along an s-axis. Find the distance traveled by the particle over the time interval $0\le t\le 1$.

24. A particle moves with a velocity of $v(t)=3\cos 2t$ m/s along an s-axis. Find the distance traveled by the particle over the time interval $0\le t\le \pi/8$.

25. Find the area under the curve $y=9/(x+2)^2$ over the interval $[-1,1]$.

26. Find the area under the curve $y=1/(3x+1)^2$ over the interval $[0,1]$.

27. Find the area of the region enclosed by the graphs of $y=1/\sqrt{1-9x^2}$, $y=0$, $x=0$, and $x=\tfrac16$.

28. Find the area of the region enclosed by the graphs of $y=\sin^{-1}x$, $x=0$, and $y=\pi/2$.

29–48 Evaluate the integrals by any method. ▪

29. $\displaystyle\int_1^5 \frac{dx}{\sqrt{2x-1}}$

30. $\displaystyle\int_1^2 \sqrt{5x-1}\,dx$

31. $\displaystyle\int_{-1}^1 \frac{x^2\,dx}{\sqrt{x^3+9}}$

32. $\displaystyle\int_{\pi/2}^{\pi} 6\sin x(\cos x+1)^5\,dx$

33. $\displaystyle\int_1^3 \frac{x+2}{\sqrt{x^2+4x+7}}\,dx$

34. $\displaystyle\int_1^2 \frac{dx}{x^2-6x+9}$

35. $\displaystyle\int_0^{\pi/4} 4\sin x\cos x\,dx$

36. $\displaystyle\int_0^{\pi/4} \sqrt{\tan x}\,\sec^2 x\,dx$

37. $\displaystyle\int_0^{\sqrt\pi} 5x\cos(x^2)\,dx$

38. $\displaystyle\int_{\pi^2}^{4\pi^2} \frac{1}{\sqrt x}\sin\sqrt x\,dx$

39. $\displaystyle\int_{\pi/12}^{\pi/9} \sec^2 3\theta\,d\theta$

40. $\displaystyle\int_0^{\pi/6} \tan 2\theta\,d\theta$

41. $\displaystyle\int_0^1 \frac{y^2\,dy}{\sqrt{4-3y}}$

42. $\displaystyle\int_{-1}^4 \frac{x\,dx}{\sqrt{5+x}}$

43. $\displaystyle\int_0^e \frac{dx}{2x+e}$

44. $\displaystyle\int_1^{\sqrt2} xe^{-x^2}\,dx$

45. $\displaystyle\int_0^1 \frac{x}{\sqrt{4-3x^4}}\,dx$

46. $\displaystyle\int_1^2 \frac{1}{\sqrt x\sqrt{4-x}}\,dx$

47. $\displaystyle\int_0^{1/\sqrt{3}} \frac{1}{1+9x^2}\,dx$ **48.** $\displaystyle\int_1^{\sqrt{2}} \frac{x}{3+x^4}\,dx$

c 49. (a) Use a CAS to find the exact value of the integral

$$\int_0^{\pi/6} \sin^4 x \cos^3 x\,dx$$

(b) Confirm the exact value by hand calculation.
   [*Hint:* Use the identity $\cos^2 x = 1 - \sin^2 x$.]

c 50. (a) Use a CAS to find the exact value of the integral

$$\int_{-\pi/4}^{\pi/4} \tan^4 x\,dx$$

(b) Confirm the exact value by hand calculation.
   [*Hint:* Use the identity $1 + \tan^2 x = \sec^2 x$.]

51. (a) Find $\displaystyle\int_0^1 f(3x+1)\,dx$ if $\displaystyle\int_1^4 f(x)\,dx = 5$.

(b) Find $\displaystyle\int_0^3 f(3x)\,dx$ if $\displaystyle\int_0^9 f(x)\,dx = 5$.

(c) Find $\displaystyle\int_{-2}^0 xf(x^2)\,dx$ if $\displaystyle\int_0^4 f(x)\,dx = 1$.

52. Given that m and n are positive integers, show that

$$\int_0^1 x^m(1-x)^n\,dx = \int_0^1 x^n(1-x)^m\,dx$$

by making a substitution. Do not attempt to evaluate the integrals.

53. Given that n is a positive integer, show that

$$\int_0^{\pi/2} \sin^n x\,dx = \int_0^{\pi/2} \cos^n x\,dx$$

by using a trigonometric identity and making a substitution. Do not attempt to evaluate the integrals.

54. Given that n is a positive integer, evaluate the integral

$$\int_0^1 x(1-x)^n\,dx$$

55. Suppose that at time $t = 0$ there are 750 bacteria in a growth medium and the bacteria population $y(t)$ grows at the rate $y'(t) = 802.137e^{1.528t}$ bacteria per hour. How many bacteria will there be in 12 hours?

56. Suppose that a particle moving along a coordinate line has velocity $v(t) = 25 + 10e^{-0.05t}$ ft/s.

(a) What is the distance traveled by the particle from time $t = 0$ to time $t = 10$?

(b) Does the term $10e^{-0.05t}$ have much effect on the distance traveled by the particle over that time interval? Explain your reasoning.

57. (a) The accompanying table shows the fraction of the Moon that is illuminated (as seen from Earth) at midnight (Eastern Standard Time) for the first week of 2005. Find the average fraction of the Moon illuminated during the first week of 2005.

   Source: Data from the U.S Naval Observatory Astronomical Applications Department.

(b) The function $f(x) = 0.5 + 0.5\sin(0.213x + 2.481)$ models data for illumination of the Moon for the first 60 days of 2005. Find the average value of this illumination function over the interval $[0, 7]$.

DAY	1	2	3	4	5	6	7
ILLUMINATION	0.74	0.65	0.56	0.45	0.35	0.25	0.16

▲ **Table Ex-57**

58. Electricity is supplied to homes in the form of ***alternating current***, which means that the voltage has a sinusoidal waveform described by an equation of the form

$$V = V_p \sin(2\pi f t)$$

(see the accompanying figure). In this equation, V_p is called the ***peak voltage*** or ***amplitude*** of the current, f is called its ***frequency***, and $1/f$ is called its ***period***. The voltages V and V_p are measured in volts (V), the time t is measured in seconds (s), and the frequency is measured in hertz (Hz). (1 Hz = 1 cycle per second; a ***cycle*** is the electrical term for one period of the waveform.) Most alternating-current voltmeters read what is called the ***rms*** or ***root-mean-square*** value of V. By definition, this is the square root of the average value of V^2 over one period.

(a) Show that
$$V_{\text{rms}} = \frac{V_p}{\sqrt{2}}$$

   [*Hint:* Compute the average over the cycle from $t = 0$ to $t = 1/f$, and use the identity $\sin^2\theta = \frac{1}{2}(1 - \cos 2\theta)$ to help evaluate the integral.]

(b) In the United States, electrical outlets supply alternating current with an rms voltage of 120 V at a frequency of 60 Hz. What is the peak voltage at such an outlet?

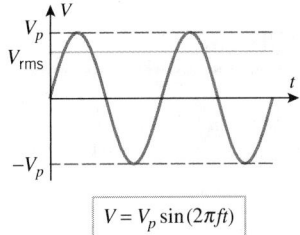

$V = V_p \sin(2\pi f t)$

◀ **Figure Ex-58**

59. Find a positive value of k such that the area under the graph of $y = e^{2x}$ over the interval $[0, k]$ is 3 square units.

60. Use a graphing utility to estimate the value of k ($k > 0$) so that the region enclosed by $y = 1/(1 + kx^2)$, $y = 0$, $x = 0$, and $x = 2$ has an area of 0.6 square unit.

c 61. (a) Find the limit

$$\lim_{n \to +\infty} \sum_{k=1}^n \frac{\sin(k\pi/n)}{n}$$

   by evaluating an appropriate definite integral over the interval $[0, 1]$.

(b) Check your answer to part (a) by evaluating the limit directly with a CAS.

FOCUS ON CONCEPTS

62. Let

$$I = \int_{-1}^{1} \frac{1}{1+x^2}\, dx$$

(a) Explain why $I > 0$.

(b) Show that the substitution $x = 1/u$ results in

$$I = -\int_{-1}^{1} \frac{1}{1+x^2}\, dx = -I$$

Thus, $2I = 0$, which implies that $I = 0$. But this contradicts part (a). What is the error?

63. (a) Prove that if f is an odd function, then

$$\int_{-a}^{a} f(x)\, dx = 0$$

and give a geometric explanation of this result. [*Hint:* One way to prove that a quantity q is zero is to show that $q = -q$.]

(b) Prove that if f is an even function, then

$$\int_{-a}^{a} f(x)\, dx = 2\int_{0}^{a} f(x)\, dx$$

and give a geometric explanation of this result. [*Hint:* Split the interval of integration from $-a$ to a into two parts at 0.]

64. Show that if f and g are continuous functions, then

$$\int_{0}^{t} f(t-x)g(x)\, dx = \int_{0}^{t} f(x)g(t-x)\, dx$$

65. (a) Let

$$I = \int_{0}^{a} \frac{f(x)}{f(x) + f(a-x)}\, dx$$

Show that $I = a/2$.

[*Hint:* Let $u = a - x$, and then note the difference between the resulting integrand and 1.]

(b) Use the result of part (a) to find

$$\int_{0}^{3} \frac{\sqrt{x}}{\sqrt{x} + \sqrt{3-x}}\, dx$$

(c) Use the result of part (a) to find

$$\int_{0}^{\pi/2} \frac{\sin x}{\sin x + \cos x}\, dx$$

66. Evaluate

(a) $\displaystyle\int_{-1}^{1} x\sqrt{\cos(x^2)}\, dx$

(b) $\displaystyle\int_{0}^{\pi} \sin^8 x \cos^5 x\, dx.$

[*Hint:* Use the substitution $u = x - (\pi/2)$.]

67. Writing   The two substitution methods discussed in this section yield the same result when used to evaluate a definite integral. Write a short paragraph that carefully explains why this is the case.

68. Writing   In some cases, the second method for the evaluation of definite integrals has distinct advantages over the first. Provide some illustrations, and write a short paragraph that discusses the advantages of the second method in each case. [*Hint:* To get started, consider the results in Exercises 52–54, 63, and 65.]

✓ **QUICK CHECK ANSWERS 5.9**

1. $F(g(b)) - F(g(a))$ **2.** (a) $\displaystyle\int_{1}^{9} u^3\, du$ (b) $\displaystyle\int_{1}^{5} \frac{1}{2\sqrt{u}}\, du$ (c) $\displaystyle\int_{0}^{1} 2e^u\, du$ **3.** (a) $\dfrac{2}{3}$ (b) $\dfrac{1}{2}\ln\left(\dfrac{7}{2}\right)$ (c) $\dfrac{3}{4}$

5.10   **LOGARITHMIC AND OTHER FUNCTIONS DEFINED BY INTEGRALS**

In Section 0.5 we defined the natural logarithm function $\ln x$ to be the inverse of e^x. Although this was convenient and enabled us to deduce many properties of $\ln x$, the mathematical foundation was shaky in that we accepted the continuity of e^x and of all exponential functions without proof. In this section we will show that $\ln x$ can be defined as a certain integral, and we will use this new definition to prove that exponential functions are continuous. This integral definition is also important in applications because it provides a way of recognizing when integrals that appear in solutions of problems can be expressed as natural logarithms.

■ **THE CONNECTION BETWEEN NATURAL LOGARITHMS AND INTEGRALS**

The connection between natural logarithms and integrals was made in the middle of the seventeenth century in the course of investigating areas under the curve $y = 1/t$. The problem being considered was to find values of $t_1, t_2, t_3, \ldots, t_n, \ldots$ for which the areas $A_1, A_2, A_3, \ldots, A_n, \ldots$ in Figure 5.10.1a would be equal. Through the combined work of Isaac Newton, the Belgian Jesuit priest Gregory of St. Vincent (1584–1667), and Gregory's student Alfons A. de Sarasa (1618–1667), it was shown that by taking the points to be

$$t_1 = e, \quad t_2 = e^2, \quad t_3 = e^3, \ldots, \quad t_n = e^n, \ldots$$

each of the areas would be 1 (Figure 5.10.1b). Thus, in modern integral notation

$$\int_1^{e^n} \frac{1}{t}\, dt = n$$

which can be expressed as

$$\int_1^{e^n} \frac{1}{t}\, dt = \ln(e^n)$$

By comparing the upper limit of the integral and the expression inside the logarithm, it is a natural leap to the more general result

$$\int_1^x \frac{1}{t}\, dt = \ln x$$

which today we take as the formal definition of the natural logarithm.

$y = \dfrac{1}{t}$

A_1 A_2 A_3 A_4

1 t_1 t_2 t_3 t_4

(a)

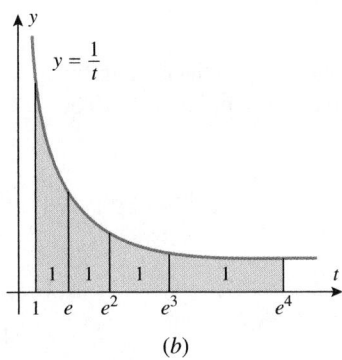

$y = \dfrac{1}{t}$

1 1 1 1

1 e e^2 e^3 e^4

(b)

Not drawn to scale

▲ **Figure 5.10.1**

5.10.1   DEFINITION   The **natural logarithm** of x is denoted by $\ln x$ and is defined by the integral

$$\ln x = \int_1^x \frac{1}{t}\, dt, \quad x > 0 \tag{1}$$

Review Theorem 5.5.8 and then explain why x is required to be positive in Definition 5.10.1.

None of the properties of $\ln x$ obtained in this section should be new, but now, for the first time, we give them a sound mathematical footing.

Our strategy for putting the study of logarithmic and exponential functions on a sound mathematical footing is to use (1) as a starting point and then define e^x as the inverse of $\ln x$. This is the exact opposite of our previous approach in which we defined $\ln x$ to be the inverse of e^x. However, whereas previously we had to *assume* that e^x is continuous, the continuity of e^x will now follow from our definitions as a *theorem*. Our first challenge is to demonstrate that the properties of $\ln x$ resulting from Definition 5.10.1 are consistent with those obtained earlier. To start, observe that Part 2 of the Fundamental Theorem of Calculus (5.6.3) implies that $\ln x$ is differentiable and

$$\frac{d}{dx}[\ln x] = \frac{d}{dx}\left[\int_1^x \frac{1}{t}\, dt\right] = \frac{1}{x} \quad (x > 0) \tag{2}$$

This is consistent with the derivative formula for $\ln x$ that we obtained previously. Moreover, because differentiability implies continuity, it follows that $\ln x$ is a continuous function on the interval $(0, +\infty)$.

Other properties of $\ln x$ can be obtained by interpreting the integral in (1) geometrically: In the case where $x > 1$, this integral represents the area under the curve $y = 1/t$ from $t = 1$ to $t = x$ (Figure 5.10.2a); in the case where $0 < x < 1$, the integral represents the negative of the area under the curve $y = 1/t$ from $t = x$ to $t = 1$ (Figure 5.10.2b); and in the case where $x = 1$, the integral has value 0 because its upper and lower limits of integration are the same. These geometric observations imply that

$$\ln x > 0 \quad \text{if} \quad x > 1$$
$$\ln x < 0 \quad \text{if} \quad 0 < x < 1$$
$$\ln x = 0 \quad \text{if} \quad x = 1$$

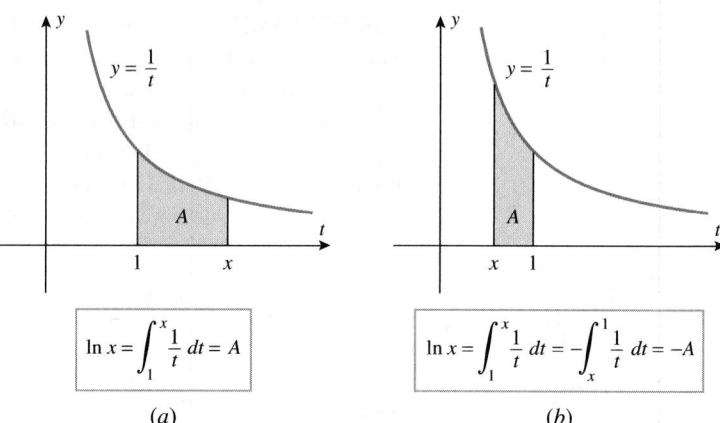

$$\ln x = \int_1^x \frac{1}{t}\, dt = A$$

$$\ln x = \int_1^x \frac{1}{t}\, dt = -\int_x^1 \frac{1}{t}\, dt = -A$$

▶ **Figure 5.10.2** (a) $\qquad\qquad (b)$

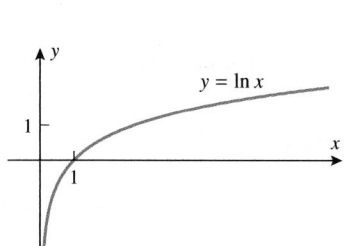

▲ **Figure 5.10.3**

Also, since $1/x$ is positive for $x > 0$, it follows from (2) that $\ln x$ is an increasing function on the interval $(0, +\infty)$. This is all consistent with the graph of $\ln x$ in Figure 5.10.3.

■ ALGEBRAIC PROPERTIES OF ln x

We can use (1) to show that Definition 5.10.1 produces the standard algebraic properties of logarithms.

5.10.2 **THEOREM** *For any positive numbers a and c and any rational number r:*

(a) $\ln ac = \ln a + \ln c$ $\qquad$ (b) $\ln \dfrac{1}{c} = -\ln c$

(c) $\ln \dfrac{a}{c} = \ln a - \ln c$ $\qquad$ (d) $\ln a^r = r \ln a$

PROOF (a) Treating a as a constant, consider the function $f(x) = \ln(ax)$. Then

$$f'(x) = \frac{1}{ax} \cdot \frac{d}{dx}(ax) = \frac{1}{ax} \cdot a = \frac{1}{x}$$

Thus, $\ln ax$ and $\ln x$ have the same derivative on $(0, +\infty)$, so these functions must differ by a constant on this interval. That is, there is a constant k such that

$$\ln ax - \ln x = k \tag{3}$$

on $(0, +\infty)$. Substituting $x = 1$ into this equation we conclude that $\ln a = k$ (verify). Thus, (3) can be written as

$$\ln ax - \ln x = \ln a$$

Setting $x = c$ establishes that

$$\ln ac - \ln c = \ln a \quad \text{or} \quad \ln ac = \ln a + \ln c$$

PROOFS (b) **AND** (c) Part (b) follows immediately from part (a) by substituting $1/c$ for a (verify). Then

$$\ln \frac{a}{c} = \ln\left(a \cdot \frac{1}{c}\right) = \ln a + \ln \frac{1}{c} = \ln a - \ln c$$

PROOF (d) First, we will argue that part (d) is satisfied if r is any nonnegative integer. If $r = 1$, then (d) is clearly satisfied; if $r = 0$, then (d) follows from the fact that $\ln 1 = 0$. Suppose that we know (d) is satisfied for r equal to some integer n. It then follows from part (a) that

$$\ln a^{n+1} = \ln[a \cdot a^n] = \ln a + \ln a^n = \ln a + n \ln a = (n + 1) \ln a$$

That is, if (d) is valid for r equal to some integer n, then it is also valid for $r = n + 1$. However, since we know (d) is satisfied if $r = 1$, it follows that (d) is valid for $r = 2$. But this implies that (d) is satisfied for $r = 3$, which in turn implies that (d) is valid for $r = 4$, and so forth. We conclude that (d) is satisfied if r is any nonnegative integer.

Next, suppose that $r = -m$ is a negative integer. Then

$$\ln a^r = \ln a^{-m} = \ln \frac{1}{a^m} = -\ln a^m \qquad \boxed{\text{By part } (b)}$$

$$= -m \ln a \qquad \boxed{\text{Part } (d) \text{ is valid for positive powers.}}$$

$$= r \ln a$$

which shows that (d) is valid for any negative integer r. Combining this result with our previous conclusion that (d) is satisfied for a nonnegative integer r shows that (d) is valid if r is *any* integer.

Finally, suppose that $r = m/n$ is any rational number, where $m \neq 0$ and $n \neq 0$ are integers. Then

$$\ln a^r = \frac{n \ln a^r}{n} = \frac{\ln[(a^r)^n]}{n} \qquad \boxed{\text{Part } (d) \text{ is valid for integer powers.}}$$

$$= \frac{\ln a^{rn}}{n} \qquad \boxed{\text{Property of exponents}}$$

$$= \frac{\ln a^m}{n} \qquad \boxed{\text{Definition of } r}$$

$$= \frac{m \ln a}{n} \qquad \boxed{\text{Part } (d) \text{ is valid for integer powers.}}$$

$$= \frac{m}{n} \ln a = r \ln a$$

which shows that (d) is valid for any rational number r. ■

> How is the proof of Theorem 5.10.2(d) for the case where r is a nonnegative integer analogous to a row of falling dominos? (This "domino" argument uses an informal version of a property of the integers known as the *principle of mathematical induction*.)

■ APPROXIMATING ln *x* NUMERICALLY

For specific values of x, the value of $\ln x$ can be approximated numerically by approximating the definite integral in (1), say by using the midpoint approximation that was discussed in Section 5.4.

Table 5.10.1

$n = 10$
$\Delta t = (b - a)/n = (2 - 1)/10 = 0.1$

k	t_k^*	$1/t_k^*$
1	1.05	0.952381
2	1.15	0.869565
3	1.25	0.800000
4	1.35	0.740741
5	1.45	0.689655
6	1.55	0.645161
7	1.65	0.606061
8	1.75	0.571429
9	1.85	0.540541
10	1.95	0.512821
		6.928355

$$\Delta t \sum_{k=1}^{n} f(t_k^*) \approx (0.1)(6.928355)$$
$$\approx 0.692836$$

▶ **Example 1** Approximate $\ln 2$ using the midpoint approximation with $n = 10$.

Solution. From (1), the exact value of $\ln 2$ is represented by the integral

$$\ln 2 = \int_1^2 \frac{1}{t} \, dt$$

The midpoint rule is given in Formulas (5) and (6) of Section 5.4. Expressed in terms of t, the latter formula is

$$\int_a^b f(t) \, dt \approx \Delta t \sum_{k=1}^{n} f(t_k^*)$$

where Δt is the common width of the subintervals and $t_1^*, t_2^*, \ldots, t_n^*$ are the midpoints. In this case we have 10 subintervals, so $\Delta t = (2 - 1)/10 = 0.1$. The computations to six decimal places are shown in Table 5.10.1. By comparison, a calculator set to display six decimal places gives $\ln 2 \approx 0.693147$, so the magnitude of the error in the midpoint approximation is about 0.000311. Greater accuracy in the midpoint approximation can be obtained by increasing n. For example, the midpoint approximation with $n = 100$ yields $\ln 2 \approx 0.693144$, which is correct to five decimal places. ◀

■ DOMAIN, RANGE, AND END BEHAVIOR OF ln x

5.10.3 THEOREM

(a) *The domain of* $\ln x$ *is* $(0, +\infty)$.

(b) $\displaystyle\lim_{x \to 0^+} \ln x = -\infty$ *and* $\displaystyle\lim_{x \to +\infty} \ln x = +\infty$

(c) *The range of* $\ln x$ *is* $(-\infty, +\infty)$.

PROOFS (*a*) AND (*b*) We have already shown that $\ln x$ is defined and increasing on the interval $(0, +\infty)$. To prove that $\ln x \to +\infty$ as $x \to +\infty$, we must show that given any number $M > 0$, the value of $\ln x$ exceeds M for sufficiently large values of x. To do this, let N be any integer. If $x > 2^N$, then

$$\ln x > \ln 2^N = N \ln 2 \tag{4}$$

by Theorem 5.10.2(*d*). Since

$$\ln 2 = \int_1^2 \frac{1}{t}\, dt > 0$$

it follows that $N \ln 2$ can be made arbitrarily large by choosing N sufficiently large. In particular, we can choose N so that $N \ln 2 > M$. It now follows from (4) that if $x > 2^N$, then $\ln x > M$, and this proves that

$$\lim_{x \to +\infty} \ln x = +\infty$$

Furthermore, by observing that $v = 1/x \to +\infty$ as $x \to 0^+$, we can use the preceding limit and Theorem 5.10.2(*b*) to conclude that

$$\lim_{x \to 0^+} \ln x = \lim_{v \to +\infty} \ln \frac{1}{v} = \lim_{v \to +\infty} (-\ln v) = -\infty$$

PROOF (*c*) It follows from part (*a*), the continuity of $\ln x$, and the Intermediate-Value Theorem (1.5.7) that $\ln x$ assumes every real value as x varies over the interval $(0, +\infty)$ (why?). ■

■ DEFINITION OF e^x

In Chapter 0 we defined $\ln x$ to be the inverse of the natural exponential function e^x. Now that we have a formal definition of $\ln x$ in terms of an integral, we will define the natural exponential function to be the inverse of $\ln x$.

Since $\ln x$ is increasing and continuous on $(0, +\infty)$ with range $(-\infty, +\infty)$, there is exactly one (positive) solution to the equation $\ln x = 1$. We *define* e to be the unique solution to $\ln x = 1$, so

$$\ln e = 1 \tag{5}$$

Furthermore, if x is any real number, there is a unique positive solution y to $\ln y = x$, so for irrational values of x we *define* e^x to be this solution. That is, when x is irrational, e^x is defined by

$$\ln e^x = x \tag{6}$$

Note that for rational values of x, we also have $\ln e^x = x \ln e = x$ from Theorem 5.10.2(*d*). Moreover, it follows immediately that $e^{\ln x} = x$ for any $x > 0$. Thus, (6) defines the exponential function for all real values of x as the inverse of the natural logarithm function.

5.10.4 DEFINITION The inverse of the natural logarithm function $\ln x$ is denoted by e^x and is called the ***natural exponential function***.

We can now establish the differentiability of e^x and confirm that

$$\frac{d}{dx}[e^x] = e^x$$

5.10.5 **THEOREM** *The natural exponential function e^x is differentiable, and hence continuous, on $(-\infty, +\infty)$, and its derivative is*

$$\frac{d}{dx}[e^x] = e^x$$

PROOF Because $\ln x$ is differentiable and

$$\frac{d}{dx}[\ln x] = \frac{1}{x} > 0$$

for all x in $(0, +\infty)$, it follows from Theorem 3.3.1, with $f(x) = \ln x$ and $f^{-1}(x) = e^x$, that e^x is differentiable on $(-\infty, +\infty)$ and its derivative is

$$\frac{d}{dx} \underbrace{[e^x]}_{f^{-1}(x)} = \underbrace{\frac{1}{1/e^x}}_{f'(f^{-1}(x))} = e^x \quad \blacksquare$$

▨ IRRATIONAL EXPONENTS

Recall from Theorem 5.10.2(d) that if $a > 0$ and r is a rational number, then $\ln a^r = r \ln a$. Then $a^r = e^{\ln a^r} = e^{r \ln a}$ for any positive value of a and any rational number r. But the expression $e^{r \ln a}$ makes sense for *any* real number r, whether rational or irrational, so it is a good candidate to give meaning to a^r for any real number r.

Use Definition 5.10.6 to prove that if $a > 0$ and r is a real number, then $\ln a^r = r \ln a$.

5.10.6 **DEFINITION** If $a > 0$ and r is a real number, a^r is defined by

$$a^r = e^{r \ln a} \tag{7}$$

With this definition it can be shown that the standard algebraic properties of exponents, such as

$$a^p a^q = a^{p+q}, \quad \frac{a^p}{a^q} = a^{p-q}, \quad (a^p)^q = a^{pq}, \quad (a^p)(b^p) = (ab)^p$$

hold for any real values of a, b, p, and q, where a and b are positive. In addition, using (7) for a real exponent r, we can define the power function x^r whose domain consists of all positive real numbers, and for a positive base b we can define the *base b exponential function b^x* whose domain consists of all real numbers.

5.10.7 **THEOREM**

(a) *For any real number r, the power function x^r is differentiable on $(0, +\infty)$ and its derivative is*
$$\frac{d}{dx}[x^r] = rx^{r-1}$$

(b) *For $b > 0$ and $b \neq 1$, the base b exponential function b^x is differentiable on $(-\infty, +\infty)$ and its derivative is*
$$\frac{d}{dx}[b^x] = b^x \ln b$$

PROOF The differentiability of $x^r = e^{r \ln x}$ and $b^x = e^{x \ln b}$ on their domains follows from the differentiability of $\ln x$ on $(0, +\infty)$ and of e^x on $(-\infty, +\infty)$:

$$\frac{d}{dx}[x^r] = \frac{d}{dx}[e^{r \ln x}] = e^{r \ln x} \cdot \frac{d}{dx}[r \ln x] = x^r \cdot \frac{r}{x} = rx^{r-1}$$

$$\frac{d}{dx}[b^x] = \frac{d}{dx}[e^{x \ln b}] = e^{x \ln b} \cdot \frac{d}{dx}[x \ln b] = b^x \ln b \quad \blacksquare$$

We expressed e as the value of a limit in Formulas (7) and (8) of Section 1.3 and in Formula (1) of Section 3.2. We now have the mathematical tools necessary to prove the existence of these limits.

5.10.8 THEOREM

(a) $\displaystyle \lim_{x \to 0} (1 + x)^{1/x} = e$ *(b)* $\displaystyle \lim_{x \to +\infty} \left(1 + \frac{1}{x}\right)^x = e$ *(c)* $\displaystyle \lim_{x \to -\infty} \left(1 + \frac{1}{x}\right)^x = e$

PROOF We will prove part *(a)*; the proofs of parts *(b)* and *(c)* follow from this limit and are left as exercises. We first observe that

$$\frac{d}{dx}[\ln(x + 1)]\bigg|_{x=0} = \frac{1}{x + 1} \cdot 1 \bigg|_{x=0} = 1$$

However, using the definition of the derivative, we obtain

$$1 = \frac{d}{dx}[\ln(x + 1)]\bigg|_{x=0} = \lim_{h \to 0} \frac{\ln(0 + h + 1) - \ln(0 + 1)}{h}$$

$$= \lim_{h \to 0}\left[\frac{1}{h} \cdot \ln(1 + h)\right]$$

or, equivalently,

$$\lim_{x \to 0} \frac{1}{x} \cdot \ln(1 + x) = 1 \tag{8}$$

Now

$$\lim_{x \to 0}(1 + x)^{1/x} = \lim_{x \to 0} e^{(\ln(1+x))/x} \qquad \boxed{\text{Definition 5.10.6}}$$

$$= e^{\lim_{x \to 0}[(\ln(1+x))/x]} \qquad \boxed{\text{Theorem 1.5.5}}$$

$$= e^1 \qquad \boxed{\text{Equation (8)}}$$

$$= e \quad \blacksquare$$

■ **GENERAL LOGARITHMS**

We note that for $b > 0$ and $b \neq 1$, the function b^x is one-to-one and so has an inverse function. Using the definition of b^x, we can solve $y = b^x$ for x as a function of y:

$$y = b^x = e^{x \ln b}$$

$$\ln y = \ln(e^{x \ln b}) = x \ln b$$

$$\frac{\ln y}{\ln b} = x$$

Thus, the inverse function for b^x is $(\ln x)/(\ln b)$.

5.10.9 DEFINITION For $b > 0$ and $b \neq 1$, the **base b logarithm** function, denoted $\log_b x$, is defined by

$$\log_b x = \frac{\ln x}{\ln b} \tag{9}$$

It follows immediately from this definition that $\log_b x$ is the inverse function for b^x and satisfies the properties in Table 0.5.3. Furthermore, $\log_b x$ is differentiable, and hence continuous, on $(0, +\infty)$, and its derivative is

$$\frac{d}{dx}[\log_b x] = \frac{1}{x \ln b}$$

As a final note of consistency, we observe that $\log_e x = \ln x$.

■ FUNCTIONS DEFINED BY INTEGRALS

The functions we have dealt with thus far in this text are called *elementary functions*; they include polynomial, rational, power, exponential, logarithmic, trigonometric, and inverse trigonometric functions, and all other functions that can be obtained from these by addition, subtraction, multiplication, division, root extraction, and composition.

However, there are many important functions that do not fall into this category. Such functions occur in many ways, but they commonly arise in the course of solving initial-value problems of the form

$$\frac{dy}{dx} = f(x), \quad y(x_0) = y_0 \tag{10}$$

Recall from Example 6 of Section 5.2 and the discussion preceding it that the basic method for solving (10) is to integrate $f(x)$, and then use the initial condition to determine the constant of integration. It can be proved that if f is continuous, then (10) has a unique solution and that this procedure produces it. However, there is another approach: Instead of solving each initial-value problem individually, we can find a general formula for the solution of (10), and then apply that formula to solve specific problems. We will now show that

$$y(x) = y_0 + \int_{x_0}^{x} f(t)\, dt \tag{11}$$

is a formula for the solution of (10). To confirm this we must show that $dy/dx = f(x)$ and that $y(x_0) = y_0$. The computations are as follows:

$$\frac{dy}{dx} = \frac{d}{dx}\left[y_0 + \int_{x_0}^{x} f(t)\, dt \right] = 0 + f(x) = f(x)$$

$$y(x_0) = y_0 + \int_{x_0}^{x_0} f(t)\, dt = y_0 + 0 = y_0$$

▶ **Example 2** In Example 6 of Section 5.2 we showed that the solution of the initial-value problem

$$\frac{dy}{dx} = \cos x, \quad y(0) = 1$$

is $y(x) = 1 + \sin x$. This initial-value problem can also be solved by applying Formula (11) with $f(x) = \cos x$, $x_0 = 0$, and $y_0 = 1$. This yields

$$y(x) = 1 + \int_{0}^{x} \cos t\, dt = 1 + \left[\sin t\right]_{t=0}^{x} = 1 + \sin x \quad ◀$$

In the last example we were able to perform the integration in Formula (11) and express the solution of the initial-value problem as an elementary function. However, sometimes this will not be possible, in which case the solution of the initial-value problem must be left in terms of an "unevaluated" integral. For example, from (11), the solution of the initial-value problem

$$\frac{dy}{dx} = e^{-x^2}, \quad y(0) = 1$$

is

$$y(x) = 1 + \int_0^x e^{-t^2}\, dt$$

However, it can be shown that there is no way to express the integral in this solution as an elementary function. Thus, we have encountered a *new* function, which we regard to be *defined* by the integral. A close relative of this function, known as the **error function**, plays an important role in probability and statistics; it is denoted by erf(x) and is defined as

$$\text{erf}(x) = \frac{2}{\sqrt{\pi}} \int_0^x e^{-t^2}\, dt \tag{12}$$

Indeed, many of the most important functions in science and engineering are defined as integrals that have special names and notations associated with them. For example, the functions defined by

$$S(x) = \int_0^x \sin\left(\frac{\pi t^2}{2}\right) dt \quad \text{and} \quad C(x) = \int_0^x \cos\left(\frac{\pi t^2}{2}\right) dt \tag{13–14}$$

are called the **Fresnel sine and cosine functions**, respectively, in honor of the French physicist Augustin Fresnel (1788–1827), who first encountered them in his study of diffraction of light waves.

■ EVALUATING AND GRAPHING FUNCTIONS DEFINED BY INTEGRALS

The following values of $S(1)$ and $C(1)$ were produced by a CAS that has a built-in algorithm for approximating definite integrals:

$$S(1) = \int_0^1 \sin\left(\frac{\pi t^2}{2}\right) dt \approx 0.438259, \qquad C(1) = \int_0^1 \cos\left(\frac{\pi t^2}{2}\right) dt \approx 0.779893$$

To generate graphs of functions defined by integrals, computer programs choose a set of x-values in the domain, approximate the integral for each of those values, and then plot the resulting points. Thus, there is a lot of computation involved in generating such graphs, since each plotted point requires the approximation of an integral. The graphs of the Fresnel functions in Figure 5.10.4 were generated in this way using a CAS.

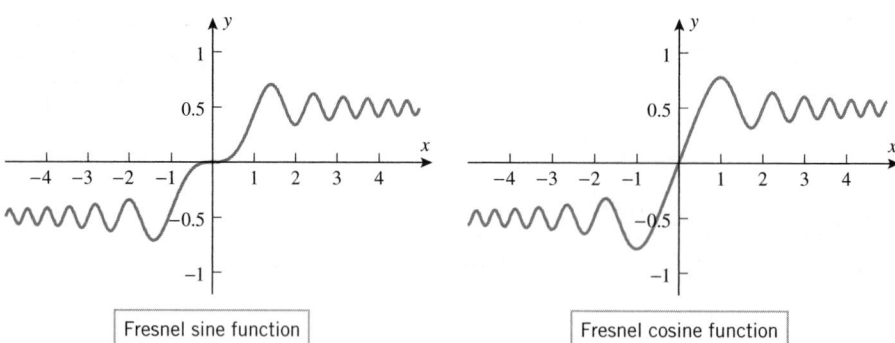

▶ **Figure 5.10.4**

Fresnel sine function   Fresnel cosine function

REMARK | Although it required a considerable amount of computation to generate the graphs of the Fresnel functions, the derivatives of $S(x)$ and $C(x)$ are easy to obtain using Part 2 of the Fundamental Theorem of Calculus (5.6.3); they are

$$S'(x) = \sin\left(\frac{\pi x^2}{2}\right) \quad \text{and} \quad C'(x) = \cos\left(\frac{\pi x^2}{2}\right) \tag{15–16}$$

These derivatives can be used to determine the locations of the relative extrema and inflection points and to investigate other properties of $S(x)$ and $C(x)$.

■ INTEGRALS WITH FUNCTIONS AS LIMITS OF INTEGRATION

Various applications can lead to integrals in which at least one of the limits of integration is a function of x. Some examples are

$$\int_x^1 \sqrt{\sin t}\, dt, \qquad \int_{x^2}^{\sin x} \sqrt{t^3 + 1}\, dt, \qquad \int_{\ln x}^{\pi} \frac{dt}{t^7 - 8}$$

We will complete this section by showing how to differentiate integrals of the form

$$\int_a^{g(x)} f(t)\, dt \tag{17}$$

where a is constant. Derivatives of other kinds of integrals with functions as limits of integration will be discussed in the exercises.

To differentiate (17) we can view the integral as a composition $F(g(x))$, where

$$F(x) = \int_a^x f(t)\, dt$$

If we now apply the chain rule, we obtain

$$\frac{d}{dx}\left[\int_a^{g(x)} f(t)\, dt\right] = \frac{d}{dx}[F(g(x))] = F'(g(x))g'(x) = f(g(x))g'(x)$$

$$\boxed{\text{Theorem 5.6.3}}$$

Thus,

$$\frac{d}{dx}\left[\int_a^{g(x)} f(t)\, dt\right] = f(g(x))g'(x) \tag{18}$$

In words:

> *To differentiate an integral with a constant lower limit and a function as the upper limit, substitute the upper limit into the integrand, and multiply by the derivative of the upper limit.*

▶ Example 3

$$\frac{d}{dx}\left[\int_1^{\sin x} (1 - t^2)\, dt\right] = (1 - \sin^2 x)\cos x = \cos^3 x \quad ◄$$

✔ QUICK CHECK EXERCISES 5.10   (See page 408 for answers.)

1. $\displaystyle\int_1^{1/e} \frac{1}{t}\, dt = $ _____

2. Estimate $\ln 2$ using Definition 5.10.1 and
   (a) a left endpoint approximation with $n = 2$
   (b) a right endpoint approximation with $n = 2$.

3. $\pi^{1/(\ln \pi)} = $ _____

4. A solution to the initial-value problem

$$\frac{dy}{dx} = \cos x^3, \quad y(0) = 2$$

   that is defined by an integral is $y = $ _____.

5. $\displaystyle\frac{d}{dx}\left[\int_0^{e^{-x}} \frac{1}{1 + t^4}\, dt\right] = $ _____

EXERCISE SET 5.10   ~ Graphing Utility   C CAS

1. Sketch the curve $y = 1/t$, and shade a region under the curve whose area is
   (a) $\ln 2$ (b) $-\ln 0.5$ (c) 2.

2. Sketch the curve $y = 1/t$, and shade two different regions under the curve whose areas are $\ln 1.5$.

3. Given that $\ln a = 2$ and $\ln c = 5$, find
   (a) $\displaystyle\int_1^{ac} \frac{1}{t}\,dt$ (b) $\displaystyle\int_1^{1/c} \frac{1}{t}\,dt$
   (c) $\displaystyle\int_1^{a/c} \frac{1}{t}\,dt$ (d) $\displaystyle\int_1^{a^3} \frac{1}{t}\,dt$.

4. Given that $\ln a = 9$, find
   (a) $\displaystyle\int_1^{\sqrt{a}} \frac{1}{t}\,dt$ (b) $\displaystyle\int_1^{2a} \frac{1}{t}\,dt$
   (c) $\displaystyle\int_1^{2/a} \frac{1}{t}\,dt$ (d) $\displaystyle\int_2^{a} \frac{1}{t}\,dt$.

5. Approximate $\ln 5$ using the midpoint rule with $n = 10$, and estimate the magnitude of the error by comparing your answer to that produced directly by a calculating utility.

6. Approximate $\ln 3$ using the midpoint rule with $n = 20$, and estimate the magnitude of the error by comparing your answer to that produced directly by a calculating utility.

7. Simplify the expression and state the values of x for which your simplification is valid.
   (a) $e^{-\ln x}$ (b) $e^{\ln x^2}$
   (c) $\ln\left(e^{-x^2}\right)$ (d) $\ln(1/e^x)$
   (e) $\exp(3\ln x)$ (f) $\ln(xe^x)$
   (g) $\ln\left(e^{x - \sqrt[3]{x}}\right)$ (h) $e^{x - \ln x}$

8. (a) Let $f(x) = e^{-2x}$. Find the simplest exact value of the function $f(\ln 3)$.
   (b) Let $f(x) = e^x + 3e^{-x}$. Find the simplest exact value of the function $f(\ln 2)$.

9–10 Express the given quantity as a power of e. ■

9. (a) 3^π (b) $2^{\sqrt{2}}$

10. (a) π^{-x} (b) x^{2x}, $x > 0$

11–12 Find the limits by making appropriate substitutions in the limits given in Theorem 5.10.8. ■

11. (a) $\displaystyle\lim_{x \to +\infty} \left(1 + \frac{1}{2x}\right)^x$ (b) $\displaystyle\lim_{x \to 0} (1 + 2x)^{1/x}$

12. (a) $\displaystyle\lim_{x \to +\infty} \left(1 + \frac{3}{x}\right)^x$ (b) $\displaystyle\lim_{x \to 0} (1 + x)^{1/(3x)}$

13–14 Find $g'(x)$ using Part 2 of the Fundamental Theorem of Calculus, and check your answer by evaluating the integral and then differentiating. ■

13. $g(x) = \displaystyle\int_1^x (t^2 - t)\,dt$ 14. $g(x) = \displaystyle\int_\pi^x (1 - \cos t)\,dt$

15–16 Find the derivative using Formula (18), and check your answer by evaluating the integral and then differentiating the result. ■

15. (a) $\displaystyle\frac{d}{dx} \int_1^{x^3} \frac{1}{t}\,dt$ (b) $\displaystyle\frac{d}{dx} \int_1^{\ln x} e^t\,dt$

16. (a) $\displaystyle\frac{d}{dx} \int_{-1}^{x^2} \sqrt{t + 1}\,dt$ (b) $\displaystyle\frac{d}{dx} \int_\pi^{1/x} \sin t\,dt$

17. Let $F(x) = \displaystyle\int_0^x \frac{\sin t}{t^2 + 1}\,dt$. Find
   (a) $F(0)$ (b) $F'(0)$ (c) $F''(0)$.

18. Let $F(x) = \displaystyle\int_2^x \sqrt{3t^2 + 1}\,dt$. Find
   (a) $F(2)$ (b) $F'(2)$ (c) $F''(2)$.

19–22 True–False Determine whether the equation is true or false. Explain your answer. ■

19. $\displaystyle\int_1^{1/a} \frac{1}{t}\,dt = -\int_1^a \frac{1}{t}\,dt$,   for $0 < a$

20. $\displaystyle\int_1^{\sqrt{a}} \frac{1}{t}\,dt = \frac{1}{2}\int_1^a \frac{1}{t}\,dt$,   for $0 < a$

21. $\displaystyle\int_{-1}^e \frac{1}{t}\,dt = 1$

22. $\displaystyle\int \frac{2x}{1 + x^2}\,dx = \int_1^{1+x^2} \frac{1}{t}\,dt + C$

C 23. (a) Use Formula (18) to find
   $$\frac{d}{dx} \int_1^{x^2} t\sqrt{1 + t}\,dt$$
   (b) Use a CAS to evaluate the integral and differentiate the resulting function.
   (c) Use the simplification command of the CAS, if necessary, to confirm that the answers in parts (a) and (b) are the same.

24. Show that
   (a) $\displaystyle\frac{d}{dx} \left[\int_x^a f(t)\,dt\right] = -f(x)$
   (b) $\displaystyle\frac{d}{dx} \left[\int_{g(x)}^a f(t)\,dt\right] = -f(g(x))g'(x)$.

25–26 Use the results in Exercise 24 to find the derivative. ■

25. (a) $\displaystyle\frac{d}{dx} \int_x^\pi \cos(t^3)\,dt$ (b) $\displaystyle\frac{d}{dx} \int_{\tan x}^3 \frac{t^2}{1 + t^2}\,dt$

26. (a) $\displaystyle\frac{d}{dx} \int_x^0 \frac{1}{(t^2 + 1)^2}\,dt$ (b) $\displaystyle\frac{d}{dx} \int_{1/x}^\pi \cos^3 t\,dt$

27. Find
   $$\frac{d}{dx} \left[\int_{3x}^{x^2} \frac{t - 1}{t^2 + 1}\,dt\right]$$
   by writing
   $$\int_{3x}^{x^2} \frac{t - 1}{t^2 + 1}\,dt = \int_{3x}^0 \frac{t - 1}{t^2 + 1}\,dt + \int_0^{x^2} \frac{t - 1}{t^2 + 1}\,dt$$

28. Use Exercise 24(b) and the idea in Exercise 27 to show that

$$\frac{d}{dx} \int_{h(x)}^{g(x)} f(t)\, dt = f(g(x))g'(x) - f(h(x))h'(x)$$

29. Use the result obtained in Exercise 28 to perform the following differentiations:

(a) $\dfrac{d}{dx} \displaystyle\int_{x^2}^{x^3} \sin^2 t\, dt$ (b) $\dfrac{d}{dx} \displaystyle\int_{-x}^{x} \dfrac{1}{1+t}\, dt.$

30. Prove that the function

$$F(x) = \int_{x}^{5x} \frac{1}{t}\, dt$$

is constant on the interval $(0, +\infty)$ by using Exercise 28 to find $F'(x)$. What is that constant?

FOCUS ON CONCEPTS

31. Let $F(x) = \int_0^x f(t)\, dt$, where f is the function whose graph is shown in the accompanying figure.
   (a) Find $F(0)$, $F(3)$, $F(5)$, $F(7)$, and $F(10)$.
   (b) On what subintervals of the interval $[0, 10]$ is F increasing? Decreasing?
   (c) Where does F have its maximum value? Its minimum value?
   (d) Sketch the graph of F.

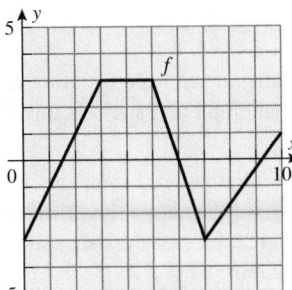

◀ Figure Ex-31

32. Determine the inflection point(s) for the graph of F in Exercise 31.

33–34 Express $F(x)$ in a piecewise form that does not involve an integral. ■

33. $F(x) = \displaystyle\int_{-1}^{x} |t|\, dt$

34. $F(x) = \displaystyle\int_{0}^{x} f(t)\, dt$, where $f(x) = \begin{cases} x, & 0 \le x \le 2 \\ 2, & x > 2 \end{cases}$

35–38 Use Formula (11) to solve the initial-value problem. ■

35. $\dfrac{dy}{dx} = \dfrac{2x^2 + 1}{x}$, $y(1) = 2$ **36.** $\dfrac{dy}{dx} = \dfrac{x+1}{\sqrt{x}}$, $y(1) = 0$

37. $\dfrac{dy}{dx} = \sec^2 x - \sin x$, $y(\pi/4) = 1$

38. $\dfrac{dy}{dx} = \dfrac{1}{x \ln x}$, $y(e) = 1$

39. Suppose that at time $t = 0$ there are P_0 individuals who have disease X, and suppose that a certain model for the spread

of the disease predicts that the disease will spread at the rate of $r(t)$ individuals per day. Write a formula for the number of individuals who will have disease X after x days.

40. Suppose that $v(t)$ is the velocity function of a particle moving along an s-axis. Write a formula for the coordinate of the particle at time T if the particle is at s_1 at time $t = 1$.

FOCUS ON CONCEPTS

41. The accompanying figure shows the graphs of $y = f(x)$ and $y = \int_0^x f(t)\, dt$. Determine which graph is which, and explain your reasoning.

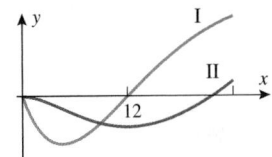

◀ Figure Ex-41

42. (a) Make a conjecture about the value of the limit

$$\lim_{k \to 0} \int_{1}^{b} t^{k-1}\, dt \quad (b > 0)$$

   (b) Check your conjecture by evaluating the integral and finding the limit. [*Hint:* Interpret the limit as the definition of the derivative of an exponential function.]

43. Let $F(x) = \int_0^x f(t)\, dt$, where f is the function graphed in the accompanying figure.
   (a) Where do the relative minima of F occur?
   (b) Where do the relative maxima of F occur?
   (c) Where does the absolute maximum of F on the interval $[0, 5]$ occur?
   (d) Where does the absolute minimum of F on the interval $[0, 5]$ occur?
   (e) Where is F concave up? Concave down?
   (f) Sketch the graph of F.

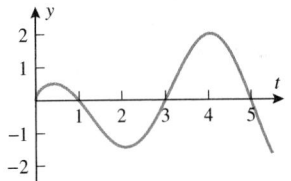

◀ Figure Ex-43

44. CAS programs have commands for working with most of the important nonelementary functions. Check your CAS documentation for information about the error function erf(x) [see Formula (12)], and then complete the following.
   (a) Generate the graph of erf(x).
   (b) Use the graph to make a conjecture about the existence and location of any relative maxima and minima of erf(x).
   (c) Check your conjecture in part (b) using the derivative of erf(x).

(cont.)

(d) Use the graph to make a conjecture about the existence and location of any inflection points of erf(x).

(e) Check your conjecture in part (d) using the second derivative of erf(x).

(f) Use the graph to make a conjecture about the existence of horizontal asymptotes of erf(x).

(g) Check your conjecture in part (f) by using the CAS to find the limits of erf(x) as $x \to \pm\infty$.

45. The Fresnel sine and cosine functions $S(x)$ and $C(x)$ were defined in Formulas (13) and (14) and graphed in Figure 5.10.4. Their derivatives were given in Formulas (15) and (16).

(a) At what points does $C(x)$ have relative minima? Relative maxima?

(b) Where do the inflection points of $C(x)$ occur?

(c) Confirm that your answers in parts (a) and (b) are consistent with the graph of $C(x)$.

46. Find the limit

$$\lim_{h \to 0} \frac{1}{h} \int_x^{x+h} \ln t \, dt$$

47. Find a function f and a number a such that

$$4 + \int_a^x f(t) \, dt = e^{2x}$$

48. (a) Give a geometric argument to show that

$$\frac{1}{x+1} < \int_x^{x+1} \frac{1}{t} \, dt < \frac{1}{x}, \quad x > 0$$

(b) Use the result in part (a) to prove that

$$\frac{1}{x+1} < \ln\left(1 + \frac{1}{x}\right) < \frac{1}{x}, \quad x > 0$$

(c) Use the result in part (b) to prove that

$$e^{x/(x+1)} < \left(1 + \frac{1}{x}\right)^x < e, \quad x > 0$$

and hence that

$$\lim_{x \to +\infty} \left(1 + \frac{1}{x}\right)^x = e$$

(d) Use the result in part (b) to prove that

$$\left(1 + \frac{1}{x}\right)^x < e < \left(1 + \frac{1}{x}\right)^{x+1}, \quad x > 0$$

49. Use a graphing utility to generate the graph of

$$y = \left(1 + \frac{1}{x}\right)^{x+1} - \left(1 + \frac{1}{x}\right)^x$$

in the window $[0, 100] \times [0, 0.2]$, and use that graph and part (d) of Exercise 48 to make a rough estimate of the error in the approximation

$$e \approx \left(1 + \frac{1}{50}\right)^{50}$$

50. Prove: If f is continuous on an open interval and a is any point in that interval, then

$$F(x) = \int_a^x f(t) \, dt$$

is continuous on the interval.

51. **Writing** A student objects that it is circular reasoning to make the definition

$$\ln x = \int_1^x \frac{1}{t} \, dt$$

since to evaluate the integral we need to know the value of $\ln x$. Write a short paragraph that answers this student's objection.

52. **Writing** Write a short paragraph that compares Definition 5.10.1 with the definition of the natural logarithm function given in Chapter 0. Be sure to discuss the issues surrounding continuity and differentiability.

✔ **QUICK CHECK ANSWERS 5.10**

1. -1 **2.** (a) $\frac{5}{6}$ (b) $\frac{7}{12}$ **3.** e **4.** $y = 2 + \int_0^x \cos t^3 \, dt$ **5.** $-\dfrac{e^{-x}}{1 + e^{-4x}}$

CHAPTER 5 REVIEW EXERCISES 〜 Graphing Utility [c] CAS

1–8 Evaluate the integrals. ▪

1. $\displaystyle\int \left[\frac{1}{2x^3} + 4\sqrt{x}\right] dx$

2. $\displaystyle\int [u^3 - 2u + 7] \, du$

3. $\displaystyle\int [4 \sin x + 2 \cos x] \, dx$

4. $\displaystyle\int \sec x (\tan x + \cos x) \, dx$

5. $\displaystyle\int [x^{-2/3} - 5e^x] \, dx$

6. $\displaystyle\int \left[\frac{3}{4x} - \sec^2 x\right] dx$

7. $\displaystyle\int \left[\frac{1}{1 + x^2} + \frac{2}{\sqrt{1 - x^2}}\right] dx$

8. $\displaystyle\int \left[\frac{12}{x\sqrt{x^2 - 1}} + \frac{1 - x^4}{1 + x^2}\right] dx$

9. Solve the initial-value problems.

(a) $\dfrac{dy}{dx} = \dfrac{1 - x}{\sqrt{x}}$, $y(1) = 0$

(b) $\dfrac{dy}{dx} = \cos x - 5e^x$, $y(0) = 0$

(c) $\dfrac{dy}{dx} = \sqrt[3]{x}$, $y(1) = 2$

(d) $\dfrac{dy}{dx} = xe^{x^2}$, $y(0) = 0$

10. The accompanying figure shows the slope field for a differential equation $dy/dx = f(x)$. Which of the following functions is most likely to be $f(x)$?

$$\sqrt{x}, \quad \sin x, \quad x^4, \quad x$$

Explain your reasoning.

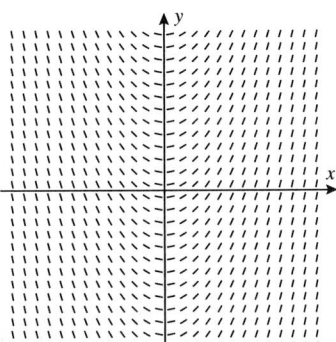

◄ **Figure Ex-10**

11. (a) Show that the substitutions $u = \sec x$ and $u = \tan x$ produce different values for the integral

$$\int \sec^2 x \tan x \, dx$$

(b) Explain why both are correct.

12. Use the two substitutions in Exercise 11 to evaluate the definite integral

$$\int_0^{\pi/4} \sec^2 x \tan x \, dx$$

and confirm that they produce the same result.

13. Evaluate the integral

$$\int \frac{x}{(x^2 - 1)\sqrt{x^4 - 2x^2}} \, dx$$

by making the substitution $u = x^2 - 1$.

14. Evaluate the integral

$$\int \sqrt{1 + x^{-2/3}} \, dx$$

by making the substitution $u = 1 + x^{2/3}$.

c **15–18** Evaluate the integrals by hand, and check your answers with a CAS if you have one. ■

15. $\displaystyle\int \frac{\cos 3x}{\sqrt{5 + 2\sin 3x}} \, dx$ **16.** $\displaystyle\int \frac{\sqrt{3 + \sqrt{x}}}{\sqrt{x}} \, dx$

17. $\displaystyle\int \frac{x^2}{(ax^3 + b)^2} \, dx$ **18.** $\displaystyle\int x \sec^2(ax^2) \, dx$

19. Express

$$\sum_{k=4}^{18} k(k - 3)$$

in sigma notation with
(a) $k = 0$ as the lower limit of summation
(b) $k = 5$ as the lower limit of summation.

20. (a) Fill in the blank:

$$1 + 3 + 5 + \cdots + (2n - 1) = \sum_{k=1}^{n} \underline{\quad\quad}$$

(b) Use part (a) to prove that the sum of the first n consecutive odd integers is a perfect square.

21. Find the area under the graph of $f(x) = 4x - x^2$ over the interval $[0, 4]$ using Definition 5.4.3 with x_k^* as the *right* endpoint of each subinterval.

22. Find the area under the graph of $f(x) = 5x - x^2$ over the interval $[0, 5]$ using Definition 5.4.3 with x_k^* as the *left* endpoint of each subinterval.

23–24 Use a calculating utility to find the left endpoint, right endpoint, and midpoint approximations to the area under the curve $y = f(x)$ over the stated interval using $n = 10$ subintervals. ■

23. $y = \ln x$; $[1, 2]$ **24.** $y = e^x$; $[0, 1]$

25. The *definite integral* of f over the interval $[a, b]$ is defined as the limit

$$\int_a^b f(x) \, dx = \lim_{\max \Delta x_k \to 0} \sum_{k=1}^{n} f(x_k^*) \Delta x_k$$

Explain what the various symbols on the right side of this equation mean.

26. Use a geometric argument to evaluate

$$\int_0^1 |2x - 1| \, dx$$

27. Suppose that

$$\int_0^1 f(x) \, dx = \tfrac{1}{2}, \quad \int_1^2 f(x) \, dx = \tfrac{1}{4},$$

$$\int_0^3 f(x) \, dx = -1, \quad \int_0^1 g(x) \, dx = 2$$

In each part, use this information to evaluate the given integral, if possible. If there is not enough information to evaluate the integral, then say so.

(a) $\displaystyle\int_0^2 f(x) \, dx$ **(b)** $\displaystyle\int_1^3 f(x) \, dx$ **(c)** $\displaystyle\int_2^3 5f(x) \, dx$

(d) $\displaystyle\int_1^0 g(x) \, dx$ **(e)** $\displaystyle\int_0^1 g(2x) \, dx$ **(f)** $\displaystyle\int_0^1 [g(x)]^2 \, dx$

28. In parts (a)–(d), use the information in Exercise 27 to evaluate the given integral. If there is not enough information to evaluate the integral, then say so.   *(cont.)*

(a) $\displaystyle\int_0^1 [f(x) + g(x)]\,dx$ (b) $\displaystyle\int_0^1 f(x)g(x)\,dx$

(c) $\displaystyle\int_0^1 \frac{f(x)}{g(x)}\,dx$ (d) $\displaystyle\int_0^1 [4g(x) - 3f(x)]\,dx$

29. In each part, evaluate the integral. Where appropriate, you may use a geometric formula.

(a) $\displaystyle\int_{-1}^1 (1 + \sqrt{1 - x^2})\,dx$

(b) $\displaystyle\int_0^3 (x\sqrt{x^2 + 1} - \sqrt{9 - x^2})\,dx$

(c) $\displaystyle\int_0^1 x\sqrt{1 - x^4}\,dx$

30. In each part, find the limit by interpreting it as a limit of Riemann sums in which the interval $[0, 1]$ is divided into n subintervals of equal length.

(a) $\displaystyle\lim_{n \to +\infty} \frac{\sqrt{1} + \sqrt{2} + \sqrt{3} + \cdots + \sqrt{n}}{n^{3/2}}$

(b) $\displaystyle\lim_{n \to +\infty} \frac{1^4 + 2^4 + 3^4 + \cdots + n^4}{n^5}$

(c) $\displaystyle\lim_{n \to +\infty} \frac{e^{1/n} + e^{2/n} + e^{3/n} + \cdots + e^{n/n}}{n}$

31–38 Evaluate the integrals using the Fundamental Theorem of Calculus and (if necessary) properties of the definite integral. ■

31. $\displaystyle\int_{-3}^0 (x^2 - 4x + 7)\,dx$ **32.** $\displaystyle\int_{-1}^2 x(1 + x^3)\,dx$

33. $\displaystyle\int_1^3 \frac{1}{x^2}\,dx$ **34.** $\displaystyle\int_1^8 (5x^{2/3} - 4x^{-2})\,dx$

35. $\displaystyle\int_0^1 (x - \sec x \tan x)\,dx$

36. $\displaystyle\int_1^4 \left(\frac{3}{\sqrt{t}} - 5\sqrt{t} - t^{-3/2}\right)dt$

37. $\displaystyle\int_0^2 |2x - 3|\,dx$ **38.** $\displaystyle\int_0^{\pi/2} \left|\tfrac{1}{2} - \sin x\right|\,dx$

39–42 Find the area under the curve $y = f(x)$ over the stated interval. ■

39. $f(x) = \sqrt{x};\ [1, 9]$ **40.** $f(x) = x^{-3/5};\ [1, 4]$

41. $f(x) = e^x;\ [1, 3]$ **42.** $f(x) = \dfrac{1}{x};\ [1, e^3]$

43. Find the area that is above the x-axis but below the curve $y = (1 - x)(x - 2)$. Make a sketch of the region.

c 44. Use a CAS to find the area of the region in the first quadrant that lies below the curve $y = x + x^2 - x^3$ and above the x-axis.

45–46 Sketch the curve and find the total area between the curve and the given interval on the x-axis. ■

45. $y = x^2 - 1;\ [0, 3]$ **46.** $y = \sqrt{x + 1} - 1;\ [-1, 1]$

47. Define $F(x)$ by

$$F(x) = \int_1^x (t^3 + 1)\,dt$$

(a) Use Part 2 of the Fundamental Theorem of Calculus to find $F'(x)$.

(b) Check the result in part (a) by first integrating and then differentiating.

48. Define $F(x)$ by

$$F(x) = \int_4^x \frac{1}{\sqrt{t}}\,dt$$

(a) Use Part 2 of the Fundamental Theorem of Calculus to find $F'(x)$.

(b) Check the result in part (a) by first integrating and then differentiating.

49–54 Use Part 2 of the Fundamental Theorem of Calculus and (where necessary) Formula (18) of Section 5.10 to find the derivatives. ■

49. $\dfrac{d}{dx}\left[\displaystyle\int_0^x e^{t^2}\,dt\right]$ **50.** $\dfrac{d}{dx}\left[\displaystyle\int_0^x \frac{t}{\cos t^2}\,dt\right]$

51. $\dfrac{d}{dx}\left[\displaystyle\int_0^x |t - 1|\,dt\right]$ **52.** $\dfrac{d}{dx}\left[\displaystyle\int_\pi^x \cos\sqrt{t}\,dt\right]$

53. $\dfrac{d}{dx}\left[\displaystyle\int_2^{\sin x} \frac{1}{1 + t^3}\,dt\right]$ **54.** $\dfrac{d}{dx}\left[\displaystyle\int_e^{\sqrt{x}} (\ln t)^2\,dt\right]$

55. State the two parts of the Fundamental Theorem of Calculus, and explain what is meant by the statement "Differentiation and integration are inverse processes."

c 56. Let $F(x) = \displaystyle\int_0^x \frac{t^2 - 3}{t^4 + 7}\,dt$.

(a) Find the intervals on which F is increasing and those on which F is decreasing.

(b) Find the open intervals on which F is concave up and those on which F is concave down.

(c) Find the x-values, if any, at which the function F has absolute extrema.

(d) Use a CAS to graph F, and confirm that the results in parts (a), (b), and (c) are consistent with the graph.

57. (a) Use differentiation to prove that the function

$$F(x) = \int_0^x \frac{1}{1 + t^2}\,dt + \int_0^{1/x} \frac{1}{1 + t^2}\,dt$$

is constant on the interval $(0, +\infty)$.

(b) Determine the constant value of the function in part (a) and then interpret (a) as an identity involving the inverse tangent function.

58. What is the natural domain of the function

$$F(x) = \int_1^x \frac{1}{t^2 - 9}\,dt?$$

Explain your reasoning.

59. In each part, determine the values of x for which $F(x)$ is positive, negative, or zero without performing the integration; explain your reasoning.

(a) $F(x) = \int_1^x \dfrac{t^4}{t^2 + 3}\, dt$ (b) $F(x) = \int_{-1}^x \sqrt{4 - t^2}\, dt$

c **60.** Use a CAS to approximate the largest and smallest values of the integral
$$\int_{-1}^x \frac{t}{\sqrt{2 + t^3}}\, dt$$
for $1 \le x \le 3$.

61. Find all values of x^* in the stated interval that are guaranteed to exist by the Mean-Value Theorem for Integrals, and explain what these numbers represent.

(a) $f(x) = \sqrt{x}$; $[0, 3]$ (b) $f(x) = 1/x$; $[1, e]$

62. A 10-gram tumor is discovered in a laboratory rat on March 1. The tumor is growing at a rate of $r(t) = t/7$ grams per week, where t denotes the number of weeks since March 1. What will be the mass of the tumor on June 7?

63. Use the graph of f shown in the accompanying figure to find the average value of f on the interval $[0, 10]$.

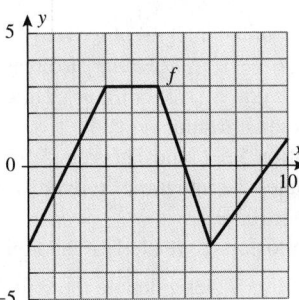

◀ **Figure Ex-63**

64. Find the average value of $f(x) = e^x + e^{-x}$ over the interval $\left[\ln \frac{1}{2}, \ln 2\right]$.

65. Derive the formulas for the position and velocity functions of a particle that moves with constant acceleration along a coordinate line.

66. The velocity of a particle moving along an s-axis is measured at 5 s intervals for 40 s, and the velocity function is modeled by a smooth curve. (The curve and the data points are shown in the accompanying figure.) Use this model in each part.

(a) Does the particle have constant acceleration? Explain your reasoning.

(b) Is there any 15 s time interval during which the acceleration is constant? Explain your reasoning.

(c) Estimate the distance traveled by the particle from time $t = 0$ to time $t = 40$.

(d) Estimate the average velocity of the particle over the 40 s time period.

(e) Is the particle ever slowing down during the 40 s time period? Explain your reasoning.

(f) Is there sufficient information for you to determine the s-coordinate of the particle at time $t = 10$? If so,

find it. If not, explain what additional information you need.

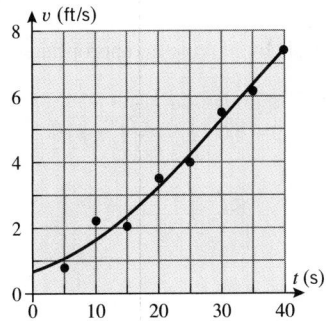

◀ **Figure Ex-66**

67–70 A particle moves along an s-axis. Use the given information to find the position function of the particle. ◾

67. $v(t) = t^3 - 2t^2 + 1$; $s(0) = 1$

68. $a(t) = 4 \cos 2t$; $v(0) = -1, s(0) = -3$

69. $v(t) = 2t - 3$; $s(1) = 5$

70. $a(t) = \cos t - 2t$; $v(0) = 0, s(0) = 0$

71–74 A particle moves with a velocity of $v(t)$ m/s along an s-axis. Find the displacement and the distance traveled by the particle during the given time interval. ◾

71. $v(t) = 2t - 4$; $0 \le t \le 6$

72. $v(t) = |t - 3|$; $0 \le t \le 5$

73. $v(t) = \dfrac{1}{2} - \dfrac{1}{t^2}$; $1 \le t \le 3$

74. $v(t) = \dfrac{3}{\sqrt{t}}$; $4 \le t \le 9$

75–76 A particle moves with acceleration $a(t)$ m/s^2 along an s-axis and has velocity v_0 m/s at time $t = 0$. Find the displacement and the distance traveled by the particle during the given time interval. ◾

75. $a(t) = -2$; $v_0 = 3$; $1 \le t \le 4$

76. $a(t) = \dfrac{1}{\sqrt{5t + 1}}$; $v_0 = 2$; $0 \le t \le 3$

77. A car traveling 60 mi/h (= 88 ft/s) along a straight road decelerates at a constant rate of 10 ft/s^2.

(a) How long will it take until the speed is 45 mi/h?

(b) How far will the car travel before coming to a stop?

78. Suppose that the velocity function of a particle moving along an s-axis is $v(t) = 20t^2 - 100t + 50$ ft/s and that the particle is at the origin at time $t = 0$. Use a graphing utility to generate the graphs of $s(t)$, $v(t)$, and $a(t)$ for the first 6 s of motion.

79. A ball is thrown vertically upward from a height of s_0 ft with an initial velocity of v_0 ft/s. If the ball is caught at height s_0, determine its average speed through the air using the free-fall model.

80. A rock, dropped from an unknown height, strikes the ground with a speed of 24 m/s. Find the height from which the rock was dropped.

81–88 Evaluate the integrals by making an appropriate substitution. ■

81. $\displaystyle\int_0^1 (2x+1)^4 \, dx$

82. $\displaystyle\int_{-5}^0 x\sqrt{4-x}\, dx$

83. $\displaystyle\int_0^1 \frac{dx}{\sqrt{3x+1}}$

84. $\displaystyle\int_0^{\sqrt{\pi}} x \sin x^2 \, dx$

85. $\displaystyle\int_0^1 \sin^2(\pi x)\cos(\pi x)\, dx$

86. $\displaystyle\int_e^{e^2} \frac{dx}{x \ln x}$

87. $\displaystyle\int_0^1 \frac{dx}{\sqrt{e^x}}$

88. $\displaystyle\int_0^{2/\sqrt{3}} \frac{1}{4+9x^2}\, dx$

89. Evaluate the limits.

(a) $\displaystyle\lim_{x\to+\infty}\left(1+\frac{1}{x}\right)^{2x}$

(b) $\displaystyle\lim_{x\to+\infty}\left(1+\frac{1}{3x}\right)^{x}$

90. Find a function f and a number a such that

$$2 + \int_a^x f(t)\, dt = e^{3x}$$

CHAPTER 5 MAKING CONNECTIONS

1. Consider a Riemann sum

$$\sum_{k=1}^n 2x_k^* \Delta x_k$$

for the integral of $f(x) = 2x$ over an interval $[a, b]$.

(a) Show that if x_k^* is the midpoint of the kth subinterval, the Riemann sum is a telescoping sum. (See Exercises 57–60 of Section 5.4 for other examples of telescoping sums.)

(b) Use part (a), Definition 5.5.1, and Theorem 5.5.2 to evaluate the definite integral of $f(x) = 2x$ over $[a, b]$.

2. The function $f(x) = \sqrt{x}$ is continuous on $[0, 4]$ and therefore integrable on this interval. Evaluate

$$\int_0^4 \sqrt{x}\, dx$$

by using Definition 5.5.1. Use subintervals of unequal length given by the partition

$$0 < 4(1)^2/n^2 < 4(2)^2/n^2 < \cdots < 4(n-1)^2/n^2 < 4$$

and let x_k^* be the right endpoint of the kth subinterval.

3. Make appropriate modifications and repeat Exercise 2 for

$$\int_0^8 \sqrt[3]{x}\, dx$$

4. Given a continuous function f and a positive real number m, let g denote the function defined by the composition $g(x) = f(mx)$.

(a) Suppose that

$$\sum_{k=1}^n g(x_k^*) \Delta x_k$$

is any Riemann sum for the integral of g over $[0, 1]$. Use the correspondence $u_k = mx_k$, $u_k^* = mx_k^*$ to create a Riemann sum for the integral of f over $[0, m]$. How are the values of the two Riemann sums related?

(b) Use part (a), Definition 5.5.1, and Theorem 5.5.2 to find an equation that relates the integral of g over $[0, 1]$ with the integral of f over $[0, m]$.

(c) How is your answer to part (b) related to Theorem 5.9.1?

5. Given a continuous function f, let g denote the function defined by $g(x) = 2xf(x^2)$.

(a) Suppose that

$$\sum_{k=1}^n g(x_k^*) \Delta x_k$$

is any Riemann sum for the integral of g over $[2, 3]$, with $x_k^* = (x_k + x_{k-1})/2$ the midpoint of the kth subinterval. Use the correspondence $u_k = x_k^2$, $u_k^* = (x_k^*)^2$ to create a Riemann sum for the integral of f over $[4, 9]$. How are the values of the two Riemann sums related?

(b) Use part (a), Definition 5.5.1, and Theorem 5.5.2 to find an equation that relates the integral of g over $[2, 3]$ with the integral of f over $[4, 9]$.

(c) How is your answer to part (b) related to Theorem 5.9.1?

Courtesy NASA

6

APPLICATIONS OF THE DEFINITE INTEGRAL IN GEOMETRY, SCIENCE, AND ENGINEERING

Calculus is essential for the computations required to land an astronaut on the moon.

In the last chapter we introduced the definite integral as the limit of Riemann sums in the context of finding areas. However, Riemann sums and definite integrals have applications that extend far beyond the area problem. In this chapter we will show how Riemann sums and definite integrals arise in such problems as finding the volume and surface area of a solid, finding the length of a plane curve, calculating the work done by a force, finding the center of gravity of a planar region, finding the pressure and force exerted by a fluid on a submerged object, and finding properties of suspended cables.

Although these problems are diverse, the required calculations can all be approached by the same procedure that we used to find areas—breaking the required calculation into "small parts," making an approximation for each part, adding the approximations from the parts to produce a Riemann sum that approximates the entire quantity to be calculated, and then taking the limit of the Riemann sums to produce an exact result.

6.1 AREA BETWEEN TWO CURVES

In the last chapter we showed how to find the area between a curve $y = f(x)$ and an interval on the x-axis. Here we will show how to find the area between two curves.

■ A REVIEW OF RIEMANN SUMS

Before we consider the problem of finding the area between two curves it will be helpful to review the basic principle that underlies the calculation of area as a definite integral. Recall that if f is continuous and nonnegative on $[a, b]$, then the definite integral for the area A under $y = f(x)$ over the interval $[a, b]$ is obtained in four steps (Figure 6.1.1):

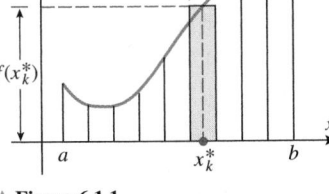

▲ **Figure 6.1.1**

- Divide the interval $[a, b]$ into n subintervals, and use those subintervals to divide the region under the curve $y = f(x)$ into n strips.

- Assuming that the width of the kth strip is Δx_k, approximate the area of that strip by the area $f(x_k^*)\Delta x_k$ of a rectangle of width Δx_k and height $f(x_k^*)$, where x_k^* is a point in the kth subinterval.

- Add the approximate areas of the strips to approximate the entire area A by the Riemann sum:

$$A \approx \sum_{k=1}^{n} f(x_k^*)\Delta x_k$$

413

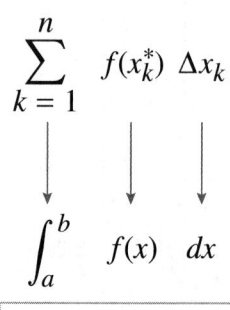

$$\sum_{k=1}^{n} f(x_k^*)\,\Delta x_k$$

$$\int_{a}^{b} f(x)\ dx$$

Effect of the limit process on the Riemann sum

▲ **Figure 6.1.2**

- Take the limit of the Riemann sums as the number of subintervals increases and all their widths approach zero. This causes the error in the approximations to approach zero and produces the following definite integral for the exact area A:

$$A = \lim_{\max \Delta x_k \to 0} \sum_{k=1}^{n} f(x_k^*)\Delta x_k = \int_{a}^{b} f(x)\,dx$$

Figure 6.1.2 illustrates the effect that the limit process has on the various parts of the Riemann sum:

- The quantity x_k^* in the Riemann sum becomes the variable x in the definite integral.
- The interval width Δx_k in the Riemann sum becomes the dx in the definite integral.
- The interval $[a, b]$, which is the union of the subintervals with widths $\Delta x_1, \Delta x_2, \dots, \Delta x_n$, does not appear explicitly in the Riemann sum but is represented by the upper and lower limits of integration in the definite integral.

■ AREA BETWEEN $y = f(x)$ AND $y = g(x)$

We will now consider the following extension of the area problem.

6.1.1 **FIRST AREA PROBLEM** Suppose that f and g are continuous functions on an interval $[a, b]$ and

$$f(x) \geq g(x) \quad \text{for} \quad a \leq x \leq b$$

[This means that the curve $y = f(x)$ lies above the curve $y = g(x)$ and that the two can touch but not cross.] Find the area A of the region bounded above by $y = f(x)$, below by $y = g(x)$, and on the sides by the lines $x = a$ and $x = b$ (Figure 6.1.3a).

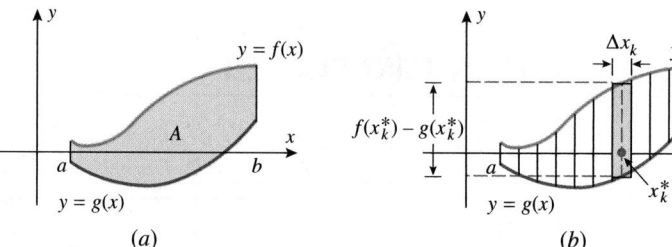

▶ **Figure 6.1.3**   *(a)*   *(b)*

To solve this problem we divide the interval $[a, b]$ into n subintervals, which has the effect of subdividing the region into n strips (Figure 6.1.3b). If we assume that the width of the kth strip is Δx_k, then the area of the strip can be approximated by the area of a rectangle of width Δx_k and height $f(x_k^*) - g(x_k^*)$, where x_k^* is a point in the kth subinterval. Adding these approximations yields the following Riemann sum that approximates the area A:

$$A \approx \sum_{k=1}^{n} [f(x_k^*) - g(x_k^*)]\Delta x_k$$

Taking the limit as n increases and the widths of all the subintervals approach zero yields the following definite integral for the area A between the curves:

$$A = \lim_{\max \Delta x_k \to 0} \sum_{k=1}^{n} [f(x_k^*) - g(x_k^*)]\Delta x_k = \int_{a}^{b} [f(x) - g(x)]\,dx$$

In summary, we have the following result.

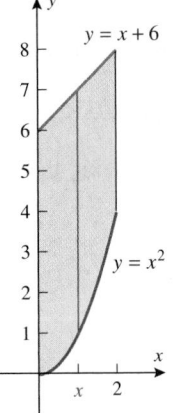

▲ Figure 6.1.4

> **6.1.2   AREA FORMULA**   If f and g are continuous functions on the interval $[a, b]$, and if $f(x) \geq g(x)$ for all x in $[a, b]$, then the area of the region bounded above by $y = f(x)$, below by $y = g(x)$, on the left by the line $x = a$, and on the right by the line $x = b$ is
>
> $$A = \int_a^b [f(x) - g(x)]\, dx \tag{1}$$

▶ **Example 1**   Find the area of the region bounded above by $y = x + 6$, bounded below by $y = x^2$, and bounded on the sides by the lines $x = 0$ and $x = 2$.

Solution.   The region and a cross section are shown in Figure 6.1.4. The cross section extends from $g(x) = x^2$ on the bottom to $f(x) = x + 6$ on the top. If the cross section is moved through the region, then its leftmost position will be $x = 0$ and its rightmost position will be $x = 2$. Thus, from (1)

$$A = \int_0^2 [(x + 6) - x^2]\, dx = \left[\frac{x^2}{2} + 6x - \frac{x^3}{3}\right]_0^2 = \frac{34}{3} - 0 = \frac{34}{3} \quad ◀$$

What does the integral in (1) represent if the graphs of f and g cross each other over the interval $[a, b]$? How would you find the area between the curves in this case?

It is possible that the upper and lower boundaries of a region may intersect at one or both endpoints, in which case the sides of the region will be points, rather than vertical line segments (Figure 6.1.5). When that occurs you will have to determine the points of intersection to obtain the limits of integration.

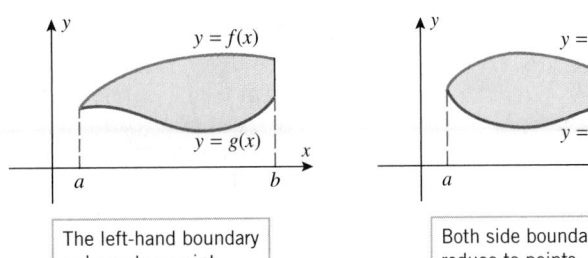

The left-hand boundary reduces to a point.

Both side boundaries reduce to points.

▶ Figure 6.1.5

▶ **Example 2**   Find the area of the region that is enclosed between the curves $y = x^2$ and $y = x + 6$.

Solution.   A sketch of the region (Figure 6.1.6) shows that the lower boundary is $y = x^2$ and the upper boundary is $y = x + 6$. At the endpoints of the region, the upper and lower boundaries have the same y-coordinates; thus, to find the endpoints we equate

$$y = x^2 \quad \text{and} \quad y = x + 6 \tag{2}$$

This yields

$$x^2 = x + 6 \quad \text{or} \quad x^2 - x - 6 = 0 \quad \text{or} \quad (x + 2)(x - 3) = 0$$

from which we obtain

$$x = -2 \quad \text{and} \quad x = 3$$

Although the y-coordinates of the endpoints are not essential to our solution, they may be obtained from (2) by substituting $x = -2$ and $x = 3$ in either equation. This yields $y = 4$ and $y = 9$, so the upper and lower boundaries intersect at $(-2, 4)$ and $(3, 9)$.

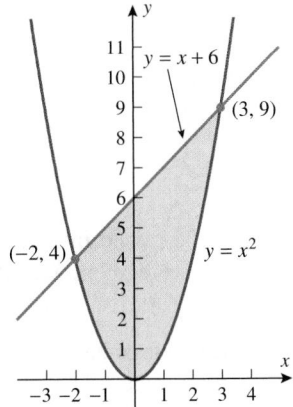

▲ Figure 6.1.6

From (1) with $f(x) = x + 6$, $g(x) = x^2$, $a = -2$, and $b = 3$, we obtain the area

$$A = \int_{-2}^{3} [(x + 6) - x^2] \, dx = \left[\frac{x^2}{2} + 6x - \frac{x^3}{3} \right]_{-2}^{3} = \frac{27}{2} - \left(-\frac{22}{3} \right) = \frac{125}{6} \blacktriangleleft$$

In the case where f and g are *nonnegative* on the interval $[a, b]$, the formula

$$A = \int_{a}^{b} [f(x) - g(x)] \, dx = \int_{a}^{b} f(x) \, dx - \int_{a}^{b} g(x) \, dx$$

states that the area A between the curves can be obtained by subtracting the area under $y = g(x)$ from the area under $y = f(x)$ (Figure 6.1.7).

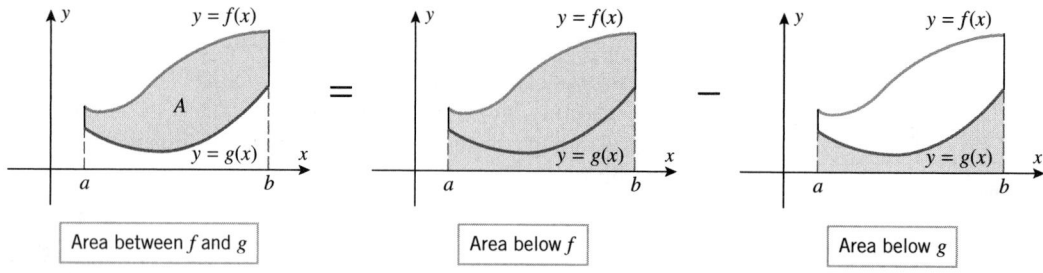

▲ **Figure 6.1.7**

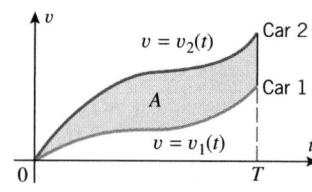

▲ **Figure 6.1.8**

▶ **Example 3**   Figure 6.1.8 shows velocity versus time curves for two race cars that move along a straight track, starting from rest at the same time. Give a physical interpretation of the area A between the curves over the interval $0 \le t \le T$.

Solution.   From (1)

$$A = \int_{0}^{T} [v_2(t) - v_1(t)] \, dt = \int_{0}^{T} v_2(t) \, dt - \int_{0}^{T} v_1(t) \, dt$$

Since v_1 and v_2 are nonnegative functions on $[0, T]$, it follows from Formula (4) of Section 5.7 that the integral of v_1 over $[0, T]$ is the distance traveled by car 1 during the time interval $0 \le t \le T$, and the integral of v_2 over $[0, T]$ is the distance traveled by car 2 during the same time interval. Since $v_1(t) \le v_2(t)$ on $[0, T]$, car 2 travels farther than car 1 does over the time interval $0 \le t \le T$, and the area A represents the distance by which car 2 is ahead of car 1 at time T. ◀

Some regions may require careful thought to determine the integrand and limits of integration in (1). Here is a systematic procedure that you can follow to set up this formula.

It is not necessary to make an extremely accurate sketch in Step 1; the only purpose of the sketch is to determine which curve is the upper boundary and which is the lower boundary.

Finding the Limits of Integration for the Area Between Two Curves

Step 1. Sketch the region and then draw a vertical line segment through the region at an arbitrary point x on the x-axis, connecting the top and bottom boundaries (Figure 6.1.9a).

Step 2. The y-coordinate of the top endpoint of the line segment sketched in Step 1 will be $f(x)$, the bottom one $g(x)$, and the length of the line segment will be $f(x) - g(x)$. This is the integrand in (1).

Step 3. To determine the limits of integration, imagine moving the line segment left and then right. The leftmost position at which the line segment intersects the region is $x = a$ and the rightmost is $x = b$ (Figures 6.1.9b and 6.1.9c).

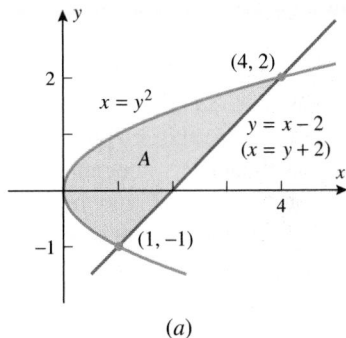

▲ **Figure 6.1.9**

There is a useful way of thinking about this procedure:

> *If you view the vertical line segment as the "cross section" of the region at the point x, then Formula (1) states that the area between the curves is obtained by integrating the length of the cross section over the interval [a, b].*

It is possible for the upper or lower boundary of a region to consist of two or more different curves, in which case it will be convenient to subdivide the region into smaller pieces in order to apply Formula (1). This is illustrated in the next example.

▶ **Example 4**   Find the area of the region enclosed by $x = y^2$ and $y = x - 2$.

Solution.   To determine the appropriate boundaries of the region, we need to know where the curves $x = y^2$ and $y = x - 2$ intersect. In Example 2 we found intersections by equating the expressions for y. Here it is easier to rewrite the latter equation as $x = y + 2$ and equate the expressions for x, namely,

$$x = y^2 \quad \text{and} \quad x = y + 2 \tag{3}$$

This yields

$$y^2 = y + 2 \quad \text{or} \quad y^2 - y - 2 = 0 \quad \text{or} \quad (y + 1)(y - 2) = 0$$

from which we obtain $y = -1$, $y = 2$. Substituting these values in either equation in (3) we see that the corresponding x-values are $x = 1$ and $x = 4$, respectively, so the points of intersection are $(1, -1)$ and $(4, 2)$ (Figure 6.1.10*a*).

To apply Formula (1), the equations of the boundaries must be written so that y is expressed explicitly as a function of x. The upper boundary can be written as $y = \sqrt{x}$ (rewrite $x = y^2$ as $y = \pm\sqrt{x}$ and choose the $+$ for the upper portion of the curve). The lower boundary consists of two parts:

$$y = -\sqrt{x} \quad \text{for} \quad 0 \le x \le 1 \qquad \text{and} \qquad y = x - 2 \quad \text{for} \quad 1 \le x \le 4$$

(Figure 6.1.10*b*). Because of this change in the formula for the lower boundary, it is necessary to divide the region into two parts and find the area of each part separately.

From (1) with $f(x) = \sqrt{x}$, $g(x) = -\sqrt{x}$, $a = 0$, and $b = 1$, we obtain

$$A_1 = \int_0^1 [\sqrt{x} - (-\sqrt{x})]\,dx = 2\int_0^1 \sqrt{x}\,dx = 2\left[\frac{2}{3}x^{3/2}\right]_0^1 = \frac{4}{3} - 0 = \frac{4}{3}$$

From (1) with $f(x) = \sqrt{x}$, $g(x) = x - 2$, $a = 1$, and $b = 4$, we obtain

$$A_2 = \int_1^4 [\sqrt{x} - (x - 2)]\,dx = \int_1^4 (\sqrt{x} - x + 2)\,dx$$

$$= \left[\frac{2}{3}x^{3/2} - \frac{1}{2}x^2 + 2x\right]_1^4 = \left(\frac{16}{3} - 8 + 8\right) - \left(\frac{2}{3} - \frac{1}{2} + 2\right) = \frac{19}{6}$$

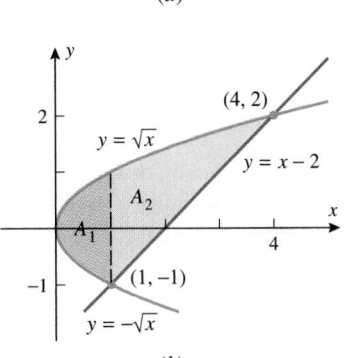

▲ **Figure 6.1.10**

Thus, the area of the entire region is

$$A = A_1 + A_2 = \frac{4}{3} + \frac{19}{6} = \frac{9}{2} \blacktriangleleft$$

■ REVERSING THE ROLES OF *x* AND *y*

Sometimes it is much easier to find the area of a region by integrating with respect to y rather than x. We will now show how this can be done.

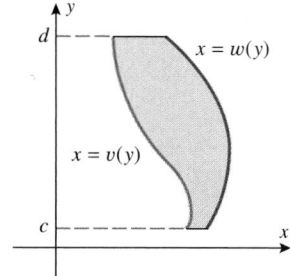

▲ **Figure 6.1.11**

6.1.3 SECOND AREA PROBLEM Suppose that w and v are continuous functions of y on an interval $[c, d]$ and that

$$w(y) \geq v(y) \quad \text{for} \quad c \leq y \leq d$$

[This means that the curve $x = w(y)$ lies to the right of the curve $x = v(y)$ and that the two can touch but not cross.] Find the area A of the region bounded on the left by $x = v(y)$, on the right by $x = w(y)$, and above and below by the lines $y = d$ and $y = c$ (Figure 6.1.11).

Proceeding as in the derivation of (1), but with the roles of x and y reversed, leads to the following analog of 6.1.2.

6.1.4 AREA FORMULA If w and v are continuous functions and if $w(y) \geq v(y)$ for all y in $[c, d]$, then the area of the region bounded on the left by $x = v(y)$, on the right by $x = w(y)$, below by $y = c$, and above by $y = d$ is

$$A = \int_c^d [w(y) - v(y)] \, dy \tag{4}$$

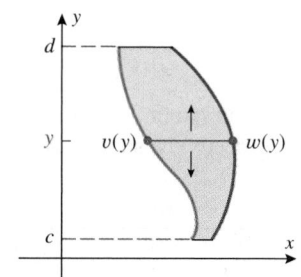

▲ **Figure 6.1.12**

The guiding principle in applying this formula is the same as with (1): The integrand in (4) can be viewed as the length of the horizontal cross section at an arbitrary point y on the y-axis, in which case Formula (4) states that the area can be obtained by integrating the length of the horizontal cross section over the interval $[c, d]$ on the y-axis (Figure 6.1.12).

In Example 4, we split the region into two parts to facilitate integrating with respect to x. In the next example we will see that splitting this region can be avoided if we integrate with respect to y.

▶ **Example 5** Find the area of the region enclosed by $x = y^2$ and $y = x - 2$, integrating with respect to y.

Solution. As indicated in Figure 6.1.10 the left boundary is $x = y^2$, the right boundary is $y = x - 2$, and the region extends over the interval $-1 \leq y \leq 2$. However, to apply (4) the equations for the boundaries must be written so that x is expressed explicitly as a function of y. Thus, we rewrite $y = x - 2$ as $x = y + 2$. It now follows from (4) that

$$A = \int_{-1}^{2} [(y + 2) - y^2] \, dy = \left[\frac{y^2}{2} + 2y - \frac{y^3}{3} \right]_{-1}^{2} = \frac{9}{2}$$

which agrees with the result obtained in Example 4. ◀

The choice between Formulas (1) and (4) is usually dictated by the shape of the region and which formula requires the least amount of splitting. However, sometimes one might choose the formula that requires more splitting because it is easier to evaluate the resulting integrals.

QUICK CHECK EXERCISES 6.1   *(See page 421 for answers.)*

1. An integral expression for the area of the region between the curves $y = 20 - 3x^2$ and $y = e^x$ and bounded on the sides by $x = 0$ and $x = 2$ is _____.

2. An integral expression for the area of the parallelogram bounded by $y = 2x + 8$, $y = 2x - 3$, $x = -1$, and $x = 5$ is _____. The value of this integral is _____.

3. (a) The points of intersection for the circle $x^2 + y^2 = 4$ and the line $y = x + 2$ are _____ and _____.

(b) Expressed as a definite integral with respect to x, _____ gives the area of the region inside the circle $x^2 + y^2 = 4$ and above the line $y = x + 2$.

(c) Expressed as a definite integral with respect to y, _____ gives the area of the region described in part (b).

4. The area of the region enclosed by the curves $y = x^2$ and $y = \sqrt[3]{x}$ is _____.

EXERCISE SET 6.1   ⌒ Graphing Utility   C CAS

1–4 Find the area of the shaded region. ▪

1.
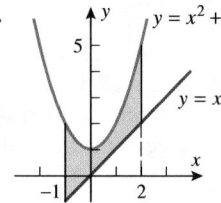

2.
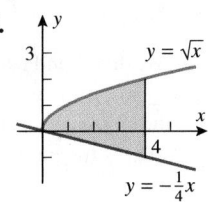

3.
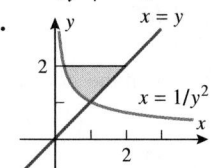

4.
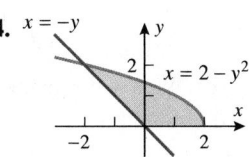

5–6 Find the area of the shaded region by (a) integrating with respect to x and (b) integrating with respect to y. ▪

5.
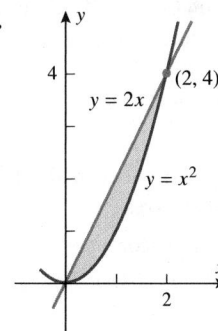

6.
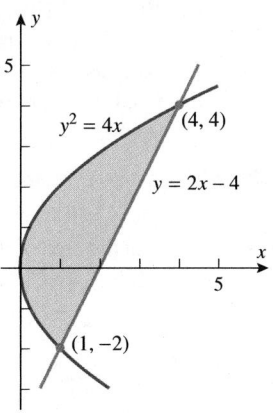

7–18 Sketch the region enclosed by the curves and find its area. ▪

7. $y = x^2$, $y = \sqrt{x}$, $x = \frac{1}{4}$, $x = 1$

8. $y = x^3 - 4x$, $y = 0$, $x = 0$, $x = 2$

9. $y = \cos 2x$, $y = 0$, $x = \pi/4$, $x = \pi/2$

10. $y = \sec^2 x$, $y = 2$, $x = -\pi/4$, $x = \pi/4$

11. $x = \sin y$, $x = 0$, $y = \pi/4$, $y = 3\pi/4$

12. $x^2 = y$, $x = y - 2$

13. $y = e^x$, $y = e^{2x}$, $x = 0$, $x = \ln 2$

14. $x = 1/y$, $x = 0$, $y = 1$, $y = e$

15. $y = \dfrac{2}{1 + x^2}$, $y = |x|$ 16. $y = \dfrac{1}{\sqrt{1 - x^2}}$, $y = 2$

17. $y = 2 + |x - 1|$, $y = -\frac{1}{5}x + 7$

18. $y = x$, $y = 4x$, $y = -x + 2$

⌒ **19–26** Use a graphing utility, where helpful, to find the area of the region enclosed by the curves. ▪

19. $y = x^3 - 4x^2 + 3x$, $y = 0$

20. $y = x^3 - 2x^2$, $y = 2x^2 - 3x$

21. $y = \sin x$, $y = \cos x$, $x = 0$, $x = 2\pi$

22. $y = x^3 - 4x$, $y = 0$ 23. $x = y^3 - y$, $x = 0$

24. $x = y^3 - 4y^2 + 3y$, $x = y^2 - y$

25. $y = xe^{x^2}$, $y = 2|x|$

26. $y = \dfrac{1}{x\sqrt{1 - (\ln x)^2}}$, $y = \dfrac{3}{x}$

27–30 True–False Determine whether the statement is true or false. Explain your answer. [In each exercise, assume that f and g are distinct continuous functions on $[a, b]$ and that A denotes the area of the region bounded by the graphs of $y = f(x)$, $y = g(x)$, $x = a$, and $x = b$.] ▪

27. If f and g differ by a positive constant c, then $A = c(b - a)$.

28. If
$$\int_a^b [f(x) - g(x)]\, dx = -3$$
then $A = 3$.

29. If
$$\int_a^b [f(x) - g(x)]\, dx = 0$$
then the graphs of $y = f(x)$ and $y = g(x)$ cross at least once on $[a, b]$.

30. If
$$A = \left| \int_a^b [f(x) - g(x)]\, dx \right|$$

then the graphs of $y = f(x)$ and $y = g(x)$ don't cross on $[a, b]$.

31. Estimate the value of k $(0 < k < 1)$ so that the region enclosed by $y = 1/\sqrt{1 - x^2}$, $y = x$, $x = 0$, and $x = k$ has an area of 1 square unit.

32. Estimate the area of the region in the first quadrant enclosed by $y = \sin 2x$ and $y = \sin^{-1} x$.

33. Use a CAS to find the area enclosed by $y = 3 - 2x$ and $y = x^6 + 2x^5 - 3x^4 + x^2$.

34. Use a CAS to find the exact area enclosed by the curves $y = x^5 - 2x^3 - 3x$ and $y = x^3$.

35. Find a horizontal line $y = k$ that divides the area between $y = x^2$ and $y = 9$ into two equal parts.

36. Find a vertical line $x = k$ that divides the area enclosed by $x = \sqrt{y}$, $x = 2$, and $y = 0$ into two equal parts.

37. (a) Find the area of the region enclosed by the parabola $y = 2x - x^2$ and the x-axis.
(b) Find the value of m so that the line $y = mx$ divides the region in part (a) into two regions of equal area.

38. Find the area between the curve $y = \sin x$ and the line segment joining the points $(0, 0)$ and $(5\pi/6, 1/2)$ on the curve.

39–42 Use Newton's Method (Section 4.7), where needed, to approximate the x-coordinates of the intersections of the curves to at least four decimal places, and then use those approximations to approximate the area of the region. ■

39. The region that lies below the curve $y = \sin x$ and above the line $y = 0.2x$, where $x \geq 0$.

40. The region enclosed by the graphs of $y = x^2$ and $y = \cos x$.

41. The region enclosed by the graphs of $y = (\ln x)/x$ and $y = x - 2$.

42. The region enclosed by the graphs of $y = 3 - 2\cos x$ and $y = 2/(1 + x^2)$.

43. Find the area of the region that is enclosed by the curves $y = x^2 - 1$ and $y = 2\sin x$.

44. Referring to the accompanying figure, use a CAS to estimate the value of k so that the areas of the shaded regions are equal.

Source: This exercise is based on Problem A1 that was posed in the Fifty-Fourth Annual William Lowell Putnam Mathematical Competition.

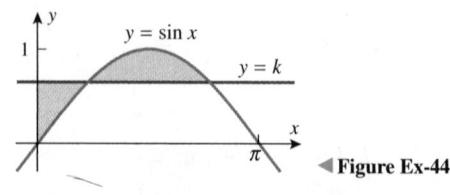

$y = \sin x$

$y = k$

◀ **Figure Ex-44**

45. Two racers in adjacent lanes move with velocity functions $v_1(t)$ m/s and $v_2(t)$ m/s, respectively. Suppose that the racers are even at time $t = 60$ s. Interpret the

value of the integral

$$\int_0^{60} [v_2(t) - v_1(t)]\, dt$$

in this context.

46. The accompanying figure shows acceleration versus time curves for two cars that move along a straight track, accelerating from rest at the starting line. What does the area A between the curves over the interval $0 \leq t \leq T$ represent? Justify your answer.

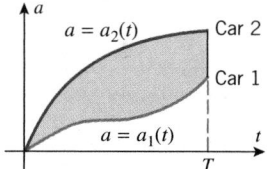

$a = a_2(t)$ Car 2

Car 1

$a = a_1(t)$

◀ **Figure Ex-46**

47. Suppose that f and g are integrable on $[a, b]$, but neither $f(x) \geq g(x)$ nor $g(x) \geq f(x)$ holds for all x in $[a, b]$ [i.e., the curves $y = f(x)$ and $y = g(x)$ are intertwined].
(a) What is the geometric significance of the integral

$$\int_a^b [f(x) - g(x)]\, dx?$$

(b) What is the geometric significance of the integral

$$\int_a^b |f(x) - g(x)|\, dx?$$

48. Let $A(n)$ be the area in the first quadrant enclosed by the curves $y = \sqrt[n]{x}$ and $y = x$.
(a) By considering how the graph of $y = \sqrt[n]{x}$ changes as n increases, make a conjecture about the limit of $A(n)$ as $n \to +\infty$.
(b) Confirm your conjecture by calculating the limit.

49. Find the area of the region enclosed between the curve $x^{1/2} + y^{1/2} = a^{1/2}$ and the coordinate axes.

50. Show that the area of the ellipse in the accompanying figure is πab. [*Hint:* Use a formula from geometry.]

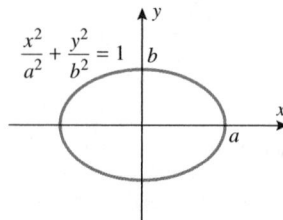

$\dfrac{x^2}{a^2} + \dfrac{y^2}{b^2} = 1$

◀ **Figure Ex-50**

51. **Writing** Suppose that f and g are continuous on $[a, b]$ but that the graphs of $y = f(x)$ and $y = g(x)$ cross several times. Describe a step-by-step procedure for determining the area bounded by the graphs of $y = f(x)$, $y = g(x)$, $x = a$, and $x = b$.

52. **Writing** Suppose that R and S are two regions in the xy-plane that lie between a pair of lines L_1 and L_2 that are parallel to the y-axis. Assume that each line between L_1 and L_2 that is parallel to the y-axis intersects R and S in line segments of equal length. Give an informal argument that the area of R is equal to the area of S. (Make reasonable assumptions about the boundaries of R and S.)

✔ **QUICK CHECK ANSWERS 6.1**

1. $\displaystyle\int_0^2 [(20 - 3x^2) - e^x]\,dx$ 2. $\displaystyle\int_{-1}^5 [(2x + 8) - (2x - 3)]\,dx;\ 66$ 3. (a) $(-2, 0);\ (0, 2)$ (b) $\displaystyle\int_{-2}^0 [\sqrt{4 - x^2} - (x + 2)]\,dx$

(c) $\displaystyle\int_0^2 [(y - 2) + \sqrt{4 - y^2}]\,dy$ 4. $\dfrac{5}{12}$

6.2 VOLUMES BY SLICING; DISKS AND WASHERS

In the last section we showed that the area of a plane region bounded by two curves can be obtained by integrating the length of a general cross section over an appropriate interval. In this section we will see that the same basic principle can be used to find volumes of certain three-dimensional solids.

■ VOLUMES BY SLICING

Recall that the underlying principle for finding the area of a plane region is to divide the region into thin strips, approximate the area of each strip by the area of a rectangle, add the approximations to form a Riemann sum, and take the limit of the Riemann sums to produce an integral for the area. Under appropriate conditions, the same strategy can be used to find the volume of a solid. The idea is to divide the solid into thin slabs, approximate the volume of each slab, add the approximations to form a Riemann sum, and take the limit of the Riemann sums to produce an integral for the volume (Figure 6.2.1).

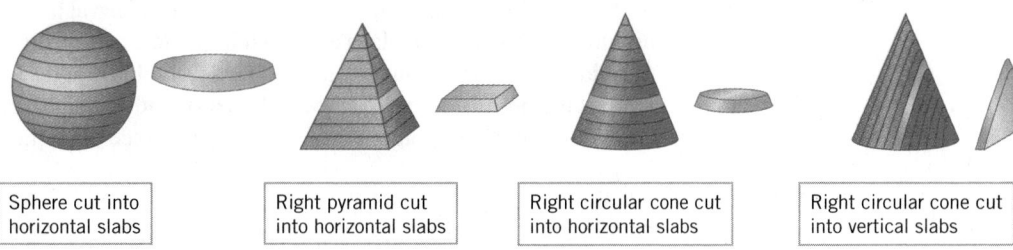

| Sphere cut into horizontal slabs | Right pyramid cut into horizontal slabs | Right circular cone cut into horizontal slabs | Right circular cone cut into vertical slabs |

▲ **Figure 6.2.1**

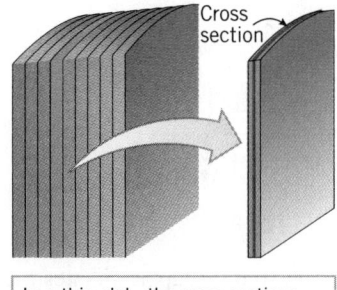

In a thin slab, the cross sections do not vary much in size and shape.

▲ **Figure 6.2.2**

What makes this method work is the fact that a *thin* slab has a cross section that does not vary much in size or shape, which, as we will see, makes its volume easy to approximate (Figure 6.2.2). Moreover, the thinner the slab, the less variation in its cross sections and the better the approximation. Thus, once we approximate the volumes of the slabs, we can set up a Riemann sum whose limit is the volume of the entire solid. We will give the details shortly, but first we need to discuss how to find the volume of a solid whose cross sections do not vary in size and shape (i.e., are congruent).

One of the simplest examples of a solid with congruent cross sections is a right circular cylinder of radius r, since all cross sections taken perpendicular to the central axis are circular regions of radius r. The volume V of a right circular cylinder of radius r and height h can be expressed in terms of the height and the area of a cross section as

$$V = \pi r^2 h = [\text{area of a cross section}] \times [\text{height}] \qquad (1)$$

This is a special case of a more general volume formula that applies to solids called *right cylinders*. A **right cylinder** is a solid that is generated when a plane region is translated along a line or **axis** that is perpendicular to the region (Figure 6.2.3).

Some Right Cylinders

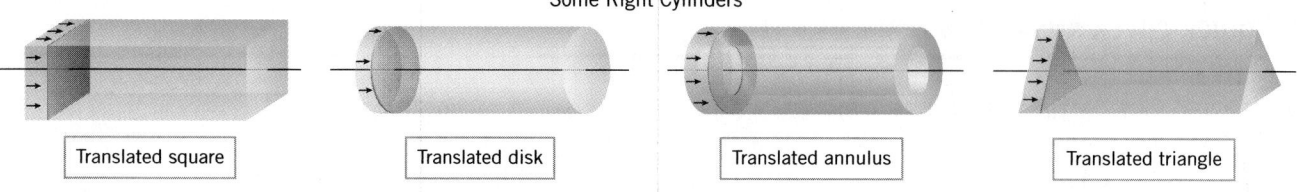

Translated square   Translated disk   Translated annulus   Translated triangle

▲ **Figure 6.2.3**

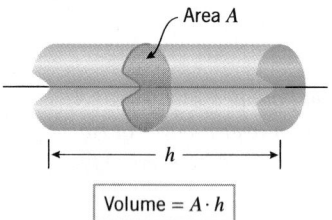

Area A

h

Volume = $A \cdot h$

▲ **Figure 6.2.4**

If a right cylinder is generated by translating a region of area A through a distance h, then h is called the **height** (or sometimes the **width**) of the cylinder, and the volume V of the cylinder is defined to be

$$V = A \cdot h = [\text{area of a cross section}] \times [\text{height}] \tag{2}$$

(Figure 6.2.4). Note that this is consistent with Formula (1) for the volume of a right *circular* cylinder.

We now have all of the tools required to solve the following problem.

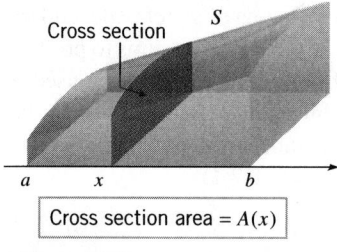

Cross section S

a x b

Cross section area = $A(x)$

▲ **Figure 6.2.5**

6.2.1   PROBLEM   Let S be a solid that extends along the x-axis and is bounded on the left and right, respectively, by the planes that are perpendicular to the x-axis at $x = a$ and $x = b$ (Figure 6.2.5). Find the volume V of the solid, assuming that its cross-sectional area $A(x)$ is known at each x in the interval $[a, b]$.

To solve this problem we begin by dividing the interval $[a, b]$ into n subintervals, thereby dividing the solid into n slabs as shown in the left part of Figure 6.2.6. If we assume that the width of the kth subinterval is Δx_k, then the volume of the kth slab can be approximated by the volume $A(x_k^*)\Delta x_k$ of a right cylinder of width (height) Δx_k and cross-sectional area $A(x_k^*)$, where x_k^* is a point in the kth subinterval (see the right part of Figure 6.2.6).

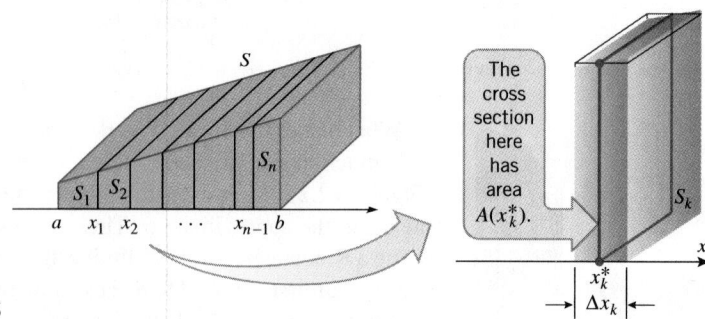

S

S_1 S_2 S_n

a x_1 x_2 $\cdots$ x_{n-1} b

The cross section here has area $A(x_k^*)$.

S_k

x

x_k^*

Δx_k

▶ **Figure 6.2.6**

Adding these approximations yields the following Riemann sum that approximates the volume V:

$$V \approx \sum_{k=1}^{n} A(x_k^*)\Delta x_k$$

Taking the limit as n increases and the widths of all the subintervals approach zero yields the definite integral

$$V = \lim_{\max \Delta x_k \to 0} \sum_{k=1}^{n} A(x_k^*) \Delta x_k = \int_a^b A(x)\, dx$$

In summary, we have the following result.

It is understood in our calculations of volume that the units of volume are the cubed units of length [e.g., cubic inches (in^3) or cubic meters (m^3)].

6.2.2 VOLUME FORMULA Let S be a solid bounded by two parallel planes perpendicular to the x-axis at $x = a$ and $x = b$. If, for each x in $[a, b]$, the cross-sectional area of S perpendicular to the x-axis is $A(x)$, then the volume of the solid is

$$V = \int_a^b A(x)\, dx \tag{3}$$

provided $A(x)$ is integrable.

There is a similar result for cross sections perpendicular to the y-axis.

6.2.3 VOLUME FORMULA Let S be a solid bounded by two parallel planes perpendicular to the y-axis at $y = c$ and $y = d$. If, for each y in $[c, d]$, the cross-sectional area of S perpendicular to the y-axis is $A(y)$, then the volume of the solid is

$$V = \int_c^d A(y)\, dy \tag{4}$$

provided $A(y)$ is integrable.

In words, these formulas state:

The volume of a solid can be obtained by integrating the cross-sectional area from one end of the solid to the other.

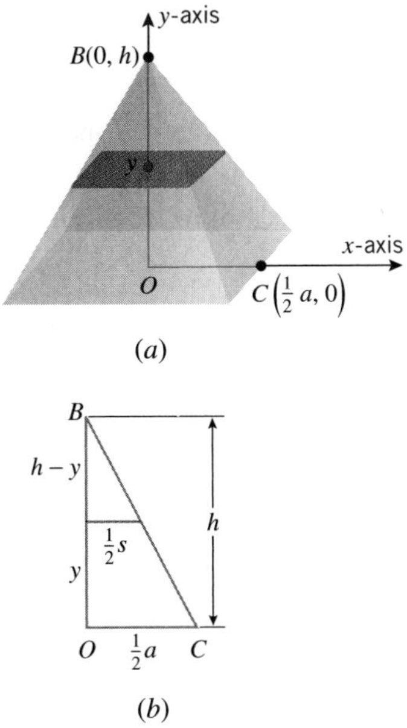

▶ **Example 1** Derive the formula for the volume of a right pyramid whose altitude is h and whose base is a square with sides of length a.

Solution. As illustrated in Figure 6.2.7a, we introduce a rectangular coordinate system in which the y-axis passes through the apex and is perpendicular to the base, and the x-axis passes through the base and is parallel to a side of the base.

At any y in the interval $[0, h]$ on the y-axis, the cross section perpendicular to the y-axis is a square. If s denotes the length of a side of this square, then by similar triangles (Figure 6.2.7b)

$$\frac{\frac{1}{2}s}{\frac{1}{2}a} = \frac{h - y}{h} \quad \text{or} \quad s = \frac{a}{h}(h - y)$$

Thus, the area $A(y)$ of the cross section at y is

$$A(y) = s^2 = \frac{a^2}{h^2}(h - y)^2$$

(a)

(b)

▲ **Figure 6.2.7**

and by (4) the volume is

$$V = \int_0^h A(y)\, dy = \int_0^h \frac{a^2}{h^2}(h-y)^2\, dy = \frac{a^2}{h^2}\int_0^h (h-y)^2\, dy$$

$$= \frac{a^2}{h^2}\left[-\frac{1}{3}(h-y)^3\right]_{y=0}^h = \frac{a^2}{h^2}\left[0+\frac{1}{3}h^3\right] = \frac{1}{3}a^2 h$$

That is, the volume is $\frac{1}{3}$ of the area of the base times the altitude. ◄

■ SOLIDS OF REVOLUTION

A *solid of revolution* is a solid that is generated by revolving a plane region about a line that lies in the same plane as the region; the line is called the *axis of revolution*. Many familiar solids are of this type (Figure 6.2.8).

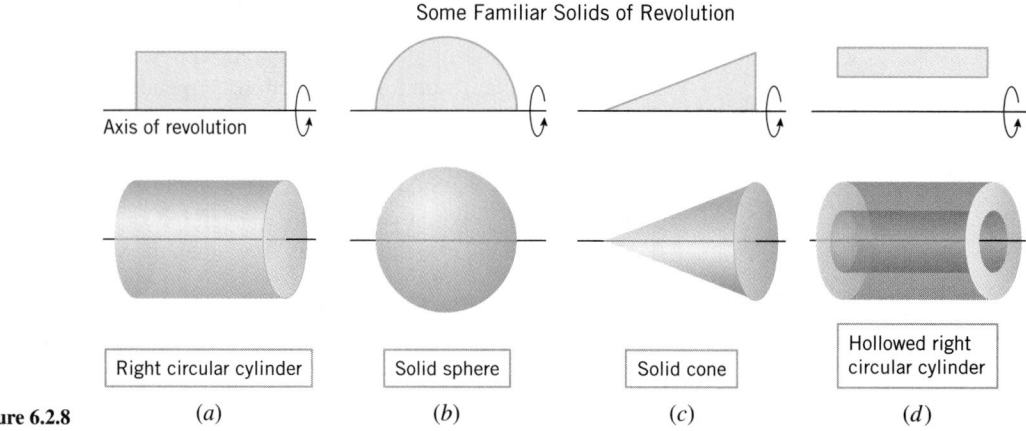

Some Familiar Solids of Revolution

| Right circular cylinder | Solid sphere | Solid cone | Hollowed right circular cylinder |

▶ **Figure 6.2.8**   (*a*)   (*b*)   (*c*)   (*d*)

■ VOLUMES BY DISKS PERPENDICULAR TO THE *x*-AXIS

We will be interested in the following general problem.

6.2.4 **PROBLEM**   Let f be continuous and nonnegative on $[a, b]$, and let R be the region that is bounded above by $y = f(x)$, below by the x-axis, and on the sides by the lines $x = a$ and $x = b$ (Figure 6.2.9*a*). Find the volume of the solid of revolution that is generated by revolving the region R about the x-axis.

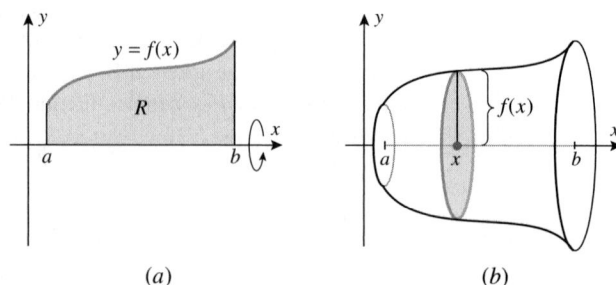

▶ **Figure 6.2.9**   (*a*)   (*b*)

We can solve this problem by slicing. For this purpose, observe that the cross section of the solid taken perpendicular to the x-axis at the point x is a circular disk of radius $f(x)$ (Figure 6.2.9b). The area of this region is

$$A(x) = \pi[f(x)]^2$$

Thus, from (3) the volume of the solid is

$$V = \int_a^b \pi[f(x)]^2\, dx \qquad (5)$$

Because the cross sections are disk shaped, the application of this formula is called the *method of disks*.

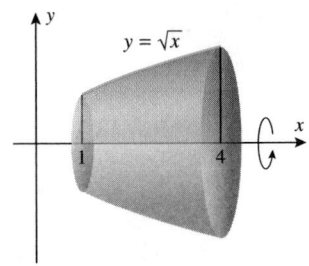

▲ **Figure 6.2.10**

▶ **Example 2** Find the volume of the solid that is obtained when the region under the curve $y = \sqrt{x}$ over the interval $[1, 4]$ is revolved about the x-axis (Figure 6.2.10).

Solution. From (5), the volume is

$$V = \int_a^b \pi[f(x)]^2\, dx = \int_1^4 \pi x\, dx = \left. \frac{\pi x^2}{2} \right]_1^4 = 8\pi - \frac{\pi}{2} = \frac{15\pi}{2} \;\blacktriangleleft$$

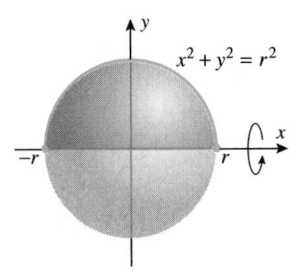

▲ **Figure 6.2.11**

▶ **Example 3** Derive the formula for the volume of a sphere of radius r.

Solution. As indicated in Figure 6.2.11, a sphere of radius r can be generated by revolving the upper semicircular disk enclosed between the x-axis and

$$x^2 + y^2 = r^2$$

about the x-axis. Since the upper half of this circle is the graph of $y = f(x) = \sqrt{r^2 - x^2}$, it follows from (5) that the volume of the sphere is

$$V = \int_a^b \pi[f(x)]^2\, dx = \int_{-r}^r \pi(r^2 - x^2)\, dx = \pi\left[r^2 x - \frac{x^3}{3} \right]_{-r}^r = \frac{4}{3}\pi r^3 \;\blacktriangleleft$$

▇ VOLUMES BY WASHERS PERPENDICULAR TO THE x-AXIS

Not all solids of revolution have solid interiors; some have holes or channels that create interior surfaces, as in Figure 6.2.8d. So we will also be interested in problems of the following type.

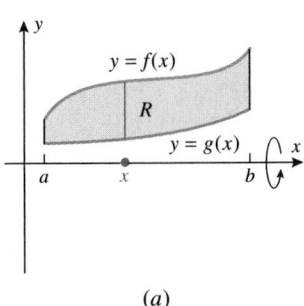

(a)

(b)

▲ **Figure 6.2.12**

> **6.2.5** **PROBLEM** Let f and g be continuous and nonnegative on $[a, b]$, and suppose that $f(x) \geq g(x)$ for all x in the interval $[a, b]$. Let R be the region that is bounded above by $y = f(x)$, below by $y = g(x)$, and on the sides by the lines $x = a$ and $x = b$ (Figure 6.2.12a). Find the volume of the solid of revolution that is generated by revolving the region R about the x-axis (Figure 6.2.12b).

We can solve this problem by slicing. For this purpose, observe that the cross section of the solid taken perpendicular to the x-axis at the point x is the annular or "washer-shaped" region with inner radius $g(x)$ and outer radius $f(x)$ (Figure 6.2.12b); its area is

$$A(x) = \pi[f(x)]^2 - \pi[g(x)]^2 = \pi([f(x)]^2 - [g(x)]^2)$$

Thus, from (3) the volume of the solid is

$$V = \int_a^b \pi([f(x)]^2 - [g(x)]^2)\,dx \qquad (6)$$

Because the cross sections are washer shaped, the application of this formula is called the *method of washers*.

▶ **Example 4** Find the volume of the solid generated when the region between the graphs of the equations $f(x) = \frac{1}{2} + x^2$ and $g(x) = x$ over the interval $[0, 2]$ is revolved about the x-axis.

Solution. First sketch the region (Figure 6.2.13a); then imagine revolving it about the x-axis (Figure 6.2.13b). From (6) the volume is

$$V = \int_a^b \pi([f(x)]^2 - [g(x)]^2)\,dx = \int_0^2 \pi\left(\left[\tfrac{1}{2} + x^2\right]^2 - x^2\right)\,dx$$

$$= \int_0^2 \pi\left(\frac{1}{4} + x^4\right)\,dx = \pi\left[\frac{x}{4} + \frac{x^5}{5}\right]_0^2 = \frac{69\pi}{10} \quad ◀$$

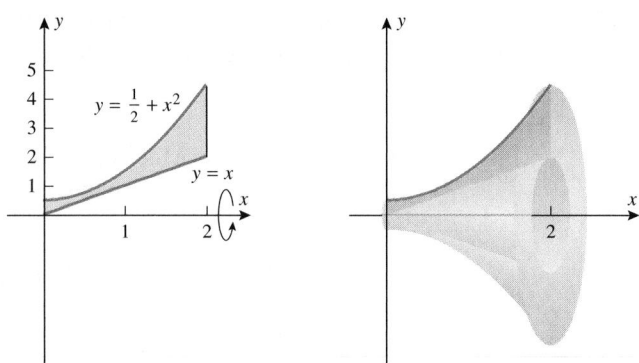

Unequal scales on axes

| Region defined by f and g | The resulting solid of revolution |

▶ **Figure 6.2.13**   (a)   (b)

■ **VOLUMES BY DISKS AND WASHERS PERPENDICULAR TO THE y-AXIS**

The methods of disks and washers have analogs for regions that are revolved about the y-axis (Figures 6.2.14 and 6.2.15). Using the method of slicing and Formula (4), you should be able to deduce the following formulas for the volumes of the solids in the figures.

$$V = \int_c^d \pi[u(y)]^2\,dy \qquad\qquad V = \int_c^d \pi([w(y)]^2 - [v(y)]^2)\,dy \qquad (7\text{–}8)$$

$$\text{Disks} \qquad\qquad\qquad\qquad\qquad\qquad \text{Washers}$$

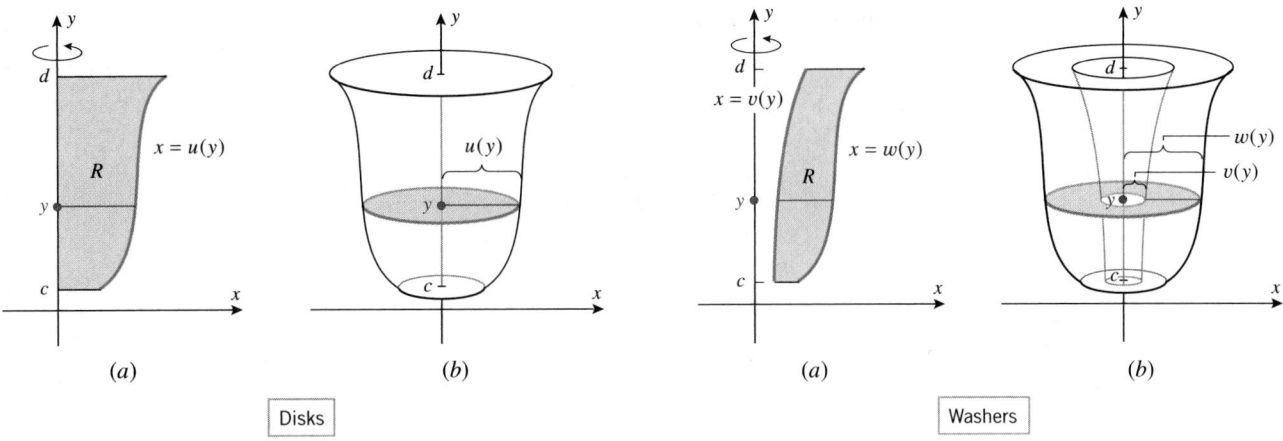

Disks
Washers

▲ **Figure 6.2.14**   ▲ **Figure 6.2.15**

▶ **Example 5**   Find the volume of the solid generated when the region enclosed by $y = \sqrt{x}$, $y = 2$, and $x = 0$ is revolved about the y-axis.

Solution.   First sketch the region and the solid (Figure 6.2.16). The cross sections taken perpendicular to the y-axis are disks, so we will apply (7). But first we must rewrite $y = \sqrt{x}$ as $x = y^2$. Thus, from (7) with $u(y) = y^2$, the volume is

$$V = \int_c^d \pi[u(y)]^2 \, dy = \int_0^2 \pi y^4 \, dy = \frac{\pi y^5}{5}\Big]_0^2 = \frac{32\pi}{5} \quad \blacktriangleleft$$

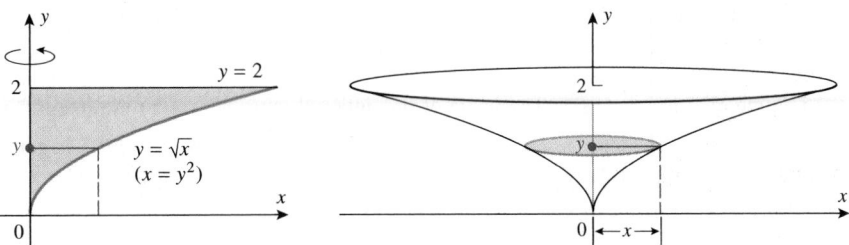

▶ **Figure 6.2.16**

■ OTHER AXES OF REVOLUTION

It is possible to use the method of disks and the method of washers to find the volume of a solid of revolution whose axis of revolution is a line other than one of the coordinate axes. Instead of developing a new formula for each situation, we will appeal to Formulas (3) and (4) and integrate an appropriate cross-sectional area to find the volume.

▶ **Example 6**   Find the volume of the solid generated when the region under the curve $y = x^2$ over the interval $[0, 2]$ is rotated about the line $y = -1$.

Solution.   First sketch the region and the axis of revolution; then imagine revolving the region about the axis (Figure 6.2.17). At each x in the interval $0 \le x \le 2$, the cross section of the solid perpendicular to the axis $y = -1$ is a washer with outer radius $x^2 + 1$ and inner radius 1. Since the area of this washer is

$$A(x) = \pi([x^2 + 1]^2 - 1^2) = \pi(x^4 + 2x^2)$$

it follows by (3) that the volume of the solid is

$$V = \int_0^2 A(x)\,dx = \int_0^2 \pi\left(x^4 + 2x^2\right) dx = \pi\left[\frac{1}{5}x^5 + \frac{2}{3}x^3\right]_0^2 = \frac{176\pi}{15} \quad \blacktriangleleft$$

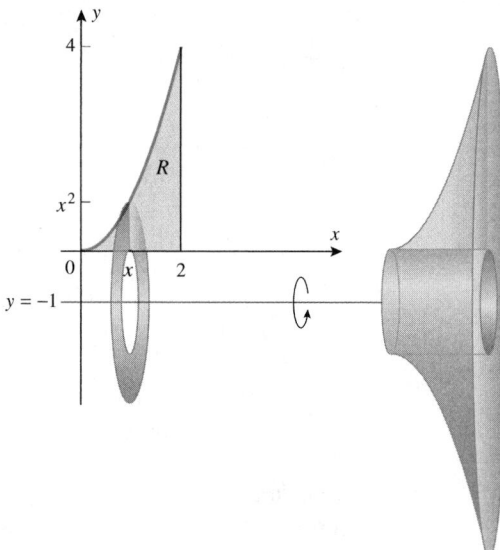

▶ **Figure 6.2.17**

✔ QUICK CHECK EXERCISES 6.2   (See page 431 for answers.)

1. A solid S extends along the x-axis from $x = 1$ to $x = 3$. For x between 1 and 3, the cross-sectional area of S perpendicular to the x-axis is $3x^2$. An integral expression for the volume of S is _____. The value of this integral is _____.

2. A solid S is generated by revolving the region between the x-axis and the curve $y = \sqrt{\sin x}$ $(0 \le x \le \pi)$ about the x-axis.
  (a) For x between 0 and π, the cross-sectional area of S perpendicular to the x-axis at x is $A(x) = $ _____.
  (b) An integral expression for the volume of S is _____.
  (c) The value of the integral in part (b) is _____.

3. A solid S is generated by revolving the region enclosed by the line $y = 2x + 1$ and the curve $y = x^2 + 1$ about the x-axis.

  (a) For x between _____ and _____, the cross-sectional area of S perpendicular to the x-axis at x is $A(x) = $ _____.
  (b) An integral expression for the volume of S is _____.

4. A solid S is generated by revolving the region enclosed by the line $y = x + 1$ and the curve $y = x^2 + 1$ about the y-axis.
  (a) For y between _____ and _____, the cross-sectional area of S perpendicular to the y-axis at y is $A(y) = $ _____.
  (b) An integral expression for the volume of S is _____.

EXERCISE SET 6.2   ⊂ CAS

1–8 Find the volume of the solid that results when the shaded region is revolved about the indicated axis. ■

1.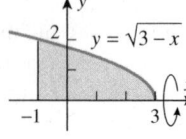

2.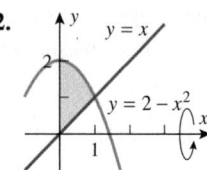

3.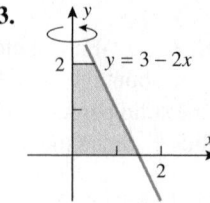

4.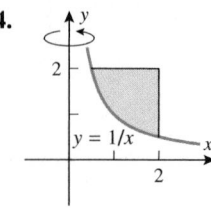

5.

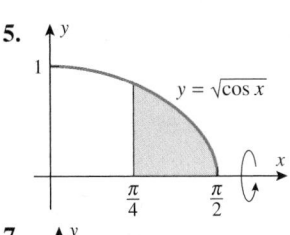

6.

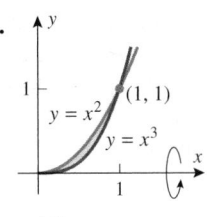

7.

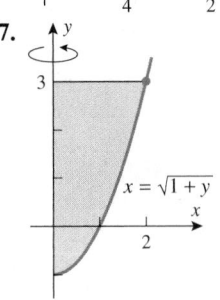

8.

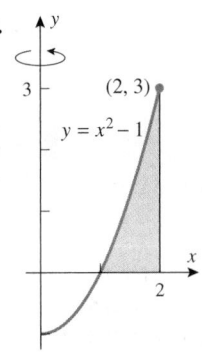

9. Find the volume of the solid whose base is the region bounded between the curve $y = x^2$ and the x-axis from $x = 0$ to $x = 2$ and whose cross sections taken perpendicular to the x-axis are squares.

10. Find the volume of the solid whose base is the region bounded between the curve $y = \sec x$ and the x-axis from $x = \pi/4$ to $x = \pi/3$ and whose cross sections taken perpendicular to the x-axis are squares.

11–18 Find the volume of the solid that results when the region enclosed by the given curves is revolved about the x-axis. ■

11. $y = \sqrt{25 - x^2}$, $y = 3$

12. $y = 9 - x^2$, $y = 0$ 13. $x = \sqrt{y}$, $x = y/4$

14. $y = \sin x$, $y = \cos x$, $x = 0$, $x = \pi/4$
[*Hint:* Use the identity $\cos 2x = \cos^2 x - \sin^2 x$.]

15. $y = e^x$, $y = 0$, $x = 0$, $x = \ln 3$

16. $y = e^{-2x}$, $y = 0$, $x = 0$, $x = 1$

17. $y = \dfrac{1}{\sqrt{4 + x^2}}$, $x = -2$, $x = 2$, $y = 0$

18. $y = \dfrac{e^{3x}}{\sqrt{1 + e^{6x}}}$, $x = 0$, $x = 1$, $y = 0$

19. Find the volume of the solid whose base is the region bounded between the curve $y = x^3$ and the y-axis from $y = 0$ to $y = 1$ and whose cross sections taken perpendicular to the y-axis are squares.

20. Find the volume of the solid whose base is the region enclosed between the curve $x = 1 - y^2$ and the y-axis and whose cross sections taken perpendicular to the y-axis are squares.

21–26 Find the volume of the solid that results when the region enclosed by the given curves is revolved about the y-axis. ■

21. $x = \csc y$, $y = \pi/4$, $y = 3\pi/4$, $x = 0$

22. $y = x^2$, $x = y^2$

23. $x = y^2$, $x = y + 2$

24. $x = 1 - y^2$, $x = 2 + y^2$, $y = -1$, $y = 1$

25. $y = \ln x$, $x = 0$, $y = 0$, $y = 1$

26. $y = \sqrt{\dfrac{1 - x^2}{x^2}}$ $(x > 0)$, $x = 0$, $y = 0$, $y = 2$

27–30 True–False Determine whether the statement is true or false. Explain your answer. [In these exercises, assume that a solid S of volume V is bounded by two parallel planes perpendicular to the x-axis at $x = a$ and $x = b$ and that for each x in $[a, b]$, $A(x)$ denotes the cross-sectional area of S perpendicular to the x-axis.] ■

27. If each cross section of S perpendicular to the x-axis is a square, then S is a rectangular parallelepiped (i.e., is box shaped).

28. If each cross section of S is a disk or a washer, then S is a solid of revolution.

29. If x is in centimeters (cm), then $A(x)$ must be a quadratic function of x, since units of $A(x)$ will be square centimeters (cm²).

30. The average value of $A(x)$ on the interval $[a, b]$ is given by $V/(b - a)$.

31. Find the volume of the solid that results when the region above the x-axis and below the ellipse

$$\frac{x^2}{a^2} + \frac{y^2}{b^2} = 1 \quad (a > 0, b > 0)$$

is revolved about the x-axis.

32. Let V be the volume of the solid that results when the region enclosed by $y = 1/x$, $y = 0$, $x = 2$, and $x = b$ $(0 < b < 2)$ is revolved about the x-axis. Find the value of b for which $V = 3$.

33. Find the volume of the solid generated when the region enclosed by $y = \sqrt{x + 1}$, $y = \sqrt{2x}$, and $y = 0$ is revolved about the x-axis. [*Hint:* Split the solid into two parts.]

34. Find the volume of the solid generated when the region enclosed by $y = \sqrt{x}$, $y = 6 - x$, and $y = 0$ is revolved about the x-axis. [*Hint:* Split the solid into two parts.]

FOCUS ON CONCEPTS

35. Suppose that f is a continuous function on $[a, b]$, and let R be the region between the curve $y = f(x)$ and the line $y = k$ from $x = a$ to $x = b$. Using the method of disks, derive with explanation a formula for the volume of a solid generated by revolving R about the line $y = k$. State and explain additional assumptions, if any, that you need about f for your formula.

36. Suppose that v and w are continuous functions on $[c, d]$, and let R be the region between the curves $x = v(y)$ and $x = w(y)$ from $y = c$ to $y = d$. Using the method of washers, derive with explanation a formula for the volume of a solid generated by revolving R about the line

$x = k$. State and explain additional assumptions, if any, that you need about v and w for your formula.

37. Consider the solid generated by revolving the shaded region in Exercise 1 about the line $y = 2$.
(a) Make a conjecture as to which is larger: the volume of this solid or the volume of the solid in Exercise 1. Explain the basis of your conjecture.
(b) Check your conjecture by calculating this volume and comparing it to the volume obtained in Exercise 1.

38. Consider the solid generated by revolving the shaded region in Exercise 4 about the line $x = 2.5$.
(a) Make a conjecture as to which is larger: the volume of this solid or the volume of the solid in Exercise 4. Explain the basis of your conjecture.
(b) Check your conjecture by calculating this volume and comparing it to the volume obtained in Exercise 4.

39. Find the volume of the solid that results when the region enclosed by $y = \sqrt{x}$, $y = 0$, and $x = 9$ is revolved about the line $x = 9$.

40. Find the volume of the solid that results when the region in Exercise 39 is revolved about the line $y = 3$.

41. Find the volume of the solid that results when the region enclosed by $x = y^2$ and $x = y$ is revolved about the line $y = -1$.

42. Find the volume of the solid that results when the region in Exercise 41 is revolved about the line $x = -1$.

43. Find the volume of the solid that results when the region enclosed by $y = x^2$ and $y = x^3$ is revolved about the line $x = 1$.

44. Find the volume of the solid that results when the region in Exercise 43 is revolved about the line $y = -1$.

45. A nose cone for a space reentry vehicle is designed so that a cross section, taken x ft from the tip and perpendicular to the axis of symmetry, is a circle of radius $\frac{1}{4}x^2$ ft. Find the volume of the nose cone given that its length is 20 ft.

46. A certain solid is 1 ft high, and a horizontal cross section taken x ft above the bottom of the solid is an annulus of inner radius x^2 ft and outer radius $\sqrt{x}$ ft. Find the volume of the solid.

47. Find the volume of the solid whose base is the region bounded between the curves $y = x$ and $y = x^2$, and whose cross sections perpendicular to the x-axis are squares.

48. The base of a certain solid is the region enclosed by $y = \sqrt{x}$, $y = 0$, and $x = 4$. Every cross section perpendicular to the x-axis is a semicircle with its diameter across the base. Find the volume of the solid.

49. In parts (a)–(c) find the volume of the solid whose base is enclosed by the circle $x^2 + y^2 = 1$ and whose cross sections taken perpendicular to the x-axis are
(a) semicircles   (b) squares
(c) equilateral triangles.

(a)   (b)   (c)

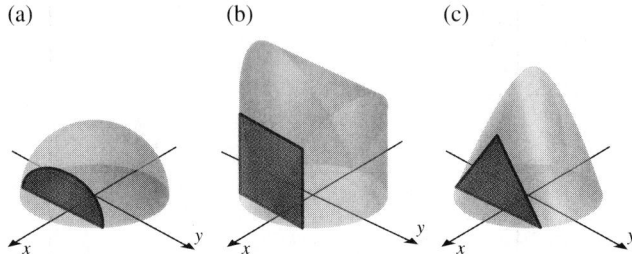

50. As shown in the accompanying figure, a cathedral dome is designed with three semicircular supports of radius r so that each horizontal cross section is a regular hexagon. Show that the volume of the dome is $r^3\sqrt{3}$.

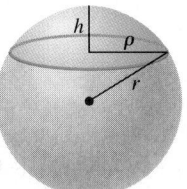

◄ **Figure Ex-50**

[C] **51–54** Use a CAS to estimate the volume of the solid that results when the region enclosed by the curves is revolved about the stated axis. ■

51. $y = \sin^8 x$, $y = 2x/\pi$, $x = 0$, $x = \pi/2$; x-axis

52. $y = \pi^2 \sin x \cos^3 x$, $y = 4x^2$, $x = 0$, $x = \pi/4$; x-axis

53. $y = e^x$, $x = 1$, $y = 1$; y-axis

54. $y = x\sqrt{\tan^{-1} x}$, $y = x$; x-axis

55. The accompanying figure shows a *spherical cap* of radius ρ and height h cut from a sphere of radius r. Show that the volume V of the spherical cap can be expressed as
(a) $V = \frac{1}{3}\pi h^2(3r - h)$ (b) $V = \frac{1}{6}\pi h(3\rho^2 + h^2)$.

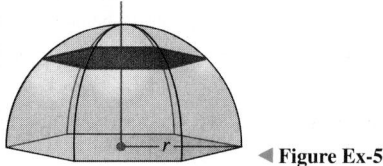

◄ **Figure Ex-55**

56. If fluid enters a hemispherical bowl with a radius of 10 ft at a rate of $\frac{1}{2}$ ft^3/min, how fast will the fluid be rising when the depth is 5 ft? [*Hint:* See Exercise 55.]

57. The accompanying figure (on the next page) shows the dimensions of a small lightbulb at 10 equally spaced points.
(a) Use formulas from geometry to make a rough estimate of the volume enclosed by the glass portion of the bulb.

(cont.)

(b) Use the average of left and right endpoint approximations to approximate the volume.

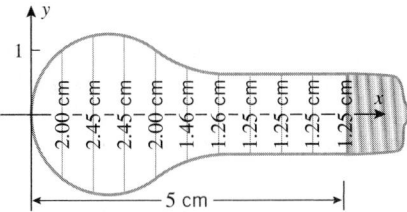

▲ **Figure Ex-57**

58. Use the result in Exercise 55 to find the volume of the solid that remains when a hole of radius $r/2$ is drilled through the center of a sphere of radius r, and then check your answer by integrating.

59. As shown in the accompanying figure, a cocktail glass with a bowl shaped like a hemisphere of diameter 8 cm contains a cherry with a diameter of 2 cm. If the glass is filled to a depth of h cm, what is the volume of liquid it contains? [*Hint:* First consider the case where the cherry is partially submerged, then the case where it is totally submerged.]

◀ **Figure Ex-59**

60. Find the volume of the torus that results when the region enclosed by the circle of radius r with center at $(h, 0)$, $h > r$, is revolved about the y-axis. [*Hint:* Use an appropriate formula from plane geometry to help evaluate the definite integral.]

61. A wedge is cut from a right circular cylinder of radius r by two planes, one perpendicular to the axis of the cylinder and the other making an angle θ with the first. Find the volume of the wedge by slicing perpendicular to the y-axis as shown in the accompanying figure.

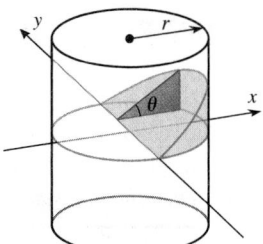

◀ **Figure Ex-61**

62. Find the volume of the wedge described in Exercise 61 by slicing perpendicular to the x-axis.

63. Two right circular cylinders of radius r have axes that intersect at right angles. Find the volume of the solid common to the two cylinders. [*Hint:* One-eighth of the solid is sketched in the accompanying figure.]

64. In 1635 Bonaventura Cavalieri, a student of Galileo, stated the following result, called *Cavalieri's principle*: *If two solids have the same height, and if the areas of their cross sections taken parallel to and at equal distances from their bases are always equal, then the solids have the same volume.* Use this result to find the volume of the oblique cylinder in the accompanying figure. (See Exercise 52 of Section 6.1 for a planar version of Cavalieri's principle.)

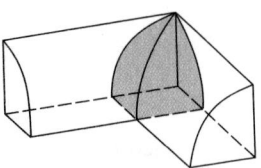   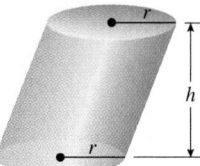

▲ **Figure Ex-63**   ▲ **Figure Ex-64**

65. **Writing** Use the results of this section to derive Cavalieri's principle (Exercise 64).

66. **Writing** Write a short paragraph that explains how Formulas (4)–(8) may all be viewed as consequences of Formula (3).

✔ **QUICK CHECK ANSWERS 6.2**

1. $\displaystyle\int_{1}^{3} 3x^2 \, dx$; 26   **2.** (a) $\pi \sin x$ (b) $\displaystyle\int_{0}^{\pi} \pi \sin x \, dx$ (c) 2π **3.** (a) 0; 2; $\pi[(2x+1)^2 - (x^2+1)^2] = \pi[-x^4 + 2x^2 + 4x]$

(b) $\displaystyle\int_{0}^{2} \pi[-x^4 + 2x^2 + 4x] \, dx$ **4.** (a) 1; 2; $\pi[(y-1) - (y-1)^2] = \pi[-y^2 + 3y - 2]$ (b) $\displaystyle\int_{1}^{2} \pi[-y^2 + 3y - 2] \, dy$

6.3   VOLUMES BY CYLINDRICAL SHELLS

The methods for computing volumes that have been discussed so far depend on our ability to compute the cross-sectional area of the solid and to integrate that area across the solid. In this section we will develop another method for finding volumes that may be applicable when the cross-sectional area cannot be found or the integration is too difficult.

■ **CYLINDRICAL SHELLS**
In this section we will be interested in the following problem.

6.3.1   PROBLEM   Let f be continuous and nonnegative on $[a, b]$ $(0 \leq a < b)$, and let R be the region that is bounded above by $y = f(x)$, below by the x-axis, and on the sides by the lines $x = a$ and $x = b$. Find the volume V of the solid of revolution S that is generated by revolving the region R about the y-axis (Figure 6.3.1).

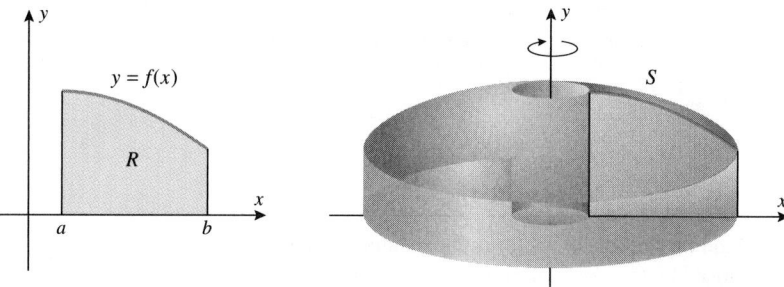

▶ **Figure 6.3.1**

Sometimes problems of the above type can be solved by the method of disks or washers perpendicular to the y-axis, but when that method is not applicable or the resulting integral is difficult, the *method of cylindrical shells*, which we will discuss here, will often work.

A *cylindrical shell* is a solid enclosed by two concentric right circular cylinders (Figure 6.3.2). The volume V of a cylindrical shell with inner radius r_1, outer radius r_2, and height h can be written as

$$V = [\text{area of cross section}] \cdot [\text{height}]$$
$$= (\pi r_2^2 - \pi r_1^2)h$$
$$= \pi(r_2 + r_1)(r_2 - r_1)h$$
$$= 2\pi \cdot \left[\tfrac{1}{2}(r_1 + r_2)\right] \cdot h \cdot (r_2 - r_1)$$

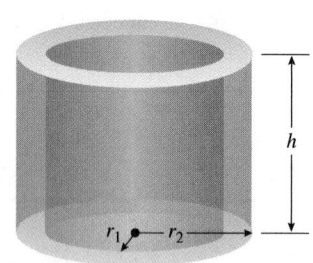

▲ **Figure 6.3.2**

But $\tfrac{1}{2}(r_1 + r_2)$ is the average radius of the shell and $r_2 - r_1$ is its thickness, so

$$V = 2\pi \cdot [\text{average radius}] \cdot [\text{height}] \cdot [\text{thickness}] \tag{1}$$

We will now show how this formula can be used to solve Problem 6.3.1. The underlying idea is to divide the interval $[a, b]$ into n subintervals, thereby subdividing the region R into n strips, $R_1, R_2, \ldots, R_n$ (Figure 6.3.3a). When the region R is revolved about the y-axis, these strips generate "tube-like" solids $S_1, S_2, \ldots, S_n$ that are nested one inside the other and together comprise the entire solid S (Figure 6.3.3b). Thus, the volume V of the solid can be obtained by adding together the volumes of the tubes; that is,

$$V = V(S_1) + V(S_2) + \cdots + V(S_n)$$

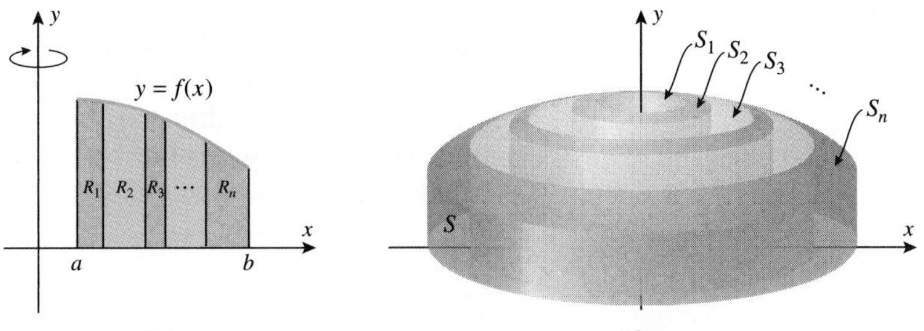

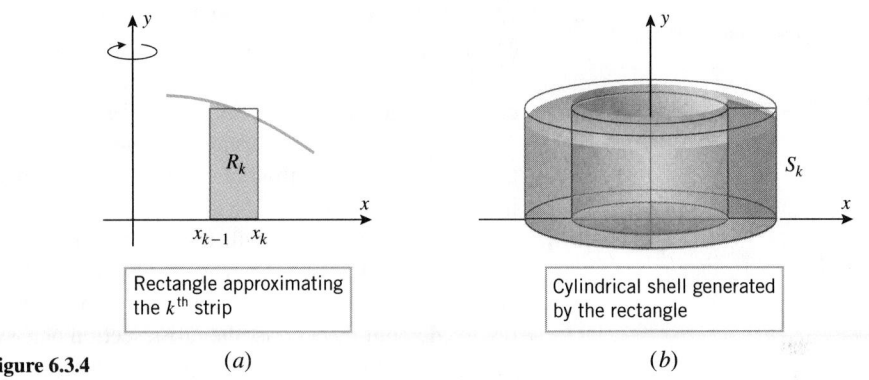

▶ **Figure 6.3.3**   (a)   (b)

As a rule, the tubes will have curved upper surfaces, so there will be no simple formulas for their volumes. However, if the strips are thin, then we can approximate each strip by a rectangle (Figure 6.3.4a). These rectangles, when revolved about the y-axis, will produce cylindrical shells whose volumes closely approximate the volumes of the tubes generated by the original strips (Figure 6.3.4b). We will show that by adding the volumes of the cylindrical shells we can obtain a Riemann sum that approximates the volume V, and by taking the limit of the Riemann sums we can obtain an integral for the exact volume V.

| Rectangle approximating the kth strip | Cylindrical shell generated by the rectangle |

▶ **Figure 6.3.4**   (a)   (b)

To implement this idea, suppose that the kth strip extends from x_{k-1} to x_k and that the width of this strip is

$$\Delta x_k = x_k - x_{k-1}$$

If we let x_k^* be the *midpoint* of the interval $[x_{k-1}, x_k]$, and if we construct a rectangle of height $f(x_k^*)$ over the interval, then revolving this rectangle about the y-axis produces a cylindrical shell of average radius x_k^*, height $f(x_k^*)$, and thickness Δx_k (Figure 6.3.5). From (1), the volume V_k of this cylindrical shell is

$$V_k = 2\pi x_k^* f(x_k^*) \Delta x_k$$

Adding the volumes of the n cylindrical shells yields the following Riemann sum that approximates the volume V:

$$V \approx \sum_{k=1}^{n} 2\pi x_k^* f(x_k^*) \Delta x_k$$

Taking the limit as n increases and the widths of all the subintervals approach zero yields the definite integral

$$V = \lim_{\max \Delta x_k \to 0} \sum_{k=1}^{n} 2\pi x_k^* f(x_k^*) \Delta x_k = \int_a^b 2\pi x f(x)\, dx$$

In summary, we have the following result.

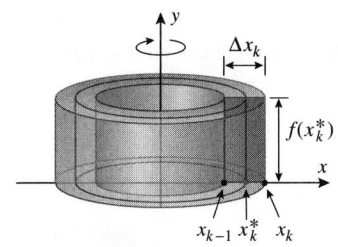

▲ **Figure 6.3.5**

6.3.2 **VOLUME BY CYLINDRICAL SHELLS ABOUT THE y-AXIS** Let f be continuous and nonnegative on $[a, b]$ $(0 \leq a < b)$, and let R be the region that is bounded above by $y = f(x)$, below by the x-axis, and on the sides by the lines $x = a$ and $x = b$. Then the volume V of the solid of revolution that is generated by revolving the region R about the y-axis is given by

$$V = \int_a^b 2\pi x f(x)\, dx \qquad (2)$$

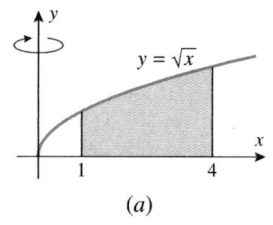

(a)

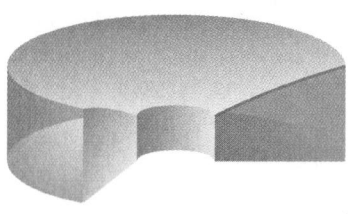

Cutaway view of the solid

(b)

▲ **Figure 6.3.6**

▶ **Example 1** Use cylindrical shells to find the volume of the solid generated when the region enclosed between $y = \sqrt{x}$, $x = 1$, $x = 4$, and the x-axis is revolved about the y-axis.

Solution. First sketch the region (Figure 6.3.6a); then imagine revolving it about the y-axis (Figure 6.3.6b). Since $f(x) = \sqrt{x}$, $a = 1$, and $b = 4$, Formula (2) yields

$$V = \int_1^4 2\pi x \sqrt{x}\, dx = 2\pi \int_1^4 x^{3/2}\, dx = \left[2\pi \cdot \frac{2}{5} x^{5/2} \right]_1^4 = \frac{4\pi}{5}[32 - 1] = \frac{124\pi}{5} \quad ◀$$

■ **VARIATIONS OF THE METHOD OF CYLINDRICAL SHELLS**

The method of cylindrical shells is applicable in a variety of situations that do not fit the conditions required by Formula (2). For example, the region may be enclosed between two curves, or the axis of revolution may be some line other than the y-axis. However, rather than develop a separate formula for every possible situation, we will give a general way of thinking about the method of cylindrical shells that can be adapted to each new situation as it arises.

For this purpose, we will need to reexamine the integrand in Formula (2): At each x in the interval $[a, b]$, the vertical line segment from the x-axis to the curve $y = f(x)$ can be viewed as the cross section of the region R at x (Figure 6.3.7a). When the region R is revolved about the y-axis, the cross section at x sweeps out the *surface* of a right circular cylinder of height $f(x)$ and radius x (Figure 6.3.7b). The area of this surface is

$$2\pi x f(x)$$

(Figure 6.3.7c), which is the integrand in (2). Thus, Formula (2) can be viewed informally in the following way.

6.3.3 **AN INFORMAL VIEWPOINT ABOUT CYLINDRICAL SHELLS** The volume V of a solid of revolution that is generated by revolving a region R about an axis can be obtained by integrating the area of the surface generated by an arbitrary cross section of R taken parallel to the axis of revolution.

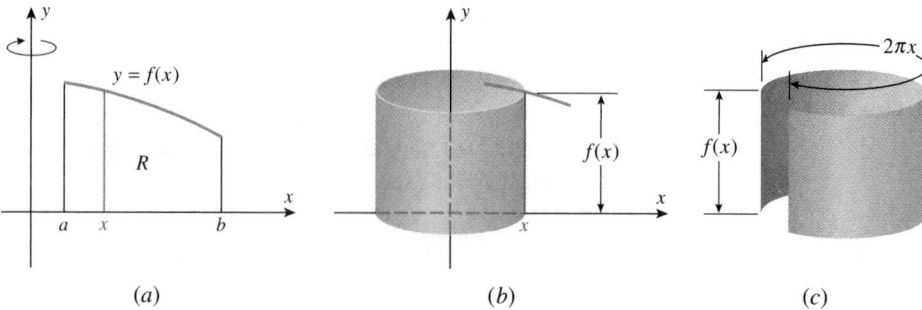

▶ **Figure 6.3.7**

(a)   (b)   (c)

The following examples illustrate how to apply this result in situations where Formula (2) is not applicable.

▶ **Example 2**   Use cylindrical shells to find the volume of the solid generated when the region R in the first quadrant enclosed between $y = x$ and $y = x^2$ is revolved about the y-axis (Figure 6.3.8a).

Solution.   As illustrated in part (b) of Figure 6.3.8, at each x in [0, 1] the cross section of R parallel to the y-axis generates a cylindrical surface of height $x - x^2$ and radius x. Since the area of this surface is

$$2\pi x(x - x^2)$$

the volume of the solid is

$$V = \int_0^1 2\pi x(x - x^2)\,dx = 2\pi \int_0^1 (x^2 - x^3)\,dx$$

$$= 2\pi\left[\frac{x^3}{3} - \frac{x^4}{4}\right]_0^1 = 2\pi\left[\frac{1}{3} - \frac{1}{4}\right] = \frac{\pi}{6} \blacktriangleleft$$

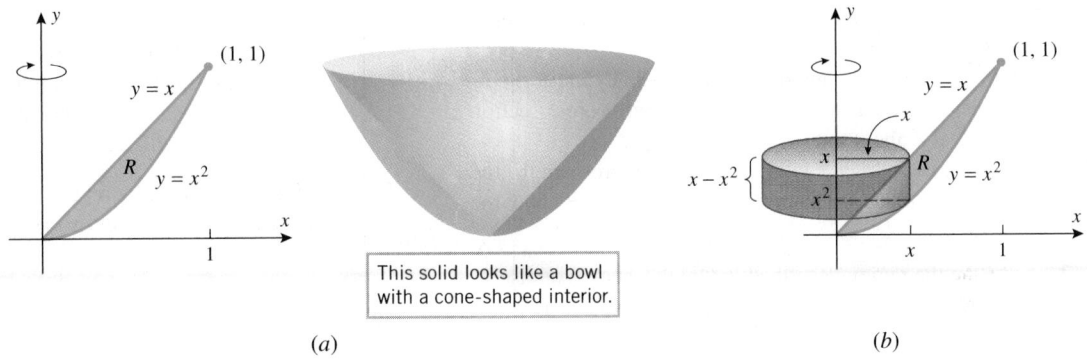

This solid looks like a bowl with a cone-shaped interior.

(a)   (b)

▲ **Figure 6.3.8**

▶ **Example 3**   Use cylindrical shells to find the volume of the solid generated when the region R under $y = x^2$ over the interval [0, 2] is revolved about the line $y = -1$.

Solution.   First draw the axis of revolution; then imagine revolving the region about the axis (Figure 6.3.9a). As illustrated in Figure 6.3.9b, at each y in the interval $0 \le y \le 4$, the cross section of R parallel to the x-axis generates a cylindrical surface of height $2 - \sqrt{y}$ and radius $y + 1$. Since the area of this surface is

$$2\pi(y + 1)(2 - \sqrt{y})$$

Note that the volume found in Example 3 agrees with the volume of the same solid found by the method of washers in Example 6 of Section 6.2. Confirm that the volume in Example 2 found by the method of cylindrical shells can also be obtained by the method of washers.

it follows that the volume of the solid is

$$\int_0^4 2\pi(y + 1)(2 - \sqrt{y})\,dy = 2\pi \int_0^4 (2y - y^{3/2} + 2 - y^{1/2})\,dy$$

$$= 2\pi\left[y^2 - \frac{2}{5}y^{5/2} + 2y - \frac{2}{3}y^{3/2}\right]_0^4 = \frac{176\pi}{15} \blacktriangleleft$$

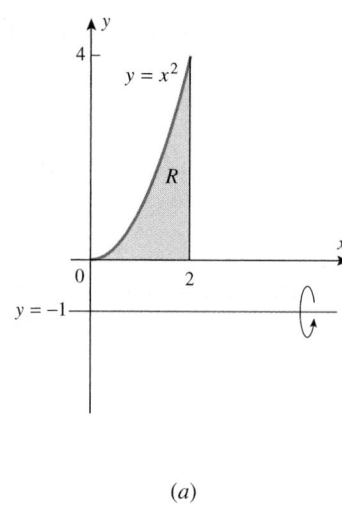

(a)

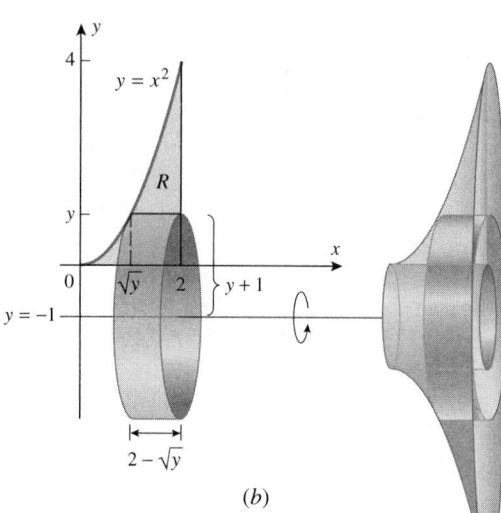

(b)

▶ **Figure 6.3.9**

✔ **QUICK CHECK EXERCISES 6.3**   *(See page 438 for answers.)*

1. Let R be the region between the x-axis and the curve $y = 1 + \sqrt{x}$ for $1 \leq x \leq 4$.
   (a) For x between 1 and 4, the area of the cylindrical surface generated by revolving the vertical cross section of R at x about the y-axis is _____.
   (b) Using cylindrical shells, an integral expression for the volume of the solid generated by revolving R about the y-axis is _____.

2. Let R be the region described in Quick Check Exercise 1.
   (a) For x between 1 and 4, the area of the cylindrical sur-

face generated by revolving the vertical cross section of R at x about the line $x = 5$ is _____.
   (b) Using cylindrical shells, an integral expression for the volume of the solid generated by revolving R about the line $x = 5$ is _____.

3. A solid S is generated by revolving the region enclosed by the curves $x = (y - 2)^2$ and $x = 4$ about the x-axis. Using cylindrical shells, an integral expression for the volume of S is _____.

EXERCISE SET 6.3   [C] CAS

1–4 Use cylindrical shells to find the volume of the solid generated when the shaded region is revolved about the indicated axis. ■

1.
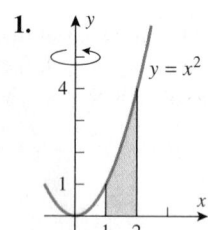

2.
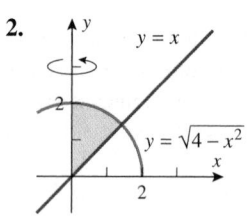

3.
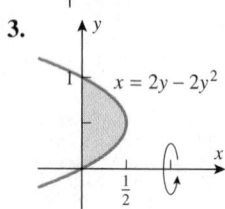

4.
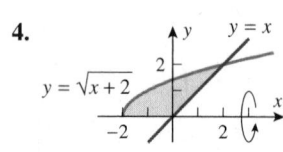

5–12 Use cylindrical shells to find the volume of the solid generated when the region enclosed by the given curves is revolved about the y-axis. ■

5. $y = x^3$, $x = 1$, $y = 0$

6. $y = \sqrt{x}$, $x = 4$, $x = 9$, $y = 0$

7. $y = 1/x$, $y = 0$, $x = 1$, $x = 3$

8. $y = \cos(x^2)$, $x = 0$, $x = \frac{1}{2}\sqrt{\pi}$, $y = 0$

9. $y = 2x - 1$, $y = -2x + 3$, $x = 2$

10. $y = 2x - x^2$, $y = 0$

11. $y = \dfrac{1}{x^2 + 1}$, $x = 0$, $x = 1$, $y = 0$

12. $y = e^{x^2}$, $x = 1$, $x = \sqrt{3}$, $y = 0$

13–16 Use cylindrical shells to find the volume of the solid generated when the region enclosed by the given curves is revolved about the x-axis. ■

13. $y^2 = x$, $y = 1$, $x = 0$

14. $x = 2y$, $y = 2$, $y = 3$, $x = 0$

15. $y = x^2$, $x = 1$, $y = 0$ **16.** $xy = 4$, $x + y = 5$

17–20 True–False Determine whether the statement is true or false. Explain your answer. ■

17. The volume of a cylindrical shell is equal to the product of the thickness of the shell with the surface area of a cylinder whose height is that of the shell and whose radius is equal to the average of the inner and outer radii of the shell.

18. The method of cylindrical shells is a special case of the method of integration of cross-sectional area that was discussed in Section 6.2.

19. In the method of cylindrical shells, integration is over an interval on a coordinate axis that is *perpendicular* to the axis of revolution of the solid.

20. The Riemann sum approximation

$$V \approx \sum_{k=1}^{n} 2\pi x_k^* f(x_k^*)\Delta x_k \quad \left(\text{where } x_k^* = \frac{x_k + x_{k-1}}{2}\right)$$

for the volume of a solid of revolution is exact when f is a constant function.

C **21.** Use a CAS to find the volume of the solid generated when the region enclosed by $y = e^x$ and $y = 0$ for $1 \le x \le 2$ is revolved about the y-axis.

C **22.** Use a CAS to find the volume of the solid generated when the region enclosed by $y = \cos x$, $y = 0$, and $x = 0$ for $0 \le x \le \pi/2$ is revolved about the y-axis.

C **23.** Consider the region to the right of the y-axis, to the left of the vertical line $x = k$ ($0 < k < \pi$), and between the curve $y = \sin x$ and the x-axis. Use a CAS to estimate the value of k so that the solid generated by revolving the region about the y-axis has a volume of 8 cubic units.

FOCUS ON CONCEPTS

24. Let R_1 and R_2 be regions of the form shown in the accompanying figure. Use cylindrical shells to find a formula for the volume of the solid that results when
 (a) region R_1 is revolved about the y-axis
 (b) region R_2 is revolved about the x-axis.

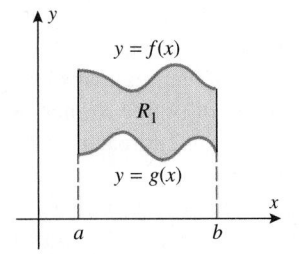
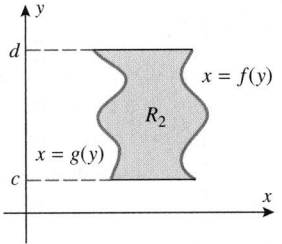

▲ **Figure Ex-24**

25. (a) Use cylindrical shells to find the volume of the solid that is generated when the region under the curve

$$y = x^3 - 3x^2 + 2x$$

over [0, 1] is revolved about the y-axis.
 (b) For this problem, is the method of cylindrical shells easier or harder than the method of slicing discussed in the last section? Explain.

26. Let f be continuous and nonnegative on $[a, b]$, and let R be the region that is enclosed by $y = f(x)$ and $y = 0$ for $a \le x \le b$. Using the method of cylindrical shells, derive with explanation a formula for the volume of the solid generated by revolving R about the line $x = k$, where $k \le a$.

27–28 Using the method of cylindrical shells, set up but do not evaluate an integral for the volume of the solid generated when the region R is revolved about (a) the line $x = 1$ and (b) the line $y = -1$. ■

27. R is the region bounded by the graphs of $y = x$, $y = 0$, and $x = 1$.

28. R is the region in the first quadrant bounded by the graphs of $y = \sqrt{1 - x^2}$, $y = 0$, and $x = 0$.

29. Use cylindrical shells to find the volume of the solid that is generated when the region that is enclosed by $y = 1/x^3$, $x = 1$, $x = 2$, $y = 0$ is revolved about the line $x = -1$.

30. Use cylindrical shells to find the volume of the solid that is generated when the region that is enclosed by $y = x^3$, $y = 1$, $x = 0$ is revolved about the line $y = 1$.

31. Use cylindrical shells to find the volume of the cone generated when the triangle with vertices $(0, 0)$, $(0, r)$, $(h, 0)$, where $r > 0$ and $h > 0$, is revolved about the x-axis.

32. The region enclosed between the curve $y^2 = kx$ and the line $x = \frac{1}{4}k$ is revolved about the line $x = \frac{1}{2}k$. Use cylindrical shells to find the volume of the resulting solid. (Assume $k > 0$.)

33. As shown in the accompanying figure, a cylindrical hole is drilled all the way through the center of a sphere. Show that the volume of the remaining solid depends only on the length L of the hole, not on the size of the sphere.

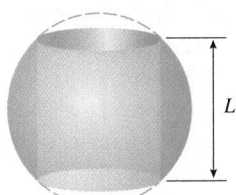

◀ **Figure Ex-33**

34. Use cylindrical shells to find the volume of the torus obtained by revolving the circle $x^2 + y^2 = a^2$ about the line

$x = b$, where $b > a > 0$. [*Hint:* It may help in the integration to think of an integral as an area.]

35. Let V_x and V_y be the volumes of the solids that result when the region enclosed by $y = 1/x$, $y = 0$, $x = \frac{1}{2}$, and $x = b$ $(b > \frac{1}{2})$ is revolved about the x-axis and y-axis, respectively. Is there a value of b for which $V_x = V_y$?

36. (a) Find the volume V of the solid generated when the region bounded by $y = 1/(1 + x^4)$, $y = 0$, $x = 1$, and $x = b$ $(b > 1)$ is revolved about the y-axis.
   (b) Find $\lim\limits_{b \to +\infty} V$.

37. Writing   Faced with the problem of computing the volume of a solid of revolution, how would you go about deciding whether to use the method of disks/washers or the method of cylindrical shells?

38. Writing   With both the method of disks/washers and with the method of cylindrical shells, we integrate an "area" to get the volume of a solid of revolution. However, these two approaches differ in very significant ways. Write a brief paragraph that discusses these differences.

✔ **QUICK CHECK ANSWERS 6.3**

1. (a) $2\pi x(1 + \sqrt{x})$ (b) $\int_1^4 2\pi x(1 + \sqrt{x})\,dx$ **2.** (a) $2\pi(5 - x)(1 + \sqrt{x})$ (b) $\int_1^4 2\pi(5 - x)(1 + \sqrt{x})\,dx$

3. $\int_0^4 2\pi y[4 - (y - 2)^2]\,dy$

6.4   LENGTH OF A PLANE CURVE

In this section we will use the tools of calculus to study the problem of finding the length of a plane curve.

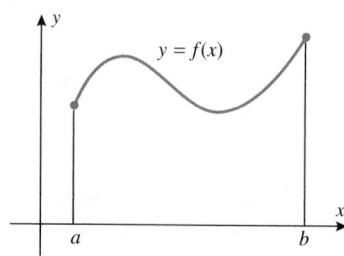

▲ **Figure 6.4.1**

Intuitively, you might think of the arc length of a curve as the number obtained by aligning a piece of string with the curve and then measuring the length of the string after it is straightened out.

■ **ARC LENGTH**

Our first objective is to define what we mean by the *length* (also called the *arc length*) of a plane curve $y = f(x)$ over an interval $[a, b]$ (Figure 6.4.1). Once that is done we will be able to focus on the problem of computing arc lengths. To avoid some complications that would otherwise occur, we will impose the requirement that f' be continuous on $[a, b]$, in which case we will say that $y = f(x)$ is a *smooth curve* on $[a, b]$ or that f is a *smooth function* on $[a, b]$. Thus, we will be concerned with the following problem.

> **6.4.1   ARC LENGTH PROBLEM**   Suppose that $y = f(x)$ is a smooth curve on the interval $[a, b]$. Define and find a formula for the arc length L of the curve $y = f(x)$ over the interval $[a, b]$.

To define the arc length of a curve we start by breaking the curve into small segments. Then we approximate the curve segments by line segments and add the lengths of the line segments to form a Riemann sum. Figure 6.4.2 illustrates how such line segments tend to become better and better approximations to a curve as the number of segments increases. As the number of segments increases, the corresponding Riemann sums approach a definite integral whose value we will take to be the arc length L of the curve.

To implement our idea for solving Problem 6.4.1, divide the interval $[a, b]$ into n subintervals by inserting points $x_1, x_2, \ldots, x_{n-1}$ between $a = x_0$ and $b = x_n$. As shown in Figure 6.4.3a, let $P_0, P_1, \ldots, P_n$ be the points on the curve with x-coordinates $a = x_0$,

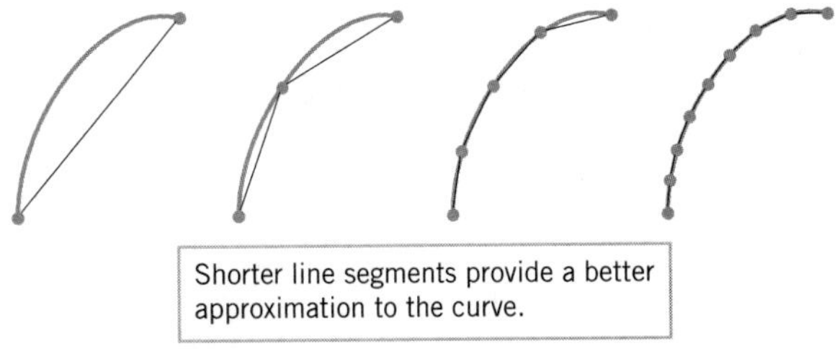

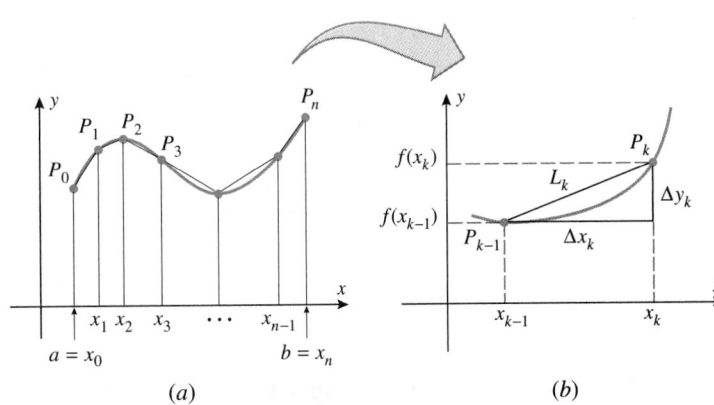

Shorter line segments provide a better approximation to the curve.

▶ **Figure 6.4.2**

▶ **Figure 6.4.3**   *(a)*   *(b)*

$x_1, x_2, \ldots, x_{n-1}, b = x_n$ and join these points with straight line segments. These line segments form a ***polygonal path*** that we can regard as an approximation to the curve $y = f(x)$. As indicated in Figure 6.4.3b, the length L_k of the kth line segment in the polygonal path is

$$L_k = \sqrt{(\Delta x_k)^2 + (\Delta y_k)^2} = \sqrt{(\Delta x_k)^2 + [f(x_k) - f(x_{k-1})]^2} \tag{1}$$

If we now add the lengths of these line segments, we obtain the following approximation to the length L of the curve

$$L \approx \sum_{k=1}^{n} L_k = \sum_{k=1}^{n} \sqrt{(\Delta x_k)^2 + [f(x_k) - f(x_{k-1})]^2} \tag{2}$$

To put this in the form of a Riemann sum we will apply the Mean-Value Theorem (4.8.2). This theorem implies that there is a point x_k^* between x_{k-1} and x_k such that

$$\frac{f(x_k) - f(x_{k-1})}{x_k - x_{k-1}} = f'(x_k^*) \quad \text{or} \quad f(x_k) - f(x_{k-1}) = f'(x_k^*) \Delta x_k$$

and hence we can rewrite (2) as

$$L \approx \sum_{k=1}^{n} \sqrt{(\Delta x_k)^2 + [f'(x_k^*)]^2 (\Delta x_k)^2} = \sum_{k=1}^{n} \sqrt{1 + [f'(x_k^*)]^2} \, \Delta x_k$$

Explain why the approximation in (2) cannot be greater than L.

Thus, taking the limit as n increases and the widths of all the subintervals approach zero yields the following integral that defines the arc length L:

$$L = \lim_{\max \Delta x_k \to 0} \sum_{k=1}^{n} \sqrt{1 + [f'(x_k^*)]^2} \, \Delta x_k = \int_a^b \sqrt{1 + [f'(x)]^2} \, dx$$

In summary, we have the following definition.

> **6.4.2   DEFINITION**   If $y = f(x)$ is a smooth curve on the interval $[a, b]$, then the arc length L of this curve over $[a, b]$ is defined as
>
> $$L = \int_a^b \sqrt{1 + [f'(x)]^2}\, dx \qquad (3)$$

This result provides both a definition and a formula for computing arc lengths. Where convenient, (3) can also be expressed as

$$L = \int_a^b \sqrt{1 + [f'(x)]^2}\, dx = \int_a^b \sqrt{1 + \left(\frac{dy}{dx}\right)^2}\, dx \qquad (4)$$

Moreover, for a curve expressed in the form $x = g(y)$, where g' is continuous on $[c, d]$, the arc length L from $y = c$ to $y = d$ can be expressed as

$$L = \int_c^d \sqrt{1 + [g'(y)]^2}\, dy = \int_c^d \sqrt{1 + \left(\frac{dx}{dy}\right)^2}\, dy \qquad (5)$$

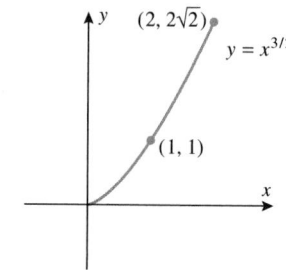

▲ **Figure 6.4.4**

▶ **Example 1**   Find the arc length of the curve $y = x^{3/2}$ from $(1, 1)$ to $(2, 2\sqrt{2})$ (Figure 6.4.4) in two ways: (a) using Formula (4) and (b) using Formula (5).

Solution (a).
$$\frac{dy}{dx} = \frac{3}{2}x^{1/2}$$

and since the curve extends from $x = 1$ to $x = 2$, it follows from (4) that

$$L = \int_1^2 \sqrt{1 + \left(\tfrac{3}{2}x^{1/2}\right)^2}\, dx = \int_1^2 \sqrt{1 + \tfrac{9}{4}x}\, dx$$

To evaluate this integral we make the u-substitution

$$u = 1 + \tfrac{9}{4}x, \quad du = \tfrac{9}{4}\, dx$$

and then change the x-limits of integration $(x = 1, x = 2)$ to the corresponding u-limits $\left(u = \tfrac{13}{4}, u = \tfrac{22}{4}\right)$:

$$L = \frac{4}{9}\int_{13/4}^{22/4} u^{1/2}\, du = \frac{8}{27}u^{3/2}\Big]_{13/4}^{22/4} = \frac{8}{27}\left[\left(\frac{22}{4}\right)^{3/2} - \left(\frac{13}{4}\right)^{3/2}\right]$$

$$= \frac{22\sqrt{22} - 13\sqrt{13}}{27} \approx 2.09$$

Solution (b).   To apply Formula (5) we must first rewrite the equation $y = x^{3/2}$ so that x is expressed as a function of y. This yields $x = y^{2/3}$ and

$$\frac{dx}{dy} = \frac{2}{3}y^{-1/3}$$

Since the curve extends from $y = 1$ to $y = 2\sqrt{2}$, it follows from (5) that

$$L = \int_1^{2\sqrt{2}} \sqrt{1 + \tfrac{4}{9}y^{-2/3}}\, dy = \frac{1}{3}\int_1^{2\sqrt{2}} y^{-1/3}\sqrt{9y^{2/3} + 4}\, dy$$

To evaluate this integral we make the u-substitution

$$u = 9y^{2/3} + 4, \quad du = 6y^{-1/3}\,dy$$

and change the y-limits of integration ($y = 1$, $y = 2\sqrt{2}$) to the corresponding u-limits ($u = 13$, $u = 22$). This gives

$$L = \frac{1}{18}\int_{13}^{22} u^{1/2}\,du = \frac{1}{27}u^{3/2}\Big]_{13}^{22} = \frac{1}{27}[(22)^{3/2} - (13)^{3/2}] = \frac{22\sqrt{22} - 13\sqrt{13}}{27}$$

The answer in part (b) agrees with that in part (a); however, the integration in part (b) is more tedious. In problems where there is a choice between using (4) or (5), it is often the case that one of the formulas leads to a simpler integral than the other. ◄

> The arc from the point $(1, 1)$ to the point $(2, 2\sqrt{2})$ in Figure 6.4.4 is nearly a straight line, so the arc length should be only slightly larger than the straight-line distance between these points. Show that this is so.

■ FINDING ARC LENGTH BY NUMERICAL METHODS

In the next chapter we will develop some techniques of integration that will enable us to find exact values of more integrals encountered in arc length calculations; however, generally speaking, most such integrals are impossible to evaluate in terms of elementary functions. In these cases one usually approximates the integral using a numerical method such as the midpoint rule discussed in Section 5.4.

TECHNOLOGY MASTERY

If your calculating utility has a numerical integration capability, use it to confirm that the arc length L in Example 2 is approximately $L \approx 3.8202$.

▶ **Example 2**   From (4), the arc length of $y = \sin x$ from $x = 0$ to $x = \pi$ is given by the integral

$$L = \int_0^\pi \sqrt{1 + (\cos x)^2}\,dx$$

This integral cannot be evaluated in terms of elementary functions; however, using a calculating utility with a numerical integration capability yields the approximation $L \approx 3.8202$. ◄

✔ **QUICK CHECK EXERCISES 6.4**   *(See page 443 for answers.)*

1. A function f is smooth on $[a, b]$ if f' is _____ on $[a, b]$.

2. If a function f is smooth on $[a, b]$, then the length of the curve $y = f(x)$ over $[a, b]$ is _____.

3. The distance between points $(1, 0)$ and $(e, 1)$ is _____.

4. Let L be the length of the curve $y = \ln x$ from $(1, 0)$ to $(e, 1)$.
   (a) Integrating with respect to x, an integral expression for L is _____.
   (b) Integrating with respect to y, an integral expression for L is _____.

EXERCISE SET 6.4   [c] CAS

1. Use the Theorem of Pythagoras to find the length of the line segment $y = 2x$ from $(1, 2)$ to $(2, 4)$, and confirm that the value is consistent with the length computed using
   (a) Formula (4)   (b) Formula (5).

2. Use the Theorem of Pythagoras to find the length of the line segment $y = 5x$ from $(0, 0)$ and $(1, 5)$, and confirm that the value is consistent with the length computed using
   (a) Formula (4)   (b) Formula (5).

3–8 Find the exact arc length of the curve over the interval. ■

3. $y = 3x^{3/2} - 1$ from $x = 0$ to $x = 1$

4. $x = \frac{1}{3}(y^2 + 2)^{3/2}$ from $y = 0$ to $y = 1$

5. $y = x^{2/3}$ from $x = 1$ to $x = 8$

6. $y = (x^6 + 8)/(16x^2)$ from $x = 2$ to $x = 3$

7. $24xy = y^4 + 48$ from $y = 2$ to $y = 4$

8. $x = \frac{1}{8}y^4 + \frac{1}{4}y^{-2}$ from $y = 1$ to $y = 4$

9–12 True–False Determine whether the statement is true or false. Explain your answer. ■

9. The graph of $y = \sqrt{1 - x^2}$ is a smooth curve on $[-1, 1]$.

10. The approximation

$$L \approx \sum_{k=1}^{n} \sqrt{(\Delta x_k)^2 + [f(x_k) - f(x_{k-1})]^2}$$

for arc length is not expressed in the form of a Riemann sum.

11. The approximation

$$L \approx \sum_{k=1}^{n} \sqrt{1 + [f'(x_k^*)]^2}\, \Delta x_k$$

for arc length is exact when f is a linear function of x.

12. In our definition of the arc length for the graph of $y = f(x)$, we need $f'(x)$ to be a continuous function in order for f to satisfy the hypotheses of the Mean-Value Theorem (4.8.2).

[C] **13–14** Express the exact arc length of the curve over the given interval as an integral that has been simplified to eliminate the radical, and then evaluate the integral using a CAS. ■

13. $y = \ln(\sec x)$ from $x = 0$ to $x = \pi/4$

14. $y = \ln(\sin x)$ from $x = \pi/4$ to $x = \pi/2$

FOCUS ON CONCEPTS

15. Consider the curve $y = x^{2/3}$.
  (a) Sketch the portion of the curve between $x = -1$ and $x = 8$.
  (b) Explain why Formula (4) cannot be used to find the arc length of the curve sketched in part (a).
  (c) Find the arc length of the curve sketched in part (a).

16. The curve segment $y = x^2$ from $x = 1$ to $x = 2$ may also be expressed as the graph of $x = \sqrt{y}$ from $y = 1$ to $y = 4$. Set up two integrals that give the arc length of this curve segment, one by integrating with respect to x, and the other by integrating with respect to y. Demonstrate a substitution that verifies that these two integrals are equal.

17. Consider the curve segments $y = x^2$ from $x = \frac{1}{2}$ to $x = 2$ and $y = \sqrt{x}$ from $x = \frac{1}{4}$ to $x = 4$.
  (a) Graph the two curve segments and use your graphs to explain why the lengths of these two curve segments should be equal.
  (b) Set up integrals that give the arc lengths of the curve segments by integrating with respect to x. Demonstrate a substitution that verifies that these two integrals are equal.
  (c) Set up integrals that give the arc lengths of the curve segments by integrating with respect to y.
  (d) Approximate the arc length of each curve segment using Formula (2) with $n = 10$ equal subintervals.
  (e) Which of the two approximations in part (d) is more accurate? Explain.
  (f) Use the midpoint approximation with $n = 10$ subintervals to approximate each arc length integral in part (b).

  (g) Use a calculating utility with numerical integration capabilities to approximate the arc length integrals in part (b) to four decimal places.

18. Follow the directions of Exercise 17 for the curve segments $y = x^{8/3}$ from $x = 10^{-3}$ to $x = 1$ and $y = x^{3/8}$ from $x = 10^{-8}$ to $x = 1$.

19. Follow the directions of Exercise 17 for the curve segment $y = \tan x$ from $x = 0$ to $x = \pi/3$ and for the curve segment $y = \tan^{-1} x$ from $x = 0$ to $x = \sqrt{3}$.

20. Let $y = f(x)$ be a smooth curve on the closed interval $[a, b]$. Prove that if m and M are nonnegative numbers such that $m \le |f'(x)| \le M$ for all x in $[a, b]$, then the arc length L of $y = f(x)$ over the interval $[a, b]$ satisfies the inequalities

$$(b - a)\sqrt{1 + m^2} \le L \le (b - a)\sqrt{1 + M^2}$$

21. Use the result of Exercise 20 to show that the arc length L of $y = \sec x$ over the interval $0 \le x \le \pi/3$ satisfies

$$\frac{\pi}{3} \le L \le \frac{\pi}{3}\sqrt{13}$$

[C] **22.** A basketball player makes a successful shot from the free throw line. Suppose that the path of the ball from the moment of release to the moment it enters the hoop is described by

$$y = 2.15 + 2.09x - 0.41x^2, \quad 0 \le x \le 4.6$$

where x is the horizontal distance (in meters) from the point of release, and y is the vertical distance (in meters) above the floor. Use a CAS or a scientific calculator with a numerical integration capability to approximate the distance the ball travels from the moment it is released to the moment it enters the hoop. Round your answer to two decimal places.

[C] **23.** Find a positive value of k (to two decimal places) such that the curve $y = k \sin x$ has an arc length of $L = 5$ units over the interval from $x = 0$ to $x = \pi$. [*Hint:* Find an integral for the arc length L in terms of k, and then use a CAS or a scientific calculator with a numerical integration capability to find integer values of k at which the values of $L - 5$ have opposite signs. Complete the solution by using the Intermediate-Value Theorem (1.5.7) to approximate the value of k to two decimal places.]

[C] **24.** As shown in the accompanying figure on the next page, a horizontal beam with dimensions 2 in × 6 in × 16 ft is fixed at both ends and is subjected to a uniformly distributed load of 120 lb/ft. As a result of the load, the centerline of the beam undergoes a deflection that is described by

$$y = -1.67 \times 10^{-8}(x^4 - 2Lx^3 + L^2x^2)$$

($0 \le x \le 192$), where $L = 192$ in is the length of the unloaded beam, x is the horizontal distance along the beam measured in inches from the left end, and y is the deflection of the centerline in inches.
  (a) Graph y versus x for $0 \le x \le 192$.
  (b) Find the maximum deflection of the centerline.   *(cont.)*

(c) Use a CAS or a calculator with a numerical integration capability to find the length of the centerline of the loaded beam. Round your answer to two decimal places.

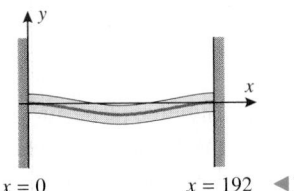

$x = 0$ $x = 192$ ◀ Figure Ex-24

[c] 25. A golfer makes a successful chip shot to the green. Suppose that the path of the ball from the moment it is struck to the moment it hits the green is described by

$$y = 12.54x - 0.41x^2$$

where x is the horizontal distance (in yards) from the point where the ball is struck, and y is the vertical distance (in yards) above the fairway. Use a CAS or a calculating utility with a numerical integration capability to find the distance the ball travels from the moment it is struck to the moment it hits the green. Assume that the fairway and green are at the same level and round your answer to two decimal places.

26–34 These exercises assume familiarity with the basic concepts of parametric curves. If needed, an introduction to this material is provided in Web Appendix I. ■

[c] 26. Assume that no segment of the curve

$$x = x(t), \quad y = y(t), \quad (a \le t \le b)$$

is traced more than once as t increases from a to b. Divide the interval $[a, b]$ into n subintervals by inserting points $t_1, t_2, \dots, t_{n-1}$ between $a = t_0$ and $b = t_n$. Let L denote the arc length of the curve. Give an informal argument for the approximation

$$L \approx \sum_{k=1}^{n} \sqrt{[x(t_k) - x(t_{k-1})]^2 + [y(t_k) - y(t_{k-1})]^2}$$

If dx/dt and dy/dt are continuous functions for $a \le t \le b$, then it can be shown that as max $\Delta t_k \to 0$, this sum converges to

$$L = \int_a^b \sqrt{\left(\frac{dx}{dt}\right)^2 + \left(\frac{dy}{dt}\right)^2} \, dt$$

27–32 Use the arc length formula from Exercise 26 to find the arc length of the curve. ■

27. $x = \frac{1}{3}t^3, \quad y = \frac{1}{2}t^2 \quad (0 \le t \le 1)$

28. $x = (1 + t)^2, \quad y = (1 + t)^3 \quad (0 \le t \le 1)$

29. $x = \cos 2t, \quad y = \sin 2t \quad (0 \le t \le \pi/2)$

30. $x = \cos t + t \sin t, \quad y = \sin t - t \cos t \quad (0 \le t \le \pi)$

31. $x = e^t \cos t, \quad y = e^t \sin t \quad (0 \le t \le \pi/2)$

32. $x = e^t(\sin t + \cos t), \quad y = e^t(\cos t - \sin t) \quad (1 \le t \le 4)$

[c] 33. (a) Show that the total arc length of the ellipse

$$x = 2\cos t, \quad y = \sin t \quad (0 \le t \le 2\pi)$$

is given by

$$4 \int_0^{\pi/2} \sqrt{1 + 3\sin^2 t} \, dt$$

(b) Use a CAS or a scientific calculator with a numerical integration capability to approximate the arc length in part (a). Round your answer to two decimal places.

(c) Suppose that the parametric equations in part (a) describe the path of a particle moving in the xy-plane, where t is time in seconds and x and y are in centimeters. Use a CAS or a scientific calculator with a numerical integration capability to approximate the distance traveled by the particle from $t = 1.5$ s to $t = 4.8$ s. Round your answer to two decimal places.

34. Show that the total arc length of the ellipse $x = a\cos t$, $y = b\sin t, 0 \le t \le 2\pi$ for $a > b > 0$ is given by

$$4a \int_0^{\pi/2} \sqrt{1 - k^2 \cos^2 t} \, dt$$

where $k = \sqrt{a^2 - b^2}/a$.

35. **Writing** In our discussion of Arc Length Problem 6.4.1, we derived the approximation

$$L \approx \sum_{k=1}^{n} \sqrt{1 + [f'(x_k^*)]^2} \, \Delta x_k$$

Discuss the geometric meaning of this approximation. (Be sure to address the appearance of the derivative f'.)

36. **Writing** Give examples in which Formula (4) for arc length cannot be applied directly, and describe how you would go about finding the arc length of the curve in each case. (Discuss both the use of alternative formulas and the use of numerical methods.)

✔**QUICK CHECK ANSWERS 6.4**

1. continuous   2. $\int_a^b \sqrt{1 + [f'(x)]^2} \, dx$ 3. $\sqrt{(e-1)^2 + 1}$ 4. (a) $\int_1^e \sqrt{1 + (1/x)^2} \, dx$ (b) $\int_0^1 \sqrt{1 + e^{2y}} \, dy$

6.5 AREA OF A SURFACE OF REVOLUTION

In this section we will consider the problem of finding the area of a surface that is generated by revolving a plane curve about a line.

■ SURFACE AREA

A *surface of revolution* is a surface that is generated by revolving a plane curve about an axis that lies in the same plane as the curve. For example, the surface of a sphere can be generated by revolving a semicircle about its diameter, and the lateral surface of a right circular cylinder can be generated by revolving a line segment about an axis that is parallel to it (Figure 6.5.1).

Some Surfaces of Revolution

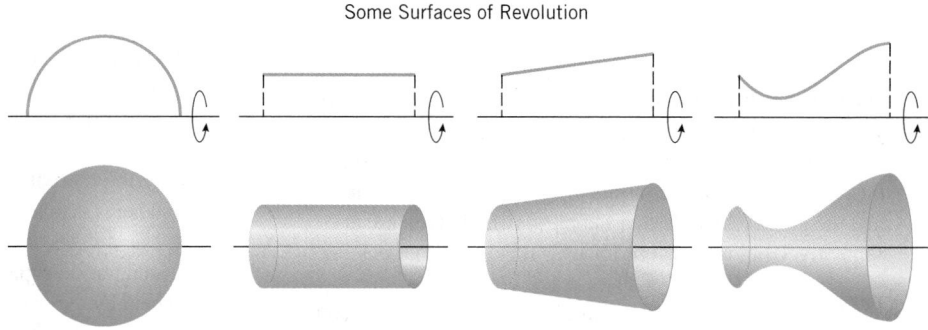

▶ **Figure 6.5.1**

In this section we will be concerned with the following problem.

6.5.1   SURFACE AREA PROBLEM   Suppose that f is a smooth, nonnegative function on $[a, b]$ and that a surface of revolution is generated by revolving the portion of the curve $y = f(x)$ between $x = a$ and $x = b$ about the x-axis (Figure 6.5.2). Define what is meant by the *area S* of the surface, and find a formula for computing it.

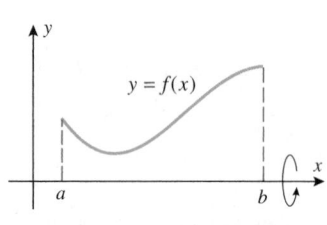

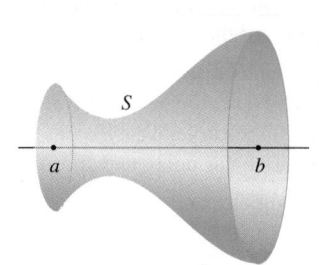

▲ **Figure 6.5.2**

To motivate an appropriate definition for the area S of a surface of revolution, we will decompose the surface into small sections whose areas can be approximated by elementary formulas, add the approximations of the areas of the sections to form a Riemann sum that approximates S, and then take the limit of the Riemann sums to obtain an integral for the exact value of S.

To implement this idea, divide the interval $[a, b]$ into n subintervals by inserting points x_1, $x_2, \ldots, x_{n-1}$ between $a = x_0$ and $b = x_n$. As illustrated in Figure 6.5.3a, the corresponding points on the graph of f define a polygonal path that approximates the curve $y = f(x)$ over the interval $[a, b]$. As illustrated in Figure 6.5.3b, when this polygonal path is revolved about the x-axis, it generates a surface consisting of n parts, each of which is a portion of a right circular cone called a *frustum* (from the Latin meaning "bit" or "piece"). Thus, the area of each part of the approximating surface can be obtained from the formula

$$S = \pi(r_1 + r_2)l \tag{1}$$

for the lateral area S of a frustum of slant height l and base radii r_1 and r_2 (Figure 6.5.4). As suggested by Figure 6.5.5, the kth frustum has radii $f(x_{k-1})$ and $f(x_k)$ and height Δx_k. Its slant height is the length L_k of the kth line segment in the polygonal path, which from Formula (1) of Section 6.4 is

$$L_k = \sqrt{(\Delta x_k)^2 + [f(x_k) - f(x_{k-1})]^2}$$

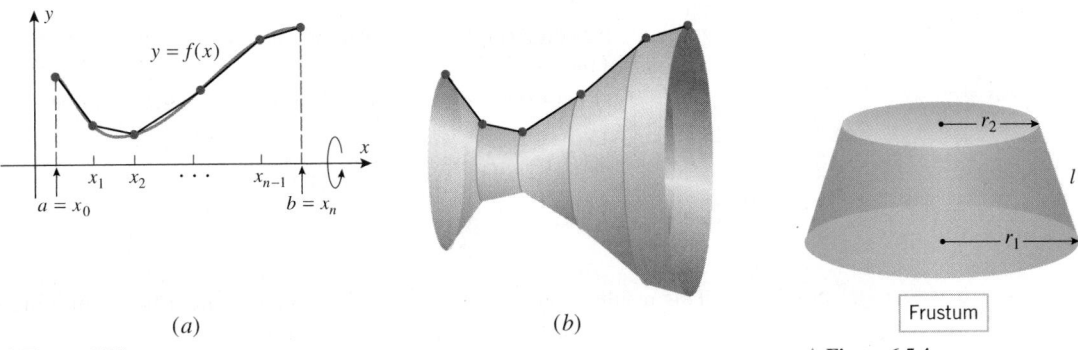

(a)

▲ Figure 6.5.3

(b)

Frustum

▲ Figure 6.5.4

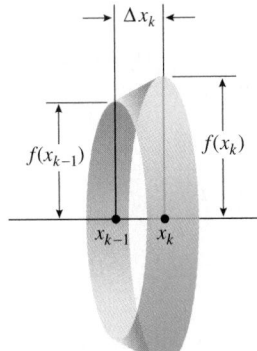

▲ Figure 6.5.5

This makes the lateral area S_k of the kth frustum

$$S_k = \pi[f(x_{k-1}) + f(x_k)]\sqrt{(\Delta x_k)^2 + [f(x_k) - f(x_{k-1})]^2}$$

If we add these areas, we obtain the following approximation to the area S of the entire surface:

$$S \approx \sum_{k=1}^{n} \pi[f(x_{k-1}) + f(x_k)]\sqrt{(\Delta x_k)^2 + [f(x_k) - f(x_{k-1})]^2} \qquad (2)$$

To put this in the form of a Riemann sum we will apply the Mean-Value Theorem (4.8.2). This theorem implies that there is a point x_k^* between x_{k-1} and x_k such that

$$\frac{f(x_k) - f(x_{k-1})}{x_k - x_{k-1}} = f'(x_k^*) \quad \text{or} \quad f(x_k) - f(x_{k-1}) = f'(x_k^*)\Delta x_k$$

and hence we can rewrite (2) as

$$S \approx \sum_{k=1}^{n} \pi[f(x_{k-1}) + f(x_k)]\sqrt{(\Delta x_k)^2 + [f'(x_k^*)]^2(\Delta x_k)^2}$$

$$= \sum_{k=1}^{n} \pi[f(x_{k-1}) + f(x_k)]\sqrt{1 + [f'(x_k^*)]^2}\,\Delta x_k \qquad (3)$$

However, this is not yet a Riemann sum because it involves the variables x_{k-1} and x_k. To eliminate these variables from the expression, observe that the average value of the numbers $f(x_{k-1})$ and $f(x_k)$ lies between these numbers, so the continuity of f and the Intermediate-Value Theorem (1.5.7) imply that there is a point x_k^{**} between x_{k-1} and x_k such that

$$\tfrac{1}{2}[f(x_{k-1}) + f(x_k)] = f(x_k^{**})$$

Thus, (2) can be expressed as

$$S \approx \sum_{k=1}^{n} 2\pi f(x_k^{**})\sqrt{1 + [f'(x_k^*)]^2}\,\Delta x_k$$

Although this expression is close to a Riemann sum in form, it is not a true Riemann sum because it involves two variables x_k^* and x_k^{**}, rather than x_k^* alone. However, it is proved in advanced calculus courses that this has no effect on the limit because of the continuity of f. Thus, we can assume that $x_k^{**} = x_k^*$ when taking the limit, and this suggests that S can be defined as

$$S = \lim_{\max \Delta x_k \to 0} \sum_{k=1}^{n} 2\pi f(x_k^{**})\sqrt{1 + [f'(x_k^*)]^2}\,\Delta x_k = \int_a^b 2\pi f(x)\sqrt{1 + [f'(x)]^2}\,dx$$

In summary, we have the following definition.

6.5.2   DEFINITION   If f is a smooth, nonnegative function on $[a, b]$, then the surface area S of the surface of revolution that is generated by revolving the portion of the curve $y = f(x)$ between $x = a$ and $x = b$ about the x-axis is defined as

$$S = \int_a^b 2\pi f(x)\sqrt{1 + [f'(x)]^2}\, dx$$

This result provides both a definition and a formula for computing surface areas. Where convenient, this formula can also be expressed as

$$S = \int_a^b 2\pi f(x)\sqrt{1 + [f'(x)]^2}\, dx = \int_a^b 2\pi y\sqrt{1 + \left(\frac{dy}{dx}\right)^2}\, dx \qquad (4)$$

Moreover, if g is nonnegative and $x = g(y)$ is a smooth curve on the interval $[c, d]$, then the area of the surface that is generated by revolving the portion of a curve $x = g(y)$ between $y = c$ and $y = d$ about the y-axis can be expressed as

$$S = \int_c^d 2\pi g(y)\sqrt{1 + [g'(y)]^2}\, dy = \int_c^d 2\pi x\sqrt{1 + \left(\frac{dx}{dy}\right)^2}\, dy \qquad (5)$$

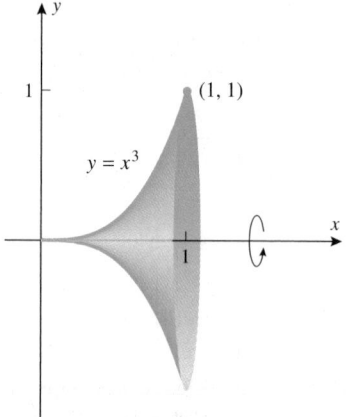

▲ **Figure 6.5.6**

▶ **Example 1**   Find the area of the surface that is generated by revolving the portion of the curve $y = x^3$ between $x = 0$ and $x = 1$ about the x-axis.

Solution.   First sketch the curve; then imagine revolving it about the x-axis (Figure 6.5.6). Since $y = x^3$, we have $dy/dx = 3x^2$, and hence from (4) the surface area S is

$$S = \int_0^1 2\pi y\sqrt{1 + \left(\frac{dy}{dx}\right)^2}\, dx$$

$$= \int_0^1 2\pi x^3\sqrt{1 + (3x^2)^2}\, dx$$

$$= 2\pi \int_0^1 x^3(1 + 9x^4)^{1/2}\, dx$$

$$= \frac{2\pi}{36} \int_1^{10} u^{1/2}\, du \qquad \boxed{\begin{array}{l} u = 1 + 9x^4 \\ du = 36x^3\, dx \end{array}}$$

$$= \frac{2\pi}{36} \cdot \frac{2}{3} u^{3/2}\Big]_{u=1}^{10} = \frac{\pi}{27}(10^{3/2} - 1) \approx 3.56 \blacktriangleleft$$

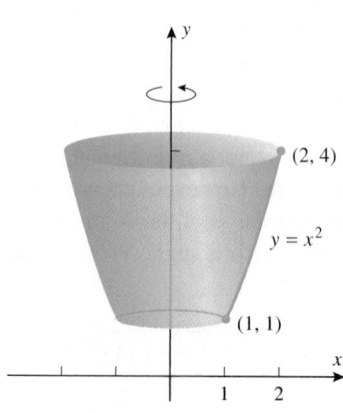

▲ **Figure 6.5.7**

▶ **Example 2**   Find the area of the surface that is generated by revolving the portion of the curve $y = x^2$ between $x = 1$ and $x = 2$ about the y-axis.

Solution.   First sketch the curve; then imagine revolving it about the y-axis (Figure 6.5.7). Because the curve is revolved about the y-axis we will apply Formula (5). Toward this end, we rewrite $y = x^2$ as $x = \sqrt{y}$ and observe that the y-values corresponding to $x = 1$ and

$x = 2$ are $y = 1$ and $y = 4$. Since $x = \sqrt{y}$, we have $dx/dy = 1/(2\sqrt{y})$, and hence from (5) the surface area S is

$$S = \int_1^4 2\pi x \sqrt{1 + \left(\frac{dx}{dy}\right)^2}\, dy$$

$$= \int_1^4 2\pi \sqrt{y} \sqrt{1 + \left(\frac{1}{2\sqrt{y}}\right)^2}\, dy$$

$$= \pi \int_1^4 \sqrt{4y + 1}\, dy$$

$$= \frac{\pi}{4} \int_5^{17} u^{1/2}\, du \qquad \boxed{\begin{array}{l} u = 4y + 1 \\ du = 4\,dy \end{array}}$$

$$= \frac{\pi}{4} \cdot \frac{2}{3} u^{3/2} \Big]_{u=5}^{17} = \frac{\pi}{6}(17^{3/2} - 5^{3/2}) \approx 30.85 \blacktriangleleft$$

✔ QUICK CHECK EXERCISES 6.5   (See page 449 for answers.)

1. If f is a smooth, nonnegative function on $[a, b]$, then the surface area S of the surface of revolution generated by revolving the portion of the curve $y = f(x)$ between $x = a$ and $x = b$ about the x-axis is _____.

2. The lateral area of the frustum with slant height $\sqrt{10}$ and base radii $r_1 = 1$ and $r_2 = 2$ is _____.

3. An integral expression for the area of the surface generated by rotating the line segment joining $(3, 1)$ and $(6, 2)$ about the x-axis is _____.

4. An integral expression for the area of the surface generated by rotating the line segment joining $(3, 1)$ and $(6, 2)$ about the y-axis is _____.

EXERCISE SET 6.5   [c] CAS

1–4 Find the area of the surface generated by revolving the given curve about the x-axis. ■

1. $y = 7x,\ 0 \le x \le 1$

2. $y = \sqrt{x},\ 1 \le x \le 4$

3. $y = \sqrt{4 - x^2},\ -1 \le x \le 1$

4. $x = \sqrt[3]{y},\ 1 \le y \le 8$

5–8 Find the area of the surface generated by revolving the given curve about the y-axis. ■

5. $x = 9y + 1,\ 0 \le y \le 2$

6. $x = y^3,\ 0 \le y \le 1$

7. $x = \sqrt{9 - y^2},\ -2 \le y \le 2$

8. $x = 2\sqrt{1 - y},\ -1 \le y \le 0$

[c] 9–12 Use a CAS to find the exact area of the surface generated by revolving the curve about the stated axis. ■

9. $y = \sqrt{x} - \frac{1}{3}x^{3/2},\ 1 \le x \le 3$; x-axis

10. $y = \frac{1}{3}x^3 + \frac{1}{4}x^{-1},\ 1 \le x \le 2$; x-axis

11. $8xy^2 = 2y^6 + 1,\ 1 \le y \le 2$; y-axis

12. $x = \sqrt{16 - y},\ 0 \le y \le 15$; y-axis

[c] 13–16 Use a CAS or a calculating utility with a numerical integration capability to approximate the area of the surface generated by revolving the curve about the stated axis. Round your answer to two decimal places. ■

13. $y = \sin x,\ 0 \le x \le \pi$; x-axis

14. $x = \tan y,\ 0 \le y \le \pi/4$; y-axis

15. $y = e^x,\ 0 \le x \le 1$; x-axis

16. $y = e^x,\ 1 \le y \le e$; y-axis

17–20 True–False Determine whether the statement is true or false. Explain your answer. ■

17. The lateral surface area S of a right circular cone with height h and base radius r is $S = \pi r \sqrt{r^2 + h^2}$.

18. The lateral surface area of a frustum of slant height l and base radii r_1 and r_2 is equal to the lateral surface area of a right circular cylinder of height l and radius equal to the average of r_1 and r_2.

19. The approximation

$$S \approx \sum_{k=1}^{n} 2\pi f(x_k^{**})\sqrt{1 + [f'(x_k^*)]^2}\, \Delta x_k$$

for surface area is exact if f is a positive-valued constant function.

20. The expression

$$\sum_{k=1}^{n} 2\pi f(x_k^{**})\sqrt{1 + [f'(x_k^*)]^2}\, \Delta x_k$$

is not a true Riemann sum for

$$\int_a^b 2\pi f(x)\sqrt{1 + [f'(x)]^2}\, dx$$

21–22 Approximate the area of the surface using Formula (2) with $n = 20$ subintervals of equal width. Round your answer to two decimal places. ■

21. The surface of Exercise 13.

22. The surface of Exercise 16.

FOCUS ON CONCEPTS

23. Assume that $y = f(x)$ is a smooth curve on the interval $[a, b]$ and assume that $f(x) \geq 0$ for $a \leq x \leq b$. Derive a formula for the surface area generated when the curve $y = f(x)$, $a \leq x \leq b$, is revolved about the line $y = -k \ (k > 0)$.

24. Would it be circular reasoning to use Definition 6.5.2 to find the surface area of a frustum of a right circular cone? Explain your answer.

---

25. Show that the area of the surface of a sphere of radius r is $4\pi r^2$. [*Hint:* Revolve the semicircle $y = \sqrt{r^2 - x^2}$ about the x-axis.]

26. The accompanying figure shows a spherical cap of height h cut from a sphere of radius r. Show that the surface area S of the cap is $S = 2\pi rh$. [*Hint:* Revolve an appropriate portion of the circle $x^2 + y^2 = r^2$ about the y-axis.]

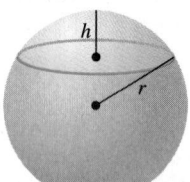

◀ **Figure Ex-26**

27. The portion of a sphere that is cut by two parallel planes is called a **zone**. Use the result of Exercise 26 to show that the surface area of a zone depends on the radius of the sphere and the distance between the planes, but not on the location of the zone.

28. Let $y = f(x)$ be a smooth curve on the interval $[a, b]$ and assume that $f(x) \geq 0$ for $a \leq x \leq b$. By the Extreme-Value

Theorem (4.4.2), the function f has a maximum value K and a minimum value k on $[a, b]$. Prove: If L is the arc length of the curve $y = f(x)$ between $x = a$ and $x = b$, and if S is the area of the surface that is generated by revolving this curve about the x-axis, then

$$2\pi k L \leq S \leq 2\pi K L$$

29. Use the results of Exercise 28 above and Exercise 21 in Section 6.4 to show that the area S of the surface generated by revolving the curve $y = \sec x$, $0 \leq x \leq \pi/3$, about the x-axis satisfies

$$\frac{2\pi^2}{3} \leq S \leq \frac{4\pi^2}{3}\sqrt{13}$$

30. Let $y = f(x)$ be a smooth curve on $[a, b]$ and assume that $f(x) \geq 0$ for $a \leq x \leq b$. Let A be the area under the curve $y = f(x)$ between $x = a$ and $x = b$, and let S be the area of the surface obtained when this section of curve is revolved about the x-axis.
  (a) Prove that $2\pi A \leq S$.
  (b) For what functions f is $2\pi A = S$?

31–37 These exercises assume familiarity with the basic concepts of parametric curves. If needed, an introduction to this material is provided in Web Appendix I. ■

31–32 For these exercises, divide the interval $[a, b]$ into n subintervals by inserting points $t_1, t_2, \ldots, t_{n-1}$ between $a = t_0$ and $b = t_n$, and assume that $x'(t)$ and $y'(t)$ are continuous functions and that no segment of the curve

$$x = x(t), \quad y = y(t) \qquad (a \leq t \leq b)$$

is traced more than once. ■

31. Let S be the area of the surface generated by revolving the curve $x = x(t)$, $y = y(t)$ $(a \leq t \leq b)$ about the x-axis. Explain how S can be approximated by

$$S \approx \sum_{k=1}^{n} (\pi[y(t_{k-1}) + y(t_k)]$$
$$\times \sqrt{[x(t_k) - x(t_{k-1})]^2 + [y(t_k) - y(t_{k-1})]^2})$$

Using results from advanced calculus, it can be shown that as $\max \Delta t_k \to 0$, this sum converges to

$$S = \int_a^b 2\pi y(t)\sqrt{[x'(t)]^2 + [y'(t)]^2}\, dt \qquad (A)$$

32. Let S be the area of the surface generated by revolving the curve $x = x(t)$, $y = y(t)$ $(a \leq t \leq b)$ about the y-axis. Explain how S can be approximated by

$$S \approx \sum_{k=1}^{n} (\pi[x(t_{k-1}) + x(t_k)]$$
$$\times \sqrt{[x(t_k) - x(t_{k-1})]^2 + [y(t_k) - y(t_{k-1})]^2})$$

Using results from advanced calculus, it can be shown that as $\max \Delta t_k \to 0$, this sum converges to

$$S = \int_a^b 2\pi x(t)\sqrt{[x'(t)]^2 + [y'(t)]^2}\, dt \qquad (B)$$

33–37 Use Formulas (A) and (B) from Exercises 31 and 32. ▪

33. Find the area of the surface generated by revolving the parametric curve $x = t^2$, $y = 2t$ $(0 \le t \le 4)$ about the x-axis.

C **34.** Use a CAS to find the area of the surface generated by revolving the parametric curve
$$x = \cos^2 t, \quad y = 5 \sin t \quad (0 \le t \le \pi/2)$$
about the x-axis.

35. Find the area of the surface generated by revolving the parametric curve $x = t$, $y = 2t^2$ $(0 \le t \le 1)$ about the y-axis.

36. Find the area of the surface generated by revolving the parametric curve $x = \cos^2 t$, $y = \sin^2 t$ $(0 \le t \le \pi/2)$ about the y-axis.

37. By revolving the semicircle
$$x = r \cos t, \quad y = r \sin t \quad (0 \le t \le \pi)$$
about the x-axis, show that the surface area of a sphere of radius r is $4\pi r^2$.

38. **Writing** Compare the derivation of Definition 6.5.2 with that of Definition 6.4.2. Discuss the geometric features that result in similarities in the two definitions.

39. **Writing** Discuss what goes wrong if we replace the frustums of right circular cones by right circular cylinders in the derivation of Definition 6.5.2.

✔ **QUICK CHECK ANSWERS 6.5**

1. $\displaystyle\int_a^b 2\pi f(x)\sqrt{1 + [f'(x)]^2}\,dx$ **2.** $3\sqrt{10}\,\pi$ **3.** $\displaystyle\int_3^6 (2\pi)\left(\frac{x}{3}\right)\sqrt{\frac{10}{9}}\,dx = \int_3^6 \frac{2\sqrt{10}\,\pi}{9}x\,dx$ **4.** $\displaystyle\int_1^2 (2\pi)(3y)\sqrt{10}\,dy$

6.6 WORK

In this section we will use the integration tools developed in the preceding chapter to study some of the basic principles of "work," which is one of the fundamental concepts in physics and engineering.

■ **THE ROLE OF WORK IN PHYSICS AND ENGINEERING**

In this section we will be concerned with two related concepts, *work* and *energy*. To put these ideas in a familiar setting, when you push a stalled car for a certain distance you are performing work, and the effect of your work is to make the car move. The energy of motion caused by the work is called the *kinetic energy* of the car. The exact connection between work and kinetic energy is governed by a principle of physics called the *work–energy relationship*. Although we will touch on this idea in this section, a detailed study of the relationship between work and energy will be left for courses in physics and engineering. Our primary goal here will be to explain the role of integration in the study of work.

■ **WORK DONE BY A CONSTANT FORCE APPLIED IN THE DIRECTION OF MOTION**

When a stalled car is pushed, the speed that the car attains depends on the force F with which it is pushed and the distance d over which that force is applied (Figure 6.6.1). Force and distance appear in the following definition of work.

▶ **Figure 6.6.1**

> **6.6.1   DEFINITION**   If a constant force of magnitude F is applied in the direction of motion of an object, and if that object moves a distance d, then we define the **work** W performed by the force on the object to be
>
> $$W = F \cdot d \tag{1}$$

If you push against an immovable object, such as a brick wall, you may tire yourself out, but you will not perform any work. Why?

Common units for measuring force are newtons (N) in the International System of Units (SI), dynes (dyn) in the centimeter-gram-second (CGS) system, and pounds (lb) in the British Engineering (BE) system. One newton is the force required to give a mass of 1 kg an acceleration of 1 m/s^2, one dyne is the force required to give a mass of 1 g an acceleration of 1 cm/s^2, and one pound of force is the force required to give a mass of 1 slug an acceleration of 1 ft/s^2.

It follows from Definition 6.6.1 that work has units of force times distance. The most common units of work are newton-meters (N·m), dyne-centimeters (dyn·cm), and foot-pounds (ft·lb). As indicated in Table 6.6.1, one newton-meter is also called a **joule** (J), and one dyne-centimeter is also called an **erg**. One foot-pound is approximately 1.36 J.

Table 6.6.1

SYSTEM	FORCE	×	DISTANCE	=	WORK
SI	newton (N)		meter (m)		joule (J)
CGS	dyne (dyn)		centimeter (cm)		erg
BE	pound (lb)		foot (ft)		foot-pound (ft·lb)

CONVERSION FACTORS:

$1 \text{ N} = 10^5 \text{ dyn} \approx 0.225 \text{ lb}$ $1 \text{ lb} \approx 4.45 \text{ N}$

$1 \text{ J} = 10^7 \text{ erg} \approx 0.738 \text{ ft·lb}$ $1 \text{ ft·lb} \approx 1.36 \text{ J} = 1.36 \times 10^7 \text{ erg}$

▶ **Example 1**   An object moves 5 ft along a line while subjected to a constant force of 100 lb in its direction of motion. The work done is

$$W = F \cdot d = 100 \cdot 5 = 500 \text{ ft·lb}$$

An object moves 25 m along a line while subjected to a constant force of 4 N in its direction of motion. The work done is

$$W = F \cdot d = 4 \cdot 25 = 100 \text{ N·m} = 100 \text{ J} \quad ◀$$

▶ **Example 2**   In the 1976 Olympics, Vasili Alexeev astounded the world by lifting a record-breaking 562 lb from the floor to above his head (about 2 m). Equally astounding was the feat of strongman Paul Anderson, who in 1957 braced himself on the floor and used his back to lift 6270 lb of lead and automobile parts a distance of 1 cm. Who did more work?

Solution.   To lift an object one must apply sufficient force to overcome the gravitational force that the Earth exerts on that object. The force that the Earth exerts on an object is that object's weight; thus, in performing their feats, Alexeev applied a force of 562 lb over a distance of 2 m and Anderson applied a force of 6270 lb over a distance of 1 cm. Pounds are units in the BE system, meters are units in SI, and centimeters are units in the CGS system. We will need to decide on the measurement system we want to use and be consistent. Let us agree to use SI and express the work of the two men in joules. Using the conversion factor in Table 6.6.1 we obtain

$$562 \text{ lb} \approx 562 \text{ lb} \times 4.45 \text{ N/lb} \approx 2500 \text{ N}$$

$$6270 \text{ lb} \approx 6270 \text{ lb} \times 4.45 \text{ N/lb} \approx 27{,}900 \text{ N}$$

Vasili Alexeev shown lifting a record-breaking 562 lb in the 1976 Olympics. In eight successive years he won olympic gold medals, captured six world championships, and broke 80 world records. In 1999 he was honored in Greece as the best sportsman of the 20th Century.

Using these values and the fact that 1 cm = 0.01 m we obtain

$$\text{Alexeev's work} = (2500 \text{ N}) \times (2 \text{ m}) = 5000 \text{ J}$$
$$\text{Anderson's work} = (27{,}900 \text{ N}) \times (0.01 \text{ m}) = 279 \text{ J}$$

Therefore, even though Anderson's lift required a tremendous upward force, it was applied over such a short distance that Alexeev did more work. ◄

■ WORK DONE BY A VARIABLE FORCE APPLIED IN THE DIRECTION OF MOTION

Many important problems are concerned with finding the work done by a *variable* force that is applied in the direction of motion. For example, Figure 6.6.2*a* shows a spring in its natural state (neither compressed nor stretched). If we want to pull the block horizontally (Figure 6.6.2*b*), then we would have to apply more and more force to the block to overcome the increasing force of the stretching spring. Thus, our next objective is to define what is meant by the work performed by a variable force and to find a formula for computing it. This will require calculus.

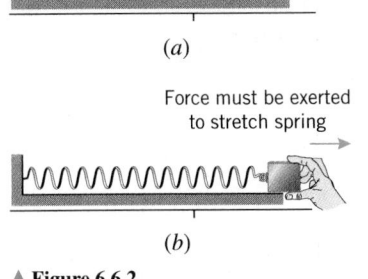

Natural position

(*a*)

Force must be exerted
to stretch spring

(*b*)

▲ **Figure 6.6.2**

6.6.2 PROBLEM Suppose that an object moves in the positive direction along a co-ordinate line while subjected to a variable force $F(x)$ that is applied in the direction of motion. Define what is meant by the *work* W performed by the force on the object as the object moves from $x = a$ to $x = b$, and find a formula for computing the work.

The basic idea for solving this problem is to break up the interval $[a, b]$ into subintervals that are sufficiently small that the force does not vary much on each subinterval. This will allow us to treat the force as constant on each subinterval and to approximate the work on each subinterval using Formula (1). By adding the approximations to the work on the subintervals, we will obtain a Riemann sum that approximates the work W over the entire interval, and by taking the limit of the Riemann sums we will obtain an integral for W.

To implement this idea, divide the interval $[a, b]$ into n subintervals by inserting points $x_1, x_2, \ldots, x_{n-1}$ between $a = x_0$ and $b = x_n$. We can use Formula (1) to approximate the work W_k done in the kth subinterval by choosing any point x_k^* in this interval and regarding the force to have a constant value $F(x_k^*)$ throughout the interval. Since the width of the kth subinterval is $x_k - x_{k-1} = \Delta x_k$, this yields the approximation

$$W_k \approx F(x_k^*)\Delta x_k$$

Adding these approximations yields the following Riemann sum that approximates the work W done over the entire interval:

$$W \approx \sum_{k=1}^{n} F(x_k^*)\Delta x_k$$

Taking the limit as n increases and the widths of all the subintervals approach zero yields the definite integral

$$W = \lim_{\max \Delta x_k \to 0} \sum_{k=1}^{n} F(x_k^*)\Delta x_k = \int_a^b F(x)\,dx$$

In summary, we have the following result.

6.6.3   **DEFINITION**   Suppose that an object moves in the positive direction along a coordinate line over the interval $[a, b]$ while subjected to a variable force $F(x)$ that is applied in the direction of motion. Then we define the **work** W performed by the force on the object to be

$$W = \int_a^b F(x)\,dx \tag{2}$$

Hooke's law [Robert Hooke (1635–1703), English physicist] states that under appropriate conditions a spring that is stretched x units beyond its natural length pulls back with a force

$$F(x) = kx$$

where k is a constant (called the **spring constant** or **spring stiffness**). The value of k depends on such factors as the thickness of the spring and the material used in its composition. Since $k = F(x)/x$, the constant k has units of force per unit length.

▶ **Example 3**   A spring exerts a force of 5 N when stretched 1 m beyond its natural length.

(a) Find the spring constant k.

(b) How much work is required to stretch the spring 1.8 m beyond its natural length?

Solution (a).   From Hooke's law,

$$F(x) = kx$$

From the data, $F(x) = 5$ N when $x = 1$ m, so $5 = k \cdot 1$. Thus, the spring constant is $k = 5$ newtons per meter (N/m). This means that the force $F(x)$ required to stretch the spring x meters is

$$F(x) = 5x \tag{3}$$

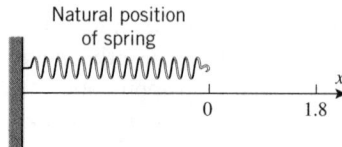

Natural position
of spring

▲ **Figure 6.6.3**

Solution (b).   Place the spring along a coordinate line as shown in Figure 6.6.3. We want to find the work W required to stretch the spring over the interval from $x = 0$ to $x = 1.8$. From (2) and (3) the work W required is

$$W = \int_a^b F(x)\,dx = \int_0^{1.8} 5x\,dx = \left.\frac{5x^2}{2}\right]_0^{1.8} = 8.1 \text{ J} \blacktriangleleft$$

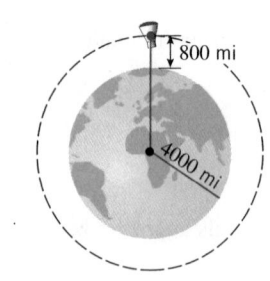

800 mi

4000 mi

▲ **Figure 6.6.4**

▶ **Example 4**   An astronaut's *weight* (or more precisely, *Earth weight*) is the force exerted on the astronaut by the Earth's gravity. As the astronaut moves upward into space, the gravitational pull of the Earth decreases, and hence so does his or her weight. If the Earth is assumed to be a sphere of radius 4000 mi, then it can be shown using physics that an astronaut who weighs 150 lb on Earth will have a weight of

$$w(x) = \frac{2{,}400{,}000{,}000}{x^2} \text{ lb}, \quad x \geq 4000$$

at a distance of x mi from the Earth's center (Exercise 25). Use this formula to determine the work in foot-pounds required to lift the astronaut to a point that is 800 mi above the surface of the Earth (Figure 6.6.4).

Solution.   Since the Earth has a radius of 4000 mi, the astronaut is lifted from a point that is 4000 mi from the Earth's center to a point that is 4800 mi from the Earth's center. Thus, from (2), the work W required to lift the astronaut is

$$
\begin{aligned}
W &= \int_{4000}^{4800} \frac{2,400,000,000}{x^2}\, dx \\
&= -\frac{2,400,000,000}{x} \Bigg]_{4000}^{4800} \\
&= -500,000 + 600,000 \\
&= 100,000 \text{ mile-pounds} \\
&= (100,000 \text{ mi·lb}) \times (5280 \text{ ft/mi}) \\
&= 5.28 \times 10^8 \text{ ft·lb} \quad \blacktriangleleft
\end{aligned}
$$

■ CALCULATING WORK FROM BASIC PRINCIPLES

Some problems cannot be solved by mechanically substituting into formulas, and one must return to basic principles to obtain solutions. This is illustrated in the next example.

▶ **Example 5**   Figure 6.6.5a shows a conical container of radius 10 ft and height 30 ft. Suppose that this container is filled with water to a depth of 15 ft. How much work is required to pump all of the water out through a hole in the top of the container?

Solution.   Our strategy will be to divide the water into thin layers, approximate the work required to move each layer to the top of the container, add the approximations for the layers to obtain a Riemann sum that approximates the total work, and then take the limit of the Riemann sums to produce an integral for the total work.

To implement this idea, introduce an x-axis as shown in Figure 6.6.5a, and divide the water into n layers with Δx_k denoting the thickness of the kth layer. This division induces a partition of the interval $[15, 30]$ into n subintervals. Although the upper and lower surfaces of the kth layer are at different distances from the top, the difference will be small if the layer is thin, and we can reasonably assume that the entire layer is concentrated at a single point x_k^* (Figure 6.6.5a). Thus, the work W_k required to move the kth layer to the top of the container is approximately

$$
W_k \approx F_k x_k^* \tag{4}
$$

where F_k is the force required to lift the kth layer. But the force required to lift the kth layer is the force needed to overcome gravity, and this is the same as the weight of the layer. If the layer is very thin, we can approximate the volume of the kth layer with the volume of a cylinder of height Δx_k and radius r_k, where (by similar triangles)

$$
\frac{r_k}{x_k^*} = \frac{10}{30} = \frac{1}{3}
$$

or, equivalently, $r_k = x_k^*/3$ (Figure 6.6.5b). Therefore, the volume of the kth layer of water is approximately

$$
\pi r_k^2 \Delta x_k = \pi (x_k^*/3)^2 \Delta x_k = \frac{\pi}{9} (x_k^*)^2 \Delta x_k
$$

Since the weight density of water is 62.4 lb/ft³, it follows that

$$
F_k \approx \frac{62.4\pi}{9} (x_k^*)^2 \Delta x_k
$$

Thus, from (4)

$$
W_k \approx \left(\frac{62.4\pi}{9} (x_k^*)^2 \Delta x_k \right) x_k^* = \frac{62.4\pi}{9} (x_k^*)^3 \Delta x_k
$$

and hence the work W required to move all n layers has the approximation

$$W = \sum_{k=1}^{n} W_k \approx \sum_{k=1}^{n} \frac{62.4\pi}{9}(x_k^*)^3 \Delta x_k$$

To find the *exact* value of the work we take the limit as max $\Delta x_k \to 0$. This yields

$$W = \lim_{\max \Delta x_k \to 0} \sum_{k=1}^{n} \frac{62.4\pi}{9}(x_k^*)^3 \Delta x_k = \int_{15}^{30} \frac{62.4\pi}{9} x^3 \, dx$$

$$= \frac{62.4\pi}{9}\left(\frac{x^4}{4}\right)\Bigg]_{15}^{30} = 1{,}316{,}250\pi \approx 4{,}135{,}000 \text{ ft·lb} \blacktriangleleft$$

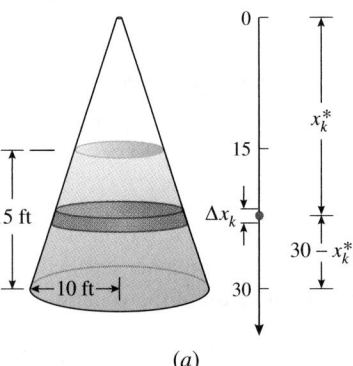

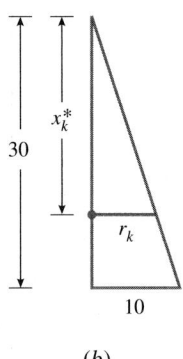

▶ **Figure 6.6.5**   (*a*)   (*b*)

■ THE WORK–ENERGY RELATIONSHIP

Mike Brinson/Getty Images

The work performed by the skater's stick in a brief interval of time produces the blinding speed of the hockey puck.

When you see an object in motion, you can be certain that somehow work has been expended to create that motion. For example, when you drop a stone from a building, the stone gathers speed because the force of the Earth's gravity is performing work on it, and when a hockey player strikes a puck with a hockey stick, the work performed on the puck during the brief period of contact with the stick creates the enormous speed of the puck across the ice. However, experience shows that the speed obtained by an object depends not only on the amount of work done, but also on the mass of the object. For example, the work required to throw a 5 oz baseball 50 mi/h would accelerate a 10 lb bowling ball to less than 9 mi/h.

Using the method of substitution for definite integrals, we will derive a simple equation that relates the work done on an object to the object's mass and velocity. Furthermore, this equation will allow us to motivate an appropriate definition for the "energy of motion" of an object. As in Definition 6.6.3, we will assume that an object moves in the positive direction along a coordinate line over the interval $[a, b]$ while subjected to a force $F(x)$ that is applied in the direction of motion. We let m denote the mass of the object, and we let $x = x(t)$, $v = v(t) = x'(t)$, and $a = a(t) = v'(t)$ denote the respective position, velocity, and acceleration of the object at time t. We will need the following important result from physics that relates the force acting on an object with the mass and acceleration of the object.

6.6.4   NEWTON'S SECOND LAW OF MOTION   If an object with mass m is subjected to a force F, then the object undergoes an acceleration a that satisfies the equation

$$F = ma \tag{5}$$

It follows from Newton's Second Law of Motion that

$$F(x(t)) = ma(t) = mv'(t)$$

Assume that

$$x(t_0) = a \quad \text{and} \quad x(t_1) = b$$

with

$$v(t_0) = v_i \quad \text{and} \quad v(t_1) = v_f$$

the initial and final velocities of the object, respectively. Then

$$W = \int_a^b F(x)\, dx = \int_{x(t_0)}^{x(t_1)} F(x)\, dx$$

$$= \int_{t_0}^{t_1} F(x(t))x'(t)\, dt \qquad \boxed{\text{By Theorem 5.9.1 with } x = x(t),\, dx = x'(t)\, dt}$$

$$= \int_{t_0}^{t_1} mv'(t)v(t)\, dt = \int_{t_0}^{t_1} mv(t)v'(t)\, dt$$

$$= \int_{v(t_0)}^{v(t_1)} mv\, dv \qquad \boxed{\text{By Theorem 5.9.1 with } v = v(t),\, dv = v'(t)\, dt}$$

$$= \int_{v_i}^{v_f} mv\, dv = \tfrac{1}{2}mv^2 \Big|_{v_i}^{v_f} = \tfrac{1}{2}mv_f^2 - \tfrac{1}{2}mv_i^2$$

We see from the equation

$$W = \tfrac{1}{2}mv_f^2 - \tfrac{1}{2}mv_i^2 \tag{6}$$

that the work done on the object is equal to the change in the quantity $\frac{1}{2}mv^2$ from its initial value to its final value. We will refer to Equation (6) as the **work–energy relationship**. If we define the "energy of motion" or **kinetic energy** of our object to be given by

$$K = \tfrac{1}{2}mv^2 \tag{7}$$

then Equation (6) tells us that the work done on an object is equal to the *change* in the object's kinetic energy. Loosely speaking, we may think of work done on an object as being "transformed" into kinetic energy of the object. The units of kinetic energy are the same as the units of work. For example, in SI kinetic energy is measured in joules (J).

▶ **Example 6**   A space probe of mass $m = 5.00 \times 10^4$ kg travels in deep space subjected only to the force of its own engine. Starting at a time when the speed of the probe is $v = 1.10 \times 10^4$ m/s, the engine is fired continuously over a distance of 2.50×10^6 m with a constant force of 4.00×10^5 N in the direction of motion. What is the final speed of the probe?

Solution.   Since the force applied by the engine is constant and in the direction of motion, the work W expended by the engine on the probe is

$$W = \text{force} \times \text{distance} = (4.00 \times 10^5 \text{ N}) \times (2.50 \times 10^6 \text{ m}) = 1.00 \times 10^{12} \text{ J}$$

From (6), the final kinetic energy $K_f = \frac{1}{2}mv_f^2$ of the probe can be expressed in terms of the work W and the initial kinetic energy $K_i = \frac{1}{2}mv_i^2$ as

$$K_f = W + K_i$$

Thus, from the known mass and initial speed we have

$$K_f = (1.00 \times 10^{12} \text{ J}) + \tfrac{1}{2}(5.00 \times 10^4 \text{ kg})(1.10 \times 10^4 \text{ m/s})^2 = 4.025 \times 10^{12} \text{ J}$$

The final kinetic energy is $K_f = \frac{1}{2}mv_f^2$, so the final speed of the probe is

$$v_f = \sqrt{\frac{2K_f}{m}} = \sqrt{\frac{2(4.025 \times 10^{12})}{5.00 \times 10^4}} \approx 1.27 \times 10^4 \text{ m/s} \blacktriangleleft$$

✔ QUICK CHECK EXERCISES 6.6 *(See page 458 for answers.)*

1. If a constant force of 5 lb moves an object 10 ft, then the work done by the force on the object is _____.

2. A newton-meter is also called a _____. A dyne-centimeter is also called an _____.

3. Suppose that an object moves in the positive direction along a coordinate line over the interval $[a, b]$. The work per-formed on the object by a variable force $F(x)$ applied in the direction of motion is $W =$ _____.

4. A force $F(x) = 10 - 2x$ N applied in the positive x-direc-tion moves an object 3 m from $x = 2$ to $x = 5$. The work done by the force on the object is _____.

EXERCISE SET 6.6

FOCUS ON CONCEPTS

1. A variable force $F(x)$ in the positive x-direction is graphed in the accompanying figure. Find the work done by the force on a particle that moves from $x = 0$ to $x = 3$.

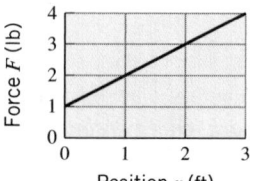

Position x (ft) ◀ **Figure Ex-1**

2. A variable force $F(x)$ in the positive x-direction is graphed in the accompanying figure. Find the work done by the force on a particle that moves from $x = 0$ to $x = 5$.

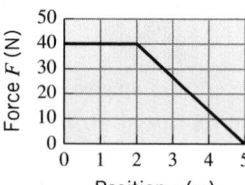

Position x (m) ◀ **Figure Ex-2**

3. For the variable force $F(x)$ in Exercise 2, consider the distance d for which the work done by the force on the particle when the particle moves from $x = 0$ to $x = d$ is half of the work done when the particle moves from $x = 0$ to $x = 5$. By inspecting the graph of F, is d more or less than 2.5? Explain, and then find the exact value of d.

4. Suppose that a variable force $F(x)$ is applied in the pos-itive x-direction so that an object moves from $x = a$ to $x = b$. Relate the work done by the force on the object and the average value of F over $[a, b]$, and illustrate this relationship graphically.

5. A constant force of 10 lb in the positive x-direction is applied to a particle whose velocity versus time curve is shown in the accompanying figure. Find the work done by the force on the particle from time $t = 0$ to $t = 5$.

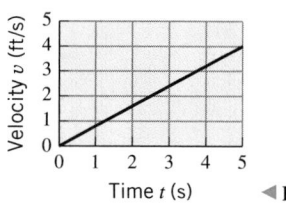

Time t (s) ◀ **Figure Ex-5**

6. A spring exerts a force of 6 N when it is stretched from its natural length of 4 m to a length of $4\frac{1}{2}$ m. Find the work required to stretch the spring from its natural length to a length of 6 m.

7. A spring exerts a force of 100 N when it is stretched 0.2 m beyond its natural length. How much work is required to stretch the spring 0.8 m beyond its natural length?

8. A spring whose natural length is 15 cm exerts a force of 45 N when stretched to a length of 20 cm.
   (a) Find the spring constant (in newtons/meter).
   (b) Find the work that is done in stretching the spring 3 cm beyond its natural length.
   (c) Find the work done in stretching the spring from a length of 20 cm to a length of 25 cm.

9. Assume that 10 ft·lb of work is required to stretch a spring 1 ft beyond its natural length. What is the spring constant?

10–13 True–False Determine whether the statement is true or false. Explain your answer. ■

10. In order to support the weight of a parked automobile, the surface of a driveway must do work against the force of gravity on the vehicle.

11. A force of 10 lb in the direction of motion of an object that moves 5 ft in 2 s does six times the work of a force of 10 lb in the direction of motion of an object that moves 5 ft in 12 s.

12. It follows from Hooke's law that in order to double the dis-tance a spring is stretched beyond its natural length, four times as much work is required.

13. In the International System of Units, work and kinetic en-ergy have the same units.

14. A cylindrical tank of radius 5 ft and height 9 ft is two-thirds filled with water. Find the work required to pump all the water over the upper rim.

15. Solve Exercise 14 assuming that the tank is half-filled with water.

16. A cone-shaped water reservoir is 20 ft in diameter across the top and 15 ft deep. If the reservoir is filled to a depth of 10 ft, how much work is required to pump all the water to the top of the reservoir?

17. The vat shown in the accompanying figure contains water to a depth of 2 m. Find the work required to pump all the water to the top of the vat. [Use 9810 N/m^3 as the weight density of water.]

18. The cylindrical tank shown in the accompanying figure is filled with a liquid weighing 50 lb/ft^3. Find the work required to pump all the liquid to a level 1 ft above the top of the tank.

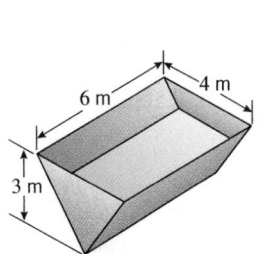

▲ Figure Ex-17   ▲ Figure Ex-18

19. A swimming pool is built in the shape of a rectangular parallelepiped 10 ft deep, 15 ft wide, and 20 ft long.
    (a) If the pool is filled to 1 ft below the top, how much work is required to pump all the water into a drain at the top edge of the pool?
    (b) A one-horsepower motor can do 550 ft·lb of work per second. What size motor is required to empty the pool in 1 hour?

20. How much work is required to fill the swimming pool in Exercise 19 to 1 ft below the top if the water is pumped in through an opening located at the bottom of the pool?

21. A 100 ft length of steel chain weighing 15 lb/ft is dangling from a pulley. How much work is required to wind the chain onto the pulley?

22. A 3 lb bucket containing 20 lb of water is hanging at the end of a 20 ft rope that weighs 4 oz/ft. The other end of the rope is attached to a pulley. How much work is required to wind the length of rope onto the pulley, assuming that the rope is wound onto the pulley at a rate of 2 ft/s and that as the bucket is being lifted, water leaks from the bucket at a rate of 0.5 lb/s?

23. A rocket weighing 3 tons is filled with 40 tons of liquid fuel. In the initial part of the flight, fuel is burned off at a constant rate of 2 tons per 1000 ft of vertical height. How much work in foot-tons (ft·ton) is done lifting the rocket 3000 ft?

24. It follows from Coulomb's law in physics that two like electrostatic charges repel each other with a force inversely proportional to the square of the distance between them. Suppose that two charges A and B repel with a force of k newtons when they are positioned at points $A(-a, 0)$ and $B(a, 0)$, where a is measured in meters. Find the work W required to move charge A along the x-axis to the origin if charge B remains stationary.

25. It is a law of physics that the gravitational force exerted by the Earth on an object above the Earth's surface varies inversely as the square of its distance from the Earth's center. Thus, an object's weight $w(x)$ is related to its distance x from the Earth's center by a formula of the form

$$w(x) = \frac{k}{x^2}$$

where k is a constant of proportionality that depends on the mass of the object.
    (a) Use this fact and the assumption that the Earth is a sphere of radius 4000 mi to obtain the formula for $w(x)$ in Example 4.
    (b) Find a formula for the weight $w(x)$ of a satellite that is x mi from the Earth's surface if its weight on Earth is 6000 lb.
    (c) How much work is required to lift the satellite from the surface of the Earth to an orbital position that is 1000 mi high?

26. (a) The formula $w(x) = k/x^2$ in Exercise 25 is applicable to all celestial bodies. Assuming that the Moon is a sphere of radius 1080 mi, find the force that the Moon exerts on an astronaut who is x mi from the surface of the Moon if her weight on the Moon's surface is 20 lb.
    (b) How much work is required to lift the astronaut to a point that is 10.8 mi above the Moon's surface?

27. The world's first commercial high-speed magnetic levitation (MAGLEV) train, a 30 km double-track project connecting Shanghai, China, to Pudong International Airport, began full revenue service in 2003. Suppose that a MAGLEV train has a mass $m = 4.00 \times 10^5$ kg and that starting at a time when the train has a speed of 20 m/s the engine applies a force of 6.40×10^5 N in the direction of motion over a distance of 3.00×10^3 m. Use the work–energy relationship (6) to find the final speed of the train.

28. Assume that a Mars probe of mass $m = 2.00 \times 10^3$ kg is subjected only to the force of its own engine. Starting at a time when the speed of the probe is $v = 1.00 \times 10^4$ m/s, the engine is fired continuously over a distance of 1.50×10^5 m with a constant force of 2.00×10^5 N in the direction of motion. Use the work–energy relationship (6) to find the final speed of the probe.

29. On August 10, 1972 a meteorite with an estimated mass of 4×10^6 kg and an estimated speed of 15 km/s skipped across the atmosphere above the western United States and Canada but fortunately did not hit the Earth. *(cont.)*

(a) Assuming that the meteorite had hit the Earth with a speed of 15 km/s, what would have been its change in kinetic energy in joules (J)?

(b) Express the energy as a multiple of the explosive energy of 1 megaton of TNT, which is 4.2×10^{15} J.

(c) The energy associated with the Hiroshima atomic bomb was 13 kilotons of TNT. To how many such bombs would the meteorite impact have been equivalent?

30. Writing After reading Examples 3–5, a student classifies work problems as either "pushing/pulling" or "pumping."

Describe these categories in your own words and discuss the methods used to solve each type. Give examples to illustrate that these categories are not mutually exclusive.

31. Writing How might you recognize that a problem can be solved by means of the work–energy relationship? That is, what sort of "givens" and "unknowns" would suggest such a solution? Discuss two or three examples.

✔ **QUICK CHECK ANSWERS 6.6**

---

1. 50 ft·lb   **2.** joule; erg   **3.** $\displaystyle\int_a^b F(x)\,dx$ **4.** 9 J

6.7 MOMENTS, CENTERS OF GRAVITY, AND CENTROIDS

*Suppose that a rigid physical body is acted on by a constant gravitational field. Because the body is composed of many particles, each of which is affected by gravity, the action of the gravitational field on the body consists of a large number of forces distributed over the entire body. However, it is a fact of physics that these individual forces can be replaced by a single force acting at a point called the **center of gravity** of the body. In this section we will show how integrals can be used to locate centers of gravity.*

■ **DENSITY AND MASS OF A LAMINA**

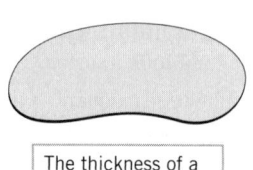

The thickness of a lamina is negligible.

▲ **Figure 6.7.1**

Let us consider an idealized flat object that is thin enough to be viewed as a two-dimensional plane region (Figure 6.7.1). Such an object is called a ***lamina***. A lamina is called ***homogeneous*** if its composition is uniform throughout and ***inhomogeneous*** otherwise. We will consider homogeneous laminas in this section. Inhomogeneous laminas will be discussed in Chapter 14. The ***density*** of a *homogeneous* lamina is defined to be its mass per unit area. Thus, the density δ of a homogeneous lamina of mass M and area A is given by $\delta = M/A$. Notice that the mass M of a homogeneous lamina can be expressed as

$$M = \delta A \tag{1}$$

The units in Equation (1) are consistent since mass = (mass/area) × area.

▶ **Example 1**   A triangular lamina with vertices (0, 0), (0, 1), and (1, 0) has density $\delta = 3$. Find its total mass.

Solution.   Referring to (1) and Figure 6.7.2, the mass M of the lamina is

$$M = \delta A = 3 \cdot \frac{1}{2} = \frac{3}{2} \text{ (unit of mass) } \blacktriangleleft$$

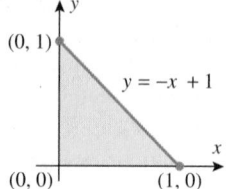

▲ **Figure 6.7.2**

■ **CENTER OF GRAVITY OF A LAMINA**

Assume that the acceleration due to the force of gravity is constant and acts downward, and suppose that a lamina occupies a region R in a horizontal xy-plane. It can be shown that there exists a unique point $(\bar{x}, \bar{y})$ (which may or may not belong to R) such that the effect of gravity on the lamina is "equivalent" to that of a single force acting at the point $(\bar{x}, \bar{y})$. This point is called the ***center of gravity*** of the lamina, and if it is in R, then the lamina will balance horizontally on the point of a support placed at $(\bar{x}, \bar{y})$. For example, the center of gravity of a homogeneous disk is at the center of the disk, and the center of gravity of a homogeneous rectangular region is at the center of the rectangle. For an irregularly shaped homogeneous lamina, locating the center of gravity requires calculus.

6.7.1   PROBLEM   Let f be a positive continuous function on the interval $[a, b]$. Suppose that a homogeneous lamina with constant density δ occupies a region R in a horizontal xy-plane bounded by the graphs of $y = f(x)$, $y = 0$, $x = a$, and $x = b$. Find the coordinates $(\bar{x}, \bar{y})$ of the center of gravity of the lamina.

To motivate the solution, consider what happens if we try to balance the lamina on a knife-edge parallel to the x-axis. Suppose the lamina in Figure 6.7.3 is placed on a knife-edge along a line $y = c$ that does not pass through the center of gravity. Because the lamina behaves as if its entire mass is concentrated at the center of gravity $(\bar{x}, \bar{y})$, the lamina will be rotationally unstable and the force of gravity will cause a rotation about $y = c$. Similarly, the lamina will undergo a rotation if placed on a knife-edge along $y = d$. However, if the knife-edge runs along the line $y = \bar{y}$ through the center of gravity, the lamina will be in perfect balance. Similarly, the lamina will be in perfect balance on a knife-edge along the line $x = \bar{x}$ through the center of gravity. This suggests that the center of gravity of a lamina can be determined as the intersection of two lines of balance, one parallel to the x-axis and the other parallel to the y-axis. In order to find these lines of balance, we will need some preliminary results about rotations.

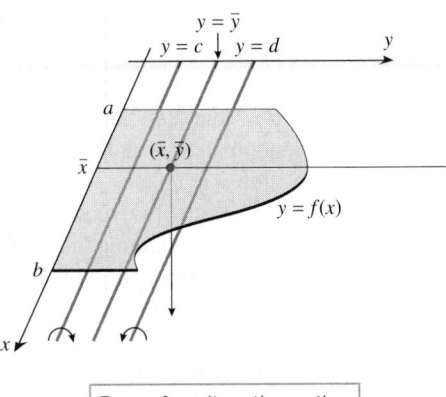

Force of gravity acting on the center of gravity of the lamina

▶ **Figure 6.7.3**

Children on a seesaw learn by experience that a lighter child can balance a heavier one by sitting farther from the fulcrum or pivot point. This is because the tendency for an object to produce rotation is proportional not only to its mass but also to the distance between the object and the fulcrum. To make this more precise, consider an x-axis, which we view as a weightless beam. If a mass m is located on the axis at x, then the tendency for that mass to produce a rotation of the beam about a point a on the axis is measured by the following quantity, called the ***moment of m about $x = a$***:

$$\begin{bmatrix} \text{moment of } m \\ \text{about } a \end{bmatrix} = m(x - a)$$

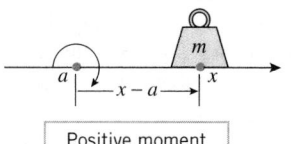

Positive moment
about a
(clockwise rotation)

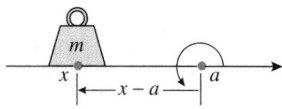

Negative moment
about a
(counterclockwise rotation)

▲ **Figure 6.7.4**

The number $x - a$ is called the **lever arm**. Depending on whether the mass is to the right or left of a, the lever arm is either the distance between x and a or the negative of this distance (Figure 6.7.4). Positive lever arms result in positive moments and clockwise rotations, and negative lever arms result in negative moments and counterclockwise rotations.

Suppose that masses $m_1, m_2, \ldots, m_n$ are located at $x_1, x_2, \ldots, x_n$ on a coordinate axis and a fulcrum is positioned at the point a (Figure 6.7.5). Depending on whether the sum of the moments about a,

$$\sum_{k=1}^{n} m_k(x_k - a) = m_1(x_1 - a) + m_2(x_2 - a) + \cdots + m_n(x_n - a)$$

is positive, negative, or zero, a weightless beam along the axis will rotate clockwise about a, rotate counterclockwise about a, or balance perfectly. In the last case, the system of masses is said to be in **equilibrium**.

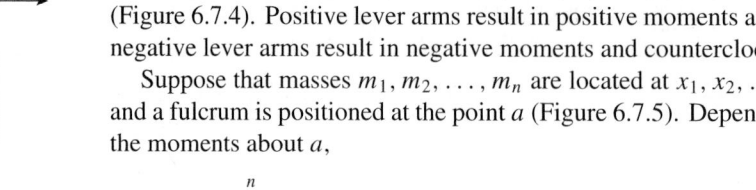

▶ **Figure 6.7.5**

Fulcrum

The preceding ideas can be extended to masses distributed in two-dimensional space. If we imagine the xy-plane to be a weightless sheet supporting a mass m located at a point (x, y), then the tendency for the mass to produce a rotation of the sheet about the line $x = a$ is $m(x - a)$, called the **moment of m about $x = a$**, and the tendency for the mass to produce a rotation about the line $y = c$ is $m(y - c)$, called the **moment of m about $y = c$** (Figure 6.7.6). In summary,

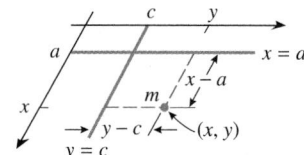

▲ **Figure 6.7.6**

$$\begin{bmatrix} \text{moment of } m \\ \text{about the} \\ \text{line } x = a \end{bmatrix} = m(x - a) \quad \text{and} \quad \begin{bmatrix} \text{moment of } m \\ \text{about the} \\ \text{line } y = c \end{bmatrix} = m(y - c) \qquad (2\text{--}3)$$

If a number of masses are distributed throughout the xy-plane, then the plane (viewed as a weightless sheet) will balance on a knife-edge along the line $x = a$ if the sum of the moments about the line is zero. Similarly, the plane will balance on a knife-edge along the line $y = c$ if the sum of the moments about that line are zero.

We are now ready to solve Problem 6.7.1. The basic idea for solving this problem is to divide the lamina into strips whose areas may be approximated by the areas of rectangles. These area approximations, along with Formulas (2) and (3), will allow us to create a Riemann sum that approximates the moment of the lamina about a horizontal or vertical line. By taking the limit of Riemann sums we will then obtain an integral for the moment of a lamina about a horizontal or vertical line. We observe that since the lamina balances on the lines $x = \bar{x}$ and $y = \bar{y}$, the moment of the lamina about those lines should be zero. This observation will enable us to calculate $\bar{x}$ and $\bar{y}$.

To implement this idea, we divide the interval $[a, b]$ into n subintervals by inserting the points $x_1, x_2, \ldots, x_{n-1}$ between $a = x_0$ and $b = x_n$. This has the effect of dividing the lamina R into n strips $R_1, R_2, \ldots, R_n$ (Figure 6.7.7a). Suppose that the kth strip extends from x_{k-1} to x_k and that the width of this strip is

$$\Delta x_k = x_k - x_{k-1}$$

We will let x_k^* be the midpoint of the kth subinterval and we will approximate R_k by a rectangle of width Δx_k and height $f(x_k^*)$. From (1), the mass ΔM_k of this rectangle is $\Delta M_k = \delta f(x_k^*)\Delta x_k$, and we will assume that the rectangle behaves as if its entire mass is concentrated at its center $(x_k^*, y_k^*) = (x_k^*, \frac{1}{2}f(x_k^*))$ (Figure 6.7.7b). It then follows from (2) and (3) that the moments of R_k about the lines $x = \bar{x}$ and $y = \bar{y}$ may be approximated

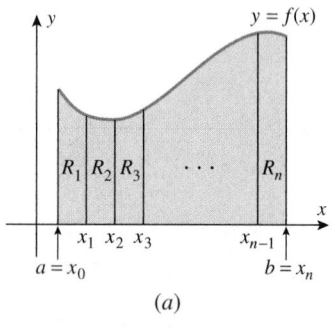

(a)

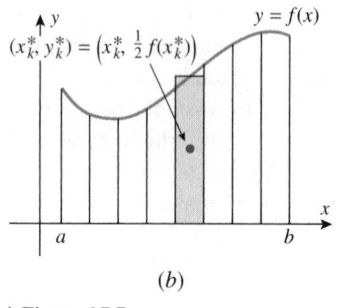

(b)

▲ **Figure 6.7.7**

by $(x_k^* - \bar{x})\Delta M_k$ and $(y_k^* - \bar{y})\Delta M_k$, respectively. Adding these approximations yields the following Riemann sums that approximate the moment of the entire lamina about the lines $x = \bar{x}$ and $y = \bar{y}$:

$$\sum_{k=1}^{n}(x_k^* - \bar{x})\Delta M_k = \sum_{k=1}^{n}(x_k^* - \bar{x})\delta f(x_k^*)\Delta x_k$$

$$\sum_{k=1}^{n}(y_k^* - \bar{y})\Delta M_k = \sum_{k=1}^{n}\left(\frac{f(x_k^*)}{2} - \bar{y}\right)\delta f(x_k^*)\Delta x_k$$

Taking the limits as n increases and the widths of all the rectangles approach zero yields the definite integrals

$$\int_a^b (x - \bar{x})\delta f(x)\,dx \quad \text{and} \quad \int_a^b \left(\frac{f(x)}{2} - \bar{y}\right)\delta f(x)\,dx$$

that represent the moments of the lamina about the lines $x = \bar{x}$ and $y = \bar{y}$. Since the lamina balances on those lines, the moments of the lamina about those lines should be zero:

$$\int_a^b (x - \bar{x})\delta f(x)\,dx = \int_a^b \left(\frac{f(x)}{2} - \bar{y}\right)\delta f(x)\,dx = 0$$

Since $\bar{x}$ and $\bar{y}$ are constant, these equations can be rewritten as

$$\int_a^b \delta x f(x)\,dx = \bar{x}\int_a^b \delta f(x)\,dx$$

$$\int_a^b \frac{1}{2}\delta(f(x))^2\,dx = \bar{y}\int_a^b \delta f(x)\,dx$$

from which we obtain the following formulas for the center of gravity of the lamina:

Center of Gravity $(\bar{x}, \bar{y})$ of a Lamina

$$\bar{x} = \frac{\displaystyle\int_a^b \delta x f(x)\,dx}{\displaystyle\int_a^b \delta f(x)\,dx}, \qquad \bar{y} = \frac{\displaystyle\int_a^b \frac{1}{2}\delta(f(x))^2\,dx}{\displaystyle\int_a^b \delta f(x)\,dx} \tag{4–5}$$

Observe that in both formulas the denominator is the mass M of the lamina. The numerator in the formula for $\bar{x}$ is denoted by M_y and is called the **first moment of the lamina about the y-axis**; the numerator of the formula for $\bar{y}$ is denoted by M_x and is called the **first moment of the lamina about the x-axis**. Thus, we can write (4) and (5) as

---

Alternative Formulas for Center of Gravity $(\bar{x}, \bar{y})$ of a Lamina

$$\bar{x} = \frac{M_y}{M} = \frac{1}{\text{mass of } R}\int_a^b \delta x f(x)\,dx \tag{6}$$

$$\bar{y} = \frac{M_x}{M} = \frac{1}{\text{mass of } R}\int_a^b \frac{1}{2}\delta(f(x))^2\,dx \tag{7}$$

▶ **Example 2** Find the center of gravity of the triangular lamina with vertices $(0, 0)$, $(0, 1)$, and $(1, 0)$ and density $\delta = 3$.

Solution. The lamina is shown in Figure 6.7.2. In Example 1 we found the mass of the lamina to be

$$M = \frac{3}{2}$$

The moment of the lamina about the y-axis is

$$M_y = \int_0^1 \delta x f(x) \, dx = \int_0^1 3x(-x+1) \, dx$$

$$= \int_0^1 (-3x^2 + 3x) \, dx = \left(-x^3 + \frac{3}{2}x^2 \right) \Big]_0^1 = -1 + \frac{3}{2} = \frac{1}{2}$$

and the moment about the x-axis is

$$M_x = \int_0^1 \frac{1}{2}\delta(f(x))^2 \, dx = \int_0^1 \frac{3}{2}(-x+1)^2 \, dx$$

$$= \int_0^1 \frac{3}{2}(x^2 - 2x + 1) \, dx = \frac{3}{2}\left(\frac{1}{3}x^3 - x^2 + x \right) \Big]_0^1 = \frac{3}{2}\left(\frac{1}{3} \right) = \frac{1}{2}$$

From (6) and (7),

$$\bar{x} = \frac{M_y}{M} = \frac{1/2}{3/2} = \frac{1}{3}, \qquad \bar{y} = \frac{M_x}{M} = \frac{1/2}{3/2} = \frac{1}{3}$$

so the center of gravity is $\left(\frac{1}{3}, \frac{1}{3} \right)$. ◄

In the case of a *homogeneous* lamina, the center of gravity of a lamina occupying the region R is called the **centroid of the region R**. Since the lamina is homogeneous, δ is constant. The factor δ in (4) and (5) may thus be moved through the integral signs and canceled, and (4) and (5) can be expressed as

> Since the density factor has canceled, we may interpret the centroid as a *geometric property* of the region, and distinguish it from the center of gravity, which is a *physical property* of an idealized object that occupies the region.

Centroid of a Region R

$$\bar{x} = \frac{\displaystyle\int_a^b xf(x) \, dx}{\displaystyle\int_a^b f(x) \, dx} = \frac{1}{\text{area of } R} \int_a^b xf(x) \, dx \qquad (8)$$

$$\bar{y} = \frac{\displaystyle\int_a^b \frac{1}{2}(f(x))^2 \, dx}{\displaystyle\int_a^b f(x) \, dx} = \frac{1}{\text{area of } R} \int_a^b \frac{1}{2}(f(x))^2 \, dx \qquad (9)$$

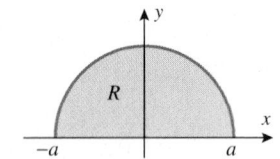

▲ **Figure 6.7.8**

► **Example 3**   Find the centroid of the semicircular region in Figure 6.7.8.

Solution.   By symmetry, $\bar{x} = 0$ since the y-axis is obviously a line of balance. To find $\bar{y}$, first note that the equation of the semicircle is $y = f(x) = \sqrt{a^2 - x^2}$. From (9),

$$\bar{y} = \frac{1}{\text{area of } R} \int_{-a}^a \frac{1}{2}(f(x))^2 \, dx = \frac{1}{\frac{1}{2}\pi a^2} \int_{-a}^a \frac{1}{2}(a^2 - x^2) \, dx$$

$$= \frac{1}{\pi a^2}\left(a^2 x - \frac{1}{3}x^3 \right) \Big]_{-a}^a$$

$$= \frac{1}{\pi a^2}\left[\left(a^3 - \frac{1}{3}a^3 \right) - \left(-a^3 + \frac{1}{3}a^3 \right) \right]$$

$$= \frac{1}{\pi a^2}\left(\frac{4a^3}{3} \right) = \frac{4a}{3\pi}$$

so the centroid is $(0, 4a/3\pi)$. ◄

■ **OTHER TYPES OF REGIONS**

The strategy used to find the center of gravity of the region in Problem 6.7.1 can be used to find the center of gravity of regions that are not of that form.

Consider a homogeneous lamina that occupies the region R between two continuous functions $f(x)$ and $g(x)$ over the interval $[a, b]$, where $f(x) \geq g(x)$ for $a \leq x \leq b$. To find the center of gravity of this lamina we can subdivide it into n strips using lines parallel to the x-axis. If x_k^* is the midpoint of the kth strip, the strip can be approximated by a rectangle of width Δx_k and height $f(x_k^*) - g(x_k^*)$. We assume that the entire mass of the kth rectangle is concentrated at its center $(x_k^*, y_k^*) = (x_k^*, \frac{1}{2}(f(x_k^*) + g(x_k^*)))$ (Figure 6.7.9). Continuing the argument as in the solution of Problem 6.7.1, we find that the center of gravity of the lamina is

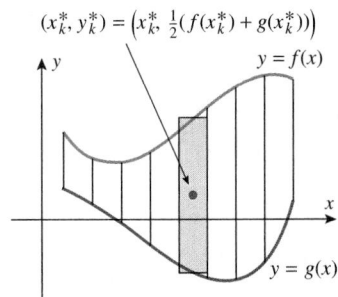

$(x_k^*, y_k^*) = \left(x_k^*, \frac{1}{2}(f(x_k^*) + g(x_k^*))\right)$

$y = f(x)$

$y = g(x)$

▲ **Figure 6.7.9**

$$\bar{x} = \frac{\displaystyle\int_a^b x(f(x) - g(x))\, dx}{\displaystyle\int_a^b (f(x) - g(x))\, dx} = \frac{1}{\text{area of } R}\int_a^b x(f(x) - g(x))\, dx \qquad (10)$$

$$\bar{y} = \frac{\displaystyle\int_a^b \frac{1}{2}\left([f(x)]^2 - [g(x)]^2\right) dx}{\displaystyle\int_a^b (f(x) - g(x))\, dx} = \frac{1}{\text{area of } R}\int_a^b \frac{1}{2}\left([f(x)]^2 - [g(x)]^2\right) dx \quad (11)$$

Note that the density of the lamina does not appear in Equations (10) and (11). This reflects the fact that the centroid is a geometric property of R.

▶ **Example 4**   Find the centroid of the region R enclosed between the curves $y = x^2$ and $y = x + 6$.

Solution.   To begin, we note that the two curves intersect when $x = -2$ and $x = 3$ and that $x + 6 \geq x^2$ over that interval (Figure 6.7.10). The area of R is

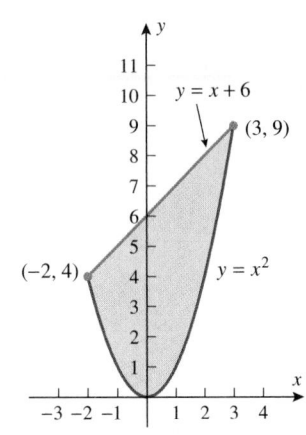

▲ **Figure 6.7.10**

$$\int_{-2}^3 [(x + 6) - x^2]\, dx = \frac{125}{6}$$

From (10) and (11),

$$\bar{x} = \frac{1}{\text{area of } R}\int_{-2}^3 x[(x + 6) - x^2]\, dx$$

$$= \frac{6}{125}\left(\frac{1}{3}x^3 + 3x^2 - \frac{1}{4}x^4\right)\Big]_{-2}^3$$

$$= \frac{6}{125} \cdot \frac{125}{12} = \frac{1}{2}$$

and

$$\bar{y} = \frac{1}{\text{area of } R}\int_{-2}^3 \frac{1}{2}((x + 6)^2 - (x^2)^2)\, dx$$

$$= \frac{6}{125}\int_{-2}^3 \frac{1}{2}(x^2 + 12x + 36 - x^4)\, dx$$

$$= \frac{6}{125} \cdot \frac{1}{2}\left(\frac{1}{3}x^3 + 6x^2 + 36x - \frac{1}{5}x^5\right)\Big]_{-2}^3$$

$$= \frac{6}{125} \cdot \frac{250}{3} = 4$$

so the centroid of R is $(\frac{1}{2}, 4)$. ◀

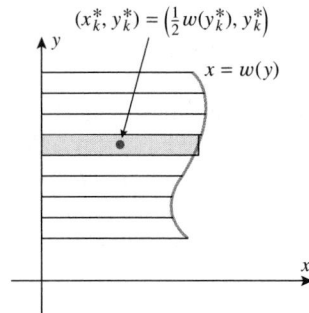

▲ **Figure 6.7.11**

Suppose that w is a continuous function of y on an interval $[c, d]$ with $w(y) \geq 0$ for $c \leq y \leq d$. Consider a lamina that occupies a region R bounded above by $y = d$, below by $y = c$, on the left by the y-axis, and on the right by $x = w(y)$ (Figure 6.7.11). To find the center of gravity of this lamina, we note that the roles of x and y in Problem 6.7.1 have been reversed. We now imagine the lamina to be subdivided into n strips using lines parallel to the x-axis. We let y_k^* be the midpoint of the kth subinterval and approximate the strip by a rectangle of width Δy_k and height $w(y_k^*)$. We assume that the entire mass of the kth rectangle is concentrated at its center $(x_k^*, y_k^*) = (\frac{1}{2}w(y_k^*), y_k^*)$ (Figure 6.7.11). Continuing the argument as in the solution of Problem 6.7.1, we find that the center of gravity of the lamina is

$$\bar{x} = \frac{\int_c^d \frac{1}{2}(w(y))^2\, dy}{\int_c^d w(y)\, dy} = \frac{1}{\text{area of } R}\int_c^d \frac{1}{2}(w(y))^2\, dy \qquad (12)$$

$$\bar{y} = \frac{\int_c^d y\,w(y)\, dy}{\int_c^d w(y)\, dy} = \frac{1}{\text{area of } R}\int_c^d y\,w(y)\, dy \qquad (13)$$

Once again, the absence of the density in Equations (12) and (13) reflects the geometric nature of the centroid.

▶ **Example 5**   Find the centroid of the region R enclosed between the curves $y = \sqrt{x}$, $y = 1$, $y = 2$, and the y-axis (Figure 6.7.12).

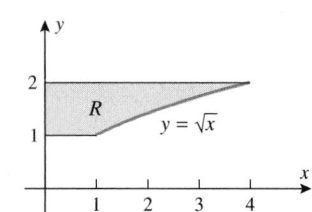

▲ **Figure 6.7.12**

Solution.   Note that $x = w(y) = y^2$ and that the area of R is

$$\int_1^2 y^2\, dy = \frac{7}{3}$$

From (12) and (13),

$$\bar{x} = \frac{1}{\text{area of } R}\int_1^2 \frac{1}{2}(y^2)^2\, dy = \frac{3}{7}\cdot\frac{1}{10}y^5\Big]_1^2 = \frac{3}{7}\cdot\frac{31}{10} = \frac{93}{70}$$

$$\bar{y} = \frac{1}{\text{area of } R}\int_1^2 y(y^2)\, dy = \frac{3}{7}\cdot\frac{1}{4}y^4\Big]_1^2 = \frac{3}{7}\cdot\frac{15}{4} = \frac{45}{28}$$

so the centroid of R is $(93/70, 45/28) \approx (1.329, 1.607)$. ◀

■ **THEOREM OF PAPPUS**

The following theorem, due to the Greek mathematician Pappus, gives an important relationship between the centroid of a plane region R and the volume of the solid generated when the region is revolved about a line.

6.7.2   **THEOREM** (*Theorem of Pappus*)   *If R is a bounded plane region and L is a line that lies in the plane of R such that R is entirely on one side of L, then the volume of the solid formed by revolving R about L is given by*

$$volume = (area\ of\ R) \cdot \binom{distance\ traveled}{by\ the\ centroid}$$

PROOF   We prove this theorem in the special case where L is the y-axis, the region R is in the first quadrant, and the region R is of the form given in Problem 6.7.1. (A more general proof will be outlined in the Exercises of Section 14.8.) In this case, the volume V of the solid formed by revolving R about L can be found by the method of cylindrical shells (Section 6.3) to be

$$V = 2\pi \int_a^b x f(x)\, dx$$

Thus, it follows from (8) that

$$V = 2\pi \bar{x}[\text{area of } R]$$

This completes the proof since $2\pi\bar{x}$ is the distance traveled by the centroid when R is revolved about the y-axis. ■

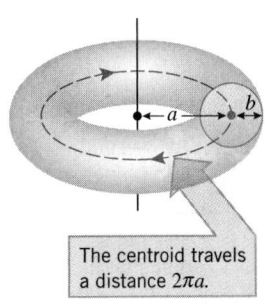

The centroid travels a distance $2\pi a$.

▲ **Figure 6.7.13**

▶ **Example 6**   Use Pappus' Theorem to find the volume V of the torus generated by revolving a circular region of radius b about a line at a distance a (greater than b) from the center of the circle (Figure 6.7.13).

Solution.   By symmetry, the centroid of a circular region is its center. Thus, the distance traveled by the centroid is $2\pi a$. Since the area of a circle of radius b is πb^2, it follows from Pappus' Theorem that the volume of the torus is

$$V = (2\pi a)(\pi b^2) = 2\pi^2 ab^2 \quad \blacktriangleleft$$

✔ **QUICK CHECK EXERCISES 6.7**   (*See page 467 for answers.*)

1. The total mass of a homogeneous lamina of area A and density δ is _____.

2. A homogeneous lamina of mass M and density δ occupies a region in the xy-plane bounded by the graphs of $y = f(x)$, $y = 0$, $x = a$, and $x = b$, where f is a nonnegative continuous function defined on an interval $[a, b]$. The x-coordinate of the center of gravity of the lamina is M_y/M, where M_y is called the _____ and is given by the integral _____.

3. Let R be the region between the graphs of $y = x^2$ and $y = 2 - x$ for $0 \le x \le 1$. The area of R is $\frac{7}{6}$ and the centroid of R is _____.

4. If the region R in Quick Check Exercise 3 is used to generate a solid G by rotating R about a horizontal line 6 units above its centroid, then the volume of G is _____.

EXERCISE SET 6.7   [C] CAS

FOCUS ON CONCEPTS

1. Masses $m_1 = 5$, $m_2 = 10$, and $m_3 = 20$ are positioned on a weightless beam as shown in the accompanying figure.

   (a) Suppose that the fulcrum is positioned at $x = 5$. Without computing the sum of moments about 5, determine whether the sum is positive, zero, or negative. Explain.

   (b) Where should the fulcrum be placed so that the beam is in equilibrium?

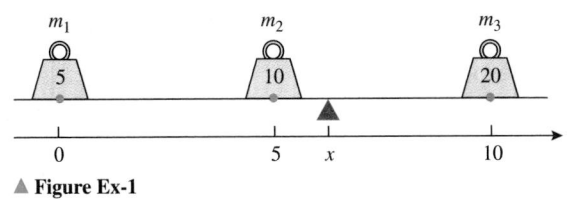

▲ **Figure Ex-1**

Pappus of Alexandria (4th century A.D.) Greek mathematician. Pappus lived during the early Christian era when mathematical activity was in a period of decline. His main contributions to mathematics appeared in a series of eight books called *The Collection* (written about 340 A.D.). This work, which survives only partially, contained some original results but was devoted mostly to statements, refinements, and proofs of results by earlier mathematicians. Pappus' Theorem, stated without proof in Book VII of *The Collection*, was probably known and proved in earlier times. This result is sometimes called Guldin's Theorem in recognition of the Swiss mathematician, Paul Guldin (1577–1643), who rediscovered it independently.

2. Masses $m_1 = 10$, $m_2 = 3$, $m_3 = 4$, and m are positioned on a weightless beam, with the fulcrum positioned at point 4, as shown in the accompanying figure.

(a) Suppose that $m = 14$. Without computing the sum of the moments about 4, determine whether the sum is positive, zero, or negative. Explain.

(b) For what value of m is the beam in equilibrium?

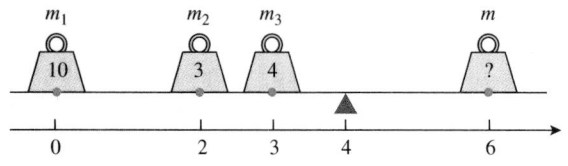

▲ **Figure Ex-2**

3–6 Find the centroid of the region by inspection and confirm your answer by integrating. ■

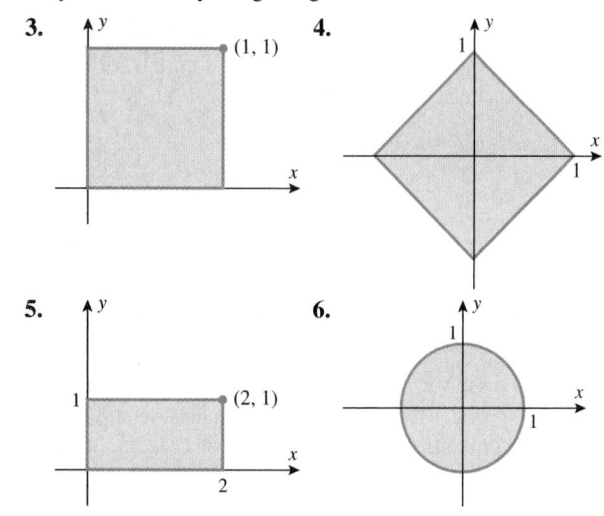

7–20 Find the centroid of the region. ■

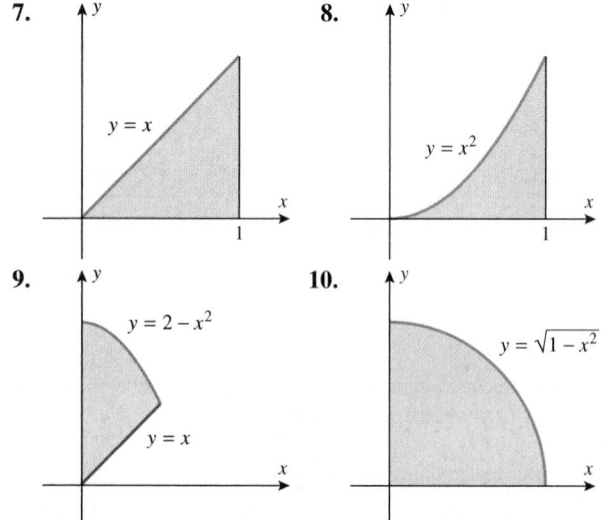

11. The triangle with vertices $(0, 0)$, $(2, 0)$, and $(0, 1)$.

12. The triangle with vertices $(0, 0)$, $(1, 1)$, and $(2, 0)$.

13. The region bounded by the graphs of $y = x^2$ and $x + y = 6$.

14. The region bounded on the left by the y-axis, on the right by the line $x = 2$, below by the parabola $y = x^2$, and above by the line $y = x + 6$.

15. The region bounded by the graphs of $y = x^2$ and $y = x + 2$.

16. The region bounded by the graphs of $y = x^2$ and $y = 1$.

17. The region bounded by the graphs of $y = \sqrt{x}$ and $y = x^2$.

18. The region bounded by the graphs of $x = 1/y$, $x = 0$, $y = 1$, and $y = 2$.

19. The region bounded by the graphs of $y = x$, $x = 1/y^2$, and $y = 2$.

20. The region bounded by the graphs of $xy = 4$ and $x + y = 5$.

FOCUS ON CONCEPTS

21. Use symmetry considerations to argue that the centroid of an isosceles triangle lies on the median to the base of the triangle.

22. Use symmetry considerations to argue that the centroid of an ellipse lies at the intersection of the major and minor axes of the ellipse.

23–26 Find the mass and center of gravity of the lamina with density δ. ■

23. A lamina bounded by the x-axis, the line $x = 1$, and the curve $y = \sqrt{x}$; $\delta = 2$.

24. A lamina bounded by the graph of $x = y^4$ and the line $x = 1$; $\delta = 15$.

25. A lamina bounded by the graph of $y = |x|$ and the line $y = 1$; $\delta = 3$.

26. A lamina bounded by the x-axis and the graph of the equation $y = 1 - x^2$; $\delta = 3$.

[C] **27–30** Use a CAS to find the mass and center of gravity of the lamina with density δ. ■

27. A lamina bounded by $y = \sin x$, $y = 0$, $x = 0$, and $x = \pi$; $\delta = 4$.

28. A lamina bounded by $y = e^x$, $y = 0$, $x = 0$, and $x = 1$; $\delta = 1/(e - 1)$.

29. A lamina bounded by the graph of $y = \ln x$, the x-axis, and the line $x = 2$; $\delta = 1$.

30. A lamina bounded by the graphs of $y = \cos x$, $y = \sin x$, $x = 0$, and $x = \pi/4$; $\delta = 1 + \sqrt{2}$.

31–34 True–False Determine whether the statement is true or false. Explain your answer. [In Exercise 34, assume that the (rotated) square lies in the xy-plane to the right of the y-axis.] ■

31. The centroid of a rectangle is the intersection of the diagonals of the rectangle.

32. The centroid of a rhombus is the intersection of the diagonals of the rhombus.

33. The centroid of an equilateral triangle is the intersection of the medians of the triangle.

34. By rotating a square about its center, it is possible to change the volume of the solid of revolution generated by revolving the square about the y-axis.

35. Find the centroid of the triangle with vertices $(0, 0)$, (a, b), and $(a, -b)$.

36. Prove that the centroid of a triangle is the point of intersection of the three medians of the triangle. [*Hint:* Choose coordinates so that the vertices of the triangle are located at $(0, -a)$, $(0, a)$, and (b, c).]

37. Find the centroid of the isosceles trapezoid with vertices $(-a, 0)$, $(a, 0)$, $(-b, c)$, and (b, c).

38. Prove that the centroid of a parallelogram is the point of intersection of the diagonals of the parallelogram. [*Hint:* Choose coordinates so that the vertices of the parallelogram are located at $(0, 0)$, $(0, a)$, (b, c), and $(b, a + c)$.]

39. Use the Theorem of Pappus and the fact that the volume of a sphere of radius a is $V = \frac{4}{3}\pi a^3$ to show that the centroid of the lamina that is bounded by the x-axis and the semicircle $y = \sqrt{a^2 - x^2}$ is $(0, 4a/(3\pi))$. (This problem was solved directly in Example 3.)

40. Use the Theorem of Pappus and the result of Exercise 39 to find the volume of the solid generated when the region bounded by the x-axis and the semicircle $y = \sqrt{a^2 - x^2}$ is revolved about

(a) the line $y = -a$ (b) the line $y = x - a$.

41. Use the Theorem of Pappus and the fact that the area of an ellipse with semiaxes a and b is πab to find the volume of the elliptical torus generated by revolving the ellipse

$$\frac{(x - k)^2}{a^2} + \frac{y^2}{b^2} = 1$$

about the y-axis. Assume that $k > a$.

42. Use the Theorem of Pappus to find the volume of the solid that is generated when the region enclosed by $y = x^2$ and $y = 8 - x^2$ is revolved about the x-axis.

43. Use the Theorem of Pappus to find the centroid of the triangular region with vertices $(0, 0)$, $(a, 0)$, and $(0, b)$, where $a > 0$ and $b > 0$. [*Hint:* Revolve the region about the x-axis to obtain $\bar{y}$ and about the y-axis to obtain $\bar{x}$.]

44. Writing Suppose that a region R in the plane is decomposed into two regions R_1 and R_2 whose areas are A_1 and A_2, respectively, and whose centroids are $(\bar{x}_1, \bar{y}_1)$ and $(\bar{x}_2, \bar{y}_2)$, respectively. Investigate the problem of expressing the centroid of R in terms of A_1, A_2, $(\bar{x}_1, \bar{y}_1)$, and $(\bar{x}_2, \bar{y}_2)$. Write a short report on your investigations, supporting your reasoning with plausible arguments. Can you extend your results to decompositions of R into more than two regions?

45. Writing How might you recognize that a problem can be solved by means of the Theorem of Pappus? That is, what sort of "givens" and "unknowns" would suggest such a solution? Discuss two or three examples.

✔ **QUICK CHECK ANSWERS 6.7**

1. δA **2.** first moment about the y-axis; $\displaystyle\int_a^b \delta x f(x)\, dx$ **3.** $\left(\dfrac{5}{14}, \dfrac{32}{35}\right)$ **4.** 14π

6.8 FLUID PRESSURE AND FORCE

In this section we will use the integration tools developed in the preceding chapter to study the pressures and forces exerted by fluids on submerged objects.

■ **WHAT IS A FLUID?**

A *fluid* is a substance that flows to conform to the boundaries of any container in which it is placed. Fluids include *liquids*, such as water, oil, and mercury, as well as *gases*, such as helium, oxygen, and air. The study of fluids falls into two categories: *fluid statics* (the study of fluids at rest) and *fluid dynamics* (the study of fluids in motion). In this section we will be concerned only with fluid statics; toward the end of this text we will investigate problems in fluid dynamics.

■ THE CONCEPT OF PRESSURE

Jupiter Images Corp.

Snowshoes prevent the woman from sinking by spreading her weight over a large area to reduce her pressure on the snow.

The effect that a force has on an object depends on how that force is spread over the surface of the object. For example, when you walk on soft snow with boots, the weight of your body crushes the snow and you sink into it. However, if you put on a pair of snowshoes to spread the weight of your body over a greater surface area, then the weight of your body has less of a crushing effect on the snow. The concept that accounts for both the magnitude of a force and the area over which it is applied is called *pressure*.

6.8.1   DEFINITION   If a force of magnitude F is applied to a surface of area A, then we define the **pressure** P exerted by the force on the surface to be

$$P = \frac{F}{A} \tag{1}$$

It follows from this definition that pressure has units of force per unit area. The most common units of pressure are newtons per square meter (N/m^2) in SI and pounds per square inch (lb/in^2) or pounds per square foot (lb/ft^2) in the BE system. As indicated in Table 6.8.1, one newton per square meter is called a *pascal* (Pa). A pressure of 1 Pa is quite small (1 Pa $= 1.45 \times 10^{-4}$ lb/in^2), so in countries using SI, tire pressure gauges are usually calibrated in kilopascals (kPa), which is 1000 pascals.

Table 6.8.1

UNITS OF FORCE AND PRESSURE

SYSTEM	FORCE	÷	AREA	=	PRESSURE
SI	newton (N)		square meter (m^2)		pascal (Pa)
BE	pound (lb)		square foot (ft^2)		lb/ft^2
BE	pound (lb)		square inch (in^2)		lb/in^2 (psi)

CONVERSION FACTORS:
1 Pa $\approx 1.45 \times 10^{-4}$ $lb/in^2 \approx 2.09 \times 10^{-2}$ lb/ft^2
1 $lb/in^2 \approx 6.89 \times 10^3$ Pa   1 $lb/ft^2 \approx 47.9$ Pa

Blaise Pascal (1623–1662) French mathematician and scientist. Pascal's mother died when he was three years old and his father, a highly educated magistrate, personally provided the boy's early education. Although Pascal showed an inclination for science and mathematics, his father refused to tutor him in those subjects until he mastered Latin and Greek. Pascal's sister and primary biographer claimed that he independently discovered the first thirty-two propositions of Euclid without ever reading a book on geometry. (However, it is generally agreed that the story is apocryphal.) Nevertheless, the precocious Pascal published a highly respected essay on conic sections by the time he was sixteen years old. Descartes, who read the essay, thought it so brilliant that he could not believe that it was written by such a young man. By age 18 his health began to fail and

until his death he was in frequent pain. However, his creativity was unimpaired.

Pascal's contributions to physics include the discovery that air pressure decreases with altitude and the principle of fluid pressure that bears his name. However, the originality of his work is questioned by some historians. Pascal made major contributions to a branch of mathematics called "projective geometry," and he helped to develop probability theory through a series of letters with Fermat.

In 1646, Pascal's health problems resulted in a deep emotional crisis that led him to become increasingly concerned with religious matters. Although born a Catholic, he converted to a religious doctrine called Jansenism and spent most of his final years writing on religion and philosophy.

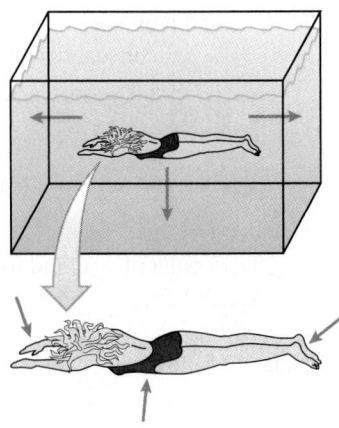

Fluid forces always act perpendicular to the surface of a submerged object.

▲ **Figure 6.8.1**

In this section we will be interested in pressures and forces on objects submerged in fluids. Pressures themselves have no directional characteristics, but the forces that they create always act perpendicular to the face of the submerged object. Thus, in Figure 6.8.1 the water pressure creates horizontal forces on the sides of the tank, vertical forces on the bottom of the tank, and forces that vary in direction, so as to be perpendicular to the different parts of the swimmer's body.

▶ **Example 1** Referring to Figure 6.8.1, suppose that the back of the swimmer's hand has a surface area of 8.4×10^{-3} m^2 and that the pressure acting on it is 5.1×10^4 Pa (a realistic value near the bottom of a deep diving pool). Find the force that acts on the swimmer's hand.

Solution. From (1), the force F is

$$F = PA = (5.1 \times 10^4 \text{ N/m}^2)(8.4 \times 10^{-3} \text{ m}^2) \approx 4.3 \times 10^2 \text{ N}$$

This is quite a large force (nearly 100 lb in the BE system). ◀

■ FLUID DENSITY

Scuba divers know that the pressure and forces on their bodies increase with the depth they dive. This is caused by the weight of the water and air above—the deeper the diver goes, the greater the weight above and so the greater the pressure and force exerted on the diver.

To calculate pressures and forces on submerged objects, we need to know something about the characteristics of the fluids in which they are submerged. For simplicity, we will assume that the fluids under consideration are *homogeneous*, by which we mean that any two samples of the fluid with the same volume have the same mass. It follows from this assumption that the mass per unit volume is a constant δ that depends on the physical characteristics of the fluid but not on the size or location of the sample; we call

$$\delta = \frac{m}{V} \qquad (2)$$

the ***mass density*** of the fluid. Sometimes it is more convenient to work with weight per unit volume than with mass per unit volume. Thus, we define the ***weight density*** ρ of a fluid to be

$$\rho = \frac{w}{V} \qquad (3)$$

where w is the weight of a fluid sample of volume V. Thus, if the weight density of a fluid is known, then the weight w of a fluid sample of volume V can be computed from the formula $w = \rho V$. Table 6.8.2 shows some typical weight densities.

Table 6.8.2

WEIGHT DENSITIES

SI	N/m^3
Machine oil	4708
Gasoline	6602
Fresh water	9810
Seawater	10,045
Mercury	133,416

BE SYSTEM	lb/ft^3
Machine oil	30.0
Gasoline	42.0
Fresh water	62.4
Seawater	64.0
Mercury	849.0

All densities are affected by variations in temperature and pressure. Weight densities are also affected by variations in g.

■ FLUID PRESSURE

To calculate fluid pressures and forces we will need to make use of an experimental observation. Suppose that a flat surface of area A is submerged in a homogeneous fluid of weight density ρ such that the entire surface lies between depths h_1 and h_2, where $h_1 \leq h_2$ (Figure 6.8.2). Experiments show that on both sides of the surface, the fluid exerts a force that is perpendicular to the surface and whose magnitude F satisfies the inequalities

$$\rho h_1 A \leq F \leq \rho h_2 A \qquad (4)$$

Thus, it follows from (1) that the pressure $P = F/A$ on a given side of the surface satisfies the inequalities

$$\rho h_1 \leq P \leq \rho h_2 \qquad (5)$$

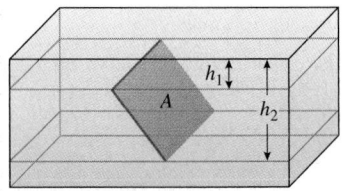

▲ **Figure 6.8.2**

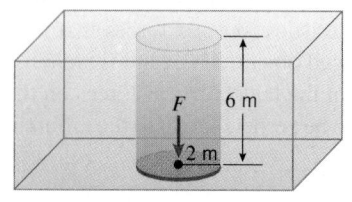

The fluid force is the fluid pressure times the area.

▲ **Figure 6.8.3**

Note that it is now a straightforward matter to calculate fluid force and pressure on a flat surface that is submerged *horizontally* at depth h, for then $h = h_1 = h_2$ and inequalities (4) and (5) become the *equalities*

$$F = \rho h A \tag{6}$$

and

$$P = \rho h \tag{7}$$

▶ **Example 2**   Find the fluid pressure and force on the top of a flat circular plate of radius 2 m that is submerged horizontally in water at a depth of 6 m (Figure 6.8.3).

Solution.   Since the weight density of water is $\rho = 9810 \text{ N/m}^3$, it follows from (7) that the fluid pressure is

$$P = \rho h = (9810)(6) = 58{,}860 \text{ Pa}$$

and it follows from (6) that the fluid force is

$$F = \rho h A = \rho h(\pi r^2) = (9810)(6)(4\pi) = 235{,}440\pi \approx 739{,}700 \text{ N} \blacktriangleleft$$

■ FLUID FORCE ON A VERTICAL SURFACE

It was easy to calculate the fluid force on the horizontal plate in Example 2 because each point on the plate was at the same depth. The problem of finding the fluid force on a vertical surface is more complicated because the depth, and hence the pressure, is not constant over the surface. To find the fluid force on a vertical surface we will need calculus.

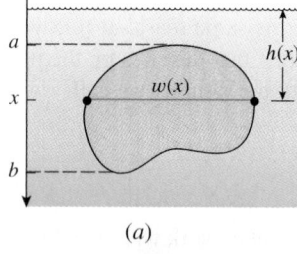

(a)

6.8.2   PROBLEM   Suppose that a flat surface is immersed vertically in a fluid of weight density ρ and that the submerged portion of the surface extends from $x = a$ to $x = b$ along an x-axis whose positive direction is down (Figure 6.8.4a). For $a \leq x \leq b$, suppose that $w(x)$ is the width of the surface and that $h(x)$ is the depth of the point x. Define what is meant by the *fluid force* F on the surface, and find a formula for computing it.

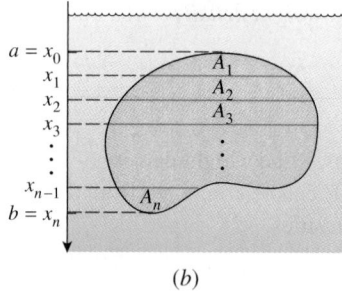

(b)

The basic idea for solving this problem is to divide the surface into horizontal strips whose areas may be approximated by areas of rectangles. These area approximations, along with inequalities (4), will allow us to create a Riemann sum that approximates the total force on the surface. By taking a limit of Riemann sums we will then obtain an integral for F.

To implement this idea, we divide the interval $[a, b]$ into n subintervals by inserting the points $x_1, x_2, \ldots, x_{n-1}$ between $a = x_0$ and $b = x_n$. This has the effect of dividing the surface into n strips of area A_k, $k = 1, 2, \ldots, n$ (Figure 6.8.4b). It follows from (4) that the force F_k on the kth strip satisfies the inequalities

$$\rho h(x_{k-1}) A_k \leq F_k \leq \rho h(x_k) A_k$$

or, equivalently,

$$h(x_{k-1}) \leq \frac{F_k}{\rho A_k} \leq h(x_k)$$

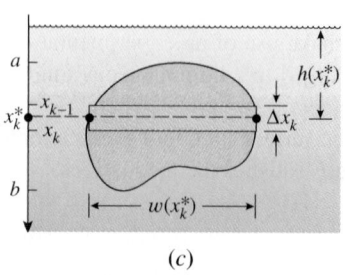

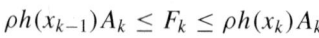

(c)

▲ **Figure 6.8.4**

Since the depth function $h(x)$ increases linearly, there must exist a point x_k^* between x_{k-1} and x_k such that

$$h(x_k^*) = \frac{F_k}{\rho A_k}$$

or, equivalently,

$$F_k = \rho h(x_k^*) A_k$$

We now approximate the area A_k of the kth strip of the surface by the area of a rectangle of width $w(x_k^*)$ and height $\Delta x_k = x_k - x_{k-1}$ (Figure 6.8.4c). It follows that F_k may be approximated as

$$F_k = \rho h(x_k^*)A_k \approx \rho h(x_k^*) \cdot \underbrace{w(x_k^*)\Delta x_k}_{\text{Area of rectangle}}$$

Adding these approximations yields the following Riemann sum that approximates the total force F on the surface:

$$F = \sum_{k=1}^{n} F_k \approx \sum_{k=1}^{n} \rho h(x_k^*)w(x_k^*)\Delta x_k$$

Taking the limit as n increases and the widths of all the subintervals approach zero yields the definite integral

$$F = \lim_{\max \Delta x_k \to 0} \sum_{k=1}^{n} \rho h(x_k^*)w(x_k^*)\Delta x_k = \int_a^b \rho h(x)w(x)\,dx$$

In summary, we have the following result.

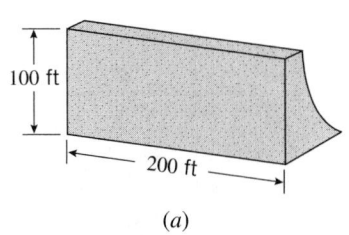

6.8.3   DEFINITION   Suppose that a flat surface is immersed vertically in a fluid of weight density ρ and that the submerged portion of the surface extends from $x = a$ to $x = b$ along an x-axis whose positive direction is down (Figure 6.8.4a). For $a \leq x \leq b$, suppose that $w(x)$ is the width of the surface and that $h(x)$ is the depth of the point x. Then we define the *fluid force* F on the surface to be

$$F = \int_a^b \rho h(x)w(x)\,dx \qquad (8)$$

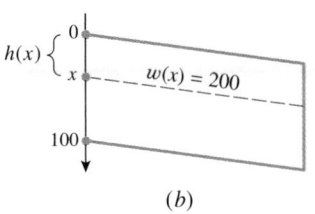

▲ **Figure 6.8.5**

▶ **Example 3**   The face of a dam is a vertical rectangle of height 100 ft and width 200 ft (Figure 6.8.5a). Find the total fluid force exerted on the face when the water surface is level with the top of the dam.

Solution.   Introduce an x-axis with its origin at the water surface as shown in Figure 6.8.5b. At a point x on this axis, the width of the dam in feet is $w(x) = 200$ and the depth in feet is $h(x) = x$. Thus, from (8) with $\rho = 62.4$ lb/ft^3 (the weight density of water) we obtain as the total force on the face

$$F = \int_0^{100} (62.4)(x)(200)\,dx = 12{,}480 \int_0^{100} x\,dx$$

$$= 12{,}480 \left. \frac{x^2}{2} \right]_0^{100} = 62{,}400{,}000 \text{ lb} \blacktriangleleft$$

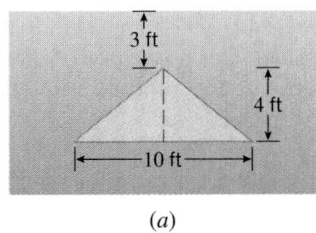

▲ **Figure 6.8.6**

▶ **Example 4**   A plate in the form of an isosceles triangle with base 10 ft and altitude 4 ft is submerged vertically in machine oil as shown in Figure 6.8.6a. Find the fluid force F against the plate surface if the oil has weight density $\rho = 30$ lb/ft^3.

Solution.   Introduce an x-axis as shown in Figure 6.8.6b. By similar triangles, the width of the plate, in feet, at a depth of $h(x) = (3 + x)$ ft satisfies

$$\frac{w(x)}{10} = \frac{x}{4}, \quad \text{so} \quad w(x) = \frac{5}{2}x$$

Thus, it follows from (8) that the force on the plate is

$$F = \int_a^b \rho h(x)w(x)\,dx = \int_0^4 (30)(3+x)\left(\frac{5}{2}x\right)dx$$

$$= 75\int_0^4 (3x + x^2)\,dx = 75\left[\frac{3x^2}{2} + \frac{x^3}{3}\right]_0^4 = 3400\text{ lb} \blacktriangleleft$$

✔ QUICK CHECK EXERCISES 6.8 *(See page 473 for answers.)*

1. The pressure unit equivalent to a newton per square meter (N/m^2) is called a _____. The pressure unit psi stands for _____.

2. Given that the weight density of water is 9810 N/m^3, the fluid pressure on a rectangular $2\text{ m} \times 3\text{ m}$ flat plate submerged horizontally in water at a depth of 10 m is _____. The fluid force on the plate is _____.

3. Suppose that a flat surface is immersed vertically in a fluid of weight density ρ and that the submerged portion of the surface extends from $x = a$ to $x = b$ along an x-axis whose positive direction is down. If, for $a \le x \le b$, the surface has width $w(x)$ and depth $h(x)$, then the fluid force on the surface is $F =$ _____.

4. A rectangular plate 2 m wide and 3 m high is submerged vertically in water so that the top of the plate is 5 m below the water surface. An integral expression for the force of the water on the plate surface is $F =$ _____.

EXERCISE SET 6.8

In this exercise set, refer to Table 6.8.2 for weight densities of fluids, where needed. ■

1. A flat rectangular plate is submerged horizontally in water.
   (a) Find the force (in lb) and the pressure (in lb/ft^2) on the top surface of the plate if its area is 100 ft^2 and the surface is at a depth of 5 ft.
   (b) Find the force (in N) and the pressure (in Pa) on the top surface of the plate if its area is 25 m^2 and the surface is at a depth of 10 m.

2. (a) Find the force (in N) on the deck of a sunken ship if its area is 160 m^2 and the pressure acting on it is $6.0 \times 10^5\text{ Pa}$.
   (b) Find the force (in lb) on a diver's face mask if its area is 60 in^2 and the pressure acting on it is 100 lb/in^2.

3–8 The flat surfaces shown are submerged vertically in water. Find the fluid force against each surface. ■

3.
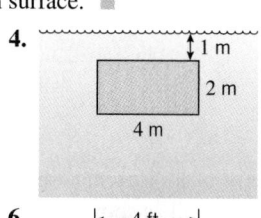

4.
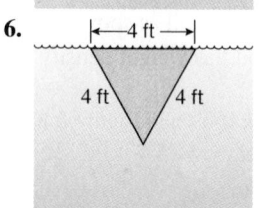

5.
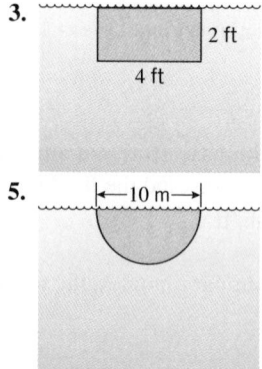

6.

7.
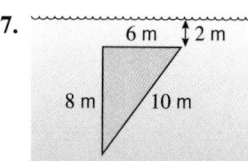

8.
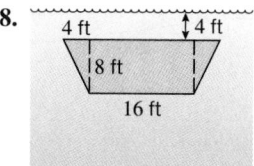

9. Suppose that a flat surface is immersed vertically in a fluid of weight density ρ. If ρ is doubled, is the force on the plate also doubled? Explain your reasoning.

10. An oil tank is shaped like a right circular cylinder of diameter 4 ft. Find the total fluid force against one end when the axis is horizontal and the tank is half filled with oil of weight density 50 lb/ft^3.

11. A square plate of side a feet is dipped in a liquid of weight density $\rho\text{ lb/ft}^3$. Find the fluid force on the plate if a vertex is at the surface and a diagonal is perpendicular to the surface.

12–15 True–False Determine whether the statement is true or false. Explain your answer. ■

12. In the International System of Units, pressure and force have the same units.

13. In a cylindrical water tank (with vertical axis), the fluid force on the base of the tank is equal to the weight of water in the tank.

14. In a rectangular water tank, the fluid force on any side of the tank must be less than the fluid force on the base of the tank.

15. In any water tank with a flat base, no matter what the shape of the tank, the fluid force on the base is at most equal to the weight of water in the tank.

16–19 Formula (8) gives the fluid force on a flat surface immersed vertically in a fluid. More generally, if a flat surface is immersed so that it makes an angle of $0 \leq \theta < \pi/2$ with the vertical, then the fluid force on the surface is given by

$$F = \int_a^b \rho h(x)w(x)\sec\theta\,dx$$

Use this formula in these exercises. ■

16. Derive the formula given above for the fluid force on a flat surface immersed at an angle in a fluid.

17. The accompanying figure shows a rectangular swimming pool whose bottom is an inclined plane. Find the fluid force on the bottom when the pool is filled to the top.

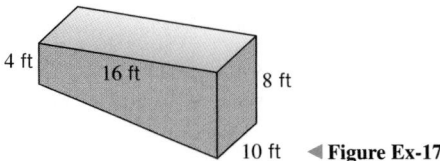

4 ft   16 ft   8 ft
10 ft   ◄ **Figure Ex-17**

18. By how many feet should the water in the pool of Exercise 17 be lowered in order for the force on the bottom to be reduced by a factor of $\frac{1}{2}$?

19. The accompanying figure shows a dam whose face is an inclined rectangle. Find the fluid force on the face when the water is level with the top of this dam.

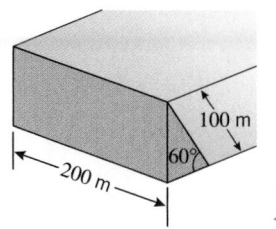

100 m
60°
200 m
◄ **Figure Ex-19**

20. An observation window on a submarine is a square with 2 ft sides. Using ρ_0 for the weight density of seawater, find the fluid force on the window when the submarine has descended so that the window is vertical and its top is at a depth of h feet.

FOCUS ON CONCEPTS

21. (a) Show: If the submarine in Exercise 20 descends vertically at a constant rate, then the fluid force on the window increases at a constant rate.
(b) At what rate is the force on the window increasing if the submarine is descending vertically at 20 ft/min?

22. (a) Let $D = D_a$ denote a disk of radius a submerged in a fluid of weight density ρ such that the center of D is h units below the surface of the fluid. For each value of r in the interval $(0, a]$, let D_r denote the disk of radius r that is concentric with D. Select a side of the disk D and define $P(r)$ to be the fluid pressure on the chosen side of D_r. Use (5) to prove that

$$\lim_{r \to 0^+} P(r) = \rho h$$

(b) Explain why the result in part (a) may be interpreted to mean that *fluid pressure at a given depth is the same in all directions*. (This statement is one version of a result known as ***Pascal's Principle***.)

23. **Writing** Suppose that we model the Earth's atmosphere as a "fluid." Atmospheric pressure at sea level is $P = 14.7$ lb/in^2 and the weight density of air at sea level is about $\rho = 4.66 \times 10^{-5}$ lb/in^3. With these numbers, what would Formula (7) yield as the height of the atmosphere above the Earth? Do you think this answer is reasonable? If not, explain how we might modify our assumptions to yield a more plausible answer.

24. **Writing** Suppose that the weight density ρ of a fluid is a function $\rho = \rho(x)$ of the depth x within the fluid. How do you think that Formula (7) for fluid pressure will need to be modified? Support your answer with plausible arguments.

✔**QUICK CHECK ANSWERS 6.8**

1. pascal; pounds per square inch   **2.** 98,100 Pa; 588,600 N   **3.** $\int_a^b \rho h(x)w(x)\,dx$ **4.** $\int_0^3 9810\,[(5+x)2]\,dx$

6.9 HYPERBOLIC FUNCTIONS AND HANGING CABLES

In this section we will study certain combinations of e^x and e^{-x}, called "hyperbolic functions." These functions, which arise in various engineering applications, have many properties in common with the trigonometric functions. This similarity is somewhat surprising, since there is little on the surface to suggest that there should be any relationship between exponential and trigonometric functions. This is because the relationship occurs within the context of complex numbers, a topic which we will leave for more advanced courses.

■ DEFINITIONS OF HYPERBOLIC FUNCTIONS

To introduce the hyperbolic functions, observe from Exercise 61 in Section 0.2 that the function e^x can be expressed in the following way as the sum of an even function and an odd function:

$$e^x = \underbrace{\frac{e^x + e^{-x}}{2}}_{\text{Even}} + \underbrace{\frac{e^x - e^{-x}}{2}}_{\text{Odd}}$$

These functions are sufficiently important that there are names and notation associated with them: the odd function is called the *hyperbolic sine* of x and the even function is called the *hyperbolic cosine* of x. They are denoted by

$$\sinh x = \frac{e^x - e^{-x}}{2} \quad \text{and} \quad \cosh x = \frac{e^x + e^{-x}}{2}$$

where sinh is pronounced "cinch" and cosh rhymes with "gosh." From these two building blocks we can create four more functions to produce the following set of six *hyperbolic functions*.

6.9.1 DEFINITION

Hyperbolic sine	$\sinh x = \dfrac{e^x - e^{-x}}{2}$	
Hyperbolic cosine	$\cosh x = \dfrac{e^x + e^{-x}}{2}$	
Hyperbolic tangent	$\tanh x = \dfrac{\sinh x}{\cosh x} = \dfrac{e^x - e^{-x}}{e^x + e^{-x}}$	
Hyperbolic cotangent	$\coth x = \dfrac{\cosh x}{\sinh x} = \dfrac{e^x + e^{-x}}{e^x - e^{-x}}$	
Hyperbolic secant	$\operatorname{sech} x = \dfrac{1}{\cosh x} = \dfrac{2}{e^x + e^{-x}}$	
Hyperbolic cosecant	$\operatorname{csch} x = \dfrac{1}{\sinh x} = \dfrac{2}{e^x - e^{-x}}$	

The terms "tanh," "sech," and "csch" are pronounced "tanch," "seech," and "coseech," respectively.

TECHNOLOGY MASTERY

Computer algebra systems have built-in capabilities for evaluating hyperbolic functions directly, but some calculators do not. However, if you need to evaluate a hyperbolic function on a calculator, you can do so by expressing it in terms of exponential functions, as in Example 1.

► **Example 1**

$$\sinh 0 = \frac{e^0 - e^{-0}}{2} = \frac{1 - 1}{2} = 0$$

$$\cosh 0 = \frac{e^0 + e^{-0}}{2} = \frac{1 + 1}{2} = 1$$

$$\sinh 2 = \frac{e^2 - e^{-2}}{2} \approx 3.6269 \blacktriangleleft$$

■ GRAPHS OF THE HYPERBOLIC FUNCTIONS

The graphs of the hyperbolic functions, which are shown in Figure 6.9.1, can be generated with a graphing utility, but it is worthwhile to observe that the general shape of the graph of $y = \cosh x$ can be obtained by sketching the graphs of $y = \frac{1}{2}e^x$ and $y = \frac{1}{2}e^{-x}$ separately and adding the corresponding y-coordinates [see part (a) of the figure]. Similarly, the general shape of the graph of $y = \sinh x$ can be obtained by sketching the graphs of $y = \frac{1}{2}e^x$ and $y = -\frac{1}{2}e^{-x}$ separately and adding corresponding y-coordinates [see part (b) of the figure].

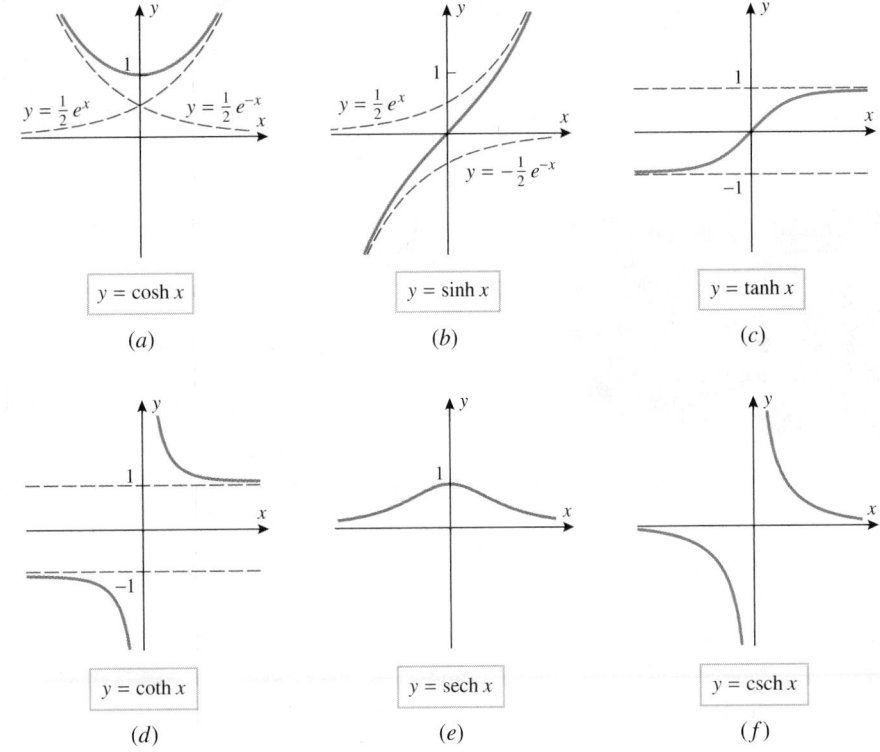

▲ **Figure 6.9.1**

Glen Allison/Stone/Getty Images

The design of the Gateway Arch near St. Louis is based on an inverted hyperbolic cosine curve (Exercise 73).

Observe that $\sinh x$ has a domain of $(-\infty, +\infty)$ and a range of $(-\infty, +\infty)$, whereas $\cosh x$ has a domain of $(-\infty, +\infty)$ and a range of $[1, +\infty)$. Observe also that $y = \frac{1}{2}e^x$ and $y = \frac{1}{2}e^{-x}$ are *curvilinear asymptotes* for $y = \cosh x$ in the sense that the graph of $y = \cosh x$ gets closer and closer to the graph of $y = \frac{1}{2}e^x$ as $x \to +\infty$ and gets closer and closer to the graph of $y = \frac{1}{2}e^{-x}$ as $x \to -\infty$. (See Section 4.3.) Similarly, $y = \frac{1}{2}e^x$ is a curvilinear asymptote for $y = \sinh x$ as $x \to +\infty$ and $y = -\frac{1}{2}e^{-x}$ is a curvilinear asymptote as $x \to -\infty$. Other properties of the hyperbolic functions are explored in the exercises.

■ HANGING CABLES AND OTHER APPLICATIONS

Hyperbolic functions arise in vibratory motions inside elastic solids and more generally in many problems where mechanical energy is gradually absorbed by a surrounding medium. They also occur when a homogeneous, flexible cable is suspended between two points, as with a telephone line hanging between two poles. Such a cable forms a curve, called a *catenary* (from the Latin *catena*, meaning "chain"). If, as in Figure 6.9.2, a coordinate system is introduced so that the low point of the cable lies on the y-axis, then it can be shown using principles of physics that the cable has an equation of the form

$$y = a \cosh\left(\frac{x}{a}\right) + c$$

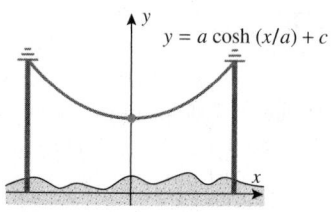

▲ **Figure 6.9.2**

where the parameters a and c are determined by the distance between the poles and the composition of the cable.

■ **HYPERBOLIC IDENTITIES**

The hyperbolic functions satisfy various identities that are similar to identities for trigonometric functions. The most fundamental of these is

$$\cosh^2 x - \sinh^2 x = 1 \tag{1}$$

which can be proved by writing

$$\cosh^2 x - \sinh^2 x = (\cosh x + \sinh x)(\cosh x - \sinh x)$$

$$= \left(\frac{e^x + e^{-x}}{2} + \frac{e^x - e^{-x}}{2} \right) \left(\frac{e^x + e^{-x}}{2} - \frac{e^x - e^{-x}}{2} \right)$$

$$= e^x \cdot e^{-x} = 1$$

Larry Auippy/Mira.com/Digital Railroad, Inc.

A flexible cable suspended between two poles forms a catenary.

Other hyperbolic identities can be derived in a similar manner or, alternatively, by performing algebraic operations on known identities. For example, if we divide (1) by $\cosh^2 x$, we obtain

$$1 - \tanh^2 x = \text{sech}^2 x$$

and if we divide (1) by $\sinh^2 x$, we obtain

$$\coth^2 x - 1 = \text{csch}^2 x$$

The following theorem summarizes some of the more useful hyperbolic identities. The proofs of those not already obtained are left as exercises.

6.9.2   THEOREM

$\cosh x + \sinh x = e^x$	$\sinh(x + y) = \sinh x \cosh y + \cosh x \sinh y$
$\cosh x - \sinh x = e^{-x}$	$\cosh(x + y) = \cosh x \cosh y + \sinh x \sinh y$
$\cosh^2 x - \sinh^2 x = 1$	$\sinh(x - y) = \sinh x \cosh y - \cosh x \sinh y$
$1 - \tanh^2 x = \text{sech}^2 x$	$\cosh(x - y) = \cosh x \cosh y - \sinh x \sinh y$
$\coth^2 x - 1 = \text{csch}^2 x$	$\sinh 2x = 2 \sinh x \cosh x$
$\cosh(-x) = \cosh x$	$\cosh 2x = \cosh^2 x + \sinh^2 x$
$\sinh(-x) = -\sinh x$	$\cosh 2x = 2\sinh^2 x + 1 = 2\cosh^2 x - 1$

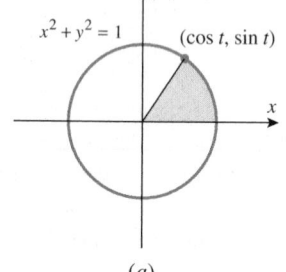

(a)

■ **WHY THEY ARE CALLED HYPERBOLIC FUNCTIONS**

Recall that the parametric equations

$$x = \cos t, \quad y = \sin t \quad (0 \le t \le 2\pi)$$

represent the unit circle $x^2 + y^2 = 1$ (Figure 6.9.3a), as may be seen by writing

$$x^2 + y^2 = \cos^2 t + \sin^2 t = 1$$

If $0 \le t \le 2\pi$, then the parameter t can be interpreted as the angle in radians from the positive x-axis to the point $(\cos t, \sin t)$ or, alternatively, as twice the shaded area of the sector in Figure 6.9.3a (verify). Analogously, the parametric equations

$$x = \cosh t, \quad y = \sinh t \quad (-\infty < t < +\infty)$$

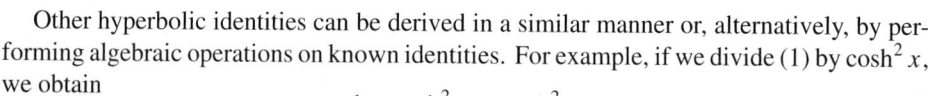

(b)

▲ **Figure 6.9.3**

represent a portion of the curve $x^2 - y^2 = 1$, as may be seen by writing

$$x^2 - y^2 = \cosh^2 t - \sinh^2 t = 1$$

and observing that $x = \cosh t > 0$. This curve, which is shown in Figure 6.9.3b, is the right half of a larger curve called the ***unit hyperbola***; this is the reason why the functions in this section are called *hyperbolic* functions. It can be shown that if $t \geq 0$, then the parameter t can be interpreted as twice the shaded area in Figure 6.9.3b. (We omit the details.)

■ DERIVATIVE AND INTEGRAL FORMULAS

Derivative formulas for $\sinh x$ and $\cosh x$ can be obtained by expressing these functions in terms of e^x and e^{-x}:

$$\frac{d}{dx}[\sinh x] = \frac{d}{dx}\left[\frac{e^x - e^{-x}}{2}\right] = \frac{e^x + e^{-x}}{2} = \cosh x$$

$$\frac{d}{dx}[\cosh x] = \frac{d}{dx}\left[\frac{e^x + e^{-x}}{2}\right] = \frac{e^x - e^{-x}}{2} = \sinh x$$

Derivatives of the remaining hyperbolic functions can be obtained by expressing them in terms of sinh and cosh and applying appropriate identities. For example,

$$\frac{d}{dx}[\tanh x] = \frac{d}{dx}\left[\frac{\sinh x}{\cosh x}\right] = \frac{\cosh x \dfrac{d}{dx}[\sinh x] - \sinh x \dfrac{d}{dx}[\cosh x]}{\cosh^2 x}$$

$$= \frac{\cosh^2 x - \sinh^2 x}{\cosh^2 x} = \frac{1}{\cosh^2 x} = \operatorname{sech}^2 x$$

The following theorem provides a complete list of the generalized derivative formulas and corresponding integration formulas for the hyperbolic functions.

6.9.3   THEOREM

$$\frac{d}{dx}[\sinh u] = \cosh u \frac{du}{dx} \qquad\qquad \int \cosh u \, du = \sinh u + C$$

$$\frac{d}{dx}[\cosh u] = \sinh u \frac{du}{dx} \qquad\qquad \int \sinh u \, du = \cosh u + C$$

$$\frac{d}{dx}[\tanh u] = \operatorname{sech}^2 u \frac{du}{dx} \qquad\qquad \int \operatorname{sech}^2 u \, du = \tanh u + C$$

$$\frac{d}{dx}[\coth u] = -\operatorname{csch}^2 u \frac{du}{dx} \qquad\qquad \int \operatorname{csch}^2 u \, du = -\coth u + C$$

$$\frac{d}{dx}[\operatorname{sech} u] = -\operatorname{sech} u \tanh u \frac{du}{dx} \qquad\qquad \int \operatorname{sech} u \tanh u \, du = -\operatorname{sech} u + C$$

$$\frac{d}{dx}[\operatorname{csch} u] = -\operatorname{csch} u \coth u \frac{du}{dx} \qquad\qquad \int \operatorname{csch} u \coth u \, du = -\operatorname{csch} u + C$$

▶ **Example 2**

$$\frac{d}{dx}[\cosh(x^3)] = \sinh(x^3) \cdot \frac{d}{dx}[x^3] = 3x^2 \sinh(x^3)$$

$$\frac{d}{dx}[\ln(\tanh x)] = \frac{1}{\tanh x} \cdot \frac{d}{dx}[\tanh x] = \frac{\operatorname{sech}^2 x}{\tanh x} \quad ◀$$

▶ **Example 3**

$$\int \sinh^5 x \cosh x \, dx = \tfrac{1}{6} \sinh^6 x + C \qquad \boxed{\begin{array}{l} u = \sinh x \\ du = \cosh x \, dx \end{array}}$$

$$\int \tanh x \, dx = \int \frac{\sinh x}{\cosh x} \, dx$$

$$= \ln |\cosh x| + C \qquad \boxed{\begin{array}{l} u = \cosh x \\ du = \sinh x \, dx \end{array}}$$

$$= \ln(\cosh x) + C$$

We were justified in dropping the absolute value signs since $\cosh x > 0$ for all x. ◀

▶ **Example 4**   A 100 ft wire is attached at its ends to the tops of two 50 ft poles that are positioned 90 ft apart. How high above the ground is the middle of the wire?

Solution.   From above, the wire forms a catenary curve with equation

$$y = a \cosh\left(\frac{x}{a}\right) + c$$

where the origin is on the ground midway between the poles. Using Formula (4) of Section 6.4 for the length of the catenary, we have

$$100 = \int_{-45}^{45} \sqrt{1 + \left(\frac{dy}{dx}\right)^2} \, dx$$

$$= 2 \int_{0}^{45} \sqrt{1 + \left(\frac{dy}{dx}\right)^2} \, dx \qquad \boxed{\begin{array}{l} \text{By symmetry} \\ \text{about the } y\text{-axis} \end{array}}$$

$$= 2 \int_{0}^{45} \sqrt{1 + \sinh^2\left(\frac{x}{a}\right)} \, dx$$

$$= 2 \int_{0}^{45} \cosh\left(\frac{x}{a}\right) dx \qquad \boxed{\begin{array}{l} \text{By (1) and the fact} \\ \text{that } \cosh x > 0 \end{array}}$$

$$= 2a \sinh\left(\frac{x}{a}\right)\Big]_{0}^{45} = 2a \sinh\left(\frac{45}{a}\right)$$

Using a calculating utility's numeric solver to solve

$$100 = 2a \sinh\left(\frac{45}{a}\right)$$

for a gives $a \approx 56.01$. Then

$$50 = y(45) = 56.01 \cosh\left(\frac{45}{56.01}\right) + c \approx 75.08 + c$$

so $c \approx -25.08$. Thus, the middle of the wire is $y(0) \approx 56.01 - 25.08 = 30.93$ ft above the ground (Figure 6.9.4). ◀

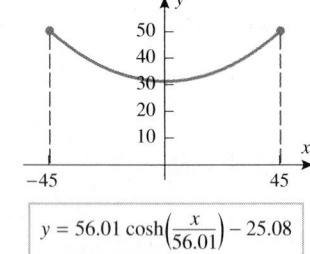

$$y = 56.01 \cosh\left(\frac{x}{56.01}\right) - 25.08$$

▲ **Figure 6.9.4**

■ INVERSES OF HYPERBOLIC FUNCTIONS

Referring to Figure 6.9.1, it is evident that the graphs of $\sinh x$, $\tanh x$, $\coth x$, and $\operatorname{csch} x$ pass the horizontal line test, but the graphs of $\cosh x$ and $\operatorname{sech} x$ do not. In the latter case, restricting x to be nonnegative makes the functions invertible (Figure 6.9.5). The graphs of the six inverse hyperbolic functions in Figure 6.9.6 were obtained by reflecting the graphs of the hyperbolic functions (with the appropriate restrictions) about the line $y = x$.

Table 6.9.1 summarizes the basic properties of the inverse hyperbolic functions. You should confirm that the domains and ranges listed in this table agree with the graphs in Figure 6.9.6.

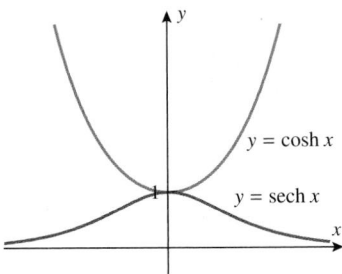

With the restriction that $x \geq 0$, the curves $y = \cosh x$ and $y = \operatorname{sech} x$ pass the horizontal line test.

▲ **Figure 6.9.5**

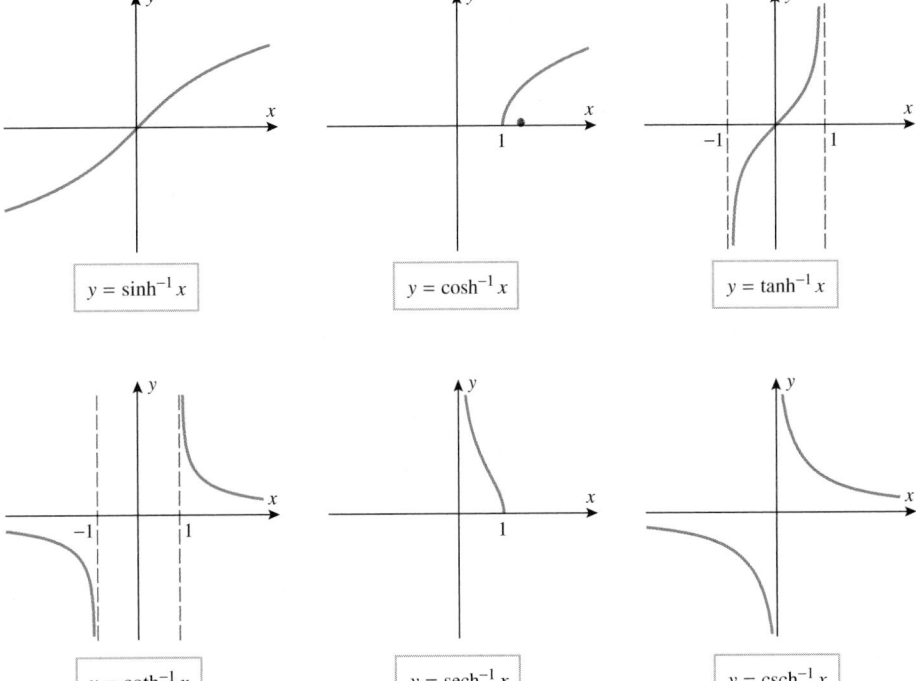

▶ **Figure 6.9.6**

Table 6.9.1

PROPERTIES OF INVERSE HYPERBOLIC FUNCTIONS

FUNCTION	DOMAIN	RANGE	BASIC RELATIONSHIPS
$\sinh^{-1} x$	$(-\infty, +\infty)$	$(-\infty, +\infty)$	$\sinh^{-1}(\sinh x) = x$ if $-\infty < x < +\infty$ $\sinh(\sinh^{-1} x) = x$ if $-\infty < x < +\infty$
$\cosh^{-1} x$	$[1, +\infty)$	$[0, +\infty)$	$\cosh^{-1}(\cosh x) = x$ if $x \geq 0$ $\cosh(\cosh^{-1} x) = x$ if $x \geq 1$
$\tanh^{-1} x$	$(-1, 1)$	$(-\infty, +\infty)$	$\tanh^{-1}(\tanh x) = x$ if $-\infty < x < +\infty$ $\tanh(\tanh^{-1} x) = x$ if $-1 < x < 1$
$\coth^{-1} x$	$(-\infty, -1) \cup (1, +\infty)$	$(-\infty, 0) \cup (0, +\infty)$	$\coth^{-1}(\coth x) = x$ if $x < 0$ or $x > 0$ $\coth(\coth^{-1} x) = x$ if $x < -1$ or $x > 1$
$\operatorname{sech}^{-1} x$	$(0, 1]$	$[0, +\infty)$	$\operatorname{sech}^{-1}(\operatorname{sech} x) = x$ if $x \geq 0$ $\operatorname{sech}(\operatorname{sech}^{-1} x) = x$ if $0 < x \leq 1$
$\operatorname{csch}^{-1} x$	$(-\infty, 0) \cup (0, +\infty)$	$(-\infty, 0) \cup (0, +\infty)$	$\operatorname{csch}^{-1}(\operatorname{csch} x) = x$ if $x < 0$ or $x > 0$ $\operatorname{csch}(\operatorname{csch}^{-1} x) = x$ if $x < 0$ or $x > 0$

■ LOGARITHMIC FORMS OF INVERSE HYPERBOLIC FUNCTIONS

Because the hyperbolic functions are expressible in terms of e^x, it should not be surprising that the inverse hyperbolic functions are expressible in terms of natural logarithms; the next theorem shows that this is so.

6.9.4 THEOREM *The following relationships hold for all x in the domains of the stated inverse hyperbolic functions:*

$$\sinh^{-1} x = \ln(x + \sqrt{x^2 + 1}) \qquad \cosh^{-1} x = \ln(x + \sqrt{x^2 - 1})$$

$$\tanh^{-1} x = \frac{1}{2}\ln\left(\frac{1+x}{1-x}\right) \qquad \coth^{-1} x = \frac{1}{2}\ln\left(\frac{x+1}{x-1}\right)$$

$$\operatorname{sech}^{-1} x = \ln\left(\frac{1 + \sqrt{1-x^2}}{x}\right) \qquad \operatorname{csch}^{-1} x = \ln\left(\frac{1}{x} + \frac{\sqrt{1+x^2}}{|x|}\right)$$

We will show how to derive the first formula in this theorem and leave the rest as exercises. The basic idea is to write the equation $x = \sinh y$ in terms of exponential functions and solve this equation for y as a function of x. This will produce the equation $y = \sinh^{-1} x$ with $\sinh^{-1} x$ expressed in terms of natural logarithms. Expressing $x = \sinh y$ in terms of exponentials yields

$$x = \sinh y = \frac{e^y - e^{-y}}{2}$$

which can be rewritten as

$$e^y - 2x - e^{-y} = 0$$

Multiplying this equation through by e^y we obtain

$$e^{2y} - 2xe^y - 1 = 0$$

and applying the quadratic formula yields

$$e^y = \frac{2x \pm \sqrt{4x^2 + 4}}{2} = x \pm \sqrt{x^2 + 1}$$

Since $e^y > 0$, the solution involving the minus sign is extraneous and must be discarded. Thus,

$$e^y = x + \sqrt{x^2 + 1}$$

Taking natural logarithms yields

$$y = \ln(x + \sqrt{x^2 + 1}) \quad \text{or} \quad \sinh^{-1} x = \ln(x + \sqrt{x^2 + 1})$$

▶ **Example 5**

$$\sinh^{-1} 1 = \ln(1 + \sqrt{1^2 + 1}) = \ln(1 + \sqrt{2}) \approx 0.8814$$

$$\tanh^{-1}\left(\frac{1}{2}\right) = \frac{1}{2}\ln\left(\frac{1 + \frac{1}{2}}{1 - \frac{1}{2}}\right) = \frac{1}{2}\ln 3 \approx 0.5493 \blacktriangleleft$$

DERIVATIVES AND INTEGRALS INVOLVING INVERSE HYPERBOLIC FUNCTIONS

Formulas for the derivatives of the inverse hyperbolic functions can be obtained from Theorem 6.9.4. For example,

$$\frac{d}{dx}[\sinh^{-1} x] = \frac{d}{dx}[\ln(x + \sqrt{x^2 + 1})] = \frac{1}{x + \sqrt{x^2 + 1}}\left(1 + \frac{x}{\sqrt{x^2 + 1}}\right)$$

$$= \frac{\sqrt{x^2 + 1} + x}{(x + \sqrt{x^2 + 1})(\sqrt{x^2 + 1})} = \frac{1}{\sqrt{x^2 + 1}}$$

> Show that the derivative of the function $\sinh^{-1} x$ can also be obtained by letting $y = \sinh^{-1} x$ and then differentiating $x = \sinh y$ implicitly.

This computation leads to two integral formulas, a formula that involves $\sinh^{-1} x$ and an equivalent formula that involves logarithms:

$$\int \frac{dx}{\sqrt{x^2 + 1}} = \sinh^{-1} x + C = \ln(x + \sqrt{x^2 + 1}) + C$$

The following two theorems list the generalized derivative formulas and corresponding integration formulas for the inverse hyperbolic functions. Some of the proofs appear as exercises.

6.9.5   THEOREM

$$\frac{d}{dx}(\sinh^{-1} u) = \frac{1}{\sqrt{1 + u^2}}\frac{du}{dx} \qquad\qquad \frac{d}{dx}(\coth^{-1} u) = \frac{1}{1 - u^2}\frac{du}{dx}, \quad |u| > 1$$

$$\frac{d}{dx}(\cosh^{-1} u) = \frac{1}{\sqrt{u^2 - 1}}\frac{du}{dx}, \quad u > 1 \qquad\qquad \frac{d}{dx}(\text{sech}^{-1} u) = -\frac{1}{u\sqrt{1 - u^2}}\frac{du}{dx}, \quad 0 < u < 1$$

$$\frac{d}{dx}(\tanh^{-1} u) = \frac{1}{1 - u^2}\frac{du}{dx}, \quad |u| < 1 \qquad\qquad \frac{d}{dx}(\text{csch}^{-1} u) = -\frac{1}{|u|\sqrt{1 + u^2}}\frac{du}{dx}, \quad u \neq 0$$

6.9.6   THEOREM   *If $a > 0$, then*

$$\int \frac{du}{\sqrt{a^2 + u^2}} = \sinh^{-1}\left(\frac{u}{a}\right) + C \quad or \quad \ln(u + \sqrt{u^2 + a^2}) + C$$

$$\int \frac{du}{\sqrt{u^2 - a^2}} = \cosh^{-1}\left(\frac{u}{a}\right) + C \quad or \quad \ln(u + \sqrt{u^2 - a^2}) + C, \quad u > a$$

$$\int \frac{du}{a^2 - u^2} = \begin{cases} \dfrac{1}{a}\tanh^{-1}\left(\dfrac{u}{a}\right) + C, \quad |u| < a \\[2mm] \dfrac{1}{a}\coth^{-1}\left(\dfrac{u}{a}\right) + C, \quad |u| > a \end{cases} \quad or \quad \frac{1}{2a}\ln\left|\frac{a + u}{a - u}\right| + C, \quad |u| \neq a$$

$$\int \frac{du}{u\sqrt{a^2 - u^2}} = -\frac{1}{a}\text{sech}^{-1}\left|\frac{u}{a}\right| + C \quad or \quad -\frac{1}{a}\ln\left(\frac{a + \sqrt{a^2 - u^2}}{|u|}\right) + C, \quad 0 < |u| < a$$

$$\int \frac{du}{u\sqrt{a^2 + u^2}} = -\frac{1}{a}\text{csch}^{-1}\left|\frac{u}{a}\right| + C \quad or \quad -\frac{1}{a}\ln\left(\frac{a + \sqrt{a^2 + u^2}}{|u|}\right) + C, \quad u \neq 0$$

▶ **Example 6**   Evaluate $\displaystyle\int \frac{dx}{\sqrt{4x^2 - 9}}$, $x > \dfrac{3}{2}$.

Solution.   Let $u = 2x$. Thus, $du = 2\,dx$ and

$$\int \frac{dx}{\sqrt{4x^2 - 9}} = \frac{1}{2} \int \frac{2\,dx}{\sqrt{4x^2 - 9}} = \frac{1}{2} \int \frac{du}{\sqrt{u^2 - 3^2}}$$

$$= \frac{1}{2} \cosh^{-1}\left(\frac{u}{3}\right) + C = \frac{1}{2} \cosh^{-1}\left(\frac{2x}{3}\right) + C$$

Alternatively, we can use the logarithmic equivalent of $\cosh^{-1}(2x/3)$,

$$\cosh^{-1}\left(\frac{2x}{3}\right) = \ln(2x + \sqrt{4x^2 - 9}) - \ln 3$$

(verify), and express the answer as

$$\int \frac{dx}{\sqrt{4x^2 - 9}} = \frac{1}{2} \ln(2x + \sqrt{4x^2 - 9}) + C \quad \blacktriangleleft$$

✔**QUICK CHECK EXERCISES 6.9**   (See page 485 for answers.)

1. $\cosh x =$ _____ $\sinh x =$ _____
   $\tanh x =$ _____

2. Complete the table.

	cosh x	sinh x	tanh x	coth x	sech x	csch x
DOMAIN						
RANGE						

3. The parametric equations

   $$x = \cosh t, \quad y = \sinh t \quad (-\infty < t < +\infty)$$

   represent the right half of the curve called a _____. Eliminating the parameter, the equation of this curve is _____.

4. $\dfrac{d}{dx}[\cosh x] =$ _____ $\dfrac{d}{dx}[\sinh x] =$ _____
   $\dfrac{d}{dx}[\tanh x] =$ _____

5. $\displaystyle\int \cosh x\, dx =$ _____ $\displaystyle\int \sinh x\, dx =$ _____
   $\displaystyle\int \tanh x\, dx =$ _____

6. $\dfrac{d}{dx}[\cosh^{-1} x] =$ _____ $\dfrac{d}{dx}[\sinh^{-1} x] =$ _____
   $\dfrac{d}{dx}[\tanh^{-1} x] =$ _____

EXERCISE SET 6.9   ⊠ Graphing Utility

1–2 Approximate the expression to four decimal places. ▪

1. (a) $\sinh 3$ (b) $\cosh(-2)$ (c) $\tanh(\ln 4)$
   (d) $\sinh^{-1}(-2)$ (e) $\cosh^{-1} 3$ (f) $\tanh^{-1} \frac{3}{4}$

2. (a) $\operatorname{csch}(-1)$ (b) $\operatorname{sech}(\ln 2)$ (c) $\coth 1$
   (d) $\operatorname{sech}^{-1} \frac{1}{2}$ (e) $\coth^{-1} 3$ (f) $\operatorname{csch}^{-1}(-\sqrt{3})$

3. Find the exact numerical value of each expression.
   (a) $\sinh(\ln 3)$ (b) $\cosh(-\ln 2)$
   (c) $\tanh(2 \ln 5)$ (d) $\sinh(-3 \ln 2)$

4. In each part, rewrite the expression as a ratio of polynomials.
   (a) $\cosh(\ln x)$ (b) $\sinh(\ln x)$
   (c) $\tanh(2 \ln x)$ (d) $\cosh(-\ln x)$

5. In each part, a value for one of the hyperbolic functions is given at an unspecified positive number x_0. Use appropri-

ate identities to find the exact values of the remaining five hyperbolic functions at x_0.
   (a) $\sinh x_0 = 2$ (b) $\cosh x_0 = \frac{5}{4}$ (c) $\tanh x_0 = \frac{4}{5}$

6. Obtain the derivative formulas for $\operatorname{csch} x$, $\operatorname{sech} x$, and $\coth x$ from the derivative formulas for $\sinh x$, $\cosh x$, and $\tanh x$.

7. Find the derivatives of $\cosh^{-1} x$ and $\tanh^{-1} x$ by differentiating the formulas in Theorem 6.9.4.

8. Find the derivatives of $\sinh^{-1} x$, $\cosh^{-1} x$, and $\tanh^{-1} x$ by differentiating the equations $x = \sinh y$, $x = \cosh y$, and $x = \tanh y$ implicitly.

9–28 Find dy/dx. ▪

9. $y = \sinh(4x - 8)$ 10. $y = \cosh(x^4)$

11. $y = \coth(\ln x)$

12. $y = \ln(\tanh 2x)$

13. $y = \operatorname{csch}(1/x)$

14. $y = \operatorname{sech}(e^{2x})$

15. $y = \sqrt{4x + \cosh^2(5x)}$

16. $y = \sinh^3(2x)$

17. $y = x^3 \tanh^2(\sqrt{x})$

18. $y = \sinh(\cos 3x)$

19. $y = \sinh^{-1}\left(\frac{1}{3}x\right)$

20. $y = \sinh^{-1}(1/x)$

21. $y = \ln(\cosh^{-1} x)$

22. $y = \cosh^{-1}(\sinh^{-1} x)$

23. $y = \dfrac{1}{\tanh^{-1} x}$

24. $y = (\coth^{-1} x)^2$

25. $y = \cosh^{-1}(\cosh x)$

26. $y = \sinh^{-1}(\tanh x)$

27. $y = e^x \operatorname{sech}^{-1} \sqrt{x}$

28. $y = (1 + x \operatorname{csch}^{-1} x)^{10}$

29–44 Evaluate the integrals. ■

29. $\displaystyle\int \sinh^6 x \cosh x\, dx$

30. $\displaystyle\int \cosh(2x - 3)\, dx$

31. $\displaystyle\int \sqrt{\tanh x}\, \operatorname{sech}^2 x\, dx$

32. $\displaystyle\int \operatorname{csch}^2(3x)\, dx$

33. $\displaystyle\int \tanh x\, dx$

34. $\displaystyle\int \coth^2 x \operatorname{csch}^2 x\, dx$

35. $\displaystyle\int_{\ln 2}^{\ln 3} \tanh x \operatorname{sech}^3 x\, dx$

36. $\displaystyle\int_0^{\ln 3} \frac{e^x - e^{-x}}{e^x + e^{-x}}\, dx$

37. $\displaystyle\int \frac{dx}{\sqrt{1 + 9x^2}}$

38. $\displaystyle\int \frac{dx}{\sqrt{x^2 - 2}}\quad (x > \sqrt{2})$

39. $\displaystyle\int \frac{dx}{\sqrt{1 - e^{2x}}}\quad (x < 0)$

40. $\displaystyle\int \frac{\sin\theta\, d\theta}{\sqrt{1 + \cos^2\theta}}$

41. $\displaystyle\int \frac{dx}{x\sqrt{1 + 4x^2}}$

42. $\displaystyle\int \frac{dx}{\sqrt{9x^2 - 25}}\quad (x > 5/3)$

43. $\displaystyle\int_0^{1/2} \frac{dx}{1 - x^2}$

44. $\displaystyle\int_0^{\sqrt{3}} \frac{dt}{\sqrt{t^2 + 1}}$

45–48 True–False Determine whether the statement is true or false. Explain your answer. ■

45. The equation $\cosh x = \sinh x$ has no solutions.

46. Exactly two of the hyperbolic functions are bounded.

47. There is exactly one hyperbolic function $f(x)$ such that for all real numbers a, the equation $f(x) = a$ has a unique solution x.

48. The identities in Theorem 6.9.2 may be obtained from the corresponding trigonometric identities by replacing each trigonometric function with its hyperbolic analogue.

49. Find the area enclosed by $y = \sinh 2x$, $y = 0$, and $x = \ln 3$.

50. Find the volume of the solid that is generated when the region enclosed by $y = \operatorname{sech} x$, $y = 0$, $x = 0$, and $x = \ln 2$ is revolved about the x-axis.

51. Find the volume of the solid that is generated when the region enclosed by $y = \cosh 2x$, $y = \sinh 2x$, $x = 0$, and $x = 5$ is revolved about the x-axis.

52. Approximate the positive value of the constant a such that the area enclosed by $y = \cosh ax$, $y = 0$, $x = 0$, and $x = 1$

is 2 square units. Express your answer to at least five decimal places.

53. Find the arc length of the catenary $y = \cosh x$ between $x = 0$ and $x = \ln 2$.

54. Find the arc length of the catenary $y = a\cosh(x/a)$ between $x = 0$ and $x = x_1$ ($x_1 > 0$).

55. In parts (a)–(f) find the limits, and confirm that they are consistent with the graphs in Figures 6.9.1 and 6.9.6.

(a) $\displaystyle\lim_{x \to +\infty} \sinh x$

(b) $\displaystyle\lim_{x \to -\infty} \sinh x$

(c) $\displaystyle\lim_{x \to +\infty} \tanh x$

(d) $\displaystyle\lim_{x \to -\infty} \tanh x$

(e) $\displaystyle\lim_{x \to +\infty} \sinh^{-1} x$

(f) $\displaystyle\lim_{x \to 1^-} \tanh^{-1} x$

FOCUS ON CONCEPTS

56. Explain how to obtain the asymptotes for $y = \tanh x$ from the curvilinear asymptotes for $y = \cosh x$ and $y = \sinh x$.

57. Prove that $\sinh x$ is an odd function of x and that $\cosh x$ is an even function of x, and check that this is consistent with the graphs in Figure 6.9.1.

58–59 Prove the identities. ■

58. (a) $\cosh x + \sinh x = e^x$

(b) $\cosh x - \sinh x = e^{-x}$

(c) $\sinh(x + y) = \sinh x \cosh y + \cosh x \sinh y$

(d) $\sinh 2x = 2\sinh x \cosh x$

(e) $\cosh(x + y) = \cosh x \cosh y + \sinh x \sinh y$

(f) $\cosh 2x = \cosh^2 x + \sinh^2 x$

(g) $\cosh 2x = 2\sinh^2 x + 1$

(h) $\cosh 2x = 2\cosh^2 x - 1$

59. (a) $1 - \tanh^2 x = \operatorname{sech}^2 x$

(b) $\tanh(x + y) = \dfrac{\tanh x + \tanh y}{1 + \tanh x \tanh y}$

(c) $\tanh 2x = \dfrac{2\tanh x}{1 + \tanh^2 x}$

60. Prove:

(a) $\cosh^{-1} x = \ln(x + \sqrt{x^2 - 1}),\quad x \geq 1$

(b) $\tanh^{-1} x = \dfrac{1}{2}\ln\left(\dfrac{1 + x}{1 - x}\right),\quad -1 < x < 1.$

61. Use Exercise 60 to obtain the derivative formulas for $\cosh^{-1} x$ and $\tanh^{-1} x$.

62. Prove:

$$\operatorname{sech}^{-1} x = \cosh^{-1}(1/x),\quad 0 < x \leq 1$$

$$\coth^{-1} x = \tanh^{-1}(1/x),\quad |x| > 1$$

$$\operatorname{csch}^{-1} x = \sinh^{-1}(1/x),\quad x \neq 0$$

63. Use Exercise 62 to express the integral

$$\int \frac{du}{1 - u^2}$$

entirely in terms of $\tanh^{-1}$.

64. Show that

(a) $\dfrac{d}{dx}[\text{sech}^{-1}|x|] = -\dfrac{1}{x\sqrt{1-x^2}}$

(b) $\dfrac{d}{dx}[\text{csch}^{-1}|x|] = -\dfrac{1}{x\sqrt{1+x^2}}$.

65. In each part, find the limit.

(a) $\displaystyle\lim_{x \to +\infty} (\cosh^{-1} x - \ln x)$ (b) $\displaystyle\lim_{x \to +\infty} \dfrac{\cosh x}{e^x}$

66. Use the first and second derivatives to show that the graph of $y = \tanh^{-1} x$ is always increasing and has an inflection point at the origin.

67. The integration formulas for $1/\sqrt{u^2 - a^2}$ in Theorem 6.9.6 are valid for $u > a$. Show that the following formula is valid for $u < -a$:

$$\int \frac{du}{\sqrt{u^2 - a^2}} = -\cosh^{-1}\left(-\frac{u}{a}\right) + C \quad \text{or} \quad \ln\left|u + \sqrt{u^2 - a^2}\right| + C$$

68. Show that $(\sinh x + \cosh x)^n = \sinh nx + \cosh nx$.

69. Show that

$$\int_{-a}^{a} e^{tx}\, dx = \frac{2\sinh at}{t}$$

70. A cable is suspended between two poles as shown in Figure 6.9.2. Assume that the equation of the curve formed by the cable is $y = a\cosh(x/a)$, where a is a positive constant. Suppose that the x-coordinates of the points of support are $x = -b$ and $x = b$, where $b > 0$.

(a) Show that the length L of the cable is given by

$$L = 2a\sinh\frac{b}{a}$$

(b) Show that the sag S (the vertical distance between the highest and lowest points on the cable) is given by

$$S = a\cosh\frac{b}{a} - a$$

71–72 These exercises refer to the hanging cable described in Exercise 70. ■

71. Assuming that the poles are 400 ft apart and the sag in the cable is 30 ft, approximate the length of the cable by approximating a. Express your final answer to the nearest tenth of a foot. [*Hint:* First let $u = 200/a$.]

72. Assuming that the cable is 120 ft long and the poles are 100 ft apart, approximate the sag in the cable by approximating a. Express your final answer to the nearest tenth of a foot. [*Hint:* First let $u = 50/a$.]

73. The design of the Gateway Arch in St. Louis, Missouri, by architect Eero Saarinen was implemented using equations provided by Dr. Hannskarl Badel. The equation used for the centerline of the arch was

$$y = 693.8597 - 68.7672\cosh(0.0100333x)\ \text{ft}$$

for x between -299.2239 and 299.2239.

(a) Use a graphing utility to graph the centerline of the arch.

(b) Find the length of the centerline to four decimal places.

(c) For what values of x is the height of the arch 100 ft? Round your answers to four decimal places.

(d) Approximate, to the nearest degree, the acute angle that the tangent line to the centerline makes with the ground at the ends of the arch.

74. Suppose that a hollow tube rotates with a constant angular velocity of ω rad/s about a horizontal axis at one end of the tube, as shown in the accompanying figure. Assume that an object is free to slide without friction in the tube while the tube is rotating. Let r be the distance from the object to the pivot point at time $t \geq 0$, and assume that the object is at rest and $r = 0$ when $t = 0$. It can be shown that if the tube is horizontal at time $t = 0$ and rotating as shown in the figure, then

$$r = \frac{g}{2\omega^2}[\sinh(\omega t) - \sin(\omega t)]$$

during the period that the object is in the tube. Assume that t is in seconds and r is in meters, and use $g = 9.8$ m/s^2 and $\omega = 2$ rad/s.

(a) Graph r versus t for $0 \leq t \leq 1$.

(b) Assuming that the tube has a length of 1 m, approximately how long does it take for the object to reach the end of the tube?

(c) Use the result of part (b) to approximate dr/dt at the instant that the object reaches the end of the tube.

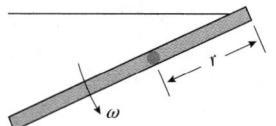

◀ **Figure Ex-74**

75. The accompanying figure (on the next page) shows a person pulling a boat by holding a rope of length a attached to the bow and walking along the edge of a dock. If we assume that the rope is always tangent to the curve traced by the bow of the boat, then this curve, which is called a **tractrix**, has the property that the segment of the tangent line between the curve and the y-axis has a constant length a. It can be proved that the equation of this tractrix is

$$y = a\,\text{sech}^{-1}\frac{x}{a} - \sqrt{a^2 - x^2}$$

(a) Show that to move the bow of the boat to a point (x, y), the person must walk a distance

$$D = a\,\text{sech}^{-1}\frac{x}{a}$$

from the origin.

(b) If the rope has a length of 15 m, how far must the person walk from the origin to bring the boat 10 m from the dock? Round your answer to two decimal places.

(c) Find the distance traveled by the bow along the tractrix as it moves from its initial position to the point where it is 5 m from the dock.

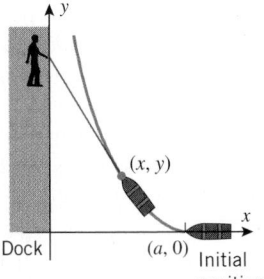

Dock | (a, 0) Initial position ◄ **Figure Ex-75**

76. Writing Suppose that, by analogy with the trigonometric functions, we *define* cosh t and sinh t geometrically using Figure 6.9.3b:

"For any real number t, define $x = \cosh t$ and $y = \sinh t$ to be the unique values of x and y such that

(i) $P(x, y)$ is on the right branch of the unit hyperbola $x^2 - y^2 = 1$;

(ii) t and y have the same sign (or are both 0);

(iii) the area of the region bounded by the x-axis, the right branch of the unit hyperbola, and the segment from the origin to P is $|t|/2$."

Discuss what properties would first need to be verified in order for this to be a legitimate definition.

77. Writing Investigate what properties of cosh t and sinh t can be proved directly from the geometric definition in Exercise 76. Write a short description of the results of your investigation.

✔ QUICK CHECK ANSWERS 6.9

1. $\dfrac{e^x + e^{-x}}{2}$; $\dfrac{e^x - e^{-x}}{2}$; $\dfrac{e^x - e^{-x}}{e^x + e^{-x}}$

2.

	cosh x	sinh x	tanh x	coth x	sech x	csch x
DOMAIN	$(-\infty, +\infty)$	$(-\infty, +\infty)$	$(-\infty, +\infty)$	$(-\infty, 0) \cup (0, +\infty)$	$(-\infty, +\infty)$	$(-\infty, 0) \cup (0, +\infty)$
RANGE	$[1, +\infty)$	$(-\infty, +\infty)$	$(-1, 1)$	$(-\infty, -1) \cup (1, +\infty)$	$(0, 1]$	$(-\infty, 0) \cup (0, +\infty)$

3. unit hyperbola; $x^2 - y^2 = 1$ **4.** $\sinh x$; $\cosh x$; $\mathrm{sech}^2 x$ **5.** $\sinh x + C$; $\cosh x + C$; $\ln(\cosh x) + C$

6. $\dfrac{1}{\sqrt{x^2 - 1}}$; $\dfrac{1}{\sqrt{1 + x^2}}$; $\dfrac{1}{1 - x^2}$

CHAPTER 6 REVIEW EXERCISES

---

1. Describe the method of slicing for finding volumes, and use that method to derive an integral formula for finding volumes by the method of disks.

2. State an integral formula for finding a volume by the method of cylindrical shells, and use Riemann sums to derive the formula.

3. State an integral formula for finding the arc length of a smooth curve $y = f(x)$ over an interval $[a, b]$, and use Riemann sums to derive the formula.

4. State an integral formula for the work W done by a variable force $F(x)$ applied in the direction of motion to an object moving from $x = a$ to $x = b$, and use Riemann sums to derive the formula.

5. State an integral formula for the fluid force F exerted on a vertical flat surface immersed in a fluid of weight density ρ, and use Riemann sums to derive the formula.

6. Let R be the region in the first quadrant enclosed by $y = x^2$, $y = 2 + x$, and $x = 0$. In each part, set up, but *do not eval-*

uate, an integral or a sum of integrals that will solve the problem.

(a) Find the area of R by integrating with respect to x.

(b) Find the area of R by integrating with respect to y.

(c) Find the volume of the solid generated by revolving R about the x-axis by integrating with respect to x.

(d) Find the volume of the solid generated by revolving R about the x-axis by integrating with respect to y.

(e) Find the volume of the solid generated by revolving R about the y-axis by integrating with respect to x.

(f) Find the volume of the solid generated by revolving R about the y-axis by integrating with respect to y.

(g) Find the volume of the solid generated by revolving R about the line $y = -3$ by integrating with respect to x.

(h) Find the volume of the solid generated by revolving R about the line $x = 5$ by integrating with respect to x.

7. (a) Set up a sum of definite integrals that represents the total shaded area between the curves $y = f(x)$ and $y = g(x)$ in the accompanying figure on the next page. *(cont.)*

(b) Find the total area enclosed between $y = x^3$ and $y = x$ over the interval $[-1, 2]$.

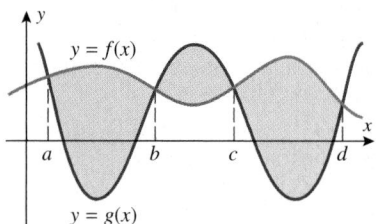

◀ **Figure Ex-7**

8. The accompanying figure shows velocity versus time curves for two cars that move along a straight track, accelerating from rest at a common starting line.
   (a) How far apart are the cars after 60 seconds?
   (b) How far apart are the cars after T seconds, where $0 \leq T \leq 60$?

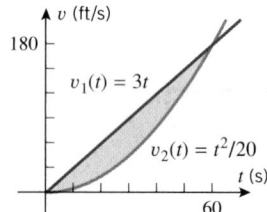

◀ **Figure Ex-8**

9. Let R be the region enclosed by the curves $y = x^2 + 4$, $y = x^3$, and the y-axis. Find and evaluate a definite integral that represents the volume of the solid generated by revolving R about the x-axis.

10. A football has the shape of the solid generated by revolving the region bounded between the x-axis and the parabola $y = 4R(x^2 - \frac{1}{4}L^2)/L^2$ about the x-axis. Find its volume.

11. Find the volume of the solid whose base is the region bounded between the curves $y = \sqrt{x}$ and $y = 1/\sqrt{x}$ for $1 \leq x \leq 4$ and whose cross sections perpendicular to the x-axis are squares.

12. Consider the region enclosed by $y = \sin^{-1} x$, $y = 0$, and $x = 1$. Set up, but *do not evaluate*, an integral that represents the volume of the solid generated by revolving the region about the x-axis using
    (a) disks   (b) cylindrical shells.

13. Find the arc length in the second quadrant of the curve $x^{2/3} + y^{2/3} = 4$ from $x = -8$ to $x = -1$.

14. Let C be the curve $y = e^x$ between $x = 0$ and $x = \ln 10$. In each part, set up, but *do not evaluate*, an integral that solves the problem.
    (a) Find the arc length of C by integrating with respect to x.
    (b) Find the arc length of C by integrating with respect to y.

15. Find the area of the surface generated by revolving the curve $y = \sqrt{25 - x}$, $9 \leq x \leq 16$, about the x-axis.

16. Let C be the curve $27x - y^3 = 0$ between $y = 0$ and $y = 2$. In each part, set up, but *do not evaluate*, an integral or a sum of integrals that solves the problem.

(a) Find the area of the surface generated by revolving C about the x-axis by integrating with respect to x.
(b) Find the area of the surface generated by revolving C about the y-axis by integrating with respect to y.
(c) Find the area of the surface generated by revolving C about the line $y = -2$ by integrating with respect to y.

17. (a) A spring exerts a force of 0.5 N when stretched 0.25 m beyond its natural length. Assuming that Hooke's law applies, how much work was performed in stretching the spring to this length?
    (b) How far beyond its natural length can the spring be stretched with 25 J of work?

18. A boat is anchored so that the anchor is 150 ft below the surface of the water. In the water, the anchor weighs 2000 lb and the chain weighs 30 lb/ft. How much work is required to raise the anchor to the surface?

19–20 Find the centroid of the region. ■

19. The region bounded by $y^2 = 4x$ and $y^2 = 8(x - 2)$.

20. The upper half of the ellipse $(x/a)^2 + (y/b)^2 = 1$.

21. In each part, set up, but *do not evaluate*, an integral that solves the problem.
    (a) Find the fluid force exerted on a side of a box that has a 3 m square base and is filled to a depth of 1 m with a liquid of weight density ρ N/m^3.
    (b) Find the fluid force exerted by a liquid of weight density ρ lb/ft^3 on a face of the vertical plate shown in part (a) of the accompanying figure.
    (c) Find the fluid force exerted on the parabolic dam in part (b) of the accompanying figure by water that extends to the top of the dam.

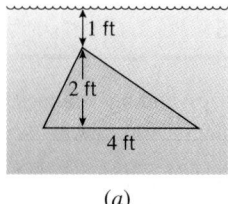

(a)   (b)

▲ **Figure Ex-21**

22. Show that for any constant a, the function $y = \sinh(ax)$ satisfies the equation $y'' = a^2 y$.

23. In each part, prove the identity.
    (a) $\cosh 3x = 4\cosh^3 x - 3\cosh x$
    (b) $\cosh \frac{1}{2}x = \sqrt{\frac{1}{2}(\cosh x + 1)}$
    (c) $\sinh \frac{1}{2}x = \pm\sqrt{\frac{1}{2}(\cosh x - 1)}$

CHAPTER 6 MAKING CONNECTIONS

1. Suppose that f is a nonnegative function defined on $[0, 1]$ such that the area between the graph of f and the interval $[0, 1]$ is A_1 and such that the area of the region R between the graph of $g(x) = f(x^2)$ and the interval $[0, 1]$ is A_2. In each part, express your answer in terms of A_1 and A_2.
   (a) What is the volume of the solid of revolution generated by revolving R about the y-axis?
   (b) Find a value of a such that if the xy-plane were horizontal, the region R would balance on the line $x = a$.

2. A water tank has the shape of a conical frustum with radius of the base 5 ft, radius of the top 10 ft and (vertical) height 15 ft. Suppose the tank is filled with water and consider the problem of finding the work required to pump all the water out through a hole in the top of the tank.
   (a) Solve this problem using the method of Example 5 in Section 6.6.
   (b) Solve this problem using Definition 6.6.3. [*Hint:* Think of the base as the head of a piston that expands to a watertight fit against the sides of the tank as the piston is pushed upward. What important result about water pressure do you need to use?]

3. A disk of radius a is an inhomogeneous lamina whose density is a function $f(r)$ of the distance r to the center of the lamina.

Modify the argument used to derive the method of cylindrical shells to find a formula for the mass of the lamina.

4. Compare Formula (10) in Section 6.7 with Formula (8) in Section 6.8. Then give a plausible argument that the force on a flat surface immersed vertically in a fluid of constant weight density is equal to the product of the area of the surface and the pressure at the centroid of the surface. Conclude that the force on the surface is the same as if the surface were immersed horizontally at the depth of the centroid.

5. *Archimedes' Principle* states that a solid immersed in a fluid experiences a buoyant force equal to the weight of the fluid displaced by the solid.
   (a) Use the results of Section 6.8 to verify Archimedes' Principle in the case of (i) a box-shaped solid with a pair of faces parallel to the surface of the fluid, (ii) a solid cylinder with vertical axis, and (iii) a cylindrical shell with vertical axis.
   (b) Give a plausible argument for Archimedes' Principle in the case of a solid of revolution immersed in fluid such that the axis of revolution of the solid is vertical. [*Hint:* Approximate the solid by a union of cylindrical shells and use the result from part (a).]

© AP/Wide World Photos

7

PRINCIPLES OF INTEGRAL EVALUATION

The floating roof on the Stade de France sports complex is an ellipse. Finding the arc length of an ellipse involves numerical integration techniques introduced in this chapter.

In earlier chapters we obtained many basic integration formulas as an immediate consequence of the corresponding differentiation formulas. For example, knowing that the derivative of sin x is cos x enabled us to deduce that the integral of cos x is sin x. Subsequently, we expanded our integration repertoire by introducing the method of u-substitution. That method enabled us to integrate many functions by transforming the integrand of an unfamiliar integral into a familiar form. However, u-substitution alone is not adequate to handle the wide variety of integrals that arise in applications, so additional integration techniques are still needed. In this chapter we will discuss some of those techniques, and we will provide a more systematic procedure for attacking unfamiliar integrals. We will talk more about numerical approximations of definite integrals, and we will explore the idea of integrating over infinite intervals.

7.1 AN OVERVIEW OF INTEGRATION METHODS

In this section we will give a brief overview of methods for evaluating integrals, and we will review the integration formulas that were discussed in earlier sections.

■ METHODS FOR APPROACHING INTEGRATION PROBLEMS

There are three basic approaches for evaluating unfamiliar integrals:

- **Technology**—CAS programs such as *Mathematica*, *Maple*, and the open source program *Sage* are capable of evaluating extremely complicated integrals, and such programs are increasingly available for both computers and handheld calculators.

- **Tables**—Prior to the development of CAS programs, scientists relied heavily on tables to evaluate difficult integrals arising in applications. Such tables were compiled over many years, incorporating the skills and experience of many people. One such table appears in the endpapers of this text, but more comprehensive tables appear in various reference books such as the *CRC Standard Mathematical Tables and Formulae*, CRC Press, Inc., 2002.

- **Transformation Methods**—Transformation methods are methods for converting unfamiliar integrals into familiar integrals. These include u-substitution, algebraic manipulation of the integrand, and other methods that we will discuss in this chapter.

None of the three methods is perfect; for example, CAS programs often encounter integrals that they cannot evaluate and they sometimes produce answers that are unnecessarily complicated, tables are not exhaustive and may not include a particular integral of interest, and transformation methods rely on human ingenuity that may prove to be inadequate in difficult problems.

In this chapter we will focus on transformation methods and tables, so it will *not be necessary* to have a CAS such as *Mathematica*, *Maple*, or *Sage*. However, if you have a CAS, then you can use it to confirm the results in the examples, and there are exercises that are designed to be solved with a CAS. If you have a CAS, keep in mind that many of the algorithms that it uses are based on the methods we will discuss here, so an understanding of these methods will help you to use your technology in a more informed way.

■ A REVIEW OF FAMILIAR INTEGRATION FORMULAS

The following is a list of basic integrals that we have encountered thus far:

CONSTANTS, POWERS, EXPONENTIALS

1. $\displaystyle\int du = u + C$

2. $\displaystyle\int a\,du = a\int du = au + C$

3. $\displaystyle\int u^r\,du = \frac{u^{r+1}}{r+1} + C,\ r \neq -1$

4. $\displaystyle\int \frac{du}{u} = \ln|u| + C$

5. $\displaystyle\int e^u\,du = e^u + C$

6. $\displaystyle\int b^u\,du = \frac{b^u}{\ln b} + C,\ b > 0, b \neq 1$

TRIGONOMETRIC FUNCTIONS

7. $\displaystyle\int \sin u\,du = -\cos u + C$

8. $\displaystyle\int \cos u\,du = \sin u + C$

9. $\displaystyle\int \sec^2 u\,du = \tan u + C$

10. $\displaystyle\int \csc^2 u\,du = -\cot u + C$

11. $\displaystyle\int \sec u \tan u\,du = \sec u + C$

12. $\displaystyle\int \csc u \cot u\,du = -\csc u + C$

13. $\displaystyle\int \tan u\,du = -\ln|\cos u| + C$

14. $\displaystyle\int \cot u\,du = \ln|\sin u| + C$

HYPERBOLIC FUNCTIONS

15. $\displaystyle\int \sinh u\,du = \cosh u + C$

16. $\displaystyle\int \cosh u\,du = \sinh u + C$

17. $\displaystyle\int \operatorname{sech}^2 u\,du = \tanh u + C$

18. $\displaystyle\int \operatorname{csch}^2 u\,du = -\coth u + C$

19. $\displaystyle\int \operatorname{sech} u \tanh u\,du = -\operatorname{sech} u + C$

20. $\displaystyle\int \operatorname{csch} u \coth u\,du = -\operatorname{csch} u + C$

ALGEBRAIC FUNCTIONS ($a > 0$)

21. $\displaystyle\int \frac{du}{\sqrt{a^2 - u^2}} = \sin^{-1}\frac{u}{a} + C \qquad (|u| < a)$

22. $\displaystyle\int \frac{du}{a^2 + u^2} = \frac{1}{a}\tan^{-1}\frac{u}{a} + C$

23. $\displaystyle\int \frac{du}{u\sqrt{u^2 - a^2}} = \frac{1}{a}\sec^{-1}\left|\frac{u}{a}\right| + C \qquad (0 < a < |u|)$

24. $\int \dfrac{du}{\sqrt{a^2 + u^2}} = \ln(u + \sqrt{u^2 + a^2}) + C$

25. $\int \dfrac{du}{\sqrt{u^2 - a^2}} = \ln\left|u + \sqrt{u^2 - a^2}\right| + C \qquad (0 < a < |u|)$

26. $\int \dfrac{du}{a^2 - u^2} = \dfrac{1}{2a} \ln\left|\dfrac{a + u}{a - u}\right| + C$

27. $\int \dfrac{du}{u\sqrt{a^2 - u^2}} = -\dfrac{1}{a} \ln\left|\dfrac{a + \sqrt{a^2 - u^2}}{u}\right| + C \qquad (0 < |u| < a)$

28. $\int \dfrac{du}{u\sqrt{a^2 + u^2}} = -\dfrac{1}{a} \ln\left|\dfrac{a + \sqrt{a^2 + u^2}}{u}\right| + C$

REMARK | Formula 25 is a generalization of a result in Theorem 6.9.6. Readers who did not cover Section 6.9 can ignore Formulas 24–28 for now, since we will develop other methods for obtaining them in this chapter.

✓ QUICK CHECK EXERCISES 7.1   (See page 491 for answers.)

1. Use algebraic manipulation and (if necessary) u-substitution to integrate the function.

(a) $\int \dfrac{x + 1}{x} \, dx = \underline{\hspace{2cm}}$

(b) $\int \dfrac{x + 2}{x + 1} \, dx = \underline{\hspace{2cm}}$

(c) $\int \dfrac{2x + 1}{x^2 + 1} \, dx = \underline{\hspace{2cm}}$

(d) $\int x e^{3 \ln x} \, dx = \underline{\hspace{2cm}}$

2. Use trigonometric identities and (if necessary) u-substitution to integrate the function.

(a) $\int \dfrac{1}{\csc x} \, dx = \underline{\hspace{2cm}}$

(b) $\int \dfrac{1}{\cos^2 x} \, dx = \underline{\hspace{2cm}}$

(c) $\int (\cot^2 x + 1) \, dx = \underline{\hspace{2cm}}$

(d) $\int \dfrac{1}{\sec x + \tan x} \, dx = \underline{\hspace{2cm}}$

3. Integrate the function.

(a) $\int \sqrt{x - 1} \, dx = \underline{\hspace{2cm}}$

(b) $\int e^{2x+1} \, dx = \underline{\hspace{2cm}}$

(c) $\int (\sin^3 x \cos x + \sin x \cos^3 x) \, dx = \underline{\hspace{2cm}}$

(d) $\int \dfrac{1}{(e^x + e^{-x})^2} \, dx = \underline{\hspace{2cm}}$

EXERCISE SET 7.1

1–30 Evaluate the integrals by making appropriate u-substitutions and applying the formulas reviewed in this section.

1. $\int (4 - 2x)^3 \, dx$

2. $\int 3\sqrt{4 + 2x} \, dx$

3. $\int x \sec^2(x^2) \, dx$

4. $\int 4x \tan(x^2) \, dx$

5. $\int \dfrac{\sin 3x}{2 + \cos 3x} \, dx$

6. $\int \dfrac{1}{9 + 4x^2} \, dx$

7. $\int e^x \sinh(e^x) \, dx$

8. $\int \dfrac{\sec(\ln x) \tan(\ln x)}{x} \, dx$

9. $\int e^{\tan x} \sec^2 x \, dx$

10. $\int \dfrac{x}{\sqrt{1 - x^4}} \, dx$

11. $\int \cos^5 5x \sin 5x \, dx$

12. $\int \dfrac{\cos x}{\sin x \sqrt{\sin^2 x + 1}} \, dx$

13. $\int \dfrac{e^x}{\sqrt{4 + e^{2x}}} \, dx$

14. $\int \dfrac{e^{\tan^{-1} x}}{1 + x^2} \, dx$

15. $\int \dfrac{e^{\sqrt{x-1}}}{\sqrt{x - 1}} \, dx$

16. $\int (x + 1) \cot(x^2 + 2x) \, dx$

17. $\int \dfrac{\cosh \sqrt{x}}{\sqrt{x}} \, dx$

18. $\int \dfrac{dx}{x (\ln x)^2}$

19. $\int \dfrac{dx}{\sqrt{x}\, 3^{\sqrt{x}}}$

20. $\displaystyle\int \sec(\sin\theta)\tan(\sin\theta)\cos\theta\,d\theta$

21. $\displaystyle\int \frac{\operatorname{csch}^2(2/x)}{x^2}\,dx$

22. $\displaystyle\int \frac{dx}{\sqrt{x^2-4}}$

23. $\displaystyle\int \frac{e^{-x}}{4-e^{-2x}}\,dx$

24. $\displaystyle\int \frac{\cos(\ln x)}{x}\,dx$

25. $\displaystyle\int \frac{e^x}{\sqrt{1-e^{2x}}}\,dx$

26. $\displaystyle\int \frac{\sinh(x^{-1/2})}{x^{3/2}}\,dx$

27. $\displaystyle\int \frac{x}{\csc(x^2)}\,dx$

28. $\displaystyle\int \frac{e^x}{\sqrt{4-e^{2x}}}\,dx$

29. $\displaystyle\int x4^{-x^2}\,dx$

30. $\displaystyle\int 2^{\pi x}\,dx$

FOCUS ON CONCEPTS

31. (a) Evaluate the integral $\int \sin x\cos x\,dx$ using the substitution $u=\sin x$.
(b) Evaluate the integral $\int \sin x\cos x\,dx$ using the identity $\sin 2x=2\sin x\cos x$.
(c) Explain why your answers to parts (a) and (b) are consistent.

32. (a) Derive the identity

$$\frac{\operatorname{sech}^2 x}{1+\tanh^2 x}=\operatorname{sech} 2x$$

(b) Use the result in part (a) to evaluate $\int \operatorname{sech} x\,dx$.
(c) Derive the identity

$$\operatorname{sech} x=\frac{2e^x}{e^{2x}+1}$$

(d) Use the result in part (c) to evaluate $\int \operatorname{sech} x\,dx$.
(e) Explain why your answers to parts (b) and (d) are consistent.

33. (a) Derive the identity

$$\frac{\sec^2 x}{\tan x}=\frac{1}{\sin x\cos x}$$

(b) Use the identity $\sin 2x=2\sin x\cos x$ along with the result in part (a) to evaluate $\int \csc x\,dx$.
(c) Use the identity $\cos x=\sin[(\pi/2)-x]$ along with your answer to part (a) to evaluate $\int \sec x\,dx$.

✔ **QUICK CHECK ANSWERS 7.1**

1. (a) $x+\ln|x|+C$ (b) $x+\ln|x+1|+C$ (c) $\ln(x^2+1)+\tan^{-1}x+C$ (d) $\dfrac{x^5}{5}+C$ **2.** (a) $-\cos x+C$ (b) $\tan x+C$

(c) $-\cot x+C$ (d) $\ln(1+\sin x)+C$ **3.** (a) $\frac{2}{3}(x-1)^{3/2}+C$ (b) $\frac{1}{2}e^{2x+1}+C$ (c) $\frac{1}{2}\sin^2 x+C$ (d) $\frac{1}{4}\tanh x+C$

7.2 INTEGRATION BY PARTS

In this section we will discuss an integration technique that is essentially an antiderivative formulation of the formula for differentiating a product of two functions.

■ **THE PRODUCT RULE AND INTEGRATION BY PARTS**

Our primary goal in this section is to develop a general method for attacking integrals of the form

$$\int f(x)g(x)\,dx$$

As a first step, let $G(x)$ be *any* antiderivative of $g(x)$. In this case $G'(x)=g(x)$, so the product rule for differentiating $f(x)G(x)$ can be expressed as

$$\frac{d}{dx}[f(x)G(x)]=f(x)G'(x)+f'(x)G(x)=f(x)g(x)+f'(x)G(x) \qquad (1)$$

This implies that $f(x)G(x)$ is an antiderivative of the function on the right side of (1), so we can express (1) in integral form as

$$\int [f(x)g(x)+f'(x)G(x)]\,dx=f(x)G(x)$$

or, equivalently, as

$$\int f(x)g(x)\,dx = f(x)G(x) - \int f'(x)G(x)\,dx \qquad (2)$$

This formula allows us to integrate $f(x)g(x)$ by integrating $f'(x)G(x)$ instead, and in many cases the net effect is to replace a difficult integration with an easier one. The application of this formula is called **integration by parts**.

In practice, we usually rewrite (2) by letting

$$u = f(x), \quad du = f'(x)\,dx$$
$$v = G(x), \quad dv = G'(x)\,dx = g(x)\,dx$$

This yields the following alternative form for (2):

$$\int u\,dv = uv - \int v\,du \qquad (3)$$

> Note that in Example 1 we omitted the constant of integration in calculating v from dv. Had we included a constant of integration, it would have eventually dropped out. This is always the case in integration by parts [Exercise 68(b)], so it is common to omit the constant at this stage of the computation. However, there are certain cases in which making a clever choice of a constant of integration to include with v can simplify the computation of $\int v\,du$ (Exercises 69–71).

▶ **Example 1** Use integration by parts to evaluate $\displaystyle\int x\cos x\,dx$.

Solution. We will apply Formula (3). The first step is to make a choice for u and dv to put the given integral in the form $\int u\,dv$. We will let

$$u = x \quad \text{and} \quad dv = \cos x\,dx$$

(Other possibilities will be considered later.) The second step is to compute du from u and v from dv. This yields

$$du = dx \quad \text{and} \quad v = \int dv = \int \cos x\,dx = \sin x$$

The third step is to apply Formula (3). This yields

$$\int \underbrace{x}_{u}\,\underbrace{\cos x\,dx}_{dv} = \underbrace{x}_{u}\,\underbrace{\sin x}_{v} - \int \underbrace{\sin x}_{v}\,\underbrace{dx}_{du}$$
$$= x\sin x - (-\cos x) + C = x\sin x + \cos x + C \quad ◀$$

■ **GUIDELINES FOR INTEGRATION BY PARTS**

The main goal in integration by parts is to choose u and dv to obtain a new integral that is easier to evaluate than the original. In general, there are no hard and fast rules for doing this; it is mainly a matter of experience that comes from lots of practice. A strategy that often works is to choose u and dv so that u becomes "simpler" when differentiated, while leaving a dv that can be readily integrated to obtain v. Thus, for the integral $\int x\cos x\,dx$ in Example 1, both goals were achieved by letting $u = x$ and $dv = \cos x\,dx$. In contrast, $u = \cos x$ would not have been a good first choice in that example, since $du/dx = -\sin x$ is no simpler than u. Indeed, had we chosen

$$u = \cos x \qquad dv = x\,dx$$
$$du = -\sin x\,dx \qquad v = \int x\,dx = \frac{x^2}{2}$$

then we would have obtained

$$\int x\cos x\,dx = \frac{x^2}{2}\cos x - \int \frac{x^2}{2}(-\sin x)\,dx = \frac{x^2}{2}\cos x + \frac{1}{2}\int x^2\sin x\,dx$$

For this choice of u and dv, the new integral is actually more complicated than the original.

The LIATE method is discussed in the article "A Technique for Integration by Parts," *American Mathematical Monthly*, Vol. 90, 1983, pp. 210–211, by Herbert Kasube.

There is another useful strategy for choosing u and dv that can be applied when the integrand is a product of two functions from *different* categories in the list

Logarithmic, **I**nverse trigonometric, **A**lgebraic, **T**rigonometric, **E**xponential

In this case you will often be successful if you take u to be the function whose category occurs earlier in the list and take dv to be the rest of the integrand. The acronym LIATE will help you to remember the order. The method does not work all the time, but it works often enough to be useful.

Note, for example, that the integrand in Example 1 consists of the product of the *algebraic* function x and the *trigonometric* function $\cos x$. Thus, the LIATE method suggests that we should let $u = x$ and $dv = \cos x \, dx$, which proved to be a successful choice.

▶ **Example 2**   Evaluate $\int xe^x \, dx$.

Solution.   In this case the integrand is the product of the algebraic function x with the exponential function e^x. According to LIATE we should let

$$u = x \quad \text{and} \quad dv = e^x \, dx$$

so that

$$du = dx \quad \text{and} \quad v = \int e^x \, dx = e^x$$

Thus, from (3)

$$\int xe^x \, dx = \int u \, dv = uv - \int v \, du = xe^x - \int e^x \, dx = xe^x - e^x + C \ \blacktriangleleft$$

▶ **Example 3**   Evaluate $\int \ln x \, dx$.

Solution.   One choice is to let $u = 1$ and $dv = \ln x \, dx$. But with this choice finding v is equivalent to evaluating $\int \ln x \, dx$ and we have gained nothing. Therefore, the only reasonable choice is to let

$$u = \ln x \qquad dv = dx$$
$$du = \frac{1}{x} \, dx \qquad v = \int dx = x$$

With this choice it follows from (3) that

$$\int \ln x \, dx = \int u \, dv = uv - \int v \, du = x \ln x - \int dx = x \ln x - x + C \ \blacktriangleleft$$

■ **REPEATED INTEGRATION BY PARTS**

It is sometimes necessary to use integration by parts more than once in the same problem.

▶ **Example 4**   Evaluate $\int x^2 e^{-x} \, dx$.

Solution.   Let

$$u = x^2, \quad dv = e^{-x} \, dx, \quad du = 2x \, dx, \quad v = \int e^{-x} \, dx = -e^{-x}$$

so that from (3)

$$\int x^2 e^{-x}\, dx = \int u\, dv = uv - \int v\, du$$

$$= x^2(-e^{-x}) - \int -e^{-x}(2x)\, dx$$

$$= -x^2 e^{-x} + 2\int x e^{-x}\, dx \tag{4}$$

The last integral is similar to the original except that we have replaced x^2 by x. Another integration by parts applied to $\int x e^{-x}\, dx$ will complete the problem. We let

$$u = x, \quad dv = e^{-x}\, dx, \quad du = dx, \quad v = \int e^{-x}\, dx = -e^{-x}$$

so that

$$\int x e^{-x}\, dx = x(-e^{-x}) - \int -e^{-x}\, dx = -x e^{-x} + \int e^{-x}\, dx = -x e^{-x} - e^{-x} + C$$

Finally, substituting this into the last line of (4) yields

$$\int x^2 e^{-x}\, dx = -x^2 e^{-x} + 2\int x e^{-x}\, dx = -x^2 e^{-x} + 2(-x e^{-x} - e^{-x}) + C$$

$$= -(x^2 + 2x + 2)e^{-x} + C \blacktriangleleft$$

The LIATE method suggests that integrals of the form

$$\int e^{ax} \sin bx\, dx \quad \text{and} \quad \int e^{ax} \cos bx\, dx$$

can be evaluated by letting $u = \sin bx$ or $u = \cos bx$ and $dv = e^{ax}\, dx$. However, this will require a technique that deserves special attention.

▶ **Example 5**   Evaluate $\int e^x \cos x\, dx$.

Solution.   Let

$$u = \cos x, \quad dv = e^x\, dx, \quad du = -\sin x\, dx, \quad v = \int e^x\, dx = e^x$$

Thus,

$$\int e^x \cos x\, dx = \int u\, dv = uv - \int v\, du = e^x \cos x + \int e^x \sin x\, dx \tag{5}$$

Since the integral $\int e^x \sin x\, dx$ is similar in form to the original integral $\int e^x \cos x\, dx$, it seems that nothing has been accomplished. However, let us integrate this new integral by parts. We let

$$u = \sin x, \quad dv = e^x\, dx, \quad du = \cos x\, dx, \quad v = \int e^x\, dx = e^x$$

Thus,

$$\int e^x \sin x\, dx = \int u\, dv = uv - \int v\, du = e^x \sin x - \int e^x \cos x\, dx$$

Together with Equation (5) this yields

$$\int e^x \cos x\, dx = e^x \cos x + e^x \sin x - \int e^x \cos x\, dx \tag{6}$$

which is an equation we can solve for the unknown integral. We obtain

$$2 \int e^x \cos x \, dx = e^x \cos x + e^x \sin x$$

and hence

$$\int e^x \cos x \, dx = \tfrac{1}{2} e^x \cos x + \tfrac{1}{2} e^x \sin x + C \blacktriangleleft$$

■ A TABULAR METHOD FOR REPEATED INTEGRATION BY PARTS

Integrals of the form

$$\int p(x) f(x) \, dx$$

More information on tabular integration by parts can be found in the articles "Tabular Integration by Parts," *College Mathematics Journal*, Vol. 21, 1990, pp. 307–311, by David Horowitz and "More on Tabular Integration by Parts," *College Mathematics Journal*, Vol. 22, 1991, pp. 407–410, by Leonard Gillman.

where $p(x)$ is a polynomial, can sometimes be evaluated using repeated integration by parts in which u is taken to be $p(x)$ or one of its derivatives at each stage. Since du is computed by differentiating u, the repeated differentiation of $p(x)$ will eventually produce 0, at which point you may be left with a simplified integration problem. A convenient method for organizing the computations into two columns is called *tabular integration by parts*.

Tabular Integration by Parts

Step 1. Differentiate $p(x)$ repeatedly until you obtain 0, and list the results in the first column.

Step 2. Integrate $f(x)$ repeatedly and list the results in the second column.

Step 3. Draw an arrow from each entry in the first column to the entry that is one row down in the second column.

Step 4. Label the arrows with alternating $+$ and $-$ signs, starting with a $+$.

Step 5. For each arrow, form the product of the expressions at its tip and tail and then multiply that product by $+1$ or -1 in accordance with the sign on the arrow. Add the results to obtain the value of the integral.

This process is illustrated in Figure 7.2.1 for the integral $\int (x^2 - x) \cos x \, dx$.

REPEATED DIFFERENTIATION		REPEATED INTEGRATION
$x^2 - x$	$+$	$\cos x$
$2x - 1$	$-$	$\sin x$
2	$+$	$-\cos x$
0		$-\sin x$

$$\int (x^2 - x) \cos x \, dx = (x^2 - x) \sin x + (2x - 1) \cos x - 2 \sin x + C$$
$$= (x^2 - x - 2) \sin x + (2x - 1) \cos x + C$$

▶ **Figure 7.2.1**

▶ **Example 6** In Example 11 of Section 5.3 we evaluated $\int x^2 \sqrt{x-1} \, dx$ using u-substitution. Evaluate this integral using tabular integration by parts.

Solution.

REPEATED DIFFERENTIATION		REPEATED INTEGRATION
x^2	$+$	$(x-1)^{1/2}$
$2x$	$-$	$\frac{2}{3}(x-1)^{3/2}$
2	$+$	$\frac{4}{15}(x-1)^{5/2}$
0		$\frac{8}{105}(x-1)^{7/2}$

> The result obtained in Example 6 looks quite different from that obtained in Example 11 of Section 5.3. Show that the two answers are equivalent.

Thus, it follows that

$$\int x^2\sqrt{x-1}\,dx = \tfrac{2}{3}x^2(x-1)^{3/2} - \tfrac{8}{15}x(x-1)^{5/2} + \tfrac{16}{105}(x-1)^{7/2} + C \blacktriangleleft$$

■ INTEGRATION BY PARTS FOR DEFINITE INTEGRALS

For definite integrals the formula corresponding to (3) is

$$\int_a^b u\,dv = uv\Big]_a^b - \int_a^b v\,du \tag{7}$$

REMARK   It is important to keep in mind that the variables u and v in this formula are functions of x and that the limits of integration in (7) are limits on the variable x. Sometimes it is helpful to emphasize this by writing (7) as

$$\int_{x=a}^b u\,dv = uv\Big]_{x=a}^b - \int_{x=a}^b v\,du \tag{8}$$

The next example illustrates how integration by parts can be used to integrate the inverse trigonometric functions.

▶ **Example 7**   Evaluate $\displaystyle\int_0^1 \tan^{-1} x\,dx$.

Solution.   Let

$$u = \tan^{-1}x, \quad dv = dx, \quad du = \frac{1}{1+x^2}\,dx, \quad v = x$$

Thus,

$$\int_0^1 \tan^{-1} x\,dx = \int_0^1 u\,dv = uv\Big]_0^1 - \int_0^1 v\,du$$

> The limits of integration refer to x; that is, $x = 0$ and $x = 1$.

$$= x\tan^{-1}x\Big]_0^1 - \int_0^1 \frac{x}{1+x^2}\,dx$$

But

$$\int_0^1 \frac{x}{1+x^2}\,dx = \frac{1}{2}\int_0^1 \frac{2x}{1+x^2}\,dx = \frac{1}{2}\ln(1+x^2)\Big]_0^1 = \frac{1}{2}\ln 2$$

so

$$\int_0^1 \tan^{-1} x\,dx = x\tan^{-1}x\Big]_0^1 - \frac{1}{2}\ln 2 = \left(\frac{\pi}{4} - 0\right) - \frac{1}{2}\ln 2 = \frac{\pi}{4} - \ln\sqrt{2} \blacktriangleleft$$

■ REDUCTION FORMULAS

Integration by parts can be used to derive *reduction formulas* for integrals. These are formulas that express an integral involving a power of a function in terms of an integral that involves a *lower* power of that function. For example, if n is a positive integer and $n \geq 2$, then integration by parts can be used to obtain the reduction formulas

$$\int \sin^n x \, dx = -\frac{1}{n} \sin^{n-1} x \cos x + \frac{n-1}{n} \int \sin^{n-2} x \, dx \qquad (9)$$

$$\int \cos^n x \, dx = \frac{1}{n} \cos^{n-1} x \sin x + \frac{n-1}{n} \int \cos^{n-2} x \, dx \qquad (10)$$

To illustrate how such formulas can be obtained, let us derive (10). We begin by writing $\cos^n x$ as $\cos^{n-1} x \cdot \cos x$ and letting

$$u = \cos^{n-1} x \qquad\qquad dv = \cos x \, dx$$

$$du = (n-1) \cos^{n-2} x(-\sin x) \, dx \qquad v = \sin x$$

$$= -(n-1) \cos^{n-2} x \sin x \, dx$$

so that

$$\int \cos^n x \, dx = \int \cos^{n-1} x \cos x \, dx = \int u \, dv = uv - \int v \, du$$

$$= \cos^{n-1} x \sin x + (n-1) \int \sin^2 x \cos^{n-2} x \, dx$$

$$= \cos^{n-1} x \sin x + (n-1) \int (1 - \cos^2 x) \cos^{n-2} x \, dx$$

$$= \cos^{n-1} x \sin x + (n-1) \int \cos^{n-2} x \, dx - (n-1) \int \cos^n x \, dx$$

Moving the last term on the right to the left side yields

$$n \int \cos^n x \, dx = \cos^{n-1} x \sin x + (n-1) \int \cos^{n-2} x \, dx$$

from which (10) follows. The derivation of reduction formula (9) is similar (Exercise 63).

Reduction formulas (9) and (10) reduce the exponent of sine (or cosine) by 2. Thus, if the formulas are applied repeatedly, the exponent can eventually be reduced to 0 if n is even or 1 if n is odd, at which point the integration can be completed. We will discuss this method in more detail in the next section, but for now, here is an example that illustrates how reduction formulas work.

▶ **Example 8**   Evaluate $\int \cos^4 x \, dx$.

Solution.   From (10) with $n = 4$

$$\int \cos^4 x \, dx = \tfrac{1}{4} \cos^3 x \sin x + \tfrac{3}{4} \int \cos^2 x \, dx \qquad \boxed{\text{Now apply (10) with } n = 2.}$$

$$= \tfrac{1}{4} \cos^3 x \sin x + \tfrac{3}{4} \left(\tfrac{1}{2} \cos x \sin x + \tfrac{1}{2} \int dx \right)$$

$$= \tfrac{1}{4} \cos^3 x \sin x + \tfrac{3}{8} \cos x \sin x + \tfrac{3}{8} x + C \quad ◀$$

✓ **QUICK CHECK EXERCISES 7.2** *(See page 500 for answers.)*

1. (a) If $G'(x) = g(x)$, then

$$\int f(x)g(x)\, dx = f(x)G(x) - \underline{\hspace{1cm}}$$

(b) If $u = f(x)$ and $v = G(x)$, then the formula in part (a) can be written in the form $\int u\, dv = \underline{\hspace{1cm}}$.

2. Find an appropriate choice of u and dv for integration by parts of each integral. Do not evaluate the integral.

(a) $\int x \ln x\, dx$; $u = \underline{\hspace{1cm}}$, $dv = \underline{\hspace{1cm}}$

(b) $\int (x-2) \sin x\, dx$; $u = \underline{\hspace{1cm}}$, $dv = \underline{\hspace{1cm}}$

(c) $\int \sin^{-1} x\, dx$; $u = \underline{\hspace{1cm}}$, $dv = \underline{\hspace{1cm}}$

(d) $\int \dfrac{x}{\sqrt{x-1}}\, dx$; $u = \underline{\hspace{1cm}}$, $dv = \underline{\hspace{1cm}}$

3. Use integration by parts to evaluate the integral.

(a) $\int x e^{2x}\, dx$

(b) $\int \ln(x-1)\, dx$

(c) $\int_0^{\pi/6} x \sin 3x\, dx$

4. Use a reduction formula to evaluate $\int \sin^3 x\, dx$.

EXERCISE SET 7.2

1–38 Evaluate the integral. ■

1. $\int x e^{-2x}\, dx$

2. $\int x e^{3x}\, dx$

3. $\int x^2 e^x\, dx$

4. $\int x^2 e^{-2x}\, dx$

5. $\int x \sin 3x\, dx$

6. $\int x \cos 2x\, dx$

7. $\int x^2 \cos x\, dx$

8. $\int x^2 \sin x\, dx$

9. $\int x \ln x\, dx$

10. $\int \sqrt{x} \ln x\, dx$

11. $\int (\ln x)^2\, dx$

12. $\int \dfrac{\ln x}{\sqrt{x}}\, dx$

13. $\int \ln(3x - 2)\, dx$

14. $\int \ln(x^2 + 4)\, dx$

15. $\int \sin^{-1} x\, dx$

16. $\int \cos^{-1}(2x)\, dx$

17. $\int \tan^{-1}(3x)\, dx$

18. $\int x \tan^{-1} x\, dx$

19. $\int e^x \sin x\, dx$

20. $\int e^{3x} \cos 2x\, dx$

21. $\int \sin(\ln x)\, dx$

22. $\int \cos(\ln x)\, dx$

23. $\int x \sec^2 x\, dx$

24. $\int x \tan^2 x\, dx$

25. $\int x^3 e^{x^2}\, dx$

26. $\int \dfrac{x e^x}{(x+1)^2}\, dx$

27. $\int_0^2 x e^{2x}\, dx$

28. $\int_0^1 x e^{-5x}\, dx$

29. $\int_1^e x^2 \ln x\, dx$

30. $\int_{\sqrt{e}}^e \dfrac{\ln x}{x^2}\, dx$

31. $\int_{-1}^1 \ln(x+2)\, dx$

32. $\int_0^{\sqrt{3}/2} \sin^{-1} x\, dx$

33. $\int_2^4 \sec^{-1} \sqrt{\theta}\, d\theta$

34. $\int_1^2 x \sec^{-1} x\, dx$

35. $\int_0^\pi x \sin 2x\, dx$

36. $\int_0^\pi (x + x \cos x)\, dx$

37. $\int_1^3 \sqrt{x} \tan^{-1} \sqrt{x}\, dx$

38. $\int_0^2 \ln(x^2 + 1)\, dx$

39–42 True–False Determine whether the statement is true or false. Explain your answer. ■

39. The main goal in integration by parts is to choose u and dv to obtain a new integral that is easier to evaluate than the original.

40. Applying the LIATE strategy to evaluate $\int x^3 \ln x\, dx$, we should choose $u = x^3$ and $dv = \ln x\, dx$.

41. To evaluate $\int \ln e^x\, dx$ using integration by parts, choose $dv = e^x\, dx$.

42. Tabular integration by parts is useful for integrals of the form $\int p(x)f(x)\, dx$, where $p(x)$ is a polynomial and $f(x)$ can be repeatedly integrated.

43–44 Evaluate the integral by making a u-substitution and then integrating by parts. ■

43. $\int e^{\sqrt{x}}\, dx$

44. $\int \cos \sqrt{x}\, dx$

45. Prove that tabular integration by parts gives the correct answer for

$$\int p(x) f(x)\, dx$$

where $p(x)$ is any *quadratic polynomial* and $f(x)$ is any function that can be repeatedly integrated.

46. The computations of any integral evaluated by repeated integration by parts can be organized using tabular integration by parts. Use this organization to evaluate $\int e^x \cos x\, dx$ in

two ways: first by repeated differentiation of $\cos x$ (compare Example 5), and then by repeated differentiation of e^x.

47–52 Evaluate the integral using tabular integration by parts.

47. $\displaystyle\int (3x^2 - x + 2)e^{-x}\,dx$ **48.** $\displaystyle\int (x^2 + x + 1)\sin x\,dx$

49. $\displaystyle\int 4x^4 \sin 2x\,dx$ **50.** $\displaystyle\int x^3\sqrt{2x+1}\,dx$

51. $\displaystyle\int e^{ax}\sin bx\,dx$ **52.** $\displaystyle\int e^{-3\theta}\sin 5\theta\,d\theta$

53. Consider the integral $\int \sin x \cos x\,dx$.
(a) Evaluate the integral two ways: first using integration by parts, and then using the substitution $u = \sin x$.
(b) Show that the results of part (a) are equivalent.
(c) Which of the two methods do you prefer? Discuss the reasons for your preference.

54. Evaluate the integral
$$\int_0^1 \frac{x^3}{\sqrt{x^2+1}}\,dx$$
using
(a) integration by parts
(b) the substitution $u = \sqrt{x^2+1}$.

55. (a) Find the area of the region enclosed by $y = \ln x$, the line $x = e$, and the x-axis.
(b) Find the volume of the solid generated when the region in part (a) is revolved about the x-axis.

56. Find the area of the region between $y = x \sin x$ and $y = x$ for $0 \le x \le \pi/2$.

57. Find the volume of the solid generated when the region between $y = \sin x$ and $y = 0$ for $0 \le x \le \pi$ is revolved about the y-axis.

58. Find the volume of the solid generated when the region enclosed between $y = \cos x$ and $y = 0$ for $0 \le x \le \pi/2$ is revolved about the y-axis.

59. A particle moving along the x-axis has velocity function $v(t) = t^3 \sin t$. How far does the particle travel from time $t = 0$ to $t = \pi$?

60. The study of sawtooth waves in electrical engineering leads to integrals of the form
$$\int_{-\pi/\omega}^{\pi/\omega} t \sin(k\omega t)\,dt$$
where k is an integer and ω is a nonzero constant. Evaluate the integral.

61. Use reduction formula (9) to evaluate
(a) $\displaystyle\int \sin^4 x\,dx$ (b) $\displaystyle\int_0^{\pi/2} \sin^5 x\,dx$.

62. Use reduction formula (10) to evaluate
(a) $\displaystyle\int \cos^5 x\,dx$ (b) $\displaystyle\int_0^{\pi/2} \cos^6 x\,dx$.

63. Derive reduction formula (9).

64. In each part, use integration by parts or other methods to derive the reduction formula.
(a) $\displaystyle\int \sec^n x\,dx = \frac{\sec^{n-2}x \tan x}{n-1} + \frac{n-2}{n-1}\int \sec^{n-2}x\,dx$
(b) $\displaystyle\int \tan^n x\,dx = \frac{\tan^{n-1}x}{n-1} - \int \tan^{n-2}x\,dx$
(c) $\displaystyle\int x^n e^x\,dx = x^n e^x - n\int x^{n-1}e^x\,dx$

65–66 Use the reduction formulas in Exercise 64 to evaluate the integrals.

65. (a) $\displaystyle\int \tan^4 x\,dx$ (b) $\displaystyle\int \sec^4 x\,dx$ (c) $\displaystyle\int x^3 e^x\,dx$

66. (a) $\displaystyle\int x^2 e^{3x}\,dx$ (b) $\displaystyle\int_0^1 xe^{-\sqrt{x}}\,dx$
[*Hint:* First make a substitution.]

67. Let f be a function whose second derivative is continuous on $[-1, 1]$. Show that
$$\int_{-1}^1 xf''(x)\,dx = f'(1) + f'(-1) - f(1) + f(-1)$$

FOCUS ON CONCEPTS

68. (a) In the integral $\int x \cos x\,dx$, let
$$u = x, \quad dv = \cos x\,dx,$$
$$du = dx, \quad v = \sin x + C_1$$
Show that the constant C_1 cancels out, thus giving the same solution obtained by omitting C_1.
(b) Show that in general
$$uv - \int v\,du = u(v + C_1) - \int (v + C_1)\,du$$
thereby justifying the omission of the constant of integration when calculating v in integration by parts.

69. Evaluate $\int \ln(x+1)\,dx$ using integration by parts. Simplify the computation of $\int v\,du$ by introducing a constant of integration $C_1 = 1$ when going from dv to v.

70. Evaluate $\int \ln(3x - 2)\,dx$ using integration by parts. Simplify the computation of $\int v\,du$ by introducing a constant of integration $C_1 = -\frac{2}{3}$ when going from dv to v. Compare your solution with your answer to Exercise 13.

71. Evaluate $\int x \tan^{-1} x\,dx$ using integration by parts. Simplify the computation of $\int v\,du$ by introducing a constant of integration $C_1 = \frac{1}{2}$ when going from dv to v.

72. What equation results if integration by parts is applied to the integral
$$\int \frac{1}{x \ln x}\,dx$$
with the choices
$$u = \frac{1}{\ln x} \quad \text{and} \quad dv = \frac{1}{x}\,dx?$$
In what sense is this equation true? In what sense is it false?

73. Writing   Explain how the product rule for derivatives and the technique of integration by parts are related.

74. Writing   For what sort of problems are the integration techniques of substitution and integration by parts "competing"

techniques? Describe situations, with examples, where each of these techniques would be preferred over the other.

✔ **QUICK CHECK ANSWERS 7.2**

1. (a) $\int f'(x)G(x)\,dx$ (b) $uv - \int v\,du$ **2.** (a) $\ln x$; $x\,dx$ (b) $x - 2$; $\sin x\,dx$ (c) $\sin^{-1} x$; dx (d) x; $\dfrac{1}{\sqrt{x-1}}\,dx$

3. (a) $\left(\dfrac{x}{2} - \dfrac{1}{4}\right)e^{2x} + C$ (b) $(x-1)\ln(x-1) - x + C$ (c) $\frac{1}{9}$ **4.** $-\frac{1}{3}\sin^2 x \cos x - \frac{2}{3}\cos x + C$

7.3 INTEGRATING TRIGONOMETRIC FUNCTIONS

In the last section we derived reduction formulas for integrating positive integer powers of sine, cosine, tangent, and secant. In this section we will show how to work with those reduction formulas, and we will discuss methods for integrating other kinds of integrals that involve trigonometric functions.

■ INTEGRATING POWERS OF SINE AND COSINE

We begin by recalling two reduction formulas from the preceding section.

$$\int \sin^n x\,dx = -\frac{1}{n}\sin^{n-1} x \cos x + \frac{n-1}{n}\int \sin^{n-2} x\,dx \tag{1}$$

$$\int \cos^n x\,dx = \frac{1}{n}\cos^{n-1} x \sin x + \frac{n-1}{n}\int \cos^{n-2} x\,dx \tag{2}$$

In the case where $n = 2$, these formulas yield

$$\int \sin^2 x\,dx = -\tfrac{1}{2}\sin x \cos x + \tfrac{1}{2}\int dx = \tfrac{1}{2}x - \tfrac{1}{2}\sin x \cos x + C \tag{3}$$

$$\int \cos^2 x\,dx = \tfrac{1}{2}\cos x \sin x + \tfrac{1}{2}\int dx = \tfrac{1}{2}x + \tfrac{1}{2}\sin x \cos x + C \tag{4}$$

Alternative forms of these integration formulas can be derived from the trigonometric identities

$$\sin^2 x = \tfrac{1}{2}(1 - \cos 2x) \quad \text{and} \quad \cos^2 x = \tfrac{1}{2}(1 + \cos 2x) \tag{5-6}$$

which follow from the double-angle formulas

$$\cos 2x = 1 - 2\sin^2 x \quad \text{and} \quad \cos 2x = 2\cos^2 x - 1$$

These identities yield

$$\int \sin^2 x\,dx = \tfrac{1}{2}\int (1 - \cos 2x)\,dx = \tfrac{1}{2}x - \tfrac{1}{4}\sin 2x + C \tag{7}$$

$$\int \cos^2 x\,dx = \tfrac{1}{2}\int (1 + \cos 2x)\,dx = \tfrac{1}{2}x + \tfrac{1}{4}\sin 2x + C \tag{8}$$

Observe that the antiderivatives in Formulas (3) and (4) involve both sines and cosines, whereas those in (7) and (8) involve sines alone. However, the apparent discrepancy is easy to resolve by using the identity

$$\sin 2x = 2 \sin x \cos x$$

to rewrite (7) and (8) in forms (3) and (4), or conversely.

In the case where $n = 3$, the reduction formulas for integrating $\sin^3 x$ and $\cos^3 x$ yield

$$\int \sin^3 x \, dx = -\tfrac{1}{3} \sin^2 x \cos x + \tfrac{2}{3} \int \sin x \, dx = -\tfrac{1}{3} \sin^2 x \cos x - \tfrac{2}{3} \cos x + C \qquad (9)$$

$$\int \cos^3 x \, dx = \tfrac{1}{3} \cos^2 x \sin x + \tfrac{2}{3} \int \cos x \, dx = \tfrac{1}{3} \cos^2 x \sin x + \tfrac{2}{3} \sin x + C \qquad (10)$$

If desired, Formula (9) can be expressed in terms of cosines alone by using the identity $\sin^2 x = 1 - \cos^2 x$, and Formula (10) can be expressed in terms of sines alone by using the identity $\cos^2 x = 1 - \sin^2 x$. We leave it for you to do this and confirm that

$$\int \sin^3 x \, dx = \tfrac{1}{3} \cos^3 x - \cos x + C \qquad (11)$$

$$\int \cos^3 x \, dx = \sin x - \tfrac{1}{3} \sin^3 x + C \qquad (12)$$

We leave it as an exercise to obtain the following formulas by first applying the reduction formulas, and then using appropriate trigonometric identities.

$$\int \sin^4 x \, dx = \tfrac{3}{8}x - \tfrac{1}{4} \sin 2x + \tfrac{1}{32} \sin 4x + C \qquad (13)$$

$$\int \cos^4 x \, dx = \tfrac{3}{8}x + \tfrac{1}{4} \sin 2x + \tfrac{1}{32} \sin 4x + C \qquad (14)$$

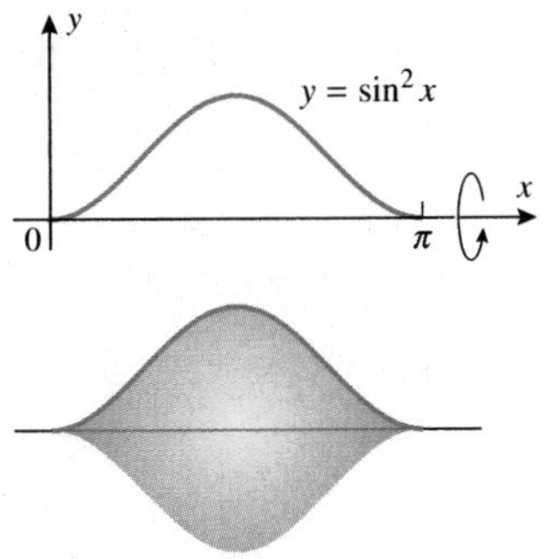

▶ **Example 1** Find the volume V of the solid that is obtained when the region under the curve $y = \sin^2 x$ over the interval $[0, \pi]$ is revolved about the x-axis (Figure 7.3.1).

Solution. Using the method of disks, Formula (5) of Section 6.2, and Formula (13) above yields

$$V = \int_0^\pi \pi \sin^4 x \, dx = \pi \left[\tfrac{3}{8}x - \tfrac{1}{4} \sin 2x + \tfrac{1}{32} \sin 4x \right]_0^\pi = \tfrac{3}{8}\pi^2 \quad ◀$$

$y = \sin^2 x$

▲ **Figure 7.3.1**

■ **INTEGRATING PRODUCTS OF SINES AND COSINES**

If m and n are positive integers, then the integral

$$\int \sin^m x \cos^n x \, dx$$

can be evaluated by one of the three procedures stated in Table 7.3.1, depending on whether m and n are odd or even.

▶ **Example 2** Evaluate

(a) $\displaystyle\int \sin^4 x \cos^5 x \, dx$ (b) $\displaystyle\int \sin^4 x \cos^4 x \, dx$

Table 7.3.1

INTEGRATING PRODUCTS OF SINES AND COSINES

$\int \sin^m x \cos^n x \, dx$	PROCEDURE	RELEVANT IDENTITIES
n odd	• Split off a factor of $\cos x$. • Apply the relevant identity. • Make the substitution $u = \sin x$.	$\cos^2 x = 1 - \sin^2 x$
m odd	• Split off a factor of $\sin x$. • Apply the relevant identity. • Make the substitution $u = \cos x$.	$\sin^2 x = 1 - \cos^2 x$
$\begin{cases} m \text{ even} \\ n \text{ even} \end{cases}$	• Use the relevant identities to reduce the powers on $\sin x$ and $\cos x$.	$\begin{cases} \sin^2 x = \frac{1}{2}(1 - \cos 2x) \\ \cos^2 x = \frac{1}{2}(1 + \cos 2x) \end{cases}$

Solution (a). Since $n = 5$ is odd, we will follow the first procedure in Table 7.3.1:

$$\int \sin^4 x \cos^5 x \, dx = \int \sin^4 x \cos^4 x \cos x \, dx$$

$$= \int \sin^4 x (1 - \sin^2 x)^2 \cos x \, dx$$

$$= \int u^4 (1 - u^2)^2 \, du$$

$$= \int (u^4 - 2u^6 + u^8) \, du$$

$$= \tfrac{1}{5} u^5 - \tfrac{2}{7} u^7 + \tfrac{1}{9} u^9 + C$$

$$= \tfrac{1}{5} \sin^5 x - \tfrac{2}{7} \sin^7 x + \tfrac{1}{9} \sin^9 x + C$$

Solution (b). Since $m = n = 4$, both exponents are even, so we will follow the third procedure in Table 7.3.1:

$$\int \sin^4 x \cos^4 x \, dx = \int (\sin^2 x)^2 (\cos^2 x)^2 \, dx$$

$$= \int \left(\tfrac{1}{2}[1 - \cos 2x] \right)^2 \left(\tfrac{1}{2}[1 + \cos 2x] \right)^2 \, dx$$

$$= \tfrac{1}{16} \int (1 - \cos^2 2x)^2 \, dx$$

$$= \tfrac{1}{16} \int \sin^4 2x \, dx \qquad \boxed{\begin{array}{l}\text{Note that this can be obtained more directly} \\ \text{from the original integral using the identity} \\ \sin x \cos x = \tfrac{1}{2} \sin 2x.\end{array}}$$

$$= \tfrac{1}{32} \int \sin^4 u \, du \qquad \boxed{\begin{array}{l} u = 2x \\ du = 2\,dx \text{ or } dx = \tfrac{1}{2}\,du \end{array}}$$

$$= \tfrac{1}{32} \left(\tfrac{3}{8} u - \tfrac{1}{4} \sin 2u + \tfrac{1}{32} \sin 4u \right) + C \qquad \boxed{\text{Formula (13)}}$$

$$= \tfrac{3}{128} x - \tfrac{1}{128} \sin 4x + \tfrac{1}{1024} \sin 8x + C \; \blacktriangleleft$$

Integrals of the form

$$\int \sin mx \cos nx \, dx, \quad \int \sin mx \sin nx \, dx, \quad \int \cos mx \cos nx \, dx \qquad (15)$$

can be found by using the trigonometric identities

$$\sin \alpha \cos \beta = \tfrac{1}{2}[\sin(\alpha - \beta) + \sin(\alpha + \beta)] \qquad (16)$$

$$\sin \alpha \sin \beta = \tfrac{1}{2}[\cos(\alpha - \beta) - \cos(\alpha + \beta)] \qquad (17)$$

$$\cos \alpha \cos \beta = \tfrac{1}{2}[\cos(\alpha - \beta) + \cos(\alpha + \beta)] \qquad (18)$$

to express the integrand as a sum or difference of sines and cosines.

▶ **Example 3** Evaluate $\int \sin 7x \cos 3x \, dx$.

Solution. Using (16) yields

$$\int \sin 7x \cos 3x \, dx = \tfrac{1}{2} \int (\sin 4x + \sin 10x) \, dx = -\tfrac{1}{8} \cos 4x - \tfrac{1}{20} \cos 10x + C \quad ◄$$

■ **INTEGRATING POWERS OF TANGENT AND SECANT**

The procedures for integrating powers of tangent and secant closely parallel those for sine and cosine. The idea is to use the following reduction formulas (which were derived in Exercise 64 of Section 7.2) to reduce the exponent in the integrand until the resulting integral can be evaluated:

$$\int \tan^n x \, dx = \frac{\tan^{n-1} x}{n-1} - \int \tan^{n-2} x \, dx \qquad (19)$$

$$\int \sec^n x \, dx = \frac{\sec^{n-2} x \tan x}{n-1} + \frac{n-2}{n-1} \int \sec^{n-2} x \, dx \qquad (20)$$

In the case where n is odd, the exponent can be reduced to 1, leaving us with the problem of integrating $\tan x$ or $\sec x$. These integrals are given by

$$\int \tan x \, dx = \ln |\sec x| + C \qquad (21)$$

$$\int \sec x \, dx = \ln |\sec x + \tan x| + C \qquad (22)$$

Formula (21) can be obtained by writing

$$\int \tan x \, dx = \int \frac{\sin x}{\cos x} \, dx$$

$$= -\ln |\cos x| + C \qquad \boxed{\begin{array}{l} u = \cos x \\ du = -\sin x \, dx \end{array}}$$

$$= \ln |\sec x| + C \qquad \boxed{\ln|\cos x| = -\ln \frac{1}{|\cos x|}}$$

To obtain Formula (22) we write

$$\int \sec x \, dx = \int \sec x \left(\frac{\sec x + \tan x}{\sec x + \tan x} \right) dx = \int \frac{\sec^2 x + \sec x \tan x}{\sec x + \tan x} \, dx$$

$$= \ln |\sec x + \tan x| + C \qquad \boxed{\begin{array}{l} u = \sec x + \tan x \\ du = (\sec^2 x + \sec x \tan x) \, dx \end{array}}$$

The following basic integrals occur frequently and are worth noting:

$$\int \tan^2 x \, dx = \tan x - x + C \tag{23}$$

$$\int \sec^2 x \, dx = \tan x + C \tag{24}$$

Formula (24) is already known to us, since the derivative of $\tan x$ is $\sec^2 x$. Formula (23) can be obtained by applying reduction formula (19) with $n = 2$ (verify) or, alternatively, by using the identity

$$1 + \tan^2 x = \sec^2 x$$

to write

$$\int \tan^2 x \, dx = \int (\sec^2 x - 1) \, dx = \tan x - x + C$$

The formulas

$$\int \tan^3 x \, dx = \tfrac{1}{2} \tan^2 x - \ln |\sec x| + C \tag{25}$$

$$\int \sec^3 x \, dx = \tfrac{1}{2} \sec x \tan x + \tfrac{1}{2} \ln |\sec x + \tan x| + C \tag{26}$$

can be deduced from (21), (22), and reduction formulas (19) and (20) as follows:

$$\int \tan^3 x \, dx = \tfrac{1}{2} \tan^2 x - \int \tan x \, dx = \tfrac{1}{2} \tan^2 x - \ln |\sec x| + C$$

$$\int \sec^3 x \, dx = \tfrac{1}{2} \sec x \tan x + \tfrac{1}{2} \int \sec x \, dx = \tfrac{1}{2} \sec x \tan x + \tfrac{1}{2} \ln |\sec x + \tan x| + C$$

■ INTEGRATING PRODUCTS OF TANGENTS AND SECANTS

If m and n are positive integers, then the integral

$$\int \tan^m x \sec^n x \, dx$$

can be evaluated by one of the three procedures stated in Table 7.3.2, depending on whether m and n are odd or even.

Table 7.3.2

INTEGRATING PRODUCTS OF TANGENTS AND SECANTS

$\int \tan^m x \sec^n x \, dx$	PROCEDURE	RELEVANT IDENTITIES
n even	• Split off a factor of $\sec^2 x$. • Apply the relevant identity. • Make the substitution $u = \tan x$.	$\sec^2 x = \tan^2 x + 1$
m odd	• Split off a factor of $\sec x \tan x$. • Apply the relevant identity. • Make the substitution $u = \sec x$.	$\tan^2 x = \sec^2 x - 1$
$\begin{cases} m \text{ even} \\ n \text{ odd} \end{cases}$	• Use the relevant identities to reduce the integrand to powers of $\sec x$ alone. • Then use the reduction formula for powers of $\sec x$.	$\tan^2 x = \sec^2 x - 1$

▶ **Example 4** Evaluate

(a) $\int \tan^2 x \sec^4 x \, dx$ (b) $\int \tan^3 x \sec^3 x \, dx$ (c) $\int \tan^2 x \sec x \, dx$

Solution (a).   Since $n = 4$ is even, we will follow the first procedure in Table 7.3.2:

$$\int \tan^2 x \sec^4 x \, dx = \int \tan^2 x \sec^2 x \sec^2 x \, dx$$

$$= \int \tan^2 x (\tan^2 x + 1) \sec^2 x \, dx$$

$$= \int u^2 (u^2 + 1) \, du$$

$$= \tfrac{1}{5} u^5 + \tfrac{1}{3} u^3 + C = \tfrac{1}{5} \tan^5 x + \tfrac{1}{3} \tan^3 x + C$$

Solution (b).   Since $m = 3$ is odd, we will follow the second procedure in Table 7.3.2:

$$\int \tan^3 x \sec^3 x \, dx = \int \tan^2 x \sec^2 x (\sec x \tan x) \, dx$$

$$= \int (\sec^2 x - 1) \sec^2 x (\sec x \tan x) \, dx$$

$$= \int (u^2 - 1) u^2 \, du$$

$$= \tfrac{1}{5} u^5 - \tfrac{1}{3} u^3 + C = \tfrac{1}{5} \sec^5 x - \tfrac{1}{3} \sec^3 x + C$$

Solution (c).   Since $m = 2$ is even and $n = 1$ is odd, we will follow the third procedure in Table 7.3.2:

$$\int \tan^2 x \sec x \, dx = \int (\sec^2 x - 1) \sec x \, dx$$

$$= \int \sec^3 x \, dx - \int \sec x \, dx \qquad \boxed{\text{See (26) and (22).}}$$

$$= \tfrac{1}{2} \sec x \tan x + \tfrac{1}{2} \ln|\sec x + \tan x| - \ln|\sec x + \tan x| + C$$

$$= \tfrac{1}{2} \sec x \tan x - \tfrac{1}{2} \ln|\sec x + \tan x| + C \blacktriangleleft$$

■ **AN ALTERNATIVE METHOD FOR INTEGRATING POWERS OF SINE, COSINE, TANGENT, AND SECANT**

The methods in Tables 7.3.1 and 7.3.2 can sometimes be applied if $m = 0$ or $n = 0$ to integrate positive integer powers of sine, cosine, tangent, and secant without reduction formulas. For example, instead of using the reduction formula to integrate $\sin^3 x$, we can apply the second procedure in Table 7.3.1:

$$\int \sin^3 x \, dx = \int (\sin^2 x) \sin x \, dx$$

$$= \int (1 - \cos^2 x) \sin x \, dx \qquad \boxed{\begin{aligned} u &= \cos x \\ du &= -\sin x \, dx \end{aligned}}$$

$$= - \int (1 - u^2) \, du$$

$$= \tfrac{1}{3} u^3 - u + C = \tfrac{1}{3} \cos^3 x - \cos x + C$$

which agrees with (11).

With the aid of the identity

$$1 + \cot^2 x = \csc^2 x$$

the techniques in Table 7.3.2 can be adapted to evaluate integrals of the form

$$\int \cot^m x \csc^n x \, dx$$

It is also possible to derive reduction formulas for powers of cot and csc that are analogous to Formulas (19) and (20).

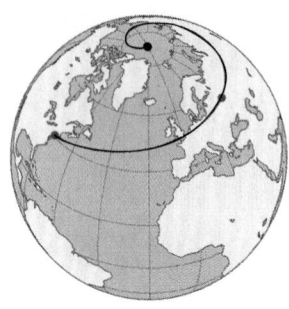

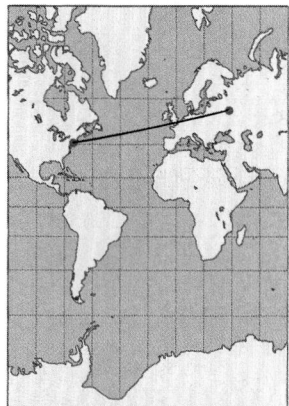

Figure 7.3.2   A flight path with constant compass heading from New York City to Moscow follows a spiral toward the North Pole but is a straight line segment on a Mercator projection.

MERCATOR'S MAP OF THE WORLD

The integral of $\sec x$ plays an important role in the design of navigational maps for charting nautical and aeronautical courses. Sailors and pilots usually chart their courses along paths with constant compass headings; for example, the course might be 30° northeast or 135° southeast. Except for courses that are parallel to the equator or run due north or south, a course with constant compass heading spirals around the Earth toward one of the poles (as in the top part of Figure 7.3.2). In 1569 the Flemish mathematician and geographer Gerhard Kramer (1512–1594) (better known by the Latin name Mercator) devised a world map, called the *Mercator projection*, in which spirals of constant compass headings appear as straight lines. This was extremely important because it enabled sailors to determine compass headings between two points by connecting them with a straight line on a map (as in the bottom part of Figure 7.3.2).

If the Earth is assumed to be a sphere of radius 4000 mi, then the lines of latitude at 1° increments are equally spaced about 70 mi apart (why?). However, in the Mercator projection, the lines of latitude become wider apart toward the poles, so that two widely spaced latitude lines near the poles may be actually the same distance apart on the Earth as two closely spaced latitude lines near the equator. It can be proved that on a Mercator map in which the equatorial line has length L, the vertical distance D_β on the map between the equator (latitude 0°) and the line of latitude $\beta°$ is

$$D_\beta = \frac{L}{2\pi} \int_0^{\beta\pi/180} \sec x \, dx \qquad (27)$$

✔ **QUICK CHECK EXERCISES 7.3**   (*See page 508 for answers.*)

---

1. Complete each trigonometric identity with an expression involving $\cos 2x$.
   (a) $\sin^2 x = $ _____   (b) $\cos^2 x = $ _____
   (c) $\cos^2 x - \sin^2 x = $ _____

2. Evaluate the integral.
   (a) $\displaystyle\int \sec^2 x \, dx = $ _____

   (b) $\displaystyle\int \tan^2 x \, dx = $ _____

   (c) $\displaystyle\int \sec x \, dx = $ _____

   (d) $\displaystyle\int \tan x \, dx = $ _____

3. Use the indicated substitution to rewrite the integral in terms of u. Do not evaluate the integral.
   (a) $\displaystyle\int \sin^2 x \cos x \, dx$; $u = \sin x$

   (b) $\displaystyle\int \sin^3 x \cos^2 x \, dx$; $u = \cos x$

   (c) $\displaystyle\int \tan^3 x \sec^2 x \, dx$; $u = \tan x$

   (d) $\displaystyle\int \tan^3 x \sec x \, dx$; $u = \sec x$

EXERCISE SET 7.3

1–52 Evaluate the integral. ■

1. $\displaystyle\int \cos^3 x \sin x \, dx$

2. $\displaystyle\int \sin^5 3x \cos 3x \, dx$

3. $\displaystyle\int \sin^2 5\theta \, d\theta$

4. $\displaystyle\int \cos^2 3x \, dx$

5. $\displaystyle\int \sin^3 a\theta \, d\theta$

6. $\displaystyle\int \cos^3 at \, dt$

7. $\displaystyle\int \sin ax \cos ax \, dx$

8. $\displaystyle\int \sin^3 x \cos^3 x \, dx$

9. $\displaystyle\int \sin^2 t \cos^3 t \, dt$

10. $\displaystyle\int \sin^3 x \cos^2 x \, dx$

11. $\int \sin^2 x \cos^2 x \, dx$

12. $\int \sin^2 x \cos^4 x \, dx$

13. $\int \sin 2x \cos 3x \, dx$

14. $\int \sin 3\theta \cos 2\theta \, d\theta$

15. $\int \sin x \cos(x/2) \, dx$

16. $\int \cos^{1/3} x \sin x \, dx$

17. $\int_0^{\pi/2} \cos^3 x \, dx$

18. $\int_0^{\pi/2} \sin^2 \frac{x}{2} \cos^2 \frac{x}{2} \, dx$

19. $\int_0^{\pi/3} \sin^4 3x \cos^3 3x \, dx$

20. $\int_{-\pi}^{\pi} \cos^2 5\theta \, d\theta$

21. $\int_0^{\pi/6} \sin 4x \cos 2x \, dx$

22. $\int_0^{2\pi} \sin^2 kx \, dx$

23. $\int \sec^2(2x - 1) \, dx$

24. $\int \tan 5x \, dx$

25. $\int e^{-x} \tan(e^{-x}) \, dx$

26. $\int \cot 3x \, dx$

27. $\int \sec 4x \, dx$

28. $\int \frac{\sec(\sqrt{x})}{\sqrt{x}} \, dx$

29. $\int \tan^2 x \sec^2 x \, dx$

30. $\int \tan^5 x \sec^4 x \, dx$

31. $\int \tan 4x \sec^4 4x \, dx$

32. $\int \tan^4 \theta \sec^4 \theta \, d\theta$

33. $\int \sec^5 x \tan^3 x \, dx$

34. $\int \tan^5 \theta \sec \theta \, d\theta$

35. $\int \tan^4 x \sec x \, dx$

36. $\int \tan^2 x \sec^3 x \, dx$

37. $\int \tan t \sec^3 t \, dt$

38. $\int \tan x \sec^5 x \, dx$

39. $\int \sec^4 x \, dx$

40. $\int \sec^5 x \, dx$

41. $\int \tan^3 4x \, dx$

42. $\int \tan^4 x \, dx$

43. $\int \sqrt{\tan x} \sec^4 x \, dx$

44. $\int \tan x \sec^{3/2} x \, dx$

45. $\int_0^{\pi/8} \tan^2 2x \, dx$

46. $\int_0^{\pi/6} \sec^3 2\theta \tan 2\theta \, d\theta$

47. $\int_0^{\pi/2} \tan^5 \frac{x}{2} \, dx$

48. $\int_0^{1/4} \sec \pi x \tan \pi x \, dx$

49. $\int \cot^3 x \csc^3 x \, dx$

50. $\int \cot^2 3t \sec 3t \, dt$

51. $\int \cot^3 x \, dx$

52. $\int \csc^4 x \, dx$

53–56 True–False Determine whether the statement is true or false. Explain your answer. ■

53. To evaluate $\int \sin^5 x \cos^8 x \, dx$, use the trigonometric identity $\sin^2 x = 1 - \cos^2 x$ and the substitution $u = \cos x$.

54. To evaluate $\int \sin^8 x \cos^5 x \, dx$, use the trigonometric identity $\sin^2 x = 1 - \cos^2 x$ and the substitution $u = \cos x$.

55. The trigonometric identity
$$\sin \alpha \cos \beta = \tfrac{1}{2}[\sin(\alpha - \beta) + \sin(\alpha + \beta)]$$
is often useful for evaluating integrals of the form $\int \sin^m x \cos^n x \, dx$.

56. The integral $\int \tan^4 x \sec^5 x \, dx$ is equivalent to one whose integrand is a polynomial in $\sec x$.

57. Let m, n be distinct nonnegative integers. Use Formulas (16)–(18) to prove:

(a) $\int_0^{2\pi} \sin mx \cos nx \, dx = 0$

(b) $\int_0^{2\pi} \cos mx \cos nx \, dx = 0$

(c) $\int_0^{2\pi} \sin mx \sin nx \, dx = 0$.

58. Evaluate the integrals in Exercise 57 when m and n denote the *same* nonnegative integer.

59. Find the arc length of the curve $y = \ln(\cos x)$ over the interval $[0, \pi/4]$.

60. Find the volume of the solid generated when the region enclosed by $y = \tan x$, $y = 1$, and $x = 0$ is revolved about the x-axis.

61. Find the volume of the solid that results when the region enclosed by $y = \cos x$, $y = \sin x$, $x = 0$, and $x = \pi/4$ is revolved about the x-axis.

62. The region bounded below by the x-axis and above by the portion of $y = \sin x$ from $x = 0$ to $x = \pi$ is revolved about the x-axis. Find the volume of the resulting solid.

63. Use Formula (27) to show that if the length of the equatorial line on a Mercator projection is L, then the vertical distance D between the latitude lines at $\alpha°$ and $\beta°$ on the same side of the equator (where $\alpha < \beta$) is
$$D = \frac{L}{2\pi} \ln \left| \frac{\sec \beta° + \tan \beta°}{\sec \alpha° + \tan \alpha°} \right|$$

64. Suppose that the equator has a length of 100 cm on a Mercator projection. In each part, use the result in Exercise 63 to answer the question.

(a) What is the vertical distance on the map between the equator and the line at $25°$ north latitude?

(b) What is the vertical distance on the map between New Orleans, Louisiana, at $30°$ north latitude and Winnipeg, Canada, at $50°$ north latitude?

FOCUS ON CONCEPTS

65. (a) Show that
$$\int \csc x \, dx = -\ln |\csc x + \cot x| + C$$

(b) Show that the result in part (a) can also be written as
$$\int \csc x \, dx = \ln |\csc x - \cot x| + C$$
and
$$\int \csc x \, dx = \ln \left| \tan \tfrac{1}{2} x \right| + C$$

66. Rewrite $\sin x + \cos x$ in the form
$$A \sin(x + \phi)$$
and use your result together with Exercise 65 to evaluate
$$\int \frac{dx}{\sin x + \cos x}$$

67. Use the method of Exercise 66 to evaluate
$$\int \frac{dx}{a \sin x + b \cos x} \quad (a, b \text{ not both zero})$$

68. (a) Use Formula (9) in Section 7.2 to show that
$$\int_0^{\pi/2} \sin^n x \, dx = \frac{n-1}{n} \int_0^{\pi/2} \sin^{n-2} x \, dx \quad (n \geq 2)$$

(b) Use this result to derive the *Wallis sine formulas*:
$$\int_0^{\pi/2} \sin^n x \, dx = \frac{\pi}{2} \cdot \frac{1 \cdot 3 \cdot 5 \cdots (n-1)}{2 \cdot 4 \cdot 6 \cdots n} \quad \begin{pmatrix} n \text{ even} \\ \text{and} \geq 2 \end{pmatrix}$$

$$\int_0^{\pi/2} \sin^n x \, dx = \frac{2 \cdot 4 \cdot 6 \cdots (n-1)}{3 \cdot 5 \cdot 7 \cdots n} \quad \begin{pmatrix} n \text{ odd} \\ \text{and} \geq 3 \end{pmatrix}$$

69. Use the Wallis formulas in Exercise 68 to evaluate

(a) $\int_0^{\pi/2} \sin^3 x \, dx$ (b) $\int_0^{\pi/2} \sin^4 x \, dx$

(c) $\int_0^{\pi/2} \sin^5 x \, dx$ (d) $\int_0^{\pi/2} \sin^6 x \, dx$.

70. Use Formula (10) in Section 7.2 and the method of Exercise 68 to derive the *Wallis cosine formulas*:
$$\int_0^{\pi/2} \cos^n x \, dx = \frac{\pi}{2} \cdot \frac{1 \cdot 3 \cdot 5 \cdots (n-1)}{2 \cdot 4 \cdot 6 \cdots n} \quad \begin{pmatrix} n \text{ even} \\ \text{and} \geq 2 \end{pmatrix}$$

$$\int_0^{\pi/2} \cos^n x \, dx = \frac{2 \cdot 4 \cdot 6 \cdots (n-1)}{3 \cdot 5 \cdot 7 \cdots n} \quad \begin{pmatrix} n \text{ odd} \\ \text{and} \geq 3 \end{pmatrix}$$

71. Writing Describe the various approaches for evaluating integrals of the form
$$\int \sin^m x \cos^n x \, dx$$
Into what cases do these types of integrals fall? What procedures and identities are used in each case?

72. Writing Describe the various approaches for evaluating integrals of the form
$$\int \tan^m x \sec^n x \, dx$$
Into what cases do these types of integrals fall? What procedures and identities are used in each case?

✔ **QUICK CHECK ANSWERS 7.3**

1. (a) $\dfrac{1 - \cos 2x}{2}$ (b) $\dfrac{1 + \cos 2x}{2}$ (c) $\cos 2x$ **2.** (a) $\tan x + C$ (b) $\tan x - x + C$ (c) $\ln|\sec x + \tan x| + C$ (d) $\ln|\sec x| + C$

3. (a) $\displaystyle\int u^2 \, du$ (b) $\displaystyle\int (u^2 - 1)u^2 \, du$ (c) $\displaystyle\int u^3 \, du$ (d) $\displaystyle\int (u^2 - 1) \, du$

7.4 TRIGONOMETRIC SUBSTITUTIONS

In this section we will discuss a method for evaluating integrals containing radicals by making substitutions involving trigonometric functions. We will also show how integrals containing quadratic polynomials can sometimes be evaluated by completing the square.

■ **THE METHOD OF TRIGONOMETRIC SUBSTITUTION**
To start, we will be concerned with integrals that contain expressions of the form
$$\sqrt{a^2 - x^2}, \quad \sqrt{x^2 + a^2}, \quad \sqrt{x^2 - a^2}$$

in which a is a positive constant. The basic idea for evaluating such integrals is to make a substitution for x that will eliminate the radical. For example, to eliminate the radical in the expression $\sqrt{a^2 - x^2}$, we can make the substitution
$$x = a \sin \theta, \quad -\pi/2 \leq \theta \leq \pi/2 \tag{1}$$

which yields
$$\sqrt{a^2 - x^2} = \sqrt{a^2 - a^2 \sin^2 \theta} = \sqrt{a^2(1 - \sin^2 \theta)}$$

$$= a\sqrt{\cos^2 \theta} = a|\cos \theta| = a \cos \theta \qquad \boxed{\cos \theta \geq 0 \text{ since } -\pi/2 \leq \theta \leq \pi/2}$$

The restriction on θ in (1) serves two purposes—it enables us to replace $|\cos\theta|$ by $\cos\theta$ to simplify the calculations, and it also ensures that the substitutions can be rewritten as $\theta = \sin^{-1}(x/a)$, if needed.

▶ **Example 1** Evaluate $\displaystyle\int \frac{dx}{x^2\sqrt{4-x^2}}$.

Solution. To eliminate the radical we make the substitution

$$x = 2\sin\theta, \quad dx = 2\cos\theta\,d\theta$$

This yields

$$\int \frac{dx}{x^2\sqrt{4-x^2}} = \int \frac{2\cos\theta\,d\theta}{(2\sin\theta)^2\sqrt{4-4\sin^2\theta}}$$

$$= \int \frac{2\cos\theta\,d\theta}{(2\sin\theta)^2(2\cos\theta)} = \frac{1}{4}\int \frac{d\theta}{\sin^2\theta}$$

$$= \frac{1}{4}\int \csc^2\theta\,d\theta = -\frac{1}{4}\cot\theta + C \tag{2}$$

At this point we have completed the integration; however, because the original integral was expressed in terms of x, it is desirable to express $\cot\theta$ in terms of x as well. This can be done using trigonometric identities, but the expression can also be obtained by writing the substitution $x = 2\sin\theta$ as $\sin\theta = x/2$ and representing it geometrically as in Figure 7.4.1. From that figure we obtain

$$\cot\theta = \frac{\sqrt{4-x^2}}{x}$$

Substituting this in (2) yields

$$\int \frac{dx}{x^2\sqrt{4-x^2}} = -\frac{1}{4}\frac{\sqrt{4-x^2}}{x} + C \blacktriangleleft$$

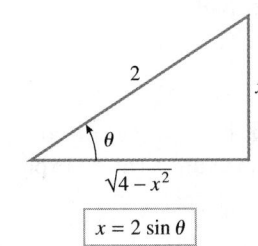

▲ **Figure 7.4.1**

▶ **Example 2** Evaluate $\displaystyle\int_1^{\sqrt{2}} \frac{dx}{x^2\sqrt{4-x^2}}$.

Solution. There are two possible approaches: we can make the substitution in the indefinite integral (as in Example 1) and then evaluate the definite integral using the x-limits of integration, or we can make the substitution in the definite integral and convert the x-limits to the corresponding θ-limits.

Method 1.

Using the result from Example 1 with the x-limits of integration yields

$$\int_1^{\sqrt{2}} \frac{dx}{x^2\sqrt{4-x^2}} = -\frac{1}{4}\left[\frac{\sqrt{4-x^2}}{x}\right]_1^{\sqrt{2}} = -\frac{1}{4}\left[1-\sqrt{3}\right] = \frac{\sqrt{3}-1}{4}$$

Method 2.

The substitution $x = 2\sin\theta$ can be expressed as $x/2 = \sin\theta$ or $\theta = \sin^{-1}(x/2)$, so the θ-limits that correspond to $x = 1$ and $x = \sqrt{2}$ are

$$x = 1: \quad \theta = \sin^{-1}(1/2) = \pi/6$$

$$x = \sqrt{2}: \quad \theta = \sin^{-1}(\sqrt{2}/2) = \pi/4$$

Thus, from (2) in Example 1 we obtain

$$\int_{1}^{\sqrt{2}} \frac{dx}{x^2\sqrt{4-x^2}} = \frac{1}{4}\int_{\pi/6}^{\pi/4} \csc^2\theta \, d\theta \qquad \boxed{\text{Convert } x\text{-limits to } \theta\text{-limits.}}$$

$$= -\frac{1}{4}\Big[\cot\theta\Big]_{\pi/6}^{\pi/4} = -\frac{1}{4}\Big[1-\sqrt{3}\Big] = \frac{\sqrt{3}-1}{4} \quad \blacktriangleleft$$

▶ **Example 3**   Find the area of the ellipse

$$\frac{x^2}{a^2} + \frac{y^2}{b^2} = 1$$

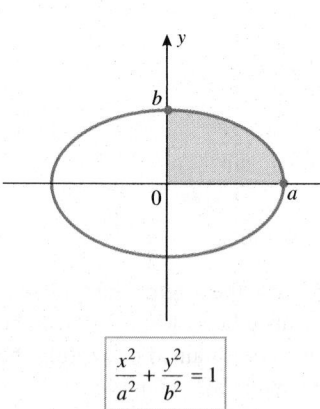

$$\boxed{\dfrac{x^2}{a^2} + \dfrac{y^2}{b^2} = 1}$$

▲ **Figure 7.4.2**

Solution.   Because the ellipse is symmetric about both axes, its area A is four times the area in the first quadrant (Figure 7.4.2). If we solve the equation of the ellipse for y in terms of x, we obtain

$$y = \pm\frac{b}{a}\sqrt{a^2-x^2}$$

where the positive square root gives the equation of the upper half. Thus, the area A is given by

$$A = 4\int_{0}^{a} \frac{b}{a}\sqrt{a^2-x^2}\, dx = \frac{4b}{a}\int_{0}^{a}\sqrt{a^2-x^2}\, dx$$

To evaluate this integral, we will make the substitution $x = a\sin\theta$ (so $dx = a\cos\theta \, d\theta$) and convert the x-limits of integration to θ-limits. Since the substitution can be expressed as $\theta = \sin^{-1}(x/a)$, the θ-limits of integration are

$$x = 0: \quad \theta = \sin^{-1}(0) = 0$$

$$x = a: \quad \theta = \sin^{-1}(1) = \pi/2$$

Thus, we obtain

$$A = \frac{4b}{a}\int_{0}^{a}\sqrt{a^2-x^2}\, dx = \frac{4b}{a}\int_{0}^{\pi/2}\sqrt{a^2-a^2\sin^2\theta}\cdot a\cos\theta \, d\theta$$

$$= \frac{4b}{a}\int_{0}^{\pi/2} a\cos\theta \cdot a\cos\theta \, d\theta$$

$$= 4ab\int_{0}^{\pi/2}\cos^2\theta \, d\theta = 4ab\int_{0}^{\pi/2}\frac{1}{2}(1+\cos 2\theta)\, d\theta$$

$$= 2ab\Big[\theta + \frac{1}{2}\sin 2\theta\Big]_{0}^{\pi/2} = 2ab\Big[\frac{\pi}{2}-0\Big] = \pi ab \quad \blacktriangleleft$$

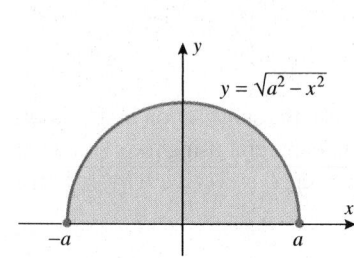

▲ **Figure 7.4.3**

REMARK   In the special case where $a = b$, the ellipse becomes a circle of radius a, and the area formula becomes $A = \pi a^2$, as expected. It is worth noting that

$$\int_{-a}^{a}\sqrt{a^2-x^2}\, dx = \tfrac{1}{2}\pi a^2 \qquad (3)$$

since this integral represents the area of the upper semicircle (Figure 7.4.3).

TECHNOLOGY MASTERY

If you have a calculating utility with a numerical integration capability, use it and Formula (3) to approximate π to three decimal places.

Thus far, we have focused on using the substitution $x = a\sin\theta$ to evaluate integrals involving radicals of the form $\sqrt{a^2-x^2}$. Table 7.4.1 summarizes this method and describes some other substitutions of this type.

Table 7.4.1

TRIGONOMETRIC SUBSTITUTIONS

EXPRESSION IN THE INTEGRAND	SUBSTITUTION	RESTRICTION ON θ	SIMPLIFICATION
$\sqrt{a^2 - x^2}$	$x = a\sin\theta$	$-\pi/2 \le \theta \le \pi/2$	$a^2 - x^2 = a^2 - a^2\sin^2\theta = a^2\cos^2\theta$
$\sqrt{a^2 + x^2}$	$x = a\tan\theta$	$-\pi/2 < \theta < \pi/2$	$a^2 + x^2 = a^2 + a^2\tan^2\theta = a^2\sec^2\theta$
$\sqrt{x^2 - a^2}$	$x = a\sec\theta$	$\begin{cases} 0 \le \theta < \pi/2 & \text{(if } x \ge a) \\ \pi/2 < \theta \le \pi & \text{(if } x \le -a) \end{cases}$	$x^2 - a^2 = a^2\sec^2\theta - a^2 = a^2\tan^2\theta$

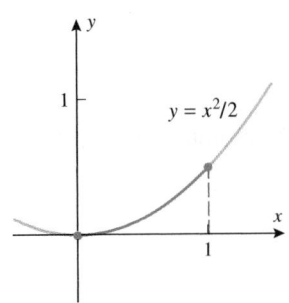

▲ **Figure 7.4.4**

▶ **Example 4**   Find the arc length of the curve $y = x^2/2$ from $x = 0$ to $x = 1$ (Figure 7.4.4).

Solution.   From Formula (4) of Section 6.4 the arc length L of the curve is

$$L = \int_0^1 \sqrt{1 + \left(\frac{dy}{dx}\right)^2}\, dx = \int_0^1 \sqrt{1 + x^2}\, dx$$

The integrand involves a radical of the form $\sqrt{a^2 + x^2}$ with $a = 1$, so from Table 7.4.1 we make the substitution

$$x = \tan\theta, \quad -\pi/2 < \theta < \pi/2$$
$$\frac{dx}{d\theta} = \sec^2\theta \quad \text{or} \quad dx = \sec^2\theta\, d\theta$$

Since this substitution can be expressed as $\theta = \tan^{-1} x$, the θ-limits of integration that correspond to the x-limits, $x = 0$ and $x = 1$, are

$$x = 0: \quad \theta = \tan^{-1} 0 = 0$$
$$x = 1: \quad \theta = \tan^{-1} 1 = \pi/4$$

Thus,

$$L = \int_0^1 \sqrt{1 + x^2}\, dx = \int_0^{\pi/4} \sqrt{1 + \tan^2\theta}\, \sec^2\theta\, d\theta$$

$$= \int_0^{\pi/4} \sqrt{\sec^2\theta}\, \sec^2\theta\, d\theta \qquad \boxed{1 + \tan^2\theta = \sec^2\theta}$$

$$= \int_0^{\pi/4} |\sec\theta|\sec^2\theta\, d\theta$$

$$= \int_0^{\pi/4} \sec^3\theta\, d\theta \qquad \boxed{\sec\theta > 0 \text{ since } -\pi/2 < \theta < \pi/2}$$

$$= \left[\tfrac{1}{2}\sec\theta\tan\theta + \tfrac{1}{2}\ln|\sec\theta + \tan\theta|\right]_0^{\pi/4} \qquad \boxed{\begin{array}{l}\text{Formula (26)} \\ \text{of Section 7.3}\end{array}}$$

$$= \tfrac{1}{2}\left[\sqrt{2} + \ln(\sqrt{2} + 1)\right] \approx 1.148 \blacktriangleleft$$

▶ **Example 5**   Evaluate $\displaystyle\int \frac{\sqrt{x^2 - 25}}{x}\, dx$, assuming that $x \ge 5$.

Solution.   The integrand involves a radical of the form $\sqrt{x^2 - a^2}$ with $a = 5$, so from Table 7.4.1 we make the substitution

$$x = 5 \sec \theta, \quad 0 \leq \theta < \pi/2$$

$$\frac{dx}{d\theta} = 5 \sec \theta \tan \theta \quad \text{or} \quad dx = 5 \sec \theta \tan \theta \, d\theta$$

Thus,

$$\int \frac{\sqrt{x^2 - 25}}{x} \, dx = \int \frac{\sqrt{25 \sec^2 \theta - 25}}{5 \sec \theta} (5 \sec \theta \tan \theta) \, d\theta$$

$$= \int \frac{5|\tan \theta|}{5 \sec \theta} (5 \sec \theta \tan \theta) \, d\theta$$

$$= 5 \int \tan^2 \theta \, d\theta \qquad \boxed{\tan \theta \geq 0 \text{ since } 0 \leq \theta < \pi/2}$$

$$= 5 \int (\sec^2 \theta - 1) \, d\theta = 5 \tan \theta - 5\theta + C$$

To express the solution in terms of x, we will represent the substitution $x = 5 \sec \theta$ geometrically by the triangle in Figure 7.4.5, from which we obtain

$$\tan \theta = \frac{\sqrt{x^2 - 25}}{5}$$

From this and the fact that the substitution can be expressed as $\theta = \sec^{-1}(x/5)$, we obtain

$$\int \frac{\sqrt{x^2 - 25}}{x} \, dx = \sqrt{x^2 - 25} - 5 \sec^{-1}\left(\frac{x}{5}\right) + C \blacktriangleleft$$

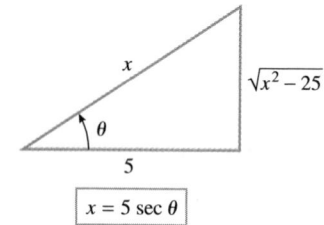

$$x = 5 \sec \theta$$

▲ **Figure 7.4.5**

■ **INTEGRALS INVOLVING** $ax^2 + bx + c$

Integrals that involve a quadratic expression $ax^2 + bx + c$, where $a \neq 0$ and $b \neq 0$, can often be evaluated by first completing the square, then making an appropriate substitution. The following example illustrates this idea.

▶ **Example 6**   Evaluate $\displaystyle\int \frac{x}{x^2 - 4x + 8} \, dx$.

Solution.   Completing the square yields

$$x^2 - 4x + 8 = (x^2 - 4x + 4) + 8 - 4 = (x - 2)^2 + 4$$

Thus, the substitution

$$u = x - 2, \quad du = dx$$

yields

$$\int \frac{x}{x^2 - 4x + 8} \, dx = \int \frac{x}{(x - 2)^2 + 4} \, dx = \int \frac{u + 2}{u^2 + 4} \, du$$

$$= \int \frac{u}{u^2 + 4} \, du + 2 \int \frac{du}{u^2 + 4}$$

$$= \frac{1}{2} \int \frac{2u}{u^2 + 4} \, du + 2 \int \frac{du}{u^2 + 4}$$

$$= \frac{1}{2} \ln(u^2 + 4) + 2 \left(\frac{1}{2}\right) \tan^{-1} \frac{u}{2} + C$$

$$= \frac{1}{2} \ln[(x - 2)^2 + 4] + \tan^{-1}\left(\frac{x - 2}{2}\right) + C \blacktriangleleft$$

✓ QUICK CHECK EXERCISES 7.4   (See page 514 for answers.)

1. For each expression, give a trigonometric substitution that will eliminate the radical.
   (a) $\sqrt{a^2 - x^2}$ _____   (b) $\sqrt{a^2 + x^2}$ _____
   (c) $\sqrt{x^2 - a^2}$ _____

2. If $x = 2 \sec \theta$ and $0 < \theta < \pi/2$, then
   (a) $\sin \theta =$ _____   (b) $\cos \theta =$ _____
   (c) $\tan \theta =$ _____.

3. In each part, state the trigonometric substitution that you would try first to evaluate the integral. Do not evaluate the integral.
   (a) $\int \sqrt{9 + x^2}\, dx$ _____

   (b) $\int \sqrt{9 - x^2}\, dx$ _____

   (c) $\int \sqrt{1 - 9x^2}\, dx$ _____

(d) $\int \sqrt{x^2 - 9}\, dx$ _____

(e) $\int \sqrt{9 + 3x^2}\, dx$ _____

(f) $\int \sqrt{1 + (9x)^2}\, dx$ _____

4. In each part, determine the substitution u.
   (a) $\int \dfrac{1}{x^2 - 2x + 10}\, dx = \int \dfrac{1}{u^2 + 3^2}\, du$;

   $u =$ _____

   (b) $\int \sqrt{x^2 - 6x + 8}\, dx = \int \sqrt{u^2 - 1}\, du$;

   $u =$ _____

   (c) $\int \sqrt{12 - 4x - x^2}\, dx = \int \sqrt{4^2 - u^2}\, du$;

   $u =$ _____

EXERCISE SET 7.4   [C] CAS

1–26 Evaluate the integral. ▨

1. $\int \sqrt{4 - x^2}\, dx$

2. $\int \sqrt{1 - 4x^2}\, dx$

3. $\int \dfrac{x^2}{\sqrt{16 - x^2}}\, dx$

4. $\int \dfrac{dx}{x^2 \sqrt{9 - x^2}}$

5. $\int \dfrac{dx}{(4 + x^2)^2}$

6. $\int \dfrac{x^2}{\sqrt{5 + x^2}}\, dx$

7. $\int \dfrac{\sqrt{x^2 - 9}}{x}\, dx$

8. $\int \dfrac{dx}{x^2 \sqrt{x^2 - 16}}$

9. $\int \dfrac{3x^3}{\sqrt{1 - x^2}}\, dx$

10. $\int x^3 \sqrt{5 - x^2}\, dx$

11. $\int \dfrac{dx}{x^2 \sqrt{9x^2 - 4}}$

12. $\int \dfrac{\sqrt{1 + t^2}}{t}\, dt$

13. $\int \dfrac{dx}{(1 - x^2)^{3/2}}$

14. $\int \dfrac{dx}{x^2 \sqrt{x^2 + 25}}$

15. $\int \dfrac{dx}{\sqrt{x^2 - 9}}$

16. $\int \dfrac{dx}{1 + 2x^2 + x^4}$

17. $\int \dfrac{dx}{(4x^2 - 9)^{3/2}}$

18. $\int \dfrac{3x^3}{\sqrt{x^2 - 25}}\, dx$

19. $\int e^x \sqrt{1 - e^{2x}}\, dx$

20. $\int \dfrac{\cos \theta}{\sqrt{2 - \sin^2 \theta}}\, d\theta$

21. $\int_0^1 5x^3 \sqrt{1 - x^2}\, dx$

22. $\int_0^{1/2} \dfrac{dx}{(1 - x^2)^2}$

23. $\int_{\sqrt{2}}^2 \dfrac{dx}{x^2 \sqrt{x^2 - 1}}$

24. $\int_{\sqrt{2}}^2 \dfrac{\sqrt{2x^2 - 4}}{x}\, dx$

25. $\int_1^3 \dfrac{dx}{x^4 \sqrt{x^2 + 3}}$

26. $\int_0^3 \dfrac{x^3}{(3 + x^2)^{5/2}}\, dx$

27–30 True–False Determine whether the statement is true or false. Explain your answer. ▨

27. An integrand involving a radical of the form $\sqrt{a^2 - x^2}$ suggests the substitution $x = a \sin \theta$.

28. The trigonometric substitution $x = a \sin \theta$ is made with the restriction $0 \le \theta \le \pi$.

29. An integrand involving a radical of the form $\sqrt{x^2 - a^2}$ suggests the substitution $x = a \cos \theta$.

30. The area enclosed by the ellipse $x^2 + 4y^2 = 1$ is $\pi/2$.

FOCUS ON CONCEPTS

31. The integral
    $$\int \dfrac{x}{x^2 + 4}\, dx$$
    can be evaluated either by a trigonometric substitution or by the substitution $u = x^2 + 4$. Do it both ways and show that the results are equivalent.

32. The integral
    $$\int \dfrac{x^2}{x^2 + 4}\, dx$$
    can be evaluated either by a trigonometric substitution or by algebraically rewriting the numerator of the integrand as $(x^2 + 4) - 4$. Do it both ways and show that the results are equivalent.

33. Find the arc length of the curve $y = \ln x$ from $x = 1$ to $x = 2$.

34. Find the arc length of the curve $y = x^2$ from $x = 0$ to $x = 1$.

35. Find the area of the surface generated when the curve in Exercise 34 is revolved about the x-axis.

36. Find the volume of the solid generated when the region enclosed by $x = y(1 - y^2)^{1/4}$, $y = 0$, $y = 1$, and $x = 0$ is revolved about the y-axis.

37–48 Evaluate the integral. ■

37. $\displaystyle\int \frac{dx}{x^2 - 4x + 5}$

38. $\displaystyle\int \frac{dx}{\sqrt{2x - x^2}}$

39. $\displaystyle\int \frac{dx}{\sqrt{3 + 2x - x^2}}$

40. $\displaystyle\int \frac{dx}{16x^2 + 16x + 5}$

41. $\displaystyle\int \frac{dx}{\sqrt{x^2 - 6x + 10}}$

42. $\displaystyle\int \frac{x}{x^2 + 2x + 2}\,dx$

43. $\displaystyle\int \sqrt{3 - 2x - x^2}\,dx$

44. $\displaystyle\int \frac{e^x}{\sqrt{1 + e^x + e^{2x}}}\,dx$

45. $\displaystyle\int \frac{dx}{2x^2 + 4x + 7}$

46. $\displaystyle\int \frac{2x + 3}{4x^2 + 4x + 5}\,dx$

47. $\displaystyle\int_1^2 \frac{dx}{\sqrt{4x - x^2}}$

48. $\displaystyle\int_0^4 \sqrt{x(4 - x)}\,dx$

C **49–50** There is a good chance that your CAS will not be able to evaluate these integrals as stated. If this is so, make a substitution that converts the integral into one that your CAS can evaluate. ■

49. $\displaystyle\int \cos x \sin x \sqrt{1 - \sin^4 x}\,dx$

50. $\displaystyle\int (x \cos x + \sin x)\sqrt{1 + x^2 \sin^2 x}\,dx$

51. (a) Use the **hyperbolic substitution** $x = 3 \sinh u$, the identity $\cosh^2 u - \sinh^2 u = 1$, and Theorem 6.9.4 to evaluate

$$\int \frac{dx}{\sqrt{x^2 + 9}}$$

(b) Evaluate the integral in part (a) using a trigonometric substitution and show that the result agrees with that obtained in part (a).

52. Use the hyperbolic substitutionn $x = \cosh u$, the identity $\sinh^2 u = \frac{1}{2}(\cosh 2u - 1)$, and the results referenced in Exercise 51 to evaluate

$$\int \sqrt{x^2 - 1}\,dx, \quad x \geq 1$$

53. Writing The trigonometric substitution $x = a \sin \theta$, $-\pi/2 \leq \theta \leq \pi/2$, is suggested for an integral whose integrand involves $\sqrt{a^2 - x^2}$. Discuss the implications of restricting θ to $\pi/2 \leq \theta \leq 3\pi/2$, and explain why the restriction $-\pi/2 \leq \theta \leq \pi/2$ should be preferred.

54. Writing The trigonometric substitution $x = a \cos \theta$ could also be used for an integral whose integrand involves $\sqrt{a^2 - x^2}$. Determine an appropriate restriction for θ with the substitution $x = a \cos \theta$, and discuss how to apply this substitution in appropriate integrals. Illustrate your discussion by evaluating the integral in Example 1 using a substitution of this type.

✔ **QUICK CHECK ANSWERS 7.4**

1. (a) $x = a \sin \theta$ **(b)** $x = a \tan \theta$ **(c)** $x = a \sec \theta$ **2. (a)** $\dfrac{\sqrt{x^2 - 4}}{x}$ **(b)** $\dfrac{2}{x}$ **(c)** $\dfrac{\sqrt{x^2 - 4}}{2}$ **3. (a)** $x = 3 \tan \theta$ **(b)** $x = 3 \sin \theta$ **(c)** $x = \frac{1}{3} \sin \theta$ **(d)** $x = 3 \sec \theta$ **(e)** $x = \sqrt{3} \tan \theta$ **(f)** $x = \frac{1}{9} \tan \theta$ **4. (a)** $x - 1$ **(b)** $x - 3$ **(c)** $x + 2$

7.5 INTEGRATING RATIONAL FUNCTIONS BY PARTIAL FRACTIONS

Recall that a rational function is a ratio of two polynomials. In this section we will give a general method for integrating rational functions that is based on the idea of decomposing a rational function into a sum of simple rational functions that can be integrated by the methods studied in earlier sections.

■ **PARTIAL FRACTIONS**

In algebra, one learns to combine two or more fractions into a single fraction by finding a common denominator. For example,

$$\frac{2}{x - 4} + \frac{3}{x + 1} = \frac{2(x + 1) + 3(x - 4)}{(x - 4)(x + 1)} = \frac{5x - 10}{x^2 - 3x - 4} \tag{1}$$

However, for purposes of integration, the left side of (1) is preferable to the right side since each of the terms is easy to integrate:

$$\int \frac{5x - 10}{x^2 - 3x - 4} \, dx = \int \frac{2}{x - 4} \, dx + \int \frac{3}{x + 1} \, dx = 2 \ln |x - 4| + 3 \ln |x + 1| + C$$

Thus, it is desirable to have some method that will enable us to obtain the left side of (1), starting with the right side. To illustrate how this can be done, we begin by noting that on the left side the numerators are constants and the denominators are the factors of the denominator on the right side. Thus, to find the left side of (1), starting from the right side, we could factor the denominator of the right side and look for constants A and B such that

$$\frac{5x - 10}{(x - 4)(x + 1)} = \frac{A}{x - 4} + \frac{B}{x + 1} \tag{2}$$

One way to find the constants A and B is to multiply (2) through by $(x - 4)(x + 1)$ to clear fractions. This yields

$$5x - 10 = A(x + 1) + B(x - 4) \tag{3}$$

This relationship holds for all x, so it holds in particular if $x = 4$ or $x = -1$. Substituting $x = 4$ in (3) makes the second term on the right drop out and yields the equation $10 = 5A$ or $A = 2$; and substituting $x = -1$ in (3) makes the first term on the right drop out and yields the equation $-15 = -5B$ or $B = 3$. Substituting these values in (2) we obtain

$$\frac{5x - 10}{(x - 4)(x + 1)} = \frac{2}{x - 4} + \frac{3}{x + 1} \tag{4}$$

which agrees with (1).

A second method for finding the constants A and B is to multiply out the right side of (3) and collect like powers of x to obtain

$$5x - 10 = (A + B)x + (A - 4B)$$

Since the polynomials on the two sides are identical, their corresponding coefficients must be the same. Equating the corresponding coefficients on the two sides yields the following system of equations in the unknowns A and B:

$$A + B = 5$$
$$A - 4B = -10$$

Solving this system yields $A = 2$ and $B = 3$ as before (verify).

The terms on the right side of (4) are called *partial fractions* of the expression on the left side because they each constitute *part* of that expression. To find those partial fractions we first had to make a guess about their form, and then we had to find the unknown constants. Our next objective is to extend this idea to general rational functions. For this purpose, suppose that $P(x)/Q(x)$ is a *proper rational function*, by which we mean that the degree of the numerator is less than the degree of the denominator. There is a theorem in advanced algebra which states that every proper rational function can be expressed as a sum

$$\frac{P(x)}{Q(x)} = F_1(x) + F_2(x) + \cdots + F_n(x)$$

where $F_1(x), F_2(x), \ldots, F_n(x)$ are rational functions of the form

$$\frac{A}{(ax + b)^k} \quad \text{or} \quad \frac{Ax + B}{(ax^2 + bx + c)^k}$$

in which the denominators are factors of $Q(x)$. The sum is called the *partial fraction decomposition* of $P(x)/Q(x)$, and the terms are called *partial fractions*. As in our opening example, there are two parts to finding a partial fraction decomposition: determining the exact form of the decomposition and finding the unknown constants.

■ FINDING THE FORM OF A PARTIAL FRACTION DECOMPOSITION

The first step in finding the form of the partial fraction decomposition of a proper rational function $P(x)/Q(x)$ is to factor $Q(x)$ completely into linear and irreducible quadratic factors, and then collect all repeated factors so that $Q(x)$ is expressed as a product of *distinct* factors of the form

$$(ax + b)^m \quad \text{and} \quad (ax^2 + bx + c)^m$$

From these factors we can determine the form of the partial fraction decomposition using two rules that we will now discuss.

■ LINEAR FACTORS

If all of the factors of $Q(x)$ are linear, then the partial fraction decomposition of $P(x)/Q(x)$ can be determined by using the following rule:

LINEAR FACTOR RULE   For each factor of the form $(ax + b)^m$, the partial fraction decomposition contains the following sum of m partial fractions:

$$\frac{A_1}{ax + b} + \frac{A_2}{(ax + b)^2} + \cdots + \frac{A_m}{(ax + b)^m}$$

where $A_1, A_2, \ldots, A_m$ are constants to be determined. In the case where $m = 1$, only the first term in the sum appears.

▶ **Example 1**   Evaluate $\displaystyle\int \frac{dx}{x^2 + x - 2}$.

Solution.   The integrand is a proper rational function that can be written as

$$\frac{1}{x^2 + x - 2} = \frac{1}{(x - 1)(x + 2)}$$

The factors $x - 1$ and $x + 2$ are both linear and appear to the first power, so each contributes one term to the partial fraction decomposition by the linear factor rule. Thus, the decomposition has the form

$$\frac{1}{(x - 1)(x + 2)} = \frac{A}{x - 1} + \frac{B}{x + 2} \tag{5}$$

where A and B are constants to be determined. Multiplying this expression through by $(x - 1)(x + 2)$ yields

$$1 = A(x + 2) + B(x - 1) \tag{6}$$

As discussed earlier, there are two methods for finding A and B: we can substitute values of x that are chosen to make terms on the right drop out, or we can multiply out on the right and equate corresponding coefficients on the two sides to obtain a system of equations that can be solved for A and B. We will use the first approach.

Setting $x = 1$ makes the second term in (6) drop out and yields $1 = 3A$ or $A = \frac{1}{3}$; and setting $x = -2$ makes the first term in (6) drop out and yields $1 = -3B$ or $B = -\frac{1}{3}$. Substituting these values in (5) yields the partial fraction decomposition

$$\frac{1}{(x - 1)(x + 2)} = \frac{\frac{1}{3}}{x - 1} + \frac{-\frac{1}{3}}{x + 2}$$

The integration can now be completed as follows:

$$\int \frac{dx}{(x-1)(x+2)} = \frac{1}{3} \int \frac{dx}{x-1} - \frac{1}{3} \int \frac{dx}{x+2}$$

$$= \frac{1}{3} \ln|x-1| - \frac{1}{3} \ln|x+2| + C = \frac{1}{3} \ln \left| \frac{x-1}{x+2} \right| + C \blacktriangleleft$$

If the factors of $Q(x)$ are linear and none are repeated, as in the last example, then the recommended method for finding the constants in the partial fraction decomposition is to substitute appropriate values of x to make terms drop out. However, if some of the linear factors are repeated, then it will not be possible to find all of the constants in this way. In this case the recommended procedure is to find as many constants as possible by substitution and then find the rest by equating coefficients. This is illustrated in the next example.

▶ **Example 2** Evaluate $\displaystyle\int \frac{2x+4}{x^3 - 2x^2} \, dx$.

Solution. The integrand can be rewritten as

$$\frac{2x+4}{x^3 - 2x^2} = \frac{2x+4}{x^2(x-2)}$$

Although x^2 is a quadratic factor, it is *not* irreducible since $x^2 = xx$. Thus, by the linear factor rule, x^2 introduces two terms (since $m = 2$) of the form

$$\frac{A}{x} + \frac{B}{x^2}$$

and the factor $x-2$ introduces one term (since $m = 1$) of the form

$$\frac{C}{x-2}$$

so the partial fraction decomposition is

$$\frac{2x+4}{x^2(x-2)} = \frac{A}{x} + \frac{B}{x^2} + \frac{C}{x-2} \qquad (7)$$

Multiplying by $x^2(x-2)$ yields

$$2x + 4 = Ax(x-2) + B(x-2) + Cx^2 \qquad (8)$$

which, after multiplying out and collecting like powers of x, becomes

$$2x + 4 = (A+C)x^2 + (-2A+B)x - 2B \qquad (9)$$

Setting $x = 0$ in (8) makes the first and third terms drop out and yields $B = -2$, and setting $x = 2$ in (8) makes the first and second terms drop out and yields $C = 2$ (verify). However, there is no substitution in (8) that produces A directly, so we look to Equation (9) to find this value. This can be done by equating the coefficients of x^2 on the two sides to obtain

$$A + C = 0 \quad \text{or} \quad A = -C = -2$$

Substituting the values $A = -2$, $B = -2$, and $C = 2$ in (7) yields the partial fraction decomposition

$$\frac{2x+4}{x^2(x-2)} = \frac{-2}{x} + \frac{-2}{x^2} + \frac{2}{x-2}$$

Thus,

$$\int \frac{2x+4}{x^2(x-2)} \, dx = -2 \int \frac{dx}{x} - 2 \int \frac{dx}{x^2} + 2 \int \frac{dx}{x-2}$$

$$= -2 \ln|x| + \frac{2}{x} + 2 \ln|x-2| + C = 2 \ln \left| \frac{x-2}{x} \right| + \frac{2}{x} + C \blacktriangleleft$$

■ **QUADRATIC FACTORS**

If some of the factors of $Q(x)$ are irreducible quadratics, then the contribution of those factors to the partial fraction decomposition of $P(x)/Q(x)$ can be determined from the following rule:

QUADRATIC FACTOR RULE   For each factor of the form $(ax^2 + bx + c)^m$, the partial fraction decomposition contains the following sum of m partial fractions:

$$\frac{A_1 x + B_1}{ax^2 + bx + c} + \frac{A_2 x + B_2}{(ax^2 + bx + c)^2} + \cdots + \frac{A_m x + B_m}{(ax^2 + bx + c)^m}$$

where $A_1, A_2, \ldots, A_m, B_1, B_2, \ldots, B_m$ are constants to be determined. In the case where $m = 1$, only the first term in the sum appears.

▶ **Example 3**   Evaluate $\displaystyle\int \frac{x^2 + x - 2}{3x^3 - x^2 + 3x - 1}\, dx$.

Solution.   The denominator in the integrand can be factored by grouping:

$$3x^3 - x^2 + 3x - 1 = x^2(3x - 1) + (3x - 1) = (3x - 1)(x^2 + 1)$$

By the linear factor rule, the factor $3x - 1$ introduces one term, namely,

$$\frac{A}{3x - 1}$$

and by the quadratic factor rule, the factor $x^2 + 1$ introduces one term, namely,

$$\frac{Bx + C}{x^2 + 1}$$

Thus, the partial fraction decomposition is

$$\frac{x^2 + x - 2}{(3x - 1)(x^2 + 1)} = \frac{A}{3x - 1} + \frac{Bx + C}{x^2 + 1} \tag{10}$$

Multiplying by $(3x - 1)(x^2 + 1)$ yields

$$x^2 + x - 2 = A(x^2 + 1) + (Bx + C)(3x - 1) \tag{11}$$

We could find A by substituting $x = \frac{1}{3}$ to make the last term drop out, and then find the rest of the constants by equating corresponding coefficients. However, in this case it is just as easy to find *all* of the constants by equating coefficients and solving the resulting system. For this purpose we multiply out the right side of (11) and collect like terms:

$$x^2 + x - 2 = (A + 3B)x^2 + (-B + 3C)x + (A - C)$$

Equating corresponding coefficients gives

$$
\begin{aligned}
A + 3B \qquad\;\; &= \;\;1 \\
-\,B + 3C &= \;\;1 \\
A \qquad\; -\,C &= -2
\end{aligned}
$$

To solve this system, subtract the third equation from the first to eliminate A. Then use the resulting equation together with the second equation to solve for B and C. Finally, determine A from the first or third equation. This yields (verify)

$$A = -\frac{7}{5}, \quad B = \frac{4}{5}, \quad C = \frac{3}{5}$$

Thus, (10) becomes

$$\frac{x^2 + x - 2}{(3x - 1)(x^2 + 1)} = \frac{-\frac{7}{5}}{3x - 1} + \frac{\frac{4}{5}x + \frac{3}{5}}{x^2 + 1}$$

and

$$\int \frac{x^2 + x - 2}{(3x - 1)(x^2 + 1)} \, dx = -\frac{7}{5} \int \frac{dx}{3x - 1} + \frac{4}{5} \int \frac{x}{x^2 + 1} \, dx + \frac{3}{5} \int \frac{dx}{x^2 + 1}$$

$$= -\frac{7}{15} \ln |3x - 1| + \frac{2}{5} \ln(x^2 + 1) + \frac{3}{5} \tan^{-1} x + C \blacktriangleleft$$

TECHNOLOGY MASTERY

Computer algebra systems have built-in capabilities for finding partial fraction decompositions. If you have a CAS, use it to find the decompositions in Examples 1, 2, and 3.

▶ **Example 4** Evaluate $\displaystyle\int \frac{3x^4 + 4x^3 + 16x^2 + 20x + 9}{(x + 2)(x^2 + 3)^2} \, dx$.

Solution. Observe that the integrand is a proper rational function since the numerator has degree 4 and the denominator has degree 5. Thus, the method of partial fractions is applicable. By the linear factor rule, the factor $x + 2$ introduces the single term

$$\frac{A}{x + 2}$$

and by the quadratic factor rule, the factor $(x^2 + 3)^2$ introduces two terms (since $m = 2$):

$$\frac{Bx + C}{x^2 + 3} + \frac{Dx + E}{(x^2 + 3)^2}$$

Thus, the partial fraction decomposition of the integrand is

$$\frac{3x^4 + 4x^3 + 16x^2 + 20x + 9}{(x + 2)(x^2 + 3)^2} = \frac{A}{x + 2} + \frac{Bx + C}{x^2 + 3} + \frac{Dx + E}{(x^2 + 3)^2} \qquad (12)$$

Multiplying by $(x + 2)(x^2 + 3)^2$ yields

$$3x^4 + 4x^3 + 16x^2 + 20x + 9$$
$$= A(x^2 + 3)^2 + (Bx + C)(x^2 + 3)(x + 2) + (Dx + E)(x + 2) \qquad (13)$$

which, after multiplying out and collecting like powers of x, becomes

$$3x^4 + 4x^3 + 16x^2 + 20x + 9$$
$$= (A + B)x^4 + (2B + C)x^3 + (6A + 3B + 2C + D)x^2$$
$$+ (6B + 3C + 2D + E)x + (9A + 6C + 2E) \qquad (14)$$

Equating corresponding coefficients in (14) yields the following system of five linear equations in five unknowns:

$$\begin{array}{rcl} A + B &=& 3 \\ 2B + C &=& 4 \\ 6A + 3B + 2C + D &=& 16 \\ 6B + 3C + 2D + E &=& 20 \\ 9A + 6C + 2E &=& 9 \end{array} \qquad (15)$$

Efficient methods for solving systems of linear equations such as this are studied in a branch of mathematics called ***linear algebra***; those methods are outside the scope of this text. However, as a practical matter most linear systems of any size are solved by computer, and most computer algebra systems have commands that in many cases can solve linear systems exactly. In this particular case we can simplify the work by first substituting $x = -2$

in (13), which yields $A = 1$. Substituting this known value of A in (15) yields the simpler system

$$
\begin{aligned}
B &= 2 \\
2B + C &= 4 \\
3B + 2C + D &= 10 \\
6B + 3C + 2D + E &= 20 \\
6C + 2E &= 0
\end{aligned}
\tag{16}
$$

This system can be solved by starting at the top and working down, first substituting $B = 2$ in the second equation to get $C = 0$, then substituting the known values of B and C in the third equation to get $D = 4$, and so forth. This yields

$$
A = 1, \quad B = 2, \quad C = 0, \quad D = 4, \quad E = 0
$$

Thus, (12) becomes

$$
\frac{3x^4 + 4x^3 + 16x^2 + 20x + 9}{(x + 2)(x^2 + 3)^2} = \frac{1}{x + 2} + \frac{2x}{x^2 + 3} + \frac{4x}{(x^2 + 3)^2}
$$

and so

$$
\int \frac{3x^4 + 4x^3 + 16x^2 + 20x + 9}{(x + 2)(x^2 + 3)^2} \, dx
$$

$$
= \int \frac{dx}{x + 2} + \int \frac{2x}{x^2 + 3} \, dx + 4 \int \frac{x}{(x^2 + 3)^2} \, dx
$$

$$
= \ln |x + 2| + \ln(x^2 + 3) - \frac{2}{x^2 + 3} + C \blacktriangleleft
$$

■ INTEGRATING IMPROPER RATIONAL FUNCTIONS

Although the method of partial fractions only applies to proper rational functions, an improper rational function can be integrated by performing a long division and expressing the function as the quotient plus the remainder over the divisor. The remainder over the divisor will be a proper rational function, which can then be decomposed into partial fractions. This idea is illustrated in the following example.

▶ **Example 5** Evaluate $\displaystyle\int \frac{3x^4 + 3x^3 - 5x^2 + x - 1}{x^2 + x - 2} \, dx$.

Solution. The integrand is an improper rational function since the numerator has degree 4 and the denominator has degree 2. Thus, we first perform the long division

$$
\begin{array}{r}
3x^2 + 1 \\
x^2 + x - 2 \,\big)\, \overline{3x^4 + 3x^3 - 5x^2 + x - 1} \\
\underline{3x^4 + 3x^3 - 6x^2 } \\
x^2 + x - 1 \\
\underline{x^2 + x - 2} \\
1
\end{array}
$$

It follows that the integrand can be expressed as

$$
\frac{3x^4 + 3x^3 - 5x^2 + x - 1}{x^2 + x - 2} = (3x^2 + 1) + \frac{1}{x^2 + x - 2}
$$

and hence

$$
\int \frac{3x^4 + 3x^3 - 5x^2 + x - 1}{x^2 + x - 2} \, dx = \int (3x^2 + 1) \, dx + \int \frac{dx}{x^2 + x - 2}
$$

The second integral on the right now involves a proper rational function and can thus be evaluated by a partial fraction decomposition. Using the result of Example 1 we obtain

$$\int \frac{3x^4 + 3x^3 - 5x^2 + x - 1}{x^2 + x - 2}\,dx = x^3 + x + \frac{1}{3}\ln\left|\frac{x-1}{x+2}\right| + C \blacktriangleleft$$

▓ CONCLUDING REMARKS

There are some cases in which the method of partial fractions is inappropriate. For example, it would be inefficient to use partial fractions to perform the integration

$$\int \frac{3x^2 + 2}{x^3 + 2x - 8}\,dx = \ln|x^3 + 2x - 8| + C$$

since the substitution $u = x^3 + 2x - 8$ is more direct. Similarly, the integration

$$\int \frac{2x - 1}{x^2 + 1}\,dx = \int \frac{2x}{x^2 + 1}\,dx - \int \frac{dx}{x^2 + 1} = \ln(x^2 + 1) - \tan^{-1}x + C$$

requires only a little algebra since the integrand is already in partial fraction form.

✔ QUICK CHECK EXERCISES 7.5   (See page 523 for answers.)

1. A partial fraction is a rational function of the form _____ or of the form _____.

2. (a) What is a proper rational function?
   (b) What condition must the degree of the numerator and the degree of the denominator of a rational function satisfy for the method of partial fractions to be applicable directly?
   (c) If the condition in part (b) is not satisfied, what must you do if you want to use partial fractions?

3. Suppose that the function $f(x) = P(x)/Q(x)$ is a proper rational function.
   (a) For each factor of $Q(x)$ of the form $(ax + b)^m$, the partial fraction decomposition of f contains the following sum of m partial fractions: _____

   (b) For each factor of $Q(x)$ of the form $(ax^2 + bx + c)^m$, where $ax^2 + bx + c$ is an irreducible quadratic, the partial fraction decomposition of f contains the following sum of m partial fractions: _____

4. Complete the partial fraction decomposition.
   (a) $\dfrac{-3}{(x+1)(2x-1)} = \dfrac{A}{x+1} - \dfrac{2}{2x-1}$
   (b) $\dfrac{2x^2 - 3x}{(x^2+1)(3x+2)} = \dfrac{B}{3x+2} - \dfrac{1}{x^2+1}$

5. Evaluate the integral.
   (a) $\displaystyle\int \frac{3}{(x+1)(1-2x)}\,dx$ (b) $\displaystyle\int \frac{2x^2-3x}{(x^2+1)(3x+2)}\,dx$

EXERCISE SET 7.5   ⓒ CAS

1–8 Write out the form of the partial fraction decomposition. (Do not find the numerical values of the coefficients.) ▪

1. $\dfrac{3x - 1}{(x-3)(x+4)}$

2. $\dfrac{5}{x(x^2-4)}$

3. $\dfrac{2x - 3}{x^3 - x^2}$

4. $\dfrac{x^2}{(x+2)^3}$

5. $\dfrac{1 - x^2}{x^3(x^2+2)}$

6. $\dfrac{3x}{(x-1)(x^2+6)}$

7. $\dfrac{4x^3 - x}{(x^2+5)^2}$

8. $\dfrac{1 - 3x^4}{(x-2)(x^2+1)^2}$

9–34 Evaluate the integral. ▪

9. $\displaystyle\int \frac{dx}{x^2 - 3x - 4}$

10. $\displaystyle\int \frac{dx}{x^2 - 6x - 7}$

11. $\displaystyle\int \frac{11x + 17}{2x^2 + 7x - 4}\,dx$

12. $\displaystyle\int \frac{5x - 5}{3x^2 - 8x - 3}\,dx$

13. $\displaystyle\int \frac{2x^2 - 9x - 9}{x^3 - 9x}\,dx$

14. $\displaystyle\int \frac{dx}{x(x^2 - 1)}$

15. $\displaystyle\int \frac{x^2 - 8}{x + 3}\,dx$

16. $\displaystyle\int \frac{x^2 + 1}{x - 1}\,dx$

17. $\displaystyle\int \frac{3x^2 - 10}{x^2 - 4x + 4}\,dx$

18. $\displaystyle\int \frac{x^2}{x^2 - 3x + 2}\,dx$

19. $\displaystyle\int \frac{2x - 3}{x^2 - 3x - 10}\,dx$

20. $\displaystyle\int \frac{3x + 1}{3x^2 + 2x - 1}\,dx$

21. $\displaystyle\int \frac{x^5 + x^2 + 2}{x^3 - x}\,dx$

22. $\displaystyle\int \frac{x^5 - 4x^3 + 1}{x^3 - 4x}\,dx$

23. $\displaystyle\int \frac{2x^2 + 3}{x(x-1)^2}\,dx$

24. $\displaystyle\int \frac{3x^2 - x + 1}{x^3 - x^2}\,dx$

25. $\displaystyle\int \frac{2x^2 - 10x + 4}{(x+1)(x-3)^2} \, dx$ **26.** $\displaystyle\int \frac{2x^2 - 2x - 1}{x^3 - x^2} \, dx$

27. $\displaystyle\int \frac{x^2}{(x+1)^3} \, dx$ **28.** $\displaystyle\int \frac{2x^2 + 3x + 3}{(x+1)^3} \, dx$

29. $\displaystyle\int \frac{2x^2 - 1}{(4x-1)(x^2+1)} \, dx$ **30.** $\displaystyle\int \frac{dx}{x^3 + 2x}$

31. $\displaystyle\int \frac{x^3 + 3x^2 + x + 9}{(x^2+1)(x^2+3)} \, dx$ **32.** $\displaystyle\int \frac{x^3 + x^2 + x + 2}{(x^2+1)(x^2+2)} \, dx$

33. $\displaystyle\int \frac{x^3 - 2x^2 + 2x - 2}{x^2 + 1} \, dx$

34. $\displaystyle\int \frac{x^4 + 6x^3 + 10x^2 + x}{x^2 + 6x + 10} \, dx$

35–38 True–False Determine whether the statement is true or false. Explain your answer. ■

35. The technique of partial fractions is used for integrals whose integrands are ratios of polynomials.

36. The integrand in
$$\int \frac{3x^4 + 5}{(x^2+1)^2} \, dx$$
is a proper rational function.

37. The partial fraction decomposition of
$$\frac{2x+3}{x^2} \quad \text{is} \quad \frac{2}{x} + \frac{3}{x^2}$$

38. If $f(x) = P(x)/(x+5)^3$ is a proper rational function, then the partial fraction decomposition of $f(x)$ has terms with constant numerators and denominators $(x+5)$, $(x+5)^2$, and $(x+5)^3$.

39–42 Evaluate the integral by making a substitution that converts the integrand to a rational function. ■

39. $\displaystyle\int \frac{\cos\theta}{\sin^2\theta + 4\sin\theta - 5} \, d\theta$ **40.** $\displaystyle\int \frac{e^t}{e^{2t} - 4} \, dt$

41. $\displaystyle\int \frac{e^{3x}}{e^{2x} + 4} \, dx$ **42.** $\displaystyle\int \frac{5 + 2\ln x}{x(1 + \ln x)^2} \, dx$

43. Find the volume of the solid generated when the region enclosed by $y = x^2/(9 - x^2)$, $y = 0$, $x = 0$, and $x = 2$ is revolved about the x-axis.

44. Find the area of the region under the curve $y = 1/(1 + e^x)$, over the interval $[-\ln 5, \ln 5]$. [*Hint:* Make a substitution that converts the integrand to a rational function.]

C **45–46** Use a CAS to evaluate the integral in two ways: (i) integrate directly; (ii) use the CAS to find the partial fraction decomposition and integrate the decomposition. Integrate by hand to check the results. ■

45. $\displaystyle\int \frac{x^2 + 1}{(x^2 + 2x + 3)^2} \, dx$

46. $\displaystyle\int \frac{x^5 + x^4 + 4x^3 + 4x^2 + 4x + 4}{(x^2 + 2)^3} \, dx$

C **47–48** Integrate by hand and check your answers using a CAS. ■

47. $\displaystyle\int \frac{dx}{x^4 - 3x^3 - 7x^2 + 27x - 18}$

48. $\displaystyle\int \frac{dx}{16x^3 - 4x^2 + 4x - 1}$

FOCUS ON CONCEPTS

49. Show that
$$\int_0^1 \frac{x}{x^4 + 1} \, dx = \frac{\pi}{8}$$

50. Use partial fractions to derive the integration formula
$$\int \frac{1}{a^2 - x^2} \, dx = \frac{1}{2a} \ln\left|\frac{a+x}{a-x}\right| + C$$

51. Suppose that $ax^2 + bx + c$ is a quadratic polynomial and that the integration
$$\int \frac{1}{ax^2 + bx + c} \, dx$$
produces a function with no inverse tangent terms. What does this tell you about the roots of the polynomial?

52. Suppose that $ax^2 + bx + c$ is a quadratic polynomial and that the integration
$$\int \frac{1}{ax^2 + bx + c} \, dx$$
produces a function with neither logarithmic nor inverse tangent terms. What does this tell you about the roots of the polynomial?

53. Does there exist a quadratic polynomial $ax^2 + bx + c$ such that the integration
$$\int \frac{x}{ax^2 + bx + c} \, dx$$
produces a function with no logarithmic terms? If so, give an example; if not, explain why no such polynomial can exist.

54. **Writing** Suppose that $P(x)$ is a cubic polynomial. State the general form of the partial fraction decomposition for
$$f(x) = \frac{P(x)}{(x+5)^4}$$
and state the implications of this decomposition for evaluating the integral $\int f(x) \, dx$.

55. **Writing** Consider the functions
$$f(x) = \frac{1}{x^2 - 4} \quad \text{and} \quad g(x) = \frac{x}{x^2 - 4}$$
Each of the integrals $\int f(x) \, dx$ and $\int g(x) \, dx$ can be evaluated using partial fractions and using at least one other integration technique. Demonstrate two different techniques for evaluating each of these integrals, and then discuss the considerations that would determine which technique you would use.

1. $\dfrac{A}{(ax+b)^k}$; $\dfrac{Ax+B}{(ax^2+bx+c)^k}$ 2. (a) A proper rational function is a rational function in which the degree of the numerator is less than the degree of the denominator. (b) The degree of the numerator must be less than the degree of the denominator. (c) Divide the denominator into the numerator, which results in the sum of a polynomial and a proper rational function.

3. (a) $\dfrac{A_1}{ax+b}+\dfrac{A_2}{(ax+b)^2}+\cdots+\dfrac{A_m}{(ax+b)^m}$ (b) $\dfrac{A_1x+B_1}{ax^2+bx+c}+\dfrac{A_2x+B_2}{(ax^2+bx+c)^2}+\cdots+\dfrac{A_mx+B_m}{(ax^2+bx+c)^m}$

4. (a) $A=1$ (b) $B=2$

5. (a) $\displaystyle\int\dfrac{3}{(x+1)(1-2x)}\,dx=\ln\left|\dfrac{x+1}{1-2x}\right|+C$ (b) $\displaystyle\int\dfrac{2x^2-3x}{(x^2+1)(3x+2)}\,dx=\dfrac{2}{3}\ln|3x+2|-\tan^{-1}x+C$

7.6 USING COMPUTER ALGEBRA SYSTEMS AND TABLES OF INTEGRALS

In this section we will discuss how to integrate using tables, and we will see some special substitutions to try when an integral doesn't match any of the forms in an integral table. In particular, we will discuss a method for integrating rational functions of sin x *and* cos x. *We will also address some of the issues that relate to using computer algebra systems for integration. Readers who are not using computer algebra systems can skip that material.*

■ INTEGRAL TABLES

Tables of integrals are useful for eliminating tedious hand computation. The endpapers of this text contain a relatively brief table of integrals that we will refer to as the **Endpaper Integral Table**; more comprehensive tables are published in standard reference books such as the *CRC Standard Mathematical Tables and Formulae*, CRC Press, Inc., 2002.

All integral tables have their own scheme for classifying integrals according to the form of the integrand. For example, the Endpaper Integral Table classifies the integrals into 15 categories; *Basic Functions, Reciprocals of Basic Functions, Powers of Trigonometric Functions, Products of Trigonometric Functions*, and so forth. The first step in working with tables is to read through the classifications so that you understand the classification scheme and know where to look in the table for integrals of different types.

■ PERFECT MATCHES

If you are lucky, the integral you are attempting to evaluate will match up perfectly with one of the forms in the table. However, when looking for matches you may have to make an adjustment for the variable of integration. For example, the integral

$$\int x^2 \sin x \, dx$$

is a perfect match with Formula (46) in the Endpaper Integral Table, except for the letter used for the variable of integration. Thus, to apply Formula (46) to the given integral we need to change the variable of integration in the formula from u to x. With that minor modification we obtain

$$\int x^2 \sin x \, dx = 2x \sin x + (2 - x^2) \cos x + C$$

Here are some more examples of perfect matches.

▶ **Example 1**   Use the Endpaper Integral Table to evaluate

$$\text{(a)} \int \sin 7x \cos 2x \, dx \qquad \text{(b)} \int x^2 \sqrt{7 + 3x} \, dx$$

$$\text{(c)} \int \frac{\sqrt{2 - x^2}}{x} \, dx \qquad \text{(d)} \int (x^3 + 7x + 1) \sin \pi x \, dx$$

Solution (a).   The integrand can be classified as a product of trigonometric functions. Thus, from Formula (40) with $m = 7$ and $n = 2$ we obtain

$$\int \sin 7x \cos 2x \, dx = -\frac{\cos 9x}{18} - \frac{\cos 5x}{10} + C$$

Solution (b).   The integrand can be classified as a power of x multiplying $\sqrt{a + bx}$. Thus, from Formula (103) with $a = 7$ and $b = 3$ we obtain

$$\int x^2 \sqrt{7 + 3x} \, dx = \frac{2}{2835} (135x^2 - 252x + 392)(7 + 3x)^{3/2} + C$$

Solution (c).   The integrand can be classified as a power of x dividing $\sqrt{a^2 - x^2}$. Thus, from Formula (79) with $a = \sqrt{2}$ we obtain

$$\int \frac{\sqrt{2 - x^2}}{x} \, dx = \sqrt{2 - x^2} - \sqrt{2} \ln \left| \frac{\sqrt{2} + \sqrt{2 - x^2}}{x} \right| + C$$

Solution (d).   The integrand can be classified as a polynomial multiplying a trigonometric function. Thus, we apply Formula (58) with $p(x) = x^3 + 7x + 1$ and $a = \pi$. The successive nonzero derivatives of $p(x)$ are

$$p'(x) = 3x^2 + 7, \quad p''(x) = 6x, \quad p'''(x) = 6$$

and so

$$\int (x^3 + 7x + 1) \sin \pi x \, dx$$

$$= -\frac{x^3 + 7x + 1}{\pi} \cos \pi x + \frac{3x^2 + 7}{\pi^2} \sin \pi x + \frac{6x}{\pi^3} \cos \pi x - \frac{6}{\pi^4} \sin \pi x + C \blacktriangleleft$$

■ **MATCHES REQUIRING SUBSTITUTIONS**

Sometimes an integral that does not match any table entry can be made to match by making an appropriate substitution.

▶ **Example 2**   Use the Endpaper Integral Table to evaluate

$$\text{(a)} \int e^{\pi x} \sin^{-1}(e^{\pi x}) \, dx \qquad \text{(b)} \int x \sqrt{x^2 - 4x + 5} \, dx$$

Solution (a).   The integrand does not even come close to matching any of the forms in the table. However, a little thought suggests the substitution

$$u = e^{\pi x}, \quad du = \pi e^{\pi x} \, dx$$

from which we obtain

$$\int e^{\pi x} \sin^{-1}(e^{\pi x})\, dx = \frac{1}{\pi} \int \sin^{-1} u\, du$$

The integrand is now a basic function, and Formula (7) yields

$$\int e^{\pi x} \sin^{-1}(e^{\pi x})\, dx = \frac{1}{\pi}\left[u \sin^{-1} u + \sqrt{1 - u^2}\right] + C$$

$$= \frac{1}{\pi}\left[e^{\pi x} \sin^{-1}(e^{\pi x}) + \sqrt{1 - e^{2\pi x}}\right] + C$$

Solution (b).   Again, the integrand does not closely match any of the forms in the table. However, a little thought suggests that it may be possible to bring the integrand closer to the form $x\sqrt{x^2 + a^2}$ by completing the square to eliminate the term involving x inside the radical. Doing this yields

$$\int x\sqrt{x^2 - 4x + 5}\, dx = \int x\sqrt{(x^2 - 4x + 4) + 1}\, dx = \int x\sqrt{(x - 2)^2 + 1}\, dx \quad (1)$$

At this point we are closer to the form $x\sqrt{x^2 + a^2}$, but we are not quite there because of the $(x - 2)^2$ rather than x^2 inside the radical. However, we can resolve that problem with the substitution

$$u = x - 2, \quad du = dx$$

With this substitution we have $x = u + 2$, so (1) can be expressed in terms of u as

$$\int x\sqrt{x^2 - 4x + 5}\, dx = \int (u + 2)\sqrt{u^2 + 1}\, du = \int u\sqrt{u^2 + 1}\, du + 2\int \sqrt{u^2 + 1}\, du$$

The first integral on the right is now a perfect match with Formula (84) with $a = 1$, and the second is a perfect match with Formula (72) with $a = 1$. Thus, applying these formulas we obtain

$$\int x\sqrt{x^2 - 4x + 5}\, dx = \tfrac{1}{3}(u^2 + 1)^{3/2} + 2\left[\tfrac{1}{2}u\sqrt{u^2 + 1} + \tfrac{1}{2}\ln(u + \sqrt{u^2 + 1})\right] + C$$

If we now replace u by $x - 2$ (in which case $u^2 + 1 = x^2 - 4x + 5$), we obtain

$$\int x\sqrt{x^2 - 4x + 5}\, dx = \tfrac{1}{3}(x^2 - 4x + 5)^{3/2} + (x - 2)\sqrt{x^2 - 4x + 5}$$

$$+ \ln\left(x - 2 + \sqrt{x^2 - 4x + 5}\right) + C$$

Although correct, this form of the answer has an unnecessary mixture of radicals and fractional exponents. If desired, we can "clean up" the answer by writing

$$(x^2 - 4x + 5)^{3/2} = (x^2 - 4x + 5)\sqrt{x^2 - 4x + 5}$$

from which it follows that (verify)

$$\int x\sqrt{x^2 - 4x + 5}\, dx = \tfrac{1}{3}(x^2 - x - 1)\sqrt{x^2 - 4x + 5}$$

$$+ \ln\left(x - 2 + \sqrt{x^2 - 4x + 5}\right) + C \blacktriangleleft$$

■ **MATCHES REQUIRING REDUCTION FORMULAS**

In cases where the entry in an integral table is a reduction formula, that formula will have to be applied first to reduce the given integral to a form in which it can be evaluated.

▶ **Example 3** Use the Endpaper Integral Table to evaluate $\int \dfrac{x^3}{\sqrt{1+x}}\,dx$.

Solution. The integrand can be classified as a power of x multiplying the reciprocal of $\sqrt{a+bx}$. Thus, from Formula (107) with $a = 1$, $b = 1$, and $n = 3$, followed by Formula (106), we obtain

$$\int \frac{x^3}{\sqrt{1+x}}\,dx = \frac{2x^3\sqrt{1+x}}{7} - \frac{6}{7}\int \frac{x^2}{\sqrt{1+x}}\,dx$$

$$= \frac{2x^3\sqrt{1+x}}{7} - \frac{6}{7}\left[\frac{2}{15}(3x^2 - 4x + 8)\sqrt{1+x}\right] + C$$

$$= \left(\frac{2x^3}{7} - \frac{12x^2}{35} + \frac{16x}{35} - \frac{32}{35}\right)\sqrt{1+x} + C \;\blacktriangleleft$$

■ **SPECIAL SUBSTITUTIONS**

The Endpaper Integral Table has numerous entries involving an exponent of $3/2$ or involving square roots (exponent $1/2$), but it has no entries with other fractional exponents. However, integrals involving fractional powers of x can often be simplified by making the substitution $u = x^{1/n}$ in which n is the least common multiple of the denominators of the exponents. The resulting integral will then involve integer powers of u.

▶ **Example 4** Evaluate

$$\text{(a)} \int \frac{\sqrt{x}}{1 + \sqrt[3]{x}}\,dx \qquad \text{(b)} \int \sqrt{1 + e^x}\,dx$$

Solution (a). The integrand contains $x^{1/2}$ and $x^{1/3}$, so we make the substitution $u = x^{1/6}$, from which we obtain

$$x = u^6, \quad dx = 6u^5\,du$$

Thus,

$$\int \frac{\sqrt{x}}{1 + \sqrt[3]{x}}\,dx = \int \frac{(u^6)^{1/2}}{1 + (u^6)^{1/3}}(6u^5)\,du = 6\int \frac{u^8}{1 + u^2}\,du$$

By long division

$$\frac{u^8}{1 + u^2} = u^6 - u^4 + u^2 - 1 + \frac{1}{1 + u^2}$$

from which it follows that

$$\int \frac{\sqrt{x}}{1 + \sqrt[3]{x}}\,dx = 6\int \left(u^6 - u^4 + u^2 - 1 + \frac{1}{1 + u^2}\right)du$$

$$= \tfrac{6}{7}u^7 - \tfrac{6}{5}u^5 + 2u^3 - 6u + 6\tan^{-1}u + C$$

$$= \tfrac{6}{7}x^{7/6} - \tfrac{6}{5}x^{5/6} + 2x^{1/2} - 6x^{1/6} + 6\tan^{-1}(x^{1/6}) + C$$

Solution (b). The integral does not match any of the forms in the Endpaper Integral Table. However, the table does include several integrals containing $\sqrt{a + bu}$. This suggests the substitution $u = e^x$, from which we obtain

$$x = \ln u, \quad dx = \frac{1}{u}\,du$$

Thus, from Formula (110) with $a = 1$ and $b = 1$, followed by Formula (108), we obtain

$$\int \sqrt{1 + e^x}\, dx = \int \frac{\sqrt{1+u}}{u}\, du$$

$$= 2\sqrt{1+u} + \int \frac{du}{u\sqrt{1+u}}$$

$$= 2\sqrt{1+u} + \ln \left| \frac{\sqrt{1+u}-1}{\sqrt{1+u}+1} \right| + C$$

$$= 2\sqrt{1+e^x} + \ln \left[\frac{\sqrt{1+e^x}-1}{\sqrt{1+e^x}+1} \right] + C \qquad \boxed{\text{Absolute value not needed}} \blacktriangleleft$$

Try finding the antiderivative in Example 4(b) using the substitution

$$u = \sqrt{1 + e^x}$$

Functions that consist of finitely many sums, differences, quotients, and products of $\sin x$ and $\cos x$ are called **rational functions of sin x and cos x**. Some examples are

$$\frac{\sin x + 3\cos^2 x}{\cos x + 4 \sin x}, \qquad \frac{\sin x}{1 + \cos x - \cos^2 x}, \qquad \frac{3 \sin^5 x}{1 + 4 \sin x}$$

The Endpaper Integral Table gives a few formulas for integrating rational functions of $\sin x$ and $\cos x$ under the heading *Reciprocals of Basic Functions*. For example, it follows from Formula (18) that

$$\int \frac{1}{1 + \sin x}\, dx = \tan x - \sec x + C \qquad (2)$$

However, since the integrand is a rational function of $\sin x$, it may be desirable in a particular application to express the value of the integral in terms of $\sin x$ and $\cos x$ and rewrite (2) as

$$\int \frac{1}{1 + \sin x}\, dx = \frac{\sin x - 1}{\cos x} + C$$

Many rational functions of $\sin x$ and $\cos x$ can be evaluated by an ingenious method that was discovered by the mathematician Karl Weierstrass (see p. 102 for biography). The idea is to make the substitution

$$u = \tan(x/2), \quad -\pi/2 < x/2 < \pi/2$$

from which it follows that

$$x = 2 \tan^{-1} u, \quad dx = \frac{2}{1 + u^2}\, du$$

To implement this substitution we need to express $\sin x$ and $\cos x$ in terms of u. For this purpose we will use the identities

$$\sin x = 2 \sin(x/2) \cos(x/2) \qquad (3)$$
$$\cos x = \cos^2(x/2) - \sin^2(x/2) \qquad (4)$$

and the following relationships suggested by Figure 7.6.1:

$$\sin(x/2) = \frac{u}{\sqrt{1+u^2}} \quad \text{and} \quad \cos(x/2) = \frac{1}{\sqrt{1+u^2}}$$

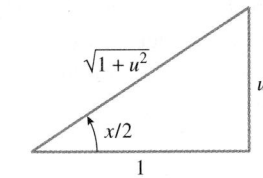

▲ **Figure 7.6.1**

Substituting these expressions in (3) and (4) yields

$$\sin x = 2 \left(\frac{u}{\sqrt{1+u^2}} \right) \left(\frac{1}{\sqrt{1+u^2}} \right) = \frac{2u}{1+u^2}$$

$$\cos x = \left(\frac{1}{\sqrt{1+u^2}} \right)^2 - \left(\frac{u}{\sqrt{1+u^2}} \right)^2 = \frac{1 - u^2}{1 + u^2}$$

In summary, we have shown that the substitution $u = \tan(x/2)$ can be implemented in a rational function of $\sin x$ and $\cos x$ by letting

$$\sin x = \frac{2u}{1 + u^2}, \quad \cos x = \frac{1 - u^2}{1 + u^2}, \quad dx = \frac{2}{1 + u^2}\,du \tag{5}$$

▶ **Example 5** Evaluate $\displaystyle\int \frac{dx}{1 - \sin x + \cos x}$.

Solution. The integrand is a rational function of $\sin x$ and $\cos x$ that does not match any of the formulas in the Endpaper Integral Table, so we make the substitution $u = \tan(x/2)$. Thus, from (5) we obtain

$$\int \frac{dx}{1 - \sin x + \cos x} = \int \frac{\dfrac{2\,du}{1 + u^2}}{1 - \left(\dfrac{2u}{1 + u^2}\right) + \left(\dfrac{1 - u^2}{1 + u^2}\right)}$$

$$= \int \frac{2\,du}{(1 + u^2) - 2u + (1 - u^2)}$$

$$= \int \frac{du}{1 - u} = -\ln|1 - u| + C = -\ln|1 - \tan(x/2)| + C \blacktriangleleft$$

> The substitution $u = \tan(x/2)$ will convert any rational function of $\sin x$ and $\cos x$ to an ordinary rational function of u. However, the method can lead to cumbersome partial fraction decompositions, so it may be worthwhile to consider other methods as well when hand computations are being used.

■ **INTEGRATING WITH COMPUTER ALGEBRA SYSTEMS**

Integration tables are rapidly giving way to computerized integration using computer algebra systems. However, as with many powerful tools, a knowledgeable operator is an important component of the system.

Sometimes computer algebra systems do not produce the most general form of the indefinite integral. For example, the integral formula

$$\int \frac{dx}{x - 1} = \ln|x - 1| + C$$

which can be obtained by inspection or by using the substitution $u = x - 1$, is valid for $x > 1$ or for $x < 1$. However, not all computer algebra systems produce this form of the answer. Some typical answers produced by various implementations of *Mathematica*, *Maple*, and the CAS on a handheld calculator are

$$\ln(-1 + x), \quad \ln(x - 1), \quad \ln(|x - 1|)$$

Observe that none of the systems include the constant of integration—the answer produced is a particular antiderivative and not the most general antiderivative (indefinite integral). Observe also that only one of these answers includes the absolute value signs; the antiderivatives produced by the other systems are valid only for $x > 1$. All systems, however, are able to calculate the definite integral

$$\int_0^{1/2} \frac{dx}{x - 1} = -\ln 2$$

correctly. Now let us examine how these systems handle the integral

$$\int x\sqrt{x^2 - 4x + 5}\,dx = \tfrac{1}{3}(x^2 - x - 1)\sqrt{x^2 - 4x + 5}$$

$$+ \ln(x - 2 + \sqrt{x^2 - 4x + 5}) \tag{6}$$

which we obtained in Example 2(b) (with the constant of integration included). Some CAS implementations produce this result in slightly different algebraic forms, but a version of *Maple* produces the result

$$\int x\sqrt{x^2 - 4x + 5}\,dx = \tfrac{1}{3}(x^2 - 4x + 5)^{3/2} + \tfrac{1}{2}(2x - 4)\sqrt{x^2 - 4x + 5} + \sinh^{-1}(x - 2)$$

This can be rewritten as (6) by expressing the fractional exponent in radical form and expressing $\sinh^{-1}(x - 2)$ in logarithmic form using Theorem 6.9.4 (verify). A version of *Mathematica* produces the result

$$\int x\sqrt{x^2 - 4x + 5}\,dx = \tfrac{1}{3}(x^2 - x - 1)\sqrt{x^2 - 4x + 5} - \sinh^{-1}(2 - x)$$

which can be rewritten in form (6) by using Theorem 6.9.4 together with the identity $\sinh^{-1}(-x) = -\sinh^{-1} x$ (verify).

Computer algebra systems can sometimes produce inconvenient or unnatural answers to integration problems. For example, various computer algebra systems produced the following results when asked to integrate $(x + 1)^7$:

$$\frac{(x + 1)^8}{8}, \qquad \frac{1}{8}x^8 + x^7 + \frac{7}{2}x^6 + 7x^5 + \frac{35}{4}x^4 + 7x^3 + \frac{7}{2}x^2 + x \tag{7}$$

The first form is in keeping with the hand computation

$$\int (x + 1)^7\,dx = \frac{(x + 1)^8}{8} + C$$

that uses the substitution $u = x + 1$, whereas the second form is based on expanding $(x + 1)^7$ and integrating term by term.

In Example 2(a) of Section 7.3 we showed that

$$\int \sin^4 x \cos^5 x\,dx = \tfrac{1}{5}\sin^5 x - \tfrac{2}{7}\sin^7 x + \tfrac{1}{9}\sin^9 x + C$$

However, a version of *Mathematica* integrates this as

$$\tfrac{3}{128}\sin x - \tfrac{1}{192}\sin 3x - \tfrac{1}{320}\sin 5x + \tfrac{1}{1792}\sin 7x + \tfrac{1}{2304}\sin 9x$$

whereas other computer algebra systems essentially integrate it as

$$-\tfrac{1}{9}\sin^3 x \cos^6 x - \tfrac{1}{21}\sin x \cos^6 x + \tfrac{1}{105}\cos^4 x \sin x + \tfrac{4}{315}\cos^2 x \sin x + \tfrac{8}{315}\sin x$$

Although these three results look quite different, they can be obtained from one another using appropriate trigonometric identities.

■ COMPUTER ALGEBRA SYSTEMS HAVE LIMITATIONS

A computer algebra system combines a set of integration rules (such as substitution) with a library of functions that it can use to construct antiderivatives. Such libraries contain elementary functions, such as polynomials, rational functions, trigonometric functions, as well as various nonelementary functions that arise in engineering, physics, and other applied fields. Just as our Endpaper Integral Table has only 121 indefinite integrals, these libraries are not exhaustive of all possible integrands. If the system cannot manipulate the integrand to a form matching one in its library, the program will give some indication that it cannot evaluate the integral. For example, when asked to evaluate the integral

$$\int (1 + \ln x)\sqrt{1 + (x \ln x)^2}\,dx \tag{8}$$

all of the systems mentioned above respond by displaying some form of the unevaluated integral as an answer, indicating that they could not perform the integration.

Sometimes computer algebra systems respond by expressing an integral in terms of another integral. For example, if you try to integrate e^{x^2} using *Mathematica*, *Maple*, or

---

Expanding the expression

$$\frac{(x + 1)^8}{8}$$

produces a constant term of $\tfrac{1}{8}$, whereas the second expression in (7) has no constant term. What is the explanation?

TECHNOLOGY MASTERY

Sometimes integrals that cannot be evaluated by a CAS in their given form can be evaluated by first rewriting them in a different form or by making a substitution. If you have a CAS, make a u-substitution in (8) that will enable you to evaluate the integral with your CAS. Then evaluate the integral.

Sage, you will obtain an expression involving erf (which stands for *error function*). The function erf(x) is defined as

$$\text{erf}(x) = \frac{2}{\sqrt{\pi}} \int_0^x e^{-t^2}\, dt$$

so all three programs essentially rewrite the given integral in terms of a closely related integral. From one point of view this is what we did in integrating $1/x$, since the natural logarithm function is (formally) defined as

$$\ln x = \int_1^x \frac{1}{t}\, dt$$

(see Section 5.10).

▶ **Example 6** A particle moves along an x-axis in such a way that its velocity $v(t)$ at time t is

$$v(t) = 30\cos^7 t \sin^4 t \quad (t \geq 0)$$

Graph the position versus time curve for the particle, given that the particle is at $x = 1$ when $t = 0$.

Solution. Since $dx/dt = v(t)$ and $x = 1$ when $t = 0$, the position function $x(t)$ is given by

$$x(t) = 1 + \int_0^t v(s)\, ds$$

Some computer algebra systems will allow this expression to be entered directly into a command for plotting functions, but it is often more efficient to perform the integration first. The authors' integration utility yields

$$x = \int 30\cos^7 t \sin^4 t\, dt$$

$$= -\tfrac{30}{11}\sin^{11} t + 10\sin^9 t - \tfrac{90}{7}\sin^7 t + 6\sin^5 t + C$$

where we have added the required constant of integration. Using the initial condition $x(0) = 1$, we substitute the values $x = 1$ and $t = 0$ into this equation to find that $C = 1$, so

$$x(t) = -\tfrac{30}{11}\sin^{11} t + 10\sin^9 t - \tfrac{90}{7}\sin^7 t + 6\sin^5 t + 1 \quad (t \geq 0)$$

The graph of x versus t is shown in Figure 7.6.2. ◀

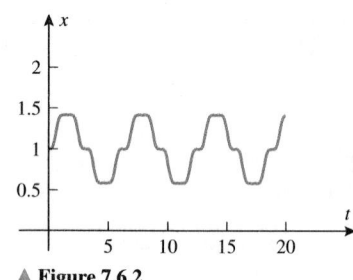

▲ **Figure 7.6.2**

✔ QUICK CHECK EXERCISES 7.6 (*See page 533 for answers.*)

1. Find an integral formula in the Endpaper Integral Table that can be used to evaluate the integral. Do not evaluate the integral.

(a) $\displaystyle\int \frac{2x}{3x+4}\, dx$ _____

(b) $\displaystyle\int \frac{1}{x\sqrt{5x-4}}\, dx$ _____

(c) $\displaystyle\int x\sqrt{3x+2}\, dx$ _____

(d) $\displaystyle\int x^2 \ln x\, dx$ _____

2. In each part, make the indicated u-substitution, and then find an integral formula in the Endpaper Integral Table that

can be used to evaluate the integral. Do not evaluate the integral.

(a) $\displaystyle\int \frac{x}{1+e^{x^2}}\, dx; \ u = x^2$ _____

(b) $\displaystyle\int e^{\sqrt{x}}\, dx; \ u = \sqrt{x}$ _____

(c) $\displaystyle\int \frac{e^x}{1+\sin(e^x)}\, dx; \ u = e^x$ _____

(d) $\displaystyle\int \frac{1}{(1-4x^2)^{3/2}}\, dx; \ u = 2x$ _____

3. In each part, use the Endpaper Integral Table to evaluate the integral. (If necessary, first make an appropriate substitution or complete the square.) *(cont.)*

(a) $\displaystyle\int \frac{1}{4-x^2}\,dx = $ _____

(b) $\displaystyle\int \cos 2x \cos x\,dx = $ _____

(c) $\displaystyle\int \frac{e^{3x}}{\sqrt{1-e^{2x}}}\,dx = $ _____

(d) $\displaystyle\int \frac{x}{x^2-4x+8}\,dx = $ _____

EXERCISE SET 7.6   C CAS

C **1–24** (a) Use the Endpaper Integral Table to evaluate the given integral. (b) If you have a CAS, use it to evaluate the integral, and then confirm that the result is equivalent to the one that you found in part (a). ■

1. $\displaystyle\int \frac{4x}{3x-1}\,dx$

2. $\displaystyle\int \frac{x}{(4-5x)^2}\,dx$

3. $\displaystyle\int \frac{1}{x(2x+5)}\,dx$

4. $\displaystyle\int \frac{1}{x^2(1-5x)}\,dx$

5. $\displaystyle\int x\sqrt{2x+3}\,dx$

6. $\displaystyle\int \frac{x}{\sqrt{2-x}}\,dx$

7. $\displaystyle\int \frac{1}{x\sqrt{4-3x}}\,dx$

8. $\displaystyle\int \frac{1}{x\sqrt{3x-4}}\,dx$

9. $\displaystyle\int \frac{1}{16-x^2}\,dx$

10. $\displaystyle\int \frac{1}{x^2-9}\,dx$

11. $\displaystyle\int \sqrt{x^2-3}\,dx$

12. $\displaystyle\int \frac{\sqrt{x^2-5}}{x^2}\,dx$

13. $\displaystyle\int \frac{x^2}{\sqrt{x^2+4}}\,dx$

14. $\displaystyle\int \frac{1}{x^2\sqrt{x^2-2}}\,dx$

15. $\displaystyle\int \sqrt{9-x^2}\,dx$

16. $\displaystyle\int \frac{\sqrt{4-x^2}}{x^2}\,dx$

17. $\displaystyle\int \frac{\sqrt{4-x^2}}{x}\,dx$

18. $\displaystyle\int \frac{1}{x\sqrt{6x-x^2}}\,dx$

19. $\displaystyle\int \sin 3x \sin 4x\,dx$

20. $\displaystyle\int \sin 2x \cos 5x\,dx$

21. $\displaystyle\int x^3 \ln x\,dx$

22. $\displaystyle\int \frac{\ln x}{\sqrt{x^3}}\,dx$

23. $\displaystyle\int e^{-2x}\sin 3x\,dx$

24. $\displaystyle\int e^x \cos 2x\,dx$

C **25–36** (a) Make the indicated u-substitution, and then use the Endpaper Integral Table to evaluate the integral. (b) If you have a CAS, use it to evaluate the integral, and then confirm that the result is equivalent to the one that you found in part (a). ■

25. $\displaystyle\int \frac{e^{4x}}{(4-3e^{2x})^2}\,dx,\ u = e^{2x}$

26. $\displaystyle\int \frac{\sin 2x}{(\cos 2x)(3-\cos 2x)}\,dx,\ u = \cos 2x$

27. $\displaystyle\int \frac{1}{\sqrt{x}(9x+4)}\,dx,\ u = 3\sqrt{x}$

28. $\displaystyle\int \frac{\cos 4x}{9+\sin^2 4x}\,dx,\ u = \sin 4x$

29. $\displaystyle\int \frac{1}{\sqrt{4x^2-9}}\,dx,\ u = 2x$

30. $\displaystyle\int x\sqrt{2x^4+3}\,dx,\ u = \sqrt{2}x^2$

31. $\displaystyle\int \frac{4x^5}{\sqrt{2-4x^4}}\,dx,\ u = 2x^2$

32. $\displaystyle\int \frac{1}{x^2\sqrt{3-4x^2}}\,dx,\ u = 2x$

33. $\displaystyle\int \frac{\sin^2(\ln x)}{x}\,dx,\ u = \ln x$

34. $\displaystyle\int e^{-2x}\cos^2(e^{-2x})\,dx,\ u = e^{-2x}$

35. $\displaystyle\int xe^{-2x}\,dx,\ u = -2x$

36. $\displaystyle\int \ln(3x+1)\,dx,\ u = 3x+1$

C **37–48** (a) Make an appropriate u-substitution, and then use the Endpaper Integral Table to evaluate the integral. (b) If you have a CAS, use it to evaluate the integral (no substitution), and then confirm that the result is equivalent to that in part (a). ■

37. $\displaystyle\int \frac{\cos 3x}{(\sin 3x)(\sin 3x + 1)^2}\,dx$

38. $\displaystyle\int \frac{\ln x}{x\sqrt{4\ln x - 1}}\,dx$

39. $\displaystyle\int \frac{x}{16x^4-1}\,dx$

40. $\displaystyle\int \frac{e^x}{3-4e^{2x}}\,dx$

41. $\displaystyle\int e^x\sqrt{3-4e^{2x}}\,dx$

42. $\displaystyle\int \frac{\sqrt{4-9x^2}}{x^2}\,dx$

43. $\displaystyle\int \sqrt{5x-9x^2}\,dx$

44. $\displaystyle\int \frac{1}{x\sqrt{x-5x^2}}\,dx$

45. $\displaystyle\int 4x\sin 2x\,dx$

46. $\displaystyle\int \cos\sqrt{x}\,dx$

47. $\displaystyle\int e^{-\sqrt{x}}\,dx$

48. $\displaystyle\int x\ln(2+x^2)\,dx$

C **49–52** (a) Complete the square, make an appropriate u-substitution, and then use the Endpaper Integral Table to evaluate the integral. (b) If you have a CAS, use it to evaluate the integral (no substitution or square completion), and then confirm that the result is equivalent to that in part (a). ■

49. $\displaystyle\int \frac{1}{x^2+6x-7}\,dx$

50. $\displaystyle\int \sqrt{3-2x-x^2}\,dx$

51. $\displaystyle\int \frac{x}{\sqrt{5+4x-x^2}}\,dx$ **52.** $\displaystyle\int \frac{x}{x^2+6x+13}\,dx$

$\boxed{c}$ **53–64** (a) Make an appropriate u-substitution of the form $u = x^{1/n}$ or $u = (x+a)^{1/n}$, and then evaluate the integral. (b) If you have a CAS, use it to evaluate the integral, and then confirm that the result is equivalent to the one that you found in part (a). ■

53. $\displaystyle\int x\sqrt{x-2}\,dx$ **54.** $\displaystyle\int \frac{x}{\sqrt{x+1}}\,dx$

55. $\displaystyle\int x^5\sqrt{x^3+1}\,dx$ **56.** $\displaystyle\int \frac{1}{x\sqrt{x^3-1}}\,dx$

57. $\displaystyle\int \frac{dx}{x-\sqrt[3]{x}}$ **58.** $\displaystyle\int \frac{dx}{\sqrt{x}+\sqrt[3]{x}}$

59. $\displaystyle\int \frac{dx}{x(1-x^{1/4})}$ **60.** $\displaystyle\int \frac{\sqrt{x}}{x+1}\,dx$

61. $\displaystyle\int \frac{dx}{x^{1/2}-x^{1/3}}$ **62.** $\displaystyle\int \frac{1+\sqrt{x}}{1-\sqrt{x}}\,dx$

63. $\displaystyle\int \frac{x^3}{\sqrt{1+x^2}}\,dx$ **64.** $\displaystyle\int \frac{x}{(x+3)^{1/5}}\,dx$

$\boxed{c}$ **65–70** (a) Make u-substitution (5) to convert the integrand to a rational function of u, and then evaluate the integral. (b) If you have a CAS, use it to evaluate the integral (no substitution), and then confirm that the result is equivalent to that in part (a). ■

65. $\displaystyle\int \frac{dx}{1+\sin x+\cos x}$ **66.** $\displaystyle\int \frac{dx}{2+\sin x}$

67. $\displaystyle\int \frac{d\theta}{1-\cos\theta}$ **68.** $\displaystyle\int \frac{dx}{4\sin x-3\cos x}$

69. $\displaystyle\int \frac{dx}{\sin x+\tan x}$ **70.** $\displaystyle\int \frac{\sin x}{\sin x+\tan x}\,dx$

71–72 Use any method to solve for x. ■

71. $\displaystyle\int_2^x \frac{1}{t(4-t)}\,dt = 0.5,\ 2 < x < 4$

72. $\displaystyle\int_1^x \frac{1}{t\sqrt{2t-1}}\,dt = 1,\ x > \tfrac{1}{2}$

73–76 Use any method to find the area of the region enclosed by the curves. ■

73. $y=\sqrt{25-x^2},\ y=0,\ x=0,\ x=4$

74. $y=\sqrt{9x^2-4},\ y=0,\ x=2$

75. $y=\dfrac{1}{25-16x^2},\ y=0,\ x=0,\ x=1$

76. $y=\sqrt{x}\ln x,\ y=0,\ x=4$

77–80 Use any method to find the volume of the solid generated when the region enclosed by the curves is revolved about the y-axis. ■

77. $y=\cos x,\ y=0,\ x=0,\ x=\pi/2$

78. $y=\sqrt{x-4},\ y=0,\ x=8$

79. $y=e^{-x},\ y=0,\ x=0,\ x=3$

80. $y=\ln x,\ y=0,\ x=5$

81–82 Use any method to find the arc length of the curve. ■

81. $y=2x^2,\ 0\le x\le 2$ **82.** $y=3\ln x,\ 1\le x\le 3$

83–84 Use any method to find the area of the surface generated by revolving the curve about the x-axis. ■

83. $y=\sin x,\ 0\le x\le\pi$ **84.** $y=1/x,\ 1\le x\le 4$

$\boxed{c}$ **85–86** Information is given about the motion of a particle moving along a coordinate line.
(a) Use a CAS to find the position function of the particle for $t\ge 0$.
(b) Graph the position versus time curve. ■

85. $v(t)=20\cos^6 t\sin^3 t,\ s(0)=2$

86. $a(t)=e^{-t}\sin 2t\sin 4t,\ v(0)=0,\ s(0)=10$

FOCUS ON CONCEPTS

87. (a) Use the substitution $u=\tan(x/2)$ to show that
$$\int \sec x\,dx = \ln\left|\frac{1+\tan(x/2)}{1-\tan(x/2)}\right| + C$$
and confirm that this is consistent with Formula (22) of Section 7.3.
(b) Use the result in part (a) to show that
$$\int \sec x\,dx = \ln\left|\tan\left(\frac{\pi}{4}+\frac{x}{2}\right)\right| + C$$

88. Use the substitution $u=\tan(x/2)$ to show that
$$\int \csc x\,dx = \frac{1}{2}\ln\left[\frac{1-\cos x}{1+\cos x}\right] + C$$
and confirm that this is consistent with the result in Exercise 65(a) of Section 7.3.

89. Find a substitution that can be used to integrate rational functions of $\sinh x$ and $\cosh x$ and use your substitution to evaluate
$$\int \frac{dx}{2\cosh x+\sinh x}$$
without expressing the integrand in terms of e^x and e^{-x}.

$\boxed{c}$ **90–93** Some integrals that can be evaluated by hand cannot be evaluated by all computer algebra systems. Evaluate the integral by hand, and determine if it can be evaluated on your CAS. ■

90. $\displaystyle\int \frac{x^3}{\sqrt{1-x^8}}\,dx$

91. $\displaystyle\int (\cos^{32}x\sin^{30}x - \cos^{30}x\sin^{32}x)\,dx$

92. $\displaystyle\int \sqrt{x-\sqrt{x^2-4}}\,dx$ [Hint: $\tfrac{1}{2}(\sqrt{x+2}-\sqrt{x-2})^2 = ?$]

93. $\int \dfrac{1}{x^{10} + x}\,dx$

[*Hint:* Rewrite the denominator as $x^{10}(1 + x^{-9})$.]

c **94.** Let

$$f(x) = \frac{-2x^5 + 26x^4 + 15x^3 + 6x^2 + 20x + 43}{x^6 - x^5 - 18x^4 - 2x^3 - 39x^2 - x - 20}$$

(a) Use a CAS to factor the denominator, and then write down the form of the partial fraction decomposition. You need not find the values of the constants.

(b) Check your answer in part (a) by using the CAS to find the partial fraction decomposition of f.

(c) Integrate f by hand, and then check your answer by integrating with the CAS.

✔ **QUICK CHECK ANSWERS 7.6**

1. (a) Formula (60) (b) Formula (108) (c) Formula (102) (d) Formula (50)   **2.** (a) Formula (25) (b) Formula (51)

(c) Formula (18) (d) Formula (97)   **3.** (a) $\dfrac{1}{4} \ln \left| \dfrac{x+2}{x-2} \right| + C$ (b) $\dfrac{1}{6} \sin 3x + \dfrac{1}{2} \sin x + C$ (c) $-\dfrac{e^x}{2} \sqrt{1 - e^{2x}} + \dfrac{1}{2} \sin^{-1} e^x + C$

(d) $\dfrac{1}{2} \ln \left(x^2 - 4x + 8 \right) + \tan^{-1} \dfrac{x-2}{2} + C$

7.7 NUMERICAL INTEGRATION; SIMPSON'S RULE

If it is necessary to evaluate a definite integral of a function for which an antiderivative cannot be found, then one must settle for some kind of numerical approximation of the integral. In Section 5.4 we considered three such approximations in the context of areas—left endpoint approximation, right endpoint approximation, and midpoint approximation. In this section we will extend those methods to general definite integrals, and we will develop some new methods that often provide more accuracy with less computation. We will also discuss the errors that arise in integral approximations.

■ **A REVIEW OF RIEMANN SUM APPROXIMATIONS**

Recall from Section 5.5 that the definite integral of a continuous function f over an interval $[a, b]$ may be computed as

$$\int_a^b f(x)\,dx = \lim_{\max \Delta x_k \to 0} \sum_{k=1}^n f(x_k^*) \Delta x_k$$

where the sum that appears on the right side is called a Riemann sum. In this formula, Δx_k is the width of the kth subinterval of a partition $a = x_0 < x_1 < x_2 < \cdots < x_n = b$ of $[a, b]$ into n subintervals, and x_k^* denotes an arbitrary point in the kth subinterval. If we take all subintervals of the same width, so that $\Delta x_k = (b - a)/n$, then as n increases the Riemann sum will eventually be a good approximation to the definite integral. We denote this by writing

$$\int_a^b f(x)\,dx \approx \left(\frac{b - a}{n} \right) [f(x_1^*) + f(x_2^*) + \cdots + f(x_n^*)] \tag{1}$$

If we denote the values of f at the endpoints of the subintervals by

$$y_0 = f(a), \quad y_1 = f(x_1), \quad y_2 = f(x_2), \ldots, y_{n-1} = f(x_{n-1}), \quad y_n = f(x_n)$$

and the values of f at the midpoints of the subintervals by

$$y_{m_1}, y_{m_2}, \ldots, y_{m_n}$$

then it follows from (1) that the left endpoint, right endpoint, and midpoint approximations discussed in Section 5.4 can be expressed as shown in Table 7.7.1. Although we originally

Table 7.7.1

LEFT ENDPOINT APPROXIMATION	RIGHT ENDPOINT APPROXIMATION	MIDPOINT APPROXIMATION
$\int_a^b f(x)\,dx \approx \left(\dfrac{b-a}{n}\right)[y_0 + y_1 + \cdots + y_{n-1}]$	$\int_a^b f(x)\,dx \approx \left(\dfrac{b-a}{n}\right)[y_1 + y_2 + \cdots + y_n]$	$\int_a^b f(x)\,dx \approx \left(\dfrac{b-a}{n}\right)[y_{m_1} + y_{m_2} + \cdots + y_{m_n}]$

obtained these results for nonnegative functions in the context of approximating areas, they are applicable to any function that is continuous on $[a, b]$.

■ **TRAPEZOIDAL APPROXIMATION**

It will be convenient in this section to denote the left endpoint, right endpoint, and midpoint approximations with n subintervals by L_n, R_n, and M_n, respectively. Of the three approximations, the midpoint approximation is most widely used in applications. If we take the average of L_n and R_n, then we obtain another important approximation denoted by

$$T_n = \tfrac{1}{2}(L_n + R_n)$$

called the ***trapezoidal approximation***:

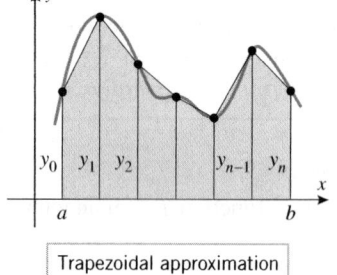

Trapezoidal approximation

▲ **Figure 7.7.1**

> ***Trapezoidal Approximation***
>
> $$\int_a^b f(x)\,dx \approx T_n = \left(\frac{b-a}{2n}\right)[y_0 + 2y_1 + \cdots + 2y_{n-1} + y_n] \tag{2}$$

The name "trapezoidal approximation" results from the fact that in the case where f is nonnegative on the interval of integration, the approximation T_n is the sum of the trapezoidal areas shown in Figure 7.7.1 (see Exercise 51).

▶ **Example 1** In Table 7.7.2 we have approximated

$$\ln 2 = \int_1^2 \frac{1}{x}\,dx$$

using the midpoint approximation and the trapezoidal approximation.[*] In each case we used $n = 10$ subdivisions of the interval $[1, 2]$, so that

$$\underbrace{\frac{b-a}{n} = \frac{2-1}{10} = 0.1}_{\text{Midpoint}} \quad\text{and}\quad \underbrace{\frac{b-a}{2n} = \frac{2-1}{20} = 0.05}_{\text{Trapezoidal}} \quad ◀$$

---

[*]Throughout this section we will show numerical values to nine places to the right of the decimal point. If your calculating utility does not show this many places, then you will need to make the appropriate adjustments. What is important here is that you understand the principles being discussed.

Table 7.7.2

MIDPOINT AND TRAPEZOIDAL APPROXIMATIONS FOR $\int_1^2 \frac{1}{x} dx$

	MIDPOINT APPROXIMATION			TRAPEZOIDAL APPROXIMATION			
i	MIDPOINT m_i	$y_{m_i} = f(m_i) = 1/m_i$	i	ENDPOINT x_i	$y_i = f(x_i) = 1/x_i$	MULTIPLIER w_i	$w_i y_i$
1	1.05	0.952380952	0	1.0	1.000000000	1	1.000000000
2	1.15	0.869565217	1	1.1	0.909090909	2	1.818181818
3	1.25	0.800000000	2	1.2	0.833333333	2	1.666666667
4	1.35	0.740740741	3	1.3	0.769230769	2	1.538461538
5	1.45	0.689655172	4	1.4	0.714285714	2	1.428571429
6	1.55	0.645161290	5	1.5	0.666666667	2	1.333333333
7	1.65	0.606060606	6	1.6	0.625000000	2	1.250000000
8	1.75	0.571428571	7	1.7	0.588235294	2	1.176470588
9	1.85	0.540540541	8	1.8	0.555555556	2	1.111111111
10	1.95	0.512820513	9	1.9	0.526315789	2	1.052631579
		6.928353603	10	2.0	0.500000000	1	0.500000000
							13.875428063

$$\int_1^2 \frac{1}{x} dx \approx (0.1)(6.928353603) \approx 0.692835360$$

$$\int_1^2 \frac{1}{x} dx \approx (0.05)(13.875428063) \approx 0.693771403$$

■ COMPARISON OF THE MIDPOINT AND TRAPEZOIDAL APPROXIMATIONS

We define the *errors* in the midpoint and trapezoidal approximations to be

By rewriting (3) and (4) in the form
$$\int_a^b f(x) dx = \text{approximation} + \text{error}$$
we see that positive values of E_M and E_T correspond to underestimates and negative values to overestimates.

$$E_M = \int_a^b f(x) dx - M_n \quad \text{and} \quad E_T = \int_a^b f(x) dx - T_n \qquad (3\text{–}4)$$

respectively, and we define $|E_M|$ and $|E_T|$ to be the *absolute errors* in these approximations. The absolute errors are nonnegative and do not distinguish between underestimates and overestimates.

▶ **Example 2** The value of ln 2 to nine decimal places is

$$\ln 2 = \int_1^2 \frac{1}{x} dx \approx 0.693147181 \qquad (5)$$

so we see from Tables 7.7.2 and 7.7.3 that the absolute errors in approximating ln 2 by M_{10} and T_{10} are

$$|E_M| = |\ln 2 - M_{10}| \approx 0.000311821$$
$$|E_T| = |\ln 2 - T_{10}| \approx 0.000624222$$

Thus, the midpoint approximation is more accurate than the trapezoidal approximation in this case. ◀

Table 7.7.3

ln 2 (NINE DECIMAL PLACES)	APPROXIMATION	ERROR
0.693147181	$M_{10} \approx 0.692835360$	$E_M = \ln 2 - M_{10} \approx 0.000311821$
0.693147181	$T_{10} \approx 0.693771403$	$E_T = \ln 2 - T_{10} \approx -0.000624222$

It is not accidental in Example 2 that the midpoint approximation of $\ln 2$ was more accurate than the trapezoidal approximation. To see why this is so, we first need to look at the midpoint approximation from another point of view. To simplify our explanation, we will assume that f is nonnegative on $[a, b]$, though the conclusions we reach will be true without this assumption.

If f is a differentiable function, then the midpoint approximation is sometimes called the *tangent line approximation* because for each subinterval of $[a, b]$ the area of the rectangle used in the midpoint approximation is equal to the area of the trapezoid whose upper boundary is the tangent line to $y = f(x)$ at the midpoint of the subinterval (Figure 7.7.2). The equality of these areas follows from the fact that the shaded areas in the figure are congruent. We will now show how this point of view about midpoint approximations can be used to establish useful criteria for determining which of M_n or T_n produces the better approximation of a given integral.

In Figure 7.7.3a we have isolated a subinterval of $[a, b]$ on which the graph of a function f is concave down, and we have shaded the areas that represent the errors in the midpoint and trapezoidal approximations over the subinterval. In Figure 7.7.3b we show a succession of four illustrations which make it evident that the error from the midpoint approximation is less than that from the trapezoidal approximation. If the graph of f were concave up, analogous figures would lead to the same conclusion. (This argument, due to Frank Buck, appeared in *The College Mathematics Journal*, Vol. 16, No. 1, 1985.)

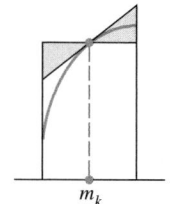

m_k

The shaded triangles have equal areas.

▲ **Figure 7.7.2**

Justify the conclusions in each step of Figure 7.7.3b.

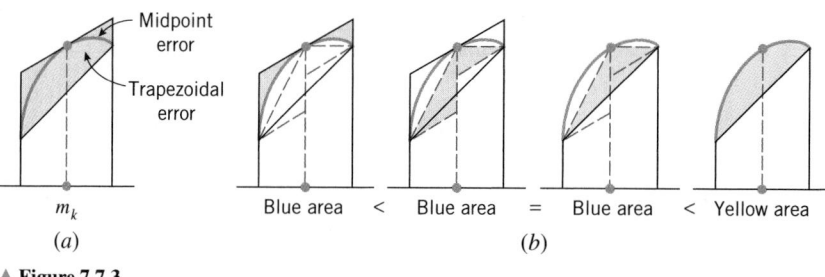

Midpoint error

Trapezoidal error

m_k

(a)

Blue area $<$ Blue area $=$ Blue area $<$ Yellow area

(b)

▲ **Figure 7.7.3**

Figure 7.7.3a also suggests that on a subinterval where the graph is concave down, the midpoint approximation is larger than the value of the integral and the trapezoidal approximation is smaller. On an interval where the graph is concave up it is the other way around. In summary, we have the following result, which we state without formal proof:

7.7.1   THEOREM   *Let f be continuous on $[a, b]$, and let $|E_M|$ and $|E_T|$ be the absolute errors that result from the midpoint and trapezoidal approximations of $\int_a^b f(x)\,dx$ using n subintervals.*

(a) *If the graph of f is either concave up or concave down on (a, b), then $|E_M| < |E_T|$, that is, the absolute error from the midpoint approximation is less than that from the trapezoidal approximation.*

(b) *If the graph of f is concave down on (a, b), then*

$$T_n < \int_a^b f(x)\,dx < M_n$$

(c) *If the graph of f is concave up on (a, b), then*

$$M_n < \int_a^b f(x)\,dx < T_n$$

▶ **Example 3**   Since the graph of $f(x) = 1/x$ is continuous on the interval $[1, 2]$ and concave up on the interval $(1, 2)$, it follows from part (a) of Theorem 7.7.1 that M_n will always provide a better approximation than T_n for

$$\int_1^2 \frac{1}{x}\, dx = \ln 2$$

Moreover, if follows from part (c) of Theorem 7.7.1 that $M_n < \ln 2 < T_n$ for every positive integer n. Note that this is consistent with our computations in Example 2.   ◀

WARNING

Do not conclude that the midpoint approximation is always better than the trapezoidal approximation; the trapezoidal approximation may be better if the function changes concavity on the interval of integration.

▶ **Example 4**   The midpoint and trapezoidal approximations can be used to approximate $\sin 1$ by using the integral

$$\sin 1 = \int_0^1 \cos x\, dx$$

Since $f(x) = \cos x$ is continuous on $[0, 1]$ and concave down on $(0, 1)$, it follows from parts (a) and (b) of Theorem 7.7.1 that the absolute error in M_n will be less than that in T_n, and that $T_n < \sin 1 < M_n$ for every positive integer n. This is consistent with the results in Table 7.7.4 for $n = 5$ (intermediate computations are omitted).   ◀

Table 7.7.4

sin 1 (NINE DECIMAL PLACES)	APPROXIMATION	ERROR
0.841470985	$M_5 \approx 0.842875074$	$E_M = \sin 1 - M_5 \approx -0.001404089$
0.841470985	$T_5 \approx 0.838664210$	$E_T = \sin 1 - T_5 \approx 0.002806775$

▶ **Example 5**   Table 7.7.5 shows approximations for $\sin 3 = \int_0^3 \cos x\, dx$ using the midpoint and trapezoidal approximations with $n = 10$ subdivisions of the interval $[0, 3]$. Note that $|E_M| < |E_T|$ and $T_{10} < \sin 3 < M_{10}$, although these results are not guaranteed by Theorem 7.7.1 since $f(x) = \cos x$ changes concavity on the interval $[0, 3]$.   ◀

Table 7.7.5

sin 3 (NINE DECIMAL PLACES)	APPROXIMATION	ERROR
0.141120008	$M_{10} \approx 0.141650601$	$E_M = \sin 3 - M_{10} \approx -0.000530592$
0.141120008	$T_{10} \approx 0.140060017$	$E_T = \sin 3 - T_{10} \approx 0.001059991$

■ **SIMPSON'S RULE**

When the left and right endpoint approximations are averaged to produce the trapezoidal approximation, a better approximation often results. We now see how a weighted average of the midpoint and trapezoidal approximations can yield an even better approximation.

The numerical evidence in Tables 7.7.3, 7.7.4, and 7.7.5 reveals that $E_T \approx -2E_M$, so that $2E_M + E_T \approx 0$ in these instances. This suggests that

$$3\int_a^b f(x)\, dx = 2\int_a^b f(x)\, dx + \int_a^b f(x)\, dx$$

$$= 2(M_k + E_M) + (T_k + E_T)$$

$$= (2M_k + T_k) + (2E_M + E_T)$$

$$\approx 2M_k + T_k$$

This gives

$$\int_a^b f(x)\,dx \approx \tfrac{1}{3}(2M_k + T_k) \tag{6}$$

The midpoint approximation M_k in (6) requires the evaluation of f at k points in the interval $[a, b]$, and the trapezoidal approximation T_k in (6) requires the evaluation of f at $k + 1$ points in $[a, b]$. Thus, $\tfrac{1}{3}(2M_k + T_k)$ uses $2k + 1$ values of f, taken at equally spaced points in the interval $[a, b]$. These points are obtained by partitioning $[a, b]$ into $2k$ equal subintervals indicated by the left endpoints, right endpoints, and midpoints used in T_k and M_k, respectively. Setting $n = 2k$, we use S_n to denote the weighted average of M_k and T_k in (6). That is,

$$S_n = S_{2k} = \tfrac{1}{3}(2M_k + T_k) \quad \text{or} \quad S_n = \tfrac{1}{3}(2M_{n/2} + T_{n/2}) \tag{7}$$

Table 7.7.6 displays the approximations S_n corresponding to the data in Tables 7.7.3 to 7.7.5.

Table 7.7.6

FUNCTION VALUE (NINE DECIMAL PLACES)	APPROXIMATION	ERROR
$\ln 2 \approx 0.693147181$	$\int_1^2 (1/x)\,dx \approx S_{20} = \tfrac{1}{3}(2M_{10} + T_{10}) \approx 0.693147375$	-0.000000194
$\sin 1 \approx 0.841470985$	$\int_0^1 \cos x\,dx \approx S_{10} = \tfrac{1}{3}(2M_5 + T_5) \approx 0.841471453$	-0.000000468
$\sin 3 \approx 0.141120008$	$\int_0^3 \cos x\,dx \approx S_{20} = \tfrac{1}{3}(2M_{10} + T_{10}) \approx 0.141120406$	-0.000000398

Using the midpoint approximation formula in Table 7.7.1 and Formula (2) for the trapezoidal approximation, we can derive a similar formula for S_n. We start by partitioning the interval $[a, b]$ into an *even* number of equal subintervals. If n is the number of subintervals, then each subinterval has length $(b - a)/n$. Label the endpoints of these subintervals successively by $a = x_0, x_1, x_2, \ldots, x_n = b$. Then $x_0, x_2, x_4, \ldots, x_n$ define a partition of $[a, b]$ into $n/2$ equal intervals, each of length $2(b - a)/n$, and the midpoints of these subintervals are $x_1, x_3, x_5, \ldots, x_{n-1}$, respectively, as illustrated in Figure 7.7.4. Using $y_i = f(x_i)$, we have

$$2M_{n/2} = 2\left(\frac{2(b - a)}{n}\right)[y_1 + y_3 + \cdots + y_{n-1}]$$

$$= \left(\frac{b - a}{n}\right)[4y_1 + 4y_3 + \cdots + 4y_{n-1}]$$

Noting that $(b - a)/[2(n/2)] = (b - a)/n$, we can express $T_{n/2}$ as

$$T_{n/2} = \left(\frac{b - a}{n}\right)[y_0 + 2y_2 + 2y_4 + \cdots + 2y_{n-2} + y_n]$$

Thus, $S_n = \tfrac{1}{3}(2M_{n/2} + T_{n/2})$ can be expressed as

$$S_n = \frac{1}{3}\left(\frac{b - a}{n}\right)[y_0 + 4y_1 + 2y_2 + 4y_3 + 2y_4 + \cdots + 2y_{n-2} + 4y_{n-1} + y_n] \tag{8}$$

The approximation

$$\int_a^b f(x)\,dx \approx S_n \tag{9}$$

with S_n as given in (8) is known as **Simpson's rule**. We denote the error in this approximation by

$$E_S = \int_a^b f(x)\,dx - S_n \tag{10}$$

As before, the absolute error in the approximation (9) is given by $|E_S|$.

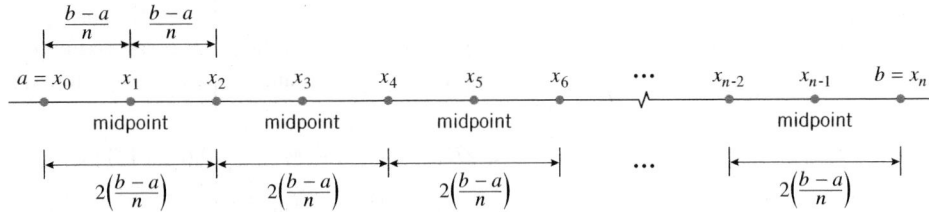

▶ **Figure 7.7.4**

▶ **Example 6**   In Table 7.7.7 we have used Simpson's rule with $n = 10$ subintervals to obtain the approximation

$$\ln 2 = \int_1^2 \frac{1}{x}\,dx \approx S_{10} = 0.693150231$$

For this approximation,

$$\frac{1}{3}\left(\frac{b-a}{n}\right) = \frac{1}{3}\left(\frac{2-1}{10}\right) = \frac{1}{30}$$

Table 7.7.7

AN APPROXIMATION TO $\ln 2$ USING SIMPSON'S RULE

i	ENDPOINT x_i	$y_i = f(x_i) = 1/x_i$	MULTIPLIER w_i	$w_i y_i$
0	1.0	1.000000000	1	1.000000000
1	1.1	0.909090909	4	3.636363636
2	1.2	0.833333333	2	1.666666667
3	1.3	0.769230769	4	3.076923077
4	1.4	0.714285714	2	1.428571429
5	1.5	0.666666667	4	2.666666667
6	1.6	0.625000000	2	1.250000000
7	1.7	0.588235294	4	2.352941176
8	1.8	0.555555556	2	1.111111111
9	1.9	0.526315789	4	2.105263158
10	2.0	0.500000000	1	0.500000000
				20.794506921

$$\int_1^2 \frac{1}{x}\,dx \approx \left(\tfrac{1}{30}\right)(20.794506921) \approx 0.693150231$$

Thomas Simpson (1710–1761) English mathematician. Simpson was the son of a weaver. He was trained to follow in his father's footsteps and had little formal education in his early life. His interest in science and mathematics was aroused in 1724, when he witnessed an eclipse of the Sun and received two books from a peddler, one on astrology and the other on arithmetic. Simpson quickly absorbed their contents and soon became a successful local fortune teller. His improved financial situation enabled him to give up weaving and marry his landlady. Then in 1733 some mysterious "unfortunate incident" forced him to move. He settled in Derby, where he taught in an evening school and worked at weaving during the day. In 1736 he moved to London and published his first mathematical work in a periodical called the *Ladies' Diary* (of which he later became the editor). In 1737 he published a successful calculus textbook that enabled him to give up weaving completely and concentrate on textbook writing and teaching. His fortunes improved further in 1740 when one Robert Heath accused him of plagiarism. The publicity was marvelous, and Simpson proceeded to dash off a succession of best-selling textbooks: *Algebra* (ten editions plus translations), *Geometry* (twelve editions plus translations), *Trigonometry* (five editions plus translations), and numerous others. It is interesting to note that Simpson did not discover the rule that bears his name—it was a well-known result by Simpson's time.

Although S_{10} is a weighted average of M_5 and T_5, it makes sense to compare S_{10} to M_{10} and T_{10}, since the sums for these three approximations involve the same number of terms. Using the values for M_{10} and T_{10} from Example 2 and the value for S_{10} in Table 7.7.7, we have

$$|E_M| = |\ln 2 - M_{10}| \approx |0.693147181 - 0.692835360| = 0.000311821$$

$$|E_T| = |\ln 2 - T_{10}| \approx |0.693147181 - 0.693771403| = 0.000624222$$

$$|E_S| = |\ln 2 - S_{10}| \approx |0.693147181 - 0.693150231| = 0.000003050$$

Comparing these absolute errors, it is clear that S_{10} is a much more accurate approximation of $\ln 2$ than either M_{10} or T_{10}. ◄

■ GEOMETRIC INTERPRETATION OF SIMPSON'S RULE

The midpoint (or tangent line) approximation and the trapezoidal approximation for a definite integral are based on approximating a segment of the curve $y = f(x)$ by line segments. Intuition suggests that we might improve on these approximations using parabolic arcs rather than line segments, thereby accounting for concavity of the curve $y = f(x)$ more closely.

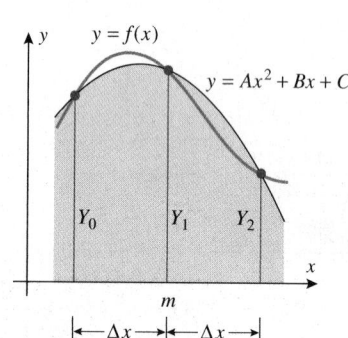

▲ Figure 7.7.5

At the heart of this idea is a formula, sometimes called the ***one-third rule***. The one-third rule expresses a definite integral of a quadratic function $g(x) = Ax^2 + Bx + C$ in terms of the values Y_0, Y_1, and Y_2 of g at the left endpoint, midpoint, and right endpoint, respectively, of the interval of integration $[m - \Delta x, m + \Delta x]$ (see Figure 7.7.5):

$$\int_{m-\Delta x}^{m+\Delta x} (Ax^2 + Bx + C)\, dx = \frac{\Delta x}{3}[Y_0 + 4Y_1 + Y_2] \tag{11}$$

Verification of the one-third rule is left for the reader (Exercise 53). By applying the one-third rule to subintervals $[x_{2k-2}, x_{2k}]$, $k = 1, \ldots, n/2$, one arrives at Formula (8) for Simpson's rule (Exercise 54). Thus, Simpson's rule corresponds to the integral of a piecewise-quadratic approximation to $f(x)$.

■ ERROR BOUNDS

With all the methods studied in this section, there are two sources of error: the *intrinsic* or *truncation error* due to the approximation formula, and the *roundoff error* introduced in the calculations. In general, increasing n reduces the truncation error but increases the roundoff error, since more computations are required for larger n. In practical applications, it is important to know how large n must be taken to ensure that a specified degree of accuracy is obtained. The analysis of roundoff error is complicated and will not be considered here. However, the following theorems, which are proved in books on numerical analysis, provide upper bounds on the truncation errors in the midpoint, trapezoidal, and Simpson's rule approximations.

7.7.2   THEOREM (*Midpoint and Trapezoidal Error Bounds*)   *If f'' is continuous on $[a, b]$ and if K_2 is the maximum value of $|f''(x)|$ on $[a, b]$, then*

$$(a)\ \ |E_M| = \left| \int_a^b f(x)\, dx - M_n \right| \leq \frac{(b-a)^3 K_2}{24n^2} \tag{12}$$

$$(b)\ \ |E_T| = \left| \int_a^b f(x)\, dx - T_n \right| \leq \frac{(b-a)^3 K_2}{12n^2} \tag{13}$$

7.7.3   THEOREM (Simpson Error Bound)   *If $f^{(4)}$ is continuous on $[a, b]$ and if K_4 is the maximum value of $|f^{(4)}(x)|$ on $[a, b]$, then*

$$|E_S| = \left| \int_a^b f(x)\, dx - S_n \right| \leq \frac{(b-a)^5 K_4}{180n^4} \tag{14}$$

▶ **Example 7**   Find an upper bound on the absolute error that results from approximating

$$\ln 2 = \int_1^2 \frac{1}{x}\, dx$$

using (a) the midpoint approximation M_{10}, (b) the trapezoidal approximation T_{10}, and (c) Simpson's rule S_{10}, each with $n = 10$ subintervals.

Solution.   We will apply Formulas (12), (13), and (14) with

$$f(x) = \frac{1}{x}, \quad a = 1, \quad b = 2, \quad \text{and} \quad n = 10$$

We have

$$f'(x) = -\frac{1}{x^2}, \quad f''(x) = \frac{2}{x^3}, \quad f'''(x) = -\frac{6}{x^4}, \quad f^{(4)}(x) = \frac{24}{x^5}$$

Thus,

$$|f''(x)| = \left| \frac{2}{x^3} \right| = \frac{2}{x^3}, \quad |f^{(4)}(x)| = \left| \frac{24}{x^5} \right| = \frac{24}{x^5}$$

where we have dropped the absolute values because $f''(x)$ and $f^{(4)}(x)$ have positive values for $1 \leq x \leq 2$. Since $|f''(x)|$ and $|f^4(x)|$ are continuous and decreasing on $[1, 2]$, both functions have their maximum values at $x = 1$; for $|f''(x)|$ this maximum value is 2 and for $|f^4(x)|$ the maximum value is 24. Thus we can take $K_2 = 2$ in (12) and (13), and $K_4 = 24$ in (14). This yields

> Note that the upper bounds calculated in Example 7 are consistent with the values $|E_M|$, $|E_T|$, and $|E_S|$ calculated in Example 6 but are considerably greater than those values. It is quite common that the upper bounds on the absolute errors given in Theorems 7.7.2 and 7.7.3 substantially exceed the actual absolute errors. However, that does not diminish the utility of these bounds.

$$|E_M| \leq \frac{(b-a)^3 K_2}{24n^2} = \frac{1^3 \cdot 2}{24 \cdot 10^2} \approx 0.000833333$$

$$|E_T| \leq \frac{(b-a)^3 K_2}{12n^2} = \frac{1^3 \cdot 2}{12 \cdot 10^2} \approx 0.001666667$$

$$|E_S| \leq \frac{(b-a)^5 K_4}{180n^4} = \frac{1^5 \cdot 24}{180 \cdot 10^4} \approx 0.000013333 \quad ◀$$

▶ **Example 8**   How many subintervals should be used in approximating

$$\ln 2 = \int_1^2 \frac{1}{x}\, dx$$

by Simpson's rule for five decimal-place accuracy?

Solution.   To obtain five decimal-place accuracy, we must choose the number of subintervals so that

$$|E_S| \leq 0.000005 = 5 \times 10^{-6}$$

From (14), this can be achieved by taking n in Simpson's rule to satisfy

$$\frac{(b-a)^5 K_4}{180n^4} \leq 5 \times 10^{-6}$$

Taking $a = 1$, $b = 2$, and $K_4 = 24$ (found in Example 7) in this inequality yields

$$\frac{1^5 \cdot 24}{180 \cdot n^4} \leq 5 \times 10^{-6}$$

which, on taking reciprocals, can be rewritten as

$$n^4 \geq \frac{2 \times 10^6}{75} = \frac{8 \times 10^4}{3}$$

Thus,

$$n \geq \frac{20}{\sqrt[4]{6}} \approx 12.779$$

Since n must be an even integer, the smallest value of n that satisfies this requirement is $n = 14$. Thus, the approximation S_{14} using 14 subintervals will produce five decimal-place accuracy. ◄

REMARK   In cases where it is difficult to find the values of K_2 and K_4 in Formulas (12), (13), and (14), these constants may be replaced by any larger constants. For example, suppose that a constant K can be easily found with the certainty that $|f''(x)| < K$ on the interval. Then $K_2 \leq K$ and

$$|E_T| \leq \frac{(b-a)^3 K_2}{12n^2} \leq \frac{(b-a)^3 K}{12n^2} \tag{15}$$

so the right side of (15) is also an upper bound on the value of $|E_T|$. Using K, however, will likely increase the computed value of n needed for a given error tolerance. Many applications involve the resolution of competing practical issues, illustrated here through the trade-off between the convenience of finding a crude bound for $|f''(x)|$ versus the efficiency of using the smallest possible n for a desired accuracy.

▶ **Example 9**   How many subintervals should be used in approximating

$$\int_0^1 \cos(x^2)\, dx$$

by the midpoint approximation for three decimal-place accuracy?

Solution.   To obtain three decimal-place accuracy, we must choose n so that

$$|E_M| \leq 0.0005 = 5 \times 10^{-4} \tag{16}$$

From (12) with $f(x) = \cos(x^2)$, $a = 0$, and $b = 1$, an upper bound on $|E_M|$ is given by

$$|E_M| \leq \frac{K_2}{24n^2} \tag{17}$$

where $|K_2|$ is the maximum value of $|f''(x)|$ on the interval $[0, 1]$. However,

$$f'(x) = -2x \sin(x^2)$$
$$f''(x) = -4x^2 \cos(x^2) - 2\sin(x^2) = -[4x^2 \cos(x^2) + 2\sin(x^2)]$$

so that

$$|f''(x)| = |4x^2 \cos(x^2) + 2\sin(x^2)| \tag{18}$$

It would be tedious to look for the maximum value of this function on the interval $[0, 1]$. For x in $[0, 1]$, it is easy to see that each of the expressions x^2, $\cos(x^2)$, and $\sin(x^2)$ is bounded in absolute value by 1, so $|4x^2 \cos(x^2) + 2\sin(x^2)| \leq 4 + 2 = 6$ on $[0, 1]$. We can improve on this by using a graphing utility to sketch $|f''(x)|$, as shown in Figure 7.7.6. It is evident from the graph that

$$|f''(x)| < 4 \quad \text{for} \quad 0 \leq x \leq 1$$

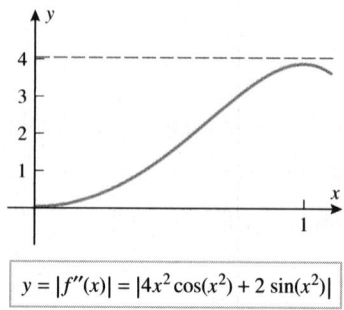

$$y = |f''(x)| = |4x^2 \cos(x^2) + 2\sin(x^2)|$$

▲ **Figure 7.7.6**

Thus, it follows from (17) that

$$|E_M| \le \frac{K_2}{24n^2} < \frac{4}{24n^2} = \frac{1}{6n^2}$$

and hence we can satisfy (16) by choosing n so that

$$\frac{1}{6n^2} < 5 \times 10^{-4}$$

which, on taking reciprocals, can be written as

$$n^2 > \frac{10^4}{30} \quad \text{or} \quad n > \frac{10^2}{\sqrt{30}} \approx 18.257$$

The smallest integer value of n satisfying this inequality is $n = 19$. Thus, the midpoint approximation M_{19} using 19 subintervals will produce three decimal-place accuracy. ◄

■ A COMPARISON OF THE THREE METHODS

Of the three methods studied in this section, Simpson's rule generally produces more accurate results than the midpoint or trapezoidal approximations for the same amount of work. To make this plausible, let us express (12), (13), and (14) in terms of the subinterval width

$$\Delta x = \frac{b - a}{n}$$

We obtain

$$|E_M| \le \frac{1}{24} K_2 (b - a)(\Delta x)^2 \tag{19}$$

$$|E_T| \le \frac{1}{12} K_2 (b - a)(\Delta x)^2 \tag{20}$$

$$|E_S| \le \frac{1}{180} K_4 (b - a)(\Delta x)^4 \tag{21}$$

(verify). For Simpson's rule, the upper bound on the absolute error is proportional to $(\Delta x)^4$, whereas the upper bound on the absolute error for the midpoint and trapezoidal approximations is proportional to $(\Delta x)^2$. Thus, reducing the interval width by a factor of 10, for example, reduces the error bound by a factor of 100 for the midpoint and trapezoidal approximations but reduces the error bound by a factor of 10,000 for Simpson's rule. This suggests that, as n increases, the accuracy of Simpson's rule improves much more rapidly than that of the other approximations.

As a final note, observe that if $f(x)$ is a polynomial of degree 3 or less, then we have $f^{(4)}(x) = 0$ for all x, so $K_4 = 0$ in (14) and consequently $|E_S| = 0$. Thus, Simpson's rule gives exact results for polynomials of degree 3 or less. Similarly, the midpoint and trapezoidal approximations give exact results for polynomials of degree 1 or less. (You should also be able to see that this is so geometrically.)

✔ QUICK CHECK EXERCISES 7.7   (See page 547 for answers.)

1. Let T_n be the trapezoidal approximation for the definite integral of $f(x)$ over an interval $[a, b]$ using n subintervals.
   (a) Expressed in terms of L_n and R_n (the left and right endpoint approximations), $T_n =$ _____.
   (b) Expressed in terms of the function values $y_0, y_1, \ldots, y_n$ at the endpoints of the subintervals, $T_n =$ _____.

2. Let I denote the definite integral of f over an interval $[a, b]$ with T_n and M_n the respective trapezoidal and midpoint approximations of I for a given n. Assume that the graph of f is concave up on the interval $[a, b]$ and order the quantities T_n, M_n, and I from smallest to largest:
   _____ < _____ < _____.

3. Let S_6 be the Simpson's rule approximation for $\int_a^b f(x)\,dx$ using $n = 6$ subintervals.
   (a) Expressed in terms of M_3 and T_3 (the midpoint and trapezoidal approximations), $S_6 = $ _____.
   (b) Using the function values $y_0, y_1, y_2, \ldots, y_6$ at the endpoints of the subintervals, $S_6 = $ _____.

4. Assume that $f^{(4)}$ is continuous on $[0, 1]$ and that $f^{(k)}(x)$ satisfies $|f^{(k)}(x)| \le 1$ on $[0, 1]$, $k = 1, 2, 3, 4$. Find an upper bound on the absolute error that results from approximating the integral of f over $[0, 1]$ using (a) the midpoint approximation M_{10}; (b) the trapezoidal approximation T_{10}; and (c) Simpson's rule S_{10}.

5. Approximate $\displaystyle\int_1^3 \frac{1}{x^2}\,dx$ using the indicated method.
   (a) $M_1 = $ _____   (b) $T_1 = $ _____
   (c) $S_2 = $ _____

EXERCISE SET 7.7   C CAS

1–6 Approximate the integral using (a) the midpoint approximation M_{10}, (b) the trapezoidal approximation T_{10}, and (c) Simpson's rule approximation S_{20} using Formula (7). In each case, find the exact value of the integral and approximate the absolute error. Express your answers to at least four decimal places. ■

1. $\displaystyle\int_0^3 \sqrt{x+1}\,dx$ 2. $\displaystyle\int_4^9 \frac{1}{\sqrt{x}}\,dx$ 3. $\displaystyle\int_0^{\pi/2} \cos x\,dx$

4. $\displaystyle\int_0^2 \sin x\,dx$ 5. $\displaystyle\int_1^3 e^{-2x}\,dx$ 6. $\displaystyle\int_0^3 \frac{1}{3x+1}\,dx$

7–12 Use inequalities (12), (13), and (14) to find upper bounds on the errors in parts (a), (b), or (c) of the indicated exercise. ■

7. Exercise 1   8. Exercise 2   9. Exercise 3

10. Exercise 4   11. Exercise 5   12. Exercise 6

13–18 Use inequalities (12), (13), and (14) to find a number n of subintervals for (a) the midpoint approximation M_n, (b) the trapezoidal approximation T_n, and (c) Simpson's rule approximation S_n to ensure that the absolute error will be less than the given value. ■

13. Exercise 1; 5×10^{-4} 14. Exercise 2; 5×10^{-4}

15. Exercise 3; 10^{-3} 16. Exercise 4; 10^{-3}

17. Exercise 5; 10^{-4} 18. Exercise 6; 10^{-4}

19–22 True–False Determine whether the statement is true or false. Explain your answer. ■

19. The midpoint approximation, M_n, is the average of the left and right endpoint approximations, L_n and R_n, respectively.

20. If $f(x)$ is concave down on the interval (a, b), then the trapezoidal approximation T_n underestimates $\int_a^b f(x)\,dx$.

21. The Simpson's rule approximation S_{50} for $\int_a^b f(x)\,dx$ is a weighted average of the approximations M_{50} and T_{50}, where M_{50} is given twice the weight of T_{50} in the average.

22. Simpson's rule approximation S_{50} for $\int_a^b f(x)\,dx$ corresponds to $\int_a^b q(x)\,dx$, where the graph of q is composed of 25 parabolic segments joined at points on the graph of f.

23–24 Find a function $g(x)$ of the form
$$g(x) = Ax^2 + Bx + C$$
whose graph contains the points $(m - \Delta x, f(m - \Delta x))$, $(m, f(m))$, and $(m + \Delta x, f(m + \Delta x))$, for the given function $f(x)$ and the given values of m and Δx. Then verify Formula (11):
$$\int_{m-\Delta x}^{m+\Delta x} g(x)\,dx = \frac{\Delta x}{3}[Y_0 + 4Y_1 + Y_2]$$
where $Y_0 = f(m - \Delta x)$, $Y_1 = f(m)$, and $Y_2 = f(m + \Delta x)$. ■

23. $f(x) = \dfrac{1}{x}$; $m = 3$, $\Delta x = 1$

24. $f(x) = \sin^2(\pi x)$; $m = \frac{1}{6}$, $\Delta x = \frac{1}{6}$

25–30 Approximate the integral using Simpson's rule S_{10} and compare your answer to that produced by a calculating utility with a numerical integration capability. Express your answers to at least four decimal places. ■

25. $\displaystyle\int_{-1}^1 e^{-x^2}\,dx$ 26. $\displaystyle\int_0^3 \frac{x}{\sqrt{2x^3+1}}\,dx$

27. $\displaystyle\int_{-1}^2 x\sqrt{2+x^3}\,dx$ 28. $\displaystyle\int_0^\pi \frac{x}{2+\sin x}\,dx$

29. $\displaystyle\int_0^1 \cos(x^2)\,dx$ 30. $\displaystyle\int_1^2 (\ln x)^{3/2}\,dx$

31–32 The exact value of the given integral is π (verify). Approximate the integral using (a) the midpoint approximation M_{10}, (b) the trapezoidal approximation T_{10}, and (c) Simpson's rule approximation S_{20} using Formula (7). Approximate the absolute error and express your answers to at least four decimal places. ■

31. $\displaystyle\int_0^2 \frac{8}{x^2+4}\,dx$ 32. $\displaystyle\int_0^3 \frac{4}{9}\sqrt{9-x^2}\,dx$

33. In Example 8 we showed that taking $n = 14$ subdivisions ensures that the approximation of
$$\ln 2 = \int_1^2 \frac{1}{x}\,dx$$
by Simpson's rule is accurate to five decimal places. Confirm this by comparing the approximation of $\ln 2$ produced by Simpson's rule with $n = 14$ to the value produced directly by your calculating utility.

34. In each part, determine whether a trapezoidal approximation would be an underestimate or an overestimate for the definite integral.

(a) $\int_0^1 \cos(x^2)\, dx$ (b) $\int_{3/2}^2 \cos(x^2)\, dx$

35–36 Find a value of n to ensure that the absolute error in approximating the integral by the midpoint approximation will be less than 10^{-4}. Estimate the absolute error, and express your answers to at least four decimal places. ■

35. $\int_0^2 x \sin x\, dx$ **36.** $\int_0^1 e^{\cos x}\, dx$

37–38 Show that the inequalities (12) and (13) are of no value in finding an upper bound on the absolute error that results from approximating the integral using either the midpoint approximation or the trapezoidal approximation. ■

37. $\int_0^1 x\sqrt{x}\, dx$ **38.** $\int_0^1 \sin\sqrt{x}\, dx$

39–40 Use Simpson's rule approximation S_{10} to approximate the length of the curve over the stated interval. Express your answers to at least four decimal places. ■

39. $y = \sin x$ from $x = 0$ to $x = \pi$

40. $y = x^{-2}$ from $x = 1$ to $x = 2$

FOCUS ON CONCEPTS

41. A graph of the speed v versus time t curve for a test run of a Mitsubishi Galant ES is shown in the accompanying figure. Estimate the speeds at times $t = 0$, 2.5, 5, 7.5, 10, 12.5, 15 s from the graph, convert to ft/s using $1 \text{ mi/h} = \frac{22}{15}$ ft/s, and use these speeds and Simpson's rule to approximate the number of feet traveled during the first 15 s. Round your answer to the nearest foot. [*Hint:* Distance traveled $= \int_0^{15} v(t)\, dt$.]

Source: Data from *Car and Driver*, November 2003.

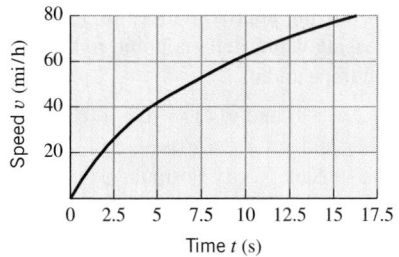

◀ **Figure Ex-41**

42. A graph of the acceleration a versus time t for an object moving on a straight line is shown in the accompanying figure. Estimate the accelerations at $t = 0, 1, 2, \ldots, 8$ seconds (s) from the graph and use Simpson's rule to approximate the change in velocity from $t = 0$ to $t = 8$ s. Round your answer to the nearest tenth cm/s. [*Hint:* Change in velocity $= \int_0^8 a(t)\, dt$.]

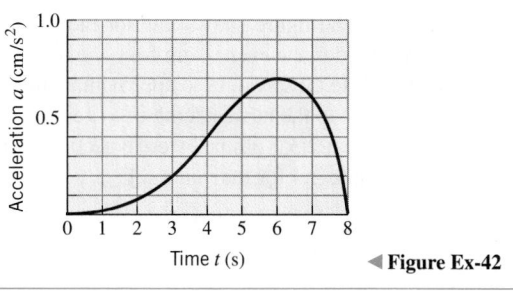

◀ **Figure Ex-42**

43–46 Numerical integration methods can be used in problems where only measured or experimentally determined values of the integrand are available. Use Simpson's rule to estimate the value of the relevant integral in these exercises. ■

43. The accompanying table gives the speeds, in miles per second, at various times for a test rocket that was fired upward from the surface of the Earth. Use these values to approximate the number of miles traveled during the first 180 s. Round your answer to the nearest tenth of a mile. [*Hint:* Distance traveled $= \int_0^{180} v(t)\, dt$.]

TIME t (s)	SPEED v (mi/s)
0	0.00
30	0.03
60	0.08
90	0.16
120	0.27
150	0.42
180	0.65

◀ **Table Ex-43**

44. The accompanying table gives the speeds of a bullet at various distances from the muzzle of a rifle. Use these values to approximate the number of seconds for the bullet to travel 1800 ft. Express your answer to the nearest hundredth of a second. [*Hint:* If v is the speed of the bullet and x is the distance traveled, then $v = dx/dt$ so that $dt/dx = 1/v$ and $t = \int_0^{1800} (1/v)\, dx$.]

DISTANCE x (ft)	SPEED v (ft/s)
0	3100
300	2908
600	2725
900	2549
1200	2379
1500	2216
1800	2059

◀ **Table Ex-44**

45. Measurements of a pottery shard recovered from an archaeological dig reveal that the shard came from a pot with a flat bottom and circular cross sections (see the accompanying figure below). The figure shows interior radius measurements of the shard made every 4 cm from the bottom of the pot to the top. Use those values to approximate the interior volume of the pot to the nearest tenth of a liter (1 L = 1000 cm^3). [*Hint:* Use 6.2.3 (volume by cross sections) to set up an appropriate integral for the volume.]

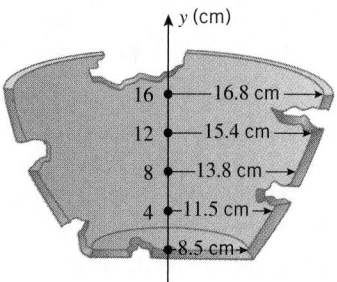

◀ **Figure Ex-45**

46. Engineers want to construct a straight and level road 600 ft long and 75 ft wide by making a vertical cut through an intervening hill (see the accompanying figure). Heights of the hill above the centerline of the proposed road, as obtained at various points from a contour map of the region, are shown in the accompanying figure. To estimate the construction costs, the engineers need to know the volume of earth that must be removed. Approximate this volume, rounded to the nearest cubic foot. [*Hint:* First set up an integral for the cross-sectional area of the cut along the centerline of the road, then assume that the height of the hill does not vary between the centerline and edges of the road.]

HORIZONTAL DISTANCE x (ft)	HEIGHT h (ft)
0	0
100	7
200	16
300	24
400	25
500	16
600	0

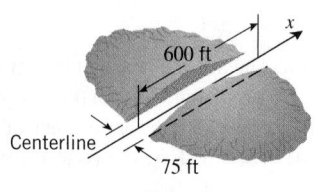

▲ **Figure Ex-46**

C **47.** Let $f(x) = \cos(x^2)$.
  (a) Use a CAS to approximate the maximum value of $|f''(x)|$ on the interval $[0, 1]$.
  (b) How large must n be in the midpoint approximation of $\int_0^1 f(x)\,dx$ to ensure that the absolute error is less than 5×10^{-4}? Compare your result with that obtained in Example 9.
  (c) Estimate the integral using the midpoint approximation with the value of n obtained in part (b).

C **48.** Let $f(x) = \sqrt{1 + x^3}$.
  (a) Use a CAS to approximate the maximum value of $|f''(x)|$ on the interval $[0, 1]$.

(b) How large must n be in the trapezoidal approximation of $\int_0^1 f(x)\,dx$ to ensure that the absolute error is less than 10^{-3}?
  (c) Estimate the integral using the trapezoidal approximation with the value of n obtained in part (b).

C **49.** Let $f(x) = \cos(x - x^2)$.
  (a) Use a CAS to approximate the maximum value of $|f^{(4)}(x)|$ on the interval $[0, 1]$.
  (b) How large must the value of n be in the approximation S_n of $\int_0^1 f(x)\,dx$ by Simpson's rule to ensure that the absolute error is less than 10^{-4}?
  (c) Estimate the integral using Simpson's rule approximation S_n with the value of n obtained in part (b).

C **50.** Let $f(x) = \sqrt{2 + x^3}$.
  (a) Use a CAS to approximate the maximum value of $|f^{(4)}(x)|$ on the interval $[0, 1]$.
  (b) How large must the value of n be in the approximation S_n of $\int_0^1 f(x)\,dx$ by Simpson's rule to ensure that the absolute error is less than 10^{-6}?
  (c) Estimate the integral using Simpson's rule approximation S_n with the value of n obtained in part (b).

FOCUS ON CONCEPTS

51. (a) Verify that the average of the left and right endpoint approximations as given in Table 7.7.1 gives Formula (2) for the trapezoidal approximation.
  (b) Suppose that f is a continuous nonnegative function on the interval $[a, b]$ and partition $[a, b]$ with equally spaced points, $a = x_0 < x_1 < \cdots < x_n = b$. Find the area of the trapezoid under the line segment joining points $(x_k, f(x_k))$ and $(x_{k+1}, f(x_{k+1}))$ and above the interval $[x_k, x_{k+1}]$. Show that the right side of Formula (2) is the sum of these trapezoidal areas (Figure 7.7.1).

52. Let f be a function that is positive, continuous, decreasing, and concave down on the interval $[a, b]$. Assuming that $[a, b]$ is subdivided into n equal subintervals, arrange the following approximations of $\int_a^b f(x)\,dx$ in order of increasing value: left endpoint, right endpoint, midpoint, and trapezoidal.

53. Suppose that $\Delta x > 0$ and $g(x) = Ax^2 + Bx + C$. Let m be a number and set $Y_0 = g(m - \Delta x)$, $Y_1 = g(m)$, and $Y_2 = g(m + \Delta x)$. Verify Formula (11):
$$\int_{m-\Delta x}^{m+\Delta x} g(x)\,dx = \frac{\Delta x}{3}[Y_0 + 4Y_1 + Y_2]$$

54. Suppose that f is a continuous nonnegative function on the interval $[a, b]$, n is even, and $[a, b]$ is partitioned using $n + 1$ equally spaced points, $a = x_0 < x_1 < \cdots < x_n = b$. Set $y_0 = f(x_0)$, $y_1 = f(x_1)$, ..., $y_n = f(x_n)$. Let $g_1, g_2, \ldots, g_{n/2}$ be the quadratic functions of the form $g_i(x) = Ax^2 + Bx + C$ so that   *(cont.)*

- the graph of g_1 passes through the points (x_0, y_0), (x_1, y_1), and (x_2, y_2);
- the graph of g_2 passes through the points (x_2, y_2), (x_3, y_3), and (x_4, y_4);
- $\ldots$
- the graph of $g_{n/2}$ passes through the points (x_{n-2}, y_{n-2}), (x_{n-1}, y_{n-1}), and (x_n, y_n).

Verify that Formula (8) computes the area under a piecewise quadratic function by showing that

$$\sum_{j=1}^{n/2} \left(\int_{x_{2j-2}}^{x_{2j}} g_j(x)\, dx \right)$$
$$= \frac{1}{3}\left(\frac{b-a}{n}\right) [y_0 + 4y_1 + 2y_2 + 4y_3 + 2y_4 + \cdots$$
$$+ 2y_{n-2} + 4y_{n-1} + y_n]$$

55. Writing Discuss two different circumstances under which numerical integration is necessary.

56. Writing For the numerical integration methods of this section, better accuracy of an approximation was obtained by increasing the number of subdivisions of the interval. Another strategy is to use the same number of subintervals, but to select subintervals of differing lengths. Discuss a scheme for doing this to approximate $\int_0^4 \sqrt{x}\, dx$ using a trapezoidal approximation with 4 subintervals. Comment on the advantages and disadvantages of your scheme.

✔ **QUICK CHECK ANSWERS 7.7**

1. (a) $\frac{1}{2}(L_n + R_n)$ (b) $\left(\dfrac{b-a}{2n}\right)[y_0 + 2y_1 + \cdots + 2y_{n-1} + y_n]$ **2.** $M_n < I < T_n$ **3.** (a) $\frac{2}{3}M_3 + \frac{1}{3}T_3$

(b) $\left(\dfrac{b-a}{18}\right)(y_0 + 4y_1 + 2y_2 + 4y_3 + 2y_4 + 4y_5 + y_6)$ **4.** (a) $\dfrac{1}{2400}$ (b) $\dfrac{1}{1200}$ (c) $\dfrac{1}{1,800,000}$

5. (a) $M_1 = \frac{1}{2}$ (b) $T_1 = \frac{10}{9}$ (c) $S_2 = \frac{19}{27}$

7.8 IMPROPER INTEGRALS

Up to now we have focused on definite integrals with continuous integrands and finite intervals of integration. In this section we will extend the concept of a definite integral to include infinite intervals of integration and integrands that become infinite within the interval of integration.

■ IMPROPER INTEGRALS

It is assumed in the definition of the definite integral

$$\int_a^b f(x)\, dx$$

that $[a, b]$ is a finite interval and that the limit that defines the integral exists; that is, the function f is integrable. We observed in Theorems 5.5.2 and 5.5.8 that continuous functions are integrable, as are bounded functions with finitely many points of discontinuity. We also observed in Theorem 5.5.8 that functions that are not bounded on the interval of integration are not integrable. Thus, for example, a function with a vertical asymptote within the interval of integration would not be integrable.

Our main objective in this section is to extend the concept of a definite integral to allow for infinite intervals of integration and integrands with vertical asymptotes within the interval of integration. We will call the vertical asymptotes *infinite discontinuities*, and we will call integrals with infinite intervals of integration or infinite discontinuities within the interval of integration ***improper integrals***. Here are some examples:

- Improper integrals with infinite intervals of integration:

$$\int_1^{+\infty} \frac{dx}{x^2}, \quad \int_{-\infty}^0 e^x \, dx, \quad \int_{-\infty}^{+\infty} \frac{dx}{1+x^2}$$

- Improper integrals with infinite discontinuities in the interval of integration:

$$\int_{-3}^3 \frac{dx}{x^2}, \quad \int_1^2 \frac{dx}{x-1}, \quad \int_0^\pi \tan x \, dx$$

- Improper integrals with infinite discontinuities and infinite intervals of integration:

$$\int_0^{+\infty} \frac{dx}{\sqrt{x}}, \quad \int_{-\infty}^{+\infty} \frac{dx}{x^2-9}, \quad \int_1^{+\infty} \sec x \, dx$$

■ INTEGRALS OVER INFINITE INTERVALS

To motivate a reasonable definition for improper integrals of the form

$$\int_a^{+\infty} f(x) \, dx$$

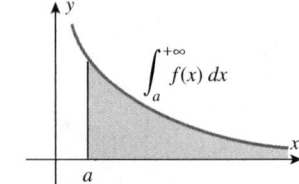

▲ **Figure 7.8.1**

let us begin with the case where f is continuous and nonnegative on $[a, +\infty)$, so we can think of the integral as the area under the curve $y = f(x)$ over the interval $[a, +\infty)$ (Figure 7.8.1). At first, you might be inclined to argue that this area is infinite because the region has infinite extent. However, such an argument would be based on vague intuition rather than precise mathematical logic, since the concept of area has only been defined over intervals of *finite extent*. Thus, before we can make any reasonable statements about the area of the region in Figure 7.8.1, we need to begin by defining what we mean by the area of this region. For that purpose, it will help to focus on a specific example.

Suppose we are interested in the area A of the region that lies below the curve $y = 1/x^2$ and above the interval $[1, +\infty)$ on the x-axis. Instead of trying to find the entire area at once, let us begin by calculating the portion of the area that lies above a finite interval $[1, b]$, where $b > 1$ is arbitrary. That area is

$$\int_1^b \frac{dx}{x^2} = -\frac{1}{x} \Big]_1^b = 1 - \frac{1}{b}$$

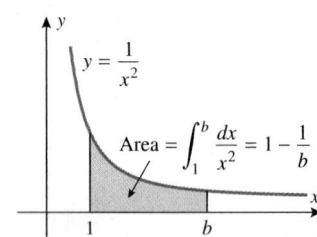

▲ **Figure 7.8.2**

(Figure 7.8.2). If we now allow b to increase so that $b \to +\infty$, then the portion of the area over the interval $[1, b]$ will begin to fill out the area over the entire interval $[1, +\infty)$ (Figure 7.8.3), and hence we can reasonably define the area A under $y = 1/x^2$ over the interval $[1, +\infty)$ to be

$$A = \int_1^{+\infty} \frac{dx}{x^2} = \lim_{b \to +\infty} \int_1^b \frac{dx}{x^2} = \lim_{b \to +\infty} \left(1 - \frac{1}{b}\right) = 1 \tag{1}$$

Thus, the area has a finite value of 1 and is not infinite as we first conjectured.

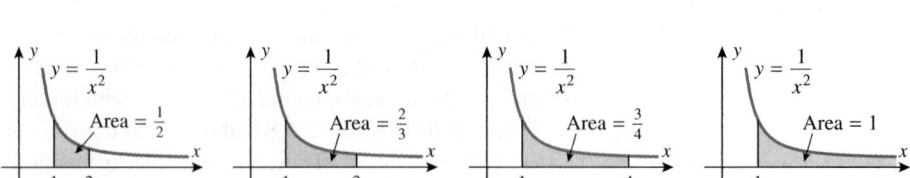

▶ **Figure 7.8.3**

With the preceding discussion as our guide, we make the following definition (which is applicable to functions with both positive and negative values).

If f is nonnegative over the interval $[a, +\infty)$, then the improper integral in Definition 7.8.1 can be interpreted to be the area under the graph of f over the interval $[a, +\infty)$. If the integral converges, then the area is finite and equal to the value of the integral, and if the integral diverges, then the area is regarded to be infinite.

7.8.1   DEFINITION   The *improper integral of f over the interval* $[a, +\infty)$ is defined to be

$$\int_a^{+\infty} f(x)\, dx = \lim_{b \to +\infty} \int_a^b f(x)\, dx$$

In the case where the limit exists, the improper integral is said to **converge**, and the limit is defined to be the value of the integral. In the case where the limit does not exist, the improper integral is said to **diverge**, and it is not assigned a value.

▶ **Example 1**   Evaluate

$$\text{(a)}\ \int_1^{+\infty} \frac{dx}{x^3} \qquad \text{(b)}\ \int_1^{+\infty} \frac{dx}{x}$$

Solution (a).   Following the definition, we replace the infinite upper limit by a finite upper limit b, and then take the limit of the resulting integral. This yields

$$\int_1^{+\infty} \frac{dx}{x^3} = \lim_{b \to +\infty} \int_1^b \frac{dx}{x^3} = \lim_{b \to +\infty} \left[-\frac{1}{2x^2} \right]_1^b = \lim_{b \to +\infty} \left(\frac{1}{2} - \frac{1}{2b^2} \right) = \frac{1}{2}$$

Since the limit is finite, the integral converges and its value is $1/2$.

Solution (b).

$$\int_1^{+\infty} \frac{dx}{x} = \lim_{b \to +\infty} \int_1^b \frac{dx}{x} = \lim_{b \to +\infty} \left[\ln x \right]_1^b = \lim_{b \to +\infty} \ln b = +\infty$$

In this case the integral diverges and hence has no value. ◀

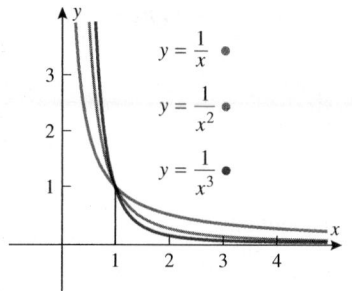

▲ **Figure 7.8.4**

Because the functions $1/x^3$, $1/x^2$, and $1/x$ are nonnegative over the interval $[1, +\infty)$, it follows from (1) and the last example that over this interval the area under $y = 1/x^3$ is $\frac{1}{2}$, the area under $y = 1/x^2$ is 1, and the area under $y = 1/x$ is infinite. However, on the surface the graphs of the three functions seem very much alike (Figure 7.8.4), and there is nothing to suggest why one of the areas should be infinite and the other two finite. One explanation is that $1/x^3$ and $1/x^2$ approach zero more rapidly than $1/x$ as $x \to +\infty$, so that the area over the interval $[1, b]$ accumulates less rapidly under the curves $y = 1/x^3$ and $y = 1/x^2$ than under $y = 1/x$ as $b \to +\infty$, and the difference is just enough that the first two areas are finite and the third is infinite.

▶ **Example 2**   For what values of p does the integral $\displaystyle\int_1^{+\infty} \frac{dx}{x^p}$ converge?

Solution.   We know from the preceding example that the integral diverges if $p = 1$, so let us assume that $p \neq 1$. In this case we have

$$\int_1^{+\infty} \frac{dx}{x^p} = \lim_{b \to +\infty} \int_1^b x^{-p}\, dx = \lim_{b \to +\infty} \frac{x^{1-p}}{1-p} \bigg]_1^b = \lim_{b \to +\infty} \left[\frac{b^{1-p}}{1-p} - \frac{1}{1-p} \right]$$

If $p > 1$, then the exponent $1 - p$ is negative and $b^{1-p} \to 0$ as $b \to +\infty$; and if $p < 1$, then the exponent $1 - p$ is positive and $b^{1-p} \to +\infty$ as $b \to +\infty$. Thus, the integral converges if $p > 1$ and diverges otherwise. In the convergent case the value of the integral is

$$\int_1^{+\infty} \frac{dx}{x^p} = \left[0 - \frac{1}{1-p} \right] = \frac{1}{p-1} \quad (p > 1) \ ◀$$

The following theorem summarizes this result.

7.8.2   THEOREM

$$\int_{1}^{+\infty} \frac{dx}{x^p} = \begin{cases} \dfrac{1}{p-1} & \text{if } p > 1 \\ \text{diverges} & \text{if } p \leq 1 \end{cases}$$

▶ **Example 3**   Evaluate $\displaystyle\int_{0}^{+\infty} (1-x)e^{-x}\, dx$.

Solution.   We begin by evaluating the indefinite integral using integration by parts. Setting $u = 1-x$ and $dv = e^{-x}\, dx$ yields

$$\int (1-x)e^{-x}\, dx = -e^{-x}(1-x) - \int e^{-x}\, dx = -e^{-x} + xe^{-x} + e^{-x} + C = xe^{-x} + C$$

Thus,

$$\int_{0}^{+\infty} (1-x)e^{-x}\, dx = \lim_{b \to +\infty} \int_{0}^{b} (1-x)e^{-x}\, dx = \lim_{b \to +\infty} \left[xe^{-x} \right]_{0}^{b} = \lim_{b \to +\infty} \frac{b}{e^{b}}$$

The limit is an indeterminate form of type ∞/∞, so we will apply L'Hôpital's rule by differentiating the numerator and denominator with respect to b. This yields

$$\int_{0}^{+\infty} (1-x)e^{-x}\, dx = \lim_{b \to +\infty} \frac{1}{e^{b}} = 0$$

We can interpret this to mean that the net signed area between the graph of $y = (1-x)e^{-x}$ and the interval $[0, +\infty)$ is 0 (Figure 7.8.5). ◀

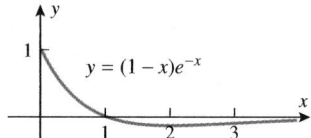

y = (1 − x)e^{−x}

The net signed area between the graph and the interval $[0, +\infty)$ is zero.

▲ **Figure 7.8.5**

If f is nonnegative over the interval $(-\infty, +\infty)$, then the improper integral

$$\int_{-\infty}^{+\infty} f(x)\, dx$$

can be interpreted to be the area under the graph of f over the interval $(-\infty, +\infty)$. The area is finite and equal to the value of the integral if the integral converges and is infinite if it diverges.

7.8.3   DEFINITION   The ***improper integral of f over the interval*** $(-\infty, b]$ is defined to be

$$\int_{-\infty}^{b} f(x)\, dx = \lim_{a \to -\infty} \int_{a}^{b} f(x)\, dx \tag{2}$$

The integral is said to ***converge*** if the limit exists and ***diverge*** if it does not.

The ***improper integral of f over the interval*** $(-\infty, +\infty)$ is defined as

$$\int_{-\infty}^{+\infty} f(x)\, dx = \int_{-\infty}^{c} f(x)\, dx + \int_{c}^{+\infty} f(x)\, dx \tag{3}$$

where c is any real number. The improper integral is said to ***converge*** if *both* terms converge and ***diverge*** if *either* term diverges.

Although we usually choose $c = 0$ in (3), the choice does not matter because it can be proved that neither the convergence nor the value of the integral is affected by the choice of c.

▶ **Example 4**   Evaluate $\displaystyle\int_{-\infty}^{+\infty} \frac{dx}{1+x^2}$.

Solution.   We will evaluate the integral by choosing $c = 0$ in (3). With this value for c we obtain

$$\int_{0}^{+\infty} \frac{dx}{1+x^2} = \lim_{b \to +\infty} \int_{0}^{b} \frac{dx}{1+x^2} = \lim_{b \to +\infty} \left[\tan^{-1} x \right]_{0}^{b} = \lim_{b \to +\infty} (\tan^{-1} b) = \frac{\pi}{2}$$

$$\int_{-\infty}^{0} \frac{dx}{1+x^2} = \lim_{a \to -\infty} \int_{a}^{0} \frac{dx}{1+x^2} = \lim_{a \to -\infty} \left[\tan^{-1} x \right]_{a}^{0} = \lim_{a \to -\infty} (-\tan^{-1} a) = \frac{\pi}{2}$$

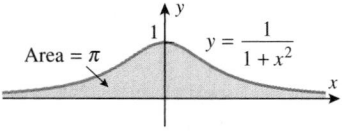

Figure 7.8.6

Thus, the integral converges and its value is

$$\int_{-\infty}^{+\infty} \frac{dx}{1+x^2} = \int_{-\infty}^{0} \frac{dx}{1+x^2} + \int_{0}^{+\infty} \frac{dx}{1+x^2} = \frac{\pi}{2} + \frac{\pi}{2} = \pi$$

Since the integrand is nonnegative on the interval $(-\infty, +\infty)$, the integral represents the area of the region shown in Figure 7.8.6. ◄

■ INTEGRALS WHOSE INTEGRANDS HAVE INFINITE DISCONTINUITIES

Next we will consider improper integrals whose integrands have infinite discontinuities. We will start with the case where the interval of integration is a finite interval $[a, b]$ and the infinite discontinuity occurs at the right-hand endpoint.

To motivate an appropriate definition for such an integral let us consider the case where f is nonnegative on $[a, b]$, so we can interpret the improper integral $\int_{a}^{b} f(x)\,dx$ as the area of the region in Figure 7.8.7a. The problem of finding the area of this region is complicated by the fact that it extends indefinitely in the positive y-direction. However, instead of trying to find the entire area at once, we can proceed indirectly by calculating the portion of the area over the interval $[a, k]$, where $a \le k < b$, and then letting k approach b to fill out the area of the entire region (Figure 7.8.7b). Motivated by this idea, we make the following definition.

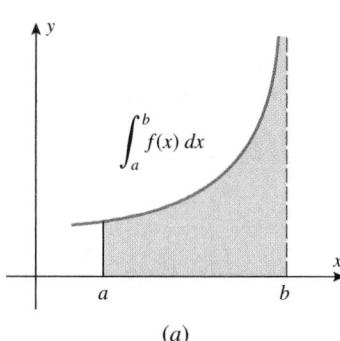

(a)

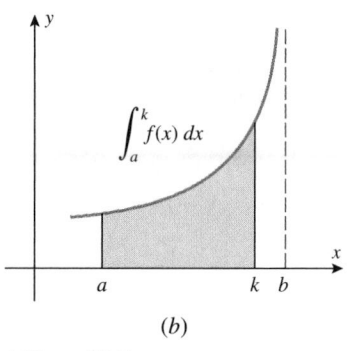

(b)

Figure 7.8.7

7.8.4 DEFINITION If f is continuous on the interval $[a, b]$, except for an infinite discontinuity at b, then the ***improper integral of f over the interval $[a, b]$*** is defined as

$$\int_{a}^{b} f(x)\,dx = \lim_{k \to b^-} \int_{a}^{k} f(x)\,dx \qquad (4)$$

In the case where the indicated limit exists, the improper integral is said to ***converge***, and the limit is defined to be the value of the integral. In the case where the limit does not exist, the improper integral is said to ***diverge***, and it is not assigned a value.

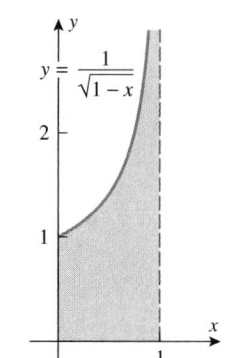

Figure 7.8.8

▶ **Example 5** Evaluate $\int_{0}^{1} \frac{dx}{\sqrt{1-x}}$.

Solution. The integral is improper because the integrand approaches $+\infty$ as x approaches the upper limit 1 from the left (Figure 7.8.8). From (4),

$$\int_{0}^{1} \frac{dx}{\sqrt{1-x}} = \lim_{k \to 1^-} \int_{0}^{k} \frac{dx}{\sqrt{1-x}} = \lim_{k \to 1^-} \left[-2\sqrt{1-x} \right]_{0}^{k}$$

$$= \lim_{k \to 1^-} \left[-2\sqrt{1-k} + 2 \right] = 2 \quad ◄$$

Improper integrals with an infinite discontinuity at the left-hand endpoint or inside the interval of integration are defined as follows.

7.8.5   **DEFINITION**   If f is continuous on the interval $[a, b]$, except for an infinite discontinuity at a, then the ***improper integral of f over the interval $[a, b]$*** is defined as

$$\int_a^b f(x)\,dx = \lim_{k \to a^+} \int_k^b f(x)\,dx \tag{5}$$

The integral is said to ***converge*** if the indicated limit exists and ***diverge*** if it does not.

If f is continuous on the interval $[a, b]$, except for an infinite discontinuity at a point c in (a, b), then the ***improper integral of f over the interval $[a, b]$*** is defined as

$$\int_a^b f(x)\,dx = \int_a^c f(x)\,dx + \int_c^b f(x)\,dx \tag{6}$$

where the two integrals on the right side are themselves improper. The improper integral on the left side is said to ***converge*** if *both* terms on the right side converge and ***diverge*** if *either* term on the right side diverges (Figure 7.8.9).

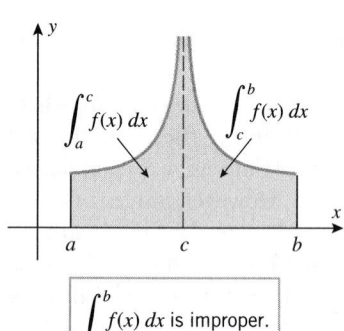

$\int_a^b f(x)\,dx$ is improper.

▲ **Figure 7.8.9**

▶ **Example 6**   Evaluate

$$\text{(a)}\ \int_1^2 \frac{dx}{1 - x} \qquad \text{(b)}\ \int_1^4 \frac{dx}{(x - 2)^{2/3}}$$

Solution (a).   The integral is improper because the integrand approaches $-\infty$ as x approaches the lower limit 1 from the right (Figure 7.8.10). From Definition 7.8.5 we obtain

$$\int_1^2 \frac{dx}{1 - x} = \lim_{k \to 1^+} \int_k^2 \frac{dx}{1 - x} = \lim_{k \to 1^+} \left[-\ln|1 - x| \right]_k^2$$

$$= \lim_{k \to 1^+} \left[-\ln|-1| + \ln|1 - k| \right] = \lim_{k \to 1^+} \ln|1 - k| = -\infty$$

so the integral diverges.

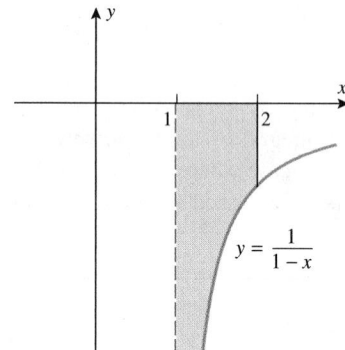

▲ **Figure 7.8.10**

Solution (b).   The integral is improper because the integrand approaches $+\infty$ at $x = 2$, which is inside the interval of integration. From Definition 7.8.5 we obtain

$$\int_1^4 \frac{dx}{(x - 2)^{2/3}} = \int_1^2 \frac{dx}{(x - 2)^{2/3}} + \int_2^4 \frac{dx}{(x - 2)^{2/3}} \tag{7}$$

and we must investigate the convergence of both improper integrals on the right. Since

$$\int_1^2 \frac{dx}{(x - 2)^{2/3}} = \lim_{k \to 2^-} \int_1^k \frac{dx}{(x - 2)^{2/3}} = \lim_{k \to 2^-} \left[3(k - 2)^{1/3} - 3(1 - 2)^{1/3} \right] = 3$$

$$\int_2^4 \frac{dx}{(x - 2)^{2/3}} = \lim_{k \to 2^+} \int_k^4 \frac{dx}{(x - 2)^{2/3}} = \lim_{k \to 2^+} \left[3(4 - 2)^{1/3} - 3(k - 2)^{1/3} \right] = 3\sqrt[3]{2}$$

we have from (7) that

$$\int_1^4 \frac{dx}{(x - 2)^{2/3}} = 3 + 3\sqrt[3]{2} \ \blacktriangleleft$$

WARNING | It is sometimes tempting to apply the Fundamental Theorem of Calculus directly to an improper integral without taking the appropriate limits. To illustrate what can go wrong with this procedure, suppose we fail to recognize that the integral

$$\int_0^2 \frac{dx}{(x-1)^2} \tag{8}$$

is improper and mistakenly evaluate this integral as

$$-\frac{1}{x-1}\bigg]_0^2 = -1 - (1) = -2$$

This result is clearly incorrect because the integrand is never negative and hence the integral cannot be negative! To evaluate (8) correctly we should first write

$$\int_0^2 \frac{dx}{(x-1)^2} = \int_0^1 \frac{dx}{(x-1)^2} + \int_1^2 \frac{dx}{(x-1)^2}$$

and then treat each term as an improper integral. For the first term,

$$\int_0^1 \frac{dx}{(x-1)^2} = \lim_{k \to 1^-} \int_0^k \frac{dx}{(x-1)^2} = \lim_{k \to 1^-}\left[-\frac{1}{k-1} - 1\right] = +\infty$$

so (8) diverges.

■ ARC LENGTH AND SURFACE AREA USING IMPROPER INTEGRALS

In Definitions 6.4.2 and 6.5.2 for arc length and surface area we required the function f to be smooth (continuous first derivative) to ensure the integrability in the resulting formula. However, smoothness is overly restrictive since some of the most basic formulas in geometry involve functions that are not smooth but lead to convergent improper integrals. Accordingly, let us agree to extend the definitions of arc length and surface area to allow functions that are not smooth, but for which the resulting integral in the formula converges.

▶ **Example 7** Derive the formula for the circumference of a circle of radius r.

Solution. For convenience, let us assume that the circle is centered at the origin, in which case its equation is $x^2 + y^2 = r^2$. We will find the arc length of the portion of the circle that lies in the first quadrant and then multiply by 4 to obtain the total circumference (Figure 7.8.11).

Since the equation of the upper semicircle is $y = \sqrt{r^2 - x^2}$, it follows from Formula (4) of Section 6.4 that the circumference C is

$$C = 4\int_0^r \sqrt{1 + (dy/dx)^2}\,dx = 4\int_0^r \sqrt{1 + \left(-\frac{x}{\sqrt{r^2 - x^2}}\right)^2}\,dx$$
$$= 4r\int_0^r \frac{dx}{\sqrt{r^2 - x^2}}$$

This integral is improper because of the infinite discontinuity at $x = r$, and hence we evaluate it by writing

$$C = 4r \lim_{k \to r^-} \int_0^k \frac{dx}{\sqrt{r^2 - x^2}}$$
$$= 4r \lim_{k \to r^-}\left[\sin^{-1}\left(\frac{x}{r}\right)\right]_0^k \quad \boxed{\text{Formula (77) in the Endpaper Integral Table}}$$
$$= 4r \lim_{k \to r^-}\left[\sin^{-1}\left(\frac{k}{r}\right) - \sin^{-1} 0\right]$$
$$= 4r[\sin^{-1} 1 - \sin^{-1} 0] = 4r\left(\frac{\pi}{2} - 0\right) = 2\pi r \ ◀$$

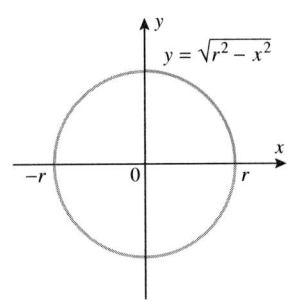

▲ **Figure 7.8.11**

$y = \sqrt{r^2 - x^2}$

✔ **QUICK CHECK EXERCISES 7.8**   *(See page 557 for answers.)*

1. In each part, determine whether the integral is improper, and if so, explain why. Do not evaluate the integrals.

   (a) $\displaystyle\int_{\pi/4}^{3\pi/4} \cot x\, dx$ (b) $\displaystyle\int_{\pi/4}^{\pi} \cot x\, dx$

   (c) $\displaystyle\int_{0}^{+\infty} \frac{1}{x^2+1}\, dx$ (d) $\displaystyle\int_{1}^{+\infty} \frac{1}{x^2-1}\, dx$

2. Express each improper integral in Quick Check Exercise 1 in terms of one or more appropriate limits. Do not evaluate the limits.

3. The improper integral

   $$\int_{1}^{+\infty} x^{-p}\, dx$$

   converges to _____ provided _____.

4. Evaluate the integrals that converge.

   (a) $\displaystyle\int_{0}^{+\infty} e^{-x}\, dx$ (b) $\displaystyle\int_{0}^{+\infty} e^{x}\, dx$

   (c) $\displaystyle\int_{0}^{1} \frac{1}{x^3}\, dx$ (d) $\displaystyle\int_{0}^{1} \frac{1}{\sqrt[3]{x^2}}\, dx$

EXERCISE SET 7.8   ∼ Graphing Utility   [c] CAS

---

1. In each part, determine whether the integral is improper, and if so, explain why.

   (a) $\displaystyle\int_{1}^{5} \frac{dx}{x-3}$ (b) $\displaystyle\int_{1}^{5} \frac{dx}{x+3}$ (c) $\displaystyle\int_{0}^{1} \ln x\, dx$

   (d) $\displaystyle\int_{1}^{+\infty} e^{-x}\, dx$ (e) $\displaystyle\int_{-\infty}^{+\infty} \frac{dx}{\sqrt[3]{x-1}}$ (f) $\displaystyle\int_{0}^{\pi/4} \tan x\, dx$

2. In each part, determine all values of p for which the integral is improper.

   (a) $\displaystyle\int_{0}^{1} \frac{dx}{x^p}$ (b) $\displaystyle\int_{1}^{2} \frac{dx}{x-p}$ (c) $\displaystyle\int_{0}^{1} e^{-px}\, dx$

3–32 Evaluate the integrals that converge. ▨

3. $\displaystyle\int_{0}^{+\infty} e^{-2x}\, dx$ 4. $\displaystyle\int_{-1}^{+\infty} \frac{x}{1+x^2}\, dx$

5. $\displaystyle\int_{3}^{+\infty} \frac{2}{x^2-1}\, dx$ 6. $\displaystyle\int_{0}^{+\infty} xe^{-x^2}\, dx$

7. $\displaystyle\int_{e}^{+\infty} \frac{1}{x\ln^3 x}\, dx$ 8. $\displaystyle\int_{2}^{+\infty} \frac{1}{x\sqrt{\ln x}}\, dx$

9. $\displaystyle\int_{-\infty}^{0} \frac{dx}{(2x-1)^3}$ 10. $\displaystyle\int_{-\infty}^{3} \frac{dx}{x^2+9}$

11. $\displaystyle\int_{-\infty}^{0} e^{3x}\, dx$ 12. $\displaystyle\int_{-\infty}^{0} \frac{e^x\, dx}{3-2e^x}$

13. $\displaystyle\int_{-\infty}^{+\infty} x\, dx$ 14. $\displaystyle\int_{-\infty}^{+\infty} \frac{x}{\sqrt{x^2+2}}\, dx$

15. $\displaystyle\int_{-\infty}^{+\infty} \frac{x}{(x^2+3)^2}\, dx$ 16. $\displaystyle\int_{-\infty}^{+\infty} \frac{e^{-t}}{1+e^{-2t}}\, dt$

17. $\displaystyle\int_{0}^{4} \frac{dx}{(x-4)^2}$ 18. $\displaystyle\int_{0}^{8} \frac{dx}{\sqrt[3]{x}}$

19. $\displaystyle\int_{0}^{\pi/2} \tan x\, dx$ 20. $\displaystyle\int_{0}^{4} \frac{dx}{\sqrt{4-x}}$

21. $\displaystyle\int_{0}^{1} \frac{dx}{\sqrt{1-x^2}}$ 22. $\displaystyle\int_{-3}^{1} \frac{x\, dx}{\sqrt{9-x^2}}$

23. $\displaystyle\int_{\pi/3}^{\pi/2} \frac{\sin x}{\sqrt{1-2\cos x}}\, dx$ 24. $\displaystyle\int_{0}^{\pi/4} \frac{\sec^2 x}{1-\tan x}\, dx$

25. $\displaystyle\int_{0}^{3} \frac{dx}{x-2}$ 26. $\displaystyle\int_{-2}^{2} \frac{dx}{x^2}$

27. $\displaystyle\int_{-1}^{8} x^{-1/3}\, dx$ 28. $\displaystyle\int_{0}^{1} \frac{dx}{(x-1)^{2/3}}$

29. $\displaystyle\int_{0}^{+\infty} \frac{1}{x^2}\, dx$ 30. $\displaystyle\int_{1}^{+\infty} \frac{dx}{x\sqrt{x^2-1}}$

31. $\displaystyle\int_{0}^{1} \frac{dx}{\sqrt{x}(x+1)}$ 32. $\displaystyle\int_{0}^{+\infty} \frac{dx}{\sqrt{x}(x+1)}$

33–36 True–False Determine whether the statement is true or false. Explain your answer. ▨

33. $\displaystyle\int_{1}^{+\infty} x^{-4/3}\, dx$ converges to 3.

34. If f is continuous on $[a, +\infty]$ and $\lim_{x\to+\infty} f(x) = 1$, then $\int_{a}^{+\infty} f(x)\, dx$ converges.

35. $\displaystyle\int_{1}^{2} \frac{1}{x(x-3)}\, dx$ is an improper integral.

36. $\displaystyle\int_{-1}^{1} \frac{1}{x^3}\, dx = 0$

37–40 Make the u-substitution and evaluate the resulting definite integral. ▨

37. $\displaystyle\int_{0}^{+\infty} \frac{e^{-\sqrt{x}}}{\sqrt{x}}\, dx;\ u = \sqrt{x}$ [*Note:* $u \to +\infty$ as $x \to +\infty$.]

38. $\displaystyle\int_{12}^{+\infty} \frac{dx}{\sqrt{x}(x+4)};\ u = \sqrt{x}$ [*Note:* $u \to +\infty$ as $x \to +\infty$.]

39. $\displaystyle\int_{0}^{+\infty} \frac{e^{-x}}{\sqrt{1-e^{-x}}}\, dx;\ u = 1 - e^{-x}$
   [*Note:* $u \to 1$ as $x \to +\infty$.]

40. $\displaystyle\int_0^{+\infty} \frac{e^{-x}}{\sqrt{1-e^{-2x}}}\,dx; \quad u = e^{-x}$

C **41–42** Express the improper integral as a limit, and then evaluate that limit with a CAS. Confirm the answer by evaluating the integral directly with the CAS. ■

41. $\displaystyle\int_0^{+\infty} e^{-x}\cos x\,dx$ **42.** $\displaystyle\int_0^{+\infty} xe^{-3x}\,dx$

C **43.** In each part, try to evaluate the integral exactly with a CAS. If your result is not a simple numerical answer, then use the CAS to find a numerical approximation of the integral.

(a) $\displaystyle\int_{-\infty}^{+\infty} \frac{1}{x^8+x+1}\,dx$ (b) $\displaystyle\int_0^{+\infty} \frac{1}{\sqrt{1+x^3}}\,dx$

(c) $\displaystyle\int_1^{+\infty} \frac{\ln x}{e^x}\,dx$ (d) $\displaystyle\int_1^{+\infty} \frac{\sin x}{x^2}\,dx$

C **44.** In each part, confirm the result with a CAS.

(a) $\displaystyle\int_0^{+\infty} \frac{\sin x}{\sqrt{x}}\,dx = \sqrt{\frac{\pi}{2}}$ (b) $\displaystyle\int_{-\infty}^{+\infty} e^{-x^2}\,dx = \sqrt{\pi}$

(c) $\displaystyle\int_0^1 \frac{\ln x}{1+x}\,dx = -\frac{\pi^2}{12}$

45. Find the length of the curve $y = (4 - x^{2/3})^{3/2}$ over the interval $[0, 8]$.

46. Find the length of the curve $y = \sqrt{4-x^2}$ over the interval $[0, 2]$.

47–48 Use L'Hôpital's rule to help evaluate the improper integral. ■

47. $\displaystyle\int_0^1 \ln x\,dx$ **48.** $\displaystyle\int_1^{+\infty} \frac{\ln x}{x^2}\,dx$

49. Find the area of the region between the x-axis and the curve $y = e^{-3x}$ for $x \geq 0$.

50. Find the area of the region between the x-axis and the curve $y = 8/(x^2 - 4)$ for $x \geq 4$.

51. Suppose that the region between the x-axis and the curve $y = e^{-x}$ for $x \geq 0$ is revolved about the x-axis.
(a) Find the volume of the solid that is generated.
(b) Find the surface area of the solid.

FOCUS ON CONCEPTS

52. Suppose that f and g are continuous functions and that

$$0 \leq f(x) \leq g(x)$$

if $x \geq a$. Give a reasonable informal argument using areas to explain why the following results are true.
(a) If $\int_a^{+\infty} f(x)\,dx$ diverges, then $\int_a^{+\infty} g(x)\,dx$ diverges.
(b) If $\int_a^{+\infty} g(x)\,dx$ converges, then $\int_a^{+\infty} f(x)\,dx$ converges and $\int_a^{+\infty} f(x)\,dx \leq \int_a^{+\infty} g(x)\,dx$.
[*Note:* The results in this exercise are sometimes called **comparison tests** for improper integrals.]

53–56 Use the results in Exercise 52. ■

53. (a) Confirm graphically and algebraically that

$$e^{-x^2} \leq e^{-x} \quad (x \geq 1)$$

(b) Evaluate the integral

$$\int_1^{+\infty} e^{-x}\,dx$$

(c) What does the result obtained in part (b) tell you about the integral

$$\int_1^{+\infty} e^{-x^2}\,dx?$$

54. (a) Confirm graphically and algebraically that

$$\frac{1}{2x+1} \leq \frac{e^x}{2x+1} \quad (x \geq 0)$$

(b) Evaluate the integral

$$\int_0^{+\infty} \frac{dx}{2x+1}$$

(c) What does the result obtained in part (b) tell you about the integral

$$\int_0^{+\infty} \frac{e^x}{2x+1}\,dx?$$

55. Let R be the region to the right of $x = 1$ that is bounded by the x-axis and the curve $y = 1/x$. When this region is revolved about the x-axis it generates a solid whose surface is known as **Gabriel's Horn** (for reasons that should be clear from the accompanying figure). Show that the solid has a finite volume but its surface has an infinite area. [*Note:* It has been suggested that if one could saturate the interior of the solid with paint and allow it to seep through to the surface, then one could paint an infinite surface with a finite amount of paint! What do you think?]

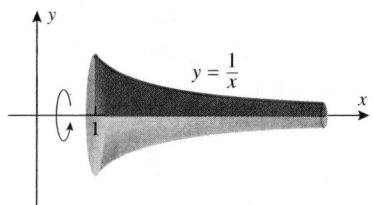

$y = \dfrac{1}{x}$

◀ **Figure Ex-55**

56. In each part, use Exercise 52 to determine whether the integral converges or diverges. If it converges, then use part (b) of that exercise to find an upper bound on the value of the integral.

(a) $\displaystyle\int_2^{+\infty} \frac{\sqrt{x^3+1}}{x}\,dx$ (b) $\displaystyle\int_2^{+\infty} \frac{x}{x^5+1}\,dx$

(c) $\displaystyle\int_0^{+\infty} \frac{xe^x}{2x+1}\,dx$

FOCUS ON CONCEPTS

57. Sketch the region whose area is
$$\int_0^{+\infty} \frac{dx}{1+x^2}$$
and use your sketch to show that
$$\int_0^{+\infty} \frac{dx}{1+x^2} = \int_0^1 \sqrt{\frac{1-y}{y}}\, dy$$

58. (a) Give a reasonable informal argument, based on areas, that explains why the integrals
$$\int_0^{+\infty} \sin x\, dx \quad \text{and} \quad \int_0^{+\infty} \cos x\, dx$$
diverge.
(b) Show that $\displaystyle\int_0^{+\infty} \frac{\cos\sqrt{x}}{\sqrt{x}}\, dx$ diverges.

59. In electromagnetic theory, the magnetic potential at a point on the axis of a circular coil is given by
$$u = \frac{2\pi N I r}{k} \int_a^{+\infty} \frac{dx}{(r^2+x^2)^{3/2}}$$
where N, I, r, k, and a are constants. Find u.

C 60. The *average speed*, $\bar{v}$, of the molecules of an ideal gas is given by
$$\bar{v} = \frac{4}{\sqrt{\pi}}\left(\frac{M}{2RT}\right)^{3/2}\int_0^{+\infty} v^3 e^{-Mv^2/(2RT)}\, dv$$
and the *root-mean-square speed*, v_{rms}, by
$$v_{\mathrm{rms}}^2 = \frac{4}{\sqrt{\pi}}\left(\frac{M}{2RT}\right)^{3/2}\int_0^{+\infty} v^4 e^{-Mv^2/(2RT)}\, dv$$
where v is the molecular speed, T is the gas temperature, M is the molecular weight of the gas, and R is the gas constant.
(a) Use a CAS to show that
$$\int_0^{+\infty} x^3 e^{-a^2 x^2}\, dx = \frac{1}{2a^4}, \quad a > 0$$
and use this result to show that $\bar{v} = \sqrt{8RT/(\pi M)}$.
(b) Use a CAS to show that
$$\int_0^{+\infty} x^4 e^{-a^2 x^2}\, dx = \frac{3\sqrt{\pi}}{8a^5}, \quad a > 0$$
and use this result to show that $v_{\mathrm{rms}} = \sqrt{3RT/M}$.

61. In Exercise 25 of Section 6.6, we determined the work required to lift a 6000 lb satellite to an orbital position that is 1000 mi above the Earth's surface. The ideas discussed in that exercise will be needed here.
(a) Find a definite integral that represents the work required to lift a 6000 lb satellite to a position b miles above the Earth's surface.
(b) Find a definite integral that represents the work required to lift a 6000 lb satellite an "infinite distance" above the Earth's surface. Evaluate the integral. [*Note:* The result obtained here is sometimes called the work required to "escape" the Earth's gravity.]

62–63 A *transform* is a formula that converts or "transforms" one function into another. Transforms are used in applications to convert a difficult problem into an easier problem whose solution can then be used to solve the original difficult problem. The *Laplace transform* of a function $f(t)$, which plays an important role in the study of differential equations, is denoted by $\mathcal{L}\{f(t)\}$ and is defined by
$$\mathcal{L}\{f(t)\} = \int_0^{+\infty} e^{-st} f(t)\, dt$$
In this formula s is treated as a constant in the integration process; thus, the Laplace transform has the effect of transforming $f(t)$ into a function of s. Use this formula in these exercises. ■

62. Show that
(a) $\mathcal{L}\{1\} = \dfrac{1}{s}, \; s > 0$ (b) $\mathcal{L}\{e^{2t}\} = \dfrac{1}{s-2}, \; s > 2$
(c) $\mathcal{L}\{\sin t\} = \dfrac{1}{s^2+1}, \; s > 0$
(d) $\mathcal{L}\{\cos t\} = \dfrac{s}{s^2+1}, \; s > 0$.

63. In each part, find the Laplace transform.
(a) $f(t) = t, \; s > 0$ (b) $f(t) = t^2, \; s > 0$
(c) $f(t) = \begin{cases} 0, & t < 3 \\ 1, & t \geq 3 \end{cases}, \; s > 0$

C 64. Later in the text, we will show that
$$\int_0^{+\infty} e^{-x^2}\, dx = \tfrac{1}{2}\sqrt{\pi}$$
Confirm that this is reasonable by using a CAS or a calculator with a numerical integration capability.

65. Use the result in Exercise 64 to show that
(a) $\displaystyle\int_{-\infty}^{+\infty} e^{-ax^2}\, dx = \sqrt{\dfrac{\pi}{a}}, \; a > 0$
(b) $\dfrac{1}{\sqrt{2\pi}\sigma}\displaystyle\int_{-\infty}^{+\infty} e^{-x^2/2\sigma^2}\, dx = 1, \; \sigma > 0$.

66–67 A convergent improper integral over an infinite interval can be approximated by first replacing the infinite limit(s) of integration by finite limit(s), then using a numerical integration technique, such as Simpson's rule, to approximate the integral with finite limit(s). This technique is illustrated in these exercises. ■

66. Suppose that the integral in Exercise 64 is approximated by first writing it as
$$\int_0^{+\infty} e^{-x^2}\, dx = \int_0^K e^{-x^2}\, dx + \int_K^{+\infty} e^{-x^2}\, dx$$
then dropping the second term, and then applying Simpson's rule to the integral
$$\int_0^K e^{-x^2}\, dx$$
The resulting approximation has two sources of error: the error from Simpson's rule and the error
$$E = \int_K^{+\infty} e^{-x^2}\, dx$$
(cont.)

that results from discarding the second term. We call E the *truncation error*.

(a) Approximate the integral in Exercise 64 by applying Simpson's rule with $n = 10$ subdivisions to the integral

$$\int_0^3 e^{-x^2}\, dx$$

Round your answer to four decimal places and compare it to $\frac{1}{2}\sqrt{\pi}$ rounded to four decimal places.

(b) Use the result that you obtained in Exercise 52 and the fact that $e^{-x^2} \le \frac{1}{3}xe^{-x^2}$ for $x \ge 3$ to show that the truncation error for the approximation in part (a) satisfies $0 < E < 2.1 \times 10^{-5}$.

67. (a) It can be shown that

$$\int_0^{+\infty} \frac{1}{x^6 + 1}\, dx = \frac{\pi}{3}$$

Approximate this integral by applying Simpson's rule with $n = 20$ subdivisions to the integral

$$\int_0^4 \frac{1}{x^6 + 1}\, dx$$

Round your answer to three decimal places and compare it to $\pi/3$ rounded to three decimal places.

(b) Use the result that you obtained in Exercise 52 and the fact that $1/(x^6 + 1) < 1/x^6$ for $x \ge 4$ to show that the truncation error for the approximation in part (a) satisfies $0 < E < 2 \times 10^{-4}$.

68. For what values of p does $\displaystyle\int_0^{+\infty} e^{px}\, dx$ converge?

69. Show that $\displaystyle\int_0^1 dx/x^p$ converges if $p < 1$ and diverges if $p \ge 1$.

c 70. It is sometimes possible to convert an improper integral into a "proper" integral having the same value by making an appropriate substitution. Evaluate the following integral by making the indicated substitution, and investigate what happens if you evaluate the integral directly using a CAS.

$$\int_0^1 \sqrt{\frac{1+x}{1-x}}\, dx; \quad u = \sqrt{1-x}$$

71–72 Transform the given improper integral into a proper integral by making the stated u-substitution; then approximate the proper integral by Simpson's rule with $n = 10$ subdivisions. Round your answer to three decimal places. ■

71. $\displaystyle\int_0^1 \frac{\cos x}{\sqrt{x}}\, dx; \quad u = \sqrt{x}$

72. $\displaystyle\int_0^1 \frac{\sin x}{\sqrt{1-x}}\, dx; \quad u = \sqrt{1-x}$

73. Writing What is "improper" about an integral over an infinite interval? Explain why Definition 5.5.1 for $\int_a^b f(x)\, dx$ fails for $\int_a^{+\infty} f(x)\, dx$. Discuss a strategy for assigning a value to $\int_a^{+\infty} f(x)\, dx$.

74. Writing What is "improper" about a definite integral over an interval on which the integrand has an infinite discontinuity? Explain why Definition 5.5.1 for $\int_a^b f(x)\, dx$ fails if the graph of f has a vertical asymptote at $x = a$. Discuss a strategy for assigning a value to $\int_a^b f(x)\, dx$ in this circumstance.

✔ QUICK CHECK ANSWERS 7.8

1. (a) proper (b) improper, since $\cot x$ has an infinite discontinuity at $x = \pi$ (c) improper, since there is an infinite interval of integration (d) improper, since there is an infinite interval of integration and the integrand has an infinite discontinuity at $x = 1$

2. (b) $\displaystyle\lim_{b \to \pi^-} \int_{\pi/4}^b \cot x\, dx$ (c) $\displaystyle\lim_{b \to +\infty} \int_0^b \frac{1}{x^2 + 1}\, dx$ (d) $\displaystyle\lim_{a \to 1^+} \int_a^2 \frac{1}{x^2 - 1}\, dx + \lim_{b \to +\infty} \int_2^b \frac{1}{x^2 - 1}\, dx$ **3.** $\displaystyle\frac{1}{p-1}$; $p > 1$

4. (a) 1 (b) diverges (c) diverges (d) 3

CHAPTER 7 REVIEW EXERCISES

1–6 Evaluate the given integral with the aid of an appropriate u-substitution. ■

1. $\displaystyle\int \sqrt{4 + 9x}\, dx$

2. $\displaystyle\int \frac{1}{\sec \pi x}\, dx$

3. $\displaystyle\int \sqrt{\cos x}\, \sin x\, dx$

4. $\displaystyle\int \frac{dx}{x \ln x}$

5. $\displaystyle\int x \tan^2(x^2) \sec^2(x^2)\, dx$

6. $\displaystyle\int_0^9 \frac{\sqrt{x}}{x + 9}\, dx$

7. (a) Evaluate the integral

$$\int \frac{1}{\sqrt{2x - x^2}}\, dx$$

three ways: using the substitution $u = \sqrt{x}$, using the substitution $u = \sqrt{2 - x}$, and completing the square.

(b) Show that the answers in part (a) are equivalent.

8. Evaluate the integral $\int_0^1 \frac{x^3}{\sqrt{x^2+1}}\,dx$

(a) using integration by parts

(b) using the substitution $u = \sqrt{x^2+1}$.

9–12 Use integration by parts to evaluate the integral. ■

9. $\int xe^{-x}\,dx$

10. $\int x\sin 2x\,dx$

11. $\int \ln(2x+3)\,dx$

12. $\int_0^{1/2} \tan^{-1}(2x)\,dx$

13. Evaluate $\int 8x^4 \cos 2x\,dx$ using tabular integration by parts.

14. A particle moving along the x-axis has velocity function $v(t) = t^2 e^{-t}$. How far does the particle travel from time $t = 0$ to $t = 5$?

15–20 Evaluate the integral. ■

15. $\int \sin^2 5\theta\,d\theta$

16. $\int \sin^3 2x \cos^2 2x\,dx$

17. $\int \sin x \cos 2x\,dx$

18. $\int_0^{\pi/6} \sin 2x \cos 4x\,dx$

19. $\int \sin^4 2x\,dx$

20. $\int x \cos^5(x^2)\,dx$

21–26 Evaluate the integral by making an appropriate trigonometric substitution. ■

21. $\int \frac{x^2}{\sqrt{9-x^2}}\,dx$

22. $\int \frac{dx}{x^2\sqrt{16-x^2}}$

23. $\int \frac{dx}{\sqrt{x^2-1}}$

24. $\int \frac{x^2}{\sqrt{x^2-25}}\,dx$

25. $\int \frac{x^2}{\sqrt{9+x^2}}\,dx$

26. $\int \frac{\sqrt{1+4x^2}}{x}\,dx$

27–32 Evaluate the integral using the method of partial fractions. ■

27. $\int \frac{dx}{x^2+3x-4}$

28. $\int \frac{dx}{x^2+8x+7}$

29. $\int \frac{x^2+2}{x+2}\,dx$

30. $\int \frac{x^2+x-16}{(x-1)(x-3)^2}\,dx$

31. $\int \frac{x^2}{(x+2)^3}\,dx$

32. $\int \frac{dx}{x^3+x}$

33. Consider the integral $\int \frac{1}{x^3-x}\,dx$.

(a) Evaluate the integral using the substitution $x = \sec\theta$. For what values of x is your result valid?

(b) Evaluate the integral using the substitution $x = \sin\theta$. For what values of x is your result valid?

(c) Evaluate the integral using the method of partial fractions. For what values of x is your result valid?

34. Find the area of the region that is enclosed by the curves $y = (x-3)/(x^3+x^2)$, $y = 0$, $x = 1$, and $x = 2$.

35–40 Use the Endpaper Integral Table to evaluate the integral. ■

35. $\int \sin 7x \cos 9x\,dx$

36. $\int (x^3-x^2)e^{-x}\,dx$

37. $\int x\sqrt{x-x^2}\,dx$

38. $\int \frac{dx}{x\sqrt{4x+3}}$

39. $\int \tan^2 2x\,dx$

40. $\int \frac{3x-1}{2+x^2}\,dx$

41–42 Approximate the integral using (a) the midpoint approximation M_{10}, (b) the trapezoidal approximation T_{10}, and (c) Simpson's rule approximation S_{20}. In each case, find the exact value of the integral and approximate the absolute error. Express your answers to at least four decimal places. ■

41. $\int_1^3 \frac{1}{\sqrt{x+1}}\,dx$

42. $\int_{-1}^1 \frac{1}{1+x^2}\,dx$

43–44 Use inequalities (12), (13), and (14) of Section 7.7 to find upper bounds on the errors in parts (a), (b), or (c) of the indicated exercise. ■

43. Exercise 41

44. Exercise 42

45–46 Use inequalities (12), (13), and (14) of Section 7.7 to find a number n of subintervals for (a) the midpoint approximation M_n, (b) the trapezoidal approximation T_n, and (c) Simpson's rule approximation S_n to ensure the absolute error will be less than 10^{-4}. ■

45. Exercise 41

46. Exercise 42

47–50 Evaluate the integral if it converges. ■

47. $\int_0^{+\infty} e^{-x}\,dx$

48. $\int_{-\infty}^2 \frac{dx}{x^2+4}$

49. $\int_0^9 \frac{dx}{\sqrt{9-x}}$

50. $\int_0^1 \frac{1}{2x-1}\,dx$

51. Find the area that is enclosed between the x-axis and the curve $y = (\ln x - 1)/x^2$ for $x \geq e$.

52. Find the volume of the solid that is generated when the region between the x-axis and the curve $y = e^{-x}$ for $x \geq 0$ is revolved about the y-axis.

53. Find a positive value of a that satisfies the equation

$$\int_0^{+\infty} \frac{1}{x^2+a^2}\,dx = 1$$

54. Consider the following methods for evaluating integrals: u-substitution, integration by parts, partial fractions, reduction formulas, and trigonometric substitutions. In each part, state the approach that you would try first to evaluate the integral. If none of them seems appropriate, then say so. You need not evaluate the integral.

(a) $\int x \sin x\,dx$

(b) $\int \cos x \sin x\,dx$

(cont.)

(c) $\int \tan^7 x \, dx$

(d) $\int \tan^7 x \sec^2 x \, dx$

(e) $\int \dfrac{3x^2}{x^3+1} \, dx$

(f) $\int \dfrac{3x^2}{(x+1)^3} \, dx$

(g) $\int \tan^{-1} x \, dx$

(h) $\int \sqrt{4-x^2} \, dx$

(i) $\int x\sqrt{4-x^2} \, dx$

55–74 Evaluate the integral.

55. $\int \dfrac{dx}{(3+x^2)^{3/2}}$

56. $\int x \cos 3x \, dx$

57. $\int_0^{\pi/4} \tan^7 \theta \, d\theta$

58. $\int \dfrac{\cos\theta}{\sin^2\theta - 6\sin\theta + 12} \, d\theta$

59. $\int \sin^2 2x \cos^3 2x \, dx$

60. $\int_0^4 \dfrac{1}{(x-3)^2} \, dx$

61. $\int e^{2x} \cos 3x \, dx$

62. $\int_{-1/\sqrt{2}}^{1/\sqrt{2}} (1-2x^2)^{3/2} \, dx$

63. $\int \dfrac{dx}{(x-1)(x+2)(x-3)}$

64. $\int_0^{1/3} \dfrac{dx}{(4-9x^2)^2}$

65. $\int_4^8 \dfrac{\sqrt{x-4}}{x} \, dx$

66. $\int_0^{\ln 2} \sqrt{e^x - 1} \, dx$

67. $\int \dfrac{1}{\sqrt{e^x + 1}} \, dx$

68. $\int \dfrac{dx}{x(x^2+x+1)}$

69. $\int_0^{1/2} \sin^{-1} x \, dx$

70. $\int \tan^5 4x \sec^4 4x \, dx$

71. $\int \dfrac{x+3}{\sqrt{x^2+2x+2}} \, dx$

72. $\int \dfrac{\sec^2\theta}{\tan^3\theta - \tan^2\theta} \, d\theta$

73. $\int_a^{+\infty} \dfrac{x}{(x^2+1)^2} \, dx$

74. $\int_0^{+\infty} \dfrac{dx}{a^2+b^2x^2}, \quad a,b>0$

CHAPTER 7 MAKING CONNECTIONS   C CAS

1. Recall from Theorem 3.3.1 and the discussion preceding it that if $f'(x)>0$, then the function f is increasing and has an inverse function. Parts (a), (b), and (c) of this problem show that if this condition is satisfied and if f' is continuous, then a definite integral of f^{-1} can be expressed in terms of a definite integral of f.

(a) Use integration by parts to show that
$$\int_a^b f(x)\,dx = bf(b) - af(a) - \int_a^b xf'(x)\,dx$$

(b) Use the result in part (a) to show that if $y = f(x)$, then
$$\int_a^b f(x)\,dx = bf(b) - af(a) - \int_{f(a)}^{f(b)} f^{-1}(y)\,dy$$

(c) Show that if we let $\alpha = f(a)$ and $\beta = f(b)$, then the result in part (b) can be written as
$$\int_\alpha^\beta f^{-1}(x)\,dx = \beta f^{-1}(\beta) - \alpha f^{-1}(\alpha) - \int_{f^{-1}(\alpha)}^{f^{-1}(\beta)} f(x)\,dx$$

2. In each part, use the result in Exercise 1 to obtain the equation, and then confirm that the equation is correct by performing the integrations.

(a) $\int_0^{1/2} \sin^{-1} x \, dx = \frac{1}{2}\sin^{-1}\left(\frac{1}{2}\right) - \int_0^{\pi/6} \sin x \, dx$

(b) $\int_e^{e^2} \ln x \, dx = (2e^2 - e) - \int_1^2 e^x \, dx$

3. The *Gamma function*, $\Gamma(x)$, is defined as
$$\Gamma(x) = \int_0^{+\infty} t^{x-1}e^{-t}\,dt$$
It can be shown that this improper integral converges if and only if $x>0$.

(a) Find $\Gamma(1)$.

(b) Prove: $\Gamma(x+1) = x\Gamma(x)$ for all $x>0$. [*Hint:* Use integration by parts.]

(c) Use the results in parts (a) and (b) to find $\Gamma(2)$, $\Gamma(3)$, and $\Gamma(4)$; and then make a conjecture about $\Gamma(n)$ for positive integer values of n.

(d) Show that $\Gamma\left(\frac{1}{2}\right) = \sqrt{\pi}$. [*Hint:* See Exercise 64 of Section 7.8.]

(e) Use the results obtained in parts (b) and (d) to show that $\Gamma\left(\frac{3}{2}\right) = \frac{1}{2}\sqrt{\pi}$ and $\Gamma\left(\frac{5}{2}\right) = \frac{3}{4}\sqrt{\pi}$.

4. Refer to the Gamma function defined in Exercise 3 to show that

(a) $\int_0^1 (\ln x)^n \, dx = (-1)^n \Gamma(n+1), \quad n>0$

[*Hint:* Let $t = -\ln x$.]

(b) $\int_0^{+\infty} e^{-x^n} \, dx = \Gamma\left(\dfrac{n+1}{n}\right), \quad n>0$.

[*Hint:* Let $t = x^n$. Use the result in Exercise 3(b).]

C 5. A *simple pendulum* consists of a mass that swings in a vertical plane at the end of a massless rod of length L, as shown in the accompanying figure. Suppose that a simple pendulum is displaced through an angle θ_0 and released from rest. It can be shown that in the absence of friction, the time T required for the pendulum to make one complete back-and-forth swing, called the *period*, is given by

$$T = \sqrt{\frac{8L}{g}} \int_0^{\theta_0} \frac{1}{\sqrt{\cos\theta - \cos\theta_0}} \, d\theta \qquad (1)$$

where $\theta = \theta(t)$ is the angle the pendulum makes with the vertical at time t. The improper integral in (1) is difficult to evaluate numerically. By a substitution outlined below it can be shown that the period can be expressed as

$$T = 4\sqrt{\frac{L}{g}} \int_0^{\pi/2} \frac{1}{\sqrt{1 - k^2 \sin^2\phi}} \, d\phi \qquad (2)$$

where $k = \sin(\theta_0/2)$. The integral in (2) is called a ***complete elliptic integral of the first kind*** and is more easily evaluated by numerical methods.

(a) Obtain (2) from (1) by substituting

$$\cos\theta = 1 - 2\sin^2(\theta/2)$$
$$\cos\theta_0 = 1 - 2\sin^2(\theta_0/2)$$
$$k = \sin(\theta_0/2)$$

and then making the change of variable

$$\sin\phi = \frac{\sin(\theta/2)}{\sin(\theta_0/2)} = \frac{\sin(\theta/2)}{k}$$

(b) Use (2) and the numerical integration capability of your CAS to estimate the period of a simple pendulum for which $L = 1.5$ ft, $\theta_0 = 20°$, and $g = 32$ ft/s^2.

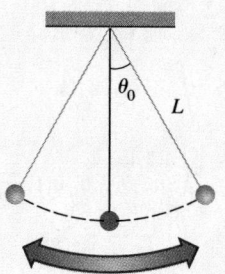

◀ **Figure Ex-5**

 **EXPANDING THE CALCULUS HORIZON**

To learn how numerical integration can be applied to the cost analysis of an engineering project, see the module entitled **Railroad Design** at:

www.wiley.com/college/anton

Photo by Milton Bell, Texas Archeological Research Laboratory, The University of Texas at Austin.

8

MATHEMATICAL MODELING WITH DIFFERENTIAL EQUATIONS

In the 1920's, excavation of an archeological site in Folsom, N.M. uncovered a collection of prehistoric stone spearheads now known as "Folsom points." In 1950, carbon dating of charred bison bones found nearby confirmed that human hunters lived in the area between 9000 B.C. and 8000 B.C. We will study carbon dating in this chapter.

Many of the principles in science and engineering concern relationships between changing quantities. Since rates of change are represented mathematically by derivatives, it should not be surprising that such principles are often expressed in terms of differential equations. We introduced the concept of a differential equation in Section 5.2, but in this chapter we will go into more detail. We will discuss some important mathematical models that involve differential equations, and we will discuss some methods for solving and approximating solutions of some of the basic types of differential equations. However, we will only be able to touch the surface of this topic, leaving many important topics in differential equations to courses that are devoted completely to the subject.

8.1 MODELING WITH DIFFERENTIAL EQUATIONS

In this section we will introduce some basic terminology and concepts concerning differential equations. We will also discuss the general idea of modeling with differential equations, and we will encounter important models that can be applied to demography, medicine, ecology, and physics. In later sections of this chapter we will investigate methods that may be used to solve these differential equations.

■ TERMINOLOGY

Recall from Section 5.2 that a ***differential equation*** is an equation involving one or more derivatives of an unknown function. In this section we will denote the unknown function by $y = y(x)$ unless the differential equation arises from an applied problem involving time, in which case we will denote it by $y = y(t)$. The ***order*** of a differential equation is the order of the highest derivative that it contains. Some examples are given in Table 8.1.1. The last two equations in that table are expressed in "prime" notation, which does not specify the independent variable explicitly. However, you will usually be able to tell from the equation itself or from the context in which it arises whether to interpret y' as dy/dx or dy/dt.

Table 8.1.1

DIFFERENTIAL EQUATION	ORDER
$\dfrac{dy}{dx} = 3y$	1
$\dfrac{d^2y}{dx^2} - 6\dfrac{dy}{dx} + 8y = 0$	2
$\dfrac{d^3y}{dt^3} - t\dfrac{dy}{dt} + (t^2 - 1)y = e^t$	3
$y' - y = e^{2x}$	1
$y'' + y' = \cos t$	2

■ SOLUTIONS OF DIFFERENTIAL EQUATIONS

A function $y = y(x)$ is a ***solution*** of a differential equation on an open interval if the equation is satisfied identically on the interval when y and its derivatives are substituted into the equation. For example, $y = e^{2x}$ is a solution of the differential equation

$$\frac{dy}{dx} - y = e^{2x} \tag{1}$$

on the interval $(-\infty, +\infty)$, since substituting y and its derivative into the left side of this equation yields

$$\frac{dy}{dx} - y = \frac{d}{dx}[e^{2x}] - e^{2x} = 2e^{2x} - e^{2x} = e^{2x}$$

for all real values of x. However, this is not the only solution on $(-\infty, +\infty)$; for example, the function

$$y = e^{2x} + Ce^x \tag{2}$$

is also a solution for every real value of the constant C, since

$$\frac{dy}{dx} - y = \frac{d}{dx}[e^{2x} + Ce^x] - (e^{2x} + Ce^x) = (2e^{2x} + Ce^x) - (e^{2x} + Ce^x) = e^{2x}$$

After developing some techniques for solving equations such as (1), we will be able to show that *all* solutions of (1) on $(-\infty, +\infty)$ can be obtained by substituting values for the constant C in (2). On a given interval, a solution of a differential equation from which all solutions on that interval can be derived by substituting values for arbitrary constants is called a ***general solution*** of the equation on the interval. Thus (2) is a general solution of (1) on the interval $(-\infty, +\infty)$.

The graph of a solution of a differential equation is called an ***integral curve*** for the equation, so the general solution of a differential equation produces a family of integral curves corresponding to the different possible choices for the arbitrary constants. For example, Figure 8.1.1 shows some integral curves for (1), which were obtained by assigning values to the arbitrary constant in (2).

> The first-order equation (1) has a single arbitrary constant in its general solution (2). Usually, the general solution of an nth-order differential equation will contain n arbitrary constants. This is plausible, since n integrations are needed to recover a function from its nth derivative.

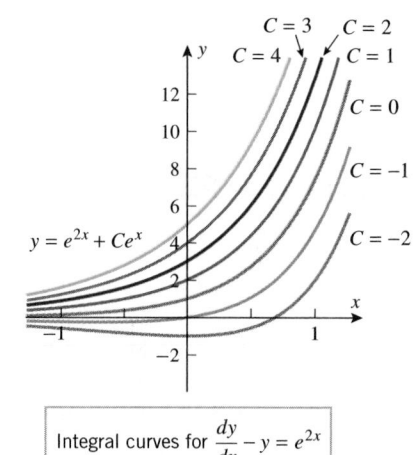

$$y = e^{2x} + Ce^x$$

Integral curves for $\dfrac{dy}{dx} - y = e^{2x}$

▶ **Figure 8.1.1**

■ INITIAL-VALUE PROBLEMS

When an applied problem leads to a differential equation, there are usually conditions in the problem that determine specific values for the arbitrary constants. As a rule of thumb, it requires n conditions to determine values for all n arbitrary constants in the general solution of an nth-order differential equation (one condition for each constant). For a first-order equation, the single arbitrary constant can be determined by specifying the value of the unknown function $y(x)$ at an arbitrary x-value x_0, say $y(x_0) = y_0$. This is called an ***initial condition***, and the problem of solving a first-order equation subject to an initial condition is called a ***first-order initial-value problem***. Geometrically, the initial condition $y(x_0) = y_0$ has the effect of isolating the integral curve that passes through the point (x_0, y_0) from the complete family of integral curves.

▶ **Example 1**   The solution of the initial-value problem

$$\frac{dy}{dx} - y = e^{2x}, \quad y(0) = 3$$

can be obtained by substituting the initial condition $x = 0$, $y = 3$ in the general solution (2) to find C. We obtain

$$3 = e^0 + Ce^0 = 1 + C$$

Thus, $C = 2$, and the solution of the initial-value problem, which is obtained by substituting this value of C in (2), is

$$y = e^{2x} + 2e^x$$

Geometrically, this solution is realized as the integral curve in Figure 8.1.1 that passes through the point $(0, 3)$. ◀

Since many of the fundamental laws of the physical and social sciences involve rates of change, it should not be surprising that such laws are modeled by differential equations. Here are some examples of the modeling process.

■ UNINHIBITED POPULATION GROWTH

One of the simplest models of population growth is based on the observation that when populations (people, plants, bacteria, and fruit flies, for example) are not constrained by environmental limitations, they tend to grow at a rate that is proportional to the size of the population—the larger the population, the more rapidly it grows.

To translate this principle into a mathematical model, suppose that $y = y(t)$ denotes the population at time t. At each point in time, the rate of increase of the population with respect to time is dy/dt, so the assumption that the rate of growth is proportional to the population is described by the differential equation

$$\frac{dy}{dt} = ky \tag{3}$$

where k is a positive constant of proportionality that can usually be determined experimentally. Thus, if the population is known at some point in time, say $y = y_0$ at time $t = 0$, then a formula for the population $y(t)$ can be obtained by solving the initial-value problem

$$\frac{dy}{dt} = ky, \quad y(0) = y_0$$

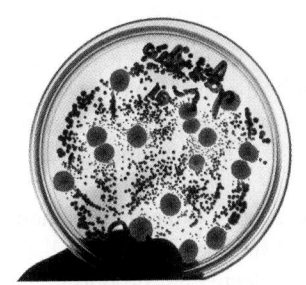

Hank Morgan–Rainbow/Getty Images
When the number of bacteria is small, an uninhibited population growth model can be used to model the growth of bacteria in a petri dish.

■ INHIBITED POPULATION GROWTH; LOGISTIC MODELS

The uninhibited population growth model was predicated on the assumption that the population $y = y(t)$ was not constrained by the environment. While this assumption is reasonable as long as the size of the population is relatively small, environmental effects become increasingly important as the population grows. In general, populations grow within ecological systems that can only support a certain number of individuals; the number L of such individuals is called the **carrying capacity** of the system. When $y > L$, the population exceeds the capacity of the ecological system and tends to decrease toward L; when $y < L$, the population is below the capacity of the ecological system and tends to increase toward L; when $y = L$, the population is in balance with the capacity of the ecological system and tends to remain stable.

To translate this into a mathematical model, we must look for a differential equation in which $y > 0$, $L > 0$, and

$$\frac{dy}{dt} < 0 \quad \text{if} \quad \frac{y}{L} > 1, \qquad \frac{dy}{dt} > 0 \quad \text{if} \quad \frac{y}{L} < 1, \qquad \frac{dy}{dt} = 0 \quad \text{if} \quad \frac{y}{L} = 1$$

Moreover, when the population is far below the carrying capacity (i.e., $y/L \approx 0$), then the environmental constraints should have little effect, and the growth rate should behave like the uninhibited population model. Thus, we want

$$\frac{dy}{dt} \approx ky \quad \text{if} \quad \frac{y}{L} \approx 0$$

A simple differential equation that meets all of these requirements is

$$\frac{dy}{dt} = k\left(1 - \frac{y}{L}\right)y$$

where k is a positive constant of proportionality. Thus if k and L can be determined experimentally, and if the population is known at some point, say $y(0) = y_0$, then a formula for the population $y(t)$ can be determined by solving the initial-value problem

$$\frac{dy}{dt} = k\left(1 - \frac{y}{L}\right)y, \quad y(0) = y_0 \tag{4}$$

This theory of population growth is due to the Belgian mathematician P. F. Verhulst (1804–1849), who introduced it in 1838 and described it as "logistic growth."[*] Thus, the differential equation in (4) is called the ***logistic differential equation***, and the growth model described by (4) is called the ***logistic model***.

■ PHARMACOLOGY

When a drug (say, penicillin or aspirin) is administered to an individual, it enters the bloodstream and then is absorbed by the body over time. Medical research has shown that the amount of a drug that is present in the bloodstream tends to decrease at a rate that is proportional to the amount of the drug present—the more of the drug that is present in the bloodstream, the more rapidly it is absorbed by the body.

To translate this principle into a mathematical model, suppose that $y = y(t)$ is the amount of the drug present in the bloodstream at time t. At each point in time, the rate of change in y with respect to t is dy/dt, so the assumption that the rate of decrease is proportional to the amount y in the bloodstream translates into the differential equation

$$\frac{dy}{dt} = -ky \tag{5}$$

where k is a positive constant of proportionality that depends on the drug and can be determined experimentally. The negative sign is required because y decreases with time. Thus, if the initial dosage of the drug is known, say $y = y_0$ at time $t = 0$, then a formula for $y(t)$ can be obtained by solving the initial-value problem

$$\frac{dy}{dt} = -ky, \quad y(0) = y_0$$

■ SPREAD OF DISEASE

Suppose that a disease begins to spread in a population of L individuals. Logic suggests that at each point in time the rate at which the disease spreads will depend on how many individuals are already affected and how many are not—as more individuals are affected, the opportunity to spread the disease tends to increase, but at the same time there are fewer individuals who are not affected, so the opportunity to spread the disease tends to decrease. Thus, there are two conflicting influences on the rate at which the disease spreads.

---

[*]Verhulst's model fell into obscurity for nearly a hundred years because he did not have sufficient census data to test its validity. However, interest in the model was revived during the 1930s when biologists used it successfully to describe the growth of fruit fly and flour beetle populations. Verhulst himself used the model to predict that an upper limit of Belgium's population would be approximately 9,400,000. In 2006 the population was about 10,379,000.

To translate this into a mathematical model, suppose that $y = y(t)$ is the number of individuals who have the disease at time t, so of necessity the number of individuals who do not have the disease at time t is $L - y$. As the value of y increases, the value of $L - y$ decreases, so the conflicting influences of the two factors on the rate of spread dy/dt are taken into account by the differential equation

$$\frac{dy}{dt} = ky(L - y)$$

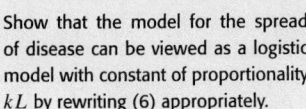

Show that the model for the spread of disease can be viewed as a logistic model with constant of proportionality kL by rewriting (6) appropriately.

where k is a positive constant of proportionality that depends on the nature of the disease and the behavior patterns of the individuals and can be determined experimentally. Thus, if the number of affected individuals is known at some point in time, say $y = y_0$ at time $t = 0$, then a formula for $y(t)$ can be obtained by solving the initial-value problem

$$\frac{dy}{dt} = ky(L - y), \quad y(0) = y_0 \tag{6}$$

■ NEWTON'S LAW OF COOLING

If a hot object is placed into a cool environment, the object will cool at a rate proportional to the difference in temperature between the object and the environment. Similarly, if a cold object is placed into a warm environment, the object will warm at a rate that is again proportional to the difference in temperature between the object and the environment. Together, these observations comprise a result known as *Newton's Law of Cooling*. (Newton's Law of Cooling appeared previously in the exercises of Section 2.2 and was mentioned briefly in Section 5.8.) To translate this into a mathematical model, suppose that $T = T(t)$ is the temperature of the object at time t and that T_e is the temperature of the environment, which is assumed to be constant. Since the rate of change dT/dt is proportional to $T - T_e$, we have

$$\frac{dT}{dt} = k(T - T_e)$$

where k is a constant of proportionality. Moreover, since dT/dt is positive when $T < T_e$, and is negative when $T > T_e$, the sign of k must be *negative*. Thus if the temperature of the object is known at some time, say $T = T_0$ at time $t = 0$, then a formula for the temperature $T(t)$ can be obtained by solving the initial-value problem

$$\frac{dT}{dt} = k(T - T_e), \quad T(0) = T_0 \tag{7}$$

■ VIBRATIONS OF SPRINGS

We conclude this section with an engineering model that leads to a second-order differential equation.

As shown in Figure 8.1.2, consider a block of mass m attached to the end of a horizontal spring. Assume that the block is set into vibratory motion by pulling the spring beyond its natural position and releasing it at time $t = 0$. We will be interested in finding a mathematical model that describes the vibratory motion of the block over time.

To translate this problem into mathematical form, we introduce a horizontal x-axis whose positive direction is to the right and whose origin is at the right end of the spring when the spring is in its natural position (Figure 8.1.3). Our goal is to find a model for the coordinate $x = x(t)$ of the point of attachment of the block to the spring as a function of time. In developing this model, we will assume that the only force on the mass m is the restoring force of the spring, and we will ignore the influence of other forces such as friction, air resistance, and so forth. Recall from Hooke's Law (Section 6.6) that when the connection point has coordinate $x(t)$, the restoring force is $-kx(t)$, where k is the spring constant. [The negative sign is due to the fact that the restoring force is to the left when $x(t)$ is positive, and the restoring force is to the right when $x(t)$ is negative.] It follows from Newton's

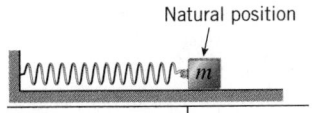

Natural position

Stretched

Released

▲ Figure 8.1.2

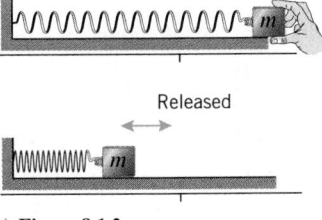

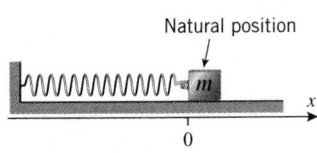

Natural position

x

0

▲ Figure 8.1.3

Second Law of Motion [Equation (5) of Section 6.6] that this restoring force is equal to the product of the mass m and the acceleration d^2x/dt^2 of the mass. In other words, we have

$$m\frac{d^2x}{dt^2} = -kx$$

which is a second-order differential equation for x. If at time $t = 0$ the mass is released from rest at position $x(0) = x_0$, then a formula for $x(t)$ can be found by solving the initial-value problem

$$m\frac{d^2x}{dt^2} = -kx, \quad x(0) = x_0, \quad x'(0) = 0 \tag{8}$$

[If at time $t = 0$ the mass is given an initial velocity $v_0 \neq 0$, then the condition $x'(0) = 0$ must be replaced by $x'(0) = v_0$.]

✔ QUICK CHECK EXERCISES 8.1   (See page 568 for answers.)

1. Match each differential equation with its family of solutions.

   (a) $x\dfrac{dy}{dx} = y$ _____

   (b) $y'' = 4y$ _____

   (c) $\dfrac{dy}{dx} = 2x$ _____

   (d) $\dfrac{d^2y}{dx^2} = -4y$ _____

   (i) $y = x^2 + C$

   (ii) $y = C_1 \sin 2x + C_2 \cos 2x$

   (iii) $y = C_1 e^{2x} + C_2 e^{-2x}$

   (iv) $y = Cx$

2. If $y = C_1 e^{2x} + C_2 x e^{2x}$ is the general solution of a differential equation, then the order of the equation is _____, and a solution to the differential equation that satisfies the initial conditions $y(0) = 1$, $y'(0) = 4$ is given by $y =$ _____.

3. The graph of a differentiable function $y = y(x)$ passes through the point $(0, 1)$ and at every point $P(x, y)$ on the graph the tangent line is perpendicular to the line through P and the origin. Find an initial-value problem whose solution is $y(x)$.

4. A glass of ice water with a temperature of $36°F$ is placed in a room with a constant temperature of $68°F$. Assuming that Newton's Law of Cooling applies, find an initial-value problem whose solution is the temperature of water t minutes after it is placed in the room. [*Note:* The differential equation will involve a constant of proportionality.]

EXERCISE SET 8.1

1. Confirm that $y = 3e^{x^3}$ is a solution of the initial-value problem $y' = 3x^2 y$, $y(0) = 3$.

2. Confirm that $y = \frac{1}{4}x^4 + 2\cos x + 1$ is a solution of the initial-value problem $y' = x^3 - 2\sin x$, $y(0) = 3$.

3–4 State the order of the differential equation, and confirm that the functions in the given family are solutions. ■

3. (a) $(1+x)\dfrac{dy}{dx} = y$; $y = c(1+x)$

   (b) $y'' + y = 0$; $y = c_1 \sin t + c_2 \cos t$

4. (a) $2\dfrac{dy}{dx} + y = x - 1$; $y = ce^{-x/2} + x - 3$

   (b) $y'' - y = 0$; $y = c_1 e^t + c_2 e^{-t}$

5–8 True–False Determine whether the statement is true or false. Explain your answer. ■

5. The equation

   $$\left(\frac{dy}{dx}\right)^2 = \frac{dy}{dx} + 2y$$

   is an example of a second-order differential equation.

6. The differential equation

   $$\frac{dy}{dx} = 2y + 1$$

   has a solution that is constant.

7. We expect the general solution of the differential equation

   $$\frac{d^3y}{dx^3} + 3\frac{d^2y}{dx^2} - \frac{dy}{dx} + 4y = 0$$

   to involve three arbitrary constants.

8. If every solution to a differential equation can be expressed in the form $y = Ae^{x+b}$ for some choice of constants A and b, then the differential equation must be of second order.

9–14 In each part, verify that the functions are solutions of the differential equation by substituting the functions into the equation. ■

9. $y'' + y' - 2y = 0$

   (a) e^{-2x} and e^x

   (b) $c_1 e^{-2x} + c_2 e^x$ (c_1, c_2 constants)

10. $y'' - y' - 6y = 0$
   (a) e^{-2x} and e^{3x}
   (b) $c_1 e^{-2x} + c_2 e^{3x}$ (c_1, c_2 constants)

11. $y'' - 4y' + 4y = 0$
   (a) e^{2x} and xe^{2x}
   (b) $c_1 e^{2x} + c_2 xe^{2x}$ (c_1, c_2 constants)

12. $y'' - 8y' + 16y = 0$
   (a) e^{4x} and xe^{4x}
   (b) $c_1 e^{4x} + c_2 xe^{4x}$ (c_1, c_2 constants)

13. $y'' + 4y = 0$
   (a) $\sin 2x$ and $\cos 2x$
   (b) $c_1 \sin 2x + c_2 \cos 2x$ (c_1, c_2 constants)

14. $y'' + 4y' + 13y = 0$
   (a) $e^{-2x} \sin 3x$ and $e^{-2x} \cos 3x$
   (b) $e^{-2x}(c_1 \sin 3x + c_2 \cos 3x)$ (c_1, c_2 constants)

15–20 Use the results of Exercises 9–14 to find a solution to the initial-value problem. ◼

15. $y'' + y' - 2y = 0$, $y(0) = -1$, $y'(0) = -4$

16. $y'' - y' - 6y = 0$, $y(0) = 1$, $y'(0) = 8$

17. $y'' - 4y' + 4y = 0$, $y(0) = 2$, $y'(0) = 2$

18. $y'' - 8y' + 16y = 0$, $y(0) = 1$, $y'(0) = 1$

19. $y'' + 4y = 0$, $y(0) = 1$, $y'(0) = 2$

20. $y'' + 4y' + 13y = 0$, $y(0) = -1$, $y'(0) = -1$

21–26 Find a solution to the initial-value problem. ◼

21. $y' + 4x = 2$, $y(0) = 3$

22. $y'' + 6x = 0$, $y(0) = 1$, $y'(0) = 2$

23. $y' - y^2 = 0$, $y(1) = 2$ [*Hint:* Assume the solution has an inverse function $x = x(y)$. Find, and solve, a differential equation that involves $x'(y)$.]

24. $y' = 1 + y^2$, $y(0) = 0$ (See Exercise 23.)

25. $x^2 y' + 2xy = 0$, $y(1) = 2$ [*Hint:* Interpret the left-hand side of the equation as the derivative of a product of two functions.]

26. $xy' + y = e^x$, $y(1) = 1 + e$ (See Exercise 25.)

FOCUS ON CONCEPTS

27. (a) Suppose that a quantity $y = y(t)$ increases at a rate that is proportional to the square of the amount present, and suppose that at time $t = 0$, the amount present is y_0. Find an initial-value problem whose solution is $y(t)$.
   (b) Suppose that a quantity $y = y(t)$ decreases at a rate that is proportional to the square of the amount present, and suppose that at a time $t = 0$, the amount present is y_0. Find an initial-value problem whose solution is $y(t)$.

28. (a) Suppose that a quantity $y = y(t)$ changes in such a way that $dy/dt = k\sqrt{y}$, where $k > 0$. Describe how y changes in words.

   (b) Suppose that a quantity $y = y(t)$ changes in such a way that $dy/dt = -ky^3$, where $k > 0$. Describe how y changes in words.

29. (a) Suppose that a particle moves along an s-axis in such a way that its velocity $v(t)$ is always half of $s(t)$. Find a differential equation whose solution is $s(t)$.
   (b) Suppose that an object moves along an s-axis in such a way that its acceleration $a(t)$ is always twice the velocity. Find a differential equation whose solution is $s(t)$.

30. Suppose that a body moves along an s-axis through a resistive medium in such a way that the velocity $v = v(t)$ decreases at a rate that is twice the square of the velocity.
   (a) Find a differential equation whose solution is the velocity $v(t)$.
   (b) Find a differential equation whose solution is the position $s(t)$.

31. Consider a solution $y = y(t)$ to the uninhibited population growth model.
   (a) Use Equation (3) to explain why y will be an increasing function of t.
   (b) Use Equation (3) to explain why the graph $y = y(t)$ will be concave up.

32. Consider the logistic model for population growth.
   (a) Explain why there are two constant solutions to this model.
   (b) For what size of the population will the population be growing most rapidly?

33. Consider the model for the spread of disease.
   (a) Explain why there are two constant solutions to this model.
   (b) For what size of the infected population is the disease spreading most rapidly?

34. Explain why there is exactly one constant solution to the Newton's Law of Cooling model.

35. Show that if c_1 and c_2 are any constants, the function

$$x = x(t) = c_1 \cos\left(\sqrt{\frac{k}{m}}\, t\right) + c_2 \sin\left(\sqrt{\frac{k}{m}}\, t\right)$$

is a solution to the differential equation for the vibrating spring. (The corresponding motion of the spring is referred to as *simple harmonic motion*.)

36. (a) Use the result of Exercise 35 to solve the initial-value problem in (8).
   (b) Find the amplitude, period, and frequency of your answer to part (a), and interpret each of these in terms of the motion of the spring.

37. **Writing** Select one of the models in this section and write a paragraph that discusses conditions under which the model would not be appropriate. How might you modify the model to take those conditions into account?

1. (a) (iv) (b) (iii) (c) (i) (d) (ii) **2.** 2; $e^{2x} + 2xe^{2x}$ **3.** $\dfrac{dy}{dx} = -\dfrac{x}{y}$, $y(0) = 1$ **4.** $\dfrac{dT}{dt} = k(T - 68)$, $T(0) = 36$

8.2 SEPARATION OF VARIABLES

In this section we will discuss a method, called "separation of variables," that can be used to solve a large class of first-order differential equations of a particular form. We will use this method to investigate mathematical models for exponential growth and decay, including population models and carbon dating.

■ FIRST-ORDER SEPARABLE EQUATIONS

We will now consider a method of solution that can often be applied to first-order equations that are expressible in the form

$$h(y)\frac{dy}{dx} = g(x) \tag{1}$$

Such first-order equations are said to be **separable**. Some examples of separable equations are given in Table 8.2.1. The name "separable" arises from the fact that Equation (1) can be rewritten in the differential form

$$h(y)\,dy = g(x)\,dx \tag{2}$$

in which the expressions involving x and y appear on opposite sides. The process of rewriting (1) in form (2) is called **separating variables**.

Some writers define a separable equation to be one that can be written in the form $dy/dx = G(x)H(y)$. Explain why this is equivalent to our definition.

Table 8.2.1

EQUATION	FORM (1)	$h(y)$	$g(x)$
$\dfrac{dy}{dx} = \dfrac{x}{y}$	$y\dfrac{dy}{dx} = x$	y	x
$\dfrac{dy}{dx} = x^2 y^3$	$\dfrac{1}{y^3}\dfrac{dy}{dx} = x^2$	$\dfrac{1}{y^3}$	x^2
$\dfrac{dy}{dx} = y$	$\dfrac{1}{y}\dfrac{dy}{dx} = 1$	$\dfrac{1}{y}$	1
$\dfrac{dy}{dx} = y - \dfrac{y}{x}$	$\dfrac{1}{y}\dfrac{dy}{dx} = 1 - \dfrac{1}{x}$	$\dfrac{1}{y}$	$1 - \dfrac{1}{x}$

To motivate a method for solving separable equations, assume that $h(y)$ and $g(x)$ are continuous functions of their respective variables, and let $H(y)$ and $G(x)$ denote antiderivatives of $h(y)$ and $g(x)$, respectively. Consider the equation that results if we integrate both sides of (2), the left side with respect to y and the right side with respect to x. We then have

$$\int h(y)\,dy = \int g(x)\,dx \tag{3}$$

or, equivalently,

$$H(y) = G(x) + C \tag{4}$$

where C denotes a constant. We claim that a differentiable function $y = y(x)$ is a solution to (1) if and only if y satisfies Equation (4) for some choice of the constant C.

Suppose that $y = y(x)$ is a solution to (1). It then follows from the chain rule that

$$\frac{d}{dx}[H(y)] = \frac{dH}{dy}\frac{dy}{dx} = h(y)\frac{dy}{dx} = g(x) = \frac{dG}{dx} \qquad (5)$$

Since the functions $H(y)$ and $G(x)$ have the same derivative with respect to x, they must differ by a constant (Theorem 4.8.3). It then follows that y satisfies (4) for an appropriate choice of C. Conversely, if $y = y(x)$ is defined implicitly by Equation (4), then implicit differentiation shows that (5) is satisfied, and thus $y(x)$ is a solution to (1) (Exercise 67). Because of this, it is common practice to refer to Equation (4) as the "solution" to (1).

In summary, we have the following procedure for solving (1), called *separation of variables*:

Separation of Variables

Step 1. Separate the variables in (1) by rewriting the equation in the differential form

$$h(y)\,dy = g(x)\,dx$$

Step 2. Integrate both sides of the equation in Step 1 (the left side with respect to y and the right side with respect to x):

$$\int h(y)\,dy = \int g(x)\,dx$$

Step 3. If $H(y)$ is any antiderivative of $h(y)$ and $G(x)$ is any antiderivative of $g(x)$, then the equation

$$H(y) = G(x) + C$$

will generally define a family of solutions implicitly. In some cases it may be possible to solve this equation explicitly for y.

▶ **Example 1** Solve the differential equation

$$\frac{dy}{dx} = -4xy^2$$

and then solve the initial-value problem

$$\frac{dy}{dx} = -4xy^2, \quad y(0) = 1$$

For an initial-value problem in which the differential equation is separable, you can either use the initial condition to solve for C, as in Example 1, or replace the indefinite integrals in Step 2 by definite integrals (Exercise 68).

Solution.   For $y \neq 0$ we can write the differential equation in form (1) as

$$\frac{1}{y^2}\frac{dy}{dx} = -4x$$

Separating variables and integrating yields

$$\frac{1}{y^2}\,dy = -4x\,dx$$

$$\int \frac{1}{y^2}\,dy = \int -4x\,dx$$

or

$$-\frac{1}{y} = -2x^2 + C$$

Solving for y as a function of x, we obtain

$$y = \frac{1}{2x^2 - C}$$

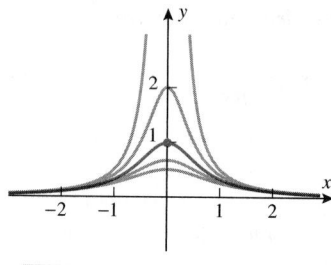

Integral curves for $\dfrac{dy}{dx} = -4xy^2$

▲ **Figure 8.2.1**

The initial condition $y(0) = 1$ requires that $y = 1$ when $x = 0$. Substituting these values into our solution yields $C = -1$ (verify). Thus, a solution to the initial-value problem is

$$y = \frac{1}{2x^2 + 1} \tag{6}$$

Some integral curves and our solution of the initial-value problem are graphed in Figure 8.2.1. ◄

One aspect of our solution to Example 1 deserves special comment. Had the initial condition been $y(0) = 0$ instead of $y(0) = 1$, the method we used would have failed to yield a solution to the resulting initial-value problem (Exercise 25). This is due to the fact that we assumed $y \neq 0$ in order to rewrite the equation $dy/dx = -4xy^2$ in the form

$$\frac{1}{y^2}\frac{dy}{dx} = -4x$$

It is important to be aware of such assumptions when manipulating a differential equation algebraically.

▶ **Example 2**   Solve the initial-value problem

$$(4y - \cos y)\frac{dy}{dx} - 3x^2 = 0, \quad y(0) = 0$$

Solution.   We can write the differential equation in form (1) as

$$(4y - \cos y)\frac{dy}{dx} = 3x^2$$

Separating variables and integrating yields

$$(4y - \cos y)\,dy = 3x^2\,dx$$

$$\int (4y - \cos y)\,dy = \int 3x^2\,dx$$

or

$$2y^2 - \sin y = x^3 + C \tag{7}$$

The solution of an initial-value problem in x and y can sometimes be expressed explicitly as a function of x [as in Formula (6) of Example 1], or explicitly as a function of y [as in Formula (8) of Example 2]. However, sometimes the solution cannot be expressed in either such form, so the only option is to express it implicitly as an equation in x and y.

For the initial-value problem, the initial condition $y(0) = 0$ requires that $y = 0$ if $x = 0$. Substituting these values into (7) to determine the constant of integration yields $C = 0$ (verify). Thus, the solution of the initial-value problem is

$$2y^2 - \sin y = x^3$$

or

$$x = \sqrt[3]{2y^2 - \sin y} \quad ◄ \tag{8}$$

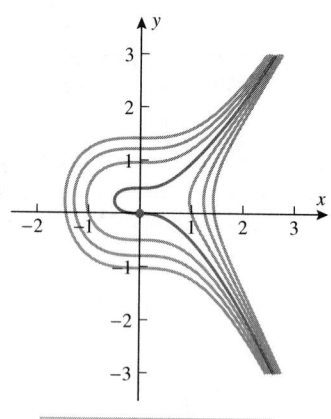

Integral curves for
$(4y - \cos y)\dfrac{dy}{dx} - 3x^2 = 0$

▲ **Figure 8.2.2**

Some integral curves and the solution of the initial-value problem in Example 2 are graphed in Figure 8.2.2.

Initial-value problems often result from geometrical questions, as in the following example.

▶ **Example 3**   Find a curve in the xy-plane that passes through $(0, 3)$ and whose tangent line at a point (x, y) has slope $2x/y^2$.

Solution. Since the slope of the tangent line is dy/dx, we have

$$\frac{dy}{dx} = \frac{2x}{y^2} \tag{9}$$

and, since the curve passes through $(0, 3)$, we have the initial condition

$$y(0) = 3$$

Equation (9) is separable and can be written as

$$y^2 \, dy = 2x \, dx$$

so

$$\int y^2 \, dy = \int 2x \, dx \quad \text{or} \quad \tfrac{1}{3} y^3 = x^2 + C$$

It follows from the initial condition that $y = 3$ if $x = 0$. Substituting these values into the last equation yields $C = 9$ (verify), so the equation of the desired curve is

$$\tfrac{1}{3} y^3 = x^2 + 9 \quad \text{or} \quad y = (3x^2 + 27)^{1/3} \quad \blacktriangleleft$$

■ **EXPONENTIAL GROWTH AND DECAY MODELS**

The population growth and pharmacology models developed in Section 8.1 are examples of a general class of models called *exponential models*. In general, exponential models arise in situations where a quantity increases or decreases at a rate that is proportional to the amount of the quantity present. More precisely, we make the following definition.

8.2.1 **DEFINITION** A quantity $y = y(t)$ is said to have an ***exponential growth model*** if it increases at a rate that is proportional to the amount of the quantity present, and it is said to have an ***exponential decay model*** if it decreases at a rate that is proportional to the amount of the quantity present. Thus, for an exponential growth model, the quantity $y(t)$ satisfies an equation of the form

$$\frac{dy}{dt} = ky \quad (k > 0) \tag{10}$$

and for an exponential decay model, the quantity $y(t)$ satisfies an equation of the form

$$\frac{dy}{dt} = -ky \quad (k > 0) \tag{11}$$

The constant k is called the ***growth constant*** or the ***decay constant***, as appropriate.

Equations (10) and (11) are separable since they have the form of (1), but with t rather than x as the independent variable. To illustrate how these equations can be solved, suppose that a positive quantity $y = y(t)$ has an exponential growth model and that we know the amount of the quantity at some point in time, say $y = y_0$ when $t = 0$. Thus, a formula for $y(t)$ can be obtained by solving the initial-value problem

$$\frac{dy}{dt} = ky, \quad y(0) = y_0$$

Separating variables and integrating yields

$$\int \frac{1}{y} \, dy = \int k \, dt$$

or (since $y > 0$)

$$\ln y = kt + C \tag{12}$$

The initial condition implies that $y = y_0$ when $t = 0$. Substituting these values in (12) yields $C = \ln y_0$ (verify). Thus,

$$\ln y = kt + \ln y_0$$

from which it follows that

$$y = e^{\ln y} = e^{kt + \ln y_0}$$

or, equivalently,

$$y = y_0 e^{kt} \tag{13}$$

We leave it for you to show that if $y = y(t)$ has an exponential decay model, and if $y(0) = y_0$, then

$$y = y_0 e^{-kt} \tag{14}$$

■ INTERPRETING THE GROWTH AND DECAY CONSTANTS

The significance of the constant k in Formulas (13) and (14) can be understood by reexamining the differential equations that gave rise to these formulas. For example, in the case of the exponential growth model, Equation (10) can be rewritten as

$$k = \frac{dy/dt}{y} \tag{15}$$

which states that the growth rate as a fraction of the entire population remains constant over time, and this constant is k. For this reason, k is called the ***relative growth rate*** of the population. It is usual to express the relative growth rate as a percentage. Thus, a relative growth rate of 3% per unit of time in an exponential growth model means that $k = 0.03$. Similarly, the constant k in an exponential decay model is called the ***relative decay rate***.

> It is standard practice in applications to call (15) the *growth rate*, even though it is misleading (the growth rate is dy/dt). However, the practice is so common that we will follow it here.

▶ **Example 4** According to United Nations data, the world population in 1998 was approximately 5.9 billion and growing at a rate of about 1.33% per year. Assuming an exponential growth model, estimate the world population at the beginning of the year 2023.

Solution. We assume that the population at the beginning of 1998 was 5.9 billion and let

$$t = \text{time elapsed from the beginning of 1998 (in years)}$$
$$y = \text{world population (in billions)}$$

Since the beginning of 1998 corresponds to $t = 0$, it follows from the given data that

$$y_0 = y(0) = 5.9 \text{ (billion)}$$

Since the growth rate is 1.33% ($k = 0.0133$), it follows from (13) that the world population at time t will be

$$y(t) = y_0 e^{kt} = 5.9 e^{0.0133t} \tag{16}$$

> In Example 4 the growth rate was given, so there was no need to calculate it. If the growth rate or decay rate is unknown, then it can be calculated using the initial condition and the value of y at another point in time (Exercise 44).

Since the beginning of the year 2023 corresponds to an elapsed time of $t = 25$ years ($2023 - 1998 = 25$), it follows from (16) that the world population by the year 2023 will be

$$y(25) = 5.9 e^{0.0133(25)} \approx 8.2$$

which is a population of approximately 8.2 billion. ◀

■ DOUBLING TIME AND HALF-LIFE

If a quantity y has an exponential growth model, then the time required for the original size to double is called the ***doubling time***, and if y has an exponential decay model, then the time required for the original size to reduce by half is called the ***half-life***. As it turns out, doubling time and half-life depend only on the growth or decay rate and not on the amount present initially. To see why this is so, suppose that $y = y(t)$ has an exponential growth model

$$y = y_0 e^{kt} \tag{17}$$

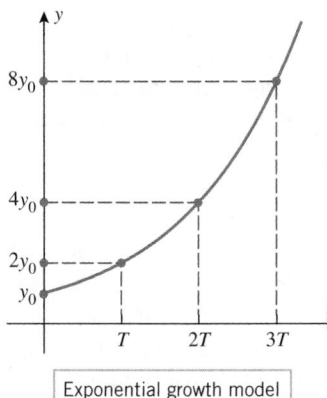

Exponential growth model with doubling time T

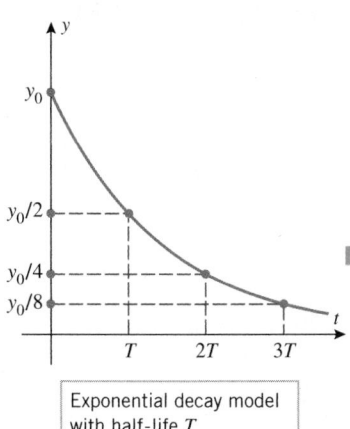

Exponential decay model with half-life T

▲ **Figure 8.2.3**

and let T denote the amount of time required for y to double in size. Thus, at time $t = T$ the value of y will be $2y_0$, and hence from (17)

$$2y_0 = y_0 e^{kT} \quad \text{or} \quad e^{kT} = 2$$

Taking the natural logarithm of both sides yields $kT = \ln 2$, which implies that the doubling time is

$$T = \frac{1}{k} \ln 2 \tag{18}$$

We leave it as an exercise to show that Formula (18) also gives the half-life of an exponential decay model. Observe that this formula does not involve the initial amount y_0, so that in an exponential growth or decay model, the quantity y doubles (or reduces by half) every T units (Figure 8.2.3).

▶ **Example 5** It follows from (18) that with a continued growth rate of 1.33% per year, the doubling time for the world population will be

$$T = \frac{1}{0.0133} \ln 2 \approx 52.116$$

or approximately 52 years. Thus, with a continued 1.33% annual growth rate the population of 5.9 billion in 1998 will double to 11.8 billion by the year 2050 and will double again to 23.6 billion by 2102. ◀

■ RADIOACTIVE DECAY

It is a fact of physics that radioactive elements disintegrate spontaneously in a process called *radioactive decay*. Experimentation has shown that the rate of disintegration is proportional to the amount of the element present, which implies that the amount $y = y(t)$ of a radioactive element present as a function of time has an exponential decay model.

Every radioactive element has a specific half-life; for example, the half-life of radioactive carbon-14 is about 5730 years. Thus, from (18), the decay constant for this element is

$$k = \frac{1}{T} \ln 2 = \frac{\ln 2}{5730} \approx 0.000121$$

and this implies that if there are y_0 units of carbon-14 present at time $t = 0$, then the number of units present after t years will be approximately

$$y(t) = y_0 e^{-0.000121t} \tag{19}$$

▶ **Example 6** If 100 grams of radioactive carbon-14 are stored in a cave for 1000 years, how many grams will be left at that time?

Solution. From (19) with $y_0 = 100$ and $t = 1000$, we obtain

$$y(1000) = 100 e^{-0.000121(1000)} = 100 e^{-0.121} \approx 88.6$$

Thus, about 88.6 grams will be left. ◀

■ CARBON DATING

When the nitrogen in the Earth's upper atmosphere is bombarded by cosmic radiation, the radioactive element carbon-14 is produced. This carbon-14 combines with oxygen to form carbon dioxide, which is ingested by plants, which in turn are eaten by animals. In this way all living plants and animals absorb quantities of radioactive carbon-14. In 1947 the American nuclear scientist W. F. Libby[*] proposed the theory that the percentage of

---

[*]W. F. Libby, "Radiocarbon Dating," *American Scientist*, Vol. 44, 1956, pp. 98–112.

carbon-14 in the atmosphere and in living tissues of plants is the same. When a plant or animal dies, the carbon-14 in the tissue begins to decay. Thus, the age of an artifact that contains plant or animal material can be estimated by determining what percentage of its original carbon-14 content remains. Various procedures, called **carbon dating** or **carbon-14 dating**, have been developed for measuring this percentage.

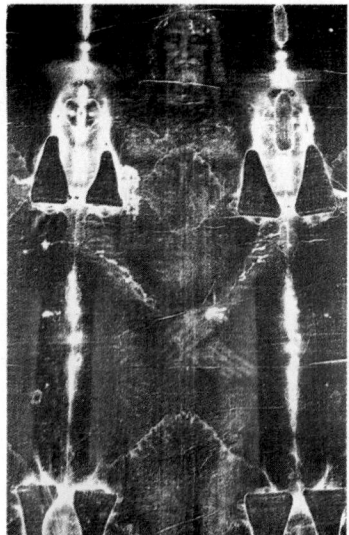

Patrick Mesner/Liaison Agency, Inc./Getty Images
The Shroud of Turin

▶ **Example 7**   In 1988 the Vatican authorized the British Museum to date a cloth relic known as the Shroud of Turin, possibly the burial shroud of Jesus of Nazareth. This cloth, which first surfaced in 1356, contains the negative image of a human body that was widely believed to be that of Jesus. The report of the British Museum showed that the fibers in the cloth contained between 92% and 93% of their original carbon-14. Use this information to estimate the age of the shroud.

Solution.   From (19), the fraction of the original carbon-14 that remains after t years is

$$\frac{y(t)}{y_0} = e^{-0.000121t}$$

Taking the natural logarithm of both sides and solving for t, we obtain

$$t = -\frac{1}{0.000121} \ln\left(\frac{y(t)}{y_0}\right)$$

Thus, taking $y(t)/y_0$ to be 0.93 and 0.92, we obtain

$$t = -\frac{1}{0.000121} \ln(0.93) \approx 600$$

$$t = -\frac{1}{0.000121} \ln(0.92) \approx 689$$

This means that when the test was done in 1988, the shroud was between 600 and 689 years old, thereby placing its origin between 1299 A.D. and 1388 A.D. Thus, if one accepts the validity of carbon-14 dating, the Shroud of Turin cannot be the burial shroud of Jesus of Nazareth. ◀

✔ **QUICK CHECK EXERCISES 8.2**   *(See page 579 for answers.)*

1. Solve the first-order separable equation

$$h(y)\frac{dy}{dx} = g(x)$$

by completing the following steps:

Step 1. Separate the variables by writing the equation in the differential form _____.

Step 2. Integrate both sides of the equation in Step 1: _____.

Step 3. If $H(y)$ is any antiderivative of $h(y)$, $G(x)$ is any antiderivative of $g(x)$, and C is an unspecified constant, then, as suggested by Step 2, the equation _____ will generally define a family of solutions to $h(y)\, dy/dx = g(x)$ implicitly.

2. Suppose that a quantity $y = y(t)$ has an exponential growth model with growth constant $k > 0$.
   (a) $y(t)$ satisfies a first-order differential equation of the form $dy/dt =$ _____.
   (b) In terms of k, the doubling time of the quantity is _____.
   (c) If $y_0 = y(0)$ is the initial amount of the quantity, then an explicit formula for $y(t)$ is given by $y(t) =$ _____.

3. Suppose that a quantity $y = y(t)$ has an exponential decay model with decay constant $k > 0$.
   (a) $y(t)$ satisfies a first-order differential equation of the form $dy/dt =$ _____.
   (b) In terms of k, the half-life of the quantity is _____.
   (c) If $y_0 = y(0)$ is the initial amount of the quantity, then an explicit formula for $y(t)$ is given by $y(t) =$ _____.

4. The initial-value problem

$$\frac{dy}{dx} = -\frac{x}{y}, \quad y(0) = 1$$

has solution $y(x) = $ _____ .

EXERCISE SET 8.2   ∼ Graphing Utility   [c] CAS

1–10 Solve the differential equation by separation of variables. Where reasonable, express the family of solutions as explicit functions of x. ■

1. $\dfrac{dy}{dx} = \dfrac{y}{x}$

2. $\dfrac{dy}{dx} = 2(1 + y^2)x$

3. $\dfrac{\sqrt{1 + x^2}}{1 + y}\dfrac{dy}{dx} = -x$

4. $(1 + x^4)\dfrac{dy}{dx} = \dfrac{x^3}{y}$

5. $(2 + 2y^2)y' = e^x y$

6. $y' = -xy$

7. $e^{-y} \sin x - y' \cos^2 x = 0$

8. $y' - (1 + x)(1 + y^2) = 0$

9. $\dfrac{dy}{dx} - \dfrac{y^2 - y}{\sin x} = 0$

10. $y - \dfrac{dy}{dx} \sec x = 0$

11–14 Solve the initial-value problem by separation of variables. ■

11. $y' = \dfrac{3x^2}{2y + \cos y}, \quad y(0) = \pi$

12. $y' - xe^y = 2e^y, \quad y(0) = 0$

13. $\dfrac{dy}{dt} = \dfrac{2t + 1}{2y - 2}, \quad y(0) = -1$

14. $y' \cosh^2 x - y \cosh 2x = 0, \quad y(0) = 3$

15. (a) Sketch some typical integral curves of the differential equation $y' = y/2x$.
   (b) Find an equation for the integral curve that passes through the point $(2, 1)$.

16. (a) Sketch some typical integral curves of the differential equation $y' = -x/y$.
   (b) Find an equation for the integral curve that passes through the point $(3, 4)$.

∼ 17–18 Solve the differential equation and then use a graphing utility to generate five integral curves for the equation. ■

17. $(x^2 + 4)\dfrac{dy}{dx} + xy = 0$

18. $(\cos y)y' = \cos x$

[c] 19–20 Solve the differential equation. If you have a CAS with implicit plotting capability, use the CAS to generate five integral curves for the equation. ■

19. $y' = \dfrac{x^2}{1 - y^2}$

20. $y' = \dfrac{y}{1 + y^2}$

21–24 True–False Determine whether the statement is true or false. Explain your answer. ■

21. Every differential equation of the form $y' = f(y)$ is separable.

22. A differential equation of the form

$$h(x)\frac{dy}{dx} = g(y)$$

is not separable.

23. If a radioactive element has a half-life of 1 minute, and if a container holds 32 g of the element at 1:00 P.M., then the amount remaining at 1:05 P.M. will be 1 g.

24. If a population is growing exponentially, then the time it takes the population to quadruple is independent of the size of the population.

25. Suppose that the initial condition in Example 1 had been $y(0) = 0$. Show that none of the solutions generated in Example 1 satisfy this initial condition, and then solve the initial-value problem

$$\frac{dy}{dx} = -4xy^2, \quad y(0) = 0$$

Why does the method of Example 1 fail to produce this particular solution?

26. Find all ordered pairs (x_0, y_0) such that if the initial condition in Example 1 is replaced by $y(x_0) = y_0$, the solution of the resulting initial-value problem is defined for all real numbers.

27. Find an equation of a curve with x-intercept 2 whose tangent line at any point (x, y) has slope xe^{-y}.

∼ 28. Use a graphing utility to generate a curve that passes through the point $(1, 1)$ and whose tangent line at (x, y) is perpendicular to the line through (x, y) with slope $-2y/(3x^2)$.

29. Suppose that an initial population of 10,000 bacteria grows exponentially at a rate of 2% per hour and that $y = y(t)$ is the number of bacteria present t hours later.
   (a) Find an initial-value problem whose solution is $y(t)$.
   (b) Find a formula for $y(t)$.
   (c) How long does it take for the initial population of bacteria to double?
   (d) How long does it take for the population of bacteria to reach 45,000?

30. A cell of the bacterium $E.$ $coli$ divides into two cells every 20 minutes when placed in a nutrient culture. Let $y = y(t)$ be the number of cells that are present t minutes after a single cell is placed in the culture. Assume that the growth of the bacteria is approximated by an exponential growth model.
   (a) Find an initial-value problem whose solution is $y(t)$.
   (b) Find a formula for $y(t)$.   (cont.)

(c) How many cells are present after 2 hours?

(d) How long does it take for the number of cells to reach 1,000,000?

31. Radon-222 is a radioactive gas with a half-life of 3.83 days. This gas is a health hazard because it tends to get trapped in the basements of houses, and many health officials suggest that homeowners seal their basements to prevent entry of the gas. Assume that 5.0×10^7 radon atoms are trapped in a basement at the time it is sealed and that $y(t)$ is the number of atoms present t days later.

(a) Find an initial-value problem whose solution is $y(t)$.

(b) Find a formula for $y(t)$.

(c) How many atoms will be present after 30 days?

(d) How long will it take for 90% of the original quantity of gas to decay?

32. Polonium-210 is a radioactive element with a half-life of 140 days. Assume that 10 milligrams of the element are placed in a lead container and that $y(t)$ is the number of milligrams present t days later.

(a) Find an initial-value problem whose solution is $y(t)$.

(b) Find a formula for $y(t)$.

(c) How many milligrams will be present after 10 weeks?

(d) How long will it take for 70% of the original sample to decay?

33. Suppose that 100 fruit flies are placed in a breeding container that can support at most 10,000 flies. Assuming that the population grows exponentially at a rate of 2% per day, how long will it take for the container to reach capacity?

34. Suppose that the town of Grayrock had a population of 10,000 in 1998 and a population of 12,000 in 2003. Assuming an exponential growth model, in what year will the population reach 20,000?

35. A scientist wants to determine the half-life of a certain radioactive substance. She determines that in exactly 5 days a 10.0-milligram sample of the substance decays to 3.5 milligrams. Based on these data, what is the half-life?

36. Suppose that 30% of a certain radioactive substance decays in 5 years.

(a) What is the half-life of the substance in years?

(b) Suppose that a certain quantity of this substance is stored in a cave. What percentage of it will remain after t years?

FOCUS ON CONCEPTS

37. (a) Make a conjecture about the effect on the graphs of $y = y_0 e^{kt}$ and $y = y_0 e^{-kt}$ of varying k and keeping y_0 fixed. Confirm your conjecture with a graphing utility.

(b) Make a conjecture about the effect on the graphs of $y = y_0 e^{kt}$ and $y = y_0 e^{-kt}$ of varying y_0 and keeping k fixed. Confirm your conjecture with a graphing utility.

38. (a) What effect does increasing y_0 and keeping k fixed have on the doubling time or half-life of an exponential model? Justify your answer.

(b) What effect does increasing k and keeping y_0 fixed have on the doubling time and half-life of an exponential model? Justify your answer.

39. (a) There is a trick, called the **Rule of 70**, that can be used to get a quick estimate of the doubling time or half-life of an exponential model. According to this rule, the doubling time or half-life is roughly 70 divided by the percentage growth or decay rate. For example, we showed in Example 5 that with a continued growth rate of 1.33% per year the world population would double every 52 years. This result agrees with the Rule of 70, since $70/1.33 \approx 52.6$. Explain why this rule works.

(b) Use the Rule of 70 to estimate the doubling time of a population that grows exponentially at a rate of 1% per year.

(c) Use the Rule of 70 to estimate the half-life of a population that decreases exponentially at a rate of 3.5% per hour.

(d) Use the Rule of 70 to estimate the growth rate that would be required for a population growing exponentially to double every 10 years.

40. Find a formula for the tripling time of an exponential growth model.

41. In 1950, a research team digging near Folsom, New Mexico, found charred bison bones along with some leaf-shaped projectile points (called the "Folsom points") that had been made by a Paleo-Indian hunting culture. It was clear from the evidence that the bison had been cooked and eaten by the makers of the points, so that carbon-14 dating of the bones made it possible for the researchers to determine when the hunters roamed North America. Tests showed that the bones contained between 27% and 30% of their original carbon-14. Use this information to show that the hunters lived roughly between 9000 B.C. and 8000 B.C.

42. (a) Use a graphing utility to make a graph of p_{rem} versus t, where p_{rem} is the percentage of carbon-14 that remains in an artifact after t years.

(b) Use the graph to estimate the percentage of carbon-14 that would have to have been present in the 1988 test of the Shroud of Turin for it to have been the burial shroud of Jesus of Nazareth (see Example 7).

43. (a) It is currently accepted that the half-life of carbon-14 might vary ± 40 years from its nominal value of 5730 years. Does this variation make it possible that the Shroud of Turin dates to the time of Jesus of Nazareth (see Example 7)?

(b) Review the subsection of Section 3.5 entitled Error Propagation, and then estimate the percentage error that results in the computed age of an artifact from an $r\%$ error in the half-life of carbon-14.

44. Suppose that a quantity y has an exponential growth model $y = y_0 e^{kt}$ or an exponential decay model $y = y_0 e^{-kt}$, and it is known that $y = y_1$ if $t = t_1$. In each case find a formula for k in terms of y_0, y_1, and t_1, assuming that $t_1 \neq 0$.

45. (a) Show that if a quantity $y = y(t)$ has an exponential model, and if $y(t_1) = y_1$ and $y(t_2) = y_2$, then the doubling time or the half-life T is

$$T = \left| \frac{(t_2 - t_1) \ln 2}{\ln(y_2/y_1)} \right|$$

(b) In a certain 1-hour period the number of bacteria in a colony increases by 25%. Assuming an exponential growth model, what is the doubling time for the colony?

46. Suppose that P dollars is invested at an annual interest rate of $r \times 100\%$. If the accumulated interest is credited to the account at the end of the year, then the interest is said to be *compounded annually*; if it is credited at the end of each 6-month period, then it is said to be *compounded semiannually*; and if it is credited at the end of each 3-month period, then it is said to be *compounded quarterly*. The more frequently the interest is compounded, the better it is for the investor since more of the interest is itself earning interest.

(a) Show that if interest is compounded n times a year at equally spaced intervals, then the value A of the investment after t years is

$$A = P \left(1 + \frac{r}{n}\right)^{nt}$$

(b) One can imagine interest to be compounded each day, each hour, each minute, and so forth. Carried to the limit one can conceive of interest compounded at each instant of time; this is called *continuous compounding*. Thus, from part (a), the value A of P dollars after t years when invested at an annual rate of $r \times 100\%$, compounded continuously, is

$$A = \lim_{n \to +\infty} P \left(1 + \frac{r}{n}\right)^{nt}$$

Use the fact that $\lim_{x \to 0} (1 + x)^{1/x} = e$ to prove that $A = Pe^{rt}$.

(c) Use the result in part (b) to show that money invested at continuous compound interest increases at a rate proportional to the amount present.

47. (a) If $1000 is invested at 8% per year compounded continuously (Exercise 46), what will the investment be worth after 5 years?

(b) If it is desired that an investment at 8% per year compounded continuously should have a value of $10,000 after 10 years, how much should be invested now?

(c) How long does it take for an investment at 8% per year compounded continuously to double in value?

48. What is the effective annual interest rate for an interest rate of $r\%$ per year compounded continuously?

49. Assume that $y = y(t)$ satisfies the logistic equation with $y_0 = y(0)$ the initial value of y.

(a) Use separation of variables to derive the solution

$$y = \frac{y_0 L}{y_0 + (L - y_0)e^{-kt}}$$

(b) Use part (a) to show that $\lim_{t \to +\infty} y(t) = L$.

50. Use your answer to Exercise 49 to derive a solution to the model for the spread of disease [Equation (6) of Section 8.1].

51. The graph of a solution to the logistic equation is known as a *logistic curve*, and if $y_0 > 0$, it has one of four general shapes, depending on the relationship between y_0 and L. In each part, assume that $k = 1$ and use a graphing utility to plot a logistic curve satisfying the given condition.
   (a) $y_0 > L$ (b) $y_0 = L$
   (c) $L/2 \le y_0 < L$ (d) $0 < y_0 < L/2$

52–53 The graph of a logistic model

$$y = \frac{y_0 L}{y_0 + (L - y_0)e^{-kt}}$$

is shown. Estimate y_0, L, and k.

52.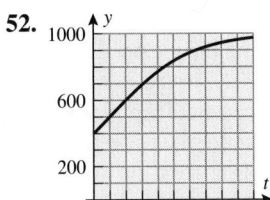

53.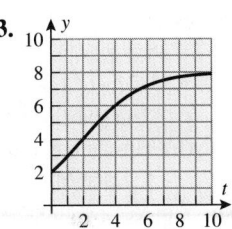

54. Plot a solution to the initial-value problem

$$\frac{dy}{dt} = 0.98 \left(1 - \frac{y}{5}\right) y, \quad y_0 = 1$$

55. Suppose that the growth of a population $y = y(t)$ is given by the logistic equation

$$y = \frac{60}{5 + 7e^{-t}}$$

(a) What is the population at time $t = 0$?
(b) What is the carrying capacity L?
(c) What is the constant k?
(d) When does the population reach half of the carrying capacity?
(e) Find an initial-value problem whose solution is $y(t)$.

56. Suppose that the growth of a population $y = y(t)$ is given by the logistic equation

$$y = \frac{1000}{1 + 999e^{-0.9t}}$$

(a) What is the population at time $t = 0$?
(b) What is the carrying capacity L?
(c) What is the constant k?   *(cont.)*

(d) When does the population reach 75% of the carrying capacity?

(e) Find an initial-value problem whose solution is $y(t)$.

57. Suppose that a university residence hall houses 1000 students. Following the semester break, 20 students in the hall return with the flu, and 5 days later 35 students have the flu.

(a) Use the result of Exercise 50 to find the number of students who will have the flu t days after returning to school.

(b) Make a table that illustrates how the flu spreads day to day over a 2-week period.

(c) Use a graphing utility to generate a graph that illustrates how the flu spreads over a 2-week period.

58. Suppose that at time $t = 0$ an object with temperature T_0 is placed in a room with constant temperature T_a. If $T_0 < T_a$, then the temperature of the object will increase, and if $T_0 > T_a$, then the temperature will decrease. Assuming that Newton's Law of Cooling applies, show that in both cases the temperature $T(t)$ at time t is given by

$$T(t) = T_a + (T_0 - T_a)e^{-kt}$$

where k is a positive constant.

59. A cup of water with a temperature of $95°C$ is placed in a room with a constant temperature of $21°C$.

(a) Assuming that Newton's Law of Cooling applies, use the result of Exercise 58 to find the temperature of the water t minutes after it is placed in the room. [*Note:* The solution will involve a constant of proportionality.]

(b) How many minutes will it take for the water to reach a temperature of $51°C$ if it cools to $85°C$ in 1 minute?

60. A glass of lemonade with a temperature of $40°F$ is placed in a room with a constant temperature of $70°F$, and 1 hour later its temperature is $52°F$. Show that t hours after the lemonade is placed in the room its temperature is approximated by $T = 70 - 30e^{-0.5t}$.

61. A rocket, fired upward from rest at time $t = 0$, has an initial mass of m_0 (including its fuel). Assuming that the fuel is consumed at a constant rate k, the mass m of the rocket, while fuel is being burned, will be given by $m = m_0 - kt$. It can be shown that if air resistance is neglected and the fuel gases are expelled at a constant speed c relative to the rocket, then the velocity v of the rocket will satisfy the equation

$$m\frac{dv}{dt} = ck - mg$$

where g is the acceleration due to gravity.

(a) Find $v(t)$ keeping in mind that the mass m is a function of t.

(b) Suppose that the fuel accounts for 80% of the initial mass of the rocket and that all of the fuel is consumed in 100 s. Find the velocity of the rocket in meters per second at the instant the fuel is exhausted. [*Note:* Take $g = 9.8 \text{ m/s}^2$ and $c = 2500 \text{ m/s}$.]

62. A bullet of mass m, fired straight up with an initial velocity of v_0, is slowed by the force of gravity and a drag force of air resistance kv^2, where k is a positive constant. As the bullet moves upward, its velocity v satisfies the equation

$$m\frac{dv}{dt} = -(kv^2 + mg)$$

where g is the constant acceleration due to gravity.

(a) Show that if $x = x(t)$ is the height of the bullet above the barrel opening at time t, then

$$mv\frac{dv}{dx} = -(kv^2 + mg)$$

(b) Express x in terms of v given that $x = 0$ when $v = v_0$.

(c) Assuming that

$$v_0 = 988 \text{ m/s}, \quad g = 9.8 \text{ m/s}^2$$
$$m = 3.56 \times 10^{-3} \text{ kg}, \quad k = 7.3 \times 10^{-6} \text{ kg/m}$$

use the result in part (b) to find out how high the bullet rises. [*Hint:* Find the velocity of the bullet at its highest point.]

63–64 Suppose that a tank containing a liquid is vented to the air at the top and has an outlet at the bottom through which the liquid can drain. It follows from *Torricelli's law* in physics that if the outlet is opened at time $t = 0$, then at each instant the depth of the liquid $h(t)$ and the area $A(h)$ of the liquid's surface are related by

$$A(h)\frac{dh}{dt} = -k\sqrt{h}$$

where k is a positive constant that depends on such factors as the viscosity of the liquid and the cross-sectional area of the outlet. Use this result in these exercises, assuming that h is in feet, $A(h)$ is in square feet, and t is in seconds. ■

63. Suppose that the cylindrical tank in the accompanying figure is filled to a depth of 4 feet at time $t = 0$ and that the constant in Torricelli's law is $k = 0.025$.

(a) Find $h(t)$.

(b) How many minutes will it take for the tank to drain completely?

64. Follow the directions of Exercise 63 for the cylindrical tank in the accompanying figure, assuming that the tank is filled to a depth of 4 feet at time $t = 0$ and that the constant in Torricelli's law is $k = 0.025$.

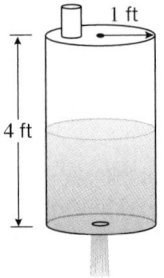

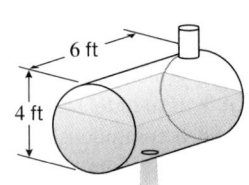

▲ Figure Ex-63   ▲ Figure Ex-64

65. Suppose that a particle moving along the x-axis encounters a resisting force that results in an acceleration of $a = dv/dt = -\frac{1}{32}v^2$. If $x = 0$ cm and $v = 128$ cm/s at time $t = 0$, find the velocity v and position x as a function of t for $t \geq 0$.

66. Suppose that a particle moving along the x-axis encounters a resisting force that results in an acceleration of $a = dv/dt = -0.02\sqrt{v}$. Given that $x = 0$ cm and $v = 9$ cm/s at time $t = 0$, find the velocity v and position x as a function of t for $t \geq 0$.

FOCUS ON CONCEPTS

67. Use implicit differentiation to prove that any differentiable function defined implicitly by Equation (4) will be a solution to (1).

68. Prove that a solution to the initial-value problem

$$h(y)\frac{dy}{dx} = g(x), \quad y(x_0) = y_0$$

is defined implicitly by the equation

$$\int_{y_0}^{y} h(r)\,dr = \int_{x_0}^{x} g(s)\,ds$$

69. Let L denote a tangent line at (x, y) to a solution of Equation (1), and let (x_1, y_1), (x_2, y_2) denote any two points on L. Prove that Equation (2) is satisfied by $dy = \Delta y = y_2 - y_1$ and $dx = \Delta x = x_2 - x_1$.

70. Writing A student objects to the method of separation of variables because it often produces an equation in x and y instead of an explicit function $y = f(x)$. Discuss the pros and cons of this student's position.

71. Writing A student objects to Step 2 in the method of separation of variables because one side of the equation is integrated with respect to x while the other side is integrated with respect to y. Answer this student's objection. [*Hint:* Recall the method of integration by substitution.]

✔**QUICK CHECK ANSWERS 8.2**

1. Step 1: $h(y)\,dy = g(x)\,dx$; Step 2: $\int h(y)\,dy = \int g(x)\,dx$; Step 3: $H(y) = G(x) + C$ **2.** (a) ky (b) $\dfrac{\ln 2}{k}$ (c) $y_0 e^{kt}$

3. (a) $-ky$ (b) $\dfrac{\ln 2}{k}$ (c) $y_0 e^{-kt}$ **4.** $y = \sqrt{1 - x^2}$

8.3 SLOPE FIELDS; EULER'S METHOD

In this section we will reexamine the concept of a slope field and we will discuss a method for approximating solutions of first-order equations numerically. Numerical approximations are important in cases where the differential equation cannot be solved exactly.

■ FUNCTIONS OF TWO VARIABLES

We will be concerned here with first-order equations that are expressed with the derivative by itself on one side of the equation. For example,

$$y' = x^3 \quad \text{and} \quad y' = \sin(xy)$$

In applied problems involving time, it is usual to use t as the independent variable, in which case one would be concerned with equations of the form $y' = f(t, y)$, where $y' = dy/dt$.

The first of these equations involves only x on the right side, so it has the form $y' = f(x)$. However, the second equation involves both x and y on the right side, so it has the form $y' = f(x, y)$, where the symbol $f(x, y)$ stands for a function of the two variables x and y. Later in the text we will study functions of two variables in more depth, but for now it will suffice to think of $f(x, y)$ as a formula that produces a unique output when values of x and y are given as inputs. For example, if

$$f(x, y) = x^2 + 3y$$

and if the inputs are $x = 2$ and $y = -4$, then the output is

$$f(2, -4) = 2^2 + 3(-4) = 4 - 12 = -8$$

■ SLOPE FIELDS

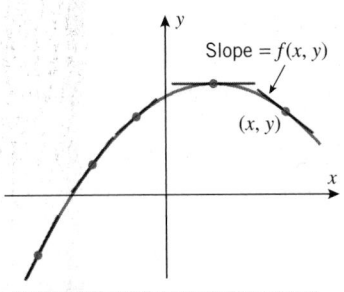

At each point (x, y) on an integral curve of $y' = f(x, y)$, the tangent line has slope $f(x, y)$.

▲ **Figure 8.3.1**

In Section 5.2 we introduced the concept of a slope field in the context of differential equations of the form $y' = f(x)$; the same principles apply to differential equations of the form

$$y' = f(x, y)$$

To see why this is so, let us review the basic idea. If we interpret y' as the slope of a tangent line, then the differential equation states that at each point (x, y) on an integral curve, the slope of the tangent line is equal to the value of f at that point (Figure 8.3.1). For example, suppose that $f(x, y) = y - x$, in which case we have the differential equation

$$y' = y - x \tag{1}$$

A geometric description of the set of integral curves can be obtained by choosing a rectangular grid of points in the xy-plane, calculating the slopes of the tangent lines to the integral curves at the gridpoints, and drawing small segments of the tangent lines through those points. The resulting picture is called a **slope field** or a **direction field** for the differential equation because it shows the "slope" or "direction" of the integral curves at the gridpoints. The more gridpoints that are used, the better the description of the integral curves. For example, Figure 8.3.2 shows two slope fields for (1)—the first was obtained by hand calculation using the 49 gridpoints shown in the accompanying table, and the second, which gives a clearer picture of the integral curves, was obtained using 625 gridpoints and a CAS.

VALUES OF $f(x, y) = y - x$

	$y = -3$	$y = -2$	$y = -1$	$y = 0$	$y = 1$	$y = 2$	$y = 3$
$x = -3$	0	1	2	3	4	5	6
$x = -2$	-1	0	1	2	3	4	5
$x = -1$	-2	-1	0	1	2	3	4
$x = 0$	-3	-2	-1	0	1	2	3
$x = 1$	-4	-3	-2	-1	0	1	2
$x = 2$	-5	-4	-3	-2	-1	0	1
$x = 3$	-6	-5	-4	-3	-2	-1	0

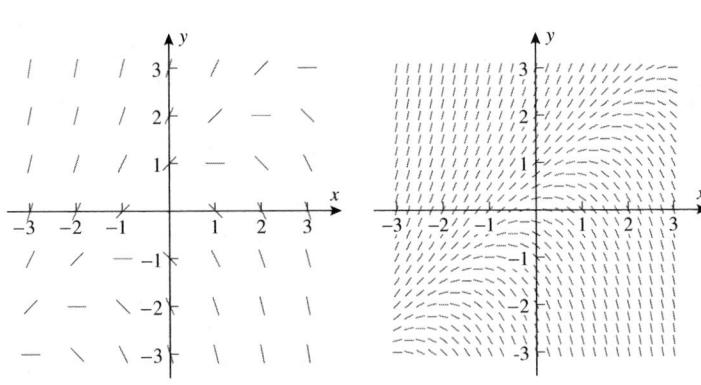

▲ **Figure 8.3.2**

It so happens that Equation (1) can be solved exactly using a method we will introduce in Section 8.4. We leave it for you to confirm that the general solution of this equation is

$$y = x + 1 + Ce^x \tag{2}$$

Confirm that the first slope field in Figure 8.3.2 is consistent with the accompanying table in that figure.

Figure 8.3.3 shows some of the integral curves superimposed on the slope field. Note that it was not necessary to have the general solution to construct the slope field. Indeed, slope fields are important precisely because they can be constructed in cases where the differential equation cannot be solved exactly.

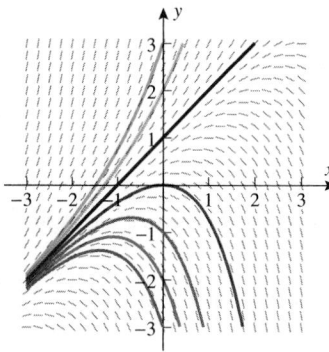

▲ **Figure 8.3.3**

■ EULER'S METHOD

Consider an initial-value problem of the form

$$y' = f(x, y), \quad y(x_0) = y_0$$

The slope field for the differential equation $y' = f(x, y)$ gives us a way to visualize the solution of the initial-value problem, since the graph of the solution is the integral curve that passes through the point (x_0, y_0). The slope field will also help us to develop a method for approximating the solution to the initial-value problem numerically.

We will not attempt to approximate $y(x)$ for all values of x; rather, we will choose some small increment Δx and focus on approximating the values of $y(x)$ at a succession of x-values spaced Δx units apart, starting from x_0. We will denote these x-values by

$$x_1 = x_0 + \Delta x, \quad x_2 = x_1 + \Delta x, \quad x_3 = x_2 + \Delta x, \quad x_4 = x_3 + \Delta x, \dots$$

and we will denote the approximations of $y(x)$ at these points by

$$y_1 \approx y(x_1), \quad y_2 \approx y(x_2), \quad y_3 \approx y(x_3), \quad y_4 \approx y(x_4), \dots$$

The technique that we will describe for obtaining these approximations is called ***Euler's Method***. Although there are better approximation methods available, many of them use Euler's Method as a starting point, so the underlying concepts are important to understand.

The basic idea behind Euler's Method is to start at the known initial point (x_0, y_0) and draw a line segment in the direction determined by the slope field until we reach the point (x_1, y_1) with x-coordinate $x_1 = x_0 + \Delta x$ (Figure 8.3.4). If Δx is small, then it is reasonable to expect that this line segment will not deviate much from the integral curve $y = y(x)$, and thus y_1 should closely approximate $y(x_1)$. To obtain the subsequent approximations, we repeat the process using the slope field as a guide at each step. Starting at the endpoint (x_1, y_1), we draw a line segment determined by the slope field until we reach the point (x_2, y_2) with x-coordinate $x_2 = x_1 + \Delta x$, and from that point we draw a line segment determined by the slope field to the point (x_3, y_3) with x-coordinate $x_3 = x_2 + \Delta x$, and so forth. As indicated in Figure 8.3.4, this procedure produces a polygonal path that tends to follow the integral curve closely, so it is reasonable to expect that the y-values $y_2, y_3, y_4, \dots$ will closely approximate $y(x_2), y(x_3), y(x_4), \dots$.

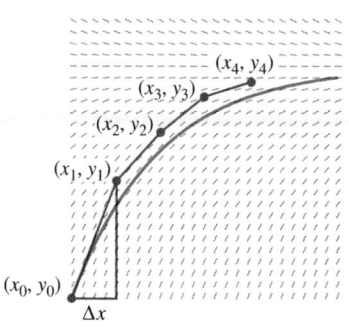

▲ **Figure 8.3.4**

To explain how the approximations $y_1, y_2, y_3, \dots$ can be computed, let us focus on a typical line segment. As indicated in Figure 8.3.5, assume that we have found the point (x_n, y_n), and we are trying to determine the next point (x_{n+1}, y_{n+1}), where $x_{n+1} = x_n + \Delta x$. Since the slope of the line segment joining the points is determined by the slope field at the starting point, the slope is $f(x_n, y_n)$, and hence

$$\frac{y_{n+1} - y_n}{x_{n+1} - x_n} = \frac{y_{n+1} - y_n}{\Delta x} = f(x_n, y_n)$$

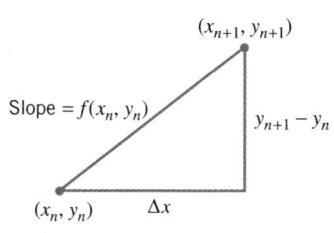

▲ **Figure 8.3.5**

which we can rewrite as

$$y_{n+1} = y_n + f(x_n, y_n)\Delta x$$

This formula, which is the heart of Euler's Method, tells us how to use each approximation to compute the next approximation.

Euler's Method

To approximate the solution of the initial-value problem

$$y' = f(x, y), \quad y(x_0) = y_0$$

proceed as follows:

Step 1. Choose a nonzero number Δx to serve as an *increment* or *step size* along the x-axis, and let

$$x_1 = x_0 + \Delta x, \quad x_2 = x_1 + \Delta x, \quad x_3 = x_2 + \Delta x, \ldots$$

Step 2. Compute successively

$$
\begin{aligned}
y_1 &= y_0 + f(x_0, y_0)\Delta x \\
y_2 &= y_1 + f(x_1, y_1)\Delta x \\
y_3 &= y_2 + f(x_2, y_2)\Delta x \\
&\ \ \vdots \\
y_{n+1} &= y_n + f(x_n, y_n)\Delta x
\end{aligned}
$$

The numbers $y_1, y_2, y_3, \ldots$ in these equations are the approximations of $y(x_1)$, $y(x_2), y(x_3), \ldots$.

▶ **Example 1**   Use Euler's Method with a step size of 0.1 to make a table of approximate values of the solution of the initial-value problem

$$y' = y - x, \quad y(0) = 2 \tag{3}$$

over the interval $0 \le x \le 1$.

Solution.   In this problem we have $f(x, y) = y - x$, $x_0 = 0$, and $y_0 = 2$. Moreover, since the step size is 0.1, the x-values at which the approximate values will be obtained are

$$x_1 = 0.1, \quad x_2 = 0.2, \quad x_3 = 0.3, \ldots, \quad x_9 = 0.9, \quad x_{10} = 1$$

The first three approximations are

$$
\begin{aligned}
y_1 &= y_0 + f(x_0, y_0)\Delta x = 2 + (2 - 0)(0.1) = 2.2 \\
y_2 &= y_1 + f(x_1, y_1)\Delta x = 2.2 + (2.2 - 0.1)(0.1) = 2.41 \\
y_3 &= y_2 + f(x_2, y_2)\Delta x = 2.41 + (2.41 - 0.2)(0.1) = 2.631
\end{aligned}
$$

Here is a way of organizing all 10 approximations rounded to five decimal places:

EULER'S METHOD FOR $y' = y - x$, $y(0) = 2$ WITH $\Delta x = 0.1$

n	x_n	y_n	$f(x_n, y_n)\Delta x$	$y_{n+1} = y_n + f(x_n, y_n)\Delta x$
0	0	2.00000	0.20000	2.20000
1	0.1	2.20000	0.21000	2.41000
2	0.2	2.41000	0.22100	2.63100
3	0.3	2.63100	0.23310	2.86410
4	0.4	2.86410	0.24641	3.11051
5	0.5	3.11051	0.26105	3.37156
6	0.6	3.37156	0.27716	3.64872
7	0.7	3.64872	0.29487	3.94359
8	0.8	3.94359	0.31436	4.25795
9	0.9	4.25795	0.33579	4.59374
10	1.0	4.59374	—	—

Observe that each entry in the last column becomes the next entry in the third column. This is reminiscent of Newton's Method in which each successive approximation is used to find the next. ◀

■ ACCURACY OF EULER'S METHOD

As a rule of thumb, the absolute error in an approximation produced by Euler's Method is proportional to the step size. Thus, reducing the step size by half reduces the absolute and percentage errors by roughly half. However, reducing the step size increases the amount of computation, thereby increasing the potential for more roundoff error. Such matters are discussed in courses on differential equations or numerical analysis.

It follows from (3) and the initial condition $y(0) = 2$ that the exact solution of the initial-value problem in Example 1 is
$$y = x + 1 + e^x$$

Thus, in this case we can compare the approximate values of $y(x)$ produced by Euler's Method with decimal approximations of the exact values (Table 8.3.1). In Table 8.3.1 the *absolute error* is calculated as

$$|\text{exact value} - \text{approximation}|$$

and the *percentage error* as

$$\frac{|\text{exact value} - \text{approximation}|}{|\text{exact value}|} \times 100\%$$

Table 8.3.1

x	EXACT SOLUTION	EULER APPROXIMATION	ABSOLUTE ERROR	PERCENTAGE ERROR
0	2.00000	2.00000	0.00000	0.00
0.1	2.20517	2.20000	0.00517	0.23
0.2	2.42140	2.41000	0.01140	0.47
0.3	2.64986	2.63100	0.01886	0.71
0.4	2.89182	2.86410	0.02772	0.96
0.5	3.14872	3.11051	0.03821	1.21
0.6	3.42212	3.37156	0.05056	1.48
0.7	3.71375	3.64872	0.06503	1.75
0.8	4.02554	3.94359	0.08195	2.04
0.9	4.35960	4.25795	0.10165	2.33
1.0	4.71828	4.59374	0.12454	2.64

Notice that the absolute error tends to increase as x moves away from x_0.

✔ QUICK CHECK EXERCISES 8.3   (See page 586 for answers.)

1. Match each differential equation with its slope field.
   (a) $y' = 2xy^2$ _____
   (b) $y' = e^{-y}$ _____
   (c) $y' = y$ _____
   (d) $y' = 2xy$ _____

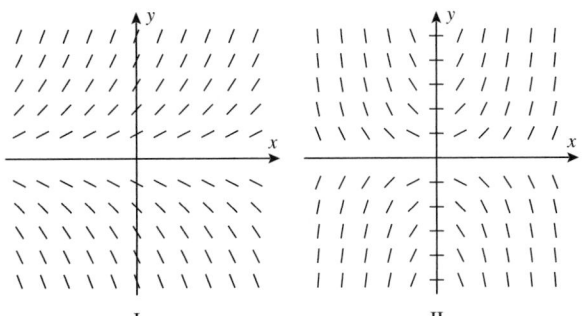

▲ Figure Ex-1

2. The slope field for $y' = y/x$ at the 16 gridpoints (x, y), where $x = -2, -1, 1, 2$ and $y = -2, -1, 1, 2$ is shown in

the accompanying figure. Use this slope field and geometric reasoning to find the integral curve that passes through the point (1, 2).

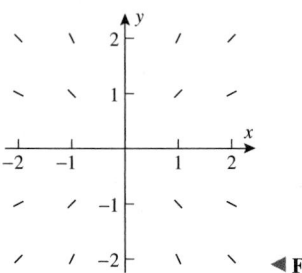

◀ **Figure Ex-2**

3. When using Euler's Method on the initial-value problem $y' = f(x, y)$, $y(x_0) = y_0$, we obtain y_{n+1} from y_n, x_n, and Δx by means of the formula $y_{n+1} = $ ———.

4. Consider the initial-value problem $y' = y$, $y(0) = 1$.
   (a) Use Euler's Method with two steps to approximate $y(1)$.
   (b) What is the exact value of $y(1)$?

EXERCISE SET 8.3   ⬚ Graphing Utility

1. Sketch the slope field for $y' = xy/4$ at the 25 gridpoints (x, y), where $x = -2, -1, \ldots, 2$ and $y = -2, -1, \ldots, 2$.

2. Sketch the slope field for $y' + y = 2$ at the 25 gridpoints (x, y), where $x = 0, 1, \ldots, 4$ and $y = 0, 1, \ldots, 4$.

3. A slope field for the differential equation $y' = 1 - y$ is shown in the accompanying figure. In each part, sketch the graph of the solution that satisfies the initial condition.
   (a) $y(0) = -1$ (b) $y(0) = 1$ (c) $y(0) = 2$

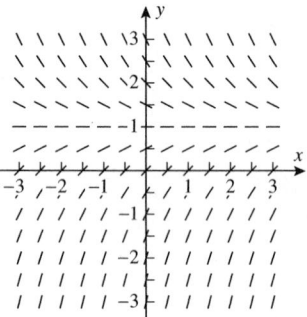

◀ **Figure Ex-3**

4. Solve the initial-value problems in Exercise 3, and use a graphing utility to confirm that the integral curves for these solutions are consistent with the sketches you obtained from the slope field.

FOCUS ON CONCEPTS

5. Use the slope field in Exercise 3 to make a conjecture about the behavior of the solutions of $y' = 1 - y$ as $x \to +\infty$, and confirm your conjecture by examining the general solution of the equation.

6. In parts (a)–(f), match the differential equation with the slope field, and explain your reasoning.
   (a) $y' = 1/x$ (b) $y' = 1/y$
   (c) $y' = e^{-x^2}$ (d) $y' = y^2 - 1$

(e) $y' = \dfrac{x + y}{x - y}$ (f) $y' = (\sin x)(\sin y)$

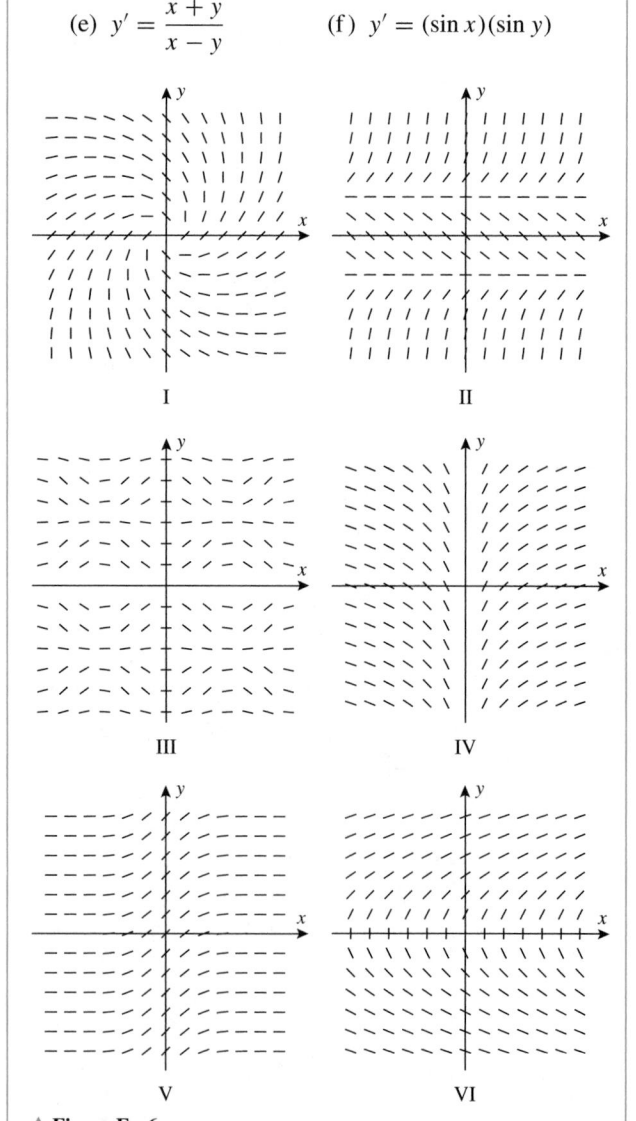

▲ **Figure Ex-6**

7–10 Use Euler's Method with the given step size Δx or Δt to approximate the solution of the initial-value problem over the stated interval. Present your answer as a table and as a graph. ■

7. $dy/dx = \sqrt[3]{y}$, $y(0) = 1$, $0 \le x \le 4$, $\Delta x = 0.5$

8. $dy/dx = x - y^2$, $y(0) = 1$, $0 \le x \le 2$, $\Delta x = 0.25$

9. $dy/dt = \cos y$, $y(0) = 1$, $0 \le t \le 2$, $\Delta t = 0.5$

10. $dy/dt = e^{-y}$, $y(0) = 0$, $0 \le t \le 1$, $\Delta t = 0.1$

11. Consider the initial-value problem
$$y' = \sin \pi t, \quad y(0) = 0$$
Use Euler's Method with five steps to approximate $y(1)$.

12–15 True–False Determine whether the statement is true or false. Explain your answer. ■

12. If the graph of $y = f(x)$ is an integral curve for a slope field, then so is any vertical translation of this graph.

13. Every integral curve for the slope field $dy/dx = e^{xy}$ is the graph of an increasing function of x.

14. Every integral curve for the slope field $dy/dx = e^y$ is concave up.

15. If $p(y)$ is a cubic polynomial in y, then the slope field $dy/dx = p(y)$ has an integral curve that is a horizontal line.

FOCUS ON CONCEPTS

16. (a) Show that the solution of the initial-value problem
$$y' = e^{-x^2}, y(0) = 0 \text{ is}$$
$$y(x) = \int_0^x e^{-t^2} dt$$

(b) Use Euler's Method with $\Delta x = 0.05$ to approximate the value of
$$y(1) = \int_0^1 e^{-t^2} dt$$
and compare the answer to that produced by a calculating utility with a numerical integration capability.

17. The accompanying figure shows a slope field for the differential equation $y' = -x/y$.
(a) Use the slope field to estimate $y\left(\frac{1}{2}\right)$ for the solution that satisfies the given initial condition $y(0) = 1$.
(b) Compare your estimate to the exact value of $y\left(\frac{1}{2}\right)$.

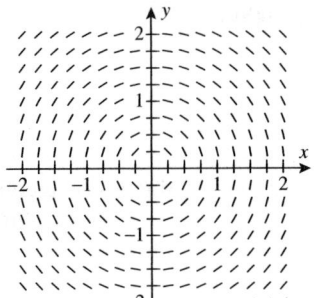
◀ **Figure Ex-17**

18. Refer to slope field II in Quick Check Exercise 1.
(a) Does the slope field appear to have a horizontal line as an integral curve?
(b) Use the differential equation for the slope field to verify your answer to part (a).

19. Refer to the slope field in Exercise 3 and consider the integral curve through $(0, -1)$.
(a) Use the slope field to estimate where the integral curve intersects the x-axis.
(b) Compare your estimate in part (a) with the exact value of the x-intercept for the integral curve.

20. Consider the initial-value problem
$$\frac{dy}{dx} = \frac{\sqrt{y}}{2}, \quad y(0) = 1$$
(a) Use Euler's Method with step sizes of $\Delta x = 0.2$, 0.1, and 0.05 to obtain three approximations of $y(1)$.
(b) Find $y(1)$ exactly.

21. A slope field of the form $y' = f(y)$ is said to be *autonomous*.
(a) Explain why the tangent segments along any horizontal line will be parallel for an autonomous slope field.
(b) The word *autonomous* means "independent." In what sense is an autonomous slope field independent?
(c) Suppose that $G(y)$ is an antiderivative of $1/[f(y)]$ and that C is a constant. Explain why any differentiable function defined implicitly by $G(y) - x = C$ will be a solution to the equation $y' = f(y)$.

22. (a) Solve the equation $y' = \sqrt{y}$ and show that every nonconstant solution has a graph that is everywhere concave up.
(b) Explain how the conclusion in part (a) may be obtained directly from the equation $y' = \sqrt{y}$ without solving.

23. (a) Find a slope field whose integral curve through $(1, 1)$ satisfies $xy^3 - x^2y = 0$ by differentiating this equation implicitly.
(b) Prove that if $y(x)$ is any integral curve of the slope field in part (a), then $x[y(x)]^3 - x^2y(x)$ will be a constant function.
(c) Find an equation that implicitly defines the integral curve through $(-1, -1)$ of the slope field in part (a).

24. (a) Find a slope field whose integral curve through $(0, 0)$ satisfies $xe^y + ye^x = 0$ by differentiating this equation implicitly.
(b) Prove that if $y(x)$ is any integral curve of the slope field in part (a), then $xe^{y(x)} + y(x)e^x$ will be a constant function.
(c) Find an equation that implicitly defines the integral curve through $(1, 1)$ of the slope field in part (a).

25. Consider the initial-value problem $y' = y$, $y(0) = 1$, and let y_n denote the approximation of $y(1)$ using Euler's Method with n steps.

    (a) What would you conjecture is the exact value of $\lim_{n \to +\infty} y_n$? Explain your reasoning.

    (b) Find an explicit formula for y_n and use it to verify your conjecture in part (a).

26. **Writing** Explain the connection between Euler's Method and the local linear approximation discussed in Section 3.5.

27. **Writing** Given a slope field, what features of an integral curve might be discussed from the slope field? Apply your ideas to the slope field in Exercise 3.

✔ QUICK CHECK ANSWERS 8.3

1. (a) IV (b) III (c) I (d) II   **2.** $y = 2x, x > 0$ **3.** $y_n + f(x_n, y_n)\Delta x$ **4.** (a) 2.25 (b) e

---

8.4 FIRST-ORDER DIFFERENTIAL EQUATIONS AND APPLICATIONS

In this section we will discuss a general method that can be used to solve a large class of first-order differential equations. We will use this method to solve differential equations related to the problems of mixing liquids and free fall retarded by air resistance.

◼ FIRST-ORDER LINEAR EQUATIONS

The simplest first-order equations are those that can be written in the form

$$\frac{dy}{dx} = q(x) \tag{1}$$

Such equations can often be solved by integration. For example, if

$$\frac{dy}{dx} = x^3 \tag{2}$$

then

$$y = \int x^3 \, dx = \frac{x^4}{4} + C$$

is the general solution of (2) on the interval $(-\infty, +\infty)$. More generally, a first-order differential equation is called **linear** if it is expressible in the form

$$\frac{dy}{dx} + p(x)y = q(x) \tag{3}$$

Equation (1) is the special case of (3) that results when the function $p(x)$ is identically 0. Some other examples of first-order linear differential equations are

$$\frac{dy}{dx} + x^2 y = e^x, \qquad \frac{dy}{dx} + (\sin x)y + x^3 = 0, \qquad \frac{dy}{dx} + 5y = 2$$

$$\boxed{p(x) = x^2, q(x) = e^x} \qquad \boxed{p(x) = \sin x, q(x) = -x^3} \qquad \boxed{p(x) = 5, q(x) = 2}$$

We will assume that the functions $p(x)$ and $q(x)$ in (3) are continuous on a common interval, and we will look for a general solution that is valid on that interval. One method for doing this is based on the observation that if we define $\mu = \mu(x)$ by

$$\mu = e^{\int p(x)\,dx} \tag{4}$$

then

$$\frac{d\mu}{dx} = e^{\int p(x)\,dx} \cdot \frac{d}{dx} \int p(x)\,dx = \mu p(x)$$

Thus,

$$\frac{d}{dx}(\mu y) = \mu \frac{dy}{dx} + \frac{d\mu}{dx} y = \mu \frac{dy}{dx} + \mu p(x) y \tag{5}$$

If (3) is multiplied through by μ, it becomes

$$\mu \frac{dy}{dx} + \mu p(x) y = \mu q(x)$$

Combining this with (5) we have

$$\frac{d}{dx}(\mu y) = \mu q(x) \tag{6}$$

This equation can be solved for y by integrating both sides with respect to x and then dividing through by μ to obtain

$$y = \frac{1}{\mu} \int \mu q(x)\,dx \tag{7}$$

which is a general solution of (3) on the interval. The function μ in (4) is called an *integrating factor* for (3), and this method for finding a general solution of (3) is called the *method of integrating factors*. Although one could simply memorize Formula (7), we recommend solving first-order linear equations by actually carrying out the steps used to derive this formula:

The Method of Integrating Factors

Step 1. Calculate the integrating factor

$$\mu = e^{\int p(x)\,dx}$$

Since any μ will suffice, we can take the constant of integration to be zero in this step.

Step 2. Multiply both sides of (3) by μ and express the result as

$$\frac{d}{dx}(\mu y) = \mu q(x)$$

Step 3. Integrate both sides of the equation obtained in Step 2 and then solve for y. Be sure to include a constant of integration in this step.

▶ **Example 1**   Solve the differential equation

$$\frac{dy}{dx} - y = e^{2x}$$

Solution.   Comparing the given equation to (3), we see that we have a first-order linear equation with $p(x) = -1$ and $q(x) = e^{2x}$. These coefficients are continuous on the interval $(-\infty, +\infty)$, so the method of integrating factors will produce a general solution on this interval. The first step is to compute the integrating factor. This yields

$$\mu = e^{\int p(x)\,dx} = e^{\int (-1)\,dx} = e^{-x}$$

Next we multiply both sides of the given equation by μ to obtain

$$e^{-x}\frac{dy}{dx} - e^{-x}y = e^{-x}e^{2x}$$

which we can rewrite as

$$\frac{d}{dx}[e^{-x}y] = e^x$$

Integrating both sides of this equation with respect to x we obtain

$$e^{-x}y = e^x + C$$

Finally, solving for y yields the general solution

$$y = e^{2x} + Ce^x \quad \blacktriangleleft$$

> Confirm that the solution obtained in Example 1 agrees with that obtained by substituting the integrating factor into Formula (7).

A differential equation of the form

$$P(x)\frac{dy}{dx} + Q(x)y = R(x)$$

can be solved by dividing through by $P(x)$ to put the equation in the form of (3) and then applying the method of integrating factors. However, the resulting solution will only be valid on intervals where $p(x) = Q(x)/P(x)$ and $q(x) = R(x)/P(x)$ are both continuous.

▶ **Example 2** Solve the initial-value problem

$$x\frac{dy}{dx} - y = x, \quad y(1) = 2$$

Solution. This differential equation can be written in the form of (3) by dividing through by x. This yields

$$\frac{dy}{dx} - \frac{1}{x}y = 1 \tag{8}$$

where $q(x) = 1$ is continuous on $(-\infty, +\infty)$ and $p(x) = -1/x$ is continuous on $(-\infty, 0)$ and $(0, +\infty)$. Since we need $p(x)$ and $q(x)$ to be continuous on a common interval, and since our initial condition requires a solution for $x = 1$, we will find a general solution of (8) on the interval $(0, +\infty)$. On this interval we have $|x| = x$, so that

$$\int p(x)\,dx = -\int \frac{1}{x}\,dx = -\ln|x| = -\ln x \qquad \boxed{\begin{array}{l}\text{Taking the constant of}\\ \text{integration to be 0}\end{array}}$$

Thus, an integrating factor that will produce a general solution on the interval $(0, +\infty)$ is

$$\mu = e^{\int p(x)\,dx} = e^{-\ln x} = e^{\ln(1/x)} = \frac{1}{x}$$

Multiplying both sides of Equation (8) by this integrating factor yields

$$\frac{1}{x}\frac{dy}{dx} - \frac{1}{x^2}y = \frac{1}{x}$$

or

$$\frac{d}{dx}\left[\frac{1}{x}y\right] = \frac{1}{x}$$

Therefore, on the interval $(0, +\infty)$,

$$\frac{1}{x}y = \int \frac{1}{x}\,dx = \ln x + C$$

from which it follows that

$$y = x \ln x + Cx \qquad (9)$$

The initial condition $y(1) = 2$ requires that $y = 2$ if $x = 1$. Substituting these values into (9) and solving for C yields $C = 2$ (verify), so the solution of the initial-value problem is

$$y = x \ln x + 2x \quad \blacktriangleleft$$

We conclude this section with some applications of first-order differential equations.

> It is not accidental that the initial-value problem in Example 2 has a unique solution. If the coefficients of (3) are continuous on an open interval that contains the point x_0, then for any y_0 there will be a unique solution of (3) on that interval that satisfies the initial condition $y(x_0) = y_0$ [Exercise 29(b)].

■ MIXING PROBLEMS

In a typical mixing problem, a tank is filled to a specified level with a solution that contains a known amount of some soluble substance (say salt). The thoroughly stirred solution is allowed to drain from the tank at a known rate, and at the same time a solution with a known concentration of the soluble substance is added to the tank at a known rate that may or may not differ from the draining rate. As time progresses, the amount of the soluble substance in the tank will generally change, and the usual mixing problem seeks to determine the amount of the substance in the tank at a specified time. This type of problem serves as a model for many kinds of problems: discharge and filtration of pollutants in a river, injection and absorption of medication in the bloodstream, and migrations of species into and out of an ecological system, for example.

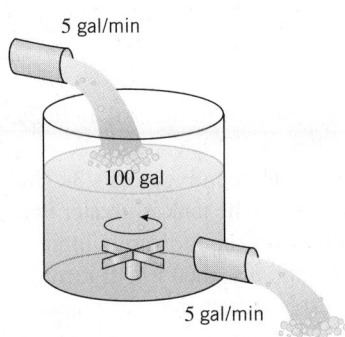

5 gal/min

100 gal

5 gal/min

▲ **Figure 8.4.1**

▶ **Example 3** At time $t = 0$, a tank contains 4 lb of salt dissolved in 100 gal of water. Suppose that brine containing 2 lb of salt per gallon of brine is allowed to enter the tank at a rate of 5 gal/min and that the mixed solution is drained from the tank at the same rate (Figure 8.4.1). Find the amount of salt in the tank after 10 minutes.

Solution. Let $y(t)$ be the amount of salt (in pounds) after t minutes. We are given that $y(0) = 4$, and we want to find $y(10)$. We will begin by finding a differential equation that is satisfied by $y(t)$. To do this, observe that dy/dt, which is the rate at which the amount of salt in the tank changes with time, can be expressed as

$$\frac{dy}{dt} = \text{rate in} - \text{rate out} \qquad (10)$$

where *rate in* is the rate at which salt enters the tank and *rate out* is the rate at which salt leaves the tank. But the rate at which salt enters the tank is

$$\text{rate in} = (2 \text{ lb/gal}) \cdot (5 \text{ gal/min}) = 10 \text{ lb/min}$$

Since brine enters and drains from the tank at the same rate, the volume of brine in the tank stays constant at 100 gal. Thus, after t minutes have elapsed, the tank contains $y(t)$ lb of salt per 100 gal of brine, and hence the rate at which salt leaves the tank at that instant is

$$\text{rate out} = \left(\frac{y(t)}{100} \text{ lb/gal}\right) \cdot (5 \text{ gal/min}) = \frac{y(t)}{20} \text{ lb/min}$$

Therefore, (10) can be written as

$$\frac{dy}{dt} = 10 - \frac{y}{20} \qquad \text{or} \qquad \frac{dy}{dt} + \frac{y}{20} = 10$$

which is a first-order linear differential equation satisfied by $y(t)$. Since we are given that $y(0) = 4$, the function $y(t)$ can be obtained by solving the initial-value problem

$$\frac{dy}{dt} + \frac{y}{20} = 10, \quad y(0) = 4$$

The integrating factor for the differential equation is

$$\mu = e^{\int (1/20)\, dt} = e^{t/20}$$

If we multiply the differential equation through by μ, then we obtain

$$\frac{d}{dt}(e^{t/20}y) = 10e^{t/20}$$

$$e^{t/20}y = \int 10e^{t/20}\, dt = 200e^{t/20} + C$$

$$y(t) = 200 + Ce^{-t/20} \tag{11}$$

The initial condition states that $y = 4$ when $t = 0$. Substituting these values into (11) and solving for C yields $C = -196$ (verify), so

$$y(t) = 200 - 196e^{-t/20} \tag{12}$$

The graph of (12) is shown in Figure 8.4.2. At time $t = 10$ the amount of salt in the tank is

$$y(10) = 200 - 196e^{-0.5} \approx 81.1 \text{ lb} \blacktriangleleft$$

Notice that it follows from (11) that

$$\lim_{t \to +\infty} y(t) = 200$$

for all values of C, so regardless of the amount of salt that is present in the tank initially, the amount of salt in the tank will eventually stabilize at 200 lb. This can also be seen geometrically from the slope field for the differential equation shown in Figure 8.4.3. This slope field suggests the following: If the amount of salt present in the tank is greater than 200 lb initially, then the amount of salt will decrease steadily over time toward a limiting value of 200 lb; and if the amount of salt is less than 200 lb initially, then it will increase steadily toward a limiting value of 200 lb. The slope field also suggests that if the amount present initially is exactly 200 lb, then the amount of salt in the tank will stay constant at 200 lb. This can also be seen from (11), since $C = 0$ in this case (verify).

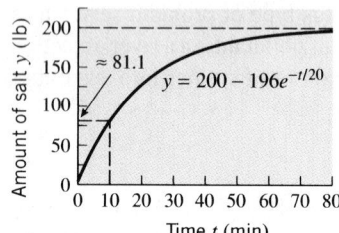

▲ **Figure 8.4.2**

The graph shown in Figure 8.4.2 suggests that $y(t) \to 200$ as $t \to +\infty$. This means that over an extended period of time the amount of salt in the tank tends toward 200 lb. Give an informal physical argument to explain why this result is to be expected.

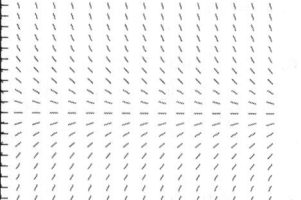

▲ **Figure 8.4.3**

■ A MODEL OF FREE-FALL MOTION RETARDED BY AIR RESISTANCE

In Section 5.7 we considered the free-fall model of an object moving along a vertical axis near the surface of the Earth. It was assumed in that model that there is no air resistance and that the only force acting on the object is the Earth's gravity. Our goal here is to find a model that takes air resistance into account. For this purpose we make the following assumptions:

- The object moves along a vertical s-axis whose origin is at the surface of the Earth and whose positive direction is up (Figure 5.7.7).

- At time $t = 0$ the height of the object is s_0 and the velocity is v_0.

- The only forces on the object are the force $F_G = -mg$ of the Earth's gravity acting down and the force F_R of air resistance acting opposite to the direction of motion. The force F_R is called the **drag force**.

In the case of free-fall motion retarded by air resistance, the net force acting on the object is

$$F_G + F_R = -mg + F_R$$

and the acceleration is d^2s/dt^2, so Newton's Second Law of Motion [Equation (5) of Section 6.6] implies that

$$-mg + F_R = m\frac{d^2s}{dt^2} \tag{13}$$

Experimentation has shown that the force F_R of air resistance depends on the shape of the object and its speed—the greater the speed, the greater the drag force. There are many possible models for air resistance, but one of the most basic assumes that the drag force F_R is proportional to the velocity of the object, that is,

$$F_R = -cv$$

where c is a positive constant that depends on the object's shape and properties of the air.[*] (The minus sign ensures that the drag force is opposite to the direction of motion.) Substituting this in (13) and writing d^2s/dt^2 as dv/dt, we obtain

$$-mg - cv = m\frac{dv}{dt}$$

Dividing by m and rearranging we obtain

$$\frac{dv}{dt} + \frac{c}{m}v = -g$$

which is a first-order linear differential equation in the unknown function $v = v(t)$ with $p(t) = c/m$ and $q(t) = -g$ [see (3)]. For a specific object, the coefficient c can be determined experimentally, so we will assume that m, g, and c are known constants. Thus, the velocity function $v = v(t)$ can be obtained by solving the initial-value problem

$$\frac{dv}{dt} + \frac{c}{m}v = -g, \quad v(0) = v_0 \tag{14}$$

Once the velocity function is found, the position function $s = s(t)$ can be obtained by solving the initial-value problem

$$\frac{ds}{dt} = v(t), \quad s(0) = s_0 \tag{15}$$

In Exercise 25 we will ask you to solve (14) and show that

$$v(t) = e^{-ct/m}\left(v_0 + \frac{mg}{c}\right) - \frac{mg}{c} \tag{16}$$

Note that

$$\lim_{t \to +\infty} v(t) = -\frac{mg}{c} \tag{17}$$

(verify). Thus, the speed $|v(t)|$ does not increase indefinitely, as in free fall; rather, because of the air resistance, it approaches a finite limiting speed v_τ given by

$$v_\tau = \left|-\frac{mg}{c}\right| = \frac{mg}{c} \tag{18}$$

This is called the ***terminal speed*** of the object, and (17) is called its ***terminal velocity***.

REMARK   Intuition suggests that near the limiting velocity, the velocity $v(t)$ changes very slowly; that is, $dv/dt \approx 0$. Thus, it should not be surprising that the limiting velocity can be obtained informally from (14) by setting $dv/dt = 0$ in the differential equation and solving for v. This yields

$$v = -\frac{mg}{c}$$

which agrees with (17).

---

[*]Other common models assume that $F_R = -cv^2$ or, more generally, $F_R = -cv^p$ for some value of p.

✔ QUICK CHECK EXERCISES 8.4   *(See page 594 for answers.)*

1. Solve the first-order linear differential equation

$$\frac{dy}{dx} + p(x)y = q(x)$$

by completing the following steps:

Step 1. Calculate the integrating factor $\mu =$ _____.

Step 2. Multiply both sides of the equation by the integrating factor and express the result as

$$\frac{d}{dx}[\underline{\qquad}] = \underline{\qquad}$$

Step 3. Integrate both sides of the equation obtained in Step 2 and solve for $y =$ _____.

2. An integrating factor for

$$\frac{dy}{dx} + \frac{y}{x} = q(x)$$

is _____.

3. At time $t = 0$, a tank contains 30 oz of salt dissolved in 60 gal of water. Then brine containing 5 oz of salt per gallon of brine is allowed to enter the tank at a rate of 3 gal/min and the mixed solution is drained from the tank at the same rate. Give an initial-value problem satisfied by the amount of salt $y(t)$ in the tank at time t. Do not solve the problem.

EXERCISE SET 8.4    Graphing Utility

1–6 Solve the differential equation by the method of integrating factors. ▪

1. $\dfrac{dy}{dx} + 4y = e^{-3x}$

2. $\dfrac{dy}{dx} + 2xy = x$

3. $y' + y = \cos(e^x)$

4. $2\dfrac{dy}{dx} + 4y = 1$

5. $(x^2 + 1)\dfrac{dy}{dx} + xy = 0$

6. $\dfrac{dy}{dx} + y + \dfrac{1}{1 - e^x} = 0$

7–10 Solve the initial-value problem. ▪

7. $x\dfrac{dy}{dx} + y = x, \quad y(1) = 2$

8. $x\dfrac{dy}{dx} - y = x^2, \quad y(1) = -1$

9. $\dfrac{dy}{dx} - 2xy = 2x, \quad y(0) = 3$

10. $\dfrac{dy}{dt} + y = 2, \quad y(0) = 1$

11–14 True–False Determine whether the statement is true or false. Explain your answer. ▪

11. If y_1 and y_2 are two solutions to a first-order linear differential equation, then $y = y_1 + y_2$ is also a solution.

12. If the first-order linear differential equation

$$\frac{dy}{dx} + p(x)y = q(x)$$

has a solution that is a constant function, then $q(x)$ is a constant multiple of $p(x)$.

13. In a mixing problem, we expect the concentration of the dissolved substance within the tank to approach a finite limit over time.

14. In our model for free-fall motion retarded by air resistance, the terminal velocity is proportional to the weight of the falling object.

15. A slope field for the differential equation $y' = 2y - x$ is shown in the accompanying figure. In each part, sketch the graph of the solution that satisfies the initial condition.
   (a) $y(1) = 1$ (b) $y(0) = -1$ (c) $y(-1) = 0$

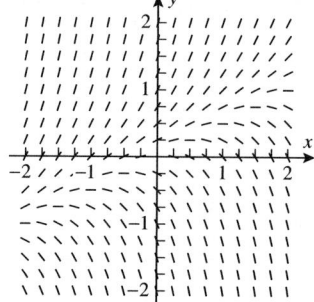

◀ **Figure Ex-15**

16. Solve the initial-value problems in Exercise 15, and use a graphing utility to confirm that the integral curves for these solutions are consistent with the sketches you obtained from the slope field.

FOCUS ON CONCEPTS

17. Use the slope field in Exercise 15 to make a conjecture about the effect of y_0 on the behavior of the solution of the initial-value problem $y' = 2y - x$, $y(0) = y_0$ as $x \to +\infty$, and check your conjecture by examining the solution of the initial-value problem.

18. Consider the slope field in Exercise 15.
   (a) Use Euler's Method with $\Delta x = 0.1$ to estimate $y\left(\frac{1}{2}\right)$ for the solution that satisfies the initial condition $y(0) = 1$.

(b) Would you conjecture your answer in part (a) to be greater than or less than the actual value of $y\left(\frac{1}{2}\right)$? Explain.

(c) Check your conjecture in part (b) by finding the exact value of $y\left(\frac{1}{2}\right)$.

19. (a) Use Euler's Method with a step size of $\Delta x = 0.2$ to approximate the solution of the initial-value problem

$$y' = x + y, \quad y(0) = 1$$

over the interval $0 \le x \le 1$.

(b) Solve the initial-value problem exactly, and calculate the error and the percentage error in each of the approximations in part (a).

(c) Sketch the exact solution and the approximate solution together.

20. It was stated at the end of Section 8.3 that reducing the step size in Euler's Method by half reduces the error in each approximation by about half. Confirm that the error in $y(1)$ is reduced by about half if a step size of $\Delta x = 0.1$ is used in Exercise 19.

21. At time $t = 0$, a tank contains 25 oz of salt dissolved in 50 gal of water. Then brine containing 4 oz of salt per gallon of brine is allowed to enter the tank at a rate of 2 gal/min and the mixed solution is drained from the tank at the same rate.
(a) How much salt is in the tank at an arbitrary time t?
(b) How much salt is in the tank after 25 min?

22. A tank initially contains 200 gal of pure water. Then at time $t = 0$ brine containing 5 lb of salt per gallon of brine is allowed to enter the tank at a rate of 20 gal/min and the mixed solution is drained from the tank at the same rate.
(a) How much salt is in the tank at an arbitrary time t?
(b) How much salt is in the tank after 30 min?

23. A tank with a 1000 gal capacity initially contains 500 gal of water that is polluted with 50 lb of particulate matter. At time $t = 0$, pure water is added at a rate of 20 gal/min and the mixed solution is drained off at a rate of 10 gal/min. How much particulate matter is in the tank when it reaches the point of overflowing?

24. The water in a polluted lake initially contains 1 lb of mercury salts per 100,000 gal of water. The lake is circular with diameter 30 m and uniform depth 3 m. Polluted water is pumped from the lake at a rate of 1000 gal/h and is replaced with fresh water at the same rate. Construct a table that shows the amount of mercury in the lake (in lb) at the end of each hour over a 12-hour period. Discuss any assumptions you made. [*Note:* Use 1 m³ = 264 gal.]

25. (a) Use the method of integrating factors to derive solution (16) to the initial-value problem (14). [*Note:* Keep in mind that c, m, and g are constants.]
(b) Show that (16) can be expressed in terms of the terminal speed (18) as

$$v(t) = e^{-gt/v_\tau}(v_0 + v_\tau) - v_\tau$$

(c) Show that if $s(0) = s_0$, then the position function of the object can be expressed as

$$s(t) = s_0 - v_\tau t + \frac{v_\tau}{g}(v_0 + v_\tau)(1 - e^{-gt/v_\tau})$$

26. Suppose a fully equipped skydiver weighing 240 lb has a terminal speed of 120 ft/s with a closed parachute and 24 ft/s with an open parachute. Suppose further that this skydiver is dropped from an airplane at an altitude of 10,000 ft, falls for 25 s with a closed parachute, and then falls the rest of the way with an open parachute.
(a) Assuming that the skydiver's initial vertical velocity is zero, use Exercise 25 to find the skydiver's vertical velocity and height at the time the parachute opens. [*Note:* Take $g = 32$ ft/s².]
(b) Use a calculating utility to find a numerical solution for the total time that the skydiver is in the air.

27. The accompanying figure is a schematic diagram of a basic *RL* series electrical circuit that contains a power source with a time-dependent voltage of $V(t)$ volts (V), a resistor with a constant resistance of R ohms (Ω), and an inductor with a constant inductance of L henrys (H). If you don't know anything about electrical circuits, don't worry; all you need to know is that electrical theory states that a current of $I(t)$ amperes (A) flows through the circuit where $I(t)$ satisfies the differential equation

$$L\frac{dI}{dt} + RI = V(t)$$

(a) Find $I(t)$ if $R = 10\,\Omega$, $L = 5$ H, V is a constant 20 V, and $I(0) = 0$ A.
(b) What happens to the current over a long period of time?

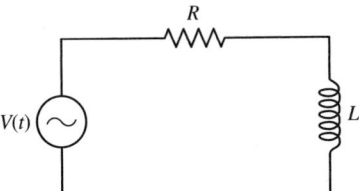

◄ **Figure Ex-27**

28. Find $I(t)$ for the electrical circuit in Exercise 27 if $R = 6\,\Omega$, $L = 3$ H, $V(t) = 3\sin t$ V, and $I(0) = 15$ A.

FOCUS ON CONCEPTS

29. (a) Prove that any function $y = y(x)$ defined by Equation (7) will be a solution to (3).
(b) Consider the initial-value problem

$$\frac{dy}{dx} + p(x)y = q(x), \quad y(x_0) = y_0$$

where the functions $p(x)$ and $q(x)$ are both continuous on some open interval. Using the general solution for a first-order linear equation, prove that this initial-value problem has a unique solution on the interval.

30. (a) Prove that solutions need not be unique for nonlinear initial-value problems by finding two solutions to

$$y\frac{dy}{dx} = x, \quad y(0) = 0$$

(b) Prove that solutions need not exist for nonlinear initial-value problems by showing that there is no solution for

$$y\frac{dy}{dx} = -x, \quad y(0) = 0$$

31. **Writing** Explain why the quantity μ in the *Method of Integrating Factors* is called an "integrating factor" and explain its role in this method.

32. **Writing** Suppose that a given first-order differential equation can be solved both by the method of integrating factors and by separation of variables. Discuss the advantages and disadvantages of each method.

✔ QUICK CHECK ANSWERS 8.4

1. Step 1: $e^{\int p(x)\,dx}$; Step 2: $\mu y, \mu q(x)$; Step 3: $\dfrac{1}{\mu}\displaystyle\int \mu q(x)\,dx$ **2.** x **3.** $\dfrac{dy}{dt} + \dfrac{y}{20} = 15, \; y(0) = 30$

CHAPTER 8 REVIEW EXERCISES   C CAS

1. Give an informal explanation of why one might expect the number of arbitrary constants in the general solution of a differential equation to be equal to the order of the equation.

2. Which of the given differential equations are separable?

(a) $\dfrac{dy}{dx} = f(x)g(y)$ (b) $\dfrac{dy}{dx} = \dfrac{f(x)}{g(y)}$

(c) $\dfrac{dy}{dx} = f(x) + g(y)$ (d) $\dfrac{dy}{dx} = \sqrt{f(x)g(y)}$

3–5 Solve the differential equation by the method of separation of variables.

3. $\dfrac{dy}{dx} = (1 + y^2)x^2$ **4.** $3\tan y - \dfrac{dy}{dx}\sec x = 0$

5. $(1 + y^2)y' = e^x y$

6–8 Solve the initial-value problem by the method of separation of variables. ■

6. $y' = 1 + y^2, \; y(0) = 1$ **7.** $y' = \dfrac{y^5}{x(1 + y^4)}, \; y(1) = 1$

8. $y' = 4y^2 \sec^2 2x, \; y(\pi/8) = 1$

9. Sketch the integral curve of $y' = -2xy^2$ that passes through the point $(0, 1)$.

10. Sketch the integral curve of $2yy' = 1$ that passes through the point $(0, 1)$ and the integral curve that passes through the point $(0, -1)$.

11. Sketch the slope field for $y' = xy/8$ at the 25 gridpoints (x, y), where $x = 0, 1, \ldots, 4$ and $y = 0, 1, \ldots, 4$.

12. Solve the differential equation $y' = xy/8$, and find a family of integral curves for the slope field in Exercise 11.

13–14 Use Euler's Method with the given step size Δx to approximate the solution of the initial-value problem over the stated interval. Present your answer as a table and as a graph. ■

13. $dy/dx = \sqrt{y}, \; y(0) = 1, \; 0 \le x \le 4, \; \Delta x = 0.5$

14. $dy/dx = \sin y, \; y(0) = 1, \; 0 \le x \le 2, \; \Delta x = 0.5$

15. Consider the initial-value problem

$$y' = \cos 2\pi t, \quad y(0) = 1$$

Use Euler's Method with five steps to approximate $y(1)$.

16. Use Euler's Method with a step size of $\Delta t = 0.1$ to approximate the solution of the initial-value problem

$$y' = 1 + 5t - y, \quad y(1) = 5$$

over the interval $[1, 2]$.

17. Cloth found in an Egyptian pyramid contains 78.5% of its original carbon-14. Estimate the age of the cloth.

18. Suppose that an initial population of 5000 bacteria grows exponentially at a rate of 1% per hour and that $y = y(t)$ is the number of bacteria present after t hours.
(a) Find an initial-value problem whose solution is $y(t)$.
(b) Find a formula for $y(t)$.
(c) What is the doubling time for the population?
(d) How long does it take for the population of bacteria to reach 30,000?

19–20 Solve the differential equation by the method of integrating factors. ■

19. $\dfrac{dy}{dx} + 3y = e^{-2x}$ **20.** $\dfrac{dy}{dx} + y - \dfrac{1}{1 + e^x} = 0$

21–23 Solve the initial-value problem by the method of integrating factors. ■

21. $y' - xy = x, \ y(0) = 3$

22. $xy' + 2y = 4x^2, \ y(1) = 2$

23. $y' \cosh x + y \sinh x = \cosh^2 x, \ y(0) = 2$

C **24.** (a) Solve the initial-value problem
$$y' - y = x \sin 3x, \quad y(0) = 1$$
by the method of integrating factors, using a CAS to perform any difficult integrations.

(b) Use the CAS to solve the initial-value problem directly, and confirm that the answer is consistent with that obtained in part (a).

(c) Graph the solution.

25. Classify the following first-order differential equations as separable, linear, both, or neither.

(a) $\dfrac{dy}{dx} - 3y = \sin x$ (b) $\dfrac{dy}{dx} + xy = x$

(c) $y\dfrac{dy}{dx} - x = 1$ (d) $\dfrac{dy}{dx} + xy^2 = \sin(xy)$

26. Determine whether the methods of integrating factors and separation of variables produce the same solutions of the differential equation
$$\frac{dy}{dx} - 4xy = x$$

27. A tank contains 1000 gal of fresh water. At time $t = 0$ min, brine containing 5 oz of salt per gallon of brine is poured into the tank at a rate of 10 gal/min, and the mixed solution is drained from the tank at the same rate. After 15 min that process is stopped and fresh water is poured into the tank at the rate of 5 gal/min, and the mixed solution is drained from the tank at the same rate. Find the amount of salt in the tank at time $t = 30$ min.

28. Suppose that a room containing 1200 ft³ of air is free of carbon monoxide. At time $t = 0$ cigarette smoke containing 4% carbon monoxide is introduced at the rate of 0.1 ft³/min, and the well-circulated mixture is vented from the room at the same rate.

(a) Find a formula for the percentage of carbon monoxide in the room at time t.

(b) Extended exposure to air containing 0.012% carbon monoxide is considered dangerous. How long will it take to reach this level?

Source: This is based on a problem from William E. Boyce and Richard C. DiPrima, *Elementary Differential Equations*, 7th ed., John Wiley & Sons, New York, 2001.

CHAPTER 8 MAKING CONNECTIONS

1. Consider the first-order differential equation
$$\frac{dy}{dx} + py = q$$
where p and q are constants. If $y = y(x)$ is a solution to this equation, define $u = u(x) = q - py(x)$.

(a) Without solving the differential equation, show that u grows exponentially as a function of x if $p < 0$, and decays exponentially as a function of x if $0 < p$.

(b) Use the result of part (a) and Equations (13–14) of Section 8.2 to solve the initial-value problem
$$\frac{dy}{dx} + 2y = 4, \quad y(0) = -1$$

2. Consider a differential equation of the form
$$\frac{dy}{dx} = f(ax + by + c)$$
where f is a function of a single variable. If $y = y(x)$ is a solution to this equation, define $u = u(x) = ax + by(x) + c$.

(a) Find a separable differential equation that is satisfied by the function u.

(b) Use your answer to part (a) to solve
$$\frac{dy}{dx} = \frac{1}{x + y}$$

3. A first-order differential equation is *homogeneous* if it can be written in the form
$$\frac{dy}{dx} = f\left(\frac{y}{x}\right) \quad \text{for } x \neq 0$$
where f is a function of a single variable. If $y = y(x)$ is a solution to a first-order homogeneous differential equation, define $u = u(x) = y(x)/x$.

(a) Find a separable differential equation that is satisfied by the function u.

(b) Use your answer to part (a) to solve
$$\frac{dy}{dx} = \frac{x - y}{x + y}$$

4. A first-order differential equation is called a *Bernoulli equation* if it can be written in the form
$$\frac{dy}{dx} + p(x)y = q(x)y^n \quad \text{for } n \neq 0, 1$$
If $y = y(x)$ is a solution to a Bernoulli equation, define $u = u(x) = [y(x)]^{1-n}$.

(a) Find a first-order linear differential equation that is satisfied by u.

(b) Use your answer to part (a) to solve the initial-value problem
$$x\frac{dy}{dx} - y = -2xy^2, \quad y(1) = \frac{1}{2}$$

INFINITE SERIES

Perspective creates the illusion that the sequence of railroad ties continues indefinitely but converges toward a single point infinitely far away.

In this chapter we will be concerned with infinite series, which are sums that involve infinitely many terms. Infinite series play a fundamental role in both mathematics and science—they are used, for example, to approximate trigonometric functions and logarithms, to solve differential equations, to evaluate difficult integrals, to create new functions, and to construct mathematical models of physical laws. Since it is impossible to add up infinitely many numbers directly, one goal will be to define exactly what we mean by the sum of an infinite series. However, unlike finite sums, it turns out that not all infinite series actually have a sum, so we will need to develop tools for determining which infinite series have sums and which do not. Once the basic ideas have been developed we will begin to apply our work; we will show how infinite series are used to evaluate such quantities as ln 2, e, sin 3°, and π, how they are used to create functions, and finally, how they are used to model physical laws.

9.1 SEQUENCES

In everyday language, the term "sequence" means a succession of things in a definite order—chronological order, size order, or logical order, for example. In mathematics, the term "sequence" is commonly used to denote a succession of numbers whose order is determined by a rule or a function. In this section, we will develop some of the basic ideas concerning sequences of numbers.

■ DEFINITION OF A SEQUENCE

Stated informally, an *infinite sequence*, or more simply a *sequence*, is an unending succession of numbers, called *terms*. It is understood that the terms have a definite order; that is, there is a first term a_1, a second term a_2, a third term a_3, a fourth term a_4, and so forth. Such a sequence would typically be written as

$$a_1, a_2, a_3, a_4, \ldots$$

where the dots are used to indicate that the sequence continues indefinitely. Some specific examples are

$$1, 2, 3, 4, \ldots, \qquad 1, \tfrac{1}{2}, \tfrac{1}{3}, \tfrac{1}{4}, \ldots,$$
$$2, 4, 6, 8, \ldots, \qquad 1, -1, 1, -1, \ldots$$

Each of these sequences has a definite pattern that makes it easy to generate additional terms if we assume that those terms follow the same pattern as the displayed terms. However, such patterns can be deceiving, so it is better to have a rule or formula for generating the terms. One way of doing this is to look for a function that relates each term in the sequence to its term number. For example, in the sequence

$$2, 4, 6, 8, \ldots$$

each term is twice the term number; that is, the nth term in the sequence is given by the formula $2n$. We denote this by writing the sequence as

$$2, 4, 6, 8, \ldots, 2n, \ldots$$

We call the function $f(n) = 2n$ the *general term* of this sequence. Now, if we want to know a specific term in the sequence, we need only substitute its term number in the formula for the general term. For example, the 37th term in the sequence is $2 \cdot 37 = 74$.

▶ **Example 1** In each part, find the general term of the sequence.

(a) $\frac{1}{2}, \frac{2}{3}, \frac{3}{4}, \frac{4}{5}, \ldots$ (b) $\frac{1}{2}, \frac{1}{4}, \frac{1}{8}, \frac{1}{16}, \ldots$

(c) $\frac{1}{2}, -\frac{2}{3}, \frac{3}{4}, -\frac{4}{5}, \ldots$ (d) $1, 3, 5, 7, \ldots$

Table 9.1.1

TERM NUMBER	1	2	3	4	⋯	n	⋯
TERM	$\frac{1}{2}$	$\frac{2}{3}$	$\frac{3}{4}$	$\frac{4}{5}$	⋯	$\frac{n}{n+1}$	⋯

Solution (a). In Table 9.1.1, the four known terms have been placed below their term numbers, from which we see that the numerator is the same as the term number and the denominator is one greater than the term number. This suggests that the nth term has numerator n and denominator $n + 1$, as indicated in the table. Thus, the sequence can be expressed as

$$\frac{1}{2}, \frac{2}{3}, \frac{3}{4}, \frac{4}{5}, \ldots, \frac{n}{n+1}, \ldots$$

Table 9.1.2

TERM NUMBER	1	2	3	4	⋯	n	⋯
TERM	$\frac{1}{2}$	$\frac{1}{2^2}$	$\frac{1}{2^3}$	$\frac{1}{2^4}$	⋯	$\frac{1}{2^n}$	⋯

Solution (b). In Table 9.1.2, the denominators of the four known terms have been expressed as powers of 2 and the first four terms have been placed below their term numbers, from which we see that the exponent in the denominator is the same as the term number. This suggests that the denominator of the nth term is 2^n, as indicated in the table. Thus, the sequence can be expressed as

$$\frac{1}{2}, \frac{1}{4}, \frac{1}{8}, \frac{1}{16}, \ldots, \frac{1}{2^n}, \ldots$$

Solution (c). This sequence is identical to that in part (a), except for the alternating signs. Thus, the nth term in the sequence can be obtained by multiplying the nth term in part (a) by $(-1)^{n+1}$. This factor produces the correct alternating signs, since its successive values, starting with $n = 1$, are $1, -1, 1, -1, \ldots$. Thus, the sequence can be written as

$$\frac{1}{2}, -\frac{2}{3}, \frac{3}{4}, -\frac{4}{5}, \ldots, (-1)^{n+1}\frac{n}{n+1}, \ldots$$

Table 9.1.3

TERM NUMBER	1	2	3	4	⋯	n	⋯
TERM	1	3	5	7	⋯	$2n-1$	⋯

Solution (d). In Table 9.1.3, the four known terms have been placed below their term numbers, from which we see that each term is one less than twice its term number. This suggests that the nth term in the sequence is $2n - 1$, as indicated in the table. Thus, the sequence can be expressed as

$$1, 3, 5, 7, \ldots, 2n - 1, \ldots \quad ◀$$

When the general term of a sequence

$$a_1, a_2, a_3, \ldots, a_n, \ldots \tag{1}$$

is known, there is no need to write out the initial terms, and it is common to write only the general term enclosed in braces. Thus, (1) might be written as

$$\{a_n\}_{n=1}^{+\infty} \quad \text{or as} \quad \{a_n\}_{n=1}^{\infty}$$

For example, here are the four sequences in Example 1 expressed in brace notation.

A sequence cannot be uniquely determined from a few initial terms. For example, the sequence whose general term is

$$f(n) = \tfrac{1}{3}(3 - 5n + 6n^2 - n^3)$$

has 1, 3, and 5 as its first three terms, but its fourth term is also 5.

SEQUENCE	BRACE NOTATION
$\dfrac{1}{2}, \dfrac{2}{3}, \dfrac{3}{4}, \dfrac{4}{5}, \dots, \dfrac{n}{n+1}, \dots$	$\left\{\dfrac{n}{n+1}\right\}_{n=1}^{+\infty}$
$\dfrac{1}{2}, \dfrac{1}{4}, \dfrac{1}{8}, \dfrac{1}{16}, \dots, \dfrac{1}{2^n}, \dots$	$\left\{\dfrac{1}{2^n}\right\}_{n=1}^{+\infty}$
$\dfrac{1}{2}, -\dfrac{2}{3}, \dfrac{3}{4}, -\dfrac{4}{5}, \dots, (-1)^{n+1}\dfrac{n}{n+1}, \dots$	$\left\{(-1)^{n+1}\dfrac{n}{n+1}\right\}_{n=1}^{+\infty}$
$1, 3, 5, 7, \dots, 2n - 1, \dots$	$\{2n - 1\}_{n=1}^{+\infty}$

The letter n in (1) is called the **index** for the sequence. It is not essential to use n for the index; any letter not reserved for another purpose can be used. For example, we might view the general term of the sequence $a_1, a_2, a_3, \dots$ to be the kth term, in which case we would denote this sequence as $\{a_k\}_{k=1}^{+\infty}$. Moreover, it is not essential to start the index at 1; sometimes it is more convenient to start it at 0 (or some other integer). For example, consider the sequence

$$1, \frac{1}{2}, \frac{1}{2^2}, \frac{1}{2^3}, \dots$$

One way to write this sequence is

$$\left\{\frac{1}{2^{n-1}}\right\}_{n=1}^{+\infty}$$

However, the general term will be simpler if we think of the initial term in the sequence as the zeroth term, in which case we can write the sequence as

$$\left\{\frac{1}{2^n}\right\}_{n=0}^{+\infty}$$

We began this section by describing a sequence as an unending succession of numbers. Although this conveys the general idea, it is not a satisfactory mathematical definition because it relies on the term "succession," which is itself an undefined term. To motivate a precise definition, consider the sequence

$$2, 4, 6, 8, \dots, 2n, \dots$$

If we denote the general term by $f(n) = 2n$, then we can write this sequence as

$$f(1), f(2), f(3), \dots, f(n), \dots$$

which is a "list" of values of the function

$$f(n) = 2n, \quad n = 1, 2, 3, \dots$$

whose domain is the set of positive integers. This suggests the following definition.

9.1.1   DEFINITION   A **sequence** is a function whose domain is a set of integers.

Typically, the domain of a sequence is the set of positive integers or the set of nonnegative integers. We will regard the expression $\{a_n\}_{n=1}^{+\infty}$ to be an alternative notation for the function $f(n) = a_n, n = 1, 2, 3, \dots$, and we will regard $\{a_n\}_{n=0}^{+\infty}$ to be an alternative notation for the function $f(n) = a_n, n = 0, 1, 2, 3, \dots$.

■ GRAPHS OF SEQUENCES

Since sequences are functions, it makes sense to talk about the graph of a sequence. For example, the graph of the sequence $\{1/n\}_{n=1}^{+\infty}$ is the graph of the equation

$$y = \frac{1}{n}, \quad n = 1, 2, 3, \ldots$$

Because the right side of this equation is defined only for positive integer values of n, the graph consists of a succession of isolated points (Figure 9.1.1a). This is different from the graph of

$$y = \frac{1}{x}, \quad x \geq 1$$

which is a continuous curve (Figure 9.1.1b).

> When the starting value for the index of a sequence is not relevant to the discussion, it is common to use a notation such as $\{a_n\}$ in which there is no reference to the starting value of n. We can distinguish between different sequences by using different letters for their general terms; thus, $\{a_n\}$, $\{b_n\}$, and $\{c_n\}$ denote three different sequences.

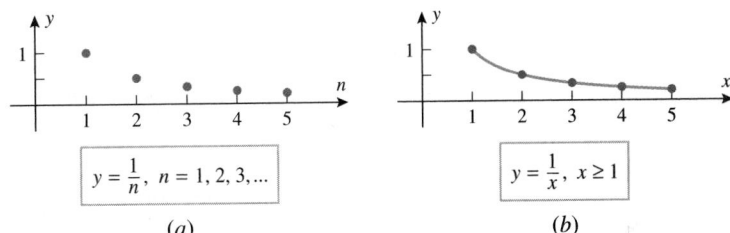

▶ **Figure 9.1.1**   (a)   (b)

■ LIMIT OF A SEQUENCE

Since sequences are functions, we can inquire about their limits. However, because a sequence $\{a_n\}$ is only defined for integer values of n, the only limit that makes sense is the limit of a_n as $n \to +\infty$. In Figure 9.1.2 we have shown the graphs of four sequences, each of which behaves differently as $n \to +\infty$:

- The terms in the sequence $\{n + 1\}$ increase without bound.
- The terms in the sequence $\{(-1)^{n+1}\}$ oscillate between -1 and 1.
- The terms in the sequence $\{n/(n + 1)\}$ increase toward a "limiting value" of 1.
- The terms in the sequence $\left\{1 + \left(-\frac{1}{2}\right)^n\right\}$ also tend toward a "limiting value" of 1, but do so in an oscillatory fashion.

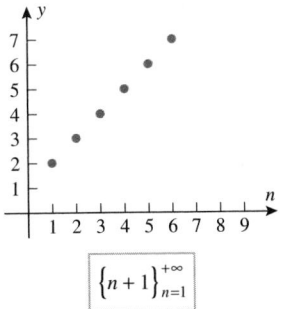
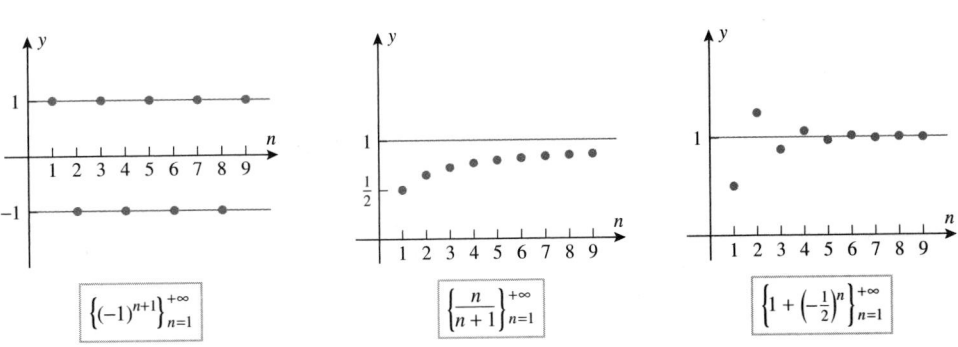

▲ **Figure 9.1.2**

Informally speaking, the limit of a sequence $\{a_n\}$ is intended to describe how a_n behaves as $n \to +\infty$. To be more specific, we will say that *a sequence $\{a_n\}$ approaches a limit L if the terms in the sequence eventually become arbitrarily close to L.* Geometrically, this

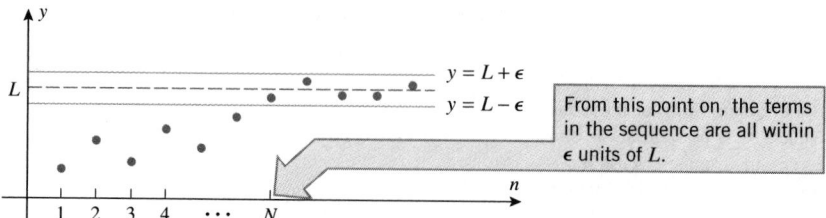

▶ **Figure 9.1.3**

means that for any positive number ϵ there is a point in the sequence after which all terms lie between the lines $y = L - \epsilon$ and $y = L + \epsilon$ (Figure 9.1.3).

The following definition makes these ideas precise.

<table>
<tr><td>

How would you define these limits?

$$\lim_{n \to +\infty} a_n = +\infty$$

$$\lim_{n \to +\infty} a_n = -\infty$$

</td></tr>
</table>

9.1.2   DEFINITION   A sequence $\{a_n\}$ is said to **converge** to the **limit** L if given any $\epsilon > 0$, there is a positive integer N such that $|a_n - L| < \epsilon$ for $n \geq N$. In this case we write

$$\lim_{n \to +\infty} a_n = L$$

A sequence that does not converge to some finite limit is said to **diverge**.

▶ **Example 2**   The first two sequences in Figure 9.1.2 diverge, and the second two converge to 1; that is,

$$\lim_{n \to +\infty} \frac{n}{n+1} = 1 \quad \text{and} \quad \lim_{n \to +\infty} \left[1 + \left(-\tfrac{1}{2}\right)^n\right] = 1 \quad ◀$$

The following theorem, which we state without proof, shows that the familiar properties of limits apply to sequences. This theorem ensures that the algebraic techniques used to find limits of the form $\lim_{x \to +\infty}$ can also be used for limits of the form $\lim_{n \to +\infty}$.

9.1.3   THEOREM   *Suppose that the sequences $\{a_n\}$ and $\{b_n\}$ converge to limits L_1 and L_2, respectively, and c is a constant. Then:*

$(a) \quad \lim_{n \to +\infty} c = c$

$(b) \quad \lim_{n \to +\infty} ca_n = c \lim_{n \to +\infty} a_n = cL_1$

$(c) \quad \lim_{n \to +\infty} (a_n + b_n) = \lim_{n \to +\infty} a_n + \lim_{n \to +\infty} b_n = L_1 + L_2$

$(d) \quad \lim_{n \to +\infty} (a_n - b_n) = \lim_{n \to +\infty} a_n - \lim_{n \to +\infty} b_n = L_1 - L_2$

$(e) \quad \lim_{n \to +\infty} (a_n b_n) = \lim_{n \to +\infty} a_n \cdot \lim_{n \to +\infty} b_n = L_1 L_2$

<table>
<tr><td>

Additional limit properties follow from those in Theorem 9.1.3. For example, use part (e) to show that if $a_n \to L$ and m is a positive integer, then

$$\lim_{n \to +\infty} (a_n)^m = L^m$$

</td></tr>
</table>

$(f) \quad \lim_{n \to +\infty} \left(\dfrac{a_n}{b_n}\right) = \dfrac{\lim_{n \to +\infty} a_n}{\lim_{n \to +\infty} b_n} = \dfrac{L_1}{L_2} \quad (\text{if } L_2 \neq 0)$

If the general term of a sequence is $f(n)$, where $f(x)$ is a function defined on the entire interval $[1, +\infty)$, then the values of $f(n)$ can be viewed as "sample values" of $f(x)$ taken

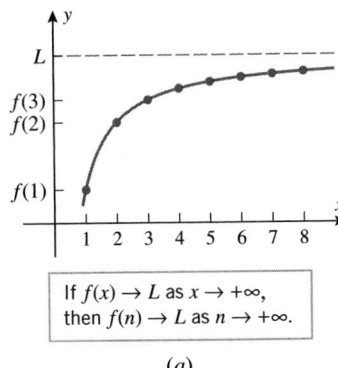

If $f(x) \to L$ as $x \to +\infty$,
then $f(n) \to L$ as $n \to +\infty$.

(a)

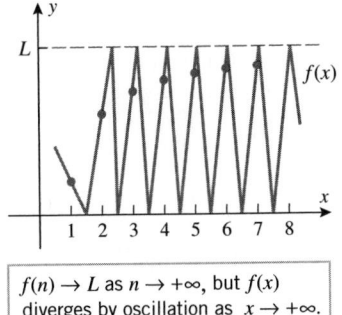

$f(n) \to L$ as $n \to +\infty$, but $f(x)$
diverges by oscillation as $x \to +\infty$.

(b)

▲ Figure 9.1.4

at the positive integers. Thus,

$$\text{if } f(x) \to L \text{ as } x \to +\infty, \quad \text{then} \quad f(n) \to L \text{ as } n \to +\infty$$

(Figure 9.1.4a). However, the converse is not true; that is, one cannot infer that $f(x) \to L$ as $x \to +\infty$ from the fact that $f(n) \to L$ as $n \to +\infty$ (Figure 9.1.4b).

▶ **Example 3**   In each part, determine whether the sequence converges or diverges by examining the limit as $n \to +\infty$.

(a) $\left\{ \dfrac{n}{2n+1} \right\}_{n=1}^{+\infty}$ (b) $\left\{ (-1)^{n+1} \dfrac{n}{2n+1} \right\}_{n=1}^{+\infty}$

(c) $\left\{ (-1)^{n+1} \dfrac{1}{n} \right\}_{n=1}^{+\infty}$ (d) $\{8 - 2n\}_{n=1}^{+\infty}$

Solution (a).   Dividing numerator and denominator by n and using Theorem 9.1.3 yields

$$\lim_{n \to +\infty} \frac{n}{2n+1} = \lim_{n \to +\infty} \frac{1}{2 + 1/n} = \frac{\displaystyle \lim_{n \to +\infty} 1}{\displaystyle \lim_{n \to +\infty} (2 + 1/n)} = \frac{\displaystyle \lim_{n \to +\infty} 1}{\displaystyle \lim_{n \to +\infty} 2 + \lim_{n \to +\infty} 1/n}$$

$$= \frac{1}{2+0} = \frac{1}{2}$$

Thus, the sequence converges to $\frac{1}{2}$.

Solution (b).   This sequence is the same as that in part (a), except for the factor of $(-1)^{n+1}$, which oscillates between $+1$ and -1. Thus, the terms in this sequence oscillate between positive and negative values, with the odd-numbered terms being identical to those in part (a) and the even-numbered terms being the negatives of those in part (a). Since the sequence in part (a) has a limit of $\frac{1}{2}$, it follows that the odd-numbered terms in this sequence approach $\frac{1}{2}$, and the even-numbered terms approach $-\frac{1}{2}$. Therefore, this sequence has no limit—it diverges.

Solution (c).   Since $1/n \to 0$, the product $(-1)^{n+1}(1/n)$ oscillates between positive and negative values, with the odd-numbered terms approaching 0 through positive values and the even-numbered terms approaching 0 through negative values. Thus,

$$\lim_{n \to +\infty} (-1)^{n+1} \frac{1}{n} = 0$$

so the sequence converges to 0.

Solution (d). $\displaystyle \lim_{n \to +\infty} (8 - 2n) = -\infty$, so the sequence $\{8 - 2n\}_{n=1}^{+\infty}$ diverges.   ◀

▶ **Example 4**   In each part, determine whether the sequence converges, and if so, find its limit.

(a) $1, \dfrac{1}{2}, \dfrac{1}{2^2}, \dfrac{1}{2^3}, \ldots, \dfrac{1}{2^n}, \ldots$ (b) $1, 2, 2^2, 2^3, \ldots, 2^n, \ldots$

Solution.   Replacing n by x in the first sequence produces the power function $(1/2)^x$, and replacing n by x in the second sequence produces the power function 2^x. Now recall that if $0 < b < 1$, then $b^x \to 0$ as $x \to +\infty$, and if $b > 1$, then $b^x \to +\infty$ as $x \to +\infty$ (Figure 0.5.1).

Thus,

$$\lim_{n \to +\infty} \frac{1}{2^n} = 0 \quad \text{and} \quad \lim_{n \to +\infty} 2^n = +\infty$$

So, the sequence $\{1/2^n\}$ converges to 0, but the sequence $\{2^n\}$ diverges. ◄

▶ **Example 5**   Find the limit of the sequence $\left\{ \dfrac{n}{e^n} \right\}_{n=1}^{+\infty}$.

Solution.   The expression

$$\lim_{n \to +\infty} \frac{n}{e^n}$$

is an indeterminate form of type ∞/∞, so L'Hôpital's rule is indicated. However, we cannot apply this rule directly to n/e^n because the functions n and e^n have been defined here only at the positive integers, and hence are not differentiable functions. To circumvent this problem we extend the domains of these functions to all real numbers, here implied by replacing n by x, and apply L'Hôpital's rule to the limit of the quotient x/e^x. This yields

$$\lim_{x \to +\infty} \frac{x}{e^x} = \lim_{x \to +\infty} \frac{1}{e^x} = 0$$

from which we can conclude that

$$\lim_{n \to +\infty} \frac{n}{e^n} = 0 \quad ◄$$

▶ **Example 6**   Show that $\lim_{n \to +\infty} \sqrt[n]{n} = 1$.

Solution.

$$\lim_{n \to +\infty} \sqrt[n]{n} = \lim_{n \to +\infty} n^{1/n} = \lim_{n \to +\infty} e^{(1/n)\ln n} = e^0 = 1 \qquad \boxed{\begin{array}{l}\text{By L'Hôpital's rule} \\ \text{applied to } (1/x)\ln x\end{array}} \quad ◄$$

Sometimes the even-numbered and odd-numbered terms of a sequence behave sufficiently differently that it is desirable to investigate their convergence separately. The following theorem, whose proof is omitted, is helpful for that purpose.

> **9.1.4   THEOREM**   *A sequence converges to a limit L if and only if the sequences of even-numbered terms and odd-numbered terms both converge to L.*

▶ **Example 7**   The sequence

$$\frac{1}{2}, \frac{1}{3}, \frac{1}{2^2}, \frac{1}{3^2}, \frac{1}{2^3}, \frac{1}{3^3}, \dots$$

converges to 0, since the even-numbered terms and the odd-numbered terms both converge to 0, and the sequence

$$1, \frac{1}{2}, 1, \frac{1}{3}, 1, \frac{1}{4}, \dots$$

diverges, since the odd-numbered terms converge to 1 and the even-numbered terms converge to 0. ◄

■ **THE SQUEEZING THEOREM FOR SEQUENCES**

The following theorem, illustrated in Figure 9.1.5, is an adaptation of the Squeezing Theorem (1.6.4) to sequences. This theorem will be useful for finding limits of sequences that cannot be obtained directly. The proof is omitted.

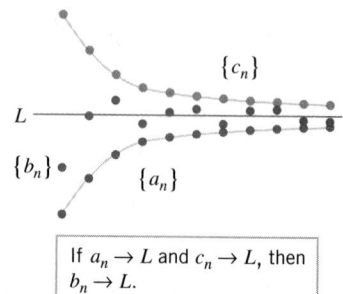

$\{c_n\}$

L

$\{b_n\}$ $\{a_n\}$

If $a_n \to L$ and $c_n \to L$, then $b_n \to L$.

▲ **Figure 9.1.5**

9.1.5   **THEOREM** (*The Squeezing Theorem for Sequences*)   *Let $\{a_n\}$, $\{b_n\}$, and $\{c_n\}$ be sequences such that*

$$a_n \leq b_n \leq c_n \quad (\text{for all values of } n \text{ beyond some index } N)$$

If the sequences $\{a_n\}$ and $\{c_n\}$ have a common limit L as $n \to +\infty$, then $\{b_n\}$ also has the limit L as $n \to +\infty$.

Recall that if n is a positive integer, then $n!$ (read "n factorial") is the product of the first n positive integers. In addition, it is convenient to define $0! = 1$.

▶ **Example 8**   Use numerical evidence to make a conjecture about the limit of the sequence

$$\left\{\frac{n!}{n^n}\right\}_{n=1}^{+\infty}$$

and then confirm that your conjecture is correct.

Solution.   Table 9.1.4, which was obtained with a calculating utility, suggests that the limit of the sequence may be 0. To confirm this we need to examine the limit of

$$a_n = \frac{n!}{n^n}$$

as $n \to +\infty$. Although this is an indeterminate form of type ∞/∞, L'Hôpital's rule is not helpful because we have no definition of $x!$ for values of x that are not integers. However, let us write out some of the initial terms and the general term in the sequence:

$$a_1 = 1, \quad a_2 = \frac{1 \cdot 2}{2 \cdot 2} = \frac{1}{2}, \quad a_3 = \frac{1 \cdot 2 \cdot 3}{3 \cdot 3 \cdot 3} = \frac{2}{9} < \frac{1}{3}, \quad a_4 = \frac{1 \cdot 2 \cdot 3 \cdot 4}{4 \cdot 4 \cdot 4 \cdot 4} = \frac{3}{32} < \frac{1}{4}, \cdots$$

If $n > 1$, the general term of the sequence can be rewritten as

$$a_n = \frac{1 \cdot 2 \cdot 3 \cdots n}{n \cdot n \cdot n \cdots n} = \frac{1}{n}\left(\frac{2 \cdot 3 \cdots n}{n \cdot n \cdots n}\right)$$

from which it follows that $a_n \leq 1/n$ (why?). It is now evident that

$$0 \leq a_n \leq \frac{1}{n}$$

However, the two outside expressions have a limit of 0 as $n \to +\infty$; thus, the Squeezing Theorem for Sequences implies that $a_n \to 0$ as $n \to +\infty$, which confirms our conjecture. ◀

Table 9.1.4

n	$\dfrac{n!}{n^n}$
1	1.0000000000
2	0.5000000000
3	0.2222222222
4	0.0937500000
5	0.0384000000
6	0.0154320988
7	0.0061198990
8	0.0024032593
9	0.0009366567
10	0.0003628800
11	0.0001399059
12	0.0000537232

The following theorem is often useful for finding the limit of a sequence with both positive and negative terms—it states that if the sequence $\{|a_n|\}$ that is obtained by taking the absolute value of each term in the sequence $\{a_n\}$ converges to 0, then $\{a_n\}$ also converges to 0.

9.1.6   **THEOREM**   *If* $\displaystyle\lim_{n \to +\infty} |a_n| = 0$, *then* $\displaystyle\lim_{n \to +\infty} a_n = 0$.

PROOF   Depending on the sign of a_n, either $a_n = |a_n|$ or $a_n = -|a_n|$. Thus, in all cases we have

$$-|a_n| \leq a_n \leq |a_n|$$

However, the limit of the two outside terms is 0, and hence the limit of a_n is 0 by the Squeezing Theorem for Sequences. ■

▶ **Example 9** Consider the sequence

$$1, -\frac{1}{2}, \frac{1}{2^2}, -\frac{1}{2^3}, \ldots, (-1)^n \frac{1}{2^n}, \ldots$$

If we take the absolute value of each term, we obtain the sequence

$$1, \frac{1}{2}, \frac{1}{2^2}, \frac{1}{2^3}, \ldots, \frac{1}{2^n}, \ldots$$

which, as shown in Example 4, converges to 0. Thus, from Theorem 9.1.6 we have

$$\lim_{n \to +\infty} \left[(-1)^n \frac{1}{2^n} \right] = 0 \quad \blacktriangleleft$$

■ **SEQUENCES DEFINED RECURSIVELY**

Some sequences do not arise from a formula for the general term, but rather from a formula or set of formulas that specify how to generate each term in the sequence from terms that precede it; such sequences are said to be defined *recursively*, and the defining formulas are called *recursion formulas*. A good example is the mechanic's rule for approximating square roots. In Exercise 25 of Section 4.7 you were asked to show that

$$x_1 = 1, \quad x_{n+1} = \frac{1}{2}\left(x_n + \frac{a}{x_n}\right) \tag{2}$$

describes the sequence produced by Newton's Method to approximate $\sqrt{a}$ as a zero of the function $f(x) = x^2 - a$. Table 9.1.5 shows the first five terms in an application of the mechanic's rule to approximate $\sqrt{2}$.

Table 9.1.5

n	$x_1 = 1, \quad x_{n+1} = \frac{1}{2}\left(x_n + \frac{2}{x_n}\right)$	DECIMAL APPROXIMATION
	$x_1 = 1$ (Starting value)	1.00000000000
1	$x_2 = \frac{1}{2}\left[1 + \frac{2}{1}\right] = \frac{3}{2}$	1.50000000000
2	$x_3 = \frac{1}{2}\left[\frac{3}{2} + \frac{2}{3/2}\right] = \frac{17}{12}$	1.41666666667
3	$x_4 = \frac{1}{2}\left[\frac{17}{12} + \frac{2}{17/12}\right] = \frac{577}{408}$	1.41421568627
4	$x_5 = \frac{1}{2}\left[\frac{577}{408} + \frac{2}{577/408}\right] = \frac{665,857}{470,832}$	1.41421356237
5	$x_6 = \frac{1}{2}\left[\frac{665,857}{470,832} + \frac{2}{665,857/470,832}\right] = \frac{886,731,088,897}{627,013,566,048}$	1.41421356237

It would take us too far afield to investigate the convergence of sequences defined recursively, but we will conclude this section with a useful technique that can sometimes be used to compute limits of such sequences.

▶ **Example 10** Assuming that the sequence in Table 9.1.5 converges, show that the limit is $\sqrt{2}$.

Solution. Assume that $x_n \to L$, where L is to be determined. Since $n+1 \to +\infty$ as $n \to +\infty$, it is also true that $x_{n+1} \to L$ as $n \to +\infty$. Thus, if we take the limit of the expression

$$x_{n+1} = \frac{1}{2}\left(x_n + \frac{2}{x_n}\right)$$

as $n \to +\infty$, we obtain

$$L = \frac{1}{2}\left(L + \frac{2}{L}\right)$$

which can be rewritten as $L^2 = 2$. The negative solution of this equation is extraneous because $x_n > 0$ for all n, so $L = \sqrt{2}$. ◄

✔ QUICK CHECK EXERCISES 9.1   (See page 607 for answers.)

1. Consider the sequence $4, 6, 8, 10, 12, \ldots$.
   (a) If $\{a_n\}_{n=1}^{+\infty}$ denotes this sequence, then $a_1 =$ _____, $a_4 =$ _____, and $a_7 =$ _____. The general term is $a_n =$ _____.
   (b) If $\{b_n\}_{n=0}^{+\infty}$ denotes this sequence, then $b_0 =$ _____, $b_4 =$ _____, and $b_8 =$ _____. The general term is $b_n =$ _____.

2. What does it mean to say that a sequence $\{a_n\}$ converges?

3. Consider sequences $\{a_n\}$ and $\{b_n\}$, where $a_n \to 2$ as $n \to +\infty$ and $b_n = (-1)^n$. Determine which of the following sequences converge and which diverge. If a sequence converges, indicate its limit.
   (a) $\{b_n\}$ (b) $\{3a_n - 1\}$ (c) $\{b_n^2\}$
   (d) $\{a_n + b_n\}$ (e) $\left\{\dfrac{1}{a_n^2 + 3}\right\}$ (f) $\left\{\dfrac{b_n}{1000}\right\}$

4. Suppose that $\{a_n\}$, $\{b_n\}$, and $\{c_n\}$ are sequences such that $a_n \leq b_n \leq c_n$ for all $n \geq 10$, and that $\{a_n\}$ and $\{c_n\}$ both converge to 12. Then the _____ Theorem for Sequences implies that $\{b_n\}$ converges to _____.

EXERCISE SET 9.1   ⌇ Graphing Utility

1. In each part, find a formula for the general term of the sequence, starting with $n = 1$.
   (a) $1, \dfrac{1}{3}, \dfrac{1}{9}, \dfrac{1}{27}, \ldots$ (b) $1, -\dfrac{1}{3}, \dfrac{1}{9}, -\dfrac{1}{27}, \ldots$
   (c) $\dfrac{1}{2}, \dfrac{3}{4}, \dfrac{5}{6}, \dfrac{7}{8}, \ldots$ (d) $\dfrac{1}{\sqrt{\pi}}, \dfrac{4}{\sqrt[3]{\pi}}, \dfrac{9}{\sqrt[4]{\pi}}, \dfrac{16}{\sqrt[5]{\pi}}, \ldots$

2. In each part, find two formulas for the general term of the sequence, one starting with $n = 1$ and the other with $n = 0$.
   (a) $1, -r, r^2, -r^3, \ldots$ (b) $r, -r^2, r^3, -r^4, \ldots$

3. (a) Write out the first four terms of the sequence $\{1 + (-1)^n\}$, starting with $n = 0$.
   (b) Write out the first four terms of the sequence $\{\cos n\pi\}$, starting with $n = 0$.
   (c) Use the results in parts (a) and (b) to express the general term of the sequence $4, 0, 4, 0, \ldots$ in two different ways, starting with $n = 0$.

4. In each part, find a formula for the general term using factorials and starting with $n = 1$.
   (a) $1 \cdot 2, 1 \cdot 2 \cdot 3 \cdot 4, 1 \cdot 2 \cdot 3 \cdot 4 \cdot 5 \cdot 6,$ $1 \cdot 2 \cdot 3 \cdot 4 \cdot 5 \cdot 6 \cdot 7 \cdot 8, \ldots$
   (b) $1, 1 \cdot 2 \cdot 3, 1 \cdot 2 \cdot 3 \cdot 4 \cdot 5, 1 \cdot 2 \cdot 3 \cdot 4 \cdot 5 \cdot 6 \cdot 7, \ldots$

5-6 Let f be the function $f(x) = \cos\left(\dfrac{\pi}{2}x\right)$ and define sequences $\{a_n\}$ and $\{b_n\}$ by $a_n = f(2n)$ and $b_n = f(2n+1)$. ■

5. (a) Does $\lim_{x \to +\infty} f(x)$ exist? Explain.
   (b) Evaluate $a_1, a_2, a_3, a_4,$ and a_5.
   (c) Does $\{a_n\}$ converge? If so, find its limit.

6. (a) Evaluate $b_1, b_2, b_3, b_4,$ and b_5.
   (b) Does $\{b_n\}$ converge? If so, find its limit.
   (c) Does $\{f(n)\}$ converge? If so, find its limit.

7-22 Write out the first five terms of the sequence, determine whether the sequence converges, and if so find its limit. ■

7. $\left\{\dfrac{n}{n+2}\right\}_{n=1}^{+\infty}$ 8. $\left\{\dfrac{n^2}{2n+1}\right\}_{n=1}^{+\infty}$ 9. $\{2\}_{n=1}^{+\infty}$

10. $\left\{\ln\left(\dfrac{1}{n}\right)\right\}_{n=1}^{+\infty}$ 11. $\left\{\dfrac{\ln n}{n}\right\}_{n=1}^{+\infty}$ 12. $\left\{n\sin\dfrac{\pi}{n}\right\}_{n=1}^{+\infty}$

13. $\{1 + (-1)^n\}_{n=1}^{+\infty}$ 14. $\left\{\dfrac{(-1)^{n+1}}{n^2}\right\}_{n=1}^{+\infty}$

15. $\left\{(-1)^n \dfrac{2n^3}{n^3+1}\right\}_{n=1}^{+\infty}$ 16. $\left\{\dfrac{n}{2^n}\right\}_{n=1}^{+\infty}$

17. $\left\{\dfrac{(n+1)(n+2)}{2n^2}\right\}_{n=1}^{+\infty}$ 18. $\left\{\dfrac{\pi^n}{4^n}\right\}_{n=1}^{+\infty}$

19. $\{n^2 e^{-n}\}_{n=1}^{+\infty}$ 20. $\{\sqrt{n^2 + 3n} - n\}_{n=1}^{+\infty}$

21. $\left\{\left(\dfrac{n+3}{n+1}\right)^n\right\}_{n=1}^{+\infty}$

22. $\left\{\left(1-\dfrac{2}{n}\right)^n\right\}_{n=1}^{+\infty}$

23–30 Find the general term of the sequence, starting with $n=1$, determine whether the sequence converges, and if so find its limit. ■

23. $\dfrac{1}{2}, \dfrac{3}{4}, \dfrac{5}{6}, \dfrac{7}{8}, \ldots$

24. $0, \dfrac{1}{2^2}, \dfrac{2}{3^2}, \dfrac{3}{4^2}, \ldots$

25. $\dfrac{1}{3}, -\dfrac{1}{9}, \dfrac{1}{27}, -\dfrac{1}{81}, \ldots$

26. $-1, 2, -3, 4, -5, \ldots$

27. $\left(1-\dfrac{1}{2}\right), \left(\dfrac{1}{3}-\dfrac{1}{2}\right), \left(\dfrac{1}{3}-\dfrac{1}{4}\right), \left(\dfrac{1}{5}-\dfrac{1}{4}\right), \ldots$

28. $3, \dfrac{3}{2}, \dfrac{3}{2^2}, \dfrac{3}{2^3}, \ldots$

29. $(\sqrt{2}-\sqrt{3}), (\sqrt{3}-\sqrt{4}), (\sqrt{4}-\sqrt{5}), \ldots$

30. $\dfrac{1}{3^5}, -\dfrac{1}{3^6}, \dfrac{1}{3^7}, -\dfrac{1}{3^8}, \ldots$

31–34 True–False Determine whether the statement is true or false. Explain your answer. ■

31. Sequences are functions.

32. If $\{a_n\}$ and $\{b_n\}$ are sequences such that $\{a_n + b_n\}$ converges, then $\{a_n\}$ and $\{b_n\}$ converge.

33. If $\{a_n\}$ diverges, then $a_n \to +\infty$ or $a_n \to -\infty$.

34. If the graph of $y = f(x)$ has a horizontal asymptote as $x \to +\infty$, then the sequence $\{f(n)\}$ converges.

35–36 Use numerical evidence to make a conjecture about the limit of the sequence, and then use the Squeezing Theorem for Sequences (Theorem 9.1.5) to confirm that your conjecture is correct. ■

35. $\displaystyle\lim_{n\to+\infty} \dfrac{\sin^2 n}{n}$

36. $\displaystyle\lim_{n\to+\infty} \left(\dfrac{1+n}{2n}\right)^n$

FOCUS ON CONCEPTS

37. Give two examples of sequences, all of whose terms are between -10 and 10, that do not converge. Use graphs of your sequences to explain their properties.

38. (a) Suppose that f satisfies $\lim_{x\to 0^+} f(x) = +\infty$. Is it possible that the sequence $\{f(1/n)\}$ converges? Explain.

(b) Find a function f such that $\lim_{x\to 0^+} f(x)$ does not exist but the sequence $\{f(1/n)\}$ converges.

39. (a) Starting with $n=1$, write out the first six terms of the sequence $\{a_n\}$, where

$$a_n = \begin{cases} 1, & \text{if } n \text{ is odd} \\ n, & \text{if } n \text{ is even} \end{cases}$$

(b) Starting with $n=1$, and considering the even and odd terms separately, find a formula for the general term of the sequence

$$1, \dfrac{1}{2^2}, 3, \dfrac{1}{2^4}, 5, \dfrac{1}{2^6}, \ldots$$

(c) Starting with $n=1$, and considering the even and odd terms separately, find a formula for the general term of the sequence

$$1, \dfrac{1}{3}, \dfrac{1}{3}, \dfrac{1}{5}, \dfrac{1}{5}, \dfrac{1}{7}, \dfrac{1}{7}, \dfrac{1}{9}, \dfrac{1}{9}, \ldots$$

(d) Determine whether the sequences in parts (a), (b), and (c) converge. For those that do, find the limit.

40. For what positive values of b does the sequence $b, 0, b^2, 0, b^3, 0, b^4, \ldots$ converge? Justify your answer.

41. Assuming that the sequence given in Formula (2) of this section converges, use the method of Example 10 to show that the limit of this sequence is $\sqrt{a}$.

42. Consider the sequence

$$a_1 = \sqrt{6}$$

$$a_2 = \sqrt{6+\sqrt{6}}$$

$$a_3 = \sqrt{6+\sqrt{6+\sqrt{6}}}$$

$$a_4 = \sqrt{6+\sqrt{6+\sqrt{6+\sqrt{6}}}}$$

$$\vdots$$

(a) Find a recursion formula for a_{n+1}.

(b) Assuming that the sequence converges, use the method of Example 10 to find the limit.

43. (a) A bored student enters the number 0.5 in a calculator display and then repeatedly computes the square of the number in the display. Taking $a_0 = 0.5$, find a formula for the general term of the sequence $\{a_n\}$ of numbers that appear in the display.

(b) Try this with a calculator and make a conjecture about the limit of a_n.

(c) Confirm your conjecture by finding the limit of a_n.

(d) For what values of a_0 will this procedure produce a convergent sequence?

44. Let

$$f(x) = \begin{cases} 2x, & 0 \le x < 0.5 \\ 2x-1, & 0.5 \le x < 1 \end{cases}$$

Does the sequence $f(0.2), f(f(0.2)), f(f(f(0.2))), \ldots$ converge? Justify your reasoning.

45. (a) Use a graphing utility to generate the graph of the equation $y = (2^x + 3^x)^{1/x}$, and then use the graph to make a conjecture about the limit of the sequence

$$\{(2^n + 3^n)^{1/n}\}_{n=1}^{+\infty}$$

(b) Confirm your conjecture by calculating the limit.

46. Consider the sequence $\{a_n\}_{n=1}^{+\infty}$ whose nth term is

$$a_n = \dfrac{1}{n}\sum_{k=1}^{n} \dfrac{1}{1+(k/n)}$$

Show that $\lim_{n\to+\infty} a_n = \ln 2$ by interpreting a_n as the Riemann sum of a definite integral.

47. The sequence whose terms are 1, 1, 2, 3, 5, 8, 13, 21, . . . is called the **Fibonacci sequence** in honor of the Italian mathematician Leonardo ("Fibonacci") da Pisa (c. 1170–1250). This sequence has the property that after starting with two 1's, each term is the sum of the preceding two.

(a) Denoting the sequence by $\{a_n\}$ and starting with $a_1 = 1$ and $a_2 = 1$, show that

$$\frac{a_{n+2}}{a_{n+1}} = 1 + \frac{a_n}{a_{n+1}} \quad \text{if } n \geq 1$$

(b) Give a reasonable informal argument to show that if the sequence $\{a_{n+1}/a_n\}$ converges to some limit L, then the sequence $\{a_{n+2}/a_{n+1}\}$ must also converge to L.

(c) Assuming that the sequence $\{a_{n+1}/a_n\}$ converges, show that its limit is $(1 + \sqrt{5})/2$.

48. If we accept the fact that the sequence $\{1/n\}_{n=1}^{+\infty}$ converges to the limit $L = 0$, then according to Definition 9.1.2, for every $\epsilon > 0$, there exists a positive integer N such that $|a_n - L| = |(1/n) - 0| < \epsilon$ when $n \geq N$. In each part, find the smallest possible value of N for the given value of ϵ.

(a) $\epsilon = 0.5$ (b) $\epsilon = 0.1$ (c) $\epsilon = 0.001$

49. If we accept the fact that the sequence

$$\left\{ \frac{n}{n+1} \right\}_{n=1}^{+\infty}$$

converges to the limit $L = 1$, then according to Definition 9.1.2, for every $\epsilon > 0$ there exists an integer N such that

$$|a_n - L| = \left| \frac{n}{n+1} - 1 \right| < \epsilon$$

when $n \geq N$. In each part, find the smallest value of N for the given value of ϵ.

(a) $\epsilon = 0.25$ (b) $\epsilon = 0.1$ (c) $\epsilon = 0.001$

50. Use Definition 9.1.2 to prove that

(a) the sequence $\{1/n\}_{n=1}^{+\infty}$ converges to 0

(b) the sequence $\left\{ \dfrac{n}{n+1} \right\}_{n=1}^{+\infty}$ converges to 1.

51. Writing Discuss, with examples, various ways that a sequence could diverge.

52. Writing Discuss the convergence of the sequence $\{r^n\}$ considering the cases $|r| < 1$, $|r| > 1$, $r = 1$, and $r = -1$ separately.

✔ **QUICK CHECK ANSWERS 9.1**

1. (a) 4; 10; 16; $2n + 2$ (b) 4; 12; 20; $2n + 4$ **2.** $\lim\limits_{n \to +\infty} a_n$ exists   **3.** (a) diverges   (b) converges to 5   (c) converges to 1

(d) diverges   (e) converges to $\frac{1}{7}$ (f) diverges   **4.** Squeezing; 12

9.2 MONOTONE SEQUENCES

There are many situations in which it is important to know whether a sequence converges, but the value of the limit is not relevant to the problem at hand. In this section we will study several techniques that can be used to determine whether a sequence converges.

■ TERMINOLOGY

We begin with some terminology.

9.2.1 DEFINITION A sequence $\{a_n\}_{n=1}^{+\infty}$ is called

> **strictly increasing** if $a_1 < a_2 < a_3 < \cdots < a_n < \cdots$
>
> **increasing** if $a_1 \leq a_2 \leq a_3 \leq \cdots \leq a_n \leq \cdots$
>
> **strictly decreasing** if $a_1 > a_2 > a_3 > \cdots > a_n > \cdots$
>
> **decreasing** if $a_1 \geq a_2 \geq a_3 \geq \cdots \geq a_n \geq \cdots$

A sequence that is either increasing or decreasing is said to be **monotone**, and a sequence that is either strictly increasing or strictly decreasing is said to be **strictly monotone**.

> Note that an increasing sequence need not be strictly increasing, and a decreasing sequence need not be strictly decreasing.

Some examples are given in Table 9.2.1 and their corresponding graphs are shown in Figure 9.2.1. The first and second sequences in Table 9.2.1 are strictly monotone; the third and fourth sequences are monotone but not strictly monotone; and the fifth sequence is neither strictly monotone nor monotone.

Table 9.2.1

SEQUENCE	DESCRIPTION
$\frac{1}{2}, \frac{2}{3}, \frac{3}{4}, \ldots, \frac{n}{n+1}, \ldots$	Strictly increasing
$1, \frac{1}{2}, \frac{1}{3}, \ldots, \frac{1}{n}, \ldots$	Strictly decreasing
$1, 1, 2, 2, 3, 3, \ldots$	Increasing; not strictly increasing
$1, 1, \frac{1}{2}, \frac{1}{2}, \frac{1}{3}, \frac{1}{3}, \ldots$	Decreasing; not strictly decreasing
$1, -\frac{1}{2}, \frac{1}{3}, -\frac{1}{4}, \ldots, (-1)^{n+1}\frac{1}{n}, \ldots$	Neither increasing nor decreasing

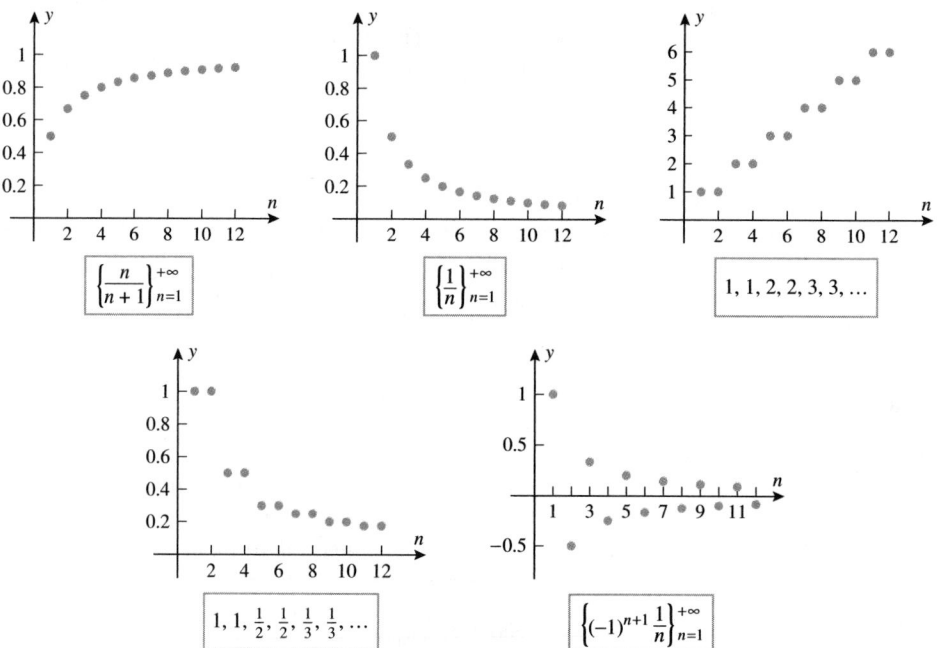

Can a sequence be both increasing and decreasing? Explain.

▲ **Figure 9.2.1**

■ TESTING FOR MONOTONICITY

Frequently, one can *guess* whether a sequence is monotone or strictly monotone by writing out some of the initial terms. However, to be certain that the guess is correct, one must give a precise mathematical argument. Table 9.2.2 provides two ways of doing this, one based

Table 9.2.2

DIFFERENCE BETWEEN SUCCESSIVE TERMS	RATIO OF SUCCESSIVE TERMS	CONCLUSION
$a_{n+1} - a_n > 0$	$a_{n+1}/a_n > 1$	Strictly increasing
$a_{n+1} - a_n < 0$	$a_{n+1}/a_n < 1$	Strictly decreasing
$a_{n+1} - a_n \geq 0$	$a_{n+1}/a_n \geq 1$	Increasing
$a_{n+1} - a_n \leq 0$	$a_{n+1}/a_n \leq 1$	Decreasing

on differences of successive terms and the other on ratios of successive terms. It is assumed in the latter case that the terms are positive. One must show that the specified conditions hold for *all* pairs of successive terms.

▶ **Example 1** Use differences of successive terms to show that

$$\frac{1}{2}, \frac{2}{3}, \frac{3}{4}, \ldots, \frac{n}{n+1}, \ldots$$

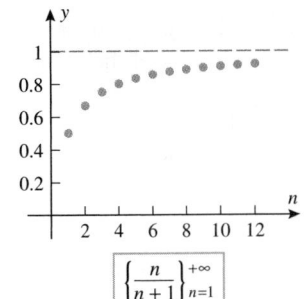

(Figure 9.2.2) is a strictly increasing sequence.

$$\left\{\frac{n}{n+1}\right\}_{n=1}^{+\infty}$$

▲ **Figure 9.2.2**

Solution. The pattern of the initial terms suggests that the sequence is strictly increasing. To prove that this is so, let

$$a_n = \frac{n}{n+1}$$

We can obtain a_{n+1} by replacing n by $n+1$ in this formula. This yields

$$a_{n+1} = \frac{n+1}{(n+1)+1} = \frac{n+1}{n+2}$$

Thus, for $n \geq 1$

$$a_{n+1} - a_n = \frac{n+1}{n+2} - \frac{n}{n+1} = \frac{n^2 + 2n + 1 - n^2 - 2n}{(n+1)(n+2)} = \frac{1}{(n+1)(n+2)} > 0$$

which proves that the sequence is strictly increasing. ◀

▶ **Example 2** Use ratios of successive terms to show that the sequence in Example 1 is strictly increasing.

Solution. As shown in the solution of Example 1,

$$a_n = \frac{n}{n+1} \quad \text{and} \quad a_{n+1} = \frac{n+1}{n+2}$$

Forming the ratio of successive terms we obtain

$$\frac{a_{n+1}}{a_n} = \frac{(n+1)/(n+2)}{n/(n+1)} = \frac{n+1}{n+2} \cdot \frac{n+1}{n} = \frac{n^2 + 2n + 1}{n^2 + 2n} \tag{1}$$

from which we see that $a_{n+1}/a_n > 1$ for $n \geq 1$. This proves that the sequence is strictly increasing. ◀

The following example illustrates still a third technique for determining whether a sequence is strictly monotone.

▶ **Example 3** In Examples 1 and 2 we proved that the sequence

$$\frac{1}{2}, \frac{2}{3}, \frac{3}{4}, \ldots, \frac{n}{n+1}, \ldots$$

is strictly increasing by considering the difference and ratio of successive terms. Alternatively, we can proceed as follows. Let

$$f(x) = \frac{x}{x+1}$$

so that the nth term in the given sequence is $a_n = f(n)$. The function f is increasing for $x \geq 1$ since

$$f'(x) = \frac{(x+1)(1) - x(1)}{(x+1)^2} = \frac{1}{(x+1)^2} > 0$$

Table 9.2.3

DERIVATIVE OF f FOR $x \geq 1$	CONCLUSION FOR THE SEQUENCE WITH $a_n = f(n)$
$f'(x) > 0$	Strictly increasing
$f'(x) < 0$	Strictly decreasing
$f'(x) \geq 0$	Increasing
$f'(x) \leq 0$	Decreasing

Thus,

$$a_n = f(n) < f(n+1) = a_{n+1}$$

which proves that the given sequence is strictly increasing. ◄

In general, if $f(n) = a_n$ is the nth term of a sequence, and if f is differentiable for $x \geq 1$, then the results in Table 9.2.3 can be used to investigate the monotonicity of the sequence.

■ PROPERTIES THAT HOLD EVENTUALLY

Sometimes a sequence will behave erratically at first and then settle down into a definite pattern. For example, the sequence

$$9, -8, -17, 12, 1, 2, 3, 4, \ldots \tag{2}$$

is strictly increasing from the fifth term on, but the sequence as a whole cannot be classified as strictly increasing because of the erratic behavior of the first four terms. To describe such sequences, we introduce the following terminology.

9.2.2   DEFINITION   If discarding finitely many terms from the beginning of a sequence produces a sequence with a certain property, then the original sequence is said to have that property **eventually**.

For example, although we cannot say that sequence (2) is strictly increasing, we can say that it is eventually strictly increasing.

▶ **Example 4**   Show that the sequence $\left\{ \dfrac{10^n}{n!} \right\}_{n=1}^{+\infty}$ is eventually strictly decreasing.

Solution.   We have

$$a_n = \frac{10^n}{n!} \quad \text{and} \quad a_{n+1} = \frac{10^{n+1}}{(n+1)!}$$

so

$$\frac{a_{n+1}}{a_n} = \frac{10^{n+1}/(n+1)!}{10^n/n!} = \frac{10^{n+1}n!}{10^n(n+1)!} = 10\frac{n!}{(n+1)n!} = \frac{10}{n+1} \tag{3}$$

From (3), $a_{n+1}/a_n < 1$ for all $n \geq 10$, so the sequence is eventually strictly decreasing, as confirmed by the graph in Figure 9.2.3. ◄

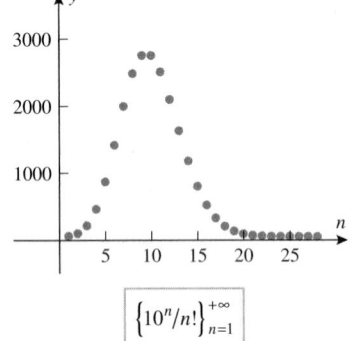

$\left\{ 10^n/n! \right\}_{n=1}^{+\infty}$

▲ **Figure 9.2.3**

■ AN INTUITIVE VIEW OF CONVERGENCE

Informally stated, the convergence or divergence of a sequence does not depend on the behavior of its *initial terms*, but rather on how the terms behave *eventually*. For example, the sequence

$$3, -9, -13, 17, 1, \frac{1}{2}, \frac{1}{3}, \frac{1}{4}, \ldots$$

eventually behaves like the sequence

$$1, \frac{1}{2}, \frac{1}{3}, \ldots, \frac{1}{n}, \ldots$$

and hence has a limit of 0.

■ CONVERGENCE OF MONOTONE SEQUENCES

The following two theorems, whose proofs are discussed at the end of this section, show that a monotone sequence either converges or becomes infinite—divergence by oscillation cannot occur.

9.2.3   THEOREM   *If a sequence $\{a_n\}$ is eventually increasing, then there are two possibilities:*

(a)   *There is a constant M, called an **upper bound** for the sequence, such that $a_n \leq M$ for all n, in which case the sequence converges to a limit L satisfying $L \leq M$.*

(b)   *No upper bound exists, in which case $\lim\limits_{n \to +\infty} a_n = +\infty$.*

9.2.4   THEOREM   *If a sequence $\{a_n\}$ is eventually decreasing, then there are two possibilities:*

(a)   *There is a constant M, called a **lower bound** for the sequence, such that $a_n \geq M$ for all n, in which case the sequence converges to a limit L satisfying $L \geq M$.*

(b)   *No lower bound exists, in which case $\lim\limits_{n \to +\infty} a_n = -\infty$.*

Theorems 9.2.3 and 9.2.4 are examples of *existence theorems*; they tell us whether a limit exists, but they do not provide a method for finding it.

▶ **Example 5**   Show that the sequence $\left\{\dfrac{10^n}{n!}\right\}_{n=1}^{+\infty}$ converges and find its limit.

Solution.   We showed in Example 4 that the sequence is eventually strictly decreasing. Since all terms in the sequence are positive, it is bounded below by $M = 0$, and hence Theorem 9.2.4 guarantees that it converges to a nonnegative limit L. However, the limit is not evident directly from the formula $10^n/n!$ for the nth term, so we will need some ingenuity to obtain it.

It follows from Formula (3) of Example 4 that successive terms in the given sequence are related by the recursion formula

$$a_{n+1} = \frac{10}{n+1} a_n \tag{4}$$

where $a_n = 10^n/n!$. We will take the limit as $n \to +\infty$ of both sides of (4) and use the fact that

$$\lim_{n \to +\infty} a_{n+1} = \lim_{n \to +\infty} a_n = L$$

We obtain

$$L = \lim_{n \to +\infty} a_{n+1} = \lim_{n \to +\infty} \left(\frac{10}{n+1} a_n\right) = \lim_{n \to +\infty} \frac{10}{n+1} \lim_{n \to +\infty} a_n = 0 \cdot L = 0$$

so that

$$L = \lim_{n \to +\infty} \frac{10^n}{n!} = 0 \blacktriangleleft$$

In the exercises we will show that the technique illustrated in the last example can be adapted to obtain

$$\lim_{n \to +\infty} \frac{x^n}{n!} = 0 \tag{5}$$

for any real value of x (Exercise 29). This result will be useful in our later work.

■ THE COMPLETENESS AXIOM

In this text we have accepted the familiar properties of real numbers without proof, and indeed, we have not even attempted to define the term *real number*. Although this is sufficient for many purposes, it was recognized by the late nineteenth century that the study of limits and functions in calculus requires a precise axiomatic formulation of the real numbers analogous to the axiomatic development of Euclidean geometry. Although we will not attempt to pursue this development, we will need to discuss one of the axioms about real numbers in order to prove Theorems 9.2.3 and 9.2.4. But first we will introduce some terminology.

If S is a nonempty set of real numbers, then we call u an **upper bound** for S if u is greater than or equal to every number in S, and we call l a **lower bound** for S if l is smaller than or equal to every number in S. For example, if S is the set of numbers in the interval $(1, 3)$, then $u = 10, 4, 3.2$, and 3 are upper bounds for S and $l = -10, 0, 0.5$, and 1 are lower bounds for S. Observe also that $u = 3$ is the smallest of all upper bounds and $l = 1$ is the largest of all lower bounds. The existence of a smallest upper bound and a largest lower bound for S is not accidental; it is a consequence of the following axiom.

9.2.5 AXIOM (*The Completeness Axiom*) *If a nonempty set S of real numbers has an upper bound, then it has a smallest upper bound (called the **least upper bound**), and if a nonempty set S of real numbers has a lower bound, then it has a largest lower bound (called the **greatest lower bound**).*

PROOF OF THEOREM 9.2.3

(a) We will prove the result for increasing sequences, and leave it for the reader to adapt the argument to sequences that are eventually increasing. Assume there exists a number M such that $a_n \leq M$ for $n = 1, 2, \ldots$. Then M is an upper bound for the set of terms in the sequence. By the Completeness Axiom there is a least upper bound for the terms; call it L. Now let ϵ be any positive number. Since L is the least upper bound for the terms, $L - \epsilon$ is not an upper bound for the terms, which means that there is at least one term a_N such that

$$a_N > L - \epsilon$$

Moreover, since $\{a_n\}$ is an increasing sequence, we must have

$$a_n \geq a_N > L - \epsilon \tag{6}$$

when $n \geq N$. But a_n cannot exceed L since L is an upper bound for the terms. This observation together with (6) tells us that $L \geq a_n > L - \epsilon$ for $n \geq N$, so all terms from the Nth on are within ϵ units of L. This is exactly the requirement to have

$$\lim_{n \to +\infty} a_n = L$$

Finally, $L \leq M$ since M is an upper bound for the terms and L is the least upper bound. This proves part (a).

(b) If there is no number M such that $a_n \leq M$ for $n = 1, 2, \ldots$, then no matter how large we choose M, there is a term a_N such that

$$a_N > M$$

and, since the sequence is increasing,

$$a_n \geq a_N > M$$

when $n \geq N$. Thus, the terms in the sequence become arbitrarily large as n increases. That is,

$$\lim_{n \to +\infty} a_n = +\infty \quad \blacksquare$$

We omit the proof of Theorem 9.2.4 since it is similar to that of 9.2.3.

✔ QUICK CHECK EXERCISES 9.2   *(See page 614 for answers.)*

1. Classify each sequence as (I) increasing, (D) decreasing, or (N) neither increasing nor decreasing.

_____ $\{2n\}$ _____ $\{2^{-n}\}$

_____ $\left\{\dfrac{5-n}{n^2}\right\}$ _____ $\left\{\dfrac{-1}{n^2}\right\}$

_____ $\left\{\dfrac{(-1)^n}{n^2}\right\}$

2. Classify each sequence as (M) monotonic, (S) strictly monotonic, or (N) not monotonic.

_____ $\{n + (-1)^n\}$ _____ $\{2n + (-1)^n\}$

_____ $\{3n + (-1)^n\}$

3. Since

$$\frac{n/[2(n+1)]}{(n-1)/(2n)} = \frac{n^2}{n^2-1} > \underline{\quad\quad}$$

the sequence $\{(n-1)/(2n)\}$ is strictly _____.

4. Since

$$\frac{d}{dx}[(x-8)^2] > 0 \text{ for } x > \underline{\quad\quad}$$

the sequence $\{(n-8)^2\}$ is _____ strictly _____.

EXERCISE SET 9.2

1–6 Use the difference $a_{n+1} - a_n$ to show that the given sequence $\{a_n\}$ is strictly increasing or strictly decreasing. ■

1. $\left\{\dfrac{1}{n}\right\}_{n=1}^{+\infty}$ 2. $\left\{1 - \dfrac{1}{n}\right\}_{n=1}^{+\infty}$ 3. $\left\{\dfrac{n}{2n+1}\right\}_{n=1}^{+\infty}$

4. $\left\{\dfrac{n}{4n-1}\right\}_{n=1}^{+\infty}$ 5. $\{n - 2^n\}_{n=1}^{+\infty}$ 6. $\{n - n^2\}_{n=1}^{+\infty}$

7–12 Use the ratio a_{n+1}/a_n to show that the given sequence $\{a_n\}$ is strictly increasing or strictly decreasing. ■

7. $\left\{\dfrac{n}{2n+1}\right\}_{n=1}^{+\infty}$ 8. $\left\{\dfrac{2^n}{1+2^n}\right\}_{n=1}^{+\infty}$ 9. $\{ne^{-n}\}_{n=1}^{+\infty}$

10. $\left\{\dfrac{10^n}{(2n)!}\right\}_{n=1}^{+\infty}$ 11. $\left\{\dfrac{n^n}{n!}\right\}_{n=1}^{+\infty}$ 12. $\left\{\dfrac{5^n}{2^{(n^2)}}\right\}_{n=1}^{+\infty}$

13–16 True–False Determine whether the statement is true or false. Explain your answer. ■

13. If $a_{n+1} - a_n > 0$ for all $n \geq 1$, then the sequence $\{a_n\}$ is strictly increasing.

14. A sequence $\{a_n\}$ is monotone if $a_{n+1} - a_n \neq 0$ for all $n \geq 1$.

15. Any bounded sequence converges.

16. If $\{a_n\}$ is eventually increasing, then $a_{100} < a_{200}$.

17–20 Use differentiation to show that the given sequence is strictly increasing or strictly decreasing. ■

17. $\left\{\dfrac{n}{2n+1}\right\}_{n=1}^{+\infty}$ 18. $\left\{\dfrac{\ln(n+2)}{n+2}\right\}_{n=1}^{+\infty}$

19. $\{\tan^{-1} n\}_{n=1}^{+\infty}$ 20. $\{ne^{-2n}\}_{n=1}^{+\infty}$

21–24 Show that the given sequence is eventually strictly increasing or eventually strictly decreasing. ■

21. $\{2n^2 - 7n\}_{n=1}^{+\infty}$ 22. $\{n^3 - 4n^2\}_{n=1}^{+\infty}$

23. $\left\{\dfrac{n!}{3^n}\right\}_{n=1}^{+\infty}$ 24. $\{n^5 e^{-n}\}_{n=1}^{+\infty}$

FOCUS ON CONCEPTS

25. Suppose that $\{a_n\}$ is a monotone sequence such that $1 \leq a_n \leq 2$ for all n. Must the sequence converge? If so, what can you say about the limit?

26. Suppose that $\{a_n\}$ is a monotone sequence such that $a_n \leq 2$ for all n. Must the sequence converge? If so, what can you say about the limit?

27. Let $\{a_n\}$ be the sequence defined recursively by $a_1 = \sqrt{2}$ and $a_{n+1} = \sqrt{2 + a_n}$ for $n \geq 1$.
    (a) List the first three terms of the sequence.
    (b) Show that $a_n < 2$ for $n \geq 1$.
    (c) Show that $a_{n+1}^2 - a_n^2 = (2 - a_n)(1 + a_n)$ for $n \geq 1$.
    (d) Use the results in parts (b) and (c) to show that $\{a_n\}$ is a strictly increasing sequence. [*Hint:* If x and y are positive real numbers such that $x^2 - y^2 > 0$, then it follows by factoring that $x - y > 0$.]
    (e) Show that $\{a_n\}$ converges and find its limit L.

28. Let $\{a_n\}$ be the sequence defined recursively by $a_1 = 1$ and $a_{n+1} = \frac{1}{2}[a_n + (3/a_n)]$ for $n \geq 1$.
    (a) Show that $a_n \geq \sqrt{3}$ for $n \geq 2$. [*Hint:* What is the minimum value of $\frac{1}{2}[x + (3/x)]$ for $x > 0$?]
    (b) Show that $\{a_n\}$ is eventually decreasing. [*Hint:* Examine $a_{n+1} - a_n$ or a_{n+1}/a_n and use the result in part (a).]
    (c) Show that $\{a_n\}$ converges and find its limit L.

29. The goal of this exercise is to establish Formula (5), namely,
$$\lim_{n \to +\infty} \frac{x^n}{n!} = 0$$
Let $a_n = |x|^n/n!$ and observe that the case where $x = 0$ is obvious, so we will focus on the case where $x \neq 0$.
    (a) Show that
$$a_{n+1} = \frac{|x|}{n+1} a_n$$
    (b) Show that the sequence $\{a_n\}$ is eventually strictly decreasing.   *(cont.)*

(c) Show that the sequence $\{a_n\}$ converges.

30. (a) Compare appropriate areas in the accompanying figure to deduce the following inequalities for $n \geq 2$:

$$\int_1^n \ln x \, dx < \ln n! < \int_1^{n+1} \ln x \, dx$$

(b) Use the result in part (a) to show that

$$\frac{n^n}{e^{n-1}} < n! < \frac{(n+1)^{n+1}}{e^n}, \quad n > 1$$

(c) Use the Squeezing Theorem for Sequences (Theorem 9.1.5) and the result in part (b) to show that

$$\lim_{n \to +\infty} \frac{\sqrt[n]{n!}}{n} = \frac{1}{e}$$

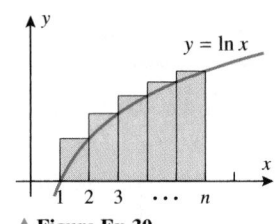
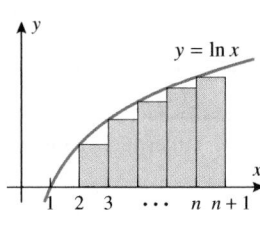

▲ **Figure Ex-30**

31. Use the left inequality in Exercise 30(b) to show that

$$\lim_{n \to +\infty} \sqrt[n]{n!} = +\infty$$

32. Writing Give an example of an increasing sequence that is not eventually strictly increasing. What can you conclude about the terms of any such sequence? Explain.

33. Writing Discuss the appropriate use of "eventually" for various properties of sequences. For example, which is a useful expression: "eventually bounded" or "eventually monotone"?

✔ **QUICK CHECK ANSWERS 9.2**

1. I; D; N; I; N **2.** N; M; S **3.** 1; increasing **4.** 8; eventually; increasing

---

9.3 INFINITE SERIES

The purpose of this section is to discuss sums that contain infinitely many terms. The most familiar examples of such sums occur in the decimal representations of real numbers. For example, when we write $\frac{1}{3}$ in the decimal form $\frac{1}{3} = 0.3333\ldots$, we mean

$$\frac{1}{3} = 0.3 + 0.03 + 0.003 + 0.0003 + \cdots$$

which suggests that the decimal representation of $\frac{1}{3}$ can be viewed as a sum of infinitely many real numbers.

■ SUMS OF INFINITE SERIES

Our first objective is to define what is meant by the "sum" of infinitely many real numbers. We begin with some terminology.

9.3.1 DEFINITION An ***infinite series*** is an expression that can be written in the form

$$\sum_{k=1}^{\infty} u_k = u_1 + u_2 + u_3 + \cdots + u_k + \cdots$$

The numbers $u_1, u_2, u_3, \ldots$ are called the ***terms*** of the series.

Since it is impossible to add infinitely many numbers together directly, sums of infinite series are defined and computed by an indirect limiting process. To motivate the basic idea, consider the decimal

$$0.3333\ldots \tag{1}$$

This can be viewed as the infinite series

$$0.3 + 0.03 + 0.003 + 0.0003 + \cdots$$

or, equivalently,

$$\frac{3}{10} + \frac{3}{10^2} + \frac{3}{10^3} + \frac{3}{10^4} + \cdots \tag{2}$$

Since (1) is the decimal expansion of $\frac{1}{3}$, any reasonable definition for the sum of an infinite series should yield $\frac{1}{3}$ for the sum of (2). To obtain such a definition, consider the following sequence of (finite) sums:

$$s_1 = \frac{3}{10} = 0.3$$

$$s_2 = \frac{3}{10} + \frac{3}{10^2} = 0.33$$

$$s_3 = \frac{3}{10} + \frac{3}{10^2} + \frac{3}{10^3} = 0.333$$

$$s_4 = \frac{3}{10} + \frac{3}{10^2} + \frac{3}{10^3} + \frac{3}{10^4} = 0.3333$$

$$\vdots$$

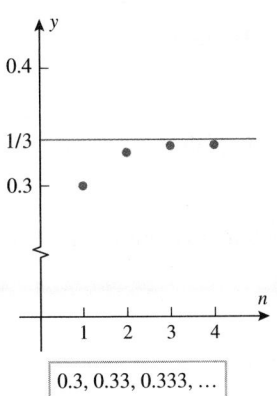

0.3, 0.33, 0.333, ...

▲ **Figure 9.3.1**

The sequence of numbers s_1, s_2, s_3, s_4, ... (Figure 9.3.1) can be viewed as a succession of approximations to the "sum" of the infinite series, which we want to be $\frac{1}{3}$. As we progress through the sequence, more and more terms of the infinite series are used, and the approximations get better and better, suggesting that the desired sum of $\frac{1}{3}$ might be the *limit* of this sequence of approximations. To see that this is so, we must calculate the limit of the general term in the sequence of approximations, namely,

$$s_n = \frac{3}{10} + \frac{3}{10^2} + \cdots + \frac{3}{10^n} \tag{3}$$

The problem of calculating

$$\lim_{n \to +\infty} s_n = \lim_{n \to +\infty} \left(\frac{3}{10} + \frac{3}{10^2} + \cdots + \frac{3}{10^n} \right)$$

is complicated by the fact that both the last term and the number of terms in the sum change with n. It is best to rewrite such limits in a closed form in which the number of terms does not vary, if possible. (See the discussion of closed form and open form following Example 2 in Section 5.4.) To do this, we multiply both sides of (3) by $\frac{1}{10}$ to obtain

$$\frac{1}{10} s_n = \frac{3}{10^2} + \frac{3}{10^3} + \cdots + \frac{3}{10^n} + \frac{3}{10^{n+1}} \tag{4}$$

and then subtract (4) from (3) to obtain

$$s_n - \frac{1}{10} s_n = \frac{3}{10} - \frac{3}{10^{n+1}}$$

$$\frac{9}{10} s_n = \frac{3}{10} \left(1 - \frac{1}{10^n} \right)$$

$$s_n = \frac{1}{3} \left(1 - \frac{1}{10^n} \right)$$

Since $1/10^n \to 0$ as $n \to +\infty$, it follows that

$$\lim_{n \to +\infty} s_n = \lim_{n \to +\infty} \frac{1}{3} \left(1 - \frac{1}{10^n} \right) = \frac{1}{3}$$

which we denote by writing

$$\frac{1}{3} = \frac{3}{10} + \frac{3}{10^2} + \frac{3}{10^3} + \cdots + \frac{3}{10^n} + \cdots$$

Motivated by the preceding example, we are now ready to define the general concept of the "sum" of an infinite series

$$u_1 + u_2 + u_3 + \cdots + u_k + \cdots$$

We begin with some terminology: Let s_n denote the sum of the initial terms of the series, up to and including the term with index n. Thus,

$$s_1 = u_1$$
$$s_2 = u_1 + u_2$$
$$s_3 = u_1 + u_2 + u_3$$
$$\vdots$$
$$s_n = u_1 + u_2 + u_3 + \cdots + u_n = \sum_{k=1}^{n} u_k$$

The number s_n is called the ***nth partial sum*** of the series and the sequence $\{s_n\}_{n=1}^{+\infty}$ is called the ***sequence of partial sums***.

As n increases, the partial sum $s_n = u_1 + u_2 + \cdots + u_n$ includes more and more terms of the series. Thus, if s_n tends toward a limit as $n \to +\infty$, it is reasonable to view this limit as the sum of *all* the terms in the series. This suggests the following definition.

9.3.2 **DEFINITION**   Let $\{s_n\}$ be the sequence of partial sums of the series

$$u_1 + u_2 + u_3 + \cdots + u_k + \cdots$$

If the sequence $\{s_n\}$ converges to a limit S, then the series is said to ***converge*** to S, and S is called the ***sum*** of the series. We denote this by writing

$$S = \sum_{k=1}^{\infty} u_k$$

If the sequence of partial sums diverges, then the series is said to ***diverge***. A divergent series has no sum.

▶ **Example 1**   Determine whether the series

$$1 - 1 + 1 - 1 + 1 - 1 + \cdots$$

converges or diverges. If it converges, find the sum.

Solution.   It is tempting to conclude that the sum of the series is zero by arguing that the positive and negative terms cancel one another. However, this is *not correct*; the problem is that algebraic operations that hold for finite sums do not carry over to infinite series in all cases. Later, we will discuss conditions under which familiar algebraic operations can be applied to infinite series, but for this example we turn directly to Definition 9.3.2. The partial sums are

$$s_1 = 1$$
$$s_2 = 1 - 1 = 0$$
$$s_3 = 1 - 1 + 1 = 1$$
$$s_4 = 1 - 1 + 1 - 1 = 0$$

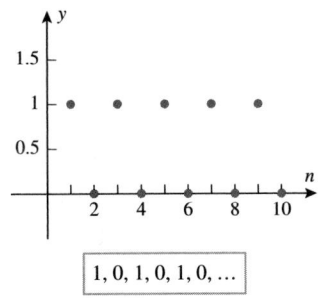

1, 0, 1, 0, 1, 0, ...

▲ **Figure 9.3.2**

and so forth. Thus, the sequence of partial sums is

$$1, 0, 1, 0, 1, 0, \ldots$$

(Figure 9.3.2). Since this is a divergent sequence, the given series diverges and consequently has no sum. ◄

■ GEOMETRIC SERIES

In many important series, each term is obtained by multiplying the preceding term by some fixed constant. Thus, if the initial term of the series is a and each term is obtained by multiplying the preceding term by r, then the series has the form

$$\sum_{k=0}^{\infty} ar^k = a + ar + ar^2 + ar^3 + \cdots + ar^k + \cdots \quad (a \neq 0) \tag{5}$$

Such series are called *geometric series*, and the number r is called the *ratio* for the series. Here are some examples:

$$1 + 2 + 4 + 8 + \cdots + 2^k + \cdots \qquad \boxed{a = 1, r = 2}$$

$$\frac{3}{10} + \frac{3}{10^2} + \frac{3}{10^3} + \cdots + \frac{3}{10^k} + \cdots \qquad \boxed{a = \frac{3}{10}, r = \frac{1}{10}}$$

$$\frac{1}{2} - \frac{1}{4} + \frac{1}{8} - \frac{1}{16} + \cdots + (-1)^{k+1}\frac{1}{2^k} + \cdots \qquad \boxed{a = \frac{1}{2}, r = -\frac{1}{2}}$$

$$1 + 1 + 1 + \cdots + 1 + \cdots \qquad \boxed{a = 1, r = 1}$$

$$1 - 1 + 1 - 1 + \cdots + (-1)^{k+1} + \cdots \qquad \boxed{a = 1, r = -1}$$

$$1 + x + x^2 + x^3 + \cdots + x^k + \cdots \qquad \boxed{a = 1, r = x}$$

The following theorem is the fundamental result on convergence of geometric series.

Sometimes it is desirable to start the index of summation of an infinite series at $k = 0$ rather than $k = 1$, in which case we would call u_0 the *zeroth term* and $s_0 = u_0$ the *zeroth partial sum*. One can prove that changing the starting value for the index of summation of an infinite series has no effect on the convergence, the divergence, or the sum. If we had started the index at $k = 1$ in (5), then the series would be expressed as

$$\sum_{k=1}^{\infty} ar^{k-1}$$

Since this expression is more complicated than (5), we started the index at $k = 0$.

9.3.3 THEOREM *A geometric series*

$$\sum_{k=0}^{\infty} ar^k = a + ar + ar^2 + \cdots + ar^k + \cdots \quad (a \neq 0)$$

converges if $|r| < 1$ and diverges if $|r| \geq 1$. If the series converges, then the sum is

$$\sum_{k=0}^{\infty} ar^k = \frac{a}{1-r}$$

PROOF Let us treat the case $|r| = 1$ first. If $r = 1$, then the series is

$$a + a + a + a + \cdots$$

so the nth partial sum is $s_n = (n+1)a$ and

$$\lim_{n \to +\infty} s_n = \lim_{n \to +\infty} (n+1)a = \pm\infty$$

(the sign depending on whether a is positive or negative). This proves divergence. If $r = -1$, the series is

$$a - a + a - a + \cdots$$

so the sequence of partial sums is

$$a, 0, a, 0, a, 0, \ldots$$

which diverges.

Now let us consider the case where $|r| \neq 1$. The nth partial sum of the series is

$$s_n = a + ar + ar^2 + \cdots + ar^n \tag{6}$$

Multiplying both sides of (6) by r yields

$$rs_n = ar + ar^2 + \cdots + ar^n + ar^{n+1} \tag{7}$$

and subtracting (7) from (6) gives

$$s_n - rs_n = a - ar^{n+1}$$

or

$$(1 - r)s_n = a - ar^{n+1} \tag{8}$$

Since $r \neq 1$ in the case we are considering, this can be rewritten as

$$s_n = \frac{a - ar^{n+1}}{1 - r} = \frac{a}{1 - r}(1 - r^{n+1}) \tag{9}$$

> Note that (6) is an open form for s_n, while (9) is a closed form for s_n. In general, one needs a closed form to calculate the limit.

If $|r| < 1$, then r^{n+1} goes to 0 as $n \to +\infty$ (can you see why?), so $\{s_n\}$ converges. From (9)

$$\lim_{n \to +\infty} s_n = \frac{a}{1 - r}$$

If $|r| > 1$, then either $r > 1$ or $r < -1$. In the case $r > 1$, r^{n+1} increases without bound as $n \to +\infty$, and in the case $r < -1$, r^{n+1} oscillates between positive and negative values that grow in magnitude, so $\{s_n\}$ diverges in both cases. ∎

Partial sums for $\displaystyle\sum_{k=0}^{\infty} \frac{5}{4^k}$

▲ **Figure 9.3.3**

▶ **Example 2** In each part, determine whether the series converges, and if so find its sum.

(a) $\displaystyle\sum_{k=0}^{\infty} \frac{5}{4^k}$ (b) $\displaystyle\sum_{k=1}^{\infty} 3^{2k}5^{1-k}$

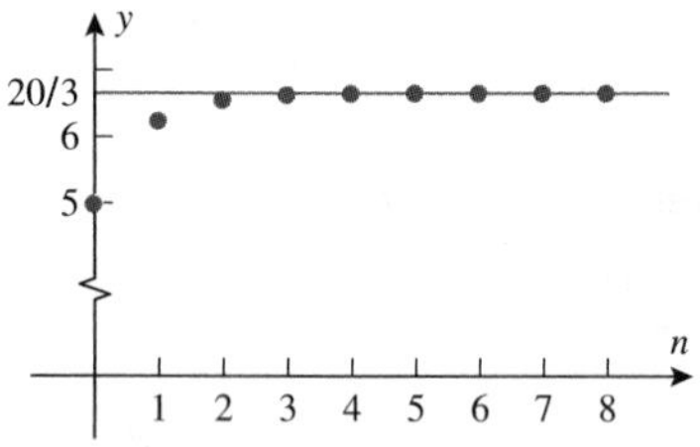

Solution (a). This is a geometric series with $a = 5$ and $r = \frac{1}{4}$. Since $|r| = \frac{1}{4} < 1$, the series converges and the sum is

$$\frac{a}{1 - r} = \frac{5}{1 - \frac{1}{4}} = \frac{20}{3}$$

(Figure 9.3.3).

Solution (b). This is a geometric series in concealed form, since we can rewrite it as

$$\sum_{k=1}^{\infty} 3^{2k}5^{1-k} = \sum_{k=1}^{\infty} \frac{9^k}{5^{k-1}} = \sum_{k=1}^{\infty} 9 \left(\frac{9}{5} \right)^{k-1}$$

Since $r = \frac{9}{5} > 1$, the series diverges. ◀

▶ **Example 3** Find the rational number represented by the repeating decimal

$$0.784784784\ldots$$

TECHNOLOGY MASTERY

Computer algebra systems have commands for finding sums of convergent series. If you have a CAS, use it to compute the sums in Examples 2 and 3.

Solution. We can write

$$0.784784784\ldots = 0.784 + 0.000784 + 0.000000784 + \cdots$$

so the given decimal is the sum of a geometric series with $a = 0.784$ and $r = 0.001$. Thus,

$$0.784784784\ldots = \frac{a}{1 - r} = \frac{0.784}{1 - 0.001} = \frac{0.784}{0.999} = \frac{784}{999} \quad ◀$$

▶ **Example 4** In each part, find all values of x for which the series converges, and find the sum of the series for those values of x.

(a) $\displaystyle\sum_{k=0}^{\infty} x^k$ (b) $3 - \dfrac{3x}{2} + \dfrac{3x^2}{4} - \dfrac{3x^3}{8} + \cdots + \dfrac{3(-1)^k}{2^k}x^k + \cdots$

Solution (a). The expanded form of the series is

$$\sum_{k=0}^{\infty} x^k = 1 + x + x^2 + \cdots + x^k + \cdots$$

The series is a geometric series with $a = 1$ and $r = x$, so it converges if $|x| < 1$ and diverges otherwise. When the series converges its sum is

$$\sum_{k=0}^{\infty} x^k = \frac{1}{1-x}$$

Solution (b). This is a geometric series with $a = 3$ and $r = -x/2$. It converges if $|-x/2| < 1$, or equivalently, when $|x| < 2$. When the series converges its sum is

$$\sum_{k=0}^{\infty} 3\left(-\frac{x}{2}\right)^k = \frac{3}{1 - \left(-\dfrac{x}{2}\right)} = \frac{6}{2+x} \quad ◀$$

■ **TELESCOPING SUMS**

▶ **Example 5** Determine whether the series

$$\sum_{k=1}^{\infty} \frac{1}{k(k+1)} = \frac{1}{1 \cdot 2} + \frac{1}{2 \cdot 3} + \frac{1}{3 \cdot 4} + \frac{1}{4 \cdot 5} + \cdots$$

converges or diverges. If it converges, find the sum.

Solution. The nth partial sum of the series is

$$s_n = \sum_{k=1}^{n} \frac{1}{k(k+1)} = \frac{1}{1 \cdot 2} + \frac{1}{2 \cdot 3} + \frac{1}{3 \cdot 4} + \cdots + \frac{1}{n(n+1)}$$

We will begin by rewriting s_n in closed form. This can be accomplished by using the method of partial fractions to obtain (verify)

$$\frac{1}{k(k+1)} = \frac{1}{k} - \frac{1}{k+1}$$

from which we obtain the sum

$$s_n = \sum_{k=1}^{n} \left(\frac{1}{k} - \frac{1}{k+1}\right)$$

$$= \left(1 - \frac{1}{2}\right) + \left(\frac{1}{2} - \frac{1}{3}\right) + \left(\frac{1}{3} - \frac{1}{4}\right) + \cdots + \left(\frac{1}{n} - \frac{1}{n+1}\right)$$

$$= 1 + \left(-\frac{1}{2} + \frac{1}{2}\right) + \left(-\frac{1}{3} + \frac{1}{3}\right) + \cdots + \left(-\frac{1}{n} + \frac{1}{n}\right) - \frac{1}{n+1}$$

$$= 1 - \frac{1}{n+1} \tag{10}$$

The sum in (10) is an example of a *telescoping sum*. The name is derived from the fact that in simplifying the sum, one term in each parenthetical expression cancels one term in the next parenthetical expression, until the entire sum collapses (like a folding telescope) into just two terms.

Thus,

$$\sum_{k=1}^{\infty} \frac{1}{k(k+1)} = \lim_{n \to +\infty} s_n = \lim_{n \to +\infty} \left(1 - \frac{1}{n+1}\right) = 1 \blacktriangleleft$$

■ HARMONIC SERIES

One of the most important of all diverging series is the *harmonic series*,

$$\sum_{k=1}^{\infty} \frac{1}{k} = 1 + \frac{1}{2} + \frac{1}{3} + \frac{1}{4} + \frac{1}{5} + \cdots$$

which arises in connection with the overtones produced by a vibrating musical string. It is not immediately evident that this series diverges. However, the divergence will become apparent when we examine the partial sums in detail. Because the terms in the series are all positive, the partial sums

$$s_1 = 1, \quad s_2 = 1 + \frac{1}{2}, \quad s_3 = 1 + \frac{1}{2} + \frac{1}{3}, \quad s_4 = 1 + \frac{1}{2} + \frac{1}{3} + \frac{1}{4}, \ldots$$

form a strictly increasing sequence

$$s_1 < s_2 < s_3 < \cdots < s_n < \cdots$$

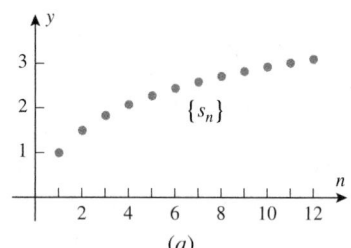

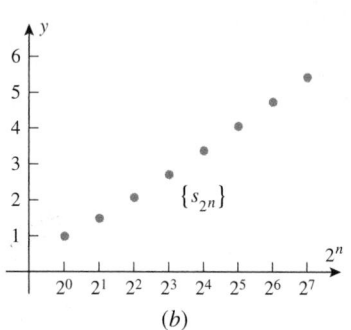

Partial sums for the harmonic series

▲ **Figure 9.3.4**

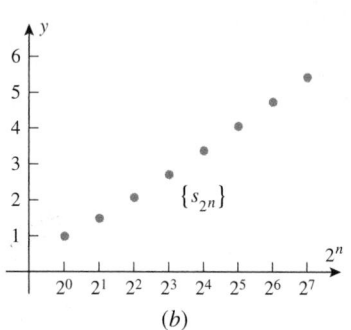

Courtesy Lilly Library, Indiana University

This is a proof of the divergence of the harmonic series, as it appeared in an appendix of Jakob Bernoulli's posthumous publication, Ars Conjectandi, which appeared in 1713.

(Figure 9.3.4*a*). Thus, by Theorem 9.2.3 we can prove divergence by demonstrating that there is no constant M that is greater than or equal to *every* partial sum. To this end, we will consider some selected partial sums, namely, $s_2, s_4, s_8, s_{16}, s_{32}, \ldots$. Note that the subscripts are successive powers of 2, so that these are the partial sums of the form s_{2^n} (Figure 9.3.4*b*). These partial sums satisfy the inequalities

$$s_2 = 1 + \tfrac{1}{2} > \tfrac{1}{2} + \tfrac{1}{2} = \tfrac{2}{2}$$

$$s_4 = s_2 + \tfrac{1}{3} + \tfrac{1}{4} > s_2 + \left(\tfrac{1}{4} + \tfrac{1}{4}\right) = s_2 + \tfrac{1}{2} > \tfrac{3}{2}$$

$$s_8 = s_4 + \tfrac{1}{5} + \tfrac{1}{6} + \tfrac{1}{7} + \tfrac{1}{8} > s_4 + \left(\tfrac{1}{8} + \tfrac{1}{8} + \tfrac{1}{8} + \tfrac{1}{8}\right) = s_4 + \tfrac{1}{2} > \tfrac{4}{2}$$

$$s_{16} = s_8 + \tfrac{1}{9} + \tfrac{1}{10} + \tfrac{1}{11} + \tfrac{1}{12} + \tfrac{1}{13} + \tfrac{1}{14} + \tfrac{1}{15} + \tfrac{1}{16}$$

$$> s_8 + \left(\tfrac{1}{16} + \tfrac{1}{16} + \tfrac{1}{16} + \tfrac{1}{16} + \tfrac{1}{16} + \tfrac{1}{16} + \tfrac{1}{16} + \tfrac{1}{16}\right) = s_8 + \tfrac{1}{2} > \tfrac{5}{2}$$

$$\vdots$$

$$s_{2^n} > \frac{n+1}{2}$$

If M is any constant, we can find a positive integer n such that $(n+1)/2 > M$. But for this n

$$s_{2^n} > \frac{n+1}{2} > M$$

so that no constant M is greater than or equal to *every* partial sum of the harmonic series. This proves divergence.

This divergence proof, which predates the discovery of calculus, is due to a French bishop and teacher, Nicole Oresme (1323–1382). This series eventually attracted the interest of Johann and Jakob Bernoulli (p. 700) and led them to begin thinking about the general concept of convergence, which was a new idea at that time.

✔ **QUICK CHECK EXERCISES 9.3**   *(See page 623 for answers.)*

1. In mathematics, the terms "sequence" and "series" have different meanings: a _____ is a succession, whereas a _____ is a sum.

2. Consider the series

$$\sum_{k=1}^{\infty} \frac{1}{2^k}$$

If $\{s_n\}$ is the sequence of partial sums for this series, then $s_1 =$ _____, $s_2 =$ _____, $s_3 =$ _____, $s_4 =$ _____, and $s_n =$ _____.

3. What does it mean to say that a series $\sum u_k$ *converges*?

4. A geometric series is a series of the form

$$\sum_{k=0}^{\infty} \underline{\hspace{1cm}}$$

This series converges to _____ if _____. This series diverges if _____.

5. The harmonic series has the form

$$\sum_{k=1}^{\infty} \underline{\hspace{1cm}}$$

Does the harmonic series converge or diverge?

EXERCISE SET 9.3   ⊂ CAS

1–2 In each part, find exact values for the first four partial sums, find a closed form for the nth partial sum, and determine whether the series converges by calculating the limit of the nth partial sum. If the series converges, then state its sum. ■

1. (a) $2 + \dfrac{2}{5} + \dfrac{2}{5^2} + \cdots + \dfrac{2}{5^{k-1}} + \cdots$

   (b) $\dfrac{1}{4} + \dfrac{2}{4} + \dfrac{2^2}{4} + \cdots + \dfrac{2^{k-1}}{4} + \cdots$

   (c) $\dfrac{1}{2 \cdot 3} + \dfrac{1}{3 \cdot 4} + \dfrac{1}{4 \cdot 5} + \cdots + \dfrac{1}{(k+1)(k+2)} + \cdots$

2. (a) $\displaystyle\sum_{k=1}^{\infty} \left(\frac{1}{4}\right)^k$ (b) $\displaystyle\sum_{k=1}^{\infty} 4^{k-1}$ (c) $\displaystyle\sum_{k=1}^{\infty} \left(\frac{1}{k+3} - \frac{1}{k+4}\right)$

3–14 Determine whether the series converges, and if so find its sum. ■

3. $\displaystyle\sum_{k=1}^{\infty} \left(-\frac{3}{4}\right)^{k-1}$

4. $\displaystyle\sum_{k=1}^{\infty} \left(\frac{2}{3}\right)^{k+2}$

5. $\displaystyle\sum_{k=1}^{\infty} (-1)^{k-1} \frac{7}{6^{k-1}}$

6. $\displaystyle\sum_{k=1}^{\infty} \left(-\frac{3}{2}\right)^{k+1}$

7. $\displaystyle\sum_{k=1}^{\infty} \frac{1}{(k+2)(k+3)}$

8. $\displaystyle\sum_{k=1}^{\infty} \left(\frac{1}{2^k} - \frac{1}{2^{k+1}}\right)$

9. $\displaystyle\sum_{k=1}^{\infty} \frac{1}{9k^2 + 3k - 2}$

10. $\displaystyle\sum_{k=2}^{\infty} \frac{1}{k^2 - 1}$

11. $\displaystyle\sum_{k=3}^{\infty} \frac{1}{k - 2}$

12. $\displaystyle\sum_{k=5}^{\infty} \left(\frac{e}{\pi}\right)^{k-1}$

13. $\displaystyle\sum_{k=1}^{\infty} \frac{4^{k+2}}{7^{k-1}}$

14. $\displaystyle\sum_{k=1}^{\infty} 5^{3k} 7^{1-k}$

15. Match a series from one of Exercises 3, 5, 7, or 9 with the graph of its sequence of partial sums.

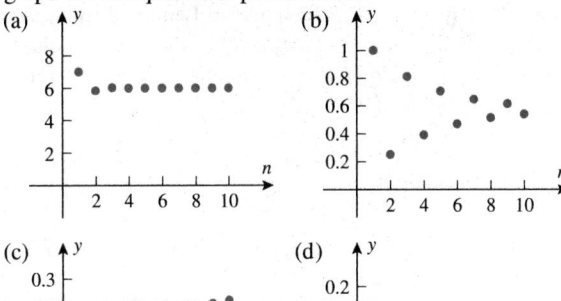

16. Match a series from one of Exercises 4, 6, 8, or 10 with the graph of its sequence of partial sums.

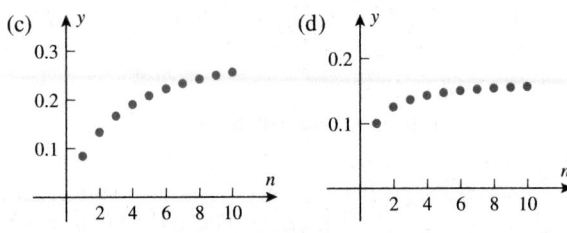
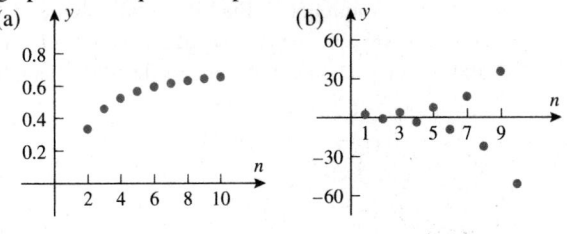
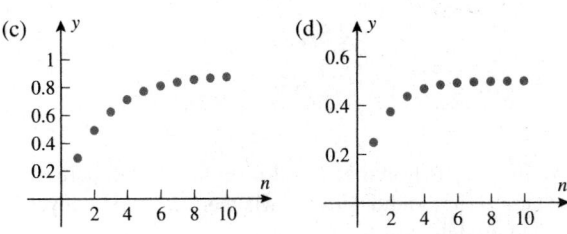

17–20 True–False Determine whether the statement is true or false. Explain your answer. ■

17. An infinite series converges if its sequence of terms converges.

18. The geometric series $a + ar + ar^2 + \cdots + ar^n + \cdots$ converges provided $|r| < 1$.

19. The harmonic series diverges.

20. An infinite series converges if its sequence of partial sums is bounded and monotone.

21–24 Express the repeating decimal as a fraction. ■

21. $0.9999\ldots$ **22.** $0.4444\ldots$

23. $5.373737\ldots$ **24.** $0.451141414\ldots$

25. Recall that a *terminating decimal* is a decimal whose digits are all 0 from some point on ($0.5 = 0.50000\ldots$, for example). Show that a decimal of the form $0.a_1 a_2 \ldots a_n 9999\ldots$, where $a_n \neq 9$, can be expressed as a terminating decimal.

FOCUS ON CONCEPTS

26. The great Swiss mathematician Leonhard Euler (biography on p. 3) sometimes reached incorrect conclusions in his pioneering work on infinite series. For example, Euler deduced that

$$\tfrac{1}{2} = 1 - 1 + 1 - 1 + \cdots$$

and

$$-1 = 1 + 2 + 4 + 8 + \cdots$$

by substituting $x = -1$ and $x = 2$ in the formula

$$\frac{1}{1-x} = 1 + x + x^2 + x^3 + \cdots$$

What was the problem with his reasoning?

27. A ball is dropped from a height of 10 m. Each time it strikes the ground it bounces vertically to a height that is $\frac{3}{4}$ of the preceding height. Find the total distance the ball will travel if it is assumed to bounce infinitely often.

28. The accompanying figure shows an "infinite staircase" constructed from cubes. Find the total volume of the staircase, given that the largest cube has a side of length 1 and each successive cube has a side whose length is half that of the preceding cube.

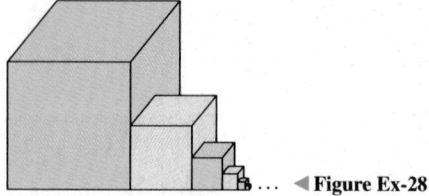

◄ **Figure Ex-28**

29. In each part, find a closed form for the *n*th partial sum of the series, and determine whether the series converges. If so, find its sum.

(a) $\ln \dfrac{1}{2} + \ln \dfrac{2}{3} + \ln \dfrac{3}{4} + \cdots + \ln \dfrac{k}{k+1} + \cdots$

(b) $\ln\left(1 - \dfrac{1}{4}\right) + \ln\left(1 - \dfrac{1}{9}\right) + \ln\left(1 - \dfrac{1}{16}\right) + \cdots$
$$+ \ln\left(1 - \dfrac{1}{(k+1)^2}\right) + \cdots$$

30. Use geometric series to show that

(a) $\displaystyle\sum_{k=0}^{\infty}(-1)^k x^k = \dfrac{1}{1+x}$ if $-1 < x < 1$

(b) $\displaystyle\sum_{k=0}^{\infty}(x - 3)^k = \dfrac{1}{4-x}$ if $2 < x < 4$

(c) $\displaystyle\sum_{k=0}^{\infty}(-1)^k x^{2k} = \dfrac{1}{1+x^2}$ if $-1 < x < 1$.

31. In each part, find all values of x for which the series converges, and find the sum of the series for those values of x.

(a) $x - x^3 + x^5 - x^7 + x^9 - \cdots$

(b) $\dfrac{1}{x^2} + \dfrac{2}{x^3} + \dfrac{4}{x^4} + \dfrac{8}{x^5} + \dfrac{16}{x^6} + \cdots$

(c) $e^{-x} + e^{-2x} + e^{-3x} + e^{-4x} + e^{-5x} + \cdots$

32. Show that for all real values of x

$$\sin x - \frac{1}{2}\sin^2 x + \frac{1}{4}\sin^3 x - \frac{1}{8}\sin^4 x + \cdots = \frac{2\sin x}{2 + \sin x}$$

33. Let a_1 be any real number, and let $\{a_n\}$ be the sequence defined recursively by

$$a_{n+1} = \tfrac{1}{2}(a_n + 1)$$

Make a conjecture about the limit of the sequence, and confirm your conjecture by expressing a_n in terms of a_1 and taking the limit.

34. Show: $\displaystyle\sum_{k=1}^{\infty} \frac{\sqrt{k+1} - \sqrt{k}}{\sqrt{k^2 + k}} = 1$.

35. Show: $\displaystyle\sum_{k=1}^{\infty} \left(\frac{1}{k} - \frac{1}{k+2}\right) = \frac{3}{2}$.

36. Show: $\dfrac{1}{1\cdot 3} + \dfrac{1}{2\cdot 4} + \dfrac{1}{3\cdot 5} + \cdots = \dfrac{3}{4}$.

37. Show: $\dfrac{1}{1\cdot 3} + \dfrac{1}{3\cdot 5} + \dfrac{1}{5\cdot 7} + \cdots = \dfrac{1}{2}$.

38. In his *Treatise on the Configurations of Qualities and Motions* (written in the 1350s), the French Bishop of Lisieux, Nicole Oresme, used a geometric method to find the sum of the series

$$\sum_{k=1}^{\infty} \frac{k}{2^k} = \frac{1}{2} + \frac{2}{4} + \frac{3}{8} + \frac{4}{16} + \cdots$$

In part (*a*) of the accompanying figure, each term in the series is represented by the area of a rectangle, and in part (b) the configuration in part (a) has been divided into rectangles with areas A_1, A_2, A_3, ... Find the sum $A_1 + A_2 + A_3 + \cdots$.

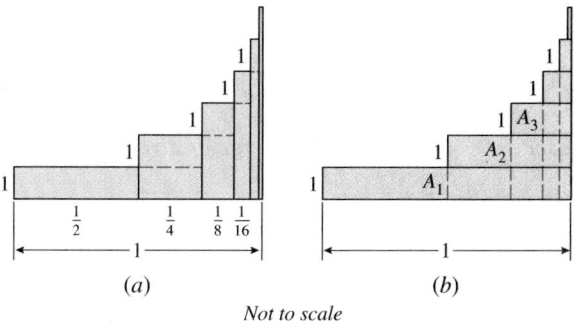

1

1

1

1

1

1

1

1

1 A_3

1 A_2

A_1

$\frac{1}{2}$ $\frac{1}{4}$ $\frac{1}{8}$ $\frac{1}{16}$

1

1

(a)

(b)

Not to scale

▲ Figure Ex-38

39. As shown in the accompanying figure, suppose that an angle θ is bisected using a straightedge and compass to produce ray R_1, then the angle between R_1 and the initial side is bisected to produce ray R_2. Thereafter, rays R_3, R_4, R_5, ... are constructed in succession by bisecting the angle between the preceding two rays. Show that the sequence of angles that these rays make with the initial side has a limit of $\theta/3$.

Source: This problem is based on "Trisection of an Angle in an Infinite Number of Steps" by Eric Kincannon, which appeared in *The College Mathematics Journal*, Vol. 21, No. 5, November 1990.

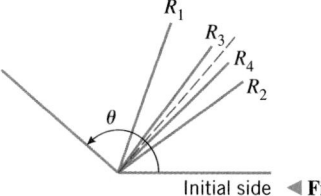

R_1

R_3

R_4

R_2

θ

Initial side   ◄ Figure Ex-39

C 40. In each part, use a CAS to find the sum of the series if it converges, and then confirm the result by hand calculation.

(a) $\displaystyle\sum_{k=1}^{\infty}(-1)^{k+1}2^k 3^{2-k}$ (b) $\displaystyle\sum_{k=1}^{\infty}\frac{3^{3k}}{5^{k-1}}$ (c) $\displaystyle\sum_{k=1}^{\infty}\frac{1}{4k^2-1}$

41. **Writing** Discuss the similarities and differences between what it means for a sequence to converge and what it means for a series to converge.

42. **Writing** Read about Zeno's dichotomy paradox in an appropriate reference work and relate the paradox in a setting that is familiar to you. Discuss a connection between the paradox and geometric series.

✔ **QUICK CHECK ANSWERS 9.3**

1. sequence; series   2. $\dfrac{1}{2}$; $\dfrac{3}{4}$; $\dfrac{7}{8}$; $\dfrac{15}{16}$; $1 - \dfrac{1}{2^n}$ 3. The sequence of partial sums converges.

4. $ar^k\ (a \neq 0)$; $\dfrac{a}{1-r}$; $|r| < 1$; $|r| \geq 1$ 5. $\dfrac{1}{k}$; diverge

9.4 CONVERGENCE TESTS

In the last section we showed how to find the sum of a series by finding a closed form for the nth partial sum and taking its limit. However, it is relatively rare that one can find a closed form for the nth partial sum of a series, so alternative methods are needed for finding the sum of a series. One possibility is to prove that the series converges, and then to approximate the sum by a partial sum with sufficiently many terms to achieve the desired degree of accuracy. In this section we will develop various tests that can be used to determine whether a given series converges or diverges.

■ THE DIVERGENCE TEST

In stating general results about convergence or divergence of series, it is convenient to use the notation $\sum u_k$ as a generic notation for a series, thus avoiding the issue of whether the sum begins with $k = 0$ or $k = 1$ or some other value. Indeed, we will see shortly that the starting index value is irrelevant to the issue of convergence. The kth term in an infinite series $\sum u_k$ is called the **general term** of the series. The following theorem establishes a relationship between the limit of the general term and the convergence properties of a series.

9.4.1   **THEOREM** (*The Divergence Test*)

(*a*)   *If* $\lim\limits_{k \to +\infty} u_k \neq 0$, *then the series* $\sum u_k$ *diverges.*

(*b*)   *If* $\lim\limits_{k \to +\infty} u_k = 0$, *then the series* $\sum u_k$ *may either converge or diverge.*

PROOF (*a*)   To prove this result, it suffices to show that if the series converges, then $\lim_{k \to +\infty} u_k = 0$ (why?). We will prove this alternative form of (*a*).

Let us assume that the series converges. The general term u_k can be written as

$$u_k = s_k - s_{k-1} \tag{1}$$

where s_k is the sum of the terms through u_k and s_{k-1} is the sum of the terms through u_{k-1}. If S denotes the sum of the series, then $\lim_{k \to +\infty} s_k = S$, and since $(k-1) \to +\infty$ as $k \to +\infty$, we also have $\lim_{k \to +\infty} s_{k-1} = S$. Thus, from (1)

$$\lim_{k \to +\infty} u_k = \lim_{k \to +\infty} (s_k - s_{k-1}) = S - S = 0$$

PROOF (*b*)   To prove this result, it suffices to produce both a convergent series and a divergent series for which $\lim_{k \to +\infty} u_k = 0$. The following series both have this property:

$$\frac{1}{2} + \frac{1}{2^2} + \cdots + \frac{1}{2^k} + \cdots \quad \text{and} \quad 1 + \frac{1}{2} + \frac{1}{3} + \cdots + \frac{1}{k} + \cdots$$

The first is a convergent geometric series and the second is the divergent harmonic series. ■

WARNING

The converse of Theorem 9.4.2 is false; i.e., showing that

$$\lim_{k \to +\infty} u_k = 0$$

does not prove that $\sum u_k$ converges, since this property may hold for divergent as well as convergent series. This is illustrated in the proof of part (*b*) of Theorem 9.4.1.

The alternative form of part (*a*) given in the preceding proof is sufficiently important that we state it separately for future reference.

9.4.2   **THEOREM**   *If the series* $\sum u_k$ *converges, then* $\lim\limits_{k \to +\infty} u_k = 0$.

▶ **Example 1**   The series

$$\sum_{k=1}^{\infty} \frac{k}{k+1} = \frac{1}{2} + \frac{2}{3} + \frac{3}{4} + \cdots + \frac{k}{k+1} + \cdots$$

diverges since

$$\lim_{k \to +\infty} \frac{k}{k+1} = \lim_{k \to +\infty} \frac{1}{1 + 1/k} = 1 \neq 0 \quad ◀$$

■ **ALGEBRAIC PROPERTIES OF INFINITE SERIES**

For brevity, the proof of the following result is omitted.

See Exercises 27 and 28 for an exploration of what happens when $\sum u_k$ or $\sum v_k$ diverge.

9.4.3   THEOREM

(a)   *If $\sum u_k$ and $\sum v_k$ are convergent series, then $\sum(u_k + v_k)$ and $\sum(u_k - v_k)$ are convergent series and the sums of these series are related by*

$$\sum_{k=1}^{\infty}(u_k + v_k) = \sum_{k=1}^{\infty} u_k + \sum_{k=1}^{\infty} v_k$$

$$\sum_{k=1}^{\infty}(u_k - v_k) = \sum_{k=1}^{\infty} u_k - \sum_{k=1}^{\infty} v_k$$

(b)   *If c is a nonzero constant, then the series $\sum u_k$ and $\sum cu_k$ both converge or both diverge. In the case of convergence, the sums are related by*

$$\sum_{k=1}^{\infty} cu_k = c \sum_{k=1}^{\infty} u_k$$

(c)   *Convergence or divergence is unaffected by deleting a finite number of terms from a series; in particular, for any positive integer K, the series*

$$\sum_{k=1}^{\infty} u_k = u_1 + u_2 + u_3 + \cdots$$

$$\sum_{k=K}^{\infty} u_k = u_K + u_{K+1} + u_{K+2} + \cdots$$

both converge or both diverge.

WARNING

Do not read too much into part (c) of Theorem 9.4.3. Although convergence is not affected when finitely many terms are deleted from the beginning of a convergent series, the *sum* of the series is changed by the removal of those terms.

▶ **Example 2**   Find the sum of the series

$$\sum_{k=1}^{\infty}\left(\frac{3}{4^k} - \frac{2}{5^{k-1}}\right)$$

Solution.   The series

$$\sum_{k=1}^{\infty} \frac{3}{4^k} = \frac{3}{4} + \frac{3}{4^2} + \frac{3}{4^3} + \cdots$$

is a convergent geometric series $\left(a = \frac{3}{4}, r = \frac{1}{4}\right)$, and the series

$$\sum_{k=1}^{\infty} \frac{2}{5^{k-1}} = 2 + \frac{2}{5} + \frac{2}{5^2} + \frac{2}{5^3} + \cdots$$

is also a convergent geometric series $\left(a = 2, r = \frac{1}{5}\right)$. Thus, from Theorems 9.4.3(a) and 9.3.3 the given series converges and

$$\sum_{k=1}^{\infty}\left(\frac{3}{4^k} - \frac{2}{5^{k-1}}\right) = \sum_{k=1}^{\infty} \frac{3}{4^k} - \sum_{k=1}^{\infty} \frac{2}{5^{k-1}}$$

$$= \frac{\frac{3}{4}}{1 - \frac{1}{4}} - \frac{2}{1 - \frac{1}{5}} = -\frac{3}{2} \quad ◀$$

▶ **Example 3**   Determine whether the following series converge or diverge.

$$\text{(a)} \sum_{k=1}^{\infty} \frac{5}{k} = 5 + \frac{5}{2} + \frac{5}{3} + \cdots + \frac{5}{k} + \cdots \qquad \text{(b)} \sum_{k=10}^{\infty} \frac{1}{k} = \frac{1}{10} + \frac{1}{11} + \frac{1}{12} + \cdots$$

Solution.   The first series is a constant times the divergent harmonic series, and hence diverges by part (*b*) of Theorem 9.4.3. The second series results by deleting the first nine terms from the divergent harmonic series, and hence diverges by part (*c*) of Theorem 9.4.3.

◀

■ **THE INTEGRAL TEST**

The expressions

$$\sum_{k=1}^{\infty} \frac{1}{k^2} \quad \text{and} \quad \int_{1}^{+\infty} \frac{1}{x^2}\, dx$$

are related in that the integrand in the improper integral results when the index k in the general term of the series is replaced by x and the limits of summation in the series are replaced by the corresponding limits of integration. The following theorem shows that there is a relationship between the convergence of the series and the integral.

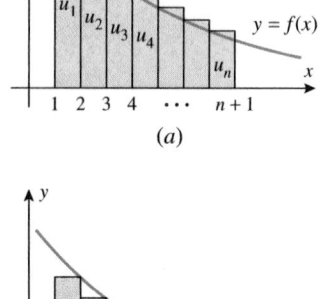

(*a*)

(*b*)

▲ **Figure 9.4.1**

9.4.4   **THEOREM** (*The Integral Test*)   *Let* $\sum u_k$ *be a series with positive terms. If f is a function that is decreasing and continuous on an interval $[a, +\infty)$ and such that $u_k = f(k)$ for all $k \geq a$, then*

$$\sum_{k=1}^{\infty} u_k \quad \text{and} \quad \int_{a}^{+\infty} f(x)\, dx$$

both converge or both diverge.

The proof of the integral test is deferred to the end of this section. However, the gist of the proof is captured in Figure 9.4.1: if the integral diverges, then so does the series (Figure 9.4.1*a*), and if the integral converges, then so does the series (Figure 9.4.1*b*).

▶ **Example 4**   Show that the integral test applies, and use the integral test to determine whether the following series converge or diverge.

$$\text{(a)} \sum_{k=1}^{\infty} \frac{1}{k} \qquad \text{(b)} \sum_{k=1}^{\infty} \frac{1}{k^2}$$

Solution (a).   We already know that this is the divergent harmonic series, so the integral test will simply illustrate another way of establishing the divergence.

Note first that the series has positive terms, so the integral test is applicable. If we replace k by x in the general term $1/k$, we obtain the function $f(x) = 1/x$, which is decreasing and continuous for $x \geq 1$ (as required to apply the integral test with $a = 1$). Since

$$\int_{1}^{+\infty} \frac{1}{x}\, dx = \lim_{b \to +\infty} \int_{1}^{b} \frac{1}{x}\, dx = \lim_{b \to +\infty} [\ln b - \ln 1] = +\infty$$

the integral diverges and consequently so does the series.

Solution (b).   Note first that the series has positive terms, so the integral test is applicable. If we replace k by x in the general term $1/k^2$, we obtain the function $f(x) = 1/x^2$, which is decreasing and continuous for $x \geq 1$. Since

$$\int_1^{+\infty} \frac{1}{x^2}\,dx = \lim_{b \to +\infty} \int_1^b \frac{dx}{x^2} = \lim_{b \to +\infty} \left[-\frac{1}{x}\right]_1^b = \lim_{b \to +\infty} \left[1 - \frac{1}{b}\right] = 1$$

the integral converges and consequently the series converges by the integral test with $a = 1$. ◄

■ *p*-SERIES

The series in Example 4 are special cases of a class of series called ***p*-series** or ***hyperharmonic series***. A p-series is an infinite series of the form

$$\sum_{k=1}^{\infty} \frac{1}{k^p} = 1 + \frac{1}{2^p} + \frac{1}{3^p} + \cdots + \frac{1}{k^p} + \cdots$$

where $p > 0$. Examples of p-series are

$$\sum_{k=1}^{\infty} \frac{1}{k} = 1 + \frac{1}{2} + \frac{1}{3} + \cdots + \frac{1}{k} + \cdots \qquad \boxed{p = 1}$$

$$\sum_{k=1}^{\infty} \frac{1}{k^2} = 1 + \frac{1}{2^2} + \frac{1}{3^2} + \cdots + \frac{1}{k^2} + \cdots \qquad \boxed{p = 2}$$

$$\sum_{k=1}^{\infty} \frac{1}{\sqrt{k}} = 1 + \frac{1}{\sqrt{2}} + \frac{1}{\sqrt{3}} + \cdots + \frac{1}{\sqrt{k}} + \cdots \qquad \boxed{p = \tfrac{1}{2}}$$

The following theorem tells when a p-series converges.

9.4.5   THEOREM (*Convergence of p-Series*)

$$\sum_{k=1}^{\infty} \frac{1}{k^p} = 1 + \frac{1}{2^p} + \frac{1}{3^p} + \cdots + \frac{1}{k^p} + \cdots$$

converges if $p > 1$ and diverges if $0 < p \leq 1$.

PROOF   To establish this result when $p \neq 1$, we will use the integral test.

$$\int_1^{+\infty} \frac{1}{x^p}\,dx = \lim_{b \to +\infty} \int_1^b x^{-p}\,dx = \lim_{b \to +\infty} \frac{x^{1-p}}{1-p}\bigg]_1^b = \lim_{b \to +\infty} \left[\frac{b^{1-p}}{1-p} - \frac{1}{1-p}\right]$$

Assume first that $p > 1$. Then $1 - p < 0$, so $b^{1-p} \to 0$ as $b \to +\infty$. Thus, the integral converges [its value is $-1/(1-p)$] and consequently the series also converges.

Now assume that $0 < p < 1$. It follows that $1 - p > 0$ and $b^{1-p} \to +\infty$ as $b \to +\infty$, so the integral and the series diverge. The case $p = 1$ is the harmonic series, which was previously shown to diverge. ■

► **Example 5**

$$1 + \frac{1}{\sqrt[3]{2}} + \frac{1}{\sqrt[3]{3}} + \cdots + \frac{1}{\sqrt[3]{k}} + \cdots$$

diverges since it is a p-series with $p = \frac{1}{3} < 1$. ◄

■ PROOF OF THE INTEGRAL TEST

Before we can prove the integral test, we need a basic result about convergence of series with *nonnegative* terms. If $u_1 + u_2 + u_3 + \cdots + u_k + \cdots$ is such a series, then its sequence of partial sums is increasing, that is,

$$s_1 \leq s_2 \leq s_3 \leq \cdots \leq s_n \leq \cdots$$

Thus, from Theorem 9.2.3 the sequence of partial sums converges to a limit S if and only if it has some upper bound M, in which case $S \leq M$. If no upper bound exists, then the sequence of partial sums diverges. Since convergence of the sequence of partial sums corresponds to convergence of the series, we have the following theorem.

9.4.6   THEOREM   *If $\sum u_k$ is a series with nonnegative terms, and if there is a constant M such that*

$$s_n = u_1 + u_2 + \cdots + u_n \leq M$$

for every n, then the series converges and the sum S satisfies $S \leq M$. If no such M exists, then the series diverges.

In words, this theorem implies that *a series with nonnegative terms converges if and only if its sequence of partial sums is bounded above.*

PROOF OF THEOREM 9.4.4   We need only show that the series converges when the integral converges and that the series diverges when the integral diverges. For simplicity, we will limit the proof to the case where $a = 1$. Assume that $f(x)$ satisfies the hypotheses of the theorem for $x \geq 1$. Since

$$f(1) = u_1, \ f(2) = u_2, \ldots, f(n) = u_n, \ldots$$

the values of $u_1, u_2, \ldots, u_n, \ldots$ can be interpreted as the areas of the rectangles shown in Figure 9.4.2.

The following inequalities result by comparing the areas under the curve $y = f(x)$ to the areas of the rectangles in Figure 9.4.2 for $n > 1$:

$$\int_1^{n+1} f(x)\,dx < u_1 + u_2 + \cdots + u_n = s_n \qquad \boxed{\text{Figure 9.4.2}a}$$

$$s_n - u_1 = u_2 + u_3 + \cdots + u_n < \int_1^n f(x)\,dx \qquad \boxed{\text{Figure 9.4.2}b}$$

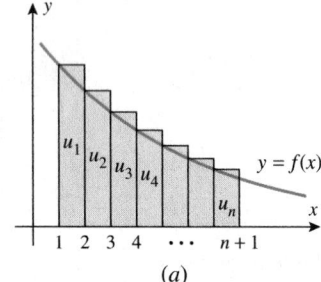

(a)

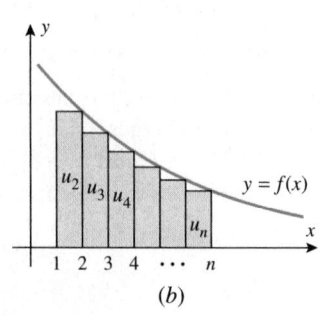

(b)

▲ **Figure 9.4.2**

These inequalities can be combined as

$$\int_1^{n+1} f(x)\,dx < s_n < u_1 + \int_1^n f(x)\,dx \tag{2}$$

If the integral $\int_1^{+\infty} f(x)\,dx$ converges to a finite value L, then from the right-hand inequality in (2)

$$s_n < u_1 + \int_1^n f(x)\,dx < u_1 + \int_1^{+\infty} f(x)\,dx = u_1 + L$$

Thus, each partial sum is less than the finite constant $u_1 + L$, and the series converges by Theorem 9.4.6. On the other hand, if the integral $\int_1^{+\infty} f(x)\,dx$ diverges, then

$$\lim_{n \to +\infty} \int_1^{n+1} f(x)\,dx = +\infty$$

so that from the left-hand inequality in (2), $s_n \to +\infty$ as $n \to +\infty$. This implies that the series also diverges. ■

✔ **QUICK CHECK EXERCISES 9.4**   *(See page 631 for answers.)*

1. The divergence test says that if _____ $\neq 0$, then the series $\sum u_k$ diverges.

2. Given that
$$a_1 = 3, \quad \sum_{k=1}^{\infty} a_k = 1, \quad \text{and} \quad \sum_{k=1}^{\infty} b_k = 5$$
it follows that
$$\sum_{k=2}^{\infty} a_k = \underline{\quad\quad} \quad \text{and} \quad \sum_{k=1}^{\infty}(2a_k + b_k) = \underline{\quad\quad}.$$

3. Since $\int_1^{+\infty}(1/\sqrt{x})\,dx = +\infty$, the _____ test applied to the series $\sum_{k=1}^{\infty}$ _____ shows that this series _____.

4. A p-series is a series of the form
$$\sum_{k=1}^{\infty} \underline{\quad\quad}$$
This series converges if _____. This series diverges if _____.

EXERCISE SET 9.4    Graphing Utility   C CAS

1. Use Theorem 9.4.3 to find the sum of each series.
   (a) $\left(\dfrac{1}{2} + \dfrac{1}{4}\right) + \left(\dfrac{1}{2^2} + \dfrac{1}{4^2}\right) + \cdots + \left(\dfrac{1}{2^k} + \dfrac{1}{4^k}\right) + \cdots$
   (b) $\displaystyle\sum_{k=1}^{\infty}\left(\dfrac{1}{5^k} - \dfrac{1}{k(k+1)}\right)$

2. Use Theorem 9.4.3 to find the sum of each series.
   (a) $\displaystyle\sum_{k=2}^{\infty}\left[\dfrac{1}{k^2-1} - \dfrac{7}{10^{k-1}}\right]$ (b) $\displaystyle\sum_{k=1}^{\infty}\left[7^{-k}3^{k+1} - \dfrac{2^{k+1}}{5^k}\right]$

3–4 For each given p-series, identify p and determine whether the series converges.

3. (a) $\displaystyle\sum_{k=1}^{\infty}\dfrac{1}{k^3}$ (b) $\displaystyle\sum_{k=1}^{\infty}\dfrac{1}{\sqrt{k}}$ (c) $\displaystyle\sum_{k=1}^{\infty}k^{-1}$ (d) $\displaystyle\sum_{k=1}^{\infty}k^{-2/3}$

4. (a) $\displaystyle\sum_{k=1}^{\infty}k^{-4/3}$ (b) $\displaystyle\sum_{k=1}^{\infty}\dfrac{1}{\sqrt[4]{k}}$ (c) $\displaystyle\sum_{k=1}^{\infty}\dfrac{1}{\sqrt[3]{k^5}}$ (d) $\displaystyle\sum_{k=1}^{\infty}\dfrac{1}{k^{\pi}}$

5–6 Apply the divergence test and state what it tells you about the series. ■

5. (a) $\displaystyle\sum_{k=1}^{\infty}\dfrac{k^2+k+3}{2k^2+1}$ (b) $\displaystyle\sum_{k=1}^{\infty}\left(1+\dfrac{1}{k}\right)^k$
   (c) $\displaystyle\sum_{k=1}^{\infty}\cos k\pi$ (d) $\displaystyle\sum_{k=1}^{\infty}\dfrac{1}{k!}$

6. (a) $\displaystyle\sum_{k=1}^{\infty}\dfrac{k}{e^k}$ (b) $\displaystyle\sum_{k=1}^{\infty}\ln k$
   (c) $\displaystyle\sum_{k=1}^{\infty}\dfrac{1}{\sqrt{k}}$ (d) $\displaystyle\sum_{k=1}^{\infty}\dfrac{\sqrt{k}}{\sqrt{k}+3}$

7–8 Confirm that the integral test is applicable and use it to determine whether the series converges. ■

7. (a) $\displaystyle\sum_{k=1}^{\infty}\dfrac{1}{5k+2}$ (b) $\displaystyle\sum_{k=1}^{\infty}\dfrac{1}{1+9k^2}$

8. (a) $\displaystyle\sum_{k=1}^{\infty}\dfrac{k}{1+k^2}$ (b) $\displaystyle\sum_{k=1}^{\infty}\dfrac{1}{(4+2k)^{3/2}}$

9–24 Determine whether the series converges. ■

9. $\displaystyle\sum_{k=1}^{\infty}\dfrac{1}{k+6}$ 10. $\displaystyle\sum_{k=1}^{\infty}\dfrac{3}{5k}$ 11. $\displaystyle\sum_{k=1}^{\infty}\dfrac{1}{\sqrt{k+5}}$

12. $\displaystyle\sum_{k=1}^{\infty}\dfrac{1}{\sqrt[k]{e}}$ 13. $\displaystyle\sum_{k=1}^{\infty}\dfrac{1}{\sqrt[3]{2k-1}}$ 14. $\displaystyle\sum_{k=3}^{\infty}\dfrac{\ln k}{k}$

15. $\displaystyle\sum_{k=1}^{\infty}\dfrac{k}{\ln(k+1)}$ 16. $\displaystyle\sum_{k=1}^{\infty}ke^{-k^2}$ 17. $\displaystyle\sum_{k=1}^{\infty}\left(1+\dfrac{1}{k}\right)^{-k}$

18. $\displaystyle\sum_{k=1}^{\infty}\dfrac{k^2+1}{k^2+3}$ 19. $\displaystyle\sum_{k=1}^{\infty}\dfrac{\tan^{-1}k}{1+k^2}$ 20. $\displaystyle\sum_{k=1}^{\infty}\dfrac{1}{\sqrt{k^2+1}}$

21. $\displaystyle\sum_{k=1}^{\infty}k^2\sin^2\left(\dfrac{1}{k}\right)$ 22. $\displaystyle\sum_{k=1}^{\infty}k^2e^{-k^3}$

23. $\displaystyle\sum_{k=5}^{\infty}7k^{-1.01}$ 24. $\displaystyle\sum_{k=1}^{\infty}\text{sech}^2 k$

25–26 Use the integral test to investigate the relationship between the value of p and the convergence of the series. ■

25. $\displaystyle\sum_{k=2}^{\infty}\dfrac{1}{k(\ln k)^p}$ 26. $\displaystyle\sum_{k=3}^{\infty}\dfrac{1}{k(\ln k)[\ln(\ln k)]^p}$

FOCUS ON CONCEPTS

27. Suppose that the series $\sum u_k$ converges and the series $\sum v_k$ diverges. Show that the series $\sum(u_k + v_k)$ and $\sum(u_k - v_k)$ both diverge. [*Hint:* Assume that $\sum(u_k + v_k)$ converges and use Theorem 9.4.3 to obtain a contradiction.]

28. Find examples to show that if the series $\sum u_k$ and $\sum v_k$ both diverge, then the series $\sum(u_k + v_k)$ and $\sum(u_k - v_k)$ may either converge or diverge.

29–30 Use the results of Exercises 27 and 28, if needed, to determine whether each series converges or diverges. ▪

29. (a) $\sum\limits_{k=1}^{\infty}\left[\left(\dfrac{2}{3}\right)^{k-1} + \dfrac{1}{k}\right]$ (b) $\sum\limits_{k=1}^{\infty}\left[\dfrac{1}{3k+2} - \dfrac{1}{k^{3/2}}\right]$

30. (a) $\sum\limits_{k=2}^{\infty}\left[\dfrac{1}{k(\ln k)^2} - \dfrac{1}{k^2}\right]$ (b) $\sum\limits_{k=2}^{\infty}\left[ke^{-k^2} + \dfrac{1}{k\ln k}\right]$

31–34 True–False Determine whether the statement is true or false. Explain your answer. ▪

31. If $\sum u_k$ converges to L, then $\sum(1/u_k)$ converges to $1/L$.

32. If $\sum cu_k$ diverges for some constant c, then $\sum u_k$ must diverge.

33. The integral test can be used to prove that a series diverges.

34. The series $\sum\limits_{k=1}^{\infty}\dfrac{1}{p^k}$ is a p-series.

C **35.** Use a CAS to confirm that

$$\sum_{k=1}^{\infty}\frac{1}{k^2} = \frac{\pi^2}{6} \quad \text{and} \quad \sum_{k=1}^{\infty}\frac{1}{k^4} = \frac{\pi^4}{90}$$

and then use these results in each part to find the sum of the series.

(a) $\sum\limits_{k=1}^{\infty}\dfrac{3k^2 - 1}{k^4}$ (b) $\sum\limits_{k=3}^{\infty}\dfrac{1}{k^2}$ (c) $\sum\limits_{k=2}^{\infty}\dfrac{1}{(k-1)^4}$

36–40 Exercise 36 will show how a partial sum can be used to obtain upper and lower bounds on the sum of a series when the hypotheses of the integral test are satisfied. This result will be needed in Exercises 37–40. ▪

36. (a) Let $\sum_{k=1}^{\infty} u_k$ be a convergent series with positive terms, and let f be a function that is decreasing and continuous on $[n, +\infty)$ and such that $u_k = f(k)$ for $k \geq n$. Use an area argument and the accompanying figure to show that

$$\int_{n+1}^{+\infty} f(x)\,dx < \sum_{k=n+1}^{\infty} u_k < \int_{n}^{+\infty} f(x)\,dx$$

(b) Show that if S is the sum of the series $\sum_{k=1}^{\infty} u_k$ and s_n is the nth partial sum, then

$$s_n + \int_{n+1}^{+\infty} f(x)\,dx < S < s_n + \int_{n}^{+\infty} f(x)\,dx$$

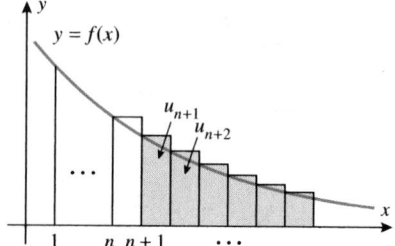

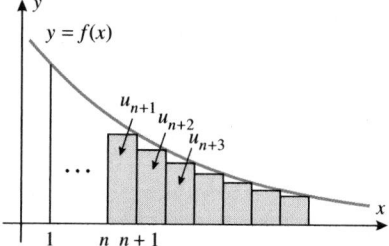

◀ **Figure Ex-36**

37. (a) It was stated in Exercise 35 that

$$\sum_{k=1}^{\infty}\frac{1}{k^2} = \frac{\pi^2}{6}$$

Show that if s_n is the nth partial sum of this series, then

$$s_n + \frac{1}{n+1} < \frac{\pi^2}{6} < s_n + \frac{1}{n}$$

(b) Calculate s_3 exactly, and then use the result in part (a) to show that

$$\frac{29}{18} < \frac{\pi^2}{6} < \frac{61}{36}$$

(c) Use a calculating utility to confirm that the inequalities in part (b) are correct.

(d) Find upper and lower bounds on the error that results if the sum of the series is approximated by the 10th partial sum.

38. In each part, find upper and lower bounds on the error that results if the sum of the series is approximated by the 10th partial sum.

(a) $\sum\limits_{k=1}^{\infty}\dfrac{1}{(2k+1)^2}$ (b) $\sum\limits_{k=1}^{\infty}\dfrac{1}{k^2+1}$ (c) $\sum\limits_{k=1}^{\infty}\dfrac{k}{e^k}$

39. It was stated in Exercise 35 that

$$\sum_{k=1}^{\infty}\frac{1}{k^4} = \frac{\pi^4}{90}$$

(a) Let s_n be the nth partial sum of the series above. Show that

$$s_n + \frac{1}{3(n+1)^3} < \frac{\pi^4}{90} < s_n + \frac{1}{3n^3}$$

(b) We can use a partial sum of the series to approximate $\pi^4/90$ to three decimal-place accuracy by capturing the sum of the series in an interval of length 0.001 (or less). Find the smallest value of n such that the interval containing $\pi^4/90$ in part (a) has a length of 0.001 or less.

(c) Approximate $\pi^4/90$ to three decimal places using the midpoint of an interval of width at most 0.001 that contains the sum of the series. Use a calculating utility to confirm that your answer is within 0.0005 of $\pi^4/90$.

40. We showed in Section 9.3 that the harmonic series $\sum_{k=1}^{\infty} 1/k$ diverges. Our objective in this problem is to demonstrate that although the partial sums of this series approach $+\infty$, they increase extremely slowly.

(a) Use inequality (2) to show that for $n \geq 2$

$$\ln(n+1) < s_n < 1 + \ln n$$

(b) Use the inequalities in part (a) to find upper and lower bounds on the sum of the first million terms in the series.

(c) Show that the sum of the first billion terms in the series is less than 22.

(d) Find a value of n so that the sum of the first n terms is greater than 100.

41. Use a graphing utility to confirm that the integral test applies to the series $\sum_{k=1}^{\infty} k^2 e^{-k}$, and then determine whether the series converges.

42. (a) Show that the hypotheses of the integral test are satisfied by the series $\sum_{k=1}^{\infty} 1/(k^3+1)$.

(b) Use a CAS and the integral test to confirm that the series converges.

(c) Construct a table of partial sums for $n = 10, 20, 30, \ldots, 100$, showing at least six decimal places.

(d) Based on your table, make a conjecture about the sum of the series to three decimal-place accuracy.

(e) Use part (b) of Exercise 36 to check your conjecture.

✔ QUICK CHECK ANSWERS 9.4

1. $\lim\limits_{k \to +\infty} u_k$ 2. $-2; 7$ 3. integral; $\dfrac{1}{\sqrt{k}}$; diverges   4. $\dfrac{1}{k^p}; p > 1; 0 < p \leq 1$

9.5 THE COMPARISON, RATIO, AND ROOT TESTS

In this section we will develop some more basic convergence tests for series with nonnegative terms. Later, we will use some of these tests to study the convergence of Taylor series.

■ THE COMPARISON TEST

We will begin with a test that is useful in its own right and is also the building block for other important convergence tests. The underlying idea of this test is to use the known convergence or divergence of a series to deduce the convergence or divergence of another series.

> **9.5.1 THEOREM (*The Comparison Test*)** Let $\sum_{k=1}^{\infty} a_k$ and $\sum_{k=1}^{\infty} b_k$ be series with non-negative terms and suppose that
>
> $$a_1 \leq b_1, \ a_2 \leq b_2, \ a_3 \leq b_3, \ldots, a_k \leq b_k, \ldots$$
>
> (a) If the "bigger series" Σb_k converges, then the "smaller series" Σa_k also converges.
>
> (b) If the "smaller series" Σa_k diverges, then the "bigger series" Σb_k also diverges.

It is not essential in Theorem 9.5.1 that the condition $a_k \leq b_k$ hold for all k, as stated; the conclusions of the theorem remain true if this condition is eventually true.

We have left the proof of this theorem for the exercises; however, it is easy to visualize why the theorem is true by interpreting the terms in the series as areas of rectangles

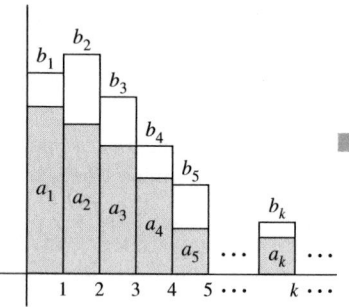

For each rectangle, a_k denotes the area of the blue portion and b_k denotes the combined area of the white and blue portions.

▲ **Figure 9.5.1**

(Figure 9.5.1). The comparison test states that if the total area $\sum b_k$ is finite, then the total area $\sum a_k$ must also be finite; and if the total area $\sum a_k$ is infinite, then the total area $\sum b_k$ must also be infinite.

■ **USING THE COMPARISON TEST**

There are two steps required for using the comparison test to determine whether a series $\sum u_k$ with positive terms converges:

Step 1. Guess at whether the series $\sum u_k$ converges or diverges.

Step 2. Find a series that proves the guess to be correct. That is, if we guess that $\sum u_k$ diverges, we must find a divergent series whose terms are "smaller" than the corresponding terms of $\sum u_k$, and if we guess that $\sum u_k$ converges, we must find a convergent series whose terms are "bigger" than the corresponding terms of $\sum u_k$.

In most cases, the series $\sum u_k$ being considered will have its general term u_k expressed as a fraction. To help with the guessing process in the first step, we have formulated two principles that are based on the form of the denominator for u_k. These principles sometimes *suggest* whether a series is likely to converge or diverge. We have called these "informal principles" because they are not intended as formal theorems. In fact, we will not guarantee that they *always* work. However, they work often enough to be useful.

9.5.2 INFORMAL PRINCIPLE *Constant terms in the denominator of u_k can usually be deleted without affecting the convergence or divergence of the series.*

9.5.3 INFORMAL PRINCIPLE *If a polynomial in k appears as a factor in the numerator or denominator of u_k, all but the leading term in the polynomial can usually be discarded without affecting the convergence or divergence of the series.*

▶ **Example 1** Use the comparison test to determine whether the following series converge or diverge.

$$\text{(a)} \sum_{k=1}^{\infty} \frac{1}{\sqrt{k} - \frac{1}{2}} \qquad \text{(b)} \sum_{k=1}^{\infty} \frac{1}{2k^2 + k}$$

Solution (a). According to Principle 9.5.2, we should be able to drop the constant in the denominator without affecting the convergence or divergence. Thus, the given series is likely to behave like

$$\sum_{k=1}^{\infty} \frac{1}{\sqrt{k}} \qquad (1)$$

which is a divergent p-series $\left(p = \frac{1}{2}\right)$. Thus, we will guess that the given series diverges and try to prove this by finding a divergent series that is "smaller" than the given series. However, series (1) does the trick since

$$\frac{1}{\sqrt{k} - \frac{1}{2}} > \frac{1}{\sqrt{k}} \qquad \text{for } k = 1, 2, \ldots$$

Thus, we have proved that the given series diverges.

Solution (b). According to Principle 9.5.3, we should be able to discard all but the leading term in the polynomial without affecting the convergence or divergence. Thus, the given series is likely to behave like

$$\sum_{k=1}^{\infty} \frac{1}{2k^2} = \frac{1}{2} \sum_{k=1}^{\infty} \frac{1}{k^2} \tag{2}$$

which converges since it is a constant times a convergent *p*-series ($p = 2$). Thus, we will guess that the given series converges and try to prove this by finding a convergent series that is "bigger" than the given series. However, series (2) does the trick since

$$\frac{1}{2k^2 + k} < \frac{1}{2k^2} \quad \text{for } k = 1, 2, \ldots$$

Thus, we have proved that the given series converges. ◄

■ **THE LIMIT COMPARISON TEST**

In the last example, Principles 9.5.2 and 9.5.3 provided the guess about convergence or divergence as well as the series needed to apply the comparison test. Unfortunately, it is not always so straightforward to find the series required for comparison, so we will now consider an alternative to the comparison test that is usually easier to apply. The proof is given in Appendix J.

9.5.4 THEOREM (*The Limit Comparison Test*) Let $\sum a_k$ and $\sum b_k$ be series with positive terms and suppose that

$$\rho = \lim_{k \to +\infty} \frac{a_k}{b_k}$$

If ρ is finite and $\rho > 0$, then the series both converge or both diverge.

The cases where $\rho = 0$ or $\rho = +\infty$ are discussed in the exercises (Exercise 54).

To use the limit comparison test we must again first guess at the convergence or divergence of $\sum a_k$ and then find a series $\sum b_k$ that supports our guess. The following example illustrates this principle.

▶ **Example 2** Use the limit comparison test to determine whether the following series converge or diverge.

(a) $\displaystyle\sum_{k=1}^{\infty} \frac{1}{\sqrt{k} + 1}$ (b) $\displaystyle\sum_{k=1}^{\infty} \frac{1}{2k^2 + k}$ (c) $\displaystyle\sum_{k=1}^{\infty} \frac{3k^3 - 2k^2 + 4}{k^7 - k^3 + 2}$

Solution (a). As in Example 1, Principle 9.5.2 suggests that the series is likely to behave like the divergent *p*-series (1). To prove that the given series diverges, we will apply the limit comparison test with

$$a_k = \frac{1}{\sqrt{k} + 1} \quad \text{and} \quad b_k = \frac{1}{\sqrt{k}}$$

We obtain

$$\rho = \lim_{k \to +\infty} \frac{a_k}{b_k} = \lim_{k \to +\infty} \frac{\sqrt{k}}{\sqrt{k} + 1} = \lim_{k \to +\infty} \frac{1}{1 + \dfrac{1}{\sqrt{k}}} = 1$$

Since ρ is finite and positive, it follows from Theorem 9.5.4 that the given series diverges.

Solution (b). As in Example 1, Principle 9.5.3 suggests that the series is likely to behave like the convergent series (2). To prove that the given series converges, we will apply the limit comparison test with

$$a_k = \frac{1}{2k^2 + k} \quad \text{and} \quad b_k = \frac{1}{2k^2}$$

We obtain

$$\rho = \lim_{k \to +\infty} \frac{a_k}{b_k} = \lim_{k \to +\infty} \frac{2k^2}{2k^2 + k} = \lim_{k \to +\infty} \frac{2}{2 + \dfrac{1}{k}} = 1$$

Since ρ is finite and positive, it follows from Theorem 9.5.4 that the given series converges, which agrees with the conclusion reached in Example 1 using the comparison test.

Solution (c). From Principle 9.5.3, the series is likely to behave like

$$\sum_{k=1}^{\infty} \frac{3k^3}{k^7} = \sum_{k=1}^{\infty} \frac{3}{k^4} \tag{3}$$

which converges since it is a constant times a convergent *p*-series. Thus, the given series is likely to converge. To prove this, we will apply the limit comparison test to series (3) and the given series. We obtain

$$\rho = \lim_{k \to +\infty} \frac{\dfrac{3k^3 - 2k^2 + 4}{k^7 - k^3 + 2}}{\dfrac{3}{k^4}} = \lim_{k \to +\infty} \frac{3k^7 - 2k^6 + 4k^4}{3k^7 - 3k^3 + 6} = 1$$

Since ρ is finite and nonzero, it follows from Theorem 9.5.4 that the given series converges, since (3) converges. ◄

■ THE RATIO TEST

The comparison test and the limit comparison test hinge on first making a guess about convergence and then finding an appropriate series for comparison, both of which can be difficult tasks in cases where Principles 9.5.2 and 9.5.3 cannot be applied. In such cases the next test can often be used, since it works exclusively with the terms of the given series—it requires neither an initial guess about convergence nor the discovery of a series for comparison. Its proof is given in Appendix J.

9.5.5 **THEOREM** (*The Ratio Test*) *Let $\sum u_k$ be a series with positive terms and suppose that*

$$\rho = \lim_{k \to +\infty} \frac{u_{k+1}}{u_k}$$

(*a*) *If $\rho < 1$, the series converges.*

(*b*) *If $\rho > 1$ or $\rho = +\infty$, the series diverges.*

(*c*) *If $\rho = 1$, the series may converge or diverge, so that another test must be tried.*

▶ **Example 3** Each of the following series has positive terms, so the ratio test applies. In each part, use the ratio test to determine whether the following series converge or diverge.

(a) $\displaystyle\sum_{k=1}^{\infty} \frac{1}{k!}$ (b) $\displaystyle\sum_{k=1}^{\infty} \frac{k}{2^k}$ (c) $\displaystyle\sum_{k=1}^{\infty} \frac{k^k}{k!}$ (d) $\displaystyle\sum_{k=3}^{\infty} \frac{(2k)!}{4^k}$ (e) $\displaystyle\sum_{k=1}^{\infty} \frac{1}{2k - 1}$

Solution (a). The series converges, since

$$\rho = \lim_{k \to +\infty} \frac{u_{k+1}}{u_k} = \lim_{k \to +\infty} \frac{1/(k+1)!}{1/k!} = \lim_{k \to +\infty} \frac{k!}{(k+1)!} = \lim_{k \to +\infty} \frac{1}{k+1} = 0 < 1$$

Solution (b). The series converges, since

$$\rho = \lim_{k \to +\infty} \frac{u_{k+1}}{u_k} = \lim_{k \to +\infty} \frac{k+1}{2^{k+1}} \cdot \frac{2^k}{k} = \frac{1}{2} \lim_{k \to +\infty} \frac{k+1}{k} = \frac{1}{2} < 1$$

Solution (c). The series diverges, since

$$\rho = \lim_{k \to +\infty} \frac{u_{k+1}}{u_k} = \lim_{k \to +\infty} \frac{(k+1)^{k+1}}{(k+1)!} \cdot \frac{k!}{k^k} = \lim_{k \to +\infty} \frac{(k+1)^k}{k^k} = \lim_{k \to +\infty} \left(1 + \frac{1}{k}\right)^k = e > 1$$

> See Formula (7)
> of Section 1.3

Solution (d). The series diverges, since

$$\rho = \lim_{k \to +\infty} \frac{u_{k+1}}{u_k} = \lim_{k \to +\infty} \frac{[2(k+1)]!}{4^{k+1}} \cdot \frac{4^k}{(2k)!} = \lim_{k \to +\infty} \left(\frac{(2k+2)!}{(2k)!} \cdot \frac{1}{4}\right)$$

$$= \lim_{k \to +\infty} \left(\frac{(2k+2)(2k+1)(2k)!}{(2k)!} \cdot \frac{1}{4}\right) = \frac{1}{4} \lim_{k \to +\infty} (2k+2)(2k+1) = +\infty$$

Solution (e). The ratio test is of no help since

$$\rho = \lim_{k \to +\infty} \frac{u_{k+1}}{u_k} = \lim_{k \to +\infty} \frac{1}{2(k+1)-1} \cdot \frac{2k-1}{1} = \lim_{k \to +\infty} \frac{2k-1}{2k+1} = 1$$

However, the integral test proves that the series diverges since

$$\int_1^{+\infty} \frac{dx}{2x-1} = \lim_{b \to +\infty} \int_1^b \frac{dx}{2x-1} = \lim_{b \to +\infty} \frac{1}{2} \ln(2x-1) \Big]_1^b = +\infty$$

Both the comparison test and the limit comparison test would also have worked here (verify). ◄

■ **THE ROOT TEST**

In cases where it is difficult or inconvenient to find the limit required for the ratio test, the next test is sometimes useful. Since its proof is similar to the proof of the ratio test, we will omit it.

9.5.6   THEOREM (*The Root Test*) *Let $\sum u_k$ be a series with positive terms and suppose that*
$$\rho = \lim_{k \to +\infty} \sqrt[k]{u_k} = \lim_{k \to +\infty} (u_k)^{1/k}$$

(a) *If $\rho < 1$, the series converges.*

(b) *If $\rho > 1$ or $\rho = +\infty$, the series diverges.*

(c) *If $\rho = 1$, the series may converge or diverge, so that another test must be tried.*

▶ **Example 4** Use the root test to determine whether the following series converge or diverge.

$$\text{(a) } \sum_{k=2}^{\infty} \left(\frac{4k-5}{2k+1}\right)^k \qquad \text{(b) } \sum_{k=1}^{\infty} \frac{1}{(\ln(k+1))^k}$$

Solution (a).   The series diverges, since

$$\rho = \lim_{k \to +\infty} (u_k)^{1/k} = \lim_{k \to +\infty} \frac{4k - 5}{2k + 1} = 2 > 1$$

Solution (b).   The series converges, since

$$\rho = \lim_{k \to +\infty} (u_k)^{1/k} = \lim_{k \to +\infty} \frac{1}{\ln(k + 1)} = 0 < 1 \ \blacktriangleleft$$

✔ **QUICK CHECK EXERCISES 9.5**   (*See page 637 for answers.*)

1–4 Select between *converges* or *diverges* to fill the first blank. ▪

1. The series

$$\sum_{k=1}^{\infty} \frac{2k^2 + 1}{2k^{8/3} - 1}$$

_____ by comparison with the *p*-series $\sum_{k=1}^{\infty}$ _____.

2. Since

$$\lim_{k \to +\infty} \frac{(k + 1)^3/3^{k+1}}{k^3/3^k} = \lim_{k \to +\infty} \frac{\left(1 + \frac{1}{k}\right)^3}{3} = \frac{1}{3}$$

the series $\sum_{k=1}^{\infty} k^3/3^k$ _____ by the _____ test.

3. Since

$$\lim_{k \to +\infty} \frac{(k + 1)!/3^{k+1}}{k!/3^k} = \lim_{k \to +\infty} \frac{k + 1}{3} = +\infty$$

the series $\sum_{k=1}^{\infty} k!/3^k$ _____ by the _____ test.

4. Since

$$\lim_{k \to +\infty} \left(\frac{1}{k^{k/2}}\right)^{1/k} = \lim_{k \to +\infty} \frac{1}{k^{1/2}} = 0$$

the series $\sum_{k=1}^{\infty} 1/k^{k/2}$ _____ by the _____ test.

EXERCISE SET 9.5

1–2 Make a guess about the convergence or divergence of the series, and confirm your guess using the comparison test. ▪

1. (a) $\displaystyle\sum_{k=1}^{\infty} \frac{1}{5k^2 - k}$ (b) $\displaystyle\sum_{k=1}^{\infty} \frac{3}{k - \frac{1}{4}}$

2. (a) $\displaystyle\sum_{k=2}^{\infty} \frac{k + 1}{k^2 - k}$ (b) $\displaystyle\sum_{k=1}^{\infty} \frac{2}{k^4 + k}$

3. In each part, use the comparison test to show that the series converges.

(a) $\displaystyle\sum_{k=1}^{\infty} \frac{1}{3^k + 5}$ (b) $\displaystyle\sum_{k=1}^{\infty} \frac{5 \sin^2 k}{k!}$

4. In each part, use the comparison test to show that the series diverges.

(a) $\displaystyle\sum_{k=1}^{\infty} \frac{\ln k}{k}$ (b) $\displaystyle\sum_{k=1}^{\infty} \frac{k}{k^{3/2} - \frac{1}{2}}$

5–10 Use the limit comparison test to determine whether the series converges. ▪

5. $\displaystyle\sum_{k=1}^{\infty} \frac{4k^2 - 2k + 6}{8k^7 + k - 8}$ **6.** $\displaystyle\sum_{k=1}^{\infty} \frac{1}{9k + 6}$

7. $\displaystyle\sum_{k=1}^{\infty} \frac{5}{3^k + 1}$ **8.** $\displaystyle\sum_{k=1}^{\infty} \frac{k(k + 3)}{(k + 1)(k + 2)(k + 5)}$

9. $\displaystyle\sum_{k=1}^{\infty} \frac{1}{\sqrt[3]{8k^2 - 3k}}$ **10.** $\displaystyle\sum_{k=1}^{\infty} \frac{1}{(2k + 3)^{17}}$

11–16 Use the ratio test to determine whether the series converges. If the test is inconclusive, then say so. ▪

11. $\displaystyle\sum_{k=1}^{\infty} \frac{3^k}{k!}$ **12.** $\displaystyle\sum_{k=1}^{\infty} \frac{4^k}{k^2}$ **13.** $\displaystyle\sum_{k=1}^{\infty} \frac{1}{5k}$

14. $\displaystyle\sum_{k=1}^{\infty} k\left(\frac{1}{2}\right)^k$ **15.** $\displaystyle\sum_{k=1}^{\infty} \frac{k!}{k^3}$ **16.** $\displaystyle\sum_{k=1}^{\infty} \frac{k}{k^2 + 1}$

17–20 Use the root test to determine whether the series converges. If the test is inconclusive, then say so. ▪

17. $\displaystyle\sum_{k=1}^{\infty} \left(\frac{3k + 2}{2k - 1}\right)^k$ **18.** $\displaystyle\sum_{k=1}^{\infty} \left(\frac{k}{100}\right)^k$

19. $\displaystyle\sum_{k=1}^{\infty} \frac{k}{5^k}$ **20.** $\displaystyle\sum_{k=1}^{\infty} (1 - e^{-k})^k$

21–24 True–False Determine whether the statement is true or false. Explain your answer. ▪

21. The limit comparison test decides convergence based on a limit of the quotient of consecutive terms in a series.

22. If $\lim_{k \to +\infty}(u_{k+1}/u_k) = 5$, then $\sum u_k$ diverges.

23. If $\lim_{k \to +\infty}(k^2 u_k) = 5$, then $\sum u_k$ converges.

24. The root test decides convergence based on a limit of kth roots of terms in the sequence of partial sums for a series.

25–47 Use any method to determine whether the series converges. ■

25. $\displaystyle\sum_{k=0}^{\infty} \frac{7^k}{k!}$

26. $\displaystyle\sum_{k=1}^{\infty} \frac{1}{2k+1}$

27. $\displaystyle\sum_{k=1}^{\infty} \frac{k^2}{5^k}$

28. $\displaystyle\sum_{k=1}^{\infty} \frac{k!10^k}{3^k}$

29. $\displaystyle\sum_{k=1}^{\infty} k^{50}e^{-k}$

30. $\displaystyle\sum_{k=1}^{\infty} \frac{k^2}{k^3+1}$

31. $\displaystyle\sum_{k=1}^{\infty} \frac{\sqrt{k}}{k^3+1}$

32. $\displaystyle\sum_{k=1}^{\infty} \frac{4}{2+3^k k}$

33. $\displaystyle\sum_{k=1}^{\infty} \frac{1}{\sqrt{k(k+1)}}$

34. $\displaystyle\sum_{k=1}^{\infty} \frac{2+(-1)^k}{5^k}$

35. $\displaystyle\sum_{k=1}^{\infty} \frac{1}{1+\sqrt{k}}$

36. $\displaystyle\sum_{k=1}^{\infty} \frac{k!}{k^k}$

37. $\displaystyle\sum_{k=1}^{\infty} \frac{\ln k}{e^k}$

38. $\displaystyle\sum_{k=1}^{\infty} \frac{k!}{e^{k^2}}$

39. $\displaystyle\sum_{k=0}^{\infty} \frac{(k+4)!}{4!k!4^k}$

40. $\displaystyle\sum_{k=1}^{\infty} \left(\frac{k}{k+1}\right)^{k^2}$

41. $\displaystyle\sum_{k=1}^{\infty} \frac{1}{4+2^{-k}}$

42. $\displaystyle\sum_{k=1}^{\infty} \frac{\sqrt{k}\ln k}{k^3+1}$

43. $\displaystyle\sum_{k=1}^{\infty} \frac{\tan^{-1}k}{k^2}$

44. $\displaystyle\sum_{k=1}^{\infty} \frac{5^k+k}{k!+3}$

45. $\displaystyle\sum_{k=0}^{\infty} \frac{(k!)^2}{(2k)!}$

46. $\displaystyle\sum_{k=1}^{\infty} \frac{[\pi(k+1)]^k}{k^{k+1}}$

47. $\displaystyle\sum_{k=1}^{\infty} \frac{\ln k}{3^k}$

48. For what positive values of α does the series $\sum_{k=1}^{\infty}(\alpha^k/k^\alpha)$ converge?

49–50 Find the general term of the series and use the ratio test to show that the series converges. ■

49. $1 + \dfrac{1\cdot 2}{1\cdot 3} + \dfrac{1\cdot 2\cdot 3}{1\cdot 3\cdot 5} + \dfrac{1\cdot 2\cdot 3\cdot 4}{1\cdot 3\cdot 5\cdot 7} + \cdots$

50. $1 + \dfrac{1\cdot 3}{3!} + \dfrac{1\cdot 3\cdot 5}{5!} + \dfrac{1\cdot 3\cdot 5\cdot 7}{7!} + \cdots$

51. Show that $\ln x < \sqrt{x}$ if $x > 0$, and use this result to investigate the convergence of

(a) $\displaystyle\sum_{k=1}^{\infty} \frac{\ln k}{k^2}$

(b) $\displaystyle\sum_{k=2}^{\infty} \frac{1}{(\ln k)^2}$

FOCUS ON CONCEPTS

52. (a) Make a conjecture about the convergence of the series $\sum_{k=1}^{\infty} \sin(\pi/k)$ by considering the local linear approximation of $\sin x$ at $x = 0$.

(b) Try to confirm your conjecture using the limit comparison test.

53. (a) We will see later that the polynomial $1 - x^2/2$ is the "local quadratic" approximation for $\cos x$ at $x = 0$. Make a conjecture about the convergence of the series

$$\sum_{k=1}^{\infty}\left[1 - \cos\left(\frac{1}{k}\right)\right]$$

by considering this approximation.

(b) Try to confirm your conjecture using the limit comparison test.

54. Let $\sum a_k$ and $\sum b_k$ be series with positive terms. Prove:

(a) If $\lim_{k \to +\infty}(a_k/b_k) = 0$ and $\sum b_k$ converges, then $\sum a_k$ converges.

(b) If $\lim_{k \to +\infty}(a_k/b_k) = +\infty$ and $\sum b_k$ diverges, then $\sum a_k$ diverges.

55. Use Theorem 9.4.6 to prove the comparison test (Theorem 9.5.1).

56. **Writing** What does the ratio test tell you about the convergence of a geometric series? Discuss similarities between geometric series and series to which the ratio test applies.

57. **Writing** Given an infinite series, discuss a strategy for deciding what convergence test to use.

✔ **QUICK CHECK ANSWERS 9.5**

1. diverges; $1/k^{2/3}$ **2.** converges; ratio   **3.** diverges; ratio   **4.** converges; root

Up to now we have focused exclusively on series with nonnegative terms. In this section we will discuss series that contain both positive and negative terms.

◼ ALTERNATING SERIES

Series whose terms alternate between positive and negative, called **alternating series**, are of special importance. Some examples are

$$\sum_{k=1}^{\infty}(-1)^{k+1}\frac{1}{k} = 1 - \frac{1}{2} + \frac{1}{3} - \frac{1}{4} + \frac{1}{5} - \cdots$$

$$\sum_{k=1}^{\infty}(-1)^{k}\frac{1}{k} = -1 + \frac{1}{2} - \frac{1}{3} + \frac{1}{4} - \frac{1}{5} + \cdots$$

In general, an alternating series has one of the following two forms:

$$\sum_{k=1}^{\infty}(-1)^{k+1}a_k = a_1 - a_2 + a_3 - a_4 + \cdots \tag{1}$$

$$\sum_{k=1}^{\infty}(-1)^{k}a_k = -a_1 + a_2 - a_3 + a_4 - \cdots \tag{2}$$

where the a_k's are assumed to be positive in both cases.

The following theorem is the key result on convergence of alternating series.

9.6.1 **THEOREM** (*Alternating Series Test*) *An alternating series of either form* (1) *or form* (2) *converges if the following two conditions are satisfied:*

(*a*) $\quad a_1 \geq a_2 \geq a_3 \geq \cdots \geq a_k \geq \cdots$

(*b*) $\quad \lim_{k \to +\infty} a_k = 0$

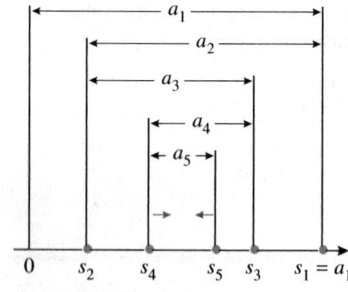

▲ **Figure 9.6.1**

It is not essential for condition (*a*) in Theorem 9.6.1 to hold for all terms; an alternating series will converge if condition (*b*) is true and condition (*a*) holds eventually.

PROOF We will consider only alternating series of form (1). The idea of the proof is to show that if conditions (*a*) and (*b*) hold, then the sequences of even-numbered and odd-numbered partial sums converge to a common limit S. It will then follow from Theorem 9.1.4 that the entire sequence of partial sums converges to S.

Figure 9.6.1 shows how successive partial sums satisfying conditions (*a*) and (*b*) appear when plotted on a horizontal axis. The even-numbered partial sums

$$s_2, s_4, s_6, s_8, \ldots, s_{2n}, \ldots$$

form an increasing sequence bounded above by a_1, and the odd-numbered partial sums

$$s_1, s_3, s_5, \ldots, s_{2n-1}, \ldots$$

form a decreasing sequence bounded below by 0. Thus, by Theorems 9.2.3 and 9.2.4, the even-numbered partial sums converge to some limit S_E and the odd-numbered partial sums converge to some limit S_O. To complete the proof we must show that $S_E = S_O$. But the

If an alternating series violates condition (*b*) of the alternating series test, then the series must diverge by the divergence test (Theorem 9.4.1).

$(2n)$-th term in the series is $-a_{2n}$, so that $s_{2n} - s_{2n-1} = -a_{2n}$, which can be written as

$$s_{2n-1} = s_{2n} + a_{2n}$$

However, $2n \to +\infty$ and $2n - 1 \to +\infty$ as $n \to +\infty$, so that

$$S_O = \lim_{n \to +\infty} s_{2n-1} = \lim_{n \to +\infty} (s_{2n} + a_{2n}) = S_E + 0 = S_E$$

which completes the proof. ∎

▶ **Example 1**   Use the alternating series test to show that the following series converge.

$$\text{(a)} \sum_{k=1}^{\infty} (-1)^{k+1} \frac{1}{k} \qquad \text{(b)} \sum_{k=1}^{\infty} (-1)^{k+1} \frac{k+3}{k(k+1)}$$

The series in part (a) of Example 1 is called the *alternating harmonic series*. Note that this series converges, whereas the harmonic series diverges.

Solution (a).   The two conditions in the alternating series test are satisfied since

$$a_k = \frac{1}{k} > \frac{1}{k+1} = a_{k+1} \quad \text{and} \quad \lim_{k \to +\infty} a_k = \lim_{k \to +\infty} \frac{1}{k} = 0$$

Solution (b).   The two conditions in the alternating series test are satisfied since

$$\frac{a_{k+1}}{a_k} = \frac{k+4}{(k+1)(k+2)} \cdot \frac{k(k+1)}{k+3} = \frac{k^2 + 4k}{k^2 + 5k + 6} = \frac{k^2 + 4k}{(k^2 + 4k) + (k+6)} < 1$$

so

$$a_k > a_{k+1}$$

and

$$\lim_{k \to +\infty} a_k = \lim_{k \to +\infty} \frac{k+3}{k(k+1)} = \lim_{k \to +\infty} \frac{\dfrac{1}{k} + \dfrac{3}{k^2}}{1 + \dfrac{1}{k}} = 0 \blacktriangleleft$$

■ **APPROXIMATING SUMS OF ALTERNATING SERIES**

The following theorem is concerned with the error that results when the sum of an alternating series is approximated by a partial sum.

9.6.2   THEOREM   *If an alternating series satisfies the hypotheses of the alternating series test, and if S is the sum of the series, then:*

(*a*)   *S lies between any two successive partial sums; that is, either*

$$s_n \leq S \leq s_{n+1} \quad \text{or} \quad s_{n+1} \leq S \leq s_n \qquad (3)$$

depending on which partial sum is larger.

(*b*)   *If S is approximated by s_n, then the absolute error $|S - s_n|$ satisfies*

$$|S - s_n| \leq a_{n+1} \qquad (4)$$

Moreover, the sign of the error $S - s_n$ is the same as that of the coefficient of a_{n+1}.

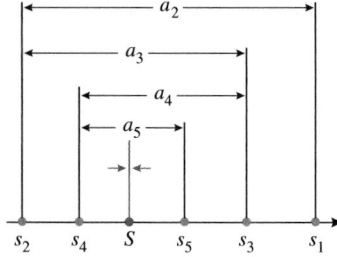

▲ Figure 9.6.2

PROOF We will prove the theorem for series of form (1). Referring to Figure 9.6.2 and keeping in mind our observation in the proof of Theorem 9.6.1 that the odd-numbered partial sums form a decreasing sequence converging to S and the even-numbered partial sums form an increasing sequence converging to S, we see that successive partial sums oscillate from one side of S to the other in smaller and smaller steps with the odd-numbered partial sums being larger than S and the even-numbered partial sums being smaller than S. Thus, depending on whether n is even or odd, we have

$$s_n \leq S \leq s_{n+1} \quad \text{or} \quad s_{n+1} \leq S \leq s_n$$

which proves (3). Moreover, in either case we have

$$|S - s_n| \leq |s_{n+1} - s_n| \tag{5}$$

But $s_{n+1} - s_n = \pm a_{n+1}$ (the sign depending on whether n is even or odd). Thus, it follows from (5) that $|S - s_n| \leq a_{n+1}$, which proves (4). Finally, since the odd-numbered partial sums are larger than S and the even-numbered partial sums are smaller than S, it follows that $S - s_n$ has the same sign as the coefficient of a_{n+1} (verify). ■

REMARK | In words, inequality (4) states that for a series satisfying the hypotheses of the alternating series test, the magnitude of the error that results from approximating S by s_n is at most that of the first term that is *not* included in the partial sum. Also, note that if $a_1 > a_2 > \cdots > a_k > \cdots$, then inequality (4) can be strengthened to $|S - s_n| < a_{n+1}$.

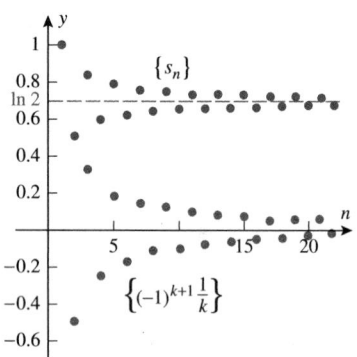

Graph of the sequences of terms and nth partial sums for the alternating harmonic series

▲ Figure 9.6.3

▶ **Example 2** Later in this chapter we will show that the sum of the alternating harmonic series is

$$\ln 2 = 1 - \frac{1}{2} + \frac{1}{3} - \frac{1}{4} + \cdots + (-1)^{k+1}\frac{1}{k} + \cdots$$

This is illustrated in Figure 9.6.3.

(a) Accepting this to be so, find an upper bound on the magnitude of the error that results if $\ln 2$ is approximated by the sum of the first eight terms in the series.

(b) Find a partial sum that approximates $\ln 2$ to one decimal-place accuracy (the nearest tenth).

Solution (a). It follows from the strengthened form of (4) that

$$|\ln 2 - s_8| < a_9 = \frac{1}{9} < 0.12 \tag{6}$$

As a check, let us compute s_8 exactly. We obtain

$$s_8 = 1 - \frac{1}{2} + \frac{1}{3} - \frac{1}{4} + \frac{1}{5} - \frac{1}{6} + \frac{1}{7} - \frac{1}{8} = \frac{533}{840}$$

Thus, with the help of a calculator

$$|\ln 2 - s_8| = \left|\ln 2 - \frac{533}{840}\right| \approx 0.059$$

This shows that the error is well under the estimate provided by upper bound (6).

Solution (b). For one decimal-place accuracy, we must choose a value of n for which $|\ln 2 - s_n| \leq 0.05$. However, it follows from the strengthened form of (4) that

$$|\ln 2 - s_n| < a_{n+1}$$

so it suffices to choose n so that $a_{n+1} \leq 0.05$.

One way to find n is to use a calculating utility to obtain numerical values for a_1, a_2, a_3, ... until you encounter the first value that is less than or equal to 0.05. If you do this, you will find that it is $a_{20} = 0.05$; this tells us that partial sum s_{19} will provide the desired accuracy. Another way to find n is to solve the inequality

$$\frac{1}{n+1} \leq 0.05$$

algebraically. We can do this by taking reciprocals, reversing the sense of the inequality, and then simplifying to obtain $n \geq 19$. Thus, s_{19} will provide the required accuracy, which is consistent with the previous result.

With the help of a calculating utility, the value of s_{19} is approximately $s_{19} \approx 0.7$ and the value of ln 2 obtained directly is approximately $\ln 2 \approx 0.69$, which agrees with s_{19} when rounded to one decimal place. ◄

> As Example 2 illustrates, the alternating harmonic series does not provide an efficient way to approximate ln 2, since too many terms and hence too much computation is required to achieve reasonable accuracy. Later, we will develop better ways to approximate logarithms.

■ ABSOLUTE CONVERGENCE
The series

$$1 - \frac{1}{2} - \frac{1}{2^2} + \frac{1}{2^3} + \frac{1}{2^4} - \frac{1}{2^5} - \frac{1}{2^6} + \cdots$$

does not fit in any of the categories studied so far—it has mixed signs but is not alternating. We will now develop some convergence tests that can be applied to such series.

9.6.3 DEFINITION   A series

$$\sum_{k=1}^{\infty} u_k = u_1 + u_2 + \cdots + u_k + \cdots$$

is said to *converge absolutely* if the series of absolute values

$$\sum_{k=1}^{\infty} |u_k| = |u_1| + |u_2| + \cdots + |u_k| + \cdots$$

converges and is said to *diverge absolutely* if the series of absolute values diverges.

► **Example 3**   Determine whether the following series converge absolutely.

$$\text{(a) } 1 - \frac{1}{2} - \frac{1}{2^2} + \frac{1}{2^3} + \frac{1}{2^4} - \frac{1}{2^5} - \cdots \qquad \text{(b) } 1 - \frac{1}{2} + \frac{1}{3} - \frac{1}{4} + \frac{1}{5} - \cdots$$

Solution (a).   The series of absolute values is the convergent geometric series

$$1 + \frac{1}{2} + \frac{1}{2^2} + \frac{1}{2^3} + \frac{1}{2^4} + \frac{1}{2^5} + \cdots$$

so the given series converges absolutely.

Solution (b).   The series of absolute values is the divergent harmonic series

$$1 + \frac{1}{2} + \frac{1}{3} + \frac{1}{4} + \frac{1}{5} + \cdots$$

so the given series diverges absolutely. ◄

It is important to distinguish between the notions of convergence and absolute convergence. For example, the series in part (b) of Example 3 converges, since it is the alternating harmonic series, yet we demonstrated that it does not converge absolutely. However, the following theorem shows that *if a series converges absolutely, then it converges.*

Theorem 9.6.4 provides a way of inferring convergence of a series with positive and negative terms from a related series with nonnegative terms (the series of absolute values). This is important because most of the convergence tests that we have developed apply only to series with nonnegative terms.

9.6.4   THEOREM   *If the series*

$$\sum_{k=1}^{\infty} |u_k| = |u_1| + |u_2| + \cdots + |u_k| + \cdots$$

converges, then so does the series

$$\sum_{k=1}^{\infty} u_k = u_1 + u_2 + \cdots + u_k + \cdots$$

PROOF   We will write the series $\sum u_k$ as

$$\sum_{k=1}^{\infty} u_k = \sum_{k=1}^{\infty} [(u_k + |u_k|) - |u_k|] \tag{7}$$

We are assuming that $\sum |u_k|$ converges, so that if we can show that $\sum (u_k + |u_k|)$ converges, then it will follow from (7) and Theorem 9.4.3(a) that $\sum u_k$ converges. However, the value of $u_k + |u_k|$ is either 0 or $2|u_k|$, depending on the sign of u_k. Thus, in all cases it is true that

$$0 \le u_k + |u_k| \le 2|u_k|$$

But $\sum 2|u_k|$ converges, since it is a constant times the convergent series $\sum |u_k|$; hence $\sum (u_k + |u_k|)$ converges by the comparison test. ■

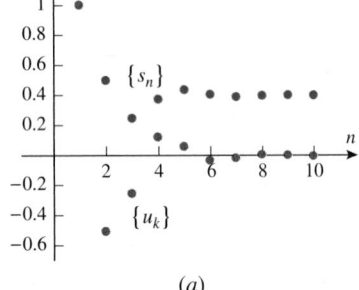

(a)

► **Example 4**   Show that the following series converge.

$$\text{(a)} \quad 1 - \frac{1}{2} - \frac{1}{2^2} + \frac{1}{2^3} + \frac{1}{2^4} - \frac{1}{2^5} - \frac{1}{2^6} + \cdots \qquad \text{(b)} \quad \sum_{k=1}^{\infty} \frac{\cos k}{k^2}$$

Solution (a).   Observe that this is not an alternating series because the signs alternate in pairs after the first term. Thus, we have no convergence test that can be applied directly. However, we showed in Example 3(a) that the series converges absolutely, so Theorem 9.6.4 implies that it converges (Figure 9.6.4a).

Solution (b).   With the help of a calculating utility, you will be able to verify that the signs of the terms in this series vary irregularly. Thus, we will test for absolute convergence. The series of absolute values is

$$\sum_{k=1}^{\infty} \left| \frac{\cos k}{k^2} \right|$$

However,

$$\left| \frac{\cos k}{k^2} \right| \le \frac{1}{k^2}$$

(b)

Graphs of the sequences of terms and nth partial sums for the series in Example 4

▲ **Figure 9.6.4**

But $\sum 1/k^2$ is a convergent p-series ($p = 2$), so the series of absolute values converges by the comparison test. Thus, the given series converges absolutely and hence converges (Figure 9.6.4b). ◄

■ CONDITIONAL CONVERGENCE

Although Theorem 9.6.4 is a useful tool for series that converge absolutely, it provides no information about the convergence or divergence of a series that diverges absolutely. For example, consider the two series

$$1 - \frac{1}{2} + \frac{1}{3} - \frac{1}{4} + \cdots + (-1)^{k+1}\frac{1}{k} + \cdots \tag{8}$$

$$-1 - \frac{1}{2} - \frac{1}{3} - \frac{1}{4} - \cdots - \frac{1}{k} - \cdots \tag{9}$$

Both of these series diverge absolutely, since in each case the series of absolute values is the divergent harmonic series

$$1 + \frac{1}{2} + \frac{1}{3} + \cdots + \frac{1}{k} + \cdots$$

However, series (8) converges, since it is the alternating harmonic series, and series (9) diverges, since it is a constant times the divergent harmonic series. As a matter of terminology, a series that converges but diverges absolutely is said to *converge conditionally* (or to be *conditionally convergent*). Thus, (8) is a conditionally convergent series.

► **Example 5** In Example 1(b) we used the alternating series test to show that the series

$$\sum_{k=1}^{\infty}(-1)^{k+1}\frac{k+3}{k(k+1)}$$

converges. Determine whether this series converges absolutely or converges conditionally.

Solution. We test the series for absolute convergence by examining the series of absolute values:

$$\sum_{k=1}^{\infty}\left|(-1)^{k+1}\frac{k+3}{k(k+1)}\right| = \sum_{k=1}^{\infty}\frac{k+3}{k(k+1)}$$

Principle 9.5.3 suggests that the series of absolute values should behave like the divergent p-series with $p = 1$. To prove that the series of absolute values diverges, we will apply the limit comparison test with

$$a_k = \frac{k+3}{k(k+1)} \quad \text{and} \quad b_k = \frac{1}{k}$$

We obtain

$$\rho = \lim_{k\to+\infty}\frac{a_k}{b_k} = \lim_{k\to+\infty}\frac{k(k+3)}{k(k+1)} = \lim_{k\to+\infty}\frac{k+3}{k+1} = 1$$

Since ρ is finite and positive, it follows from the limit comparison test that the series of absolute values diverges. Thus, the original series converges and also diverges absolutely, and so converges conditionally. ◄

■ THE RATIO TEST FOR ABSOLUTE CONVERGENCE

Although one cannot generally infer convergence or divergence of a series from absolute divergence, the following variation of the ratio test provides a way of deducing divergence from absolute divergence in certain situations. We omit the proof.

9.6.5 **THEOREM** (*Ratio Test for Absolute Convergence*) Let $\sum u_k$ be a series with nonzero terms and suppose that

$$\rho = \lim_{k \to +\infty} \frac{|u_{k+1}|}{|u_k|}$$

(a) *If $\rho < 1$, then the series $\sum u_k$ converges absolutely and therefore converges.*

(b) *If $\rho > 1$ or if $\rho = +\infty$, then the series $\sum u_k$ diverges.*

(c) *If $\rho = 1$, no conclusion about convergence or absolute convergence can be drawn from this test.*

▶ **Example 6** Use the ratio test for absolute convergence to determine whether the series converges.

$$(a)\ \sum_{k=1}^{\infty}(-1)^k\frac{2^k}{k!} \qquad (b)\ \sum_{k=1}^{\infty}(-1)^k\frac{(2k-1)!}{3^k}$$

Solution (a). Taking the absolute value of the general term u_k we obtain

$$|u_k| = \left|(-1)^k\frac{2^k}{k!}\right| = \frac{2^k}{k!}$$

Thus,

$$\rho = \lim_{k \to +\infty} \frac{|u_{k+1}|}{|u_k|} = \lim_{k \to +\infty} \frac{2^{k+1}}{(k+1)!} \cdot \frac{k!}{2^k} = \lim_{k \to +\infty} \frac{2}{k+1} = 0 < 1$$

which implies that the series converges absolutely and therefore converges.

Solution (b). Taking the absolute value of the general term u_k we obtain

$$|u_k| = \left|(-1)^k\frac{(2k-1)!}{3^k}\right| = \frac{(2k-1)!}{3^k}$$

Thus,

$$\rho = \lim_{k \to +\infty} \frac{|u_{k+1}|}{|u_k|} = \lim_{k \to +\infty} \frac{[2(k+1)-1]!}{3^{k+1}} \cdot \frac{3^k}{(2k-1)!}$$

$$= \lim_{k \to +\infty} \frac{1}{3} \cdot \frac{(2k+1)!}{(2k-1)!} = \frac{1}{3}\lim_{k \to +\infty}(2k)(2k+1) = +\infty$$

which implies that the series diverges. ◀

■ SUMMARY OF CONVERGENCE TESTS

We conclude this section with a summary of convergence tests that can be used for reference. The skill of selecting a good test is developed through lots of practice. In some instances a test may be inconclusive, so another test must be tried.

Summary of Convergence Tests

NAME	STATEMENT	COMMENTS
Divergence Test (9.4.1)	If $\lim\limits_{k \to +\infty} u_k \neq 0$, then $\sum u_k$ diverges.	If $\lim\limits_{k \to +\infty} u_k = 0$, then $\sum u_k$ may or may not converge.
Integral Test (9.4.4)	Let $\sum u_k$ be a series with positive terms. If f is a function that is decreasing and continuous on an interval $[a, +\infty)$ and such that $u_k = f(k)$ for all $k \geq a$, then $$\sum_{k=1}^{\infty} u_k \quad \text{and} \quad \int_a^{+\infty} f(x)\, dx$$ both converge or both diverge.	This test only applies to series that have positive terms. Try this test when $f(x)$ is easy to integrate.
Comparison Test (9.5.1)	Let $\sum_{k=1}^{\infty} a_k$ and $\sum_{k=1}^{\infty} b_k$ be series with nonnegative terms such that $$a_1 \leq b_1,\ a_2 \leq b_2, \ldots, a_k \leq b_k, \ldots$$ If $\sum b_k$ converges, then $\sum a_k$ converges, and if $\sum a_k$ diverges, then $\sum b_k$ diverges.	This test only applies to series with nonnegative terms. Try this test as a last resort; other tests are often easier to apply.
Limit Comparison Test (9.5.4)	Let $\sum a_k$ and $\sum b_k$ be series with positive terms and let $$\rho = \lim_{k \to +\infty} \frac{a_k}{b_k}$$ If $0 < \rho < +\infty$, then both series converge or both diverge.	This is easier to apply than the comparison test, but still requires some skill in choosing the series $\sum b_k$ for comparison.
Ratio Test (9.5.5)	Let $\sum u_k$ be a series with positive terms and suppose that $$\rho = \lim_{k \to +\infty} \frac{u_{k+1}}{u_k}$$ (a) Series converges if $\rho < 1$. (b) Series diverges if $\rho > 1$ or $\rho = +\infty$. (c) The test is inconclusive if $\rho = 1$.	Try this test when u_k involves factorials or kth powers.
Root Test (9.5.6)	Let $\sum u_k$ be a series with positive terms and suppose that $$\rho = \lim_{k \to +\infty} \sqrt[k]{u_k}$$ (a) The series converges if $\rho < 1$. (b) The series diverges if $\rho > 1$ or $\rho = +\infty$. (c) The test is inconclusive if $\rho = 1$.	Try this test when u_k involves kth powers.
Alternating Series Test (9.6.1)	If $a_k > 0$ for $k = 1, 2, 3, \ldots$, then the series $$a_1 - a_2 + a_3 - a_4 + \cdots$$ $$-a_1 + a_2 - a_3 + a_4 - \cdots$$ converge if the following conditions hold: (a) $a_1 \geq a_2 \geq a_3 \geq \cdots$ (b) $\lim\limits_{k \to +\infty} a_k = 0$	This test applies only to alternating series.
Ratio Test for Absolute Convergence (9.6.5)	Let $\sum u_k$ be a series with nonzero terms and suppose that $$\rho = \lim_{k \to +\infty} \frac{|u_{k+1}|}{|u_k|}$$ (a) The series converges absolutely if $\rho < 1$. (b) The series diverges if $\rho > 1$ or $\rho = +\infty$. (c) The test is inconclusive if $\rho = 1$.	The series need not have positive terms and need not be alternating to use this test.

✔ **QUICK CHECK EXERCISES 9.6**   (*See page 648 for answers.*)

1. What characterizes an *alternating* series?

2. (a) The series

$$\sum_{k=1}^{\infty} \frac{(-1)^{k+1}}{k^2}$$

converges by the alternating series test since _____ and _____.

(b) If

$$S = \sum_{k=1}^{\infty} \frac{(-1)^{k+1}}{k^2} \quad \text{and} \quad s_9 = \sum_{k=1}^{9} \frac{(-1)^{k+1}}{k^2}$$

then $|S - s_9| < $ _____.

3. Classify each sequence as conditionally convergent, absolutely convergent, or divergent.

(a) $\displaystyle\sum_{k=1}^{\infty}(-1)^{k+1}\frac{1}{k}$: _____

(b) $\displaystyle\sum_{k=1}^{\infty}(-1)^{k}\frac{3k-1}{9k+15}$: _____

(c) $\displaystyle\sum_{k=1}^{\infty}(-1)^{k}\frac{1}{k(k+2)}$: _____

(d) $\displaystyle\sum_{k=1}^{\infty}(-1)^{k+1}\frac{1}{\sqrt[4]{k^3}}$: _____

4. Given that

$$\lim_{k \to +\infty} \frac{(k+1)^4/4^{k+1}}{k^4/4^k} = \lim_{k \to +\infty} \frac{\left(1+\frac{1}{k}\right)^4}{4} = \frac{1}{4}$$

is the series $\sum_{k=1}^{\infty}(-1)^k k^4/4^k$ conditionally convergent, absolutely convergent, or divergent?

EXERCISE SET 9.6   C CAS

1–2 Show that the series converges by confirming that it satisfies the hypotheses of the alternating series test (Theorem 9.6.1). ■

1. $\displaystyle\sum_{k=1}^{\infty} \frac{(-1)^{k+1}}{2k+1}$

2. $\displaystyle\sum_{k=1}^{\infty}(-1)^{k+1}\frac{k}{3^k}$

3–6 Determine whether the alternating series converges; justify your answer. ■

3. $\displaystyle\sum_{k=1}^{\infty}(-1)^{k+1}\frac{k+1}{3k+1}$

4. $\displaystyle\sum_{k=1}^{\infty}(-1)^{k+1}\frac{k+1}{\sqrt{k}+1}$

5. $\displaystyle\sum_{k=1}^{\infty}(-1)^{k+1}e^{-k}$

6. $\displaystyle\sum_{k=3}^{\infty}(-1)^k\frac{\ln k}{k}$

7–12 Use the ratio test for absolute convergence (Theorem 9.6.5) to determine whether the series converges or diverges. If the test is inconclusive, say so. ■

7. $\displaystyle\sum_{k=1}^{\infty}\left(-\frac{3}{5}\right)^k$

8. $\displaystyle\sum_{k=1}^{\infty}(-1)^{k+1}\frac{2^k}{k!}$

9. $\displaystyle\sum_{k=1}^{\infty}(-1)^{k+1}\frac{3^k}{k^2}$

10. $\displaystyle\sum_{k=1}^{\infty}(-1)^k\frac{k}{5^k}$

11. $\displaystyle\sum_{k=1}^{\infty}(-1)^k\frac{k^3}{e^k}$

12. $\displaystyle\sum_{k=1}^{\infty}(-1)^{k+1}\frac{k^k}{k!}$

13–28 Classify each series as absolutely convergent, conditionally convergent, or divergent. ■

13. $\displaystyle\sum_{k=1}^{\infty}\frac{(-1)^{k+1}}{3k}$

14. $\displaystyle\sum_{k=1}^{\infty}\frac{(-1)^{k+1}}{k^{4/3}}$

15. $\displaystyle\sum_{k=1}^{\infty}\frac{(-4)^k}{k^2}$

16. $\displaystyle\sum_{k=1}^{\infty}\frac{(-1)^{k+1}}{k!}$

17. $\displaystyle\sum_{k=1}^{\infty}\frac{\cos k\pi}{k}$

18. $\displaystyle\sum_{k=3}^{\infty}\frac{(-1)^k\ln k}{k}$

19. $\displaystyle\sum_{k=1}^{\infty}(-1)^{k+1}\frac{k+2}{k(k+3)}$

20. $\displaystyle\sum_{k=1}^{\infty}\frac{(-1)^{k+1}k^2}{k^3+1}$

21. $\displaystyle\sum_{k=1}^{\infty}\sin\frac{k\pi}{2}$

22. $\displaystyle\sum_{k=1}^{\infty}\frac{\sin k}{k^3}$

23. $\displaystyle\sum_{k=2}^{\infty}\frac{(-1)^k}{k\ln k}$

24. $\displaystyle\sum_{k=1}^{\infty}\frac{(-1)^k}{\sqrt{k(k+1)}}$

25. $\displaystyle\sum_{k=2}^{\infty}\left(-\frac{1}{\ln k}\right)^k$

26. $\displaystyle\sum_{k=1}^{\infty}\frac{k\cos k\pi}{k^2+1}$

27. $\displaystyle\sum_{k=1}^{\infty}\frac{(-1)^{k+1}k!}{(2k-1)!}$

28. $\displaystyle\sum_{k=1}^{\infty}(-1)^{k+1}\frac{3^{2k-1}}{k^2+1}$

29–32 True–False Determine whether the statement is true or false. Explain your answer. ■

29. An alternating series is one whose terms alternate between even and odd.

30. If a series satisfies the hypothesis of the alternating series test, then the sequence of partial sums of the series oscillates between overestimates and underestimates for the sum of the series.

31. If a series converges, then either it converges absolutely or it converges conditionally.

32. If $\sum(u_k)^2$ converges, then $\sum u_k$ converges absolutely.

33–36 Each series satisfies the hypotheses of the alternating series test. For the stated value of n, find an upper bound on the absolute error that results if the sum of the series is approximated by the nth partial sum.

33. $\displaystyle\sum_{k=1}^{\infty} \frac{(-1)^{k+1}}{k}; \ n = 7$ **34.** $\displaystyle\sum_{k=1}^{\infty} \frac{(-1)^{k+1}}{k!}; \ n = 5$

35. $\displaystyle\sum_{k=1}^{\infty} \frac{(-1)^{k+1}}{\sqrt{k}}; \ n = 99$

36. $\displaystyle\sum_{k=1}^{\infty} \frac{(-1)^{k+1}}{(k+1)\ln(k+1)}; \ n = 3$

37–40 Each series satisfies the hypotheses of the alternating series test. Find a value of n for which the nth partial sum is ensured to approximate the sum of the series to the stated accuracy.

37. $\displaystyle\sum_{k=1}^{\infty} \frac{(-1)^{k+1}}{k}; \ |\text{error}| < 0.0001$

38. $\displaystyle\sum_{k=1}^{\infty} \frac{(-1)^{k+1}}{k!}; \ |\text{error}| < 0.00001$

39. $\displaystyle\sum_{k=1}^{\infty} \frac{(-1)^{k+1}}{\sqrt{k}}; \ \text{two decimal places}$

40. $\displaystyle\sum_{k=1}^{\infty} \frac{(-1)^{k+1}}{(k+1)\ln(k+1)}; \ \text{one decimal place}$

41–42 Find an upper bound on the absolute error that results if s_{10} is used to approximate the sum of the given *geometric* series. Compute s_{10} rounded to four decimal places and compare this value with the exact sum of the series.

41. $\dfrac{3}{4} - \dfrac{3}{8} + \dfrac{3}{16} - \dfrac{3}{32} + \cdots$ **42.** $1 - \dfrac{2}{3} + \dfrac{4}{9} - \dfrac{8}{27} + \cdots$

43–46 Each series satisfies the hypotheses of the alternating series test. Approximate the sum of the series to two decimal-place accuracy.

43. $1 - \dfrac{1}{3!} + \dfrac{1}{5!} - \dfrac{1}{7!} + \cdots$ **44.** $1 - \dfrac{1}{2!} + \dfrac{1}{4!} - \dfrac{1}{6!} + \cdots$

45. $\dfrac{1}{1 \cdot 2} - \dfrac{1}{2 \cdot 2^2} + \dfrac{1}{3 \cdot 2^3} - \dfrac{1}{4 \cdot 2^4} + \cdots$

46. $\dfrac{1}{1^5 + 4 \cdot 1} - \dfrac{1}{3^5 + 4 \cdot 3} + \dfrac{1}{5^5 + 4 \cdot 5} - \dfrac{1}{7^5 + 4 \cdot 7} + \cdots$

FOCUS ON CONCEPTS

C **47.** The purpose of this exercise is to show that the error bound in part (b) of Theorem 9.6.2 can be overly conservative in certain cases.
  (a) Use a CAS to confirm that
  $$\frac{\pi}{4} = 1 - \frac{1}{3} + \frac{1}{5} - \frac{1}{7} + \cdots$$
  (b) Use the CAS to show that $|(\pi/4) - s_{25}| < 10^{-2}$.

  (c) According to the error bound in part (b) of Theorem 9.6.2, what value of n is required to ensure that $|(\pi/4) - s_n| < 10^{-2}$?

48. Prove: If a series $\sum a_k$ converges absolutely, then the series $\sum a_k^2$ converges.

49. (a) Find examples to show that if $\sum a_k$ converges, then $\sum a_k^2$ may diverge or converge.
  (b) Find examples to show that if $\sum a_k^2$ converges, then $\sum a_k$ may diverge or converge.

50. Let $\sum u_k$ be a series and define series $\sum p_k$ and $\sum q_k$ so that
$$p_k = \begin{cases} u_k, & u_k > 0 \\ 0, & u_k \le 0 \end{cases} \quad \text{and} \quad q_k = \begin{cases} 0, & u_k \ge 0 \\ -u_k, & u_k < 0 \end{cases}$$

  (a) Show that $\sum u_k$ converges absolutely if and only if $\sum p_k$ and $\sum q_k$ both converge.
  (b) Show that if one of $\sum p_k$ or $\sum q_k$ converges and the other diverges, then $\sum u_k$ diverges.
  (c) Show that if $\sum u_k$ converges conditionally, then both $\sum p_k$ and $\sum q_k$ diverge.

51. It can be proved that the terms of any conditionally convergent series can be rearranged to give either a divergent series or a conditionally convergent series whose sum is any given number S. For example, we stated in Example 2 that
$$\ln 2 = 1 - \frac{1}{2} + \frac{1}{3} - \frac{1}{4} + \frac{1}{5} - \frac{1}{6} + \cdots$$
Show that we can rearrange this series so that its sum is $\frac{1}{2}\ln 2$ by rewriting it as
$$\left(1 - \frac{1}{2} - \frac{1}{4}\right) + \left(\frac{1}{3} - \frac{1}{6} - \frac{1}{8}\right) + \left(\frac{1}{5} - \frac{1}{10} - \frac{1}{12}\right) + \cdots$$
[*Hint:* Add the first two terms in each grouping.]

52–54 Exercise 51 illustrates that one of the nuances of "conditional" convergence is that the sum of a series that converges conditionally depends on the order that the terms of the series are summed. Absolutely convergent series are more dependable, however. It can be proved that any series that is constructed from an absolutely convergent series by rearranging the terms will also be absolutely convergent and has the same sum as the original series. Use this fact together with parts (a) and (b) of Theorem 9.4.3 in these exercises.

52. It was stated in Exercise 35 of Section 9.4 that
$$\frac{\pi^2}{6} = 1 + \frac{1}{2^2} + \frac{1}{3^2} + \frac{1}{4^2} + \cdots$$
Use this to show that
$$\frac{\pi^2}{8} = 1 + \frac{1}{3^2} + \frac{1}{5^2} + \frac{1}{7^2} + \cdots$$

53. Use the series for $\pi^2/6$ given in the preceding exercise to show that
$$\frac{\pi^2}{12} = 1 - \frac{1}{2^2} + \frac{1}{3^2} - \frac{1}{4^2} + \cdots$$

54. It was stated in Exercise 35 of Section 9.4 that
$$\frac{\pi^4}{90} = 1 + \frac{1}{2^4} + \frac{1}{3^4} + \frac{1}{4^4} + \cdots$$
Use this to show that
$$\frac{\pi^4}{96} = 1 + \frac{1}{3^4} + \frac{1}{5^4} + \frac{1}{7^4} + \cdots$$

55. Writing Consider the series
$$1 - \frac{1}{2} + \frac{2}{3} - \frac{1}{3} + \frac{2}{4} - \frac{1}{4} + \frac{2}{5} - \frac{1}{5} + \cdots$$

Determine whether this series converges and use this series as an example in a discussion of the importance of hypotheses (a) and (b) of the alternating series test (Theorem 9.6.1).

56. Writing Discuss the ways that conditional convergence is "conditional." In particular, describe how one could rearrange the terms of a conditionally convergent series $\sum u_k$ so that the resulting series diverges, either to $+\infty$ or to $-\infty$. [*Hint:* See Exercise 50.]

✔**QUICK CHECK ANSWERS 9.6**

1. Terms alternate between positive and negative.   **2.** (a) $1 \geq \frac{1}{4} \geq \frac{1}{9} \geq \cdots \geq \frac{1}{k^2} \geq \frac{1}{(k+1)^2} \geq \cdots;\ \lim\limits_{k \to +\infty} \frac{1}{k^2} = 0$ (b) $\frac{1}{100}$
3. (a) conditionally convergent (b) divergent (c) absolutely convergent (d) conditionally convergent   **4.** absolutely convergent

---

9.7 MACLAURIN AND TAYLOR POLYNOMIALS

In a local linear approximation the tangent line to the graph of a function is used to obtain a linear approximation of the function near the point of tangency. In this section we will consider how one might improve on the accuracy of local linear approximations by using higher-order polynomials as approximating functions. We will also investigate the error associated with such approximations.

■ LOCAL QUADRATIC APPROXIMATIONS
Recall from Formula (1) in Section 3.5 that the local linear approximation of a function f at x_0 is
$$f(x) \approx f(x_0) + f'(x_0)(x - x_0) \tag{1}$$
In this formula, the approximating function
$$p(x) = f(x_0) + f'(x_0)(x - x_0)$$
is a first-degree polynomial satisfying $p(x_0) = f(x_0)$ and $p'(x_0) = f'(x_0)$ (verify). Thus, the local linear approximation of f at x_0 has the property that its value and the value of its first derivative match those of f at x_0.

If the graph of a function f has a pronounced "bend" at x_0, then we can expect that the accuracy of the local linear approximation of f at x_0 will decrease rapidly as we progress away from x_0 (Figure 9.7.1). One way to deal with this problem is to approximate the function f at x_0 by a polynomial p of degree 2 with the property that the value of p and the values of its first two derivatives match those of f at x_0. This ensures that the graphs of f and p not only have the same tangent line at x_0, but they also bend in the same direction at x_0 (both concave up or concave down). As a result, we can expect that the graph of p will remain close to the graph of f over a larger interval around x_0 than the graph of the local linear approximation. The polynomial p is called the *local quadratic approximation of f at $x = x_0$.*

To illustrate this idea, let us try to find a formula for the local quadratic approximation of a function f at $x = 0$. This approximation has the form
$$f(x) \approx c_0 + c_1 x + c_2 x^2 \tag{2}$$
where c_0, c_1, and c_2 must be chosen so that the values of
$$p(x) = c_0 + c_1 x + c_2 x^2$$

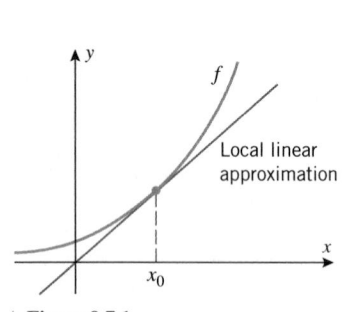

Local linear
approximation

▲ **Figure 9.7.1**

and its first two derivatives match those of f at 0. Thus, we want

$$p(0) = f(0), \quad p'(0) = f'(0), \quad p''(0) = f''(0) \tag{3}$$

But the values of $p(0)$, $p'(0)$, and $p''(0)$ are as follows:

$$
\begin{aligned}
p(x) &= c_0 + c_1 x + c_2 x^2 & p(0) &= c_0 \\
p'(x) &= c_1 + 2c_2 x & p'(0) &= c_1 \\
p''(x) &= 2c_2 & p''(0) &= 2c_2
\end{aligned}
$$

Thus, it follows from (3) that

$$c_0 = f(0), \quad c_1 = f'(0), \quad c_2 = \frac{f''(0)}{2}$$

and substituting these in (2) yields the following formula for the local quadratic approximation of f at $x = 0$:

$$f(x) \approx f(0) + f'(0)x + \frac{f''(0)}{2}x^2 \tag{4}$$

▶ **Example 1** Find the local linear and quadratic approximations of e^x at $x = 0$, and graph e^x and the two approximations together.

Solution. If we let $f(x) = e^x$, then $f'(x) = f''(x) = e^x$; and hence

$$f(0) = f'(0) = f''(0) = e^0 = 1$$

Thus, from (4) the local quadratic approximation of e^x at $x = 0$ is

$$e^x \approx 1 + x + \frac{x^2}{2}$$

and the local linear approximation (which is the linear part of the local quadratic approximation) is

$$e^x \approx 1 + x$$

The graphs of e^x and the two approximations are shown in Figure 9.7.2. As expected, the local quadratic approximation is more accurate than the local linear approximation near $x = 0$. ◀

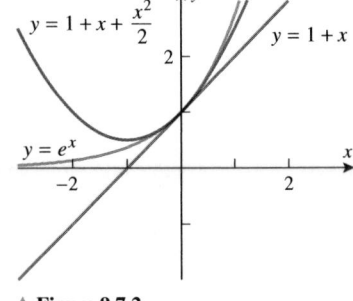

$y = 1 + x + \dfrac{x^2}{2}$

$y = 1 + x$

$y = e^x$

▲ **Figure 9.7.2**

■ MACLAURIN POLYNOMIALS

It is natural to ask whether one can improve on the accuracy of a local quadratic approximation by using a polynomial of degree 3. Specifically, one might look for a polynomial of degree 3 with the property that its value and the values of its first three derivatives match

---

Colin Maclaurin (1698–1746) Scottish mathematician. Maclaurin's father, a minister, died when the boy was only six months old, and his mother when he was nine years old. He was then raised by an uncle who was also a minister. Maclaurin entered Glasgow University as a divinity student but switched to mathematics after one year. He received his Master's degree at age 17 and, in spite of his youth, began teaching at Marischal College in Aberdeen, Scotland. He met Isaac Newton during a visit to London in 1719 and from that time on became Newton's disciple. During that era, some of Newton's analytic methods were bitterly attacked by major

mathematicians and much of Maclaurin's important mathematical work resulted from his efforts to defend Newton's ideas geometrically. Maclaurin's work, *A Treatise of Fluxions* (1742), was the first systematic formulation of Newton's methods. The treatise was so carefully done that it was a standard of mathematical rigor in calculus until the work of Cauchy in 1821. Maclaurin was also an outstanding experimentalist; he devised numerous ingenious mechanical devices, made important astronomical observations, performed actuarial computations for insurance societies, and helped to improve maps of the islands around Scotland.

those of f at a point; and if this provides an improvement in accuracy, why not go on to polynomials of even higher degree? Thus, we are led to consider the following general problem.

9.7.1 PROBLEM Given a function f that can be differentiated n times at $x = x_0$, find a polynomial p of degree n with the property that the value of p and the values of its first n derivatives match those of f at x_0.

We will begin by solving this problem in the case where $x_0 = 0$. Thus, we want a polynomial

$$p(x) = c_0 + c_1 x + c_2 x^2 + c_3 x^3 + \cdots + c_n x^n \tag{5}$$

such that

$$f(0) = p(0), \quad f'(0) = p'(0), \quad f''(0) = p''(0), \ldots, \quad f^{(n)}(0) = p^{(n)}(0) \tag{6}$$

But

$$
\begin{aligned}
p(x) &= c_0 + c_1 x + c_2 x^2 + c_3 x^3 + \cdots + c_n x^n \\
p'(x) &= c_1 + 2c_2 x + 3c_3 x^2 + \cdots + nc_n x^{n-1} \\
p''(x) &= 2c_2 + 3 \cdot 2c_3 x + \cdots + n(n-1)c_n x^{n-2} \\
p'''(x) &= 3 \cdot 2c_3 + \cdots + n(n-1)(n-2)c_n x^{n-3} \\
&\quad \vdots \\
p^{(n)}(x) &= n(n-1)(n-2) \cdots (1)c_n
\end{aligned}
$$

Thus, to satisfy (6) we must have

$$
\begin{aligned}
f(0) &= p(0) &&= c_0 \\
f'(0) &= p'(0) &&= c_1 \\
f''(0) &= p''(0) &&= 2c_2 = 2!c_2 \\
f'''(0) &= p'''(0) &&= 3 \cdot 2c_3 = 3!c_3 \\
&\quad \vdots \\
f^{(n)}(0) &= p^{(n)}(0) = n(n-1)(n-2) \cdots (1)c_n = n!c_n
\end{aligned}
$$

which yields the following values for the coefficients of $p(x)$:

$$c_0 = f(0), \quad c_1 = f'(0), \quad c_2 = \frac{f''(0)}{2!}, \quad c_3 = \frac{f'''(0)}{3!}, \ldots, \quad c_n = \frac{f^{(n)}(0)}{n!}$$

The polynomial that results by using these coefficients in (5) is called the *nth Maclaurin polynomial for f*.

Local linear approximations and local quadratic approximations at $x = 0$ of a function f are special cases of the MacLaurin polynomials for f. Verify that $f(x) \approx p_1(x)$ is the local linear approximation of f at $x = 0$, and $f(x) \approx p_2(x)$ is the local quadratic approximation at $x = 0$.

9.7.2 DEFINITION If f can be differentiated n times at 0, then we define the **nth Maclaurin polynomial for f** to be

$$p_n(x) = f(0) + f'(0)x + \frac{f''(0)}{2!}x^2 + \frac{f'''(0)}{3!}x^3 + \cdots + \frac{f^{(n)}(0)}{n!}x^n \tag{7}$$

Note that the polynomial in (7) has the property that its value and the values of its first n derivatives match the values of f and its first n derivatives at $x = 0$.

▶ **Example 2**   Find the Maclaurin polynomials p_0, p_1, p_2, p_3, and p_n for e^x.

Solution.   Let $f(x) = e^x$. Thus,

$$f'(x) = f''(x) = f'''(x) = \cdots = f^{(n)}(x) = e^x$$

and

$$f(0) = f'(0) = f''(0) = f'''(0) = \cdots = f^{(n)}(0) = e^0 = 1$$

Therefore,

$$p_0(x) = f(0) = 1$$

$$p_1(x) = f(0) + f'(0)x = 1 + x$$

$$p_2(x) = f(0) + f'(0)x + \frac{f''(0)}{2!}x^2 = 1 + x + \frac{x^2}{2!} = 1 + x + \frac{1}{2}x^2$$

$$p_3(x) = f(0) + f'(0)x + \frac{f''(0)}{2!}x^2 + \frac{f'''(0)}{3!}x^3$$

$$= 1 + x + \frac{x^2}{2!} + \frac{x^3}{3!} = 1 + x + \frac{1}{2}x^2 + \frac{1}{6}x^3$$

$$p_n(x) = f(0) + f'(0)x + \frac{f''(0)}{2!}x^2 + \cdots + \frac{f^{(n)}(0)}{n!}x^n$$

$$= 1 + x + \frac{x^2}{2!} + \cdots + \frac{x^n}{n!} \quad ◀$$

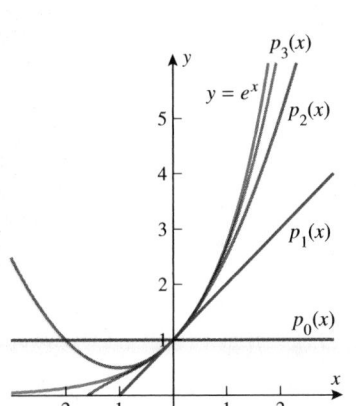

▲ **Figure 9.7.3**

Figure 9.7.3 shows the graph of e^x (in blue) and the graph of the first four Maclaurin polynomials. Note that the graphs of $p_1(x)$, $p_2(x)$, and $p_3(x)$ are virtually indistinguishable from the graph of e^x near $x = 0$, so these polynomials are good approximations of e^x for x near 0. However, the farther x is from 0, the poorer these approximations become. This is typical of the Maclaurin polynomials for a function $f(x)$; they provide good approximations of $f(x)$ near 0, but the accuracy diminishes as x progresses away from 0. It is usually the case that the higher the degree of the polynomial, the larger the interval on which it provides a specified accuracy. Accuracy issues will be investigated later.

Augustin Louis Cauchy (1789–1857) French mathematician. Cauchy's early education was acquired from his father, a barrister and master of the classics. Cauchy entered L'Ecole Polytechnique in 1805 to study engineering, but because of poor health, was advised to concentrate on mathematics. His major mathematical work began in 1811 with a series of brilliant solutions to some difficult outstanding problems. In 1814 he wrote a treatise on integrals that was to become the basis for modern complex variable theory; in 1816 there followed a classic paper on wave propagation in liquids that won a prize from the French Academy; and in 1822 he wrote a paper that formed the basis of modern elasticity theory. Cauchy's mathematical contributions for the next 35 years were brilliant and staggering in quantity, over 700 papers filling 26 modern volumes. Cauchy's work initiated the era of modern analysis. He brought to mathematics standards of precision and rigor undreamed of by Leibniz and Newton.

Cauchy's life was inextricably tied to the political upheavals of the time. A strong partisan of the Bourbons, he left his wife and children in 1830 to follow the Bourbon king Charles X into exile. For his loyalty he was made a baron by the ex-king. Cauchy eventually returned to France, but refused to accept a university position until the government waived its requirement that he take a loyalty oath.

It is difficult to get a clear picture of the man. Devoutly Catholic, he sponsored charitable work for unwed mothers, criminals, and relief for Ireland. Yet other aspects of his life cast him in an unfavorable light. The Norwegian mathematician Abel described him as, "mad, infinitely Catholic, and bigoted." Some writers praise his teaching, yet others say he rambled incoherently and, according to a report of the day, he once devoted an entire lecture to extracting the square root of seventeen to ten decimal places by a method well known to his students. In any event, Cauchy is undeniably one of the greatest minds in the history of science.

▶ **Example 3**   Find the *n*th Maclaurin polynomials for

$$\text{(a) } \sin x \qquad \text{(b) } \cos x$$

Solution (a).   In the Maclaurin polynomials for $\sin x$, only the odd powers of x appear explicitly. To see this, let $f(x) = \sin x$; thus,

$$
\begin{aligned}
f(x) &= \sin x & f(0) &= 0 \\
f'(x) &= \cos x & f'(0) &= 1 \\
f''(x) &= -\sin x & f''(0) &= 0 \\
f'''(x) &= -\cos x & f'''(0) &= -1
\end{aligned}
$$

Since $f^{(4)}(x) = \sin x = f(x)$, the pattern $0, 1, 0, -1$ will repeat as we evaluate successive derivatives at 0. Therefore, the successive Maclaurin polynomials for $\sin x$ are

$$p_0(x) = 0$$
$$p_1(x) = 0 + x$$
$$p_2(x) = 0 + x + 0$$
$$p_3(x) = 0 + x + 0 - \frac{x^3}{3!}$$
$$p_4(x) = 0 + x + 0 - \frac{x^3}{3!} + 0$$
$$p_5(x) = 0 + x + 0 - \frac{x^3}{3!} + 0 + \frac{x^5}{5!}$$
$$p_6(x) = 0 + x + 0 - \frac{x^3}{3!} + 0 + \frac{x^5}{5!} + 0$$
$$p_7(x) = 0 + x + 0 - \frac{x^3}{3!} + 0 + \frac{x^5}{5!} + 0 - \frac{x^7}{7!}$$

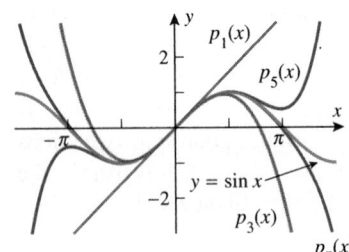

▲ **Figure 9.7.4**

Because of the zero terms, each even-order Maclaurin polynomial [after $p_0(x)$] is the same as the preceding odd-order Maclaurin polynomial. That is,

$$p_{2k+1}(x) = p_{2k+2}(x) = x - \frac{x^3}{3!} + \frac{x^5}{5!} - \frac{x^7}{7!} + \cdots + (-1)^k \frac{x^{2k+1}}{(2k+1)!} \quad (k = 0, 1, 2, \ldots)$$

The graphs of $\sin x$, $p_1(x)$, $p_3(x)$, $p_5(x)$, and $p_7(x)$ are shown in Figure 9.7.4.

Solution (b).   In the Maclaurin polynomials for $\cos x$, only the even powers of x appear explicitly; the computations are similar to those in part (a). The reader should be able to show that

$$p_0(x) = p_1(x) = 1$$
$$p_2(x) = p_3(x) = 1 - \frac{x^2}{2!}$$
$$p_4(x) = p_5(x) = 1 - \frac{x^2}{2!} + \frac{x^4}{4!}$$
$$p_6(x) = p_7(x) = 1 - \frac{x^2}{2!} + \frac{x^4}{4!} - \frac{x^6}{6!}$$

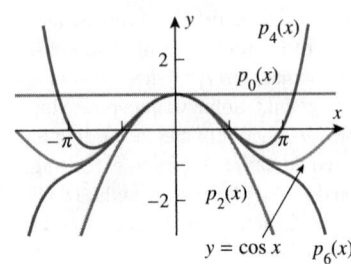

▲ **Figure 9.7.5**

In general, the Maclaurin polynomials for $\cos x$ are given by

$$p_{2k}(x) = p_{2k+1}(x) = 1 - \frac{x^2}{2!} + \frac{x^4}{4!} - \frac{x^6}{6!} + \cdots + (-1)^k \frac{x^{2k}}{(2k)!} \quad (k = 0, 1, 2, \ldots)$$

The graphs of $\cos x$, $p_0(x)$, $p_2(x)$, $p_4(x)$, and $p_6(x)$ are shown in Figure 9.7.5.   ◀

■ **TAYLOR POLYNOMIALS**

Up to now we have focused on approximating a function f in the vicinity of $x = 0$. Now we will consider the more general case of approximating f in the vicinity of an arbitrary domain value x_0. The basic idea is the same as before; we want to find an nth-degree polynomial p with the property that its value and the values of its first n derivatives match those of f at x_0. However, rather than expressing $p(x)$ in powers of x, it will simplify the computations if we express it in powers of $x - x_0$; that is,

$$p(x) = c_0 + c_1(x - x_0) + c_2(x - x_0)^2 + \cdots + c_n(x - x_0)^n \tag{8}$$

We will leave it as an exercise for you to imitate the computations used in the case where $x_0 = 0$ to show that

$$c_0 = f(x_0), \quad c_1 = f'(x_0), \quad c_2 = \frac{f''(x_0)}{2!}, \quad c_3 = \frac{f'''(x_0)}{3!}, \ldots, \quad c_n = \frac{f^{(n)}(x_0)}{n!}$$

Substituting these values in (8) we obtain a polynomial called the *nth Taylor polynomial about $x = x_0$ for f*.

Local linear approximations and local quadratic approximations at $x = x_0$ of a function f are special cases of the Taylor polynomials for f. Verify that $f(x) \approx p_1(x)$ is the local linear approximation of f at $x = x_0$, and $f(x) \approx p_2(x)$ is the local quadratic approximation at $x = x_0$.

9.7.3 **DEFINITION** If f can be differentiated n times at x_0, then we define the *nth Taylor polynomial for f about $x = x_0$* to be

$$p_n(x) = f(x_0) + f'(x_0)(x - x_0) + \frac{f''(x_0)}{2!}(x - x_0)^2$$
$$+ \frac{f'''(x_0)}{3!}(x - x_0)^3 + \cdots + \frac{f^{(n)}(x_0)}{n!}(x - x_0)^n \tag{9}$$

The Maclaurin polynomials are the special cases of the Taylor polynomials in which $x_0 = 0$. Thus, theorems about Taylor polynomials also apply to Maclaurin polynomials.

▶ **Example 4** Find the first four Taylor polynomials for $\ln x$ about $x = 2$.

Solution. Let $f(x) = \ln x$. Thus,

$$\begin{array}{ll} f(x) = \ln x & f(2) = \ln 2 \\ f'(x) = 1/x & f'(2) = 1/2 \\ f''(x) = -1/x^2 & f''(2) = -1/4 \\ f'''(x) = 2/x^3 & f'''(2) = 1/4 \end{array}$$

Brook Taylor (1685–1731) English mathematician. Taylor was born of well-to-do parents. Musicians and artists were entertained frequently in the Taylor home, which undoubtedly had a lasting influence on him. In later years, Taylor published a definitive work on the mathematical theory of perspective and obtained major mathematical results about the vibrations of strings. There also exists an unpublished work, *On Musick*, that was intended to be part of a joint paper with Isaac Newton. Taylor's life was scarred with unhappiness, illness, and tragedy. Because his first wife was not rich enough to suit his father, the two men argued bitterly and parted ways. Subsequently, his wife died in childbirth. Then, after he remarried, his second wife also died in childbirth, though his daughter survived. Taylor's most productive period was from 1714 to 1719, during which time he wrote on a wide range of subjects—magnetism, capillary action, thermometers, perspective, and calculus. In his final years, Taylor devoted his writing efforts to religion and philosophy. According to Taylor, the results that bear his name were motivated by coffeehouse conversations about works of Newton on planetary motion and works of Halley ("Halley's comet") on roots of polynomials. Unfortunately, Taylor's writing style was so terse and hard to understand that he never received credit for many of his innovations.

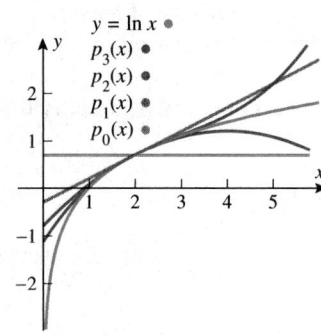

▲ **Figure 9.7.6**

Substituting in (9) with $x_0 = 2$ yields

$$p_0(x) = f(2) = \ln 2$$

$$p_1(x) = f(2) + f'(2)(x - 2) = \ln 2 + \tfrac{1}{2}(x - 2)$$

$$p_2(x) = f(2) + f'(2)(x - 2) + \frac{f''(2)}{2!}(x - 2)^2 = \ln 2 + \tfrac{1}{2}(x - 2) - \tfrac{1}{8}(x - 2)^2$$

$$p_3(x) = f(2) + f'(2)(x - 2) + \frac{f''(2)}{2!}(x - 2)^2 + \frac{f'''(2)}{3!}(x - 2)^3$$

$$= \ln 2 + \tfrac{1}{2}(x - 2) - \tfrac{1}{8}(x - 2)^2 + \tfrac{1}{24}(x - 2)^3$$

The graph of $\ln x$ (in blue) and its first four Taylor polynomials about $x = 2$ are shown in Figure 9.7.6. As expected, these polynomials produce their best approximations of $\ln x$ near 2. ◄

■ SIGMA NOTATION FOR TAYLOR AND MACLAURIN POLYNOMIALS

Frequently, we will want to express Formula (9) in sigma notation. To do this, we use the notation $f^{(k)}(x_0)$ to denote the kth derivative of f at $x = x_0$, and we make the convention that $f^{(0)}(x_0)$ denotes $f(x_0)$. This enables us to write

$$\sum_{k=0}^{n} \frac{f^{(k)}(x_0)}{k!}(x - x_0)^k = f(x_0) + f'(x_0)(x - x_0)$$

$$+ \frac{f''(x_0)}{2!}(x - x_0)^2 + \cdots + \frac{f^{(n)}(x_0)}{n!}(x - x_0)^n \quad (10)$$

In particular, we can write the nth Maclaurin polynomial for $f(x)$ as

$$\sum_{k=0}^{n} \frac{f^{(k)}(0)}{k!}x^k = f(0) + f'(0)x + \frac{f''(0)}{2!}x^2 + \cdots + \frac{f^{(n)}(0)}{n!}x^n \quad (11)$$

▶ **Example 5**   Find the nth Maclaurin polynomial for

$$\frac{1}{1 - x}$$

and express it in sigma notation.

Solution.   Let $f(x) = 1/(1 - x)$. The values of f and its first k derivatives at $x = 0$ are as follows:

$$f(x) = \frac{1}{1 - x} \qquad f(0) = 1 = 0!$$

$$f'(x) = \frac{1}{(1 - x)^2} \qquad f'(0) = 1 = 1!$$

$$f''(x) = \frac{2}{(1 - x)^3} \qquad f''(0) = 2 = 2!$$

$$f'''(x) = \frac{3 \cdot 2}{(1 - x)^4} \qquad f'''(0) = 3!$$

$$f^{(4)}(x) = \frac{4 \cdot 3 \cdot 2}{(1 - x)^5} \qquad f^{(4)}(0) = 4!$$

$$\vdots \qquad\qquad \vdots$$

$$f^{(k)}(x) = \frac{k!}{(1 - x)^{k+1}} \qquad f^{(k)}(0) = k!$$

TECHNOLOGY MASTERY

Computer algebra systems have commands for generating Taylor polynomials of any specified degree. If you have a CAS, use it to find some of the Maclaurin and Taylor polynomials in Examples 3, 4, and 5.

Thus, substituting $f^{(k)}(0) = k!$ into Formula (11) yields the nth Maclaurin polynomial for $1/(1-x)$:

$$p_n(x) = \sum_{k=0}^{n} x^k = 1 + x + x^2 + \cdots + x^n \quad (n = 0, 1, 2, \ldots) \; \blacktriangleleft$$

▶ **Example 6** Find the nth Taylor polynomial for $1/x$ about $x = 1$ and express it in sigma notation.

Solution. Let $f(x) = 1/x$. The computations are similar to those in Example 5. We leave it for you to show that

$$f(1) = 1, \quad f'(1) = -1, \quad f''(1) = 2!, \quad f'''(1) = -3!,$$
$$f^{(4)}(1) = 4!, \ldots, \quad f^{(k)}(1) = (-1)^k k!$$

Thus, substituting $f^{(k)}(1) = (-1)^k k!$ into Formula (10) with $x_0 = 1$ yields the nth Taylor polynomial for $1/x$:

$$\sum_{k=0}^{n} (-1)^k (x-1)^k = 1 - (x-1) + (x-1)^2 - (x-1)^3 + \cdots + (-1)^n (x-1)^n \; \blacktriangleleft$$

■ **THE nTH REMAINDER**

It will be convenient to have a notation for the error in the approximation $f(x) \approx p_n(x)$. Accordingly, we will let $R_n(x)$ denote the difference between $f(x)$ and its nth Taylor polynomial; that is,

$$R_n(x) = f(x) - p_n(x) = f(x) - \sum_{k=0}^{n} \frac{f^{(k)}(x_0)}{k!} (x-x_0)^k \tag{12}$$

This can also be written as

$$f(x) = p_n(x) + R_n(x) = \sum_{k=0}^{n} \frac{f^{(k)}(x_0)}{k!} (x-x_0)^k + R_n(x) \tag{13}$$

The function $R_n(x)$ is called the ***nth remainder*** for the Taylor series of f, and Formula (13) is called ***Taylor's formula with remainder***.

Finding a bound for $R_n(x)$ gives an indication of the accuracy of the approximation $p_n(x) \approx f(x)$. The following theorem, which is proved in Appendix J, provides such a bound.

The bound for $|R_n(x)|$ in (14) is called the *Lagrange error bound*.

> **9.7.4** **THEOREM (*The Remainder Estimation Theorem*)** *If the function f can be differentiated $n+1$ times on an interval containing the number x_0, and if M is an upper bound for $|f^{(n+1)}(x)|$ on the interval, that is, $|f^{(n+1)}(x)| \leq M$ for all x in the interval, then*
>
> $$|R_n(x)| \leq \frac{M}{(n+1)!} |x - x_0|^{n+1} \tag{14}$$
>
> *for all x in the interval.*

▶ **Example 7**   Use an nth Maclaurin polynomial for e^x to approximate e to five decimal-place accuracy.

Solution.   We note first that the exponential function e^x has derivatives of all orders for every real number x. From Example 2, the nth Maclaurin polynomial for e^x is

$$\sum_{k=0}^{n} \frac{x^k}{k!} = 1 + x + \frac{x^2}{2!} + \cdots + \frac{x^n}{n!}$$

from which we have

$$e = e^1 \approx \sum_{k=0}^{n} \frac{1^k}{k!} = 1 + 1 + \frac{1}{2!} + \cdots + \frac{1}{n!}$$

Thus, our problem is to determine how many terms to include in a Maclaurin polynomial for e^x to achieve five decimal-place accuracy; that is, we want to choose n so that the absolute value of the nth remainder at $x = 1$ satisfies

$$|R_n(1)| \leq 0.000005$$

To determine n we use the Remainder Estimation Theorem with $f(x) = e^x$, $x = 1$, $x_0 = 0$, and the interval $[0, 1]$. In this case it follows from (14) that

$$|R_n(1)| \leq \frac{M}{(n+1)!} \cdot |1 - 0|^{n+1} = \frac{M}{(n+1)!} \qquad (15)$$

where M is an upper bound on the value of $f^{(n+1)}(x) = e^x$ for x in the interval $[0, 1]$. However, e^x is an increasing function, so its maximum value on the interval $[0, 1]$ occurs at $x = 1$; that is, $e^x \leq e$ on this interval. Thus, we can take $M = e$ in (15) to obtain

$$|R_n(1)| \leq \frac{e}{(n+1)!} \qquad (16)$$

Unfortunately, this inequality is not very useful because it involves e, which is the very quantity we are trying to approximate. However, if we accept that $e < 3$, then we can replace (16) with the following less precise, but more easily applied, inequality:

$$|R_n(1)| \leq \frac{3}{(n+1)!}$$

Thus, we can achieve five decimal-place accuracy by choosing n so that

$$\frac{3}{(n+1)!} \leq 0.000005 \quad \text{or} \quad (n+1)! \geq 600{,}000$$

Since $9! = 362{,}880$ and $10! = 3{,}628{,}800$, the smallest value of n that meets this criterion is $n = 9$. Thus, to five decimal-place accuracy

$$e \approx 1 + 1 + \frac{1}{2!} + \frac{1}{3!} + \frac{1}{4!} + \frac{1}{5!} + \frac{1}{6!} + \frac{1}{7!} + \frac{1}{8!} + \frac{1}{9!} \approx 2.71828$$

As a check, a calculator's 12-digit representation of e is $e \approx 2.71828182846$, which agrees with the preceding approximation when rounded to five decimal places. ◀

▶ **Example 8**   Use the Remainder Estimation Theorem to find an interval containing $x = 0$ throughout which $f(x) = \cos x$ can be approximated by $p(x) = 1 - (x^2/2!)$ to three decimal-place accuracy.

Solution.   We note first that $f(x) = \cos x$ has derivatives of all orders for every real number x, so the first hypothesis of the Remainder Estimation Theorem is satisfied over any interval that we choose. The given polynomial $p(x)$ is both the second and the third

Maclaurin polynomial for $\cos x$; we will choose the degree n of the polynomial to be as large as possible, so we will take $n = 3$. Our problem is to determine an interval on which the absolute value of the third remainder at x satisfies

$$|R_3(x)| \leq 0.0005$$

We will use the Remainder Estimation Theorem with $f(x) = \cos x$, $n = 3$, and $x_0 = 0$. It follows from (14) that

$$|R_3(x)| \leq \frac{M}{(3 + 1)!}|x - 0|^{3+1} = \frac{M|x|^4}{24} \tag{17}$$

where M is an upper bound for $|f^{(4)}(x)| = |\cos x|$. Since $|\cos x| \leq 1$ for every real number x, we can take $M = 1$ in (17) to obtain

$$|R_3(x)| \leq \frac{|x|^4}{24} \tag{18}$$

Thus we can achieve three decimal-place accuracy by choosing values of x for which

$$\frac{|x|^4}{24} \leq 0.0005 \quad \text{or} \quad |x| \leq 0.3309$$

so the interval $[-0.3309, 0.3309]$ is one option. We can check this answer by graphing $|f(x) - p(x)|$ over the interval $[-0.3309, 0.3309]$ (Figure 9.7.7). ◄

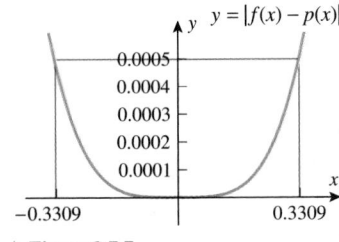

▲ **Figure 9.7.7**

✔ **QUICK CHECK EXERCISES 9.7**   *(See page 659 for answers.)*

1. If f can be differentiated three times at 0, then the third Maclaurin polynomial for f is $p_3(x) = $ _____.

2. The third Maclaurin polynomial for $f(x) = e^{2x}$ is
$$p_3(x) = \underline{\qquad} + \underline{\qquad} x$$
$$+ \underline{\qquad} x^2 + \underline{\qquad} x^3$$

3. If $f(2) = 3$, $f'(2) = -4$, and $f''(2) = 10$, then the second Taylor polynomial for f about $x = 2$ is $p_2(x) = $ _____.

4. The third Taylor polynomial for $f(x) = x^5$ about $x = -1$ is
$$p_3(x) = \underline{\qquad} + \underline{\qquad} (x + 1)$$
$$+ \underline{\qquad} (x + 1)^2 + \underline{\qquad} (x + 1)^3$$

5. (a) If a function f has nth Taylor polynomial $p_n(x)$ about $x = x_0$, then the nth remainder $R_n(x)$ is defined by $R_n(x) = $ _____.

   (b) Suppose that a function f can be differentiated five times on an interval containing $x_0 = 2$ and that $|f^{(5)}(x)| \leq 20$ for all x in the interval. Then the fourth remainder satisfies $|R_4(x)| \leq $ _____ for all x in the interval.

EXERCISE SET 9.7   ⊠ Graphing Utility

⊠ **1–2** In each part, find the local quadratic approximation of f at $x = x_0$, and use that approximation to find the local linear approximation of f at x_0. Use a graphing utility to graph f and the two approximations on the same screen. ■

1. (a) $f(x) = e^{-x}$; $x_0 = 0$ (b) $f(x) = \cos x$; $x_0 = 0$

2. (a) $f(x) = \sin x$; $x_0 = \pi/2$ (b) $f(x) = \sqrt{x}$; $x_0 = 1$

3. (a) Find the local quadratic approximation of $\sqrt{x}$ at $x_0 = 1$.
   (b) Use the result obtained in part (a) to approximate $\sqrt{1.1}$, and compare your approximation to that produced directly by your calculating utility. [*Note:* See Example 1 of Section 3.5.]

4. (a) Find the local quadratic approximation of $\cos x$ at $x_0 = 0$.
   (b) Use the result obtained in part (a) to approximate $\cos 2°$, and compare the approximation to that produced directly by your calculating utility.

5. Use an appropriate local quadratic approximation to approximate $\tan 61°$, and compare the result to that produced directly by your calculating utility.

6. Use an appropriate local quadratic approximation to approximate $\sqrt{36.03}$, and compare the result to that produced directly by your calculating utility.

7–16 Find the Maclaurin polynomials of orders $n = 0, 1, 2, 3$, and 4, and then find the nth Maclaurin polynomials for the function in sigma notation. ▪

7. e^{-x} **8.** e^{ax} **9.** $\cos \pi x$

10. $\sin \pi x$ **11.** $\ln(1 + x)$ **12.** $\dfrac{1}{1 + x}$

13. $\cosh x$ **14.** $\sinh x$ **15.** $x \sin x$

16. xe^x

17–24 Find the Taylor polynomials of orders $n = 0, 1, 2, 3$, and 4 about $x = x_0$, and then find the nth Taylor polynomial for the function in sigma notation. ▪

17. e^x; $x_0 = 1$ **18.** e^{-x}; $x_0 = \ln 2$

19. $\dfrac{1}{x}$; $x_0 = -1$ **20.** $\dfrac{1}{x + 2}$; $x_0 = 3$

21. $\sin \pi x$; $x_0 = \dfrac{1}{2}$ **22.** $\cos x$; $x_0 = \dfrac{\pi}{2}$

23. $\ln x$; $x_0 = 1$ **24.** $\ln x$; $x_0 = e$

25. (a) Find the third Maclaurin polynomial for
$$f(x) = 1 + 2x - x^2 + x^3$$
  (b) Find the third Taylor polynomial about $x = 1$ for
$$f(x) = 1 + 2(x - 1) - (x - 1)^2 + (x - 1)^3$$

26. (a) Find the nth Maclaurin polynomial for
$$f(x) = c_0 + c_1 x + c_2 x^2 + \cdots + c_n x^n$$
  (b) Find the nth Taylor polynomial about $x = 1$ for
$$f(x) = c_0 + c_1(x - 1) + c_2(x - 1)^2 + \cdots + c_n(x - 1)^n$$

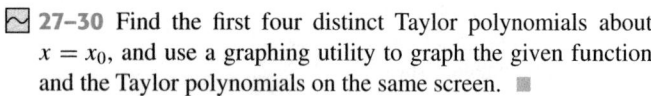 **27–30** Find the first four distinct Taylor polynomials about $x = x_0$, and use a graphing utility to graph the given function and the Taylor polynomials on the same screen. ▪

27. $f(x) = e^{-2x}$; $x_0 = 0$ **28.** $f(x) = \sin x$; $x_0 = \pi/2$

29. $f(x) = \cos x$; $x_0 = \pi$ **30.** $\ln(x + 1)$; $x_0 = 0$

31–34 True–False Determine whether the statement is true or false. Explain your answer. ▪

31. The equation of a tangent line to a differentiable function is a first-degree Taylor polynomial for that function.

32. The graph of a function f and the graph of its Maclaurin polynomial have a common y-intercept.

33. If $p_6(x)$ is the sixth-degree Taylor polynomial for a function f about $x = x_0$, then $p_6^{(4)}(x_0) = 4! f^{(4)}(x_0)$.

34. If $p_4(x)$ is the fourth-degree Maclaurin polynomial for e^x, then
$$|e^2 - p_4(2)| \le \frac{9}{5!}$$

35–36 Use the method of Example 7 to approximate the given expression to the specified accuracy. Check your answer to that produced directly by your calculating utility. ▪

35. $\sqrt{e}$; four decimal-place accuracy

36. $1/e$; three decimal-place accuracy

37. Which of the functions graphed in the following figure is most likely to have $p(x) = 1 - x + 2x^2$ as its second-order Maclaurin polynomial? Explain your reasoning.

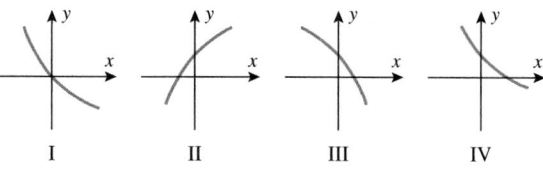

I   II   III   IV

38. Suppose that the values of a function f and its first three derivatives at $x = 1$ are
$$f(1) = 2, \quad f'(1) = -3, \quad f''(1) = 0, \quad f'''(1) = 6$$
Find as many Taylor polynomials for f as you can about $x = 1$.

39. Let $p_1(x)$ and $p_2(x)$ be the local linear and local quadratic approximations of $f(x) = e^{\sin x}$ at $x = 0$.
  (a) Use a graphing utility to generate the graphs of $f(x)$, $p_1(x)$, and $p_2(x)$ on the same screen for $-1 \le x \le 1$.
  (b) Construct a table of values of $f(x)$, $p_1(x)$, and $p_2(x)$ for $x = -1.00, -0.75, -0.50, -0.25, 0, 0.25, 0.50, 0.75, 1.00$. Round the values to three decimal places.
  (c) Generate the graph of $|f(x) - p_1(x)|$, and use the graph to determine an interval on which $p_1(x)$ approximates $f(x)$ with an error of at most ± 0.01. [*Suggestion:* Review the discussion relating to Figure 3.5.4.]
  (d) Generate the graph of $|f(x) - p_2(x)|$, and use the graph to determine an interval on which $p_2(x)$ approximates $f(x)$ with an error of at most ± 0.01.

40. (a) The accompanying figure shows a sector of radius r and central angle 2α. Assuming that the angle α is small, use the local quadratic approximation of $\cos \alpha$ at $\alpha = 0$ to show that $x \approx r\alpha^2/2$.
  (b) Assuming that the Earth is a sphere of radius 4000 mi, use the result in part (a) to approximate the maximum amount by which a 100 mi arc along the equator will diverge from its chord.

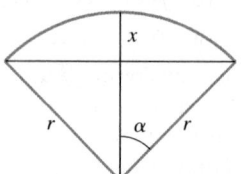

◄ **Figure Ex-40**

41. (a) Find an interval $[0, b]$ over which e^x can be approximated by $1 + x + (x^2/2!)$ to three decimal-place accuracy throughout the interval.

(b) Check your answer in part (a) by graphing

$$\left| e^x - \left(1 + x + \frac{x^2}{2!} \right) \right|$$

over the interval you obtained.

42. Show that the nth Taylor polynomial for $\sinh x$ about $x = \ln 4$ is

$$\sum_{k=0}^{n} \frac{16 - (-1)^k}{8k!} (x - \ln 4)^k$$

43–46 Use the Remainder Estimation Theorem to find an interval containing $x = 0$ over which $f(x)$ can be approximated by $p(x)$ to three decimal-place accuracy throughout the interval. Check your answer by graphing $|f(x) - p(x)|$ over the interval you obtained. ■

43. $f(x) = \sin x;\ \ p(x) = x - \dfrac{x^3}{3!}$

44. $f(x) = \cos x;\ \ p(x) = 1 - \dfrac{x^2}{2!} + \dfrac{x^4}{4!}$

45. $f(x) = \dfrac{1}{1 + x^2};\ \ p(x) = 1 - x^2 + x^4$

46. $f(x) = \ln(1 + x);\ \ p(x) = x - \dfrac{x^2}{2} + \dfrac{x^3}{3}$

✔ **QUICK CHECK ANSWERS 9.7**

1. $f(0) + f'(0)x + \dfrac{f''(0)}{2!} x^2 + \dfrac{f'''(0)}{3!} x^3$ **2.** $1; 2; 2; \frac{4}{3}$ **3.** $3 - 4(x - 2) + 5(x - 2)^2$ **4.** $-1; 5; -10; 10$

5. (a) $f(x) - p_n(x)$ (b) $\frac{1}{6}|x - 2|^5$

9.8 MACLAURIN AND TAYLOR SERIES; POWER SERIES

Recall from the last section that the nth Taylor polynomial $p_n(x)$ at $x = x_0$ for a function f was defined so its value and the values of its first n derivatives match those of f at x_0. This being the case, it is reasonable to expect that for values of x near x_0 the values of $p_n(x)$ will become better and better approximations of $f(x)$ as n increases, and may possibly converge to $f(x)$ as $n \to +\infty$. We will explore this idea in this section.

■ **MACLAURIN AND TAYLOR SERIES**

In Section 9.7 we defined the nth Maclaurin polynomial for a function f as

$$\sum_{k=0}^{n} \frac{f^{(k)}(0)}{k!} x^k = f(0) + f'(0)x + \frac{f''(0)}{2!} x^2 + \cdots + \frac{f^{(n)}(0)}{n!} x^n$$

and the nth Taylor polynomial for f about $x = x_0$ as

$$\sum_{k=0}^{n} \frac{f^{(k)}(x_0)}{k!} (x - x_0)^k = f(x_0) + f'(x_0)(x - x_0)$$

$$+ \frac{f''(x_0)}{2!} (x - x_0)^2 + \cdots + \frac{f^{(n)}(x_0)}{n!} (x - x_0)^n$$

It is not a big step to extend the notions of Maclaurin and Taylor polynomials to series by not stopping the summation index at n. Thus, we have the following definition.

9.8.1 **DEFINITION** If f has derivatives of all orders at x_0, then we call the series

$$\sum_{k=0}^{\infty} \frac{f^{(k)}(x_0)}{k!}(x - x_0)^k = f(x_0) + f'(x_0)(x - x_0) + \frac{f''(x_0)}{2!}(x - x_0)^2$$

$$+ \cdots + \frac{f^{(k)}(x_0)}{k!}(x - x_0)^k + \cdots \quad (1)$$

the **Taylor series for f about $x = x_0$**. In the special case where $x_0 = 0$, this series becomes

$$\sum_{k=0}^{\infty} \frac{f^{(k)}(0)}{k!}x^k = f(0) + f'(0)x + \frac{f''(0)}{2!}x^2 + \cdots + \frac{f^{(k)}(0)}{k!}x^k + \cdots \quad (2)$$

in which case we call it the **Maclaurin series for f**.

Note that the nth Maclaurin and Taylor polynomials are the nth partial sums for the corresponding Maclaurin and Taylor series.

▶ **Example 1** Find the Maclaurin series for

$$\text{(a) } e^x \quad \text{(b) } \sin x \quad \text{(c) } \cos x \quad \text{(d) } \frac{1}{1 - x}$$

Solution (a). In Example 2 of Section 9.7 we found that the nth Maclaurin polynomial for e^x is

$$p_n(x) = \sum_{k=0}^{n} \frac{x^k}{k!} = 1 + x + \frac{x^2}{2!} + \cdots + \frac{x^n}{n!}$$

Thus, the Maclaurin series for e^x is

$$\sum_{k=0}^{\infty} \frac{x^k}{k!} = 1 + x + \frac{x^2}{2!} + \cdots + \frac{x^k}{k!} + \cdots$$

Solution (b). In Example 3(a) of Section 9.7 we found that the Maclaurin polynomials for $\sin x$ are given by

$$p_{2k+1}(x) = p_{2k+2}(x) = x - \frac{x^3}{3!} + \frac{x^5}{5!} - \frac{x^7}{7!} + \cdots + (-1)^k \frac{x^{2k+1}}{(2k + 1)!} \quad (k = 0, 1, 2, \ldots)$$

Thus, the Maclaurin series for $\sin x$ is

$$\sum_{k=0}^{\infty} (-1)^k \frac{x^{2k+1}}{(2k + 1)!} = x - \frac{x^3}{3!} + \frac{x^5}{5!} - \frac{x^7}{7!} + \cdots + (-1)^k \frac{x^{2k+1}}{(2k + 1)!} + \cdots$$

Solution (c). In Example 3(b) of Section 9.7 we found that the Maclaurin polynomials for $\cos x$ are given by

$$p_{2k}(x) = p_{2k+1}(x) = 1 - \frac{x^2}{2!} + \frac{x^4}{4!} - \frac{x^6}{6!} + \cdots + (-1)^k \frac{x^{2k}}{(2k)!} \quad (k = 0, 1, 2, \ldots)$$

Thus, the Maclaurin series for $\cos x$ is

$$\sum_{k=0}^{\infty} (-1)^k \frac{x^{2k}}{(2k)!} = 1 - \frac{x^2}{2!} + \frac{x^4}{4!} - \frac{x^6}{6!} + \cdots + (-1)^k \frac{x^{2k}}{(2k)!} + \cdots$$

Solution (d). In Example 5 of Section 9.7 we found that the nth Maclaurin polynomial for $1/(1-x)$ is

$$p_n(x) = \sum_{k=0}^{n} x^k = 1 + x + x^2 + \cdots + x^n \quad (n = 0, 1, 2, \ldots)$$

Thus, the Maclaurin series for $1/(1-x)$ is

$$\sum_{k=0}^{\infty} x^k = 1 + x + x^2 + \cdots + x^k + \cdots \quad \blacktriangleleft$$

▶ **Example 2** Find the Taylor series for $1/x$ about $x = 1$.

Solution. In Example 6 of Section 9.7 we found that the nth Taylor polynomial for $1/x$ about $x = 1$ is

$$\sum_{k=0}^{n} (-1)^k (x-1)^k = 1 - (x-1) + (x-1)^2 - (x-1)^3 + \cdots + (-1)^n (x-1)^n$$

Thus, the Taylor series for $1/x$ about $x = 1$ is

$$\sum_{k=0}^{\infty} (-1)^k (x-1)^k = 1 - (x-1) + (x-1)^2 - (x-1)^3 + \cdots + (-1)^k (x-1)^k + \cdots \quad \blacktriangleleft$$

■ **POWER SERIES IN x**

Maclaurin and Taylor series differ from the series that we have considered in Sections 9.3 to 9.6 in that their terms are not merely constants, but instead involve a variable. These are examples of *power series*, which we now define.

If $c_0, c_1, c_2, \ldots$ are constants and x is a variable, then a series of the form

$$\sum_{k=0}^{\infty} c_k x^k = c_0 + c_1 x + c_2 x^2 + \cdots + c_k x^k + \cdots \tag{3}$$

is called a ***power series in x***. Some examples are

$$\sum_{k=0}^{\infty} x^k = 1 + x + x^2 + x^3 + \cdots$$

$$\sum_{k=0}^{\infty} \frac{x^k}{k!} = 1 + x + \frac{x^2}{2!} + \frac{x^3}{3!} + \cdots$$

$$\sum_{k=0}^{\infty} (-1)^k \frac{x^{2k}}{(2k)!} = 1 - \frac{x^2}{2!} + \frac{x^4}{4!} - \frac{x^6}{6!} + \cdots$$

From Example 1, these are the Maclaurin series for the functions $1/(1-x)$, e^x, and $\cos x$, respectively. Indeed, every Maclaurin series

$$\sum_{k=0}^{\infty} \frac{f^{(k)}(0)}{k!} x^k = f(0) + f'(0)x + \frac{f''(0)}{2!} x^2 + \cdots + \frac{f^{(k)}(0)}{k!} x^k + \cdots$$

is a power series in x.

■ RADIUS AND INTERVAL OF CONVERGENCE

If a numerical value is substituted for x in a power series $\sum c_k x^k$, then the resulting series of numbers may either converge or diverge. This leads to the problem of determining the set of x-values for which a given power series converges; this is called its **convergence set**.

Observe that every power series in x converges at $x = 0$, since substituting this value in (3) produces the series

$$c_0 + 0 + 0 + 0 + \cdots + 0 + \cdots$$

whose sum is c_0. In some cases $x = 0$ may be the only number in the convergence set; in other cases the convergence set is some finite or infinite interval containing $x = 0$. This is the content of the following theorem, whose proof will be omitted.

9.8.2   THEOREM   *For any power series in x, exactly one of the following is true:*

(a) *The series converges only for $x = 0$.*

(b) *The series converges absolutely (and hence converges) for all real values of x.*

(c) *The series converges absolutely (and hence converges) for all x in some finite open interval $(-R, R)$ and diverges if $x < -R$ or $x > R$. At either of the values $x = R$ or $x = -R$, the series may converge absolutely, converge conditionally, or diverge, depending on the particular series.*

This theorem states that the convergence set for a power series in x is always an interval centered at $x = 0$ (possibly just the value $x = 0$ itself or possibly infinite). For this reason, the convergence set of a power series in x is called the **interval of convergence**. In the case where the convergence set is the single value $x = 0$ we say that the series has **radius of convergence 0**, in the case where the convergence set is $(-\infty, +\infty)$ we say that the series has **radius of convergence $+\infty$**, and in the case where the convergence set extends between $-R$ and R we say that the series has **radius of convergence R** (Figure 9.8.1).

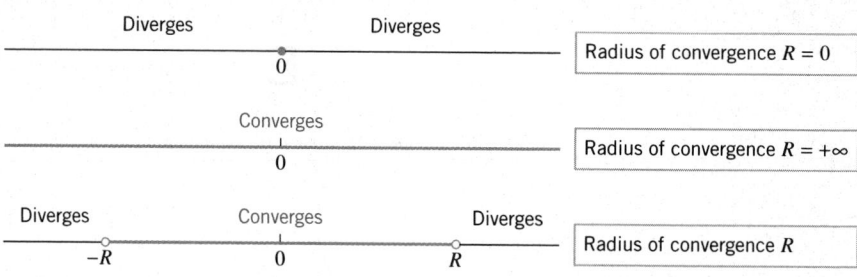

▶ **Figure 9.8.1**

■ FINDING THE INTERVAL OF CONVERGENCE

The usual procedure for finding the interval of convergence of a power series is to apply the ratio test for absolute convergence (Theorem 9.6.5). The following example illustrates how this works.

▶ **Example 3**   Find the interval of convergence and radius of convergence of the following power series.

$$\text{(a) } \sum_{k=0}^{\infty} x^k \qquad \text{(b) } \sum_{k=0}^{\infty} \frac{x^k}{k!} \qquad \text{(c) } \sum_{k=0}^{\infty} k! x^k \qquad \text{(d) } \sum_{k=0}^{\infty} \frac{(-1)^k x^k}{3^k (k+1)}$$

Solution (a). Applying the ratio test for absolute convergence to the given series, we obtain

$$\rho = \lim_{k \to +\infty} \left| \frac{u_{k+1}}{u_k} \right| = \lim_{k \to +\infty} \left| \frac{x^{k+1}}{x^k} \right| = \lim_{k \to +\infty} |x| = |x|$$

so the series converges absolutely if $\rho = |x| < 1$ and diverges if $\rho = |x| > 1$. The test is inconclusive if $|x| = 1$ (i.e., if $x = 1$ or $x = -1$), which means that we will have to investigate convergence at these values separately. At these values the series becomes

$$\sum_{k=0}^{\infty} 1^k = 1 + 1 + 1 + 1 + \cdots \qquad \boxed{x = 1}$$

$$\sum_{k=0}^{\infty} (-1)^k = 1 - 1 + 1 - 1 + \cdots \qquad \boxed{x = -1}$$

both of which diverge; thus, the interval of convergence for the given power series is $(-1, 1)$, and the radius of convergence is $R = 1$.

Solution (b). Applying the ratio test for absolute convergence to the given series, we obtain

$$\rho = \lim_{k \to +\infty} \left| \frac{u_{k+1}}{u_k} \right| = \lim_{k \to +\infty} \left| \frac{x^{k+1}}{(k+1)!} \cdot \frac{k!}{x^k} \right| = \lim_{k \to +\infty} \left| \frac{x}{k+1} \right| = 0$$

Since $\rho < 1$ for all x, the series converges absolutely for all x. Thus, the interval of convergence is $(-\infty, +\infty)$ and the radius of convergence is $R = +\infty$.

Solution (c). If $x \neq 0$, then the ratio test for absolute convergence yields

$$\rho = \lim_{k \to +\infty} \left| \frac{u_{k+1}}{u_k} \right| = \lim_{k \to +\infty} \left| \frac{(k+1)! x^{k+1}}{k! x^k} \right| = \lim_{k \to +\infty} |(k+1)x| = +\infty$$

Therefore, the series diverges for all nonzero values of x. Thus, the interval of convergence is the single value $x = 0$ and the radius of convergence is $R = 0$.

Solution (d). Since $|(-1)^k| = |(-1)^{k+1}| = 1$, we obtain

$$\rho = \lim_{k \to +\infty} \left| \frac{u_{k+1}}{u_k} \right| = \lim_{k \to +\infty} \left| \frac{x^{k+1}}{3^{k+1}(k+2)} \cdot \frac{3^k(k+1)}{x^k} \right|$$

$$= \lim_{k \to +\infty} \left[\frac{|x|}{3} \cdot \left(\frac{k+1}{k+2} \right) \right]$$

$$= \frac{|x|}{3} \lim_{k \to +\infty} \left(\frac{1 + (1/k)}{1 + (2/k)} \right) = \frac{|x|}{3}$$

The ratio test for absolute convergence implies that the series converges absolutely if $|x| < 3$ and diverges if $|x| > 3$. The ratio test fails to provide any information when $|x| = 3$, so the cases $x = -3$ and $x = 3$ need separate analyses. Substituting $x = -3$ in the given series yields

$$\sum_{k=0}^{\infty} \frac{(-1)^k(-3)^k}{3^k(k+1)} = \sum_{k=0}^{\infty} \frac{(-1)^k(-1)^k 3^k}{3^k(k+1)} = \sum_{k=0}^{\infty} \frac{1}{k+1}$$

which is the divergent harmonic series $1 + \frac{1}{2} + \frac{1}{3} + \frac{1}{4} + \cdots$. Substituting $x = 3$ in the given series yields

$$\sum_{k=0}^{\infty} \frac{(-1)^k 3^k}{3^k(k+1)} = \sum_{k=0}^{\infty} \frac{(-1)^k}{k+1} = 1 - \frac{1}{2} + \frac{1}{3} - \frac{1}{4} + \cdots$$

which is the conditionally convergent alternating harmonic series. Thus, the interval of convergence for the given series is $(-3, 3]$ and the radius of convergence is $R = 3$. ◄

■ POWER SERIES IN $x - x_0$

If x_0 is a constant, and if x is replaced by $x - x_0$ in (3), then the resulting series has the form

$$\sum_{k=0}^{\infty} c_k (x - x_0)^k = c_0 + c_1(x - x_0) + c_2(x - x_0)^2 + \cdots + c_k(x - x_0)^k + \cdots$$

This is called a ***power series in*** $x - x_0$. Some examples are

$$\sum_{k=0}^{\infty} \frac{(x-1)^k}{k+1} = 1 + \frac{(x-1)}{2} + \frac{(x-1)^2}{3} + \frac{(x-1)^3}{4} + \cdots \qquad \boxed{x_0 = 1}$$

$$\sum_{k=0}^{\infty} \frac{(-1)^k (x+3)^k}{k!} = 1 - (x+3) + \frac{(x+3)^2}{2!} - \frac{(x+3)^3}{3!} + \cdots \qquad \boxed{x_0 = -3}$$

The first of these is a power series in $x - 1$ and the second is a power series in $x + 3$. Note that a power series in x is a power series in $x - x_0$ in which $x_0 = 0$. More generally, the Taylor series

$$\sum_{k=0}^{\infty} \frac{f^{(k)}(x_0)}{k!}(x - x_0)^k$$

is a power series in $x - x_0$.

The main result on convergence of a power series in $x - x_0$ can be obtained by substituting $x - x_0$ for x in Theorem 9.8.2. This leads to the following theorem.

9.8.3 THEOREM *For a power series* $\sum c_k (x - x_0)^k$, *exactly one of the following statements is true:*

(a) *The series converges only for* $x = x_0$.

(b) *The series converges absolutely (and hence converges) for all real values of* x.

(c) *The series converges absolutely (and hence converges) for all* x *in some finite open interval* $(x_0 - R, x_0 + R)$ *and diverges if* $x < x_0 - R$ *or* $x > x_0 + R$. *At either of the values* $x = x_0 - R$ *or* $x = x_0 + R$, *the series may converge absolutely, converge conditionally, or diverge, depending on the particular series.*

It follows from this theorem that the set of values for which a power series in $x - x_0$ converges is always an interval centered at $x = x_0$; we call this the ***interval of convergence*** (Figure 9.8.2). In part (*a*) of Theorem 9.8.3 the interval of convergence reduces to the single value $x = x_0$, in which case we say that the series has ***radius of convergence* $R = 0$**; in part

▶ **Figure 9.8.2**

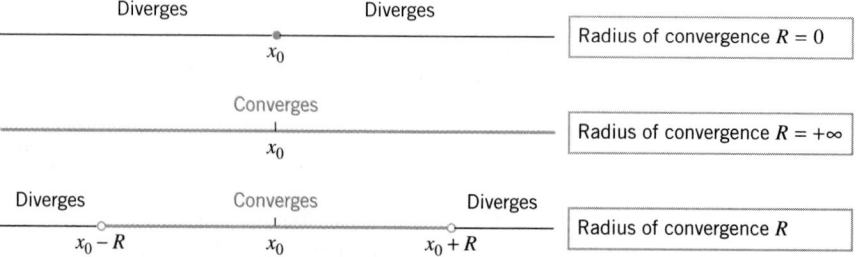

(b) the interval of convergence is infinite (the entire real line), in which case we say that the series has ***radius of convergence*** $R = +\infty$; and in part (c) the interval extends between $x_0 - R$ and $x_0 + R$, in which case we say that the series has ***radius of convergence R***.

▶ **Example 4** Find the interval of convergence and radius of convergence of the series

$$\sum_{k=1}^{\infty} \frac{(x-5)^k}{k^2}$$

Solution. We apply the ratio test for absolute convergence.

$$\rho = \lim_{k \to +\infty} \left| \frac{u_{k+1}}{u_k} \right| = \lim_{k \to +\infty} \left| \frac{(x-5)^{k+1}}{(k+1)^2} \cdot \frac{k^2}{(x-5)^k} \right|$$

$$= \lim_{k \to +\infty} \left[|x-5| \left(\frac{k}{k+1} \right)^2 \right]$$

$$= |x-5| \lim_{k \to +\infty} \left(\frac{1}{1+(1/k)} \right)^2 = |x-5|$$

Thus, the series converges absolutely if $|x - 5| < 1$, or $-1 < x - 5 < 1$, or $4 < x < 6$. The series diverges if $x < 4$ or $x > 6$.

To determine the convergence behavior at the endpoints $x = 4$ and $x = 6$, we substitute these values in the given series. If $x = 6$, the series becomes

$$\sum_{k=1}^{\infty} \frac{1^k}{k^2} = \sum_{k=1}^{\infty} \frac{1}{k^2} = 1 + \frac{1}{2^2} + \frac{1}{3^2} + \frac{1}{4^2} + \cdots$$

which is a convergent p-series ($p = 2$). If $x = 4$, the series becomes

$$\sum_{k=1}^{\infty} \frac{(-1)^k}{k^2} = -1 + \frac{1}{2^2} - \frac{1}{3^2} + \frac{1}{4^2} - \cdots$$

Since this series converges absolutely, the interval of convergence for the given series is $[4, 6]$. The radius of convergence is $R = 1$ (Figure 9.8.3). ◀

It will always be a waste of time to test for convergence at the endpoints of the interval of convergence using the ratio test, since ρ will always be 1 at those points if

$$\lim_{k \to +\infty} \left| \frac{u_{k+1}}{u_k} \right|$$

exists. Explain why this must be so.

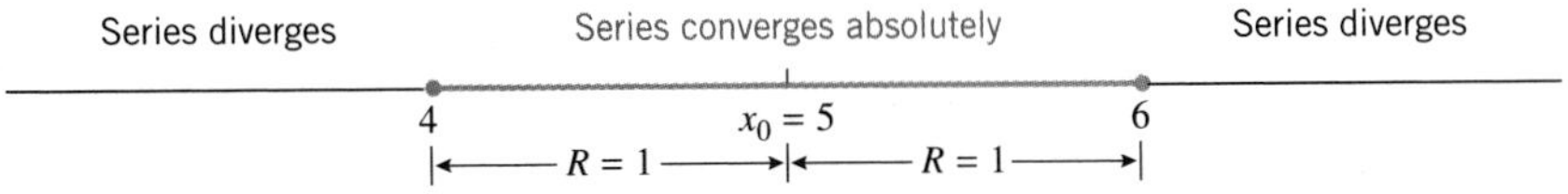

Series diverges   Series converges absolutely   Series diverges

▶ **Figure 9.8.3**

■ **FUNCTIONS DEFINED BY POWER SERIES**

If a function f is expressed as a power series on some interval, then we say that the power series ***represents*** f on that interval. For example, we saw in Example 4(a) of Section 9.3 that

$$\frac{1}{1-x} = \sum_{k=0}^{\infty} x^k$$

if $|x| < 1$, so this power series represents the function $1/(1-x)$ on the interval $-1 < x < 1$.

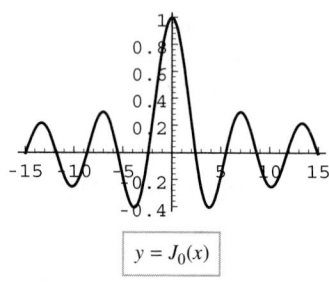

$y = J_0(x)$

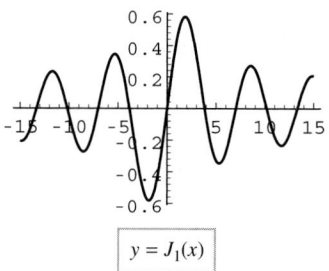

$y = J_1(x)$

Generated by Mathematica

▲ **Figure 9.8.4**

TECHNOLOGY MASTERY

Many computer algebra systems have the Bessel functions as part of their libraries. If you have a CAS with Bessel functions, use it to generate the graphs in Figure 9.8.4.

Sometimes new functions actually originate as power series, and the properties of the functions are developed by working with their power series representations. For example, the functions

$$J_0(x) = \sum_{k=0}^{\infty} \frac{(-1)^k x^{2k}}{2^{2k}(k!)^2} = 1 - \frac{x^2}{2^2(1!)^2} + \frac{x^4}{2^4(2!)^2} - \frac{x^6}{2^6(3!)^2} + \cdots \quad (4)$$

and

$$J_1(x) = \sum_{k=0}^{\infty} \frac{(-1)^k x^{2k+1}}{2^{2k+1}(k!)(k+1)!} = \frac{x}{2} - \frac{x^3}{2^3(1!)(2!)} + \frac{x^5}{2^5(2!)(3!)} - \cdots \quad (5)$$

which are called **Bessel functions** in honor of the German mathematician and astronomer Friedrich Wilhelm Bessel (1784–1846), arise naturally in the study of planetary motion and in various problems that involve heat flow.

To find the domains of these functions, we must determine where their defining power series converge. For example, in the case of $J_0(x)$ we have

$$\rho = \lim_{k \to +\infty} \left| \frac{u_{k+1}}{u_k} \right| = \lim_{k \to +\infty} \left| \frac{x^{2(k+1)}}{2^{2(k+1)}[(k+1)!]^2} \cdot \frac{2^{2k}(k!)^2}{x^{2k}} \right|$$

$$= \lim_{k \to +\infty} \left| \frac{x^2}{4(k+1)^2} \right| = 0 < 1$$

so the series converges for all x; that is, the domain of $J_0(x)$ is $(-\infty, +\infty)$. We leave it as an exercise (Exercise 59) to show that the power series for $J_1(x)$ also converges for all x. Computer-generated graphs of $J_0(x)$ and $J_1(x)$ are shown in Figure 9.8.4.

✔ **QUICK CHECK EXERCISES 9.8**   *(See page 668 for answers.)*

1. If f has derivatives of all orders at x_0, then the Taylor series for f about $x = x_0$ is defined to be

$$\sum_{k=0}^{\infty} \underline{\qquad}$$

2. Since

$$\lim_{k \to +\infty} \left| \frac{2^{k+1} x^{k+1}}{2^k x^k} \right| = 2|x|$$

the radius of convergence for the infinite series $\sum_{k=0}^{\infty} 2^k x^k$ is _____.

3. Since

$$\lim_{k \to +\infty} \left| \frac{(3^{k+1} x^{k+1})/(k+1)!}{(3^k x^k)/k!} \right| = \lim_{k \to +\infty} \left| \frac{3x}{k+1} \right| = 0$$

the interval of convergence for the series $\sum_{k=0}^{\infty} (3^k/k!) x^k$ is _____.

4. (a) Since

$$\lim_{k \to +\infty} \left| \frac{(x-4)^{k+1}/\sqrt{k+1}}{(x-4)^k/\sqrt{k}} \right| = \lim_{k \to +\infty} \left| \sqrt{\frac{k}{k+1}} (x-4) \right|$$

$$= |x - 4|$$

the radius of convergence for the infinite series $\sum_{k=1}^{\infty} (1/\sqrt{k})(x-4)^k$ is _____.

(b) When $x = 3$,

$$\sum_{k=1}^{\infty} \frac{1}{\sqrt{k}} (x-4)^k = \sum_{k=1}^{\infty} \frac{1}{\sqrt{k}} (-1)^k$$

Does this series converge or diverge?

(c) When $x = 5$,

$$\sum_{k=1}^{\infty} \frac{1}{\sqrt{k}} (x-4)^k = \sum_{k=1}^{\infty} \frac{1}{\sqrt{k}}$$

Does this series converge or diverge?

(d) The interval of convergence for the infinite series $\sum_{k=1}^{\infty} (1/\sqrt{k})(x-4)^k$ is _____.

EXERCISE SET 9.8   ~ Graphing Utility   [C] CAS

1–10 Use sigma notation to write the Maclaurin series for the function. ■

1. e^{-x} 2. e^{ax} 3. $\cos \pi x$ 4. $\sin \pi x$

5. $\ln(1 + x)$ 6. $\dfrac{1}{1 + x}$ 7. $\cosh x$

8. $\sinh x$ 9. $x \sin x$ 10. xe^x

11–18 Use sigma notation to write the Taylor series about $x = x_0$ for the function. ■

11. e^x; $x_0 = 1$ 12. e^{-x}; $x_0 = \ln 2$

13. $\dfrac{1}{x}$; $x_0 = -1$ 14. $\dfrac{1}{x + 2}$; $x_0 = 3$

15. $\sin \pi x$; $x_0 = \dfrac{1}{2}$ 16. $\cos x$; $x_0 = \dfrac{\pi}{2}$

17. $\ln x$; $x_0 = 1$ 18. $\ln x$; $x_0 = e$

19–22 Find the interval of convergence of the power series, and find a familiar function that is represented by the power series on that interval. ■

19. $1 - x + x^2 - x^3 + \cdots + (-1)^k x^k + \cdots$

20. $1 + x^2 + x^4 + \cdots + x^{2k} + \cdots$

21. $1 + (x - 2) + (x - 2)^2 + \cdots + (x - 2)^k + \cdots$

22. $1 - (x + 3) + (x + 3)^2 - (x + 3)^3$
$$+ \cdots + (-1)^k (x + 3)^k| \cdots .$$

23. Suppose that the function f is represented by the power series
$$f(x) = 1 - \frac{x}{2} + \frac{x^2}{4} - \frac{x^3}{8} + \cdots + (-1)^k \frac{x^k}{2^k} + \cdots$$
   (a) Find the domain of f.   (b) Find $f(0)$ and $f(1)$.

24. Suppose that the function f is represented by the power series
$$f(x) = 1 - \frac{x - 5}{3} + \frac{(x - 5)^2}{3^2} - \frac{(x - 5)^3}{3^3} + \cdots$$
   (a) Find the domain of f.   (b) Find $f(3)$ and $f(6)$.

25–28 True–False Determine whether the statement is true or false. Explain your answer. ■

25. If a power series in x converges conditionally at $x = 3$, then the series converges if $|x| < 3$ and diverges if $|x| > 3$.

26. The ratio test is often useful to determine convergence at the endpoints of the interval of convergence of a power series.

27. The Maclaurin series for a polynomial function has radius of convergence $+\infty$.

28. The series $\displaystyle\sum_{k=0}^{\infty} \frac{x^k}{k!}$ converges if $|x| < 1$.

29–48 Find the radius of convergence and the interval of convergence. ■

29. $\displaystyle\sum_{k=0}^{\infty} \frac{x^k}{k + 1}$ 30. $\displaystyle\sum_{k=0}^{\infty} 3^k x^k$ 31. $\displaystyle\sum_{k=0}^{\infty} \frac{(-1)^k x^k}{k!}$

32. $\displaystyle\sum_{k=0}^{\infty} \frac{k!}{2^k} x^k$ 33. $\displaystyle\sum_{k=1}^{\infty} \frac{5^k}{k^2} x^k$ 34. $\displaystyle\sum_{k=2}^{\infty} \frac{x^k}{\ln k}$

35. $\displaystyle\sum_{k=1}^{\infty} \frac{x^k}{k(k + 1)}$ 36. $\displaystyle\sum_{k=0}^{\infty} \frac{(-2)^k x^{k+1}}{k + 1}$

37. $\displaystyle\sum_{k=1}^{\infty} (-1)^{k-1} \frac{x^k}{\sqrt{k}}$ 38. $\displaystyle\sum_{k=0}^{\infty} \frac{(-1)^k x^{2k}}{(2k)!}$

39. $\displaystyle\sum_{k=0}^{\infty} \frac{3^k}{k!} x^k$ 40. $\displaystyle\sum_{k=2}^{\infty} (-1)^{k+1} \frac{x^k}{k(\ln k)^2}$

41. $\displaystyle\sum_{k=0}^{\infty} \frac{x^k}{1 + k^2}$ 42. $\displaystyle\sum_{k=0}^{\infty} \frac{(x - 3)^k}{2^k}$

43. $\displaystyle\sum_{k=1}^{\infty} (-1)^{k+1} \frac{(x + 1)^k}{k}$ 44. $\displaystyle\sum_{k=0}^{\infty} (-1)^k \frac{(x - 4)^k}{(k + 1)^2}$

45. $\displaystyle\sum_{k=0}^{\infty} \left(\frac{3}{4}\right)^k (x + 5)^k$ 46. $\displaystyle\sum_{k=1}^{\infty} \frac{(2k + 1)!}{k^3} (x - 2)^k$

47. $\displaystyle\sum_{k=0}^{\infty} \frac{\pi^k (x - 1)^{2k}}{(2k + 1)!}$ 48. $\displaystyle\sum_{k=0}^{\infty} \frac{(2x - 3)^k}{4^{2k}}$

49. Use the root test to find the interval of convergence of
$$\sum_{k=2}^{\infty} \frac{x^k}{(\ln k)^k}$$

50. Find the domain of the function
$$f(x) = \sum_{k=1}^{\infty} \frac{1 \cdot 3 \cdot 5 \cdots (2k - 1)}{(2k - 2)!} x^k$$

51. Show that the series
$$1 - \frac{x}{2!} + \frac{x^2}{4!} - \frac{x^3}{6!} + \cdots$$
is the Maclaurin series for the function
$$f(x) = \begin{cases} \cos \sqrt{x}, & x \geq 0 \\ \cosh \sqrt{-x}, & x < 0 \end{cases}$$
[Hint: Use the Maclaurin series for $\cos x$ and $\cosh x$ to obtain series for $\cos \sqrt{x}$, where $x \geq 0$, and $\cosh \sqrt{-x}$, where $x \leq 0$.]

FOCUS ON CONCEPTS

~ 52. If a function f is represented by a power series on an interval, then the graphs of the partial sums can be used as approximations to the graph of f.
   (a) Use a graphing utility to generate the graph of $1/(1 - x)$ together with the graphs of the first four partial sums of its Maclaurin series over the interval $(-1, 1)$.
   (b) In general terms, where are the graphs of the partial sums the most accurate?

53. Prove:
  (a) If f is an even function, then all odd powers of x in its Maclaurin series have coefficient 0.
  (b) If f is an odd function, then all even powers of x in its Maclaurin series have coefficient 0.

54. Suppose that the power series $\sum c_k(x - x_0)^k$ has radius of convergence R and p is a nonzero constant. What can you say about the radius of convergence of the power series $\sum pc_k(x - x_0)^k$? Explain your reasoning. [*Hint:* See Theorem 9.4.3.]

55. Suppose that the power series $\sum c_k(x - x_0)^k$ has a finite radius of convergence R, and the power series $\sum d_k(x - x_0)^k$ has a radius of convergence of $+\infty$. What can you say about the radius of convergence of $\sum (c_k + d_k)(x - x_0)^k$? Explain your reasoning.

56. Suppose that the power series $\sum c_k(x - x_0)^k$ has a finite radius of convergence R_1 and the power series $\sum d_k(x - x_0)^k$ has a finite radius of convergence R_2. What can you say about the radius of convergence of $\sum (c_k + d_k)(x - x_0)^k$? Explain your reasoning. [*Hint:* The case $R_1 = R_2$ requires special attention.]

57. Show that if p is a positive integer, then the power series
$$\sum_{k=0}^{\infty} \frac{(pk)!}{(k!)^p} x^k$$
has a radius of convergence of $1/p^p$.

58. Show that if p and q are positive integers, then the power series
$$\sum_{k=0}^{\infty} \frac{(k+p)!}{k!(k+q)!} x^k$$
has a radius of convergence of $+\infty$.

59. Show that the power series representation of the Bessel function $J_1(x)$ converges for all x [Formula (5)].

60. Approximate the values of the Bessel functions $J_0(x)$ and $J_1(x)$ at $x = 1$, each to four decimal-place accuracy.

C **61.** If the constant p in the general p-series is replaced by a variable x for $x > 1$, then the resulting function is called the ***Riemann zeta function*** and is denoted by
$$\zeta(x) = \sum_{k=1}^{\infty} \frac{1}{k^x}$$
  (a) Let s_n be the nth partial sum of the series for $\zeta(3.7)$. Find n such that s_n approximates $\zeta(3.7)$ to two decimal-place accuracy, and calculate s_n using this value of n. [*Hint:* Use the right inequality in Exercise 36(b) of Section 9.4 with $f(x) = 1/x^{3.7}$.]
  (b) Determine whether your CAS can evaluate the Riemann zeta function directly. If so, compare the value produced by the CAS to the value of s_n obtained in part (a).

62. Prove: If $\lim_{k \to +\infty} |c_k|^{1/k} = L$, where $L \neq 0$, then $1/L$ is the radius of convergence of the power series $\sum_{k=0}^{\infty} c_k x^k$.

63. Prove: If the power series $\sum_{k=0}^{\infty} c_k x^k$ has radius of convergence R, then the series $\sum_{k=0}^{\infty} c_k x^{2k}$ has radius of convergence $\sqrt{R}$.

64. Prove: If the interval of convergence of the series $\sum_{k=0}^{\infty} c_k(x - x_0)^k$ is $(x_0 - R, x_0 + R]$, then the series converges conditionally at $x_0 + R$.

65. **Writing** The sine function can be defined geometrically from the unit circle or analytically from its Maclaurin series. Discuss the advantages of each representation with regard to providing information about the sine function.

✔ **QUICK CHECK ANSWERS 9.8**

1. $\dfrac{f^{(k)}(x_0)}{k!}(x - x_0)^k$ **2.** $\dfrac{1}{2}$ **3.** $(-\infty, +\infty)$ **4.** (a) 1 (b) converges (c) diverges (d) $[3, 5)$

9.9 **CONVERGENCE OF TAYLOR SERIES**

In this section we will investigate when a Taylor series for a function converges to that function on some interval, and we will consider how Taylor series can be used to approximate values of trigonometric, exponential, and logarithmic functions.

■ **THE CONVERGENCE PROBLEM FOR TAYLOR SERIES**
Recall that the nth Taylor polynomial for a function f about $x = x_0$ has the property that its value and the values of its first n derivatives match those of f at x_0. As n increases,

more and more derivatives match up, so it is reasonable to hope that for values of x near x_0 the values of the Taylor polynomials might converge to the value of $f(x)$; that is,

$$f(x) = \lim_{n \to +\infty} \sum_{k=0}^{n} \frac{f^{(k)}(x_0)}{k!} (x - x_0)^k \tag{1}$$

However, the nth Taylor polynomial for f is the nth partial sum of the Taylor series for f, so (1) is equivalent to stating that the Taylor series for f converges at x, and its sum is $f(x)$. Thus, we are led to consider the following problem.

Problem 9.9.1 is concerned not only with whether the Taylor series of a function f converges, but also whether it converges to the function f itself. Indeed, it is possible for a Taylor series of a function f to converge to values different from $f(x)$ for certain values of x (Exercise 14).

9.9.1   PROBLEM   Given a function f that has derivatives of all orders at $x = x_0$, determine whether there is an open interval containing x_0 such that $f(x)$ is the sum of its Taylor series about $x = x_0$ at each point in the interval; that is,

$$f(x) = \sum_{k=0}^{\infty} \frac{f^{(k)}(x_0)}{k!} (x - x_0)^k \tag{2}$$

for all values of x in the interval.

One way to show that (1) holds is to show that

$$\lim_{n \to +\infty} \left[f(x) - \sum_{k=0}^{n} \frac{f^{(k)}(x_0)}{k!} (x - x_0)^k \right] = 0$$

However, the difference appearing on the left side of this equation is the nth remainder for the Taylor series [Formula (12) of Section 9.7]. Thus, we have the following result.

9.9.2   THEOREM   *The equality*

$$f(x) = \sum_{k=0}^{\infty} \frac{f^{(k)}(x_0)}{k!} (x - x_0)^k$$

holds at a point x if and only if $\lim_{n \to +\infty} R_n(x) = 0$.

■ ESTIMATING THE nTH REMAINDER

It is relatively rare that one can prove directly that $R_n(x) \to 0$ as $n \to +\infty$. Usually, this is proved indirectly by finding appropriate bounds on $|R_n(x)|$ and applying the Squeezing Theorem for Sequences. The Remainder Estimation Theorem (Theorem 9.7.4) provides a useful bound for this purpose. Recall that this theorem asserts that if M is an upper bound for $|f^{(n+1)}(x)|$ on an interval containing x_0, then

$$|R_n(x)| \le \frac{M}{(n+1)!} |x - x_0|^{n+1} \tag{3}$$

for all x in that interval.

The following example illustrates how the Remainder Estimation Theorem is applied.

▶ **Example 1**   Show that the Maclaurin series for $\cos x$ converges to $\cos x$ for all x; that is,

$$\cos x = \sum_{k=0}^{\infty} (-1)^k \frac{x^{2k}}{(2k)!} = 1 - \frac{x^2}{2!} + \frac{x^4}{4!} - \frac{x^6}{6!} + \cdots \qquad (-\infty < x < +\infty)$$

Solution.   From Theorem 9.9.2 we must show that $R_n(x) \to 0$ for all x as $n \to +\infty$. For this purpose let $f(x) = \cos x$, so that for all x we have

$$f^{(n+1)}(x) = \pm \cos x \quad \text{or} \quad f^{(n+1)}(x) = \pm \sin x$$

In all cases we have $|f^{(n+1)}(x)| \leq 1$, so we can apply (3) with $M = 1$ and $x_0 = 0$ to conclude that

$$0 \leq |R_n(x)| \leq \frac{|x|^{n+1}}{(n+1)!} \tag{4}$$

However, it follows from Formula (5) of Section 9.2 with $n + 1$ in place of n and $|x|$ in place of x that

$$\lim_{n \to +\infty} \frac{|x|^{n+1}}{(n+1)!} = 0 \tag{5}$$

Using this result and the Squeezing Theorem for Sequences (Theorem 9.1.5), it follows from (4) that $|R_n(x)| \to 0$ and hence that $R_n(x) \to 0$ as $n \to +\infty$ (Theorem 9.1.6). Since this is true for all x, we have proved that the Maclaurin series for $\cos x$ converges to $\cos x$ for all x. This is illustrated in Figure 9.9.1, where we can see how successive partial sums approximate the cosine curve more and more closely. ◄

The method of Example 1 can be easily modified to prove that the Taylor series for $\sin x$ and $\cos x$ about any point $x = x_0$ converge to $\sin x$ and $\cos x$, respectively, for all x (Exercises 21 and 22). For reference, some of the most important Maclaurin series are listed in Table 9.9.1 at the end of this section.

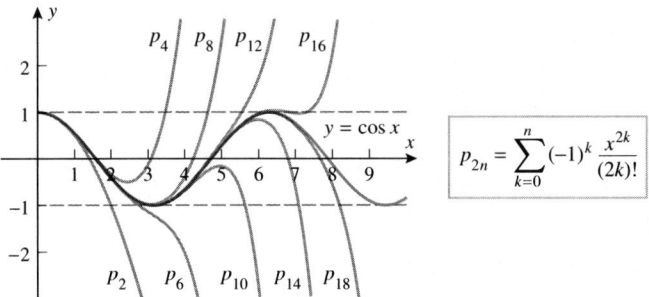

▶ **Figure 9.9.1**

$$P_{2n} = \sum_{k=0}^{n} (-1)^k \frac{x^{2k}}{(2k)!}$$

■ **APPROXIMATING TRIGONOMETRIC FUNCTIONS**

In general, to approximate the value of a function f at a point x using a Taylor series, there are two basic questions that must be answered:

- About what point x_0 should the Taylor series be expanded?
- How many terms in the series should be used to achieve the desired accuracy?

In response to the first question, x_0 needs to be a point at which the derivatives of f can be evaluated easily, since these values are needed for the coefficients in the Taylor series. Furthermore, if the function f is being evaluated at x, then x_0 should be chosen as close as possible to x, since Taylor series tend to converge more rapidly near x_0. For example, to approximate $\sin 3°$ ($= \pi/60$ radians), it would be reasonable to take $x_0 = 0$, since $\pi/60$ is close to 0 and the derivatives of $\sin x$ are easy to evaluate at 0. On the other hand, to approximate $\sin 85°$ ($= 17\pi/36$ radians), it would be more natural to take $x_0 = \pi/2$, since $17\pi/36$ is close to $\pi/2$ and the derivatives of $\sin x$ are easy to evaluate at $\pi/2$.

In response to the second question posed above, the number of terms required to achieve a specific accuracy needs to be determined on a problem-by-problem basis. The next example gives two methods for doing this.

▶ **Example 2**   Use the Maclaurin series for $\sin x$ to approximate $\sin 3°$ to five decimal-place accuracy.

Solution.   In the Maclaurin series

$$\sin x = \sum_{k=0}^{\infty} (-1)^k \frac{x^{2k+1}}{(2k+1)!} = x - \frac{x^3}{3!} + \frac{x^5}{5!} - \frac{x^7}{7!} + \cdots \tag{6}$$

the angle x is assumed to be in radians (because the differentiation formulas for the trigonometric functions were derived with this assumption). Since $3° = \pi/60$ radians, it follows from (6) that

$$\sin 3° = \sin \frac{\pi}{60} = \left(\frac{\pi}{60}\right) - \frac{(\pi/60)^3}{3!} + \frac{(\pi/60)^5}{5!} - \frac{(\pi/60)^7}{7!} + \cdots \tag{7}$$

We must now determine how many terms in the series are required to achieve five decimal-place accuracy. We will consider two possible approaches, one using the Remainder Estimation Theorem (Theorem 9.7.4) and the other using the fact that (7) satisfies the hypotheses of the alternating series test (Theorem 9.6.1).

Method 1. (*The Remainder Estimation Theorem*)

Since we want to achieve five decimal-place accuracy, our goal is to choose n so that the absolute value of the nth remainder at $x = \pi/60$ does not exceed $0.000005 = 5 \times 10^{-6}$; that is,

$$\left| R_n\left(\frac{\pi}{60}\right) \right| \leq 0.000005 \tag{8}$$

However, if we let $f(x) = \sin x$, then $f^{(n+1)}(x)$ is either $\pm \sin x$ or $\pm \cos x$, and in either case $|f^{(n+1)}(x)| \leq 1$ for all x. Thus, it follows from the Remainder Estimation Theorem with $M = 1$, $x_0 = 0$, and $x = \pi/60$ that

$$\left| R_n\left(\frac{\pi}{60}\right) \right| \leq \frac{(\pi/60)^{n+1}}{(n+1)!}$$

Thus, we can satisfy (8) by choosing n so that

$$\frac{(\pi/60)^{n+1}}{(n+1)!} \leq 0.000005$$

With the help of a calculating utility you can verify that the smallest value of n that meets this criterion is $n = 3$. Thus, to achieve five decimal-place accuracy we need only keep terms up to the third power in (7). This yields

$$\sin 3° \approx \left(\frac{\pi}{60}\right) - \frac{(\pi/60)^3}{3!} \approx 0.05234 \tag{9}$$

(verify). As a check, a calculator gives $\sin 3° \approx 0.05233595624$, which agrees with (9) when rounded to five decimal places.

Method 2. (*The Alternating Series Test*)

We leave it for you to check that (7) satisfies the hypotheses of the alternating series test (Theorem 9.6.1).

Let s_n denote the sum of the terms in (7) up to and including the nth power of $\pi/60$. Since the exponents in the series are odd integers, the integer n must be odd, and the exponent of the first term *not* included in the sum s_n must be $n + 2$. Thus, it follows from part (*b*) of Theorem 9.6.2 that

$$|\sin 3° - s_n| < \frac{(\pi/60)^{n+2}}{(n+2)!}$$

This means that for five decimal-place accuracy we must look for the first positive odd integer n such that

$$\frac{(\pi/60)^{n+2}}{(n+2)!} \leq 0.000005$$

With the help of a calculating utility you can verify that the smallest value of n that meets this criterion is $n = 3$. This agrees with the result obtained above using the Remainder Estimation Theorem and hence leads to approximation (9) as before. ◄

■ ROUNDOFF AND TRUNCATION ERROR

There are two types of errors that occur when computing with series. The first, called ***truncation error***, is the error that results when a series is approximated by a partial sum; and the second, called ***roundoff error***, is the error that arises from approximations in numerical computations. For example, in our derivation of (9) we took $n = 3$ to keep the truncation error below 0.000005. However, to evaluate the partial sum we had to approximate π, thereby introducing roundoff error. Had we not exercised some care in choosing this approximation, the roundoff error could easily have degraded the final result.

Methods for estimating and controlling roundoff error are studied in a branch of mathematics called ***numerical analysis***. However, as a rule of thumb, to achieve n decimal-place accuracy in a final result, all intermediate calculations must be accurate to at least $n + 1$ decimal places. Thus, in (9) at least six decimal-place accuracy in π is required to achieve the five decimal-place accuracy in the final numerical result. As a practical matter, a good working procedure is to perform all intermediate computations with the maximum number of digits that your calculating utility can handle and then round at the end.

■ APPROXIMATING EXPONENTIAL FUNCTIONS

▶ **Example 3**   Show that the Maclaurin series for e^x converges to e^x for all x; that is,

$$e^x = \sum_{k=0}^{\infty} \frac{x^k}{k!} = 1 + x + \frac{x^2}{2!} + \frac{x^3}{3!} + \cdots + \frac{x^k}{k!} + \cdots \qquad (-\infty < x < +\infty)$$

Solution.   Let $f(x) = e^x$, so that

$$f^{(n+1)}(x) = e^x$$

We want to show that $R_n(x) \to 0$ as $n \to +\infty$ for all x in the interval $-\infty < x < +\infty$. However, it will be helpful here to consider the cases $x \le 0$ and $x > 0$ separately. If $x \le 0$, then we will take the interval in the Remainder Estimation Theorem (Theorem 9.7.4) to be $[x, 0]$, and if $x > 0$, then we will take it to be $[0, x]$. Since $f^{(n+1)}(x) = e^x$ is an increasing function, it follows that if c is in the interval $[x, 0]$, then

$$|f^{(n+1)}(c)| \le |f^{(n+1)}(0)| = e^0 = 1$$

and if c is in the interval $[0, x]$, then

$$|f^{(n+1)}(c)| \le |f^{(n+1)}(x)| = e^x$$

Thus, we can apply Theorem 9.7.4 with $M = 1$ in the case where $x \le 0$ and with $M = e^x$ in the case where $x > 0$. This yields

$$0 \le |R_n(x)| \le \frac{|x|^{n+1}}{(n+1)!} \qquad \text{if } x \le 0$$

$$0 \le |R_n(x)| \le e^x \frac{|x|^{n+1}}{(n+1)!} \qquad \text{if } x > 0$$

Thus, in both cases it follows from (5) and the Squeezing Theorem for Sequences that $|R_n(x)| \to 0$ as $n \to +\infty$, which in turn implies that $R_n(x) \to 0$ as $n \to +\infty$. Since this is true for all x, we have proved that the Maclaurin series for e^x converges to e^x for all x. ◄

Since the Maclaurin series for e^x converges to e^x for all x, we can use partial sums of the Maclaurin series to approximate powers of e to arbitrary precision. Recall that in Example 7 of Section 9.7 we were able to use the Remainder Estimation Theorem to determine that evaluating the ninth Maclaurin polynomial for e^x at $x = 1$ yields an approximation for e with five decimal-place accuracy:

$$e \approx 1 + 1 + \frac{1}{2!} + \frac{1}{3!} + \frac{1}{4!} + \frac{1}{5!} + \frac{1}{6!} + \frac{1}{7!} + \frac{1}{8!} + \frac{1}{9!} \approx 2.71828$$

■ APPROXIMATING LOGARITHMS

The Maclaurin series

$$\ln(1 + x) = x - \frac{x^2}{2} + \frac{x^3}{3} - \frac{x^4}{4} + \cdots \qquad (-1 < x \le 1) \qquad (10)$$

is the starting point for the approximation of natural logarithms. Unfortunately, the usefulness of this series is limited because of its slow convergence and the restriction $-1 < x \le 1$. However, if we replace x by $-x$ in this series, we obtain

$$\ln(1 - x) = -x - \frac{x^2}{2} - \frac{x^3}{3} - \frac{x^4}{4} - \cdots \qquad (-1 \le x < 1) \qquad (11)$$

and on subtracting (11) from (10) we obtain

$$\ln\left(\frac{1 + x}{1 - x}\right) = 2\left(x + \frac{x^3}{3} + \frac{x^5}{5} + \frac{x^7}{7} + \cdots\right) \qquad (-1 < x < 1) \qquad (12)$$

Series (12), first obtained by James Gregory in 1668, can be used to compute the natural logarithm of any positive number y by letting

$$y = \frac{1 + x}{1 - x}$$

or, equivalently,

$$x = \frac{y - 1}{y + 1} \qquad (13)$$

and noting that $-1 < x < 1$. For example, to compute $\ln 2$ we let $y = 2$ in (13), which yields $x = \frac{1}{3}$. Substituting this value in (12) gives

$$\ln 2 = 2\left[\frac{1}{3} + \frac{\left(\frac{1}{3}\right)^3}{3} + \frac{\left(\frac{1}{3}\right)^5}{5} + \frac{\left(\frac{1}{3}\right)^7}{7} + \cdots\right] \qquad (14)$$

In Exercise 19 we will ask you to show that five decimal-place accuracy can be achieved using the partial sum with terms up to and including the 13th power of $\frac{1}{3}$. Thus, to five decimal-place accuracy

$$\ln 2 \approx 2\left[\frac{1}{3} + \frac{\left(\frac{1}{3}\right)^3}{3} + \frac{\left(\frac{1}{3}\right)^5}{5} + \frac{\left(\frac{1}{3}\right)^7}{7} + \cdots + \frac{\left(\frac{1}{3}\right)^{13}}{13}\right] \approx 0.69315$$

(verify). As a check, a calculator gives $\ln 2 \approx 0.69314718056$, which agrees with the preceding approximation when rounded to five decimal places.

■ APPROXIMATING π

In the next section we will show that

$$\tan^{-1} x = x - \frac{x^3}{3} + \frac{x^5}{5} - \frac{x^7}{7} + \cdots \qquad (-1 \le x \le 1) \qquad (15)$$

Letting $x = 1$, we obtain

$$\frac{\pi}{4} = \tan^{-1} 1 = 1 - \frac{1}{3} + \frac{1}{5} - \frac{1}{7} + \cdots$$

In Example 2 of Section 9.6, we stated without proof that

$$\ln 2 = 1 - \frac{1}{2} + \frac{1}{3} - \frac{1}{4} + \frac{1}{5} - \cdots$$

This result can be obtained by letting $x = 1$ in (10), but as indicated in the text discussion, this series converges too slowly to be of practical use.

James Gregory (1638–1675) Scottish mathematician and astronomer. Gregory, the son of a minister, was famous in his time as the inventor of the Gregorian reflecting telescope, so named in his honor. Although he is not generally ranked with the great mathematicians, much of his work relating to calculus was studied by Leibniz and Newton and undoubtedly influenced some of their discoveries. There is a manuscript, discovered posthumously, which shows that Gregory had anticipated Taylor series well before Taylor.

or

$$\pi = 4\left[1 - \frac{1}{3} + \frac{1}{5} - \frac{1}{7} + \cdots\right]$$

This famous series, obtained by Leibniz in 1674, converges too slowly to be of computational value. A more practical procedure for approximating π uses the identity

$$\frac{\pi}{4} = \tan^{-1}\frac{1}{2} + \tan^{-1}\frac{1}{3} \qquad (16)$$

which was derived in Exercise 58 of Section 0.4. By using this identity and series (15) to approximate $\tan^{-1}\frac{1}{2}$ and $\tan^{-1}\frac{1}{3}$, the value of π can be approximated efficiently to any degree of accuracy.

■ BINOMIAL SERIES

If m is a real number, then the Maclaurin series for $(1 + x)^m$ is called the ***binomial series***; it is given by

$$1 + mx + \frac{m(m-1)}{2!}x^2 + \frac{m(m-1)(m-2)}{3!}x^3 + \cdots + \frac{m(m-1)\cdots(m-k+1)}{k!}x^k + \cdots$$

In the case where m is a nonnegative integer, the function $f(x) = (1 + x)^m$ is a polynomial of degree m, so

$$f^{(m+1)}(0) = f^{(m+2)}(0) = f^{(m+3)}(0) = \cdots = 0$$

and the binomial series reduces to the familiar binomial expansion

$$(1 + x)^m = 1 + mx + \frac{m(m-1)}{2!}x^2 + \frac{m(m-1)(m-2)}{3!}x^3 + \cdots + x^m$$

which is valid for $-\infty < x < +\infty$.

It can be proved that if m is not a nonnegative integer, then the binomial series converges to $(1 + x)^m$ if $|x| < 1$. Thus, for such values of x

$$(1 + x)^m = 1 + mx + \frac{m(m-1)}{2!}x^2 + \cdots + \frac{m(m-1)\cdots(m-k+1)}{k!}x^k + \cdots \qquad (17)$$

or in sigma notation,

$$(1 + x)^m = 1 + \sum_{k=1}^{\infty}\frac{m(m-1)\cdots(m-k+1)}{k!}x^k \quad \text{if } |x| < 1 \qquad (18)$$

> Let $f(x) = (1 + x)^m$. Verify that
> $$f(0) = 1$$
> $$f'(0) = m$$
> $$f''(0) = m(m-1)$$
> $$f'''(0) = m(m-1)(m-2)$$
> $$\vdots$$
> $$f^{(k)}(0) = m(m-1)\cdots(m-k+1)$$

▶ **Example 4** Find binomial series for

$$\text{(a) } \frac{1}{(1+x)^2} \qquad \text{(b) } \frac{1}{\sqrt{1+x}}$$

Solution (a). Since the general term of the binomial series is complicated, you may find it helpful to write out some of the beginning terms of the series, as in Formula (17), to see developing patterns. Substituting $m = -2$ in this formula yields

$$\frac{1}{(1+x)^2} = (1 + x)^{-2} = 1 + (-2)x + \frac{(-2)(-3)}{2!}x^2$$

$$+ \frac{(-2)(-3)(-4)}{3!}x^3 + \frac{(-2)(-3)(-4)(-5)}{4!}x^4 + \cdots$$

$$= 1 - 2x + \frac{3!}{2!}x^2 - \frac{4!}{3!}x^3 + \frac{5!}{4!}x^4 - \cdots$$

$$= 1 - 2x + 3x^2 - 4x^3 + 5x^4 - \cdots$$

$$= \sum_{k=0}^{\infty}(-1)^k(k+1)x^k$$

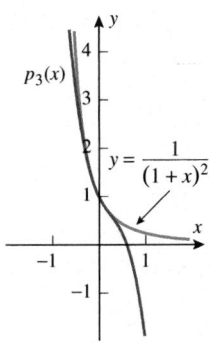

$$p_3(x) = 1 - 2x + 3x^2 - 4x^3$$

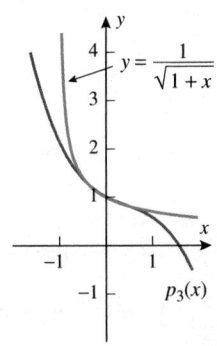

$$p_3(x) = 1 - \frac{1}{2}x + \frac{3}{8}x^2 - \frac{5}{16}x^3$$

▲ **Figure 9.9.2**

Solution (b). Substituting $m = -\frac{1}{2}$ in (17) yields

$$\frac{1}{\sqrt{1+x}} = 1 - \frac{1}{2}x + \frac{\left(-\frac{1}{2}\right)\left(-\frac{1}{2}-1\right)}{2!}x^2 + \frac{\left(-\frac{1}{2}\right)\left(-\frac{1}{2}-1\right)\left(-\frac{1}{2}-2\right)}{3!}x^3 + \cdots$$

$$= 1 - \frac{1}{2}x + \frac{1 \cdot 3}{2^2 \cdot 2!}x^2 - \frac{1 \cdot 3 \cdot 5}{2^3 \cdot 3!}x^3 + \cdots$$

$$= 1 + \sum_{k=1}^{\infty}(-1)^k \frac{1 \cdot 3 \cdot 5 \cdots (2k-1)}{2^k k!}x^k \quad ◀$$

Figure 9.9.2 shows the graphs of the functions in Example 4 compared to their third-degree Maclaurin polynomials.

■ SOME IMPORTANT MACLAURIN SERIES

For reference, Table 9.9.1 lists the Maclaurin series for some of the most important functions, together with a specification of the intervals over which the Maclaurin series converge to those functions. Some of these results are derived in the exercises and others will be derived in the next section using some special techniques that we will develop.

Table 9.9.1

SOME IMPORTANT MACLAURIN SERIES

MACLAURIN SERIES	INTERVAL OF CONVERGENCE
$\dfrac{1}{1-x} = \sum_{k=0}^{\infty} x^k = 1 + x + x^2 + x^3 + \cdots$	$-1 < x < 1$
$\dfrac{1}{1+x^2} = \sum_{k=0}^{\infty}(-1)^k x^{2k} = 1 - x^2 + x^4 - x^6 + \cdots$	$-1 < x < 1$
$e^x = \sum_{k=0}^{\infty} \dfrac{x^k}{k!} = 1 + x + \dfrac{x^2}{2!} + \dfrac{x^3}{3!} + \dfrac{x^4}{4!} + \cdots$	$-\infty < x < +\infty$
$\sin x = \sum_{k=0}^{\infty}(-1)^k \dfrac{x^{2k+1}}{(2k+1)!} = x - \dfrac{x^3}{3!} + \dfrac{x^5}{5!} - \dfrac{x^7}{7!} + \cdots$	$-\infty < x < +\infty$
$\cos x = \sum_{k=0}^{\infty}(-1)^k \dfrac{x^{2k}}{(2k)!} = 1 - \dfrac{x^2}{2!} + \dfrac{x^4}{4!} - \dfrac{x^6}{6!} + \cdots$	$-\infty < x < +\infty$
$\ln(1+x) = \sum_{k=1}^{\infty}(-1)^{k+1} \dfrac{x^k}{k} = x - \dfrac{x^2}{2} + \dfrac{x^3}{3} - \dfrac{x^4}{4} + \cdots$	$-1 < x \le 1$
$\tan^{-1} x = \sum_{k=0}^{\infty}(-1)^k \dfrac{x^{2k+1}}{2k+1} = x - \dfrac{x^3}{3} + \dfrac{x^5}{5} - \dfrac{x^7}{7} + \cdots$	$-1 \le x \le 1$
$\sinh x = \sum_{k=0}^{\infty} \dfrac{x^{2k+1}}{(2k+1)!} = x + \dfrac{x^3}{3!} + \dfrac{x^5}{5!} + \dfrac{x^7}{7!} + \cdots$	$-\infty < x < +\infty$
$\cosh x = \sum_{k=0}^{\infty} \dfrac{x^{2k}}{(2k)!} = 1 + \dfrac{x^2}{2!} + \dfrac{x^4}{4!} + \dfrac{x^6}{6!} + \cdots$	$-\infty < x < +\infty$
$(1+x)^m = 1 + \sum_{k=1}^{\infty} \dfrac{m(m-1)\cdots(m-k+1)}{k!}x^k$	$-1 < x < 1^{*}$ $(m \ne 0, 1, 2, \ldots)$

---

*The behavior at the endpoints depends on m: For $m > 0$ the series converges absolutely at both endpoints; for $m \le -1$ the series diverges at both endpoints; and for $-1 < m < 0$ the series converges conditionally at $x = 1$ and diverges at $x = -1$.

✔ **QUICK CHECK EXERCISES 9.9**   (*See page 677 for answers.*)

1. $\cos x = \displaystyle\sum_{k=0}^{\infty}$ _____

2. $e^x = \displaystyle\sum_{k=0}^{\infty}$ _____

3. $\ln(1+x) = \displaystyle\sum_{k=1}^{\infty}$ _____ for x in the interval _____.

4. If m is a real number but not a nonnegative integer, the *binomial series*

$$1 + \sum_{k=1}^{\infty} \text{_____}$$

converges to $(1+x)^m$ if $|x| <$ _____.

EXERCISE SET 9.9   Graphing Utility   [C] CAS

1. Use the Remainder Estimation Theorem and the method of Example 1 to prove that the Taylor series for $\sin x$ about $x = \pi/4$ converges to $\sin x$ for all x.

2. Use the Remainder Estimation Theorem and the method of Example 3 to prove that the Taylor series for e^x about $x = 1$ converges to e^x for all x.

3–10 Approximate the specified function value as indicated and check your work by comparing your answer to the function value produced directly by your calculating utility. ■

3. Approximate $\sin 4°$ to five decimal-place accuracy using both of the methods given in Example 2.

4. Approximate $\cos 3°$ to three decimal-place accuracy using both of the methods given in Example 2.

5. Approximate $\cos 0.1$ to five decimal-place accuracy using the Maclaurin series for $\cos x$.

6. Approximate $\tan^{-1} 0.1$ to three decimal-place accuracy using the Maclaurin series for $\tan^{-1} x$.

7. Approximate $\sin 85°$ to four decimal-place accuracy using an appropriate Taylor series.

8. Approximate $\cos(-175°)$ to four decimal-place accuracy using a Taylor series.

9. Approximate $\sinh 0.5$ to three decimal-place accuracy using the Maclaurin series for $\sinh x$.

10. Approximate $\cosh 0.1$ to three decimal-place accuracy using the Maclaurin series for $\cosh x$.

11. (a) Use Formula (12) in the text to find a series that converges to $\ln 1.25$.
(b) Approximate $\ln 1.25$ using the first two terms of the series. Round your answer to three decimal places, and compare the result to that produced directly by your calculating utility.

12. (a) Use Formula (12) to find a series that converges to $\ln 3$.
(b) Approximate $\ln 3$ using the first two terms of the series. Round your answer to three decimal places, and compare the result to that produced directly by your calculating utility.

FOCUS ON CONCEPTS

13. (a) Use the Maclaurin series for $\tan^{-1} x$ to approximate $\tan^{-1} \frac{1}{2}$ and $\tan^{-1} \frac{1}{3}$ to three decimal-place accuracy.
(b) Use the results in part (a) and Formula (16) to approximate π.
(c) Would you be willing to guarantee that your answer in part (b) is accurate to three decimal places? Explain your reasoning.
(d) Compare your answer in part (b) to that produced by your calculating utility.

14. The purpose of this exercise is to show that the Taylor series of a function f may possibly converge to a value different from $f(x)$ for certain values of x. Let

$$f(x) = \begin{cases} e^{-1/x^2}, & x \neq 0 \\ 0, & x = 0 \end{cases}$$

(a) Use the definition of a derivative to show that $f'(0) = 0$.
(b) With some difficulty it can be shown that if $n \geq 2$ then $f^{(n)}(0) = 0$. Accepting this fact, show that the Maclaurin series of f converges for all x, but converges to $f(x)$ only at $x = 0$.

15. (a) Find an upper bound on the error that can result if $\cos x$ is approximated by $1 - (x^2/2!) + (x^4/4!)$ over the interval $[-0.2, 0.2]$.
(b) Check your answer in part (a) by graphing

$$\left| \cos x - \left(1 - \frac{x^2}{2!} + \frac{x^4}{4!} \right) \right|$$

over the interval.

16. (a) Find an upper bound on the error that can result if $\ln(1+x)$ is approximated by x over the interval $[-0.01, 0.01]$.
(b) Check your answer in part (a) by graphing

$$|\ln(1+x) - x|$$

over the interval.

17. Use Formula (17) for the binomial series to obtain the Maclaurin series for

(a) $\dfrac{1}{1+x}$ (b) $\sqrt[3]{1+x}$ (c) $\dfrac{1}{(1+x)^3}$.

18. If m is any real number, and k is a nonnegative integer, then we define the **binomial coefficient** $\dbinom{m}{k}$ by the formulas $\dbinom{m}{0} = 1$ and

$$\binom{m}{k} = \frac{m(m-1)(m-2)\cdots(m-k+1)}{k!}$$

for $k \geq 1$. Express Formula (17) in the text in terms of binomial coefficients.

19. In this exercise we will use the Remainder Estimation Theorem to determine the number of terms that are required in Formula (14) to approximate $\ln 2$ to five decimal-place accuracy. For this purpose let

$$f(x) = \ln\frac{1+x}{1-x} = \ln(1+x) - \ln(1-x) \quad (-1 < x < 1)$$

(a) Show that

$$f^{(n+1)}(x) = n!\left[\frac{(-1)^n}{(1+x)^{n+1}} + \frac{1}{(1-x)^{n+1}}\right]$$

(b) Use the triangle inequality [Theorem 0.1.4(d)] to show that

$$|f^{(n+1)}(x)| \leq n!\left[\frac{1}{(1+x)^{n+1}} + \frac{1}{(1-x)^{n+1}}\right]$$

(c) Since we want to achieve five decimal-place accuracy, our goal is to choose n so that the absolute value of the nth remainder at $x = \frac{1}{3}$ does not exceed the value $0.000005 = 0.5 \times 10^{-5}$; that is, $\left|R_n\left(\frac{1}{3}\right)\right| \leq 0.000005$. Use the Remainder Estimation Theorem to show that this condition will be satisfied if n is chosen so that

$$\frac{M}{(n+1)!}\left(\frac{1}{3}\right)^{n+1} \leq 0.000005$$

where $|f^{(n+1)}(x)| \leq M$ on the interval $\left[0, \frac{1}{3}\right]$.

(d) Use the result in part (b) to show that M can be taken as

$$M = n!\left[1 + \frac{1}{\left(\frac{2}{3}\right)^{n+1}}\right]$$

(e) Use the results in parts (c) and (d) to show that five decimal-place accuracy will be achieved if n satisfies

$$\frac{1}{n+1}\left[\left(\frac{1}{3}\right)^{n+1} + \left(\frac{1}{2}\right)^{n+1}\right] \leq 0.000005$$

and then show that the smallest value of n that satisfies this condition is $n = 13$.

20. Use Formula (12) and the method of Exercise 19 to approximate $\ln\left(\frac{5}{3}\right)$ to five decimal-place accuracy. Then check your work by comparing your answer to that produced directly by your calculating utility.

21. Prove: The Taylor series for $\cos x$ about any value $x = x_0$ converges to $\cos x$ for all x.

22. Prove: The Taylor series for $\sin x$ about any value $x = x_0$ converges to $\sin x$ for all x.

23. Research has shown that the proportion p of the population with IQs (intelligence quotients) between α and β is approximately

$$p = \frac{1}{16\sqrt{2\pi}}\int_\alpha^\beta e^{-\frac{1}{2}\left(\frac{x-100}{16}\right)^2}\,dx$$

Use the first three terms of an appropriate Maclaurin series to estimate the proportion of the population that has IQs between 100 and 110.

C **24.** (a) In 1706 the British astronomer and mathematician John Machin discovered the following formula for $\pi/4$, called **Machin's formula**:

$$\frac{\pi}{4} = 4\tan^{-1}\frac{1}{5} - \tan^{-1}\frac{1}{239}$$

Use a CAS to approximate $\pi/4$ using Machin's formula to 25 decimal places.

(b) In 1914 the brilliant Indian mathematician Srinivasa Ramanujan (1887–1920) showed that

$$\frac{1}{\pi} = \frac{\sqrt{8}}{9801}\sum_{k=0}^\infty \frac{(4k)!(1103 + 26{,}390k)}{(k!)^4 396^{4k}}$$

Use a CAS to compute the first four partial sums in **Ramanujan's formula**.

✔ **QUICK CHECK ANSWERS 9.9**

1. $(-1)^k\dfrac{x^{2k}}{(2k)!}$ **2.** $\dfrac{x^k}{k!}$ **3.** $(-1)^{k+1}\dfrac{x^k}{k}$; $(-1, 1]$ **4.** $\dfrac{m(m-1)\cdots(m-k+1)}{k!}x^k$; 1

9.10 **DIFFERENTIATING AND INTEGRATING POWER SERIES; MODELING WITH TAYLOR SERIES**

In this section we will discuss methods for finding power series for derivatives and integrals of functions, and we will discuss some practical methods for finding Taylor series that can be used in situations where it is difficult or impossible to find the series directly.

■ **DIFFERENTIATING POWER SERIES**

We begin by considering the following problem.

> **9.10.1** **PROBLEM** Suppose that a function f is represented by a power series on an open interval. How can we use the power series to find the derivative of f on that interval?

The solution to this problem can be motivated by considering the Maclaurin series for $\sin x$:

$$\sin x = x - \frac{x^3}{3!} + \frac{x^5}{5!} - \frac{x^7}{7!} + \cdots \qquad (-\infty < x < +\infty)$$

Of course, we already know that the derivative of $\sin x$ is $\cos x$; however, we are concerned here with using the Maclaurin series to deduce this. The solution is easy—all we need to do is differentiate the Maclaurin series term by term and observe that the resulting series is the Maclaurin series for $\cos x$:

$$\frac{d}{dx}\left[x - \frac{x^3}{3!} + \frac{x^5}{5!} - \frac{x^7}{7!} + \cdots\right] = 1 - 3\frac{x^2}{3!} + 5\frac{x^4}{5!} - 7\frac{x^6}{7!} + \cdots$$

$$= 1 - \frac{x^2}{2!} + \frac{x^4}{4!} - \frac{x^6}{6!} + \cdots = \cos x$$

Here is another example.

$$\frac{d}{dx}[e^x] = \frac{d}{dx}\left[1 + x + \frac{x^2}{2!} + \frac{x^3}{3!} + \frac{x^4}{4!} + \cdots\right]$$

$$= 1 + 2\frac{x}{2!} + 3\frac{x^2}{3!} + 4\frac{x^3}{4!} + \cdots = 1 + x + \frac{x^2}{2!} + \frac{x^3}{3!} + \cdots = e^x$$

The preceding computations suggest that if a function f is represented by a power series on an open interval, then a power series representation of f' on that interval can be obtained by differentiating the power series for f term by term. This is stated more precisely in the following theorem, which we give without proof.

> **9.10.2** **THEOREM** (*Differentiation of Power Series*) *Suppose that a function f is represented by a power series in $x - x_0$ that has a nonzero radius of convergence R; that is,*
>
> $$f(x) = \sum_{k=0}^{\infty} c_k (x - x_0)^k \qquad (x_0 - R < x < x_0 + R)$$
>
> *Then:*
>
> (*a*) *The function f is differentiable on the interval $(x_0 - R, x_0 + R)$.*
>
> (*b*) *If the power series representation for f is differentiated term by term, then the resulting series has radius of convergence R and converges to f' on the interval $(x_0 - R, x_0 + R)$; that is,*
>
> $$f'(x) = \sum_{k=0}^{\infty} \frac{d}{dx}[c_k(x - x_0)^k] \qquad (x_0 - R < x < x_0 + R)$$

This theorem has an important implication about the differentiability of functions that are represented by power series. According to the theorem, the power series for f' has the same radius of convergence as the power series for f, and this means that the theorem can be applied to f' as well as f. However, if we do this, then we conclude that f' is differentiable on the interval $(x_0 - R, x_0 + R)$, and the power series for f'' has the same radius of convergence as the power series for f and f'. We can now repeat this process ad infinitum, applying the theorem successively to f'', f''', ..., $f^{(n)}$, ... to conclude that f has derivatives of all orders on the interval $(x_0 - R, x_0 + R)$. Thus, we have established the following result.

9.10.3 THEOREM *If a function f can be represented by a power series in $x - x_0$ with a nonzero radius of convergence R, then f has derivatives of all orders on the interval $(x_0 - R, x_0 + R)$.*

In short, it is only the most "well-behaved" functions that can be represented by power series; that is, if a function f does not possess derivatives of all orders on an interval $(x_0 - R, x_0 + R)$, then it cannot be represented by a power series in $x - x_0$ on that interval.

▶ **Example 1** In Section 9.8, we showed that the Bessel function $J_0(x)$, represented by the power series

$$J_0(x) = \sum_{k=0}^{\infty} \frac{(-1)^k x^{2k}}{2^{2k}(k!)^2} \tag{1}$$

has radius of convergence $+\infty$ [see Formula (7) of that section and the related discussion]. Thus, $J_0(x)$ has derivatives of all orders on the interval $(-\infty, +\infty)$, and these can be obtained by differentiating the series term by term. For example, if we write (1) as

$$J_0(x) = 1 + \sum_{k=1}^{\infty} \frac{(-1)^k x^{2k}}{2^{2k}(k!)^2}$$

and differentiate term by term, we obtain

$$J_0'(x) = \sum_{k=1}^{\infty} \frac{(-1)^k (2k) x^{2k-1}}{2^{2k}(k!)^2} = \sum_{k=1}^{\infty} \frac{(-1)^k x^{2k-1}}{2^{2k-1} k!(k-1)!} ◀$$

See Exercise 45 for a relationship between $J_0'(x)$ and $J_1(x)$.

REMARK The computations in this example use some techniques that are worth noting. First, when a power series is expressed in sigma notation, the formula for the general term of the series will often not be of a form that can be used for differentiating the constant term. Thus, if the series has a nonzero constant term, as here, it is usually a good idea to split it off from the summation before differentiating. Second, observe how we simplified the final formula by canceling the factor k from one of the factorials in the denominator. This is a standard simplification technique.

■ **INTEGRATING POWER SERIES**

Since the derivative of a function that is represented by a power series can be obtained by differentiating the series term by term, it should not be surprising that an antiderivative of a function represented by a power series can be obtained by integrating the series term by term. For example, we know that $\sin x$ is an antiderivative of $\cos x$. Here is how this result can be obtained by integrating the Maclaurin series for $\cos x$ term by term:

$$\int \cos x \, dx = \int \left[1 - \frac{x^2}{2!} + \frac{x^4}{4!} - \frac{x^6}{6!} + \cdots \right] dx$$

$$= \left[x - \frac{x^3}{3(2!)} + \frac{x^5}{5(4!)} - \frac{x^7}{7(6!)} + \cdots \right] + C$$

$$= \left[x - \frac{x^3}{3!} + \frac{x^5}{5!} - \frac{x^7}{7!} + \cdots \right] + C = \sin x + C$$

The same idea applies to definite integrals. For example, by direct integration we have

$$\int_0^1 \frac{dx}{1 + x^2} = \tan^{-1} x \Big]_0^1 = \tan^{-1} 1 - \tan 0 = \frac{\pi}{4} - 0 = \frac{\pi}{4}$$

and we will show later in this section that

$$\frac{\pi}{4} = 1 - \frac{1}{3} + \frac{1}{5} - \frac{1}{7} + \cdots \tag{2}$$

Thus,

$$\int_0^1 \frac{dx}{1 + x^2} = 1 - \frac{1}{3} + \frac{1}{5} - \frac{1}{7} + \cdots$$

Here is how this result can be obtained by integrating the Maclaurin series for $1/(1 + x^2)$ term by term (see Table 9.9.1):

$$\int_0^1 \frac{dx}{1 + x^2} = \int_0^1 [1 - x^2 + x^4 - x^6 + \cdots] \, dx$$

$$= x - \frac{x^3}{3} + \frac{x^5}{5} - \frac{x^7}{7} + \cdots \Big]_0^1 = 1 - \frac{1}{3} + \frac{1}{5} - \frac{1}{7} + \cdots$$

The preceding computations are justified by the following theorem, which we give without proof.

Theorems 9.10.2 and 9.10.4 tell us how to use a power series representation of a function f to produce power series representations of $f'(x)$ and $\int f(x)\,dx$ that have the same radius of convergence as f. However, the *intervals* of convergence for these series may not be the same because their convergence behavior may differ at the endpoints of the interval. (See Exercises 25 and 26.)

9.10.4   THEOREM (*Integration of Power Series*)   *Suppose that a function f is represented by a power series in $x - x_0$ that has a nonzero radius of convergence R; that is,*

$$f(x) = \sum_{k=0}^{\infty} c_k (x - x_0)^k \qquad (x_0 - R < x < x_0 + R)$$

(a) *If the power series representation of f is integrated term by term, then the resulting series has radius of convergence R and converges to an antiderivative for $f(x)$ on the interval $(x_0 - R, x_0 + R)$; that is,*

$$\int f(x) \, dx = \sum_{k=0}^{\infty} \left[\frac{c_k}{k + 1} (x - x_0)^{k+1} \right] + C \qquad (x_0 - R < x < x_0 + R)$$

(b) *If α and β are points in the interval $(x_0 - R, x_0 + R)$, and if the power series representation of f is integrated term by term from α to β, then the resulting series converges absolutely on the interval $(x_0 - R, x_0 + R)$ and*

$$\int_\alpha^\beta f(x) \, dx = \sum_{k=0}^{\infty} \left[\int_\alpha^\beta c_k (x - x_0)^k \, dx \right]$$

■ **POWER SERIES REPRESENTATIONS MUST BE TAYLOR SERIES**

For many functions it is difficult or impossible to find the derivatives that are required to obtain a Taylor series. For example, to find the Maclaurin series for $1/(1 + x^2)$ directly would require some tedious derivative computations (try it). A more practical approach is to substitute $-x^2$ for x in the geometric series

$$\frac{1}{1-x} = 1 + x + x^2 + x^3 + x^4 + \cdots \qquad (-1 < x < 1)$$

to obtain

$$\frac{1}{1+x^2} = 1 - x^2 + x^4 - x^6 + x^8 - \cdots$$

However, there are two questions of concern with this procedure:

- Where does the power series that we obtained for $1/(1 + x^2)$ actually converge to $1/(1 + x^2)$?

- How do we know that the power series we have obtained is actually the Maclaurin series for $1/(1 + x^2)$?

The first question is easy to resolve. Since the geometric series converges to $1/(1 - x)$ if $|x| < 1$, the second series will converge to $1/(1 + x^2)$ if $|-x^2| < 1$ or $|x^2| < 1$. However, this is true if and only if $|x| < 1$, so the power series we obtained for the function $1/(1 + x^2)$ converges to this function if $-1 < x < 1$.

The second question is more difficult to answer and leads us to the following general problem.

9.10.5 PROBLEM Suppose that a function f is represented by a power series in $x - x_0$ that has a nonzero radius of convergence. What relationship exists between the given power series and the Taylor series for f about $x = x_0$?

The answer is that they are the same; and here is the theorem that proves it.

Theorem 9.10.6 tells us that no matter how we arrive at a power series representation of a function f, be it by substitution, by differentiation, by integration, or by some algebraic process, that series will be the Taylor series for f about $x = x_0$, provided the series converges to f on some open interval containing x_0.

9.10.6 THEOREM *If a function f is represented by a power series in $x - x_0$ on some open interval containing x_0, then that power series is the Taylor series for f about $x = x_0$.*

PROOF Suppose that

$$f(x) = c_0 + c_1(x - x_0) + c_2(x - x_0)^2 + \cdots + c_k(x - x_0)^k + \cdots$$

for all x in some open interval containing x_0. To prove that this is the Taylor series for f about $x = x_0$, we must show that

$$c_k = \frac{f^{(k)}(x_0)}{k!} \qquad \text{for} \quad k = 0, 1, 2, 3, \ldots$$

However, the assumption that the series converges to $f(x)$ on an open interval containing x_0 ensures that it has a nonzero radius of convergence R; hence we can differentiate term by term in accordance with Theorem 9.10.2. Thus,

$$f(x) = c_0 + c_1(x - x_0) + c_2(x - x_0)^2 + c_3(x - x_0)^3 + c_4(x - x_0)^4 + \cdots$$

$$f'(x) = c_1 + 2c_2(x - x_0) + 3c_3(x - x_0)^2 + 4c_4(x - x_0)^3 + \cdots$$

$$f''(x) = 2!c_2 + (3 \cdot 2)c_3(x - x_0) + (4 \cdot 3)c_4(x - x_0)^2 + \cdots$$

$$f'''(x) = 3!c_3 + (4 \cdot 3 \cdot 2)c_4(x - x_0) + \cdots$$

$$\vdots$$

On substituting $x = x_0$, all the powers of $x - x_0$ drop out, leaving

$$f(x_0) = c_0, \quad f'(x_0) = c_1, \quad f''(x_0) = 2!c_2, \quad f'''(x_0) = 3!c_3, \ldots$$

from which we obtain

$$c_0 = f(x_0), \quad c_1 = f'(x_0), \quad c_2 = \frac{f''(x_0)}{2!}, \quad c_3 = \frac{f'''(x_0)}{3!}, \ldots$$

which shows that the coefficients $c_0, c_1, c_2, c_3, \ldots$ are precisely the coefficients in the Taylor series about x_0 for $f(x)$. ■

SOME PRACTICAL WAYS TO FIND TAYLOR SERIES

▶ **Example 2**   Find Taylor series for the given functions about the given x_0.

(a) e^{-x^2}, $x_0 = 0$ (b) $\ln x$, $x_0 = 1$ (c) $\dfrac{1}{x}$, $x_0 = 1$

Solution (a).   The simplest way to find the Maclaurin series for e^{-x^2} is to substitute $-x^2$ for x in the Maclaurin series

$$e^x = 1 + x + \frac{x^2}{2!} + \frac{x^3}{3!} + \frac{x^4}{4!} + \cdots \tag{3}$$

to obtain

$$e^{-x^2} = 1 - x^2 + \frac{x^4}{2!} - \frac{x^6}{3!} + \frac{x^8}{4!} - \cdots$$

Since (3) converges for all values of x, so will the series for e^{-x^2}.

Solution (b).   We begin with the Maclaurin series for $\ln(1 + x)$, which can be found in Table 9.9.1:

$$\ln(1 + x) = x - \frac{x^2}{2} + \frac{x^3}{3} - \frac{x^4}{4} + \cdots \quad (-1 < x \leq 1)$$

Substituting $x - 1$ for x in this series gives

$$\ln(1 + [x - 1]) = \ln x = (x - 1) - \frac{(x - 1)^2}{2} + \frac{(x - 1)^3}{3} - \frac{(x - 1)^4}{4} + \cdots \tag{4}$$

Since the original series converges when $-1 < x \leq 1$, the interval of convergence for (4) will be $-1 < x - 1 \leq 1$ or, equivalently, $0 < x \leq 2$.

Solution (c).   Since $1/x$ is the derivative of $\ln x$, we can differentiate the series for $\ln x$ found in (b) to obtain

$$\frac{1}{x} = 1 - \frac{2(x - 1)}{2} + \frac{3(x - 1)^2}{3} - \frac{4(x - 1)^3}{4} + \cdots$$

$$= 1 - (x - 1) + (x - 1)^2 - (x - 1)^3 + \cdots \tag{5}$$

By Theorem 9.10.2, we know that the radius of convergence for (5) is the same as that for (4), which is $R = 1$. Thus the interval of convergence for (5) must be at least $0 < x < 2$. Since the behaviors of (4) and (5) may differ at the endpoints $x = 0$ and $x = 2$, those must be checked separately. When $x = 0$, (5) becomes

$$1 - (-1) + (-1)^2 - (-1)^3 + \cdots = 1 + 1 + 1 + 1 + \cdots$$

which diverges by the divergence test. Similarly, when $x = 2$, (5) becomes

$$1 - 1 + 1^2 - 1^3 + \cdots = 1 - 1 + 1 - 1 + \cdots$$

which also diverges by the divergence test. Thus the interval of convergence for (5) is $0 < x < 2$. ◄

▶ **Example 3** Find the Maclaurin series for $\tan^{-1} x$.

Solution. It would be tedious to find the Maclaurin series directly. A better approach is to start with the formula

$$\int \frac{1}{1 + x^2} \, dx = \tan^{-1} x + C$$

and integrate the Maclaurin series

$$\frac{1}{1 + x^2} = 1 - x^2 + x^4 - x^6 + x^8 - \cdots \qquad (-1 < x < 1)$$

term by term. This yields

$$\tan^{-1} x + C = \int \frac{1}{1 + x^2} \, dx = \int [1 - x^2 + x^4 - x^6 + x^8 - \cdots] \, dx$$

or

$$\tan^{-1} x = \left[x - \frac{x^3}{3} + \frac{x^5}{5} - \frac{x^7}{7} + \frac{x^9}{9} - \cdots \right] - C$$

The constant of integration can be evaluated by substituting $x = 0$ and using the condition $\tan^{-1} 0 = 0$. This gives $C = 0$, so that

$$\tan^{-1} x = x - \frac{x^3}{3} + \frac{x^5}{5} - \frac{x^7}{7} + \frac{x^9}{9} - \cdots \qquad (-1 < x < 1) \qquad (6)$$

◄

REMARK Observe that neither Theorem 9.10.2 nor Theorem 9.10.3 addresses what happens at the endpoints of the interval of convergence. However, it can be proved that if the Taylor series for f about $x = x_0$ converges to $f(x)$ for all x in the interval $(x_0 - R, x_0 + R)$, and if the Taylor series converges at the right endpoint $x_0 + R$, then the value that it converges to at that point is the limit of $f(x)$ as $x \to x_0 + R$ from the left; and if the Taylor series converges at the left endpoint $x_0 - R$, then the value that it converges to at that point is the limit of $f(x)$ as $x \to x_0 - R$ from the right.

For example, the Maclaurin series for $\tan^{-1} x$ given in (6) converges at both $x = -1$ and $x = 1$, since the hypotheses of the alternating series test (Theorem 9.6.1) are satisfied at those points. Thus, the continuity of $\tan^{-1} x$ on the interval $[-1, 1]$ implies that at $x = 1$ the Maclaurin series converges to

$$\lim_{x \to 1^-} \tan^{-1} x = \tan^{-1} 1 = \frac{\pi}{4}$$

and at $x = -1$ it converges to

$$\lim_{x \to -1^+} \tan^{-1} x = \tan^{-1}(-1) = -\frac{\pi}{4}$$

This shows that the Maclaurin series for $\tan^{-1} x$ actually converges to $\tan^{-1} x$ on the closed interval $-1 \le x \le 1$. Moreover, the convergence at $x = 1$ establishes Formula (2).

■ **APPROXIMATING DEFINITE INTEGRALS USING TAYLOR SERIES**

Taylor series provide an alternative to Simpson's rule and other numerical methods for approximating definite integrals.

▶ **Example 4** Approximate the integral

$$\int_0^1 e^{-x^2} \, dx$$

to three decimal-place accuracy by expanding the integrand in a Maclaurin series and integrating term by term.

Solution. We found in Example 2(a) that the Maclaurin series for e^{-x^2} is

$$e^{-x^2} = 1 - x^2 + \frac{x^4}{2!} - \frac{x^6}{3!} + \frac{x^8}{4!} - \cdots$$

Therefore,

$$\int_0^1 e^{-x^2} \, dx = \int_0^1 \left[1 - x^2 + \frac{x^4}{2!} - \frac{x^6}{3!} + \frac{x^8}{4!} - \cdots \right] dx$$

$$= \left[x - \frac{x^3}{3} + \frac{x^5}{5(2!)} - \frac{x^7}{7(3!)} + \frac{x^9}{9(4!)} - \cdots \right]_0^1$$

$$= 1 - \frac{1}{3} + \frac{1}{5 \cdot 2!} - \frac{1}{7 \cdot 3!} + \frac{1}{9 \cdot 4!} - \cdots$$

$$= \sum_{k=0}^{\infty} \frac{(-1)^k}{(2k+1)k!}$$

Since this series clearly satisfies the hypotheses of the alternating series test (Theorem 9.6.1), it follows from Theorem 9.6.2 that if we approximate the integral by s_n (the nth partial sum of the series), then

$$\left| \int_0^1 e^{-x^2} \, dx - s_n \right| < \frac{1}{[2(n+1)+1](n+1)!} = \frac{1}{(2n+3)(n+1)!}$$

Thus, for three decimal-place accuracy we must choose n such that

$$\frac{1}{(2n+3)(n+1)!} \le 0.0005 = 5 \times 10^{-4}$$

With the help of a calculating utility you can show that the smallest value of n that satisfies this condition is $n = 5$. Thus, the value of the integral to three decimal-place accuracy is

$$\int_0^1 e^{-x^2} \, dx \approx 1 - \frac{1}{3} + \frac{1}{5 \cdot 2!} - \frac{1}{7 \cdot 3!} + \frac{1}{9 \cdot 4!} - \frac{1}{11 \cdot 5!} \approx 0.747$$

What advantages does the method of Example 4 have over Simpson's rule? What are its disadvantages?

As a check, a calculator with a built-in numerical integration capability produced the approximation 0.746824, which agrees with our result when rounded to three decimal places. ◀

■ **FINDING TAYLOR SERIES BY MULTIPLICATION AND DIVISION**

The following examples illustrate some algebraic techniques that are sometimes useful for finding Taylor series.

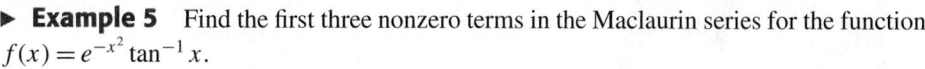

In the left margin:

$$
\begin{array}{r}
1 - x^2 + \dfrac{x^4}{2} - \cdots \\
\times \quad x - \dfrac{x^3}{3} + \dfrac{x^5}{5} - \cdots \\
\hline
x - x^3 + \dfrac{x^5}{2} - \cdots \\
- \dfrac{x^3}{3} + \dfrac{x^5}{3} - \dfrac{x^7}{6} + \cdots \\
\dfrac{x^5}{5} - \dfrac{x^7}{5} + \cdots \\
\hline
x - \dfrac{4}{3}x^3 + \dfrac{31}{30}x^5 - \cdots
\end{array}
$$

$$
\begin{array}{r}
x + \dfrac{x^3}{3} + \dfrac{2x^5}{15} + \cdots \\
\end{array}
$$

$$
1 - \dfrac{x^2}{2} + \dfrac{x^4}{24} - \cdots \Big) \overline{\; x - \dfrac{x^3}{6} + \dfrac{x^5}{120} - \cdots \;}
$$

$$
\begin{array}{r}
x - \dfrac{x^3}{2} + \dfrac{x^5}{24} - \cdots \\
\hline
\dfrac{x^3}{3} - \dfrac{x^5}{30} + \cdots \\
\dfrac{x^3}{3} - \dfrac{x^5}{6} + \cdots \\
\hline
\dfrac{2x^5}{15} + \cdots
\end{array}
$$

TECHNOLOGY MASTERY

If you have a CAS, use its capability for multiplying and dividing polynomials to perform the computations in Examples 5 and 6.

▶ **Example 5** Find the first three nonzero terms in the Maclaurin series for the function $f(x) = e^{-x^2} \tan^{-1} x$.

Solution. Using the series for e^{-x^2} and $\tan^{-1} x$ obtained in Examples 2 and 3 gives

$$
e^{-x^2} \tan^{-1} x = \left(1 - x^2 + \frac{x^4}{2} - \cdots \right)\left(x - \frac{x^3}{3} + \frac{x^5}{5} - \cdots \right)
$$

Multiplying, as shown in the margin, we obtain

$$
e^{-x^2} \tan^{-1} x = x - \frac{4}{3}x^3 + \frac{31}{30}x^5 - \cdots
$$

More terms in the series can be obtained by including more terms in the factors. Moreover, one can prove that a series obtained by this method converges at each point in the intersection of the intervals of convergence of the factors (and possibly on a larger interval). Thus, we can be certain that the series we have obtained converges for all x in the interval $-1 \leq x \leq 1$ (why?). ◀

▶ **Example 6** Find the first three nonzero terms in the Maclaurin series for $\tan x$.

Solution. Using the first three terms in the Maclaurin series for $\sin x$ and $\cos x$, we can express $\tan x$ as

$$
\tan x = \frac{\sin x}{\cos x} = \frac{x - \dfrac{x^3}{3!} + \dfrac{x^5}{5!} - \cdots}{1 - \dfrac{x^2}{2!} + \dfrac{x^4}{4!} - \cdots}
$$

Dividing, as shown in the margin, we obtain

$$
\tan x = x + \frac{x^3}{3} + \frac{2x^5}{15} + \cdots \quad ◀
$$

■ **MODELING PHYSICAL LAWS WITH TAYLOR SERIES**

Taylor series provide an important way of modeling physical laws. To illustrate the idea we will consider the problem of modeling the period of a simple pendulum (Figure 9.10.1). As explained in Chapter 7 Making Connections Exercise 5, the period T of such a pendulum is given by

$$
T = 4\sqrt{\frac{L}{g}} \int_0^{\pi/2} \frac{1}{\sqrt{1 - k^2 \sin^2 \phi}}\, d\phi \tag{7}
$$

where

$L = $ length of the supporting rod

$g = $ acceleration due to gravity

$k = \sin(\theta_0/2)$, where θ_0 is the initial angle of displacement from the vertical

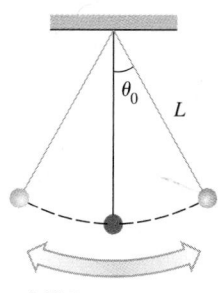

▲ **Figure 9.10.1**

The integral, which is called a *complete elliptic integral of the first kind*, cannot be expressed in terms of elementary functions and is often approximated by numerical methods. Unfortunately, numerical values are so specific that they often give little insight into general physical principles. However, if we expand the integrand of (7) in a series and integrate term by term, then we can generate an infinite series that can be used to construct various mathematical models for the period T that give a deeper understanding of the behavior of the pendulum.

© ACE STOCK LIMITED/Alamy

Understanding the motion of a pendulum played a critical role in the advance of accurate time-keeping with the development of the pendulum clock in the 17th century.

To obtain a series for the integrand, we will substitute $-k^2 \sin^2 \phi$ for x in the binomial series for $1/\sqrt{1+x}$ that we derived in Example 4(*b*) of Section 9.9. If we do this, then we can rewrite (7) as

$$T = 4\sqrt{\frac{L}{g}} \int_0^{\pi/2} \left[1 + \frac{1}{2}k^2 \sin^2 \phi + \frac{1 \cdot 3}{2^2 2!}k^4 \sin^4 \phi + \frac{1 \cdot 3 \cdot 5}{2^3 3!}k^6 \sin^6 \phi + \cdots \right] d\phi \quad (8)$$

If we integrate term by term, then we can produce a series that converges to the period T. However, one of the most important cases of pendulum motion occurs when the initial displacement is small, in which case all subsequent displacements are small, and we can assume that $k = \sin(\theta_0/2) \approx 0$. In this case we expect the convergence of the series for T to be rapid, and we can approximate the sum of the series by dropping all but the constant term in (8). This yields

$$T = 2\pi\sqrt{\frac{L}{g}} \quad (9)$$

which is called the **first-order model** of T or the model for **small vibrations**. This model can be improved on by using more terms in the series. For example, if we use the first two terms in the series, we obtain the **second-order model**

$$T = 2\pi\sqrt{\frac{L}{g}}\left(1 + \frac{k^2}{4}\right) \quad (10)$$

(verify).

✔ QUICK CHECK EXERCISES 9.10   (*See page 689 for answers.*)

1. The Maclaurin series for e^{-x^2} obtained by substituting $-x^2$ for x in the series

$$e^x = \sum_{k=0}^{\infty} \frac{x^k}{k!}$$

is $e^{-x^2} = \sum_{k=0}^{\infty}$ _____.

2. $\dfrac{d}{dx}\left[\displaystyle\sum_{k=1}^{\infty}(-1)^{k+1}\frac{x^k}{k}\right] =$ _____ + _____ x

$+$ _____ $x^2 +$ _____ $x^3 + \cdots$

$= \displaystyle\sum_{k=0}^{\infty}$ _____

3. $\left(\displaystyle\sum_{k=0}^{\infty}\frac{x^k}{k!}\right)\left(\displaystyle\sum_{k=0}^{\infty}\frac{x^k}{k+1}\right)$

$= \left(1 + x + \dfrac{x^2}{2!} + \cdots\right)\left(1 + \dfrac{x}{2} + \dfrac{x^2}{3} + \cdots\right)$

$=$ _____ $+$ _____ $x +$ _____ $x^2 + \cdots$

4. Suppose that $f(1) = 4$ and $f'(x) = \displaystyle\sum_{k=0}^{\infty}\frac{(-1)^k}{(k+1)!}(x-1)^k$

(a) $f''(1) =$ _____

(b) $f(x) =$ _____ $+$ _____ $(x-1)$

$+$ _____ $(x-1)^2 +$ _____ $(x-1)^3 + \cdots$

$=$ _____ $+ \displaystyle\sum_{k=1}^{\infty}$ _____

EXERCISE SET 9.10   [C] CAS

1. In each part, obtain the Maclaurin series for the function by making an appropriate substitution in the Maclaurin series for $1/(1-x)$. Include the general term in your answer, and state the radius of convergence of the series.

(a) $\dfrac{1}{1+x}$ (b) $\dfrac{1}{1-x^2}$ (c) $\dfrac{1}{1-2x}$ (d) $\dfrac{1}{2-x}$

2. In each part, obtain the Maclaurin series for the function by making an appropriate substitution in the Maclaurin series for $\ln(1+x)$. Include the general term in your answer, and

state the radius of convergence of the series.

(a) $\ln(1-x)$ (b) $\ln(1+x^2)$

(c) $\ln(1+2x)$ (d) $\ln(2+x)$

3. In each part, obtain the first four nonzero terms of the Maclaurin series for the function by making an appropriate substitution in one of the binomial series obtained in Example 4 of Section 9.9.

(a) $(2+x)^{-1/2}$ (b) $(1-x^2)^{-2}$

4. (a) Use the Maclaurin series for $1/(1-x)$ to find the Maclaurin series for $1/(a-x)$, where $a \neq 0$, and state the radius of convergence of the series.

   (b) Use the binomial series for $1/(1+x)^2$ obtained in Example 4 of Section 9.9 to find the first four nonzero terms in the Maclaurin series for $1/(a+x)^2$, where $a \neq 0$, and state the radius of convergence of the series.

5–8 Find the first four nonzero terms of the Maclaurin series for the function by making an appropriate substitution in a known Maclaurin series and performing any algebraic operations that are required. State the radius of convergence of the series. ■

5. (a) $\sin 2x$ (b) e^{-2x} (c) e^{x^2} (d) $x^2 \cos \pi x$

6. (a) $\cos 2x$ (b) $x^2 e^x$ (c) $x e^{-x}$ (d) $\sin(x^2)$

7. (a) $\dfrac{x^2}{1+3x}$ (b) $x \sinh 2x$ (c) $x(1-x^2)^{3/2}$

8. (a) $\dfrac{x}{x-1}$ (b) $3 \cosh(x^2)$ (c) $\dfrac{x}{(1+2x)^3}$

9–10 Find the first four nonzero terms of the Maclaurin series for the function by using an appropriate trigonometric identity or property of logarithms and then substituting in a known Maclaurin series. ■

9. (a) $\sin^2 x$ (b) $\ln[(1+x^3)^{12}]$

10. (a) $\cos^2 x$ (b) $\ln\left(\dfrac{1-x}{1+x}\right)$

11. (a) Use a known Maclaurin series to find the Taylor series of $1/x$ about $x = 1$ by expressing this function as
$$\frac{1}{x} = \frac{1}{1-(1-x)}$$

   (b) Find the interval of convergence of the Taylor series.

12. Use the method of Exercise 11 to find the Taylor series of $1/x$ about $x = x_0$, and state the interval of convergence of the Taylor series.

13–14 Find the first four nonzero terms of the Maclaurin series for the function by multiplying the Maclaurin series of the factors. ■

13. (a) $e^x \sin x$ (b) $\sqrt{1+x} \ln(1+x)$

14. (a) $e^{-x^2} \cos x$ (b) $(1+x^2)^{4/3}(1+x)^{1/3}$

15–16 Find the first four nonzero terms of the Maclaurin series for the function by dividing appropriate Maclaurin series. ■

15. (a) $\sec x$ $\left(= \dfrac{1}{\cos x}\right)$ (b) $\dfrac{\sin x}{e^x}$

16. (a) $\dfrac{\tan^{-1} x}{1+x}$ (b) $\dfrac{\ln(1+x)}{1-x}$

17. Use the Maclaurin series for e^x and e^{-x} to derive the Maclaurin series for $\sinh x$ and $\cosh x$. Include the general terms in your answers and state the radius of convergence of each series.

18. Use the Maclaurin series for $\sinh x$ and $\cosh x$ to obtain the first four nonzero terms in the Maclaurin series for $\tanh x$.

19–20 Find the first five nonzero terms of the Maclaurin series for the function by using partial fractions and a known Maclaurin series. ■

19. $\dfrac{4x-2}{x^2-1}$ 20. $\dfrac{x^3+x^2+2x-2}{x^2-1}$

21–22 Confirm the derivative formula by differentiating the appropriate Maclaurin series term by term. ■

21. (a) $\dfrac{d}{dx}[\cos x] = -\sin x$ (b) $\dfrac{d}{dx}[\ln(1+x)] = \dfrac{1}{1+x}$

22. (a) $\dfrac{d}{dx}[\sinh x] = \cosh x$ (b) $\dfrac{d}{dx}[\tan^{-1} x] = \dfrac{1}{1+x^2}$

23–24 Confirm the integration formula by integrating the appropriate Maclaurin series term by term. ■

23. (a) $\displaystyle\int e^x \, dx = e^x + C$

    (b) $\displaystyle\int \sinh x \, dx = \cosh x + C$

24. (a) $\displaystyle\int \sin x \, dx = -\cos x + C$

    (b) $\displaystyle\int \dfrac{1}{1+x} \, dx = \ln(1+x) + C$

25. Consider the series
$$\sum_{k=0}^{\infty} \frac{x^{k+1}}{(k+1)(k+2)}$$
Determine the intervals of convergence for this series and for the series obtained by differentiating this series term by term.

26. Consider the series
$$\sum_{k=1}^{\infty} \frac{(-3)^k}{k} x^k$$
Determine the intervals of convergence for this series and for the series obtained by integrating this series term by term.

27. (a) Use the Maclaurin series for $1/(1-x)$ to find the Maclaurin series for
$$f(x) = \frac{x}{1-x^2}$$

    (b) Use the Maclaurin series obtained in part (a) to find $f^{(5)}(0)$ and $f^{(6)}(0)$.

    (c) What can you say about the value of $f^{(n)}(0)$?

28. Let $f(x) = x^2 \cos 2x$. Use the method of Exercise 27 to find $f^{(99)}(0)$.

29–30 The limit of an indeterminate form as $x \to x_0$ can sometimes be found by expanding the functions involved in Taylor series about $x = x_0$ and taking the limit of the series term by term. Use this method to find the limits in these exercises. ■

29. (a) $\displaystyle\lim_{x \to 0} \frac{\sin x}{x}$ (b) $\displaystyle\lim_{x \to 0} \frac{\tan^{-1} x - x}{x^3}$

30. (a) $\displaystyle\lim_{x \to 0} \frac{1 - \cos x}{\sin x}$ (b) $\displaystyle\lim_{x \to 0} \frac{\ln\sqrt{1+x} - \sin 2x}{x}$

31–34 Use Maclaurin series to approximate the integral to three decimal-place accuracy. ■

31. $\displaystyle\int_0^1 \sin(x^2)\,dx$ **32.** $\displaystyle\int_0^{1/2} \tan^{-1}(2x^2)\,dx$

33. $\displaystyle\int_0^{0.2} \sqrt[3]{1+x^4}\,dx$ **34.** $\displaystyle\int_0^{1/2} \frac{dx}{\sqrt[4]{x^2+1}}$

FOCUS ON CONCEPTS

35. (a) Find the Maclaurin series for e^{x^4}. What is the radius of convergence?

   (b) Explain two different ways to use the Maclaurin series for e^{x^4} to find a series for $x^3 e^{x^4}$. Confirm that both methods produce the same series.

36. (a) Differentiate the Maclaurin series for $1/(1-x)$, and use the result to show that

$$\sum_{k=1}^{\infty} k x^k = \frac{x}{(1-x)^2} \quad \text{for } -1 < x < 1$$

   (b) Integrate the Maclaurin series for $1/(1-x)$, and use the result to show that

$$\sum_{k=1}^{\infty} \frac{x^k}{k} = -\ln(1-x) \quad \text{for } -1 < x < 1$$

   (c) Use the result in part (b) to show that

$$\sum_{k=1}^{\infty} (-1)^{k+1} \frac{x^k}{k} = \ln(1+x) \quad \text{for } -1 < x < 1$$

   (d) Show that the series in part (c) converges if $x = 1$.

   (e) Use the remark following Example 3 to show that

$$\sum_{k=1}^{\infty} (-1)^{k+1} \frac{x^k}{k} = \ln(1+x) \quad \text{for } -1 < x \le 1$$

---

37. Use the results in Exercise 36 to find the sum of the series.

   (a) $\displaystyle\sum_{k=1}^{\infty} \frac{k}{3^k} = \frac{1}{3} + \frac{2}{3^2} + \frac{3}{3^3} + \frac{4}{3^4} + \cdots$

   (b) $\displaystyle\sum_{k=1}^{\infty} \frac{1}{k(4^k)} = \frac{1}{4} + \frac{1}{2(4^2)} + \frac{1}{3(4^3)} + \frac{1}{4(4^4)} + \cdots$

38. Use the results in Exercise 36 to find the sum of each series.

   (a) $\displaystyle\sum_{k=1}^{\infty} (-1)^{k+1} \frac{1}{k} = 1 - \frac{1}{2} + \frac{1}{3} - \frac{1}{4} + \cdots$

   (b) $\displaystyle\sum_{k=1}^{\infty} \frac{(e-1)^k}{k e^k} = \frac{e-1}{e} + \frac{(e-1)^2}{2(e^2)} - \frac{(e-1)^3}{3(e^3)} + \cdots$

39. (a) Use the relationship

$$\int \frac{1}{\sqrt{1+x^2}}\,dx = \sinh^{-1} x + C$$

   to find the first four nonzero terms in the Maclaurin series for $\sinh^{-1} x$.

   (b) Express the series in sigma notation.

   (c) What is the radius of convergence?

40. (a) Use the relationship

$$\int \frac{1}{\sqrt{1-x^2}}\,dx = \sin^{-1} x + C$$

   to find the first four nonzero terms in the Maclaurin series for $\sin^{-1} x$.

   (b) Express the series in sigma notation.

   (c) What is the radius of convergence?

41. We showed by Formula (19) of Section 8.2 that if there are y_0 units of radioactive carbon-14 present at time $t = 0$, then the number of units present t years later is

$$y(t) = y_0 e^{-0.000121t}$$

   (a) Express $y(t)$ as a Maclaurin series.

   (b) Use the first two terms in the series to show that the number of units present after 1 year is approximately $(0.999879)y_0$.

   (c) Compare this to the value produced by the formula for $y(t)$.

42. Suppose that a simple pendulum with a length of $L = 1$ meter is given an initial displacement of $\theta_0 = 5°$ from the vertical.

   (a) Approximate the period T of the pendulum using Formula (9) for the first-order model of T. [*Note:* Take $g = 9.8$ m/s^2.]

   (b) Approximate the period of the pendulum using Formula (10) for the second-order model.

   (c) Use the numerical integration capability of a CAS to approximate the period of the pendulum from Formula (7), and compare it to the values obtained in parts (a) and (b).

43. Use the first three nonzero terms in Formula (8) and the Wallis sine formula in the Endpaper Integral Table (Formula 122) to obtain a model for the period of a simple pendulum.

44. Recall that the gravitational force exerted by the Earth on an object is called the object's *weight* (or more precisely, its *Earth weight*). If an object of mass m is on the surface of the Earth (mean sea level), then the magnitude of its weight is mg, where g is the acceleration due to gravity at the Earth's surface. A more general formula for the magnitude of the gravitational force that the Earth exerts on an object of mass m is

$$F = \frac{mgR^2}{(R+h)^2}$$

   where R is the radius of the Earth and h is the height of the object above the Earth's surface.

   (a) Use the binomial series for $1/(1+x)^2$ obtained in Example 4 of Section 9.9 to express F as a Maclaurin series in powers of h/R.

   (b) Show that if $h = 0$, then $F = mg$.

   (c) Show that if $h/R \approx 0$, then $F \approx mg - (2mgh/R)$. [*Note:* The quantity $2mgh/R$ can be thought of as a "correction term" for the weight that takes the object's height above the Earth's surface into account.]

   (d) If we assume that the Earth is a sphere of radius $R = 4000$ mi at mean sea level, by approximately what percentage does a person's weight change in going from mean sea level to the top of Mt. Everest (29,028 ft)?

45. (a) Show that the Bessel function $J_0(x)$ given by Formula (4) of Section 9.8 satisfies the differential equation $xy'' + y' + xy = 0$. (This is called the **Bessel equation of order zero**.)

(b) Show that the Bessel function $J_1(x)$ given by Formula (5) of Section 9.8 satisfies the differential equation $x^2 y'' + xy' + (x^2 - 1)y = 0$. (This is called the **Bessel equation of order one**.)

(c) Show that $J_0'(x) = -J_1(x)$.

46. Prove: If the power series $\sum_{k=0}^{\infty} a_k x^k$ and $\sum_{k=0}^{\infty} b_k x^k$ have the same sum on an interval $(-r, r)$, then $a_k = b_k$ for all values of k.

47. **Writing** Evaluate the limit

$$\lim_{x \to 0} \frac{x - \sin x}{x^3}$$

in two ways: using L'Hôpital's rule and by replacing $\sin x$ by its Maclaurin series. Discuss how the use of a series can give qualitative information about how the value of an indeterminate limit is approached.

✔ QUICK CHECK ANSWERS 9.10

1. $(-1)^k \dfrac{x^{2k}}{k!}$ **2.** $1; -1; 1; -1; (-1)^k x^k$ **3.** $1; \dfrac{3}{2}; \dfrac{4}{3}$ **4.** (a) $-\dfrac{1}{2}$ (b) $4; 1; -\dfrac{1}{4}; \dfrac{1}{18}; 4; (-1)^{k+1} \dfrac{(x-1)^k}{k \cdot (k!)}$

CHAPTER 9 REVIEW EXERCISES

1. What is the difference between an infinite sequence and an infinite series?

2. What is meant by the sum of an infinite series?

3. (a) What is a geometric series? Give some examples of convergent and divergent geometric series.

(b) What is a *p*-series? Give some examples of convergent and divergent *p*-series.

4. State conditions under which an alternating series is guaranteed to converge.

5. (a) What does it mean to say that an infinite series converges absolutely?

(b) What relationship exists between convergence and absolute convergence of an infinite series?

6. State the Remainder Estimation Theorem, and describe some of its uses.

7. If a power series in $x - x_0$ has radius of convergence R, what can you say about the set of x-values at which the series converges?

8. (a) Write down the formula for the Maclaurin series for f in sigma notation.

(b) Write down the formula for the Taylor series for f about $x = x_0$ in sigma notation.

9. Are the following statements true or false? If true, state a theorem to justify your conclusion; if false, then give a counterexample.

(a) If $\sum u_k$ converges, then $u_k \to 0$ as $k \to +\infty$.

(b) If $u_k \to 0$ as $k \to +\infty$, then $\sum u_k$ converges.

(c) If $f(n) = a_n$ for $n = 1, 2, 3, \ldots$, and if $a_n \to L$ as $n \to +\infty$, then $f(x) \to L$ as $x \to +\infty$.

(d) If $f(n) = a_n$ for $n = 1, 2, 3, \ldots$, and if $f(x) \to L$ as $x \to +\infty$, then $a_n \to L$ as $n \to +\infty$.

(e) If $0 < a_n < 1$, then $\{a_n\}$ converges.

(f) If $0 < u_k < 1$, then $\sum u_k$ converges.

(g) If $\sum u_k$ and $\sum v_k$ converge, then $\sum (u_k + v_k)$ diverges.

(h) If $\sum u_k$ and $\sum v_k$ diverge, then $\sum (u_k - v_k)$ converges.

(i) If $0 \le u_k \le v_k$ and $\sum v_k$ converges, then $\sum u_k$ converges.

(j) If $0 \le u_k \le v_k$ and $\sum u_k$ diverges, then $\sum v_k$ diverges.

(k) If an infinite series converges, then it converges absolutely.

(l) If an infinite series diverges absolutely, then it diverges.

10. State whether each of the following is true or false. Justify your answers.

(a) The function $f(x) = x^{1/3}$ has a Maclaurin series.

(b) $1 + \frac{1}{2} - \frac{1}{2} + \frac{1}{3} - \frac{1}{3} + \frac{1}{4} - \frac{1}{4} + \cdots = 1$

(c) $1 + \frac{1}{2} - \frac{1}{2} + \frac{1}{2} - \frac{1}{2} + \frac{1}{2} - \frac{1}{2} + \cdots = 1$

11. Find the general term of the sequence, starting with $n = 1$, determine whether the sequence converges, and if so find its limit.

(a) $\dfrac{3}{2^2 - 1^2}, \dfrac{4}{3^2 - 2^2}, \dfrac{5}{4^2 - 3^2}, \ldots$

(b) $\dfrac{1}{3}, -\dfrac{2}{5}, \dfrac{3}{7}, -\dfrac{4}{9}, \ldots$

12. Suppose that the sequence $\{a_k\}$ is defined recursively by

$$a_0 = c, \quad a_{k+1} = \sqrt{a_k}$$

Assuming that the sequence converges, find its limit if

(a) $c = \frac{1}{2}$ \hspace{2cm} (b) $c = \frac{3}{2}$.

13. Show that the sequence is eventually strictly monotone.

(a) $\left\{ (n - 10)^4 \right\}_{n=0}^{+\infty}$ \hspace{1cm} (b) $\left\{ \dfrac{100^n}{(2n)!(n!)} \right\}_{n=1}^{+\infty}$

14. (a) Give an example of a bounded sequence that diverges.

(b) Give an example of a monotonic sequence that diverges.

15–20 Use any method to determine whether the series converge. ■

15. (a) $\displaystyle\sum_{k=1}^{\infty} \frac{1}{5^k}$ (b) $\displaystyle\sum_{k=1}^{\infty} \frac{1}{5^k + 1}$

16. (a) $\displaystyle\sum_{k=1}^{\infty} (-1)^k \frac{k+4}{k^2 + k}$ (b) $\displaystyle\sum_{k=1}^{\infty} (-1)^{k+1} \left(\frac{k+2}{3k-1} \right)^k$

17. (a) $\displaystyle\sum_{k=1}^{\infty} \frac{1}{k^3 + 2k + 1}$ (b) $\displaystyle\sum_{k=1}^{\infty} \frac{1}{(3+k)^{2/5}}$

18. (a) $\displaystyle\sum_{k=1}^{\infty} \frac{\ln k}{k\sqrt{k}}$ (b) $\displaystyle\sum_{k=1}^{\infty} \frac{k^{4/3}}{8k^2 + 5k + 1}$

19. (a) $\displaystyle\sum_{k=1}^{\infty} \frac{9}{\sqrt{k} + 1}$ (b) $\displaystyle\sum_{k=1}^{\infty} \frac{\cos(1/k)}{k^2}$

20. (a) $\displaystyle\sum_{k=1}^{\infty} \frac{k^{-1/2}}{2 + \sin^2 k}$ (b) $\displaystyle\sum_{k=1}^{\infty} \frac{(-1)^{k+1}}{k^2 + 1}$

21. Find a formula for the exact error that results when the sum of the geometric series $\sum_{k=0}^{\infty}(1/5)^k$ is approximated by the sum of the first 100 terms in the series.

22. Suppose that $\displaystyle\sum_{k=1}^{n} u_k = 2 - \frac{1}{n}$. Find

(a) u_{100} (b) $\displaystyle\lim_{k \to +\infty} u_k$ (c) $\displaystyle\sum_{k=1}^{\infty} u_k$.

23. In each part, determine whether the series converges; if so, find its sum.

(a) $\displaystyle\sum_{k=1}^{\infty} \left(\frac{3}{2^k} - \frac{2}{3^k} \right)$ (b) $\displaystyle\sum_{k=1}^{\infty} [\ln(k+1) - \ln k]$

(c) $\displaystyle\sum_{k=1}^{\infty} \frac{1}{k(k+2)}$ (d) $\displaystyle\sum_{k=1}^{\infty} [\tan^{-1}(k+1) - \tan^{-1} k]$

24. It can be proved that

$$\lim_{n \to +\infty} \sqrt[n]{n!} = +\infty \quad \text{and} \quad \lim_{n \to +\infty} \frac{\sqrt[n]{n!}}{n} = \frac{1}{e}$$

In each part, use these limits and the root test to determine whether the series converges.

(a) $\displaystyle\sum_{k=0}^{\infty} \frac{2^k}{k!}$ (b) $\displaystyle\sum_{k=0}^{\infty} \frac{k^k}{k!}$

25. Let a, b, and p be positive constants. For which values of p does the series $\displaystyle\sum_{k=1}^{\infty} \frac{1}{(a + bk)^p}$ converge?

26. Find the interval of convergence of

$$\sum_{k=0}^{\infty} \frac{(x - x_0)^k}{b^k} \quad (b > 0)$$

27. (a) Show that $k^k \geq k!$.

(b) Use the comparison test to show that $\sum_{k=1}^{\infty} k^{-k}$ converges.

(c) Use the root test to show that the series converges.

28. Does the series $1 - \frac{2}{3} + \frac{3}{5} - \frac{4}{7} + \frac{5}{9} + \cdots$ converge? Justify your answer.

29. (a) Find the first five Maclaurin polynomials of the function $p(x) = 1 - 7x + 5x^2 + 4x^3$.

(b) Make a general statement about the Maclaurin polynomials of a polynomial of degree n.

30. Show that the approximation

$$\sin x \approx x - \frac{x^3}{3!} + \frac{x^5}{5!}$$

is accurate to four decimal places if $0 \leq x \leq \pi/4$.

31. Use a Maclaurin series and properties of alternating series to show that $|\ln(1 + x) - x| \leq x^2/2$ if $0 < x < 1$.

32. Use Maclaurin series to approximate the integral

$$\int_0^1 \frac{1 - \cos x}{x} \, dx$$

to three decimal-place accuracy.

33. In parts (a)–(d), find the sum of the series by associating it with some Maclaurin series.

(a) $2 + \dfrac{4}{2!} + \dfrac{8}{3!} + \dfrac{16}{4!} + \cdots$

(b) $\pi - \dfrac{\pi^3}{3!} + \dfrac{\pi^5}{5!} - \dfrac{\pi^7}{7!} + \cdots$

(c) $1 - \dfrac{e^2}{2!} + \dfrac{e^4}{4!} - \dfrac{e^6}{6!} + \cdots$

(d) $1 - \ln 3 + \dfrac{(\ln 3)^2}{2!} - \dfrac{(\ln 3)^3}{3!} + \cdots$

34. In each part, write out the first four terms of the series, and then find the radius of convergence.

(a) $\displaystyle\sum_{k=1}^{\infty} \frac{1 \cdot 2 \cdot 3 \cdots k}{1 \cdot 4 \cdot 7 \cdots (3k-2)} x^k$

(b) $\displaystyle\sum_{k=1}^{\infty} (-1)^k \frac{1 \cdot 2 \cdot 3 \cdots k}{1 \cdot 3 \cdot 5 \cdots (2k-1)} x^{2k+1}$

35. Use an appropriate Taylor series for $\sqrt[3]{x}$ to approximate $\sqrt[3]{28}$ to three decimal-place accuracy, and check your answer by comparing it to that produced directly by your calculating utility.

36. Differentiate the Maclaurin series for xe^x and use the result to show that

$$\sum_{k=0}^{\infty} \frac{k+1}{k!} = 2e$$

37. Use the supplied Maclaurin series for $\sin x$ and $\cos x$ to find the first four nonzero terms of the Maclaurin series for the given functions.

$$\sin x = \sum_{k=0}^{\infty} (-1)^k \frac{x^{2k+1}}{(2k+1)!}$$

$$\cos x = \sum_{k=0}^{\infty} (-1)^k \frac{x^{2k}}{(2k)!}$$

(a) $\sin x \cos x$ (b) $\frac{1}{2} \sin 2x$

CHAPTER 9 MAKING CONNECTIONS

1. As shown in the accompanying figure, suppose that lines L_1 and L_2 form an angle θ, $0 < \theta < \pi/2$, at their point of intersection P. A point P_0 is chosen that is on L_1 and a units from P. Starting from P_0 a zig-zag path is constructed by successively going back and forth between L_1 and L_2 along a perpendicular from one line to the other. Find the following sums in terms of θ and a.

   (a) $P_0P_1 + P_1P_2 + P_2P_3 + \cdots$

   (b) $P_0P_1 + P_2P_3 + P_4P_5 + \cdots$

   (c) $P_1P_2 + P_3P_4 + P_5P_6 + \cdots$

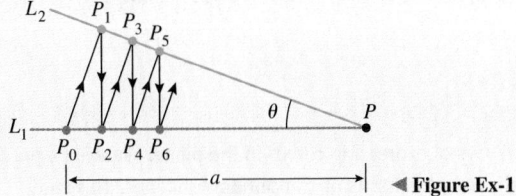

◀ Figure Ex-1

2. (a) Find A and B such that
$$\frac{6^k}{(3^{k+1} - 2^{k+1})(3^k - 2^k)} = \frac{2^k A}{3^k - 2^k} + \frac{2^k B}{3^{k+1} - 2^{k+1}}$$

   (b) Use the result in part (a) to find a closed form for the nth partial sum of the series
$$\sum_{k=1}^{\infty} \frac{6^k}{(3^{k+1} - 2^{k+1})(3^k - 2^k)}$$
   and then find the sum of the series.

   Source: This exercise is adapted from a problem that appeared in the Forty-Fifth Annual William Lowell Putnam Competition.

3. Show that the alternating p-series
$$1 - \frac{1}{2^p} + \frac{1}{3^p} - \frac{1}{4^p} + \cdots + (-1)^{k+1}\frac{1}{k^p} + \cdots$$
   converges absolutely if $p > 1$, converges conditionally if $0 < p \leq 1$, and diverges if $p \leq 0$.

4. As illustrated in the accompanying figure, a bug, starting at point A on a 180 cm wire, walks the length of the wire, stops and walks in the opposite direction for half the length of the wire, stops again and walks in the opposite direction for one-third the length of the wire, stops again and walks in the opposite direction for one-fourth the length of the wire, and so forth until it stops for the 1000th time.

   (a) Give upper and lower bounds on the distance between the bug and point A when it finally stops. [*Hint:* As stated in Example 2 of Section 9.6, assume that the sum of the alternating harmonic series is $\ln 2$.]

   (b) Give upper and lower bounds on the total distance that the bug has traveled when it finally stops. [*Hint:* Use inequality (2) of Section 9.4.]

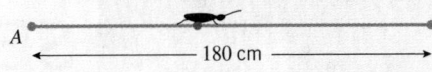

▲ Figure Ex-4

5. In Section 6.6 we defined the kinetic energy K of a particle with mass m and velocity v to be $K = \frac{1}{2}mv^2$ [see Formula (7) of that section]. In this formula the mass m is assumed to be constant, and K is called the **Newtonian kinetic energy**. However, in Albert Einstein's relativity theory the mass m increases with the velocity and the kinetic energy K is given by the formula
$$K = m_0c^2\left[\frac{1}{\sqrt{1 - (v/c)^2}} - 1\right]$$
   in which m_0 is the mass of the particle when its velocity is zero, and c is the speed of light. This is called the **relativistic kinetic energy**. Use an appropriate binomial series to show that if the velocity is small compared to the speed of light (i.e., $v/c \approx 0$), then the Newtonian and relativistic kinetic energies are in close agreement.

6. In Section 8.4 we studied the motion of a falling object that has mass m and is retarded by air resistance. We showed that if the initial velocity is v_0 and the drag force F_R is proportional to the velocity, that is, $F_R = -cv$, then the velocity of the object at time t is
$$v(t) = e^{-ct/m}\left(v_0 + \frac{mg}{c}\right) - \frac{mg}{c}$$
   where g is the acceleration due to gravity [see Formula (16) of Section 8.4].

   (a) Use a Maclaurin series to show that if $ct/m \approx 0$, then the velocity can be approximated as
$$v(t) \approx v_0 - \left(\frac{cv_0}{m} + g\right)t$$

   (b) Improve on the approximation in part (a).

 ## EXPANDING THE CALCULUS HORIZON

To learn how ecologists use mathematical models based on the process of iteration to study the growth and decline of animal populations, see the module entitled **Iteration and Dynamical Systems** at:

www.wiley.com/college/anton

Dwight R. Kuhn

10

PARAMETRIC AND POLAR CURVES; CONIC SECTIONS

In this chapter we will study alternative ways of expressing curves in the plane. We will begin by studying parametric curves: curves described in terms of component functions. This study will include methods for finding tangent lines to parametric curves. We will then introduce polar coordinate systems and discuss methods for finding tangent lines to polar curves, arc length of polar curves, and areas enclosed by polar curves. Our attention will then turn to a review of the basic properties of conic sections: parabolas, ellipses, and hyperbolas. Finally, we will consider conic sections in the context of polar coordinates and discuss some applications in astronomy.

Mathematical curves, such as the spirals in the center of a sunflower, can be described conveniently using ideas developed in this chapter.

10.1 PARAMETRIC EQUATIONS; TANGENT LINES AND ARC LENGTH FOR PARAMETRIC CURVES

Graphs of functions must pass the vertical line test, a limitation that excludes curves with self-intersections or even such basic curves as circles. In this section we will study an alternative method for describing curves algebraically that is not subject to the severe restriction of the vertical line test. We will then derive formulas required to find slopes, tangent lines, and arc lengths of these parametric curves. We will conclude with an investigation of a classic parametric curve known as the cycloid.

■ PARAMETRIC EQUATIONS

Suppose that a particle moves along a curve C in the xy-plane in such a way that its x- and y-coordinates, as functions of time, are

$$x = f(t), \quad y = g(t)$$

We call these the ***parametric equations*** of motion for the particle and refer to C as the ***trajectory*** of the particle or the ***graph*** of the equations (Figure 10.1.1). The variable t is called the ***parameter*** for the equations.

A moving particle with trajectory C

▲ **Figure 10.1.1**

▶ **Example 1** Sketch the trajectory over the time interval $0 \leq t \leq 10$ of the particle whose parametric equations of motion are

$$x = t - 3\sin t, \quad y = 4 - 3\cos t \tag{1}$$

Solution. One way to sketch the trajectory is to choose a representative succession of times, plot the (x, y) coordinates of points on the trajectory at those times, and connect the points with a smooth curve. The trajectory in Figure 10.1.2 was obtained in this way from the data in Table 10.1.1 in which the approximate coordinates of the particle are given at time increments of 1 unit. Observe that there is no t-axis in the picture; the values of t appear only as labels on the plotted points, and even these are usually omitted unless it is important to emphasize the locations of the particle at specific times. ◄

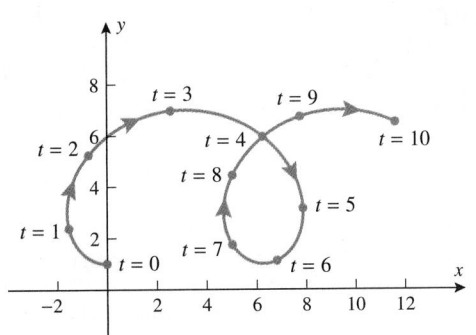

▲ **Figure 10.1.2**

Table 10.1.1

t	x	y
0	0.0	1.0
1	−1.5	2.4
2	−0.7	5.2
3	2.6	7.0
4	6.3	6.0
5	7.9	3.1
6	6.8	1.1
7	5.0	1.7
8	5.0	4.4
9	7.8	6.7
10	11.6	6.5

Although parametric equations commonly arise in problems of motion with time as the parameter, they arise in other contexts as well. Thus, unless the problem dictates that the parameter t in the equations

$$x = f(t), \quad y = g(t)$$

represents time, it should be viewed simply as an independent variable that varies over some interval of real numbers. (In fact, there is no need to use the letter t for the parameter; any letter not reserved for another purpose can be used.) If no restrictions on the parameter are stated explicitly or implied by the equations, then it is understood that it varies from $-\infty$ to $+\infty$. To indicate that a parameter t is restricted to an interval $[a, b]$, we will write

$$x = f(t), \quad y = g(t) \qquad (a \le t \le b)$$

► **Example 2** Find the graph of the parametric equations

$$x = \cos t, \quad y = \sin t \qquad (0 \le t \le 2\pi) \tag{2}$$

Solution. One way to find the graph is to eliminate the parameter t by noting that

$$x^2 + y^2 = \sin^2 t + \cos^2 t = 1$$

Thus, the graph is contained in the unit circle $x^2 + y^2 = 1$. Geometrically, the parameter t can be interpreted as the angle swept out by the radial line from the origin to the point $(x, y) = (\cos t, \sin t)$ on the unit circle (Figure 10.1.3). As t increases from 0 to 2π, the point traces the circle counterclockwise, starting at $(1, 0)$ when $t = 0$ and completing one full revolution when $t = 2\pi$. One can obtain different portions of the circle by varying the interval over which the parameter varies. For example,

$$x = \cos t, \quad y = \sin t \qquad (0 \le t \le \pi) \tag{3}$$

represents just the upper semicircle in Figure 10.1.3. ◄

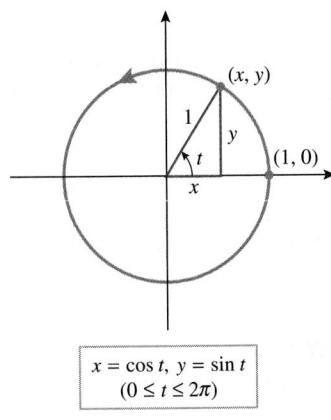

$x = \cos t, y = \sin t$
$(0 \le t \le 2\pi)$

▲ **Figure 10.1.3**

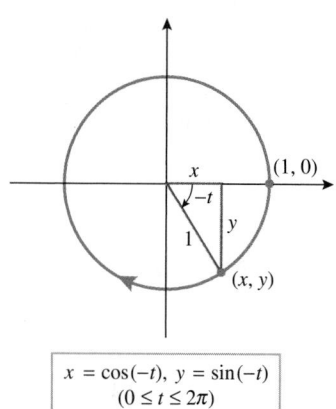

$$x = \cos(-t), \; y = \sin(-t)$$
$$(0 \le t \le 2\pi)$$

▲ **Figure 10.1.4**

■ ORIENTATION

The direction in which the graph of a pair of parametric equations is traced as the parameter increases is called the ***direction of increasing parameter*** or sometimes the ***orientation*** imposed on the curve by the equations. Thus, we make a distinction between a ***curve***, which is a set of points, and a ***parametric curve***, which is a curve with an orientation imposed on it by a set of parametric equations. For example, we saw in Example 2 that the circle represented parametrically by (2) is traced counterclockwise as t increases and hence has *counterclockwise orientation*. As shown in Figures 10.1.2 and 10.1.3, the orientation of a parametric curve can be indicated by arrowheads.

To obtain parametric equations for the unit circle with *clockwise orientation*, we can replace t by $-t$ in (2) and use the identities $\cos(-t) = \cos t$ and $\sin(-t) = -\sin t$. This yields

$$x = \cos t, \quad y = -\sin t \qquad (0 \le t \le 2\pi)$$

Here, the circle is traced clockwise by a point that starts at $(1, 0)$ when $t = 0$ and completes one full revolution when $t = 2\pi$ (Figure 10.1.4).

TECHNOLOGY MASTERY | When parametric equations are graphed using a calculator, the orientation can often be determined by watching the direction in which the graph is traced on the screen. However, many computers graph so fast that it is often hard to discern the orientation. See if you can use your graphing utility to confirm that (3) has a counterclockwise orientation.

▶ **Example 3** Graph the parametric curve

$$x = 2t - 3, \quad y = 6t - 7$$

by eliminating the parameter, and indicate the orientation on the graph.

Solution. To eliminate the parameter we will solve the first equation for t as a function of x, and then substitute this expression for t into the second equation:

$$t = \left(\tfrac{1}{2}\right)(x + 3)$$
$$y = 6\left(\tfrac{1}{2}\right)(x + 3) - 7$$
$$y = 3x + 2$$

Thus, the graph is a line of slope 3 and y-intercept 2. To find the orientation we must look to the original equations; the direction of increasing t can be deduced by observing that x increases as t increases *or* by observing that y increases as t increases. Either piece of information tells us that the line is traced left to right as shown in Figure 10.1.5. ◀

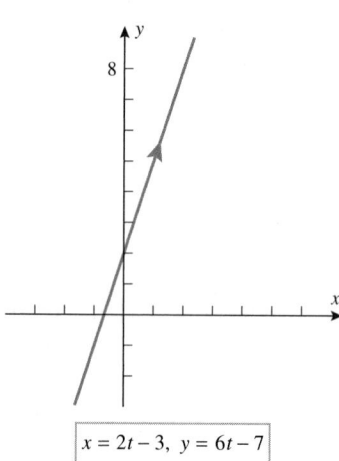

$$x = 2t - 3, \; y = 6t - 7$$

▲ **Figure 10.1.5**

REMARK | Not all parametric equations produce curves with definite orientations; if the equations are badly behaved, then the point tracing the curve may leap around sporadically or move back and forth, failing to determine a definite direction. For example, if

$$x = \sin t, \quad y = \sin^2 t$$

then the point (x, y) moves along the parabola $y = x^2$. However, the value of x varies periodically between -1 and 1, so the point (x, y) moves periodically back and forth along the parabola between the points $(-1, 1)$ and $(1, 1)$ (as shown in Figure 10.1.6). Later in the text we will discuss restrictions that eliminate such erratic behavior, but for now we will just avoid such complications.

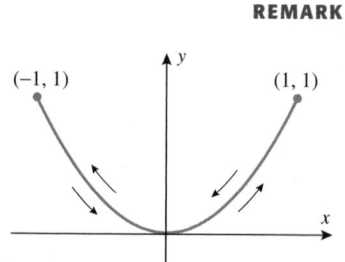

▲ **Figure 10.1.6**

■ EXPRESSING ORDINARY FUNCTIONS PARAMETRICALLY

An equation $y = f(x)$ can be expressed in parametric form by introducing the parameter $t = x$; this yields the parametric equations

$$x = t, \quad y = f(t)$$

For example, the portion of the curve $y = \cos x$ over the interval $[-2\pi, 2\pi]$ can be expressed parametrically as

$$x = t, \quad y = \cos t \quad (-2\pi \le t \le 2\pi)$$

(Figure 10.1.7).

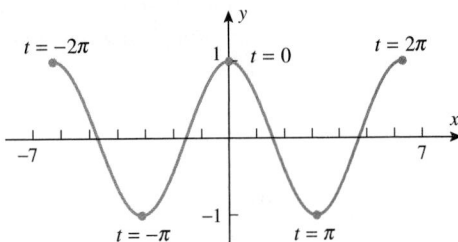

▶ **Figure 10.1.7**

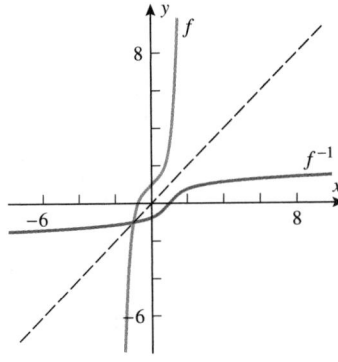

▲ **Figure 10.1.8**

If a function f is one-to-one, then it has an inverse function f^{-1}. In this case the equation $y = f^{-1}(x)$ is equivalent to $x = f(y)$. We can express the graph of f^{-1} in parametric form by introducing the parameter $y = t$; this yields the parametric equations

$$x = f(t), \quad y = t$$

For example, Figure 10.1.8 shows the graph of $f(x) = x^5 + x + 1$ and its inverse. The graph of f can be repesented parametrically as

$$x = t, \quad y = t^5 + t + 1$$

and the graph of f^{-1} can be represented parametrically as

$$x = t^5 + t + 1, \quad y = t$$

■ TANGENT LINES TO PARAMETRIC CURVES

We will be concerned with curves that are given by parametric equations

$$x = f(t), \quad y = g(t)$$

in which $f(t)$ and $g(t)$ have continuous first derivatives with respect to t. It can be proved that if $dx/dt \ne 0$, then y is a differentiable function of x, in which case the chain rule implies that

$$\frac{dy}{dx} = \frac{dy/dt}{dx/dt} \tag{4}$$

This formula makes it possible to find dy/dx directly from the parametric equations without eliminating the parameter.

▶ **Example 4** Find the slope of the tangent line to the unit circle

$$x = \cos t, \quad y = \sin t \quad (0 \le t \le 2\pi)$$

at the point where $t = \pi/6$ (Figure 10.1.9).

Solution. From (4), the slope at a general point on the circle is

$$\frac{dy}{dx} = \frac{dy/dt}{dx/dt} = \frac{\cos t}{-\sin t} = -\cot t \tag{5}$$

Thus, the slope at $t = \pi/6$ is

$$\left. \frac{dy}{dx} \right|_{t=\pi/6} = -\cot \frac{\pi}{6} = -\sqrt{3} \quad ◀$$

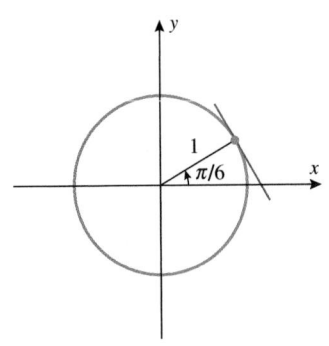

▲ **Figure 10.1.9**

Note that Formula (5) makes sense geometrically because the radius from the origin to the point $P(\cos t, \sin t)$ has slope $m = \tan t$. Thus the tangent line at P, being perpendicular to the radius, has slope

$$-\frac{1}{m} = -\frac{1}{\tan t} = -\cot t$$

(Figure 10.1.10).

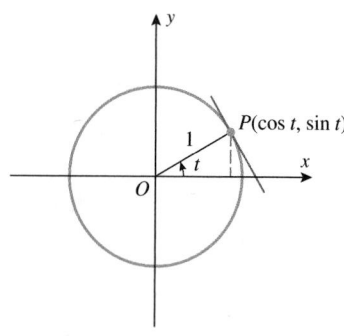

Radius OP has slope $m = \tan t$.

▲ **Figure 10.1.10**

Stanislovas Kairys/iStockphoto
The complicated motion of a paper airplane is best described mathematically using parametric equations.

It follows from Formula (4) that the tangent line to a parametric curve will be horizontal at those points where $dy/dt = 0$ and $dx/dt \neq 0$, since $dy/dx = 0$ at such points. Two different situations occur when $dx/dt = 0$. At points where $dx/dt = 0$ and $dy/dt \neq 0$, the right side of (4) has a nonzero numerator and a zero denominator; we will agree that the curve has **infinite slope** and a **vertical tangent line** at such points. At points where dx/dt and dy/dt are both zero, the right side of (4) becomes an indeterminate form; we call such points **singular points**. No general statement can be made about the behavior of parametric curves at singular points; they must be analyzed case by case.

▶ **Example 5** In a disastrous first flight, an experimental paper airplane follows the trajectory of the particle in Example 1:

$$x = t - 3\sin t, \quad y = 4 - 3\cos t \quad (t \geq 0)$$

but crashes into a wall at time $t = 10$ (Figure 10.1.11).

(a) At what times was the airplane flying horizontally?

(b) At what times was it flying vertically?

Solution (a). The airplane was flying horizontally at those times when $dy/dt = 0$ and $dx/dt \neq 0$. From the given trajectory we have

$$\frac{dy}{dt} = 3\sin t \quad \text{and} \quad \frac{dx}{dt} = 1 - 3\cos t \tag{6}$$

Setting $dy/dt = 0$ yields the equation $3\sin t = 0$, or, more simply, $\sin t = 0$. This equation has four solutions in the time interval $0 \leq t \leq 10$:

$$t = 0, \quad t = \pi, \quad t = 2\pi, \quad t = 3\pi$$

Since $dx/dt = 1 - 3\cos t \neq 0$ for these values of t (verify), the airplane was flying horizontally at times

$$t = 0, \quad t = \pi \approx 3.14, \quad t = 2\pi \approx 6.28, \quad \text{and} \quad t = 3\pi \approx 9.42$$

which is consistent with Figure 10.1.11.

Solution (b). The airplane was flying vertically at those times when $dx/dt = 0$ and $dy/dt \neq 0$. Setting $dx/dt = 0$ in (6) yields the equation

$$1 - 3\cos t = 0 \quad \text{or} \quad \cos t = \tfrac{1}{3}$$

This equation has three solutions in the time interval $0 \leq t \leq 10$ (Figure 10.1.12):

$$t = \cos^{-1}\tfrac{1}{3}, \quad t = 2\pi - \cos^{-1}\tfrac{1}{3}, \quad t = 2\pi + \cos^{-1}\tfrac{1}{3}$$

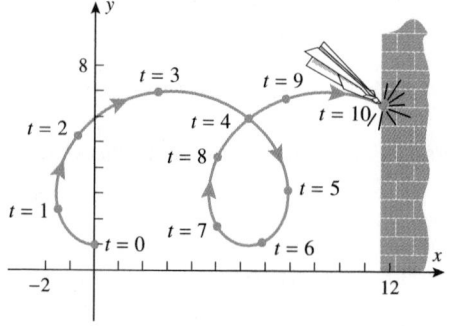

▲ **Figure 10.1.11**

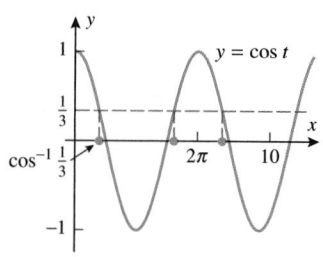

▲ **Figure 10.1.12**

Since $dy/dt = 3 \sin t$ is not zero at these points (why?), it follows that the airplane was flying vertically at times

$$t = \cos^{-1} \tfrac{1}{3} \approx 1.23, \quad t \approx 2\pi - 1.23 \approx 5.05, \quad t \approx 2\pi + 1.23 \approx 7.51$$

which again is consistent with Figure 10.1.11. ◄

▶ **Example 6** The curve represented by the parametric equations

$$x = t^2, \quad y = t^3 \qquad (-\infty < t < +\infty)$$

is called a *semicubical parabola*. The parameter t can be eliminated by cubing x and squaring y, from which it follows that $y^2 = x^3$. The graph of this equation, shown in Figure 10.1.13, consists of two branches: an upper branch obtained by graphing $y = x^{3/2}$ and a lower branch obtained by graphing $y = -x^{3/2}$. The two branches meet at the origin, which corresponds to $t = 0$ in the parametric equations. This is a singular point because the derivatives $dx/dt = 2t$ and $dy/dt = 3t^2$ are both zero there. ◄

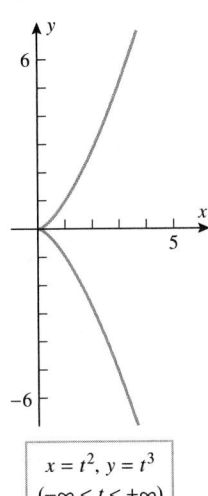

$$x = t^2, \, y = t^3$$
$$(-\infty < t < +\infty)$$

▲ **Figure 10.1.13**

▶ **Example 7** Without eliminating the parameter, find dy/dx and d^2y/dx^2 at $(1, 1)$ and $(1, -1)$ on the semicubical parabola given by the parametric equations in Example 6.

Solution. From (4) we have

$$\frac{dy}{dx} = \frac{dy/dt}{dx/dt} = \frac{3t^2}{2t} = \frac{3}{2}t \qquad (t \neq 0) \tag{7}$$

and from (4) applied to $y' = dy/dx$ we have

$$\frac{d^2y}{dx^2} = \frac{dy'}{dx} = \frac{dy'/dt}{dx/dt} = \frac{3/2}{2t} = \frac{3}{4t} \tag{8}$$

Since the point $(1, 1)$ on the curve corresponds to $t = 1$ in the parametric equations, it follows from (7) and (8) that

$$\left.\frac{dy}{dx}\right|_{t=1} = \frac{3}{2} \quad \text{and} \quad \left.\frac{d^2y}{dx^2}\right|_{t=1} = \frac{3}{4}$$

Similarly, the point $(1, -1)$ corresponds to $t = -1$ in the parametric equations, so applying (7) and (8) again yields

$$\left.\frac{dy}{dx}\right|_{t=-1} = -\frac{3}{2} \quad \text{and} \quad \left.\frac{d^2y}{dx^2}\right|_{t=-1} = -\frac{3}{4}$$

Note that the values we obtained for the first and second derivatives are consistent with the graph in Figure 10.1.13, since at $(1, 1)$ on the upper branch the tangent line has positive slope and the curve is concave up, and at $(1, -1)$ on the lower branch the tangent line has negative slope and the curve is concave down.

Finally, observe that we were able to apply Formulas (7) and (8) for both $t = 1$ and $t = -1$, even though the points $(1, 1)$ and $(1, -1)$ lie on different branches. In contrast, had we chosen to perform the same computations by eliminating the parameter, we would have had to obtain separate derivative formulas for $y = x^{3/2}$ and $y = -x^{3/2}$. ◄

WARNING

Although it is true that

$$\frac{dy}{dx} = \frac{dy/dt}{dx/dt}$$

you cannot conclude that d^2y/dx^2 is the quotient of d^2y/dt^2 and d^2x/dt^2. To illustrate that this conclusion is erroneous, show that for the parametric curve in Example 7,

$$\left.\frac{d^2y}{dx^2}\right|_{t=1} \neq \left.\frac{d^2y/dt^2}{d^2x/dt^2}\right|_{t=1}$$

■ **ARC LENGTH OF PARAMETRIC CURVES**

The following result provides a formula for finding the arc length of a curve from parametric equations for the curve. Its derivation is similar to that of Formula (3) in Section 6.4 and will be omitted.

Formulas (4) and (5) in Section 6.4 can be viewed as special cases of (9). For example, Formula (4) in Section 6.4 can be obtained from (9) by writing $y = f(x)$ parametrically as

$$x = t, \quad y = f(t)$$

and Formula (5) in Section 6.4 can be obtained by writing $x = g(y)$ parametrically as

$$x = g(t), \quad y = t$$

10.1.1   ARC LENGTH FORMULA FOR PARAMETRIC CURVES   If no segment of the curve represented by the parametric equations

$$x = x(t), \quad y = y(t) \quad (a \le t \le b)$$

is traced more than once as t increases from a to b, and if dx/dt and dy/dt are continuous functions for $a \le t \le b$, then the arc length L of the curve is given by

$$L = \int_a^b \sqrt{\left(\frac{dx}{dt}\right)^2 + \left(\frac{dy}{dt}\right)^2}\, dt \tag{9}$$

▶ **Example 8**   Use (9) to find the circumference of a circle of radius a from the parametric equations

$$x = a\cos t, \quad y = a\sin t \quad (0 \le t \le 2\pi)$$

Solution.

$$L = \int_0^{2\pi} \sqrt{\left(\frac{dx}{dt}\right)^2 + \left(\frac{dy}{dt}\right)^2}\, dt = \int_0^{2\pi} \sqrt{(-a\sin t)^2 + (a\cos t)^2}\, dt$$

$$= \int_0^{2\pi} a\, dt = at\Big]_0^{2\pi} = 2\pi a \blacktriangleleft$$

■ **THE CYCLOID (THE APPLE OF DISCORD)**

The results of this section can be used to investigate a curve known as a *cycloid*. This curve, which is one of the most significant in the history of mathematics, can be generated by a point on a circle that rolls along a straight line (Figure 10.1.14). This curve has a fascinating history, which we will discuss shortly; but first we will show how to obtain parametric equations for it. For this purpose, let us assume that the circle has radius a and rolls along the positive x-axis of a rectangular coordinate system. Let $P(x, y)$ be the point on the circle that traces the cycloid, and assume that P is initially at the origin. We will take as our parameter the angle θ that is swept out by the radial line to P as the circle rolls (Figure 10.1.14). It is standard here to regard θ as positive, even though it is generated by a clockwise rotation.

The motion of P is a combination of the movement of the circle's center parallel to the x-axis and the rotation of P about the center. As the radial line sweeps out an angle θ, the point P traverses an arc of length $a\theta$, and the circle moves a distance $a\theta$ along the x-axis. Thus, as suggested by Figure 10.1.15, the center moves to the point $(a\theta, a)$, and the coordinates of P are

$$x = a\theta - a\sin\theta, \quad y = a - a\cos\theta \tag{10}$$

These are the equations of the cycloid in terms of the parameter θ.

One of the reasons the cycloid is important in the history of mathematics is that the study of its properties helped to spur the development of early versions of differentiation and integration. Work on the cycloid was carried out by some of the most famous names in seventeenth century mathematics, including Johann and Jakob Bernoulli, Descartes, L'Hôpital, Newton, and Leibniz. The curve was named the "cycloid" by the Italian mathematician and astronomer, Galileo, who spent over 40 years investigating its properties. An early problem of interest was that of constructing tangent lines to the cycloid. This problem was first solved by Descartes, and then by Fermat, whom Descartes had challenged with the question. A modern solution to this problem follows directly from the parametric equations (10) and Formula (4). For example, using Formula (4), it is straightforward to show that the x-intercepts of the cycloid are cusps and that there is a horizontal tangent line to the cycloid halfway between adjacent x-intercepts (Exercise 60).

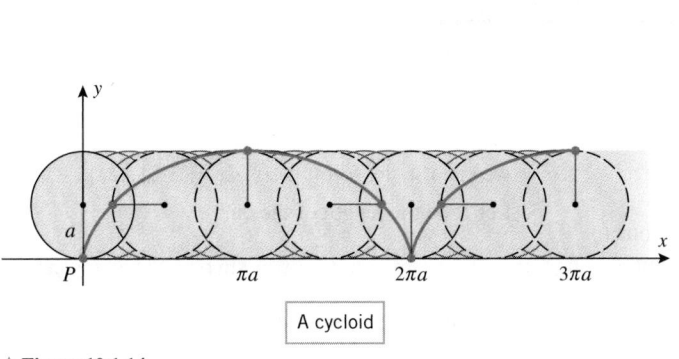

A cycloid

▲ **Figure 10.1.14**

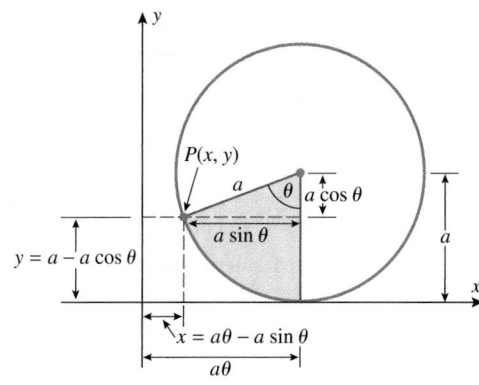

▲ **Figure 10.1.15**

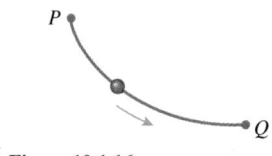

▲ **Figure 10.1.16**

Another early problem was determining the arc length of an arch of the cycloid. This was solved in 1658 by the famous British architect and mathematician, Sir Christopher Wren. He showed that the arc length of one arch of the cycloid is exactly eight times the radius of the generating circle. [For a solution to this problem using Formula (9), see Exercise 71.]

The cycloid is also important historically because it provides the solution to two famous mathematical problems—the ***brachistochrone problem*** (from Greek words meaning "shortest time") and the ***tautochrone problem*** (from Greek words meaning "equal time"). The brachistochrone problem is to determine the shape of a wire along which a bead might slide from a point P to another point Q, not directly below, in the *shortest time*. The tautochrone problem is to find the shape of a wire from P to Q such that two beads started at any points on the wire between P and Q reach Q in the *same amount of time*. The solution to both problems turns out to be an inverted cycloid (Figure 10.1.16).

In June of 1696, Johann Bernoulli posed the brachistochrone problem in the form of a challenge to other mathematicians. At first, one might conjecture that the wire should form a straight line, since that shape results in the shortest distance from P to Q. However, the inverted cycloid allows the bead to fall more rapidly at first, building up sufficient speed to reach Q in the shortest time, even though it travels a longer distance. The problem was solved by Newton, Leibniz, and L'Hôpital, as well as by Johann Bernoulli and his older brother Jakob; it was formulated and solved *incorrectly* years earlier by Galileo, who thought the answer was a circular arc. In fact, Johann was so impressed with his brother Jakob's solution that he claimed it to be his own. (This was just one of many disputes about the cycloid that eventually led to the curve being known as the "apple of discord.") One solution of the brachistochrone problem leads to the differential equation

$$\left(1 + \left(\frac{dy}{dx}\right)^2\right) y = 2a \tag{11}$$

where a is a positive constant. We leave it as an exercise (Exercise 72) to show that the cycloid provides a solution to this differential equation.

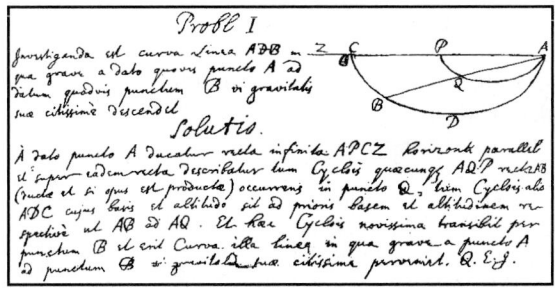

Newton's solution of the brachistochrone problem in his own handwriting

✔ QUICK CHECK EXERCISES 10.1   *(See page 705 for answers.)*

1. Find parametric equations for a circle of radius 2, centered at $(3, 5)$.

2. The graph of the curve described by the parametric equations $x = 4t - 1$, $y = 3t + 2$ is a straight line with slope _____ and y-intercept _____.

3. Suppose that a parametric curve C is given by the equations $x = f(t)$, $y = g(t)$ for $0 \leq t \leq 1$. Find parametric equations for C that reverse the direction the curve is traced as the parameter increases from 0 to 1.

4. To find dy/dx directly from the parametric equations

$$x = f(t), \quad y = g(t)$$

we can use the formula $dy/dx =$ _____.

5. Let L be the length of the curve

$$x = \ln t, \quad y = \sin t \quad (1 \leq t \leq \pi)$$

An integral expression for L is _____.

EXERCISE SET 10.1    Graphing Utility   CAS

1. (a) By eliminating the parameter, sketch the trajectory over the time interval $0 \leq t \leq 5$ of the particle whose parametric equations of motion are

$$x = t - 1, \quad y = t + 1$$

 (b) Indicate the direction of motion on your sketch.
 (c) Make a table of x- and y-coordinates of the particle at times $t = 0, 1, 2, 3, 4, 5$.
 (d) Mark the position of the particle on the curve at the times in part (c), and label those positions with the values of t.

 **Johann** (left) **and Jakob** (right) **Bernoulli** Members of an amazing Swiss family that included several generations of outstanding mathematicians and scientists. Nikolaus Bernoulli (1623–1708), a druggist, fled from Antwerp to escape religious persecution and ultimately settled in Basel, Switzerland. There he had three sons, Jakob I (also called Jacques or James), Nikolaus, and Johann I (also called Jean or John). The Roman numerals are used to distinguish family members with identical names (see the family tree below). Following Newton and Leibniz, the Bernoulli brothers, Jakob I and Johann I, are considered by some to be the two most important founders of calculus. Jakob I was self-taught in mathematics. His father wanted him to study for the ministry, but he turned to mathematics and in 1686 became a professor at the University of Basel. When he started working in mathematics, he knew nothing of Newton's and Leibniz' work. He eventually became familiar with Newton's results, but because so little of Leibniz' work was published, Jakob duplicated many of Leibniz' results.

Jakob's younger brother Johann I was urged to enter into business by his father. Instead, he turned to medicine and studied mathematics under the guidance of his older brother. He eventually became a mathematics professor at Gröningen in Holland, and then, when Jakob died in 1705, Johann succeeded him as mathematics professor at Basel. Throughout their lives, Jakob I and Johann I had a mutual passion for criticizing each other's work, which frequently erupted into ugly confrontations. Leibniz tried to mediate the disputes, but Jakob, who resented Leibniz' superior intellect, accused him of siding with Johann, and thus Leibniz became entangled in the arguments. The brothers often worked on common problems that they posed as challenges to one another. Johann, interested in gaining fame, often used unscrupulous means to make himself appear the originator of his brother's results; Jakob occasionally retaliated. Thus, it is often difficult to determine who deserves credit for many results. However, both men made major contributions

to the development of calculus. In addition to his work on calculus, Jakob helped establish fundamental principles in probability, including the Law of Large Numbers, which is a cornerstone of modern probability theory.

Among the other members of the Bernoulli family, Daniel, son of Johann I, is the most famous. He was a professor of mathematics at St. Petersburg Academy in Russia and subsequently a professor of anatomy and then physics at Basel. He did work in calculus and probability, but is best known for his work in physics. A basic law of fluid flow, called Bernoulli's principle, is named in his honor. He won the annual prize of the French Academy 10 times for work on vibrating strings, tides of the sea, and kinetic theory of gases.

Johann II succeeded his father as professor of mathematics at Basel. His research was on the theory of heat and sound. Nikolaus I was a mathematician and law scholar who worked on probability and series. On the recommendation of Leibniz, he was appointed professor of mathematics at Padua and then went to Basel as a professor of logic and then law. Nikolaus II was professor of jurisprudence in Switzerland and then professor of mathematics at St. Petersburg Academy. Johann III was a professor of mathematics and astronomy in Berlin and Jakob II succeeded his uncle Daniel as professor of mathematics at St. Petersburg Academy in Russia. Truly an incredible family!

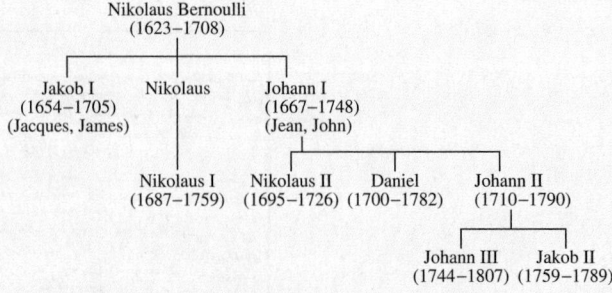

2. (a) By eliminating the parameter, sketch the trajectory over the time interval $0 \leq t \leq 1$ of the particle whose parametric equations of motion are

$$x = \cos(\pi t), \quad y = \sin(\pi t)$$

(b) Indicate the direction of motion on your sketch.

(c) Make a table of x- and y-coordinates of the particle at times $t = 0, 0.25, 0.5, 0.75, 1$.

(d) Mark the position of the particle on the curve at the times in part (c), and label those positions with the values of t.

3–12 Sketch the curve by eliminating the parameter, and indicate the direction of increasing t. ◼

3. $x = 3t - 4, \; y = 6t + 2$

4. $x = t - 3, \; y = 3t - 7 \quad (0 \leq t \leq 3)$

5. $x = 2\cos t, \; y = 5\sin t \quad (0 \leq t \leq 2\pi)$

6. $x = \sqrt{t}, \; y = 2t + 4$

7. $x = 3 + 2\cos t, \; y = 2 + 4\sin t \quad (0 \leq t \leq 2\pi)$

8. $x = \sec t, \; y = \tan t \quad (\pi \leq t < 3\pi/2)$

9. $x = \cos 2t, \; y = \sin t \quad (-\pi/2 \leq t \leq \pi/2)$

10. $x = 4t + 3, \; y = 16t^2 - 9$

11. $x = 2\sin^2 t, \; y = 3\cos^2 t \quad (0 \leq t \leq \pi/2)$

12. $x = \sec^2 t, \; y = \tan^2 t \quad (0 \leq t < \pi/2)$

13–18 Find parametric equations for the curve, and check your work by generating the curve with a graphing utility. ◼

13. A circle of radius 5, centered at the origin, oriented clockwise.

14. The portion of the circle $x^2 + y^2 = 1$ that lies in the third quadrant, oriented counterclockwise.

15. A vertical line intersecting the x-axis at $x = 2$, oriented upward.

16. The ellipse $x^2/4 + y^2/9 = 1$, oriented counterclockwise.

17. The portion of the parabola $x = y^2$ joining $(1, -1)$ and $(1, 1)$, oriented down to up.

18. The circle of radius 4, centered at $(1, -3)$, oriented counterclockwise.

19. (a) Use a graphing utility to generate the trajectory of a particle whose equations of motion over the time interval $0 \leq t \leq 5$ are

$$x = 6t - \tfrac{1}{2}t^3, \quad y = 1 + \tfrac{1}{2}t^2$$

(b) Make a table of x- and y-coordinates of the particle at times $t = 0, 1, 2, 3, 4, 5$.

(c) At what times is the particle on the y-axis?

(d) During what time interval is $y < 5$?

(e) At what time does the x-coordinate of the particle reach a maximum?

20. (a) Use a graphing utility to generate the trajectory of a paper airplane whose equations of motion for $t \geq 0$ are

$$x = t - 2\sin t, \quad y = 3 - 2\cos t$$

(b) Assuming that the plane flies in a room in which the floor is at $y = 0$, explain why the plane will not crash into the floor. [For simplicity, ignore the physical size of the plane by treating it as a particle.]

(c) How high must the ceiling be to ensure that the plane does not touch or crash into it?

21–22 Graph the equation using a graphing utility. ◼

21. (a) $x = y^2 + 2y + 1$
(b) $x = \sin y, \; -2\pi \leq y \leq 2\pi$

22. (a) $x = y + 2y^3 - y^5$
(b) $x = \tan y, \; -\pi/2 < y < \pi/2$

FOCUS ON CONCEPTS

23. In each part, match the parametric equation with one of the curves labeled (I)–(VI), and explain your reasoning.
(a) $x = \sqrt{t}, \; y = \sin 3t$ (b) $x = 2\cos t, \; y = 3\sin t$
(c) $x = t\cos t, \; y = t\sin t$

(d) $x = \dfrac{3t}{1 + t^3}, \; y = \dfrac{3t^2}{1 + t^3}$

(e) $x = \dfrac{t^3}{1 + t^2}, \; y = \dfrac{2t^2}{1 + t^2}$

(f) $x = \tfrac{1}{2}\cos t, \; y = \sin 2t$

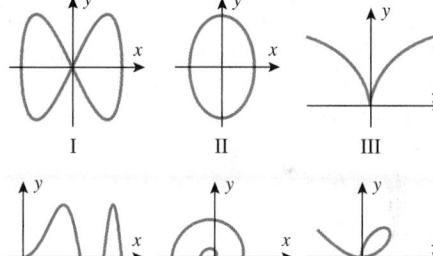

I   II   III

IV   V   VI

▲ **Figure Ex-23**

24. (a) Identify the orientation of the curves in Exercise 23.
(b) Explain why the parametric curve

$$x = t^2, \quad y = t^4 \quad (-1 \leq t \leq 1)$$

does not have a definite orientation.

25. (a) Suppose that the line segment from the point $P(x_0, y_0)$ to $Q(x_1, y_1)$ is represented parametrically by

$$x = x_0 + (x_1 - x_0)t,$$
$$y = y_0 + (y_1 - y_0)t \quad (0 \leq t \leq 1)$$

and that $R(x, y)$ is the point on the line segment corresponding to a specified value of t (see the accompanying figure on the next page). Show that $t = r/q$, where r is the distance from P to R and q is the distance from P to Q.

(cont.)

(b) What value of t produces the midpoint between points P and Q?

(c) What value of t produces the point that is three-fourths of the way from P to Q?

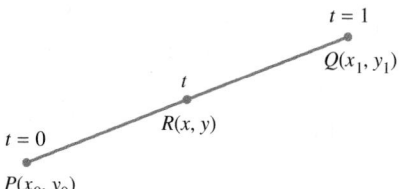

◀ **Figure Ex-25**

26. Find parametric equations for the line segment joining $P(2, -1)$ and $Q(3, 1)$, and use the result in Exercise 25 to find

(a) the midpoint between P and Q

(b) the point that is one-fourth of the way from P to Q

(c) the point that is three-fourths of the way from P to Q.

27. (a) Show that the line segment joining the points (x_0, y_0) and (x_1, y_1) can be represented parametrically as

$$x = x_0 + (x_1 - x_0)\frac{t - t_0}{t_1 - t_0},$$

$$y = y_0 + (y_1 - y_0)\frac{t - t_0}{t_1 - t_0} \quad (t_0 \le t \le t_1)$$

(b) Which way is the line segment oriented?

(c) Find parametric equations for the line segment traced from $(3, -1)$ to $(1, 4)$ as t varies from 1 to 2, and check your result with a graphing utility.

28. (a) By eliminating the parameter, show that if a and c are not both zero, then the graph of the parametric equations

$$x = at + b, \quad y = ct + d \quad (t_0 \le t \le t_1)$$

is a line segment.

(b) Sketch the parametric curve

$$x = 2t - 1, \quad y = t + 1 \quad (1 \le t \le 2)$$

and indicate its orientation.

(c) What can you say about the line in part (a) if a or c (but not both) is zero?

(d) What do the equations represent if a and c are both zero?

29–32 Use a graphing utility and parametric equations to display the graphs of f and f^{-1} on the same screen. ■

29. $f(x) = x^3 + 0.2x - 1, \quad -1 \le x \le 2$

30. $f(x) = \sqrt{x^2 + 2} + x, \quad -5 \le x \le 5$

31. $f(x) = \cos(\cos 0.5x), \quad 0 \le x \le 3$

32. $f(x) = x + \sin x, \quad 0 \le x \le 6$

33–36 True–False Determine whether the statement is true or false. Explain your answer. ■

33. The equation $y = 1 - x^2$ can be described parametrically by $x = \sin t$, $y = \cos^2 t$.

34. The graph of the parametric equations $x = f(t)$, $y = t$ is the reflection of the graph of $y = f(x)$ about the x-axis.

35. For the parametric curve $x = x(t)$, $y = 3t^4 - 2t^3$, the derivative of y with respect to x is computed by

$$\frac{dy}{dx} = \frac{12t^3 - 6t^2}{x'(t)}$$

36. The curve represented by the parametric equations

$$x = t^3, \quad y = t + t^6 \quad (-\infty < t < +\infty)$$

is concave down for $t < 0$.

37. Parametric curves can be defined piecewise by using different formulas for different values of the parameter. Sketch the curve that is represented piecewise by the parametric equations

$$\begin{cases} x = 2t, & y = 4t^2 & \left(0 \le t \le \tfrac{1}{2}\right) \\ x = 2 - 2t, & y = 2t & \left(\tfrac{1}{2} \le t \le 1\right) \end{cases}$$

38. Find parametric equations for the rectangle in the accompanying figure, assuming that the rectangle is traced counterclockwise as t varies from 0 to 1, starting at $\left(\tfrac{1}{2}, \tfrac{1}{2}\right)$ when $t = 0$. [*Hint:* Represent the rectangle piecewise, letting t vary from 0 to $\tfrac{1}{4}$ for the first edge, from $\tfrac{1}{4}$ to $\tfrac{1}{2}$ for the second edge, and so forth.]

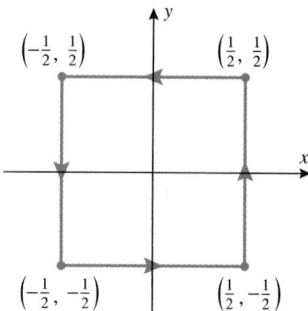

◀ **Figure Ex-38**

39. (a) Find parametric equations for the ellipse that is centered at the origin and has intercepts $(4, 0)$, $(-4, 0)$, $(0, 3)$, and $(0, -3)$.

(b) Find parametric equations for the ellipse that results by translating the ellipse in part (a) so that its center is at $(-1, 2)$.

(c) Confirm your results in parts (a) and (b) using a graphing utility.

40. We will show later in the text that if a projectile is fired from ground level with an initial speed of v_0 meters per second at an angle α with the horizontal, and if air resistance is neglected, then its position after t seconds, relative to the coordinate system in the accompanying figure on the next page is

$$x = (v_0 \cos \alpha)t, \quad y = (v_0 \sin \alpha)t - \tfrac{1}{2}gt^2$$

where $g \approx 9.8 \text{ m/s}^2$.

(a) By eliminating the parameter, show that the trajectory lies on the graph of a quadratic polynomial.

(b) Use a graphing utility to sketch the trajectory if $\alpha = 30°$ and $v_0 = 1000$ m/s.

(c) Using the trajectory in part (b), how high does the shell rise?

(cont.)

(d) Using the trajectory in part (b), how far does the shell travel horizontally?

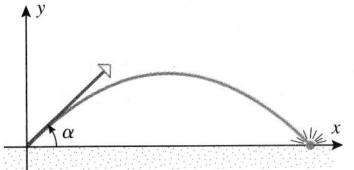

◀ **Figure Ex-40**

41. (a) Find the slope of the tangent line to the parametric curve $x = t/2$, $y = t^2 + 1$ at $t = -1$ and at $t = 1$ without eliminating the parameter.
   (b) Check your answers in part (a) by eliminating the parameter and differentiating an appropriate function of x.

42. (a) Find the slope of the tangent line to the parametric curve $x = 3\cos t$, $y = 4\sin t$ at $t = \pi/4$ and at $t = 7\pi/4$ without eliminating the parameter.
   (b) Check your answers in part (a) by eliminating the parameter and differentiating an appropriate function of x.

43. For the parametric curve in Exercise 41, make a conjecture about the sign of d^2y/dx^2 at $t = -1$ and at $t = 1$, and confirm your conjecture without eliminating the parameter.

44. For the parametric curve in Exercise 42, make a conjecture about the sign of d^2y/dx^2 at $t = \pi/4$ and at $t = 7\pi/4$, and confirm your conjecture without eliminating the parameter.

45–50 Find dy/dx and d^2y/dx^2 at the given point without eliminating the parameter. ■

45. $x = \sqrt{t}$, $y = 2t + 4$; $t = 1$

46. $x = \frac{1}{2}t^2 + 1$, $y = \frac{1}{3}t^3 - t$; $t = 2$

47. $x = \sec t$, $y = \tan t$; $t = \pi/3$

48. $x = \sinh t$, $y = \cosh t$; $t = 0$

49. $x = \theta + \cos\theta$, $y = 1 + \sin\theta$; $\theta = \pi/6$

50. $x = \cos\phi$, $y = 3\sin\phi$; $\phi = 5\pi/6$

51. (a) Find the equation of the tangent line to the curve
$$x = e^t, \quad y = e^{-t}$$
at $t = 1$ without eliminating the parameter.
   (b) Find the equation of the tangent line in part (a) by eliminating the parameter.

52. (a) Find the equation of the tangent line to the curve
$$x = 2t + 4, \quad y = 8t^2 - 2t + 4$$
at $t = 1$ without eliminating the parameter.
   (b) Find the equation of the tangent line in part (a) by eliminating the parameter.

53–54 Find all values of t at which the parametric curve has (a) a horizontal tangent line and (b) a vertical tangent line. ■

53. $x = 2\sin t$, $y = 4\cos t$ $(0 \leq t \leq 2\pi)$

54. $x = 2t^3 - 15t^2 + 24t + 7$, $y = t^2 + t + 1$

55. In the mid-1850s the French physicist Jules Antoine Lissajous (1822–1880) became interested in parametric equations of the form
$$x = \sin at, \quad y = \sin bt$$
in the course of studying vibrations that combine two perpendicular sinusoidal motions. If a/b is a rational number, then the combined effect of the oscillations is a periodic motion along a path called a *Lissajous curve*.
   (a) Use a graphing utility to generate the complete graph of the Lissajous curves corresponding to $a = 1, b = 2$; $a = 2, b = 3$; $a = 3, b = 4$; and $a = 4, b = 5$.
   (b) The Lissajous curve
$$x = \sin t, \quad y = \sin 2t \quad (0 \leq t \leq 2\pi)$$
crosses itself at the origin (see Figure Ex-55). Find equations for the two tangent lines at the origin.

56. The *prolate cycloid*
$$x = 2 - \pi\cos t, \quad y = 2t - \pi\sin t \quad (-\pi \leq t \leq \pi)$$
crosses itself at a point on the x-axis (see the accompanying figure). Find equations for the two tangent lines at that point.

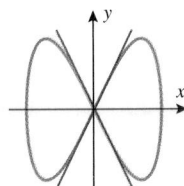

▲ **Figure Ex-55**   ▲ **Figure Ex-56**

57. Show that the curve $x = t^2$, $y = t^3 - 4t$ intersects itself at the point $(4, 0)$, and find equations for the two tangent lines to the curve at the point of intersection.

58. Show that the curve with parametric equations
$$x = t^2 - 3t + 5, \quad y = t^3 + t^2 - 10t + 9$$
intersects itself at the point $(3, 1)$, and find equations for the two tangent lines to the curve at the point of intersection.

59. (a) Use a graphing utility to generate the graph of the parametric curve
$$x = \cos^3 t, \quad y = \sin^3 t \quad (0 \leq t \leq 2\pi)$$
and make a conjecture about the values of t at which singular points occur.
   (b) Confirm your conjecture in part (a) by calculating appropriate derivatives.

60. Verify that the cycloid described by Formula (10) has cusps at its x-intercepts and horizontal tangent lines at midpoints between adjacent x-intercepts (see Figure 10.1.14).

61. (a) What is the slope of the tangent line at time t to the trajectory of the paper airplane in Example 5?

(b) What was the airplane's approximate angle of inclination when it crashed into the wall?

62. Suppose that a bee follows the trajectory

$$x = t - 2\cos t, \quad y = 2 - 2\sin t \quad (0 \le t \le 10)$$

(a) At what times was the bee flying horizontally?

(b) At what times was the bee flying vertically?

63. Consider the family of curves described by the parametric equations

$$x = a\cos t + h, \quad y = b\sin t + k \quad (0 \le t < 2\pi)$$

where $a \ne 0$ and $b \ne 0$. Describe the curves in this family if

(a) h and k are fixed but a and b can vary

(b) a and b are fixed but h and k can vary

(c) $a = 1$ and $b = 1$, but h and k vary so that $h = k + 1$.

64. (a) Use a graphing utility to study how the curves in the family

$$x = 2a\cos^2 t, \quad y = 2a\cos t \sin t \quad (-2\pi < t < 2\pi)$$

change as a varies from 0 to 5.

(b) Confirm your conclusion algebraically.

(c) Write a brief paragraph that describes your findings.

65–70 Find the exact arc length of the curve over the stated interval. ■

65. $x = t^2$, $y = \frac{1}{3}t^3$ $(0 \le t \le 1)$

66. $x = \sqrt{t} - 2$, $y = 2t^{3/4}$ $(1 \le t \le 16)$

67. $x = \cos 3t$, $y = \sin 3t$ $(0 \le t \le \pi)$

68. $x = \sin t + \cos t$, $y = \sin t - \cos t$ $(0 \le t \le \pi)$

69. $x = e^{2t}(\sin t + \cos t)$, $y = e^{2t}(\sin t - \cos t)$ $(-1 \le t \le 1)$

70. $x = 2\sin^{-1} t$, $y = \ln(1 - t^2)$ $\left(0 \le t \le \frac{1}{2}\right)$

71. (a) Use Formula (9) to show that the length L of one arch of a cycloid is given by

$$L = a \int_0^{2\pi} \sqrt{2(1 - \cos\theta)}\, d\theta$$

(b) Use a CAS to show that L is eight times the radius of the wheel that generates the cycloid (see the accompanying figure).

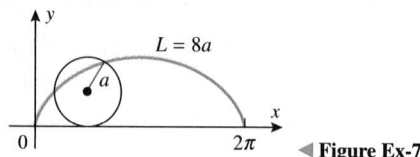

◄ **Figure Ex-71**

72. Use the parametric equations in Formula (10) to verify that the cycloid provides one solution to the differential equation

$$\left(1 + \left(\frac{dy}{dx}\right)^2\right) y = 2a$$

where a is a positive constant.

FOCUS ON CONCEPTS

73. The amusement park rides illustrated in the accompanying figure consist of two connected rotating arms of length 1—an inner arm that rotates counterclockwise at 1 radian per second and an outer arm that can be programmed to rotate either clockwise at 2 radians per second (the Scrambler ride) or counterclockwise at 2 radians per second (the Calypso ride). The center of the rider cage is at the end of the outer arm.

(a) Show that in the Scrambler ride the center of the cage has parametric equations

$$x = \cos t + \cos 2t, \quad y = \sin t - \sin 2t$$

(b) Find parametric equations for the center of the cage in the Calypso ride, and use a graphing utility to confirm that the center traces the curve shown in the accompanying figure.

(c) Do you think that a rider travels the same distance in one revolution of the Scrambler ride as in one revolution of the Calypso ride? Justify your conclusion.

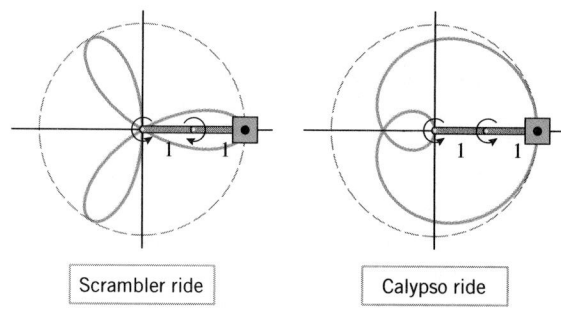

Scrambler ride   Calypso ride

▲ **Figure Ex-73**

74. (a) If a thread is unwound from a fixed circle while being held taut (i.e., tangent to the circle), then the end of the thread traces a curve called an ***involute of a circle***. Show that if the circle is centered at the origin, has radius a, and the end of the thread is initially at the point $(a, 0)$, then the involute can be expressed parametrically as

$$x = a(\cos\theta + \theta\sin\theta), \quad y = a(\sin\theta - \theta\cos\theta)$$

where θ is the angle shown in part (a) of the accompanying figure on the next page.

(b) Assuming that the dog in part (b) of the accompanying figure on the next page unwinds its leash while keeping it taut, for what values of θ in the interval $0 \le \theta \le 2\pi$ will the dog be walking North? South? East? West?

(c) Use a graphing utility to generate the curve traced by the dog, and show that it is consistent with your answer in part (b).

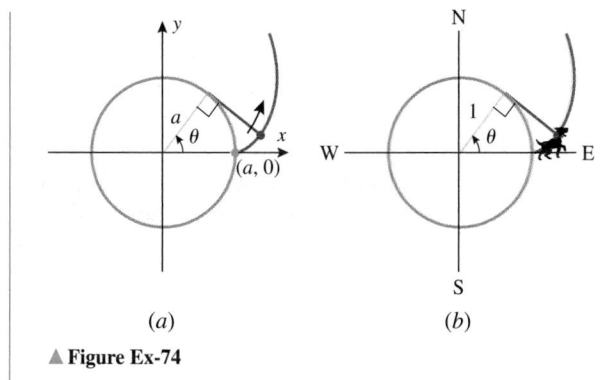

(a)   (b)

▲ **Figure Ex-74**

75–80 If $f'(t)$ and $g'(t)$ are continuous functions, and if no segment of the curve

$$x = f(t), \quad y = g(t) \quad (a \le t \le b)$$

is traced more than once, then it can be shown that the area of the surface generated by revolving this curve about the x-axis is

$$S = \int_a^b 2\pi y \sqrt{\left(\frac{dx}{dt}\right)^2 + \left(\frac{dy}{dt}\right)^2} \, dt$$

and the area of the surface generated by revolving the curve about the y-axis is

$$S = \int_a^b 2\pi x \sqrt{\left(\frac{dx}{dt}\right)^2 + \left(\frac{dy}{dt}\right)^2} \, dt$$

[The derivations are similar to those used to obtain Formulas (4) and (5) in Section 6.5.] Use the formulas above in these exercises. ■

75. Find the area of the surface generated by revolving $x = t^2$, $y = 3t$ ($0 \le t \le 2$) about the x-axis.

76. Find the area of the surface generated by revolving the curve $x = e^t \cos t$, $y = e^t \sin t$ ($0 \le t \le \pi/2$) about the x-axis.

77. Find the area of the surface generated by revolving the curve $x = \cos^2 t$, $y = \sin^2 t$ ($0 \le t \le \pi/2$) about the y-axis.

78. Find the area of the surface generated by revolving $x = 6t$, $y = 4t^2$ ($0 \le t \le 1$) about the y-axis.

79. By revolving the semicircle

$$x = r \cos t, \quad y = r \sin t \quad (0 \le t \le \pi)$$

about the x-axis, show that the surface area of a sphere of radius r is $4\pi r^2$.

80. The equations

$$x = a\phi - a \sin \phi, \quad y = a - a \cos \phi \quad (0 \le \phi \le 2\pi)$$

represent one arch of a cycloid. Show that the surface area generated by revolving this curve about the x-axis is given by $S = 64\pi a^2/3$.

81. Writing Consult appropriate reference works and write an essay on American mathematician Nathaniel Bowditch (1773–1838) and his investigation of **Bowditch curves** (better known as Lissajous curves; see Exercise 55).

82. Writing What are some of the advantages of expressing a curve parametrically rather than in the form $y = f(x)$?

✔ **QUICK CHECK ANSWERS 10.1**

1. $x = 3 + 2\cos t$, $y = 5 + 2\sin t$ $(0 \le t \le 2\pi)$ **2.** $\frac{3}{4}$; 2.75   **3.** $x = f(1-t)$, $y = g(1-t)$ **4.** $\dfrac{dy/dt}{dx/dt} = \dfrac{g'(t)}{f'(t)}$

5. $\displaystyle\int_1^\pi \sqrt{(1/t)^2 + \cos^2 t} \, dt$

10.2 POLAR COORDINATES

Up to now we have specified the location of a point in the plane by means of coordinates relative to two perpendicular coordinate axes. However, sometimes a moving point has a special affinity for some fixed point, such as a planet moving in an orbit under the central attraction of the Sun. In such cases, the path of the particle is best described by its angular direction and its distance from the fixed point. In this section we will discuss a new kind of coordinate system that is based on this idea.

■ **POLAR COORDINATE SYSTEMS**

A *polar coordinate system* in a plane consists of a fixed point O, called the *pole* (or *origin*), and a ray emanating from the pole, called the *polar axis*. In such a coordinate system

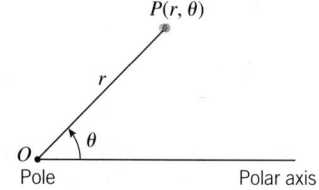

▲ **Figure 10.2.1**

we can associate with each point P in the plane a pair of ***polar coordinates*** (r, θ), where r is the distance from P to the pole and θ is an angle from the polar axis to the ray OP (Figure 10.2.1). The number r is called the ***radial coordinate*** of P and the number θ the ***angular coordinate*** (or ***polar angle***) of P. In Figure 10.2.2, the points $(6, \pi/4)$, $(5, 2\pi/3)$, $(3, 5\pi/4)$, and $(4, 11\pi/6)$ are plotted in polar coordinate systems. If P is the pole, then $r = 0$, but there is no clearly defined polar angle. We will agree that an arbitrary angle can be used in this case; that is, $(0, \theta)$ are polar coordinates of the pole for all choices of θ.

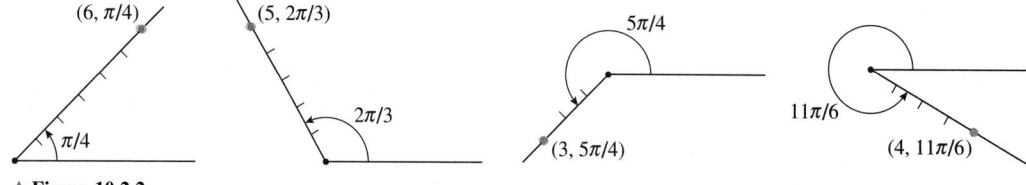

▲ **Figure 10.2.2**

The polar coordinates of a point are not unique. For example, the polar coordinates

$$(1, 7\pi/4), \quad (1, -\pi/4), \quad \text{and} \quad (1, 15\pi/4)$$

all represent the same point (Figure 10.2.3).

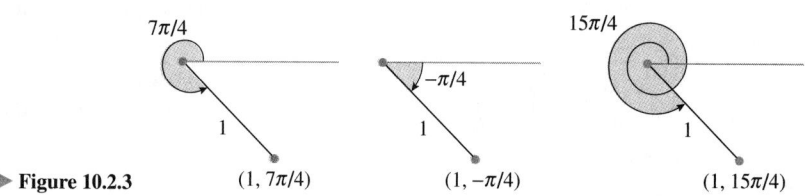

▶ **Figure 10.2.3** $(1, 7\pi/4)$ $(1, -\pi/4)$ $(1, 15\pi/4)$

In general, if a point P has polar coordinates (r, θ), then

$$(r, \theta + 2n\pi) \quad \text{and} \quad (r, \theta - 2n\pi)$$

are also polar coordinates of P for any nonnegative integer n. Thus, every point has infinitely many pairs of polar coordinates.

As defined above, the radial coordinate r of a point P is nonnegative, since it represents the distance from P to the pole. However, it will be convenient to allow for negative values of r as well. To motivate an appropriate definition, consider the point P with polar coordinates $(3, 5\pi/4)$. As shown in Figure 10.2.4, we can reach this point by rotating the polar axis through an angle of $5\pi/4$ and then moving 3 units from the pole along the terminal side of the angle, or we can reach the point P by rotating the polar axis through an angle of $\pi/4$ and then moving 3 units from the pole along the extension of the terminal side. This suggests that the point $(3, 5\pi/4)$ might also be denoted by $(-3, \pi/4)$, with the minus sign serving to indicate that the point is on the *extension* of the angle's terminal side rather than on the terminal side itself.

In general, the terminal side of the angle $\theta + \pi$ is the extension of the terminal side of θ, so we define negative radial coordinates by agreeing that

$$(-r, \theta) \quad \text{and} \quad (r, \theta + \pi)$$

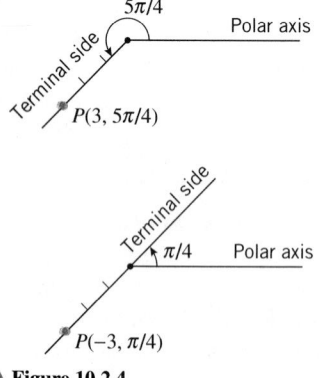

▲ **Figure 10.2.4**

are polar coordinates of the same point.

▬ RELATIONSHIP BETWEEN POLAR AND RECTANGULAR COORDINATES

Frequently, it will be useful to superimpose a rectangular xy-coordinate system on top of a polar coordinate system, making the positive x-axis coincide with the polar axis. If this is done, then every point P will have both rectangular coordinates (x, y) and polar coordinates

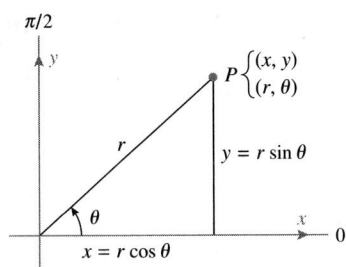

▲ **Figure 10.2.5**

(r, θ). As suggested by Figure 10.2.5, these coordinates are related by the equations

$$x = r\cos\theta, \quad y = r\sin\theta \tag{1}$$

These equations are well suited for finding x and y when r and θ are known. However, to find r and θ when x and y are known, it is preferable to use the identities $\sin^2\theta + \cos^2\theta = 1$ and $\tan\theta = \sin\theta/\cos\theta$ to rewrite (1) as

$$r^2 = x^2 + y^2, \quad \tan\theta = \frac{y}{x} \tag{2}$$

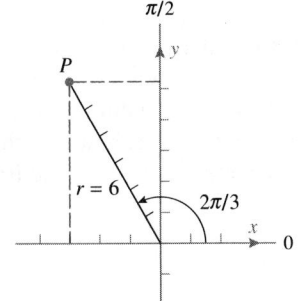

▲ **Figure 10.2.6**

▶ **Example 1** Find the rectangular coordinates of the point P whose polar coordinates are $(r, \theta) = (6, 2\pi/3)$ (Figure 10.2.6).

Solution. Substituting the polar coordinates $r = 6$ and $\theta = 2\pi/3$ in (1) yields

$$x = 6\cos\frac{2\pi}{3} = 6\left(-\frac{1}{2}\right) = -3$$

$$y = 6\sin\frac{2\pi}{3} = 6\left(\frac{\sqrt{3}}{2}\right) = 3\sqrt{3}$$

Thus, the rectangular coordinates of P are $(x, y) = (-3, 3\sqrt{3})$. ◀

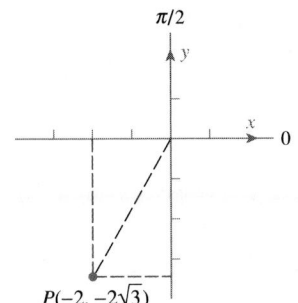

▲ **Figure 10.2.7**

▶ **Example 2** Find polar coordinates of the point P whose rectangular coordinates are $(-2, -2\sqrt{3})$ (Figure 10.2.7).

Solution. We will find the polar coordinates (r, θ) of P that satisfy the conditions $r > 0$ and $0 \le \theta < 2\pi$. From the first equation in (2),

$$r^2 = x^2 + y^2 = (-2)^2 + (-2\sqrt{3})^2 = 4 + 12 = 16$$

so $r = 4$. From the second equation in (2),

$$\tan\theta = \frac{y}{x} = \frac{-2\sqrt{3}}{-2} = \sqrt{3}$$

From this and the fact that $(-2, -2\sqrt{3})$ lies in the third quadrant, it follows that the angle satisfying the requirement $0 \le \theta < 2\pi$ is $\theta = 4\pi/3$. Thus, $(r, \theta) = (4, 4\pi/3)$ are polar coordinates of P. All other polar coordinates of P are expressible in the form

$$\left(4, \frac{4\pi}{3} + 2n\pi\right) \quad \text{or} \quad \left(-4, \frac{\pi}{3} + 2n\pi\right)$$

where n is an integer. ◀

■ **GRAPHS IN POLAR COORDINATES**

We will now consider the problem of graphing equations in r and θ, where θ is assumed to be measured in radians. Some examples of such equations are

$$r = 1, \quad \theta = \pi/4, \quad r = \theta, \quad r = \sin\theta, \quad r = \cos 2\theta$$

In a rectangular coordinate system the graph of an equation in x and y consists of all points whose coordinates (x, y) satisfy the equation. However, in a polar coordinate system, points have infinitely many different pairs of polar coordinates, so that a given point may have some polar coordinates that satisfy an equation and others that do not. Given an equation in r and θ, we define its *graph in polar coordinates* to consist of all points with *at least one* pair of coordinates (r, θ) that satisfy the equation.

▶ **Example 3**   Sketch the graphs of

$$\text{(a) } r = 1 \qquad \text{(b) } \theta = \frac{\pi}{4}$$

in polar coordinates.

Solution (a).   For all values of θ, the point $(1, \theta)$ is 1 unit away from the pole. Since θ is arbitrary, the graph is the circle of radius 1 centered at the pole (Figure 10.2.8a).

Solution (b).   For all values of r, the point $(r, \pi/4)$ lies on a line that makes an angle of $\pi/4$ with the polar axis (Figure 10.2.8b). Positive values of r correspond to points on the line in the first quadrant and negative values of r to points on the line in the third quadrant. Thus, in absence of any restriction on r, the graph is the entire line. Observe, however, that had we imposed the restriction $r \geq 0$, the graph would have been just the ray in the first quadrant. ◀

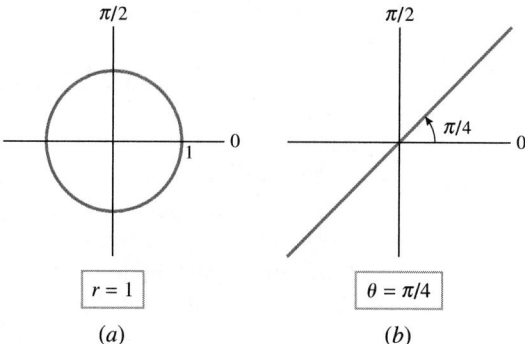

▶ **Figure 10.2.8**   (*a*)   (*b*)

Equations $r = f(\theta)$ that express r as a function of θ are especially important. One way to graph such an equation is to choose some typical values of θ, calculate the corresponding values of r, and then plot the resulting pairs (r, θ) in a polar coordinate system. The next two examples illustrate this process.

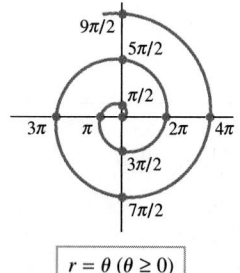

▲ **Figure 10.2.9**

▶ **Example 4**   Sketch the graph of $r = \theta$ $(\theta \geq 0)$ in polar coordinates by plotting points.

Solution.   Observe that as θ increases, so does r; thus, the graph is a curve that spirals out from the pole as θ increases. A reasonably accurate sketch of the spiral can be obtained by plotting the points that correspond to values of θ that are integer multiples of $\pi/2$, keeping in mind that the value of r is always equal to the value of θ (Figure 10.2.9). ◀

Graph the spiral $r = \theta$ $(\theta \leq 0)$. Compare your graph to that in Figure 10.2.9.

▶ **Example 5**   Sketch the graph of the equation $r = \sin\theta$ in polar coordinates by plotting points.

Solution.   Table 10.2.1 shows the coordinates of points on the graph at increments of $\pi/6$.

These points are plotted in Figure 10.2.10. Note, however, that there are 13 points listed in the table but only 6 distinct plotted points. This is because the pairs from $\theta = \pi$ on yield duplicates of the preceding points. For example, $(-1/2, 7\pi/6)$ and $(1/2, \pi/6)$ represent the same point. ◄

Table 10.2.1

θ (RADIANS)	0	$\frac{\pi}{6}$	$\frac{\pi}{3}$	$\frac{\pi}{2}$	$\frac{2\pi}{3}$	$\frac{5\pi}{6}$	π	$\frac{7\pi}{6}$	$\frac{4\pi}{3}$	$\frac{3\pi}{2}$	$\frac{5\pi}{3}$	$\frac{11\pi}{6}$	2π
$r = \sin\theta$	0	$\frac{1}{2}$	$\frac{\sqrt{3}}{2}$	1	$\frac{\sqrt{3}}{2}$	$\frac{1}{2}$	0	$-\frac{1}{2}$	$-\frac{\sqrt{3}}{2}$	-1	$-\frac{\sqrt{3}}{2}$	$-\frac{1}{2}$	0
(r, θ)	$(0,0)$	$\left(\frac{1}{2},\frac{\pi}{6}\right)$	$\left(\frac{\sqrt{3}}{2},\frac{\pi}{3}\right)$	$\left(1,\frac{\pi}{2}\right)$	$\left(\frac{\sqrt{3}}{2},\frac{2\pi}{3}\right)$	$\left(\frac{1}{2},\frac{5\pi}{6}\right)$	$(0,\pi)$	$\left(-\frac{1}{2},\frac{7\pi}{6}\right)$	$\left(-\frac{\sqrt{3}}{2},\frac{4\pi}{3}\right)$	$\left(-1,\frac{3\pi}{2}\right)$	$\left(-\frac{\sqrt{3}}{2},\frac{5\pi}{3}\right)$	$\left(-\frac{1}{2},\frac{11\pi}{6}\right)$	$(0,2\pi)$

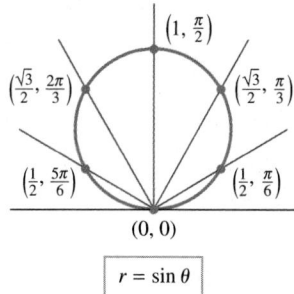

$r = \sin\theta$

▲ Figure 10.2.10

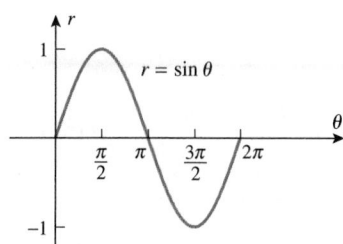

▲ Figure 10.2.11

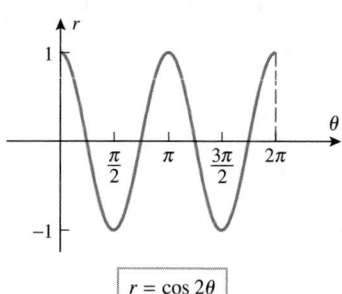

$r = \cos 2\theta$

▲ Figure 10.2.12

Observe that the points in Figure 10.2.10 appear to lie on a circle. We can confirm that this is so by expressing the polar equation $r = \sin\theta$ in terms of x and y. To do this, we multiply the equation through by r to obtain

$$r^2 = r \sin\theta$$

which now allows us to apply Formulas (1) and (2) to rewrite the equation as

$$x^2 + y^2 = y$$

Rewriting this equation as $x^2 + y^2 - y = 0$ and then completing the square yields

$$x^2 + \left(y - \tfrac{1}{2}\right)^2 = \tfrac{1}{4}$$

which is a circle of radius $\frac{1}{2}$ centered at the point $\left(0, \frac{1}{2}\right)$ in the xy-plane.

It is often useful to view the equation $r = f(\theta)$ as an equation in rectangular coordinates (rather than polar coordinates) and graphed in a rectangular θr-coordinate system. For example, Figure 10.2.11 shows the graph of $r = \sin\theta$ displayed using rectangular θr-coordinates. This graph can actually help to visualize how the polar graph in Figure 10.2.10 is generated:

- At $\theta = 0$ we have $r = 0$, which corresponds to the pole $(0, 0)$ on the polar graph.
- As θ varies from 0 to $\pi/2$, the value of r increases from 0 to 1, so the point (r, θ) moves along the circle from the pole to the high point at $(1, \pi/2)$.
- As θ varies from $\pi/2$ to π, the value of r decreases from 1 back to 0, so the point (r, θ) moves along the circle from the high point back to the pole.
- As θ varies from π to $3\pi/2$, the values of r are negative, varying from 0 to -1. Thus, the point (r, θ) moves along the circle from the pole to the high point at $(1, \pi/2)$, which is the same as the point $(-1, 3\pi/2)$. This duplicates the motion that occurred for $0 \leq \theta \leq \pi/2$.
- As θ varies from $3\pi/2$ to 2π, the value of r varies from -1 to 0. Thus, the point (r, θ) moves along the circle from the high point back to the pole, duplicating the motion that occurred for $\pi/2 \leq \theta \leq \pi$.

▶ **Example 6**   Sketch the graph of $r = \cos 2\theta$ in polar coordinates.

Solution.   Instead of plotting points, we will use the graph of $r = \cos 2\theta$ in rectangular coordinates (Figure 10.2.12) to visualize how the polar graph of this equation is generated. The analysis and the resulting polar graph are shown in Figure 10.2.13. This curve is called a *four-petal rose*. ◄

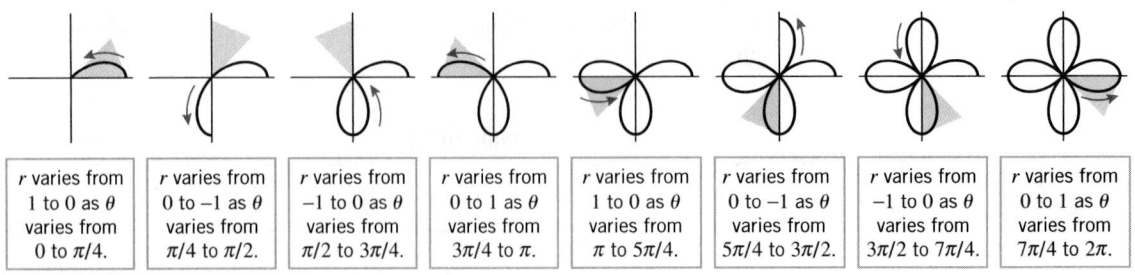

| r varies from 1 to 0 as θ varies from 0 to $\pi/4$. | r varies from 0 to -1 as θ varies from $\pi/4$ to $\pi/2$. | r varies from -1 to 0 as θ varies from $\pi/2$ to $3\pi/4$. | r varies from 0 to 1 as θ varies from $3\pi/4$ to π. | r varies from 1 to 0 as θ varies from π to $5\pi/4$. | r varies from 0 to -1 as θ varies from $5\pi/4$ to $3\pi/2$. | r varies from -1 to 0 as θ varies from $3\pi/2$ to $7\pi/4$. | r varies from 0 to 1 as θ varies from $7\pi/4$ to 2π. |

▲ **Figure 10.2.13**

■ SYMMETRY TESTS

Observe that the polar graph of $r = \cos 2\theta$ in Figure 10.2.13 is symmetric about the x-axis and the y-axis. This symmetry could have been predicted from the following theorem, which is suggested by Figure 10.2.14 (we omit the proof).

10.2.1   THEOREM (Symmetry Tests)

(a) *A curve in polar coordinates is symmetric about the x-axis if replacing θ by $-\theta$ in its equation produces an equivalent equation (Figure 10.2.14a).*

(b) *A curve in polar coordinates is symmetric about the y-axis if replacing θ by $\pi - \theta$ in its equation produces an equivalent equation (Figure 10.2.14b).*

(c) *A curve in polar coordinates is symmetric about the origin if replacing θ by $\theta + \pi$, or replacing r by $-r$ in its equation produces an equivalent equation (Figure 10.2.14c).*

The converse of each part of Theorem 10.2.1 is false. See Exercise 79.

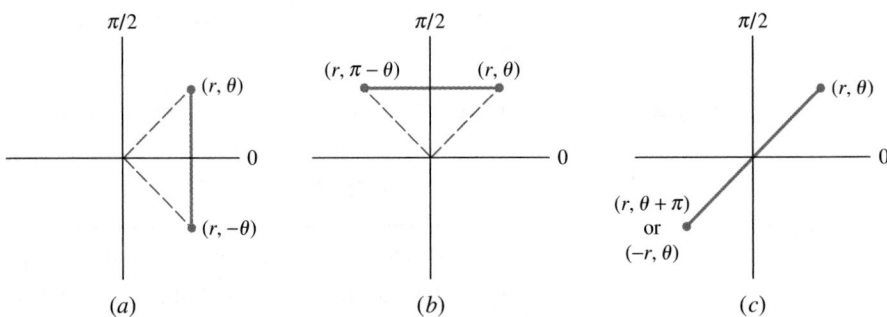

▶ **Figure 10.2.14**   (a)   (b)   (c)

▶ **Example 7**   Use Theorem 10.2.1 to confirm that the graph of $r = \cos 2\theta$ in Figure 10.2.13 is symmetric about the x-axis and y-axis.

A graph that is symmetric about both the x-axis and the y-axis is also symmetric about the origin. Use Theorem 10.2.1(c) to verify that the curve in Example 7 is symmetric about the origin.

Solution.   To test for symmetry about the x-axis, we replace θ by $-\theta$. This yields

$$r = \cos(-2\theta) = \cos 2\theta$$

Thus, replacing θ by $-\theta$ does not alter the equation.

To test for symmetry about the y-axis, we replace θ by $\pi - \theta$. This yields

$$r = \cos 2(\pi - \theta) = \cos(2\pi - 2\theta) = \cos(-2\theta) = \cos 2\theta$$

Thus, replacing θ by $\pi - \theta$ does not alter the equation. ◀

▶ **Example 8**   Sketch the graph of $r = a(1 - \cos\theta)$ in polar coordinates, assuming a to be a positive constant.

Solution.   Observe first that replacing θ by $-\theta$ does not alter the equation, so we know in advance that the graph is symmetric about the polar axis. Thus, if we graph the upper half of the curve, then we can obtain the lower half by reflection about the polar axis.

As in our previous examples, we will first graph the equation in rectangular θr-coordinates. This graph, which is shown in Figure 10.2.15a, can be obtained by rewriting the given equation as $r = a - a\cos\theta$, from which we see that the graph in rectangular θr-coordinates can be obtained by first reflecting the graph of $r = a\cos\theta$ about the x-axis to obtain the graph of $r = -a\cos\theta$, and then translating that graph up a units to obtain the graph of $r = a - a\cos\theta$. Now we can see the following:

- As θ varies from 0 to $\pi/3$, r increases from 0 to $a/2$.
- As θ varies from $\pi/3$ to $\pi/2$, r increases from $a/2$ to a.
- As θ varies from $\pi/2$ to $2\pi/3$, r increases from a to $3a/2$.
- As θ varies from $2\pi/3$ to π, r increases from $3a/2$ to $2a$.

This produces the polar curve shown in Figure 10.2.15b. The rest of the curve can be obtained by continuing the preceding analysis from π to 2π or, as noted above, by reflecting the portion already graphed about the x-axis (Figure 10.2.15c). This heart-shaped curve is called a **cardioid** (from the Greek word *kardia* meaning "heart").   ◀

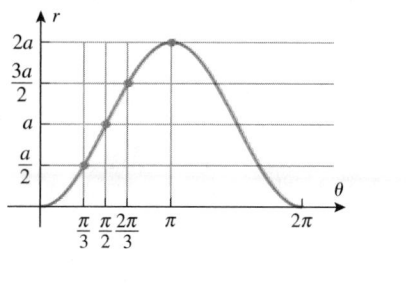

$$r = a(1 - \cos\theta)$$

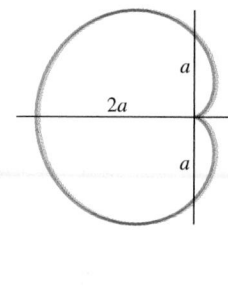

(a)   (b)   (c)

▲ **Figure 10.2.15**

▶ **Example 9**   Sketch the graph of $r^2 = 4\cos 2\theta$ in polar coordinates.

Solution.   This equation does not express r as a function of θ, since solving for r in terms of θ yields two functions:

$$r = 2\sqrt{\cos 2\theta} \quad \text{and} \quad r = -2\sqrt{\cos 2\theta}$$

Thus, to graph the equation $r^2 = 4\cos 2\theta$ we will have to graph the two functions separately and then combine those graphs.

We will start with the graph of $r = 2\sqrt{\cos 2\theta}$. Observe first that this equation is not changed if we replace θ by $-\theta$ or if we replace θ by $\pi - \theta$. Thus, the graph is symmetric about the x-axis and the y-axis. This means that the entire graph can be obtained by graphing the portion in the first quadrant, reflecting that portion about the y-axis to obtain the portion in the second quadrant, and then reflecting those two portions about the x-axis to obtain the portions in the third and fourth quadrants.

To begin the analysis, we will graph the equation $r = 2\sqrt{\cos 2\theta}$ in rectangular θr-coordinates (see Figure 10.2.16a). Note that there are gaps in that graph over the intervals $\pi/4 < \theta < 3\pi/4$ and $5\pi/4 < \theta < 7\pi/4$ because $\cos 2\theta$ is negative for those values of θ. From this graph we can see the following:

- As θ varies from 0 to $\pi/4$, r decreases from 2 to 0.
- As θ varies from $\pi/4$ to $\pi/2$, no points are generated on the polar graph.

This produces the portion of the graph shown in Figure 10.2.16b. As noted above, we can complete the graph by a reflection about the y-axis followed by a reflection about the x-axis (Figure 10.2.16c). The resulting propeller-shaped graph is called a **lemniscate** (from the Greek word *lemniscos* for a looped ribbon resembling the number 8). We leave it for you to verify that the equation $r = 2\sqrt{\cos 2\theta}$ has the same graph as $r = -2\sqrt{\cos 2\theta}$, but traced in a diagonally opposite manner. Thus, the graph of the equation $r^2 = 4 \cos 2\theta$ consists of two identical superimposed lemniscates. ◄

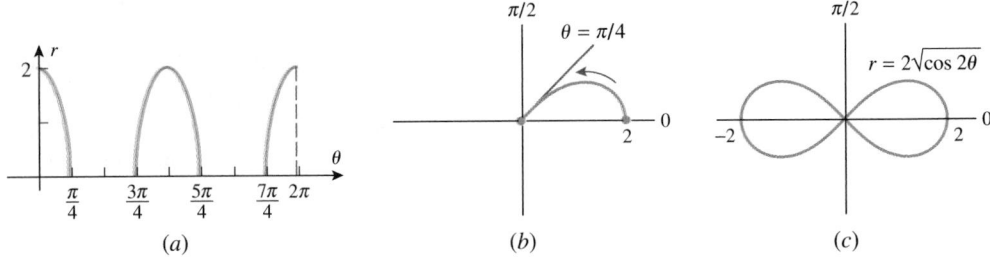

▲ **Figure 10.2.16**

▦ FAMILIES OF LINES AND RAYS THROUGH THE POLE

If θ_0 is a fixed angle, then for all values of r the point (r, θ_0) lies on the line that makes an angle of $\theta = \theta_0$ with the polar axis; and, conversely, every point on this line has a pair of polar coordinates of the form (r, θ_0). Thus, the equation $\theta = \theta_0$ represents the line that passes through the pole and makes an angle of θ_0 with the polar axis (Figure 10.2.17a). If r is restricted to be nonnegative, then the graph of the equation $\theta = \theta_0$ is the ray that emanates from the pole and makes an angle of θ_0 with the polar axis (Figure 10.2.17b). Thus, as θ_0 varies, the equation $\theta = \theta_0$ produces either a family of lines through the pole or a family of rays through the pole, depending on the restrictions on r.

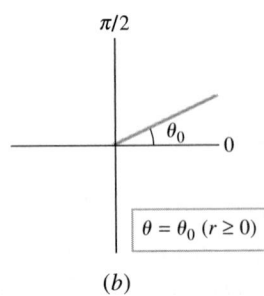

▲ **Figure 10.2.17**

▦ FAMILIES OF CIRCLES

We will consider three families of circles in which a is assumed to be a positive constant:

$$r = a \qquad r = 2a \cos \theta \qquad r = 2a \sin \theta \qquad (3\text{–}5)$$

The equation $r = a$ represents a circle of radius a centered at the pole (Figure 10.2.18a). Thus, as a varies, this equation produces a family of circles centered at the pole. For families (4) and (5), recall from plane geometry that a triangle that is inscribed in a circle with a diameter of the circle for a side must be a right triangle. Thus, as indicated in Figures 10.2.18b and 10.2.18c, the equation $r = 2a \cos \theta$ represents a circle of radius a, centered on the x-axis and tangent to the y-axis at the origin; similarly, the equation $r = 2a \sin \theta$ represents a circle of radius a, centered on the y-axis and tangent to the x-axis at the origin. Thus, as a varies, Equations (4) and (5) produce the families illustrated in Figures 10.2.18d and 10.2.18e.

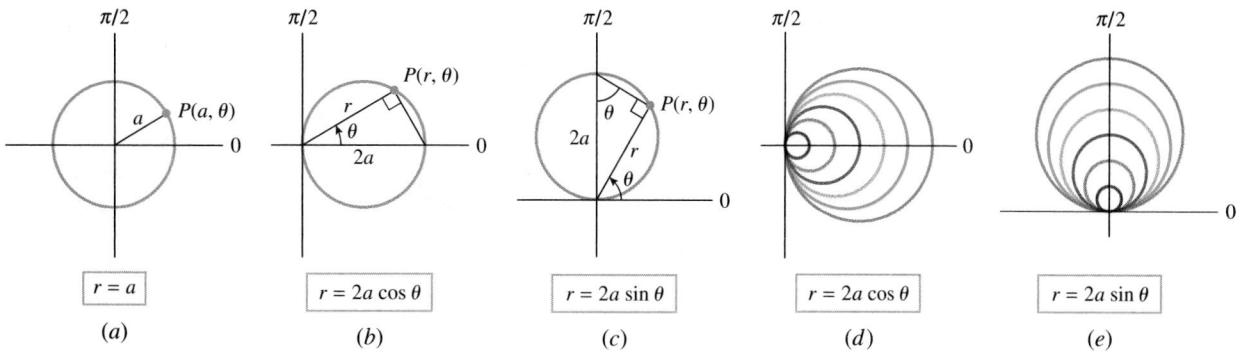

Figure 10.2.18

FAMILIES OF ROSE CURVES

Observe that replacing θ by $-\theta$ does not change the equation $r = 2a\cos\theta$ and that replacing θ by $\pi - \theta$ does not change the equation $r = 2a\sin\theta$. This explains why the circles in Figure 10.2.18d are symmetric about the x-axis and those in Figure 10.2.18e are symmetric about the y-axis.

What do the graphs of one-petal roses look like?

In polar coordinates, equations of the form

$$r = a \sin n\theta \qquad r = a \cos n\theta \qquad (6\text{–}7)$$

in which $a > 0$ and n is a positive integer represent families of flower-shaped curves called **roses** (Figure 10.2.19). The rose consists of n equally spaced petals of radius a if n is odd and $2n$ equally spaced petals of radius a if n is even. It can be shown that a rose with an even number of petals is traced out exactly once as θ varies over the interval $0 \le \theta < 2\pi$ and a rose with an odd number of petals is traced out exactly once as θ varies over the interval $0 \le \theta < \pi$ (Exercise 78). A four-petal rose of radius 1 was graphed in Example 6.

ROSE CURVES

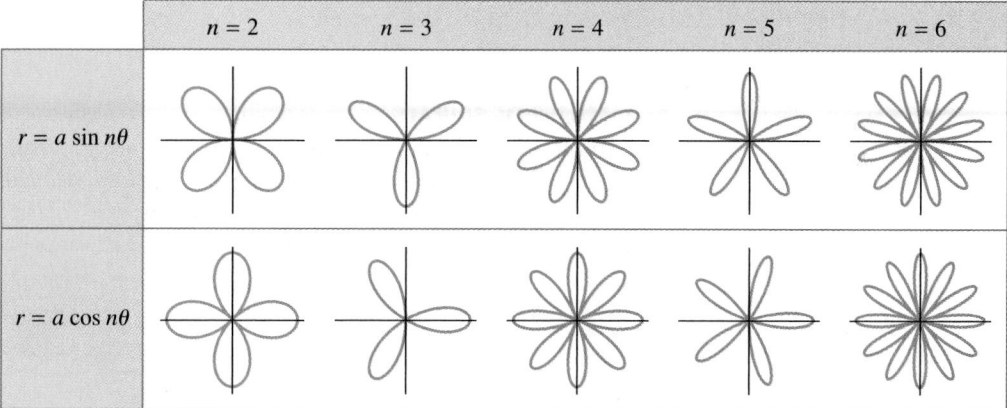

Figure 10.2.19

FAMILIES OF CARDIOIDS AND LIMAÇONS

Equations with any of the four forms

$$r = a \pm b \sin\theta \qquad r = a \pm b \cos\theta \qquad (8\text{–}9)$$

in which $a > 0$ and $b > 0$ represent polar curves called **limaçons** (from the Latin word *limax* for a snail-like creature that is commonly called a "slug"). There are four possible shapes for a limaçon that are determined by the ratio a/b (Figure 10.2.20). If $a = b$ (the case $a/b = 1$), then the limaçon is called a **cardioid** because of its heart-shaped appearance, as noted in Example 8.

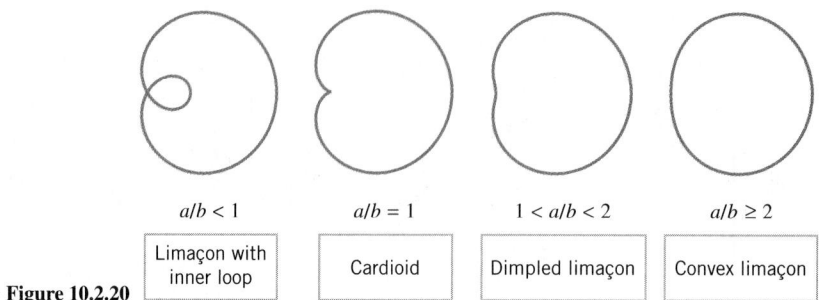

▶ **Figure 10.2.20**

▶ **Example 10**   Figure 10.2.21 shows the family of limaçons $r = a + \cos\theta$ with the constant a varying from 0.25 to 2.50 in steps of 0.25. In keeping with Figure 10.2.20, the limaçons evolve from the loop type to the convex type. As a increases from the starting value of 0.25, the loops get smaller and smaller until the cardioid is reached at $a = 1$. As a increases further, the limaçons evolve through the dimpled type into the convex type. ◀

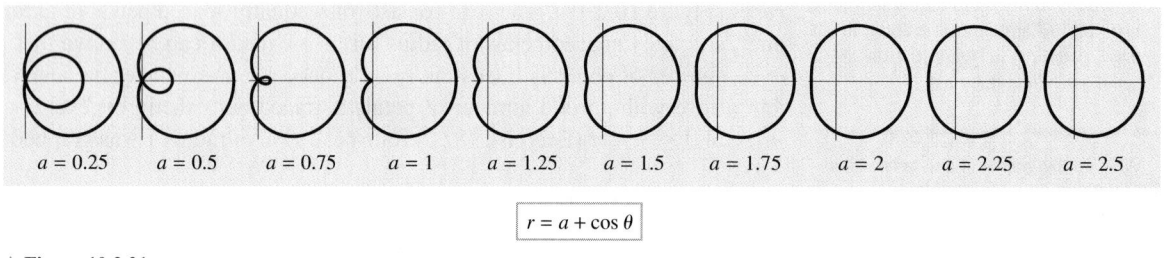

$$r = a + \cos\theta$$

▲ **Figure 10.2.21**

FAMILIES OF SPIRALS

A *spiral* is a curve that coils around a central point. Spirals generally have "left-hand" and "right-hand" versions that coil in opposite directions, depending on the restrictions on the polar angle and the signs of constants that appear in their equations. Some of the more common types of spirals are shown in Figure 10.2.22 for nonnegative values of θ, a, and b.

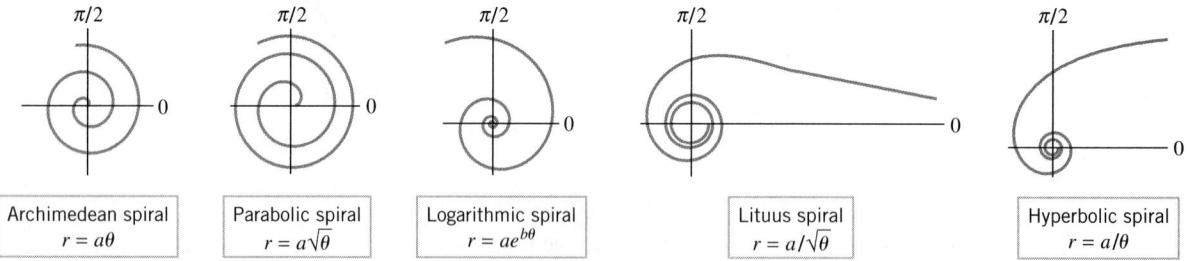

▲ **Figure 10.2.22**

SPIRALS IN NATURE

Spirals of many kinds occur in nature. For example, the shell of the chambered nautilus (below) forms a logarithmic spiral, and a coiled sailor's rope forms an Archimedean spiral. Spirals also occur in flowers, the tusks of certain animals, and in the shapes of galaxies.

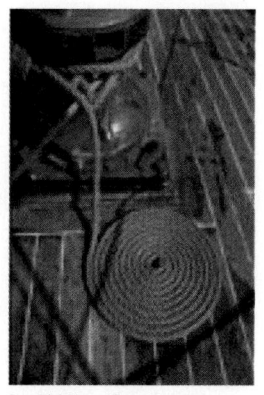

Thomas Taylor/Photo Researchers

The shell of the chambered nautilus reveals a logarithmic spiral. The animal lives in the outermost chamber.

Rex Ziak/Stone/Getty Images

A sailor's coiled rope forms an Archimedean spiral.

Courtesy NASA & The Hubble Heritage Team

A spiral galaxy.

■ GENERATING POLAR CURVES WITH GRAPHING UTILITIES

For polar curves that are too complicated for hand computation, graphing utilities can be used. Although many graphing utilities are capable of graphing polar curves directly, some are not. However, if a graphing utility is capable of graphing parametric equations, then it can be used to graph a polar curve $r = f(\theta)$ by converting this equation to parametric form. This can be done by substituting $f(\theta)$ for r in (1). This yields

$$x = f(\theta) \cos \theta, \quad y = f(\theta) \sin \theta \qquad (10)$$

which is a pair of parametric equations for the polar curve in terms of the parameter θ.

▶ **Example 11**   Express the polar equation

$$r = 2 + \cos \frac{5\theta}{2}$$

parametrically, and generate the polar graph from the parametric equations using a graphing utility.

Solution.   Substituting the given expression for r in $x = r \cos \theta$ and $y = r \sin \theta$ yields the parametric equations

$$x = \left[2 + \cos \frac{5\theta}{2} \right] \cos \theta, \quad y = \left[2 + \cos \frac{5\theta}{2} \right] \sin \theta$$

Next, we need to find an interval over which to vary θ to produce the entire graph. To find such an interval, we will look for the smallest number of complete revolutions that must occur until the value of r begins to repeat. Algebraically, this amounts to finding the smallest positive integer n such that

$$2 + \cos \left(\frac{5(\theta + 2n\pi)}{2} \right) = 2 + \cos \frac{5\theta}{2}$$

or

$$\cos \left(\frac{5\theta}{2} + 5n\pi \right) = \cos \frac{5\theta}{2}$$

TECHNOLOGY MASTERY

Use a graphing utility to duplicate the curve in Figure 10.2.23. If your graphing utility requires that t be used as the parameter, then you will have to replace θ by t in (10) to generate the graph.

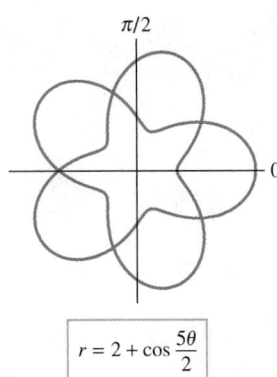

$r = 2 + \cos \dfrac{5\theta}{2}$

▲ **Figure 10.2.23**

For this equality to hold, the quantity $5n\pi$ must be an even multiple of π; the smallest n for which this occurs is $n = 2$. Thus, the entire graph will be traced in two revolutions, which means it can be generated from the parametric equations

$$x = \left[2 + \cos \frac{5\theta}{2}\right] \cos \theta, \quad y = \left[2 + \cos \frac{5\theta}{2}\right] \sin \theta \qquad (0 \le \theta \le 4\pi)$$

This yields the graph in Figure 10.2.23. ◄

✔ **QUICK CHECK EXERCISES 10.2**   *(See page 719 for answers.)*

1. (a) Rectangular coordinates of a point (x, y) may be recovered from its polar coordinates (r, θ) by means of the equations $x = $ _____ and $y = $ _____.

   (b) Polar coordinates (r, θ) may be recovered from rectangular coordinates (x, y) by means of the equations $r^2 = $ _____ and $\tan \theta = $ _____.

2. Find the rectangular coordinates of the points whose polar coordinates are given.
   (a) $(4, \pi/3)$ (b) $(2, -\pi/6)$
   (c) $(6, -2\pi/3)$ (d) $(4, 5\pi/4)$

3. In each part, find polar coordinates satisfying the stated conditions for the point whose rectangular coordinates are $(1, \sqrt{3})$.
   (a) $r \ge 0$ and $0 \le \theta < 2\pi$
   (b) $r \le 0$ and $0 \le \theta < 2\pi$

4. In each part, state the name that describes the polar curve most precisely: a rose, a line, a circle, a limaçon, a cardioid, a spiral, a lemniscate, or none of these.
   (a) $r = 1 - \theta$ (b) $r = 1 + 2 \sin \theta$
   (c) $r = \sin 2\theta$ (d) $r = \cos^2 \theta$
   (e) $r = \csc \theta$ (f) $r = 2 + 2 \cos \theta$
   (g) $r = -2 \sin \theta$

EXERCISE SET 10.2    Graphing Utility

1–2 Plot the points in polar coordinates. ■

1. (a) $(3, \pi/4)$ (b) $(5, 2\pi/3)$ (c) $(1, \pi/2)$
   (d) $(4, 7\pi/6)$ (e) $(-6, -\pi)$ (f) $(-1, 9\pi/4)$

2. (a) $(2, -\pi/3)$ (b) $(3/2, -7\pi/4)$ (c) $(-3, 3\pi/2)$
   (d) $(-5, -\pi/6)$ (e) $(2, 4\pi/3)$ (f) $(0, \pi)$

3–4 Find the rectangular coordinates of the points whose polar coordinates are given. ■

3. (a) $(6, \pi/6)$ (b) $(7, 2\pi/3)$ (c) $(-6, -5\pi/6)$
   (d) $(0, -\pi)$ (e) $(7, 17\pi/6)$ (f) $(-5, 0)$

4. (a) $(-2, \pi/4)$ (b) $(6, -\pi/4)$ (c) $(4, 9\pi/4)$
   (d) $(3, 0)$ (e) $(-4, -3\pi/2)$ (f) $(0, 3\pi)$

5. In each part, a point is given in rectangular coordinates. Find two pairs of polar coordinates for the point, one pair satisfying $r \ge 0$ and $0 \le \theta < 2\pi$, and the second pair satisfying $r \ge 0$ and $-2\pi < \theta \le 0$.
   (a) $(-5, 0)$ (b) $(2\sqrt{3}, -2)$ (c) $(0, -2)$
   (d) $(-8, -8)$ (e) $(-3, 3\sqrt{3})$ (f) $(1, 1)$

6. In each part, find polar coordinates satisfying the stated conditions for the point whose rectangular coordinates are $(-\sqrt{3}, 1)$.

   (a) $r \ge 0$ and $0 \le \theta < 2\pi$
   (b) $r \le 0$ and $0 \le \theta < 2\pi$
   (c) $r \ge 0$ and $-2\pi < \theta \le 0$
   (d) $r \le 0$ and $-\pi < \theta \le \pi$

7–8 Use a calculating utility, where needed, to approximate the polar coordinates of the points whose rectangular coordinates are given. ■

7. (a) $(3, 4)$ (b) $(6, -8)$ (c) $(-1, \tan^{-1} 1)$

8. (a) $(-3, 4)$ (b) $(-3, 1.7)$ (c) $\left(2, \sin^{-1} \frac{1}{2}\right)$

9–10 Identify the curve by transforming the given polar equation to rectangular coordinates. ■

9. (a) $r = 2$ (b) $r \sin \theta = 4$
    (c) $r = 3 \cos \theta$ (d) $r = \dfrac{6}{3 \cos \theta + 2 \sin \theta}$

10. (a) $r = 5 \sec \theta$ (b) $r = 2 \sin \theta$
    (c) $r = 4 \cos \theta + 4 \sin \theta$ (d) $r = \sec \theta \tan \theta$

11–12 Express the given equations in polar coordinates. ■

11. (a) $x = 3$ (b) $x^2 + y^2 = 7$
    (c) $x^2 + y^2 + 6y = 0$ (d) $9xy = 4$

12. (a) $y = -3$ (b) $x^2 + y^2 = 5$
(c) $x^2 + y^2 + 4x = 0$ (d) $x^2(x^2 + y^2) = y^2$

FOCUS ON CONCEPTS

13–16 A graph is given in a rectangular θr-coordinate system. Sketch the corresponding graph in polar coordinates. ■

13.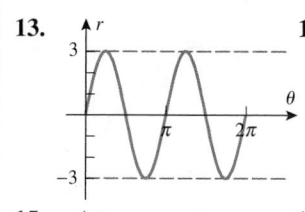

14.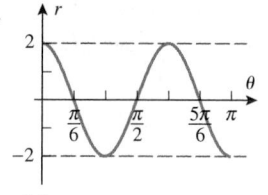

15.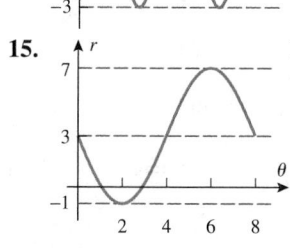

16.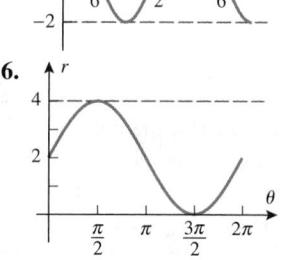

17–20 Find an equation for the given polar graph. [*Note:* Numeric labels on these graphs represent distances to the origin.] ■

17. (a) 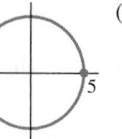 (b) 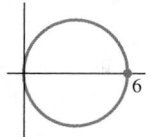 (c)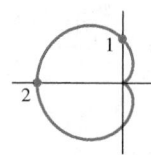

Circle　　　　Circle　　　　Cardioid

18. (a) 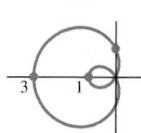 (b) 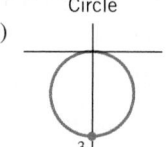 (c)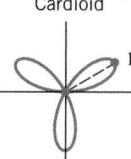

Limaçon　　　　Circle　　　　Three-petal rose

19. (a) 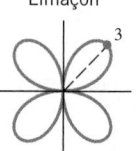 (b) (c)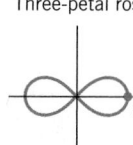

Four-petal rose　　　Limaçon　　　Lemniscate

20. (a) 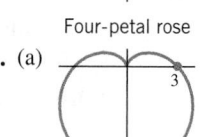 (b) 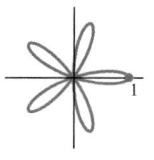 (c)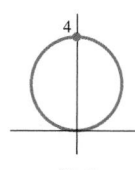

Cardioid　　　Five-petal rose　　　Circle

21–46 Sketch the curve in polar coordinates. ■

21. $\theta = \dfrac{\pi}{3}$　　**22.** $\theta = -\dfrac{3\pi}{4}$　　**23.** $r = 3$

24. $r = 4\cos\theta$　　**25.** $r = 6\sin\theta$　　**26.** $r - 2 = 2\cos\theta$

27. $r = 3(1 + \sin\theta)$ **28.** $r = 5 - 5\sin\theta$

29. $r = 4 - 4\cos\theta$ **30.** $r = 1 + 2\sin\theta$

31. $r = -1 - \cos\theta$ **32.** $r = 4 + 3\cos\theta$

33. $r = 3 - \sin\theta$ **34.** $r = 3 + 4\cos\theta$

35. $r - 5 = 3\sin\theta$ **36.** $r = 5 - 2\cos\theta$

37. $r = -3 - 4\sin\theta$ **38.** $r^2 = \cos 2\theta$

39. $r^2 = 16\sin 2\theta$ **40.** $r = 4\theta \quad (\theta \geq 0)$

41. $r = 4\theta \quad (\theta \leq 0)$ **42.** $r = 4\theta$

43. $r = -2\cos 2\theta$ **44.** $r = 3\sin 2\theta$

45. $r = 9\sin 4\theta$ **46.** $r = 2\cos 3\theta$

47–50 True–False Determine whether the statement is true or false. Explain your answer. ■

47. The polar coordinate pairs $(-1, \pi/3)$ and $(1, -2\pi/3)$ describe the same point.

48. If the graph of $r = f(\theta)$ drawn in rectangular θr-coordinates is symmetric about the r-axis, then the graph of $r = f(\theta)$ drawn in polar coordinates is symmetric about the x-axis.

49. The portion of the polar graph of $r = \sin 2\theta$ for values of θ between $\pi/2$ and π is contained in the second quadrant.

50. The graph of a dimpled limaçon passes through the polar origin.

51–55 Determine a shortest parameter interval on which a complete graph of the polar equation can be generated, and then use a graphing utility to generate the polar graph. ■

51. $r = \cos\dfrac{\theta}{2}$ **52.** $r = \sin\dfrac{\theta}{2}$

53. $r = 1 - 2\sin\dfrac{\theta}{4}$ **54.** $r = 0.5 + \cos\dfrac{\theta}{3}$

55. $r = \cos\dfrac{\theta}{5}$

56. The accompanying figure shows the graph of the "butterfly curve"
$$r = e^{\cos\theta} - 2\cos 4\theta + \sin^3\dfrac{\theta}{4}$$
Determine a shortest parameter interval on which the complete butterfly can be generated, and then check your answer using a graphing utility.

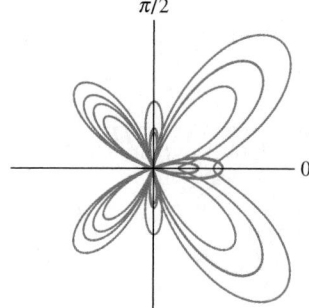

◀ **Figure Ex-56**

57. The accompanying figure shows the Archimedean spiral $r = \theta/2$ produced with a graphing calculator.
   (a) What interval of values for θ do you think was used to generate the graph?
   (b) Duplicate the graph with your own graphing utility.

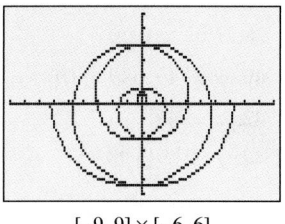

[−9, 9] × [−6, 6]
xScl = 1, yScl = 1   ◀ **Figure Ex-57**

58. Find equations for the two families of circles in the accompanying figure.

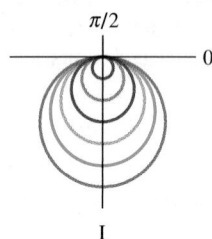

I   II

▲ **Figure Ex-58**

59. (a) Show that if a varies, then the polar equation
$$r = a \sec \theta \quad (-\pi/2 < \theta < \pi/2)$$
   describes a family of lines perpendicular to the polar axis.
   (b) Show that if b varies, then the polar equation
$$r = b \csc \theta \quad (0 < \theta < \pi)$$
   describes a family of lines parallel to the polar axis.

FOCUS ON CONCEPTS

60. The accompanying figure shows graphs of the Archimedean spiral $r = \theta$ and the parabolic spiral $r = \sqrt{\theta}$. Which is which? Explain your reasoning.

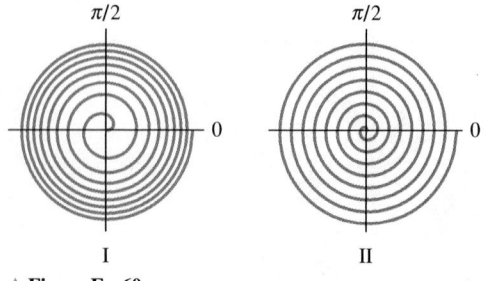

I   II

▲ **Figure Ex-60**

61–62 A polar graph of $r = f(\theta)$ is given over the stated interval. Sketch the graph of
   (a) $r = f(-\theta)$ (b) $r = f\left(\theta - \dfrac{\pi}{2}\right)$
   (c) $r = f\left(\theta + \dfrac{\pi}{2}\right)$ (d) $r = -f(\theta)$. ■

61. $0 \le \theta \le \pi/2$ **62.** $\pi/2 \le \theta \le \pi$

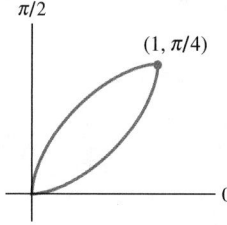   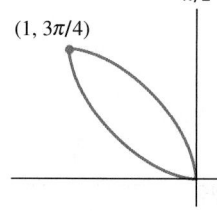

▲ **Figure Ex-61**   ▲ **Figure Ex-62**

63–64 Use the polar graph from the indicated exercise to sketch the graph of
   (a) $r = f(\theta) + 1$ (b) $r = 2f(\theta) - 1$. ■

63. Exercise 61   **64.** Exercise 62

65. Show that if the polar graph of $r = f(\theta)$ is rotated counterclockwise around the origin through an angle α, then $r = f(\theta - \alpha)$ is an equation for the rotated curve. [*Hint:* If (r_0, θ_0) is any point on the original graph, then $(r_0, \theta_0 + \alpha)$ is a point on the rotated graph.]

66. Use the result in Exercise 65 to find an equation for the lemniscate that results when the lemniscate in Example 9 is rotated counterclockwise through an angle of $\pi/2$.

67. Use the result in Exercise 65 to find an equation for the cardioid $r = 1 + \cos \theta$ after it has been rotated through the given angle, and check your answer with a graphing utility.
   (a) $\dfrac{\pi}{4}$ (b) $\dfrac{\pi}{2}$ (c) π (d) $\dfrac{5\pi}{4}$

68. (a) Show that if A and B are not both zero, then the graph of the polar equation
$$r = A \sin \theta + B \cos \theta$$
   is a circle. Find its radius.
   (b) Derive Formulas (4) and (5) from the formula given in part (a).

69. Find the highest point on the cardioid $r = 1 + \cos \theta$.

70. Find the leftmost point on the upper half of the cardioid $r = 1 + \cos \theta$.

71. Show that in a polar coordinate system the distance d between the points (r_1, θ_1) and (r_2, θ_2) is
$$d = \sqrt{r_1^2 + r_2^2 - 2r_1 r_2 \cos(\theta_1 - \theta_2)}$$

72–74 Use the formula obtained in Exercise 71 to find the distance between the two points indicated in polar coordinates. ■

72. $(3, \pi/6)$ and $(2, \pi/3)$

73. Successive tips of the four-petal rose $r = \cos 2\theta$. Check your answer using geometry.

74. Successive tips of the three-petal rose $r = \sin 3\theta$. Check your answer using trigonometry.

75. In the late seventeenth century the Italian astronomer Giovanni Domenico Cassini (1625–1712) introduced the family of curves

$$(x^2 + y^2 + a^2)^2 - b^4 - 4a^2 x^2 = 0 \quad (a > 0, b > 0)$$

in his studies of the relative motions of the Earth and the Sun. These curves, which are called **Cassini ovals**, have one of the three basic shapes shown in the accompanying figure.

(a) Show that if $a = b$, then the polar equation of the Cassini oval is $r^2 = 2a^2 \cos 2\theta$, which is a lemniscate.

(b) Use the formula in Exercise 71 to show that the lemniscate in part (a) is the curve traced by a point that moves in such a way that the product of its distances from the polar points $(a, 0)$ and (a, π) is a^2.

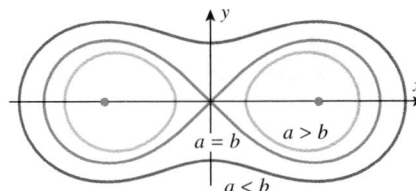

▲ **Figure Ex-75**

76–77 Vertical and horizontal asymptotes of polar curves can sometimes be detected by investigating the behavior of $x = r \cos \theta$ and $y = r \sin \theta$ as θ varies. This idea is used in these exercises. ■

76. Show that the **hyperbolic spiral** $r = 1/\theta$ $(\theta > 0)$ has a horizontal asymptote at $y = 1$ by showing that $y \to 1$ and $x \to +\infty$ as $\theta \to 0^+$. Confirm this result by generating the spiral with a graphing utility.

77. Show that the spiral $r = 1/\theta^2$ does not have any horizontal asymptotes.

78. Prove that a rose with an even number of petals is traced out exactly once as θ varies over the interval $0 \le \theta < 2\pi$ and a rose with an odd number of petals is traced out exactly once as θ varies over the interval $0 \le \theta < \pi$.

79. (a) Use a graphing utility to confirm that the graph of $r = 2 - \sin(\theta/2)$ $(0 \le \theta \le 4\pi)$ is symmetric about the x-axis.

(b) Show that replacing θ by $-\theta$ in the polar equation $r = 2 - \sin(\theta/2)$ does not produce an equivalent equation. Why does this not contradict the symmetry demonstrated in part (a)?

80. **Writing** Use a graphing utility to investigate how the family of polar curves $r = 1 + a \cos n\theta$ is affected by changing the values of a and n, where a is a positive real number and n is a positive integer. Write a brief paragraph to explain your conclusions.

81. **Writing** Why do you think the adjective "polar" was chosen in the name "polar coordinates"?

✔ QUICK CHECK ANSWERS 10.2

1. (a) $r \cos \theta$; $r \sin \theta$ (b) $x^2 + y^2$; y/x **2.** (a) $(2, 2\sqrt{3})$ (b) $(\sqrt{3}, -1)$ (c) $(-3, -3\sqrt{3})$ (d) $(-2\sqrt{2}, -2\sqrt{2})$
3. (a) $(2, \pi/3)$ (b) $(-2, 4\pi/3)$ **4.** (a) spiral (b) limaçon (c) rose (d) none of these (e) line (f) cardioid (g) circle

10.3 TANGENT LINES, ARC LENGTH, AND AREA FOR POLAR CURVES

In this section we will derive the formulas required to find slopes, tangent lines, and arc lengths of polar curves. We will then show how to find areas of regions that are bounded by polar curves.

■ **TANGENT LINES TO POLAR CURVES**

Our first objective in this section is to find a method for obtaining slopes of tangent lines to polar curves of the form $r = f(\theta)$ in which r is a differentiable function of θ. We showed in the last section that a curve of this form can be expressed parametrically in terms of the parameter θ by substituting $f(\theta)$ for r in the equations $x = r \cos \theta$ and $y = r \sin \theta$. This yields

$$x = f(\theta) \cos \theta, \quad y = f(\theta) \sin \theta$$

from which we obtain

$$\frac{dx}{d\theta} = -f(\theta)\sin\theta + f'(\theta)\cos\theta = -r\sin\theta + \frac{dr}{d\theta}\cos\theta$$

$$\frac{dy}{d\theta} = f(\theta)\cos\theta + f'(\theta)\sin\theta = r\cos\theta + \frac{dr}{d\theta}\sin\theta$$

(1)

Thus, if $dx/d\theta$ and $dy/d\theta$ are continuous and if $dx/d\theta \neq 0$, then y is a differentiable function of x, and Formula (4) in Section 10.1 with θ in place of t yields

$$\frac{dy}{dx} = \frac{dy/d\theta}{dx/d\theta} = \frac{r\cos\theta + \sin\theta\dfrac{dr}{d\theta}}{-r\sin\theta + \cos\theta\dfrac{dr}{d\theta}}$$

(2)

▶ **Example 1**   Find the slope of the tangent line to the circle $r = 4\cos\theta$ at the point where $\theta = \pi/4$.

Solution.   From (2) with $r = 4\cos\theta$, so that $dr/d\theta = -4\sin\theta$, we obtain

$$\frac{dy}{dx} = \frac{4\cos^2\theta - 4\sin^2\theta}{-8\sin\theta\cos\theta} = -\frac{\cos^2\theta - \sin^2\theta}{2\sin\theta\cos\theta}$$

Using the double-angle formulas for sine and cosine,

$$\frac{dy}{dx} = -\frac{\cos 2\theta}{\sin 2\theta} = -\cot 2\theta$$

Thus, at the point where $\theta = \pi/4$ the slope of the tangent line is

$$m = \left.\frac{dy}{dx}\right|_{\theta=\pi/4} = -\cot\frac{\pi}{2} = 0$$

which implies that the circle has a horizontal tangent line at the point where $\theta = \pi/4$ (Figure 10.3.1). ◀

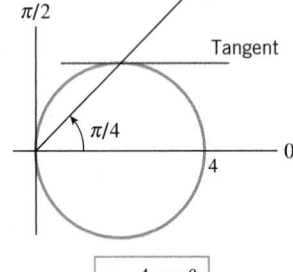

$r = 4\cos\theta$

▲ **Figure 10.3.1**

▶ **Example 2**   Find the points on the cardioid $r = 1 - \cos\theta$ at which there is a horizontal tangent line, a vertical tangent line, or a singular point.

Solution.   A horizontal tangent line will occur where $dy/d\theta = 0$ and $dx/d\theta \neq 0$, a vertical tangent line where $dy/d\theta \neq 0$ and $dx/d\theta = 0$, and a singular point where $dy/d\theta = 0$ and $dx/d\theta = 0$. We could find these derivatives from the formulas in (1). However, an alternative approach is to go back to basic principles and express the cardioid parametrically by substituting $r = 1 - \cos\theta$ in the conversion formulas $x = r\cos\theta$ and $y = r\sin\theta$. This yields

$$x = (1 - \cos\theta)\cos\theta, \quad y = (1 - \cos\theta)\sin\theta \qquad (0 \leq \theta \leq 2\pi)$$

Differentiating these equations with respect to θ and then simplifying yields (verify)

$$\frac{dx}{d\theta} = \sin\theta(2\cos\theta - 1), \quad \frac{dy}{d\theta} = (1 - \cos\theta)(1 + 2\cos\theta)$$

Thus, $dx/d\theta = 0$ if $\sin\theta = 0$ or $\cos\theta = \frac{1}{2}$, and $dy/d\theta = 0$ if $\cos\theta = 1$ or $\cos\theta = -\frac{1}{2}$. We leave it for you to solve these equations and show that the solutions of $dx/d\theta = 0$ on the interval $0 \leq \theta \leq 2\pi$ are

$$\frac{dx}{d\theta} = 0: \quad \theta = 0, \ \frac{\pi}{3}, \ \pi, \ \frac{5\pi}{3}, \ 2\pi$$

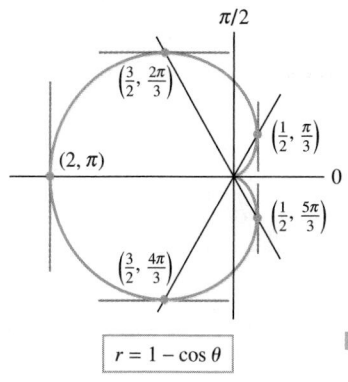

$r = 1 - \cos\theta$

▲ Figure 10.3.2

and the solutions of $dy/d\theta = 0$ on the interval $0 \leq \theta \leq 2\pi$ are

$$\frac{dy}{d\theta} = 0: \quad \theta = 0, \quad \frac{2\pi}{3}, \quad \frac{4\pi}{3}, \quad 2\pi$$

Thus, horizontal tangent lines occur at $\theta = 2\pi/3$ and $\theta = 4\pi/3$; vertical tangent lines occur at $\theta = \pi/3$, π, and $5\pi/3$; and singular points occur at $\theta = 0$ and $\theta = 2\pi$ (Figure 10.3.2). Note, however, that $r = 0$ at both singular points, so there is really only one singular point on the cardioid—the pole. ◄

■ TANGENT LINES TO POLAR CURVES AT THE ORIGIN

Formula (2) reveals some useful information about the behavior of a polar curve $r = f(\theta)$ that passes through the origin. If we assume that $r = 0$ and $dr/d\theta \neq 0$ when $\theta = \theta_0$, then it follows from Formula (2) that the slope of the tangent line to the curve at $\theta = \theta_0$ is

$$\frac{dy}{dx} = \frac{0 + \sin\theta_0 \dfrac{dr}{d\theta}}{0 + \cos\theta_0 \dfrac{dr}{d\theta}} = \frac{\sin\theta_0}{\cos\theta_0} = \tan\theta_0$$

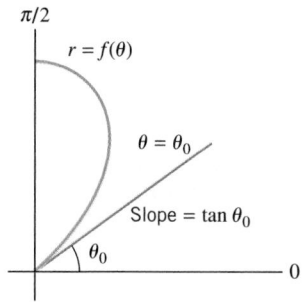

▲ Figure 10.3.3

(Figure 10.3.3). However, $\tan\theta_0$ is also the slope of the line $\theta = \theta_0$, so we can conclude that this line is tangent to the curve at the origin. Thus, we have established the following result.

10.3.1 THEOREM *If the polar curve $r = f(\theta)$ passes through the origin at $\theta = \theta_0$, and if $dr/d\theta \neq 0$ at $\theta = \theta_0$, then the line $\theta = \theta_0$ is tangent to the curve at the origin.*

This theorem tells us that equations of the tangent lines at the origin to the curve $r = f(\theta)$ can be obtained by solving the equation $f(\theta) = 0$. It is important to keep in mind, however, that $r = f(\theta)$ may be zero for more than one value of θ, so there may be more than one tangent line at the origin. This is illustrated in the next example.

▶ **Example 3** The three-petal rose $r = \sin 3\theta$ in Figure 10.3.4 has three tangent lines at the origin, which can be found by solving the equation

$$\sin 3\theta = 0$$

It was shown in Exercise 78 of Section 10.2 that the complete rose is traced once as θ varies over the interval $0 \leq \theta < \pi$, so we need only look for solutions in this interval. We leave it for you to confirm that these solutions are

$$\theta = 0, \quad \theta = \frac{\pi}{3}, \quad \text{and} \quad \theta = \frac{2\pi}{3}$$

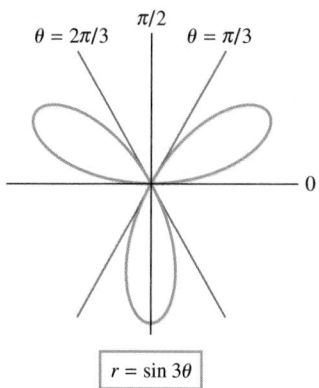

$r = \sin 3\theta$

▲ Figure 10.3.4

Since $dr/d\theta = 3\cos 3\theta \neq 0$ for these values of θ, these three lines are tangent to the rose at the origin, which is consistent with the figure. ◄

■ ARC LENGTH OF A POLAR CURVE

A formula for the arc length of a polar curve $r = f(\theta)$ can be derived by expressing the curve in parametric form and applying Formula (9) of Section 10.1 for the arc length of a parametric curve. We leave it as an exercise to show the following.

10.3.2 ARC LENGTH FORMULA FOR POLAR CURVES If no segment of the polar curve $r = f(\theta)$ is traced more than once as θ increases from α to β, and if $dr/d\theta$ is continuous for $\alpha \le \theta \le \beta$, then the arc length L from $\theta = \alpha$ to $\theta = \beta$ is

$$L = \int_\alpha^\beta \sqrt{[f(\theta)]^2 + [f'(\theta)]^2}\, d\theta = \int_\alpha^\beta \sqrt{r^2 + \left(\frac{dr}{d\theta}\right)^2}\, d\theta \qquad (3)$$

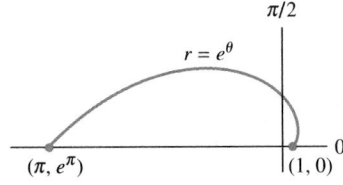

▲ **Figure 10.3.5**

▶ **Example 4** Find the arc length of the spiral $r = e^\theta$ in Figure 10.3.5 between $\theta = 0$ and $\theta = \pi$.

Solution.
$$L = \int_\alpha^\beta \sqrt{r^2 + \left(\frac{dr}{d\theta}\right)^2}\, d\theta = \int_0^\pi \sqrt{(e^\theta)^2 + (e^\theta)^2}\, d\theta$$
$$= \int_0^\pi \sqrt{2}\, e^\theta\, d\theta = \sqrt{2}\, e^\theta \bigg]_0^\pi = \sqrt{2}(e^\pi - 1) \approx 31.3 \blacktriangleleft$$

▶ **Example 5** Find the total arc length of the cardioid $r = 1 + \cos\theta$.

Solution. The cardioid is traced out once as θ varies from $\theta = 0$ to $\theta = 2\pi$. Thus,

$$L = \int_\alpha^\beta \sqrt{r^2 + \left(\frac{dr}{d\theta}\right)^2}\, d\theta = \int_0^{2\pi} \sqrt{(1 + \cos\theta)^2 + (-\sin\theta)^2}\, d\theta$$
$$= \sqrt{2} \int_0^{2\pi} \sqrt{1 + \cos\theta}\, d\theta$$
$$= 2 \int_0^{2\pi} \sqrt{\cos^2 \tfrac{1}{2}\theta}\, d\theta \qquad \boxed{\text{Identity (45) of Appendix B}}$$
$$= 2 \int_0^{2\pi} \left|\cos \tfrac{1}{2}\theta\right| d\theta$$

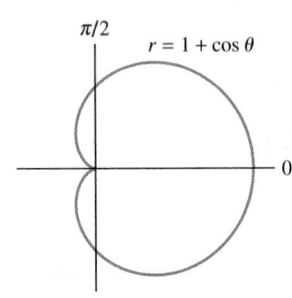

▲ **Figure 10.3.6**

Since $\cos \tfrac{1}{2}\theta$ changes sign at π, we must split the last integral into the sum of two integrals: the integral from 0 to π plus the integral from π to 2π. However, the integral from π to 2π is equal to the integral from 0 to π, since the cardioid is symmetric about the polar axis (Figure 10.3.6). Thus,

$$L = 2 \int_0^{2\pi} \left|\cos \tfrac{1}{2}\theta\right| d\theta = 4 \int_0^\pi \cos \tfrac{1}{2}\theta\, d\theta = 8 \sin \tfrac{1}{2}\theta \bigg]_0^\pi = 8 \blacktriangleleft$$

■ **AREA IN POLAR COORDINATES**

We begin our investigation of area in polar coordinates with a simple case.

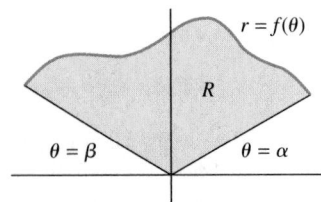

▲ **Figure 10.3.7**

10.3.3 AREA PROBLEM IN POLAR COORDINATES Suppose that α and β are angles that satisfy the condition
$$\alpha < \beta \le \alpha + 2\pi$$
and suppose that $f(\theta)$ is continuous and nonnegative for $\alpha \le \theta \le \beta$. Find the area of the region R enclosed by the polar curve $r = f(\theta)$ and the rays $\theta = \alpha$ and $\theta = \beta$ (Figure 10.3.7).

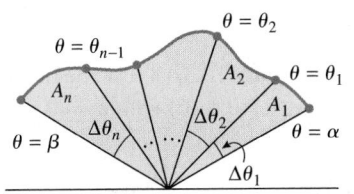

▲ **Figure 10.3.8**

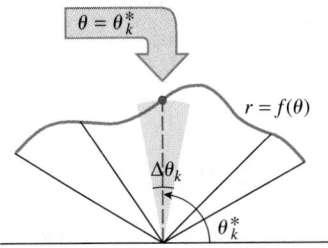

▲ **Figure 10.3.9**

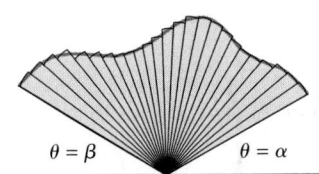

▲ **Figure 10.3.10**

In rectangular coordinates we obtained areas under curves by dividing the region into an increasing number of vertical strips, approximating the strips by rectangles, and taking a limit. In polar coordinates rectangles are clumsy to work with, and it is better to partition the region into *wedges* by using rays

$$\theta = \theta_1, \ \theta = \theta_2, \ldots, \ \theta = \theta_{n-1}$$

such that

$$\alpha < \theta_1 < \theta_2 < \cdots < \theta_{n-1} < \beta$$

(Figure 10.3.8). As shown in that figure, the rays divide the region R into n wedges with areas $A_1, A_2, \ldots, A_n$ and central angles $\Delta\theta_1, \Delta\theta_2, \ldots, \Delta\theta_n$. The area of the entire region can be written as

$$A = A_1 + A_2 + \cdots + A_n = \sum_{k=1}^{n} A_k \qquad (4)$$

If $\Delta\theta_k$ is small, then we can approximate the area A_k of the kth wedge by the area of a sector with central angle $\Delta\theta_k$ and radius $f(\theta_k^*)$, where $\theta = \theta_k^*$ is any ray that lies in the kth wedge (Figure 10.3.9). Thus, from (4) and Formula (5) of Appendix B for the area of a sector, we obtain

$$A = \sum_{k=1}^{n} A_k \approx \sum_{k=1}^{n} \tfrac{1}{2}[f(\theta_k^*)]^2 \Delta\theta_k \qquad (5)$$

If we now increase n in such a way that $\max \Delta\theta_k \to 0$, then the sectors will become better and better approximations of the wedges and it is reasonable to expect that (5) will approach the exact value of the area A (Figure 10.3.10); that is,

$$A = \lim_{\max \Delta\theta_k \to 0} \sum_{k=1}^{n} \tfrac{1}{2}[f(\theta_k^*)]^2 \Delta\theta_k = \int_{\alpha}^{\beta} \tfrac{1}{2}[f(\theta)]^2 \, d\theta$$

Note that the discussion above can easily be adapted to the case where $f(\theta)$ is nonpositive for $\alpha \leq \theta \leq \beta$. We summarize this result below.

10.3.4   AREA IN POLAR COORDINATES   If α and β are angles that satisfy the condition

$$\alpha < \beta \leq \alpha + 2\pi$$

and if $f(\theta)$ is continuous and either nonnegative or nonpositive for $\alpha \leq \theta \leq \beta$, then the area A of the region R enclosed by the polar curve $r = f(\theta)$ ($\alpha \leq \theta \leq \beta$) and the lines $\theta = \alpha$ and $\theta = \beta$ is

$$A = \int_{\alpha}^{\beta} \tfrac{1}{2}[f(\theta)]^2 \, d\theta = \int_{\alpha}^{\beta} \tfrac{1}{2} r^2 \, d\theta \qquad (6)$$

The hardest part of applying (6) is determining the limits of integration. This can be done as follows:

Area in Polar Coordinates: Limits of Integration

Step 1. Sketch the region R whose area is to be determined.

Step 2. Draw an arbitrary "radial line" from the pole to the boundary curve $r = f(\theta)$.

Step 3. Ask, "Over what interval of values must θ vary in order for the radial line to sweep out the region R?"

Step 4. Your answer in Step 3 will determine the lower and upper limits of integration.

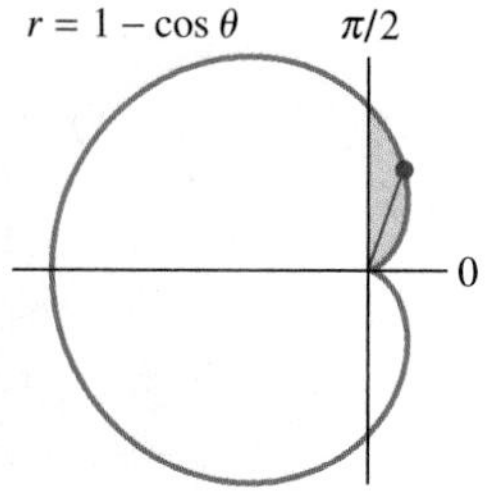

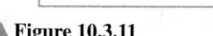

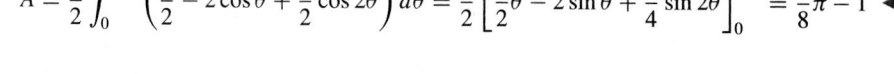

The shaded region is swept out by the radial line as θ varies from 0 to $\pi/2$.

▲ **Figure 10.3.11**

▶ **Example 6** Find the area of the region in the first quadrant that is within the cardioid $r = 1 - \cos\theta$.

Solution. The region and a typical radial line are shown in Figure 10.3.11. For the radial line to sweep out the region, θ must vary from 0 to $\pi/2$. Thus, from (6) with $\alpha = 0$ and $\beta = \pi/2$, we obtain

$$A = \int_0^{\pi/2} \frac{1}{2} r^2 \, d\theta = \frac{1}{2} \int_0^{\pi/2} (1 - \cos\theta)^2 \, d\theta = \frac{1}{2} \int_0^{\pi/2} (1 - 2\cos\theta + \cos^2\theta) \, d\theta$$

With the help of the identity $\cos^2\theta = \frac{1}{2}(1 + \cos 2\theta)$, this can be rewritten as

$$A = \frac{1}{2} \int_0^{\pi/2} \left(\frac{3}{2} - 2\cos\theta + \frac{1}{2}\cos 2\theta \right) d\theta = \frac{1}{2}\left[\frac{3}{2}\theta - 2\sin\theta + \frac{1}{4}\sin 2\theta \right]_0^{\pi/2} = \frac{3}{8}\pi - 1 \blacktriangleleft$$

▶ **Example 7** Find the entire area within the cardioid of Example 6.

Solution. For the radial line to sweep out the entire cardioid, θ must vary from 0 to 2π. Thus, from (6) with $\alpha = 0$ and $\beta = 2\pi$,

$$A = \int_0^{2\pi} \frac{1}{2} r^2 \, d\theta = \frac{1}{2} \int_0^{2\pi} (1 - \cos\theta)^2 \, d\theta$$

If we proceed as in Example 6, this reduces to

$$A = \frac{1}{2} \int_0^{2\pi} \left(\frac{3}{2} - 2\cos\theta + \frac{1}{2}\cos 2\theta \right) d\theta = \frac{3\pi}{2}$$

Alternative Solution. Since the cardioid is symmetric about the x-axis, we can calculate the portion of the area above the x-axis and double the result. In the portion of the cardioid above the x-axis, θ ranges from 0 to π, so that

$$A = 2 \int_0^{\pi} \frac{1}{2} r^2 \, d\theta = \int_0^{\pi} (1 - \cos\theta)^2 \, d\theta = \frac{3\pi}{2} \blacktriangleleft$$

■ **USING SYMMETRY**

Although Formula (6) is applicable if $r = f(\theta)$ is negative, area computations can sometimes be simplified by using symmetry to restrict the limits of integration to intervals where $r \geq 0$. This is illustrated in the next example.

▶ **Example 8** Find the area of the region enclosed by the rose curve $r = \cos 2\theta$.

Solution. Referring to Figure 10.2.13 and using symmetry, the area in the first quadrant that is swept out for $0 \leq \theta \leq \pi/4$ is one-eighth of the total area inside the rose. Thus, from Formula (6)

$$A = 8 \int_0^{\pi/4} \frac{1}{2} r^2 \, d\theta = 4 \int_0^{\pi/4} \cos^2 2\theta \, d\theta$$

$$= 4 \int_0^{\pi/4} \frac{1}{2}(1 + \cos 4\theta) \, d\theta = 2 \int_0^{\pi/4} (1 + \cos 4\theta) \, d\theta$$

$$= 2\theta + \frac{1}{2}\sin 4\theta \Big]_0^{\pi/4} = \frac{\pi}{2} \blacktriangleleft$$

Sometimes the most natural way to satisfy the restriction $\alpha < \beta \leq \alpha + 2\pi$ required by Formula (6) is to use a negative value for α. For example, suppose that we are interested in finding the area of the shaded region in Figure 10.3.12a. The first step would be to determine the intersections of the cardioid $r = 4 + 4\cos\theta$ and the circle $r = 6$, since this information is needed for the limits of integration. To find the points of intersection, we can equate the two expressions for r. This yields

$$4 + 4\cos\theta = 6 \quad \text{or} \quad \cos\theta = \frac{1}{2}$$

which is satisfied by the positive angles

$$\theta = \frac{\pi}{3} \quad \text{and} \quad \theta = \frac{5\pi}{3}$$

However, there is a problem here because the radial lines to the circle and cardioid do not sweep through the shaded region shown in Figure 10.3.12b as θ varies over the interval $\pi/3 \leq \theta \leq 5\pi/3$. There are two ways to circumvent this problem—one is to take advantage of the symmetry by integrating over the interval $0 \leq \theta \leq \pi/3$ and doubling the result, and the second is to use a negative lower limit of integration and integrate over the interval $-\pi/3 \leq \theta \leq \pi/3$ (Figure 10.3.12c). The two methods are illustrated in the next example.

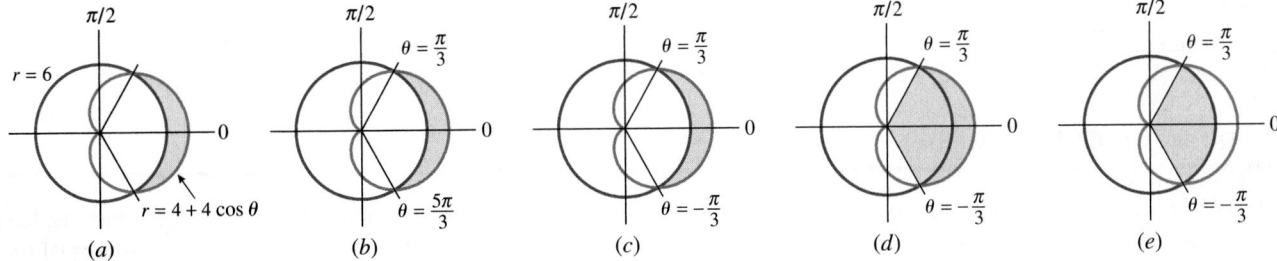

(a) (b) (c) (d) (e)

▲ **Figure 10.3.12**

▶ **Example 9** Find the area of the region that is inside of the cardioid $r = 4 + 4\cos\theta$ and outside of the circle $r = 6$.

Solution Using a Negative Angle.   The area of the region can be obtained by subtracting the areas in Figures 10.3.12d and 10.3.12e:

$$A = \int_{-\pi/3}^{\pi/3} \frac{1}{2}(4 + 4\cos\theta)^2 \, d\theta - \int_{-\pi/3}^{\pi/3} \frac{1}{2}(6)^2 \, d\theta \qquad \boxed{\begin{array}{l}\text{Area inside cardioid}\\ \text{minus area inside circle.}\end{array}}$$

$$= \int_{-\pi/3}^{\pi/3} \frac{1}{2}[(4 + 4\cos\theta)^2 - 36] \, d\theta = \int_{-\pi/3}^{\pi/3} (16\cos\theta + 8\cos^2\theta - 10) \, d\theta$$

$$= \left[16\sin\theta + (4\theta + 2\sin 2\theta) - 10\theta\right]_{-\pi/3}^{\pi/3} = 18\sqrt{3} - 4\pi$$

Solution Using Symmetry.   Using symmetry, we can calculate the area above the polar axis and double it. This yields (verify)

$$A = 2\int_{0}^{\pi/3} \frac{1}{2}[(4 + 4\cos\theta)^2 - 36] \, d\theta = 2(9\sqrt{3} - 2\pi) = 18\sqrt{3} - 4\pi$$

which agrees with the preceding result. ◀

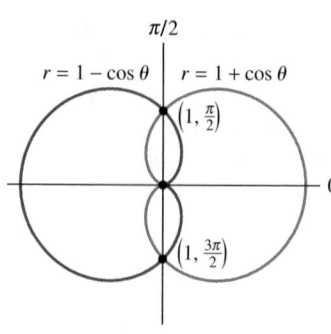

$r = 1 - \cos\theta$ $r = 1 + \cos\theta$

$\left(1, \frac{\pi}{2}\right)$

$\left(1, \frac{3\pi}{2}\right)$

▲ **Figure 10.3.13**

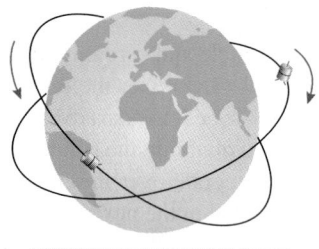

The orbits intersect, but the satellites do not collide.

▲ **Figure 10.3.14**

■ INTERSECTIONS OF POLAR GRAPHS

In the last example we found the intersections of the cardioid and circle by equating their expressions for r and solving for θ. However, because a point can be represented in different ways in polar coordinates, this procedure will not always produce all of the intersections. For example, the cardioids

$$r = 1 - \cos\theta \quad \text{and} \quad r = 1 + \cos\theta \qquad (7)$$

intersect at three points: the pole, the point $(1, \pi/2)$, and the point $(1, 3\pi/2)$ (Figure 10.3.13). Equating the right-hand sides of the equations in (7) yields $1 - \cos\theta = 1 + \cos\theta$ or $\cos\theta = 0$, so

$$\theta = \frac{\pi}{2} + k\pi, \quad k = 0, \pm 1, \pm 2, \ldots$$

Substituting any of these values in (7) yields $r = 1$, so that we have found only two distinct points of intersection, $(1, \pi/2)$ and $(1, 3\pi/2)$; the pole has been missed. This problem occurs because the two cardioids pass through the pole at different values of θ—the cardioid $r = 1 - \cos\theta$ passes through the pole at $\theta = 0$, and the cardioid $r = 1 + \cos\theta$ passes through the pole at $\theta = \pi$.

The situation with the cardioids is analogous to two satellites circling the Earth in intersecting orbits (Figure 10.3.14). The satellites will not collide unless they reach the same point at the same time. In general, when looking for intersections of polar curves, it is a good idea to graph the curves to determine how many intersections there should be.

✔ QUICK CHECK EXERCISES 10.3   *(See page 729 for answers.)*

1. (a) To obtain dy/dx directly from the polar equation $r = f(\theta)$, we can use the formula

$$\frac{dy}{dx} = \frac{dy/d\theta}{dx/d\theta} = \underline{\hspace{2cm}}$$

(b) Use the formula in part (a) to find dy/dx directly from the polar equation $r = \csc\theta$.

2. (a) What conditions on $f(\theta_0)$ and $f'(\theta_0)$ guarantee that the line $\theta = \theta_0$ is tangent to the polar curve $r = f(\theta)$ at the origin?

(b) What are the values of θ_0 in $[0, 2\pi]$ at which the lines $\theta = \theta_0$ are tangent at the origin to the four-petal rose $r = \cos 2\theta$?

3. (a) To find the arc length L of the polar curve $r = f(\theta)$ $(\alpha \le \theta \le \beta)$, we can use the formula $L = \underline{\hspace{2cm}}$.

(b) The polar curve $r = \sec\theta$ $(0 \le \theta \le \pi/4)$ has arc length $L = \underline{\hspace{2cm}}$.

4. The area of the region enclosed by a nonnegative polar curve $r = f(\theta)$ $(\alpha \le \theta \le \beta)$ and the lines $\theta = \alpha$ and $\theta = \beta$ is given by the definite integral $\underline{\hspace{2cm}}$.

5. Find the area of the circle $r = a$ by integration.

EXERCISE SET 10.3   ⬚ Graphing Utility   ⊡ CAS

1–6 Find the slope of the tangent line to the polar curve for the given value of θ. ■

1. $r = 2\sin\theta$; $\theta = \pi/6$

2. $r = 1 + \cos\theta$; $\theta = \pi/2$

3. $r = 1/\theta$; $\theta = 2$

4. $r = a\sec 2\theta$; $\theta = \pi/6$

5. $r = \sin 3\theta$; $\theta = \pi/4$

6. $r = 4 - 3\sin\theta$; $\theta = \pi$

7–8 Calculate the slopes of the tangent lines indicated in the accompanying figures. ■

7. $r = 2 + 2\sin\theta$

8. $r = 1 - 2\sin\theta$

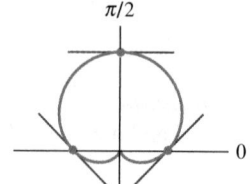

▲ **Figure Ex-7**

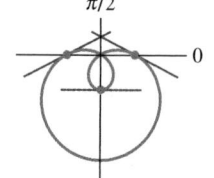

▲ **Figure Ex-8**

9–10 Find polar coordinates of all points at which the polar curve has a horizontal or a vertical tangent line. ■

9. $r = a(1 + \cos\theta)$

10. $r = a\sin\theta$

11–12 Use a graphing utility to make a conjecture about the number of points on the polar curve at which there is a horizontal tangent line, and confirm your conjecture by finding appropriate derivatives. ■

11. $r = \sin\theta\cos^2\theta$ **12.** $r = 1 - 2\sin\theta$

13–18 Sketch the polar curve and find polar equations of the tangent lines to the curve at the pole. ■

13. $r = 2\cos 3\theta$ **14.** $r = 4\sin\theta$ **15.** $r = 4\sqrt{\cos 2\theta}$

16. $r = \sin 2\theta$ **17.** $r = 1 - 2\cos\theta$ **18.** $r = 2\theta$

19–22 Use Formula (3) to calculate the arc length of the polar curve. ■

19. The entire circle $r = a$

20. The entire circle $r = 2a\cos\theta$

21. The entire cardioid $r = a(1 - \cos\theta)$

22. $r = e^{3\theta}$ from $\theta = 0$ to $\theta = 2$

23. (a) Show that the arc length of one petal of the rose $r = \cos n\theta$ is given by

$$2\int_0^{\pi/(2n)}\sqrt{1 + (n^2 - 1)\sin^2 n\theta}\, d\theta$$

(b) Use the numerical integration capability of a calculating utility to approximate the arc length of one petal of the four-petal rose $r = \cos 2\theta$.

(c) Use the numerical integration capability of a calculating utility to approximate the arc length of one petal of the n-petal rose $r = \cos n\theta$ for $n = 2, 3, 4, \ldots, 20$; then make a conjecture about the limit of these arc lengths as $n \to +\infty$.

24. (a) Sketch the spiral $r = e^{-\theta/8}$ $(0 \le \theta < +\infty)$.

(b) Find an improper integral for the total arc length of the spiral.

(c) Show that the integral converges and find the total arc length of the spiral.

25. Write down, but do not evaluate, an integral for the area of each shaded region.

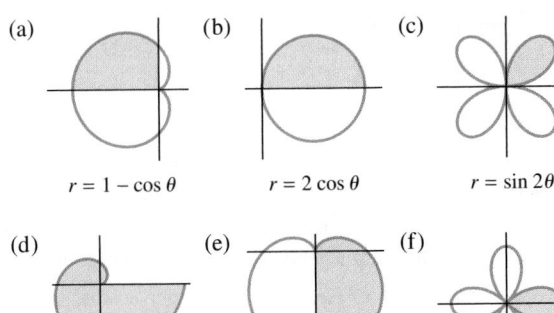

(a) $r = 1 - \cos\theta$ (b) $r = 2\cos\theta$ (c) $r = \sin 2\theta$

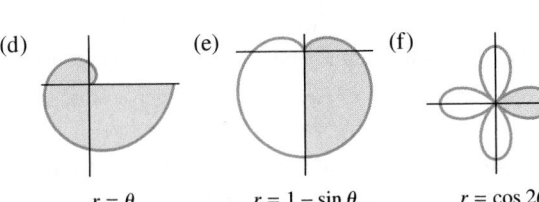

(d) $r = \theta$ (e) $r = 1 - \sin\theta$ (f) $r = \cos 2\theta$

26. Find the area of the shaded region in Exercise 25(d).

27. In each part, find the area of the circle by integration.
(a) $r = 2a\sin\theta$ (b) $r = 2a\cos\theta$

28. (a) Show that $r = 2\sin\theta + 2\cos\theta$ is a circle.
(b) Find the area of the circle using a geometric formula and then by integration.

29–34 Find the area of the region described. ■

29. The region that is enclosed by the cardioid $r = 2 + 2\sin\theta$.

30. The region in the first quadrant within the cardioid $r = 1 + \cos\theta$.

31. The region enclosed by the rose $r = 4\cos 3\theta$.

32. The region enclosed by the rose $r = 2\sin 2\theta$.

33. The region enclosed by the inner loop of the limaçon $r = 1 + 2\cos\theta$. [*Hint:* $r \le 0$ over the interval of integration.]

34. The region swept out by a radial line from the pole to the curve $r = 2/\theta$ as θ varies over the interval $1 \le \theta \le 3$.

35–38 Find the area of the shaded region. ■

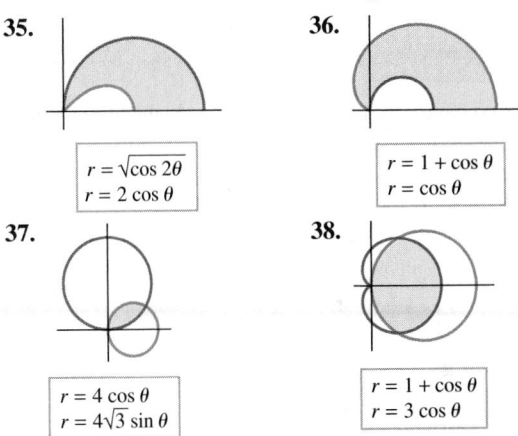

35.
$r = \sqrt{\cos 2\theta}$
$r = 2\cos\theta$

36.
$r = 1 + \cos\theta$
$r = \cos\theta$

37.
$r = 4\cos\theta$
$r = 4\sqrt{3}\sin\theta$

38.
$r = 1 + \cos\theta$
$r = 3\cos\theta$

39–46 Find the area of the region described. ■

39. The region inside the circle $r = 3\sin\theta$ and outside the cardioid $r = 1 + \sin\theta$.

40. The region outside the cardioid $r = 2 - 2\cos\theta$ and inside the circle $r = 4$.

41. The region inside the cardioid $r = 2 + 2\cos\theta$ and outside the circle $r = 3$.

42. The region that is common to the circles $r = 2\cos\theta$ and $r = 2\sin\theta$.

43. The region between the loops of the limaçon $r = \frac{1}{2} + \cos\theta$.

44. The region inside the cardioid $r = 2 + 2\cos\theta$ and to the right of the line $r\cos\theta = \frac{3}{2}$.

45. The region inside the circle $r = 2$ and to the right of the line $r = \sqrt{2}\sec\theta$.

46. The region inside the rose $r = 2a\cos 2\theta$ and outside the circle $r = a\sqrt{2}$.

47–50 True–False Determine whether the statement is true or false. Explain your answer. ■

47. The x-axis is tangent to the polar curve $r = \cos(\theta/2)$ at $\theta = 3\pi$.

48. The arc length of the polar curve $r = \sqrt{\theta}$ for $0 \le \theta \le \pi/2$ is given by

$$L = \int_0^{\pi/2} \sqrt{1 + \frac{1}{4\theta}}\, d\theta$$

49. The area of a sector with central angle θ taken from a circle of radius r is θr^2.

50. The expression

$$\frac{1}{2}\int_{-\pi/4}^{\pi/4} (1 - \sqrt{2}\cos\theta)^2\, d\theta$$

computes the area enclosed by the inner loop of the limaçon $r = 1 - \sqrt{2}\cos\theta$.

FOCUS ON CONCEPTS

51. (a) Find the error: The area that is inside the lemniscate $r^2 = a^2\cos 2\theta$ is

$$A = \int_0^{2\pi} \tfrac{1}{2}r^2\, d\theta = \int_0^{2\pi} \tfrac{1}{2}a^2\cos 2\theta\, d\theta$$

$$= \tfrac{1}{4}a^2 \sin 2\theta \Big]_0^{2\pi} = 0$$

(b) Find the correct area.

(c) Find the area inside the lemniscate $r^2 = 4\cos 2\theta$ and outside the circle $r = \sqrt{2}$.

52. Find the area inside the curve $r^2 = \sin 2\theta$.

53. A radial line is drawn from the origin to the spiral $r = a\theta$ ($a > 0$ and $\theta \ge 0$). Find the area swept out during the second revolution of the radial line that was not swept out during the first revolution.

54. As illustrated in the accompanying figure, suppose that a rod with one end fixed at the pole of a polar coordinate system rotates counterclockwise at the constant rate of 1 rad/s. At time $t = 0$ a bug on the rod is 10 mm from the pole and is moving outward along the rod at the constant speed of 2 mm/s.
(a) Find an equation of the form $r = f(\theta)$ for the path of motion of the bug, assuming that $\theta = 0$ when $t = 0$.
(b) Find the distance the bug travels along the path in part (a) during the first 5 s. Round your answer to the nearest tenth of a millimeter.

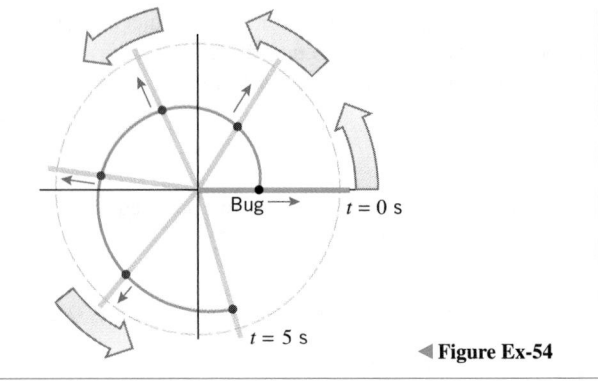

Bug ⟶ $t = 0$ s

$t = 5$ s   ◀ **Figure Ex-54**

55. (a) Show that the Folium of Descartes $x^3 - 3xy + y^3 = 0$ can be expressed in polar coordinates as

$$r = \frac{3\sin\theta\cos\theta}{\cos^3\theta + \sin^3\theta}$$

(b) Use a CAS to show that the area inside of the loop is $\frac{3}{2}$ (Figure 3.1.3a).

56. (a) What is the area that is enclosed by one petal of the rose $r = a\cos n\theta$ if n is an even integer?
(b) What is the area that is enclosed by one petal of the rose $r = a\cos n\theta$ if n is an odd integer?
(c) Use a CAS to show that the total area enclosed by the rose $r = a\cos n\theta$ is $\pi a^2/2$ if the number of petals is even. [*Hint:* See Exercise 78 of Section 10.2.]
(d) Use a CAS to show that the total area enclosed by the rose $r = a\cos n\theta$ is $\pi a^2/4$ if the number of petals is odd.

57. One of the most famous problems in Greek antiquity was "squaring the circle," that is, using a straightedge and compass to construct a square whose area is equal to that of a given circle. It was proved in the nineteenth century that no such construction is possible. However, show that the shaded areas in the accompanying figure are equal, thereby "squaring the crescent."

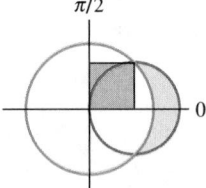

◀ **Figure Ex-57**

58. Use a graphing utility to generate the polar graph of the equation $r = \cos 3\theta + 2$, and find the area that it encloses.

59. Use a graphing utility to generate the graph of the *bifolium* $r = 2\cos\theta\sin^2\theta$, and find the area of the upper loop.

60. Use Formula (9) of Section 10.1 to derive the arc length formula for polar curves, Formula (3).

61. As illustrated in the accompanying figure, let $P(r, \theta)$ be a point on the polar curve $r = f(\theta)$, let ψ be the smallest counterclockwise angle from the extended radius OP to the tangent line at P, and let ϕ be the angle of inclination of the tangent line. Derive the formula

$$\tan \psi = \frac{r}{dr/d\theta}$$

by substituting $\tan \phi$ for dy/dx in Formula (2) and applying the trigonometric identity

$$\tan(\phi - \theta) = \frac{\tan \phi - \tan \theta}{1 + \tan \phi \tan \theta}$$

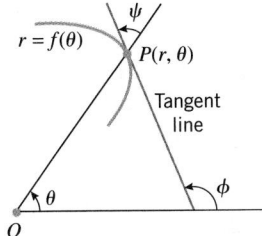

◀ **Figure Ex-61**

62–63 Use the formula for ψ obtained in Exercise 61. ▨

62. (a) Use the trigonometric identity

$$\tan \frac{\theta}{2} = \frac{1 - \cos \theta}{\sin \theta}$$

to show that if (r, θ) is a point on the cardioid

$$r = 1 - \cos \theta \qquad (0 \leq \theta < 2\pi)$$

then $\psi = \theta/2$.

(b) Sketch the cardioid and show the angle ψ at the points where the cardioid crosses the y-axis.

(c) Find the angle ψ at the points where the cardioid crosses the y-axis.

63. Show that for a logarithmic spiral $r = ae^{b\theta}$, the angle from the radial line to the tangent line is constant along the spiral (see the accompanying figure). [*Note:* For this reason, logarithmic spirals are sometimes called **equiangular spirals**.]

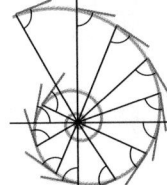

◀ **Figure Ex-63**

64. (a) In the discussion associated with Exercises 75–80 of Section 10.1, formulas were given for the area of the

surface of revolution that is generated by revolving a parametric curve about the x-axis or y-axis. Use those formulas to derive the following formulas for the areas of the surfaces of revolution that are generated by revolving the portion of the polar curve $r = f(\theta)$ from $\theta = \alpha$ to $\theta = \beta$ about the polar axis and about the line $\theta = \pi/2$:

$$S = \int_\alpha^\beta 2\pi r \sin\theta \sqrt{r^2 + \left(\frac{dr}{d\theta}\right)^2} \, d\theta \qquad \boxed{\text{About } \theta = 0}$$

$$S = \int_\alpha^\beta 2\pi r \cos\theta \sqrt{r^2 + \left(\frac{dr}{d\theta}\right)^2} \, d\theta \qquad \boxed{\text{About } \theta = \pi/2}$$

(b) State conditions under which these formulas hold.

65–68 Sketch the surface, and use the formulas in Exercise 64 to find the surface area. ▨

65. The surface generated by revolving the circle $r = \cos\theta$ about the line $\theta = \pi/2$.

66. The surface generated by revolving the spiral $r = e^\theta$ $(0 \leq \theta \leq \pi/2)$ about the line $\theta = \pi/2$.

67. The "apple" generated by revolving the upper half of the cardioid $r = 1 - \cos\theta$ $(0 \leq \theta \leq \pi)$ about the polar axis.

68. The sphere of radius a generated by revolving the semicircle $r = a$ in the upper half-plane about the polar axis.

69. Writing
(a) Show that if $0 \leq \theta_1 < \theta_2 \leq \pi$ and if r_1 and r_2 are positive, then the area A of a triangle with vertices $(0, 0)$, (r_1, θ_1), and (r_2, θ_2) is

$$A = \tfrac{1}{2} r_1 r_2 \sin(\theta_2 - \theta_1)$$

(b) Use the formula obtained in part (a) to describe an approach to answer Area Problem 10.3.3 that uses an approximation of the region R by triangles instead of circular wedges. Reconcile your approach with Formula (6).

70. Writing In order to find the area of a region bounded by two polar curves it is often necessary to determine their points of intersection. Give an example to illustrate that the points of intersection of curves $r = f(\theta)$ and $r = g(\theta)$ may not coincide with solutions to $f(\theta) = g(\theta)$. Discuss some strategies for determining intersection points of polar curves and provide examples to illustrate your strategies.

✔QUICK CHECK ANSWERS 10.3

1. (a) $\dfrac{r \cos\theta + \sin\theta \dfrac{dr}{d\theta}}{-r \sin\theta + \cos\theta \dfrac{dr}{d\theta}}$ (b) $\dfrac{dy}{dx} = 0$ **2.** (a) $f(\theta_0) = 0$, $f'(\theta_0) \neq 0$ (b) $\theta_0 = \dfrac{\pi}{4}, \dfrac{3\pi}{4}, \dfrac{5\pi}{4}, \dfrac{7\pi}{4}$

3. (a) $\displaystyle\int_\alpha^\beta \sqrt{r^2 + \left(\frac{dr}{d\theta}\right)^2} \, d\theta$ (b) 1   **4.** $\displaystyle\int_\alpha^\beta \tfrac{1}{2}[f(\theta)]^2 \, d\theta = \int_\alpha^\beta \tfrac{1}{2} r^2 \, d\theta$ **5.** $\displaystyle\int_0^{2\pi} \tfrac{1}{2} a^2 \, d\theta = \pi a^2$

10.4 CONIC SECTIONS

In this section[*] we will discuss some of the basic geometric properties of parabolas, ellipses, and hyperbolas. These curves play an important role in calculus and also arise naturally in a broad range of applications in such fields as planetary motion, design of telescopes and antennas, geodetic positioning, and medicine, to name a few.

■ CONIC SECTIONS

Circles, ellipses, parabolas, and hyperbolas are called *conic sections* or *conics* because they can be obtained as intersections of a plane with a double-napped circular cone (Figure 10.4.1). If the plane passes through the vertex of the double-napped cone, then the intersection is a point, a pair of intersecting lines, or a single line. These are called *degenerate conic sections*.

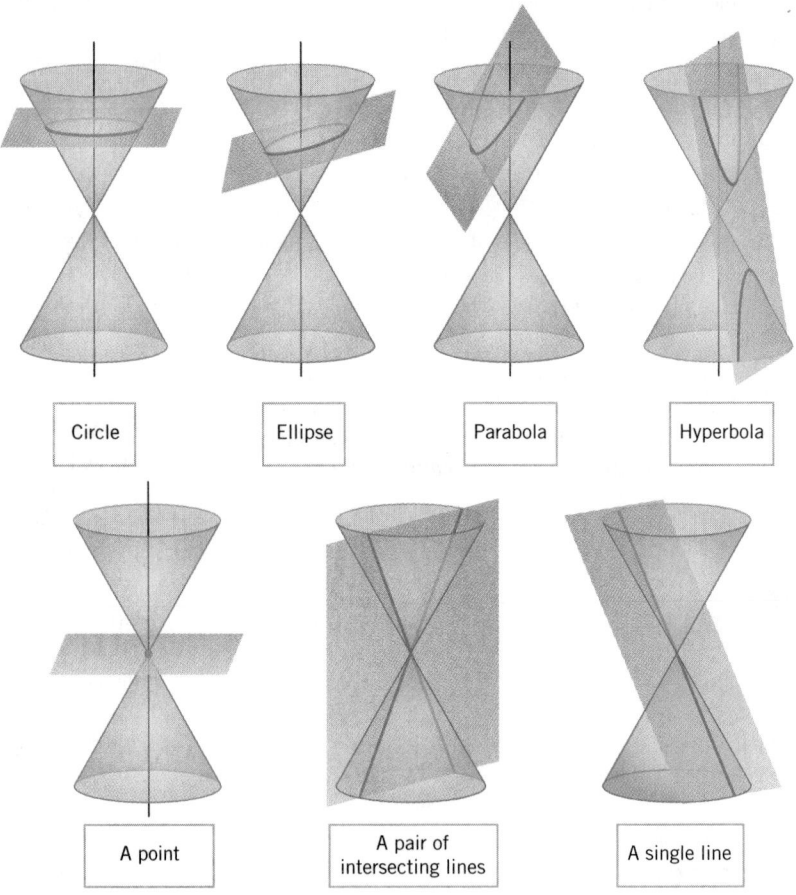

| Circle | Ellipse | Parabola | Hyperbola |

| A point | A pair of intersecting lines | A single line |

▲ **Figure 10.4.1**

---

[*]Some students may already be familiar with the material in this section, in which case it can be treated as a review. Instructors who want to spend some additional time on precalculus review may want to allocate more than one lecture on this material.

■ DEFINITIONS OF THE CONIC SECTIONS

Although we could derive properties of parabolas, ellipses, and hyperbolas by defining them as intersections with a double-napped cone, it will be better suited to calculus if we begin with equivalent definitions that are based on their geometric properties.

10.4.1   DEFINITION   A *parabola* is the set of all points in the plane that are equidistant from a fixed line and a fixed point not on the line.

The line is called the ***directrix*** of the parabola, and the point is called the ***focus*** (Figure 10.4.2). A parabola is symmetric about the line that passes through the focus at right angles to the directrix. This line, called the ***axis*** or the ***axis of symmetry*** of the parabola, intersects the parabola at a point called the ***vertex***.

10.4.2   DEFINITION   An *ellipse* is the set of all points in the plane, the sum of whose distances from two fixed points is a given positive constant that is greater than the distance between the fixed points.

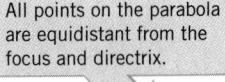

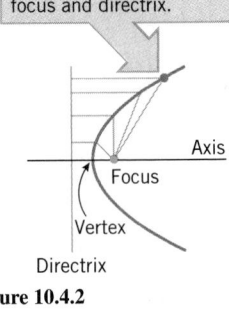

▲ **Figure 10.4.2**

The two fixed points are called the ***foci*** (plural of "focus") of the ellipse, and the midpoint of the line segment joining the foci is called the ***center*** (Figure 10.4.3a). To help visualize Definition 10.4.2, imagine that two ends of a string are tacked to the foci and a pencil traces a curve as it is held tight against the string (Figure 10.4.3b). The resulting curve will be an ellipse since the sum of the distances to the foci is a constant, namely, the total length of the string. Note that if the foci coincide, the ellipse reduces to a circle. For ellipses other than circles, the line segment through the foci and across the ellipse is called the ***major axis*** (Figure 10.4.3c), and the line segment across the ellipse, through the center, and perpendicular to the major axis is called the ***minor axis***. The endpoints of the major axis are called ***vertices***.

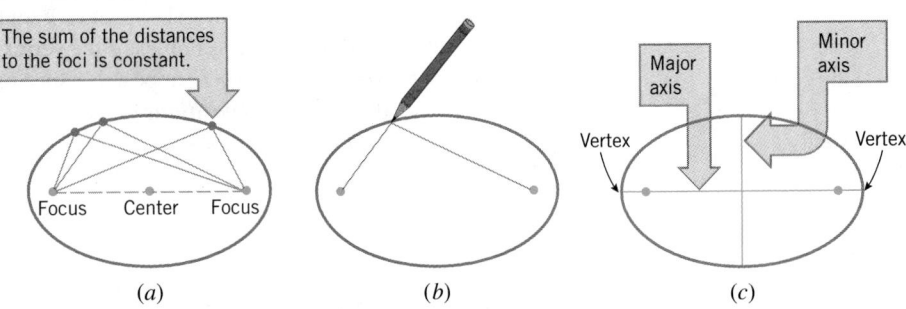

▶ **Figure 10.4.3**

10.4.3   DEFINITION   A *hyperbola* is the set of all points in the plane, the difference of whose distances from two fixed distinct points is a given positive constant that is less than the distance between the fixed points.

The two fixed points are called the ***foci*** of the hyperbola, and the term "difference" that is used in the definition is understood to mean the distance to the farther focus minus the distance to the closer focus. As a result, the points on the hyperbola form two ***branches***, each "wrapping around" the closer focus (Figure 10.4.4a). The midpoint of the line segment joining the foci is called the **center** of the hyperbola, the line through the foci is called the **focal axis**, and the line through the center that is perpendicular to the focal axis is called the **conjugate axis**. The hyperbola intersects the focal axis at two points called the **vertices**.

Associated with every hyperbola is a pair of lines, called the **asymptotes** of the hyperbola. These lines intersect at the center of the hyperbola and have the property that as a point P moves along the hyperbola away from the center, the vertical distance between P and one of the asymptotes approaches zero (Figure 10.4.4b).

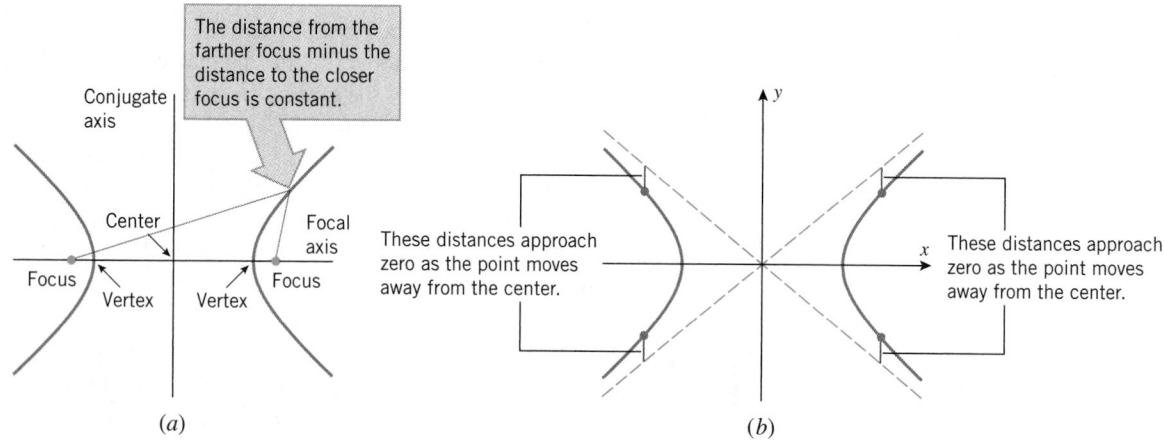

(a)

▲ **Figure 10.4.4**

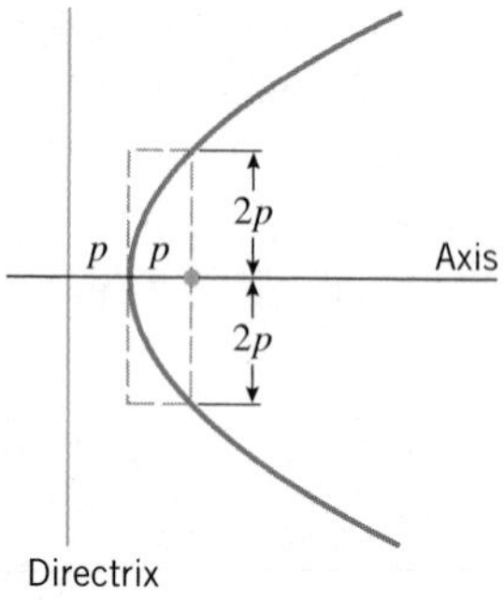

(b)

■ EQUATIONS OF PARABOLAS IN STANDARD POSITION

It is traditional in the study of parabolas to denote the distance between the focus and the vertex by p. The vertex is equidistant from the focus and the directrix, so the distance between the vertex and the directrix is also p; consequently, the distance between the focus and the directrix is $2p$ (Figure 10.4.5). As illustrated in that figure, the parabola passes through two of the corners of a box that extends from the vertex to the focus along the axis of symmetry and extends $2p$ units above and $2p$ units below the axis of symmetry.

The equation of a parabola is simplest if the vertex is the origin and the axis of symmetry is along the x-axis or y-axis. The four possible such orientations are shown in Figure 10.4.6. These are called the **standard positions** of a parabola, and the resulting equations are called the **standard equations** of a parabola.

▲ **Figure 10.4.5**

PARABOLAS IN STANDARD POSITION

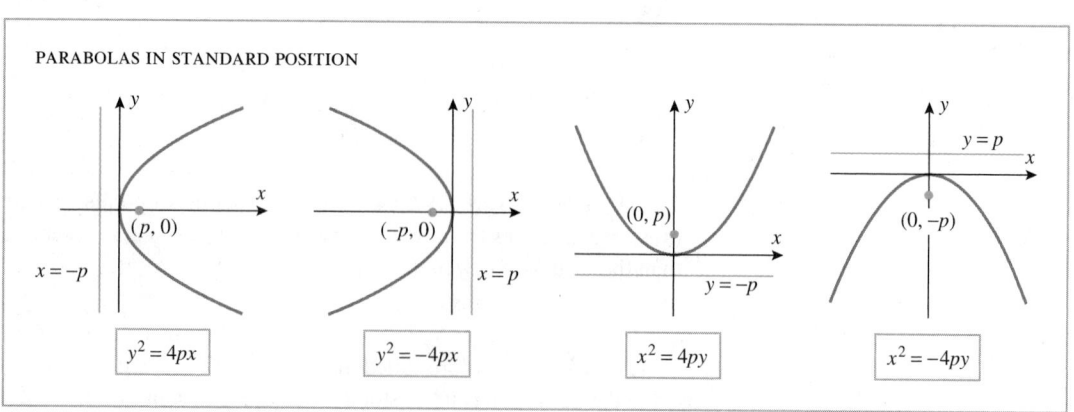

▲ **Figure 10.4.6**

To illustrate how the equations in Figure 10.4.6 are obtained, we will derive the equation for the parabola with focus $(p, 0)$ and directrix $x = -p$. Let $P(x, y)$ be any point on the parabola. Since P is equidistant from the focus and directrix, the distances PF and PD in Figure 10.4.7 are equal; that is,

$$PF = PD \tag{1}$$

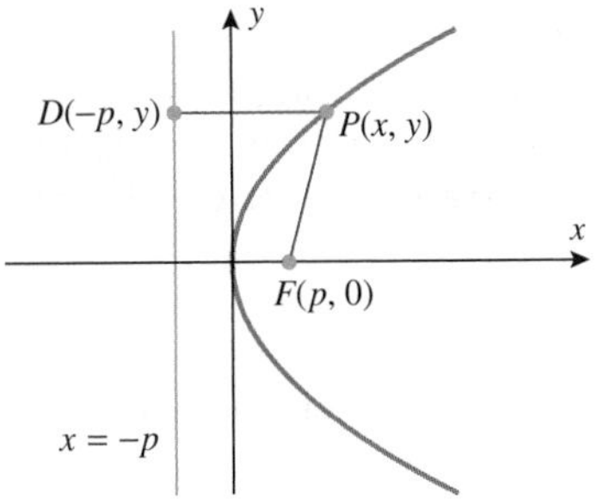

where $D(-p, y)$ is the foot of the perpendicular from P to the directrix. From the distance formula, the distances PF and PD are

$$PF = \sqrt{(x - p)^2 + y^2} \quad \text{and} \quad PD = \sqrt{(x + p)^2} \tag{2}$$

Substituting in (1) and squaring yields

$$(x - p)^2 + y^2 = (x + p)^2 \tag{3}$$

and after simplifying

$$y^2 = 4px \tag{4}$$

The derivations of the other equations in Figure 10.4.6 are similar.

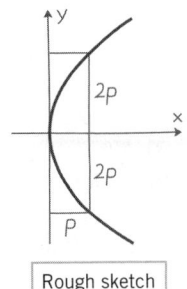

▲ **Figure 10.4.7**

■ **A TECHNIQUE FOR SKETCHING PARABOLAS**

Parabolas can be sketched from their *standard equations* using four basic steps:

Sketching a Parabola from Its Standard Equation

Step 1. Determine whether the axis of symmetry is along the x-axis or the y-axis. Referring to Figure 10.4.6, the axis of symmetry is along the x-axis if the equation has a y^2-term, and it is along the y-axis if it has an x^2-term.

Step 2. Determine which way the parabola opens. If the axis of symmetry is along the x-axis, then the parabola opens to the right if the coefficient of x is positive, and it opens to the left if the coefficient is negative. If the axis of symmetry is along the y-axis, then the parabola opens up if the coefficient of y is positive, and it opens down if the coefficient is negative.

Step 3. Determine the value of p and draw a box extending p units from the origin along the axis of symmetry in the direction in which the parabola opens and extending $2p$ units on each side of the axis of symmetry.

Step 4. Using the box as a guide, sketch the parabola so that its vertex is at the origin and it passes through the corners of the box (Figure 10.4.8).

▲ **Figure 10.4.8**

Rough sketch

▶ **Example 1** Sketch the graphs of the parabolas

(a) $x^2 = 12y$ (b) $y^2 + 8x = 0$

and show the focus and directrix of each.

Solution (a). This equation involves x^2, so the axis of symmetry is along the y-axis, and the coefficient of y is positive, so the parabola opens upward. From the coefficient of y, we obtain $4p = 12$ or $p = 3$. Drawing a box extending $p = 3$ units up from the origin and $2p = 6$ units to the left and $2p = 6$ units to the right of the y-axis, then using corners of the box as a guide, yields the graph in Figure 10.4.9.

The focus is $p = 3$ units from the vertex along the axis of symmetry in the direction in which the parabola opens, so its coordinates are $(0, 3)$. The directrix is perpendicular to the axis of symmetry at a distance of $p = 3$ units from the vertex on the opposite side from the focus, so its equation is $y = -3$.

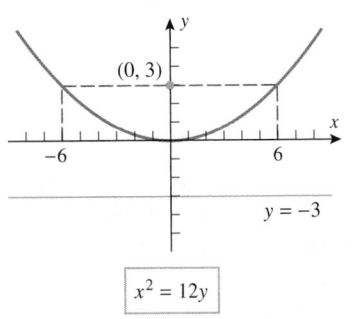

▲ **Figure 10.4.9**

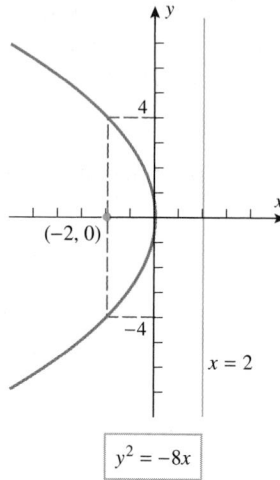

$$y^2 = -8x$$

▲ Figure 10.4.10

Solution (b).   We first rewrite the equation in the standard form

$$y^2 = -8x$$

This equation involves y^2, so the axis of symmetry is along the x-axis, and the coefficient of x is negative, so the parabola opens to the left. From the coefficient of x we obtain $4p = 8$, so $p = 2$. Drawing a box extending $p = 2$ units left from the origin and $2p = 4$ units above and $2p = 4$ units below the x-axis, then using corners of the box as a guide, yields the graph in Figure 10.4.10. ◄

▶ **Example 2**   Find an equation of the parabola that is symmetric about the y-axis, has its vertex at the origin, and passes through the point $(5, 2)$.

Solution.   Since the parabola is symmetric about the y-axis and has its vertex at the origin, the equation is of the form

$$x^2 = 4py \quad \text{or} \quad x^2 = -4py$$

where the sign depends on whether the parabola opens up or down. But the parabola must open up since it passes through the point $(5, 2)$, which lies in the first quadrant. Thus, the equation is of the form

$$x^2 = 4py \tag{5}$$

Since the parabola passes through $(5, 2)$, we must have $5^2 = 4p \cdot 2$ or $4p = \frac{25}{2}$. Therefore, (5) becomes

$$x^2 = \tfrac{25}{2}y \quad ◄$$

■ EQUATIONS OF ELLIPSES IN STANDARD POSITION

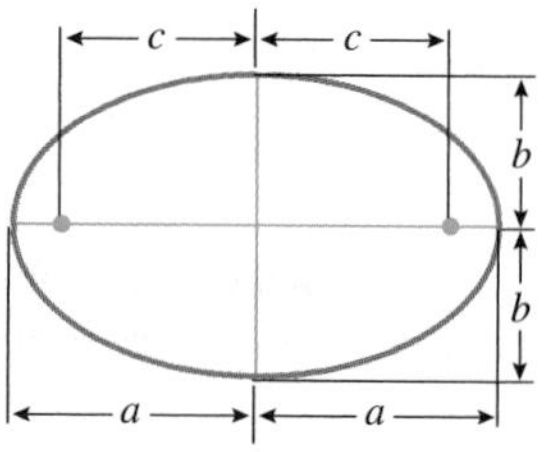

It is traditional in the study of ellipses to denote the length of the major axis by $2a$, the length of the minor axis by $2b$, and the distance between the foci by $2c$ (Figure 10.4.11). The number a is called the **semimajor axis** and the number b the **semiminor axis** (standard but odd terminology, since a and b are numbers, not geometric axes).

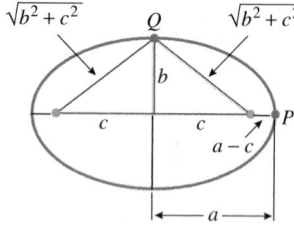

▲ Figure 10.4.11

There is a basic relationship between the numbers a, b, and c that can be obtained by examining the sum of the distances to the foci from a point P at the end of the major axis and from a point Q at the end of the minor axis (Figure 10.4.12). From Definition 10.4.2, these sums must be equal, so we obtain

$$2\sqrt{b^2 + c^2} = (a - c) + (a + c)$$

from which it follows that

$$a = \sqrt{b^2 + c^2} \tag{6}$$

or, equivalently,

$$c = \sqrt{a^2 - b^2} \tag{7}$$

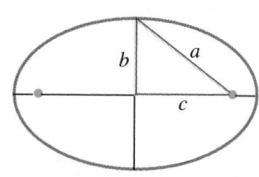

▲ Figure 10.4.12

From (6), the distance from a focus to an end of the minor axis is a (Figure 10.4.13), which implies that for *all* points on the ellipse the sum of the distances to the foci is $2a$.

It also follows from (6) that $a \geq b$ with the equality holding only when $c = 0$. Geometrically, this means that the major axis of an ellipse is at least as large as the minor axis and that the two axes have equal length only when the foci coincide, in which case the ellipse is a circle.

The equation of an ellipse is simplest if the center of the ellipse is at the origin and the foci are on the x-axis or y-axis. The two possible such orientations are shown in Figure 10.4.14.

▲ Figure 10.4.13

These are called the *standard positions* of an ellipse, and the resulting equations are called the *standard equations* of an ellipse.

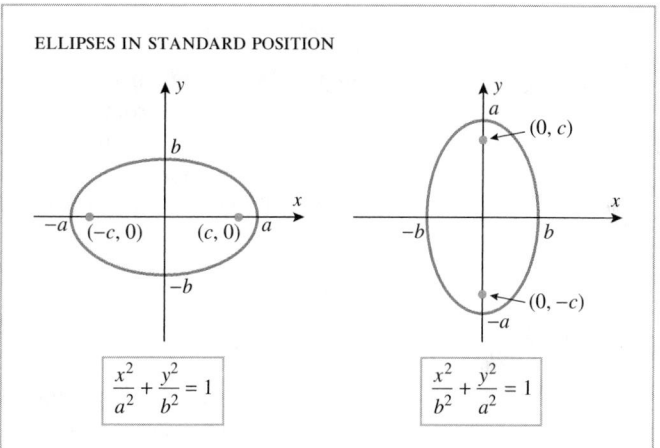

ELLIPSES IN STANDARD POSITION

$$\frac{x^2}{a^2} + \frac{y^2}{b^2} = 1$$

$$\frac{x^2}{b^2} + \frac{y^2}{a^2} = 1$$

▶ **Figure 10.4.14**

To illustrate how the equations in Figure 10.4.14 are obtained, we will derive the equation for the ellipse with foci on the x-axis. Let $P(x, y)$ be any point on that ellipse. Since the sum of the distances from P to the foci is $2a$, it follows (Figure 10.4.15) that

$$PF' + PF = 2a$$

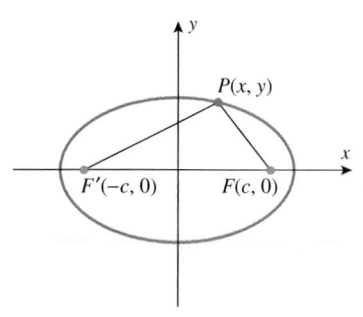

▲ **Figure 10.4.15**

so

$$\sqrt{(x + c)^2 + y^2} + \sqrt{(x - c)^2 + y^2} = 2a$$

Transposing the second radical to the right side of the equation and squaring yields

$$(x + c)^2 + y^2 = 4a^2 - 4a\sqrt{(x - c)^2 + y^2} + (x - c)^2 + y^2$$

and, on simplifying,

$$\sqrt{(x - c)^2 + y^2} = a - \frac{c}{a}x \qquad (8)$$

Squaring again and simplifying yields

$$\frac{x^2}{a^2} + \frac{y^2}{a^2 - c^2} = 1$$

which, by virtue of (6), can be written as

$$\frac{x^2}{a^2} + \frac{y^2}{b^2} = 1 \qquad (9)$$

Conversely, it can be shown that any point whose coordinates satisfy (9) has $2a$ as the sum of its distances from the foci, so that such a point is on the ellipse.

■ **A TECHNIQUE FOR SKETCHING ELLIPSES**

Ellipses can be sketched from their *standard equations* using three basic steps:

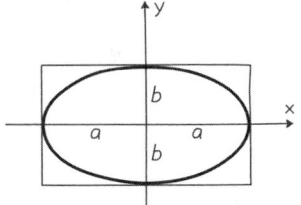

Rough sketch

▲ **Figure 10.4.16**

Sketching an Ellipse from Its Standard Equation

Step 1. Determine whether the major axis is on the x-axis or the y-axis. This can be ascertained from the sizes of the denominators in the equation. Referring to Figure 10.4.14, and keeping in mind that $a^2 > b^2$ (since $a > b$), the major axis is along the x-axis if x^2 has the larger denominator, and it is along the y-axis if y^2 has the larger denominator. If the denominators are equal, the ellipse is a circle.

Step 2. Determine the values of a and b and draw a box extending a units on each side of the center along the major axis and b units on each side of the center along the minor axis.

Step 3. Using the box as a guide, sketch the ellipse so that its center is at the origin and it touches the sides of the box where the sides intersect the coordinate axes (Figure 10.4.16).

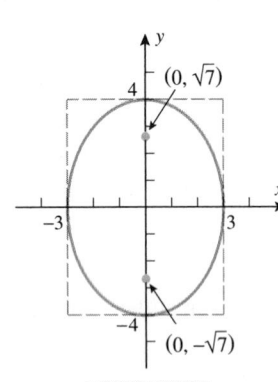

$$\frac{x^2}{9} + \frac{y^2}{16} = 1$$

▲ **Figure 10.4.17**

▶ **Example 3**   Sketch the graphs of the ellipses

$$\text{(a)} \ \frac{x^2}{9} + \frac{y^2}{16} = 1 \qquad \text{(b)} \ x^2 + 2y^2 = 4$$

showing the foci of each.

Solution (a).   Since y^2 has the larger denominator, the major axis is along the y-axis. Moreover, since $a^2 > b^2$, we must have $a^2 = 16$ and $b^2 = 9$, so

$$a = 4 \quad \text{and} \quad b = 3$$

Drawing a box extending 4 units on each side of the origin along the y-axis and 3 units on each side of the origin along the x-axis as a guide yields the graph in Figure 10.4.17.

The foci lie c units on each side of the center along the major axis, where c is given by (7). From the values of a^2 and b^2 above, we obtain

$$c = \sqrt{a^2 - b^2} = \sqrt{16 - 9} = \sqrt{7} \approx 2.6$$

Thus, the coordinates of the foci are $(0, \sqrt{7})$ and $(0, -\sqrt{7})$, since they lie on the y-axis.

Solution (b).   We first rewrite the equation in the standard form

$$\frac{x^2}{4} + \frac{y^2}{2} = 1$$

Since x^2 has the larger denominator, the major axis lies along the x-axis, and we have $a^2 = 4$ and $b^2 = 2$. Drawing a box extending $a = 2$ units on each side of the origin along the x-axis and extending $b = \sqrt{2} \approx 1.4$ units on each side of the origin along the y-axis as a guide yields the graph in Figure 10.4.18.

From (7), we obtain

$$c = \sqrt{a^2 - b^2} = \sqrt{2} \approx 1.4$$

Thus, the coordinates of the foci are $(\sqrt{2}, 0)$ and $(-\sqrt{2}, 0)$, since they lie on the x-axis. ◀

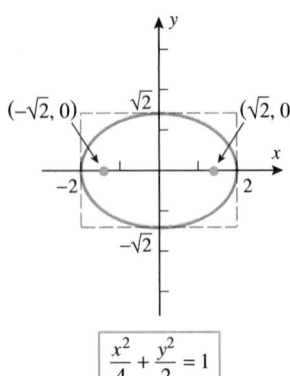

$$\frac{x^2}{4} + \frac{y^2}{2} = 1$$

▲ **Figure 10.4.18**

▶ **Example 4** Find an equation for the ellipse with foci $(0, \pm 2)$ and major axis with endpoints $(0, \pm 4)$.

Solution. From Figure 10.4.14, the equation has the form

$$\frac{x^2}{b^2} + \frac{y^2}{a^2} = 1$$

and from the given information, $a = 4$ and $c = 2$. It follows from (6) that

$$b^2 = a^2 - c^2 = 16 - 4 = 12$$

so the equation of the ellipse is

$$\frac{x^2}{12} + \frac{y^2}{16} = 1 \quad ◄$$

■ EQUATIONS OF HYPERBOLAS IN STANDARD POSITION

It is traditional in the study of hyperbolas to denote the distance between the vertices by $2a$, the distance between the foci by $2c$ (Figure 10.4.19), and to define the quantity b as

$$b = \sqrt{c^2 - a^2} \tag{10}$$

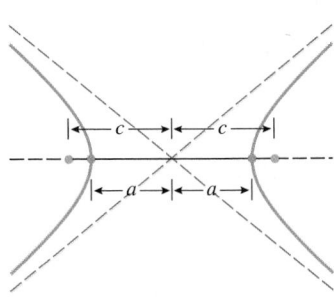

▲ **Figure 10.4.19**

This relationship, which can also be expressed as

$$c = \sqrt{a^2 + b^2} \tag{11}$$

is pictured geometrically in Figure 10.4.20. As illustrated in that figure, and as we will show later in this section, the asymptotes pass through the corners of a box extending b units on each side of the center along the conjugate axis and a units on each side of the center along the focal axis. The number a is called the ***semifocal axis*** of the hyperbola and the number b the ***semiconjugate axis***. (As with the semimajor and semiminor axes of an ellipse, these are numbers, not geometric axes.)

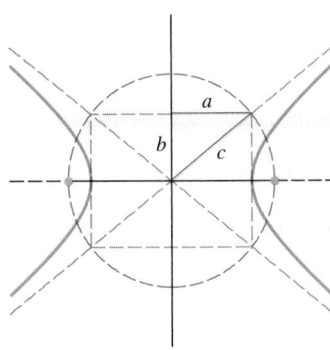

▲ **Figure 10.4.20**

If V is one vertex of a hyperbola, then, as illustrated in Figure 10.4.21, the distance from V to the farther focus minus the distance from V to the closer focus is

$$[(c - a) + 2a] - (c - a) = 2a$$

Thus, for *all* points on a hyperbola, the distance to the farther focus minus the distance to the closer focus is $2a$.

The equation of a hyperbola has an especially convenient form if the center of the hyperbola is at the origin and the foci are on the x-axis or y-axis. The two possible such orientations are shown in Figure 10.4.22. These are called the ***standard positions*** of a hyperbola, and the resulting equations are called the ***standard equations*** of a hyperbola.

The derivations of these equations are similar to those already given for parabolas and ellipses, so we will leave them as exercises. However, to illustrate how the equations of the asymptotes are derived, we will derive those equations for the hyperbola

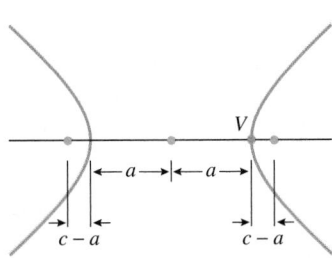

▲ **Figure 10.4.21**

$$\frac{x^2}{a^2} - \frac{y^2}{b^2} = 1$$

We can rewrite this equation as

$$y^2 = \frac{b^2}{a^2}(x^2 - a^2)$$

which is equivalent to the pair of equations

$$y = \frac{b}{a}\sqrt{x^2 - a^2} \quad \text{and} \quad y = -\frac{b}{a}\sqrt{x^2 - a^2}$$

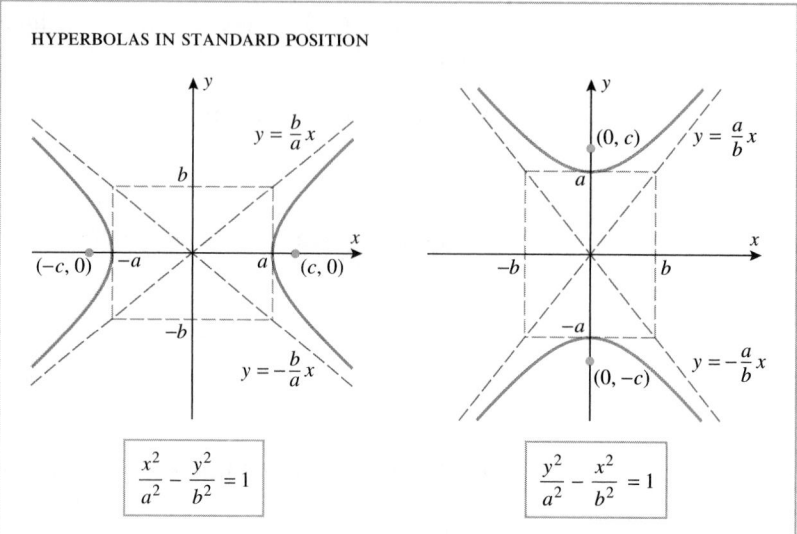

► Figure 10.4.22

Thus, in the first quadrant, the vertical distance between the line $y = (b/a)x$ and the hyperbola can be written as

$$\frac{b}{a}x - \frac{b}{a}\sqrt{x^2 - a^2}$$

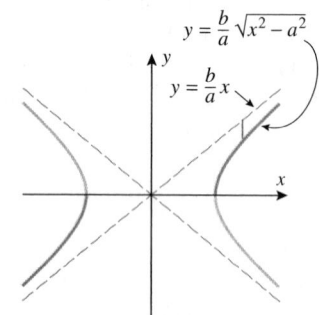

▲ Figure 10.4.23

(Figure 10.4.23). But this distance tends to zero as $x \to +\infty$ since

$$\lim_{x \to +\infty}\left(\frac{b}{a}x - \frac{b}{a}\sqrt{x^2 - a^2}\right) = \lim_{x \to +\infty}\frac{b}{a}\left(x - \sqrt{x^2 - a^2}\right)$$

$$= \lim_{x \to +\infty}\frac{b}{a}\frac{\left(x - \sqrt{x^2 - a^2}\right)\left(x + \sqrt{x^2 - a^2}\right)}{x + \sqrt{x^2 - a^2}}$$

$$= \lim_{x \to +\infty}\frac{ab}{x + \sqrt{x^2 - a^2}} = 0$$

The analysis in the remaining quadrants is similar.

■ A QUICK WAY TO FIND ASYMPTOTES

There is a trick that can be used to avoid memorizing the equations of the asymptotes of a hyperbola. They can be obtained, when needed, by replacing 1 by 0 on the right side of the hyperbola equation, and then solving for y in terms of x. For example, for the hyperbola

$$\frac{x^2}{a^2} - \frac{y^2}{b^2} = 1$$

we would write

$$\frac{x^2}{a^2} - \frac{y^2}{b^2} = 0 \quad \text{or} \quad y^2 = \frac{b^2}{a^2}x^2 \quad \text{or} \quad y = \pm\frac{b}{a}x$$

which are the equations for the asymptotes.

■ A TECHNIQUE FOR SKETCHING HYPERBOLAS

Hyperbolas can be sketched from their *standard equations* using four basic steps:

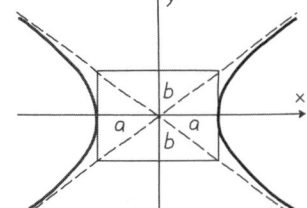

Rough sketch

▲ **Figure 10.4.24**

> *Sketching a Hyperbola from Its Standard Equation*
>
> **Step 1.** Determine whether the focal axis is on the x-axis or the y-axis. This can be ascertained from the location of the minus sign in the equation. Referring to Figure 10.4.22, the focal axis is along the x-axis when the minus sign precedes the y^2-term, and it is along the y-axis when the minus sign precedes the x^2-term.
>
> **Step 2.** Determine the values of a and b and draw a box extending a units on either side of the center along the focal axis and b units on either side of the center along the conjugate axis. (The squares of a and b can be read directly from the equation.)
>
> **Step 3.** Draw the asymptotes along the diagonals of the box.
>
> **Step 4.** Using the box and the asymptotes as a guide, sketch the graph of the hyperbola (Figure 10.4.24).

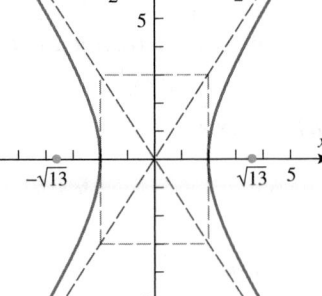

▲ **Figure 10.4.25**

▶ **Example 5** Sketch the graphs of the hyperbolas

$$\text{(a) } \frac{x^2}{4} - \frac{y^2}{9} = 1 \qquad \text{(b) } y^2 - x^2 = 1$$

showing their vertices, foci, and asymptotes.

Solution (a). The minus sign precedes the y^2-term, so the focal axis is along the x-axis. From the denominators in the equation we obtain

$$a^2 = 4 \quad \text{and} \quad b^2 = 9$$

Since a and b are positive, we must have $a = 2$ and $b = 3$. Recalling that the vertices lie a units on each side of the center on the focal axis, it follows that their coordinates in this case are $(2, 0)$ and $(-2, 0)$. Drawing a box extending $a = 2$ units along the x-axis on each side of the origin and $b = 3$ units on each side of the origin along the y-axis, then drawing the asymptotes along the diagonals of the box as a guide, yields the graph in Figure 10.4.25.

To obtain equations for the asymptotes, we replace 1 by 0 in the given equation; this yields

$$\frac{x^2}{4} - \frac{y^2}{9} = 0 \quad \text{or} \quad y = \pm \frac{3}{2}x$$

The foci lie c units on each side of the center along the focal axis, where c is given by (11). From the values of a^2 and b^2 above we obtain

$$c = \sqrt{a^2 + b^2} = \sqrt{4 + 9} = \sqrt{13} \approx 3.6$$

Since the foci lie on the x-axis in this case, their coordinates are $(\sqrt{13}, 0)$ and $(-\sqrt{13}, 0)$.

Solution (b). The minus sign precedes the x^2-term, so the focal axis is along the y-axis. From the denominators in the equation we obtain $a^2 = 1$ and $b^2 = 1$, from which it follows that

$$a = 1 \quad \text{and} \quad b = 1$$

Thus, the vertices are at $(0, -1)$ and $(0, 1)$. Drawing a box extending $a = 1$ unit on either side of the origin along the y-axis and $b = 1$ unit on either side of the origin along the x-axis, then drawing the asymptotes, yields the graph in Figure 10.4.26. Since the box is actually

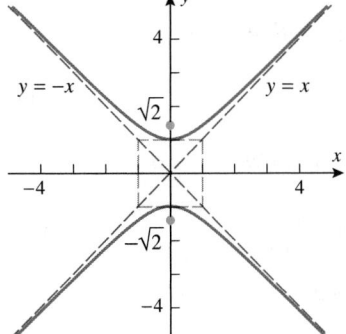

▲ **Figure 10.4.26**

A hyperbola in which $a = b$, as in part (b) of Example 5, is called an *equilateral hyperbola*. Such hyperbolas always have perpendicular asymptotes.

a square, the asymptotes are perpendicular and have equations $y = \pm x$. This can also be seen by replacing 1 by 0 in the given equation, which yields $y^2 - x^2 = 0$ or $y = \pm x$. Also,

$$c = \sqrt{a^2 + b^2} = \sqrt{1 + 1} = \sqrt{2}$$

so the foci, which lie on the y-axis, are $(0, -\sqrt{2})$ and $(0, \sqrt{2})$. ◄

▶ **Example 6**   Find the equation of the hyperbola with vertices $(0, \pm 8)$ and asymptotes $y = \pm \frac{4}{3}x$.

Solution.   Since the vertices are on the y-axis, the equation of the hyperbola has the form $(y^2/a^2) - (x^2/b^2) = 1$ and the asymptotes are

$$y = \pm \frac{a}{b}x$$

From the locations of the vertices we have $a = 8$, so the given equations of the asymptotes yield

$$y = \pm \frac{a}{b}x = \pm \frac{8}{b}x = \pm \frac{4}{3}x$$

from which it follows that $b = 6$. Thus, the hyperbola has the equation

$$\frac{y^2}{64} - \frac{x^2}{36} = 1 \quad ◄$$

■ **TRANSLATED CONICS**

Equations of conics that are translated from their standard positions can be obtained by replacing x by $x - h$ and y by $y - k$ in their standard equations. For a parabola, this translates the vertex from the origin to the point (h, k); and for ellipses and hyperbolas, this translates the center from the origin to the point (h, k).

Parabolas with vertex (h, k) and axis parallel to x-axis

$$(y - k)^2 = 4p(x - h) \quad \text{[Opens right]} \tag{12}$$

$$(y - k)^2 = -4p(x - h) \quad \text{[Opens left]} \tag{13}$$

Parabolas with vertex (h, k) and axis parallel to y-axis

$$(x - h)^2 = 4p(y - k) \quad \text{[Opens up]} \tag{14}$$

$$(x - h)^2 = -4p(y - k) \quad \text{[Opens down]} \tag{15}$$

Ellipse with center (h, k) and major axis parallel to x-axis

$$\frac{(x - h)^2}{a^2} + \frac{(y - k)^2}{b^2} = 1 \quad [b < a] \tag{16}$$

Ellipse with center (h, k) and major axis parallel to y-axis

$$\frac{(x - h)^2}{b^2} + \frac{(y - k)^2}{a^2} = 1 \quad [b < a] \tag{17}$$

Hyperbola with center (h, k) and focal axis parallel to x-axis

$$\frac{(x - h)^2}{a^2} - \frac{(y - k)^2}{b^2} = 1 \tag{18}$$

Hyperbola with center (h, k) and focal axis parallel to y-axis

$$\frac{(y - k)^2}{a^2} - \frac{(x - h)^2}{b^2} = 1 \tag{19}$$

▶ **Example 7**   Find an equation for the parabola that has its vertex at $(1, 2)$ and its focus at $(4, 2)$.

Solution.   Since the focus and vertex are on a horizontal line, and since the focus is to the right of the vertex, the parabola opens to the right and its equation has the form

$$(y - k)^2 = 4p(x - h)$$

Since the vertex and focus are 3 units apart, we have $p = 3$, and since the vertex is at $(h, k) = (1, 2)$, we obtain

$$(y - 2)^2 = 12(x - 1) \ \blacktriangleleft$$

Sometimes the equations of translated conics occur in expanded form, in which case we are faced with the problem of identifying the graph of a quadratic equation in x and y:

$$Ax^2 + Cy^2 + Dx + Ey + F = 0 \qquad (20)$$

The basic procedure for determining the nature of such a graph is to complete the squares of the quadratic terms and then try to match up the resulting equation with one of the forms of a translated conic.

▶ **Example 8**   Describe the graph of the equation

$$y^2 - 8x - 6y - 23 = 0$$

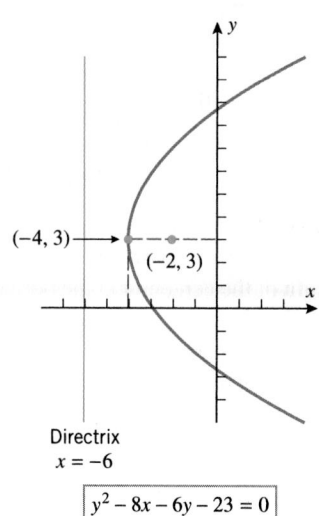

Directrix
$x = -6$

$y^2 - 8x - 6y - 23 = 0$

▲ **Figure 10.4.27**

Solution.   The equation involves quadratic terms in y but none in x, so we first take all of the y-terms to one side:

$$y^2 - 6y = 8x + 23$$

Next, we complete the square on the y-terms by adding 9 to both sides:

$$(y - 3)^2 = 8x + 32$$

Finally, we factor out the coefficient of the x-term to obtain

$$(y - 3)^2 = 8(x + 4)$$

This equation is of form (12) with $h = -4$, $k = 3$, and $p = 2$, so the graph is a parabola with vertex $(-4, 3)$ opening to the right. Since $p = 2$, the focus is 2 units to the right of the vertex, which places it at the point $(-2, 3)$; and the directrix is 2 units to the left of the vertex, which means that its equation is $x = -6$. The parabola is shown in Figure 10.4.27. ◀

▶ **Example 9**   Describe the graph of the equation

$$16x^2 + 9y^2 - 64x - 54y + 1 = 0$$

Solution.   This equation involves quadratic terms in both x and y, so we will group the x-terms and the y-terms on one side and put the constant on the other:

$$(16x^2 - 64x) + (9y^2 - 54y) = -1$$

Next, factor out the coefficients of x^2 and y^2 and complete the squares:

$$16(x^2 - 4x + 4) + 9(y^2 - 6y + 9) = -1 + 64 + 81$$

or

$$16(x - 2)^2 + 9(y - 3)^2 = 144$$

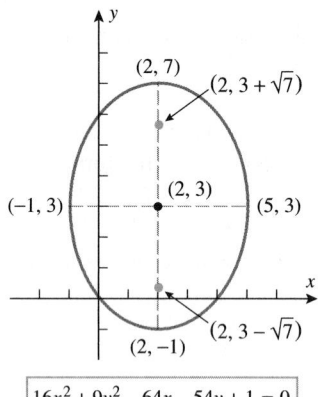

$$16x^2 + 9y^2 - 64x - 54y + 1 = 0$$

▲ **Figure 10.4.28**

Finally, divide through by 144 to introduce a 1 on the right side:

$$\frac{(x-2)^2}{9} + \frac{(y-3)^2}{16} = 1$$

This is an equation of form (17), with $h = 2$, $k = 3$, $a^2 = 16$, and $b^2 = 9$. Thus, the graph of the equation is an ellipse with center $(2, 3)$ and major axis parallel to the y-axis. Since $a = 4$, the major axis extends 4 units above and 4 units below the center, so its endpoints are $(2, 7)$ and $(2, -1)$ (Figure 10.4.28). Since $b = 3$, the minor axis extends 3 units to the left and 3 units to the right of the center, so its endpoints are $(-1, 3)$ and $(5, 3)$. Since

$$c = \sqrt{a^2 - b^2} = \sqrt{16 - 9} = \sqrt{7}$$

the foci lie $\sqrt{7}$ units above and below the center, placing them at the points $(2, 3 + \sqrt{7})$ and $(2, 3 - \sqrt{7})$. ◄

▶ **Example 10**   Describe the graph of the equation

$$x^2 - y^2 - 4x + 8y - 21 = 0$$

Solution.   This equation involves quadratic terms in both x and y, so we will group the x-terms and the y-terms on one side and put the constant on the other:

$$(x^2 - 4x) - (y^2 - 8y) = 21$$

We leave it for you to verify by completing the squares that this equation can be written as

$$\frac{(x-2)^2}{9} - \frac{(y-4)^2}{9} = 1 \qquad (21)$$

This is an equation of form (18) with $h = 2$, $k = 4$, $a^2 = 9$, and $b^2 = 9$. Thus, the equation represents a hyperbola with center $(2, 4)$ and focal axis parallel to the x-axis. Since $a = 3$, the vertices are located 3 units to the left and 3 units to the right of the center, or at the points $(-1, 4)$ and $(5, 4)$. From (11), $c = \sqrt{a^2 + b^2} = \sqrt{9 + 9} = 3\sqrt{2}$, so the foci are located $3\sqrt{2}$ units to the left and right of the center, or at the points $(2 - 3\sqrt{2}, 4)$ and $(2 + 3\sqrt{2}, 4)$.

The equations of the asymptotes may be found using the trick of replacing 1 by 0 in (21) to obtain

$$\frac{(x-2)^2}{9} - \frac{(y-4)^2}{9} = 0$$

This can be written as $y - 4 = \pm(x - 2)$, which yields the asymptotes

$$y = x + 2 \quad \text{and} \quad y = -x + 6$$

With the aid of a box extending $a = 3$ units left and right of the center and $b = 3$ units above and below the center, we obtain the sketch in Figure 10.4.29. ◄

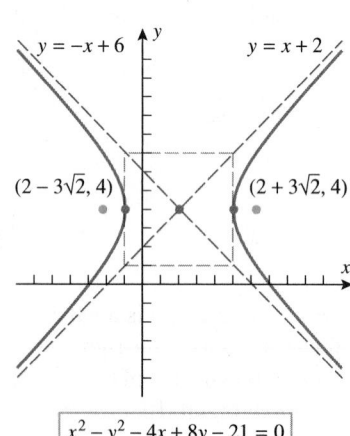

$$x^2 - y^2 - 4x + 8y - 21 = 0$$

▲ **Figure 10.4.29**

■ **REFLECTION PROPERTIES OF THE CONIC SECTIONS**

Parabolas, ellipses, and hyperbolas have certain reflection properties that make them extremely valuable in various applications. In the exercises we will ask you to prove the following results.

10.4.4   THEOREM (*Reflection Property of Parabolas*)   *The tangent line at a point P on a parabola makes equal angles with the line through P parallel to the axis of symmetry and the line through P and the focus (Figure 10.4.30a).*

10.4.5 **THEOREM** (*Reflection Property of Ellipses*) *A line tangent to an ellipse at a point P makes equal angles with the lines joining P to the foci (Figure 10.4.30b).*

10.4.6 **THEOREM** (*Reflection Property of Hyperbolas*) *A line tangent to a hyperbola at a point P makes equal angles with the lines joining P to the foci (Figure 10.4.30c).*

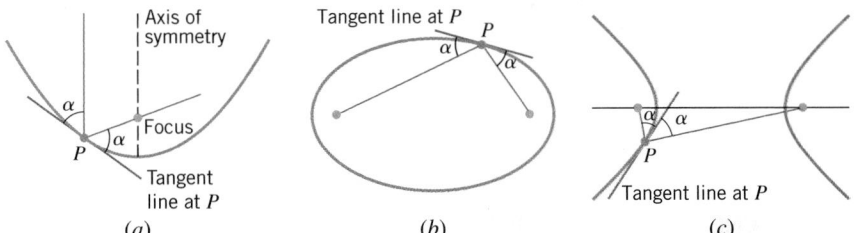

▶ **Figure 10.4.30**

(a)   (b)   (c)

■ APPLICATIONS OF THE CONIC SECTIONS

John Mead/Science Photo Library/Photo Researchers
Incoming signals are reflected by the parabolic antenna to the receiver at the focus.

Fermat's principle in optics implies that light reflects off of a surface at an angle equal to its angle of incidence. (See Exercise 62 in Section 4.5.) In particular, if a reflecting surface is generated by revolving a parabola about its axis of symmetry, it follows from Theorem 10.4.4 that all light rays entering parallel to the axis will be reflected to the focus (Figure 10.4.31a); conversely, if a light source is located at the focus, then the reflected rays will all be parallel to the axis (Figure 10.4.31b). This principle is used in certain telescopes to reflect the approximately parallel rays of light from the stars and planets off of a parabolic mirror to an eyepiece at the focus; and the parabolic reflectors in flashlights and automobile headlights utilize this principle to form a parallel beam of light rays from a bulb placed at the focus. The same optical principles apply to radar signals and sound waves, which explains the parabolic shape of many antennas.

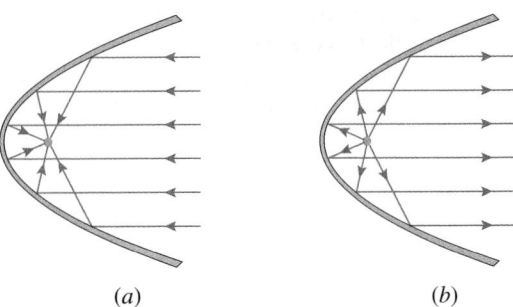

▶ **Figure 10.4.31**   (a)   (b)

Visitors to various rooms in the United States Capitol Building and in St. Paul's Cathedral in London are often astonished by the "whispering gallery" effect in which two people at opposite ends of the room can hear one another's whispers very clearly. Such rooms have ceilings with elliptical cross sections and common foci. Thus, when the two people stand at the foci, their whispers are reflected directly to one another off of the elliptical ceiling.

Hyperbolic navigation systems, which were developed in World War II as navigational aids to ships, are based on the definition of a hyperbola. With these systems the ship receives

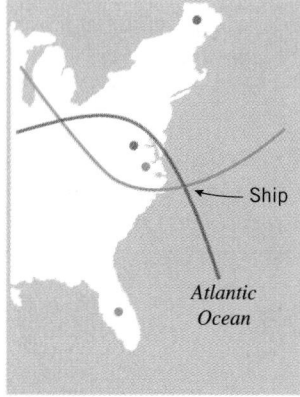

synchronized radio signals from two widely spaced transmitters with known positions. The ship's electronic receiver measures the difference in reception times between the signals and then uses that difference to compute the difference $2a$ between its distances from the two transmitters. This information places the ship somewhere on the hyperbola whose foci are at the transmitters and whose points have $2a$ as the difference in their distances from the foci. By repeating the process with a second set of transmitters, the position of the ship can be approximated as the intersection of two hyperbolas (Figure 10.4.32). (The modern global positioning system (GPS) is based on the same principle.)

▲ **Figure 10.4.32**

✔ QUICK CHECK EXERCISES 10.4   *(See page 748 for answers.)*

1. Identify the conic.
   (a) The set of points in the plane, the sum of whose distances to two fixed points is a positive constant greater than the distance between the fixed points is _____.
   (b) The set of points in the plane, the difference of whose distances to two fixed points is a positive constant less than the distance between the fixed points is _____.
   (c) The set of points in the plane that are equidistant from a fixed line and a fixed point not on the line is _____.

2. (a) The equation of the parabola with focus $(p, 0)$ and directrix $x = -p$ is _____.
   (b) The equation of the parabola with focus $(0, p)$ and directrix $y = -p$ is _____.

3. (a) Suppose that an ellipse has semimajor axis a and semiminor axis b. Then for all points on the ellipse, the sum of the distances to the foci is equal to _____.
   (b) The two standard equations of an ellipse with semimajor axis a and semiminor axis b are _____ and _____.

(c) Suppose that an ellipse has semimajor axis a, semiminor axis b, and foci $(\pm c, 0)$. Then c may be obtained from a and b by the equation $c =$ _____.

4. (a) Suppose that a hyperbola has semifocal axis a and semiconjugate axis b. Then for all points on the hyperbola, the difference of the distance to the farther focus minus the distance to the closer focus is equal to _____.
   (b) The two standard equations of a hyperbola with semifocal axis a and semiconjugate axis b are _____ and _____.
   (c) Suppose that a hyperbola in standard position has semifocal axis a, semiconjugate axis b, and foci $(\pm c, 0)$. Then c may be obtained from a and b by the equation $c =$ _____. The equations of the asymptotes of this hyperbola are $y = \pm$ _____.

EXERCISE SET 10.4   ◪ Graphing Utility

FOCUS ON CONCEPTS

1. In parts (a)–(f), find the equation of the conic.

(a)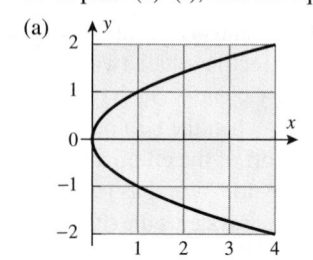

(b)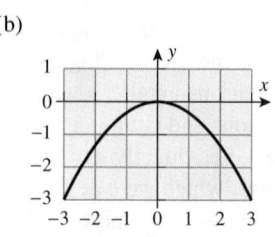

(c)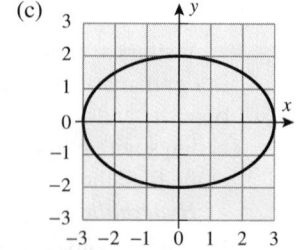

(d)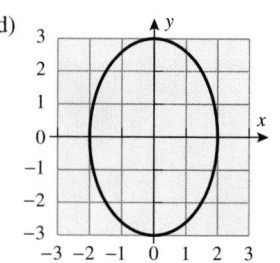

(e)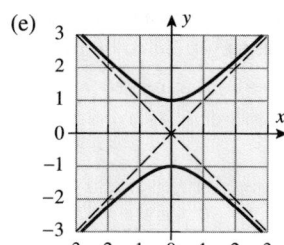

(f)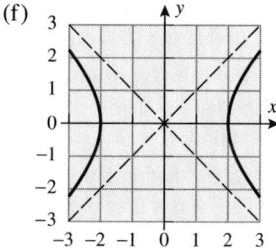

2. (a) Find the focus and directrix for each parabola in Exercise 1.

(b) Find the foci of the ellipses in Exercise 1.

(c) Find the foci and the equations of the asymptotes of the hyperbolas in Exercise 1.

3–6 Sketch the parabola, and label the focus, vertex, and directrix. ◼

3. (a) $y^2 = 4x$ (b) $x^2 = -8y$

4. (a) $y^2 = -10x$ (b) $x^2 = 4y$

5. (a) $(y - 1)^2 = -12(x + 4)$ (b) $(x - 1)^2 = 2\left(y - \frac{1}{2}\right)$

6. (a) $y^2 - 6y - 2x + 1 = 0$ (b) $y = 4x^2 + 8x + 5$

7–10 Sketch the ellipse, and label the foci, vertices, and ends of the minor axis. ◼

7. (a) $\dfrac{x^2}{16} + \dfrac{y^2}{9} = 1$ (b) $9x^2 + y^2 = 9$

8. (a) $\dfrac{x^2}{25} + \dfrac{y^2}{4} = 1$ (b) $4x^2 + y^2 = 36$

9. (a) $(x + 3)^2 + 4(y - 5)^2 = 16$

(b) $\frac{1}{4}x^2 + \frac{1}{9}(y + 2)^2 - 1 = 0$

10. (a) $9x^2 + 4y^2 - 18x + 24y + 9 = 0$

(b) $5x^2 + 9y^2 + 20x - 54y = -56$

11–14 Sketch the hyperbola, and label the vertices, foci, and asymptotes. ◼

11. (a) $\dfrac{x^2}{16} - \dfrac{y^2}{9} = 1$ (b) $9y^2 - x^2 = 36$

12. (a) $\dfrac{y^2}{9} - \dfrac{x^2}{25} = 1$ (b) $16x^2 - 25y^2 = 400$

13. (a) $\dfrac{(y + 4)^2}{3} - \dfrac{(x - 2)^2}{5} = 1$

(b) $16(x + 1)^2 - 8(y - 3)^2 = 16$

14. (a) $x^2 - 4y^2 + 2x + 8y - 7 = 0$

(b) $16x^2 - y^2 - 32x - 6y = 57$

15–18 Find an equation for the parabola that satisfies the given conditions. ◼

15. (a) Vertex $(0, 0)$; focus $(3, 0)$.

(b) Vertex $(0, 0)$; directrix $y = \frac{1}{4}$.

16. (a) Focus $(6, 0)$; directrix $x = -6$.

(b) Focus $(1, 1)$; directrix $y = -2$.

17. Axis $y = 0$; passes through $(3, 2)$ and $(2, -\sqrt{2})$.

18. Vertex $(5, -3)$; axis parallel to the y-axis; passes through $(9, 5)$.

19–22 Find an equation for the ellipse that satisfies the given conditions. ◼

19. (a) Ends of major axis $(\pm 3, 0)$; ends of minor axis $(0, \pm 2)$.

(b) Length of minor axis 8; foci $(0, \pm 3)$.

20. (a) Foci $(\pm 1, 0)$; $b = \sqrt{2}$.

(b) $c = 2\sqrt{3}$; $a = 4$; center at the origin; foci on a coordinate axis (two answers).

21. (a) Ends of major axis $(0, \pm 6)$; passes through $(-3, 2)$.

(b) Foci $(-1, 1)$ and $(-1, 3)$; minor axis of length 4.

22. (a) Center at $(0, 0)$; major and minor axes along the coordinate axes; passes through $(3, 2)$ and $(1, 6)$.

(b) Foci $(2, 1)$ and $(2, -3)$; major axis of length 6.

23–26 Find an equation for a hyperbola that satisfies the given conditions. [*Note:* In some cases there may be more than one hyperbola.] ◼

23. (a) Vertices $(\pm 2, 0)$; foci $(\pm 3, 0)$.

(b) Vertices $(0, \pm 2)$; asymptotes $y = \pm\frac{2}{3}x$.

24. (a) Asymptotes $y = \pm\frac{3}{2}x$; $b = 4$.

(b) Foci $(0, \pm 5)$; asymptotes $y = \pm 2x$.

25. (a) Asymptotes $y = \pm\frac{3}{4}x$; $c = 5$.

(b) Foci $(\pm 3, 0)$; asymptotes $y = \pm 2x$.

26. (a) Vertices $(0, 6)$ and $(6, 6)$; foci 10 units apart.

(b) Asymptotes $y = x - 2$ and $y = -x + 4$; passes through the origin.

27–30 True–False Determine whether the statement is true or false. Explain your answer. ◼

27. A hyperbola is the set of all points in the plane that are equidistant from a fixed line and a fixed point not on the line.

28. If an ellipse is not a circle, then the foci of an ellipse lie on the major axis of the ellipse.

29. If a parabola has equation $y^2 = 4px$, where p is a positive constant, then the perpendicular distance from the parabola's focus to its directrix is p.

30. The hyperbola $(y^2/a^2) - x^2 = 1$ has asymptotes the lines $y = \pm x/a$.

31. (a) As illustrated in the accompanying figure, a parabolic arch spans a road 40 ft wide. How high is the arch if a center section of the road 20 ft wide has a minimum clearance of 12 ft?

(b) How high would the center be if the arch were the upper half of an ellipse?

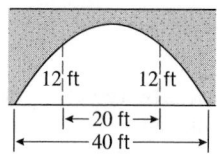

◀ **Figure Ex-31**

32. (a) Find an equation for the parabolic arch with base b and height h, shown in the accompanying figure.

(b) Find the area under the arch.

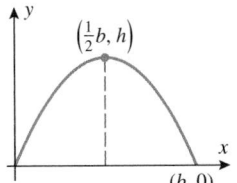

◄ **Figure Ex-32**

33. Show that the vertex is the closest point on a parabola to the focus. [*Suggestion:* Introduce a convenient coordinate system and use Definition 10.4.1.]

34. As illustrated in the accompanying figure, suppose that a comet moves in a parabolic orbit with the Sun at its focus and that the line from the Sun to the comet makes an angle of 60° with the axis of the parabola when the comet is 40 million miles from the center of the Sun. Use the result in Exercise 33 to determine how close the comet will come to the center of the Sun.

35. For the parabolic reflector in the accompanying figure, how far from the vertex should the light source be placed to produce a beam of parallel rays?

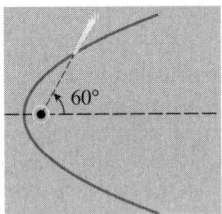

▲ **Figure Ex-34**

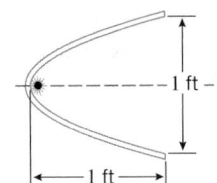

▲ **Figure Ex-35**

36. (a) Show that the right and left branches of the hyperbola

$$\frac{x^2}{a^2} - \frac{y^2}{b^2} = 1$$

can be represented parametrically as

$$x = a \cosh t, \quad y = b \sinh t \quad (-\infty < t < +\infty)$$
$$x = -a \cosh t, \quad y = b \sinh t \quad (-\infty < t < +\infty)$$

(b) Use a graphing utility to generate both branches of the hyperbola $x^2 - y^2 = 1$ on the same screen.

37. (a) Show that the right and left branches of the hyperbola

$$\frac{x^2}{a^2} - \frac{y^2}{b^2} = 1$$

can be represented parametrically as

$$x = a \sec t, \quad y = b \tan t \quad (-\pi/2 < t < \pi/2)$$
$$x = -a \sec t, \quad y = b \tan t \quad (-\pi/2 < t < \pi/2)$$

(b) Use a graphing utility to generate both branches of the hyperbola $x^2 - y^2 = 1$ on the same screen.

38. Find an equation of the parabola traced by a point that moves so that its distance from $(2, 4)$ is the same as its distance to the x-axis.

39. Find an equation of the ellipse traced by a point that moves so that the sum of its distances to $(4, 1)$ and $(4, 5)$ is 12.

40. Find the equation of the hyperbola traced by a point that moves so that the difference between its distances to $(0, 0)$ and $(1, 1)$ is 1.

41. Show that an ellipse with semimajor axis a and semiminor axis b has area $A = \pi ab$.

FOCUS ON CONCEPTS

42. Show that if a plane is not parallel to the axis of a right circular cylinder, then the intersection of the plane and cylinder is an ellipse (possibly a circle). [*Hint:* Let θ be the angle shown in the accompanying figure, introduce coordinate axes as shown, and express x' and y' in terms of x and y.]

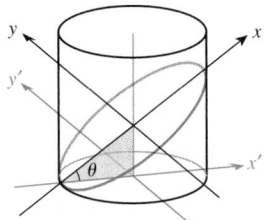

◄ **Figure Ex-42**

43. As illustrated in the accompanying figure, a carpenter needs to cut an elliptical hole in a sloped roof through which a circular vent pipe of diameter D is to be inserted vertically. The carpenter wants to draw the outline of the hole on the roof using a pencil, two tacks, and a piece of string (as in Figure 10.4.3b). The center point of the ellipse is known, and common sense suggests that its major axis must be perpendicular to the drip line of the roof. The carpenter needs to determine the length L of the string and the distance T between a tack and the center point. The architect's plans show that the pitch of the roof is p (pitch = rise over run; see the accompanying figure). Find T and L in terms of D and p.

Source: This exercise is based on an article by William H. Enos, which appeared in the *Mathematics Teacher*, Feb. 1991, p. 148.

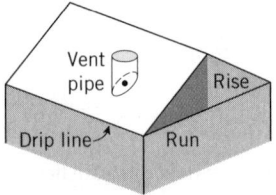

◄ **Figure Ex-43**

44. As illustrated in the accompanying figure on the next page, suppose that two observers are stationed at the points $F_1(c, 0)$ and $F_2(-c, 0)$ in an xy-coordinate system. Suppose also that the sound of an explosion in the xy-plane is heard by the F_1 observer t seconds before it is heard by the F_2 observer. Assuming that the speed of sound is a constant v, show that the explosion occurred somewhere on the hyperbola

$$\frac{x^2}{v^2t^2/4} - \frac{y^2}{c^2 - (v^2t^2/4)} = 1$$

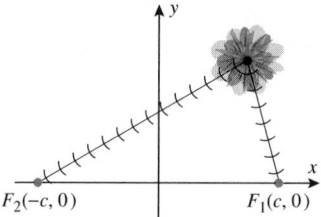

$F_2(-c, 0)$ $F_1(c, 0)$ ◀ **Figure Ex-44**

45. As illustrated in the accompanying figure, suppose that two transmitting stations are positioned 100 km apart at points $F_1(50, 0)$ and $F_2(-50, 0)$ on a straight shoreline in an xy-coordinate system. Suppose also that a ship is traveling parallel to the shoreline but 200 km at sea. Find the coordinates of the ship if the stations transmit a pulse simultaneously, but the pulse from station F_1 is received by the ship 100 microseconds sooner than the pulse from station F_2. [*Hint:* Use the formula obtained in Exercise 44, assuming that the pulses travel at the speed of light (299,792,458 m/s).]

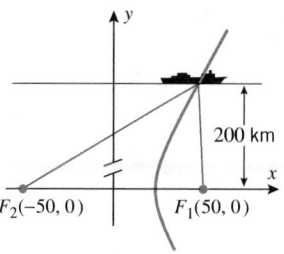

200 km

$F_2(-50, 0)$ $F_1(50, 0)$

◀ **Figure Ex-45**

46. A nuclear cooling tower is to have a height of h feet and the shape of the solid that is generated by revolving the region R enclosed by the right branch of the hyperbola $1521x^2 - 225y^2 = 342,225$ and the lines $x = 0$, $y = -h/2$, and $y = h/2$ about the y-axis.
    (a) Find the volume of the tower.
    (b) Find the lateral surface area of the tower.

47. Let R be the region that is above the x-axis and enclosed between the curve $b^2x^2 - a^2y^2 = a^2b^2$ and the line $x = \sqrt{a^2 + b^2}$.
    (a) Sketch the solid generated by revolving R about the x-axis, and find its volume.
    (b) Sketch the solid generated by revolving R about the y-axis, and find its volume.

48. Prove: The line tangent to the parabola $x^2 = 4py$ at the point (x_0, y_0) is $x_0x = 2p(y + y_0)$.

49. Prove: The line tangent to the ellipse

$$\frac{x^2}{a^2} + \frac{y^2}{b^2} = 1$$

at the point (x_0, y_0) has the equation

$$\frac{xx_0}{a^2} + \frac{yy_0}{b^2} = 1$$

50. Prove: The line tangent to the hyperbola

$$\frac{x^2}{a^2} - \frac{y^2}{b^2} = 1$$

at the point (x_0, y_0) has the equation

$$\frac{xx_0}{a^2} - \frac{yy_0}{b^2} = 1$$

51. Use the results in Exercises 49 and 50 to show that if an ellipse and a hyperbola have the same foci, then at each point of intersection their tangent lines are perpendicular.

52. Consider the second-degree equation

$$Ax^2 + Cy^2 + Dx + Ey + F = 0$$

where A and C are not both 0. Show by completing the square:
    (a) If $AC > 0$, then the equation represents an ellipse, a circle, a point, or has no graph.
    (b) If $AC < 0$, then the equation represents a hyperbola or a pair of intersecting lines.
    (c) If $AC = 0$, then the equation represents a parabola, a pair of parallel lines, or has no graph.

53. In each part, use the result in Exercise 52 to make a statement about the graph of the equation, and then check your conclusion by completing the square and identifying the graph.
    (a) $x^2 - 5y^2 - 2x - 10y - 9 = 0$
    (b) $x^2 - 3y^2 - 6y - 3 = 0$
    (c) $4x^2 + 8y^2 + 16x + 16y + 20 = 0$
    (d) $3x^2 + y^2 + 12x + 2y + 13 = 0$
    (e) $x^2 + 8x + 2y + 14 = 0$
    (f) $5x^2 + 40x + 2y + 94 = 0$

54. Derive the equation $x^2 = 4py$ in Figure 10.4.6.

55. Derive the equation $(x^2/b^2) + (y^2/a^2) = 1$ given in Figure 10.4.14.

56. Derive the equation $(x^2/a^2) - (y^2/b^2) = 1$ given in Figure 10.4.22.

57. Prove Theorem 10.4.4. [*Hint:* Choose coordinate axes so that the parabola has the equation $x^2 = 4py$. Show that the tangent line at $P(x_0, y_0)$ intersects the y-axis at $Q(0, -y_0)$ and that the triangle whose three vertices are at P, Q, and the focus is isosceles.]

58. Given two intersecting lines, let L_2 be the line with the larger angle of inclination ϕ_2, and let L_1 be the line with the smaller angle of inclination ϕ_1. We define the **angle θ between L_1 and L_2** by $\theta = \phi_2 - \phi_1$. (See the accompanying figure on the next page.)
    (a) Prove: If L_1 and L_2 are not perpendicular, then

    $$\tan \theta = \frac{m_2 - m_1}{1 + m_1m_2}$$

    where L_1 and L_2 have slopes m_1 and m_2.
    (b) Prove Theorem 10.4.5. [*Hint:* Introduce coordinates so that the equation $(x^2/a^2) + (y^2/b^2) = 1$ describes the ellipse, and use part (a).]   *(cont.)*

(c) Prove Theorem 10.4.6. [*Hint:* Introduce coordinates so that the equation $(x^2/a^2) - (y^2/b^2) = 1$ describes the hyperbola, and use part (a).]

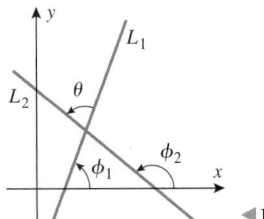

◀ **Figure Ex-58**

59. **Writing** Suppose that you want to draw an ellipse that has given values for the lengths of the major and minor axes by using the method shown in Figure 10.4.3*b*. Assuming that the axes are drawn, explain how a compass can be used to locate the positions for the tacks.

60. **Writing** List the forms for standard equations of parabolas, ellipses, and hyperbolas, and write a summary of techniques for sketching conic sections from their standard equations.

✔ **QUICK CHECK ANSWERS 10.4**

1. (a) an ellipse (b) a hyperbola (c) a parabola   **2.** (a) $y^2 = 4px$ (b) $x^2 = 4py$

3. (a) $2a$ (b) $\dfrac{x^2}{a^2} + \dfrac{y^2}{b^2} = 1$; $\dfrac{x^2}{b^2} + \dfrac{y^2}{a^2} = 1$ (c) $\sqrt{a^2 - b^2}$ **4.** (a) $2a$ (b) $\dfrac{x^2}{a^2} - \dfrac{y^2}{b^2} = 1$; $\dfrac{y^2}{a^2} - \dfrac{x^2}{b^2} = 1$ (c) $\sqrt{a^2 + b^2}$; $\dfrac{b}{a}x$

10.5 ROTATION OF AXES; SECOND-DEGREE EQUATIONS

In the preceding section we obtained equations of conic sections with axes parallel to the coordinate axes. In this section we will study the equations of conics that are "tilted" relative to the coordinate axes. This will lead us to investigate rotations of coordinate axes.

■ QUADRATIC EQUATIONS IN x AND y

We saw in Examples 8 to 10 of the preceding section that equations of the form

$$Ax^2 + Cy^2 + Dx + Ey + F = 0 \tag{1}$$

can represent conic sections. Equation (1) is a special case of the more general equation

$$Ax^2 + Bxy + Cy^2 + Dx + Ey + F = 0 \tag{2}$$

which, if A, B, and C are not all zero, is called a ***quadratic equation*** in x and y. It is usually the case that the graph of any second-degree equation is a conic section. If $B = 0$, then (2) reduces to (1) and the conic section has its axis or axes parallel to the coordinate axes. However, if $B \neq 0$, then (2) contains a ***cross-product term*** Bxy, and the graph of the conic section represented by the equation has its axis or axes "tilted" relative to the coordinate axes. As an illustration, consider the ellipse with foci $F_1(1, 2)$ and $F_2(-1, -2)$ and such that the sum of the distances from each point $P(x, y)$ on the ellipse to the foci is 6 units. Expressing this condition as an equation, we obtain (Figure 10.5.1)

$$\sqrt{(x - 1)^2 + (y - 2)^2} + \sqrt{(x + 1)^2 + (y + 2)^2} = 6$$

Squaring both sides, then isolating the remaining radical, then squaring again ultimately yields

$$8x^2 - 4xy + 5y^2 = 36$$

as the equation of the ellipse. This is of form (2) with $A = 8$, $B = -4$, $C = 5$, $D = 0$, $E = 0$, and $F = -36$.

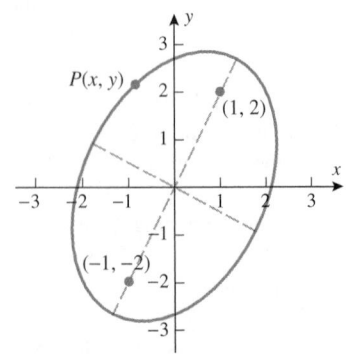

▲ **Figure 10.5.1**

■ ROTATION OF AXES

To study conics that are tilted relative to the coordinate axes it is frequently helpful to rotate the coordinate axes, so that the rotated coordinate axes are parallel to the axes of the conic. Before we can discuss the details, we need to develop some ideas about rotation of coordinate axes.

In Figure 10.5.2a the axes of an xy-coordinate system have been rotated about the origin through an angle θ to produce a new $x'y'$-coordinate system. As shown in the figure, each point P in the plane has coordinates (x', y') as well as coordinates (x, y). To see how the two are related, let r be the distance from the common origin to the point P, and let α be the angle shown in Figure 10.5.2b. It follows that

$$x = r\cos(\theta + \alpha), \quad y = r\sin(\theta + \alpha) \tag{3}$$

and

$$x' = r\cos\alpha, \quad y' = r\sin\alpha \tag{4}$$

Using familiar trigonometric identities, the relationships in (3) can be written as

$$x = r\cos\theta\cos\alpha - r\sin\theta\sin\alpha$$
$$y = r\sin\theta\cos\alpha + r\cos\theta\sin\alpha$$

and on substituting (4) in these equations we obtain the following relationships called the *rotation equations*:

$$\begin{aligned}x &= x'\cos\theta - y'\sin\theta\\ y &= x'\sin\theta + y'\cos\theta\end{aligned} \tag{5}$$

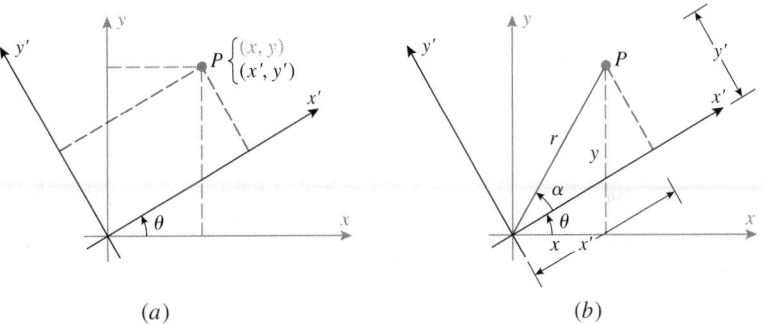

▶ **Figure 10.5.2**   (a)   (b)

▶ **Example 1**   Suppose that the axes of an xy-coordinate system are rotated through an angle of $\theta = 45°$ to obtain an $x'y'$-coordinate system. Find the equation of the curve

$$x^2 - xy + y^2 - 6 = 0$$

in $x'y'$-coordinates.

Solution.   Substituting $\sin\theta = \sin 45° = 1/\sqrt{2}$ and $\cos\theta = \cos 45° = 1/\sqrt{2}$ in (5) yields the rotation equations

$$x = \frac{x'}{\sqrt{2}} - \frac{y'}{\sqrt{2}} \quad \text{and} \quad y = \frac{x'}{\sqrt{2}} + \frac{y'}{\sqrt{2}}$$

Substituting these into the given equation yields

$$\left(\frac{x'}{\sqrt{2}} - \frac{y'}{\sqrt{2}}\right)^2 - \left(\frac{x'}{\sqrt{2}} - \frac{y'}{\sqrt{2}}\right)\left(\frac{x'}{\sqrt{2}} + \frac{y'}{\sqrt{2}}\right) + \left(\frac{x'}{\sqrt{2}} + \frac{y'}{\sqrt{2}}\right)^2 - 6 = 0$$

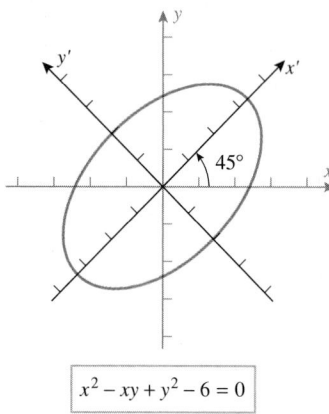

$$x^2 - xy + y^2 - 6 = 0$$

▲ **Figure 10.5.3**

or

$$\frac{x'^2 - 2x'y' + y'^2 - x'^2 + y'^2 + x'^2 + 2x'y' + y'^2}{2} = 6$$

or

$$\frac{x'^2}{12} + \frac{y'^2}{4} = 1$$

which is the equation of an ellipse (Figure 10.5.3). ◄

If the rotation equations (5) are solved for x' and y' in terms of x and y, one obtains (Exercise 16):

$$\begin{aligned} x' &= x \cos\theta + y \sin\theta \\ y' &= -x \sin\theta + y \cos\theta \end{aligned} \tag{6}$$

▶ **Example 2**   Find the new coordinates of the point $(2, 4)$ if the coordinate axes are rotated through an angle of $\theta = 30°$.

Solution.   Using the rotation equations in (6) with $x = 2$, $y = 4$, $\cos\theta = \cos 30° = \sqrt{3}/2$, and $\sin\theta = \sin 30° = 1/2$, we obtain

$$\begin{aligned} x' &= 2(\sqrt{3}/2) + 4(1/2) = \sqrt{3} + 2 \\ y' &= -2(1/2) + 4(\sqrt{3}/2) = -1 + 2\sqrt{3} \end{aligned}$$

Thus, the new coordinates are $(\sqrt{3} + 2, -1 + 2\sqrt{3})$. ◄

■ **ELIMINATING THE CROSS-PRODUCT TERM**

In Example 1 we were able to identify the curve $x^2 - xy + y^2 - 6 = 0$ as an ellipse because the rotation of axes eliminated the xy-term, thereby reducing the equation to a familiar form. This occurred because the new $x'y'$-axes were aligned with the axes of the ellipse. The following theorem tells how to determine an appropriate rotation of axes to eliminate the cross-product term of a second-degree equation in x and y.

10.5.1   THEOREM   *If the equation*

$$Ax^2 + Bxy + Cy^2 + Dx + Ey + F = 0 \tag{7}$$

is such that $B \neq 0$, and if an $x'y'$-coordinate system is obtained by rotating the xy-axes through an angle θ satisfying

$$\cot 2\theta = \frac{A - C}{B} \tag{8}$$

then, in $x'y'$-coordinates, Equation (7) will have the form

$$A'x'^2 + C'y'^2 + D'x' + E'y' + F' = 0$$

It is always possible to satisfy (8) with an angle θ in the interval

$$0 < \theta < \pi/2$$

We will always choose θ in this way.

PROOF   Substituting (5) into (7) and simplifying yields

$$A'x'^2 + B'x'y' + C'y'^2 + D'x' + E'y' + F' = 0$$

where
$$A' = A\cos^2\theta + B\cos\theta\sin\theta + C\sin^2\theta$$
$$B' = B(\cos^2\theta - \sin^2\theta) + 2(C - A)\sin\theta\cos\theta$$
$$C' = A\sin^2\theta - B\sin\theta\cos\theta + C\cos^2\theta$$
$$D' = D\cos\theta + E\sin\theta \tag{9}$$
$$E' = -D\sin\theta + E\cos\theta$$
$$F' = F$$

(Verify.) To complete the proof we must show that $B' = 0$ if

$$\cot 2\theta = \frac{A - C}{B}$$

or, equivalently,

$$\frac{\cos 2\theta}{\sin 2\theta} = \frac{A - C}{B} \tag{10}$$

However, by using the trigonometric double-angle formulas, we can rewrite B' in the form

$$B' = B\cos 2\theta - (A - C)\sin 2\theta$$

Thus, $B' = 0$ if θ satisfies (10). ∎

▶ **Example 3** Identify and sketch the curve $xy = 1$.

Solution. As a first step, we will rotate the coordinate axes to eliminate the cross-product term. Comparing the given equation to (7), we have

$$A = 0, \quad B = 1, \quad C = 0$$

Thus, the desired angle of rotation must satisfy

$$\cot 2\theta = \frac{A - C}{B} = \frac{0 - 0}{1} = 0$$

This condition can be met by taking $2\theta = \pi/2$ or $\theta = \pi/4 = 45°$. Making the substitutions $\cos\theta = \cos 45° = 1/\sqrt{2}$ and $\sin\theta = \sin 45° = 1/\sqrt{2}$ in (5) yields

$$x = \frac{x'}{\sqrt{2}} - \frac{y'}{\sqrt{2}} \quad \text{and} \quad y = \frac{x'}{\sqrt{2}} + \frac{y'}{\sqrt{2}}$$

Substituting these in the equation $xy = 1$ yields

$$\left(\frac{x'}{\sqrt{2}} - \frac{y'}{\sqrt{2}}\right)\left(\frac{x'}{\sqrt{2}} + \frac{y'}{\sqrt{2}}\right) = 1 \quad \text{or} \quad \frac{x'^2}{2} - \frac{y'^2}{2} = 1$$

which is the equation in the $x'y'$-coordinate system of an equilateral hyperbola with vertices at $(\sqrt{2}, 0)$ and $(-\sqrt{2}, 0)$ in that coordinate system (Figure 10.5.4). ◀

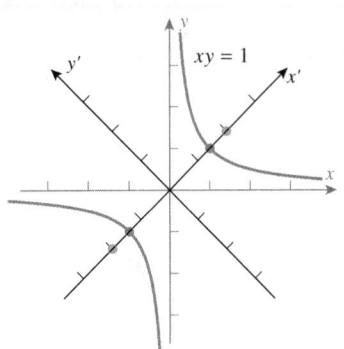

▲ **Figure 10.5.4**

In problems where it is inconvenient to solve

$$\cot 2\theta = \frac{A - C}{B}$$

for θ, the values of $\sin\theta$ and $\cos\theta$ needed for the rotation equations can be obtained by first calculating $\cos 2\theta$ and then computing $\sin\theta$ and $\cos\theta$ from the identities

$$\sin\theta = \sqrt{\frac{1 - \cos 2\theta}{2}} \quad \text{and} \quad \cos\theta = \sqrt{\frac{1 + \cos 2\theta}{2}}$$

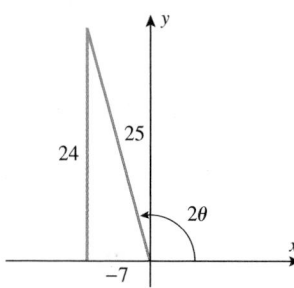

▲ **Figure 10.5.5**

▶ **Example 4**   Identify and sketch the curve

$$153x^2 - 192xy + 97y^2 - 30x - 40y - 200 = 0$$

Solution.   We have $A = 153$, $B = -192$, and $C = 97$, so

$$\cot 2\theta = \frac{A - C}{B} = -\frac{56}{192} = -\frac{7}{24}$$

Since θ is to be chosen in the range $0 < \theta < \pi/2$, this relationship is represented by the triangle in Figure 10.5.5. From that triangle we obtain $\cos 2\theta = -\frac{7}{25}$, which implies that

$$\cos \theta = \sqrt{\frac{1 + \cos 2\theta}{2}} = \sqrt{\frac{1 - \frac{7}{25}}{2}} = \frac{3}{5}$$

$$\sin \theta = \sqrt{\frac{1 - \cos 2\theta}{2}} = \sqrt{\frac{1 + \frac{7}{25}}{2}} = \frac{4}{5}$$

Substituting these values in (5) yields the rotation equations

$$x = \tfrac{3}{5}x' - \tfrac{4}{5}y' \quad \text{and} \quad y = \tfrac{4}{5}x' + \tfrac{3}{5}y'$$

and substituting these in turn in the given equation yields

$$\tfrac{153}{25}(3x' - 4y')^2 - \tfrac{192}{25}(3x' - 4y')(4x' + 3y') + \tfrac{97}{25}(4x' + 3y')^2$$

$$-\tfrac{30}{5}(3x' - 4y') - \tfrac{40}{5}(4x' + 3y') - 200 = 0$$

which simplifies to

$$25x'^2 + 225y'^2 - 50x' - 200 = 0$$

or

$$x'^2 + 9y'^2 - 2x' - 8 = 0$$

Completing the square yields

$$\frac{(x' - 1)^2}{9} + y'^2 = 1$$

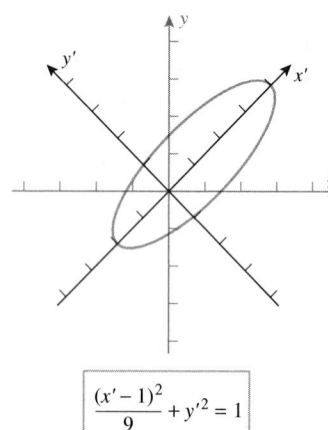

$$\frac{(x' - 1)^2}{9} + y'^2 = 1$$

▲ **Figure 10.5.6**

which is the equation in the $x'y'$-coordinate system of an ellipse with center $(1, 0)$ in that coordinate system and semiaxes $a = 3$ and $b = 1$ (Figure 10.5.6). ◀

There is a method for deducing the kind of curve represented by a second-degree equation directly from the equation itself without rotating coordinate axes. For a discussion of this topic, see the section on the ***discriminant*** that appears in Web Appendix K.

✔**QUICK CHECK EXERCISES 10.5**   (*See page 754 for answers.*)

1. Suppose that an xy-coordinate system is rotated θ radians to produce a new $x'y'$-coordinate system.
   (a) x and y may be obtained from x', y', and θ using the rotation equations $x = $ _____ and $y = $ _____.
   (b) x' and y' may be obtained from x, y, and θ using the equations $x' = $ _____ and $y' = $ _____.

2. If the equation

$$Ax^2 + Bxy + Cy^2 + Dx + Ey + F = 0$$

is such that $B \neq 0$, then the xy-term in this equation can be eliminated by a rotation of axes through an angle θ satisfying $\cot 2\theta = $ _____.

3. In each part, determine a rotation angle θ that will eliminate the xy-term.
   (a) $2x^2 + xy + 2y^2 + x - y = 0$
   (b) $x^2 + 2\sqrt{3}xy + 3y^2 - 2x + y = 1$
   (c) $3x^2 + \sqrt{3}xy + 2y^2 + y = 0$

4. Express $2x^2 + xy + 2y^2 = 1$ in the $x'y'$-coordinate system obtained by rotating the xy-coordinate system through the angle $\theta = \pi/4$.

EXERCISE SET 10.5

1. Let an $x'y'$-coordinate system be obtained by rotating an xy-coordinate system through an angle of $\theta = 60°$.
   (a) Find the $x'y'$-coordinates of the point whose xy-coordinates are $(-2, 6)$.
   (b) Find an equation of the curve $\sqrt{3}xy + y^2 = 6$ in $x'y'$-coordinates.
   (c) Sketch the curve in part (b), showing both xy-axes and $x'y'$-axes.

2. Let an $x'y'$-coordinate system be obtained by rotating an xy-coordinate system through an angle of $\theta = 30°$.
   (a) Find the $x'y'$-coordinates of the point whose xy-coordinates are $(1, -\sqrt{3})$.
   (b) Find an equation of the curve $2x^2 + 2\sqrt{3}xy = 3$ in $x'y'$-coordinates.
   (c) Sketch the curve in part (b), showing both xy-axes and $x'y'$-axes.

3–12 Rotate the coordinate axes to remove the xy-term. Then identify the type of conic and sketch its graph. ■

3. $xy = -9$

4. $x^2 - xy + y^2 - 2 = 0$

5. $x^2 + 4xy - 2y^2 - 6 = 0$

6. $31x^2 + 10\sqrt{3}xy + 21y^2 - 144 = 0$

7. $x^2 + 2\sqrt{3}xy + 3y^2 + 2\sqrt{3}x - 2y = 0$

8. $34x^2 - 24xy + 41y^2 - 25 = 0$

9. $9x^2 - 24xy + 16y^2 - 80x - 60y + 100 = 0$

10. $5x^2 - 6xy + 5y^2 - 8\sqrt{2}x + 8\sqrt{2}y = 8$

11. $52x^2 - 72xy + 73y^2 + 40x + 30y - 75 = 0$

12. $6x^2 + 24xy - y^2 - 12x + 26y + 11 = 0$

13. Let an $x'y'$-coordinate system be obtained by rotating an xy-coordinate system through an angle of $45°$. Use (6) to find an equation of the curve $3x'^2 + y'^2 = 6$ in xy-coordinates.

14. Let an $x'y'$-coordinate system be obtained by rotating an xy-coordinate system through an angle of $30°$. Use (5) to find an equation in $x'y'$-coordinates of the curve $y = x^2$.

FOCUS ON CONCEPTS

15. Let an $x'y'$-coordinate system be obtained by rotating an xy-coordinate system through an angle θ. Prove: For every value of θ, the equation $x^2 + y^2 = r^2$ becomes the equation $x'^2 + y'^2 = r^2$. Give a geometric explanation.

16. Derive (6) by solving the rotation equations in (5) for x' and y' in terms of x and y.

17. Let an $x'y'$-coordinate system be obtained by rotating an xy-coordinate system through an angle θ. Explain how to find the xy-coordinates of a point whose $x'y'$-coordinates are known.

18. Let an $x'y'$-coordinate system be obtained by rotating an xy-coordinate system through an angle θ. Explain how to find the xy-equation of a line whose $x'y'$-equation is known.

19–22 Show that the graph of the given equation is a parabola. Find its vertex, focus, and directrix. ■

19. $x^2 + 2xy + y^2 + 4\sqrt{2}x - 4\sqrt{2}y = 0$

20. $x^2 - 2\sqrt{3}xy + 3y^2 - 8\sqrt{3}x - 8y = 0$

21. $9x^2 - 24xy + 16y^2 - 80x - 60y + 100 = 0$

22. $x^2 + 2\sqrt{3}xy + 3y^2 + 16\sqrt{3}x - 16y - 96 = 0$

23–26 Show that the graph of the given equation is an ellipse. Find its foci, vertices, and the ends of its minor axis. ■

23. $288x^2 - 168xy + 337y^2 - 3600 = 0$

24. $25x^2 - 14xy + 25y^2 - 288 = 0$

25. $31x^2 + 10\sqrt{3}xy + 21y^2 - 32x + 32\sqrt{3}y - 80 = 0$

26. $43x^2 - 14\sqrt{3}xy + 57y^2 - 36\sqrt{3}x - 36y - 540 = 0$

27–30 Show that the graph of the given equation is a hyperbola. Find its foci, vertices, and asymptotes. ■

27. $x^2 - 10\sqrt{3}xy + 11y^2 + 64 = 0$

28. $17x^2 - 312xy + 108y^2 - 900 = 0$

29. $32y^2 - 52xy - 7x^2 + 72\sqrt{5}x - 144\sqrt{5}y + 900 = 0$

30. $2\sqrt{2}y^2 + 5\sqrt{2}xy + 2\sqrt{2}x^2 + 18x + 18y + 36\sqrt{2} = 0$

31. Show that the graph of the equation

$$\sqrt{x} + \sqrt{y} = 1$$

is a portion of a parabola. [*Hint:* First rationalize the equation and then perform a rotation of axes.]

FOCUS ON CONCEPTS

32. Derive the expression for B' in (9).

33. Use (9) to prove that $B^2 - 4AC = B'^2 - 4A'C'$ for all values of θ.

34. Use (9) to prove that $A + C = A' + C'$ for all values of θ.

35. Prove: If $A = C$ in (7), then the cross-product term can be eliminated by rotating through $45°$.

36. Prove: If $B \neq 0$, then the graph of $x^2 + Bxy + F = 0$ is a hyperbola if $F \neq 0$ and two intersecting lines if $F = 0$.

1. (a) $x' \cos\theta - y' \sin\theta$; $x' \sin\theta + y' \cos\theta$ (b) $x \cos\theta + y \sin\theta$; $-x \sin\theta + y \cos\theta$ **2.** $\dfrac{A - C}{B}$ **3.** (a) $\dfrac{\pi}{4}$ (b) $\dfrac{\pi}{3}$ (c) $\dfrac{\pi}{6}$
4. $5x'^2 + 3y'^2 = 2$

10.6 CONIC SECTIONS IN POLAR COORDINATES

It will be shown later in the text that if an object moves in a gravitational field that is directed toward a fixed point (such as the center of the Sun), then the path of that object must be a conic section with the fixed point at a focus. For example, planets in our solar system move along elliptical paths with the Sun at a focus, and the comets move along parabolic, elliptical, or hyperbolic paths with the Sun at a focus, depending on the conditions under which they were born. For applications of this type it is usually desirable to express the equations of the conic sections in polar coordinates with the pole at a focus. In this section we will show how to do this.

■ THE FOCUS–DIRECTRIX CHARACTERIZATION OF CONICS

To obtain polar equations for the conic sections we will need the following theorem.

It is an unfortunate historical accident that the letter *e* is used for the base of the natural logarithm as well as for the eccentricity of conic sections. However, as a practical matter the appropriate interpretation will usually be clear from the context in which the letter is used.

> **10.6.1 THEOREM (*Focus–Directrix Property of Conics*)** *Suppose that a point P moves in the plane determined by a fixed point (called the **focus**) and a fixed line (called the **directrix**), where the focus does not lie on the directrix. If the point moves in such a way that its distance to the focus divided by its distance to the directrix is some constant e (called the **eccentricity**), then the curve traced by the point is a conic section. Moreover, the conic is*
>
> (a) *a parabola if* $e = 1$ (b) *an ellipse if* $0 < e < 1$ (c) *a hyperbola if* $e > 1$.

We will not give a formal proof of this theorem; rather, we will use the specific cases in Figure 10.6.1 to illustrate the basic ideas. For the parabola, we will take the directrix to be $x = -p$, as usual; and for the ellipse and the hyperbola we will take the directrix to be $x = a^2/c$. We want to show in all three cases that if P is a point on the graph, F is the focus, and D is the directrix, then the ratio PF/PD is some constant e, where $e = 1$ for the parabola, $0 < e < 1$ for the ellipse, and $e > 1$ for the hyperbola. We will give the arguments for the parabola and ellipse and leave the argument for the hyperbola as an exercise.

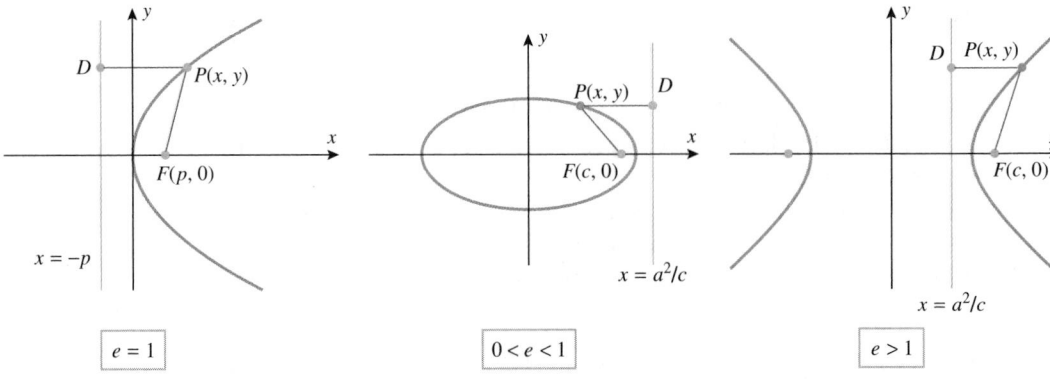

▲ **Figure 10.6.1**

For the parabola, the distance PF to the focus is equal to the distance PD to the directrix, so that $PF/PD = 1$, which is what we wanted to show. For the ellipse, we rewrite Equation (8) of Section 10.4 as

$$\sqrt{(x-c)^2 + y^2} = a - \frac{c}{a}x = \frac{c}{a}\left(\frac{a^2}{c} - x\right)$$

But the expression on the left side is the distance PF, and the expression in the parentheses on the right side is the distance PD, so we have shown that

$$PF = \frac{c}{a}PD$$

Thus, PF/PD is constant, and the eccentricity is

$$e = \frac{c}{a} \tag{1}$$

If we rule out the degenerate case where $a = 0$ or $c = 0$, then it follows from Formula (7) of Section 10.4 that $0 < c < a$, so $0 < e < 1$, which is what we wanted to show.

We will leave it as an exercise to show that the eccentricity of the hyperbola in Figure 10.6.1 is also given by Formula (1), but in this case it follows from Formula (11) of Section 10.4 that $c > a$, so $e > 1$.

■ ECCENTRICITY OF AN ELLIPSE AS A MEASURE OF FLATNESS

The eccentricity of an ellipse can be viewed as a measure of its flatness—as e approaches 0 the ellipses become more and more circular, and as e approaches 1 they become more and more flat (Figure 10.6.2). Table 10.6.1 shows the orbital eccentricities of various celestial objects. Note that most of the planets actually have fairly circular orbits.

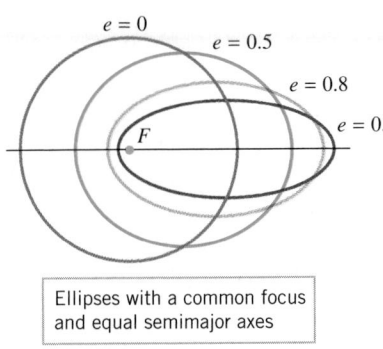

Ellipses with a common focus and equal semimajor axes

▲ **Figure 10.6.2**

Table 10.6.1

CELESTIAL BODY	ECCENTRICITY
Mercury	0.206
Venus	0.007
Earth	0.017
Mars	0.093
Jupiter	0.048
Saturn	0.056
Uranus	0.046
Neptune	0.010
Pluto	0.249
Halley's comet	0.970

■ POLAR EQUATIONS OF CONICS

Our next objective is to derive polar equations for the conic sections from their focus–directrix characterizations. We will assume that the focus is at the pole and the directrix is either parallel or perpendicular to the polar axis. If the directrix is parallel to the polar axis, then it can be above or below the pole; and if the directrix is perpendicular to the polar axis, then it can be to the left or right of the pole. Thus, there are four cases to consider. We will derive the formulas for the case in which the directrix is perpendicular to the polar axis and to the right of the pole.

As illustrated in Figure 10.6.3, let us assume that the directrix is perpendicular to the polar axis and d units to the right of the pole, where the constant d is known. If P is a point

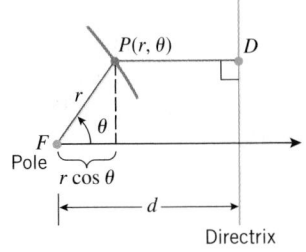

▲ **Figure 10.6.3**

on the conic and if the eccentricity of the conic is e, then it follows from Theorem 10.6.1 that $PF/PD = e$ or, equivalently, that

$$PF = ePD \tag{2}$$

However, it is evident from Figure 10.6.3 that $PF = r$ and $PD = d - r\cos\theta$. Thus, (2) can be written as

$$r = e(d - r\cos\theta)$$

which can be solved for r and expressed as

$$r = \frac{ed}{1 + e\cos\theta}$$

(verify). Observe that this single polar equation can represent a parabola, an ellipse, or a hyperbola, depending on the value of e. In contrast, the rectangular equations for these conics all have different forms. The derivations in the other three cases are similar.

10.6.2   THEOREM   *If a conic section with eccentricity e is positioned in a polar co-ordinate system so that its focus is at the pole and the corresponding directrix is d units from the pole and is either parallel or perpendicular to the polar axis, then the equation of the conic has one of four possible forms, depending on its orientation:*

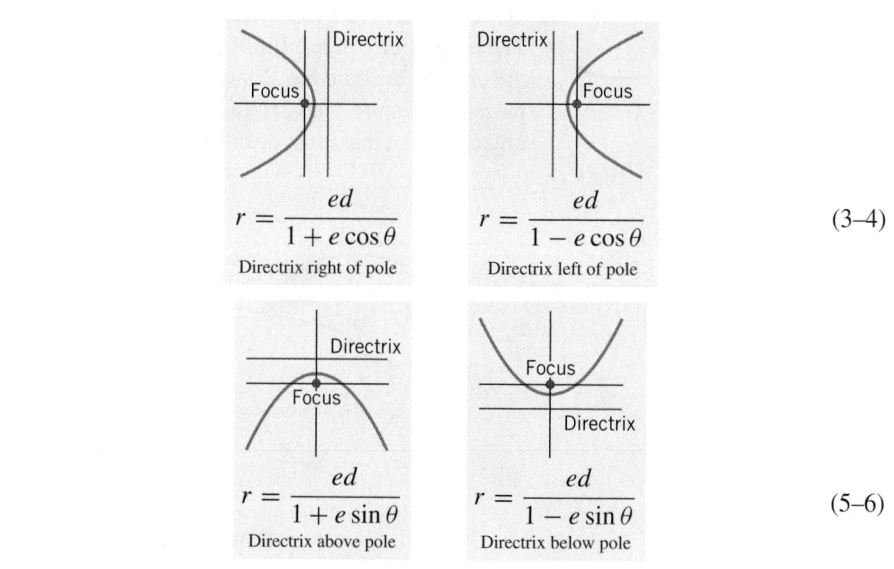

$$r = \frac{ed}{1 + e\cos\theta}$$
Directrix right of pole

$$r = \frac{ed}{1 - e\cos\theta}$$
Directrix left of pole

$$(3\text{--}4)$$

$$r = \frac{ed}{1 + e\sin\theta}$$
Directrix above pole

$$r = \frac{ed}{1 - e\sin\theta}$$
Directrix below pole

$$(5\text{--}6)$$

SKETCHING CONICS IN POLAR COORDINATES

Precise graphs of conic sections in polar coordinates can be generated with graphing utilities. However, it is often useful to be able to make quick sketches of these graphs that show their orientations and give some sense of their dimensions. The orientation of a conic relative to the polar axis can be deduced by matching its equation with one of the four forms in Theorem 10.6.2. The key dimensions of a parabola are determined by the constant p (Figure 10.4.5) and those of ellipses and hyperbolas by the constants a, b, and c (Figures 10.4.11 and 10.4.20). Thus, we need to show how these constants can be obtained from the polar equations.

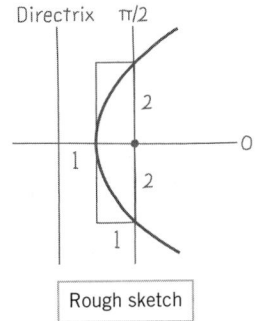

Rough sketch

▲ **Figure 10.6.4**

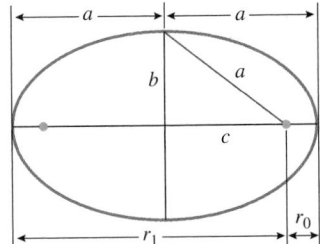

▲ **Figure 10.6.5**

In words, Formula (8) states that a is the *arithmetic average* (also called the *arithmetic mean*) of r_0 and r_1, and Formula (10) states that b is the *geometric mean* of r_0 and r_1.

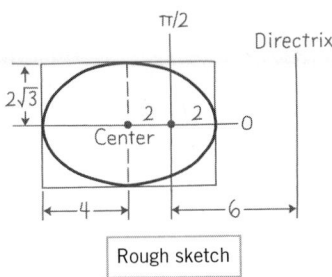

Rough sketch

▲ **Figure 10.6.6**

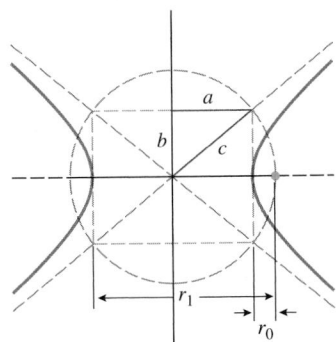

▲ **Figure 10.6.7**

▶ **Example 1** Sketch the graph of $r = \dfrac{2}{1 - \cos\theta}$ in polar coordinates.

Solution. The equation is an exact match to (4) with $d = 2$ and $e = 1$. Thus, the graph is a parabola with the focus at the pole and the directrix 2 units to the left of the pole. This tells us that the parabola opens to the right along the polar axis and $p = 1$. Thus, the parabola looks roughly like that sketched in Figure 10.6.4. ◀

All of the important geometric information about an ellipse can be obtained from the values of a, b, and c in Figure 10.6.5. One way to find these values from the polar equation of an ellipse is based on finding the distances from the focus to the vertices. As shown in the figure, let r_0 be the distance from the focus to the closest vertex and r_1 the distance to the farthest vertex. Thus,

$$r_0 = a - c \quad \text{and} \quad r_1 = a + c \tag{7}$$

from which it follows that

$$a = \tfrac{1}{2}(r_1 + r_0) \qquad c = \tfrac{1}{2}(r_1 - r_0) \tag{8–9}$$

Moreover, it also follows from (7) that

$$r_0 r_1 = a^2 - c^2 = b^2$$

Thus,

$$b = \sqrt{r_0 r_1} \tag{10}$$

▶ **Example 2** Find the constants a, b, and c for the ellipse $r = \dfrac{6}{2 + \cos\theta}$.

Solution. This equation does not match any of the forms in Theorem 10.6.2 because they all require a constant term of 1 in the denominator. However, we can put the equation into one of these forms by dividing the numerator and denominator by 2 to obtain

$$r = \dfrac{3}{1 + \tfrac{1}{2}\cos\theta}$$

This is an exact match to (3) with $d = 6$ and $e = \tfrac{1}{2}$, so the graph is an ellipse with the directrix 6 units to the right of the pole. The distance r_0 from the focus to the closest vertex can be obtained by setting $\theta = 0$ in this equation, and the distance r_1 to the farthest vertex can be obtained by setting $\theta = \pi$. This yields

$$r_0 = \dfrac{3}{1 + \tfrac{1}{2}\cos 0} = \dfrac{3}{\tfrac{3}{2}} = 2, \quad r_1 = \dfrac{3}{1 + \tfrac{1}{2}\cos\pi} = \dfrac{3}{\tfrac{1}{2}} = 6$$

Thus, from Formulas (8), (10), and (9), respectively, we obtain

$$a = \tfrac{1}{2}(r_1 + r_0) = 4, \quad b = \sqrt{r_0 r_1} = 2\sqrt{3}, \quad c = \tfrac{1}{2}(r_1 - r_0) = 2$$

The ellipse looks roughly like that sketched in Figure 10.6.6. ◀

All of the important information about a hyperbola can be obtained from the values of a, b, and c in Figure 10.6.7. As with the ellipse, one way to find these values from the polar equation of a hyperbola is based on finding the distances from the focus to the vertices. As shown in the figure, let r_0 be the distance from the focus to the closest vertex and r_1 the distance to the farthest vertex. Thus,

$$r_0 = c - a \quad \text{and} \quad r_1 = c + a \tag{11}$$

from which it follows that

$$a = \tfrac{1}{2}(r_1 - r_0) \qquad c = \tfrac{1}{2}(r_1 + r_0) \tag{12–13}$$

In words, Formula (13) states that c is the **arithmetic mean** of r_0 and r_1, and Formula (14) states that b is the **geometric mean** of r_0 and r_1.

Moreover, it also follows from (11) that

$$r_0 r_1 = c^2 - a^2 = b^2$$

from which it follows that

$$b = \sqrt{r_0 r_1} \tag{14}$$

▶ **Example 3**   Sketch the graph of $r = \dfrac{2}{1 + 2\sin\theta}$ in polar coordinates.

Solution.   This equation is an exact match to (5) with $d = 1$ and $e = 2$. Thus, the graph is a hyperbola with its directrix 1 unit above the pole. However, it is not so straightforward to compute the values of r_0 and r_1, since hyperbolas in polar coordinates are generated in a strange way as θ varies from 0 to 2π. This can be seen from Figure 10.6.8a, which is the graph of the given equation in rectangular θr-coordinates. It follows from this graph that the corresponding polar graph is generated in pieces (see Figure 10.6.8b):

- As θ varies over the interval $0 \le \theta < 7\pi/6$, the value of r is positive and varies from 2 down to 2/3 and then to $+\infty$, which generates part of the lower branch.
- As θ varies over the interval $7\pi/6 < \theta \le 3\pi/2$, the value of r is negative and varies from $-\infty$ to -2, which generates the right part of the upper branch.
- As θ varies over the interval $3\pi/2 \le \theta < 11\pi/6$, the value of r is negative and varies from -2 to $-\infty$, which generates the left part of the upper branch.
- As θ varies over the interval $11\pi/6 < \theta \le 2\pi$, the value of r is positive and varies from $+\infty$ to 2, which fills in the missing piece of the lower right branch.

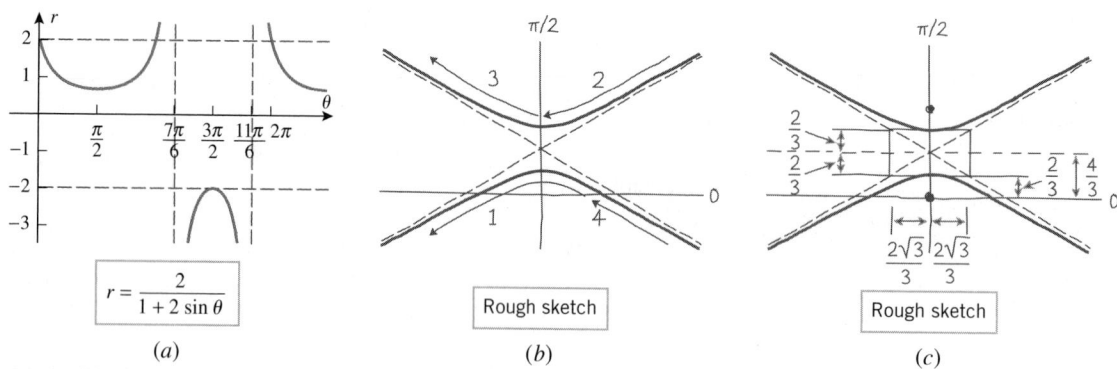

$r = \dfrac{2}{1 + 2\sin\theta}$

(a)   Rough sketch (b)   Rough sketch (c)

▲ **Figure 10.6.8**

To obtain a rough sketch of a hyperbola, it is generally sufficient to locate the center, the asymptotes, and the points where $\theta = 0$, $\theta = \pi/2$, $\theta = \pi$, and $\theta = 3\pi/2$.

It is now clear that we can obtain r_0 by setting $\theta = \pi/2$ and r_1 by setting $\theta = 3\pi/2$. Keeping in mind that r_0 and r_1 are positive, this yields

$$r_0 = \frac{2}{1 + 2\sin(\pi/2)} = \frac{2}{3}, \quad r_1 = \left| \frac{2}{1 + 2\sin(3\pi/2)} \right| = \left| \frac{2}{-1} \right| = 2$$

Thus, from Formulas (12), (14), and (13), respectively, we obtain

$$a = \frac{1}{2}(r_1 - r_0) = \frac{2}{3}, \quad b = \sqrt{r_0 r_1} = \frac{2\sqrt{3}}{3}, \quad c = \frac{1}{2}(r_1 + r_0) = \frac{4}{3}$$

Thus, the hyperbola looks roughly like that sketched in Figure 10.6.8c. ◄

■ APPLICATIONS IN ASTRONOMY

In 1609 Johannes Kepler published a book known as *Astronomia Nova* (or sometimes *Commentaries on the Motions of Mars*) in which he succeeded in distilling thousands of years of observational astronomy into three beautiful laws of planetary motion (Figure 10.6.9).

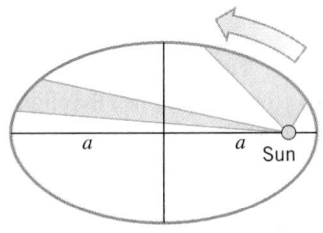

Equal areas are swept out in equal times, and the square of the period T is proportional to a^3.

▲ **Figure 10.6.9**

10.6.3 KEPLER'S LAWS

- First law (*Law of Orbits*). Each planet moves in an elliptical orbit with the Sun at a focus.

- Second law (*Law of Areas*). The radial line from the center of the Sun to the center of a planet sweeps out equal areas in equal times.

- Third law (*Law of Periods*). The square of a planet's period (the time it takes the planet to complete one orbit about the Sun) is proportional to the cube of the semimajor axis of its orbit.

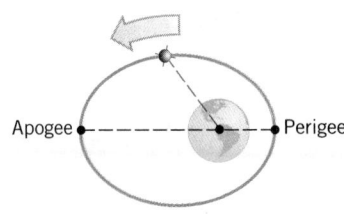

Apogee ●————————● Perigee

▲ **Figure 10.6.10**

Kepler's laws, although stated for planetary motion around the Sun, apply to all orbiting celestial bodies that are subjected to a *single* central gravitational force—artificial satellites subjected only to the central force of Earth's gravity and moons subjected only to the central gravitational force of a planet, for example. Later in the text we will derive Kepler's laws from basic principles, but for now we will show how they can be used in basic astronomical computations.

In an elliptical orbit, the closest point to the focus is called the *perigee* and the farthest point the *apogee* (Figure 10.6.10). The distances from the focus to the perigee and apogee

---

Johannes Kepler (1571–1630) German astronomer and physicist. Kepler, whose work provided our contemporary view of planetary motion, led a fascinating but ill-starred life. His alcoholic father made him work in a family-owned tavern as a child, later withdrawing him from elementary school and hiring him out as a field laborer, where the boy contracted smallpox, permanently crippling his hands and impairing his eyesight. In later years, Kepler's first wife and several children died, his mother was accused of witchcraft, and being a Protestant he was often subjected to persecution by Catholic authorities. He was often impoverished, eking out a living as an astrologer and prognosticator. Looking back on his unhappy childhood, Kepler described his father as "criminally inclined" and "quarrelsome" and his mother as "garrulous" and "bad-tempered." However, it was his mother who left an indelible mark on the six-year-old Kepler by showing him the comet of 1577; and in later life he personally prepared her defense against the witchcraft charges. Kepler became acquainted with the work of Copernicus as a student at the University of Tübingen, where he received his master's degree in 1591. He continued on as a theological student, but at the urging of the university officials he abandoned his clerical studies and accepted a position as a mathematician and teacher in Graz, Austria. However, he was expelled from the city when it came under Catholic control, and in 1600 he finally moved on to Prague, where he became an assistant at the observatory of the famous Danish astronomer Tycho Brahe. Brahe was a brilliant and meticulous astronomical observer who amassed the most accurate astronomical data known at that time; and when Brahe died in 1601 Kepler inherited the treasure-trove of data. After eight years of intense labor, Kepler deciphered the underlying principles buried in the data and in 1609 published his monumental work, *Astronomia Nova*, in which he stated his first two laws of planetary motion. Commenting on his discovery of elliptical orbits, Kepler wrote, "I was almost driven to madness in considering and calculating this matter. I could not find out why the planet would rather go on an elliptical orbit (rather than a circle). Oh ridiculous me!" It ultimately remained for Isaac Newton to discover the laws of gravitation that explained the reason for elliptical orbits.

are called the *perigee distance* and *apogee distance*, respectively. For orbits around the Sun, it is more common to use the terms *perihelion* and *aphelion*, rather than perigee and apogee, and to measure time in Earth years and distances in astronomical units (AU), where 1 AU is the semimajor axis a of the Earth's orbit (approximately 150×10^6 km or 92.9×10^6 mi). With this choice of units, the constant of proportionality in Kepler's third law is 1, since $a = 1$ AU produces a period of $T = 1$ Earth year. In this case Kepler's third law can be expressed as

$$T = a^{3/2} \tag{15}$$

Shapes of elliptical orbits are often specified by giving the eccentricity e and the semimajor axis a, so it is useful to express the polar equations of an ellipse in terms of these constants. Figure 10.6.11, which can be obtained from the ellipse in Figure 10.6.1 and the relationship $c = ea$, implies that the distance d between the focus and the directrix is

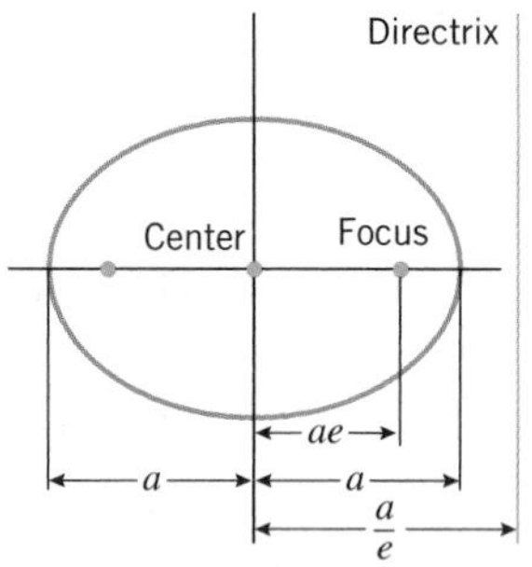

$$d = \frac{a}{e} - c = \frac{a}{e} - ea = \frac{a(1 - e^2)}{e} \tag{16}$$

from which it follows that $ed = a(1 - e^2)$. Thus, depending on the orientation of the ellipse, the formulas in Theorem 10.6.2 can be expressed in terms of a and e as

$$r = \frac{a(1 - e^2)}{1 \pm e \cos \theta} \qquad r = \frac{a(1 - e^2)}{1 \pm e \sin \theta} \tag{17–18}$$

+: Directrix right of pole   +: Directrix above pole
−: Directrix left of pole   −: Directrix below pole

Moreover, it is evident from Figure 10.6.11 that the distances from the focus to the closest and farthest vertices can be expressed in terms of a and e as

$$r_0 = a - ea = a(1 - e) \quad \text{and} \quad r_1 = a + ea = a(1 + e) \tag{19–20}$$

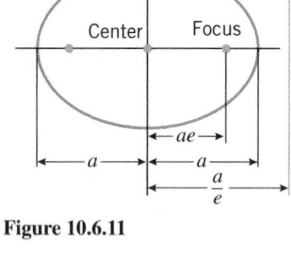

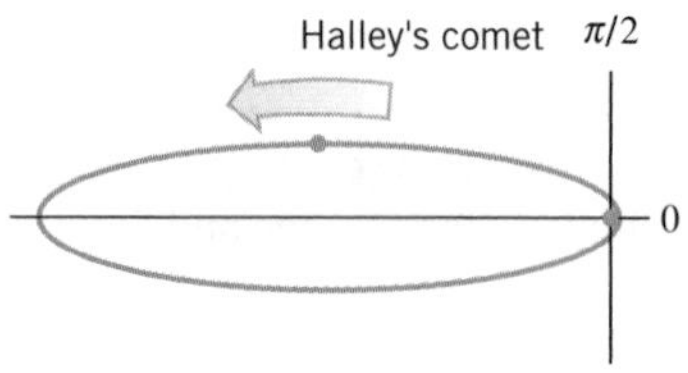

Directrix

Center   Focus

$\leftarrow ae \rightarrow$

$\leftarrow a \rightarrow \leftarrow a \rightarrow$

$\frac{a}{e}$

▲ **Figure 10.6.11**

Halley's comet $\pi/2$

0

▲ **Figure 10.6.12**

Science Photo Library/Photo Researchers
Halley's comet photographed April 21, 1910 in Peru.

▶ **Example 4** Halley's comet (last seen in 1986) has an eccentricity of 0.97 and a semimajor axis of $a = 18.1$ AU.

(a) Find the equation of its orbit in the polar coordinate system shown in Figure 10.6.12.

(b) Find the period of its orbit.

(c) Find its perihelion and aphelion distances.

Solution (a). From (17), the polar equation of the orbit has the form

$$r = \frac{a(1 - e^2)}{1 + e \cos \theta}$$

But $a(1 - e^2) = 18.1[1 - (0.97)^2] \approx 1.07$. Thus, the equation of the orbit is

$$r = \frac{1.07}{1 + 0.97 \cos \theta}$$

Solution (b). From (15), with $a = 18.1$, the period of the orbit is

$$T = (18.1)^{3/2} \approx 77 \text{ years}$$

Solution (c). Since the perihelion and aphelion distances are the distances to the closest and farthest vertices, respectively, it follows from (19) and (20) that

$$r_0 = a - ea = a(1 - e) = 18.1(1 - 0.97) \approx 0.543 \text{ AU}$$
$$r_1 = a + ea = a(1 + e) = 18.1(1 + 0.97) \approx 35.7 \text{ AU}$$

or since $1 \text{ AU} \approx 150 \times 10^6$ km, the perihelion and aphelion distances in kilometers are

$$r_0 = 18.1(1 - 0.97)(150 \times 10^6) \approx 81{,}500{,}000 \text{ km}$$
$$r_1 = 18.1(1 + 0.97)(150 \times 10^6) \approx 5{,}350{,}000{,}000 \text{ km} \blacktriangleleft$$

Minimum distance

Maximum distance

▲ **Figure 10.6.13**

▶ **Example 5**   An Apollo lunar lander orbits the Moon in an elliptic orbit with eccentricity $e = 0.12$ and semimajor axis $a = 2015$ km. Assuming the Moon to be a sphere of radius 1740 km, find the minimum and maximum heights of the lander above the lunar surface (Figure 10.6.13).

Solution.   If we let r_0 and r_1 denote the minimum and maximum distances from the center of the Moon, then the minimum and maximum distances from the surface of the Moon will be

$$d_{\min} = r_0 - 1740$$
$$d_{\max} = r_1 - 1740$$

or from Formulas (19) and (20)

$$d_{\min} = r_0 - 1740 = a(1 - e) - 1740 = 2015(0.88) - 1740 = 33.2 \text{ km}$$
$$d_{\max} = r_1 - 1740 = a(1 + e) - 1740 = 2015(1.12) - 1740 = 516.8 \text{ km} \blacktriangleleft$$

✔ **QUICK CHECK EXERCISES 10.6**   (See page 763 for answers.)

1. In each part, name the conic section described.
   (a) The set of points whose distance to the point $(2, 3)$ is half the distance to the line $x + y = 1$ is _____.
   (b) The set of points whose distance to the point $(2, 3)$ is equal to the distance to the line $x + y = 1$ is _____.
   (c) The set of points whose distance to the point $(2, 3)$ is twice the distance to the line $x + y = 1$ is _____.

2. In each part: (i) Identify the polar graph as a parabola, an ellipse, or a hyperbola; (ii) state whether the directrix is above, below, to the left, or to the right of the pole; and (iii) find the distance from the pole to the directrix.
   (a) $r = \dfrac{1}{4 + \cos \theta}$ (b) $r = \dfrac{1}{1 - 4 \cos \theta}$

   (c) $r = \dfrac{1}{4 + 4 \sin \theta}$ (d) $r = \dfrac{4}{1 - \sin \theta}$

3. If the distance from a vertex of an ellipse to the nearest focus is r_0, and if the distance from that vertex to the farthest focus is r_1, then the semimajor axis is $a =$ _____ and the semiminor axis is $b =$ _____.

4. If the distance from a vertex of a hyperbola to the nearest focus is r_0, and if the distance from that vertex to the farthest focus is r_1, then the semifocal axis is $a =$ _____ and the semiconjugate axis is $b =$ _____.

EXERCISE SET 10.6   ☒ Graphing Utility

1–2 Find the eccentricity and the distance from the pole to the directrix, and sketch the graph in polar coordinates. ■

1. (a) $r = \dfrac{3}{2 - 2 \cos \theta}$ (b) $r = \dfrac{3}{2 + \sin \theta}$

2. (a) $r = \dfrac{4}{2 + 3 \cos \theta}$ (b) $r = \dfrac{5}{3 + 3 \sin \theta}$

☒ **3–4** Use Formulas (3)–(6) to identify the type of conic and its orientation. Check your answer by generating the graph with a graphing utility. ■

3. (a) $r = \dfrac{8}{1 - \sin \theta}$ (b) $r = \dfrac{16}{4 + 3 \sin \theta}$

4. (a) $r = \dfrac{4}{2 - 3 \sin \theta}$ (b) $r = \dfrac{12}{4 + \cos \theta}$

5–6 Find a polar equation for the conic that has its focus at the pole and satisfies the stated conditions. Points are in polar coordinates and directrices in rectangular coordinates for simplicity. (In some cases there may be more than one conic that satisfies the conditions.) ■

5. (a) Ellipse; $e = \frac{3}{4}$; directrix $x = 2$.
   (b) Parabola; directrix $x = 1$.
   (c) Hyperbola; $e = \frac{4}{3}$; directrix $y = 3$.

6. (a) Ellipse; ends of major axis $(2, \pi/2)$ and $(6, 3\pi/2)$.
(b) Parabola; vertex $(2, \pi)$.
(c) Hyperbola; $e = \sqrt{2}$; vertex $(2, 0)$.

7–8 Find the distances from the pole to the vertices, and then apply Formulas (8)–(10) to find the equation of the ellipse in rectangular coordinates. ■

7. (a) $r = \dfrac{6}{2 + \sin \theta}$ 　　(b) $r = \dfrac{1}{2 - \cos \theta}$

8. (a) $r = \dfrac{6}{5 + 2\cos \theta}$ 　　(b) $r = \dfrac{8}{4 - 3\sin \theta}$

9–10 Find the distances from the pole to the vertices, and then apply Formulas (12)–(14) to find the equation of the hyperbola in rectangular coordinates. ■

9. (a) $r = \dfrac{3}{1 + 2\sin \theta}$ 　　(b) $r = \dfrac{5}{2 - 3\cos \theta}$

10. (a) $r = \dfrac{4}{1 - 2\sin \theta}$ 　　(b) $r = \dfrac{15}{2 + 8\cos \theta}$

11–12 Find a polar equation for the ellipse that has its focus at the pole and satisfies the stated conditions. ■

11. (a) Directrix to the right of the pole; $a = 8$; $e = \frac{1}{2}$.
(b) Directrix below the pole; $a = 4$; $e = \frac{3}{5}$.

12. (a) Directrix to the left of the pole; $b = 4$; $e = \frac{3}{5}$.
(b) Directrix above the pole; $c = 5$; $e = \frac{1}{5}$.

13. Find the polar equation of an equilateral hyperbola with a focus at the pole and vertex $(5, 0)$.

FOCUS ON CONCEPTS

14. Prove that a hyperbola is an equilateral hyperbola if and only if $e = \sqrt{2}$.

15. (a) Show that the coordinates of the point P on the hyperbola in Figure 10.6.1 satisfy the equation

$$\sqrt{(x - c)^2 + y^2} = \frac{c}{a}x - a$$

(b) Use the result obtained in part (a) to show that $PF/PD = c/a$.

16. (a) Show that the eccentricity of an ellipse can be expressed in terms of r_0 and r_1 as

$$e = \frac{r_1 - r_0}{r_1 + r_0}$$

(b) Show that

$$\frac{r_1}{r_0} = \frac{1 + e}{1 - e}$$

17. (a) Show that the eccentricity of a hyperbola can be expressed in terms of r_0 and r_1 as

$$e = \frac{r_1 + r_0}{r_1 - r_0}$$

(b) Show that

$$\frac{r_1}{r_0} = \frac{e + 1}{e - 1}$$

18. (a) Sketch the curves

$$r = \frac{1}{1 + \cos \theta} \quad \text{and} \quad r = \frac{1}{1 - \cos \theta}$$

(b) Find polar coordinates of the intersections of the curves in part (a).
(c) Show that the curves are *orthogonal*, that is, their tangent lines are perpendicular at the points of intersection.

19–22 True–False Determine whether the statement is true or false. Explain your answer. ■

19. If an ellipse is not a circle, then the eccentricity of the ellipse is less than one.

20. A parabola has eccentricity greater than one.

21. If one ellipse has foci that are farther apart than those of a second ellipse, then the eccentricity of the first is greater than that of the second.

22. If d is a positive constant, then the conic section with polar equation

$$r = \frac{d}{1 + \cos \theta}$$

is a parabola.

23–28 Use the following values, where needed:

radius of the Earth $= 4000$ mi $= 6440$ km
1 year (Earth year) $= 365$ days (Earth days)
1 AU $= 92.9 \times 10^6$ mi $= 150 \times 10^6$ km ■

23. The dwarf planet Pluto has eccentricity $e = 0.249$ and semi-major axis $a = 39.5$ AU.
(a) Find the period T in years.
(b) Find the perihelion and aphelion distances.
(c) Choose a polar coordinate system with the center of the Sun at the pole, and find a polar equation of Pluto's orbit in that coordinate system.
(d) Make a sketch of the orbit with reasonably accurate proportions.

24. (a) Let a be the semimajor axis of a planet's orbit around the Sun, and let T be its period. Show that if T is measured in days and a is measured in kilometers, then $T = (365 \times 10^{-9})(a/150)^{3/2}$.
(b) Use the result in part (a) to find the period of the planet Mercury in days, given that its semimajor axis is $a = 57.95 \times 10^6$ km.
(c) Choose a polar coordinate system with the Sun at the pole, and find an equation for the orbit of Mercury in that coordinate system given that the eccentricity of the orbit is $e = 0.206$.
(d) Use a graphing utility to generate the orbit of Mercury from the equation obtained in part (c).

25. The Hale–Bopp comet, discovered independently on July 23, 1995 by Alan Hale and Thomas Bopp, has an orbital eccentricity of $e = 0.9951$ and a period of 2380 years.
(a) Find its semimajor axis in astronomical units (AU).
(b) Find its perihelion and aphelion distances. *(cont.)*

(c) Choose a polar coordinate system with the center of the Sun at the pole, and find an equation for the Hale–Bopp orbit in that coordinate system.

(d) Make a sketch of the Hale–Bopp orbit with reasonably accurate proportions.

26. Mars has a perihelion distance of 204,520,000 km and an aphelion distance of 246,280,000 km.
(a) Use these data to calculate the eccentricity, and compare your answer to the value given in Table 10.6.1.
(b) Find the period of Mars.
(c) Choose a polar coordinate system with the center of the Sun at the pole, and find an equation for the orbit of Mars in that coordinate system.
(d) Use a graphing utility to generate the orbit of Mars from the equation obtained in part (c).

27. *Vanguard 1* was launched in March 1958 into an orbit around the Earth with eccentricity $e = 0.21$ and semimajor axis 8864.5 km. Find the minimum and maximum heights of *Vanguard 1* above the surface of the Earth.

28. The planet Jupiter is believed to have a rocky core of radius 10,000 km surrounded by two layers of hydrogen—a 40,000 km thick layer of compressed metallic-like hydrogen and a 20,000 km thick layer of ordinary molecular hydrogen. The visible features, such as the Great Red Spot, are at the outer surface of the molecular hydrogen layer.

On November 6, 1997 the spacecraft *Galileo* was placed in a Jovian orbit to study the moon Europa. The orbit had eccentricity 0.814580 and semimajor axis 3,514,918.9 km. Find *Galileo*'s minimum and maximum heights above the molecular hydrogen layer (see the accompanying figure).

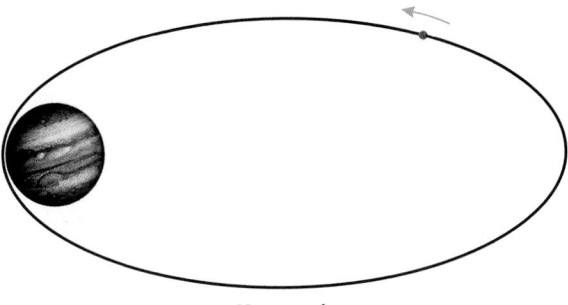

Not to scale

▲ **Figure Ex-28**

29. **Writing** Discuss how a hyperbola's eccentricity e affects the shape of the hyperbola. How is the shape affected as e approaches 1? As e approaches $+\infty$? Draw some pictures to illustrate your conclusions.

30. **Writing** Discuss the relationship between the eccentricity e of an ellipse and the distance z between the directrix and center of the ellipse. For example, if the foci remain fixed, what happens to z as e approaches 0?

✔ QUICK CHECK ANSWERS 10.6

1. (a) an ellipse (b) a parabola (c) a hyperbola **2.** (a) (i) ellipse (ii) to the right of the pole (iii) distance $= 1$
(b) (i) hyperbola (ii) to the left of the pole (iii) distance $= \frac{1}{4}$ (c) (i) parabola (ii) above the pole (iii) distance $= \frac{1}{4}$
(d) (i) parabola (ii) below the pole (iii) distance $= 4$ **3.** $\frac{1}{2}(r_1 + r_0)$; $\sqrt{r_0 r_1}$ **4.** $\frac{1}{2}(r_1 - r_0)$; $\sqrt{r_0 r_1}$

CHAPTER 10 REVIEW EXERCISES   ⌐ Graphing Utility

1. Find parametric equations for the portion of the circle $x^2 + y^2 = 2$ that lies outside the first quadrant, oriented clockwise. Check your work by generating the curve with a graphing utility.

2. (a) Suppose that the equations $x = f(t)$, $y = g(t)$ describe a curve C as t increases from 0 to 1. Find parametric equations that describe the same curve C but traced in the opposite direction as t increases from 0 to 1.
(b) Check your work using the parametric graphing feature of a graphing utility by generating the line segment between $(1, 2)$ and $(4, 0)$ in both possible directions as t increases from 0 to 1.

3. (a) Find the slope of the tangent line to the parametric curve $x = t^2 + 1$, $y = t/2$ at $t = -1$ and $t = 1$ without eliminating the parameter.
(b) Check your answers in part (a) by eliminating the parameter and differentiating a function of x.

4. Find dy/dx and d^2y/dx^2 at $t = 2$ for the parametric curve $x = \frac{1}{2}t^2$, $y = \frac{1}{3}t^3$.

5. Find all values of t at which a tangent line to the parametric curve $x = 2\cos t$, $y = 4\sin t$ is
(a) horizontal (b) vertical.

6. Find the exact arc length of the curve
$$x = 1 - 5t^4, \quad y = 4t^5 - 1 \quad (0 \le t \le 1)$$

7. In each part, find the rectangular coordinates of the point whose polar coordinates are given.
(a) $(-8, \pi/4)$ (b) $(7, -\pi/4)$ (c) $(8, 9\pi/4)$
(d) $(5, 0)$ (e) $(-2, -3\pi/2)$ (f) $(0, \pi)$

8. Express the point whose xy-coordinates are $(-1, 1)$ in polar coordinates with
(a) $r > 0$, $0 \le \theta < 2\pi$ (b) $r < 0$, $0 \le \theta < 2\pi$
(c) $r > 0$, $-\pi < \theta \le \pi$ (d) $r < 0$, $-\pi < \theta \le \pi$.

9. In each part, use a calculating utility to approximate the polar coordinates of the point whose rectangular coordinates are given.
(a) $(4, 3)$ (b) $(2, -5)$ (c) $(1, \tan^{-1} 1)$

10. In each part, state the name that describes the polar curve most precisely: a rose, a line, a circle, a limaçon, a cardioid, a spiral, a lemniscate, or none of these.
(a) $r = 3 \cos \theta$ (b) $r = \cos 3\theta$
(c) $r = \dfrac{3}{\cos \theta}$ (d) $r = 3 - \cos \theta$
(e) $r = 1 - 3 \cos \theta$ (f) $r^2 = 3 \cos \theta$
(g) $r = (3 \cos \theta)^2$ (h) $r = 1 + 3\theta$

11. In each part, identify the curve by converting the polar equation to rectangular coordinates. Assume that $a > 0$.
(a) $r = a \sec^2 \dfrac{\theta}{2}$ (b) $r^2 \cos 2\theta = a^2$

(c) $r = 4 \csc \left(\theta - \dfrac{\pi}{4} \right)$ (d) $r = 4 \cos \theta + 8 \sin \theta$

12. In each part, express the given equation in polar coordinates.
(a) $x = 7$ (b) $x^2 + y^2 = 9$
(c) $x^2 + y^2 - 6y = 0$ (d) $4xy = 9$

13–17 Sketch the curve in polar coordinates. ■

13. $\theta = \dfrac{\pi}{6}$ **14.** $r = 6 \cos \theta$

15. $r = 3(1 - \sin \theta)$ **16.** $r^2 = \sin 2\theta$

17. $r = 3 - \cos \theta$

18. (a) Show that the maximum value of the y-coordinate of points on the curve $r = 1/\sqrt{\theta}$ for θ in the interval $(0, \pi]$ occurs when $\tan \theta = 2\theta$.
(b) Use a calculating utility to solve the equation in part (a) to at least four decimal-place accuracy.
(c) Use the result of part (b) to approximate the maximum value of y for $0 < \theta \leq \pi$.

19. (a) Find the minimum and maximum x-coordinates of points on the cardioid $r = 1 - \cos \theta$.
(b) Find the minimum and maximum y-coordinates of points on the cardioid in part (a).

20. Determine the slope of the tangent line to the polar curve $r = 1 + \sin \theta$ at $\theta = \pi/4$.

21. A parametric curve of the form

$$x = a \cot t + b \cos t, \quad y = a + b \sin t \quad (0 < t < 2\pi)$$

is called a **conchoid of Nicomedes** (see the accompanying figure for the case $0 < a < b$).
(a) Describe how the conchoid

$$x = \cot t + 4 \cos t, \quad y = 1 + 4 \sin t$$

is generated as t varies over the interval $0 < t < 2\pi$.
(b) Find the horizontal asymptote of the conchoid given in part (a).
(c) For what values of t does the conchoid in part (a) have a horizontal tangent line? A vertical tangent line?

(d) Find a polar equation $r = f(\theta)$ for the conchoid in part (a), and then find polar equations for the tangent lines to the conchoid at the pole.

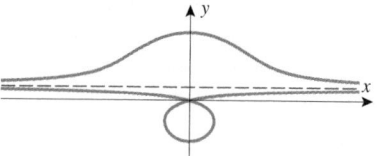

◀ **Figure Ex-21**

22. (a) Find the arc length of the polar curve $r = 1/\theta$ for $\pi/4 \leq \theta \leq \pi/2$.
(b) What can you say about the arc length of the portion of the curve that lies inside the circle $r = 1$?

23. Find the area of the region that is enclosed by the cardioid $r = 2 + 2 \cos \theta$.

24. Find the area of the region in the first quadrant within the cardioid $r = 1 + \sin \theta$.

25. Find the area of the region that is common to the circles $r = 1$, $r = 2 \cos \theta$, and $r = 2 \sin \theta$.

26. Find the area of the region that is inside the cardioid $r = a(1 + \sin \theta)$ and outside the circle $r = a \sin \theta$.

27–30 Sketch the parabola, and label the focus, vertex, and directrix. ■

27. $y^2 = 6x$ **28.** $x^2 = -9y$

29. $(y + 1)^2 = -7(x - 4)$ **30.** $\left(x - \tfrac{1}{2} \right)^2 = 2(y - 1)$

31–34 Sketch the ellipse, and label the foci, the vertices, and the ends of the minor axis. ■

31. $\dfrac{x^2}{4} + \dfrac{y^2}{25} = 1$ **32.** $4x^2 + 9y^2 = 36$

33. $9(x - 1)^2 + 16(y - 3)^2 = 144$

34. $3(x + 2)^2 + 4(y + 1)^2 = 12$

35–37 Sketch the hyperbola, and label the vertices, foci, and asymptotes. ■

35. $\dfrac{x^2}{16} - \dfrac{y^2}{4} = 1$ **36.** $9y^2 - 4x^2 = 36$

37. $\dfrac{(x - 2)^2}{9} - \dfrac{(y - 4)^2}{4} = 1$

38. In each part, sketch the graph of the conic section with reasonably accurate proportions.
(a) $x^2 - 4x + 8y + 36 = 0$
(b) $3x^2 + 4y^2 - 30x - 8y + 67 = 0$
(c) $4x^2 - 5y^2 - 8x - 30y - 21 = 0$

39–41 Find an equation for the conic described. ■

39. A parabola with vertex $(0, 0)$ and focus $(0, -4)$.

40. An ellipse with the ends of the major axis $(0, \pm\sqrt{5})$ and the ends of the minor axis $(\pm 1, 0)$.

41. A hyperbola with vertices $(0, \pm 3)$ and asymptotes $y = \pm x$.

Craig Aurness/Corbis Images

11

THREE-DIMENSIONAL SPACE; VECTORS

To describe fully the motion of a boat, one must specify its speed and direction of motion at each instant. Speed and direction together describe a "vector" quantity. We will study vectors in this chapter.

In this chapter we will discuss rectangular coordinate systems in three dimensions, and we will study the analytic geometry of lines, planes, and other basic surfaces. The second theme of this chapter is the study of vectors. These are the mathematical objects that physicists and engineers use to study forces, displacements, and velocities of objects moving on curved paths. More generally, vectors are used to represent all physical entities that involve both a magnitude and a direction for their complete description. We will introduce various algebraic operations on vectors, and we will apply these operations to problems involving force, work, and rotational tendencies in two and three dimensions. Finally, we will discuss cylindrical and spherical coordinate systems, which are appropriate in problems that involve various kinds of symmetries and also have specific applications in navigation and celestial mechanics.

11.1 RECTANGULAR COORDINATES IN 3-SPACE; SPHERES; CYLINDRICAL SURFACES

In this section we will discuss coordinate systems in three-dimensional space and some basic facts about surfaces in three dimensions.

■ RECTANGULAR COORDINATE SYSTEMS

In the remainder of this text we will call three-dimensional space *3-space*, two-dimensional space (a plane) *2-space*, and one-dimensional space (a line) *1-space*. Just as points in 2-space can be placed in one-to-one correspondence with pairs of real numbers using two perpendicular coordinate lines, so points in 3-space can be placed in one-to-one correspondence with triples of real numbers by using three mutually perpendicular coordinate lines, called the *x-axis*, the *y-axis*, and the *z-axis*, positioned so that their origins coincide (Figure 11.1.1). The three coordinate axes form a three-dimensional *rectangular coordinate system* (or *Cartesian coordinate system*). The point of intersection of the coordinate axes is called the *origin* of the coordinate system.

Rectangular coordinate systems in 3-space fall into two categories: *left-handed* and *right-handed*. A right-handed system has the property that when the fingers of the right hand are cupped so that they curve from the positive *x*-axis toward the positive *y*-axis, the thumb points (roughly) in the direction of the positive *z*-axis (Figure 11.1.2). A similar

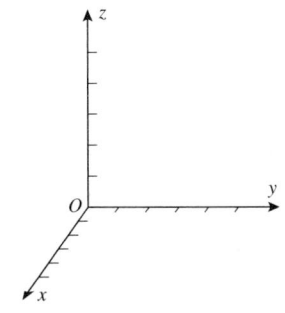

▲ **Figure 11.1.1**

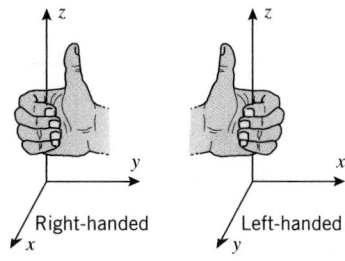

▲ **Figure 11.1.2**

property holds for a left-handed coordinate system (Figure 11.1.2). We will use only right-handed coordinate systems in this text.

The coordinate axes, taken in pairs, determine three **coordinate planes**: the **xy-plane**, the **xz-plane**, and the **yz-plane** (Figure 11.1.3). To each point P in 3-space we can assign a triple of real numbers by passing three planes through P parallel to the coordinate planes and letting a, b, and c be the coordinates of the intersections of those planes with the x-axis, y-axis, and z-axis, respectively (Figure 11.1.4). We call a, b, and c the **x-coordinate**, **y-coordinate**, and **z-coordinate** of P, respectively, and we denote the point P by (a, b, c) or by $P(a, b, c)$. Figure 11.1.5 shows the points $(4, 5, 6)$ and $(-3, 2, -4)$.

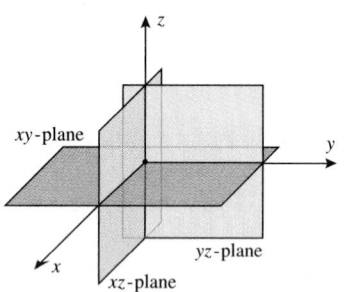

▲ **Figure 11.1.3**

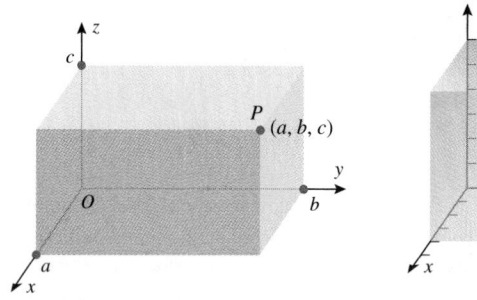

▲ **Figure 11.1.4**

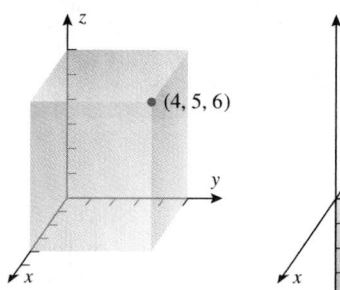

▲ **Figure 11.1.5**

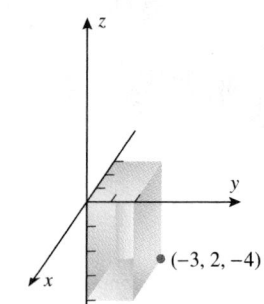

Just as the coordinate axes in a two-dimensional coordinate system divide 2-space into four quadrants, so the coordinate planes of a three-dimensional coordinate system divide 3-space into eight parts, called **octants**. The set of points with three positive coordinates forms the **first octant**; the remaining octants have no standard numbering.

You should be able to visualize the following facts about three-dimensional rectangular coordinate systems:

REGION	DESCRIPTION
xy-plane	Consists of all points of the form $(x, y, 0)$
xz-plane	Consists of all points of the form $(x, 0, z)$
yz-plane	Consists of all points of the form $(0, y, z)$
x-axis	Consists of all points of the form $(x, 0, 0)$
y-axis	Consists of all points of the form $(0, y, 0)$
z-axis	Consists of all points of the form $(0, 0, z)$

■ DISTANCE IN 3-SPACE; SPHERES

Recall that in 2-space the distance d between the points $P_1(x_1, y_1)$ and $P_2(x_2, y_2)$ is

$$d = \sqrt{(x_2 - x_1)^2 + (y_2 - y_1)^2} \tag{1}$$

The distance formula in 3-space has the same form, but it has a third term to account for the added dimension. (We will see that this is a common occurrence in extending formulas from 2-space to 3-space.) The distance between the points $P_1(x_1, y_1, z_1)$ and $P_2(x_2, y_2, z_2)$ is

$$d = \sqrt{(x_2 - x_1)^2 + (y_2 - y_1)^2 + (z_2 - z_1)^2} \tag{2}$$

We leave the proof of (2) as an exercise (Exercise 7).

▶ **Example 1**   Find the distance d between the points $(2, 3, -1)$ and $(4, -1, 3)$.

Solution.   From Formula (2)

$$d = \sqrt{(4-2)^2 + (-1-3)^2 + (3+1)^2} = \sqrt{36} = 6 \blacktriangleleft$$

In an xy-coordinate system, the set of points (x, y) whose coordinates satisfy an equation in x and y is called the ***graph*** of the equation. Analogously, in an xyz-coordinate system, the set of points (x, y, z) whose coordinates satisfy an equation in x, y, and z is called the ***graph*** of the equation.

Recall that the standard equation of the circle in 2-space that has center (x_0, y_0) and radius r is

$$(x - x_0)^2 + (y - y_0)^2 = r^2 \tag{3}$$

This follows from distance formula (1) and the fact that the circle consists of all points in 2-space whose distance from (x_0, y_0) is r. Analogously, the ***standard equation of the sphere*** in 3-space that has center (x_0, y_0, z_0) and radius r is

$$(x - x_0)^2 + (y - y_0)^2 + (z - z_0)^2 = r^2 \tag{4}$$

This follows from distance formula (2) and the fact that the sphere consists of all points in 3-space whose distance from (x_0, y_0, z_0) is r. Note that (4) has the same form as the standard equation for the circle in 2-space, but with an additional term to account for the third coordinate. Some examples of the standard equation of the sphere are given in the following table:

EQUATION	GRAPH
$(x-3)^2 + (y-2)^2 + (z-1)^2 = 9$	Sphere with center $(3, 2, 1)$ and radius 3
$(x+1)^2 + y^2 + (z+4)^2 = 5$	Sphere with center $(-1, 0, -4)$ and radius $\sqrt{5}$
$x^2 + y^2 + z^2 = 1$	Sphere with center $(0, 0, 0)$ and radius 1

If the terms in (4) are expanded and like terms are collected, then the resulting equation has the form

$$x^2 + y^2 + z^2 + Gx + Hy + Iz + J = 0 \tag{5}$$

The following example shows how the center and radius of a sphere that is expressed in this form can be obtained by completing the squares.

▶ **Example 2**   Find the center and radius of the sphere

$$x^2 + y^2 + z^2 - 2x - 4y + 8z + 17 = 0$$

Solution.   We can put the equation in the form of (4) by completing the squares:

$$(x^2 - 2x) + (y^2 - 4y) + (z^2 + 8z) = -17$$
$$(x^2 - 2x + 1) + (y^2 - 4y + 4) + (z^2 + 8z + 16) = -17 + 21$$
$$(x - 1)^2 + (y - 2)^2 + (z + 4)^2 = 4$$

which is the equation of the sphere with center $(1, 2, -4)$ and radius 2. ◀

In general, completing the squares in (5) produces an equation of the form

$$(x - x_0)^2 + (y - y_0)^2 + (z - z_0)^2 = k$$

If $k > 0$, then the graph of this equation is a sphere with center (x_0, y_0, z_0) and radius $\sqrt{k}$. If $k = 0$, then the sphere has radius zero, so the graph is the single point (x_0, y_0, z_0). If $k < 0$, the equation is not satisfied by any values of x, y, and z (why?), so it has no graph.

> **11.1.1**   **THEOREM**   *An equation of the form*
>
> $$x^2 + y^2 + z^2 + Gx + Hy + Iz + J = 0$$
>
> *represents a sphere, a point, or has no graph.*

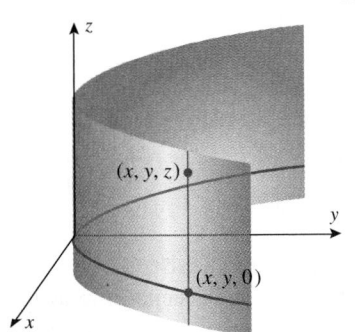

▲ **Figure 11.1.6**

CYLINDRICAL SURFACES

Although it is natural to graph equations in two variables in 2-space and equations in three variables in 3-space, it is also possible to graph equations in two variables in 3-space. For example, the graph of the equation $y = x^2$ in an xy-coordinate system is a parabola; however, there is nothing to prevent us from inquiring about its graph in an xyz-coordinate system. To obtain this graph we need only observe that the equation $y = x^2$ does not impose any restrictions on z. Thus, if we find values of x and y that satisfy this equation, then the coordinates of the point (x, y, z) will also satisfy the equation for *arbitrary* values of z. Geometrically, the point (x, y, z) lies on the vertical line through the point $(x, y, 0)$ in the xy-plane, which means that we can obtain the graph of $y = x^2$ in an xyz-coordinate system by first graphing the equation in the xy-plane and then translating that graph parallel to the z-axis to generate the entire graph (Figure 11.1.6).

The process of generating a surface by translating a plane curve parallel to some line is called *extrusion*, and surfaces that are generated by extrusion are called *cylindrical surfaces*. A familiar example is the surface of a right circular cylinder, which can be generated by translating a circle parallel to the axis of the cylinder. The following theorem provides basic information about graphing equations in two variables in 3-space:

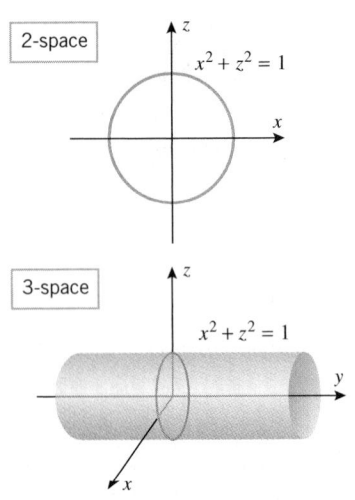

▲ **Figure 11.1.7**

> **11.1.2**   **THEOREM**   *An equation that contains only two of the variables x, y, and z represents a cylindrical surface in an xyz-coordinate system. The surface can be obtained by graphing the equation in the coordinate plane of the two variables that appear in the equation and then translating that graph parallel to the axis of the missing variable.*

▶ **Example 3**   Sketch the graph of $x^2 + z^2 = 1$ in 3-space.

Solution.   Since y does not appear in this equation, the graph is a cylindrical surface generated by extrusion parallel to the y-axis. In the xz-plane the graph of the equation $x^2 + z^2 = 1$ is a circle. Thus, in 3-space the graph is a right circular cylinder along the y-axis (Figure 11.1.7). ◀

▶ **Example 4**   Sketch the graph of $z = \sin y$ in 3-space.

Solution.   (See Figure 11.1.8.) ◀

In an xy-coordinate system, the graph of the equation $x = 1$ is a line parallel to the y-axis. What is the graph of this equation in an xyz-coordinate system?

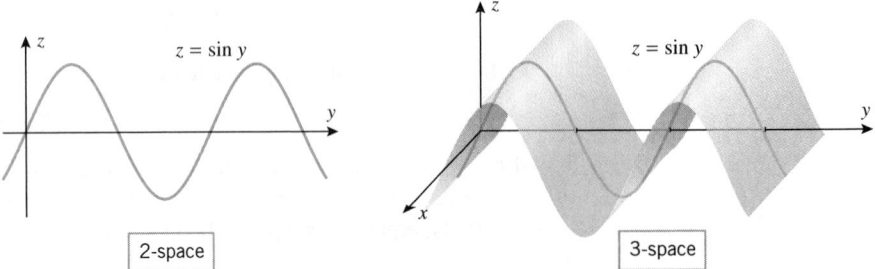

▶ **Figure 11.1.8**

✔ QUICK CHECK EXERCISES 11.1   *(See page 773 for answers.)*

1. The distance between the points $(1, -2, 0)$ and $(4, 0, 5)$ is _____.

2. The graph of $(x - 3)^2 + (y - 2)^2 + (z + 1)^2 = 16$ is a _____ of radius _____ centered at _____.

3. The shortest distance from the point $(4, 0, 5)$ to the sphere $(x - 1)^2 + (y + 2)^2 + z^2 = 36$ is _____.

4. Let S be the graph of $x^2 + z^2 + 6z = 16$ in 3-space.
   (a) The intersection of S with the xz-plane is a circle with center _____ and radius _____.
   (b) The intersection of S with the xy-plane is two lines, $x = $ _____ and $x = $ _____.
   (c) The intersection of S with the yz-plane is two lines, $z = $ _____ and $z = $ _____.

EXERCISE SET 11.1    Graphing Utility

1. In each part, find the coordinates of the eight corners of the box.

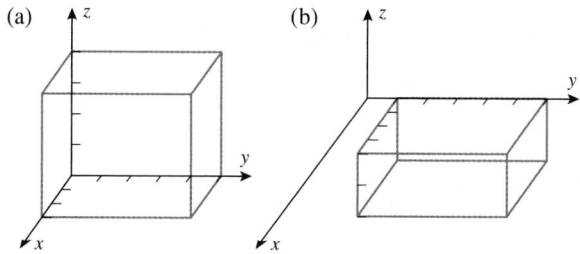

2. A cube of side 4 has its geometric center at the origin and its faces parallel to the coordinate planes. Sketch the cube and give the coordinates of the corners.

FOCUS ON CONCEPTS

3. Suppose that a box has its faces parallel to the coordinate planes and the points $(4, 2, -2)$ and $(-6, 1, 1)$ are endpoints of a diagonal. Sketch the box and give the coordinates of the remaining six corners.

4. Suppose that a box has its faces parallel to the coordinate planes and the points (x_1, y_1, z_1) and (x_2, y_2, z_2) are endpoints of a diagonal.
   (a) Find the coordinates of the remaining six corners.
   (b) Show that the midpoint of the line segment joining (x_1, y_1, z_1) and (x_2, y_2, z_2) is

   $$\left(\tfrac{1}{2}(x_1 + x_2), \tfrac{1}{2}(y_1 + y_2), \tfrac{1}{2}(z_1 + z_2)\right)$$

   [*Suggestion:* Apply Theorem H.2 in Web Appendix H to three appropriate edges of the box.]

5. Interpret the graph of $x = 1$ in the contexts of
   (a) a number line   (b) 2-space   (c) 3-space.

6. Consider the points $P(3, 1, 0)$ and $Q(1, 4, 4)$.
   (a) Sketch the triangle with vertices P, Q, and $(1, 4, 0)$. Without computing distances, explain why this triangle is a right triangle, and then apply the Theorem of Pythagoras twice to find the distance from P to Q.
   (b) Repeat part (a) using the points P, Q, and $(3, 4, 0)$.
   (c) Repeat part (a) using the points P, Q, and $(1, 1, 4)$.

7. (a) Consider a box whose sides have lengths a, b, and c. Use the Theorem of Pythagoras to show that a diagonal of the box has length $d = \sqrt{a^2 + b^2 + c^2}$. [*Hint:* Use the Theorem of Pythagoras to find the length of a diagonal of the base and then again to find the length of a diagonal of the entire box.]
   (b) Use the result of part (a) to derive formula (2).

8. (a) Make a conjecture about the set of points in 3-space that are equidistant from the origin and the point $(1, 0, 0)$.
   (b) Confirm your conjecture in part (a) by using distance formula (2).

9. Find the center and radius of the sphere that has $(1, -2, 4)$ and $(3, 4, -12)$ as endpoints of a diameter. [See Exercise 4.]

10. Show that $(4, 5, 2)$, $(1, 7, 3)$, and $(2, 4, 5)$ are vertices of an equilateral triangle.

11. (a) Show that $(2, 1, 6)$, $(4, 7, 9)$, and $(8, 5, -6)$ are the vertices of a right triangle.
    (b) Which vertex is at the 90° angle?
    (c) Find the area of the triangle.

12. Find the distance from the point $(-5, 2, -3)$ to the
    (a) xy-plane   (b) xz-plane   (c) yz-plane
    (d) x-axis   (e) y-axis   (f) z-axis.

13. In each part, find the standard equation of the sphere that satisfies the stated conditions.
    (a) Center $(1, 0, -1)$; diameter $= 8$.
    (b) Center $(-1, 3, 2)$ and passing through the origin.
    (c) A diameter has endpoints $(-1, 2, 1)$ and $(0, 2, 3)$.

14. Find equations of two spheres that are centered at the origin and are tangent to the sphere of radius 1 centered at $(3, -2, 4)$.

15. In each part, find an equation of the sphere with center $(2, -1, -3)$ and satisfying the given condition.
    (a) Tangent to the xy-plane
    (b) Tangent to the xz-plane
    (c) Tangent to the yz-plane

16. (a) Find an equation of the sphere that is inscribed in the cube that is centered at the point $(-2, 1, 3)$ and has sides of length 1 that are parallel to the coordinate planes.

(cont.)

(b) Find an equation of the sphere that is circumscribed about the cube in part (a).

17. A sphere has center in the first octant and is tangent to each of the three coordinate planes. Show that the center of the sphere is at a point of the form (r, r, r), where r is the radius of the sphere.

18. A sphere has center in the first octant and is tangent to each of the three coordinate planes. The distance from the origin to the sphere is $3 - \sqrt{3}$ units. Find an equation for the sphere.

19–22 True–False Determine whether the statement is true or false. Explain your answer. ■

19. By definition, a "cylindrical surface" is a right circular cylinder whose axis is parallel to one of the coordinate axes.

20. The graph of $x^2 + y^2 = 1$ in 3-space is a circle of radius 1 centered at the origin.

21. If a point belongs to both the xy-plane and the xz-plane, then the point lies on the x-axis.

22. A sphere with center $P(x_0, y_0, z_0)$ and radius r consists of all points (x, y, z) that satisfy the inequality

$$(x - x_0)^2 + (y - y_0)^2 + (z - z_0)^2 \leq r^2$$

23–28 Describe the surface whose equation is given. ■

23. $x^2 + y^2 + z^2 + 10x + 4y + 2z - 19 = 0$

24. $x^2 + y^2 + z^2 - y = 0$

25. $2x^2 + 2y^2 + 2z^2 - 2x - 3y + 5z - 2 = 0$

26. $x^2 + y^2 + z^2 + 2x - 2y + 2z + 3 = 0$

27. $x^2 + y^2 + z^2 - 3x + 4y - 8z + 25 = 0$

28. $x^2 + y^2 + z^2 - 2x - 6y - 8z + 1 = 0$

29. In each part, sketch the portion of the surface that lies in the first octant.
    (a) $y = x$ (b) $y = z$ (c) $x = z$

30. In each part, sketch the graph of the equation in 3-space.
    (a) $x = 1$ (b) $y = 1$ (c) $z = 1$

31. In each part, sketch the graph of the equation in 3-space.
    (a) $x^2 + y^2 = 25$ (b) $y^2 + z^2 = 25$ (c) $x^2 + z^2 = 25$

32. In each part, sketch the graph of the equation in 3-space.
    (a) $x = y^2$ (b) $z = x^2$ (c) $y = z^2$

33. In each part, write an equation for the surface.
    (a) The plane that contains the x-axis and the point $(0, 1, 2)$.
    (b) The plane that contains the y-axis and the point $(1, 0, 2)$.
    (c) The right circular cylinder that has radius 1 and is centered on the line parallel to the z-axis that passes through the point $(1, 1, 0)$.
    (d) The right circular cylinder that has radius 1 and is centered on the line parallel to the y-axis that passes through the point $(1, 0, 1)$.

34. Find equations for the following right circular cylinders. Each cylinder has radius a and is tangent to two coordinate planes.

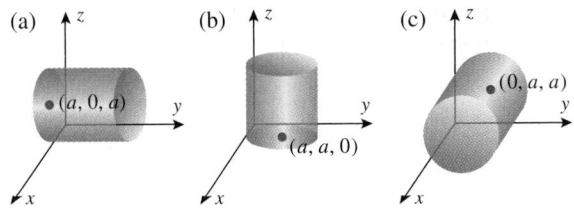

35–44 Sketch the surface in 3-space. ■

35. $y = \sin x$

36. $y = e^x$

37. $z = 1 - y^2$

38. $z = \cos x$

39. $2x + z = 3$

40. $2x + 3y = 6$

41. $4x^2 + 9z^2 = 36$

42. $z = \sqrt{3 - x}$

43. $y^2 - 4z^2 = 4$

44. $yz = 1$

45. Use a graphing utility to generate the curve $y = x^3/(1 + x^2)$ in the xy-plane, and then use the graph to help sketch the surface $z = y^3/(1 + y^2)$ in 3-space.

46. Use a graphing utility to generate the curve $y = x/(1 + x^4)$ in the xy-plane, and then use the graph to help sketch the surface $z = y/(1 + y^4)$ in 3-space.

47. If a bug walks on the sphere

$$x^2 + y^2 + z^2 + 2x - 2y - 4z - 3 = 0$$

how close and how far can it get from the origin?

48. Describe the set of all points in 3-space whose coordinates satisfy the inequality $x^2 + y^2 + z^2 - 2x + 8z \leq 8$.

49. Describe the set of all points in 3-space whose coordinates satisfy the inequality $y^2 + z^2 + 6y - 4z > 3$.

50. The distance between a point $P(x, y, z)$ and the point $A(1, -2, 0)$ is twice the distance between P and the point $B(0, 1, 1)$. Show that the set of all such points is a sphere, and find the center and radius of the sphere.

51. As shown in the accompanying figure, a bowling ball of radius R is placed inside a box just large enough to hold it, and it is secured for shipping by packing a Styrofoam sphere into each corner of the box. Find the radius of the largest Styrofoam sphere that can be used. [*Hint:* Take the origin of a Cartesian coordinate system at a corner of the box with the coordinate axes along the edges.]

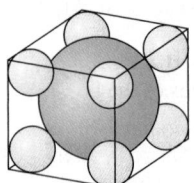

◀ **Figure Ex-51**

52. Consider the equation

$$x^2 + y^2 + z^2 + Gx + Hy + Iz + J = 0$$

and let $K = G^2 + H^2 + I^2 - 4J$.
    (a) Prove that the equation represents a sphere if $K > 0$, a point if $K = 0$, and has no graph if $K < 0$. *(cont.)*

(b) In the case where $K > 0$, find the center and radius of the sphere.

53. (a) The accompanying figure shows a surface of revolution that is generated by revolving the curve $y = f(x)$ in the xy-plane about the x-axis. Show that the equation of this surface is $y^2 + z^2 = [f(x)]^2$. [*Hint:* Each point on the curve traces a circle as it revolves about the x-axis.]

(b) Find an equation of the surface of revolution that is generated by revolving the curve $y = e^x$ in the xy-plane about the x-axis.

(c) Show that the ellipsoid $3x^2 + 4y^2 + 4z^2 = 16$ is a surface of revolution about the x-axis by finding a curve $y = f(x)$ in the xy-plane that generates it.

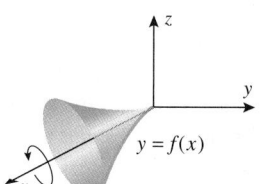

$y = f(x)$

◀ **Figure Ex-53**

54. In each part, use the idea in Exercise 53(a) to derive a formula for the stated surface of revolution.

(a) The surface generated by revolving the curve $x = f(y)$ in the xy-plane about the y-axis.

(b) The surface generated by revolving the curve $y = f(z)$ in the yz-plane about the z-axis.

(c) The surface generated by revolving the curve $z = f(x)$ in the xz-plane about the x-axis.

55. Show that for all values of θ and ϕ, the point

$$(a \sin \phi \cos \theta, a \sin \phi \sin \theta, a \cos \phi)$$

lies on the sphere $x^2 + y^2 + z^2 = a^2$.

56. **Writing** Explain how you might determine whether a set of points in 3-space is the graph of an equation involving at most two of the variables x, y, and z.

57. **Writing** Discuss what happens geometrically when equations in x, y, and z are replaced by inequalities. For example, compare the graph of $x^2 + y^2 + z^2 = 1$ with the set of points that satisfy the inequality $x^2 + y^2 + z^2 \leq 1$.

✔ **QUICK CHECK ANSWERS 11.1**

1. $\sqrt{38}$ 2. sphere; 4; $(3, 2, -1)$ 3. $\sqrt{38} - 6$ 4. (a) $(0, 0, -3)$; 5 (b) 4; -4 (c) 2; -8

11.2 VECTORS

Many physical quantities such as area, length, mass, and temperature are completely described once the magnitude of the quantity is given. Such quantities are called "scalars." Other physical quantities, called "vectors," are not completely determined until both a magnitude and a direction are specified. For example, winds are usually described by giving their speed and direction, say 20 mi/h northeast. The wind speed and wind direction together form a vector quantity called the wind velocity. Other examples of vectors are force and displacement. In this section we will develop the basic mathematical properties of vectors.

■ VECTORS IN PHYSICS AND ENGINEERING

A particle that moves along a line can move in only two directions, so its direction of motion can be described by taking one direction to be positive and the other negative. Thus, the *displacement* or *change in position* of the point can be described by a signed real number. For example, a displacement of 3 (= +3) describes a position change of 3 units in the positive direction, and a displacement of -3 describes a position change of 3 units in the negative direction. However, for a particle that moves in two dimensions or three dimensions, a plus or minus sign is no longer sufficient to specify the direction of motion—other methods are required. One method is to use an arrow, called a *vector*, that points in the direction of motion and whose length represents the distance from the starting point to the ending point; this is called the *displacement vector* for the motion. For example, Figure 11.2.1a shows the displacement vector of a particle that moves from point A to point B along a circuitous path. Note that the length of the arrow describes the

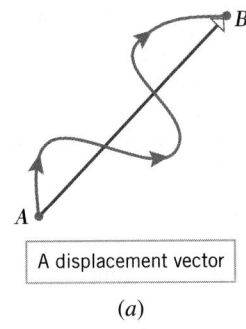

A displacement vector

(a)

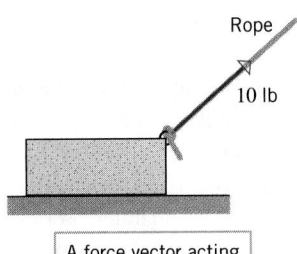

A force vector acting on a block

(b)

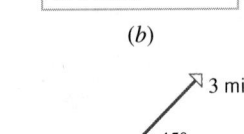

Two velocity vectors that affect the motion of the boat

(c)

▲ **Figure 11.2.1**

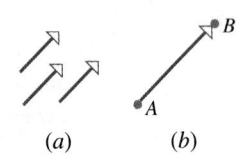

(a)   *(b)*

▲ **Figure 11.2.2**

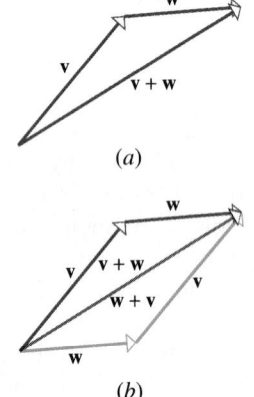

(a)

(b)

▲ **Figure 11.2.3**

distance between the starting and ending points and not the actual distance traveled by the particle.

Arrows are not limited to describing displacements—they can be used to describe any physical quantity that involves both a magnitude and a direction. Two important examples are forces and velocities. For example, the arrow in Figure 11.2.1*b* represents a force vector of 10 lb acting in a specific direction on a block, and the arrows in Figure 11.2.1*c* show the velocity vector of a boat whose motor propels it parallel to the shore at 2 mi/h and the velocity vector of a 3 mi/h wind acting at an angle of 45° with the shoreline. Intuition suggests that the two velocity vectors will combine to produce some net velocity for the boat at an angle to the shoreline. Thus, our first objective in this section is to define mathematical operations on vectors that can be used to determine the combined effect of vectors.

■ **VECTORS VIEWED GEOMETRICALLY**

Vectors can be represented geometrically by arrows in 2-space or 3-space; the direction of the arrow specifies the direction of the vector, and the length of the arrow describes its magnitude. The tail of the arrow is called the *initial point* of the vector, and the tip of the arrow the *terminal point*. We will denote vectors with lowercase boldface type such as **a**, **k**, **v**, **w**, and **x**. When discussing vectors, we will refer to real numbers as *scalars*. Scalars will be denoted by lowercase italic type such as a, k, v, w, and x. Two vectors, **v** and **w**, are considered to be *equal* (also called *equivalent*) if they have the same length and same direction, in which case we write **v** = **w**. Geometrically, two vectors are equal if they are translations of one another; thus, the three vectors in Figure 11.2.2*a* are equal, even though they are in different positions.

Because vectors are not affected by translation, the initial point of a vector **v** can be moved to any convenient point A by making an appropriate translation. If the initial point of **v** is A and the terminal point is B, then we write $\mathbf{v} = \overrightarrow{AB}$ when we want to emphasize the initial and terminal points (Figure 11.2.2*b*). If the initial and terminal points of a vector coincide, then the vector has length zero; we call this the *zero vector* and denote it by **0**. The zero vector does not have a specific direction, so we will agree that it can be assigned any convenient direction in a specific problem.

There are various algebraic operations that are performed on vectors, all of whose definitions originated in physics. We begin with vector addition.

11.2.1 **DEFINITION** If **v** and **w** are vectors, then the *sum* **v** + **w** is the vector from the initial point of **v** to the terminal point of **w** when the vectors are positioned so the initial point of **w** is at the terminal point of **v** (Figure 11.2.3*a*).

In Figure 11.2.3*b* we have constructed two sums, **v** + **w** (from purple arrows) and **w** + **v** (from green arrows). It is evident that

$$\mathbf{v} + \mathbf{w} = \mathbf{w} + \mathbf{v}$$

and that the sum (gray arrow) coincides with the diagonal of the parallelogram determined by **v** and **w** when these vectors are positioned so they have the same initial point.

Since the initial and terminal points of **0** coincide, it follows that

$$\mathbf{0} + \mathbf{v} = \mathbf{v} + \mathbf{0} = \mathbf{v}$$

11.2.2 **DEFINITION** If **v** is a nonzero vector and k is a nonzero real number (a scalar), then the *scalar multiple* $k\mathbf{v}$ is defined to be the vector whose length is $|k|$ times the length of **v** and whose direction is the same as that of **v** if $k > 0$ and opposite to that of **v** if $k < 0$. We define $k\mathbf{v} = \mathbf{0}$ if $k = 0$ or $\mathbf{v} = \mathbf{0}$.

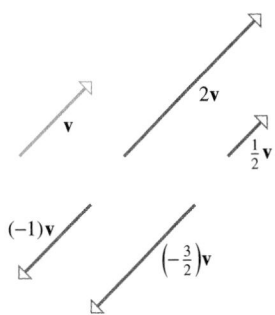

▲ Figure 11.2.4

Figure 11.2.4 shows the geometric relationship between a vector **v** and various scalar multiples of it. Observe that if k and **v** are nonzero, then the vectors **v** and $k\mathbf{v}$ lie on the same line if their initial points coincide and lie on parallel or coincident lines if they do not. Thus, we say that **v** and $k\mathbf{v}$ are *parallel vectors*. Observe also that the vector $(-1)\mathbf{v}$ has the same length as **v** but is oppositely directed. We call $(-1)\mathbf{v}$ the *negative* of **v** and denote it by $-\mathbf{v}$ (Figure 11.2.5). In particular, $-\mathbf{0} = (-1)\mathbf{0} = \mathbf{0}$.

Vector subtraction is defined in terms of addition and scalar multiplication by

$$\mathbf{v} - \mathbf{w} = \mathbf{v} + (-\mathbf{w})$$

The difference $\mathbf{v} - \mathbf{w}$ can be obtained geometrically by first constructing the vector $-\mathbf{w}$ and then adding **v** and $-\mathbf{w}$, say by the parallelogram method (Figure 11.2.6*a*). However, if **v** and **w** are positioned so their initial points coincide, then $\mathbf{v} - \mathbf{w}$ can be formed more directly, as shown in Figure 11.2.6*b*, by drawing the vector from the terminal point of **w** (the second term) to the terminal point of **v** (the first term). In the special case where $\mathbf{v} = \mathbf{w}$ the terminal points of the vectors coincide, so their difference is **0**; that is,

$$\mathbf{v} + (-\mathbf{v}) = \mathbf{v} - \mathbf{v} = \mathbf{0}$$

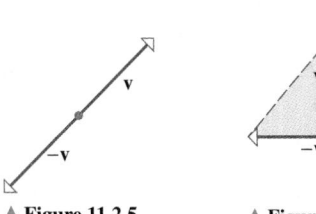

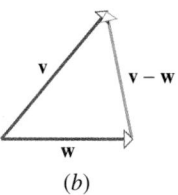

▲ Figure 11.2.5   ▲ Figure 11.2.6

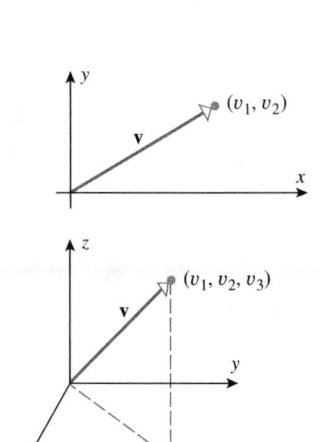

▲ Figure 11.2.7

Note the difference in notation between a *point* (v_1, v_2) and a *vector* $\langle v_1, v_2 \rangle$.

■ VECTORS IN COORDINATE SYSTEMS

Problems involving vectors are often best solved by introducing a rectangular coordinate system. If a vector **v** is positioned with its initial point at the origin of a rectangular coordinate system, then its terminal point will have coordinates of the form (v_1, v_2) or (v_1, v_2, v_3), depending on whether the vector is in 2-space or 3-space (Figure 11.2.7). We call these coordinates the *components* of **v**, and we write **v** in *component form* using the *bracket notation*

$$\mathbf{v} = \langle v_1, v_2 \rangle \quad \text{or} \quad \mathbf{v} = \langle v_1, v_2, v_3 \rangle$$

$$\underset{\boxed{\text{2-space}}}{} \qquad \underset{\boxed{\text{3-space}}}{}$$

In particular, the zero vectors in 2-space and 3-space are

$$\mathbf{0} = \langle 0, 0 \rangle \quad \text{and} \quad \mathbf{0} = \langle 0, 0, 0 \rangle$$

respectively.

Components provide a simple way of identifying equivalent vectors. For example, consider the vectors $\mathbf{v} = \langle v_1, v_2 \rangle$ and $\mathbf{w} = \langle w_1, w_2 \rangle$ in 2-space. If $\mathbf{v} = \mathbf{w}$, then the vectors have the same length and same direction, and this means that their terminal points coincide when their initial points are placed at the origin. It follows that $v_1 = w_1$ and $v_2 = w_2$, so we have shown that equivalent vectors have the same components. Conversely, if $v_1 = w_1$ and $v_2 = w_2$, then the terminal points of the vectors coincide when their initial points are placed at the origin. It follows that the vectors have the same length and same direction, so we have shown that vectors with the same components are equivalent. A similar argument holds for vectors in 3-space, so we have the following result.

> **11.2.3 THEOREM**   *Two vectors are equivalent if and only if their corresponding components are equal.*

For example,

$$\langle a, b, c \rangle = \langle 1, -4, 2 \rangle$$

if and only if $a = 1$, $b = -4$, and $c = 2$.

■ **ARITHMETIC OPERATIONS ON VECTORS**

The next theorem shows how to perform arithmetic operations on vectors using components.

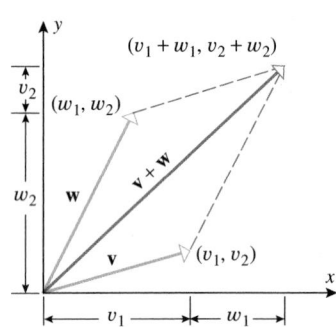

> **11.2.4 THEOREM**   *If* $\mathbf{v} = \langle v_1, v_2 \rangle$ *and* $\mathbf{w} = \langle w_1, w_2 \rangle$ *are vectors in 2-space and* k *is any scalar, then*
>
> $$\mathbf{v} + \mathbf{w} = \langle v_1 + w_1, v_2 + w_2 \rangle \qquad (1)$$
> $$\mathbf{v} - \mathbf{w} = \langle v_1 - w_1, v_2 - w_2 \rangle \qquad (2)$$
> $$k\mathbf{v} = \langle kv_1, kv_2 \rangle \qquad (3)$$
>
> *Similarly, if* $\mathbf{v} = \langle v_1, v_2, v_3 \rangle$ *and* $\mathbf{w} = \langle w_1, w_2, w_3 \rangle$ *are vectors in 3-space and* k *is any scalar, then*
>
> $$\mathbf{v} + \mathbf{w} = \langle v_1 + w_1, v_2 + w_2, v_3 + w_3 \rangle \qquad (4)$$
> $$\mathbf{v} - \mathbf{w} = \langle v_1 - w_1, v_2 - w_2, v_3 - w_3 \rangle \qquad (5)$$
> $$k\mathbf{v} = \langle kv_1, kv_2, kv_3 \rangle \qquad (6)$$

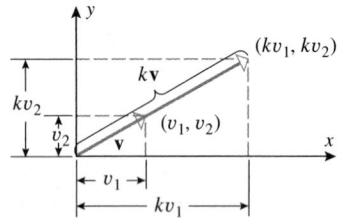

▲ **Figure 11.2.8**

We will not prove this theorem. However, results (1) and (3) should be evident from Figure 11.2.8. Similar figures in 3-space can be used to motivate (4) and (6). Formulas (2) and (5) can be obtained by writing $\mathbf{v} + \mathbf{w} = \mathbf{v} + (-1)\mathbf{w}$.

▶ **Example 1**   If $\mathbf{v} = \langle -2, 0, 1 \rangle$ and $\mathbf{w} = \langle 3, 5, -4 \rangle$, then

$$\mathbf{v} + \mathbf{w} = \langle -2, 0, 1 \rangle + \langle 3, 5, -4 \rangle = \langle 1, 5, -3 \rangle$$
$$3\mathbf{v} = \langle -6, 0, 3 \rangle$$
$$-\mathbf{w} = \langle -3, -5, 4 \rangle$$
$$\mathbf{w} - 2\mathbf{v} = \langle 3, 5, -4 \rangle - \langle -4, 0, 2 \rangle = \langle 7, 5, -6 \rangle \quad ◀$$

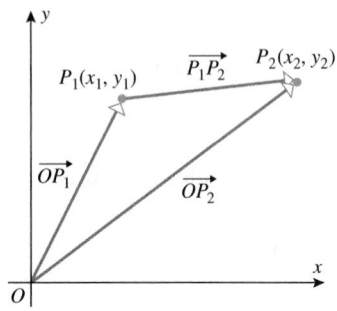

▲ **Figure 11.2.9**

■ **VECTORS WITH INITIAL POINT NOT AT THE ORIGIN**

Recall that we defined the components of a vector to be the coordinates of its terminal point when its initial point is at the origin. We will now consider the problem of finding the components of a vector whose initial point is not at the origin. To be specific, suppose that $P_1(x_1, y_1)$ and $P_2(x_2, y_2)$ are points in 2-space and we are interested in finding the components of the vector $\overrightarrow{P_1 P_2}$. As illustrated in Figure 11.2.9, we can write this vector as

$$\overrightarrow{P_1 P_2} = \overrightarrow{OP_2} - \overrightarrow{OP_1} = \langle x_2, y_2 \rangle - \langle x_1, y_1 \rangle = \langle x_2 - x_1, y_2 - y_1 \rangle$$

Thus, we have shown that the components of the vector $\overrightarrow{P_1P_2}$ can be obtained by subtracting the coordinates of its initial point from the coordinates of its terminal point. Similar computations hold in 3-space, so we have established the following result.

11.2.5 THEOREM *If $\overrightarrow{P_1P_2}$ is a vector in 2-space with initial point $P_1(x_1, y_1)$ and terminal point $P_2(x_2, y_2)$, then*

$$\overrightarrow{P_1P_2} = \langle x_2 - x_1, y_2 - y_1 \rangle \tag{7}$$

Similarly, if $\overrightarrow{P_1P_2}$ is a vector in 3-space with initial point $P_1(x_1, y_1, z_1)$ and terminal point $P_2(x_2, y_2, z_2)$, then

$$\overrightarrow{P_1P_2} = \langle x_2 - x_1, y_2 - y_1, z_2 - z_1 \rangle \tag{8}$$

▶ **Example 2**   In 2-space the vector from $P_1(1, 3)$ to $P_2(4, -2)$ is

$$\overrightarrow{P_1P_2} = \langle 4 - 1, -2 - 3 \rangle = \langle 3, -5 \rangle$$

and in 3-space the vector from $A(0, -2, 5)$ to $B(3, 4, -1)$ is

$$\overrightarrow{AB} = \langle 3 - 0, 4 - (-2), -1 - 5 \rangle = \langle 3, 6, -6 \rangle \quad ◀$$

■ **RULES OF VECTOR ARITHMETIC**

The following theorem shows that many of the familiar rules of ordinary arithmetic also hold for vector arithmetic.

> It follows from part (*b*) of Theorem 11.2.6 that the expression
>
> $$\mathbf{u} + \mathbf{v} + \mathbf{w}$$
>
> is unambiguous since the same vector results no matter how the terms are grouped.

11.2.6 THEOREM   *For any vectors $\mathbf{u}$, $\mathbf{v}$, and $\mathbf{w}$ and any scalars k and l, the following relationships hold:*

(*a*) $\mathbf{u} + \mathbf{v} = \mathbf{v} + \mathbf{u}$	(*e*) $k(l\mathbf{u}) = (kl)\mathbf{u}$
(*b*) $(\mathbf{u} + \mathbf{v}) + \mathbf{w} = \mathbf{u} + (\mathbf{v} + \mathbf{w})$	(*f*) $k(\mathbf{u} + \mathbf{v}) = k\mathbf{u} + k\mathbf{v}$
(*c*) $\mathbf{u} + \mathbf{0} = \mathbf{0} + \mathbf{u} = \mathbf{u}$	(*g*) $(k + l)\mathbf{u} = k\mathbf{u} + l\mathbf{u}$
(*d*) $\mathbf{u} + (-\mathbf{u}) = \mathbf{0}$	(*h*) $1\mathbf{u} = \mathbf{u}$

The results in this theorem can be proved either algebraically by using components or geometrically by treating the vectors as arrows. We will prove part (*b*) both ways and leave some of the remaining proofs as exercises.

> Observe that in Figure 11.2.10 the vectors $\mathbf{u}$, $\mathbf{v}$, and $\mathbf{w}$ are positioned "tip to tail" and that
>
> $$\mathbf{u} + \mathbf{v} + \mathbf{w}$$
>
> is the vector from the initial point of $\mathbf{u}$ (the first term in the sum) to the terminal point of $\mathbf{w}$ (the last term in the sum). This "tip to tail" method of vector addition also works for four or more vectors (Figure 11.2.11).

PROOF (*b*) (ALGEBRAIC IN 2-SPACE)   Let $\mathbf{u} = \langle u_1, u_2 \rangle$, $\mathbf{v} = \langle v_1, v_2 \rangle$, and $\mathbf{w} = \langle w_1, w_2 \rangle$. Then

$$(\mathbf{u} + \mathbf{v}) + \mathbf{w} = (\langle u_1, u_2 \rangle + \langle v_1, v_2 \rangle) + \langle w_1, w_2 \rangle$$

$$= \langle u_1 + v_1, u_2 + v_2 \rangle + \langle w_1, w_2 \rangle$$

$$= \langle (u_1 + v_1) + w_1, (u_2 + v_2) + w_2 \rangle$$

$$= \langle u_1 + (v_1 + w_1), u_2 + (v_2 + w_2) \rangle$$

$$= \langle u_1, u_2 \rangle + \langle v_1 + w_1, v_2 + w_2 \rangle$$

$$= \mathbf{u} + (\mathbf{v} + \mathbf{w})$$

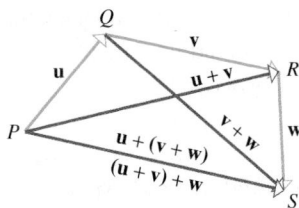

▲ Figure 11.2.10

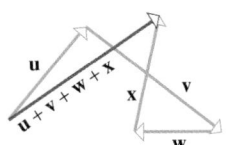

▲ Figure 11.2.11

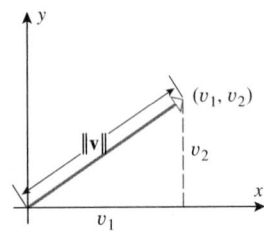

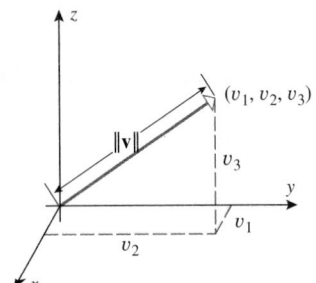

▲ Figure 11.2.12

PROOF (*b*) (GEOMETRIC) Let **u**, **v**, and **w** be represented by $\overrightarrow{PQ}$, $\overrightarrow{QR}$, and $\overrightarrow{RS}$ as shown in Figure 11.2.10. Then

$$\mathbf{v} + \mathbf{w} = \overrightarrow{QS} \quad \text{and} \quad \mathbf{u} + (\mathbf{v} + \mathbf{w}) = \overrightarrow{PS}$$
$$\mathbf{u} + \mathbf{v} = \overrightarrow{PR} \quad \text{and} \quad (\mathbf{u} + \mathbf{v}) + \mathbf{w} = \overrightarrow{PS}$$

Therefore,

$$(\mathbf{u} + \mathbf{v}) + \mathbf{w} = \mathbf{u} + (\mathbf{v} + \mathbf{w}) \quad \blacksquare$$

■ NORM OF A VECTOR

The distance between the initial and terminal points of a vector **v** is called the **length**, the **norm**, or the **magnitude** of **v** and is denoted by $\|\mathbf{v}\|$. This distance does not change if the vector is translated, so for purposes of calculating the norm we can assume that the vector is positioned with its initial point at the origin (Figure 11.2.12). This makes it evident that the norm of a vector $\mathbf{v} = \langle v_1, v_2 \rangle$ in 2-space is given by

$$\|\mathbf{v}\| = \sqrt{v_1^2 + v_2^2} \tag{9}$$

and the norm of a vector $\mathbf{v} = \langle v_1, v_2, v_3 \rangle$ in 3-space is given by

$$\|\mathbf{v}\| = \sqrt{v_1^2 + v_2^2 + v_3^2} \tag{10}$$

▶ **Example 3** Find the norms of $\mathbf{v} = \langle -2, 3 \rangle$, $10\mathbf{v} = \langle -20, 30 \rangle$, and $\mathbf{w} = \langle 2, 3, 6 \rangle$.

Solution. From (9) and (10)

$$\|\mathbf{v}\| = \sqrt{(-2)^2 + 3^2} = \sqrt{13}$$
$$\|10\mathbf{v}\| = \sqrt{(-20)^2 + 30^2} = \sqrt{1300} = 10\sqrt{13}$$
$$\|\mathbf{w}\| = \sqrt{2^2 + 3^2 + 6^2} = \sqrt{49} = 7 \quad \blacktriangleleft$$

Note that $\|10\mathbf{v}\| = 10\|\mathbf{v}\|$ in Example 3. This is consistent with Definition 11.2.2, which stipulated that for any vector **v** and scalar k, the length of $k\mathbf{v}$ must be $|k|$ times the length of **v**; that is,

$$\|k\mathbf{v}\| = |k| \|\mathbf{v}\| \tag{11}$$

Thus, for example,

$$\|3\mathbf{v}\| = |3| \|\mathbf{v}\| = 3\|\mathbf{v}\|$$
$$\|-2\mathbf{v}\| = |-2| \|\mathbf{v}\| = 2\|\mathbf{v}\|$$
$$\|-1\mathbf{v}\| = |-1| \|\mathbf{v}\| = \|\mathbf{v}\|$$

This applies to vectors in 2-space and 3-space.

■ UNIT VECTORS

A vector of length 1 is called a **unit vector**. In an *xy*-coordinate system the unit vectors along the *x*- and *y*-axes are denoted by **i** and **j**, respectively; and in an *xyz*-coordinate system the unit vectors along the *x*-, *y*-, and *z*-axes are denoted by **i**, **j**, and **k**, respectively (Figure 11.2.13). Thus,

$$\mathbf{i} = \langle 1, 0 \rangle, \quad \mathbf{j} = \langle 0, 1 \rangle \qquad \boxed{\text{In 2-space}}$$
$$\mathbf{i} = \langle 1, 0, 0 \rangle, \quad \mathbf{j} = \langle 0, 1, 0 \rangle, \quad \mathbf{k} = \langle 0, 0, 1 \rangle \qquad \boxed{\text{In 3-space}}$$

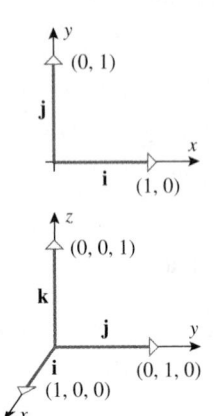

▲ Figure 11.2.13

Every vector in 2-space is expressible uniquely in terms of **i** and **j**, and every vector in 3-space is expressible uniquely in terms of **i**, **j**, and **k** as follows:

$$\mathbf{v} = \langle v_1, v_2 \rangle = \langle v_1, 0 \rangle + \langle 0, v_2 \rangle = v_1 \langle 1, 0 \rangle + v_2 \langle 0, 1 \rangle = v_1 \mathbf{i} + v_2 \mathbf{j}$$

$$\mathbf{v} = \langle v_1, v_2, v_3 \rangle = v_1 \langle 1, 0, 0 \rangle + v_2 \langle 0, 1, 0 \rangle + v_3 \langle 0, 0, 1 \rangle = v_1 \mathbf{i} + v_2 \mathbf{j} + v_3 \mathbf{k}$$

▶ **Example 4**   The following table provides some examples of vector notation in 2-space and 3-space.

The two notations for vectors illustrated in Example 4 are completely interchangeable, the choice being a matter of convenience or personal preference.

2-SPACE	3-SPACE
$\langle 2, 3 \rangle = 2\mathbf{i} + 3\mathbf{j}$	$\langle 2, -3, 4 \rangle = 2\mathbf{i} - 3\mathbf{j} + 4\mathbf{k}$
$\langle -4, 0 \rangle = -4\mathbf{i} + 0\mathbf{j} = -4\mathbf{i}$	$\langle 0, 3, 0 \rangle = 3\mathbf{j}$
$\langle 0, 0 \rangle = 0\mathbf{i} + 0\mathbf{j} = \mathbf{0}$	$\langle 0, 0, 0 \rangle = 0\mathbf{i} + 0\mathbf{j} + 0\mathbf{k} = \mathbf{0}$
$(3\mathbf{i} + 2\mathbf{j}) + (4\mathbf{i} + \mathbf{j}) = 7\mathbf{i} + 3\mathbf{j}$	$(3\mathbf{i} + 2\mathbf{j} - \mathbf{k}) - (4\mathbf{i} - \mathbf{j} + 2\mathbf{k}) = -\mathbf{i} + 3\mathbf{j} - 3\mathbf{k}$
$5(6\mathbf{i} - 2\mathbf{j}) = 30\mathbf{i} - 10\mathbf{j}$	$2(\mathbf{i} + \mathbf{j} - \mathbf{k}) + 4(\mathbf{i} - \mathbf{j}) = 6\mathbf{i} - 2\mathbf{j} - 2\mathbf{k}$
$\lVert 2\mathbf{i} - 3\mathbf{j} \rVert = \sqrt{2^2 + (-3)^2} = \sqrt{13}$	$\lVert \mathbf{i} + 2\mathbf{j} - 3\mathbf{k} \rVert = \sqrt{1^2 + 2^2 + (-3)^2} = \sqrt{14}$
$\lVert v_1 \mathbf{i} + v_2 \mathbf{j} \rVert = \sqrt{v_1^2 + v_2^2}$	$\lVert \langle v_1, v_2, v_3 \rangle \rVert = \sqrt{v_1^2 + v_2^2 + v_3^2}$

◀

■ NORMALIZING A VECTOR

A common problem in applications is to find a unit vector **u** that has the same direction as some given nonzero vector **v**. This can be done by multiplying **v** by the reciprocal of its length; that is,

$$\mathbf{u} = \frac{1}{\lVert \mathbf{v} \rVert} \mathbf{v} = \frac{\mathbf{v}}{\lVert \mathbf{v} \rVert}$$

is a unit vector with the same direction as **v**—the direction is the same because $k = 1/\lVert \mathbf{v} \rVert$ is a positive scalar, and the length is 1 because

$$\lVert \mathbf{u} \rVert = \lVert k\mathbf{v} \rVert = |k| \lVert \mathbf{v} \rVert = k \lVert \mathbf{v} \rVert = \frac{1}{\lVert \mathbf{v} \rVert} \lVert \mathbf{v} \rVert = 1$$

The process of multiplying a vector **v** by the reciprocal of its length to obtain a unit vector with the same direction is called **normalizing v**.

TECHNOLOGY MASTERY

Many calculating utilities can perform vector operations, and some have built-in norm and normalization operations. If your calculator has these capabilities, use it to check the computations in Examples 1, 3, and 5.

▶ **Example 5**   Find the unit vector that has the same direction as $\mathbf{v} = 2\mathbf{i} + 2\mathbf{j} - \mathbf{k}$.

Solution.   The vector **v** has length

$$\lVert \mathbf{v} \rVert = \sqrt{2^2 + 2^2 + (-1)^2} = 3$$

so the unit vector **u** in the same direction as **v** is

$$\mathbf{u} = \tfrac{1}{3} \mathbf{v} = \tfrac{2}{3} \mathbf{i} + \tfrac{2}{3} \mathbf{j} - \tfrac{1}{3} \mathbf{k} \quad ◀$$

■ VECTORS DETERMINED BY LENGTH AND ANGLE

If **v** is a nonzero vector with its initial point at the origin of an xy-coordinate system, and if θ is the angle from the positive x-axis to the radial line through **v**, then the x-component of **v** can be written as $\lVert \mathbf{v} \rVert \cos\theta$ and the y-component as $\lVert \mathbf{v} \rVert \sin\theta$ (Figure 11.2.14); and hence **v** can be expressed in trigonometric form as

$$\mathbf{v} = \lVert \mathbf{v} \rVert \langle \cos\theta, \sin\theta \rangle \quad \text{or} \quad \mathbf{v} = \lVert \mathbf{v} \rVert \cos\theta \, \mathbf{i} + \lVert \mathbf{v} \rVert \sin\theta \, \mathbf{j} \qquad (12)$$

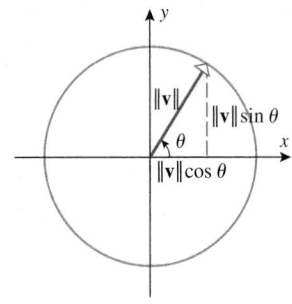

▲ **Figure 11.2.14**

In the special case of a unit vector **u** this simplifies to

$$\mathbf{u} = \langle \cos\theta, \sin\theta \rangle \quad \text{or} \quad \mathbf{u} = \cos\theta\,\mathbf{i} + \sin\theta\,\mathbf{j} \tag{13}$$

▶ **Example 6**

(a) Find the vector of length 2 that makes an angle of $\pi/4$ with the positive x-axis.

(b) Find the angle that the vector $\mathbf{v} = -\sqrt{3}\,\mathbf{i} + \mathbf{j}$ makes with the positive x-axis.

Solution (a). From (12)

$$\mathbf{v} = 2\cos\frac{\pi}{4}\mathbf{i} + 2\sin\frac{\pi}{4}\mathbf{j} = \sqrt{2}\,\mathbf{i} + \sqrt{2}\,\mathbf{j}$$

Solution (b). We will normalize **v**, then use (13) to find $\sin\theta$ and $\cos\theta$, and then use these values to find θ. Normalizing **v** yields

$$\frac{\mathbf{v}}{\|\mathbf{v}\|} = \frac{-\sqrt{3}\,\mathbf{i} + \mathbf{j}}{\sqrt{\left(-\sqrt{3}\right)^2 + 1^2}} = -\frac{\sqrt{3}}{2}\mathbf{i} + \frac{1}{2}\mathbf{j}$$

Thus, $\cos\theta = -\sqrt{3}/2$ and $\sin\theta = 1/2$, from which we conclude that $\theta = 5\pi/6$. ◀

■ **VECTORS DETERMINED BY LENGTH AND A VECTOR IN THE SAME DIRECTION**

It is a common problem in many applications that a direction in 2-space or 3-space is determined by some known unit vector **u**, and it is of interest to find the components of a vector **v** that has the same direction as **u** and some specified length $\|\mathbf{v}\|$. This can be done by expressing **v** as

$$\mathbf{v} = \|\mathbf{v}\|\mathbf{u} \qquad \boxed{\text{v is equal to its length times a unit vector in the same direction.}}$$

and then reading off the components of $\|\mathbf{v}\|\mathbf{u}$.

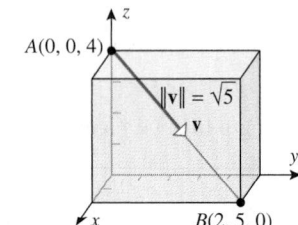

▲ **Figure 11.2.15**

▶ **Example 7** Figure 11.2.15 shows a vector **v** of length $\sqrt{5}$ that extends along the line through A and B. Find the components of **v**.

Solution. First we will find the components of the vector $\overrightarrow{AB}$, then we will normalize this vector to obtain a unit vector in the direction of **v**, and then we will multiply this unit vector by $\|\mathbf{v}\|$ to obtain the vector **v**. The computations are as follows:

$$\overrightarrow{AB} = \langle 2, 5, 0 \rangle - \langle 0, 0, 4 \rangle = \langle 2, 5, -4 \rangle$$

$$\|\overrightarrow{AB}\| = \sqrt{2^2 + 5^2 + (-4)^2} = \sqrt{45} = 3\sqrt{5}$$

$$\frac{\overrightarrow{AB}}{\|\overrightarrow{AB}\|} = \left\langle \frac{2}{3\sqrt{5}}, \frac{5}{3\sqrt{5}}, -\frac{4}{3\sqrt{5}} \right\rangle$$

$$\mathbf{v} = \|\mathbf{v}\|\left(\frac{\overrightarrow{AB}}{\|\overrightarrow{AB}\|}\right) = \sqrt{5}\left\langle \frac{2}{3\sqrt{5}}, \frac{5}{3\sqrt{5}}, -\frac{4}{3\sqrt{5}} \right\rangle = \left\langle \frac{2}{3}, \frac{5}{3}, -\frac{4}{3} \right\rangle \blacktriangleleft$$

■ **RESULTANT OF TWO CONCURRENT FORCES**

The effect that a force has on an object depends on the magnitude and direction of the force and the point at which it is applied. Thus, forces are regarded to be vector quantities and, indeed, the algebraic operations on vectors that we have defined in this section have their origin in the study of forces. For example, it is a fact of physics that if two forces $\mathbf{F}_1$ and

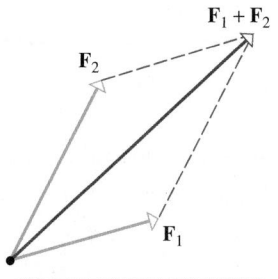

The single force $\mathbf{F}_1 + \mathbf{F}_2$ has the same effect as the two forces $\mathbf{F}_1$ and $\mathbf{F}_2$.

▲ **Figure 11.2.16**

$\mathbf{F}_2$ are applied at the same point on an object, then the two forces have the same effect on the object as the single force $\mathbf{F}_1 + \mathbf{F}_2$ applied at the point (Figure 11.2.16). Physicists and engineers call $\mathbf{F}_1 + \mathbf{F}_2$ the *resultant* of $\mathbf{F}_1$ and $\mathbf{F}_2$, and they say that the forces $\mathbf{F}_1$ and $\mathbf{F}_2$ are *concurrent* to indicate that they are applied at the same point.

In many applications, the magnitudes of two concurrent forces and the angle between them are known, and the problem is to find the magnitude and direction of the resultant. One approach to solving this problem is to use (12) to find the components of the concurrent forces, and then use (1) to find the components of the resultant. The next example illustrates this method.

▶ **Example 8**   Suppose that two forces are applied to an eye bracket, as shown in Figure 11.2.17. Find the magnitude of the resultant and the angle θ that it makes with the positive x-axis.

Solution.   Note that $\mathbf{F}_1$ makes an angle of $30°$ with the positive x-axis and $\mathbf{F}_2$ makes an angle of $30° + 40° = 70°$ with the positive x-axis. Since we are given that $\|\mathbf{F}_1\| = 200$ N and $\|\mathbf{F}_2\| = 300$ N, (12) yields

$$\mathbf{F}_1 = 200\langle \cos 30°, \sin 30° \rangle = \langle 100\sqrt{3}, 100 \rangle$$

and

$$\mathbf{F}_2 = 300\langle \cos 70°, \sin 70° \rangle = \langle 300\cos 70°, 300\sin 70° \rangle$$

Therefore, the resultant $\mathbf{F} = \mathbf{F}_1 + \mathbf{F}_2$ has component form

$$\mathbf{F} = \mathbf{F}_1 + \mathbf{F}_2 = \langle 100\sqrt{3} + 300\cos 70°, 100 + 300\sin 70° \rangle$$
$$= 100\langle \sqrt{3} + 3\cos 70°, 1 + 3\sin 70° \rangle \approx \langle 275.8, 381.9 \rangle$$

The magnitude of the resultant is then

$$\|\mathbf{F}\| = 100\sqrt{\left(\sqrt{3} + 3\cos 70°\right)^2 + \left(1 + 3\sin 70°\right)^2} \approx 471 \text{ N}$$

Let θ denote the angle $\mathbf{F}$ makes with the positive x-axis when the initial point of $\mathbf{F}$ is at the origin. Using (12) and equating the x-components of $\mathbf{F}$ yield

$$\|\mathbf{F}\|\cos\theta = 100\sqrt{3} + 300\cos 70° \quad \text{or} \quad \cos\theta = \frac{100\sqrt{3} + 300\cos 70°}{\|\mathbf{F}\|}$$

Since the terminal point of $\mathbf{F}$ is in the first quadrant, we have

$$\theta = \cos^{-1}\left(\frac{100\sqrt{3} + 300\cos 70°}{\|\mathbf{F}\|}\right) \approx 54.2°$$

(Figure 11.2.18). ◀

The resultant of three or more concurrent forces can be found by working in pairs. For example, the resultant of three forces can be found by finding the resultant of any two of the forces and then finding the resultant of that resultant with the third force.

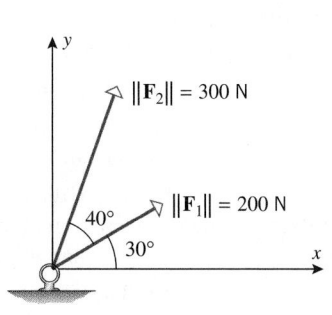

▲ **Figure 11.2.17**

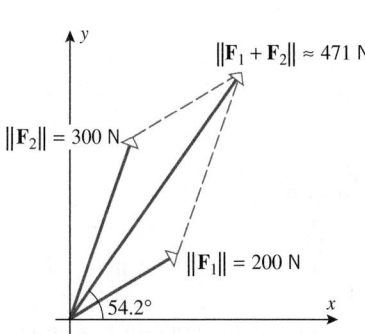

▲ **Figure 11.2.18**

✔**QUICK CHECK EXERCISES 11.2** *(See page 784 for answers.)*

1. If $\mathbf{v} = \langle 3, -1, 7 \rangle$ and $\mathbf{w} = \langle 4, 10, -5 \rangle$, then
   (a) $\|\mathbf{v}\| = $ _____
   (b) $\mathbf{v} + \mathbf{w} = $ _____
   (c) $\mathbf{v} - \mathbf{w} = $ _____
   (d) $2\mathbf{v} = $ _____.

2. The unit vector in the direction of $\mathbf{v} = \langle 3, -1, 7 \rangle$ is _____.

3. The unit vector in 2-space that makes an angle of $\pi/3$ with the positive x-axis is _____.

4. Consider points $A(3, 4, 0)$ and $B(0, 0, 5)$.
   (a) $\overrightarrow{AB} = $ _____
   (b) If $\mathbf{v}$ is a vector in the same direction as $\overrightarrow{AB}$ and the length of $\mathbf{v}$ is $\sqrt{2}$, then $\mathbf{v} = $ _____.

EXERCISE SET 11.2

1–4 Sketch the vectors with their initial points at the origin.

1. (a) $\langle 2, 5 \rangle$ (b) $\langle -5, -4 \rangle$ (c) $\langle 2, 0 \rangle$
   (d) $-5\mathbf{i} + 3\mathbf{j}$ (e) $3\mathbf{i} - 2\mathbf{j}$ (f) $-6\mathbf{j}$

2. (a) $\langle -3, 7 \rangle$ (b) $\langle 6, -2 \rangle$ (c) $\langle 0, -8 \rangle$
   (d) $4\mathbf{i} + 2\mathbf{j}$ (e) $-2\mathbf{i} - \mathbf{j}$ (f) $4\mathbf{i}$

3. (a) $\langle 1, -2, 2 \rangle$ (b) $\langle 2, 2, -1 \rangle$
   (c) $-\mathbf{i} + 2\mathbf{j} + 3\mathbf{k}$ (d) $2\mathbf{i} + 3\mathbf{j} - \mathbf{k}$

4. (a) $\langle -1, 3, 2 \rangle$ (b) $\langle 3, 4, 2 \rangle$
   (c) $2\mathbf{j} - \mathbf{k}$ (d) $\mathbf{i} - \mathbf{j} + 2\mathbf{k}$

5–6 Find the components of the vector, and sketch an equivalent vector with its initial point at the origin.

5. (a) 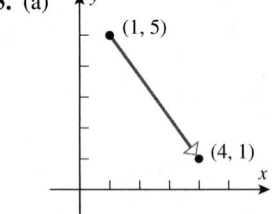   (b)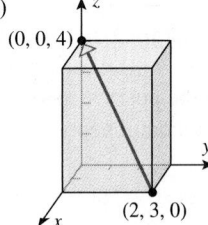

6. (a) 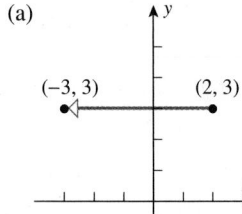   (b)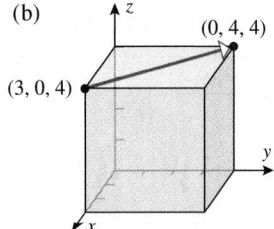

7–8 Find the components of the vector $\overrightarrow{P_1 P_2}$. ■

7. (a) $P_1(3, 5)$, $P_2(2, 8)$ (b) $P_1(7, -2)$, $P_2(0, 0)$
   (c) $P_1(5, -2, 1)$, $P_2(2, 4, 2)$

8. (a) $P_1(-6, -2)$, $P_2(-4, -1)$
   (b) $P_1(0, 0, 0)$, $P_2(-1, 6, 1)$
   (c) $P_1(4, 1, -3)$, $P_2(9, 1, -3)$

9. (a) Find the terminal point of $\mathbf{v} = 3\mathbf{i} - 2\mathbf{j}$ if the initial point is $(1, -2)$.
   (b) Find the initial point of $\mathbf{v} = \langle -3, 1, 2 \rangle$ if the terminal point is $(5, 0, -1)$.

10. (a) Find the terminal point of $\mathbf{v} = \langle 7, 6 \rangle$ if the initial point is $(2, -1)$.
    (b) Find the terminal point of $\mathbf{v} = \mathbf{i} + 2\mathbf{j} - 3\mathbf{k}$ if the initial point is $(-2, 1, 4)$.

11–12 Perform the stated operations on the given vectors $\mathbf{u}$, $\mathbf{v}$, and $\mathbf{w}$. ■

11. $\mathbf{u} = 3\mathbf{i} - \mathbf{k}$, $\mathbf{v} = \mathbf{i} - \mathbf{j} + 2\mathbf{k}$, $\mathbf{w} = 3\mathbf{j}$
    (a) $\mathbf{w} - \mathbf{v}$ (b) $6\mathbf{u} + 4\mathbf{w}$
    (c) $-\mathbf{v} - 2\mathbf{w}$ (d) $4(3\mathbf{u} + \mathbf{v})$
    (e) $-8(\mathbf{v} + \mathbf{w}) + 2\mathbf{u}$ (f) $3\mathbf{w} - (\mathbf{v} - \mathbf{w})$

12. $\mathbf{u} = \langle 2, -1, 3 \rangle$, $\mathbf{v} = \langle 4, 0, -2 \rangle$, $\mathbf{w} = \langle 1, 1, 3 \rangle$
    (a) $\mathbf{u} - \mathbf{w}$ (b) $7\mathbf{v} + 3\mathbf{w}$ (c) $-\mathbf{w} + \mathbf{v}$
    (d) $3(\mathbf{u} - 7\mathbf{v})$ (e) $-3\mathbf{v} - 8\mathbf{w}$ (f) $2\mathbf{v} - (\mathbf{u} + \mathbf{w})$

13–14 Find the norm of $\mathbf{v}$. ■

13. (a) $\mathbf{v} = \langle 1, -1 \rangle$ (b) $\mathbf{v} = -\mathbf{i} + 7\mathbf{j}$
    (c) $\mathbf{v} = \langle -1, 2, 4 \rangle$ (d) $\mathbf{v} = -3\mathbf{i} + 2\mathbf{j} + \mathbf{k}$

14. (a) $\mathbf{v} = \langle 3, 4 \rangle$ (b) $\mathbf{v} = \sqrt{2}\mathbf{i} - \sqrt{7}\mathbf{j}$
    (c) $\mathbf{v} = \langle 0, -3, 0 \rangle$ (d) $\mathbf{v} = \mathbf{i} + \mathbf{j} + \mathbf{k}$

15. Let $\mathbf{u} = \mathbf{i} - 3\mathbf{j} + 2\mathbf{k}$, $\mathbf{v} = \mathbf{i} + \mathbf{j}$, and $\mathbf{w} = 2\mathbf{i} + 2\mathbf{j} - 4\mathbf{k}$. Find
    (a) $\|\mathbf{u} + \mathbf{v}\|$ (b) $\|\mathbf{u}\| + \|\mathbf{v}\|$
    (c) $\|-2\mathbf{u}\| + 2\|\mathbf{v}\|$ (d) $\|3\mathbf{u} - 5\mathbf{v} + \mathbf{w}\|$
    (e) $\dfrac{1}{\|\mathbf{w}\|}\mathbf{w}$ (f) $\left\|\dfrac{1}{\|\mathbf{w}\|}\mathbf{w}\right\|$.

16. Is it possible to have $\|\mathbf{u} - \mathbf{v}\| = \|\mathbf{u} + \mathbf{v}\|$ if $\mathbf{u}$ and $\mathbf{v}$ are nonzero vectors? Justify your conclusion geometrically.

17–20 True–False Determine whether the statement is true or false. Explain your answer. ■

17. The norm of the sum of two vectors is equal to the sum of the norms of the two vectors.

18. If two distinct vectors $\mathbf{v}$ and $\mathbf{w}$ are drawn with the same initial point, then a vector drawn between the terminal points of $\mathbf{v}$ and $\mathbf{w}$ will be either $\mathbf{v} - \mathbf{w}$ or $\mathbf{w} - \mathbf{v}$.

19. There are exactly two unit vectors that are parallel to a given nonzero vector.

20. Given a nonzero scalar c and vectors $\mathbf{b}$ and $\mathbf{d}$, the vector equation $c\mathbf{a} + \mathbf{b} = \mathbf{d}$ has a unique solution $\mathbf{a}$.

21–22 Find unit vectors that satisfy the stated conditions.

21. (a) Same direction as $-\mathbf{i} + 4\mathbf{j}$.
   (b) Oppositely directed to $6\mathbf{i} - 4\mathbf{j} + 2\mathbf{k}$.
   (c) Same direction as the vector from the point $A(-1, 0, 2)$ to the point $B(3, 1, 1)$.

22. (a) Oppositely directed to $3\mathbf{i} - 4\mathbf{j}$.
   (b) Same direction as $2\mathbf{i} - \mathbf{j} - 2\mathbf{k}$.
   (c) Same direction as the vector from the point $A(-3, 2)$ to the point $B(1, -1)$.

23–24 Find the vectors that satisfy the stated conditions.

23. (a) Oppositely directed to $\mathbf{v} = \langle 3, -4 \rangle$ and half the length of $\mathbf{v}$.
   (b) Length $\sqrt{17}$ and same direction as $\mathbf{v} = \langle 7, 0, -6 \rangle$.

24. (a) Same direction as $\mathbf{v} = -2\mathbf{i} + 3\mathbf{j}$ and three times the length of $\mathbf{v}$.
   (b) Length 2 and oppositely directed to $\mathbf{v} = -3\mathbf{i} + 4\mathbf{j} + \mathbf{k}$.

25. In each part, find the component form of the vector $\mathbf{v}$ in 2-space that has the stated length and makes the stated angle θ with the positive x-axis.
   (a) $\|\mathbf{v}\| = 3$; $\theta = \pi/4$ (b) $\|\mathbf{v}\| = 2$; $\theta = 90°$
   (c) $\|\mathbf{v}\| = 5$; $\theta = 120°$ (d) $\|\mathbf{v}\| = 1$; $\theta = \pi$

26. Find the component forms of $\mathbf{v} + \mathbf{w}$ and $\mathbf{v} - \mathbf{w}$ in 2-space, given that $\|\mathbf{v}\| = 1$, $\|\mathbf{w}\| = 1$, $\mathbf{v}$ makes an angle of $\pi/6$ with the positive x-axis, and $\mathbf{w}$ makes an angle of $3\pi/4$ with the positive x-axis.

27–28 Find the component form of $\mathbf{v} + \mathbf{w}$, given that $\mathbf{v}$ and $\mathbf{w}$ are unit vectors.

27. 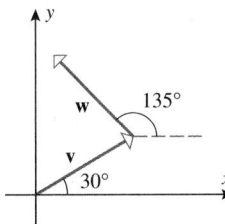   **28.**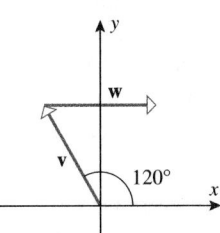

29. In each part, sketch the vector $\mathbf{u} + \mathbf{v} + \mathbf{w}$ and express it in component form.
   (a) 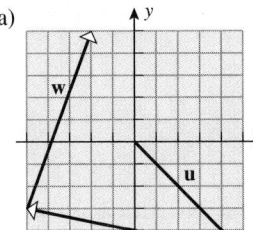   (b)

30. In each part of Exercise 29, sketch the vector $\mathbf{u} - \mathbf{v} + \mathbf{w}$ and express it in component form.

31. Let $\mathbf{u} = \langle 1, 3 \rangle$, $\mathbf{v} = \langle 2, 1 \rangle$, $\mathbf{w} = \langle 4, -1 \rangle$. Find the vector $\mathbf{x}$ that satisfies $2\mathbf{u} - \mathbf{v} + \mathbf{x} = 7\mathbf{x} + \mathbf{w}$.

32. Let $\mathbf{u} = \langle -1, 1 \rangle$, $\mathbf{v} = \langle 0, 1 \rangle$, and $\mathbf{w} = \langle 3, 4 \rangle$. Find the vector $\mathbf{x}$ that satisfies $\mathbf{u} - 2\mathbf{x} = \mathbf{x} - \mathbf{w} + 3\mathbf{v}$.

33. Find $\mathbf{u}$ and $\mathbf{v}$ if $\mathbf{u} + 2\mathbf{v} = 3\mathbf{i} - \mathbf{k}$ and $3\mathbf{u} - \mathbf{v} = \mathbf{i} + \mathbf{j} + \mathbf{k}$.

34. Find $\mathbf{u}$ and $\mathbf{v}$ if $\mathbf{u} + \mathbf{v} = \langle 2, -3 \rangle$ and $3\mathbf{u} + 2\mathbf{v} = \langle -1, 2 \rangle$.

35. Use vectors to find the lengths of the diagonals of the parallelogram that has $\mathbf{i} + \mathbf{j}$ and $\mathbf{i} - 2\mathbf{j}$ as adjacent sides.

36. Use vectors to find the fourth vertex of a parallelogram, three of whose vertices are $(0, 0)$, $(1, 3)$, and $(2, 4)$. [*Note:* There is more than one answer.]

37. (a) Given that $\|\mathbf{v}\| = 3$, find all values of k such that $\|k\mathbf{v}\| = 5$.
   (b) Given that $k = -2$ and $\|k\mathbf{v}\| = 6$, find $\|\mathbf{v}\|$.

38. What do you know about k and $\mathbf{v}$ if $\|k\mathbf{v}\| = 0$?

39. In each part, find two unit vectors in 2-space that satisfy the stated condition.
   (a) Parallel to the line $y = 3x + 2$
   (b) Parallel to the line $x + y = 4$
   (c) Perpendicular to the line $y = -5x + 1$

40. In each part, find two unit vectors in 3-space that satisfy the stated condition.
   (a) Perpendicular to the xy-plane
   (b) Perpendicular to the xz-plane
   (c) Perpendicular to the yz-plane

FOCUS ON CONCEPTS

41. Let $\mathbf{r} = \langle x, y \rangle$ be an arbitrary vector. In each part, describe the set of all points (x, y) in 2-space that satisfy the stated condition.
   (a) $\|\mathbf{r}\| = 1$ (b) $\|\mathbf{r}\| \le 1$ (c) $\|\mathbf{r}\| > 1$

42. Let $\mathbf{r} = \langle x, y \rangle$ and $\mathbf{r}_0 = \langle x_0, y_0 \rangle$. In each part, describe the set of all points (x, y) in 2-space that satisfy the stated condition.
   (a) $\|\mathbf{r} - \mathbf{r}_0\| = 1$ (b) $\|\mathbf{r} - \mathbf{r}_0\| \le 1$ (c) $\|\mathbf{r} - \mathbf{r}_0\| > 1$

43. Let $\mathbf{r} = \langle x, y, z \rangle$ be an arbitrary vector. In each part, describe the set of all points (x, y, z) in 3-space that satisfy the stated condition.
   (a) $\|\mathbf{r}\| = 1$ (b) $\|\mathbf{r}\| \le 1$ (c) $\|\mathbf{r}\| > 1$

44. Let $\mathbf{r}_1 = \langle x_1, y_1 \rangle$, $\mathbf{r}_2 = \langle x_2, y_2 \rangle$, and $\mathbf{r} = \langle x, y \rangle$. Assuming that $k > \|\mathbf{r}_2 - \mathbf{r}_1\|$, describe the set of all points (x, y) for which $\|\mathbf{r} - \mathbf{r}_1\| + \|\mathbf{r} - \mathbf{r}_2\| = k$.

45–50 Find the magnitude of the resultant force and the angle that it makes with the positive x-axis.

45. 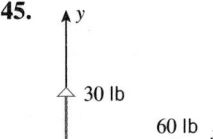   **46.**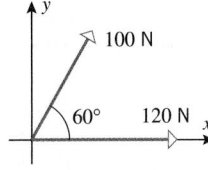

47.   **48.**

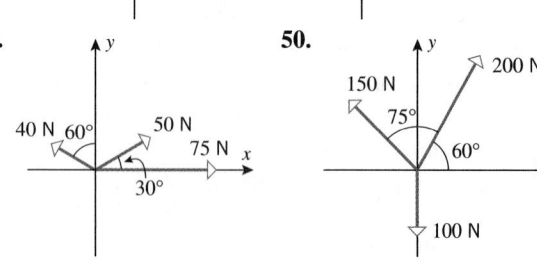

49.   **50.**

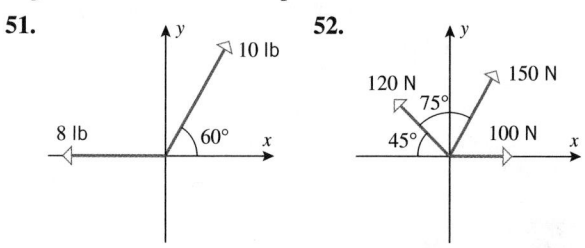

51–52 A particle is said to be in *static equilibrium* if the resultant of all forces applied to it is zero. In these exercises, find the force **F** that must be applied to the point to produce static equilibrium. Describe **F** by specifying its magnitude and the angle that it makes with the positive *x*-axis. ▨

51.   **52.**

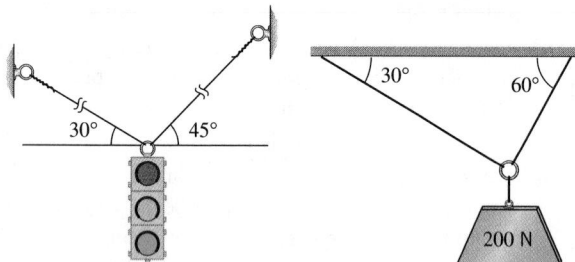

53. The accompanying figure shows a 250 lb traffic light supported by two flexible cables. The magnitudes of the forces that the cables apply to the eye ring are called the cable *tensions*. Find the tensions in the cables if the traffic light is in static equilibrium (defined above Exercise 51).

54. Find the tensions in the cables shown in the accompanying figure if the block is in static equilibrium (see Exercise 53).

▲ **Figure Ex-53**   ▲ **Figure Ex-54**

55. A vector **w** is said to be a *linear combination* of the vectors v_1 and v_2 if **w** can be expressed as $w = c_1 v_1 + c_2 v_2$, where c_1 and c_2 are scalars.
  (a) Find scalars c_1 and c_2 to express the vector $4\mathbf{j}$ as a linear combination of the vectors $v_1 = 2\mathbf{i} - \mathbf{j}$ and $v_2 = 4\mathbf{i} + 2\mathbf{j}$.
  (b) Show that the vector $\langle 3, 5 \rangle$ cannot be expressed as a linear combination of the vectors $v_1 = \langle 1, -3 \rangle$ and $v_2 = \langle -2, 6 \rangle$.

56. A vector **w** is a *linear combination* of the vectors v_1, v_2, and v_3 if **w** can be expressed as $w = c_1 v_1 + c_2 v_2 + c_3 v_3$, where c_1, c_2, and c_3 are scalars.
  (a) Find scalars c_1, c_2, and c_3 to express $\langle -1, 1, 5 \rangle$ as a linear combination of $v_1 = \langle 1, 0, 1 \rangle$, $v_2 = \langle 3, 2, 0 \rangle$, and $v_3 = \langle 0, 1, 1 \rangle$.
  (b) Show that the vector $2\mathbf{i} + \mathbf{j} - \mathbf{k}$ cannot be expressed as a linear combination of $v_1 = \mathbf{i} - \mathbf{j}$, $v_2 = 3\mathbf{i} + \mathbf{k}$, and $v_3 = 4\mathbf{i} - \mathbf{j} + \mathbf{k}$.

57. Use a theorem from plane geometry to show that if **u** and **v** are vectors in 2-space or 3-space, then

$$\|\mathbf{u} + \mathbf{v}\| \le \|\mathbf{u}\| + \|\mathbf{v}\|$$

which is called the *triangle inequality for vectors*. Give some examples to illustrate this inequality.

58. Prove parts (*a*), (*c*), and (*e*) of Theorem 11.2.6 algebraically in 2-space.

59. Prove parts (*d*), (*g*), and (*h*) of Theorem 11.2.6 algebraically in 2-space.

60. Prove part (*f*) of Theorem 11.2.6 geometrically.

FOCUS ON CONCEPTS

61. Use vectors to prove that the line segment joining the midpoints of two sides of a triangle is parallel to the third side and half as long.

62. Use vectors to prove that the midpoints of the sides of a quadrilateral are the vertices of a parallelogram.

63. Writing Do some research and then write a few paragraphs on the early history of the use of vectors in mathematics.

64. Writing Write a paragraph that discusses some of the similarities and differences between the rules of "vector arithmetic" and the rules of arithmetic of real numbers.

✔ **QUICK CHECK ANSWERS 11.2**

1. (a) $\sqrt{59}$ (b) $\langle 7, 9, 2 \rangle$ (c) $\langle -1, -11, 12 \rangle$ (d) $\langle 6, -2, 14 \rangle$ **2.** $\dfrac{1}{\sqrt{59}} v = \left\langle \dfrac{3}{\sqrt{59}}, -\dfrac{1}{\sqrt{59}}, \dfrac{7}{\sqrt{59}} \right\rangle$ **3.** $\left\langle \dfrac{1}{2}, \dfrac{\sqrt{3}}{2} \right\rangle = \dfrac{1}{2}\mathbf{i} + \dfrac{\sqrt{3}}{2}\mathbf{j}$

4. (a) $\langle -3, -4, 5 \rangle$ (b) $\dfrac{1}{5}\overrightarrow{AB} = \left\langle -\dfrac{3}{5}, -\dfrac{4}{5}, 1 \right\rangle$

11.3 DOT PRODUCT; PROJECTIONS

In the last section we defined three operations on vectors—addition, subtraction, and scalar multiplication. In scalar multiplication a vector is multiplied by a scalar and the result is a vector. In this section we will define a new kind of multiplication in which two vectors are multiplied to produce a scalar. This multiplication operation has many uses, some of which we will also discuss in this section.

■ **DEFINITION OF THE DOT PRODUCT**

11.3.1 DEFINITION   If $\mathbf{u} = \langle u_1, u_2 \rangle$ and $\mathbf{v} = \langle v_1, v_2 \rangle$ are vectors in 2-space, then the *dot product* of $\mathbf{u}$ and $\mathbf{v}$ is written as $\mathbf{u} \cdot \mathbf{v}$ and is defined as

$$\mathbf{u} \cdot \mathbf{v} = u_1 v_1 + u_2 v_2$$

Similarly, if $\mathbf{u} = \langle u_1, u_2, u_3 \rangle$ and $\mathbf{v} = \langle v_1, v_2, v_3 \rangle$ are vectors in 3-space, then their dot product is defined as

$$\mathbf{u} \cdot \mathbf{v} = u_1 v_1 + u_2 v_2 + u_3 v_3$$

In words, the dot product of two vectors is formed by multiplying their corresponding components and adding the resulting products. Note that the dot product of two vectors is a scalar.

▶ **Example 1**

$$\langle 3, 5 \rangle \cdot \langle -1, 2 \rangle = 3(-1) + 5(2) = 7$$
$$\langle 2, 3 \rangle \cdot \langle -3, 2 \rangle = 2(-3) + 3(2) = 0$$
$$\langle 1, -3, 4 \rangle \cdot \langle 1, 5, 2 \rangle = 1(1) + (-3)(5) + 4(2) = -6$$

Here are the same computations expressed another way:

$$(3\mathbf{i} + 5\mathbf{j}) \cdot (-\mathbf{i} + 2\mathbf{j}) = 3(-1) + 5(2) = 7$$
$$(2\mathbf{i} + 3\mathbf{j}) \cdot (-3\mathbf{i} + 2\mathbf{j}) = 2(-3) + 3(2) = 0$$
$$(\mathbf{i} - 3\mathbf{j} + 4\mathbf{k}) \cdot (\mathbf{i} + 5\mathbf{j} + 2\mathbf{k}) = 1(1) + (-3)(5) + 4(2) = -6 \quad ◀$$

TECHNOLOGY MASTERY

Many calculating utilities have a built-in dot product operation. If your calculating utility has this capability, use it to check the computations in Example 1.

■ **ALGEBRAIC PROPERTIES OF THE DOT PRODUCT**

The following theorem provides some of the basic algebraic properties of the dot product.

11.3.2 THEOREM   *If $\mathbf{u}$, $\mathbf{v}$, and $\mathbf{w}$ are vectors in 2- or 3-space and k is a scalar, then:*

(*a*) $\mathbf{u} \cdot \mathbf{v} = \mathbf{v} \cdot \mathbf{u}$

(*b*) $\mathbf{u} \cdot (\mathbf{v} + \mathbf{w}) = \mathbf{u} \cdot \mathbf{v} + \mathbf{u} \cdot \mathbf{w}$

(*c*) $k(\mathbf{u} \cdot \mathbf{v}) = (k\mathbf{u}) \cdot \mathbf{v} = \mathbf{u} \cdot (k\mathbf{v})$

(*d*) $\mathbf{v} \cdot \mathbf{v} = \|\mathbf{v}\|^2$

(*e*) $\mathbf{0} \cdot \mathbf{v} = 0$

Note the difference between the two zeros that appear in part (*e*) of Theorem 11.3.2—the zero on the left side is the *zero vector* (boldface), whereas the zero on the right side is the *zero scalar* (lightface).

We will prove parts (*c*) and (*d*) for vectors in 3-space and leave some of the others as exercises.

PROOF (*c*)   Let $\mathbf{u} = \langle u_1, u_2, u_3 \rangle$ and $\mathbf{v} = \langle v_1, v_2, v_3 \rangle$. Then

$$k(\mathbf{u} \cdot \mathbf{v}) = k(u_1 v_1 + u_2 v_2 + u_3 v_3) = (k u_1)v_1 + (k u_2)v_2 + (k u_3)v_3 = (k\mathbf{u}) \cdot \mathbf{v}$$

Similarly, $k(\mathbf{u} \cdot \mathbf{v}) = \mathbf{u} \cdot (k\mathbf{v})$.

PROOF (*d*) $\mathbf{v} \cdot \mathbf{v} = v_1 v_1 + v_2 v_2 + v_3 v_3 = v_1^2 + v_2^2 + v_3^2 = \|\mathbf{v}\|^2$. ∎

The following alternative form of the formula in part (*d*) of Theorem 11.3.2 provides a useful way of expressing the norm of a vector in terms of a dot product:

$$\|\mathbf{v}\| = \sqrt{\mathbf{v} \cdot \mathbf{v}} \tag{1}$$

ANGLE BETWEEN VECTORS

Suppose that $\mathbf{u}$ and $\mathbf{v}$ are nonzero vectors in 2-space or 3-space that are positioned so their initial points coincide. We define the ***angle between* $\mathbf{u}$ *and* $\mathbf{v}$** to be the angle θ determined by the vectors that satisfies the condition $0 \le \theta \le \pi$ (Figure 11.3.1). In 2-space, θ is the smallest counterclockwise angle through which one of the vectors can be rotated until it aligns with the other.

The next theorem provides a way of calculating the angle between two vectors from their components.

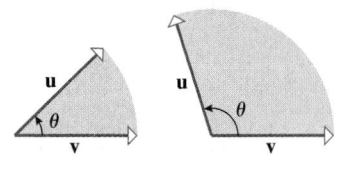

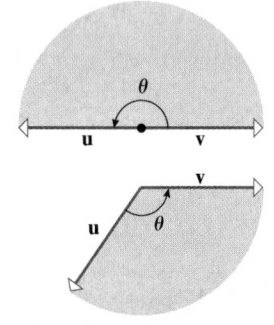

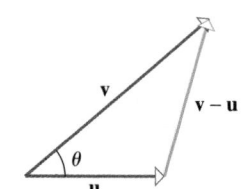

θ is the angle between $\mathbf{u}$ and $\mathbf{v}$.

▲ **Figure 11.3.1**

> **11.3.3   THEOREM**   *If* $\mathbf{u}$ *and* $\mathbf{v}$ *are nonzero vectors in 2-space or 3-space, and if* θ *is the angle between them, then*
> $$\cos\theta = \frac{\mathbf{u} \cdot \mathbf{v}}{\|\mathbf{u}\|\|\mathbf{v}\|} \tag{2}$$

PROOF   Suppose that the vectors $\mathbf{u}$, $\mathbf{v}$, and $\mathbf{v} - \mathbf{u}$ are positioned to form three sides of a triangle, as shown in Figure 11.3.2. It follows from the law of cosines that

$$\|\mathbf{v} - \mathbf{u}\|^2 = \|\mathbf{u}\|^2 + \|\mathbf{v}\|^2 - 2\|\mathbf{u}\|\|\mathbf{v}\|\cos\theta \tag{3}$$

Using the properties of the dot product in Theorem 11.3.2, we can rewrite the left side of this equation as

$$
\begin{aligned}
\|\mathbf{v} - \mathbf{u}\|^2 &= (\mathbf{v} - \mathbf{u}) \cdot (\mathbf{v} - \mathbf{u}) \\
&= (\mathbf{v} - \mathbf{u}) \cdot \mathbf{v} - (\mathbf{v} - \mathbf{u}) \cdot \mathbf{u} \\
&= \mathbf{v} \cdot \mathbf{v} - \mathbf{u} \cdot \mathbf{v} - \mathbf{v} \cdot \mathbf{u} + \mathbf{u} \cdot \mathbf{u} \\
&= \|\mathbf{v}\|^2 - 2\mathbf{u} \cdot \mathbf{v} + \|\mathbf{u}\|^2
\end{aligned}
$$

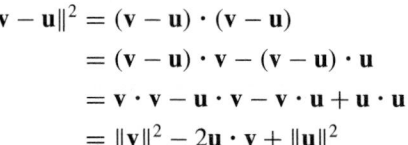

▲ **Figure 11.3.2**

Substituting this back into (3) yields

$$\|\mathbf{v}\|^2 - 2\mathbf{u} \cdot \mathbf{v} + \|\mathbf{u}\|^2 = \|\mathbf{u}\|^2 + \|\mathbf{v}\|^2 - 2\|\mathbf{u}\|\|\mathbf{v}\|\cos\theta$$

which we can simplify and rewrite as

$$\mathbf{u} \cdot \mathbf{v} = \|\mathbf{u}\|\|\mathbf{v}\|\cos\theta$$

Finally, dividing both sides of this equation by $\|\mathbf{u}\|\|\mathbf{v}\|$ yields (2). ∎

▶ **Example 2**   Find the angle between the vector $\mathbf{u} = \mathbf{i} - 2\mathbf{j} + 2\mathbf{k}$ and

(a) $\mathbf{v} = -3\mathbf{i} + 6\mathbf{j} + 2\mathbf{k}$ (b) $\mathbf{w} = 2\mathbf{i} + 7\mathbf{j} + 6\mathbf{k}$ (c) $\mathbf{z} = -3\mathbf{i} + 6\mathbf{j} - 6\mathbf{k}$

Solution (*a*).

$$\cos\theta = \frac{\mathbf{u} \cdot \mathbf{v}}{\|\mathbf{u}\|\|\mathbf{v}\|} = \frac{-11}{(3)(7)} = -\frac{11}{21}$$

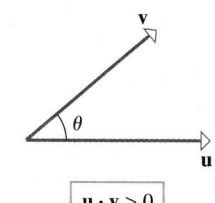

$$\boxed{\mathbf{u} \cdot \mathbf{v} > 0}$$

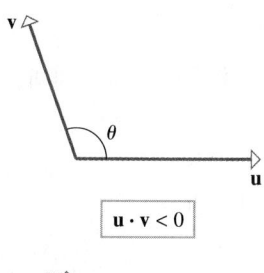

$$\boxed{\mathbf{u} \cdot \mathbf{v} < 0}$$

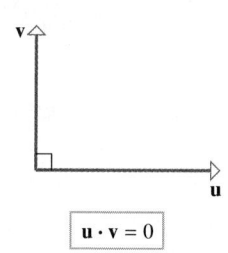

$$\boxed{\mathbf{u} \cdot \mathbf{v} = 0}$$

▲ **Figure 11.3.3**

Thus,

$$\theta = \cos^{-1}\left(-\tfrac{11}{21}\right) \approx 2.12 \text{ radians} \approx 121.6°$$

Solution (b).

$$\cos\theta = \frac{\mathbf{u} \cdot \mathbf{w}}{\|\mathbf{u}\| \|\mathbf{w}\|} = \frac{0}{\|\mathbf{u}\| \|\mathbf{w}\|} = 0$$

Thus, $\theta = \pi/2$, which means that the vectors are perpendicular.

Solution (c).

$$\cos\theta = \frac{\mathbf{u} \cdot \mathbf{z}}{\|\mathbf{u}\| \|\mathbf{z}\|} = \frac{-27}{(3)(9)} = -1$$

Thus, $\theta = \pi$, which means that the vectors are oppositely directed. (In retrospect, we could have seen this without computing θ, since $\mathbf{z} = -3\mathbf{u}$.) ◄

■ **INTERPRETING THE SIGN OF THE DOT PRODUCT**
It will often be convenient to express Formula (2) as

$$\mathbf{u} \cdot \mathbf{v} = \|\mathbf{u}\| \|\mathbf{v}\| \cos\theta \tag{4}$$

which expresses the dot product of $\mathbf{u}$ and $\mathbf{v}$ in terms of the lengths of these vectors and the angle between them. Since $\mathbf{u}$ and $\mathbf{v}$ are assumed to be nonzero vectors, this version of the formula makes it clear that the sign of $\mathbf{u} \cdot \mathbf{v}$ is the same as the sign of $\cos\theta$. Thus, we can tell from the dot product whether the angle between two vectors is acute or obtuse or whether the vectors are perpendicular (Figure 11.3.3).

REMARK The terms "perpendicular," "orthogonal," and "normal" are all commonly used to describe geometric objects that meet at right angles. For consistency, we will say that two vectors are *orthogonal*, a vector is *normal* to a plane, and two planes are *perpendicular*. Moreover, although the zero vector does not make a well-defined angle with other vectors, we will consider **0** to be orthogonal to *all* vectors. This convention allows us to say that $\mathbf{u}$ and $\mathbf{v}$ are orthogonal vectors if and only if $\mathbf{u} \cdot \mathbf{v} = 0$, and makes Formula (4) valid if $\mathbf{u}$ or $\mathbf{v}$ (or both) is zero.

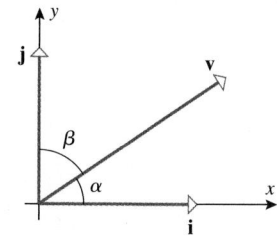

▲ **Figure 11.3.4**

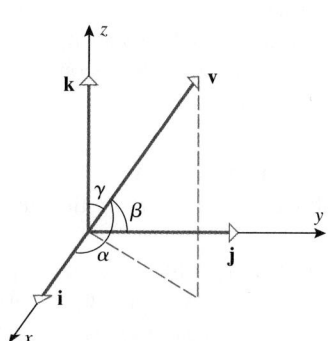

▲ **Figure 11.3.5**

■ **DIRECTION ANGLES**
In an xy-coordinate system, the direction of a nonzero vector $\mathbf{v}$ is completely determined by the angles α and β between $\mathbf{v}$ and the unit vectors $\mathbf{i}$ and $\mathbf{j}$ (Figure 11.3.4), and in an xyz-coordinate system the direction is completely determined by the angles α, β, and γ between $\mathbf{v}$ and the unit vectors $\mathbf{i}$, $\mathbf{j}$, and $\mathbf{k}$ (Figure 11.3.5). In both 2-space and 3-space the angles between a nonzero vector $\mathbf{v}$ and the vectors $\mathbf{i}$, $\mathbf{j}$, and $\mathbf{k}$ are called the ***direction angles*** of $\mathbf{v}$, and the cosines of those angles are called the ***direction cosines*** of $\mathbf{v}$. Formulas for the direction cosines of a vector can be obtained from Formula (2). For example, if $\mathbf{v} = v_1\mathbf{i} + v_2\mathbf{j} + v_3\mathbf{k}$, then

$$\cos\alpha = \frac{\mathbf{v} \cdot \mathbf{i}}{\|\mathbf{v}\| \|\mathbf{i}\|} = \frac{v_1}{\|\mathbf{v}\|}, \quad \cos\beta = \frac{\mathbf{v} \cdot \mathbf{j}}{\|\mathbf{v}\| \|\mathbf{j}\|} = \frac{v_2}{\|\mathbf{v}\|}, \quad \cos\gamma = \frac{\mathbf{v} \cdot \mathbf{k}}{\|\mathbf{v}\| \|\mathbf{k}\|} = \frac{v_3}{\|\mathbf{v}\|}$$

Thus, we have the following theorem.

11.3.4   THEOREM   *The direction cosines of a nonzero vector* $\mathbf{v} = v_1\mathbf{i} + v_2\mathbf{j} + v_3\mathbf{k}$ *are*

$$\cos\alpha = \frac{v_1}{\|\mathbf{v}\|}, \quad \cos\beta = \frac{v_2}{\|\mathbf{v}\|}, \quad \cos\gamma = \frac{v_3}{\|\mathbf{v}\|}$$

The direction cosines of a vector $\mathbf{v} = v_1\mathbf{i} + v_2\mathbf{j} + v_3\mathbf{k}$ can be computed by normalizing $\mathbf{v}$ and reading off the components of $\mathbf{v}/\|\mathbf{v}\|$, since

$$\frac{\mathbf{v}}{\|\mathbf{v}\|} = \frac{v_1}{\|\mathbf{v}\|}\mathbf{i} + \frac{v_2}{\|\mathbf{v}\|}\mathbf{j} + \frac{v_3}{\|\mathbf{v}\|}\mathbf{k} = (\cos\alpha)\mathbf{i} + (\cos\beta)\mathbf{j} + (\cos\gamma)\mathbf{k}$$

We leave it as an exercise for you to show that the direction cosines of a vector satisfy the equation

$$\cos^2\alpha + \cos^2\beta + \cos^2\gamma = 1 \tag{5}$$

▶ **Example 3**   Find the direction cosines of the vector $\mathbf{v} = 2\mathbf{i} - 4\mathbf{j} + 4\mathbf{k}$, and approximate the direction angles to the nearest degree.

Solution.   First we will normalize the vector $\mathbf{v}$ and then read off the components. We have $\|\mathbf{v}\| = \sqrt{4 + 16 + 16} = 6$, so that $\mathbf{v}/\|\mathbf{v}\| = \frac{1}{3}\mathbf{i} - \frac{2}{3}\mathbf{j} + \frac{2}{3}\mathbf{k}$. Thus,

$$\cos\alpha = \tfrac{1}{3}, \quad \cos\beta = -\tfrac{2}{3}, \quad \cos\gamma = \tfrac{2}{3}$$

With the help of a calculating utility we obtain

$$\alpha = \cos^{-1}\left(\tfrac{1}{3}\right) \approx 71°, \quad \beta = \cos^{-1}\left(-\tfrac{2}{3}\right) \approx 132°, \quad \gamma = \cos^{-1}\left(\tfrac{2}{3}\right) \approx 48° \quad ◀$$

▶ **Example 4**   Find the angle between a diagonal of a cube and one of its edges.

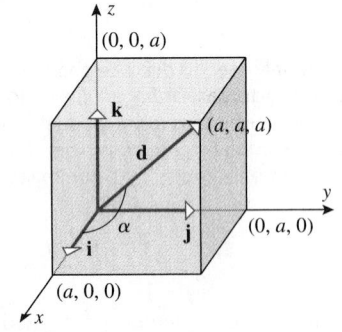

▲ **Figure 11.3.6**

Solution.   Assume that the cube has side a, and introduce a coordinate system as shown in Figure 11.3.6. In this coordinate system the vector

$$\mathbf{d} = a\mathbf{i} + a\mathbf{j} + a\mathbf{k}$$

is a diagonal of the cube and the unit vectors $\mathbf{i}$, $\mathbf{j}$, and $\mathbf{k}$ run along the edges. By symmetry, the diagonal makes the same angle with each edge, so it is sufficient to find the angle between $\mathbf{d}$ and $\mathbf{i}$ (the direction angle α). Thus,

$$\cos\alpha = \frac{\mathbf{d}\cdot\mathbf{i}}{\|\mathbf{d}\|\,\|\mathbf{i}\|} = \frac{a}{\|\mathbf{d}\|} = \frac{a}{\sqrt{3a^2}} = \frac{1}{\sqrt{3}}$$

and hence

$$\alpha = \cos^{-1}\left(\frac{1}{\sqrt{3}}\right) \approx 0.955 \text{ radian} \approx 54.7° \quad ◀$$

◼ DECOMPOSING VECTORS INTO ORTHOGONAL COMPONENTS

In many applications it is desirable to "decompose" a vector into a sum of two orthogonal vectors with convenient specified directions. For example, Figure 11.3.7 shows a block on an inclined plane. The downward force $\mathbf{F}$ that gravity exerts on the block can be decomposed into the sum

$$\mathbf{F} = \mathbf{F}_1 + \mathbf{F}_2$$

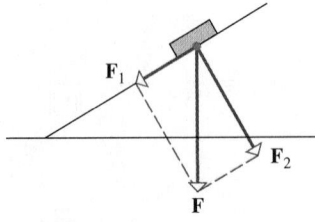

The force of gravity pulls the block against the ramp and down the ramp.

▲ **Figure 11.3.7**

where the force $\mathbf{F}_1$ is parallel to the ramp and the force $\mathbf{F}_2$ is perpendicular to the ramp. The forces $\mathbf{F}_1$ and $\mathbf{F}_2$ are useful because $\mathbf{F}_1$ is the force that pulls the block *along* the ramp, and $\mathbf{F}_2$ is the force that the block exerts *against* the ramp.

Thus, our next objective is to develop a computational procedure for decomposing a vector into a sum of orthogonal vectors. For this purpose, suppose that $\mathbf{e}_1$ and $\mathbf{e}_2$ are two orthogonal *unit* vectors in 2-space, and suppose that we want to express a given vector $\mathbf{v}$ as a sum

$$\mathbf{v} = \mathbf{w}_1 + \mathbf{w}_2$$

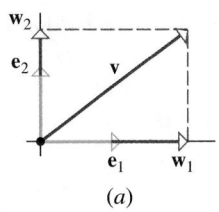

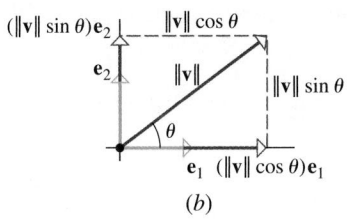

▲ **Figure 11.3.8**

so that $\mathbf{w}_1$ is a scalar multiple of $\mathbf{e}_1$ and $\mathbf{w}_2$ is a scalar multiple of $\mathbf{e}_2$ (Figure 11.3.8a). That is, we want to find scalars k_1 and k_2 such that

$$\mathbf{v} = k_1\mathbf{e}_1 + k_2\mathbf{e}_2 \qquad (6)$$

We can find k_1 by taking the dot product of $\mathbf{v}$ with $\mathbf{e}_1$. This yields

$$\begin{aligned}
\mathbf{v} \cdot \mathbf{e}_1 &= (k_1\mathbf{e}_1 + k_2\mathbf{e}_2) \cdot \mathbf{e}_1 \\
&= k_1(\mathbf{e}_1 \cdot \mathbf{e}_1) + k_2(\mathbf{e}_2 \cdot \mathbf{e}_1) \\
&= k_1\|\mathbf{e}_1\|^2 + 0 = k_1
\end{aligned}$$

Similarly,

$$\mathbf{v} \cdot \mathbf{e}_2 = (k_1\mathbf{e}_1 + k_2\mathbf{e}_2) \cdot \mathbf{e}_2 = k_1(\mathbf{e}_1 \cdot \mathbf{e}_2) + k_2(\mathbf{e}_2 \cdot \mathbf{e}_2) = 0 + k_2\|\mathbf{e}_2\|^2 = k_2$$

Substituting these expressions for k_1 and k_2 in (6) yields

$$\mathbf{v} = (\mathbf{v} \cdot \mathbf{e}_1)\mathbf{e}_1 + (\mathbf{v} \cdot \mathbf{e}_2)\mathbf{e}_2 \qquad (7)$$

In this formula we call $(\mathbf{v} \cdot \mathbf{e}_1)\mathbf{e}_1$ and $(\mathbf{v} \cdot \mathbf{e}_2)\mathbf{e}_2$ the *vector components* of $\mathbf{v}$ along $\mathbf{e}_1$ and $\mathbf{e}_2$, respectively; and we call $\mathbf{v} \cdot \mathbf{e}_1$ and $\mathbf{v} \cdot \mathbf{e}_2$ the *scalar components* of $\mathbf{v}$ along $\mathbf{e}_1$ and $\mathbf{e}_2$, respectively. If θ denotes the angle between $\mathbf{v}$ and $\mathbf{e}_1$, and the angle between $\mathbf{v}$ and $\mathbf{e}_2$ is $\pi/2$ or less, then the scalar components of $\mathbf{v}$ can be written in trigonometric form as

$$\mathbf{v} \cdot \mathbf{e}_1 = \|\mathbf{v}\|\cos\theta \quad \text{and} \quad \mathbf{v} \cdot \mathbf{e}_2 = \|\mathbf{v}\|\sin\theta \qquad (8)$$

> Note that the vector components of $\mathbf{v}$ along $\mathbf{e}_1$ and $\mathbf{e}_2$ are *vectors*, whereas the scalar components of $\mathbf{v}$ along $\mathbf{e}_1$ and $\mathbf{e}_2$ are *numbers*.

(Figure 11.3.8b). Moreover, the vector components of $\mathbf{v}$ can be expressed as

$$(\mathbf{v} \cdot \mathbf{e}_1)\mathbf{e}_1 = (\|\mathbf{v}\|\cos\theta)\mathbf{e}_1 \quad \text{and} \quad (\mathbf{v} \cdot \mathbf{e}_2)\mathbf{e}_2 = (\|\mathbf{v}\|\sin\theta)\mathbf{e}_2 \qquad (9)$$

and the decomposition (6) can be expressed as

$$\mathbf{v} = (\|\mathbf{v}\|\cos\theta)\mathbf{e}_1 + (\|\mathbf{v}\|\sin\theta)\mathbf{e}_2 \qquad (10)$$

provided the angle between $\mathbf{v}$ and $\mathbf{e}_2$ is at most $\pi/2$.

▶ **Example 5**   Let

$$\mathbf{v} = \langle 2, 3 \rangle, \quad \mathbf{e}_1 = \left\langle \frac{1}{\sqrt{2}}, \frac{1}{\sqrt{2}} \right\rangle, \quad \text{and} \quad \mathbf{e}_2 = \left\langle -\frac{1}{\sqrt{2}}, \frac{1}{\sqrt{2}} \right\rangle$$

Find the scalar components of $\mathbf{v}$ along $\mathbf{e}_1$ and $\mathbf{e}_2$ and the vector components of $\mathbf{v}$ along $\mathbf{e}_1$ and $\mathbf{e}_2$.

Solution.   The scalar components of $\mathbf{v}$ along $\mathbf{e}_1$ and $\mathbf{e}_2$ are

$$\mathbf{v} \cdot \mathbf{e}_1 = 2\left(\frac{1}{\sqrt{2}}\right) + 3\left(\frac{1}{\sqrt{2}}\right) = \frac{5}{\sqrt{2}}$$

$$\mathbf{v} \cdot \mathbf{e}_2 = 2\left(-\frac{1}{\sqrt{2}}\right) + 3\left(\frac{1}{\sqrt{2}}\right) = \frac{1}{\sqrt{2}}$$

so the vector components are

> Notice that in Example 5
> $(\mathbf{v} \cdot \mathbf{e}_1)\mathbf{e}_1 + (\mathbf{v} \cdot \mathbf{e}_2)\mathbf{e}_2 = \langle 2, 3 \rangle = \mathbf{v}$
> as guaranteed by (7).

$$(\mathbf{v} \cdot \mathbf{e}_1)\mathbf{e}_1 = \frac{5}{\sqrt{2}}\left\langle \frac{1}{\sqrt{2}}, \frac{1}{\sqrt{2}} \right\rangle = \left\langle \frac{5}{2}, \frac{5}{2} \right\rangle$$

$$(\mathbf{v} \cdot \mathbf{e}_2)\mathbf{e}_2 = \frac{1}{\sqrt{2}}\left\langle -\frac{1}{\sqrt{2}}, \frac{1}{\sqrt{2}} \right\rangle = \left\langle -\frac{1}{2}, \frac{1}{2} \right\rangle \quad ◀$$

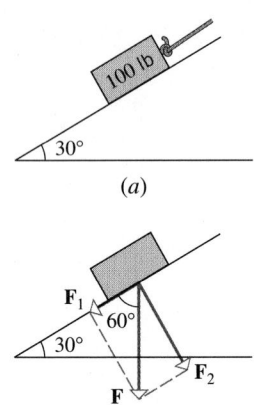

▲ **Figure 11.3.9**

▶ **Example 6**   A rope is attached to a 100 lb block on a ramp that is inclined at an angle of 30° with the ground (Figure 11.3.9a). How much force does the block exert against the ramp, and how much force must be applied to the rope in a direction parallel to the ramp to prevent the block from sliding down the ramp? (Assume that the ramp is smooth, that is, exerts no frictional forces.)

Solution.   Let **F** denote the downward force of gravity on the block (so $\|\mathbf{F}\| = 100$ lb), and let $\mathbf{F}_1$ and $\mathbf{F}_2$ be the vector components of **F** parallel and perpendicular to the ramp (as shown in Figure 11.3.9b). The lengths of $\mathbf{F}_1$ and $\mathbf{F}_2$ are

$$\|\mathbf{F}_1\| = \|\mathbf{F}\|\cos 60° = 100\left(\frac{1}{2}\right) = 50 \text{ lb}$$

$$\|\mathbf{F}_2\| = \|\mathbf{F}\|\sin 60° = 100\left(\frac{\sqrt{3}}{2}\right) \approx 86.6 \text{ lb}$$

Thus, the block exerts a force of approximately 86.6 lb against the ramp, and it requires a force of 50 lb to prevent the block from sliding down the ramp. ◀

■ **ORTHOGONAL PROJECTIONS**

The vector components of **v** along $\mathbf{e}_1$ and $\mathbf{e}_2$ in (7) are also called the *orthogonal projections* of **v** on $\mathbf{e}_1$ and $\mathbf{e}_2$ and are commonly denoted by

$$\text{proj}_{\mathbf{e}_1}\mathbf{v} = (\mathbf{v} \cdot \mathbf{e}_1)\mathbf{e}_1 \quad \text{and} \quad \text{proj}_{\mathbf{e}_2}\mathbf{v} = (\mathbf{v} \cdot \mathbf{e}_2)\mathbf{e}_2$$

In general, if **e** is a unit vector, then we define the ***orthogonal projection of* v *on* e** to be

$$\text{proj}_{\mathbf{e}}\mathbf{v} = (\mathbf{v} \cdot \mathbf{e})\mathbf{e} \tag{11}$$

The orthogonal projection of **v** on an arbitrary nonzero vector **b** can be obtained by normalizing **b** and then applying Formula (11); that is,

$$\text{proj}_{\mathbf{b}}\mathbf{v} = \left(\mathbf{v} \cdot \frac{\mathbf{b}}{\|\mathbf{b}\|}\right)\left(\frac{\mathbf{b}}{\|\mathbf{b}\|}\right)$$

which can be rewritten as

$$\text{proj}_{\mathbf{b}}\mathbf{v} = \frac{\mathbf{v} \cdot \mathbf{b}}{\|\mathbf{b}\|^2}\mathbf{b} \tag{12}$$

Geometrically, if **b** and **v** have a common initial point, then $\text{proj}_{\mathbf{b}}\mathbf{v}$ is the vector that is determined when a perpendicular is dropped from the terminal point of **v** to the line through **b** (illustrated in Figure 11.3.10 in two cases).

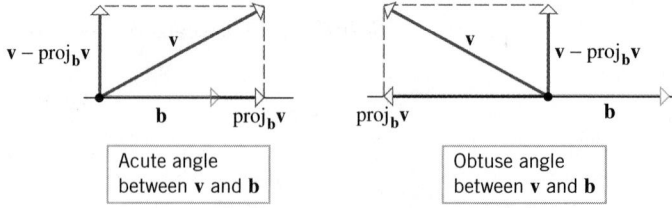

▶ **Figure 11.3.10**

Moreover, it is evident from Figure 11.3.10 that if we subtract $\text{proj}_{\mathbf{b}}\mathbf{v}$ from **v**, then the resulting vector

$$\mathbf{v} - \text{proj}_{\mathbf{b}}\mathbf{v}$$

will be orthogonal to **b**; we call this the ***vector component of* v *orthogonal to* b**.

▶ **Example 7**   Find the orthogonal projection of $v = i + j + k$ on $b = 2i + 2j$, and then find the vector component of v orthogonal to b.

Solution.   We have

$$v \cdot b = (i + j + k) \cdot (2i + 2j) = 2 + 2 + 0 = 4$$
$$\|b\|^2 = 2^2 + 2^2 = 8$$

Thus, the orthogonal projection of v on b is

$$\text{proj}_b v = \frac{v \cdot b}{\|b\|^2} b = \frac{4}{8}(2i + 2j) = i + j$$

and the vector component of v orthogonal to b is

$$v - \text{proj}_b v = (i + j + k) - (i + j) = k$$

These results are consistent with Figure 11.3.11. ◀

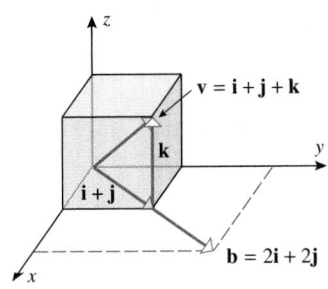

Stated informally, the orthogonal projection $\text{proj}_b v$ is the "shadow" that v casts on the line through b.

▲ **Figure 11.3.11**

■ WORK

In Section 6.6 we discussed the work done by a constant force acting on an object that moves along a line. We defined the work W done on the object by a constant force of magnitude F acting in the direction of motion over a distance d to be

$$W = Fd = \text{force} \times \text{distance} \qquad (13)$$

If we let F denote a force vector of magnitude $\|F\| = F$ *acting in the direction of motion,* then we can write (13) as

$$W = \|F\|d$$

Furthermore, if we assume that the object moves along a line from point P to point Q, then $d = \|\overrightarrow{PQ}\|$, so that the work can be expressed entirely in vector form as

$$W = \|F\|\|\overrightarrow{PQ}\|$$

(Figure 11.3.12*a*). The vector $\overrightarrow{PQ}$ is called the *displacement vector* for the object. In the case where a constant force F is not in the direction of motion, but rather makes an angle θ with the displacement vector, then we *define* the work W done by F to be

$$W = (\|F\|\cos\theta)\|\overrightarrow{PQ}\| = F \cdot \overrightarrow{PQ} \qquad (14)$$

(Figure 11.3.12*b*).

Note that in Formula (14) the quantity $\|F\|\cos\theta$ is the scalar component of force along the displacement vector. Thus, in the case where $\cos\theta > 0$, a force of magnitude $\|F\|$ acting at an angle θ does the same work as a force of magnitude $\|F\|\cos\theta$ acting in the direction of motion.

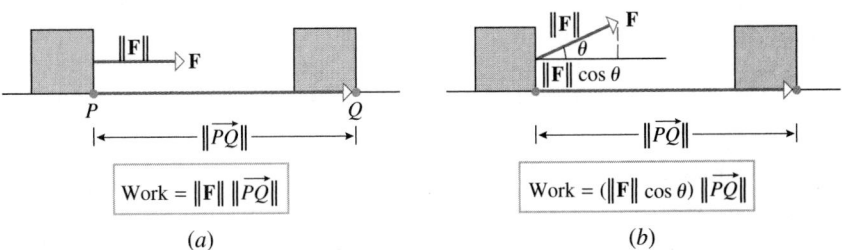

▲ **Figure 11.3.12**

▶ **Example 8**   A wagon is pulled horizontally by exerting a constant force of 10 lb on the handle at an angle of 60° with the horizontal. How much work is done in moving the wagon 50 ft?

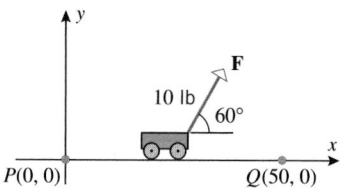

▲ Figure 11.3.13

Solution. Introduce an xy-coordinate system so that the wagon moves from $P(0, 0)$ to $Q(50, 0)$ along the x-axis (Figure 11.3.13). In this coordinate system

$$\overrightarrow{PQ} = 50\mathbf{i}$$

and

$$\mathbf{F} = (10\cos 60°)\mathbf{i} + (10\sin 60°)\mathbf{j} = 5\mathbf{i} + 5\sqrt{3}\mathbf{j}$$

so the work done is

$$W = \mathbf{F} \cdot \overrightarrow{PQ} = (5\mathbf{i} + 5\sqrt{3}\mathbf{j}) \cdot (50\mathbf{i}) = 250 \text{ ft·lb} \blacktriangleleft$$

✔QUICK CHECK EXERCISES 11.3   (See page 794 for answers.)

1. $\langle 3, 1, -2 \rangle \cdot \langle 6, 0, 5 \rangle = $ _____

2. Suppose that $\mathbf{u}$, $\mathbf{v}$, and $\mathbf{w}$ are vectors in 3-space such that $\|\mathbf{u}\| = 5$, $\mathbf{u} \cdot \mathbf{v} = 7$, and $\mathbf{u} \cdot \mathbf{w} = -3$.
   (a) $\mathbf{u} \cdot \mathbf{u} = $ _____   (b) $\mathbf{v} \cdot \mathbf{u} = $ _____
   (c) $\mathbf{u} \cdot (\mathbf{v} - \mathbf{w}) = $ _____   (d) $\mathbf{u} \cdot (2\mathbf{w}) = $ _____

3. For the vectors $\mathbf{u}$ and $\mathbf{v}$ in the preceding exercise, if the angle between $\mathbf{u}$ and $\mathbf{v}$ is $\pi/3$, then $\|\mathbf{v}\| = $ _____.

4. The direction cosines of $\langle 2, -1, 3 \rangle$ are $\cos\alpha = $ _____, $\cos\beta = $ _____, and $\cos\gamma = $ _____.

5. The orthogonal projection of $\mathbf{v} = 10\mathbf{i}$ on $\mathbf{b} = -3\mathbf{i} + \mathbf{j}$ is _____.

EXERCISE SET 11.3   [C] CAS

1. In each part, find the dot product of the vectors and the cosine of the angle between them.
   (a) $\mathbf{u} = \mathbf{i} + 2\mathbf{j}$, $\mathbf{v} = 6\mathbf{i} - 8\mathbf{j}$
   (b) $\mathbf{u} = \langle -7, -3 \rangle$, $\mathbf{v} = \langle 0, 1 \rangle$
   (c) $\mathbf{u} = \mathbf{i} - 3\mathbf{j} + 7\mathbf{k}$, $\mathbf{v} = 8\mathbf{i} - 2\mathbf{j} - 2\mathbf{k}$
   (d) $\mathbf{u} = \langle -3, 1, 2 \rangle$, $\mathbf{v} = \langle 4, 2, -5 \rangle$

2. In each part use the given information to find $\mathbf{u} \cdot \mathbf{v}$.
   (a) $\|\mathbf{u}\| = 1$, $\|\mathbf{v}\| = 2$, the angle between $\mathbf{u}$ and $\mathbf{v}$ is $\pi/6$.
   (b) $\|\mathbf{u}\| = 2$, $\|\mathbf{v}\| = 3$, the angle between $\mathbf{u}$ and $\mathbf{v}$ is $135°$.

3. In each part, determine whether $\mathbf{u}$ and $\mathbf{v}$ make an acute angle, an obtuse angle, or are orthogonal.
   (a) $\mathbf{u} = 7\mathbf{i} + 3\mathbf{j} + 5\mathbf{k}$, $\mathbf{v} = -8\mathbf{i} + 4\mathbf{j} + 2\mathbf{k}$
   (b) $\mathbf{u} = 6\mathbf{i} + \mathbf{j} + 3\mathbf{k}$, $\mathbf{v} = 4\mathbf{i} - 6\mathbf{k}$
   (c) $\mathbf{u} = \langle 1, 1, 1 \rangle$, $\mathbf{v} = \langle -1, 0, 0 \rangle$
   (d) $\mathbf{u} = \langle 4, 1, 6 \rangle$, $\mathbf{v} = \langle -3, 0, 2 \rangle$

FOCUS ON CONCEPTS

4. Does the triangle in 3-space with vertices $(-1, 2, 3)$, $(2, -2, 0)$, and $(3, 1, -4)$ have an obtuse angle? Justify your answer.

5. The accompanying figure shows eight vectors that are equally spaced around a circle of radius 1. Find the dot product of $\mathbf{v}_0$ with each of the other seven vectors.

6. The accompanying figure shows six vectors that are equally spaced around a circle of radius 5. Find the dot product of $\mathbf{v}_0$ with each of the other five vectors.

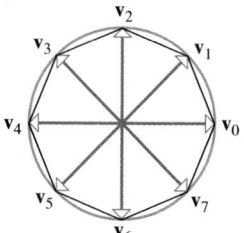

▲ Figure Ex-5

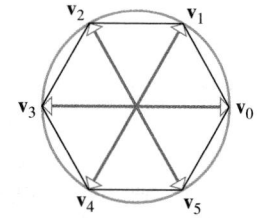

▲ Figure Ex-6

7. (a) Use vectors to show that $A(2, -1, 1)$, $B(3, 2, -1)$, and $C(7, 0, -2)$ are vertices of a right triangle. At which vertex is the right angle?
   (b) Use vectors to find the interior angles of the triangle with vertices $(-1, 0)$, $(2, -1)$, and $(1, 4)$. Express your answers to the nearest degree.

8. (a) Show that if $\mathbf{v} = a\mathbf{i} + b\mathbf{j}$ is a vector in 2-space, then the vectors
   $$\mathbf{v}_1 = -b\mathbf{i} + a\mathbf{j} \quad \text{and} \quad \mathbf{v}_2 = b\mathbf{i} - a\mathbf{j}$$
   are both orthogonal to $\mathbf{v}$.
   (b) Use the result in part (a) to find two unit vectors that are orthogonal to the vector $\mathbf{v} = 3\mathbf{i} - 2\mathbf{j}$. Sketch the vectors $\mathbf{v}$, $\mathbf{v}_1$, and $\mathbf{v}_2$.

9. Explain why each of the following expressions makes no sense.
   (a) $\mathbf{u} \cdot (\mathbf{v} \cdot \mathbf{w})$ (b) $(\mathbf{u} \cdot \mathbf{v}) + \mathbf{w}$
   (c) $\|\mathbf{u} \cdot \mathbf{v}\|$ (d) $k \cdot (\mathbf{u} + \mathbf{v})$

10. Explain why each of the following expressions makes sense.
   (a) $(\mathbf{u} \cdot \mathbf{v})\mathbf{w}$
   (b) $(\mathbf{u} \cdot \mathbf{v})(\mathbf{v} \cdot \mathbf{w})$
   (c) $\mathbf{u} \cdot \mathbf{v} + k$
   (d) $(k\mathbf{u}) \cdot \mathbf{v}$

11. Verify parts (b) and (c) of Theorem 11.3.2 for the vectors $\mathbf{u} = 6\mathbf{i} - \mathbf{j} + 2\mathbf{k}$, $\mathbf{v} = 2\mathbf{i} + 7\mathbf{j} + 4\mathbf{k}$, $\mathbf{w} = \mathbf{i} + \mathbf{j} - 3\mathbf{k}$ and $k = -5$.

12. Let $\mathbf{u} = \langle 1, 2 \rangle$, $\mathbf{v} = \langle 4, -2 \rangle$, and $\mathbf{w} = \langle 6, 0 \rangle$. Find
   (a) $\mathbf{u} \cdot (7\mathbf{v} + \mathbf{w})$
   (b) $\|(\mathbf{u} \cdot \mathbf{w})\mathbf{w}\|$
   (c) $\|\mathbf{u}\|(\mathbf{v} \cdot \mathbf{w})$
   (d) $(\|\mathbf{u}\|\mathbf{v}) \cdot \mathbf{w}$.

13. Find r so that the vector from the point $A(1, -1, 3)$ to the point $B(3, 0, 5)$ is orthogonal to the vector from A to the point $P(r, r, r)$.

14. Find two unit vectors in 2-space that make an angle of $45°$ with $4\mathbf{i} + 3\mathbf{j}$.

15–16 Find the direction cosines of $\mathbf{v}$ and confirm that they satisfy Equation (5). Then use the direction cosines to approximate the direction angles to the nearest degree. ■

15. (a) $\mathbf{v} = \mathbf{i} + \mathbf{j} - \mathbf{k}$
   (b) $\mathbf{v} = 2\mathbf{i} - 2\mathbf{j} + \mathbf{k}$

16. (a) $\mathbf{v} = 3\mathbf{i} - 2\mathbf{j} - 6\mathbf{k}$
   (b) $\mathbf{v} = 3\mathbf{i} - 4\mathbf{k}$

FOCUS ON CONCEPTS

17. Show that the direction cosines of a vector satisfy
$$\cos^2 \alpha + \cos^2 \beta + \cos^2 \gamma = 1$$

18. Let θ and λ be the angles shown in the accompanying figure. Show that the direction cosines of $\mathbf{v}$ can be expressed as
$$\cos \alpha = \cos \lambda \cos \theta$$
$$\cos \beta = \cos \lambda \sin \theta$$
$$\cos \gamma = \sin \lambda$$

[*Hint:* Express $\mathbf{v}$ in component form and normalize.]

19. The accompanying figure shows a cube.
   (a) Find the angle between the vectors $\mathbf{d}$ and $\mathbf{u}$ to the nearest degree.
   (b) Make a conjecture about the angle between the vectors $\mathbf{d}$ and $\mathbf{v}$, and confirm your conjecture by computing the angle.

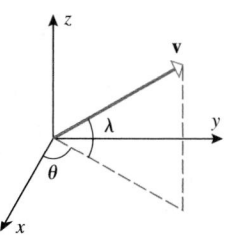

▲ **Figure Ex-18**

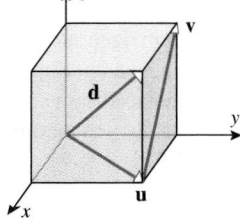

▲ **Figure Ex-19**

20. Show that two nonzero vectors $\mathbf{v}_1$ and $\mathbf{v}_2$ are orthogonal if and only if their direction cosines satisfy
$$\cos \alpha_1 \cos \alpha_2 + \cos \beta_1 \cos \beta_2 + \cos \gamma_1 \cos \gamma_2 = 0$$

21. Use the result in Exercise 18 to find the direction angles of the vector shown in the accompanying figure to the nearest degree.

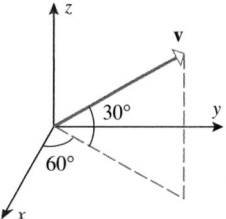

◀ **Figure Ex-21**

22. Find, to the nearest degree, the acute angle formed by two diagonals of a cube.

23. Find, to the nearest degree, the angles that a diagonal of a box with dimensions 10 cm by 15 cm by 25 cm makes with the edges of the box.

24. In each part, find the vector component of $\mathbf{v}$ along $\mathbf{b}$ and the vector component of $\mathbf{v}$ orthogonal to $\mathbf{b}$. Then sketch the vectors $\mathbf{v}$, $\text{proj}_\mathbf{b}\mathbf{v}$, and $\mathbf{v} - \text{proj}_\mathbf{b}\mathbf{v}$.
   (a) $\mathbf{v} = 2\mathbf{i} - \mathbf{j}$, $\mathbf{b} = 3\mathbf{i} + 4\mathbf{j}$
   (b) $\mathbf{v} = \langle 4, 5 \rangle$, $\mathbf{b} = \langle 1, -2 \rangle$
   (c) $\mathbf{v} = -3\mathbf{i} - 2\mathbf{j}$, $\mathbf{b} = 2\mathbf{i} + \mathbf{j}$

25. In each part, find the vector component of $\mathbf{v}$ along $\mathbf{b}$ and the vector component of $\mathbf{v}$ orthogonal to $\mathbf{b}$.
   (a) $\mathbf{v} = 2\mathbf{i} - \mathbf{j} + 3\mathbf{k}$, $\mathbf{b} = \mathbf{i} + 2\mathbf{j} + 2\mathbf{k}$
   (b) $\mathbf{v} = \langle 4, -1, 7 \rangle$, $\mathbf{b} = \langle 2, 3, -6 \rangle$

26–27 Express the vector $\mathbf{v}$ as the sum of a vector parallel to $\mathbf{b}$ and a vector orthogonal to $\mathbf{b}$. ■

26. (a) $\mathbf{v} = 2\mathbf{i} - 4\mathbf{j}$, $\mathbf{b} = \mathbf{i} + \mathbf{j}$
   (b) $\mathbf{v} = 3\mathbf{i} + \mathbf{j} - 2\mathbf{k}$, $\mathbf{b} = 2\mathbf{i} - \mathbf{k}$
   (c) $\mathbf{v} = 4\mathbf{i} - 2\mathbf{j} + 6\mathbf{k}$, $\mathbf{b} = -2\mathbf{i} + \mathbf{j} - 3\mathbf{k}$

27. (a) $\mathbf{v} = \langle -3, 5 \rangle$, $\mathbf{b} = \langle 1, 1 \rangle$
   (b) $\mathbf{v} = \langle -2, 1, 6 \rangle$, $\mathbf{b} = \langle 0, -2, 1 \rangle$
   (c) $\mathbf{v} = \langle 1, 4, 1 \rangle$, $\mathbf{b} = \langle 3, -2, 5 \rangle$

28–31 True–False Determine whether the statement is true or false. Explain your answer. ■

28. If $\mathbf{a} \cdot \mathbf{b} = \mathbf{a} \cdot \mathbf{c}$ and $\mathbf{a} \neq \mathbf{0}$, then $\mathbf{b} = \mathbf{c}$.

29. If $\mathbf{v}$ and $\mathbf{w}$ are nonzero orthogonal vectors, then $\mathbf{v} + \mathbf{w} \neq \mathbf{0}$.

30. If $\mathbf{u}$ is a unit vector that is parallel to a nonzero vector $\mathbf{v}$, then $\mathbf{u} \cdot \mathbf{v} = \pm\|\mathbf{v}\|$.

31. If $\mathbf{v}$ and $\mathbf{b}$ are nonzero vectors, then the orthogonal projection of $\mathbf{v}$ on $\mathbf{b}$ is a vector that is parallel to $\mathbf{b}$.

32. If L is a line in 2-space or 3-space that passes through the points A and B, then the distance from a point P to the line L is equal to the length of the component of the vector $\overrightarrow{AP}$ that is orthogonal to the vector $\overrightarrow{AB}$ (see the accompanying figure). Use this result to find the distance from the point $P(1, 0)$ to the line through $A(2, -3)$ and $B(5, 1)$.

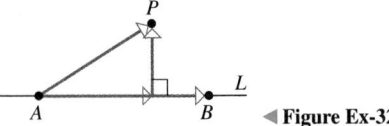

◀ **Figure Ex-32**

33. Use the method of Exercise 32 to find the distance from the point $P(-3, 1, 2)$ to the line through $A(1, 1, 0)$ and $B(-2, 3, -4)$.

34. As shown in the accompanying figure, a child with mass 34 kg is seated on a smooth (frictionless) playground slide that is inclined at an angle of $27°$ with the horizontal. How much force does the child exert on the slide, and how much force must be applied in the direction of **P** to prevent the child from sliding down the slide? Take the acceleration due to gravity to be 9.8 m/s^2.

35. For the child in Exercise 34, how much force must be applied in the direction of **Q** (shown in the accompanying figure) to prevent the child from sliding down the slide?

▲ **Figure Ex-34**

▲ **Figure Ex-35**

36. Find the work done by a force $\mathbf{F} = -3\mathbf{j}$ pounds applied to a point that moves on a line from $(1, 3)$ to $(4, 7)$. Assume that distance is measured in feet.

37. A force of $\mathbf{F} = 4\mathbf{i} - 6\mathbf{j} + \mathbf{k}$ newtons is applied to a point that moves a distance of 15 meters in the direction of the vector $\mathbf{i} + \mathbf{j} + \mathbf{k}$. How much work is done?

38. A boat travels 100 meters due north while the wind exerts a force of 500 newtons toward the northeast. How much work does the wind do?

FOCUS ON CONCEPTS

39. Let **u** and **v** be adjacent sides of a parallelogram. Use vectors to prove that the diagonals of the parallelogram are perpendicular if the sides are equal in length.

40. Let **u** and **v** be adjacent sides of a parallelogram. Use vectors to prove that the parallelogram is a rectangle if the diagonals are equal in length.

41. Prove that
$$\|\mathbf{u} + \mathbf{v}\|^2 + \|\mathbf{u} - \mathbf{v}\|^2 = 2\|\mathbf{u}\|^2 + 2\|\mathbf{v}\|^2$$
and interpret the result geometrically by translating it into a theorem about parallelograms.

42. Prove: $\mathbf{u} \cdot \mathbf{v} = \frac{1}{4}\|\mathbf{u} + \mathbf{v}\|^2 - \frac{1}{4}\|\mathbf{u} - \mathbf{v}\|^2$.

43. Show that if $\mathbf{v}_1$, $\mathbf{v}_2$, and $\mathbf{v}_3$ are mutually orthogonal nonzero vectors in 3-space, and if a vector **v** in 3-space is expressed as
$$\mathbf{v} = c_1\mathbf{v}_1 + c_2\mathbf{v}_2 + c_3\mathbf{v}_3$$
then the scalars c_1, c_2, and c_3 are given by the formulas
$$c_i = (\mathbf{v} \cdot \mathbf{v}_i)/\|\mathbf{v}_i\|^2, \quad i = 1, 2, 3$$

44. Show that the three vectors
$$\mathbf{v}_1 = 3\mathbf{i} - \mathbf{j} + 2\mathbf{k}, \quad \mathbf{v}_2 = \mathbf{i} + \mathbf{j} - \mathbf{k}, \quad \mathbf{v}_3 = \mathbf{i} - 5\mathbf{j} - 4\mathbf{k}$$
are mutually orthogonal, and then use the result of Exercise 43 to find scalars c_1, c_2, and c_3 so that
$$c_1\mathbf{v}_1 + c_2\mathbf{v}_2 + c_3\mathbf{v}_3 = \mathbf{i} - \mathbf{j} + \mathbf{k}$$

C 45. For each x in $(-\infty, +\infty)$, let $\mathbf{u}(x)$ be the vector from the origin to the point $P(x, y)$ on the curve $y = x^2 + 1$, and $\mathbf{v}(x)$ the vector from the origin to the point $Q(x, y)$ on the line $y = -x - 1$.
(a) Use a CAS to find, to the nearest degree, the minimum angle between $\mathbf{u}(x)$ and $\mathbf{v}(x)$ for x in $(-\infty, +\infty)$.
(b) Determine whether there are any real values of x for which $\mathbf{u}(x)$ and $\mathbf{v}(x)$ are orthogonal.

C 46. Let **u** be a unit vector in the xy-plane of an xyz-coordinate system, and let **v** be a unit vector in the yz-plane. Let θ_1 be the angle between **u** and **i**, let θ_2 be the angle between **v** and **k**, and let θ be the angle between **u** and **v**.
(a) Show that $\cos\theta = \pm\sin\theta_1\sin\theta_2$.
(b) Find θ if θ is acute and $\theta_1 = \theta_2 = 45°$.
(c) Use a CAS to find, to the nearest degree, the maximum and minimum values of θ if θ is acute and $\theta_2 = 2\theta_1$.

47. Prove parts (b) and (e) of Theorem 11.3.2 for vectors in 3-space.

48. **Writing** Discuss some of the similarities and differences between the multiplication properties of real numbers and those of the dot product of vectors.

49. **Writing** Discuss the merits of the following claim: "Suppose an algebraic identity involves only the addition, subtraction, and multiplication of real numbers. If the numbers are replaced by vectors, and the multiplication is replaced by the dot product, then an identity involving vectors will result."

✔ **QUICK CHECK ANSWERS 11.3**

1. 8 **2.** (a) 25 (b) 7 (c) 10 (d) -6 **3.** $\frac{14}{5}$ **4.** $\dfrac{2}{\sqrt{14}}; -\dfrac{1}{\sqrt{14}}; \dfrac{3}{\sqrt{14}}$ **5.** $9\mathbf{i} - 3\mathbf{j}$

11.4 CROSS PRODUCT

In many applications of vectors in mathematics, physics, and engineering, there is a need to find a vector that is orthogonal to two given vectors. In this section we will discuss a new type of vector multiplication that can be used for this purpose.

■ DETERMINANTS

Some of the concepts that we will develop in this section require basic ideas about ***determinants***, which are functions that assign numerical values to square arrays of numbers. For example, if a_1, a_2, b_1, and b_2 are real numbers, then we define a **2×2 *determinant*** by

$$\begin{vmatrix} a_1 & a_2 \\ b_1 & b_2 \end{vmatrix} = a_1 b_2 - a_2 b_1 \tag{1}$$

The purpose of the arrows is to help you remember the formula—the determinant is the product of the entries on the rightward arrow minus the product of the entries on the leftward arrow. For example,

$$\begin{vmatrix} 3 & -2 \\ 4 & 5 \end{vmatrix} = (3)(5) - (-2)(4) = 15 + 8 = 23$$

A **3×3 *determinant*** is defined in terms of 2×2 determinants by

$$\begin{vmatrix} a_1 & a_2 & a_3 \\ b_1 & b_2 & b_3 \\ c_1 & c_2 & c_3 \end{vmatrix} = a_1 \begin{vmatrix} b_2 & b_3 \\ c_2 & c_3 \end{vmatrix} - a_2 \begin{vmatrix} b_1 & b_3 \\ c_1 & c_3 \end{vmatrix} + a_3 \begin{vmatrix} b_1 & b_2 \\ c_1 & c_2 \end{vmatrix} \tag{2}$$

The right side of this formula is easily remembered by noting that a_1, a_2, and a_3 are the entries in the first "row" of the left side, and the 2×2 determinants on the right side arise by deleting the first row and an appropriate column from the left side. The pattern is as follows:

$$\begin{vmatrix} a_1 & a_2 & a_3 \\ b_1 & b_2 & b_3 \\ c_1 & c_2 & c_3 \end{vmatrix} = a_1 \begin{vmatrix} a_1 & a_2 & a_3 \\ b_1 & b_2 & b_3 \\ c_1 & c_2 & c_3 \end{vmatrix} - a_2 \begin{vmatrix} a_1 & a_2 & a_3 \\ b_1 & b_2 & b_3 \\ c_1 & c_2 & c_3 \end{vmatrix} + a_3 \begin{vmatrix} a_1 & a_2 & a_3 \\ b_1 & b_2 & b_3 \\ c_1 & c_2 & c_3 \end{vmatrix}$$

For example,

$$\begin{vmatrix} 3 & -2 & -5 \\ 1 & 4 & -4 \\ 0 & 3 & 2 \end{vmatrix} = 3 \begin{vmatrix} 4 & -4 \\ 3 & 2 \end{vmatrix} - (-2) \begin{vmatrix} 1 & -4 \\ 0 & 2 \end{vmatrix} + (-5) \begin{vmatrix} 1 & 4 \\ 0 & 3 \end{vmatrix}$$

$$= 3(20) + 2(2) - 5(3) = 49$$

There are also definitions of 4×4 determinants, 5×5 determinants, and higher, but we will not need them in this text. Properties of determinants are studied in a branch of mathematics called ***linear algebra***, but we will only need the two properties stated in the following theorem.

11.4.1   THEOREM

(a)   If two rows in the array of a determinant are the same, then the value of the determinant is 0.

(b)   Interchanging two rows in the array of a determinant multiplies its value by -1.

We will give the proofs of parts (a) and (b) for 2×2 determinants and leave the proofs for 3×3 determinants as exercises.

PROOF (a)

$$\begin{vmatrix} a_1 & a_2 \\ a_1 & a_2 \end{vmatrix} = a_1 a_2 - a_2 a_1 = 0$$

PROOF (b)

$$\begin{vmatrix} b_1 & b_2 \\ a_1 & a_2 \end{vmatrix} = b_1 a_2 - b_2 a_1 = -(a_1 b_2 - a_2 b_1) = - \begin{vmatrix} a_1 & a_2 \\ b_1 & b_2 \end{vmatrix} \quad \blacksquare$$

■ CROSS PRODUCT

We now turn to the main concept in this section.

11.4.2   **DEFINITION**   If $\mathbf{u} = \langle u_1, u_2, u_3 \rangle$ and $\mathbf{v} = \langle v_1, v_2, v_3 \rangle$ are vectors in 3-space, then the *cross product* $\mathbf{u} \times \mathbf{v}$ is the vector defined by

$$\mathbf{u} \times \mathbf{v} = \begin{vmatrix} u_2 & u_3 \\ v_2 & v_3 \end{vmatrix} \mathbf{i} - \begin{vmatrix} u_1 & u_3 \\ v_1 & v_3 \end{vmatrix} \mathbf{j} + \begin{vmatrix} u_1 & u_2 \\ v_1 & v_2 \end{vmatrix} \mathbf{k} \tag{3}$$

or, equivalently,

$$\mathbf{u} \times \mathbf{v} = (u_2 v_3 - u_3 v_2)\mathbf{i} - (u_1 v_3 - u_3 v_1)\mathbf{j} + (u_1 v_2 - u_2 v_1)\mathbf{k} \tag{4}$$

Observe that the right side of Formula (3) has the same form as the right side of Formula (2), the difference being notation and the order of the factors in the three terms. Thus, we can rewrite (3) as

$$\mathbf{u} \times \mathbf{v} = \begin{vmatrix} \mathbf{i} & \mathbf{j} & \mathbf{k} \\ u_1 & u_2 & u_3 \\ v_1 & v_2 & v_3 \end{vmatrix} \tag{5}$$

However, this is just a mnemonic device and not a true determinant since the entries in a determinant are numbers, not vectors.

▶ **Example 1**   Let $\mathbf{u} = \langle 1, 2, -2 \rangle$ and $\mathbf{v} = \langle 3, 0, 1 \rangle$. Find

$$\text{(a) } \mathbf{u} \times \mathbf{v} \qquad \text{(b) } \mathbf{v} \times \mathbf{u}$$

Solution (a).

$$\mathbf{u} \times \mathbf{v} = \begin{vmatrix} \mathbf{i} & \mathbf{j} & \mathbf{k} \\ 1 & 2 & -2 \\ 3 & 0 & 1 \end{vmatrix}$$

$$= \begin{vmatrix} 2 & -2 \\ 0 & 1 \end{vmatrix} \mathbf{i} - \begin{vmatrix} 1 & -2 \\ 3 & 1 \end{vmatrix} \mathbf{j} + \begin{vmatrix} 1 & 2 \\ 3 & 0 \end{vmatrix} \mathbf{k} = 2\mathbf{i} - 7\mathbf{j} - 6\mathbf{k}$$

Solution (b).   We could use the method of part (a), but it is really not necessary to perform any computations. We need only observe that reversing $\mathbf{u}$ and $\mathbf{v}$ interchanges the second and third rows in (5), which in turn interchanges the rows in the arrays for the 2×2 determinants in (3). But interchanging the rows in the array of a 2×2 determinant reverses its sign, so the net effect of reversing the factors in a cross product is to reverse the signs of the components. Thus, by inspection

$$\mathbf{v} \times \mathbf{u} = -(\mathbf{u} \times \mathbf{v}) = -2\mathbf{i} + 7\mathbf{j} + 6\mathbf{k} \blacktriangleleft$$

▶ **Example 2**   Show that $\mathbf{u} \times \mathbf{u} = \mathbf{0}$ for any vector $\mathbf{u}$ in 3-space.

Solution.   We could let $\mathbf{u} = u_1\mathbf{i} + u_2\mathbf{j} + u_3\mathbf{k}$ and apply the method in part (a) of Example 1 to show that

$$\mathbf{u} \times \mathbf{u} = \begin{vmatrix} \mathbf{i} & \mathbf{j} & \mathbf{k} \\ u_1 & u_2 & u_3 \\ u_1 & u_2 & u_3 \end{vmatrix} = 0$$

However, the actual computations are unnecessary. We need only observe that if the two factors in a cross product are the same, then each 2×2 determinant in (3) is zero because its array has identical rows. Thus, $\mathbf{u} \times \mathbf{u} = \mathbf{0}$ by inspection. ◄

■ ALGEBRAIC PROPERTIES OF THE CROSS PRODUCT

Our next goal is to establish some of the basic algebraic properties of the cross product. As you read the discussion, keep in mind the essential differences between the cross product and the dot product:

- The cross product is defined only for vectors in 3-space, whereas the dot product is defined for vectors in 2-space and 3-space.

- The cross product of two vectors is a vector, whereas the dot product of two vectors is a scalar.

The main algebraic properties of the cross product are listed in the next theorem.

11.4.3   THEOREM   *If* $\mathbf{u}$, $\mathbf{v}$, *and* $\mathbf{w}$ *are any vectors in 3-space and* k *is any scalar, then:*

(*a*) $\mathbf{u} \times \mathbf{v} = -(\mathbf{v} \times \mathbf{u})$

(*b*) $\mathbf{u} \times (\mathbf{v} + \mathbf{w}) = (\mathbf{u} \times \mathbf{v}) + (\mathbf{u} \times \mathbf{w})$

(*c*) $(\mathbf{u} + \mathbf{v}) \times \mathbf{w} = (\mathbf{u} \times \mathbf{w}) + (\mathbf{v} \times \mathbf{w})$

(*d*) $k(\mathbf{u} \times \mathbf{v}) = (k\mathbf{u}) \times \mathbf{v} = \mathbf{u} \times (k\mathbf{v})$

(*e*) $\mathbf{u} \times \mathbf{0} = \mathbf{0} \times \mathbf{u} = \mathbf{0}$

(*f*) $\mathbf{u} \times \mathbf{u} = \mathbf{0}$

Whereas the order of the factors does not matter for ordinary multiplication, or for dot products, it does matter for cross products. Specifically, part (*a*) of Theorem 11.4.3 shows that reversing the order of the factors in a cross product reverses the direction of the resulting vector.

Parts (*a*) and (*f*) were addressed in Examples 1 and 2. The other proofs are left as exercises.

The following cross products occur so frequently that it is helpful to be familiar with them:

$$\begin{array}{lll} \mathbf{i} \times \mathbf{j} = \mathbf{k} & \mathbf{j} \times \mathbf{k} = \mathbf{i} & \mathbf{k} \times \mathbf{i} = \mathbf{j} \\ \mathbf{j} \times \mathbf{i} = -\mathbf{k} & \mathbf{k} \times \mathbf{j} = -\mathbf{i} & \mathbf{i} \times \mathbf{k} = -\mathbf{j} \end{array} \qquad (6)$$

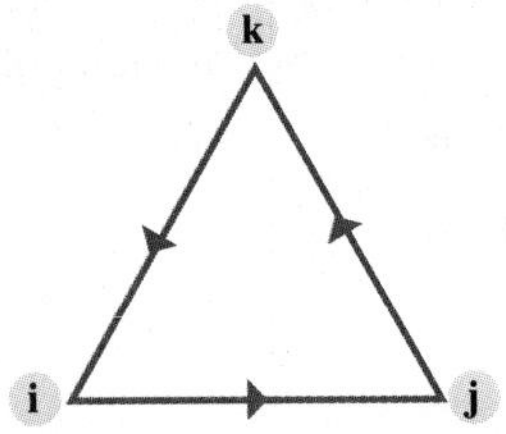

▲ Figure 11.4.1

These results are easy to obtain; for example,

$$\mathbf{i} \times \mathbf{j} = \begin{vmatrix} \mathbf{i} & \mathbf{j} & \mathbf{k} \\ 1 & 0 & 0 \\ 0 & 1 & 0 \end{vmatrix} = \begin{vmatrix} 0 & 0 \\ 1 & 0 \end{vmatrix} \mathbf{i} - \begin{vmatrix} 1 & 0 \\ 0 & 0 \end{vmatrix} \mathbf{j} + \begin{vmatrix} 1 & 0 \\ 0 & 1 \end{vmatrix} \mathbf{k} = \mathbf{k}$$

However, rather than computing these cross products each time you need them, you can use the diagram in Figure 11.4.1. In this diagram, the cross product of two consecutive vectors in the counterclockwise direction is the next vector around, and the cross product of two consecutive vectors in the clockwise direction is the negative of the next vector around.

WARNING We can write a product of three real numbers as uvw since the associative law $u(vw) = (uv)w$ ensures that the same value for the product results no matter how the factors are grouped. However, the associative law *does not* hold for cross products. For example,

$$\mathbf{i} \times (\mathbf{j} \times \mathbf{j}) = \mathbf{i} \times \mathbf{0} = \mathbf{0} \quad \text{and} \quad (\mathbf{i} \times \mathbf{j}) \times \mathbf{j} = \mathbf{k} \times \mathbf{j} = -\mathbf{i}$$

so that $\mathbf{i} \times (\mathbf{j} \times \mathbf{j}) \neq (\mathbf{i} \times \mathbf{j}) \times \mathbf{j}$. Thus, we cannot write a cross product with three vectors as $\mathbf{u} \times \mathbf{v} \times \mathbf{w}$, since this expression is ambiguous without parentheses.

■ **GEOMETRIC PROPERTIES OF THE CROSS PRODUCT**

The following theorem shows that the cross product of two vectors is orthogonal to both factors. This property of the cross product will be used many times in the following sections.

11.4.4 THEOREM *If* $\mathbf{u}$ *and* $\mathbf{v}$ *are vectors in 3-space, then:*

(a) $\mathbf{u} \cdot (\mathbf{u} \times \mathbf{v}) = 0$ ($\mathbf{u} \times \mathbf{v}$ *is orthogonal to* $\mathbf{u}$)

(b) $\mathbf{v} \cdot (\mathbf{u} \times \mathbf{v}) = 0$ ($\mathbf{u} \times \mathbf{v}$ *is orthogonal to* $\mathbf{v}$)

We will prove part (*a*). The proof of part (*b*) is similar.

PROOF (*a*) Let $\mathbf{u} = \langle u_1, u_2, u_3 \rangle$ and $\mathbf{v} = \langle v_1, v_2, v_3 \rangle$. Then from (4)

$$\mathbf{u} \times \mathbf{v} = \langle u_2 v_3 - u_3 v_2, u_3 v_1 - u_1 v_3, u_1 v_2 - u_2 v_1 \rangle \qquad (7)$$

so that

$$\mathbf{u} \cdot (\mathbf{u} \times \mathbf{v}) = u_1(u_2 v_3 - u_3 v_2) + u_2(u_3 v_1 - u_1 v_3) + u_3(u_1 v_2 - u_2 v_1) = 0 \quad ■$$

▶ **Example 3** Find a vector that is orthogonal to both of the vectors $\mathbf{u} = \langle 2, -1, 3 \rangle$ and $\mathbf{v} = \langle -7, 2, -1 \rangle$.

Solution. By Theorem 11.4.4, the vector $\mathbf{u} \times \mathbf{v}$ will be orthogonal to both $\mathbf{u}$ and $\mathbf{v}$. We compute that

$$\mathbf{u} \times \mathbf{v} = \begin{vmatrix} \mathbf{i} & \mathbf{j} & \mathbf{k} \\ 2 & -1 & 3 \\ -7 & 2 & -1 \end{vmatrix}$$

$$= \begin{vmatrix} -1 & 3 \\ 2 & -1 \end{vmatrix} \mathbf{i} - \begin{vmatrix} 2 & 3 \\ -7 & -1 \end{vmatrix} \mathbf{j} + \begin{vmatrix} 2 & -1 \\ -7 & 2 \end{vmatrix} \mathbf{k} = -5\mathbf{i} - 19\mathbf{j} - 3\mathbf{k} \quad ◀$$

Confirm that $\mathbf{u} \times \mathbf{v}$ in Example 3 is orthogonal to both $\mathbf{u}$ and $\mathbf{v}$ by computing $\mathbf{u} \cdot (\mathbf{u} \times \mathbf{v})$ and $\mathbf{v} \cdot (\mathbf{u} \times \mathbf{v})$.

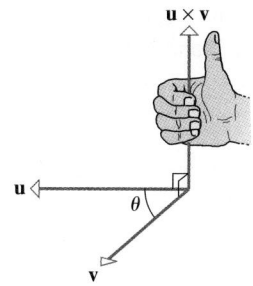

▲ Figure 11.4.2

It can be proved that if **u** and **v** are nonzero and nonparallel vectors, then the direction of **u** × **v** relative to **u** and **v** is determined by a right-hand rule;* that is, if the fingers of the right hand are cupped so they curl from **u** toward **v** in the direction of rotation that takes **u** into **v** in less than 180°, then the thumb will point (roughly) in the direction of **u** × **v** (Figure 11.4.2). For example, we stated in (6) that

$$\mathbf{i} \times \mathbf{j} = \mathbf{k}, \quad \mathbf{j} \times \mathbf{k} = \mathbf{i}, \quad \mathbf{k} \times \mathbf{i} = \mathbf{j}$$

all of which are consistent with the right-hand rule (verify).

The next theorem lists some more important geometric properties of the cross product.

11.4.5   THEOREM   *Let* **u** *and* **v** *be nonzero vectors in 3-space, and let* θ *be the angle between these vectors when they are positioned so their initial points coincide.*

(a) $\|\mathbf{u} \times \mathbf{v}\| = \|\mathbf{u}\| \|\mathbf{v}\| \sin \theta$

(b)   *The area A of the parallelogram that has* **u** *and* **v** *as adjacent sides is*

$$A = \|\mathbf{u} \times \mathbf{v}\| \tag{8}$$

(c)   **u** × **v** = **0** *if and only if* **u** *and* **v** *are parallel vectors, that is, if and only if they are scalar multiples of one another.*

PROOF *(a)*

$$\|\mathbf{u}\| \|\mathbf{v}\| \sin \theta = \|\mathbf{u}\| \|\mathbf{v}\| \sqrt{1 - \cos^2 \theta}$$

$$= \|\mathbf{u}\| \|\mathbf{v}\| \sqrt{1 - \frac{(\mathbf{u} \cdot \mathbf{v})^2}{\|\mathbf{u}\|^2 \|\mathbf{v}\|^2}} \qquad \boxed{\text{Theorem 11.3.3}}$$

$$= \sqrt{\|\mathbf{u}\|^2 \|\mathbf{v}\|^2 - (\mathbf{u} \cdot \mathbf{v})^2}$$

$$= \sqrt{(u_1^2 + u_2^2 + u_3^2)(v_1^2 + v_2^2 + v_3^2) - (u_1 v_1 + u_2 v_2 + u_3 v_3)^2}$$

$$= \sqrt{(u_2 v_3 - u_3 v_2)^2 + (u_1 v_3 - u_3 v_1)^2 + (u_1 v_2 - u_2 v_1)^2}$$

$$= \|\mathbf{u} \times \mathbf{v}\| \qquad \boxed{\text{See Formula (4).}}$$

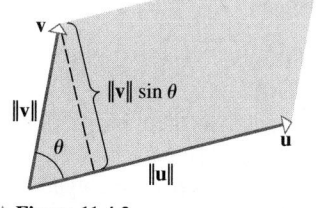

▲ Figure 11.4.3

PROOF *(b)*   Referring to Figure 11.4.3, the parallelogram that has **u** and **v** as adjacent sides can be viewed as having base $\|\mathbf{u}\|$ and altitude $\|\mathbf{v}\| \sin \theta$. Thus, its area A is

$$A = (\text{base})(\text{altitude}) = \|\mathbf{u}\| \|\mathbf{v}\| \sin \theta = \|\mathbf{u} \times \mathbf{v}\|$$

PROOF *(c)*   Since **u** and **v** are assumed to be nonzero vectors, it follows from part *(a)* that **u** × **v** = **0** if and only if $\sin \theta = 0$; this is true if and only if $\theta = 0$ or $\theta = \pi$ (since $0 \leq \theta \leq \pi$). Geometrically, this means that **u** × **v** = **0** if and only if **u** and **v** are parallel vectors. ∎

▶ **Example 4**   Find the area of the triangle that is determined by the points $P_1(2, 2, 0)$, $P_2(-1, 0, 2)$, and $P_3(0, 4, 3)$.

---

*Recall that we agreed to consider only right-handed coordinate systems in this text. Had we used left-handed systems instead, a "left-hand rule" would apply here.

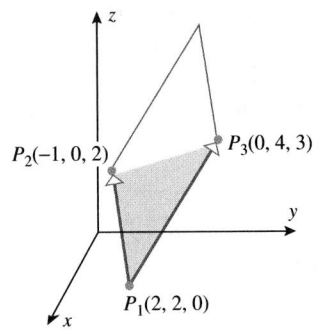

▲ **Figure 11.4.4**

Solution.   The area A of the triangle is half the area of the parallelogram determined by the vectors $\overrightarrow{P_1P_2}$ and $\overrightarrow{P_1P_3}$ (Figure 11.4.4). But $\overrightarrow{P_1P_2} = \langle -3, -2, 2 \rangle$ and $\overrightarrow{P_1P_3} = \langle -2, 2, 3 \rangle$, so

$$\overrightarrow{P_1P_2} \times \overrightarrow{P_1P_3} = \langle -10, 5, -10 \rangle$$

(verify), and consequently

$$A = \tfrac{1}{2} \| \overrightarrow{P_1P_2} \times \overrightarrow{P_1P_3} \| = \tfrac{15}{2} \quad \blacktriangleleft$$

■ SCALAR TRIPLE PRODUCTS

If $\mathbf{u} = \langle u_1, u_2, u_3 \rangle$, $\mathbf{v} = \langle v_1, v_2, v_3 \rangle$, and $\mathbf{w} = \langle w_1, w_2, w_3 \rangle$ are vectors in 3-space, then the number

$$\mathbf{u} \cdot (\mathbf{v} \times \mathbf{w})$$

is called the *scalar triple product* of $\mathbf{u}$, $\mathbf{v}$, and $\mathbf{w}$. It is not necessary to compute the dot product and cross product to evaluate a scalar triple product—the value can be obtained directly from the formula

$$\mathbf{u} \cdot (\mathbf{v} \times \mathbf{w}) = \begin{vmatrix} u_1 & u_2 & u_3 \\ v_1 & v_2 & v_3 \\ w_1 & w_2 & w_3 \end{vmatrix} \tag{9}$$

the validity of which can be seen by writing

$$\mathbf{u} \cdot (\mathbf{v} \times \mathbf{w}) = \mathbf{u} \cdot \left(\begin{vmatrix} v_2 & v_3 \\ w_2 & w_3 \end{vmatrix} \mathbf{i} - \begin{vmatrix} v_1 & v_3 \\ w_1 & w_3 \end{vmatrix} \mathbf{j} + \begin{vmatrix} v_1 & v_2 \\ w_1 & w_2 \end{vmatrix} \mathbf{k} \right)$$

$$= u_1 \begin{vmatrix} v_2 & v_3 \\ w_2 & w_3 \end{vmatrix} - u_2 \begin{vmatrix} v_1 & v_3 \\ w_1 & w_3 \end{vmatrix} + u_3 \begin{vmatrix} v_1 & v_2 \\ w_1 & w_2 \end{vmatrix}$$

$$= \begin{vmatrix} u_1 & u_2 & u_3 \\ v_1 & v_2 & v_3 \\ w_1 & w_2 & w_3 \end{vmatrix}$$

TECHNOLOGY MASTERY

Many calculating utilities have built-in cross product and determinant operations. If your calculating utility has these capabilities, use it to check the computations in Examples 1 and 5.

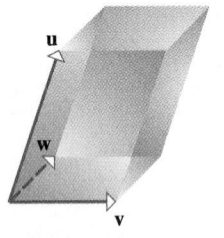

▲ **Figure 11.4.5**

It follows from Formula (10) that

$$\mathbf{u} \cdot (\mathbf{v} \times \mathbf{w}) = \pm V$$

The $+$ occurs when $\mathbf{u}$ makes an acute angle with $\mathbf{v} \times \mathbf{w}$ and the $-$ occurs when it makes an obtuse angle.

▶ **Example 5**   Calculate the scalar triple product $\mathbf{u} \cdot (\mathbf{v} \times \mathbf{w})$ of the vectors

$$\mathbf{u} = 3\mathbf{i} - 2\mathbf{j} - 5\mathbf{k}, \quad \mathbf{v} = \mathbf{i} + 4\mathbf{j} - 4\mathbf{k}, \quad \mathbf{w} = 3\mathbf{j} + 2\mathbf{k}$$

Solution.

$$\mathbf{u} \cdot (\mathbf{v} \times \mathbf{w}) = \begin{vmatrix} 3 & -2 & -5 \\ 1 & 4 & -4 \\ 0 & 3 & 2 \end{vmatrix} = 49 \quad \blacktriangleleft$$

■ GEOMETRIC PROPERTIES OF THE SCALAR TRIPLE PRODUCT

If $\mathbf{u}$, $\mathbf{v}$, and $\mathbf{w}$ are nonzero vectors in 3-space that are positioned so their initial points coincide, then these vectors form the adjacent sides of a parallelepiped (Figure 11.4.5). The following theorem establishes a relationship between the volume of this parallelepiped and the scalar triple product of the sides.

11.4.6   THEOREM   *Let $\mathbf{u}$, $\mathbf{v}$, and $\mathbf{w}$ be nonzero vectors in 3-space.*

(a)   The volume V of the parallelepiped that has $\mathbf{u}$, $\mathbf{v}$, and $\mathbf{w}$ as adjacent edges is

$$V = |\mathbf{u} \cdot (\mathbf{v} \times \mathbf{w})| \tag{10}$$

(b) $\mathbf{u} \cdot (\mathbf{v} \times \mathbf{w}) = 0$ if and only if $\mathbf{u}$, $\mathbf{v}$, and $\mathbf{w}$ lie in the same plane.

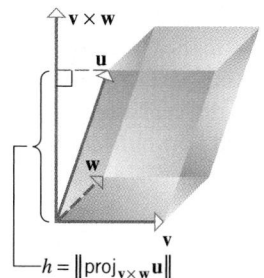

▲ Figure 11.4.6

PROOF (*a*) Referring to Figure 11.4.6, let us regard the base of the parallelepiped with **u**, **v**, and **w** as adjacent sides to be the parallelogram determined by **v** and **w**. Thus, the area of the base is $\|\mathbf{v} \times \mathbf{w}\|$, and the altitude h of the parallelepiped (shown in the figure) is the length of the orthogonal projection of **u** on the vector $\mathbf{v} \times \mathbf{w}$. Therefore, from Formula (12) of Section 11.3 we have

$$h = \|\text{proj}_{\mathbf{v} \times \mathbf{w}}\mathbf{u}\| = \frac{|\mathbf{u} \cdot (\mathbf{v} \times \mathbf{w})|}{\|\mathbf{v} \times \mathbf{w}\|^2}\|\mathbf{v} \times \mathbf{w}\| = \frac{|\mathbf{u} \cdot (\mathbf{v} \times \mathbf{w})|}{\|\mathbf{v} \times \mathbf{w}\|}$$

It now follows that the volume of the parallelepiped is

$$V = (\text{area of base})(\text{height}) = \|\mathbf{v} \times \mathbf{w}\|h = |\mathbf{u} \cdot (\mathbf{v} \times \mathbf{w})|$$

PROOF (*b*) The vectors **u**, **v**, and **w** lie in the same plane if and only if the parallelepiped with these vectors as adjacent sides has volume zero (why?). Thus, from part (*a*) the vectors lie in the same plane if and only if $\mathbf{u} \cdot (\mathbf{v} \times \mathbf{w}) = 0$. ■

ALGEBRAIC PROPERTIES OF THE SCALAR TRIPLE PRODUCT

We observed earlier in this section that the expression $\mathbf{u} \times \mathbf{v} \times \mathbf{w}$ must be avoided because it is ambiguous without parentheses. However, the expression $\mathbf{u} \cdot \mathbf{v} \times \mathbf{w}$ is not ambiguous—it has to mean $\mathbf{u} \cdot (\mathbf{v} \times \mathbf{w})$ and not $(\mathbf{u} \cdot \mathbf{v}) \times \mathbf{w}$ because we cannot form the cross product of a scalar and a vector. Similarly, the expression $\mathbf{u} \times \mathbf{v} \cdot \mathbf{w}$ must mean $(\mathbf{u} \times \mathbf{v}) \cdot \mathbf{w}$ and not $\mathbf{u} \times (\mathbf{v} \cdot \mathbf{w})$. Thus, when you see an expression of the form $\mathbf{u} \cdot \mathbf{v} \times \mathbf{w}$ or $\mathbf{u} \times \mathbf{v} \cdot \mathbf{w}$, the cross product is formed first and the dot product second.

Since interchanging two rows of a determinant multiplies its value by -1, making two row interchanges in a determinant has no effect on its value. This being the case, it follows that

$$\mathbf{u} \cdot (\mathbf{v} \times \mathbf{w}) = \mathbf{w} \cdot (\mathbf{u} \times \mathbf{v}) = \mathbf{v} \cdot (\mathbf{w} \times \mathbf{u}) \tag{11}$$

since the 3×3 determinants that are used to compute these scalar triple products can be obtained from one another by two row interchanges (verify).

Another useful formula can be obtained by rewriting the first equality in (11) as

$$\mathbf{u} \cdot (\mathbf{v} \times \mathbf{w}) = (\mathbf{u} \times \mathbf{v}) \cdot \mathbf{w}$$

and then omitting the superfluous parentheses to obtain

$$\mathbf{u} \cdot \mathbf{v} \times \mathbf{w} = \mathbf{u} \times \mathbf{v} \cdot \mathbf{w} \tag{12}$$

In words, this formula states that the dot and cross in a scalar triple product can be interchanged (provided the factors are grouped appropriately).

> A good way to remember Formula (11) is to observe that the second expression in the formula can be obtained from the first by leaving the dot, cross, and parentheses fixed, moving the first two vectors to the right, and bringing the third vector to the first position. The same procedure produces the third expression from the second and the first expression from the third (verify).

DOT AND CROSS PRODUCTS ARE COORDINATE INDEPENDENT

In Definitions 11.3.1 and 11.4.2 we defined the dot product and the cross product of two vectors in terms of the components of those vectors in a coordinate system. Thus, it is theoretically possible that changing the coordinate system might change $\mathbf{u} \cdot \mathbf{v}$ or $\mathbf{u} \times \mathbf{v}$, since the components of a vector depend on the coordinate system that is chosen. However, the relationships

$$\mathbf{u} \cdot \mathbf{v} = \|\mathbf{u}\|\|\mathbf{v}\|\cos\theta \tag{13}$$

$$\|\mathbf{u} \times \mathbf{v}\| = \|\mathbf{u}\|\|\mathbf{v}\|\sin\theta \tag{14}$$

> This independence of a coordinate system is important in applications because it allows us to choose any convenient coordinate system for solving a problem with full confidence that the choice will not affect computations that involve dot products or cross products.

that were obtained in Theorems 11.3.3 and 11.4.5 show that this is not the case. Formula (13) shows that the value of $\mathbf{u} \cdot \mathbf{v}$ depends only on the lengths of the vectors and the angle between them—not on the coordinate system. Similarly, Formula (14), in combination with the right-hand rule and Theorem 11.4.4, shows that $\mathbf{u} \times \mathbf{v}$ does not depend on the coordinate system (as long as it is right-handed).

World Perspectives/Getty Images

Astronauts use tools that are designed to limit forces that would impart unintended rotational motion to a satellite.

▮ MOMENTS AND ROTATIONAL MOTION IN 3-SPACE

Cross products play an important role in describing rotational motion in 3-space. For example, suppose that an astronaut on a satellite repair mission in space applies a force **F** at a point Q on the surface of a spherical satellite. If the force is directed along a line that passes through the center P of the satellite, then Newton's Second Law of Motion implies that the force will accelerate the satellite in the direction of **F**. However, if the astronaut applies the same force at an angle θ with the vector $\overrightarrow{PQ}$, then **F** will tend to cause a rotation, as well as an acceleration in the direction of **F**. To see why this is so, let us resolve **F** into a sum of orthogonal components $\mathbf{F} = \mathbf{F}_1 + \mathbf{F}_2$, where $\mathbf{F}_1$ is the orthogonal projection of **F** on the vector $\overrightarrow{PQ}$ and $\mathbf{F}_2$ is the component of **F** orthogonal to $\overrightarrow{PQ}$ (Figure 11.4.7). Since the force $\mathbf{F}_1$ acts along the line through the center of the satellite, it contributes to the linear acceleration of the satellite but does not cause any rotation. However, the force $\mathbf{F}_2$ is tangent to the circle around the satellite in the plane of **F** and $\overrightarrow{PQ}$, so it causes the satellite to rotate about an axis that is perpendicular to that plane.

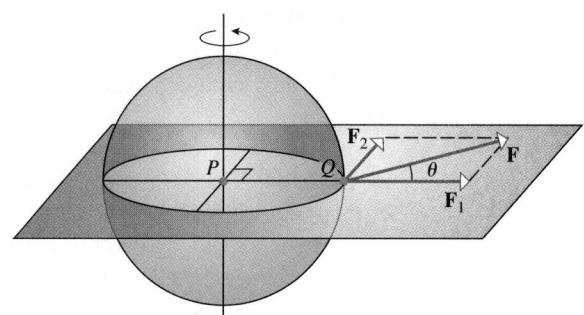

▶ **Figure 11.4.7**

You know from your own experience that the "tendency" for rotation about an axis depends both on the amount of force and how far from the axis it is applied. For example, it is easier to close a door by pushing on its outer edge than applying the same force close to the hinges. In fact, the tendency of rotation of the satellite can be measured by

$$\|\overrightarrow{PQ}\|\|\mathbf{F}_2\| \qquad \boxed{\text{distance from the center} \times \text{magnitude of the force}} \qquad (15)$$

However, $\|\mathbf{F}_2\| = \|\mathbf{F}\|\sin\theta$, so we can rewrite (15) as

$$\|\overrightarrow{PQ}\|\|\mathbf{F}\|\sin\theta = \|\overrightarrow{PQ} \times \mathbf{F}\|$$

This is called the *scalar moment* or *torque* of **F** about the point P. Scalar moments have units of force times distance—pound-feet or newton-meters, for example. The vector $\overrightarrow{PQ} \times \mathbf{F}$ is called the *vector moment* or *torque vector* of **F** about P.

Recalling that the direction of $\overrightarrow{PQ} \times \mathbf{F}$ is determined by the right-hand rule, it follows that the direction of rotation about P that results by applying the force **F** at the point Q is counterclockwise looking down the axis of $\overrightarrow{PQ} \times \mathbf{F}$ (Figure 11.4.7). Thus, the vector moment $\overrightarrow{PQ} \times \mathbf{F}$ captures the essential information about the rotational effect of the force—the magnitude of the cross product provides the scalar moment of the force, and the cross product vector itself provides the axis and direction of rotation.

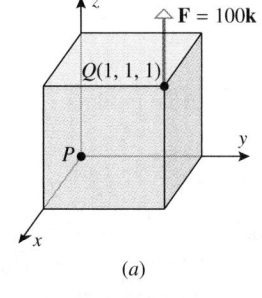

(a)

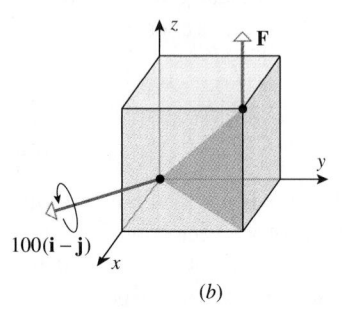

(b)

▲ **Figure 11.4.8**

▶ **Example 6** Figure 11.4.8a shows a force **F** of 100 N applied in the positive z-direction at the point $Q(1, 1, 1)$ of a cube whose sides have a length of 1 m. Assuming that the cube is free to rotate about the point $P(0, 0, 0)$ (the origin), find the scalar moment of the force about P, and describe the direction of rotation.

Solution. The force vector is $\mathbf{F} = 100\mathbf{k}$, and the vector from P to Q is $\overrightarrow{PQ} = \mathbf{i} + \mathbf{j} + \mathbf{k}$, so the vector moment of $\mathbf{F}$ about P is

$$\overrightarrow{PQ} \times \mathbf{F} = \begin{vmatrix} \mathbf{i} & \mathbf{j} & \mathbf{k} \\ 1 & 1 & 1 \\ 0 & 0 & 100 \end{vmatrix} = 100\mathbf{i} - 100\mathbf{j}$$

Thus, the scalar moment of $\mathbf{F}$ about P is $\|100\mathbf{i} - 100\mathbf{j}\| = 100\sqrt{2} \approx 141$ N·m, and the direction of rotation is counterclockwise looking along the vector $100\mathbf{i} - 100\mathbf{j} = 100(\mathbf{i} - \mathbf{j})$ toward its initial point (Figure 11.4.8*b*). ◄

✔QUICK CHECK EXERCISES 11.4   (*See page 805 for answers.*)

1. (a) $\begin{vmatrix} 3 & 2 \\ 4 & 5 \end{vmatrix} = $ _____   (b) $\begin{vmatrix} 3 & 2 & 1 \\ 3 & 2 & 1 \\ 5 & 5 & 5 \end{vmatrix} = $ _____

2. $\langle 1, 2, 0 \rangle \times \langle 3, 0, 4 \rangle = $ _____

3. Suppose that $\mathbf{u}$, $\mathbf{v}$, and $\mathbf{w}$ are vectors in 3-space such that $\mathbf{u} \times \mathbf{v} = \langle 2, 7, 3 \rangle$ and $\mathbf{u} \times \mathbf{w} = \langle -5, 4, 0 \rangle$.
   (a) $\mathbf{u} \times \mathbf{u} = $ _____   (b) $\mathbf{v} \times \mathbf{u} = $ _____

(c) $\mathbf{u} \times (\mathbf{v} + \mathbf{w}) = $ _____
(d) $\mathbf{u} \times (2\mathbf{w}) = $ _____

4. Let $\mathbf{u} = \mathbf{i} - 5\mathbf{k}$, $\mathbf{v} = 2\mathbf{i} - 4\mathbf{j} + \mathbf{k}$, and $\mathbf{w} = 3\mathbf{i} - 2\mathbf{j} + 5\mathbf{k}$.
   (a) $\mathbf{u} \cdot (\mathbf{v} \times \mathbf{w}) = $ _____
   (b) The volume of the parallelepiped that has $\mathbf{u}$, $\mathbf{v}$, and $\mathbf{w}$ as adjacent edges is $V = $ _____.

EXERCISE SET 11.4   [c] CAS

1. (a) Use a determinant to find the cross product

$$\mathbf{i} \times (\mathbf{i} + \mathbf{j} + \mathbf{k})$$

(b) Check your answer in part (a) by rewriting the cross product as

$$\mathbf{i} \times (\mathbf{i} + \mathbf{j} + \mathbf{k}) = (\mathbf{i} \times \mathbf{i}) + (\mathbf{i} \times \mathbf{j}) + (\mathbf{i} \times \mathbf{k})$$

and evaluating each term.

2. In each part, use the two methods in Exercise 1 to find
   (a) $\mathbf{j} \times (\mathbf{i} + \mathbf{j} + \mathbf{k})$ (b) $\mathbf{k} \times (\mathbf{i} + \mathbf{j} + \mathbf{k})$.

3–6 Find $\mathbf{u} \times \mathbf{v}$ and check that it is orthogonal to both $\mathbf{u}$ and $\mathbf{v}$. ■

3. $\mathbf{u} = \langle 1, 2, -3 \rangle$, $\mathbf{v} = \langle -4, 1, 2 \rangle$

4. $\mathbf{u} = 3\mathbf{i} + 2\mathbf{j} - \mathbf{k}$, $\mathbf{v} = -\mathbf{i} - 3\mathbf{j} + \mathbf{k}$

5. $\mathbf{u} = \langle 0, 1, -2 \rangle$, $\mathbf{v} = \langle 3, 0, -4 \rangle$

6. $\mathbf{u} = 4\mathbf{i} + \mathbf{k}$, $\mathbf{v} = 2\mathbf{i} - \mathbf{j}$

7. Let $\mathbf{u} = \langle 2, -1, 3 \rangle$, $\mathbf{v} = \langle 0, 1, 7 \rangle$, and $\mathbf{w} = \langle 1, 4, 5 \rangle$. Find
   (a) $\mathbf{u} \times (\mathbf{v} \times \mathbf{w})$ (b) $(\mathbf{u} \times \mathbf{v}) \times \mathbf{w}$
   (c) $(\mathbf{u} \times \mathbf{v}) \times (\mathbf{v} \times \mathbf{w})$ (d) $(\mathbf{v} \times \mathbf{w}) \times (\mathbf{u} \times \mathbf{v})$.

[c] **8.** Use a CAS or a calculating utility that can compute determinants or cross products to solve Exercise 7.

9. Find the direction cosines of $\mathbf{u} \times \mathbf{v}$ for the vectors $\mathbf{u}$ and $\mathbf{v}$ in the accompanying figure.

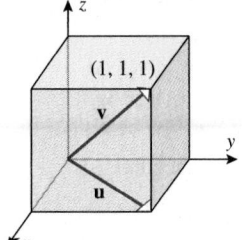

◄ Figure Ex-9

10. Find two unit vectors that are orthogonal to both

$$\mathbf{u} = -7\mathbf{i} + 3\mathbf{j} + \mathbf{k}, \quad \mathbf{v} = 2\mathbf{i} + 4\mathbf{k}$$

11. Find two unit vectors that are normal to the plane determined by the points $A(0, -2, 1)$, $B(1, -1, -2)$, and $C(-1, 1, 0)$.

12. Find two unit vectors that are parallel to the yz-plane and are orthogonal to the vector $3\mathbf{i} - \mathbf{j} + 2\mathbf{k}$.

13–16 True–False Determine whether the statement is true or false. Explain your answer. ■

13. If the cross product of two nonzero vectors is the zero vector, then each of the two vectors is a scalar multiple of the other.

14. For any three vectors $\mathbf{a}$, $\mathbf{b}$, and $\mathbf{c}$, we have $\mathbf{a} \times (\mathbf{b} \times \mathbf{c}) = (\mathbf{a} \times \mathbf{b}) \times \mathbf{c}$.

15. If $\mathbf{v} \times \mathbf{u} = \mathbf{v} \times \mathbf{w}$ and if $\mathbf{v} \neq \mathbf{0}$, then $\mathbf{u} = \mathbf{w}$.

16. If $\mathbf{u} = a\mathbf{v} + b\mathbf{w}$, then $\mathbf{u} \cdot \mathbf{v} \times \mathbf{w} = 0$.

17–18 Find the area of the parallelogram that has **u** and **v** as adjacent sides. ■

17. $\mathbf{u} = \mathbf{i} - \mathbf{j} + 2\mathbf{k},\quad \mathbf{v} = 3\mathbf{j} + \mathbf{k}$

18. $\mathbf{u} = 2\mathbf{i} + 3\mathbf{j},\quad \mathbf{v} = -\mathbf{i} + 2\mathbf{j} - 2\mathbf{k}$

19–20 Find the area of the triangle with vertices P, Q, and R. ■

19. $P(1, 5, -2),\quad Q(0, 0, 0),\quad R(3, 5, 1)$

20. $P(2, 0, -3),\quad Q(1, 4, 5),\quad R(7, 2, 9)$

21–24 Find $\mathbf{u} \cdot (\mathbf{v} \times \mathbf{w})$. ■

21. $\mathbf{u} = 2\mathbf{i} - 3\mathbf{j} + \mathbf{k},\quad \mathbf{v} = 4\mathbf{i} + \mathbf{j} - 3\mathbf{k},\quad \mathbf{w} = \mathbf{j} + 5\mathbf{k}$

22. $\mathbf{u} = \langle 1, -2, 2 \rangle,\quad \mathbf{v} = \langle 0, 3, 2 \rangle,\quad \mathbf{w} = \langle -4, 1, -3 \rangle$

23. $\mathbf{u} = \langle 2, 1, 0 \rangle,\quad \mathbf{v} = \langle 1, -3, 1 \rangle,\quad \mathbf{w} = \langle 4, 0, 1 \rangle$

24. $\mathbf{u} = \mathbf{i},\quad \mathbf{v} = \mathbf{i} + \mathbf{j},\quad \mathbf{w} = \mathbf{i} + \mathbf{j} + \mathbf{k}$

25–26 Use a scalar triple product to find the volume of the parallelepiped that has **u**, **v**, and **w** as adjacent edges. ■

25. $\mathbf{u} = \langle 2, -6, 2 \rangle,\quad \mathbf{v} = \langle 0, 4, -2 \rangle,\quad \mathbf{w} = \langle 2, 2, -4 \rangle$

26. $\mathbf{u} = 3\mathbf{i} + \mathbf{j} + 2\mathbf{k},\quad \mathbf{v} = 4\mathbf{i} + 5\mathbf{j} + \mathbf{k},\quad \mathbf{w} = \mathbf{i} + 2\mathbf{j} + 4\mathbf{k}$

27. In each part, use a scalar triple product to determine whether the vectors lie in the same plane.
(a) $\mathbf{u} = \langle 1, -2, 1 \rangle,\quad \mathbf{v} = \langle 3, 0, -2 \rangle,\quad \mathbf{w} = \langle 5, -4, 0 \rangle$
(b) $\mathbf{u} = 5\mathbf{i} - 2\mathbf{j} + \mathbf{k},\quad \mathbf{v} = 4\mathbf{i} - \mathbf{j} + \mathbf{k},\quad \mathbf{w} = \mathbf{i} - \mathbf{j}$
(c) $\mathbf{u} = \langle 4, -8, 1 \rangle,\quad \mathbf{v} = \langle 2, 1, -2 \rangle,\quad \mathbf{w} = \langle 3, -4, 12 \rangle$

28. Suppose that $\mathbf{u} \cdot (\mathbf{v} \times \mathbf{w}) = 3$. Find
(a) $\mathbf{u} \cdot (\mathbf{w} \times \mathbf{v})$ (b) $(\mathbf{v} \times \mathbf{w}) \cdot \mathbf{u}$
(c) $\mathbf{w} \cdot (\mathbf{u} \times \mathbf{v})$ (d) $\mathbf{v} \cdot (\mathbf{u} \times \mathbf{w})$
(e) $(\mathbf{u} \times \mathbf{w}) \cdot \mathbf{v}$ (f) $\mathbf{v} \cdot (\mathbf{w} \times \mathbf{w})$.

29. Consider the parallelepiped with adjacent edges

$$\mathbf{u} = 3\mathbf{i} + 2\mathbf{j} + \mathbf{k}$$
$$\mathbf{v} = \mathbf{i} + \mathbf{j} + 2\mathbf{k}$$
$$\mathbf{w} = \mathbf{i} + 3\mathbf{j} + 3\mathbf{k}$$

(a) Find the volume.
(b) Find the area of the face determined by **u** and **w**.
(c) Find the angle between **u** and the plane containing the face determined by **v** and **w**.

30. Show that in 3-space the distance d from a point P to the line L through points A and B can be expressed as

$$d = \frac{\|\overrightarrow{AP} \times \overrightarrow{AB}\|}{\|\overrightarrow{AB}\|}$$

31. Use the result in Exercise 30 to find the distance between the point P and the line through the points A and B.
(a) $P(-3, 1, 2),\quad A(1, 1, 0),\quad B(-2, 3, -4)$
(b) $P(4, 3),\quad A(2, 1),\quad B(0, 2)$

32. It is a theorem of solid geometry that the volume of a tetrahedron is $\frac{1}{3}$(area of base) · (height). Use this result to prove that the volume of a tetrahedron with adjacent edges given by the vectors **u**, **v**, and **w** is $\frac{1}{6}|\mathbf{u} \cdot (\mathbf{v} \times \mathbf{w})|$.

33. Use the result of Exercise 32 to find the volume of the tetrahedron with vertices

$$P(-1, 2, 0),\quad Q(2, 1, -3),\quad R(1, 0, 1),\quad S(3, -2, 3)$$

34. Let θ be the angle between the vectors $\mathbf{u} = 2\mathbf{i} + 3\mathbf{j} - 6\mathbf{k}$ and $\mathbf{v} = 2\mathbf{i} + 3\mathbf{j} + 6\mathbf{k}$.
(a) Use the dot product to find $\cos\theta$.
(b) Use the cross product to find $\sin\theta$.
(c) Confirm that $\sin^2\theta + \cos^2\theta = 1$.

FOCUS ON CONCEPTS

35. Let A, B, C, and D be four distinct points in 3-space. If $\overrightarrow{AB} \times \overrightarrow{CD} \neq \mathbf{0}$ and $\overrightarrow{AC} \cdot (\overrightarrow{AB} \times \overrightarrow{CD}) = 0$, explain why the line through A and B must intersect the line through C and D.

36. Let A, B, and C be three distinct noncollinear points in 3-space. Describe the set of all points P that satisfy the vector equation $\overrightarrow{AP} \cdot (\overrightarrow{AB} \times \overrightarrow{AC}) = 0$.

37. What can you say about the angle between nonzero vectors **u** and **v** if $\mathbf{u} \cdot \mathbf{v} = \|\mathbf{u} \times \mathbf{v}\|$?

38. Show that if **u** and **v** are vectors in 3-space, then

$$\|\mathbf{u} \times \mathbf{v}\|^2 = \|\mathbf{u}\|^2 \|\mathbf{v}\|^2 - (\mathbf{u} \cdot \mathbf{v})^2$$

[*Note:* This result is sometimes called **Lagrange's identity**.]

---

39. The accompanying figure shows a force **F** of 10 lb applied in the positive y-direction to the point $Q(1, 1, 1)$ of a cube whose sides have a length of 1 ft. In each part, find the scalar moment of **F** about the point P, and describe the direction of rotation, if any, if the cube is free to rotate about P.
(a) P is the point $(0, 0, 0)$.   (b) P is the point $(1, 0, 0)$.
(c) P is the point $(1, 0, 1)$.

40. The accompanying figure shows a force **F** of 1000 N applied to the corner of a box.
(a) Find the scalar moment of **F** about the point P.
(b) Find the direction angles of the vector moment of **F** about the point P to the nearest degree.

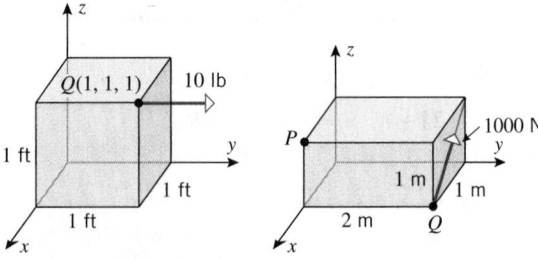

▲ **Figure Ex-39**   ▲ **Figure Ex-40**

41. As shown in the accompanying figure on the next page, a force of 200 N is applied at an angle of 18° to a point near the end of a monkey wrench. Find the scalar moment of the force about the center of the bolt. [*Note:* Treat this as a problem in two dimensions.]

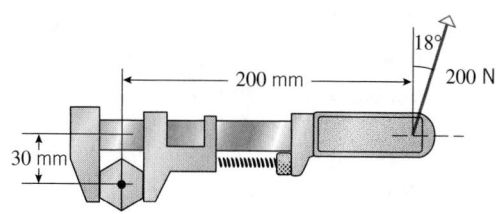

▲ Figure Ex-41

42. Prove parts (*b*) and (*c*) of Theorem 11.4.3.

43. Prove parts (*d*) and (*e*) of Theorem 11.4.3.

44. Prove part (*b*) of Theorem 11.4.1 for 3×3 determinants. [*Note:* Just give the proof for the first two rows.] Then use (*b*) to prove (*a*).

FOCUS ON CONCEPTS

45. Expressions of the form

$$\mathbf{u} \times (\mathbf{v} \times \mathbf{w}) \quad \text{and} \quad (\mathbf{u} \times \mathbf{v}) \times \mathbf{w}$$

are called **vector triple products**. It can be proved with some effort that

$$\mathbf{u} \times (\mathbf{v} \times \mathbf{w}) = (\mathbf{u} \cdot \mathbf{w})\mathbf{v} - (\mathbf{u} \cdot \mathbf{v})\mathbf{w}$$
$$(\mathbf{u} \times \mathbf{v}) \times \mathbf{w} = (\mathbf{w} \cdot \mathbf{u})\mathbf{v} - (\mathbf{w} \cdot \mathbf{v})\mathbf{u}$$

These expressions can be summarized with the following mnemonic rule:

vector triple product = (outer · remote)adjacent
$$\qquad - \text{(outer · adjacent)remote}$$

See if you can figure out what the expressions "outer," "remote," and "adjacent" mean in this rule, and then use the rule to find the two vector triple products of the vectors

$$\mathbf{u} = \mathbf{i} + 3\mathbf{j} - \mathbf{k}, \quad \mathbf{v} = \mathbf{i} + \mathbf{j} + 2\mathbf{k}, \quad \mathbf{w} = 3\mathbf{i} - \mathbf{j} + 2\mathbf{k}$$

46. (a) Use the result in Exercise 45 to show that
   $\mathbf{u} \times (\mathbf{v} \times \mathbf{w})$ lies in the same plane as $\mathbf{v}$ and $\mathbf{w}$, and
   $(\mathbf{u} \times \mathbf{v}) \times \mathbf{w}$ lies in the same plane as $\mathbf{u}$ and $\mathbf{v}$.
   (b) Use a geometrical argument to justify the results in part (a).

47. In each part, use the result in Exercise 45 to prove the vector identity.
   (a) $(\mathbf{a} \times \mathbf{b}) \times (\mathbf{c} \times \mathbf{d}) = (\mathbf{a} \times \mathbf{b} \cdot \mathbf{d})\mathbf{c} - (\mathbf{a} \times \mathbf{b} \cdot \mathbf{c})\mathbf{d}$
   (b) $(\mathbf{a} \times \mathbf{b}) \times \mathbf{c} + (\mathbf{b} \times \mathbf{c}) \times \mathbf{a} + (\mathbf{c} \times \mathbf{a}) \times \mathbf{b} = 0$

48. Prove: If $\mathbf{a}, \mathbf{b}, \mathbf{c}$, and $\mathbf{d}$ lie in the same plane when positioned with a common initial point, then

$$(\mathbf{a} \times \mathbf{b}) \times (\mathbf{c} \times \mathbf{d}) = 0$$

C 49. Use a CAS to approximate the minimum area of a triangle if two of its vertices are $(2, -1, 0)$ and $(3, 2, 2)$ and its third vertex is on the curve $y = \ln x$ in the *xy*-plane.

50. If a force $\mathbf{F}$ is applied to an object at a point Q, then the line through Q parallel to $\mathbf{F}$ is called the **line of action** of the force. We defined the vector moment of $\mathbf{F}$ about a point P to be $\overrightarrow{PQ} \times \mathbf{F}$. Show that if Q' is any point on the line of action of $\mathbf{F}$, then $\overrightarrow{PQ} \times \mathbf{F} = \overrightarrow{PQ'} \times \mathbf{F}$; that is, it is not essential to use the point of application to compute the vector moment—any point on the line of action will do. [*Hint:* Write $\overrightarrow{PQ'} = \overrightarrow{PQ} + \overrightarrow{QQ'}$ and use properties of the cross product.]

51. Writing Discuss some of the similarities and differences between the multiplication of real numbers and the cross product of vectors.

52. Writing In your own words, describe what it means to say that the cross-product operation is "coordinate independent," and state why this fact is significant.

✔ QUICK CHECK ANSWERS 11.4

1. (a) 7 (b) 0   **2.** $8\mathbf{i} - 4\mathbf{j} - 6\mathbf{k}$ **3.** (a) $\langle 0, 0, 0 \rangle$ (b) $\langle -2, -7, -3 \rangle$ (c) $\langle -3, 11, 3 \rangle$ (d) $\langle -10, 8, 0 \rangle$ **4.** (a) -58 (b) 58

11.5 PARAMETRIC EQUATIONS OF LINES

In this section we will discuss parametric equations of lines in 2-space and 3-space. In 3-space, parametric equations of lines are especially important because they generally provide the most convenient form for representing lines algebraically.

■ LINES DETERMINED BY A POINT AND A VECTOR

A line in 2-space or 3-space can be determined uniquely by specifying a point on the line and a nonzero vector parallel to the line (Figure 11.5.1). For example, consider a line *L*

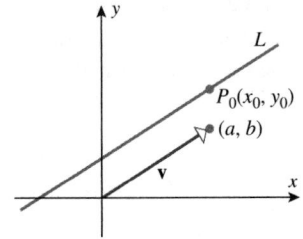

A unique line L passes through P_0 and is parallel to $\mathbf{v}$.

▲ **Figure 11.5.1**

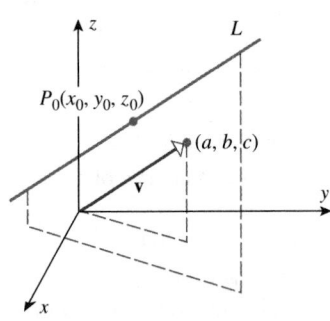

▲ **Figure 11.5.2**

in 3-space that passes through the point $P_0(x_0, y_0, z_0)$ and is parallel to the nonzero vector $\mathbf{v} = \langle a, b, c \rangle$. Then L consists precisely of those points $P(x, y, z)$ for which the vector $\overrightarrow{P_0P}$ is parallel to $\mathbf{v}$ (Figure 11.5.2). In other words, the point $P(x, y, z)$ is on L if and only if $\overrightarrow{P_0P}$ is a scalar multiple of $\mathbf{v}$, say

$$\overrightarrow{P_0P} = t\mathbf{v}$$

This equation can be written as

$$\langle x - x_0, y - y_0, z - z_0 \rangle = \langle ta, tb, tc \rangle$$

which implies that

$$x - x_0 = ta, \quad y - y_0 = tb, \quad z - z_0 = tc$$

Thus, L can be described by the parametric equations

$$x = x_0 + at, \quad y = y_0 + bt, \quad z = z_0 + ct$$

A similar description applies to lines in 2-space. We summarize these descriptions in the following theorem.

11.5.1 THEOREM

(a) *The line in 2-space that passes through the point $P_0(x_0, y_0)$ and is parallel to the nonzero vector $\mathbf{v} = \langle a, b \rangle = a\mathbf{i} + b\mathbf{j}$ has parametric equations*

$$x = x_0 + at, \quad y = y_0 + bt \tag{1}$$

(b) *The line in 3-space that passes through the point $P_0(x_0, y_0, z_0)$ and is parallel to the nonzero vector $\mathbf{v} = \langle a, b, c \rangle = a\mathbf{i} + b\mathbf{j} + c\mathbf{k}$ has parametric equations*

$$x = x_0 + at, \quad y = y_0 + bt, \quad z = z_0 + ct \tag{2}$$

REMARK Although it is not stated explicitly, it is understood in Equations (1) and (2) that $-\infty < t < +\infty$, which reflects the fact that lines extend indefinitely.

▶ **Example 1** Find parametric equations of the line

(a) passing through $(4, 2)$ and parallel to $\mathbf{v} = \langle -1, 5 \rangle$;

(b) passing through $(1, 2, -3)$ and parallel to $\mathbf{v} = 4\mathbf{i} + 5\mathbf{j} - 7\mathbf{k}$;

(c) passing through the origin in 3-space and parallel to $\mathbf{v} = \langle 1, 1, 1 \rangle$.

Solution (a). From (1) with $x_0 = 4$, $y_0 = 2$, $a = -1$, and $b = 5$ we obtain

$$x = 4 - t, \quad y = 2 + 5t$$

Solution (b). From (2) we obtain

$$x = 1 + 4t, \quad y = 2 + 5t, \quad z = -3 - 7t$$

Solution (c). From (2) with $x_0 = 0$, $y_0 = 0$, $z_0 = 0$, $a = 1$, $b = 1$, and $c = 1$ we obtain

$$x = t, \quad y = t, \quad z = t \quad ◀$$

► **Example 2**

(a) Find parametric equations of the line L passing through the points $P_1(2, 4, -1)$ and $P_2(5, 0, 7)$.

(b) Where does the line intersect the xy-plane?

Solution (a). The vector $\overrightarrow{P_1P_2} = \langle 3, -4, 8 \rangle$ is parallel to L and the point $P_1(2, 4, -1)$ lies on L, so it follows from (2) that L has parametric equations

$$x = 2 + 3t, \quad y = 4 - 4t, \quad z = -1 + 8t \tag{3}$$

Had we used P_2 as the point on L rather than P_1, we would have obtained the equations

$$x = 5 + 3t, \quad y = -4t, \quad z = 7 + 8t$$

Although these equations look different from those obtained using P_1, the two sets of equations are actually equivalent in that both generate L as t varies from $-\infty$ to $+\infty$. To see this, note that if t_1 gives a point

$$(x, y, z) = (2 + 3t_1, 4 - 4t_1, -1 + 8t_1)$$

on L using the first set of equations, then $t_2 = t_1 - 1$ gives the *same* point

$$\begin{aligned}(x, y, z) &= (5 + 3t_2, -4t_2, 7 + 8t_2) \\ &= (5 + 3(t_1 - 1), -4(t_1 - 1), 7 + 8(t_1 - 1)) \\ &= (2 + 3t_1, 4 - 4t_1, -1 + 8t_1)\end{aligned}$$

on L using the second set of equations. Conversely, if t_2 gives a point on L using the second set of equations, then $t_1 = t_2 + 1$ gives the same point using the first set.

Solution (b). It follows from (3) in part (a) that the line intersects the xy-plane at the point where $z = -1 + 8t = 0$, that is, when $t = \frac{1}{8}$. Substituting this value of t in (3) yields the point of intersection $(x, y, z) = \left(\frac{19}{8}, \frac{7}{2}, 0\right)$. ◄

► **Example 3** Let L_1 and L_2 be the lines

$$L_1: x = 1 + 4t, \quad y = 5 - 4t, \quad z = -1 + 5t$$
$$L_2: x = 2 + 8t, \quad y = 4 - 3t, \quad z = 5 + t$$

(a) Are the lines parallel?

(b) Do the lines intersect?

Solution (a). The line L_1 is parallel to the vector $4\mathbf{i} - 4\mathbf{j} + 5\mathbf{k}$, and the line L_2 is parallel to the vector $8\mathbf{i} - 3\mathbf{j} + \mathbf{k}$. These vectors are not parallel since neither is a scalar multiple of the other. Thus, the lines are not parallel.

Solution (b). For L_1 and L_2 to intersect at some point (x_0, y_0, z_0) these coordinates would have to satisfy the equations of both lines. In other words, there would have to exist values t_1 and t_2 for the parameters such that

$$x_0 = 1 + 4t_1, \quad y_0 = 5 - 4t_1, \quad z_0 = -1 + 5t_1$$

and

$$x_0 = 2 + 8t_2, \quad y_0 = 4 - 3t_2, \quad z_0 = 5 + t_2$$

This leads to three conditions on t_1 and t_2,

$$1 + 4t_1 = 2 + 8t_2$$
$$5 - 4t_1 = 4 - 3t_2 \qquad (4)$$
$$-1 + 5t_1 = 5 + t_2$$

Thus, the lines intersect if there are values of t_1 and t_2 that satisfy all three equations, and the lines do not intersect if there are no such values. You should be familiar with methods for solving systems of two linear equations in two unknowns; however, this is a system of three linear equations in two unknowns. To determine whether this system has a solution we will solve the first two equations for t_1 and t_2 and then check whether these values satisfy the third equation.

We will solve the first two equations by the method of elimination. We can eliminate the unknown t_1 by adding the equations. This yields the equation

$$6 = 6 + 5t_2$$

from which we obtain $t_2 = 0$. We can now find t_1 by substituting this value of t_2 in either the first or second equation. This yields $t_1 = \frac{1}{4}$. However, the values $t_1 = \frac{1}{4}$ and $t_2 = 0$ do not satisfy the third equation in (4), so the lines do not intersect. ◄

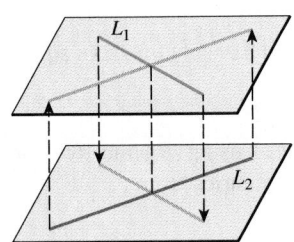

Parallel planes containing skew lines L_1 and L_2 can be determined by translating each line until it intersects the other.

▲ **Figure 11.5.3**

Two lines in 3-space that are not parallel and do not intersect (such as those in Example 3) are called *skew* lines. As illustrated in Figure 11.5.3, any two skew lines lie in parallel planes.

■ LINE SEGMENTS

Sometimes one is not interested in an entire line, but rather some *segment* of a line. Parametric equations of a line segment can be obtained by finding parametric equations for the entire line, and then restricting the parameter appropriately so that only the desired segment is generated.

▶ **Example 4** Find parametric equations describing the line segment joining the points $P_1(2, 4, -1)$ and $P_2(5, 0, 7)$.

Solution. From Example 2, the line through the points P_1 and P_2 has parametric equations $x = 2 + 3t$, $y = 4 - 4t$, $z = -1 + 8t$. With these equations, the point P_1 corresponds to $t = 0$ and P_2 to $t = 1$. Thus, the line segment that joins P_1 and P_2 is given by

$$x = 2 + 3t, \quad y = 4 - 4t, \quad z = -1 + 8t \qquad (0 \le t \le 1) \ ◄$$

■ VECTOR EQUATIONS OF LINES

We will now show how vector notation can be used to express the parametric equations of a line more compactly. Because two vectors are equal if and only if their components are equal, (1) and (2) can be written in vector form as

$$\langle x, y \rangle = \langle x_0 + at, y_0 + bt \rangle$$
$$\langle x, y, z \rangle = \langle x_0 + at, y_0 + bt, z_0 + ct \rangle$$

or, equivalently, as

$$\langle x, y \rangle = \langle x_0, y_0 \rangle + t \langle a, b \rangle \qquad (5)$$

$$\langle x, y, z \rangle = \langle x_0, y_0, z_0 \rangle + t \langle a, b, c \rangle \qquad (6)$$

For the equation in 2-space we define the vectors $\mathbf{r}$, $\mathbf{r}_0$, and $\mathbf{v}$ as

$$\mathbf{r} = \langle x, y \rangle, \quad \mathbf{r}_0 = \langle x_0, y_0 \rangle, \quad \mathbf{v} = \langle a, b \rangle \tag{7}$$

and for the equation in 3-space we define them as

$$\mathbf{r} = \langle x, y, z \rangle, \quad \mathbf{r}_0 = \langle x_0, y_0, z_0 \rangle, \quad \mathbf{v} = \langle a, b, c \rangle \tag{8}$$

Substituting (7) and (8) in (5) and (6), respectively, yields the equation

$$\mathbf{r} = \mathbf{r}_0 + t\mathbf{v} \tag{9}$$

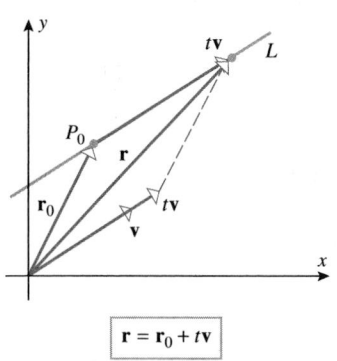

$$\boxed{\mathbf{r} = \mathbf{r}_0 + t\mathbf{v}}$$

▲ **Figure 11.5.4**

in both cases. We call this the ***vector equation of a line*** in 2-space or 3-space. In this equation, $\mathbf{v}$ is a nonzero vector parallel to the line, and $\mathbf{r}_0$ is a vector whose components are the coordinates of a point on the line.

We can interpret Equation (9) geometrically by positioning the vectors $\mathbf{r}_0$ and $\mathbf{v}$ with their initial points at the origin and the vector $t\mathbf{v}$ with its initial point at P_0 (Figure 11.5.4). The vector $t\mathbf{v}$ is a scalar multiple of $\mathbf{v}$ and hence is parallel to $\mathbf{v}$ and L. Moreover, since the initial point of $t\mathbf{v}$ is at the point P_0 on L, this vector actually runs along L; hence, the vector $\mathbf{r} = \mathbf{r}_0 + t\mathbf{v}$ can be interpreted as the vector from the origin to a point on L. As the parameter t varies from 0 to $+\infty$, the terminal point of $\mathbf{r}$ traces out the portion of L that extends from P_0 in the direction of $\mathbf{v}$, and as t varies from 0 to $-\infty$, the terminal point of $\mathbf{r}$ traces out the portion of L that extends from P_0 in the direction that is opposite to $\mathbf{v}$. Thus, the entire line is traced as t varies over the interval $(-\infty, +\infty)$, and it is traced in the direction of $\mathbf{v}$ as t increases.

▶ **Example 5** The equation

$$\langle x, y, z \rangle = \langle -1, 0, 2 \rangle + t\langle 1, 5, -4 \rangle$$

is of form (9) with

$$\mathbf{r}_0 = \langle -1, 0, 2 \rangle \quad \text{and} \quad \mathbf{v} = \langle 1, 5, -4 \rangle$$

Thus, the equation represents the line in 3-space that passes through the point $(-1, 0, 2)$ and is parallel to the vector $\langle 1, 5, -4 \rangle$. ◀

▶ **Example 6** Find an equation of the line in 3-space that passes through the points $P_1(2, 4, -1)$ and $P_2(5, 0, 7)$.

Solution. The vector

$$\overrightarrow{P_1P_2} = \langle 3, -4, 8 \rangle$$

is parallel to the line, so it can be used as $\mathbf{v}$ in (9). For $\mathbf{r}_0$ we can use either the vector from the origin to P_1 or the vector from the origin to P_2. Using the former yields

$$\mathbf{r}_0 = \langle 2, 4, -1 \rangle$$

Thus, a vector equation of the line through P_1 and P_2 is

$$\langle x, y, z \rangle = \langle 2, 4, -1 \rangle + t\langle 3, -4, 8 \rangle$$

If needed, we can express the line parametrically by equating corresponding components on the two sides of this vector equation, in which case we obtain the parametric equations in Example 2 (verify). ◀

✓ **QUICK CHECK EXERCISES 11.5**   *(See page 812 for answers.)*

1. Let L be the line through $(2, 5)$ and parallel to $\mathbf{v} = \langle 3, -1 \rangle$.
 (a) Parametric equations of L are

$$x = \underline{\hspace{1cm}} \qquad y = \underline{\hspace{1cm}}$$

 (b) A vector equation of L is $\langle x, y \rangle = \underline{\hspace{1cm}}$.

2. Parametric equations for the line through $(5, 3, 7)$ and parallel to the line $x = 3 - t, y = 2, z = 8 + 4t$ are

$$x = \underline{\hspace{1cm}}, \qquad y = \underline{\hspace{1cm}}, \qquad z = \underline{\hspace{1cm}}$$

3. Parametric equations for the line segment joining the points $(3, 0, 11)$ and $(2, 6, 7)$ are

$$x = \underline{\hspace{1cm}}, \qquad y = \underline{\hspace{1cm}}, \qquad z = \underline{\hspace{1cm}} \quad (\underline{\hspace{1cm}})$$

4. The line through the points $(-3, 8, -4)$ and $(1, 0, 8)$ intersects the yz-plane at $\underline{\hspace{1cm}}$.

EXERCISE SET 11.5    Graphing Utility   CAS

1. (a) Find parametric equations for the lines through the corner of the unit square shown in part (a) of the accompanying figure.
 (b) Find parametric equations for the lines through the corner of the unit cube shown in part (b) of the accompanying figure.

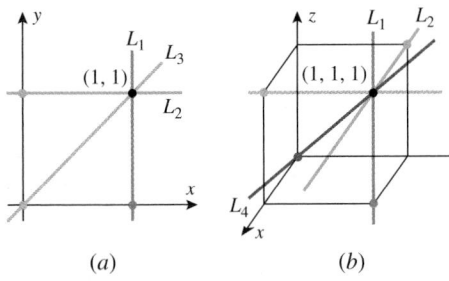

(a)   *(b)*

▲ **Figure Ex-1**

2. (a) Find parametric equations for the line segments in the unit square in part (a) of the accompanying figure.
 (b) Find parametric equations for the line segments in the unit cube shown in part (b) of the accompanying figure.

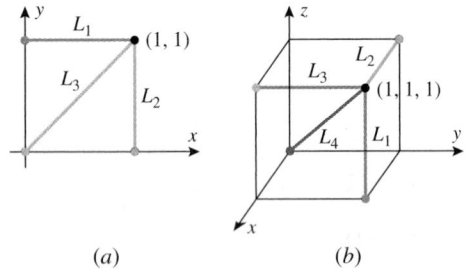

(a)   *(b)*

▲ **Figure Ex-2**

3–4 Find parametric equations for the line through P_1 and P_2 and also for the line segment joining those points. ■

3. (a) $P_1(3, -2)$, $P_2(5, 1)$ (b) $P_1(5, -2, 1)$, $P_2(2, 4, 2)$

4. (a) $P_1(0, 1)$, $P_2(-3, -4)$
 (b) $P_1(-1, 3, 5)$, $P_2(-1, 3, 2)$

5–6 Find parametric equations for the line whose vector equation is given. ■

5. (a) $\langle x, y \rangle = \langle 2, -3 \rangle + t \langle 1, -4 \rangle$
 (b) $x\mathbf{i} + y\mathbf{j} + z\mathbf{k} = \mathbf{k} + t(\mathbf{i} - \mathbf{j} + \mathbf{k})$

6. (a) $x\mathbf{i} + y\mathbf{j} = (3\mathbf{i} - 4\mathbf{j}) + t(2\mathbf{i} + \mathbf{j})$
 (b) $\langle x, y, z \rangle = \langle -1, 0, 2 \rangle + t \langle -1, 3, 0 \rangle$

7–8 Find a point P on the line and a vector $\mathbf{v}$ parallel to the line by inspection. ■

7. (a) $x\mathbf{i} + y\mathbf{j} = (2\mathbf{i} - \mathbf{j}) + t(4\mathbf{i} - \mathbf{j})$
 (b) $\langle x, y, z \rangle = \langle -1, 2, 4 \rangle + t \langle 5, 7, -8 \rangle$

8. (a) $\langle x, y \rangle = \langle -1, 5 \rangle + t \langle 2, 3 \rangle$
 (b) $x\mathbf{i} + y\mathbf{j} + z\mathbf{k} = (\mathbf{i} + \mathbf{j} - 2\mathbf{k}) + t\mathbf{j}$

9–10 Express the given parametric equations of a line using bracket notation and also using $\mathbf{i}, \mathbf{j}, \mathbf{k}$ notation. ■

9. (a) $x = -3 + t, \ y = 4 + 5t$
 (b) $x = 2 - t, \ y = -3 + 5t, \ z = t$

10. (a) $x = t, \ y = -2 + t$
 (b) $x = 1 + t, \ y = -7 + 3t, \ z = 4 - 5t$

11–14 True–False Determine whether the statement is true or false. Explain your answer. In these exercises L_0 and L_1 are lines in 3-space whose parametric equations are

$$L_0 : x = x_0 + a_0 t, \quad y = y_0 + b_0 t, \quad z = z_0 + c_0 t$$
$$L_1 : x = x_1 + a_1 t, \quad y = y_1 + b_1 t, \quad z = z_1 + c_1 t \quad ■$$

11. By definition, if L_1 and L_2 do not intersect, then L_1 and L_2 are parallel.

12. If L_1 and L_2 are parallel, then $\mathbf{v}_0 = \langle a_0, b_0, c_0 \rangle$ is a scalar multiple of $\mathbf{v}_1 = \langle a_1, b_1, c_1 \rangle$.

13. If L_1 and L_2 intersect at a point (x, y, z), then there exists a single value of t such that

$$L_0 : x = x_0 + a_0 t, \quad y = y_0 + b_0 t, \quad z = z_0 + c_0 t$$
$$L_1 : x = x_1 + a_1 t, \quad y = y_1 + b_1 t, \quad z = z_1 + c_1 t$$

are satisfied.

14. If L_0 passes through the origin, then the vectors $\langle a_0, b_0, c_0 \rangle$ and $\langle x_0, y_0, z_0 \rangle$ are parallel.

15–22 Find parametric equations of the line that satisfies the stated conditions. ■

15. The line through $(-5, 2)$ that is parallel to $2\mathbf{i} - 3\mathbf{j}$.

16. The line through $(0, 3)$ that is parallel to the line $x = -5 + t$, $y = 1 - 2t$.

17. The line that is tangent to the circle $x^2 + y^2 = 25$ at the point $(3, -4)$.

18. The line that is tangent to the parabola $y = x^2$ at the point $(-2, 4)$.

19. The line through $(-1, 2, 4)$ that is parallel to $3\mathbf{i} - 4\mathbf{j} + \mathbf{k}$.

20. The line through $(2, -1, 5)$ that is parallel to $\langle -1, 2, 7 \rangle$.

21. The line through $(-2, 0, 5)$ that is parallel to the line given by $x = 1 + 2t$, $y = 4 - t$, $z = 6 + 2t$.

22. The line through the origin that is parallel to the line given by $x = t$, $y = -1 + t$, $z = 2$.

23. Where does the line $x = 1 + 3t$, $y = 2 - t$ intersect
(a) the x-axis   (b) the y-axis
(c) the parabola $y = x^2$?

24. Where does the line $\langle x, y \rangle = \langle 4t, 3t \rangle$ intersect the circle $x^2 + y^2 = 25$?

25–26 Find the intersections of the lines with the xy-plane, the xz-plane, and the yz-plane. ■

25. $x = -2$, $y = 4 + 2t$, $z = -3 + t$

26. $x = -1 + 2t$, $y = 3 + t$, $z = 4 - t$

27. Where does the line $x = 1 + t$, $y = 3 - t$, $z = 2t$ intersect the cylinder $x^2 + y^2 = 16$?

28. Where does the line $x = 2 - t$, $y = 3t$, $z = -1 + 2t$ intersect the plane $2y + 3z = 6$?

29–30 Show that the lines L_1 and L_2 intersect, and find their point of intersection. ■

29. L_1: $x = 2 + t$, $y = 2 + 3t$, $z = 3 + t$
L_2: $x = 2 + t$, $y = 3 + 4t$, $z = 4 + 2t$

30. L_1: $x + 1 = 4t$, $y - 3 = t$, $z - 1 = 0$
L_2: $x + 13 = 12t$, $y - 1 = 6t$, $z - 2 = 3t$

31–32 Show that the lines L_1 and L_2 are skew. ■

31. L_1: $x = 1 + 7t$, $y = 3 + t$, $z = 5 - 3t$
L_2: $x = 4 - t$, $y = 6$, $z = 7 + 2t$

32. L_1: $x = 2 + 8t$, $y = 6 - 8t$, $z = 10t$
L_2: $x = 3 + 8t$, $y = 5 - 3t$, $z = 6 + t$

33–34 Determine whether the lines L_1 and L_2 are parallel. ■

33. L_1: $x = 3 - 2t$, $y = 4 + t$, $z = 6 - t$
L_2: $x = 5 - 4t$, $y = -2 + 2t$, $z = 7 - 2t$

34. L_1: $x = 5 + 3t$, $y = 4 - 2t$, $z = -2 + 3t$
L_2: $x = -1 + 9t$, $y = 5 - 6t$, $z = 3 + 8t$

35–36 Determine whether the points P_1, P_2, and P_3 lie on the same line. ■

35. $P_1(6, 9, 7)$, $P_2(9, 2, 0)$, $P_3(0, -5, -3)$

36. $P_1(1, 0, 1)$, $P_2(3, -4, -3)$, $P_3(4, -6, -5)$

37–38 Show that the lines L_1 and L_2 are the same. ■

37. L_1: $x = 3 - t$, $y = 1 + 2t$
L_2: $x = -1 + 3t$, $y = 9 - 6t$

38. L_1: $x = 1 + 3t$, $y = -2 + t$, $z = 2t$
L_2: $x = 4 - 6t$, $y = -1 - 2t$, $z = 2 - 4t$

FOCUS ON CONCEPTS

39. Sketch the vectors $\mathbf{r}_0 = \langle -1, 2 \rangle$ and $\mathbf{v} = \langle 1, 1 \rangle$, and then sketch the six vectors $\mathbf{r}_0 \pm \mathbf{v}$, $\mathbf{r}_0 \pm 2\mathbf{v}$, $\mathbf{r}_0 \pm 3\mathbf{v}$. Draw the line L: $x = -1 + t$, $y = 2 + t$, and describe the relationship between L and the vectors you sketched. What is the vector equation of L?

40. Sketch the vectors $\mathbf{r}_0 = \langle 0, 2, 1 \rangle$ and $\mathbf{v} = \langle 1, 0, 1 \rangle$, and then sketch the vectors $\mathbf{r}_0 + \mathbf{v}$, $\mathbf{r}_0 + 2\mathbf{v}$, and $\mathbf{r}_0 + 3\mathbf{v}$. Draw the line L: $x = t$, $y = 2$, $z = 1 + t$, and describe the relationship between L and the vectors you sketched. What is the vector equation of L?

41. Sketch the vectors $\mathbf{r}_0 = \langle -2, 0 \rangle$ and $\mathbf{r}_1 = \langle 1, 3 \rangle$, and then sketch the vectors
$$\tfrac{1}{3}\mathbf{r}_0 + \tfrac{2}{3}\mathbf{r}_1, \quad \tfrac{1}{2}\mathbf{r}_0 + \tfrac{1}{2}\mathbf{r}_1, \quad \tfrac{2}{3}\mathbf{r}_0 + \tfrac{1}{3}\mathbf{r}_1$$
Draw the line segment $(1 - t)\mathbf{r}_0 + t\mathbf{r}_1$ ($0 \le t \le 1$). If n is a positive integer, what is the position of the point on this line segment corresponding to $t = 1/n$, relative to the points $(-2, 0)$ and $(1, 3)$?

42. Sketch the vectors $\mathbf{r}_0 = \langle 2, 0, 4 \rangle$ and $\mathbf{r}_1 = \langle 0, 4, 0 \rangle$, and then sketch the vectors
$$\tfrac{1}{4}\mathbf{r}_0 + \tfrac{3}{4}\mathbf{r}_1, \quad \tfrac{1}{2}\mathbf{r}_0 + \tfrac{1}{2}\mathbf{r}_1, \quad \tfrac{3}{4}\mathbf{r}_0 + \tfrac{1}{4}\mathbf{r}_1$$
Draw the line segment $(1 - t)\mathbf{r}_0 + t\mathbf{r}_1$ ($0 \le t \le 1$). If n is a positive integer, what is the position of the point on this line segment corresponding to $t = 1/n$, relative to the points $(2, 0, 4)$ and $(0, 4, 0)$?

43–44 Describe the line segment represented by the vector equation. ■

43. $\langle x, y \rangle = \langle 1, 0 \rangle + t\langle -2, 3 \rangle$ ($0 \le t \le 2$)

44. $\langle x, y, z \rangle = \langle -2, 1, 4 \rangle + t\langle 3, 0, -1 \rangle$ ($0 \le t \le 3$)

45. Find the point on the line segment joining $P_1(3, 6)$ and $P_2(8, -4)$ that is $\tfrac{2}{5}$ of the way from P_1 to P_2.

46. Find the point on the line segment joining $P_1(1, 4, -3)$ and $P_2(1, 5, -1)$ that is $\tfrac{2}{3}$ of the way from P_1 to P_2.

47–48 Use the method in Exercise 32 of Section 11.3 to find the distance from the point P to the line L, and then check your answer using the method in Exercise 30 of Section 11.4. ■

47. $P(-2, 1, 1)$
L: $x = 3 - t$, $y = t$, $z = 1 + 2t$

48. $P(1, 4, -3)$
$L: x = 2 + t, \ y = -1 - t, \ z = 3t$

49–50 Show that the lines L_1 and L_2 are parallel, and find the distance between them. ■

49. $L_1: x = 2 - t, \ y = 2t, \ z = 1 + t$
$L_2: x = 1 + 2t, \ y = 3 - 4t, \ z = 5 - 2t$

50. $L_1: x = 2t, \ y = 3 + 4t, \ z = 2 - 6t$
$L_2: x = 1 + 3t, \ y = 6t, \ z = -9t$

51. (a) Find parametric equations for the line through the points (x_0, y_0, z_0) and (x_1, y_1, z_1).
(b) Find parametric equations for the line through the point (x_1, y_1, z_1) and parallel to the line
$$x = x_0 + at, \quad y = y_0 + bt, \quad z = z_0 + ct$$

52. Let L be the line that passes through the point (x_0, y_0, z_0) and is parallel to the vector $\mathbf{v} = \langle a, b, c \rangle$, where a, b, and c are nonzero. Show that a point (x, y, z) lies on the line L if and only if
$$\frac{x - x_0}{a} = \frac{y - y_0}{b} = \frac{z - z_0}{c}$$
These equations, which are called the **symmetric equations** of L, provide a nonparametric representation of L.

53. (a) Describe the line whose symmetric equations are
$$\frac{x - 1}{2} = \frac{y + 3}{4} = z - 5$$
(see Exercise 52).
(b) Find parametric equations for the line in part (a).

54. Consider the lines L_1 and L_2 whose symmetric equations are
$$L_1: \frac{x - 1}{2} = \frac{y + \frac{3}{2}}{1} = \frac{z + 1}{2}$$
$$L_2: \frac{x - 4}{-1} = \frac{y - 3}{-2} = \frac{z + 4}{2}$$
(see Exercise 52).
(a) Are L_1 and L_2 parallel? Perpendicular?
(b) Find parametric equations for L_1 and L_2.
(c) Do L_1 and L_2 intersect? If so, where?

55. Let L_1 and L_2 be the lines whose parametric equations are
$$L_1: x = 1 + 2t, \quad y = 2 - t, \quad z = 4 - 2t$$
$$L_2: x = 9 + t, \quad y = 5 + 3t, \quad z = -4 - t$$
(a) Show that L_1 and L_2 intersect at the point $(7, -1, -2)$.
(b) Find, to the nearest degree, the acute angle between L_1 and L_2 at their intersection.
(c) Find parametric equations for the line that is perpendicular to L_1 and L_2 and passes through their point of intersection.

56. Let L_1 and L_2 be the lines whose parametric equations are
$$L_1: x = 4t, \qquad y = 1 - 2t, \quad z = 2 + 2t$$
$$L_2: x = 1 + t, \qquad y = 1 - t, \qquad z = -1 + 4t$$
(a) Show that L_1 and L_2 intersect at the point $(2, 0, 3)$.
(b) Find, to the nearest degree, the acute angle between L_1 and L_2 at their intersection.
(c) Find parametric equations for the line that is perpendicular to L_1 and L_2 and passes through their point of intersection.

57–58 Find parametric equations of the line that contains the point P and intersects the line L at a right angle, and find the distance between P and L. ■

57. $P(0, 2, 1)$
$L: x = 2t, \ y = 1 - t, \ z = 2 + t$

58. $P(3, 1, -2)$
$L: x = -2 + 2t, \ y = 4 + 2t, \ z = 2 + t$

59. Two bugs are walking along lines in 3-space. At time t bug 1 is at the point (x, y, z) on the line
$$x = 4 - t, \quad y = 1 + 2t, \quad z = 2 + t$$
and at the same time t bug 2 is at the point (x, y, z) on the line
$$x = t, \quad y = 1 + t, \quad z = 1 + 2t$$
Assume that distance is in centimeters and that time is in minutes.
(a) Find the distance between the bugs at time $t = 0$.
(b) Use a graphing utility to graph the distance between the bugs as a function of time from $t = 0$ to $t = 5$.
(c) What does the graph tell you about the distance between the bugs?
(d) How close do the bugs get?

60. Suppose that the temperature T at a point (x, y, z) on the line $x = t, y = 1 + t, z = 3 - 2t$ is $T = 25x^2yz$. Use a CAS or a calculating utility with a root-finding capability to approximate the maximum temperature on that portion of the line that extends from the xz-plane to the xy-plane.

61. Writing Give some examples of geometric problems that can be solved using the parametric equations of a line, and describe their solution. For example, how would you find the points of intersection of a line and a sphere?

62. Writing Discuss how the vector equation of a line can be used to model the motion of a point that is moving with constant velocity in 3-space.

✔**QUICK CHECK ANSWERS 11.5**

1. (a) $2 + 3t$; $5 - t$ (b) $\langle 2, 5 \rangle + t\langle 3, -1 \rangle$ **2.** $5 - t$; 3; $7 + 4t$ **3.** $3 - t$; $6t$; $11 - 4t$; $0 \leq t \leq 1$ **4.** $(0, 2, 5)$

11.6 PLANES IN 3-SPACE

In this section we will use vectors to derive equations of planes in 3-space, and then we will use these equations to solve various geometric problems.

■ PLANES PARALLEL TO THE COORDINATE PLANES

The graph of the equation $x = a$ in an xyz-coordinate system consists of all points of the form (a, y, z), where y and z are arbitrary. One such point is $(a, 0, 0)$, and all others are in the plane that passes through this point and is parallel to the yz-plane (Figure 11.6.1). Similarly, the graph of $y = b$ is the plane through $(0, b, 0)$ that is parallel to the xz-plane, and the graph of $z = c$ is the plane through $(0, 0, c)$ that is parallel to the xy-plane.

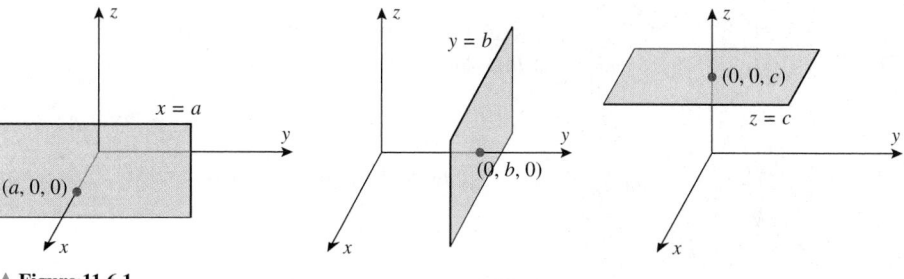

▲ **Figure 11.6.1**

■ PLANES DETERMINED BY A POINT AND A NORMAL VECTOR

A plane in 3-space can be determined uniquely by specifying a point in the plane and a vector perpendicular to the plane (Figure 11.6.2). A vector perpendicular to a plane is called a **normal** to the plane.

Suppose that we want to find an equation of the plane passing through $P_0(x_0, y_0, z_0)$ and perpendicular to the vector $\mathbf{n} = \langle a, b, c \rangle$. Define the vectors $\mathbf{r}_0$ and $\mathbf{r}$ as

$$\mathbf{r}_0 = \langle x_0, y_0, z_0 \rangle \quad \text{and} \quad \mathbf{r} = \langle x, y, z \rangle$$

It should be evident from Figure 11.6.3 that the plane consists precisely of those points $P(x, y, z)$ for which the vector $\mathbf{r} - \mathbf{r}_0$ is orthogonal to $\mathbf{n}$; or, expressed as an equation,

$$\mathbf{n} \cdot (\mathbf{r} - \mathbf{r}_0) = 0 \tag{1}$$

If preferred, we can express this vector equation in terms of components as

$$\langle a, b, c \rangle \cdot \langle x - x_0, y - y_0, z - z_0 \rangle = 0 \tag{2}$$

from which we obtain

$$a(x - x_0) + b(y - y_0) + c(z - z_0) = 0 \tag{3}$$

This is called the ***point-normal form*** of the equation of a plane. Formulas (1) and (2) are vector versions of this formula.

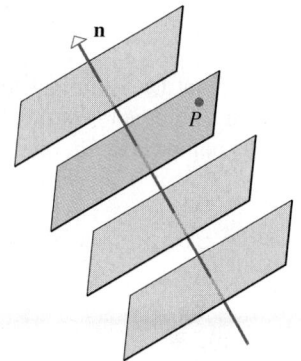

The colored plane is determined uniquely by the point P and the vector $\mathbf{n}$ perpendicular to the plane.

▲ **Figure 11.6.2**

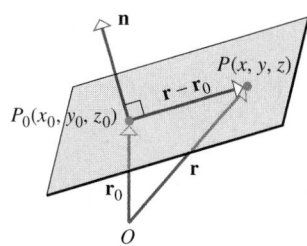

▲ **Figure 11.6.3**

What does Equation (1) represent if

$\mathbf{n} = \langle a, b \rangle$, $\mathbf{r}_0 = \langle x_0, y_0 \rangle$, $\mathbf{r} = \langle x, y \rangle$

are vectors in an xy-plane in 2-space? Draw a picture.

▶ **Example 1** Find an equation of the plane passing through the point $(3, -1, 7)$ and perpendicular to the vector $\mathbf{n} = \langle 4, 2, -5 \rangle$.

Solution. From (3), a point-normal form of the equation is

$$4(x - 3) + 2(y + 1) - 5(z - 7) = 0 \tag{4}$$

If preferred, this equation can be written in vector form as

$$\langle 4, 2, -5 \rangle \cdot \langle x - 3, y + 1, z - 7 \rangle = 0 \blacktriangleleft$$

Observe that if we multiply out the terms in (3) and simplify, we obtain an equation of the form

$$ax + by + cz + d = 0 \tag{5}$$

For example, Equation (4) in Example 1 can be rewritten as

$$4x + 2y - 5z + 25 = 0$$

The following theorem shows that every equation of form (5) represents a plane in 3-space.

11.6.1   THEOREM   *If a, b, c, and d are constants, and a, b, and c are not all zero, then the graph of the equation*

$$ax + by + cz + d = 0 \tag{6}$$

is a plane that has the vector $\mathbf{n} = \langle a, b, c \rangle$ *as a normal.*

PROOF   Since $a, b,$ and c are not all zero, there is at least one point (x_0, y_0, z_0) whose coordinates satisfy Equation (6). For example, if $a \neq 0$, then such a point is $(-d/a, 0, 0)$, and similarly if $b \neq 0$ or $c \neq 0$ (verify). Thus, let (x_0, y_0, z_0) be any point whose coordinates satisfy (6); that is,

$$ax_0 + by_0 + cz_0 + d = 0$$

Subtracting this equation from (6) yields

$$a(x - x_0) + b(y - y_0) + c(z - z_0) = 0$$

which is the point-normal form of a plane with normal $\mathbf{n} = \langle a, b, c \rangle$. ∎

Equation (6) is called the **_general form_** of the equation of a plane.

▶ **Example 2**   Determine whether the planes

$$3x - 4y + 5z = 0 \quad \text{and} \quad -6x + 8y - 10z - 4 = 0$$

are parallel.

Solution.   It is clear geometrically that two planes are parallel if and only if their normals are parallel vectors. A normal to the first plane is

$$\mathbf{n}_1 = \langle 3, -4, 5 \rangle$$

and a normal to the second plane is

$$\mathbf{n}_2 = \langle -6, 8, -10 \rangle$$

Since $\mathbf{n}_2$ is a scalar multiple of $\mathbf{n}_1$, the normals are parallel, and hence so are the planes. ◀

We have seen that a unique plane is determined by a point in the plane and a nonzero vector normal to the plane. In contrast, a unique plane is not determined by a point in the plane and a nonzero vector *parallel* to the plane (Figure 11.6.4). However, a unique plane

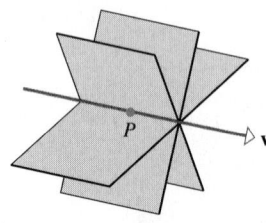

There are infinitely many planes containing P and parallel to $\mathbf{v}$.

▲ **Figure 11.6.4**

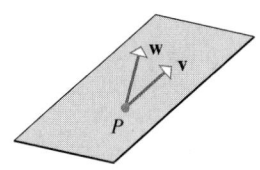

There is a unique plane through P that is parallel to both $\mathbf{v}$ and $\mathbf{w}$.

▲ **Figure 11.6.5**

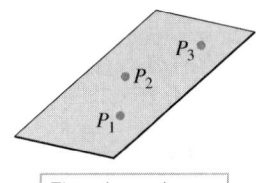

There is a unique plane through three noncollinear points.

▲ **Figure 11.6.6**

is determined by a point in the plane and two nonparallel vectors that are parallel to the plane (Figure 11.6.5). A unique plane is also determined by three noncollinear points that lie in the plane (Figure 11.6.6).

▶ **Example 3** Find an equation of the plane through the points $P_1(1, 2, -1)$, $P_2(2, 3, 1)$, and $P_3(3, -1, 2)$.

Solution. Since the points P_1, P_2, and P_3 lie in the plane, the vectors $\overrightarrow{P_1P_2} = \langle 1, 1, 2 \rangle$ and $\overrightarrow{P_1P_3} = \langle 2, -3, 3 \rangle$ are parallel to the plane. Therefore,

$$\overrightarrow{P_1P_2} \times \overrightarrow{P_1P_3} = \begin{vmatrix} \mathbf{i} & \mathbf{j} & \mathbf{k} \\ 1 & 1 & 2 \\ 2 & -3 & 3 \end{vmatrix} = 9\mathbf{i} + \mathbf{j} - 5\mathbf{k}$$

is normal to the plane, since it is orthogonal to both $\overrightarrow{P_1P_2}$ and $\overrightarrow{P_1P_3}$. By using this normal and the point $P_1(1, 2, -1)$ in the plane, we obtain the point-normal form

$$9(x - 1) + (y - 2) - 5(z + 1) = 0$$

which can be rewritten as
$$9x + y - 5z - 16 = 0 \quad \blacktriangleleft$$

▶ **Example 4** Determine whether the line

$$x = 3 + 8t, \quad y = 4 + 5t, \quad z = -3 - t$$

is parallel to the plane $x - 3y + 5z = 12$.

Solution. The vector $\mathbf{v} = \langle 8, 5, -1 \rangle$ is parallel to the line and the vector $\mathbf{n} = \langle 1, -3, 5 \rangle$ is normal to the plane. For the line and plane to be parallel, the vectors $\mathbf{v}$ and $\mathbf{n}$ must be orthogonal. But this is not so, since the dot product

$$\mathbf{v} \cdot \mathbf{n} = (8)(1) + (5)(-3) + (-1)(5) = -12$$

is nonzero. Thus, the line and plane are not parallel. ◀

▶ **Example 5** Find the intersection of the line and plane in Example 4.

Solution. If we let (x_0, y_0, z_0) be the point of intersection, then the coordinates of this point satisfy both the equation of the plane and the parametric equations of the line. Thus,

$$x_0 - 3y_0 + 5z_0 = 12 \tag{7}$$

and for some value of t, say $t = t_0$,

$$x_0 = 3 + 8t_0, \quad y_0 = 4 + 5t_0, \quad z_0 = -3 - t_0 \tag{8}$$

Substituting (8) in (7) yields

$$(3 + 8t_0) - 3(4 + 5t_0) + 5(-3 - t_0) = 12$$

Solving for t_0 yields $t_0 = -3$ and on substituting this value in (8), we obtain

$$(x_0, y_0, z_0) = (-21, -11, 0) \quad \blacktriangleleft$$

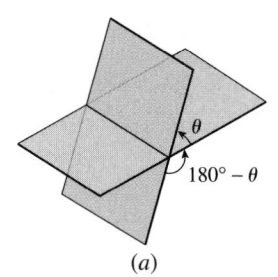

(a)

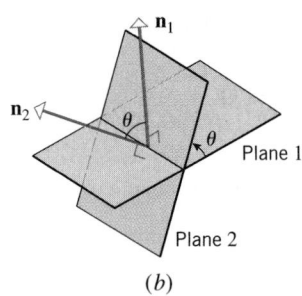

(b)

▲ **Figure 11.6.7**

■ INTERSECTING PLANES

Two distinct intersecting planes determine two positive angles of intersection—an (acute) angle θ that satisfies the condition $0 \leq \theta \leq \pi/2$ and the supplement of that angle (Figure 11.6.7a). If $\mathbf{n}_1$ and $\mathbf{n}_2$ are normals to the planes, then depending on the directions of $\mathbf{n}_1$ and $\mathbf{n}_2$, the angle θ is either the angle between $\mathbf{n}_1$ and $\mathbf{n}_2$ or the angle between $\mathbf{n}_1$ and $-\mathbf{n}_2$ (Figure 11.6.7b). In both cases, Theorem 11.3.3 yields the following formula for the *acute angle θ between the planes*:

$$\cos \theta = \frac{|\mathbf{n}_1 \cdot \mathbf{n}_2|}{\|\mathbf{n}_1\| \|\mathbf{n}_2\|} \tag{9}$$

▶ **Example 6**   Find the acute angle of intersection between the two planes

$$2x - 4y + 4z = 6 \quad \text{and} \quad 6x + 2y - 3z = 4$$

Solution.   The given equations yield the normals $\mathbf{n}_1 = \langle 2, -4, 4 \rangle$ and $\mathbf{n}_2 = \langle 6, 2, -3 \rangle$. Thus, Formula (9) yields

$$\cos \theta = \frac{|\mathbf{n}_1 \cdot \mathbf{n}_2|}{\|\mathbf{n}_1\| \|\mathbf{n}_2\|} = \frac{|-8|}{\sqrt{36}\sqrt{49}} = \frac{4}{21}$$

from which we obtain

$$\theta = \cos^{-1}\left(\frac{4}{21}\right) \approx 79° \quad ◀$$

▶ **Example 7**   Find an equation for the line L of intersection of the planes in Example 6.

Solution.   First compute $\mathbf{v} = \mathbf{n}_1 \times \mathbf{n}_2 = \langle 2, -4, 4 \rangle \times \langle 6, 2, -3 \rangle = \langle 4, 30, 28 \rangle$. Since $\mathbf{v}$ is orthogonal to $\mathbf{n}_1$, it is parallel to the first plane, and since $\mathbf{v}$ is orthogonal to $\mathbf{n}_2$, it is parallel to the second plane. That is, $\mathbf{v}$ is parallel to L, the intersection of the two planes. To find a point on L we observe that L must intersect the xy-plane, $z = 0$, since $\mathbf{v} \cdot \langle 0, 0, 1 \rangle = 28 \neq 0$. Substituting $z = 0$ in the equations of both planes yields

$$2x - 4y = 6$$
$$6x + 2y = 4$$

with solution $x = 1$, $y = -1$. Thus, $P(1, -1, 0)$ is a point on L. A vector equation for L is

$$\langle x, y, z \rangle = \langle 1, -1, 0 \rangle + t \langle 4, 30, 28 \rangle \quad ◀$$

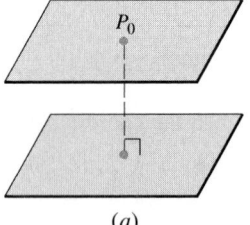

(a)

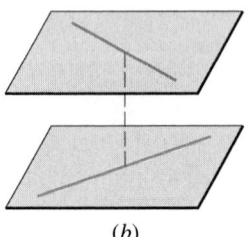

(b)

▲ **Figure 11.6.8**

■ DISTANCE PROBLEMS INVOLVING PLANES

Next we will consider three basic distance problems in 3-space:

- Find the distance between a point and a plane.
- Find the distance between two parallel planes.
- Find the distance between two skew lines.

The three problems are related. If we can find the distance between a point and a plane, then we can find the distance between parallel planes by computing the distance between one of the planes and an arbitrary point P_0 in the other plane (Figure 11.6.8a). Moreover, we can find the distance between two skew lines by computing the distance between parallel planes containing them (Figure 11.6.8b).

> **11.6.2   THEOREM**   *The distance D between a point $P_0(x_0, y_0, z_0)$ and the plane $ax + by + cz + d = 0$ is*
>
> $$D = \frac{|ax_0 + by_0 + cz_0 + d|}{\sqrt{a^2 + b^2 + c^2}} \tag{10}$$

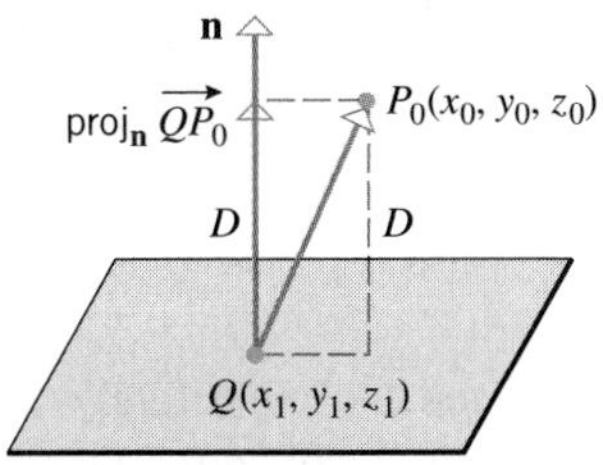

PROOF   Let $Q(x_1, y_1, z_1)$ be any point in the plane, and position the normal $\mathbf{n} = \langle a, b, c \rangle$ so that its initial point is at Q. As illustrated in Figure 11.6.9, the distance D is equal to the length of the orthogonal projection of $\overrightarrow{QP_0}$ on $\mathbf{n}$. Thus, from (12) of Section 11.3,

$$D = \| \text{proj}_{\mathbf{n}} \overrightarrow{QP_0} \| = \left\| \frac{\overrightarrow{QP_0} \cdot \mathbf{n}}{\|\mathbf{n}\|^2} \mathbf{n} \right\| = \frac{|\overrightarrow{QP_0} \cdot \mathbf{n}|}{\|\mathbf{n}\|^2} \|\mathbf{n}\| = \frac{|\overrightarrow{QP_0} \cdot \mathbf{n}|}{\|\mathbf{n}\|}$$

▲ **Figure 11.6.9**

But

$$\overrightarrow{QP_0} = \langle x_0 - x_1, y_0 - y_1, z_0 - z_1 \rangle$$
$$\overrightarrow{QP_0} \cdot \mathbf{n} = a(x_0 - x_1) + b(y_0 - y_1) + c(z_0 - z_1)$$
$$\|\mathbf{n}\| = \sqrt{a^2 + b^2 + c^2}$$

Thus,

$$D = \frac{|a(x_0 - x_1) + b(y_0 - y_1) + c(z_0 - z_1)|}{\sqrt{a^2 + b^2 + c^2}} \tag{11}$$

Since the point $Q(x_1, y_1, z_1)$ lies in the plane, its coordinates satisfy the equation of the plane; that is,
$$ax_1 + by_1 + cz_1 + d = 0$$

or

$$d = -ax_1 - by_1 - cz_1$$

Combining this expression with (11) yields (10).   ∎

There is an analog of Formula (10) in 2-space that can be used to compute the distance between a point and a line (see Exercise 52).

▶ **Example 8**   Find the distance D between the point $(1, -4, -3)$ and the plane

$$2x - 3y + 6z = -1$$

Solution.   Formula (10) requires the plane be rewritten in the form $ax + by + cz + d = 0$. Thus, we rewrite the equation of the given plane as

$$2x - 3y + 6z + 1 = 0$$

from which we obtain $a = 2$, $b = -3$, $c = 6$, and $d = 1$. Substituting these values and the coordinates of the given point in (10), we obtain

$$D = \frac{|(2)(1) + (-3)(-4) + 6(-3) + 1|}{\sqrt{2^2 + (-3)^2 + 6^2}} = \frac{|-3|}{7} = \frac{3}{7} \blacktriangleleft$$

▶ **Example 9**   The planes

$$x + 2y - 2z = 3 \quad \text{and} \quad 2x + 4y - 4z = 7$$

are parallel since their normals, $\langle 1, 2, -2 \rangle$ and $\langle 2, 4, -4 \rangle$, are parallel vectors. Find the distance between these planes.

Solution.   To find the distance D between the planes, we can select an *arbitrary* point in one of the planes and compute its distance to the other plane. By setting $y = z = 0$ in the equation $x + 2y - 2z = 3$, we obtain the point $P_0(3, 0, 0)$ in this plane. From (10), the distance from P_0 to the plane $2x + 4y - 4z = 7$ is

$$D = \frac{|(2)(3) + 4(0) + (-4)(0) - 7|}{\sqrt{2^2 + 4^2 + (-4)^2}} = \frac{1}{6} \blacktriangleleft$$

▶ **Example 10**   It was shown in Example 3 of Section 11.5 that the lines

$$L_1: x = 1 + 4t, \quad y = 5 - 4t, \quad z = -1 + 5t$$
$$L_2: x = 2 + 8t, \quad y = 4 - 3t, \quad z = 5 + t$$

are skew. Find the distance between them.

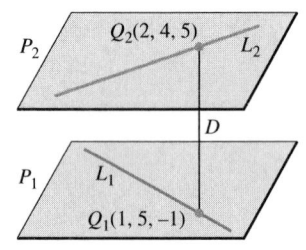

▲ **Figure 11.6.10**

Solution.   Let P_1 and P_2 denote parallel planes containing L_1 and L_2, respectively (Figure 11.6.10). To find the distance D between L_1 and L_2, we will calculate the distance from a point in P_1 to the plane P_2. Since L_1 lies in plane P_1, we can find a point in P_1 by finding a point on the line L_1; we can do this by substituting any convenient value of t in the parametric equations of L_1. The simplest choice is $t = 0$, which yields the point $Q_1(1, 5, -1)$.

The next step is to find an equation for the plane P_2. For this purpose, observe that the vector $\mathbf{u}_1 = \langle 4, -4, 5 \rangle$ is parallel to line L_1, and therefore also parallel to planes P_1 and P_2. Similarly, $\mathbf{u}_2 = \langle 8, -3, 1 \rangle$ is parallel to L_2 and hence parallel to P_1 and P_2. Therefore, the cross product

$$\mathbf{n} = \mathbf{u}_1 \times \mathbf{u}_2 = \begin{vmatrix} \mathbf{i} & \mathbf{j} & \mathbf{k} \\ 4 & -4 & 5 \\ 8 & -3 & 1 \end{vmatrix} = 11\mathbf{i} + 36\mathbf{j} + 20\mathbf{k}$$

is normal to both P_1 and P_2. Using this normal and the point $Q_2(2, 4, 5)$ found by setting $t = 0$ in the equations of L_2, we obtain an equation for P_2:

$$11(x - 2) + 36(y - 4) + 20(z - 5) = 0$$

or

$$11x + 36y + 20z - 266 = 0$$

The distance between $Q_1(1, 5, -1)$ and this plane is

$$D = \frac{|(11)(1) + (36)(5) + (20)(-1) - 266|}{\sqrt{11^2 + 36^2 + 20^2}} = \frac{95}{\sqrt{1817}}$$

which is also the distance between L_1 and L_2. ◀

✔ **QUICK CHECK EXERCISES 11.6**   *(See page 821 for answers.)*

1. The point-normal form of the equation of the plane through $(0, 3, 5)$ and perpendicular to $\langle -4, 1, 7 \rangle$ is _____.

2. A normal vector for the plane $4x - 2y + 7z - 11 = 0$ is _____.

3. A normal vector for the plane through the points $(2, 5, 1)$, $(3, 7, 0)$, and $(2, 5, 2)$ is _____.

4. The acute angle of intersection of the planes $x + y - 2z = 5$ and $3y - 4z = 6$ is _____.

5. The distance between the point $(9, 8, 3)$ and the plane $x + y - 2z = 5$ is _____.

EXERCISE SET 11.6

1. Find equations of the planes P_1, P_2, and P_3 that are parallel to the coordinate planes and pass through the corner $(3, 4, 5)$ of the box shown in the accompanying figure.

2. Find equations of the planes P_1, P_2, and P_3 that are parallel to the coordinate planes and pass through the corner (x_0, y_0, z_0) of the box shown in the accompanying figure.

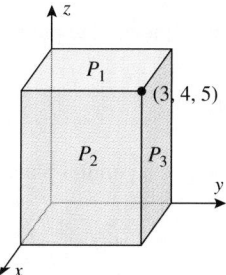

▲ **Figure Ex-1**

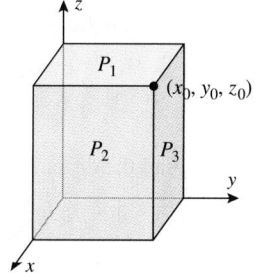

▲ **Figure Ex-2**

3–6 Find an equation of the plane that passes through the point P and has the vector $\mathbf{n}$ as a normal.

3. $P(2, 6, 1)$; $\mathbf{n} = \langle 1, 4, 2 \rangle$

4. $P(-1, -1, 2)$; $\mathbf{n} = \langle -1, 7, 6 \rangle$

5. $P(1, 0, 0)$; $\mathbf{n} = \langle 0, 0, 1 \rangle$

6. $P(0, 0, 0)$; $\mathbf{n} = \langle 2, -3, -4 \rangle$

7–10 Find an equation of the plane indicated in the figure. ■

7.

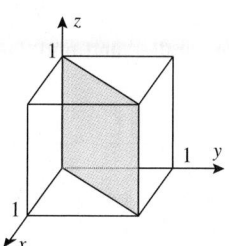

8.

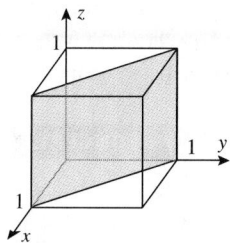

9.

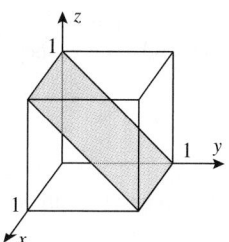

10.

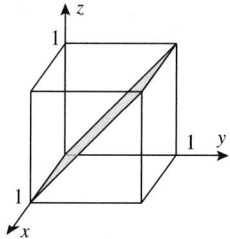

11–12 Find an equation of the plane that passes through the given points. ■

11. $(-2, 1, 1)$, $(0, 2, 3)$, and $(1, 0, -1)$

12. $(3, 2, 1)$, $(2, 1, -1)$, and $(-1, 3, 2)$

13–14 Determine whether the planes are parallel, perpendicular, or neither. ■

13. (a) $2x - 8y - 6z - 2 = 0$ (b) $3x - 2y + z = 1$
    $-x + 4y + 3z - 5 = 0$ $4x + 5y - 2z = 4$
    (c) $x - y + 3z - 2 = 0$
    $2x + z = 1$

14. (a) $3x - 2y + z = 4$ (b) $y = 4x - 2z + 3$
    $6x - 4y + 3z = 7$ $x = \frac{1}{4}y + \frac{1}{2}z$
    (c) $x + 4y + 7z = 3$
    $5x - 3y + z = 0$

15–16 Determine whether the line and plane are parallel, perpendicular, or neither. ■

15. (a) $x = 4 + 2t$, $y = -t$, $z = -1 - 4t$;
    $3x + 2y + z - 7 = 0$
    (b) $x = t$, $y = 2t$, $z = 3t$;
    $x - y + 2z = 5$
    (c) $x = -1 + 2t$, $y = 4 + t$, $z = 1 - t$;
    $4x + 2y - 2z = 7$

16. (a) $x = 3 - t$, $y = 2 + t$, $z = 1 - 3t$;
    $2x + 2y - 5 = 0$
    (b) $x = 1 - 2t$, $y = t$, $z = -t$;
    $6x - 3y + 3z = 1$
    (c) $x = t$, $y = 1 - t$, $z = 2 + t$;
    $x + y + z = 1$

17–18 Determine whether the line and plane intersect; if so, find the coordinates of the intersection. ■

17. (a) $x = t$, $y = t$, $z = t$;
    $3x - 2y + z - 5 = 0$
    (b) $x = 2 - t$, $y = 3 + t$, $z = t$;
    $2x + y + z = 1$

18. (a) $x = 3t$, $y = 5t$, $z = -t$;
    $2x - y + z + 1 = 0$
    (b) $x = 1 + t$, $y = -1 + 3t$, $z = 2 + 4t$;
    $x - y + 4z = 7$

19–20 Find the acute angle of intersection of the planes to the nearest degree. ■

19. $x = 0$ and $2x - y + z - 4 = 0$

20. $x + 2y - 2z = 5$ and $6x - 3y + 2z = 8$

21–24 True–False Determine whether the statement is true or false. Explain your answer. ■

21. Every plane has exactly two unit normal vectors.

22. If a plane is parallel to one of the coordinate planes, then its normal vector is parallel to one of the three vectors $\mathbf{i}$, $\mathbf{j}$, or $\mathbf{k}$.

23. If two planes intersect in a line L, then L is parallel to the cross product of the normals to the two planes.

24. If $a^2 + b^2 + c^2 = 1$, then the distance from $P(x_0, y_0, z_0)$ to the plane $ax + by + cz = 0$ is $|\langle a, b, c \rangle \cdot \langle x_0, y_0, z_0 \rangle|$.

25–34 Find an equation of the plane that satisfies the stated conditions. ■

25. The plane through the origin that is parallel to the plane $4x - 2y + 7z + 12 = 0$.

26. The plane that contains the line $x = -2 + 3t$, $y = 4 + 2t$, $z = 3 - t$ and is perpendicular to the plane $x - 2y + z = 5$.

27. The plane through the point $(-1, 4, 2)$ that contains the line of intersection of the planes $4x - y + z - 2 = 0$ and $2x + y - 2z - 3 = 0$.

28. The plane through $(-1, 4, -3)$ that is perpendicular to the line $x - 2 = t$, $y + 3 = 2t$, $z = -t$.

29. The plane through $(1, 2, -1)$ that is perpendicular to the line of intersection of the planes $2x + y + z = 2$ and $x + 2y + z = 3$.

30. The plane through the points $P_1(-2, 1, 4)$, $P_2(1, 0, 3)$ that is perpendicular to the plane $4x - y + 3z = 2$.

31. The plane through $(-1, 2, -5)$ that is perpendicular to the planes $2x - y + z = 1$ and $x + y - 2z = 3$.

32. The plane that contains the point $(2, 0, 3)$ and the line $x = -1 + t$, $y = t$, $z = -4 + 2t$.

33. The plane whose points are equidistant from $(2, -1, 1)$ and $(3, 1, 5)$.

34. The plane that contains the line $x = 3t$, $y = 1 + t$, $z = 2t$ and is parallel to the intersection of the planes $y + z = -1$ and $2x - y + z = 0$.

35. Find parametric equations of the line through the point $(5, 0, -2)$ that is parallel to the planes $x - 4y + 2z = 0$ and $2x + 3y - z + 1 = 0$.

36. Let L be the line $x = 3t + 1$, $y = -5t$, $z = t$.
(a) Show that L lies in the plane $2x + y - z = 2$.
(b) Show that L is parallel to the plane $x + y + 2z = 0$. Is the line above, below, or on this plane?

37. Show that the lines

$$x = -2 + t, \quad y = 3 + 2t, \quad z = 4 - t$$
$$x = 3 - t, \quad y = 4 - 2t, \quad z = t$$

are parallel and find an equation of the plane they determine.

38. Show that the lines

$$L_1: x + 1 = 4t, \quad y - 3 = t, \quad z - 1 = 0$$
$$L_2: x + 13 = 12t, \quad y - 1 = 6t, \quad z - 2 = 3t$$

intersect and find an equation of the plane they determine.

39. Do the points $(1, 0, -1)$, $(0, 2, 3)$, $(-2, 1, 1)$, and $(4, 2, 3)$ lie in the same plane? Justify your answer two different ways.

40. Show that if a, b, and c are nonzero, then the plane whose intercepts with the coordinate axes are $x = a$,

$y = b$, and $z = c$ is given by the equation

$$\frac{x}{a} + \frac{y}{b} + \frac{z}{c} = 1$$

41–42 Find parametric equations of the line of intersection of the planes. ■

41. $-2x + 3y + 7z + 2 = 0$ **42.** $3x - 5y + 2z = 0$
     $x + 2y - 3z + 5 = 0$ $z = 0$

43–44 Find the distance between the point and the plane. ■

43. $(1, -2, 3)$; $2x - 2y + z = 4$

44. $(0, 1, 5)$; $3x + 6y - 2z - 5 = 0$

45–46 Find the distance between the given parallel planes. ■

45. $-2x + y + z = 0$ **46.** $x + y + z = 1$
     $6x - 3y - 3z - 5 = 0$ $x + y + z = -1$

47–48 Find the distance between the given skew lines. ■

47. $x = 1 + 7t$, $y = 3 + t$, $z = 5 - 3t$
      $x = 4 - t$, $y = 6$, $z = 7 + 2t$

48. $x = 3 - t$, $y = 4 + 4t$, $z = 1 + 2t$
      $x = t$, $y = 3$, $z = 2t$

49. Find an equation of the sphere with center $(2, 1, -3)$ that is tangent to the plane $x - 3y + 2z = 4$.

50. Locate the point of intersection of the plane $2x + y - z = 0$ and the line through $(3, 1, 0)$ that is perpendicular to the plane.

51. Show that the line $x = -1 + t$, $y = 3 + 2t$, $z = -t$ and the plane $2x - 2y - 2z + 3 = 0$ are parallel, and find the distance between them.

52. Formulas (1), (2), (3), (5), and (10), which apply to planes in 3-space, have analogs for lines in 2-space.
(a) Draw an analog of Figure 11.6.3 in 2-space to illustrate that the equation of the line that passes through the point $P(x_0, y_0)$ and is perpendicular to the vector $\mathbf{n} = \langle a, b \rangle$ can be expressed as

$$\mathbf{n} \cdot (\mathbf{r} - \mathbf{r}_0) = 0$$

where $\mathbf{r} = \langle x, y \rangle$ and $\mathbf{r}_0 = \langle x_0, y_0 \rangle$.
(b) Show that the vector equation in part (a) can be expressed as

$$a(x - x_0) + b(y - y_0) = 0$$

This is called the ***point-normal form of a line***.
(c) Using the proof of Theorem 11.6.1 as a guide, show that if a and b are not both zero, then the graph of the equation

$$ax + by + c = 0$$

is a line that has $\mathbf{n} = \langle a, b \rangle$ as a normal.   *(cont.)*

(d) Using the proof of Theorem 11.6.2 as a guide, show that the distance D between a point $P(x_0, y_0)$ and the line $ax + by + c = 0$ is

$$D = \frac{|ax_0 + by_0 + c|}{\sqrt{a^2 + b^2}}$$

(e) Use the formula in part (d) to find the distance between the point $P(-3, 5)$ and the line $y = -2x + 1$.

53. (a) Show that the distance D between parallel planes

$$ax + by + cz + d_1 = 0$$
$$ax + by + cz + d_2 = 0$$

is

$$D = \frac{|d_1 - d_2|}{\sqrt{a^2 + b^2 + c^2}}$$

(b) Use the formula in part (a) to solve Exercise 45.

54. Writing Explain why any line in 3-space must lie in some vertical plane. Must any line in 3-space also lie in some horizontal plane?

55. Writing Given two planes, discuss the various possibilities for the set of points they have in common. Then consider the set of points that three planes can have in common.

✔ **QUICK CHECK ANSWERS 11.6**

1. $-4x + (y - 3) + 7(z - 5) = 0$ **2.** $\langle 4, -2, 7 \rangle$ **3.** $\langle 2, -1, 0 \rangle$ **4.** $\cos^{-1} \dfrac{11}{5\sqrt{6}} \approx 26°$ **5.** $\sqrt{6}$

11.7 QUADRIC SURFACES

In this section we will study an important class of surfaces that are the three-dimensional analogs of the conic sections.

■ TRACES OF SURFACES

Although the general shape of a curve in 2-space can be obtained by plotting points, this method is not usually helpful for surfaces in 3-space because too many points are required. It is more common to build up the shape of a surface with a network of ***mesh lines***, which are curves obtained by cutting the surface with well-chosen planes. For example, Figure 11.7.1, which was generated by a CAS, shows the graph of $z = x^3 - 3xy^2$ rendered with a combination of mesh lines and colorization to produce the surface detail. This surface is called a "monkey saddle" because a monkey sitting astride the surface has a place for its two legs and tail.

The mesh line that results when a surface is cut by a plane is called the ***trace*** of the surface in the plane (Figure 11.7.2). One way to deduce the shape of a surface is by examining its traces in planes parallel to the coordinate planes. For example, consider the surface

$$z = x^2 + y^2 \tag{1}$$

To find its trace in the plane $z = k$, we substitute this value of z into (1), which yields

$$x^2 + y^2 = k \qquad (z = k) \tag{2}$$

If $k < 0$, this equation has no real solutions, so there is no trace. However, if $k \geq 0$, then the graph of (2) is a circle of radius $\sqrt{k}$ centered at the point $(0, 0, k)$ on the z-axis (Figure 11.7.3a). Thus, for nonnegative values of k the traces parallel to the xy-plane form a family of circles, centered on the z-axis, whose radii start at zero and increase with k. This suggests that the surface has the form shown in Figure 11.7.3b.

To obtain more detailed information about the shape of this surface, we can examine the traces of (1) in planes parallel to the yz-plane. Such planes have equations of the form $x = k$, so we substitute this in (1) to obtain

$$z = k^2 + y^2 \qquad (x = k)$$

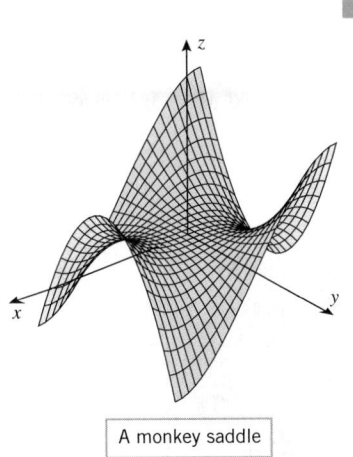

A monkey saddle

▲ **Figure 11.7.1**

The parenthetical part of Equation (2) is a reminder that the z-coordinate of each point in the trace is $z = k$. This needs to be stated explicitly because the variable z does not appear in the equation $x^2 + y^2 = k$.

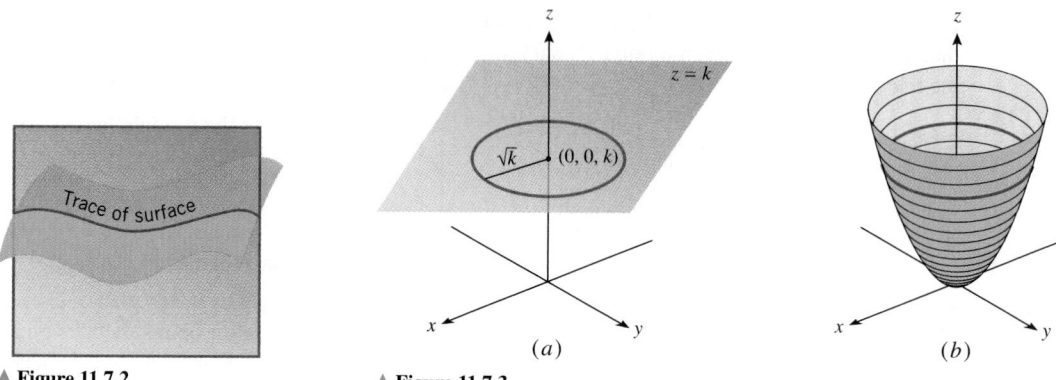

▲ **Figure 11.7.2**

▲ **Figure 11.7.3**

which we can rewrite as

$$z - k^2 = y^2 \qquad (x = k) \qquad (3)$$

For simplicity, let us start with the case where $k = 0$ (the trace in the yz-plane), in which case the trace has the equation

$$z = y^2 \qquad (x = 0)$$

You should be able to recognize that this is a parabola in the plane $x = 0$ that has its vertex at the origin, opens in the positive z-direction, and is symmetric about the z-axis (the blue parabola in Figure 11.7.4a). You should also be able to recognize that the $-k^2$ term in (3) has the effect of translating the parabola $z = y^2$ in the positive z-direction, so its new vertex in the plane $x = k$ is at the point $(k, 0, k^2)$. This is the red parabola in Figure 11.7.4a. Thus, the traces in planes parallel to the yz-plane form a family of parabolas whose vertices move upward as k^2 increases (Figure 11.7.4b). Similarly, the traces in planes parallel to the xz-plane have equations of the form

$$z - k^2 = x^2 \qquad (y = k)$$

which again is a family of parabolas whose vertices move upward as k^2 increases (Figure 11.7.4c).

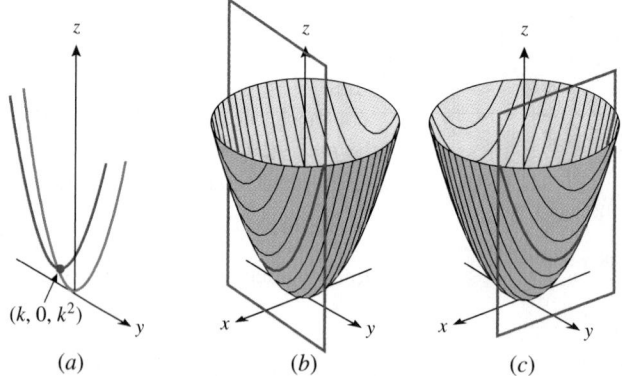

▶ **Figure 11.7.4** (a) (b) (c)

■ **THE QUADRIC SURFACES**

In the discussion of Formula (2) in Section 10.5 we noted that a second-degree equation

$$Ax^2 + Bxy + Cy^2 + Dx + Ey + F = 0$$

represents a conic section (possibly degenerate). The analog of this equation in an xyz-coordinate system is

$$Ax^2 + By^2 + Cz^2 + Dxy + Exz + Fyz + Gx + Hy + Iz + J = 0 \qquad (4)$$

which is called a **second-degree equation in x, y, and z**. The graphs of such equations are called **quadric surfaces** or sometimes **quadrics**.

Six common types of quadric surfaces are shown in Table 11.7.1—*ellipsoids, hyperboloids of one sheet, hyperboloids of two sheets, elliptic cones, elliptic paraboloids,* and *hyperbolic paraboloids.* (The constants a, b, and c that appear in the equations in the table are assumed to be positive.) Observe that none of the quadric surfaces in the table have cross-product terms in their equations. This is because of their orientations relative

Table 11.7.1

SURFACE	EQUATION	SURFACE	EQUATION
ELLIPSOID	$$\frac{x^2}{a^2} + \frac{y^2}{b^2} + \frac{z^2}{c^2} = 1$$ The traces in the coordinate planes are ellipses, as are the traces in those planes that are parallel to the coordinate planes and intersect the surface in more than one point.	ELLIPTIC CONE	$$z^2 = \frac{x^2}{a^2} + \frac{y^2}{b^2}$$ The trace in the xy-plane is a point (the origin), and the traces in planes parallel to the xy-plane are ellipses. The traces in the yz- and xz-planes are pairs of lines intersecting at the origin. The traces in planes parallel to these are hyperbolas.
HYPERBOLOID OF ONE SHEET	$$\frac{x^2}{a^2} + \frac{y^2}{b^2} - \frac{z^2}{c^2} = 1$$ The trace in the xy-plane is an ellipse, as are the traces in planes parallel to the xy-plane. The traces in the yz-plane and xz-plane are hyperbolas, as are the traces in those planes that are parallel to these and do not pass through the x- or y-intercepts. At these intercepts the traces are pairs of intersecting lines.	ELLIPTIC PARABOLOID	$$z = \frac{x^2}{a^2} + \frac{y^2}{b^2}$$ The trace in the xy-plane is a point (the origin), and the traces in planes parallel to and above the xy-plane are ellipses. The traces in the yz- and xz-planes are parabolas, as are the traces in planes parallel to these.
HYPERBOLOID OF TWO SHEETS	$$\frac{z^2}{c^2} - \frac{x^2}{a^2} - \frac{y^2}{b^2} = 1$$ There is no trace in the xy-plane. In planes parallel to the xy-plane that intersect the surface in more than one point the traces are ellipses. In the yz- and xz-planes, the traces are hyperbolas, as are the traces in those planes that are parallel to these.	HYPERBOLIC PARABOLOID	$$z = \frac{y^2}{b^2} - \frac{x^2}{a^2}$$ The trace in the xy-plane is a pair of lines intersecting at the origin. The traces in planes parallel to the xy-plane are hyperbolas. The hyperbolas above the xy-plane open in the y-direction, and those below in the x-direction. The traces in the yz- and xz-planes are parabolas, as are the traces in planes parallel to these.

to the coordinate axes. Later in this section we will discuss other possible orientations that produce equations of the quadric surfaces with no cross-product terms. In the special case where the elliptic cross sections of an elliptic cone or an elliptic paraboloid are circles, the terms *circular cone* and *circular paraboloid* are used.

■ TECHNIQUES FOR GRAPHING QUADRIC SURFACES

Accurate graphs of quadric surfaces are best left for graphing utilities. However, the techniques that we will now discuss can be used to generate rough sketches of these surfaces that are useful for various purposes.

A rough sketch of an ellipsoid

$$\frac{x^2}{a^2} + \frac{y^2}{b^2} + \frac{z^2}{c^2} = 1 \qquad (a > 0, b > 0, c > 0) \tag{5}$$

can be obtained by first plotting the intersections with the coordinate axes, and then sketching the elliptical traces in the coordinate planes. Example 1 illustrates this technique.

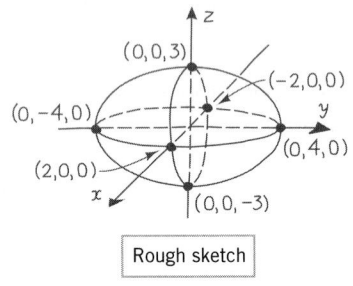

Rough sketch

▲ **Figure 11.7.5**

▶ **Example 1**   Sketch the ellipsoid

$$\frac{x^2}{4} + \frac{y^2}{16} + \frac{z^2}{9} = 1 \tag{6}$$

Solution.   The *x*-intercepts can be obtained by setting $y = 0$ and $z = 0$ in (6). This yields $x = \pm 2$. Similarly, the *y*-intercepts are $y = \pm 4$, and the *z*-intercepts are $z = \pm 3$. Sketching the elliptical traces in the coordinate planes yields the graph in Figure 11.7.5. ◀

A rough sketch of a hyperboloid of one sheet

$$\frac{x^2}{a^2} + \frac{y^2}{b^2} - \frac{z^2}{c^2} = 1 \qquad (a > 0, b > 0, c > 0) \tag{7}$$

can be obtained by first sketching the elliptical trace in the *xy*-plane, then the elliptical traces in the planes $z = \pm c$, and then the hyperbolic curves that join the endpoints of the axes of these ellipses. The next example illustrates this technique.

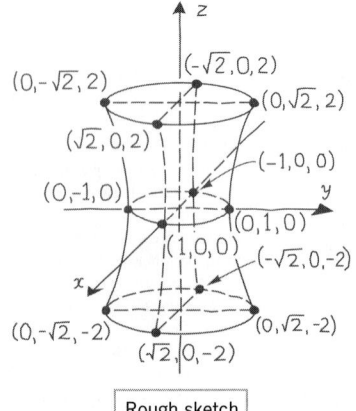

Rough sketch

▲ **Figure 11.7.6**

▶ **Example 2**   Sketch the graph of the hyperboloid of one sheet

$$x^2 + y^2 - \frac{z^2}{4} = 1 \tag{8}$$

Solution.   The trace in the *xy*-plane, obtained by setting $z = 0$ in (8), is

$$x^2 + y^2 = 1 \qquad (z = 0)$$

which is a circle of radius 1 centered on the *z*-axis. The traces in the planes $z = 2$ and $z = -2$, obtained by setting $z = \pm 2$ in (8), are given by

$$x^2 + y^2 = 2 \qquad (z = \pm 2)$$

which are circles of radius $\sqrt{2}$ centered on the *z*-axis. Joining these circles by the hyperbolic traces in the vertical coordinate planes yields the graph in Figure 11.7.6. ◀

A rough sketch of the hyperboloid of two sheets

$$\frac{z^2}{c^2} - \frac{x^2}{a^2} - \frac{y^2}{b^2} = 1 \qquad (a > 0, b > 0, c > 0) \tag{9}$$

can be obtained by first plotting the intersections with the z-axis, then sketching the elliptical traces in the planes $z = \pm 2c$, and then sketching the hyperbolic traces that connect the z-axis intersections and the endpoints of the axes of the ellipses. (It is not essential to use the planes $z = \pm 2c$, but these are good choices since they simplify the calculations slightly and have the right spacing for a good sketch.) The next example illustrates this technique.

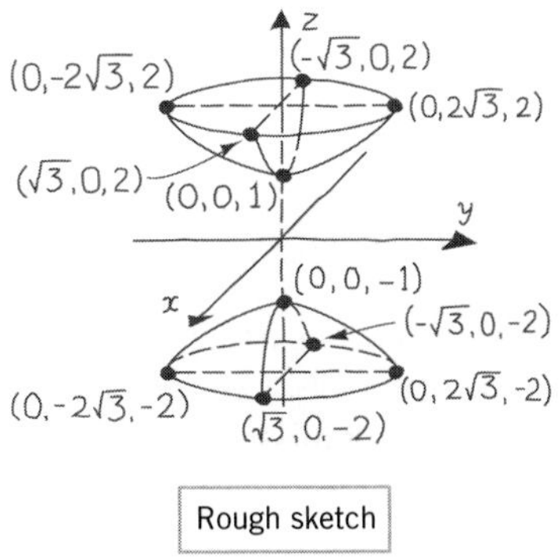

▶ **Example 3**   Sketch the graph of the hyperboloid of two sheets

$$z^2 - x^2 - \frac{y^2}{4} = 1 \tag{10}$$

Solution.   The z-intercepts, obtained by setting $x = 0$ and $y = 0$ in (10), are $z = \pm 1$. The traces in the planes $z = 2$ and $z = -2$, obtained by setting $z = \pm 2$ in (10), are given by

$$\frac{x^2}{3} + \frac{y^2}{12} = 1 \qquad (z = \pm 2)$$

Sketching these ellipses and the hyperbolic traces in the vertical coordinate planes yields Figure 11.7.7. ◀

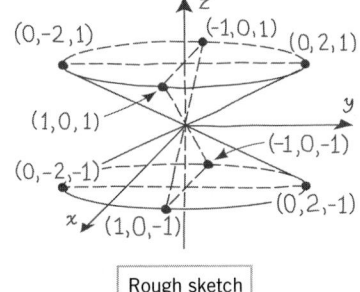

$(0,-2\sqrt{3},2)$ $(-\sqrt{3},0,2)$ $(0,2\sqrt{3},2)$
$(\sqrt{3},0,2)$ $(0,0,1)$
$(0,0,-1)$
$(-\sqrt{3},0,-2)$
$(0,-2\sqrt{3},-2)$ $(0,2\sqrt{3},-2)$
$(\sqrt{3},0,-2)$

Rough sketch

▲ **Figure 11.7.7**

A rough sketch of the elliptic cone

$$z^2 = \frac{x^2}{a^2} + \frac{y^2}{b^2} \qquad (a > 0, b > 0) \tag{11}$$

can be obtained by first sketching the elliptical traces in the planes $z = \pm 1$ and then sketching the linear traces that connect the endpoints of the axes of the ellipses. The next example illustrates this technique.

▶ **Example 4**   Sketch the graph of the elliptic cone

$$z^2 = x^2 + \frac{y^2}{4} \tag{12}$$

Solution.   The traces of (12) in the planes $z = \pm 1$ are given by

$$x^2 + \frac{y^2}{4} = 1 \qquad (z = \pm 1)$$

Sketching these ellipses and the linear traces in the vertical coordinate planes yields the graph in Figure 11.7.8. ◀

$(0,-2,1)$ $(-1,0,1)$ $(0,2,1)$
$(1,0,1)$
$(-1,0,-1)$
$(0,-2,-1)$
$(0,2,-1)$
$(1,0,-1)$

Rough sketch

▲ **Figure 11.7.8**

In the special cases of (11) and (13) where $a = b$, the traces parallel to the xy-plane are circles. In these cases, we call (11) a *circular cone* and (13) a *circular paraboloid.*

A rough sketch of the elliptic paraboloid

$$z = \frac{x^2}{a^2} + \frac{y^2}{b^2} \qquad (a > 0, b > 0) \tag{13}$$

can be obtained by first sketching the elliptical trace in the plane $z = 1$ and then sketching the parabolic traces in the vertical coordinate planes to connect the origin to the ends of the axes of the ellipse. The next example illustrates this technique.

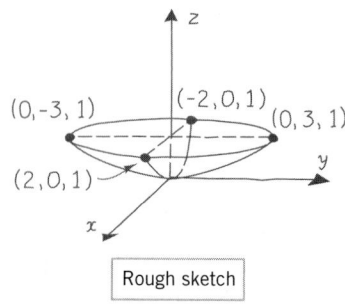

Rough sketch

▲ **Figure 11.7.9**

▶ **Example 5** Sketch the graph of the elliptic paraboloid

$$z = \frac{x^2}{4} + \frac{y^2}{9} \qquad (14)$$

Solution. The trace of (14) in the plane $z = 1$ is

$$\frac{x^2}{4} + \frac{y^2}{9} = 1 \qquad (z = 1)$$

Sketching this ellipse and the parabolic traces in the vertical coordinate planes yields the graph in Figure 11.7.9. ◀

A rough sketch of the hyperbolic paraboloid

$$z = \frac{y^2}{b^2} - \frac{x^2}{a^2} \qquad (a > 0, b > 0) \qquad (15)$$

can be obtained by first sketching the two parabolic traces that pass through the origin (one in the plane $x = 0$ and the other in the plane $y = 0$). After the parabolic traces are drawn, sketch the hyperbolic traces in the planes $z = \pm 1$ and then fill in any missing edges. The next example illustrates this technique.

▶ **Example 6** Sketch the graph of the hyperbolic paraboloid

$$z = \frac{y^2}{4} - \frac{x^2}{9} \qquad (16)$$

Solution. Setting $x = 0$ in (16) yields

$$z = \frac{y^2}{4} \qquad (x = 0)$$

which is a parabola in the yz-plane with vertex at the origin and opening in the positive z-direction (since $z \geq 0$), and setting $y = 0$ yields

$$z = -\frac{x^2}{9} \qquad (y = 0)$$

which is a parabola in the xz-plane with vertex at the origin and opening in the negative z-direction.

The trace in the plane $z = 1$ is

$$\frac{y^2}{4} - \frac{x^2}{9} = 1 \qquad (z = 1)$$

which is a hyperbola that opens along a line parallel to the y-axis (verify), and the trace in the plane $z = -1$ is

$$\frac{x^2}{9} - \frac{y^2}{4} = 1 \qquad (z = -1)$$

which is a hyperbola that opens along a line parallel to the x-axis. Combining all of the above information leads to the sketch in Figure 11.7.10. ◀

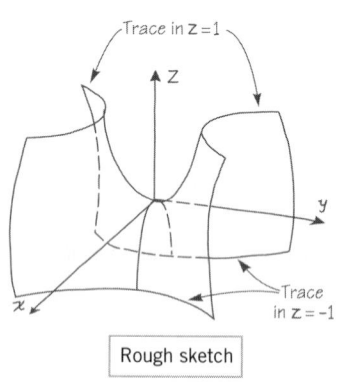

Rough sketch

▲ **Figure 11.7.10**

REMARK The hyperbolic paraboloid in Figure 11.7.10 has an interesting behavior at the origin—the trace in the xz-plane has a relative maximum at $(0, 0, 0)$, and the trace in the yz-plane has a relative minimum at $(0, 0, 0)$. Thus, a bug walking on the surface may view the origin as a highest point if traveling along one path, or may view the origin as a lowest point if traveling along a different path. A point with this property is commonly called a *saddle point* or a *minimax point*.

Figure 11.7.11 shows two computer-generated views of the hyperbolic paraboloid in Example 6. The first view, which is much like our rough sketch in Figure 11.7.10, has cuts at the top and bottom that are hyperbolic traces parallel to the xy-plane. In the second view the top horizontal cut has been omitted; this helps to emphasize the parabolic traces parallel to the xz-plane.

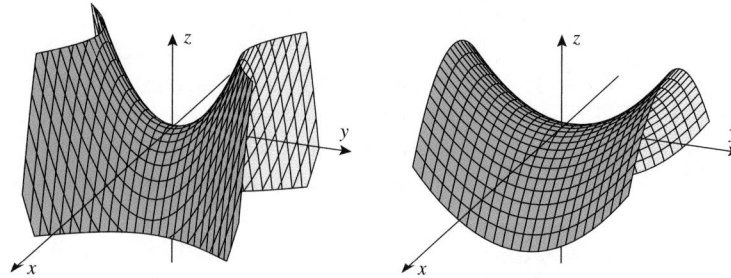

▶ **Figure 11.7.11**

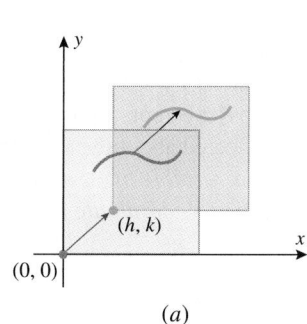

(a)

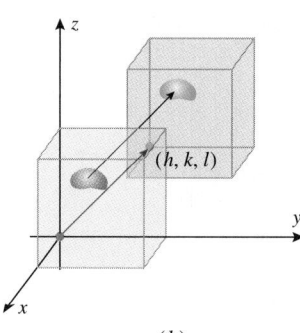

(b)

▲ **Figure 11.7.12**

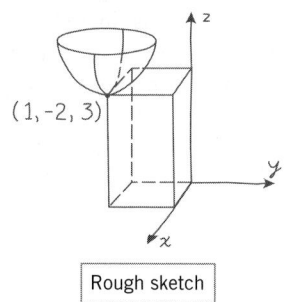

Rough sketch

▲ **Figure 11.7.13**

■ **TRANSLATIONS OF QUADRIC SURFACES**

In Section 10.4 we saw that a conic in an xy-coordinate system can be translated by substituting $x - h$ for x and $y - k$ for y in its equation. To understand why this works, think of the xy-axes as fixed and think of the plane as a transparent sheet of plastic on which all graphs are drawn. When the coordinates of points are modified by substituting $(x - h, y - k)$ for (x, y), the geometric effect is to translate the sheet of plastic (and hence all curves) so that the point on the plastic that was initially at $(0, 0)$ is moved to the point (h, k) (see Figure 11.7.12a).

For the analog in three dimensions, think of the xyz-axes as fixed and think of 3-space as a transparent block of plastic in which all surfaces are embedded. When the coordinates of points are modified by substituting $(x - h, y - k, z - l)$ for (x, y, z), the geometric effect is to translate the block of plastic (and hence all surfaces) so that the point in the plastic block that was initially at $(0, 0, 0)$ is moved to the point (h, k, l) (see Figure 11.7.12b).

▶ **Example 7** Describe the surface $z = (x - 1)^2 + (y + 2)^2 + 3$.

Solution. The equation can be rewritten as

$$z - 3 = (x - 1)^2 + (y + 2)^2$$

This surface is the paraboloid that results by translating the paraboloid

$$z = x^2 + y^2$$

in Figure 11.7.3 so that the new "vertex" is at the point $(1, -2, 3)$. A rough sketch of this paraboloid is shown in Figure 11.7.13. ◀

▶ **Example 8** Describe the surface

$$4x^2 + 4y^2 + z^2 + 8y - 4z = -4$$

Solution. Completing the squares yields

$$4x^2 + 4(y + 1)^2 + (z - 2)^2 = -4 + 4 + 4$$

or

$$x^2 + (y + 1)^2 + \frac{(z - 2)^2}{4} = 1$$

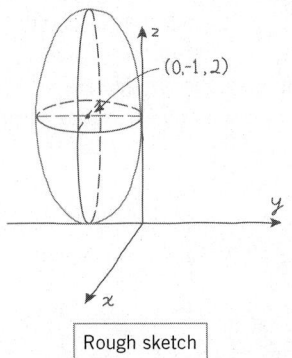

Rough sketch

▲ **Figure 11.7.14**

In Figure 11.7.14, the cross section in the yz-plane is shown tangent to both the y- and z-axes. Confirm that this is correct.

Thus, the surface is the ellipsoid that results when the ellipsoid

$$x^2 + y^2 + \frac{z^2}{4} = 1$$

is translated so that the new "center" is at the point $(0, -1, 2)$. A rough sketch of this ellipsoid is shown in Figure 11.7.14. ◄

■ **REFLECTIONS OF SURFACES IN 3-SPACE**

Recall that in an xy-coordinate system a point (x, y) is reflected about the x-axis if y is replaced by $-y$, and it is reflected about the y-axis if x is replaced by $-x$. In an xyz-coordinate system, a point (x, y, z) is reflected about the xy-plane if z is replaced by $-z$, it is reflected about the yz-plane if x is replaced by $-x$, and it is reflected about the xz-plane if y is replaced by $-y$ (Figure 11.7.15). It follows that *replacing a variable by its negative in the equation of a surface causes that surface to be reflected about a coordinate plane.*

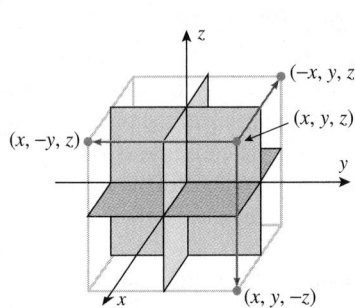

▲ **Figure 11.7.15**

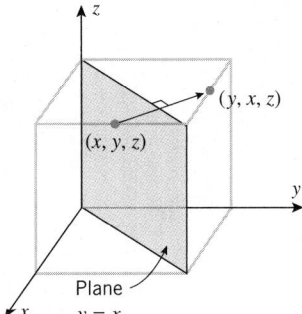

▲ **Figure 11.7.16**

Recall also that in an xy-coordinate system a point (x, y) is reflected about the line $y = x$ if x and y are interchanged. However, in an xyz-coordinate system, interchanging x and y reflects the point (x, y, z) about the plane $y = x$ (Figure 11.7.16). Similarly, interchanging x and z reflects the point about the plane $x = z$, and interchanging y and z reflects it about the plane $y = z$. Thus, it follows that *interchanging two variables in the equation of a surface reflects that surface about a plane that makes a 45° angle with two of the coordinate planes.*

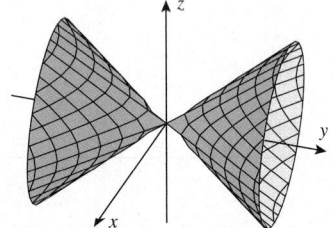

▲ **Figure 11.7.17**

▶ **Example 9**   Describe the surfaces

(a) $y^2 = x^2 + z^2$ (b) $z = -(x^2 + y^2)$

Solution (a).   The graph of the equation $y^2 = x^2 + z^2$ results from interchanging y and z in the equation $z^2 = x^2 + y^2$. Thus, the graph of the equation $y^2 = x^2 + z^2$ can be obtained by reflecting the graph of $z^2 = x^2 + y^2$ about the plane $y = z$. Since the graph of $z^2 = x^2 + y^2$ is a circular cone opening along the z-axis (see Table 11.7.1), it follows that the graph of $y^2 = x^2 + z^2$ is a circular cone opening along the y-axis (Figure 11.7.17).

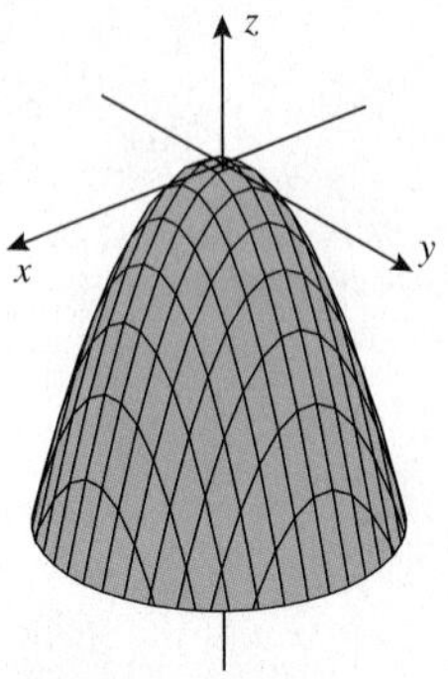

Solution (b).   The graph of the equation $z = -(x^2 + y^2)$ can be written as $-z = x^2 + y^2$, which can be obtained by replacing z with $-z$ in the equation $z = x^2 + y^2$. Since the graph of $z = x^2 + y^2$ is a circular paraboloid opening in the positive z-direction (see Table 11.7.1), it follows that the graph of $z = -(x^2 + y^2)$ is a circular paraboloid opening in the negative z-direction (Figure 11.7.18). ◄

▲ **Figure 11.7.18**

■ A TECHNIQUE FOR IDENTIFYING QUADRIC SURFACES

The equations of the quadric surfaces in Table 11.7.1 have certain characteristics that make it possible to identify quadric surfaces that are derived from these equations by reflections. These identifying characteristics, which are shown in Table 11.7.2, are based on writing the equation of the quadric surface so that all of the variable terms are on the left side of the equation and there is a 1 or a 0 on the right side. These characteristics do not change when the surface is reflected about a coordinate plane or planes of the form $x = y$, $x = z$, or $y = z$, thereby making it possible to identify the reflected quadric surface from the form of its equation.

Table 11.7.2

IDENTIFYING A QUADRIC SURFACE FROM THE FORM OF ITS EQUATION

EQUATION	$\dfrac{x^2}{a^2} + \dfrac{y^2}{b^2} + \dfrac{z^2}{c^2} = 1$	$\dfrac{x^2}{a^2} + \dfrac{y^2}{b^2} - \dfrac{z^2}{c^2} = 1$	$\dfrac{z^2}{c^2} - \dfrac{x^2}{a^2} - \dfrac{y^2}{b^2} = 1$	$z^2 - \dfrac{x^2}{a^2} - \dfrac{y^2}{b^2} = 0$	$z - \dfrac{x^2}{a^2} - \dfrac{y^2}{b^2} = 0$	$z - \dfrac{y^2}{b^2} + \dfrac{x^2}{a^2} = 0$
CHARACTERISTIC	No minus signs	One minus sign	Two minus signs	No linear terms	One linear term; two quadratic terms with the same sign	One linear term; two quadratic terms with opposite signs
CLASSIFICATION	Ellipsoid	Hyperboloid of one sheet	Hyperboloid of two sheets	Elliptic cone	Elliptic paraboloid	Hyperbolic paraboloid

▶ **Example 10**   Identify the surfaces

(a) $3x^2 - 4y^2 + 12z^2 + 12 = 0$ (b) $4x^2 - 4y + z^2 = 0$

Solution (a).   The equation can be rewritten as

$$\frac{y^2}{3} - \frac{x^2}{4} - z^2 = 1$$

This equation has a 1 on the right side and two negative terms on the left side, so its graph is a hyperboloid of two sheets.

Solution (b).   The equation has one linear term and two quadratic terms with the same sign, so its graph is an elliptic paraboloid. ◄

✔ QUICK CHECK EXERCISES 11.7   (See page 832 for answers.)

1. For the surface $4x^2 + y^2 + z^2 = 9$, classify the indicated trace as an ellipse, hyperbola, or parabola.
   (a) $x = 0$ (b) $y = 0$ (c) $z = 1$

2. For the surface $4x^2 + z^2 - y^2 = 9$, classify the indicated trace as an ellipse, hyperbola, or parabola.
   (a) $x = 0$ (b) $y = 0$ (c) $z = 1$

3. For the surface $4x^2 + y^2 - z = 0$, classify the indicated trace as an ellipse, hyperbola, or parabola.
   (a) $x = 0$ (b) $y = 0$ (c) $z = 1$

4. Classify each surface as an ellipsoid, hyperboloid of one sheet, hyperboloid of two sheets, elliptic cone, elliptic paraboloid, or hyperbolic paraboloid.

   (a) $\dfrac{x^2}{36} + \dfrac{y^2}{25} - z = 0$ (b) $\dfrac{x^2}{36} + \dfrac{y^2}{25} + z^2 = 1$

   (c) $\dfrac{x^2}{36} - \dfrac{y^2}{25} + z = 0$ (d) $\dfrac{x^2}{36} + \dfrac{y^2}{25} - z^2 = 1$

   (e) $\dfrac{x^2}{36} + \dfrac{y^2}{25} - z^2 = 0$ (f) $z^2 - \dfrac{x^2}{36} - \dfrac{y^2}{25} = 1$

EXERCISE SET 11.7

1–2 Identify the quadric surface as an ellipsoid, hyperboloid of one sheet, hyperboloid of two sheets, elliptic cone, elliptic paraboloid, or hyperbolic paraboloid by matching the equation with one of the forms given in Table 11.7.1. State the values of a, b, and c in each case. ■

1. (a) $z = \dfrac{x^2}{4} + \dfrac{y^2}{9}$ (b) $z = \dfrac{y^2}{25} - x^2$

     (c) $x^2 + y^2 - z^2 = 16$ (d) $x^2 + y^2 - z^2 = 0$

     (e) $4z = x^2 + 4y^2$ (f) $z^2 - x^2 - y^2 = 1$

2. (a) $6x^2 + 3y^2 + 4z^2 = 12$ (b) $y^2 - x^2 - z = 0$

     (c) $9x^2 + y^2 - 9z^2 = 9$ (d) $4x^2 + y^2 - 4z^2 = -4$

     (e) $2z - x^2 - 4y^2 = 0$ (f) $12z^2 - 3x^2 = 4y^2$

3. Find an equation for and sketch the surface that results when the circular paraboloid $z = x^2 + y^2$ is reflected about the plane

     (a) $z = 0$ (b) $x = 0$ (c) $y = 0$

     (d) $y = x$ (e) $x = z$ (f) $y = z$.

4. Find an equation for and sketch the surface that results when the hyperboloid of one sheet $x^2 + y^2 - z^2 = 1$ is reflected about the plane

     (a) $z = 0$ (b) $x = 0$ (c) $y = 0$

     (d) $y = x$ (e) $x = z$ (f) $y = z$.

FOCUS ON CONCEPTS

5. The given equations represent quadric surfaces whose orientations are different from those in Table 11.7.1. In each part, identify the quadric surface, and give a verbal description of its orientation (e.g., an elliptic cone opening along the z-axis or a hyperbolic paraboloid straddling the y-axis).

     (a) $\dfrac{z^2}{c^2} - \dfrac{y^2}{b^2} + \dfrac{x^2}{a^2} = 1$ (b) $\dfrac{x^2}{a^2} - \dfrac{y^2}{b^2} - \dfrac{z^2}{c^2} = 1$

     (c) $x = \dfrac{y^2}{b^2} + \dfrac{z^2}{c^2}$ (d) $x^2 = \dfrac{y^2}{b^2} + \dfrac{z^2}{c^2}$

     (e) $y = \dfrac{z^2}{c^2} - \dfrac{x^2}{a^2}$ (f) $y = -\left(\dfrac{x^2}{a^2} + \dfrac{z^2}{c^2}\right)$

6. For each of the surfaces in Exercise 5, find the equation of the surface that results if the given surface is reflected about the xz-plane and that surface is then reflected about the plane $z = 0$.

7–8 Find equations of the traces in the coordinate planes and sketch the traces in an xyz-coordinate system. [*Suggestion:* If you have trouble sketching a trace directly in three dimensions, start with a sketch in two dimensions by placing the coordinate plane in the plane of the paper, then transfer the sketch to three dimensions.] ■

7. (a) $\dfrac{x^2}{9} + \dfrac{y^2}{25} + \dfrac{z^2}{4} = 1$ (b) $z = x^2 + 4y^2$

     (c) $\dfrac{x^2}{9} + \dfrac{y^2}{16} - \dfrac{z^2}{4} = 1$

8. (a) $y^2 + 9z^2 = x$ (b) $4x^2 - y^2 + 4z^2 = 4$

     (c) $z^2 = x^2 + \dfrac{y^2}{4}$

9–10 In these exercises, traces of the surfaces in the planes are conic sections. In each part, find an equation of the trace, and state whether it is an ellipse, a parabola, or a hyperbola. ■

9. (a) $4x^2 + y^2 + z^2 = 4$; $y = 1$

     (b) $4x^2 + y^2 + z^2 = 4$; $x = \frac{1}{2}$

     (c) $9x^2 - y^2 - z^2 = 16$; $x = 2$

     (d) $9x^2 - y^2 - z^2 = 16$; $z = 2$

     (e) $z = 9x^2 + 4y^2$; $y = 2$

     (f) $z = 9x^2 + 4y^2$; $z = 4$

10. (a) $9x^2 - y^2 + 4z^2 = 9$; $x = 2$

     (b) $9x^2 - y^2 + 4z^2 = 9$; $y = 4$

     (c) $x^2 + 4y^2 - 9z^2 = 0$; $y = 1$

     (d) $x^2 + 4y^2 - 9z^2 = 0$; $z = 1$

     (e) $z = x^2 - 4y^2$; $x = 1$

     (f) $z = x^2 - 4y^2$; $z = 4$

11–14 True–False Determine whether the statement is true or false. Explain your answer. ■

11. A quadric surface is the graph of a fourth-degree polynomial in x, y, and z.

12. Every ellipsoid will intersect the z-axis in exactly two points.

13. Every ellipsoid is a surface of revolution.

14. The hyperbolic paraboloid

$$z = \frac{y^2}{b^2} - \frac{x^2}{a^2}$$

intersects the xy-plane in a pair of intersecting lines.

15–26 Identify and sketch the quadric surface. ■

15. $x^2 + \dfrac{y^2}{4} + \dfrac{z^2}{9} = 1$ **16.** $x^2 + 4y^2 + 9z^2 = 36$

17. $\dfrac{x^2}{4} + \dfrac{y^2}{9} - \dfrac{z^2}{16} = 1$ **18.** $x^2 + y^2 - z^2 = 9$

19. $4z^2 = x^2 + 4y^2$ **20.** $9x^2 + 4y^2 - 36z^2 = 0$

21. $9z^2 - 4y^2 - 9x^2 = 36$ **22.** $y^2 - \dfrac{x^2}{4} - \dfrac{z^2}{9} = 1$

23. $z = y^2 - x^2$ **24.** $16z = y^2 - x^2$

25. $4z = x^2 + 2y^2$ **26.** $z - 3x^2 - 3y^2 = 0$

27–32 The given equation represents a quadric surface whose orientation is different from that in Table 11.7.1. Identify and sketch the surface. ■

27. $x^2 - 3y^2 - 3z^2 = 0$ **28.** $x - y^2 - 4z^2 = 0$

29. $2y^2 - x^2 + 2z^2 = 8$ **30.** $x^2 - 3y^2 - 3z^2 = 9$

31. $z = \dfrac{x^2}{4} - \dfrac{y^2}{9}$ **32.** $4x^2 - y^2 + 4z^2 = 16$

33–36 Sketch the surface. ■

33. $z = \sqrt{x^2 + y^2}$

34. $z = \sqrt{1 - x^2 - y^2}$

35. $z = \sqrt{x^2 + y^2 - 1}$

36. $z = \sqrt{1 + x^2 + y^2}$

37–40 Identify the surface and make a rough sketch that shows its position and orientation. ■

37. $z = (x + 2)^2 + (y - 3)^2 - 9$

38. $4x^2 - y^2 + 16(z - 2)^2 = 100$

39. $9x^2 + y^2 + 4z^2 - 18x + 2y + 16z = 10$

40. $z^2 = 4x^2 + y^2 + 8x - 2y + 4z$

41–42 Use the ellipsoid $4x^2 + 9y^2 + 18z^2 = 72$ in these exercises. ■

41. (a) Find an equation of the elliptical trace in the plane $z = \sqrt{2}$.
  (b) Find the lengths of the major and minor axes of the ellipse in part (a).
  (c) Find the coordinates of the foci of the ellipse in part (a).
  (d) Describe the orientation of the focal axis of the ellipse in part (a) relative to the coordinate axes.

42. (a) Find an equation of the elliptical trace in the plane $x = 3$.
  (b) Find the lengths of the major and minor axes of the ellipse in part (a).
  (c) Find the coordinates of the foci of the ellipse in part (a).
  (d) Describe the orientation of the focal axis of the ellipse in part (a) relative to the coordinate axes.

43–46 These exercises refer to the hyperbolic paraboloid $z = y^2 - x^2$. ■

43. (a) Find an equation of the hyperbolic trace in the plane $z = 4$.
  (b) Find the vertices of the hyperbola in part (a).
  (c) Find the foci of the hyperbola in part (a).
  (d) Describe the orientation of the focal axis of the hyperbola in part (a) relative to the coordinate axes.

44. (a) Find an equation of the hyperbolic trace in the plane $z = -4$.
  (b) Find the vertices of the hyperbola in part (a).
  (c) Find the foci of the hyperbola in part (a).
  (d) Describe the orientation of the focal axis of the hyperbola in part (a) relative to the coordinate axes.

45. (a) Find an equation of the parabolic trace in the plane $x = 2$.
  (b) Find the vertices of the parabola in part (a).
  (c) Find the focus of the parabola in part (a).
  (d) Describe the orientation of the focal axis of the parabola in part (a) relative to the coordinate axes.

46. (a) Find an equation of the parabolic trace in the plane $y = 2$.
  (b) Find the vertex of the parabola in part (a).
  (c) Find the focus of the parabola in part (a).

  (d) Describe the orientation of the focal axis of the parabola in part (a) relative to the coordinate axes.

47–48 Sketch the region enclosed between the surfaces and describe their curve of intersection. ■

47. The paraboloids $z = x^2 + y^2$ and $z = 4 - x^2 - y^2$

48. The ellipsoid $2x^2 + 2y^2 + z^2 = 3$ and the paraboloid $z = x^2 + y^2$.

49–50 Find an equation for the surface generated by revolving the curve about the y-axis. ■

49. $y = 4x^2$ $(z = 0)$

50. $y = 2x$ $(z = 0)$

51. Find an equation of the surface consisting of all points $P(x, y, z)$ that are equidistant from the point $(0, 0, 1)$ and the plane $z = -1$. Identify the surface.

52. Find an equation of the surface consisting of all points $P(x, y, z)$ that are twice as far from the plane $z = -1$ as from the point $(0, 0, 1)$. Identify the surface.

53. If a sphere
$$\frac{x^2}{a^2} + \frac{y^2}{a^2} + \frac{z^2}{a^2} = 1$$
of radius a is compressed in the z-direction, then the resulting surface, called an **oblate spheroid**, has an equation of the form
$$\frac{x^2}{a^2} + \frac{y^2}{a^2} + \frac{z^2}{c^2} = 1$$
where $c < a$. Show that the oblate spheroid has a circular trace of radius a in the xy-plane and an elliptical trace in the xz-plane with major axis of length $2a$ along the x-axis and minor axis of length $2c$ along the z-axis.

54. The Earth's rotation causes a flattening at the poles, so its shape is often modeled as an oblate spheroid rather than a sphere (see Exercise 53 for terminology). One of the models used by global positioning satellites is the **World Geodetic System of 1984** (WGS-84), which treats the Earth as an oblate spheroid whose equatorial radius is 6378.1370 km and whose polar radius (the distance from the Earth's center to the poles) is 6356.5231 km. Use the WGS-84 model to find an equation for the surface of the Earth relative to the coordinate system shown in the accompanying figure.

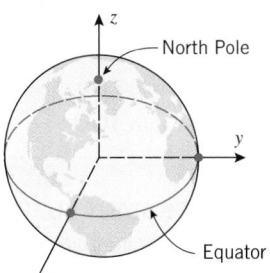

◀ **Figure Ex-54**

55. Use the method of slicing to show that the volume of the ellipsoid
$$\frac{x^2}{a^2} + \frac{y^2}{b^2} + \frac{z^2}{c^2} = 1$$
is $\frac{4}{3}\pi abc$.

56. Writing Discuss some of the connections between conic sections and traces of quadric surfaces.

57. Writing Give a sequence of steps for determining the type of quadric surface that is associated with a quadratic equation in x, y, and z.

✔ **QUICK CHECK ANSWERS 11.7**

1. (a) ellipse (b) ellipse (c) ellipse   2. (a) hyperbola (b) ellipse (c) hyperbola   3. (a) parabola (b) parabola (c) ellipse
4. (a) elliptic paraboloid (b) ellipsoid (c) hyperbolic paraboloid (d) hyperboloid of one sheet (e) elliptic cone
(f) hyperboloid of two sheets

11.8 CYLINDRICAL AND SPHERICAL COORDINATES

In this section we will discuss two new types of coordinate systems in 3-space that are often more useful than rectangular coordinate systems for studying surfaces with symmetries. These new coordinate systems also have important applications in navigation, astronomy, and the study of rotational motion about an axis.

CYLINDRICAL AND SPHERICAL COORDINATE SYSTEMS

Three coordinates are required to establish the location of a point in 3-space. We have already done this using rectangular coordinates. However, Figure 11.8.1 shows two other possibilities: part (*a*) of the figure shows the *rectangular coordinates* (x, y, z) of a point P, part (*b*) shows the *cylindrical coordinates* (r, θ, z) of P, and part (*c*) shows the *spherical coordinates* (ρ, θ, ϕ) of P. In a rectangular coordinate system the coordinates can be any real numbers, but in cylindrical and spherical coordinate systems there are restrictions on the allowable values of the coordinates (as indicated in Figure 11.8.1).

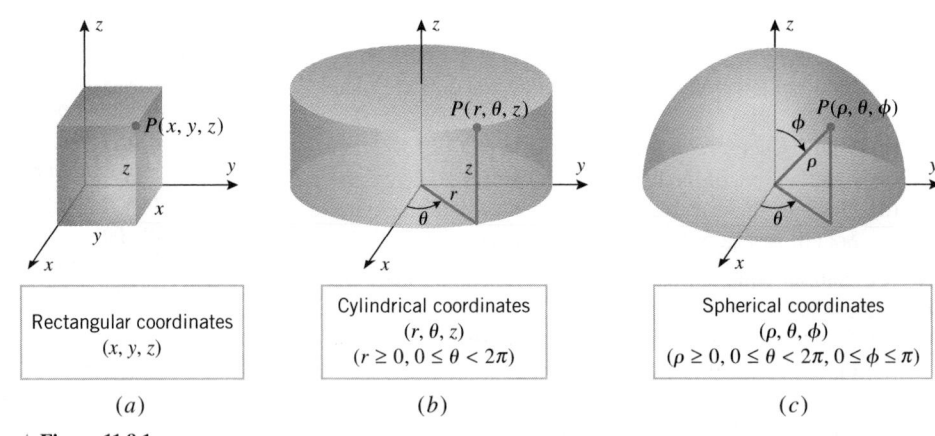

Rectangular coordinates (x, y, z)	Cylindrical coordinates (r, θ, z) $(r \geq 0, 0 \leq \theta < 2\pi)$	Spherical coordinates (ρ, θ, ϕ) $(\rho \geq 0, 0 \leq \theta < 2\pi, 0 \leq \phi \leq \pi)$
(*a*)	(*b*)	(*c*)

▲ **Figure 11.8.1**

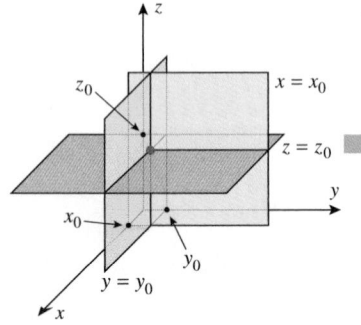

▲ **Figure 11.8.2**

CONSTANT SURFACES

In rectangular coordinates the surfaces represented by equations of the form

$$x = x_0, \quad y = y_0, \quad \text{and} \quad z = z_0$$

where x_0, y_0, and z_0 are constants, are planes parallel to the yz-plane, xz-plane, and xy-plane, respectively (Figure 11.8.2). In cylindrical coordinates the surfaces represented by equations of the form

$$r = r_0, \quad \theta = \theta_0, \quad \text{and} \quad z = z_0$$

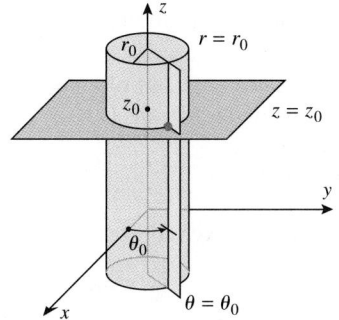

▲ **Figure 11.8.3**

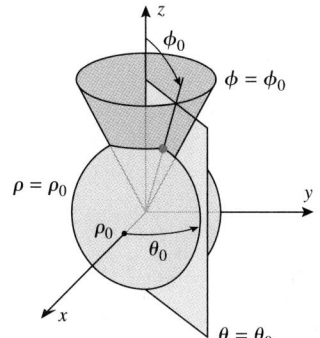

▲ **Figure 11.8.4**

where r_0, θ_0, and z_0 are constants, are shown in Figure 11.8.3:

- The surface $r = r_0$ is a right circular cylinder of radius r_0 centered on the z-axis.
- The surface $\theta = \theta_0$ is a half-plane attached along the z-axis and making an angle θ_0 with the positive x-axis.
- The surface $z = z_0$ is a horizontal plane.

In spherical coordinates the surfaces represented by equations of the form

$$\rho = \rho_0, \quad \theta = \theta_0, \quad \text{and} \quad \phi = \phi_0$$

where ρ_0, θ_0, and ϕ_0 are constants, are shown in Figure 11.8.4:

- The surface $\rho = \rho_0$ consists of all points whose distance ρ from the origin is ρ_0. Assuming ρ_0 to be nonnegative, this is a sphere of radius ρ_0 centered at the origin.
- As in cylindrical coordinates, the surface $\theta = \theta_0$ is a half-plane attached along the z-axis, making an angle of θ_0 with the positive x-axis.
- The surface $\phi = \phi_0$ consists of all points from which a line segment to the origin makes an angle of ϕ_0 with the positive z-axis. If $0 < \phi_0 < \pi/2$, this will be the nappe of a cone opening up, while if $\pi/2 < \phi_0 < \pi$, this will be the nappe of a cone opening down. (If $\phi_0 = \pi/2$, then the cone is flat, and the surface is the xy-plane.)

■ CONVERTING COORDINATES

Just as we needed to convert between rectangular and polar coordinates in 2-space, so we will need to be able to convert between rectangular, cylindrical, and spherical coordinates in 3-space. Table 11.8.1 provides formulas for making these conversions.

Table 11.8.1

CONVERSION FORMULAS FOR COORDINATE SYSTEMS

CONVERSION		FORMULAS	RESTRICTIONS
Cylindrical to rectangular	$(r, \theta, z) \rightarrow (x, y, z)$	$x = r\cos\theta, \quad y = r\sin\theta, \quad z = z$	
Rectangular to cylindrical	$(x, y, z) \rightarrow (r, \theta, z)$	$r = \sqrt{x^2 + y^2}, \quad \tan\theta = y/x, \quad z = z$	
Spherical to cylindrical	$(\rho, \theta, \phi) \rightarrow (r, \theta, z)$	$r = \rho\sin\phi, \quad \theta = \theta, \quad z = \rho\cos\phi$	$r \geq 0, \rho \geq 0$ $0 \leq \theta < 2\pi$
Cylindrical to spherical	$(r, \theta, z) \rightarrow (\rho, \theta, \phi)$	$\rho = \sqrt{r^2 + z^2}, \quad \theta = \theta, \quad \tan\phi = r/z$	$0 \leq \phi \leq \pi$
Spherical to rectangular	$(\rho, \theta, \phi) \rightarrow (x, y, z)$	$x = \rho\sin\phi\cos\theta, \quad y = \rho\sin\phi\sin\theta, \quad z = \rho\cos\phi$	
Rectangular to spherical	$(x, y, z) \rightarrow (\rho, \theta, \phi)$	$\rho = \sqrt{x^2 + y^2 + z^2}, \quad \tan\theta = y/x, \quad \cos\phi = z/\sqrt{x^2 + y^2 + z^2}$	

The diagrams in Figure 11.8.5 will help you to understand how the formulas in Table 11.8.1 are derived. For example, part (a) of the figure shows that in converting between rectangular coordinates (x, y, z) and cylindrical coordinates (r, θ, z), we can interpret (r, θ) as polar coordinates of (x, y). Thus, the polar-to-rectangular and rectangular-to-polar

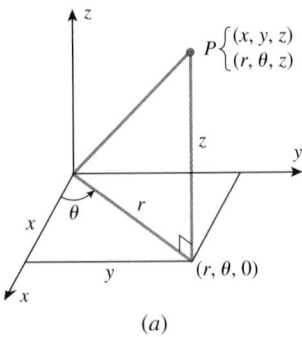

(a)

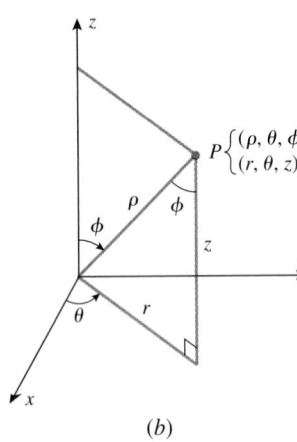

(b)

Comparison of coordinate systems

▲ **Figure 11.8.5**

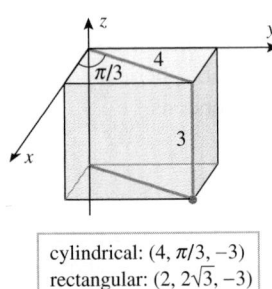

cylindrical: $(4, \pi/3, -3)$
rectangular: $(2, 2\sqrt{3}, -3)$

▲ **Figure 11.8.6**

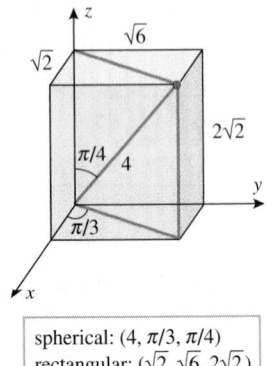

spherical: $(4, \pi/3, \pi/4)$
rectangular: $(\sqrt{2}, \sqrt{6}, 2\sqrt{2})$

▲ **Figure 11.8.7**

conversion formulas (1) and (2) of Section 10.2 provide the conversion formulas between rectangular and cylindrical coordinates in the table.

Part (b) of Figure 11.8.5 suggests that the spherical coordinates (ρ, θ, ϕ) of a point P can be converted to cylindrical coordinates (r, θ, z) by the conversion formulas

$$r = \rho \sin \phi, \quad \theta = \theta, \quad z = \rho \cos \phi \tag{1}$$

Moreover, since the cylindrical coordinates (r, θ, z) of P can be converted to rectangular coordinates (x, y, z) by the conversion formulas

$$x = r \cos \theta, \quad y = r \sin \theta, \quad z = z \tag{2}$$

we can obtain direct conversion formulas from spherical coordinates to rectangular coordinates by substituting (1) in (2). This yields

$$x = \rho \sin \phi \cos \theta, \quad y = \rho \sin \phi \sin \theta, \quad z = \rho \cos \phi \tag{3}$$

The other conversion formulas in Table 11.8.1 are left as exercises.

▶ **Example 1**

(a) Find the rectangular coordinates of the point with cylindrical coordinates

$$(r, \theta, z) = (4, \pi/3, -3)$$

(b) Find the rectangular coordinates of the point with spherical coordinates

$$(\rho, \theta, \phi) = (4, \pi/3, \pi/4)$$

Solution (a).   Applying the cylindrical-to-rectangular conversion formulas in Table 11.8.1 yields

$$x = r \cos \theta = 4 \cos \frac{\pi}{3} = 2, \quad y = r \sin \theta = 4 \sin \frac{\pi}{3} = 2\sqrt{3}, \quad z = -3$$

Thus, the rectangular coordinates of the point are $(x, y, z) = (2, 2\sqrt{3}, -3)$ (Figure 11.8.6).

Solution (b).   Applying the spherical-to-rectangular conversion formulas in Table 12.8.1 yields
$$x = \rho \sin \phi \cos \theta = 4 \sin \frac{\pi}{4} \cos \frac{\pi}{3} = \sqrt{2}$$
$$y = \rho \sin \phi \sin \theta = 4 \sin \frac{\pi}{4} \sin \frac{\pi}{3} = \sqrt{6}$$
$$z = \rho \cos \phi = 4 \cos \frac{\pi}{4} = 2\sqrt{2}$$

The rectangular coordinates of the point are $(x, y, z) = (\sqrt{2}, \sqrt{6}, 2\sqrt{2})$ (Figure 11.8.7).   ◀

Since the interval $0 \leq \theta < 2\pi$ covers two periods of the tangent function, the conversion formula $\tan \theta = y/x$ does not completely determine θ. The following example shows how to deal with this ambiguity.

▶ **Example 2**   Find the spherical coordinates of the point that has rectangular coordinates

$$(x, y, z) = (4, -4, 4\sqrt{6})$$

How should θ be chosen if $x = 0$?
How should θ be chosen if $y = 0$?

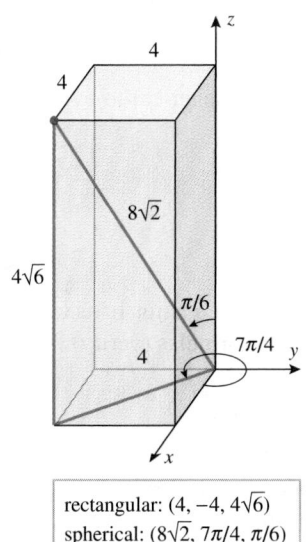

rectangular: $(4, -4, 4\sqrt{6})$
spherical: $(8\sqrt{2}, 7\pi/4, \pi/6)$

▲ **Figure 11.8.8**

Solution. From the rectangular-to-spherical conversion formulas in Table 11.8.1 we obtain

$$\rho = \sqrt{x^2 + y^2 + z^2} = \sqrt{16 + 16 + 96} = \sqrt{128} = 8\sqrt{2}$$

$$\tan \theta = \frac{y}{x} = -1$$

$$\cos \phi = \frac{z}{\sqrt{x^2 + y^2 + z^2}} = \frac{4\sqrt{6}}{8\sqrt{2}} = \frac{\sqrt{3}}{2}$$

From the restriction $0 \le \theta < 2\pi$ and the computed value of $\tan \theta$, the possibilities for θ are $\theta = 3\pi/4$ and $\theta = 7\pi/4$. However, the given point has a negative y-coordinate, so we must have $\theta = 7\pi/4$. Moreover, from the restriction $0 \le \phi \le \pi$ and the computed value of $\cos \phi$, the only possibility for ϕ is $\phi = \pi/6$. Thus, the spherical coordinates of the point are $(\rho, \theta, \phi) = (8\sqrt{2}, 7\pi/4, \pi/6)$ (Figure 11.8.8). ◄

■ **EQUATIONS OF SURFACES IN CYLINDRICAL AND SPHERICAL COORDINATES**
Surfaces of revolution about the z-axis of a rectangular coordinate system usually have simpler equations in cylindrical coordinates than in rectangular coordinates, and the equations of surfaces with symmetry about the origin are usually simpler in spherical coordinates than in rectangular coordinates. For example, consider the upper nappe of the circular cone whose equation in rectangular coordinates is

$$z = \sqrt{x^2 + y^2}$$

(Table 11.8.2). The corresponding equation in cylindrical coordinates can be obtained from the cylindrical-to-rectangular conversion formulas in Table 11.8.1. This yields

$$z = \sqrt{(r \cos \theta)^2 + (r \sin \theta)^2} = \sqrt{r^2} = |r| = r$$

so the equation of the cone in cylindrical coordinates is $z = r$. Going a step further, the equation of the cone in spherical coordinates can be obtained from the spherical-to-cylindrical conversion formulas from Table 11.8.1. This yields

$$\rho \cos \phi = \rho \sin \phi$$

which, if $\rho \ne 0$, can be rewritten as

$$\tan \phi = 1 \quad \text{or} \quad \phi = \frac{\pi}{4}$$

Geometrically, this tells us that the radial line from the origin to any point on the cone makes an angle of $\pi/4$ with the z-axis.

Table 11.8.2

	CONE	CYLINDER	SPHERE	PARABOLOID	HYPERBOLOID
RECTANGULAR	$z = \sqrt{x^2 + y^2}$	$x^2 + y^2 = 1$	$x^2 + y^2 + z^2 = 1$	$z = x^2 + y^2$	$x^2 + y^2 - z^2 = 1$
CYLINDRICAL	$z = r$	$r = 1$	$z^2 = 1 - r^2$	$z = r^2$	$z^2 = r^2 - 1$
SPHERICAL	$\phi = \pi/4$	$\rho = \csc \phi$	$\rho = 1$	$\rho = \cos \phi \csc^2 \phi$	$\rho^2 = -\sec 2\phi$

▶ **Example 3**   Find equations of the paraboloid $z = x^2 + y^2$ in cylindrical and spherical coordinates.

Solution.   The rectangular-to-cylindrical conversion formulas in Table 11.8.1 yield

$$z = r^2 \qquad (4)$$

which is the equation in cylindrical coordinates. Now applying the spherical-to-cylindrical conversion formulas to (4) yields

$$\rho \cos \phi = \rho^2 \sin^2 \phi$$

which we can rewrite as

$$\rho = \cos \phi \csc^2 \phi$$

Alternatively, we could have obtained this equation directly from the equation in rectangular coordinates by applying the spherical-to-rectangular conversion formulas (verify). ◀

> Verify the equations given in Table 11.8.2 for the cylinder and hyperboloid in cylindrical and spherical coordinates.

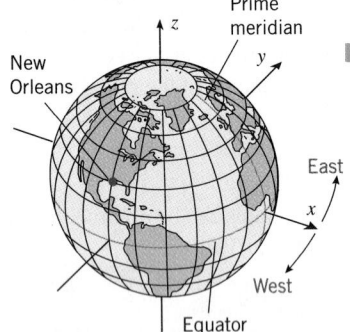

▲ **Figure 11.8.9**

■ SPHERICAL COORDINATES IN NAVIGATION

Spherical coordinates are related to longitude and latitude coordinates used in navigation. To see why this is so, let us construct a right-hand rectangular coordinate system with its origin at the center of the Earth, its positive z-axis passing through the North Pole, and its positive x-axis passing through the prime meridian (Figure 11.8.9). If we assume the Earth to be a sphere of radius $\rho = 4000$ miles, then each point on the Earth has spherical coordinates of the form $(4000, \theta, \phi)$, where ϕ and θ determine the latitude and longitude of the point. It is common to specify longitudes in degrees east or west of the prime meridian and latitudes in degrees north or south of the equator. However, the next example shows that it is a simple matter to determine ϕ and θ from such data.

Jon Arnold/Danita Delimont

Modern navigation systems use multiple coordinate representations to calculate position.

▶ **Example 4**   The city of New Orleans is located at $90°$ west longitude and $30°$ north latitude. Find its spherical and rectangular coordinates relative to the coordinate axes of Figure 11.8.9. (Assume that distance is in miles.)

Solution.   A longitude of $90°$ west corresponds to $\theta = 360° - 90° = 270°$ or $\theta = 3\pi/2$ radians; and a latitude of $30°$ north corresponds to $\phi = 90° - 30° = 60°$ or $\phi = \pi/3$ radians. Thus, the spherical coordinates (ρ, θ, ϕ) of New Orleans are $(4000, 3\pi/2, \pi/3)$.

To find the rectangular coordinates we apply the spherical-to-rectangular conversion formulas in Table 11.8.1. This yields

$$x = 4000 \sin \frac{\pi}{3} \cos \frac{3\pi}{2} = 4000 \frac{\sqrt{3}}{2}(0) = 0 \text{ mi}$$

$$y = 4000 \sin \frac{\pi}{3} \sin \frac{3\pi}{2} = 4000 \frac{\sqrt{3}}{2}(-1) = -2000\sqrt{3} \text{ mi}$$

$$z = 4000 \cos \frac{\pi}{3} = 4000 \left(\frac{1}{2} \right) = 2000 \text{ mi} \quad ◀$$

✔ QUICK CHECK EXERCISES 11.8   *(See page 838 for answers.)*

1. The conversion formulas from cylindrical coordinates (r, θ, z) to rectangular coordinates (x, y, z) are

$$x = \underline{\hspace{1cm}}, \quad y = \underline{\hspace{1cm}}, \quad z = \underline{\hspace{1cm}}$$

2. The conversion formulas from spherical coordinates (ρ, θ, ϕ) to rectangular coordinates (x, y, z) are

$$x = \underline{\hspace{1cm}}, \quad y = \underline{\hspace{1cm}}, \quad z = \underline{\hspace{1cm}}$$

3. The conversion formulas from spherical coordinates (ρ, θ, ϕ) to cylindrical coordinates (r, θ, z) are

$$r = \underline{\hspace{1cm}}, \qquad \theta = \underline{\hspace{1cm}}, \qquad z = \underline{\hspace{1cm}}$$

4. Let P be the point in 3-space with rectangular coordinates $(\sqrt{2}, -\sqrt{2}, 2\sqrt{3})$.
   (a) Cylindrical coordinates for P are $(r, \theta, z) = \underline{\hspace{1cm}}$.
   (b) Spherical coordinates for P are $(\rho, \theta, \phi) = \underline{\hspace{1cm}}$.

5. Give an equation of a sphere of radius 5, centered at the origin, in
   (a) rectangular coordinates
   (b) cylindrical coordinates
   (c) spherical coordinates.

EXERCISE SET 11.8 $\sim$ Graphing Utility   [c] CAS

1–2 Convert from rectangular to cylindrical coordinates. ∎

1. (a) $(4\sqrt{3}, 4, -4)$ (b) $(-5, 5, 6)$
   (c) $(0, 2, 0)$ (d) $(4, -4\sqrt{3}, 6)$

2. (a) $(\sqrt{2}, -\sqrt{2}, 1)$ (b) $(0, 1, 1)$
   (c) $(-4, 4, -7)$ (d) $(2, -2, -2)$

3–4 Convert from cylindrical to rectangular coordinates. ∎

3. (a) $(4, \pi/6, 3)$ (b) $(8, 3\pi/4, -2)$
   (c) $(5, 0, 4)$ (d) $(7, \pi, -9)$

4. (a) $(6, 5\pi/3, 7)$ (b) $(1, \pi/2, 0)$
   (c) $(3, \pi/2, 5)$ (d) $(4, \pi/2, -1)$

5–6 Convert from rectangular to spherical coordinates. ∎

5. (a) $(1, \sqrt{3}, -2)$ (b) $(1, -1, \sqrt{2})$
   (c) $(0, 3\sqrt{3}, 3)$ (d) $(-5\sqrt{3}, 5, 0)$

6. (a) $(4, 4, 4\sqrt{6})$ (b) $(1, -\sqrt{3}, -2)$
   (c) $(2, 0, 0)$ (d) $(\sqrt{3}, 1, 2\sqrt{3})$

7–8 Convert from spherical to rectangular coordinates. ∎

7. (a) $(5, \pi/6, \pi/4)$ (b) $(7, 0, \pi/2)$
   (c) $(1, \pi, 0)$ (d) $(2, 3\pi/2, \pi/2)$

8. (a) $(1, 2\pi/3, 3\pi/4)$ (b) $(3, 7\pi/4, 5\pi/6)$
   (c) $(8, \pi/6, \pi/4)$ (d) $(4, \pi/2, \pi/3)$

9–10 Convert from cylindrical to spherical coordinates. ∎

9. (a) $(\sqrt{3}, \pi/6, 3)$ (b) $(1, \pi/4, -1)$
   (c) $(2, 3\pi/4, 0)$ (d) $(6, 1, -2\sqrt{3})$

10. (a) $(4, 5\pi/6, 4)$ (b) $(2, 0, -2)$
   (c) $(4, \pi/2, 3)$ (d) $(6, \pi, 2)$

11–12 Convert from spherical to cylindrical coordinates. ∎

11. (a) $(5, \pi/4, 2\pi/3)$ (b) $(1, 7\pi/6, \pi)$
   (c) $(3, 0, 0)$ (d) $(4, \pi/6, \pi/2)$

12. (a) $(5, \pi/2, 0)$ (b) $(6, 0, 3\pi/4)$
   (c) $(\sqrt{2}, 3\pi/4, \pi)$ (d) $(5, 2\pi/3, 5\pi/6)$

[c] **13.** Use a CAS or a programmable calculating utility to set up the conversion formulas in Table 11.8.1, and then use the CAS or calculating utility to solve the problems in Exercises 1, 3, 5, 7, 9, and 11.

[c] **14.** Use a CAS or a programmable calculating utility to set up the conversion formulas in Table 11.8.1, and then use the CAS or calculating utility to solve the problems in Exercises 2, 4, 6, 8, 10, and 12.

15–18 True–False Determine whether the statement is true or false. Explain your answer. ∎

15. In cylindrical coordinates for a point, r is the distance from the point to the z-axis.

16. In spherical coordinates for a point, ρ is the distance from the point to the origin.

17. The graph of $\theta = \theta_0$ in cylindrical coordinates is the same as the graph of $\theta = \theta_0$ in spherical coordinates.

18. The graph of $r = f(\theta)$ in cylindrical coordinates can always be obtained by extrusion of the polar graph of $r = f(\theta)$ in the xy-plane.

19–26 An equation is given in cylindrical coordinates. Express the equation in rectangular coordinates and sketch the graph. ∎

19. $r = 3$ **20.** $\theta = \pi/4$ **21.** $z = r^2$

22. $z = r\cos\theta$ **23.** $r = 4\sin\theta$ **24.** $r = 2\sec\theta$

25. $r^2 + z^2 = 1$ **26.** $r^2\cos 2\theta = z$

27–34 An equation is given in spherical coordinates. Express the equation in rectangular coordinates and sketch the graph. ∎

27. $\rho = 3$ **28.** $\theta = \pi/3$ **29.** $\phi = \pi/4$

30. $\rho = 2\sec\phi$ **31.** $\rho = 4\cos\phi$ **32.** $\rho\sin\phi = 1$

33. $\rho\sin\phi = 2\cos\theta$ **34.** $\rho - 2\sin\phi\cos\theta = 0$

35–46 An equation of a surface is given in rectangular coordinates. Find an equation of the surface in (a) cylindrical coordinates and (b) spherical coordinates. ∎

35. $z = 3$ **36.** $y = 2$

37. $z = 3x^2 + 3y^2$ **38.** $z = \sqrt{3x^2 + 3y^2}$

39. $x^2 + y^2 = 4$ **40.** $x^2 + y^2 - 6y = 0$

41. $x^2 + y^2 + z^2 = 9$ **42.** $z^2 = x^2 - y^2$

43. $2x + 3y + 4z = 1$ **44.** $x^2 + y^2 - z^2 = 1$

45. $x^2 = 16 - z^2$ **46.** $x^2 + y^2 + z^2 = 2z$

FOCUS ON CONCEPTS

47–50 Describe the region in 3-space that satisfies the given inequalities. ■

47. $r^2 \le z \le 4$

48. $0 \le r \le 2\sin\theta, \quad 0 \le z \le 3$

49. $1 \le \rho \le 3$

50. $0 \le \phi \le \pi/6, \quad 0 \le \rho \le 2$

51. St. Petersburg (Leningrad), Russia, is located at 30° east longitude and 60° north latitude. Find its spherical and rectangular coordinates relative to the coordinate axes of Figure 11.8.9. Take miles as the unit of distance and assume the Earth to be a sphere of radius 4000 miles.

52. (a) Show that the curve of intersection of the surfaces $z = \sin\theta$ and $r = a$ (cylindrical coordinates) is an ellipse.

(b) Sketch the surface $z = \sin\theta$ for $0 \le \theta \le \pi/2$.

53. The accompanying figure shows a right circular cylinder of radius 10 cm spinning at 3 revolutions per minute about the z-axis. At time $t = 0$ s, a bug at the point $(0, 10, 0)$ begins walking straight up the face of the cylinder at the rate of 0.5 cm/min.

(a) Find the cylindrical coordinates of the bug after 2 min.

(b) Find the rectangular coordinates of the bug after 2 min.

(c) Find the spherical coordinates of the bug after 2 min.

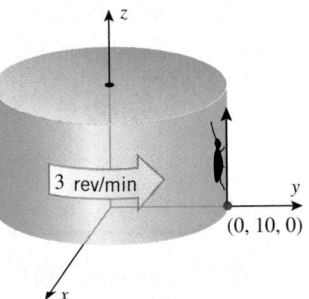

◀ **Figure Ex-53**

54. Referring to Exercise 53, use a graphing utility to graph the bug's distance from the origin as a function of time.

55. **Writing** Discuss some practical applications in which non-rectangular coordinate systems are useful.

56. **Writing** The terms "zenith" and "azimuth" are used in celestial navigation. How do these terms relate to spherical coordinates?

✔ **QUICK CHECK ANSWERS 11.8**

1. $r\cos\theta; \ r\sin\theta; \ z$ **2.** $\rho\sin\phi\cos\theta; \ \rho\sin\phi\sin\theta; \ \rho\cos\phi$ **3.** $\rho\sin\phi; \ \theta; \ \rho\cos\theta$

4. (a) $(2, 7\pi/4, 2\sqrt{3})$ (b) $(4, 7\pi/4, \pi/6)$ **5.** (a) $x^2 + y^2 + z^2 = 25$ (b) $r^2 + z^2 = 25$ (c) $\rho = 5$

CHAPTER 11 REVIEW EXERCISES

1. (a) What is the difference between a vector and a scalar? Give a physical example of each.

(b) How can you determine whether or not two vectors are orthogonal?

(c) How can you determine whether or not two vectors are parallel?

(d) How can you determine whether or not three vectors with a common initial point lie in the same plane in 3-space?

2. (a) Sketch vectors **u** and **v** for which **u** + **v** and **u** − **v** are orthogonal.

(b) How can you use vectors to determine whether four points in 3-space lie in the same plane?

(c) If forces $\mathbf{F}_1 = \mathbf{i}$ and $\mathbf{F}_2 = \mathbf{j}$ are applied at a point in 2-space, what force would you apply at that point to cancel the combined effect of $\mathbf{F}_1$ and $\mathbf{F}_2$?

(d) Write an equation of the sphere with center $(1, -2, 2)$ that passes through the origin.

3. (a) Draw a picture that shows the direction angles $\alpha, \beta,$ and γ of a vector.

(b) What are the components of a unit vector in 2-space that makes an angle of 120° with the vector **i** (two answers)?

(c) How can you use vectors to determine whether a triangle with known vertices $P_1, P_2,$ and P_3 has an obtuse angle?

(d) True or false: The cross product of orthogonal unit vectors is a unit vector. Explain your reasoning.

4. (a) Make a table that shows all possible cross products of the vectors **i**, **j**, and **k**.

(b) Give a geometric interpretation of $\|\mathbf{u} \times \mathbf{v}\|$.

(c) Give a geometric interpretation of $|\mathbf{u} \cdot (\mathbf{v} \times \mathbf{w})|$.

(d) Write an equation of the plane that passes through the origin and is perpendicular to the line $x = t, \ y = 2t, \ z = -t$.

5. In each part, find an equation of the sphere with center $(-3, 5, -4)$ and satisfying the given condition.

(a) Tangent to the xy-plane

(b) Tangent to the xz-plane

(c) Tangent to the yz-plane

6. Find the largest and smallest distances between the point $P(1, 1, 1)$ and the sphere

$$x^2 + y^2 + z^2 - 2y + 6z - 6 = 0$$

7. Given the points $P(3, 4)$, $Q(1, 1)$, and $R(5, 2)$, use vector methods to find the coordinates of the fourth vertex of the parallelogram whose adjacent sides are $\overrightarrow{PQ}$ and $\overrightarrow{QR}$.

8. Let $\mathbf{u} = \langle 3, 5, -1 \rangle$ and $\mathbf{v} = \langle 2, -2, 3 \rangle$. Find

(a) $2\mathbf{u} + 5\mathbf{v}$ (b) $\dfrac{1}{\|\mathbf{v}\|}\mathbf{v}$

(c) $\|\mathbf{u}\|$ (d) $\|\mathbf{u} - \mathbf{v}\|$.

9. Let $\mathbf{a} = c\mathbf{i} + \mathbf{j}$ and $\mathbf{b} = 4\mathbf{i} + 3\mathbf{j}$. Find c so that
(a) $\mathbf{a}$ and $\mathbf{b}$ are orthogonal
(b) the angle between $\mathbf{a}$ and $\mathbf{b}$ is $\pi/4$
(c) the angle between $\mathbf{a}$ and $\mathbf{b}$ is $\pi/6$
(d) $\mathbf{a}$ and $\mathbf{b}$ are parallel.

10. Let $\mathbf{r}_0 = \langle x_0, y_0, z_0 \rangle$ and $\mathbf{r} = \langle x, y, z \rangle$. Describe the set of all points (x, y, z) for which
(a) $\mathbf{r} \cdot \mathbf{r}_0 = 0$ (b) $(\mathbf{r} - \mathbf{r}_0) \cdot \mathbf{r}_0 = 0$.

11. Show that if $\mathbf{u}$ and $\mathbf{v}$ are unit vectors and θ is the angle between them, then $\|\mathbf{u} - \mathbf{v}\| = 2 \sin \frac{1}{2}\theta$.

12. Find the vector with length 5 and direction angles $\alpha = 60°$, $\beta = 120°$, $\gamma = 135°$.

13. Assuming that force is in pounds and distance is in feet, find the work done by a constant force $\mathbf{F} = 3\mathbf{i} - 4\mathbf{j} + \mathbf{k}$ acting on a particle that moves on a straight line from $P(5, 7, 0)$ to $Q(6, 6, 6)$.

14. Assuming that force is in newtons and distance is in meters, find the work done by the resultant of the constant forces $\mathbf{F}_1 = \mathbf{i} - 3\mathbf{j} + \mathbf{k}$ and $\mathbf{F}_2 = \mathbf{i} + 2\mathbf{j} + 2\mathbf{k}$ acting on a particle that moves on a straight line from $P(-1, -2, 3)$ to $Q(0, 2, 0)$.

15. (a) Find the area of the triangle with vertices $A(1, 0, 1)$, $B(0, 2, 3)$, and $C(2, 1, 0)$.
(b) Use the result in part (a) to find the length of the altitude from vertex C to side AB.

16. True or false? Explain your reasoning.
(a) If $\mathbf{u} \cdot \mathbf{v} = 0$, then $\mathbf{u} = \mathbf{0}$ or $\mathbf{v} = \mathbf{0}$.
(b) If $\mathbf{u} \times \mathbf{v} = \mathbf{0}$, then $\mathbf{u} = \mathbf{0}$ or $\mathbf{v} = \mathbf{0}$.
(c) If $\mathbf{u} \cdot \mathbf{v} = 0$ and $\mathbf{u} \times \mathbf{v} = \mathbf{0}$, then $\mathbf{u} = \mathbf{0}$ or $\mathbf{v} = \mathbf{0}$.

17. Consider the points

$$A(1, -1, 2), \quad B(2, -3, 0), \quad C(-1, -2, 0), \quad D(2, 1, -1)$$

(a) Find the volume of the parallelepiped that has the vectors $\overrightarrow{AB}$, $\overrightarrow{AC}$, $\overrightarrow{AD}$ as adjacent edges.
(b) Find the distance from D to the plane containing A, B, and C.

18. Suppose that a force $\mathbf{F}$ with a magnitude of 9 lb is applied to the lever–shaft assembly shown in the accompanying figure.
(a) Express the force $\mathbf{F}$ in component form.
(b) Find the vector moment of $\mathbf{F}$ about the origin.

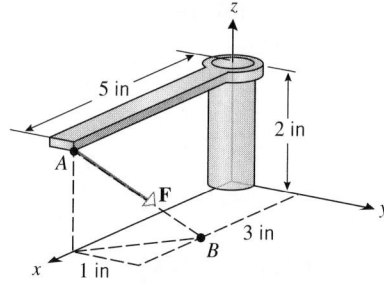

◀ **Figure Ex-18**

19. Let P be the point $(4, 1, 2)$. Find parametric equations for the line through P and parallel to the vector $\langle 1, -1, 0 \rangle$.

20. (a) Find parametric equations for the intersection of the planes $2x + y - z = 3$ and $x + 2y + z = 3$.
(b) Find the acute angle between the two planes.

21. Find an equation of the plane that is parallel to the plane $x + 5y - z + 8 = 0$ and contains the point $(1, 1, 4)$.

22. Find an equation of the plane through the point $(4, 3, 0)$ and parallel to the vectors $\mathbf{i} + \mathbf{k}$ and $2\mathbf{j} - \mathbf{k}$.

23. What condition must the constants satisfy for the planes

$$a_1 x + b_1 y + c_1 z = d_1 \quad \text{and} \quad a_2 x + b_2 y + c_2 z = d_2$$

to be perpendicular?

24. (a) List six common types of quadric surfaces, and describe their traces in planes parallel to the coordinate planes.
(b) Give the coordinates of the points that result when the point (x, y, z) is reflected about the plane $y = x$, the plane $y = z$, and the plane $x = z$.
(c) Describe the intersection of the surfaces $r = 5$ and $z = 1$ in cylindrical coordinates.
(d) Describe the intersection of the surfaces $\phi = \pi/4$ and $\theta = 0$ in spherical coordinates.

25. In each part, identify the surface by completing the squares.
(a) $x^2 + 4y^2 - z^2 - 6x + 8y + 4z = 0$
(b) $x^2 + y^2 + z^2 + 6x - 4y + 12z = 0$
(c) $x^2 + y^2 - z^2 - 2x + 4y + 5 = 0$

26. In each part, express the equation in cylindrical and spherical coordinates.
(a) $x^2 + y^2 = z$ (b) $x^2 - y^2 - z^2 = 0$

27. In each part, express the equation in rectangular coordinates.
(a) $z = r^2 \cos 2\theta$ (b) $\rho^2 \sin \phi \cos \phi \cos \theta = 1$

28–29 Sketch the solid in 3-space that is described in cylindrical coordinates by the stated inequalities. ■

28. (a) $1 \leq r \leq 2$ (b) $2 \leq z \leq 3$ (c) $\pi/6 \leq \theta \leq \pi/3$
(d) $1 \leq r \leq 2$, $2 \leq z \leq 3$, and $\pi/6 \leq \theta \leq \pi/3$

29. (a) $r^2 + z^2 \leq 4$ (b) $r \leq 1$
(c) $r^2 + z^2 \leq 4$ and $r > 1$

30–31 Sketch the solid in 3-space that is described in spherical coordinates by the stated inequalities. ■

30. (a) $0 \leq \rho \leq 2$ (b) $0 \leq \phi \leq \pi/6$
    (c) $0 \leq \rho \leq 2$ and $0 \leq \phi \leq \pi/6$

31. (a) $0 \leq \rho \leq 5$, $0 \leq \phi \leq \pi/2$, and $0 \leq \theta \leq \pi/2$
    (b) $0 \leq \phi \leq \pi/3$ and $0 \leq \rho \leq 2 \sec \phi$
    (c) $0 \leq \rho \leq 2$ and $\pi/6 \leq \phi \leq \pi/3$

32. Sketch the surface whose equation in spherical coordinates is $\rho = a(1 - \cos \phi)$. [*Hint:* The surface is shaped like a familiar fruit.]

CHAPTER 11 MAKING CONNECTIONS

1. Define a "rotation operator" R on vectors in the xy-plane by the formula
$$R(x\mathbf{i} + y\mathbf{j}) = -y\mathbf{i} + x\mathbf{j}$$

(a) Verify that R rotates vectors $90°$ counterclockwise.
(b) Prove that R has the following linearity properties:

$$R(c\mathbf{v}) = cR(\mathbf{v}) \quad \text{and} \quad R(\mathbf{v} + \mathbf{w}) = R(\mathbf{v}) + R(\mathbf{w})$$

2. (a) Given a triangle in the xy-plane, assign to each side of the triangle an outward normal vector whose length is the same as that of the corresponding side. Prove that the sum of the resulting three normal vectors is the zero vector.
(b) Extend the result of part (a) to a polygon of n sides in the xy-plane. [*Hint:* Use the results of the preceding exercise.]

3. (a) Given a tetrahedron in 3-space, assign to each face of the tetrahedron an outward normal vector whose length is numerically the same as the area of the corresponding face. Prove that the sum of the resulting four normal vectors is the zero vector. [*Hint:* Use cross products.]
(b) Extend your result from part (a) to a pyramid with a four-sided base. [*Hint:* Divide the base into two triangles and use the result from part (a) on each of the two resulting tetrahedra.]
(c) Can you extend the results of parts (a) and (b) to other polyhedra?

4. Given a tetrahedron in 3-space, pick a vertex and label the three faces that meet at that vertex as A, B, and C. Let a, b, and c denote the respective areas of those faces, and let d denote the area of the fourth face of the tetrahedron. Let α denote the (internal) angle between faces A and B, β the angle between B and C, and γ the angle between A and C.
(a) Prove that

$$d^2 = a^2 + b^2 + c^2 - 2ab \cos \alpha - 2bc \cos \beta - 2ac \cos \gamma$$

This result is sometimes referred to as the *law of cosines for a tetrahedron*. [*Hint:* Use the result in part (a) of the preceding exercise.]
(b) With the result in part (a) as motivation, state and prove a "Theorem of Pythagoras for a Tetrahedron."

5. Any circle that lies on a sphere can be realized as the intersection of the sphere and a plane. If the plane passes through the center of the sphere, then the circle is referred to as a *great circle*. Given two points on a sphere, the *great circle distance* between the two points is the length of the smallest arc of a great circle that contains both points. Assume that Σ is a sphere of radius ρ centered at the origin in 3-space. If points P and Q lie on Σ and have spherical coordinates (ρ, θ_1, ϕ_1) and (ρ, θ_2, ϕ_2), respectively, prove that the great circle distance between P and Q is

$$\rho \cos^{-1}(\cos \phi_1 \cos \phi_2 + \cos(\theta_1 - \theta_2) \sin \phi_1 \sin \phi_2)$$

6. A ship at sea is at point A that is $60°$ west longitude and $40°$ north latitude. The ship travels to point B that is $40°$ west longitude and $20°$ north latitude. Assuming that the Earth is a sphere with radius 6370 kilometers, find the shortest distance the ship can travel in going from A to B, given that the shortest distance between two points on a sphere is along the arc of the great circle joining the points. [*Suggestion:* Introduce an xyz-coordinate system as in Figure 11.8.9, and use the result of the preceding exercise.]

Courtesy Cedar Point

12

VECTOR-VALUED FUNCTIONS

The design of a roller coaster requires an understanding of the mathematical principles governing the motion of objects that move with varying speed and direction.

In this chapter we will consider functions whose values are vectors. Such functions provide a unified way of studying parametric curves in 2-space and 3-space and are a basic tool for analyzing the motion of particles along curved paths. We will begin by developing the calculus of vector-valued functions—we will show how to differentiate and integrate such functions, and we will develop some of the basic properties of these operations. We will then apply these calculus tools to define three fundamental vectors that can be used to describe such basic characteristics of curves as curvature and twisting tendencies. Once this is done, we will develop the concepts of velocity and acceleration for such motion, and we will apply these concepts to explain various physical phenomena. Finally, we will use the calculus of vector-valued functions to develop basic principles of gravitational attraction and to derive Kepler's laws of planetary motion.

12.1 INTRODUCTION TO VECTOR-VALUED FUNCTIONS

In Section 11.5 we discussed parametric equations of lines in 3-space. In this section we will discuss more general parametric curves in 3-space, and we will show how vector notation can be used to express parametric equations in 2-space and 3-space in a more compact form. This will lead us to consider a new kind of function—namely, functions that associate vectors with real numbers. Such functions have many important applications in physics and engineering.

PARAMETRIC CURVES IN 3-SPACE

Recall from Section 10.1 that if f and g are well-behaved functions, then the pair of parametric equations

$$x = f(t), \quad y = g(t) \tag{1}$$

generates a curve in 2-space that is traced in a specific direction as the parameter t increases. We defined this direction to be the *orientation* of the curve or the *direction of increasing parameter*, and we called the curve together with its orientation the *graph* of the parametric equations or the *parametric curve* represented by the equations. Analogously, if f, g, and h are three well-behaved functions, then the parametric equations

$$x = f(t), \quad y = g(t), \quad z = h(t) \tag{2}$$

generate a curve in 3-space that is traced in a specific direction as t increases. As in 2-space, this direction is called the ***orientation*** or ***direction of increasing parameter***, and

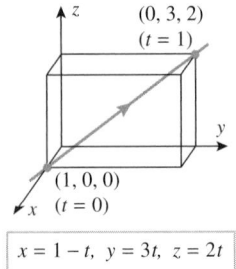

$$x = 1 - t, \ y = 3t, \ z = 2t$$

▲ **Figure 12.1.1**

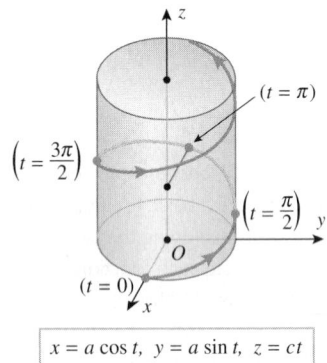

$$x = a \cos t, \ y = a \sin t, \ z = ct$$

. ▲ **Figure 12.1.2**

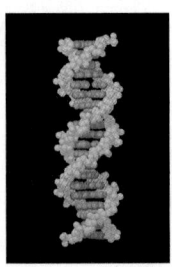

The circular helix described in Example 2 occurs in nature. Above is a computer representation of the twin helix DNA molecule (deoxyribonucleic acid). This structure contains all the inherited instructions necessary for the development of a living organism.

TECHNOLOGY MASTERY

If you have a CAS, use it to generate the tricuspoid in Figure 12.1.3, and show that this parametric curve is oriented counterclockwise.

the curve together with its orientation is called the ***graph*** of the parametric equations or the ***parametric curve*** represented by the equations. If no restrictions are stated explicitly or are implied by the equations, then it will be understood that t varies over the interval $(-\infty, +\infty)$.

▶ **Example 1** The parametric equations

$$x = 1 - t, \quad y = 3t, \quad z = 2t$$

represent a line in 3-space that passes through the point $(1, 0, 0)$ and is parallel to the vector $\langle -1, 3, 2 \rangle$. Since x decreases as t increases, the line has the orientation shown in Figure 12.1.1. ◀

▶ **Example 2** Describe the parametric curve represented by the equations

$$x = a \cos t, \quad y = a \sin t, \quad z = ct$$

where a and c are positive constants.

Solution. As the parameter t increases, the value of $z = ct$ also increases, so the point (x, y, z) moves upward. However, as t increases, the point (x, y, z) also moves in a path directly over the circle

$$x = a \cos t, \quad y = a \sin t$$

in the xy-plane. The combination of these upward and circular motions produces a corkscrew-shaped curve that wraps around a right circular cylinder of radius a centered on the z-axis (Figure 12.1.2). This curve is called a ***circular helix***. ◀

■ **PARAMETRIC CURVES GENERATED WITH TECHNOLOGY**

Except in the simplest cases, parametric curves can be difficult to visualize and draw without the help of a graphing utility. For example, the ***tricuspoid*** is the graph of the parametric equations

$$x = 2 \cos t + \cos 2t, \quad y = 2 \sin t - \sin 2t$$

Although it would be tedious to plot the tricuspoid by hand, a computer rendering is easy to obtain and reveals the significance of the name of the curve (Figure 12.1.3). However, note that the depiction of the tricuspoid in Figure 12.1.3 is incomplete, since the orientation of the curve is not indicated. This is often the case for curves that are generated with a graphing utility. (Some graphing utilities plot parametric curves slowly enough for the orientation to be discerned, or provide a feature for tracing the points along the curve in the direction of increasing parameter.)

Parametric curves in 3-space can be difficult to visualize correctly even with the help of a graphing utility. For example, Figure 12.1.4*a* shows a parametric curve called a *torus knot* that was produced with a CAS. However, it is unclear from this computer-generated figure whether the points of overlap are intersections or whether one portion of the curve is in front of the other. To resolve the visualization problem, some graphing utilities provide the capability of enclosing the curve within a thin tube, as in Figure 12.1.4*b*. Such graphs are called ***tube plots***.

■ **PARAMETRIC EQUATIONS FOR INTERSECTIONS OF SURFACES**

Curves in 3-space often arise as intersections of surfaces. For example, Figure 12.1.5*a* shows a portion of the intersection of the cylinders $z = x^3$ and $y = x^2$. One method for finding parametric equations for the curve of intersection is to choose one of the variables as the parameter and use the two equations to express the remaining two variables in terms

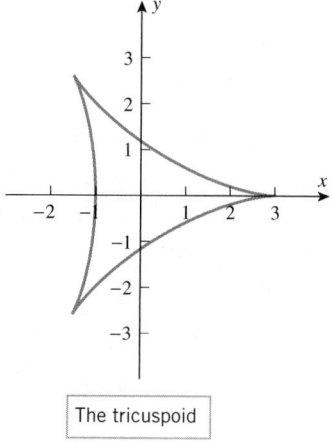

The tricuspoid

▲ **Figure 12.1.3**

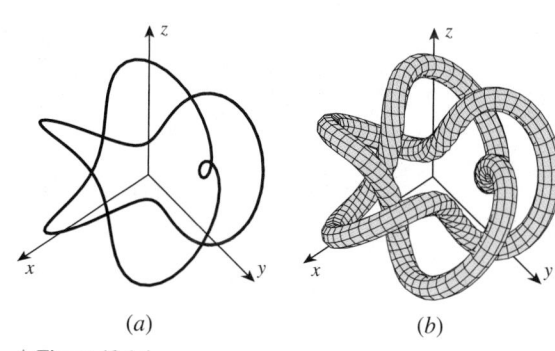

(a)   (b)

▲ **Figure 12.1.4**

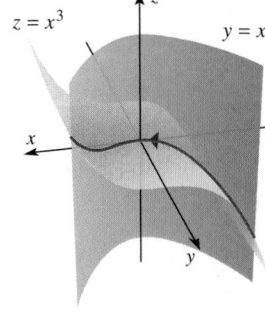

$z = x^3$ $y = x^2$

$x = t, y = t^2, z = t^3$

(a)

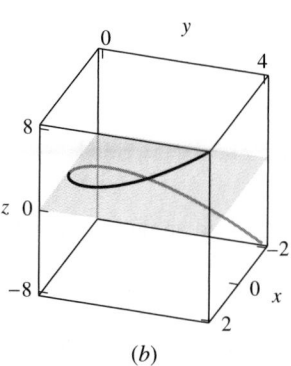

(b)

▲ **Figure 12.1.5**

of that parameter. In particular, if we choose $x = t$ as the parameter and substitute this into the equations $z = x^3$ and $y = x^2$, we obtain the parametric equations

$$x = t, \quad y = t^2, \quad z = t^3 \tag{3}$$

This curve is called a ***twisted cubic***. The portion of the twisted cubic shown in Figure 12.1.5a corresponds to $t \geq 0$; a computer-generated graph of the twisted cubic for positive and negative values of t is shown in Figure 12.1.5b. Some other examples and techniques for finding intersections of surfaces are discussed in the exercises.

■ **VECTOR-VALUED FUNCTIONS**

The twisted cubic defined by the equations in (3) is the set of points of the form (t, t^2, t^3) for real values of t. If we view each of these points as a terminal point for a vector $\mathbf{r}$ whose initial point is at the origin,

$$\mathbf{r} = \langle x, y, z \rangle = \langle t, t^2, t^3 \rangle = t\mathbf{i} + t^2\mathbf{j} + t^3\mathbf{k}$$

then we obtain $\mathbf{r}$ as a function of the parameter t, that is, $\mathbf{r} = \mathbf{r}(t)$. Since this function produces a *vector*, we say that $\mathbf{r} = \mathbf{r}(t)$ defines $\mathbf{r}$ as a ***vector-valued function of a real variable***, or more simply, a ***vector-valued function***. The vectors that we will consider in this text are either in 2-space or 3-space, so we will say that a vector-valued function is in 2-space or in 3-space according to the kind of vectors that it produces.

If $\mathbf{r}(t)$ is a vector-valued function in 3-space, then for each allowable value of t the vector $\mathbf{r} = \mathbf{r}(t)$ can be represented in terms of components as

$$\mathbf{r} = \mathbf{r}(t) = \langle x(t), y(t), z(t) \rangle = x(t)\mathbf{i} + y(t)\mathbf{j} + z(t)\mathbf{k} \tag{4}$$

The functions $x(t)$, $y(t)$, and $z(t)$ are called the ***component functions*** or the ***components*** of $\mathbf{r}(t)$.

Whereas a vector-valued function in 3-space, such as (4), has three components, a vector-valued function in 2-space has only two components and hence has the form

$$r(t) = \langle x(t), y(t) \rangle$$
$$= x(t)\mathbf{i} + y(t)\mathbf{j}$$

Find the vector-valued function in 2-space whose component functions are $x(t) = t$ and $y(t) = t^2$.

▶ **Example 3**   The component functions of

$$\mathbf{r}(t) = \langle t, t^2, t^3 \rangle = t\mathbf{i} + t^2\mathbf{j} + t^3\mathbf{k}$$

are

$$x(t) = t, \quad y(t) = t^2, \quad z(t) = t^3 \ \blacktriangleleft$$

The ***domain*** of a vector-valued function $\mathbf{r}(t)$ is the set of allowable values for t. If $\mathbf{r}(t)$ is defined in terms of component functions and the domain is not specified explicitly, then it will be understood that the domain is the intersection of the natural domains of the component functions; this is called the ***natural domain*** of $\mathbf{r}(t)$.

▶ **Example 4** Find the natural domain of

$$\mathbf{r}(t) = \langle \ln |t - 1|, e^t, \sqrt{t} \rangle = (\ln |t - 1|)\mathbf{i} + e^t\mathbf{j} + \sqrt{t}\mathbf{k}$$

Solution. The natural domains of the component functions

$$x(t) = \ln |t - 1|, \quad y(t) = e^t, \quad z(t) = \sqrt{t}$$

are

$$(-\infty, 1) \cup (1, +\infty), \quad (-\infty, +\infty), \quad [0, +\infty)$$

respectively. The intersection of these sets is

$$[0, 1) \cup (1, +\infty)$$

(verify), so the natural domain of $\mathbf{r}(t)$ consists of all values of t such that

$$0 \leq t < 1 \quad \text{or} \quad t > 1 \blacktriangleleft$$

■ **GRAPHS OF VECTOR-VALUED FUNCTIONS**

If $\mathbf{r}(t)$ is a vector-valued function in 2-space or 3-space, then we define the *graph* of $\mathbf{r}(t)$ to be the parametric curve described by the component functions for $\mathbf{r}(t)$. For example, if

$$\mathbf{r}(t) = \langle 1 - t, 3t, 2t \rangle = (1 - t)\mathbf{i} + 3t\mathbf{j} + 2t\mathbf{k} \tag{5}$$

then the graph of $\mathbf{r} = \mathbf{r}(t)$ is the graph of the parametric equations

$$x = 1 - t, \quad y = 3t, \quad z = 2t$$

Thus, the graph of (5) is the line in Figure 12.1.1.

▶ **Example 5** Describe the graph of the vector-valued function

$$\mathbf{r}(t) = \langle \cos t, \sin t, t \rangle = \cos t\mathbf{i} + \sin t\mathbf{j} + t\mathbf{k}$$

Solution. The corresponding parametric equations are

$$x = \cos t, \quad y = \sin t, \quad z = t$$

Thus, as we saw in Example 2, the graph is a circular helix wrapped around a cylinder of radius 1. ◀

Up to now we have considered parametric curves to be paths traced by moving points. However, if a parametric curve is viewed as the graph of a vector-valued function, then we can also imagine the graph to be traced by the tip of a moving vector. For example, if the curve C in 3-space is the graph of

$$\mathbf{r}(t) = x(t)\mathbf{i} + y(t)\mathbf{j} + z(t)\mathbf{k}$$

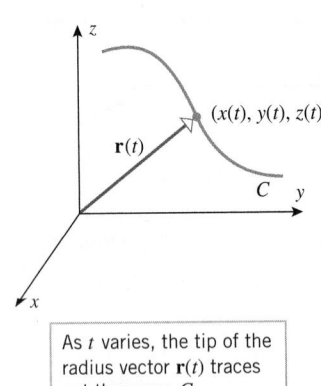

As t varies, the tip of the radius vector $\mathbf{r}(t)$ traces out the curve C.

▲ **Figure 12.1.6**

and if we position $\mathbf{r}(t)$ so its initial point is at the origin, then its terminal point will fall on the curve C (as shown in Figure 12.1.6). Thus, when $\mathbf{r}(t)$ is positioned with its initial point at the origin, its terminal point will trace out the curve C as the parameter t varies, in which case we call $\mathbf{r}(t)$ the *radius vector* or the *position vector* for C. For simplicity, we will sometimes let the dependence on t be understood and write $\mathbf{r}$ rather than $\mathbf{r}(t)$ for a radius vector.

▶ **Example 6** Sketch the graph and a radius vector of

(a) $\mathbf{r}(t) = \cos t\mathbf{i} + \sin t\mathbf{j}, \quad 0 \leq t \leq 2\pi$

(b) $\mathbf{r}(t) = \cos t\mathbf{i} + \sin t\mathbf{j} + 2\mathbf{k}, \quad 0 \leq t \leq 2\pi$

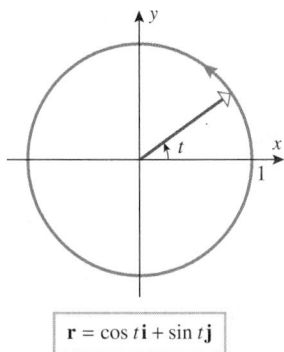

$$\mathbf{r} = \cos t\,\mathbf{i} + \sin t\,\mathbf{j}$$

▲ Figure 12.1.7

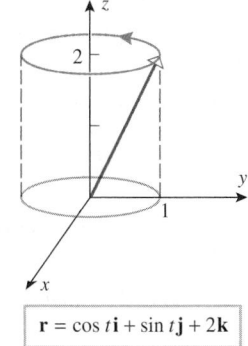

$$\mathbf{r} = \cos t\,\mathbf{i} + \sin t\,\mathbf{j} + 2\mathbf{k}$$

▲ Figure 12.1.8

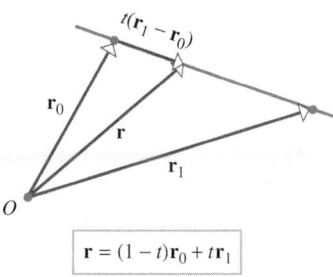

$$\mathbf{r} = (1 - t)\mathbf{r}_0 + t\mathbf{r}_1$$

▲ Figure 12.1.9

Solution (a). The corresponding parametric equations are

$$x = \cos t, \quad y = \sin t \qquad (0 \le t \le 2\pi)$$

so the graph is a circle of radius 1, centered at the origin, and oriented counterclockwise. The graph and a radius vector are shown in Figure 12.1.7.

Solution (b). The corresponding parametric equations are

$$x = \cos t, \quad y = \sin t, \quad z = 2 \qquad (0 \le t \le 2\pi)$$

From the third equation, the tip of the radius vector traces a curve in the plane $z = 2$, and from the first two equations, the curve is a circle of radius 1 centered at the point $(0, 0, 2)$ and traced counterclockwise looking down the z-axis. The graph and a radius vector are shown in Figure 12.1.8. ◄

■ VECTOR FORM OF A LINE SEGMENT

Recall from Formula (9) of Section 11.5 that if $\mathbf{r}_0$ is a vector in 2-space or 3-space with its initial point at the origin, then the line that passes through the terminal point of $\mathbf{r}_0$ and is parallel to the vector $\mathbf{v}$ can be expressed in vector form as

$$\mathbf{r} = \mathbf{r}_0 + t\mathbf{v}$$

In particular, if $\mathbf{r}_0$ and $\mathbf{r}_1$ are vectors in 2-space or 3-space with their initial points at the origin, then the line that passes through the terminal points of these vectors can be expressed in vector form as

$$\mathbf{r} = \mathbf{r}_0 + t(\mathbf{r}_1 - \mathbf{r}_0) \qquad \text{or} \qquad \mathbf{r} = (1 - t)\mathbf{r}_0 + t\mathbf{r}_1 \qquad (6\text{--}7)$$

as indicated in Figure 12.1.9.

It is common to call either (6) or (7) the ***two-point vector form of a line*** and to say, for simplicity, that the line passes through the *points* $\mathbf{r}_0$ and $\mathbf{r}_1$ (as opposed to saying that it passes through the *terminal points* of $\mathbf{r}_0$ and $\mathbf{r}_1$).

It is understood in (6) and (7) that t varies from $-\infty$ to $+\infty$. However, if we restrict t to vary over the interval $0 \le t \le 1$, then $\mathbf{r}$ will vary from $\mathbf{r}_0$ to $\mathbf{r}_1$. Thus, the equation

$$\mathbf{r} = (1 - t)\mathbf{r}_0 + t\mathbf{r}_1 \qquad (0 \le t \le 1) \tag{8}$$

represents the line segment in 2-space or 3-space that is traced from $\mathbf{r}_0$ to $\mathbf{r}_1$.

✔ QUICK CHECK EXERCISES 12.1   *(See page 847 for answers.)*

1. (a) Express the parametric equations

$$x = \frac{1}{t}, \quad y = \sqrt{t}, \quad z = \sin^{-1} t$$

as a single vector equation of the form

$$\mathbf{r} = x(t)\mathbf{i} + y(t)\mathbf{j} + z(t)\mathbf{k}$$

   (b) The vector equation in part (a) defines $\mathbf{r} = \mathbf{r}(t)$ as a vector-valued function. The domain of $\mathbf{r}(t)$ is _____ and $\mathbf{r}\left(\frac{1}{2}\right) = $ _____.

2. Describe the graph of $\mathbf{r}(t) = \langle 1 + 2t, -1 + 3t \rangle$.

3. Describe the graph of $\mathbf{r}(t) = \sin^2 t\,\mathbf{i} + \cos^2 t\,\mathbf{j}$.

4. Find a vector equation for the curve of intersection of the surfaces $y = x^2$ and $z = y$ in terms of the parameter $x = t$.

EXERCISE SET 12.1   ◺ Graphing Utility

1–4 Find the domain of $\mathbf{r}(t)$ and the value of $\mathbf{r}(t_0)$. ■

1. $\mathbf{r}(t) = \cos t\,\mathbf{i} - 3t\,\mathbf{j}; \quad t_0 = \pi$

2. $\mathbf{r}(t) = \langle \sqrt{3t + 1}, t^2 \rangle; \quad t_0 = 1$

3. $\mathbf{r}(t) = \cos \pi t\,\mathbf{i} - \ln t\,\mathbf{j} + \sqrt{t - 2}\,\mathbf{k}; \quad t_0 = 3$

4. $\mathbf{r}(t) = \langle 2e^{-t}, \sin^{-1} t, \ln(1-t)\rangle$; $t_0 = 0$

5–6 Express the parametric equations as a single vector equation of the form

$$\mathbf{r} = x(t)\mathbf{i} + y(t)\mathbf{j} \quad \text{or} \quad \mathbf{r} = x(t)\mathbf{i} + y(t)\mathbf{j} + z(t)\mathbf{k} \; \blacksquare$$

5. $x = 3\cos t, \; y = t + \sin t$

6. $x = 2t, \; y = 2\sin 3t, \; z = 5\cos 3t$

7–8 Find the parametric equations that correspond to the given vector equation. $\blacksquare$

7. $\mathbf{r} = 3t^2\mathbf{i} - 2\mathbf{j}$

8. $\mathbf{r} = (2t-1)\mathbf{i} - 3\sqrt{t}\mathbf{j} + \sin 3t\mathbf{k}$

9–14 Describe the graph of the equation. $\blacksquare$

9. $\mathbf{r} = (3 - 2t)\mathbf{i} + 5t\mathbf{j}$ **10.** $\mathbf{r} = 2\sin 3t\mathbf{i} - 2\cos 3t\mathbf{j}$

11. $\mathbf{r} = 2t\mathbf{i} - 3\mathbf{j} + (1 + 3t)\mathbf{k}$

12. $\mathbf{r} = 3\mathbf{i} + 2\cos t\mathbf{j} + 2\sin t\mathbf{k}$

13. $\mathbf{r} = 2\cos t\mathbf{i} - 3\sin t\mathbf{j} + \mathbf{k}$

14. $\mathbf{r} = -3\mathbf{i} + (1 - t^2)\mathbf{j} + t\mathbf{k}$

15. (a) Find the slope of the line in 2-space that is represented by the vector equation $\mathbf{r} = (1 - 2t)\mathbf{i} - (2 - 3t)\mathbf{j}$.
   (b) Find the coordinates of the point where the line

$$\mathbf{r} = (2 + t)\mathbf{i} + (1 - 2t)\mathbf{j} + 3t\mathbf{k}$$

   intersects the xz-plane.

16. (a) Find the y-intercept of the line in 2-space that is represented by the vector equation $\mathbf{r} = (3 + 2t)\mathbf{i} + 5t\mathbf{j}$.
   (b) Find the coordinates of the point where the line

$$\mathbf{r} = t\mathbf{i} + (1 + 2t)\mathbf{j} - 3t\mathbf{k}$$

   intersects the plane $3x - y - z = 2$.

17–18 Sketch the line segment represented by each vector equation. $\blacksquare$

17. (a) $\mathbf{r} = (1 - t)\mathbf{i} + t\mathbf{j}$; $0 \le t \le 1$
   (b) $\mathbf{r} = (1 - t)(\mathbf{i} + \mathbf{j}) + t(\mathbf{i} - \mathbf{j})$; $0 \le t \le 1$

18. (a) $\mathbf{r} = (1 - t)(\mathbf{i} + \mathbf{j}) + t\mathbf{k}$; $0 \le t \le 1$
   (b) $\mathbf{r} = (1 - t)(\mathbf{i} + \mathbf{j} + \mathbf{k}) + t(\mathbf{i} + \mathbf{j})$; $0 \le t \le 1$

19–20 Write a vector equation for the line segment from P to Q. $\blacksquare$

19. 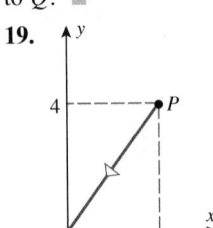   **20.**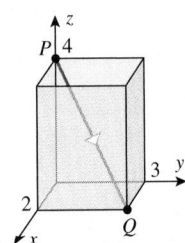

21–30 Sketch the graph of $\mathbf{r}(t)$ and show the direction of increasing t. $\blacksquare$

21. $\mathbf{r}(t) = 2\mathbf{i} + t\mathbf{j}$ **22.** $\mathbf{r}(t) = \langle 3t - 4, 6t + 2\rangle$

23. $\mathbf{r}(t) = (1 + \cos t)\mathbf{i} + (3 - \sin t)\mathbf{j}$; $0 \le t \le 2\pi$

24. $\mathbf{r}(t) = \langle 2\cos t, 5\sin t\rangle$; $0 \le t \le 2\pi$

25. $\mathbf{r}(t) = \cosh t\mathbf{i} + \sinh t\mathbf{j}$ **26.** $\mathbf{r}(t) = \sqrt{t}\mathbf{i} + (2t + 4)\mathbf{j}$

27. $\mathbf{r}(t) = 2\cos t\mathbf{i} + 2\sin t\mathbf{j} + t\mathbf{k}$

28. $\mathbf{r}(t) = 9\cos t\mathbf{i} + 4\sin t\mathbf{j} + t\mathbf{k}$

29. $\mathbf{r}(t) = t\mathbf{i} + t^2\mathbf{j} + 2\mathbf{k}$

30. $\mathbf{r}(t) = t\mathbf{i} + t\mathbf{j} + \sin t\mathbf{k}$; $0 \le t \le 2\pi$

31–34 True–False Determine whether the statement is true or false. Explain your answer. $\blacksquare$

31. The natural domain of a vector-valued function is the union of the domains of its component functions.

32. If $\mathbf{r}(t) = \langle x(t), y(t)\rangle$ is a vector-valued function in 2-space, then the graph of $\mathbf{r}(t)$ is a surface in 3-space.

33. If $\mathbf{r}_0$ and $\mathbf{r}_1$ are vectors in 3-space, then the graph of the vector-valued function

$$\mathbf{r}(t) = (1 - t)\mathbf{r}_0 + t\mathbf{r}_1 \quad (0 \le t \le 1)$$

is the straight line segment joining the terminal points of $\mathbf{r}_0$ and $\mathbf{r}_1$.

34. The graph of $\mathbf{r}(t) = \langle 2\cos t, 2\sin t, t\rangle$ is a circular helix.

35–36 Sketch the curve of intersection of the surfaces, and find parametric equations for the intersection in terms of parameter $x = t$. Check your work with a graphing utility by generating the parametric curve over the interval $-1 \le t \le 1$. $\blacksquare$

35. $z = x^2 + y^2, \; x - y = 0$

36. $y + x = 0, \; z = \sqrt{2 - x^2 - y^2}$

37–38 Sketch the curve of intersection of the surfaces, and find a vector equation for the curve in terms of the parameter $x = t$. $\blacksquare$

37. $9x^2 + y^2 + 9z^2 = 81, \; y = x^2 \quad (z > 0)$

38. $y = x, \; x + y + z = 1$

39. Show that the graph of

$$\mathbf{r} = t\sin t\mathbf{i} + t\cos t\mathbf{j} + t^2\mathbf{k}$$

lies on the paraboloid $z = x^2 + y^2$.

40. Show that the graph of

$$\mathbf{r} = t\mathbf{i} + \frac{1 + t}{t}\mathbf{j} + \frac{1 - t^2}{t}\mathbf{k}, \quad t > 0$$

lies in the plane $x - y + z + 1 = 0$.

FOCUS ON CONCEPTS

41. Show that the graph of

$$\mathbf{r} = \sin t\mathbf{i} + 2\cos t\mathbf{j} + \sqrt{3}\sin t\mathbf{k}$$

is a circle, and find its center and radius. [*Hint:* Show that the curve lies on both a sphere and a plane.]

42. Show that the graph of
$$\mathbf{r} = 3\cos t\,\mathbf{i} + 3\sin t\,\mathbf{j} + 3\sin t\,\mathbf{k}$$
is an ellipse, and find the lengths of the major and minor axes. [*Hint:* Show that the graph lies on both a circular cylinder and a plane and use the result in Exercise 42 of Section 10.4.]

43. For the helix $\mathbf{r} = a\cos t\,\mathbf{i} + a\sin t\,\mathbf{j} + ct\,\mathbf{k}$, find the value of c ($c > 0$) so that the helix will make one complete turn in a distance of 3 units measured along the z-axis.

44. How many revolutions will the circular helix
$$\mathbf{r} = a\cos t\,\mathbf{i} + a\sin t\,\mathbf{j} + 0.2t\,\mathbf{k}$$
make in a distance of 10 units measured along the z-axis?

45. Show that the curve $\mathbf{r} = t\cos t\,\mathbf{i} + t\sin t\,\mathbf{j} + t\,\mathbf{k}$, $t \geq 0$, lies on the cone $z = \sqrt{x^2 + y^2}$. Describe the curve.

46. Describe the curve $\mathbf{r} = a\cos t\,\mathbf{i} + b\sin t\,\mathbf{j} + ct\,\mathbf{k}$, where a, b, and c are positive constants such that $a \neq b$.

47. In each part, match the vector equation with one of the accompanying graphs, and explain your reasoning.
(a) $\mathbf{r} = t\mathbf{i} - t\mathbf{j} + \sqrt{2 - t^2}\,\mathbf{k}$
(b) $\mathbf{r} = \sin \pi t\,\mathbf{i} - t\mathbf{j} + t\,\mathbf{k}$
(c) $\mathbf{r} = \sin t\,\mathbf{i} + \cos t\,\mathbf{j} + \sin 2t\,\mathbf{k}$
(d) $\mathbf{r} = \frac{1}{2}t\mathbf{i} + \cos 3t\,\mathbf{j} + \sin 3t\,\mathbf{k}$

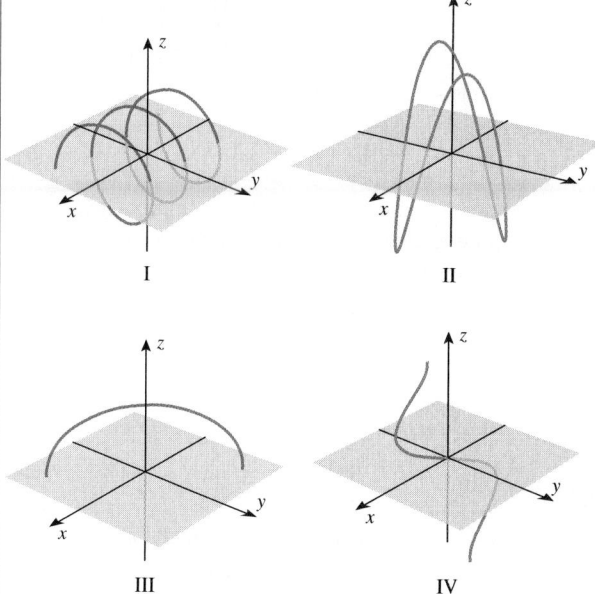

I   II

III   IV

48. Check your conclusions in Exercise 47 by generating the curves with a graphing utility. [*Note:* Your graphing utility may look at the curve from a different viewpoint. Read the documentation for your graphing utility to determine how to control the viewpoint, and see if you can generate a reasonable facsimile of the graphs shown in the figure by adjusting the viewpoint and choosing the interval of t-values appropriately.]

49. (a) Find parametric equations for the curve of intersection of the circular cylinder $x^2 + y^2 = 9$ and the parabolic cylinder $z = x^2$ in terms of a parameter t for which $x = 3\cos t$.
(b) Use a graphing utility to generate the curve of intersection in part (a).

50. (a) Sketch the graph of
$$\mathbf{r}(t) = \left\langle 2t, \frac{2}{1 + t^2} \right\rangle$$
(b) Prove that the curve in part (a) is also the graph of the function
$$y = \frac{8}{4 + x^2}$$
[The graphs of $y = a^3/(a^2 + x^2)$, where a denotes a constant, were first studied by the French mathematician Pierre de Fermat, and later by the Italian mathematicians Guido Grandi and Maria Agnesi. Any such curve is now known as a "witch of Agnesi." There are a number of theories for the origin of this name. Some suggest there was a mistranslation by either Grandi or Agnesi of some less colorful Latin name into Italian. Others lay the blame on a translation into English of Agnesi's 1748 treatise, *Analytical Institutions*.]

51. Writing Consider the curve C of intersection of the cone $z = \sqrt{x^2 + y^2}$ and the plane $z = y + 2$. Sketch and identify the curve C, and describe a procedure for finding a vector-valued function $\mathbf{r}(t)$ whose graph is C.

52. Writing Suppose that $\mathbf{r}_1(t)$ and $\mathbf{r}_2(t)$ are vector-valued functions in 2-space. Explain why solving the equation $\mathbf{r}_1(t) = \mathbf{r}_2(t)$ may not produce all of the points where the graphs of these functions intersect.

✔**QUICK CHECK ANSWERS 12.1**

1. (a) $\mathbf{r} = \frac{1}{t}\mathbf{i} + \sqrt{t}\,\mathbf{j} + \sin^{-1} t\,\mathbf{k}$ (b) $0 < t \leq 1$; $2\mathbf{i} + \frac{\sqrt{2}}{2}\mathbf{j} + \frac{\pi}{6}\mathbf{k}$ **2.** The graph is a line through $(1, -1)$ with direction vector $2\mathbf{i} + 3\mathbf{j}$.   **3.** The graph is the line segment in the xy-plane from $(0, 1)$ to $(1, 0)$.   **4.** $\mathbf{r} = \langle t, t^2, t^2 \rangle$

12.2 CALCULUS OF VECTOR-VALUED FUNCTIONS

In this section we will define limits, derivatives, and integrals of vector-valued functions and discuss their properties.

■ LIMITS AND CONTINUITY

Our first goal in this section is to develop a notion of what it means for a vector-valued function $\mathbf{r}(t)$ in 2-space or 3-space to approach a limiting vector $\mathbf{L}$ as t approaches a number a. That is, we want to define

$$\lim_{t \to a} \mathbf{r}(t) = \mathbf{L} \tag{1}$$

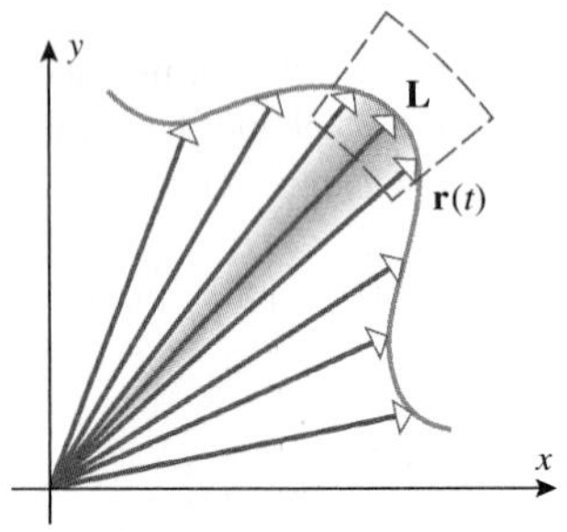

One way to motivate a reasonable definition of (1) is to position $\mathbf{r}(t)$ and $\mathbf{L}$ with their initial points at the origin and interpret this limit to mean that the terminal point of $\mathbf{r}(t)$ approaches the terminal point of $\mathbf{L}$ as t approaches a or, equivalently, that the vector $\mathbf{r}(t)$ approaches the vector $\mathbf{L}$ in both length and direction at t approaches a (Figure 12.2.1). Algebraically, this is equivalent to stating that

$$\lim_{t \to a} \|\mathbf{r}(t) - \mathbf{L}\| = 0 \tag{2}$$

(Figure 12.2.2). Thus, we make the following definition.

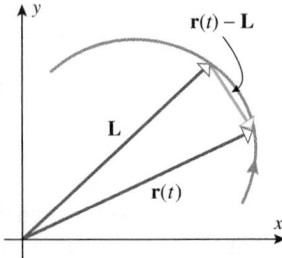

r(t) approaches **L** in length
and direction if $\lim\limits_{t \to a} \mathbf{r}(t) = \mathbf{L}$.

▲ **Figure 12.2.1**

12.2.1 DEFINITION   Let $\mathbf{r}(t)$ be a vector-valued function that is defined for all t in some open interval containing the number a, except that $\mathbf{r}(t)$ need not be defined at a. We will write

$$\lim_{t \to a} \mathbf{r}(t) = \mathbf{L}$$

if and only if

$$\lim_{t \to a} \|\mathbf{r}(t) - \mathbf{L}\| = 0$$

$\|\mathbf{r}(t) - \mathbf{L}\|$ is the distance between terminal points for vectors $\mathbf{r}(t)$ and $\mathbf{L}$ when positioned with the same initial points.

▲ **Figure 12.2.2**

It is clear intuitively that $\mathbf{r}(t)$ will approach a limiting vector $\mathbf{L}$ as t approaches a if and only if the component functions of $\mathbf{r}(t)$ approach the corresponding components of $\mathbf{L}$. This suggests the following theorem, whose formal proof is omitted.

Note that $\|\mathbf{r}(t) - \mathbf{L}\|$ is a real number for each value of t, so even though this expression involves a vector-valued function, the limit

$$\lim_{t \to a} \|\mathbf{r}(t) - \mathbf{L}\|$$

is an ordinary limit of a real-valued function.

12.2.2 THEOREM

(a) *If* $\mathbf{r}(t) = \langle x(t), y(t) \rangle = x(t)\mathbf{i} + y(t)\mathbf{j}$, *then*

$$\lim_{t \to a} \mathbf{r}(t) = \left\langle \lim_{t \to a} x(t), \lim_{t \to a} y(t) \right\rangle = \lim_{t \to a} x(t)\mathbf{i} + \lim_{t \to a} y(t)\mathbf{j}$$

provided the limits of the component functions exist. Conversely, the limits of the component functions exist provided $\mathbf{r}(t)$ *approaches a limiting vector as t approaches a.*

(b) *If* $\mathbf{r}(t) = \langle x(t), y(t), z(t) \rangle = x(t)\mathbf{i} + y(t)\mathbf{j} + z(t)\mathbf{k}$, *then*

$$\lim_{t \to a} \mathbf{r}(t) = \left\langle \lim_{t \to a} x(t), \lim_{t \to a} y(t), \lim_{t \to a} z(t) \right\rangle$$

$$= \lim_{t \to a} x(t)\mathbf{i} + \lim_{t \to a} y(t)\mathbf{j} + \lim_{t \to a} z(t)\mathbf{k}$$

provided the limits of the component functions exist. Conversely, the limits of the component functions exist provided $\mathbf{r}(t)$ *approaches a limiting vector as t approaches a.*

How would you define the one-sided limits

$$\lim_{t \to a^+} \mathbf{r}(t) \quad \text{and} \quad \lim_{t \to a^-} \mathbf{r}(t)?$$

Limits of vector-valued functions have many of the same properties as limits of real-valued functions. For example, assuming that the limits exist, the limit of a sum is the sum of the limits, the limit of a difference is the difference of the limits, and a constant scalar factor can be moved through a limit symbol.

▶ **Example 1** Let $\mathbf{r}(t) = t^2\mathbf{i} + e^t\mathbf{j} - (2\cos \pi t)\mathbf{k}$. Then

$$\lim_{t \to 0} \mathbf{r}(t) = \left(\lim_{t \to 0} t^2 \right) \mathbf{i} + \left(\lim_{t \to 0} e^t \right) \mathbf{j} - \left(\lim_{t \to 0} 2\cos \pi t \right) \mathbf{k} = \mathbf{j} - 2\mathbf{k}$$

Alternatively, using the angle bracket notation for vectors,

$$\lim_{t \to 0} \mathbf{r}(t) = \lim_{t \to 0} \langle t^2, e^t, -2\cos \pi t \rangle = \left\langle \lim_{t \to 0} t^2, \lim_{t \to 0} e^t, \lim_{t \to 0}(-2\cos \pi t) \right\rangle = \langle 0, 1, -2 \rangle \quad ◀$$

Motivated by the definition of continuity for real-valued functions, we define a vector-valued function $\mathbf{r}(t)$ to be ***continuous*** at $t = a$ if

$$\lim_{t \to a} \mathbf{r}(t) = \mathbf{r}(a) \tag{3}$$

That is, $\mathbf{r}(a)$ is defined, the limit of $\mathbf{r}(t)$ as $t \to a$ exists, and the two are equal. As in the case for real-valued functions, we say that $\mathbf{r}(t)$ is ***continuous on an interval*** I if it is continuous at each point of I [with the understanding that at an endpoint in I the two-sided limit in (3) is replaced by the appropriate one-sided limit]. It follows from Theorem 12.2.2 that a vector-valued function is continuous at $t = a$ if and only if its component functions are continuous at $t = a$.

■ **DERIVATIVES**

The derivative of a vector-valued function is defined by a limit similar to that for the derivative of a real-valued function.

12.2.3 DEFINITION   If $\mathbf{r}(t)$ is a vector-valued function, we define the ***derivative of r with respect to t*** to be the vector-valued function $\mathbf{r}'$ given by

$$\mathbf{r}'(t) = \lim_{h \to 0} \frac{\mathbf{r}(t + h) - \mathbf{r}(t)}{h} \tag{4}$$

The domain of $\mathbf{r}'$ consists of all values of t in the domain of $\mathbf{r}(t)$ for which the limit exists.

The function $\mathbf{r}(t)$ is ***differentiable*** at t if the limit in (4) exists. All of the standard notations for derivatives continue to apply. For example, the derivative of $\mathbf{r}(t)$ can be expressed as

$$\frac{d}{dt}[\mathbf{r}(t)], \quad \frac{d\mathbf{r}}{dt}, \quad \mathbf{r}'(t), \quad \text{or} \quad \mathbf{r}'$$

It is important to keep in mind that $\mathbf{r}'(t)$ is a vector, not a number, and hence has a magnitude and a direction for each value of t [except if $\mathbf{r}'(t) = \mathbf{0}$, in which case $\mathbf{r}'(t)$ has magnitude zero but no specific direction]. In the next section we will consider the significance of the magnitude of $\mathbf{r}'(t)$, but for now our goal is to obtain a geometric interpretation of the direction of $\mathbf{r}'(t)$. For this purpose, consider parts (a) and (b) of Figure 12.2.3. These illustrations show the graph C of $\mathbf{r}(t)$ (with its orientation) and the vectors $\mathbf{r}(t)$, $\mathbf{r}(t + h)$, and $\mathbf{r}(t + h) - \mathbf{r}(t)$ for positive h and for negative h. In both cases, the vector $\mathbf{r}(t + h) - \mathbf{r}(t)$ runs along the secant line joining the terminal points of $\mathbf{r}(t + h)$ and $\mathbf{r}(t)$, but with opposite directions in the two cases. In the case where h is positive the vector $\mathbf{r}(t + h) - \mathbf{r}(t)$ points in the direction of increasing parameter, and in the case where h is

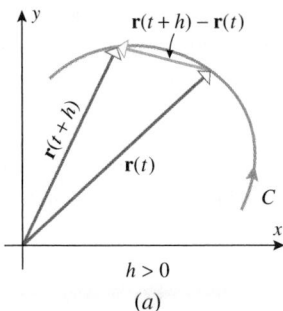

$h > 0$

(a)

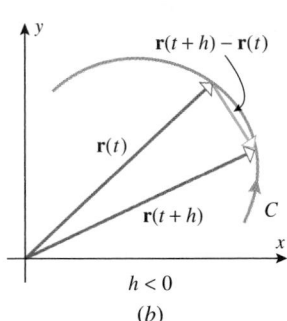

$h < 0$

(b)

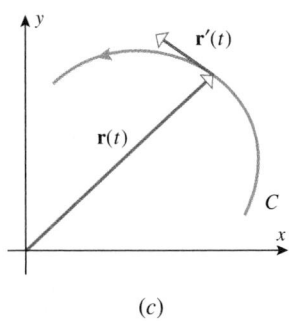

(c)

▲ **Figure 12.2.3**

negative it points in the opposite direction. However, in the case where h is negative the direction gets reversed when we multiply by $1/h$, so in both cases the vector

$$\frac{1}{h}[\mathbf{r}(t+h) - \mathbf{r}(t)] = \frac{\mathbf{r}(t+h) - \mathbf{r}(t)}{h}$$

points in the direction of increasing parameter and runs along the secant line. As $h \to 0$, the secant line approaches the tangent line at the terminal point of $\mathbf{r}(t)$, so we can conclude that the limit

$$\mathbf{r}'(t) = \lim_{h \to 0} \frac{\mathbf{r}(t+h) - \mathbf{r}(t)}{h}$$

(if it exists and is nonzero) is a vector that is tangent to the curve C at the tip of $\mathbf{r}(t)$ and points in the direction of increasing parameter (Figure 12.2.3c).

We can summarize all of this as follows.

12.2.4   **GEOMETRIC INTERPRETATION OF THE DERIVATIVE**   Suppose that C is the graph of a vector-valued function $\mathbf{r}(t)$ in 2-space or 3-space and that $\mathbf{r}'(t)$ exists and is nonzero for a given value of t. If the vector $\mathbf{r}'(t)$ is positioned with its initial point at the terminal point of the radius vector $\mathbf{r}(t)$, then $\mathbf{r}'(t)$ is tangent to C and points in the direction of increasing parameter.

Since limits of vector-valued functions can be computed componentwise, it seems reasonable that we should be able to compute derivatives in terms of component functions as well. This is the result of the next theorem.

12.2.5   **THEOREM**   *If* $\mathbf{r}(t)$ *is a vector-valued function, then* $\mathbf{r}$ *is differentiable at* t *if and only if each of its component functions is differentiable at* t, *in which case the component functions of* $\mathbf{r}'(t)$ *are the derivatives of the corresponding component functions of* $\mathbf{r}(t)$.

PROOF   For simplicity, we give the proof in 2-space; the proof in 3-space is identical, except for the additional component. Assume that $\mathbf{r}(t) = x(t)\mathbf{i} + y(t)\mathbf{j}$. Then

$$\mathbf{r}'(t) = \lim_{h \to 0} \frac{\mathbf{r}(t+h) - \mathbf{r}(t)}{h}$$

$$= \lim_{h \to 0} \frac{[x(t+h)\mathbf{i} + y(t+h)\mathbf{j}] - [x(t)\mathbf{i} + y(t)\mathbf{j}]}{h}$$

$$= \left(\lim_{h \to 0} \frac{x(t+h) - x(t)}{h} \right)\mathbf{i} + \left(\lim_{h \to 0} \frac{y(t+h) - y(t)}{h} \right)\mathbf{j}$$

$$= x'(t)\mathbf{i} + y'(t)\mathbf{j} \quad \blacksquare$$

▶ **Example 2**   Let $\mathbf{r}(t) = t^2\mathbf{i} + e^t\mathbf{j} - (2\cos \pi t)\mathbf{k}$. Then

$$\mathbf{r}'(t) = \frac{d}{dt}(t^2)\mathbf{i} + \frac{d}{dt}(e^t)\mathbf{j} - \frac{d}{dt}(2\cos \pi t)\mathbf{k}$$

$$= 2t\mathbf{i} + e^t\mathbf{j} + (2\pi \sin \pi t)\mathbf{k} \quad ◀$$

■ **DERIVATIVE RULES**

Many of the rules for differentiating real-valued functions have analogs in the context of differentiating vector-valued functions. We state some of these in the following theorem.

12.2.6   **THEOREM** (*Rules of Differentiation*)   *Let* $\mathbf{r}(t)$, $\mathbf{r}_1(t)$, *and* $\mathbf{r}_2(t)$ *be differentiable vector-valued functions that are all in 2-space or all in 3-space, and let* $f(t)$ *be a differentiable real-valued function, k a scalar, and* $\mathbf{c}$ *a constant vector (that is, a vector whose value does not depend on t). Then the following rules of differentiation hold:*

(a) $\dfrac{d}{dt}[\mathbf{c}] = \mathbf{0}$

(b) $\dfrac{d}{dt}[k\mathbf{r}(t)] = k\dfrac{d}{dt}[\mathbf{r}(t)]$

(c) $\dfrac{d}{dt}[\mathbf{r}_1(t) + \mathbf{r}_2(t)] = \dfrac{d}{dt}[\mathbf{r}_1(t)] + \dfrac{d}{dt}[\mathbf{r}_2(t)]$

(d) $\dfrac{d}{dt}[\mathbf{r}_1(t) - \mathbf{r}_2(t)] = \dfrac{d}{dt}[\mathbf{r}_1(t)] - \dfrac{d}{dt}[\mathbf{r}_2(t)]$

(e) $\dfrac{d}{dt}[f(t)\mathbf{r}(t)] = f(t)\dfrac{d}{dt}[\mathbf{r}(t)] + \dfrac{d}{dt}[f(t)]\mathbf{r}(t)$

The proofs of most of these rules are immediate consequences of Definition 12.2.3, although the last rule can be seen more easily by application of the product rule for real-valued functions to the component functions. The proof of Theorem 12.2.6 is left as an exercise.

■ TANGENT LINES TO GRAPHS OF VECTOR-VALUED FUNCTIONS

Motivated by the discussion of the geometric interpretation of the derivative of a vector-valued function, we make the following definition.

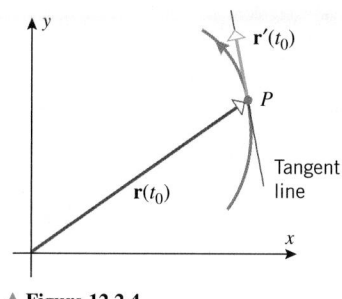

▲ **Figure 12.2.4**

12.2.7   **DEFINITION**   Let P be a point on the graph of a vector-valued function $\mathbf{r}(t)$, and let $\mathbf{r}(t_0)$ be the radius vector from the origin to P (Figure 12.2.4). If $\mathbf{r}'(t_0)$ exists and $\mathbf{r}'(t_0) \neq \mathbf{0}$, then we call $\mathbf{r}'(t_0)$ a *tangent vector* to the graph of $\mathbf{r}(t)$ at $\mathbf{r}(t_0)$, and we call the line through P that is parallel to the tangent vector the *tangent line* to the graph of $\mathbf{r}(t)$ at $\mathbf{r}(t_0)$.

Let $\mathbf{r}_0 = \mathbf{r}(t_0)$ and $\mathbf{v}_0 = \mathbf{r}'(t_0)$. It follows from Formula (9) of Section 11.5 that the tangent line to the graph of $\mathbf{r}(t)$ at $\mathbf{r}_0$ is given by the vector equation

$$\mathbf{r} = \mathbf{r}_0 + t\mathbf{v}_0 \tag{5}$$

▶ **Example 3**   Find parametric equations of the tangent line to the circular helix

$$x = \cos t, \quad y = \sin t, \quad z = t$$

where $t = t_0$, and use that result to find parametric equations for the tangent line at the point where $t = \pi$.

Solution.   The vector equation of the helix is

$$\mathbf{r}(t) = \cos t\,\mathbf{i} + \sin t\,\mathbf{j} + t\,\mathbf{k}$$

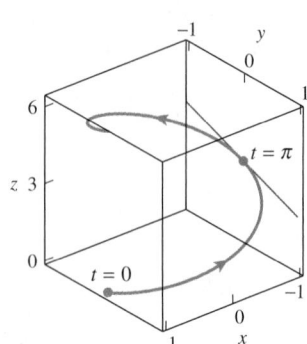

▲ **Figure 12.2.5**

so we have

$$\mathbf{r}_0 = \mathbf{r}(t_0) = \cos t_0 \mathbf{i} + \sin t_0 \mathbf{j} + t_0 \mathbf{k}$$

$$\mathbf{v}_0 = \mathbf{r}'(t_0) = (-\sin t_0)\mathbf{i} + \cos t_0 \mathbf{j} + \mathbf{k}$$

It follows from (5) that the vector equation of the tangent line at $t = t_0$ is

$$\mathbf{r} = \cos t_0 \mathbf{i} + \sin t_0 \mathbf{j} + t_0 \mathbf{k} + t[(-\sin t_0)\mathbf{i} + \cos t_0 \mathbf{j} + \mathbf{k}]$$

$$= (\cos t_0 - t \sin t_0)\mathbf{i} + (\sin t_0 + t \cos t_0)\mathbf{j} + (t_0 + t)\mathbf{k}$$

Thus, the parametric equations of the tangent line at $t = t_0$ are

$$x = \cos t_0 - t \sin t_0, \quad y = \sin t_0 + t \cos t_0, \quad z = t_0 + t$$

In particular, the tangent line at the point where $t = \pi$ has parametric equations

$$x = -1, \quad y = -t, \quad z = \pi + t$$

The graph of the helix and this tangent line are shown in Figure 12.2.5. ◄

▶ **Example 4**   Let

$$\mathbf{r}_1(t) = (\tan^{-1} t)\mathbf{i} + (\sin t)\mathbf{j} + t^2 \mathbf{k}$$

and

$$\mathbf{r}_2(t) = (t^2 - t)\mathbf{i} + (2t - 2)\mathbf{j} + (\ln t)\mathbf{k}$$

The graphs of $\mathbf{r}_1(t)$ and $\mathbf{r}_2(t)$ intersect at the origin. Find the degree measure of the acute angle between the tangent lines to the graphs of $\mathbf{r}_1(t)$ and $\mathbf{r}_2(t)$ at the origin.

Solution.   The graph of $\mathbf{r}_1(t)$ passes through the origin at $t = 0$, where its tangent vector is

$$\mathbf{r}_1'(0) = \left\langle \frac{1}{1 + t^2}, \cos t, 2t \right\rangle \bigg|_{t=0} = \langle 1, 1, 0 \rangle$$

The graph of $\mathbf{r}_2(t)$ passes through the origin at $t = 1$ (verify), where its tangent vector is

$$\mathbf{r}_2'(1) = \left\langle 2t - 1, 2, \frac{1}{t} \right\rangle \bigg|_{t=1} = \langle 1, 2, 1 \rangle$$

By Theorem 11.3.3, the angle θ between these two tangent vectors satisfies

$$\cos \theta = \frac{\langle 1, 1, 0 \rangle \cdot \langle 1, 2, 1 \rangle}{\| \langle 1, 1, 0 \rangle \| \, \| \langle 1, 2, 1 \rangle \|} = \frac{1 + 2 + 0}{\sqrt{2}\sqrt{6}} = \frac{3}{\sqrt{12}} = \frac{\sqrt{3}}{2}$$

It follows that $\theta = \pi/6$ radians, or $30°$. ◄

■ **DERIVATIVES OF DOT AND CROSS PRODUCTS**

The following rules, which are derived in the exercises, provide a method for differentiating dot products in 2-space and 3-space and cross products in 3-space.

Note that in (6) the order of the factors in each term on the right does not matter, but in (7) it does.

$$\frac{d}{dt}[\mathbf{r}_1(t) \cdot \mathbf{r}_2(t)] = \mathbf{r}_1(t) \cdot \frac{d\mathbf{r}_2}{dt} + \frac{d\mathbf{r}_1}{dt} \cdot \mathbf{r}_2(t) \tag{6}$$

$$\frac{d}{dt}[\mathbf{r}_1(t) \times \mathbf{r}_2(t)] = \mathbf{r}_1(t) \times \frac{d\mathbf{r}_2}{dt} + \frac{d\mathbf{r}_1}{dt} \times \mathbf{r}_2(t) \tag{7}$$

In plane geometry one learns that a tangent line to a circle is perpendicular to the radius at the point of tangency. Consequently, if a point moves along a circle in 2-space that is centered at the origin, then one would expect the radius vector and the tangent vector at any point on the circle to be orthogonal. This is the motivation for the following useful theorem, which is applicable in both 2-space and 3-space.

12.2.8   THEOREM   *If* $\mathbf{r}(t)$ *is a differentiable vector-valued function in 2-space or 3-space and* $\|\mathbf{r}(t)\|$ *is constant for all* t, *then*

$$\mathbf{r}(t) \cdot \mathbf{r}'(t) = 0 \tag{8}$$

that is, $\mathbf{r}(t)$ *and* $\mathbf{r}'(t)$ *are orthogonal vectors for all* t.

PROOF   It follows from (6) with $\mathbf{r}_1(t) = \mathbf{r}_2(t) = \mathbf{r}(t)$ that

$$\frac{d}{dt}[\mathbf{r}(t) \cdot \mathbf{r}(t)] = \mathbf{r}(t) \cdot \frac{d\mathbf{r}}{dt} + \frac{d\mathbf{r}}{dt} \cdot \mathbf{r}(t)$$

or, equivalently,

$$\frac{d}{dt}[\|\mathbf{r}(t)\|^2] = 2\mathbf{r}(t) \cdot \frac{d\mathbf{r}}{dt} \tag{9}$$

But $\|\mathbf{r}(t)\|^2$ is constant, so its derivative is zero. Thus

$$2\mathbf{r}(t) \cdot \frac{d\mathbf{r}}{dt} = 0$$

from which (8) follows.   ■

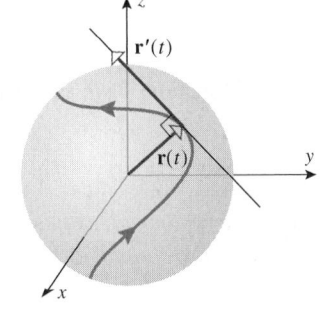

▲ **Figure 12.2.6**

▶ **Example 5**   Just as a tangent line to a circle in 2-space is perpendicular to the radius at the point of tangency, so a tangent vector to a curve on the surface of a sphere in 3-space that is centered at the origin is orthogonal to the radius vector at the point of tangency (Figure 12.2.6). To see that this is so, suppose that the graph of $\mathbf{r}(t)$ lies on the surface of a sphere of positive radius k centered at the origin. For each value of t we have $\|\mathbf{r}(t)\| = k$, so by Theorem 12.2.8

$$\mathbf{r}(t) \cdot \mathbf{r}'(t) = 0$$

and hence the radius vector $\mathbf{r}(t)$ and the tangent vector $\mathbf{r}'(t)$ are orthogonal.   ◀

■ **DEFINITE INTEGRALS OF VECTOR-VALUED FUNCTIONS**

If $\mathbf{r}(t)$ is a vector-valued function that is continuous on the interval $a \le t \le b$, then we define the ***definite integral*** of $\mathbf{r}(t)$ over this interval as a limit of Riemann sums, just as in Definition 5.5.1, except here the integrand is a vector-valued function. Specifically, we define

$$\int_a^b \mathbf{r}(t)\, dt = \lim_{\max \Delta t_k \to 0} \sum_{k=1}^n \mathbf{r}(t_k^*)\Delta t_k \tag{10}$$

It follows from (10) that the definite integral of $\mathbf{r}(t)$ over the interval $a \le t \le b$ can be expressed as a vector whose components are the definite integrals of the component functions of $\mathbf{r}(t)$. For example, if $\mathbf{r}(t) = x(t)\mathbf{i} + y(t)\mathbf{j}$, then

$$\int_a^b \mathbf{r}(t)\, dt = \lim_{\max \Delta t_k \to 0} \sum_{k=1}^n \mathbf{r}(t_k^*)\Delta t_k$$

$$= \lim_{\max \Delta t_k \to 0} \left[\left(\sum_{k=1}^n x(t_k^*)\Delta t_k \right)\mathbf{i} + \left(\sum_{k=1}^n y(t_k^*)\Delta t_k \right)\mathbf{j} \right]$$

$$= \left(\lim_{\max \Delta t_k \to 0} \sum_{k=1}^n x(t_k^*)\Delta t_k \right)\mathbf{i} + \left(\lim_{\max \Delta t_k \to 0} \sum_{k=1}^n y(t_k^*)\Delta t_k \right)\mathbf{j}$$

$$= \left(\int_a^b x(t)\, dt \right)\mathbf{i} + \left(\int_a^b y(t)\, dt \right)\mathbf{j}$$

Rewrite Formulas (11) and (12) in bracket notation with

$$\mathbf{r}(t) = \langle x(t), y(t) \rangle$$

and

$$\mathbf{r}(t) = \langle x(t), y(t), z(t) \rangle$$

respectively.

In general, we have

$$\int_a^b \mathbf{r}(t)\,dt = \left(\int_a^b x(t)\,dt \right) \mathbf{i} + \left(\int_a^b y(t)\,dt \right) \mathbf{j} \qquad \boxed{\text{2-space}} \qquad (11)$$

$$\int_a^b \mathbf{r}(t)\,dt = \left(\int_a^b x(t)\,dt \right) \mathbf{i} + \left(\int_a^b y(t)\,dt \right) \mathbf{j} + \left(\int_a^b z(t)\,dt \right) \mathbf{k} \qquad \boxed{\text{3-space}} \qquad (12)$$

▶ **Example 6**   Let $\mathbf{r}(t) = t^2 \mathbf{i} + e^t \mathbf{j} - (2 \cos \pi t)\mathbf{k}$. Then

$$\int_0^1 \mathbf{r}(t)\,dt = \left(\int_0^1 t^2\,dt \right) \mathbf{i} + \left(\int_0^1 e^t\,dt \right) \mathbf{j} - \left(\int_0^1 2 \cos \pi t\,dt \right) \mathbf{k}$$

$$= \frac{t^3}{3} \Bigg]_0^1 \mathbf{i} + e^t \Bigg]_0^1 \mathbf{j} - \frac{2}{\pi} \sin \pi t \Bigg]_0^1 \mathbf{k} = \frac{1}{3}\mathbf{i} + (e-1)\mathbf{j} \blacktriangleleft$$

RULES OF INTEGRATION

As with differentiation, many of the rules for integrating real-valued functions have analogs for vector-valued functions.

12.2.9   **THEOREM** (*Rules of Integration*)   *Let* $\mathbf{r}(t)$, $\mathbf{r}_1(t)$, *and* $\mathbf{r}_2(t)$ *be vector-valued functions in 2-space or 3-space that are continuous on the interval* $a \le t \le b$, *and let k be a scalar. Then the following rules of integration hold:*

(a) $\displaystyle \int_a^b k\mathbf{r}(t)\,dt = k \int_a^b \mathbf{r}(t)\,dt$

(b) $\displaystyle \int_a^b [\mathbf{r}_1(t) + \mathbf{r}_2(t)]\,dt = \int_a^b \mathbf{r}_1(t)\,dt + \int_a^b \mathbf{r}_2(t)\,dt$

(c) $\displaystyle \int_a^b [\mathbf{r}_1(t) - \mathbf{r}_2(t)]\,dt = \int_a^b \mathbf{r}_1(t)\,dt - \int_a^b \mathbf{r}_2(t)\,dt$

We omit the proof.

ANTIDERIVATIVES OF VECTOR-VALUED FUNCTIONS

An ***antiderivative*** for a vector-valued function $\mathbf{r}(t)$ is a vector-valued function $\mathbf{R}(t)$ such that

$$\mathbf{R}'(t) = \mathbf{r}(t) \qquad (13)$$

As in Chapter 5, we express Equation (13) using integral notation as

$$\int \mathbf{r}(t)\,dt = \mathbf{R}(t) + \mathbf{C} \qquad (14)$$

where $\mathbf{C}$ represents an arbitrary constant *vector*.

Since differentiation of vector-valued functions can be performed componentwise, it follows that antidifferentiation can be done this way as well. This is illustrated in the next example.

▶ **Example 7**

$$\int (2t\mathbf{i} + 3t^2\mathbf{j})\, dt = \left(\int 2t\, dt \right)\mathbf{i} + \left(\int 3t^2\, dt \right)\mathbf{j}$$

$$= (t^2 + C_1)\mathbf{i} + (t^3 + C_2)\mathbf{j}$$

$$= (t^2\mathbf{i} + t^3\mathbf{j}) + (C_1\mathbf{i} + C_2\mathbf{j}) = (t^2\mathbf{i} + t^3\mathbf{j}) + \mathbf{C}$$

where $\mathbf{C} = C_1\mathbf{i} + C_2\mathbf{j}$ is an arbitrary vector constant of integration. ◀

Most of the familiar integration properties have vector counterparts. For example, vector differentiation and integration are inverse operations in the sense that

$$\frac{d}{dt}\left[\int \mathbf{r}(t)\, dt \right] = \mathbf{r}(t) \qquad \text{and} \qquad \int \mathbf{r}'(t)\, dt = \mathbf{r}(t) + \mathbf{C} \qquad (15\text{--}16)$$

Moreover, if $\mathbf{R}(t)$ is an antiderivative of $\mathbf{r}(t)$ on an interval containing $t = a$ and $t = b$, then we have the following vector form of the Fundamental Theorem of Calculus:

$$\int_a^b \mathbf{r}(t)\, dt = \mathbf{R}(t) \bigg]_a^b = \mathbf{R}(b) - \mathbf{R}(a) \qquad (17)$$

▶ **Example 8** Evaluate the definite integral $\int_0^2 (2t\mathbf{i} + 3t^2\mathbf{j})\, dt$.

Solution. Integrating the components yields

$$\int_0^2 (2t\mathbf{i} + 3t^2\mathbf{j})\, dt = t^2 \bigg]_0^2 \mathbf{i} + t^3 \bigg]_0^2 \mathbf{j} = 4\mathbf{i} + 8\mathbf{j}$$

Alternative Solution. The function $\mathbf{R}(t) = t^2\mathbf{i} + t^3\mathbf{j}$ is an antiderivative of the integrand since $\mathbf{R}'(t) = 2t\mathbf{i} + 3t^2\mathbf{j}$. Thus, it follows from (17) that

$$\int_0^2 (2t\mathbf{i} + 3t^2\mathbf{j})\, dt = \mathbf{R}(t) \bigg]_0^2 = t^2\mathbf{i} + t^3\mathbf{j} \bigg]_0^2 = (4\mathbf{i} + 8\mathbf{j}) - (0\mathbf{i} + 0\mathbf{j}) = 4\mathbf{i} + 8\mathbf{j} \blacktriangleleft$$

▶ **Example 9** Find $\mathbf{r}(t)$ given that $\mathbf{r}'(t) = \langle 3, 2t \rangle$ and $\mathbf{r}(1) = \langle 2, 5 \rangle$.

Solution. Integrating $\mathbf{r}'(t)$ to obtain $\mathbf{r}(t)$ yields

$$\mathbf{r}(t) = \int \mathbf{r}'(t)\, dt = \int \langle 3, 2t \rangle\, dt = \langle 3t, t^2 \rangle + \mathbf{C}$$

where $\mathbf{C}$ is a vector constant of integration. To find the value of $\mathbf{C}$ we substitute $t = 1$ and use the given value of $\mathbf{r}(1)$ to obtain

$$\mathbf{r}(1) = \langle 3, 1 \rangle + \mathbf{C} = \langle 2, 5 \rangle$$

so that $\mathbf{C} = \langle -1, 4 \rangle$. Thus,

$$\mathbf{r}(t) = \langle 3t, t^2 \rangle + \langle -1, 4 \rangle = \langle 3t - 1, t^2 + 4 \rangle \blacktriangleleft$$

✔**QUICK CHECK EXERCISES 12.2** (*See page 858 for answers.*)

1. (a) $\lim_{t \to 3}(t^2\mathbf{i} + 2t\mathbf{j}) = $ _____

   (b) $\lim_{t \to \pi/4} \langle \cos t, \sin t \rangle = $ _____

2. Find $\mathbf{r}'(t)$.

   (a) $\mathbf{r}(t) = (4 + 5t)\mathbf{i} + (t - t^2)\mathbf{j}$

   (b) $\mathbf{r}(t) = \left\langle \dfrac{1}{t}, \tan t, e^{2t} \right\rangle$

3. Suppose that $\mathbf{r}_1(0) = \langle 3, 2, 1 \rangle$, $\mathbf{r}_2(0) = \langle 1, 2, 3 \rangle$, $\mathbf{r}'_1(0) = \langle 0, 0, 0 \rangle$, and $\mathbf{r}'_2(0) = \langle -6, -4, -2 \rangle$. Use this in-

formation to evaluate the derivative of each function at $t = 0$.

   (a) $\mathbf{r}(t) = 2\mathbf{r}_1(t) - \mathbf{r}_2(t)$

   (b) $\mathbf{r}(t) = \cos t \, \mathbf{r}_1(t) + e^{2t}\mathbf{r}_2(t)$

   (c) $\mathbf{r}(t) = \mathbf{r}_1(t) \times \mathbf{r}_2(t)$

   (d) $f(t) = \mathbf{r}_1(t) \cdot \mathbf{r}_2(t)$

4. (a) $\displaystyle\int_0^1 \langle 2t, t^2, \sin \pi t \rangle \, dt = $ _____

   (b) $\displaystyle\int (t\mathbf{i} - 3t^2\mathbf{j} + e^t\mathbf{k}) \, dt = $ _____

EXERCISE SET 12.2   ⬚ Graphing Utility

1–4 Find the limit. ▨

1. $\displaystyle\lim_{t \to +\infty} \left\langle \dfrac{t^2 + 1}{3t^2 + 2}, \dfrac{1}{t} \right\rangle$ 2. $\displaystyle\lim_{t \to 0^+} \left(\sqrt{t}\,\mathbf{i} + \dfrac{\sin t}{t}\mathbf{j} \right)$

3. $\displaystyle\lim_{t \to 2}(t\mathbf{i} - 3\mathbf{j} + t^2\mathbf{k})$ 4. $\displaystyle\lim_{t \to 1} \left\langle \dfrac{3}{t^2}, \dfrac{\ln t}{t^2 - 1}, \sin 2t \right\rangle$

5–6 Determine whether $\mathbf{r}(t)$ is continuous at $t = 0$. Explain your reasoning. ▨

5. (a) $\mathbf{r}(t) = 3\sin t\,\mathbf{i} - 2t\mathbf{j}$ (b) $\mathbf{r}(t) = t^2\mathbf{i} + \dfrac{1}{t}\mathbf{j} + t\mathbf{k}$

6. (a) $\mathbf{r}(t) = e^t\mathbf{i} + \mathbf{j} + \csc t\,\mathbf{k}$

   (b) $\mathbf{r}(t) = 5\mathbf{i} - \sqrt{3t + 1}\,\mathbf{j} + e^{2t}\mathbf{k}$

7. Sketch the circle $\mathbf{r}(t) = \cos t\,\mathbf{i} + \sin t\,\mathbf{j}$, and in each part draw the vector with its correct length.

   (a) $\mathbf{r}'(\pi/4)$ (b) $\mathbf{r}''(\pi)$ (c) $\mathbf{r}(2\pi) - \mathbf{r}(3\pi/2)$

8. Sketch the circle $\mathbf{r}(t) = \cos t\,\mathbf{i} - \sin t\,\mathbf{j}$, and in each part draw the vector with its correct length.

   (a) $\mathbf{r}'(\pi/4)$ (b) $\mathbf{r}''(\pi)$ (c) $\mathbf{r}(2\pi) - \mathbf{r}(3\pi/2)$

9–10 Find $\mathbf{r}'(t)$. ▨

9. $\mathbf{r}(t) = 4\mathbf{i} - \cos t\,\mathbf{j}$

10. $\mathbf{r}(t) = (\tan^{-1} t)\mathbf{i} + t\cos t\,\mathbf{j} - \sqrt{t}\,\mathbf{k}$

11–14 Find the vector $\mathbf{r}'(t_0)$; then sketch the graph of $\mathbf{r}(t)$ in 2-space and draw the tangent vector $\mathbf{r}'(t_0)$. ▨

11. $\mathbf{r}(t) = \langle t, t^2 \rangle$; $t_0 = 2$ 12. $\mathbf{r}(t) = t^3\mathbf{i} + t^2\mathbf{j}$; $t_0 = 1$

13. $\mathbf{r}(t) = \sec t\,\mathbf{i} + \tan t\,\mathbf{j}$; $t_0 = 0$

14. $\mathbf{r}(t) = 2\sin t\,\mathbf{i} + 3\cos t\,\mathbf{j}$; $t_0 = \pi/6$

15–16 Find the vector $\mathbf{r}'(t_0)$; then sketch the graph of $\mathbf{r}(t)$ in 3-space and draw the tangent vector $\mathbf{r}'(t_0)$. ▨

15. $\mathbf{r}(t) = 2\sin t\,\mathbf{i} + \mathbf{j} + 2\cos t\,\mathbf{k}$; $t_0 = \pi/2$

16. $\mathbf{r}(t) = \cos t\,\mathbf{i} + \sin t\,\mathbf{j} + t\mathbf{k}$; $t_0 = \pi/4$

〜17–18 Use a graphing utility to generate the graph of $\mathbf{r}(t)$ and the graph of the tangent line at t_0 on the same screen. ▨

17. $\mathbf{r}(t) = \sin \pi t\,\mathbf{i} + t^2\mathbf{j}$; $t_0 = \frac{1}{2}$

18. $\mathbf{r}(t) = 3\sin t\,\mathbf{i} + 4\cos t\,\mathbf{j}$; $t_0 = \pi/4$

19–22 Find parametric equations of the line tangent to the graph of $\mathbf{r}(t)$ at the point where $t = t_0$. ▨

19. $\mathbf{r}(t) = t^2\mathbf{i} + (2 - \ln t)\mathbf{j}$; $t_0 = 1$

20. $\mathbf{r}(t) = e^{2t}\mathbf{i} - 2\cos 3t\,\mathbf{j}$; $t_0 = 0$

21. $\mathbf{r}(t) = 2\cos \pi t\,\mathbf{i} + 2\sin \pi t\,\mathbf{j} + 3t\mathbf{k}$; $t_0 = \frac{1}{3}$

22. $\mathbf{r}(t) = \ln t\,\mathbf{i} + e^{-t}\mathbf{j} + t^3\mathbf{k}$; $t_0 = 2$

23–26 Find a vector equation of the line tangent to the graph of $\mathbf{r}(t)$ at the point P_0 on the curve. ▨

23. $\mathbf{r}(t) = (2t - 1)\mathbf{i} + \sqrt{3t + 4}\,\mathbf{j}$; $P_0(-1, 2)$

24. $\mathbf{r}(t) = 4\cos t\,\mathbf{i} - 3t\mathbf{j}$; $P_0(2, -\pi)$

25. $\mathbf{r}(t) = t^2\mathbf{i} - \dfrac{1}{t + 1}\mathbf{j} + (4 - t^2)\mathbf{k}$; $P_0(4, 1, 0)$

26. $\mathbf{r}(t) = \sin t\,\mathbf{i} + \cosh t\,\mathbf{j} + (\tan^{-1} t)\mathbf{k}$; $P_0(0, 1, 0)$

27. Let $\mathbf{r}(t) = \cos t\,\mathbf{i} + \sin t\,\mathbf{j} + \mathbf{k}$. Find

   (a) $\displaystyle\lim_{t \to 0}(\mathbf{r}(t) - \mathbf{r}'(t))$ (b) $\displaystyle\lim_{t \to 0}(\mathbf{r}(t) \times \mathbf{r}'(t))$

   (c) $\displaystyle\lim_{t \to 0}(\mathbf{r}(t) \cdot \mathbf{r}'(t))$.

28. Let $\mathbf{r}(t) = t\mathbf{i} + t^2\mathbf{j} + t^3\mathbf{k}$. Find

$$\lim_{t \to 1} \mathbf{r}(t) \cdot (\mathbf{r}'(t) \times \mathbf{r}''(t))$$

29–30 Calculate

$$\dfrac{d}{dt}[\mathbf{r}_1(t) \cdot \mathbf{r}_2(t)] \quad \text{and} \quad \dfrac{d}{dt}[\mathbf{r}_1(t) \times \mathbf{r}_2(t)]$$

first by differentiating the product directly and then by applying Formulas (6) and (7). ▨

29. $\mathbf{r}_1(t) = 2t\mathbf{i} + 3t^2\mathbf{j} + t^3\mathbf{k}$, $\mathbf{r}_2(t) = t^4\mathbf{k}$

30. $\mathbf{r}_1(t) = \cos t\,\mathbf{i} + \sin t\,\mathbf{j} + t\mathbf{k}$, $\mathbf{r}_2(t) = \mathbf{i} + t\mathbf{k}$

31–34 Evaluate the indefinite integral. ▨

31. $\int (3\mathbf{i} + 4t\mathbf{j})\, dt$

32. $\int \left(t^2\mathbf{i} - 2t\mathbf{j} + \frac{1}{t}\mathbf{k} \right) dt$

33. $\int \langle \sin t, -\cos t \rangle\, dt$

34. $\int \langle e^{-t}, e^t, 3t^2 \rangle\, dt$

35–40 Evaluate the definite integral. ▨

35. $\int_0^{\pi/2} \langle \cos 2t, \sin 2t \rangle\, dt$

36. $\int_0^1 (t^2\mathbf{i} + t^3\mathbf{j})\, dt$

37. $\int_0^2 \|t\mathbf{i} + t^2\mathbf{j}\|\, dt$

38. $\int_{-3}^3 \langle (3-t)^{3/2}, (3+t)^{3/2}, 1 \rangle\, dt$

39. $\int_1^9 (t^{1/2}\mathbf{i} + t^{-1/2}\mathbf{j})\, dt$

40. $\int_0^1 (e^{2t}\mathbf{i} + e^{-t}\mathbf{j} + t\mathbf{k})\, dt$

41–44 True–False Determine whether the statement is true or false. Explain your answer. ▨

41. If a vector-valued function $\mathbf{r}(t)$ is continuous at $t = a$, then the limit
$$\lim_{h \to 0} \frac{\mathbf{r}(a+h) - \mathbf{r}(a)}{h}$$
exists.

42. If $\mathbf{r}(t)$ is a vector-valued function in 2-space and $\|\mathbf{r}(t)\|$ is constant, then $\mathbf{r}(t)$ and $\mathbf{r}'(t)$ are parallel vectors for all t.

43. If $\mathbf{r}(t)$ is a vector-valued function that is continuous on the interval $a \le t \le b$, then
$$\int_a^b \mathbf{r}(t)\, dt$$
is a vector.

44. If $\mathbf{r}(t)$ is a vector-valued function that is continuous on the interval $[a, b]$, then for $a < t < b$,
$$\frac{d}{dt} \left[\int_a^t \mathbf{r}(u)\, du \right] = \mathbf{r}(t)$$

45–48 Solve the vector initial-value problem for $\mathbf{y}(t)$ by integrating and using the initial conditions to find the constants of integration. ▨

45. $\mathbf{y}'(t) = 2t\mathbf{i} + 3t^2\mathbf{j}, \quad \mathbf{y}(0) = \mathbf{i} - \mathbf{j}$

46. $\mathbf{y}'(t) = \cos t\mathbf{i} + \sin t\mathbf{j}, \quad \mathbf{y}(0) = \mathbf{i} - \mathbf{j}$

47. $\mathbf{y}''(t) = \mathbf{i} + e^t\mathbf{j}, \quad \mathbf{y}(0) = 2\mathbf{i}, \quad \mathbf{y}'(0) = \mathbf{j}$

48. $\mathbf{y}''(t) = 12t^2\mathbf{i} - 2t\mathbf{j}, \quad \mathbf{y}(0) = 2\mathbf{i} - 4\mathbf{j}, \quad \mathbf{y}'(0) = \mathbf{0}$

49. (a) Find the points where the curve
$$\mathbf{r} = t\mathbf{i} + t^2\mathbf{j} - 3t\mathbf{k}$$
intersects the plane $2x - y + z = -2$.
(b) For the curve and plane in part (a), find, to the nearest degree, the acute angle that the tangent line to the curve makes with a line normal to the plane at each point of intersection.

50. Find where the tangent line to the curve
$$\mathbf{r} = e^{-2t}\mathbf{i} + \cos t\mathbf{j} + 3 \sin t\mathbf{k}$$
at the point $(1, 1, 0)$ intersects the yz-plane.

51–52 Show that the graphs of $\mathbf{r}_1(t)$ and $\mathbf{r}_2(t)$ intersect at the point P. Find, to the nearest degree, the acute angle between the tangent lines to the graphs of $\mathbf{r}_1(t)$ and $\mathbf{r}_2(t)$ at the point P. ▨

51. $\mathbf{r}_1(t) = t^2\mathbf{i} + t\mathbf{j} + 3t^3\mathbf{k}$
$\mathbf{r}_2(t) = (t-1)\mathbf{i} + \frac{1}{4}t^2\mathbf{j} + (5-t)\mathbf{k}; \quad P(1, 1, 3)$

52. $\mathbf{r}_1(t) = 2e^{-t}\mathbf{i} + \cos t\mathbf{j} + (t^2 + 3)\mathbf{k}$
$\mathbf{r}_2(t) = (1-t)\mathbf{i} + t^2\mathbf{j} + (t^3 + 4)\mathbf{k}; \quad P(2, 1, 3)$

FOCUS ON CONCEPTS

53. Use Formula (7) to derive the differentiation formula
$$\frac{d}{dt}[\mathbf{r}(t) \times \mathbf{r}'(t)] = \mathbf{r}(t) \times \mathbf{r}''(t)$$

54. Let $\mathbf{u} = \mathbf{u}(t)$, $\mathbf{v} = \mathbf{v}(t)$, and $\mathbf{w} = \mathbf{w}(t)$ be differentiable vector-valued functions. Use Formulas (6) and (7) to show that
$$\frac{d}{dt}[\mathbf{u} \cdot (\mathbf{v} \times \mathbf{w})]$$
$$= \frac{d\mathbf{u}}{dt} \cdot [\mathbf{v} \times \mathbf{w}] + \mathbf{u} \cdot \left[\frac{d\mathbf{v}}{dt} \times \mathbf{w} \right] + \mathbf{u} \cdot \left[\mathbf{v} \times \frac{d\mathbf{w}}{dt} \right]$$

55. Let $u_1, u_2, u_3, v_1, v_2, v_3, w_1, w_2,$ and w_3 be differentiable functions of t. Use Exercise 54 to show that
$$\frac{d}{dt} \begin{vmatrix} u_1 & u_2 & u_3 \\ v_1 & v_2 & v_3 \\ w_1 & w_2 & w_3 \end{vmatrix}$$
$$= \begin{vmatrix} u_1' & u_2' & u_3' \\ v_1 & v_2 & v_3 \\ w_1 & w_2 & w_3 \end{vmatrix} + \begin{vmatrix} u_1 & u_2 & u_3 \\ v_1' & v_2' & v_3' \\ w_1 & w_2 & w_3 \end{vmatrix} + \begin{vmatrix} u_1 & u_2 & u_3 \\ v_1 & v_2 & v_3 \\ w_1' & w_2' & w_3' \end{vmatrix}$$

56. Prove Theorem 12.2.6 for 2-space.

57. Derive Formulas (6) and (7) for 3-space.

58. Prove Theorem 12.2.9 for 2-space.

59. Writing Explain what it means for a vector-valued function $\mathbf{r}(t)$ to be differentiable, and discuss geometric interpretations of $\mathbf{r}'(t)$.

60. Writing Let $\mathbf{r}(t) = \langle t^2, t^3 + 1 \rangle$ and define $\theta(t)$ to be the angle between $\mathbf{r}(t)$ and $\mathbf{r}'(t)$. The graph of $\theta = \theta(t)$ is shown in the accompanying figure. Interpret important features of this graph in terms of information about $\mathbf{r}(t)$ and $\mathbf{r}'(t)$. Accompany your discussion with a graph of $\mathbf{r}(t)$, highlighting particular instances of the vectors $\mathbf{r}(t)$ and $\mathbf{r}'(t)$.

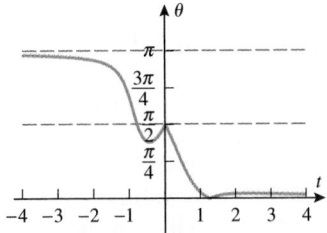

◀ **Figure Ex-60**

1. (a) $9\mathbf{i} + 6\mathbf{j}$ (b) $\left\langle \dfrac{\sqrt{2}}{2}, \dfrac{\sqrt{2}}{2} \right\rangle$ **2.** (a) $\mathbf{r}'(t) = 5\mathbf{i} + (1 - 2t)\mathbf{j}$ (b) $\mathbf{r}'(t) = \left\langle -\dfrac{1}{t^2}, \sec^2 t, 2e^{2t} \right\rangle$ **3.** (a) $\langle 6, 4, 2 \rangle$ (b) $\langle -4, 0, 4 \rangle$

(c) $\mathbf{0}$ (d) -28 **4.** (a) $\left\langle 1, \dfrac{1}{3}, \dfrac{2}{\pi} \right\rangle$ (b) $\dfrac{t^2}{2}\mathbf{i} - t^3\mathbf{j} + e^t\mathbf{k} + \mathbf{C}$

12.3 CHANGE OF PARAMETER; ARC LENGTH

We observed in earlier sections that a curve in 2-space or 3-space can be represented parametrically in more than one way. For example, in Section 10.1 we gave two parametric representations of a circle—one in which the circle was traced clockwise and the other in which it was traced counterclockwise. Sometimes it will be desirable to change the parameter for a parametric curve to a different parameter that is better suited for the problem at hand. In this section we will investigate issues associated with changes of parameter, and we will show that arc length plays a special role in parametric representations of curves.

■ SMOOTH PARAMETRIZATIONS

Graphs of vector-valued functions range from continuous and smooth to discontinuous and wildly erratic. In this text we will not be concerned with graphs of the latter type, so we will need to impose restrictions to eliminate the unwanted behavior. We will say that a curve represented by $\mathbf{r}(t)$ is *smoothly parametrized* by $\mathbf{r}(t)$, or that $\mathbf{r}(t)$ is a *smooth function* of t if $\mathbf{r}'(t)$ is continuous and $\mathbf{r}'(t) \neq \mathbf{0}$ for any allowable value of t. Geometrically, this means that a smoothly parametrized curve can have no abrupt changes in direction as the parameter increases.

> Mathematically, "smoothness" is a property of the *parametrization* and not of the curve itself. Exercise 38 gives an example of a curve that is well-behaved geometrically and has one parametrization that is smooth and another that is not.

▶ **Example 1**   Determine whether the following vector-valued functions are smooth.

(a) $\mathbf{r}(t) = a\cos t\,\mathbf{i} + a\sin t\,\mathbf{j} + ct\,\mathbf{k}$ $(a > 0, c > 0)$

(b) $\mathbf{r}(t) = t^2\mathbf{i} + t^3\mathbf{j}$

Solution (a).   We have

$$\mathbf{r}'(t) = -a\sin t\,\mathbf{i} + a\cos t\,\mathbf{j} + c\,\mathbf{k}$$

The components are continuous functions, and there is no value of t for which all three of them are zero (verify), so $\mathbf{r}(t)$ is a smooth function. The graph of $\mathbf{r}(t)$ is the circular helix in Figure 12.1.2.

Solution (b).   We have
$$\mathbf{r}'(t) = 2t\,\mathbf{i} + 3t^2\,\mathbf{j}$$

Although the components are continuous functions, they are both equal to zero if $t = 0$, so $\mathbf{r}(t)$ is not a smooth function. The graph of $\mathbf{r}(t)$, which is shown in Figure 12.3.1, is a semicubical parabola traced in the upward direction (see Example 6 of Section 10.1). Observe that for values of t slightly less than zero the angle between $\mathbf{r}'(t)$ and $\mathbf{i}$ is near π, and for values of t slightly larger than zero the angle is near 0; hence there is a sudden reversal in the direction of the tangent vector as t increases through $t = 0$ (see Exercise 44). ◀

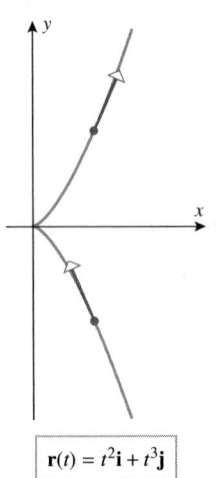

$$\mathbf{r}(t) = t^2\mathbf{i} + t^3\mathbf{j}$$

▲ **Figure 12.3.1**

■ **ARC LENGTH FROM THE VECTOR VIEWPOINT**

Recall from Theorem 10.1.1 that the arc length L of a parametric curve

$$x = x(t), \quad y = y(t) \qquad (a \le t \le b) \tag{1}$$

is given by the formula

$$L = \int_a^b \sqrt{\left(\frac{dx}{dt}\right)^2 + \left(\frac{dy}{dt}\right)^2} \, dt \tag{2}$$

Analogously, the arc length L of a parametric curve

$$x = x(t), \quad y = y(t), \quad z = z(t) \qquad (a \le t \le b) \tag{3}$$

in 3-space is given by the formula

$$L = \int_a^b \sqrt{\left(\frac{dx}{dt}\right)^2 + \left(\frac{dy}{dt}\right)^2 + \left(\frac{dz}{dt}\right)^2} \, dt \tag{4}$$

Formulas (2) and (4) have vector forms that we can obtain by letting

$$\mathbf{r}(t) = x(t)\mathbf{i} + y(t)\mathbf{j} \quad \text{or} \quad \mathbf{r}(t) = x(t)\mathbf{i} + y(t)\mathbf{j} + z(t)\mathbf{k}$$

| 2-space | | 3-space |

It follows that

$$\frac{d\mathbf{r}}{dt} = \frac{dx}{dt}\mathbf{i} + \frac{dy}{dt}\mathbf{j} \quad \text{or} \quad \frac{d\mathbf{r}}{dt} = \frac{dx}{dt}\mathbf{i} + \frac{dy}{dt}\mathbf{j} + \frac{dz}{dt}\mathbf{k}$$

| 2-space | | 3-space |

and hence

$$\left\| \frac{d\mathbf{r}}{dt} \right\| = \sqrt{\left(\frac{dx}{dt}\right)^2 + \left(\frac{dy}{dt}\right)^2} \quad \text{or} \quad \left\| \frac{d\mathbf{r}}{dt} \right\| = \sqrt{\left(\frac{dx}{dt}\right)^2 + \left(\frac{dy}{dt}\right)^2 + \left(\frac{dz}{dt}\right)^2}$$

| 2-space | | 3-space |

Substituting these expressions in (2) and (4) leads us to the following theorem.

12.3.1 THEOREM *If C is the graph in 2-space or 3-space of a smooth vector-valued function $\mathbf{r}(t)$, then its arc length L from $t = a$ to $t = b$ is*

$$L = \int_a^b \left\| \frac{d\mathbf{r}}{dt} \right\| \, dt \tag{5}$$

▶ **Example 2** Find the arc length of that portion of the circular helix

$$x = \cos t, \quad y = \sin t, \quad z = t$$

from $t = 0$ to $t = \pi$.

Solution. Set $\mathbf{r}(t) = (\cos t)\mathbf{i} + (\sin t)\mathbf{j} + t\mathbf{k} = \langle \cos t, \sin t, t \rangle$. Then

$$\mathbf{r}'(t) = \langle -\sin t, \cos t, 1 \rangle \quad \text{and} \quad \|\mathbf{r}'(t)\| = \sqrt{(-\sin t)^2 + (\cos t)^2 + 1} = \sqrt{2}$$

From Theorem 12.3.1 the arc length of the helix is

$$L = \int_0^{\pi} \left\| \frac{d\mathbf{r}}{dt} \right\| dt = \int_0^{\pi} \sqrt{2}\, dt = \sqrt{2}\pi \blacktriangleleft$$

■ ARC LENGTH AS A PARAMETER

For many purposes the best parameter to use for representing a curve in 2-space or 3-space parametrically is the length of arc measured along the curve from some fixed reference point. This can be done as follows:

> ***Using Arc Length as a Parameter***
>
> **Step 1.** Select an arbitrary point on the curve C to serve as a ***reference point***.
>
> **Step 2.** Starting from the reference point, choose one direction along the curve to be the ***positive direction*** and the other to be the ***negative direction***.
>
> **Step 3.** If P is a point on the curve, let s be the "signed" arc length along C from the reference point to P, where s is positive if P is in the positive direction from the reference point and s is negative if P is in the negative direction. Figure 12.3.2 illustrates this idea.

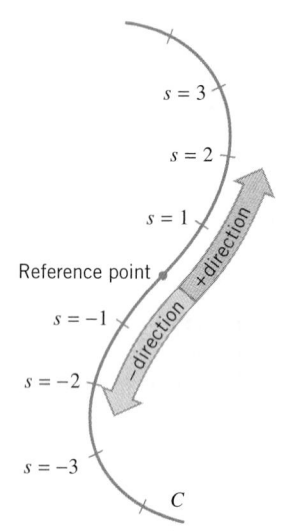

▲ **Figure 12.3.2**

By this procedure, a unique point P on the curve is determined when a value for s is given. For example, $s = 2$ determines the point that is 2 units along the curve in the positive direction from the reference point, and $s = -\frac{3}{2}$ determines the point that is $\frac{3}{2}$ units along the curve in the negative direction from the reference point.

Let us now treat s as a variable. As the value of s changes, the corresponding point P moves along C and the coordinates of P become functions of s. Thus, in 2-space the coordinates of P are $(x(s), y(s))$, and in 3-space they are $(x(s), y(s), z(s))$. Therefore, in 2-space or 3-space the curve C is given by the parametric equations

$$x = x(s), \quad y = y(s) \quad \text{or} \quad x = x(s), \quad y = y(s), \quad z = z(s)$$

A parametric representation of a curve with arc length as the parameter is called an ***arc length parametrization*** of the curve. Note that a given curve will generally have infinitely many different arc length parametrizations, since the reference point and orientation can be chosen arbitrarily.

▶ **Example 3** Find the arc length parametrization of the circle $x^2 + y^2 = a^2$ with counterclockwise orientation and $(a, 0)$ as the reference point.

Solution. The circle with counterclockwise orientation can be represented by the parametric equations

$$x = a\cos t, \quad y = a\sin t \quad (0 \leq t \leq 2\pi) \tag{6}$$

in which t can be interpreted as the angle in radian measure from the positive x-axis to the radius from the origin to the point $P(x, y)$ (Figure 12.3.3). If we take the positive direction for measuring the arc length to be counterclockwise, and we take $(a, 0)$ to be the reference point, then s and t are related by

$$s = at \quad \text{or} \quad t = s/a$$

Making this change of variable in (6) and noting that s increases from 0 to $2\pi a$ as t increases from 0 to 2π yields the following arc length parametrization of the circle:

$$x = a\cos(s/a), \quad y = a\sin(s/a) \quad (0 \leq s \leq 2\pi a) \blacktriangleleft$$

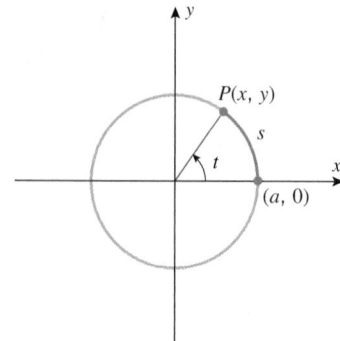

▲ **Figure 12.3.3**

■ CHANGE OF PARAMETER

In many situations the solution of a problem can be simplified by choosing the parameter in a vector-valued function or a parametric curve in the right way. The two most common parameters for curves in 2-space or 3-space are time and arc length. However, there are other useful possibilities as well. For example, in analyzing the motion of a particle in 2-space, it is often desirable to parametrize its trajectory in terms of the angle ϕ between the tangent vector and the positive x-axis (Figure 12.3.4). Thus, our next objective is to develop methods for changing the parameter in a vector-valued function or parametric curve. This will allow us to move freely between different possible parametrizations.

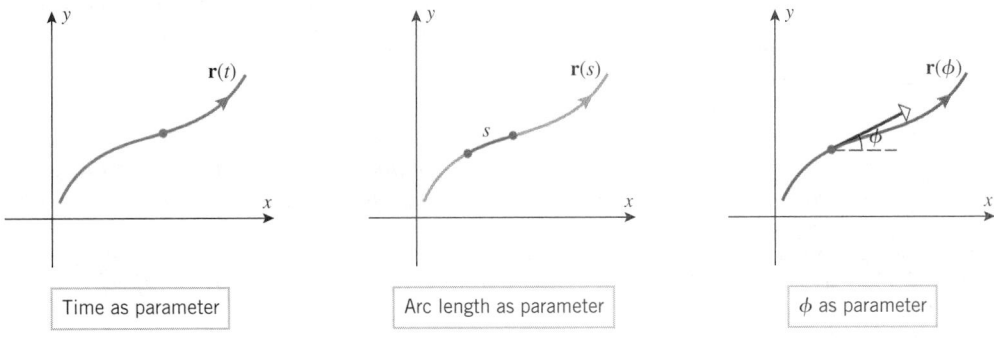

Time as parameter   Arc length as parameter ϕ as parameter

▲ Figure 12.3.4

A *change of parameter* in a vector-valued function $\mathbf{r}(t)$ is a substitution $t = g(\tau)$ that produces a new vector-valued function $\mathbf{r}(g(\tau))$ having the same graph as $\mathbf{r}(t)$, but possibly traced differently as the parameter τ increases.

▶ **Example 4**   Find a change of parameter $t = g(\tau)$ for the circle

$$\mathbf{r}(t) = \cos t\mathbf{i} + \sin t\mathbf{j} \qquad (0 \le t \le 2\pi)$$

such that

(a) the circle is traced counterclockwise as τ increases over the interval $[0, 1]$;

(b) the circle is traced clockwise as τ increases over the interval $[0, 1]$.

Solution (a).   The given circle is traced counterclockwise as t increases. Thus, if we choose g to be an increasing function, then it will follow from the relationship $t = g(\tau)$ that t increases when τ increases, thereby ensuring that the circle will be traced counterclockwise as τ increases. We also want to choose g so that t increases from 0 to 2π as τ increases from 0 to 1. A simple choice of g that satisfies all of the required criteria is the linear function graphed in Figure 12.3.5a. The equation of this line is

$$t = g(\tau) = 2\pi\tau \tag{7}$$

which is the desired change of parameter. The resulting representation of the circle in terms of the parameter τ is

$$\mathbf{r}(g(\tau)) = \cos 2\pi\tau\mathbf{i} + \sin 2\pi\tau\,\mathbf{j} \qquad (0 \le \tau \le 1)$$

Solution (b).   To ensure that the circle is traced clockwise, we will choose g to be a decreasing function such that t decreases from 2π to 0 as τ increases from 0 to 1. A simple choice of g that achieves this is the linear function

$$t = g(\tau) = 2\pi(1 - \tau) \tag{8}$$

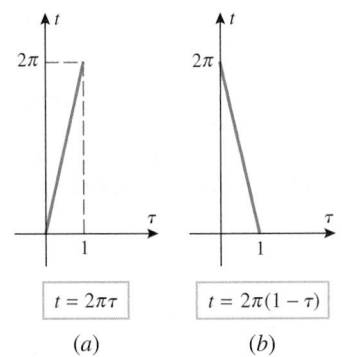

$t = 2\pi\tau$ $t = 2\pi(1 - \tau)$

(a) (b)

▲ Figure 12.3.5

graphed in Figure 12.3.5*b*. The resulting representation of the circle in terms of the parameter τ is

$$\mathbf{r}(g(\tau)) = \cos(2\pi(1 - \tau))\mathbf{i} + \sin(2\pi(1 - \tau))\mathbf{j} \qquad (0 \leq \tau \leq 1)$$

which simplifies to (verify)

$$\mathbf{r}(g(\tau)) = \cos 2\pi\tau\,\mathbf{i} - \sin 2\pi\tau\,\mathbf{j} \qquad (0 \leq \tau \leq 1) \ \blacktriangleleft$$

When making a change of parameter $t = g(\tau)$ in a vector-valued function $\mathbf{r}(t)$, it will be important to ensure that the new vector-valued function $\mathbf{r}(g(\tau))$ is smooth if $\mathbf{r}(t)$ is smooth. To establish conditions under which this happens, we will need the following version of the chain rule for vector-valued functions. The proof is left as an exercise.

Strictly speaking, since $d\mathbf{r}/dt$ is a vector and $dt/d\tau$ is a scalar, Formula (9) should be written in the form

$$\frac{d\mathbf{r}}{d\tau} = \frac{dt}{d\tau}\frac{d\mathbf{r}}{dt}$$

(scalar first). However, reversing the order of the factors makes the formula easier to remember, and we will continue to do so.

12.3.2   THEOREM (*Chain Rule*)   Let $\mathbf{r}(t)$ be a vector-valued function in 2-space or 3-space that is differentiable with respect to t. If $t = g(\tau)$ is a change of parameter in which g is differentiable with respect to τ, then $\mathbf{r}(g(\tau))$ is differentiable with respect to τ and

$$\frac{d\mathbf{r}}{d\tau} = \frac{d\mathbf{r}}{dt}\frac{dt}{d\tau} \tag{9}$$

A change of parameter $t = g(\tau)$ in which $\mathbf{r}(g(\tau))$ is smooth if $\mathbf{r}(t)$ is smooth is called a ***smooth change of parameter***. It follows from (9) that $t = g(\tau)$ will be a smooth change of parameter if $dt/d\tau$ is continuous and $dt/d\tau \neq 0$ for all values of τ, since these conditions imply that $d\mathbf{r}/d\tau$ is continuous and nonzero if $d\mathbf{r}/dt$ is continuous and nonzero. Smooth changes of parameter fall into two categories—those for which $dt/d\tau > 0$ for all τ (called ***positive changes of parameter***) and those for which $dt/d\tau < 0$ for all τ (called ***negative changes of parameter***). A positive change of parameter preserves the orientation of a parametric curve, and a negative change of parameter reverses it.

▶ **Example 5**   In Example 4 the change of parameter in Formula (7) is positive since $dt/d\tau = 2\pi > 0$, and the change of parameter given by Formula (8) is negative since $dt/d\tau = -2\pi < 0$. The positive change of parameter preserved the orientation of the circle, and the negative change of parameter reversed it. ◀

■ **FINDING ARC LENGTH PARAMETRIZATIONS**

Next we will consider the problem of finding an arc length parametrization of a vector-valued function that is expressed initially in terms of some other parameter t. The following theorem will provide a general method for doing this.

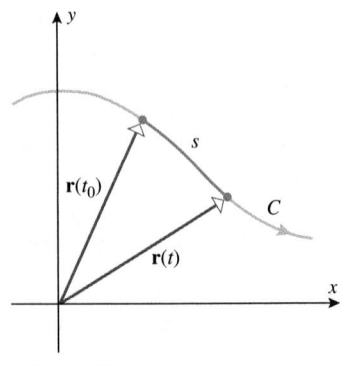

▲ **Figure 12.3.6**

12.3.3   THEOREM   Let C be the graph of a smooth vector-valued function $\mathbf{r}(t)$ in 2-space or 3-space, and let $\mathbf{r}(t_0)$ be any point on C. Then the following formula defines a positive change of parameter from t to s, where s is an arc length parameter having $\mathbf{r}(t_0)$ as its reference point (Figure 12.3.6):

$$s = \int_{t_0}^{t} \left\| \frac{d\mathbf{r}}{du} \right\| du \tag{10}$$

PROOF From (5) with u as the variable of integration instead of t, the integral represents the arc length of that portion of C between $\mathbf{r}(t_0)$ and $\mathbf{r}(t)$ if $t > t_0$ and the negative of that arc length if $t < t_0$. Thus, s is the arc length parameter with $\mathbf{r}(t_0)$ as its reference point and its positive direction in the direction of increasing t. ■

When needed, Formula (10) can be expressed in component form as

$$s = \int_{t_0}^{t} \sqrt{\left(\frac{dx}{du}\right)^2 + \left(\frac{dy}{du}\right)^2}\, du \qquad \boxed{\text{2-space}} \qquad (11)$$

$$s = \int_{t_0}^{t} \sqrt{\left(\frac{dx}{du}\right)^2 + \left(\frac{dy}{du}\right)^2 + \left(\frac{dz}{du}\right)^2}\, du \qquad \boxed{\text{3-space}} \qquad (12)$$

▶ **Example 6** Find the arc length parametrization of the circular helix

$$\mathbf{r} = \cos t\,\mathbf{i} + \sin t\,\mathbf{j} + t\,\mathbf{k} \qquad (13)$$

that has reference point $\mathbf{r}(0) = (1, 0, 0)$ and the same orientation as the given helix.

Solution. Replacing t by u in $\mathbf{r}$ for integration purposes and taking $t_0 = 0$ in Formula (10), we obtain

$$\mathbf{r} = \cos u\,\mathbf{i} + \sin u\,\mathbf{j} + u\,\mathbf{k}$$

$$\frac{d\mathbf{r}}{du} = (-\sin u)\mathbf{i} + \cos u\,\mathbf{j} + \mathbf{k}$$

$$\left\|\frac{d\mathbf{r}}{du}\right\| = \sqrt{(-\sin u)^2 + \cos^2 u + 1} = \sqrt{2}$$

$$s = \int_0^t \left\|\frac{d\mathbf{r}}{du}\right\| du = \int_0^t \sqrt{2}\, du = \sqrt{2}u\bigg]_0^t = \sqrt{2}t$$

Thus, $t = s/\sqrt{2}$, so (13) can be reparametrized in terms of s as

$$\mathbf{r} = \cos\left(\frac{s}{\sqrt{2}}\right)\mathbf{i} + \sin\left(\frac{s}{\sqrt{2}}\right)\mathbf{j} + \frac{s}{\sqrt{2}}\mathbf{k}$$

We are guaranteed that this reparametrization preserves the orientation of the helix since Formula (10) produces a positive change of parameter. ◀

▶ **Example 7** A bug walks along the trunk of a tree following a path modeled by the circular helix in Example 6. The bug starts at the reference point $(1, 0, 0)$ and walks up the helix for a distance of 10 units. What are the bug's final coordinates?

Solution. From Example 6, the arc length parametrization of the helix relative to the reference point $(1, 0, 0)$ is

$$\mathbf{r} = \cos\left(\frac{s}{\sqrt{2}}\right)\mathbf{i} + \sin\left(\frac{s}{\sqrt{2}}\right)\mathbf{j} + \frac{s}{\sqrt{2}}\mathbf{k}$$

or, expressed parametrically,

$$x = \cos\left(\frac{s}{\sqrt{2}}\right), \quad y = \sin\left(\frac{s}{\sqrt{2}}\right), \quad z = \frac{s}{\sqrt{2}}$$

Thus, at $s = 10$ the coordinates are

$$\left(\cos\left(\frac{10}{\sqrt{2}}\right), \sin\left(\frac{10}{\sqrt{2}}\right), \frac{10}{\sqrt{2}}\right) \approx (0.705, 0.709, 7.07) \blacktriangleleft$$

▶ **Example 8**   Recall from Formula (9) of Section 11.5 that the equation

$$\mathbf{r} = \mathbf{r}_0 + t\mathbf{v} \tag{14}$$

is the vector form of the line that passes through the terminal point of $\mathbf{r}_0$ and is parallel to the vector $\mathbf{v}$. Find the arc length parametrization of the line that has reference point $\mathbf{r}_0$ and the same orientation as the given line.

Solution.   Replacing t by u in (14) for integration purposes and taking $t_0 = 0$ in Formula (10), we obtain

$$\mathbf{r} = \mathbf{r}_0 + u\mathbf{v} \quad \text{and} \quad \frac{d\mathbf{r}}{du} = \mathbf{v} \quad \boxed{\text{Since } \mathbf{r}_0 \text{ is constant}}$$

It follows from this that

$$s = \int_0^t \left\|\frac{d\mathbf{r}}{du}\right\| du = \int_0^t \|\mathbf{v}\| \, du = \|\mathbf{v}\| u \Big]_0^t = t\|\mathbf{v}\|$$

This implies that $t = s/\|\mathbf{v}\|$, so (14) can be reparametrized in terms of s as

$$\mathbf{r} = \mathbf{r}_0 + s\left(\frac{\mathbf{v}}{\|\mathbf{v}\|}\right) \blacktriangleleft \tag{15}$$

In words, Formula (15) tells us that the line represented by Equation (14) can be reparametrized in terms of arc length with $\mathbf{r}_0$ as the reference point by normalizing $\mathbf{v}$ and then replacing t by s.

▶ **Example 9**   Find the arc length parametrization of the line

$$x = 2t + 1, \quad y = 3t - 2$$

that has the same orientation as the given line and uses $(1, -2)$ as the reference point.

Solution.   The line passes through the point $(1, -2)$ and is parallel to $\mathbf{v} = 2\mathbf{i} + 3\mathbf{j}$. To find the arc length parametrization of the line, we need only rewrite the given equations using $\mathbf{v}/\|\mathbf{v}\|$ rather than $\mathbf{v}$ to determine the direction and replace t by s. Since

$$\frac{\mathbf{v}}{\|\mathbf{v}\|} = \frac{2\mathbf{i} + 3\mathbf{j}}{\sqrt{13}} = \frac{2}{\sqrt{13}}\mathbf{i} + \frac{3}{\sqrt{13}}\mathbf{j}$$

it follows that the parametric equations for the line in terms of s are

$$x = \frac{2}{\sqrt{13}}s + 1, \quad y = \frac{3}{\sqrt{13}}s - 2 \blacktriangleleft$$

■ PROPERTIES OF ARC LENGTH PARAMETRIZATIONS

Because arc length parameters for a curve C are intimately related to the geometric characteristics of C, arc length parametrizations have properties that are not enjoyed by other parametrizations. For example, the following theorem shows that if a smooth curve is represented parametrically using an arc length parameter, then the tangent vectors all have length 1.

12.3.4 THEOREM

(a) *If C is the graph of a smooth vector-valued function* $\mathbf{r}(t)$ *in 2-space or 3-space, where t is a general parameter, and if s is the arc length parameter for C defined by Formula (10), then for every value of t the tangent vector has length*

$$\left\| \frac{d\mathbf{r}}{dt} \right\| = \frac{ds}{dt} \tag{16}$$

(b) *If C is the graph of a smooth vector-valued function* $\mathbf{r}(s)$ *in 2-space or 3-space, where s is an arc length parameter, then for every value of s the tangent vector to C has length*

$$\left\| \frac{d\mathbf{r}}{ds} \right\| = 1 \tag{17}$$

(c) *If C is the graph of a smooth vector-valued function* $\mathbf{r}(t)$ *in 2-space or 3-space, and if* $\|d\mathbf{r}/dt\| = 1$ *for every value of t, then for any value of* t_0 *in the domain of* $\mathbf{r}$, *the parameter* $s = t - t_0$ *is an arc length parameter that has its reference point at the point on C where* $t = t_0$.

PROOF (a) This result follows by applying the Fundamental Theorem of Calculus (Theorem 5.6.3) to Formula (10).

PROOF (b) Let $t = s$ in part (a).

PROOF (c) It follows from Theorem 12.3.3 that the formula

$$s = \int_{t_0}^{t} \left\| \frac{d\mathbf{r}}{du} \right\| du$$

defines an arc length parameter for C with reference point $\mathbf{r}(0)$. However, $\|d\mathbf{r}/du\| = 1$ by hypothesis, so we can rewrite the formula for s as

$$s = \int_{t_0}^{t} du = u \Big]_{t_0}^{t} = t - t_0 \quad \blacksquare$$

The component forms of Formulas (16) and (17) will be of sufficient interest in later sections that we provide them here for reference:

$$\frac{ds}{dt} = \left\| \frac{d\mathbf{r}}{dt} \right\| = \sqrt{\left(\frac{dx}{dt} \right)^2 + \left(\frac{dy}{dt} \right)^2} \qquad \text{2-space} \tag{18}$$

$$\frac{ds}{dt} = \left\| \frac{d\mathbf{r}}{dt} \right\| = \sqrt{\left(\frac{dx}{dt} \right)^2 + \left(\frac{dy}{dt} \right)^2 + \left(\frac{dz}{dt} \right)^2} \qquad \text{3-space} \tag{19}$$

$$\left\| \frac{d\mathbf{r}}{ds} \right\| = \sqrt{\left(\frac{dx}{ds} \right)^2 + \left(\frac{dy}{ds} \right)^2} = 1 \qquad \text{2-space} \tag{20}$$

$$\left\| \frac{d\mathbf{r}}{ds} \right\| = \sqrt{\left(\frac{dx}{ds} \right)^2 + \left(\frac{dy}{ds} \right)^2 + \left(\frac{dz}{ds} \right)^2} = 1 \qquad \text{3-space} \tag{21}$$

Note that Formulas (18) and (19) do not involve t_0, and hence do not depend on where the reference point for s is chosen. This is to be expected since changing the reference point shifts s by a constant (the arc length between the two reference points), and this constant drops out on differentiating.

✔ **QUICK CHECK EXERCISES 12.3** (*See page 868 for answers.*)

1. If $\mathbf{r}(t)$ is a smooth vector-valued function, then the integral

$$\int_a^b \left\| \frac{d\mathbf{r}}{dt} \right\| dt$$

may be interpreted geometrically as the _____.

2. If $\mathbf{r}(s)$ is a smooth vector-valued function parametrized by arc length s, then

$$\left\| \frac{d\mathbf{r}}{ds} \right\| = \underline{\hspace{1cm}}$$

and the arc length of the graph of $\mathbf{r}$ over the interval $a \le s \le b$ is _____.

3. If $\mathbf{r}(t)$ is a smooth vector-valued function, then the arc length parameter s having $\mathbf{r}(t_0)$ as the reference point may be defined by the integral

$$s = \int_{t_0}^t \underline{\hspace{1cm}} du$$

4. Suppose that $\mathbf{r}(t)$ is a smooth vector-valued function of t with $\mathbf{r}'(1) = \langle \sqrt{3}, -\sqrt{3}, -1 \rangle$, and let $\mathbf{r}_1(t)$ be defined by the equation $\mathbf{r}_1(t) = \mathbf{r}(2 \cos t)$. Then $\mathbf{r}_1'(\pi/3) = $ _____.

EXERCISE SET 12.3

1–4 Determine whether $\mathbf{r}(t)$ is a smooth function of the parameter t. ▪

1. $\mathbf{r}(t) = t^3 \mathbf{i} + (3t^2 - 2t)\mathbf{j} + t^2 \mathbf{k}$

2. $\mathbf{r}(t) = \cos t^2 \mathbf{i} + \sin t^2 \mathbf{j} + e^{-t} \mathbf{k}$

3. $\mathbf{r}(t) = te^{-t} \mathbf{i} + (t^2 - 2t)\mathbf{j} + \cos \pi t \mathbf{k}$

4. $\mathbf{r}(t) = \sin \pi t \mathbf{i} + (2t - \ln t)\mathbf{j} + (t^2 - t)\mathbf{k}$

5–8 Find the arc length of the parametric curve. ▪

5. $x = \cos^3 t,\ y = \sin^3 t, z = 2;\ 0 \le t \le \pi/2$

6. $x = 3 \cos t,\ y = 3 \sin t, z = 4t;\ 0 \le t \le \pi$

7. $x = e^t,\ y = e^{-t}, z = \sqrt{2}t;\ 0 \le t \le 1$

8. $x = \frac{1}{2}t,\ y = \frac{1}{3}(1-t)^{3/2}, z = \frac{1}{3}(1+t)^{3/2};\ -1 \le t \le 1$

9–12 Find the arc length of the graph of $\mathbf{r}(t)$. ▪

9. $\mathbf{r}(t) = t^3 \mathbf{i} + t\mathbf{j} + \frac{1}{2}\sqrt{6}t^2 \mathbf{k};\ 1 \le t \le 3$

10. $\mathbf{r}(t) = (4 + 3t)\mathbf{i} + (2 - 2t)\mathbf{j} + (5 + t)\mathbf{k};\ 3 \le t \le 4$

11. $\mathbf{r}(t) = 3 \cos t \mathbf{i} + 3 \sin t \mathbf{j} + t\mathbf{k};\ 0 \le t \le 2\pi$

12. $\mathbf{r}(t) = t^2 \mathbf{i} + (\cos t + t \sin t)\mathbf{j} + (\sin t - t \cos t)\mathbf{k};$ $0 \le t \le \pi$

13–16 Calculate $d\mathbf{r}/d\tau$ by the chain rule, and then check your result by expressing $\mathbf{r}$ in terms of τ and differentiating. ▪

13. $\mathbf{r} = t\mathbf{i} + t^2 \mathbf{j};\ t = 4\tau + 1$

14. $\mathbf{r} = \langle 3 \cos t, 3 \sin t \rangle;\ t = \pi \tau$

15. $\mathbf{r} = e^t \mathbf{i} + 4e^{-t} \mathbf{j};\ t = \tau^2$

16. $\mathbf{r} = \mathbf{i} + 3t^{3/2} \mathbf{j} + t\mathbf{k};\ t = 1/\tau$

17–20 True–False Determine whether the statement is true or false. Explain your answer. ▪

17. If $\mathbf{r}(t)$ is a smooth vector-valued function in 2-space, then

$$\int_a^b \|\mathbf{r}'(t)\| dt$$

is a vector.

18. If the line $y = x$ is parametrized by the vector-valued function $\mathbf{r}(t)$, then $\mathbf{r}(t)$ is smooth.

19. If $\mathbf{r}(s)$ parametrizes the graph of $y = |x|$ in 2-space by arc length, then $\mathbf{r}(s)$ is smooth.

20. If a curve C in the plane is parametrized by the smooth vector-valued function $\mathbf{r}(s)$, where s is an arc length parameter, then

$$\int_{-1}^3 \|\mathbf{r}'(s)\| ds = 4$$

21. (a) Find the arc length parametrization of the line

$$x = t, \quad y = t$$

that has the same orientation as the given line and has reference point $(0, 0)$.

(b) Find the arc length parametrization of the line

$$x = t, \quad y = t, \quad z = t$$

that has the same orientation as the given line and has reference point $(0, 0, 0)$.

22. Find arc length parametrizations of the lines in Exercise 21 that have the stated reference points but are oriented opposite to the given lines.

23. (a) Find the arc length parametrization of the line

$$x = 1 + t, \quad y = 3 - 2t, \quad z = 4 + 2t$$

that has the same direction as the given line and has reference point $(1, 3, 4)$.

(b) Use the parametric equations obtained in part (a) to find the point on the line that is 25 units from the reference point in the direction of increasing parameter.

24. (a) Find the arc length parametrization of the line
$$x = -5 + 3t, \quad y = 2t, \quad z = 5 + t$$
that has the same direction as the given line and has reference point $(-5, 0, 5)$.

(b) Use the parametric equations obtained in part (a) to find the point on the line that is 10 units from the reference point in the direction of increasing parameter.

25–30 Find an arc length parametrization of the curve that has the same orientation as the given curve and for which the reference point corresponds to $t = 0$. ■

25. $\mathbf{r}(t) = (3 + \cos t)\mathbf{i} + (2 + \sin t)\mathbf{j}; \ 0 \le t \le 2\pi$

26. $\mathbf{r}(t) = \cos^3 t\mathbf{i} + \sin^3 t\mathbf{j}; \ 0 \le t \le \pi/2$

27. $\mathbf{r}(t) = \frac{1}{3}t^3\mathbf{i} + \frac{1}{2}t^2\mathbf{j}; \ t \ge 0$

28. $\mathbf{r}(t) = (1 + t)^2\mathbf{i} + (1 + t)^3\mathbf{j}; \ 0 \le t \le 1$

29. $\mathbf{r}(t) = e^t \cos t\mathbf{i} + e^t \sin t\mathbf{j}; \ 0 \le t \le \pi/2$

30. $\mathbf{r}(t) = \sin e^t\mathbf{i} + \cos e^t\mathbf{j} + \sqrt{3}e^t\mathbf{k}; \ t \ge 0$

31. Show that the arc length of the circular helix $x = a \cos t$, $y = a \sin t$, $z = ct$ for $0 \le t \le t_0$ is $t_0\sqrt{a^2 + c^2}$.

32. Use the result in Exercise 31 to show the circular helix
$$\mathbf{r} = a \cos t\mathbf{i} + a \sin t\mathbf{j} + ct\mathbf{k}$$
can be expressed as
$$\mathbf{r} = \left(a \cos \frac{s}{w}\right)\mathbf{i} + \left(a \sin \frac{s}{w}\right)\mathbf{j} + \frac{cs}{w}\mathbf{k}$$
where $w = \sqrt{a^2 + c^2}$ and s is an arc length parameter with reference point at $(a, 0, 0)$.

33. Find an arc length parametrization of the cycloid
$$\begin{aligned} x &= at - a \sin t \\ y &= a - a \cos t \end{aligned} \quad (0 \le t \le 2\pi)$$
with $(0, 0)$ as the reference point.

34. Show that in cylindrical coordinates a curve given by the parametric equations $r = r(t)$, $\theta = \theta(t)$, $z = z(t)$ for $a \le t \le b$ has arc length
$$L = \int_a^b \sqrt{\left(\frac{dr}{dt}\right)^2 + r^2\left(\frac{d\theta}{dt}\right)^2 + \left(\frac{dz}{dt}\right)^2}\, dt$$
[*Hint:* Use the relationships $x = r \cos \theta$, $y = r \sin \theta$.]

35. In each part, use the formula in Exercise 34 to find the arc length of the curve.

(a) $r = e^{2t}, \theta = t, z = e^{2t}; \ 0 \le t \le \ln 2$

(b) $r = t^2, \theta = \ln t, z = \frac{1}{3}t^3; \ 1 \le t \le 2$

36. Show that in spherical coordinates a curve given by the parametric equations $\rho = \rho(t)$, $\theta = \theta(t)$, $\phi = \phi(t)$ for $a \le t \le b$ has arc length
$$L = \int_a^b \sqrt{\left(\frac{d\rho}{dt}\right)^2 + \rho^2 \sin^2 \phi \left(\frac{d\theta}{dt}\right)^2 + \rho^2\left(\frac{d\phi}{dt}\right)^2}\, dt$$
[*Hint:* $x = \rho \sin \phi \cos \theta$, $y = \rho \sin \phi \sin \theta$, $z = \rho \cos \phi$.]

37. In each part, use the formula in Exercise 36 to find the arc length of the curve.

(a) $\rho = e^{-t}, \theta = 2t, \phi = \pi/4; \ 0 \le t \le 2$

(b) $\rho = 2t, \theta = \ln t, \phi = \pi/6; \ 1 \le t \le 5$

FOCUS ON CONCEPTS

38. (a) Sketch the graph of $\mathbf{r}(t) = t\mathbf{i} + t^2\mathbf{j}$. Show that $\mathbf{r}(t)$ is a smooth vector-valued function but the change of parameter $t = \tau^3$ produces a vector-valued function that is not smooth, yet has the same graph as $\mathbf{r}(t)$.

(b) Examine how the two vector-valued functions are traced, and see if you can explain what causes the problem.

39. Find a change of parameter $t = g(\tau)$ for the semicircle
$$\mathbf{r}(t) = \cos t\mathbf{i} + \sin t\mathbf{j} \quad (0 \le t \le \pi)$$
such that

(a) the semicircle is traced counterclockwise as τ varies over the interval $[0, 1]$

(b) the semicircle is traced clockwise as τ varies over the interval $[0, 1]$.

40. What change of parameter $t = g(\tau)$ would you make if you wanted to trace the graph of $\mathbf{r}(t)$ ($0 \le t \le 1$) in the opposite direction with τ varying from 0 to 1?

41. As illustrated in the accompanying figure, copper cable with a diameter of $\frac{1}{2}$ inch is to be wrapped in a circular helix around a cylinder that has a 12-inch diameter. What length of cable (measured along its centerline) will make one complete turn around the cylinder in a distance of 20 inches (between centerlines) measured parallel to the axis of the cylinder?

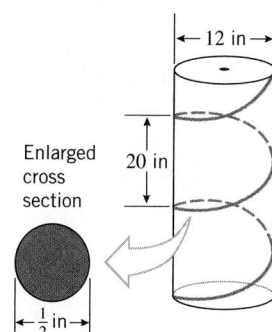

◄ **Figure Ex-41**

42. Let $\mathbf{r}(t) = \langle \cos t, \sin t, t^{3/2} \rangle$. Find

(a) $\|\mathbf{r}'(t)\|$ (b) $\dfrac{ds}{dt}$ (c) $\displaystyle\int_0^2 \|\mathbf{r}'(t)\|\, dt$.

43. Let $\mathbf{r}(t) = \ln t\mathbf{i} + 2t\mathbf{j} + t^2\mathbf{k}$. Find

(a) $\|\mathbf{r}'(t)\|$ (b) $\dfrac{ds}{dt}$ (c) $\displaystyle\int_1^3 \|\mathbf{r}'(t)\|\, dt$.

44. Let $\mathbf{r}(t) = t^2\mathbf{i} + t^3\mathbf{j}$ (see Figure 12.3.1). Let $\theta(t)$ be the angle between $\mathbf{r}'(t)$ and $\mathbf{i}$. Show that
$$\theta(t) \to \pi \text{ as } t \to 0^- \quad \text{and} \quad \theta(t) \to 0 \text{ as } t \to 0^+$$

45. Prove: If $\mathbf{r}(t)$ is a smoothly parametrized function, then the angles between $\mathbf{r}'(t)$ and the vectors $\mathbf{i}$, $\mathbf{j}$, and $\mathbf{k}$ are continuous functions of t.

46. Prove the vector form of the chain rule for 2-space (Theorem 12.3.2) by expressing $\mathbf{r}(t)$ in terms of components.

47. Writing The triangle with vertices $(0, 0)$, $(1, 0)$, and $(0, 1)$ has three "corners." Discuss whether it is possible to have a smooth vector-valued function whose graph is this triangle. Also discuss whether it is possible to have a differentiable vector-valued function whose graph is this triangle.

✔ QUICK CHECK ANSWERS 12.3

1. arc length of the graph of $\mathbf{r}(t)$ from $t = a$ to $t = b$ **2.** 1; $b - a$ **3.** $\left\| \dfrac{d\mathbf{r}}{du} \right\|$ **4.** $\langle -3, 3, \sqrt{3} \rangle$

12.4 UNIT TANGENT, NORMAL, AND BINORMAL VECTORS

In this section we will discuss some of the fundamental geometric properties of vector-valued functions. Our work here will have important applications to the study of motion along a curved path in 2-space or 3-space and to the study of the geometric properties of curves and surfaces.

■ UNIT TANGENT VECTORS

Recall that if C is the graph of a *smooth* vector-valued function $\mathbf{r}(t)$ in 2-space or 3-space, then the vector $\mathbf{r}'(t)$ is nonzero, tangent to C, and points in the direction of increasing parameter. Thus, by normalizing $\mathbf{r}'(t)$ we obtain a unit vector

As a general rule, we will position $\mathbf{T}(t)$ with its initial point at the terminal point of $\mathbf{r}(t)$, as in Figure 12.4.1. This will ensure that $\mathbf{T}(t)$ is actually tangent to the graph of $\mathbf{r}(t)$ and not simply parallel to the tangent line.

$$\mathbf{T}(t) = \frac{\mathbf{r}'(t)}{\|\mathbf{r}'(t)\|} \qquad (1)$$

that is tangent to C and points in the direction of increasing parameter. We call $\mathbf{T}(t)$ the *unit tangent vector* to C at t.

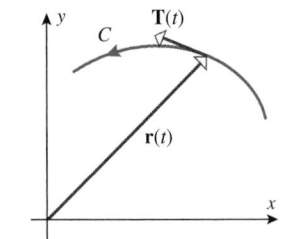

▲ Figure 12.4.1

▶ **Example 1** Find the unit tangent vector to the graph of $\mathbf{r}(t) = t^2\mathbf{i} + t^3\mathbf{j}$ at the point where $t = 2$.

Solution. Since

$$\mathbf{r}'(t) = 2t\mathbf{i} + 3t^2\mathbf{j}$$

we obtain

$$\mathbf{T}(2) = \frac{\mathbf{r}'(2)}{\|\mathbf{r}'(2)\|} = \frac{4\mathbf{i} + 12\mathbf{j}}{\sqrt{160}} = \frac{4\mathbf{i} + 12\mathbf{j}}{4\sqrt{10}} = \frac{1}{\sqrt{10}}\mathbf{i} + \frac{3}{\sqrt{10}}\mathbf{j}$$

The graph of $\mathbf{r}(t)$ and the vector $\mathbf{T}(2)$ are shown in Figure 12.4.2. ◀

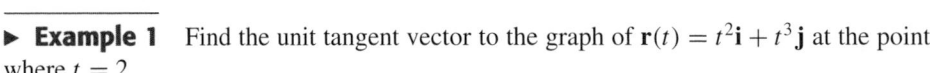

■ UNIT NORMAL VECTORS

Recall from Theorem 12.2.8 that if a vector-valued function $\mathbf{r}(t)$ has constant norm, then $\mathbf{r}(t)$ and $\mathbf{r}'(t)$ are orthogonal vectors. In particular, $\mathbf{T}(t)$ has constant norm 1, so $\mathbf{T}(t)$ and $\mathbf{T}'(t)$ are orthogonal vectors. This implies that $\mathbf{T}'(t)$ is perpendicular to the tangent line to C at t, so we say that $\mathbf{T}'(t)$ is *normal* to C at t. It follows that if $\mathbf{T}'(t) \neq \mathbf{0}$, and if we normalize $\mathbf{T}'(t)$, then we obtain a unit vector

$$\mathbf{N}(t) = \frac{\mathbf{T}'(t)}{\|\mathbf{T}'(t)\|} \qquad (2)$$

▲ Figure 12.4.2

that is normal to C and points in the same direction as $\mathbf{T}'(t)$. We call $\mathbf{N}(t)$ the ***principal unit normal vector*** to C at t, or more simply, the ***unit normal vector***. Observe that the unit normal vector is defined only at points where $\mathbf{T}'(t) \neq \mathbf{0}$. Unless stated otherwise, we will assume that this condition is satisfied. In particular, this *excludes* straight lines.

REMARK In 2-space there are two unit vectors that are orthogonal to $\mathbf{T}(t)$, and in 3-space there are infinitely many such vectors (Figure 12.4.3). In both cases the principal unit normal is that particular normal that points in the direction of $\mathbf{T}'(t)$. After the next example we will show that for a nonlinear parametric curve in 2-space the principal unit normal is the one that points "inward" toward the concave side of the curve.

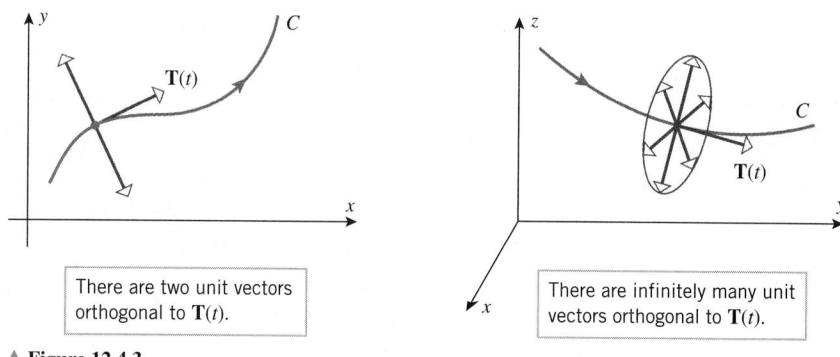

There are two unit vectors orthogonal to $\mathbf{T}(t)$.

There are infinitely many unit vectors orthogonal to $\mathbf{T}(t)$.

▲ **Figure 12.4.3**

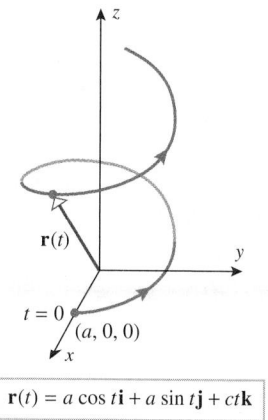

$\mathbf{r}(t) = a \cos t\, \mathbf{i} + a \sin t\, \mathbf{j} + ct\mathbf{k}$

▲ **Figure 12.4.4**

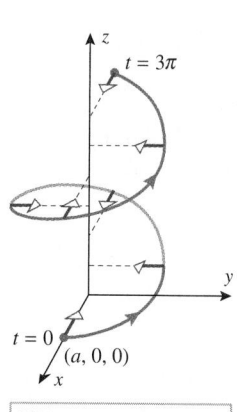

$\mathbf{N}(t) = -(\cos t\, \mathbf{i} + \sin t\, \mathbf{j})$

▲ **Figure 12.4.5**

▶ **Example 2** Find $\mathbf{T}(t)$ and $\mathbf{N}(t)$ for the circular helix

$$x = a \cos t, \quad y = a \sin t, \quad z = ct$$

where $a > 0$.

Solution. The radius vector for the helix is

$$\mathbf{r}(t) = a \cos t\, \mathbf{i} + a \sin t\, \mathbf{j} + ct\mathbf{k}$$

(Figure 12.4.4). Thus,

$$\mathbf{r}'(t) = (-a \sin t)\mathbf{i} + a \cos t\, \mathbf{j} + c\mathbf{k}$$

$$\|\mathbf{r}'(t)\| = \sqrt{(-a \sin t)^2 + (a \cos t)^2 + c^2} = \sqrt{a^2 + c^2}$$

$$\mathbf{T}(t) = \frac{\mathbf{r}'(t)}{\|\mathbf{r}'(t)\|} = -\frac{a \sin t}{\sqrt{a^2 + c^2}}\mathbf{i} + \frac{a \cos t}{\sqrt{a^2 + c^2}}\mathbf{j} + \frac{c}{\sqrt{a^2 + c^2}}\mathbf{k}$$

$$\mathbf{T}'(t) = -\frac{a \cos t}{\sqrt{a^2 + c^2}}\mathbf{i} - \frac{a \sin t}{\sqrt{a^2 + c^2}}\mathbf{j}$$

$$\|\mathbf{T}'(t)\| = \sqrt{\left(-\frac{a \cos t}{\sqrt{a^2 + c^2}}\right)^2 + \left(-\frac{a \sin t}{\sqrt{a^2 + c^2}}\right)^2} = \sqrt{\frac{a^2}{a^2 + c^2}} = \frac{a}{\sqrt{a^2 + c^2}}$$

$$\mathbf{N}(t) = \frac{\mathbf{T}'(t)}{\|\mathbf{T}'(t)\|} = (-\cos t)\mathbf{i} - (\sin t)\mathbf{j} = -(\cos t\, \mathbf{i} + \sin t\, \mathbf{j})$$

Note that the $\mathbf{k}$ component of the principal unit normal $\mathbf{N}(t)$ is zero for every value of t, so this vector always lies in a horizontal plane, as illustrated in Figure 12.4.5. We leave it as an exercise to show that this vector actually always points toward the z-axis. ◀

■ INWARD UNIT NORMAL VECTORS IN 2-SPACE

Our next objective is to show that for a nonlinear parametric curve C in 2-space the unit normal vector always points toward the concave side of C. For this purpose, let $\phi(t)$ be the angle from the positive x-axis to $\mathbf{T}(t)$, and let $\mathbf{n}(t)$ be the unit vector that results when $\mathbf{T}(t)$ is rotated counterclockwise through an angle of $\pi/2$ (Figure 12.4.6). Since $\mathbf{T}(t)$ and $\mathbf{n}(t)$ are unit vectors, it follows from Formula (13) of Section 11.2 that these vectors can be expressed as

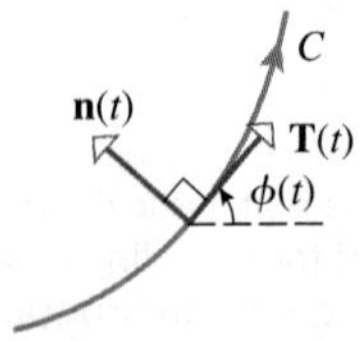

$$\mathbf{T}(t) = \cos\phi(t)\mathbf{i} + \sin\phi(t)\mathbf{j} \tag{3}$$

and

$$\mathbf{n}(t) = \cos[\phi(t) + \pi/2]\mathbf{i} + \sin[\phi(t) + \pi/2]\mathbf{j} = -\sin\phi(t)\mathbf{i} + \cos\phi(t)\mathbf{j} \tag{4}$$

Observe that on intervals where $\phi(t)$ is increasing the vector $\mathbf{n}(t)$ points *toward* the concave side of C, and on intervals where $\phi(t)$ is decreasing it points *away* from the concave side (Figure 12.4.7).

▲ **Figure 12.4.6**

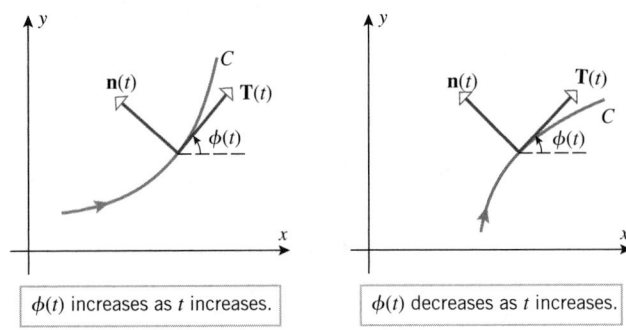

▶ **Figure 12.4.7**

$\phi(t)$ increases as t increases. $\phi(t)$ decreases as t increases.

Now let us differentiate $\mathbf{T}(t)$ by using Formula (3) and applying the chain rule. This yields

$$\frac{d\mathbf{T}}{dt} = \frac{d\mathbf{T}}{d\phi}\frac{d\phi}{dt} = [(-\sin\phi)\mathbf{i} + (\cos\phi)\mathbf{j}]\frac{d\phi}{dt}$$

and thus from (4)

$$\frac{d\mathbf{T}}{dt} = \mathbf{n}(t)\frac{d\phi}{dt} \tag{5}$$

But $d\phi/dt > 0$ on intervals where $\phi(t)$ is increasing and $d\phi/dt < 0$ on intervals where $\phi(t)$ is decreasing. Thus, it follows from (5) that $d\mathbf{T}/dt$ has the same direction as $\mathbf{n}(t)$ on intervals where $\phi(t)$ is increasing and the opposite direction on intervals where $\phi(t)$ is decreasing. Therefore, $\mathbf{T}'(t) = d\mathbf{T}/dt$ points "inward" toward the concave side of the curve in all cases, and hence so does $\mathbf{N}(t)$. For this reason, $\mathbf{N}(t)$ is also called the ***inward unit normal*** when applied to curves in 2-space.

■ COMPUTING T AND N FOR CURVES PARAMETRIZED BY ARC LENGTH

In the case where $\mathbf{r}(s)$ is parametrized by arc length, the procedures for computing the unit tangent vector $\mathbf{T}(s)$ and the unit normal vector $\mathbf{N}(s)$ are simpler than in the general case. For example, we showed in Theorem 12.3.4 that if s is an arc length parameter, then $\|\mathbf{r}'(s)\| = 1$. Thus, Formula (1) for the unit tangent vector simplifies to

$$\mathbf{T}(s) = \mathbf{r}'(s) \tag{6}$$

and consequently Formula (2) for the unit normal vector simplifies to

$$\mathbf{N}(s) = \frac{\mathbf{r}''(s)}{\|\mathbf{r}''(s)\|} \tag{7}$$

WARNING

Formulas (6) and (7) are only applicable when the curve is parametrized by an arc length parameter s. For other parametrizations Formulas (1) and (2) can be used.

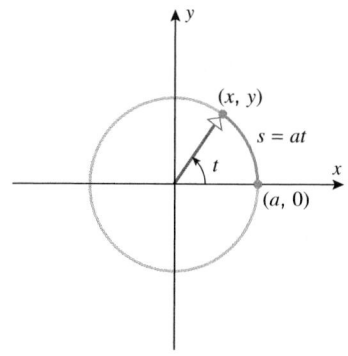

▲ **Figure 12.4.8**

▶ **Example 3**   The circle of radius a with counterclockwise orientation and centered at the origin can be represented by the vector-valued function

$$\mathbf{r} = a\cos t\mathbf{i} + a\sin t\mathbf{j} \qquad (0 \le t \le 2\pi) \tag{8}$$

Parametrize this circle by arc length and find $\mathbf{T}(s)$ and $\mathbf{N}(s)$.

Solution.   In (8) we can interpret t as the angle in radian measure from the positive x-axis to the radius vector (Figure 12.4.8). This angle subtends an arc of length $s = at$ on the circle, so we can reparametrize the circle in terms of s by substituting s/a for t in (8). This yields

$$\mathbf{r}(s) = a\cos(s/a)\mathbf{i} + a\sin(s/a)\mathbf{j} \qquad (0 \le s \le 2\pi a)$$

To find $\mathbf{T}(s)$ and $\mathbf{N}(s)$ from Formulas (6) and (7), we must compute $\mathbf{r}'(s)$, $\mathbf{r}''(s)$, and $\|\mathbf{r}''(s)\|$. Doing so, we obtain

$$\mathbf{r}'(s) = -\sin(s/a)\mathbf{i} + \cos(s/a)\mathbf{j}$$

$$\mathbf{r}''(s) = -(1/a)\cos(s/a)\mathbf{i} - (1/a)\sin(s/a)\mathbf{j}$$

$$\|\mathbf{r}''(s)\| = \sqrt{(-1/a)^2\cos^2(s/a) + (-1/a)^2\sin^2(s/a)} = 1/a$$

Thus,

$$\mathbf{T}(s) = \mathbf{r}'(s) = -\sin(s/a)\mathbf{i} + \cos(s/a)\mathbf{j}$$

$$\mathbf{N}(s) = \mathbf{r}''(s)/\|\mathbf{r}''(s)\| = -\cos(s/a)\mathbf{i} - \sin(s/a)\mathbf{j}$$

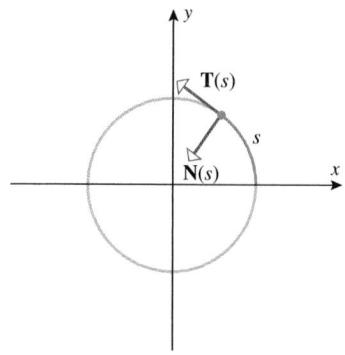

▲ **Figure 12.4.9**

so $\mathbf{N}(s)$ points toward the center of the circle for all s (Figure 12.4.9). This makes sense geometrically and is also consistent with our earlier observation that in 2-space the unit normal vector is the inward normal. ◀

■ **BINORMAL VECTORS IN 3-SPACE**
If C is the graph of a vector-valued function $\mathbf{r}(t)$ in 3-space, then we define the *binormal vector* to C at t to be

$$\mathbf{B}(t) = \mathbf{T}(t) \times \mathbf{N}(t) \tag{9}$$

It follows from properties of the cross product that $\mathbf{B}(t)$ is orthogonal to both $\mathbf{T}(t)$ and $\mathbf{N}(t)$ and is oriented relative to $\mathbf{T}(t)$ and $\mathbf{N}(t)$ by the right-hand rule. Moreover, $\mathbf{T}(t) \times \mathbf{N}(t)$ is a unit vector since

$$\|\mathbf{T}(t) \times \mathbf{N}(t)\| = \|\mathbf{T}(t)\|\|\mathbf{N}(t)\|\sin(\pi/2) = 1$$

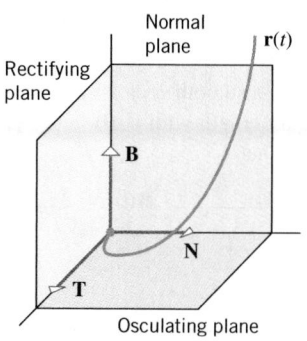

▲ **Figure 12.4.10**

Thus, $\{\mathbf{T}(t), \mathbf{N}(t), \mathbf{B}(t)\}$ is a set of three mutually orthogonal unit vectors.

Just as the vectors $\mathbf{i}$, $\mathbf{j}$, and $\mathbf{k}$ determine a right-handed coordinate system in 3-space, so do the vectors $\mathbf{T}(t)$, $\mathbf{N}(t)$, and $\mathbf{B}(t)$. At each point on a smooth parametric curve C in 3-space, these vectors determine three mutually perpendicular planes that pass through the point—the **TB**-plane (called the *rectifying plane*), the **TN**-plane (called the *osculating plane*), and the **NB**-plane (called the *normal plane*) (Figure 12.4.10). Moreover, one can show that a coordinate system determined by $\mathbf{T}(t)$, $\mathbf{N}(t)$, and $\mathbf{B}(t)$ is right-handed in the sense that each of these vectors is related to the other two by the right-hand rule (Figure 12.4.11):

$$\mathbf{B}(t) = \mathbf{T}(t) \times \mathbf{N}(t), \quad \mathbf{N}(t) = \mathbf{B}(t) \times \mathbf{T}(t), \quad \mathbf{T}(t) = \mathbf{N}(t) \times \mathbf{B}(t) \tag{10}$$

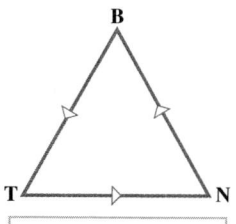

In (10), the vectors $\mathbf{B}$, $\mathbf{N}$, and $\mathbf{T}$ are each expressed as the cross product of the other two taken in the counterclockwise direction around the above triangle.

▲ **Figure 12.4.11**

The coordinate system determined by $\mathbf{T}(t)$, $\mathbf{N}(t)$, and $\mathbf{B}(t)$ is called the **TNB-*frame*** or sometimes the *Frenet frame* in honor of the French mathematician Jean Frédéric Frenet (1816–1900) who pioneered its application to the study of space curves. Typically, the *xyz*-coordinate system determined by the unit vectors $\mathbf{i}$, $\mathbf{j}$, and $\mathbf{k}$ remains fixed, whereas the **TNB**-frame changes as its origin moves along the curve C (Figure 12.4.12).

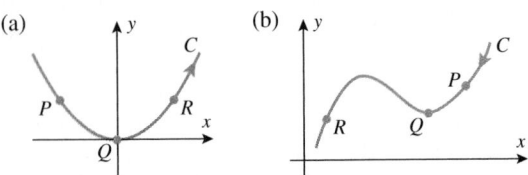

▶ **Figure 12.4.12**

Formula (9) expresses $\mathbf{B}(t)$ in terms of $\mathbf{T}(t)$ and $\mathbf{N}(t)$. Alternatively, the binormal $\mathbf{B}(t)$ can be expressed directly in terms of $\mathbf{r}(t)$ as

$$\mathbf{B}(t) = \frac{\mathbf{r}'(t) \times \mathbf{r}''(t)}{\|\mathbf{r}'(t) \times \mathbf{r}''(t)\|} \tag{11}$$

and in the case where the parameter is arc length it can be expressed in terms of $\mathbf{r}(s)$ as

$$\mathbf{B}(s) = \frac{\mathbf{r}'(s) \times \mathbf{r}''(s)}{\|\mathbf{r}''(s)\|} \tag{12}$$

We omit the proof.

✔ QUICK CHECK EXERCISES 12.4   *(See page 873 for answers.)*

1. If C is the graph of a smooth vector-valued function $\mathbf{r}(t)$, then the unit tangent, unit normal, and binormal to C at t are defined, respectively, by

$\mathbf{T}(t) = $ _____ , $\mathbf{N}(t) = $ _____ , $\mathbf{B}(t) = $ _____

2. If C is the graph of a smooth vector-valued function $\mathbf{r}(s)$ parametrized by arc length, then the definitions of the unit tangent and unit normal to C at s simplify, respectively, to

$\mathbf{T}(s) = $ _____   and $\mathbf{N}(s) = $ _____

3. If C is the graph of a smooth vector-valued function $\mathbf{r}(t)$, then the unit binormal vector to C at t may be computed directly in terms of $\mathbf{r}'(t)$ and $\mathbf{r}''(t)$ by the formula $\mathbf{B}(t) = $ _____ . When $t = s$ is the arc length parameter, this formula simplifies to $\mathbf{B}(s) = $ _____ .

4. Suppose that C is the graph of a smooth vector-valued function $\mathbf{r}(s)$ parametrized by arc length with $\mathbf{r}'(0) = \left\langle \frac{2}{3}, \frac{1}{3}, \frac{2}{3} \right\rangle$ and $\mathbf{r}''(0) = \langle -3, 12, -3 \rangle$. Then

$\mathbf{T}(0) = $ _____ , $\mathbf{N}(0) = $ _____ , $\mathbf{B}(0) = $ _____

EXERCISE SET 12.4

FOCUS ON CONCEPTS

1. In each part, sketch the unit tangent and normal vectors at the points P, Q, and R, taking into account the orientation of the curve C.

(a)   (b)

2. Make a rough sketch that shows the ellipse

$$\mathbf{r}(t) = 3 \cos t \mathbf{i} + 2 \sin t \mathbf{j}$$

for $0 \le t \le 2\pi$ and the unit tangent and normal vectors at the points $t = 0$, $t = \pi/4$, $t = \pi/2$, and $t = \pi$.

3. In the marginal note associated with Example 8 of Section 12.3, we observed that a line $\mathbf{r} = \mathbf{r}_0 + t\mathbf{v}$ can be parametrized in terms of an arc length parameter s with reference point $\mathbf{r}_0$ by normalizing $\mathbf{v}$. Use this result to show that the tangent line to the graph of $\mathbf{r}(t)$ at the point t_0 can be expressed as

$$\mathbf{r} = \mathbf{r}(t_0) + s\mathbf{T}(t_0)$$

where s is an arc length parameter with reference point $\mathbf{r}(t_0)$.

4. Use the result in Exercise 3 to show that the tangent line to the parabola

$$x = t, \quad y = t^2$$

at the point $(1, 1)$ can be expressed parametrically as

$$x = 1 + \frac{s}{\sqrt{5}}, \quad y = 1 + \frac{2s}{\sqrt{5}}$$

5–12 Find $\mathbf{T}(t)$ and $\mathbf{N}(t)$ at the given point. ▨

5. $\mathbf{r}(t) = (t^2 - 1)\mathbf{i} + t\mathbf{j}$; $t = 1$

6. $\mathbf{r}(t) = \frac{1}{2}t^2\mathbf{i} + \frac{1}{3}t^3\mathbf{j}$; $t = 1$

7. $\mathbf{r}(t) = 5\cos t\mathbf{i} + 5\sin t\mathbf{j}$; $t = \pi/3$

8. $\mathbf{r}(t) = \ln t\mathbf{i} + t\mathbf{j}$; $t = e$

9. $\mathbf{r}(t) = 4\cos t\mathbf{i} + 4\sin t\mathbf{j} + t\mathbf{k}$; $t = \pi/2$

10. $\mathbf{r}(t) = t\mathbf{i} + \frac{1}{2}t^2\mathbf{j} + \frac{1}{3}t^3\mathbf{k}$; $t = 0$

11. $x = e^t\cos t$, $y = e^t\sin t$, $z = e^t$; $t = 0$

12. $x = \cosh t$, $y = \sinh t$, $z = t$; $t = \ln 2$

13–14 Use the result in Exercise 3 to find parametric equations for the tangent line to the graph of $\mathbf{r}(t)$ at t_0 in terms of an arc length parameter s. ▨

13. $\mathbf{r}(t) = \sin t\mathbf{i} + \cos t\mathbf{j} + \frac{1}{2}t^2\mathbf{k}$; $t_0 = 0$

14. $\mathbf{r}(t) = t\mathbf{i} + t\mathbf{j} + \sqrt{9 - t^2}\mathbf{k}$; $t_0 = 1$

15–18 Use the formula $\mathbf{B}(t) = \mathbf{T}(t) \times \mathbf{N}(t)$ to find $\mathbf{B}(t)$, and then check your answer by using Formula (11) to find $\mathbf{B}(t)$ directly from $\mathbf{r}(t)$. ▨

15. $\mathbf{r}(t) = 3\sin t\mathbf{i} + 3\cos t\mathbf{j} + 4t\mathbf{k}$

16. $\mathbf{r}(t) = e^t\sin t\mathbf{i} + e^t\cos t\mathbf{j} + 3\mathbf{k}$

17. $\mathbf{r}(t) = (\sin t - t\cos t)\mathbf{i} + (\cos t + t\sin t)\mathbf{j} + \mathbf{k}$

18. $\mathbf{r}(t) = a\cos t\mathbf{i} + a\sin t\mathbf{j} + ct\mathbf{k}$ $(a \neq 0, c \neq 0)$

19–20 Find $\mathbf{T}(t)$, $\mathbf{N}(t)$, and $\mathbf{B}(t)$ for the given value of t. Then find equations for the osculating, normal, and rectifying planes at the point that corresponds to that value of t. ▨

19. $\mathbf{r}(t) = \cos t\mathbf{i} + \sin t\mathbf{j} + \mathbf{k}$; $t = \pi/4$

20. $\mathbf{r}(t) = e^t\mathbf{i} + e^t\cos t\mathbf{j} + e^t\sin t\mathbf{k}$; $t = 0$

21–24 True–False Determine whether the statement is true or false. Explain your answer. ▨

21. If C is the graph of a smooth vector-valued function $\mathbf{r}(t)$ in 2-space, then the unit tangent vector $\mathbf{T}(t)$ to C is orthogonal to $\mathbf{r}(t)$ and points in the direction of increasing parameter.

22. If C is the graph of a smooth vector-valued function $\mathbf{r}(t)$ in 2-space, then the angle measured in the counterclockwise direction from the unit tangent vector $\mathbf{T}(t)$ to the unit normal vector $\mathbf{N}(t)$ is $\pi/2$.

23. If the smooth vector-valued function $\mathbf{r}(s)$ is parametrized by arc length and $\mathbf{r}''(s)$ is defined, then $\mathbf{r}'(s)$ and $\mathbf{r}''(s)$ are orthogonal vectors.

24. The binormal vector $\mathbf{B}(t)$ to the graph of a vector-valued function $\mathbf{r}(t)$ in 3-space is the dot product of unit tangent and unit normal vectors, $\mathbf{T}(t)$ and $\mathbf{N}(t)$.

25. Writing Look up the definition of "osculating" in a dictionary and discuss why "osculating plane" is an appropriate term for the TN-plane.

26. Writing Discuss some of the advantages of parametrizing a curve by arc length.

✔ **QUICK CHECK ANSWERS 12.4**

1. $\dfrac{\mathbf{r}'(t)}{\|\mathbf{r}'(t)\|}$; $\dfrac{\mathbf{T}'(t)}{\|\mathbf{T}'(t)\|}$; $\mathbf{T}(t) \times \mathbf{N}(t)$ **2.** $\mathbf{r}'(s)$; $\dfrac{\mathbf{r}''(s)}{\|\mathbf{r}''(s)\|}$ **3.** $\dfrac{\mathbf{r}'(t) \times \mathbf{r}''(t)}{\|\mathbf{r}'(t) \times \mathbf{r}''(t)\|}$; $\dfrac{\mathbf{r}'(s) \times \mathbf{r}''(s)}{\|\mathbf{r}''(s)\|}$

4. $\left\langle \dfrac{2}{3}, \dfrac{1}{3}, \dfrac{2}{3} \right\rangle$; $\left\langle -\dfrac{1}{3\sqrt{2}}, \dfrac{4}{3\sqrt{2}}, -\dfrac{1}{3\sqrt{2}} \right\rangle$; $\left\langle -\dfrac{1}{\sqrt{2}}, 0, \dfrac{1}{\sqrt{2}} \right\rangle$

12.5 CURVATURE

In this section we will consider the problem of obtaining a numerical measure of how sharply a curve in 2-space or 3-space bends. Our results will have applications in geometry and in the study of motion along a curved path.

▨ **DEFINITION OF CURVATURE**

Suppose that C is the graph of a smooth vector-valued function in 2-space or 3-space that is parametrized in terms of arc length. Figure 12.5.1 suggests that for a curve in 2-space the "sharpness" of the bend in C is closely related to $d\mathbf{T}/ds$, which is the rate of change of the unit tangent vector $\mathbf{T}$ with respect to s. (Keep in mind that $\mathbf{T}$ has constant length, so only its direction changes.) If C is a straight line (no bend), then the direction of $\mathbf{T}$ remains constant (Figure 12.5.1a); if C bends slightly, then $\mathbf{T}$ undergoes a gradual change of direction (Figure 12.5.1b); and if C bends sharply, then $\mathbf{T}$ undergoes a rapid change of direction (Figure 12.5.1c).

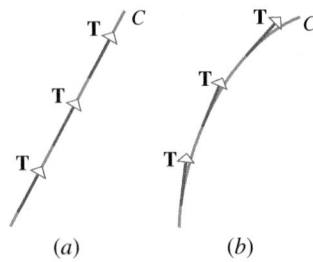

(a)   *(b)*

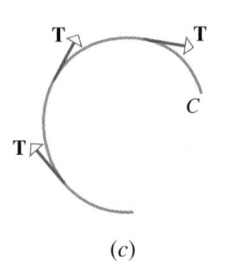

(c)

▲ **Figure 12.5.1**

The situation in 3-space is more complicated because bends in a curve are not limited to a single plane—they can occur in all directions, as illustrated by the complicated tube plot in Figure 12.1.4. To describe the bending characteristics of a curve in 3-space completely, one must take into account $d\mathbf{T}/ds$, $d\mathbf{N}/ds$, and $d\mathbf{B}/ds$. A complete study of this topic would take us too far afield, so we will limit our discussion to $d\mathbf{T}/ds$, which is the most important of these derivatives in applications.

12.5.1 **DEFINITION** If C is a smooth curve in 2-space or 3-space that is parametrized by arc length, then the ***curvature*** of C, denoted by $\kappa = \kappa(s)$ (κ = Greek "kappa"), is defined by

$$\kappa(s) = \left\| \frac{d\mathbf{T}}{ds} \right\| = \| \mathbf{r}''(s) \| \tag{1}$$

Observe that $\kappa(s)$ is a real-valued function of s, since it is the *length* of $d\mathbf{T}/ds$ that measures the curvature. In general, the curvature will vary from point to point along a curve; however, the following example shows that the curvature is constant for circles in 2-space, as you might expect.

▶ **Example 1** In Example 3 of Section 12.4 we showed that the circle of radius a, centered at the origin, can be parametrized in terms of arc length as

$$\mathbf{r}(s) = a \cos\left(\frac{s}{a}\right) \mathbf{i} + a \sin\left(\frac{s}{a}\right) \mathbf{j} \qquad (0 \le s \le 2\pi a)$$

Thus,

$$\mathbf{r}''(s) = -\frac{1}{a} \cos\left(\frac{s}{a}\right) \mathbf{i} - \frac{1}{a} \sin\left(\frac{s}{a}\right) \mathbf{j}$$

and hence from (1)

$$\kappa(s) = \| \mathbf{r}''(s) \| = \sqrt{\left[-\frac{1}{a} \cos\left(\frac{s}{a}\right)\right]^2 + \left[-\frac{1}{a} \sin\left(\frac{s}{a}\right)\right]^2} = \frac{1}{a}$$

so the circle has constant curvature $1/a$. ◀

The next example shows that lines have zero curvature, which is consistent with the fact that they do not bend.

▶ **Example 2** Recall from Formula (15) of Section 12.3 that a line in 2-space or 3-space can be parametrized in terms of arc length as

$$\mathbf{r} = \mathbf{r}_0 + s\mathbf{u}$$

where the terminal point of $\mathbf{r}_0$ is a point on the line and $\mathbf{u}$ is a unit vector parallel to the line. Since $\mathbf{u}$ and $\mathbf{r}_0$ are constant, their derivatives with respect to s are zero, and hence

$$\mathbf{r}'(s) = \frac{d\mathbf{r}}{ds} = \frac{d}{ds}[\mathbf{r}_0 + s\mathbf{u}] = \mathbf{0} + \mathbf{u} = \mathbf{u}$$

$$\mathbf{r}''(s) = \frac{d\mathbf{r}'}{ds} = \frac{d}{ds}[\mathbf{u}] = \mathbf{0}$$

Thus,

$$\kappa(s) = \| \mathbf{r}''(s) \| = 0 \ ◀$$

■ **FORMULAS FOR CURVATURE**

Formula (1) is only applicable if the curve is parametrized in terms of arc length. The following theorem provides two formulas for curvature in terms of a general parameter t.

12.5.2   THEOREM   *If $\mathbf{r}(t)$ is a smooth vector-valued function in 2-space or 3-space, then for each value of t at which $\mathbf{T}'(t)$ and $\mathbf{r}''(t)$ exist, the curvature κ can be expressed as*

(a) $$\kappa(t) = \frac{\|\mathbf{T}'(t)\|}{\|\mathbf{r}'(t)\|} \tag{2}$$

(b) $$\kappa(t) = \frac{\|\mathbf{r}'(t) \times \mathbf{r}''(t)\|}{\|\mathbf{r}'(t)\|^3} \tag{3}$$

PROOF (a) It follows from Formula (1) and Formula (16) of Section 12.3 that

$$\kappa(t) = \left\|\frac{d\mathbf{T}}{ds}\right\| = \left\|\frac{d\mathbf{T}/dt}{ds/dt}\right\| = \left\|\frac{d\mathbf{T}/dt}{\|d\mathbf{r}/dt\|}\right\| = \frac{\|\mathbf{T}'(t)\|}{\|\mathbf{r}'(t)\|}$$

PROOF (b) It follows from Formula (1) of Section 12.4 that

$$\mathbf{r}'(t) = \|\mathbf{r}'(t)\|\mathbf{T}(t) \tag{4}$$
$$\mathbf{r}''(t) = \|\mathbf{r}'(t)\|'\mathbf{T}(t) + \|\mathbf{r}'(t)\|\mathbf{T}'(t) \tag{5}$$

But from Formula (2) of Section 12.4 and part (a) of this theorem we have

$$\mathbf{T}'(t) = \|\mathbf{T}'(t)\|\mathbf{N}(t) \quad \text{and} \quad \|\mathbf{T}'(t)\| = \kappa(t)\|\mathbf{r}'(t)\|$$

so

$$\mathbf{T}'(t) = \kappa(t)\|\mathbf{r}'(t)\|\mathbf{N}(t)$$

Substituting this into (5) yields

$$\mathbf{r}''(t) = \|\mathbf{r}'(t)\|'\mathbf{T}(t) + \kappa(t)\|\mathbf{r}'(t)\|^2\mathbf{N}(t) \tag{6}$$

Thus, from (4) and (6)

$$\mathbf{r}'(t) \times \mathbf{r}''(t) = \|\mathbf{r}'(t)\|\|\mathbf{r}'(t)\|'(\mathbf{T}(t) \times \mathbf{T}(t)) + \kappa(t)\|\mathbf{r}'(t)\|^3(\mathbf{T}(t) \times \mathbf{N}(t))$$

But the cross product of a vector with itself is zero, so this equation simplifies to

$$\mathbf{r}'(t) \times \mathbf{r}''(t) = \kappa(t)\|\mathbf{r}'(t)\|^3(\mathbf{T}(t) \times \mathbf{N}(t)) = \kappa(t)\|\mathbf{r}'(t)\|^3\mathbf{B}(t)$$

It follows from this equation and the fact that $\mathbf{B}(t)$ is a unit vector that

$$\|\mathbf{r}'(t) \times \mathbf{r}''(t)\| = \kappa(t)\|\mathbf{r}'(t)\|^3$$

Formula (3) now follows.   ■

REMARK | Formula (2) is useful if $\mathbf{T}(t)$ is known or is easy to obtain; however, Formula (3) will usually be easier to apply, since it involves only $\mathbf{r}(t)$ and its derivatives. We also note that cross products were defined only for vectors in 3-space, so to use Formula (3) in 2-space we must first write the 2-space function $\mathbf{r}(t) = x(t)\mathbf{i} + y(t)\mathbf{j}$ as the 3-space function $\mathbf{r}(t) = x(t)\mathbf{i} + y(t)\mathbf{j} + 0\mathbf{k}$ with a zero $\mathbf{k}$ component.

▶ **Example 3**   Find $\kappa(t)$ for the circular helix

$$x = a\cos t, \quad y = a\sin t, \quad z = ct$$

where $a > 0$.

Solution.   The radius vector for the helix is

$$\mathbf{r}(t) = a \cos t\,\mathbf{i} + a \sin t\,\mathbf{j} + ct\,\mathbf{k}$$

Thus,

$$\mathbf{r}'(t) = (-a \sin t)\mathbf{i} + a \cos t\,\mathbf{j} + c\mathbf{k}$$
$$\mathbf{r}''(t) = (-a \cos t)\mathbf{i} + (-a \sin t)\mathbf{j}$$

$$\mathbf{r}'(t) \times \mathbf{r}''(t) = \begin{vmatrix} \mathbf{i} & \mathbf{j} & \mathbf{k} \\ -a \sin t & a \cos t & c \\ -a \cos t & -a \sin t & 0 \end{vmatrix} = (ac \sin t)\mathbf{i} - (ac \cos t)\mathbf{j} + a^2\mathbf{k}$$

Therefore,

$$\|\mathbf{r}'(t)\| = \sqrt{(-a \sin t)^2 + (a \cos t)^2 + c^2} = \sqrt{a^2 + c^2}$$

and

$$\|\mathbf{r}'(t) \times \mathbf{r}''(t)\| = \sqrt{(ac \sin t)^2 + (-ac \cos t)^2 + a^4}$$
$$= \sqrt{a^2 c^2 + a^4} = a\sqrt{a^2 + c^2}$$

so

$$\kappa(t) = \frac{\|\mathbf{r}'(t) \times \mathbf{r}''(t)\|}{\|\mathbf{r}'(t)\|^3} = \frac{a\sqrt{a^2 + c^2}}{\left(\sqrt{a^2 + c^2}\right)^3} = \frac{a}{a^2 + c^2}$$

Note that κ does not depend on t, which tells us that the helix has constant curvature. ◄

▶ **Example 4**   The graph of the vector equation

$$\mathbf{r} = 2 \cos t\,\mathbf{i} + 3 \sin t\,\mathbf{j} \quad (0 \le t \le 2\pi)$$

is the ellipse in Figure 12.5.2. Find the curvature of the ellipse at the endpoints of the major and minor axes, and use a graphing utility to generate the graph of $\kappa(t)$.

Solution.   To apply Formula (3), we must treat the ellipse as a curve in the xy-plane of an xyz-coordinate system by adding a zero $\mathbf{k}$ component and writing its equation as

$$\mathbf{r} = 2 \cos t\,\mathbf{i} + 3 \sin t\,\mathbf{j} + 0\mathbf{k}$$

It is not essential to write the zero $\mathbf{k}$ component explicitly as long as you assume it to be there when you calculate a cross product. Thus,

$$\mathbf{r}'(t) = (-2 \sin t)\mathbf{i} + 3 \cos t\,\mathbf{j}$$
$$\mathbf{r}''(t) = (-2 \cos t)\mathbf{i} + (-3 \sin t)\mathbf{j}$$

$$\mathbf{r}'(t) \times \mathbf{r}''(t) = \begin{vmatrix} \mathbf{i} & \mathbf{j} & \mathbf{k} \\ -2 \sin t & 3 \cos t & 0 \\ -2 \cos t & -3 \sin t & 0 \end{vmatrix} = [(6 \sin^2 t) + (6 \cos^2 t)]\mathbf{k} = 6\mathbf{k}$$

Therefore,

$$\|\mathbf{r}'(t)\| = \sqrt{(-2 \sin t)^2 + (3 \cos t)^2} = \sqrt{4 \sin^2 t + 9 \cos^2 t}$$
$$\|\mathbf{r}'(t) \times \mathbf{r}''(t)\| = 6$$

so

$$\kappa(t) = \frac{\|\mathbf{r}'(t) \times \mathbf{r}''(t)\|}{\|\mathbf{r}'(t)\|^3} = \frac{6}{[4 \sin^2 t + 9 \cos^2 t]^{3/2}} \tag{7}$$

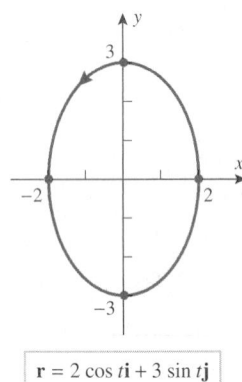

$$\mathbf{r} = 2 \cos t\,\mathbf{i} + 3 \sin t\,\mathbf{j}$$

▲ **Figure 12.5.2**

The endpoints of the minor axis are $(2, 0)$ and $(-2, 0)$, which correspond to $t = 0$ and $t = \pi$, respectively. Substituting these values in (7) yields the same curvature at both points, namely,

$$\kappa = \kappa(0) = \kappa(\pi) = \frac{6}{9^{3/2}} = \frac{6}{27} = \frac{2}{9}$$

The endpoints of the major axis are $(0, 3)$ and $(0, -3)$, which correspond to $t = \pi/2$ and $t = 3\pi/2$, respectively; from (7) the curvature at these points is

$$\kappa = \kappa\left(\frac{\pi}{2}\right) = \kappa\left(\frac{3\pi}{2}\right) = \frac{6}{4^{3/2}} = \frac{3}{4}$$

Observe that the curvature is greater at the ends of the major axis than at the ends of the minor axis, as you might expect. Figure 12.5.3 shows the graph of κ versus t. This graph illustrates clearly that the curvature is minimum at $t = 0$ (the right end of the minor axis), increases to a maximum at $t = \pi/2$ (the top of the major axis), decreases to a minimum again at $t = \pi$ (the left end of the minor axis), and continues cyclically in this manner. Figure 12.5.4 provides another way of picturing the curvature. ◄

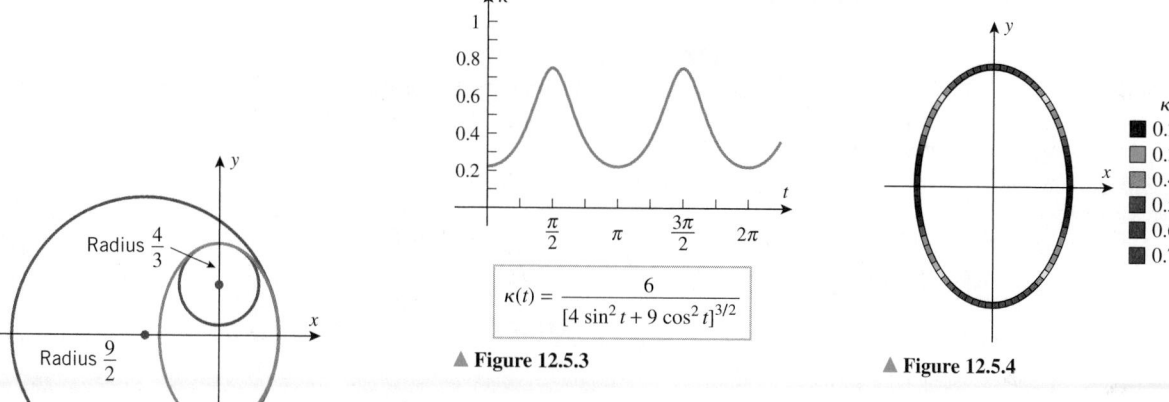

▲ Figure 12.5.3

▲ Figure 12.5.4

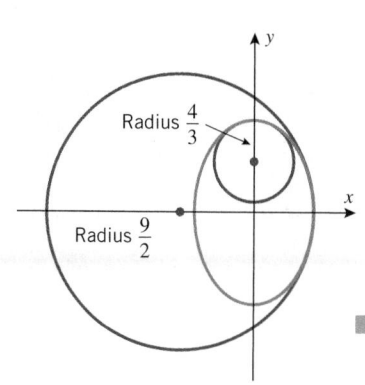

▲ Figure 12.5.5

RADIUS OF CURVATURE

In the last example we found the curvature at the ends of the minor axis to be $\frac{2}{9}$ and the curvature at the ends of the major axis to be $\frac{3}{4}$. To obtain a better understanding of the meaning of these numbers, recall from Example 1 that a circle of radius a has a constant curvature of $1/a$; thus, the curvature of the ellipse at the ends of the minor axis is the same as that of a circle of radius $\frac{9}{2}$, and the curvature at the ends of the major axis is the same as that of a circle of radius $\frac{4}{3}$ (Figure 12.5.5).

In general, if a curve C in 2-space has nonzero curvature κ at a point P, then the circle of radius $\rho = 1/\kappa$ sharing a common tangent with C at P, and centered on the concave side of the curve at P, is called the *osculating circle* or *circle of curvature* at P (Figure 12.5.6). The osculating circle and the curve C not only touch at P but they have equal curvatures at that point. In this sense, the osculating circle is the circle that best approximates the curve C near P. The radius ρ of the osculating circle at P is called the *radius of curvature* at P, and the center of the circle is called the *center of curvature* at P (Figure 12.5.6).

Osculating circle

Center of
curvature

$\rho = \frac{1}{\kappa}$

C

P

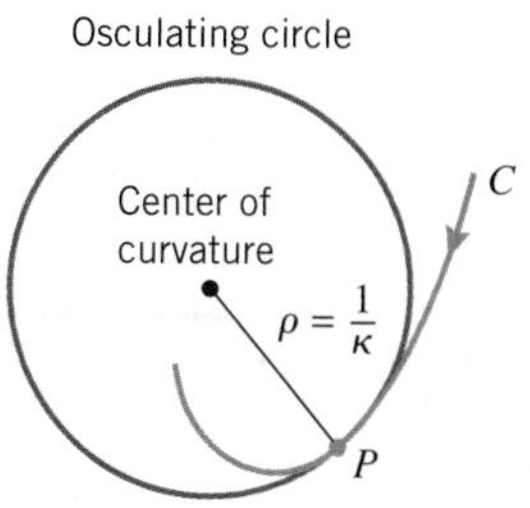

▲ Figure 12.5.6

AN INTERPRETATION OF CURVATURE IN 2-SPACE

A useful geometric interpretation of curvature in 2-space can be obtained by considering the angle ϕ measured counterclockwise from the direction of the positive x-axis to the unit tangent vector $\mathbf{T}$ (Figure 12.5.7). By Formula (13) of Section 11.2, we can express $\mathbf{T}$ in terms of ϕ as

$$\mathbf{T}(\phi) = \cos\phi\,\mathbf{i} + \sin\phi\,\mathbf{j}$$

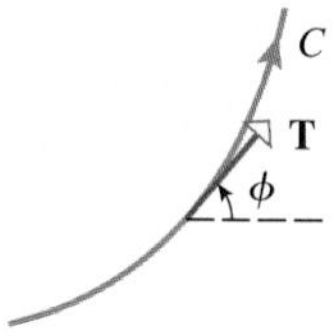

C

$\mathbf{T}$

ϕ

▲ Figure 12.5.7

Thus,

$$\frac{d\mathbf{T}}{d\phi} = (-\sin\phi)\mathbf{i} + \cos\phi\,\mathbf{j}$$

$$\frac{d\mathbf{T}}{ds} = \frac{d\mathbf{T}}{d\phi}\frac{d\phi}{ds}$$

from which we obtain

$$\kappa(s) = \left\|\frac{d\mathbf{T}}{ds}\right\| = \left|\frac{d\phi}{ds}\right|\left\|\frac{d\mathbf{T}}{d\phi}\right\| = \left|\frac{d\phi}{ds}\right|\sqrt{(-\sin\phi)^2 + \cos^2\phi} = \left|\frac{d\phi}{ds}\right|$$

In summary, we have shown that

$$\kappa(s) = \left|\frac{d\phi}{ds}\right| \tag{8}$$

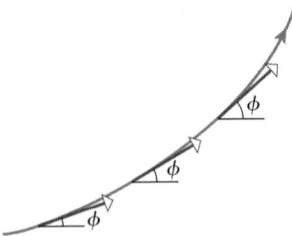

In 2-space, $\kappa(s)$ is the magnitude of the rate of change of ϕ with respect to s.

▲ **Figure 12.5.8**

which tells us that curvature in 2-space can be interpreted as the magnitude of the rate of change of ϕ with respect to s—the greater the curvature, the more rapidly ϕ changes with s (Figure 12.5.8). In the case of a straight line, the angle ϕ is constant (Figure 12.5.9) and consequently $\kappa(s) = |d\phi/ds| = 0$, which is consistent with the fact that a straight line has zero curvature at every point.

■ FORMULA SUMMARY

We conclude this section with a summary of formulas for **T**, **N**, and **B**. These formulas have either been derived in the text or are easily derivable from formulas we have already established.

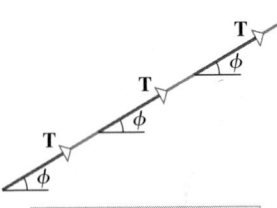

ϕ is constant, so the line has zero curvature.

▲ **Figure 12.5.9**

$$\mathbf{T}(s) = \mathbf{r}'(s) \tag{9}$$

$$\mathbf{N}(s) = \frac{1}{\kappa(s)}\frac{d\mathbf{T}}{ds} = \frac{\mathbf{r}''(s)}{\|\mathbf{r}''(s)\|} = \frac{\mathbf{r}''(s)}{\kappa(s)} \tag{10}$$

$$\mathbf{B}(s) = \frac{\mathbf{r}'(s) \times \mathbf{r}''(s)}{\|\mathbf{r}''(s)\|} = \frac{\mathbf{r}'(s) \times \mathbf{r}''(s)}{\kappa(s)} \tag{11}$$

$$\mathbf{T}(t) = \frac{\mathbf{r}'(t)}{\|\mathbf{r}'(t)\|} \tag{12}$$

$$\mathbf{B}(t) = \frac{\mathbf{r}'(t) \times \mathbf{r}''(t)}{\|\mathbf{r}'(t) \times \mathbf{r}''(t)\|} \tag{13}$$

$$\mathbf{N}(t) = \mathbf{B}(t) \times \mathbf{T}(t) \tag{14}$$

✔ QUICK CHECK EXERCISES 12.5   (See page 881 for answers.)

1. If C is a smooth curve parametrized by arc length, then the curvature is defined by $\kappa(s) =$ _____.

2. Let $\mathbf{r}(t)$ be a smooth vector-valued function with curvature $\kappa(t)$.
   (a) The curvature may be expressed in terms of $\mathbf{T}'(t)$ and $\mathbf{r}'(t)$ as $\kappa(t) =$ _____.
   (b) The curvature may be expressed directly in terms of $\mathbf{r}'(t)$ and $\mathbf{r}''(t)$ as $\kappa(t) =$ _____.

3. Suppose that C is the graph of a smooth vector-valued function $\mathbf{r}(s) = \langle x(s), y(s)\rangle$ parametrized by arc length and that the unit tangent $\mathbf{T}(s) = \langle\cos\phi(s), \sin\phi(s)\rangle$. Then the curvature can be expressed in terms of $\phi(s)$ as $\kappa(s) =$ _____.

4. Suppose that C is a smooth curve and that $x^2 + y^2 = 4$ is the osculating circle to C at $P(1, \sqrt{3})$. Then the curvature of C at P is _____.

EXERCISE SET 12.5   ⟋ Graphing Utility   [C] CAS

FOCUS ON CONCEPTS

1–2 Use the osculating circle shown in the figure to estimate the curvature at the indicated point. ▧

1.

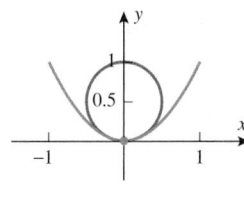

2.

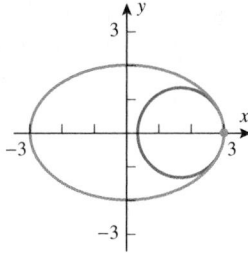

3–4 For a plane curve $y = f(x)$ the curvature at $(x, f(x))$ is a function $\kappa(x)$. In these exercises the graphs of $f(x)$ and $\kappa(x)$ are shown. Determine which is which and explain your reasoning. ▧

3. (a)

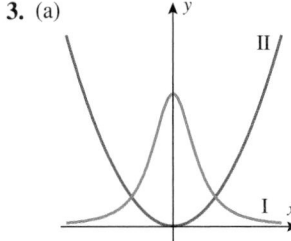

(b)

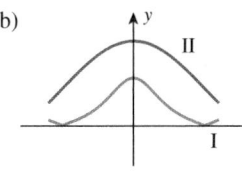

4. (a)

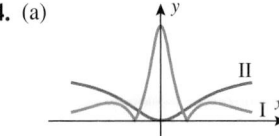

(b)

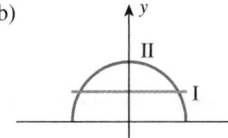

5–12 Use Formula (3) to find $\kappa(t)$. ▧

5. $\mathbf{r}(t) = t^2\mathbf{i} + t^3\mathbf{j}$

6. $\mathbf{r}(t) = 4\cos t\,\mathbf{i} + \sin t\,\mathbf{j}$

7. $\mathbf{r}(t) = e^{3t}\mathbf{i} + e^{-t}\mathbf{j}$

8. $x = 1 - t^3$, $y = t - t^2$

9. $\mathbf{r}(t) = 4\cos t\,\mathbf{i} + 4\sin t\,\mathbf{j} + t\mathbf{k}$

10. $\mathbf{r}(t) = t\mathbf{i} + \frac{1}{2}t^2\mathbf{j} + \frac{1}{3}t^3\mathbf{k}$

11. $x = \cosh t$, $y = \sinh t$, $z = t$

12. $\mathbf{r}(t) = \mathbf{i} + t\mathbf{j} + t^2\mathbf{k}$

13–16 Find the curvature and the radius of curvature at the stated point. ▧

13. $\mathbf{r}(t) = 3\cos t\,\mathbf{i} + 4\sin t\,\mathbf{j} + t\mathbf{k}$; $t = \pi/2$

14. $\mathbf{r}(t) = e^t\mathbf{i} + e^{-t}\mathbf{j} + t\mathbf{k}$; $t = 0$

15. $x = e^t\cos t$, $y = e^t\sin t$, $z = e^t$; $t = 0$

16. $x = \sin t$, $y = \cos t$, $z = \frac{1}{2}t^2$; $t = 0$

17–18 Confirm that s is an arc length parameter by showing that $\|d\mathbf{r}/ds\| = 1$, and then apply Formula (1) to find $\kappa(s)$. ▧

17. $\mathbf{r} = \sin\left(1 + \dfrac{s}{2}\right)\mathbf{i} + \cos\left(1 + \dfrac{s}{2}\right)\mathbf{j} + \sqrt{3}\left(1 + \dfrac{s}{2}\right)\mathbf{k}$

18. $\mathbf{r} = \left(1 - \frac{2}{3}s\right)^{3/2}\mathbf{i} + \left(\frac{2}{3}s\right)^{3/2}\mathbf{j}$ $\left(0 \le s \le \frac{3}{2}\right)$

19–22 True–False Determine whether the statement is true or false. Explain your answer. ▧

19. A circle of radius 2 has constant curvature $\frac{1}{2}$.

20. A vertical line in 2-space has undefined curvature.

21. If $\mathbf{r}(s)$ is parametrized by arc length, then the curvature of the graph of $\mathbf{r}(s)$ is the length of $\mathbf{r}'(s)$.

22. If C is a curve in 2-space, then the osculating circle to C at a point P has radius equal to the curvature of C at P.

23. (a) Use Formula (3) to show that in 2-space the curvature of a smooth parametric curve

$$x = x(t), \quad y = y(t)$$

is

$$\kappa(t) = \frac{|x'y'' - y'x''|}{(x'^2 + y'^2)^{3/2}}$$

where primes denote differentiation with respect to t.

(b) Use the result in part (a) to show that in 2-space the curvature of the plane curve given by $y = f(x)$ is

$$\kappa(x) = \frac{|d^2y/dx^2|}{[1 + (dy/dx)^2]^{3/2}}$$

[*Hint:* Express $y = f(x)$ parametrically with $x = t$ as the parameter.]

24. Use part (b) of Exercise 23 to show that the curvature of $y = f(x)$ can be expressed in terms of the angle of inclination of the tangent line as

$$\kappa(\phi) = \left|\frac{d^2y}{dx^2}\cos^3\phi\right|$$

[*Hint:* $\tan\phi = dy/dx$.]

25–28 Use the result in Exercise 23(b) to find the curvature at the stated point. ▧

25. $y = \sin x$; $x = \pi/2$

26. $y = x^3/3$; $x = 0$

27. $y = e^{-x}$; $x = 1$

28. $y^2 - 4x^2 = 9$; $(2, 5)$

29–32 Use the result in Exercise 23(a) to find the curvature at the stated point. ▧

29. $x = t^2, y = t^3$; $t = \frac{1}{2}$

30. $x = e^{3t}, y = e^{-t}$; $t = 0$

31. $x = t, y = 1/t$; $t = 1$

32. $x = 2\sin 2t, y = 3\sin t$; $t = \pi/2$

33. In each part, use the formulas in Exercise 23 to help find the radius of curvature at the stated points. Then sketch the graph together with the osculating circles at those points.
(a) $y = \cos x$ at $x = 0$ and $x = \pi$
(b) $x = 2\cos t$, $y = \sin t$ $(0 \le t \le 2\pi)$ at $t = 0$ and $t = \pi/2$

34. Use the formula in Exercise 23(a) to find $\kappa(t)$ for the curve $x = e^{-t}\cos t$, $y = e^{-t}\sin t$. Then sketch the graph of $\kappa(t)$.

35–36 Generate the graph of $y = f(x)$ using a graphing utility, and then make a conjecture about the shape of the graph of $y = \kappa(x)$. Check your conjecture by generating the graph of $y = \kappa(x)$. ■

35. $f(x) = xe^{-x}$ for $0 \le x \le 5$

36. $f(x) = x^3 - x$ for $-1 \le x \le 1$

c **37.** (a) If you have a CAS, read the documentation on calculating higher-order derivatives. Then use the CAS and part (b) of Exercise 23 to find $\kappa(x)$ for $f(x) = x^4 - 2x^2$.
  (b) Use the CAS to generate the graphs of $f(x) = x^4 - 2x^2$ and $\kappa(x)$ on the same screen for $-2 \le x \le 2$.
  (c) Find the radius of curvature at each relative extremum.
  (d) Make a reasonably accurate hand-drawn sketch that shows the graph of $f(x) = x^4 - 2x^2$ and the osculating circles in their correct proportions at the relative extrema.

c **38.** (a) Use a CAS to graph the parametric curve $x = t \cos t$, $y = t \sin t$ for $t \ge 0$.
  (b) Make a conjecture about the behavior of the curvature $\kappa(t)$ as $t \to +\infty$.
  (c) Use the CAS and part (a) of Exercise 23 to find $\kappa(t)$.
  (d) Check your conjecture by finding the limit of $\kappa(t)$ as $t \to +\infty$.

39. Use the formula in Exercise 23(a) to show that for a curve in polar coordinates described by $r = f(\theta)$ the curvature is

$$\kappa(\theta) = \frac{\left| r^2 + 2\left(\dfrac{dr}{d\theta}\right)^2 - r\dfrac{d^2 r}{d\theta^2}\right|}{\left[r^2 + \left(\dfrac{dr}{d\theta}\right)^2\right]^{3/2}}$$

[*Hint:* Let θ be the parameter and use the relationships $x = r \cos\theta$, $y = r \sin\theta$.]

40. Use the result in Exercise 39 to show that a circle has constant curvature.

41–44 Use the formula in Exercise 39 to find the curvature at the indicated point. ■

41. $r = 1 + \cos\theta$; $\theta = \pi/2$ **42.** $r = e^{2\theta}$; $\theta = 1$

43. $r = \sin 3\theta$; $\theta = 0$ **44.** $r = \theta$; $\theta = 1$

45. Find the radius of curvature of the parabola $y^2 = 4px$ at $(0, 0)$.

46. At what point(s) does $y = e^x$ have maximum curvature?

47. At what point(s) does $4x^2 + 9y^2 = 36$ have minimum radius of curvature?

48. Find the maximum and minimum values of the radius of curvature for the curve $x = \cos t$, $y = \sin t$, $z = \cos t$.

49. Use the formula in Exercise 39 to show that the curvature of the polar curve $r = e^{a\theta}$ is inversely proportional to r.

c **50.** Use the formula in Exercise 39 and a CAS to show that the curvature of the lemniscate $r = \sqrt{a \cos 2\theta}$ is directly proportional to r.

51. (a) Use the result in Exercise 24 to show that for the parabola $y = x^2$ the curvature $\kappa(\phi)$ at points where the tangent line has an angle of inclination of ϕ is

$$\kappa(\phi) = |2\cos^3 \phi|$$

  (b) Use the result in part (a) to find the radius of curvature of the parabola at the point on the parabola where the tangent line has slope 1.
  (c) Make a sketch with reasonably accurate proportions that shows the osculating circle at the point on the parabola where the tangent line has slope 1.

52. The **evolute** of a smooth parametric curve C in 2-space is the curve formed from the centers of curvature of C. The accompanying figure shows the ellipse $x = 3\cos t$, $y = 2\sin t$ ($0 \le t \le 2\pi$) and its evolute graphed together.
  (a) Which points on the evolute correspond to $t = 0$ and $t = \pi/2$?
  (b) In what direction is the evolute traced as t increases from 0 to 2π?
  (c) What does the evolute of a circle look like? Explain your reasoning.

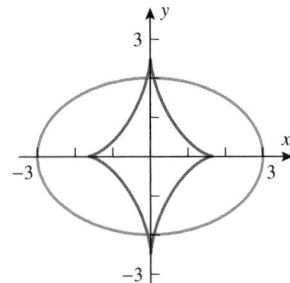

◀ **Figure Ex-52**

FOCUS ON CONCEPTS

53–57 These exercises are concerned with the problem of creating a single smooth curve by piecing together two separate smooth curves. If two smooth curves C_1 and C_2 are joined at a point P to form a curve C, then we will say that C_1 and C_2 make a **smooth transition** at P if the curvature of C is continuous at P. ■

53. Show that the transition at $x = 0$ from the horizontal line $y = 0$ for $x \le 0$ to the parabola $y = x^2$ for $x > 0$ is not smooth, whereas the transition to $y = x^3$ for $x > 0$ is smooth.

54. (a) Sketch the graph of the curve defined piecewise by $y = x^2$ for $x < 0$, $y = x^4$ for $x \ge 0$.
  (b) Show that for the curve in part (a) the transition at $x = 0$ is not smooth.

55. The accompanying figure on the next page shows the arc of a circle of radius r with center at $(0, r)$. Find the value of a so that there is a smooth transition from the circle to the parabola $y = ax^2$ at the point where $x = 0$.

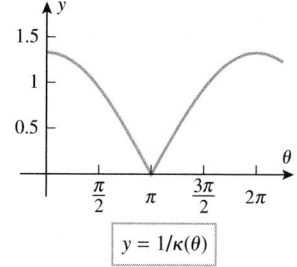
Arc of circle $(0, r)$
$y = ax^2$

◀ **Figure Ex-55**

56. Find $a, b,$ and c so that there is a smooth transition at $x = 0$ from the curve $y = e^x$ for $x \le 0$ to the parabola $y = ax^2 + bx + c$ for $x > 0$. [*Hint:* The curvature is continuous at those points where y'' is continuous.]

57. Assume that f is a function for which $f'''(x)$ is defined for all $x \le 0$. Explain why it is always possible to find numbers $a, b,$ and c such that there is a smooth transition at $x = 0$ from the curve $y = f(x)$, $x \le 0$, to the parabola $y = ax^2 + bx + c$.

58–61 Assume that s is an arc length parameter for a smooth vector-valued function $\mathbf{r}(s)$ in 3-space and that $d\mathbf{T}/ds$ and $d\mathbf{N}/ds$ exist at each point on the curve. (This implies that $d\mathbf{B}/ds$ exists as well, since $\mathbf{B} = \mathbf{T} \times \mathbf{N}$.) ▪

58. Show that
$$\frac{d\mathbf{T}}{ds} = \kappa(s)\mathbf{N}(s)$$
and use this result to obtain the formulas in (10).

59. (a) Show that $d\mathbf{B}/ds$ is perpendicular to $\mathbf{B}(s)$.
(b) Show that $d\mathbf{B}/ds$ is perpendicular to $\mathbf{T}(s)$. [*Hint:* Use the fact that $\mathbf{B}(s)$ is perpendicular to both $\mathbf{T}(s)$ and $\mathbf{N}(s)$, and differentiate $\mathbf{B} \cdot \mathbf{T}$ with respect to s.]
(c) Use the results in parts (a) and (b) to show that $d\mathbf{B}/ds$ is a scalar multiple of $\mathbf{N}(s)$. The *negative* of this scalar is called the ***torsion*** of $\mathbf{r}(s)$ and is denoted by $\tau(s)$. Thus,
$$\frac{d\mathbf{B}}{ds} = -\tau(s)\mathbf{N}(s)$$
(d) Show that $\tau(s) = 0$ for all s if the graph of $\mathbf{r}(s)$ lies in a plane. [*Note:* For reasons that we cannot discuss here, the torsion is related to the "twisting" properties of the curve, and $\tau(s)$ is regarded as a numerical measure of the tendency for the curve to twist out of the osculating plane.]

60. Let κ be the curvature of C and τ the torsion (defined in Exercise 59). By differentiating $\mathbf{N} = \mathbf{B} \times \mathbf{T}$ with respect to s, show that $d\mathbf{N}/ds = -\kappa\mathbf{T} + \tau\mathbf{B}$.

61. The following derivatives, known as the ***Frenet–Serret formulas***, are fundamental in the theory of curves in 3-space:

$$d\mathbf{T}/ds = \kappa\mathbf{N} \qquad \text{[Exercise 58]}$$
$$d\mathbf{N}/ds = -\kappa\mathbf{T} + \tau\mathbf{B} \quad \text{[Exercise 60]}$$
$$d\mathbf{B}/ds = -\tau\mathbf{N} \qquad \text{[Exercise 59(c)]}$$

Use the first two Frenet–Serret formulas and the fact that $\mathbf{r}'(s) = \mathbf{T}$ if $\mathbf{r} = \mathbf{r}(s)$ to show that
$$\tau = \frac{[\mathbf{r}'(s) \times \mathbf{r}''(s)] \cdot \mathbf{r}'''(s)}{\|\mathbf{r}''(s)\|^2} \quad \text{and} \quad \mathbf{B} = \frac{\mathbf{r}'(s) \times \mathbf{r}''(s)}{\|\mathbf{r}''(s)\|}$$

62. (a) Use the chain rule and the first two Frenet–Serret formulas in Exercise 61 to show that
$$\mathbf{T}' = \kappa s'\mathbf{N} \quad \text{and} \quad \mathbf{N}' = -\kappa s'\mathbf{T} + \tau s'\mathbf{B}$$
where primes denote differentiation with respect to t.
(b) Show that Formulas (4) and (6) can be written in the form
$$\mathbf{r}'(t) = s'\mathbf{T} \quad \text{and} \quad \mathbf{r}''(t) = s''\mathbf{T} + \kappa(s')^2\mathbf{N}$$
(c) Use the results in parts (a) and (b) to show that
$$\mathbf{r}'''(t) = [s''' - \kappa^2(s')^3]\mathbf{T}$$
$$+ [3\kappa s's'' + \kappa'(s')^2]\mathbf{N} + \kappa\tau(s')^3\mathbf{B}$$
(d) Use the results in parts (b) and (c) to show that
$$\tau(t) = \frac{[\mathbf{r}'(t) \times \mathbf{r}''(t)] \cdot \mathbf{r}'''(t)}{\|\mathbf{r}'(t) \times \mathbf{r}''(t)\|^2}$$

63–66 Use the formula in Exercise 62(d) to find the torsion $\tau = \tau(t)$. ▪

63. The twisted cubic $\mathbf{r}(t) = 2t\mathbf{i} + t^2\mathbf{j} + \frac{1}{3}t^3\mathbf{k}$

64. The circular helix $\mathbf{r}(t) = a\cos t\mathbf{i} + a\sin t\mathbf{j} + ct\mathbf{k}$

65. $\mathbf{r}(t) = e^t\mathbf{i} + e^{-t}\mathbf{j} + \sqrt{2}t\mathbf{k}$

66. $\mathbf{r}(t) = (t - \sin t)\mathbf{i} + (1 - \cos t)\mathbf{j} + t\mathbf{k}$

67. **Writing** One property of a twice-differentiable function $f(x)$ is that an inflection point on the graph is a point at which the tangent line crosses the graph of f. Consider the analogous issue in 2-space for an osculating circle to a curve C at a point P: What does it mean for the osculating circle to cross (or not to cross) C at P? Investigate this issue through some examples of your own and write a brief essay, with illustrations, supporting your conclusions.

68. **Writing** The accompanying figure is the graph of the radius of curvature versus θ in rectangular coordinates for the cardioid $r = 1 + \cos\theta$. In words, explain what the graph tells you about the cardioid.

y
1.5
1
0.5
$\frac{\pi}{2}$ π $\frac{3\pi}{2}$ 2π θ

$y = 1/\kappa(\theta)$

◀ **Figure Ex-68**

✔ **QUICK CHECK ANSWERS 12.5**

1. $\left\|\dfrac{d\mathbf{T}}{ds}\right\| = \|\mathbf{r}''(s)\|$ **2.** (a) $\dfrac{\|\mathbf{T}'(t)\|}{\|\mathbf{r}'(t)\|}$ (b) $\dfrac{\|\mathbf{r}'(t) \times \mathbf{r}''(t)\|}{\|\mathbf{r}'(t)\|^3}$ **3.** $\left|\dfrac{d\phi}{ds}\right|$ **4.** $\dfrac{1}{2}$

12.6 MOTION ALONG A CURVE

In earlier sections we considered the motion of a particle along a line. In that situation there are only two directions in which the particle can move—the positive direction or the negative direction. Motion in 2-space or 3-space is more complicated because there are infinitely many directions in which a particle can move. In this section we will show how vectors can be used to analyze motion along curves in 2-space or 3-space.

■ VELOCITY, ACCELERATION, AND SPEED

Let us assume that the motion of a particle in 2-space or 3-space is described by a smooth vector-valued function $\mathbf{r}(t)$ in which the parameter t denotes time; we will call this the **position function** or **trajectory** of the particle. As the particle moves along its trajectory, its direction of motion and its speed can vary from instant to instant. Thus, before we can undertake any analysis of such motion, we must have clear answers to the following questions:

- What is the direction of motion of the particle at an instant of time?
- What is the speed of the particle at an instant of time?

We will define the direction of motion at time t to be the direction of the unit tangent vector $\mathbf{T}(t)$, and we will define the speed to be ds/dt—the instantaneous rate of change of the arc length traveled by the particle from an arbitrary reference point. Taking this a step further, we will combine the speed and the direction of motion to form the vector

$$\mathbf{v}(t) = \frac{ds}{dt}\mathbf{T}(t) \tag{1}$$

which we call the **velocity** of the particle at time t. Thus, at each instant of time the velocity vector $\mathbf{v}(t)$ points in the direction of motion and has a magnitude that is equal to the speed of the particle (Figure 12.6.1).

Recall that for motion along a coordinate line the velocity function is the derivative of the position function. The same is true for motion along a curve, since

$$\frac{d\mathbf{r}}{dt} = \frac{d\mathbf{r}}{ds}\frac{ds}{dt} = \frac{ds}{dt}\mathbf{T}(t) = \mathbf{v}(t)$$

For motion along a coordinate line, the acceleration function was defined to be the derivative of the velocity function. The definition is the same for motion along a curve.

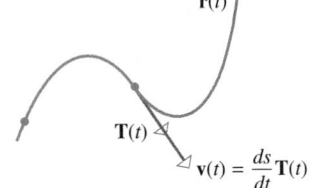

The length of the velocity vector is the speed of the particle, and the direction of the velocity vector is the direction of motion.

▲ **Figure 12.6.1**

12.6.1 DEFINITION If $\mathbf{r}(t)$ is the position function of a particle moving along a curve in 2-space or 3-space, then the **instantaneous velocity**, **instantaneous acceleration**, and **instantaneous speed** of the particle at time t are defined by

$$\text{velocity} = \mathbf{v}(t) = \frac{d\mathbf{r}}{dt} \tag{2}$$

$$\text{acceleration} = \mathbf{a}(t) = \frac{d\mathbf{v}}{dt} = \frac{d^2\mathbf{r}}{dt^2} \tag{3}$$

$$\text{speed} = \|\mathbf{v}(t)\| = \frac{ds}{dt} \tag{4}$$

As shown in Table 12.6.1, the position, velocity, acceleration, and speed can also be expressed in component form.

Table 12.6.1

FORMULAS FOR POSITION, VELOCITY, ACCELERATION, AND SPEED

	2-SPACE	3-SPACE
POSITION	$\mathbf{r}(t) = x(t)\mathbf{i} + y(t)\mathbf{j}$	$\mathbf{r}(t) = x(t)\mathbf{i} + y(t)\mathbf{j} + z(t)\mathbf{k}$
VELOCITY	$\mathbf{v}(t) = \dfrac{dx}{dt}\mathbf{i} + \dfrac{dy}{dt}\mathbf{j}$	$\mathbf{v}(t) = \dfrac{dx}{dt}\mathbf{i} + \dfrac{dy}{dt}\mathbf{j} + \dfrac{dz}{dt}\mathbf{k}$
ACCELERATION	$\mathbf{a}(t) = \dfrac{d^2x}{dt^2}\mathbf{i} + \dfrac{d^2y}{dt^2}\mathbf{j}$	$\mathbf{a}(t) = \dfrac{d^2x}{dt^2}\mathbf{i} + \dfrac{d^2y}{dt^2}\mathbf{j} + \dfrac{d^2z}{dt^2}\mathbf{k}$
SPEED	$\|\mathbf{v}(t)\| = \sqrt{\left(\dfrac{dx}{dt}\right)^2 + \left(\dfrac{dy}{dt}\right)^2}$	$\|\mathbf{v}(t)\| = \sqrt{\left(\dfrac{dx}{dt}\right)^2 + \left(\dfrac{dy}{dt}\right)^2 + \left(\dfrac{dz}{dt}\right)^2}$

▶ **Example 1** A particle moves along a circular path in such a way that its x- and y-coordinates at time t are

$$x = 2\cos t, \quad y = 2\sin t$$

(a) Find the instantaneous velocity and speed of the particle at time t.

(b) Sketch the path of the particle, and show the position and velocity vectors at time $t = \pi/4$ with the velocity vector drawn so that its initial point is at the tip of the position vector.

(c) Show that at each instant the acceleration vector is perpendicular to the velocity vector.

Solution (a). At time t, the position vector is

$$\mathbf{r}(t) = 2\cos t\,\mathbf{i} + 2\sin t\,\mathbf{j}$$

so the instantaneous velocity and speed are

$$\mathbf{v}(t) = \frac{d\mathbf{r}}{dt} = -2\sin t\,\mathbf{i} + 2\cos t\,\mathbf{j}$$

$$\|\mathbf{v}(t)\| = \sqrt{(-2\sin t)^2 + (2\cos t)^2} = 2$$

Solution (b). The graph of the parametric equations is a circle of radius 2 centered at the origin. At time $t = \pi/4$ the position and velocity vectors of the particle are

$$\mathbf{r}(\pi/4) = 2\cos(\pi/4)\mathbf{i} + 2\sin(\pi/4)\mathbf{j} = \sqrt{2}\mathbf{i} + \sqrt{2}\mathbf{j}$$

$$\mathbf{v}(\pi/4) = -2\sin(\pi/4)\mathbf{i} + 2\cos(\pi/4)\mathbf{j} = -\sqrt{2}\mathbf{i} + \sqrt{2}\mathbf{j}$$

These vectors and the circle are shown in Figure 12.6.2.

Solution (c). At time t, the acceleration vector is

$$\mathbf{a}(t) = \frac{d\mathbf{v}}{dt} = -2\cos t\,\mathbf{i} - 2\sin t\,\mathbf{j}$$

One way of showing that $\mathbf{v}(t)$ and $\mathbf{a}(t)$ are perpendicular is to show that their dot product is zero (try it). However, it is easier to observe that $\mathbf{a}(t)$ is the negative of $\mathbf{r}(t)$, which implies that $\mathbf{v}(t)$ and $\mathbf{a}(t)$ are perpendicular, since at each point on a circle the radius and tangent line are perpendicular. ◀

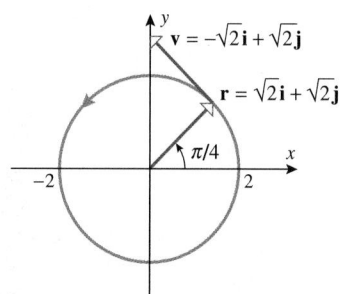

▲ **Figure 12.6.2**

How could you apply Theorem 12.2.8 to answer part (c) of Example 1?

Since $\mathbf{v}(t)$ can be obtained by differentiating $\mathbf{r}(t)$, and since $\mathbf{a}(t)$ can be obtained by differentiating $\mathbf{v}(t)$, it follows that $\mathbf{r}(t)$ can be obtained by integrating $\mathbf{v}(t)$, and $\mathbf{v}(t)$ can be obtained by integrating $\mathbf{a}(t)$. However, such integrations do not produce unique functions because constants of integration occur. Typically, initial conditions are required to determine these constants.

▶ **Example 2** A particle moves through 3-space in such a way that its velocity is

$$\mathbf{v}(t) = \mathbf{i} + t\mathbf{j} + t^2\mathbf{k}$$

Find the coordinates of the particle at time $t = 1$ given that the particle is at the point $(-1, 2, 4)$ at time $t = 0$.

Solution. Integrating the velocity function to obtain the position function yields

$$\mathbf{r}(t) = \int \mathbf{v}(t)\, dt = \int (\mathbf{i} + t\mathbf{j} + t^2\mathbf{k})\, dt = t\mathbf{i} + \frac{t^2}{2}\mathbf{j} + \frac{t^3}{3}\mathbf{k} + \mathbf{C} \qquad (5)$$

where $\mathbf{C}$ is a vector constant of integration. Since the coordinates of the particle at time $t = 0$ are $(-1, 2, 4)$, the position vector at time $t = 0$ is

$$\mathbf{r}(0) = -\mathbf{i} + 2\mathbf{j} + 4\mathbf{k} \qquad (6)$$

It follows on substituting $t = 0$ in (5) and equating the result with (6) that

$$\mathbf{C} = -\mathbf{i} + 2\mathbf{j} + 4\mathbf{k}$$

Substituting this value of $\mathbf{C}$ in (5) and simplifying yields

$$\mathbf{r}(t) = (t - 1)\mathbf{i} + \left(\frac{t^2}{2} + 2\right)\mathbf{j} + \left(\frac{t^3}{3} + 4\right)\mathbf{k}$$

Thus, at time $t = 1$ the position vector of the particle is

$$\mathbf{r}(1) = 0\mathbf{i} + \frac{5}{2}\mathbf{j} + \frac{13}{3}\mathbf{k}$$

so its coordinates at that instant are $\left(0, \frac{5}{2}, \frac{13}{3}\right)$. ◀

DISPLACEMENT AND DISTANCE TRAVELED

If a particle travels along a curve C in 2-space or 3-space, the ***displacement*** of the particle over the time interval $t_1 \le t \le t_2$ is commonly denoted by $\Delta\mathbf{r}$ and is defined as

$$\Delta\mathbf{r} = \mathbf{r}(t_2) - \mathbf{r}(t_1) \qquad (7)$$

(Figure 12.6.3). The displacement vector, which describes the change in position of the particle during the time interval, can be obtained by integrating the velocity function from t_1 to t_2:

$$\Delta\mathbf{r} = \int_{t_1}^{t_2} \mathbf{v}(t)\, dt = \int_{t_1}^{t_2} \frac{d\mathbf{r}}{dt}\, dt = \mathbf{r}(t)\Big]_{t_1}^{t_2} = \mathbf{r}(t_2) - \mathbf{r}(t_1) \qquad \boxed{\text{Displacement}} \qquad (8)$$

It follows from Theorem 12.3.1 that we can find the distance s traveled by a particle over a time interval $t_1 \le t \le t_2$ by integrating the speed over that interval, since

$$s = \int_{t_1}^{t_2} \left\| \frac{d\mathbf{r}}{dt} \right\| dt = \int_{t_1}^{t_2} \|\mathbf{v}(t)\|\, dt \qquad \boxed{\text{Distance traveled}} \qquad (9)$$

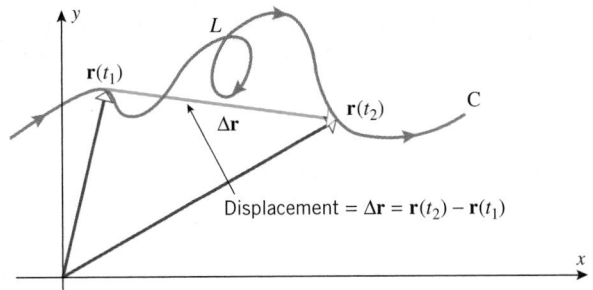

Figure 12.6.3

▶ **Example 3**   Suppose that a particle moves along a circular helix in 3-space so that its position vector at time t is

$$\mathbf{r}(t) = (4\cos \pi t)\mathbf{i} + (4\sin \pi t)\mathbf{j} + t\mathbf{k}$$

Find the distance traveled and the displacement of the particle during the time interval $1 \leq t \leq 5$.

Solution.   We have

$$\mathbf{v}(t) = \frac{d\mathbf{r}}{dt} = (-4\pi \sin \pi t)\mathbf{i} + (4\pi \cos \pi t)\mathbf{j} + \mathbf{k}$$

$$\|\mathbf{v}(t)\| = \sqrt{(-4\pi \sin \pi t)^2 + (4\pi \cos \pi t)^2 + 1} = \sqrt{16\pi^2 + 1}$$

Thus, it follows from (9) that the distance traveled by the particle from time $t = 1$ to $t = 5$ is

$$s = \int_1^5 \sqrt{16\pi^2 + 1}\, dt = 4\sqrt{16\pi^2 + 1}$$

Moreover, it follows from (8) that the displacement over the time interval is

$$\Delta\mathbf{r} = \mathbf{r}(5) - \mathbf{r}(1)$$

$$= (4\cos 5\pi \mathbf{i} + 4\sin 5\pi \mathbf{j} + 5\mathbf{k}) - (4\cos \pi \mathbf{i} + 4\sin \pi \mathbf{j} + \mathbf{k})$$

$$= (-4\mathbf{i} + 5\mathbf{k}) - (-4\mathbf{i} + \mathbf{k}) = 4\mathbf{k}$$

which tells us that the change in the position of the particle over the time interval was 4 units straight up. ◀

■ NORMAL AND TANGENTIAL COMPONENTS OF ACCELERATION

You know from your experience as an automobile passenger that if a car speeds up rapidly, then your body is thrown back against the backrest of the seat. You also know that if the car rounds a turn in the road, then your body is thrown toward the outside of the curve—the greater the curvature in the road, the greater this effect. The explanation of these effects can be understood by resolving the velocity and acceleration components of the motion into vector components that are parallel to the unit tangent and unit normal vectors. The following theorem explains how to do this.

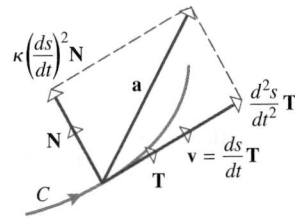

▲ **Figure 12.6.4**

12.6.2   THEOREM   *If a particle moves along a smooth curve C in 2-space or 3-space, then at each point on the curve velocity and acceleration vectors can be written as*

$$\mathbf{v} = \frac{ds}{dt}\mathbf{T} \qquad \mathbf{a} = \frac{d^2s}{dt^2}\mathbf{T} + \kappa\left(\frac{ds}{dt}\right)^2\mathbf{N} \qquad (10\text{–}11)$$

where s is an arc length parameter for the curve, and $\mathbf{T}$, $\mathbf{N}$, and κ denote the unit tangent vector, unit normal vector, and curvature at the point (Figure 12.6.4).

PROOF   Formula (10) is just a restatement of (1). To obtain (11), we differentiate both sides of (10) with respect to t; this yields

$$\mathbf{a} = \frac{d}{dt}\left(\frac{ds}{dt}\mathbf{T}\right) = \frac{d^2s}{dt^2}\mathbf{T} + \frac{ds}{dt}\frac{d\mathbf{T}}{dt}$$

$$= \frac{d^2s}{dt^2}\mathbf{T} + \frac{ds}{dt}\frac{d\mathbf{T}}{ds}\frac{ds}{dt}$$

$$= \frac{d^2s}{dt^2}\mathbf{T} + \left(\frac{ds}{dt}\right)^2\frac{d\mathbf{T}}{ds}$$

$$= \frac{d^2s}{dt^2}\mathbf{T} + \left(\frac{ds}{dt}\right)^2\kappa\mathbf{N} \qquad \boxed{\text{Formula (10) of Section 12.5}}$$

from which (11) follows. ∎

The coefficients of **T** and **N** in (11) are commonly denoted by

$$a_T = \frac{d^2s}{dt^2} \qquad a_N = \kappa\left(\frac{ds}{dt}\right)^2 \tag{12–13}$$

in which case Formula (11) is expressed as

$$\mathbf{a} = a_T\mathbf{T} + a_N\mathbf{N} \tag{14}$$

> Formula (14) applies to motion in both 2-space and 3-space. What is interesting is that the 3-space formula does not involve the binormal vector **B**, so the acceleration vector always lies in the plane of **T** and **N** (the osculating plane), even for highly twisting paths of motion (Figure 12.6.5).

In this formula the scalars a_T and a_N are called the ***tangential scalar component of acceleration*** and the ***normal scalar component of acceleration***, and the vectors $a_T\mathbf{T}$ and $a_N\mathbf{N}$ are called the ***tangential vector component of acceleration*** and the ***normal vector component of acceleration***.

The scalar components of acceleration explain the effect that you experience when a car speeds up rapidly or rounds a turn. The rapid increase in speed produces a large value for d^2s/dt^2, which results in a large tangential scalar component of acceleration; and by Newton's second law this corresponds to a large tangential force on the car in the direction of motion. To understand the effect of rounding a turn, observe that the normal scalar component of acceleration has the curvature κ and the square of the speed ds/dt as factors. Thus, sharp turns or turns taken at high speed both correspond to large normal forces on the car.

Although Formulas (12) and (13) provide useful insight into the behavior of particles moving along curved paths, they are not always the best formulas for computations. The following theorem provides some more useful formulas that relate a_T, a_N, and κ to the velocity **v** and acceleration **a**.

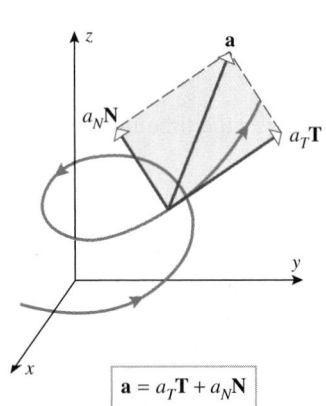

$$\boxed{\mathbf{a} = a_T\mathbf{T} + a_N\mathbf{N}}$$

▲ **Figure 12.6.5**

> Theorem 12.6.3 applies to motion in 2-space and 3-space, but for motion in 2-space you will have to add a zero **k** component to **v** to calculate the cross product.

12.6.3   THEOREM   *If a particle moves along a smooth curve C in 2-space or 3-space, then at each point on the curve the velocity **v** and the acceleration **a** are related to a_T, a_N, and κ by the formulas*

$$a_T = \frac{\mathbf{v}\cdot\mathbf{a}}{\|\mathbf{v}\|} \qquad a_N = \frac{\|\mathbf{v}\times\mathbf{a}\|}{\|\mathbf{v}\|} \qquad \kappa = \frac{\|\mathbf{v}\times\mathbf{a}\|}{\|\mathbf{v}\|^3} \tag{15–17}$$

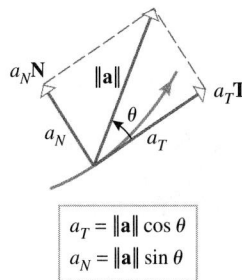

$$a_T = \|\mathbf{a}\|\cos\theta$$
$$a_N = \|\mathbf{a}\|\sin\theta$$

▲ Figure 12.6.6

PROOF As illustrated in Figure 12.6.6, let θ be the angle between the vector $\mathbf{a}$ and the vector $a_T\mathbf{T}$. Thus,

$$a_T = \|\mathbf{a}\|\cos\theta \quad\text{and}\quad a_N = \|\mathbf{a}\|\sin\theta$$

from which we obtain

$$a_T = \|\mathbf{a}\|\cos\theta = \frac{\|\mathbf{v}\|\|\mathbf{a}\|\cos\theta}{\|\mathbf{v}\|} = \frac{\mathbf{v}\cdot\mathbf{a}}{\|\mathbf{v}\|}$$

$$a_N = \|\mathbf{a}\|\sin\theta = \frac{\|\mathbf{v}\|\|\mathbf{a}\|\sin\theta}{\|\mathbf{v}\|} = \frac{\|\mathbf{v}\times\mathbf{a}\|}{\|\mathbf{v}\|}$$

$$\kappa = \frac{a_N}{(ds/dt)^2} = \frac{a_N}{\|\mathbf{v}\|^2} = \frac{1}{\|\mathbf{v}\|^2}\frac{\|\mathbf{v}\times\mathbf{a}\|}{\|\mathbf{v}\|} = \frac{\|\mathbf{v}\times\mathbf{a}\|}{\|\mathbf{v}\|^3} \quad\blacksquare$$

> Recall that for nonlinear smooth curves in 2-space the unit normal vector $\mathbf{N}$ is the inward normal (points toward the concave side of the curve). Explain why the same is true for $a_N\mathbf{N}$.

▶ **Example 4** Suppose that a particle moves through 3-space so that its position vector at time t is

$$\mathbf{r}(t) = t\mathbf{i} + t^2\mathbf{j} + t^3\mathbf{k}$$

(The path is the twisted cubic shown in Figure 12.1.5.)

(a) Find the scalar tangential and normal components of acceleration at time t.

(b) Find the scalar tangential and normal components of acceleration at time $t = 1$.

(c) Find the vector tangential and normal components of acceleration at time $t = 1$.

(d) Find the curvature of the path at the point where the particle is located at time $t = 1$.

Solution (a). We have

$$\mathbf{v}(t) = \mathbf{r}'(t) = \mathbf{i} + 2t\mathbf{j} + 3t^2\mathbf{k}$$
$$\mathbf{a}(t) = \mathbf{v}'(t) = 2\mathbf{j} + 6t\mathbf{k}$$
$$\|\mathbf{v}(t)\| = \sqrt{1 + 4t^2 + 9t^4}$$
$$\mathbf{v}(t)\cdot\mathbf{a}(t) = 4t + 18t^3$$
$$\mathbf{v}(t)\times\mathbf{a}(t) = \begin{vmatrix} \mathbf{i} & \mathbf{j} & \mathbf{k} \\ 1 & 2t & 3t^2 \\ 0 & 2 & 6t \end{vmatrix} = 6t^2\mathbf{i} - 6t\mathbf{j} + 2\mathbf{k}$$

Thus, from (15) and (16)

$$a_T = \frac{\mathbf{v}\cdot\mathbf{a}}{\|\mathbf{v}\|} = \frac{4t + 18t^3}{\sqrt{1 + 4t^2 + 9t^4}}$$

$$a_N = \frac{\|\mathbf{v}\times\mathbf{a}\|}{\|\mathbf{v}\|} = \frac{\sqrt{36t^4 + 36t^2 + 4}}{\sqrt{1 + 4t^2 + 9t^4}} = 2\sqrt{\frac{9t^4 + 9t^2 + 1}{9t^4 + 4t^2 + 1}}$$

Solution (b). At time $t = 1$, the components a_T and a_N in part (a) are

$$a_T = \frac{22}{\sqrt{14}} \approx 5.88 \quad\text{and}\quad a_N = 2\sqrt{\frac{19}{14}} \approx 2.33$$

Solution (c). Since $\mathbf{T}$ and $\mathbf{v}$ have the same direction, $\mathbf{T}$ can be obtained by normalizing $\mathbf{v}$, that is,

$$\mathbf{T}(t) = \frac{\mathbf{v}(t)}{\|\mathbf{v}(t)\|}$$

At time $t = 1$ we have

$$\mathbf{T}(1) = \frac{\mathbf{v}(1)}{\|\mathbf{v}(1)\|} = \frac{\mathbf{i} + 2\mathbf{j} + 3\mathbf{k}}{\|\mathbf{i} + 2\mathbf{j} + 3\mathbf{k}\|} = \frac{1}{\sqrt{14}}(\mathbf{i} + 2\mathbf{j} + 3\mathbf{k})$$

From this and part (b) we obtain the vector tangential component of acceleration:

$$a_T(1)\mathbf{T}(1) = \frac{22}{\sqrt{14}}\mathbf{T}(1) = \frac{11}{7}(\mathbf{i} + 2\mathbf{j} + 3\mathbf{k}) = \frac{11}{7}\mathbf{i} + \frac{22}{7}\mathbf{j} + \frac{33}{7}\mathbf{k}$$

To find the normal vector component of acceleration, we rewrite $\mathbf{a} = a_T\mathbf{T} + a_N\mathbf{N}$ as

$$a_N\mathbf{N} = \mathbf{a} - a_T\mathbf{T}$$

Thus, at time $t = 1$ the normal vector component of acceleration is

$$a_N(1)\mathbf{N}(1) = \mathbf{a}(1) - a_T(1)\mathbf{T}(1)$$

$$= (2\mathbf{j} + 6\mathbf{k}) - \left(\frac{11}{7}\mathbf{i} + \frac{22}{7}\mathbf{j} + \frac{33}{7}\mathbf{k} \right)$$

$$= -\frac{11}{7}\mathbf{i} - \frac{8}{7}\mathbf{j} + \frac{9}{7}\mathbf{k}$$

Solution (d).   We will apply Formula (17) with $t = 1$. From part (a)

$$\|\mathbf{v}(1)\| = \sqrt{14} \quad \text{and} \quad \mathbf{v}(1) \times \mathbf{a}(1) = 6\mathbf{i} - 6\mathbf{j} + 2\mathbf{k}$$

Thus, at time $t = 1$

$$\kappa = \frac{\|\mathbf{v} \times \mathbf{a}\|}{\|\mathbf{v}\|^3} = \frac{\sqrt{76}}{(\sqrt{14})^3} = \frac{1}{14}\sqrt{\frac{38}{7}} \approx 0.17 \blacktriangleleft$$

In the case where $\|\mathbf{a}\|$ and a_T are known, there is a useful alternative to Formula (16) for a_N that does not require the calculation of a cross product. It follows algebraically from Formula (14) (see Exercise 51) or geometrically from Figure 12.6.6 and the Theorem of Pythagoras that

Confirm that the value of a_N computed in Example 4 agrees with the value that results by applying Formula (18).

$$a_N = \sqrt{\|\mathbf{a}\|^2 - a_T^2} \tag{18}$$

■ A MODEL OF PROJECTILE MOTION

Earlier in this text we examined various problems concerned with objects moving *vertically* in the Earth's gravitational field (see the subsection of Section 5.7 entitled Free-Fall Model and the subsection of Section 8.4 entitled A Model of Free-Fall Motion Retarded by Air Resistance). Now we will consider the motion of a projectile launched along a *curved* path in the Earth's gravitational field. For this purpose we will need the following *vector version* of Newton's Second Law of Motion (6.6.4)

$$\mathbf{F} = m\mathbf{a} \tag{19}$$

and we will need to make three modeling assumptions:

- The mass m of the object is constant.
- The only force acting on the object after it is launched is the force of the Earth's gravity. (Thus, air resistance and the gravitational effect of other planets and celestial objects are ignored.)
- The object remains sufficiently close to the Earth that we can assume the force of gravity to be constant.

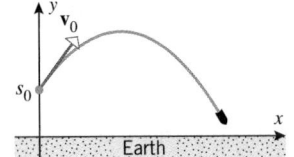

▲ **Figure 12.6.7**

Let us assume that at time $t = 0$ an object of mass m is launched from a height of s_0 above the Earth with an initial velocity vector of $\mathbf{v}_0$. Furthermore, let us introduce an xy-coordinate system as shown in Figure 12.6.7. In this coordinate system the positive y-direction is up, the origin is at the surface of the Earth, and the initial location of the object is $(0, s_0)$. Our objective is to use basic principles of physics to derive the velocity function $\mathbf{v}(t)$ and the position function $\mathbf{r}(t)$ from the acceleration function $\mathbf{a}(t)$ of the object. Our starting point is the physical observation that the downward force $\mathbf{F}$ of the Earth's gravity on an object of mass m is

$$\mathbf{F} = -mg\mathbf{j}$$

where g is the acceleration due to gravity. It follows from this fact and Newton's second law (19) that

$$m\mathbf{a} = -mg\mathbf{j}$$

or on canceling m from both sides

$$\mathbf{a} = -g\mathbf{j} \tag{20}$$

Observe that this acceleration function does not involve t and hence is constant. We can now obtain the velocity function $\mathbf{v}(t)$ by integrating this acceleration function and using the initial condition $\mathbf{v}(0) = \mathbf{v}_0$ to find the constant of integration. Integrating (20) with respect to t and keeping in mind that $-g\mathbf{j}$ is constant yields

$$\mathbf{v}(t) = \int -g\mathbf{j}\, dt = -gt\mathbf{j} + \mathbf{c}_1$$

where $\mathbf{c}_1$ is a vector constant of integration. Substituting $t = 0$ in this equation and using the initial condition $\mathbf{v}(0) = \mathbf{v}_0$ yields $\mathbf{v}_0 = \mathbf{c}_1$. Thus, the velocity function of the object is

$$\mathbf{v}(t) = -gt\mathbf{j} + \mathbf{v}_0 \tag{21}$$

To obtain the position function $\mathbf{r}(t)$ of the object, we will integrate the velocity function and use the known initial position of the object to find the constant of integration. For this purpose observe that the object has coordinates $(0, s_0)$ at time $t = 0$, so the position vector at that time is

$$\mathbf{r}(0) = 0\mathbf{i} + s_0\mathbf{j} = s_0\mathbf{j} \tag{22}$$

This is the initial condition that we will need to find the constant of integration. Integrating (21) with respect to t yields

$$\mathbf{r}(t) = \int (-gt\mathbf{j} + \mathbf{v}_0)\, dt = -\tfrac{1}{2}gt^2\mathbf{j} + t\mathbf{v}_0 + \mathbf{c}_2 \tag{23}$$

where $\mathbf{c}_2$ is another vector constant of integration. Substituting $t = 0$ in (23) and using initial condition (22) yields

$$s_0\mathbf{j} = \mathbf{c}_2$$

so that (23) can be written as

$$\mathbf{r}(t) = \left(-\tfrac{1}{2}gt^2 + s_0\right)\mathbf{j} + t\mathbf{v}_0 \tag{24}$$

This formula expresses the position function of the object in terms of its known initial position and velocity.

Observe that the mass m does not appear in Formulas (21) and (24) and hence has no influence on the velocity or the trajectory of the object. This explains the famous observation of Galileo that two objects of different mass that are released from the same height reach the ground at the same time if air resistance is neglected.

■ **PARAMETRIC EQUATIONS OF PROJECTILE MOTION**

Formulas (21) and (24) can be used to obtain parametric equations for the position and velocity in terms of the initial speed of the object and the angle that the initial velocity vector makes with the positive x-axis. For this purpose, let $v_0 = \|\mathbf{v}_0\|$ be the initial speed, let α be the angle that the initial velocity vector $\mathbf{v}_0$ makes with the positive x-axis, let v_x and v_y be the horizontal and vertical scalar components of $\mathbf{v}(t)$ at time t, and let x and y

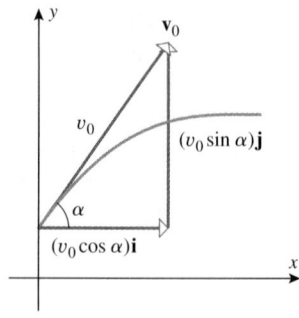

▲ **Figure 12.6.8**

be the horizontal and vertical components of $\mathbf{r}(t)$ at time t. As illustrated in Figure 12.6.8, the initial velocity vector can be expressed as

$$\mathbf{v}_0 = (v_0 \cos \alpha)\mathbf{i} + (v_0 \sin \alpha)\mathbf{j} \tag{25}$$

Substituting this expression in (24) and combining like components yields (verify)

$$\mathbf{r}(t) = (v_0 \cos \alpha)t\mathbf{i} + \left(s_0 + (v_0 \sin \alpha)t - \tfrac{1}{2}gt^2\right)\mathbf{j} \tag{26}$$

which is equivalent to the parametric equations

$$x = (v_0 \cos \alpha)t, \quad y = s_0 + (v_0 \sin \alpha)t - \tfrac{1}{2}gt^2 \tag{27}$$

Similarly, substituting (25) in (21) and combining like components yields

$$\mathbf{v}(t) = (v_0 \cos \alpha)\mathbf{i} + (v_0 \sin \alpha - gt)\mathbf{j}$$

which is equivalent to the parametric equations

$$v_x = v_0 \cos \alpha, \quad v_y = v_0 \sin \alpha - gt \tag{28}$$

The parameter t can be eliminated in (27) by solving the first equation for t and substituting in the second equation. We leave it for you to show that this yields

$$y = s_0 + (\tan \alpha)x - \left(\frac{g}{2v_0^2 \cos^2 \alpha}\right)x^2 \tag{29}$$

which is the equation of a parabola, since the right side is a quadratic polynomial in x. Thus, we have shown that the trajectory of the projectile is a parabolic arc.

▶ **Example 5** A shell, fired from a cannon, has a muzzle speed (the speed as it leaves the barrel) of 800 ft/s. The barrel makes an angle of 45° with the horizontal and, for simplicity, the barrel opening is assumed to be at ground level.

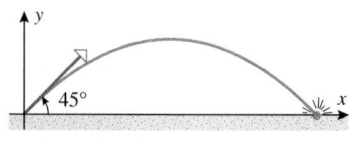

▲ **Figure 12.6.9**

(a) Find parametric equations for the shell's trajectory relative to the coordinate system in Figure 12.6.9.

(b) How high does the shell rise?

(c) How far does the shell travel horizontally?

(d) What is the speed of the shell at its point of impact with the ground?

Solution (a). From (27) with $v_0 = 800$ ft/s, $\alpha = 45°$, $s_0 = 0$ ft (since the shell starts at ground level), and $g = 32$ ft/s², we obtain the parametric equations

$$x = (800 \cos 45°)t, \quad y = (800 \sin 45°)t - 16t^2 \quad (t \geq 0)$$

which simplify to

$$x = 400\sqrt{2}t, \quad y = 400\sqrt{2}t - 16t^2 \quad (t \geq 0) \tag{30}$$

Solution (b). The maximum height of the shell is the maximum value of y in (30), which occurs when $dy/dt = 0$, that is, when

$$400\sqrt{2} - 32t = 0 \quad \text{or} \quad t = \frac{25\sqrt{2}}{2}$$

Substituting this value of t in (30) yields

$$y = 5000 \text{ ft}$$

as the maximum height of the shell.

Solution (c). The shell will hit the ground when $y = 0$. From (30), this occurs when

$$400\sqrt{2}t - 16t^2 = 0 \quad \text{or} \quad t(400\sqrt{2} - 16t) = 0$$

The solution $t = 0$ corresponds to the initial position of the shell and the solution $t = 25\sqrt{2}$ to the time of impact. Substituting the latter value in the equation for x in (30) yields

$$x = 20{,}000 \text{ ft}$$

as the horizontal distance traveled by the shell.

Solution (d). From (30), the position function of the shell is

$$\mathbf{r}(t) = 400\sqrt{2}t\mathbf{i} + (400\sqrt{2}t - 16t^2)\mathbf{j}$$

so that the velocity function is

$$\mathbf{v}(t) = \mathbf{r}'(t) = 400\sqrt{2}\mathbf{i} + (400\sqrt{2} - 32t)\mathbf{j}$$

From part (c), impact occurs when $t = 25\sqrt{2}$, so the velocity vector at this point is

$$\mathbf{v}(25\sqrt{2}) = 400\sqrt{2}\mathbf{i} + [400\sqrt{2} - 32(25\sqrt{2})]\mathbf{j} = 400\sqrt{2}\mathbf{i} - 400\sqrt{2}\mathbf{j}$$

The speed at impact and the muzzle speed of the shell in Example 5 are the same. Is this an expected result? Explain.

Thus, the speed at impact is

$$\|\mathbf{v}(25\sqrt{2})\| = \sqrt{(400\sqrt{2})^2 + (-400\sqrt{2})^2} = 800 \text{ ft/s} \blacktriangleleft$$

✔ QUICK CHECK EXERCISES 12.6   (See page 895 for answers.)

1. If $\mathbf{r}(t)$ is the position function of a particle, then the velocity, acceleration, and speed of the particle at time t are given, respectively, by

   $$\mathbf{v}(t) = \underline{\hspace{1cm}}, \quad \mathbf{a}(t) = \underline{\hspace{1cm}}, \quad \frac{ds}{dt} = \underline{\hspace{1cm}}$$

2. If $\mathbf{r}(t)$ is the position function of a particle, then the displacement of the particle over the time interval $t_1 \le t \le t_2$ is _____, and the distance s traveled by the particle during this time interval is given by the integral _____.

3. The tangential scalar component of acceleration is given by the formula _____, and the normal scalar component of acceleration is given by the formula _____.

4. The projectile motion model

   $$\mathbf{r}(t) = \left(-\tfrac{1}{2}gt^2 + s_0\right)\mathbf{j} + t\mathbf{v}_0$$

   describes the motion of an object with constant acceleration $\mathbf{a} = \underline{\hspace{1cm}}$ and velocity function $\mathbf{v}(t) = \underline{\hspace{1cm}}$. The initial position of the object is _____ and its initial velocity is _____.

EXERCISE SET 12.6   ◪ Graphing Utility   © CAS

1–4 In these exercises $\mathbf{r}(t)$ is the position vector of a particle moving in the plane. Find the velocity, acceleration, and speed at an arbitrary time t. Then sketch the path of the particle together with the velocity and acceleration vectors at the indicated time t. ■

1. $\mathbf{r}(t) = 3\cos t\mathbf{i} + 3\sin t\mathbf{j}; \ t = \pi/3$

2. $\mathbf{r}(t) = t\mathbf{i} + t^2\mathbf{j}; \ t = 2$

3. $\mathbf{r}(t) = e^t\mathbf{i} + e^{-t}\mathbf{j}; \ t = 0$

4. $\mathbf{r}(t) = (2 + 4t)\mathbf{i} + (1 - t)\mathbf{j}; \ t = 1$

5–8 Find the velocity, speed, and acceleration at the given time t of a particle moving along the given curve. ■

5. $\mathbf{r}(t) = t\mathbf{i} + \tfrac{1}{2}t^2\mathbf{j} + \tfrac{1}{3}t^3\mathbf{k}; \ t = 1$

6. $x = 1 + 3t, \ y = 2 - 4t, \ z = 7 + t; \ t = 2$

7. $x = 2\cos t, \ y = 2\sin t, \ z = t; \ t = \pi/4$

8. $\mathbf{r}(t) = e^t\sin t\mathbf{i} + e^t\cos t\mathbf{j} + t\mathbf{k}; \ t = \pi/2$

FOCUS ON CONCEPTS

9. As illustrated in the accompanying figure on the next page, suppose that the equations of motion of a particle moving along an elliptic path are $x = a\cos\omega t$, $y = b\sin\omega t$.
   (a) Show that the acceleration is directed toward the origin.   *(cont.)*

(b) Show that the magnitude of the acceleration is proportional to the distance from the particle to the origin.

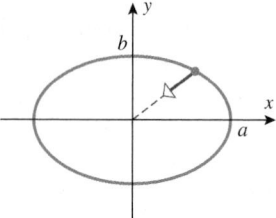

◀ **Figure Ex-9**

10. Suppose that a particle vibrates in such a way that its position function is $\mathbf{r}(t) = 16 \sin \pi t\, \mathbf{i} + 4 \cos 2\pi t\, \mathbf{j}$, where distance is in millimeters and t is in seconds.
   (a) Find the velocity and acceleration at time $t = 1$ s.
   (b) Show that the particle moves along a parabolic curve.
   (c) Show that the particle moves back and forth along the curve.

11. What can you say about the trajectory of a particle that moves in 2-space or 3-space with zero acceleration? Justify your answer.

12. Recall from Theorem 12.2.8 that if $\mathbf{r}(t)$ is a vector-valued function in 2-space or 3-space, and if $\|\mathbf{r}(t)\|$ is constant for all t, then $\mathbf{r}(t) \cdot \mathbf{r}'(t) = 0$.
   (a) Translate this theorem into a statement about the motion of a particle in 2-space or 3-space.
   (b) Replace $\mathbf{r}(t)$ by $\mathbf{r}'(t)$ in the theorem, and translate the result into a statement about the motion of a particle in 2-space or 3-space.

13. Suppose that the position vector of a particle moving in the plane is $\mathbf{r} = 12\sqrt{t}\,\mathbf{i} + t^{3/2}\,\mathbf{j}$, $t > 0$. Find the minimum speed of the particle and its location when it has this speed.

14. Suppose that the motion of a particle is described by the position vector $\mathbf{r} = (t - t^2)\mathbf{i} - t^2\,\mathbf{j}$. Find the minimum speed of the particle and its location when it has this speed.

⊠ 15. Suppose that the position function of a particle moving in 2-space is $\mathbf{r} = \sin 3t\mathbf{i} - 2\cos 3t\mathbf{j}$, $0 \le t \le 2\pi/3$.
   (a) Use a graphing utility to graph the speed of the particle versus time from $t = 0$ to $t = 2\pi/3$.
   (b) What are the maximum and minimum speeds of the particle?
   (c) Use the graph to estimate the time at which the maximum speed first occurs.
   (d) Find the exact time at which the maximum speed first occurs.

⊠ 16. Suppose that the position function of a particle moving in 3-space is $\mathbf{r} = 3\cos 2t\mathbf{i} + \sin 2t\mathbf{j} + 4t\mathbf{k}$.
   (a) Use a graphing utility to graph the speed of the particle versus time from $t = 0$ to $t = \pi$.

   (b) Use the graph to estimate the maximum and minimum speeds of the particle.
   (c) Use the graph to estimate the time at which the maximum speed first occurs.
   (d) Find the exact values of the maximum and minimum speeds and the exact time at which the maximum speed first occurs.

17–20 Use the given information to find the position and velocity vectors of the particle. ■

17. $\mathbf{a}(t) = -\cos t\mathbf{i} - \sin t\mathbf{j}$; $\mathbf{v}(0) = \mathbf{i}$; $\mathbf{r}(0) = \mathbf{j}$

18. $\mathbf{a}(t) = \mathbf{i} + e^{-t}\mathbf{j}$; $\mathbf{v}(0) = 2\mathbf{i} + \mathbf{j}$; $\mathbf{r}(0) = \mathbf{i} - \mathbf{j}$

19. $\mathbf{a}(t) = \sin t\mathbf{i} + \cos t\mathbf{j} + e^t\mathbf{k}$; $\mathbf{v}(0) = \mathbf{k}$; $\mathbf{r}(0) = -\mathbf{i} + \mathbf{k}$

20. $\mathbf{a}(t) = (t + 1)^{-2}\mathbf{j} - e^{-2t}\mathbf{k}$; $\mathbf{v}(0) = 3\mathbf{i} - \mathbf{j}$; $\mathbf{r}(0) = 2\mathbf{k}$

21. Find, to the nearest degree, the angle between $\mathbf{v}$ and $\mathbf{a}$ for $\mathbf{r} = t^3\mathbf{i} + t^2\mathbf{j}$ when $t = 1$.

22. Show that the angle between $\mathbf{v}$ and $\mathbf{a}$ is constant for the position vector $\mathbf{r} = e^t \cos t\mathbf{i} + e^t \sin t\mathbf{j}$. Find the angle.

23. (a) Suppose that at time $t = t_0$ an electron has a position vector of $\mathbf{r} = 3.5\mathbf{i} - 1.7\mathbf{j} + \mathbf{k}$, and at a later time $t = t_1$ it has a position vector of $\mathbf{r} = 4.2\mathbf{i} + \mathbf{j} - 2.4\mathbf{k}$. What is the displacement of the electron during the time interval from t_0 to t_1?
   (b) Suppose that during a certain time interval a proton has a displacement of $\Delta \mathbf{r} = 0.7\mathbf{i} + 2.9\mathbf{j} - 1.2\mathbf{k}$ and its final position vector is known to be $\mathbf{r} = 3.6\mathbf{k}$. What was the initial position vector of the proton?

24. Suppose that the position function of a particle moving along a circle in the xy-plane is $\mathbf{r} = 5\cos 2\pi t\mathbf{i} + 5\sin 2\pi t\mathbf{j}$.
   (a) Sketch some typical displacement vectors over the time interval from $t = 0$ to $t = 1$.
   (b) What is the distance traveled by the particle during the time interval?

25–28 Find the displacement and the distance traveled over the indicated time interval. ■

25. $\mathbf{r} = t^2\mathbf{i} + \frac{1}{3}t^3\mathbf{j}$; $1 \le t \le 3$

26. $\mathbf{r} = (1 - 3\sin t)\mathbf{i} + 3\cos t\mathbf{j}$; $0 \le t \le 3\pi/2$

27. $\mathbf{r} = e^t\mathbf{i} + e^{-t}\mathbf{j} + \sqrt{2}t\mathbf{k}$; $0 \le t \le \ln 3$

28. $\mathbf{r} = \cos 2t\mathbf{i} + (1 - \cos 2t)\mathbf{j} + \left(3 + \frac{1}{2}\cos 2t\right)\mathbf{k}$; $0 \le t \le \pi$

29–30 The position vectors $\mathbf{r}_1$ and $\mathbf{r}_2$ of two particles are given. Show that the particles move along the same path but the speed of the first is constant and the speed of the second is not. ■

29. $\mathbf{r}_1 = 2\cos 3t\mathbf{i} + 2\sin 3t\mathbf{j}$
   $\mathbf{r}_2 = 2\cos(t^2)\mathbf{i} + 2\sin(t^2)\mathbf{j}$ $(t \ge 0)$

30. $\mathbf{r}_1 = (3 + 2t)\mathbf{i} + t\mathbf{j} + (1 - t)\mathbf{k}$
   $\mathbf{r}_2 = (5 - 2t^3)\mathbf{i} + (1 - t^3)\mathbf{j} + t^3\mathbf{k}$

31–36 The position function of a particle is given. Use Theorem 12.6.3 to find

(a) the scalar tangential and normal components of acceleration at the stated time t;

(b) the vector tangential and normal components of acceleration at the stated time t;

(c) the curvature of the path at the point where the particle is located at the stated time t. ■

31. $\mathbf{r} = e^{-t}\mathbf{i} + e^t\mathbf{j}$; $t = 0$

32. $\mathbf{r} = \cos(t^2)\mathbf{i} + \sin(t^2)\mathbf{j}$; $t = \sqrt{\pi}/2$

33. $\mathbf{r} = (t^3 - 2t)\mathbf{i} + (t^2 - 4)\mathbf{j}$; $t = 1$

34. $\mathbf{r} = e^t\cos t\mathbf{i} + e^t\sin t\mathbf{j}$; $t = \pi/4$

35. $\mathbf{r} = e^t\mathbf{i} + e^{-2t}\mathbf{j} + t\mathbf{k}$; $t = 0$

36. $\mathbf{r} = 3\sin t\mathbf{i} + 2\cos t\mathbf{j} - \sin 2t\mathbf{k}$; $t = \pi/2$

37–38 In these exercises $\mathbf{v}$ and $\mathbf{a}$ are given at a certain instant of time. Find a_T, a_N, $\mathbf{T}$, and $\mathbf{N}$ at this instant. ■

37. $\mathbf{v} = -4\mathbf{j}$, $\mathbf{a} = 2\mathbf{i} + 3\mathbf{j}$

38. $\mathbf{v} = 3\mathbf{i} - 4\mathbf{k}$, $\mathbf{a} = \mathbf{i} - \mathbf{j} + 2\mathbf{k}$

39–40 The speed $\|\mathbf{v}\|$ of a particle at an arbitrary time t is given. Find the scalar tangential component of acceleration at the indicated time. ■

39. $\|\mathbf{v}\| = \sqrt{t^2 + e^{-3t}}$; $t = 0$

40. $\|\mathbf{v}\| = \sqrt{(4t - 1)^2 + \cos^2 \pi t}$; $t = \frac{1}{4}$

41. The nuclear accelerator at the Enrico Fermi Laboratory is circular with a radius of 1 km. Find the scalar normal component of acceleration of a proton moving around the accelerator with a constant speed of 2.9×10^5 km/s.

42. Suppose that a particle moves with nonzero acceleration along the curve $y = f(x)$. Use part (b) of Exercise 23 in Section 12.5 to show that the acceleration vector is tangent to the curve at each point where $f''(x) = 0$.

43–44 Use the given information and Exercise 23 of Section 12.5 to find the normal scalar component of acceleration as a function of x. ■

43. A particle moves along the parabola $y = x^2$ with a constant speed of 3 units per second.

44. A particle moves along the curve $x = \ln y$ with a constant speed of 2 units per second.

45–46 Use the given information to find the normal scalar component of acceleration at time $t = 1$. ■

45. $\mathbf{a}(1) = \mathbf{i} + 2\mathbf{j} - 2\mathbf{k}$; $a_T(1) = 3$

46. $\|\mathbf{a}(1)\| = 9$; $a_T(1)\mathbf{T}(1) = 2\mathbf{i} - 2\mathbf{j} + \mathbf{k}$

47–50 True–False Determine whether the statement is true or false. Explain your answer. ■

47. The velocity and unit tangent vectors for a moving particle are parallel.

48. If a particle moves along a smooth curve C in 3-space, then at each point on C the normal scalar component of acceleration for the particle is the product of the curvature of C and speed of the particle at the point.

49. If a particle is moving along a smooth curve C and passes through a point at which the curvature is zero, then the velocity and acceleration vectors have the same direction at that point.

50. The distance traveled by a particle over a time interval is the magnitude of the displacement vector for the particle during that time interval.

51. Derive Formula (18) from Formula (14).

52. An automobile travels at a constant speed around a curve whose radius of curvature is 1000 m. What is the maximum allowable speed if the maximum acceptable value for the normal scalar component of acceleration is 1.5 m/s²?

53. If an automobile of mass m rounds a curve, then its inward vector component of acceleration $a_N\mathbf{N}$ is caused by the frictional force $\mathbf{F}$ of the road. Thus, it follows from the vector form of Newton's second law [Equation (19)] that the frictional force and the normal scalar component of acceleration are related by the equation $\mathbf{F} = ma_N\mathbf{N}$. Thus,

$$\|\mathbf{F}\| = m\kappa \left(\frac{ds}{dt}\right)^2$$

Use this result to find the magnitude of the frictional force in newtons exerted by the road on a 500 kg go-cart driven at a speed of 10 km/h around a circular track of radius 15 m. [*Note:* $1\,\text{N} = 1\,\text{kg·m/s}^2$.]

54. A shell is fired from ground level with a muzzle speed of 320 ft/s and elevation angle of 60°. Find

(a) parametric equations for the shell's trajectory

(b) the maximum height reached by the shell

(c) the horizontal distance traveled by the shell

(d) the speed of the shell at impact.

55. A rock is thrown downward from the top of a building, 168 ft high, at an angle of 60° with the horizontal. How far from the base of the building will the rock land if its initial speed is 80 ft/s?

56. Solve Exercise 55 assuming that the rock is thrown horizontally at a speed of 80 ft/s.

57. A shell is to be fired from ground level at an elevation angle of 30°. What should the muzzle speed be in order for the maximum height of the shell to be 2500 ft?

58. A shell, fired from ground level at an elevation angle of 45°, hits the ground 24,500 m away. Calculate the muzzle speed of the shell.

59. Find two elevation angles that will enable a shell, fired from ground level with a muzzle speed of 800 ft/s, to hit a ground-level target 10,000 ft away.

60. A ball rolls off a table 4 ft high while moving at a constant speed of 5 ft/s. *(cont.)*

(a) How long does it take for the ball to hit the floor after it leaves the table?

(b) At what speed does the ball hit the floor?

(c) If a ball were dropped from rest at table height just as the rolling ball leaves the table, which ball would hit the ground first? Justify your answer.

61. As illustrated in the accompanying figure, a fire hose sprays water with an initial velocity of 40 ft/s at an angle of 60° with the horizontal.

(a) Confirm that the water will clear corner point A.

(b) Confirm that the water will hit the roof.

(c) How far from corner point A will the water hit the roof?

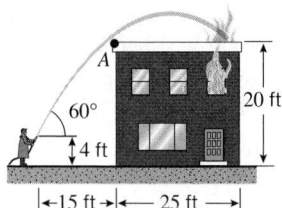

◀ Figure Ex-61

62. What is the minimum initial velocity that will allow the water in Exercise 61 to hit the roof?

63. As shown in the accompanying figure, water is sprayed from a hose with an initial velocity of 35 m/s at an angle of 45° with the horizontal.

(a) What is the radius of curvature of the stream at the point where it leaves the hose?

(b) What is the maximum height of the stream above the nozzle of the hose?

64. As illustrated in the accompanying figure, a train is traveling on a curved track. At a point where the train is traveling at a speed of 132 ft/s and the radius of curvature of the track is 3000 ft, the engineer hits the brakes to make the train slow down at a constant rate of 7.5 ft/s².

(a) Find the magnitude of the acceleration vector at the instant the engineer hits the brakes.

(b) Approximate the angle between the acceleration vector and the unit tangent vector **T** at the instant the engineer hits the brakes.

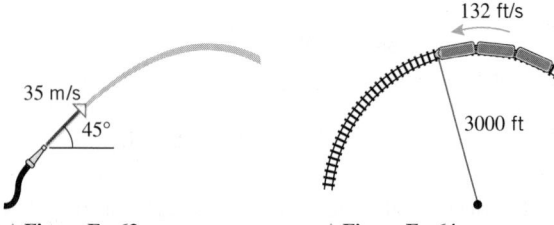

▲ Figure Ex-63   ▲ Figure Ex-64

65. A shell is fired from ground level at an elevation angle of α and a muzzle speed of v_0.

(a) Show that the maximum height reached by the shell is

$$\text{maximum height} = \frac{(v_0 \sin \alpha)^2}{2g}$$

(b) The ***horizontal range*** R of the shell is the horizontal distance traveled when the shell returns to ground level. Show that $R = (v_0^2 \sin 2\alpha)/g$. For what elevation angle will the range be maximum? What is the maximum range?

66. A shell is fired from ground level with an elevation angle α and a muzzle speed of v_0. Find two angles that can be used to hit a target at ground level that is a distance of three-fourths the maximum range of the shell. Express your answer to the nearest tenth of a degree. [*Hint:* See Exercise 65(b).]

67. At time $t = 0$ a baseball that is 5 ft above the ground is hit with a bat. The ball leaves the bat with a speed of 80 ft/s at an angle of 30° above the horizontal.

(a) How long will it take for the baseball to hit the ground? Express your answer to the nearest hundredth of a second.

(b) Use the result in part (a) to find the horizontal distance traveled by the ball. Express your answer to the nearest tenth of a foot.

68. Repeat Exercise 67, assuming that the ball leaves the bat with a speed of 70 ft/s at an angle of 60° above the horizontal.

C 69. At time $t = 0$ a skier leaves the end of a ski jump with a speed of v_0 ft/s at an angle α with the horizontal (see the accompanying figure). The skier lands 259 ft down the incline 2.9 s later.

(a) Approximate v_0 to the nearest ft/s and α to the nearest degree. [*Note:* Use $g = 32$ ft/s² as the acceleration due to gravity.]

(b) Use a CAS or a calculating utility with a numerical integration capability to approximate the distance traveled by the skier.

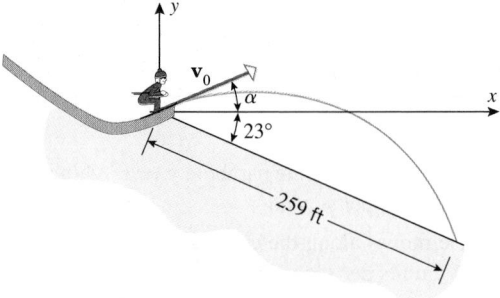

▲ Figure Ex-69

70. At time $t = 0$ a projectile is fired from a height h above level ground at an elevation angle of α with a speed v. Let R be the horizontal distance to the point where the projectile hits the ground.

(a) Show that α and R must satisfy the equation

$$g(\sec^2 \alpha)R^2 - 2v^2(\tan \alpha)R - 2v^2 h = 0 \qquad \text{(cont.)}$$

(b) If $g, h,$ and v are constant, then the equation in part (a) defines R implicitly as a function of α. Let R_0 be the maximum value of R and α_0 the value of α when $R = R_0$. Use implicit differentiation to find $dR/d\alpha$ and show that
$$\tan \alpha_0 = \frac{v^2}{g R_0}$$
[*Hint:* Assume that $dR/d\alpha = 0$ when R attains a maximum.]

(c) Use the results in parts (a) and (b) to show that
$$R_0 = \frac{v}{g}\sqrt{v^2 + 2gh}$$
and
$$\alpha_0 = \tan^{-1}\frac{v}{\sqrt{v^2 + 2gh}}$$

71. Writing Consider the various forces that a passenger in a car would sense while traveling over the crest of a hill or around a curve. Relate these sensations to the tangential and normal vector components of the acceleration vector for the car's motion. Discuss how speeding up or slowing down (e.g., doubling or halving the car's speed) affects these components.

72. Writing The formula
$$\mathbf{r}(t) = (v_0 \cos\alpha)t\,\mathbf{i} + (s_0 + (v_0 \sin\alpha)t - \tfrac{1}{2}gt^2)\mathbf{j}$$
models a position function for projectile motion [Formula (26)]. Identify the various quantities (v_0, α, s_0, and g) in this formula and discuss how the formula is derived, including any assumptions that are made.

✔ QUICK CHECK ANSWERS 12.6

1. $\dfrac{d\mathbf{r}}{dt}$; $\dfrac{d\mathbf{v}}{dt} = \dfrac{d^2\mathbf{r}}{dt^2}$; $\|\mathbf{v}(t)\|$ **2.** $\mathbf{r}(t_2) - \mathbf{r}(t_1)$; $\displaystyle\int_{t_1}^{t_2} \|\mathbf{v}(t)\|\,dt$ **3.** $\dfrac{d^2 s}{dt^2}$; $\kappa(ds/dt)^2$ **4.** $-g\mathbf{j}$; $-gt\mathbf{j} + \mathbf{v}_0$; $s_0\mathbf{j}$; $\mathbf{v}_0$

12.7 KEPLER'S LAWS OF PLANETARY MOTION

One of the great advances in the history of astronomy occurred in the early 1600s when Johannes Kepler* deduced from empirical data that all planets in our solar system move in elliptical orbits with the Sun at a focus. Subsequently, Isaac Newton showed mathematically that such planetary motion is the consequence of an inverse-square law of gravitational attraction. In this section we will use the concepts developed in the preceding sections of this chapter to derive three basic laws of planetary motion, known as **Kepler's laws***.*

■ KEPLER'S LAWS

In Section 10.6 we stated the following laws of planetary motion that were published by Johannes Kepler in 1609 in his book known as *Astronomia Nova*.

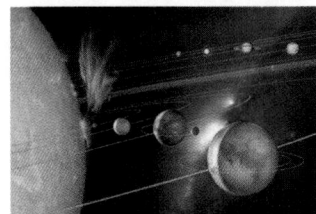

The planets in our solar system move in accordance with Kepler's three laws.

12.7.1 KEPLER'S LAWS

- First law (**Law of Orbits**). Each planet moves in an elliptical orbit with the Sun at a focus.

- Second law (**Law of Areas**). Equal areas are swept out in equal times by the line from the Sun to a planet.

- Third law (**Law of Periods**). The square of a planet's period (the time it takes the planet to complete one orbit about the Sun) is proportional to the cube of the semimajor axis of its orbit.

---

*See biography on p. 759.

■ CENTRAL FORCES

If a particle moves under the influence of a *single* force that is always directed toward a fixed point O, then the particle is said to be moving in a **central force field**. The force is called a **central force**, and the point O is called the **center of force**. For example, in the simplest model of planetary motion, it is assumed that the only force acting on a planet is the force of the Sun's gravity, directed toward the center of the Sun. This model, which produces Kepler's laws, ignores the forces that other celestial objects exert on the planet as well as the minor effect that the planet's gravity has on the Sun. Central force models are also used to study the motion of comets, asteroids, planetary moons, and artificial satellites. They also have important applications in electromagnetics. Our objective in this section is to develop some basic principles about central force fields and then use those results to derive Kepler's laws.

Suppose that a particle P of mass m moves in a central force field due to a force $\mathbf{F}$ that is directed toward a fixed point O, and let $\mathbf{r} = \mathbf{r}(t)$ be the position vector from O to P (Figure 12.7.1). Let $\mathbf{v} = \mathbf{v}(t)$ and $\mathbf{a} = \mathbf{a}(t)$ be the velocity and acceleration functions of the particle, and assume that $\mathbf{F}$ and $\mathbf{a}$ are related by Newton's second law ($\mathbf{F} = m\mathbf{a}$).

Our first objective is to show that the particle P moves in a plane containing the point O. For this purpose observe that $\mathbf{a}$ has the same direction as $\mathbf{F}$ by Newton's second law, and this implies that $\mathbf{a}$ and $\mathbf{r}$ are oppositely directed vectors. Thus, it follows from part (c) of Theorem 11.4.5 that

$$\mathbf{r} \times \mathbf{a} = \mathbf{0}$$

Since the velocity and acceleration of the particle are given by $\mathbf{v} = d\mathbf{r}/dt$ and $\mathbf{a} = d\mathbf{v}/dt$, respectively, we have

$$\frac{d}{dt}(\mathbf{r} \times \mathbf{v}) = \mathbf{r} \times \frac{d\mathbf{v}}{dt} + \frac{d\mathbf{r}}{dt} \times \mathbf{v} = (\mathbf{r} \times \mathbf{a}) + (\mathbf{v} \times \mathbf{v}) = \mathbf{0} + \mathbf{0} = \mathbf{0} \qquad (1)$$

Integrating the left and right sides of this equation with respect to t yields

$$\mathbf{r} \times \mathbf{v} = \mathbf{b} \qquad (2)$$

where $\mathbf{b}$ is a constant (independent of t). However, $\mathbf{b}$ is orthogonal to both $\mathbf{r}$ and $\mathbf{v}$, so we can conclude that $\mathbf{r} = \mathbf{r}(t)$ and $\mathbf{v} = \mathbf{v}(t)$ lie in a fixed plane containing the point O.

■ NEWTON'S LAW OF UNIVERSAL GRAVITATION

Our next objective is to derive the position function of a particle moving under a central force in a polar coordinate system. For this purpose we will need the following result, known as **Newton's Law of Universal Gravitation**.

12.7.2   NEWTON'S LAW OF UNIVERSAL GRAVITATION   Every particle of matter in the Universe attracts every other particle of matter in the Universe with a force that is proportional to the product of their masses and inversely proportional to the square of the distance between them. Specifically, if a particle of mass M and a particle of mass m are at a distance r from each other, then they attract each other with equal and opposite forces, $\mathbf{F}$ and $-\mathbf{F}$, of magnitude

$$\|\mathbf{F}\| = \frac{GMm}{r^2} \qquad (3)$$

where G is a constant called the **universal gravitational constant**.

To obtain a formula for the vector force $\mathbf{F}$ that mass M exerts on mass m, we will let $\mathbf{r}$ be the radius vector from mass M to mass m (Figure 12.7.2). Thus, the distance r between

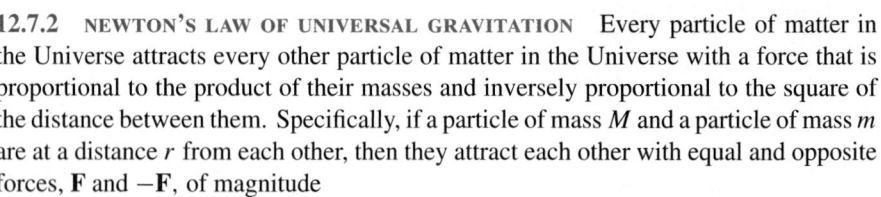

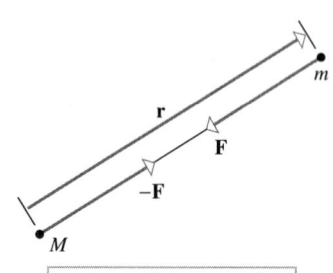

▲ Figure 12.7.1

Astronomers call the plane containing the orbit of a planet the *ecliptic* of the planet.

M exerts force **F** on *m*, and *m* exerts force −**F** on *M*.

▲ Figure 12.7.2

the masses is $\|\mathbf{r}\|$, and the force $\mathbf{F}$ can be expressed in terms of $\mathbf{r}$ as

$$\mathbf{F} = \|\mathbf{F}\| \left(-\frac{\mathbf{r}}{\|\mathbf{r}\|} \right) = \|\mathbf{F}\| \left(-\frac{\mathbf{r}}{r} \right)$$

which from (3) can be expressed as

$$\mathbf{F} = -\frac{GMm}{r^3}\mathbf{r} \tag{4}$$

We start by finding a formula for the acceleration function. To do this we use Formula (4) and Newton's second law to obtain

$$m\mathbf{a} = -\frac{GMm}{r^3}\mathbf{r}$$

from which we obtain

$$\mathbf{a} = -\frac{GM}{r^3}\mathbf{r} \tag{5}$$

> Observe in Formula (5) that the acceleration $\mathbf{a}$ does not involve m. Thus, the mass of a planet has no effect on its acceleration.

To obtain a formula for the position function of the mass m, we will need to introduce a coordinate system and make some assumptions about the initial conditions:

- The distance r from m to M is minimum at time $t = 0$.
- The mass m has nonzero position and velocity vectors $\mathbf{r}_0$ and $\mathbf{v}_0$ at time $t = 0$.
- A polar coordinate system is introduced with its pole at mass M and oriented so $\theta = 0$ at time $t = 0$.
- The vector $\mathbf{v}_0$ is perpendicular to the polar axis at time $t = 0$.

Moreover, to ensure that the polar angle θ increases with t, let us agree to observe this polar coordinate system looking toward the pole from the terminal point of the vector $\mathbf{b} = \mathbf{r}_0 \times \mathbf{v}_0$. We will also find it useful to superimpose an xyz-coordinate system on the polar coordinate system with the positive z-axis in the direction of $\mathbf{b}$ (Figure 12.7.3).

For computational purposes, it will be helpful to denote $\|\mathbf{r}_0\|$ by r_0 and $\|\mathbf{v}_0\|$ by v_0, in which case we can express the vectors $\mathbf{r}_0$ and $\mathbf{v}_0$ in xyz-coordinates as

$$\mathbf{r}_0 = r_0\mathbf{i} \quad \text{and} \quad \mathbf{v}_0 = v_0\mathbf{j}$$

and the vector $\mathbf{b}$ as

$$\mathbf{b} = \mathbf{r}_0 \times \mathbf{v}_0 = r_0\mathbf{i} \times v_0\mathbf{j} = r_0 v_0\mathbf{k} \tag{6}$$

(Figure 12.7.4). It will also be useful to introduce the unit vector

$$\mathbf{u} = \cos\theta\,\mathbf{i} + \sin\theta\,\mathbf{j} \tag{7}$$

which will allow us to express the polar form of the position vector $\mathbf{r}$ as

$$\mathbf{r} = r\cos\theta\,\mathbf{i} + r\sin\theta\,\mathbf{j} = r(\cos\theta\,\mathbf{i} + \sin\theta\,\mathbf{j}) = r\mathbf{u} \tag{8}$$

and to express the acceleration vector $\mathbf{a}$ in terms of $\mathbf{u}$ by rewriting (5) as

$$\mathbf{a} = -\frac{GM}{r^2}\mathbf{u} \tag{9}$$

We are now ready to derive the position function of the mass m in polar coordinates. For this purpose, recall from (2) that the vector $\mathbf{b} = \mathbf{r} \times \mathbf{v}$ is constant, so it follows from (6) that the relationship

$$\mathbf{b} = \mathbf{r} \times \mathbf{v} = r_0 v_0\mathbf{k} \tag{10}$$

holds for *all* values of t. Now let us examine $\mathbf{b}$ from another point of view. It follows from (8) that

$$\mathbf{v} = \frac{d\mathbf{r}}{dt} = \frac{d}{dt}(r\mathbf{u}) = r\frac{d\mathbf{u}}{dt} + \frac{dr}{dt}\mathbf{u}$$

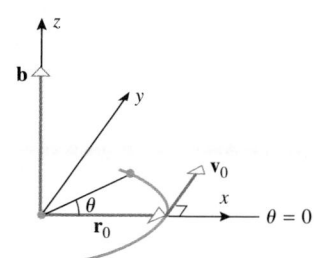

▲ **Figure 12.7.3**

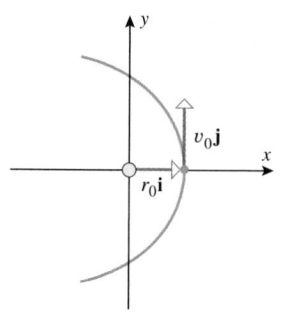

▲ **Figure 12.7.4**

and hence

$$\mathbf{b} = \mathbf{r} \times \mathbf{v} = (r\mathbf{u}) \times \left(r\frac{d\mathbf{u}}{dt} + \frac{dr}{dt}\mathbf{u} \right) = r^2\mathbf{u} \times \frac{d\mathbf{u}}{dt} + r\frac{dr}{dt}\mathbf{u} \times \mathbf{u} = r^2\mathbf{u} \times \frac{d\mathbf{u}}{dt} \quad (11)$$

But (7) implies that

$$\frac{d\mathbf{u}}{dt} = \frac{d\mathbf{u}}{d\theta}\frac{d\theta}{dt} = (-\sin\theta\mathbf{i} + \cos\theta\mathbf{j})\frac{d\theta}{dt}$$

so

$$\mathbf{u} \times \frac{d\mathbf{u}}{dt} = \frac{d\theta}{dt}\mathbf{k} \quad (12)$$

Substituting (12) in (11) yields

$$\mathbf{b} = r^2\frac{d\theta}{dt}\mathbf{k} \quad (13)$$

Thus, it follows from (7), (9), and (13) that

$$\mathbf{a} \times \mathbf{b} = -\frac{GM}{r^2}(\cos\theta\mathbf{i} + \sin\theta\mathbf{j}) \times \left(r^2\frac{d\theta}{dt}\mathbf{k} \right)$$

$$= GM(-\sin\theta\mathbf{i} + \cos\theta\mathbf{j})\frac{d\theta}{dt} = GM\frac{d\mathbf{u}}{dt} \quad (14)$$

From this formula and the fact that $d\mathbf{b}/dt = \mathbf{0}$ (since $\mathbf{b}$ is constant), we obtain

$$\frac{d}{dt}(\mathbf{v} \times \mathbf{b}) = \mathbf{v} \times \frac{d\mathbf{b}}{dt} + \frac{d\mathbf{v}}{dt} \times \mathbf{b} = \mathbf{a} \times \mathbf{b} = GM\frac{d\mathbf{u}}{dt}$$

Integrating both sides of this equation with respect to t yields

$$\mathbf{v} \times \mathbf{b} = GM\mathbf{u} + \mathbf{C} \quad (15)$$

where $\mathbf{C}$ is a vector constant of integration. This constant can be obtained by evaluating both sides of the equation at $t = 0$. We leave it as an exercise to show that

$$\mathbf{C} = (r_0 v_0^2 - GM)\mathbf{i} \quad (16)$$

from which it follows that

$$\mathbf{v} \times \mathbf{b} = GM\mathbf{u} + (r_0 v_0^2 - GM)\mathbf{i} \quad (17)$$

We can now obtain the position function by computing the scalar triple product $\mathbf{r} \cdot (\mathbf{v} \times \mathbf{b})$ in two ways. First we use (10) and property (11) of Section 11.4 to obtain

$$\mathbf{r} \cdot (\mathbf{v} \times \mathbf{b}) = (\mathbf{r} \times \mathbf{v}) \cdot \mathbf{b} = \mathbf{b} \cdot \mathbf{b} = r_0^2 v_0^2 \quad (18)$$

and next we use (17) to obtain

$$\mathbf{r} \cdot (\mathbf{v} \times \mathbf{b}) = \mathbf{r} \cdot (GM\mathbf{u}) + \mathbf{r} \cdot (r_0 v_0^2 - GM)\mathbf{i}$$

$$= \mathbf{r} \cdot \left(GM\frac{\mathbf{r}}{r} \right) + r\mathbf{u} \cdot (r_0 v_0^2 - GM)\mathbf{i}$$

$$= GMr + r(r_0 v_0^2 - GM)\cos\theta$$

If we now equate this to (18), we obtain

$$r_0^2 v_0^2 = GMr + r(r_0 v_0^2 - GM)\cos\theta$$

which when solved for r gives

$$r = \frac{r_0^2 v_0^2}{GM + (r_0 v_0^2 - GM)\cos\theta} = \frac{\dfrac{r_0^2 v_0^2}{GM}}{1 + \left(\dfrac{r_0 v_0^2}{GM} - 1 \right)\cos\theta} \quad (19)$$

or more simply

$$r = \frac{k}{1 + e\cos\theta} \quad (20)$$

where

$$k = \frac{r_0^2 v_0^2}{GM} \quad \text{and} \quad e = \frac{r_0 v_0^2}{GM} - 1 \tag{21–22}$$

We will leave it as an exercise to show that $e \geq 0$. Accepting this to be so, it follows by comparing (20) to Formula (3) of Section 10.6 that the trajectory is a conic section with eccentricity e, the focus at the pole, and $d = k/e$. Thus, depending on whether $e < 1$, $e = 1$, or $e > 1$, the trajectory will be, respectively, an ellipse, a parabola, or a hyperbola (Figure 12.7.5).

Note from Formula (22) that e depends on r_0 and v_0, so the exact form of the trajectory is determined by the mass M and the initial conditions. If the initial conditions are such that $e < 1$, then the mass m becomes trapped in an elliptical orbit; otherwise the mass m "escapes" and never returns to its initial position. Accordingly, the initial velocity that produces an eccentricity of $e = 1$ is called the **escape speed** and is denoted by v_{esc}. Thus, it follows from (22) that

$$v_{esc} = \sqrt{\frac{2GM}{r_0}} \tag{23}$$

(verify).

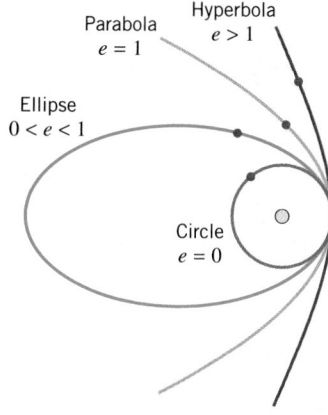

▲ **Figure 12.7.5**

Parabola $e = 1$

Hyperbola $e > 1$

Ellipse $0 < e < 1$

Circle $e = 0$

◼ KEPLER'S FIRST AND SECOND LAWS

It follows from our general discussion of central force fields that the planets have elliptical orbits with the Sun at the focus, which is Kepler's first law. To derive Kepler's second law, we begin by equating (10) and (13) to obtain

$$r^2 \frac{d\theta}{dt} = r_0 v_0 \tag{24}$$

To prove that the radial line from the center of the Sun to the center of a planet sweeps out equal areas in equal times, let $r = f(\theta)$ denote the polar equation of the planet, and let A denote the area swept out by the radial line as it varies from any fixed angle θ_0 to an angle θ. It follows from the area formula in 10.3.4 that A can be expressed as

$$A = \int_{\theta_0}^{\theta} \frac{1}{2} [f(\phi)]^2 \, d\phi$$

where the dummy variable ϕ is introduced for the integration to reserve θ for the upper limit. It now follows from Part 2 of the Fundamental Theorem of Calculus and the chain rule that

$$\frac{dA}{dt} = \frac{dA}{d\theta} \frac{d\theta}{dt} = \frac{1}{2} [f(\theta)]^2 \frac{d\theta}{dt} = \frac{1}{2} r^2 \frac{d\theta}{dt}$$

Thus, it follows from (24) that

$$\frac{dA}{dt} = \frac{1}{2} r_0 v_0 \tag{25}$$

which shows that A changes at a constant rate. This implies that equal areas are swept out in equal times.

◼ KEPLER'S THIRD LAW

To derive Kepler's third law, we let a and b be the semimajor and semiminor axes of the elliptical orbit, and we recall that the area of this ellipse is πab. It follows by integrating (25) that in t units of time the radial line will sweep out an area of $A = \frac{1}{2} r_0 v_0 t$. Thus, if T denotes the time required for the planet to make one revolution around the Sun (the period), then the radial line will sweep out the area of the entire ellipse during that time and hence

$$\pi ab = \frac{1}{2} r_0 v_0 T$$

from which we obtain

$$T^2 = \frac{4\pi^2 a^2 b^2}{r_0^2 v_0^2} \tag{26}$$

However, it follows from Formula (1) of Section 10.6 and the relationship $c^2 = a^2 - b^2$ for an ellipse that

$$e = \frac{c}{a} = \frac{\sqrt{a^2 - b^2}}{a}$$

Thus, $b^2 = a^2(1 - e^2)$ and hence (26) can be written as

$$T^2 = \frac{4\pi^2 a^4 (1 - e^2)}{r_0^2 v_0^2} \tag{27}$$

But comparing Equation (20) to Equation (17) of Section 10.6 shows that

$$k = a(1 - e^2)$$

Finally, substituting this expression and (21) in (27) yields

$$T^2 = \frac{4\pi^2 a^3}{r_0^2 v_0^2} k = \frac{4\pi^2 a^3}{r_0^2 v_0^2} \frac{r_0^2 v_0^2}{GM} = \frac{4\pi^2}{GM} a^3 \tag{28}$$

Thus, we have proved that T^2 is proportional to a^3, which is Kepler's third law. When convenient, Formula (28) can also be expressed as

$$T = \frac{2\pi}{\sqrt{GM}} a^{3/2} \tag{29}$$

ARTIFICIAL SATELLITES

Kepler's second and third laws and Formula (23) also apply to satellites that orbit a celestial body; we need only interpret M to be the mass of the body exerting the force and m to be the mass of the satellite. Values of GM that are required in many of the formulas in this section have been determined experimentally for various attracting bodies (Table 12.7.1).

Table 12.7.1

ATTRACTING BODY	INTERNATIONAL SYSTEM	BRITISH ENGINEERING SYSTEM
Earth	$GM = 3.99 \times 10^{14} \text{ m}^3/\text{s}^2$ $GM = 3.99 \times 10^{5} \text{ km}^3/\text{s}^2$	$GM = 1.41 \times 10^{16} \text{ ft}^3/\text{s}^2$ $GM = 1.24 \times 10^{12} \text{ mi}^3/\text{h}^2$
Sun	$GM = 1.33 \times 10^{20} \text{ m}^3/\text{s}^2$ $GM = 1.33 \times 10^{11} \text{ km}^3/\text{s}^2$	$GM = 4.69 \times 10^{21} \text{ ft}^3/\text{s}^2$ $GM = 4.13 \times 10^{17} \text{ mi}^3/\text{h}^2$
Moon	$GM = 4.90 \times 10^{12} \text{ m}^3/\text{s}^2$ $GM = 4.90 \times 10^{3} \text{ km}^3/\text{s}^2$	$GM = 1.73 \times 10^{14} \text{ ft}^3/\text{s}^2$ $GM = 1.53 \times 10^{10} \text{ mi}^3/\text{h}^2$

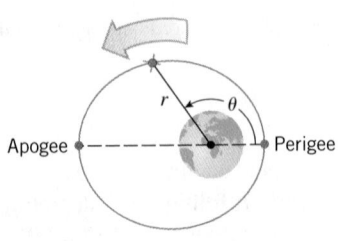

Apogee · — — — — · Perigee

▲ **Figure 12.7.6**

Recall that for orbits of planets around the Sun, the point at which the distance between the center of the planet and the center of the Sun is maximum is called the *aphelion* and the point at which it is minimum the *perihelion*. For satellites orbiting the Earth, the point at which the maximum distance occurs is called the **apogee**, and the point at which the minimum distance occurs is called the **perigee** (Figure 12.7.6). The actual distances between the centers at apogee and perigee are called the **apogee distance** and the **perigee distance**.

▶ **Example 1**   A geosynchronous orbit for a satellite is a circular orbit about the equator of the Earth in which the satellite stays fixed over a point on the equator. Use the fact that the Earth makes one revolution about its axis every 24 hours to find the altitude in miles of a communications satellite in geosynchronous orbit. Assume the Earth to be a sphere of radius 4000 mi.

Solution.   To remain fixed over a point on the equator, the satellite must have a period of $T = 24$ h. It follows from (28) or (29) and the Earth value of $GM = 1.24 \times 10^{12}$ mi^3/h^2 from Table 12.7.1 that

$$a = \sqrt[3]{\frac{GMT^2}{4\pi^2}} = \sqrt[3]{\frac{(1.24 \times 10^{12})(24)^2}{4\pi^2}} \approx 26{,}250 \text{ mi}$$

and hence the altitude h of the satellite is

$$h \approx 26{,}250 - 4000 = 22{,}250 \text{ mi} \blacktriangleleft$$

✔ QUICK CHECK EXERCISES 12.7   (See page 902 for answers.)

1. Let G denote the universal gravitational constant and let M and m denote masses a distance r apart.
   (a) According to Newton's Law of Universal Gravitation, M and m attract each other with a force of magnitude _____.
   (b) If **r** is the radius vector from M to m, then the force of attraction that mass M exerts on mass m is _____.

2. Suppose that a mass m is in an orbit about a mass M and that r_0 is the minimum distance from m to M. If G is the universal gravitational constant, then the "escape" speed of m is _____.

3. For a planet in an elliptical orbit about the Sun, the square of the planet's period is proportional to what power of the semimajor axis of its orbit?

4. Suppose that a mass m is in an orbit about a mass M and that r_0 is the minimum distance from m to M. If v_0 is the speed of mass m when it is a distance r_0 from M, and if G denotes the universal gravitational constant, then the eccentricity of the orbit is _____.

EXERCISE SET 12.7

1–14 In exercises that require numerical values, use Table 12.7.1 and the following values, where needed:

radius of Earth = 4000 mi = 6440 km
radius of Moon = 1080 mi = 1740 km
1 year (Earth year) = 365 days ■

FOCUS ON CONCEPTS

1. (a) Obtain the value of **C** given in Formula (16) by setting $t = 0$ in (15).
   (b) Use Formulas (7), (17), and (22) to show that
   $$\mathbf{v} \times \mathbf{b} = GM[(e + \cos\theta)\mathbf{i} + \sin\theta\,\mathbf{j}]$$
   (c) Show that $\|\mathbf{v} \times \mathbf{b}\| = \|\mathbf{v}\|\|\mathbf{b}\|$.
   (d) Use the results in parts (b) and (c) to show that the speed of a particle in an elliptical orbit is
   $$v = \frac{v_0}{1+e}\sqrt{e^2 + 2e\cos\theta + 1}$$
   (e) Suppose that a particle is in an elliptical orbit. Use part (d) to conclude that the distance from the particle to the center of force is a minimum if and only if the speed of the particle is a maximum. Similarly,

argue that the distance from the particle to the center of force is a maximum if and only if the speed of the particle is a minimum.

2. Use the result in Exercise 1(d) to show that when a particle in an elliptical orbit with eccentricity e reaches an end of the minor axis, its speed is
   $$v = v_0\sqrt{\frac{1-e}{1+e}}$$

3. Use the result in Exercise 1(d) to show that for a particle in an elliptical orbit with eccentricity e, the maximum and minimum speeds are related by
   $$v_{\max} = v_{\min}\frac{1+e}{1-e}$$

4. Use Formula (22) and the result in Exercise 1(d) to show that the speed v of a particle in a circular orbit of radius r_0 is constant and is given by
   $$v = \sqrt{\frac{GM}{r_0}}$$

5. Suppose that a particle is in an elliptical orbit in a central force field in which the center of force is at a focus, and let $\mathbf{r} = \mathbf{r}(t)$ and $\mathbf{v} = \mathbf{v}(t)$ be the position and velocity functions of the particle, respectively. Let r_{min} and r_{max} denote the minimum and maximum distances from the particle to the center of force, and let v_{min} and v_{max} denote the minimum and maximum speeds of the particle.

(a) Review the discussion of ellipses in polar coordinates in Section 10.6, and show that if the ellipse has eccentricity e and semimajor axis a, then $r_{min} = a(1 - e)$ and $r_{max} = a(1 + e)$.

(b) Explain why r_{min} and r_{max} occur at points at which $\mathbf{r}$ and $\mathbf{v}$ are orthogonal. [*Hint:* First argue that the extreme values of $\|\mathbf{r}\|$ occur at critical points of the function $\|\mathbf{r}\|^2 = \mathbf{r} \cdot \mathbf{r}$.]

(c) Explain why v_{min} and v_{max} occur at points at which $\mathbf{r}$ and $\mathbf{v}$ are orthogonal. [*Hint:* First argue that the extreme values of $\|\mathbf{v}\|$ occur at critical points of the function $\|\mathbf{v}\|^2 = \mathbf{v} \cdot \mathbf{v}$. Then use Equation (5).]

(d) Use Equation (2) and parts (b) and (c) to conclude that $r_{max}v_{min} = r_{min}v_{max}$.

6. Use the results in parts (a) and (d) of Exercise 5 to give a derivation of the equation in Exercise 3.

7. Use the result in Exercise 4 to find the speed in km/s of a satellite in a circular orbit that is 200 km above the surface of the Earth.

8. Use the result in Exercise 4 to find the speed in mi/h of a communications satellite that is in geosynchronous orbit around the Earth (see Example 1).

9. Find the escape speed in km/s for a space probe in a circular orbit that is 300 km above the surface of the Earth.

10. The universal gravitational constant is approximately
$$G = 6.67 \times 10^{-11} \text{ m}^3/\text{kg·s}^2$$
and the semimajor axis of the Earth's orbit is approximately
$$a = 149.6 \times 10^6 \text{ km}$$
Estimate the mass of the Sun in kg.

11. (a) The eccentricity of the Moon's orbit around the Earth is 0.055, and its semimajor axis is $a = 238,900$ mi. Find the maximum and minimum distances between the surface of the Earth and the surface of the Moon.

(b) Find the period of the Moon's orbit in days.

12. (a) *Vanguard 1* was launched in March 1958 with perigee and apogee altitudes above the Earth of 649 km and 4340 km, respectively. Find the length of the semimajor axis of its orbit.

(b) Use the result in part (a) of Exercise 16 in Section 10.6 to find the eccentricity of its orbit.

(c) Find the period of *Vanguard 1* in minutes.

13. (a) Suppose that a space probe is in a circular orbit at an altitude of 180 mi above the surface of the Earth. Use the result in Exercise 4 to find its speed.

(b) During a very short period of time, a thruster rocket on the space probe is fired to increase the speed of the probe by 600 mi/h in its direction of motion. Find the eccentricity of the resulting elliptical orbit, and use the result in part (a) of Exercise 5 to find the apogee altitude.

14. Show that the quantity e defined by Formula (22) is nonnegative. [*Hint:* The polar axis was chosen so that r is minimum when $\theta = 0$.]

✔QUICK CHECK ANSWERS 12.7

1. (a) $\dfrac{GMm}{r^2}$ (b) $-\dfrac{GMm}{r^3}\mathbf{r}$ **2.** $\sqrt{\dfrac{2GM}{r_0}}$ **3.** 3 **4.** $e = \dfrac{r_0 v_0^2}{GM} - 1$

CHAPTER 12 REVIEW EXERCISES

1. In words, what is meant by the graph of a vector-valued function?

2–5 Describe the graph of the equation. ■

2. $\mathbf{r} = (2 - 3t)\mathbf{i} - 4t\mathbf{j}$ **3.** $\mathbf{r} = 3\sin 2t\mathbf{i} + 3\cos 2t\mathbf{j}$

4. $\mathbf{r} = 3\cos t\mathbf{i} + 2\sin t\mathbf{j} - \mathbf{k}$ **5.** $\mathbf{r} = -2\mathbf{i} + t\mathbf{j} + (t^2 - 1)\mathbf{k}$

6. Describe the graph of the vector-valued function.

(a) $\mathbf{r} = \mathbf{r}_0 + t(\mathbf{r}_1 - \mathbf{r}_0)$

(b) $\mathbf{r} = \mathbf{r}_0 + t(\mathbf{r}_1 - \mathbf{r}_0)$ $(0 \le t \le 1)$

(c) $\mathbf{r} = \mathbf{r}_0 + t\mathbf{r}'(t_0)$

7. Show that the graph of $\mathbf{r}(t) = t\sin \pi t\mathbf{i} + t\mathbf{j} + t\cos \pi t\mathbf{k}$ lies on the surface of a cone, and sketch the cone.

8. Find parametric equations for the intersection of the surfaces
$$y = x^2 \quad \text{and} \quad 2x^2 + y^2 + 6z^2 = 24$$
and sketch the intersection.

9. In words, give a geometric description of the statement $\lim_{t \to a} \mathbf{r}(t) = \mathbf{L}$.

10. Evaluate $\lim\limits_{t \to 0} \left(e^{-t}\mathbf{i} + \dfrac{1 - \cos t}{t}\mathbf{j} + t^2\mathbf{k} \right)$.

11. Find parametric equations of the line tangent to the graph of

$$\mathbf{r}(t) = (t + \cos 2t)\mathbf{i} - (t^2 + t)\mathbf{j} + \sin t\mathbf{k}$$

at the point where $t = 0$.

12. Suppose that $\mathbf{r}_1(t)$ and $\mathbf{r}_2(t)$ are smooth vector-valued functions such that $\mathbf{r}_1(0) = \langle -1, 1, 2 \rangle$, $\mathbf{r}_2(0) = \langle 1, 2, 1 \rangle$, $\mathbf{r}_1'(0) = \langle 1, 0, 1 \rangle$, and $\mathbf{r}_2'(0) = \langle 4, 0, 2 \rangle$. Use this information to evaluate the derivative at $t = 0$ of each function.
 (a) $\mathbf{r}(t) = 3\mathbf{r}_1(t) + 2\mathbf{r}_2(t)$ (b) $\mathbf{r}(t) = [\ln(t + 1)]\mathbf{r}_1(t)$
 (c) $\mathbf{r}(t) = \mathbf{r}_1(t) \times \mathbf{r}_2(t)$ (d) $f(t) = \mathbf{r}_1(t) \cdot \mathbf{r}_2(t)$

13. Evaluate $\displaystyle\int (\cos t\mathbf{i} + \sin t\mathbf{j})\, dt$.

14. Evaluate $\displaystyle\int_0^{\pi/3} \langle \cos 3t, -\sin 3t \rangle\, dt$.

15. Solve the vector initial-value problem

$$\mathbf{y}'(t) = t^2\mathbf{i} + 2t\mathbf{j}, \quad \mathbf{y}(0) = \mathbf{i} + \mathbf{j}$$

16. Solve the vector initial-value problem

$$\frac{d\mathbf{r}}{dt} = \mathbf{r}, \quad \mathbf{r}(0) = \mathbf{r}_0$$

for the unknown vector-valued function $\mathbf{r}(t)$.

17. Find the arc length of the graph of

$$\mathbf{r}(t) = e^{\sqrt{2}t}\mathbf{i} + e^{-\sqrt{2}t}\mathbf{j} + 2t\mathbf{k} \quad (0 \le t \le \sqrt{2}\ln 2)$$

18. Suppose that $\mathbf{r}(t)$ is a smooth vector-valued function of t with $\mathbf{r}'(0) = 3\mathbf{i} - \mathbf{j} + \mathbf{k}$ and that $\mathbf{r}_1(t) = \mathbf{r}(2 - e^{t\ln 2})$. Find $\mathbf{r}_1'(1)$.

19. Find the arc length parametrization of the line through $P(-1, 4, 3)$ and $Q(0, 2, 5)$ that has reference point P and orients the line in the direction from P to Q.

20. Find an arc length parametrization of the curve

$$\mathbf{r}(t) = \langle e^t \cos t, -e^t \sin t \rangle \quad (0 \le t \le \pi/2)$$

which has the same orientation and has $\mathbf{r}(0)$ as the reference point.

21. Suppose that $\mathbf{r}(t)$ is a smooth vector-valued function. State the definitions of $\mathbf{T}(t)$, $\mathbf{N}(t)$, and $\mathbf{B}(t)$.

22. Find $\mathbf{T}(0)$, $\mathbf{N}(0)$, and $\mathbf{B}(0)$ for the curve

$$\mathbf{r}(t) = \left\langle 2\cos t, \, 2\cos t + \frac{3}{\sqrt{5}}\sin t, \, \cos t - \frac{6}{\sqrt{5}}\sin t \right\rangle$$

23. State the definition of "curvature" and explain what it means geometrically.

24. Suppose that $\mathbf{r}(t)$ is a smooth curve with $\mathbf{r}'(0) = \mathbf{i}$ and $\mathbf{r}''(0) = \mathbf{i} + 2\mathbf{j}$. Find the curvature at $t = 0$.

25–28 Find the curvature of the curve at the stated point. ■

25. $\mathbf{r}(t) = 2\cos t\mathbf{i} + 3\sin t\mathbf{j} - t\mathbf{k}; \; t = \pi/2$

26. $\mathbf{r}(t) = \langle 2t, e^{2t}, e^{-2t} \rangle; \; t = 0$

27. $y = \cos x; \; x = \pi/2$ 28. $y = \ln x; \; x = 1$

29. Suppose that $\mathbf{r}(t)$ is the position function of a particle moving in 2-space or 3-space. In each part, explain what the given quantity represents physically.
 (a) $\left\| \dfrac{d\mathbf{r}}{dt} \right\|$ (b) $\displaystyle\int_{t_0}^{t_1} \left\| \dfrac{d\mathbf{r}}{dt} \right\| dt$ (c) $\|\mathbf{r}(t)\|$

30. (a) What does Theorem 12.2.8 tell you about the velocity vector of a particle that moves over a sphere?
 (b) What does Theorem 12.2.8 tell you about the acceleration vector of a particle that moves with constant speed?
 (c) Show that the particle with position function

$$\mathbf{r}(t) = \sqrt{1 - \tfrac{1}{4}\cos^2 t}\,\cos t\mathbf{i} + \sqrt{1 - \tfrac{1}{4}\cos^2 t}\,\sin t\mathbf{j} + \tfrac{1}{2}\cos t\mathbf{k}$$

  moves over a sphere.

31. As illustrated in the accompanying figure, suppose that a particle moves counterclockwise around a circle of radius R centered at the origin at a constant rate of ω radians per second. This is called **uniform circular motion**. If we assume that the particle is at the point $(R, 0)$ at time $t = 0$, then its position function will be

$$\mathbf{r}(t) = R\cos \omega t\mathbf{i} + R\sin \omega t\mathbf{j}$$

 (a) Show that the velocity vector $\mathbf{v}(t)$ is always tangent to the circle and that the particle has constant speed v given by

$$v = R\omega$$

 (b) Show that the acceleration vector $\mathbf{a}(t)$ is always directed toward the center of the circle and has constant magnitude a given by

$$a = R\omega^2$$

 (c) Show that the time T required for the particle to make one complete revolution is

$$T = \frac{2\pi}{\omega} = \frac{2\pi R}{v}$$

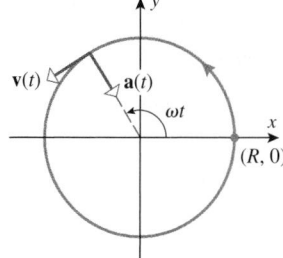

◀ Figure Ex-31

32. If a particle of mass m has uniform circular motion (see Exercise 31), then the acceleration vector $\mathbf{a}(t)$ is called the **centripetal acceleration**. According to Newton's second law, this acceleration must be produced by some force $\mathbf{F}(t)$, called the **centripetal force**, that is related to $\mathbf{a}(t)$ by the equation $\mathbf{F}(t) = m\mathbf{a}(t)$. If this force is not present, then the particle cannot undergo uniform circular motion. *(cont.)*

(a) Show that the direction of the centripetal force varies with time but that it has constant magnitude F given by

$$F = \frac{mv^2}{R}$$

(b) An astronaut with a mass of $m = 60$ kg orbits the Earth at an altitude of $h = 3200$ km with a constant speed of $v = 6.43$ km/s. Find her centripetal acceleration assuming that the radius of the Earth is 6440 km.

(c) What centripetal gravitational force in newtons does the Earth exert on the astronaut?

33. At time $t = 0$ a particle at the origin of an xyz-coordinate system has a velocity vector of $\mathbf{v}_0 = \mathbf{i} + 2\mathbf{j} - \mathbf{k}$. The acceleration function of the particle is $\mathbf{a}(t) = 2t^2\mathbf{i} + \mathbf{j} + \cos 2t\mathbf{k}$.

(a) Find the position function of the particle.

(b) Find the speed of the particle at time $t = 1$.

34. Let $\mathbf{v} = \mathbf{v}(t)$ and $\mathbf{a} = \mathbf{a}(t)$ be the velocity and acceleration vectors for a particle moving in 2-space or 3-space. Show that the rate of change of its speed can be expressed as

$$\frac{d}{dt}(\|\mathbf{v}\|) = \frac{1}{\|\mathbf{v}\|}(\mathbf{v} \cdot \mathbf{a})$$

35. Use Formula (23) in Section 12.7 and refer to Table 12.7.1 to find the escape speed (in km/s) for a space probe 600 km above the surface of the Earth.

36. As illustrated in the accompanying figure, the polar coordinates of a rocket are tracked by radar from a point that is b units from the launching pad. Show that the speed v of the rocket can be expressed in terms b, θ, and $d\theta/dt$ as

$$v = b \sec^2 \theta \frac{d\theta}{dt}$$

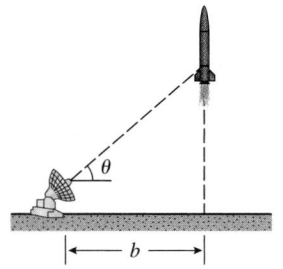

◄ **Figure Ex-34**

37. A player throws a ball with an initial speed of 60 ft/s at an unknown angle α with the horizontal from a point that is 4 ft above the floor of a gymnasium. Given that the ceiling of the gymnasium is 25 ft high, determine the maximum height h at which the ball can hit a wall that is 60 ft away (see the accompanying figure).

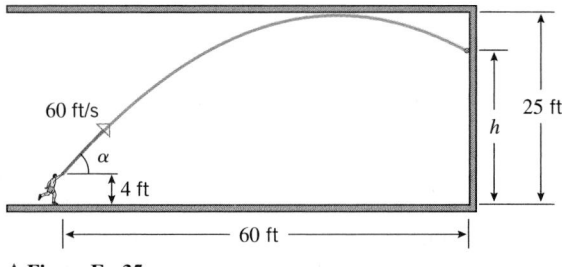

▲ **Figure Ex-35**

CHAPTER 12 MAKING CONNECTIONS [C] CAS

1. (a) Use the formulas

$$\mathbf{N}(t) = \mathbf{B}(t) \times \mathbf{T}(t)$$
$$\mathbf{T}(t) = \mathbf{r}'(t)/\|\mathbf{r}'(t)\|$$

and

$$\mathbf{B}(t) = \frac{\mathbf{r}'(t) \times \mathbf{r}''(t)}{\|\mathbf{r}'(t) \times \mathbf{r}''(t)\|}$$

to show that $\mathbf{N}(t)$ can be expressed in terms of $\mathbf{r}(t)$ as

$$\mathbf{N}(t) = \frac{\mathbf{r}'(t) \times \mathbf{r}''(t)}{\|\mathbf{r}'(t) \times \mathbf{r}''(t)\|} \times \frac{\mathbf{r}'(t)}{\|\mathbf{r}'(t)\|}$$

(b) Use properties of cross products to show that the formula in part (a) can be expressed as

$$\mathbf{N}(t) = \frac{(\mathbf{r}'(t) \times \mathbf{r}''(t)) \times \mathbf{r}'(t)}{\|(\mathbf{r}'(t) \times \mathbf{r}''(t)) \times \mathbf{r}'(t)\|}$$

(c) Use the result in part (b) to find $\mathbf{N}(t)$ at the given point.
   (i) $\mathbf{r}(t) = (t^2 - 1)\mathbf{i} + t\mathbf{j}$; $t = 1$
   (ii) $\mathbf{r}(t) = 4\cos t\mathbf{i} + 4\sin t\mathbf{j} + t\mathbf{k}$; $t = \pi/2$

2. (a) Use the result in Exercise 1(b) and Exercise 45 of Section 11.4 to show that $\mathbf{N}(t)$ can be expressed directly in terms of $\mathbf{r}(t)$ as

$$\mathbf{N}(t) = \frac{\mathbf{u}(t)}{\|\mathbf{u}(t)\|}$$

where

$$\mathbf{u}(t) = \|\mathbf{r}'(t)\|^2\mathbf{r}''(t) - (\mathbf{r}'(t) \cdot \mathbf{r}''(t))\mathbf{r}'(t)$$

(b) Use the result in part (a) to find $\mathbf{N}(t)$.
   (i) $\mathbf{r}(t) = \sin t\mathbf{i} + \cos t\mathbf{j} + t\mathbf{k}$
   (ii) $\mathbf{r}(t) = t\mathbf{i} + t^2\mathbf{j} + t^3\mathbf{k}$

3. In Making Connections Exercise 1 of Chapter 10 we defined the Cornu spiral parametrically as

$$x = \int_0^t \cos\left(\frac{\pi u^2}{2}\right) du, \quad y = \int_0^t \sin\left(\frac{\pi u^2}{2}\right) du$$

This curve, which is graphed in the accompanying figure, is used in highway design to create a gradual transition from a straight road (zero curvature) to an exit ramp with positive curvature. *(cont.)*

(a) Express the Cornu spiral as a vector-valued function $\mathbf{r}(t)$, and then use Theorem 12.3.4 to show that $s = t$ is the arc length parameter with reference point $(0, 0)$.

(b) Replace t by s and use Formula (1) of Section 12.5 to show that $\kappa(s) = \pi|s|$. [*Note*: If $s \geq 0$, then the curvature $\kappa(s) = \pi s$ increases from 0 at a constant rate with respect to s. This makes the spiral ideal for joining a curved road to a straight road.]

(c) What happens to the curvature of the Cornu spiral as $s \to +\infty$? In words, explain why this is consistent with the graph.

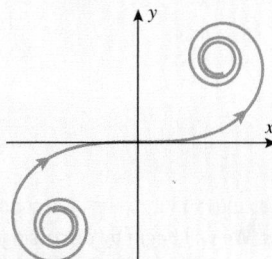

◀ **Figure Ex-3**

C **4.** In 1975, German engineer Werner Stengel pioneered the use of Cornu spirals (see Exercise 3) in the design of loops for roller coasters with the *Revolution* at Six Flags Magic Mountain in California. For this design, the top of the loop is a circular arc, joined at either end to Cornu spirals that ease the transitions to horizontal track. The accompanying figure illustrates this design when the circular arc (in red) is a semicircle, quarter-circle, or a single point, respectively. Suppose that a roller-coaster loop is designed to be 45 feet across at its widest point. For each case in Figure Ex-4, find the vertical distance between the level of the horizontal track and the top of the loop. Use the numerical integration capability of your CAS to estimate integrals, as necessary.

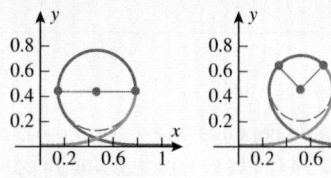

▲ **Figure Ex-4**

5. Use the results in Exercise 61 of Section 12.5 and the results in Exercise 32 of Section 12.3 to show that for the circular helix
$$\mathbf{r} = a\cos t\,\mathbf{i} + a\sin t\,\mathbf{j} + ct\,\mathbf{k}$$
with $a > 0$, the torsion and the binormal vector are
$$\tau = \frac{c}{w^2}$$

and
$$\mathbf{B} = \left(\frac{c}{w}\sin\frac{s}{w}\right)\mathbf{i} - \left(\frac{c}{w}\cos\frac{s}{w}\right)\mathbf{j} + \left(\frac{a}{w}\right)\mathbf{k}$$
where $w = \sqrt{a^2 + c^2}$ and s has reference point $(a, 0, 0)$.

6. Suppose that the position function of a point moving in the xy-plane is
$$\mathbf{r} = x(t)\mathbf{i} + y(t)\mathbf{j}$$
This equation can be expressed in polar coordinates by making the substitution
$$x(t) = r(t)\cos\theta(t), \quad y(t) = r(t)\sin\theta(t)$$
This yields
$$\mathbf{r} = r(t)\cos\theta(t)\mathbf{i} + r(t)\sin\theta(t)\mathbf{j}$$
which can be expressed as
$$\mathbf{r} = r(t)\mathbf{e}_r(t)$$
where $\mathbf{e}_r(t) = \cos\theta(t)\mathbf{i} + \sin\theta(t)\mathbf{j}$.

(a) Show that $\mathbf{e}_r(t)$ is a unit vector in the same direction as the radius vector $\mathbf{r}$ if $r(t) > 0$. Also, show that $\mathbf{e}_\theta(t) = -\sin\theta(t)\mathbf{i} + \cos\theta(t)\mathbf{j}$ is the unit vector that results when $\mathbf{e}_r(t)$ is rotated counterclockwise through an angle of $\pi/2$. The vector $\mathbf{e}_r(t)$ is called the **radial unit vector** and the vector $\mathbf{e}_\theta(t)$ is called the **transverse unit vector** (see the accompanying figure).

(b) Show that the velocity function $\mathbf{v} = \mathbf{v}(t)$ can be expressed in terms of radial and transverse components as
$$\mathbf{v} = \frac{dr}{dt}\mathbf{e}_r + r\frac{d\theta}{dt}\mathbf{e}_\theta$$

(c) Show that the acceleration function $\mathbf{a} = \mathbf{a}(t)$ can be expressed in terms of radial and transverse components as
$$\mathbf{a} = \left[\frac{d^2r}{dt^2} - r\left(\frac{d\theta}{dt}\right)^2\right]\mathbf{e}_r + \left[r\frac{d^2\theta}{dt^2} + 2\frac{dr}{dt}\frac{d\theta}{dt}\right]\mathbf{e}_\theta$$

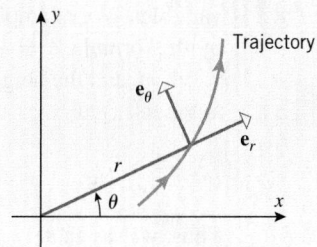

◀ **Figure Ex-6**

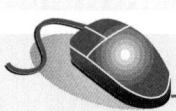

Expanding the Calculus Horizon

For a practical application of projectile motion in a whimsical setting, see the module entitled **Blammo the Human Cannonball** at:

www.wiley.com/college/anton

13

PARTIAL DERIVATIVES

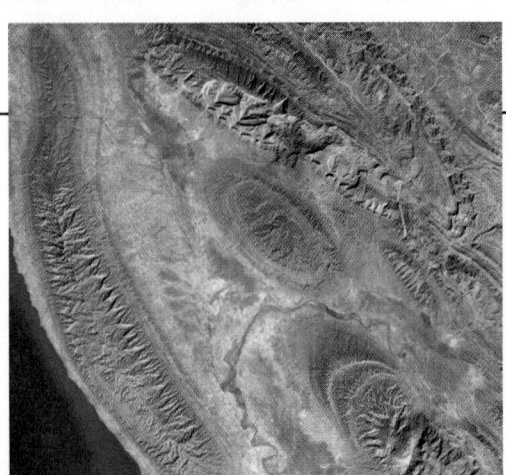

© Science Photo Library

Three-dimensional surfaces have high points and low points that are analogous to the peaks and valleys of a mountain range. In this chapter we will use derivatives to locate these points and to study other features of such surfaces.

In this chapter we will extend many of the basic concepts of calculus to functions of two or more variables, commonly called functions of several variables. We will begin by discussing limits and continuity for functions of two and three variables, then we will define derivatives of such functions, and then we will use these derivatives to study tangent planes, rates of change, slopes of surfaces, and maximization and minimization problems. Although many of the basic ideas that we developed for functions of one variable will carry over in a natural way, functions of several variables are intrinsically more complicated than functions of one variable, so we will need to develop new tools and new ideas to deal with such functions.

13.1 FUNCTIONS OF TWO OR MORE VARIABLES

In previous sections we studied real-valued functions of a real variable and vector-valued functions of a real variable. In this section we will consider real-valued functions of two or more real variables.

■ NOTATION AND TERMINOLOGY

There are many familiar formulas in which a given variable depends on two or more other variables. For example, the area A of a triangle depends on the base length b and height h by the formula $A = \frac{1}{2}bh$; the volume V of a rectangular box depends on the length l, the width w, and the height h by the formula $V = lwh$; and the arithmetic average $\bar{x}$ of n real numbers, $x_1, x_2, \ldots, x_n$, depends on those numbers by the formula

$$\bar{x} = \frac{1}{n}(x_1 + x_2 + \cdots + x_n)$$

Thus, we say that

A is a function of the two variables b and h;

V is a function of the three variables l, w, and h;

$\bar{x}$ is a function of the n variables $x_1, x_2, \ldots, x_n$.

The terminology and notation for functions of two or more variables is similar to that for functions of one variable. For example, the expression

$$z = f(x, y)$$

means that z is a function of x and y in the sense that a unique value of the dependent variable z is determined by specifying values for the independent variables x and y. Similarly,

$$w = f(x, y, z)$$

expresses w as a function of x, y, and z, and

$$u = f(x_1, x_2, \ldots, x_n)$$

expresses u as a function of $x_1, x_2, \ldots, x_n$.

As with functions of one variable, the independent variables of a function of two or more variables may be restricted to lie in some set D, which we call the *domain* of f. Sometimes the domain will be determined by physical restrictions on the variables. If the function is defined by a formula and if there are no physical restrictions or other restrictions stated explicitly, then it is understood that the domain consists of all points for which the formula yields a real value for the dependent variable. We call this the *natural domain* of the function. The following definitions summarize this discussion.

By extension, one can define the notion of "n-dimensional space" in which a "point" is a sequence of n real numbers $(x_1, x_2, \ldots, x_n)$, and a function of n real variables is a rule that assigns a unique real number $f(x_1, x_2, \ldots, x_n)$ to each point in some set in this space.

13.1.1 DEFINITION A *function f of two variables*, x and y, is a rule that assigns a unique real number $f(x, y)$ to each point (x, y) in some set D in the xy-plane.

13.1.2 DEFINITION A *function f of three variables*, x, y, and z, is a rule that assigns a unique real number $f(x, y, z)$ to each point (x, y, z) in some set D in three-dimensional space.

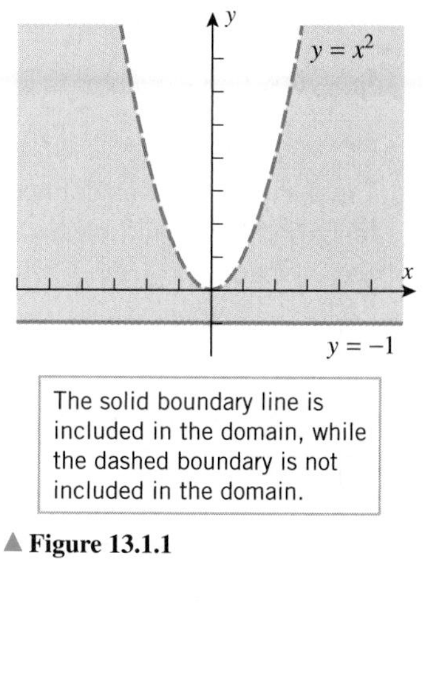

The solid boundary line is included in the domain, while the dashed boundary is not included in the domain.

▲ **Figure 13.1.1**

▶ **Example 1** Let $f(x, y) = \sqrt{y + 1} + \ln(x^2 - y)$. Find $f(e, 0)$ and sketch the natural domain of f.

Solution. By substitution,

$$f(e, 0) = \sqrt{0 + 1} + \ln(e^2 - 0) = \sqrt{1} + \ln(e^2) = 1 + 2 = 3$$

To find the natural domain of f, we note that $\sqrt{y + 1}$ is defined only when $y \geq -1$, while $\ln(x^2 - y)$ is defined only when $0 < x^2 - y$ or $y < x^2$. Thus, the natural domain of f consists of all points in the xy-plane for which $-1 \leq y < x^2$. To sketch the natural domain, we first sketch the parabola $y = x^2$ as a "dashed" curve and the line $y = -1$ as a solid curve. The natural domain of f is then the region lying above or on the line $y = -1$ and below the parabola $y = x^2$ (Figure 13.1.1.) ◀

▶ **Example 2** Let

$$f(x, y, z) = \sqrt{1 - x^2 - y^2 - z^2}$$

Find $f\left(0, \frac{1}{2}, -\frac{1}{2}\right)$ and the natural domain of f.

Solution. By substitution,

$$f\left(0, \tfrac{1}{2}, -\tfrac{1}{2}\right) = \sqrt{1 - (0)^2 - \left(\tfrac{1}{2}\right)^2 - \left(-\tfrac{1}{2}\right)^2} = \sqrt{\tfrac{1}{2}}$$

Because of the square root sign, we must have $0 \leq 1 - x^2 - y^2 - z^2$ in order to have a real value for $f(x, y, z)$. Rewriting this inequality in the form

$$x^2 + y^2 + z^2 \leq 1$$

we see that the natural domain of f consists of all points on or within the sphere

$$x^2 + y^2 + z^2 = 1 \quad \blacktriangleleft$$

FUNCTIONS DESCRIBED BY TABLES

Sometimes it is either desirable or necessary to represent a function of two variables in table form, rather than as an explicit formula. For example, the U.S. National Weather Service uses the formula

$$W = 35.74 + 0.6215T + (0.4275T - 35.75)v^{0.16} \tag{1}$$

The wind chill index is that temperature (in °F) which would produce the same sensation on exposed skin at a wind speed of 3 mi/h as the temperature and wind speed combination in current weather conditions.

to model the wind chill index W (in °F) as a function of the temperature T (in °F) and the wind speed v (in mi/h) for wind speeds greater than 3 mi/h. This formula is sufficiently complex that it is difficult to get an intuitive feel for the relationship between the variables. One can get a clearer sense of the relationship by selecting sample values of T and v and constructing a table, such as Table 13.1.1, in which we have rounded the values of W to the nearest integer. For example, if the temperature is 30°F and the wind speed is 5 mi/h, it feels as if the temperature is 25°F. If the wind speed increases to 15 mi/h, the temperature then feels as if it has dropped to 19°F. Note that in this case, an increase in wind speed of 10 mi/h causes a 6°F decrease in the wind chill index. To estimate wind chill values not displayed in the table, we can use **linear interpolation**. For example, suppose that the temperature is 30°F and the wind speed is 7 mi/h. A reasonable estimate for the drop in the wind chill index from its value when the wind speed is 5 mi/h would be $\frac{2}{10} \cdot 6°F = 1.2°F$. (Why?) The resulting estimate in wind chill would then be $25° - 1.2° = 23.8°F$.

In some cases, tables for functions of two variables arise directly from experimental data, in which case one must either work directly with the table or else use some technique to construct a formula that models the data in the table. Such modeling techniques are developed in statistics and numerical analysis texts.

Table 13.1.1

TEMPERATURE T (°F)

WIND SPEED v (mi/h)	20	25	30	35
5	13	19	25	31
15	6	13	19	25
25	3	9	16	23
35	0	7	14	21
45	-2	5	12	19

GRAPHS OF FUNCTIONS OF TWO VARIABLES

Recall that for a function f of one variable, the graph of $f(x)$ in the xy-plane was defined to be the graph of the equation $y = f(x)$. Similarly, if f is a function of two variables, we define the **graph** of $f(x, y)$ in xyz-space to be the graph of the equation $z = f(x, y)$. In general, such a graph will be a surface in 3-space.

▶ **Example 3** In each part, describe the graph of the function in an xyz-coordinate system.

(a) $f(x, y) = 1 - x - \frac{1}{2}y$ (b) $f(x, y) = \sqrt{1 - x^2 - y^2}$
(c) $f(x, y) = -\sqrt{x^2 + y^2}$

Solution (a). By definition, the graph of the given function is the graph of the equation

$$z = 1 - x - \frac{1}{2}y$$

which is a plane. A triangular portion of the plane can be sketched by plotting the intersections with the coordinate axes and joining them with line segments (Figure 13.1.2a).

Solution (b). By definition, the graph of the given function is the graph of the equation

$$z = \sqrt{1 - x^2 - y^2} \tag{2}$$

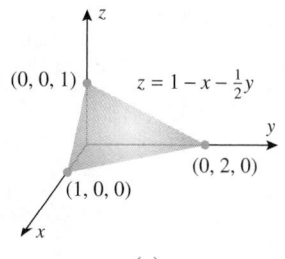

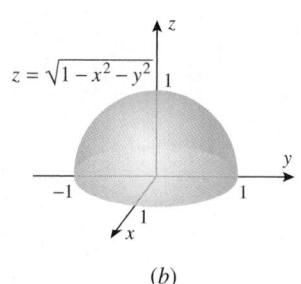

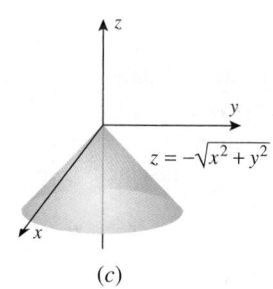

▲ Figure 13.1.2

After squaring both sides, this can be rewritten as

$$x^2 + y^2 + z^2 = 1$$

which represents a sphere of radius 1, centered at the origin. Since (2) imposes the added condition that $z \geq 0$, the graph is just the upper hemisphere (Figure 13.1.2b).

Solution (c).   The graph of the given function is the graph of the equation

$$z = -\sqrt{x^2 + y^2} \qquad (3)$$

After squaring, we obtain

$$z^2 = x^2 + y^2$$

which is the equation of a circular cone (see Table 11.7.1). Since (3) imposes the condition that $z \leq 0$, the graph is just the lower nappe of the cone (Figure 13.1.2c). ◄

■ LEVEL CURVES

We are all familiar with the topographic (or contour) maps in which a three-dimensional landscape, such as a mountain range, is represented by two-dimensional contour lines or curves of constant elevation. Consider, for example, the model hill and its contour map shown in Figure 13.1.3. The contour map is constructed by passing planes of constant elevation through the hill, projecting the resulting contours onto a flat surface, and labeling the contours with their elevations. In Figure 13.1.3, note how the two gullies appear as indentations in the contour lines and how the curves are close together on the contour map where the hill has a steep slope and become more widely spaced where the slope is gradual.

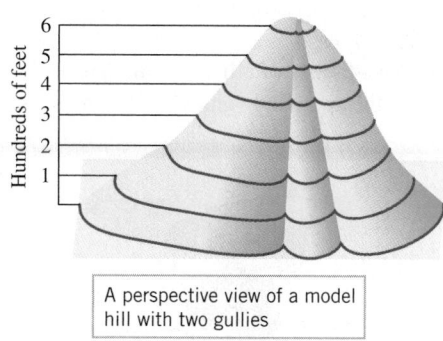

A perspective view of a model hill with two gullies

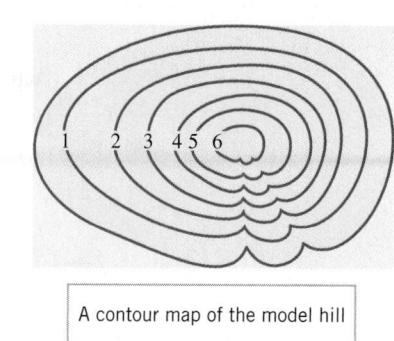

A contour map of the model hill

▲ Figure 13.1.3

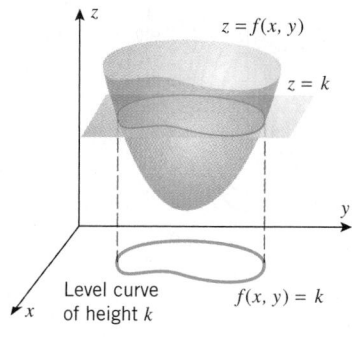

▲ Figure 13.1.4

Contour maps are also useful for studying functions of two variables. If the surface $z = f(x, y)$ is cut by the horizontal plane $z = k$, then at all points on the intersection we have $f(x, y) = k$. The projection of this intersection onto the xy-plane is called the ***level curve of height k*** or the ***level curve with constant k*** (Figure 13.1.4). A set of level curves for $z = f(x, y)$ is called a ***contour plot*** or ***contour map*** of f.

▶ **Example 4**   The graph of the function $f(x, y) = y^2 - x^2$ in xyz-space is the hyperbolic paraboloid (saddle surface) shown in Figure 13.1.5a. The level curves have equations of the form $y^2 - x^2 = k$. For $k > 0$ these curves are hyperbolas opening along lines parallel to the y-axis; for $k < 0$ they are hyperbolas opening along lines parallel to the x-axis; and for $k = 0$ the level curve consists of the intersecting lines $y + x = 0$ and $y - x = 0$ (Figure 13.1.5b). ◄

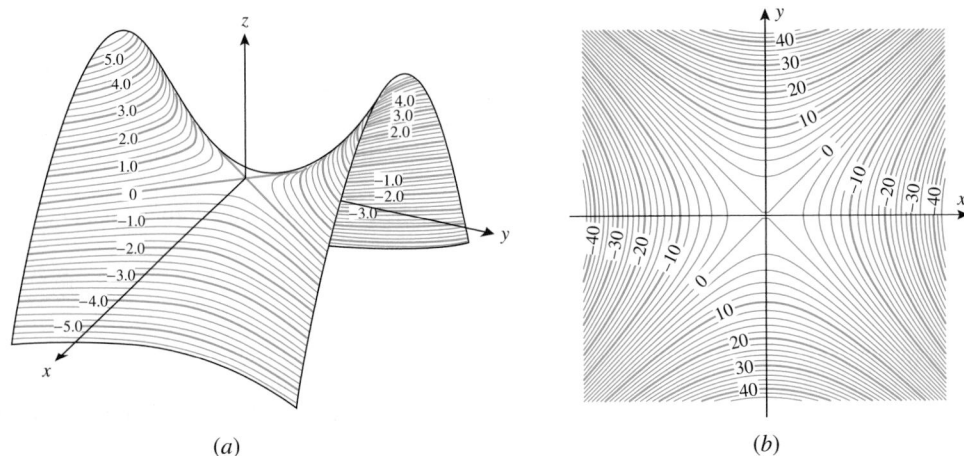

(a)   (b)

▲ **Figure 13.1.5**

▶ **Example 5**   Sketch the contour plot of $f(x, y) = 4x^2 + y^2$ using level curves of height $k = 0, 1, 2, 3, 4, 5$.

Solution.   The graph of the surface $z = 4x^2 + y^2$ is the paraboloid shown in the left part of Figure 13.1.6, so we can reasonably expect the contour plot to be a family of ellipses centered at the origin. The level curve of height k has the equation $4x^2 + y^2 = k$. If $k = 0$, then the graph is the single point $(0, 0)$. For $k > 0$ we can rewrite the equation as

$$\frac{x^2}{k/4} + \frac{y^2}{k} = 1$$

which represents a family of ellipses with x-intercepts $\pm\sqrt{k}/2$ and y-intercepts $\pm\sqrt{k}$. The contour plot for the specified values of k is shown in the right part of Figure 13.1.6. ◀

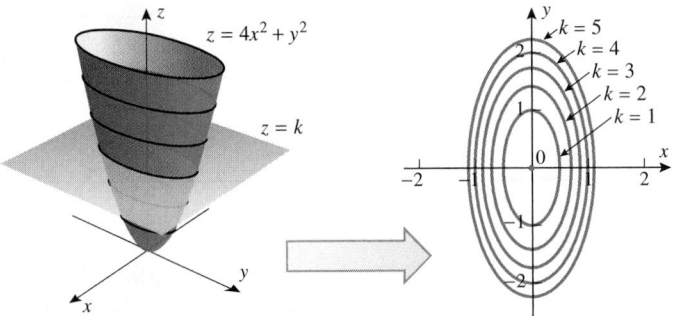

▶ **Figure 13.1.6**

▶ **Example 6**   Sketch the contour plot of $f(x, y) = 2 - x - y$ using level curves of height $k = -6, -4, -2, 0, 2, 4, 6$.

Solution.   The graph of the surface $z = 2 - x - y$ is the plane shown in the left part of Figure 13.1.7, so we can reasonably expect the contour plot to be a family of parallel lines. The level curve of height k has the equation $2 - x - y = k$, which we can rewrite as

$$y = -x + (2 - k)$$

This represents a family of parallel lines of slope -1. The contour plot for the specified values of k is shown in the right part of Figure 13.1.7. ◀

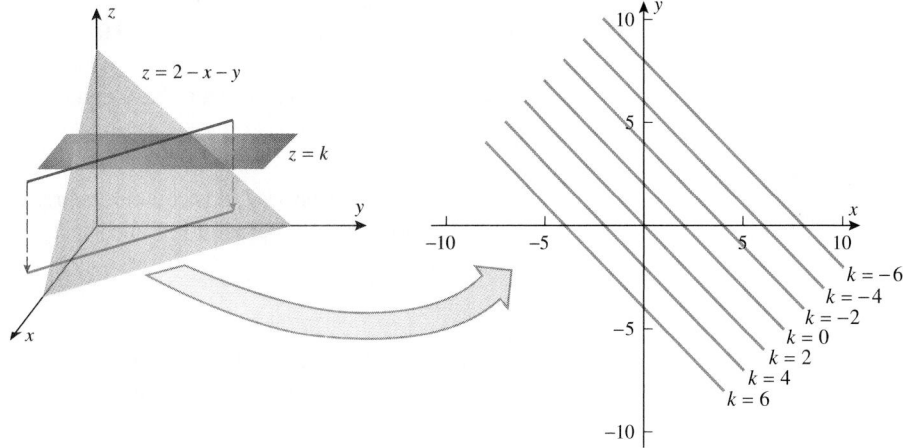

▲ Figure 13.1.7

▇ CONTOUR PLOTS USING TECHNOLOGY

Except in the simplest cases, contour plots can be difficult to produce without the help of a graphing utility. Figure 13.1.8 illustrates how graphing technology can be used to display level curves. The table shows two graphical representations of the level curves of the function $f(x, y) = |\sin x \sin y|$ produced with a CAS over the domain $0 \leq x \leq 2\pi$, $0 \leq y \leq 2\pi$.

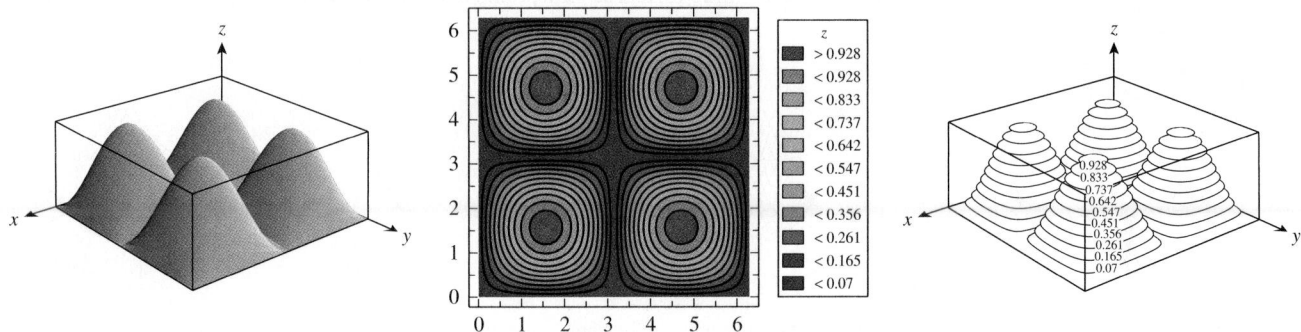

▲ Figure 13.1.8

▇ LEVEL SURFACES

> The term "level surface" is standard but confusing, since a level surface need *not* be level in the sense of being horizontal—it is simply a surface on which all values of f are the same.

Observe that the graph of $y = f(x)$ is a curve in 2-space, and the graph of $z = f(x, y)$ is a surface in 3-space, so the number of dimensions required for these graphs is one greater than the number of independent variables. Accordingly, there is no "direct" way to graph a function of three variables since four dimensions are required. However, if k is a constant, then the graph of the equation $f(x, y, z) = k$ will generally be a surface in 3-space (e.g., the graph of $x^2 + y^2 + z^2 = 1$ is a sphere), which we call the ***level surface with constant k***. Some geometric insight into the behavior of the function f can sometimes be obtained by graphing these level surfaces for various values of k.

▶ **Example 7** Describe the level surfaces of

(a) $f(x, y, z) = x^2 + y^2 + z^2$ (b) $f(x, y, z) = z^2 - x^2 - y^2$

Solution (a).   The level surfaces have equations of the form

$$x^2 + y^2 + z^2 = k$$

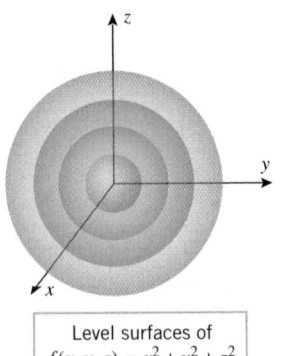

Level surfaces of
$f(x, y, z) = x^2 + y^2 + z^2$

▲ **Figure 13.1.9**

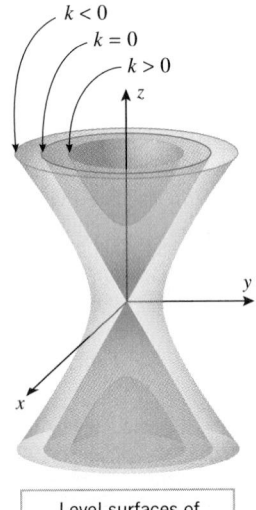

Level surfaces of
$f(x, y, z) = z^2 - x^2 - y^2$

▲ **Figure 13.1.10**

TECHNOLOGY MASTERY

If you have a graphing utility that can generate surfaces in 3-space, read the documentation and try to duplicate some of the surfaces in Figures 13.1.11 and 13.1.12 and Table 13.1.2.

For $k > 0$ the graph of this equation is a sphere of radius $\sqrt{k}$, centered at the origin; for $k = 0$ the graph is the single point $(0, 0, 0)$; and for $k < 0$ there is no level surface (Figure 13.1.9).

Solution (b). The level surfaces have equations of the form

$$z^2 - x^2 - y^2 = k$$

As discussed in Section 11.7, this equation represents a cone if $k = 0$, a hyperboloid of two sheets if $k > 0$, and a hyperboloid of one sheet if $k < 0$ (Figure 13.1.10). ◄

■ **GRAPHING FUNCTIONS OF TWO VARIABLES USING TECHNOLOGY**

Generating surfaces with a graphing utility is more complicated than generating plane curves because there are more factors that must be taken into account. We can only touch on the ideas here, so if you want to use a graphing utility, its documentation will be your main source of information.

Graphing utilities can only show a portion of xyz-space in a viewing screen, so the first step in graphing a surface is to determine which portion of xyz-space you want to display. This region is called the ***viewing box*** or ***viewing window***. For example, Figure 13.1.11 shows the effect of graphing the paraboloid $z = x^2 + y^2$ in three different viewing windows. However, within a fixed viewing box, the appearance of the surface is also affected by the ***viewpoint***, that is, the direction from which the surface is viewed, and the distance from the viewer to the surface. For example, Figure 13.1.12 shows the graph of the paraboloid $z = x^2 + y^2$ from three different viewpoints using the first viewing box in Figure 13.1.11.

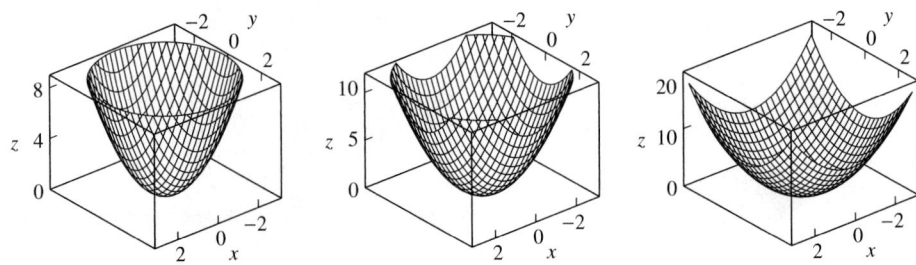

▲ **Figure 13.1.11** Varying the viewing box.

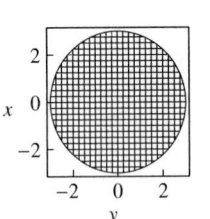 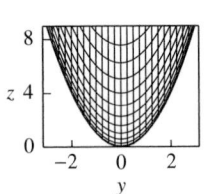 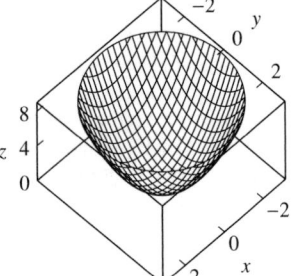

▲ **Figure 13.1.12** Varying the viewpoint.

Table 13.1.2 shows six surfaces in 3-space along with their associated contour plots. Note that the mesh lines on the surface are traces in vertical planes, whereas the level curves correspond to traces in horizontal planes. In these contour plots the color gradation is from dark to light as z increases.

Table 13.1.2

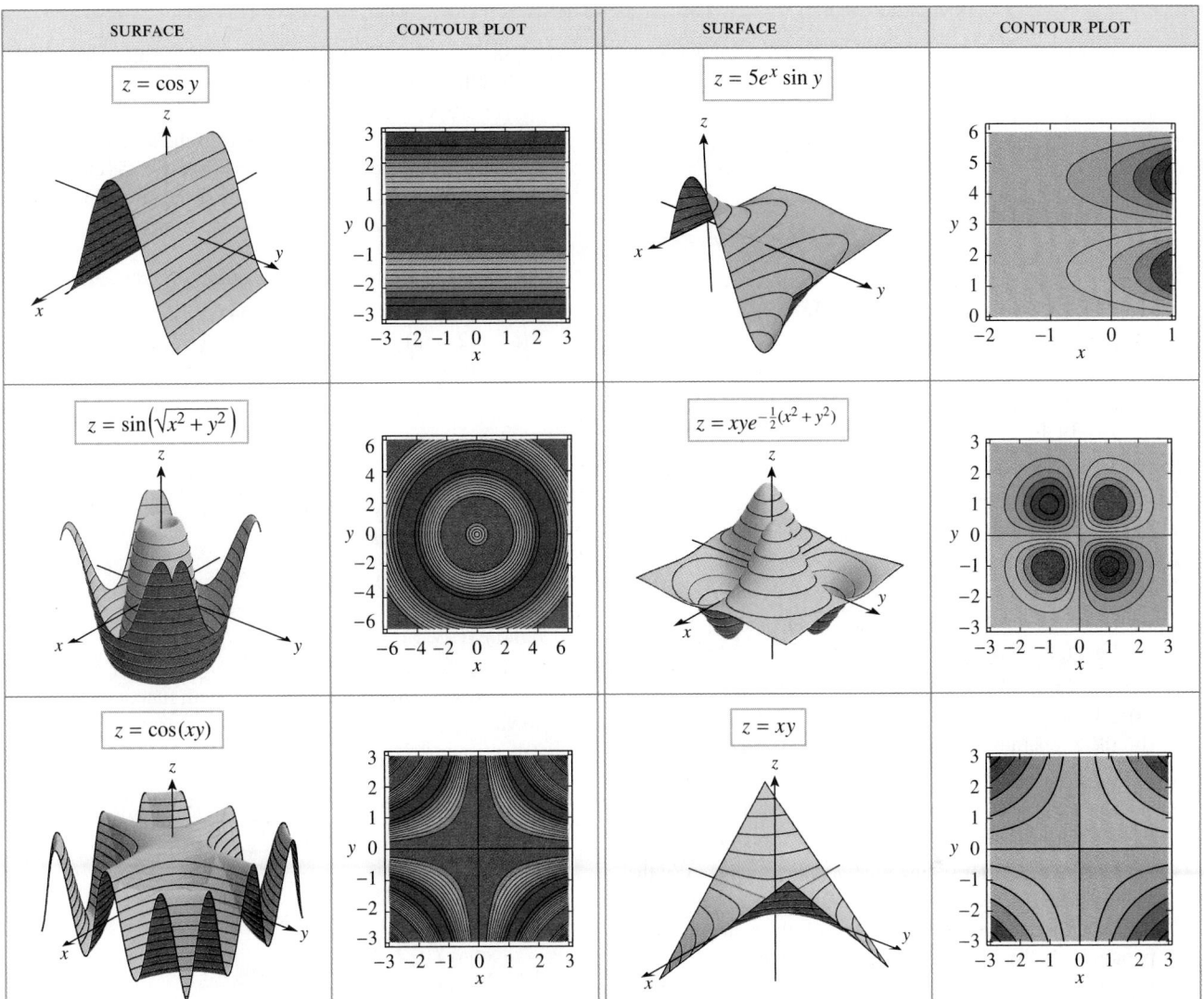

SURFACE	CONTOUR PLOT	SURFACE	CONTOUR PLOT
$z = \cos y$		$z = 5e^x \sin y$	
$z = \sin\left(\sqrt{x^2 + y^2}\right)$		$z = xye^{-\frac{1}{2}(x^2 + y^2)}$	
$z = \cos(xy)$		$z = xy$	

✔ **QUICK CHECK EXERCISES 13.1** (See page 917 for answers.)

1. The domain of $f(x, y) = \ln xy$ is _____ and the domain of $g(x, y) = \ln x + \ln y$ is _____.

2. Let $f(x, y) = \dfrac{x - y}{x + y + 1}$.
   (a) $f(2, 1) = $ _____ (b) $f(1, 2) = $ _____
   (c) $f(a, a) = $ _____ (d) $f(y + 1, y) = $ _____

3. Let $f(x, y) = e^{x+y}$.
   (a) For what values of k will the graph of the level curve $f(x, y) = k$ be nonempty?

(b) Describe the level curves $f(x, y) = k$ for the values of k obtained in part (a).

4. Let $f(x, y, z) = \dfrac{1}{x^2 + y^2 + z^2 + 1}$.
   (a) For what values of k will the graph of the level surface $f(x, y, z) = k$ be nonempty?
   (b) Describe the level surfaces $f(x, y, z) = k$ for the values of k obtained in part (a).

EXERCISE SET 13.1   ~ Graphing Utility   [C] CAS

1–8 These exercises are concerned with functions of two variables.

1. Let $f(x, y) = x^2 y + 1$. Find
   (a) $f(2, 1)$ (b) $f(1, 2)$ (c) $f(0, 0)$
   (d) $f(1, -3)$ (e) $f(3a, a)$ (f) $f(ab, a - b)$.

2. Let $f(x, y) = x + \sqrt[3]{xy}$. Find
   (a) $f(t, t^2)$ (b) $f(x, x^2)$ (c) $f(2y^2, 4y)$.

3. Let $f(x, y) = xy + 3$. Find
   (a) $f(x + y, x - y)$ (b) $f(xy, 3x^2 y^3)$.

4. Let $g(x) = x \sin x$. Find
   (a) $g(x/y)$ (b) $g(xy)$ (c) $g(x - y)$.

5. Find $F(g(x), h(y))$ if $F(x, y) = xe^{xy}$, $g(x) = x^3$, and $h(y) = 3y + 1$.

6. Find $g(u(x, y), v(x, y))$ if $g(x, y) = y \sin(x^2 y)$, $u(x, y) = x^2 y^3$, and $v(x, y) = \pi xy$.

7. Let $f(x, y) = x + 3x^2 y^2$, $x(t) = t^2$, and $y(t) = t^3$. Find
   (a) $f(x(t), y(t))$ (b) $f(x(0), y(0))$
   (c) $f(x(2), y(2))$.

8. Let $g(x, y) = ye^{-3x}$, $x(t) = \ln(t^2 + 1)$, and $y(t) = \sqrt{t}$. Find $g(x(t), y(t))$.

9. Refer to Table 13.1.1 to estimate the wind chill index when
   (a) the temperature is $25°$F and the wind speed is 7 mi/h
   (b) the temperature is $28°$F and the wind speed is 5 mi/h.

10. Refer to Table 13.1.1 to estimate the wind chill index when
    (a) the temperature is $35°$F and the wind speed is 14 mi/h
    (b) the temperature is $32°$F and the wind speed is 15 mi/h.

11. One method for determining relative humidity is to wet the bulb of a thermometer, whirl it through the air, and then compare the thermometer reading with the actual air temperature. If the relative humidity is less than 100%, the reading on the thermometer will be less than the temperature of the air. This difference in temperature is known as the *wet-bulb depression*. The accompanying table gives the relative humidity as a function of the air temperature and the wet-bulb depression. Use the table to complete parts (a)–(c).
    (a) What is the relative humidity if the air temperature is $20°$C and the wet-bulb thermometer reads $16°$C?
    (b) Estimate the relative humidity if the air temperature is $25°$C and the wet-bulb depression is $3.5°$C.
    (c) Estimate the relative humidity if the air temperature is $22°$C and the wet-bulb depression is $5°$C.

12. Use the table in Exercise 11 to complete parts (a)–(c).
    (a) What is the wet-bulb depression if the air temperature is $30°$C and the relative humidity is 73%?
    (b) Estimate the relative humidity if the air temperature is $15°$C and the wet-bulb depression is $4.25°$C.
    (c) Estimate the relative humidity if the air temperature is $26°$C and the wet-bulb depression is $3°$C.

13–16 These exercises involve functions of three variables.

13. Let $f(x, y, z) = xy^2 z^3 + 3$. Find
    (a) $f(2, 1, 2)$ (b) $f(-3, 2, 1)$
    (c) $f(0, 0, 0)$ (d) $f(a, a, a)$
    (e) $f(t, t^2, -t)$ (f) $f(a + b, a - b, b)$.

14. Let $f(x, y, z) = zxy + x$. Find
    (a) $f(x + y, x - y, x^2)$ (b) $f(xy, y/x, xz)$.

15. Find $F(f(x), g(y), h(z))$ if $F(x, y, z) = ye^{xyz}$, $f(x) = x^2$, $g(y) = y + 1$, and $h(z) = z^2$.

16. Find $g(u(x, y, z), v(x, y, z), w(x, y, z))$ if $g(x, y, z) = z \sin xy$, $u(x, y, z) = x^2 z^3$, $v(x, y, z) = \pi xyz$, and $w(x, y, z) = xy/z$.

17–18 These exercises are concerned with functions of four or more variables.

17. (a) Let $f(x, y, z, t) = x^2 y^3 \sqrt{z + t}$. Find $f(\sqrt{5}, 2, \pi, 3\pi)$.
    (b) Let $f(x_1, x_2, \ldots, x_n) = \sum_{k=1}^{n} kx_k$. Find $f(1, 1, \ldots, 1)$.

18. (a) Let $f(u, v, \lambda, \phi) = e^{u+v} \cos \lambda \tan \phi$. Find $f(-2, 2, 0, \pi/4)$.
    (b) Let $f(x_1, x_2, \ldots, x_n) = x_1^2 + x_2^2 + \cdots + x_n^2$. Find $f(1, 2, \ldots, n)$.

19–22 Sketch the domain of f. Use solid lines for portions of the boundary included in the domain and dashed lines for portions not included.

19. $f(x, y) = \ln(1 - x^2 - y^2)$ 20. $f(x, y) = \sqrt{x^2 + y^2 - 4}$

21. $f(x, y) = \dfrac{1}{x - y^2}$ 22. $f(x, y) = \ln xy$

23–24 Describe the domain of f in words.

23. (a) $f(x, y) = xe^{-\sqrt{y+2}}$
    (b) $f(x, y, z) = \sqrt{25 - x^2 - y^2 - z^2}$
    (c) $f(x, y, z) = e^{xyz}$

24. (a) $f(x, y) = \dfrac{\sqrt{4 - x^2}}{y^2 + 3}$ (b) $f(x, y) = \ln(y - 2x)$
    (c) $f(x, y, z) = \dfrac{xyz}{x + y + z}$

AIR TEMPERATURE (°C)

WET-BULB DEPRESSION (°C)	15	20	25	30
3	71	74	77	79
4	62	66	70	73
5	53	59	63	67

▲ Table Ex-11

25–28 True–False Determine whether the statement is true or false. Explain your answer. ■

25. If the domain of $f(x, y)$ is the xy-plane, then the domain of $f(\sin^{-1} t, \sqrt{t})$ is the interval $[0, 1]$.

26. If $f(x, y) = y/x$, then a contour $f(x, y) = m$ is the straight line $y = mx$.

27. The natural domain of $f(x, y, z) = \sqrt{1 - x^2 - y^2}$ is a disk of radius 1 centered at the origin in the xy-plane.

28. Every level surface of $f(x, y, z) = x + 2y + 3z$ is a plane.

29–38 Sketch the graph of f. ■

29. $f(x, y) = 3$

30. $f(x, y) = \sqrt{9 - x^2 - y^2}$

31. $f(x, y) = \sqrt{x^2 + y^2}$

32. $f(x, y) = x^2 + y^2$

33. $f(x, y) = x^2 - y^2$

34. $f(x, y) = 4 - x^2 - y^2$

35. $f(x, y) = \sqrt{x^2 + y^2 + 1}$

36. $f(x, y) = \sqrt{x^2 + y^2 - 1}$

37. $f(x, y) = y + 1$

38. $f(x, y) = x^2$

FOCUS ON CONCEPTS

39. In each part, match the contour plot with one of the functions

$$f(x, y) = \sqrt{x^2 + y^2}, \quad f(x, y) = x^2 + y^2,$$
$$f(x, y) = 1 - x^2 - y^2$$

by inspection, and explain your reasoning. Larger values of z are indicated by lighter colors in the contour plot, and the concentric contours correspond to equally spaced values of z.

(a) 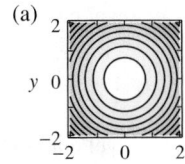 (b) 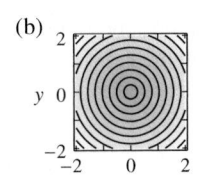 (c)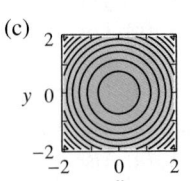

40. In each part, match the contour plot with one of the surfaces in the accompanying figure by inspection, and explain your reasoning. The larger the value of z, the lighter the color in the contour plot.

(a) 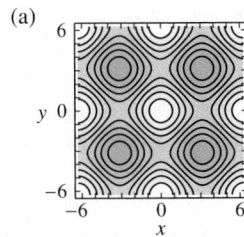 (b)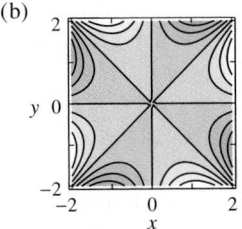

(c) 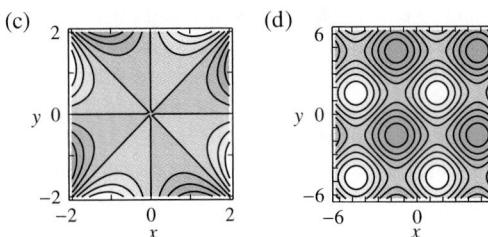 (d)

(I) (II)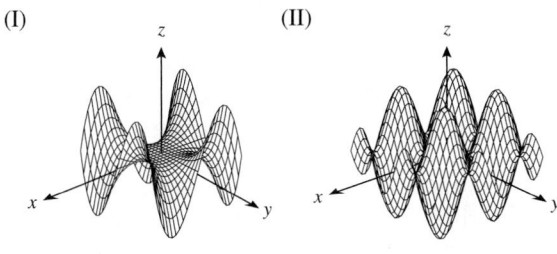

(III) (IV)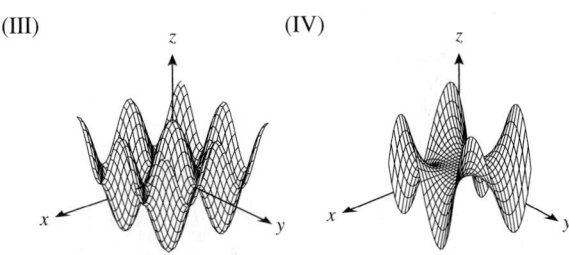

▲ **Figure Ex-40**

41. In each part, the questions refer to the contour map in the accompanying figure.
   (a) Is A or B the higher point? Explain your reasoning.
   (b) Is the slope steeper at point A or at point B? Explain your reasoning.
   (c) Starting at A and moving so that y remains constant and x increases, will the elevation begin to increase or decrease?
   (d) Starting at B and moving so that y remains constant and x increases, will the elevation begin to increase or decrease?
   (e) Starting at A and moving so that x remains constant and y decreases, will the elevation begin to increase or decrease?
   (f) Starting at B and moving so that x remains constant and y decreases, will the elevation begin to increase or decrease?

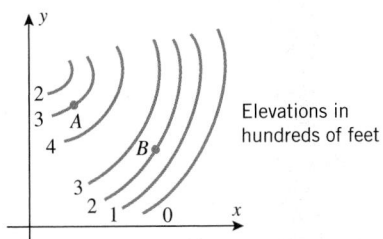

Elevations in hundreds of feet

◀ **Figure Ex-41**

42. A curve connecting points of equal atmospheric pressure on a weather map is called an **isobar**. On a typical weather map the isobars refer to pressure at mean sea level and are given in units of **millibars** (mb). Mathematically, isobars are level curves for the pressure function $p(x, y)$ defined at the geographic points (x, y) represented on the map. Tightly packed isobars correspond to steep slopes on the graph of the pressure function, and these are usually associated with strong winds—the steeper the slope, the greater the speed of the wind.

  (a) Referring to the accompanying weather map, is the wind speed greater in Medicine Hat, Alberta or in Chicago? Explain your reasoning.

  (b) Estimate the average rate of change in atmospheric pressure (in mb/mi) from Medicine Hat to Chicago, given that the distance between the two cities is approximately 1400 mi.

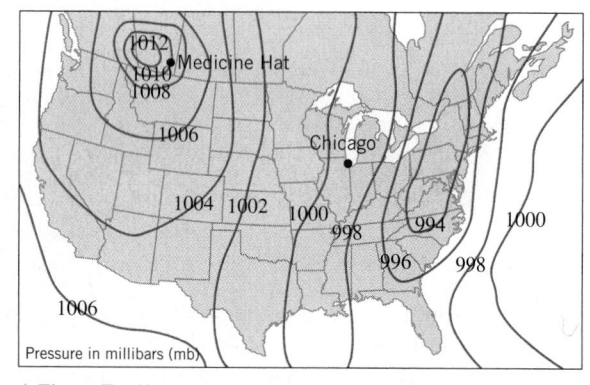

▲ **Figure Ex-42**

43–48 Sketch the level curve $z = k$ for the specified values of k. ■

43. $z = x^2 + y^2$; $k = 0, 1, 2, 3, 4$

44. $z = y/x$; $k = -2, -1, 0, 1, 2$

45. $z = x^2 + y$; $k = -2, -1, 0, 1, 2$

46. $z = x^2 + 9y^2$; $k = 0, 1, 2, 3, 4$

47. $z = x^2 - y^2$; $k = -2, -1, 0, 1, 2$

48. $z = y \csc x$; $k = -2, -1, 0, 1, 2$

49–52 Sketch the level surface $f(x, y, z) = k$. ■

49. $f(x, y, z) = 4x^2 + y^2 + 4z^2$; $k = 16$

50. $f(x, y, z) = x^2 + y^2 - z^2$; $k = 0$

51. $f(x, y, z) = z - x^2 - y^2 + 4$; $k = 7$

52. $f(x, y, z) = 4x - 2y + z$; $k = 1$

53–56 Describe the level surfaces in words. ■

53. $f(x, y, z) = (x - 2)^2 + y^2 + z^2$

54. $f(x, y, z) = 3x - y + 2z$ **55.** $f(x, y, z) = x^2 + z^2$

56. $f(x, y, z) = z - x^2 - y^2$

57. Let $f(x, y) = x^2 - 2x^3 + 3xy$. Find an equation of the level curve that passes through the point
  (a) $(-1, 1)$ (b) $(0, 0)$ (c) $(2, -1)$.

58. Let $f(x, y) = ye^x$. Find an equation of the level curve that passes through the point
  (a) $(\ln 2, 1)$ (b) $(0, 3)$ (c) $(1, -2)$.

59. Let $f(x, y, z) = x^2 + y^2 - z$. Find an equation of the level surface that passes through the point
  (a) $(1, -2, 0)$ (b) $(1, 0, 3)$ (c) $(0, 0, 0)$.

60. Let $f(x, y, z) = xyz + 3$. Find an equation of the level surface that passes through the point
  (a) $(1, 0, 2)$ (b) $(-2, 4, 1)$ (c) $(0, 0, 0)$.

61. If $T(x, y)$ is the temperature at a point (x, y) on a thin metal plate in the xy-plane, then the level curves of T are called **isothermal curves**. All points on such a curve are at the same temperature. Suppose that a plate occupies the first quadrant and $T(x, y) = xy$.
  (a) Sketch the isothermal curves on which $T = 1$, $T = 2$, and $T = 3$.
  (b) An ant, initially at $(1, 4)$, wants to walk on the plate so that the temperature along its path remains constant. What path should the ant take and what is the temperature along that path?

62. If $V(x, y)$ is the voltage or potential at a point (x, y) in the xy-plane, then the level curves of V are called **equipotential curves**. Along such a curve, the voltage remains constant. Given that
$$V(x, y) = \frac{8}{\sqrt{16 + x^2 + y^2}}$$
sketch the equipotential curves at which $V = 2.0$, $V = 1.0$, and $V = 0.5$.

63. Let $f(x, y) = x^2 + y^3$.
  (a) Use a graphing utility to generate the level curve that passes through the point $(2, -1)$.
  (b) Generate the level curve of height 1.

64. Let $f(x, y) = 2\sqrt{xy}$.
  (a) Use a graphing utility to generate the level curve that passes through the point $(2, 2)$.
  (b) Generate the level curve of height 8.

65. Let $f(x, y) = xe^{-(x^2+y^2)}$.
  (a) Use a CAS to generate the graph of f for $-2 \le x \le 2$ and $-2 \le y \le 2$.
  (b) Generate a contour plot for the surface, and confirm visually that it is consistent with the surface obtained in part (a).
  (c) Read the appropriate documentation and explore the effect of generating the graph of f from various viewpoints.

66. Let $f(x, y) = \frac{1}{10}e^x \sin y$.
  (a) Use a CAS to generate the graph of f for $0 \le x \le 4$ and $0 \le y \le 2\pi$.
  (b) Generate a contour plot for the surface, and confirm visually that it is consistent with the surface obtained in part (a).
  (cont.)

(c) Read the appropriate documentation and explore the effect of generating the graph of f from various viewpoints.

67. In each part, describe in words how the graph of g is related to the graph of f.
(a) $g(x, y) = f(x - 1, y)$ (b) $g(x, y) = 1 + f(x, y)$
(c) $g(x, y) = -f(x, y + 1)$

68. (a) Sketch the graph of $f(x, y) = e^{-(x^2+y^2)}$.
(b) Describe in words how the graph of the function $g(x, y) = e^{-a(x^2+y^2)}$ is related to the graph of f for positive values of a.

69. **Writing** Find a few practical examples of functions of two and three variables, and discuss how physical considerations affect their domains.

70. **Writing** Describe two different ways in which a function $f(x, y)$ can be represented geometrically. Discuss some of the advantages and disadvantages of each representation.

✔ **QUICK CHECK ANSWERS 13.1**

1. points (x, y) in the first or third quadrants; points (x, y) in the first quadrant   **2.** (a) $\frac{1}{4}$ (b) $-\frac{1}{4}$ (c) 0 (d) $1/(2y + 2)$
3. (a) $k > 0$ (b) the lines $x + y = \ln k$ **4.** (a) $0 < k \leq 1$ (b) spheres of radius $\sqrt{(1 - k)/k}$ for $0 < k < 1$, the single point $(0, 0, 0)$ for $k = 1$

13.2 LIMITS AND CONTINUITY

In this section we will introduce the notions of limit and continuity for functions of two or more variables. We will not go into great detail—our objective is to develop the basic concepts accurately and to obtain results needed in later sections. A more extensive study of these topics is usually given in advanced calculus.

■ LIMITS ALONG CURVES

For a function of one variable there are two one-sided limits at a point x_0, namely,

$$\lim_{x \to x_0^+} f(x) \quad \text{and} \quad \lim_{x \to x_0^-} f(x)$$

reflecting the fact that there are only two directions from which x can approach x_0, the right or the left. For functions of two or three variables the situation is more complicated because there are infinitely many different curves along which one point can approach another (Figure 13.2.1). Our first objective in this section is to define the limit of $f(x, y)$ as (x, y) approaches a point (x_0, y_0) along a curve C (and similarly for functions of three variables).

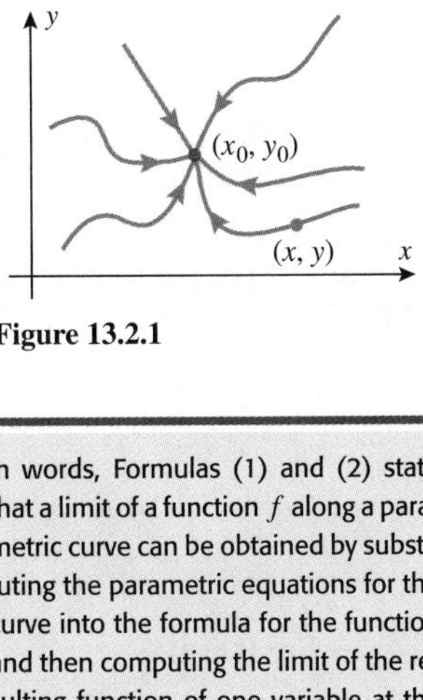

If C is a smooth parametric curve in 2-space or 3-space that is represented by the equations

$$x = x(t), \quad y = y(t) \quad \text{or} \quad x = x(t), \quad y = y(t), \quad z = z(t)$$

and if $x_0 = x(t_0)$, $y_0 = y(t_0)$, and $z_0 = z(t_0)$, then the limits

$$\lim_{\substack{(x, y) \to (x_0, y_0) \\ (\text{along } C)}} f(x, y) \quad \text{and} \quad \lim_{\substack{(x, y, z) \to (x_0, y_0, z_0) \\ (\text{along } C)}} f(x, y, z)$$

are defined by

$$\lim_{\substack{(x, y) \to (x_0, y_0) \\ (\text{along } C)}} f(x, y) = \lim_{t \to t_0} f(x(t), y(t)) \tag{1}$$

$$\lim_{\substack{(x, y, z) \to (x_0, y_0, z_0) \\ (\text{along } C)}} f(x, y, z) = \lim_{t \to t_0} f(x(t), y(t), z(t)) \tag{2}$$

▲ **Figure 13.2.1**

In words, Formulas (1) and (2) state that a limit of a function f along a parametric curve can be obtained by substituting the parametric equations for the curve into the formula for the function and then computing the limit of the resulting function of one variable at the appropriate point.

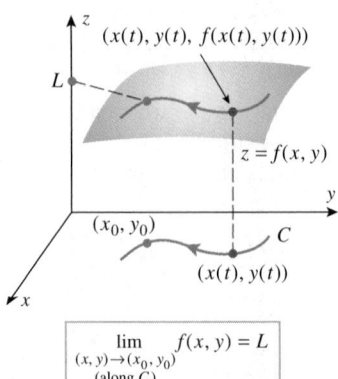

$$\lim_{\substack{(x,\,y)\to(x_0,\,y_0) \\ (\text{along } C)}} f(x, y) = L$$

▲ **Figure 13.2.2**

In these formulas the limit of the function of t must be treated as a one-sided limit if (x_0, y_0) or (x_0, y_0, z_0) is an endpoint of C.

A geometric interpretation of the limit along a curve for a function of two variables is shown in Figure 13.2.2: As the point $(x(t), y(t))$ moves along the curve C in the xy-plane toward (x_0, y_0), the point $(x(t), y(t), f(x(t), y(t)))$ moves directly above it along the graph of $z = f(x, y)$ with $f(x(t), y(t))$ approaching the limiting value L. In the figure we followed a common practice of omitting the zero z-coordinate for points in the xy-plane.

▶ **Example 1**   Figure 13.2.3*a* shows a computer-generated graph of the function

$$f(x, y) = -\frac{xy}{x^2 + y^2}$$

The graph reveals that the surface has a ridge above the line $y = -x$, which is to be expected since $f(x, y)$ has a constant value of $\frac{1}{2}$ for $y = -x$, except at $(0, 0)$ where f is undefined (verify). Moreover, the graph suggests that the limit of $f(x, y)$ as $(x, y) \to (0, 0)$ along a line through the origin varies with the direction of the line. Find this limit along

    (a) the x-axis   (b) the y-axis   (c) the line $y = x$

    (d) the line $y = -x$ (e) the parabola $y = x^2$

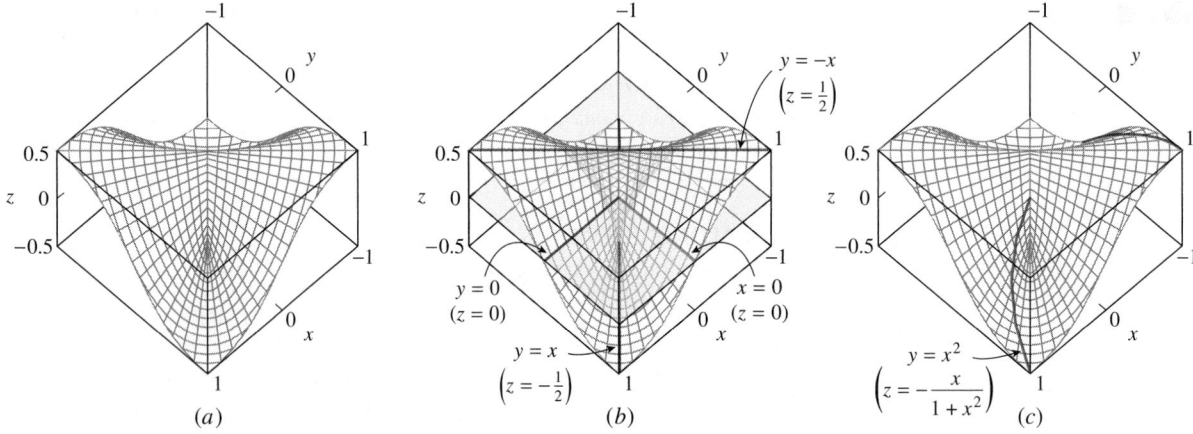

▲ **Figure 13.2.3**

Solution (a).   The x-axis has parametric equations $x = t$, $y = 0$, with $(0, 0)$ corresponding to $t = 0$, so

$$\lim_{(x,\,y)\to(0,\,0) \atop (\text{along } y=0)} f(x, y) = \lim_{t\to 0} f(t, 0) = \lim_{t\to 0}\left(-\frac{0}{t^2}\right) = \lim_{t\to 0} 0 = 0$$

which is consistent with Figure 13.2.3*b*.

Solution (b).   The y-axis has parametric equations $x = 0$, $y = t$, with $(0, 0)$ corresponding to $t = 0$, so

$$\lim_{(x,\,y)\to(0,\,0) \atop (\text{along } x=0)} f(x, y) = \lim_{t\to 0} f(0, t) = \lim_{t\to 0}\left(-\frac{0}{t^2}\right) = \lim_{t\to 0} 0 = 0$$

which is consistent with Figure 13.2.3*b*.

Solution (c). The line $y = x$ has parametric equations $x = t$, $y = t$, with $(0, 0)$ corresponding to $t = 0$, so

$$\lim_{\substack{(x, y) \to (0, 0) \\ \text{(along } y = x)}} f(x, y) = \lim_{t \to 0} f(t, t) = \lim_{t \to 0} \left(-\frac{t^2}{2t^2} \right) = \lim_{t \to 0} \left(-\frac{1}{2} \right) = -\frac{1}{2}$$

which is consistent with Figure 13.2.3*b*.

Solution (d). The line $y = -x$ has parametric equations $x = t$, $y = -t$, with $(0, 0)$ corresponding to $t = 0$, so

$$\lim_{\substack{(x, y) \to (0, 0) \\ \text{(along } y = -x)}} f(x, y) = \lim_{t \to 0} f(t, -t) = \lim_{t \to 0} \frac{t^2}{2t^2} = \lim_{t \to 0} \frac{1}{2} = \frac{1}{2}$$

which is consistent with Figure 13.2.3*b*.

Solution (e). The parabola $y = x^2$ has parametric equations $x = t$, $y = t^2$, with $(0, 0)$ corresponding to $t = 0$, so

$$\lim_{\substack{(x, y) \to (0, 0) \\ \text{(along } y = x^2)}} f(x, y) = \lim_{t \to 0} f(t, t^2) = \lim_{t \to 0} \left(-\frac{t^3}{t^2 + t^4} \right) = \lim_{t \to 0} \left(-\frac{t}{1 + t^2} \right) = 0$$

This is consistent with Figure 13.2.3*c*, which shows the parametric curve

$$x = t, \quad y = t^2, \quad z = -\frac{t}{1 + t^2}$$

superimposed on the surface. ◄

> For uniformity, we have chosen the same parameter t in each part of Example 1. We could have used x or y as the parameter, according to the context. For example, part (b) could be computed using
>
> $$\lim_{y \to 0} f(0, y)$$
>
> and part (e) could be computed using
>
> $$\lim_{x \to 0} f(x, x^2)$$

■ OPEN AND CLOSED SETS

Although limits along specific curves are useful for many purposes, they do not always tell the complete story about the limiting behavior of a function at a point; what is required is a limit concept that accounts for the behavior of the function in an *entire vicinity* of a point, not just along smooth curves passing through the point. For this purpose, we start by introducing some terminology.

Let C be a circle in 2-space that is centered at (x_0, y_0) and has positive radius δ. The set of points that are enclosed by the circle, but do not lie on the circle, is called the ***open disk*** of radius δ centered at (x_0, y_0), and the set of points that lie on the circle together with those enclosed by the circle is called the ***closed disk*** of radius δ centered at (x_0, y_0) (Figure 13.2.4). Analogously, if S is a sphere in 3-space that is centered at (x_0, y_0, z_0) and has positive radius δ, then the set of points that are enclosed by the sphere, but do not lie on the sphere, is called the ***open ball*** of radius δ centered at (x_0, y_0, z_0), and the set of points that lie on the sphere together with those enclosed by the sphere is called the ***closed ball*** of radius δ centered at (x_0, y_0, z_0). Disks and balls are the two-dimensional and three-dimensional analogs of intervals on a line.

The notions of "open" and "closed" can be extended to more general sets in 2-space and 3-space. If D is a set of points in 2-space, then a point (x_0, y_0) is called an ***interior point*** of D if there is *some* open disk centered at (x_0, y_0) that contains only points of D, and (x_0, y_0) is called a ***boundary point*** of D if *every* open disk centered at (x_0, y_0) contains both points in D and points not in D. The same terminology applies to sets in 3-space, but in that case the definitions use balls rather than disks (Figure 13.2.5).

For a set D in either 2-space or 3-space, the set of all interior points is called the ***interior*** of D and the set of all boundary points is called the ***boundary*** of D. Moreover, just as for disks, we say that D is ***closed*** if it contains all of its boundary points and ***open*** if it contains *none* of its boundary points. The set of all points in 2-space and the set of all points in

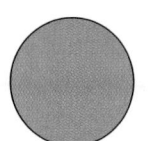

A closed disk includes all of the points on its bounding circle.

An open disk contains none of the points on its bounding circle.

▲ Figure 13.2.4

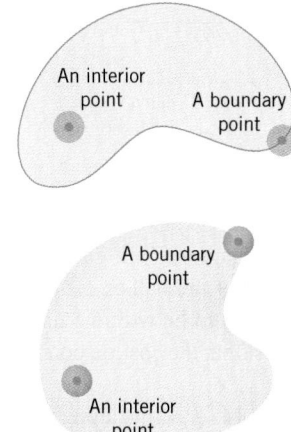

An interior point

A boundary point

A boundary point

An interior point

▲ Figure 13.2.5

3-space have no boundary points (why?), so by agreement they are regarded to be both open and closed.

■ GENERAL LIMITS OF FUNCTIONS OF TWO VARIABLES

The statement

$$\lim_{(x,y)\to(x_0,y_0)} f(x,y) = L$$

is intended to convey the idea that the value of $f(x, y)$ can be made as close as we like to the number L by restricting the point (x, y) to be sufficiently close to (but different from) the point (x_0, y_0). This idea has a formal expression in the following definition and is illustrated in Figure 13.2.6.

13.2.1 DEFINITION Let f be a function of two variables, and assume that f is defined at all points of some open disk centered at (x_0, y_0), except possibly at (x_0, y_0). We will write

$$\lim_{(x,y)\to(x_0,y_0)} f(x,y) = L \qquad (3)$$

if given any number $\epsilon > 0$, we can find a number $\delta > 0$ such that $f(x, y)$ satisfies

$$|f(x, y) - L| < \epsilon$$

whenever the distance between (x, y) and (x_0, y_0) satisfies

$$0 < \sqrt{(x - x_0)^2 + (y - y_0)^2} < \delta$$

When convenient, (3) can also be written as

$$\lim_{\substack{x\to x_0 \\ y\to y_0}} f(x,y) = L$$

or as

$$f(x, y) \to L \quad \text{as} \quad (x, y) \to (x_0, y_0)$$

In Figure 13.2.6, the condition

$$|f(x, y) - L| < \epsilon$$

is satisfied at each point (x, y) within the circular region. However, the fact that this condition is satisfied at the center of the circular region is not relevant to the limit.

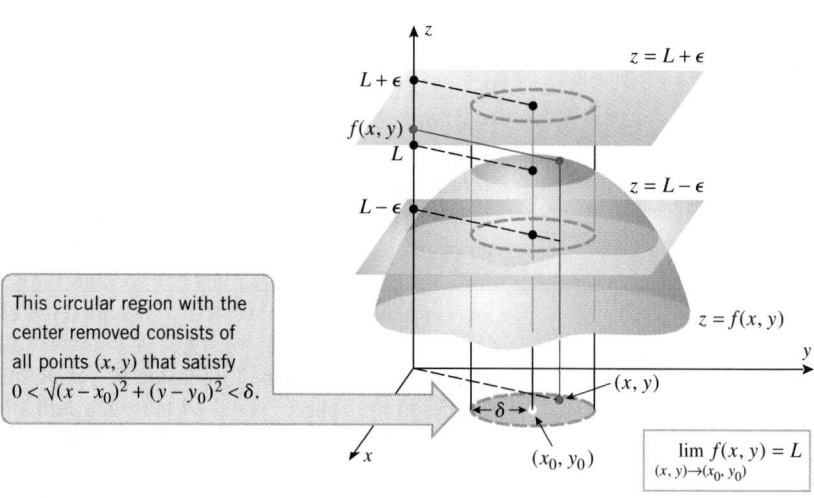

This circular region with the center removed consists of all points (x, y) that satisfy $0 < \sqrt{(x - x_0)^2 + (y - y_0)^2} < \delta$.

$$\lim_{(x,y)\to(x_0,y_0)} f(x,y) = L$$

▲ **Figure 13.2.6**

Another illustration of Definition 13.2.1 is shown in the "arrow diagram" of Figure 13.2.7. As in Figure 13.2.6, this figure is intended to convey the idea that the values of $f(x, y)$ can be forced within ϵ units of L on the z-axis by restricting (x, y) to lie within δ units of (x_0, y_0) in the xy-plane. We used a white dot at (x_0, y_0) to suggest that the epsilon condition need not hold at this point.

We note without proof that the standard properties of limits hold for limits along curves and for general limits of functions of two variables, so that computations involving such limits can be performed in the usual way.

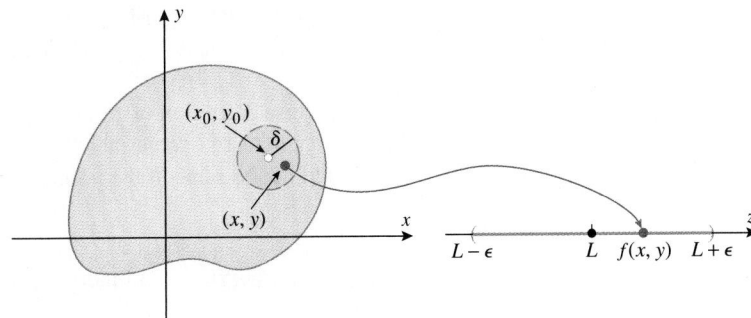

▶ **Figure 13.2.7**

▶ **Example 2**

$$\lim_{(x,y)\to(1,4)} [5x^3y^2 - 9] = \lim_{(x,y)\to(1,4)} [5x^3y^2] - \lim_{(x,y)\to(1,4)} 9$$

$$= 5\left[\lim_{(x,y)\to(1,4)} x\right]^3 \left[\lim_{(x,y)\to(1,4)} y\right]^2 - 9$$

$$= 5(1)^3(4)^2 - 9 = 71 \ \blacktriangleleft$$

■ **RELATIONSHIPS BETWEEN GENERAL LIMITS AND LIMITS ALONG SMOOTH CURVES**

Stated informally, if $f(x, y)$ has limit L as (x, y) approaches (x_0, y_0), then the value of $f(x, y)$ gets closer and closer to L as the distance between (x, y) and (x_0, y_0) approaches zero. Since this statement imposes no restrictions on the direction in which (x, y) approaches (x_0, y_0), it is plausible that the function $f(x, y)$ will also have the limit L as (x, y) approaches (x_0, y_0) along *any* smooth curve C. This is the implication of the following theorem, which we state without proof.

WARNING

In general, one cannot show that

$$\lim_{(x,y)\to(x_0,y_0)} f(x, y) = L$$

by showing that this limit holds along a specific curve, or even some specific family of curves. The problem is there may be some other curve along which the limit does not exist or has a value different from L (see Exercise 34, for example).

13.2.2 THEOREM

(a) *If $f(x, y) \to L$ as $(x, y) \to (x_0, y_0)$, then $f(x, y) \to L$ as $(x, y) \to (x_0, y_0)$ along any smooth curve.*

(b) *If the limit of $f(x, y)$ fails to exist as $(x, y) \to (x_0, y_0)$ along some smooth curve, or if $f(x, y)$ has different limits as $(x, y) \to (x_0, y_0)$ along two different smooth curves, then the limit of $f(x, y)$ does not exist as $(x, y) \to (x_0, y_0)$.*

▶ **Example 3** The limit

$$\lim_{(x,y)\to(0,0)} -\frac{xy}{x^2 + y^2}$$

does not exist because in Example 1 we found two different smooth curves along which this limit had different values. Specifically,

$$\lim_{\substack{(x,y)\to(0,0) \\ (\text{along } x=0)}} -\frac{xy}{x^2+y^2} = 0 \quad \text{and} \quad \lim_{\substack{(x,y)\to(0,0) \\ (\text{along } y=x)}} -\frac{xy}{x^2+y^2} = -\frac{1}{2} \ \blacktriangleleft$$

■ **CONTINUITY**

Stated informally, a function of one variable is continuous if its graph is an unbroken curve without jumps or holes. To extend this idea to functions of two variables, imagine that the graph of $z = f(x, y)$ is formed from a thin sheet of clay that has been molded into peaks

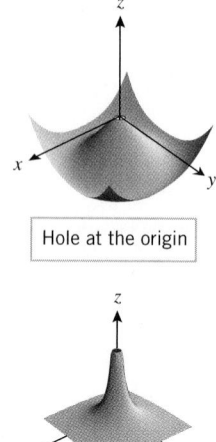

Hole at the origin

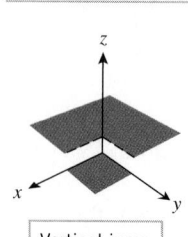

Infinite at the origin

Vertical jump at the origin

▲ **Figure 13.2.8**

and valleys. We will regard f as being continuous if the clay surface has no tears or holes. The functions graphed in Figure 13.2.8 fail to be continuous because of their behavior at $(0, 0)$.

The precise definition of continuity at a point for functions of two variables is similar to that for functions of one variable—we require the limit of the function and the value of the function to be the same at the point.

13.2.3   **DEFINITION**   A function $f(x, y)$ is said to be ***continuous at*** (x_0, y_0) if $f(x_0, y_0)$ is defined and if

$$\lim_{(x,y) \to (x_0, y_0)} f(x, y) = f(x_0, y_0)$$

In addition, if f is continuous at every point in an open set D, then we say that f is ***continuous on*** D, and if f is continuous at every point in the xy-plane, then we say that f is ***continuous everywhere***.

The following theorem, which we state without proof, illustrates some of the ways in which continuous functions can be combined to produce new continuous functions.

13.2.4   **THEOREM**

(a)   If $g(x)$ is continuous at x_0 and $h(y)$ is continuous at y_0, then $f(x, y) = g(x)h(y)$ is continuous at (x_0, y_0).

(b)   If $h(x, y)$ is continuous at (x_0, y_0) and $g(u)$ is continuous at $u = h(x_0, y_0)$, then the composition $f(x, y) = g(h(x, y))$ is continuous at (x_0, y_0).

(c)   If $f(x, y)$ is continuous at (x_0, y_0), and if $x(t)$ and $y(t)$ are continuous at t_0 with $x(t_0) = x_0$ and $y(t_0) = y_0$, then the composition $f(x(t), y(t))$ is continuous at t_0.

▶ **Example 4**   Use Theorem 13.2.4 to show that the functions $f(x, y) = 3x^2y^5$ and $f(x, y) = \sin(3x^2y^5)$ are continuous everywhere.

Solution.   The polynomials $g(x) = 3x^2$ and $h(y) = y^5$ are continuous at every real number, and therefore by part (*a*) of Theorem 13.2.4, the function $f(x, y) = 3x^2y^5$ is continuous at every point (x, y) in the xy-plane. Since $3x^2y^5$ is continuous at every point in the xy-plane and $\sin u$ is continuous at every real number u, it follows from part (*b*) of Theorem 13.2.4 that the composition $f(x, y) = \sin(3x^2y^5)$ is continuous everywhere. ◀

Theorem 13.2.4 is one of a whole class of theorems about continuity of functions in two or more variables. The content of these theorems can be summarized informally with three basic principles:

Recognizing Continuous Functions

- A composition of continuous functions is continuous.
- A sum, difference, or product of continuous functions is continuous.
- A quotient of continuous functions is continuous, except where the denominator is zero.

By using these principles and Theorem 13.2.4, you should be able to confirm that the following functions are all continuous everywhere:

$$xe^{xy} + y^{2/3}, \quad \cosh(xy^3) - |xy|, \quad \frac{xy}{1 + x^2 + y^2}$$

▶ **Example 5** Evaluate $\displaystyle\lim_{(x,y) \to (-1,2)} \frac{xy}{x^2 + y^2}$.

Solution. Since $f(x, y) = xy/(x^2 + y^2)$ is continuous at $(-1, 2)$ (why?), it follows from the definition of continuity for functions of two variables that

$$\lim_{(x,y) \to (-1,2)} \frac{xy}{x^2 + y^2} = \frac{(-1)(2)}{(-1)^2 + (2)^2} = -\frac{2}{5} \quad \blacktriangleleft$$

▶ **Example 6** Since the function

$$f(x, y) = \frac{x^3 y^2}{1 - xy}$$

is a quotient of continuous functions, it is continuous except where $1 - xy = 0$. Thus, $f(x, y)$ is continuous everywhere except on the hyperbola $xy = 1$. ◀

■ LIMITS AT DISCONTINUITIES

Sometimes it is easy to recognize when a limit does not exist. For example, it is evident that

$$\lim_{(x,y) \to (0,0)} \frac{1}{x^2 + y^2} = +\infty$$

which implies that the values of the function approach $+\infty$ as $(x, y) \to (0, 0)$ along any smooth curve (Figure 13.2.9). However, it is not evident whether the limit

$$\lim_{(x,y) \to (0,0)} (x^2 + y^2) \ln(x^2 + y^2)$$

exists because it is an indeterminate form of type $0 \cdot \infty$. Although L'Hôpital's rule cannot be applied directly, the following example illustrates a method for finding this limit by converting to polar coordinates.

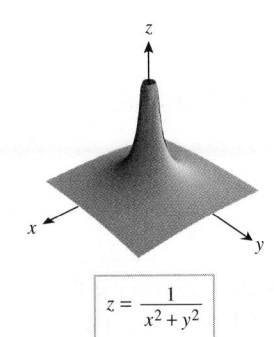

$$z = \frac{1}{x^2 + y^2}$$

▲ **Figure 13.2.9**

▶ **Example 7** Find $\displaystyle\lim_{(x,y) \to (0,0)} (x^2 + y^2) \ln(x^2 + y^2)$.

Solution. Let (r, θ) be polar coordinates of the point (x, y) with $r \geq 0$. Then we have

$$x = r \cos\theta, \quad y = r \sin\theta, \quad r^2 = x^2 + y^2$$

Moreover, since $r \geq 0$ we have $r = \sqrt{x^2 + y^2}$, so that $r \to 0^+$ if and only if $(x, y) \to (0, 0)$. Thus, we can rewrite the given limit as

$$\lim_{(x,y) \to (0,0)} (x^2 + y^2) \ln(x^2 + y^2) = \lim_{r \to 0^+} r^2 \ln r^2$$

$$= \lim_{r \to 0^+} \frac{2 \ln r}{1/r^2} \qquad \boxed{\text{This converts the limit to an indeterminate form of type } \infty/\infty.}$$

$$= \lim_{r \to 0^+} \frac{2/r}{-2/r^3} \qquad \boxed{\text{L'Hôpital's rule}}$$

$$= \lim_{r \to 0^+} (-r^2) = 0 \quad \blacktriangleleft$$

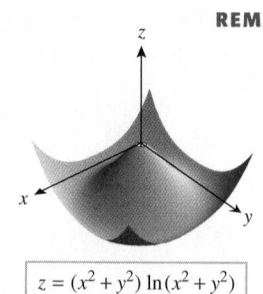

$$z = (x^2 + y^2) \ln(x^2 + y^2)$$

▲ **Figure 13.2.10**

REMARK The graph of $f(x, y) = (x^2 + y^2) \ln(x^2 + y^2)$ in Example 7 is a surface with a hole (sometimes called a *puncture*) at the origin (Figure 13.2.10). We can remove this discontinuity by *defining* $f(0, 0)$ to be 0. (See Exercises 39 and 40, which also deal with the notion of a "removable" discontinuity.)

■ CONTINUITY AT BOUNDARY POINTS

Recall that in our study of continuity for functions of one variable, we first defined continuity at a point, then continuity on an open interval, and then, by using one-sided limits, we extended the notion of continuity to include the boundary points of the interval. Similarly, for functions of two variables one can extend the notion of continuity of $f(x, y)$ to the boundary of its domain by modifying Definition 13.2.1 appropriately so that (x, y) is restricted to approach (x_0, y_0) through points lying wholly in the domain of f. We will omit the details.

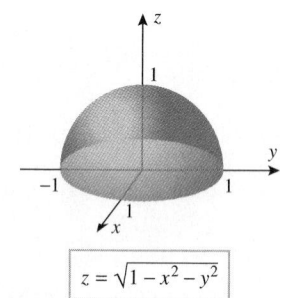

$$z = \sqrt{1 - x^2 - y^2}$$

▲ **Figure 13.2.11**

▶ **Example 8** The graph of the function $f(x, y) = \sqrt{1 - x^2 - y^2}$ is the upper hemisphere shown in Figure 13.2.11, and the natural domain of f is the closed unit disk

$$x^2 + y^2 \leq 1$$

The graph of f has no tears or holes, so it passes our "intuitive test" of continuity. In this case the continuity at a point (x_0, y_0) on the boundary reflects the fact that

$$\lim_{(x,y) \to (x_0, y_0)} \sqrt{1 - x^2 - y^2} = \sqrt{1 - x_0^2 - y_0^2} = 0$$

when (x, y) is restricted to points on the closed unit disk $x^2 + y^2 \leq 1$. It follows that f is continuous on its domain. ◀

■ EXTENSIONS TO THREE VARIABLES

All of the results in this section can be extended to functions of three or more variables. For example, the distance between the points (x, y, z) and (x_0, y_0, z_0) in 3-space is

$$\sqrt{(x - x_0)^2 + (y - y_0)^2 + (z - z_0)^2}$$

so the natural extension of Definition 13.2.1 to 3-space is as follows:

13.2.5 **DEFINITION** Let f be a function of three variables, and assume that f is defined at all points within a ball centered at (x_0, y_0, z_0), except possibly at (x_0, y_0, z_0). We will write

$$\lim_{(x,y,z) \to (x_0, y_0, z_0)} f(x, y, z) = L \tag{4}$$

if given any number $\epsilon > 0$, we can find a number $\delta > 0$ such that $f(x, y, z)$ satisfies

$$|f(x, y, z) - L| < \epsilon$$

whenever the distance between (x, y, z) and (x_0, y_0, z_0) satisfies

$$0 < \sqrt{(x - x_0)^2 + (y - y_0)^2 + (z - z_0)^2} < \delta$$

As with functions of one and two variables, we define a function $f(x, y, z)$ of three variables to be continuous at a point (x_0, y_0, z_0) if the limit of the function and the value of the function are the same at this point; that is,

$$\lim_{(x,y,z) \to (x_0, y_0, z_0)} f(x, y, z) = f(x_0, y_0, z_0)$$

Although we will omit the details, the properties of limits and continuity that we discussed for functions of two variables, including the notion of continuity at boundary points, carry over to functions of three variables.

QUICK CHECK EXERCISES 13.2 (See page 927 for answers.)

1. Let

$$f(x, y) = \frac{x^2 - y^2}{x^2 + y^2}$$

Determine the limit of $f(x, y)$ as (x, y) approaches $(0, 0)$ along the curve C.
(a) $C: x = 0$ (b) $C: y = 0$
(c) $C: y = x$ (d) $C: y = x^2$

2. (a) $\lim\limits_{(x,y) \to (3,2)} x \cos \pi y = $ _____

(b) $\lim\limits_{(x,y) \to (0,1)} e^{xy^2} = $ _____

(c) $\lim\limits_{(x,y) \to (0,0)} (x^2 + y^2) \sin\left(\dfrac{1}{x^2 + y^2}\right) = $ _____

3. A function $f(x, y)$ is continuous at (x_0, y_0) provided $f(x_0, y_0)$ exists and provided $f(x, y)$ has limit _____ as (x, y) approaches _____.

4. Determine all values of the constant a such that the function $f(x, y) = \sqrt{x^2 - ay^2 + 1}$ is continuous everywhere.

EXERCISE SET 13.2

1–6 Use limit laws and continuity properties to evaluate the limit. ■

1. $\lim\limits_{(x,y) \to (1,3)} (4xy^2 - x)$

2. $\lim\limits_{(x,y) \to (1/2,\pi)} (xy^2 \sin xy)$

3. $\lim\limits_{(x,y) \to (-1,2)} \dfrac{xy^3}{x + y}$

4. $\lim\limits_{(x,y) \to (1,-3)} e^{2x - y^2}$

5. $\lim\limits_{(x,y) \to (0,0)} \ln(1 + x^2 y^3)$

6. $\lim\limits_{(x,y) \to (4,-2)} x \sqrt[3]{y^3 + 2x}$

7–8 Show that the limit does not exist by considering the limits as $(x, y) \to (0, 0)$ along the coordinate axes. ■

7. (a) $\lim\limits_{(x,y) \to (0,0)} \dfrac{3}{x^2 + 2y^2}$

(b) $\lim\limits_{(x,y) \to (0,0)} \dfrac{x + y}{2x^2 + y^2}$

8. (a) $\lim\limits_{(x,y) \to (0,0)} \dfrac{x - y}{x^2 + y^2}$

(b) $\lim\limits_{(x,y) \to (0,0)} \dfrac{\cos xy}{x^2 + y^2}$

9–12 Evaluate the limit using the substitution $z = x^2 + y^2$ and observing that $z \to 0^+$ if and only if $(x, y) \to (0, 0)$. ■

9. $\lim\limits_{(x,y) \to (0,0)} \dfrac{\sin(x^2 + y^2)}{x^2 + y^2}$

10. $\lim\limits_{(x,y) \to (0,0)} \dfrac{1 - \cos(x^2 + y^2)}{x^2 + y^2}$

11. $\lim\limits_{(x,y) \to (0,0)} e^{-1/(x^2 + y^2)}$

12. $\lim\limits_{(x,y) \to (0,0)} \dfrac{e^{-1/\sqrt{x^2 + y^2}}}{\sqrt{x^2 + y^2}}$

13–22 Determine whether the limit exists. If so, find its value. ■

13. $\lim\limits_{(x,y) \to (0,0)} \dfrac{x^4 - y^4}{x^2 + y^2}$

14. $\lim\limits_{(x,y) \to (0,0)} \dfrac{x^4 - 16y^4}{x^2 + 4y^2}$

15. $\lim\limits_{(x,y) \to (0,0)} \dfrac{xy}{3x^2 + 2y^2}$

16. $\lim\limits_{(x,y) \to (0,0)} \dfrac{1 - x^2 - y^2}{x^2 + y^2}$

17. $\lim\limits_{(x,y,z) \to (2,-1,2)} \dfrac{xz^2}{\sqrt{x^2 + y^2 + z^2}}$

18. $\lim\limits_{(x,y,z) \to (2,0,-1)} \ln(2x + y - z)$

19. $\lim\limits_{(x,y,z) \to (0,0,0)} \dfrac{\sin(x^2 + y^2 + z^2)}{\sqrt{x^2 + y^2 + z^2}}$

20. $\lim\limits_{(x,y,z) \to (0,0,0)} \dfrac{\sin\sqrt{x^2 + y^2 + z^2}}{x^2 + y^2 + z^2}$

21. $\lim\limits_{(x,y,z) \to (0,0,0)} \dfrac{e^{\sqrt{x^2 + y^2 + z^2}}}{\sqrt{x^2 + y^2 + z^2}}$

22. $\lim\limits_{(x,y,z) \to (0,0,0)} \tan^{-1}\left[\dfrac{1}{x^2 + y^2 + z^2}\right]$

23–26 Evaluate the limits by converting to polar coordinates, as in Example 7. ■

23. $\lim\limits_{(x,y) \to (0,0)} \sqrt{x^2 + y^2} \ln(x^2 + y^2)$

24. $\lim\limits_{(x,y) \to (0,0)} y \ln(x^2 + y^2)$

25. $\lim\limits_{(x,y) \to (0,0)} \dfrac{x^2 y^2}{\sqrt{x^2 + y^2}}$

26. $\lim\limits_{(x,y) \to (0,0)} \dfrac{xy}{\sqrt{x^2 + 2y^2}}$

27–28 Evaluate the limits by converting to spherical coordinates (ρ, θ, ϕ) and by observing that $\rho \to 0^+$ if and only if $(x, y, z) \to (0, 0, 0)$. ■

27. $\lim\limits_{(x,y,z) \to (0,0,0)} \dfrac{xyz}{x^2 + y^2 + z^2}$

28. $\lim\limits_{(x,y,z) \to (0,0,0)} \dfrac{\sin x \sin y}{\sqrt{x^2 + 2y^2 + 3z^2}}$

29–32 True–False Determine whether the statement is true or false. Explain your answer. ■

29. If D is an open set in 2-space or in 3-space, then every point in D is an interior point of D.

30. If $f(x, y) \to L$ as (x, y) approaches $(0, 0)$ along the x-axis, and if $f(x, y) \to L$ as (x, y) approaches $(0, 0)$ along the y-axis, then $\lim_{(x,y) \to (0,0)} f(x, y) = L$.

31. If f and g are functions of two variables such that $f + g$ and fg are both continuous, then f and g are themselves continuous.

32. If $\lim_{x \to 0^+} f(x) = L \neq 0$, then

$$\lim_{(x,y) \to (0,0)} \frac{x^2 + y^2}{f(x^2 + y^2)} = 0$$

FOCUS ON CONCEPTS

33. The accompanying figure shows a portion of the graph of

$$f(x, y) = \frac{x^2 y}{x^4 + y^2}$$

(a) Based on the graph in the figure, does $f(x, y)$ have a limit as $(x, y) \to (0, 0)$? Explain your reasoning.

(b) Show that $f(x, y) \to 0$ as $(x, y) \to (0, 0)$ along any line $y = mx$. Does this imply that $f(x, y) \to 0$ as $(x, y) \to (0, 0)$? Explain.

(c) Show that $f(x, y) \to \frac{1}{2}$ as $(x, y) \to (0, 0)$ along the parabola $y = x^2$, and confirm visually that this is consistent with the graph of $f(x, y)$.

(d) Based on parts (b) and (c), does $f(x, y)$ have a limit as $(x, y) \to (0, 0)$? Is this consistent with your answer to part (a)?

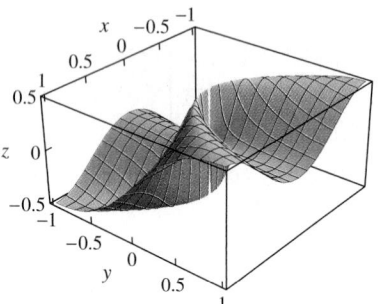

◀ **Figure Ex-33**

34. (a) Show that the value of

$$\frac{x^3 y}{2x^6 + y^2}$$

approaches 0 as $(x, y) \to (0, 0)$ along any straight line $y = mx$, or along any parabola $y = kx^2$.

(b) Show that

$$\lim_{(x,y) \to (0,0)} \frac{x^3 y}{2x^6 + y^2}$$

does not exist by letting $(x, y) \to (0, 0)$ along the curve $y = x^3$.

35. (a) Show that the value of

$$\frac{xyz}{x^2 + y^4 + z^4}$$

approaches 0 as $(x, y, z) \to (0, 0, 0)$ along any line $x = at$, $y = bt$, $z = ct$.

(b) Show that the limit

$$\lim_{(x,y,z) \to (0,0,0)} \frac{xyz}{x^2 + y^4 + z^4}$$

does not exist by letting $(x, y, z) \to (0, 0, 0)$ along the curve $x = t^2$, $y = t$, $z = t$.

36. Find $\displaystyle\lim_{(x,y) \to (0,1)} \tan^{-1}\left[\frac{x^2 + 1}{x^2 + (y-1)^2}\right]$.

37. Find $\displaystyle\lim_{(x,y) \to (0,1)} \tan^{-1}\left[\frac{x^2 - 1}{x^2 + (y-1)^2}\right]$.

38. Let $f(x, y) = \begin{cases} \dfrac{\sin(x^2 + y^2)}{x^2 + y^2}, & (x, y) \neq (0, 0) \\ 1, & (x, y) = (0, 0). \end{cases}$

Show that f is continuous at $(0, 0)$.

39–40 A function $f(x, y)$ is said to have a ***removable discontinuity*** at (x_0, y_0) if $\lim_{(x,y) \to (x_0, y_0)} f(x, y)$ exists but f is not continuous at (x_0, y_0), either because f is not defined at (x_0, y_0) or because $f(x_0, y_0)$ differs from the value of the limit. Determine whether $f(x, y)$ has a removable discontinuity at $(0, 0)$. ■

39. $f(x, y) = \dfrac{x^2}{x^2 + y^2}$

40. $f(x, y) = xy \ln(x^2 + y^2)$

41–48 Sketch the largest region on which the function f is continuous. ■

41. $f(x, y) = y \ln(1 + x)$

42. $f(x, y) = \sqrt{x - y}$

43. $f(x, y) = \dfrac{x^2 y}{\sqrt{25 - x^2 - y^2}}$

44. $f(x, y) = \ln(2x - y + 1)$

45. $f(x, y) = \cos\left(\dfrac{xy}{1 + x^2 + y^2}\right)$

46. $f(x, y) = e^{1-xy}$

47. $f(x, y) = \sin^{-1}(xy)$

48. $f(x, y) = \tan^{-1}(y - x)$

49–52 Describe the largest region on which the function f is continuous. ■

49. $f(x, y, z) = 3x^2 e^{yz} \cos(xyz)$

50. $f(x, y, z) = \ln(4 - x^2 - y^2 - z^2)$

51. $f(x, y, z) = \dfrac{y + 1}{x^2 + z^2 - 1}$

52. $f(x, y, z) = \sin\sqrt{x^2 + y^2 + 3z^2}$

53. Writing Describe the procedure you would use to determine whether or not the limit

$$\lim_{(x,y) \to (x_0, y_0)} f(x, y)$$

exists.

54. Writing In your own words, state the geometric interpretations of ϵ and δ in the definition of

$$\lim_{(x,y) \to (x_0, y_0)} f(x, y) = L$$

given in Definition 13.2.1.

✔ **QUICK CHECK ANSWERS 13.2**

1. (a) -1 (b) 1 (c) 0 (d) 1   2. (a) 3 (b) 1 (c) 0   3. $f(x_0, y_0)$; (x_0, y_0) 4. $a \leq 0$

13.3 PARTIAL DERIVATIVES

In this section we will develop the mathematical tools for studying rates of change that involve two or more independent variables.

◼ PARTIAL DERIVATIVES OF FUNCTIONS OF TWO VARIABLES

If $z = f(x, y)$, then one can inquire how the value of z changes if y is held fixed and x is allowed to vary, or if x is held fixed and y is allowed to vary. For example, the ideal gas law in physics states that under appropriate conditions the pressure exerted by a gas is a function of the volume of the gas and its temperature. Thus, a physicist studying gases might be interested in the rate of change of the pressure if the volume is held fixed and the temperature is allowed to vary, or if the temperature is held fixed and the volume is allowed to vary. We now define a derivative that describes such rates of change.

Suppose that (x_0, y_0) is a point in the domain of a function $f(x, y)$. If we fix $y = y_0$, then $f(x, y_0)$ is a function of the variable x alone. The value of the derivative

$$\frac{d}{dx}[f(x, y_0)]$$

at x_0 then gives us a measure of the instantaneous rate of change of f with respect to x at the point (x_0, y_0). Similarly, the value of the derivative

$$\frac{d}{dy}[f(x_0, y)]$$

at y_0 gives us a measure of the instantaneous rate of change of f with respect to y at the point (x_0, y_0). These derivatives are so basic to the study of differential calculus of multivariable functions that they have their own name and notation.

13.3.1 DEFINITION If $z = f(x, y)$ and (x_0, y_0) is a point in the domain of f, then the ***partial derivative of f with respect to x*** at (x_0, y_0) [also called the ***partial derivative of z with respect to x*** at (x_0, y_0)] is the derivative at x_0 of the function that results when $y = y_0$ is held fixed and x is allowed to vary. This partial derivative is denoted by $f_x(x_0, y_0)$ and is given by

$$f_x(x_0, y_0) = \frac{d}{dx}[f(x, y_0)]\bigg|_{x=x_0} = \lim_{\Delta x \to 0} \frac{f(x_0 + \Delta x, y_0) - f(x_0, y_0)}{\Delta x} \quad (1)$$

Similarly, the ***partial derivative of f with respect to y*** at (x_0, y_0) [also called the ***partial derivative of z with respect to y*** at (x_0, y_0)] is the derivative at y_0 of the function that results when $x = x_0$ is held fixed and y is allowed to vary. This partial derivative is denoted by $f_y(x_0, y_0)$ and is given by

$$f_y(x_0, y_0) = \frac{d}{dy}[f(x_0, y)]\bigg|_{y=y_0} = \lim_{\Delta y \to 0} \frac{f(x_0, y_0 + \Delta y) - f(x_0, y_0)}{\Delta y} \quad (2)$$

The limits in (1) and (2) show the relationship between partial derivatives and derivatives of functions of one variable. In practice, our usual method for computing partial derivatives is to hold one variable fixed and then differentiate the resulting function using the derivative rules for functions of one variable.

▶ **Example 1** Find $f_x(1, 3)$ and $f_y(1, 3)$ for the function $f(x, y) = 2x^3y^2 + 2y + 4x$.

Solution. Since

$$f_x(x, 3) = \frac{d}{dx}[f(x, 3)] = \frac{d}{dx}[18x^3 + 4x + 6] = 54x^2 + 4$$

we have $f_x(1, 3) = 54 + 4 = 58$. Also, since

$$f_y(1, y) = \frac{d}{dy}[f(1, y)] = \frac{d}{dy}[2y^2 + 2y + 4] = 4y + 2$$

we have $f_y(1, 3) = 4(3) + 2 = 14$. ◀

◼ THE PARTIAL DERIVATIVE FUNCTIONS

Formulas (1) and (2) define the partial derivatives of a function at a specific point (x_0, y_0). However, often it will be desirable to omit the subscripts and think of the partial derivatives as functions of the variables x and y. These functions are

$$f_x(x, y) = \lim_{\Delta x \to 0} \frac{f(x + \Delta x, y) - f(x, y)}{\Delta x} \qquad f_y(x, y) = \lim_{\Delta y \to 0} \frac{f(x, y + \Delta y) - f(x, y)}{\Delta y}$$

The following example gives an alternative way of performing the computations in Example 1.

▶ **Example 2** Find $f_x(x, y)$ and $f_y(x, y)$ for $f(x, y) = 2x^3y^2 + 2y + 4x$, and use those partial derivatives to compute $f_x(1, 3)$ and $f_y(1, 3)$.

Solution. Keeping y fixed and differentiating with respect to x yields

$$f_x(x, y) = \frac{d}{dx}[2x^3y^2 + 2y + 4x] = 6x^2y^2 + 4$$

and keeping x fixed and differentiating with respect to y yields

$$f_y(x, y) = \frac{d}{dy}[2x^3y^2 + 2y + 4x] = 4x^3y + 2$$

Thus,

$$f_x(1, 3) = 6(1^2)(3^2) + 4 = 58 \quad \text{and} \quad f_y(1, 3) = 4(1^3)3 + 2 = 14$$

which agree with the results in Example 1. ◀

TECHNOLOGY MASTERY

Computer algebra systems have specific commands for calculating partial derivatives. If you have a CAS, use it to find the partial derivatives $f_x(x, y)$ and $f_y(x, y)$ in Example 2.

◼ PARTIAL DERIVATIVE NOTATION

If $z = f(x, y)$, then the partial derivatives f_x and f_y are also denoted by the symbols

The symbol ∂ is called a partial derivative sign. It is derived from the Cyrillic alphabet.

$$\frac{\partial f}{\partial x}, \quad \frac{\partial z}{\partial x} \qquad \text{and} \qquad \frac{\partial f}{\partial y}, \quad \frac{\partial z}{\partial y}$$

Some typical notations for the partial derivatives of $z = f(x, y)$ at a point (x_0, y_0) are

$$\left.\frac{\partial f}{\partial x}\right|_{x=x_0, y=y_0}, \quad \left.\frac{\partial z}{\partial x}\right|_{(x_0, y_0)}, \quad \left.\frac{\partial f}{\partial x}\right|_{(x_0, y_0)}, \quad \frac{\partial f}{\partial x}(x_0, y_0), \quad \frac{\partial z}{\partial x}(x_0, y_0)$$

▶ **Example 3**   Find $\partial z/\partial x$ and $\partial z/\partial y$ if $z = x^4 \sin(xy^3)$.

Solution.

$$\frac{\partial z}{\partial x} = \frac{\partial}{\partial x}[x^4 \sin(xy^3)] = x^4 \frac{\partial}{\partial x}[\sin(xy^3)] + \sin(xy^3) \cdot \frac{\partial}{\partial x}(x^4)$$

$$= x^4 \cos(xy^3) \cdot y^3 + \sin(xy^3) \cdot 4x^3 = x^4 y^3 \cos(xy^3) + 4x^3 \sin(xy^3)$$

$$\frac{\partial z}{\partial y} = \frac{\partial}{\partial y}[x^4 \sin(xy^3)] = x^4 \frac{\partial}{\partial y}[\sin(xy^3)] + \sin(xy^3) \cdot \frac{\partial}{\partial y}(x^4)$$

$$= x^4 \cos(xy^3) \cdot 3xy^2 + \sin(xy^3) \cdot 0 = 3x^5 y^2 \cos(xy^3) \quad ◀$$

■ **PARTIAL DERIVATIVES VIEWED AS RATES OF CHANGE AND SLOPES**

Recall that if $y = f(x)$, then the value of $f'(x_0)$ can be interpreted either as the rate of change of y with respect to x at x_0 or as the slope of the tangent line to the graph of f at x_0. Partial derivatives have analogous interpretations. To see that this is so, suppose that C_1 is the intersection of the surface $z = f(x, y)$ with the plane $y = y_0$ and that C_2 is its intersection with the plane $x = x_0$ (Figure 13.3.1). Thus, $f_x(x, y_0)$ can be interpreted as the rate of change of z with respect to x along the curve C_1, and $f_y(x_0, y)$ can be interpreted as the rate of change of z with respect to y along the curve C_2. In particular, $f_x(x_0, y_0)$ is the rate of change of z with respect to x along the curve C_1 at the point (x_0, y_0), and $f_y(x_0, y_0)$ is the rate of change of z with respect to y along the curve C_2 at the point (x_0, y_0).

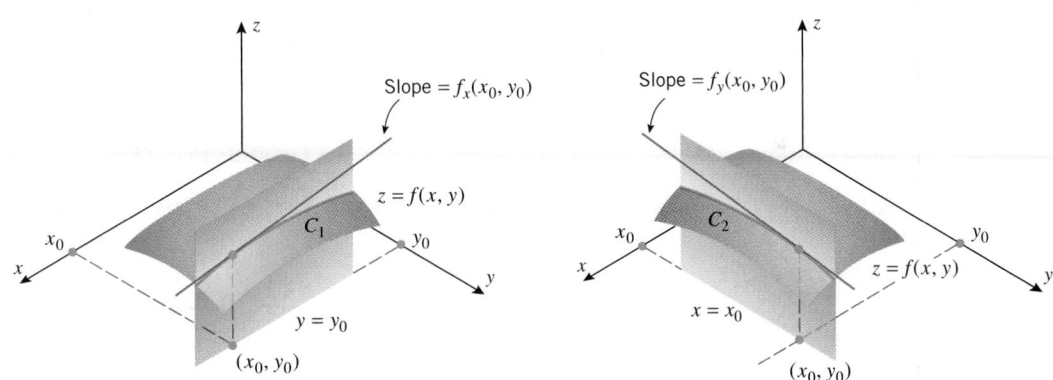

▲ **Figure 13.3.1**

▶ **Example 4**   Recall that the wind chill temperature index is given by the formula

$$W = 35.74 + 0.6215T + (0.4275T - 35.75)v^{0.16}$$

Compute the partial derivative of W with respect to v at the point $(T, v) = (25, 10)$ and interpret this partial derivative as a rate of change.

Solution.   Holding T fixed and differentiating with respect to v yields

$$\frac{\partial W}{\partial v}(T, v) = 0 + 0 + (0.4275T - 35.75)(0.16)v^{0.16-1} = (0.4275T - 35.75)(0.16)v^{-0.84}$$

Since W is in degrees Fahrenheit and v is in miles per hour, a rate of change of W with respect to v will have units $°F/(mi/h)$ (which may also be written as $°F·h/mi$). Substituting

In an applied problem, the interpretations of $f_x(x_0, y_0)$ and $f_y(x_0, y_0)$ must be accompanied by the proper units. See Example 4.

Confirm the conclusion of Example 4 by calculating

$$\frac{W(25, 10 + \Delta v) - W(25, 10)}{\Delta v}$$

for values of Δv near 0.

$T = 25$ and $v = 10$ gives

$$\frac{\partial W}{\partial v}(25, 10) = (-4.01)10^{-0.84} \approx -0.58 \ \frac{°F}{mi/h}$$

as the instantaneous rate of change of W with respect to v at $(T, v) = (25, 10)$. We conclude that if the air temperature is a constant $25°F$ and the wind speed changes by a small amount from an initial speed of 10 mi/h, then the ratio of the change in the wind chill index to the change in wind speed should be about $-0.58°F/(mi/h)$. ◄

Geometrically, $f_x(x_0, y_0)$ can be viewed as the slope of the tangent line to the curve C_1 at the point (x_0, y_0), and $f_y(x_0, y_0)$ can be viewed as the slope of the tangent line to the curve C_2 at the point (x_0, y_0) (Figure 13.3.1). We will call $f_x(x_0, y_0)$ the **slope of the surface in the x-direction** at (x_0, y_0) and $f_y(x_0, y_0)$ the **slope of the surface in the y-direction** at (x_0, y_0).

▶ **Example 5** Let $f(x, y) = x^2 y + 5y^3$.

(a) Find the slope of the surface $z = f(x, y)$ in the x-direction at the point $(1, -2)$.

(b) Find the slope of the surface $z = f(x, y)$ in the y-direction at the point $(1, -2)$.

Solution (a).   Differentiating f with respect to x with y held fixed yields

$$f_x(x, y) = 2xy$$

Thus, the slope in the x-direction is $f_x(1, -2) = -4$; that is, z is decreasing at the rate of 4 units per unit increase in x.

Solution (b).   Differentiating f with respect to y with x held fixed yields

$$f_y(x, y) = x^2 + 15y^2$$

Thus, the slope in the y-direction is $f_y(1, -2) = 61$; that is, z is increasing at the rate of 61 units per unit increase in y. ◄

■ ESTIMATING PARTIAL DERIVATIVES FROM TABULAR DATA

For functions that are presented in tabular form, we can estimate partial derivatives by using adjacent entries within the table.

Table 13.3.1

TEMPERATURE T (°F)

WIND SPEED v (mi/h)	20	25	30	35
5	13	19	25	31
10	9	15	21	27
15	6	13	19	25
20	4	11	17	24

▶ **Example 6**   Use the values of the wind chill index function $W(T, v)$ displayed in Table 13.3.1 to estimate the partial derivative of W with respect to v at $(T, v) = (25, 10)$. Compare this estimate with the value of the partial derivative obtained in Example 4.

Solution.   Since

$$\frac{\partial W}{\partial v}(25, 10) = \lim_{\Delta v \to 0} \frac{W(25, 10 + \Delta v) - W(25, 10)}{\Delta v} = \lim_{\Delta v \to 0} \frac{W(25, 10 + \Delta v) - 15}{\Delta v}$$

we can approximate the partial derivative by

$$\frac{\partial W}{\partial v}(25, 10) \approx \frac{W(25, 10 + \Delta v) - 15}{\Delta v}$$

With $\Delta v = 5$ this approximation is

$$\frac{\partial W}{\partial v}(25, 10) \approx \frac{W(25, 10 + 5) - 15}{5} = \frac{W(25, 15) - 15}{5} = \frac{13 - 15}{5} = -\frac{2}{5} \ \frac{°F}{mi/h}$$

and with $\Delta v = -5$ this approximation is

$$\frac{\partial W}{\partial v}(25, 10) \approx \frac{W(25, 10 - 5) - 15}{-5} = \frac{W(25, 5) - 15}{-5} = \frac{19 - 15}{-5} = -\frac{4}{5}\ \frac{^\circ F}{mi/h}$$

We will take the average, $-\frac{3}{5} = -0.6^\circ F/(mi/h)$, of these two approximations as our estimate of $(\partial W/\partial v)(25, 10)$. This is close to the value

$$\frac{\partial W}{\partial v}(25, 10) = (-4.01)10^{-0.84} \approx -0.58\ \frac{^\circ F}{mi/h}$$

found in Example 4. ◄

■ IMPLICIT PARTIAL DIFFERENTIATION

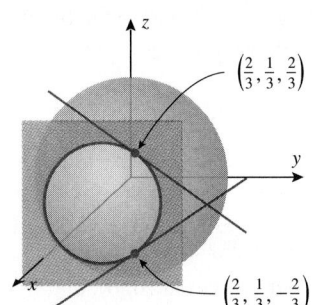

▲ **Figure 13.3.2**

▶ **Example 7**   Find the slope of the sphere $x^2 + y^2 + z^2 = 1$ in the y-direction at the points $\left(\frac{2}{3}, \frac{1}{3}, \frac{2}{3}\right)$ and $\left(\frac{2}{3}, \frac{1}{3}, -\frac{2}{3}\right)$ (Figure 13.3.2).

Solution.   The point $\left(\frac{2}{3}, \frac{1}{3}, \frac{2}{3}\right)$ lies on the upper hemisphere $z = \sqrt{1 - x^2 - y^2}$, and the point $\left(\frac{2}{3}, \frac{1}{3}, -\frac{2}{3}\right)$ lies on the lower hemisphere $z = -\sqrt{1 - x^2 - y^2}$. We could find the slopes by differentiating each expression for z separately with respect to y and then evaluating the derivatives at $x = \frac{2}{3}$ and $y = \frac{1}{3}$. However, it is more efficient to differentiate the given equation

$$x^2 + y^2 + z^2 = 1$$

implicitly with respect to y, since this will give us both slopes with one differentiation. To perform the implicit differentiation, we view z as a function of x and y and differentiate both sides with respect to y, taking x to be fixed. The computations are as follows:

$$\frac{\partial}{\partial y}[x^2 + y^2 + z^2] = \frac{\partial}{\partial y}[1]$$

$$0 + 2y + 2z\frac{\partial z}{\partial y} = 0$$

$$\frac{\partial z}{\partial y} = -\frac{y}{z}$$

Substituting the y- and z-coordinates of the points $\left(\frac{2}{3}, \frac{1}{3}, \frac{2}{3}\right)$ and $\left(\frac{2}{3}, \frac{1}{3}, -\frac{2}{3}\right)$ in this expression, we find that the slope at the point $\left(\frac{2}{3}, \frac{1}{3}, \frac{2}{3}\right)$ is $-\frac{1}{2}$ and the slope at $\left(\frac{2}{3}, \frac{1}{3}, -\frac{2}{3}\right)$ is $\frac{1}{2}$. ◄

Check the results in Example 7 by differentiating the functions

$$z = \sqrt{1 - x^2 - y^2}$$

and

$$z = -\sqrt{1 - x^2 - y^2}$$

directly.

▶ **Example 8**   Suppose that $D = \sqrt{x^2 + y^2}$ is the length of the diagonal of a rectangle whose sides have lengths x and y that are allowed to vary. Find a formula for the rate of change of D with respect to x if x varies with y held constant, and use this formula to find the rate of change of D with respect to x at the point where $x = 3$ and $y = 4$.

Solution.   Differentiating both sides of the equation $D^2 = x^2 + y^2$ with respect to x yields

$$2D\frac{\partial D}{\partial x} = 2x \quad \text{and thus} \quad D\frac{\partial D}{\partial x} = x$$

Since $D = 5$ when $x = 3$ and $y = 4$, it follows that

$$5\left.\frac{\partial D}{\partial x}\right|_{x=3,\,y=4} = 3 \quad \text{or} \quad \left.\frac{\partial D}{\partial x}\right|_{x=3,\,y=4} = \frac{3}{5}$$

Thus, D is increasing at a rate of $\frac{3}{5}$ unit per unit increase in x at the point $(3, 4)$. ◄

■ **PARTIAL DERIVATIVES AND CONTINUITY**

In contrast to the case of functions of a single variable, the existence of partial derivatives for a multivariable function does not guarantee the continuity of the function. This fact is shown in the following example.

▶ **Example 9**   Let

$$f(x, y) = \begin{cases} -\dfrac{xy}{x^2 + y^2}, & (x, y) \neq (0, 0) \\ 0, & (x, y) = (0, 0) \end{cases} \tag{3}$$

(a) Show that $f_x(x, y)$ and $f_y(x, y)$ exist at all points (x, y).

(b) Explain why f is not continuous at $(0, 0)$.

Solution (a).   Figure 13.3.3 shows the graph of f. Note that f is similar to the function considered in Example 1 of Section 13.2, except that here we have assigned f a value of 0 at $(0, 0)$. Except at this point, the partial derivatives of f are

$$f_x(x, y) = -\frac{(x^2 + y^2)y - xy(2x)}{(x^2 + y^2)^2} = \frac{x^2y - y^3}{(x^2 + y^2)^2} \tag{4}$$

$$f_y(x, y) = -\frac{(x^2 + y^2)x - xy(2y)}{(x^2 + y^2)^2} = \frac{xy^2 - x^3}{(x^2 + y^2)^2} \tag{5}$$

It is not evident from Formula (3) whether f has partial derivatives at $(0, 0)$, and if so, what the values of those derivatives are. To answer that question we will have to use the definitions of the partial derivatives (Definition 13.3.1). Applying Formulas (1) and (2) to (3) we obtain

$$f_x(0, 0) = \lim_{\Delta x \to 0} \frac{f(\Delta x, 0) - f(0, 0)}{\Delta x} = \lim_{\Delta x \to 0} \frac{0 - 0}{\Delta x} = 0$$

$$f_y(0, 0) = \lim_{\Delta y \to 0} \frac{f(0, \Delta y) - f(0, 0)}{\Delta y} = \lim_{\Delta y \to 0} \frac{0 - 0}{\Delta y} = 0$$

This shows that f has partial derivatives at $(0, 0)$ and the values of both partial derivatives are 0 at that point.

Solution (b).   We saw in Example 3 of Section 13.2 that

$$\lim_{(x,y) \to (0,0)} -\frac{xy}{x^2 + y^2}$$

does not exist. Thus, f is not continuous at $(0, 0)$. ◀

We will study the relationship between the continuity of a function and the properties of its partial derivatives in the next section.

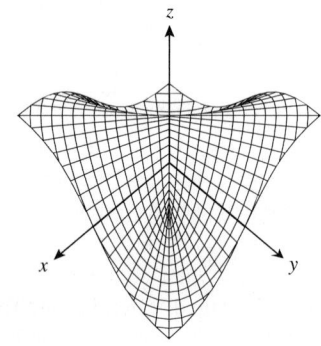

▲ **Figure 13.3.3**

■ **PARTIAL DERIVATIVES OF FUNCTIONS WITH MORE THAN TWO VARIABLES**

For a function $f(x, y, z)$ of three variables, there are three *partial derivatives*:

$$f_x(x, y, z), \quad f_y(x, y, z), \quad f_z(x, y, z)$$

The partial derivative f_x is calculated by holding y and z constant and differentiating with respect to x. For f_y the variables x and z are held constant, and for f_z the variables x and y are held constant. If a dependent variable

$$w = f(x, y, z)$$

is used, then the three partial derivatives of f can be denoted by

$$\frac{\partial w}{\partial x}, \quad \frac{\partial w}{\partial y}, \quad \text{and} \quad \frac{\partial w}{\partial z}$$

▶ **Example 10** If $f(x, y, z) = x^3 y^2 z^4 + 2xy + z$, then

$$f_x(x, y, z) = 3x^2 y^2 z^4 + 2y$$
$$f_y(x, y, z) = 2x^3 y z^4 + 2x$$
$$f_z(x, y, z) = 4x^3 y^2 z^3 + 1$$
$$f_z(-1, 1, 2) = 4(-1)^3(1)^2(2)^3 + 1 = -31 \quad ◀$$

▶ **Example 11** If $f(\rho, \theta, \phi) = \rho^2 \cos\phi \sin\theta$, then

$$f_\rho(\rho, \theta, \phi) = 2\rho \cos\phi \sin\theta$$
$$f_\theta(\rho, \theta, \phi) = \rho^2 \cos\phi \cos\theta$$
$$f_\phi(\rho, \theta, \phi) = -\rho^2 \sin\phi \sin\theta \quad ◀$$

In general, if $f(v_1, v_2, \ldots, v_n)$ is a function of n variables, there are n partial derivatives of f, each of which is obtained by holding $n - 1$ of the variables fixed and differentiating the function f with respect to the remaining variable. If $w = f(v_1, v_2, \ldots, v_n)$, then these partial derivatives are denoted by

$$\frac{\partial w}{\partial v_1}, \frac{\partial w}{\partial v_2}, \ldots, \frac{\partial w}{\partial v_n}$$

where $\partial w / \partial v_i$ is obtained by holding all variables except v_i fixed and differentiating with respect to v_i.

■ HIGHER-ORDER PARTIAL DERIVATIVES

Suppose that f is a function of two variables x and y. Since the partial derivatives $\partial f / \partial x$ and $\partial f / \partial y$ are also functions of x and y, these functions may themselves have partial derivatives. This gives rise to four possible *second-order* partial derivatives of f, which are defined by

$$\frac{\partial^2 f}{\partial x^2} = \frac{\partial}{\partial x}\left(\frac{\partial f}{\partial x}\right) = f_{xx} \qquad \frac{\partial^2 f}{\partial y^2} = \frac{\partial}{\partial y}\left(\frac{\partial f}{\partial y}\right) = f_{yy}$$

> Differentiate twice with respect to x.

> Differentiate twice with respect to y.

$$\frac{\partial^2 f}{\partial y \partial x} = \frac{\partial}{\partial y}\left(\frac{\partial f}{\partial x}\right) = f_{xy} \qquad \frac{\partial^2 f}{\partial x \partial y} = \frac{\partial}{\partial x}\left(\frac{\partial f}{\partial y}\right) = f_{yx}$$

> Differentiate first with respect to x and then with respect to y.

> Differentiate first with respect to y and then with respect to x.

The last two cases are called the *mixed second-order partial derivatives* or the *mixed second partials*. Also, the derivatives $\partial f / \partial x$ and $\partial f / \partial y$ are often called the *first-order partial derivatives* when it is necessary to distinguish them from higher-order partial derivatives. Similar conventions apply to the second-order partial derivatives of a function of three variables.

WARNING | Observe that the two notations for the mixed second partials have opposite conventions for the order of differentiation. In the "∂" notation the derivatives are taken right to left, and in the "subscript" notation they are taken left to right. The conventions are logical if you insert parentheses:

$$\frac{\partial^2 f}{\partial y \partial x} = \frac{\partial}{\partial y}\left(\frac{\partial f}{\partial x}\right)$$

Right to left. Differentiate inside the parentheses first.

$$f_{xy} = (f_x)_y$$

Left to right. Differentiate inside the parentheses first.

▶ **Example 12** Find the second-order partial derivatives of $f(x, y) = x^2 y^3 + x^4 y$.

Solution. We have

$$\frac{\partial f}{\partial x} = 2xy^3 + 4x^3 y \quad \text{and} \quad \frac{\partial f}{\partial y} = 3x^2 y^2 + x^4$$

so that

$$\frac{\partial^2 f}{\partial x^2} = \frac{\partial}{\partial x}\left(\frac{\partial f}{\partial x}\right) = \frac{\partial}{\partial x}(2xy^3 + 4x^3 y) = 2y^3 + 12x^2 y$$

$$\frac{\partial^2 f}{\partial y^2} = \frac{\partial}{\partial y}\left(\frac{\partial f}{\partial y}\right) = \frac{\partial}{\partial y}(3x^2 y^2 + x^4) = 6x^2 y$$

$$\frac{\partial^2 f}{\partial x \partial y} = \frac{\partial}{\partial x}\left(\frac{\partial f}{\partial y}\right) = \frac{\partial}{\partial x}(3x^2 y^2 + x^4) = 6xy^2 + 4x^3$$

$$\frac{\partial^2 f}{\partial y \partial x} = \frac{\partial}{\partial y}\left(\frac{\partial f}{\partial x}\right) = \frac{\partial}{\partial y}(2xy^3 + 4x^3 y) = 6xy^2 + 4x^3 \quad ◀$$

Third-order, fourth-order, and higher-order partial derivatives can be obtained by successive differentiation. Some possibilities are

$$\frac{\partial^3 f}{\partial x^3} = \frac{\partial}{\partial x}\left(\frac{\partial^2 f}{\partial x^2}\right) = f_{xxx} \qquad \frac{\partial^4 f}{\partial y^4} = \frac{\partial}{\partial y}\left(\frac{\partial^3 f}{\partial y^3}\right) = f_{yyyy}$$

$$\frac{\partial^3 f}{\partial y^2 \partial x} = \frac{\partial}{\partial y}\left(\frac{\partial^2 f}{\partial y \partial x}\right) = f_{xyy} \qquad \frac{\partial^4 f}{\partial y^2 \partial x^2} = \frac{\partial}{\partial y}\left(\frac{\partial^3 f}{\partial y \partial x^2}\right) = f_{xxyy}$$

▶ **Example 13** Let $f(x, y) = y^2 e^x + y$. Find f_{xyy}.

Solution.

$$f_{xyy} = \frac{\partial^3 f}{\partial y^2 \partial x} = \frac{\partial^2}{\partial y^2}\left(\frac{\partial f}{\partial x}\right) = \frac{\partial^2}{\partial y^2}(y^2 e^x) = \frac{\partial}{\partial y}(2y e^x) = 2e^x \quad ◀$$

■ **EQUALITY OF MIXED PARTIALS**

For a function $f(x, y)$ it might be expected that there would be four distinct second-order partial derivatives: $f_{xx}, f_{xy}, f_{yx},$ and f_{yy}. However, observe that the mixed second-order partial derivatives in Example 12 are equal. The following theorem (proved in Appendix D) explains why this is so.

If f is a function of three variables, then the analog of Theorem 13.3.2 holds for each pair of mixed second-order partials if we replace "open disk" by "open ball." How many second-order partials does $f(x, y, z)$ have?

13.3.2 THEOREM *Let f be a function of two variables. If f_{xy} and f_{yx} are continuous on some open disk, then $f_{xy} = f_{yx}$ on that disk.*

It follows from this theorem that if $f_{xy}(x, y)$ and $f_{yx}(x, y)$ are continuous everywhere, then $f_{xy}(x, y) = f_{yx}(x, y)$ for all values of x and y. Since polynomials are continuous everywhere, this explains why the mixed second-order partials in Example 12 are equal.

■ THE WAVE EQUATION

Consider a string of length L that is stretched taut between $x = 0$ and $x = L$ on an x-axis, and suppose that the string is set into vibratory motion by "plucking" it at time $t = 0$ (Figure 13.3.4a). The displacement of a point on the string depends both on its coordinate x and the elapsed time t, and hence is described by a function $u(x, t)$ of two variables. For a fixed value t, the function $u(x, t)$ depends on x alone, and the graph of u versus x describes the shape of the string—think of it as a "snapshot" of the string at time t (Figure 13.3.4b). It follows that at a fixed time t, the partial derivative $\partial u/\partial x$ represents the slope of the string at x, and the sign of the second partial derivative $\partial^2 u/\partial x^2$ tells us whether the string is concave up or concave down at x (Figure 13.3.4c).

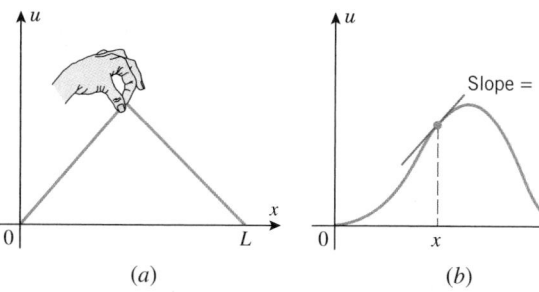

(a)　　　　　(b)　　　　　(c)

▲ **Figure 13.3.4**

Leverett Bradley/Getty Images
The vibration of a plucked string is governed by the wave equation.

For a fixed value of x, the function $u(x, t)$ depends on t alone, and the graph of u versus t is the position versus time curve of the point on the string with coordinate x. Thus, for a fixed value of x, the partial derivative $\partial u/\partial t$ is the velocity of the point with coordinate x, and $\partial^2 u/\partial t^2$ is the acceleration of that point.

It can be proved that under appropriate conditions the function $u(x, t)$ satisfies an equation of the form

$$\frac{\partial^2 u}{\partial t^2} = c^2 \frac{\partial^2 u}{\partial x^2} \tag{6}$$

where c is a positive constant that depends on the physical characteristics of the string. This equation, which is called the ***one-dimensional wave equation***, involves partial derivatives of the unknown function $u(x, t)$ and hence is classified as a ***partial differential equation***. Techniques for solving partial differential equations are studied in advanced courses and will not be discussed in this text.

▶ **Example 14** Show that the function $u(x, t) = \sin(x - ct)$ is a solution of Equation (6).

Solution. We have

$$\frac{\partial u}{\partial x} = \cos(x - ct), \qquad \frac{\partial^2 u}{\partial x^2} = -\sin(x - ct)$$

$$\frac{\partial u}{\partial t} = -c\cos(x - ct), \qquad \frac{\partial^2 u}{\partial t^2} = -c^2 \sin(x - ct)$$

Thus, $u(x, t)$ satisfies (6). ◀

✔ QUICK CHECK EXERCISES 13.3 *(See page 940 for answers.)*

1. Let $f(x, y) = x \sin xy$. Then $f_x(x, y) =$ _____ and $f_y(x, y) =$ _____.

2. The slope of the surface $z = xy^2$ in the x-direction at the point $(2, 3)$ is _____, and the slope of this surface in the y-direction at the point $(2, 3)$ is _____.

3. The volume V of a right circular cone of radius r and height h is given by $V = \frac{1}{3}\pi r^2 h$.

(a) Find a formula for the instantaneous rate of change of V with respect to r if r changes and h remains constant.

(b) Find a formula for the instantaneous rate of change of V with respect to h if h changes and r remains constant.

4. Find all second-order partial derivatives for the function $f(x, y) = x^2 y^3$.

EXERCISE SET 13.3 ◪ Graphing Utility

1. Let $f(x, y) = 3x^3 y^2$. Find
   (a) $f_x(x, y)$ (b) $f_y(x, y)$ (c) $f_x(1, y)$
   (d) $f_x(x, 1)$ (e) $f_y(1, y)$ (f) $f_y(x, 1)$
   (g) $f_x(1, 2)$ (h) $f_y(1, 2)$.

2. Let $z = e^{2x} \sin y$. Find
   (a) $\partial z / \partial x$ (b) $\partial z / \partial y$ (c) $\partial z / \partial x|_{(0,y)}$
   (d) $\partial z / \partial x|_{(x,0)}$ (e) $\partial z / \partial y|_{(0,y)}$ (f) $\partial z / \partial y|_{(x,0)}$
   (g) $\partial z / \partial x|_{(\ln 2, 0)}$ (h) $\partial z / \partial y|_{(\ln 2, 0)}$.

3. Let $f(x, y) = \sqrt{3x + 2y}$.
   (a) Find the slope of the surface $z = f(x, y)$ in the x-direction at the point $(4, 2)$.
   (b) Find the slope of the surface $z = f(x, y)$ in the y-direction at the point $(4, 2)$.

4. Let $f(x, y) = xe^{-y} + 5y$.
   (a) Find the slope of the surface $z = f(x, y)$ in the x-direction at the point $(3, 0)$.
   (b) Find the slope of the surface $z = f(x, y)$ in the y-direction at the point $(3, 0)$.

5. Let $z = \sin(y^2 - 4x)$.
   (a) Find the rate of change of z with respect to x at the point $(2, 1)$ with y held fixed.
   (b) Find the rate of change of z with respect to y at the point $(2, 1)$ with x held fixed.

6. Let $z = (x + y)^{-1}$.
   (a) Find the rate of change of z with respect to x at the point $(-2, 4)$ with y held fixed.
   (b) Find the rate of change of z with respect to y at the point $(-2, 4)$ with x held fixed.

FOCUS ON CONCEPTS

7. Use the information in the accompanying figure to find the values of the first-order partial derivatives of f at the point $(1, 2)$.

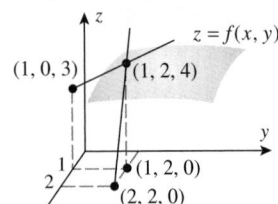

◀ **Figure Ex-7**

8. The accompanying figure shows a contour plot for an unspecified function $f(x, y)$. Make a conjecture about the signs of the partial derivatives $f_x(x_0, y_0)$ and $f_y(x_0, y_0)$, and explain your reasoning.

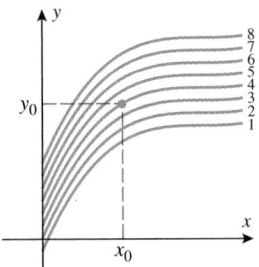

◀ **Figure Ex-8**

9. Suppose that Nolan throws a baseball to Ryan and that the baseball leaves Nolan's hand at the same height at which it is caught by Ryan. It we ignore air resistance, the horizontal range r of the baseball is a function of the initial speed v of the ball when it leaves Nolan's hand and the angle θ above the horizontal at which it is thrown. Use the accompanying table and the method of Example 6 to estimate
   (a) the partial derivative of r with respect to v when $v = 80$ ft/s and $\theta = 40°$
   (b) the partial derivative of r with respect to θ when $v = 80$ ft/s and $\theta = 40°$.

SPEED v (ft/s)

ANGLE θ (degrees)	75	80	85	90
35	165	188	212	238
40	173	197	222	249
45	176	200	226	253
50	173	197	222	249

◀ **Table Ex-9**

10. Use the table in Exercise 9 and the method of Example 6 to estimate
    (a) the partial derivative of r with respect to v when $v = 85$ ft/s and $\theta = 45°$
    (b) the partial derivative of r with respect to θ when $v = 85$ ft/s and $\theta = 45°$.

11. The accompanying figure shows the graphs of an unspecified function $f(x, y)$ and its partial derivatives $f_x(x, y)$ and $f_y(x, y)$. Determine which is which, and explain your reasoning.

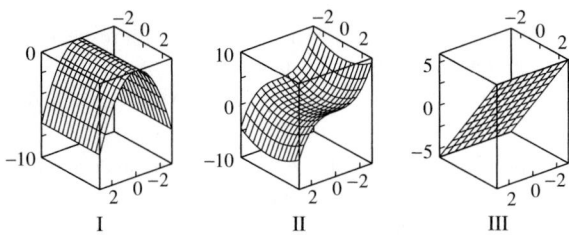

I   II   III

▲ **Figure Ex-11**

12. What can you say about the signs of $\partial z/\partial x$, $\partial^2 z/\partial x^2$, $\partial z/\partial y$, and $\partial^2 z/\partial y^2$ at the point P in the accompanying figure? Explain your reasoning.

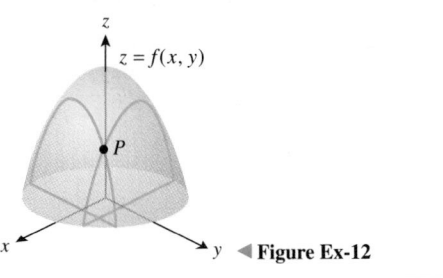

$z = f(x, y)$

◀ **Figure Ex-12**

13–16 True–False Determine whether the statement is true or false. Explain your answer. ■

13. If the line $y = 2$ is a contour of $f(x, y)$ through $(4, 2)$, then $f_x(4, 2) = 0$.

14. If the plane $x = 3$ intersects the surface $z = f(x, y)$ in a curve that passes through $(3, 4, 16)$ and satisfies $z = y^2$, then $f_y(3, 4) = 8$.

15. If the graph of $z = f(x, y)$ is a plane in 3-space, then both f_x and f_y are constant functions.

16. There exists a polynomial $f(x, y)$ that satisfies the equations $f_x(x, y) = 3x^2 + y^2 + 2y$ and $f_y(x, y) = 2xy + 2y$.

17–22 Find $\partial z/\partial x$ and $\partial z/\partial y$. ■

17. $z = 4e^{x^2 y^3}$

18. $z = \cos(x^5 y^4)$

19. $z = x^3 \ln(1 + xy^{-3/5})$

20. $z = e^{xy} \sin 4y^2$

21. $z = \dfrac{xy}{x^2 + y^2}$

22. $z = \dfrac{x^2 y^3}{\sqrt{x + y}}$

23–28 Find $f_x(x, y)$ and $f_y(x, y)$. ■

23. $f(x, y) = \sqrt{3x^5 y - 7x^3 y}$

24. $f(x, y) = \dfrac{x + y}{x - y}$

25. $f(x, y) = y^{-3/2} \tan^{-1}(x/y)$

26. $f(x, y) = x^3 e^{-y} + y^3 \sec \sqrt{x}$

27. $f(x, y) = (y^2 \tan x)^{-4/3}$

28. $f(x, y) = \cosh(\sqrt{x}) \sinh^2(xy^2)$

29–32 Evaluate the indicated partial derivatives. ■

29. $f(x, y) = 9 - x^2 - 7y^3$; $f_x(3, 1)$, $f_y(3, 1)$

30. $f(x, y) = x^2 y e^{xy}$; $\partial f/\partial x(1, 1)$, $\partial f/\partial y(1, 1)$

31. $z = \sqrt{x^2 + 4y^2}$; $\partial z/\partial x(1, 2)$, $\partial z/\partial y(1, 2)$

32. $w = x^2 \cos xy$; $\partial w/\partial x \left(\frac{1}{2}, \pi\right)$, $\partial w/\partial y \left(\frac{1}{2}, \pi\right)$

33. Let $f(x, y, z) = x^2 y^4 z^3 + xy + z^2 + 1$. Find
(a) $f_x(x, y, z)$ (b) $f_y(x, y, z)$ (c) $f_z(x, y, z)$
(d) $f_x(1, y, z)$ (e) $f_y(1, 2, z)$ (f) $f_z(1, 2, 3)$.

34. Let $w = x^2 y \cos z$. Find
(a) $\partial w/\partial x(x, y, z)$ (b) $\partial w/\partial y(x, y, z)$
(c) $\partial w/\partial z(x, y, z)$ (d) $\partial w/\partial x(2, y, z)$
(e) $\partial w/\partial y(2, 1, z)$ (f) $\partial w/\partial z(2, 1, 0)$.

35–38 Find f_x, f_y, and f_z. ■

35. $f(x, y, z) = z \ln(x^2 y \cos z)$

36. $f(x, y, z) = y^{-3/2} \sec\left(\dfrac{xz}{y}\right)$

37. $f(x, y, z) = \tan^{-1}\left(\dfrac{1}{xy^2 z^3}\right)$

38. $f(x, y, z) = \cosh(\sqrt{z}) \sinh^2(x^2 y z)$

39–42 Find $\partial w/\partial x$, $\partial w/\partial y$, and $\partial w/\partial z$. ■

39. $w = ye^z \sin xz$

40. $w = \dfrac{x^2 - y^2}{y^2 + z^2}$

41. $w = \sqrt{x^2 + y^2 + z^2}$

42. $w = y^3 e^{2x + 3z}$

43. Let $f(x, y, z) = y^2 e^{xz}$. Find
(a) $\partial f/\partial x|_{(1,1,1)}$ (b) $\partial f/\partial y|_{(1,1,1)}$ (c) $\partial f/\partial z|_{(1,1,1)}$.

44. Let $w = \sqrt{x^2 + 4y^2 - z^2}$. Find
(a) $\partial w/\partial x|_{(2,1,-1)}$ (b) $\partial w/\partial y|_{(2,1,-1)}$
(c) $\partial w/\partial z|_{(2,1,-1)}$.

45. Let $f(x, y) = e^x \cos y$. Use a graphing utility to graph the functions $f_x(0, y)$ and $f_y(x, \pi/2)$.

46. Let $f(x, y) = e^x \sin y$. Use a graphing utility to graph the functions $f_x(0, y)$ and $f_y(x, 0)$.

47. A point moves along the intersection of the elliptic paraboloid $z = x^2 + 3y^2$ and the plane $y = 1$. At what rate is z changing with respect to x when the point is at $(2, 1, 7)$?

48. A point moves along the intersection of the elliptic paraboloid $z = x^2 + 3y^2$ and the plane $x = 2$. At what rate is z changing with respect to y when the point is at $(2, 1, 7)$?

49. A point moves along the intersection of the plane $y = 3$ and the surface $z = \sqrt{29 - x^2 - y^2}$. At what rate is z changing with respect to x when the point is at $(4, 3, 2)$?

50. Find the slope of the tangent line at $(-1, 1, 5)$ to the curve of intersection of the surface $z = x^2 + 4y^2$ and
(a) the plane $x = -1$ (b) the plane $y = 1$.

51. The volume V of a right circular cylinder is given by the formula $V = \pi r^2 h$, where r is the radius and h is the height.
(a) Find a formula for the instantaneous rate of change of V with respect to r if r changes and h remains constant.

(cont.)

(b) Find a formula for the instantaneous rate of change of V with respect to h if h changes and r remains constant.

(c) Suppose that h has a constant value of 4 in, but r varies. Find the rate of change of V with respect to r at the point where $r = 6$ in.

(d) Suppose that r has a constant value of 8 in, but h varies. Find the instantaneous rate of change of V with respect to h at the point where $h = 10$ in.

52. The volume V of a right circular cone is given by

$$V = \frac{\pi}{24} d^2 \sqrt{4s^2 - d^2}$$

where s is the slant height and d is the diameter of the base.

(a) Find a formula for the instantaneous rate of change of V with respect to s if d remains constant.

(b) Find a formula for the instantaneous rate of change of V with respect to d if s remains constant.

(c) Suppose that d has a constant value of 16 cm, but s varies. Find the rate of change of V with respect to s when $s = 10$ cm.

(d) Suppose that s has a constant value of 10 cm, but d varies. Find the rate of change of V with respect to d when $d = 16$ cm.

53. According to the ideal gas law, the pressure, temperature, and volume of a gas are related by $P = kT/V$, where k is a constant of proportionality. Suppose that V is measured in cubic inches (in^3), T is measured in kelvins (K), and that for a certain gas the constant of proportionality is $k = 10$ in·lb/K.

(a) Find the instantaneous rate of change of pressure with respect to temperature if the temperature is 80 K and the volume remains fixed at 50 in^3.

(b) Find the instantaneous rate of change of volume with respect to pressure if the volume is 50 in^3 and the temperature remains fixed at 80 K.

54. The temperature at a point (x, y) on a metal plate in the xy-plane is $T(x, y) = x^3 + 2y^2 + x$ degrees Celsius. Assume that distance is measured in centimeters and find the rate at which temperature changes with respect to distance if we start at the point $(1, 2)$ and move

(a) to the right and parallel to the x-axis

(b) upward and parallel to the y-axis.

55. The length, width, and height of a rectangular box are $l = 5$, $w = 2$, and $h = 3$, respectively.

(a) Find the instantaneous rate of change of the volume of the box with respect to the length if w and h are held constant.

(b) Find the instantaneous rate of change of the volume of the box with respect to the width if l and h are held constant.

(c) Find the instantaneous rate of change of the volume of the box with respect to the height if l and w are held constant.

56. The area A of a triangle is given by $A = \frac{1}{2} ab \sin \theta$, where a and b are the lengths of two sides and θ is the angle between these sides. Suppose that $a = 5$, $b = 10$, and $\theta = \pi/3$.

(a) Find the rate at which A changes with respect to a if b and θ are held constant.

(b) Find the rate at which A changes with respect to θ if a and b are held constant.

(c) Find the rate at which b changes with respect to a if A and θ are held constant.

57. The volume of a right circular cone of radius r and height h is $V = \frac{1}{3} \pi r^2 h$. Show that if the height remains constant while the radius changes, then the volume satisfies

$$\frac{\partial V}{\partial r} = \frac{2V}{r}$$

58. Find parametric equations for the tangent line at $(1, 3, 3)$ to the curve of intersection of the surface $z = x^2 y$ and

(a) the plane $x = 1$ (b) the plane $y = 3$.

59. (a) By differentiating implicitly, find the slope of the hyperboloid $x^2 + y^2 - z^2 = 1$ in the x-direction at the points $(3, 4, 2\sqrt{6})$ and $(3, 4, -2\sqrt{6})$.

(b) Check the results in part (a) by solving for z and differentiating the resulting functions directly.

60. (a) By differentiating implicitly, find the slope of the hyperboloid $x^2 + y^2 - z^2 = 1$ in the y-direction at the points $(3, 4, 2\sqrt{6})$ and $(3, 4, -2\sqrt{6})$.

(b) Check the results in part (a) by solving for z and differentiating the resulting functions directly.

61–64 Calculate $\partial z/\partial x$ and $\partial z/\partial y$ using implicit differentiation. Leave your answers in terms of x, y, and z. ■

61. $(x^2 + y^2 + z^2)^{3/2} = 1$ **62.** $\ln(2x^2 + y - z^3) = x$

63. $x^2 + z \sin xyz = 0$ **64.** $e^{xy} \sinh z - z^2 x + 1 = 0$

65–66 Find $\partial w/\partial x$, $\partial w/\partial y$, and $\partial w/\partial z$ using implicit differentiation. Leave your answers in terms of x, y, z, and w. ■

65. $(x^2 + y^2 + z^2 + w^2)^{3/2} = 4$

66. $\ln(2x^2 + y - z^3 + 3w) = z$

67. $w^2 + w \sin xyz = 1$

68. $e^{xy} \sinh w - z^2 w + 1 = 0$

69–72 Find f_x and f_y. ■

69. $f(x, y) = \displaystyle\int_y^x e^{t^2}\, dt$ **70.** $f(x, y) = \displaystyle\int_1^{xy} e^{t^2}\, dt$

71. $f(x, y) = \displaystyle\int_0^{x^2 y^3} \sin t^3\, dt$ **72.** $f(x, y) = \displaystyle\int_{x+y}^{x-y} \sin t^3\, dt$

73. Let $z = \sqrt{x} \cos y$. Find

(a) $\partial^2 z/\partial x^2$ (b) $\partial^2 z/\partial y^2$

(c) $\partial^2 z/\partial x \partial y$ (d) $\partial^2 z/\partial y \partial x$.

74. Let $f(x, y) = 4x^2 - 2y + 7x^4 y^5$. Find

(a) f_{xx} (b) f_{yy} (c) f_{xy} (d) f_{yx}.

75–82 Confirm that the mixed second-order partial derivatives of f are the same. ■

75. $f(x, y) = 4x^2 - 8xy^4 + 7y^5 - 3$

76. $f(x, y) = \sqrt{x^2 + y^2}$ **77.** $f(x, y) = e^x \cos y$

78. $f(x, y) = e^{x-y^2}$ **79.** $f(x, y) = \ln(4x - 5y)$

80. $f(x, y) = \ln(x^2 + y^2)$

81. $f(x, y) = (x - y)/(x + y)$

82. $f(x, y) = (x^2 - y^2)/(x^2 + y^2)$

83. Express the following derivatives in "∂" notation.

(a) f_{xxx} (b) f_{xyy} (c) f_{yyxx} (d) f_{xyyy}

84. Express the derivatives in "subscript" notation.

(a) $\dfrac{\partial^3 f}{\partial y^2 \partial x}$ (b) $\dfrac{\partial^4 f}{\partial x^4}$ (c) $\dfrac{\partial^4 f}{\partial y^2 \partial x^2}$ (d) $\dfrac{\partial^5 f}{\partial x^2 \partial y^3}$

85. Given $f(x, y) = x^3 y^5 - 2x^2 y + x$, find

(a) f_{xxy} (b) f_{yxy} (c) f_{yyy}.

86. Given $z = (2x - y)^5$, find

(a) $\dfrac{\partial^3 z}{\partial y \partial x \partial y}$ (b) $\dfrac{\partial^3 z}{\partial x^2 \partial y}$ (c) $\dfrac{\partial^4 z}{\partial x^2 \partial y^2}$.

87. Given $f(x, y) = y^3 e^{-5x}$, find

(a) $f_{xyy}(0, 1)$ (b) $f_{xxx}(0, 1)$ (c) $f_{yyxx}(0, 1)$.

88. Given $w = e^y \cos x$, find

(a) $\dfrac{\partial^3 w}{\partial y^2 \partial x}\bigg|_{(\pi/4, 0)}$ (b) $\dfrac{\partial^3 w}{\partial x^2 \partial y}\bigg|_{(\pi/4, 0)}$

89. Let $f(x, y, z) = x^3 y^5 z^7 + xy^2 + y^3 z$. Find

(a) f_{xy} (b) f_{yz} (c) f_{xz} (d) f_{zz}

(e) f_{zyy} (f) f_{xxy} (g) f_{zyx} (h) f_{xxyz}.

90. Let $w = (4x - 3y + 2z)^5$. Find

(a) $\dfrac{\partial^2 w}{\partial x \partial z}$ (b) $\dfrac{\partial^3 w}{\partial x \partial y \partial z}$ (c) $\dfrac{\partial^4 w}{\partial z^2 \partial y \partial x}$.

91. Show that the function satisfies **Laplace's equation**

$$\frac{\partial^2 z}{\partial x^2} + \frac{\partial^2 z}{\partial y^2} = 0$$

(a) $z = x^2 - y^2 + 2xy$

(b) $z = e^x \sin y + e^y \cos x$

(c) $z = \ln(x^2 + y^2) + 2\tan^{-1}(y/x)$

92. Show that the function satisfies the **heat equation**

$$\frac{\partial z}{\partial t} = c^2 \frac{\partial^2 z}{\partial x^2} \quad (c > 0, \text{ constant})$$

(a) $z = e^{-t} \sin(x/c)$ (b) $z = e^{-t} \cos(x/c)$

93. Show that the function $u(x, t) = \sin c\omega t \sin \omega x$ satisfies the wave equation [Equation (6)] for all real values of ω.

94. In each part, show that $u(x, y)$ and $v(x, y)$ satisfy the **Cauchy–Riemann equations**

$$\frac{\partial u}{\partial x} = \frac{\partial v}{\partial y} \quad \text{and} \quad \frac{\partial u}{\partial y} = -\frac{\partial v}{\partial x}$$

(a) $u = x^2 - y^2$, $v = 2xy$

(b) $u = e^x \cos y$, $v = e^x \sin y$

(c) $u = \ln(x^2 + y^2)$, $v = 2\tan^{-1}(y/x)$

95. Show that if $u(x, y)$ and $v(x, y)$ each have equal mixed second partials, and if u and v satisfy the Cauchy–Riemann equations (Exercise 94), then u, v, and $u + v$ satisfy Laplace's equation (Exercise 91).

96. When two resistors having resistances R_1 ohms and R_2 ohms are connected in parallel, their combined resistance R in ohms is $R = R_1 R_2/(R_1 + R_2)$. Show that

$$\frac{\partial^2 R}{\partial R_1^2} \frac{\partial^2 R}{\partial R_2^2} = \frac{4R^2}{(R_1 + R_2)^4}$$

97–100 Find the indicated partial derivatives. ■

97. $f(v, w, x, y) = 4v^2 w^3 x^4 y^5$;

$\partial f/\partial v, \ \partial f/\partial w, \ \partial f/\partial x, \ \partial f/\partial y$

98. $w = r \cos st + e^u \sin ur$;

$\partial w/\partial r, \ \partial w/\partial s, \ \partial w/\partial t, \ \partial w/\partial u$

99. $f(v_1, v_2, v_3, v_4) = \dfrac{v_1^2 - v_2^2}{v_3^2 + v_4^2}$;

$\partial f/\partial v_1, \ \partial f/\partial v_2, \ \partial f/\partial v_3, \ \partial f/\partial v_4$

100. $V = xe^{2x-y} + we^{zw} + yw$;

$\partial V/\partial x, \ \partial V/\partial y, \ \partial V/\partial z, \ \partial V/\partial w$

101. Let $u(w, x, y, z) = xe^{yw} \sin^2 z$. Find

(a) $\dfrac{\partial u}{\partial x}(0, 0, 1, \pi)$ (b) $\dfrac{\partial u}{\partial y}(0, 0, 1, \pi)$

(c) $\dfrac{\partial u}{\partial w}(0, 0, 1, \pi)$ (d) $\dfrac{\partial u}{\partial z}(0, 0, 1, \pi)$

(e) $\dfrac{\partial^4 u}{\partial x \partial y \partial w \partial z}$ (f) $\dfrac{\partial^4 u}{\partial w \partial z \partial y^2}$.

102. Let $f(v, w, x, y) = 2v^{1/2} w^4 x^{1/2} y^{2/3}$. Find $f_v(1, -2, 4, 8)$, $f_w(1, -2, 4, 8)$, $f_x(1, -2, 4, 8)$, and $f_y(1, -2, 4, 8)$.

103–104 Find $\partial w/\partial x_i$ for $i = 1, 2, \ldots, n$. ■

103. $w = \cos(x_1 + 2x_2 + \cdots + nx_n)$

104. $w = \left(\displaystyle\sum_{k=1}^{n} x_k\right)^{1/n}$

105–106 Describe the largest set on which Theorem 13.3.2 can be used to prove that f_{xy} and f_{yx} are equal on that set. Then confirm by direct computation that $f_{xy} = f_{yx}$ on the given set. ■

105. (a) $f(x, y) = 4x^3 y + 3x^2 y$ (b) $f(x, y) = x^3/y$

106. (a) $f(x, y) = \sqrt{x^2 + y^2 - 1}$

(b) $f(x, y) = \sin(x^2 + y^3)$

107. Let $f(x, y) = 2x^2 - 3xy + y^2$. Find $f_x(2, -1)$ and $f_y(2, -1)$ by evaluating the limits in Definition 13.3.1. Then check your work by calculating the derivative in the usual way.

108. Let $f(x, y) = (x^2 + y^2)^{2/3}$. Show that

$$f_x(x, y) = \begin{cases} \dfrac{4x}{3(x^2 + y^2)^{1/3}}, & (x, y) \neq (0, 0) \\ 0, & (x, y) = (0, 0) \end{cases}$$

Source: This problem, due to Don Cohen, appeared in *Mathematics and Computer Education*, Vol. 25, No. 2, 1991, p. 179.

109. Let $f(x, y) = (x^3 + y^3)^{1/3}$.
 (a) Show that $f_y(0, 0) = 1$.
 (b) At what points, if any, does $f_y(x, y)$ fail to exist?

110. Writing Explain how one might use the graph of the equation $z = f(x, y)$ to determine the signs of $f_x(x_0, y_0)$ and $f_y(x_0, y_0)$ by inspection.

111. Writing Explain how one might use the graphs of some appropriate contours of $z = f(x, y)$ to determine the signs of $f_x(x_0, y_0)$ and $f_y(x_0, y_0)$ by inspection.

✔ **QUICK CHECK ANSWERS 13.3**

1. $\sin xy + xy \cos xy$; $x^2 \cos xy$ **2.** 9; 12   **3.** (a) $\frac{2}{3}\pi rh$ (b) $\frac{1}{3}\pi r^2 s$
4. $f_{xx}(x, y) = 2y^3$, $f_{yy}(x, y) = 6x^2y$, $f_{xy}(x, y) = f_{yx}(x, y) = 6xy^2$

13.4 DIFFERENTIABILITY, DIFFERENTIALS, AND LOCAL LINEARITY

In this section we will extend the notion of differentiability to functions of two or three variables. Our definition of differentiability will be based on the idea that a function is differentiable at a point provided it can be very closely approximated by a linear function near that point. In the process, we will expand the concept of a "differential" to functions of more than one variable and define the "local linear approximation" of a function.

■ DIFFERENTIABILITY

Recall that a function f of one variable is called differentiable at x_0 if it has a derivative at x_0, that is, if the limit

$$f'(x_0) = \lim_{\Delta x \to 0} \frac{f(x_0 + \Delta x) - f(x_0)}{\Delta x} \tag{1}$$

exists. As a consequence of (1) a differentiable function enjoys a number of other important properties:

- The graph of $y = f(x)$ has a nonvertical tangent line at the point $(x_0, f(x_0))$;
- f may be closely approximated by a linear function near x_0 (Section 3.5);
- f is continuous at x_0.

Our primary objective in this section is to extend the notion of differentiability to functions of two or three variables in such a way that the natural analogs of these properties hold. For example, if a function $f(x, y)$ of two variables is differentiable at a point (x_0, y_0), we want it to be the case that

- the surface $z = f(x, y)$ has a nonvertical tangent plane at the point $(x_0, y_0, f(x_0, y_0))$ (Figure 13.4.1);
- the values of f at points near (x_0, y_0) can be very closely approximated by the values of a linear function;
- f is continuous at (x_0, y_0).

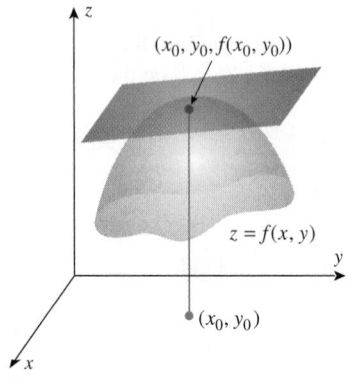

▲ **Figure 13.4.1**

One could reasonably conjecture that a function f of two or three variables should be called differentiable at a point if all the first-order partial derivatives of the function exist at that point. Unfortunately, this condition is not strong enough to guarantee that the properties above hold. For instance, we saw in Example 9 of Section 13.3 that the mere existence of both first-order partial derivatives for a function is not sufficient to guarantee the continuity of the function. To determine what else we should include in our definition, it will be helpful to reexamine one of the consequences of differentiability for a *single-variable* function $f(x)$. Suppose that $f(x)$ is differentiable at $x = x_0$ and let

$$\Delta f = f(x_0 + \Delta x) - f(x_0)$$

denote the change in f that corresponds to the change Δx in x from x_0 to $x_0 + \Delta x$. We saw in Section 3.5 that

$$\Delta f \approx f'(x_0)\Delta x$$

provided Δx is close to 0. In fact, for Δx close to 0 the error $\Delta f - f'(x_0)\Delta x$ in this approximation will have magnitude much smaller than that of Δx because

$$\lim_{\Delta x \to 0} \frac{\Delta f - f'(x_0)\Delta x}{\Delta x} = \lim_{\Delta x \to 0} \left(\frac{f(x_0 + \Delta x) - f(x_0)}{\Delta x} - f'(x_0) \right) = f'(x_0) - f'(x_0) = 0$$

Since the magnitude of Δx is just the distance between the points x_0 and $x_0 + \Delta x$, we see that when the two points are close together, the magnitude of the error in the approximation will be much smaller than the distance between the two points (Figure 13.4.2). The extension of this idea to functions of two or three variables is the "extra ingredient" needed in our definition of differentiability for multivariable functions.

For a function $f(x, y)$, the symbol Δf, called the **increment** of f, denotes the change in the value of $f(x, y)$ that results when (x, y) varies from some initial position (x_0, y_0) to some new position $(x_0 + \Delta x, y_0 + \Delta y)$; thus

$$\Delta f = f(x_0 + \Delta x, y_0 + \Delta y) - f(x_0, y_0) \tag{2}$$

(see Figure 13.4.3). [If a dependent variable $z = f(x, y)$ is used, then we will sometimes write Δz rather than Δf.] Let us assume that both $f_x(x_0, y_0)$ and $f_y(x_0, y_0)$ exist and (by analogy with the one-variable case) make the approximation

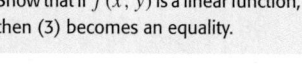

Show that if $f(x, y)$ is a linear function, then (3) becomes an equality.

$$\Delta f \approx f_x(x_0, y_0)\Delta x + f_y(x_0, y_0)\Delta y \tag{3}$$

For Δx and Δy close to 0, we would like the error

$$\Delta f - f_x(x_0, y_0)\Delta x - f_y(x_0, y_0)\Delta y$$

in this approximation to be much smaller than the distance $\sqrt{(\Delta x)^2 + (\Delta y)^2}$ between (x_0, y_0) and $(x_0 + \Delta x, y_0 + \Delta y)$. We can guarantee this by requiring that

$$\lim_{(\Delta x, \Delta y) \to (0,0)} \frac{\Delta f - f_x(x_0, y_0)\Delta x - f_y(x_0, y_0)\Delta y}{\sqrt{(\Delta x)^2 + (\Delta y)^2}} = 0$$

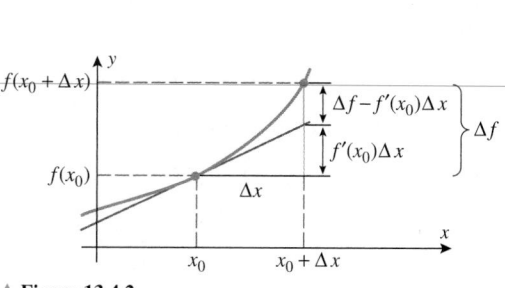

▲ Figure 13.4.2

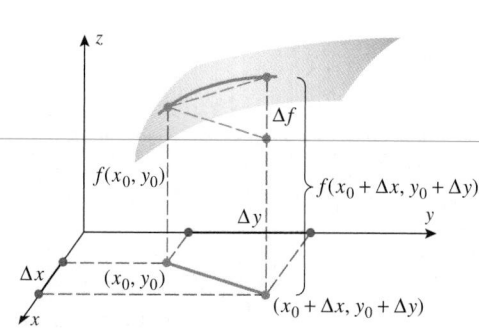

▲ Figure 13.4.3

Based on these ideas, we can now give our definition of differentiability for functions of two variables.

13.4.1 DEFINITION   A function f of two variables is said to be **differentiable** at (x_0, y_0) provided $f_x(x_0, y_0)$ and $f_y(x_0, y_0)$ both exist and

$$\lim_{(\Delta x, \Delta y) \to (0,0)} \frac{\Delta f - f_x(x_0, y_0)\Delta x - f_y(x_0, y_0)\Delta y}{\sqrt{(\Delta x)^2 + (\Delta y)^2}} = 0 \tag{4}$$

As with the one-variable case, verification of differentiability using this definition involves the computation of a limit.

▶ **Example 1**   Use Definition 13.4.1 to prove that $f(x, y) = x^2 + y^2$ is differentiable at $(0, 0)$.

Solution.   The increment is

$$\Delta f = f(0 + \Delta x, 0 + \Delta y) - f(0, 0) = (\Delta x)^2 + (\Delta y)^2$$

Since $f_x(x, y) = 2x$ and $f_y(x, y) = 2y$, we have $f_x(0, 0) = f_y(0, 0) = 0$, and (4) becomes

$$\lim_{(\Delta x, \Delta y) \to (0,0)} \frac{(\Delta x)^2 + (\Delta y)^2}{\sqrt{(\Delta x)^2 + (\Delta y)^2}} = \lim_{(\Delta x, \Delta y) \to (0,0)} \sqrt{(\Delta x)^2 + (\Delta y)^2} = 0$$

Therefore, f is differentiable at $(0, 0)$. ◀

We now derive an important consequence of limit (4). Define a function

$$\epsilon = \epsilon(\Delta x, \Delta y) = \frac{\Delta f - f_x(x_0, y_0)\Delta x - f_y(x_0, y_0)\Delta y}{\sqrt{(\Delta x)^2 + (\Delta y)^2}} \quad \text{for } (\Delta x, \Delta y) \neq (0, 0)$$

and define $\epsilon(0, 0)$ to be 0. Equation (4) then implies that

$$\lim_{(\Delta x, \Delta y) \to (0,0)} \epsilon(\Delta x, \Delta y) = 0$$

Furthermore, it immediately follows from the definition of ϵ that

$$\Delta f = f_x(x_0, y_0)\Delta x + f_y(x_0, y_0)\Delta y + \epsilon\sqrt{(\Delta x)^2 + (\Delta y)^2} \tag{5}$$

In other words, if f is differentiable at (x_0, y_0), then Δf may be expressed as shown in (5), where $\epsilon \to 0$ as $(\Delta x, \Delta y) \to (0, 0)$ and where $\epsilon = 0$ if $(\Delta x, \Delta y) = (0, 0)$.

For functions of three variables we have an analogous definition of differentiability in terms of the increment

$$\Delta f = f(x_0 + \Delta x, y_0 + \Delta y, z_0 + \Delta z) - f(x_0, y_0, z_0)$$

13.4.2 DEFINITION   A function f of three variables is said to be **differentiable** at (x_0, y_0, z_0) provided $f_x(x_0, y_0, z_0)$, $f_y(x_0, y_0, z_0)$, and $f_z(x_0, y_0, z_0)$ exist and

$$\lim_{(\Delta x, \Delta y, \Delta z) \to (0,0,0)} \frac{\Delta f - f_x(x_0, y_0, z_0)\Delta x - f_y(x_0, y_0, z_0)\Delta y - f_z(x_0, y_0, z_0)\Delta z}{\sqrt{(\Delta x)^2 + (\Delta y)^2 + (\Delta z)^2}} = 0 \tag{6}$$

In a manner similar to the two-variable case, we can express the limit (6) in terms of a function $\epsilon(\Delta x, \Delta y, \Delta z)$ that vanishes at $(\Delta x, \Delta y, \Delta z) = (0, 0, 0)$ and is continuous there. The details are left as an exercise for the reader.

If a function f of two variables is differentiable at each point of a region R in the xy-plane, then we say that f is ***differentiable on R***; and if f is differentiable at every point in the xy-plane, then we say that f is ***differentiable everywhere***. For a function f of three variables we have corresponding conventions.

■ **DIFFERENTIABILITY AND CONTINUITY**

Recall that we want a function to be continuous at every point at which it is differentiable. The next result shows this to be the case.

13.4.3 THEOREM *If a function is differentiable at a point, then it is continuous at that point.*

PROOF We will give the proof for $f(x, y)$, a function of two variables, since that will reveal the essential ideas. Assume that f is differentiable at (x_0, y_0). To prove that f is continuous at (x_0, y_0) we must show that

$$\lim_{(x, y) \to (x_0, y_0)} f(x, y) = f(x_0, y_0)$$

which, on letting $x = x_0 + \Delta x$ and $y = y_0 + \Delta y$, is equivalent to

$$\lim_{(\Delta x, \Delta y) \to (0, 0)} f(x_0 + \Delta x, y_0 + \Delta y) = f(x_0, y_0)$$

By Equation (2) this is equivalent to

$$\lim_{(\Delta x, \Delta y) \to (0, 0)} \Delta f = 0$$

However, from Equation (5)

$$\lim_{(\Delta x, \Delta y) \to (0, 0)} \Delta f = \lim_{(\Delta x, \Delta y) \to (0, 0)} \left[f_x(x_0, y_0) \Delta x + f_y(x_0, y_0) \Delta y \right.$$
$$\left. + \epsilon(\Delta x, \Delta y) \sqrt{(\Delta x)^2 + (\Delta y)^2} \right]$$
$$= 0 + 0 + 0 \cdot 0 = 0 \quad ■$$

The converse of Theorem 13.4.3 is false. For example, the function

$$f(x, y) = \sqrt{x^2 + y^2}$$

is continuous at $(0, 0)$ but is not differentiable at $(0, 0)$. Why not?

It can be difficult to verify that a function is differentiable at a point directly from the definition. The next theorem, whose proof is usually studied in more advanced courses, provides simple conditions for a function to be differentiable at a point.

13.4.4 THEOREM *If all first-order partial derivatives of f exist and are continuous at a point, then f is differentiable at that point.*

For example, consider the function

$$f(x, y, z) = x + yz$$

Since $f_x(x, y, z) = 1$, $f_y(x, y, z) = z$, and $f_z(x, y, z) = y$ are defined and continuous everywhere, we conclude from Theorem 13.4.4 that f is differentiable everywhere.

■ **DIFFERENTIALS**

As with the one-variable case, the approximations

$$\Delta f \approx f_x(x_0, y_0)\Delta x + f_y(x_0, y_0)\Delta y$$

for a function of two variables and the approximation

$$\Delta f \approx f_x(x_0, y_0, z_0)\Delta x + f_y(x_0, y_0, z_0)\Delta y + f_z(x_0, y_0, z_0)\Delta z \tag{7}$$

for a function of three variables have a convenient formulation in the language of differentials. If $z = f(x, y)$ is differentiable at a point (x_0, y_0), we let

$$dz = f_x(x_0, y_0)\, dx + f_y(x_0, y_0)\, dy \tag{8}$$

denote a new function with dependent variable dz and independent variables dx and dy. We refer to this function (also denoted df) as the ***total differential of z*** at (x_0, y_0) or as the ***total differential of f*** at (x_0, y_0). Similarly, for a function $w = f(x, y, z)$ of three variables we have the ***total differential of w*** at (x_0, y_0, z_0),

$$dw = f_x(x_0, y_0, z_0)\, dx + f_y(x_0, y_0, z_0)\, dy + f_z(x_0, y_0, z_0)\, dz \tag{9}$$

which is also referred to as the ***total differential of f*** at (x_0, y_0, z_0). It is common practice to omit the subscripts and write Equations (8) and (9) as

$$dz = f_x(x, y)\, dx + f_y(x, y)\, dy \tag{10}$$

and

$$dw = f_x(x, y, z)\, dx + f_y(x, y, z)\, dy + f_z(x, y, z)\, dz \tag{11}$$

In the two-variable case, the approximation

$$\Delta f \approx f_x(x_0, y_0)\Delta x + f_y(x_0, y_0)\Delta y$$

can be written in the form

$$\Delta f \approx df \tag{12}$$

for $dx = \Delta x$ and $dy = \Delta y$. Equivalently, we can write approximation (12) as

$$\Delta z \approx dz \tag{13}$$

In other words, we can estimate the change Δz in z by the value of the differential dz where dx is the change in x and dy is the change in y. Furthermore, it follows from (4) that if Δx and Δy are close to 0, then the magnitude of the error in approximation (13) will be much smaller than the distance $\sqrt{(\Delta x)^2 + (\Delta y)^2}$ between (x_0, y_0) and $(x_0 + \Delta x, y_0 + \Delta y)$.

▶ **Example 2** Use (13) to approximate the change in $z = xy^2$ from its value at $(0.5, 1.0)$ to its value at $(0.503, 1.004)$. Compare the magnitude of the error in this approximation with the distance between the points $(0.5, 1.0)$ and $(0.503, 1.004)$.

Solution. For $z = xy^2$ we have $dz = y^2\, dx + 2xy\, dy$. Evaluating this differential at $(x, y) = (0.5, 1.0)$, $dx = \Delta x = 0.503 - 0.5 = 0.003$, and $dy = \Delta y = 1.004 - 1.0 = 0.004$ yields

$$dz = 1.0^2(0.003) + 2(0.5)(1.0)(0.004) = 0.007$$

Since $z = 0.5$ at $(x, y) = (0.5, 1.0)$ and $z = 0.507032048$ at $(x, y) = (0.503, 1.004)$, we have

$$\Delta z = 0.507032048 - 0.5 = 0.007032048$$

and the error in approximating Δz by dz has magnitude

$$|dz - \Delta z| = |0.007 - 0.007032048| = 0.000032048$$

Since the distance between $(0.5, 1.0)$ and $(0.503, 1.004) = (0.5 + \Delta x, 1.0 + \Delta y)$ is

$$\sqrt{(\Delta x)^2 + (\Delta y)^2} = \sqrt{(0.003)^2 + (0.004)^2} = \sqrt{0.000025} = 0.005$$

we have

$$\frac{|dz - \Delta z|}{\sqrt{(\Delta x)^2 + (\Delta y)^2}} = \frac{0.000032048}{0.005} = 0.0064096 < \frac{1}{150}$$

Thus, the magnitude of the error in our approximation is less than $\frac{1}{150}$ of the distance between the two points. ◄

With the appropriate changes in notation, the preceding analysis can be extended to functions of three or more variables.

───────

▶ **Example 3**   The length, width, and height of a rectangular box are measured with an error of at most 5%. Use a total differential to estimate the maximum percentage error that results if these quantities are used to calculate the diagonal of the box.

Solution.   The diagonal D of a box with length x, width y, and height z is given by

$$D = \sqrt{x^2 + y^2 + z^2}$$

Let x_0, y_0, z_0, and $D_0 = \sqrt{x_0^2 + y_0^2 + z_0^2}$ denote the actual values of the length, width, height, and diagonal of the box. The total differential dD of D at (x_0, y_0, z_0) is given by

$$dD = \frac{x_0}{\sqrt{x_0^2 + y_0^2 + z_0^2}}\, dx + \frac{y_0}{\sqrt{x_0^2 + y_0^2 + z_0^2}}\, dy + \frac{z_0}{\sqrt{x_0^2 + y_0^2 + z_0^2}}\, dz$$

If x, y, z, and $D = \sqrt{x^2 + y^2 + z^2}$ are the measured and computed values of the length, width, height, and diagonal, respectively, then

$$\Delta x = x - x_0, \quad \Delta y = y - y_0, \quad \Delta z = z - z_0$$

and

$$\left| \frac{\Delta x}{x_0} \right| \le 0.05, \quad \left| \frac{\Delta y}{y_0} \right| \le 0.05, \quad \left| \frac{\Delta z}{z_0} \right| \le 0.05$$

We are seeking an estimate for the maximum size of $\Delta D / D_0$. With the aid of Equation (11) we have

$$\frac{\Delta D}{D_0} \approx \frac{dD}{D_0} = \frac{1}{x_0^2 + y_0^2 + z_0^2}[x_0 \Delta x + y_0 \Delta y + z_0 \Delta z]$$

$$= \frac{1}{x_0^2 + y_0^2 + z_0^2}\left[x_0^2 \frac{\Delta x}{x_0} + y_0^2 \frac{\Delta y}{y_0} + z_0^2 \frac{\Delta z}{z_0} \right]$$

Since

$$\left| \frac{dD}{D_0} \right| = \frac{1}{x_0^2 + y_0^2 + z_0^2}\left| x_0^2 \frac{\Delta x}{x_0} + y_0^2 \frac{\Delta y}{y_0} + z_0^2 \frac{\Delta z}{z_0} \right|$$

$$\le \frac{1}{x_0^2 + y_0^2 + z_0^2}\left(x_0^2 \left| \frac{\Delta x}{x_0} \right| + y_0^2 \left| \frac{\Delta y}{y_0} \right| + z_0^2 \left| \frac{\Delta z}{z_0} \right| \right)$$

$$\le \frac{1}{x_0^2 + y_0^2 + z_0^2}\left(x_0^2 (0.05) + y_0^2 (0.05) + z_0^2 (0.05) \right) = 0.05$$

we estimate the maximum percentage error in D to be 5%. ◄

LOCAL LINEAR APPROXIMATIONS

We now show that if a function f is differentiable at a point, then it can be very closely approximated by a linear function near that point. For example, suppose that $f(x, y)$ is differentiable at the point (x_0, y_0). Then approximation (3) can be written in the form

$$f(x_0 + \Delta x, y_0 + \Delta y) \approx f(x_0, y_0) + f_x(x_0, y_0)\Delta x + f_y(x_0, y_0)\Delta y$$

If we let $x = x_0 + \Delta x$ and $y = x_0 + \Delta y$, this approximation becomes

$$f(x, y) \approx f(x_0, y_0) + f_x(x_0, y_0)(x - x_0) + f_y(x_0, y_0)(y - y_0) \tag{14}$$

which yields a linear approximation of $f(x, y)$. Since the error in this approximation is equal to the error in approximation (3), we conclude that for (x, y) close to (x_0, y_0), the error in (14) will be much smaller than the distance between these two points. When $f(x, y)$ is differentiable at (x_0, y_0) we get

$$L(x, y) = f(x_0, y_0) + f_x(x_0, y_0)(x - x_0) + f_y(x_0, y_0)(y - y_0) \tag{15}$$

and refer to $L(x, y)$ as the ***local linear approximation to f at*** (x_0, y_0).

> Show that if $f(x, y)$ is a linear function, then (14) becomes an equality.

> Explain why the error in approximation (14) is the same as the error in approximation (3).

▶ **Example 4** Let $L(x, y)$ denote the local linear approximation to $f(x, y) = \sqrt{x^2 + y^2}$ at the point $(3, 4)$. Compare the error in approximating

$$f(3.04, 3.98) = \sqrt{(3.04)^2 + (3.98)^2}$$

by $L(3.04, 3.98)$ with the distance between the points $(3, 4)$ and $(3.04, 3.98)$.

Solution. We have

$$f_x(x, y) = \frac{x}{\sqrt{x^2 + y^2}} \quad \text{and} \quad f_y(x, y) = \frac{y}{\sqrt{x^2 + y^2}}$$

with $f_x(3, 4) = \frac{3}{5}$ and $f_y(3, 4) = \frac{4}{5}$. Therefore, the local linear approximation to f at $(3, 4)$ is given by

$$L(x, y) = 5 + \tfrac{3}{5}(x - 3) + \tfrac{4}{5}(y - 4)$$

Consequently,

$$f(3.04, 3.98) \approx L(3.04, 3.98) = 5 + \tfrac{3}{5}(0.04) + \tfrac{4}{5}(-0.02) = 5.008$$

Since

$$f(3.04, 3.98) = \sqrt{(3.04)^2 + (3.98)^2} \approx 5.00819$$

the error in the approximation is about $5.00819 - 5.008 = 0.00019$. This is less than $\frac{1}{200}$ of the distance

$$\sqrt{(3.04 - 3)^2 + (3.98 - 4)^2} \approx 0.045$$

between the points $(3, 4)$ and $(3.04, 3.98)$. ◀

For a function $f(x, y, z)$ that is differentiable at (x_0, y_0, z_0), the local linear approximation is

$$
\begin{aligned}
L(x, y, z) = f(x_0, y_0, z_0) &+ f_x(x_0, y_0, z_0)(x - x_0) \\
&+ f_y(x_0, y_0, z_0)(y - y_0) + f_z(x_0, y_0, z_0)(z - z_0)
\end{aligned} \tag{16}
$$

We have formulated our definitions in this section in such a way that continuity and local linearity are consequences of differentiability. In Section 13.7 we will show that if a function $f(x, y)$ is differentiable at a point (x_0, y_0), then the graph of $L(x, y)$ is a nonvertical tangent plane to the graph of f at the point $(x_0, y_0, f(x_0, y_0))$.

✔ **QUICK CHECK EXERCISES 13.4**   (See page 949 for answers.)

1. Assume that $f(x, y)$ is differentiable at (x_0, y_0) and let Δf denote the change in f from its value at (x_0, y_0) to its value at $(x_0 + \Delta x, y_0 + \Delta y)$.

   (a) $\Delta f \approx$ _____

   (b) The limit that guarantees the error in the approximation in part (a) is very small when both Δx and Δy are close to 0 is _____.

2. Compute the differential of each function.

   (a) $z = xe^{y^2}$ (b) $w = x\sin(yz)$

3. If f is differentiable at (x_0, y_0), then the local linear approximation to f at (x_0, y_0) is $L(x) =$ _____.

4. Assume that $f(1, -2) = 4$ and $f(x, y)$ is differentiable at $(1, -2)$ with $f_x(1, -2) = 2$ and $f_y(1, -2) = -3$. Estimate the value of $f(0.9, -1.950)$.

EXERCISE SET 13.4

FOCUS ON CONCEPTS

1. Suppose that a function $f(x, y)$ is differentiable at the point $(3, 4)$ with $f_x(3, 4) = 2$ and $f_y(3, 4) = -1$. If $f(3, 4) = 5$, estimate the value of $f(3.01, 3.98)$.

2. Suppose that a function $f(x, y)$ is differentiable at the point $(-1, 2)$ with $f_x(-1, 2) = 1$ and $f_y(-1, 2) = 3$. If $f(-1, 2) = 2$, estimate the value of $f(-0.99, 2.02)$.

3. Suppose that a function $f(x, y, z)$ is differentiable at the point $(1, 2, 3)$ with $f_x(1, 2, 3) = 1$, $f_y(1, 2, 3) = 2$, and $f_z(1, 2, 3) = 3$. If $f(1, 2, 3) = 4$, estimate the value of $f(1.01, 2.02, 3.03)$.

4. Suppose that a function $f(x, y, z)$ is differentiable at the point $(2, 1, -2)$, $f_x(2, 1, -2) = -1$, $f_y(2, 1, -2) = 1$, and $f_z(2, 1, -2) = -2$. If $f(2, 1, -2) = 0$, estimate the value of $f(1.98, 0.99, -1.97)$.

5. Use Definitions 13.4.1 and 13.4.2 to prove that a constant function of two or three variables is differentiable everywhere.

6. Use Definitions 13.4.1 and 13.4.2 to prove that a linear function of two or three variables is differentiable everywhere.

7. Use Definition 13.4.2 to prove that
$$f(x, y, z) = x^2 + y^2 + z^2$$
is differentiable at $(0, 0, 0)$.

8. Use Definition 13.4.2 to determine all values of r such that $f(x, y, z) = (x^2 + y^2 + z^2)^r$ is differentiable at $(0, 0, 0)$.

9–20 Compute the differential dz or dw of the function. ■

9. $z = 7x - 2y$ 10. $z = e^{xy}$ 11. $z = x^3y^2$

12. $z = 5x^2y^5 - 2x + 4y + 7$

13. $z = \tan^{-1}xy$ 14. $z = \sec^2(x - 3y)$

15. $w = 8x - 3y + 4z$ 16. $w = e^{xyz}$

17. $w = x^3y^2z$

18. $w = 4x^2y^3z^7 - 3xy + z + 5$

19. $w = \tan^{-1}(xyz)$ 20. $w = \sqrt{x} + \sqrt{y} + \sqrt{z}$

21–26 Use a total differential to approximate the change in the values of f from P to Q. Compare your estimate with the actual change in f. ■

21. $f(x, y) = x^2 + 2xy - 4x$; $P(1, 2)$, $Q(1.01, 2.04)$

22. $f(x, y) = x^{1/3}y^{1/2}$; $P(8, 9)$, $Q(7.78, 9.03)$

23. $f(x, y) = \dfrac{x + y}{xy}$; $P(-1, -2)$, $Q(-1.02, -2.04)$

24. $f(x, y) = \ln\sqrt{1 + xy}$; $P(0, 2)$, $Q(-0.09, 1.98)$

25. $f(x, y, z) = 2xy^2z^3$; $P(1, -1, 2)$, $Q(0.99, -1.02, 2.02)$

26. $f(x, y, z) = \dfrac{xyz}{x + y + z}$; $P(-1, -2, 4)$,
$Q(-1.04, -1.98, 3.97)$

27–30 True–False Determine whether the statement is true or false. Explain your answer. ■

27. By definition, a function $f(x, y)$ is differentiable at (x_0, y_0) provided both $f_x(x_0, y_0)$ and $f_y(x_0, y_0)$ are defined.

28. For any point (x_0, y_0) in the domain of a function $f(x, y)$, we have
$$\lim_{(\Delta x, \Delta y) \to (0,0)} \Delta f = 0$$
where
$$\Delta f = f(x_0 + \Delta x, y_0 + \Delta y) - f(x_0, y_0)$$

29. If f_x and f_y are both continuous at (x_0, y_0), then so is f.

30. The graph of a local linear approximation to a function $f(x, y)$ is a plane.

31. In the accompanying figure a rectangle with initial length x_0 and initial width y_0 has been enlarged, resulting in a rectangle with length $x_0 + \Delta x$ and width $y_0 + \Delta y$. What portion of the figure represents the increase in the area of the rectangle? What portion of the figure represents an approximation of the increase in area by a total differential?

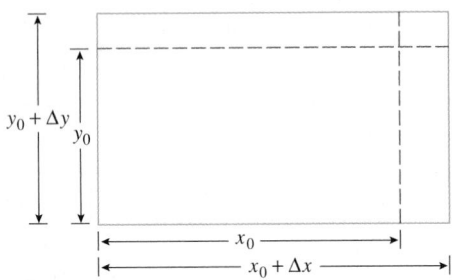

▲ **Figure Ex-31**

32. The volume V of a right circular cone of radius r and height h is given by $V = \frac{1}{3}\pi r^2 h$. Suppose that the height decreases from 20 in to 19.95 in and the radius increases from 4 in to 4.05 in. Compare the change in volume of the cone with an approximation of this change using a total differential.

33–40 (a) Find the local linear approximation L to the specified function f at the designated point P. (b) Compare the error in approximating f by L at the specified point Q with the distance between P and Q. ■

33. $f(x, y) = \dfrac{1}{\sqrt{x^2 + y^2}}$; $P(4, 3)$, $Q(3.92, 3.01)$

34. $f(x, y) = x^{0.5}y^{0.3}$; $P(1, 1)$, $Q(1.05, 0.97)$

35. $f(x, y) = x \sin y$; $P(0, 0)$, $Q(0.003, 0.004)$

36. $f(x, y) = \ln xy$; $P(1, 2)$, $Q(1.01, 2.02)$

37. $f(x, y, z) = xyz$; $P(1, 2, 3)$, $Q(1.001, 2.002, 3.003)$

38. $f(x, y, z) = \dfrac{x + y}{y + z}$; $P(-1, 1, 1)$, $Q(-0.99, 0.99, 1.01)$

39. $f(x, y, z) = xe^{yz}$; $P(1, -1, -1)$, $Q(0.99, -1.01, -0.99)$

40. $f(x, y, z) = \ln(x + yz)$; $P(2, 1, -1)$, $Q(2.02, 0.97, -1.01)$

41. In each part, confirm that the stated formula is the local linear approximation at $(0, 0)$.

(a) $e^x \sin y \approx y$ (b) $\dfrac{2x + 1}{y + 1} \approx 1 + 2x - y$

42. Show that the local linear approximation of the function $f(x, y) = x^\alpha y^\beta$ at $(1, 1)$ is

$$x^\alpha y^\beta \approx 1 + \alpha(x - 1) + \beta(y - 1)$$

43. In each part, confirm that the stated formula is the local linear approximation at $(1, 1, 1)$.

(a) $xyz + 2 \approx x + y + z$ (b) $\dfrac{4x}{y + z} \approx 2x - y - z + 2$

44. Based on Exercise 42, what would you conjecture is the local linear approximation to $x^\alpha y^\beta z^\gamma$ at $(1, 1, 1)$? Verify your conjecture by finding this local linear approximation.

45. Suppose that a function $f(x, y)$ is differentiable at the point $(1, 1)$ with $f_x(1, 1) = 2$ and $f(1, 1) = 3$. Let $L(x, y)$ denote the local linear approximation of f at $(1, 1)$. If $L(1.1, 0.9) = 3.15$, find the value of $f_y(1, 1)$.

46. Suppose that a function $f(x, y)$ is differentiable at the point $(0, -1)$ with $f_y(0, -1) = -2$ and $f(0, -1) = 3$. Let $L(x, y)$ denote the local linear approximation of f at $(0, -1)$. If $L(0.1, -1.1) = 3.3$, find the value of $f_x(0, -1)$.

47. Suppose that a function $f(x, y, z)$ is differentiable at the point $(3, 2, 1)$ and $L(x, y, z) = x - y + 2z - 2$ is the local linear approximation to f at $(3, 2, 1)$. Find $f(3, 2, 1)$, $f_x(3, 2, 1)$, $f_y(3, 2, 1)$, and $f_z(3, 2, 1)$.

48. Suppose that a function $f(x, y, z)$ is differentiable at the point $(0, -1, -2)$ and $L(x, y, z) = x + 2y + 3z + 4$ is the local linear approximation to f at $(0, -1, -2)$. Find $f(0, -1, -2)$, $f_x(0, -1, -2)$, $f_y(0, -1, -2)$, and $f_z(0, -1, -2)$.

49–52 A function f is given along with a local linear approximation L to f at a point P. Use the information given to determine point P. ■

49. $f(x, y) = x^2 + y^2$; $L(x, y) = 2y - 2x - 2$

50. $f(x, y) = x^2 y$; $L(x, y) = 4y - 4x + 8$

51. $f(x, y, z) = xy + z^2$; $L(x, y, z) = y + 2z - 1$

52. $f(x, y, z) = xyz$; $L(x, y, z) = x - y - z - 2$

53. The length and width of a rectangle are measured with errors of at most 3% and 5%, respectively. Use differentials to approximate the maximum percentage error in the calculated area.

54. The radius and height of a right circular cone are measured with errors of at most 1% and 4%, respectively. Use differentials to approximate the maximum percentage error in the calculated volume.

55. The length and width of a rectangle are measured with errors of at most $r\%$, where r is small. Use differentials to approximate the maximum percentage error in the calculated length of the diagonal.

56. The legs of a right triangle are measured to be 3 cm and 4 cm, with a maximum error of 0.05 cm in each measurement. Use differentials to approximate the maximum possible error in the calculated value of (a) the hypotenuse and (b) the area of the triangle.

57. The period T of a simple pendulum with small oscillations is calculated from the formula $T = 2\pi\sqrt{L/g}$, where L is the length of the pendulum and g is the acceleration due to gravity. Suppose that measured values of L and g have errors of at most 0.5% and 0.1%, respectively. Use differentials to approximate the maximum percentage error in the calculated value of T.

58. According to the ideal gas law, the pressure, temperature, and volume of a confined gas are related by $P = kT/V$, where k is a constant. Use differentials to approximate the percentage change in pressure if the temperature of a gas is increased 3% and the volume is increased 5%.

59. Suppose that certain measured quantities x and y have errors of at most $r\%$ and $s\%$, respectively. For each of the following formulas in x and y, use differentials to approximate the maximum possible error in the calculated result.
(a) xy (b) x/y (c) x^2y^3 (d) $x^3\sqrt{y}$

60. The total resistance R of three resistances R_1, R_2, and R_3, connected in parallel, is given by

$$\frac{1}{R} = \frac{1}{R_1} + \frac{1}{R_2} + \frac{1}{R_3}$$

Suppose that R_1, R_2, and R_3 are measured to be 100 ohms, 200 ohms, and 500 ohms, respectively, with a maximum error of 10% in each. Use differentials to approximate the maximum percentage error in the calculated value of R.

61. The area of a triangle is to be computed from the formula $A = \frac{1}{2}ab\sin\theta$, where a and b are the lengths of two sides and θ is the included angle. Suppose that a, b, and θ are measured to be 40 ft, 50 ft, and $30°$, respectively. Use differentials to approximate the maximum error in the calculated value of A if the maximum errors in a, b, and θ are $\frac{1}{2}$ ft, $\frac{1}{4}$ ft, and $2°$, respectively.

62. The length, width, and height of a rectangular box are measured with errors of at most $r\%$ (where r is small). Use differentials to approximate the maximum percentage error in the computed value of the volume.

63. Use Theorem 13.4.4 to prove that $f(x, y) = x^2\sin y$ is differentiable everywhere.

64. Use Theorem 13.4.4 to prove that $f(x, y, z) = xy\sin z$ is differentiable everywhere.

65. Suppose that $f(x, y)$ is differentiable at the point (x_0, y_0) and let $z_0 = f(x_0, y_0)$. Prove that $g(x, y, z) = z - f(x, y)$ is differentiable at (x_0, y_0, z_0).

66. Suppose that Δf satisfies an equation in the form of (5), where $\epsilon(\Delta x, \Delta y)$ is continuous at $(\Delta x, \Delta y) = (0, 0)$ with $\epsilon(0, 0) = 0$. Prove that f is differentiable at (x_0, y_0).

67. Writing Discuss the similarities and differences between the definition of "differentiability" for a function of a single variable and the definition of "differentiability" for a function of two variables.

68. Writing Discuss the use of differentials in the approximation of increments and in the estimation of errors.

✔ **QUICK CHECK ANSWERS 13.4**

1. (a) $f_x(x_0, y_0)\Delta x + f_y(x_0, y_0)\Delta y$ (b) $\displaystyle\lim_{(\Delta x, \Delta y)\to(0,0)} \frac{\Delta f - f_x(x_0, y_0)\Delta x - f_y(x_0, y_0)\Delta y}{\sqrt{(\Delta x)^2 + (\Delta y)^2}} = 0$ **2.** (a) $dz = e^{y^2}dx + 2xye^{y^2}dy$

(b) $dw = \sin(yz)\,dx + xz\cos(yz)\,dy + xy\cos(yz)\,dz$ **3.** $f(x_0, y_0) + f_x(x_0, y_0)(x - x_0) + f_y(x_0, y_0)(y - y_0)$ **4.** 3.65

13.5 THE CHAIN RULE

In this section we will derive versions of the chain rule for functions of two or three variables. These new versions will allow us to generate useful relationships among the derivatives and partial derivatives of various functions.

■ CHAIN RULES FOR DERIVATIVES

If y is a differentiable function of x and x is a differentiable function of t, then the chain rule for functions of one variable states that, under composition, y becomes a differentiable function of t with

$$\frac{dy}{dt} = \frac{dy}{dx}\frac{dx}{dt}$$

We will now derive a version of the chain rule for functions of two variables.

Assume that $z = f(x, y)$ is a function of x and y, and suppose that x and y are in turn functions of a single variable t, say

$$x = x(t), \quad y = y(t)$$

The composition $z = f(x(t), y(t))$ then expresses z as a function of the single variable t. Thus, we can ask for the derivative dz/dt and we can inquire about its relationship to the derivatives $\partial z/\partial x$, $\partial z/\partial y$, dx/dt, and dy/dt. Letting Δx, Δy, and Δz denote the changes in x, y, and z, respectively, that correspond to a change of Δt in t, we have

$$\frac{dz}{dt} = \lim_{\Delta t \to 0} \frac{\Delta z}{\Delta t}, \quad \frac{dx}{dt} = \lim_{\Delta t \to 0} \frac{\Delta x}{\Delta t}, \quad \text{and} \quad \frac{dy}{dt} = \lim_{\Delta t \to 0} \frac{\Delta y}{\Delta t}$$

It follows from (3) of Section 13.4 that

$$\Delta z \approx \frac{\partial z}{\partial x} \Delta x + \frac{\partial z}{\partial y} \Delta y \tag{1}$$

where the partial derivatives are evaluated at $(x(t), y(t))$. Dividing both sides of (1) by Δt yields

$$\frac{\Delta z}{\Delta t} \approx \frac{\partial z}{\partial x} \frac{\Delta x}{\Delta t} + \frac{\partial z}{\partial y} \frac{\Delta y}{\Delta t} \tag{2}$$

Similarly, we can produce the analog of (2) for functions of three variables as follows: assume that $w = f(x, y, z)$ is a function of x, y, and z, and suppose that x, y, and z are functions of a single variable t. As above we define Δw, Δx, Δy, and Δz to be the changes in w, x, y, and z that correspond to a change of Δt in t. Then (7) in Section 13.4 implies that

$$\Delta w \approx \frac{\partial w}{\partial x} \Delta x + \frac{\partial w}{\partial y} \Delta y + \frac{\partial w}{\partial z} \Delta z \tag{3}$$

and dividing both sides of (3) by Δt yields

$$\frac{\Delta w}{\Delta t} \approx \frac{\partial w}{\partial x} \frac{\Delta x}{\Delta t} + \frac{\partial w}{\partial y} \frac{\Delta y}{\Delta t} + \frac{\partial w}{\partial z} \frac{\Delta z}{\Delta t} \tag{4}$$

Taking the limit as $\Delta t \to 0$ of both sides of (2) and (4) suggests the following results. (A complete proof of the two-variable case can be found in Appendix D.)

13.5.1 THEOREM (*Chain Rules for Derivatives*) *If $x = x(t)$ and $y = y(t)$ are differentiable at t, and if $z = f(x, y)$ is differentiable at the point $(x, y) = (x(t), y(t))$, then $z = f(x(t), y(t))$ is differentiable at t and*

$$\frac{dz}{dt} = \frac{\partial z}{\partial x} \frac{dx}{dt} + \frac{\partial z}{\partial y} \frac{dy}{dt} \tag{5}$$

where the ordinary derivatives are evaluated at t and the partial derivatives are evaluated at (x, y).

If each of the functions $x = x(t)$, $y = y(t)$, and $z = z(t)$ is differentiable at t, and if $w = f(x, y, z)$ is differentiable at the point $(x, y, z) = (x(t), y(t), z(t))$, then the function $w = f(x(t), y(t), z(t))$ is differentiable at t and

$$\frac{dw}{dt} = \frac{\partial w}{\partial x} \frac{dx}{dt} + \frac{\partial w}{\partial y} \frac{dy}{dt} + \frac{\partial w}{\partial z} \frac{dz}{dt} \tag{6}$$

where the ordinary derivatives are evaluated at t and the partial derivatives are evaluated at (x, y, z).

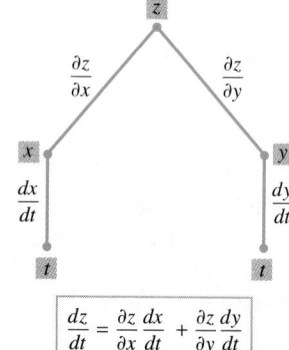

$$\frac{dz}{dt} = \frac{\partial z}{\partial x} \frac{dx}{dt} + \frac{\partial z}{\partial y} \frac{dy}{dt}$$

▲ **Figure 13.5.1**

Formula (5) can be represented schematically by a "tree diagram" that is constructed as follows (Figure 13.5.1). Starting with z at the top of the tree and moving downward, join each variable by lines (or branches) to those variables on which it depends *directly*. Thus, z is joined to x and y and these in turn are joined to t. Next, label each branch with a derivative whose "numerator" contains the variable at the top end of that branch and whose "denominator" contains the variable at the bottom end of that branch. This completes the "tree." To find the formula for dz/dt, follow the two paths through the tree that start with z and end with t. Each such path corresponds to a term in Formula (5).

Create a tree diagram for Formula (6).

▶ **Example 1** Suppose that

$$z = x^2 y, \quad x = t^2, \quad y = t^3$$

Use the chain rule to find dz/dt, and check the result by expressing z as a function of t and differentiating directly.

Solution. By the chain rule [Formula (5)],

$$\frac{dz}{dt} = \frac{\partial z}{\partial x}\frac{dx}{dt} + \frac{\partial z}{\partial y}\frac{dy}{dt} = (2xy)(2t) + (x^2)(3t^2)$$

$$= (2t^5)(2t) + (t^4)(3t^2) = 7t^6$$

Alternatively, we can express z directly as a function of t,

$$z = x^2 y = (t^2)^2(t^3) = t^7$$

and then differentiate to obtain $dz/dt = 7t^6$. However, this procedure may not always be convenient. ◀

▶ **Example 2** Suppose that

$$w = \sqrt{x^2 + y^2 + z^2}, \quad x = \cos\theta, \quad y = \sin\theta, \quad z = \tan\theta$$

Use the chain rule to find $dw/d\theta$ when $\theta = \pi/4$.

Solution. From Formula (6) with θ in the place of t, we obtain

$$\frac{dw}{d\theta} = \frac{\partial w}{\partial x}\frac{dx}{d\theta} + \frac{\partial w}{\partial y}\frac{dy}{d\theta} + \frac{\partial w}{\partial z}\frac{dz}{d\theta}$$

$$= \frac{1}{2}(x^2 + y^2 + z^2)^{-1/2}(2x)(-\sin\theta) + \frac{1}{2}(x^2 + y^2 + z^2)^{-1/2}(2y)(\cos\theta)$$

$$+ \frac{1}{2}(x^2 + y^2 + z^2)^{-1/2}(2z)(\sec^2\theta)$$

When $\theta = \pi/4$, we have

$$x = \cos\frac{\pi}{4} = \frac{1}{\sqrt{2}}, \quad y = \sin\frac{\pi}{4} = \frac{1}{\sqrt{2}}, \quad z = \tan\frac{\pi}{4} = 1$$

Substituting $x = 1/\sqrt{2}$, $y = 1/\sqrt{2}$, $z = 1$, $\theta = \pi/4$ in the formula for $dw/d\theta$ yields

Confirm the result of Example 2 by expressing w directly as a function of θ.

$$\frac{dw}{d\theta}\bigg|_{\theta=\pi/4} = \frac{1}{2}\left(\frac{1}{\sqrt{2}}\right)(\sqrt{2})\left(-\frac{1}{\sqrt{2}}\right) + \frac{1}{2}\left(\frac{1}{\sqrt{2}}\right)(\sqrt{2})\left(\frac{1}{\sqrt{2}}\right) + \frac{1}{2}\left(\frac{1}{\sqrt{2}}\right)(2)(2)$$

$$= \sqrt{2} \quad ◀$$

REMARK There are many variations in derivative notations, each of which gives the chain rule a different look. If $z = f(x, y)$, where x and y are functions of t, then some possibilities are

$$\frac{dz}{dt} = f_x \frac{dx}{dt} + f_y \frac{dy}{dt}$$

$$\frac{df}{dt} = \frac{\partial f}{\partial x} \frac{dx}{dt} + \frac{\partial f}{\partial y} \frac{dy}{dt}$$

$$\frac{df}{dt} = f_x x'(t) + f_y y'(t)$$

■ CHAIN RULES FOR PARTIAL DERIVATIVES

In Formula (5) the variables x and y are each functions of a single variable t. We now consider the case where x and y are each functions of two variables. Let $z = f(x, y)$ and suppose that x and y are functions of u and v, say

$$x = x(u, v), \quad y = y(u, v)$$

The composition $z = f(x(u, v), y(u, v))$ expresses z as a function of the two variables u and v. Thus, we can ask for the partial derivatives $\partial z/\partial u$ and $\partial z/\partial v$; and we can inquire about the relationship between these derivatives and the derivatives $\partial z/\partial x$, $\partial z/\partial y$, $\partial x/\partial u$, $\partial x/\partial v$, $\partial y/\partial u$, and $\partial y/\partial v$.

Similarly, if $w = f(x, y, z)$ and x, y, and z are each functions of u and v, then the composition $w = f(x(u, v), y(u, v), z(u, v))$ expresses w as a function of u and v. Thus we can also ask for the derivatives $\partial w/\partial u$ and $\partial w/\partial v$; and we can investigate the relationship between these derivatives, the partial derivatives $\partial w/\partial x$, $\partial w/\partial y$, and $\partial w/\partial z$, and the partial derivatives of x, y, and z with respect to u and v.

13.5.2   **THEOREM** (*Chain Rules for Partial Derivatives*)   *If $x = x(u, v)$ and $y = y(u, v)$ have first-order partial derivatives at the point (u, v), and if $z = f(x, y)$ is differentiable at the point $(x, y) = (x(u, v), y(u, v))$, then $z = f(x(u, v), y(u, v))$ has first-order partial derivatives at the point (u, v) given by*

$$\frac{\partial z}{\partial u} = \frac{\partial z}{\partial x} \frac{\partial x}{\partial u} + \frac{\partial z}{\partial y} \frac{\partial y}{\partial u} \quad \text{and} \quad \frac{\partial z}{\partial v} = \frac{\partial z}{\partial x} \frac{\partial x}{\partial v} + \frac{\partial z}{\partial y} \frac{\partial y}{\partial v} \qquad (7\text{–}8)$$

If each function $x = x(u, v)$, $y = y(u, v)$, and $z = z(u, v)$ has first-order partial derivatives at the point (u, v), and if the function $w = f(x, y, z)$ is differentiable at the point $(x, y, z) = (x(u, v), y(u, v), z(u, v))$, then $w = f(x(u, v), y(u, v), z(u, v))$ has first-order partial derivatives at the point (u, v) given by

$$\frac{\partial w}{\partial u} = \frac{\partial w}{\partial x} \frac{\partial x}{\partial u} + \frac{\partial w}{\partial y} \frac{\partial y}{\partial u} + \frac{\partial w}{\partial z} \frac{\partial z}{\partial u} \quad \text{and} \quad \frac{\partial w}{\partial v} = \frac{\partial w}{\partial x} \frac{\partial x}{\partial v} + \frac{\partial w}{\partial y} \frac{\partial y}{\partial v} + \frac{\partial w}{\partial z} \frac{\partial z}{\partial v}$$

$$(9\text{–}10)$$

PROOF   We will prove Formula (7); the other formulas are derived similarly. If v is held fixed, then $x = x(u, v)$ and $y = y(u, v)$ become functions of u alone. Thus, we are back to the case of Theorem 13.5.1. If we apply that theorem with u in place of t, and if we use ∂ rather than d to indicate that the variable v is fixed, we obtain

$$\frac{\partial z}{\partial u} = \frac{\partial z}{\partial x} \frac{\partial x}{\partial u} + \frac{\partial z}{\partial y} \frac{\partial y}{\partial u} \quad ■$$

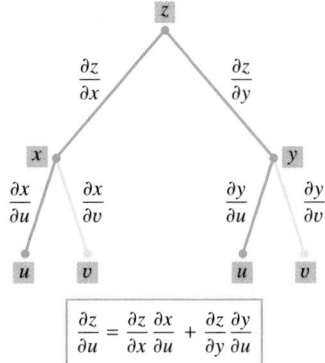

$$\frac{\partial z}{\partial u} = \frac{\partial z}{\partial x}\frac{\partial x}{\partial u} + \frac{\partial z}{\partial y}\frac{\partial y}{\partial u}$$

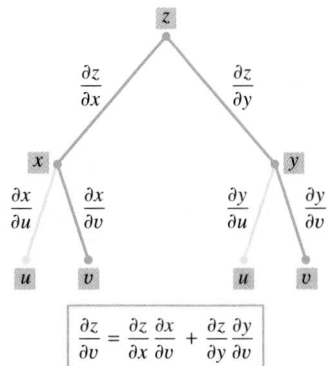

$$\frac{\partial z}{\partial v} = \frac{\partial z}{\partial x}\frac{\partial x}{\partial v} + \frac{\partial z}{\partial y}\frac{\partial y}{\partial v}$$

▲ Figure 13.5.2

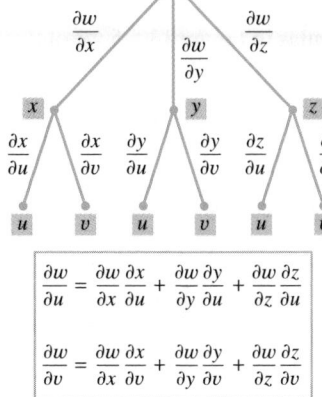

$$\frac{\partial w}{\partial u} = \frac{\partial w}{\partial x}\frac{\partial x}{\partial u} + \frac{\partial w}{\partial y}\frac{\partial y}{\partial u} + \frac{\partial w}{\partial z}\frac{\partial z}{\partial u}$$

$$\frac{\partial w}{\partial v} = \frac{\partial w}{\partial x}\frac{\partial x}{\partial v} + \frac{\partial w}{\partial y}\frac{\partial y}{\partial v} + \frac{\partial w}{\partial z}\frac{\partial z}{\partial v}$$

▲ Figure 13.5.3

Figures 13.5.2 and 13.5.3 show tree diagrams for the formulas in Theorem 13.5.2. As illustrated in Figure 13.5.2, the formula for $\partial z/\partial u$ can be obtained by tracing all paths through the tree that start with z and end with u, and the formula for $\partial z/\partial v$ can be obtained by tracing all paths through the tree that start with z and end with v. Figure 13.5.3 displays analogous results for $\partial w/\partial u$ and $\partial w/\partial v$.

▶ **Example 3** Given that

$$z = e^{xy}, \quad x = 2u + v, \quad y = u/v$$

find $\partial z/\partial u$ and $\partial z/\partial v$ using the chain rule.

Solution.

$$\frac{\partial z}{\partial u} = \frac{\partial z}{\partial x}\frac{\partial x}{\partial u} + \frac{\partial z}{\partial y}\frac{\partial y}{\partial u} = (ye^{xy})(2) + (xe^{xy})\left(\frac{1}{v}\right) = \left[2y + \frac{x}{v}\right]e^{xy}$$

$$= \left[\frac{2u}{v} + \frac{2u+v}{v}\right]e^{(2u+v)(u/v)} = \left[\frac{4u}{v} + 1\right]e^{(2u+v)(u/v)}$$

$$\frac{\partial z}{\partial v} = \frac{\partial z}{\partial x}\frac{\partial x}{\partial v} + \frac{\partial z}{\partial y}\frac{\partial y}{\partial v} = (ye^{xy})(1) + (xe^{xy})\left(-\frac{u}{v^2}\right)$$

$$= \left[y - x\left(\frac{u}{v^2}\right)\right]e^{xy} = \left[\frac{u}{v} - (2u+v)\left(\frac{u}{v^2}\right)\right]e^{(2u+v)(u/v)}$$

$$= -\frac{2u^2}{v^2}e^{(2u+v)(u/v)} \quad \blacktriangleleft$$

▶ **Example 4** Suppose that

$$w = e^{xyz}, \quad x = 3u + v, \quad y = 3u - v, \quad z = u^2 v$$

Use appropriate forms of the chain rule to find $\partial w/\partial u$ and $\partial w/\partial v$.

Solution. From the tree diagram and corresponding formulas in Figure 13.5.3 we obtain

$$\frac{\partial w}{\partial u} = yze^{xyz}(3) + xze^{xyz}(3) + xye^{xyz}(2uv) = e^{xyz}(3yz + 3xz + 2xyuv)$$

and

$$\frac{\partial w}{\partial v} = yze^{xyz}(1) + xze^{xyz}(-1) + xye^{xyz}(u^2) = e^{xyz}(yz - xz + xyu^2)$$

If desired, we can express $\partial w/\partial u$ and $\partial w/\partial v$ in terms of u and v alone by replacing x, y, and z by their expressions in terms of u and v. ◀

■ **OTHER VERSIONS OF THE CHAIN RULE**

Although we will not prove it, the chain rule extends to functions $w = f(v_1, v_2, \ldots, v_n)$ of n variables. For example, if each v_i is a function of t, $i = 1, 2, \ldots, n$, the relevant formula is

$$\frac{dw}{dt} = \frac{\partial w}{\partial v_1}\frac{dv_1}{dt} + \frac{\partial w}{\partial v_2}\frac{dv_2}{dt} + \cdots + \frac{\partial w}{\partial v_n}\frac{dv_n}{dt} \tag{11}$$

Note that (11) is a natural extension of Formulas (5) and (6) in Theorem 13.5.1.

There are infinitely many variations of the chain rule, depending on the number of variables and the choice of independent and dependent variables. A good working procedure is to use tree diagrams to derive new versions of the chain rule as needed.

▶ **Example 5** Suppose that $w = x^2 + y^2 - z^2$ and

$$x = \rho \sin \phi \cos \theta, \quad y = \rho \sin \phi \sin \theta, \quad z = \rho \cos \phi$$

Use appropriate forms of the chain rule to find $\partial w / \partial \rho$ and $\partial w / \partial \theta$.

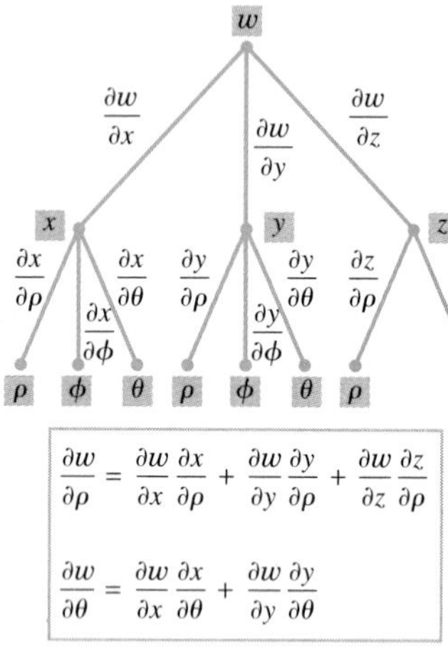

Solution. From the tree diagram and corresponding formulas in Figure 13.5.4 we obtain

$$\frac{\partial w}{\partial \rho} = 2x \sin \phi \cos \theta + 2y \sin \phi \sin \theta - 2z \cos \phi$$
$$= 2\rho \sin^2 \phi \cos^2 \theta + 2\rho \sin^2 \phi \sin^2 \theta - 2\rho \cos^2 \phi$$
$$= 2\rho \sin^2 \phi (\cos^2 \theta + \sin^2 \theta) - 2\rho \cos^2 \phi$$
$$= 2\rho (\sin^2 \phi - \cos^2 \phi)$$
$$= -2\rho \cos 2\phi$$

$$\frac{\partial w}{\partial \theta} = (2x)(-\rho \sin \phi \sin \theta) + (2y)\rho \sin \phi \cos \theta$$
$$= -2\rho^2 \sin^2 \phi \sin \theta \cos \theta + 2\rho^2 \sin^2 \phi \sin \theta \cos \theta$$
$$= 0$$

This result is explained by the fact that w does not vary with θ. You can see this directly by expressing the variables x, y, and z in terms of ρ, ϕ, and θ in the formula for w. (Verify that $w = -\rho^2 \cos 2\phi$.) ◀

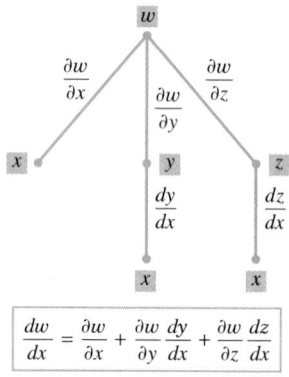

$$\frac{\partial w}{\partial \rho} = \frac{\partial w}{\partial x}\frac{\partial x}{\partial \rho} + \frac{\partial w}{\partial y}\frac{\partial y}{\partial \rho} + \frac{\partial w}{\partial z}\frac{\partial z}{\partial \rho}$$

$$\frac{\partial w}{\partial \theta} = \frac{\partial w}{\partial x}\frac{\partial x}{\partial \theta} + \frac{\partial w}{\partial y}\frac{\partial y}{\partial \theta}$$

▲ **Figure 13.5.4**

▶ **Example 6** Suppose that

$$w = xy + yz, \quad y = \sin x, \quad z = e^x$$

Use an appropriate form of the chain rule to find dw/dx.

Solution. From the tree diagram and corresponding formulas in Figure 13.5.5 we obtain

$$\frac{dw}{dx} = y + (x + z)\cos x + ye^x$$
$$= \sin x + (x + e^x)\cos x + e^x \sin x$$

This result can also be obtained by first expressing w explicitly in terms of x as

$$w = x \sin x + e^x \sin x$$

and then differentiating with respect to x; however, such direct substitution is not always possible. ◀

$$\frac{dw}{dx} = \frac{\partial w}{\partial x} + \frac{\partial w}{\partial y}\frac{dy}{dx} + \frac{\partial w}{\partial z}\frac{dz}{dx}$$

▲ **Figure 13.5.5**

WARNING The symbol ∂z, unlike the differential dz, has no meaning of its own. For example, if we were to "cancel" partial symbols in the chain-rule formula

$$\frac{\partial z}{\partial u} = \frac{\partial z}{\partial x}\frac{\partial x}{\partial u} + \frac{\partial z}{\partial y}\frac{\partial y}{\partial u}$$

we would obtain

$$\frac{\partial z}{\partial u} = \frac{\partial z}{\partial u} + \frac{\partial z}{\partial u}$$

which is false in cases where $\partial z / \partial u \neq 0$.

One of the principal uses of the chain rule for functions of a *single* variable was to compute formulas for the derivatives of compositions of functions. Theorems 13.5.1 and 13.5.2 are important not so much for the computation of formulas but because they allow us to express *relationships* among various derivatives. As an illustration, we revisit the topic of implicit differentiation.

■ IMPLICIT DIFFERENTIATION

Consider the special case where $z = f(x, y)$ is a function of x and y and y is a differentiable function of x. Equation (5) then becomes

$$\frac{dz}{dx} = \frac{\partial f}{\partial x}\frac{dx}{dx} + \frac{\partial f}{\partial y}\frac{dy}{dx} = \frac{\partial f}{\partial x} + \frac{\partial f}{\partial y}\frac{dy}{dx} \tag{12}$$

This result can be used to find derivatives of functions that are defined implicitly. For example, suppose that the equation

$$f(x, y) = c \tag{13}$$

defines y implicitly as a differentiable function of x and we are interested in finding dy/dx. Differentiating both sides of (13) with respect to x and applying (12) yields

$$\frac{\partial f}{\partial x} + \frac{\partial f}{\partial y}\frac{dy}{dx} = 0$$

Thus, if $\partial f/\partial y \neq 0$, we obtain

$$\frac{dy}{dx} = -\frac{\partial f/\partial x}{\partial f/\partial y}$$

In summary, we have the following result.

> Show that the function $y = x$ is defined implicitly by the equation
>
> $$x^2 - 2xy + y^2 = 0$$
>
> but that Theorem 13.5.3 is not applicable for finding dy/dx.

13.5.3   THEOREM   *If the equation $f(x, y) = c$ defines y implicitly as a differentiable function of x, and if $\partial f/\partial y \neq 0$, then*

$$\frac{dy}{dx} = -\frac{\partial f/\partial x}{\partial f/\partial y} \tag{14}$$

▶ **Example 7**   Given that

$$x^3 + y^2x - 3 = 0$$

find dy/dx using (14), and check the result using implicit differentiation.

Solution.   By (14) with $f(x, y) = x^3 + y^2x - 3$,

$$\frac{dy}{dx} = -\frac{\partial f/\partial x}{\partial f/\partial y} = -\frac{3x^2 + y^2}{2yx}$$

Alternatively, differentiating implicitly yields

$$3x^2 + y^2 + x\left(2y\frac{dy}{dx}\right) - 0 = 0 \quad \text{or} \quad \frac{dy}{dx} = -\frac{3x^2 + y^2}{2yx}$$

which agrees with the result obtained by (14). ◀

The chain rule also applies to implicit partial differentiation. Consider the case where $w = f(x, y, z)$ is a function of x, y, and z and z is a differentiable function of x and y. It follows from Theorem 13.5.2 that

$$\frac{\partial w}{\partial x} = \frac{\partial f}{\partial x} + \frac{\partial f}{\partial z}\frac{\partial z}{\partial x} \tag{15}$$

If the equation

$$f(x, y, z) = c \tag{16}$$

defines z implicitly as a differentiable function of x and y, then taking the partial derivative of each side of (16) with respect to x and applying (15) gives

$$\frac{\partial f}{\partial x} + \frac{\partial f}{\partial z}\frac{\partial z}{\partial x} = 0$$

If $\partial f/\partial z \neq 0$, then

$$\frac{\partial z}{\partial x} = -\frac{\partial f/\partial x}{\partial f/\partial z}$$

A similar result holds for $\partial z/\partial y$.

13.5.4 THEOREM *If the equation $f(x, y, z) = c$ defines z implicitly as a differentiable function of x and y, and if $\partial f/\partial z \neq 0$, then*

$$\frac{\partial z}{\partial x} = -\frac{\partial f/\partial x}{\partial f/\partial z} \qquad and \qquad \frac{\partial z}{\partial y} = -\frac{\partial f/\partial y}{\partial f/\partial z}$$

▶ **Example 8** Consider the sphere $x^2 + y^2 + z^2 = 1$. Find $\partial z/\partial x$ and $\partial z/\partial y$ at the point $\left(\frac{2}{3}, \frac{1}{3}, \frac{2}{3}\right)$.

Solution. By Theorem 13.5.4 with $f(x, y, z) = x^2 + y^2 + z^2$,

$$\frac{\partial z}{\partial x} = -\frac{\partial f/\partial x}{\partial f/\partial z} = -\frac{2x}{2z} = -\frac{x}{z} \quad \text{and} \quad \frac{\partial z}{\partial y} = -\frac{\partial f/\partial y}{\partial f/\partial z} = -\frac{2y}{2z} = -\frac{y}{z}$$

At the point $\left(\frac{2}{3}, \frac{1}{3}, \frac{2}{3}\right)$, evaluating these derivatives gives $\partial z/\partial x = -1$ and $\partial z/\partial y = -\frac{1}{2}$. ◀

> Note the similarity between the expression for $\partial z/\partial y$ found in Example 8 and that found in Example 7 of Section 13.3.

✔ **QUICK CHECK EXERCISES 13.5** *(See page 959 for answers.)*

1. Suppose that $z = xy^2$ and x and y are differentiable functions of t with $x = 1$, $y = -1$, $dx/dt = -2$, and $dy/dt = 3$ when $t = -1$. Then $dz/dt = $ _____ when $t = -1$.

2. Suppose that C is the graph of the equation $f(x, y) = 1$ and that this equation defines y implicitly as a differentiable function of x. If the point $(2, 1)$ belongs to C with $f_x(2, 1) = 3$ and $f_y(2, 1) = -1$, then the tangent line to C at the point $(2, 1)$ has slope _____.

3. A rectangle is growing in such a way that when its length is 5 ft and its width is 2 ft, the length is increasing at a rate of 3 ft/s and its width is increasing at a rate of 4 ft/s. At this instant the area of the rectangle is growing at a rate of _____.

4. Suppose that $z = x/y$, where x and y are differentiable functions of u and v such that $x = 3$, $y = 1$, $\partial x/\partial u = 4$, $\partial x/\partial v = -2$, $\partial y/\partial u = 1$, and $\partial y/\partial v = -1$ when $u = 2$ and $v = 1$. When $u = 2$ and $v = 1$, $\partial z/\partial u = $ _____ and $\partial z/\partial v = $ _____.

EXERCISE SET 13.5

1–6 Use an appropriate form of the chain rule to find dz/dt. ■

1. $z = 3x^2y^3$; $x = t^4$, $y = t^2$

2. $z = \ln(2x^2 + y)$; $x = \sqrt{t}$, $y = t^{2/3}$

3. $z = 3\cos x - \sin xy$; $x = 1/t$, $y = 3t$

4. $z = \sqrt{1 + x - 2xy^4}$; $x = \ln t$, $y = t$

5. $z = e^{1-xy}$; $x = t^{1/3}$, $y = t^3$

6. $z = \cosh^2 xy$; $x = t/2$, $y = e^t$

7–10 Use an appropriate form of the chain rule to find dw/dt. ■

7. $w = 5x^2y^3z^4$; $x = t^2$, $y = t^3$, $z = t^5$

8. $w = \ln(3x^2 - 2y + 4z^3)$; $x = t^{1/2}$, $y = t^{2/3}$, $z = t^{-2}$

9. $w = 5\cos xy - \sin xz$; $x = 1/t$, $y = t$, $z = t^3$

10. $w = \sqrt{1 + x - 2yz^4x}$; $x = \ln t$, $y = t$, $z = 4t$

FOCUS ON CONCEPTS

11. Suppose that
$$w = x^3y^2z^4; \quad x = t^2, \quad y = t + 2, \quad z = 2t^4$$
Find the rate of change of w with respect to t at $t = 1$ by using the chain rule, and then check your work by expressing w as a function of t and differentiating.

12. Suppose that
$$w = x \sin yz^2; \quad x = \cos t, \quad y = t^2, \quad z = e^t$$
Find the rate of change of w with respect to t at $t = 0$ by using the chain rule, and then check your work by expressing w as a function of t and differentiating.

13. Suppose that $z = f(x, y)$ is differentiable at the point $(4, 8)$ with $f_x(4, 8) = 3$ and $f_y(4, 8) = -1$. If $x = t^2$ and $y = t^3$, find dz/dt when $t = 2$.

14. Suppose that $w = f(x, y, z)$ is differentiable at the point $(1, 0, 2)$ with $f_x(1, 0, 2) = 1$, $f_y(1, 0, 2) = 2$, and $f_z(1, 0, 2) = 3$. If $x = t$, $y = \sin(\pi t)$, and $z = t^2 + 1$, find dw/dt when $t = 1$.

15. Explain how the product rule for functions of a single variable may be viewed as a consequence of the chain rule applied to a particular function of two variables.

16. A student attempts to differentiate the function x^x using the power rule, mistakenly getting $x \cdot x^{x-1}$. A second student attempts to differentiate x^x by treating it as an exponential function, mistakenly getting $(\ln x)x^x$. Use the chain rule to explain why the correct derivative is the sum of these two incorrect results.

17–22 Use appropriate forms of the chain rule to find $\partial z/\partial u$ and $\partial z/\partial v$. ■

17. $z = 8x^2y - 2x + 3y$; $x = uv$, $y = u - v$

18. $z = x^2 - y \tan x$; $x = u/v$, $y = u^2v^2$

19. $z = x/y$; $x = 2\cos u$, $y = 3\sin v$

20. $z = 3x - 2y$; $x = u + v \ln u$, $y = u^2 - v \ln v$

21. $z = e^{x^2y}$; $x = \sqrt{uv}$, $y = 1/v$

22. $z = \cos x \sin y$; $x = u - v$, $y = u^2 + v^2$

23–30 Use appropriate forms of the chain rule to find the derivatives. ■

23. Let $T = x^2y - xy^3 + 2$; $x = r\cos\theta$, $y = r\sin\theta$. Find $\partial T/\partial r$ and $\partial T/\partial\theta$.

24. Let $R = e^{2s-t^2}$; $s = 3\phi$, $t = \phi^{1/2}$. Find $dR/d\phi$.

25. Let $t = u/v$; $u = x^2 - y^2$, $v = 4xy^3$. Find $\partial t/\partial x$ and $\partial t/\partial y$.

26. Let $w = rs/(r^2 + s^2)$; $r = uv$, $s = u - 2v$. Find $\partial w/\partial u$ and $\partial w/\partial v$.

27. Let $z = \ln(x^2 + 1)$, where $x = r\cos\theta$. Find $\partial z/\partial r$ and $\partial z/\partial\theta$.

28. Let $u = rs^2 \ln t$, $r = x^2$, $s = 4y + 1$, $t = xy^3$. Find $\partial u/\partial x$ and $\partial u/\partial y$.

29. Let $w = 4x^2 + 4y^2 + z^2$, $x = \rho\sin\phi\cos\theta$, $y = \rho\sin\phi\sin\theta$, $z = \rho\cos\phi$. Find $\partial w/\partial\rho$, $\partial w/\partial\phi$, and $\partial w/\partial\theta$.

30. Let $w = 3xy^2z^3$, $y = 3x^2 + 2$, $z = \sqrt{x - 1}$. Find dw/dx.

31. Use a chain rule to find the value of $\dfrac{dw}{ds}\Big|_{s=1/4}$ if $w = r^2 - r\tan\theta$; $r = \sqrt{s}$, $\theta = \pi s$.

32. Use a chain rule to find the values of
$$\frac{\partial f}{\partial u}\Big|_{u=1, v=-2} \quad \text{and} \quad \frac{\partial f}{\partial v}\Big|_{u=1, v=-2}$$
if $f(x, y) = x^2y^2 - x + 2y$; $x = \sqrt{u}$, $y = uv^3$.

33. Use a chain rule to find the values of
$$\frac{\partial z}{\partial r}\Big|_{r=2, \theta=\pi/6} \quad \text{and} \quad \frac{\partial z}{\partial\theta}\Big|_{r=2, \theta=\pi/6}$$
if $z = xye^{x/y}$; $x = r\cos\theta$, $y = r\sin\theta$.

34. Use a chain rule to find $\dfrac{dz}{dt}\Big|_{t=3}$ if $z = x^2y$; $x = t^2$, $y = t + 7$.

35–38 True–False Determine whether the statement is true or false. Explain your answer. ■

35. The symbols ∂z and ∂x are defined in such a way that the partial derivative $\partial z/\partial x$ can be interpreted as a ratio.

36. If z is a differentiable function of x_1, x_2, and x_3, and if x_i is a differentiable function of t for $i = 1, 2, 3$, then z is a differentiable function of t and
$$\frac{dz}{dt} = \sum_{i=1}^{3} \frac{\partial z}{\partial x_i}\frac{dx_i}{dt}$$

37. If z is a differentiable function of x and y, and if x and y are twice differentiable functions of t, then z is a twice differentiable function of t and
$$\frac{d^2z}{dt^2} = \frac{\partial z}{\partial x}\frac{d^2x}{dt^2} + \frac{\partial z}{\partial y}\frac{d^2y}{dt^2}$$

38. If z is a differentiable function of x and y such that $z = 2$ when $x = y = 1$ and such that
$$x\frac{\partial z}{\partial x} - y\frac{\partial z}{\partial y} = 0$$
then $z = 2xy$.

39–42 Use Theorem 13.5.3 to find dy/dx and check your result using implicit differentiation. ■

39. $x^2 y^3 + \cos y = 0$

40. $x^3 - 3xy^2 + y^3 = 5$

41. $e^{xy} + ye^y = 1$

42. $x - \sqrt{xy} + 3y = 4$

43–46 Find $\partial z/\partial x$ and $\partial z/\partial y$ by implicit differentiation, and confirm that the results obtained agree with those predicted by the formulas in Theorem 13.5.4. ■

43. $x^2 - 3yz^2 + xyz - 2 = 0$

44. $\ln(1+z) + xy^2 + z = 1$

45. $ye^x - 5\sin 3z = 3z$

46. $e^{xy}\cos yz - e^{yz}\sin xz + 2 = 0$

47. (a) Suppose that $z = f(u)$ and $u = g(x, y)$. Draw a tree diagram, and use it to construct chain rules that express $\partial z/\partial x$ and $\partial z/\partial y$ in terms of dz/du, $\partial u/\partial x$, and $\partial u/\partial y$.

(b) Show that
$$\frac{\partial^2 z}{\partial x^2} = \frac{dz}{du}\frac{\partial^2 u}{\partial x^2} + \frac{d^2 z}{du^2}\left(\frac{\partial u}{\partial x}\right)^2$$
$$\frac{\partial^2 z}{\partial y^2} = \frac{dz}{du}\frac{\partial^2 u}{\partial y^2} + \frac{d^2 z}{du^2}\left(\frac{\partial u}{\partial y}\right)^2$$
$$\frac{\partial^2 z}{\partial y\partial x} = \frac{dz}{du}\frac{\partial^2 u}{\partial y\partial x} + \frac{d^2 z}{du^2}\frac{\partial u}{\partial x}\frac{\partial u}{\partial y}$$

48. (a) Let $z = f(x^2 - y^2)$. Use the result in Exercise 47(a) to show that
$$y\frac{\partial z}{\partial x} + x\frac{\partial z}{\partial y} = 0$$

(b) Let $z = f(xy)$. Use the result in Exercise 47(a) to show that
$$x\frac{\partial z}{\partial x} - y\frac{\partial z}{\partial y} = 0$$

(c) Confirm the result in part (a) in the case where $z = \sin(x^2 - y^2)$.

(d) Confirm the result in part (b) in the case where $z = e^{xy}$.

49. Let f be a differentiable function of one variable, and let $z = f(x + 2y)$. Show that
$$2\frac{\partial z}{\partial x} - \frac{\partial z}{\partial y} = 0$$

50. Let f be a differentiable function of one variable, and let $z = f(x^2 + y^2)$. Show that
$$y\frac{\partial z}{\partial x} - x\frac{\partial z}{\partial y} = 0$$

51. Let f be a differentiable function of one variable, and let $w = f(u)$, where $u = x + 2y + 3z$. Show that
$$\frac{\partial w}{\partial x} + \frac{\partial w}{\partial y} + \frac{\partial w}{\partial z} = 6\frac{dw}{du}$$

52. Let f be a differentiable function of one variable, and let $w = f(\rho)$, where $\rho = (x^2 + y^2 + z^2)^{1/2}$. Show that
$$\left(\frac{\partial w}{\partial x}\right)^2 + \left(\frac{\partial w}{\partial y}\right)^2 + \left(\frac{\partial w}{\partial z}\right)^2 = \left(\frac{dw}{d\rho}\right)^2$$

53. Let $z = f(x - y, y - x)$. Show that $\partial z/\partial x + \partial z/\partial y = 0$.

54. Let f be a differentiable function of three variables and suppose that $w = f(x - y, y - z, z - x)$. Show that
$$\frac{\partial w}{\partial x} + \frac{\partial w}{\partial y} + \frac{\partial w}{\partial z} = 0$$

55. Suppose that the equation $z = f(x, y)$ is expressed in the polar form $z = g(r, \theta)$ by making the substitution $x = r\cos\theta$ and $y = r\sin\theta$.

(a) View r and θ as functions of x and y and use implicit differentiation to show that
$$\frac{\partial r}{\partial x} = \cos\theta \quad \text{and} \quad \frac{\partial\theta}{\partial x} = -\frac{\sin\theta}{r}$$

(b) View r and θ as functions of x and y and use implicit differentiation to show that
$$\frac{\partial r}{\partial y} = \sin\theta \quad \text{and} \quad \frac{\partial\theta}{\partial y} = \frac{\cos\theta}{r}$$

(c) Use the results in parts (a) and (b) to show that
$$\frac{\partial z}{\partial x} = \frac{\partial z}{\partial r}\cos\theta - \frac{1}{r}\frac{\partial z}{\partial\theta}\sin\theta$$
$$\frac{\partial z}{\partial y} = \frac{\partial z}{\partial r}\sin\theta + \frac{1}{r}\frac{\partial z}{\partial\theta}\cos\theta$$

(d) Use the result in part (c) to show that
$$\left(\frac{\partial z}{\partial x}\right)^2 + \left(\frac{\partial z}{\partial y}\right)^2 = \left(\frac{\partial z}{\partial r}\right)^2 + \frac{1}{r^2}\left(\frac{\partial z}{\partial\theta}\right)^2$$

(e) Use the result in part (c) to show that if $z = f(x, y)$ satisfies Laplace's equation
$$\frac{\partial^2 z}{\partial x^2} + \frac{\partial^2 z}{\partial y^2} = 0$$

then $z = g(r, \theta)$ satisfies the equation
$$\frac{\partial^2 z}{\partial r^2} + \frac{1}{r^2}\frac{\partial^2 z}{\partial\theta^2} + \frac{1}{r}\frac{\partial z}{\partial r} = 0$$

and conversely. The latter equation is called the *polar form of Laplace's equation*.

56. Show that the function
$$z = \tan^{-1}\frac{2xy}{x^2 - y^2}$$

satisfies Laplace's equation; then make the substitution $x = r\cos\theta$, $y = r\sin\theta$, and show that the resulting function of r and θ satisfies the polar form of Laplace's equation given in part (e) of Exercise 55.

57. (a) Show that if $u(x, y)$ and $v(x, y)$ satisfy the Cauchy–Riemann equations (Exercise 94, Section 13.3), and if $x = r\cos\theta$ and $y = r\sin\theta$, then
$$\frac{\partial u}{\partial r} = \frac{1}{r}\frac{\partial v}{\partial\theta} \quad \text{and} \quad \frac{\partial v}{\partial r} = -\frac{1}{r}\frac{\partial u}{\partial\theta}$$

This is called the *polar form of the Cauchy–Riemann equations*.

(b) Show that the functions
$$u = \ln(x^2 + y^2), \quad v = 2\tan^{-1}(y/x)$$

satisfy the Cauchy–Riemann equations; then make the substitution $x = r\cos\theta$, $y = r\sin\theta$, and show that the resulting functions of r and θ satisfy the polar form of the Cauchy–Riemann equations.

58. Recall from Formula (6) of Section 13.3 that under appropriate conditions a plucked string satisfies the wave equation

$$\frac{\partial^2 u}{\partial t^2} = c^2 \frac{\partial^2 u}{\partial x^2}$$

where c is a positive constant.

(a) Show that a function of the form $u(x, t) = f(x + ct)$ satisfies the wave equation.

(b) Show that a function of the form $u(x, t) = g(x - ct)$ satisfies the wave equation.

(c) Show that a function of the form

$$u(x, t) = f(x + ct) + g(x - ct)$$

satisfies the wave equation.

(d) It can be proved that every solution of the wave equation is expressible in the form stated in part (c). Confirm that $u(x, t) = \sin t \sin x$ satisfies the wave equation in which $c = 1$, and then use appropriate trigonometric identities to express this function in the form $f(x + t) + g(x - t)$.

59. Let f be a differentiable function of three variables, and let $w = f(x, y, z)$, $x = \rho \sin \phi \cos \theta$, $y = \rho \sin \phi \sin \theta$, and $z = \rho \cos \phi$. Express $\partial w/\partial \rho$, $\partial w/\partial \phi$, and $\partial w/\partial \theta$ in terms of $\partial w/\partial x$, $\partial w/\partial y$, and $\partial w/\partial z$.

60. Let $w = f(x, y, z)$ be differentiable, where $z = g(x, y)$. Taking x and y as the independent variables, express each of the following in terms of $\partial f/\partial x$, $\partial f/\partial y$, $\partial f/\partial z$, $\partial z/\partial x$, and $\partial z/\partial y$.

(a) $\partial w/\partial x$ (b) $\partial w/\partial y$

61. Let $w = \ln(e^r + e^s + e^t + e^u)$. Show that

$$w_{rstu} = -6e^{r+s+t+u-4w}$$

[*Hint:* Take advantage of the relationship $e^w = e^r + e^s + e^t + e^u$.]

62. Suppose that w is a differentiable function of x_1, x_2, and x_3, and

$$x_1 = a_1 y_1 + b_1 y_2$$
$$x_2 = a_2 y_1 + b_2 y_2$$
$$x_3 = a_3 y_1 + b_3 y_2$$

where the a's and b's are constants. Express $\partial w/\partial y_1$ and $\partial w/\partial y_2$ in terms of $\partial w/\partial x_1$, $\partial w/\partial x_2$, and $\partial w/\partial x_3$.

63. (a) Let w be a differentiable function of x_1, x_2, x_3, and x_4, and let each x_i be a differentiable function of t. Find a chain-rule formula for dw/dt.

(b) Let w be a differentiable function of x_1, x_2, x_3, and x_4, and let each x_i be a differentiable function of v_1, v_2, and v_3. Find chain-rule formulas for $\partial w/\partial v_1$, $\partial w/\partial v_2$, and $\partial w/\partial v_3$.

64. Let $w = (x_1^2 + x_2^2 + \cdots + x_n^2)^k$, where $n \geq 2$. For what values of k does

$$\frac{\partial^2 w}{\partial x_1^2} + \frac{\partial^2 w}{\partial x_2^2} + \cdots + \frac{\partial^2 w}{\partial x_n^2} = 0$$

hold?

65. We showed in Exercise 28 of Section 5.10 that

$$\frac{d}{dx} \int_{h(x)}^{g(x)} f(t)\, dt = f(g(x))g'(x) - f(h(x))h'(x)$$

Derive this same result by letting $u = g(x)$ and $v = h(x)$ and then differentiating the function

$$F(u, v) = \int_v^u f(t)\, dt$$

with respect to x.

66. Prove: If f, f_x, and f_y are continuous on a circular region containing $A(x_0, y_0)$ and $B(x_1, y_1)$, then there is a point (x^*, y^*) on the line segment joining A and B such that

$$f(x_1, y_1) - f(x_0, y_0)$$
$$= f_x(x^*, y^*)(x_1 - x_0) + f_y(x^*, y^*)(y_1 - y_0)$$

This result is the two-dimensional version of the Mean-Value Theorem. [*Hint:* Express the line segment joining A and B in parametric form and use the Mean-Value Theorem for functions of one variable.]

67. Prove: If $f_x(x, y) = 0$ and $f_y(x, y) = 0$ throughout a circular region, then $f(x, y)$ is constant on that region. [*Hint:* Use the result of Exercise 66.]

68. Writing   Use differentials to give an informal justification for the chain rules for derivatives.

69. Writing   Compare the use of the formula

$$\frac{dy}{dx} = -\frac{\partial f/\partial x}{\partial f/\partial y}$$

with the process of implicit differentiation.

✔ **QUICK CHECK ANSWERS 13.5**

1. -8 **2.** 3 **3.** $26\ \text{ft}^2/\text{s}$ **4.** $1;\ 1$

13.6 DIRECTIONAL DERIVATIVES AND GRADIENTS

The partial derivatives $f_x(x, y)$ and $f_y(x, y)$ represent the rates of change of $f(x, y)$ in directions parallel to the x- and y-axes. In this section we will investigate rates of change of $f(x, y)$ in other directions.

■ DIRECTIONAL DERIVATIVES

In this section we extend the concept of a *partial* derivative to the more general notion of a *directional* derivative. We have seen that the partial derivatives of a function give the instantaneous rates of change of that function in directions parallel to the coordinate axes. Directional derivatives allow us to compute the rates of change of a function with respect to distance in *any* direction.

Suppose that we wish to compute the instantaneous rate of change of a function $f(x, y)$ with respect to distance from a point (x_0, y_0) in some direction. Since there are infinitely many different directions from (x_0, y_0) in which we could move, we need a convenient method for describing a specific direction starting at (x_0, y_0). One way to do this is to use a unit vector

$$\mathbf{u} = u_1\mathbf{i} + u_2\mathbf{j}$$

that has its initial point at (x_0, y_0) and points in the desired direction (Figure 13.6.1). This vector determines a line l in the xy-plane that can be expressed parametrically as

$$x = x_0 + su_1, \quad y = y_0 + su_2 \tag{1}$$

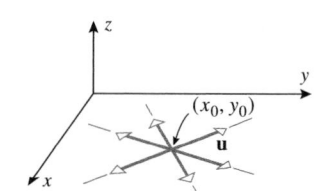

▲ Figure 13.6.1

Since u is a unit vector, s is the arc length parameter that has its reference point at (x_0, y_0) and has positive values in the direction of $\mathbf{u}$. For $s = 0$, the point (x, y) is at the reference point (x_0, y_0), and as s increases, the point (x, y) moves along l in the direction of $\mathbf{u}$. On the line l the variable $z = f(x_0 + su_1, y_0 + su_2)$ is a function of the parameter s. The value of the derivative dz/ds at $s = 0$ then gives an instantaneous rate of change of $f(x, y)$ with respect to distance from (x_0, y_0) in the direction of $\mathbf{u}$.

13.6.1 DEFINITION If $f(x, y)$ is a function of x and y, and if $\mathbf{u} = u_1\mathbf{i} + u_2\mathbf{j}$ is a unit vector, then the **directional derivative of f in the direction of $\mathbf{u}$** at (x_0, y_0) is denoted by $D_\mathbf{u}f(x_0, y_0)$ and is defined by

$$D_\mathbf{u}f(x_0, y_0) = \frac{d}{ds}\left[f(x_0 + su_1, y_0 + su_2)\right]_{s=0} \tag{2}$$

provided this derivative exists.

Slope in **u** direction = rate of change of z with respect to s

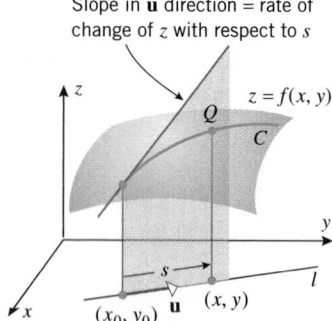

▲ Figure 13.6.2

Geometrically, $D_\mathbf{u}f(x_0, y_0)$ can be interpreted as the **slope of the surface $z = f(x, y)$ in the direction of u** at the point $(x_0, y_0, f(x_0, y_0))$ (Figure 13.6.2). Usually the value of $D_\mathbf{u}f(x_0, y_0)$ will depend on both the point (x_0, y_0) and the direction $\mathbf{u}$. Thus, at a fixed point the slope of the surface may vary with the direction (Figure 13.6.3). Analytically, the directional derivative represents the **instantaneous rate of change of $f(x, y)$ with respect to distance in the direction of u** at the point (x_0, y_0).

▶ **Example 1** Let $f(x, y) = xy$. Find and interpret $D_\mathbf{u}f(1, 2)$ for the unit vector

$$\mathbf{u} = \frac{\sqrt{3}}{2}\mathbf{i} + \frac{1}{2}\mathbf{j}$$

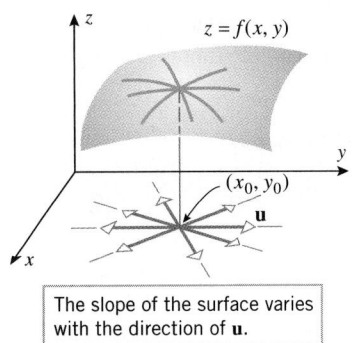

$z = f(x, y)$

(x_0, y_0)

u

The slope of the surface varies with the direction of **u**.

▲ **Figure 13.6.3**

Solution.   It follows from Equation (2) that

$$D_{\mathbf{u}} f(1, 2) = \frac{d}{ds} \left[f \left(1 + \frac{\sqrt{3}s}{2}, 2 + \frac{s}{2} \right) \right]_{s=0}$$

Since

$$f \left(1 + \frac{\sqrt{3}s}{2}, 2 + \frac{s}{2} \right) = \left(1 + \frac{\sqrt{3}s}{2} \right) \left(2 + \frac{s}{2} \right) = \frac{\sqrt{3}}{4}s^2 + \left(\frac{1}{2} + \sqrt{3} \right) s + 2$$

we have

$$D_{\mathbf{u}} f(1, 2) = \frac{d}{ds} \left[\frac{\sqrt{3}}{4}s^2 + \left(\frac{1}{2} + \sqrt{3} \right) s + 2 \right]_{s=0}$$

$$= \left[\frac{\sqrt{3}}{2}s + \frac{1}{2} + \sqrt{3} \right]_{s=0} = \frac{1}{2} + \sqrt{3}$$

Since $\frac{1}{2} + \sqrt{3} \approx 2.23$, we conclude that if we move a small distance from the point $(1, 2)$ in the direction of **u**, the function $f(x, y) = xy$ will increase by about 2.23 times the distance moved. ◄

The definition of a directional derivative for a function $f(x, y, z)$ of three variables is similar to Definition 13.6.1.

13.6.2   DEFINITION   If $\mathbf{u} = u_1 \mathbf{i} + u_2 \mathbf{j} + u_3 \mathbf{k}$ is a unit vector, and if $f(x, y, z)$ is a function of x, y, and z, then the *directional derivative of f in the direction of* **u** at (x_0, y_0, z_0) is denoted by $D_{\mathbf{u}} f(x_0, y_0, z_0)$ and is defined by

$$D_{\mathbf{u}} f(x_0, y_0, z_0) = \frac{d}{ds} \left[f(x_0 + su_1, y_0 + su_2, z_0 + su_3) \right]_{s=0} \quad (3)$$

provided this derivative exists.

Although Equation (3) does not have a convenient geometric interpretation, we can still interpret directional derivatives for functions of three variables in terms of instantaneous rates of change in a specified direction.

For a function that is differentiable at a point, directional derivatives exist in every direction from the point and can be computed directly in terms of the first-order partial derivatives of the function.

13.6.3   THEOREM

(a)   *If $f(x, y)$ is differentiable at (x_0, y_0), and if $\mathbf{u} = u_1 \mathbf{i} + u_2 \mathbf{j}$ is a unit vector, then the directional derivative $D_{\mathbf{u}} f(x_0, y_0)$ exists and is given by*

$$D_{\mathbf{u}} f(x_0, y_0) = f_x(x_0, y_0)u_1 + f_y(x_0, y_0)u_2 \quad (4)$$

(b)   *If $f(x, y, z)$ is differentiable at (x_0, y_0, z_0), and if $\mathbf{u} = u_1 \mathbf{i} + u_2 \mathbf{j} + u_3 \mathbf{k}$ is a unit vector, then the directional derivative $D_{\mathbf{u}} f(x_0, y_0, z_0)$ exists and is given by*

$$D_{\mathbf{u}} f(x_0, y_0, z_0) = f_x(x_0, y_0, z_0)u_1 + f_y(x_0, y_0, z_0)u_2 + f_z(x_0, y_0, z_0)u_3 \quad (5)$$

PROOF   We will give the proof of part (a); the proof of part (b) is similar and will be omitted. The function $z = f(x_0 + su_1, y_0 + su_2)$ is the composition of the function $z = f(x, y)$ with the functions

$$x = x(s) = x_0 + su_1 \quad \text{and} \quad y = y(s) = y_0 + su_2$$

As such, the chain rule in Formula (5) of Section 13.5 immediately gives

$$D_{\mathbf{u}} f(x_0, y_0) = \frac{d}{ds} \left[f(x_0 + su_1, y_0 + su_2) \right]_{s=0}$$

$$= \frac{dz}{ds}\bigg|_{s=0} = f_x(x_0, y_0)u_1 + f_y(x_0, y_0)u_2 \quad \blacksquare$$

We can use Theorem 13.6.3 to confirm the result of Example 1. For $f(x, y) = xy$ we have $f_x(1, 2) = 2$ and $f_y(1, 2) = 1$ (verify). With

$$\mathbf{u} = \frac{\sqrt{3}}{2}\mathbf{i} + \frac{1}{2}\mathbf{j}$$

Equation (4) becomes

$$D_{\mathbf{u}} f(1, 2) = 2 \left(\frac{\sqrt{3}}{2} \right) + \frac{1}{2} = \sqrt{3} + \frac{1}{2}$$

which agrees with our solution in Example 1.

Recall from Formula (13) of Section 11.2 that a unit vector $\mathbf{u}$ in the xy-plane can be expressed as

$$\mathbf{u} = \cos\phi\,\mathbf{i} + \sin\phi\,\mathbf{j} \tag{6}$$

where ϕ is the angle from the positive x-axis to $\mathbf{u}$. Thus, Formula (4) can also be expressed as

$$D_{\mathbf{u}} f(x_0, y_0) = f_x(x_0, y_0) \cos\phi + f_y(x_0, y_0) \sin\phi \tag{7}$$

▶ **Example 2**   Find the directional derivative of $f(x, y) = e^{xy}$ at $(-2, 0)$ in the direction of the unit vector that makes an angle of $\pi/3$ with the positive x-axis.

Solution.   The partial derivatives of f are

$$f_x(x, y) = ye^{xy}, \quad f_y(x, y) = xe^{xy}$$

$$f_x(-2, 0) = 0, \quad f_y(-2, 0) = -2$$

The unit vector $\mathbf{u}$ that makes an angle of $\pi/3$ with the positive x-axis is

$$\mathbf{u} = \cos(\pi/3)\mathbf{i} + \sin(\pi/3)\mathbf{j} = \frac{1}{2}\mathbf{i} + \frac{\sqrt{3}}{2}\mathbf{j}$$

Thus, from (7)

$$D_{\mathbf{u}} f(-2, 0) = f_x(-2, 0) \cos(\pi/3) + f_y(-2, 0) \sin(\pi/3)$$

$$= 0(1/2) + (-2)(\sqrt{3}/2) = -\sqrt{3} \quad ◀$$

Note that in Example 3 we used a *unit vector* to specify the direction of the directional derivative. This is required in order to apply either Formula (4) or Formula (5).

▶ **Example 3**   Find the directional derivative of $f(x, y, z) = x^2 y - yz^3 + z$ at the point $(1, -2, 0)$ in the direction of the vector $\mathbf{a} = 2\mathbf{i} + \mathbf{j} - 2\mathbf{k}$.

Solution. The partial derivatives of f are

$$f_x(x, y, z) = 2xy, \quad f_y(x, y, z) = x^2 - z^3, \quad f_z(x, y, z) = -3yz^2 + 1$$

$$f_x(1, -2, 0) = -4, \quad f_y(1, -2, 0) = 1, \quad f_z(1, -2, 0) = 1$$

Since **a** is not a unit vector, we normalize it, getting

$$\mathbf{u} = \frac{\mathbf{a}}{\|\mathbf{a}\|} = \frac{1}{\sqrt{9}}(2\mathbf{i} + \mathbf{j} - 2\mathbf{k}) = \frac{2}{3}\mathbf{i} + \frac{1}{3}\mathbf{j} - \frac{2}{3}\mathbf{k}$$

Formula (5) then yields

$$D_{\mathbf{u}}f(1, -2, 0) = (-4)\left(\frac{2}{3}\right) + \frac{1}{3} - \frac{2}{3} = -3 \blacktriangleleft$$

◼ THE GRADIENT

Formula (4) can be expressed in the form of a dot product as

$$D_{\mathbf{u}}f(x_0, y_0) = (f_x(x_0, y_0)\mathbf{i} + f_y(x_0, y_0)\mathbf{j}) \cdot (u_1\mathbf{i} + u_2\mathbf{j})$$
$$= (f_x(x_0, y_0)\mathbf{i} + f_y(x_0, y_0)\mathbf{j}) \cdot \mathbf{u}$$

Similarly, Formula (5) can be expressed as

$$D_{\mathbf{u}}f(x_0, y_0, z_0) = (f_x(x_0, y_0, z_0)\mathbf{i} + f_y(x_0, y_0, z_0)\mathbf{j} + f_z(x_0, y_0, z_0)\mathbf{k}) \cdot \mathbf{u}$$

In both cases the directional derivative is obtained by dotting the direction vector **u** with a new vector constructed from the first-order partial derivatives of f.

13.6.4   DEFINITION

(a)   If f is a function of x and y, then the ***gradient of*** f is defined by

$$\nabla f(x, y) = f_x(x, y)\mathbf{i} + f_y(x, y)\mathbf{j} \tag{8}$$

(b)   If f is a function of x, y, and z, then the ***gradient of*** f is defined by

$$\nabla f(x, y, z) = f_x(x, y, z)\mathbf{i} + f_y(x, y, z)\mathbf{j} + f_z(x, y, z)\mathbf{k} \tag{9}$$

> Remember that ∇f is not a product of ∇ and f. Think of ∇ as an "operator" that acts on a function f to produce the gradient ∇f.

The symbol ∇ (read "del") is an inverted delta. (It is sometimes called a "nabla" because of its similarity in form to an ancient Hebrew ten-stringed harp of that name.)

Formulas (4) and (5) can now be written as

$$D_{\mathbf{u}}f(x_0, y_0) = \nabla f(x_0, y_0) \cdot \mathbf{u} \tag{10}$$

and

$$D_{\mathbf{u}}f(x_0, y_0, z_0) = \nabla f(x_0, y_0, z_0) \cdot \mathbf{u} \tag{11}$$

respectively. For example, using Formula (11) our solution to Example 3 would take the form

$$D_{\mathbf{u}}f(1, -2, 0) = \nabla f(1, -2, 0) \cdot \mathbf{u} = (-4\mathbf{i} + \mathbf{j} + \mathbf{k}) \cdot \left(\tfrac{2}{3}\mathbf{i} + \tfrac{1}{3}\mathbf{j} - \tfrac{2}{3}\mathbf{k}\right)$$
$$= (-4)\left(\tfrac{2}{3}\right) + \tfrac{1}{3} - \tfrac{2}{3} = -3$$

Formula (10) can be interpreted to mean that the slope of the surface $z = f(x, y)$ at the point (x_0, y_0) in the direction of **u** is the dot product of the gradient with **u** (Figure 13.6.4).

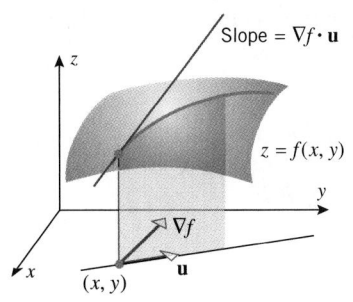

▲ **Figure 13.6.4**

■ PROPERTIES OF THE GRADIENT

The gradient is not merely a notational device to simplify the formula for the directional derivative; we will see that the length and direction of the gradient ∇f provide important information about the function f and the surface $z = f(x, y)$. For example, suppose that $\nabla f(x, y) \neq \mathbf{0}$, and let us use Formula (4) of Section 11.3 to rewrite (10) as

$$D_{\mathbf{u}} f(x, y) = \nabla f(x, y) \cdot \mathbf{u} = \|\nabla f(x, y)\| \|\mathbf{u}\| \cos \theta = \|\nabla f(x, y)\| \cos \theta \qquad (12)$$

where θ is the angle between $\nabla f(x, y)$ and $\mathbf{u}$. Equation (12) tells us that the maximum value of $D_{\mathbf{u}} f$ at the point (x, y) is $\|\nabla f(x, y)\|$, and this maximum occurs when $\theta = 0$, that is, when $\mathbf{u}$ is in the direction of $\nabla f(x, y)$. Geometrically, this means:

> *At (x, y), the surface $z = f(x, y)$ has its maximum slope in the direction of the gradient, and the maximum slope is $\|\nabla f(x, y)\|$.*

That is, the function $f(x, y)$ increases most rapidly in the direction of its gradient (Figure 13.6.5).

Similarly, (12) tells us that the minimum value of $D_{\mathbf{u}} f$ at the point (x, y) is $-\|\nabla f(x, y)\|$, and this minimum occurs when $\theta = \pi$, that is, when $\mathbf{u}$ is oppositely directed to $\nabla f(x, y)$. Geometrically, this means:

> *At (x, y), the surface $z = f(x, y)$ has its minimum slope in the direction that is opposite to the gradient, and the minimum slope is $-\|\nabla f(x, y)\|$.*

That is, the function $f(x, y)$ decreases most rapidly in the direction opposite to its gradient (Figure 13.6.5).

Finally, in the case where $\nabla f(x, y) = \mathbf{0}$, it follows from (12) that $D_{\mathbf{u}} f(x, y) = 0$ in all directions at the point (x, y). This typically occurs where the surface $z = f(x, y)$ has a "relative maximum," a "relative minimum," or a saddle point.

A similar analysis applies to functions of three variables. As a consequence, we have the following result.

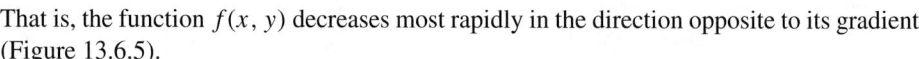

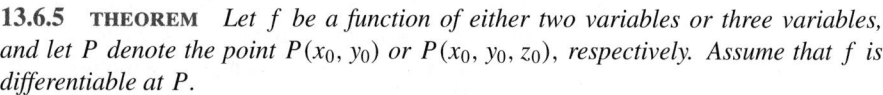

▲ **Figure 13.6.5**

> **13.6.5** **THEOREM** *Let f be a function of either two variables or three variables, and let P denote the point $P(x_0, y_0)$ or $P(x_0, y_0, z_0)$, respectively. Assume that f is differentiable at P.*
>
> *(a)* *If $\nabla f = \mathbf{0}$ at P, then all directional derivatives of f at P are zero.*
>
> *(b)* *If $\nabla f \neq \mathbf{0}$ at P, then among all possible directional derivatives of f at P, the derivative in the direction of ∇f at P has the largest value. The value of this largest directional derivative is $\|\nabla f\|$ at P.*
>
> *(c)* *If $\nabla f \neq \mathbf{0}$ at P, then among all possible directional derivatives of f at P, the derivative in the direction opposite to that of ∇f at P has the smallest value. The value of this smallest directional derivative is $-\|\nabla f\|$ at P.*

▶ **Example 4** Let $f(x, y) = x^2 e^y$. Find the maximum value of a directional derivative at $(-2, 0)$, and find the unit vector in the direction in which the maximum value occurs.

Solution.   Since

$$\nabla f(x, y) = f_x(x, y)\mathbf{i} + f_y(x, y)\mathbf{j} = 2xe^y\mathbf{i} + x^2e^y\mathbf{j}$$

the gradient of f at $(-2, 0)$ is

$$\nabla f(-2, 0) = -4\mathbf{i} + 4\mathbf{j}$$

By Theorem 13.6.5, the maximum value of the directional derivative is

$$\|\nabla f(-2, 0)\| = \sqrt{(-4)^2 + 4^2} = \sqrt{32} = 4\sqrt{2}$$

This maximum occurs in the direction of $\nabla f(-2, 0)$. The unit vector in this direction is

$$\mathbf{u} = \frac{\nabla f(-2, 0)}{\|\nabla f(-2, 0)\|} = \frac{1}{4\sqrt{2}}(-4\mathbf{i} + 4\mathbf{j}) = -\frac{1}{\sqrt{2}}\mathbf{i} + \frac{1}{\sqrt{2}}\mathbf{j} \blacktriangleleft$$

> What would be the minimum value of a directional derivative of
> $$f(x, y) = x^2e^y$$
> at $(-2, 0)$?

■ GRADIENTS ARE NORMAL TO LEVEL CURVES

We have seen that the gradient points in the direction in which a function increases most rapidly. For a function $f(x, y)$ of two variables, we will now consider how this direction of maximum rate of increase can be determined from a contour map of the function. Suppose that (x_0, y_0) is a point on a level curve $f(x, y) = c$ of f, and assume that this curve can be smoothly parametrized as

$$x = x(s), \quad y = y(s) \tag{13}$$

where s is an arc length parameter. Recall from Formula (6) of Section 12.4 that the unit tangent vector to (13) is

$$\mathbf{T} = \mathbf{T}(s) = \left(\frac{dx}{ds}\right)\mathbf{i} + \left(\frac{dy}{ds}\right)\mathbf{j}$$

Since $\mathbf{T}$ gives a direction along which f is nearly constant, we would expect the instantaneous rate of change of f with respect to distance in the direction of $\mathbf{T}$ to be 0. That is, we would expect that

$$D_{\mathbf{T}}f(x, y) = \nabla f(x, y) \cdot \mathbf{T}(s) = 0$$

To show this to be the case, we differentiate both sides of the equation $f(x, y) = c$ with respect to s. Assuming that f is differentiable at (x, y), we can use the chain rule to obtain

$$\frac{\partial f}{\partial x}\frac{dx}{ds} + \frac{\partial f}{\partial y}\frac{dy}{ds} = 0$$

which we can rewrite as

$$\left(\frac{\partial f}{\partial x}\mathbf{i} + \frac{\partial f}{\partial y}\mathbf{j}\right) \cdot \left(\frac{dx}{ds}\mathbf{i} + \frac{dy}{ds}\mathbf{j}\right) = 0$$

or, alternatively, as

$$\nabla f(x, y) \cdot \mathbf{T} = 0$$

Therefore, if $\nabla f(x, y) \neq \mathbf{0}$, then $\nabla f(x, y)$ should be normal to the level curve $f(x, y) = c$ at any point (x, y) on the curve.

It is proved in advanced courses that if $f(x, y)$ has continuous first-order partial derivatives, and if $\nabla f(x_0, y_0) \neq \mathbf{0}$, then near (x_0, y_0) the graph of $f(x, y) = c$ is indeed a smooth curve through (x_0, y_0). Furthermore, we also know from Theorem 13.4.4 that f will be differentiable at (x_0, y_0). We therefore have the following result.

> Show that the level curves for
> $$f(x, y) = x^2 + y^2$$
> are circles and verify Theorem 13.6.6 at $(x_0, y_0) = (3, 4)$.

> **13.6.6   THEOREM**   *Assume that $f(x, y)$ has continuous first-order partial derivatives in an open disk centered at (x_0, y_0) and that $\nabla f(x_0, y_0) \neq \mathbf{0}$. Then $\nabla f(x_0, y_0)$ is normal to the level curve of f through (x_0, y_0).*

When we examine a contour map, we instinctively regard the distance between adjacent contours to be measured in a normal direction. If the contours correspond to equally spaced values of f, then the closer together the contours appear to be, the more rapidly the values of f will be changing in that normal direction. It follows from Theorems 13.6.5 and 13.6.6 that this rate of change of f is given by $\|\nabla f(x, y)\|$. Thus, the closer together the contours appear to be, the greater the length of the gradient of f.

▶ **Example 5**   A contour plot of a function f is given in Figure 13.6.6a. Sketch the directions of the gradient of f at the points P, Q, and R. At which of these three points does the gradient vector have maximum length? Minimum length?

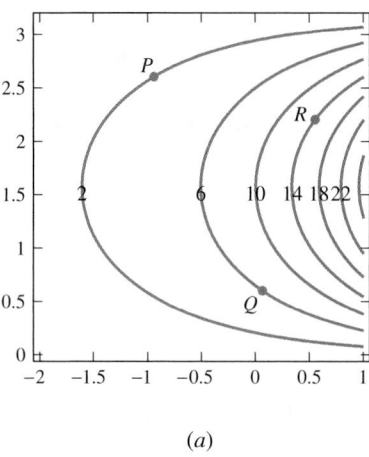
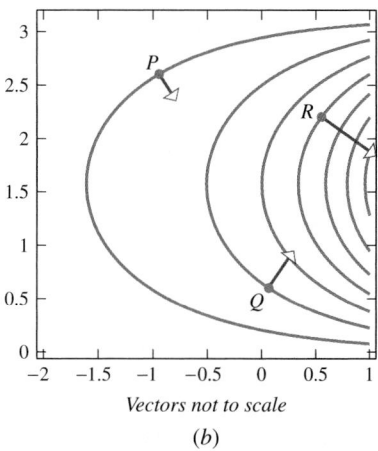

Vectors not to scale

(a)   (b)

▲ **Figure 13.6.6**

Solution.   It follows from Theorems 13.6.5 and 13.6.6 that the directions of the gradient vectors will be as given in Figure 13.6.6b. Based on the density of the contour lines, we would guess that the gradient of f has maximum length at R and minimum length at P, with the length at Q somewhere in between. ◀

REMARK | If (x_0, y_0) is a point on the level curve $f(x, y) = c$, then the slope of the surface $z = f(x, y)$ at that point in the direction of **u** is

$$D_{\mathbf{u}} f(x_0, y_0) = \nabla f(x_0, y_0) \cdot \mathbf{u}$$

If **u** is tangent to the level curve at (x_0, y_0), then $f(x, y)$ is neither increasing nor decreasing in that direction, so $D_{\mathbf{u}} f(x_0, y_0) = 0$. Thus, $\nabla f(x_0, y_0)$, $-\nabla f(x_0, y_0)$, and the tangent vector **u** mark the directions of maximum slope, minimum slope, and zero slope at a point (x_0, y_0) on a level curve (Figure 13.6.7). Good skiers use these facts intuitively to control their speed by zigzagging down ski slopes—they ski across the slope with their skis tangential to a level curve to stop their downhill motion, and they point their skis down the slope and normal to the level curve to obtain the most rapid descent.

$f(x, y) = c$

u

$\nabla f(x_0, y_0)$

(x_0, y_0)

$-\nabla f(x_0, y_0)$

▲ **Figure 13.6.7**

■ AN APPLICATION OF GRADIENTS

There are numerous applications in which the motion of an object must be controlled so that it moves toward a heat source. For example, in medical applications the operation of certain diagnostic equipment is designed to locate heat sources generated by tumors or infections, and in military applications the trajectories of heat-seeking missiles are controlled to seek and destroy enemy aircraft. The following example illustrates how gradients are used to solve such problems.

UPI Photo/Michael Ammons/Air Force/Digital Railroad, Inc

Heat-seeking missiles such as "Stinger" and "Sidewinder" use infrared sensors to measure gradients.

▶ **Example 6**   A heat-seeking particle is located at the point $(2, 3)$ on a flat metal plate whose temperature at a point (x, y) is

$$T(x, y) = 10 - 8x^2 - 2y^2$$

Find an equation for the trajectory of the particle if it moves continuously in the direction of maximum temperature increase.

Solution.   Assume that the trajectory is represented parametrically by the equations

$$x = x(t), \quad y = y(t)$$

where the particle is at the point $(2, 3)$ at time $t = 0$. Because the particle moves in the direction of maximum temperature increase, its direction of motion at time t is in the direction of the gradient of $T(x, y)$, and hence its velocity vector $\mathbf{v}(t)$ at time t points in the direction of the gradient. Thus, there is a scalar k that depends on t such that

$$\mathbf{v}(t) = k\nabla T(x, y)$$

from which we obtain

$$\frac{dx}{dt}\mathbf{i} + \frac{dy}{dt}\mathbf{j} = k(-16x\mathbf{i} - 4y\mathbf{j})$$

Equating components yields

$$\frac{dx}{dt} = -16kx, \quad \frac{dy}{dt} = -4ky$$

and dividing to eliminate k yields

$$\frac{dy}{dx} = \frac{-4ky}{-16kx} = \frac{y}{4x}$$

Thus, we can obtain the trajectory by solving the initial-value problem

$$\frac{dy}{dx} - \frac{y}{4x} = 0, \quad y(2) = 3$$

The differential equation is a separable first-order equation and hence can be solved by the method of separation of variables discussed in Section 8.2. We leave it for you to show that the solution of the initial-value problem is

$$y = \frac{3}{\sqrt[4]{2}}x^{1/4}$$

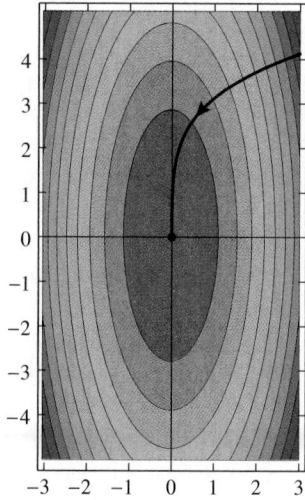

▲ **Figure 13.6.8**

The graph of the trajectory and a contour plot of the temperature function are shown in Figure 13.6.8. ◄

✔ **QUICK CHECK EXERCISES 13.6**   (See page 971 for answers.)

1. The gradient of $f(x, y, z) = xy^2z^3$ at the point $(1, 1, 1)$ is _____.

2. Suppose that the differentiable function $f(x, y)$ has the property that

$$f\left(2 + \frac{s\sqrt{3}}{2}, 1 + \frac{s}{2}\right) = 3se^s$$

The directional derivative of f in the direction of

$$\mathbf{u} = \frac{\sqrt{3}}{2}\mathbf{i} + \frac{1}{2}\mathbf{j}$$

at $(2, 1)$ is _____.

3. If the gradient of $f(x, y)$ at the origin is $6\mathbf{i} + 8\mathbf{j}$, then the directional derivative of f in the direction of $\mathbf{a} = 3\mathbf{i} + 4\mathbf{j}$ at the origin is _____. The slope of the tangent line to the level curve of f through the origin at $(0, 0)$ is _____.

4. If the gradient of $f(x, y, z)$ at $(1, 2, 3)$ is $2\mathbf{i} - 2\mathbf{j} + \mathbf{k}$, then the maximum value for a directional derivative of f at $(1, 2, 3)$ is _____ and the minimum value for a directional derivative at this point is _____.

EXERCISE SET 13.6   ⬿ Graphing Utility   [C] CAS

1–8 Find $D_{\mathbf{u}} f$ at P. ▨

1. $f(x, y) = (1 + xy)^{3/2}$; $P(3, 1)$; $\mathbf{u} = \dfrac{1}{\sqrt{2}}\mathbf{i} + \dfrac{1}{\sqrt{2}}\mathbf{j}$

2. $f(x, y) = e^{2xy}$; $P(4, 0)$; $\mathbf{u} = -\frac{3}{5}\mathbf{i} + \frac{4}{5}\mathbf{j}$

3. $f(x, y) = \ln(1 + x^2 + y)$; $P(0, 0)$;
$\mathbf{u} = -\dfrac{1}{\sqrt{10}}\mathbf{i} - \dfrac{3}{\sqrt{10}}\mathbf{j}$

4. $f(x, y) = \dfrac{cx + dy}{x - y}$; $P(3, 4)$; $\mathbf{u} = \frac{4}{5}\mathbf{i} + \frac{3}{5}\mathbf{j}$

5. $f(x, y, z) = 4x^5 y^2 z^3$; $P(2, -1, 1)$; $\mathbf{u} = \frac{1}{3}\mathbf{i} + \frac{2}{3}\mathbf{j} - \frac{2}{3}\mathbf{k}$

6. $f(x, y, z) = ye^{xz} + z^2$; $P(0, 2, 3)$; $\mathbf{u} = \frac{2}{7}\mathbf{i} - \frac{3}{7}\mathbf{j} + \frac{6}{7}\mathbf{k}$

7. $f(x, y, z) = \ln(x^2 + 2y^2 + 3z^2)$; $P(-1, 2, 4)$;
$\mathbf{u} = -\frac{3}{13}\mathbf{i} - \frac{4}{13}\mathbf{j} - \frac{12}{13}\mathbf{k}$

8. $f(x, y, z) = \sin xyz$; $P\left(\frac{1}{2}, \frac{1}{3}, \pi\right)$;
$\mathbf{u} = \dfrac{1}{\sqrt{3}}\mathbf{i} - \dfrac{1}{\sqrt{3}}\mathbf{j} + \dfrac{1}{\sqrt{3}}\mathbf{k}$

9–18 Find the directional derivative of f at P in the direction of $\mathbf{a}$. ▨

9. $f(x, y) = 4x^3 y^2$; $P(2, 1)$; $\mathbf{a} = 4\mathbf{i} - 3\mathbf{j}$

10. $f(x, y) = x^2 - 3xy + 4y^3$; $P(-2, 0)$; $\mathbf{a} = \mathbf{i} + 2\mathbf{j}$

11. $f(x, y) = y^2 \ln x$; $P(1, 4)$; $\mathbf{a} = -3\mathbf{i} + 3\mathbf{j}$

12. $f(x, y) = e^x \cos y$; $P(0, \pi/4)$; $\mathbf{a} = 5\mathbf{i} - 2\mathbf{j}$

13. $f(x, y) = \tan^{-1}(y/x)$; $P(-2, 2)$; $\mathbf{a} = -\mathbf{i} - \mathbf{j}$

14. $f(x, y) = xe^y - ye^x$; $P(0, 0)$; $\mathbf{a} = 5\mathbf{i} - 2\mathbf{j}$

15. $f(x, y, z) = x^3 z - yx^2 + z^2$; $P(2, -1, 1)$;
$\mathbf{a} = 3\mathbf{i} - \mathbf{j} + 2\mathbf{k}$

16. $f(x, y, z) = y - \sqrt{x^2 + z^2}$; $P(-3, 1, 4)$;
$\mathbf{a} = 2\mathbf{i} - 2\mathbf{j} - \mathbf{k}$

17. $f(x, y, z) = \dfrac{z - x}{z + y}$; $P(1, 0, -3)$; $\mathbf{a} = -6\mathbf{i} + 3\mathbf{j} - 2\mathbf{k}$

18. $f(x, y, z) = e^{x + y + 3z}$; $P(-2, 2, -1)$; $\mathbf{a} = 20\mathbf{i} - 4\mathbf{j} + 5\mathbf{k}$

19–22 Find the directional derivative of f at P in the direction of a vector making the counterclockwise angle θ with the positive x-axis. ▨

19. $f(x, y) = \sqrt{xy}$; $P(1, 4)$; $\theta = \pi/3$

20. $f(x, y) = \dfrac{x - y}{x + y}$; $P(-1, -2)$; $\theta = \pi/2$

21. $f(x, y) = \tan(2x + y)$; $P(\pi/6, \pi/3)$; $\theta = 7\pi/4$

22. $f(x, y) = \sinh x \cosh y$; $P(0, 0)$; $\theta = \pi$

23. Find the directional derivative of
$$f(x, y) = \frac{x}{x + y}$$
at $P(1, 0)$ in the direction of $Q(-1, -1)$.

24. Find the directional derivative of $f(x, y) = e^{-x} \sec y$ at $P(0, \pi/4)$ in the direction of the origin.

25. Find the directional derivative of $f(x, y) = \sqrt{xy}e^y$ at $P(1, 1)$ in the direction of the negative y-axis.

26. Let
$$f(x, y) = \frac{y}{x + y}$$
Find a unit vector $\mathbf{u}$ for which $D_{\mathbf{u}} f(2, 3) = 0$.

27. Find the directional derivative of
$$f(x, y, z) = \frac{y}{x + z}$$
at $P(2, 1, -1)$ in the direction from P to $Q(-1, 2, 0)$.

28. Find the directional derivative of the function
$$f(x, y, z) = x^3 y^2 z^5 - 2xz + yz + 3x$$
at $P(-1, -2, 1)$ in the direction of the negative z-axis.

FOCUS ON CONCEPTS

29. Suppose that $D_{\mathbf{u}} f(1, 2) = -5$ and $D_{\mathbf{v}} f(1, 2) = 10$, where $\mathbf{u} = \frac{3}{5}\mathbf{i} - \frac{4}{5}\mathbf{j}$ and $\mathbf{v} = \frac{4}{5}\mathbf{i} + \frac{3}{5}\mathbf{j}$. Find
(a) $f_x(1, 2)$ (b) $f_y(1, 2)$
(c) the directional derivative of f at $(1, 2)$ in the direction of the origin.

30. Given that $f_x(-5, 1) = -3$ and $f_y(-5, 1) = 2$, find the directional derivative of f at $P(-5, 1)$ in the direction of the vector from P to $Q(-4, 3)$.

31. The accompanying figure shows some level curves of an unspecified function $f(x, y)$. Which of the three vectors shown in the figure is most likely to be ∇f? Explain.

32. The accompanying figure shows some level curves of an unspecified function $f(x, y)$. Of the gradients at P and Q, which probably has the greater length? Explain.

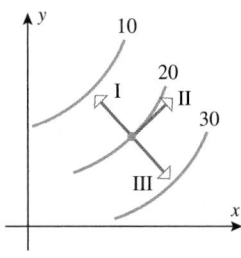

▲ Figure Ex-31

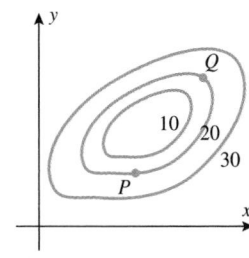

▲ Figure Ex-32

33–36 Find ∇z or ∇w. ▨

33. $z = 4x - 8y$ **34.** $z = e^{-3y} \cos 4x$

35. $w = \ln \sqrt{x^2 + y^2 + z^2}$ **36.** $w = e^{-5x} \sec x^2 yz$

37–40 Find the gradient of f at the indicated point. ▨

37. $f(x, y) = (x^2 + xy)^3$; $(-1, -1)$

38. $f(x, y) = (x^2 + y^2)^{-1/2}$; $(3, 4)$

39. $f(x, y, z) = y \ln(x + y + z)$; $(-3, 4, 0)$

40. $f(x, y, z) = y^2 z \tan^3 x$; $(\pi/4, -3, 1)$

41–44 Sketch the level curve of $f(x, y)$ that passes through P and draw the gradient vector at P. ■

41. $f(x, y) = 4x - 2y + 3;$ $P(1, 2)$

42. $f(x, y) = y/x^2;$ $P(-2, 2)$

43. $f(x, y) = x^2 + 4y^2;$ $P(-2, 0)$

44. $f(x, y) = x^2 - y^2;$ $P(2, -1)$

45. Find a unit vector $\mathbf{u}$ that is normal at $P(1, -2)$ to the level curve of $f(x, y) = 4x^2 y$ through P.

46. Find a unit vector $\mathbf{u}$ that is normal at $P(2, -3)$ to the level curve of $f(x, y) = 3x^2 y - xy$ through P.

47–54 Find a unit vector in the direction in which f increases most rapidly at P, and find the rate of change of f at P in that direction. ■

47. $f(x, y) = 4x^3 y^2;$ $P(-1, 1)$

48. $f(x, y) = 3x - \ln y;$ $P(2, 4)$

49. $f(x, y) = \sqrt{x^2 + y^2};$ $P(4, -3)$

50. $f(x, y) = \dfrac{x}{x + y};$ $P(0, 2)$

51. $f(x, y, z) = x^3 z^2 + y^3 z + z - 1;$ $P(1, 1, -1)$

52. $f(x, y, z) = \sqrt{x - 3y + 4z};$ $P(0, -3, 0)$

53. $f(x, y, z) = \dfrac{x}{z} + \dfrac{z}{y^2};$ $P(1, 2, -2)$

54. $f(x, y, z) = \tan^{-1}\left(\dfrac{x}{y + z}\right);$ $P(4, 2, 2)$

55–60 Find a unit vector in the direction in which f decreases most rapidly at P, and find the rate of change of f at P in that direction. ■

55. $f(x, y) = 20 - x^2 - y^2;$ $P(-1, -3)$

56. $f(x, y) = e^{xy};$ $P(2, 3)$

57. $f(x, y) = \cos(3x - y);$ $P(\pi/6, \pi/4)$

58. $f(x, y) = \sqrt{\dfrac{x - y}{x + y}};$ $P(3, 1)$

59. $f(x, y, z) = \dfrac{x + z}{z - y};$ $P(5, 7, 6)$

60. $f(x, y, z) = 4e^{xy} \cos z;$ $P(0, 1, \pi/4)$

61–64 True–False Determine whether the statement is true or false. Explain your answer. In each exercise, assume that f denotes a differentiable function of two variables whose domain is the xy-plane. ■

61. If $\mathbf{v} = 2\mathbf{u}$, then the directional derivative of f in the direction of $\mathbf{v}$ at a point (x_0, y_0) is twice the directional derivative of f in the direction of $\mathbf{u}$ at the point (x_0, y_0),

62. If $y = x^2$ is a contour of f, then $f_x(0, 0) = 0$.

63. If $\mathbf{u}$ is a fixed unit vector and $D_{\mathbf{u}} f(x, y) = 0$ for all points (x, y), then f is a constant function.

64. If the displacement vector from (x_0, y_0) to (x_1, y_1) is a positive multiple of $\nabla f(x_0, y_0)$, then $f(x_0, y_0) \le f(x_1, y_1)$.

FOCUS ON CONCEPTS

65. Given that $\nabla f(4, -5) = 2\mathbf{i} - \mathbf{j}$, find the directional derivative of the function f at the point $(4, -5)$ in the direction of $\mathbf{a} = 5\mathbf{i} + 2\mathbf{j}$.

66. Given that $\nabla f(x_0, y_0) = \mathbf{i} - 2\mathbf{j}$ and $D_{\mathbf{u}} f(x_0, y_0) = -2$, find $\mathbf{u}$ (two answers).

67. The accompanying figure shows some level curves of an unspecified function $f(x, y)$.
  (a) Use the available information to approximate the length of the vector $\nabla f(1, 2)$, and sketch the approximation. Explain how you approximated the length and determined the direction of the vector.
  (b) Sketch an approximation of the vector $-\nabla f(4, 4)$.

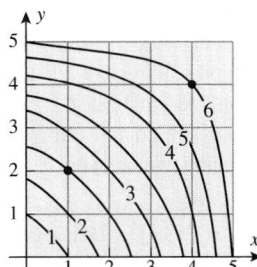

◀ **Figure Ex-67**

68. The accompanying figure shows a topographic map of a hill and a point P at the bottom of the hill. Suppose that you want to climb from the point P toward the top of the hill in such a way that you are always ascending in the direction of steepest slope. Sketch the projection of your path on the contour map. This is called the **path of steepest ascent**. Explain how you determined the path.

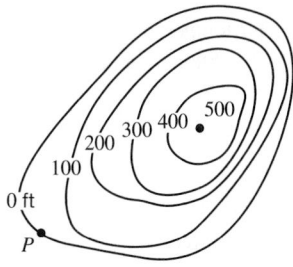

◀ **Figure Ex-68**

69. Let $z = 3x^2 - y^2$. Find all points at which $\|\nabla z\| = 6$.

70. Given that $z = 3x + y^2$, find $\nabla \|\nabla z\|$ at the point $(5, 2)$.

71. A particle moves along a path C given by the equations $x = t$ and $y = -t^2$. If $z = x^2 + y^2$, find dz/ds along C at the instant when the particle is at the point $(2, -4)$.

72. The temperature (in degrees Celsius) at a point (x, y) on a metal plate in the xy-plane is

$$T(x, y) = \dfrac{xy}{1 + x^2 + y^2} \qquad \text{(cont.)}$$

(a) Find the rate of change of temperature at $(1, 1)$ in the direction of $\mathbf{a} = 2\mathbf{i} - \mathbf{j}$.

(b) An ant at $(1, 1)$ wants to walk in the direction in which the temperature drops most rapidly. Find a unit vector in that direction.

73. If the electric potential at a point (x, y) in the xy-plane is $V(x, y)$, then the *electric intensity vector* at the point (x, y) is $\mathbf{E} = -\nabla V(x, y)$. Suppose that $V(x, y) = e^{-2x} \cos 2y$.

(a) Find the electric intensity vector at $(\pi/4, 0)$.

(b) Show that at each point in the plane, the electric potential decreases most rapidly in the direction of the vector $\mathbf{E}$.

74. On a certain mountain, the elevation z above a point (x, y) in an xy-plane at sea level is $z = 2000 - 0.02x^2 - 0.04y^2$, where x, y, and z are in meters. The positive x-axis points east, and the positive y-axis north. A climber is at the point $(-20, 5, 1991)$.

(a) If the climber uses a compass reading to walk due west, will she begin to ascend or descend?

(b) If the climber uses a compass reading to walk northeast, will she ascend or descend? At what rate?

(c) In what compass direction should the climber begin walking to travel a level path (two answers)?

75. Given that the directional derivative of $f(x, y, z)$ at the point $(3, -2, 1)$ in the direction of $\mathbf{a} = 2\mathbf{i} - \mathbf{j} - 2\mathbf{k}$ is -5 and that $\|\nabla f(3, -2, 1)\| = 5$, find $\nabla f(3, -2, 1)$.

76. The temperature (in degrees Celsius) at a point (x, y, z) in a metal solid is

$$T(x, y, z) = \frac{xyz}{1 + x^2 + y^2 + z^2}$$

(a) Find the rate of change of temperature with respect to distance at $(1, 1, 1)$ in the direction of the origin.

(b) Find the direction in which the temperature rises most rapidly at the point $(1, 1, 1)$. (Express your answer as a unit vector.)

(c) Find the rate at which the temperature rises moving from $(1, 1, 1)$ in the direction obtained in part (b).

77. Let $r = \sqrt{x^2 + y^2}$.

(a) Show that $\nabla r = \dfrac{\mathbf{r}}{r}$, where $\mathbf{r} = x\mathbf{i} + y\mathbf{j}$.

(b) Show that $\nabla f(r) = f'(r)\nabla r = \dfrac{f'(r)}{r}\mathbf{r}$.

78. Use the formula in part (b) of Exercise 77 to find

(a) $\nabla f(r)$ if $f(r) = re^{-3r}$

(b) $f(r)$ if $\nabla f(r) = 3r^2\mathbf{r}$ and $f(2) = 1$.

79. Let $\mathbf{u}_r$ be a unit vector whose counterclockwise angle from the positive x-axis is θ, and let $\mathbf{u}_\theta$ be a unit vector $90°$ counterclockwise from $\mathbf{u}_r$. Show that if $z = f(x, y)$, $x = r\cos\theta$, and $y = r\sin\theta$, then

$$\nabla z = \frac{\partial z}{\partial r}\mathbf{u}_r + \frac{1}{r}\frac{\partial z}{\partial \theta}\mathbf{u}_\theta$$

[*Hint:* Use part (c) of Exercise 55, Section 13.5.]

80. Prove: If f and g are differentiable, then

(a) $\nabla(f + g) = \nabla f + \nabla g$

(b) $\nabla(cf) = c\nabla f$ (c constant)

(c) $\nabla(fg) = f\nabla g + g\nabla f$

(d) $\nabla\left(\dfrac{f}{g}\right) = \dfrac{g\nabla f - f\nabla g}{g^2}$

(e) $\nabla(f^n) = nf^{n-1}\nabla f$.

81–82 A heat-seeking particle is located at the point P on a flat metal plate whose temperature at a point (x, y) is $T(x, y)$. Find parametric equations for the trajectory of the particle if it moves continuously in the direction of maximum temperature increase.

81. $T(x, y) = 5 - 4x^2 - y^2$; $P(1, 4)$

82. $T(x, y) = 100 - x^2 - 2y^2$; $P(5, 3)$

83. Use a graphing utility to generate the trajectory of the particle together with some representative level curves of the temperature function in Exercise 81.

84. Use a graphing utility to generate the trajectory of the particle together with some representative level curves of the temperature function in Exercise 82.

85. (a) Use a CAS to graph $f(x, y) = (x^2 + 3y^2)e^{-(x^2+y^2)}$.

(b) At how many points do you think it is true that $D_\mathbf{u} f(x, y) = 0$ for all unit vectors $\mathbf{u}$?

(c) Use a CAS to find ∇f.

(d) Use a CAS to solve the equation $\nabla f(x, y) = 0$ for x and y.

(e) Use the result in part (d) together with Theorem 13.6.5 to check your conjecture in part (b).

86. Prove: If $x = x(t)$ and $y = y(t)$ are differentiable at t, and if $z = f(x, y)$ is differentiable at the point $(x(t), y(t))$, then

$$\frac{dz}{dt} = \nabla z \cdot \mathbf{r}'(t)$$

where $\mathbf{r}(t) = x(t)\mathbf{i} + y(t)\mathbf{j}$.

87. Prove: If f, f_x, and f_y are continuous on a circular region, and if $\nabla f(x, y) = \mathbf{0}$ throughout the region, then $f(x, y)$ is constant on the region. [*Hint:* See Exercise 67, Section 13.5.]

88. Prove: If the function f is differentiable at the point (x, y) and if $D_\mathbf{u} f(x, y) = 0$ in two nonparallel directions, then $D_\mathbf{u} f(x, y) = 0$ in all directions.

89. Given that the functions $u = u(x, y, z)$, $v = v(x, y, z)$, $w = w(x, y, z)$, and $f(u, v, w)$ are all differentiable, show that

$$\nabla f(u, v, w) = \frac{\partial f}{\partial u}\nabla u + \frac{\partial f}{\partial v}\nabla v + \frac{\partial f}{\partial w}\nabla w$$

90. Writing Let f denote a differentiable function of two variables. Write a short paragraph that discusses the connections between directional derivatives of f and slopes of tangent lines to the graph of f.

91. Writing Let f denote a differentiable function of two variables. Although we have defined what it means to say that f is differentiable, we have not defined the "derivative" of f. Write a short paragraph that discusses the merits of defining the derivative of f to be the gradient ∇f.

13.7 TANGENT PLANES AND NORMAL VECTORS

In this section we will discuss tangent planes to surfaces in three-dimensional space. We will be concerned with three main questions: What is a tangent plane? When do tangent planes exist? How do we find equations of tangent planes?

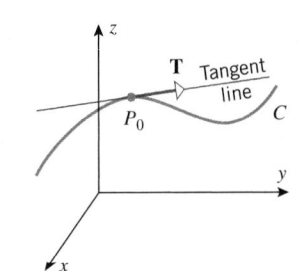
▲ Figure 13.7.1

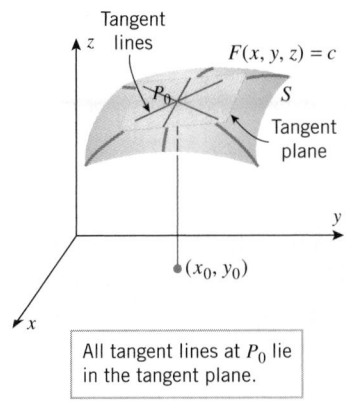

All tangent lines at P_0 lie in the tangent plane.

▲ Figure 13.7.2

■ **TANGENT PLANES AND NORMAL VECTORS TO LEVEL SURFACES $F(x, y, z) = c$**

We begin by considering the problem of finding tangent planes to level surfaces of a function $F(x, y, z)$. These surfaces are represented by equations of the form $F(x, y, z) = c$. We will assume that F has continuous first-order partial derivatives, since this has an important geometric consequence. Fix c, and suppose that $P_0(x_0, y_0, z_0)$ satisfies the equation $F(x, y, z) = c$. In advanced courses it is proved that if F has continuous first-order partial derivatives, and if $\nabla F(x_0, y_0, z_0) \neq \mathbf{0}$, then near P_0 the graph of $F(x, y, z) = c$ is indeed a "surface" rather than some possibly exotic-looking set of points in 3-space.

We will base our concept of a tangent plane to a level surface $S: F(x, y, z) = c$ on the more elementary notion of a tangent line to a curve C in 3-space (Figure 13.7.1). Intuitively, we would expect a tangent plane to S at a point P_0 to be composed of the tangent lines at P_0 of all curves on S that pass through P_0 (Figure 13.7.2). Suppose C is a curve on S through P_0 that is parametrized by $x = x(t)$, $y = y(t)$, $z = z(t)$ with $x_0 = x(t_0)$, $y_0 = y(t_0)$, and $z_0 = z(t_0)$. The tangent line l to C through P_0 is then parallel to the vector

$$\mathbf{r}' = x'(t_0)\mathbf{i} + y'(t_0)\mathbf{j} + z'(t_0)\mathbf{k}$$

where we assume that $\mathbf{r}' \neq \mathbf{0}$ (Definition 12.2.7). Since C is on the surface $F(x, y, z) = c$, we have

$$c = F(x(t), y(t), z(t)) \tag{1}$$

Computing the derivative at t_0 of both sides of (1), we have by the chain rule that

$$0 = F_x(x_0, y_0, z_0)x'(t_0) + F_y(x_0, y_0, z_0)y'(t_0) + F_z(x_0, y_0, z_0)z'(t_0)$$

We can write this equation in vector form as

$$0 = (F_x(x_0, y_0, z_0)\mathbf{i} + F_y(x_0, y_0, z_0)\mathbf{j} + F_z(x_0, y_0, z_0)\mathbf{k}) \cdot (x'(t_0)\mathbf{i} + y'(t_0)\mathbf{j} + z'(t_0)\mathbf{k})$$

or

$$0 = \nabla F(x_0, y_0, z_0) \cdot \mathbf{r}' \tag{2}$$

It follows that if $\nabla F(x_0, y_0, z_0) \neq \mathbf{0}$, then $\nabla F(x_0, y_0, z_0)$ is normal to line l. Therefore, the tangent line l to C at P_0 is contained in the plane through P_0 with normal vector $\nabla F(x_0, y_0, z_0)$. Since C was *arbitrary*, we conclude that the same is true for any curve on S through P_0 (Figure 13.7.3). Thus, it makes sense to define the tangent plane to S at P_0 to be the plane through P_0 whose normal vector is

$$\mathbf{n} = \nabla F(x_0, y_0, z_0) = \langle F_x(x_0, y_0, z_0), F_y(x_0, y_0, z_0), F_z(x_0, y_0, z_0) \rangle$$

Using the point-normal form [see Formula (3) in Section 11.6], we have the following definition.

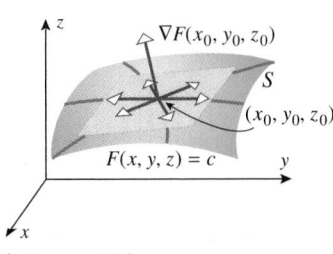
▲ Figure 13.7.3

> **13.7.1 DEFINITION** Assume that $F(x, y, z)$ has continuous first-order partial derivatives and that $P_0(x_0, y_0, z_0)$ is a point on the level surface $S: F(x, y, z) = c$. If $\nabla F(x_0, y_0, z_0) \neq \mathbf{0}$, then $\mathbf{n} = \nabla F(x_0, y_0, z_0)$ is a *normal vector* to S at P_0 and the *tangent plane* to S at P_0 is the plane with equation
>
> $$F_x(x_0, y_0, z_0)(x - x_0) + F_y(x_0, y_0, z_0)(y - y_0) + F_z(x_0, y_0, z_0)(z - z_0) = 0 \quad (3)$$

Definition 13.7.1 can be viewed as an extension of Theorem 13.6.6 from curves to surfaces.

The line through the point P_0 parallel to the normal vector $\mathbf{n}$ is perpendicular to the tangent plane (3). We will call this the *normal line*, or sometimes more simply the *normal* to the surface $F(x, y, z) = c$ at P_0. It follows that this line can be expressed parametrically as

$$x = x_0 + F_x(x_0, y_0, z_0)t, \quad y = y_0 + F_y(x_0, y_0, z_0)t, \quad z = z_0 + F_z(x_0, y_0, z_0)t \quad (4)$$

▶ **Example 1** Consider the ellipsoid $x^2 + 4y^2 + z^2 = 18$.

(a) Find an equation of the tangent plane to the ellipsoid at the point $(1, 2, 1)$.

(b) Find parametric equations of the line that is normal to the ellipsoid at the point $(1, 2, 1)$.

(c) Find the acute angle that the tangent plane at the point $(1, 2, 1)$ makes with the xy-plane.

Solution (a). We apply Definition 13.7.1 with $F(x, y, z) = x^2 + 4y^2 + z^2$ and $(x_0, y_0, z_0) = (1, 2, 1)$. Since

$$\nabla F(x, y, z) = \langle F_x(x, y, z), F_y(x, y, z), F_z(x, y, z) \rangle = \langle 2x, 8y, 2z \rangle$$

we have

$$\mathbf{n} = \nabla F(1, 2, 1) = \langle 2, 16, 2 \rangle$$

Hence, from (3) the equation of the tangent plane is

$$2(x - 1) + 16(y - 2) + 2(z - 1) = 0 \quad \text{or} \quad x + 8y + z = 18$$

Solution (b). Since $\mathbf{n} = \langle 2, 16, 2 \rangle$ at the point $(1, 2, 1)$, it follows from (4) that parametric equations for the normal line to the ellipsoid at the point $(1, 2, 1)$ are

$$x = 1 + 2t, \quad y = 2 + 16t, \quad z = 1 + 2t$$

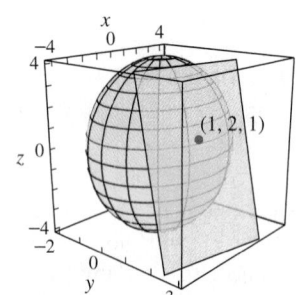

▲ **Figure 13.7.4**

Solution (c). To find the acute angle θ between the tangent plane and the xy-plane, we will apply Formula (9) of Section 11.6 with $\mathbf{n}_1 = \mathbf{n} = \langle 2, 16, 2 \rangle$ and $\mathbf{n}_2 = \langle 0, 0, 1 \rangle$. This yields

$$\cos \theta = \frac{|\langle 2, 16, 2 \rangle \cdot \langle 0, 0, 1 \rangle|}{\|\langle 2, 16, 2 \rangle\| \, \|\langle 0, 0, 1 \rangle\|} = \frac{2}{(2\sqrt{66})(1)} = \frac{1}{\sqrt{66}}$$

Thus,

$$\theta = \cos^{-1}\left(\frac{1}{\sqrt{66}}\right) \approx 83°$$

(Figure 13.7.4). ◀

■ **TANGENT PLANES TO SURFACES OF THE FORM $z = f(x, y)$**

To find a tangent plane to a surface of the form $z = f(x, y)$, we can use Equation (3) with the function $F(x, y, z) = z - f(x, y)$.

▶ **Example 2** Find an equation for the tangent plane and parametric equations for the normal line to the surface $z = x^2 y$ at the point $(2, 1, 4)$.

Solution. Let $F(x, y, z) = z - x^2 y$. Then $F(x, y, z) = 0$ on the surface, so we can find the find the gradient of F at the point $(2, 1, 4)$:

$$\nabla F(x, y, z) = -2xy\mathbf{i} - x^2\mathbf{j} + \mathbf{k}$$

$$\nabla F(2, 1, 4) = -4\mathbf{i} - 4\mathbf{j} + \mathbf{k}$$

From (3) the tangent plane has equation

$$-4(x - 2) - 4(y - 1) + 1(z - 4) = 0 \quad \text{or} \quad -4x - 4y + z = -8$$

and the normal line has equations

$$x = 2 - 4t, \qquad y = 1 - 4t, \qquad z = 4 + t \ \blacktriangleleft$$

Suppose that $f(x, y)$ is differentiable at a point (x_0, y_0) and that $z_0 = f(x_0, y_0)$. It can be shown that the procedure of Example 2 can be used to find the tangent plane to the surface $z = f(x, y)$ at the point (x_0, y_0, z_0). This yields an alternative equation for a tangent plane to the graph of a differentiable function.

13.7.2 **THEOREM** *If $f(x, y)$ is differentiable at the point (x_0, y_0), then the tangent plane to the surface $z = f(x, y)$ at the point $P_0(x_0, y_0, f(x_0, y_0))$ [or (x_0, y_0)] is the plane*

$$z = f(x_0, y_0) + f_x(x_0, y_0)(x - x_0) + f_y(x_0, y_0)(y - y_0) \tag{5}$$

PROOF Consider the function $F(x, y, z) = z - f(x, y)$. Since $F(x, y, z) = 0$ on the surface, we will apply (3) to this function. The partial derivatives of F are

$$F_x(x, y, z) = -f_x(x, y), \quad F_y(x, y, z) = -f_y(x, y), \quad F_z(x, y, z) = 1$$

Since the point at which we evaluate these derivatives lies on the surface, it will have the form $(x_0, y_0, f(x_0, y_0))$. Thus, (3) gives

$$0 = F_x(x_0, y_0, z_0)(x - x_0) + F_y(x_0, y_0, z_0)(y - y_0) + F_z(x_0, y_0, z_0)(z - f(x_0, y_0))$$

$$= -f_x(x_0, y_0)(x - x_0) - f_y(x_0, y_0)(y - y_0) + 1(z - f(x_0, y_0))$$

which is equivalent to (5). ∎

Recall from Section 13.4 that if a function $f(x, y)$ is differentiable at a point (x_0, y_0), then the local linear approximation $L(x, y)$ to f at (x_0, y_0) has the equation

$$L(x, y) = f(x_0, y_0) + f_x(x_0, y_0)(x - x_0) + f_y(x_0, y_0)(y - y_0)$$

Notice that the equation $z = L(x, y)$ is identical to that of the tangent plane to $f(x, y)$ at the point (x_0, y_0). Thus, the graph of the local linear approximation to $f(x, y)$ at the point (x_0, y_0) is the tangent plane to the surface $z = f(x, y)$ at the point (x_0, y_0).

■ TANGENT PLANES AND TOTAL DIFFERENTIALS

Recall that for a function $z = f(x, y)$ of two variables, the approximation by differentials is

$$\Delta z = \Delta f = f(x, y) - f(x_0, y_0) \approx dz = f_x(x_0, y_0)(x - x_0) + f_y(x_0, y_0)(y - y_0)$$

Note that the tangent plane in Figure 13.7.5 is analogous to the tangent line in Figure 13.4.2.

The tangent plane provides a geometric interpretation of this approximation. We see in Figure 13.7.5 that Δz is the change in z *along the surface* $z = f(x, y)$ from the point $P_0(x_0, y_0, f(x_0, y_0))$ to the point $P(x, y, f(x, y))$, and dz is the change in z *along the tangent plane* from P_0 to $Q(x, y, L(x, y))$. The small vertical displacement at (x, y) between the surface and the plane represents the error in the local linear approximation to f at (x_0, y_0). We have seen that near (x_0, y_0) this error term has magnitude much smaller than the distance between (x, y) and (x_0, y_0).

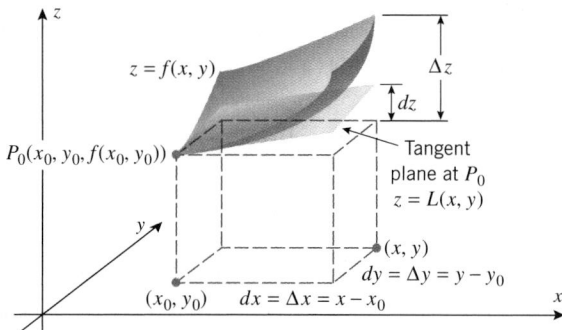

▶ **Figure 13.7.5**

USING GRADIENTS TO FIND TANGENT LINES TO INTERSECTIONS OF SURFACES

In general, the intersection of two surfaces $F(x, y, z) = 0$ and $G(x, y, z) = 0$ will be a curve in 3-space. If (x_0, y_0, z_0) is a point on this curve, then $\nabla F(x_0, y_0, z_0)$ will be normal to the surface $F(x, y, z) = 0$ at (x_0, y_0, z_0) and $\nabla G(x_0, y_0, z_0)$ will be normal to the surface $G(x, y, z) = 0$ at (x_0, y_0, z_0). Thus, if the curve of intersection can be smoothly parametrized, then its unit tangent vector $\mathbf{T}$ at (x_0, y_0, z_0) will be orthogonal to both $\nabla F(x_0, y_0, z_0)$ and $\nabla G(x_0, y_0, z_0)$ (Figure 13.7.6). Consequently, if

$$\nabla F(x_0, y_0, z_0) \times \nabla G(x_0, y_0, z_0) \neq \mathbf{0}$$

then this cross product will be parallel to $\mathbf{T}$ and hence will be tangent to the curve of intersection. This tangent vector can be used to determine the direction of the tangent line to the curve of intersection at the point (x_0, y_0, z_0).

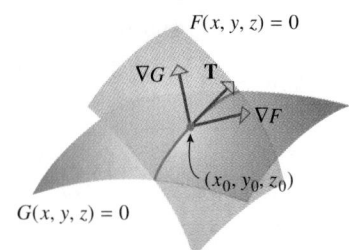

▲ **Figure 13.7.6**

▶ **Example 3**   Find parametric equations of the tangent line to the curve of intersection of the paraboloid $z = x^2 + y^2$ and the ellipsoid $3x^2 + 2y^2 + z^2 = 9$ at the point $(1, 1, 2)$ (Figure 13.7.7).

Solution.   We begin by rewriting the equations of the surfaces as

$$x^2 + y^2 - z = 0 \quad \text{and} \quad 3x^2 + 2y^2 + z^2 - 9 = 0$$

and we take

$$F(x, y, z) = x^2 + y^2 - z \quad \text{and} \quad G(x, y, z) = 3x^2 + 2y^2 + z^2 - 9$$

We will need the gradients of these functions at the point $(1, 1, 2)$. The computations are

$$\nabla F(x, y, z) = 2x\mathbf{i} + 2y\mathbf{j} - \mathbf{k}, \quad \nabla G(x, y, z) = 6x\mathbf{i} + 4y\mathbf{j} + 2z\mathbf{k}$$
$$\nabla F(1, 1, 2) = 2\mathbf{i} + 2\mathbf{j} - \mathbf{k}, \quad \nabla G(1, 1, 2) = 6\mathbf{i} + 4\mathbf{j} + 4\mathbf{k}$$

Thus, a tangent vector at $(1, 1, 2)$ to the curve of intersection is

$$\nabla F(1, 1, 2) \times \nabla G(1, 1, 2) = \begin{vmatrix} \mathbf{i} & \mathbf{j} & \mathbf{k} \\ 2 & 2 & -1 \\ 6 & 4 & 4 \end{vmatrix} = 12\mathbf{i} - 14\mathbf{j} - 4\mathbf{k}$$

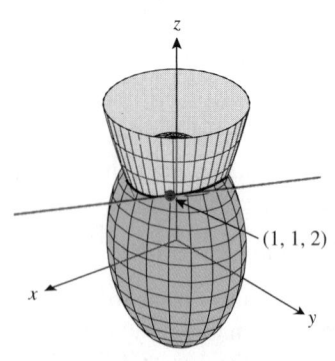

▲ **Figure 13.7.7**

Since any scalar multiple of this vector will do just as well, we can multiply by $\frac{1}{2}$ to reduce the size of the coefficients and use the vector of $6\mathbf{i} - 7\mathbf{j} - 2\mathbf{k}$ to determine the direction of the tangent line. This vector and the point $(1, 1, 2)$ yield the parametric equations

$$x = 1 + 6t, \quad y = 1 - 7t, \quad z = 2 - 2t \blacktriangleleft$$

✔ QUICK CHECK EXERCISES 13.7 *(See page 977 for answers.)*

1. Suppose that $f(1, 0, -1) = 2$, and $f(x, y, z)$ is differentiable at $(1, 0, -1)$ with $\nabla f(1, 0, -1) = \langle 2, 1, 1 \rangle$. An equation for the tangent plane to the level surface $f(x, y, z) = 2$ at the point $(1, 0, -1)$ is _____, and parametric equations for the normal line to the level surface through the point $(1, 0, -1)$ are

   $$x = \underline{\hspace{1cm}}, \quad y = \underline{\hspace{1cm}}, \quad z = \underline{\hspace{1cm}}$$

2. Suppose that $f(x, y)$ is differentiable at the point $(3, 1)$ with $f(3, 1) = 4$, $f_x(3, 1) = 2$, and $f_y(3, 1) = -3$. An equation for the tangent plane to the graph of f at the point $(3, 1, 4)$ is _____, and parametric equations for the normal line to the graph of f through the point $(3, 1, 4)$ are

   $$x = \underline{\hspace{1cm}}, \quad y = \underline{\hspace{1cm}}, \quad z = \underline{\hspace{1cm}}$$

3. An equation for the tangent plane to the graph of $z = x^2\sqrt{y}$ at the point $(2, 4, 8)$ is _____, and parametric equations for the normal line to the graph of $z = x^2\sqrt{y}$ through the point $(2, 4, 8)$ are

   $$x = \underline{\hspace{1cm}}, \quad y = \underline{\hspace{1cm}}, \quad z = \underline{\hspace{1cm}}$$

4. The sphere $x^2 + y^2 + z^2 = 9$ and the plane $x + y + z = 5$ intersect in a circle that passes through the point $(2, 1, 2)$. Parametric equations for the tangent line to this circle at $(2, 1, 2)$ are

   $$x = \underline{\hspace{1cm}}, \quad y = \underline{\hspace{1cm}}, \quad z = \underline{\hspace{1cm}}$$

EXERCISE SET 13.7 □c CAS

1. Consider the ellipsoid $x^2 + y^2 + 4z^2 = 12$.
   (a) Find an equation of the tangent plane to the ellipsoid at the point $(2, 2, 1)$.
   (b) Find parametric equations of the line that is normal to the ellipsoid at the point $(2, 2, 1)$.
   (c) Find the acute angle that the tangent plane at the point $(2, 2, 1)$ makes with the xy-plane.

2. Consider the surface $xz - yz^3 + yz^2 = 2$.
   (a) Find an equation of the tangent plane to the surface at the point $(2, -1, 1)$.
   (b) Find parametric equations of the line that is normal to the surface at the point $(2, -1, 1)$.
   (c) Find the acute angle that the tangent plane at the point $(2, -1, 1)$ makes with the xy-plane.

3–10 Find an equation for the tangent plane and parametric equations for the normal line to the surface at the point P. ■

3. $x^2 + y^2 + z^2 = 25$; $P(-3, 0, 4)$
4. $x^2y - 4z^2 = -7$; $P(-3, 1, -2)$
5. $z = 4x^3y^2 + 2y$; $P(1, -2, 12)$
6. $z = \frac{1}{2}x^7y^{-2}$; $P(2, 4, 4)$
7. $z = xe^{-y}$; $P(1, 0, 1)$
8. $z = \ln\sqrt{x^2 + y^2}$; $P(-1, 0, 0)$
9. $z = e^{3y}\sin 3x$; $P(\pi/6, 0, 1)$
10. $z = x^{1/2} + y^{1/2}$; $P(4, 9, 5)$

FOCUS ON CONCEPTS

11. Find all points on the surface at which the tangent plane is horizontal.
    (a) $z = x^3y^2$
    (b) $z = x^2 - xy + y^2 - 2x + 4y$

12. Find a point on the surface $z = 3x^2 - y^2$ at which the tangent plane is parallel to the plane $6x + 4y - z = 5$.

13. Find a point on the surface $z = 8 - 3x^2 - 2y^2$ at which the tangent plane is perpendicular to the line $x = 2 - 3t$, $y = 7 + 8t$, $z = 5 - t$.

14. Show that the surfaces
    $$z = \sqrt{x^2 + y^2} \quad \text{and} \quad z = \frac{1}{10}(x^2 + y^2) + \frac{5}{2}$$
    intersect at $(3, 4, 5)$ and have a common tangent plane at that point.

15. (a) Find all points of intersection of the line
    $$x = -1 + t, \quad y = 2 + t, \quad z = 2t + 7$$
    and the surface
    $$z = x^2 + y^2$$
    (b) At each point of intersection, find the cosine of the acute angle between the given line and the line normal to the surface.

16. Show that if f is differentiable and $z = xf(x/y)$, then all tangent planes to the graph of this equation pass through the origin.

17–20 True–False Determine whether the statement is true or false. Explain your answer. ■

17. If the tangent plane to the level surface of $F(x, y, z)$ at the point $P_0(x_0, y_0, z_0)$ is also tangent to a level surface of $G(x, y, z)$ at P_0, then $\nabla F(x_0, y_0, z_0) = \nabla G(x_0, y_0, z_0)$.

18. If the tangent plane to the graph of $z = f(x, y)$ at the point $(1, 1, 2)$ has equation $x - y + 2z = 4$, then $f_x(1, 1) = 1$ and $f_y(1, 1) = -1$.

19. If the tangent plane to the graph of $z = f(x, y)$ at the point $(1, 2, 1)$ has equation $2x + y - z = 3$, then the local linear approximation to f at $(1, 2)$ is given by the function $L(x, y) = 1 + 2(x - 1) + (y - 2)$.

20. The normal line to the surface $z = f(x, y)$ at the point $P_0(x_0, y_0, f(x_0, y_0))$ has a direction vector given by $f_x(x_0, y_0)\mathbf{i} + f_y(x_0, y_0)\mathbf{j} - \mathbf{k}$.

21–22 Find two unit vectors that are normal to the given surface at the point P. ■

21. $\sqrt{\dfrac{z + x}{y - 1}} = z^2$; $P(3, 5, 1)$

22. $\sin xz - 4\cos yz = 4$; $P(\pi, \pi, 1)$

23. Show that every line that is normal to the sphere
$$x^2 + y^2 + z^2 = 1$$
passes through the origin.

24. Find all points on the ellipsoid $2x^2 + 3y^2 + 4z^2 = 9$ at which the plane tangent to the ellipsoid is parallel to the plane $x - 2y + 3z = 5$.

25. Find all points on the surface $x^2 + y^2 - z^2 = 1$ at which the normal line is parallel to the line through $P(1, -2, 1)$ and $Q(4, 0, -1)$.

26. Show that the ellipsoid $2x^2 + 3y^2 + z^2 = 9$ and the sphere
$$x^2 + y^2 + z^2 - 6x - 8y - 8z + 24 = 0$$
have a common tangent plane at the point $(1, 1, 2)$.

27. Find parametric equations for the tangent line to the curve of intersection of the paraboloid $z = x^2 + y^2$ and the ellipsoid $x^2 + 4y^2 + z^2 = 9$ at the point $(1, -1, 2)$.

28. Find parametric equations for the tangent line to the curve of intersection of the cone $z = \sqrt{x^2 + y^2}$ and the plane $x + 2y + 2z = 20$ at the point $(4, 3, 5)$.

29. Find parametric equations for the tangent line to the curve of intersection of the cylinders $x^2 + z^2 = 25$ and $y^2 + z^2 = 25$ at the point $(3, -3, 4)$.

c **30.** The accompanying figure shows the intersection of the surfaces $z = 8 - x^2 - y^2$ and $4x + 2y - z = 0$.
   (a) Find parametric equations for the tangent line to the curve of intersection at the point $(0, 2, 4)$.
   (b) Use a CAS to generate a reasonable facsimile of the figure. You need not generate the colors, but try to obtain a similar viewpoint.

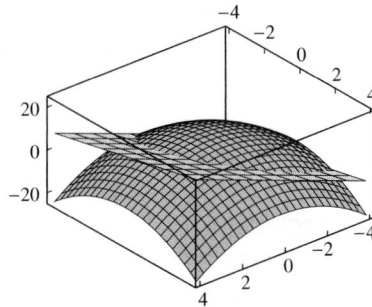

◀ **Figure Ex-30**

31. Show that the equation of the plane that is tangent to the ellipsoid
$$\frac{x^2}{a^2} + \frac{y^2}{b^2} + \frac{z^2}{c^2} = 1$$
at (x_0, y_0, z_0) can be written in the form
$$\frac{x_0 x}{a^2} + \frac{y_0 y}{b^2} + \frac{z_0 z}{c^2} = 1$$

32. Show that the equation of the plane that is tangent to the paraboloid
$$z = \frac{x^2}{a^2} + \frac{y^2}{b^2}$$
at (x_0, y_0, z_0) can be written in the form
$$z + z_0 = \frac{2x_0 x}{a^2} + \frac{2y_0 y}{b^2}$$

33. Prove: If the surfaces $z = f(x, y)$ and $z = g(x, y)$ intersect at $P(x_0, y_0, z_0)$, and if f and g are differentiable at (x_0, y_0), then the normal lines at P are perpendicular if and only if
$$f_x(x_0, y_0)g_x(x_0, y_0) + f_y(x_0, y_0)g_y(x_0, y_0) = -1$$

34. Use the result in Exercise 33 to show that the normal lines to the cones $z = \sqrt{x^2 + y^2}$ and $z = -\sqrt{x^2 + y^2}$ are perpendicular to the normal lines to the sphere $x^2 + y^2 + z^2 = a^2$ at every point of intersection (see Figure Ex-36).

35. Two surfaces $f(x, y, z) = 0$ and $g(x, y, z) = 0$ are said to be **orthogonal** at a point P of intersection if ∇f and ∇g are nonzero at P and the normal lines to the surfaces are perpendicular at P. Show that if $\nabla f(x_0, y_0, z_0) \neq \mathbf{0}$ and $\nabla g(x_0, y_0, z_0) \neq \mathbf{0}$, then the surfaces $f(x, y, z) = 0$ and $g(x, y, z) = 0$ are orthogonal at the point (x_0, y_0, z_0) if and only if
$$f_x g_x + f_y g_y + f_z g_z = 0$$
at this point. [*Note:* This is a more general version of the result in Exercise 33.]

36. Use the result of Exercise 35 to show that the sphere $x^2 + y^2 + z^2 = a^2$ and the cone $z^2 = x^2 + y^2$ are orthogonal at every point of intersection (see the accompanying figure).

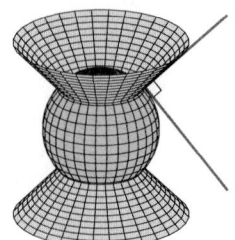

◀ **Figure Ex-36**

37. Show that the volume of the solid bounded by the coordinate planes and a plane tangent to the portion of the surface $xyz = k$, $k > 0$, in the first octant does not depend on the point of tangency.

38. *Writing* Discuss the role of the chain rule in defining a tangent plane to a level surface.

39. *Writing* Discuss the relationship between tangent planes and local linear approximations for functions of two variables.

✔ **QUICK CHECK ANSWERS 13.7**

---

1. $2(x - 1) + y + (z + 1) = 0$; $x = 1 + 2t$; $y = t$; $z = -1 + t$
2. $z = 4 + 2(x - 3) - 3(y - 1)$; $x = 3 + 2t$; $y = 1 - 3t$; $z = 4 - t$
3. $z = 8 + 8(x - 2) + (y - 4)$; $x = 2 + 8t$; $y = 4 + t$; $z = 8 - t$ **4.** $x = 2 + t$; $y = 1$; $z = 2 - t$

13.8 MAXIMA AND MINIMA OF FUNCTIONS OF TWO VARIABLES

Earlier in this text we learned how to find maximum and minimum values of a function of one variable. In this section we will develop similar techniques for functions of two variables.

■ EXTREMA

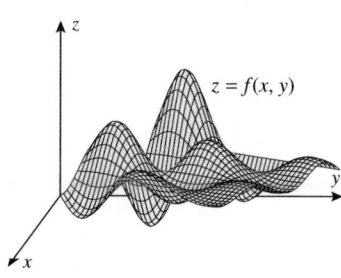

▲ **Figure 13.8.1**

If we imagine the graph of a function f of two variables to be a mountain range (Figure 13.8.1), then the mountaintops, which are the high points in their immediate vicinity, are called *relative maxima* of f, and the valley bottoms, which are the low points in their immediate vicinity, are called *relative minima* of f.

Just as a geologist might be interested in finding the highest mountain and deepest valley in an entire mountain range, so a mathematician might be interested in finding the largest and smallest values of $f(x, y)$ over the *entire* domain of f. These are called the *absolute maximum* and *absolute minimum values* of f. The following definitions make these informal ideas precise.

> **13.8.1 DEFINITION** A function f of two variables is said to have a *relative maximum* at a point (x_0, y_0) if there is a disk centered at (x_0, y_0) such that $f(x_0, y_0) \geq f(x, y)$ for all points (x, y) that lie inside the disk, and f is said to have an *absolute maximum* at (x_0, y_0) if $f(x_0, y_0) \geq f(x, y)$ for all points (x, y) in the domain of f.

> **13.8.2 DEFINITION** A function f of two variables is said to have a *relative minimum* at a point (x_0, y_0) if there is a disk centered at (x_0, y_0) such that $f(x_0, y_0) \leq f(x, y)$ for all points (x, y) that lie inside the disk, and f is said to have an *absolute minimum* at (x_0, y_0) if $f(x_0, y_0) \leq f(x, y)$ for all points (x, y) in the domain of f.

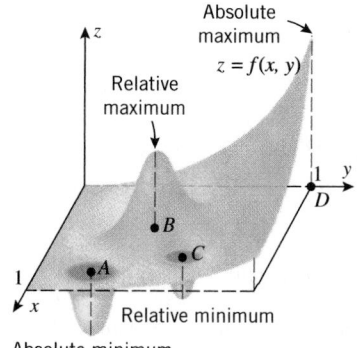

▲ **Figure 13.8.2**

If f has a relative maximum or a relative minimum at (x_0, y_0), then we say that f has a *relative extremum* at (x_0, y_0), and if f has an absolute maximum or absolute minimum at (x_0, y_0), then we say that f has an *absolute extremum* at (x_0, y_0).

Figure 13.8.2 shows the graph of a function f whose domain is the square region in the xy-plane whose points satisfy the inequalities $0 \leq x \leq 1$, $0 \leq y \leq 1$. The function f has relative minima at the points A and C and a relative maximum at B. There is an absolute minimum at A and an absolute maximum at D.

For functions of two variables we will be concerned with two important questions:

- Are there any relative or absolute extrema?
- If so, where are they located?

■ BOUNDED SETS

Just as we distinguished between finite intervals and infinite intervals on the real line, so we will want to distinguish between regions of "finite extent" and regions of "infinite extent" in 2-space and 3-space. A set of points in 2-space is called **bounded** if the entire set can be contained within some rectangle, and is called **unbounded** if there is no rectangle that contains all the points of the set. Similarly, a set of points in 3-space is **bounded** if the entire set can be contained within some box, and is unbounded otherwise (Figure 13.8.3).

> Explain why any subset of a bounded set is also bounded.

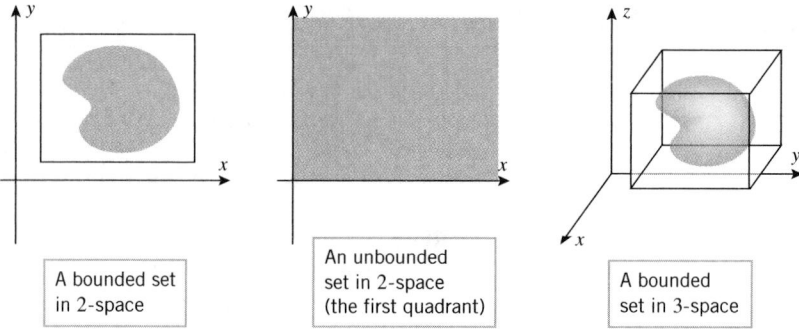

A bounded set in 2-space

An unbounded set in 2-space (the first quadrant)

A bounded set in 3-space

► **Figure 13.8.3**

■ THE EXTREME-VALUE THEOREM

For functions of one variable that are continuous on a closed interval, the Extreme-Value Theorem (Theorem 4.4.2) answered the existence question for absolute extrema. The following theorem, which we state without proof, is the corresponding result for functions of two variables.

13.8.3 THEOREM (*Extreme-Value Theorem*) *If $f(x, y)$ is continuous on a closed and bounded set R, then f has both an absolute maximum and an absolute minimum on R.*

► **Example 1** The square region R whose points satisfy the inequalities

$$0 \le x \le 1 \quad \text{and} \quad 0 \le y \le 1$$

is a closed and bounded set in the xy-plane. The function f whose graph is shown in Figure 13.8.2 is continuous on R; thus, it is guaranteed to have an absolute maximum and minimum on R by the last theorem. These occur at points D and A that are shown in the figure. ◄

REMARK If any of the conditions in the Extreme-Value Theorem fail to hold, then there is no guarantee that an absolute maximum or absolute minimum exists on the region R. Thus, a discontinuous function on a closed and bounded set need not have any absolute extrema, and a continuous function on a set that is not closed and bounded also need not have any absolute extrema.

■ FINDING RELATIVE EXTREMA

Recall that if a function g of one variable has a relative extremum at a point x_0 where g is differentiable, then $g'(x_0) = 0$. To obtain the analog of this result for functions of two variables, suppose that $f(x, y)$ has a relative maximum at a point (x_0, y_0) and that the partial derivatives of f exist at (x_0, y_0). It seems plausible geometrically that the traces of the surface $z = f(x, y)$ on the planes $x = x_0$ and $y = y_0$ have horizontal tangent lines at (x_0, y_0) (Figure 13.8.4), so

$$f_x(x_0, y_0) = 0 \quad \text{and} \quad f_y(x_0, y_0) = 0$$

The same conclusion holds if f has a relative minimum at (x_0, y_0), all of which suggests the following result, which we state without formal proof.

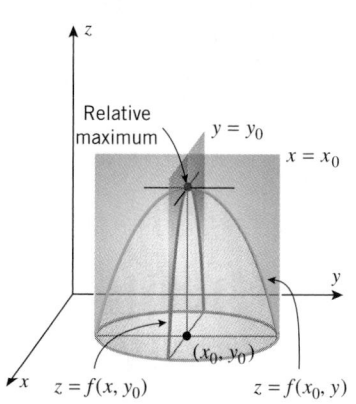

Relative maximum

$y = y_0$

$x = x_0$

(x_0, y_0)

$z = f(x, y_0)$ $z = f(x_0, y)$

▲ **Figure 13.8.4**

> **13.8.4 THEOREM** *If f has a relative extremum at a point (x_0, y_0), and if the first-order partial derivatives of f exist at this point, then*
>
> $$f_x(x_0, y_0) = 0 \quad \text{and} \quad f_y(x_0, y_0) = 0$$

Recall that the *critical points* of a function f of one variable are those values of x in the domain of f at which $f'(x) = 0$ or f is not differentiable. The following definition is the analog for functions of two variables.

Explain why

$$D_{\mathbf{u}} f(x_0, y_0) = 0$$

for all $\mathbf{u}$ if (x_0, y_0) is a critical point of f and f is differentiable at (x_0, y_0).

> **13.8.5 DEFINITION** A point (x_0, y_0) in the domain of a function $f(x, y)$ is called a ***critical point*** of the function if $f_x(x_0, y_0) = 0$ and $f_y(x_0, y_0) = 0$ or if one or both partial derivatives do not exist at (x_0, y_0).

It follows from this definition and Theorem 13.8.4 that relative extrema occur at critical points, just as for a function of one variable. However, recall that for a function of one variable a relative extremum need not occur at *every* critical point. For example, the function might have an inflection point with a horizontal tangent line at the critical point (see Figure 4.2.6). Similarly, a function of two variables need not have a relative extremum at every critical point. For example, consider the function

$$f(x, y) = y^2 - x^2$$

This function, whose graph is the hyperbolic paraboloid shown in Figure 13.8.5, has a critical point at $(0, 0)$, since

$$f_x(x, y) = -2x \quad \text{and} \quad f_y(x, y) = 2y$$

from which it follows that

$$f_x(0, 0) = 0 \quad \text{and} \quad f_y(0, 0) = 0$$

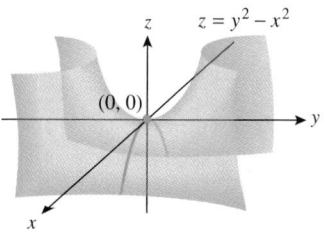

$z = y^2 - x^2$

$(0, 0)$

The function $f(x, y) = y^2 - x^2$ has neither a relative maximum nor a relative minimum at the critical point $(0, 0)$.

▲ **Figure 13.8.5**

However, the function f has neither a relative maximum nor a relative minimum at $(0, 0)$. For obvious reasons, the point $(0, 0)$ is called a *saddle point* of f. In general, we will say that a surface $z = f(x, y)$ has a ***saddle point*** at (x_0, y_0) if there are two distinct vertical planes through this point such that the trace of the surface in one of the planes has a relative maximum at (x_0, y_0) and the trace in the other has a relative minimum at (x_0, y_0).

▶ **Example 2** The three functions graphed in Figure 13.8.6 all have critical points at $(0, 0)$. For the paraboloids, the partial derivatives at the origin are zero. You can check this algebraically by evaluating the partial derivatives at $(0, 0)$, but you can see it geometrically by observing that the traces in the xz-plane and yz-plane have horizontal tangent lines at $(0, 0)$. For the cone neither partial derivative exists at the origin because the traces in the xz-plane and the yz-plane have corners there. The paraboloid in part (a) and the cone in part (c) have a relative minimum and absolute minimum at the origin, and the paraboloid in part (b) has a relative maximum and an absolute maximum at the origin. ◄

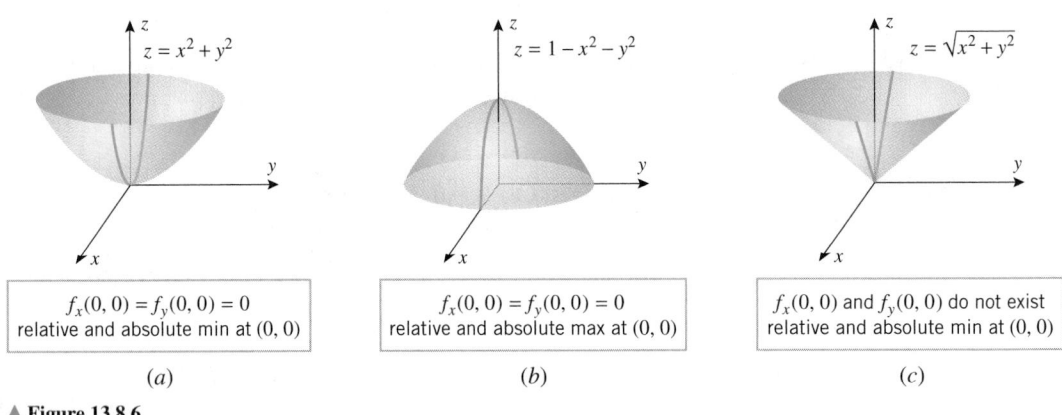

$f_x(0, 0) = f_y(0, 0) = 0$ relative and absolute min at $(0, 0)$	$f_x(0, 0) = f_y(0, 0) = 0$ relative and absolute max at $(0, 0)$	$f_x(0, 0)$ and $f_y(0, 0)$ do not exist relative and absolute min at $(0, 0)$
(a)	(b)	(c)

▲ **Figure 13.8.6**

■ **THE SECOND PARTIALS TEST**

For functions of one variable the second derivative test (Theorem 4.2.4) was used to determine the behavior of a function at a critical point. The following theorem, which is usually proved in advanced calculus, is the analog of that theorem for functions of two variables.

> **13.8.6   THEOREM** (*The Second Partials Test*)   *Let f be a function of two variables with continuous second-order partial derivatives in some disk centered at a critical point (x_0, y_0), and let*
> $$D = f_{xx}(x_0, y_0) f_{yy}(x_0, y_0) - f_{xy}^2(x_0, y_0)$$
>
> (a)   *If $D > 0$ and $f_{xx}(x_0, y_0) > 0$, then f has a relative minimum at (x_0, y_0).*
>
> (b)   *If $D > 0$ and $f_{xx}(x_0, y_0) < 0$, then f has a relative maximum at (x_0, y_0).*
>
> (c)   *If $D < 0$, then f has a saddle point at (x_0, y_0).*
>
> (d)   *If $D = 0$, then no conclusion can be drawn.*

With the notation of Theorem 13.8.6, show that if $D > 0$, then $f_{xx}(x_0, y_0)$ and $f_{yy}(x_0, y_0)$ have the same sign. Thus, we can replace $f_{xx}(x_0, y_0)$ by $f_{yy}(x_0, y_0)$ in parts (a) and (b) of the theorem.

► **Example 3**   Locate all relative extrema and saddle points of

$$f(x, y) = 3x^2 - 2xy + y^2 - 8y$$

Solution.   Since $f_x(x, y) = 6x - 2y$ and $f_y(x, y) = -2x + 2y - 8$, the critical points of f satisfy the equations

$$6x - 2y = 0$$
$$-2x + 2y - 8 = 0$$

Solving these for x and y yields $x = 2$, $y = 6$ (verify), so $(2, 6)$ is the only critical point. To apply Theorem 13.8.6 we need the second-order partial derivatives

$$f_{xx}(x, y) = 6, \quad f_{yy}(x, y) = 2, \quad f_{xy}(x, y) = -2$$

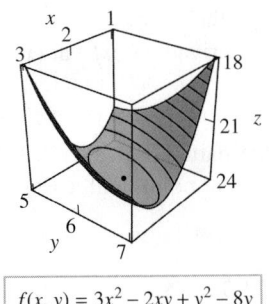

$$f(x, y) = 3x^2 - 2xy + y^2 - 8y$$

▲ **Figure 13.8.7**

At the point (2, 6) we have

$$D = f_{xx}(2, 6)f_{yy}(2, 6) - f_{xy}^2(2, 6) = (6)(2) - (-2)^2 = 8 > 0$$

and

$$f_{xx}(2, 6) = 6 > 0$$

so f has a relative minimum at (2, 6) by part (a) of the second partials test. Figure 13.8.7 shows a graph of f in the vicinity of the relative minimum. ◄

▶ **Example 4** Locate all relative extrema and saddle points of

$$f(x, y) = 4xy - x^4 - y^4$$

Solution. Since

$$f_x(x, y) = 4y - 4x^3 \qquad (1)$$
$$f_y(x, y) = 4x - 4y^3$$

the critical points of f have coordinates satisfying the equations

$$\begin{array}{cc} 4y - 4x^3 = 0 \\ 4x - 4y^3 = 0 \end{array} \quad \text{or} \quad \begin{array}{c} y = x^3 \\ x = y^3 \end{array} \qquad (2)$$

Substituting the top equation in the bottom yields $x = (x^3)^3$ or, equivalently, $x^9 - x = 0$ or $x(x^8 - 1) = 0$, which has solutions $x = 0, x = 1, x = -1$. Substituting these values in the top equation of (2), we obtain the corresponding y-values $y = 0, y = 1, y = -1$. Thus, the critical points of f are $(0, 0)$, $(1, 1)$, and $(-1, -1)$.

From (1),

$$f_{xx}(x, y) = -12x^2, \quad f_{yy}(x, y) = -12y^2, \quad f_{xy}(x, y) = 4$$

which yields the following table:

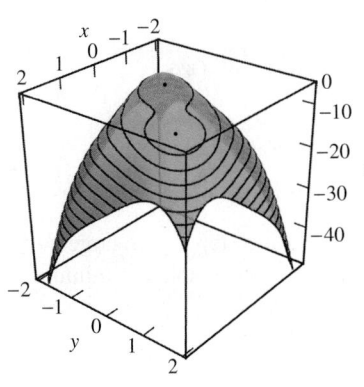

$$f(x, y) = 4xy - x^4 - y^4$$

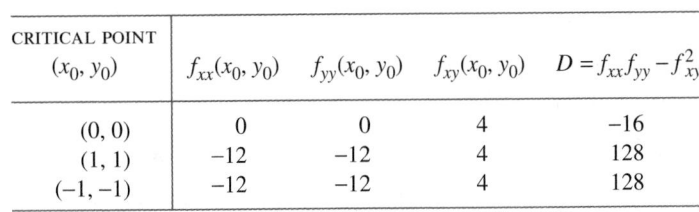

CRITICAL POINT (x_0, y_0)	$f_{xx}(x_0, y_0)$	$f_{yy}(x_0, y_0)$	$f_{xy}(x_0, y_0)$	$D = f_{xx}f_{yy} - f_{xy}^2$
(0, 0)	0	0	4	−16
(1, 1)	−12	−12	4	128
(−1, −1)	−12	−12	4	128

At the points $(1, 1)$ and $(-1, -1)$, we have $D > 0$ and $f_{xx} < 0$, so relative maxima occur at these critical points. At $(0, 0)$ there is a saddle point since $D < 0$. The surface and a contour plot are shown in Figure 13.8.8. ◄

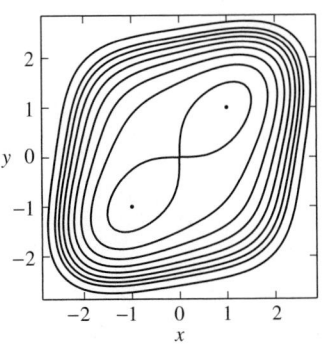

▲ **Figure 13.8.8**

The "figure eight" pattern at $(0, 0)$ in the contour plot for the surface in Figure 13.8.8 is typical for level curves that pass through a saddle point. If a bug starts at the point $(0, 0, 0)$ on the surface, in how many directions can it walk and remain in the xy-plane?

The following theorem, which is the analog for functions of two variables of Theorem 4.4.3, will lead to an important method for finding absolute extrema.

13.8.7 THEOREM *If a function f of two variables has an absolute extremum (either an absolute maximum or an absolute minimum) at an interior point of its domain, then this extremum occurs at a critical point.*

PROOF   If f has an absolute maximum at the point (x_0, y_0) in the interior of the domain of f, then f has a relative maximum at (x_0, y_0). If both partial derivatives exist at (x_0, y_0), then

$$f_x(x_0, y_0) = 0 \quad \text{and} \quad f_y(x_0, y_0) = 0$$

by Theorem 13.8.4, so (x_0, y_0) is a critical point of f. If either partial derivative does not exist, then again (x_0, y_0) is a critical point, so (x_0, y_0) is a critical point in all cases. The proof for an absolute minimum is similar. ■

■ FINDING ABSOLUTE EXTREMA ON CLOSED AND BOUNDED SETS

If $f(x, y)$ is continuous on a closed and bounded set R, then the Extreme-Value Theorem (Theorem 13.8.3) guarantees the existence of an absolute maximum and an absolute minimum of f on R. These absolute extrema can occur either on the boundary of R or in the interior of R, but if an absolute extremum occurs in the interior, then it occurs at a critical point by Theorem 13.8.7. Thus, we are led to the following procedure for finding absolute extrema:

Compare this procedure with that in Section 4.4 for finding the extreme values of $f(x)$ on a closed interval.

How to Find the Absolute Extrema of a Continuous Function f of Two Variables on a Closed and Bounded Set R

Step 1. Find the critical points of f that lie in the interior of R.

Step 2. Find all boundary points at which the absolute extrema can occur.

Step 3. Evaluate $f(x, y)$ at the points obtained in the preceding steps. The largest of these values is the absolute maximum and the smallest the absolute minimum.

▶ **Example 5**   Find the absolute maximum and minimum values of

$$f(x, y) = 3xy - 6x - 3y + 7 \tag{3}$$

on the closed triangular region R with vertices $(0, 0)$, $(3, 0)$, and $(0, 5)$.

Solution.   The region R is shown in Figure 13.8.9. We have

$$\frac{\partial f}{\partial x} = 3y - 6 \quad \text{and} \quad \frac{\partial f}{\partial y} = 3x - 3$$

so all critical points occur where

$$3y - 6 = 0 \quad \text{and} \quad 3x - 3 = 0$$

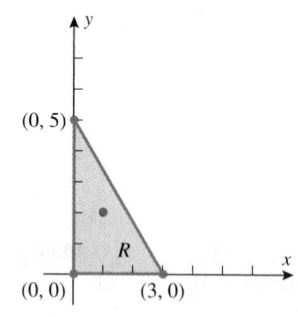

▲ **Figure 13.8.9**

Solving these equations yields $x = 1$ and $y = 2$, so $(1, 2)$ is the only critical point. As shown in Figure 13.8.9, this critical point is in the interior of R.

Next we want to determine the locations of the points on the boundary of R at which the absolute extrema might occur. The boundary of R consists of three line segments, each of which we will treat separately:

The line segment between $(0, 0)$ *and* $(3, 0)$: On this line segment we have $y = 0$, so (3) simplifies to a function of the single variable x,

$$u(x) = f(x, 0) = -6x + 7, \quad 0 \leq x \leq 3$$

This function has no critical points because $u'(x) = -6$ is nonzero for all x. Thus the extreme values of $u(x)$ occur at the endpoints $x = 0$ and $x = 3$, which correspond to the points $(0, 0)$ and $(3, 0)$ of R.

The line segment between $(0, 0)$ *and* $(0, 5)$: On this line segment we have $x = 0$, so (3) simplifies to a function of the single variable y,

$$v(y) = f(0, y) = -3y + 7, \quad 0 \le y \le 5$$

This function has no critical points because $v'(y) = -3$ is nonzero for all y. Thus, the extreme values of $v(y)$ occur at the endpoints $y = 0$ and $y = 5$, which correspond to the points $(0, 0)$ and $(0, 5)$ of R.

The line segment between $(3, 0)$ *and* $(0, 5)$: In the xy-plane, an equation for this line segment is

$$y = -\tfrac{5}{3}x + 5, \quad 0 \le x \le 3 \tag{4}$$

so (3) simplifies to a function of the single variable x,

$$\begin{aligned} w(x) = f\left(x, -\tfrac{5}{3}x + 5\right) &= 3x\left(-\tfrac{5}{3}x + 5\right) - 6x - 3\left(-\tfrac{5}{3}x + 5\right) + 7 \\ &= -5x^2 + 14x - 8, \quad 0 \le x \le 3 \end{aligned}$$

Since $w'(x) = -10x + 14$, the equation $w'(x) = 0$ yields $x = \tfrac{7}{5}$ as the only critical point of w. Thus, the extreme values of w occur either at the critical point $x = \tfrac{7}{5}$ or at the endpoints $x = 0$ and $x = 3$. The endpoints correspond to the points $(0, 5)$ and $(3, 0)$ of R, and from (4) the critical point corresponds to $\left(\tfrac{7}{5}, \tfrac{8}{3}\right)$.

Finally, Table 13.8.1 lists the values of $f(x, y)$ at the interior critical point and at the points on the boundary where an absolute extremum can occur. From the table we conclude that the absolute maximum value of f is $f(0, 0) = 7$ and the absolute minimum value is $f(3, 0) = -11$. ◄

Table 13.8.1

(x, y)	$(0, 0)$	$(3, 0)$	$(0, 5)$	$\left(\tfrac{7}{5}, \tfrac{8}{3}\right)$	$(1, 2)$
$f(x, y)$	7	−11	−8	$\tfrac{9}{5}$	1

▶ **Example 6**   Determine the dimensions of a rectangular box, open at the top, having a volume of 32 ft³, and requiring the least amount of material for its construction.

Solution.   Let

$$x = \text{length of the box (in feet)}$$
$$y = \text{width of the box (in feet)}$$
$$z = \text{height of the box (in feet)}$$
$$S = \text{surface area of the box (in square feet)}$$

We may reasonably assume that the box with least surface area requires the least amount of material, so our objective is to minimize the surface area

$$S = xy + 2xz + 2yz \tag{5}$$

(Figure 13.8.10) subject to the volume requirement

$$xyz = 32 \tag{6}$$

From (6) we obtain $z = 32/xy$, so (5) can be rewritten as

$$S = xy + \frac{64}{y} + \frac{64}{x} \tag{7}$$

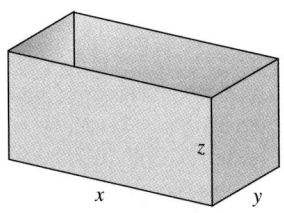

Two sides each have area xz.
Two sides each have area yz.
The base has area xy.

▲ **Figure 13.8.10**

which expresses S as a function of two variables. The dimensions x and y in this formula must be positive, but otherwise have no limitation, so our problem reduces to finding the absolute minimum value of S over the open first quadrant: $x > 0$, $y > 0$. Because this region is neither closed nor bounded, we have no mathematical guarantee at this stage that an absolute minimum exists. However, if S has an absolute minimum value in the open first quadrant, then it must occur at a critical point of S. Thus, our next step is to find the critical points of S.

Differentiating (7) we obtain

$$\frac{\partial S}{\partial x} = y - \frac{64}{x^2}, \quad \frac{\partial S}{\partial y} = x - \frac{64}{y^2} \tag{8}$$

so the coordinates of the critical points of S satisfy

$$y - \frac{64}{x^2} = 0, \quad x - \frac{64}{y^2} = 0$$

Solving the first equation for y yields

$$y = \frac{64}{x^2} \tag{9}$$

and substituting this expression in the second equation yields

$$x - \frac{64}{(64/x^2)^2} = 0$$

which can be rewritten as

$$x\left(1 - \frac{x^3}{64}\right) = 0$$

The solutions of this equation are $x = 0$ and $x = 4$. Since we require $x > 0$, the only solution of significance is $x = 4$. Substituting this value into (9) yields $y = 4$. We conclude that the point $(x, y) = (4, 4)$ is the only critical point of S in the first quadrant. Since $S = 48$ if $x = y = 4$, this suggests we try to show that the minimum value of S on the open first quadrant is 48.

It immediately follows from Equation (7) that $48 < S$ at any point in the first quadrant for which at least one of the inequalities

$$xy > 48, \quad \frac{64}{y} > 48, \quad \frac{64}{x} > 48$$

is satisfied. Therefore, to prove that $48 \leq S$, we can restrict attention to the set of points in the first quadrant that satisfy the three inequalities

$$xy \leq 48, \quad \frac{64}{y} \leq 48, \quad \frac{64}{x} \leq 48$$

These inequalities can be rewritten as

$$xy \leq 48, \quad y \geq \frac{4}{3}, \quad x \geq \frac{4}{3}$$

and they define a closed and bounded region R within the first quadrant (Figure 13.8.11). The function S is continuous on R, so Theorem 13.8.3 guarantees that S has an absolute minimum value somewhere on R. Since the point $(4, 4)$ lies within R, and $48 < S$ on the boundary of R (why?), the minimum value of S on R must occur at an interior point. It then follows from Theorem 13.8.7 that the mimimum value of S on R must occur at a critical point of S. Hence, the absolute minimum of S on R (and therefore on the entire open first quadrant) is $S = 48$ at the point $(4, 4)$. Substituting $x = 4$ and $y = 4$ into (6) yields $z = 2$, so the box using the least material has a height of 2 ft and a square base whose edges are 4 ft long. ◄

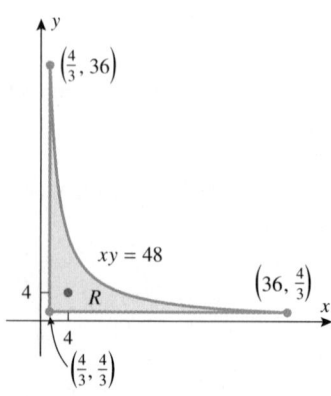

▲ Figure 13.8.11

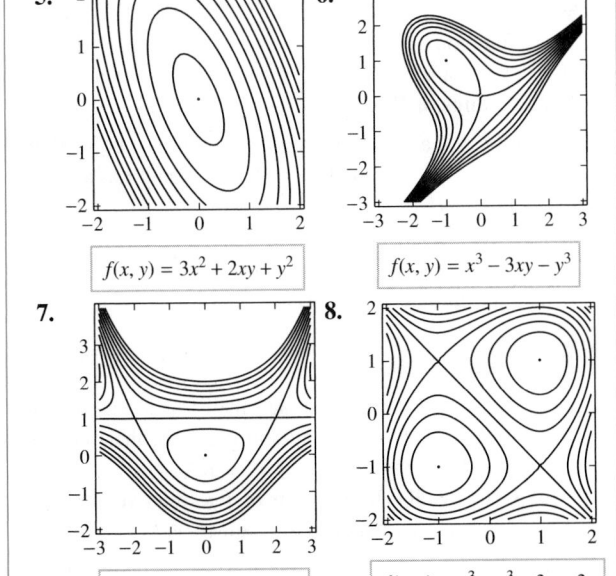

REMARK Fortunately, in our solution to Example 6 we were able to prove the existence of an absolute minimum of S in the first quadrant. The general problem of finding the absolute extrema of a function on an unbounded region, or on a region that is not closed, can be difficult and will not be considered in this text. However, in applied problems we can sometimes use physical considerations to deduce that an absolute extremum has been found. For example, the graph of Equation (7) in Figure 13.8.12 strongly suggests that the relative minimum at $x = 4$ and $y = 4$ is also an absolute minimum.

▲ Figure 13.8.12

✔ QUICK CHECK EXERCISES 13.8   *(See page 989 for answers.)*

1. The critical points of the function $f(x, y) = x^3 + xy + y^2$ are _____.

2. Suppose that $f(x, y)$ has continuous second-order partial derivatives everywhere and that the origin is a critical point for f. State what information (if any) is provided by the second partials test if
   (a) $f_{xx}(0, 0) = 2$, $f_{xy}(0, 0) = 2$, $f_{yy}(0, 0) = 2$
   (b) $f_{xx}(0, 0) = -2$, $f_{xy}(0, 0) = 2$, $f_{yy}(0, 0) = 2$
   (c) $f_{xx}(0, 0) = 3$, $f_{xy}(0, 0) = 2$, $f_{yy}(0, 0) = 2$

   (d) $f_{xx}(0, 0) = -3$, $f_{xy}(0, 0) = 2$, $f_{yy}(0, 0) = -2$.

3. For the function $f(x, y) = x^3 - 3xy + y^3$, state what information (if any) is provided by the second partials test at the point
   (a) $(0, 0)$ (b) $(-1, -1)$ (c) $(1, 1)$.

4. A rectangular box has total surface area of 2 ft^2. Express the volume of the box as a function of the dimensions x and y of the base of the box.

EXERCISE SET 13.8    Graphing Utility   [c] CAS

1–2 Locate all absolute maxima and minima, if any, by inspection. Then check your answers using calculus.

1. (a) $f(x, y) = (x - 2)^2 + (y + 1)^2$
   (b) $f(x, y) = 1 - x^2 - y^2$
   (c) $f(x, y) = x + 2y - 5$

2. (a) $f(x, y) = 1 - (x + 1)^2 - (y - 5)^2$
   (b) $f(x, y) = e^{xy}$
   (c) $f(x, y) = x^2 - y^2$

3–4 Complete the squares and locate all absolute maxima and minima, if any, by inspection. Then check your answers using calculus. ▪

3. $f(x, y) = 13 - 6x + x^2 + 4y + y^2$
4. $f(x, y) = 1 - 2x - x^2 + 4y - 2y^2$

FOCUS ON CONCEPTS

5–8 The contour plots show all significant features of the function. Make a conjecture about the number and the location of all relative extrema and saddle points, and then use calculus to check your conjecture. ▪

5.
$f(x, y) = 3x^2 + 2xy + y^2$

6.
$f(x, y) = x^3 - 3xy - y^3$

7.
$f(x, y) = x^2 + 2y^2 - x^2y$

8.
$f(x, y) = x^3 + y^3 - 3x - 3y$

9–20 Locate all relative maxima, relative minima, and saddle points, if any. ■

9. $f(x, y) = y^2 + xy + 3y + 2x + 3$

10. $f(x, y) = x^2 + xy - 2y - 2x + 1$

11. $f(x, y) = x^2 + xy + y^2 - 3x$

12. $f(x, y) = xy - x^3 - y^2$ **13.** $f(x, y) = x^2 + y^2 + \dfrac{2}{xy}$

14. $f(x, y) = xe^y$ **15.** $f(x, y) = x^2 + y - e^y$

16. $f(x, y) = xy + \dfrac{2}{x} + \dfrac{4}{y}$ **17.** $f(x, y) = e^x \sin y$

18. $f(x, y) = y \sin x$ **19.** $f(x, y) = e^{-(x^2+y^2+2x)}$

20. $f(x, y) = xy + \dfrac{a^3}{x} + \dfrac{b^3}{y}$ $(a \neq 0, b \neq 0)$

[C] **21.** Use a CAS to generate a contour plot of
$$f(x, y) = 2x^2 - 4xy + y^4 + 2$$
for $-2 \leq x \leq 2$ and $-2 \leq y \leq 2$, and use the plot to approximate the locations of all relative extrema and saddle points in the region. Check your answer using calculus, and identify the relative extrema as relative maxima or minima.

[C] **22.** Use a CAS to generate a contour plot of
$$f(x, y) = 2y^2 x - yx^2 + 4xy$$
for $-5 \leq x \leq 5$ and $-5 \leq y \leq 5$, and use the plot to approximate the locations of all relative extrema and saddle points in the region. Check your answer using calculus, and identify the relative extrema as relative maxima or minima.

23–26 True–False Determine whether the statement is true or false. Explain your answer. In these exercises, assume that $f(x, y)$ has continuous second-order partial derivatives and that
$$D(x, y) = f_{xx}(x, y) f_{yy}(x, y) - f_{xy}^2(x, y)$$ ■

23. If the function f is defined on the disk $x^2 + y^2 \leq 1$, then f has a critical point somewhere on this disk.

24. If the function f is defined on the disk $x^2 + y^2 \leq 1$, and if f is not a constant function, then f has a finite number of critical points on this disk.

25. If $P(x_0, y_0)$ is a critical point of f, and if f is defined on a disk centered at P with $D(x_0, y_0) > 0$, then f has a relative extremum at P.

26. If $P(x_0, y_0)$ is a critical point of f with $f(x_0, y_0) = 0$, and if f is defined on a disk centered at P with $D(x_0, y_0) < 0$, then f has both positive and negative values on this disk.

FOCUS ON CONCEPTS

27. (a) Show that the second partials test provides no information about the critical points of the function $f(x, y) = x^4 + y^4$.
(b) Classify all critical points of f as relative maxima, relative minima, or saddle points.

28. (a) Show that the second partials test provides no information about the critical points of the function $f(x, y) = x^4 - y^4$.

(b) Classify all critical points of f as relative maxima, relative minima, or saddle points.

29. Recall from Theorem 4.4.4 that if a continuous function of one variable has exactly one relative extremum on an interval, then that relative extremum is an absolute extremum on the interval. This exercise shows that this result does not extend to functions of two variables.
(a) Show that $f(x, y) = 3xe^y - x^3 - e^{3y}$ has only one critical point and that a relative maximum occurs there. (See the accompanying figure.)
(b) Show that f does not have an absolute maximum.

Source: This exercise is based on the article "The Only Critical Point in Town Test" by Ira Rosenholtz and Lowell Smylie, *Mathematics Magazine*, Vol. 58, No. 3, May 1985, pp. 149–150.

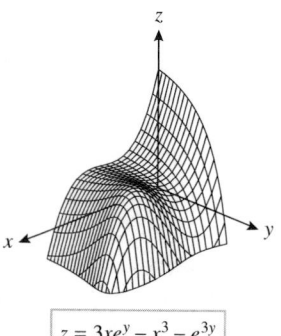

$z = 3xe^y - x^3 - e^{3y}$

◀ **Figure Ex-29**

30. If f is a continuous function of one variable with two relative maxima on an interval, then there must be a relative minimum between the relative maxima. (Convince yourself of this by drawing some pictures.) The purpose of this exercise is to show that this result does not extend to functions of two variables. Show that $f(x, y) = 4x^2 e^y - 2x^4 - e^{4y}$ has two relative maxima but no other critical points (see Figure Ex-30).

Source: This exercise is based on the problem "Two Mountains Without a Valley" proposed and solved by Ira Rosenholtz, *Mathematics Magazine*, Vol. 60, No. 1, February 1987, p. 48.

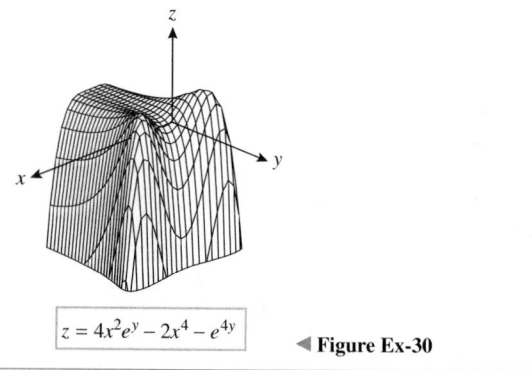

$z = 4x^2 e^y - 2x^4 - e^{4y}$

◀ **Figure Ex-30**

31–36 Find the absolute extrema of the given function on the indicated closed and bounded set R. ■

31. $f(x, y) = xy - x - 3y$; R is the triangular region with vertices $(0, 0)$, $(0, 4)$, and $(5, 0)$.

32. $f(x, y) = xy - 2x$; R is the triangular region with vertices $(0, 0)$, $(0, 4)$, and $(4, 0)$.

33. $f(x, y) = x^2 - 3y^2 - 2x + 6y$; R is the region bounded by the square with vertices $(0, 0)$, $(0, 2)$, $(2, 2)$, and $(2, 0)$.

34. $f(x, y) = xe^y - x^2 - e^y$; R is the rectangular region with vertices $(0, 0)$, $(0, 1)$, $(2, 1)$, and $(2, 0)$.

35. $f(x, y) = x^2 + 2y^2 - x$; R is the disk $x^2 + y^2 \le 4$.

36. $f(x, y) = xy^2$; R is the region that satisfies the inequalities $x \ge 0$, $y \ge 0$, and $x^2 + y^2 \le 1$.

37. Find three positive numbers whose sum is 48 and such that their product is as large as possible.

38. Find three positive numbers whose sum is 27 and such that the sum of their squares is as small as possible.

39. Find all points on the portion of the plane $x + y + z = 5$ in the first octant at which $f(x, y, z) = xy^2z^2$ has a maximum value.

40. Find the points on the surface $x^2 - yz = 5$ that are closest to the origin.

41. Find the dimensions of the rectangular box of maximum volume that can be inscribed in a sphere of radius a.

42. Find the maximum volume of a rectangular box with three faces in the coordinate planes and a vertex in the first octant on the plane $x + y + z = 1$.

43. A closed rectangular box with a volume of 16 ft^3 is made from two kinds of materials. The top and bottom are made of material costing 10¢ per square foot and the sides from material costing 5¢ per square foot. Find the dimensions of the box so that the cost of materials is minimized.

44. A manufacturer makes two models of an item, standard and deluxe. It costs $40 to manufacture the standard model and $60 for the deluxe. A market research firm estimates that if the standard model is priced at x dollars and the deluxe at y dollars, then the manufacturer will sell $500(y - x)$ of the standard items and $45{,}000 + 500(x - 2y)$ of the deluxe each year. How should the items be priced to maximize the profit?

45. Consider the function

$$f(x, y) = 4x^2 - 3y^2 + 2xy$$

over the unit square $0 \le x \le 1, 0 \le y \le 1$.
  (a) Find the maximum and minimum values of f on each edge of the square.
  (b) Find the maximum and minimum values of f on each diagonal of the square.
  (c) Find the maximum and minimum values of f on the entire square.

46. Show that among all parallelograms with perimeter l, a square with sides of length $l/4$ has maximum area. [*Hint:* The area of a parallelogram is given by the formula $A = ab \sin \alpha$, where a and b are the lengths of two adjacent sides and α is the angle between them.]

47. Determine the dimensions of a rectangular box, open at the top, having volume V, and requiring the least amount of material for its construction.

48. A length of sheet metal 27 inches wide is to be made into a water trough by bending up two sides as shown in the accompanying figure. Find x and ϕ so that the trapezoid-shaped cross section has a maximum area.

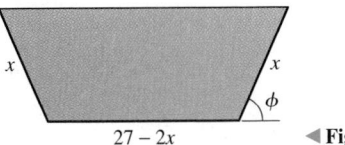

$27 - 2x$ ◀ **Figure Ex-48**

49–50 A common problem in experimental work is to obtain a mathematical relationship $y = f(x)$ between two variables x and y by "fitting" a curve to points in the plane that correspond to experimentally determined values of x and y, say

$$(x_1, y_1), (x_2, y_2), \ldots, (x_n, y_n)$$

The curve $y = f(x)$ is called a ***mathematical model*** of the data. The general form of the function f is commonly determined by some underlying physical principle, but sometimes it is just determined by the pattern of the data. We are concerned with fitting a straight line $y = mx + b$ to data. Usually, the data will not lie on a line (possibly due to experimental error or variations in experimental conditions), so the problem is to find a line that fits the data "best" according to some criterion. One criterion for selecting the line of best fit is to choose m and b to minimize the function

$$g(m, b) = \sum_{i=1}^{n} (mx_i + b - y_i)^2$$

This is called the ***method of least squares***, and the resulting line is called the ***regression line*** or the ***least squares line of best fit***. Geometrically, $|mx_i + b - y_i|$ is the vertical distance between the data point (x_i, y_i) and the line $y = mx + b$.

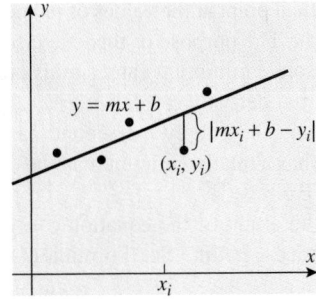

These vertical distances are called the ***residuals*** of the data points, so the effect of minimizing $g(m, b)$ is to minimize the sum of the squares of the residuals. In these exercises, we will derive a formula for the regression line. ∎

49. The purpose of this exercise is to find the values of m and b that produce the regression line.
  (a) To minimize $g(m, b)$, we start by finding values of m and b such that $\partial g / \partial m = 0$ and $\partial g / \partial b = 0$. Show

that these equations are satisfied if m and b satisfy the conditions

$$\left(\sum_{i=1}^{n} x_i^2\right) m + \left(\sum_{i=1}^{n} x_i\right) b = \sum_{i=1}^{n} x_i y_i$$

$$\left(\sum_{i=1}^{n} x_i\right) m + nb = \sum_{i=1}^{n} y_i$$

(b) Let $\bar{x} = (x_1 + x_2 + \cdots + x_n)/n$ denote the arithmetic average of $x_1, x_2, \ldots, x_n$. Use the fact that

$$\sum_{i=1}^{n} (x_i - \bar{x})^2 \geq 0$$

to show that

$$n\left(\sum_{i=1}^{n} x_i^2\right) - \left(\sum_{i=1}^{n} x_i\right)^2 \geq 0$$

with equality if and only if all the x_i's are the same.

(c) Assuming that not all the x_i's are the same, prove that the equations in part (a) have the unique solution

$$m = \frac{n\sum_{i=1}^{n} x_i y_i - \sum_{i=1}^{n} x_i \sum_{i=1}^{n} y_i}{n\sum_{i=1}^{n} x_i^2 - \left(\sum_{i=1}^{n} x_i\right)^2}$$

$$b = \frac{1}{n}\left(\sum_{i=1}^{n} y_i - m\sum_{i=1}^{n} x_i\right)$$

[*Note:* We have shown that g has a critical point at these values of m and b. In the next exercise we will show that g has an absolute minimum at this critical point. Accepting this to be so, we have shown that the line $y = mx + b$ is the regression line for these values of m and b.]

50. Assume that not all the x_i's are the same, so that $g(m, b)$ has a unique critical point at the values of m and b obtained in Exercise 49(c). The purpose of this exercise is to show that g has an absolute minimum value at this point.

(a) Find the partial derivatives $g_{mm}(m, b)$, $g_{bb}(m, b)$, and $g_{mb}(m, b)$, and then apply the second partials test to show that g has a relative minimum at the critical point obtained in Exercise 49.

(b) Show that the graph of the equation $z = g(m, b)$ is a quadric surface. [*Hint:* See Formula (4) of Section 11.7.]

(c) It can be proved that the graph of $z = g(m, b)$ is an elliptic paraboloid. Accepting this to be so, show that this paraboloid opens in the positive z-direction, and explain how this shows that g has an absolute minimum at the critical point obtained in Exercise 49.

51–54 Use the formulas obtained in Exercise 49 to find and draw the regression line. If you have a calculating utility that can calculate regression lines, use it to check your work. ■

51. 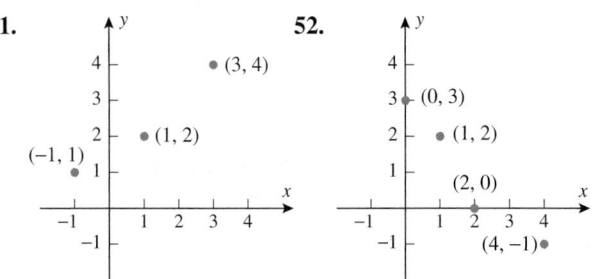 52.

53.

x	1	2	3	4
y	1.5	1.6	2.1	3.0

54.

x	1	2	3	4	5
y	4.2	3.5	3.0	2.4	2.0

55. The following table shows the life expectancy by year of birth of females in the United States:

YEAR OF BIRTH	1930	1940	1950	1960	1970	1980	1990	2000
LIFE EXPECTANCY	61.6	65.2	71.1	73.1	74.7	77.5	78.8	79.7

(a) Take $t = 0$ to be the year 1930, and let y be the life expectancy for birth year t. Use the regression capability of a calculating utility to find the regression line of y as a function of t.

(b) Use a graphing utility to make a graph that shows the data points and the regression line.

(c) Use the regression line to make a conjecture about the life expectancy of females born in the year 2010.

56. A company manager wants to establish a relationship between the sales of a certain product and the price. The company research department provides the following data:

PRICE (x) IN DOLLARS	$35.00	$40.00	$45.00	$48.00	$50.00
DAILY SALES VOLUME (y) IN UNITS	80	75	68	66	63

(a) Use a calculating utility to find the regression line of y as a function of x.

(b) Use a graphing utility to make a graph that shows the data points and the regression line.

(c) Use the regression line to make a conjecture about the number of units that would be sold at a price of $60.00.

57. If a gas is cooled with its volume held constant, then it follows from the *ideal gas law* in physics that its pressure drops proportionally to the drop in temperature. The temperature that, in theory, corresponds to a pressure of zero is called *absolute zero*. Suppose that an experiment produces the following data for pressure P versus temperature T with the volume held constant: *(cont.)*

P (KILOPASCALS)	134	142	155	160	171	184
T (°CELSIUS)	0	20	40	60	80	100

(a) Use a calculating utility to find the regression line of P as a function of T.

(b) Use a graphing utility to make a graph that shows the data points and the regression line.

(c) Use the regression line to estimate the value of absolute zero in degrees Celsius.

58. Find

(a) a continuous function $f(x, y)$ that is defined on the entire xy-plane and has no absolute extrema on the xy-plane;

(b) a function $f(x, y)$ that is defined everywhere on the rectangle $0 \le x \le 1, 0 \le y \le 1$ and has no absolute extrema on the rectangle.

59. Show that if f has a relative maximum at (x_0, y_0), then $G(x) = f(x, y_0)$ has a relative maximum at $x = x_0$ and $H(y) = f(x_0, y)$ has a relative maximum at $y = y_0$.

60. Writing Explain how to determine the location of relative extrema or saddle points of $f(x, y)$ by examining the contours of f.

61. Writing Suppose that the second partials test gives no information about a certain critical point (x_0, y_0) because $D(x_0, y_0) = 0$. Discuss what other steps you might take to determine whether there is a relative extremum at that critical point.

✔ **QUICK CHECK ANSWERS 13.8**

1. $(0, 0)$ and $\left(\frac{1}{6}, -\frac{1}{12}\right)$ **2.** (a) no information (b) a saddle point at $(0, 0)$ (c) a relative minimum at $(0, 0)$
(d) a relative maximum at $(0, 0)$ **3.** (a) a saddle point at $(0, 0)$ (b) no information, since $(-1, -1)$ is not a critical point
(c) a relative minimum at $(1, 1)$ **4.** $V = \dfrac{xy(1 - xy)}{x + y}$

13.9 LAGRANGE MULTIPLIERS

In this section we will study a powerful new method for maximizing or minimizing a function subject to constraints on the variables. This method will help us to solve certain optimization problems that are difficult or impossible to solve using the methods studied in the last section.

■ EXTREMUM PROBLEMS WITH CONSTRAINTS

In Example 6 of the last section, we solved the problem of minimizing

$$S = xy + 2xz + 2yz \tag{1}$$

subject to the constraint

$$xyz - 32 = 0 \tag{2}$$

This is a special case of the following general problem:

13.9.1 Three-Variable Extremum Problem with One Constraint
Maximize or minimize the function $f(x, y, z)$ subject to the constraint $g(x, y, z) = 0$.

We will also be interested in the following two-variable version of this problem:

13.9.2 Two-Variable Extremum Problem with One Constraint
Maximize or minimize the function $f(x, y)$ subject to the constraint $g(x, y) = 0$.

■ LAGRANGE MULTIPLIERS

One way to attack problems of these types is to solve the constraint equation for one of the variables in terms of the others and substitute the result into f. This produces a new function of one or two variables that incorporates the constraint and can be maximized or minimized by applying standard methods. For example, to solve the problem in Example 6 of the last section we substituted (2) into (1) to obtain

$$S = xy + \frac{64}{y} + \frac{64}{x}$$

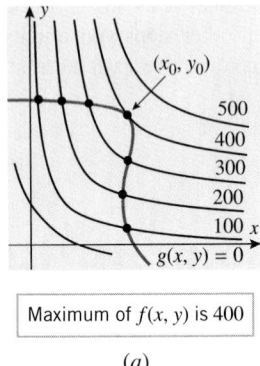

Maximum of $f(x, y)$ is 400

(a)

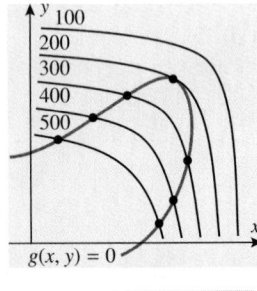

Minimum of $f(x, y)$ is 200

(b)

▲ **Figure 13.9.1**

which we then minimized by finding the critical points and applying the second partials test. However, this approach hinges on our ability to solve the constraint equation for one of the variables in terms of the others. If this cannot be done, then other methods must be used. One such method, called the *method of Lagrange multipliers*, will be discussed in this section.

To motivate the method of Lagrange multipliers, suppose that we are trying to maximize a function $f(x, y)$ subject to the constraint $g(x, y) = 0$. Geometrically, this means that we are looking for a point (x_0, y_0) on the graph of the constraint curve at which $f(x, y)$ is as large as possible. To help locate such a point, let us construct a contour plot of $f(x, y)$ in the same coordinate system as the graph of $g(x, y) = 0$. For example, Figure 13.9.1a shows some typical level curves of $f(x, y) = c$, which we have labeled $c = 100, 200, 300, 400$, and 500 for purposes of illustration. In this figure, each point of intersection of $g(x, y) = 0$ with a level curve is a candidate for a solution, since these points lie on the constraint curve. Among the seven such intersections shown in the figure, the maximum value of $f(x, y)$ occurs at the intersection (x_0, y_0) where $f(x, y)$ has a value of 400. Note that at (x_0, y_0) the constraint curve and the level curve just touch and thus have a *common* tangent line at this point. Since $\nabla f(x_0, y_0)$ is normal to the level curve $f(x, y) = 400$ at (x_0, y_0), and since $\nabla g(x_0, y_0)$ is normal to the constraint curve $g(x, y) = 0$ at (x_0, y_0), we conclude that the vectors $\nabla f(x_0, y_0)$ and $\nabla g(x_0, y_0)$ must be parallel. That is,

$$\nabla f(x_0, y_0) = \lambda \nabla g(x_0, y_0) \tag{3}$$

for some scalar λ. The same condition holds at points on the constraint curve where $f(x, y)$ has a minimum. For example, if the level curves are as shown in Figure 13.9.1b, then the minimum value of $f(x, y)$ occurs where the constraint curve just touches a level curve.

Joseph Louis Lagrange (1736–1813) French–Italian mathematician and astronomer. Lagrange, the son of a public official, was born in Turin, Italy. (Baptismal records list his name as Giuseppe Lodovico Lagrangia.) Although his father wanted him to be a lawyer, Lagrange was attracted to mathematics and astronomy after reading a memoir by the astronomer Halley. At age 16 he began to study mathematics on his own and by age 19 was appointed to a professorship at the Royal Artillery School in Turin. The following year Lagrange sent Euler solutions to some famous problems using new methods that eventually blossomed into a branch of mathematics called calculus of variations. These methods and Lagrange's applications of them to problems in celestial mechanics were so monumental that by age 25 he was regarded by many of his contemporaries as the greatest living mathematician.

In 1776, on the recommendations of Euler, he was chosen to succeed Euler as the director of the Berlin Academy. During his stay in Berlin, Lagrange distinguished himself not only in celestial me-

chanics, but also in algebraic equations and the theory of numbers. After twenty years in Berlin, he moved to Paris at the invitation of Louis XVI. He was given apartments in the Louvre and treated with great honor, even during the revolution.

Napoleon was a great admirer of Lagrange and showered him with honors—count, senator, and Legion of Honor. The years Lagrange spent in Paris were devoted primarily to didactic treatises summarizing his mathematical conceptions. One of Lagrange's most famous works is a memoir, *Mécanique Analytique*, in which he reduced the theory of mechanics to a few general formulas from which all other necessary equations could be derived.

It is an interesting historical fact that Lagrange's father speculated unsuccessfully in several financial ventures, so his family was forced to live quite modestly. Lagrange himself stated that if his family had money, he would not have made mathematics his vocation. In spite of his fame, Lagrange was always a shy and modest man. On his death, he was buried with honor in the Pantheon.

Thus, to find the maximum or minimum of $f(x, y)$ subject to the constraint $g(x, y) = 0$, we look for points at which (3) holds—this is the method of Lagrange multipliers.

Our next objective in this section is to make the preceding intuitive argument more precise. For this purpose it will help to begin with some terminology about the problem of maximizing or minimizing a function $f(x, y)$ subject to a constraint $g(x, y) = 0$. As with other kinds of maximization and minimization problems, we need to distinguish between relative and absolute extrema. We will say that f has a ***constrained absolute maximum (minimum)*** at (x_0, y_0) if $f(x_0, y_0)$ is the largest (smallest) value of f on the constraint curve, and we will say that f has a ***constrained relative maximum (minimum)*** at (x_0, y_0) if $f(x_0, y_0)$ is the largest (smallest) value of f on some segment of the constraint curve that extends on both sides of the point (x_0, y_0) (Figure 13.9.2).

Let us assume that a constrained relative maximum or minimum occurs at the point (x_0, y_0), and for simplicity let us further assume that the equation $g(x, y) = 0$ can be smoothly parametrized as

$$x = x(s), \quad y = y(s)$$

where s is an arc length parameter with reference point (x_0, y_0) at $s = 0$. Thus, the quantity

$$z = f(x(s), y(s))$$

has a relative maximum or minimum at $s = 0$, and this implies that $dz/ds = 0$ at that point. From the chain rule, this equation can be expressed as

$$\frac{dz}{ds} = \frac{\partial f}{\partial x}\frac{dx}{ds} + \frac{\partial f}{\partial y}\frac{dy}{ds} = \left(\frac{\partial f}{\partial x}\mathbf{i} + \frac{\partial f}{\partial y}\mathbf{j}\right) \cdot \left(\frac{dx}{ds}\mathbf{i} + \frac{dy}{ds}\mathbf{j}\right) = 0$$

where the derivatives are all evaluated at $s = 0$. However, the first factor in the dot product is the gradient of f, and the second factor is the unit tangent vector to the constraint curve. Since the point (x_0, y_0) corresponds to $s = 0$, it follows from this equation that

$$\nabla f(x_0, y_0) \cdot \mathbf{T}(0) = 0$$

which implies that the gradient is either $\mathbf{0}$ or is normal to the constraint curve at a constrained relative extremum. However, the constraint curve $g(x, y) = 0$ is a level curve for the function $g(x, y)$, so that if $\nabla g(x_0, y_0) \neq \mathbf{0}$, then $\nabla g(x_0, y_0)$ is normal to this curve at (x_0, y_0). It then follows that there is some scalar λ such that

$$\nabla f(x_0, y_0) = \lambda \nabla g(x_0, y_0) \tag{4}$$

This scalar is called a ***Lagrange multiplier***. Thus, the ***method of Lagrange multipliers*** for finding constrained relative extrema is to look for points on the constraint curve $g(x, y) = 0$ at which Equation (4) is satisfied for some scalar λ.

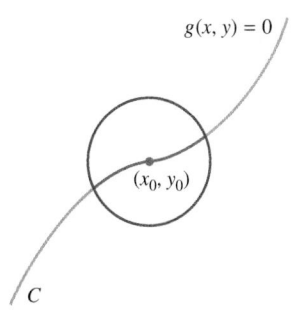

$g(x, y) = 0$

(x_0, y_0)

C

A constrained relative maximum occurs at (x_0, y_0) if $f(x_0, y_0) \geq f(x, y)$ on some segment of C that extends on both sides of (x_0, y_0).

▲ **Figure 13.9.2**

13.9.3 **THEOREM** (*Constrained-Extremum Principle for Two Variables and One Constraint*) *Let f and g be functions of two variables with continuous first partial derivatives on some open set containing the constraint curve $g(x, y) = 0$, and assume that $\nabla g \neq \mathbf{0}$ at any point on this curve. If f has a constrained relative extremum, then this extremum occurs at a point (x_0, y_0) on the constraint curve at which the gradient vectors $\nabla f(x_0, y_0)$ and $\nabla g(x_0, y_0)$ are parallel; that is, there is some number λ such that*

$$\nabla f(x_0, y_0) = \lambda \nabla g(x_0, y_0)$$

▶ **Example 1** At what point or points on the circle $x^2 + y^2 = 1$ does $f(x, y) = xy$ have an absolute maximum, and what is that maximum?

Solution.   The circle $x^2 + y^2 = 1$ is a closed and bounded set and $f(x, y) = xy$ is a continuous function, so it follows from the Extreme-Value Theorem (Theorem 13.8.3) that f has an absolute maximum and an absolute minimum on the circle. To find these extrema, we will use Lagrange multipliers to find the constrained relative extrema, and then we will evaluate f at those relative extrema to find the absolute extrema.

We want to maximize $f(x, y) = xy$ subject to the constraint

$$g(x, y) = x^2 + y^2 - 1 = 0 \tag{5}$$

First we will look for constrained *relative* extrema. For this purpose we will need the gradients

$$\nabla f = y\mathbf{i} + x\mathbf{j} \quad \text{and} \quad \nabla g = 2x\mathbf{i} + 2y\mathbf{j}$$

From the formula for ∇g we see that $\nabla g = \mathbf{0}$ if and only if $x = 0$ and $y = 0$, so $\nabla g \neq \mathbf{0}$ at any point on the circle $x^2 + y^2 = 1$. Thus, at a constrained relative extremum we must have

$$\nabla f = \lambda \nabla g \quad \text{or} \quad y\mathbf{i} + x\mathbf{j} = \lambda(2x\mathbf{i} + 2y\mathbf{j})$$

which is equivalent to the pair of equations

$$y = 2x\lambda \quad \text{and} \quad x = 2y\lambda$$

It follows from these equations that if $x = 0$, then $y = 0$, and if $y = 0$, then $x = 0$. In either case we have $x^2 + y^2 = 0$, so the constraint equation $x^2 + y^2 = 1$ is not satisfied. Thus, we can assume that x and y are nonzero, and we can rewrite the equations as

$$\lambda = \frac{y}{2x} \quad \text{and} \quad \lambda = \frac{x}{2y}$$

from which we obtain

$$\frac{y}{2x} = \frac{x}{2y}$$

or

$$y^2 = x^2 \tag{6}$$

Substituting this in (5) yields

$$2x^2 - 1 = 0$$

from which we obtain $x = \pm 1/\sqrt{2}$. Each of these values, when substituted in Equation (6), produces y-values of $y = \pm 1/\sqrt{2}$. Thus, constrained relative extrema occur at the points $(1/\sqrt{2}, 1/\sqrt{2})$, $(1/\sqrt{2}, -1/\sqrt{2})$, $(-1/\sqrt{2}, 1/\sqrt{2})$, and $(-1/\sqrt{2}, -1/\sqrt{2})$. The values of xy at these points are as follows:

(x, y)	$(1/\sqrt{2}, 1/\sqrt{2})$	$(1/\sqrt{2}, -1/\sqrt{2})$	$(-1/\sqrt{2}, 1/\sqrt{2})$	$(-1/\sqrt{2}, -1/\sqrt{2})$
xy	$1/2$	$-1/2$	$-1/2$	$1/2$

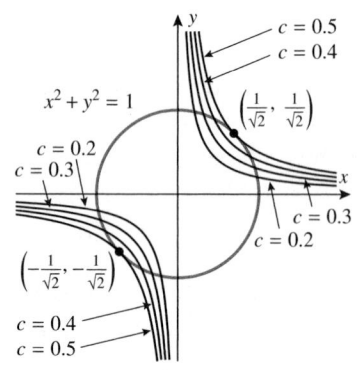

▲ **Figure 13.9.3**

Thus, the function $f(x, y) = xy$ has an absolute maximum of $\frac{1}{2}$ occurring at the two points $(1/\sqrt{2}, 1/\sqrt{2})$ and $(-1/\sqrt{2}, -1/\sqrt{2})$. Although it was not asked for, we can also see that f has an absolute minimum of $-\frac{1}{2}$ occurring at the points $(1/\sqrt{2}, -1/\sqrt{2})$ and $(-1/\sqrt{2}, 1/\sqrt{2})$. Figure 13.9.3 shows some level curves $xy = c$ and the constraint curve in the vicinity of the maxima. A similar figure for the minima can be obtained using negative values of c for the level curves $xy = c$. ◄

Give another solution to Example 1 using the parametrization

$$x = \cos\theta, \quad y = \sin\theta$$

and the identity

$$\sin 2\theta = 2 \sin\theta \cos\theta$$

REMARK   If c is a constant, then the functions $g(x, y)$ and $g(x, y) - c$ have the same gradient since the constant c drops out when we differentiate. Consequently, it is *not* essential to rewrite a constraint of the form $g(x, y) = c$ as $g(x, y) - c = 0$ in order to apply the constrained-extremum principle. Thus, in the last example, we could have kept the constraint in the form $x^2 + y^2 = 1$ and then taken $g(x, y) = x^2 + y^2$ rather than $g(x, y) = x^2 + y^2 - 1$.

▶ **Example 2**   Use the method of Lagrange multipliers to find the dimensions of a rectangle with perimeter p and maximum area.

Solution.   Let

$x =$ length of the rectangle, $y =$ width of the rectangle, $A =$ area of the rectangle

We want to maximize $A = xy$ on the line segment

$$2x + 2y = p, \quad 0 \le x, y \tag{7}$$

that corresponds to the perimeter constraint. This segment is a closed and bounded set, and since $f(x, y) = xy$ is a continuous function, it follows from the Extreme-Value Theorem (Theorem 13.8.3) that f has an absolute maximum on this segment. This absolute maximum must also be a constrained relative maximum since f is 0 at the endpoints of the segment and positive elsewhere on the segment. If $g(x, y) = 2x + 2y$, then we have

$$\nabla f = y\mathbf{i} + x\mathbf{j} \quad \text{and} \quad \nabla g = 2\mathbf{i} + 2\mathbf{j}$$

Noting that $\nabla g \neq \mathbf{0}$, it follows from (4) that

$$y\mathbf{i} + x\mathbf{j} = \lambda(2\mathbf{i} + 2\mathbf{j})$$

at a constrained relative maximum. This is equivalent to the two equations

$$y = 2\lambda \quad \text{and} \quad x = 2\lambda$$

Eliminating λ from these equations we obtain $x = y$, which shows that the rectangle is actually a square. Using this condition and constraint (7), we obtain $x = p/4$, $y = p/4$. ◀

■ THREE VARIABLES AND ONE CONSTRAINT

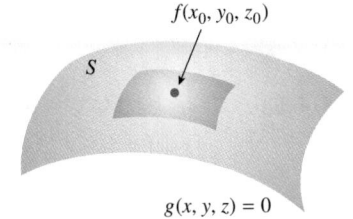

$f(x_0, y_0, z_0)$

S

$g(x, y, z) = 0$

A constrained relative maximum occurs at (x_0, y_0, z_0) if $f(x_0, y_0, z_0) \ge f(x, y, z)$ at all points of S near (x_0, y_0, z_0).

▲ **Figure 13.9.4**

The method of Lagrange multipliers can also be used to maximize or minimize a function of three variables $f(x, y, z)$ subject to a constraint $g(x, y, z) = 0$. As a rule, the graph of $g(x, y, z) = 0$ will be some surface S in 3-space. Thus, from a geometric viewpoint, the problem is to maximize or minimize $f(x, y, z)$ as (x, y, z) varies over the surface S (Figure 13.9.4). As usual, we distinguish between relative and absolute extrema. We will say that f has a ***constrained absolute maximum (minimum)*** at (x_0, y_0, z_0) if $f(x_0, y_0, z_0)$ is the largest (smallest) value of $f(x, y, z)$ on S, and we will say that f has a ***constrained relative maximum (minimum)*** at (x_0, y_0, z_0) if $f(x_0, y_0, z_0)$ is the largest (smallest) value of $f(x, y, z)$ at all points of S "near" (x_0, y_0, z_0).

The following theorem, which we state without proof, is the three-variable analog of Theorem 13.9.3.

13.9.4   THEOREM (*Constrained-Extremum Principle for Three Variables and One Constraint*)   *Let f and g be functions of three variables with continuous first partial derivatives on some open set containing the constraint surface $g(x, y, z) = 0$, and assume that $\nabla g \neq \mathbf{0}$ at any point on this surface. If f has a constrained relative extremum, then this extremum occurs at a point (x_0, y_0, z_0) on the constraint surface at which the gradient vectors $\nabla f(x_0, y_0, z_0)$ and $\nabla g(x_0, y_0, z_0)$ are parallel; that is, there is some number λ such that*

$$\nabla f(x_0, y_0, z_0) = \lambda \nabla g(x_0, y_0, z_0)$$

▶ **Example 3**   Find the points on the sphere $x^2 + y^2 + z^2 = 36$ that are closest to and farthest from the point $(1, 2, 2)$.

Solution.   To avoid radicals, we will find points on the sphere that minimize and maximize the *square* of the distance to $(1, 2, 2)$. Thus, we want to find the relative extrema of

$$f(x, y, z) = (x - 1)^2 + (y - 2)^2 + (z - 2)^2$$

subject to the constraint

$$x^2 + y^2 + z^2 = 36 \tag{8}$$

If we let $g(x, y, z) = x^2 + y^2 + z^2$, then $\nabla g = 2x\mathbf{i} + 2y\mathbf{j} + 2z\mathbf{k}$. Thus, $\nabla g = \mathbf{0}$ if and only if $x = y = z = 0$. It follows that $\nabla g \neq \mathbf{0}$ at any point of the sphere (8), and hence the constrained relative extrema must occur at points where

$$\nabla f(x, y, z) = \lambda \nabla g(x, y, z)$$

That is,

$$2(x - 1)\mathbf{i} + 2(y - 2)\mathbf{j} + 2(z - 2)\mathbf{k} = \lambda(2x\mathbf{i} + 2y\mathbf{j} + 2z\mathbf{k})$$

which leads to the equations

$$2(x - 1) = 2x\lambda, \quad 2(y - 2) = 2y\lambda, \quad 2(z - 2) = 2z\lambda \tag{9}$$

We may assume that x, y, and z are nonzero since $x = 0$ does not satisfy the first equation, $y = 0$ does not satisfy the second, and $z = 0$ does not satisfy the third. Thus, we can rewrite (9) as

$$\frac{x - 1}{x} = \lambda, \quad \frac{y - 2}{y} = \lambda, \quad \frac{z - 2}{z} = \lambda$$

The first two equations imply that

$$\frac{x - 1}{x} = \frac{y - 2}{y}$$

from which it follows that

$$y = 2x \tag{10}$$

Similarly, the first and third equations imply that

$$z = 2x \tag{11}$$

Substituting (10) and (11) in the constraint equation (8), we obtain

$$9x^2 = 36 \quad \text{or} \quad x = \pm 2$$

Substituting these values in (10) and (11) yields two points:

$$(2, 4, 4) \quad \text{and} \quad (-2, -4, -4)$$

Since $f(2, 4, 4) = 9$ and $f(-2, -4, -4) = 81$, it follows that $(2, 4, 4)$ is the point on the sphere closest to $(1, 2, 2)$, and $(-2, -4, -4)$ is the point that is farthest (Figure 13.9.5). ◄

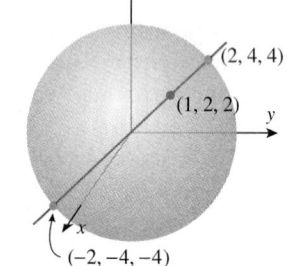

▲ **Figure 13.9.5**

REMARK   Solving nonlinear systems such as (9) usually involves trial and error. A technique that sometimes works is demonstrated in Example 3. In that example the equations were solved for a common variable (λ), and we then derived relationships between the remaining variables (x, y, and z). Substituting those relationships in the constraint equation led to the value of one of the variables, and the values of the other variables were then computed.

Next we will use Lagrange multipliers to solve the problem of Example 6 in the last section.

▶ **Example 4**   Use Lagrange multipliers to determine the dimensions of a rectangular box, open at the top, having a volume of 32 ft³, and requiring the least amount of material for its construction.

Solution. With the notation introduced in Example 6 of the last section, the problem is to minimize the surface area
$$S = xy + 2xz + 2yz$$

subject to the volume constraint
$$xyz = 32 \qquad (12)$$

If we let $f(x, y, z) = xy + 2xz + 2yz$ and $g(x, y, z) = xyz$, then
$$\nabla f = (y + 2z)\mathbf{i} + (x + 2z)\mathbf{j} + (2x + 2y)\mathbf{k} \quad \text{and} \quad \nabla g = yz\mathbf{i} + xz\mathbf{j} + xy\mathbf{k}$$

It follows that $\nabla g \neq \mathbf{0}$ at any point on the surface $xyz = 32$, since x, y, and z are all nonzero on this surface. Thus, at a constrained relative extremum we must have $\nabla f = \lambda \nabla g$, that is,
$$(y + 2z)\mathbf{i} + (x + 2z)\mathbf{j} + (2x + 2y)\mathbf{k} = \lambda(yz\mathbf{i} + xz\mathbf{j} + xy\mathbf{k})$$

This condition yields the three equations
$$y + 2z = \lambda yz, \quad x + 2z = \lambda xz, \quad 2x + 2y = \lambda xy$$

Because x, y, and z are nonzero, these equations can be rewritten as
$$\frac{1}{z} + \frac{2}{y} = \lambda, \quad \frac{1}{z} + \frac{2}{x} = \lambda, \quad \frac{2}{y} + \frac{2}{x} = \lambda$$

From the first two equations,
$$y = x \qquad (13)$$

and from the first and third equations,
$$z = \tfrac{1}{2}x \qquad (14)$$

Substituting (13) and (14) in the volume constraint (12) yields
$$\tfrac{1}{2}x^3 = 32$$

This equation, together with (13) and (14), yields
$$x = 4, \quad y = 4, \quad z = 2$$

which agrees with the result that was obtained in Example 6 of the last section. ◀

There are variations in the method of Lagrange multipliers that can be used to solve problems with two or more constraints. However, we will not discuss that topic here.

✔ **QUICK CHECK EXERCISES 13.9**   *(See page 997 for answers.)*

1. (a) Suppose that $f(x, y)$ and $g(x, y)$ are differentiable at the origin and have nonzero gradients there, and that $g(0, 0) = 0$. If the maximum value of $f(x, y)$ subject to the constraint $g(x, y) = 0$ occurs at the origin, how is the tangent line to the graph of $g(x, y) = 0$ related to the tangent line at the origin to the level curve of f through $(0, 0)$?

   (b) Suppose that $f(x, y, z)$ and $g(x, y, z)$ are differentiable at the origin and have nonzero gradients there, and that $g(0, 0, 0) = 0$. If the maximum value of $f(x, y, z)$ subject to the constraint $g(x, y, z) = 0$ occurs at the origin,

   how is the tangent plane to the graph of the constraint $g(x, y, z) = 0$ related to the tangent plane at the origin to the level surface of f through $(0, 0, 0)$?

2. The maximum value of $x + y$ subject to the constraint $x^2 + y^2 = 1$ is _____.

3. The maximum value of $x + y + z$ subject to the constraint $x^2 + y^2 + z^2 = 1$ is _____.

4. The maximum and minimum values of $2x + 3y$ subject to the constraint $x + y = 1$, where $0 \leq x, 0 \leq y$, are _____ and _____, respectively.

EXERCISE SET 13.9 　 Graphing Utility 　 C CAS

---

1. The accompanying figure shows graphs of the line $x + y = 4$ and the level curves of height $c = 2, 4, 6$, and 8 for the function $f(x, y) = xy$.
   (a) Use the figure to find the maximum value of the function $f(x, y) = xy$ subject to $x + y = 4$, and explain your reasoning.
   (b) How can you tell from the figure that your answer to part (a) is not the minimum value of f subject to the constraint?
   (c) Use Lagrange multipliers to check your work.

2. The accompanying figure shows the graphs of the line $3x + 4y = 25$ and the level curves of height $c = 9, 16, 25, 36$, and 49 for the function $f(x, y) = x^2 + y^2$.
   (a) Use the accompanying figure to find the minimum value of the function $f(x, y) = x^2 + y^2$ subject to $3x + 4y = 25$, and explain your reasoning.
   (b) How can you tell from the accompanying figure that your answer to part (a) is not the maximum value of f subject to the constraint?
   (c) Use Lagrange multipliers to check your work.

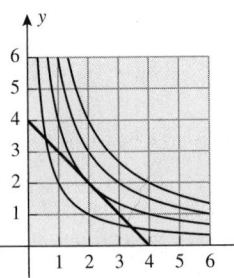

▲ Figure Ex-1   ▲ Figure Ex-2

3. (a) On a graphing utility, graph the circle $x^2 + y^2 = 25$ and two distinct level curves of $f(x, y) = x^2 - y$ that just touch the circle in a single point.
   (b) Use the results you obtained in part (a) to approximate the maximum and minimum values of f subject to the constraint $x^2 + y^2 = 25$.
   (c) Check your approximations in part (b) using Lagrange multipliers.

C 4. (a) If you have a CAS with implicit plotting capability, use it to graph the circle $(x - 4)^2 + (y - 4)^2 = 4$ and two level curves of $f(x, y) = x^3 + y^3 - 3xy$ that just touch the circle.
   (b) Use the result you obtained in part (a) to approximate the minimum value of f subject to the constraint $(x - 4)^2 + (y - 4)^2 = 4$.
   (c) Confirm graphically that you have found a minimum and not a maximum.
   (d) Check your approximation using Lagrange multipliers and solving the required equations numerically.

5–12 Use Lagrange multipliers to find the maximum and minimum values of f subject to the given constraint. Also, find the points at which these extreme values occur. ■

5. $f(x, y) = xy$; $4x^2 + 8y^2 = 16$
6. $f(x, y) = x^2 - y^2$; $x^2 + y^2 = 25$
7. $f(x, y) = 4x^3 + y^2$; $2x^2 + y^2 = 1$
8. $f(x, y) = x - 3y - 1$; $x^2 + 3y^2 = 16$
9. $f(x, y, z) = 2x + y - 2z$; $x^2 + y^2 + z^2 = 4$
10. $f(x, y, z) = 3x + 6y + 2z$; $2x^2 + 4y^2 + z^2 = 70$
11. $f(x, y, z) = xyz$; $x^2 + y^2 + z^2 = 1$
12. $f(x, y, z) = x^4 + y^4 + z^4$; $x^2 + y^2 + z^2 = 1$

13–16 True–False Determine whether the statement is true or false. Explain your answer. ■

13. A "Lagrange multiplier" is a special type of gradient vector.
14. The extrema of $f(x, y)$ subject to the constraint $g(x, y) = 0$ occur at those points for which $\nabla f = \nabla g$.
15. In the method of Lagrange mutlipliers it is necessary to solve a constraint equation $g(x, y) = 0$ for y in terms of x.
16. The extrema of $f(x, y)$ subject to the constraint $g(x, y) = 0$ occur at those points at which a contour of f is tangent to the constraint curve $g(x, y) = 0$.

17–24 Solve using Lagrange multipliers. ■

17. Find the point on the line $2x - 4y = 3$ that is closest to the origin.
18. Find the point on the line $y = 2x + 3$ that is closest to $(4, 2)$.
19. Find the point on the plane $x + 2y + z = 1$ that is closest to the origin.
20. Find the point on the plane $4x + 3y + z = 2$ that is closest to $(1, -1, 1)$.
21. Find the points on the circle $x^2 + y^2 = 45$ that are closest to and farthest from $(1, 2)$.
22. Find the points on the surface $xy - z^2 = 1$ that are closest to the origin.
23. Find a vector in 3-space whose length is 5 and whose components have the largest possible sum.
24. Suppose that the temperature at a point (x, y) on a metal plate is $T(x, y) = 4x^2 - 4xy + y^2$. An ant, walking on the plate, traverses a circle of radius 5 centered at the origin. What are the highest and lowest temperatures encountered by the ant?

25–32 Use Lagrange multipliers to solve the indicated problems from Section 13.8. ■

25. Exercise 38
26. Exercise 39

27. Exercise 40

28. Exercise 41

29. Exercise 43

30. Exercises 45(a) and (b)

31. Exercise 46

32. Exercise 47

[c] 33. Let α, β, and γ be the angles of a triangle.
   (a) Use Lagrange multipliers to find the maximum value of $f(\alpha, \beta, \gamma) = \cos\alpha \cos\beta \cos\gamma$, and determine the angles for which the maximum occurs.
   (b) Express $f(\alpha, \beta, \gamma)$ as a function of α and β alone, and use a CAS to graph this function of two variables. Confirm that the result obtained in part (a) is consistent with the graph.

34. The accompanying figure shows the intersection of the elliptic paraboloid $z = x^2 + 4y^2$ and the right circular cylinder $x^2 + y^2 = 1$. Use Lagrange multipliers to find the highest and lowest points on the curve of intersection.

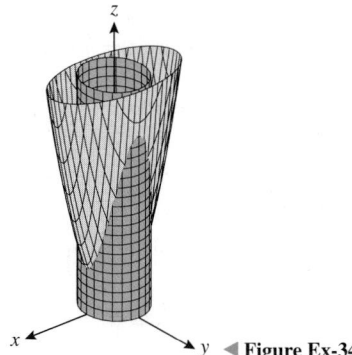

◀ **Figure Ex-34**

35. **Writing** List a sequence of steps for solving a two-variable extremum problem with one constraint using the method of Lagrange multipliers. Interpret each step geometrically.

36. **Writing** Redo Example 2 using the methods of Section 4.5, and compare your solution with that of Example 2. For example, how is the perimeter constraint used in each approach?

✔ **QUICK CHECK ANSWERS 13.9**

---

1. (a) They are the same line. (b) They are the same plane.   2. $\sqrt{2}$ 3. $\sqrt{3}$ 4. 3; 2

CHAPTER 13 REVIEW EXERCISES   〰 Graphing Utility

---

1. Let $f(x, y) = e^x \ln y$. Find
   (a) $f(\ln y, e^x)$ (b) $f(r + s, rs)$.

2. Sketch the domain of f using solid lines for portions of the boundary included in the domain and dashed lines for portions not included.
   (a) $f(x, y) = \ln(xy - 1)$ (b) $f(x, y) = (\sin^{-1} x)/e^y$

3. Show that the level curves of the cone $z = \sqrt{x^2 + y^2}$ and the paraboloid $z = x^2 + y^2$ are circles, and make a sketch that illustrates the difference between the contour plots of the two functions.

4. (a) In words, describe the level surfaces of the function $f(x, y, z) = a^2 x^2 + a^2 y^2 + z^2$, where $a > 0$.
   (b) Find a function $f(x, y, z)$ whose level surfaces form a family of circular paraboloids that open in the positive z-direction.

5–6 (a) Find the limit of $f(x, y)$ as $(x, y) \to (0, 0)$ if it exists, and (b) determine whether f is continuous at $(0, 0)$. ■

5. $f(x, y) = \dfrac{x^4 - x + y - x^3 y}{x - y}$

6. $f(x, y) = \begin{cases} \dfrac{x^4 - y^4}{x^2 + y^2} & \text{if } (x, y) \neq (0, 0) \\ 0 & \text{if } (x, y) = (0, 0) \end{cases}$

7. (a) A company manufactures two types of computer monitors: standard monitors and high resolution monitors. Suppose that $P(x, y)$ is the profit that results from producing and selling x standard monitors and y high-resolution monitors. What do the two partial derivatives $\partial P/\partial x$ and $\partial P/\partial y$ represent?
   (b) Suppose that the temperature at time t at a point (x, y) on the surface of a lake is $T(x, y, t)$. What do the partial derivatives $\partial T/\partial x$, $\partial T/\partial y$, and $\partial T/\partial t$ represent?

8. Let $z = f(x, y)$.
   (a) Express $\partial z/\partial x$ and $\partial z/\partial y$ as limits.
   (b) In words, what do the derivatives $f_x(x_0, y_0)$ and $f_y(x_0, y_0)$ tell you about the surface $z = f(x, y)$?
   (c) In words, what do the derivatives $\partial z/\partial x(x_0, y_0)$ and $\partial z/\partial y(x_0, y_0)$ tell you about the rates of change of z with respect to x and y?

9. The pressure in newtons per square meter (N/m²) of a gas in a cylinder is given by $P = 10T/V$ with T in kelvins (K) and V in cubic meters (m³).
   (a) If T is increasing at a rate of 3 K/min with V held fixed at 2.5 m³, find the rate at which the pressure is changing when $T = 50$ K.
   (b) If T is held fixed at 50 K while V is decreasing at the rate of 3 m³/min, find the rate at which the pressure is changing when $V = 2.5$ m³.

10. Find the slope of the tangent line at the point $(1, -2, -3)$ on the curve of intersection of the surface $z = 5 - 4x^2 - y^2$ with
(a) the plane $x = 1$ (b) the plane $y = -2$.

11–14 Verify the assertion. ■

11. If $w = \tan(x^2 + y^2) + x\sqrt{y}$, then $w_{xy} = w_{yx}$.

12. If $w = \ln(3x - 3y) + \cos(x + y)$, then $\partial^2 w / \partial x^2 = \partial^2 w / \partial y^2$.

13. If $F(x, y, z) = 2z^3 - 3(x^2 + y^2)z$, then F satisfies the equation $F_{xx} + F_{yy} + F_{zz} = 0$.

14. If $f(x, y, z) = xyz + x^2 + \ln(y/z)$, then $f_{xyzx} = f_{zxxy}$.

15. What do Δf and df represent, and how are they related?

16. If $w = x^2 y - 2xy + y^2 x$, find the increment Δw and the differential dw if (x, y) varies from $(1, 0)$ to $(1.1, -0.1)$.

17. Use differentials to estimate the change in the volume $V = \frac{1}{3}x^2 h$ of a pyramid with a square base when its height h is increased from 2 to 2.2 m and its base dimension x is decreased from 1 to 0.9 m. Compare this to ΔV.

18. Find the local linear approximation of $f(x, y) = \sin(xy)$ at $\left(\frac{1}{3}, \pi\right)$.

19. Suppose that z is a differentiable function of x and y with

$$\frac{\partial z}{\partial x}(1, 2) = 4 \quad \text{and} \quad \frac{\partial z}{\partial y}(1, 2) = 2$$

If $x = x(t)$ and $y = y(t)$ are differentiable functions of t with $x(0) = 1$, $y(0) = 2$, $x'(0) = -\frac{1}{2}$, and (under composition) $z'(0) = 2$, find $y'(0)$.

20. In each part, use Theorem 13.5.3 to find dy/dx.
(a) $3x^2 - 5xy + \tan xy = 0$
(b) $x \ln y + \sin(x - y) = \pi$

21. Given that $f(x, y) = 0$, use Theorem 13.5.3 to express $d^2 y / dx^2$ in terms of partial derivatives of f.

22. Let $z = f(x, y)$, where $x = g(t)$ and $y = h(t)$.
(a) Show that

$$\frac{d}{dt}\left(\frac{\partial z}{\partial x}\right) = \frac{\partial^2 z}{\partial x^2}\frac{dx}{dt} + \frac{\partial^2 z}{\partial y \partial x}\frac{dy}{dt}$$

and

$$\frac{d}{dt}\left(\frac{\partial z}{\partial y}\right) = \frac{\partial^2 z}{\partial x \partial y}\frac{dx}{dt} + \frac{\partial^2 z}{\partial y^2}\frac{dy}{dt}$$

(b) Use the formulas in part (a) to help find a formula for $d^2 z / dt^2$.

23. (a) How are the directional derivative and the gradient of a function related?
(b) Under what conditions is the directional derivative of a differentiable function 0?
(c) In what direction does the directional derivative of a differentiable function have its maximum value? Its minimum value?

24. In words, what does the derivative $D_{\mathbf{u}} f(x_0, y_0)$ tell you about the surface $z = f(x, y)$?

25. Find $D_{\mathbf{u}} f(-3, 5)$ for $f(x, y) = y \ln(x + y)$ if $\mathbf{u} = \frac{3}{5}\mathbf{i} + \frac{4}{5}\mathbf{j}$.

26. Suppose that $\nabla f(0, 0) = 2\mathbf{i} + \frac{3}{2}\mathbf{j}$.
(a) Find a unit vector $\mathbf{u}$ such that $D_{\mathbf{u}} f(0, 0)$ is a maximum. What is this maximum value?
(b) Find a unit vector $\mathbf{u}$ such that $D_{\mathbf{u}} f(0, 0)$ is a minimum. What is this minimum value?

27. At the point $(1, 2)$, the directional derivative $D_{\mathbf{u}} f$ is $2\sqrt{2}$ toward $P_1(2, 3)$ and -3 toward $P_2(1, 0)$. Find $D_{\mathbf{u}} f(1, 2)$ toward the origin.

28. Find equations for the tangent plane and normal line to the given surface at P_0.
(a) $z = x^2 e^{2y}$; $P_0(1, \ln 2, 4)$
(b) $x^2 y^3 z^4 + xyz = 2$; $P_0(2, 1, -1)$

29. Find all points P_0 on the surface $z = 2 - xy$ at which the normal line passes through the origin.

30. Show that for all tangent planes to the surface

$$x^{2/3} + y^{2/3} + z^{2/3} = 1$$

the sum of the squares of the x-, y-, and z-intercepts is 1.

31. Find all points on the paraboloid $z = 9x^2 + 4y^2$ at which the normal line is parallel to the line through the points $P(4, -2, 5)$ and $Q(-2, -6, 4)$.

32. Suppose the equations of motion of a particle are $x = t - 1$, $y = 4e^{-t}$, $z = 2 - \sqrt{t}$, where $t > 0$. Find, to the nearest tenth of a degree, the acute angle between the velocity vector and the normal line to the surface $(x^2/4) + y^2 + z^2 = 1$ at the points where the particle collides with the surface. Use a calculating utility with a root-finding capability where needed.

33–36 Locate all relative minima, relative maxima, and saddle points. ■

33. $f(x, y) = x^2 + 3xy + 3y^2 - 6x + 3y$

34. $f(x, y) = x^2 y - 6y^2 - 3x^2$

35. $f(x, y) = x^3 - 3xy + \frac{1}{2}y^2$

36. $f(x, y) = 4x^2 - 12xy + 9y^2$

37–39 Solve these exercises two ways:
(a) Use the constraint to eliminate a variable.
(b) Use Lagrange multipliers. ■

37. Find all relative extrema of $x^2 y^2$ subject to the constraint $4x^2 + y^2 = 8$.

38. Find the dimensions of the rectangular box of maximum volume that can be inscribed in the ellipsoid

$$(x/a)^2 + (y/b)^2 + (z/c)^2 = 1$$

39. As illustrated in the accompanying figure on the next page, suppose that a current I branches into currents I_1, I_2, and I_3 through resistors R_1, R_2, and R_3 in such a way that the total power dissipated in the three resistors is a minimum. Find the ratios $I_1 : I_2 : I_3$ if the power dissipated in R_i is $I_i^2 R_i$ $(i = 1, 2, 3)$ and $I_1 + I_2 + I_3 = I$.

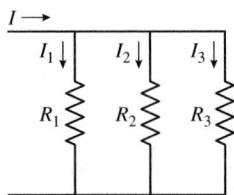

◀ **Figure Ex-39**

40–42 In economics, a ***production model*** is a mathematical relationship between the output of a company or a country and the labor and capital equipment required to produce that output. Much of the pioneering work in the field of production models occurred in the 1920s when Paul Douglas of the University of Chicago and his collaborator Charles Cobb proposed that the output P can be expressed in terms of the labor L and the capital equipment K by an equation of the form

$$P = cL^{\alpha}K^{\beta}$$

where c is a constant of proportionality and α and β are constants such that $0 < \alpha < 1$ and $0 < \beta < 1$. This is called the ***Cobb–Douglas production model***. Typically, P, L, and K are all expressed in terms of their equivalent monetary values. These exercises explore properties of this model. ■

40. (a) Consider the Cobb–Douglas production model given by the formula $P = L^{0.75}K^{0.25}$. Sketch the level curves $P(L, K) = 1$, $P(L, K) = 2$, and $P(L, K) = 3$ in an *LK*-coordinate system (L horizontal and K vertical). Your sketch need not be accurate numerically, but it should show the general shape of the curves and their relative positions.

   (b) Use a graphing utility to make a more extensive contour plot of the model.

41. (a) Find $\partial P/\partial L$ and $\partial P/\partial K$ for the Cobb–Douglas production model $P = cL^{\alpha}K^{\beta}$.

   (b) The derivative $\partial P/\partial L$ is called the ***marginal productivity of labor***, and the derivative $\partial P/\partial K$ is called the ***marginal productivity of capital***. Explain what these quantities mean in practical terms.

   (c) Show that if $\beta = 1 - \alpha$, then P satisfies the partial differential equation

$$K\frac{\partial P}{\partial K} + L\frac{\partial P}{\partial L} = P$$

42. Consider the Cobb–Douglas production model

$$P = 1000L^{0.6}K^{0.4}$$

   (a) Find the maximum output value of P if labor costs $\$50.00$ per unit, capital costs $\$100.00$ per unit, and the total cost of labor and capital is set at $\$200{,}000$.

   (b) How should the $\$200{,}000$ be allocated between labor and capital to achieve the maximum?

CHAPTER 13 MAKING CONNECTIONS

1. Suppose that a function $z = f(x, y)$ is expressed in polar form by making the substitutions $x = r\cos\theta$ and $y = r\sin\theta$. Show that

$$r\frac{\partial z}{\partial r} = x\frac{\partial z}{\partial x} + y\frac{\partial z}{\partial y}$$

$$\frac{\partial z}{\partial \theta} = -y\frac{\partial z}{\partial x} + x\frac{\partial z}{\partial y}$$

2. A function $f(x, y)$ is said to be ***homogeneous of degree n*** if $f(tx, ty) = t^{n}f(x, y)$ for $t > 0$. In each part, show that the function is homogeneous, and find its degree.

   (a) $f(x, y) = 3x^2 + y^2$ (b) $f(x, y) = \sqrt{x^2 + y^2}$

   (c) $f(x, y) = x^2 y - 2y^3$ (d) $f(x, y) = \dfrac{5}{(x^2 + 2y^2)^2}$

3. Suppose that a function $f(x, y)$ is defined for all points $(x, y) \neq (0, 0)$. Prove that f is homogeneous of degree n if and only if there exists a function $g(\theta)$ that is 2π periodic such that in polar form the equation $z = f(x, y)$ becomes

$$z = r^{n}g(\theta)$$

for $r > 0$ and $-\infty < \theta < +\infty$.

4. (a) Use the chain rule to show that if $f(x, y)$ is a homogeneous function of degree n, then

$$x\frac{\partial f}{\partial x} + y\frac{\partial f}{\partial y} = nf$$

   [*Hint:* Let $u = tx$ and $v = ty$ in $f(tx, ty)$, and differentiate both sides of $f(u, v) = t^{n}f(x, y)$ with respect to t.]

   (b) Use the results of Exercise 1 and 3 to give another derivation of the equation in part (a).

   (c) Confirm that the functions in Exercise 2 satisfy the equation in part (a).

5. Suppose that a function $f(x, y)$ is defined for all points $(x, y) \neq (0, 0)$ and satisfies

$$x\frac{\partial f}{\partial x} + y\frac{\partial f}{\partial y} = nf$$

Prove that f is homogeneous of degree n. [*Hint:* Express the function $z = f(x, y)$ in polar form and use Exercise 1 to conclude that

$$r\frac{\partial z}{\partial r} - nz = 0$$

Divide both sides of this equation by r^{n+1} and interpret the left-hand side of the resulting equation as the partial derivative with respect to r of a product of two functions.]

14

Stone/Getty Images

MULTIPLE INTEGRALS

Finding the areas of complex surfaces such as those used in the design of the Denver International Airport require integration methods studied in this chapter.

In this chapter we will extend the concept of a definite integral to functions of two and three variables. Whereas functions of one variable are usually integrated over intervals, functions of two variables are usually integrated over regions in 2-space and functions of three variables over regions in 3-space. Calculating such integrals will require some new techniques that will be a central focus in this chapter. Once we have developed the basic methods for integrating functions of two and three variables, we will show how such integrals can be used to calculate surface areas and volumes of solids; and we will also show how they can be used to find masses and centers of gravity of flat plates and three-dimensional solids. In addition to our study of integration, we will generalize the concept of a parametric curve in 2-space to a parametric surface in 3-space. This will allow us to work with a wider variety of surfaces than previously possible and will provide a powerful tool for generating surfaces using computers and other graphing utilities.

14.1 DOUBLE INTEGRALS

The notion of a definite integral can be extended to functions of two or more variables. In this section we will discuss the double integral, which is the extension to functions of two variables.

■ VOLUME

Recall that the definite integral of a function of one variable

$$\int_a^b f(x)\,dx = \lim_{\max \Delta x_k \to 0} \sum_{k=1}^n f(x_k^*)\Delta x_k = \lim_{n \to +\infty} \sum_{k=1}^n f(x_k^*)\Delta x_k \qquad (1)$$

arose from the problem of finding areas under curves. [In the rightmost expression in (1), we use the "limit as $n \to +\infty$" to encapsulate the process by which we increase the number of subintervals of $[a, b]$ in such a way that the lengths of the subintervals approach zero.] Integrals of functions of two variables arise from the problem of finding volumes under surfaces.

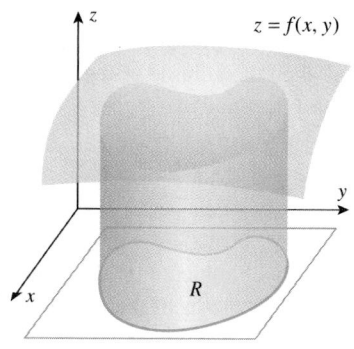

▲ Figure 14.1.1

14.1.1   THE VOLUME PROBLEM   Given a function f of two variables that is continuous and nonnegative on a region R in the xy-plane, find the volume of the solid enclosed between the surface $z = f(x, y)$ and the region R (Figure 14.1.1).

Later, we will place more restrictions on the region R, but for now we will just assume that the entire region can be enclosed within some suitably large rectangle with sides parallel to the coordinate axes. This ensures that R does not extend indefinitely in any direction.

The procedure for finding the volume V of the solid in Figure 14.1.1 will be similar to the limiting process used for finding areas, except that now the approximating elements will be rectangular parallelepipeds rather than rectangles. We proceed as follows:

- Using lines parallel to the coordinate axes, divide the rectangle enclosing the region R into subrectangles, and exclude from consideration all those subrectangles that contain any points outside of R. This leaves only rectangles that are subsets of R (Figure 14.1.2). Assume that there are n such rectangles, and denote the area of the kth such rectangle by ΔA_k.

- Choose any arbitrary point in each subrectangle, and denote the point in the kth subrectangle by (x_k^*, y_k^*). As shown in Figure 14.1.3, the product $f(x_k^*, y_k^*)\Delta A_k$ is the volume of a rectangular parallelepiped with base area ΔA_k and height $f(x_k^*, y_k^*)$, so the sum

$$\sum_{k=1}^{n} f(x_k^*, y_k^*)\Delta A_k$$

can be viewed as an approximation to the volume V of the entire solid.

- There are two sources of error in the approximation: first, the parallelepipeds have flat tops, whereas the surface $z = f(x, y)$ may be curved; second, the rectangles that form the bases of the parallelepipeds may not completely cover the region R. However, if we repeat the above process with more and more subdivisions in such a way that both the lengths and the widths of the subrectangles approach zero, then it is plausible that the errors of both types approach zero, and the exact volume of the solid will be

$$V = \lim_{n \to +\infty} \sum_{k=1}^{n} f(x_k^*, y_k^*)\Delta A_k$$

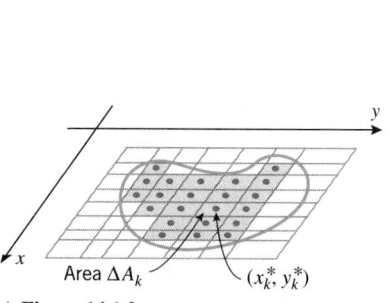

▲ Figure 14.1.2

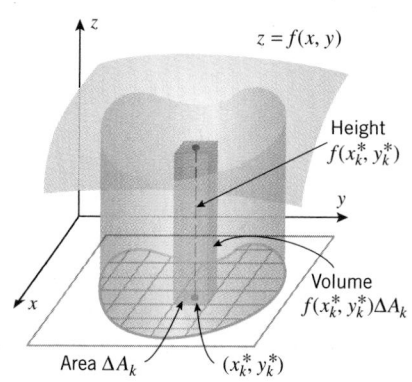

▲ Figure 14.1.3

This suggests the following definition.

Definition 14.1.2 is satisfactory for our present purposes, but some issues would have to be resolved before it could be regarded as rigorous. For example, we would have to prove that the limit actually exists and that its value does not depend on how the points $(x_1^*, y_1^*), (x_2^*, y_2^*), \ldots, (x_n^*, y_n^*)$ are chosen. These facts are true if the region R is not too "complicated" and if f is continuous on R. The details are beyond the scope of this text.

14.1.2   DEFINITION (*Volume Under a Surface*)   If f is a function of two variables that is continuous and nonnegative on a region R in the xy-plane, then the volume of the solid enclosed between the surface $z = f(x, y)$ and the region R is defined by

$$V = \lim_{n \to +\infty} \sum_{k=1}^{n} f(x_k^*, y_k^*) \Delta A_k \tag{2}$$

Here, $n \to +\infty$ indicates the process of increasing the number of subrectangles of the rectangle enclosing R in such a way that both the lengths and the widths of the subrectangles approach zero.

It is assumed in Definition 14.1.2 that f is nonnegative on the region R. If f is continuous on R and has both positive and negative values, then the limit

$$\lim_{n \to +\infty} \sum_{k=1}^{n} f(x_k^*, y_k^*) \Delta A_k \tag{3}$$

no longer represents the volume between R and the surface $z = f(x, y)$; rather, it represents a *difference* of volumes—the volume between R and the portion of the surface that is above the xy-plane minus the volume between R and the portion of the surface below the xy-plane. We call this the ***net signed volume*** between the region R and the surface $z = f(x, y)$.

DEFINITION OF A DOUBLE INTEGRAL

As in Definition 14.1.2, the notation $n \to +\infty$ in (3) encapsulates a process in which the enclosing rectangle for R is repeatedly subdivided in such a way that both the lengths and the widths of the subrectangles approach zero. Note that subdividing so that the subrectangle lengths approach zero forces the mesh of the partition of the length of the enclosing rectangle for R to approach zero. Similarly, subdividing so that the subrectangle widths approach zero forces the mesh of the partition of the width of the enclosing rectangle for R to approach zero. Thus, we have extended the notion conveyed by Formula (1) where the definite integral of a one-variable function is expressed as a limit of Riemann sums. By extension, the sums in (3) are also called ***Riemann sums***, and the limit of the Riemann sums is denoted by

$$\iint\limits_{R} f(x, y) \, dA = \lim_{n \to +\infty} \sum_{k=1}^{n} f(x_k^*, y_k^*) \Delta A_k \tag{4}$$

which is called the ***double integral*** of $f(x, y)$ over R.

If f is continuous and nonnegative on the region R, then the volume formula in (2) can be expressed as

$$V = \iint\limits_{R} f(x, y) \, dA \tag{5}$$

If f has both positive and negative values on R, then a positive value for the double integral of f over R means that there is more volume above R than below, a negative value for the double integral means that there is more volume below R than above, and a value of zero means that the volume above R is the same as the volume below R.

EVALUATING DOUBLE INTEGRALS

Except in the simplest cases, it is impractical to obtain the value of a double integral from the limit in (4). However, we will now show how to evaluate double integrals by calculating two successive single integrals. For the rest of this section we will limit our discussion to the case where R is a rectangle; in the next section we will consider double integrals over more complicated regions.

The partial derivatives of a function $f(x, y)$ are calculated by holding one of the variables fixed and differentiating with respect to the other variable. Let us consider the reverse of this process, ***partial integration***. The symbols

$$\int_a^b f(x, y)\, dx \quad \text{and} \quad \int_c^d f(x, y)\, dy$$

denote ***partial definite integrals***; the first integral, called the ***partial definite integral with respect to x***, is evaluated by holding y fixed and integrating with respect to x, and the second integral, called the ***partial definite integral with respect to y***, is evaluated by holding x fixed and integrating with respect to y. As the following example shows, the partial definite integral with respect to x is a function of y, and the partial definite integral with respect to y is a function of x.

▶ **Example 1**

$$\int_0^1 xy^2\, dx = y^2 \int_0^1 x\, dx = \frac{y^2 x^2}{2}\Bigg]_{x=0}^1 = \frac{y^2}{2}$$

$$\int_0^1 xy^2\, dy = x \int_0^1 y^2\, dy = \frac{xy^3}{3}\Bigg]_{y=0}^1 = \frac{x}{3} \quad ◀$$

A partial definite integral with respect to x is a function of y and hence can be integrated with respect to y; similarly, a partial definite integral with respect to y can be integrated with respect to x. This two-stage integration process is called ***iterated*** (or ***repeated***) ***integration***. We introduce the following notation:

$$\int_c^d \int_a^b f(x, y)\, dx\, dy = \int_c^d \left[\int_a^b f(x, y)\, dx \right] dy \tag{6}$$

$$\int_a^b \int_c^d f(x, y)\, dy\, dx = \int_a^b \left[\int_c^d f(x, y)\, dy \right] dx \tag{7}$$

These integrals are called ***iterated integrals***.

▶ **Example 2** Evaluate

(a) $\displaystyle\int_1^3 \int_2^4 (40 - 2xy)\, dy\, dx$ \quad (b) $\displaystyle\int_2^4 \int_1^3 (40 - 2xy)\, dx\, dy$

Solution (a).

$$\int_1^3 \int_2^4 (40 - 2xy)\, dy\, dx = \int_1^3 \left[\int_2^4 (40 - 2xy)\, dy \right] dx$$

$$= \int_1^3 (40y - xy^2)\Big]_{y=2}^4 dx$$

$$= \int_1^3 [(160 - 16x) - (80 - 4x)]\, dx$$

$$= \int_1^3 (80 - 12x)\, dx$$

$$= (80x - 6x^2)\Big]_1^3 = 112$$

Solution (b).

$$\int_2^4 \int_1^3 (40 - 2xy)\, dx\, dy = \int_2^4 \left[\int_1^3 (40 - 2xy)\, dx\right] dy$$

$$= \int_2^4 (40x - x^2 y)\Big]_{x=1}^{3}\, dy$$

$$= \int_2^4 [(120 - 9y) - (40 - y)]\, dy$$

$$= \int_2^4 (80 - 8y)\, dy$$

$$= (80y - 4y^2)\Big]_2^4 = 112 \quad \blacktriangleleft$$

It is no accident that both parts of Example 2 produced the same answer. Consider the solid S bounded above by the surface $z = 40 - 2xy$ and below by the rectangle R defined by $1 \le x \le 3$ and $2 \le y \le 4$. By the method of slicing discussed in Section 6.2, the volume of S is given by

$$V = \int_1^3 A(x)\, dx$$

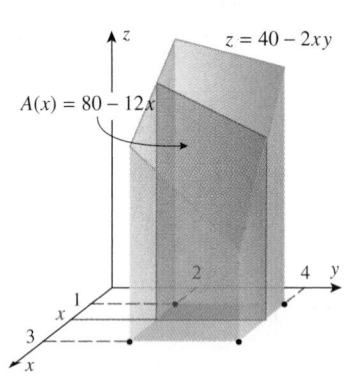

▲ **Figure 14.1.4**

where $A(x)$ is the area of a vertical cross section of S taken perpendicular to the x-axis (Figure 14.1.4). For a fixed value of x, $1 \le x \le 3$, $z = 40 - 2xy$ is a function of y, so the integral

$$A(x) = \int_2^4 (40 - 2xy)\, dy$$

represents the area under the graph of this function of y. Thus,

$$V = \int_1^3 \left[\int_2^4 (40 - 2xy)\, dy\right] dx = \int_1^3 \int_2^4 (40 - 2xy)\, dy\, dx$$

is the volume of S. Similarly, by the method of slicing with cross sections of S taken perpendicular to the y-axis, the volume of S is given by

$$V = \int_2^4 A(y)\, dy = \int_2^4 \left[\int_1^3 (40 - 2xy)\, dx\right] dy = \int_2^4 \int_1^3 (40 - 2xy)\, dx\, dy$$

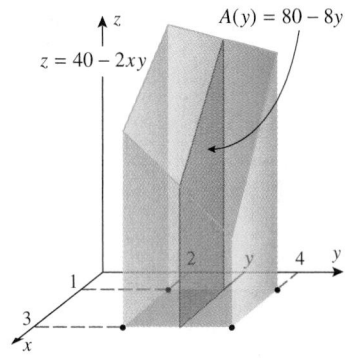

▲ **Figure 14.1.5**

(Figure 14.1.5). Thus, the iterated integrals in parts (a) and (b) of Example 2 both measure the volume of S, which by Formula (5) is the double integral of $z = 40 - 2xy$ over R. That is,

$$\int_1^3 \int_2^4 (40 - 2xy)\, dy\, dx = \iint\limits_R (40 - 2xy)\, dA = \int_2^4 \int_1^3 (40 - 2xy)\, dx\, dy$$

The geometric argument above applies to any continuous function $f(x, y)$ that is nonnegative on a rectangle $R = [a, b] \times [c, d]$, as is the case for $f(x, y) = 40 - 2xy$ on $[1, 3] \times [2, 4]$. The conclusion that the double integral of $f(x, y)$ over R has the same value as either of the two possible iterated integrals is true even when f is negative at some points in R. We state this result in the following theorem and omit a formal proof.

We will often denote the rectangle

$$\{(x, y) : a \le x \le b, c \le y \le d\}$$

as $[a, b] \times [c, d]$ for simplicity.

14.1.3   THEOREM (*Fubini's Theorem*)   *Let R be the rectangle defined by the inequalities*

$$a \le x \le b, \quad c \le y \le d$$

If $f(x, y)$ is continuous on this rectangle, then

$$\iint\limits_R f(x, y)\, dA = \int_c^d \int_a^b f(x, y)\, dx\, dy = \int_a^b \int_c^d f(x, y)\, dy\, dx$$

Theorem 14.1.3 allows us to evaluate a double integral over a rectangle by converting it to an iterated integral. This can be done in two ways, both of which produce the value of the double integral.

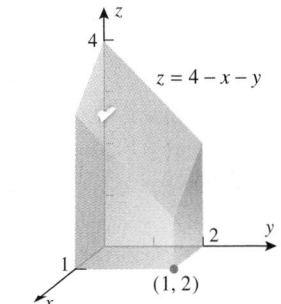

▲ **Figure 14.1.6**

▶ **Example 3** Use a double integral to find the volume of the solid that is bounded above by the plane $z = 4 - x - y$ and below by the rectangle $R = [0, 1] \times [0, 2]$ (Figure 14.1.6).

Solution. The volume is the double integral of $z = 4 - x - y$ over R. Using Theorem 14.1.3, this can be obtained from either of the iterated integrals

$$\int_0^2 \int_0^1 (4 - x - y)\, dx\, dy \quad \text{or} \quad \int_0^1 \int_0^2 (4 - x - y)\, dy\, dx \tag{8}$$

Using the first of these, we obtain

$$V = \iint_R (4 - x - y)\, dA = \int_0^2 \int_0^1 (4 - x - y)\, dx\, dy$$

$$= \int_0^2 \left[4x - \frac{x^2}{2} - xy \right]_{x=0}^1 dy = \int_0^2 \left(\frac{7}{2} - y \right) dy$$

$$= \left[\frac{7}{2}y - \frac{y^2}{2} \right]_0^2 = 5$$

You can check this result by evaluating the second integral in (8). ◀

TECHNOLOGY MASTERY

If you have a CAS with a built-in capability for computing iterated double integrals, use it to check Example 3.

Theorem 14.1.3 guarantees that the double integral in Example 4 can also be evaluated by integrating first with respect to y and then with respect to x. Verify this.

▶ **Example 4** Evaluate the double integral

$$\iint_R y^2 x\, dA$$

over the rectangle $R = \{(x, y) : -3 \le x \le 2, 0 \le y \le 1\}$.

Solution. In view of Theorem 14.1.3, the value of the double integral can be obtained by evaluating one of two possible iterated double integrals. We choose to integrate first with

Guido Fubini (1879–1943) Italian mathematician. Fubini, the son of a mathematician, showed brilliance in mathematics as a young pupil in Venice. He entered college at the Scuola Normale Superiore di Pisa in 1896 and presented his doctoral thesis on the subject of elliptic geometry in 1900 at the young age of 20. He subsequently had teaching positions at various universities, finally settling at the University of Turin where he remained for several decades. His mathematical work was diverse, and he made major contributions to many branches of mathematics. At the outbreak of World War I he shifted his attention to the accuracy of artillery fire, and following the war he worked on other applied subjects such as electrical circuits and acoustics. In 1939, as he neared age 60 and retirement, Benito Mussolini's Fascists adopted Hitler's anti-Jewish policies, so Fubini, who was Jewish, accepted a position at Princeton University, where he stayed until his death four years later. Fubini was well liked by his colleagues at Princeton and stories about him abound. He once gave a lecture on ballistics in which he showed that if you fired a projectile of a certain shape, then under the right conditions it could double back on itself and hit your own troops. Then, tongue in cheek, he suggested that one could fool the enemy by aiming this "Fubini Gun" at one's own troops and hit the unsuspecting enemy after the projectile reversed direction.

Fubini was exceptionally short, which occasionally caused problems. The story goes that one day his worried landlady called his friends to report that he had not come home. After searching everywhere, including the area near the local lake, it was discovered that Fubini was trapped in a stalled elevator and was unable to reach any of the buttons. Fubini celebrated his rescue with a party and later left a sign in his room that said, "To my landlady: When I am not home at 6:30 at night, please check the elevator...."

(photo by Wendy Wray)

respect to x and then with respect to y.

$$\iint\limits_{R} y^2x\,dA = \int_0^1 \int_{-3}^2 y^2x\,dx\,dy = \int_0^1 \left[\frac{1}{2}y^2x^2\right]_{x=-3}^2 dy$$

$$= \int_0^1 \left(-\frac{5}{2}y^2\right) dy = -\frac{5}{6}y^3\Big]_0^1 = -\frac{5}{6} \blacktriangleleft$$

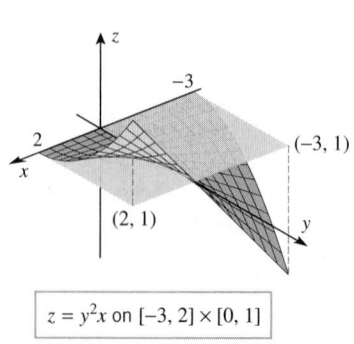

$z = y^2x$ on $[-3, 2] \times [0, 1]$

▲ **Figure 14.1.7**

The integral in Example 4 can be interpreted as the net signed volume between the rectangle $[-3, 2] \times [0, 1]$ and the surface $z = y^2x$. That is, it is the volume below $z = y^2x$ and above $[0, 2] \times [0, 1]$ minus the volume above $z = y^2x$ and below $[-3, 0] \times [0, 1]$ (Figure 14.1.7).

■ **PROPERTIES OF DOUBLE INTEGRALS**

To distinguish between double integrals of functions of two variables and definite integrals of functions of one variable, we will refer to the latter as *single integrals*. Because double integrals, like single integrals, are defined as limits, they inherit many of the properties of limits. The following results, which we state without proof, are analogs of those in Theorem 5.5.4.

$$\iint\limits_{R} cf(x, y)\,dA = c\iint\limits_{R} f(x, y)\,dA \quad (c \text{ a constant}) \tag{9}$$

$$\iint\limits_{R} [f(x, y) + g(x, y)]\,dA = \iint\limits_{R} f(x, y)\,dA + \iint\limits_{R} g(x, y)\,dA \tag{10}$$

$$\iint\limits_{R} [f(x, y) - g(x, y)]\,dA = \iint\limits_{R} f(x, y)\,dA - \iint\limits_{R} g(x, y)\,dA \tag{11}$$

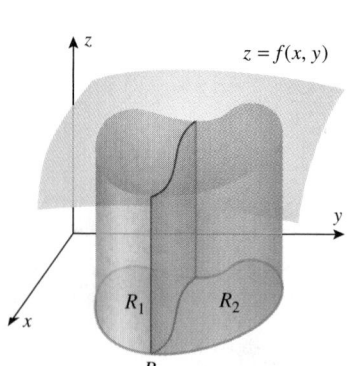

$z = f(x, y)$

The volume of the entire solid is the sum of the volumes of the solids above R_1 and R_2.

▲ **Figure 14.1.8**

It is evident intuitively that if $f(x, y)$ is nonnegative on a region R, then subdividing R into two regions R_1 and R_2 has the effect of subdividing the solid between R and $z = f(x, y)$ into two solids, the sum of whose volumes is the volume of the entire solid (Figure 14.1.8). This suggests the following result, which holds even if f has negative values:

$$\iint\limits_{R} f(x, y)\,dA = \iint\limits_{R_1} f(x, y)\,dA + \iint\limits_{R_2} f(x, y)\,dA \tag{12}$$

The proof of this result will be omitted.

✔ **QUICK CHECK EXERCISES 14.1**   *(See page 1008 for answers.)*

1. The double integral is defined as a limit of Riemann sums by

$$\iint\limits_{R} f(x, y)\,dA = \underline{\hspace{2cm}}$$

2. The iterated integral

$$\int_1^5 \int_2^4 f(x, y)\,dx\,dy$$

integrates f over the rectangle defined by

$$\underline{\hspace{1.5cm}} \leq x \leq \underline{\hspace{1.5cm}}, \quad \underline{\hspace{1.5cm}} \leq y \leq \underline{\hspace{1.5cm}}$$

3. Supply the missing integrand and limits of integration.

$$\int_1^5 \int_2^4 (3x^2 - 2xy + y^2)\,dx\,dy = \int_\square^\square \underline{\hspace{1.5cm}}\,dy$$

4. The volume of the solid enclosed by the surface $z = x/y$ and the rectangle $0 \leq x \leq 4$, $1 \leq y \leq e^2$ in the xy-plane is

$$\underline{\hspace{1.5cm}}.$$

EXERCISE SET 14.1   [C] CAS

1–12 Evaluate the iterated integrals. ■

1. $\displaystyle\int_0^1\int_0^2 (x+3)\,dy\,dx$ **2.** $\displaystyle\int_1^3\int_{-1}^1 (2x-4y)\,dy\,dx$

3. $\displaystyle\int_2^4\int_0^1 x^2y\,dx\,dy$ **4.** $\displaystyle\int_{-2}^0\int_{-1}^2 (x^2+y^2)\,dx\,dy$

5. $\displaystyle\int_0^{\ln 3}\int_0^{\ln 2} e^{x+y}\,dy\,dx$ **6.** $\displaystyle\int_0^2\int_0^1 y\sin x\,dy\,dx$

7. $\displaystyle\int_{-1}^0\int_2^5 dx\,dy$ **8.** $\displaystyle\int_4^6\int_{-3}^7 dy\,dx$

9. $\displaystyle\int_0^1\int_0^1 \frac{x}{(xy+1)^2}\,dy\,dx$ **10.** $\displaystyle\int_{\pi/2}^\pi\int_1^2 x\cos xy\,dy\,dx$

11. $\displaystyle\int_0^{\ln 2}\int_0^1 xye^{y^2x}\,dy\,dx$ **12.** $\displaystyle\int_3^4\int_1^2 \frac{1}{(x+y)^2}\,dy\,dx$

13–16 Evaluate the double integral over the rectangular region R. ■

13. $\displaystyle\iint_R 4xy^3\,dA;\ R=\{(x,y): -1\le x\le 1, -2\le y\le 2\}$

14. $\displaystyle\iint_R \frac{xy}{\sqrt{x^2+y^2+1}}\,dA;$

$R=\{(x,y): 0\le x\le 1, 0\le y\le 1\}$

15. $\displaystyle\iint_R x\sqrt{1-x^2}\,dA;\ R=\{(x,y): 0\le x\le 1, 2\le y\le 3\}$

16. $\displaystyle\iint_R (x\sin y - y\sin x)\,dA;$

$R=\{(x,y): 0\le x\le \pi/2, 0\le y\le \pi/3\}$

FOCUS ON CONCEPTS

17. (a) Let $f(x,y)=x^2+y$, and as shown in the accompanying figure, let the rectangle $R=[0,2]\times[0,2]$ be subdivided into 16 subrectangles. Take (x_k^*, y_k^*) to be the center of the kth rectangle, and approximate the double integral of f over R by the resulting Riemann sum.
(b) Compare the result in part (a) to the exact value of the integral.

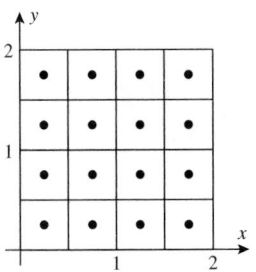
◀ **Figure Ex-17**

18. (a) Let $f(x,y)=x-2y$, and as shown in Exercise 17, let the rectangle $R=[0,2]\times[0,2]$ be subdivided into 16 subrectangles. Take (x_k^*, y_k^*) to be the center of the kth rectangle, and approximate the double integral of f over R by the resulting Riemann sum.
(b) Compare the result in part (a) to the exact value of the integral.

19–20 Each iterated integral represents the volume of a solid. Make a sketch of the solid. Use geometry to find the volume of the solid, and then evaluate the iterated integral. ■

19. $\displaystyle\int_0^5\int_1^2 4\,dx\,dy$ **20.** $\displaystyle\int_0^1\int_0^1 (2-x-y)\,dx\,dy$

21–22 Each iterated integral represents the volume of a solid. Make a sketch of the solid. (You do *not* have to find the volume.) ■

21. $\displaystyle\int_0^3\int_0^4 \sqrt{25-x^2-y^2}\,dy\,dx$

22. $\displaystyle\int_{-2}^2\int_{-2}^2 (x^2+y^2)\,dx\,dy$

23–26 True–False Determine whether the statement is true or false. Explain your answer. ■

23. In the definition of a double integral

$$\iint_R f(x,y)\,dA = \lim_{n\to+\infty}\sum_{k=1}^n f(x_k^*, y_k^*)\Delta A_k$$

the symbol ΔA_k represents a rectangular region within R from which the point (x_k^*, y_k^*) is taken.

24. If R is the rectangle $\{(x,y): 1\le x\le 4, 0\le y\le 3\}$ and $\int_0^3 f(x,y)\,dy = 2x$, then

$$\iint_R f(x,y)\,dA = 15$$

25. If R is the rectangle $\{(x,y): 1\le x\le 5, 2\le y\le 4\}$, then

$$\iint_R f(x,y)\,dA = \int_1^5\int_2^4 f(x,y)\,dx\,dy$$

26. Suppose that for some region R in the xy-plane

$$\iint_R f(x,y)\,dA = 0$$

If R is subdivided into two regions R_1 and R_2, then

$$\iint_{R_1} f(x,y)\,dA = -\iint_{R_2} f(x,y)\,dA$$

27. In this exercise, suppose that $f(x,y)=g(x)h(y)$ and $R=\{(x,y): a\le x\le b, c\le y\le d\}$. Show that

$$\iint_R f(x,y)\,dA = \left[\int_a^b g(x)\,dx\right]\left[\int_c^d h(y)\,dy\right]$$

28. Use the result in Exercise 27 evaluate the integral
$$\int_0^{\ln 2} \int_{-1}^1 \sqrt{e^y + 1} \tan x \, dx \, dy$$
by inspection. Explain your reasoning.

29–32 Use a double integral to find the volume. ◼

29. The volume under the plane $z = 2x + y$ and over the rectangle $R = \{(x, y) : 3 \le x \le 5, 1 \le y \le 2\}$.

30. The volume under the surface $z = 3x^3 + 3x^2 y$ and over the rectangle $R = \{(x, y) : 1 \le x \le 3, 0 \le y \le 2\}$.

31. The volume of the solid enclosed by the surface $z = x^2$ and the planes $x = 0$, $x = 2$, $y = 3$, $y = 0$, and $z = 0$.

32. The volume in the first octant bounded by the coordinate planes, the plane $y = 4$, and the plane $(x/3) + (z/5) = 1$.

33. Evaluate the integral by choosing a convenient order of integration:
$$\iint_R x \cos(xy) \cos^2 \pi x \, dA; \ R = \left[0, \tfrac{1}{2}\right] \times [0, \pi]$$

34. (a) Sketch the solid in the first octant that is enclosed by the planes $x = 0$, $z = 0$, $x = 5$, $z - y = 0$, and $z = -2y + 6$.
(b) Find the volume of the solid by breaking it into two parts.

35–38 The *average value* or *mean value* of a continuous function $f(x, y)$ over a rectangle $R = [a, b] \times [c, d]$ is defined as
$$f_{\text{ave}} = \frac{1}{A(R)} \iint_R f(x, y) \, dA$$
where $A(R) = (b - a)(d - c)$ is the area of the rectangle R (compare to Definition 5.8.1). Use this definition in these exercises. ◼

35. Find the average value of $f(x, y) = y \sin xy$ over the rectangle $[0, 1] \times [0, \pi/2]$.

36. Find the average value of $f(x, y) = x(x^2 + y)^{1/2}$ over the rectangle $[0, 1] \times [0, 3]$.

37. Suppose that the temperature in degrees Celsius at a point (x, y) on a flat metal plate is $T(x, y) = 10 - 8x^2 - 2y^2$,

where x and y are in meters. Find the average temperature of the rectangular portion of the plate for which $0 \le x \le 1$ and $0 \le y \le 2$.

38. Show that if $f(x, y)$ is constant on the rectangle $R = [a, b] \times [c, d]$, say $f(x, y) = k$, then $f_{\text{ave}} = k$ over R.

39–40 Most computer algebra systems have commands for approximating double integrals numerically. Read the relevant documentation and use a CAS to find a numerical approximation of the double integral in these exercises. ◼

C **39.** $\displaystyle\int_0^2 \int_0^1 \sin\sqrt{x^3 + y^3} \, dx \, dy$

C **40.** $\displaystyle\int_{-1}^1 \int_{-1}^1 e^{-(x^2 + y^2)} \, dx \, dy$

C **41.** Use a CAS to evaluate the iterated integrals
$$\int_0^1 \int_0^1 \frac{y - x}{(x + y)^3} \, dx \, dy \quad \text{and} \quad \int_0^1 \int_0^1 \frac{y - x}{(x + y)^3} \, dy \, dx$$
Does this contradict Theorem 14.1.3? Explain.

C **42.** Use a CAS to show that the volume V under the surface $z = xy^3 \sin xy$ over the rectangle shown in the accompanying figure is $V = 3/\pi$.

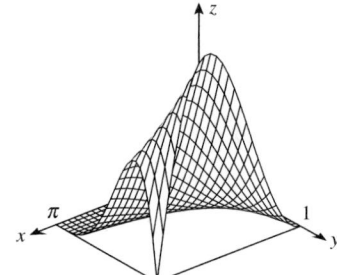

◀ **Figure Ex-42**

43. **Writing** Discuss how computing a volume using an iterated double integral corresponds to the method of computing a volume by slicing (Section 6.2).

44. **Writing** Discuss how the double integral property given in Formula (12) generalizes the single integral property in Theorem 5.5.5.

✔ **QUICK CHECK ANSWERS 14.1**

1. $\displaystyle\lim_{n \to +\infty} \sum_{k=1}^n f(x_k^*, y_k^*) \Delta A_k$ **2.** $2 \le x \le 4$, $1 \le y \le 5$ **3.** $\displaystyle\int_1^5 (56 - 12y + 2y^2) \, dy$ **4.** 16

14.2 DOUBLE INTEGRALS OVER NONRECTANGULAR REGIONS

In this section we will show how to evaluate double integrals over regions other than rectangles.

ITERATED INTEGRALS WITH NONCONSTANT LIMITS OF INTEGRATION

Later in this section we will see that double integrals over nonrectangular regions can often be evaluated as iterated integrals of the following types:

Note that in (1) and (2) the limits of integration in the outer integral are constants. This is consistent with the fact that the value of each iterated integral is a number that represents a net signed volume.

$$\int_a^b \int_{g_1(x)}^{g_2(x)} f(x, y)\, dy\, dx = \int_a^b \left[\int_{g_1(x)}^{g_2(x)} f(x, y)\, dy \right] dx \tag{1}$$

$$\int_c^d \int_{h_1(y)}^{h_2(y)} f(x, y)\, dx\, dy = \int_c^d \left[\int_{h_1(y)}^{h_2(y)} f(x, y)\, dx \right] dy \tag{2}$$

We begin with an example that illustrates how to evaluate such integrals.

▶ **Example 1**   Evaluate

$$\text{(a)} \ \int_0^1 \int_{-x}^{x^2} y^2 x\, dy\, dx \qquad \text{(b)} \ \int_0^{\pi/3} \int_0^{\cos y} x \sin y\, dx\, dy$$

Solution (a).

$$\int_0^1 \int_{-x}^{x^2} y^2 x\, dy\, dx = \int_0^1 \left[\int_{-x}^{x^2} y^2 x\, dy \right] dx = \int_0^1 \frac{y^3 x}{3} \bigg]_{y=-x}^{x^2} dx$$

$$= \int_0^1 \left[\frac{x^7}{3} + \frac{x^4}{3} \right] dx = \left(\frac{x^8}{24} + \frac{x^5}{15} \right) \bigg]_0^1 = \frac{13}{120}$$

Solution (b).

$$\int_0^{\pi/3} \int_0^{\cos y} x \sin y\, dx\, dy = \int_0^{\pi/3} \left[\int_0^{\cos y} x \sin y\, dx \right] dy = \int_0^{\pi/3} \frac{x^2}{2} \sin y \bigg]_{x=0}^{\cos y} dy$$

$$= \int_0^{\pi/3} \left[\frac{1}{2} \cos^2 y \sin y \right] dy = -\frac{1}{6} \cos^3 y \bigg]_0^{\pi/3} = \frac{7}{48} \ \blacktriangleleft$$

DOUBLE INTEGRALS OVER NONRECTANGULAR REGIONS

Plane regions can be extremely complex, and the theory of double integrals over very general regions is a topic for advanced courses in mathematics. We will limit our study of double integrals to two basic types of regions, which we will call *type I* and *type II*; they are defined as follows.

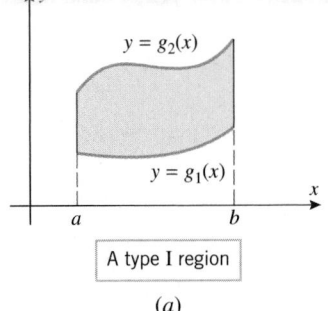

A type I region

(a)

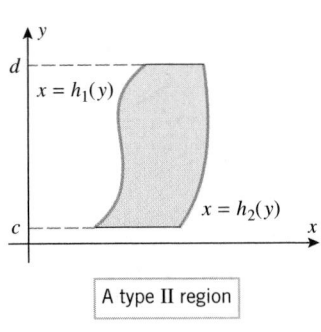

A type II region

(b)

▲ **Figure 14.2.1**

14.2.1   DEFINITION

(a)   A *type I region* is bounded on the left and right by vertical lines $x = a$ and $x = b$ and is bounded below and above by continuous curves $y = g_1(x)$ and $y = g_2(x)$, where $g_1(x) \leq g_2(x)$ for $a \leq x \leq b$ (Figure 14.2.1a).

(b)   A *type II region* is bounded below and above by horizontal lines $y = c$ and $y = d$ and is bounded on the left and right by continuous curves $x = h_1(y)$ and $x = h_2(y)$ satisfying $h_1(y) \leq h_2(y)$ for $c \leq y \leq d$ (Figure 14.2.1b).

The following theorem will enable us to evaluate double integrals over type I and type II regions using iterated integrals.

14.2.2   THEOREM

(a) *If R is a type I region on which $f(x, y)$ is continuous, then*

$$\iint_R f(x, y)\, dA = \int_a^b \int_{g_1(x)}^{g_2(x)} f(x, y)\, dy\, dx \tag{3}$$

(b) *If R is a type II region on which $f(x, y)$ is continuous, then*

$$\iint_R f(x, y)\, dA = \int_c^d \int_{h_1(y)}^{h_2(y)} f(x, y)\, dx\, dy \tag{4}$$

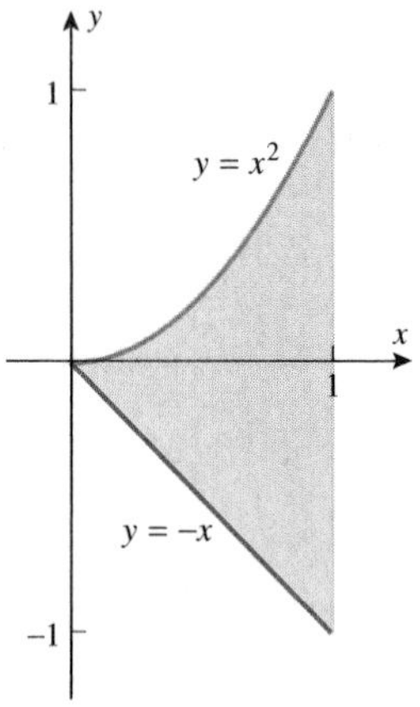

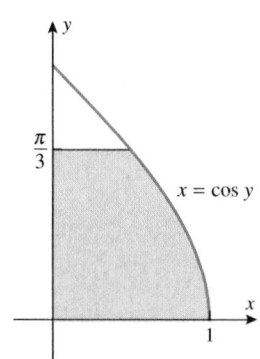

▲ **Figure 14.2.2**

▶ **Example 2**   Each of the iterated integrals in Example 1 is equal to a double integral over a region R. Identify the region R in each case.

Solution.   Using Theorem 14.2.2, the integral in Example 1(a) is the double integral of the function $f(x, y) = y^2 x$ over the type I region R bounded on the left and right by the vertical lines $x = 0$ and $x = 1$ and bounded below and above by the curves $y = -x$ and $y = x^2$ (Figure 14.2.2). The integral in Example 1(b) is the double integral of the function $f(x, y) = x \sin y$ over the type II region R bounded below and above by the horizontal lines $y = 0$ and $y = \pi/3$ and bounded on the left and right by the curves $x = 0$ and $x = \cos y$ (Figure 14.2.3). ◀

We will not prove Theorem 14.2.2, but for the case where $f(x, y)$ is nonnegative on the region R, it can be made plausible by a geometric argument that is similar to that given for Theorem 14.1.3. Since $f(x, y)$ is nonnegative, the double integral can be interpreted as the volume of the solid S that is bounded above by the surface $z = f(x, y)$ and below by the region R, so it suffices to show that the iterated integrals also represent this volume. Consider the iterated integral in (3), for example. For a fixed value of x, the function $f(x, y)$ is a function of y, and hence the integral

$$A(x) = \int_{g_1(x)}^{g_2(x)} f(x, y)\, dy$$

represents the area under the graph of this function of y between $y = g_1(x)$ and $y = g_2(x)$. This area, shown in yellow in Figure 14.2.4, is the cross-sectional area at x of the solid S, and hence by the method of slicing, the volume V of the solid S is

$$V = \int_a^b \int_{g_1(x)}^{g_2(x)} f(x, y)\, dy\, dx$$

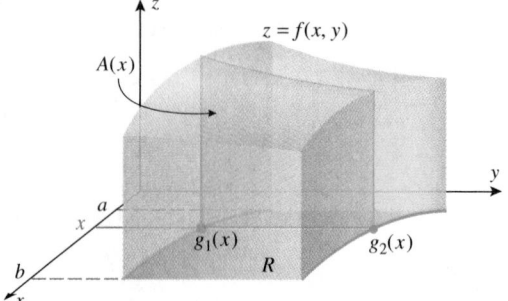

▲ **Figure 14.2.3**

▶ **Figure 14.2.4**

which shows that in (3) the iterated integral is equal to the double integral. Similarly, the iterated integral in (4) is equal to the corresponding double integral.

■ SETTING UP LIMITS OF INTEGRATION FOR EVALUATING DOUBLE INTEGRALS

To apply Theorem 14.2.2, it is helpful to start with a two-dimensional sketch of the region R. [It is not necessary to graph $f(x, y)$.] For a type I region, the limits of integration in Formula (3) can be obtained as follows:

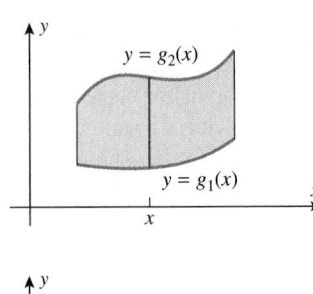

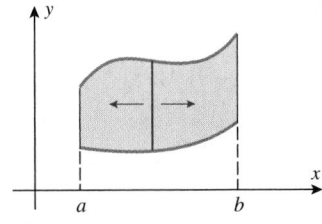

▲ Figure 14.2.5

Determining Limits of Integration: Type I Region

Step 1. Since x is held fixed for the first integration, we draw a vertical line through the region R at an arbitrary fixed value x (Figure 14.2.5). This line crosses the boundary of R twice. The lower point of intersection is on the curve $y = g_1(x)$ and the higher point is on the curve $y = g_2(x)$. These two intersections determine the lower and upper y-limits of integration in Formula (3).

Step 2. Imagine moving the line drawn in Step 1 first to the left and then to the right (Figure 14.2.5). The leftmost position where the line intersects the region R is $x = a$, and the rightmost position where the line intersects the region R is $x = b$. This yields the limits for the x-integration in Formula (3).

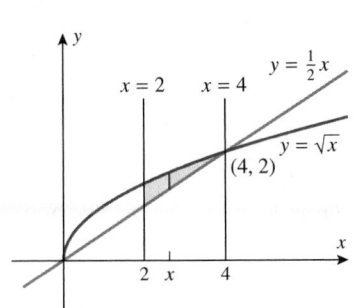

▲ Figure 14.2.6

▶ **Example 3** Evaluate

$$\iint\limits_{R} xy \, dA$$

over the region R enclosed between $y = \frac{1}{2}x$, $y = \sqrt{x}$, $x = 2$, and $x = 4$.

Solution. We view R as a type I region. The region R and a vertical line corresponding to a fixed x are shown in Figure 14.2.6. This line meets the region R at the lower boundary $y = \frac{1}{2}x$ and the upper boundary $y = \sqrt{x}$. These are the y-limits of integration. Moving this line first left and then right yields the x-limits of integration, $x = 2$ and $x = 4$. Thus,

$$\iint\limits_{R} xy \, dA = \int_2^4 \int_{x/2}^{\sqrt{x}} xy \, dy \, dx = \int_2^4 \left[\frac{xy^2}{2} \right]_{y=x/2}^{\sqrt{x}} dx = \int_2^4 \left(\frac{x^2}{2} - \frac{x^3}{8} \right) dx$$

$$= \left[\frac{x^3}{6} - \frac{x^4}{32} \right]_2^4 = \left(\frac{64}{6} - \frac{256}{32} \right) - \left(\frac{8}{6} - \frac{16}{32} \right) = \frac{11}{6} \blacktriangleleft$$

If R is a type II region, then the limits of integration in Formula (4) can be obtained as follows:

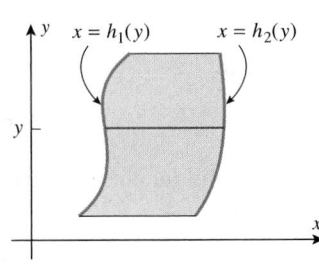

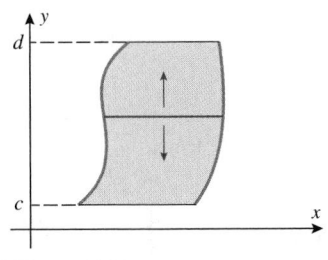

▲ Figure 14.2.7

Determining Limits of Integration: Type II Region

Step 1. Since y is held fixed for the first integration, we draw a horizontal line through the region R at a fixed value y (Figure 14.2.7). This line crosses the boundary of R twice. The leftmost point of intersection is on the curve $x = h_1(y)$ and the rightmost point is on the curve $x = h_2(y)$. These intersections determine the x-limits of integration in (4).

Step 2. Imagine moving the line drawn in Step 1 first down and then up (Figure 14.2.7). The lowest position where the line intersects the region R is $y = c$, and the highest position where the line intersects the region R is $y = d$. This yields the y-limits of integration in (4).

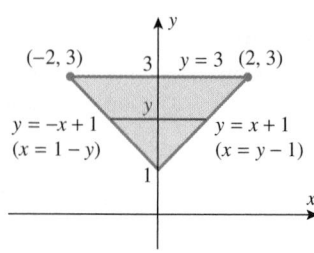

▲ **Figure 14.2.8**

To integrate over a type II region, the left- and right-hand boundaries must be expressed in the form $x = h_1(y)$ and $x = h_2(y)$. This is why we rewrote the boundary equations

$$y = -x + 1 \quad \text{and} \quad y = x + 1$$

as

$$x = 1 - y \quad \text{and} \quad x = y - 1$$

in Example 4.

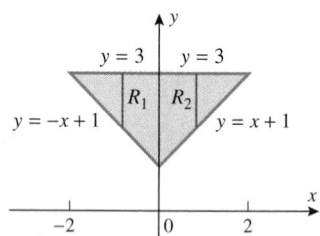

▲ **Figure 14.2.9**

▶ **Example 4**   Evaluate

$$\iint_R (2x - y^2)\, dA$$

over the triangular region R enclosed between the lines $y = -x + 1$, $y = x + 1$, and $y = 3$.

Solution.   We view R as a type II region. The region R and a horizontal line corresponding to a fixed y are shown in Figure 14.2.8. This line meets the region R at its left-hand boundary $x = 1 - y$ and its right-hand boundary $x = y - 1$. These are the x-limits of integration. Moving this line first down and then up yields the y-limits, $y = 1$ and $y = 3$. Thus,

$$\iint_R (2x - y^2)\, dA = \int_1^3 \int_{1-y}^{y-1} (2x - y^2)\, dx\, dy = \int_1^3 \left[x^2 - y^2 x \right]_{x=1-y}^{y-1} dy$$

$$= \int_1^3 [(1 - 2y + 2y^2 - y^3) - (1 - 2y + y^3)]\, dy$$

$$= \int_1^3 (2y^2 - 2y^3)\, dy = \left[\frac{2y^3}{3} - \frac{y^4}{2} \right]_1^3 = -\frac{68}{3} \quad ◀$$

In Example 4 we could have treated R as a type I region, but with an added complication. Viewed as a type I region, the upper boundary of R is the line $y = 3$ (Figure 14.2.9) and the lower boundary consists of two parts, the line $y = -x + 1$ to the left of the y-axis and the line $y = x + 1$ to the right of the y-axis. To carry out the integration it is necessary to decompose the region R into two parts, R_1 and R_2, as shown in Figure 14.2.9, and write

$$\iint_R (2x - y^2)\, dA = \iint_{R_1} (2x - y^2)\, dA + \iint_{R_2} (2x - y^2)\, dA$$

$$= \int_{-2}^0 \int_{-x+1}^3 (2x - y^2)\, dy\, dx + \int_0^2 \int_{x+1}^3 (2x - y^2)\, dy\, dx$$

This will yield the same result that was obtained in Example 4. (Verify.)

▶ **Example 5**   Use a double integral to find the volume of the tetrahedron bounded by the coordinate planes and the plane $z = 4 - 4x - 2y$.

Solution.   The tetrahedron in question is bounded above by the plane

$$z = 4 - 4x - 2y \tag{5}$$

and below by the triangular region R shown in Figure 14.2.10. Thus, the volume is given by

$$V = \iint_R (4 - 4x - 2y)\, dA$$

The region R is bounded by the x-axis, the y-axis, and the line $y = 2 - 2x$ [set $z = 0$ in (5)], so that treating R as a type I region yields

$$V = \iint_R (4 - 4x - 2y)\, dA = \int_0^1 \int_0^{2-2x} (4 - 4x - 2y)\, dy\, dx$$

$$= \int_0^1 \left[4y - 4xy - y^2 \right]_{y=0}^{2-2x} dx = \int_0^1 (4 - 8x + 4x^2)\, dx = \frac{4}{3} \quad ◀$$

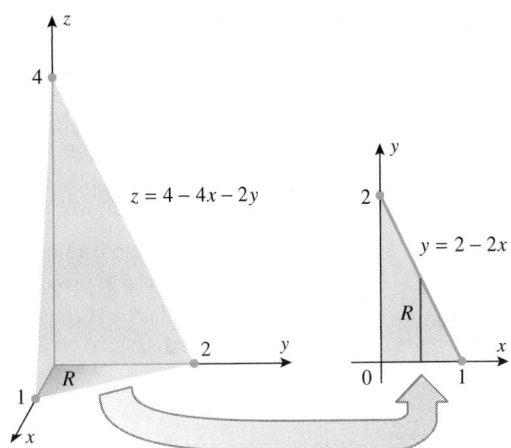

▶ **Figure 14.2.10**

▶ **Example 6**   Find the volume of the solid bounded by the cylinder $x^2 + y^2 = 4$ and the planes $y + z = 4$ and $z = 0$.

Solution.   The solid shown in Figure 14.2.11 is bounded above by the plane $z = 4 - y$ and below by the region R within the circle $x^2 + y^2 = 4$. The volume is given by

$$V = \iint\limits_{R} (4 - y)\, dA$$

Treating R as a type I region we obtain

$$V = \int_{-2}^{2} \int_{-\sqrt{4-x^2}}^{\sqrt{4-x^2}} (4 - y)\, dy\, dx = \int_{-2}^{2} \left[4y - \frac{1}{2}y^2 \right]_{y=-\sqrt{4-x^2}}^{\sqrt{4-x^2}} dx$$

$$= \int_{-2}^{2} 8\sqrt{4 - x^2}\, dx = 8(2\pi) = 16\pi \qquad \boxed{\text{See Formula (3) of Section 7.4.}} \quad ◀$$

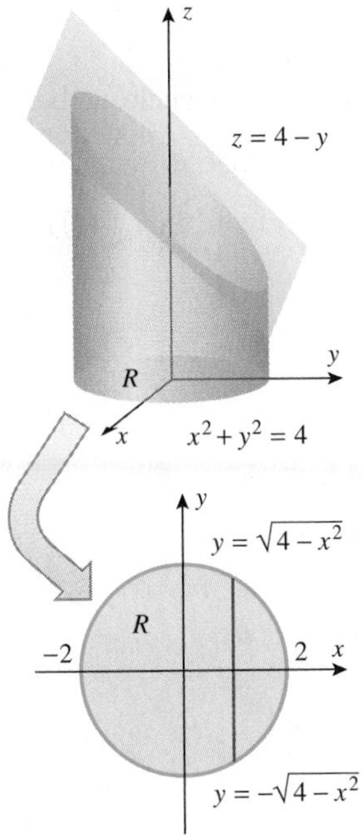

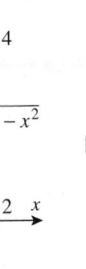

■ **REVERSING THE ORDER OF INTEGRATION**
Sometimes the evaluation of an iterated integral can be simplified by reversing the order of integration. The next example illustrates how this is done.

▶ **Example 7**   Since there is no elementary antiderivative of e^{x^2}, the integral

$$\int_{0}^{2} \int_{y/2}^{1} e^{x^2}\, dx\, dy$$

cannot be evaluated by performing the x-integration first. Evaluate this integral by expressing it as an equivalent iterated integral with the order of integration reversed.

Solution.   For the inside integration, y is fixed and x varies from the line $x = y/2$ to the line $x = 1$ (Figure 14.2.12). For the outside integration, y varies from 0 to 2, so the given iterated integral is equal to a double integral over the triangular region R in Figure 14.2.12.
To reverse the order of integration, we treat R as a type I region, which enables us to write the given integral as

$$\int_{0}^{2} \int_{y/2}^{1} e^{x^2}\, dx\, dy = \iint\limits_{R} e^{x^2}\, dA = \int_{0}^{1} \int_{0}^{2x} e^{x^2}\, dy\, dx = \int_{0}^{1} \left[e^{x^2} y \right]_{y=0}^{2x} dx$$

$$= \int_{0}^{1} 2x e^{x^2}\, dx = e^{x^2} \Big]_{0}^{1} = e - 1 \quad ◀$$

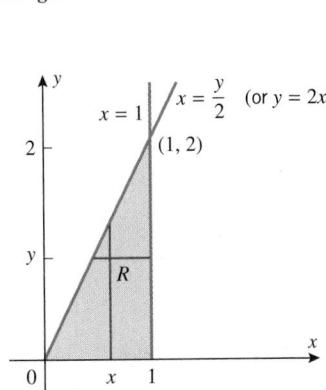

▲ **Figure 14.2.11**

▲ **Figure 14.2.12**

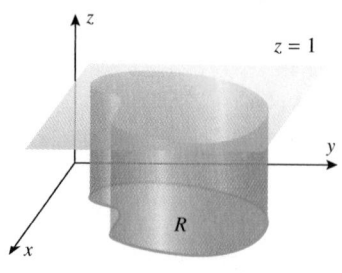

Cylinder with base R and height 1

▲ **Figure 14.2.13**

Formula (7) can be confusing because it equates an area and a volume; the formula is intended to equate only the *numerical values* of the area and volume and not the units, which must, of course, be different.

■ AREA CALCULATED AS A DOUBLE INTEGRAL

Although double integrals arose in the context of calculating volumes, they can also be used to calculate areas. To see why this is so, recall that a *right cylinder* is a solid that is generated when a plane region is translated along a line that is perpendicular to the region. In Formula (2) of Section 6.2 we stated that the volume V of a right cylinder with cross-sectional area A and height h is

$$V = A \cdot h \tag{6}$$

Now suppose that we are interested in finding the area A of a region R in the xy-plane. If we translate the region R upward 1 unit, then the resulting solid will be a right cylinder that has cross-sectional area A, base R, and the plane $z = 1$ as its top (Figure 14.2.13). Thus, it follows from (6) that

$$\iint\limits_{R} 1 \, dA = (\text{area of } R) \cdot 1$$

which we can rewrite as

$$\text{area of } R = \iint\limits_{R} 1 \, dA = \iint\limits_{R} dA \tag{7}$$

▶ **Example 8**   Use a double integral to find the area of the region R enclosed between the parabola $y = \frac{1}{2}x^2$ and the line $y = 2x$.

Solution.   The region R may be treated equally well as type I (Figure 14.2.14a) or type II (Figure 14.2.14b). Treating R as type I yields

$$\text{area of } R = \iint\limits_{R} dA = \int_{0}^{4} \int_{x^2/2}^{2x} dy \, dx = \int_{0}^{4} \left[y \right]_{y=x^2/2}^{2x} dx$$

$$= \int_{0}^{4} \left(2x - \frac{1}{2}x^2 \right) dx = \left[x^2 - \frac{x^3}{6} \right]_{0}^{4} = \frac{16}{3}$$

Treating R as type II yields

$$\text{area of } R = \iint\limits_{R} dA = \int_{0}^{8} \int_{y/2}^{\sqrt{2y}} dx \, dy = \int_{0}^{8} \left[x \right]_{x=y/2}^{\sqrt{2y}} dy$$

$$= \int_{0}^{8} \left(\sqrt{2y} - \frac{1}{2}y \right) dy = \left[\frac{2\sqrt{2}}{3} y^{3/2} - \frac{y^2}{4} \right]_{0}^{8} = \frac{16}{3} \quad ◀$$

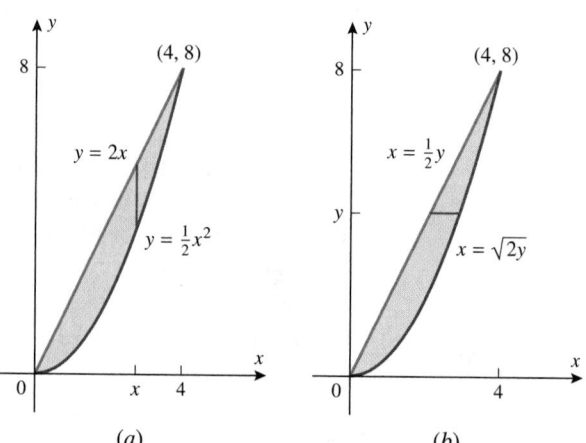

▶ **Figure 14.2.14** (a) (b)

✔ **QUICK CHECK EXERCISES 14.2**   *(See page 1018 for answers.)*

1. Supply the missing integrand and limits of integration.

   (a) $\displaystyle\int_1^5 \int_2^{y/2} 6x^2 y \, dx \, dy = \int_\square^\square \underline{\hspace{1.5cm}} dy$

   (b) $\displaystyle\int_1^5 \int_2^{x/2} 6x^2 y \, dy \, dx = \int_\square^\square \underline{\hspace{1.5cm}} dx$

2. Let R be the triangular region in the xy-plane with vertices $(0, 0)$, $(3, 0)$, and $(0, 4)$. Supply the missing portions of the integrals.

   (a) Treating R as a type I region,

   $$\iint\limits_R f(x, y) \, dA = \int_\square^\square \int_\square^\square f(x, y) \, \underline{\hspace{1cm}}$$

(b) Treating R as a type II region,

$$\iint\limits_R f(x, y) \, dA = \int_\square^\square \int_\square^\square f(x, y) \, \underline{\hspace{1cm}}$$

3. Let R be the triangular region in the xy-plane with vertices $(0, 0)$, $(3, 3)$, and $(0, 4)$. Expressed as an iterated double integral, the area of R is $A(R) = \underline{\hspace{1.5cm}}$.

4. The line $y = 2 - x$ and the parabola $y = x^2$ intersect at the points $(-2, 4)$ and $(1, 1)$. If R is the region enclosed by $y = 2 - x$ and $y = x^2$, then

$$\iint\limits_R (1 + 2y) \, dA = \underline{\hspace{1.5cm}}$$

EXERCISE SET 14.2   ⬚ Graphing Utility   © CAS

1–8 Evaluate the iterated integral. ▪

1. $\displaystyle\int_0^1 \int_{x^2}^x xy^2 \, dy \, dx$

2. $\displaystyle\int_1^{3/2} \int_y^{3-y} y \, dx \, dy$

3. $\displaystyle\int_0^3 \int_0^{\sqrt{9-y^2}} y \, dx \, dy$

4. $\displaystyle\int_{1/4}^1 \int_{x^2}^x \sqrt{\frac{x}{y}} \, dy \, dx$

5. $\displaystyle\int_{\sqrt{\pi}}^{\sqrt{2\pi}} \int_0^{x^3} \sin \frac{y}{x} \, dy \, dx$

6. $\displaystyle\int_{-1}^1 \int_{-x^2}^{x^2} (x^2 - y) \, dy \, dx$

7. $\displaystyle\int_0^1 \int_0^x y\sqrt{x^2 - y^2} \, dy \, dx$

8. $\displaystyle\int_1^2 \int_0^{y^2} e^{x/y^2} \, dx \, dy$

FOCUS ON CONCEPTS

9. Let R be the region shown in the accompanying figure. Fill in the missing limits of integration.

   (a) $\displaystyle\iint\limits_R f(x, y) \, dA = \int_\square^\square \int_\square^\square f(x, y) \, dy \, dx$

   (b) $\displaystyle\iint\limits_R f(x, y) \, dA = \int_\square^\square \int_\square^\square f(x, y) \, dx \, dy$

10. Let R be the region shown in the accompanying figure. Fill in the missing limits of integration.

    (a) $\displaystyle\iint\limits_R f(x, y) \, dA = \int_\square^\square \int_\square^\square f(x, y) \, dy \, dx$

    (b) $\displaystyle\iint\limits_R f(x, y) \, dA = \int_\square^\square \int_\square^\square f(x, y) \, dx \, dy$

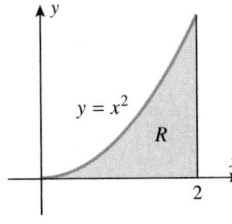

▲ **Figure Ex-9**   ▲ **Figure Ex-10**

11. Let R be the region shown in the accompanying figure. Fill in the missing limits of integration.

    (a) $\displaystyle\iint\limits_R f(x, y) \, dA = \int_1^2 \int_\square^\square f(x, y) \, dy \, dx$

    $$+ \int_2^4 \int_\square^\square f(x, y) \, dy \, dx$$

    $$+ \int_4^5 \int_\square^\square f(x, y) \, dy \, dx$$

    (b) $\displaystyle\iint\limits_R f(x, y) \, dA = \int_\square^\square \int_\square^\square f(x, y) \, dx \, dy$

12. Let R be the region shown in the accompanying figure. Fill in the missing limits of integration.

    (a) $\displaystyle\iint\limits_R f(x, y) \, dA = \int_\square^\square \int_\square^\square f(x, y) \, dy \, dx$

    (b) $\displaystyle\iint\limits_R f(x, y) \, dA = \int_\square^\square \int_\square^\square f(x, y) \, dx \, dy$

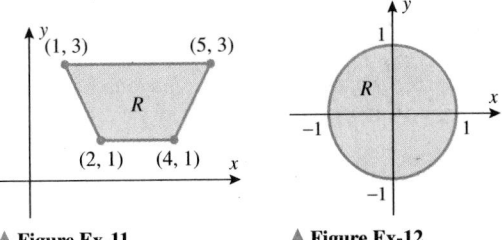

▲ **Figure Ex-11**   ▲ **Figure Ex-12**

13. Evaluate $\displaystyle\iint\limits_R xy \, dA$, where R is the region in

    (a) Exercise 9   (b) Exercise 11.

14. Evaluate $\iint\limits_{R} (x + y)\, dA$, where R is the region in

(a) Exercise 10   (b) Exercise 12.

15–18 Evaluate the double integral in two ways using iterated integrals: (a) viewing R as a type I region, and (b) viewing R as a type II region. ■

15. $\iint\limits_{R} x^2\, dA$; R is the region bounded by $y = 16/x$, $y = x$, and $x = 8$.

16. $\iint\limits_{R} xy^2\, dA$; R is the region enclosed by $y = 1$, $y = 2$, $x = 0$, and $y = x$.

17. $\iint\limits_{R} (3x - 2y)\, dA$; R is the region enclosed by the circle $x^2 + y^2 = 1$.

18. $\iint\limits_{R} y\, dA$; R is the region in the first quadrant enclosed between the circle $x^2 + y^2 = 25$ and the line $x + y = 5$.

19–24 Evaluate the double integral. ■

19. $\iint\limits_{R} x(1 + y^2)^{-1/2}\, dA$; R is the region in the first quadrant enclosed by $y = x^2$, $y = 4$, and $x = 0$.

20. $\iint\limits_{R} x \cos y\, dA$; R is the triangular region bounded by the lines $y = x$, $y = 0$, and $x = \pi$.

21. $\iint\limits_{R} xy\, dA$; R is the region enclosed by $y = \sqrt{x}$, $y = 6 - x$, and $y = 0$.

22. $\iint\limits_{R} x\, dA$; R is the region enclosed by $y = \sin^{-1} x$, $x = 1/\sqrt{2}$, and $y = 0$.

23. $\iint\limits_{R} (x - 1)\, dA$; R is the region in the first quadrant enclosed between $y = x$ and $y = x^3$.

24. $\iint\limits_{R} x^2\, dA$; R is the region in the first quadrant enclosed by $xy = 1$, $y = x$, and $y = 2x$.

25. Evaluate $\iint\limits_{R} \sin(y^3)\, dA$, where R is the region bounded by $y = \sqrt{x}$, $y = 2$, and $x = 0$. [*Hint:* Choose the order of integration carefully.]

26. Evaluate $\iint\limits_{R} x\, dA$, where R is the region bounded by $x = \ln y$, $x = 0$, and $y = e$.

27. (a) By hand or with the help of a graphing utility, make a sketch of the region R enclosed between the curves $y = x + 2$ and $y = e^x$.
(b) Estimate the intersections of the curves in part (a).
(c) Viewing R as a type I region, estimate $\iint\limits_{R} x\, dA$.
(d) Viewing R as a type II region, estimate $\iint\limits_{R} x\, dA$.

28. (a) By hand or with the help of a graphing utility, make a sketch of the region R enclosed between the curves $y = 4x^3 - x^4$ and $y = 3 - 4x + 4x^2$.
(b) Find the intersections of the curves in part (a).
(c) Find $\iint\limits_{R} x\, dA$.

29–32 Use double integration to find the area of the plane region enclosed by the given curves. ■

29. $y = \sin x$ and $y = \cos x$, for $0 \le x \le \pi/4$.

30. $y^2 = -x$ and $3y - x = 4$.

31. $y^2 = 9 - x$ and $y^2 = 9 - 9x$.

32. $y = \cosh x$, $y = \sinh x$, $x = 0$, and $x = 1$.

33–36 True–False Determine whether the statement is true or false. Explain your answer. ■

33. $\displaystyle\int_0^1 \int_{x^2}^{2x} f(x, y)\, dy\, dx = \int_{x^2}^{2x} \int_0^1 f(x, y)\, dx\, dy$

34. If a region R is bounded below by $y = g_1(x)$ and above by $y = g_2(x)$ for $a \le x \le b$, then
$$\iint\limits_{R} f(x, y)\, dA = \int_a^b \int_{g_1(x)}^{g_2(x)} f(x, y)\, dy\, dx$$

35. If R is the region in the xy-plane enclosed by $y = x^2$ and $y = 1$, then
$$\iint\limits_{R} f(x, y)\, dA = 2 \int_0^1 \int_{x^2}^1 f(x, y)\, dy\, dx$$

36. The area of a region R in the xy-plane is given by $\iint\limits_{R} xy\, dA$.

37–38 Use double integration to find the volume of the solid. ■

37.   **38.**

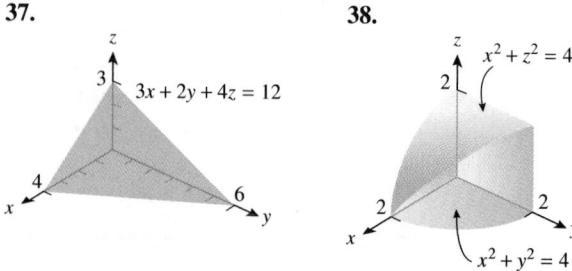

39–44 Use double integration to find the volume of each solid. ▪

39. The solid bounded by the cylinder $x^2 + y^2 = 9$ and the planes $z = 0$ and $z = 3 - x$.

40. The solid in the first octant bounded above by the paraboloid $z = x^2 + 3y^2$, below by the plane $z = 0$, and laterally by $y = x^2$ and $y = x$.

41. The solid bounded above by the paraboloid $z = 9x^2 + y^2$, below by the plane $z = 0$, and laterally by the planes $x = 0$, $y = 0$, $x = 3$, and $y = 2$.

42. The solid enclosed by $y^2 = x$, $z = 0$, and $x + z = 1$.

43. The wedge cut from the cylinder $4x^2 + y^2 = 9$ by the planes $z = 0$ and $z = y + 3$.

44. The solid in the first octant bounded above by $z = 9 - x^2$, below by $z = 0$, and laterally by $y^2 = 3x$.

C **45–46** Use a double integral and a CAS to find the volume of the solid. ▪

45. The solid bounded above by the paraboloid $z = 1 - x^2 - y^2$ and below by the xy-plane.

46. The solid in the first octant that is bounded by the paraboloid $z = x^2 + y^2$, the cylinder $x^2 + y^2 = 4$, and the coordinate planes.

47–52 Express the integral as an equivalent integral with the order of integration reversed. ▪

47. $\displaystyle\int_0^2 \int_0^{\sqrt{x}} f(x, y)\, dy\, dx$ **48.** $\displaystyle\int_0^4 \int_{2y}^8 f(x, y)\, dx\, dy$

49. $\displaystyle\int_0^2 \int_1^{e^y} f(x, y)\, dx\, dy$ **50.** $\displaystyle\int_1^e \int_0^{\ln x} f(x, y)\, dy\, dx$

51. $\displaystyle\int_0^1 \int_{\sin^{-1} y}^{\pi/2} f(x, y)\, dx\, dy$ **52.** $\displaystyle\int_0^1 \int_{y^2}^{\sqrt{y}} f(x, y)\, dx\, dy$

53–56 Evaluate the integral by first reversing the order of integration. ▪

53. $\displaystyle\int_0^1 \int_{4x}^4 e^{-y^2}\, dy\, dx$ **54.** $\displaystyle\int_0^2 \int_{y/2}^1 \cos(x^2)\, dx\, dy$

55. $\displaystyle\int_0^4 \int_{\sqrt{y}}^2 e^{x^3}\, dx\, dy$ **56.** $\displaystyle\int_1^3 \int_0^{\ln x} x\, dy\, dx$

C **57.** Try to evaluate the integral with a CAS using the stated order of integration, and then by reversing the order of integration.

(a) $\displaystyle\int_0^4 \int_{\sqrt{x}}^2 \sin \pi y^3\, dy\, dx$

(b) $\displaystyle\int_0^1 \int_{\sin^{-1} y}^{\pi/2} \sec^2(\cos x)\, dx\, dy$

58. Use the appropriate Wallis formula (see Exercise Set 7.3) to find the volume of the solid enclosed between the circular paraboloid $z = x^2 + y^2$, the right circular cylinder $x^2 + y^2 = 4$, and the xy-plane (see the accompanying figure for cut view).

59. Evaluate $\displaystyle\iint_R xy^2\, dA$ over the region R shown in the accompanying figure.

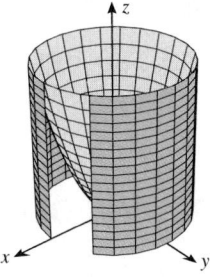
▲ Figure Ex-58

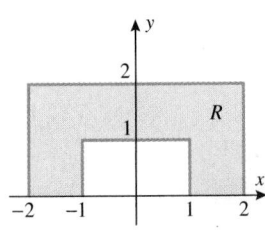
▲ Figure Ex-59

60. Give a geometric argument to show that

$$\int_0^1 \int_0^{\sqrt{1-y^2}} \sqrt{1 - x^2 - y^2}\, dx\, dy = \frac{\pi}{6}$$

61–62 The *average value* or *mean value* of a continuous function $f(x, y)$ over a region R in the xy-plane is defined as

$$f_{\text{ave}} = \frac{1}{A(R)} \iint_R f(x, y)\, dA$$

where $A(R)$ is the area of the region R (compare to the definition preceding Exercise 35 in Section 14.1). Use this definition in these exercises. ▪

61. Find the average value of $1/(1 + x^2)$ over the triangular region with vertices $(0, 0)$, $(1, 1)$, and $(0, 1)$.

62. Find the average value of $f(x, y) = x^2 - xy$ over the region enclosed by $y = x$ and $y = 3x - x^2$.

63. Suppose that the temperature in degrees Celsius at a point (x, y) on a flat metal plate is $T(x, y) = 5xy + x^2$, where x and y are in meters. Find the average temperature of the diamond-shaped portion of the plate for which $|2x + y| \le 4$ and $|2x - y| \le 4$.

64. A circular lens of radius 2 inches has thickness $1 - (r^2/4)$ inches at all points r inches from the center of the lens. Find the average thickness of the lens.

C **65.** Use a CAS to approximate the intersections of the curves $y = \sin x$ and $y = x/2$, and then approximate the volume of the solid in the first octant that is below the surface $z = \sqrt{1 + x + y}$ and above the region in the xy-plane that is enclosed by the curves.

66. Writing Describe the steps you would follow to find the limits of integration that express a double integral over a nonrectangular region as an iterated double integral. Illustrate your discussion with an example.

67. Writing Describe the steps you would follow to reverse the order of integration in an iterated double integral. Illustrate your discussion with an example.

✔️ **QUICK CHECK ANSWERS 14.2**

1. (a) $\int_1^5 \left(\frac{1}{4} y^4 - 16y \right) dy$ (b) $\int_1^5 \left(\frac{3}{4} x^4 - 12x^2 \right) dx$ 2. (a) $\int_0^3 \int_0^{-\frac{4}{3}x+4} f(x, y) \, dy \, dx$ (b) $\int_0^4 \int_0^{-\frac{3}{4}y+3} f(x, y) \, dx \, dy$

3. $\int_0^3 \int_x^{-\frac{1}{3}x+4} dy \, dx$ 4. $\int_{-2}^1 \int_{x^2}^{2-x} (1 + 2y) \, dy \, dx = 18.9$

14.3 DOUBLE INTEGRALS IN POLAR COORDINATES

In this section we will study double integrals in which the integrand and the region of integration are expressed in polar coordinates. Such integrals are important for two reasons: first, they arise naturally in many applications, and second, many double integrals in rectangular coordinates can be evaluated more easily if they are converted to polar coordinates.

■ **SIMPLE POLAR REGIONS**

Some double integrals are easier to evaluate if the region of integration is expressed in polar coordinates. This is usually true if the region is bounded by a cardioid, a rose curve, a spiral, or, more generally, by any curve whose equation is simpler in polar coordinates than in rectangular coordinates. For example, the quarter-disk in Figure 14.3.1 is described in rectangular coordinates by

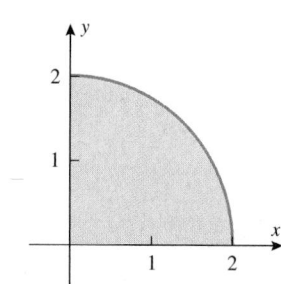

▶ **Figure 14.3.1**

$$0 \leq y \leq \sqrt{4 - x^2}, \quad 0 \leq x \leq 2$$

However, in polar coordinates the region is described more simply by

$$0 \leq r \leq 2, \quad 0 \leq \theta \leq \pi/2$$

Moreover, double integrals whose integrands involve $x^2 + y^2$ also tend to be easier to evaluate in polar coordinates because this sum simplifies to r^2 when the conversion formulas $x = r \cos \theta$ and $y = r \sin \theta$ are applied.

Figure 14.3.2*a* shows a region R in a polar coordinate system that is enclosed between two rays, $\theta = \alpha$ and $\theta = \beta$, and two polar curves, $r = r_1(\theta)$ and $r = r_2(\theta)$. If, as shown in the figure, the functions $r_1(\theta)$ and $r_2(\theta)$ are continuous and their graphs do not cross, then the region R is called a *simple polar region*. If $r_1(\theta)$ is identically zero, then the boundary $r = r_1(\theta)$ reduces to a point (the origin), and the region has the general shape shown in Figure 14.3.2*b*. If, in addition, $\beta = \alpha + 2\pi$, then the rays coincide, and the region has the

> An overview of polar coordinates can be found in Section 10.2.

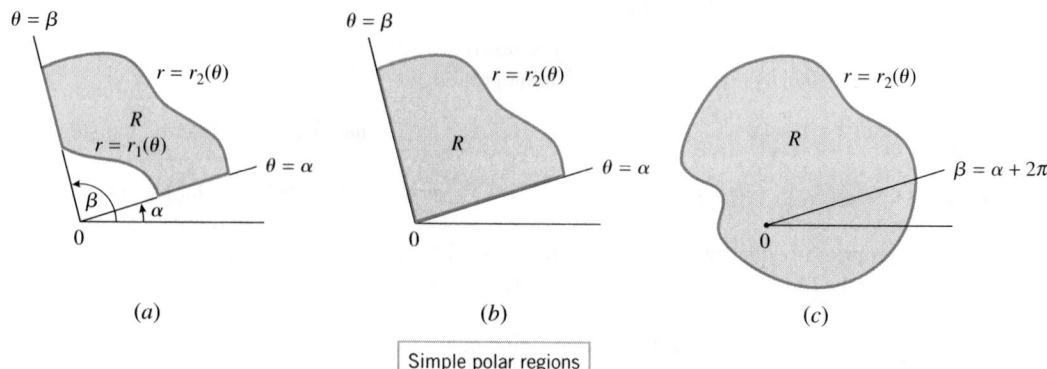

(a)   (b)   (c)

Simple polar regions

▲ **Figure 14.3.2**

general shape shown in Figure 14.3.2c. The following definition expresses these geometric ideas algebraically.

14.3.1 DEFINITION A *simple polar region* in a polar coordinate system is a region that is enclosed between two rays, $\theta = \alpha$ and $\theta = \beta$, and two continuous polar curves, $r = r_1(\theta)$ and $r = r_2(\theta)$, where the equations of the rays and the polar curves satisfy the following conditions:

(i) $\alpha \le \beta$ (ii) $\beta - \alpha \le 2\pi$ (iii) $0 \le r_1(\theta) \le r_2(\theta)$

REMARK | Conditions (i) and (ii) together imply that the ray $\theta = \beta$ can be obtained by rotating the ray $\theta = \alpha$ counterclockwise through an angle that is at most 2π radians. This is consistent with Figure 14.3.2. Condition (iii) implies that the boundary curves $r = r_1(\theta)$ and $r = r_2(\theta)$ can touch but cannot actually cross over one another (why?). Thus, in keeping with Figure 14.3.2, it is appropriate to describe $r = r_1(\theta)$ as the *inner boundary* of the region and $r = r_2(\theta)$ as the *outer boundary*.

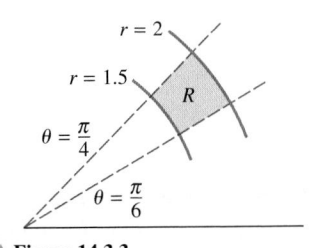

▲ **Figure 14.3.3**

A *polar rectangle* is a simple polar region for which the bounding polar curves are circular arcs. For example, Figure 14.3.3 shows the polar rectangle R given by

$$1.5 \le r \le 2, \quad \frac{\pi}{6} \le \theta \le \frac{\pi}{4}$$

■ **DOUBLE INTEGRALS IN POLAR COORDINATES**

Next we will consider the polar version of Problem 14.1.1.

14.3.2 THE VOLUME PROBLEM IN POLAR COORDINATES Given a function $f(r, \theta)$ that is continuous and nonnegative on a simple polar region R, find the volume of the solid that is enclosed between the region R and the surface whose equation in cylindrical coordinates is $z = f(r, \theta)$ (Figure 14.3.4).

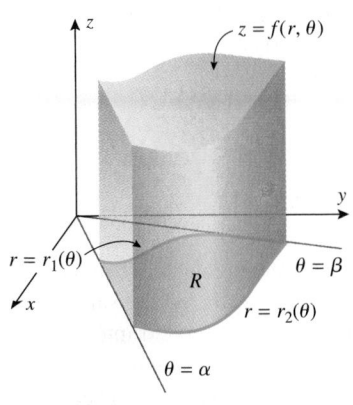

▲ **Figure 14.3.4**

To motivate a formula for the volume V of the solid in Figure 14.3.4, we will use a limit process similar to that used to obtain Formula (2) of Section 14.1, except that here we will use circular arcs and rays to subdivide the region R into polar rectangles. As shown in Figure 14.3.5, we will exclude from consideration all polar rectangles that contain any points outside of R, leaving only polar rectangles that are subsets of R. Assume that there are n such polar rectangles, and denote the area of the kth polar rectangle by ΔA_k. Let (r_k^*, θ_k^*) be any point in this polar rectangle. As shown in Figure 14.3.6, the product $f(r_k^*, \theta_k^*)\Delta A_k$ is the volume of a solid with base area ΔA_k and height $f(r_k^*, \theta_k^*)$, so the sum

$$\sum_{k=1}^{n} f(r_k^*, \theta_k^*)\Delta A_k$$

can be viewed as an approximation to the volume V of the entire solid.

If we now increase the number of subdivisions in such a way that the dimensions of the polar rectangles approach zero, then it seems plausible that the errors in the approximations approach zero, and the exact volume of the solid is

$$V = \lim_{n \to +\infty} \sum_{k=1}^{n} f(r_k^*, \theta_k^*)\Delta A_k \qquad (1)$$

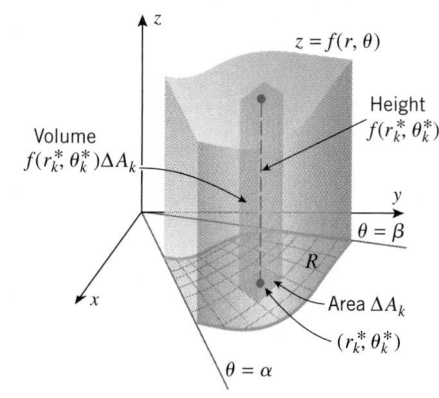

▲ **Figure 14.3.5**

▲ **Figure 14.3.6**

If $f(r, \theta)$ is continuous on R and has both positive and negative values, then the limit

$$\lim_{n \to +\infty} \sum_{k=1}^{n} f(r_k^*, \theta_k^*) \Delta A_k \tag{2}$$

represents the net signed volume between the region R and the surface $z = f(r, \theta)$ (as with double integrals in rectangular coordinates). The sums in (2) are called **polar Riemann sums**, and the limit of the polar Riemann sums is denoted by

$$\iint\limits_{R} f(r, \theta) \, dA = \lim_{n \to +\infty} \sum_{k=1}^{n} f(r_k^*, \theta_k^*) \Delta A_k \tag{3}$$

Polar double integrals are also called **double integrals in polar coordinates** to distinguish them from double integrals over regions in the xy-plane; the latter are called **double integrals in rectangular coordinates**. Double integrals in polar coordinates have the usual integral properties, such as those stated in Formulas (9), (10), and (11) of Section 14.1.

which is called the **polar double integral** of $f(r, \theta)$ over R. If $f(r, \theta)$ is continuous and nonnegative on R, then the volume formula (1) can be expressed as

$$V = \iint\limits_{R} f(r, \theta) \, dA \tag{4}$$

■ EVALUATING POLAR DOUBLE INTEGRALS

In Sections 14.1 and 14.2 we evaluated double integrals in rectangular coordinates by expressing them as iterated integrals. Polar double integrals are evaluated the same way. To motivate the formula that expresses a double polar integral as an iterated integral, we will assume that $f(r, \theta)$ is nonnegative so that we can interpret (3) as a volume. However, the results that we will obtain will also be applicable if f has negative values. To begin, let us choose the arbitrary point (r_k^*, θ_k^*) in (3) to be at the "center" of the kth polar rectangle as shown in Figure 14.3.7. Suppose also that this polar rectangle has a central angle $\Delta\theta_k$ and a "radial thickness" Δr_k. Thus, the inner radius of this polar rectangle is $r_k^* - \frac{1}{2}\Delta r_k$ and the outer radius is $r_k^* + \frac{1}{2}\Delta r_k$. Treating the area ΔA_k of this polar rectangle as the difference in area of two sectors, we obtain

$$\Delta A_k = \tfrac{1}{2}\left(r_k^* + \tfrac{1}{2}\Delta r_k\right)^2 \Delta\theta_k - \tfrac{1}{2}\left(r_k^* - \tfrac{1}{2}\Delta r_k\right)^2 \Delta\theta_k$$

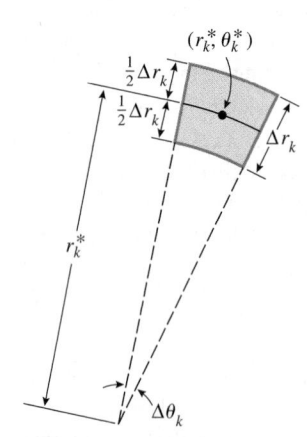

▲ **Figure 14.3.7**

which simplifies to

$$\Delta A_k = r_k^* \Delta r_k \Delta\theta_k \tag{5}$$

Thus, from (3) and (4)

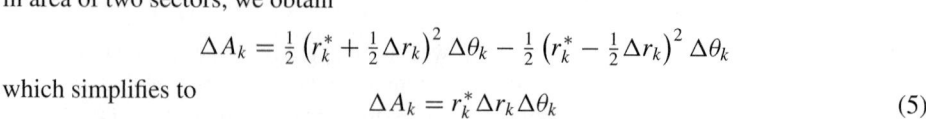

$$V = \iint\limits_{R} f(r, \theta) \, dA = \lim_{n \to +\infty} \sum_{k=1}^{n} f(r_k^*, \theta_k^*) r_k^* \Delta r_k \Delta\theta_k$$

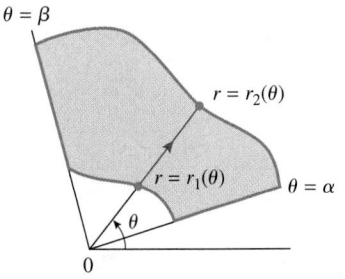

$\theta = \beta$

$r = r_2(\theta)$

$r = r_1(\theta)$

$\theta = \alpha$

θ

0

▲ **Figure 14.3.8**

which suggests that the volume V can be expressed as the iterated integral

$$V = \iint\limits_R f(r, \theta)\, dA = \int_\alpha^\beta \int_{r_1(\theta)}^{r_2(\theta)} f(r, \theta) r\, dr\, d\theta \qquad (6)$$

in which the limits of integration are chosen to cover the region R; that is, with θ fixed between α and β, the value of r varies from $r_1(\theta)$ to $r_2(\theta)$ (Figure 14.3.8).

Although we assumed $f(r, \theta)$ to be nonnegative in deriving Formula (6), it can be proved that the relationship between the polar double integral and the iterated integral in this formula also holds if f has negative values. Accepting this to be so, we obtain the following theorem, which we state without formal proof.

Note the extra factor of r that appears in the integrand when expressing a polar double integral as an iterated integral in polar coordinates.

14.3.3 THEOREM   *If R is a simple polar region whose boundaries are the rays $\theta = \alpha$ and $\theta = \beta$ and the curves $r = r_1(\theta)$ and $r = r_2(\theta)$ shown in Figure 14.3.8, and if $f(r, \theta)$ is continuous on R, then*

$$\iint\limits_R f(r, \theta)\, dA = \int_\alpha^\beta \int_{r_1(\theta)}^{r_2(\theta)} f(r, \theta) r\, dr\, d\theta \qquad (7)$$

To apply this theorem you will need to be able to find the rays and the curves that form the boundary of the region R, since these determine the limits of integration in the iterated integral. This can be done as follows:

Determining Limits of Integration for a Polar Double Integral: Simple Polar Region

Step 1. Since θ is held fixed for the first integration, draw a radial line from the origin through the region R at a fixed angle θ (Figure 14.3.9a). This line crosses the boundary of R at most twice. The innermost point of intersection is on the inner boundary curve $r = r_1(\theta)$ and the outermost point is on the outer boundary curve $r = r_2(\theta)$. These intersections determine the r-limits of integration in (7).

Step 2. Imagine rotating the radial line from Step 1 about the origin, thus sweeping out the region R. The least angle at which the radial line intersects the region R is $\theta = \alpha$ and the greatest angle is $\theta = \beta$ (Figure 14.3.9b). This determines the θ-limits of integration.

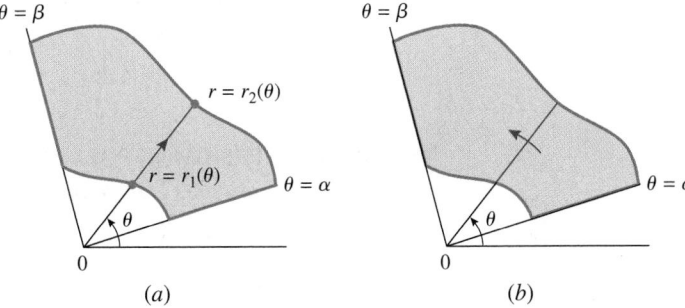

▶ **Figure 14.3.9**   (a)   (b)

▶ **Example 1**   Evaluate

$$\iint\limits_{R} \sin \theta \, dA$$

where R is the region in the first quadrant that is outside the circle $r = 2$ and inside the cardioid $r = 2(1 + \cos \theta)$.

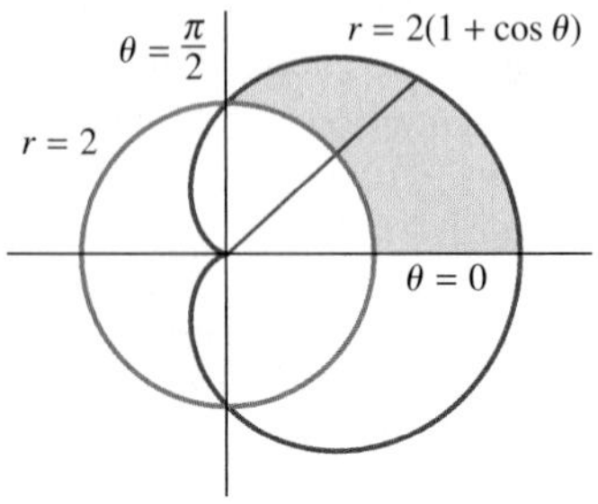

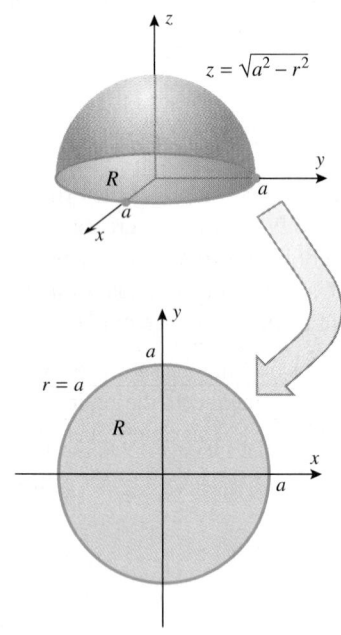

$\theta = \dfrac{\pi}{2}$ $r = 2(1 + \cos \theta)$

$r = 2$

$\theta = 0$

▲ **Figure 14.3.10**

Solution.   The region R is sketched in Figure 14.3.10. Following the two steps outlined above we obtain

$$\iint\limits_{R} \sin \theta \, dA = \int_{0}^{\pi/2} \int_{2}^{2(1+\cos\theta)} (\sin \theta) r \, dr \, d\theta$$

$$= \int_{0}^{\pi/2} \left[\frac{1}{2} r^2 \sin \theta \right]_{r=2}^{2(1+\cos\theta)} d\theta$$

$$= 2 \int_{0}^{\pi/2} [(1 + \cos \theta)^2 \sin \theta - \sin \theta] \, d\theta$$

$$= 2 \left[-\frac{1}{3}(1 + \cos \theta)^3 + \cos \theta \right]_{0}^{\pi/2}$$

$$= 2 \left[-\frac{1}{3} - \left(-\frac{5}{3} \right) \right] = \frac{8}{3} \quad ◀$$

▶ **Example 2**   The sphere of radius a centered at the origin is expressed in rectangular coordinates as $x^2 + y^2 + z^2 = a^2$, and hence its equation in cylindrical coordinates is $r^2 + z^2 = a^2$. Use this equation and a polar double integral to find the volume of the sphere.

z

$z = \sqrt{a^2 - r^2}$

R

a

a

y

x

y

a

$r = a$

R

a

x

▲ **Figure 14.3.11**

Solution.   In cylindrical coordinates the upper hemisphere is given by the equation

$$z = \sqrt{a^2 - r^2}$$

so the volume enclosed by the entire sphere is

$$V = 2 \iint\limits_{R} \sqrt{a^2 - r^2} \, dA$$

where R is the circular region shown in Figure 14.3.11. Thus,

$$V = 2 \iint\limits_{R} \sqrt{a^2 - r^2} \, dA = \int_{0}^{2\pi} \int_{0}^{a} \sqrt{a^2 - r^2} (2r) \, dr \, d\theta$$

$$= \int_{0}^{2\pi} \left[-\frac{2}{3}(a^2 - r^2)^{3/2} \right]_{r=0}^{a} d\theta = \int_{0}^{2\pi} \frac{2}{3} a^3 \, d\theta$$

$$= \left[\frac{2}{3} a^3 \theta \right]_{0}^{2\pi} = \frac{4}{3} \pi a^3 \quad ◀$$

■ **FINDING AREAS USING POLAR DOUBLE INTEGRALS**

Recall from Formula (7) of Section 14.2 that the area of a region R in the xy-plane can be expressed as

$$\text{area of } R = \iint\limits_{R} 1 \, dA = \iint\limits_{R} dA \qquad (8)$$

The argument used to derive this result can also be used to show that the formula applies to polar double integrals over regions in polar coordinates.

▶ **Example 3**   Use a polar double integral to find the area enclosed by the three-petaled rose $r = \sin 3\theta$.

Solution.   The rose is sketched in Figure 14.3.12. We will use Formula (8) to calculate the area of the petal R in the first quadrant and multiply by three.

$$A = 3 \iint\limits_R dA = 3 \int_0^{\pi/3} \int_0^{\sin 3\theta} r \, dr \, d\theta$$

$$= \frac{3}{2} \int_0^{\pi/3} \sin^2 3\theta \, d\theta = \frac{3}{4} \int_0^{\pi/3} (1 - \cos 6\theta) \, d\theta$$

$$= \frac{3}{4} \left[\theta - \frac{\sin 6\theta}{6} \right]_0^{\pi/3} = \frac{1}{4}\pi \quad ◀$$

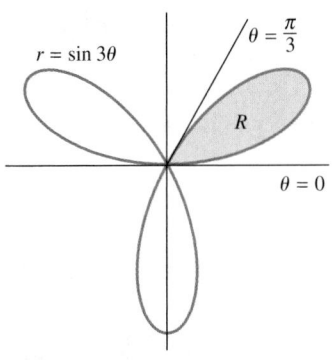

$r = \sin 3\theta$

$\theta = \frac{\pi}{3}$

R

$\theta = 0$

▲ **Figure 14.3.12**

■ **CONVERTING DOUBLE INTEGRALS FROM RECTANGULAR TO POLAR COORDINATES**

Sometimes a double integral that is difficult to evaluate in rectangular coordinates can be evaluated more easily in polar coordinates by making the substitution $x = r \cos \theta$, $y = r \sin \theta$ and expressing the region of integration in polar form; that is, we rewrite the double integral in rectangular coordinates as

$$\iint\limits_R f(x, y) \, dA = \iint\limits_R f(r \cos \theta, r \sin \theta) \, dA = \iint\limits_{\substack{\text{appropriate} \\ \text{limits}}} f(r \cos \theta, r \sin \theta) r \, dr \, d\theta \quad (9)$$

▶ **Example 4**   Use polar coordinates to evaluate $\displaystyle\int_{-1}^{1} \int_0^{\sqrt{1-x^2}} (x^2 + y^2)^{3/2} \, dy \, dx$.

Solution.   In this problem we are starting with an iterated integral in rectangular coordinates rather than a double integral, so before we can make the conversion to polar coordinates we will have to identify the region of integration. To do this, we observe that for fixed x the y-integration runs from $y = 0$ to $y = \sqrt{1 - x^2}$, which tells us that the lower boundary of the region is the x-axis and the upper boundary is a semicircle of radius 1 centered at the origin. From the x-integration we see that x varies from -1 to 1, so we conclude that the region of integration is as shown in Figure 14.3.13. In polar coordinates, this is the region swept out as r varies between 0 and 1 and θ varies between 0 and π. Thus,

$$\int_{-1}^{1} \int_0^{\sqrt{1-x^2}} (x^2 + y^2)^{3/2} \, dy \, dx = \iint\limits_R (x^2 + y^2)^{3/2} \, dA$$

$$= \int_0^{\pi} \int_0^1 (r^3) r \, dr \, d\theta = \int_0^{\pi} \frac{1}{5} \, d\theta = \frac{\pi}{5} \quad ◀$$

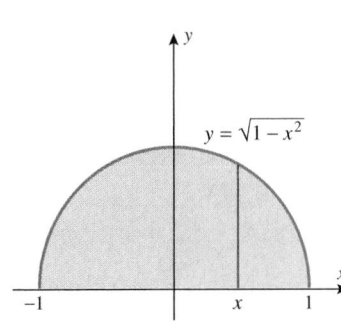

y

$y = \sqrt{1 - x^2}$

x

-1 x 1

▲ **Figure 14.3.13**

REMARK | The reason the conversion to polar coordinates worked so nicely in Example 4 is that the substitution $x = r \cos \theta$, $y = r \sin \theta$ collapsed the sum $x^2 + y^2$ into the single term r^2, thereby simplifying the integrand. Whenever you see an expression involving $x^2 + y^2$ in the integrand, you should consider the possibility of converting to polar coordinates.

✔ **QUICK CHECK EXERCISES 14.3** *(See page 1025 for answers.)*

1. The polar region inside the circle $r = 2\sin\theta$ and outside the circle $r = 1$ is a simple polar region given by the inequalities

$$\underline{\hspace{1cm}} \le r \le \underline{\hspace{1cm}}, \qquad \underline{\hspace{1cm}} \le \theta \le \underline{\hspace{1cm}}$$

2. Let R be the region in the first quadrant enclosed between the circles $x^2 + y^2 = 9$ and $x^2 + y^2 = 100$. Supply the missing limits of integration.

$$\iint\limits_{R} f(r, \theta)\, dA = \int_{\square}^{\square} \int_{\square}^{\square} f(r, \theta)\, r\, dr\, d\theta$$

3. Let V be the volume of the solid bounded above by the hemisphere $z = \sqrt{1 - r^2}$ and bounded below by the disk enclosed within the circle $r = \sin\theta$. Expressed as a double integral in polar coordinates, $V = \underline{\hspace{1cm}}$.

4. Express the iterated integral as a double integral in polar coordinates.

$$\int_{1/\sqrt{2}}^{1} \int_{\sqrt{1-x^2}}^{x} \left(\frac{1}{x^2 + y^2} \right) dy\, dx = \underline{\hspace{1cm}}$$

EXERCISE SET 14.3

1–6 Evaluate the iterated integral. ▪

1. $\displaystyle\int_{0}^{\pi/2} \int_{0}^{\sin\theta} r\cos\theta\, dr\, d\theta$

2. $\displaystyle\int_{0}^{\pi} \int_{0}^{1+\cos\theta} r\, dr\, d\theta$

3. $\displaystyle\int_{0}^{\pi/2} \int_{0}^{a\sin\theta} r^2\, dr\, d\theta$

4. $\displaystyle\int_{0}^{\pi/6} \int_{0}^{\cos 3\theta} r\, dr\, d\theta$

5. $\displaystyle\int_{0}^{\pi} \int_{0}^{1-\sin\theta} r^2\cos\theta\, dr\, d\theta$

6. $\displaystyle\int_{0}^{\pi/2} \int_{0}^{\cos\theta} r^3\, dr\, d\theta$

7–10 Use a double integral in polar coordinates to find the area of the region described. ▪

7. The region enclosed by the cardioid $r = 1 - \cos\theta$.

8. The region enclosed by the rose $r = \sin 2\theta$.

9. The region in the first quadrant bounded by $r = 1$ and $r = \sin 2\theta$, with $\pi/4 \le \theta \le \pi/2$.

10. The region inside the circle $x^2 + y^2 = 4$ and to the right of the line $x = 1$.

FOCUS ON CONCEPTS

11–12 Let R be the region described. Sketch the region R and fill in the missing limits of integration.

$$\iint\limits_{R} f(r, \theta)\, dA = \int_{\square}^{\square} \int_{\square}^{\square} f(r, \theta)\, r\, dr\, d\theta \;\; ▪$$

11. The region inside the circle $r = 4\sin\theta$ and outside the circle $r = 2$.

12. The region inside the circle $r = 1$ and outside the cardioid $r = 1 + \cos\theta$.

13–16 Express the volume of the solid described as a double integral in polar coordinates. ▪

13.

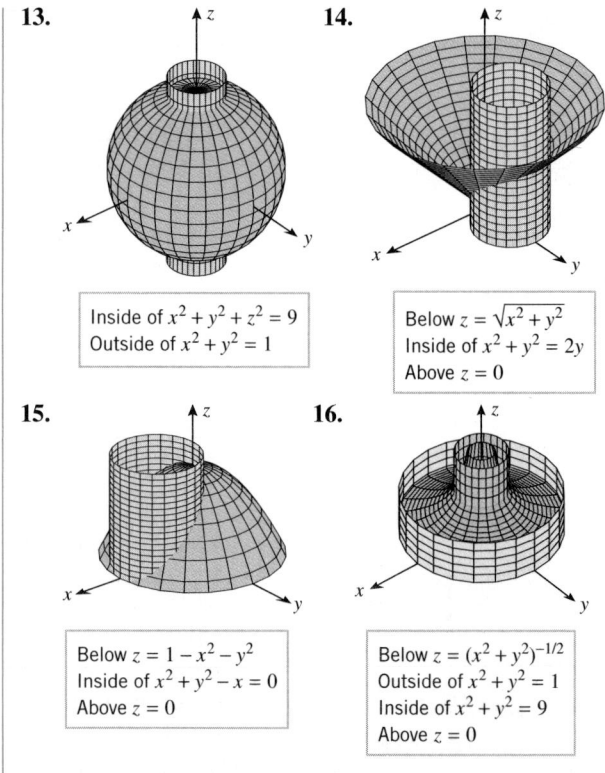

Inside of $x^2 + y^2 + z^2 = 9$
Outside of $x^2 + y^2 = 1$

14.

Below $z = \sqrt{x^2 + y^2}$
Inside of $x^2 + y^2 = 2y$
Above $z = 0$

15.

Below $z = 1 - x^2 - y^2$
Inside of $x^2 + y^2 - x = 0$
Above $z = 0$

16.

Below $z = (x^2 + y^2)^{-1/2}$
Outside of $x^2 + y^2 = 1$
Inside of $x^2 + y^2 = 9$
Above $z = 0$

17–20 Find the volume of the solid described in the indicated exercise. ▪

17. Exercise 13

18. Exercise 14

19. Exercise 15

20. Exercise 16

21. Find the volume of the solid in the first octant bounded above by the surface $z = r\sin\theta$, below by the xy-plane, and laterally by the plane $x = 0$ and the surface $r = 3\sin\theta$.

22. Find the volume of the solid inside the surface $r^2 + z^2 = 4$ and outside the surface $r = 2\cos\theta$.

23–26 Use polar coordinates to evaluate the double integral. ▪

23. $\displaystyle\iint\limits_R e^{-(x^2+y^2)}\,dA$, where R is the region enclosed by the circle $x^2 + y^2 = 1$.

24. $\displaystyle\iint\limits_R \sqrt{9 - x^2 - y^2}\,dA$, where R is the region in the first quadrant within the circle $x^2 + y^2 = 9$.

25. $\displaystyle\iint\limits_R \frac{1}{1 + x^2 + y^2}\,dA$, where R is the sector in the first quadrant bounded by $y = 0$, $y = x$, and $x^2 + y^2 = 4$.

26. $\displaystyle\iint\limits_R 2y\,dA$, where R is the region in the first quadrant bounded above by the circle $(x - 1)^2 + y^2 = 1$ and below by the line $y = x$.

27–34 Evaluate the iterated integral by converting to polar coordinates. ■

27. $\displaystyle\int_0^1 \int_0^{\sqrt{1-x^2}} (x^2 + y^2)\,dy\,dx$

28. $\displaystyle\int_{-2}^2 \int_{-\sqrt{4-y^2}}^{\sqrt{4-y^2}} e^{-(x^2+y^2)}\,dx\,dy$

29. $\displaystyle\int_0^2 \int_0^{\sqrt{2x-x^2}} \sqrt{x^2 + y^2}\,dy\,dx$

30. $\displaystyle\int_0^1 \int_0^{\sqrt{1-y^2}} \cos(x^2 + y^2)\,dx\,dy$

31. $\displaystyle\int_0^a \int_0^{\sqrt{a^2-x^2}} \frac{dy\,dx}{(1 + x^2 + y^2)^{3/2}}\quad (a > 0)$

32. $\displaystyle\int_0^1 \int_y^{\sqrt{y}} \sqrt{x^2 + y^2}\,dx\,dy$

33. $\displaystyle\int_0^{\sqrt{2}} \int_y^{\sqrt{4-y^2}} \frac{1}{\sqrt{1 + x^2 + y^2}}\,dx\,dy$

34. $\displaystyle\int_0^4 \int_3^{\sqrt{25-x^2}} dy\,dx$

35–38 True–False Determine whether the statement is true or false. Explain your answer. ■

35. The disk of radius 2 that is centered at the origin is a polar rectangle.

36. If f is continuous and nonnegative on a simple polar region R, then the volume of the solid enclosed between R and the surface $z = f(r, \theta)$ is expressed as

$$\iint\limits_R f(r, \theta)r\,dA$$

37. If R is the region in the first quadrant between the circles $r = 1$ and $r = 2$, and if f is continuous on R, then

$$\iint\limits_R f(r, \theta)\,dA = \int_0^{\pi/2} \int_1^2 f(r, \theta)\,dr\,d\theta$$

38. The area enclosed by the circle $r = \sin\theta$ is given by

$$A = \int_0^{2\pi} \int_0^{\sin\theta} r\,dr\,d\theta$$

39. Use a double integral in polar coordinates to find the volume of a cylinder of radius a and height h.

40. Suppose that a geyser, centered at the origin of a polar coordinate system, sprays water in a circular pattern in such a way that the depth D of water that reaches a point at a distance of r feet from the origin in 1 hour is $D = ke^{-r}$. Find the total volume of water that the geyser sprays inside a circle of radius R centered at the origin.

41. Evaluate $\displaystyle\iint\limits_R x^2\,dA$ over the region R shown in the accompanying figure.

42. Show that the shaded area in the accompanying figure is $a^2\phi - \frac{1}{2}a^2 \sin 2\phi$.

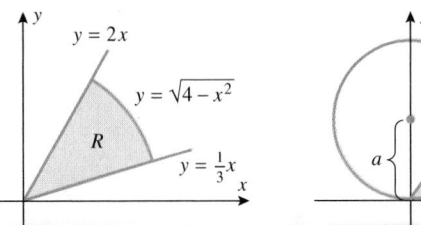

▲ **Figure Ex-41**   ▲ **Figure Ex-42**

43. (a) Use a double integral in polar coordinates to find the volume of the oblate spheroid

$$\frac{x^2}{a^2} + \frac{y^2}{a^2} + \frac{z^2}{c^2} = 1 \quad (0 < c < a)$$

   (b) Use the result in part (a) and the World Geodetic System of 1984 (WGS-84) discussed in Exercise 54 of Section 11.7 to find the volume of the Earth in cubic meters.

44. Use polar coordinates to find the volume of the solid that is above the xy-plane, inside the cylinder $x^2 + y^2 - ay = 0$, and inside the ellipsoid

$$\frac{x^2}{a^2} + \frac{y^2}{a^2} + \frac{z^2}{c^2} = 1$$

45. Find the area of the region enclosed by the lemniscate $r^2 = 2a^2 \cos 2\theta$.

46. Find the area in the first quadrant that is inside the circle $r = 4\sin\theta$ and outside the lemniscate $r^2 = 8\cos 2\theta$.

✔**QUICK CHECK ANSWERS 14.3**

1. $1 \le r \le 2\sin\theta$, $\pi/6 \le \theta \le 5\pi/6$ **2.** $\displaystyle\int_0^{\pi/2} \int_3^{10} f(r, \theta)r\,dr\,d\theta$ **3.** $\displaystyle\int_0^\pi \int_0^{\sin\theta} r\sqrt{1 - r^2}\,dr\,d\theta$ **4.** $\displaystyle\int_0^{\pi/4} \int_1^{\sec\theta} \frac{1}{r}\,dr\,d\theta$

14.4 SURFACE AREA; PARAMETRIC SURFACES

In Section 6.5 we showed how to find the surface area of a surface of revolution. In this section we will derive area formulas for surfaces with equations of the form $z = f(x, y)$ and for surfaces that are represented by parametric equations.

■ **SURFACE AREA FOR SURFACES OF THE FORM $z = f(x, y)$**

In Section 6.5 we obtained formulas for the surface area of a surface of revolution [see Formulas (4) and (5) of that section]. We now obtain a formula for the surface area S of a surface of the form $z = f(x, y)$.

Consider a surface σ of the form $z = f(x, y)$ defined over a region R in the xy-plane (Figure 14.4.1a). We will assume that f has continuous first partial derivatives at the interior points of R. (Geometrically, this means that the surface will have a nonvertical tangent plane at each interior point of R.) We begin by subdividing R into rectangular regions by lines parallel to the x- and y-axes and by discarding any nonrectangular portions that contain points on the boundary of R. Assume that what remains are n rectangles labeled $R_1, R_2, \ldots, R_n$.

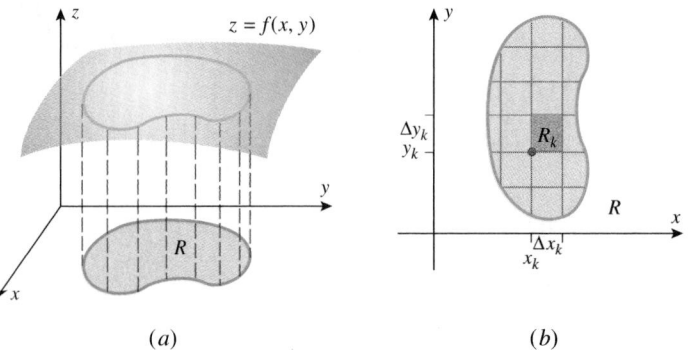

▶ **Figure 14.4.1**
      (a)   (b)

Let (x_k, y_k) be the lower left corner of the kth rectangle R_k, and assume that R_k has area $\Delta A_k = \Delta x_k \Delta y_k$, where Δx_k and Δy_k are the dimensions of R_k (Figure 14.4.1b). The portion of σ that lies over R_k will be some *curvilinear patch* on the surface that has a corner at $P_k(x_k, y_k, f(x_k, y_k))$; denote the area of this patch by ΔS_k (Figure 14.4.2a). To obtain an approximation of ΔS_k, we will replace σ by the tangent plane to σ at P_k. The equation of this tangent plane is

$$z = f(x_k, y_k) + f_x(x_k, y_k)(x - x_k) + f_y(x_k, y_k)(y - y_k)$$

(see Theorem 13.7.2). The portion of the tangent plane that lies over R_k will be a parallelogram τ_k. This parallelogram will have a vertex at P_k and adjacent sides determined by the

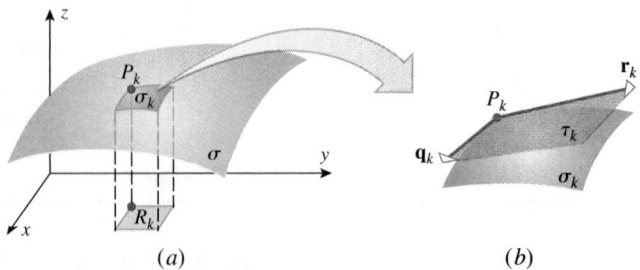

▶ **Figure 14.4.2**
      (a)   (b)

vectors

$$\mathbf{q}_k = \left\langle \Delta x_k, 0, \frac{\partial z}{\partial x} \Delta x_k \right\rangle \quad \text{and} \quad \mathbf{r}_k = \left\langle 0, \Delta y_k, \frac{\partial z}{\partial y} \Delta y_k \right\rangle$$

as illustrated in Figure 14.4.2b. [Here we use $\partial z/\partial x$ to represent $f_x(x_k, y_k)$ and $\partial z/\partial y$ to represent $f_y(x_k, y_k)$.]

If the dimensions of R_k are small, then τ_k should provide a good approximation to the curvilinear patch σ_k. By Theorem 11.4.5(b), the area of the parallelogram τ_k is the length of the cross product of $\mathbf{q}_k$ and $\mathbf{r}_k$. Thus, we expect the approximation

$$\Delta S_k \approx \text{area } \tau_k = \|\mathbf{q}_k \times \mathbf{r}_k\|$$

to be good when Δx_k and Δy_k are close to 0. Computing the cross product yields

$$\|\mathbf{q}_k \times \mathbf{r}_k\| = \begin{Vmatrix} \mathbf{i} & \mathbf{j} & \mathbf{k} \\ \Delta x_k & 0 & \dfrac{\partial z}{\partial x}\Delta x_k \\ 0 & \Delta y_k & \dfrac{\partial z}{\partial y}\Delta y_k \end{Vmatrix} = \left(-\frac{\partial z}{\partial x}\mathbf{i} - \frac{\partial z}{\partial y}\mathbf{j} + \mathbf{k} \right) \Delta x_k \Delta y_k$$

so

$$\Delta S_k \approx \left\| \left(-\frac{\partial z}{\partial x}\mathbf{i} - \frac{\partial z}{\partial y}\mathbf{j} + \mathbf{k} \right) \Delta x_k \Delta y_k \right\| = \left\| -\frac{\partial z}{\partial x}\mathbf{i} - \frac{\partial z}{\partial y}\mathbf{j} + \mathbf{k} \right\| \Delta x_k \Delta y_k$$

$$= \sqrt{\left(\frac{\partial z}{\partial x} \right)^2 + \left(\frac{\partial z}{\partial y} \right)^2 + 1} \, \Delta A_k \tag{1}$$

It follows that the surface area of the entire surface can be approximated as

$$S \approx \sum_{k=1}^{n} \sqrt{\left(\frac{\partial z}{\partial x} \right)^2 + \left(\frac{\partial z}{\partial y} \right)^2 + 1} \, \Delta A_k$$

If we assume that the errors in the approximations approach zero as n increases in such a way that the dimensions of the rectangles approach zero, then it is plausible that the exact value of S is

$$S = \lim_{n \to +\infty} \sum_{k=1}^{n} \sqrt{\left(\frac{\partial z}{\partial x} \right)^2 + \left(\frac{\partial z}{\partial y} \right)^2 + 1} \, \Delta A_k$$

or, equivalently,

$$S = \iint_R \sqrt{\left(\frac{\partial z}{\partial x} \right)^2 + \left(\frac{\partial z}{\partial y} \right)^2 + 1} \, dA \tag{2}$$

▶ **Example 1** Find the surface area of that portion of the surface $z = \sqrt{4 - x^2}$ that lies above the rectangle R in the xy-plane whose coordinates satisfy $0 \le x \le 1$ and $0 \le y \le 4$.

Solution. As shown in Figure 14.4.3, the surface is a portion of the cylinder $x^2 + z^2 = 4$. It follows from (2) that the surface area is

$$S = \iint_R \sqrt{\left(\frac{\partial z}{\partial x} \right)^2 + \left(\frac{\partial z}{\partial y} \right)^2 + 1} \, dA$$

$$= \iint_R \sqrt{\left(-\frac{x}{\sqrt{4-x^2}} \right)^2 + 0 + 1} \, dA = \int_0^4 \int_0^1 \frac{2}{\sqrt{4-x^2}} \, dx \, dy$$

$$= 2 \int_0^4 \left[\sin^{-1}\left(\frac{1}{2}x \right) \right]_{x=0}^{1} dy = 2 \int_0^4 \frac{\pi}{6} \, dy = \frac{4}{3}\pi \blacktriangleleft$$

Formula 21
of Section 7.1

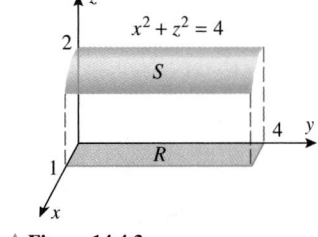

▲ **Figure 14.4.3**

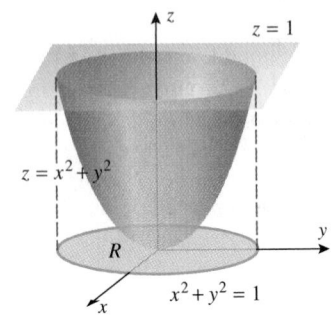

▲ **Figure 14.4.4**

▶ **Example 2**   Find the surface area of the portion of the paraboloid $z = x^2 + y^2$ below the plane $z = 1$.

Solution.   The surface $z = x^2 + y^2$ is the circular paraboloid shown in Figure 14.4.4. The trace of the paraboloid in the plane $z = 1$ projects onto the circle $x^2 + y^2 = 1$ in the xy-plane, and the portion of the paraboloid that lies below the plane $z = 1$ projects onto the region R that is enclosed by this circle. Thus, it follows from (2) that the surface area is

$$S = \iint\limits_{R} \sqrt{4x^2 + 4y^2 + 1}\, dA$$

The expression $4x^2 + 4y^2 + 1 = 4(x^2 + y^2) + 1$ in the integrand suggests that we evaluate the integral in polar coordinates. In accordance with Formula (9) of Section 14.3, we substitute $x = r\cos\theta$ and $y = r\sin\theta$ in the integrand, replace dA by $r\, dr\, d\theta$, and find the limits of integration by expressing the region R in polar coordinates. This yields

$$S = \int_0^{2\pi} \int_0^1 \sqrt{4r^2 + 1}\, r\, dr\, d\theta = \int_0^{2\pi} \left[\frac{1}{12}(4r^2 + 1)^{3/2} \right]_{r=0}^{1} d\theta$$

$$= \int_0^{2\pi} \frac{1}{12}(5\sqrt{5} - 1)\, d\theta = \frac{1}{6}\pi(5\sqrt{5} - 1) \blacktriangleleft$$

Some surfaces can't be described conveniently in terms of a function $z = f(x, y)$. For such surfaces, a parametric description may provide a simpler approach. We pause for a discussion of surfaces represented parametrically, with the ultimate goal of deriving a formula for the area of a parametric surface.

■ PARAMETRIC REPRESENTATION OF SURFACES

We have seen that curves in 3-space can be represented by three equations involving one parameter, say

$$x = x(t), \quad y = y(t), \quad z = z(t)$$

Surfaces in 3-space can be represented parametrically by three equations involving two parameters, say

$$x = x(u, v), \quad y = y(u, v), \quad z = z(u, v) \tag{3}$$

To visualize why such equations represent a surface, think of (u, v) as a point that varies over some region in a uv-plane. If u is held constant, then v is the only varying parameter in (3), and hence these equations represent a curve in 3-space. We call this a ***constant u-curve*** (Figure 14.4.5). Similarly, if v is held constant, then u is the only varying parameter in (3), so again these equations represent a curve in 3-space. We call this a ***constant v-curve***. By varying the constants we generate a family of u-curves and a family of v-curves that together form a surface.

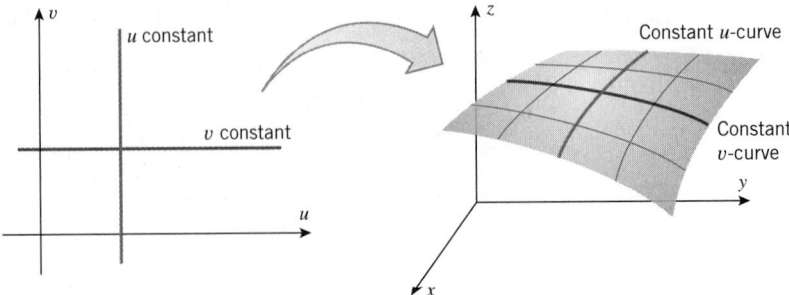

▶ **Figure 14.4.5**

▶ **Example 3**   Consider the paraboloid $z = 4 - x^2 - y^2$. One way to parametrize this surface is to take $x = u$ and $y = v$ as the parameters, in which case the surface is represented by the parametric equations

$$x = u, \quad y = v, \quad z = 4 - u^2 - v^2 \tag{4}$$

Figure 14.4.6a shows a computer-generated graph of this surface. The constant u-curves correspond to constant x-values and hence appear on the surface as traces parallel to the yz-plane. Similarly, the constant v-curves correspond to constant y-values and hence appear on the surface as traces parallel to the xz-plane. ◀

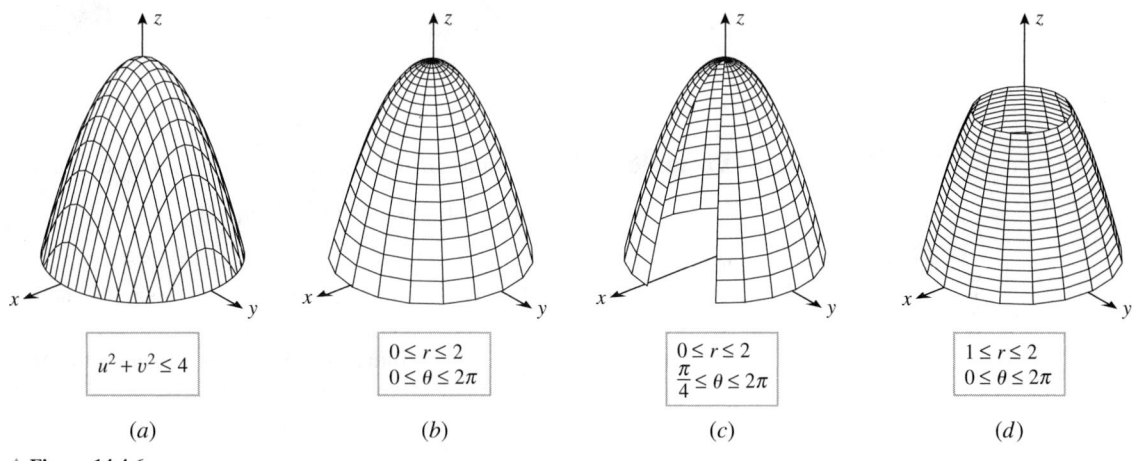

▲ **Figure 14.4.6**

▶ **Example 4**   The paraboloid $z = 4 - x^2 - y^2$ that was considered in Example 3 can also be parametrized by first expressing the equation in cylindrical coordinates. For this purpose, we make the substitution $x = r\cos\theta$, $y = r\sin\theta$, which yields $z = 4 - r^2$. Thus, the paraboloid can be represented parametrically in terms of r and θ as

$$x = r\cos\theta, \quad y = r\sin\theta, \quad z = 4 - r^2 \tag{5}$$

A computer-generated graph of this surface for $0 \le r \le 2$ and $0 \le \theta \le 2\pi$ is shown in Figure 14.4.6b. The constant r-curves correspond to constant z-values and hence appear on the surface as traces parallel to the xy-plane. The constant θ-curves appear on the surface as traces from vertical planes through the origin at varying angles with the x-axis. Parts (c) and (d) of Figure 14.4.6 show the effect of restrictions on the parameters r and θ. ◀

TECHNOLOGY MASTERY

If you have a graphing utility that can generate parametric surfaces, consult the relevant documentation and then try to generate the surfaces in Figure 14.4.6.

▶ **Example 5**   One way to generate the sphere $x^2 + y^2 + z^2 = 1$ with a graphing utility is to graph the upper and lower hemispheres

$$z = \sqrt{1 - x^2 - y^2} \quad \text{and} \quad z = -\sqrt{1 - x^2 - y^2}$$

on the same screen. However, this sometimes produces a fragmented sphere (Figure 14.4.7a) because roundoff error sporadically produces negative values inside the radical when $1 - x^2 - y^2$ is near zero. A better graph can be generated by first expressing the sphere in spherical coordinates as $\rho = 1$ and then using the spherical-to-rectangular conversion formulas in Table 11.8.1 to obtain the parametric equations

$$x = \sin\phi\cos\theta, \quad y = \sin\phi\sin\theta, \quad z = \cos\phi$$

with parameters θ and ϕ. Figure 14.4.7b shows the graph of this parametric surface for

$0 \le \theta \le 2\pi$ and $0 \le \phi \le \pi$. In the language of cartographers, the constant ϕ-curves are the *lines of latitude* and the constant θ-curves are the *lines of longitude*. ◄

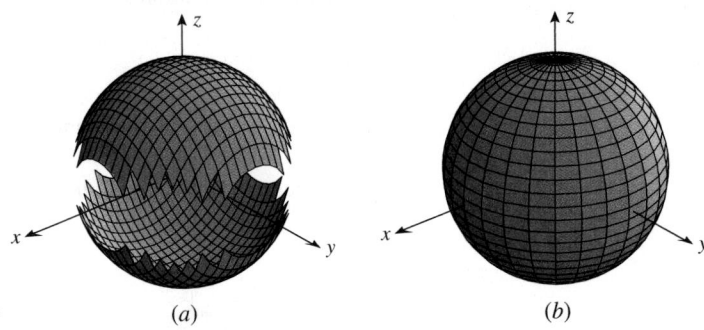

▶ **Figure 14.4.7**   (a)   (b)

▶ **Example 6**   Find parametric equations for the portion of the right circular cylinder

$$x^2 + z^2 = 9 \quad \text{for which} \quad 0 \le y \le 5$$

in terms of the parameters u and v shown in Figure 14.4.8a. The parameter u is the y-coordinate of a point $P(x, y, z)$ on the surface, and v is the angle shown in the figure.

Solution.   The radius of the cylinder is 3, so it is evident from the figure that $y = u$, $x = 3\cos v$, and $z = 3\sin v$. Thus, the surface can be represented parametrically as

$$x = 3\cos v, \quad y = u, \quad z = 3\sin v$$

To obtain the portion of the surface from $y = 0$ to $y = 5$, we let the parameter u vary over the interval $0 \le u \le 5$, and to ensure that the entire lateral surface is covered, we let the parameter v vary over the interval $0 \le v \le 2\pi$. Figure 14.4.8b shows a computer-generated graph of the surface in which u and v vary over these intervals. Constant u-curves appear as circular traces parallel to the xz-plane, and constant v-curves appear as lines parallel to the y-axis. ◄

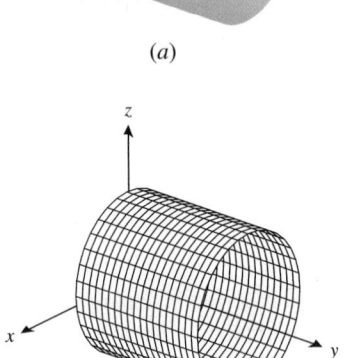

(a)

(b)

▲ **Figure 14.4.8**

■ REPRESENTING SURFACES OF REVOLUTION PARAMETRICALLY

The basic idea of Example 6 can be adapted to obtain parametric equations for surfaces of revolution. For example, suppose that we want to find parametric equations for the surface generated by revolving the plane curve $y = f(x)$ about the x-axis. Figure 14.4.9 suggests that the surface can be represented parametrically as

$$x = u, \quad y = f(u)\cos v, \quad z = f(u)\sin v \tag{6}$$

where v is the angle shown.

In the exercises we will discuss formulas analogous to (6) for surfaces of revolution about other axes.

▶ **Example 7**   Find parametric equations for the surface generated by revolving the curve $y = 1/x$ about the x-axis.

Solution.   From (6) this surface can be represented parametrically as

$$x = u, \quad y = \frac{1}{u}\cos v, \quad z = \frac{1}{u}\sin v$$

A general principle for representing surfaces of revolution parametrically is to let the variable about whose axis the curve is revolving be equal to u and let the other variables be $f(u)\cos v$ and $f(u)\sin v$.

Figure 14.4.10 shows a computer-generated graph of the surface in which $0.7 \le u \le 5$ and $0 \le v \le 2\pi$. This surface is a portion of Gabriel's horn, which was discussed in Exercise 55 of Section 7.8. ◄

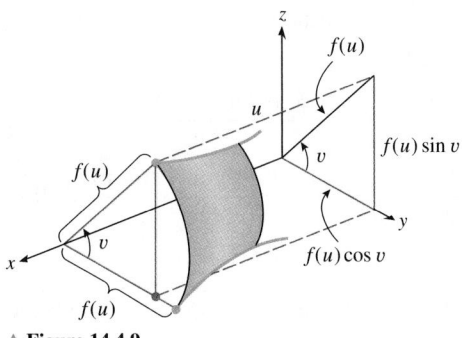

▲ **Figure 14.4.9**

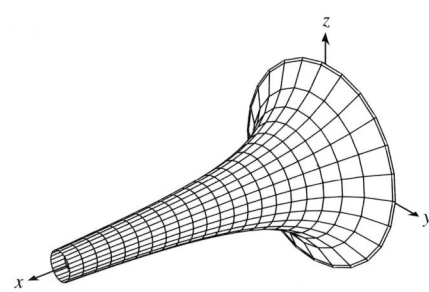

▲ **Figure 14.4.10**

■ VECTOR-VALUED FUNCTIONS OF TWO VARIABLES

Recall that the parametric equations

$$x = x(t), \quad y = y(t), \quad z = z(t)$$

can be expressed in vector form as

$$\mathbf{r} = x(t)\mathbf{i} + y(t)\mathbf{j} + z(t)\mathbf{k}$$

where $\mathbf{r} = x\mathbf{i} + y\mathbf{j} + z\mathbf{k}$ is the radius vector and $\mathbf{r}(t) = x(t)\mathbf{i} + y(t)\mathbf{j} + z(t)\mathbf{k}$ is a vector-valued function of one variable. Similarly, the parametric equations

$$x = x(u, v), \quad y = y(u, v), \quad z = z(u, v)$$

can be expressed in vector form as

$$\mathbf{r} = x(u, v)\mathbf{i} + y(u, v)\mathbf{j} + z(u, v)\mathbf{k}$$

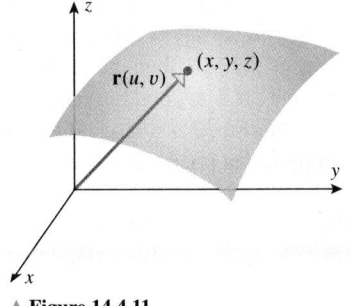

▲ **Figure 14.4.11**

Here the function $\mathbf{r}(u, v) = x(u, v)\mathbf{i} + y(u, v)\mathbf{j} + z(u, v)\mathbf{k}$ is a ***vector-valued function of two variables***. We define the ***graph*** of $\mathbf{r}(u, v)$ to be the graph of the corresponding parametric equations. Geometrically, we can view $\mathbf{r}$ as a vector from the origin to a point (x, y, z) that moves over the surface $\mathbf{r} = \mathbf{r}(u, v)$ as u and v vary (Figure 14.4.11). As with vector-valued functions of one variable, we say that $\mathbf{r}(u, v)$ is ***continuous*** if each component is continuous.

▶ **Example 8** The paraboloid in Example 3 was expressed parametrically as

$$x = u, \quad y = v, \quad z = 4 - u^2 - v^2$$

These equations can be expressed in vector form as

$$\mathbf{r} = u\mathbf{i} + v\mathbf{j} + (4 - u^2 - v^2)\mathbf{k} \quad ◀$$

■ PARTIAL DERIVATIVES OF VECTOR-VALUED FUNCTIONS

Partial derivatives of vector-valued functions of two variables are obtained by taking partial derivatives of the components. For example, if

$$\mathbf{r}(u, v) = x(u, v)\mathbf{i} + y(u, v)\mathbf{j} + z(u, v)\mathbf{k}$$

then

$$\frac{\partial \mathbf{r}}{\partial u} = \frac{\partial x}{\partial u}\mathbf{i} + \frac{\partial y}{\partial u}\mathbf{j} + \frac{\partial z}{\partial u}\mathbf{k}$$

$$\frac{\partial \mathbf{r}}{\partial v} = \frac{\partial x}{\partial v}\mathbf{i} + \frac{\partial y}{\partial v}\mathbf{j} + \frac{\partial z}{\partial v}\mathbf{k}$$

These derivatives can also be written as $\mathbf{r}_u$ and $\mathbf{r}_v$ or $\mathbf{r}_u(u, v)$ and $\mathbf{r}_v(u, v)$ and can be expressed as the limits

$$\frac{\partial \mathbf{r}}{\partial u} = \lim_{\Delta u \to 0} \frac{\mathbf{r}(u + \Delta u, v) - \mathbf{r}(u, v)}{\Delta u} = \lim_{w \to u} \frac{\mathbf{r}(w, v) - \mathbf{r}(u, v)}{w - u} \tag{7}$$

$$\frac{\partial \mathbf{r}}{\partial v} = \lim_{\Delta v \to 0} \frac{\mathbf{r}(u, v + \Delta v) - \mathbf{r}(u, v)}{\Delta v} = \lim_{w \to v} \frac{\mathbf{r}(u, w) - \mathbf{r}(u, v)}{w - v} \tag{8}$$

▶ **Example 9**   Find the partial derivatives of the vector-valued function $\mathbf{r}$ in Example 8.

Solution.

$$\frac{\partial \mathbf{r}}{\partial u} = \frac{\partial}{\partial u}[u\mathbf{i} + v\mathbf{j} + (4 - u^2 - v^2)\mathbf{k}] = \mathbf{i} - 2u\mathbf{k}$$

$$\frac{\partial \mathbf{r}}{\partial v} = \frac{\partial}{\partial v}[u\mathbf{i} + v\mathbf{j} + (4 - u^2 - v^2)\mathbf{k}] = \mathbf{j} - 2v\mathbf{k} \blacktriangleleft$$

■ **TANGENT PLANES TO PARAMETRIC SURFACES**

Our next objective is to show how to find tangent planes to parametric surfaces. Let σ denote a parametric surface in 3-space, with P_0 a point on σ. We will say that a plane is *tangent* to σ at P_0 provided a line through P_0 lies in the plane if and only if it is a tangent line at P_0 to a curve on σ. We showed in Section 13.7 that if $z = f(x, y)$, then the graph of f has a tangent plane at a point if f is differentiable at that point. It is beyond the scope of this text to obtain precise conditions under which a parametric surface has a tangent plane at a point, so we will simply assume the existence of tangent planes at points of interest and focus on finding their equations.

Suppose that the parametric surface σ is the graph of the vector-valued function $\mathbf{r}(u, v)$ and that we are interested in the tangent plane at the point (x_0, y_0, z_0) on the surface that corresponds to the parameter values $u = u_0$ and $v = v_0$; that is,

$$\mathbf{r}(u_0, v_0) = x_0\mathbf{i} + y_0\mathbf{j} + z_0\mathbf{k}$$

If $v = v_0$ is kept fixed and u is allowed to vary, then $\mathbf{r}(u, v_0)$ is a vector-valued function of one variable whose graph is the constant v-curve through the point (u_0, v_0); similarly, if $u = u_0$ is kept fixed and v is allowed to vary, then $\mathbf{r}(u_0, v)$ is a vector-valued function of one variable whose graph is the constant u-curve through the point (u_0, v_0). Moreover, it follows from the geometric interpretation of the derivative developed in Section 12.2 that if $\partial \mathbf{r}/\partial u \neq \mathbf{0}$ at (u_0, v_0), then this vector is tangent to the constant v-curve through (u_0, v_0); and if $\partial \mathbf{r}/\partial v \neq \mathbf{0}$ at (u_0, v_0), then this vector is tangent to the constant u-curve through (u_0, v_0) (Figure 14.4.12). Thus, if $\partial \mathbf{r}/\partial u \times \partial \mathbf{r}/\partial v \neq \mathbf{0}$ at (u_0, v_0), then the vector

$$\frac{\partial \mathbf{r}}{\partial u} \times \frac{\partial \mathbf{r}}{\partial v} = \begin{vmatrix} \mathbf{i} & \mathbf{j} & \mathbf{k} \\ \dfrac{\partial x}{\partial u} & \dfrac{\partial y}{\partial u} & \dfrac{\partial z}{\partial u} \\ \dfrac{\partial x}{\partial v} & \dfrac{\partial y}{\partial v} & \dfrac{\partial z}{\partial v} \end{vmatrix} \tag{9}$$

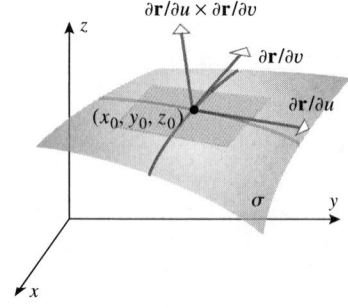

▲ **Figure 14.4.12**

is orthogonal to both tangent vectors at the point (u_0, v_0) and hence is normal to the tangent plane and the surface at this point (Figure 14.4.12). Accordingly, we make the following definition.

14.4.1 **DEFINITION** If a parametric surface σ is the graph of $\mathbf{r} = \mathbf{r}(u, v)$, and if $\partial\mathbf{r}/\partial u \times \partial\mathbf{r}/\partial v \neq \mathbf{0}$ at a point on the surface, then the **principal unit normal vector** to the surface at that point is denoted by $\mathbf{n}$ or $\mathbf{n}(u, v)$ and is defined as

$$\mathbf{n} = \frac{\dfrac{\partial\mathbf{r}}{\partial u} \times \dfrac{\partial\mathbf{r}}{\partial v}}{\left\| \dfrac{\partial\mathbf{r}}{\partial u} \times \dfrac{\partial\mathbf{r}}{\partial v} \right\|} \qquad (10)$$

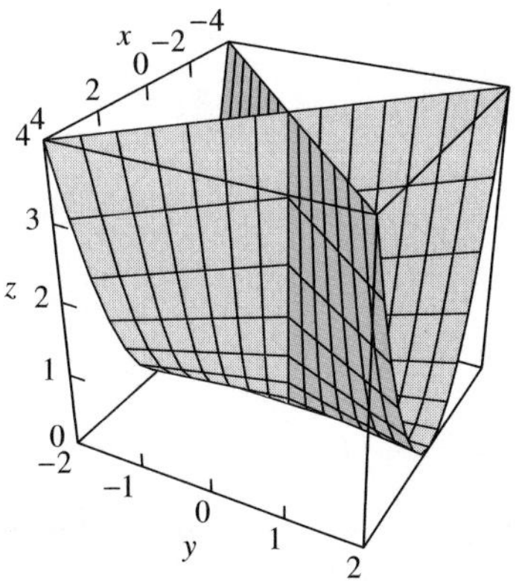

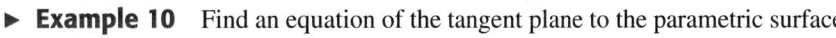

▲ **Figure 14.4.13**

▶ **Example 10** Find an equation of the tangent plane to the parametric surface

$$x = uv, \quad y = u, \quad z = v^2$$

at the point where $u = 2$ and $v = -1$. This surface, called **Whitney's umbrella**, is an example of a self-intersecting parametric surface (Figure 14.4.13).

Solution. We start by writing the equations in the vector form

$$\mathbf{r} = uv\mathbf{i} + u\mathbf{j} + v^2\mathbf{k}$$

The partial derivatives of $\mathbf{r}$ are

$$\frac{\partial\mathbf{r}}{\partial u}(u, v) = v\mathbf{i} + \mathbf{j}$$

$$\frac{\partial\mathbf{r}}{\partial v}(u, v) = u\mathbf{i} + 2v\mathbf{k}$$

and at $u = 2$ and $v = -1$ these partial derivatives are

$$\frac{\partial\mathbf{r}}{\partial u}(2, -1) = -\mathbf{i} + \mathbf{j}$$

$$\frac{\partial\mathbf{r}}{\partial v}(2, -1) = 2\mathbf{i} - 2\mathbf{k}$$

Thus, from (9) and (10) a normal to the surface at this point is

$$\frac{\partial\mathbf{r}}{\partial u}(2, -1) \times \frac{\partial\mathbf{r}}{\partial v}(2, -1) = \begin{vmatrix} \mathbf{i} & \mathbf{j} & \mathbf{k} \\ -1 & 1 & 0 \\ 2 & 0 & -2 \end{vmatrix} = -2\mathbf{i} - 2\mathbf{j} - 2\mathbf{k}$$

Since any normal will suffice to find the tangent plane, it makes sense to multiply this vector by $-\frac{1}{2}$ and use the simpler normal $\mathbf{i} + \mathbf{j} + \mathbf{k}$. It follows from the given parametric equations that the point on the surface corresponding to $u = 2$ and $v = -1$ is $(-2, 2, 1)$, so the tangent plane at this point can be expressed in point-normal form as

Convince yourself that the result obtained in Example 10 is consistent with Figure 14.4.13.

$$(x + 2) + (y - 2) + (z - 1) = 0 \quad \text{or} \quad x + y + z = 1 \quad ◀$$

▶ **Example 11** The sphere $x^2 + y^2 + z^2 = a^2$ can be expressed in spherical coordinates as $\rho = a$, and the spherical-to-rectangular conversion formulas in Table 11.8.1 can then be used to express the sphere as the graph of the vector-valued function

$$\mathbf{r}(\phi, \theta) = a \sin\phi \cos\theta\mathbf{i} + a \sin\phi \sin\theta\mathbf{j} + a \cos\phi\mathbf{k}$$

where $0 \leq \phi \leq \pi$ and $0 \leq \theta \leq 2\pi$ (verify). Use this function to show that the radius vector is normal to the tangent plane at each point on the sphere.

Solution. We will show that at each point of the sphere the unit normal vector $\mathbf{n}$ is a scalar multiple of $\mathbf{r}$ (and hence is parallel to $\mathbf{r}$). We have

$$\frac{\partial \mathbf{r}}{\partial \phi} \times \frac{\partial \mathbf{r}}{\partial \theta} = \begin{vmatrix} \mathbf{i} & \mathbf{j} & \mathbf{k} \\ \dfrac{\partial x}{\partial \phi} & \dfrac{\partial y}{\partial \phi} & \dfrac{\partial z}{\partial \phi} \\ \dfrac{\partial x}{\partial \theta} & \dfrac{\partial y}{\partial \theta} & \dfrac{\partial z}{\partial \theta} \end{vmatrix} = \begin{vmatrix} \mathbf{i} & \mathbf{j} & \mathbf{k} \\ a \cos \phi \cos \theta & a \cos \phi \sin \theta & -a \sin \phi \\ -a \sin \phi \sin \theta & a \sin \phi \cos \theta & 0 \end{vmatrix}$$

$$= a^2 \sin^2 \phi \cos \theta \mathbf{i} + a^2 \sin^2 \phi \sin \theta \mathbf{j} + a^2 \sin \phi \cos \phi \mathbf{k}$$

and hence

$$\left\| \frac{\partial \mathbf{r}}{\partial \phi} \times \frac{\partial \mathbf{r}}{\partial \theta} \right\| = \sqrt{a^4 \sin^4 \phi \cos^2 \theta + a^4 \sin^4 \phi \sin^2 \theta + a^4 \sin^2 \phi \cos^2 \phi}$$

$$= \sqrt{a^4 \sin^4 \phi + a^4 \sin^2 \phi \cos^2 \phi}$$

$$= a^2 \sqrt{\sin^2 \phi} = a^2 |\sin \phi| = a^2 \sin \phi$$

For $\phi \neq 0$ or π, it follows from (10) that

$$\mathbf{n} = \sin \phi \cos \theta \mathbf{i} + \sin \phi \sin \theta \mathbf{j} + \cos \phi \mathbf{k} = \frac{1}{a} \mathbf{r}$$

Furthermore, the tangent planes at $\phi \neq 0$ or π are horizontal, to which $\mathbf{r} = \pm a \mathbf{k}$ is clearly normal. ◄

■ SURFACE AREA OF PARAMETRIC SURFACES

We now obtain a formula for the surface area S of a parametric surface σ. Let σ be a parametric surface whose vector equation is

$$\mathbf{r} = x(u, v)\mathbf{i} + y(u, v)\mathbf{j} + z(u, v)\mathbf{k}$$

Our discussion will be analogous to the case for surfaces of the form $z = f(x, y)$. Here, R will be a region in the uv-plane that we subdivide into n rectangular regions as shown in Figure 14.4.14a. Let R_k be the kth rectangular region, and denote its area by ΔA_k. The patch σ_k is the image of R_k on σ. The patch will have a corner at $\mathbf{r}(u_k, v_k)$; denote the area of σ_k by ΔS_k (Figure 14.4.14b).

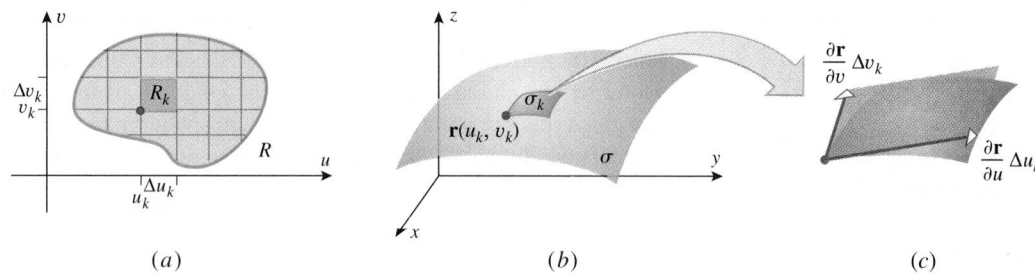

(a) (b) (c)

▲ **Figure 14.4.14**

Recall that in the case of $z = f(x, y)$ we used the area of a parallelogram in a tangent plane to the surface to approximate the area of the patch. In the parametric case, the desired parallelogram is spanned by the tangent vectors

$$\frac{\partial \mathbf{r}}{\partial u} \Delta u_k \quad \text{and} \quad \frac{\partial \mathbf{r}}{\partial v} \Delta v_k$$

where the partial derivatives are evaluated at (u_k, v_k) (Figure 14.4.14c). Thus,

$$\Delta S_k \approx \left\| \frac{\partial \mathbf{r}}{\partial u} \Delta u_k \times \frac{\partial \mathbf{r}}{\partial v} \Delta v_k \right\| = \left\| \frac{\partial \mathbf{r}}{\partial u} \times \frac{\partial \mathbf{r}}{\partial v} \right\| \Delta u_k \Delta v_k = \left\| \frac{\partial \mathbf{r}}{\partial u} \times \frac{\partial \mathbf{r}}{\partial v} \right\| \Delta A_k \qquad (11)$$

The surface area of the entire surface is the sum of the areas ΔS_k. If we assume that the errors in the approximations in (11) approach zero as n increases in such a way that the dimensions of the rectangles R_k approach zero, then it is plausible that the exact value of S is

$$S = \lim_{n \to +\infty} \sum_{k=1}^{n} \left\| \frac{\partial \mathbf{r}}{\partial u} \times \frac{\partial \mathbf{r}}{\partial v} \right\| \Delta A_k$$

or, equivalently,

$$S = \iint\limits_{R} \left\| \frac{\partial \mathbf{r}}{\partial u} \times \frac{\partial \mathbf{r}}{\partial v} \right\| dA \qquad (12)$$

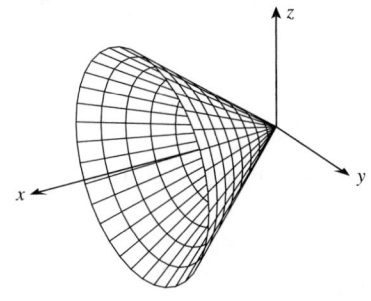

▲ **Figure 14.4.15**

▶ **Example 12** It follows from (6) that the parametric equations

$$x = u, \quad y = u \cos v, \quad z = u \sin v$$

represent the cone that results when the line $y = x$ in the xy-plane is revolved about the x-axis. Use Formula (12) to find the surface area of that portion of the cone for which $0 \le u \le 2$ and $0 \le v \le 2\pi$ (Figure 14.4.15).

Solution. The surface can be expressed in vector form as

$$\mathbf{r} = u\mathbf{i} + u \cos v\mathbf{j} + u \sin v\mathbf{k} \quad (0 \le u \le 2, \ 0 \le v \le 2\pi)$$

Thus,

$$\frac{\partial \mathbf{r}}{\partial u} = \mathbf{i} + \cos v\mathbf{j} + \sin v\mathbf{k}$$

$$\frac{\partial \mathbf{r}}{\partial v} = -u \sin v\mathbf{j} + u \cos v\mathbf{k}$$

$$\frac{\partial \mathbf{r}}{\partial u} \times \frac{\partial \mathbf{r}}{\partial v} = \begin{vmatrix} \mathbf{i} & \mathbf{j} & \mathbf{k} \\ 1 & \cos v & \sin v \\ 0 & -u \sin v & u \cos v \end{vmatrix} = u\mathbf{i} - u \cos v\mathbf{j} - u \sin v\mathbf{k}$$

$$\left\| \frac{\partial \mathbf{r}}{\partial u} \times \frac{\partial \mathbf{r}}{\partial v} \right\| = \sqrt{u^2 + (-u \cos v)^2 + (-u \sin v)^2} = |u|\sqrt{2} = u\sqrt{2}$$

Thus, from (12)

$$S = \iint\limits_{R} \left\| \frac{\partial \mathbf{r}}{\partial u} \times \frac{\partial \mathbf{r}}{\partial v} \right\| dA = \int_{0}^{2\pi} \int_{0}^{2} \sqrt{2} u \, du \, dv = 2\sqrt{2} \int_{0}^{2\pi} dv = 4\pi\sqrt{2} \blacktriangleleft$$

✔ **QUICK CHECK EXERCISES 14.4**   (*See page 1039 for answers.*)

1. The surface area of a surface of the form $z = f(x, y)$ over a region R in the xy-plane is given by

$$S = \iint\limits_{R} \underline{\hspace{2cm}} dA$$

2. Consider the surface represented parametrically by

$$\begin{aligned} x &= 1 - u \\ y &= (1 - u) \cos v \quad (0 \le u \le 1, 0 \le v \le 2\pi) \\ z &= (1 - u) \sin v \end{aligned}$$

(a) Describe the constant u-curves.
(b) Describe the constant v-curves.

3. If

$$\mathbf{r}(u, v) = (1 - u)\mathbf{i} + [(1 - u) \cos v]\mathbf{j} + [(1 - u) \sin v]\mathbf{k}$$

then

$$\frac{\partial \mathbf{r}}{\partial u} = \underline{\hspace{1cm}} \quad \text{and} \quad \frac{\partial \mathbf{r}}{\partial v} = \underline{\hspace{1cm}}.$$

4. If

$$\mathbf{r}(u, v) = (1 - u)\mathbf{i} + [(1 - u) \cos v]\mathbf{j} + [(1 - u) \sin v]\mathbf{k}$$

the principal unit normal to the graph of $\mathbf{r}$ at the point where $u = 1/2$ and $v = \pi/6$ is given by _____.

5. Suppose σ is a parametric surface with vector equation

$$\mathbf{r}(u, v) = x(u, v)\mathbf{i} + y(u, v)\mathbf{j} + z(u, v)\mathbf{k}$$

If σ has no self-intersections and σ is smooth on a region R in the uv-plane, then the surface area of σ is given by

$$S = \iint\limits_{R} \underline{\hspace{1cm}} \, dA$$

EXERCISE SET 14.4    Graphing Utility   CAS

1–4 Express the area of the given surface as an iterated double integral, and then find the surface area. ■

1. The portion of the cylinder $y^2 + z^2 = 9$ that is above the rectangle $R = \{(x, y) : 0 \le x \le 2, -3 \le y \le 3\}$.

2. The portion of the plane $2x + 2y + z = 8$ in the first octant.

3. The portion of the cone $z^2 = 4x^2 + 4y^2$ that is above the region in the first quadrant bounded by the line $y = x$ and the parabola $y = x^2$.

4. The portion of the surface $z = 2x + y^2$ that is above the triangular region with vertices $(0, 0)$, $(0, 1)$, and $(1, 1)$.

5–10 Express the area of the given surface as an iterated double integral in polar coordinates, and then find the surface area. ■

5. The portion of the cone $z = \sqrt{x^2 + y^2}$ that lies inside the cylinder $x^2 + y^2 = 2x$.

6. The portion of the paraboloid $z = 1 - x^2 - y^2$ that is above the xy-plane.

7. The portion of the surface $z = xy$ that is above the sector in the first quadrant bounded by the lines $y = x/\sqrt{3}$, $y = 0$, and the circle $x^2 + y^2 = 9$.

8. The portion of the paraboloid $2z = x^2 + y^2$ that is inside the cylinder $x^2 + y^2 = 8$.

9. The portion of the sphere $x^2 + y^2 + z^2 = 16$ between the planes $z = 1$ and $z = 2$.

10. The portion of the sphere $x^2 + y^2 + z^2 = 8$ that is inside the cone $z = \sqrt{x^2 + y^2}$.

11–12 Sketch the parametric surface. ■

11. (a) $x = u$, $y = v$, $z = \sqrt{u^2 + v^2}$
　　(b) $x = u$, $y = \sqrt{u^2 + v^2}$, $z = v$
　　(c) $x = \sqrt{u^2 + v^2}$, $y = u$, $z = v$

12. (a) $x = u$, $y = v$, $z = u^2 + v^2$
　　(b) $x = u$, $y = u^2 + v^2$, $z = v$
　　(c) $x = u^2 + v^2$, $y = u$, $z = v$

13–14 Find a parametric representation of the surface in terms of the parameters $u = x$ and $v = y$. ■

13. (a) $2z - 3x + 4y = 5$　　(b) $z = x^2$

14. (a) $z + zx^2 - y = 0$　　(b) $y^2 - 3z = 5$

15. (a) Find parametric equations for the portion of the cylinder $x^2 + y^2 = 5$ that extends between the planes $z = 0$ and $z = 1$.
　　(b) Find parametric equations for the portion of the cylinder $x^2 + z^2 = 4$ that extends between the planes $y = 1$ and $y = 3$.

16. (a) Find parametric equations for the portion of the plane $x + y = 1$ that extends between the planes $z = -1$ and $z = 1$.
　　(b) Find parametric equations for the portion of the plane $y - 2z = 5$ that extends between the planes $x = 0$ and $x = 3$.

17. Find parametric equations for the surface generated by revolving the curve $y = \sin x$ about the x-axis.

18. Find parametric equations for the surface generated by revolving the curve $y - e^x = 0$ about the x-axis.

19–24 Find a parametric representation of the surface in terms of the parameters r and θ, where (r, θ, z) are the cylindrical coordinates of a point on the surface. ■

19. $z = \dfrac{1}{1 + x^2 + y^2}$　　**20.** $z = e^{-(x^2 + y^2)}$

21. $z = 2xy$　　**22.** $z = x^2 - y^2$

23. The portion of the sphere $x^2 + y^2 + z^2 = 9$ on or above the plane $z = 2$.

24. The portion of the cone $z = \sqrt{x^2 + y^2}$ on or below the plane $z = 3$.

25. Find a parametric representation of the cone

$$z = \sqrt{3x^2 + 3y^2}$$

in terms of parameters ρ and θ, where (ρ, θ, ϕ) are spherical coordinates of a point on the surface.

26. Describe the cylinder $x^2 + y^2 = 9$ in terms of parameters θ and ϕ, where (ρ, θ, ϕ) are spherical coordinates of a point on the surface.

27–32 Eliminate the parameters to obtain an equation in rectangular coordinates, and describe the surface. ■

27. $x = 2u + v$, $y = u - v$, $z = 3v$ for $-\infty < u < +\infty$ and $-\infty < v < +\infty$.

28. $x = u \cos v$, $y = u^2$, $z = u \sin v$ for $0 \le u \le 2$ and $0 \le v < 2\pi$.

29. $x = 3 \sin u$, $y = 2 \cos u$, $z = 2v$ for $0 \le u < 2\pi$ and $1 \le v \le 2$.

30. $x = \sqrt{u} \cos v$, $y = \sqrt{u} \sin v$, $z = u$ for $0 \le u \le 4$ and $0 \le v < 2\pi$.

31. $\mathbf{r}(u, v) = 3u \cos v \mathbf{i} + 4u \sin v \mathbf{j} + u \mathbf{k}$ for $0 \le u \le 1$ and $0 \le v < 2\pi$.

32. $\mathbf{r}(u, v) = \sin u \cos v \mathbf{i} + 2 \sin u \sin v \mathbf{j} + 3 \cos u \mathbf{k}$ for $0 \le u \le \pi$ and $0 \le v < 2\pi$.

33. The accompanying figure shows the graphs of two parametric representations of the cone $z = \sqrt{x^2 + y^2}$ for $0 \le z \le 2$.
  (a) Find parametric equations that produce reasonable facsimiles of these surfaces.
  (b) Use a graphing utility to check your answer in part (a).

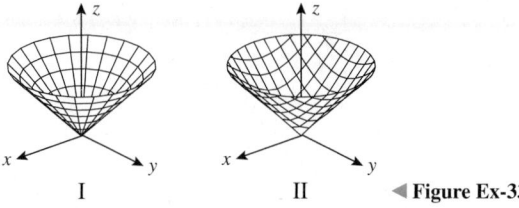

I   II   ◀ **Figure Ex-33**

34. The accompanying figure shows the graphs of two parametric representations of the paraboloid $z = x^2 + y^2$ for $0 \le z \le 2$.
  (a) Find parametric equations that produce reasonable facsimiles of these surfaces.
  (b) Use a graphing utility to check your answer in part (a).

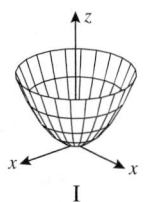 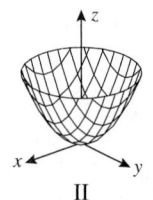

I   II   ◀ **Figure Ex-34**

35. In each part, the figure shows a portion of the parametric surface $x = 3 \cos v$, $y = u$, $z = 3 \sin v$. Find restrictions on u and v that produce the surface, and check your answer with a graphing utility.

(a)   (b)

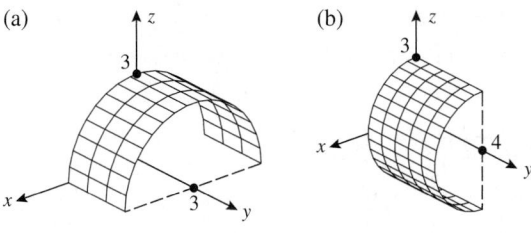

36. In each part, the figure shows a portion of the parametric surface $x = 3 \cos v$, $y = 3 \sin v$, $z = u$. Find restrictions on u and v that produce the surface, and check your answer with a graphing utility.

(a)   (b)

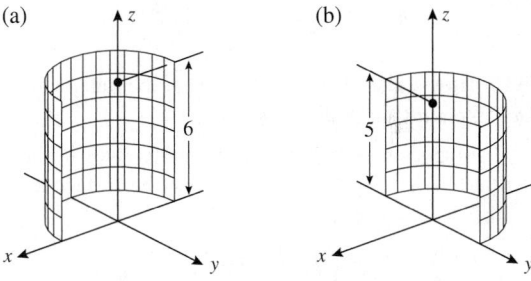

37. In each part, the figure shows a hemisphere that is a portion of the sphere $x = \sin \phi \cos \theta$, $y = \sin \phi \sin \theta$, $z = \cos \phi$. Find restrictions on ϕ and θ that produce the hemisphere, and check your answer with a graphing utility.

(a)   (b)

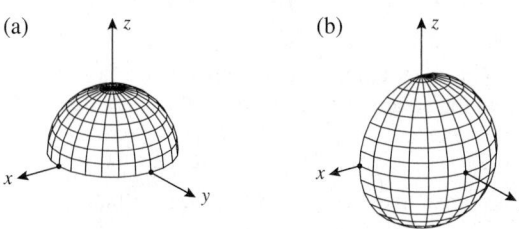

38. In each part, the figure shows a portion of the sphere $x = \sin \phi \cos \theta$, $y = \sin \phi \sin \theta$, $z = \cos \phi$. Find restrictions on ϕ and θ that produce the surface, and check your answer with a graphing utility.

(a)   (b)

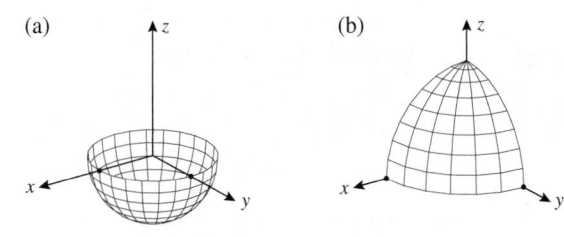

39–44 Find an equation of the tangent plane to the parametric surface at the stated point. ■

39. $x = u$, $y = v$, $z = u^2 + v^2$; $(1, 2, 5)$

40. $x = u^2$, $y = v^2$, $z = u + v$; $(1, 4, 3)$

41. $x = 3v \sin u$, $y = 2v \cos u$, $z = u^2$; $(0, 2, 0)$

42. $\mathbf{r} = uv\mathbf{i} + (u - v)\mathbf{j} + (u + v)\mathbf{k}$; $u = 1, v = 2$

43. $\mathbf{r} = u \cos v\mathbf{i} + u \sin v\mathbf{j} + v\mathbf{k}$; $u = 1/2, v = \pi/4$

44. $\mathbf{r} = uv\mathbf{i} + ue^v\mathbf{j} + ve^u\mathbf{k}$; $u = \ln 2, v = 0$

45–46 Find the area of the given surface. ■

45. The portion of the paraboloid

$$\mathbf{r}(u, v) = u \cos v\mathbf{i} + u \sin v\mathbf{j} + u^2\mathbf{k}$$

for which $1 \le u \le 2, 0 \le v \le 2\pi$.

46. The portion of the cone

$$\mathbf{r}(u, v) = u \cos v\mathbf{i} + u \sin v\mathbf{j} + u\mathbf{k}$$

for which $0 \le u \le 2v, 0 \le v \le \pi/2$.

47–50 True–False Determine whether the statement is true or false. Explain your answer. ■

47. If f has continuous first partial derivatives in the interior of a region R in the xy-plane, then the surface area of the surface $z = f(x, y)$ over R is

$$\iint\limits_R \sqrt{[f(x, y)]^2 + 1} \, dA$$

48. Suppose that $z = f(x, y)$ has continuous first partial derivatives in the interior of a region R in the xy-plane, and set $\mathbf{q} = \langle 1, 0, \partial z/\partial x \rangle$ and $\mathbf{r} = \langle 0, 1, \partial z/\partial y \rangle$. Then the surface area of the surface $z = f(x, y)$ over R is

$$\iint\limits_R \|\mathbf{q} \times \mathbf{r}\| \, dA$$

49. If $\mathbf{r}(u, v) = x(u, v)\mathbf{i} + y(u, v)\mathbf{j} + z(u, v)\mathbf{k}$ such that $\partial\mathbf{r}/\partial u$ and $\partial\mathbf{r}/\partial v$ are nonzero vectors at (u_0, v_0), then

$$\frac{\partial\mathbf{r}}{\partial u} \times \frac{\partial\mathbf{r}}{\partial v}$$

is normal to the graph of $\mathbf{r} = \mathbf{r}(u, v)$ at (u_0, v_0).

50. For the function $f(x, y) = ax + by$, the area of the surface $z = f(x, y)$ over a rectangle R in the xy-plane is the product of $\|\langle 1, 0, a \rangle \times \langle 0, 1, b \rangle\|$ and the area of R.

51. Use parametric equations to derive the formula for the surface area of a sphere of radius a.

52. Use parametric equations to derive the formula for the lateral surface area of a right circular cylinder of radius r and height h.

53. The portion of the surface

$$z = \frac{h}{a}\sqrt{x^2 + y^2} \quad (a, h > 0)$$

between the xy-plane and the plane $z = h$ is a right circular cone of height h and radius a. Use a double integral to show that the lateral surface area of this cone is $S = \pi a\sqrt{a^2 + h^2}$.

54. The accompanying figure shows the **torus** that is generated by revolving the circle

$$(x - a)^2 + z^2 = b^2 \quad (0 < b < a)$$

in the xz-plane about the z-axis.

(a) Show that this torus can be expressed parametrically as

$$x = (a + b \cos v) \cos u$$
$$y = (a + b \cos v) \sin u$$
$$z = b \sin v$$

where u and v are the parameters shown in the figure and $0 \le u \le 2\pi, 0 \le v \le 2\pi$.

(b) Use a graphing utility to generate a torus.

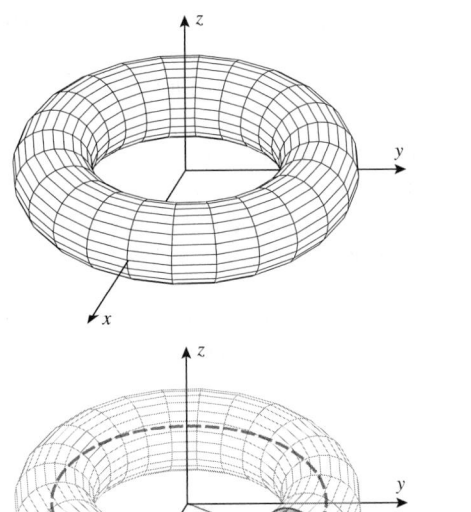

◀ **Figure Ex-54**

55. Find the surface area of the torus in Exercise 54(a).

56. Use a CAS to graph the **helicoid**

$$x = u \cos v, \quad y = u \sin v, \quad z = v$$

for $0 \le u \le 5$ and $0 \le v \le 4\pi$ (see the accompanying figure), and then use the numerical double integration operation of the CAS to approximate the surface area.

57. Use a CAS to graph the **pseudosphere**

$$x = \cos u \sin v$$
$$y = \sin u \sin v$$
$$z = \cos v + \ln\left(\tan\frac{v}{2}\right)$$

for $0 \le u \le 2\pi, 0 < v < \pi$ (see the accompanying figure on the next page), and then use the numerical double integration operation of the CAS to approximate the surface area between the planes $z = -1$ and $z = 1$.

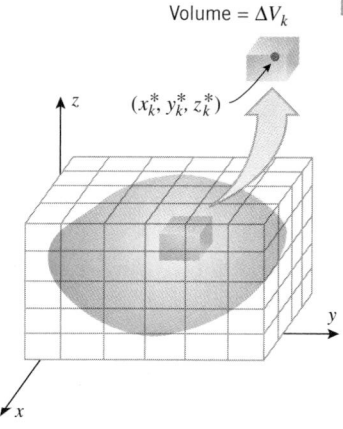

▲ Figure Ex-56   ▲ Figure Ex-57

58. (a) Find parametric equations for the surface of revolution that is generated by revolving the curve $z = f(x)$ in the xz-plane about the z-axis.

(b) Use the result obtained in part (a) to find parametric equations for the surface of revolution that is generated by revolving the curve $z = 1/x^2$ in the xz-plane about the z-axis.

(c) Use a graphing utility to check your work by graphing the parametric surface.

59–61 The parametric equations in these exercises represent a quadric surface for positive values of a, b, and c. Identify the type of surface by eliminating the parameters u and v. Check your conclusion by choosing specific values for the constants and generating the surface with a graphing utility. ■

59. $x = a \cos u \cos v$, $y = b \sin u \cos v$, $z = c \sin v$

60. $x = a \cos u \cosh v$, $y = b \sin u \cosh v$, $z = c \sinh v$

61. $x = a \sinh v$, $y = b \sinh u \cosh v$, $z = c \cosh u \cosh v$

62. **Writing** An early popular approach to defining surface area was to take a limit of surface areas of inscribed polyhedra, but an example in which this approach fails was published in 1890 by H. A. Schwartz. Frieda Zames discusses Schwartz's example in her article "Surface Area and the Cylinder Area Paradox," *The Two-Year College Mathematics Journal*, Vol. 8, No. 4, September 1977, pp. 207–211. Read the article and write a short summary.

✔ **QUICK CHECK ANSWERS 14.4**

1. $\sqrt{\left(\dfrac{\partial z}{\partial x}\right)^2 + \left(\dfrac{\partial z}{\partial y}\right)^2 + 1}$ **2.** (a) The constant u-curves are circles of radius $1 - u$ centered at $(1 - u, 0, 0)$ and parallel to the yz-plane.   (b) The constant v-curves are line segments joining the points $(1, \cos v, \sin v)$ and $(0, 0, 0)$.
3. $\dfrac{\partial \mathbf{r}}{\partial u} = -\mathbf{i} - (\cos v)\mathbf{j} - (\sin v)\mathbf{k}$; $\dfrac{\partial \mathbf{r}}{\partial v} = -[(1 - u)\sin v]\mathbf{j} + [(1 - u)\cos v]\mathbf{k}$ **4.** $\dfrac{1}{\sqrt{8}}(-2\mathbf{i} + \sqrt{3}\mathbf{j} + \mathbf{k})$ **5.** $\left\| \dfrac{\partial \mathbf{r}}{\partial u} \times \dfrac{\partial \mathbf{r}}{\partial v} \right\|$

14.5 TRIPLE INTEGRALS

In the preceding sections we defined and discussed properties of double integrals for functions of two variables. In this section we will define triple integrals for functions of three variables.

■ DEFINITION OF A TRIPLE INTEGRAL

A single integral of a function $f(x)$ is defined over a finite closed interval on the x-axis, and a double integral of a function $f(x, y)$ is defined over a finite closed region R in the xy-plane. Our first goal in this section is to define what is meant by a *triple integral* of $f(x, y, z)$ over a closed solid region G in an xyz-coordinate system. To ensure that G does not extend indefinitely in some direction, we will assume that it can be enclosed in a suitably large box whose sides are parallel to the coordinate planes (Figure 14.5.1). In this case we say that G is a **finite solid**.

To define the triple integral of $f(x, y, z)$ over G, we first divide the box into n "subboxes" by planes parallel to the coordinate planes. We then discard those subboxes that contain any points outside of G and choose an arbitrary point in each of the remaining subboxes. As shown in Figure 14.5.1, we denote the volume of the kth remaining subbox by ΔV_k and the point selected in the kth subbox by (x_k^*, y_k^*, z_k^*). Next we form the product

$$f(x_k^*, y_k^*, z_k^*)\Delta V_k$$

Volume $= \Delta V_k$

(x_k^*, y_k^*, z_k^*)

▲ Figure 14.5.1

for each subbox, then add the products for all of the subboxes to obtain the **Riemann sum**

$$\sum_{k=1}^{n} f(x_k^*, y_k^*, z_k^*)\Delta V_k$$

Finally, we repeat this process with more and more subdivisions in such a way that the length, width, and height of each subbox approach zero, and n approaches $+\infty$. The limit

$$\iiint_{G} f(x, y, z)\, dV = \lim_{n \to +\infty} \sum_{k=1}^{n} f(x_k^*, y_k^*, z_k^*)\Delta V_k \qquad (1)$$

is called the **triple integral** of $f(x, y, z)$ over the region G. Conditions under which the triple integral exists are studied in advanced calculus. However, for our purposes it suffices to say that existence is ensured when f is continuous on G and the region G is not too "complicated."

■ **PROPERTIES OF TRIPLE INTEGRALS**

Triple integrals enjoy many properties of single and double integrals:

$$\iiint_{G} cf(x, y, z)\, dV = c \iiint_{G} f(x, y, z)\, dV \quad (c \text{ a constant})$$

$$\iiint_{G} [f(x, y, z) + g(x, y, z)]\, dV = \iiint_{G} f(x, y, z)\, dV + \iiint_{G} g(x, y, z)\, dV$$

$$\iiint_{G} [f(x, y, z) - g(x, y, z)]\, dV = \iiint_{G} f(x, y, z)\, dV - \iiint_{G} g(x, y, z)\, dV$$

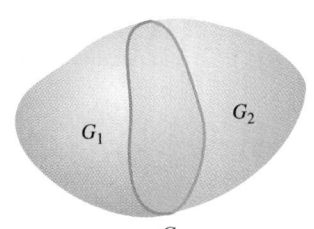

Moreover, if the region G is subdivided into two subregions G_1 and G_2 (Figure 14.5.2), then

$$\iiint_{G} f(x, y, z)\, dV = \iiint_{G_1} f(x, y, z)\, dV + \iiint_{G_2} f(x, y, z)\, dV$$

▲ **Figure 14.5.2**

We omit the proofs.

■ **EVALUATING TRIPLE INTEGRALS OVER RECTANGULAR BOXES**

Just as a double integral can be evaluated by two successive single integrations, so a triple integral can be evaluated by three successive integrations. The following theorem, which we state without proof, is the analog of Theorem 14.1.3.

There are two possible orders of integration for the iterated integrals in Theorem 14.1.3:

$$dx\, dy, \quad dy\, dx$$

Six orders of integration are possible for the iterated integral in Theorem 14.5.1:

$$dx\, dy\, dz, \quad dy\, dz\, dx, \quad dz\, dx\, dy$$
$$dx\, dz\, dy, \quad dz\, dy\, dx, \quad dy\, dx\, dz$$

> **14.5.1   THEOREM (Fubini's Theorem[*])**   *Let G be the rectangular box defined by the inequalities*
> $$a \le x \le b, \quad c \le y \le d, \quad k \le z \le l$$
> *If f is continuous on the region G, then*
> $$\iiint_{G} f(x, y, z)\, dV = \int_{a}^{b} \int_{c}^{d} \int_{k}^{l} f(x, y, z)\, dz\, dy\, dx \qquad (2)$$
> *Moreover, the iterated integral on the right can be replaced with any of the five other iterated integrals that result by altering the order of integration.*

---

[*]See the Fubini biography on p. 1005.

▶ **Example 1**   Evaluate the triple integral

$$\iiint\limits_{G} 12xy^2z^3 \, dV$$

over the rectangular box G defined by the inequalities $-1 \leq x \leq 2, 0 \leq y \leq 3, 0 \leq z \leq 2$.

Solution.   Of the six possible iterated integrals we might use, we will choose the one in (2). Thus, we will first integrate with respect to z, holding x and y fixed, then with respect to y, holding x fixed, and finally with respect to x.

$$\iiint\limits_{G} 12xy^2z^3 \, dV = \int_{-1}^{2} \int_{0}^{3} \int_{0}^{2} 12xy^2z^3 \, dz \, dy \, dx$$

$$= \int_{-1}^{2} \int_{0}^{3} \left[3xy^2z^4 \right]_{z=0}^{2} dy \, dx = \int_{-1}^{2} \int_{0}^{3} 48xy^2 \, dy \, dx$$

$$= \int_{-1}^{2} \left[16xy^3 \right]_{y=0}^{3} dx = \int_{-1}^{2} 432x \, dx$$

$$= 216x^2 \Big]_{-1}^{2} = 648 \quad \blacktriangleleft$$

■ **EVALUATING TRIPLE INTEGRALS OVER MORE GENERAL REGIONS**

Next we will consider how triple integrals can be evaluated over solids that are not rectangular boxes. For the moment we will limit our discussion to solids of the type shown in Figure 14.5.3. Specifically, we will assume that the solid G is bounded above by a surface $z = g_2(x, y)$ and below by a surface $z = g_1(x, y)$ and that the projection of the solid on the xy-plane is a type I or type II region R (see Definition 14.2.1). In addition, we will assume that $g_1(x, y)$ and $g_2(x, y)$ are continuous on R and that $g_1(x, y) \leq g_2(x, y)$ on R. Geometrically, this means that the surfaces may touch but cannot cross. We call a solid of this type a ***simple xy-solid***.

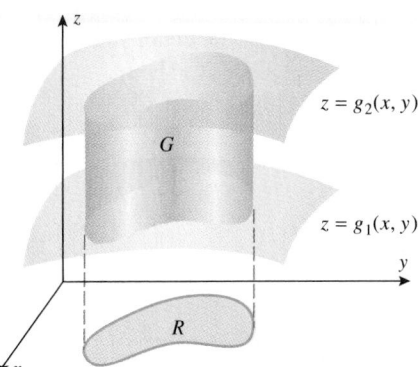

▶ **Figure 14.5.3**

The following theorem, which we state without proof, will enable us to evaluate triple integrals over simple xy-solids.

14.5.2   **THEOREM**   *Let G be a simple xy-solid with upper surface $z = g_2(x, y)$ and lower surface $z = g_1(x, y)$, and let R be the projection of G on the xy-plane. If $f(x, y, z)$ is continuous on G, then*

$$\iiint\limits_{G} f(x, y, z) \, dV = \iint\limits_{R} \left[\int_{g_1(x,y)}^{g_2(x,y)} f(x, y, z) \, dz \right] dA \qquad (3)$$

In (3), the first integration is with respect to z, after which a function of x and y remains. This function of x and y is then integrated over the region R in the xy-plane. To apply (3), it is helpful to begin with a three-dimensional sketch of the solid G. The limits of integration can be obtained from the sketch as follows:

Determining Limits of Integration: Simple xy-Solid

Step 1. Find an equation $z = g_2(x, y)$ for the upper surface and an equation $z = g_1(x, y)$ for the lower surface of G. The functions $g_1(x, y)$ and $g_2(x, y)$ determine the lower and upper z-limits of integration.

Step 2. Make a two-dimensional sketch of the projection R of the solid on the xy-plane. From this sketch determine the limits of integration for the double integral over R in (3).

▶ **Example 2**   Let G be the wedge in the first octant that is cut from the cylindrical solid $y^2 + z^2 \leq 1$ by the planes $y = x$ and $x = 0$. Evaluate

$$\iiint\limits_G z \, dV$$

Solution.   The solid G and its projection R on the xy-plane are shown in Figure 14.5.4. The upper surface of the solid is formed by the cylinder and the lower surface by the xy-plane. Since the portion of the cylinder $y^2 + z^2 = 1$ that lies above the xy-plane has the equation $z = \sqrt{1 - y^2}$, and the xy-plane has the equation $z = 0$, it follows from (3) that

$$\iiint\limits_G z \, dV = \iint\limits_R \left[\int_0^{\sqrt{1-y^2}} z \, dz \right] dA \qquad (4)$$

For the double integral over R, the x- and y-integrations can be performed in either order, since R is both a type I and type II region. We will integrate with respect to x first. With this choice, (4) yields

$$\iiint\limits_G z \, dV = \int_0^1 \int_0^y \int_0^{\sqrt{1-y^2}} z \, dz \, dx \, dy = \int_0^1 \int_0^y \frac{1}{2} z^2 \Big]_{z=0}^{\sqrt{1-y^2}} dx \, dy$$

$$= \int_0^1 \int_0^y \frac{1}{2}(1 - y^2) \, dx \, dy = \frac{1}{2} \int_0^1 (1 - y^2)x \Big]_{x=0}^y dy$$

$$= \frac{1}{2} \int_0^1 (y - y^3) \, dy = \frac{1}{2} \left[\frac{1}{2} y^2 - \frac{1}{4} y^4 \right]_0^1 = \frac{1}{8} \blacktriangleleft$$

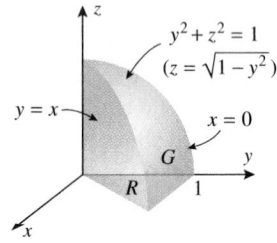

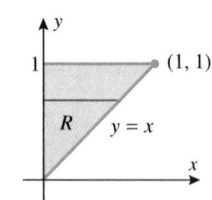

▲ **Figure 14.5.4**

TECHNOLOGY MASTERY

Most computer algebra systems have a built-in capability for computing iterated triple integrals. If you have a CAS, consult the relevant documentation and use the CAS to check Examples 1 and 2.

■ **VOLUME CALCULATED AS A TRIPLE INTEGRAL**

Triple integrals have many physical interpretations, some of which we will consider in Section 14.8. However, in the special case where $f(x, y, z) = 1$, Formula (1) yields

$$\iiint\limits_G dV = \lim_{n \to +\infty} \sum_{k=1}^n \Delta V_k$$

which Figure 14.5.1 suggests is the volume of G; that is,

$$\text{volume of } G = \iiint_G dV \tag{5}$$

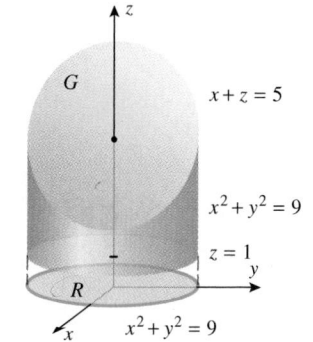

> **► Example 3** Use a triple integral to find the volume of the solid within the cylinder $x^2 + y^2 = 9$ and between the planes $z = 1$ and $x + z = 5$.

Solution. The solid G and its projection R on the xy-plane are shown in Figure 14.5.5. The lower surface of the solid is the plane $z = 1$ and the upper surface is the plane $x + z = 5$ or, equivalently, $z = 5 - x$. Thus, from (3) and (5)

$$\text{volume of } G = \iiint_G dV = \iint_R \left[\int_1^{5-x} dz \right] dA \tag{6}$$

For the double integral over R, we will integrate with respect to y first. Thus, (6) yields

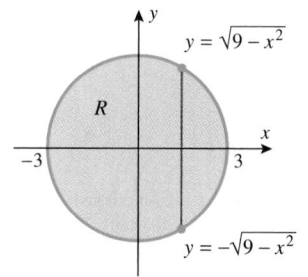

▲ Figure 14.5.5

$$\text{volume of } G = \int_{-3}^3 \int_{-\sqrt{9-x^2}}^{\sqrt{9-x^2}} \int_1^{5-x} dz\, dy\, dx = \int_{-3}^3 \int_{-\sqrt{9-x^2}}^{\sqrt{9-x^2}} z \Big]_{z=1}^{5-x} dy\, dx$$

$$= \int_{-3}^3 \int_{-\sqrt{9-x^2}}^{\sqrt{9-x^2}} (4 - x)\, dy\, dx = \int_{-3}^3 (8 - 2x)\sqrt{9 - x^2}\, dx$$

$$= 8 \int_{-3}^3 \sqrt{9 - x^2}\, dx - \int_{-3}^3 2x\sqrt{9 - x^2}\, dx \qquad \boxed{\text{For the first integral, see Formula (3) of Section 7.4.}}$$

$$= 8 \left(\frac{9}{2}\pi\right) - \int_{-3}^3 2x\sqrt{9 - x^2}\, dx \qquad \boxed{\text{The second integral is 0 because the integrand is an odd function.}}$$

$$= 8 \left(\frac{9}{2}\pi\right) - 0 = 36\pi \;◄$$

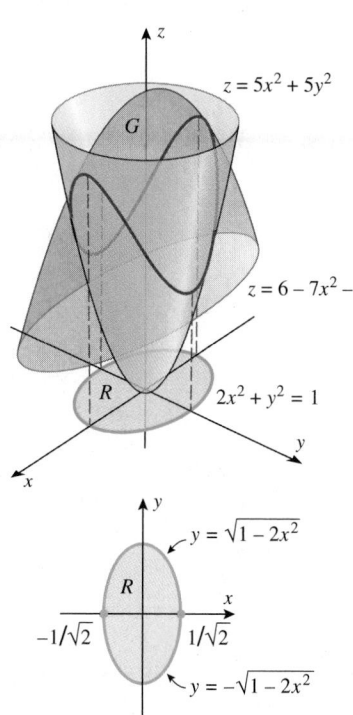

> **► Example 4** Find the volume of the solid enclosed between the paraboloids

$$z = 5x^2 + 5y^2 \quad \text{and} \quad z = 6 - 7x^2 - y^2$$

Solution. The solid G and its projection R on the xy-plane are shown in Figure 14.5.6. The projection R is obtained by solving the given equations simultaneously to determine where the paraboloids intersect. We obtain

$$5x^2 + 5y^2 = 6 - 7x^2 - y^2$$

or

$$2x^2 + y^2 = 1 \tag{7}$$

▲ Figure 14.5.6

which tells us that the paraboloids intersect in a curve on the elliptic cylinder given by (7).

The projection of this intersection on the xy-plane is an ellipse with this same equation. Therefore,

$$\text{volume of } G = \iiint\limits_{G} dV = \iint\limits_{R} \left[\int_{5x^2+5y^2}^{6-7x^2-y^2} dz \right] dA$$

$$= \int_{-1/\sqrt{2}}^{1/\sqrt{2}} \int_{-\sqrt{1-2x^2}}^{\sqrt{1-2x^2}} \int_{5x^2+5y^2}^{6-7x^2-y^2} dz\, dy\, dx$$

$$= \int_{-1/\sqrt{2}}^{1/\sqrt{2}} \int_{-\sqrt{1-2x^2}}^{\sqrt{1-2x^2}} (6 - 12x^2 - 6y^2)\, dy\, dx$$

$$= \int_{-1/\sqrt{2}}^{1/\sqrt{2}} \left[6(1 - 2x^2)y - 2y^3 \right]_{y=-\sqrt{1-2x^2}}^{\sqrt{1-2x^2}} dx$$

$$= 8 \int_{-1/\sqrt{2}}^{1/\sqrt{2}} (1 - 2x^2)^{3/2}\, dx = \frac{8}{\sqrt{2}} \int_{-\pi/2}^{\pi/2} \cos^4\theta\, d\theta = \frac{3\pi}{\sqrt{2}} \blacktriangleleft$$

Let $x = \dfrac{1}{\sqrt{2}} \sin\theta$.

Use the Wallis cosine formula in Exercise 70 of Section 7.3.

■ INTEGRATION IN OTHER ORDERS

In Formula (3) for integrating over a simple xy-solid, the z-integration was performed first. However, there are situations in which it is preferable to integrate in a different order. For example, Figure 14.5.7a shows a *simple xz-solid*, and Figure 14.5.7b shows a *simple yz-solid*. For a simple xz-solid it is usually best to integrate with respect to y first, and for a simple yz-solid it is usually best to integrate with respect to x first:

$$\iiint\limits_{\substack{G \\ \text{simple } xz\text{-solid}}} f(x, y, z)\, dV = \iint\limits_{R} \left[\int_{g_1(x,z)}^{g_2(x,z)} f(x, y, z)\, dy \right] dA \tag{8}$$

$$\iiint\limits_{\substack{G \\ \text{simple } yz\text{-solid}}} f(x, y, z)\, dV = \iint\limits_{R} \left[\int_{g_1(y,z)}^{g_2(y,z)} f(x, y, z)\, dx \right] dA \tag{9}$$

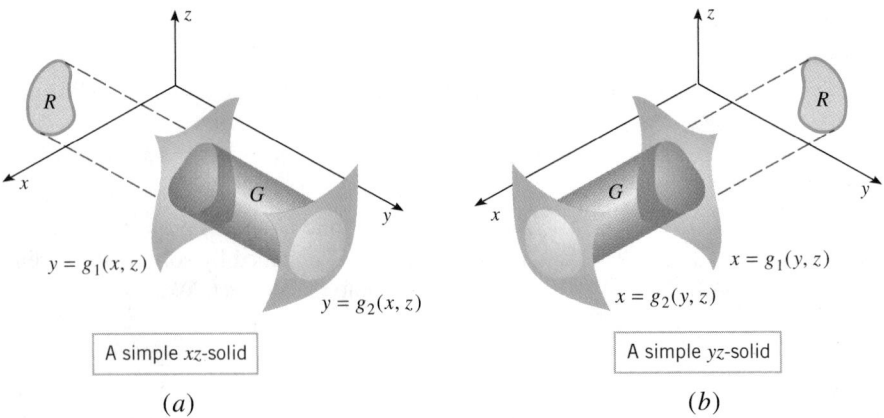

A simple xz-solid

$y = g_1(x, z)$
$y = g_2(x, z)$

A simple yz-solid

$x = g_1(y, z)$
$x = g_2(y, z)$

▶ **Figure 14.5.7**

(a) $\qquad$ (b)

Sometimes a solid G can be viewed as a simple xy-solid, a simple xz-solid, and a simple yz-solid, in which case the order of integration can be chosen to simplify the computations.

▶ **Example 5**   In Example 2 we evaluated

$$\iiint\limits_{G} z \, dV$$

over the wedge in Figure 14.5.4 by integrating first with respect to z. Evaluate this integral by integrating first with respect to x.

Solution.   The solid is bounded in the back by the plane $x = 0$ and in the front by the plane $x = y$, so

$$\iiint\limits_{G} z \, dV = \iint\limits_{R} \left[\int_{0}^{y} z \, dx \right] dA$$

where R is the projection of G on the yz-plane (Figure 14.5.8). The integration over R can be performed first with respect to z and then y or vice versa. Performing the z-integration first yields

$$\iiint\limits_{G} z \, dV = \int_{0}^{1} \int_{0}^{\sqrt{1-y^2}} \int_{0}^{y} z \, dx \, dz \, dy = \int_{0}^{1} \int_{0}^{\sqrt{1-y^2}} zx \Big]_{x=0}^{y} dz \, dy$$

$$= \int_{0}^{1} \int_{0}^{\sqrt{1-y^2}} zy \, dz \, dy = \int_{0}^{1} \frac{1}{2} z^2 y \Big]_{z=0}^{\sqrt{1-y^2}} dy = \int_{0}^{1} \frac{1}{2}(1 - y^2)y \, dy = \frac{1}{8}$$

which agrees with the result in Example 2. ◀

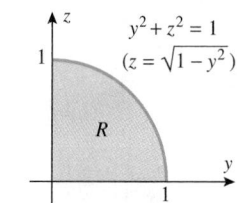

▲ **Figure 14.5.8**

In the figure: $y^2 + z^2 = 1$, $(z = \sqrt{1-y^2})$, R

✔ **QUICK CHECK EXERCISES 14.5**   *(See page 1048 for answers.)*

1. The iterated integral

$$\int_{1}^{5} \int_{2}^{4} \int_{3}^{6} f(x, y, z) \, dx \, dz \, dy$$

integrates f over the rectangular box defined by

_____ $\leq x \leq$ _____,   _____ $\leq y \leq$ _____,

_____ $\leq z \leq$ _____

2. Let G be the solid in the first octant bounded below by the surface $z = y + x^2$ and bounded above by the plane $z = 4$. Supply the missing limits of integration.

(a) $\displaystyle\iiint\limits_{G} f(x, y, z) \, dA = \int_{\square}^{\square} \int_{\square}^{\square} \int_{y+x^2}^{4} f(x, y, z) \, dz \, dx \, dy$

(b) $\displaystyle\iiint\limits_{G} f(x, y, z) \, dA = \int_{\square}^{\square} \int_{\square}^{\square} \int_{y+x^2}^{4} f(x, y, z) \, dz \, dy \, dx$

(c) $\displaystyle\iiint\limits_{G} f(x, y, z) \, dA = \int_{\square}^{\square} \int_{\square}^{\square} \int_{\square}^{\square} f(x, y, z) \, dy \, dz \, dx$

3. The volume of the solid G in Quick Check Exercise 2 is _____.

EXERCISE SET 14.5   ☐ CAS

1–8 Evaluate the iterated integral. ■

1. $\displaystyle\int_{-1}^{1} \int_{0}^{2} \int_{0}^{1} (x^2 + y^2 + z^2) \, dx \, dy \, dz$

2. $\displaystyle\int_{1/3}^{1/2} \int_{0}^{\pi} \int_{0}^{1} zx \sin xy \, dz \, dy \, dx$

3. $\displaystyle\int_{0}^{2} \int_{-1}^{y^2} \int_{-1}^{z} yz \, dx \, dz \, dy$

4. $\displaystyle\int_{0}^{\pi/4} \int_{0}^{1} \int_{0}^{x^2} x \cos y \, dz \, dx \, dy$

5. $\displaystyle\int_{0}^{3} \int_{0}^{\sqrt{9-z^2}} \int_{0}^{x} xy \, dy \, dx \, dz$

6. $\displaystyle\int_{1}^{3} \int_{x}^{x^2} \int_{0}^{\ln z} xe^y \, dy \, dz \, dx$

7. $\displaystyle\int_{0}^{2} \int_{0}^{\sqrt{4-x^2}} \int_{-5+x^2+y^2}^{3-x^2-y^2} x \, dz \, dy \, dx$

8. $\displaystyle\int_{1}^{2} \int_{z}^{2} \int_{0}^{\sqrt{3}y} \frac{y}{x^2 + y^2} \, dx \, dy \, dz$

9–12 Evaluate the triple integral. ■

9. $\iiint\limits_{G} xy \sin yz \, dV$, where G is the rectangular box defined by the inequalities $0 \le x \le \pi, 0 \le y \le 1, 0 \le z \le \pi/6$.

10. $\iiint\limits_{G} y \, dV$, where G is the solid enclosed by the plane $z = y$, the xy-plane, and the parabolic cylinder $y = 1 - x^2$.

11. $\iiint\limits_{G} xyz \, dV$, where G is the solid in the first octant that is bounded by the parabolic cylinder $z = 2 - x^2$ and the planes $z = 0, y = x$, and $y = 0$.

12. $\iiint\limits_{G} \cos(z/y) \, dV$, where G is the solid defined by the inequalities $\pi/6 \le y \le \pi/2, y \le x \le \pi/2, 0 \le z \le xy$.

c **13.** Use the numerical triple integral operation of a CAS to approximate
$$\iiint\limits_{G} \frac{\sqrt{x + z^2}}{y} \, dV$$
where G is the rectangular box defined by the inequalities $0 \le x \le 3, 1 \le y \le 2, -2 \le z \le 1$.

c **14.** Use the numerical triple integral operation of a CAS to approximate
$$\iiint\limits_{G} e^{-x^2 - y^2 - z^2} \, dV$$
where G is the spherical region $x^2 + y^2 + z^2 \le 1$.

15–18 Use a triple integral to find the volume of the solid. ■

15. The solid in the first octant bounded by the coordinate planes and the plane $3x + 6y + 4z = 12$.

16. The solid bounded by the surface $z = \sqrt{y}$ and the planes $x + y = 1, x = 0$, and $z = 0$.

17. The solid bounded by the surface $y = x^2$ and the planes $y + z = 4$ and $z = 0$.

18. The wedge in the first octant that is cut from the solid cylinder $y^2 + z^2 \le 1$ by the planes $y = x$ and $x = 0$.

FOCUS ON CONCEPTS

19. Let G be the solid enclosed by the surfaces in the accompanying figure. Fill in the missing limits of integration.

(a) $\iiint\limits_{G} f(x, y, z) \, dV$
$$= \int_{\square}^{\square} \int_{\square}^{\square} \int_{\square}^{\square} f(x, y, z) \, dz \, dy \, dx$$

(b) $\iiint\limits_{G} f(x, y, z) \, dV$
$$= \int_{\square}^{\square} \int_{\square}^{\square} \int_{\square}^{\square} f(x, y, z) \, dz \, dx \, dy$$

20. Let G be the solid enclosed by the surfaces in the accompanying figure. Fill in the missing limits of integration.

(a) $\iiint\limits_{G} f(x, y, z) \, dV$
$$= \int_{\square}^{\square} \int_{\square}^{\square} \int_{\square}^{\square} f(x, y, z) \, dz \, dy \, dx$$

(b) $\iiint\limits_{G} f(x, y, z) \, dV$
$$= \int_{\square}^{\square} \int_{\square}^{\square} \int_{\square}^{\square} f(x, y, z) \, dz \, dx \, dy$$

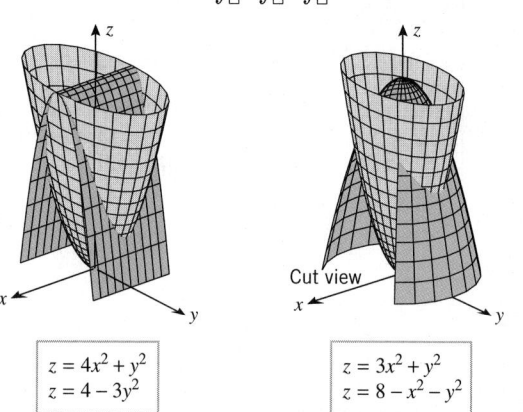

| $z = 4x^2 + y^2$ |
| $z = 4 - 3y^2$ |

| $z = 3x^2 + y^2$ |
| $z = 8 - x^2 - y^2$ |

▲ **Figure Ex-19**   ▲ **Figure Ex-20**

21–24 Set up (but do not evaluate) an iterated triple integral for the volume of the solid enclosed between the given surfaces. ■

21. The surfaces in Exercise 19.

22. The surfaces in Exercise 20.

23. The elliptic cylinder $x^2 + 9y^2 = 9$ and the planes $z = 0$ and $z = x + 3$.

24. The cylinders $x^2 + y^2 = 1$ and $x^2 + z^2 = 1$.

25–26 In each part, sketch the solid whose volume is given by the integral. ■

25. (a) $\displaystyle\int_{-1}^{1} \int_{-\sqrt{1-x^2}}^{\sqrt{1-x^2}} \int_{0}^{y+1} dz \, dy \, dx$

(b) $\displaystyle\int_{0}^{9} \int_{0}^{y/3} \int_{0}^{\sqrt{y^2 - 9x^2}} dz \, dx \, dy$

(c) $\displaystyle\int_{0}^{1} \int_{0}^{\sqrt{1-x^2}} \int_{0}^{2} dy \, dz \, dx$

26. (a) $\displaystyle\int_{0}^{3} \int_{x^2}^{9} \int_{0}^{2} dz \, dy \, dx$

(b) $\displaystyle\int_{0}^{2} \int_{0}^{2-y} \int_{0}^{2-x-y} dz \, dx \, dy$

(c) $\displaystyle\int_{-2}^{2} \int_{0}^{4-y^2} \int_{0}^{2} dx \, dz \, dy$

27–30 True–False Determine whether the statement is true or false. Explain your answer. ■

27. If G is the rectangular solid that is defined by $1 \leq x \leq 3$, $2 \leq y \leq 5$, $-1 \leq z \leq 1$, and if $f(x, y, z)$ is continuous on G, then

$$\iiint_G f(x, y, z)\, dV = \int_1^3 \int_{-1}^1 \int_2^5 f(x, y, z)\, dy\, dz\, dx$$

28. If G is a simple xy-solid and $f(x, y, z)$ is continuous on G, then the triple integral of f over G can be expressed as an iterated integral whose outermost integration is performed with respect to z.

29. If G is the portion of the unit ball in the first octant, then

$$\iiint_G f(x, y, z)\, dV = \int_0^1 \int_0^1 \int_0^{\sqrt{1-x^2-y^2}} f(x, y, z)\, dz\, dy\, dx$$

30. If G is a simple xy-solid and

$$\text{volume of } G = \iiint_G f(x, y, z)\, dV$$

then $f(x, y, z) = 1$ at every point in G.

31. Let G be the rectangular box defined by the inequalities $a \leq x \leq b, c \leq y \leq d, k \leq z \leq l$. Show that

$$\iiint_G f(x)g(y)h(z)\, dV$$

$$= \left[\int_a^b f(x)\, dx \right]\left[\int_c^d g(y)\, dy \right]\left[\int_k^l h(z)\, dz \right]$$

32. Use the result of Exercise 31 to evaluate

(a) $\displaystyle\iiint_G xy^2 \sin z\, dV$, where G is the set of points satisfying $-1 \leq x \leq 1, 0 \leq y \leq 1, 0 \leq z \leq \pi/2$;

(b) $\displaystyle\iiint_G e^{2x+y-z}\, dV$, where G is the set of points satisfying $0 \leq x \leq 1, 0 \leq y \leq \ln 3, 0 \leq z \leq \ln 2$.

33–36 The *average value* or *mean value* of a continuous function $f(x, y, z)$ over a solid G is defined as

$$f_{\text{ave}} = \frac{1}{V(G)} \iiint_G f(x, y, z)\, dV$$

where $V(G)$ is the volume of the solid G (compare to the definition preceding Exercise 61 of Section 14.2). Use this definition in these exercises. ◾

33. Find the average value of $f(x, y, z) = x + y + z$ over the tetrahedron shown in the accompanying figure.

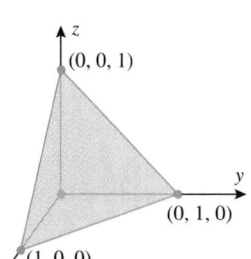

◀ **Figure Ex-33**

34. Find the average value of $f(x, y, z) = xyz$ over the spherical region $x^2 + y^2 + z^2 \leq 1$.

C 35. Use the numerical triple integral operation of a CAS to approximate the average distance from the origin to a point in the solid of Example 4.

C 36. Let $d(x, y, z)$ be the distance from the point (z, z, z) to the point $(x, y, 0)$. Use the numerical triple integral operation of a CAS to approximate the average value of d for $0 \leq x \leq 1, 0 \leq y \leq 1$, and $0 \leq z \leq 1$. Write a short explanation as to why this value may be considered to be the average distance between a point on the diagonal from $(0, 0, 0)$ to $(1, 1, 1)$ and a point on the face in the xy-plane for the unit cube $0 \leq x \leq 1, 0 \leq y \leq 1$, and $0 \leq z \leq 1$.

37. Let G be the tetrahedron in the first octant bounded by the coordinate planes and the plane

$$\frac{x}{a} + \frac{y}{b} + \frac{z}{c} = 1 \quad (a > 0, b > 0, c > 0)$$

(a) List six different iterated integrals that represent the volume of G.

(b) Evaluate any one of the six to show that the volume of G is $\frac{1}{6}abc$.

38. Use a triple integral to derive the formula for the volume of the ellipsoid

$$\frac{x^2}{a^2} + \frac{y^2}{b^2} + \frac{z^2}{c^2} = 1$$

FOCUS ON CONCEPTS

39–40 Express each integral as an equivalent integral in which the z-integration is performed first, the y-integration second, and the x-integration last. ◾

39. (a) $\displaystyle\int_0^5 \int_0^2 \int_0^{\sqrt{4-y^2}} f(x, y, z)\, dx\, dy\, dz$

(b) $\displaystyle\int_0^9 \int_0^{3-\sqrt{x}} \int_0^z f(x, y, z)\, dy\, dz\, dx$

(c) $\displaystyle\int_0^4 \int_y^{8-y} \int_0^{\sqrt{4-y}} f(x, y, z)\, dx\, dz\, dy$

40. (a) $\displaystyle\int_0^3 \int_0^{\sqrt{9-z^2}} \int_0^{\sqrt{9-y^2-z^2}} f(x, y, z)\, dx\, dy\, dz$

(b) $\displaystyle\int_0^4 \int_0^2 \int_0^{x/2} f(x, y, z)\, dy\, dz\, dx$

(c) $\displaystyle\int_0^4 \int_0^{4-y} \int_0^{\sqrt{z}} f(x, y, z)\, dx\, dz\, dy$

41. Writing The following initial steps can be used to express a triple integral over a solid G as an iterated triple integral: First project G onto one of the coordinate planes to obtain a region R, and then project R onto one of the coordinate axes. Describe how you would use these steps to find the limits of integration. Illustrate your discussion with an example.

1. $3 \leq x \leq 6, \ 1 \leq y \leq 5, \ 2 \leq z \leq 4$ 2. (a) $\int_0^4 \int_0^{\sqrt{4-y}} \int_{y+x^2}^4 f(x, y, z) \, dz \, dx \, dy$ (b) $\int_0^2 \int_0^{4-x^2} \int_{y+x^2}^4 f(x, y, z) \, dz \, dy \, dx$

(c) $\int_0^2 \int_{x^2}^4 \int_0^{z-x^2} f(x, y, z) \, dy \, dz \, dx$ 3. $\dfrac{128}{15}$

14.6   TRIPLE INTEGRALS IN CYLINDRICAL AND SPHERICAL COORDINATES

In Section 14.3 we saw that some double integrals are easier to evaluate in polar coordinates than in rectangular coordinates. Similarly, some triple integrals are easier to evaluate in cylindrical or spherical coordinates than in rectangular coordinates. In this section we will study triple integrals in these coordinate systems.

▌ TRIPLE INTEGRALS IN CYLINDRICAL COORDINATES

Recall that in rectangular coordinates the triple integral of a continuous function f over a solid region G is defined as

$$\iiint\limits_G f(x, y, z) \, dV = \lim_{n \to +\infty} \sum_{k=1}^{n} f(x_k^*, y_k^*, z_k^*) \Delta V_k$$

where ΔV_k denotes the volume of a rectangular parallelepiped interior to G and (x_k^*, y_k^*, z_k^*) is a point in this parallelepiped (see Figure 14.5.1). Triple integrals in cylindrical and spherical coordinates are defined similarly, except that the region G is divided not into rectangular parallelepipeds but into regions more appropriate to these coordinate systems.

In cylindrical coordinates, the simplest equations are of the form

$$r = \text{constant}, \quad \theta = \text{constant}, \quad z = \text{constant}$$

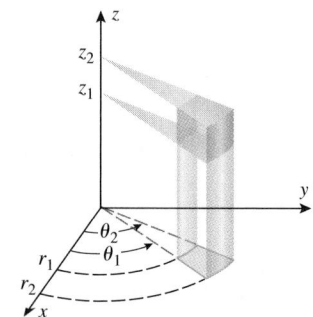

▲ Figure 14.6.1

The first equation represents a right circular cylinder centered on the z-axis, the second a vertical half-plane hinged on the z-axis, and the third a horizontal plane. (See Figure 11.8.3.) These surfaces can be paired up to determine solids called **cylindrical wedges** or **cylindrical elements of volume**. To be precise, a cylindrical wedge is a solid enclosed between six surfaces of the following form:

two cylinders (blue)	$r = r_1, \quad r = r_2$	$(r_1 < r_2)$
two vertical half-planes (yellow)	$\theta = \theta_1, \quad \theta = \theta_2$	$(\theta_1 < \theta_2)$
two horizontal planes (gray)	$z = z_1, \quad z = z_2$	$(z_1 < z_2)$

(Figure 14.6.1). The dimensions $\theta_2 - \theta_1, r_2 - r_1$, and $z_2 - z_1$ are called the **central angle**, **thickness**, and **height** of the wedge.

To define the triple integral over G of a function $f(r, \theta, z)$ in cylindrical coordinates we proceed as follows:

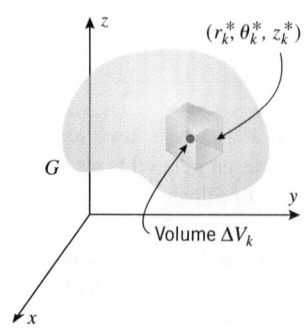

▲ Figure 14.6.2

- Subdivide G into pieces by a three-dimensional grid consisting of concentric circular cylinders centered on the z-axis, half-planes hinged on the z-axis, and horizontal planes. Exclude from consideration all pieces that contain any points outside of G, thereby leaving only cylindrical wedges that are subsets of G.

- Assume that there are n such cylindrical wedges, and denote the volume of the kth cylindrical wedge by ΔV_k. As indicated in Figure 14.6.2, let $(r_k^*, \theta_k^*, z_k^*)$ be any point in the kth cylindrical wedge.

- Repeat this process with more and more subdivisions so that as n increases, the height, thickness, and central angle of the cylindrical wedges approach zero. Define

$$\iiint\limits_{G} f(r, \theta, z)\,dV = \lim_{n \to +\infty} \sum_{k=1}^{n} f(r_k^*, \theta_k^*, z_k^*)\Delta V_k \tag{1}$$

For computational purposes, it will be helpful to express (1) as an iterated integral. Toward this end we note that the volume ΔV_k of the kth cylindrical wedge can be expressed as

$$\Delta V_k = [\text{area of base}] \cdot [\text{height}] \tag{2}$$

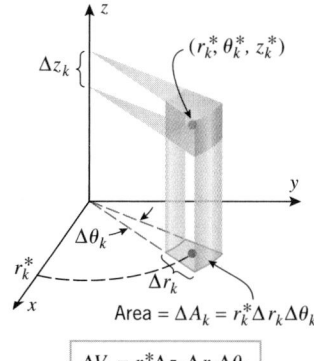

$$\Delta V_k = r_k^* \Delta z_k \Delta r_k \Delta \theta_k$$

▲ **Figure 14.6.3**

Note the extra factor of r that appears in the integrand on converting a triple integral to an iterated integral in cylindrical coordinates.

If we denote the thickness, central angle, and height of this wedge by Δr_k, $\Delta\theta_k$, and Δz_k, and if we choose the arbitrary point $(r_k^*, \theta_k^*, z_k^*)$ to lie above the "center" of the base (Figures 14.3.6 and 14.6.3), then it follows from (5) of Section 14.3 that the base has area $\Delta A_k = r_k^* \Delta r_k \Delta\theta_k$. Thus, (2) can be written as

$$\Delta V_k = r_k^* \Delta r_k \Delta\theta_k \Delta z_k = r_k^* \Delta z_k \Delta r_k \Delta\theta_k$$

Substituting this expression in (1) yields

$$\iiint\limits_{G} f(r, \theta, z)\,dV = \lim_{n \to +\infty} \sum_{k=1}^{n} f(r_k^*, \theta_k^*, z_k^*)r_k^* \Delta z_k \Delta r_k \Delta\theta_k$$

which suggests that a triple integral in cylindrical coordinates can be evaluated as an iterated integral of the form

$$\iiint\limits_{G} f(r, \theta, z)\,dV = \underset{\substack{\text{appropriate}\\ \text{limits}}}{\iiint} f(r, \theta, z)r\,dz\,dr\,d\theta \tag{3}$$

In this formula the integration with respect to z is done first, then with respect to r, and then with respect to θ, but any order of integration is allowable.

The following theorem, which we state without proof, makes the preceding ideas more precise.

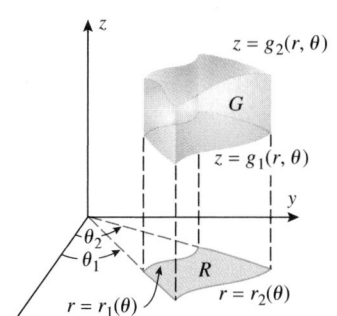

▲ **Figure 14.6.4**

14.6.1   THEOREM   *Let G be a solid region whose upper surface has the equation $z = g_2(r, \theta)$ and whose lower surface has the equation $z = g_1(r, \theta)$ in cylindrical coordinates. If the projection of the solid on the xy-plane is a simple polar region R, and if $f(r, \theta, z)$ is continuous on G, then*

$$\iiint\limits_{G} f(r, \theta, z)\,dV = \iint\limits_{R}\left[\int_{g_1(r,\theta)}^{g_2(r,\theta)} f(r, \theta, z)\,dz\right]dA \tag{4}$$

where the double integral over R is evaluated in polar coordinates. In particular, if the projection R is as shown in Figure 14.6.4, then (4) can be written as

$$\iiint\limits_{G} f(r, \theta, z)\,dV = \int_{\theta_1}^{\theta_2}\int_{r_1(\theta)}^{r_2(\theta)}\int_{g_1(r,\theta)}^{g_2(r,\theta)} f(r, \theta, z)r\,dz\,dr\,d\theta \tag{5}$$

The type of solid to which Formula (5) applies is illustrated in Figure 14.6.4. To apply (4) and (5) it is best to begin with a three-dimensional sketch of the solid G, from which the limits of integration can be obtained as follows:

Determining Limits of Integration: Cylindrical Coordinates

Step 1. Identify the upper surface $z = g_2(r, \theta)$ and the lower surface $z = g_1(r, \theta)$ of the solid. The functions $g_1(r, \theta)$ and $g_2(r, \theta)$ determine the z-limits of integration. (If the upper and lower surfaces are given in rectangular coordinates, convert them to cylindrical coordinates.)

Step 2. Make a two-dimensional sketch of the projection R of the solid on the xy-plane. From this sketch the r- and θ-limits of integration may be obtained exactly as with double integrals in polar coordinates.

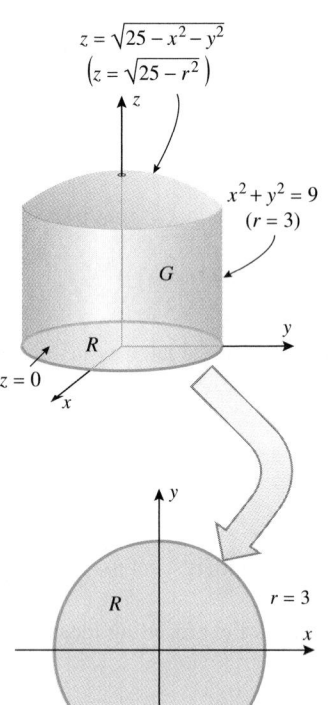

$z = \sqrt{25 - x^2 - y^2}$
$\left(z = \sqrt{25 - r^2}\right)$

$x^2 + y^2 = 9$
$(r = 3)$

G

R

$z = 0$

$r = 3$

▲ **Figure 14.6.5**

▶ **Example 1** Use triple integration in cylindrical coordinates to find the volume of the solid G that is bounded above by the hemisphere $z = \sqrt{25 - x^2 - y^2}$, below by the xy-plane, and laterally by the cylinder $x^2 + y^2 = 9$.

Solution. The solid G and its projection R on the xy-plane are shown in Figure 14.6.5. In cylindrical coordinates, the upper surface of G is the hemisphere $z = \sqrt{25 - r^2}$ and the lower surface is the plane $z = 0$. Thus, from (4), the volume of G is

$$V = \iiint_G dV = \iint_R \left[\int_0^{\sqrt{25-r^2}} dz \right] dA$$

For the double integral over R, we use polar coordinates:

$$V = \int_0^{2\pi} \int_0^3 \int_0^{\sqrt{25-r^2}} r \, dz \, dr \, d\theta = \int_0^{2\pi} \int_0^3 \left[rz \right]_{z=0}^{\sqrt{25-r^2}} dr \, d\theta$$

$$= \int_0^{2\pi} \int_0^3 r\sqrt{25 - r^2} \, dr \, d\theta = \int_0^{2\pi} \left[-\frac{1}{3}(25 - r^2)^{3/2} \right]_{r=0}^3 d\theta$$

$$= \int_0^{2\pi} \frac{61}{3} \, d\theta = \frac{122}{3}\pi \quad ◀$$

$u = 25 - r^2$
$du = -2r \, dr$

■ **CONVERTING TRIPLE INTEGRALS FROM RECTANGULAR TO CYLINDRICAL COORDINATES**

Sometimes a triple integral that is difficult to integrate in rectangular coordinates can be evaluated more easily by making the substitution $x = r\cos\theta$, $y = r\sin\theta$, $z = z$ to convert it to an integral in cylindrical coordinates. Under such a substitution, a rectangular triple integral can be expressed as an iterated integral in cylindrical coordinates as

$$\iiint_G f(x, y, z) \, dV = \iiint_{\substack{\text{appropriate} \\ \text{limits}}} f(r\cos\theta, r\sin\theta, z) r \, dz \, dr \, d\theta \qquad (6)$$

The order of integration on the right side of (6) can be changed, provided the limits of integration are adjusted accordingly.

▶ **Example 2** Use cylindrical coordinates to evaluate

$$\int_{-3}^{3} \int_{-\sqrt{9-x^2}}^{\sqrt{9-x^2}} \int_0^{9-x^2-y^2} x^2 \, dz \, dy \, dx$$

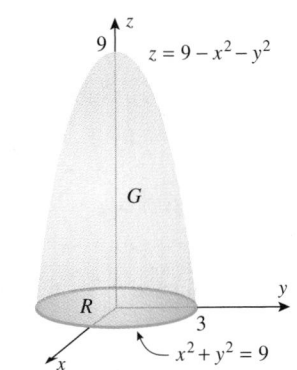

▲ Figure 14.6.6

Solution. In problems of this type, it is helpful to sketch the region of integration G and its projection R on the xy-plane. From the z-limits of integration, the upper surface of G is the paraboloid $z = 9 - x^2 - y^2$ and the lower surface is the xy-plane $z = 0$. From the x- and y-limits of integration, the projection R is the region in the xy-plane enclosed by the circle $x^2 + y^2 = 9$ (Figure 14.6.6). Thus,

$$\int_{-3}^{3}\int_{-\sqrt{9-x^2}}^{\sqrt{9-x^2}}\int_{0}^{9-x^2-y^2} x^2\, dz\, dy\, dx = \iiint_G x^2\, dV$$

$$= \iint_R \left[\int_0^{9-r^2} r^2\cos^2\theta\, dz\right] dA = \int_0^{2\pi}\int_0^3\int_0^{9-r^2} (r^2\cos^2\theta)r\, dz\, dr\, d\theta$$

$$= \int_0^{2\pi}\int_0^3\int_0^{9-r^2} r^3\cos^2\theta\, dz\, dr\, d\theta = \int_0^{2\pi}\int_0^3 \left[zr^3\cos^2\theta\right]_{z=0}^{9-r^2} dr\, d\theta$$

$$= \int_0^{2\pi}\int_0^3 (9r^3 - r^5)\cos^2\theta\, dr\, d\theta = \int_0^{2\pi}\left[\left(\frac{9r^4}{4} - \frac{r^6}{6}\right)\cos^2\theta\right]_{r=0}^{3} d\theta$$

$$= \frac{243}{4}\int_0^{2\pi}\cos^2\theta\, d\theta = \frac{243}{4}\int_0^{2\pi}\frac{1}{2}(1 + \cos 2\theta)\, d\theta = \frac{243\pi}{4} \quad \blacktriangleleft$$

■ TRIPLE INTEGRALS IN SPHERICAL COORDINATES

In spherical coordinates, the simplest equations are of the form

$$\rho = \text{constant}, \quad \theta = \text{constant}, \quad \phi = \text{constant}$$

As indicated in Figure 11.8.4, the first equation represents a sphere centered at the origin and the second a half-plane hinged on the z-axis. The graph of the third equation is a right circular cone nappe with its vertex at the origin and its line of symmetry along the z-axis for $\phi \neq \pi/2$, and is the xy-plane if $\phi = \pi/2$. By a ***spherical wedge*** or ***spherical element of volume*** we mean a solid enclosed between six surfaces of the following form:

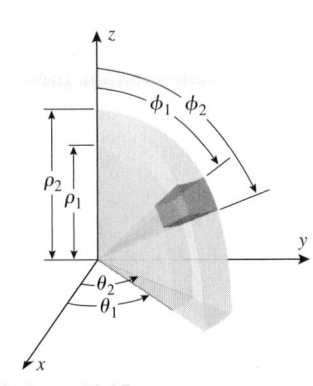

▲ Figure 14.6.7

two spheres (green)	$\rho = \rho_1$, $\rho = \rho_2$ $(\rho_1 < \rho_2)$
two vertical half-planes (yellow)	$\theta = \theta_1$, $\theta = \theta_2$ $(\theta_1 < \theta_2)$
nappes of two circular cones (pink)	$\phi = \phi_1$, $\phi = \phi_2$ $(\phi_1 < \phi_2)$

(Figure 14.6.7). We will refer to the numbers $\rho_2 - \rho_1$, $\theta_2 - \theta_1$, and $\phi_2 - \phi_1$ as the ***dimensions*** of a spherical wedge.

If G is a solid region in three-dimensional space, then the triple integral over G of a continuous function $f(\rho, \theta, \phi)$ in spherical coordinates is similar in definition to the triple integral in cylindrical coordinates, except that the solid G is partitioned into *spherical wedges* by a three-dimensional grid consisting of spheres centered at the origin, half-planes hinged on the z-axis, and nappes of right circular cones with vertices at the origin and lines of symmetry along the z-axis (Figure 14.6.8).

The defining equation of a triple integral in spherical coordinates is

$$\iiint_G f(\rho, \theta, \phi)\, dV = \lim_{n \to +\infty} \sum_{k=1}^{n} f(\rho_k^*, \theta_k^*, \phi_k^*)\Delta V_k \tag{7}$$

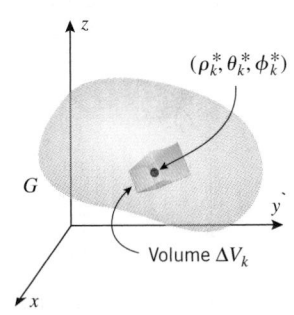

▲ Figure 14.6.8

where ΔV_k is the volume of the kth spherical wedge that is interior to G, $(\rho_k^*, \theta_k^*, \phi_k^*)$ is an arbitrary point in this wedge, and n increases in such a way that the dimensions of each interior spherical wedge tend to zero.

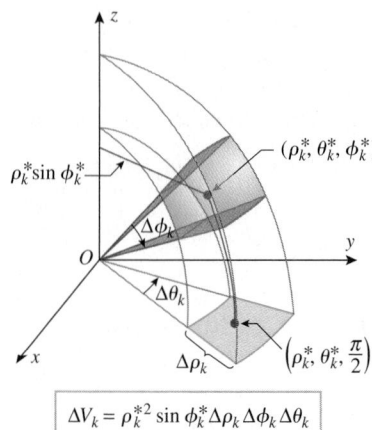

$$\Delta V_k = \rho_k^{*2} \sin \phi_k^* \Delta \rho_k \Delta \phi_k \Delta \theta_k$$

▲ **Figure 14.6.9**

Note the extra factor of $\rho^2 \sin \phi$ that appears in the integrand on converting a triple integral to an iterated integral in spherical coordinates. This is analogous to the extra factor of r that appears in an iterated integral in cylindrical coordinates.

For computational purposes, it will be desirable to express (7) as an iterated integral. In Exercise 30 we will help you to show that if the point $(\rho_k^*, \theta_k^*, \phi_k^*)$ is suitably chosen, then the volume ΔV_k in (7) can be written as

$$\Delta V_k = \rho_k^{*2} \sin \phi_k^* \Delta \rho_k \Delta \phi_k \Delta \theta_k \qquad (8)$$

where $\Delta \rho_k$, $\Delta \phi_k$, and $\Delta \theta_k$ are the dimensions of the wedge (Figure 14.6.9). Substituting this in (7) we obtain

$$\iiint\limits_{G} f(\rho, \theta, \phi) \, dV = \lim_{n \to +\infty} \sum_{k=1}^{n} f(\rho_k^*, \theta_k^*, \phi_k^*) \rho_k^{*2} \sin \phi_k^* \Delta \rho_k \Delta \phi_k \Delta \theta_k$$

which suggests that a triple integral in spherical coordinates can be evaluated as an iterated integral of the form

$$\iiint\limits_{G} f(\rho, \theta, \phi) \, dV = \iiint\limits_{\substack{\text{appropriate} \\ \text{limits}}} f(\rho, \theta, \phi) \rho^2 \sin \phi \, d\rho \, d\phi \, d\theta \qquad (9)$$

The analog of Theorem 14.6.1 for triple integrals in spherical coordinates is tedious to state, so instead we will give some examples that illustrate techniques for obtaining the limits of integration. In all of our examples we will use the same order of integration—first with respect to ρ, then ϕ, and then θ. Once you have mastered the basic ideas, there should be no trouble using other orders of integration.

Suppose that we want to integrate $f(\rho, \theta, \phi)$ over the spherical solid G enclosed by the sphere $\rho = \rho_0$. The basic idea is to choose the limits of integration so that every point of the solid is accounted for in the integration process. Figure 14.6.10 illustrates one way of doing this. Holding θ and ϕ fixed for the first integration, we let ρ vary from 0 to ρ_0. This covers a radial line from the origin to the surface of the sphere. Next, keeping θ fixed, we let ϕ vary from 0 to π so that the radial line sweeps out a fan-shaped region. Finally, we let θ vary from 0 to 2π so that the fan-shaped region makes a complete revolution, thereby sweeping out the entire sphere. Thus, the triple integral of $f(\rho, \theta, \phi)$ over the spherical solid G can be evaluated by writing

$$\iiint\limits_{G} f(\rho, \theta, \phi) \, dV = \int_{0}^{2\pi} \int_{0}^{\pi} \int_{0}^{\rho_0} f(\rho, \theta, \phi) \rho^2 \sin \phi \, d\rho \, d\phi \, d\theta$$

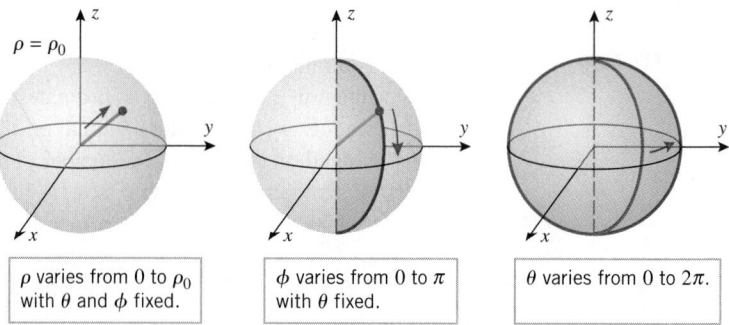

▶ **Figure 14.6.10**

Table 14.6.1 suggests how the limits of integration in spherical coordinates can be obtained for some other common solids.

Table 14.6.1

DETERMINATION OF LIMITS	INTEGRAL

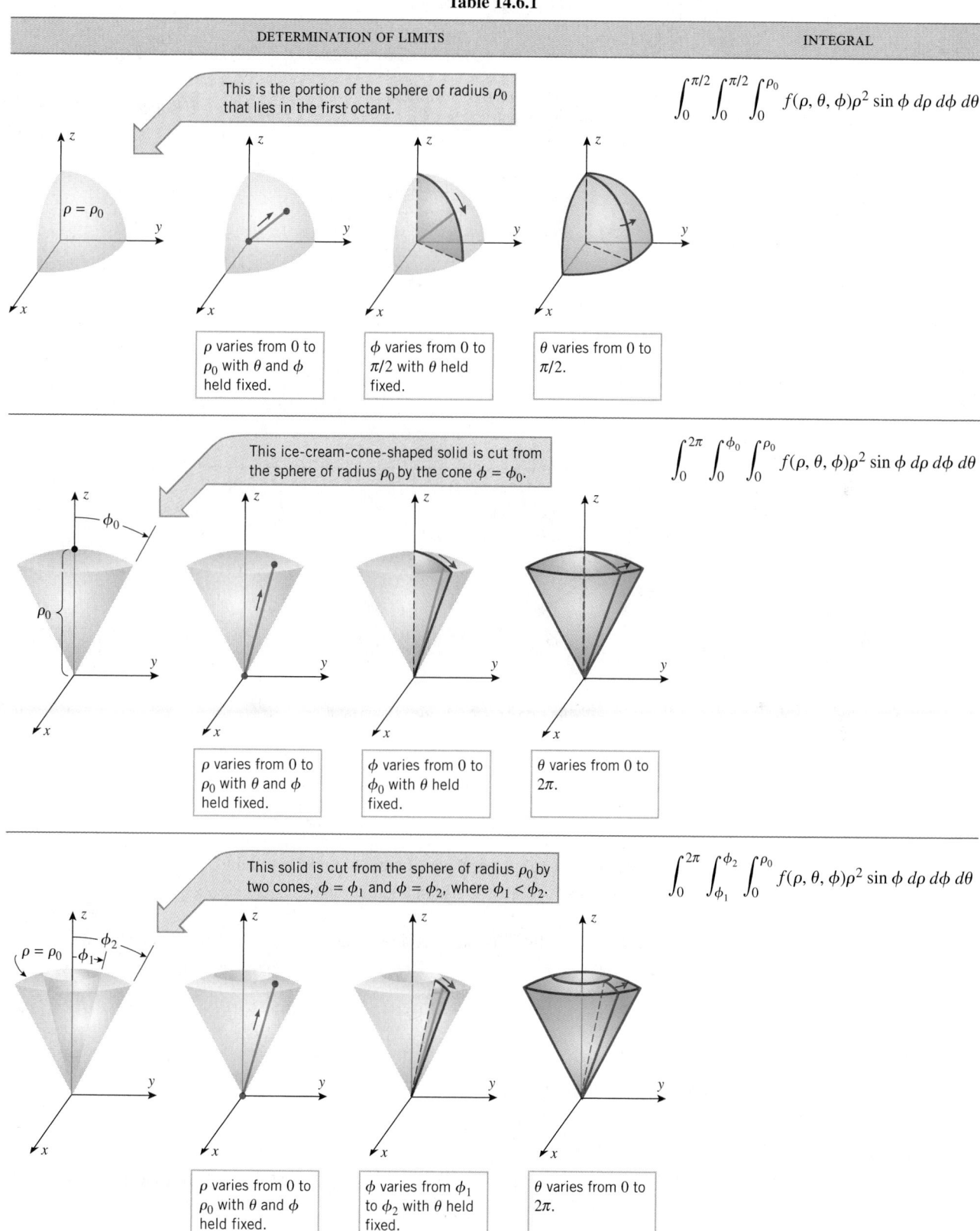

This is the portion of the sphere of radius ρ_0 that lies in the first octant.

$$\int_0^{\pi/2} \int_0^{\pi/2} \int_0^{\rho_0} f(\rho, \theta, \phi)\rho^2 \sin\phi \, d\rho \, d\phi \, d\theta$$

ρ varies from 0 to ρ_0 with θ and ϕ held fixed.

ϕ varies from 0 to $\pi/2$ with θ held fixed.

θ varies from 0 to $\pi/2$.

This ice-cream-cone-shaped solid is cut from the sphere of radius ρ_0 by the cone $\phi = \phi_0$.

$$\int_0^{2\pi} \int_0^{\phi_0} \int_0^{\rho_0} f(\rho, \theta, \phi)\rho^2 \sin\phi \, d\rho \, d\phi \, d\theta$$

ρ varies from 0 to ρ_0 with θ and ϕ held fixed.

ϕ varies from 0 to ϕ_0 with θ held fixed.

θ varies from 0 to 2π.

This solid is cut from the sphere of radius ρ_0 by two cones, $\phi = \phi_1$ and $\phi = \phi_2$, where $\phi_1 < \phi_2$.

$$\int_0^{2\pi} \int_{\phi_1}^{\phi_2} \int_0^{\rho_0} f(\rho, \theta, \phi)\rho^2 \sin\phi \, d\rho \, d\phi \, d\theta$$

ρ varies from 0 to ρ_0 with θ and ϕ held fixed.

ϕ varies from ϕ_1 to ϕ_2 with θ held fixed.

θ varies from 0 to 2π.

Table 14.6.1 (*continued*)

DETERMINATION OF LIMITS	INTEGRAL

This solid is enclosed laterally by the cone $\phi = \phi_0$, where $0 < \phi_0 < \pi/2$, and on top by the horizontal plane $z = a$.

$$\int_0^{2\pi} \int_0^{\phi_0} \int_0^{a\sec\phi} f(\rho, \theta, \phi)\rho^2 \sin\phi \, d\rho \, d\phi \, d\theta$$

ρ varies from 0 to $a \sec \phi$ with θ and ϕ held fixed.

ϕ varies from 0 to ϕ_0 with θ held fixed.

θ varies from 0 to 2π.

This solid is enclosed between two concentric spheres, $\rho = \rho_1$ and $\rho = \rho_2$, where $\rho_1 < \rho_2$.

$$\int_0^{2\pi} \int_0^{\pi} \int_{\rho_1}^{\rho_2} f(\rho, \theta, \phi)\rho^2 \sin\phi \, d\rho \, d\phi \, d\theta$$

ρ varies from ρ_1 to ρ_2 with θ and ϕ held fixed.

ϕ varies from 0 to π with θ held fixed.

θ varies from 0 to 2π.

▶ **Example 3** Use spherical coordinates to find the volume of the solid G bounded above by the sphere $x^2 + y^2 + z^2 = 16$ and below by the cone $z = \sqrt{x^2 + y^2}$.

Solution. The solid G is sketched in Figure 14.6.11. In spherical coordinates, the equation of the sphere $x^2 + y^2 + z^2 = 16$ is $\rho = 4$ and the equation of the cone $z = \sqrt{x^2 + y^2}$ is

$$\rho \cos\phi = \sqrt{\rho^2 \sin^2\phi \cos^2\theta + \rho^2 \sin^2\phi \sin^2\theta}$$

which simplifies to

$$\rho \cos\phi = \rho \sin\phi$$

Dividing both sides of this equation by $\rho \cos\phi$ yields $\tan\phi = 1$, from which it follows that

$$\phi = \pi/4$$

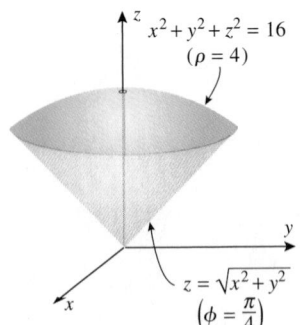

$x^2 + y^2 + z^2 = 16$
$(\rho = 4)$

$z = \sqrt{x^2 + y^2}$
$\left(\phi = \dfrac{\pi}{4}\right)$

▲ **Figure 14.6.11**

Thus, it follows from the second entry in Table 14.6.1 that the volume of G is

$$V = \iiint_G dV = \int_0^{2\pi} \int_0^{\pi/4} \int_0^4 \rho^2 \sin\phi \, d\rho \, d\phi \, d\theta$$

$$= \int_0^{2\pi} \int_0^{\pi/4} \left[\frac{\rho^3}{3} \sin\phi\right]_{\rho=0}^4 d\phi \, d\theta$$

$$= \int_0^{2\pi} \int_0^{\pi/4} \frac{64}{3} \sin\phi \, d\phi \, d\theta$$

$$= \frac{64}{3} \int_0^{2\pi} \left[-\cos\phi\right]_{\phi=0}^{\pi/4} d\theta = \frac{64}{3} \int_0^{2\pi} \left(1 - \frac{\sqrt{2}}{2}\right) d\theta$$

$$= \frac{64\pi}{3}(2 - \sqrt{2}) \approx 39.26 \blacktriangleleft$$

■ CONVERTING TRIPLE INTEGRALS FROM RECTANGULAR TO SPHERICAL COORDINATES

Referring to Table 11.8.1, triple integrals can be converted from rectangular coordinates to spherical coordinates by making the substitution $x = \rho \sin\phi \cos\theta$, $y = \rho \sin\phi \sin\theta$, $z = \rho \cos\phi$. The two integrals are related by the equation

$$\iiint_G f(x, y, z) \, dV = \iiint_{\substack{\text{appropriate} \\ \text{limits}}} f(\rho \sin\phi \cos\theta, \rho \sin\phi \sin\theta, \rho \cos\phi)\rho^2 \sin\phi \, d\rho \, d\phi \, d\theta \qquad (10)$$

▶ **Example 4**   Use spherical coordinates to evaluate

$$\int_{-2}^2 \int_{-\sqrt{4-x^2}}^{\sqrt{4-x^2}} \int_0^{\sqrt{4-x^2-y^2}} z^2 \sqrt{x^2 + y^2 + z^2} \, dz \, dy \, dx$$

Solution.   In problems like this, it is helpful to begin (when possible) with a sketch of the region G of integration. From the z-limits of integration, the upper surface of G is the hemisphere $z = \sqrt{4 - x^2 - y^2}$ and the lower surface is the xy-plane $z = 0$. From the x- and y-limits of integration, the projection of the solid G on the xy-plane is the region enclosed by the circle $x^2 + y^2 = 4$. From this information we obtain the sketch of G in Figure 14.6.12. Thus,

$$\int_{-2}^2 \int_{-\sqrt{4-x^2}}^{\sqrt{4-x^2}} \int_0^{\sqrt{4-x^2-y^2}} z^2 \sqrt{x^2 + y^2 + z^2} \, dz \, dy \, dx$$

$$= \iiint_G z^2 \sqrt{x^2 + y^2 + z^2} \, dV$$

$$= \int_0^{2\pi} \int_0^{\pi/2} \int_0^2 \rho^5 \cos^2\phi \sin\phi \, d\rho \, d\phi \, d\theta$$

$$= \int_0^{2\pi} \int_0^{\pi/2} \frac{32}{3} \cos^2\phi \sin\phi \, d\phi \, d\theta$$

$$= \frac{32}{3} \int_0^{2\pi} \left[-\frac{1}{3} \cos^3\phi\right]_{\phi=0}^{\pi/2} d\theta = \frac{32}{9} \int_0^{2\pi} d\theta = \frac{64}{9}\pi \blacktriangleleft$$

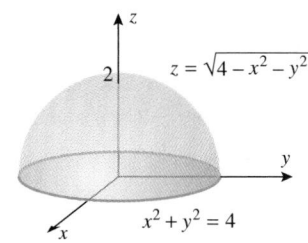

$z = \sqrt{4 - x^2 - y^2}$

$x^2 + y^2 = 4$

▲ **Figure 14.6.12**

✔ **QUICK CHECK EXERCISES 14.6**   *(See page 1058 for answers.)*

1. (a) The cylindrical wedge $1 \leq r \leq 3$, $\pi/6 \leq \theta \leq \pi/2$, $0 \leq z \leq 5$ has volume $V =$ _____.
   (b) The spherical wedge $1 \leq \rho \leq 3$, $\pi/6 \leq \theta \leq \pi/2$, $0 \leq \phi \leq \pi/3$ has volume $V =$ _____.

2. Let G be the solid region inside the sphere of radius 2 centered at the origin and above the plane $z = 1$. In each part, supply the missing integrand and limits of integration for the iterated integral in cylindrical coordinates.
   (a) The volume of G is
   $$\iiint_G dV = \int_\square^\square \int_\square^\square \int_\square^\square \underline{\quad\quad} \, dz \, dr \, d\theta$$
   (b) $$\iiint_G \frac{z}{x^2 + y^2 + z^2} \, dV$$
   $$= \int_\square^\square \int_\square^\square \int_\square^\square \underline{\quad\quad} \, dz \, dr \, d\theta$$

3. Let G be the solid region described in Quick Check Exercise 2. In each part, supply the missing integrand and limits of integration for the iterated integral in spherical coordinates.
   (a) The volume of G is
   $$\iiint_G dV = \int_\square^\square \int_\square^\square \int_\square^\square \underline{\quad\quad} \, d\rho \, d\phi \, d\theta$$
   (b) $$\iiint_G \frac{z}{x^2 + y^2 + z^2} \, dV$$
   $$= \int_\square^\square \int_\square^\square \int_\square^\square \underline{\quad\quad} \, d\rho \, d\phi \, d\theta$$

EXERCISE SET 14.6   [C] CAS

1–4 Evaluate the iterated integral.

1. $$\int_0^{2\pi} \int_0^1 \int_0^{\sqrt{1-r^2}} zr \, dz \, dr \, d\theta$$

2. $$\int_0^{\pi/2} \int_0^{\cos\theta} \int_0^{r^2} r \sin\theta \, dz \, dr \, d\theta$$

3. $$\int_0^{\pi/2} \int_0^{\pi/2} \int_0^1 \rho^3 \sin\phi \cos\phi \, d\rho \, d\phi \, d\theta$$

4. $$\int_0^{2\pi} \int_0^{\pi/4} \int_0^{a\sec\phi} \rho^2 \sin\phi \, d\rho \, d\phi \, d\theta \quad (a > 0)$$

FOCUS ON CONCEPTS

5. Sketch the region G and identify the function f so that
   $$\iiint_G f(r, \theta, z) \, dV$$
   corresponds to the iterated integral in Exercise 1.

6. Sketch the region G and identify the function f so that
   $$\iiint_G f(r, \theta, z) \, dV$$
   corresponds to the iterated integral in Exercise 2.

7. Sketch the region G and identify the function f so that
   $$\iiint_G f(\rho, \theta, \phi) \, dV$$
   corresponds to the iterated integral in Exercise 3.

8. Sketch the region G and identify the function f so that
   $$\iiint_G f(\rho, \theta, \phi) \, dV$$
   corresponds to the iterated integral in Exercise 4.

9–12 Use cylindrical coordinates to find the volume of the solid.

9. The solid enclosed by the paraboloid $z = x^2 + y^2$ and the plane $z = 9$.

10. The solid that is bounded above and below by the sphere $x^2 + y^2 + z^2 = 9$ and inside the cylinder $x^2 + y^2 = 4$.

11. The solid that is inside the surface $r^2 + z^2 = 20$ but not above the surface $z = r^2$.

12. The solid enclosed between the cone $z = (hr)/a$ and the plane $z = h$.

13–16 Use spherical coordinates to find the volume of the solid.

13. The solid bounded above by the sphere $\rho = 4$ and below by the cone $\phi = \pi/3$.

14. The solid within the cone $\phi = \pi/4$ and between the spheres $\rho = 1$ and $\rho = 2$.

15. The solid enclosed by the sphere $x^2 + y^2 + z^2 = 4a^2$ and the planes $z = 0$ and $z = a$.

16. The solid within the sphere $x^2 + y^2 + z^2 = 9$, outside the cone $z = \sqrt{x^2 + y^2}$, and above the xy-plane.

17–20 Use cylindrical or spherical coordinates to evaluate the integral. ■

17. $\displaystyle\int_0^a \int_0^{\sqrt{a^2-x^2}} \int_0^{a^2-x^2-y^2} x^2 \, dz\,dy\,dx \quad (a > 0)$

18. $\displaystyle\int_{-1}^1 \int_0^{\sqrt{1-x^2}} \int_0^{\sqrt{1-x^2-y^2}} e^{-(x^2+y^2+z^2)^{3/2}} \, dz\,dy\,dx$

19. $\displaystyle\int_0^2 \int_0^{\sqrt{4-y^2}} \int_{\sqrt{x^2+y^2}}^{\sqrt{8-x^2-y^2}} z^2 \, dz\,dx\,dy$

20. $\displaystyle\int_{-3}^3 \int_{-\sqrt{9-y^2}}^{\sqrt{9-y^2}} \int_{-\sqrt{9-x^2-y^2}}^{\sqrt{9-x^2-y^2}} \sqrt{x^2+y^2+z^2} \, dz\,dx\,dy$

21–24 True–False Determine whether the statement is true or false. Explain your answer. ■

21. A rectangular triple integral can be expressed as an iterated integral in cylindrical coordinates as

$$\iiint_G f(x,y,z)\,dV = \iiint_{\substack{\text{appropriate}\\\text{limits}}} f(r\cos\theta, r\sin\theta, z)r^2 \, dz\,dr\,d\theta$$

22. If $0 \le \rho_1 < \rho_2$, $0 \le \theta_1 < \theta_2 \le 2\pi$, and $0 \le \phi_1 < \phi_2 \le \pi$, then the volume of the spherical wedge bounded by the spheres $\rho = \rho_1$ and $\rho = \rho_2$, the half-planes $\theta = \theta_1$ and $\theta = \theta_2$, and the cones $\phi = \phi_1$ and $\phi = \phi_2$ is

$$\int_{\theta_1}^{\theta_2} \int_{\phi_1}^{\phi_2} \int_{\rho_1}^{\rho_2} \rho^2 \sin\phi \, d\rho\,d\phi\,d\theta$$

23. Let G be the solid region in 3-space between the spheres of radius 1 and 3 centered at the origin and above the cone $z = \sqrt{x^2+y^2}$. The volume of G equals

$$\int_0^{\pi/4} \int_0^{2\pi} \int_1^3 \rho^2 \sin\phi \, d\rho\,d\theta\,d\phi$$

24. If G is the solid in Exercise 23 and $f(x,y,z)$ is continuous on G, then

$$\iiint_G f(x,y,z)\,dV = \int_0^{\pi/4} \int_0^{2\pi} \int_1^3 F(\rho,\theta,\phi)\rho^2 \sin\phi \, d\rho\,d\theta\,d\phi$$

where $F(\rho,\theta,\phi) = f(\rho\sin\phi\sin\theta, \rho\sin\phi\cos\theta, \rho\cos\phi)$.

c **25.** (a) Use a CAS to evaluate

$$\int_{-2}^2 \int_1^4 \int_{\pi/6}^{\pi/3} \frac{r\tan^3\theta}{\sqrt{1+z^2}} \, d\theta\,dr\,dz$$

(b) Find a function $f(x,y,z)$ and sketch a region G in 3-space so that the triple integral in rectangular coordinates

$$\iiint_G f(x,y,z)\,dV$$

matches the iterated integral in cylindrical coordinates given in part (a).

c **26.** Use a CAS to evaluate

$$\int_0^{\pi/2} \int_0^{\pi/4} \int_0^{\cos\theta} \rho^{17} \cos\phi \cos^{19}\theta \, d\rho\,d\phi\,d\theta$$

27. Find the volume enclosed by $x^2 + y^2 + z^2 = a^2$ using
(a) cylindrical coordinates
(b) spherical coordinates.

28. Let G be the solid in the first octant bounded by the sphere $x^2 + y^2 + z^2 = 4$ and the coordinate planes. Evaluate

$$\iiint_G xyz \, dV$$

(a) using rectangular coordinates
(b) using cylindrical coordinates
(c) using spherical coordinates.

29. Find the volume of the solid in the first octant bounded by the sphere $\rho = 2$, the coordinate planes, and the cones $\phi = \pi/6$ and $\phi = \pi/3$.

30. In this exercise we will obtain a formula for the volume of the spherical wedge illustrated in Figures 14.6.7 and 14.6.9.
(a) Use a triple integral in cylindrical coordinates to show that the volume of the solid bounded above by a sphere $\rho = \rho_0$, below by a cone $\phi = \phi_0$, and on the sides by $\theta = \theta_1$ and $\theta = \theta_2$ ($\theta_1 < \theta_2$) is

$$V = \tfrac{1}{3}\rho_0^3(1 - \cos\phi_0)(\theta_2 - \theta_1)$$

[*Hint:* In cylindrical coordinates, the sphere has the equation $r^2 + z^2 = \rho_0^2$ and the cone has the equation $z = r\cot\phi_0$. For simplicity, consider only the case $0 < \phi_0 < \pi/2$.]
(b) Subtract appropriate volumes and use the result in part (a) to deduce that the volume ΔV of the spherical wedge is

$$\Delta V = \frac{\rho_2^3 - \rho_1^3}{3}(\cos\phi_1 - \cos\phi_2)(\theta_2 - \theta_1)$$

(c) Apply the Mean-Value Theorem to the functions $\cos\phi$ and ρ^3 to deduce that the formula in part (b) can be written as

$$\Delta V = \rho^{*2} \sin\phi^* \, \Delta\rho \, \Delta\phi \, \Delta\theta$$

where ρ^* is between ρ_1 and ρ_2, ϕ^* is between ϕ_1 and ϕ_2, and $\Delta\rho = \rho_2 - \rho_1$, $\Delta\phi = \phi_2 - \phi_1$, $\Delta\theta = \theta_2 - \theta_1$.

31. Writing Suppose that a triple integral is expressed in cylindrical or spherical coordinates in such a way that the outermost variable of integration is θ and none of the limits of integration involves θ. Discuss what this says about the region of integration for the integral.

1. (a) $\dfrac{20}{3}\pi$ (b) $\dfrac{13}{9}\pi$ **2.** (a) $\displaystyle\int_0^{2\pi}\int_0^{\sqrt{3}}\int_1^{\sqrt{4-r^2}} r\,dz\,dr\,d\theta$ (b) $\displaystyle\int_0^{2\pi}\int_0^{\sqrt{3}}\int_1^{\sqrt{4-r^2}} \dfrac{rz}{r^2+z^2}\,dz\,dr\,d\theta$

3. (a) $\displaystyle\int_0^{2\pi}\int_0^{\pi/3}\int_{\sec\phi}^2 \rho^2\sin\phi\,d\rho\,d\phi\,d\theta$ (b) $\displaystyle\int_0^{2\pi}\int_0^{\pi/3}\int_{\sec\phi}^2 \rho\cos\phi\sin\phi\,d\rho\,d\phi\,d\theta$

14.7 CHANGE OF VARIABLES IN MULTIPLE INTEGRALS; JACOBIANS

In this section we will discuss a general method for evaluating double and triple integrals by substitution. Most of the results in this section are very difficult to prove, so our approach will be informal and motivational. Our goal is to provide a geometric understanding of the basic principles and an exposure to computational techniques.

■ CHANGE OF VARIABLE IN A SINGLE INTEGRAL

To motivate techniques for evaluating double and triple integrals by substitution, it will be helpful to consider the effect of a substitution $x = g(u)$ on a single integral over an interval $[a, b]$. If g is differentiable and either increasing or decreasing, then g is one-to-one and

$$\int_a^b f(x)\,dx = \int_{g^{-1}(a)}^{g^{-1}(b)} f(g(u))g'(u)\,du$$

In this relationship $f(x)$ and dx are expressed in terms of u, and the u-limits of integration result from solving the equations

$$a = g(u) \quad \text{and} \quad b = g(u)$$

In the case where g is decreasing we have $g^{-1}(b) < g^{-1}(a)$, which is contrary to our usual convention of writing definite integrals with the larger limit of integration at the top. We can remedy this by reversing the limits of integration and writing

$$\int_a^b f(x)\,dx = -\int_{g^{-1}(b)}^{g^{-1}(a)} f(g(u))g'(u)\,du = \int_{g^{-1}(b)}^{g^{-1}(a)} f(g(u))|g'(u)|\,du$$

where the absolute value results from the fact that $g'(u)$ is negative. Thus, regardless of whether g is increasing or decreasing we can write

$$\int_a^b f(x)\,dx = \int_\alpha^\beta f(g(u))|g'(u)|\,du \tag{1}$$

where α and β are the u-limits of integration and $\alpha < \beta$.

The expression $g'(u)$ that appears in (1) is called the ***Jacobian*** of the change of variable $x = g(u)$ in honor of C. G. J. Jacobi, who made the first serious study of change of variables in multiple integrals in the mid-1800s. Formula (1) reveals three effects of the change of variable $x = g(u)$:

- The new integrand becomes $f(g(u))$ times the absolute value of the Jacobian.
- dx becomes du.
- The x-interval of integration is transformed into a u-interval of integration.

Our goal in this section is to show that analogous results hold for changing variables in double and triple integrals.

■ TRANSFORMATIONS OF THE PLANE

In earlier sections we considered parametric equations of three kinds:

$$x = x(t), \quad y = y(t)$$ ⬚ A curve in the plane

$$x = x(t), \quad y = y(t), \quad z = z(t)$$ ⬚ A curve in 3-space

$$x = x(u, v), \quad y = y(u, v), \quad z = z(u, v)$$ ⬚ A surface in 3-space

Now we will consider parametric equations of the form

$$x = x(u, v), \quad y = y(u, v) \tag{2}$$

Parametric equations of this type associate points in the xy-plane with points in the uv-plane. These equations can be written in vector form as

$$\mathbf{r} = \mathbf{r}(u, v) = x(u, v)\mathbf{i} + y(u, v)\mathbf{j}$$

where $\mathbf{r} = x\mathbf{i} + y\mathbf{j}$ is a position vector in the xy-plane and $\mathbf{r}(u, v)$ is a vector-valued function of the variables u and v.

It will also be useful in this section to think of the parametric equations in (2) in terms of inputs and outputs. If we think of the pair of numbers (u, v) as an input, then the two equations, in combination, produce a unique output (x, y), and hence define a function T that associates points in the xy-plane with points in the uv-plane. This function is described by the formula

$$T(u, v) = (x(u, v), y(u, v))$$

We call T a **transformation** from the uv-plane to the xy-plane and (x, y) the **image** of (u, v) under the transformation T. We also say that T **maps** (u, v) into (x, y). The set R of all images in the xy-plane of a set S in the uv-plane is called the **image of S under T**. If distinct points in the uv-plane have distinct images in the xy-plane, then T is said to be **one-to-one**. In this case the equations in (2) define u and v as functions of x and y, say

$$u = u(x, y), \quad v = v(x, y)$$

These equations, which can often be obtained by solving (2) for u and v in terms of x and y, define a transformation from the xy-plane to the uv-plane that maps the image of (u, v) under T back into (u, v). This transformation is denoted by T^{-1} and is called the **inverse of T** (Figure 14.7.1).

Carl Gustav Jacob Jacobi (1804–1851) German mathematician. Jacobi, the son of a banker, grew up in a background of wealth and culture and showed brilliance in mathematics early. He resisted studying mathematics by rote, preferring instead to learn general principles from the works of the masters, Euler and Lagrange. He entered the University of Berlin at age 16 as a student of mathematics and classical studies. However, he soon realized that he could not do both and turned fully to mathematics with a blazing intensity that he would maintain throughout his life. He received his Ph.D. in 1825 and was able to secure a position as a lecturer at the University of Berlin by giving up Judaism and becoming a Christian. However, his promotion opportunities remained limited and he moved on to the University of Königsberg. Jacobi was born to teach—he had a dynamic personality and delivered his lectures with a clarity and enthusiasm that frequently left his audience spellbound. In spite of extensive teaching commitments, he was able to publish volumes of revolutionary mathematical research that eventually made him the leading European mathematician after Gauss. His main body of research was in the area of elliptic functions, a branch of mathematics with important applications in astronomy and physics as well as in other fields of mathematics. Because of his family wealth, Jacobi was not dependent on his teaching salary in his early years. However, his comfortable world eventually collapsed. In 1840 his family went bankrupt and he was wiped out financially. In 1842 he had a nervous breakdown from overwork. In 1843 he became seriously ill with diabetes and moved to Berlin with the help of a government grant to defray his medical expenses. In 1848 he made an injudicious political speech that caused the government to withdraw the grant, eventually resulting in the loss of his home. His health continued to decline and in 1851 he finally succumbed to successive bouts of influenza and smallpox. In spite of all his problems, Jacobi was a tireless worker to the end. When a friend expressed concern about the effect of the hard work on his health, Jacobi replied, "Certainly, I have sometimes endangered my health by overwork, but what of it? Only cabbages have no nerves, no worries. And what do they get out of their perfect well-being?"

Because there are four variables involved, a three-dimensional figure is not very useful for describing the transformation geometrically. The idea here is to use the two planes to get the four dimensions needed.

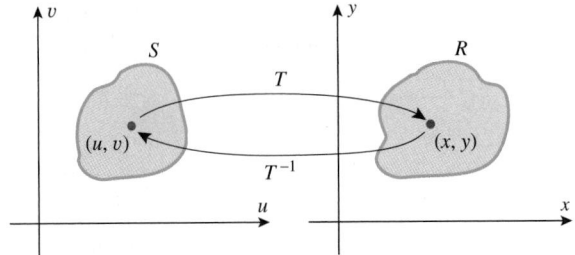

▶ **Figure 14.7.1**

One way to visualize the geometric effect of a transformation T is to determine the images in the xy-plane of the vertical and horizontal lines in the uv-plane. Following the discussion in Section 14.4, sets of points in the xy-plane that are images of horizontal lines (v constant) are called ***constant v-curves***, and sets of points that are images of vertical lines (u constant) are called ***constant u-curves*** (Figure 14.7.2).

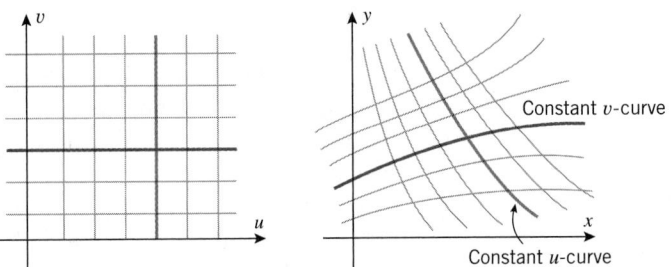

▶ **Figure 14.7.2**

▶ **Example 1**   Let T be the transformation from the uv-plane to the xy-plane defined by the equations

$$x = \tfrac{1}{4}(u + v), \quad y = \tfrac{1}{2}(u - v) \tag{3}$$

(a) Find $T(1, 3)$.

(b) Sketch the constant v-curves corresponding to $v = -2, -1, 0, 1, 2$.

(c) Sketch the constant u-curves corresponding to $u = -2, -1, 0, 1, 2$.

(d) Sketch the image under T of the square region in the uv-plane bounded by the lines $u = -2, u = 2, v = -2$, and $v = 2$.

Solution (a).   Substituting $u = 1$ and $v = 3$ in (3) yields $T(1, 3) = (1, -1)$.

Solutions (b and c).   In these parts it will be convenient to express the transformation equations with u and v as functions of x and y. From (3)

$$4x = u + v, \quad 2y = u - v$$

Combining these equations gives

$$4x + 2y = 2u, \quad 4x - 2y = 2v$$

or

$$2x + y = u, \quad 2x - y = v$$

Thus, the constant v-curves corresponding to $v = -2, -1, 0, 1$, and 2 are

$$2x - y = -2, \quad 2x - y = -1, \quad 2x - y = 0, \quad 2x - y = 1, \quad 2x - y = 2$$

and the constant u-curves corresponding to $u = -2, -1, 0, 1$, and 2 are

$$2x + y = -2, \quad 2x + y = -1, \quad 2x + y = 0, \quad 2x + y = 1, \quad 2x + y = 2$$

In Figure 14.7.3 the constant v-curves are shown in purple and the constant u-curves in gold.

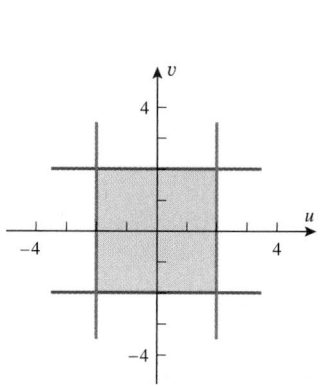

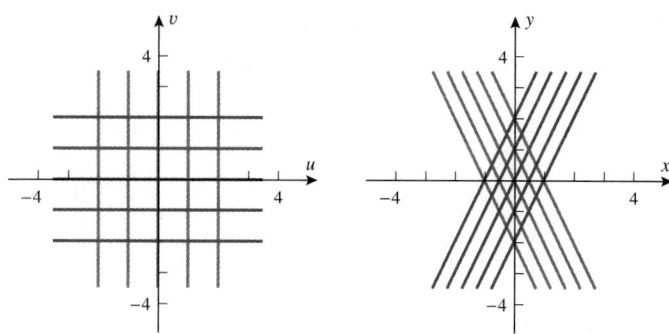

Solution (d). The image of a region can often be found by finding the image of its boundary. In this case the images of the boundary lines $u = -2$, $u = 2$, $v = -2$, and $v = 2$ enclose the diamond-shaped region in the xy-plane shown in Figure 14.7.4. ◀

■ **JACOBIANS IN TWO VARIABLES**

To derive the change of variables formula for double integrals, we will need to understand the relationship between the area of a *small* rectangular region in the uv-plane and the area of its image in the xy-plane under a transformation T given by the equations

$$x = x(u, v), \quad y = y(u, v)$$

For this purpose, suppose that Δu and Δv are positive, and consider a rectangular region S in the uv-plane enclosed by the lines

$$u = u_0, \quad u = u_0 + \Delta u, \quad v = v_0, \quad v = v_0 + \Delta v$$

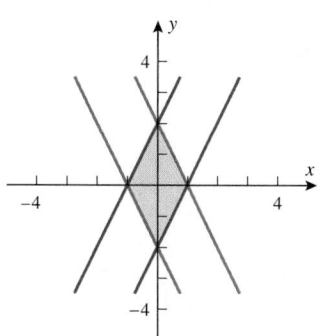

▲ **Figure 14.7.4**

If the functions $x(u, v)$ and $y(u, v)$ are continuous, and if Δu and Δv are not too large, then the image of S in the xy-plane will be a region R that looks like a slightly distorted parallelogram (Figure 14.7.5). The sides of R are the constant u-curves and v-curves that correspond to the sides of S.

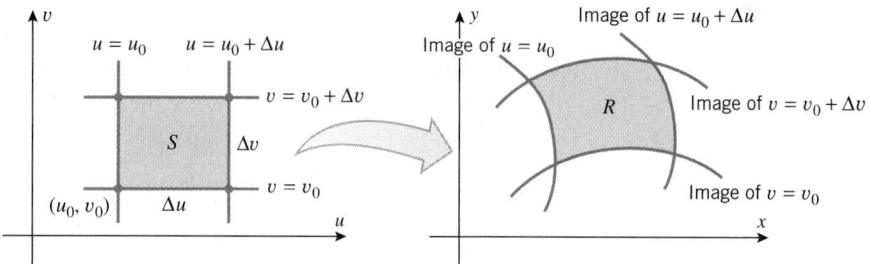

▶ **Figure 14.7.5**

If we let

$$\mathbf{r} = \mathbf{r}(u, v) = x(u, v)\mathbf{i} + y(u, v)\mathbf{j}$$

be the position vector of the point in the xy-plane that corresponds to the point (u, v) in the uv-plane, then the constant v-curve corresponding to $v = v_0$ and the constant u-curve corresponding to $u = u_0$ can be represented in vector form as

$$\mathbf{r}(u, v_0) = x(u, v_0)\mathbf{i} + y(u, v_0)\mathbf{j} \quad \boxed{\text{Constant } v\text{-curve}}$$

$$\mathbf{r}(u_0, v) = x(u_0, v)\mathbf{i} + y(u_0, v)\mathbf{j} \quad \boxed{\text{Constant } u\text{-curve}}$$

Since we are assuming Δu and Δv to be small, the region R can be approximated by a parallelogram determined by the "secant vectors"

$$\mathbf{a} = \mathbf{r}(u_0 + \Delta u, v_0) - \mathbf{r}(u_0, v_0) \quad (4)$$

$$\mathbf{b} = \mathbf{r}(u_0, v_0 + \Delta v) - \mathbf{r}(u_0, v_0) \quad (5)$$

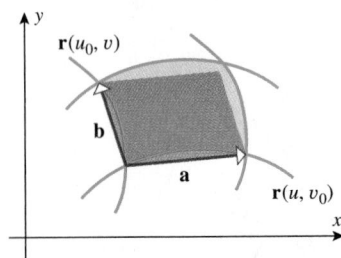

▲ **Figure 14.7.6**

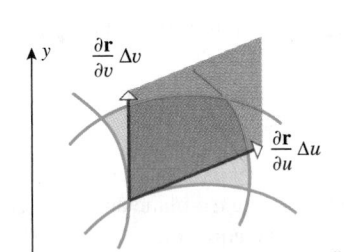

▲ **Figure 14.7.7**

shown in Figure 14.7.6. A more useful approximation of R can be obtained by using Formulas (7) and (8) of Section 14.4 to approximate these secant vectors by tangent vectors as follows:

$$\mathbf{a} = \frac{\mathbf{r}(u_0 + \Delta u, v_0) - \mathbf{r}(u_0, v_0)}{\Delta u} \Delta u$$

$$\approx \frac{\partial \mathbf{r}}{\partial u} \Delta u = \left(\frac{\partial x}{\partial u} \mathbf{i} + \frac{\partial y}{\partial u} \mathbf{j} \right) \Delta u$$

$$\mathbf{b} = \frac{\mathbf{r}(u_0, v_0 + \Delta v) - \mathbf{r}(u_0, v_0)}{\Delta v} \Delta v$$

$$\approx \frac{\partial \mathbf{r}}{\partial v} \Delta v = \left(\frac{\partial x}{\partial v} \mathbf{i} + \frac{\partial y}{\partial v} \mathbf{j} \right) \Delta v$$

where the partial derivatives are evaluated at (u_0, v_0) (Figure 14.7.7). Hence, it follows that the area of the region R, which we will denote by ΔA, can be approximated by the area of the parallelogram determined by these vectors. Thus, from Theorem 11.4.5(b) we have

$$\Delta A \approx \left\| \frac{\partial \mathbf{r}}{\partial u} \Delta u \times \frac{\partial \mathbf{r}}{\partial v} \Delta v \right\| = \left\| \frac{\partial \mathbf{r}}{\partial u} \times \frac{\partial \mathbf{r}}{\partial v} \right\| \Delta u \, \Delta v \tag{6}$$

where the derivatives are evaluated at (u_0, v_0). Computing the cross product, we obtain

$$\frac{\partial \mathbf{r}}{\partial u} \times \frac{\partial \mathbf{r}}{\partial v} = \begin{vmatrix} \mathbf{i} & \mathbf{j} & \mathbf{k} \\ \dfrac{\partial x}{\partial u} & \dfrac{\partial y}{\partial u} & 0 \\ \dfrac{\partial x}{\partial v} & \dfrac{\partial y}{\partial v} & 0 \end{vmatrix} = \begin{vmatrix} \dfrac{\partial x}{\partial u} & \dfrac{\partial y}{\partial u} \\ \dfrac{\partial x}{\partial v} & \dfrac{\partial y}{\partial v} \end{vmatrix} \mathbf{k} = \begin{vmatrix} \dfrac{\partial x}{\partial u} & \dfrac{\partial x}{\partial v} \\ \dfrac{\partial y}{\partial u} & \dfrac{\partial y}{\partial v} \end{vmatrix} \mathbf{k} \tag{7}$$

The determinant in (7) is sufficiently important that it has its own terminology and notation.

14.7.1 DEFINITION If T is the transformation from the uv-plane to the xy-plane defined by the equations $x = x(u, v)$, $y = y(u, v)$, then the *Jacobian of T* is denoted by $J(u, v)$ or by $\partial(x, y)/\partial(u, v)$ and is defined by

$$J(u, v) = \frac{\partial(x, y)}{\partial(u, v)} = \begin{vmatrix} \dfrac{\partial x}{\partial u} & \dfrac{\partial x}{\partial v} \\ \dfrac{\partial y}{\partial u} & \dfrac{\partial y}{\partial v} \end{vmatrix} = \frac{\partial x}{\partial u} \frac{\partial y}{\partial v} - \frac{\partial y}{\partial u} \frac{\partial x}{\partial v}$$

Using the notation in this definition, it follows from (6) and (7) that

$$\Delta A \approx \left\| \frac{\partial(x, y)}{\partial(u, v)} \mathbf{k} \right\| \Delta u \, \Delta v$$

or, since $\mathbf{k}$ is a unit vector,

$$\Delta A \approx \left| \frac{\partial(x, y)}{\partial(u, v)} \right| \Delta u \, \Delta v \tag{8}$$

At the point (u_0, v_0) this important formula relates the areas of the regions R and S in Figure 14.7.5; it tells us that *for small values of Δu and Δv, the area of R is approximately the absolute value of the Jacobian times the area of S.* Moreover, it is proved in advanced calculus courses that the relative error in the approximation approaches zero as $\Delta u \to 0$ and $\Delta v \to 0$.

■ CHANGE OF VARIABLES IN DOUBLE INTEGRALS

Our next objective is to provide a geometric motivation for the following result.

A precise statement of conditions under which Formula (9) holds is beyond the scope of this course. Suffice it to say that the formula holds if T is a one-to-one transformation, $f(x, y)$ is continuous on R, the partial derivatives of $x(u, v)$ and $y(u, v)$ exist and are continuous on S, and the regions R and S are not complicated.

14.7.2   CHANGE OF VARIABLES FORMULA FOR DOUBLE INTEGRALS   If the transformation $x = x(u, v)$, $y = y(u, v)$ maps the region S in the uv-plane into the region R in the xy-plane, and if the Jacobian $\partial(x, y)/\partial(u, v)$ is nonzero and does not change sign on S, then with appropriate restrictions on the transformation and the regions it follows that

$$\iint\limits_{R} f(x, y) \, dA_{xy} = \iint\limits_{S} f(x(u, v), y(u, v)) \left| \frac{\partial(x, y)}{\partial(u, v)} \right| dA_{uv} \tag{9}$$

where we have attached subscripts to the dA's to help identify the associated variables.

To motivate Formula (9), we proceed as follows:

- Subdivide the region S in the uv-plane into pieces by lines parallel to the coordinate axes, and exclude from consideration any pieces that contain points outside of S. This leaves only rectangular regions that are subsets of S. Assume that there are n such regions and denote the kth such region by S_k. Assume that S_k has dimensions Δu_k by Δv_k and, as shown in Figure 14.7.8a, let (u_k^*, v_k^*) be its "lower left corner."

- As shown in Figure 14.7.8b, the transformation T defined by the coordinate equations $x = x(u, v)$, $y = y(u, v)$ maps S_k into a curvilinear parallelogram R_k in the xy-plane and maps the point (u_k^*, v_k^*) into the point $(x_k^*, y_k^*) = (x(u_k^*, v_k^*), y(u_k^*, v_k^*))$ in R_k. Denote the area of R_k by ΔA_k.

- In rectangular coordinates the double integral of $f(x, y)$ over a region R is defined as a limit of Riemann sums in which R is subdivided into *rectangular* subregions. It is proved in advanced calculus courses that under appropriate conditions subdivisions into *curvilinear* parallelograms can be used instead. Accepting this to be so, we can approximate the double integral of $f(x, y)$ over R as

$$\iint\limits_{R} f(x, y) \, dA_{xy} \approx \sum_{k=1}^{n} f(x_k^*, y_k^*) \, \Delta A_k$$

$$\approx \sum_{k=1}^{n} f(x(u_k^*, v_k^*), y(u_k^*, v_k^*)) \left| \frac{\partial(x, y)}{\partial(u, v)} \right| \Delta u_k \, \Delta v_k$$

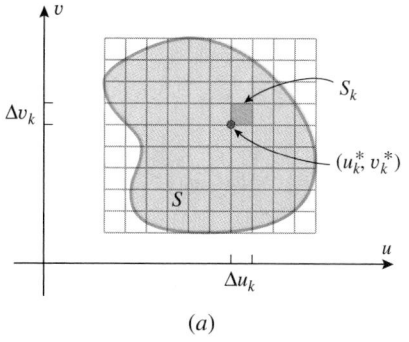

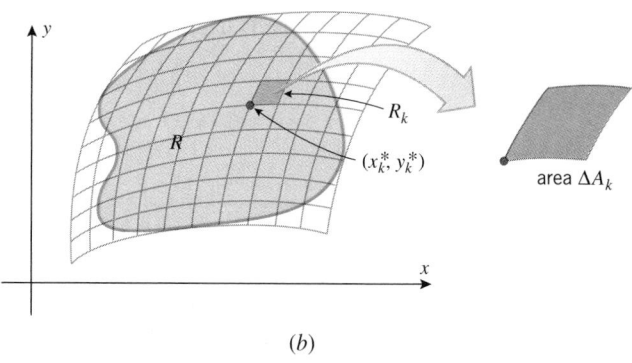

(a)   (b)

▲ **Figure 14.7.8**

where the Jacobian is evaluated at (u_k^*, v_k^*). But the last expression is a Riemann sum for the integral

$$\iint\limits_{S} f(x(u, v), y(u, v)) \left| \frac{\partial(x, y)}{\partial(u, v)} \right| dA_{uv}$$

so Formula (9) follows if we assume that the errors in the approximations approach zero as $n \to +\infty$.

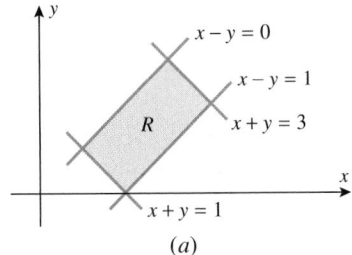

(a)

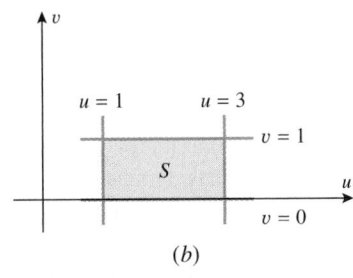

(b)

▲ **Figure 14.7.9**

▶ **Example 2** Evaluate

$$\iint\limits_{R} \frac{x - y}{x + y}\, dA$$

where R is the region enclosed by $x - y = 0$, $x - y = 1$, $x + y = 1$, and $x + y = 3$ (Figure 14.7.9a).

Solution. This integral would be tedious to evaluate directly because the region R is oriented in such a way that we would have to subdivide it and integrate over each part separately. However, the occurrence of the expressions $x - y$ and $x + y$ in the equations of the boundary suggests that the transformation

$$u = x + y, \quad v = x - y \tag{10}$$

would be helpful, since with this transformation the boundary lines

$$x + y = 1, \quad x + y = 3, \quad x - y = 0, \quad x - y = 1$$

are constant u-curves and constant v-curves corresponding to the lines

$$u = 1, \quad u = 3, \quad v = 0, \quad v = 1$$

in the uv-plane. These lines enclose the rectangular region S shown in Figure 14.7.9b. To find the Jacobian $\partial(x, y)/\partial(u, v)$ of this transformation, we first solve (10) for x and y in terms of u and v. This yields

$$x = \tfrac{1}{2}(u + v), \quad y = \tfrac{1}{2}(u - v)$$

from which we obtain

$$\frac{\partial(x, y)}{\partial(u, v)} = \begin{vmatrix} \dfrac{\partial x}{\partial u} & \dfrac{\partial x}{\partial v} \\[2mm] \dfrac{\partial y}{\partial u} & \dfrac{\partial y}{\partial v} \end{vmatrix} = \begin{vmatrix} \tfrac{1}{2} & \tfrac{1}{2} \\[2mm] \tfrac{1}{2} & -\tfrac{1}{2} \end{vmatrix} = -\tfrac{1}{4} - \tfrac{1}{4} = -\tfrac{1}{2}$$

Thus, from Formula (9), but with the notation dA rather than dA_{xy},

$$\iint\limits_{R} \frac{x - y}{x + y}\, dA = \iint\limits_{S} \frac{v}{u} \left| \frac{\partial(x, y)}{\partial(u, v)} \right| dA_{uv}$$

$$= \iint\limits_{S} \frac{v}{u} \left| -\frac{1}{2} \right| dA_{uv} = \frac{1}{2} \int_{0}^{1} \int_{1}^{3} \frac{v}{u}\, du\, dv$$

$$= \frac{1}{2} \int_{0}^{1} v \ln |u| \Big]_{u=1}^{3} dv$$

$$= \frac{1}{2} \ln 3 \int_{0}^{1} v\, dv = \frac{1}{4} \ln 3 \quad \blacktriangleleft$$

The underlying idea illustrated in Example 2 is to find a one-to-one transformation that maps a rectangle S in the uv-plane into the region R of integration, and then use that transformation as a substitution in the integral to produce an equivalent integral over S.

▶ **Example 3**   Evaluate

$$\iint\limits_R e^{xy}\, dA$$

where R is the region enclosed by the lines $y = \frac{1}{2}x$ and $y = x$ and the hyperbolas $y = 1/x$ and $y = 2/x$ (Figure 14.7.10a).

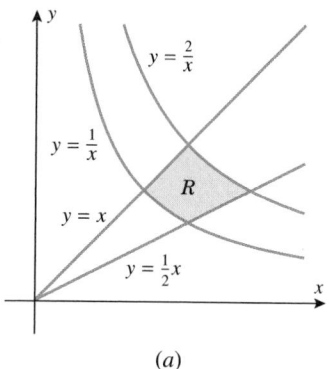

(a)

Solution.   As in the last example, we look for a transformation in which the boundary curves in the xy-plane become constant v-curves and constant u-curves. For this purpose we rewrite the four boundary curves as

$$\frac{y}{x} = \frac{1}{2}, \quad \frac{y}{x} = 1, \quad xy = 1, \quad xy = 2$$

which suggests the transformation

$$u = \frac{y}{x}, \quad v = xy \tag{11}$$

With this transformation the boundary curves in the xy-plane are constant u-curves and constant v-curves corresponding to the lines

$$u = \tfrac{1}{2}, \quad u = 1, \quad v = 1, \quad v = 2$$

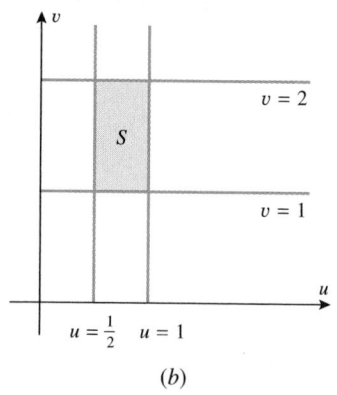

(b)

▲ **Figure 14.7.10**

in the uv-plane. These lines enclose the region S shown in Figure 14.7.10b. To find the Jacobian $\partial(x, y)/\partial(u, v)$ of this transformation, we first solve (11) for x and y in terms of u and v. This yields

$$x = \sqrt{v/u}, \quad y = \sqrt{uv}$$

from which we obtain

$$\frac{\partial(x, y)}{\partial(u, v)} = \begin{vmatrix} \dfrac{\partial x}{\partial u} & \dfrac{\partial x}{\partial v} \\[2mm] \dfrac{\partial y}{\partial u} & \dfrac{\partial y}{\partial v} \end{vmatrix} = \begin{vmatrix} -\dfrac{1}{2u}\sqrt{\dfrac{v}{u}} & \dfrac{1}{2\sqrt{uv}} \\[3mm] \dfrac{1}{2}\sqrt{\dfrac{v}{u}} & \dfrac{1}{2}\sqrt{\dfrac{u}{v}} \end{vmatrix} = -\frac{1}{4u} - \frac{1}{4u} = -\frac{1}{2u}$$

Thus, from Formula (9), but with the notation dA rather than dA_{xy},

$$\iint\limits_R e^{xy}\, dA = \iint\limits_S e^{v}\left| -\frac{1}{2u} \right| dA_{uv} = \frac{1}{2}\iint\limits_S \frac{1}{u}e^{v}\, dA_{uv}$$

$$= \frac{1}{2}\int_1^2 \int_{1/2}^1 \frac{1}{u}e^{v}\, du\, dv = \frac{1}{2}\int_1^2 e^{v} \ln|u|\Big]_{u=1/2}^1 dv$$

$$= \frac{1}{2}\ln 2 \int_1^2 e^{v}\, dv = \frac{1}{2}(e^2 - e)\ln 2 \quad ◀$$

■ **CHANGE OF VARIABLES IN TRIPLE INTEGRALS**

Equations of the form

$$x = x(u, v, w), \quad y = y(u, v, w), \quad z = z(u, v, w) \tag{12}$$

define a *transformation* T from uvw-space to xyz-space. Just as a transformation $x = x(u, v)$, $y = y(u, v)$ in two variables maps small rectangles in the uv-plane into curvilinear parallelograms in the xy-plane, so (12) maps small rectangular parallelepipeds

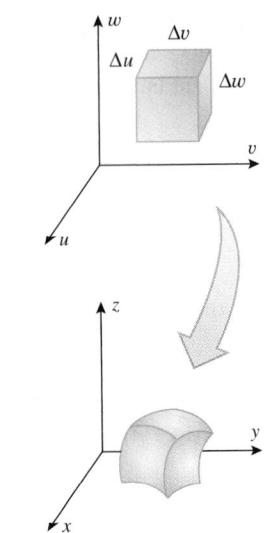

▲ **Figure 14.7.11**

in uvw-space into curvilinear parallelepipeds in xyz-space (Figure 14.7.11). The definition of the Jacobian of (12) is similar to Definition 14.7.1.

14.7.3 **DEFINITION** If T is the transformation from uvw-space to xyz-space defined by the equations $x = x(u, v, w)$, $y = y(u, v, w)$, $z = z(u, v, w)$, then the **Jacobian of T** is denoted by $J(u, v, w)$ or $\partial(x, y, z)/\partial(u, v, w)$ and is defined by

$$J(u, v, w) = \frac{\partial(x, y, z)}{\partial(u, v, w)} = \begin{vmatrix} \dfrac{\partial x}{\partial u} & \dfrac{\partial x}{\partial v} & \dfrac{\partial x}{\partial w} \\[2mm] \dfrac{\partial y}{\partial u} & \dfrac{\partial y}{\partial v} & \dfrac{\partial y}{\partial w} \\[2mm] \dfrac{\partial z}{\partial u} & \dfrac{\partial z}{\partial v} & \dfrac{\partial z}{\partial w} \end{vmatrix}$$

For small values of Δu, Δv, and Δw, the volume ΔV of the curvilinear parallelepiped in Figure 14.7.11 is related to the volume $\Delta u\, \Delta v\, \Delta w$ of the rectangular parallelepiped by

$$\Delta V \approx \left| \frac{\partial(x, y, z)}{\partial(u, v, w)} \right| \Delta u\, \Delta v\, \Delta w \tag{13}$$

which is the analog of Formula (8). Using this relationship and an argument similar to the one that led to Formula (9), we can obtain the following result.

14.7.4 **CHANGE OF VARIABLES FORMULA FOR TRIPLE INTEGRALS** If the transformation $x = x(u, v, w)$, $y = y(u, v, w)$, $z = z(u, v, w)$ maps the region S in uvw-space into the region R in xyz-space, and if the Jacobian $\partial(x, y, z)/\partial(u, v, w)$ is nonzero and does not change sign on S, then with appropriate restrictions on the transformation and the regions it follows that

$$\iiint\limits_{R} f(x, y, z)\, dV_{xyz} = \iiint\limits_{S} f(x(u, v, w),\ y(u, v, w),\ z(u, v, w)) \left| \frac{\partial(x, y, z)}{\partial(u, v, w)} \right| dV_{uvw}$$

$$\tag{14}$$

▶ **Example 4** Find the volume of the region G enclosed by the ellipsoid

$$\frac{x^2}{a^2} + \frac{y^2}{b^2} + \frac{z^2}{c^2} = 1$$

Solution. The volume V is given by the triple integral

$$V = \iiint\limits_{G} dV$$

To evaluate this integral, we make the change of variables

$$x = au, \quad y = bv, \quad z = cw \tag{15}$$

which maps the region S in uvw-space enclosed by a sphere of radius 1 into the region G in xyz-space. This can be seen from (15) by noting that

$$\frac{x^2}{a^2} + \frac{y^2}{b^2} + \frac{z^2}{c^2} = 1 \quad \text{becomes} \quad u^2 + v^2 + w^2 = 1$$

The Jacobian of (15) is

$$\frac{\partial(x, y, z)}{\partial(u, v, w)} = \begin{vmatrix} \dfrac{\partial x}{\partial u} & \dfrac{\partial x}{\partial v} & \dfrac{\partial x}{\partial w} \\[2mm] \dfrac{\partial y}{\partial u} & \dfrac{\partial y}{\partial v} & \dfrac{\partial y}{\partial w} \\[2mm] \dfrac{\partial z}{\partial u} & \dfrac{\partial z}{\partial v} & \dfrac{\partial z}{\partial w} \end{vmatrix} = \begin{vmatrix} a & 0 & 0 \\ 0 & b & 0 \\ 0 & 0 & c \end{vmatrix} = abc$$

Thus, from Formula (14), but with the notation dV rather than dV_{xyz},

$$V = \iiint\limits_{G} dV = \iiint\limits_{S} \left| \frac{\partial(x, y, z)}{\partial(u, v, w)} \right| dV_{uvw} = abc \iiint\limits_{S} dV_{uvw}$$

The last integral is the volume enclosed by a sphere of radius 1, which we know to be $\frac{4}{3}\pi$. Thus, the volume enclosed by the ellipsoid is $V = \frac{4}{3}\pi abc$. ◀

Jacobians also arise in converting triple integrals in rectangular coordinates to iterated integrals in cylindrical and spherical coordinates. For example, we will ask you to show in Exercise 48 that the Jacobian of the transformation

$$x = r\cos\theta, \quad y = r\sin\theta, \quad z = z$$

is

$$\frac{\partial(x, y, z)}{\partial(r, \theta, z)} = r$$

and the Jacobian of the transformation

$$x = \rho\sin\phi\cos\theta, \quad y = \rho\sin\phi\sin\theta, \quad z = \rho\cos\phi$$

is

$$\frac{\partial(x, y, z)}{\partial(\rho, \phi, \theta)} = \rho^2\sin\phi$$

Thus, Formulas (6) and (10) of Section 14.6 can be expressed in terms of Jacobians as

$$\iiint\limits_{G} f(x, y, z)\, dV = \iiint\limits_{\substack{\text{appropriate} \\ \text{limits}}} f(r\cos\theta, r\sin\theta, z) \frac{\partial(x, y, z)}{\partial(r, \theta, z)}\, dz\, dr\, d\theta \qquad (16)$$

The absolute-value signs are omitted from Formulas (16) and (17) because the Jacobians are nonnegative (see the restrictions in Table 11.8.1).

$$\iiint\limits_{G} f(x, y, z)\, dV = \iiint\limits_{\substack{\text{appropriate} \\ \text{limits}}} f(\rho\sin\phi\cos\theta, \rho\sin\phi\sin\theta, \rho\cos\phi) \frac{\partial(x, y, z)}{\partial(\rho, \phi, \theta)}\, d\rho\, d\phi\, d\theta$$

$$(17)$$

✔ QUICK CHECK EXERCISES 14.7   *(See page 1071 for answers.)*

1. Let T be the transformation from the uv-plane to the xy-plane defined by the equations

$$x = u - 2v, \quad y = 3u + v$$

  (a) Sketch the image under T of the rectangle $1 \leq u \leq 3$, $0 \leq v \leq 2$.
  (b) Solve for u and v in terms of x and y:

$$u = \underline{\hspace{1cm}}, \quad v = \underline{\hspace{1cm}}$$

2. State the relationship between R and S in the change of variables formula

$$\iint\limits_{R} f(x, y) \, dA_{xy} = \iint\limits_{S} f(x(u, v), y(u, v)) \left| \frac{\partial(x, y)}{\partial(u, v)} \right| dA_{uv}$$

3. Let T be the transformation in Quick Check Exercise 1.
  (a) The Jacobian $\partial(x, y)/\partial(u, v)$ of T is _____.
  (b) Let R be the region in Quick Check Exercise 1(a). Fill in the missing integrand and limits of integration for the change of variables given by T.

$$\iint\limits_{R} e^{x+2y} \, dA = \int_{\square}^{\square} \int_{\square}^{\square} \underline{\hspace{1cm}} \, du \, dv$$

4. The Jacobian of the transformation

$$x = uv, \quad y = vw, \quad z = 2w$$

is

$$\frac{\partial(x, y, z)}{\partial(u, v, w)} = \underline{\hspace{1cm}}$$

EXERCISE SET 14.7

1–4 Find the Jacobian $\partial(x, y)/\partial(u, v)$. ■

1. $x = u + 4v, \; y = 3u - 5v$

2. $x = u + 2v^2, \; y = 2u^2 - v$

3. $x = \sin u + \cos v, \; y = -\cos u + \sin v$

4. $x = \dfrac{2u}{u^2 + v^2}, \; y = -\dfrac{2v}{u^2 + v^2}$

5–8 Solve for x and y in terms of u and v, and then find the Jacobian $\partial(x, y)/\partial(u, v)$. ■

5. $u = 2x - 5y, \; v = x + 2y$

6. $u = e^x, \; v = ye^{-x}$

7. $u = x^2 - y^2, \; v = x^2 + y^2 \quad (x > 0, y > 0)$

8. $u = xy, \; v = xy^3 \quad (x > 0, y > 0)$

9–12 Find the Jacobian $\partial(x, y, z)/\partial(u, v, w)$. ■

9. $x = 3u + v, \; y = u - 2w, \; z = v + w$

10. $x = u - uv, \; y = uv - uvw, \; z = uvw$

11. $u = xy, \; v = y, \; w = x + z$

12. $u = x + y + z, \; v = x + y - z, \; w = x - y + z$

13–16 True–False Determine whether the statement is true or false. Explain your answer. ■

13. If $\mathbf{r} = x(u, v)\mathbf{i} + y(u, v)\mathbf{j}$, then evaluating $|\partial(x, y)/\partial(u, v)|$ at a point (u_0, v_0) gives the perimeter of the parallelogram generated by the vectors $\partial \mathbf{r}/\partial u$ and $\partial \mathbf{r}/\partial v$ at (u_0, v_0).

14. If $\mathbf{r} = x(u, v)\mathbf{i} + y(u, v)\mathbf{j}$ maps the rectangle $0 \leq u \leq 2$, $1 \leq v \leq 5$ to a region R in the xy-plane, then the area of R is given by

$$\int_{1}^{5} \int_{0}^{2} \left| \frac{\partial(x, y)}{\partial(u, v)} \right| du \, dv$$

15. The Jacobian of the transformation $x = r \cos \theta, \; y = r \sin \theta$ is

$$\frac{\partial(x, y)}{\partial(r, \theta)} = r^2$$

16. The Jacobian of the transformation $x = \rho \sin \phi \cos \theta$, $y = \rho \sin \phi \sin \theta, z = \rho \cos \phi$ is

$$\frac{\partial(x, y, z)}{\partial(\rho, \phi, \theta)} = \rho^2 \sin \phi$$

FOCUS ON CONCEPTS

17–20 Sketch the image in the xy-plane of the set S under the given transformation. ■

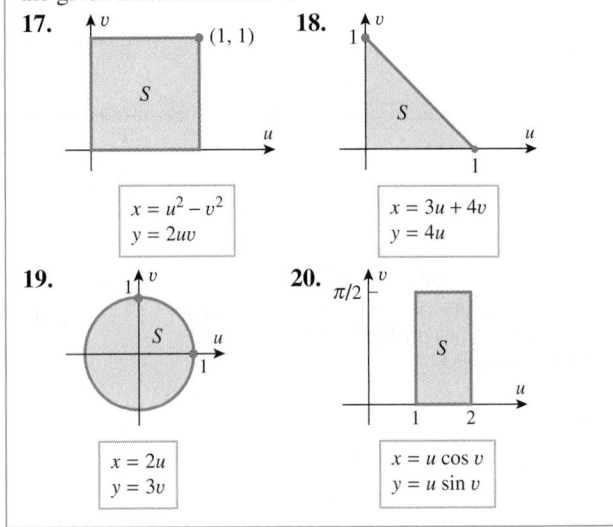

17.
$x = u^2 - v^2$
$y = 2uv$

18.
$x = 3u + 4v$
$y = 4u$

19.
$x = 2u$
$y = 3v$

20.
$x = u \cos v$
$y = u \sin v$

21. Use the transformation $u = x - 2y, v = 2x + y$ to find

$$\iint\limits_{R} \frac{x - 2y}{2x + y} \, dA$$

(cont.)

where R is the rectangular region enclosed by the lines $x - 2y = 1$, $x - 2y = 4$, $2x + y = 1$, $2x + y = 3$.

22. Use the transformation $u = x + y$, $v = x - y$ to find

$$\iint\limits_{R} (x - y)e^{x^2 - y^2}\, dA$$

over the rectangular region R enclosed by the lines $x + y = 0$, $x + y = 1$, $x - y = 1$, $x - y = 4$.

23. Use the transformation $u = \frac{1}{2}(x + y)$, $v = \frac{1}{2}(x - y)$ to find

$$\iint\limits_{R} \sin \tfrac{1}{2}(x + y) \cos \tfrac{1}{2}(x - y)\, dA$$

over the triangular region R with vertices $(0, 0)$, $(2, 0)$, $(1, 1)$.

24. Use the transformation $u = y/x$, $v = xy$ to find

$$\iint\limits_{R} xy^3\, dA$$

over the region R in the first quadrant enclosed by $y = x$, $y = 3x$, $xy = 1$, $xy = 4$.

25–27 The transformation $x = au$, $y = bv$ ($a > 0, b > 0$) can be rewritten as $x/a = u$, $y/b = v$, and hence it maps the circular region

$$u^2 + v^2 \leq 1$$

into the elliptical region

$$\frac{x^2}{a^2} + \frac{y^2}{b^2} \leq 1$$

In these exercises, perform the integration by transforming the elliptical region of integration into a circular region of integration and then evaluating the transformed integral in polar coordinates. ▪

25. $\displaystyle\iint\limits_{R} \sqrt{16x^2 + 9y^2}\, dA$, where R is the region enclosed by the ellipse $(x^2/9) + (y^2/16) = 1$.

26. $\displaystyle\iint\limits_{R} e^{-(x^2 + 4y^2)}\, dA$, where R is the region enclosed by the ellipse $(x^2/4) + y^2 = 1$.

27. $\displaystyle\iint\limits_{R} \sin(4x^2 + 9y^2)\, dA$, where R is the region in the first quadrant enclosed by the ellipse $4x^2 + 9y^2 = 1$ and the coordinate axes.

28. Show that the area of the ellipse

$$\frac{x^2}{a^2} + \frac{y^2}{b^2} = 1$$

is πab.

29–30 If a, b, and c are positive constants, then the transformation $x = au$, $y = bv$, $z = cw$ can be rewritten as $x/a = u$, $y/b = v$, $z/c = w$, and hence it maps the spherical region

$$u^2 + v^2 + w^2 \leq 1$$

into the ellipsoidal region

$$\frac{x^2}{a^2} + \frac{y^2}{b^2} + \frac{z^2}{c^2} \leq 1$$

In these exercises, perform the integration by transforming the ellipsoidal region of integration into a spherical region of integration and then evaluating the transformed integral in spherical coordinates. ▪

29. $\displaystyle\iiint\limits_{G} x^2\, dV$, where G is the region enclosed by the ellipsoid $9x^2 + 4y^2 + z^2 = 36$.

30. $\displaystyle\iiint\limits_{G} (y^2 + z^2)\, dV$, where G is the region enclosed by the ellipsoid

$$\frac{x^2}{a^2} + \frac{y^2}{b^2} + \frac{z^2}{c^2} = 1$$

FOCUS ON CONCEPTS

31–34 Find a transformation

$$u = f(x, y), \quad v = g(x, y)$$

that when applied to the region R in the xy-plane has as its image the region S in the uv-plane. ▪

31.

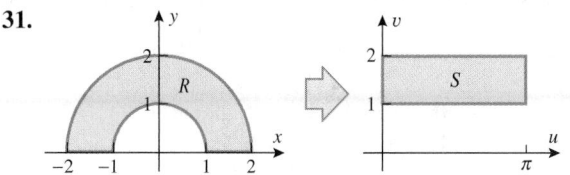

32.

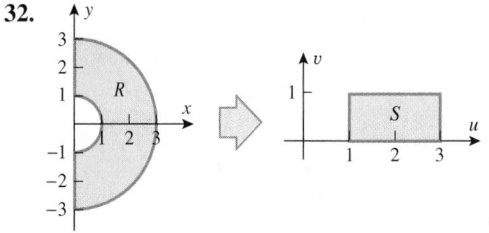

33.

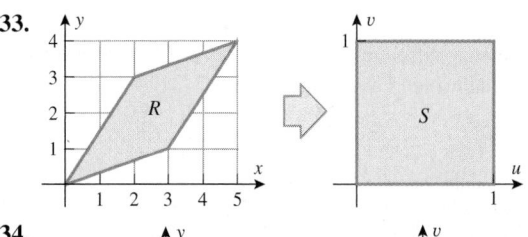

34.

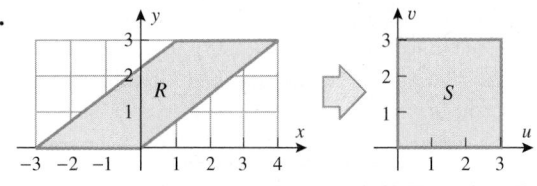

35–38 Evaluate the integral by making an appropriate change of variables. ■

35. $\iint\limits_{R} \dfrac{y - 4x}{y + 4x}\, dA$, where R is the region enclosed by the lines $y = 4x$, $y = 4x + 2$, $y = 2 - 4x$, $y = 5 - 4x$.

36. $\iint\limits_{R} (x^2 - y^2)\, dA$, where R is the rectangular region enclosed by the lines $y = -x$, $y = 1 - x$, $y = x$, $y = x + 2$.

37. $\iint\limits_{R} \dfrac{\sin(x - y)}{\cos(x + y)}\, dA$, where R is the triangular region enclosed by the lines $y = 0$, $y = x$, $x + y = \pi/4$.

38. $\iint\limits_{R} e^{(y-x)/(y+x)}\, dA$, where R is the region in the first quadrant enclosed by the trapezoid with vertices $(0, 1)$, $(1, 0)$, $(0, 4)$, $(4, 0)$.

39. Use an appropriate change of variables to find the area of the region in the first quadrant enclosed by the curves $y = x$, $y = 2x$, $x = y^2$, $x = 4y^2$.

40. Use an appropriate change of variables to find the volume of the solid bounded above by the plane $x + y + z = 9$, below by the xy-plane, and laterally by the elliptic cylinder $4x^2 + 9y^2 = 36$. [*Hint:* Express the volume as a double integral in xy-coordinates, then use polar coordinates to evaluate the transformed integral.]

41. Use the transformation $u = x$, $v = z - y$, $w = xy$ to find
$$\iiint\limits_{G} (z - y)^2 xy\, dV$$
where G is the region enclosed by the surfaces $x = 1$, $x = 3$, $z = y$, $z = y + 1$, $xy = 2$, $xy = 4$.

42. Use the transformation $u = xy$, $v = yz$, $w = xz$ to find the volume of the region in the first octant that is enclosed by the hyperbolic cylinders $xy = 1$, $xy = 2$, $yz = 1$, $yz = 3$, $xz = 1$, $xz = 4$.

43. (a) Verify that
$$\begin{vmatrix} a_1 & b_1 \\ c_1 & d_1 \end{vmatrix} \begin{vmatrix} a_2 & b_2 \\ c_2 & d_2 \end{vmatrix} = \begin{vmatrix} a_1 a_2 + b_1 c_2 & a_1 b_2 + b_1 d_2 \\ c_1 a_2 + d_1 c_2 & c_1 b_2 + d_1 d_2 \end{vmatrix}$$

(b) If $x = x(u, v)$, $y = y(u, v)$ is a one-to-one transformation, then $u = u(x, y)$, $v = v(x, y)$. Assuming the necessary differentiability, use the result in part (a) and the chain rule to show that
$$\frac{\partial(x, y)}{\partial(u, v)} \cdot \frac{\partial(u, v)}{\partial(x, y)} = 1$$

44–46 The formula obtained in part (b) of Exercise 43 is useful in integration problems where it is inconvenient or impossible to solve the transformation equations $u = f(x, y)$, $v = g(x, y)$ explicitly for x and y in terms of u and v. In these exercises, use the relationship
$$\frac{\partial(x, y)}{\partial(u, v)} = \frac{1}{\partial(u, v)/\partial(x, y)}$$
to avoid solving for x and y in terms of u and v. ■

44. Use the transformation $u = xy$, $v = xy^4$ to find
$$\iint\limits_{R} \sin(xy)\, dA$$
where R is the region enclosed by the curves $xy = \pi$, $xy = 2\pi$, $xy^4 = 1$, $xy^4 = 2$.

45. Use the transformation $u = x^2 - y^2$, $v = x^2 + y^2$ to find
$$\iint\limits_{R} xy\, dA$$
where R is the region in the first quadrant that is enclosed by the hyperbolas $x^2 - y^2 = 1$, $x^2 - y^2 = 4$ and the circles $x^2 + y^2 = 9$, $x^2 + y^2 = 16$.

46. Use the transformation $u = xy$, $v = x^2 - y^2$ to find
$$\iint\limits_{R} (x^4 - y^4)e^{xy}\, dA$$
where R is the region in the first quadrant enclosed by the hyperbolas $xy = 1$, $xy = 3$, $x^2 - y^2 = 3$, $x^2 - y^2 = 4$.

47. The three-variable analog of the formula derived in part (b) of Exercise 43 is
$$\frac{\partial(x, y, z)}{\partial(u, v, w)} \cdot \frac{\partial(u, v, w)}{\partial(x, y, z)} = 1$$
Use this result to show that the volume V of the oblique parallelepiped that is bounded by the planes $x + y + 2z = \pm 3$, $x - 2y + z = \pm 2$, $4x + y + z = \pm 6$ is $V = 16$.

48. (a) Consider the transformation
$$x = r\cos\theta, \quad y = r\sin\theta, \quad z = z$$
from cylindrical to rectangular coordinates, where $r \geq 0$. Show that
$$\frac{\partial(x, y, z)}{\partial(r, \theta, z)} = r$$

(b) Consider the transformation
$$x = \rho\sin\phi\cos\theta, \quad y = \rho\sin\phi\sin\theta, \quad z = \rho\cos\phi$$
from spherical to rectangular coordinates, where $0 \leq \phi \leq \pi$. Show that
$$\frac{\partial(x, y, z)}{\partial(\rho, \phi, \theta)} = \rho^2\sin\phi$$

49. Writing For single-variable definite integrals, the technique of substitution was generally used to simplify the integrand. Discuss some motivations for using a change of variables in a multiple integral.

50. Writing Suppose that the boundary curves of a region R in the xy-plane can be described as level curves of various functions. Discuss how this information can be used to choose an appropriate change of variables for a double integral over R. Illustrate your discussion with an example.

1. (a) The image is the region in the xy-plane enclosed by the parallelogram with vertices $(1, 3)$, $(-3, 5)$, $(-1, 11)$, and $(3, 9)$.
(b) $u = \frac{1}{7}(x + 2y)$, $v = \frac{1}{7}(y - 3x)$.   **2.** S is a region in the uv-plane and R is the image of S in the xy-plane under the
transformation $x = x(u, v)$, $y = y(u, v)$.   **3.** (a) 7 (b) $\displaystyle\int_0^2 \int_1^3 7e^{7u}\, du\, dv$ **4.** $2vw$

14.8 CENTERS OF GRAVITY USING MULTIPLE INTEGRALS

In Section 6.7 we showed how to find the mass and center of gravity of a homogeneous lamina using single integrals. In this section we will show how double and triple integrals can be used to find the mass and center of gravity of inhomogeneous laminas and three-dimensional solids.

■ DENSITY AND MASS OF AN INHOMOGENEOUS LAMINA

An idealized flat object that is thin enough to be viewed as a two-dimensional plane region is called a *lamina* (Figure 14.8.1). A lamina is called *homogeneous* if its composition is uniform throughout and *inhomogeneous* otherwise. The *density* of a *homogeneous* lamina was defined in Section 6.7 to be its mass per unit area. Thus, the density δ of a homogeneous lamina of mass M and area A is given by $\delta = M/A$.

For an inhomogeneous lamina the composition may vary from point to point, and hence an appropriate definition of "density" must reflect this. To motivate such a definition, suppose that the lamina is placed in an xy-plane. The density at a point (x, y) can be specified by a function $\delta(x, y)$, called the *density function*, which can be interpreted as follows: Construct a small rectangle centered at (x, y) and let ΔM and ΔA be the mass and area of the portion of the lamina enclosed by this rectangle (Figure 14.8.2). If the ratio $\Delta M / \Delta A$ approaches a limiting value as the dimensions (and hence the area) of the rectangle approach zero, then this limit is considered to be the density of the lamina at (x, y). Symbolically,

The thickness of a lamina is negligible.

▲ **Figure 14.8.1**

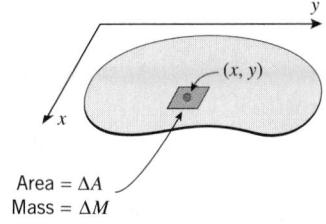

Area $= \Delta A$
Mass $= \Delta M$

▲ **Figure 14.8.2**

$$\delta(x, y) = \lim_{\Delta A \to 0} \frac{\Delta M}{\Delta A} \tag{1}$$

From this relationship we obtain the approximation

$$\Delta M \approx \delta(x, y)\Delta A \tag{2}$$

which relates the mass and area of a small rectangular portion of the lamina centered at (x, y). It is assumed that as the dimensions of the rectangle tend to zero, the error in this approximation also tends to zero.

The following result shows how to find the mass of a lamina from its density function.

14.8.1 MASS OF A LAMINA If a lamina with a continuous density function $\delta(x, y)$ occupies a region R in the xy-plane, then its total mass M is given by

$$M = \iint_R \delta(x, y)\, dA \tag{3}$$

This formula can be motivated by a familiar limiting process that can be outlined as follows: Imagine the lamina to be subdivided into rectangular pieces using lines parallel to the

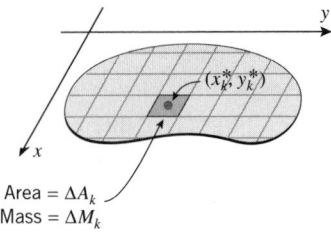

Area = ΔA_k
Mass = ΔM_k

▲ **Figure 14.8.3**

coordinate axes and excluding from consideration any nonrectangular parts at the boundary (Figure 14.8.3). Assume that there are n such rectangular pieces, and suppose that the kth piece has area ΔA_k. If we let (x_k^*, y_k^*) denote the center of the kth piece, then from Formula (2), the mass ΔM_k of this piece can be approximated by

$$\Delta M_k \approx \delta(x_k^*, y_k^*)\Delta A_k \tag{4}$$

and hence the mass M of the entire lamina can be approximated by

$$M \approx \sum_{k=1}^{n} \delta(x_k^*, y_k^*)\Delta A_k$$

If we now increase n in such a way that the dimensions of the rectangles tend to zero, then it is plausible that the errors in our approximations will approach zero, so

$$M = \lim_{n \to +\infty} \sum_{k=1}^{n} \delta(x_k^*, y_k^*)\Delta A_k = \iint\limits_{R} \delta(x, y)\, dA$$

▶ **Example 1** A triangular lamina with vertices $(0, 0)$, $(0, 1)$, and $(1, 0)$ has density function $\delta(x, y) = xy$. Find its total mass.

Solution. Referring to (3) and Figure 14.8.4, the mass M of the lamina is

$$M = \iint\limits_{R} \delta(x, y)\, dA = \iint\limits_{R} xy\, dA = \int_0^1 \int_0^{-x+1} xy\, dy\, dx$$

$$= \int_0^1 \left[\frac{1}{2}xy^2\right]_{y=0}^{-x+1} dx = \int_0^1 \left[\frac{1}{2}x^3 - x^2 + \frac{1}{2}x\right] dx = \frac{1}{24} \text{ (unit of mass)} ◀$$

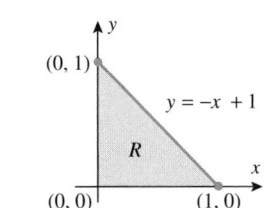

$(0, 1)$

$y = -x + 1$

R

$(0, 0)$ $(1, 0)$

▲ **Figure 14.8.4**

■ **CENTER OF GRAVITY OF AN INHOMOGENEOUS LAMINA**

Recall that the *center of gravity* of a lamina occupying a region R in the horizontal xy-plane is the point $(\bar{x}, \bar{y})$ such that the effect of gravity on the lamina is "equivalent" to that of a single force acting at $(\bar{x}, \bar{y})$. If $(\bar{x}, \bar{y})$ is in R, then the lamina will balance horizontally on a point of support placed at $(\bar{x}, \bar{y})$. In Section 6.7 we showed how to locate the center of gravity of a homogeneous lamina. We now turn to this problem for an inhomogeneous lamina.

14.8.2 PROBLEM Suppose that a lamina with a continuous density function $\delta(x, y)$ occupies a region R in a horizontal xy-plane. Find the coordinates $(\bar{x}, \bar{y})$ of the center of gravity.

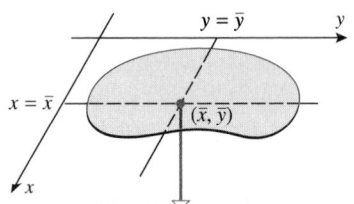

$y = \bar{y}$

$x = \bar{x}$

$(\bar{x}, \bar{y})$

▲ **Figure 14.8.5**

To motivate the solution of Problem 14.8.2, consider what happens if we try to place the lamina in Figure 14.8.5 on a knife-edge running along the line $y = \bar{y}$. Since the lamina behaves as if its entire mass is concentrated at $(\bar{x}, \bar{y})$, the lamina will be in perfect balance. Similarly, the lamina will be in perfect balance if the knife-edge runs along the line $x = \bar{x}$. To find these lines of balance we begin by reviewing some results from Section 6.7 about rotations.

Recall that if a point-mass m is located at the point (x, y), then the moment of m about $x = a$ measures the tendency of the mass to produce a rotation about the line $x = a$, and the moment of m about $y = c$ measures the tendency of the mass to produce a rotation about the line $y = c$. The moments are given by the following formulas:

$$\begin{bmatrix} \text{moment of } m \\ \text{about the} \\ \text{line } x = a \end{bmatrix} = m(x - a) \quad \text{and} \quad \begin{bmatrix} \text{moment of } m \\ \text{about the} \\ \text{line } y = c \end{bmatrix} = m(y - c) \qquad (5\text{--}6)$$

If a number of point-masses are distributed throughout the xy-plane, the sum of their moments about $x = a$ is a measure of the tendency of the masses to produce a rotation of the plane (viewed as a weightless sheet) about the line $x = a$. If the sum of these moments is zero, the collective masses will produce no net rotational effect about the line. (Intuitively, this means that the plane would balance on a knife-edge along the line $x = a$. Similarly, if the sum of the moments of the masses about $y = c$ is zero, the plane would balance on a knife-edge along the line $y = c$.)

We are now ready to solve Problem 14.8.2. We imagine the lamina to be subdivided into rectangular pieces using lines parallel to the coordinate axes and excluding from consideration any nonrectangular pieces at the boundary (Figure 14.8.3). We assume that there are n such rectangular pieces and that the kth piece has area ΔA_k and mass ΔM_k. We will let (x_k^*, y_k^*) be the center of the kth piece, and we will assume that the entire mass of the kth piece is concentrated at its center. From (4), the mass of the kth piece can be approximated by

$$\Delta M_k \approx \delta(x_k^*, y_k^*)\Delta A_k$$

Since the lamina balances on the lines $x = \bar{x}$ and $y = \bar{y}$, the sum of the moments of the rectangular pieces about those lines should be close to zero; that is,

$$\sum_{k=1}^{n}(x_k^* - \bar{x})\Delta M_k = \sum_{k=1}^{n}(x_k^* - \bar{x})\delta(x_k^*, y_k^*)\Delta A_k \approx 0$$

$$\sum_{k=1}^{n}(y_k^* - \bar{y})\Delta M_k = \sum_{k=1}^{n}(y_k^* - \bar{y})\delta(x_k^*, y_k^*)\Delta A_k \approx 0$$

If we now increase n in such a way that the dimensions of the rectangles tend to zero, then it is plausible that the errors in our approximations will approach zero, so that

$$\lim_{n \to +\infty} \sum_{k=1}^{n}(x_k^* - \bar{x})\delta(x_k^*, y_k^*)\Delta A_k = 0$$

$$\lim_{n \to +\infty} \sum_{k=1}^{n}(y_k^* - \bar{y})\delta(x_k^*, y_k^*)\Delta A_k = 0$$

from which we obtain

$$\iint\limits_{R}(x - \bar{x})\delta(x, y)\, dA = \iint\limits_{R} x\delta(x, y)\, dA - \bar{x}\iint\limits_{R}\delta(x, y)\, dA = 0 \qquad (7)$$

$$\iint\limits_{R}(y - \bar{y})\delta(x, y)\, dA = \iint\limits_{R} y\delta(x, y)\, dA - \bar{y}\iint\limits_{R}\delta(x, y)\, dA = 0 \qquad (8)$$

Solving (7) and (8) respectively for $\bar{x}$ and $\bar{y}$ gives formulas for the center of gravity of a lamina:

Center of Gravity $(\bar{x}, \bar{y})$ of a Lamina

$$\bar{x} = \frac{\iint\limits_{R} x\delta(x, y)\, dA}{\iint\limits_{R}\delta(x, y)\, dA}, \qquad \bar{y} = \frac{\iint\limits_{R} y\delta(x, y)\, dA}{\iint\limits_{R}\delta(x, y)\, dA} \qquad (9\text{--}10)$$

In both formulas the denominator is the mass M of the lamina [see (3)]. Following the terminology of Section 6.7, the numerator in the formula for $\bar{x}$ is denoted by M_y and is called the ***first moment of the lamina about the y-axis***; the numerator of the formula for $\bar{y}$ is denoted by M_x and is called the ***first moment of the lamina about the x-axis***. Thus, Formulas (9) and (10) can be expressed as

> ***Alternative Formulas for Center of Gravity*** $(\bar{x}, \bar{y})$ ***of a Lamina***
>
> $$\bar{x} = \frac{M_y}{M} = \frac{1}{\text{mass of } R} \iint\limits_{R} x\delta(x, y) \, dA \tag{11}$$
>
> $$\bar{y} = \frac{M_x}{M} = \frac{1}{\text{mass of } R} \iint\limits_{R} y\delta(x, y) \, dA \tag{12}$$

▶ **Example 2**   Find the center of gravity of the triangular lamina with vertices $(0, 0)$, $(0, 1)$, and $(1, 0)$ and density function $\delta(x, y) = xy$.

Solution.   The lamina is shown in Figure 14.8.4. In Example 1 we found the mass of the lamina to be

$$M = \iint\limits_{R} \delta(x, y) \, dA = \iint\limits_{R} xy \, dA = \frac{1}{24}$$

The moment of the lamina about the y-axis is

$$M_y = \iint\limits_{R} x\delta(x, y) \, dA = \iint\limits_{R} x^2 y \, dA = \int_0^1 \int_0^{-x+1} x^2 y \, dy \, dx$$

$$= \int_0^1 \left[\frac{1}{2} x^2 y^2 \right]_{y=0}^{-x+1} dx = \int_0^1 \left(\frac{1}{2} x^4 - x^3 + \frac{1}{2} x^2 \right) dx = \frac{1}{60}$$

and the moment about the x-axis is

$$M_x = \iint\limits_{R} y\delta(x, y) \, dA = \iint\limits_{R} xy^2 \, dA = \int_0^1 \int_0^{-x+1} xy^2 \, dy \, dx$$

$$= \int_0^1 \left[\frac{1}{3} xy^3 \right]_{y=0}^{-x+1} dx = \int_0^1 \left(-\frac{1}{3} x^4 + x^3 - x^2 + \frac{1}{3} x \right) dx = \frac{1}{60}$$

From (11) and (12),

$$\bar{x} = \frac{M_y}{M} = \frac{1/60}{1/24} = \frac{2}{5}, \quad \bar{y} = \frac{M_x}{M} = \frac{1/60}{1/24} = \frac{2}{5}$$

so the center of gravity is $\left(\frac{2}{5}, \frac{2}{5} \right)$. ◀

Recall that the center of gravity of a *homogeneous* lamina is called the ***centroid of the lamina*** or sometimes the ***centroid of the region R***. Because the density function δ is constant for a homogeneous lamina, the factor δ may be moved through the integral signs in (9) and (10) and canceled. Thus, the centroid $(\bar{x}, \bar{y})$ is a geometric property of the region R and is given by the following formulas:

Centroid of a Region R

$$
\bar{x} = \frac{\displaystyle\iint_R x\,dA}{\displaystyle\iint_R dA} = \frac{1}{\text{area of } R}\iint_R x\,dA \tag{13}
$$

$$
\bar{y} = \frac{\displaystyle\iint_R y\,dA}{\displaystyle\iint_R dA} = \frac{1}{\text{area of } R}\iint_R y\,dA \tag{14}
$$

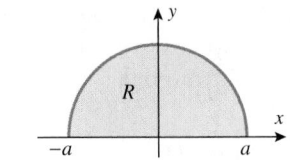

▲ **Figure 14.8.6**

▶ **Example 3**   Find the centroid of the semicircular region in Figure 14.8.6.

Solution.   By symmetry, $\bar{x} = 0$ since the y-axis is obviously a line of balance. From (14),

$$
\bar{y} = \frac{1}{\text{area of } R}\iint_R y\,dA = \frac{1}{\frac{1}{2}\pi a^2}\iint_R y\,dA
$$

$$
= \frac{1}{\frac{1}{2}\pi a^2}\int_0^\pi \int_0^a (r\sin\theta)r\,dr\,d\theta \qquad \boxed{\text{Evaluating in polar coordinates}}
$$

$$
= \frac{1}{\frac{1}{2}\pi a^2}\int_0^\pi \left[\frac{1}{3}r^3\sin\theta\right]_{r=0}^a d\theta
$$

$$
= \frac{1}{\frac{1}{2}\pi a^2}\left(\frac{1}{3}a^3\right)\int_0^\pi \sin\theta\,d\theta = \frac{1}{\frac{1}{2}\pi a^2}\left(\frac{2}{3}a^3\right) = \frac{4a}{3\pi}
$$

Compare the calculation in Example 3 to that of Example 3 in Section 6.7.

so the centroid is $\left(0, \dfrac{4a}{3\pi}\right)$. ◀

■ **CENTER OF GRAVITY AND CENTROID OF A SOLID**

For a three-dimensional solid G, the formulas for moments, center of gravity, and centroid are similar to those for laminas. If G is *homogeneous*, then its **density** is defined to be its mass per unit volume. Thus, if G is a homogeneous solid of mass M and volume V, then its density δ is given by $\delta = M/V$. If G is inhomogeneous and is in an *xyz*-coordinate system, then its density at a general point (x, y, z) is specified by a **density function** $\delta(x, y, z)$ whose value at a point can be viewed as a limit:

$$
\delta(x, y, z) = \lim_{\Delta V \to 0}\frac{\Delta M}{\Delta V}
$$

where ΔM and ΔV represent the mass and volume of a rectangular parallelepiped, centered at (x, y, z), whose dimensions tend to zero (Figure 14.8.7).

Using the discussion of laminas as a model, you should be able to show that the mass M of a solid with a continuous density function $\delta(x, y, z)$ is

$$
M = \text{ mass of } G = \iiint_G \delta(x, y, z)\,dV \tag{15}
$$

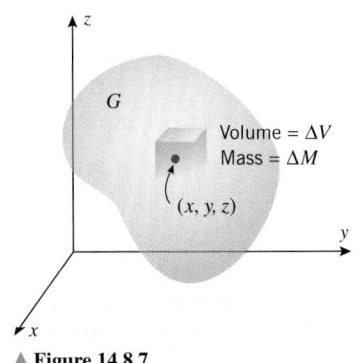

▲ **Figure 14.8.7**

The formulas for center of gravity and centroid are as follows:

Center of Gravity $(\bar{x}, \bar{y}, \bar{z})$ of a Solid G	**Centroid $(\bar{x}, \bar{y}, \bar{z})$ of a Solid G**	
$\bar{x} = \dfrac{1}{M} \iiint\limits_{G} x\delta(x, y, z)\,dV$	$\bar{x} = \dfrac{1}{V} \iiint\limits_{G} x\,dV$	
$\bar{y} = \dfrac{1}{M} \iiint\limits_{G} y\delta(x, y, z)\,dV$	$\bar{y} = \dfrac{1}{V} \iiint\limits_{G} y\,dV$	(16–17)
$\bar{z} = \dfrac{1}{M} \iiint\limits_{G} z\delta(x, y, z)\,dV$	$\bar{z} = \dfrac{1}{V} \iiint\limits_{G} z\,dV$	

▲ **Figure 14.8.8**

▶ **Example 4**   Find the mass and the center of gravity of a cylindrical solid of height h and radius a (Figure 14.8.8), assuming that the density at each point is proportional to the distance between the point and the base of the solid.

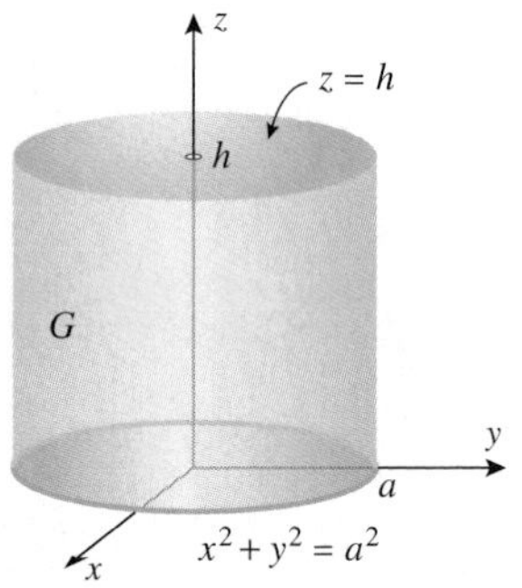

Solution.   Since the density is proportional to the distance z from the base, the density function has the form $\delta(x, y, z) = kz$, where k is some (unknown) positive constant of proportionality. From (15) the mass of the solid is

$$M = \iiint\limits_{G} \delta(x, y, z)\,dV = \int_{-a}^{a} \int_{-\sqrt{a^2-x^2}}^{\sqrt{a^2-x^2}} \int_{0}^{h} kz\,dz\,dy\,dx$$

$$= k \int_{-a}^{a} \int_{-\sqrt{a^2-x^2}}^{\sqrt{a^2-x^2}} \frac{1}{2}h^2\,dy\,dx$$

$$= kh^2 \int_{-a}^{a} \sqrt{a^2 - x^2}\,dx$$

$$= \tfrac{1}{2}kh^2\pi a^2 \qquad \boxed{\text{Interpret the integral as the area of a semicircle.}}$$

Without additional information, the constant k cannot be determined. However, as we will now see, the value of k does not affect the center of gravity.
From (16),

$$\bar{z} = \frac{1}{M} \iiint\limits_{G} z\delta(x, y, z)\,dV = \frac{1}{\frac{1}{2}kh^2\pi a^2} \iiint\limits_{G} z\delta(x, y, z)\,dV$$

$$= \frac{1}{\frac{1}{2}kh^2\pi a^2} \int_{-a}^{a} \int_{-\sqrt{a^2-x^2}}^{\sqrt{a^2-x^2}} \int_{0}^{h} z(kz)\,dz\,dy\,dx$$

$$= \frac{k}{\frac{1}{2}kh^2\pi a^2} \int_{-a}^{a} \int_{-\sqrt{a^2-x^2}}^{\sqrt{a^2-x^2}} \frac{1}{3}h^3\,dy\,dx$$

$$= \frac{\frac{1}{3}kh^3}{\frac{1}{2}kh^2\pi a^2} \int_{-a}^{a} 2\sqrt{a^2 - x^2}\,dx$$

$$= \frac{\frac{1}{3}kh^3\pi a^2}{\frac{1}{2}kh^2\pi a^2} = \frac{2}{3}h$$

Similar calculations using (16) will yield $\bar{x} = \bar{y} = 0$. However, this is evident by inspection, since it follows from the symmetry of the solid and the form of its density function that the center of gravity is on the z-axis. Thus, the center of gravity is $\left(0, 0, \tfrac{2}{3}h\right)$. ◀

▶ **Example 5**   Find the centroid of the solid G bounded below by the cone $z = \sqrt{x^2 + y^2}$ and above by the sphere $x^2 + y^2 + z^2 = 16$.

Solution.   The solid G is sketched in Figure 14.8.9. In Example 3 of Section 14.6, spherical coordinates were used to find that the volume of G is

$$V = \frac{64\pi}{3}(2 - \sqrt{2})$$

By symmetry, the centroid $(\bar{x}, \bar{y}, \bar{z})$ is on the z-axis, so $\bar{x} = \bar{y} = 0$. In spherical coordinates, the equation of the sphere $x^2 + y^2 + z^2 = 16$ is $\rho = 4$ and the equation of the cone $z = \sqrt{x^2 + y^2}$ is $\phi = \pi/4$, so from (17) we have

$$\bar{z} = \frac{1}{V} \iiint_G z\,dV = \frac{1}{V} \int_0^{2\pi} \int_0^{\pi/4} \int_0^4 (\rho\cos\phi)\rho^2\sin\phi\,d\rho\,d\phi\,d\theta$$

$$= \frac{1}{V} \int_0^{2\pi} \int_0^{\pi/4} \left[\frac{\rho^4}{4}\cos\phi\sin\phi\right]_{\rho=0}^4 d\phi\,d\theta$$

$$= \frac{64}{V} \int_0^{2\pi} \int_0^{\pi/4} \sin\phi\cos\phi\,d\phi\,d\theta = \frac{64}{V} \int_0^{2\pi} \left[\frac{1}{2}\sin^2\phi\right]_{\phi=0}^{\pi/4} d\theta$$

$$= \frac{16}{V} \int_0^{2\pi} d\theta = \frac{32\pi}{V} = \frac{3}{2(2 - \sqrt{2})}$$

The centroid of G is

$$(\bar{x}, \bar{y}, \bar{z}) = \left(0, 0, \frac{3}{2(2 - \sqrt{2})}\right) \approx (0, 0, 2.561) \ ◀$$

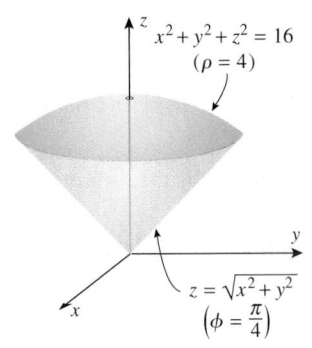

z

$x^2 + y^2 + z^2 = 16$
$(\rho = 4)$

$z = \sqrt{x^2 + y^2}$
$\left(\phi = \frac{\pi}{4}\right)$

y

x

▲ **Figure 14.8.9**

✔ QUICK CHECK EXERCISES 14.8   (See page 1080 for answers.)

1. The total mass of a lamina with continuous density function $\delta(x, y)$ that occupies a region R in the xy-plane is given by $M = $ _____.

2. Consider a lamina with mass M and continuous density function $\delta(x, y)$ that occupies a region R in the xy-plane. The x-coordinate of the center of gravity of the lamina is M_y/M, where M_y is called the _____ and is given by the double integral _____.

3. Let R be the region between the graphs of $y = x^2$ and $y = 2 - x$ for $0 \le x \le 1$. The area of R is $\frac{7}{6}$ and the centroid of R is _____.

EXERCISE SET 14.8   ⌁ Graphing Utility   [C] CAS

1–4 Find the mass and center of gravity of the lamina. ▪

1. A lamina with density $\delta(x, y) = x + y$ is bounded by the x-axis, the line $x = 1$, and the curve $y = \sqrt{x}$.

2. A lamina with density $\delta(x, y) = y$ is bounded by $y = \sin x$, $y = 0$, $x = 0$, and $x = \pi$.

3. A lamina with density $\delta(x, y) = xy$ is in the first quadrant and is bounded by the circle $x^2 + y^2 = a^2$ and the coordinate axes.

4. A lamina with density $\delta(x, y) = x^2 + y^2$ is bounded by the x-axis and the upper half of the circle $x^2 + y^2 = 1$.

FOCUS ON CONCEPTS

5–6 For the given density function, make a conjecture about the coordinates of the center of gravity and confirm your conjecture by integrating. ▪

5. $\delta(x, y) = |x + y - 1|$

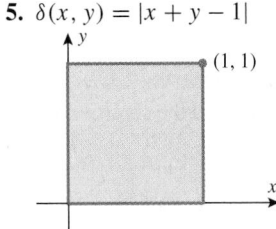

y

$(1, 1)$

x

6. $\delta(x, y) = 1 + x^2 + y^2$

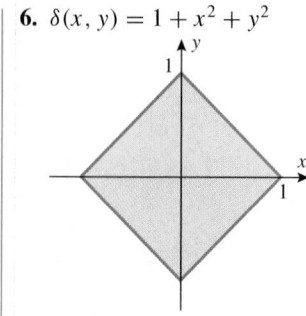

7–8 Make a conjecture about the coordinates of the centroid of the region and confirm your conjecture by integrating. ∎

7.   **8.**

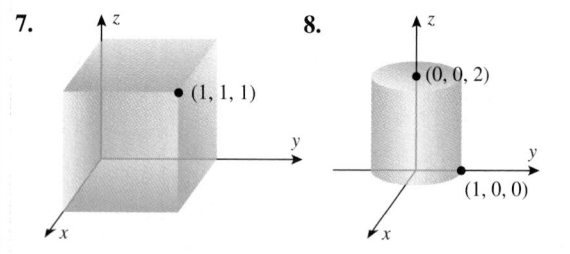

9–12 True–False Determine whether the statement is true or false. Explain your answer. ∎

9. The center of gravity of a homogeneous lamina in a plane is located at the lamina's centroid.

10. The mass of a two-dimensional lamina is the product of its area and the density of the lamia at its centroid.

11. The coordinates of the center of gravity of a two-dimensional lamina are the lamina's first moments about the y- and x-axes, respectively.

12. The density of a solid in 3-space is measured in units of mass per unit area.

13. Show that in polar coordinates the formulas for the centroid $(\bar{x}, \bar{y})$ of a region R are

$$\bar{x} = \frac{1}{\text{area of } R} \iint\limits_{R} r^2 \cos\theta \, dr \, d\theta$$

$$\bar{y} = \frac{1}{\text{area of } R} \iint\limits_{R} r^2 \sin\theta \, dr \, d\theta$$

14. Use the result of Exercise 13 to find the centroid $(\bar{x}, \bar{y})$ of the region enclosed by the cardioid $r = a(1 + \sin\theta)$.

15. Use the result of Exercise 13 to find the centroid $(\bar{x}, \bar{y})$ of the petal of the rose $r = \sin 2\theta$ in the first quadrant.

16. Let R be the rectangle bounded by the lines $x = 0$, $x = 3$, $y = 0$, and $y = 2$. By inspection, find the centroid of R and use it to evaluate

$$\iint\limits_{R} x \, dA \quad \text{and} \quad \iint\limits_{R} y \, dA$$

17–22 Find the centroid of the solid. ∎

17. The tetrahedron in the first octant enclosed by the coordinate planes and the plane $x + y + z = 1$.

18. The solid bounded by the parabolic cylinder $z = 1 - y^2$ and the planes $x + z = 1$, $x = 0$, and $z = 0$.

19. The solid bounded by the surface $z = y^2$ and the planes $x = 0$, $x = 1$, and $z = 1$.

20. The solid in the first octant bounded by the surface $z = xy$ and the planes $z = 0$, $x = 2$, and $y = 2$.

21. The solid in the first octant that is bounded by the sphere $x^2 + y^2 + z^2 = a^2$ and the coordinate planes.

22. The solid enclosed by the xy-plane and the hemisphere $z = \sqrt{a^2 - x^2 - y^2}$.

23–26 Find the mass and center of gravity of the solid. ∎

23. The cube that has density $\delta(x, y, z) = a - x$ and is defined by the inequalities $0 \le x \le a$, $0 \le y \le a$, and $0 \le z \le a$.

24. The cylindrical solid that has density $\delta(x, y, z) = h - z$ and is enclosed by $x^2 + y^2 = a^2$, $z = 0$, and $z = h$.

25. The solid that has density $\delta(x, y, z) = yz$ and is enclosed by $z = 1 - y^2$ (for $y \ge 0$), $z = 0$, $y = 0$, $x = -1$, and $x = 1$.

26. The solid that has density $\delta(x, y, z) = xz$ and is enclosed by $y = 9 - x^2$ (for $x \ge 0$), $x = 0$, $y = 0$, $z = 0$, and $z = 1$.

27. Find the center of gravity of the square lamina with vertices $(0, 0)$, $(1, 0)$, $(0, 1)$, and $(1, 1)$ if
(a) the density is proportional to the square of the distance from the origin;
(b) the density is proportional to the distance from the y-axis.

28. Find the center of gravity of the cube that is determined by the inequalities $0 \le x \le 1$, $0 \le y \le 1$, $0 \le z \le 1$ if
(a) the density is proportional to the square of the distance to the origin;
(b) the density is proportional to the sum of the distances to the faces that lie in the coordinate planes.

C **29.** Use the numerical triple integral capability of a CAS to approximate the location of the centroid of the solid that is bounded above by the surface $z = 1/(1 + x^2 + y^2)$, below by the xy-plane, and laterally by the plane $y = 0$ and the surface $y = \sin x$ for $0 \le x \le \pi$ (see the accompanying figure on the next page).

30. The accompanying figure on the next page shows the solid that is bounded above by the surface $z = 1/(x^2 + y^2 + 1)$, below by the xy-plane, and laterally by the surface $x^2 + y^2 = a^2$.
(a) By symmetry, the centroid of the solid lies on the z-axis. Make a conjecture about the behavior of the z-coordinate of the centroid as $a \to 0^+$ and as $a \to +\infty$.
(b) Find the z-coordinate of the centroid, and check your conjecture by calculating the appropriate limits. *(cont.)*

(c) Use a graphing utility to plot the z-coordinate of the centroid versus a, and use the graph to estimate the value of a for which the centroid is $(0, 0, 0.25)$.

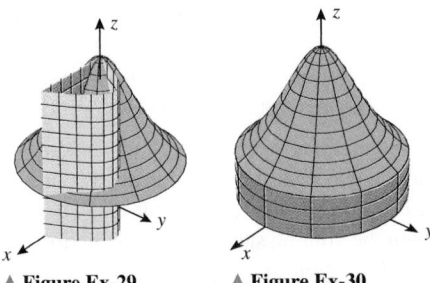

▲ **Figure Ex-29**   ▲ **Figure Ex-30**

31–32 Use cylindrical coordinates. ■

31. Find the mass of the solid with density $\delta(x, y, z) = 3 - z$ that is bounded by the cone $z = \sqrt{x^2 + y^2}$ and the plane $z = 3$.

32. Find the mass of a right circular cylinder of radius a and height h if the density is proportional to the distance from the base. (Let k be the constant of proportionality.)

33–34 Use spherical coordinates. ■

33. Find the mass of a spherical solid of radius a if the density is proportional to the distance from the center. (Let k be the constant of proportionality.)

34. Find the mass of the solid enclosed between the spheres $x^2 + y^2 + z^2 = 1$ and $x^2 + y^2 + z^2 = 4$ if the density is $\delta(x, y, z) = (x^2 + y^2 + z^2)^{-1/2}$.

35–36 Use cylindrical coordinates to find the centroid of the solid. ■

35. The solid that is bounded above by the sphere

$$x^2 + y^2 + z^2 = 2$$

and below by the paraboloid $z = x^2 + y^2$.

36. The solid that is bounded by the cone $z = \sqrt{x^2 + y^2}$ and the plane $z = 2$.

37–38 Use spherical coordinates to find the centroid of the solid. ■

37. The solid in the first octant bounded by the coordinate planes and the sphere $x^2 + y^2 + z^2 = a^2$.

38. The solid bounded above by the sphere $\rho = 4$ and below by the cone $\phi = \pi/3$.

39. Find the mass of the solid that is enclosed by the sphere $x^2 + y^2 + z^2 = 1$ and lies above the cone $z = \sqrt{x^2 + y^2}$ if the density is $\delta(x, y, z) = \sqrt{x^2 + y^2 + z^2}$.

40. Find the center of gravity of the solid bounded by the paraboloid $z = 1 - x^2 - y^2$ and the xy-plane, assuming the density to be $\delta(x, y, z) = x^2 + y^2 + z^2$.

41. Find the center of gravity of the solid that is bounded by the cylinder $x^2 + y^2 = 1$, the cone $z = \sqrt{x^2 + y^2}$, and the xy-plane if the density is $\delta(x, y, z) = z$.

42. Find the center of gravity of the solid hemisphere bounded by $z = \sqrt{a^2 - x^2 - y^2}$ and $z = 0$ if the density is proportional to the distance from the origin.

43. Find the centroid of the solid that is enclosed by the hemispheres $y = \sqrt{9 - x^2 - z^2}$, $y = \sqrt{4 - x^2 - z^2}$, and the plane $y = 0$.

44. Suppose that the density at a point in a gaseous spherical star is modeled by the formula

$$\delta = \delta_0 e^{-(\rho/R)^3}$$

where δ_0 is a positive constant, R is the radius of the star, and ρ is the distance from the point to the star's center. Find the mass of the star.

45–46 The tendency of a lamina to resist a change in rotational motion about an axis is measured by its ***moment of inertia*** about that axis. If a lamina occupies a region R of the xy-plane, and if its density function $\delta(x, y)$ is continuous on R, then the moments of inertia about the x-axis, the y-axis, and the z-axis are denoted by I_x, I_y, and I_z, respectively, and are defined by

$$I_x = \iint\limits_R y^2\, \delta(x, y)\, dA, \quad I_y = \iint\limits_R x^2\, \delta(x, y)\, dA,$$

$$I_z = \iint\limits_R (x^2 + y^2)\, \delta(x, y)\, dA$$

Use these definitions in Exercises 45 and 46. ■

45. Consider the rectangular lamina that occupies the region described by the inequalities $0 \le x \le a$ and $0 \le y \le b$. Assuming that the lamina has constant density δ, show that

$$I_x = \frac{\delta a b^3}{3}, \quad I_y = \frac{\delta a^3 b}{3}, \quad I_z = \frac{\delta a b(a^2 + b^2)}{3}$$

46. Consider the circular lamina that occupies the region described by the inequalities $0 \le x^2 + y^2 \le a^2$. Assuming that the lamina has constant density δ, show that

$$I_x = I_y = \frac{\delta \pi a^4}{4}, \quad I_z = \frac{\delta \pi a^4}{2}$$

47–50 The tendency of a solid to resist a change in rotational motion about an axis is measured by its ***moment of inertia*** about that axis. If the solid occupies a region G in an xyz-coordinate system, and if its density function $\delta(x, y, z)$ is continuous on G, then the moments of inertia about the x-axis, the y-axis, and the z-axis are denoted by I_x, I_y, and I_z, respectively, and are defined by

$$I_x = \iiint\limits_G (y^2 + z^2)\, \delta(x, y, z)\, dV$$

$$I_y = \iiint\limits_G (x^2 + z^2)\, \delta(x, y, z)\, dV$$

$$I_z = \iiint\limits_G (x^2 + y^2)\, \delta(x, y, z)\, dV$$

In these exercises, find the indicated moments of inertia of the solid, assuming that it has constant density δ. ■

47. I_z for the solid cylinder $x^2 + y^2 \leq a^2$, $0 \leq z \leq h$.

48. I_y for the solid cylinder $x^2 + y^2 \leq a^2$, $0 \leq z \leq h$.

49. I_z for the hollow cylinder $a_1^2 \leq x^2 + y^2 \leq a_2^2$, $0 \leq z \leq h$.

50. I_z for the solid sphere $x^2 + y^2 + z^2 \leq a^2$.

51–55 These exercises reference the *Theorem of Pappus*: *If R is a bounded plane region and L is a line that lies in the plane of R such that R is entirely on one side of L, then the volume of the solid formed by revolving R about L is given by*

$$volume = (\ area\ of\ R\ ) \cdot \left(\begin{array}{c} distance\ traveled \\ by\ the\ centroid \end{array} \right) \blacksquare$$

51. Perform the following steps to prove the Theorem of Pappus:

(a) Introduce an xy-coordinate system so that L is along the y-axis and the region R is in the first quadrant. Partition R into rectangular subregions in the usual way and let R_k be a typical subregion of R with center (x_k^*, y_k^*) and area $\Delta A_k = \Delta x_k \Delta y_k$. Show that the volume generated by R_k as it revolves about L is

$$2\pi x_k^* \Delta x_k \Delta y_k = 2\pi x_k^* \Delta A_k$$

(b) Show that the volume generated by R as it revolves about L is

$$V = \iint\limits_R 2\pi x \, dA = 2\pi \cdot \bar{x} \cdot [\text{area of } R]$$

52. Use the Theorem of Pappus and the result of Example 3 to find the volume of the solid generated when the region bounded by the x-axis and the semicircle $y = \sqrt{a^2 - x^2}$ is revolved about

(a) the line $y = -a$ (b) the line $y = x - a$.

53. Use the Theorem of Pappus and the fact that the area of an ellipse with semiaxes a and b is πab to find the volume of the elliptical torus generated by revolving the ellipse

$$\frac{(x - k)^2}{a^2} + \frac{y^2}{b^2} = 1$$

about the y-axis. Assume that $k > a$.

54. Use the Theorem of Pappus to find the volume of the solid that is generated when the region enclosed by $y = x^2$ and $y = 8 - x^2$ is revolved about the x-axis.

55. Use the Theorem of Pappus to find the centroid of the triangular region with vertices $(0, 0)$, $(a, 0)$, and $(0, b)$, where $a > 0$ and $b > 0$. [*Hint:* Revolve the region about the x-axis to obtain $\bar{y}$ and about the y-axis to obtain $\bar{x}$.]

56. It can be proved that if a bounded plane region slides along a helix in such a way that the region is always orthogonal to the helix (i.e., orthogonal to the unit tangent vector to the helix), then the volume swept out by the region is equal to the area of the region times the distance traveled by its centroid. Use this result to find the volume of the "tube" in the accompanying figure that is swept out by sliding a circle of radius $\frac{1}{2}$ along the helix

$$x = \cos t, \quad y = \sin t, \quad z = \frac{t}{4} \quad (0 \leq t \leq 4\pi)$$

in such a way that the circle is always centered on the helix and lies in the plane perpendicular to the helix.

◄ **Figure Ex-56**

57. Writing   Give a physical interpretation of the "center of gravity" of a lamina.

✔ **QUICK CHECK ANSWERS 14.8**

1. $\iint\limits_R \delta(x, y) \, dA$ **2.** first moment about the y-axis; $\iint\limits_R x\delta(x, y) \, dA$ **3.** $\left(\dfrac{5}{14}, \dfrac{32}{35} \right)$

CHAPTER 14 REVIEW EXERCISES

1. The double integral over a region R in the xy-plane is defined as

$$\iint\limits_R f(x, y) \, dA = \lim_{n \to +\infty} \sum_{k=1}^{n} f(x_k^*, y_k^*) \, \Delta A_k$$

Describe the procedure on which this definition is based.

2. The triple integral over a solid G in an xyz-coordinate system is defined as

$$\iiint\limits_G f(x, y, z) \, dV = \lim_{n \to +\infty} \sum_{k=1}^{n} f(x_k^*, y_k^*, z_k^*) \, \Delta V_k$$

Describe the procedure on which this definition is based.

3. (a) Express the area of a region R in the xy-plane as a double integral.

   (b) Express the volume of a region G in an xyz-coordinate system as a triple integral.

   (c) Express the area of the portion of the surface $z = f(x, y)$ that lies above the region R in the xy-plane as a double integral.

4. (a) Write down parametric equations for a sphere of radius a centered at the origin.

   (b) Write down parametric equations for the right circular cylinder of radius a and height h that is centered on the z-axis, has its base in the xy-plane, and extends in the positive z-direction.

5. Let R be the region in the accompanying figure. Fill in the missing limits of integration in the iterated integral

$$\int_{\square}^{\square} \int_{\square}^{\square} f(x, y)\, dx\, dy$$

over R.

6. Let R be the region shown in the accompanying figure. Fill in the missing limits of integration in the sum of the iterated integrals

$$\int_{0}^{2} \int_{\square}^{\square} f(x, y)\, dy\, dx + \int_{2}^{3} \int_{\square}^{\square} f(x, y)\, dy\, dx$$

over R.

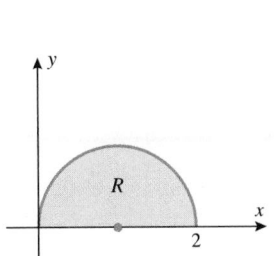

▲ Figure Ex-5   ▲ Figure Ex-6

7. (a) Find constants a, b, c, and d such that the transformation $x = au + bv$, $y = cu + dv$ maps the region S in the accompanying figure into the region R.

   (b) Find the area of the parallelogram R by integrating over the region S, and check your answer using a formula from geometry.

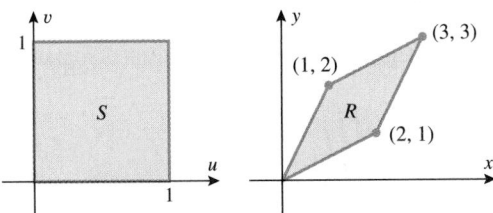

▲ Figure Ex-7

8. Give a geometric argument to show that

$$0 < \int_{0}^{\pi} \int_{0}^{\pi} \sin\sqrt{xy}\, dy\, dx < \pi^2$$

9–10 Evaluate the iterated integral. ■

9. $\displaystyle\int_{1/2}^{1} \int_{0}^{2x} \cos(\pi x^2)\, dy\, dx$ **10.** $\displaystyle\int_{0}^{2} \int_{-y}^{2y} xe^{y^3}\, dx\, dy$

11–12 Express the iterated integral as an equivalent integral with the order of integration reversed. ■

11. $\displaystyle\int_{0}^{2} \int_{0}^{x/2} e^x e^y\, dy\, dx$ **12.** $\displaystyle\int_{0}^{\pi} \int_{y}^{\pi} \frac{\sin x}{x}\, dx\, dy$

13–14 Sketch the region whose area is represented by the iterated integral. ■

13. $\displaystyle\int_{0}^{\pi/2} \int_{\tan(x/2)}^{\sin x} dy\, dx$

14. $\displaystyle\int_{\pi/6}^{\pi/2} \int_{a}^{a(1+\cos\theta)} r\, dr\, d\theta \quad (a > 0)$

15–16 Evaluate the double integral. ■

15. $\displaystyle\iint_R x^2 \sin y^2\, dA$; R is the region that is bounded by $y = x^3$, $y = -x^3$, and $y = 8$.

16. $\displaystyle\iint_R (4 - x^2 - y^2)\, dA$; R is the sector in the first quadrant bounded by the circle $x^2 + y^2 = 4$ and the coordinate axes.

17. Convert to rectangular coordinates and evaluate:

$$\int_{0}^{\pi/2} \int_{0}^{2a\sin\theta} r\sin 2\theta\, dr\, d\theta$$

18. Convert to polar coordinates and evaluate:

$$\int_{0}^{\sqrt{2}} \int_{x}^{\sqrt{4-x^2}} 4xy\, dy\, dx$$

19–20 Find the area of the region using a double integral. ■

19. The region bounded by $y = 2x^3$, $2x + y = 4$, and the x-axis.

20. The region enclosed by the rose $r = \cos 3\theta$.

21. Convert to cylindrical coordinates and evaluate:

$$\int_{-2}^{2} \int_{-\sqrt{4-x^2}}^{\sqrt{4-x^2}} \int_{(x^2+y^2)^2}^{16} x^2\, dz\, dy\, dx$$

22. Convert to spherical coordinates and evaluate:

$$\int_{0}^{1} \int_{0}^{\sqrt{1-x^2}} \int_{0}^{\sqrt{1-x^2-y^2}} \frac{1}{1 + x^2 + y^2 + z^2}\, dz\, dy\, dx$$

23. Let G be the region bounded above by the sphere $\rho = a$ and below by the cone $\phi = \pi/3$. Express

$$\iiint_G (x^2 + y^2)\, dV$$

as an iterated integral in

(a) spherical coordinates   (b) cylindrical coordinates
(c) rectangular coordinates.

24. Let $G = \{(x, y, z) : x^2 + y^2 \leq z \leq 4x\}$. Express the volume of G as an iterated integral in
   (a) rectangular coordinates   (b) cylindrical coordinates.

25–26 Find the volume of the solid using a triple integral. ■

25. The solid bounded below by the cone $\phi = \pi/6$ and above by the plane $z = a$.

26. The solid enclosed between the surfaces $x = y^2 + z^2$ and $x = 1 - y^2$.

27. Find the area of the portion of the surface $z = 3y + 2x^2 + 4$ that is above the triangular region with vertices $(0, 0)$, $(1, 1)$, and $(1, -1)$.

28. Find the surface area of the portion of the spiral ramp

$$\mathbf{r}(u, v) = u \cos v\,\mathbf{i} + u \sin v\,\mathbf{j} + v\mathbf{k}$$

   for which $0 \leq u \leq 2, 0 \leq v \leq 3u$.

29–30 Find the equation of the tangent plane to the surface at the specified point. ■

29. $\mathbf{r} = u\mathbf{i} + v\mathbf{j} + (u^2 + v^2)\mathbf{k}$; $u = 1, v = 2$

30. $x = u \cosh v, y = u \sinh v, z = u^2$; $(-3, 0, 9)$

31. Suppose that you have a double integral over a region R in the xy-plane and you want to transform that integral into an equivalent double integral over a region S in the uv-plane. Describe the procedure you would use.

32. Use the transformation $u = x - 3y, v = 3x + y$ to find

$$\iint\limits_R \frac{x - 3y}{(3x + y)^2}\, dA$$

   where R is the rectangular region enclosed by the lines $x - 3y = 0, x - 3y = 4, 3x + y = 1$, and $3x + y = 3$.

33. Let G be the solid in 3-space defined by the inequalities

$$1 - e^x \leq y \leq 3 - e^x, \quad 1 - y \leq 2z \leq 2 - y, \quad y \leq e^x \leq y + 4$$

   (a) Using the coordinate transformation

$$u = e^x + y, \quad v = y + 2z, \quad w = e^x - y$$

   calculate the Jacobian $\partial(x, y, z)/\partial(u, v, w)$. Express your answer in terms of u, v, and w.
   (b) Using a triple integral and the change of variables given in part (a), find the volume of G.

34. Find the average distance from a point inside a sphere of radius a to the center. [See the definition preceding Exercise 33 of Section 14.5.]

35–36 Find the centroid of the region. ■

35. The region bounded by $y^2 = 4x$ and $y^2 = 8(x - 2)$.

36. The upper half of the ellipse $(x/a)^2 + (y/b)^2 = 1$.

37–38 Find the centroid of the solid. ■

37. The solid cone with vertex $(0, 0, h)$ and with base the disk $x^2 + y^2 \leq a^2$ in the xy-plane.

38. The solid bounded by $y = x^2, z = 0$, and $y + z = 4$.

CHAPTER 14 MAKING CONNECTIONS   c CAS

1. The integral $\int_0^{+\infty} e^{-x^2}\, dx$, which arises in probability theory, can be evaluated using the following method. Let the value of the integral be I. Thus,

$$I = \int_0^{+\infty} e^{-x^2}\, dx = \int_0^{+\infty} e^{-y^2}\, dy$$

since the letter used for the variable of integration in a definite integral does not matter.
   (a) Give a reasonable argument to show that

$$I^2 = \int_0^{+\infty} \int_0^{+\infty} e^{-(x^2+y^2)}\, dx\, dy$$

   (b) Evaluate the iterated integral in part (a) by converting to polar coordinates.
   (c) Use the result in part (b) to show that $I = \sqrt{\pi}/2$.

2. Show that

$$\int_0^{+\infty} \int_0^{+\infty} \frac{1}{(1 + x^2 + y^2)^2}\, dx\, dy = \frac{\pi}{4}$$

   [*Hint:* See Exercise 1.]

c 3. (a) Use the numerical integration capability of a CAS to approximate the value of the double integral

$$\int_{-1}^1 \int_0^{\sqrt{1-x^2}} e^{-(x^2+y^2)^2}\, dy\, dx$$

   (b) Compare the approximation obtained in part (a) to the approximation that results if the integral is first converted to polar coordinates.

c 4. (a) Find the region G over which the triple integral

$$\iiint\limits_G (1 - x^2 - y^2 - z^2)\, dV$$

   has its maximum value.
   (b) Use the numerical triple integral operation of a CAS to approximate the maximum value.
   (c) Find the exact maximum value.

5–6 The accompanying figure shows the graph of an *astroidal sphere*

$$x^{2/3} + y^{2/3} + z^{2/3} = a^{2/3}$$

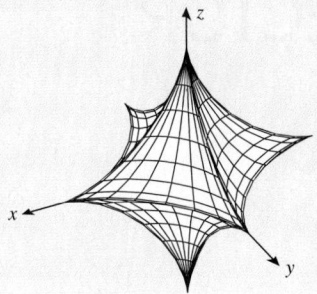

C 5. (a) Show that the astroidal sphere can be represented parametrically as

$$x = a(\sin u \cos v)^3$$
$$y = a(\sin u \sin v)^3 \qquad (0 \le u \le \pi, \ 0 \le v \le 2\pi)$$
$$z = a(\cos u)^3$$

(b) Use a CAS to approximate the surface area in the case where $a = 1$.

6. Find the volume of the astroidal sphere using a triple integral and the transformation

$$x = \rho(\sin \phi \cos \theta)^3$$
$$y = \rho(\sin \phi \sin \theta)^3$$
$$z = \rho(\cos \phi)^3$$

for which $0 \le \rho \le a, 0 \le \phi \le \pi, 0 \le \theta \le 2\pi$.

TOPICS IN VECTOR CALCULUS

NASA Goddard Space Flight Center (NASA/GSFC)

Results in this chapter provide tools for analyzing and understanding the behavior of hurricanes and other fluid flows.

The main theme of this chapter is the concept of a "flow." The body of mathematics that we will study here is concerned with analyzing flows of various types—the flow of a fluid or the flow of electricity, for example. Indeed, the early writings of Isaac Newton on calculus are replete with such nouns as "fluxion" and "fluent," which are rooted in the Latin *fluere* (to flow). We will begin this chapter by introducing the concept of a vector field, which is the mathematical description of a flow. In subsequent sections, we will introduce two new kinds of integrals that are used in a variety of applications to analyze properties of vector fields and flows. Finally, we conclude with three major theorems, Green's Theorem, the Divergence Theorem, and Stokes' Theorem. These theorems provide a deep insight into the nature of flows and are the basis for many of the most important principles in physics and engineering.

15.1 VECTOR FIELDS

In this section we will consider functions that associate vectors with points in 2-space or 3-space. We will see that such functions play an important role in the study of fluid flow, gravitational force fields, electromagnetic force fields, and a wide range of other applied problems.

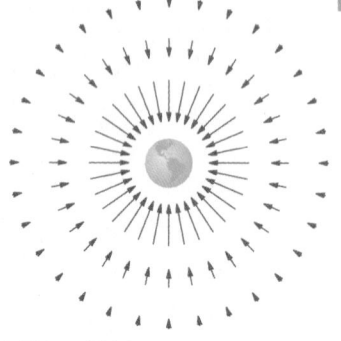

▲ **Figure 15.1.1**

■ VECTOR FIELDS

To motivate the mathematical ideas in this section, consider a *unit* point-mass located at any point in the universe. According to Newton's Law of Universal Gravitation, the Earth exerts an attractive force on the mass that is directed toward the center of the Earth and has a magnitude that is inversely proportional to the square of the distance from the mass to the Earth's center (Figure 15.1.1). This association of force vectors with points in space is called the Earth's *gravitational field*. A similar idea arises in fluid flow. Imagine a stream in which the water flows horizontally at every level, and consider the layer of water at a specific depth. At each point of the layer, the water has a certain velocity, which we can represent by a vector at that point (Figure 15.1.2). This association of velocity vectors with points in the two-dimensional layer is called the *velocity field* at that layer. These ideas are captured in the following definition.

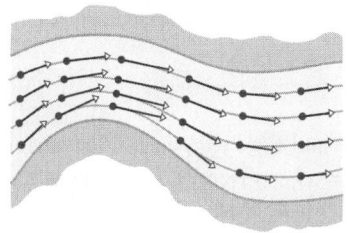

▲ Figure 15.1.2

Notice that a vector field is really just a vector-valued function. The term "vector field" is commonly used in physics and engineering.

15.1.1 DEFINITION A **vector field** in a plane is a function that associates with each point P in the plane a unique vector $\mathbf{F}(P)$ parallel to the plane. Similarly, a vector field in 3-space is a function that associates with each point P in 3-space a unique vector $\mathbf{F}(P)$ in 3-space.

Observe that in this definition there is no reference to a coordinate system. However, for computational purposes it is usually desirable to introduce a coordinate system so that vectors can be assigned components. Specifically, if $\mathbf{F}(P)$ is a vector field in an xy-coordinate system, then the point P will have some coordinates (x, y) and the associated vector will have components that are functions of x and y. Thus, the vector field $\mathbf{F}(P)$ can be expressed as

$$\mathbf{F}(x, y) = f(x, y)\mathbf{i} + g(x, y)\mathbf{j}$$

Similarly, in 3-space with an xyz-coordinate system, a vector field $\mathbf{F}(P)$ can be expressed as

$$\mathbf{F}(x, y, z) = f(x, y, z)\mathbf{i} + g(x, y, z)\mathbf{j} + h(x, y, z)\mathbf{k}$$

■ **GRAPHICAL REPRESENTATIONS OF VECTOR FIELDS**

A vector field in 2-space can be pictured geometrically by drawing representative field vectors $\mathbf{F}(x, y)$ at some well-chosen points in the xy-plane. But, just as it is usually not possible to describe a plane curve completely by plotting finitely many points, so it is usually not possible to describe a vector field completely by drawing finitely many vectors. Nevertheless, such graphical representations can provide useful information about the general behavior of the field if the vectors are chosen appropriately. However, graphical representations of vector fields require a substantial amount of computation, so they are usually created using computers. Figure 15.1.3 shows four computer-generated vector fields. The vector field in part (*a*) might describe the velocity of the current in a stream at various depths. At the bottom of the stream the velocity is zero, but the speed of the current increases as the depth decreases. Points at the same depth have the same speed. The vector field in part (*b*) might describe the velocity at points on a rotating wheel. At the center of the wheel the velocity is zero, but the speed increases with the distance from the center. Points at the same distance from the center have the same speed. The vector field in part (*c*) might describe the repulsive force of an electrical charge—the closer to the charge, the greater the force of repulsion. Part (*d*) shows a vector field in 3-space. Such pictures tend to be cluttered and hence are of lesser value than graphical representations of vector fields in 2-space. Note also that the

TECHNOLOGY MASTERY

If you have a graphing utility that can generate vector fields, read the relevant documentation and try to make reasonable duplicates of parts (*a*) and (*b*) of Figure 15.1.3.

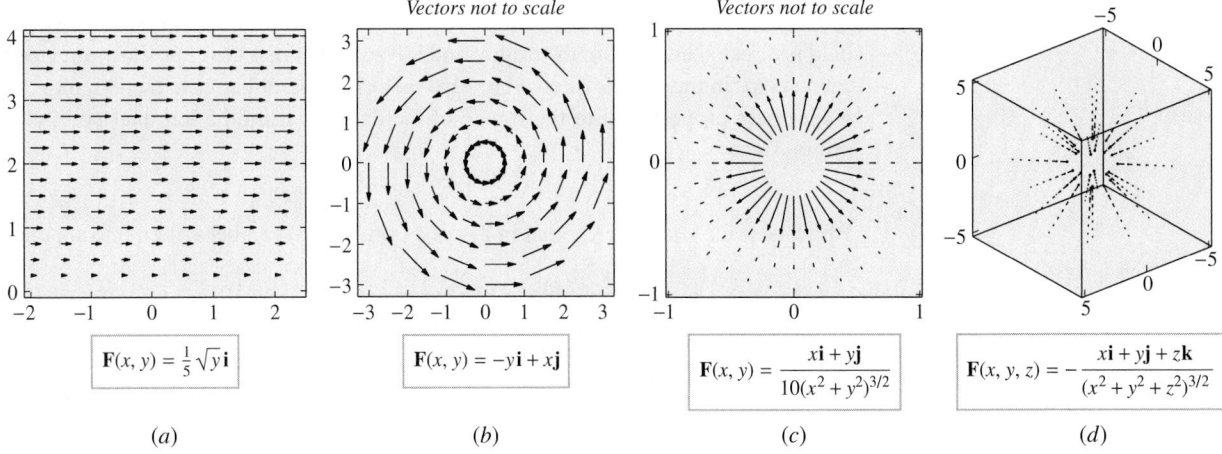

$$\mathbf{F}(x, y) = \tfrac{1}{5}\sqrt{y}\,\mathbf{i}$$

(*a*)

$$\mathbf{F}(x, y) = -y\mathbf{i} + x\mathbf{j}$$

(*b*)

$$\mathbf{F}(x, y) = \frac{x\mathbf{i} + y\mathbf{j}}{10(x^2 + y^2)^{3/2}}$$

(*c*)

$$\mathbf{F}(x, y, z) = -\frac{x\mathbf{i} + y\mathbf{j} + z\mathbf{k}}{(x^2 + y^2 + z^2)^{3/2}}$$

(*d*)

▲ Figure 15.1.3

vectors in parts (b) and (c) are not to scale—their lengths have been compressed for clarity. We will follow this procedure throughout this chapter.

■ A COMPACT NOTATION FOR VECTOR FIELDS

Sometimes it is helpful to denote the vector fields $\mathbf{F}(x, y)$ and $\mathbf{F}(x, y, z)$ entirely in vector notation by identifying (x, y) with the radius vector $\mathbf{r} = x\mathbf{i} + y\mathbf{j}$ and (x, y, z) with the radius vector $\mathbf{r} = x\mathbf{i} + y\mathbf{j} + z\mathbf{k}$. With this notation a vector field in either 2-space or 3-space can be written as $\mathbf{F}(\mathbf{r})$. When no confusion is likely to arise, we will sometimes omit the $\mathbf{r}$ altogether and denote the vector field as $\mathbf{F}$.

■ INVERSE-SQUARE FIELDS

According to Newton's Law of Universal Gravitation, particles with masses m and M attract each other with a force $\mathbf{F}$ of magnitude

$$\|\mathbf{F}\| = \frac{GmM}{r^2} \tag{1}$$

where r is the distance between the particles and G is a constant. If we assume that the particle of mass M is located at the origin of an xyz-coordinate system and $\mathbf{r}$ is the radius vector to the particle of mass m, then $r = \|\mathbf{r}\|$, and the force $\mathbf{F}(\mathbf{r})$ exerted by the particle of mass M on the particle of mass m is in the direction of the unit vector $-\mathbf{r}/\|\mathbf{r}\|$. Thus, it follows from (1) that

$$\mathbf{F}(\mathbf{r}) = -\frac{GmM}{\|\mathbf{r}\|^2} \frac{\mathbf{r}}{\|\mathbf{r}\|} = -\frac{GmM}{\|\mathbf{r}\|^3}\mathbf{r} \tag{2}$$

If m and M are constant, and we let $c = -GmM$, then this formula can be expressed as

$$\mathbf{F}(\mathbf{r}) = \frac{c}{\|\mathbf{r}\|^3}\mathbf{r}$$

Vector fields of this form arise in electromagnetic as well as gravitational problems. Such fields are so important that they have their own terminology.

15.1.2 DEFINITION If $\mathbf{r}$ is a radius vector in 2-space or 3-space, and if c is a constant, then a vector field of the form
$$\mathbf{F}(\mathbf{r}) = \frac{c}{\|\mathbf{r}\|^3}\mathbf{r} \tag{3}$$
is called an ***inverse-square field***.

Observe that if $c > 0$ in (3), then $\mathbf{F}(\mathbf{r})$ has the same direction as $\mathbf{r}$, so each vector in the field is directed away from the origin; and if $c < 0$, then $\mathbf{F}(\mathbf{r})$ is oppositely directed to $\mathbf{r}$, so each vector in the field is directed toward the origin. In either case the magnitude of $\mathbf{F}(\mathbf{r})$ is inversely proportional to the square of the distance from the terminal point of $\mathbf{r}$ to the origin, since

$$\|\mathbf{F}(\mathbf{r})\| = \frac{|c|}{\|\mathbf{r}\|^3}\|\mathbf{r}\| = \frac{|c|}{\|\mathbf{r}\|^2}$$

We leave it for you to verify that in 2-space Formula (3) can be written in component form as

$$\mathbf{F}(x, y) = \frac{c}{(x^2 + y^2)^{3/2}}(x\mathbf{i} + y\mathbf{j}) \tag{4}$$

and in 3-space as

$$\mathbf{F}(x, y, z) = \frac{c}{(x^2 + y^2 + z^2)^{3/2}}(x\mathbf{i} + y\mathbf{j} + z\mathbf{k}) \tag{5}$$

[see parts (c) and (d) of Figure 15.1.3].

▶ **Example 1**   *Coulomb's law* states that *the electrostatic force exerted by one charged particle on another is directly proportional to the product of the charges and inversely proportional to the square of the distance between them.* This has the same form as Newton's Law of Universal Gravitation, so the electrostatic force field exerted by a charged particle is an inverse-square field. Specifically, if a particle of charge Q is at the origin of a coordinate system, and if **r** is the radius vector to a particle of charge q, then the force **F(r)** that the particle of charge Q exerts on the particle of charge q is of the form

$$\mathbf{F(r)} = \frac{qQ}{4\pi\epsilon_0 \|\mathbf{r}\|^3}\mathbf{r}$$

where ϵ_0 is a positive constant (called the ***permittivity constant***). This formula is of form (3) with $c = qQ/4\pi\epsilon_0$. ◀

■ **GRADIENT FIELDS**

An important class of vector fields arises from the process of finding gradients. Recall that if ϕ is a function of three variables, then the gradient of ϕ is defined as

$$\nabla\phi = \frac{\partial\phi}{\partial x}\mathbf{i} + \frac{\partial\phi}{\partial y}\mathbf{j} + \frac{\partial\phi}{\partial z}\mathbf{k}$$

This formula defines a vector field in 3-space called the ***gradient field of*** $\boldsymbol\phi$. Similarly, the gradient of a function of two variables defines a gradient field in 2-space. At each point in a gradient field where the gradient is nonzero, the vector points in the direction in which the rate of increase of ϕ is maximum.

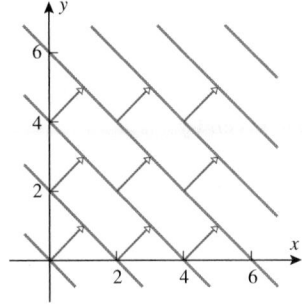

▲ **Figure 15.1.4**

▶ **Example 2**   Sketch the gradient field of $\phi(x, y) = x + y$.

Solution.   The gradient of ϕ is

$$\nabla\phi = \frac{\partial\phi}{\partial x}\mathbf{i} + \frac{\partial\phi}{\partial y}\mathbf{j} = \mathbf{i} + \mathbf{j}$$

which is constant [i.e., is the same vector at each point (x, y)]. A portion of the vector field is sketched in Figure 15.1.4 together with some level curves of ϕ. Note that at each point, $\nabla\phi$ is normal to the level curve of ϕ through the point (Theorem 13.6.6). ◀

■ **CONSERVATIVE FIELDS AND POTENTIAL FUNCTIONS**

If **F(r)** is an arbitrary vector field in 2-space or 3-space, we can ask whether it is the gradient field of some function ϕ, and if so, how we can find ϕ. This is an important problem in various applications, and we will study it in more detail later. However, there is some terminology for such fields that we will introduce now.

15.1.3   **DEFINITION**   A vector field **F** in 2-space or 3-space is said to be ***conservative*** in a region if it is the gradient field for some function ϕ in that region, that is, if

$$\mathbf{F} = \nabla\phi$$

The function ϕ is called a ***potential function*** for **F** in the region.

▶ **Example 3**   Inverse-square fields are conservative in any region that does not contain the origin. For example, in the two-dimensional case the function

$$\phi(x, y) = -\frac{c}{(x^2 + y^2)^{1/2}} \tag{6}$$

is a potential function for (4) in any region not containing the origin, since

$$
\begin{aligned}
\nabla\phi(x, y) &= \frac{\partial\phi}{\partial x}\mathbf{i} + \frac{\partial\phi}{\partial y}\mathbf{j} \\
&= \frac{cx}{(x^2 + y^2)^{3/2}}\mathbf{i} + \frac{cy}{(x^2 + y^2)^{3/2}}\mathbf{j} \\
&= \frac{c}{(x^2 + y^2)^{3/2}}(x\mathbf{i} + y\mathbf{j}) \\
&= \mathbf{F}(x, y)
\end{aligned}
$$

In a later section we will discuss methods for finding potential functions for conservative vector fields. ◀

DIVERGENCE AND CURL

We will now define two important operations on vector fields in 3-space—the *divergence* and the *curl* of the field. These names originate in the study of fluid flow, in which case the divergence relates to the way in which fluid flows toward or away from a point and the curl relates to the rotational properties of the fluid at a point. We will investigate the physical interpretations of these operations in more detail later, but for now we will focus only on their computation.

15.1.4   DEFINITION   If $\mathbf{F}(x, y, z) = f(x, y, z)\mathbf{i} + g(x, y, z)\mathbf{j} + h(x, y, z)\mathbf{k}$, then we define the *divergence of* $\mathbf{F}$, written div $\mathbf{F}$, to be the function given by

$$\operatorname{div} \mathbf{F} = \frac{\partial f}{\partial x} + \frac{\partial g}{\partial y} + \frac{\partial h}{\partial z} \tag{7}$$

15.1.5   DEFINITION   If $\mathbf{F}(x, y, z) = f(x, y, z)\mathbf{i} + g(x, y, z)\mathbf{j} + h(x, y, z)\mathbf{k}$, then we define the *curl of* $\mathbf{F}$, written curl $\mathbf{F}$, to be the vector field given by

$$\operatorname{curl} \mathbf{F} = \left(\frac{\partial h}{\partial y} - \frac{\partial g}{\partial z}\right)\mathbf{i} + \left(\frac{\partial f}{\partial z} - \frac{\partial h}{\partial x}\right)\mathbf{j} + \left(\frac{\partial g}{\partial x} - \frac{\partial f}{\partial y}\right)\mathbf{k} \tag{8}$$

REMARK   Observe that div $\mathbf{F}$ and curl $\mathbf{F}$ depend on the point at which they are computed, and hence are more properly written as div $\mathbf{F}(x, y, z)$ and curl $\mathbf{F}(x, y, z)$. However, even though these functions are expressed in terms of x, y, and z, it can be proved that their values at a fixed point depend only on the point and not on the coordinate system selected. This is important in applications, since it allows physicists and engineers to compute the curl and divergence in any convenient coordinate system.

Before proceeding to some examples, we note that div $\mathbf{F}$ has scalar values, whereas curl $\mathbf{F}$ has vector values (i.e., curl $\mathbf{F}$ is itself a vector field). Moreover, for computational purposes it is useful to note that the formula for the curl can be expressed in the determinant form

$$\text{curl } \mathbf{F} = \begin{vmatrix} \mathbf{i} & \mathbf{j} & \mathbf{k} \\ \dfrac{\partial}{\partial x} & \dfrac{\partial}{\partial y} & \dfrac{\partial}{\partial z} \\ f & g & h \end{vmatrix} \tag{9}$$

You should verify that Formula (8) results if the determinant is computed by interpreting a "product" such as $(\partial/\partial x)(g)$ to mean $\partial g/\partial x$. Keep in mind, however, that (9) is just a mnemonic device and not a true determinant, since the entries in a determinant must be numbers, not vectors and partial derivative symbols.

▶ **Example 4**   Find the divergence and the curl of the vector field

$$\mathbf{F}(x, y, z) = x^2 y \mathbf{i} + 2y^3 z \mathbf{j} + 3z \mathbf{k}$$

Solution.   From (7)

$$\text{div } \mathbf{F} = \frac{\partial}{\partial x}(x^2 y) + \frac{\partial}{\partial y}(2y^3 z) + \frac{\partial}{\partial z}(3z)$$

$$= 2xy + 6y^2 z + 3$$

and from (9)

TECHNOLOGY MASTERY

Most computer algebra systems can compute gradient fields, divergence, and curl. If you have a CAS with these capabilities, read the relevant documentation, and use your CAS to check the computations in Examples 2 and 4.

$$\text{curl } \mathbf{F} = \begin{vmatrix} \mathbf{i} & \mathbf{j} & \mathbf{k} \\ \dfrac{\partial}{\partial x} & \dfrac{\partial}{\partial y} & \dfrac{\partial}{\partial z} \\ x^2 y & 2y^3 z & 3z \end{vmatrix}$$

$$= \left[\frac{\partial}{\partial y}(3z) - \frac{\partial}{\partial z}(2y^3 z) \right] \mathbf{i} + \left[\frac{\partial}{\partial z}(x^2 y) - \frac{\partial}{\partial x}(3z) \right] \mathbf{j} + \left[\frac{\partial}{\partial x}(2y^3 z) - \frac{\partial}{\partial y}(x^2 y) \right] \mathbf{k}$$

$$= -2y^3 \mathbf{i} - x^2 \mathbf{k} \quad \blacktriangleleft$$

▶ **Example 5**   Show that the divergence of the inverse-square field

$$\mathbf{F}(x, y, z) = \frac{c}{(x^2 + y^2 + z^2)^{3/2}} (x\mathbf{i} + y\mathbf{j} + z\mathbf{k})$$

is zero.

Solution.   The computations can be simplified by letting $r = (x^2 + y^2 + z^2)^{1/2}$, in which case $\mathbf{F}$ can be expressed as

$$\mathbf{F}(x, y, z) = \frac{cx\mathbf{i} + cy\mathbf{j} + cz\mathbf{k}}{r^3} = \frac{cx}{r^3}\mathbf{i} + \frac{cy}{r^3}\mathbf{j} + \frac{cz}{r^3}\mathbf{k}$$

We leave it for you to show that

$$\frac{\partial r}{\partial x} = \frac{x}{r}, \quad \frac{\partial r}{\partial y} = \frac{y}{r}, \quad \frac{\partial r}{\partial z} = \frac{z}{r}$$

Thus

$$\operatorname{div}\mathbf{F}=c\left[\frac{\partial}{\partial x}\left(\frac{x}{r^3}\right)+\frac{\partial}{\partial y}\left(\frac{y}{r^3}\right)+\frac{\partial}{\partial z}\left(\frac{z}{r^3}\right)\right] \qquad (10)$$

But

$$\frac{\partial}{\partial x}\left(\frac{x}{r^3}\right)=\frac{r^3-x(3r^2)(x/r)}{(r^3)^2}=\frac{1}{r^3}-\frac{3x^2}{r^5}$$

$$\frac{\partial}{\partial y}\left(\frac{y}{r^3}\right)=\frac{1}{r^3}-\frac{3y^2}{r^5}$$

$$\frac{\partial}{\partial z}\left(\frac{z}{r^3}\right)=\frac{1}{r^3}-\frac{3z^2}{r^5}$$

Substituting these expressions in (10) yields

$$\operatorname{div}\mathbf{F}=c\left[\frac{3}{r^3}-\frac{3x^2+3y^2+3z^2}{r^5}\right]=c\left[\frac{3}{r^3}-\frac{3r^2}{r^5}\right]=0 \quad \blacktriangleleft$$

■ THE ∇ OPERATOR

Thus far, the symbol ∇ that appears in the gradient expression $\nabla\phi$ has not been given a meaning of its own. However, it is often convenient to view ∇ as an operator

$$\nabla=\frac{\partial}{\partial x}\mathbf{i}+\frac{\partial}{\partial y}\mathbf{j}+\frac{\partial}{\partial z}\mathbf{k} \qquad (11)$$

which when applied to $\phi(x,y,z)$ produces the gradient

$$\nabla\phi=\frac{\partial\phi}{\partial x}\mathbf{i}+\frac{\partial\phi}{\partial y}\mathbf{j}+\frac{\partial\phi}{\partial z}\mathbf{k}$$

We call (11) the **del operator**. This is analogous to the derivative operator d/dx, which when applied to $f(x)$ produces the derivative $f'(x)$.

The del operator allows us to express the divergence of a vector field

$$\mathbf{F}=f(x,y,z)\mathbf{i}+g(x,y,z)\mathbf{j}+h(x,y,z)\mathbf{k}$$

in dot product notation as

$$\operatorname{div}\mathbf{F}=\nabla\cdot\mathbf{F}=\frac{\partial f}{\partial x}+\frac{\partial g}{\partial y}+\frac{\partial h}{\partial z} \qquad (12)$$

and the curl of this field in cross-product notation as

$$\operatorname{curl}\mathbf{F}=\nabla\times\mathbf{F}=\begin{vmatrix} \mathbf{i} & \mathbf{j} & \mathbf{k} \\ \dfrac{\partial}{\partial x} & \dfrac{\partial}{\partial y} & \dfrac{\partial}{\partial z} \\ f & g & h \end{vmatrix} \qquad (13)$$

■ THE LAPLACIAN ∇^2

The operator that results by taking the dot product of the del operator with itself is denoted by ∇^2 and is called the **Laplacian operator**. This operator has the form

$$\nabla^2=\nabla\cdot\nabla=\frac{\partial^2}{\partial x^2}+\frac{\partial^2}{\partial y^2}+\frac{\partial^2}{\partial z^2} \qquad (14)$$

When applied to $\phi(x, y, z)$ the Laplacian operator produces the function

$$\nabla^2 \phi = \frac{\partial^2 \phi}{\partial x^2} + \frac{\partial^2 \phi}{\partial y^2} + \frac{\partial^2 \phi}{\partial z^2}$$

Note that $\nabla^2 \phi$ can also be expressed as div $(\nabla \phi)$. The equation $\nabla^2 \phi = 0$ or, equivalently,

$$\frac{\partial^2 \phi}{\partial x^2} + \frac{\partial^2 \phi}{\partial y^2} + \frac{\partial^2 \phi}{\partial z^2} = 0$$

is known as **Laplace's equation**. This partial differential equation plays an important role in a wide variety of applications, resulting from the fact that it is satisfied by the potential function for the inverse-square field.

✔ QUICK CHECK EXERCISES 15.1   (See page 1093 for answers.)

1. The function $\phi(x, y, z) = xy + yz + xz$ is a potential for the vector field $\mathbf{F} = $ _____.

2. The vector field $\mathbf{F}(x, y, z) = $ _____, defined for $(x, y, z) \neq (0, 0, 0)$, is always directed toward the origin and is of length equal to the distance from (x, y, z) to the origin.

3. An inverse-square field is one that can be written in the form $\mathbf{F}(\mathbf{r}) = $ _____.

4. The vector field

$$\mathbf{F}(x, y, z) = yz\mathbf{i} + xy^2\mathbf{j} + yz^2\mathbf{k}$$

has divergence _____ and curl _____.

Pierre-Simon de Laplace (1749–1827) French mathematician and physicist. Laplace is sometimes referred to as the French Isaac Newton because of his work in celestial mechanics. In a five-volume treatise entitled *Traité de Mécanique Céleste*, he solved extremely difficult problems involving gravitational interactions between the planets. In particular, he was able to show that our solar system is stable and not prone to catastrophic collapse as a result of these interactions. This was an issue of major concern at the time because Jupiter's orbit appeared to be shrinking and Saturn's expanding; Laplace showed that these were expected periodic anomalies. In addition to his work in celestial mechanics, he founded modern probability theory, showed with Lavoisier that respiration is a form of combustion, and developed methods that fostered many new branches of pure mathematics.

Laplace was born to moderately successful parents in Normandy, his father being a farmer and cider merchant. He matriculated in the theology program at the University of Caen at age 16 but left for Paris at age 18 with a letter of introduction to the influential mathematician d'Alembert, who eventually helped him undertake a career in mathematics. Laplace was a prolific writer, and after his election to the Academy of Sciences in 1773, the secretary wrote that the Academy had never received so many important research papers by so young a person in such a short time. Laplace had little interest in pure mathematics—he regarded mathematics merely as a tool for solving applied problems. In his impatience with mathematical detail, he frequently omitted complicated arguments with the statement, "It is easy to show that...." He admitted, however, that as time passed he often had trouble reconstructing the omitted details himself!

At the height of his fame, Laplace served on many government committees and held the posts of Minister of the Interior and Chancellor of the Senate. He barely escaped imprisonment and execution during the period of the Revolution, probably because he was able to convince each opposing party that he sided with them. Napoleon described him as a great mathematician but a poor administrator who "sought subtleties everywhere, had only doubtful ideas, and ... carried the spirit of the infinitely small into administration." In spite of his genius, Laplace was both egotistic and insecure, attempting to ensure his place in history by conveniently failing to credit mathematicians whose work he used—an unnecessary pettiness since his own work was so brilliant. However, on the positive side he was supportive of young mathematicians, often treating them as his own children. Laplace ranks as one of the most influential mathematicians in history.

EXERCISE SET 15.1   ⊠ Graphing Utility   C CAS

1–2 Match the vector field $\mathbf{F}(x, y)$ with one of the plots, and explain your reasoning. ■

1. (a) $\mathbf{F}(x, y) = x\mathbf{i}$ (b) $\mathbf{F}(x, y) = \sin x\mathbf{i} + \mathbf{j}$

2. (a) $\mathbf{F}(x, y) = \mathbf{i} + \mathbf{j}$

(b) $\mathbf{F}(x, y) = \dfrac{x}{\sqrt{x^2 + y^2}}\mathbf{i} + \dfrac{y}{\sqrt{x^2 + y^2}}\mathbf{j}$

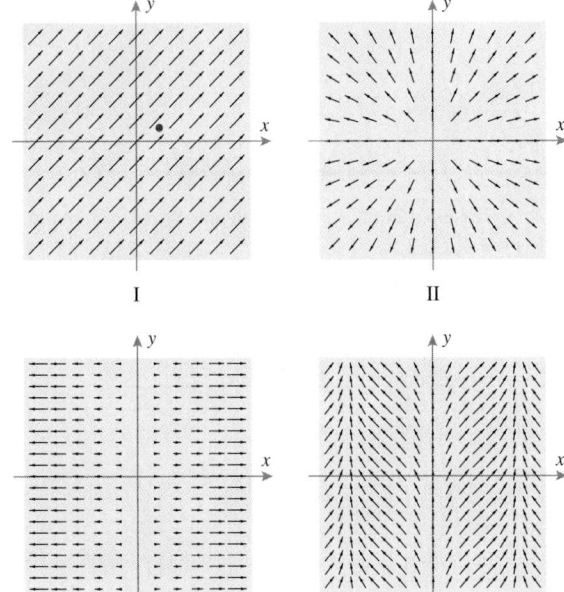

I

II

III

IV

3–4 Determine whether the statement about the vector field $\mathbf{F}(x, y)$ is true or false. If false, explain why. ■

3. $\mathbf{F}(x, y) = x^2\mathbf{i} - y\mathbf{j}$.
(a) $\|\mathbf{F}(x, y)\| \to 0$ as $(x, y) \to (0, 0)$.
(b) If (x, y) is on the positive y-axis, then the vector points in the negative y-direction.
(c) If (x, y) is in the first quadrant, then the vector points down and to the right.

4. $\mathbf{F}(x, y) = \dfrac{x}{\sqrt{x^2 + y^2}}\mathbf{i} - \dfrac{y}{\sqrt{x^2 + y^2}}\mathbf{j}$.
(a) As (x, y) moves away from the origin, the lengths of the vectors decrease.
(b) If (x, y) is a point on the positive x-axis, then the vector points up.
(c) If (x, y) is a point on the positive y-axis, the vector points to the right.

5–8 Sketch the vector field by drawing some representative nonintersecting vectors. The vectors need not be drawn to scale, but they should be in reasonably correct proportion relative to each other. ■

5. $\mathbf{F}(x, y) = 2\mathbf{i} - \mathbf{j}$ **6.** $\mathbf{F}(x, y) = y\mathbf{j}$, $y > 0$

7. $\mathbf{F}(x, y) = y\mathbf{i} - x\mathbf{j}$. [*Note:* Each vector in the field is perpendicular to the position vector $\mathbf{r} = x\mathbf{i} + y\mathbf{j}$.]

8. $\mathbf{F}(x, y) = \dfrac{x\mathbf{i} + y\mathbf{j}}{\sqrt{x^2 + y^2}}$. [*Note:* Each vector in the field is a unit vector in the same direction as the position vector $\mathbf{r} = x\mathbf{i} + y\mathbf{j}$.]

⊠ **9–10** Use a graphing utility to generate a plot of the vector field. ■

9. $\mathbf{F}(x, y) = \mathbf{i} + \cos y\mathbf{j}$ **10.** $\mathbf{F}(x, y) = y\mathbf{i} - x\mathbf{j}$

11–14 True–False Determine whether the statement is true or false. Explain your answer. ■

11. The vector-valued function
$$\mathbf{F}(x, y) = y\mathbf{i} + x^2\mathbf{j} + xy\mathbf{k}$$
is an example of a vector field in the xy-plane.

12. If $\mathbf{r}$ is a radius vector in 3-space, then a vector field of the form
$$\mathbf{F}(\mathbf{r}) = \frac{1}{\|\mathbf{r}\|^2}\mathbf{r}$$
is an example of an inverse-square field.

13. If $\mathbf{F}$ is a vector field, then so is $\nabla \times \mathbf{F}$.

14. If $\mathbf{F}$ is a vector field and $\nabla \cdot \mathbf{F} = \phi$, then ϕ is a potential function for $\mathbf{F}$.

15–16 Confirm that ϕ is a potential function for $\mathbf{F}(\mathbf{r})$ on some region, and state the region. ■

15. (a) $\phi(x, y) = \tan^{-1} xy$
$$\mathbf{F}(x, y) = \frac{y}{1 + x^2 y^2}\mathbf{i} + \frac{x}{1 + x^2 y^2}\mathbf{j}$$
(b) $\phi(x, y, z) = x^2 - 3y^2 + 4z^2$
$\mathbf{F}(x, y, z) = 2x\mathbf{i} - 6y\mathbf{j} + 8z\mathbf{k}$

16. (a) $\phi(x, y) = 2y^2 + 3x^2 y - xy^3$
$\mathbf{F}(x, y) = (6xy - y^3)\mathbf{i} + (4y + 3x^2 - 3xy^2)\mathbf{j}$
(b) $\phi(x, y, z) = x \sin z + y \sin x + z \sin y$
$\mathbf{F}(x, y, z) = (\sin z + y \cos x)\mathbf{i} + (\sin x + z \cos y)\mathbf{j}$
$\qquad\qquad\qquad\qquad + (\sin y + x \cos z)\mathbf{k}$

17–22 Find div $\mathbf{F}$ and curl $\mathbf{F}$. ■

17. $\mathbf{F}(x, y, z) = x^2\mathbf{i} - 2\mathbf{j} + yz\mathbf{k}$

18. $\mathbf{F}(x, y, z) = xz^3\mathbf{i} + 2y^4 x^2\mathbf{j} + 5z^2 y\mathbf{k}$

19. $\mathbf{F}(x, y, z) = 7y^3 z^2\mathbf{i} - 8x^2 z^5\mathbf{j} - 3xy^4\mathbf{k}$

20. $\mathbf{F}(x, y, z) = e^{xy}\mathbf{i} - \cos y\mathbf{j} + \sin^2 z\mathbf{k}$

21. $\mathbf{F}(x, y, z) = \dfrac{1}{\sqrt{x^2 + y^2 + z^2}}(x\mathbf{i} + y\mathbf{j} + z\mathbf{k})$

22. $\mathbf{F}(x, y, z) = \ln x\mathbf{i} + e^{xyz}\mathbf{j} + \tan^{-1}(z/x)\mathbf{k}$

23–24 Find $\nabla \cdot (\mathbf{F} \times \mathbf{G})$. ■

23. $\mathbf{F}(x, y, z) = 2x\mathbf{i} + \mathbf{j} + 4y\mathbf{k}$
$\mathbf{G}(x, y, z) = x\mathbf{i} + y\mathbf{j} - z\mathbf{k}$

24. $\mathbf{F}(x, y, z) = yz\mathbf{i} + xz\mathbf{j} + xy\mathbf{k}$
$\mathbf{G}(x, y, z) = xy\mathbf{j} + xyz\mathbf{k}$

25–26 Find $\nabla \cdot (\nabla \times \mathbf{F})$. ■

25. $\mathbf{F}(x, y, z) = \sin x\mathbf{i} + \cos(x - y)\mathbf{j} + z\mathbf{k}$

26. $\mathbf{F}(x, y, z) = e^{xz}\mathbf{i} + 3xe^y\mathbf{j} - e^{yz}\mathbf{k}$

27–28 Find $\nabla \times (\nabla \times \mathbf{F})$. ■

27. $\mathbf{F}(x, y, z) = xy\mathbf{j} + xyz\mathbf{k}$

28. $\mathbf{F}(x, y, z) = y^2x\mathbf{i} - 3yz\mathbf{j} + xy\mathbf{k}$

C **29.** Use a CAS to check the calculations in Exercises 23, 25, and 27.

C **30.** Use a CAS to check the calculations in Exercises 24, 26, and 28.

31–38 Let k be a constant, $\mathbf{F} = \mathbf{F}(x, y, z)$, $\mathbf{G} = \mathbf{G}(x, y, z)$, and $\phi = \phi(x, y, z)$. Prove the following identities, assuming that all derivatives involved exist and are continuous. ■

31. $\mathrm{div}(k\mathbf{F}) = k\,\mathrm{div}\,\mathbf{F}$ **32.** $\mathrm{curl}(k\mathbf{F}) = k\,\mathrm{curl}\,\mathbf{F}$

33. $\mathrm{div}(\mathbf{F} + \mathbf{G}) = \mathrm{div}\,\mathbf{F} + \mathrm{div}\,\mathbf{G}$

34. $\mathrm{curl}(\mathbf{F} + \mathbf{G}) = \mathrm{curl}\,\mathbf{F} + \mathrm{curl}\,\mathbf{G}$

35. $\mathrm{div}(\phi\mathbf{F}) = \phi\,\mathrm{div}\,\mathbf{F} + \nabla\phi \cdot \mathbf{F}$

36. $\mathrm{curl}(\phi\mathbf{F}) = \phi\,\mathrm{curl}\,\mathbf{F} + \nabla\phi \times \mathbf{F}$

37. $\mathrm{div}(\mathrm{curl}\,\mathbf{F}) = 0$ **38.** $\mathrm{curl}(\nabla\phi) = \mathbf{0}$

39. Rewrite the identities in Exercises 31, 33, 35, and 37 in an equivalent form using the notation $\nabla \cdot$ for divergence and $\nabla \times$ for curl.

40. Rewrite the identities in Exercises 32, 34, 36, and 38 in an equivalent form using the notation $\nabla \cdot$ for divergence and $\nabla \times$ for curl.

41–42 Verify that the radius vector $\mathbf{r} = x\mathbf{i} + y\mathbf{j} + z\mathbf{k}$ has the stated property. ■

41. (a) $\mathrm{curl}\,\mathbf{r} = \mathbf{0}$ (b) $\nabla\|\mathbf{r}\| = \dfrac{\mathbf{r}}{\|\mathbf{r}\|}$

42. (a) $\mathrm{div}\,\mathbf{r} = 3$ (b) $\nabla\dfrac{1}{\|\mathbf{r}\|} = -\dfrac{\mathbf{r}}{\|\mathbf{r}\|^3}$

43–44 Let $\mathbf{r} = x\mathbf{i} + y\mathbf{j} + z\mathbf{k}$, let $r = \|\mathbf{r}\|$, let f be a differentiable function of one variable, and let $\mathbf{F}(\mathbf{r}) = f(r)\mathbf{r}$. ■

43. (a) Use the chain rule and Exercise 41(b) to show that
$$\nabla f(r) = \frac{f'(r)}{r}\mathbf{r}$$
(b) Use the result in part (a) and Exercises 35 and 42(a) to show that $\mathrm{div}\,\mathbf{F} = 3f(r) + rf'(r)$.

44. (a) Use part (a) of Exercise 43, Exercise 36, and Exercise 41(a) to show that $\mathrm{curl}\,\mathbf{F} = \mathbf{0}$.
(b) Use the result in part (a) of Exercise 43 and Exercises 35 and 42(a) to show that
$$\nabla^2 f(r) = 2\frac{f'(r)}{r} + f''(r)$$

45. Use the result in Exercise 43(b) to show that the divergence of the inverse-square field $\mathbf{F} = \mathbf{r}/\|\mathbf{r}\|^3$ is zero.

46. Use the result of Exercise 43(b) to show that if $\mathbf{F}$ is a vector field of the form $\mathbf{F} = f(\|\mathbf{r}\|)\mathbf{r}$ and if $\mathrm{div}\,\mathbf{F} = 0$, then $\mathbf{F}$ is an inverse-square field. [*Suggestion:* Let $r = \|\mathbf{r}\|$ and multiply $3f(r) + rf'(r) = 0$ through by r^2. Then write the result as a derivative of a product.]

47. A curve C is called a **flow line** of a vector field $\mathbf{F}$ if $\mathbf{F}$ is a tangent vector to C at each point along C (see the accompanying figure).
(a) Let C be a flow line for $\mathbf{F}(x, y) = -y\mathbf{i} + x\mathbf{j}$, and let (x, y) be a point on C for which $y \neq 0$. Show that the flow lines satisfy the differential equation
$$\frac{dy}{dx} = -\frac{x}{y}$$
(b) Solve the differential equation in part (a) by separation of variables, and show that the flow lines are concentric circles centered at the origin.

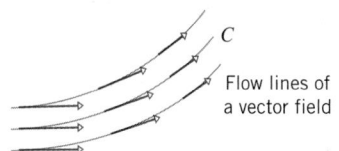

Flow lines of
a vector field

◀ **Figure Ex-47**

48–50 Find a differential equation satisfied by the flow lines of $\mathbf{F}$ (see Exercise 47), and solve it to find equations for the flow lines of $\mathbf{F}$. Sketch some typical flow lines and tangent vectors. ■

48. $\mathbf{F}(x, y) = \mathbf{i} + x\mathbf{j}$ **49.** $\mathbf{F}(x, y) = x\mathbf{i} + \mathbf{j}$, $x > 0$

50. $\mathbf{F}(x, y) = x\mathbf{i} - y\mathbf{j}$, $x > 0$ and $y > 0$

51. Writing Discuss the similarities and differences between the concepts "vector field" and "slope field."

52. Writing In physical applications it is often necessary to deal with vector quantities that depend not only on position in space but also on time. Give some examples and discuss how the concept of a vector field would need to be modified to apply to such situations.

✔ **QUICK CHECK ANSWERS 15.1**

1. $(y + z)\mathbf{i} + (x + z)\mathbf{j} + (x + y)\mathbf{k}$ **2.** $-\mathbf{r} = -x\mathbf{i} - y\mathbf{j} - z\mathbf{k}$ **3.** $\dfrac{c}{\|\mathbf{r}\|^3}\mathbf{r}$ **4.** $2xy + 2yz;\ z^2\mathbf{i} + y\mathbf{j} + (y^2 - z)\mathbf{k}$

15.2   LINE INTEGRALS

In earlier chapters we considered three kinds of integrals in rectangular coordinates: single integrals over intervals, double integrals over two-dimensional regions, and triple integrals over three-dimensional regions. In this section we will discuss integrals along curves in two- or three-dimensional space.

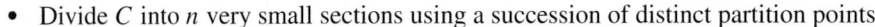

■ LINE INTEGRALS

The first goal of this section is to define what it means to integrate a function along a curve. To motivate the definition we will consider the problem of finding the mass of a very thin wire whose linear density function (mass per unit length) is known. We assume that we can model the wire by a smooth curve C between two points P and Q in 3-space (Figure 15.2.1). Given any point (x, y, z) on C, we let $f(x, y, z)$ denote the corresponding value of the density function. To compute the mass of the wire, we proceed as follows:

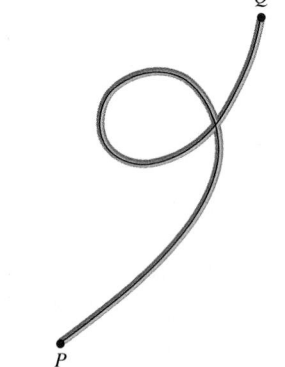

- Divide C into n very small sections using a succession of distinct partition points

$$P = P_0, P_1, P_2, \ldots, P_{n-1}, P_n = Q$$

as illustrated on the left side of Figure 15.2.2. Let ΔM_k be the mass of the kth section, and let Δs_k be the length of the arc between P_{k-1} and P_k.

▲ **Figure 15.2.1**   A bent thin wire modeled by a smooth curve

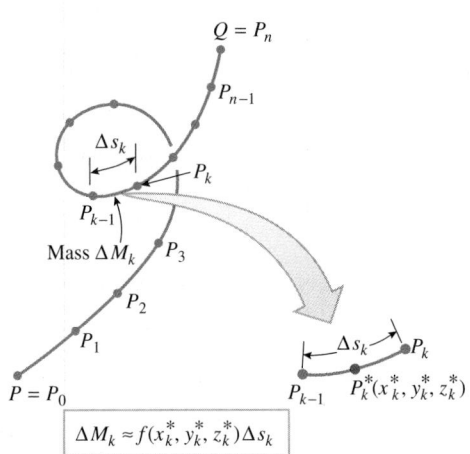

$$\Delta M_k \approx f(x_k^*, y_k^*, z_k^*)\Delta s_k$$

▶ **Figure 15.2.2**

- Choose an arbitrary sampling point $P_k^*(x_k^*, y_k^*, z_k^*)$ on the kth arc, as illustrated on the right side of Figure 15.2.2. If Δs_k is very small, the value of f will not vary much along the kth section and we can approximate f along this section by the value $f(x_k^*, y_k^*, z_k^*)$. It follows that the mass of the kth section can be approximated by

$$\Delta M_k \approx f(x_k^*, y_k^*, z_k^*)\Delta s_k$$

- The mass M of the entire wire can then be approximated by

$$M = \sum_{k=1}^{n} \Delta M_k \approx \sum_{k=1}^{n} f(x_k^*, y_k^*, z_k^*)\Delta s_k \tag{1}$$

- We will use the expression max $\Delta s_k \to 0$ to indicate the process of increasing n in such a way that the lengths of all the sections approach 0. It is plausible that the error in (1) will approach 0 as max $\Delta s_k \to 0$ and the exact value of M will be given by

$$M = \lim_{\max \Delta s_k \to 0} \sum_{k=1}^{n} f(x_k^*, y_k^*, z_k^*)\Delta s_k \tag{2}$$

The limit in (2) is similar to the limit of Riemann sums used to define the definite integral of a function over an interval (Definition 5.5.1). With this similarity in mind, we make the following definition.

15.2.1   DEFINITION   If C is a smooth curve in 2-space or 3-space, then the *line integral of f with respect to s along C* is

$$\int_C f(x, y)\, ds = \lim_{\max \Delta s_k \to 0} \sum_{k=1}^{n} f(x_k^*, y_k^*) \Delta s_k \qquad \boxed{\text{2-space}} \qquad (3)$$

or

$$\int_C f(x, y, z)\, ds = \lim_{\max \Delta s_k \to 0} \sum_{k=1}^{n} f(x_k^*, y_k^*, z_k^*) \Delta s_k \qquad \boxed{\text{3-space}} \qquad (4)$$

provided this limit exists and does not depend on the choice of partition or on the choice of sample points.

It is usually impractical to evaluate line integrals directly from Definition 15.2.1. However, the definition is important in the application and interpretation of line integrals. For example:

- If C is a curve in 3-space that models a thin wire, and if $f(x, y, z)$ is the linear density function of the wire, then it follows from (2) and Definition 15.2.1 that the mass M of the wire is given by

$$M = \int_C f(x, y, z)\, ds \qquad (5)$$

  That is, to obtain the mass of a thin wire, we integrate the linear density function over the smooth curve that models the wire.

- If C is a smooth curve of arc length L, and f is identically 1, then it immediately follows from Definition 15.2.1 that

$$\int_C ds = \lim_{\max \Delta s_k \to 0} \sum_{k=1}^{n} \Delta s_k = \lim_{\max \Delta s_k \to 0} L = L \qquad (6)$$

- If C is a curve in the xy-plane and $f(x, y)$ is a nonnegative continuous function defined on C, then $\int_C f(x, y)\, ds$ can be interpreted as the area A of the "sheet" that is swept out by a vertical line segment that extends upward from the point (x, y) to a height of $f(x, y)$ and moves along C from one endpoint to the other (Figure 15.2.3). To see why this is so, refer to Figure 15.2.4 in which $f(x_k^*, y_k^*)$ is the value of f at an arbitrary point P_k^* on the kth arc of the partition and note the approximation

$$\Delta A_k \approx f(x_k^*, y_k^*) \Delta s_k$$

It follows that

$$A = \sum_{k=1}^{n} \Delta A_k \approx \sum_{k=1}^{n} f(x_k^*, y_k^*) \Delta s_k$$

It is then plausible that

$$A = \lim_{\max \Delta s_k \to 0} \sum_{k=1}^{n} f(x_k^*, y_k^*) \Delta s_k = \int_C f(x, y)\, ds \qquad (7)$$

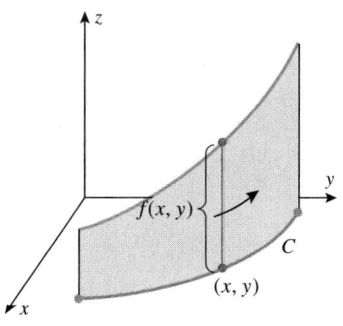

▲ **Figure 15.2.3**

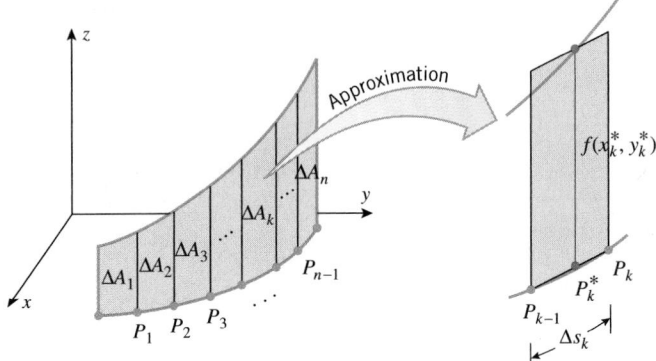

▶ **Figure 15.2.4**

Since Definition 15.2.1 is closely modeled on Definition 5.5.1, it should come as no surprise that line integrals share many of the common properties of ordinary definite integrals. For example, we have

$$\int_C [f(x, y) + g(x, y)]\, ds = \int_C f(x, y)\, ds + \int_C g(x, y)\, ds$$

provided both line integrals on the right-hand side of this equation exist. Similarly, it can be shown that if f is continuous on C, then the line integral of f with respect to s along C exists.

■ EVALUATING LINE INTEGRALS

Except in simple cases, it will not be feasible to evaluate a line integral directly from (3) or (4). However, we will now show that it is possible to express a line integral as an ordinary definite integral, so that no special methods of evaluation are required. For example, suppose that C is a curve in the xy-plane that is smoothly parametrized by

$$\mathbf{r}(t) = x(t)\mathbf{i} + y(t)\mathbf{j} \qquad (a \le t \le b)$$

Moreover, suppose that each partition point P_k of C corresponds to a parameter value of t_k in $[a, b]$. The arc length of C between points P_{k-1} and P_k is then given by

$$\Delta s_k = \int_{t_{k-1}}^{t_k} \|\mathbf{r}'(t)\|\, dt \tag{8}$$

(Theorem 12.3.1). If we let $\Delta t_k = t_k - t_{k-1}$, then it follows from (8) and the Mean-Value Theorem for Integrals (Theorem 5.6.2) that there exists a point t_k^* in $[t_{k-1}, t_k]$ such that

$$\Delta s_k = \int_{t_{k-1}}^{t_k} \|\mathbf{r}'(t)\|\, dt = \|\mathbf{r}'(t_k^*)\| \Delta t_k$$

We let $P_k^*(x_k^*, y_k^*) = P_k^*(x(t_k^*), y(t_k^*))$ correspond to the parameter value t_k^* (Figure 15.2.5).

Since the parametrization of C is smooth, it can be shown that $\max \Delta s_k \to 0$ if and only if $\max \Delta t_k \to 0$ (Exercise 53). Furthermore, the composition $f(x(t), y(t))$ is a real-valued function defined on $[a, b]$ and we have

$$\int_C f(x, y)\, ds = \lim_{\max \Delta s_k \to 0} \sum_{k=1}^n f(x_k^*, y_k^*)\, \Delta s_k \qquad \boxed{\text{Definition 15.2.1}}$$

$$= \lim_{\max \Delta s_k \to 0} \sum_{k=1}^n f(x(t_k^*), y(t_k^*)) \|\mathbf{r}'(t_k^*)\| \Delta t_k \qquad \boxed{\text{Substitution}}$$

$$= \lim_{\max \Delta t_k \to 0} \sum_{k=1}^n f(x(t_k^*), y(t_k^*)) \|\mathbf{r}'(t_k^*)\| \Delta t_k$$

$$= \int_a^b f(x(t), y(t)) \|\mathbf{r}'(t)\|\, dt \qquad \boxed{\text{Definition 5.5.1}}$$

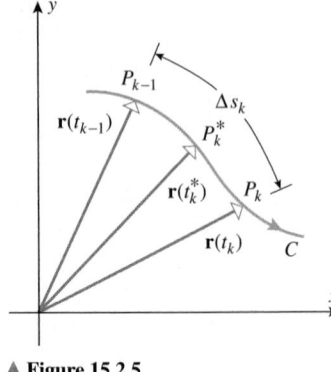

▲ **Figure 15.2.5**

Therefore, if C is smoothly parametrized by

$$\mathbf{r}(t) = x(t)\mathbf{i} + y(t)\mathbf{j} \qquad (a \le t \le b)$$

then

$$\int_C f(x, y)\, ds = \int_a^b f(x(t), y(t)) \|\mathbf{r}'(t)\|\, dt \qquad (9)$$

Similarly, if C is a curve in 3-space that is smoothly parametrized by

$$\mathbf{r}(t) = x(t)\mathbf{i} + y(t)\mathbf{j} + z(t)\mathbf{k} \qquad (a \le t \le b)$$

then

$$\int_C f(x, y, z)\, ds = \int_a^b f(x(t), y(t), z(t)) \|\mathbf{r}'(t)\|\, dt \qquad (10)$$

Explain how Formulas (9) and (10) confirm Formula (6) for arc length.

▶ **Example 1** Using the given parametrization, evaluate the line integral $\int_C (1 + xy^2)\, ds$.

(a) $C : \mathbf{r}(t) = t\mathbf{i} + 2t\mathbf{j} \quad (0 \le t \le 1)$ (see Figure 15.2.6a)

(b) $C : \mathbf{r}(t) = (1 - t)\mathbf{i} + (2 - 2t)\mathbf{j} \quad (0 \le t \le 1)$ (see Figure 15.2.6b)

Solution (a). Since $\mathbf{r}'(t) = \mathbf{i} + 2\mathbf{j}$, we have $\|\mathbf{r}'(t)\| = \sqrt{5}$ and it follows from Formula (9) that

$$\int_C (1 + xy^2)\, ds = \int_0^1 [1 + t(2t)^2]\sqrt{5}\, dt$$

$$= \int_0^1 (1 + 4t^3)\sqrt{5}\, dt$$

$$= \sqrt{5}\,[t + t^4]_0^1 = 2\sqrt{5}$$

Solution (b). Since $\mathbf{r}'(t) = -\mathbf{i} - 2\mathbf{j}$, we have $\|\mathbf{r}'(t)\| = \sqrt{5}$ and it follows from Formula (9) that

$$\int_C (1 + xy^2)\, ds = \int_0^1 [1 + (1 - t)(2 - 2t)^2]\sqrt{5}\, dt$$

$$= \int_0^1 [1 + 4(1 - t)^3]\sqrt{5}\, dt$$

$$= \sqrt{5}\,[t - (1 - t)^4]_0^1 = 2\sqrt{5} \blacktriangleleft$$

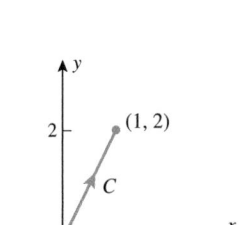

(a)

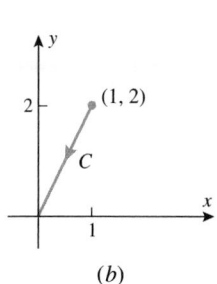

(b)

▲ **Figure 15.2.6**

Note that the integrals in parts (a) and (b) of Example 1 agree, even though the corresponding parametrizations of C have opposite orientations. This illustrates the important result that the value of a line integral of f with respect to s along C *does not depend on an orientation of C.* (This is because Δs_k is always positive; therefore, it does not matter in which *direction* along C we list the partition points of the curve in Definition 15.2.1.) Later in this section we will discuss line integrals that are defined only for oriented curves.

Formula (9) has an alternative expression for a curve C in the xy-plane that is given by parametric equations

$$x = x(t), \quad y = y(t) \qquad (a \le t \le b)$$

In this case, we write (9) in the expanded form

$$\int_C f(x, y)\, ds = \int_a^b f(x(t), y(t)) \sqrt{\left(\frac{dx}{dt}\right)^2 + \left(\frac{dy}{dt}\right)^2}\, dt \qquad (11)$$

Similarly, if C is a curve in 3-space that is parametrized by

$$x = x(t), \quad y = y(t), \quad z = z(t) \qquad (a \le t \le b)$$

then we write (10) in the form

$$\int_C f(x, y, z)\, ds = \int_a^b f(x(t), y(t), z(t)) \sqrt{\left(\frac{dx}{dt}\right)^2 + \left(\frac{dy}{dt}\right)^2 + \left(\frac{dz}{dt}\right)^2}\, dt \qquad (12)$$

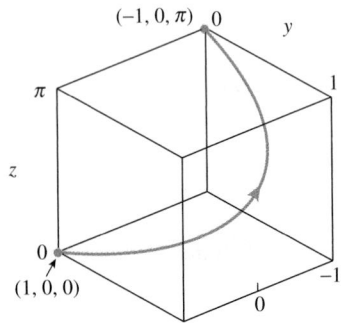

▲ **Figure 15.2.7**

▶ **Example 2**   Evaluate the line integral $\int_C (xy + z^3)\, ds$ from $(1, 0, 0)$ to $(-1, 0, \pi)$ along the helix C that is represented by the parametric equations

$$x = \cos t, \quad y = \sin t, \quad z = t \qquad (0 \le t \le \pi)$$

(Figure 15.2.7).

Solution.   From (12)

$$\int_C (xy + z^3)\, ds = \int_0^\pi (\cos t \sin t + t^3) \sqrt{\left(\frac{dx}{dt}\right)^2 + \left(\frac{dy}{dt}\right)^2 + \left(\frac{dz}{dt}\right)^2}\, dt$$

$$= \int_0^\pi (\cos t \sin t + t^3) \sqrt{(-\sin t)^2 + (\cos t)^2 + 1}\, dt$$

$$= \sqrt{2} \int_0^\pi (\cos t \sin t + t^3)\, dt$$

$$= \sqrt{2} \left[\frac{\sin^2 t}{2} + \frac{t^4}{4}\right]_0^\pi = \frac{\sqrt{2}\pi^4}{4} \qquad ◀$$

If $\delta(x, y)$ is the linear density function of a wire that is modeled by a smooth curve C in the xy-plane, then an argument similar to the derivation of Formula (5) shows that the mass of the wire is given by $\int_C \delta(x, y)\, ds$.

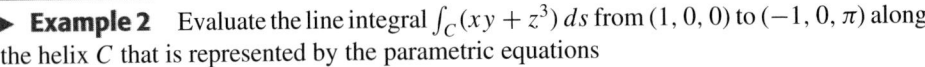

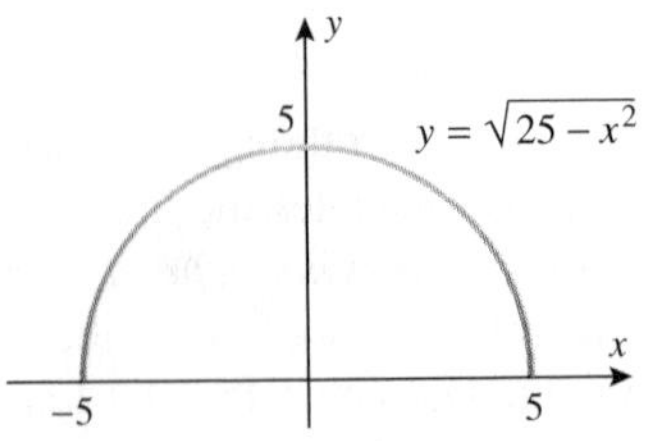

▶ **Example 3**   Suppose that a semicircular wire has the equation $y = \sqrt{25 - x^2}$ and that its mass density is $\delta(x, y) = 15 - y$ (Figure 15.2.8). Physically, this means the wire has a maximum density of 15 units at the base ($y = 0$) and that the density of the wire decreases linearly with respect to y to a value of 10 units at the top ($y = 5$). Find the mass of the wire.

Solution.   The mass M of the wire can be expressed as the line integral

$$M = \int_C \delta(x, y)\, ds = \int_C (15 - y)\, ds$$

along the semicircle C. To evaluate this integral we will express C parametrically as

$$x = 5 \cos t, \quad y = 5 \sin t \qquad (0 \le t \le \pi)$$

▲ **Figure 15.2.8**

$y = \sqrt{25 - x^2}$

Thus, it follows from (11) that

$$
\begin{aligned}
M &= \int_C (15 - y)\, ds = \int_0^\pi (15 - 5\sin t) \sqrt{\left(\frac{dx}{dt}\right)^2 + \left(\frac{dy}{dt}\right)^2}\, dt \\
&= \int_0^\pi (15 - 5\sin t) \sqrt{(-5\sin t)^2 + (5\cos t)^2}\, dt \\
&= 5 \int_0^\pi (15 - 5\sin t)\, dt \\
&= 5 \left[15t + 5\cos t \right]_0^\pi \\
&= 75\pi - 50 \approx 185.6 \text{ units of mass} \blacktriangleleft
\end{aligned}
$$

In the special case where t is an arc length parameter, say $t = s$, it follows from Formulas (20) and (21) in Section 12.3 that the radicals in (11) and (12) reduce to 1 and the equations simplify to

$$
\int_C f(x, y)\, ds = \int_a^b f(x(s), y(s))\, ds \tag{13}
$$

and

$$
\int_C f(x, y, z)\, ds = \int_a^b f(x(s), y(s), z(s))\, ds \tag{14}
$$

respectively.

▶ **Example 4**   Find the area of the surface extending upward from the circle $x^2 + y^2 = 1$ in the xy-plane to the parabolic cylinder $z = 1 - x^2$ (Figure 15.2.9).

Solution.   It follows from (7) that the area A of the surface can be expressed as the line integral

$$
A = \int_C (1 - x^2)\, ds \tag{15}
$$

where C is the circle $x^2 + y^2 = 1$. This circle can be parametrized in terms of arc length as

$$
x = \cos s, \quad y = \sin s \qquad (0 \le s \le 2\pi)
$$

Thus, it follows from (13) and (15) that

$$
\begin{aligned}
A &= \int_C (1 - x^2)\, ds = \int_0^{2\pi} (1 - \cos^2 s)\, ds \\
&= \int_0^{2\pi} \sin^2 s\, ds = \frac{1}{2} \int_0^{2\pi} (1 - \cos 2s)\, ds = \pi \blacktriangleleft
\end{aligned}
$$

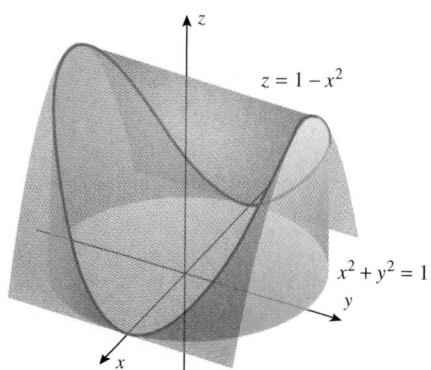

▶ **Figure 15.2.9**

■ **LINE INTEGRALS WITH RESPECT TO *x*, *y*, AND *z***

We now describe a second type of line integral in which we replace the "*ds*" in the integral by dx, dy, or dz. For example, suppose that f is a function defined on a smooth curve C in the xy-plane and that partition points of C are denoted by $P_k(x_k, y_k)$. Letting

$$\Delta x_k = x_k - x_{k-1} \quad \text{and} \quad \Delta y_k = y_k - y_{k-1}$$

we would like to define

$$\int_C f(x, y)\, dx = \lim_{\max \Delta s_k \to 0} \sum_{k=1}^n f(x_k^*, y_k^*) \Delta x_k \tag{16}$$

$$\int_C f(x, y)\, dy = \lim_{\max \Delta s_k \to 0} \sum_{k=1}^n f(x_k^*, y_k^*) \Delta y_k \tag{17}$$

However, unlike Δs_k, the values of Δx_k and Δy_k change sign if the order of the partition points along C is reversed. Therefore, in order to define the line integrals using Formulas (16) and (17), we must restrict ourselves to *oriented* curves C and to partitions of C in which the partition points are ordered in the direction of the curve. With this restriction, if the limit in (16) exists and does not depend on the choice of partition or sampling points, then we refer to (16) as the **line integral of *f* with respect to *x* along *C***. Similarly, (17) defines the **line integral of *f* with respect to *y* along *C***. If C is a smooth curve in 3-space, we can have **line integrals of *f* with respect to *x*, *y*, and *z* along *C***. For example,

$$\int_C f(x, y, z)\, dx = \lim_{\max \Delta s_k \to 0} \sum_{k=1}^n f(x_k^*, y_k^*, z_k^*) \Delta x_k$$

and so forth. As was the case with line integrals with respect to s, line integrals of f with respect to x, y, and z exist if f is continuous on C.

The basic procedure for evaluating these line integrals is to find parametric equations for C, say

$$x = x(t), \quad y = y(t), \quad z = z(t) \quad (a \le t \le b)$$

in which the orientation of C is in the direction of increasing t, and then express the integrand in terms of t. For example,

$$\int_C f(x, y, z)\, dz = \int_a^b f(x(t), y(t), z(t)) z'(t)\, dt$$

[Such a formula is easy to remember—just substitute for x, y, and z using the parametric equations and recall that $dz = z'(t)\, dt$.]

> **Example 5**   Evaluate $\int_C 3xy\, dy$, where C is the line segment joining $(0, 0)$ and $(1, 2)$ with the given orientation.

(a) Oriented from $(0, 0)$ to $(1, 2)$ as in Figure 15.2.6*a*.

(b) Oriented from $(1, 2)$ to $(0, 0)$ as in Figure 15.2.6*b*.

Solution (a).   Using the parametrization

$$x = t, \quad y = 2t \quad (0 \le t \le 1)$$

we have

$$\int_C 3xy\, dy = \int_0^1 3(t)(2t)(2)\, dt = \int_0^1 12t^2\, dt = 4t^3 \Big]_0^1 = 4$$

Explain why Formula (16) implies that $\int_C dx = x_f - x_i$, where x_f and x_i are the respective x-coordinates of the final and initial points of C. What about $\int_C dy$?

Explain why Formula (16) implies that $\int_C f(x, y)\, dx = 0$ on any oriented segment parallel to the y-axis. What can you say about $\int_C f(x, y)\, dy$ on any oriented segment parallel to the x-axis?

Solution (b).   Using the parametrization

$$x = 1 - t, \quad y = 2 - 2t \quad (0 \le t \le 1)$$

we have

$$\int_C 3xy \, dy = \int_0^1 3(1-t)(2-2t)(-2) \, dt = \int_0^1 -12(1-t)^2 \, dt = 4(1-t)^3 \Big]_0^1 = -4 \;\blacktriangleleft$$

In Example 5, note that reversing the orientation of the curve changed the sign of the line integral. This is because reversing the orientation of a curve changes the sign of Δx_k in definition (16). Thus, unlike line integrals of functions with respect to s along C, reversing the orientation of C changes the sign of a line integral with respect to x, y, and z. If C is a smooth oriented curve, we will let $-C$ denote the oriented curve consisting of the same points as C but with the opposite orientation (Figure 15.2.10). We then have

$$\int_{-C} f(x, y) \, dx = -\int_C f(x, y) \, dx \quad \text{and} \quad \int_{-C} g(x, y) \, dy = -\int_C g(x, y) \, dy$$

$$(18\text{--}19)$$

while

$$\int_{-C} f(x, y) \, ds = \int_C f(x, y) \, ds \tag{20}$$

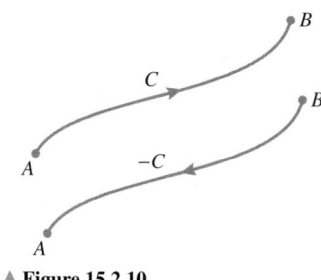

▲ **Figure 15.2.10**

Similar identities hold for line integrals in 3-space. Unless indicated otherwise, we will assume that parametric curves are oriented in the direction of increasing parameter.

Frequently, the line integrals with respect to x and y occur in combination, in which case we will dispense with one of the integral signs and write

$$\int_C f(x, y) \, dx + g(x, y) \, dy = \int_C f(x, y) \, dx + \int_C g(x, y) \, dy \tag{21}$$

We will use a similar convention for combinations of line integrals with respect to x, y, and z along curves in 3-space.

▶ **Example 6**   Evaluate

$$\int_C 2xy \, dx + (x^2 + y^2) \, dy$$

along the circular arc C given by $x = \cos t,\ y = \sin t\ (0 \le t \le \pi/2)$ (Figure 15.2.11).

Solution.   We have

$$\int_C 2xy \, dx = \int_0^{\pi/2} (2 \cos t \sin t) \left[\frac{d}{dt}(\cos t) \right] dt$$

$$= -2 \int_0^{\pi/2} \sin^2 t \cos t \, dt = -\frac{2}{3} \sin^3 t \Big]_0^{\pi/2} = -\frac{2}{3}$$

$$\int_C (x^2 + y^2) \, dy = \int_0^{\pi/2} (\cos^2 t + \sin^2 t) \left[\frac{d}{dt}(\sin t) \right] dt$$

$$= \int_0^{\pi/2} \cos t \, dt = \sin t \Big]_0^{\pi/2} = 1$$

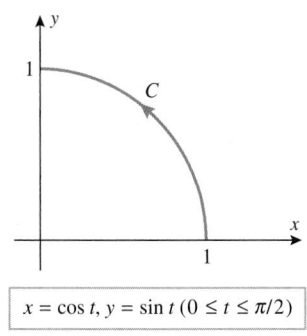

$x = \cos t,\ y = \sin t\ (0 \le t \le \pi/2)$

▲ **Figure 15.2.11**

Thus, from (21)

$$\int_C 2xy\,dx + (x^2 + y^2)\,dy = \int_C 2xy\,dx + \int_C (x^2 + y^2)\,dy$$

$$= -\frac{2}{3} + 1 = \frac{1}{3} \blacktriangleleft$$

It can be shown that if f and g are continuous functions on C, then combinations of line integrals with respect to x and y can be expressed in terms of a limit and can be evaluated together in a single step. For example, we have

$$\int_C f(x, y)\,dx + g(x, y)\,dy = \lim_{\max \Delta s_k \to 0} \sum_{k=1}^{n} [f(x_k^*, y_k^*)\Delta x_k + g(x_k^*, y_k^*)\,\Delta y_k] \qquad (22)$$

and

$$\int_C f(x, y)\,dx + g(x, y)\,dy = \int_a^b [f(x(t), y(t))x'(t) + g(x(t), y(t))y'(t)]\,dt \qquad (23)$$

Similar results hold for line integrals in 3-space. The evaluation of a line integral can sometimes be simplified by using Formula (23).

▶ **Example 7**   Evaluate

$$\int_C (3x^2 + y^2)\,dx + 2xy\,dy$$

along the circular arc C given by $x = \cos t$, $y = \sin t$ ($0 \le t \le \pi/2$) (Figure 15.2.11).

Solution.   From (23) we have

$$\int_C (3x^2 + y^2)\,dx + 2xy\,dy = \int_0^{\pi/2} [(3\cos^2 t + \sin^2 t)(-\sin t) + 2(\cos t)(\sin t)(\cos t)]\,dt$$

$$= \int_0^{\pi/2} (-3\cos^2 t \sin t - \sin^3 t + 2\cos^2 t \sin t)\,dt$$

$$= \int_0^{\pi/2} (-\cos^2 t - \sin^2 t)(\sin t)\,dt = \int_0^{\pi/2} -\sin t\,dt$$

$$= \cos t \Big]_0^{\pi/2} = -1 \blacktriangleleft$$

Compare the computations in Example 7 with those involved in computing

$$\int_C (3x^2 + y^2)\,dx + \int_C 2xy\,dy$$

It follows from (18) and (19) that

$$\int_{-C} f(x, y)\,dx + g(x, y)\,dy = -\int_C f(x, y)\,dx + g(x, y)\,dy \qquad (24)$$

so that reversing the orientation of C changes the sign of a line integral in which x and y occur in combination. Similarly,

$$\int_{-C} f(x, y, z)\,dx + g(x, y, z)\,dy + h(x, y, z)\,dz$$

$$= -\int_C f(x, y, z)\,dx + g(x, y, z)\,dy + h(x, y, z)\,dz \qquad (25)$$

■ INTEGRATING A VECTOR FIELD ALONG A CURVE

There is an alternative notation for line integrals with respect to x, y, and z that is particularly appropriate for dealing with problems involving vector fields. We will interpret $d\mathbf{r}$ as

$$d\mathbf{r} = dx\,\mathbf{i} + dy\,\mathbf{j} \quad \text{or} \quad d\mathbf{r} = dx\,\mathbf{i} + dy\,\mathbf{j} + dz\,\mathbf{k}$$

depending on whether C is in 2-space or 3-space. For an oriented curve C in 2-space and a vector field

$$\mathbf{F}(x, y) = f(x, y)\mathbf{i} + g(x, y)\mathbf{j}$$

we will write

$$\int_C \mathbf{F} \cdot d\mathbf{r} = \int_C (f(x, y)\mathbf{i} + g(x, y)\mathbf{j}) \cdot (dx\,\mathbf{i} + dy\,\mathbf{j}) = \int_C f(x, y)\,dx + g(x, y)\,dy \quad (26)$$

Similarly, for a curve C in 3-space and vector field

$$\mathbf{F}(x, y, z) = f(x, y, z)\mathbf{i} + g(x, y, z)\mathbf{j} + h(x, y, z)\mathbf{k}$$

we will write

$$\int_C \mathbf{F} \cdot d\mathbf{r} = \int_C (f(x, y, z)\mathbf{i} + g(x, y, z)\mathbf{j} + h(x, y, z)\mathbf{k}) \cdot (dx\,\mathbf{i} + dy\,\mathbf{j} + dz\,\mathbf{k})$$
$$= \int_C f(x, y, z)\,dx + g(x, y, z)\,dy + h(x, y, z)\,dz \quad (27)$$

With these conventions, we are led to the following definition.

15.2.2   DEFINITION   If $\mathbf{F}$ is a continuous vector field and C is a smooth oriented curve, then the *line integral of $\mathbf{F}$ along C* is

$$\int_C \mathbf{F} \cdot d\mathbf{r} \quad (28)$$

The notation in Definition 15.2.2 makes it easy to remember the formula for evaluating the line integral of $\mathbf{F}$ along C. For example, suppose that C is an oriented curve in the plane given in vector form by

$$\mathbf{r} = \mathbf{r}(t) = x(t)\mathbf{i} + y(t)\mathbf{j} \qquad (a \leq t \leq b)$$

If we write

$$\mathbf{F}(\mathbf{r}(t)) = f(x(t), y(t))\mathbf{i} + g(x(t), y(t))\mathbf{j}$$

then

$$\int_C \mathbf{F} \cdot d\mathbf{r} = \int_a^b \mathbf{F}(\mathbf{r}(t)) \cdot \mathbf{r}'(t)\,dt \quad (29)$$

Formula (29) is also valid for oriented curves in 3-space.

▶ **Example 8**   Evaluate $\int_C \mathbf{F} \cdot d\mathbf{r}$ where $\mathbf{F}(x, y) = \cos x\,\mathbf{i} + \sin x\,\mathbf{j}$ and where C is the given oriented curve.

(a) $C : \mathbf{r}(t) = -\dfrac{\pi}{2}\mathbf{i} + t\mathbf{j} \quad (1 \leq t \leq 2)$ (see Figure 15.2.12a)

(b) $C : \mathbf{r}(t) = t\mathbf{i} + t^2\mathbf{j} \quad (-1 \leq t \leq 2)$ (see Figure 15.2.12b)

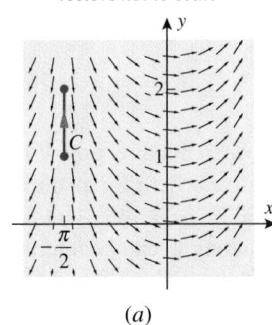

Vectors not to scale

(a)

(b)

▲ **Figure 15.2.12**

Solution (a).   Using (29) we have

$$\int_C \mathbf{F} \cdot d\mathbf{r} = \int_1^2 \mathbf{F}(\mathbf{r}(t)) \cdot \mathbf{r}'(t)\, dt = \int_1^2 (-\mathbf{j}) \cdot \mathbf{j}\, dt = \int_1^2 (-1)\, dt = -1$$

Solution (b).   Using (29) we have

$$\int_C \mathbf{F} \cdot d\mathbf{r} = \int_{-1}^2 \mathbf{F}(\mathbf{r}(t)) \cdot \mathbf{r}'(t)\, dt = \int_{-1}^2 (\cos t\,\mathbf{i} + \sin t\,\mathbf{j}) \cdot (\mathbf{i} + 2t\mathbf{j})\, dt$$

$$= \int_{-1}^2 (\cos t + 2t \sin t)\, dt = (-2t \cos t + 3 \sin t)\Big]_{-1}^2$$

$$= -2 \cos 1 - 4 \cos 2 + 3(\sin 1 + \sin 2) \approx 5.83629 \quad \blacktriangleleft$$

If we let t denote an arc length parameter, say $t = s$, with $\mathbf{T} = \mathbf{r}'(s)$ the unit tangent vector field along C, then

$$\int_C \mathbf{F} \cdot d\mathbf{r} = \int_a^b \mathbf{F}(\mathbf{r}(s)) \cdot \mathbf{r}'(s)\, ds = \int_a^b \mathbf{F}(\mathbf{r}(s)) \cdot \mathbf{T}\, ds = \int_C \mathbf{F} \cdot \mathbf{T}\, ds$$

which shows that

$$\int_C \mathbf{F} \cdot d\mathbf{r} = \int_C \mathbf{F} \cdot \mathbf{T}\, ds \tag{30}$$

In words, the integral of a vector field along a curve has the same value as the integral of the tangential component of the vector field along the curve.

We can use (30) to interpret $\int_C \mathbf{F} \cdot d\mathbf{r}$ geometrically. If θ is the angle between $\mathbf{F}$ and $\mathbf{T}$ at a point on C, then at this point

$$\mathbf{F} \cdot \mathbf{T} = \|\mathbf{F}\|\|\mathbf{T}\| \cos \theta \qquad \boxed{\text{Formula (4) in Section 11.3}}$$

$$= \|\mathbf{F}\| \cos \theta \qquad \boxed{\text{Since } \|\mathbf{T}\| = 1}$$

Thus,

$$-\|\mathbf{F}\| \le \mathbf{F} \cdot \mathbf{T} \le \|\mathbf{F}\|$$

and if $\mathbf{F} \ne \mathbf{0}$, then the sign of $\mathbf{F} \cdot \mathbf{T}$ will depend on the angle between the direction of $\mathbf{F}$ and the direction of C (Figure 15.2.13). That is, $\mathbf{F} \cdot \mathbf{T}$ will be positive where $\mathbf{F}$ has the same general direction as C, it will be 0 if $\mathbf{F}$ is normal to C, and it will be negative where $\mathbf{F}$ and C have more or less opposite directions. The line integral of $\mathbf{F}$ along C can be interpreted as the accumulated effect of the magnitude of $\mathbf{F}$ along C, the extent to which $\mathbf{F}$ and C have the same direction, and the arc length of C.

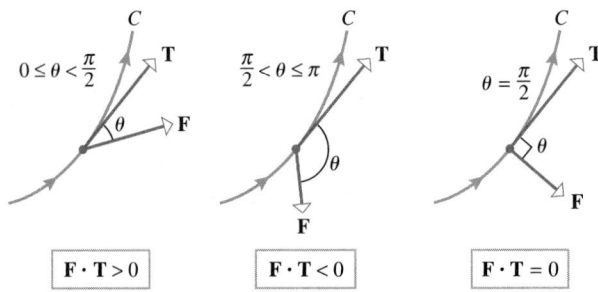

▶ **Figure 15.2.13**

▶ Example 9   Use (30) to evaluate $\int_C \mathbf{F} \cdot d\mathbf{r}$ where $\mathbf{F}(x, y) = -y\mathbf{i} + x\mathbf{j}$ and where C is the given oriented curve.

(a) $C : x^2 + y^2 = 3$ $(0 \leq x, y;$ oriented as in Figure 15.2.14*a*)

(b) $C : \mathbf{r}(t) = t\mathbf{i} + 2t\mathbf{j}$ $(0 \leq t \leq 1;$ see Figure 15.2.14*b*)

Solution (a).   At every point on C the direction of $\mathbf{F}$ and the direction of C are the same. (Why?) In addition, at every point on C

$$\|\mathbf{F}\| = \sqrt{(-y)^2 + x^2} = \sqrt{x^2 + y^2} = \sqrt{3}$$

Therefore, $\mathbf{F} \cdot \mathbf{T} = \|\mathbf{F}\| \cos(0) = \|\mathbf{F}\| = \sqrt{3}$, and

$$\int_C \mathbf{F} \cdot d\mathbf{r} = \int_C \mathbf{F} \cdot \mathbf{T}\, ds = \int_C \sqrt{3}\, ds = \sqrt{3} \int_C ds = \frac{3\pi}{2}$$

Solution (b).   The vector field $\mathbf{F}$ is normal to C at every point. (Why?) Therefore,

$$\int_C \mathbf{F} \cdot d\mathbf{r} = \int_C \mathbf{F} \cdot \mathbf{T}\, ds = \int_C 0\, ds = 0 \blacktriangleleft$$

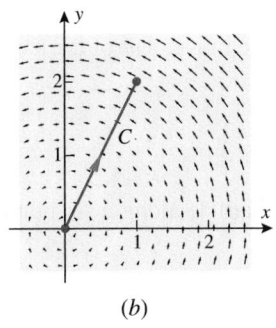

Vectors not to scale

(a)

(b)

▲ **Figure 15.2.14**

Refer to Figure 15.2.12 and explain the sign of each line integral in Example 8 geometrically. Exercises 5 and 6 take this geometric analysis further.

In light of (20) and (30), you might expect that reversing the orientation of C in $\int_C \mathbf{F} \cdot d\mathbf{r}$ would have no effect on the value of the line integral. However, reversing the orientation of C reverses the orientation of $\mathbf{T}$ in the integrand and hence reverses the sign of the integral; that is,

$$\int_{-C} \mathbf{F} \cdot \mathbf{T}\, ds = -\int_C \mathbf{F} \cdot \mathbf{T}\, ds \tag{31}$$

$$\int_{-C} \mathbf{F} \cdot d\mathbf{r} = -\int_C \mathbf{F} \cdot d\mathbf{r} \tag{32}$$

■ WORK AS A LINE INTEGRAL

An important application of line integrals with respect to x, y, and z is to the problem of defining the work performed by a variable force moving a particle along a curved path. In Section 6.6 we defined the work W performed by a force of constant magnitude acting on an object in the direction of motion (Definition 6.6.1), and later in that section we extended the definition to allow for a force of variable magnitude acting in the direction of motion (Definition 6.6.3). In Section 11.3 we took the concept of work a step further by defining the work W performed by a constant force $\mathbf{F}$ moving a particle in a straight line from point P to point Q. We defined the work to be

$$W = \mathbf{F} \cdot \overrightarrow{PQ} \tag{33}$$

[Formula (14) in Section 11.3]. Our next goal is to define a more general concept of work —the work performed by a variable force acting on a particle that moves along a curved path in 2-space or 3-space.

In many applications variable forces arise from force fields (gravitational fields, electromagnetic fields, and so forth), so we will consider the problem of work in that context. To motivate an appropriate definition for work performed by a force field, we will use a limit process, and since the procedure is the same for 2-space and 3-space, we will discuss it in detail for 2-space only. The idea is as follows:

- Assume that a force field $\mathbf{F} = \mathbf{F}(x, y)$ moves a particle along a smooth curve C from a point P to a point Q. Divide C into n arcs using the partition points

$$P = P_0(x_0, y_0),\ P_1(x_1, y_1),\ P_2(x_2, y_2),\ \ldots,\ P_{n-1}(x_{n-1}, y_{n-1}),\ P_n(x_n, y_n) = Q$$

directed along C from P to Q, and denote the length of the kth arc by Δs_k. Let (x_k^*, y_k^*) be any point on the kth arc, and let

$$\mathbf{F}_k^* = \mathbf{F}(x_k^*, y_k^*) = f(x_k^*, y_k^*)\mathbf{i} + g(x_k^*, y_k^*)\mathbf{j}$$

be the force vector at this point (Figure 15.2.15).

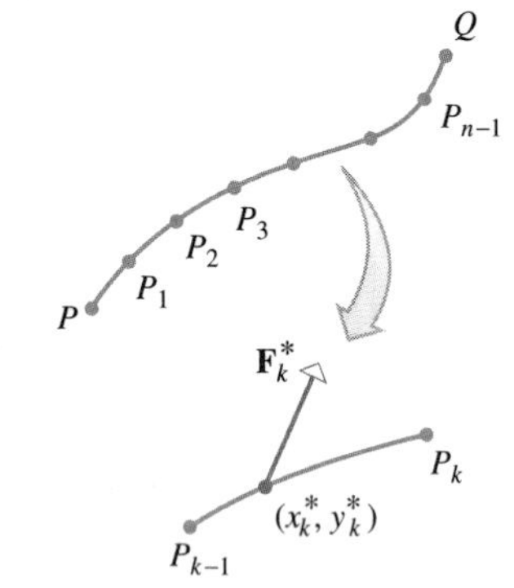

- If the kth arc is small, then the force will not vary much, so we can approximate the force by the constant value $\mathbf{F}_k^*$ on this arc. Moreover, the direction of motion will not vary much over this small arc, so we can approximate the movement of the particle by the displacement vector

$$\overrightarrow{P_{k-1}P_k} = (\Delta x_k)\mathbf{i} + (\Delta y_k)\mathbf{j}$$

where $\Delta x_k = x_k - x_{k-1}$ and $\Delta y_k = y_k - y_{k-1}$.

- Since the work done by a constant force $\mathbf{F}_k^*$ moving a particle along a straight line from P_{k-1} to P_k is

$$\mathbf{F}_k^* \cdot \overrightarrow{P_{k-1}P_k} = (f(x_k^*, y_k^*)\mathbf{i} + g(x_k^*, y_k^*)\mathbf{j}) \cdot ((\Delta x_k)\mathbf{i} + (\Delta y_k)\mathbf{j})$$
$$= f(x_k^*, y_k^*)\Delta x_k + g(x_k^*, y_k^*)\Delta y_k$$

[Formula (33)], the work ΔW_k performed by the force field along the kth arc of C can be approximated by

$$\Delta W_k \approx f(x_k^*, y_k^*)\Delta x_k + g(x_k^*, y_k^*)\Delta y_k$$

The total work W performed by the force moving the particle over the entire curve C can then be approximated as

$$W = \sum_{k=1}^{n} \Delta W_k \approx \sum_{k=1}^{n} [f(x_k^*, y_k^*)\Delta x_k + g(x_k^*, y_k^*)\Delta y_k]$$

- As max $\Delta s_k \to 0$, it is plausible that the error in this approximation approaches 0 and the exact work performed by the force field is

$$W = \lim_{\max \Delta s_k \to 0} \sum_{k=1}^{n} [f(x_k^*, y_k^*)\Delta x_k + g(x_k^*, y_k^*)\Delta y_k]$$

$$= \int_C f(x, y)\, dx + g(x, y)\, dy \qquad \boxed{\text{Formula (22)}}$$

$$= \int_C \mathbf{F} \cdot d\mathbf{r} \qquad \boxed{\text{Formula (26)}}$$

Thus, we are led to the following definition.

▲ Figure 15.2.15

Note from Formula (30) that the work performed by a force field on a particle moving along a smooth curve C is obtained by integrating the scalar tangential component of force along C. This implies that the component of force orthogonal to the direction of motion of the particle has no effect on the work done.

15.2.3 **DEFINITION** Suppose that under the influence of a continuous force field $\mathbf{F}$ a particle moves along a smooth curve C and that C is oriented in the direction of motion of the particle. Then the *work performed by the force field* on the particle is

$$\int_C \mathbf{F} \cdot d\mathbf{r} \qquad (34)$$

For example, suppose that force is measured in pounds and distance is measured in feet. It follows from part (a) of Example 9 that the work done by a force $\mathbf{F}(x, y) = -y\mathbf{i} + x\mathbf{j}$ acting on a particle moving along the circle $x^2 + y^2 = 3$ from $(\sqrt{3}, 0)$ to $(0, \sqrt{3})$ is $3\pi/2$ foot-pounds.

■ LINE INTEGRALS ALONG PIECEWISE SMOOTH CURVES

Thus far, we have only considered line integrals along smooth curves. However, the notion of a line integral can be extended to curves formed from finitely many smooth curves $C_1, C_2, \ldots, C_n$ joined end to end. Such a curve is called *piecewise smooth* (Figure 15.2.16). We define a line integral along a piecewise smooth curve C to be the sum of the integrals along the sections:

$$\int_C = \int_{C_1} + \int_{C_2} + \cdots + \int_{C_n}$$

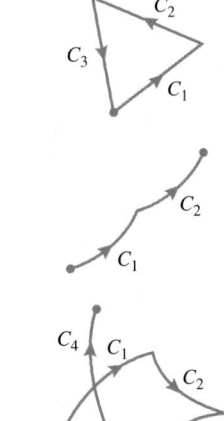

► **Example 10** Evaluate

$$\int_C x^2 y \, dx + x \, dy$$

where C is the triangular path shown in Figure 15.2.17.

Solution.   We will integrate over C_1, C_2, and C_3 separately and add the results. For each of the three integrals we must find parametric equations that trace the path of integration in the correct direction. For this purpose recall from Formula (7) of Section 12.1 that the graph of the vector-valued function

$$\mathbf{r}(t) = (1 - t)\mathbf{r}_0 + t\mathbf{r}_1 \qquad (0 \le t \le 1)$$

is the line segment joining $\mathbf{r}_0$ and $\mathbf{r}_1$, oriented in the direction from $\mathbf{r}_0$ to $\mathbf{r}_1$. Thus, the line segments C_1, C_2, and C_3 can be represented in vector notation as

$$C_1: \mathbf{r}(t) = (1 - t)\langle 0, 0 \rangle + t\langle 1, 0 \rangle = \langle t, 0 \rangle$$
$$C_2: \mathbf{r}(t) = (1 - t)\langle 1, 0 \rangle + t\langle 1, 2 \rangle = \langle 1, 2t \rangle$$
$$C_3: \mathbf{r}(t) = (1 - t)\langle 1, 2 \rangle + t\langle 0, 0 \rangle = \langle 1 - t, 2 - 2t \rangle$$

where t varies from 0 to 1 in each case. From these equations we obtain

$$\int_{C_1} x^2 y \, dx + x \, dy = \int_{C_1} x^2 y \, dx = \int_0^1 (t^2)(0)\frac{d}{dt}[t] \, dt = 0$$

$$\int_{C_2} x^2 y \, dx + x \, dy = \int_{C_2} x \, dy = \int_0^1 (1)\frac{d}{dt}[2t] \, dt = 2$$

$$\int_{C_3} x^2 y \, dx + x \, dy = \int_0^1 (1 - t)^2 (2 - 2t)\frac{d}{dt}[1 - t] \, dt + \int_0^1 (1 - t)\frac{d}{dt}[2 - 2t] \, dt$$

$$= 2\int_0^1 (t - 1)^3 \, dt + 2\int_0^1 (t - 1) \, dt = -\tfrac{1}{2} - 1 = -\tfrac{3}{2}$$

Thus,

$$\int_C x^2 y \, dx + x \, dy = 0 + 2 + \left(-\tfrac{3}{2}\right) = \tfrac{1}{2} \quad ◄$$

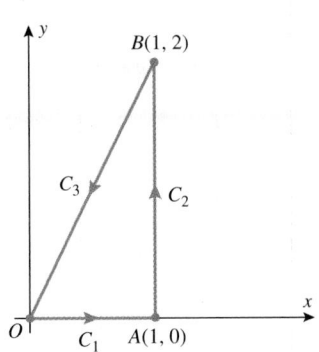

▲ **Figure 15.2.16**

▲ **Figure 15.2.17**

✔ **QUICK CHECK EXERCISES 15.2**   *(See page 1111 for answers.)*

1. The area of the surface extending upward from the line segment $y = x$ $(0 \le x \le 1)$ in the xy-plane to the plane $z = 2x + 1$ is _____.

2. Suppose that a wire has equation $y = 1 - x$ $(0 \le x \le 1)$ and that its mass density is $\delta(x, y) = 2 - x$. The mass of the wire is _____.

3. If C is the curve represented by the equations
$$x = \sin t, \quad y = \cos t, \quad z = t \quad (0 \le t \le 2\pi)$$
then $\int_C y\, dx - x\, dy + dz =$ _____.

4. If C is the unit circle $x^2 + y^2 = 1$ oriented counterclockwise and $\mathbf{F}(x, y) = x\mathbf{i} + y\mathbf{j}$, then
$$\int_C \mathbf{F} \cdot d\mathbf{r} = \underline{\qquad}$$

EXERCISE SET 15.2    Graphing Utility   c CAS

FOCUS ON CONCEPTS

1. Let C be the line segment from $(0, 0)$ to $(0, 1)$. In each part, evaluate the line integral along C by inspection, and explain your reasoning.

(a) $\displaystyle\int_C ds$ (b) $\displaystyle\int_C \sin xy\, dy$

2. Let C be the line segment from $(0, 2)$ to $(0, 4)$. In each part, evaluate the line integral along C by inspection, and explain your reasoning.

(a) $\displaystyle\int_C ds$ (b) $\displaystyle\int_C e^{xy}\, dx$

3–4 Evaluate $\int_C \mathbf{F} \cdot d\mathbf{r}$ by inspection for the force field $\mathbf{F}(x, y) = \mathbf{i} + \mathbf{j}$ and the curve C shown in the figure. Explain your reasoning. [*Note:* For clarity, the vectors in the force field are shown at less than true scale.] ■

3.   4.

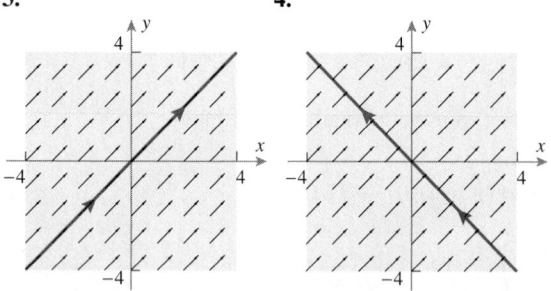

5. Use (30) to explain why the line integral in part (a) of Example 8 can be found by multiplying the length of the line segment C by -1.

~ 6. (a) Use (30) to explain why the line integral in part (b) of Example 8 should be close to, but somewhat less than, the length of the parabolic curve C.
   (b) Verify the conclusion in part (a) of this exercise by computing the length of C and comparing the length with the value of the line integral.

7. Let C be the curve represented by the equations
$$x = 2t, \quad y = 3t^2 \quad (0 \le t \le 1)$$
In each part, evaluate the line integral along C.

(a) $\displaystyle\int_C (x - y)\, ds$ (b) $\displaystyle\int_C (x - y)\, dx$

(c) $\displaystyle\int_C (x - y)\, dy$

8. Let C be the curve represented by the equations
$$x = t, \quad y = 3t^2, \quad z = 6t^3 \quad (0 \le t \le 1)$$
In each part, evaluate the line integral along C.

(a) $\displaystyle\int_C xyz^2\, ds$ (b) $\displaystyle\int_C xyz^2\, dx$

(c) $\displaystyle\int_C xyz^2\, dy$ (d) $\displaystyle\int_C xyz^2\, dz$

9. In each part, evaluate the integral
$$\int_C (3x + 2y)\, dx + (2x - y)\, dy$$
along the stated curve.
(a) The line segment from $(0, 0)$ to $(1, 1)$.
(b) The parabolic arc $y = x^2$ from $(0, 0)$ to $(1, 1)$.
(c) The curve $y = \sin(\pi x/2)$ from $(0, 0)$ to $(1, 1)$.
(d) The curve $x = y^3$ from $(0, 0)$ to $(1, 1)$.

10. In each part, evaluate the integral
$$\int_C y\, dx + z\, dy - x\, dz$$
along the stated curve.
(a) The line segment from $(0, 0, 0)$ to $(1, 1, 1)$.
(b) The twisted cubic $x = t, y = t^2, z = t^3$ from $(0, 0, 0)$ to $(1, 1, 1)$.
(c) The helix $x = \cos \pi t, y = \sin \pi t, z = t$ from $(1, 0, 0)$ to $(-1, 0, 1)$.

11–14 True–False Determine whether the statement is true or false. Explain your answer. ■

11. If C is a smooth oriented curve in the xy-plane and $f(x, y)$ is a continuous function defined on C, then

$$\int_C f(x, y)\, ds = -\int_{-C} f(x, y)\, ds$$

12. The line integral of a continuous vector field along a smooth curve C is a vector.

13. If $\mathbf{F}(x, y) = f(x, y)\mathbf{i} + g(x, y)\mathbf{j}$ along a smooth oriented curve C in the xy-plane, then

$$\int_C \mathbf{F} \cdot d\mathbf{r} = \int_C f(x, y)\, dx + g(x, y)\, dy$$

14. If a smooth oriented curve C in the xy-plane is a contour for a differentiable function $f(x, y)$, then

$$\int_C \nabla f \cdot d\mathbf{r} = 0$$

15–18 Evaluate the line integral with respect to s along the curve C. ■

15. $\displaystyle\int_C \frac{1}{1+x}\, ds$

$C : \mathbf{r}(t) = t\mathbf{i} + \frac{2}{3}t^{3/2}\mathbf{j} \quad (0 \le t \le 3)$

16. $\displaystyle\int_C \frac{x}{1+y^2}\, ds$

$C : x = 1 + 2t, \ y = t \quad (0 \le t \le 1)$

17. $\displaystyle\int_C 3x^2 yz\, ds$

$C : x = t, \ y = t^2, \ z = \frac{2}{3}t^3 \quad (0 \le t \le 1)$

18. $\displaystyle\int_C \frac{e^{-z}}{x^2 + y^2}\, ds$

$C : \mathbf{r}(t) = 2\cos t\mathbf{i} + 2\sin t\mathbf{j} + t\mathbf{k} \quad (0 \le t \le 2\pi)$

19–26 Evaluate the line integral along the curve C. ■

19. $\displaystyle\int_C (x + 2y)\, dx + (x - y)\, dy$

$C : x = 2\cos t, \ y = 4\sin t \quad (0 \le t \le \pi/4)$

20. $\displaystyle\int_C (x^2 - y^2)\, dx + x\, dy$

$C : x = t^{2/3}, \ y = t \quad (-1 \le t \le 1)$

21. $\displaystyle\int_C -y\, dx + x\, dy$

$C : y^2 = 3x$ from $(3, 3)$ to $(0, 0)$

22. $\displaystyle\int_C (y - x)\, dx + x^2 y\, dy$

$C : y^2 = x^3$ from $(1, -1)$ to $(1, 1)$

23. $\displaystyle\int_C (x^2 + y^2)\, dx - x\, dy$

$C : x^2 + y^2 = 1$, counterclockwise from $(1, 0)$ to $(0, 1)$

24. $\displaystyle\int_C (y - x)\, dx + xy\, dy$

$C :$ the line segment from $(3, 4)$ to $(2, 1)$

25. $\displaystyle\int_C yz\, dx - xz\, dy + xy\, dz$

$C : x = e^t, \ y = e^{3t}, \ z = e^{-t} \quad (0 \le t \le 1)$

26. $\displaystyle\int_C x^2\, dx + xy\, dy + z^2\, dz$

$C : x = \sin t, \ y = \cos t, \ z = t^2 \quad (0 \le t \le \pi/2)$

C **27–28** Use a CAS to evaluate the line integrals along the given curves. ■

27. (a) $\displaystyle\int_C (x^3 + y^3)\, ds$

$C : \mathbf{r}(t) = e^t \mathbf{i} + e^{-t}\mathbf{j} \quad (0 \le t \le \ln 2)$

(b) $\displaystyle\int_C xe^z\, dx + (x - z)\, dy + (x^2 + y^2 + z^2)\, dz$

$C : x = \sin t, \ y = \cos t, \ z = t \quad (0 \le t \le \pi/2)$

28. (a) $\displaystyle\int_C x^7 y^3\, ds$

$C : x = \cos^3 t, \ y = \sin^3 t \quad (0 \le t \le \pi/2)$

(b) $\displaystyle\int_C x^5 z\, dx + 7y\, dy + y^2 z\, dz$

$C : \mathbf{r}(t) = t\mathbf{i} + t^2\mathbf{j} + \ln t\mathbf{k} \quad (1 \le t \le e)$

29–30 Evaluate $\int_C y\, dx - x\, dy$ along the curve C shown in the figure. ■

29. (a) 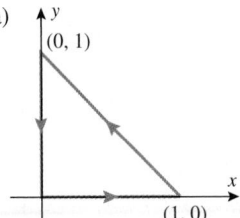 (b)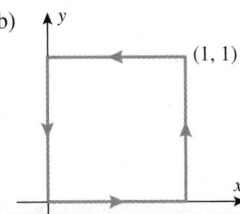

30. (a) 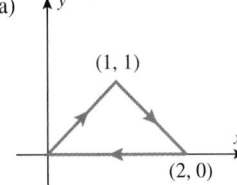 (b)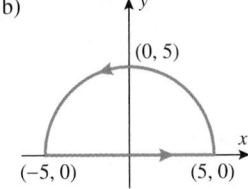

31–32 Evaluate $\int_C x^2 z\, dx - yx^2\, dy + 3\, dz$ along the curve C shown in the figure. ■

31. 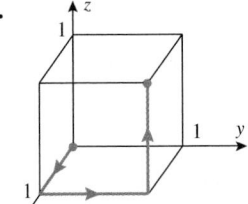 **32.**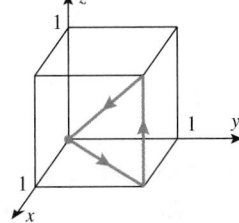

33–36 Evaluate $\int_C \mathbf{F} \cdot d\mathbf{r}$ along the curve C. ■

33. $\mathbf{F}(x, y) = x^2\mathbf{i} + xy\mathbf{j}$

$C : \mathbf{r}(t) = 2\cos t\mathbf{i} + 2\sin t\mathbf{j} \quad (0 \le t \le \pi)$

34. $\mathbf{F}(x, y) = x^2 y \mathbf{i} + 4 \mathbf{j}$
$C : \mathbf{r}(t) = e^t \mathbf{i} + e^{-t} \mathbf{j} \quad (0 \le t \le 1)$

35. $\mathbf{F}(x, y) = (x^2 + y^2)^{-3/2}(x \mathbf{i} + y \mathbf{j})$
$C : \mathbf{r}(t) = e^t \sin t \mathbf{i} + e^t \cos t \mathbf{j} \quad (0 \le t \le 1)$

36. $\mathbf{F}(x, y, z) = z \mathbf{i} + x \mathbf{j} + y \mathbf{k}$
$C : \mathbf{r}(t) = \sin t \mathbf{i} + 3 \sin t \mathbf{j} + \sin^2 t \mathbf{k} \quad (0 \le t \le \pi/2)$

37. Find the mass of a thin wire shaped in the form of the circular arc $y = \sqrt{9 - x^2}$ ($0 \le x \le 3$) if the density function is $\delta(x, y) = x\sqrt{y}$.

38. Find the mass of a thin wire shaped in the form of the curve $x = e^t \cos t$, $y = e^t \sin t$ ($0 \le t \le 1$) if the density function δ is proportional to the distance from the origin.

39. Find the mass of a thin wire shaped in the form of the helix $x = 3 \cos t$, $y = 3 \sin t$, $z = 4t$ ($0 \le t \le \pi/2$) if the density function is $\delta = kx/(1 + y^2)$ ($k > 0$).

40. Find the mass of a thin wire shaped in the form of the curve $x = 2t$, $y = \ln t$, $z = 4\sqrt{t}$ ($1 \le t \le 4$) if the density function is proportional to the distance above the xy-plane.

41–44 Find the work done by the force field $\mathbf{F}$ on a particle that moves along the curve C. ■

41. $\mathbf{F}(x, y) = xy \mathbf{i} + x^2 \mathbf{j}$
$C : x = y^2$ from $(0, 0)$ to $(1, 1)$

42. $\mathbf{F}(x, y) = (x^2 + xy) \mathbf{i} + (y - x^2 y) \mathbf{j}$
$C : x = t, \ y = 1/t \quad (1 \le t \le 3)$

43. $\mathbf{F}(x, y, z) = xy \mathbf{i} + yz \mathbf{j} + xz \mathbf{k}$
$C : \mathbf{r}(t) = t \mathbf{i} + t^2 \mathbf{j} + t^3 \mathbf{k} \quad (0 \le t \le 1)$

44. $\mathbf{F}(x, y, z) = (x + y) \mathbf{i} + xy \mathbf{j} - z^2 \mathbf{k}$
$C :$ along line segments from $(0, 0, 0)$ to $(1, 3, 1)$ to $(2, -1, 4)$

45–46 Find the work done by the force field

$$\mathbf{F}(x, y) = \frac{1}{x^2 + y^2} \mathbf{i} + \frac{4}{x^2 + y^2} \mathbf{j}$$

on a particle that moves along the curve C shown in the figure. ■

45.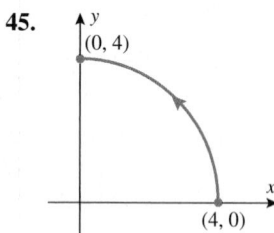
$(0, 4)$
$(4, 0)$

46.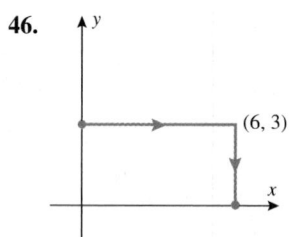
$(6, 3)$

47–48 Use a line integral to find the area of the surface. ■

47. The surface that extends upward from the parabola $y = x^2$ ($0 \le x \le 2$) in the xy-plane to the plane $z = 3x$.

48. The surface that extends upward from the semicircle $y = \sqrt{4 - x^2}$ in the xy-plane to the surface $z = x^2 y$.

49. As illustrated in the accompanying figure, a sinusoidal cut is made in the top of a cylindrical tin can. Suppose that the base is modeled by the parametric equations $x = \cos t$, $y = \sin t, z = 0$ ($0 \le t \le 2\pi$), and the height of the cut as a function of t is $z = 2 + 0.5 \sin 3t$.
   (a) Use a geometric argument to find the lateral surface area of the cut can.
   (b) Write down a line integral for the surface area.
   (c) Use the line integral to calculate the surface area.

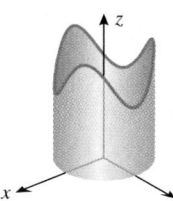
◄ **Figure Ex-49**

50. Evaluate the integral $\displaystyle\int_{-C} \frac{x \, dy - y \, dx}{x^2 + y^2}$, where C is the circle $x^2 + y^2 = a^2$ traversed counterclockwise.

51. Suppose that a particle moves through the force field $\mathbf{F}(x, y) = xy \mathbf{i} + (x - y) \mathbf{j}$ from the point $(0, 0)$ to the point $(1, 0)$ along the curve $x = t$, $y = \lambda t(1 - t)$. For what value of λ will the work done by the force field be 1?

52. A farmer weighing 150 lb carries a sack of grain weighing 20 lb up a circular helical staircase around a silo of radius 25 ft. As the farmer climbs, grain leaks from the sack at a rate of 1 lb per 10 ft of ascent. How much work is performed by the farmer in climbing through a vertical distance of 60 ft in exactly four revolutions? [*Hint:* Find a vector field that represents the force exerted by the farmer in lifting his own weight plus the weight of the sack upward at each point along his path.]

53. Suppose that a curve C in the xy-plane is smoothly parametrized by

$$\mathbf{r}(t) = x(t) \mathbf{i} + y(t) \mathbf{j} \qquad (a \le t \le b)$$

In each part, refer to the notation used in the derivation of Formula (9).
   (a) Let m and M denote the respective minimum and maximum values of $\|\mathbf{r}'(t)\|$ on $[a, b]$. Prove that

$$0 \le m(\max \Delta t_k) \le \max \Delta s_k \le M(\max \Delta t_k)$$

   (b) Use part (a) to prove that $\max \Delta s_k \to 0$ if and only if $\max \Delta t_k \to 0$.

54. **Writing** Discuss the similarities and differences between the definition of a definite integral over an interval (Definition 5.5.1) and the definition of the line integral with respect to arc length along a curve (Definition 15.2.1).

55. **Writing** Describe the different types of line integrals, and discuss how they are related.

15.3 INDEPENDENCE OF PATH; CONSERVATIVE VECTOR FIELDS

*In this section we will show that for certain kinds of vector fields **F** the line integral of **F** along a curve depends only on the endpoints of the curve and not on the curve itself. Vector fields with this property, which include gravitational and electrostatic fields, are of special importance in physics and engineering.*

■ **WORK INTEGRALS**

We saw in the last section that if **F** is a force field in 2-space or 3-space, then the work performed by the field on a particle moving along a parametric curve C from an initial point P to a final point Q is given by the integral

$$\int_C \mathbf{F} \cdot d\mathbf{r} \quad \text{or equivalently} \quad \int_C \mathbf{F} \cdot \mathbf{T}\, ds$$

Accordingly, we call an integral of this type a ***work integral***. Recall that a work integral can also be expressed in scalar form as

$$\int_C \mathbf{F} \cdot d\mathbf{r} = \int_C f(x,y)\, dx + g(x,y)\, dy \qquad \boxed{\text{2-space}} \tag{1}$$

$$\int_C \mathbf{F} \cdot d\mathbf{r} = \int_C f(x,y,z)\, dx + g(x,y,z)\, dy + h(x,y,z)\, dz \qquad \boxed{\text{3-space}} \tag{2}$$

where f, g, and h are the component functions of **F**.

■ **INDEPENDENCE OF PATH**

The parametric curve C in a work integral is called the ***path of integration***. One of the important problems in applications is to determine how the path of integration affects the work performed by a force field on a particle that moves from a fixed point P to a fixed point Q. We will show shortly that if the force field **F** is conservative (i.e., is the gradient of some potential function ϕ), then the work that the field performs on a particle that moves from P to Q does not depend on the particular path C that the particle follows. This is illustrated in the following example.

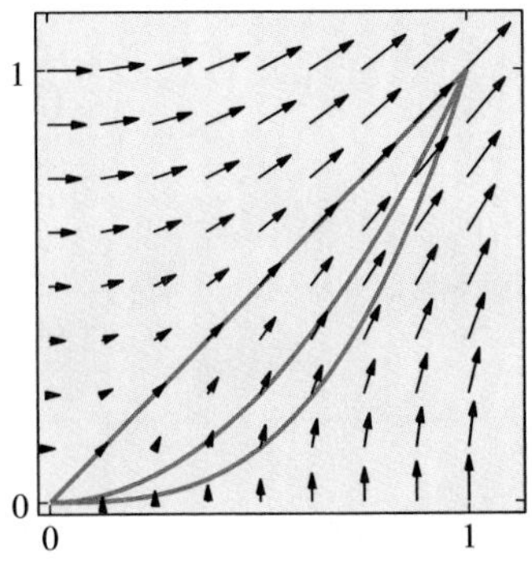

Vectors not to scale
▲ **Figure 15.3.1**

▶ **Example 1** The force field $\mathbf{F}(x,y) = y\mathbf{i} + x\mathbf{j}$ is conservative since it is the gradient of $\phi(x,y) = xy$ (verify). Thus, the preceding discussion suggests that the work performed by the field on a particle that moves from the point $(0,0)$ to the point $(1,1)$ should be the same along different paths. Confirm that the value of the work integral

$$\int_C \mathbf{F} \cdot d\mathbf{r}$$

is the same along the following paths (Figure 15.3.1):

(a) The line segment $y = x$ from $(0,0)$ to $(1,1)$.
(b) The parabola $y = x^2$ from $(0,0)$ to $(1,1)$.
(c) The cubic $y = x^3$ from $(0,0)$ to $(1,1)$.

Solution (a). With $x = t$ as the parameter, the path of integration is given by

$$x = t, \quad y = t \quad (0 \le t \le 1)$$

Thus,

$$\int_C \mathbf{F} \cdot d\mathbf{r} = \int_C (y\mathbf{i} + x\mathbf{j}) \cdot (dx\mathbf{i} + dy\mathbf{j}) = \int_C y \, dx + x \, dy$$
$$= \int_0^1 2t \, dt = 1$$

Solution (b). With $x = t$ as the parameter, the path of integration is given by

$$x = t, \quad y = t^2 \quad (0 \le t \le 1)$$

Thus,

$$\int_C \mathbf{F} \cdot d\mathbf{r} = \int_C y \, dx + x \, dy = \int_0^1 3t^2 \, dt = 1$$

Solution (c). With $x = t$ as the parameter, the path of integration is given by

$$x = t, \quad y = t^3 \quad (0 \le t \le 1)$$

Thus,

$$\int_C \mathbf{F} \cdot d\mathbf{r} = \int_C y \, dx + x \, dy = \int_0^1 4t^3 \, dt = 1 \blacktriangleleft$$

■ THE FUNDAMENTAL THEOREM OF LINE INTEGRALS

Recall from the Fundamental Theorem of Calculus (Theorem 5.6.1) that if F is an antiderivative of f, then

$$\int_a^b f(x) \, dx = F(b) - F(a)$$

The following result is the analog of that theorem for line integrals in 2-space.

15.3.1   THEOREM (*The Fundamental Theorem of Line Integrals*)   *Suppose that*

$$\mathbf{F}(x, y) = f(x, y)\mathbf{i} + g(x, y)\mathbf{j}$$

is a conservative vector field in some open region D containing the points (x_0, y_0) and (x_1, y_1) and that $f(x, y)$ and $g(x, y)$ are continuous in this region. If

$$\mathbf{F}(x, y) = \nabla\phi(x, y)$$

and if C is any piecewise smooth parametric curve that starts at (x_0, y_0), ends at (x_1, y_1), and lies in the region D, then

$$\int_C \mathbf{F}(x, y) \cdot d\mathbf{r} = \phi(x_1, y_1) - \phi(x_0, y_0) \tag{3}$$

or, equivalently,

$$\int_C \nabla\phi \cdot d\mathbf{r} = \phi(x_1, y_1) - \phi(x_0, y_0) \tag{4}$$

The value of

$$\int_C \mathbf{F} \cdot d\mathbf{r} = \int_C \mathbf{F} \cdot \mathbf{T} \, ds$$

depends on the magnitude of **F** along C, the alignment of **F** with the direction of C at each point, and the length of C. If **F** is conservative, these various factors always "balance out" so that the value of $\int_C \mathbf{F} \cdot d\mathbf{r}$ depends only on the initial and final points of C.

PROOF   We will give the proof for a smooth curve C. The proof for a piecewise smooth curve, which is left as an exercise, can be obtained by applying the theorem to each individual smooth piece and adding the results. Suppose that C is given parametrically by $x = x(t)$, $y = y(t)$ ($a \leq t \leq b$), so that the initial and final points of the curve are

$$(x_0, y_0) = (x(a), y(a)) \quad \text{and} \quad (x_1, y_1) = (x(b), y(b))$$

Since $\mathbf{F}(x, y) = \nabla\phi$, it follows that

$$\mathbf{F}(x, y) = \frac{\partial\phi}{\partial x}\mathbf{i} + \frac{\partial\phi}{\partial y}\mathbf{j}$$

so

$$\int_C \mathbf{F}(x, y) \cdot d\mathbf{r} = \int_C \frac{\partial\phi}{\partial x}\,dx + \frac{\partial\phi}{\partial y}\,dy = \int_a^b \left[\frac{\partial\phi}{\partial x}\frac{dx}{dt} + \frac{\partial\phi}{\partial y}\frac{dy}{dt}\right]dt$$

$$= \int_a^b \frac{d}{dt}[\phi(x(t), y(t))]\,dt = \phi(x(t), y(t))\Big]_{t=a}^{b}$$

$$= \phi(x(b), y(b)) - \phi(x(a), y(a))$$

$$= \phi(x_1, y_1) - \phi(x_0, y_0) \quad\blacksquare$$

Stated informally, this theorem shows that *the value of a line integral of a conservative vector field along a piecewise smooth path is **independent of the path***; that is, the value of the integral depends on the endpoints and not on the actual path C. Accordingly, for line integrals of conservative vector fields, it is common to express (3) and (4) as

$$\int_{(x_0, y_0)}^{(x_1, y_1)} \mathbf{F} \cdot d\mathbf{r} = \int_{(x_0, y_0)}^{(x_1, y_1)} \nabla\phi \cdot d\mathbf{r} = \phi(x_1, y_1) - \phi(x_0, y_0) \tag{5}$$

▶ **Example 2**

If **F** is conservative, then you have a choice of methods for evaluating $\int_C \mathbf{F} \cdot d\mathbf{r}$. You can work directly with the curve C, you can replace C with another curve that has the same endpoints as C, or you can apply Formula (3).

(a) Confirm that the force field $\mathbf{F}(x, y) = y\mathbf{i} + x\mathbf{j}$ in Example 1 is conservative by showing that $\mathbf{F}(x, y)$ is the gradient of $\phi(x, y) = xy$.

(b) Use the Fundamental Theorem of Line Integrals to evaluate $\displaystyle\int_{(0,0)}^{(1,1)} \mathbf{F} \cdot d\mathbf{r}$.

Solution (a).

$$\nabla\phi = \frac{\partial\phi}{\partial x}\mathbf{i} + \frac{\partial\phi}{\partial y}\mathbf{j} = y\mathbf{i} + x\mathbf{j}$$

Solution (b).   From (5) we obtain

$$\int_{(0,0)}^{(1,1)} \mathbf{F} \cdot d\mathbf{r} = \phi(1, 1) - \phi(0, 0) = 1 - 0 = 1$$

which agrees with the results obtained in Example 1 by integrating from $(0, 0)$ to $(1, 1)$ along specific paths. ◀

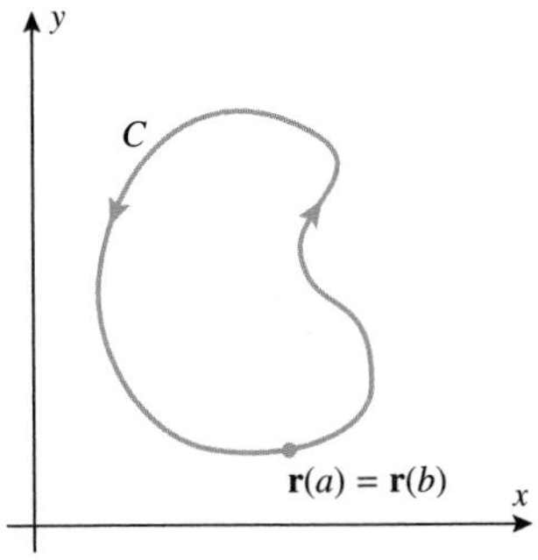

■ **LINE INTEGRALS ALONG CLOSED PATHS**

Parametric curves that begin and end at the same point play an important role in the study of vector fields, so there is some special terminology associated with them. A parametric curve C that is represented by the vector-valued function $\mathbf{r}(t)$ for $a \leq t \leq b$ is said to be ***closed*** if the initial point $\mathbf{r}(a)$ and the terminal point $\mathbf{r}(b)$ coincide; that is, $\mathbf{r}(a) = \mathbf{r}(b)$ (Figure 15.3.2).

▲ **Figure 15.3.2**

It follows from (5) that the line integral of a conservative vector field along a closed path C that begins and ends at (x_0, y_0) is zero. This is because the point (x_1, y_1) in (5) is the same as (x_0, y_0) and hence

$$\int_C \mathbf{F} \cdot d\mathbf{r} = \phi(x_1, y_1) - \phi(x_0, y_0) = 0$$

Our next objective is to show that the converse of this result is also true. That is, we want to show that under appropriate conditions a vector field whose line integral is zero along *all* closed paths must be conservative. For this to be true we will need to require that the domain D of the vector field be ***connected***, by which we mean that any two points in D can be joined by some piecewise smooth curve that lies entirely in D. Stated informally, D is connected if it does not consist of two or more separate pieces (Figure 15.3.3).

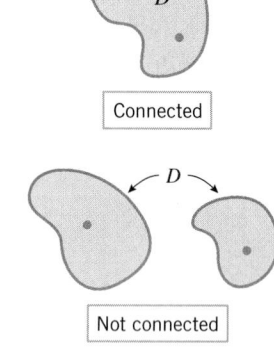

▲ Figure 15.3.3

> **15.3.2   THEOREM**   *If $f(x, y)$ and $g(x, y)$ are continuous on some open connected region D, then the following statements are equivalent (all true or all false):*
>
> (a) $\mathbf{F}(x, y) = f(x, y)\mathbf{i} + g(x, y)\mathbf{j}$ *is a conservative vector field on the region D.*
>
> (b) $\displaystyle\int_C \mathbf{F} \cdot d\mathbf{r} = 0$ *for every piecewise smooth closed curve C in D.*
>
> (c) $\displaystyle\int_C \mathbf{F} \cdot d\mathbf{r}$ *is independent of the path from any point P in D to any point Q in D for every piecewise smooth curve C in D.*

This theorem can be established by proving three implications: $(a) \Rightarrow (b)$, $(b) \Rightarrow (c)$, and $(c) \Rightarrow (a)$. Since we showed above that $(a) \Rightarrow (b)$, we need only prove the last two implications. We will prove $(c) \Rightarrow (a)$ and leave the other implication as an exercise.

PROOF $(c) \Rightarrow (a)$. We are assuming that $\int_C \mathbf{F} \cdot d\mathbf{r}$ is independent of the path for every piecewise smooth curve C in the region, and we want to show that there is a function $\phi = \phi(x, y)$ such that $\nabla\phi = \mathbf{F}(x, y)$ at each point of the region; that is,

$$\frac{\partial\phi}{\partial x} = f(x, y) \quad \text{and} \quad \frac{\partial\phi}{\partial y} = g(x, y) \tag{6}$$

Now choose a fixed point (a, b) in D, let (x, y) be any point in D, and define

$$\phi(x, y) = \int_{(a,b)}^{(x,y)} \mathbf{F} \cdot d\mathbf{r} \tag{7}$$

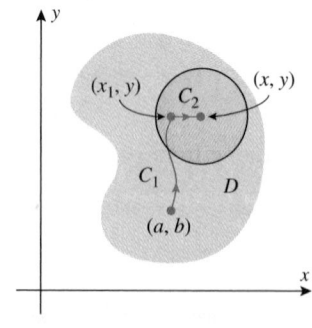

▲ Figure 15.3.4

This is an unambiguous definition because we have assumed that the integral is independent of the path. We will show that $\nabla\phi = \mathbf{F}$. Since D is open, we can find a circular disk centered at (x, y) whose points lie entirely in D. As shown in Figure 15.3.4, choose any point (x_1, y) in this disk that lies on the same horizontal line as (x, y) such that $x_1 < x$. Because the integral in (7) is independent of path, we can evaluate it by first integrating from (a, b) to (x_1, y) along an arbitrary piecewise smooth curve C_1 in D, and then continuing along the horizontal line segment C_2 from (x_1, y) to (x, y). This yields

$$\phi(x, y) = \int_{C_1} \mathbf{F} \cdot d\mathbf{r} + \int_{C_2} \mathbf{F} \cdot d\mathbf{r} = \int_{(a,b)}^{(x_1,y)} \mathbf{F} \cdot d\mathbf{r} + \int_{C_2} \mathbf{F} \cdot d\mathbf{r}$$

Since the first term does not depend on x, its partial derivative with respect to x is zero and hence

$$\frac{\partial \phi}{\partial x} = \frac{\partial}{\partial x} \int_{C_2} \mathbf{F} \cdot d\mathbf{r} = \frac{\partial}{\partial x} \int_{C_2} f(x, y)\, dx + g(x, y)\, dy$$

However, the line integral with respect to y is zero along the horizontal line segment C_2, so this equation simplifies to

$$\frac{\partial \phi}{\partial x} = \frac{\partial}{\partial x} \int_{C_2} f(x, y)\, dx \tag{8}$$

To evaluate the integral in this expression, we treat y as a constant and express the line C_2 parametrically as

$$x = t, \quad y = y \qquad (x_1 \leq t \leq x)$$

At the risk of confusion, but to avoid complicating the notation, we have used x both as the dependent variable in the parametric equations and as the endpoint of the line segment. With the latter interpretation of x, it follows that (8) can be expressed as

$$\frac{\partial \phi}{\partial x} = \frac{\partial}{\partial x} \int_{x_1}^{x} f(t, y)\, dt$$

Now we apply Part 2 of the Fundamental Theorem of Calculus (Theorem 5.6.3), treating y as constant. This yields

$$\frac{\partial \phi}{\partial x} = f(x, y)$$

which proves the first part of (6). The proof that $\partial \phi / \partial y = g(x, y)$ can be obtained in a similar manner by joining (x, y) to a point (x, y_1) with a vertical line segment (Exercise 39). ∎

A TEST FOR CONSERVATIVE VECTOR FIELDS

Although Theorem 15.3.2 is an important characterization of conservative vector fields, it is not an effective computational tool because it is usually not possible to evaluate the line integral over all possible piecewise smooth curves in D, as required in parts (b) and (c). To develop a method for determining whether a vector field is conservative, we will need to introduce some new concepts about parametric curves and connected sets. We will say that a parametric curve is *simple* if it does not intersect itself between its endpoints. A simple parametric curve may or may not be closed (Figure 15.3.5). In addition, we will say that a connected set D in 2-space is *simply connected* if no simple closed curve in D encloses points that are not in D. Stated informally, a connected set D is simply connected if it has no holes; a connected set with one or more holes is said to be *multiply connected* (Figure 15.3.6).

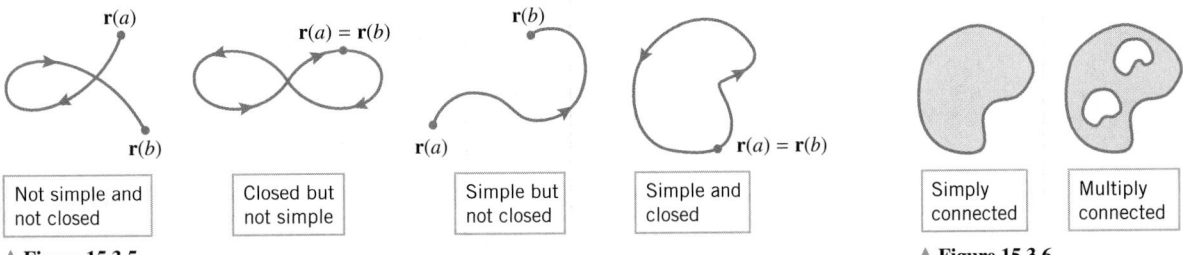

| Not simple and not closed | Closed but not simple | Simple but not closed | Simple and closed | Simply connected | Multiply connected |

▲ Figure 15.3.5   ▲ Figure 15.3.6

The following theorem is the primary tool for determining whether a vector field in 2-space is conservative.

> **15.3.3** **THEOREM** (*Conservative Field Test*)   *If $f(x, y)$ and $g(x, y)$ are continuous and have continuous first partial derivatives on some open region D, and if the vector field $\mathbf{F}(x, y) = f(x, y)\mathbf{i} + g(x, y)\mathbf{j}$ is conservative on D, then*
>
> $$\frac{\partial f}{\partial y} = \frac{\partial g}{\partial x} \tag{9}$$
>
> *at each point in D. Conversely, if D is simply connected and (9) holds at each point in D, then $\mathbf{F}(x, y) = f(x, y)\mathbf{i} + g(x, y)\mathbf{j}$ is conservative.*

A complete proof of this theorem requires results from advanced calculus and will be omitted. However, it is not hard to see why (9) must hold if $\mathbf{F}$ is conservative. For this purpose suppose that $\mathbf{F} = \nabla\phi$, in which case we can express the functions f and g as

$$\frac{\partial \phi}{\partial x} = f \quad \text{and} \quad \frac{\partial \phi}{\partial y} = g \tag{10}$$

Thus,

$$\frac{\partial f}{\partial y} = \frac{\partial}{\partial y}\left(\frac{\partial \phi}{\partial x}\right) = \frac{\partial^2 \phi}{\partial y \partial x} \quad \text{and} \quad \frac{\partial g}{\partial x} = \frac{\partial}{\partial x}\left(\frac{\partial \phi}{\partial y}\right) = \frac{\partial^2 \phi}{\partial x \partial y}$$

But the mixed partial derivatives in these equations are equal (Theorem 13.3.2), so (9) follows.

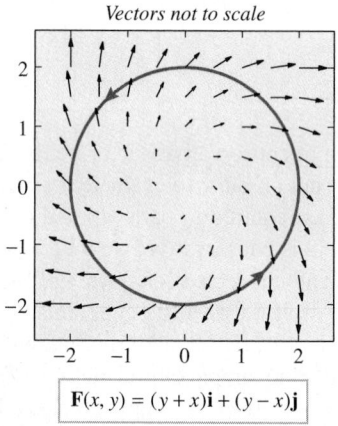

Vectors not to scale

$\mathbf{F}(x, y) = (y + x)\mathbf{i} + (y - x)\mathbf{j}$

▲ **Figure 15.3.7**

▶ **Example 3**   Use Theorem 15.3.3 to determine whether the vector field

$$\mathbf{F}(x, y) = (y + x)\mathbf{i} + (y - x)\mathbf{j}$$

is conservative on some open set.

Solution.   Let $f(x, y) = y + x$ and $g(x, y) = y - x$. Then

$$\frac{\partial f}{\partial y} = 1 \quad \text{and} \quad \frac{\partial g}{\partial x} = -1$$

Thus, there are no points in the xy-plane at which condition (9) holds, and hence $\mathbf{F}$ is not conservative on any open set. ◀

REMARK   Since the vector field $\mathbf{F}$ in Example 3 is not conservative, it follows from Theorem 15.3.2 that there must exist piecewise smooth closed curves in every open connected set in the xy-plane on which

$$\int_C \mathbf{F} \cdot d\mathbf{r} = \int_C \mathbf{F} \cdot \mathbf{T}\, ds \neq 0$$

One such curve is the oriented circle shown in Figure 15.3.7. The figure suggests that $\mathbf{F} \cdot \mathbf{T} < 0$ at each point of C (why?), so $\int_C \mathbf{F} \cdot \mathbf{T}\, ds < 0$.

Once it is established that a vector field is conservative, a potential function for the field can be obtained by first integrating either of the equations in (10). This is illustrated in the following example.

▶ **Example 4** Let $\mathbf{F}(x, y) = 2xy^3\mathbf{i} + (1 + 3x^2y^2)\mathbf{j}$.

(a) Show that $\mathbf{F}$ is a conservative vector field on the entire xy-plane.
(b) Find ϕ by first integrating $\partial\phi/\partial x$.
(c) Find ϕ by first integrating $\partial\phi/\partial y$.

Solution (a). Since $f(x, y) = 2xy^3$ and $g(x, y) = 1 + 3x^2y^2$, we have

$$\frac{\partial f}{\partial y} = 6xy^2 = \frac{\partial g}{\partial x}$$

so (9) holds for all (x, y).

Solution (b). Since the field $\mathbf{F}$ is conservative, there is a potential function ϕ such that

$$\frac{\partial\phi}{\partial x} = 2xy^3 \quad \text{and} \quad \frac{\partial\phi}{\partial y} = 1 + 3x^2y^2 \tag{11}$$

Integrating the first of these equations with respect to x (and treating y as a constant) yields

$$\phi = \int 2xy^3\,dx = x^2y^3 + k(y) \tag{12}$$

where $k(y)$ represents the "constant" of integration. We are justified in treating the constant of integration as a function of y, since y is held constant in the integration process. To find $k(y)$ we differentiate (12) with respect to y and use the second equation in (11) to obtain

$$\frac{\partial\phi}{\partial y} = 3x^2y^2 + k'(y) = 1 + 3x^2y^2$$

from which it follows that $k'(y) = 1$. Thus,

$$k(y) = \int k'(y)\,dy = \int 1\,dy = y + K$$

where K is a (numerical) constant of integration. Substituting in (12) we obtain

$$\phi = x^2y^3 + y + K$$

The appearance of the arbitrary constant K tells us that ϕ is not unique. As a check on the computations, you may want to verify that $\nabla\phi = \mathbf{F}$.

You can also use (7) to find a potential function for a conservative vector field. For example, find a potential function for the vector field in Example 4 by evaluating (7) on the line segment

$$\mathbf{r}(t) = t(x\mathbf{i}) + t(y\mathbf{j}) \quad (0 \le t \le 1)$$

from $(0, 0)$ to (x, y).

Solution (c). Integrating the second equation in (11) with respect to y (and treating x as a constant) yields

$$\phi = \int (1 + 3x^2y^2)\,dy = y + x^2y^3 + k(x) \tag{13}$$

where $k(x)$ is the "constant" of integration. Differentiating (13) with respect to x and using the first equation in (11) yields

$$\frac{\partial\phi}{\partial x} = 2xy^3 + k'(x) = 2xy^3$$

from which it follows that $k'(x) = 0$ and consequently that $k(x) = K$, where K is a numerical constant of integration. Substituting this in (13) yields

$$\phi = y + x^2y^3 + K$$

which agrees with the solution in part (b). ◀

▶ **Example 5** Use the potential function obtained in Example 4 to evaluate the integral

$$\int_{(1,4)}^{(3,1)} 2xy^3 \, dx + (1 + 3x^2y^2) \, dy$$

Solution. The integrand can be expressed as $\mathbf{F} \cdot d\mathbf{r}$, where $\mathbf{F}$ is the vector field in Example 4. Thus, using Formula (3) and the potential function $\phi = y + x^2y^3 + K$ for $\mathbf{F}$, we obtain

$$\int_{(1,4)}^{(3,1)} 2xy^3 \, dx + (1 + 3x^2y^2) \, dy = \int_{(1,4)}^{(3,1)} \mathbf{F} \cdot d\mathbf{r} = \phi(3,1) - \phi(1,4)$$

$$= (10 + K) - (68 + K) = -58 \blacktriangleleft$$

In the solution to Example 5, note that the constant K drops out. In future integration problems of the type in this example, we will often omit K from the computations. See Exercise 7 for other ways to evaluate this integral.

▶ **Example 6** Let $\mathbf{F}(x, y) = e^y\mathbf{i} + xe^y\mathbf{j}$ denote a force field in the xy-plane.

(a) Verify that the force field $\mathbf{F}$ is conservative on the entire xy-plane.

(b) Find the work done by the field on a particle that moves from $(1, 0)$ to $(-1, 0)$ along the semicircular path C shown in Figure 15.3.8.

Solution (a). For the given field we have $f(x, y) = e^y$ and $g(x, y) = xe^y$. Thus,

$$\frac{\partial}{\partial y}(e^y) = e^y = \frac{\partial}{\partial x}(xe^y)$$

so (9) holds for all (x, y) and hence $\mathbf{F}$ is conservative on the entire xy-plane.

Vectors not to scale

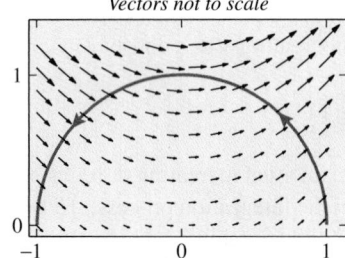

▲ **Figure 15.3.8**

Solution (b). From Formula (34) of Section 15.2, the work done by the field is

$$W = \int_C \mathbf{F} \cdot d\mathbf{r} = \int_C e^y \, dx + xe^y \, dy \tag{14}$$

However, the calculations involved in integrating along C are tedious, so it is preferable to apply Theorem 15.3.1, taking advantage of the fact that the field is conservative and the integral is independent of path. Thus, we write (14) as

$$W = \int_{(1,0)}^{(-1,0)} e^y \, dx + xe^y \, dy = \phi(-1, 0) - \phi(1, 0) \tag{15}$$

As illustrated in Example 4, we can find ϕ by integrating either of the equations

$$\frac{\partial \phi}{\partial x} = e^y \quad \text{and} \quad \frac{\partial \phi}{\partial y} = xe^y \tag{16}$$

We will integrate the first. We obtain

$$\phi = \int e^y \, dx = xe^y + k(y) \tag{17}$$

Differentiating this equation with respect to y and using the second equation in (16) yields

$$\frac{\partial \phi}{\partial y} = xe^y + k'(y) = xe^y$$

from which it follows that $k'(y) = 0$ or $k(y) = K$. Thus, from (17)

$$\phi = xe^y + K$$

and hence from (15)

$$W = \phi(-1, 0) - \phi(1, 0) = (-1)e^0 - 1e^0 = -2 \blacktriangleleft$$

■ CONSERVATIVE VECTOR FIELDS IN 3-SPACE

All of the results in this section have analogs in 3-space: Theorems 15.3.1 and 15.3.2 can be extended to vector fields in 3-space simply by adding a third variable and modifying the hypotheses appropriately. For example, in 3-space, Formula (3) becomes

$$\int_C \mathbf{F}(x, y, z) \cdot d\mathbf{r} = \phi(x_1, y_1, z_1) - \phi(x_0, y_0, z_0) \tag{18}$$

Theorem 15.3.3 can also be extended to vector fields in 3-space. We leave it for the exercises to show that if $\mathbf{F}(x, y, z) = f(x, y, z)\mathbf{i} + g(x, y, z)\mathbf{j} + h(x, y, z)\mathbf{k}$ is a conservative field, then

$$\frac{\partial f}{\partial y} = \frac{\partial g}{\partial x}, \quad \frac{\partial f}{\partial z} = \frac{\partial h}{\partial x}, \quad \frac{\partial g}{\partial z} = \frac{\partial h}{\partial y} \tag{19}$$

that is, curl $\mathbf{F} = \mathbf{0}$. Conversely, a vector field satisfying these conditions on a suitably restricted region is conservative on that region if f, g, and h are continuous and have continuous first partial derivatives in the region. Some problems involving Formulas (18) and (19) are given in the review exercises at the end of this chapter.

■ CONSERVATION OF ENERGY

If $\mathbf{F}(x, y, z)$ is a conservative force field with a potential function $\phi(x, y, z)$, then we call $V(x, y, z) = -\phi(x, y, z)$ the ***potential energy*** of the field at the point (x, y, z). Thus, it follows from the 3-space version of Theorem 15.3.1 that the work W done by $\mathbf{F}$ on a particle that moves along any path C from a point (x_0, y_0, z_0) to a point (x_1, y_1, z_1) is related to the potential energy by the equation

$$W = \int_C \mathbf{F} \cdot d\mathbf{r} = \phi(x_1, y_1, z_1) - \phi(x_0, y_0, z_0) = -[V(x_1, y_1, z_1) - V(x_0, y_0, z_0)] \tag{20}$$

That is, the work done by the field is the negative of the change in potential energy. In particular, it follows from the 3-space analog of Theorem 15.3.2 that if a particle traverses a piecewise smooth closed path in a conservative vector field, then the work done by the field is zero, and there is no change in potential energy. To take this a step further, suppose that a particle of mass m moves along any piecewise smooth curve (not necessarily closed) in a conservative force field $\mathbf{F}$, starting at (x_0, y_0, z_0) with speed v_i and ending at (x_1, y_1, z_1) with speed v_f. If $\mathbf{F}$ is the only force acting on the particle, then an argument similar to the derivation of Equation (6) in Section 6.6 shows that the work done on the particle by $\mathbf{F}$ is equal to the change in kinetic energy $\frac{1}{2}mv_f^2 - \frac{1}{2}mv_i^2$ of the particle. (An argument for smooth curves appears in the Making Connections exercises.) If we let V_i denote the potential energy at the starting point and V_f the potential energy at the final point, then it follows from (20) that

$$\tfrac{1}{2}mv_f^2 - \tfrac{1}{2}mv_i^2 = -[V_f - V_i]$$

which we can rewrite as

$$\tfrac{1}{2}mv_f^2 + V_f = \tfrac{1}{2}mv_i^2 + V_i$$

This equation states that the total energy of the particle (kinetic energy + potential energy) does not change as the particle moves along a path in a conservative vector field. This result, called the ***conservation of energy principle***, explains the origin of the term "conservative vector field."

✔ QUICK CHECK EXERCISES 15.3   (See page 1121 for answers.)

1. If C is a piecewise smooth curve from $(1, 2, 3)$ to $(4, 5, 6)$, then
$$\int_C dx + 2\,dy + 3\,dz = \underline{\hspace{1cm}}$$

2. If C is the portion of the circle $x^2 + y^2 = 1$ where $0 \le x$, oriented counterclockwise, and $f(x, y) = ye^x$, then
$$\int_C \nabla f \cdot d\mathbf{r} = \underline{\hspace{1cm}}$$

3. A potential function for the vector field
$$\mathbf{F}(x, y, z) = yz\mathbf{i} + (xz + z)\mathbf{j} + (xy + y + 1)\mathbf{k}$$
is $\phi(x, y, z) = \underline{\hspace{1cm}}$.

4. If a, b, and c are nonzero real numbers such that the vector field $x^5 y^a \mathbf{i} + x^b y^c \mathbf{j}$ is a conservative vector field, then
$$a = \underline{\hspace{1cm}}, \quad b = \underline{\hspace{1cm}}, \quad c = \underline{\hspace{1cm}}$$

EXERCISE SET 15.3   [c] CAS

1–6 Determine whether $\mathbf{F}$ is a conservative vector field. If so, find a potential function for it. ■

1. $\mathbf{F}(x, y) = x\mathbf{i} + y\mathbf{j}$ **2.** $\mathbf{F}(x, y) = 3y^2\mathbf{i} + 6xy\mathbf{j}$

3. $\mathbf{F}(x, y) = x^2 y\mathbf{i} + 5xy^2\mathbf{j}$

4. $\mathbf{F}(x, y) = e^x \cos y\mathbf{i} - e^x \sin y\mathbf{j}$

5. $\mathbf{F}(x, y) = (\cos y + y \cos x)\mathbf{i} + (\sin x - x \sin y)\mathbf{j}$

6. $\mathbf{F}(x, y) = x \ln y\mathbf{i} + y \ln x\mathbf{j}$

7. In each part, evaluate $\int_C 2xy^3\,dx + (1 + 3x^2y^2)\,dy$ over the curve C, and compare your answer with the result of Example 5.
   (a) C is the line segment from $(1, 4)$ to $(3, 1)$.
   (b) C consists of the line segment from $(1, 4)$ to $(1, 1)$, followed by the line segment from $(1, 1)$ to $(3, 1)$.

8. (a) Show that the line integral $\int_C y \sin x\,dx - \cos x\,dy$ is independent of the path.
   (b) Evaluate the integral in part (a) along the line segment from $(0, 1)$ to $(\pi, -1)$.
   (c) Evaluate the integral $\int_{(0,1)}^{(\pi,-1)} y \sin x\,dx - \cos x\,dy$ using Theorem 15.3.1, and confirm that the value is the same as that obtained in part (b).

9–14 Show that the integral is independent of the path, and use Theorem 15.3.1 to find its value. ■

9. $\int_{(1,2)}^{(4,0)} 3y\,dx + 3x\,dy$

10. $\int_{(0,0)}^{(1,\pi/2)} e^x \sin y\,dx + e^x \cos y\,dy$

11. $\int_{(0,0)}^{(3,2)} 2xe^y\,dx + x^2 e^y\,dy$

12. $\int_{(-1,2)}^{(0,1)} (3x - y + 1)\,dx - (x + 4y + 2)\,dy$

13. $\int_{(2,-2)}^{(-1,0)} 2xy^3\,dx + 3y^2x^2\,dy$

14. $\int_{(1,1)}^{(3,3)} \left(e^x \ln y - \dfrac{e^y}{x}\right) dx + \left(\dfrac{e^x}{y} - e^y \ln x\right) dy$, where x and y are positive.

15–18 Confirm that the force field $\mathbf{F}$ is conservative in some open connected region containing the points P and Q, and then find the work done by the force field on a particle moving along an arbitrary smooth curve in the region from P to Q. ■

15. $\mathbf{F}(x, y) = xy^2\mathbf{i} + x^2 y\mathbf{j}$; $P(1, 1)$, $Q(0, 0)$

16. $\mathbf{F}(x, y) = 2xy^3\mathbf{i} + 3x^2y^2\mathbf{j}$; $P(-3, 0)$, $Q(4, 1)$

17. $\mathbf{F}(x, y) = ye^{xy}\mathbf{i} + xe^{xy}\mathbf{j}$; $P(-1, 1)$, $Q(2, 0)$

18. $\mathbf{F}(x, y) = e^{-y} \cos x\mathbf{i} - e^{-y} \sin x\mathbf{j}$; $P(\pi/2, 1)$, $Q(-\pi/2, 0)$

19–22 True–False Determine whether the statement is true or false. Explain your answer. ■

19. If $\mathbf{F}$ is a vector field and there exists a closed curve C such that $\int_C \mathbf{F} \cdot d\mathbf{r} = 0$, then $\mathbf{F}$ is conservative.

20. If $\mathbf{F}(x, y) = ay\mathbf{i} + bx\mathbf{j}$ is a conservative vector field, then $a = b$.

21. If $\phi(x, y)$ is a potential function for a constant vector field, then the graph of $z = \phi(x, y)$ is a plane.

22. If $f(x, y)$ and $g(x, y)$ are differentiable functions defined on the xy-plane, and if $f_y(x, y) = g_x(x, y)$ for all (x, y), then there exists a function $\phi(x, y)$ such that $\phi_x(x, y) = f(x, y)$ and $\phi_y(x, y) = g(x, y)$.

23–24 Find the exact value of $\int_C \mathbf{F} \cdot d\mathbf{r}$ using any method. ■

23. $\mathbf{F}(x, y) = (e^y + ye^x)\mathbf{i} + (xe^y + e^x)\mathbf{j}$
   $C : \mathbf{r}(t) = \sin(\pi t/2)\mathbf{i} + \ln t\mathbf{j}$ $(1 \le t \le 2)$

24. $\mathbf{F}(x, y) = 2xy\mathbf{i} + (x^2 + \cos y)\mathbf{j}$
   $C : \mathbf{r}(t) = t\mathbf{i} + t \cos(t/3)\mathbf{j}$ $(0 \le t \le \pi)$

[c] 25. Use the numerical integration capability of a CAS or other calculating utility to approximate the value of the integral in Exercise 23 by direct integration. Confirm that the numerical approximation is consistent with the exact value.

[c] 26. Use the numerical integration capability of a CAS or other calculating utility to approximate the value of the integral in Exercise 24 by direct integration. Confirm that the numerical approximation is consistent with the exact value.

27–28 Is the vector field conservative? Explain. ■

27.

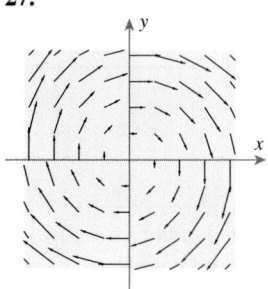

28.

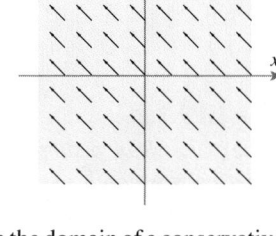

29. Suppose that C is a circle in the domain of a conservative vector field in the xy-plane whose component functions are continuous. Explain why there must be at least two points on C at which the vector field is normal to the circle.

30. Does the result in Exercise 29 remain true if the circle C is replaced by a square? Explain.

31. Prove: If
$$\mathbf{F}(x, y, z) = f(x, y, z)\mathbf{i} + g(x, y, z)\mathbf{j} + h(x, y, z)\mathbf{k}$$
is a conservative field and f, g, and h are continuous and have continuous first partial derivatives in a region, then
$$\frac{\partial f}{\partial y} = \frac{\partial g}{\partial x}, \quad \frac{\partial f}{\partial z} = \frac{\partial h}{\partial x}, \quad \frac{\partial g}{\partial z} = \frac{\partial h}{\partial y}$$
in the region.

32. Use the result in Exercise 31 to show that the integral
$$\int_C yz\,dx + xz\,dy + yx^2\,dz$$
is not independent of the path.

33. Find a nonzero function h for which
$$\mathbf{F}(x, y) = h(x)[x \sin y + y \cos y]\mathbf{i}$$
$$+ h(x)[x \cos y - y \sin y]\mathbf{j}$$
is conservative.

34. (a) In Example 3 of Section 15.1 we showed that
$$\phi(x, y) = -\frac{c}{(x^2 + y^2)^{1/2}}$$
is a potential function for the two-dimensional inverse-square field
$$\mathbf{F}(x, y) = \frac{c}{(x^2 + y^2)^{3/2}}(x\mathbf{i} + y\mathbf{j})$$
but we did not explain how the potential function $\phi(x, y)$ was obtained. Use Theorem 15.3.3 to show

that the two-dimensional inverse-square field is conservative everywhere except at the origin, and then use the method of Example 4 to derive the formula for $\phi(x, y)$.

(b) Use an appropriate generalization of the method of Example 4 to derive the potential function
$$\phi(x, y, z) = -\frac{c}{(x^2 + y^2 + z^2)^{1/2}}$$
for the three-dimensional inverse-square field given by Formula (5) of Section 15.1.

35–36 Use the result in Exercise 34(b). ■

35. In each part, find the work done by the three-dimensional inverse-square field
$$\mathbf{F}(\mathbf{r}) = \frac{1}{\|\mathbf{r}\|^3}\mathbf{r}$$
on a particle that moves along the curve C.
(a) C is the line segment from $P(1, 1, 2)$ to $Q(3, 2, 1)$.
(b) C is the curve
$$\mathbf{r}(t) = (2t^2 + 1)\mathbf{i} + (t^3 + 1)\mathbf{j} + (2 - \sqrt{t})\mathbf{k}$$
where $0 \le t \le 1$.
(c) C is the circle in the xy-plane of radius 1 centered at $(2, 0, 0)$ traversed counterclockwise.

36. Let $\mathbf{F}(x, y) = \dfrac{y}{x^2 + y^2}\mathbf{i} - \dfrac{x}{x^2 + y^2}\mathbf{j}$.
(a) Show that
$$\int_{C_1} \mathbf{F} \cdot d\mathbf{r} \neq \int_{C_2} \mathbf{F} \cdot d\mathbf{r}$$
if C_1 and C_2 are the semicircular paths from $(1, 0)$ to $(-1, 0)$ given by
$$C_1 : x = \cos t, \quad y = \sin t \qquad (0 \le t \le \pi)$$
$$C_2 : x = \cos t, \quad y = -\sin t \qquad (0 \le t \le \pi)$$
(b) Show that the components of $\mathbf{F}$ satisfy Formula (9).
(c) Do the results in parts (a) and (b) contradict Theorem 15.3.3? Explain.

37. Prove Theorem 15.3.1 if C is a piecewise smooth curve composed of smooth curves $C_1, C_2, \ldots, C_n$.

38. Prove that (*b*) implies (*c*) in Theorem 15.3.2. [*Hint:* Consider any two piecewise smooth oriented curves C_1 and C_2 in the region from a point P to a point Q, and integrate around the closed curve consisting of C_1 and $-C_2$.]

39. Complete the proof of Theorem 15.3.2 by showing that $\partial \phi / \partial y = g(x, y)$, where $\phi(x, y)$ is the function in (7).

40. **Writing** Describe the different methods available for evaluating the integral of a conservative vector field over a smooth curve.

41. **Writing** Discuss some of the ways that you can show a vector field is *not* conservative.

✔ **QUICK CHECK ANSWERS 15.3**

1. 18   **2.** 2   **3.** $xyz + yz + z$ **4.** 6, 6, 5

15.4 GREEN'S THEOREM

In this section we will discuss a remarkable and beautiful theorem that expresses a double integral over a plane region in terms of a line integral around its boundary.

■ GREEN'S THEOREM

> **15.4.1 THEOREM (*Green's Theorem*)** *Let R be a simply connected plane region whose boundary is a simple, closed, piecewise smooth curve C oriented counterclockwise. If $f(x, y)$ and $g(x, y)$ are continuous and have continuous first partial derivatives on some open set containing R, then*
>
> $$\int_C f(x, y)\, dx + g(x, y)\, dy = \iint_R \left(\frac{\partial g}{\partial x} - \frac{\partial f}{\partial y} \right) dA \qquad (1)$$

PROOF For simplicity, we will prove the theorem for regions that are simultaneously type I and type II (see Definition 14.2.1). Such a region is shown in Figure 15.4.1. The crux of the proof is to show that

$$\int_C f(x, y)\, dx = - \iint_R \frac{\partial f}{\partial y}\, dA \quad \text{and} \quad \int_C g(x, y)\, dy = \iint_R \frac{\partial g}{\partial x}\, dA \qquad (2\text{–}3)$$

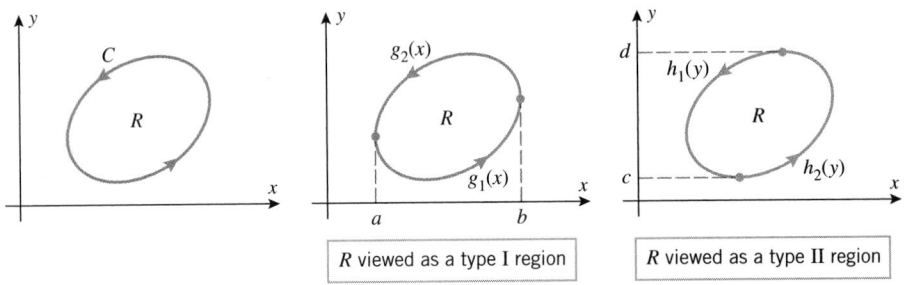

▶ **Figure 15.4.1**

R viewed as a type I region

R viewed as a type II region

To prove (2), view R as a type I region and let C_1 and C_2 be the lower and upper boundary curves, oriented as in Figure 15.4.2. Then

$$\int_C f(x, y)\, dx = \int_{C_1} f(x, y)\, dx + \int_{C_2} f(x, y)\, dx$$

or, equivalently,

$$\int_C f(x, y)\, dx = \int_{C_1} f(x, y)\, dx - \int_{-C_2} f(x, y)\, dx \qquad (4)$$

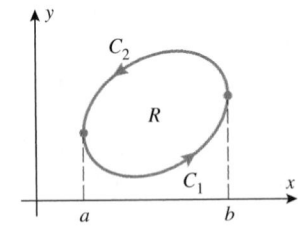

▲ **Figure 15.4.2**

(This step will help simplify our calculations since C_1 and $-C_2$ are then both oriented left to right.) The curves C_1 and $-C_2$ can be expressed parametrically as

$$C_1 : x = t, \quad y = g_1(t) \qquad (a \le t \le b)$$
$$-C_2 : x = t, \quad y = g_2(t) \qquad (a \le t \le b)$$

Thus, we can rewrite (4) as

$$\int_C f(x, y)\, dx = \int_a^b f(t, g_1(t)) x'(t)\, dt - \int_a^b f(t, g_2(t)) x'(t)\, dt$$

$$= \int_a^b f(t, g_1(t))\, dt - \int_a^b f(t, g_2(t))\, dt$$

$$= -\int_a^b [f(t, g_2(t)) - f(t, g_1(t))]\, dt$$

$$= -\int_a^b \left[f(t, y) \right]_{y=g_1(t)}^{y=g_2(t)} dt = -\int_a^b \left[\int_{g_1(t)}^{g_2(t)} \frac{\partial f}{\partial y}\, dy \right] dt$$

$$= -\int_a^b \int_{g_1(x)}^{g_2(x)} \frac{\partial f}{\partial y}\, dy\, dx = -\iint_R \frac{\partial f}{\partial y}\, dA$$

Since $x = t$

The proof of (3) is obtained similarly by treating R as a type II region. We omit the details. ∎

Supply the details for the proof of (3).

▶ **Example 1**   Use Green's Theorem to evaluate

$$\int_C x^2 y\, dx + x\, dy$$

along the triangular path shown in Figure 15.4.3.

Solution.   Since $f(x, y) = x^2 y$ and $g(x, y) = x$, it follows from (1) that

$$\int_C x^2 y\, dx + x\, dy = \iint_R \left[\frac{\partial}{\partial x}(x) - \frac{\partial}{\partial y}(x^2 y) \right] dA = \int_0^1 \int_0^{2x} (1 - x^2)\, dy\, dx$$

$$= \int_0^1 (2x - 2x^3)\, dx = \left[x^2 - \frac{x^4}{2} \right]_0^1 = \frac{1}{2}$$

This agrees with the result obtained in Example 10 of Section 15.2, where we evaluated the line integral directly. Note how much simpler this solution is. ◀

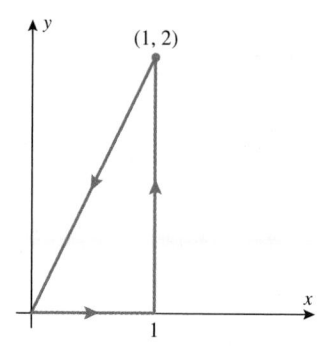
(1, 2)

▲ **Figure 15.4.3**

George Green (1793–1841) English mathematician and physicist. Green left school at an early age to work in his father's bakery and consequently had little early formal education. When his father opened a mill, the boy used the top room as a study in which he taught himself physics and mathematics from library books. In 1828 Green published his most important work, *An Essay on the Application of Mathematical Analysis to the Theories of Electricity and Magnetism.* Although Green's Theorem appeared in that paper, the result went virtually unnoticed because of the small pressrun and local distribution. Following the death of his father in 1829, Green was urged by friends to seek a college education. In 1833, after four years of self-study to close the gaps in his elementary education, Green was admitted to Caius College, Cambridge. He graduated four years later, but with a disappointing performance on his final examinations—possibly because he was more interested in his own research. After a succession of works on light and sound, he was named to be Perse Fellow at Caius College. Two years later he died. In 1845, four years after his death, his paper of 1828 was published and the theories developed therein by this obscure, self-taught baker's son helped pave the way to the modern theories of electricity and magnetism.

■ A NOTATION FOR LINE INTEGRALS AROUND SIMPLE CLOSED CURVES

It is common practice to denote a line integral around a simple closed curve by an integral sign with a superimposed circle. With this notation Formula (1) would be written as

$$\oint_C f(x, y)\, dx + g(x, y)\, dy = \iint_R \left(\frac{\partial g}{\partial x} - \frac{\partial f}{\partial y} \right) dA$$

Sometimes a direction arrow is added to the circle to indicate whether the integration is clockwise or counterclockwise. Thus, if we wanted to emphasize the counterclockwise direction of integration required by Theorem 15.4.1, we could express (1) as

$$\oint_C f(x, y)\, dx + g(x, y)\, dy = \iint_R \left(\frac{\partial g}{\partial x} - \frac{\partial f}{\partial y} \right) dA \tag{5}$$

■ FINDING WORK USING GREEN'S THEOREM

It follows from Formula (26) of Section 15.2 that the integral on the left side of (5) is the work performed by the force field $\mathbf{F}(x, y) = f(x, y)\mathbf{i} + g(x, y)\mathbf{j}$ on a particle moving counterclockwise around the simple closed curve C. In the case where this vector field is conservative, it follows from Theorem 15.3.2 that the integrand in the double integral on the right side of (5) is zero, so the work performed by the field is zero, as expected. For vector fields that are not conservative, it is often more efficient to calculate the work around simple closed curves by using Green's Theorem than by parametrizing the curve.

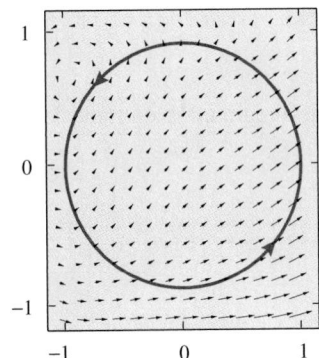

▲ **Figure 15.4.4**

▶ **Example 2** Find the work done by the force field

$$\mathbf{F}(x, y) = (e^x - y^3)\mathbf{i} + (\cos y + x^3)\mathbf{j}$$

on a particle that travels once around the unit circle $x^2 + y^2 = 1$ in the counterclockwise direction (Figure 15.4.4).

Solution. The work W performed by the field is

$$W = \oint_C \mathbf{F} \cdot d\mathbf{r} = \oint_C (e^x - y^3)\, dx + (\cos y + x^3)\, dy$$

$$= \iint_R \left[\frac{\partial}{\partial x}(\cos y + x^3) - \frac{\partial}{\partial y}(e^x - y^3) \right] dA \qquad \boxed{\text{Green's Theorem}}$$

$$= \iint_R (3x^2 + 3y^2)\, dA = 3 \iint_R (x^2 + y^2)\, dA$$

$$= 3 \int_0^{2\pi} \int_0^1 (r^2) r\, dr\, d\theta = \frac{3}{4} \int_0^{2\pi} d\theta = \frac{3\pi}{2} \quad ◄$$

> We converted to polar coordinates.

■ FINDING AREAS USING GREEN'S THEOREM

Green's Theorem leads to some useful new formulas for the area A of a region R that satisfies the conditions of the theorem. Two such formulas can be obtained as follows:

$$A = \iint_R dA = \oint_C x\, dy \quad \text{and} \quad A = \iint_R dA = \oint_C (-y)\, dx$$

> Set $f(x, y) = 0$ and $g(x, y) = x$ in (1).

> Set $f(x, y) = -y$ and $g(x, y) = 0$ in (1).

A third formula can be obtained by adding these two equations together. Thus, we have the following three formulas that express the area A of a region R in terms of line integrals around the boundary:

$$A = \oint_C x\,dy = -\oint_C y\,dx = \frac{1}{2}\oint_C -y\,dx + x\,dy \qquad (6)$$

> Although the third formula in (6) looks more complicated than the other two, it often leads to simpler integrations. Each has advantages in certain situations.

▶ **Example 3**   Use a line integral to find the area enclosed by the ellipse

$$\frac{x^2}{a^2} + \frac{y^2}{b^2} = 1$$

Solution.   The ellipse, with counterclockwise orientation, can be represented parametrically by

$$x = a\cos t, \quad y = b\sin t \qquad (0 \le t \le 2\pi)$$

If we denote this curve by C, then from the third formula in (6) the area A enclosed by the ellipse is

$$A = \frac{1}{2}\oint_C -y\,dx + x\,dy$$

$$= \frac{1}{2}\int_0^{2\pi} [(-b\sin t)(-a\sin t) + (a\cos t)(b\cos t)]\,dt$$

$$= \frac{1}{2}ab\int_0^{2\pi}(\sin^2 t + \cos^2 t)\,dt = \frac{1}{2}ab\int_0^{2\pi}dt = \pi ab \quad ◀$$

■ **GREEN'S THEOREM FOR MULTIPLY CONNECTED REGIONS**
Recall that a plane region is said to be simply connected if it has no holes and is said to be multiply connected if it has one or more holes (see Figure 15.3.6). At the beginning of this section we stated Green's Theorem for a counterclockwise integration around the boundary of a simply connected region R (Theorem 15.4.1). Our next goal is to extend this theorem to multiply connected regions. To make this extension we will need to assume that *the region lies on the left when any portion of the boundary is traversed in the direction of its orientation*. This implies that the outer boundary curve of the region is oriented counterclockwise and the boundary curves that enclose holes have clockwise orientation (Figure 15.4.5a). If all portions of the boundary of a multiply connected region R are oriented in this way, then we say that the boundary of R has ***positive orientation***.

We will now derive a version of Green's Theorem that applies to multiply connected regions with positively oriented boundaries. For simplicity, we will consider a multiply connected region R with one hole, and we will assume that $f(x, y)$ and $g(x, y)$ have continuous first partial derivatives on some open set containing R. As shown in Figure 15.4.5b, let us divide R into two regions R' and R'' by introducing two "cuts" in R. The cuts are shown as line segments, but any piecewise smooth curves will suffice. If we assume that f and g satisfy the hypotheses of Green's Theorem on R (and hence on R' and R''), then we can apply this theorem to both R' and R'' to obtain

$$\iint_R \left(\frac{\partial g}{\partial x} - \frac{\partial f}{\partial y}\right) dA = \iint_{R'} \left(\frac{\partial g}{\partial x} - \frac{\partial f}{\partial y}\right) dA + \iint_{R''} \left(\frac{\partial g}{\partial x} - \frac{\partial f}{\partial y}\right) dA$$

$$= \underbrace{\oint f(x, y)\,dx + g(x, y)\,dy}_{\substack{\text{Boundary} \\ \text{of } R'}} + \underbrace{\oint f(x, y)\,dx + g(x, y)\,dy}_{\substack{\text{Boundary} \\ \text{of } R''}}$$

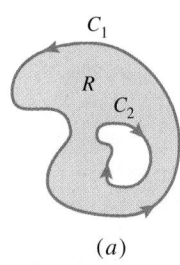

C_1

R

C_2

(a)

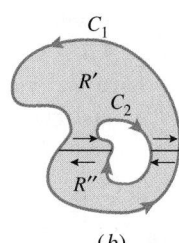

C_1

R'

C_2

R''

(b)

▲ **Figure 15.4.5**

However, the two line integrals are taken in opposite directions along the cuts, and hence cancel there, leaving only the contributions along C_1 and C_2. Thus,

$$\iint\limits_R \left(\frac{\partial g}{\partial x} - \frac{\partial f}{\partial y} \right) dA = \oint_{C_1} f(x, y)\,dx + g(x, y)\,dy + \oint_{C_2} f(x, y)\,dx + g(x, y)\,dy \quad (7)$$

which is an extension of Green's Theorem to a multiply connected region with one hole. Observe that the integral around the outer boundary is taken counterclockwise and the integral around the hole is taken clockwise. More generally, if R is a multiply connected region with n holes, then the analog of (7) involves a sum of $n + 1$ integrals, one taken counterclockwise around the outer boundary of R and the rest taken clockwise around the holes.

▶ **Example 4**   Evaluate the integral

$$\oint_C \frac{-y\,dx + x\,dy}{x^2 + y^2}$$

if C is a piecewise smooth simple closed curve oriented counterclockwise such that (a) C does not enclose the origin and (b) C encloses the origin.

Solution (a).   Let

$$f(x, y) = -\frac{y}{x^2 + y^2}, \quad g(x, y) = \frac{x}{x^2 + y^2} \quad (8)$$

so that

$$\frac{\partial g}{\partial x} = \frac{y^2 - x^2}{(x^2 + y^2)^2} = \frac{\partial f}{\partial y}$$

if x and y are not both zero. Thus, if C does not enclose the origin, we have

$$\frac{\partial g}{\partial x} - \frac{\partial f}{\partial y} = 0 \quad (9)$$

on the simply connected region enclosed by C, and hence the given integral is zero by Green's Theorem.

Solution (b).   Unlike the situation in part (a), we cannot apply Green's Theorem directly because the functions $f(x, y)$ and $g(x, y)$ in (8) are discontinuous at the origin. Our problems are further compounded by the fact that we do not have a specific curve C that we can parametrize to evaluate the integral. Our strategy for circumventing these problems will be to replace C with a specific curve that produces the same value for the integral and then use that curve for the evaluation. To obtain such a curve, we will apply Green's Theorem for multiply connected regions to a region that does not contain the origin. For this purpose we construct a circle C_a with *clockwise* orientation, centered at the origin, and with sufficiently small radius a that it lies inside the region enclosed by C (Figure 15.4.6). This creates a multiply connected region R whose boundary curves C and C_a have the orientations required by Formula (7) and such that within R the functions $f(x, y)$ and $g(x, y)$ in (8) satisfy the hypotheses of Green's Theorem (the origin does not belong to R). Thus, it follows from (7) and (9) that

$$\oint_C \frac{-y\,dx + x\,dy}{x^2 + y^2} + \oint_{C_a} \frac{-y\,dx + x\,dy}{x^2 + y^2} = \iint\limits_R 0\,dA = 0$$

It follows from this equation that

$$\oint_C \frac{-y\,dx + x\,dy}{x^2 + y^2} = -\oint_{C_a} \frac{-y\,dx + x\,dy}{x^2 + y^2}$$

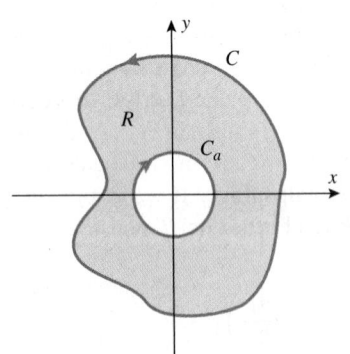

▲ **Figure 15.4.6**

which we can rewrite as

$$\oint_C \frac{-y\,dx + x\,dy}{x^2 + y^2} = \oint_{-C_a} \frac{-y\,dx + x\,dy}{x^2 + y^2}$$

> Reversing the orientation of C_a reverses the sign of the integral.

But C_a has clockwise orientation, so $-C_a$ has counterclockwise orientation. Thus, we have shown that the original integral can be evaluated by integrating counterclockwise around a circle of radius a that is centered at the origin and lies within the region enclosed by C. Such a circle can be expressed parametrically as $x = a\cos t$, $y = a\sin t$ $(0 \le t \le 2\pi)$; and hence

$$\oint_C \frac{-y\,dx + x\,dy}{x^2 + y^2} = \int_0^{2\pi} \frac{(-a\sin t)(-a\sin t)\,dt + (a\cos t)(a\cos t)\,dt}{(a\cos t)^2 + (a\sin t)^2}$$

$$= \int_0^{2\pi} 1\,dt = 2\pi$$

✔ QUICK CHECK EXERCISES 15.4   *(See page 1129 for answers.)*

1. If C is the square with vertices $(\pm 1, \pm 1)$ oriented counterclockwise, then

$$\int_C -y\,dx + x\,dy = \underline{\qquad}$$

2. If C is the triangle with vertices $(0,0)$, $(1,0)$, and $(1,1)$ oriented counterclockwise, then

$$\int_C 2xy\,dx + (x^2 + x)\,dy = \underline{\qquad}$$

3. If C is the unit circle centered at the origin and oriented counterclockwise, then

$$\int_C (y^3 - y - x)\,dx + (x^3 + x + y)\,dy = \underline{\qquad}$$

4. What region R and choice of functions $f(x, y)$ and $g(x, y)$ allow us to use Formula (1) of Theorem 15.4.1 to claim that

$$\int_0^1 \int_0^{\sqrt{1-x^2}} (2x + 2y)\,dy\,dx = \int_0^{\pi/2} (\sin^3 t + \cos^3 t)\,dt?$$

EXERCISE SET 15.4 $\boxed{c}$ CAS

1–2 Evaluate the line integral using Green's Theorem and check the answer by evaluating it directly. ▨

1. $\oint_C y^2\,dx + x^2\,dy$, where C is the square with vertices $(0, 0)$, $(1, 0)$, $(1, 1)$, and $(0, 1)$ oriented counterclockwise.

2. $\oint_C y\,dx + x\,dy$, where C is the unit circle oriented counterclockwise.

3–13 Use Green's Theorem to evaluate the integral. In each exercise, assume that the curve C is oriented counterclockwise. ▨

3. $\oint_C 3xy\,dx + 2xy\,dy$, where C is the rectangle bounded by $x = -2$, $x = 4$, $y = 1$, and $y = 2$.

4. $\oint_C (x^2 - y^2)\,dx + x\,dy$, where C is the circle $x^2 + y^2 = 9$.

5. $\oint_C x\cos y\,dx - y\sin x\,dy$, where C is the square with vertices $(0, 0)$, $(\pi/2, 0)$, $(\pi/2, \pi/2)$, and $(0, \pi/2)$.

6. $\oint_C y\tan^2 x\,dx + \tan x\,dy$, where C is the circle $x^2 + (y + 1)^2 = 1$.

7. $\oint_C (x^2 - y)\,dx + x\,dy$, where C is the circle $x^2 + y^2 = 4$.

8. $\oint_C (e^x + y^2)\,dx + (e^y + x^2)\,dy$, where C is the boundary of the region between $y = x^2$ and $y = x$.

9. $\oint_C \ln(1 + y)\,dx - \frac{xy}{1 + y}\,dy$, where C is the triangle with vertices $(0, 0)$, $(2, 0)$, and $(0, 4)$.

10. $\oint_C x^2 y\,dx - y^2 x\,dy$, where C is the boundary of the region in the first quadrant, enclosed between the coordinate axes and the circle $x^2 + y^2 = 16$.

11. $\oint_C \tan^{-1} y\,dx - \frac{y^2 x}{1 + y^2}\,dy$, where C is the square with vertices $(0, 0)$, $(1, 0)$, $(1, 1)$, and $(0, 1)$.

12. $\oint_C \cos x \sin y \, dx + \sin x \cos y \, dy$, where C is the triangle with vertices $(0, 0)$, $(3, 3)$, and $(0, 3)$.

13. $\oint_C x^2 y \, dx + (y + xy^2) \, dy$, where C is the boundary of the region enclosed by $y = x^2$ and $x = y^2$.

14. Let C be the boundary of the region enclosed between $y = x^2$ and $y = 2x$. Assuming that C is oriented counterclockwise, evaluate the following integrals by Green's Theorem:

(a) $\oint_C (6xy - y^2) \, dx$ (b) $\oint_C (6xy - y^2) \, dy$.

15–18 True–False Determine whether the statement is true or false. Explain your answer. (In Exercises 16–18, assume that C is a simple, smooth, closed curve, oriented counterclockwise.)

15. Green's Theorem allows us to replace any line integral by a double integral.

16. If

$$\int_C f(x, y) \, dx + g(x, y) \, dy = 0$$

then $\partial g / \partial x = \partial f / \partial y$ at all points in the region bounded by C.

17. It must be the case that

$$\int_C x \, dy > 0$$

18. It must be the case that

$$\int_C e^{x^2} \, dx + \sin y^3 \, dy = 0$$

c **19.** Use a CAS to check Green's Theorem by evaluating both integrals in the equation

$$\oint_C e^y \, dx + ye^x \, dy = \iint_R \left[\frac{\partial}{\partial x} (ye^x) - \frac{\partial}{\partial y} (e^y) \right] dA$$

where
(a) C is the circle $x^2 + y^2 = 1$
(b) C is the boundary of the region enclosed by $y = x^2$ and $x = y^2$.

20. In Example 3, we used Green's Theorem to obtain the area of an ellipse. Obtain this area using the first and then the second formula in (6).

21. Use a line integral to find the area of the region enclosed by the astroid

$$x = a \cos^3 \phi, \quad y = a \sin^3 \phi \quad (0 \le \phi \le 2\pi)$$

22. Use a line integral to find the area of the triangle with vertices $(0, 0)$, $(a, 0)$, and $(0, b)$, where $a > 0$ and $b > 0$.

23. Use the formula

$$A = \frac{1}{2} \oint_C -y \, dx + x \, dy$$

to find the area of the region swept out by the line from the origin to the ellipse $x = a \cos t$, $y = b \sin t$ if t varies from $t = 0$ to $t = t_0$ ($0 \le t_0 \le 2\pi$).

24. Use the formula

$$A = \frac{1}{2} \oint_C -y \, dx + x \, dy$$

to find the area of the region swept out by the line from the origin to the hyperbola $x = a \cosh t$, $y = b \sinh t$ if t varies from $t = 0$ to $t = t_0$ ($t_0 \ge 0$).

FOCUS ON CONCEPTS

25. Suppose that $\mathbf{F}(x, y) = f(x, y)\mathbf{i} + g(x, y)\mathbf{j}$ is a vector field whose component functions f and g have continuous first partial derivatives. Let C denote a simple, closed, piecewise smooth curve oriented counterclockwise that bounds a region R contained in the domain of $\mathbf{F}$. We can think of $\mathbf{F}$ as a vector field in 3-space by writing it as

$$\mathbf{F}(x, y, z) = f(x, y)\mathbf{i} + g(x, y)\mathbf{j} + 0\mathbf{k}$$

With this convention, explain why

$$\int_C \mathbf{F} \cdot d\mathbf{r} = \iint_R \text{curl } \mathbf{F} \cdot \mathbf{k} \, dA$$

26. Suppose that $\mathbf{F}(x, y) = f(x, y)\mathbf{i} + g(x, y)\mathbf{j}$ is a vector field on the xy-plane and that f and g have continuous first partial derivatives with $f_y = g_x$ everywhere. Use Green's Theorem to explain why

$$\int_{C_1} \mathbf{F} \cdot d\mathbf{r} = \int_{C_2} \mathbf{F} \cdot d\mathbf{r}$$

where C_1 and C_2 are the oriented curves in the accompanying figure. [*Note:* Compare this result with Theorems 15.3.2 and 15.3.3.]

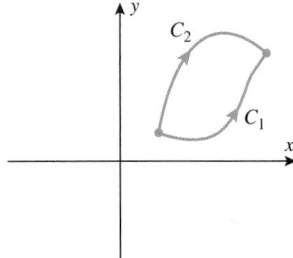

◀ **Figure Ex-26**

27. Suppose that $f(x)$ and $g(x)$ are continuous functions with $g(x) \le f(x)$. Let R denote the region bounded by the graph of f, the graph of g, and the vertical lines $x = a$ and $x = b$. Let C denote the boundary of R oriented counterclockwise. What familiar formula results from applying Green's Theorem to $\int_C (-y) \, dx$?

28. In the accompanying figure on the next page, C is a smooth oriented curve from $P(x_0, y_0)$ to $Q(x_1, y_1)$ that is contained inside the rectangle with corners at the origin and Q and outside the rectangle with corners at the origin and P.
(a) What region in the figure has area $\int_C x \, dy$?
(b) What region in the figure has area $\int_C y \, dx$?
(c) Express $\int_C x \, dy + \int_C y \, dx$ in terms of the coordinates of P and Q. *(cont.)*

(d) Interpret the result of part (c) in terms of the Fundamental Theorem of Line Integrals.
(e) Interpret the result in part (c) in terms of integration by parts.

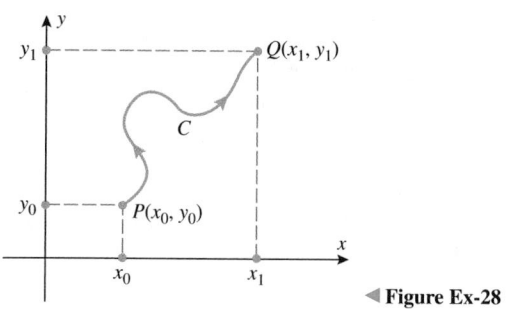

◀ Figure Ex-28

29–30 Use Green's Theorem to find the work done by the force field **F** on a particle that moves along the stated path. ■

29. $\mathbf{F}(x, y) = xy\mathbf{i} + \left(\frac{1}{2}x^2 + xy\right)\mathbf{j}$; the particle starts at $(5, 0)$, traverses the upper semicircle $x^2 + y^2 = 25$, and returns to its starting point along the x-axis.

30. $\mathbf{F}(x, y) = \sqrt{y}\,\mathbf{i} + \sqrt{x}\,\mathbf{j}$; the particle moves counterclockwise one time around the closed curve given by the equations $y = 0$, $x = 2$, and $y = x^3/4$.

31. Evaluate $\oint_C y\,dx - x\,dy$, where C is the cardioid

$$r = a(1 + \cos\theta) \quad (0 \le \theta \le 2\pi)$$

32. Let R be a plane region with area A whose boundary is a piecewise smooth, simple, closed curve C. Use Green's Theorem to prove that the centroid $(\bar{x}, \bar{y})$ of R is given by

$$\bar{x} = \frac{1}{2A}\oint_C x^2\,dy, \quad \bar{y} = -\frac{1}{2A}\oint_C y^2\,dx$$

33–36 Use the result in Exercise 32 to find the centroid of the region. ■

33.

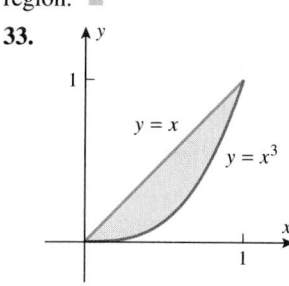

34.

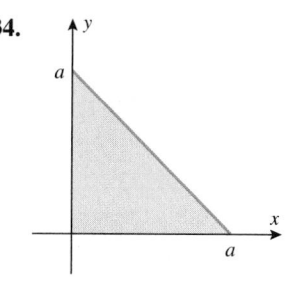

35.

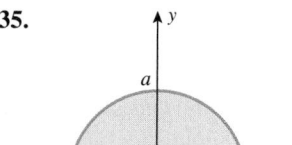

36.

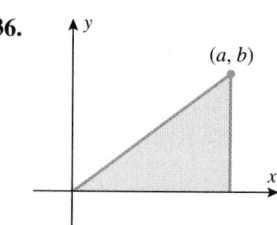

37. Find a simple closed curve C with counterclockwise orientation that maximizes the value of

$$\oint_C \frac{1}{3}y^3\,dx + \left(x - \frac{1}{3}x^3\right)\,dy$$

and explain your reasoning.

38. (a) Let C be the line segment from a point (a, b) to a point (c, d). Show that

$$\int_C -y\,dx + x\,dy = ad - bc$$

(b) Use the result in part (a) to show that the area A of a triangle with successive vertices (x_1, y_1), (x_2, y_2), and (x_3, y_3) going counterclockwise is

$$A = \frac{1}{2}[(x_1y_2 - x_2y_1) + (x_2y_3 - x_3y_2) + (x_3y_1 - x_1y_3)]$$

(c) Find a formula for the area of a polygon with successive vertices (x_1, y_1), (x_2, y_2), ..., (x_n, y_n) going counterclockwise.

(d) Use the result in part (c) to find the area of a quadrilateral with vertices $(0, 0)$, $(3, 4)$, $(-2, 2)$, $(-1, 0)$.

39–40 Evaluate the integral $\int_C \mathbf{F} \cdot d\mathbf{r}$, where C is the boundary of the region R and C is oriented so that the region is on the left when the boundary is traversed in the direction of its orientation. ■

39. $\mathbf{F}(x, y) = (x^2 + y)\mathbf{i} + (4x - \cos y)\mathbf{j}$; C is the boundary of the region R that is inside the square with vertices $(0, 0)$, $(5, 0)$, $(5, 5)$, $(0, 5)$ but is outside the rectangle with vertices $(1, 1)$, $(3, 1)$, $(3, 2)$, $(1, 2)$.

40. $\mathbf{F}(x, y) = (e^{-x} + 3y)\mathbf{i} + x\mathbf{j}$; C is the boundary of the region R inside the circle $x^2 + y^2 = 16$ and outside the circle $x^2 - 2x + y^2 = 3$.

41. Writing Discuss the role of the Fundamental Theorem of Calculus in the proof of Green's Theorem.

42. Writing Use the Internet or other sources to find information about "planimeters," and then write a paragraph that describes the relationship between these devices and Green's Theorem.

✔ **QUICK CHECK ANSWERS 15.4**

1. 8   **2.** $\frac{1}{2}$ **3.** 2π **4.** R is the region $x^2 + y^2 \le 1$ $(0 \le x, 0 \le y)$ and $f(x, y) = -y^2$, $g(x, y) = x^2$.

In previous sections we considered four kinds of integrals—integrals over intervals, double integrals over two-dimensional regions, triple integrals over three-dimensional solids, and line integrals along curves in two- or three-dimensional space. In this section we will discuss integrals over surfaces in three-dimensional space. Such integrals occur in problems involving fluid and heat flow, electricity, magnetism, mass, and center of gravity.

■ **DEFINITION OF A SURFACE INTEGRAL**

In this section we will define what it means to integrate a function $f(x, y, z)$ over a smooth parametric surface σ. To motivate the definition we will consider the problem of finding the mass of a curved lamina whose density function (mass per unit area) is known. Recall that in Section 6.7 we defined a *lamina* to be an idealized flat object that is thin enough to be viewed as a plane region. Analogously, a ***curved lamina*** is an idealized object that is thin enough to be viewed as a surface in 3-space. A curved lamina may look like a bent plate, as in Figure 15.5.1, or it may enclose a region in 3-space, like the shell of an egg. We will model the lamina by a smooth parametric surface σ. Given any point (x, y, z) on σ, we let $f(x, y, z)$ denote the corresponding value of the density function. To compute the mass of the lamina, we proceed as follows:

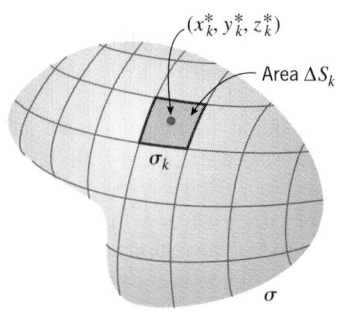

The thickness of a curved lamina is negligible.

▲ **Figure 15.5.1**

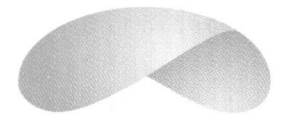

- As shown in Figure 15.5.2, we divide σ into n very small patches $\sigma_1, \sigma_2, \ldots, \sigma_n$ with areas $\Delta S_1, \Delta S_2, \ldots, \Delta S_n$, respectively. Let (x_k^*, y_k^*, z_k^*) be a sample point in the kth patch with ΔM_k the mass of the corresponding section.

- If the dimensions of σ_k are very small, the value of f will not vary much along the kth section and we can approximate f along this section by the value $f(x_k^*, y_k^*, z_k^*)$. It follows that the mass of the kth section can be approximated by

$$\Delta M_k \approx f(x_k^*, y_k^*, z_k^*)\Delta S_k$$

- The mass M of the entire lamina can then be approximated by

$$M = \sum_{k=1}^{n} \Delta M_k \approx \sum_{k=1}^{n} f(x_k^*, y_k^*, z_k^*)\Delta S_k \tag{1}$$

- We will use the expression $n \to \infty$ to indicate the process of increasing n in such a way that the maximum dimension of each patch approaches 0. It is plausible that the error in (1) will approach 0 as $n \to \infty$ and the exact value of M will be given by

$$M = \lim_{n \to \infty} \sum_{k=1}^{n} f(x_k^*, y_k^*, z_k^*)\Delta S_k \tag{2}$$

▲ **Figure 15.5.2**

The limit in (2) is very similar to the limit used to find the mass of a thin wire [Formula (2) in Section 15.2]. By analogy to Definition 15.2.1, we make the following definition.

15.5.1 **DEFINITION** If σ is a smooth parametric surface, then the ***surface integral*** of $f(x, y, z)$ over σ is

$$\iint\limits_{\sigma} f(x, y, z)\, dS = \lim_{n \to \infty} \sum_{k=1}^{n} f(x_k^*, y_k^*, z_k^*)\Delta S_k \tag{3}$$

provided this limit exists and does not depend on the way the subdivisions of σ are made or how the sample points (x_k^*, y_k^*, z_k^*) are chosen.

It can be shown that the integral of f over σ exists if f is continuous on σ.

We see from (2) and Definition 15.5.1 that if σ models a lamina and if $f(x, y, z)$ is the density function of the lamina, then the mass M of the lamina is given by

$$M = \iint\limits_{\sigma} f(x, y, z) \, dS \qquad (4)$$

That is, to obtain the mass of a lamina, we integrate the density function over the smooth surface that models the lamina.

Note that if σ is a smooth surface of surface area S, and f is identically 1, then it immediately follows from Definition 15.5.1 that

$$\iint\limits_{\sigma} dS = \lim_{n \to \infty} \sum_{k=1}^{n} \Delta S_k = \lim_{n \to \infty} S = S \qquad (5)$$

■ EVALUATING SURFACE INTEGRALS

There are various procedures for evaluating surface integrals that depend on how the surface σ is represented. The following theorem provides a method for evaluating a surface integral when σ is represented parametrically.

15.5.2 THEOREM *Let σ be a smooth parametric surface whose vector equation is*

$$\mathbf{r} = x(u, v)\mathbf{i} + y(u, v)\mathbf{j} + z(u, v)\mathbf{k}$$

where (u, v) varies over a region R in the uv-plane. If $f(x, y, z)$ is continuous on σ, then

$$\iint\limits_{\sigma} f(x, y, z) \, dS = \iint\limits_{R} f(x(u, v), y(u, v), z(u, v)) \left\| \frac{\partial \mathbf{r}}{\partial u} \times \frac{\partial \mathbf{r}}{\partial v} \right\| dA \qquad (6)$$

Explain how to use Formula (6) to confirm Formula (5).

To motivate this result, suppose that the parameter domain R is subdivided as in Figure 14.4.14, and suppose that the point (x_k^*, y_k^*, z_k^*) in (3) corresponds to parameter values of u_k^* and v_k^*. If we use Formula (11) of Section 14.4 to approximate ΔS_k, and if we assume that the errors in the approximations approach zero as $n \to +\infty$, then it follows from (3) that

$$\iint\limits_{\sigma} f(x, y, z) \, dS = \lim_{n \to +\infty} \sum_{k=1}^{n} f(x(u_k^*, v_k^*), y(u_k^*, v_k^*), z(u_k^*, v_k^*)) \left\| \frac{\partial \mathbf{r}}{\partial u} \times \frac{\partial \mathbf{r}}{\partial v} \right\| \Delta A_k$$

which suggests Formula (6).

Although Theorem 15.5.2 is stated for *smooth* parametric surfaces, Formula (6) remains valid even if $\partial \mathbf{r}/\partial u \times \partial \mathbf{r}/\partial v$ is allowed to equal $\mathbf{0}$ on the boundary of R.

▶ **Example 1**   Evaluate the surface integral $\displaystyle\iint_\sigma x^2 \, dS$ over the sphere $x^2 + y^2 + z^2 = 1$.

Solution.   As in Example 11 of Section 14.4 (with $a = 1$), the sphere is the graph of the vector-valued function

$$\mathbf{r}(\phi, \theta) = \sin\phi\cos\theta\mathbf{i} + \sin\phi\sin\theta\mathbf{j} + \cos\phi\mathbf{k} \quad (0 \le \phi \le \pi, \ 0 \le \theta \le 2\pi) \quad (7)$$

and

$$\left\| \frac{\partial \mathbf{r}}{\partial \phi} \times \frac{\partial \mathbf{r}}{\partial \theta} \right\| = \sin\phi$$

Explain why the function $\mathbf{r}(\phi, \theta)$ given in (7) fails to be smooth on its domain.

From the $\mathbf{i}$-component of $\mathbf{r}$, the integrand in the surface integral can be expressed in terms of ϕ and θ as $x^2 = \sin^2\phi\cos^2\theta$. Thus, it follows from (6) with ϕ and θ in place of u and v and R as the rectangular region in the $\phi\theta$-plane determined by the inequalities in (7) that

$$\iint_\sigma x^2 \, dS = \iint_R (\sin^2\phi\cos^2\theta) \left\| \frac{\partial \mathbf{r}}{\partial \phi} \times \frac{\partial \mathbf{r}}{\partial \theta} \right\| dA$$

$$= \int_0^{2\pi} \int_0^\pi \sin^3\phi\cos^2\theta \, d\phi \, d\theta$$

$$= \int_0^{2\pi} \left[\int_0^\pi \sin^3\phi \, d\phi \right] \cos^2\theta \, d\theta$$

$$= \int_0^{2\pi} \left[\frac{1}{3}\cos^3\phi - \cos\phi \right]_0^\pi \cos^2\theta \, d\theta \qquad \boxed{\text{Formula (11),} \atop \text{Section 7.3}}$$

$$= \frac{4}{3} \int_0^{2\pi} \cos^2\theta \, d\theta$$

$$= \frac{4}{3} \left[\frac{1}{2}\theta + \frac{1}{4}\sin 2\theta \right]_0^{2\pi} = \frac{4\pi}{3} \qquad \boxed{\text{Formula (8),} \atop \text{Section 7.3}} \quad ◀$$

■ **SURFACE INTEGRALS OVER** $z = g(x, y)$, $y = g(x, z)$, **AND** $x = g(y, z)$

In the case where σ is a surface of the form $z = g(x, y)$, we can take $x = u$ and $y = v$ as parameters and express the equation of the surface as

$$\mathbf{r} = u\mathbf{i} + v\mathbf{j} + g(u, v)\mathbf{k}$$

in which case we obtain

$$\left\| \frac{\partial \mathbf{r}}{\partial u} \times \frac{\partial \mathbf{r}}{\partial v} \right\| = \sqrt{\left(\frac{\partial z}{\partial x} \right)^2 + \left(\frac{\partial z}{\partial y} \right)^2 + 1}$$

(verify). Thus, it follows from (6) that

$$\iint_\sigma f(x, y, z) \, dS = \iint_R f(x, y, g(x, y)) \sqrt{\left(\frac{\partial z}{\partial x} \right)^2 + \left(\frac{\partial z}{\partial y} \right)^2 + 1} \, dA$$

Note that in this formula the region R lies in the xy-plane because the parameters are x and y. Geometrically, this region is the projection of σ on the xy-plane. The following theorem summarizes this result and gives analogous formulas for surface integrals over surfaces of the form $y = g(x, z)$ and $x = g(y, z)$.

15.5.3 THEOREM

(a) *Let σ be a surface with equation $z = g(x, y)$ and let R be its projection on the xy-plane. If g has continuous first partial derivatives on R and $f(x, y, z)$ is continuous on σ, then*

$$\iint_{\sigma} f(x, y, z)\, dS = \iint_{R} f(x, y, g(x, y))\sqrt{\left(\frac{\partial z}{\partial x}\right)^2 + \left(\frac{\partial z}{\partial y}\right)^2 + 1}\, dA \qquad (8)$$

(b) *Let σ be a surface with equation $y = g(x, z)$ and let R be its projection on the xz-plane. If g has continuous first partial derivatives on R and $f(x, y, z)$ is continuous on σ, then*

$$\iint_{\sigma} f(x, y, z)\, dS = \iint_{R} f(x, g(x, z), z)\sqrt{\left(\frac{\partial y}{\partial x}\right)^2 + \left(\frac{\partial y}{\partial z}\right)^2 + 1}\, dA \qquad (9)$$

(c) *Let σ be a surface with equation $x = g(y, z)$ and let R be its projection on the yz-plane. If g has continuous first partial derivatives on R and $f(x, y, z)$ is continuous on σ, then*

$$\iint_{\sigma} f(x, y, z)\, dS = \iint_{R} f(g(y, z), y, z)\sqrt{\left(\frac{\partial x}{\partial y}\right)^2 + \left(\frac{\partial x}{\partial z}\right)^2 + 1}\, dA \qquad (10)$$

Formulas (9) and (10) can be recovered from Formula (8). Explain how.

▶ **Example 2** Evaluate the surface integral

$$\iint_{\sigma} xz\, dS$$

where σ is the part of the plane $x + y + z = 1$ that lies in the first octant.

Solution. The equation of the plane can be written as

$$z = 1 - x - y$$

Consequently, we can apply Formula (8) with $z = g(x, y) = 1 - x - y$ and $f(x, y, z) = xz$. We have

$$\frac{\partial z}{\partial x} = -1 \quad \text{and} \quad \frac{\partial z}{\partial y} = -1$$

so (8) becomes

$$\iint_{\sigma} xz\, dS = \iint_{R} x(1 - x - y)\sqrt{(-1)^2 + (-1)^2 + 1}\, dA \qquad (11)$$

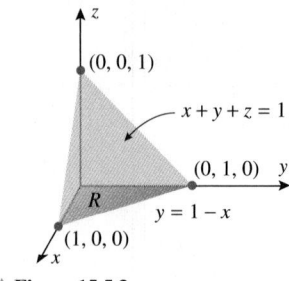

▲ **Figure 15.5.3**

where R is the projection of σ on the xy-plane (Figure 15.5.3). Rewriting the double integral in (11) as an iterated integral yields

$$\iint_\sigma xz\,dS = \sqrt{3}\int_0^1\int_0^{1-x}(x-x^2-xy)\,dy\,dx$$

$$= \sqrt{3}\int_0^1\left[xy-x^2y-\frac{xy^2}{2}\right]_{y=0}^{1-x}dx$$

$$= \sqrt{3}\int_0^1\left(\frac{x}{2}-x^2+\frac{x^3}{2}\right)dx$$

$$= \sqrt{3}\left[\frac{x^2}{4}-\frac{x^3}{3}+\frac{x^4}{8}\right]_0^1=\frac{\sqrt{3}}{24}\ \blacktriangleleft$$

▶ **Example 3** Evaluate the surface integral

$$\iint_\sigma y^2z^2\,dS$$

where σ is the part of the cone $z=\sqrt{x^2+y^2}$ that lies between the planes $z=1$ and $z=2$ (Figure 15.5.4).

Solution. We will apply Formula (8) with

$$z=g(x,y)=\sqrt{x^2+y^2}\quad\text{and}\quad f(x,y,z)=y^2z^2$$

Thus,

$$\frac{\partial z}{\partial x}=\frac{x}{\sqrt{x^2+y^2}}\quad\text{and}\quad\frac{\partial z}{\partial y}=\frac{y}{\sqrt{x^2+y^2}}$$

so

$$\sqrt{\left(\frac{\partial z}{\partial x}\right)^2+\left(\frac{\partial z}{\partial y}\right)^2+1}=\sqrt{2}$$

(verify), and (8) yields

$$\iint_\sigma y^2z^2\,dS=\iint_R y^2\left(\sqrt{x^2+y^2}\right)^2\sqrt{2}\,dA=\sqrt{2}\iint_R y^2(x^2+y^2)\,dA$$

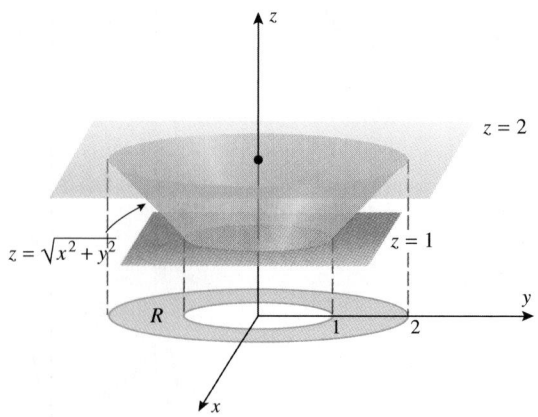

▶ **Figure 15.5.4**

where R is the annulus enclosed between $x^2 + y^2 = 1$ and $x^2 + y^2 = 4$ (Figure 15.5.4). Using polar coordinates to evaluate this double integral over the annulus R yields

$$\iint_\sigma y^2 z^2 \, dS = \sqrt{2} \int_0^{2\pi} \int_1^2 (r \sin \theta)^2 (r^2) r \, dr \, d\theta$$

$$= \sqrt{2} \int_0^{2\pi} \int_1^2 r^5 \sin^2 \theta \, dr \, d\theta$$

$$= \sqrt{2} \int_0^{2\pi} \left[\frac{r^6}{6} \sin^2 \theta \right]_{r=1}^2 d\theta = \frac{21}{\sqrt{2}} \int_0^{2\pi} \sin^2 \theta \, d\theta$$

$$= \frac{21}{\sqrt{2}} \left[\frac{1}{2}\theta - \frac{1}{4} \sin 2\theta \right]_0^{2\pi} = \frac{21\pi}{\sqrt{2}} \qquad \boxed{\begin{array}{l} \text{Formula (7),} \\ \text{Section 7.3} \end{array}} \quad \blacktriangleleft$$

Evaluate the integral in Example 3 with the help of Formula (6) and the parametrization

$$\mathbf{r} = \langle r \cos \theta, r \sin \theta, r \rangle$$
$$(1 \le r \le 2, 0 \le \theta \le 2\pi)$$

▶ **Example 4**   Suppose that a curved lamina σ with constant density $\delta(x, y, z) = \delta_0$ is the portion of the paraboloid $z = x^2 + y^2$ below the plane $z = 1$ (Figure 15.5.5). Find the mass of the lamina.

Solution.   Since $z = g(x, y) = x^2 + y^2$, it follows that

$$\frac{\partial z}{\partial x} = 2x \quad \text{and} \quad \frac{\partial z}{\partial y} = 2y$$

Therefore,

$$M = \iint_\sigma \delta_0 \, dS = \iint_R \delta_0 \sqrt{(2x)^2 + (2y)^2 + 1} \, dA = \delta_0 \iint_R \sqrt{4x^2 + 4y^2 + 1} \, dA \qquad (12)$$

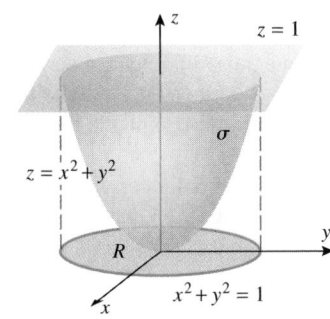

▲ **Figure 15.5.5**

where R is the circular region enclosed by $x^2 + y^2 = 1$. To evaluate (12) we use polar coordinates:

$$M = \delta_0 \int_0^{2\pi} \int_0^1 \sqrt{4r^2 + 1} \, r \, dr \, d\theta = \frac{\delta_0}{12} \int_0^{2\pi} (4r^2 + 1)^{3/2} \Big]_{r=0}^1 d\theta$$

$$= \frac{\delta_0}{12} \int_0^{2\pi} (5^{3/2} - 1) \, d\theta = \frac{\pi \delta_0}{6} (5\sqrt{5} - 1) \quad \blacktriangleleft$$

✔ **QUICK CHECK EXERCISES 15.5**   *(See page 1138 for answers.)*

1. Consider the surface integral $\iint_\sigma f(x, y, z) \, dS$.
   (a) If σ is a parametric surface whose vector equation is
   $$\mathbf{r} = x(u, v)\mathbf{i} + y(u, v)\mathbf{j} + z(u, v)\mathbf{k}$$
   to evaluate the integral replace dS by _____.
   (b) If σ is the graph of a function $z = g(x, y)$ with continuous first partial derivatives, to evaluate the integral replace dS by _____.

2. If σ is the triangular region with vertices $(1, 0, 0)$, $(0, 1, 0)$, and $(0, 0, 1)$, then
   $$\iint_\sigma (x + y + z) \, dS = \text{_____}$$

3. If σ is the sphere of radius 2 centered at the origin, then
   $$\iint_\sigma (x^2 + y^2 + z^2) \, dS = \text{_____}$$

4. If $f(x, y, z)$ is the mass density function of a curved lamina σ, then the mass of σ is given by the integral _____.

EXERCISE SET 15.5   <u>C</u> CAS

1–8 Evaluate the surface integral

$$\iint\limits_{\sigma} f(x, y, z)\, dS \; \blacksquare$$

1. $f(x, y, z) = z^2$; σ is the portion of the cone $z = \sqrt{x^2 + y^2}$ between the planes $z = 1$ and $z = 2$.

2. $f(x, y, z) = xy$; σ is the portion of the plane $x + y + z = 1$ lying in the first octant.

3. $f(x, y, z) = x^2 y$; σ is the portion of the cylinder $x^2 + z^2 = 1$ between the planes $y = 0$, $y = 1$, and above the xy-plane.

4. $f(x, y, z) = (x^2 + y^2)z$; σ is the portion of the sphere $x^2 + y^2 + z^2 = 4$ above the plane $z = 1$.

5. $f(x, y, z) = x - y - z$; σ is the portion of the plane $x + y = 1$ in the first octant between $z = 0$ and $z = 1$.

6. $f(x, y, z) = x + y$; σ is the portion of the plane $z = 6 - 2x - 3y$ in the first octant.

7. $f(x, y, z) = x + y + z$; σ is the surface of the cube defined by the inequalities $0 \le x \le 1, 0 \le y \le 1, 0 \le z \le 1$. [*Hint:* Integrate over each face separately.]

8. $f(x, y, z) = x^2 + y^2$; σ is the surface of the sphere $x^2 + y^2 + z^2 = a^2$.

9–12 True–False Determine whether the statement is true or false. Explain your answer. ■

9. If $f(x, y, z) \ge 0$ on σ, then

$$\iint\limits_{\sigma} f(x, y, z)\, dS \ge 0$$

10. If σ has surface area S, and if

$$\iint\limits_{\sigma} f(x, y, z)\, dS = S$$

then $f(x, y, z)$ is equal to 1 identically on σ.

11. If σ models a curved lamina, and if $f(x, y, z)$ is the density function of the lamina, then

$$\iint\limits_{\sigma} f(x, y, z)\, dS$$

represents the total density of the lamina.

12. If σ is the portion of a plane $z = c$ over a region R in the xy-plane, then

$$\iint\limits_{\sigma} f(x, y, z)\, dS = \iint\limits_{R} f(x, y, c)\, dA$$

for every continuous function f on σ.

13–14 Sometimes evaluating a surface integral results in an improper integral. When this happens, one can either attempt to determine the value of the integral using an appropriate limit or one can try another method. These exercises explore both approaches. ■

13. Consider the integral of $f(x, y, z) = z + 1$ over the upper hemisphere $\sigma: z = \sqrt{1 - x^2 - y^2}$ $(0 \le x^2 + y^2 \le 1)$.

  (a) Explain why evaluating this surface integral using (8) results in an improper integral.

  (b) Use (8) to evaluate the integral of f over the surface $\sigma_r : z = \sqrt{1 - x^2 - y^2}$ $(0 \le x^2 + y^2 \le r^2 < 1)$. Take the limit of this result as $r \to 1^-$ to determine the integral of f over σ.

  (c) Parametrize σ using spherical coordinates and evaluate the integral of f over σ using (6). Verify that your answer agrees with the result in part (b).

14. Consider the integral of $f(x, y, z) = \sqrt{x^2 + y^2 + z^2}$ over the cone $\sigma : z = \sqrt{x^2 + y^2}$ $(0 \le z \le 1)$.

  (a) Explain why evaluating this surface integral using (8) results in an improper integral.

  (b) Use (8) to evaluate the integral of f over the surface $\sigma_r : z = \sqrt{x^2 + y^2}$ $(0 < r^2 \le x^2 + y^2 \le 1)$. Take the limit of this result as $r \to 0^+$ to determine the integral of f over σ.

  (c) Parametrize σ using spherical coordinates and evaluate the integral of f over σ using (6). Verify that your answer agrees with the result in part (b).

FOCUS ON CONCEPTS

15–18 In some cases it is possible to use Definition 15.5.1 along with symmetry considerations to evaluate a surface integral without reference to a parametrization of the surface. In these exercises, σ denotes the unit sphere centered at the origin. ■

15. (a) Explain why it is possible to subdivide σ into patches and choose corresponding sample points (x_k^*, y_k^*, z_k^*) such that (i) the dimensions of each patch are as small as desired and (ii) for each sample point (x_k^*, y_k^*, z_k^*), there exists a sample point (x_j^*, y_j^*, z_j^*) with

$$x_k = -x_j, \quad y_k = y_j, \quad z_k = z_j$$

and with $\Delta S_k = \Delta S_j$.

  (b) Use Definition 15.5.1, the result in part (a), and the fact that surface integrals exist for continuous functions to prove that $\iint_{\sigma} x^n\, dS = 0$ for n an odd positive integer.

16. Use the argument in Exercise 15 to prove that if $f(x)$ is a continuous odd function of x, and if $g(y, z)$ is a continuous function, then

$$\iint\limits_{\sigma} f(x)g(y, z)\, dS = 0$$

17. (a) Explain why

$$\iint\limits_{\sigma} x^2\, dS = \iint\limits_{\sigma} y^2\, dS = \iint\limits_{\sigma} z^2\, dS \quad \text{(cont.)}$$

(b) Conclude from part (a) that

$$\iint\limits_{\sigma} x^2\,dS = \frac{1}{3}\left[\iint\limits_{\sigma} x^2\,dS + \iint\limits_{\sigma} y^2\,dS + \iint\limits_{\sigma} y^2\,dS\right]$$

(c) Use part (b) to evaluate

$$\iint\limits_{\sigma} x^2\,dS$$

without performing an integration.

18. Use the results of Exercises 16 and 17 to evaluate

$$\iint\limits_{\sigma} (x-y)^2\,dS$$

without performing an integration.

19–20 Set up, but do not evaluate, an iterated integral equal to the given surface integral by projecting σ on (a) the xy-plane, (b) the yz-plane, and (c) the xz-plane. ▪

19. $\displaystyle\iint\limits_{\sigma} xyz\,dS$, where σ is the portion of the plane

$2x + 3y + 4z = 12$ in the first octant.

20. $\displaystyle\iint\limits_{\sigma} xz\,dS$, where σ is the portion of the sphere

$x^2 + y^2 + z^2 = a^2$ in the first octant.

C 21. Use a CAS to confirm that the three integrals you obtained in Exercise 19 are equal, and find the exact value of the surface integral.

C 22. Try to confirm with a CAS that the three integrals you obtained in Exercise 20 are equal. If you did not succeed, what was the difficulty?

23–24 Set up, but do not evaluate, two different iterated integrals equal to the given integral. ▪

23. $\displaystyle\iint\limits_{\sigma} xyz\,dS$, where σ is the portion of the surface $y^2 = x$

between the planes $z = 0$, $z = 4$, $y = 1$, and $y = 2$.

24. $\displaystyle\iint\limits_{\sigma} x^2 y\,dS$, where σ is the portion of the cylinder

$y^2 + z^2 = a^2$ in the first octant between the planes $x = 0$, $x = 9$, $z = y$, and $z = 2y$.

C 25. Use a CAS to confirm that the two integrals you obtained in Exercise 23 are equal, and find the exact value of the surface integral.

C 26. Use a CAS to find the value of the surface integral

$$\iint\limits_{\sigma} x^2 yz\,dS$$

where the surface σ is the portion of the elliptic paraboloid $z = 5 - 3x^2 - 2y^2$ that lies above the xy-plane.

27–28 Find the mass of the lamina with constant density δ_0. ▪

27. The lamina that is the portion of the circular cylinder $x^2 + z^2 = 4$ that lies directly above the rectangle $R = \{(x, y) : 0 \le x \le 1, 0 \le y \le 4\}$ in the xy-plane.

28. The lamina that is the portion of the paraboloid $2z = x^2 + y^2$ inside the cylinder $x^2 + y^2 = 8$.

29. Find the mass of the lamina that is the portion of the surface $y^2 = 4 - z$ between the planes $x = 0$, $x = 3$, $y = 0$, and $y = 3$ if the density is $\delta(x, y, z) = y$.

30. Find the mass of the lamina that is the portion of the cone $z = \sqrt{x^2 + y^2}$ between $z = 1$ and $z = 4$ if the density is $\delta(x, y, z) = x^2 z$.

31. If a curved lamina has constant density δ_0, what relationship must exist between its mass and surface area? Explain your reasoning.

32. Show that if the density of the lamina $x^2 + y^2 + z^2 = a^2$ at each point is equal to the distance between that point and the xy-plane, then the mass of the lamina is $2\pi a^3$.

33–34 The centroid of a surface σ is defined by

$$\bar{x} = \frac{\displaystyle\iint\limits_{\sigma} x\,dS}{\text{area of } \sigma},\quad \bar{y} = \frac{\displaystyle\iint\limits_{\sigma} y\,dS}{\text{area of } \sigma},\quad \bar{z} = \frac{\displaystyle\iint\limits_{\sigma} z\,dS}{\text{area of } \sigma}$$

Find the centroid of the surface. ▪

33. The portion of the paraboloid $z = \frac{1}{2}(x^2 + y^2)$ below the plane $z = 4$.

34. The portion of the sphere $x^2 + y^2 + z^2 = 4$ above the plane $z = 1$.

35–38 Evaluate the integral $\iint_{\sigma} f(x, y, z)\,dS$ over the surface σ represented by the vector-valued function $\mathbf{r}(u, v)$. ▪

35. $f(x, y, z) = xyz$; $\mathbf{r}(u, v) = u\cos v\mathbf{i} + u\sin v\mathbf{j} + 3u\mathbf{k}$
$(1 \le u \le 2,\ 0 \le v \le \pi/2)$

36. $f(x, y, z) = \dfrac{x^2 + z^2}{y}$; $\mathbf{r}(u, v) = 2\cos v\mathbf{i} + u\mathbf{j} + 2\sin v\mathbf{k}$
$(1 \le u \le 3,\ 0 \le v \le 2\pi)$

37. $f(x, y, z) = \dfrac{1}{\sqrt{1 + 4x^2 + 4y^2}}$;
$\mathbf{r}(u, v) = u\cos v\mathbf{i} + u\sin v\mathbf{j} + u^2\mathbf{k}$
$(0 \le u \le \sin v,\ 0 \le v \le \pi)$

38. $f(x, y, z) = e^{-z}$;
$\mathbf{r}(u, v) = 2\sin u\cos v\mathbf{i} + 2\sin u\sin v\mathbf{j} + 2\cos u\mathbf{k}$
$(0 \le u \le \pi/2, 0 \le v \le 2\pi)$

C 39. Use a CAS to approximate the mass of the curved lamina $z = e^{-x^2 - y^2}$ that lies above the region in the xy-plane enclosed by $x^2 + y^2 = 9$ given that the density function is $\delta(x, y, z) = \sqrt{x^2 + y^2}$.

c **40.** The surface σ shown in the accompanying figure, called a *Möbius strip*, is represented by the parametric equations

$$x = (5 + u \cos(v/2)) \cos v$$
$$y = (5 + u \cos(v/2)) \sin v$$
$$z = u \sin(v/2)$$

where $-1 \le u \le 1$ and $0 \le v \le 2\pi$.

(a) Use a CAS to generate a reasonable facsimile of this surface.

(b) Use a CAS to approximate the location of the centroid of σ (see the definition preceding Exercise 33).

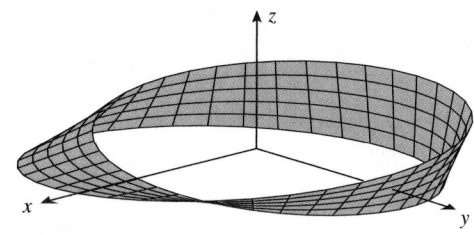

▲ **Figure Ex-40**

41. Writing Discuss the similarities and differences between the definition of a surface integral and the definition of a double integral.

42. Writing Suppose that a surface σ in 3-space and a function $f(x, y, z)$ are described geometrically. For example, σ might be the sphere of radius 1 centered at the origin and $f(x, y, z)$ might be the distance from the point (x, y, z) to the z-axis. How would you explain to a classmate a procedure for evaluating the surface integral of f over σ?

✔ **QUICK CHECK ANSWERS 15.5**

1. (a) $\left\| \dfrac{\partial \mathbf{r}}{\partial u} \times \dfrac{\partial \mathbf{r}}{\partial v} \right\| dA$ (b) $\sqrt{\left(\dfrac{\partial z}{\partial x}\right)^2 + \left(\dfrac{\partial z}{\partial y}\right)^2 + 1}\, dA$ 2. $\dfrac{\sqrt{3}}{2}$ 3. 64π 4. $\displaystyle\iint_{\sigma} f(x, y, z)\, dS$

15.6 APPLICATIONS OF SURFACE INTEGRALS; FLUX

In this section we will discuss applications of surface integrals to vector fields associated with fluid flow and electrostatic forces. However, the ideas that we will develop will be general in nature and applicable to other kinds of vector fields as well.

■ FLOW FIELDS

We will be concerned in this section with vector fields in 3-space that involve some type of "flow"—the flow of a fluid or the flow of charged particles in an electrostatic field, for example. In the case of fluid flow, the vector field $\mathbf{F}(x, y, z)$ represents the velocity of a fluid particle at the point (x, y, z), and the fluid particles flow along "streamlines" that are tangential to the velocity vectors (Figure 15.6.1a). In the case of an electrostatic field, $\mathbf{F}(x, y, z)$ is the force that the field exerts on a small unit of positive charge at the point (x, y, z), and such charges have acceleration in the directions of "electric lines" that are tangential to the force vectors (Figures 15.6.1b and 15.6.1c).

■ ORIENTED SURFACES

Our main goal in this section is to study flows of vector fields through permeable surfaces placed in the field. For this purpose we will need to consider some basic ideas about surfaces. Most surfaces that we encounter in applications have two sides—a sphere has an inside and an outside, and an infinite horizontal plane has a top side and a bottom side, for example. However, there exist mathematical surfaces with only one side. For example, Figure 15.6.2a shows the construction of a surface called a *Möbius strip* [in honor of the German mathematician August Möbius (1790–1868)]. The Möbius strip has only one side in the sense that a bug can traverse the *entire* surface without crossing an edge (Figure 15.6.2b). In contrast,

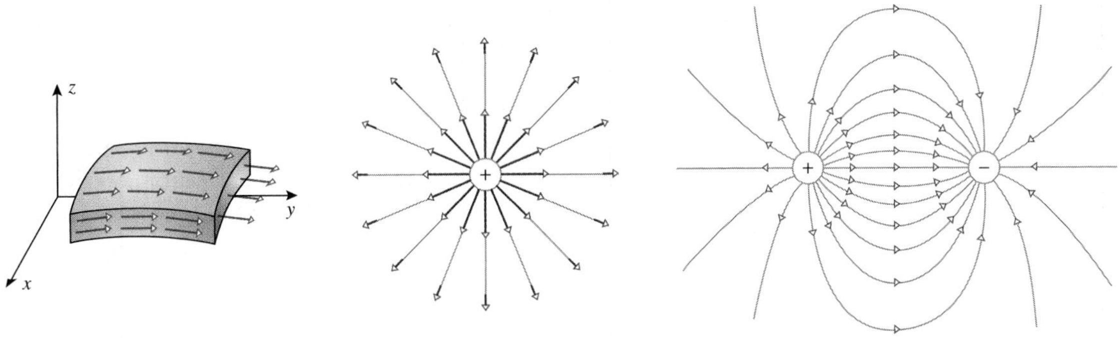

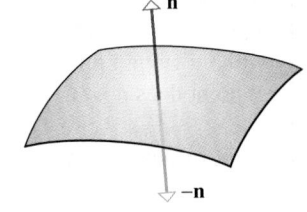

The velocity vectors of the fluid particles are tangent to the streamlines.

By Coulomb's law the electro-static field resulting from a single positive charge is an inverse-square field in which **F** is the repulsive force on a small unit positive charge.

The electrostatic field **F** that results from two charges of equal strength but opposite polarity.

(a)　　　　　　　　　　　*(b)*　　　　　　　　　　*(c)*

▲ Figure 15.6.1

If a bug starts at P with its back facing you and makes one circuit around the strip, then its back will face away from you when it returns to P.

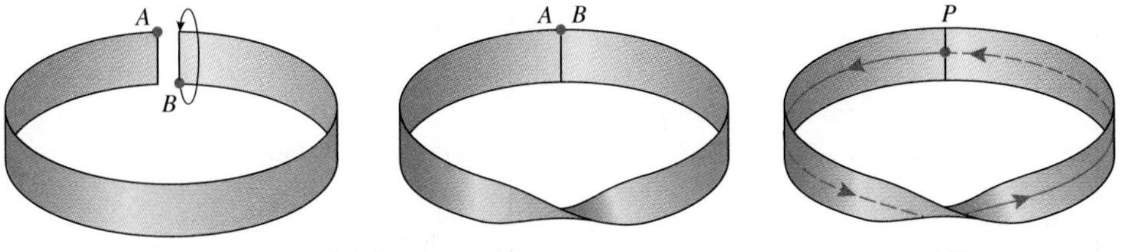

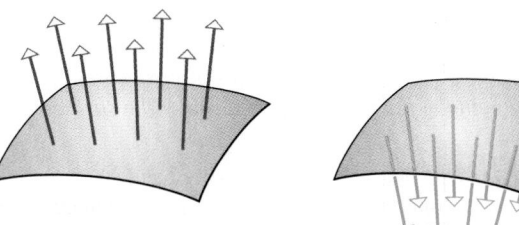

(a)　　　　　　　　　　　　　　　　　　*(b)*

▲ Figure 15.6.2

a sphere is two-sided in the sense that a bug walking on the sphere can traverse the inside surface or the outside surface but cannot traverse both without somehow passing through the sphere. A two-sided surface is said to be ***orientable***, and a one-sided surface is said to be ***nonorientable***. In the rest of this text we will only be concerned with orientable surfaces.

In applications, it is important to have some way of distinguishing between the two sides of an orientable surface. For this purpose let us suppose that σ is an orientable surface that has a unit normal vector **n** at each point. As illustrated in Figure 15.6.3, the vectors **n** and $-$**n** point to opposite sides of the surface and hence serve to distinguish between the two sides. It can be proved that if σ is a smooth orientable surface, then it is always possible to choose the direction of **n** at each point so that $\mathbf{n} = \mathbf{n}(x, y, z)$ varies continuously over the surface. These unit vectors are then said to form an ***orientation*** of the surface. It can also be proved that a smooth orientable surface has only two possible orientations. For example, the surface in Figure 15.6.4 is oriented up by the purple vectors and down by the green vectors. However, we cannot create a third orientation by mixing the two since this

▲ Figure 15.6.3

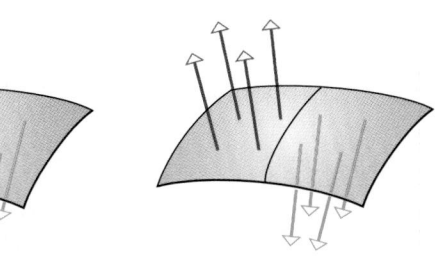

▲ Figure 15.6.4

produces points on the surface at which there is an abrupt change in direction (across the black curve in the figure, for example).

ORIENTATION OF A SMOOTH PARAMETRIC SURFACE

When a surface is expressed parametrically, the parametric equations create a natural orientation of the surface. To see why this is so, recall from Section 14.4 that if a smooth parametric surface σ is given by the vector equation

$$\mathbf{r} = x(u, v)\mathbf{i} + y(u, v)\mathbf{j} + z(u, v)\mathbf{k}$$

then the unit normal

$$\mathbf{n} = \mathbf{n}(u, v) = \frac{\dfrac{\partial \mathbf{r}}{\partial u} \times \dfrac{\partial \mathbf{r}}{\partial v}}{\left\| \dfrac{\partial \mathbf{r}}{\partial u} \times \dfrac{\partial \mathbf{r}}{\partial v} \right\|} \tag{1}$$

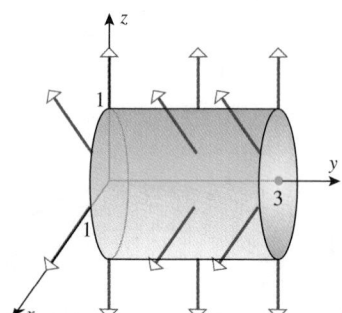

▲ **Figure 15.6.5**

See if you can find a parametrization of the cylinder in which the positive direction is inward.

is a continuous vector-valued function of u and v. Thus, Formula (1) defines an orientation of the surface; we call this the **positive orientation** of the parametric surface and we say that $\mathbf{n}$ points in the **positive direction** from the surface. The orientation determined by $-\mathbf{n}$ is called the **negative orientation** of the surface and we say that $-\mathbf{n}$ points in the **negative direction** from the surface. For example, consider the cylinder that is represented parametrically by the vector equation

$$\mathbf{r}(u, v) = \cos u\,\mathbf{i} + v\mathbf{j} - \sin u\,\mathbf{k} \qquad (0 \le u \le 2\pi, \ \ 0 \le v \le 3)$$

Then

$$\frac{\partial \mathbf{r}}{\partial u} \times \frac{\partial \mathbf{r}}{\partial v} = \cos u\,\mathbf{i} - \sin u\,\mathbf{k}$$

has unit length, so that Formula (1) becomes

$$\mathbf{n} = \frac{\partial \mathbf{r}}{\partial u} \times \frac{\partial \mathbf{r}}{\partial v} = \cos u\,\mathbf{i} - \sin u\,\mathbf{k}$$

Since $\mathbf{n}$ has the same $\mathbf{i}$- and $\mathbf{k}$-components as $\mathbf{r}$, the positive orientation of the cylinder is *outward* and the negative orientation is *inward* (Figure 15.6.5).

FLUX

In physics, the term *fluid* is used to describe both liquids and gases. Liquids are usually regarded to be **incompressible**, meaning that the liquid has a uniform density (mass per unit volume) that cannot be altered by compressive forces. Gases are regarded to be **compressible**, meaning that the density may vary from point to point and can be altered by compressive forces. In this text we will be concerned primarily with incompressible fluids. Moreover, we will assume that the velocity of the fluid at a fixed point does not vary with time. Fluid flows with this property are said to be in a **steady state**.

Our next goal in this section is to define a fundamental concept of physics known as *flux* (from the Latin word *fluxus*, meaning "flowing"). This concept is applicable to any vector field, but we will motivate it in the context of steady-state incompressible fluid flow. Imagine that fluid is flowing freely through a permeable surface, from one side of the surface to the other. In this context, you can think of flux as:

The volume of fluid that passes through the surface in one unit of time.

This idea is illustrated in Figure 15.6.6, which suggests that the volume of fluid that flows through a portion of the surface depends on three factors:

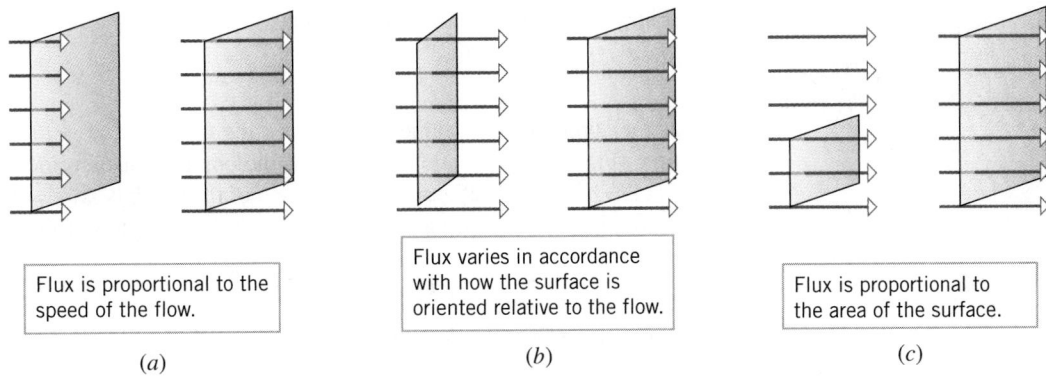

Flux is proportional to the speed of the flow.

Flux varies in accordance with how the surface is oriented relative to the flow.

Flux is proportional to the area of the surface.

(a)   (b)   (c)

▲ **Figure 15.6.6**

- The speed of the fluid; the greater the speed, the greater the volume (Figure 15.6.6a).
- How the surface is oriented relative to the flow; the more nearly orthogonal the flow is to the surface, the greater the volume (Figure 15.6.6b).
- The area of the portion of the surface; the greater the area, the greater the volume (Figure 15.6.6c).

These ideas lead us to the following problem.

15.6.1   PROBLEM   Suppose that an oriented surface σ is immersed in an incompressible, steady-state fluid flow and that the surface is permeable so that the fluid can flow through it freely in either direction. Find the net volume of fluid Φ that passes through the surface per unit of time, where the net volume is interpreted to mean the volume that passes through the surface in the positive direction minus the volume that passes through the surface in the negative direction.

To solve this problem, suppose that the velocity of the fluid at a point (x, y, z) on the surface σ is given by

$$\mathbf{F}(x, y, z) = f(x, y, z)\mathbf{i} + g(x, y, z)\mathbf{j} + h(x, y, z)\mathbf{k}$$

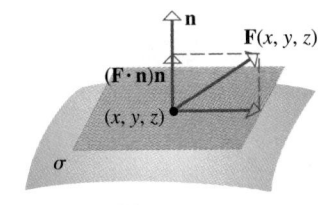

▲ **Figure 15.6.7**

Let $\mathbf{n}$ be the unit normal toward the positive side of σ at the point (x, y, z). As illustrated in Figure 15.6.7, the velocity vector $\mathbf{F}$ can be resolved into two orthogonal components—a component $(\mathbf{F} \cdot \mathbf{n})\mathbf{n}$ that is perpendicular to the surface σ and a second component that is along the "face" of σ. The component of velocity along the face of the surface does not contribute to the flow through σ and hence can be ignored in our computations. Moreover, observe that the sign of $\mathbf{F} \cdot \mathbf{n}$ determines the direction of flow—a positive value means the flow is in the direction of $\mathbf{n}$ and a negative value means that it is opposite to $\mathbf{n}$.

To solve Problem 15.6.1, we subdivide σ into n patches $\sigma_1, \sigma_2, \ldots, \sigma_n$ with areas

$$\Delta S_1, \Delta S_2, \ldots, \Delta S_n$$

If the patches are small and the flow is not too erratic, it is reasonable to assume that the velocity does not vary much on each patch. Thus, if (x_k^*, y_k^*, z_k^*) is any point in the kth patch, we can assume that $\mathbf{F}(x, y, z)$ is constant and equal to $\mathbf{F}(x_k^*, y_k^*, z_k^*)$ throughout the patch and that the component of velocity across the surface σ_k is

$$\mathbf{F}(x_k^*, y_k^*, z_k^*) \cdot \mathbf{n}(x_k^*, y_k^*, z_k^*) \tag{2}$$

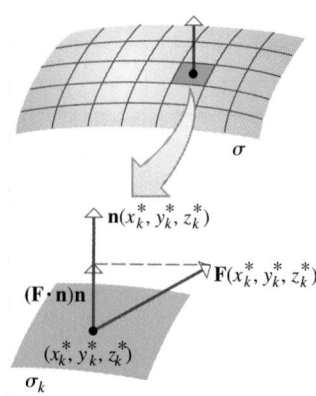

▲ **Figure 15.6.8**

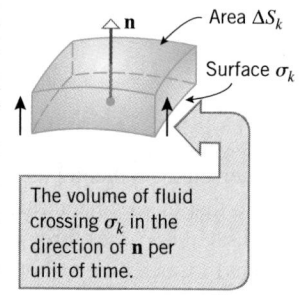

The volume of fluid crossing σ_k in the direction of **n** per unit of time.

▲ **Figure 15.6.9**

If the fluid has mass density δ, then $\Phi\delta$ (volume/time × density) represents the net mass of fluid that passes through σ per unit of time.

(Figure 15.6.8). Thus, we can interpret

$$\mathbf{F}(x_k^*, y_k^*, z_k^*) \cdot \mathbf{n}(x_k^*, y_k^*, z_k^*)\Delta S_k$$

as the approximate volume of fluid crossing the patch σ_k in the direction of **n** per unit of time (Figure 15.6.9). For example, if the component of velocity in the direction of **n** is $\mathbf{F}(x_k^*, y_k^*, z_k^*) \cdot \mathbf{n} = 25$ cm/s, and the area of the patch is $\Delta S_k = 2$ cm^2, then the volume of fluid ΔV_k crossing the patch in the direction of **n** per unit of time is approximately

$$\Delta V_k \approx \mathbf{F}(x_k^*, y_k^*, z_k^*) \cdot \mathbf{n}(x_k^*, y_k^*, z_k^*)\Delta S_k = 25 \text{ cm/s} \cdot 2 \text{ cm}^2 = 50 \text{ cm}^3/\text{s}$$

In the case where the velocity component $\mathbf{F}(x_k^*, y_k^*, z_k^*) \cdot \mathbf{n}(x_k^*, y_k^*, z_k^*)$ is negative, the flow is in the direction opposite to **n**, so that $-\mathbf{F}(x_k^*, y_k^*, z_k^*) \cdot \mathbf{n}(x_k^*, y_k^*, z_k^*)\Delta S_k$ is the approximate volume of fluid crossing the patch σ_k in the direction opposite to **n** per unit time. Thus, the sum

$$\sum_{k=1}^{n} \mathbf{F}(x_k^*, y_k^*, z_k^*) \cdot \mathbf{n}(x_k^*, y_k^*, z_k^*)\Delta S_k$$

measures the approximate net volume of fluid that crosses the surface σ in the direction of its orientation **n** per unit of time.

If we now increase n in such a way that the maximum dimension of each patch approaches zero, then it is plausible that the errors in the approximations approach zero, and the limit

$$\Phi = \lim_{n \to +\infty} \sum_{k=1}^{n} \mathbf{F}(x_k^*, y_k^*, z_k^*) \cdot \mathbf{n}(x_k^*, y_k^*, z_k^*)\Delta S_k \tag{3}$$

represents the exact net volume of fluid that crosses the surface σ in the direction of its orientation **n** per unit of time. The quantity Φ defined by Equation (3) is called the ***flux of F across*** σ. The flux can also be expressed as the surface integral

$$\Phi = \iint\limits_{\sigma} \mathbf{F}(x, y, z) \cdot \mathbf{n}(x, y, z) \, dS \tag{4}$$

A positive flux means that in one unit of time a greater volume of fluid passes through σ in the positive direction than in the negative direction, a negative flux means that a greater volume passes through the surface in the negative direction than in the positive direction, and a zero flux means that the same volume passes through the surface in each direction. Integrals of form (4) arise in other contexts as well and are called ***flux integrals***.

■ EVALUATING FLUX INTEGRALS

An effective formula for evaluating flux integrals can be obtained by applying Theorem 15.5.2 and using Formula (1) for **n**. This yields

$$\iint\limits_{\sigma} \mathbf{F} \cdot \mathbf{n} \, dS = \iint\limits_{R} \mathbf{F} \cdot \mathbf{n} \left\| \frac{\partial \mathbf{r}}{\partial u} \times \frac{\partial \mathbf{r}}{\partial v} \right\| dA$$

$$= \iint\limits_{R} \mathbf{F} \cdot \frac{\dfrac{\partial \mathbf{r}}{\partial u} \times \dfrac{\partial \mathbf{r}}{\partial v}}{\left\| \dfrac{\partial \mathbf{r}}{\partial u} \times \dfrac{\partial \mathbf{r}}{\partial v} \right\|} \left\| \frac{\partial \mathbf{r}}{\partial u} \times \frac{\partial \mathbf{r}}{\partial v} \right\| dA$$

$$= \iint\limits_{R} \mathbf{F} \cdot \left(\frac{\partial \mathbf{r}}{\partial u} \times \frac{\partial \mathbf{r}}{\partial v} \right) dA$$

In summary, we have the following result.

15.6.2   THEOREM   *Let σ be a smooth parametric surface represented by the vector equation $\mathbf{r} = \mathbf{r}(u, v)$ in which (u, v) varies over a region R in the uv-plane. If the component functions of the vector field $\mathbf{F}$ are continuous on σ, and if $\mathbf{n}$ determines the positive orientation of σ, then*

$$\Phi = \iint_\sigma \mathbf{F} \cdot \mathbf{n}\, dS = \iint_R \mathbf{F} \cdot \left(\frac{\partial \mathbf{r}}{\partial u} \times \frac{\partial \mathbf{r}}{\partial v} \right) dA \qquad (5)$$

where it is understood that the integrand on the right side of the equation is expressed in terms of u and v.

Although Theorem 15.6.2 was derived for smooth parametric surfaces, Formula (5) is valid more generally. For example, as long as σ has a continuous normal vector field $\mathbf{n}$ and the component functions of $\mathbf{r}(u, v)$ have continuous first partial derivatives, Formula (5) can be applied whenever $\partial \mathbf{r}/\partial u \times \partial \mathbf{r}/\partial v$ is a positive multiple of $\mathbf{n}$ in the *interior* of R. (That is, $\partial \mathbf{r}/\partial u \times \partial \mathbf{r}/\partial v$ is allowed to equal $\mathbf{0}$ on the boundary of R.)

▶ **Example 1**   Find the flux of the vector field $\mathbf{F}(x, y, z) = z\mathbf{k}$ across the outward-oriented sphere $x^2 + y^2 + z^2 = a^2$.

Solution.   The sphere with outward positive orientation can be represented by the vector-valued function

$$\mathbf{r}(\phi, \theta) = a \sin \phi \cos \theta \,\mathbf{i} + a \sin \phi \sin \theta \,\mathbf{j} + a \cos \phi \,\mathbf{k} \qquad (0 \le \phi \le \pi, \ 0 \le \theta \le 2\pi)$$

From this formula we obtain (see Example 11 of Section 14.4 for the computations)

$$\frac{\partial \mathbf{r}}{\partial \phi} \times \frac{\partial \mathbf{r}}{\partial \theta} = a^2 \sin^2 \phi \cos \theta \,\mathbf{i} + a^2 \sin^2 \phi \sin \theta \,\mathbf{j} + a^2 \sin \phi \cos \phi \,\mathbf{k}$$

Moreover, for points on the sphere we have $\mathbf{F} = z\mathbf{k} = a \cos \phi \,\mathbf{k}$; hence,

$$\mathbf{F} \cdot \left(\frac{\partial \mathbf{r}}{\partial \phi} \times \frac{\partial \mathbf{r}}{\partial \theta} \right) = a^3 \sin \phi \cos^2 \phi$$

Thus, it follows from (5) with the parameters u and v replaced by ϕ and θ that

$$\Phi = \iint_\sigma \mathbf{F} \cdot \mathbf{n}\, dS$$

$$= \iint_R \mathbf{F} \cdot \left(\frac{\partial \mathbf{r}}{\partial \phi} \times \frac{\partial \mathbf{r}}{\partial \theta} \right) dA$$

$$= \int_0^{2\pi} \int_0^\pi a^3 \sin \phi \cos^2 \phi \, d\phi \, d\theta$$

$$= a^3 \int_0^{2\pi} \left[-\frac{\cos^3 \phi}{3} \right]_0^\pi d\theta$$

$$= \frac{2a^3}{3} \int_0^{2\pi} d\theta = \frac{4\pi a^3}{3} \quad ◀$$

Solve Example 1 using symmetry: First argue that the vector fields $x\mathbf{i}$, $y\mathbf{j}$, and $z\mathbf{k}$ will have the same flux across the sphere. Then define

$$\mathbf{H} = x\mathbf{i} + y\mathbf{j} + z\mathbf{k}$$

and explain why

$$\mathbf{H} \cdot \mathbf{n} = a$$

Use this to compute Φ.

REMARK | Reversing the orientation of the surface σ in (5) reverses the sign of $\mathbf{n}$, hence the sign of $\mathbf{F} \cdot \mathbf{n}$, and hence reverses the sign of Φ. This can also be seen physically by interpreting the flux integral as the volume of fluid per unit time that crosses σ in the positive direction minus the volume per unit time that crosses in the negative direction—reversing the orientation of σ changes the sign of the difference. Thus, in Example 1 an inward orientation of the sphere would produce a flux of $-4\pi a^3/3$.

■ ORIENTATION OF NONPARAMETRIC SURFACES

Nonparametric surfaces of the form $z = g(x, y)$, $y = g(z, x)$, and $x = g(y, z)$ can be expressed parametrically using the independent variables as parameters. More precisely, these surfaces can be represented by the vector equations

$$\mathbf{r} = u\mathbf{i} + v\mathbf{j} + g(u, v)\mathbf{k}, \quad \mathbf{r} = v\mathbf{i} + g(u, v)\mathbf{j} + u\mathbf{k}, \quad \mathbf{r} = g(u, v)\mathbf{i} + u\mathbf{j} + v\mathbf{k} \quad (6\text{–}8)$$

$$\boxed{z = g(x, y)} \qquad\qquad \boxed{y = g(z, x)} \qquad\qquad \boxed{x = g(y, z)}$$

These representations impose positive and negative orientations on the surfaces in accordance with Formula (1). We leave it as an exercise to calculate $\mathbf{n}$ and $-\mathbf{n}$ in each case and to show that the positive and negative orientations are as shown in Table 15.6.1. (To assist with perspective, each graph is pictured as a portion of the surface of a small solid region.)

Table 15.6.1

$z = g(x, y)$	$y = g(z, x)$	$x = g(y, z)$
$\mathbf{n} = \dfrac{-\dfrac{\partial z}{\partial x}\mathbf{i} - \dfrac{\partial z}{\partial y}\mathbf{j} + \mathbf{k}}{\sqrt{\left(\dfrac{\partial z}{\partial x}\right)^2 + \left(\dfrac{\partial z}{\partial y}\right)^2 + 1}}$ Positive **k**-component Positive orientation	$\mathbf{n} = \dfrac{-\dfrac{\partial y}{\partial x}\mathbf{i} + \mathbf{j} - \dfrac{\partial y}{\partial z}\mathbf{k}}{\sqrt{\left(\dfrac{\partial y}{\partial x}\right)^2 + \left(\dfrac{\partial y}{\partial z}\right)^2 + 1}}$ Positive **j**-component Positive orientation	$\mathbf{n} = \dfrac{\mathbf{i} - \dfrac{\partial x}{\partial y}\mathbf{j} - \dfrac{\partial x}{\partial z}\mathbf{k}}{\sqrt{\left(\dfrac{\partial x}{\partial y}\right)^2 + \left(\dfrac{\partial x}{\partial z}\right)^2 + 1}}$ Positive **i**-component Positive orientation
$-\mathbf{n} = \dfrac{\dfrac{\partial z}{\partial x}\mathbf{i} + \dfrac{\partial z}{\partial y}\mathbf{j} - \mathbf{k}}{\sqrt{\left(\dfrac{\partial z}{\partial x}\right)^2 + \left(\dfrac{\partial z}{\partial y}\right)^2 + 1}}$ Negative **k**-component Negative orientation	$-\mathbf{n} = \dfrac{\dfrac{\partial y}{\partial x}\mathbf{i} - \mathbf{j} + \dfrac{\partial y}{\partial z}\mathbf{k}}{\sqrt{\left(\dfrac{\partial y}{\partial x}\right)^2 + \left(\dfrac{\partial y}{\partial z}\right)^2 + 1}}$ Negative **j**-component Negative orientation	$-\mathbf{n} = \dfrac{-\mathbf{i} + \dfrac{\partial x}{\partial y}\mathbf{j} + \dfrac{\partial x}{\partial z}\mathbf{k}}{\sqrt{\left(\dfrac{\partial x}{\partial y}\right)^2 + \left(\dfrac{\partial x}{\partial z}\right)^2 + 1}}$ Negative **i**-component Negative orientation

The results in Table 15.6.1 can also be obtained using gradients. To see how this can be done, rewrite the equations of the surfaces as

$$z - g(x, y) = 0, \quad y - g(z, x) = 0, \quad x - g(y, z) = 0$$

Each of these equations has the form $G(x, y, z) = 0$ and hence can be viewed as a level surface of a function $G(x, y, z)$. Since the gradient of G is normal to the level surface, it follows that the unit normal $\mathbf{n}$ is either $\nabla G/\|\nabla G\|$ or $-\nabla G/\|\nabla G\|$. However, if $G(x, y, z) = z - g(x, y)$, then ∇G has a $\mathbf{k}$-component of 1; if $G(x, y, z) = y - g(z, x)$,

> The dependent variable will increase as you move away from a surface
>
> $$z = g(x, y), \quad y = g(z, x)$$
>
> or
>
> $$x = g(y, z)$$
>
> in the direction of positive orientation.

then ∇G has a **j**-component of 1; and if $G(x, y, z) = x - g(y, z)$, then ∇G has an **i**-component of 1. Thus, it is evident from Table 15.6.1 that in all three cases we have

$$\mathbf{n} = \frac{\nabla G}{\|\nabla G\|} \tag{9}$$

Moreover, we leave it as an exercise to show that if the surfaces $z = g(x, y)$, $y = g(z, x)$, and $x = g(y, z)$ are expressed in vector forms (6), (7), and (8), then

$$\nabla G = \frac{\partial \mathbf{r}}{\partial u} \times \frac{\partial \mathbf{r}}{\partial v} \tag{10}$$

[compare (1) and (9)]. Thus, we are led to the following version of Theorem 15.6.2 for nonparametric surfaces.

15.6.3   THEOREM   *Let σ be a smooth surface of the form $z = g(x, y)$, $y = g(z, x)$, or $x = g(y, z)$, and suppose that the component functions of the vector field $\mathbf{F}$ are continuous on σ. Suppose also that the equation for σ is rewritten as $G(x, y, z) = 0$ by taking g to the left side of the equation, and let R be the projection of σ on the coordinate plane determined by the independent variables of g. If σ has positive orientation, then*

$$\Phi = \iint_\sigma \mathbf{F} \cdot \mathbf{n} \, dS = \iint_R \mathbf{F} \cdot \nabla G \, dA \tag{11}$$

Formula (11) can either be used directly for computations or to derive some more specific formulas for each of the three surface types. For example, if $z = g(x, y)$, then we have $G(x, y, z) = z - g(x, y)$, so

$$\nabla G = -\frac{\partial g}{\partial x}\mathbf{i} - \frac{\partial g}{\partial y}\mathbf{j} + \mathbf{k} = -\frac{\partial z}{\partial x}\mathbf{i} - \frac{\partial z}{\partial y}\mathbf{j} + \mathbf{k}$$

Substituting this expression for ∇G in (11) and taking R to be the projection of the surface $z = g(x, y)$ on the xy-plane yields

$$\iint_\sigma \mathbf{F} \cdot \mathbf{n} \, dS = \iint_R \mathbf{F} \cdot \left(-\frac{\partial z}{\partial x}\mathbf{i} - \frac{\partial z}{\partial y}\mathbf{j} + \mathbf{k}\right) dA \qquad \begin{array}{l}\sigma \text{ of the form } z = g(x, y) \\ \text{and oriented up}\end{array} \tag{12}$$

$$\iint_\sigma \mathbf{F} \cdot \mathbf{n} \, dS = \iint_R \mathbf{F} \cdot \left(\frac{\partial z}{\partial x}\mathbf{i} + \frac{\partial z}{\partial y}\mathbf{j} - \mathbf{k}\right) dA \qquad \begin{array}{l}\sigma \text{ of the form } z = g(x, y) \\ \text{and oriented down}\end{array} \tag{13}$$

The derivations of the corresponding formulas when $y = g(z, x)$ and $x = g(y, z)$ are left as exercises.

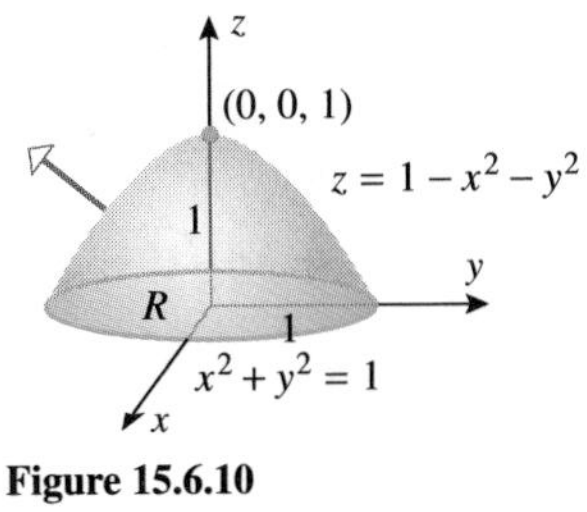

▲ Figure 15.6.10

▶ **Example 2**   Let σ be the portion of the surface $z = 1 - x^2 - y^2$ that lies above the xy-plane, and suppose that σ is oriented up, as shown in Figure 15.6.10. Find the flux of the vector field $\mathbf{F}(x, y, z) = x\mathbf{i} + y\mathbf{j} + z\mathbf{k}$ across σ.

Solution. From (12) the flux Φ is given by

$$\Phi = \iint_\sigma \mathbf{F} \cdot \mathbf{n} \, dS = \iint_R \mathbf{F} \cdot \left(-\frac{\partial z}{\partial x} \mathbf{i} - \frac{\partial z}{\partial y} \mathbf{j} + \mathbf{k} \right) dA$$

$$= \iint_R (x\mathbf{i} + y\mathbf{j} + z\mathbf{k}) \cdot (2x\mathbf{i} + 2y\mathbf{j} + \mathbf{k}) \, dA$$

$$= \iint_R (x^2 + y^2 + 1) \, dA \qquad \boxed{\text{Since } z = 1 - x^2 - y^2 \text{ on the surface}}$$

$$= \int_0^{2\pi} \int_0^1 (r^2 + 1) r \, dr \, d\theta \qquad \boxed{\text{Using polar coordinates to evaluate the integral}}$$

$$= \int_0^{2\pi} \left(\frac{3}{4} \right) d\theta = \frac{3\pi}{2} \quad \blacktriangleleft$$

✔ **QUICK CHECK EXERCISES 15.6**   *(See page 1148 for answers.)*

In these exercises, $\mathbf{F}(x, y, z)$ denotes a vector field defined on a surface σ oriented by a unit normal vector field $\mathbf{n}(x, y, z)$, and Φ denotes the flux of $\mathbf{F}$ across σ.

1. (a) Φ is the value of the surface integral _____.

(b) If σ is the unit sphere and $\mathbf{n}$ is the outward unit normal, then the flux of

$$\mathbf{F}(x, y, z) = x\mathbf{i} + y\mathbf{j} + z\mathbf{k}$$

across σ is $\Phi =$ _____.

2. (a) Assume that σ is parametrized by a vector-valued function $\mathbf{r}(u, v)$ whose domain is a region R in the uv-plane and that $\mathbf{n}$ is a positive multiple of

$$\frac{\partial \mathbf{r}}{\partial u} \times \frac{\partial \mathbf{r}}{\partial v}$$

Then the double integral over R whose value is Φ is _____.

(b) Suppose that σ is the parametric surface

$$\mathbf{r}(u, v) = u\mathbf{i} + v\mathbf{j} + (u + v)\mathbf{k} \qquad (0 \le u^2 + v^2 \le 1)$$

and that $\mathbf{n}$ is a positive multiple of

$$\frac{\partial \mathbf{r}}{\partial u} \times \frac{\partial \mathbf{r}}{\partial v}$$

Then the flux of $\mathbf{F}(x, y, z) = x\mathbf{i} + y\mathbf{j} + z\mathbf{k}$ across σ is $\Phi =$ _____.

3. (a) Assume that σ is the graph of a function $z = g(x, y)$ over a region R in the xy-plane and that $\mathbf{n}$ has a positive $\mathbf{k}$-component for every point on σ. Then a double integral over R whose value is Φ is _____.

(b) Suppose that σ is the triangular region with vertices $(1, 0, 0)$, $(0, 1, 0)$, and $(0, 0, 1)$ with upward orientation. Then the flux of

$$\mathbf{F}(x, y, z) = x\mathbf{i} + y\mathbf{j} + z\mathbf{k}$$

across σ is $\Phi =$ _____.

4. In the case of steady-state incompressible fluid flow, with $\mathbf{F}(x, y, z)$ the fluid velocity at (x, y, z) on σ, Φ can be interpreted as _____.

EXERCISE SET 15.6   ⓒ CAS

FOCUS ON CONCEPTS

1. Suppose that the surface σ of the unit cube in the accompanying figure has an outward orientation. In each part, determine whether the flux of the vector field $\mathbf{F}(x, y, z) = z\mathbf{j}$ across the specified face is positive, negative, or zero.

(a) The face $x = 1$ (b) The face $x = 0$
(c) The face $y = 1$ (d) The face $y = 0$
(e) The face $z = 1$ (f) The face $z = 0$

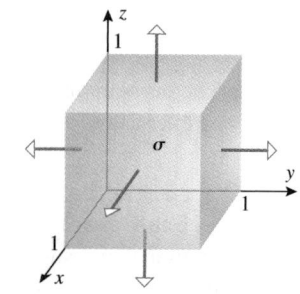

◀ **Figure Ex-1**

2. Answer the questions posed in Exercise 1 for the vector field $\mathbf{F}(x, y, z) = x\mathbf{i} - z\mathbf{k}$.

3. Answer the questions posed in Exercise 1 for the vector field $\mathbf{F}(x, y, z) = x\mathbf{i} + y\mathbf{j} + z\mathbf{k}$.

4. Find the flux of the constant vector field $\mathbf{F}(x, y, z) = \mathbf{i}$ across the entire surface σ in Figure Ex-1. Explain your reasoning.

5. Let σ be the cylindrical surface that is represented by the vector-valued function $\mathbf{r}(u, v) = \cos v\mathbf{i} + \sin v\mathbf{j} + u\mathbf{k}$ with $0 \leq u \leq 1$ and $0 \leq v \leq 2\pi$.
   (a) Find the unit normal $\mathbf{n} = \mathbf{n}(u, v)$ that defines the positive orientation of σ.
   (b) Is the positive orientation inward or outward? Justify your answer.

6. Let σ be the conical surface that is represented by the parametric equations $x = r\cos\theta$, $y = r\sin\theta$, $z = r$ with $1 \leq r \leq 2$ and $0 \leq \theta \leq 2\pi$.
   (a) Find the unit normal $\mathbf{n} = \mathbf{n}(r, \theta)$ that defines the positive orientation of σ.
   (b) Is the positive orientation upward or downward? Justify your answer.

7–12 Find the flux of the vector field $\mathbf{F}$ across σ. ■

7. $\mathbf{F}(x, y, z) = x\mathbf{i} + y\mathbf{j} + 2z\mathbf{k}$; σ is the portion of the surface $z = 1 - x^2 - y^2$ above the xy-plane, oriented by upward normals.

8. $\mathbf{F}(x, y, z) = (x + y)\mathbf{i} + (y + z)\mathbf{j} + (z + x)\mathbf{k}$; σ is the portion of the plane $x + y + z = 1$ in the first octant, oriented by unit normals with positive components.

9. $\mathbf{F}(x, y, z) = x\mathbf{i} + y\mathbf{j} + 2z\mathbf{k}$; σ is the portion of the cone $z^2 = x^2 + y^2$ between the planes $z = 1$ and $z = 2$, oriented by upward unit normals.

10. $\mathbf{F}(x, y, z) = y\mathbf{j} + \mathbf{k}$; σ is the portion of the paraboloid $z = x^2 + y^2$ below the plane $z = 4$, oriented by downward unit normals.

11. $\mathbf{F}(x, y, z) = x\mathbf{k}$; the surface σ is the portion of the paraboloid $z = x^2 + y^2$ below the plane $z = y$, oriented by downward unit normals.

12. $\mathbf{F}(x, y, z) = x^2\mathbf{i} + yx\mathbf{j} + zx\mathbf{k}$; σ is the portion of the plane $6x + 3y + 2z = 6$ in the first octant, oriented by unit normals with positive components.

13–16 Find the flux of the vector field $\mathbf{F}$ across σ in the direction of positive orientation. ■

13. $\mathbf{F}(x, y, z) = x\mathbf{i} + y\mathbf{j} + \mathbf{k}$; σ is the portion of the paraboloid
$$\mathbf{r}(u, v) = u\cos v\mathbf{i} + u\sin v\mathbf{j} + (1 - u^2)\mathbf{k}$$
with $1 \leq u \leq 2$, $0 \leq v \leq 2\pi$.

14. $\mathbf{F}(x, y, z) = e^{-y}\mathbf{i} - y\mathbf{j} + x\sin z\mathbf{k}$; σ is the portion of the elliptic cylinder
$$\mathbf{r}(u, v) = 2\cos v\mathbf{i} + \sin v\mathbf{j} + u\mathbf{k}$$
with $0 \leq u \leq 5$, $0 \leq v \leq 2\pi$.

15. $\mathbf{F}(x, y, z) = \sqrt{x^2 + y^2}\,\mathbf{k}$; σ is the portion of the cone
$$\mathbf{r}(u, v) = u\cos v\mathbf{i} + u\sin v\mathbf{j} + 2u\mathbf{k}$$
with $0 \leq u \leq \sin v$, $0 \leq v \leq \pi$.

16. $\mathbf{F}(x, y, z) = x\mathbf{i} + y\mathbf{j} + z\mathbf{k}$; σ is the portion of the sphere
$$\mathbf{r}(u, v) = 2\sin u \cos v\mathbf{i} + 2\sin u \sin v\mathbf{j} + 2\cos u\mathbf{k}$$
with $0 \leq u \leq \pi/3$, $0 \leq v \leq 2\pi$.

17. Let σ be the surface of the cube bounded by the planes $x = \pm 1$, $y = \pm 1$, $z = \pm 1$, oriented by outward unit normals. In each part, find the flux of $\mathbf{F}$ across σ.
   (a) $\mathbf{F}(x, y, z) = x\mathbf{i}$
   (b) $\mathbf{F}(x, y, z) = x\mathbf{i} + y\mathbf{j} + z\mathbf{k}$
   (c) $\mathbf{F}(x, y, z) = x^2\mathbf{i} + y^2\mathbf{j} + z^2\mathbf{k}$

18. Let σ be the closed surface consisting of the portion of the paraboloid $z = x^2 + y^2$ for which $0 \leq z \leq 1$ and capped by the disk $x^2 + y^2 \leq 1$ in the plane $z = 1$. Find the flux of the vector field $\mathbf{F}(x, y, z) = z\mathbf{j} - y\mathbf{k}$ in the outward direction across σ.

19–22 True–False Determine whether the statement is true or false. Explain your answer. ■

19. The Möbius strip is a surface that has two orientations.

20. The flux of a vector field is another vector field.

21. If the net volume of fluid that passes through a surface per unit time in the positive direction is zero, then the velocity of the fluid is everywhere tangent to the surface.

22. If a surface σ is oriented by a unit normal vector field $\mathbf{n}$, the flux of $\mathbf{n}$ across σ is numerically equal to the surface area of σ.

23–24 Find the flux of $\mathbf{F}$ across the surface σ by expressing σ parametrically. ■

23. $\mathbf{F}(x, y, z) = \mathbf{i} + \mathbf{j} + \mathbf{k}$; the surface σ is the portion of the cone $z = \sqrt{x^2 + y^2}$ between the planes $z = 1$ and $z = 2$, oriented by downward unit normals.

24. $\mathbf{F}(x, y, z) = x\mathbf{i} + y\mathbf{j} + z\mathbf{k}$; σ is the portion of the cylinder $x^2 + z^2 = 1$ between the planes $y = 1$ and $y = -2$, oriented by outward unit normals.

25. Let x, y, and z be measured in meters, and suppose that $\mathbf{F}(x, y, z) = 2x\mathbf{i} - 3y\mathbf{j} + z\mathbf{k}$ is the velocity vector (in m/s) of a fluid particle at the point (x, y, z) in a steady-state incompressible fluid flow.
   (a) Find the net volume of fluid that passes in the upward direction through the portion of the plane $x + y + z = 1$ in the first octant in 1 s.
   (b) Assuming that the fluid has a mass density of 806 kg/m³, find the net mass of fluid that passes in the upward direction through the surface in part (a) in 1 s.

26. Let x, y, and z be measured in meters, and suppose that $\mathbf{F}(x, y, z) = -y\mathbf{i} + z\mathbf{j} + 3x\mathbf{k}$ is the velocity vector (in m/s) of a fluid particle at the point (x, y, z) in a steady-state incompressible fluid flow.   *(cont.)*

(a) Find the net volume of fluid that passes in the upward direction through the hemisphere $z = \sqrt{9 - x^2 - y^2}$ in 1 s.

(b) Assuming that the fluid has a mass density of 1060 kg/m^3, find the net mass of fluid that passes in the upward direction through the surface in part (a) in 1 s.

27. (a) Derive the analogs of Formulas (12) and (13) for surfaces of the form $x = g(y, z)$.

(b) Let σ be the portion of the paraboloid $x = y^2 + z^2$ for $x \leq 1$ and $z \geq 0$ oriented by unit normals with negative x-components. Use the result in part (a) to find the flux of
$$\mathbf{F}(x, y, z) = y\mathbf{i} - z\mathbf{j} + 8\mathbf{k}$$
across σ.

28. (a) Derive the analogs of Formulas (12) and (13) for surfaces of the form $y = g(z, x)$.

(b) Let σ be the portion of the paraboloid $y = z^2 + x^2$ for $y \leq 1$ and $z \geq 0$ oriented by unit normals with positive y-components. Use the result in part (a) to find the flux of
$$\mathbf{F}(x, y, z) = x\mathbf{i} + y\mathbf{j} + z\mathbf{k}$$
across σ.

29. Let $\mathbf{F} = \|\mathbf{r}\|^k \mathbf{r}$, where $\mathbf{r} = x\mathbf{i} + y\mathbf{j} + z\mathbf{k}$ and k is a constant. (Note that if $k = -3$, this is an inverse-square field.) Let σ

be the sphere of radius a centered at the origin and oriented by the outward normal $\mathbf{n} = \mathbf{r}/\|\mathbf{r}\| = \mathbf{r}/a$.

(a) Find the flux of $\mathbf{F}$ across σ without performing any integrations. [*Hint:* The surface area of a sphere of radius a is $4\pi a^2$.]

(b) For what value of k is the flux independent of the radius of the sphere?

30. Let
$$\mathbf{F}(x, y, z) = a^2 x\mathbf{i} + (y/a)\mathbf{j} + az^2\mathbf{k}$$
and let σ be the sphere of radius 1 centered at the origin and oriented outward. Use a CAS to find all values of a such that the flux of $\mathbf{F}$ across σ is 3π.

31. Let
$$\mathbf{F}(x, y, z) = \left(\frac{6}{a} + 1\right)x\mathbf{i} - 4ay\mathbf{j} + a^2 z\mathbf{k}$$
and let σ be the sphere of radius a centered at the origin and oriented outward. Use a CAS to find all values of a such that the flux of $\mathbf{F}$ across σ is zero.

32. **Writing** Discuss the similarities and differences between the flux of a vector field across a surface and the line integral of a vector field along a curve.

33. **Writing** Write a paragraph explaining the concept of flux to someone unfamiliar with its meaning.

✔ **QUICK CHECK ANSWERS 15.6**

1. (a) $\displaystyle\iint_\sigma \mathbf{F} \cdot \mathbf{n}\, dS$ (b) 4π 2. (a) $\displaystyle\iint_R \mathbf{F} \cdot \left(\frac{\partial \mathbf{r}}{\partial u} \times \frac{\partial \mathbf{r}}{\partial v}\right) dA$ (b) 0   3. (a) $\displaystyle\iint_R \mathbf{F} \cdot \left(-\frac{\partial z}{\partial x}\mathbf{i} - \frac{\partial z}{\partial y}\mathbf{j} + \mathbf{k}\right) dA$ (b) $\dfrac{1}{2}$

4. the net volume of fluid crossing σ in the positive direction per unit time

---

15.7 THE DIVERGENCE THEOREM

In this section we will be concerned with flux across surfaces, such as spheres, that "enclose" a region of space. We will show that the flux across such surfaces can be expressed in terms of the divergence of the vector field, and we will use this result to give a physical interpretation of the concept of divergence.

■ ORIENTATION OF PIECEWISE SMOOTH CLOSED SURFACES

In the last section we studied flux across general surfaces. Here we will be concerned exclusively with surfaces that are boundaries of finite solids—the surface of a solid sphere, the surface of a solid box, or the surface of a solid cylinder, for example. Such surfaces are said to be *closed*. A closed surface may or may not be smooth, but most of the surfaces that arise in applications are *piecewise smooth*; that is, they consist of finitely many smooth surfaces joined together at the edges (a box, for example). We will limit our discussion to piecewise smooth surfaces that can be assigned an *inward orientation* (toward the interior of the solid) and an *outward orientation* (away from the interior). It is very difficult to make

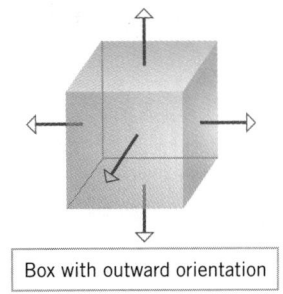

Box with outward orientation

▲ **Figure 15.7.1**

this concept mathematically precise, but the basic idea is that each piece of the surface is orientable, and oriented pieces fit together in such a way that the entire surface can be assigned an orientation (Figure 15.7.1).

■ THE DIVERGENCE THEOREM

In Section 15.1 we defined the divergence of a vector field

$$\mathbf{F}(x, y, z) = f(x, y, z)\mathbf{i} + g(x, y, z)\mathbf{j} + h(x, y, z)\mathbf{k}$$

as

$$\operatorname{div} \mathbf{F} = \frac{\partial f}{\partial x} + \frac{\partial g}{\partial y} + \frac{\partial h}{\partial z}$$

but we did not attempt to give a physical explanation of its meaning at that time. The following result, known as the *Divergence Theorem* or *Gauss's Theorem*, will provide us with a physical interpretation of divergence in the context of fluid flow.

15.7.1   THEOREM (*The Divergence Theorem*)   *Let G be a solid whose surface σ is oriented outward. If*

$$\mathbf{F}(x, y, z) = f(x, y, z)\mathbf{i} + g(x, y, z)\mathbf{j} + h(x, y, z)\mathbf{k}$$

where f, g, and h have continuous first partial derivatives on some open set containing G, and if **n** *is the outward unit normal on σ, then*

$$\iint_{\sigma} \mathbf{F} \cdot \mathbf{n} \, dS = \iiint_{G} \operatorname{div} \mathbf{F} \, dV \tag{1}$$

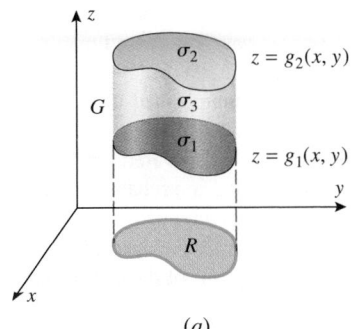

(a)

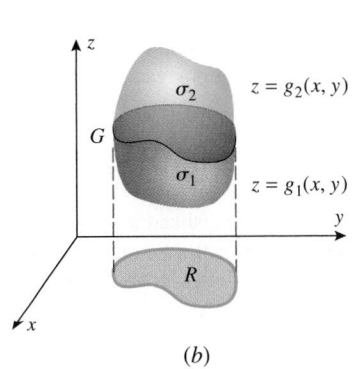

(b)

▲ **Figure 15.7.2**

The proof of this theorem for a general solid G is too difficult to present here. However, we can give a proof for the special case where G is simultaneously a simple xy-solid, a simple yz-solid, and a simple zx-solid (see Figure 14.5.3 and the related discussion for terminology).

PROOF   Formula (1) can be expressed as

$$\iint_{\sigma} [f(x, y, z)\mathbf{i} + g(x, y, z)\mathbf{j} + h(x, y, z)\mathbf{k}] \cdot \mathbf{n} \, dS = \iiint_{G} \left(\frac{\partial f}{\partial x} + \frac{\partial g}{\partial y} + \frac{\partial h}{\partial z} \right) dV$$

so it suffices to prove the three equalities

$$\iint_{\sigma} f(x, y, z)\mathbf{i} \cdot \mathbf{n} \, dS = \iiint_{G} \frac{\partial f}{\partial x} \, dV \tag{2a}$$

$$\iint_{\sigma} g(x, y, z)\mathbf{j} \cdot \mathbf{n} \, dS = \iiint_{G} \frac{\partial g}{\partial y} \, dV \tag{2b}$$

$$\iint_{\sigma} h(x, y, z)\mathbf{k} \cdot \mathbf{n} \, dS = \iiint_{G} \frac{\partial h}{\partial z} \, dV \tag{2c}$$

Since the proofs of all three equalities are similar, we will prove only the third.

Suppose that G has upper surface $z = g_2(x, y)$, lower surface $z = g_1(x, y)$, and projection R on the xy-plane. Let σ_1 denote the lower surface, σ_2 the upper surface, and σ_3 the lateral surface (Figure 15.7.2a). If the upper surface and lower surface meet as in

Figure 15.7.2*b*, then there is no lateral surface σ_3. Our proof will allow for both cases shown in those figures.

It follows from Theorem 14.5.2 that

$$\iiint\limits_{G} \frac{\partial h}{\partial z}\, dV = \iint\limits_{R} \left[\int_{g_1(x,y)}^{g_2(x,y)} \frac{\partial h}{\partial z}\, dz \right] dA = \iint\limits_{R} \left[h(x,y,z) \right]_{z=g_1(x,y)}^{g_2(x,y)} dA$$

so

$$\iiint\limits_{G} \frac{\partial h}{\partial z}\, dV = \iint\limits_{R} [h(x,y,g_2(x,y)) - h(x,y,g_1(x,y))]\, dA \qquad (3)$$

Carl Friedrich Gauss (1777–1855) German mathematician and scientist. Sometimes called the "prince of mathematicians," Gauss ranks with Newton and Archimedes as one of the three greatest mathematicians who ever lived. His father, a laborer, was an uncouth but honest man who would have liked Gauss to take up a trade such as gardening or bricklaying; but the boy's genius for mathematics was not to be denied. In the entire history of mathematics there may never have been a child so precocious as Gauss—by his own account he worked out the rudiments of arithmetic before he could talk. One day, before he was even three years old, his genius became apparent to his parents in a very dramatic way. His father was preparing the weekly payroll for the laborers under his charge while the boy watched quietly from a corner. At the end of the long and tedious calculation, Gauss informed his father that there was an error in the result and stated the answer, which he had worked out in his head. To the astonishment of his parents, a check of the computations showed Gauss to be correct!

For his elementary education Gauss was enrolled in a squalid school run by a man named Büttner whose main teaching technique was thrashing. Büttner was in the habit of assigning long addition problems which, unknown to his students, were arithmetic progressions that he could sum up using formulas. On the first day that Gauss entered the arithmetic class, the students were asked to sum the numbers from 1 to 100. But no sooner had Büttner stated the problem than Gauss turned over his slate and exclaimed in his peasant dialect, "Ligget se'." (Here it lies.) For nearly an hour Büttner glared at Gauss, who sat with folded hands while his classmates toiled away. When Büttner examined the slates at the end of the period, Gauss's slate contained a single number, 5050—the only correct solution in the class. To his credit, Büttner recognized the genius of Gauss and with the help of his assistant, John Bartels, had him brought to the attention of Karl Wilhelm Ferdinand, Duke of Brunswick. The shy and awkward boy, who was then fourteen, so captivated the Duke that he subsidized him through preparatory school, college, and the early part of his career.

From 1795 to 1798 Gauss studied mathematics at the University of Göttingen, receiving his degree in absentia from the University of Helmstadt. For his dissertation, he gave the first complete proof of the fundamental theorem of algebra, which states that every polynomial equation has as many solutions as its degree. At age 19 he solved a problem that baffled Euclid, inscribing a regular polygon of 17 sides in a circle using straightedge and compass; and in 1801, at age 24, he published his first masterpiece, *Disquisitiones Arithmeticae*, considered by many to be one of the most brilliant achievements in mathematics. In that book Gauss systematized the study of number theory (properties of the integers) and formulated the basic concepts that form the foundation of that subject.

In the same year that the *Disquisitiones* was published, Gauss again applied his phenomenal computational skills in a dramatic way. The astronomer Giuseppi Piazzi had observed the asteroid Ceres for $\frac{1}{40}$ of its orbit, but lost it in the Sun. Using only three observations and the "method of least squares" that he had developed in 1795, Gauss computed the orbit with such accuracy that astronomers had no trouble relocating it the following year. This achievement brought him instant recognition as the premier mathematician in Europe, and in 1807 he was made Professor of Astronomy and head of the astronomical observatory at Göttingen.

In the years that followed, Gauss revolutionized mathematics by bringing to it standards of precision and rigor undreamed of by his predecessors. He had a passion for perfection that drove him to polish and rework his papers rather than publish less finished work in greater numbers—his favorite saying was "Pauca, sed matura" (Few, but ripe). As a result, many of his important discoveries were squirreled away in diaries that remained unpublished until years after his death.

Among his myriad achievements, Gauss discovered the Gaussian or "bell-shaped" error curve fundamental in probability, gave the first geometric interpretation of complex numbers and established their fundamental role in mathematics, developed methods of characterizing surfaces intrinsically by means of the curves that they contain, developed the theory of conformal (angle-preserving) maps, and discovered non-Euclidean geometry 30 years before the ideas were published by others. In physics he made major contributions to the theory of lenses and capillary action, and with Wilhelm Weber he did fundamental work in electromagnetism. Gauss invented the heliotrope, bifilar magnetometer, and an electrotelegraph.

Gauss was deeply religious and aristocratic in demeanor. He mastered foreign languages with ease, read extensively, and enjoyed mineralogy and botany as hobbies. He disliked teaching and was usually cool and discouraging to other mathematicians, possibly because he had already anticipated their work. It has been said that if Gauss had published all of his discoveries, the current state of mathematics would be advanced by 50 years. He was without a doubt the greatest mathematician of the modern era.

Next we will evaluate the surface integral in (2c) by integrating over each surface of G separately. If there is a lateral surface σ_3, then at each point of this surface $\mathbf{k} \cdot \mathbf{n} = 0$ since $\mathbf{n}$ is horizontal and $\mathbf{k}$ is vertical. Thus,

$$\iint\limits_{\sigma_3} h(x, y, z)\mathbf{k} \cdot \mathbf{n} \, dS = 0$$

Therefore, regardless of whether G has a lateral surface, we can write

$$\iint\limits_{\sigma} h(x, y, z)\mathbf{k} \cdot \mathbf{n} \, dS = \iint\limits_{\sigma_1} h(x, y, z)\mathbf{k} \cdot \mathbf{n} \, dS + \iint\limits_{\sigma_2} h(x, y, z)\mathbf{k} \cdot \mathbf{n} \, dS \qquad (4)$$

On the upper surface σ_2, the outer normal is an upward normal, and on the lower surface σ_1, the outer normal is a downward normal. Thus, Formulas (12) and (13) of Section 15.6 imply that

$$\iint\limits_{\sigma_2} h(x, y, z)\mathbf{k} \cdot \mathbf{n} \, dS = \iint\limits_{R} h(x, y, g_2(x, y))\mathbf{k} \cdot \left(-\frac{\partial z}{\partial x}\mathbf{i} - \frac{\partial z}{\partial y}\mathbf{j} + \mathbf{k} \right) dA$$

$$= \iint\limits_{R} h(x, y, g_2(x, y)) \, dA \qquad (5)$$

and

$$\iint\limits_{\sigma_1} h(x, y, z)\mathbf{k} \cdot \mathbf{n} \, dS = \iint\limits_{R} h(x, y, g_1(x, y))\mathbf{k} \cdot \left(\frac{\partial z}{\partial x}\mathbf{i} + \frac{\partial z}{\partial y}\mathbf{j} - \mathbf{k} \right) dA$$

$$= -\iint\limits_{R} h(x, y, g_1(x, y)) \, dA \qquad (6)$$

Substituting (5) and (6) into (4) and combining the terms into a single integral yields

$$\iint\limits_{\sigma} h(x, y, z)\mathbf{k} \cdot \mathbf{n} \, dS = \iint\limits_{R} [h(x, y, g_2(x, y)) - h(x, y, g_1(x, y))] \, dA \qquad (7)$$

> Explain how the derivation of (2c) should be modified to yield a proof of (2a) or (2b).

Equation (2c) now follows from (3) and (7). ∎

The flux of a vector field across a closed surface with outward orientation is sometimes called the ***outward flux*** across the surface. In words, the Divergence Theorem states:

> *The outward flux of a vector field across a closed surface is equal to the triple integral of the divergence over the region enclosed by the surface.*

■ USING THE DIVERGENCE THEOREM TO FIND FLUX

Sometimes it is easier to find the flux across a closed surface by using the Divergence Theorem than by evaluating the flux integral directly. This is illustrated in the following example.

▶ **Example 1** Use the Divergence Theorem to find the outward flux of the vector field $\mathbf{F}(x, y, z) = z\mathbf{k}$ across the sphere $x^2 + y^2 + z^2 = a^2$.

Solution. Let σ denote the outward-oriented spherical surface and G the region that it encloses. The divergence of the vector field is

$$\text{div } \mathbf{F} = \frac{\partial z}{\partial z} = 1$$

so from (1) the flux across σ is

$$\Phi = \iint_{\sigma} \mathbf{F} \cdot \mathbf{n}\, dS = \iiint_{G} dV = \text{volume of } G = \frac{4\pi a^3}{3}.$$

Note how much simpler this calculation is than that in Example 1 of Section 15.6. ◄

The Divergence Theorem is usually the method of choice for finding the flux across closed piecewise smooth surfaces with multiple sections, since it eliminates the need for a separate integral evaluation over each section. This is illustrated in the next three examples.

▶ **Example 2**   Use the Divergence Theorem to find the outward flux of the vector field

$$\mathbf{F}(x, y, z) = 2x\mathbf{i} + 3y\mathbf{j} + z^2\mathbf{k}$$

across the unit cube in Figure 15.7.3.

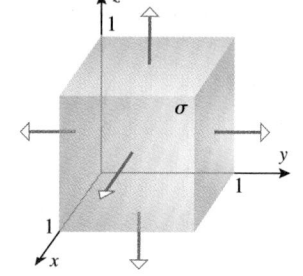

▲ **Figure 15.7.3**

Solution. Let σ denote the outward-oriented surface of the cube and G the region that it encloses. The divergence of the vector field is

$$\text{div } \mathbf{F} = \frac{\partial}{\partial x}(2x) + \frac{\partial}{\partial y}(3y) + \frac{\partial}{\partial z}(z^2) = 5 + 2z$$

so from (1) the flux across σ is

$$\Phi = \iint_{\sigma} \mathbf{F} \cdot \mathbf{n}\, dS = \iiint_{G} (5 + 2z)\, dV = \int_0^1 \int_0^1 \int_0^1 (5 + 2z)\, dz\, dy\, dx$$

$$= \int_0^1 \int_0^1 \left[5z + z^2\right]_{z=0}^1 dy\, dx = \int_0^1 \int_0^1 6\, dy\, dx = 6 \blacktriangleleft$$

Let $\mathbf{F}(x, y, z)$ be the vector field in Example 2 and show that $\mathbf{F} \cdot \mathbf{n}$ is constant on each of the six faces of the cube in Figure 15.7.3. Use your computations to confirm the result in Example 2.

▶ **Example 3**   Use the Divergence Theorem to find the outward flux of the vector field

$$\mathbf{F}(x, y, z) = x^3\mathbf{i} + y^3\mathbf{j} + z^2\mathbf{k}$$

across the surface of the region that is enclosed by the circular cylinder $x^2 + y^2 = 9$ and the planes $z = 0$ and $z = 2$ (Figure 15.7.4).

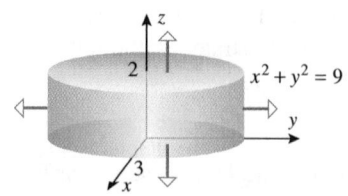

▲ **Figure 15.7.4**

Solution. Let σ denote the outward-oriented surface and G the region that it encloses. The divergence of the vector field is

$$\text{div } \mathbf{F} = \frac{\partial}{\partial x}(x^3) + \frac{\partial}{\partial y}(y^3) + \frac{\partial}{\partial z}(z^2) = 3x^2 + 3y^2 + 2z$$

so from (1) the flux across σ is

$$\Phi = \iint\limits_{\sigma} \mathbf{F} \cdot \mathbf{n}\, dS = \iiint\limits_{G} (3x^2 + 3y^2 + 2z)\, dV$$

$$= \int_0^{2\pi} \int_0^3 \int_0^2 (3r^2 + 2z)r\, dz\, dr\, d\theta \qquad \text{Using cylindrical coordinates}$$

$$= \int_0^{2\pi} \int_0^3 \left[3r^3 z + z^2 r \right]_{z=0}^{2}\, dr\, d\theta$$

$$= \int_0^{2\pi} \int_0^3 (6r^3 + 4r)\, dr\, d\theta$$

$$= \int_0^{2\pi} \left[\frac{3r^4}{2} + 2r^2 \right]_0^3\, d\theta$$

$$= \int_0^{2\pi} \frac{279}{2}\, d\theta = 279\pi \quad \blacktriangleleft$$

▶ **Example 4** Use the Divergence Theorem to find the outward flux of the vector field

$$\mathbf{F}(x, y, z) = x^3 \mathbf{i} + y^3 \mathbf{j} + z^3 \mathbf{k}$$

across the surface of the region that is enclosed by the hemisphere $z = \sqrt{a^2 - x^2 - y^2}$ and the plane $z = 0$ (Figure 15.7.5).

Solution. Let σ denote the outward-oriented surface and G the region that it encloses. The divergence of the vector field is

$$\text{div } \mathbf{F} = \frac{\partial}{\partial x}(x^3) + \frac{\partial}{\partial y}(y^3) + \frac{\partial}{\partial z}(z^3) = 3x^2 + 3y^2 + 3z^2$$

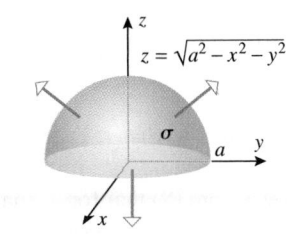

$z = \sqrt{a^2 - x^2 - y^2}$

σ

a

▲ **Figure 15.7.5**

so from (1) the flux across σ is

$$\Phi = \iint\limits_{\sigma} \mathbf{F} \cdot \mathbf{n}\, dS = \iiint\limits_{G} (3x^2 + 3y^2 + 3z^2)\, dV$$

$$= \int_0^{2\pi} \int_0^{\pi/2} \int_0^a (3\rho^2)\rho^2 \sin\phi\, d\rho\, d\phi\, d\theta \qquad \text{Using spherical coordinates}$$

$$= 3 \int_0^{2\pi} \int_0^{\pi/2} \int_0^a \rho^4 \sin\phi\, d\rho\, d\phi\, d\theta$$

$$= 3 \int_0^{2\pi} \int_0^{\pi/2} \left[\frac{\rho^5}{5} \sin\phi \right]_{\rho=0}^{a}\, d\phi\, d\theta$$

$$= \frac{3a^5}{5} \int_0^{2\pi} \int_0^{\pi/2} \sin\phi\, d\phi\, d\theta$$

$$= \frac{3a^5}{5} \int_0^{2\pi} \left[-\cos\phi \right]_0^{\pi/2}\, d\theta$$

$$= \frac{3a^5}{5} \int_0^{2\pi} d\theta = \frac{6\pi a^5}{5} \quad \blacktriangleleft$$

DIVERGENCE VIEWED AS FLUX DENSITY

The Divergence Theorem provides a way of interpreting the divergence of a vector field **F**. Suppose that G is a *small* spherical region centered at the point P_0 and that its surface, denoted by $\sigma(G)$, is oriented outward. Denote the volume of the region by vol(G) and the flux of **F** across $\sigma(G)$ by $\Phi(G)$. If div **F** is continuous on G, then across the small region G the value of div **F** will not vary much from its value div $\mathbf{F}(P_0)$ at the center, and we can reasonably approximate div **F** by the constant div $\mathbf{F}(P_0)$ on G. Thus, the Divergence Theorem implies that the flux $\Phi(G)$ of **F** across $\sigma(G)$ can be approximated by

$$\Phi(G) = \iint\limits_{\sigma(G)} \mathbf{F} \cdot \mathbf{n}\, dS = \iiint\limits_{G} \operatorname{div} \mathbf{F}\, dV \approx \operatorname{div} \mathbf{F}(P_0) \iiint\limits_{G} dV = \operatorname{div} \mathbf{F}(P_0)\, \operatorname{vol}(G)$$

from which we obtain the approximation

$$\operatorname{div} \mathbf{F}(P_0) \approx \frac{\Phi(G)}{\operatorname{vol}(G)} \tag{8}$$

The expression on the right side of (8) is called the ***outward flux density of* F *across* G**. If we now let the radius of the sphere approach zero [so that vol(G) approaches zero], then it is plausible that the error in this approximation will approach zero, and the divergence of **F** at the point P_0 will be given exactly by

$$\operatorname{div} \mathbf{F}(P_0) = \lim_{\operatorname{vol}(G) \to 0} \frac{\Phi(G)}{\operatorname{vol}(G)}$$

which we can express as

> Formula (9) is sometimes taken as the definition of divergence. This is a useful alternative to Definition 15.1.4 because it does not require a coordinate system.

$$\operatorname{div} \mathbf{F}(P_0) = \lim_{\operatorname{vol}(G) \to 0} \frac{1}{\operatorname{vol}(G)} \iint\limits_{\sigma(G)} \mathbf{F} \cdot \mathbf{n}\, dS \tag{9}$$

This limit, which is called the ***outward flux density of* F *at* P_0**, tells us that if **F** denotes the velocity field of a fluid, then *in a steady-state fluid flow* div **F** *can be interpreted as the limiting flux per unit volume at a point*. Moreover, it follows from (8) that for a small spherical region G centered at a point P_0 in the flow, the outward flux across the surface of G can be approximated by

$$\Phi(G) \approx (\operatorname{div} \mathbf{F}(P_0))(\operatorname{vol}(G)) \tag{10}$$

SOURCES AND SINKS

If P_0 is a point in an incompressible fluid at which div $\mathbf{F}(P_0) > 0$, then it follows from (8) that $\Phi(G) > 0$ for a sufficiently small sphere G centered at P_0. Thus, there is a greater volume of fluid going out through the surface of G than coming in. But this can only happen if there is some point *inside* the sphere at which fluid is entering the flow (say by condensation, melting of a solid, or a chemical reaction); otherwise the net outward flow through the surface would result in a decrease in density within the sphere, contradicting the incompressibility assumption. Similarly, if div $\mathbf{F}(P_0) < 0$, there would have to be a point *inside* the sphere at which fluid is leaving the flow (say by evaporation); otherwise the net inward flow through the surface would result in an increase in density within the sphere. In an incompressible fluid, points at which div $\mathbf{F}(P_0) > 0$ are called ***sources*** and points at which div $\mathbf{F}(P_0) < 0$ are called ***sinks***. Fluid enters the flow at a source and drains out at a sink. In an incompressible fluid without sources or sinks we must have

$$\operatorname{div} \mathbf{F}(P) = 0$$

at every point P. In hydrodynamics this is called the ***continuity equation for incompressible fluids*** and is sometimes taken as the defining characteristic of an incompressible fluid.

■ **GAUSS'S LAW FOR INVERSE-SQUARE FIELDS**

The Divergence Theorem applied to inverse-square fields (see Definition 15.1.2) produces a result called *Gauss's Law for Inverse-Square Fields*. This result is the basis for many important principles in physics.

15.7.2   GAUSS'S LAW FOR INVERSE-SQUARE FIELDS   If

$$\mathbf{F(r)} = \frac{c}{\|\mathbf{r}\|^3}\mathbf{r}$$

is an inverse-square field in 3-space, and if σ is a closed orientable surface that surrounds the origin, then the outward flux of $\mathbf{F}$ across σ is

$$\Phi = \iint_{\sigma} \mathbf{F} \cdot \mathbf{n} \, dS = 4\pi c \tag{11}$$

To derive this result, recall from Formula (5) of Section 15.1 that $\mathbf{F}$ can be expressed in component form as

$$\mathbf{F}(x, y, z) = \frac{c}{(x^2 + y^2 + z^2)^{3/2}}(x\mathbf{i} + y\mathbf{j} + z\mathbf{k}) \tag{12}$$

Since the components of $\mathbf{F}$ are not continuous at the origin, we cannot apply the Divergence Theorem across the solid enclosed by σ. However, we can circumvent this difficulty by constructing a sphere of radius a centered at the origin, where the radius is sufficiently small that the sphere lies entirely within the region enclosed by σ (Figure 15.7.6). We will denote the surface of this sphere by σ_a. The solid G enclosed between σ_a and σ is an example of a three-dimensional solid with an internal "cavity." Just as we were able to extend Green's Theorem to multiply connected regions in the plane (regions with holes), so it is possible to extend the Divergence Theorem to solids in 3-space with internal cavities, provided the surface integral in the theorem is taken over the *entire* boundary with the outside boundary of the solid oriented outward and the boundaries of the cavities oriented inward. Thus, if $\mathbf{F}$ is the inverse-square field in (12), and if σ_a is oriented inward, then the Divergence Theorem yields

$$\iiint_{G} \operatorname{div} \mathbf{F} \, dV = \iint_{\sigma} \mathbf{F} \cdot \mathbf{n} \, dS + \iint_{\sigma_a} \mathbf{F} \cdot \mathbf{n} \, dS \tag{13}$$

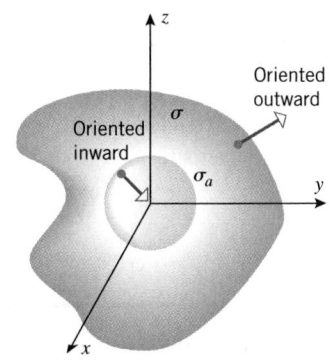

▲ **Figure 15.7.6**

But we showed in Example 5 of Section 15.1 that $\operatorname{div} \mathbf{F} = 0$, so (13) yields

$$\iint_{\sigma} \mathbf{F} \cdot \mathbf{n} \, dS = -\iint_{\sigma_a} \mathbf{F} \cdot \mathbf{n} \, dS \tag{14}$$

We can evaluate the surface integral over σ_a by expressing the integrand in terms of components; however, it is easier to leave it in vector form. At each point on the sphere the unit normal $\mathbf{n}$ points inward along a radius from the origin, and hence $\mathbf{n} = -\mathbf{r}/\|\mathbf{r}\|$. Thus, (14) yields

$$\iint_{\sigma} \mathbf{F} \cdot \mathbf{n}\, dS = -\iint_{\sigma_a} \frac{c}{\|\mathbf{r}\|^3} \mathbf{r} \cdot \left(-\frac{\mathbf{r}}{\|\mathbf{r}\|}\right) dS$$

$$= \iint_{\sigma_a} \frac{c}{\|\mathbf{r}\|^4} (\mathbf{r} \cdot \mathbf{r})\, dS$$

$$= \iint_{\sigma_a} \frac{c}{\|\mathbf{r}\|^2}\, dS$$

$$= \frac{c}{a^2} \iint_{\sigma_a} dS \qquad \boxed{\|\mathbf{r}\| = a \text{ on } \sigma_a}$$

$$= \frac{c}{a^2}(4\pi a^2) \qquad \boxed{\begin{array}{l}\text{The integral is the surface}\\\text{area of the sphere.}\end{array}}$$

$$= 4\pi c$$

which establishes (11).

■ **GAUSS'S LAW IN ELECTROSTATICS**

It follows from Example 1 of Section 15.1 with $q = 1$ that a single charged particle of charge Q located at the origin creates an inverse-square field

$$\mathbf{F}(\mathbf{r}) = \frac{Q}{4\pi\epsilon_0 \|\mathbf{r}\|^3} \mathbf{r}$$

in which $\mathbf{F}(\mathbf{r})$ is the electrical force exerted by Q on a unit positive charge ($q = 1$) located at the point with position vector $\mathbf{r}$. In this case Gauss's law (15.7.2) states that the outward flux Φ across any closed orientable surface σ that surrounds Q is

$$\Phi = \iint_{\sigma} \mathbf{F} \cdot \mathbf{n}\, dS = 4\pi \left(\frac{Q}{4\pi\epsilon_0}\right) = \frac{Q}{\epsilon_0}$$

This result, which is called **Gauss's Law for Electric Fields**, can be extended to more than one charge. It is one of the fundamental laws in electricity and magnetism.

✔**QUICK CHECK EXERCISES 15.7**   *(See page 1158 for answers.)*

1. Let G be a solid whose surface σ is oriented outward by the unit normal $\mathbf{n}$, and let $\mathbf{F}(x, y, z)$ denote a vector field whose component functions have continuous first partial derivatives on some open set containing G. The Divergence Theorem states that the surface integral _____ and the triple integral _____ have the same value.

2. The outward flux of $\mathbf{F}(x, y, z) = x\mathbf{i} + y\mathbf{j} + z\mathbf{k}$ across any unit cube is _____.

3. If $\mathbf{F}(x, y, z)$ is the velocity vector field for a steady-state incompressible fluid flow, then a point at which div $\mathbf{F}$ is positive is called a _____ and a point at which div $\mathbf{F}$ is negative is called a _____. The continuity equation for an incompressible fluid states that _____.

4. If

$$\mathbf{F}(\mathbf{r}) = \frac{c}{\|\mathbf{r}\|^3} \mathbf{r}$$

is an inverse-square field, and if σ is a closed orientable surface that surrounds the origin, then Gauss's law states that the outward flux of $\mathbf{F}$ across σ is _____. On the other hand, if σ does not surround the origin, then it follows from the Divergence Theorem that the outward flux of $\mathbf{F}$ across σ is _____.

EXERCISE SET 15.7   [c] CAS

1–4 Verify Formula (1) in the Divergence Theorem by evaluating the surface integral and the triple integral. ■

1. $\mathbf{F}(x, y, z) = x\mathbf{i} + y\mathbf{j} + z\mathbf{k}$; σ is the surface of the cube bounded by the planes $x = 0$, $x = 1$, $y = 0$, $y = 1$, $z = 0$, $z = 1$.

2. $\mathbf{F}(x, y, z) = x\mathbf{i} + y\mathbf{j} + z\mathbf{k}$; σ is the spherical surface $x^2 + y^2 + z^2 = 1$.

3. $\mathbf{F}(x, y, z) = 2x\mathbf{i} - yz\mathbf{j} + z^2\mathbf{k}$; the surface σ is the paraboloid $z = x^2 + y^2$ capped by the disk $x^2 + y^2 \le 1$ in the plane $z = 1$.

4. $\mathbf{F}(x, y, z) = xy\mathbf{i} + yz\mathbf{j} + xz\mathbf{k}$; σ is the surface of the cube bounded by the planes $x = 0$, $x = 2$, $y = 0$, $y = 2$, $z = 0$, $z = 2$.

5–8 True–False Determine whether the statement is true or false. Explain your answer. ■

5. The Divergence Theorem equates a surface integral and a line integral.

6. If G is a solid whose surface σ is oriented outward, and if div $\mathbf{F} > 0$ at all points of G, then the flux of $\mathbf{F}$ across σ is positive.

7. The continuity equation for incompressible fluids states that the divergence of the velocity vector field of the fluid is zero.

8. Since the divergence of an inverse-square field is zero, the flux of an inverse-square field across any closed orientable surface must be zero as well.

9–19 Use the Divergence Theorem to find the flux of $\mathbf{F}$ across the surface σ with outward orientation. ■

9. $\mathbf{F}(x, y, z) = (x^2 + y)\mathbf{i} + z^2\mathbf{j} + (e^y - z)\mathbf{k}$; σ is the surface of the rectangular solid bounded by the coordinate planes and the planes $x = 3$, $y = 1$, and $z = 2$.

10. $\mathbf{F}(x, y, z) = z^3\mathbf{i} - x^3\mathbf{j} + y^3\mathbf{k}$, where σ is the sphere $x^2 + y^2 + z^2 = a^2$.

11. $\mathbf{F}(x, y, z) = (x - z)\mathbf{i} + (y - x)\mathbf{j} + (z - y)\mathbf{k}$; σ is the surface of the cylindrical solid bounded by $x^2 + y^2 = a^2$, $z = 0$, and $z = 1$.

12. $\mathbf{F}(x, y, z) = x\mathbf{i} + y\mathbf{j} + z\mathbf{k}$; σ is the surface of the solid bounded by the paraboloid $z = 1 - x^2 - y^2$ and the xy-plane.

13. $\mathbf{F}(x, y, z) = x^3\mathbf{i} + y^3\mathbf{j} + z^3\mathbf{k}$; σ is the surface of the cylindrical solid bounded by $x^2 + y^2 = 4$, $z = 0$, and $z = 3$.

14. $\mathbf{F}(x, y, z) = (x^2 + y)\mathbf{i} + xy\mathbf{j} - (2xz + y)\mathbf{k}$; σ is the surface of the tetrahedron in the first octant bounded by $x + y + z = 1$ and the coordinate planes.

15. $\mathbf{F}(x, y, z) = (x^3 - e^y)\mathbf{i} + (y^3 + \sin z)\mathbf{j} + (z^3 - xy)\mathbf{k}$, where σ is the surface of the solid bounded above by $z = \sqrt{4 - x^2 - y^2}$ and below by the xy-plane. [*Hint:* Use spherical coordinates.]

16. $\mathbf{F}(x, y, z) = 2xz\mathbf{i} + yz\mathbf{j} + z^2\mathbf{k}$, where σ is the surface of the solid bounded above by $z = \sqrt{a^2 - x^2 - y^2}$ and below by the xy-plane.

17. $\mathbf{F}(x, y, z) = x^2\mathbf{i} + y^2\mathbf{j} + z^2\mathbf{k}$; σ is the surface of the conical solid bounded by $z = \sqrt{x^2 + y^2}$ and $z = 1$.

18. $\mathbf{F}(x, y, z) = x^2 y\mathbf{i} - xy^2\mathbf{j} + (z + 2)\mathbf{k}$; σ is the surface of the solid bounded above by the plane $z = 2x$ and below by the paraboloid $z = x^2 + y^2$.

19. $\mathbf{F}(x, y, z) = x^3\mathbf{i} + x^2 y\mathbf{j} + xy\mathbf{k}$; σ is the surface of the solid bounded by $z = 4 - x^2$, $y + z = 5$, $z = 0$, and $y = 0$.

20. Prove that if $\mathbf{r} = x\mathbf{i} + y\mathbf{j} + z\mathbf{k}$ and σ is the surface of a solid G oriented by outward unit normals, then

$$\text{vol}(G) = \frac{1}{3} \iint_\sigma \mathbf{r} \cdot \mathbf{n} \, dS$$

where vol(G) is the volume of G.

21. Use the result in Exercise 20 to find the outward flux of the vector field $\mathbf{F}(x, y, z) = x\mathbf{i} + y\mathbf{j} + z\mathbf{k}$ across the surface σ of the cylindrical solid bounded by $x^2 + 4x + y^2 = 5$, $z = -1$, and $z = 4$.

FOCUS ON CONCEPTS

22. Let $\mathbf{F}(x, y, z) = a\mathbf{i} + b\mathbf{j} + c\mathbf{k}$ be a constant vector field and let σ be the surface of a solid G. Use the Divergence Theorem to show that the flux of $\mathbf{F}$ across σ is zero. Give an informal physical explanation of this result.

23. Find a vector field $\mathbf{F}(x, y, z)$ that has
  (a) positive divergence everywhere
  (b) negative divergence everywhere.

24. In each part, the figure shows a horizontal layer of the vector field of a fluid flow in which the flow is parallel to the xy-plane at every point and is identical in each layer (i.e., is independent of z). For each flow, what can you say about the sign of the divergence at the origin? Explain your reasoning.

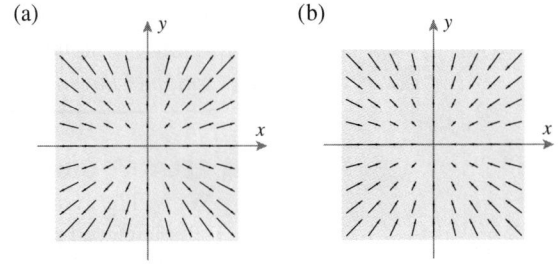

25. Let $\mathbf{F}(x, y, z)$ be a nonzero vector field in 3-space whose component functions have continuous first partial derivatives, and assume that div $\mathbf{F} = 0$ everywhere. If σ is any sphere in 3-space, explain why there are infinitely many points on σ at which $\mathbf{F}$ is tangent to the sphere.

26. Does the result in Exercise 25 remain true if the sphere σ is replaced by a cube? Explain.

27–31 Prove the identity, assuming that $\mathbf{F}$, σ, and G satisfy the hypotheses of the Divergence Theorem and that all necessary differentiability requirements for the functions $f(x, y, z)$ and $g(x, y, z)$ are met. ■

27. $\displaystyle\iint\limits_{\sigma} \text{curl } \mathbf{F} \cdot \mathbf{n} \, dS = 0$ [*Hint:* See Exercise 37, Section 15.1.]

28. $\displaystyle\iint\limits_{\sigma} \nabla f \cdot \mathbf{n} \, dS = \iiint\limits_{G} \nabla^2 f \, dV$

$$\left(\nabla^2 f = \frac{\partial^2 f}{\partial x^2} + \frac{\partial^2 f}{\partial y^2} + \frac{\partial^2 f}{\partial z^2} \right)$$

29. $\displaystyle\iint\limits_{\sigma} (f \nabla g) \cdot \mathbf{n} \, dS = \iiint\limits_{G} (f \nabla^2 g + \nabla f \cdot \nabla g) \, dV$

30. $\displaystyle\iint\limits_{\sigma} (f \nabla g - g \nabla f) \cdot \mathbf{n} \, dS = \iiint\limits_{G} (f \nabla^2 g - g \nabla^2 f) \, dV$

[*Hint:* Interchange f and g in 29.]

31. $\displaystyle\iint\limits_{\sigma} (f \mathbf{n}) \cdot \mathbf{v} \, dS = \iiint\limits_{G} \nabla f \cdot \mathbf{v} \, dV$ ($\mathbf{v}$ a fixed vector)

32. Use the Divergence Theorem to find all positive values of k such that
$$\mathbf{F}(\mathbf{r}) = \frac{\mathbf{r}}{\|\mathbf{r}\|^k}$$
satisfies the condition div $\mathbf{F} = 0$ when $\mathbf{r} \neq \mathbf{0}$. [*Hint:* Modify the proof of (11).]

33–36 Determine whether the vector field $\mathbf{F}(x, y, z)$ is free of sources and sinks. If it is not, locate them. ■

33. $\mathbf{F}(x, y, z) = (y + z)\mathbf{i} - xz^3\mathbf{j} + (x^2 \sin y)\mathbf{k}$

34. $\mathbf{F}(x, y, z) = xy\mathbf{i} - xy\mathbf{j} + y^2\mathbf{k}$

35. $\mathbf{F}(x, y, z) = x^3\mathbf{i} + y^3\mathbf{j} + z^3\mathbf{k}$

36. $\mathbf{F}(x, y, z) = (x^3 - x)\mathbf{i} + (y^3 - y)\mathbf{j} + (z^3 - z)\mathbf{k}$

C **37.** Let σ be the surface of the solid G that is enclosed by the paraboloid $z = 1 - x^2 - y^2$ and the plane $z = 0$. Use a CAS to verify Formula (1) in the Divergence Theorem for the vector field
$$\mathbf{F} = (x^2 y - z^2)\mathbf{i} + (y^3 - x)\mathbf{j} + (2x + 3z - 1)\mathbf{k}$$
by evaluating the surface integral and the triple integral.

38. Writing Discuss what it means to say that the divergence of a vector field is independent of a coordinate system. Explain how we know this to be true.

39. Writing Describe some geometrical and physical applications of the Divergence Theorem.

✔ **QUICK CHECK ANSWERS 15.7**

1. $\displaystyle\iint\limits_{\sigma} \mathbf{F} \cdot \mathbf{n} \, dS; \quad \iiint\limits_{G} \text{div } \mathbf{F} \, dV$ **2.** 3   **3.** source; sink; div $\mathbf{F} = 0$ **4.** $4\pi c$; 0

15.8 STOKES' THEOREM

In this section we will discuss a generalization of Green's Theorem to three dimensions that has important applications in the study of vector fields, particularly in the analysis of rotational motion of fluids. This theorem will also provide us with a physical interpretation of the curl of a vector field.

■ RELATIVE ORIENTATION OF CURVES AND SURFACES

We will be concerned in this section with oriented surfaces in 3-space that are bounded by simple closed parametric curves (Figure 15.8.1a). If σ is an oriented surface bounded by a simple closed parametric curve C, then there are two possible relationships between the orientations of σ and C, which can be described as follows. Imagine a person walking along the curve C with his or her head in the direction of the orientation of σ. The person is said to be walking in the ***positive direction*** of C relative to the orientation of σ if the surface is on the person's left (Figure 15.8.1b), and the person is said to be walking in the ***negative direction*** of C relative to the orientation of σ if the surface is on the person's right (Figure 15.8.1c). The positive direction of C establishes a right-hand relationship between the orientations of σ and C in the sense that if the fingers of the right hand are curled from the direction of C toward σ, then the thumb points (roughly) in the direction of the orientation of σ.

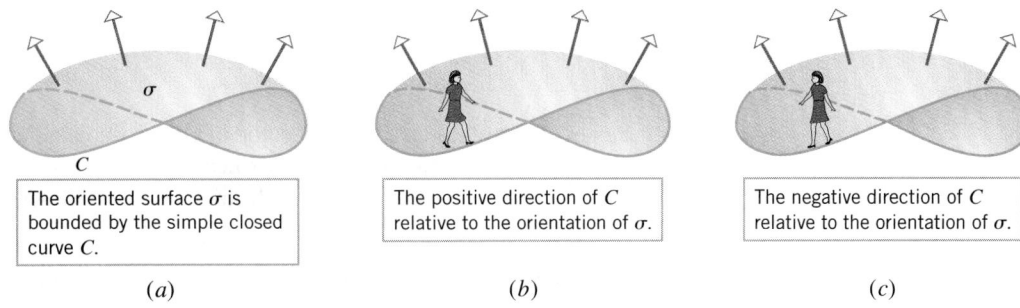

The oriented surface σ is bounded by the simple closed curve C.	The positive direction of C relative to the orientation of σ.	The negative direction of C relative to the orientation of σ.
(a)	(b)	(c)

▲ **Figure 15.8.1**

■ STOKES' THEOREM

In Section 15.1 we defined the curl of a vector field

$$\mathbf{F}(x, y, z) = f(x, y, z)\mathbf{i} + g(x, y, z)\mathbf{j} + h(x, y, z)\mathbf{k}$$

as

$$\text{curl } \mathbf{F} = \left(\frac{\partial h}{\partial y} - \frac{\partial g}{\partial z}\right)\mathbf{i} + \left(\frac{\partial f}{\partial z} - \frac{\partial h}{\partial x}\right)\mathbf{j} + \left(\frac{\partial g}{\partial x} - \frac{\partial f}{\partial y}\right)\mathbf{k} = \begin{vmatrix} \mathbf{i} & \mathbf{j} & \mathbf{k} \\ \dfrac{\partial}{\partial x} & \dfrac{\partial}{\partial y} & \dfrac{\partial}{\partial z} \\ f & g & h \end{vmatrix} \quad (1)$$

but we did not attempt to give a physical explanation of its meaning at that time. The following result, known as *Stokes' Theorem*, will provide us with a physical interpretation of the curl in the context of fluid flow.

15.8.1 THEOREM (*Stokes' Theorem*) *Let σ be a piecewise smooth oriented surface that is bounded by a simple, closed, piecewise smooth curve C with positive orientation. If the components of the vector field*

$$\mathbf{F}(x, y, z) = f(x, y, z)\mathbf{i} + g(x, y, z)\mathbf{j} + h(x, y, z)\mathbf{k}$$

are continuous and have continuous first partial derivatives on some open set containing σ, and if $\mathbf{T}$ is the unit tangent vector to C, then

$$\oint_C \mathbf{F} \cdot \mathbf{T}\, ds = \iint_\sigma (\text{curl } \mathbf{F}) \cdot \mathbf{n}\, dS \quad (2)$$

The proof of this theorem is beyond the scope of this text, so we will focus on its applications.

Recall from Formulas (30) and (34) in Section 15.2 that if $\mathbf{F}$ is a force field, the integral on the left side of (2) represents the work performed by the force field on a particle that traverses the curve C. Thus, loosely phrased, Stokes' Theorem states:

> *The work performed by a force field on a particle that traverses a simple, closed, piecewise smooth curve C in the positive direction can be obtained by integrating the normal component of the curl over an oriented surface σ bounded by C.*

■ **USING STOKES' THEOREM TO CALCULATE WORK**

For computational purposes it is usually preferable to use Formula (30) in Section 15.2 to rewrite the formula in Stokes' Theorem as

$$\oint_C \mathbf{F} \cdot d\mathbf{r} = \iint_\sigma (\text{curl } \mathbf{F}) \cdot \mathbf{n} \, dS \tag{3}$$

Stokes' Theorem is usually the method of choice for calculating work around piecewise smooth curves with multiple sections, since it eliminates the need for a separate integral evaluation over each section. This is illustrated in the following example.

▶ **Example 1**   Find the work performed by the force field

$$\mathbf{F}(x, y, z) = x^2\mathbf{i} + 4xy^3\mathbf{j} + y^2x\mathbf{k}$$

on a particle that traverses the rectangle C in the plane $z = y$ shown in Figure 15.8.2.

Solution.   The work performed by the field is

$$W = \oint_C \mathbf{F} \cdot d\mathbf{r}$$

However, to evaluate this integral directly would require four separate integrations, one over each side of the rectangle. Instead, we will use Formula (3) to express the work as the surface integral

$$W = \iint_\sigma (\text{curl } \mathbf{F}) \cdot \mathbf{n} \, dS$$

in which the plane surface σ enclosed by C is assigned a *downward* orientation to make the orientation of C positive, as required by Stokes' Theorem.

Since the surface σ has equation $z = y$ and

$$\text{curl } \mathbf{F} = \begin{vmatrix} \mathbf{i} & \mathbf{j} & \mathbf{k} \\ \dfrac{\partial}{\partial x} & \dfrac{\partial}{\partial y} & \dfrac{\partial}{\partial z} \\ x^2 & 4xy^3 & xy^2 \end{vmatrix} = 2xy\mathbf{i} - y^2\mathbf{j} + 4y^3\mathbf{k}$$

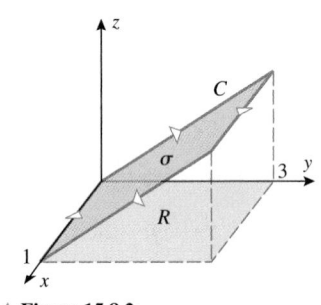

▲ **Figure 15.8.2**

George Gabriel Stokes **(1819–1903)** Irish mathematician and physicist. Born in Skreen, Ireland, Stokes came from a family deeply rooted in the Church of Ireland. His father was a rector, his mother the daughter of a rector, and three of his brothers took holy orders. He received his early education from his father and a local parish clerk. In 1837, he entered Pembroke College and after graduating with top honors accepted a fellowship at the college. In 1847 he was appointed Lucasian professor of mathematics at Cambridge, a position once held by Isaac Newton (and now held by the British physicist, Stephen Hawking), but one that had lost its esteem through the years. By virtue of his accomplishments, Stokes ultimately restored the position to the eminence it once held. Unfortunately, the position paid very little and Stokes was forced to teach at the Government School of Mines during the 1850s to supplement his income.

Stokes was one of several outstanding nineteenth century scientists who helped turn the physical sciences in a more empirical direction. He systematically studied hydrodynamics, elasticity of solids, behavior of waves in elastic solids, and diffraction of light. For Stokes, mathematics was a tool for his physical studies. He wrote classic papers on the motion of viscous fluids that laid the foundation for modern hydrodynamics; he elaborated on the wave theory of light; and he wrote papers on gravitational variation that established him as a founder of the modern science of geodesy.

Stokes was honored in his later years with degrees, medals, and memberships in foreign societies. He was knighted in 1889. Throughout his life, Stokes gave generously of his time to learned societies and readily assisted those who sought his help in solving problems. He was deeply religious and vitally concerned with the relationship between science and religion.

it follows from Formula (13) of Section 15.6 with curl **F** replacing **F** that

$$W = \iint_\sigma (\text{curl } \mathbf{F}) \cdot \mathbf{n}\, dS = \iint_R (\text{curl } \mathbf{F}) \cdot \left(\frac{\partial z}{\partial x}\mathbf{i} + \frac{\partial z}{\partial y}\mathbf{j} - \mathbf{k} \right) dA$$

$$= \iint_R (2xy\mathbf{i} - y^2\mathbf{j} + 4y^3\mathbf{k}) \cdot (0\mathbf{i} + \mathbf{j} - \mathbf{k})\, dA$$

$$= \int_0^1 \int_0^3 (-y^2 - 4y^3)\, dy\, dx$$

$$= -\int_0^1 \left[\frac{y^3}{3} + y^4 \right]_{y=0}^{3} dx$$

$$= -\int_0^1 90\, dx = -90 \quad \blacktriangleleft$$

Explain how the result in Example 1 shows that the given force field is not conservative.

▶ **Example 2**   Verify Stokes' Theorem for the vector field $\mathbf{F}(x, y, z) = 2z\mathbf{i} + 3x\mathbf{j} + 5y\mathbf{k}$, taking σ to be the portion of the paraboloid $z = 4 - x^2 - y^2$ for which $z \geq 0$ with upward orientation, and C to be the positively oriented circle $x^2 + y^2 = 4$ that forms the boundary of σ in the xy-plane (Figure 15.8.3).

Solution.   We will verify Formula (3). Since σ is oriented up, the positive orientation of C is counterclockwise looking down the positive z-axis. Thus, C can be represented parametrically (with positive orientation) by

$$x = 2\cos t, \quad y = 2\sin t, \quad z = 0 \qquad (0 \leq t \leq 2\pi) \tag{4}$$

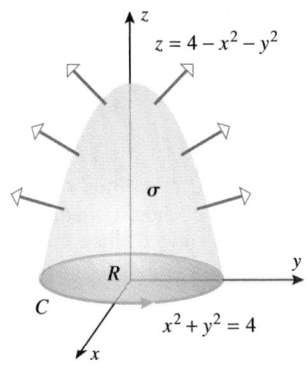

$z = 4 - x^2 - y^2$

σ

R

C

$x^2 + y^2 = 4$

▲ **Figure 15.8.3**

Therefore,

$$\oint_C \mathbf{F} \cdot d\mathbf{r} = \oint_C 2z\, dx + 3x\, dy + 5y\, dz$$

$$= \int_0^{2\pi} [0 + (6\cos t)(2\cos t) + 0]\, dt$$

$$= \int_0^{2\pi} 12\cos^2 t\, dt = 12 \left[\frac{1}{2}t + \frac{1}{4}\sin 2t \right]_0^{2\pi} = 12\pi$$

To evaluate the right side of (3), we start by finding curl **F**. We obtain

$$\text{curl } \mathbf{F} = \begin{vmatrix} \mathbf{i} & \mathbf{j} & \mathbf{k} \\ \dfrac{\partial}{\partial x} & \dfrac{\partial}{\partial y} & \dfrac{\partial}{\partial z} \\ 2z & 3x & 5y \end{vmatrix} = 5\mathbf{i} + 2\mathbf{j} + 3\mathbf{k}$$

Since σ is oriented up and is expressed in the form $z = g(x, y) = 4 - x^2 - y^2$, it follows from Formula (12) of Section 15.6 with curl **F** replacing **F** that

$$\iint_{\sigma} (\text{curl } \mathbf{F}) \cdot \mathbf{n}\, dS = \iint_{R} (\text{curl } \mathbf{F}) \cdot \left(-\frac{\partial z}{\partial x}\mathbf{i} - \frac{\partial z}{\partial y}\mathbf{j} + \mathbf{k} \right) dA$$

$$= \iint_{R} (5\mathbf{i} + 2\mathbf{j} + 3\mathbf{k}) \cdot (2x\mathbf{i} + 2y\mathbf{j} + \mathbf{k})\, dA$$

$$= \iint_{R} (10x + 4y + 3)\, dA$$

$$= \int_{0}^{2\pi} \int_{0}^{2} (10r\cos\theta + 4r\sin\theta + 3)r\, dr\, d\theta$$

$$= \int_{0}^{2\pi} \left[\frac{10r^3}{3}\cos\theta + \frac{4r^3}{3}\sin\theta + \frac{3r^2}{2} \right]_{r=0}^{2} d\theta$$

$$= \int_{0}^{2\pi} \left(\frac{80}{3}\cos\theta + \frac{32}{3}\sin\theta + 6 \right) d\theta$$

$$= \left[\frac{80}{3}\sin\theta - \frac{32}{3}\cos\theta + 6\theta \right]_{0}^{2\pi} = 12\pi$$

As guaranteed by Stokes' Theorem, the value of this surface integral is the same as the value obtained for the line integral. Note, however, that the line integral was simpler to evaluate and hence would be the method of choice in this case. ◄

REMARK Observe that in Formula (3) the only relationships required between σ and C are that C be the boundary of σ and that C be positively oriented relative to the orientation of σ. Thus, if σ_1 and σ_2 are *different* oriented surfaces but have the *same* positively oriented boundary curve C, then it follows from (3) that

$$\iint_{\sigma_1} \text{curl } \mathbf{F} \cdot \mathbf{n}\, dS = \iint_{\sigma_2} \text{curl } \mathbf{F} \cdot \mathbf{n}\, dS$$

For example, the parabolic surface in Example 2 has the same positively oriented boundary C as the disk R in Figure 15.8.3 with upper orientation. Thus, the value of the surface integral in that example would not change if σ is replaced by R (or by any other oriented surface that has the positively oriented circle C as its boundary). This can be useful in computations because it is sometimes possible to circumvent a difficult integration by changing the surface of integration.

■ **RELATIONSHIP BETWEEN GREEN'S THEOREM AND STOKES' THEOREM**

It is sometimes convenient to regard a vector field

$$\mathbf{F}(x, y) = f(x, y)\mathbf{i} + g(x, y)\mathbf{j}$$

in 2-space as a vector field in 3-space by expressing it as

$$\mathbf{F}(x, y) = f(x, y)\mathbf{i} + g(x, y)\mathbf{j} + 0\mathbf{k} \tag{5}$$

If R is a region in the xy-plane enclosed by a simple, closed, piecewise smooth curve C, then we can treat R as a *flat* surface, and we can treat a surface integral over R as an ordinary double integral over R. Thus, if we orient R up and C counterclockwise looking down the positive z-axis, then Formula (3) applied to (5) yields

$$\oint_{C} \mathbf{F} \cdot d\mathbf{r} = \iint_{R} \text{curl } \mathbf{F} \cdot \mathbf{k}\, dA \tag{6}$$

But

$$\text{curl } \mathbf{F} = \begin{vmatrix} \mathbf{i} & \mathbf{j} & \mathbf{k} \\ \dfrac{\partial}{\partial x} & \dfrac{\partial}{\partial y} & \dfrac{\partial}{\partial z} \\ f & g & 0 \end{vmatrix} = -\frac{\partial g}{\partial z}\mathbf{i} + \frac{\partial f}{\partial z}\mathbf{j} + \left(\frac{\partial g}{\partial x} - \frac{\partial f}{\partial y}\right)\mathbf{k} = \left(\frac{\partial g}{\partial x} - \frac{\partial f}{\partial y}\right)\mathbf{k}$$

since $\partial g/\partial z = \partial f/\partial z = 0$. Substituting this expression in (6) and expressing the integrals in terms of components yields

$$\oint_C f\,dx + g\,dy = \iint_R \left(\frac{\partial g}{\partial x} - \frac{\partial f}{\partial y}\right)dA$$

which is Green's Theorem [Formula (1) of Section 15.4]. Thus, we have shown that Green's Theorem can be viewed as a special case of Stokes' Theorem.

■ **CURL VIEWED AS CIRCULATION**

Stokes' Theorem provides a way of interpreting the curl of a vector field $\mathbf{F}$ in the context of fluid flow. For this purpose let σ_a be a small oriented disk of radius a centered at a point P_0 in a steady-state fluid flow, and let $\mathbf{n}$ be a unit normal vector at the center of the disk that points in the direction of orientation. Let us assume that the flow of liquid past the disk causes it to spin around the axis through $\mathbf{n}$, and let us try to find the direction of $\mathbf{n}$ that will produce the maximum rotation rate in the positive direction of the boundary curve C_a (Figure 15.8.4). For convenience, we will denote the area of the disk σ_a by $A(\sigma_a)$; that is, $A(\sigma_a) = \pi a^2$.

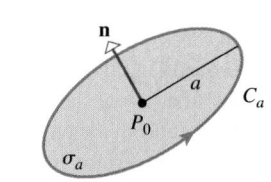
▲ **Figure 15.8.4**

If the direction of $\mathbf{n}$ is fixed, then at each point of C_a the only component of $\mathbf{F}$ that contributes to the rotation of the disk about $\mathbf{n}$ is the component $\mathbf{F} \cdot \mathbf{T}$ tangent to C_a (Figure 15.8.5). Thus, for a fixed $\mathbf{n}$ the integral

$$\oint_{C_a} \mathbf{F} \cdot \mathbf{T}\,ds \tag{7}$$

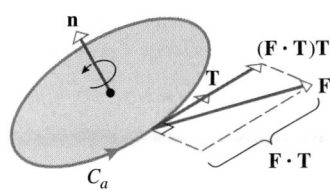
▲ **Figure 15.8.5**

can be viewed as a measure of the tendency for the fluid to flow in the positive direction around C_a. Accordingly, (7) is called the **circulation of $\mathbf{F}$ around C_a**. For example, in the extreme case where the flow is normal to the circle at each point, the circulation around C_a is zero, since $\mathbf{F} \cdot \mathbf{T} = 0$ at each point. The more closely that $\mathbf{F}$ aligns with $\mathbf{T}$ along the circle, the larger the value of $\mathbf{F} \cdot \mathbf{T}$ and the larger the value of the circulation.

To see the relationship between circulation and curl, suppose that curl $\mathbf{F}$ is continuous on σ_a, so that when σ_a is small the value of curl $\mathbf{F}$ at any point of σ_a will not vary much from the value of curl $\mathbf{F}(P_0)$ at the center. Thus, for a small disk σ_a we can reasonably approximate curl $\mathbf{F}$ on σ_a by the constant value curl $\mathbf{F}(P_0)$. Moreover, because the surface σ_a is flat, the unit normal vectors that orient σ_a are all equal. Thus, the vector quantity $\mathbf{n}$ in Formula (3) can be treated as a constant, and we can write

$$\oint_{C_a} \mathbf{F} \cdot \mathbf{T}\,ds = \iint_{\sigma_a} (\text{curl } \mathbf{F}) \cdot \mathbf{n}\,dS \approx \text{curl } \mathbf{F}(P_0) \cdot \mathbf{n} \iint_{\sigma_a} dS$$

where the line integral is taken in the positive direction of C_a. But the last double integral in this equation represents the surface area of σ_a, so

$$\oint_{C_a} \mathbf{F} \cdot \mathbf{T}\,ds \approx [\text{curl } \mathbf{F}(P_0) \cdot \mathbf{n}]A(\sigma_a)$$

from which we obtain

$$\text{curl } \mathbf{F}(P_0) \cdot \mathbf{n} \approx \frac{1}{A(\sigma_a)}\oint_{C_a} \mathbf{F} \cdot \mathbf{T}\,ds \tag{8}$$

Formula (9) is sometimes taken as a definition of curl. This is a useful alternative to Definition 15.1.5 because it does not require a coordinate system.

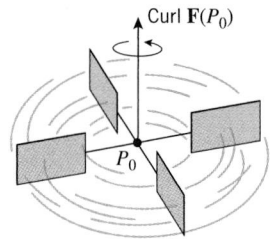

▲ **Figure 15.8.6**

The quantity on the right side of (8) is called the *circulation density of* **F** *around* C_a. If we now let the radius a of the disk approach zero (with **n** fixed), then it is plausible that the error in this approximation will approach zero and the exact value of curl $\mathbf{F}(P_0) \cdot \mathbf{n}$ will be given by

$$\text{curl } \mathbf{F}(P_0) \cdot \mathbf{n} = \lim_{a \to 0} \frac{1}{A(\sigma_a)} \oint_{C_a} \mathbf{F} \cdot \mathbf{T} \, ds \tag{9}$$

We call curl $\mathbf{F}(P_0) \cdot \mathbf{n}$ the *circulation density of* **F** *at* P_0 *in the direction of* **n**. This quantity has its maximum value when **n** is in the same direction as curl $\mathbf{F}(P_0)$; this tells us that *at each point in a steady-state fluid flow the maximum circulation density occurs in the direction of the curl.* Physically, this means that if a small paddle wheel is immersed in the fluid so that the pivot point is at P_0, then the paddles will turn most rapidly when the spindle is aligned with curl $\mathbf{F}(P_0)$ (Figure 15.8.6). If curl $\mathbf{F} = \mathbf{0}$ at each point of a region, then **F** is said to be *irrotational* in that region, since no circulation occurs about any point of the region.

✔ **QUICK CHECK EXERCISES 15.8** *(See page 1166 for answers.)*

1. Let σ be a piecewise smooth oriented surface that is bounded by a simple, closed, piecewise smooth curve C with positive orientation. If the component functions of the vector field $\mathbf{F}(x, y, z)$ have continuous first partial derivatives on some open set containing σ, and if **T** is the unit tangent vector to C, then Stokes' Theorem states that the line integral _____ and the surface integral _____ are equal.

2. We showed in Example 2 that the vector field

$$\mathbf{F}(x, y, z) = 2z\mathbf{i} + 3x\mathbf{j} + 5y\mathbf{k}$$

satisfies the equation curl $\mathbf{F} = 5\mathbf{i} + 2\mathbf{j} + 3\mathbf{k}$. It follows from Stokes' Theorem that if C is any circle of radius a in the xy-plane that is oriented counterclockwise when viewed from the positive z-axis, then

$$\int_C \mathbf{F} \cdot \mathbf{T} \, ds = \underline{\hspace{1cm}}$$

where **T** denotes the unit tangent vector to C.

3. (a) If σ_1 and σ_2 are two oriented surfaces that have the same positively oriented boundary curve C, and if the vector field $\mathbf{F}(x, y, z)$ has continuous first partial derivatives on some open set containing σ_1 and σ_2, then it follows from Stokes' Theorem that the surface integrals _____ and _____ are equal.

(b) Let $\mathbf{F}(x, y, z) = 2z\mathbf{i} + 3x\mathbf{j} + 5y\mathbf{k}$, let a be a positive number, and let σ be the portion of the paraboloid $z = a^2 - x^2 - y^2$ for which $z \geq 0$ with upward orientation. Using part (a) and Quick Check Exercise 2, it follows that

$$\iint_\sigma (\text{curl } \mathbf{F}) \cdot \mathbf{n} \, dS = \underline{\hspace{1cm}}$$

4. For steady-state flow, the maximum circulation density occurs in the direction of the _____ of the velocity vector field for the flow.

EXERCISE SET 15.8   **C** CAS

1–4 Verify Formula (2) in Stokes' Theorem by evaluating the line integral and the surface integral. Assume that the surface has an upward orientation. ■

1. $\mathbf{F}(x, y, z) = (x - y)\mathbf{i} + (y - z)\mathbf{j} + (z - x)\mathbf{k}$; σ is the portion of the plane $x + y + z = 1$ in the first octant.

2. $\mathbf{F}(x, y, z) = x^2\mathbf{i} + y^2\mathbf{j} + z^2\mathbf{k}$; σ is the portion of the cone $z = \sqrt{x^2 + y^2}$ below the plane $z = 1$.

3. $\mathbf{F}(x, y, z) = x\mathbf{i} + y\mathbf{j} + z\mathbf{k}$; σ is the upper hemisphere $z = \sqrt{a^2 - x^2 - y^2}$.

4. $\mathbf{F}(x, y, z) = (z - y)\mathbf{i} + (z + x)\mathbf{j} - (x + y)\mathbf{k}$; σ is the portion of the paraboloid $z = 9 - x^2 - y^2$ above the xy-plane.

5–12 Use Stokes' Theorem to evaluate $\oint_C \mathbf{F} \cdot d\mathbf{r}$. ■

5. $\mathbf{F}(x, y, z) = z^2\mathbf{i} + 2x\mathbf{j} - y^3\mathbf{k}$; C is the circle $x^2 + y^2 = 1$ in the xy-plane with counterclockwise orientation looking down the positive z-axis.

6. $\mathbf{F}(x, y, z) = xz\mathbf{i} + 3x^2y^2\mathbf{j} + yx\mathbf{k}$; C is the rectangle in the plane $z = y$ shown in Figure 15.8.2.

7. $\mathbf{F}(x, y, z) = 3z\mathbf{i} + 4x\mathbf{j} + 2y\mathbf{k}$; C is the boundary of the paraboloid shown in Figure 15.8.3.

8. $\mathbf{F}(x, y, z) = -3y^2\mathbf{i} + 4z\mathbf{j} + 6x\mathbf{k}$; C is the triangle in the plane $z = \frac{1}{2}y$ with vertices $(2, 0, 0)$, $(0, 2, 1)$, and $(0, 0, 0)$ with a counterclockwise orientation looking down the positive z-axis.

9. $\mathbf{F}(x, y, z) = xy\mathbf{i} + x^2\mathbf{j} + z^2\mathbf{k}$; C is the intersection of the paraboloid $z = x^2 + y^2$ and the plane $z = y$ with a counterclockwise orientation looking down the positive z-axis.

10. $\mathbf{F}(x, y, z) = xy\mathbf{i} + yz\mathbf{j} + zx\mathbf{k}$; C is the triangle in the plane $x + y + z = 1$ with vertices $(1, 0, 0)$, $(0, 1, 0)$, and $(0, 0, 1)$ with a counterclockwise orientation looking from the first octant toward the origin.

11. $\mathbf{F}(x, y, z) = (x - y)\mathbf{i} + (y - z)\mathbf{j} + (z - x)\mathbf{k}$; C is the circle $x^2 + y^2 = a^2$ in the xy-plane with counterclockwise orientation looking down the positive z-axis.

12. $\mathbf{F}(x, y, z) = (z + \sin x)\mathbf{i} + (x + y^2)\mathbf{j} + (y + e^z)\mathbf{k}$; C is the intersection of the sphere $x^2 + y^2 + z^2 = 1$ and the cone $z = \sqrt{x^2 + y^2}$ with counterclockwise orientation looking down the positive z-axis.

13–16 True–False Determine whether the statement is true or false. Explain your answer. ■

13. Stokes' Theorem equates a line integral and a surface integral.

14. Stokes' Theorem is a special case of Green's Theorem.

15. The circulation of a vector field $\mathbf{F}$ around a closed curve C is defined to be
$$\int_C (\text{curl }\mathbf{F}) \cdot \mathbf{T}\, ds$$

16. If $\mathbf{F}(x, y, z)$ is defined everywhere in 3-space, and if curl $\mathbf{F}$ has no $\mathbf{k}$-component at any point in the xy-plane, then
$$\int_C \mathbf{F} \cdot \mathbf{T}\, ds = 0$$
for every smooth, simple, closed curve in the xy-plane.

17. Consider the vector field given by the formula
$$\mathbf{F}(x, y, z) = (x - z)\mathbf{i} + (y - x)\mathbf{j} + (z - xy)\mathbf{k}$$
(a) Use Stokes' Theorem to find the circulation around the triangle with vertices $A(1, 0, 0)$, $B(0, 2, 0)$, and $C(0, 0, 1)$ oriented counterclockwise looking from the origin toward the first octant.
(b) Find the circulation density of $\mathbf{F}$ at the origin in the direction of $\mathbf{k}$.
(c) Find the unit vector $\mathbf{n}$ such that the circulation density of $\mathbf{F}$ at the origin is maximum in the direction of $\mathbf{n}$.

FOCUS ON CONCEPTS

18. (a) Let σ denote the surface of a solid G with $\mathbf{n}$ the outward unit normal vector field to σ. Assume that $\mathbf{F}$ is a vector field with continuous first-order partial derivatives on σ. Prove that
$$\iint_\sigma (\text{curl }\mathbf{F}) \cdot \mathbf{n}\, dS = 0$$
[*Hint:* Let C denote a simple closed curve on σ that separates the surface into two subsurfaces σ_1 and σ_2 that share C as their common boundary. Apply Stokes' Theorem to σ_1 and to σ_2 and add the results.]
(b) The vector field curl($\mathbf{F}$) is called the *curl field* of $\mathbf{F}$. In words, interpret the formula in part (a) as a statement about the flux of the curl field.

19–20 The figures in these exercises show a horizontal layer of the vector field of a fluid flow in which the flow is parallel to the xy-plane at every point and is identical in each layer (i.e., is independent of z). For each flow, state whether you believe that the curl is nonzero at the origin, and explain your reasoning. If you believe that it is nonzero, then state whether it points in the positive or negative z-direction. ■

19. (a)   (b)

20. (a)   (b)

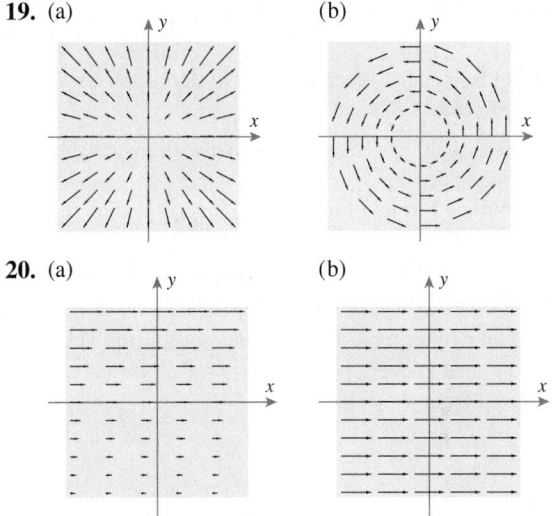

21. Let $\mathbf{F}(x, y, z)$ be a conservative vector field in 3-space whose component functions have continuous first partial derivatives. Explain how to use Formula (9) to prove that curl $\mathbf{F} = \mathbf{0}$.

22. In 1831 the physicist Michael Faraday discovered that an electric current can be produced by varying the magnetic flux through a conducting loop. His experiments showed that the electromotive force $\mathbf{E}$ is related to the magnetic induction $\mathbf{B}$ by the equation
$$\oint_C \mathbf{E} \cdot d\mathbf{r} = -\iint_\sigma \frac{\partial \mathbf{B}}{\partial t} \cdot \mathbf{n}\, dS$$
Use this result to make a conjecture about the relationship between curl $\mathbf{E}$ and $\mathbf{B}$, and explain your reasoning.

C 23. Let σ be the portion of the paraboloid $z = 1 - x^2 - y^2$ for which $z \geq 0$, and let C be the circle $x^2 + y^2 = 1$ that forms the boundary of σ in the xy-plane. Assuming that σ is oriented up, use a CAS to verify Formula (2) in Stokes' Theorem for the vector field
$$\mathbf{F} = (x^2y - z^2)\mathbf{i} + (y^3 - x)\mathbf{j} + (2x + 3z - 1)\mathbf{k}$$
by evaluating the line integral and the surface integral.

24. Writing Discuss what it means to say that the curl of a vector field is independent of a coordinate system. Explain how we know this to be true.

25. Writing Compare and contrast the Fundamental Theorem of Line Integrals, the Divergence Theorem, and Stokes' Theorem.

✔ QUICK CHECK ANSWERS 15.8

1. $\displaystyle\int_C \mathbf{F} \cdot \mathbf{T}\, ds$; $\displaystyle\iint_\sigma (\text{curl } \mathbf{F}) \cdot \mathbf{n}\, dS$ 2. $3\pi a^2$ 3. (a) $\displaystyle\iint_{\sigma_1} (\text{curl } \mathbf{F}) \cdot \mathbf{n}\, dS$; $\displaystyle\iint_{\sigma_2} (\text{curl } \mathbf{F}) \cdot \mathbf{n}\, dS$ (b) $3\pi a^2$ 4. curl

CHAPTER 15 REVIEW EXERCISES

1. In words, what is a vector field? Give some physical examples of vector fields.

2. (a) Give a physical example of an inverse-square field $\mathbf{F}(\mathbf{r})$ in 3-space.
   (b) Write a formula for a general inverse-square field $\mathbf{F}(\mathbf{r})$ in terms of the radius vector $\mathbf{r}$.
   (c) Write a formula for a general inverse-square field $\mathbf{F}(x, y, z)$ in 3-space using rectangular coordinates.

3. Find an explicit coordinate expression for the vector field $\mathbf{F}(x, y)$ that at every point $(x, y) \neq (1, 2)$ is the unit vector directed from (x, y) to $(1, 2)$.

4. Find $\nabla \left(\dfrac{x + y}{x - y} \right)$.

5. Find $\text{curl}(z\mathbf{i} + x\mathbf{j} + y\mathbf{k})$.

6. Let
$$\mathbf{F}(x, y, z) = \frac{x}{x^2 + y^2}\mathbf{i} + \frac{y}{x^2 + y^2}\mathbf{j} + \frac{z}{x^2 + y^2}\mathbf{k}$$
   Sketch the level surface $\text{div } \mathbf{F} = 1$.

7. Assume that C is the parametric curve $x = x(t)$, $y = y(t)$, where t varies from a to b. In each part, express the line integral as a definite integral with variable of integration t.
   (a) $\displaystyle\int_C f(x, y)\, dx + g(x, y)\, dy$ (b) $\displaystyle\int_C f(x, y)\, ds$

8. (a) Express the mass M of a thin wire in 3-space as a line integral.
   (b) Express the length of a curve as a line integral.

9. Give a physical interpretation of $\int_C \mathbf{F} \cdot \mathbf{T}\, ds$.

10. State some alternative notations for $\int_C \mathbf{F} \cdot \mathbf{T}\, ds$.

11–13 Evaluate the line integral. ■

11. $\displaystyle\int_C (x - y)\, ds$; $C : x^2 + y^2 = 1$

12. $\displaystyle\int_C x\, dx + z\, dy - 2y^2\, dz$;
$C : x = \cos t,\ y = \sin t,\ z = t \quad (0 \leq t \leq 2\pi)$

13. $\displaystyle\int_C \mathbf{F} \cdot d\mathbf{r}$ where $\mathbf{F}(x, y) = (x/y)\mathbf{i} - (y/x)\mathbf{j}$;
$\mathbf{r}(t) = t\mathbf{i} + 2t\mathbf{j} \quad (1 \leq t \leq 2)$

14. Find the work done by the force field
$$\mathbf{F}(x, y) = y^2\mathbf{i} + xy\mathbf{j}$$

moving a particle from $(0, 0)$ to $(1, 1)$ along the parabola $y = x^2$.

15. State the Fundamental Theorem of Line Integrals, including all required hypotheses.

16. Evaluate $\int_C \nabla f \cdot d\mathbf{r}$ where $f(x, y, z) = xy^2z^3$ and
$$\mathbf{r}(t) = t\mathbf{i} + (t^2 + t)\mathbf{j} + \sin(3\pi t/2)\mathbf{k} \quad (0 \leq t \leq 1)$$

17. Let $\mathbf{F}(x, y) = y\mathbf{i} - 2x\mathbf{j}$.
   (a) Find a nonzero function $h(x)$ such that $h(x)\mathbf{F}(x, y)$ is a conservative vector field.
   (b) Find a nonzero function $g(y)$ such that $g(y)\mathbf{F}(x, y)$ is a conservative vector field.

18. Let $\mathbf{F}(x, y) = (ye^{xy} - 1)\mathbf{i} + xe^{xy}\mathbf{j}$.
   (a) Show that $\mathbf{F}$ is a conservative vector field.
   (b) Find a potential function for $\mathbf{F}$.
   (c) Find the work performed by the force field on a particle that moves along the sawtooth curve represented by the parametric equations
$$\begin{aligned} x &= t + \sin^{-1}(\sin t) \\ y &= (2/\pi)\sin^{-1}(\sin t) \end{aligned} \quad (0 \leq t \leq 8\pi)$$
   (see the accompanying figure).

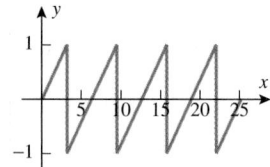

◀ Figure Ex-18

19. State Green's Theorem, including all of the required hypotheses.

20. Express the area of a plane region as a line integral.

21. Let α and β denote angles that satisfy $0 < \beta - \alpha \leq 2\pi$ and assume that $r = f(\theta)$ is a smooth polar curve with $f(\theta) > 0$ on the interval $[\alpha, \beta]$. Use the formula
$$A = \frac{1}{2}\int_C -y\, dx + x\, dy$$
   to find the area of the region R enclosed by the curve $r = f(\theta)$ and the rays $\theta = \alpha$ and $\theta = \beta$.

22. (a) Use Green's Theorem to prove that
$$\int_C f(x)\, dx + g(y)\, dy = 0$$

if f and g are differentiable functions and C is a simple, closed, piecewise smooth curve.

(b) What does this tell you about the vector field $\mathbf{F}(x, y) = f(x)\mathbf{i} + g(y)\mathbf{j}$?

23. Assume that σ is the parametric surface

$$\mathbf{r} = x(u, v)\mathbf{i} + y(u, v)\mathbf{j} + z(u, v)\mathbf{k}$$

where (u, v) varies over a region R. Express the surface integral

$$\iint_{\sigma} f(x, y, z)\, dS$$

as a double integral with variables of integration u and v.

24. Evaluate $\iint_{\sigma} z\, dS$; $\sigma : x^2 + y^2 = 1$ $(0 \leq z \leq 1)$.

25. Do you think that the surface in the accompanying figure is orientable? Explain your reasoning.

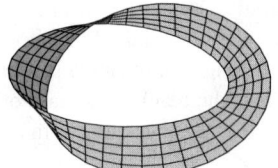

◀ **Figure Ex-25**

26. Give a physical interpretation of $\iint_{\sigma} \mathbf{F} \cdot \mathbf{n}\, dS$.

27. Find the flux of $\mathbf{F}(x, y, z) = x\mathbf{i} + y\mathbf{j} + 2z\mathbf{k}$ through the portion of the paraboloid $z = 1 - x^2 - y^2$ that is on or above the xy-plane, with upward orientation.

28. Find the flux of $\mathbf{F}(x, y, z) = x\mathbf{i} + 2y\mathbf{j} + 3z\mathbf{k}$ through the unit sphere centered at the origin with outward orientation.

29. State the Divergence Theorem and Stokes' Theorem, including all required hypotheses.

30. Let G be a solid with the surface σ oriented by outward unit normals, suppose that ϕ has continuous first and second partial derivatives in some open set containing G, and let $D_{\mathbf{n}}\phi$ be the directional derivative of ϕ, where $\mathbf{n}$ is an outward unit normal to σ. Show that

$$\iint_{\sigma} D_{\mathbf{n}}\phi\, dS = \iiint_{G} \left[\frac{\partial^2\phi}{\partial x^2} + \frac{\partial^2\phi}{\partial y^2} + \frac{\partial^2\phi}{\partial z^2} \right] dV$$

31. Let σ be the sphere $x^2 + y^2 + z^2 = 1$, let $\mathbf{n}$ be an inward unit normal, and let $D_{\mathbf{n}}f$ be the directional derivative of $f(x, y, z) = x^2 + y^2 + z^2$. Use the result in Exercise 30 to evaluate the surface integral

$$\iint_{\sigma} D_{\mathbf{n}}f\, dS$$

32. Use Stokes' Theorem to evaluate $\iint_{\sigma} \text{curl } \mathbf{F} \cdot \mathbf{n}\, dS$ where $\mathbf{F}(x, y, z) = (z - y)\mathbf{i} + (x + z)\mathbf{j} - (x + y)\mathbf{k}$ and σ is the portion of the paraboloid $z = 2 - x^2 - y^2$ on or above the plane $z = 1$, with upward orientation.

33. Let $\mathbf{F}(x, y, z) = f(x, y, z)\mathbf{i} + g(x, y, z)\mathbf{j} + h(x, y, z)\mathbf{k}$ and suppose that f, g, and h are continuous and have continuous first partial derivatives in a region. It was shown in Exercise 31 of Section 15.3 that if $\mathbf{F}$ is conservative in the region, then

$$\frac{\partial f}{\partial y} = \frac{\partial g}{\partial x}, \quad \frac{\partial f}{\partial z} = \frac{\partial h}{\partial x}, \quad \frac{\partial g}{\partial z} = \frac{\partial h}{\partial y}$$

there. Use this result to show that if $\mathbf{F}$ is conservative in an open spherical region, then curl $\mathbf{F} = \mathbf{0}$ in that region.

34–35 With the aid of Exercise 33, determine whether $\mathbf{F}$ is conservative. ▣

34. (a) $\mathbf{F}(x, y, z) = z^2\mathbf{i} + e^{-y}\mathbf{j} + 2xz\mathbf{k}$
  (b) $\mathbf{F}(x, y, z) = xy\mathbf{i} + x^2\mathbf{j} + \sin z\mathbf{k}$

35. (a) $\mathbf{F}(x, y, z) = \sin x\mathbf{i} + z\mathbf{j} + y\mathbf{k}$
  (b) $\mathbf{F}(x, y, z) = z\mathbf{i} + 2yz\mathbf{j} + y^2\mathbf{k}$

36. As discussed in Example 1 of Section 15.1, *Coulomb's law* states that the electrostatic force $\mathbf{F}(\mathbf{r})$ that a particle of charge Q exerts on a particle of charge q is given by the formula

$$\mathbf{F}(\mathbf{r}) = \frac{qQ}{4\pi\epsilon_0 \|\mathbf{r}\|^3}\mathbf{r}$$

where $\mathbf{r}$ is the radius vector from Q to q and ϵ_0 is the permittivity constant.

(a) Express the vector field $\mathbf{F}(\mathbf{r})$ in coordinate form $\mathbf{F}(x, y, z)$ with Q at the origin.

(b) Find the work performed by the force field $\mathbf{F}$ on a charge q that moves along a straight line from $(3, 0, 0)$ to $(3, 1, 5)$.

CHAPTER 15 MAKING CONNECTIONS

Assume that the motion of a particle of mass m is described by a smooth vector-valued function

$$\mathbf{r}(t) = x(t)\mathbf{i} + y(t)\mathbf{j} + z(t)\mathbf{k} \quad (a \le t \le b)$$

where t denotes time. Let C denote the graph of the vector-valued function and let $v(t)$ and $\mathbf{a}(t)$ denote the respective speed and acceleration of the particle at time t.

1. We will say that the particle is moving "freely" under the influence of a force field $\mathbf{F}(x, y, z)$, provided $\mathbf{F}$ is the *only* force acting on the particle. In this case Newton's Second Law of Motion becomes

$$\mathbf{F}(x(t), y(t), z(t)) = m\mathbf{a}(t)$$

Use Theorem 12.6.2 to prove that when the particle is moving freely

$$\int_C \mathbf{F} \cdot \mathbf{T}\, ds = \int_C m\left(\frac{dv}{dt}\right) ds = m\int_a^b v(t)\left(\frac{dv}{dt}\right) dt$$

$$= m\int_a^b \frac{d}{dt}\left(\frac{1}{2}[v(t)]^2\right) dt$$

$$= \frac{1}{2}m[v(b)]^2 - \frac{1}{2}m[v(a)]^2$$

This tells us that the work performed by $\mathbf{F}$ on the particle is equal to the change in kinetic energy of the particle.

2. Suppose that the particle moves along a *prescribed* curve C under the influence of a force field $\mathbf{F}(x, y, z)$. In addition to $\mathbf{F}$, the particle will experience a concurrent "support force" $\mathbf{S}(x(t), y(t), z(t))$ from the curve. (Imagine a roller-coaster car falling without friction under the influence of the gravitational force $\mathbf{F}$. The tracks of the coaster provide the support force $\mathbf{S}$.) In this case we will say that the particle has a "constrained" motion under the influence of $\mathbf{F}$. Prove that the work performed by $\mathbf{F}$ on a particle with constrained motion is also equal to the change in kinetic energy of the particle. [*Hint:* Apply the argument of Exercise 1 to the resultant force $\mathbf{F} + \mathbf{S}$ on the particle. Use the fact that at each point on C, $\mathbf{S}$ will be normal to the curve.]

3. Suppose that $\mathbf{F}$ is a conservative force field. Use Exercises 1 and 2, along with the discussion in Section 15.3, to develop the conservation of energy principle for both free and constrained motion under $\mathbf{F}$.

4. As shown in the accompanying figure, a girl with mass m is sliding down a smooth (frictionless) playground slide that is inclined at an angle of θ with the horizontal. If the acceleration due to gravity is g and the length of the slide is l, prove that the speed of the child when she reaches the base of the slide is $v = \sqrt{2gl\sin\theta}$. Assume that she starts from rest at the top of the slide.

◀ **Figure Ex-4**

 **EXPANDING THE CALCULUS HORIZON**

To learn how the topics in this chapter can be used to model hurricane behavior, see the module entitled **Hurricane Modeling** at:

www.wiley.com/college/anton

A

GRAPHING FUNCTIONS USING CALCULATORS AND COMPUTER ALGEBRA SYSTEMS

■ GRAPHING CALCULATORS AND COMPUTER ALGEBRA SYSTEMS

The development of new technology has significantly changed how and where mathematicians, engineers, and scientists perform their work, as well as their approach to problem solving. Among the most significant of these developments are programs called **Computer Algebra Systems** (abbreviated CAS), the most common being *Mathematica* and *Maple*.[*] Computer algebra systems not only have graphing capabilities, but, as their name suggests, they can perform many of the symbolic computations that occur in algebra, calculus, and branches of higher mathematics. For example, it is a trivial task for a CAS to perform the factorization

$$x^6 + 23x^5 + 147x^4 - 139x^3 - 3464x^2 - 2112x + 23040 = (x + 5)(x - 3)^2(x + 8)^3$$

or the exact numerical computation

$$\left(\frac{63456}{3177295} - \frac{43907}{22854377} \right)^3 = \frac{225191245716420829125932020230122866923}{3828959555819369204449565945369203764688375}$$

Technology has also made it possible to generate graphs of equations and functions in seconds that in the past might have taken hours. Figure A.1 shows the graphs of the function $f(x) = x^4 - x^3 - 2x^2$ produced with various graphing utilities; the first two were generated with the CAS programs, *Mathematica* and *Maple*, and the third with a graphing calculator. Graphing calculators produce coarser graphs than most computer programs but have the advantage of being compact and portable.

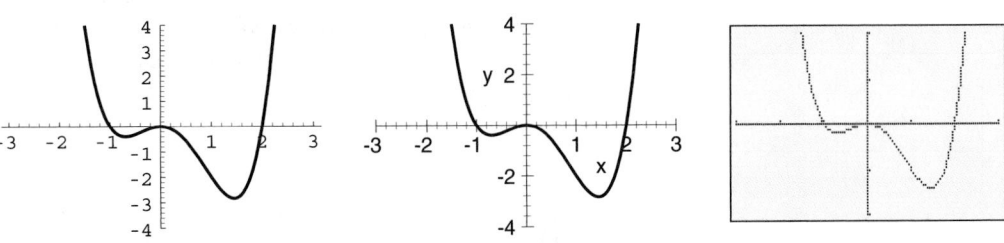

Generated by Mathematica   Generated by Maple   Generated by a graphing calculator

▲ **Figure A.1**

---

[*]*Mathematica* is a product of Wolfram Research, Inc.; *Maple* is a product of Waterloo Maple Software, Inc.

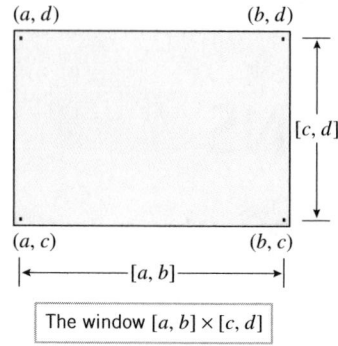

The window $[a, b] \times [c, d]$

▲ **Figure A.2**

TECHNOLOGY MASTERY

Use your graphing utility to generate the graph of the function

$$f(x) = x^4 - x^3 - 2x^2$$

in the window $[-3, 3] \times [-4, 4]$.

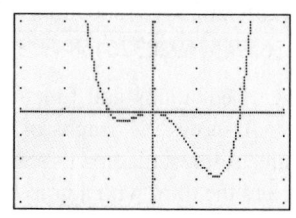

Generated by Mathematica

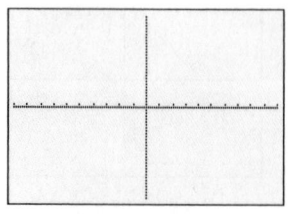

Generated by a graphing calculator

▲ **Figure A.3**

[−5, 5] × [−5, 5]
xScl = 0.5, yScl = 10

▲ **Figure A.4**

■ **VIEWING WINDOWS**

Graphing utilities can only show a portion of the xy-plane in the viewing screen, so the first step in graphing an equation is to determine which rectangular portion of the xy-plane you want to display. This region is called the ***viewing window*** (or ***viewing rectangle***). For example, in Figure A.1 the viewing window extends over the interval $[-3, 3]$ in the x-direction and over the interval $[-4, 4]$ in the y-direction, so we denote the viewing window by $[-3, 3] \times [-4, 4]$ (read "$[-3, 3]$ by $[-4, 4]$"). In general, if the viewing window is $[a, b] \times [c, d]$, then the window extends between $x = a$ and $x = b$ in the x-direction and between $y = c$ and $y = d$ in the y-direction. We will call $[a, b]$ the ***x-interval*** for the window and $[c, d]$ the ***y-interval*** for the window (Figure A.2).

Different graphing utilities designate viewing windows in different ways. For example, the first two graphs in Figure A.1 were produced by the commands

```
Plot[x^4 - x^3 -2*x^2, {x, -3, 3}, PlotRange->{-4, 4}]
```
(*Mathematica*)
```
plot(x^4 - x^3 -2*x^2, x = -3..3, y = -4..4);
```
(*Maple*)

and the last graph was produced on a graphing calculator by pressing the GRAPH button after setting the values for the variables that determine the x-interval and y-interval to be

$$x\text{Min} = -3, \quad x\text{Max} = 3, \quad y\text{Min} = -4, \quad y\text{Max} = 4$$

■ **TICK MARKS AND GRID LINES**

To help locate points in a viewing window, graphing utilities provide methods for drawing ***tick marks*** (also called ***scale marks***). With computer programs such as *Mathematica* and *Maple*, there are specific commands for designating the spacing between tick marks, but if the user does not specify the spacing, then the programs make certain *default* choices. For example, in the first two parts of Figure A.1, the tick marks shown were the default choices.

On some graphing calculators the spacing between tick marks is determined by two ***scale variables*** (also called ***scale factors***), which we will denote by

$$x\text{Scl} \quad \text{and} \quad y\text{Scl}$$

(The notation varies among calculators.) These variables specify the spacing between the tick marks in the x- and y-directions, respectively. For example, in the third part of Figure A.1 the window and tick marks were designated by the settings

$$x\text{Min} = -3 \qquad x\text{Max} = 3$$
$$y\text{Min} = -4 \qquad y\text{Max} = 4$$
$$x\text{Scl} = 1 \qquad y\text{Scl} = 1$$

Most graphing utilities allow for variations in the design and positioning of tick marks. For example, Figure A.3 shows two variations of the graphs in Figure A.1; the first was generated on a computer using an option for placing the ticks and numbers on the edges of a box, and the second was generated on a graphing calculator using an option for drawing grid lines to simulate graph paper.

▶ **Example 1**   Figure A.4 shows the window $[-5, 5] \times [-5, 5]$ with the tick marks spaced 0.5 unit apart in the x-direction and 10 units apart in the y-direction. No tick marks are actually visible in the y-direction because the tick mark at the origin is covered by the x-axis, and all other tick marks in that direction fall outside of the viewing window.   ◀

▶ **Example 2**   Figure A.5 shows the window $[-10, 10] \times [-10, 10]$ with the tick marks spaced 0.1 unit apart in the x- and y-directions. In this case the tick marks are so close together that they create thick lines on the coordinate axes. When this occurs you will usually want to increase the scale factors to reduce the number of tick marks to make them legible. ◀

TECHNOLOGY MASTERY

Graphing calculators provide a way of clearing all settings and returning them to *default values*. For example, on one calculator the default window is $[-10, 10] \times [-10, 10]$ and the default scale factors are xScl $= 1$ and yScl $= 1$. Read your documentation to determine the default values for your calculator and how to restore the default settings. If you are using a CAS, read your documentation to determine the commands for specifying the spacing between tick marks.

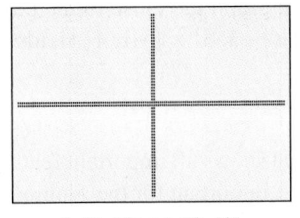

$[-10, 10] \times [-10, 10]$
xScl $= 0.1$, yScl $= 0.1$

▲ **Figure A.5**

■ CHOOSING A VIEWING WINDOW

When the graph of a function extends indefinitely in some direction, no single viewing window can show it all. In such cases the choice of the viewing window can affect one's perception of how the graph looks. For example, Figure A.6 shows a computer-generated graph of $y = 9 - x^2$, and Figure A.7 shows four views of this graph generated on a calculator.

- In part (*a*) the graph falls completely outside of the window, so the window is blank (except for the ticks and axes).
- In part (*b*) the graph is broken into two pieces because it passes in and out of the window.
- In part (*c*) the graph appears to be a straight line because we have zoomed in on a very small segment of the curve.
- In part (*d*) we have a more revealing picture of the graph shape because the window encompasses the high point on the graph and the intersections with the x-axis.

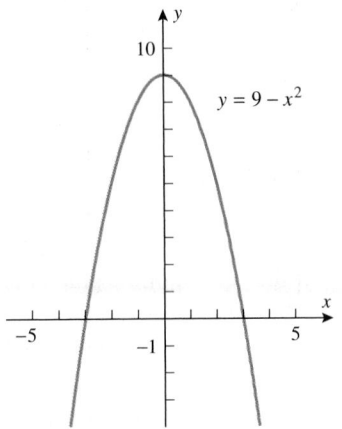

▲ **Figure A.6**

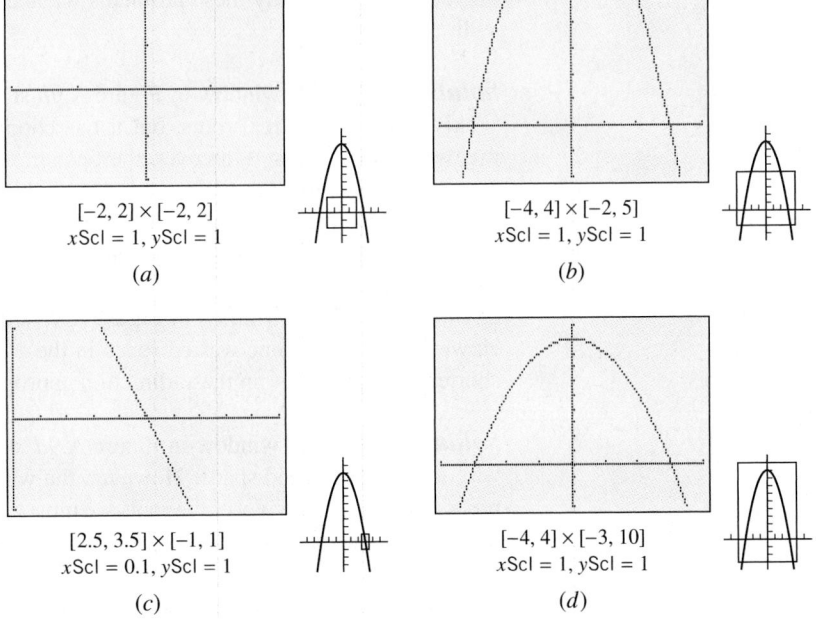

$[-2, 2] \times [-2, 2]$
xScl $= 1$, yScl $= 1$
(*a*)

$[-4, 4] \times [-2, 5]$
xScl $= 1$, yScl $= 1$
(*b*)

$[2.5, 3.5] \times [-1, 1]$
xScl $= 0.1$, yScl $= 1$
(*c*)

$[-4, 4] \times [-3, 10]$
xScl $= 1$, yScl $= 1$
(*d*)

▲ **Figure A.7** Four views of $y = 9 - x^2$

The following example illustrates how the domain and range of a function can be used to find a good viewing window when the graph of the function does not extend indefinitely in both the x- and y-directions.

▶ **Example 3** Use the domain and range of the function $f(x) = \sqrt{12 - 3x^2}$ to determine a viewing window that contains the entire graph.

Solution. The natural domain of f is $[-2, 2]$ and the range is $[0, \sqrt{12}]$ (verify), so the entire graph will be contained in the viewing window $[-2, 2] \times [0, \sqrt{12}]$. For clarity, it is desirable to use a slightly larger window to avoid having the graph too close to the edges of the screen. For example, taking the viewing window to be $[-3, 3] \times [-1, 4]$ yields the graph in Figure A.8. ◀

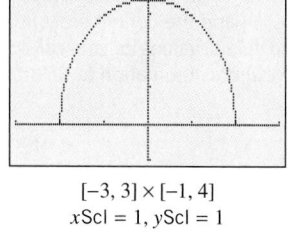

$[-3, 3] \times [-1, 4]$
xScl $= 1$, yScl $= 1$

▲ **Figure A.8**

Sometimes it will be impossible to find a single window that shows all important features of a graph, in which case you will need to decide what is most important for the problem at hand and choose the window appropriately.

▶ **Example 4** Graph the equation $y = x^3 - 12x^2 + 18$ in the following windows and discuss the advantages and disadvantages of each window.

(a) $[-10, 10] \times [-10, 10]$ with xScl $= 1$, yScl $= 1$
(b) $[-20, 20] \times [-20, 20]$ with xScl $= 1$, yScl $= 1$
(c) $[-20, 20] \times [-300, 20]$ with xScl $= 1$, yScl $= 20$
(d) $[-5, 15] \times [-300, 20]$ with xScl $= 1$, yScl $= 20$
(e) $[1, 2] \times [-1, 1]$ with xScl $= 0.1$, yScl $= 0.1$

Solution (a). The window in Figure A.9a has chopped off the portion of the graph that intersects the y-axis, and it shows only two of three possible real roots for the given cubic polynomial. To remedy these problems we need to widen the window in both the x- and y-directions.

Solution (b). The window in Figure A.9b shows the intersection of the graph with the y-axis and the three real roots, but it has chopped off the portion of the graph between the two positive roots. Moreover, the ticks in the y-direction are nearly illegible because they are so close together. We need to extend the window in the negative y-direction and increase yScl. We do not know how far to extend the window, so some experimentation will be required to obtain what we want.

Solution (c). The window in Figure A.9c shows all of the main features of the graph. However, we have some wasted space in the x-direction. We can improve the picture by shortening the window in the x-direction appropriately.

Solution (d). The window in Figure A.9d shows all of the main features of the graph without a lot of wasted space. However, the window does not provide a clear view of the roots. To get a closer view of the roots we must forget about showing all of the main features of the graph and choose windows that zoom in on the roots themselves.

Solution (e). The window in Figure A.9e displays very little of the graph, but it clearly shows that the root in the interval $[1, 2]$ is approximately 1.3. ◀

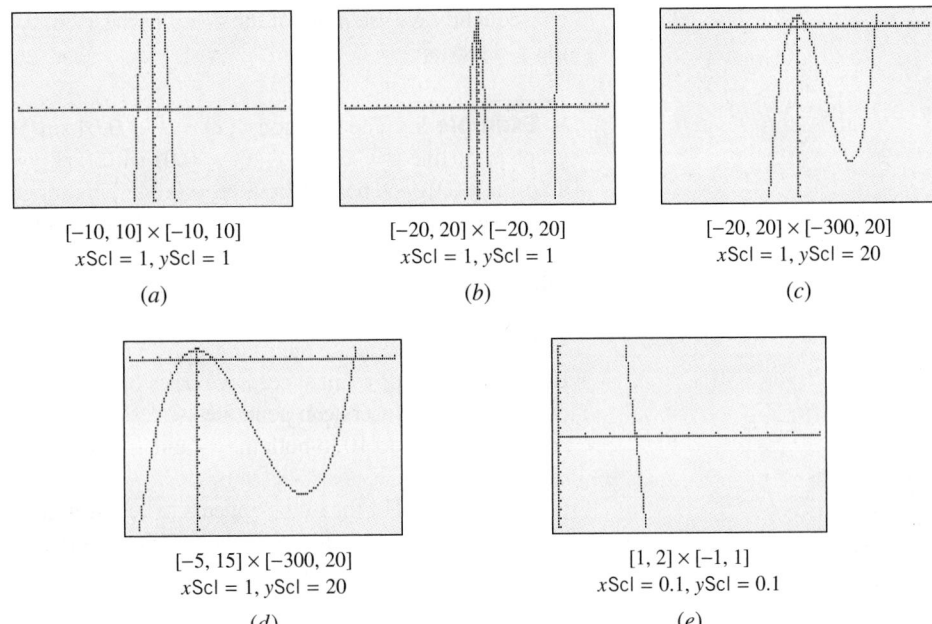

[−10, 10] × [−10, 10]
xScl = 1, yScl = 1

(*a*)

[−20, 20] × [−20, 20]
xScl = 1, yScl = 1

(*b*)

[−20, 20] × [−300, 20]
xScl = 1, yScl = 20

(*c*)

[−5, 15] × [−300, 20]
xScl = 1, yScl = 20

(*d*)

[1, 2] × [−1, 1]
xScl = 0.1, yScl = 0.1

(*e*)

▶ **Figure A.9**

**TECHNOLOGY
MASTERY**

Sometimes you will want to determine the viewing window by choosing the x-interval and allowing the graphing utility to determine a y-interval that encompasses the maximum and minimum values of the function over the x-interval. Most graphing utilities provide some method for doing this, so read your documentation to determine how to use this feature. Allowing the graphing utility to determine the y-interval of the window takes some of the guesswork out of problems like that in part (b) of the preceding example.

■ **ZOOMING**

The process of enlarging or reducing the size of a viewing window is called *zooming*. If you reduce the size of the window, you see *less* of the graph as a whole, but more detail of the part shown; this is called *zooming in*. In contrast, if you enlarge the size of the window, you see *more* of the graph as a whole, but less detail of the part shown; this is called *zooming out*. Most graphing calculators provide menu items for zooming in or zooming out by fixed factors. For example, on one calculator the amount of enlargement or reduction is controlled by setting values for two *zoom factors*, denoted by xFact and yFact. If

$$x\text{Fact} = 10 \quad \text{and} \quad y\text{Fact} = 5$$

then each time a zoom command is executed the viewing window is enlarged or reduced by a factor of 10 in the x-direction and a factor of 5 in the y-direction. With computer programs such as *Mathematica* and *Maple*, zooming is controlled by adjusting the x-interval and y-interval directly; however, there are ways to automate this by programming.

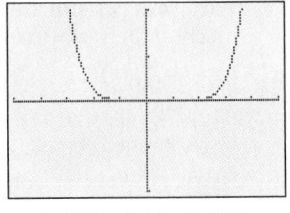

[−5, 5] × [−1000, 1000]
xScl = 1, yScl = 500

(*a*)

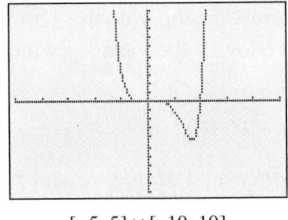

[−5, 5] × [−10, 10]
xScl = 1, yScl = 1

(*b*)

▲ **Figure A.10**

■ **COMPRESSION**

Enlarging the viewing window for a graph has the geometric effect of compressing the graph, since more of the graph is packed into the calculator screen. If the compression is sufficiently great, then some of the detail in the graph may be lost. Thus, the choice of the viewing window frequently depends on whether you want to see more of the graph or more of the detail. Figure A.10 shows two views of the equation

$$y = x^5(x - 2)$$

In part (*a*) of the figure the y-interval is very large, resulting in a vertical compression that obscures the detail in the vicinity of the x-axis. In part (*b*) the y-interval is smaller, and consequently we see more of the detail in the vicinity of the x-axis but less of the graph in the y-direction.

▶ **Example 5**   The function $f(x) = x + 0.01 \sin(50\pi x)$ is the sum of $f_1(x) = x$, whose graph is the line $y = x$, and $f_2(x) = 0.01 \sin(50\pi x)$, whose graph is a sinusoidal curve with amplitude 0.01 and period $2\pi/50\pi = 0.04$. This suggests that the graph of $f(x)$ will follow the general path of the line $y = x$ but will have bumps resulting from the contributions of the sinusoidal oscillations, as shown in part (c) of Figure A.11. Generate the four graphs shown in Figure A.11 and explain why the oscillations are visible only in part (c).

Solution.   To generate the four graphs, you first need to put your utility in radian mode.* Because the windows in successive parts of the example are decreasing in size by a factor of 10, calculator users can generate successive graphs by using the zoom feature with the zoom factors set to 10 in both the x- and y-directions.

(a) In Figure A.11a the graph appears to be a straight line because the vertical compression has hidden the small sinusoidal oscillations (their amplitude is only 0.01).

(b) In Figure A.11b small bumps begin to appear on the line because there is less vertical compression.

(c) In Figure A.11c the oscillations have become clear because the vertical scale is more in keeping with the amplitude of the oscillations.

(d) In Figure A.11d the graph appears to be a straight line because we have zoomed in on such a small portion of the curve. ◄

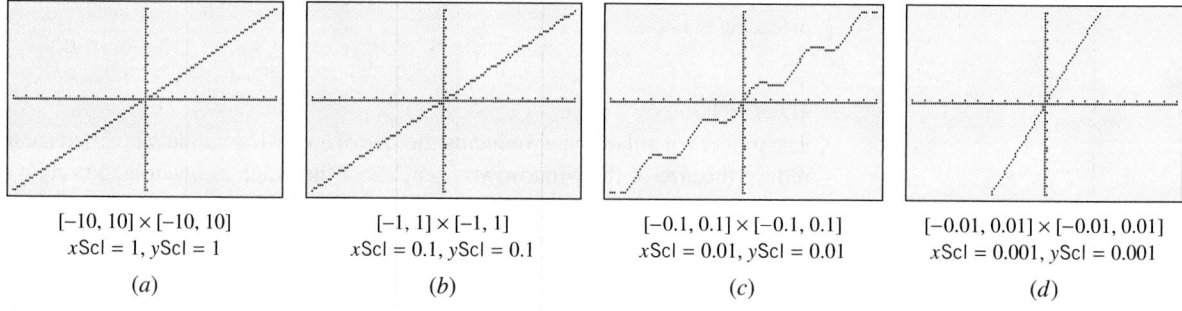

$[-10, 10] \times [-10, 10]$	$[-1, 1] \times [-1, 1]$	$[-0.1, 0.1] \times [-0.1, 0.1]$	$[-0.01, 0.01] \times [-0.01, 0.01]$
xScl = 1, yScl = 1	xScl = 0.1, yScl = 0.1	xScl = 0.01, yScl = 0.01	xScl = 0.001, yScl = 0.001
(a)	(b)	(c)	(d)

▲ **Figure A.11**

■ ASPECT RATIO DISTORTION

Figure A.12a shows a circle of radius 5 and two perpendicular lines graphed in the window $[-10, 10] \times [-10, 10]$ with xScl = 1 and yScl = 1. However, the circle is distorted and the lines do not appear perpendicular because the calculator has not used the same length for 1 unit on the x-axis and 1 unit on the y-axis. (Compare the spacing between the ticks on the axes.) This is called ***aspect ratio distortion***. Many calculators provide a menu item for automatically correcting the distortion by adjusting the viewing window appropriately. For example, one calculator makes this correction to the viewing window $[-10, 10] \times [-10, 10]$ by changing it to

$$[-16.9970674487, 16.9970674487] \times [-10, 10]$$

(Figure A.12b). With computer programs such as *Mathematica* and *Maple*, aspect ratio distortion is controlled with adjustments to the physical dimensions of the viewing window on the computer screen, rather than altering the x- and y-intervals of the viewing window.

---

*In this text we follow the convention that angles are measured in radians unless degree measure is specified.

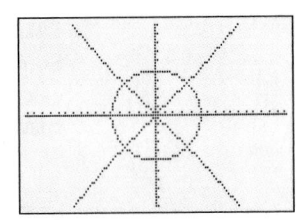

$[-10, 10] \times [-10, 10]$
$x\mathrm{Scl} = 1, y\mathrm{Scl} = 1$

(a)

$[-16.9970674487, 16.9970674487] \times [-10, 10]$
$x\mathrm{Scl} = 1, y\mathrm{Scl} = 1$

(b)

▶ **Figure A.12**

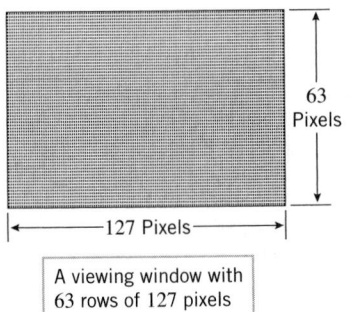

63
Pixels

127 Pixels

A viewing window with
63 rows of 127 pixels

▲ **Figure A.13**

TECHNOLOGY MASTERY

If you are using a graphing calculator,
read the documentation to determine
its resolution.

■ **SAMPLING ERROR**

The viewing window of a graphing utility is composed of a rectangular grid of small rectangular blocks called *pixels*. For black-and-white displays each pixel has two states—an activated (or dark) state and a deactivated (or light state). A graph is formed by activating appropriate pixels to produce the curve shape. In one popular calculator the grid of pixels consists of 63 rows of 127 pixels each (Figure A.13), in which case we say that the screen has a *resolution* of 127×63 (pixels in each row × number of rows). A typical resolution for a computer screen is 1280×1024. The greater the resolution, the smoother the graphs tend to appear on the screen.

The procedure that a graphing utility uses to generate a graph is similar to plotting points by hand: When an equation is entered and a window is chosen, the utility *selects* the *x*-coordinates of certain pixels (the choice of which depends on the window being used) and *computes* the corresponding *y*-coordinates. It then activates the pixels whose coordinates most closely match those of the calculated points and uses a built-in algorithm to activate additional intermediate pixels to create the curve shape. This process is not perfect, and it is possible that a particular window will produce a false impression about the graph shape because important characteristics of the graph occur between the computed points. This is called *sampling error*. For example, Figure A.14 shows the graph of $y = \cos(10\pi x)$ produced by a popular calculator in four different windows. (Your calculator may produce different results.) The graph in part (a) has the correct shape, but the other three do not because of sampling error:

- In part (b) the plotted pixels happened to fall at the peaks of the cosine curve, giving the false impression that the graph is a horizontal line.
- In part (c) the plotted pixels fell at successively higher points along the graph.
- In part (d) the plotted points fell in some regular pattern that created yet another misleading impression of the graph shape.

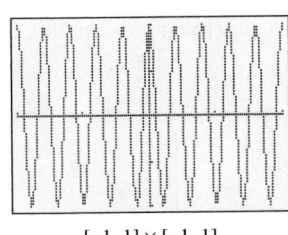

$[-1, 1] \times [-1, 1]$
$x\mathrm{Scl} = 0.5, y\mathrm{Scl} = 0.5$

(a)

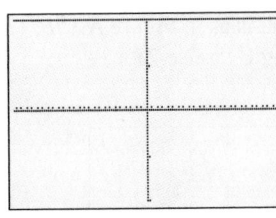

$[-12.6, 12.6] \times [-1, 1]$
$x\mathrm{Scl} = 1, y\mathrm{Scl} = 0.5$

(b)

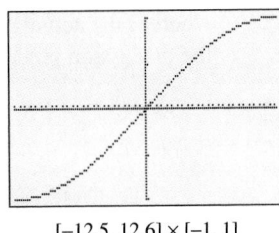

$[-12.5, 12.6] \times [-1, 1]$
$x\mathrm{Scl} = 1, y\mathrm{Scl} = 0.5$

(c)

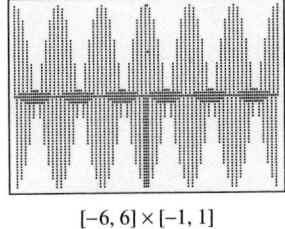

$[-6, 6] \times [-1, 1]$
$x\mathrm{Scl} = 1, y\mathrm{Scl} = 0.5$

(d)

▲ **Figure A.14**

REMARK | For trigonometric graphs with rapid oscillations, Figure A.14 suggests that restricting the x-interval to a few periods is likely to produce a more accurate representation about the graph shape.

FALSE GAPS

Sometimes graphs that are continuous appear to have gaps when they are generated on a calculator. These *false gaps* typically occur where the graph rises so rapidly that vertical space is opened up between successive pixels.

▶ **Example 6**   Figure A.15 shows the graph of the semicircle $y = \sqrt{9 - x^2}$ in two viewing windows. Although this semicircle has x-intercepts at the points $x = \pm 3$, part (a) of the figure shows false gaps at those points because there are no pixels with x-coordinates ± 3 in the window selected. In part (b) no gaps occur because there are pixels with x-coordinates $x = \pm 3$ in the window being used. ◀

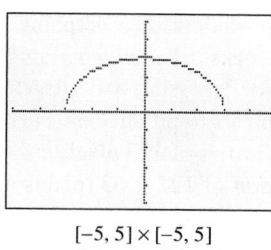

$[-5, 5] \times [-5, 5]$
xScl = 1, yScl = 1

(a)

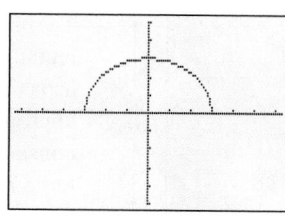

$[-6.3, 6.3] \times [-5, 5]$
xScl = 1, yScl = 1

(b)

▶ **Figure A.15**

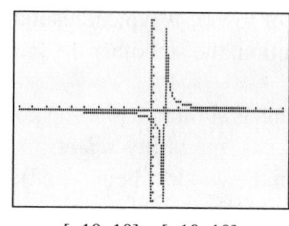

$[-10, 10] \times [-10, 10]$
xScl = 1, yScl = 1

$y = 1/(x - 1)$ with false line segments

(a)

FALSE LINE SEGMENTS

In addition to creating false gaps in continuous graphs, calculators can err in the opposite direction by placing *false line segments* in the gaps of discontinuous curves.

▶ **Example 7**   Figure A.16a shows the graph of $y = 1/(x - 1)$ in the default window on a calculator. Although the graph appears to contain vertical line segments near $x = 1$, they should not be there. There is actually a gap in the curve at $x = 1$, since a division by zero occurs at that point (Figure A.16b). ◀

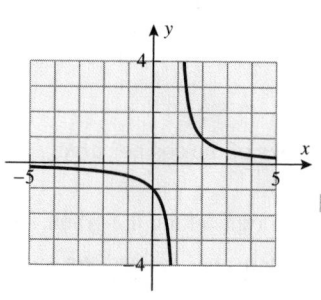

Actual curve shape of $y = 1/(x - 1)$

(b)

▲ **Figure A.16**

ERRORS OF OMISSION

Most graphing utilities use logarithms to evaluate functions with fractional exponents such as $f(x) = x^{2/3} = \sqrt[3]{x^2}$. However, because logarithms are only defined for positive numbers, many (but not all) graphing utilities will omit portions of the graphs of functions with fractional exponents. For example, one calculator graphs $y = x^{2/3}$ as in Figure A.17a, whereas the actual graph is as in Figure A.17b. (For a way to circumvent this problem, see the discussion preceding Exercise 23.)

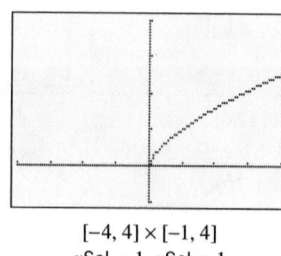

$[-4, 4] \times [-1, 4]$
xScl = 1, yScl = 1

(a)

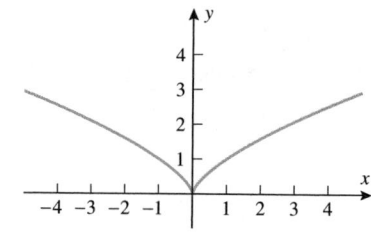

(b)

▶ **Figure A.17**

■ WHAT IS THE TRUE SHAPE OF A GRAPH?

Although graphing utilities are powerful tools for generating graphs quickly, they can produce misleading graphs as a result of compression, sampling error, false gaps, and false line segments. In short, *graphing utilities can suggest graph shapes*, *but they cannot establish them with certainty*. Thus, the more you know about the functions you are graphing, the easier it will be to choose good viewing windows, and the better you will be able to judge the reasonableness of the results produced by your graphing utility.

■ MORE INFORMATION ON GRAPHING AND CALCULATING UTILITIES

The main source of information about your graphing utility is its own documentation, and from time to time in this book we suggest that you refer to that documentation to learn some particular technique.

■ GENERATING PARAMETRIC CURVES WITH GRAPHING UTILITIES

Many graphing utilities allow you to graph equations of the form $y = f(x)$ but not equations of the form $x = g(y)$. Sometimes you will be able to rewrite $x = g(y)$ in the form $y = f(x)$; however, if this is inconvenient or impossible, then you can graph $x = g(y)$ by introducing a parameter $t = y$ and expressing the equation in the parametric form $x = g(t)$, $y = t$. (You may have to experiment with various intervals for t to produce a complete graph.)

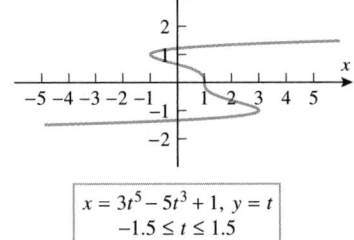

$$x = 3t^5 - 5t^3 + 1, \quad y = t$$
$$-1.5 \le t \le 1.5$$

▲ **Figure A.18**

▶ **Example 8**   Use a graphing utility to graph the equation $x = 3y^5 - 5y^3 + 1$.

Solution.   If we let $t = y$ be the parameter, then the equation can be written in parametric form as

$$x = 3t^5 - 5t^3 + 1, \quad y = t$$

Figure A.18 shows the graph of these equations for $-1.5 \le t \le 1.5$.   ◀

Some parametric curves are so complex that it is virtually impossible to visualize them without using some kind of graphing utility. Figure A.19 shows three such curves.

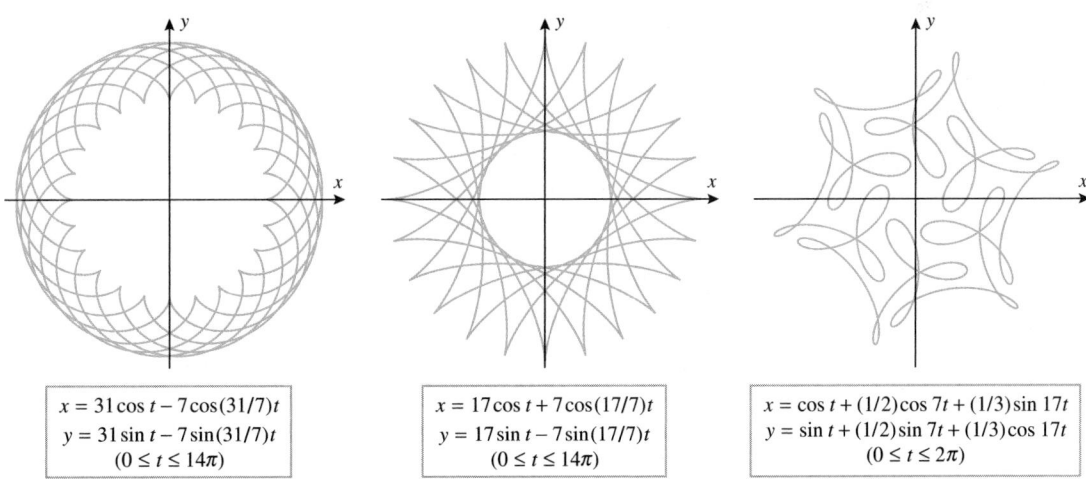

$$x = 31\cos t - 7\cos(31/7)t$$
$$y = 31\sin t - 7\sin(31/7)t$$
$$(0 \le t \le 14\pi)$$

$$x = 17\cos t + 7\cos(17/7)t$$
$$y = 17\sin t - 7\sin(17/7)t$$
$$(0 \le t \le 14\pi)$$

$$x = \cos t + (1/2)\cos 7t + (1/3)\sin 17t$$
$$y = \sin t + (1/2)\sin 7t + (1/3)\cos 17t$$
$$(0 \le t \le 2\pi)$$

▲ **Figure A.19**

■ GRAPHING INVERSE FUNCTIONS WITH GRAPHING UTILITIES

Most graphing utilities cannot graph inverse functions directly. However, there is a way of graphing inverse functions by expressing the graphs parametrically. To see how this can be done, suppose that we are interested in graphing the inverse of a one-to-one function f.

TECHNOLOGY MASTERY

Try your hand at using a graphing utility to generate some parametric curves that you think are interesting or beautiful.

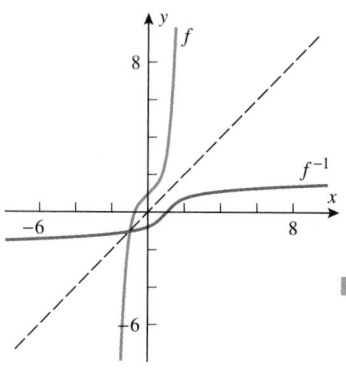

▲ **Figure A.20**

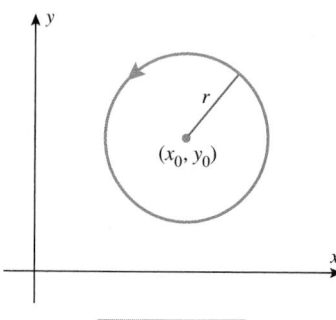

$$x = x_0 + r \cos t$$
$$y = y_0 + r \sin t$$
$$(0 \le t \le 2\pi)$$

▲ **Figure A.21**

TECHNOLOGY MASTERY

Use the parametric capability of your graphing utility to generate a circle of radius 5 that is centered at $(3, -2)$.

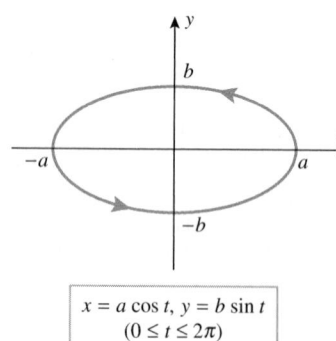

$$x = a \cos t, \ y = b \sin t$$
$$(0 \le t \le 2\pi)$$

▲ **Figure A.22**

We know that the equation $y = f(x)$ can be expressed parametrically as

$$x = t, \quad y = f(t) \tag{1}$$

and we know that the graph of f^{-1} can be obtained by interchanging x and y, since this reflects the graph of f about the line $y = x$. Thus, from (1) the graph of f^{-1} can be represented parametrically as

$$x = f(t), \quad y = t \tag{2}$$

For example, Figure A.20 shows the graph of $f(x) = x^5 + x + 1$ and its inverse generated with a graphing utility. The graph of f was generated from the parametric equations

$$x = t, \quad y = t^5 + t + 1$$

and the graph of f^{-1} was generated from the parametric equations

$$x = t^5 + t + 1, \quad y = t$$

■ TRANSLATION

If a parametric curve C is given by the equations $x = f(t)$, $y = g(t)$, then adding a constant to $f(t)$ translates the curve C in the x-direction, and adding a constant to $g(t)$ translates it in the y-direction. Thus, a circle of radius r, centered at (x_0, y_0) can be represented parametrically as

$$x = x_0 + r \cos t, \quad y = y_0 + r \sin t \quad (0 \le t \le 2\pi)$$

(Figure A.21). If desired, we can eliminate the parameter from these equations by noting that

$$(x - x_0)^2 + (y - y_0)^2 = (r \cos t)^2 + (r \sin t)^2 = r^2$$

Thus, we have obtained the familiar equation in rectangular coordinates for a circle of radius r, centered at (x_0, y_0):

$$(x - x_0)^2 + (y - y_0)^2 = r^2$$

■ SCALING

If a parametric curve C is given by the equations $x = f(t)$, $y = g(t)$, then multiplying $f(t)$ by a constant stretches or compresses C in the x-direction, and multiplying $g(t)$ by a constant stretches or compresses C in the y-direction. For example, we would expect the parametric equations

$$x = 3 \cos t, \quad y = 2 \sin t \quad (0 \le t \le 2\pi)$$

to represent an ellipse, centered at the origin, since the graph of these equations results from stretching the unit circle

$$x = \cos t, \quad y = \sin t \quad (0 \le t \le 2\pi)$$

by a factor of 3 in the x-direction and a factor of 2 in the y-direction. In general, if a and b are positive constants, then the parametric equations

$$x = a \cos t, \quad y = b \sin t \quad (0 \le t \le 2\pi) \tag{3}$$

represent an ellipse, centered at the origin, and extending between $-a$ and a on the x-axis and between $-b$ and b on the y-axis (Figure A.22). The numbers a and b are called the **semiaxes** of the ellipse. If desired, we can eliminate the parameter t in (3) and rewrite the equations in rectangular coordinates as

$$\frac{x^2}{a^2} + \frac{y^2}{b^2} = 1 \tag{4}$$

TECHNOLOGY MASTERY Use the parametric capability of your graphing utility to generate an ellipse that is centered at the origin and that extends between -4 and 4 in the x-direction and between -3 and 3 in the y-direction. Generate an ellipse with the same dimensions, but translated so that its center is at the point $(2, 3)$.

EXERCISE SET A   ⌇ Graphing Utility

⌇ **1–4** Use a graphing utility to generate the graph of f in the given viewing windows, and specify the window that you think gives the best view of the graph. ■

1. $f(x) = x^4 - x^2$
   (a) $[-50, 50] \times [-50, 50]$ (b) $[-5, 5] \times [-5, 5]$
   (c) $[-2, 2] \times [-2, 2]$ (d) $[-2, 2] \times [-1, 1]$
   (e) $[-1.5, 1.5] \times [-0.5, 0.5]$

2. $f(x) = x^5 - x^3$
   (a) $[-50, 50] \times [-50, 50]$ (b) $[-5, 5] \times [-5, 5]$
   (c) $[-2, 2] \times [-2, 2]$ (d) $[-2, 2] \times [-1, 1]$
   (e) $[-1.5, 1.5] \times [-0.5, 0.5]$

3. $f(x) = x^2 + 12$
   (a) $[-1, 1] \times [13, 15]$ (b) $[-2, 2] \times [11, 15]$
   (c) $[-4, 4] \times [10, 28]$ (d) A window of your choice

4. $f(x) = -12 - x^2$
   (a) $[-1, 1] \times [-15, -13]$ (b) $[-2, 2] \times [-15, -11]$
   (c) $[-4, 4] \times [-28, -10]$ (d) A window of your choice

⌇ **5–6** Use the domain and range of f to determine a viewing window that contains the entire graph, and generate the graph in that window. ■

5. $f(x) = \sqrt{16 - 2x^2}$ 6. $f(x) = \sqrt{3 - 2x - x^2}$

⌇ **7–14** Generate the graph of f in a viewing window that you think is appropriate. ■

7. $f(x) = x^2 - 9x - 36$ 8. $f(x) = \dfrac{x + 7}{x - 9}$

9. $f(x) = 2\cos(80x)$ 10. $f(x) = 12\sin(x/80)$

11. $f(x) = 300 - 10x^2 + 0.01x^3$

12. $f(x) = x(30 - 2x)(25 - 2x)$

13. $f(x) = x^2 + \dfrac{1}{x}$ 14. $f(x) = \sqrt{11x - 18}$

⌇ **15–16** Generate the graph of f and determine whether your graphs contain false line segments. Sketch the actual graph and see if you can make the false line segments disappear by changing the viewing window. ■

15. $f(x) = \dfrac{x}{x^2 - 1}$ 16. $f(x) = \dfrac{x^2}{4 - x^2}$

17. The graph of the equation $x^2 + y^2 = 16$ is a circle of radius 4 centered at the origin.
   (a) Find a function whose graph is the upper semicircle and graph it.
   (b) Find a function whose graph is the lower semicircle and graph it.
   (c) Graph the upper and lower semicircles together. If the combined graphs do not appear circular, see if you can adjust the viewing window to eliminate the aspect ratio distortion.
   (d) Graph the portion of the circle in the first quadrant.
   (e) Is there a function whose graph is the right half of the circle? Explain.

⌇ 18. In each part, graph the equation by solving for y in terms of x and graphing the resulting functions together.
   (a) $x^2/4 + y^2/9 = 1$ (b) $y^2 - x^2 = 1$

⌇ 19. Read the documentation for your graphing utility to determine how to graph functions involving absolute values, and graph the given equation.
   (a) $y = |x|$ (b) $y = |x - 1|$
   (c) $y = |x| - 1$ (d) $y = |\sin x|$
   (e) $y = \sin|x|$ (f) $y = |x| - |x + 1|$

⌇ 20. Based on your knowledge of the absolute value function, sketch the graph of $f(x) = |x|/x$. Check your result using a graphing utility.

21–22 Most graphing utilities provide some way of graphing functions that are defined piecewise; read the documentation for your graphing utility to find out how to do this. However, if your goal is just to find the general shape of the graph, you can graph each portion of the function separately and combine the pieces with a hand-drawn sketch. Use this method in these exercises. ■

21. Draw the graph of
$$f(x) = \begin{cases} \sqrt[3]{x - 2}, & x \le 2 \\ x^3 - 2x - 4, & x > 2 \end{cases}$$

22. Draw the graph of
$$f(x) = \begin{cases} x^3 - x^2, & x \le 1 \\ \dfrac{1}{1 - x}, & 1 < x < 4 \\ x^2 \cos\sqrt{x}, & 4 \le x \end{cases}$$

⌇ **23–24** We noted in the text that for functions involving fractional exponents (or radicals), graphing utilities sometimes omit portions of the graph. If $f(x) = x^{p/q}$, where p/q is a positive fraction in *lowest terms*, then you can circumvent this problem as follows:
   • If p is even and q is odd, then graph $g(x) = |x|^{p/q}$ instead of $f(x)$.
   • If p is odd and q is odd, then graph $g(x) = (|x|/x)|x|^{p/q}$ instead of $f(x)$. ■

23. (a) Generate the graphs of $f(x) = x^{2/5}$ and $g(x) = |x|^{2/5}$, and determine whether your graphing utility missed part of the graph of f.
   (b) Generate the graphs of the functions $f(x) = x^{1/5}$ and $g(x) = (|x|/x)|x|^{1/5}$, and determine whether your graphing utility missed part of the graph of f.
   (c) Generate a graph of the function $f(x) = (x - 1)^{4/5}$ that shows all of its important features.
   (d) Generate a graph of the function $f(x) = (x + 1)^{3/4}$ that shows all of its important features.

24. The graphs of $y = (x^2 - 4)^{2/3}$ and $y = [(x^2 - 4)^2]^{1/3}$ should be the same. Does your graphing utility produce

the same graph for both equations? If not, what do you think is happening?

25. In each part, graph the function for various values of c, and write a paragraph or two that describes how changes in c affect the graph in each case.
(a) $y = cx^2$ (b) $y = x^2 + cx$ (c) $y = x^2 + x + c$

26. The graph of an equation of the form $y^2 = x(x - a)(x - b)$ (where $0 < a < b$) is called a *bipartite cubic*. The accompanying figure shows a typical graph of this type.
(a) Graph the bipartite cubic $y^2 = x(x - 1)(x - 2)$ by solving for y in terms of x and graphing the two resulting functions.
(b) Find the x-intercepts of the bipartite cubic

$$y^2 = x(x - a)(x - b)$$

and make a conjecture about how changes in the values of a and b would affect the graph. Test your conjecture by graphing the bipartite cubic for various values of a and b.

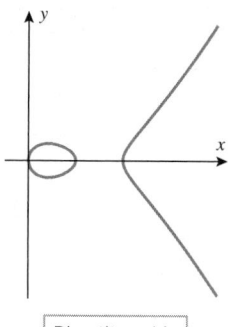

Bipartite cubic

◀ **Figure Ex-26**

27. Based on your knowledge of the graphs of $y = x$ and $y = \sin x$, make a sketch of the graph of $y = x \sin x$. Check your conclusion using a graphing utility.

28. What do you think the graph of $y = \sin(1/x)$ looks like? Test your conclusion using a graphing utility. [*Suggestion:* Examine the graph on a succession of smaller and smaller intervals centered at $x = 0$.]

29–30 Graph the equation using a graphing utility. ■

29. (a) $x = y^2 + 2y + 1$
(b) $x = \sin y, \quad -2\pi \le y \le 2\pi$

30. (a) $x = y + 2y^3 - y^5$
(b) $x = \tan y, \quad -\pi/2 < y < \pi/2$

31–34 Use a graphing utility and parametric equations to display the graphs of f and f^{-1} on the same screen. ■

31. $f(x) = x^3 + 0.2x - 1, \quad -1 \le x \le 2$

32. $f(x) = \sqrt{x^2 + 2} + x, \quad -5 \le x \le 5$

33. $f(x) = \cos(\cos 0.5x), \quad 0 \le x \le 3$

34. $f(x) = x + \sin x, \quad 0 \le x \le 6$

35. (a) Find parametric equations for the ellipse that is centered at the origin and has intercepts $(4, 0)$, $(-4, 0)$, $(0, 3)$, and $(0, -3)$.
(b) Find parametric equations for the ellipse that results by translating the ellipse in part (a) so that its center is at $(-1, 2)$.
(c) Confirm your results in parts (a) and (b) using a graphing utility.

B
TRIGONOMETRY REVIEW

■ ANGLES

Angles in the plane can be generated by rotating a ray about its endpoint. The starting position of the ray is called the ***initial side*** of the angle, the final position is called the ***terminal side*** of the angle, and the point at which the initial and terminal sides meet is called the ***vertex*** of the angle. We allow for the possibility that the ray may make more than one complete revolution. Angles are considered to be ***positive*** if generated counterclockwise and ***negative*** if generated clockwise (Figure B.1).

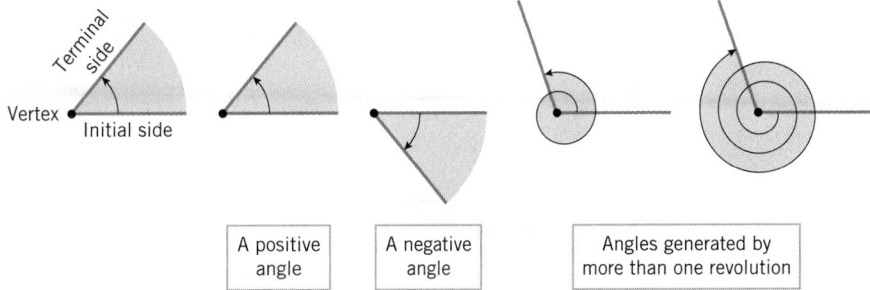

▶ **Figure B.1**

There are two standard measurement systems for describing the size of an angle: ***degree measure*** and ***radian measure***. In degree measure, one degree (written $1°$) is the measure of an angle generated by $1/360$ of one revolution. Thus, there are $360°$ in an angle of one revolution, $180°$ in an angle of one-half revolution, $90°$ in an angle of one-quarter revolution (a *right angle*), and so forth. Degrees are divided into sixty equal parts, called ***minutes***, and minutes are divided into sixty equal parts, called ***seconds***. Thus, one minute (written $1'$) is $1/60$ of a degree, and one second (written $1''$) is $1/60$ of a minute. Smaller subdivisions of a degree are expressed as fractions of a second.

In radian measure, angles are measured by the length of the arc that the angle subtends on a circle of radius 1 when the vertex is at the center. One unit of arc on a circle of radius 1 is called one ***radian*** (written 1 radian or 1 rad) (Figure B.2), and hence the entire circumference of a circle of radius 1 is 2π radians. It follows that an angle of $360°$ subtends an arc of 2π radians, an angle of $180°$ subtends an arc of π radians, an angle of $90°$ subtends an arc of $\pi/2$ radians, and so forth. Figure B.3 and Table B.1 show the relationship between degree measure and radian measure for some important positive angles.

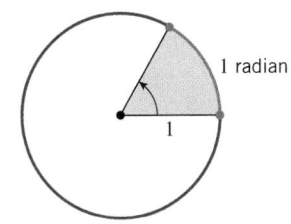

▲ **Figure B.2**

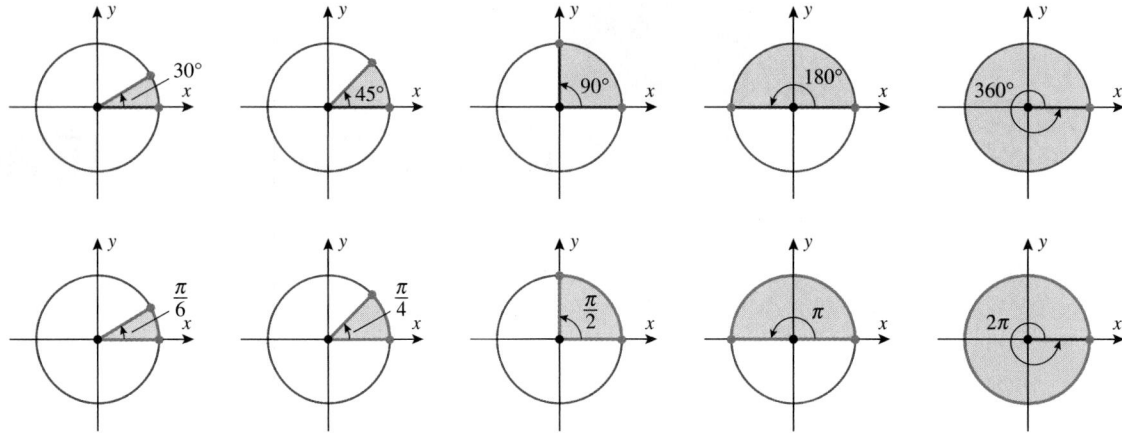

▲ **Figure B.3**

Observe that in Table B.1, angles in degrees are designated by the degree symbol, but angles in radians have no units specified. This is standard practice—when no units are specified for an angle, it is understood that the units are radians.

Table B.1

DEGREES	30°	45°	60°	90°	120°	135°	150°	180°	270°	360°
RADIANS	$\dfrac{\pi}{6}$	$\dfrac{\pi}{4}$	$\dfrac{\pi}{3}$	$\dfrac{\pi}{2}$	$\dfrac{2\pi}{3}$	$\dfrac{3\pi}{4}$	$\dfrac{5\pi}{6}$	π	$\dfrac{3\pi}{2}$	2π

From the fact that π radians corresponds to $180°$, we obtain the following formulas, which are useful for converting from degrees to radians and conversely.

$$1° = \frac{\pi}{180}\text{rad} \approx 0.01745 \text{ rad} \tag{1}$$

$$1 \text{ rad} = \left(\frac{180}{\pi}\right)° \approx 57°\,17'\,44.8'' \tag{2}$$

▶ **Example 1**

(a) Express $146°$ in radians.   (b) Express 3 radians in degrees.

Solution (a).   From (1), degrees can be converted to radians by multiplying by a conversion factor of $\pi/180$. Thus,

$$146° = \left(\frac{\pi}{180} \cdot 146\right)\text{rad} = \frac{73\pi}{90}\text{ rad} \approx 2.5482 \text{ rad}$$

Solution (b).   From (2), radians can be converted to degrees by multiplying by a conversion factor of $180/\pi$. Thus,

$$3 \text{ rad} = \left(3 \cdot \frac{180}{\pi}\right)° = \left(\frac{540}{\pi}\right)° \approx 171.9° \blacktriangleleft$$

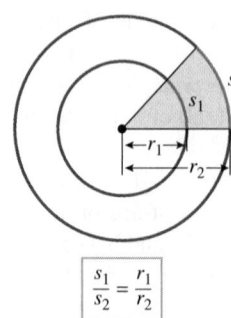

$$\frac{s_1}{s_2} = \frac{r_1}{r_2}$$

▲ **Figure B.4**

■ **RELATIONSHIPS BETWEEN ARC LENGTH, ANGLE, RADIUS, AND AREA**

There is a theorem from plane geometry which states that for two concentric circles, the ratio of the arc lengths subtended by a central angle is equal to the ratio of the corresponding radii (Figure B.4). In particular, if s is the arc length subtended on a circle of radius r by a central angle of θ radians, then by comparison with the arc length subtended by that angle on a circle of radius 1 we obtain

$$\frac{s}{\theta} = \frac{r}{1}$$

from which we obtain the following relationships between the central angle θ, the radius r, and the subtended arc length s when θ is in radians (Figure B.5):

$$\theta = s/r \qquad \text{and} \qquad s = r\theta \qquad (3\text{–}4)$$

The shaded region in Figure B.5 is called a **sector**. It is a theorem from plane geometry that the ratio of the area A of this sector to the area of the entire circle is the same as the ratio of the central angle of the sector to the central angle of the entire circle; thus, if the angles are in radians, we have

$$\frac{A}{\pi r^2} = \frac{\theta}{2\pi}$$

Solving for A yields the following formula for the area of a sector in terms of the radius r and the angle θ in radians:

$$A = \tfrac{1}{2}r^2\theta \qquad (5)$$

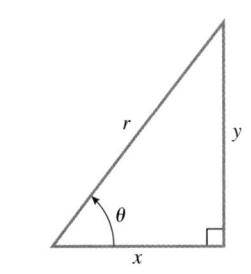

If θ is in radians, then $\theta = s/r$.

▲ **Figure B.5**

TRIGONOMETRIC FUNCTIONS FOR RIGHT TRIANGLES

The **sine**, **cosine**, **tangent**, **cosecant**, **secant**, and **cotangent** of a positive acute angle θ can be defined as ratios of the sides of a right triangle. Using the notation from Figure B.6, these definitions take the following form:

$$\sin\theta = \frac{\text{side opposite }\theta}{\text{hypotenuse}} = \frac{y}{r}, \qquad \csc\theta = \frac{\text{hypotenuse}}{\text{side opposite }\theta} = \frac{r}{y}$$

$$\cos\theta = \frac{\text{side adjacent to }\theta}{\text{hypotenuse}} = \frac{x}{r}, \qquad \sec\theta = \frac{\text{hypotenuse}}{\text{side adjacent to }\theta} = \frac{r}{x} \qquad (6)$$

$$\tan\theta = \frac{\text{side opposite }\theta}{\text{side adjacent to }\theta} = \frac{y}{x}, \qquad \cot\theta = \frac{\text{side adjacent to }\theta}{\text{side opposite }\theta} = \frac{x}{y}$$

▲ **Figure B.6**

We will call sin, cos, tan, csc, sec, and cot the **trigonometric functions**. Because similar triangles have proportional sides, the values of the trigonometric functions depend only on the size of θ and not on the particular right triangle used to compute the ratios. Moreover, in these definitions it does not matter whether θ is measured in degrees or radians.

▶ **Example 2**   Recall from geometry that the two legs of a $45°\text{–}45°\text{–}90°$ triangle are of equal size and that the hypotenuse of a $30°\text{–}60°\text{–}90°$ triangle is twice the shorter leg, where the shorter leg is opposite the $30°$ angle. These facts and the Theorem of Pythagoras yield Figure B.7. From that figure we obtain the results in Table B.2. ◀

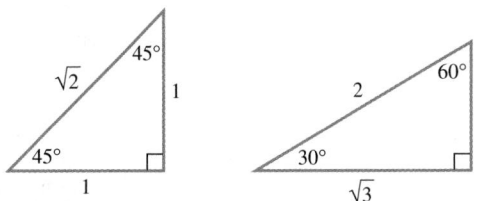

▶ **Figure B.7**

Table B.2

$\sin 45° = 1/\sqrt{2},$	$\cos 45° = 1/\sqrt{2},$	$\tan 45° = 1$
$\csc 45° = \sqrt{2},$	$\sec 45° = \sqrt{2},$	$\cot 45° = 1$
$\sin 30° = 1/2,$	$\cos 30° = \sqrt{3}/2,$	$\tan 30° = 1/\sqrt{3}$
$\csc 30° = 2,$	$\sec 30° = 2/\sqrt{3},$	$\cot 30° = \sqrt{3}$
$\sin 60° = \sqrt{3}/2,$	$\cos 60° = 1/2,$	$\tan 60° = \sqrt{3}$
$\csc 60° = 2/\sqrt{3},$	$\sec 60° = 2,$	$\cot 60° = 1/\sqrt{3}$

◼ ANGLES IN RECTANGULAR COORDINATE SYSTEMS

Because the angles of a right triangle are between $0°$ and $90°$, the formulas in (6) are not directly applicable to negative angles or to angles greater than $90°$. To extend the trigonometric functions to include these cases, it will be convenient to consider angles in rectangular coordinate systems. An angle is said to be in *standard position* in an xy-coordinate system if its vertex is at the origin and its initial side is on the positive x-axis (Figure B.8).

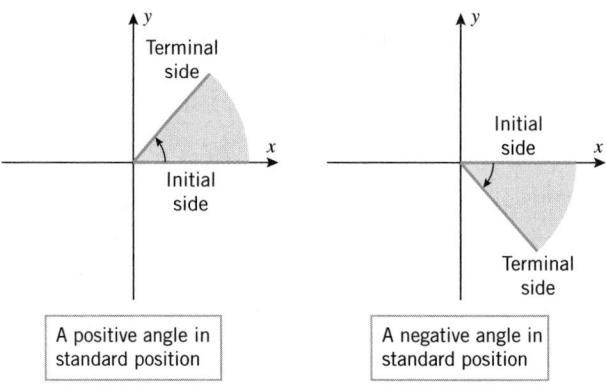

▶ **Figure B.8**

A positive angle in standard position

A negative angle in standard position

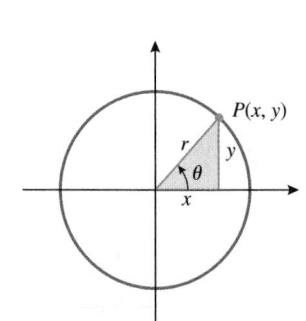

▲ **Figure B.9**

To define the trigonometric functions of an angle θ in standard position, construct a circle of radius r, centered at the origin, and let $P(x, y)$ be the intersection of the terminal side of θ with this circle (Figure B.9). We make the following definition.

B.1 **DEFINITION**

$$\sin \theta = \frac{y}{r}, \quad \cos \theta = \frac{x}{r}, \quad \tan \theta = \frac{y}{x}$$

$$\csc \theta = \frac{r}{y}, \quad \sec \theta = \frac{r}{x}, \quad \cot \theta = \frac{x}{y}$$

Note that the formulas in this definition agree with those in (6), so there is no conflict with the earlier definition of the trigonometric functions for triangles. However, this definition applies to all angles (except for cases where a zero denominator occurs).

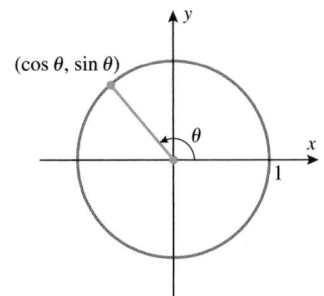

▲ **Figure B.10**

In the special case where $r = 1$, we have $\sin \theta = y$ and $\cos \theta = x$, so the terminal side of the angle θ intersects the unit circle at the point $(\cos \theta, \sin \theta)$ (Figure B.10). It follows from Definition B.1 that the remaining trigonometric functions of θ are expressible as (verify)

$$\tan \theta = \frac{\sin \theta}{\cos \theta}, \quad \cot \theta = \frac{\cos \theta}{\sin \theta} = \frac{1}{\tan \theta}, \quad \sec \theta = \frac{1}{\cos \theta}, \quad \csc \theta = \frac{1}{\sin \theta} \quad (7\text{--}10)$$

These observations suggest the following procedure for evaluating the trigonometric functions of common angles:

- Construct the angle θ in standard position in an xy-coordinate system.
- Find the coordinates of the intersection of the terminal side of the angle and the unit circle; the x- and y-coordinates of this intersection are the values of $\cos \theta$ and $\sin \theta$, respectively.
- Use Formulas (7) through (10) to find the values of the remaining trigonometric functions from the values of $\cos \theta$ and $\sin \theta$.

▶ **Example 3**   Evaluate the trigonometric functions of $\theta = 150°$.

Solution.   Construct a unit circle and place the angle $\theta = 150°$ in standard position (Figure B.11). Since $\angle AOP$ is $30°$ and $\triangle OAP$ is a $30°$–$60°$–$90°$ triangle, the leg AP has length $\frac{1}{2}$ (half the hypotenuse) and the leg OA has length $\sqrt{3}/2$ by the Theorem of Pythagoras. Thus, the coordinates of P are $(-\sqrt{3}/2, 1/2)$, from which we obtain

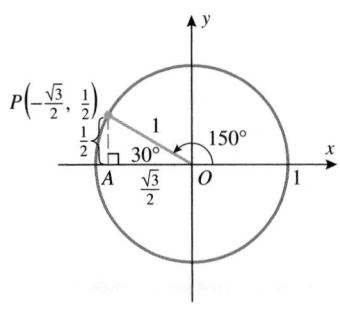

$$\sin 150° = \frac{1}{2}, \quad \cos 150° = -\frac{\sqrt{3}}{2}, \quad \tan 150° = \frac{\sin 150°}{\cos 150°} = \frac{1/2}{-\sqrt{3}/2} = -\frac{1}{\sqrt{3}}$$

$$\csc 150° = \frac{1}{\sin 150°} = 2, \quad \sec 150° = \frac{1}{\cos 150°} = -\frac{2}{\sqrt{3}}$$

$$\cot 150° = \frac{1}{\tan 150°} = -\sqrt{3} \blacktriangleleft$$

▲ **Figure B.11**

▶ **Example 4**   Evaluate the trigonometric functions of $\theta = 5\pi/6$.

Solution.   Since $5\pi/6 = 150°$, this problem is equivalent to that of Example 3. From that example we obtain

$$\sin \frac{5\pi}{6} = \frac{1}{2}, \quad \cos \frac{5\pi}{6} = -\frac{\sqrt{3}}{2}, \quad \tan \frac{5\pi}{6} = -\frac{1}{\sqrt{3}}$$

$$\csc \frac{5\pi}{6} = 2, \quad \sec \frac{5\pi}{6} = -\frac{2}{\sqrt{3}}, \quad \cot \frac{5\pi}{6} = -\sqrt{3} \blacktriangleleft$$

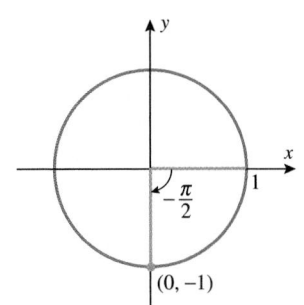

▲ **Figure B.12**

▶ **Example 5**   Evaluate the trigonometric functions of $\theta = -\pi/2$.

Solution.   As shown in Figure B.12, the terminal side of $\theta = -\pi/2$ intersects the unit circle at the point $(0, -1)$, so

$$\sin(-\pi/2) = -1, \quad \cos(-\pi/2) = 0$$

and from Formulas (7) through (10),

$$\tan(-\pi/2) = \frac{\sin(-\pi/2)}{\cos(-\pi/2)} = \frac{-1}{0} \quad \text{(undefined)}$$

$$\cot(-\pi/2) = \frac{\cos(-\pi/2)}{\sin(-\pi/2)} = \frac{0}{-1} = 0$$

$$\sec(-\pi/2) = \frac{1}{\cos(-\pi/2)} = \frac{1}{0} \quad \text{(undefined)}$$

$$\csc(-\pi/2) = \frac{1}{\sin(-\pi/2)} = \frac{1}{-1} = -1 \quad \blacktriangleleft$$

The reader should be able to obtain all of the results in Table B.3 by the methods illustrated in the last three examples. The dashes indicate quantities that are undefined.

Table B.3

	$\theta = 0$ (0°)	$\pi/6$ (30°)	$\pi/4$ (45°)	$\pi/3$ (60°)	$\pi/2$ (90°)	$2\pi/3$ (120°)	$3\pi/4$ (135°)	$5\pi/6$ (150°)	π (180°)	$3\pi/2$ (270°)	2π (360°)
$\sin\theta$	0	1/2	$1/\sqrt{2}$	$\sqrt{3}/2$	1	$\sqrt{3}/2$	$1/\sqrt{2}$	1/2	0	−1	0
$\cos\theta$	1	$\sqrt{3}/2$	$1/\sqrt{2}$	1/2	0	−1/2	$-1/\sqrt{2}$	$-\sqrt{3}/2$	−1	0	1
$\tan\theta$	0	$1/\sqrt{3}$	1	$\sqrt{3}$	—	$-\sqrt{3}$	−1	$-1/\sqrt{3}$	0	—	0
$\csc\theta$	—	2	$\sqrt{2}$	$2/\sqrt{3}$	1	$2/\sqrt{3}$	$\sqrt{2}$	2	—	−1	—
$\sec\theta$	1	$2/\sqrt{3}$	$\sqrt{2}$	2	—	−2	$-\sqrt{2}$	$-2/\sqrt{3}$	−1	—	1
$\cot\theta$	—	$\sqrt{3}$	1	$1/\sqrt{3}$	0	$-1/\sqrt{3}$	−1	$-\sqrt{3}$	—	0	—

REMARK | It is only in special cases that exact values for trigonometric functions can be obtained; usually, a calculating utility or a computer program will be required.

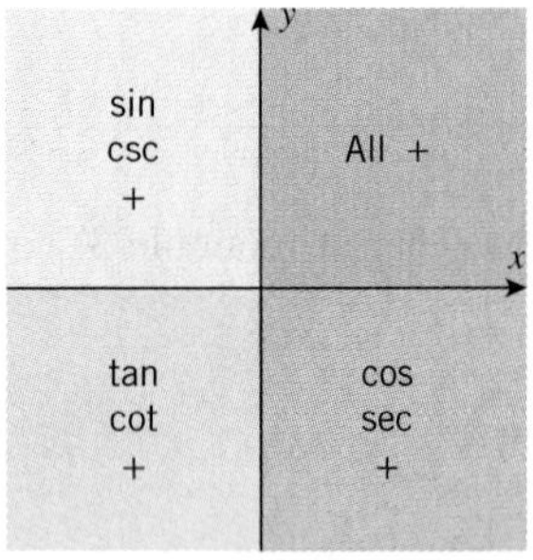

▲ **Figure B.13**

The signs of the trigonometric functions of an angle are determined by the quadrant in which the terminal side of the angle falls. For example, if the terminal side falls in the first quadrant, then x and y are positive in Definition B.1, so all of the trigonometric functions have positive values. If the terminal side falls in the second quadrant, then x is negative and y is positive, so sin and csc are positive, but all other trigonometric functions are negative. The diagram in Figure B.13 shows which trigonometric functions are positive in the various quadrants. The reader will find it instructive to check that the results in Table B.3 are consistent with Figure B.13.

■ TRIGONOMETRIC IDENTITIES

A *trigonometric identity* is an equation involving trigonometric functions that is true for all angles for which both sides of the equation are defined. One of the most important identities in trigonometry can be derived by applying the Theorem of Pythagoras to the triangle in Figure B.9 to obtain

$$x^2 + y^2 = r^2$$

Dividing both sides by r^2 and using the definitions of $\sin\theta$ and $\cos\theta$ (Definition B.1), we obtain the following fundamental result:

$$\sin^2\theta + \cos^2\theta = 1 \qquad (11)$$

The following identities can be obtained from (11) by dividing through by $\cos^2\theta$ and $\sin^2\theta$, respectively, then applying Formulas (7) through (10):

$$\tan^2\theta + 1 = \sec^2\theta \tag{12}$$

$$1 + \cot^2\theta = \csc^2\theta \tag{13}$$

If (x, y) is a point on the unit circle, then the points $(-x, y)$, $(-x, -y)$, and $(x, -y)$ also lie on the unit circle (why?), and the four points form four corners of a rectangle with sides parallel to the coordinate axes (Figure B.14a). The x- and y-coordinates of each corner represent the cosine and sine of an angle in standard position whose terminal side passes through the corner; hence we obtain the identities in parts (b), (c), and (d) of Figure B.14 for sine and cosine. Dividing those identities leads to identities for the tangent. In summary:

$$\begin{array}{lll}
\sin(\pi - \theta) = \sin\theta, & \sin(\pi + \theta) = -\sin\theta, & \sin(-\theta) = -\sin\theta \quad (14\text{--}16) \\
\cos(\pi - \theta) = -\cos\theta, & \cos(\pi + \theta) = -\cos\theta, & \cos(-\theta) = \cos\theta \quad (17\text{--}19) \\
\tan(\pi - \theta) = -\tan\theta, & \tan(\pi + \theta) = \tan\theta, & \tan(-\theta) = -\tan\theta \quad (20\text{--}22)
\end{array}$$

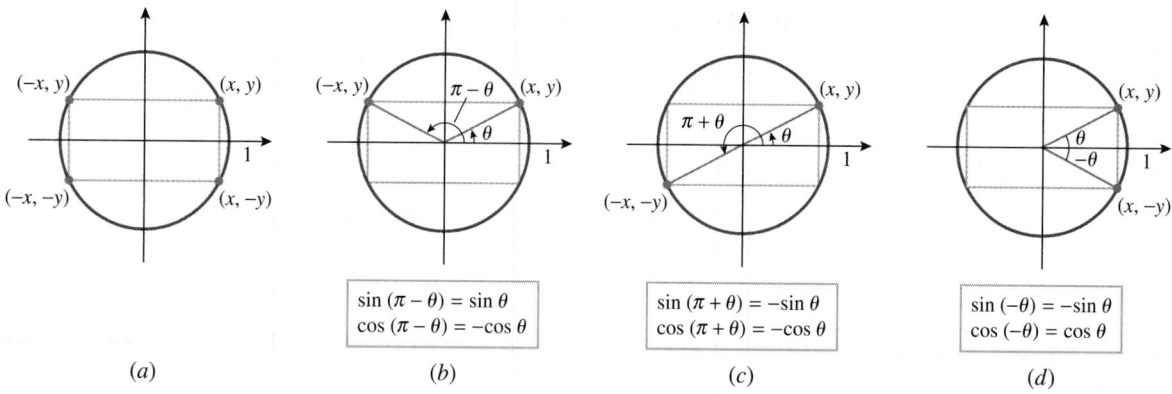

$$\begin{array}{llll}
\sin(\pi - \theta) = \sin\theta & \sin(\pi + \theta) = -\sin\theta & \sin(-\theta) = -\sin\theta \\
\cos(\pi - \theta) = -\cos\theta & \cos(\pi + \theta) = -\cos\theta & \cos(-\theta) = \cos\theta
\end{array}$$

(a) (b) (c) (d)

▲ **Figure B.14**

Two angles in standard position that have the same terminal side must have the same values for their trigonometric functions since their terminal sides intersect the unit circle at the same point. In particular, two angles whose radian measures differ by a multiple of 2π have the same terminal side and hence have the same values for their trigonometric functions. This yields the identities

$$\sin\theta = \sin(\theta + 2\pi) = \sin(\theta - 2\pi) \tag{23}$$

$$\cos\theta = \cos(\theta + 2\pi) = \cos(\theta - 2\pi) \tag{24}$$

and more generally,

$$\sin\theta = \sin(\theta \pm 2n\pi), \quad n = 0, 1, 2, \dots \tag{25}$$

$$\cos\theta = \cos(\theta \pm 2n\pi), \quad n = 0, 1, 2, \dots \tag{26}$$

Identity (21) implies that

$$\tan\theta = \tan(\theta + \pi) \quad \text{and} \quad \tan\theta = \tan(\theta - \pi) \tag{27--28}$$

Identity (27) is just (21) with the terms in the sum reversed, and identity (28) follows from (21) by substituting $\theta - \pi$ for θ. These two identities state that adding or subtracting π

from an angle does not affect the value of the tangent of the angle. It follows that the same is true for any multiple of π; thus,

$$\tan\theta = \tan(\theta \pm n\pi), \quad n = 0, 1, 2, \ldots \tag{29}$$

Figure B.15 shows complementary angles θ and $(\pi/2) - \theta$ of a right triangle. It follows from (6) that

$$\sin\theta = \frac{\text{side opposite } \theta}{\text{hypotenuse}} = \frac{\text{side adjacent to } (\pi/2) - \theta}{\text{hypotenuse}} = \cos\left(\frac{\pi}{2} - \theta\right)$$

$$\cos\theta = \frac{\text{side adjacent to } \theta}{\text{hypotenuse}} = \frac{\text{side opposite } (\pi/2) - \theta}{\text{hypotenuse}} = \sin\left(\frac{\pi}{2} - \theta\right)$$

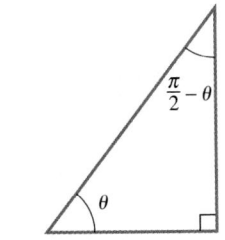

▲ **Figure B.15**

which yields the identities

$$\sin\left(\frac{\pi}{2} - \theta\right) = \cos\theta, \quad \cos\left(\frac{\pi}{2} - \theta\right) = \sin\theta, \quad \tan\left(\frac{\pi}{2} - \theta\right) = \cot\theta \tag{30–32}$$

where the third identity results from dividing the first two. These identities are also valid for angles that are not acute and for negative angles as well.

■ THE LAW OF COSINES

The next theorem, called the **law of cosines**, generalizes the Theorem of Pythagoras. This result is important in its own right and is also the starting point for some important trigonometric identities.

B.2   THEOREM (*Law of Cosines*)   *If the sides of a triangle have lengths a, b, and c, and if θ is the angle between the sides with lengths a and b, then*

$$c^2 = a^2 + b^2 - 2ab\cos\theta$$

PROOF   Introduce a coordinate system so that θ is in standard position and the side of length a falls along the positive x-axis. As shown in Figure B.16, the side of length a extends from the origin to $(a, 0)$ and the side of length b extends from the origin to some point (x, y). From the definition of $\sin\theta$ and $\cos\theta$ we have $\sin\theta = y/b$ and $\cos\theta = x/b$, so

$$y = b\sin\theta, \quad x = b\cos\theta \tag{33}$$

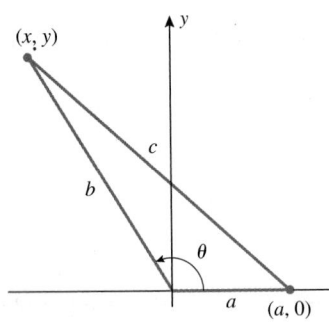

▲ **Figure B.16**

From the distance formula in Theorem H.1 of Appendix H, we obtain

$$c^2 = (x - a)^2 + (y - 0)^2$$

so that, from (33),

$$c^2 = (b\cos\theta - a)^2 + b^2\sin^2\theta$$

$$= a^2 + b^2(\cos^2\theta + \sin^2\theta) - 2ab\cos\theta$$

$$= a^2 + b^2 - 2ab\cos\theta$$

which completes the proof. ■

We will now show how the law of cosines can be used to obtain the following identities, called the **addition formulas** for sine and cosine:

$$\sin(\alpha + \beta) = \sin\alpha\cos\beta + \cos\alpha\sin\beta \tag{34}$$

$$\cos(\alpha + \beta) = \cos\alpha\cos\beta - \sin\alpha\sin\beta \tag{35}$$

$$\sin(\alpha - \beta) = \sin \alpha \cos \beta - \cos \alpha \sin \beta \tag{36}$$

$$\cos(\alpha - \beta) = \cos \alpha \cos \beta + \sin \alpha \sin \beta \tag{37}$$

We will derive (37) first. In our derivation we will assume that $0 \le \beta < \alpha < 2\pi$ (Figure B.17). As shown in the figure, the terminal sides of α and β intersect the unit circle at the points $P_1(\cos \alpha, \sin \alpha)$ and $P_2(\cos \beta, \sin \beta)$. If we denote the lengths of the sides of triangle $OP_1 P_2$ by OP_1, $P_1 P_2$, and OP_2, then $OP_1 = OP_2 = 1$ and, from the distance formula in Theorem H.1 of Appendix H,

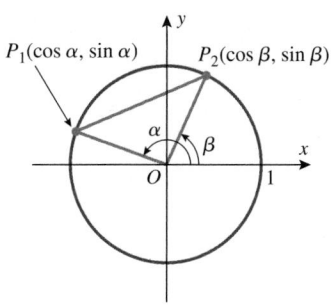

$$
\begin{aligned}
(P_1 P_2)^2 &= (\cos \beta - \cos \alpha)^2 + (\sin \beta - \sin \alpha)^2 \\
&= (\sin^2 \alpha + \cos^2 \alpha) + (\sin^2 \beta + \cos^2 \beta) - 2(\cos \alpha \cos \beta + \sin \alpha \sin \beta) \\
&= 2 - 2(\cos \alpha \cos \beta + \sin \alpha \sin \beta)
\end{aligned}
$$

▲ **Figure B.17**

But angle $P_2 O P_1 = \alpha - \beta$, so that the law of cosines yields

$$
\begin{aligned}
(P_1 P_2)^2 &= (OP_1)^2 + (OP_2)^2 - 2(OP_1)(OP_2) \cos(\alpha - \beta) \\
&= 2 - 2 \cos(\alpha - \beta)
\end{aligned}
$$

Equating the two expressions for $(P_1 P_2)^2$ and simplifying, we obtain

$$\cos(\alpha - \beta) = \cos \alpha \cos \beta + \sin \alpha \sin \beta$$

which completes the derivation of (37).

We can use (31) and (37) to derive (36) as follows:

$$
\begin{aligned}
\sin(\alpha - \beta) &= \cos \left[\frac{\pi}{2} - (\alpha - \beta) \right] = \cos \left[\left(\frac{\pi}{2} - \alpha \right) - (-\beta) \right] \\
&= \cos \left(\frac{\pi}{2} - \alpha \right) \cos(-\beta) + \sin \left(\frac{\pi}{2} - \alpha \right) \sin(-\beta) \\
&= \cos \left(\frac{\pi}{2} - \alpha \right) \cos \beta - \sin \left(\frac{\pi}{2} - \alpha \right) \sin \beta \\
&= \sin \alpha \cos \beta - \cos \alpha \sin \beta
\end{aligned}
$$

Identities (34) and (35) can be obtained from (36) and (37) by substituting $-\beta$ for β and using the identities

$$\sin(-\beta) = -\sin \beta, \quad \cos(-\beta) = \cos \beta$$

We leave it for the reader to derive the identities

$$\tan(\alpha + \beta) = \frac{\tan \alpha + \tan \beta}{1 - \tan \alpha \tan \beta} \qquad \tan(\alpha - \beta) = \frac{\tan \alpha - \tan \beta}{1 + \tan \alpha \tan \beta} \tag{38–39}$$

Identity (38) can be obtained by dividing (34) by (35) and then simplifying. Identity (39) can be obtained from (38) by substituting $-\beta$ for β and simplifying.

In the special case where $\alpha = \beta$, identities (34), (35), and (38) yield the ***double-angle formulas***

$$\sin 2\alpha = 2 \sin \alpha \cos \alpha \tag{40}$$

$$\cos 2\alpha = \cos^2 \alpha - \sin^2 \alpha \tag{41}$$

$$\tan 2\alpha = \frac{2 \tan \alpha}{1 - \tan^2 \alpha} \tag{42}$$

By using the identity $\sin^2 \alpha + \cos^2 \alpha = 1$, (41) can be rewritten in the alternative forms

$$\cos 2\alpha = 2 \cos^2 \alpha - 1 \qquad \text{and} \qquad \cos 2\alpha = 1 - 2 \sin^2 \alpha \tag{43–44}$$

If we replace α by $\alpha/2$ in (43) and (44) and use some algebra, we obtain the **half-angle formulas**

$$\cos^2 \frac{\alpha}{2} = \frac{1 + \cos\alpha}{2} \quad \text{and} \quad \sin^2 \frac{\alpha}{2} = \frac{1 - \cos\alpha}{2} \qquad (45\text{–}46)$$

We leave it for the exercises to derive the following **product-to-sum formulas** from (34) through (37):

$$\sin\alpha \cos\beta = \frac{1}{2}[\sin(\alpha - \beta) + \sin(\alpha + \beta)] \qquad (47)$$

$$\sin\alpha \sin\beta = \frac{1}{2}[\cos(\alpha - \beta) - \cos(\alpha + \beta)] \qquad (48)$$

$$\cos\alpha \cos\beta = \frac{1}{2}[\cos(\alpha - \beta) + \cos(\alpha + \beta)] \qquad (49)$$

We also leave it for the exercises to derive the following **sum-to-product formulas**:

$$\sin\alpha + \sin\beta = 2\sin\frac{\alpha + \beta}{2}\cos\frac{\alpha - \beta}{2} \qquad (50)$$

$$\sin\alpha - \sin\beta = 2\cos\frac{\alpha + \beta}{2}\sin\frac{\alpha - \beta}{2} \qquad (51)$$

$$\cos\alpha + \cos\beta = 2\cos\frac{\alpha + \beta}{2}\cos\frac{\alpha - \beta}{2} \qquad (52)$$

$$\cos\alpha - \cos\beta = -2\sin\frac{\alpha + \beta}{2}\sin\frac{\alpha - \beta}{2} \qquad (53)$$

■ FINDING AN ANGLE FROM THE VALUE OF ITS TRIGONOMETRIC FUNCTIONS

There are numerous situations in which it is necessary to find an unknown angle from a known value of one of its trigonometric functions. The following example illustrates a method for doing this.

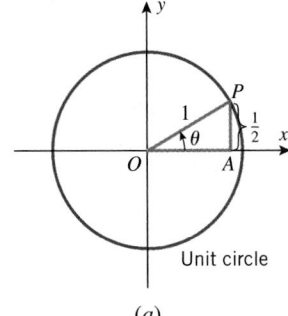

Unit circle

(a)

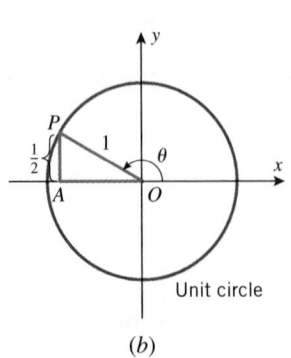

Unit circle

(b)

▲ **Figure B.18**

▶ **Example 6** Find θ if $\sin\theta = \frac{1}{2}$.

Solution. We begin by looking for positive angles that satisfy the equation. Because $\sin\theta$ is positive, the angle θ must terminate in the first or second quadrant. If it terminates in the first quadrant, then the hypotenuse of $\triangle OAP$ in Figure B.18a is double the leg AP, so

$$\theta = 30° = \frac{\pi}{6} \text{ radians}$$

If θ terminates in the second quadrant (Figure B.18b), then the hypotenuse of $\triangle OAP$ is double the leg AP, so $\angle AOP = 30°$, which implies that

$$\theta = 180° - 30° = 150° = \frac{5\pi}{6} \text{ radians}$$

Now that we have found these two solutions, all other solutions are obtained by adding or subtracting multiples of 360° (2π radians) to or from them. Thus, the entire set of solutions is given by the formulas

$$\theta = 30° \pm n \cdot 360°, \quad n = 0, 1, 2, \dots$$

and

$$\theta = 150° \pm n \cdot 360°, \quad n = 0, 1, 2, \ldots$$

or in radian measure,

$$\theta = \frac{\pi}{6} \pm n \cdot 2\pi, \quad n = 0, 1, 2, \ldots$$

and

$$\theta = \frac{5\pi}{6} \pm n \cdot 2\pi, \quad n = 0, 1, 2, \ldots \blacktriangleleft$$

◼ ANGLE OF INCLINATION

The slope of a nonvertical line L is related to the angle that L makes with the positive x-axis. If ϕ is the smallest positive angle measured counterclockwise from the x-axis to L, then the slope of the line can be expressed as

$$m = \tan \phi \tag{54}$$

(Figure B.19a). The angle ϕ, which is called the ***angle of inclination*** of the line, satisfies $0° \le \phi < 180°$ in degree measure (or, equivalently, $0 \le \phi < \pi$ in radian measure). If ϕ is an acute angle, then $m = \tan \phi$ is positive and the line slopes up to the right, and if ϕ is an obtuse angle, then $m = \tan \phi$ is negative and the line slopes down to the right. For example, a line whose angle of inclination is $45°$ has slope $m = \tan 45° = 1$, and a line whose angle of inclination is $135°$ has a slope of $m = \tan 135° = -1$ (Figure B.19b). Figure B.20 shows a convenient way of using the line $x = 1$ as a "ruler" for visualizing the relationship between lines of various slopes.

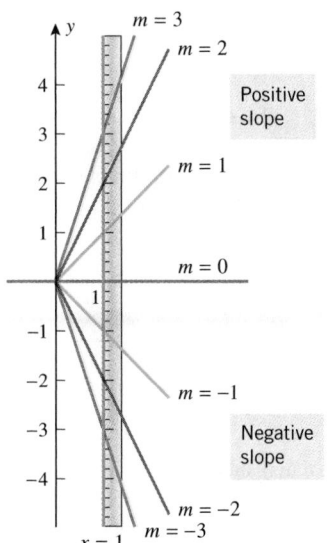

▲ **Figure B.20**

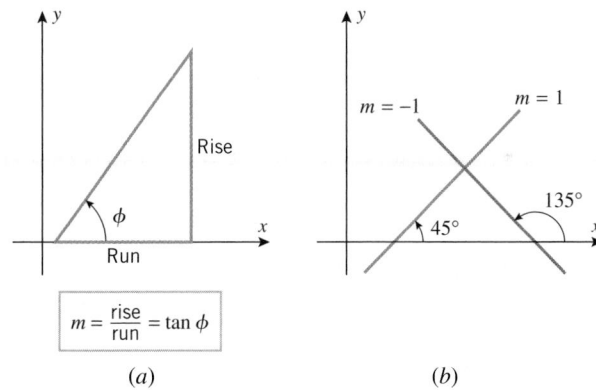

▲ **Figure B.19**

EXERCISE SET B

1–2 Express the angles in radians. ◼

1. (a) $75°$　　(b) $390°$　　(c) $20°$　　(d) $138°$

2. (a) $420°$　　(b) $15°$　　(c) $225°$　　(d) $165°$

3–4 Express the angles in degrees. ◼

3. (a) $\pi/15$　　(b) 1.5　　(c) $8\pi/5$　　(d) 3π

4. (a) $\pi/10$　　(b) 2　　(c) $2\pi/5$　　(d) $7\pi/6$

5–6 Find the exact values of all six trigonometric functions of θ. ◼

5. (a) 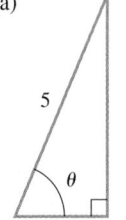　　(b) 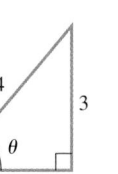　　(c)

6. (a)   (b)   (c)

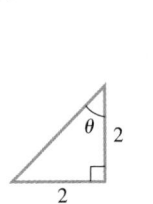 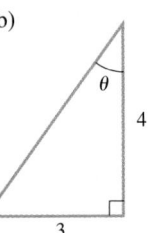 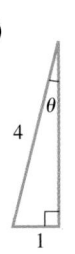

7–12 The angle θ is an acute angle of a right triangle. Solve the problems by drawing an appropriate right triangle. Do *not* use a calculator.

7. Find $\sin\theta$ and $\cos\theta$ given that $\tan\theta = 3$.

8. Find $\sin\theta$ and $\tan\theta$ given that $\cos\theta = \frac{2}{3}$.

9. Find $\tan\theta$ and $\csc\theta$ given that $\sec\theta = \frac{5}{2}$.

10. Find $\cot\theta$ and $\sec\theta$ given that $\csc\theta = 4$.

11. Find the length of the side adjacent to θ given that the hypotenuse has length 6 and $\cos\theta = 0.3$.

12. Find the length of the hypotenuse given that the side opposite θ has length 2.4 and $\sin\theta = 0.8$.

13–14 The value of an angle θ is given. Find the values of all six trigonometric functions of θ without using a calculator.

13. (a) $225°$ (b) $-210°$ (c) $5\pi/3$ (d) $-3\pi/2$

14. (a) $330°$ (b) $-120°$ (c) $9\pi/4$ (d) -3π

15–16 Use the information to find the exact values of the remaining five trigonometric functions of θ.

15. (a) $\cos\theta = \frac{3}{5},\ 0 < \theta < \pi/2$
(b) $\cos\theta = \frac{3}{5},\ -\pi/2 < \theta < 0$
(c) $\tan\theta = -1/\sqrt{3},\ \pi/2 < \theta < \pi$
(d) $\tan\theta = -1/\sqrt{3},\ -\pi/2 < \theta < 0$
(e) $\csc\theta = \sqrt{2},\ 0 < \theta < \pi/2$
(f) $\csc\theta = \sqrt{2},\ \pi/2 < \theta < \pi$

16. (a) $\sin\theta = \frac{1}{4},\ 0 < \theta < \pi/2$
(b) $\sin\theta = \frac{1}{4},\ \pi/2 < \theta < \pi$
(c) $\cot\theta = \frac{1}{3},\ 0 < \theta < \pi/2$
(d) $\cot\theta = \frac{1}{3},\ \pi < \theta < 3\pi/2$
(e) $\sec\theta = -\frac{5}{2},\ \pi/2 < \theta < \pi$
(f) $\sec\theta = -\frac{5}{2},\ \pi < \theta < 3\pi/2$

17–18 Use a calculating utility to find x to four decimal places.

17. (a)   (b)

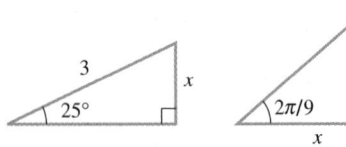

18. (a)   (b)

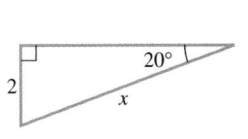 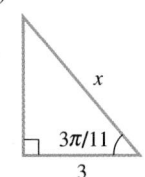

19. In each part, let θ be an acute angle of a right triangle. Express the remaining five trigonometric functions in terms of a.
(a) $\sin\theta = a/3$ (b) $\tan\theta = a/5$ (c) $\sec\theta = a$

20–27 Find all values of θ (in radians) that satisfy the given equation. Do not use a calculator.

20. (a) $\cos\theta = -1/\sqrt{2}$ (b) $\sin\theta = -1/\sqrt{2}$

21. (a) $\tan\theta = -1$ (b) $\cos\theta = \frac{1}{2}$

22. (a) $\sin\theta = -\frac{1}{2}$ (b) $\tan\theta = \sqrt{3}$

23. (a) $\tan\theta = 1/\sqrt{3}$ (b) $\sin\theta = -\sqrt{3}/2$

24. (a) $\sin\theta = -1$ (b) $\cos\theta = -1$

25. (a) $\cot\theta = -1$ (b) $\cot\theta = \sqrt{3}$

26. (a) $\sec\theta = -2$ (b) $\csc\theta = -2$

27. (a) $\csc\theta = 2/\sqrt{3}$ (b) $\sec\theta = 2/\sqrt{3}$

28–29 Find the values of all six trigonometric functions of θ.

28.   **29.**

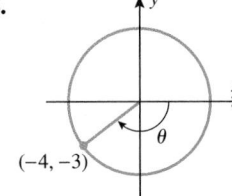 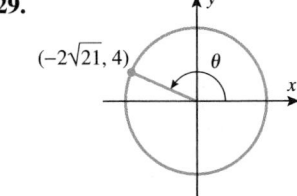

30. Find all values of θ (in radians) such that
(a) $\sin\theta = 1$ (b) $\cos\theta = 1$ (c) $\tan\theta = 1$
(d) $\csc\theta = 1$ (e) $\sec\theta = 1$ (f) $\cot\theta = 1$.

31. Find all values of θ (in radians) such that
(a) $\sin\theta = 0$ (b) $\cos\theta = 0$ (c) $\tan\theta = 0$
(d) $\csc\theta$ is undefined   (e) $\sec\theta$ is undefined
(f) $\cot\theta$ is undefined.

32. How could you use a ruler and protractor to approximate $\sin 17°$ and $\cos 17°$?

33. Find the length of the circular arc on a circle of radius 4 cm subtended by an angle of
(a) $\pi/6$ (b) $150°$.

34. Find the radius of a circular sector that has an angle of $\pi/3$ and a circular arc length of 7 units.

35. A point P moving counterclockwise on a circle of radius 5 cm traverses an arc length of 2 cm. What is the angle swept out by a radius from the center to P?

36. Find a formula for the area A of a circular sector in terms of its radius r and arc length s.

37. As shown in the accompanying figure, a right circular cone is made from a circular piece of paper of radius R by cutting out a sector of angle θ radians and gluing the cut edges of the remaining piece together. Find
(a) the radius r of the base of the cone in terms of R and θ
(b) the height h of the cone in terms of R and θ.

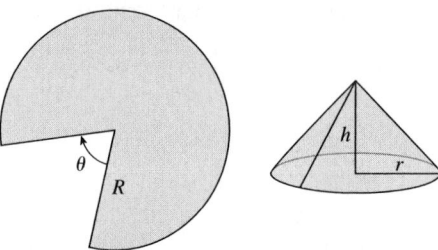

▲ **Figure Ex-37**

38. As shown in the accompanying figure, let r and L be the radius of the base and the slant height of a right circular cone. Show that the lateral surface area, S, of the cone is $S = \pi r L$. [*Hint:* As shown in the figure in Exercise 37, the lateral surface of the cone becomes a circular sector when cut along a line from the vertex to the base and flattened.]

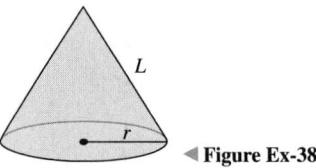

◀ **Figure Ex-38**

39. Two sides of a triangle have lengths of 3 cm and 7 cm and meet at an angle of $60°$. Find the area of the triangle.

40. Let ABC be a triangle whose angles at A and B are $30°$ and $45°$. If the side opposite the angle B has length 9, find the lengths of the remaining sides and the size of the angle C.

41. A 10-foot ladder leans against a house and makes an angle of $67°$ with level ground. How far is the top of the ladder above the ground? Express your answer to the nearest tenth of a foot.

42. From a point 120 feet on level ground from a building, the angle of elevation to the top of the building is $76°$. Find the height of the building. Express your answer to the nearest foot.

43. An observer on level ground is at a distance d from a building. The angles of elevation to the bottoms of the windows on the second and third floors are α and β, respectively. Find the distance h between the bottoms of the windows in terms of α, β, and d.

44. From a point on level ground, the angle of elevation to the top of a tower is α. From a point that is d units closer to the tower, the angle of elevation is β. Find the height h of the tower in terms of α, β, and d.

45–46 Do *not* use a calculator in these exercises. ◼

45. If $\cos\theta = \frac{2}{3}$ and $0 < \theta < \pi/2$, find
(a) $\sin 2\theta$ (b) $\cos 2\theta$.

46. If $\tan\alpha = \frac{3}{4}$ and $\tan\beta = 2$, where $0 < \alpha < \pi/2$ and $0 < \beta < \pi/2$, find
(a) $\sin(\alpha - \beta)$ (b) $\cos(\alpha + \beta)$.

47. Express $\sin 3\theta$ and $\cos 3\theta$ in terms of $\sin\theta$ and $\cos\theta$.

48–58 Derive the given identities. ◼

48. $\dfrac{\cos\theta\,\sec\theta}{1 + \tan^2\theta} = \cos^2\theta$

49. $\dfrac{\cos\theta\,\tan\theta + \sin\theta}{\tan\theta} = 2\cos\theta$

50. $2\csc 2\theta = \sec\theta\,\csc\theta$ **51.** $\tan\theta + \cot\theta = 2\csc 2\theta$

52. $\dfrac{\sin 2\theta}{\sin\theta} - \dfrac{\cos 2\theta}{\cos\theta} = \sec\theta$

53. $\dfrac{\sin\theta + \cos 2\theta - 1}{\cos\theta - \sin 2\theta} = \tan\theta$

54. $\sin 3\theta + \sin\theta = 2\sin 2\theta\cos\theta$

55. $\sin 3\theta - \sin\theta = 2\cos 2\theta\sin\theta$

56. $\tan\dfrac{\theta}{2} = \dfrac{1 - \cos\theta}{\sin\theta}$ **57.** $\tan\dfrac{\theta}{2} = \dfrac{\sin\theta}{1 + \cos\theta}$

58. $\cos\left(\dfrac{\pi}{3} + \theta\right) + \cos\left(\dfrac{\pi}{3} - \theta\right) = \cos\theta$

59–60 In these exercises, refer to an arbitrary triangle ABC in which the side of length a is opposite angle A, the side of length b is opposite angle B, and the side of length c is opposite angle C. ◼

59. Prove: The area of a triangle ABC can be written as
$$\text{area} = \tfrac{1}{2}bc\sin A$$
Find two other similar formulas for the area.

60. Prove the *law of sines*: In any triangle, the ratios of the sides to the sines of the opposite angles are equal; that is,
$$\frac{a}{\sin A} = \frac{b}{\sin B} = \frac{c}{\sin C}$$

61. Use identities (34) through (37) to express each of the following in terms of $\sin\theta$ or $\cos\theta$.
(a) $\sin\left(\dfrac{\pi}{2} + \theta\right)$ (b) $\cos\left(\dfrac{\pi}{2} + \theta\right)$
(c) $\sin\left(\dfrac{3\pi}{2} - \theta\right)$ (d) $\cos\left(\dfrac{3\pi}{2} + \theta\right)$

62. Derive identities (38) and (39).

63. Derive identity
(a) (47)   (b) (48)   (c) (49).

64. If $A = \alpha + \beta$ and $B = \alpha - \beta$, then $\alpha = \frac{1}{2}(A + B)$ and $\beta = \frac{1}{2}(A - B)$ (verify). Use this result and identities (47) through (49) to derive identity
(a) (50)   (b) (52)   (c) (53).

65. Substitute $-\beta$ for β in identity (50) to derive identity (51).

66. (a) Express $3 \sin \alpha + 5 \cos \alpha$ in the form
$$C \sin(\alpha + \phi)$$

(b) Show that a sum of the form
$$A \sin \alpha + B \cos \alpha$$
can be rewritten in the form $C \sin(\alpha + \phi)$.

67. Show that the length of the diagonal of the parallelogram in the accompanying figure is
$$d = \sqrt{a^2 + b^2 + 2ab \cos \theta}$$

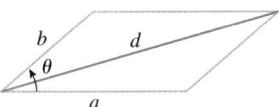

◄ **Figure Ex-67**

68–69 Find the angle of inclination of the line with slope m to the nearest degree. Use a calculating utility, where needed. ▪

68. (a) $m = \frac{1}{2}$ (b) $m = -1$
(c) $m = 2$ (d) $m = -57$

69. (a) $m = -\frac{1}{2}$ (b) $m = 1$
(c) $m = -2$ (d) $m = 57$

70–71 Find the angle of inclination of the line to the nearest degree. Use a calculating utility, where needed. ▪

70. (a) $3y = 2 - \sqrt{3}x$ (b) $y - 4x + 7 = 0$

71. (a) $y = \sqrt{3}x + 2$ (b) $y + 2x + 5 = 0$

SOLVING POLYNOMIAL EQUATIONS

We will assume in this appendix that you know how to divide polynomials using long division and synthetic division. If you need to review those techniques, refer to an algebra book.

A BRIEF REVIEW OF POLYNOMIALS

Recall that if n is a nonnegative integer, then a ***polynomial of degree n*** is a function that can be written in the following forms, depending on whether you want the powers of x in ascending or descending order:

$$c_0 + c_1 x + c_2 x^2 + \cdots + c_n x^n \quad (c_n \neq 0)$$
$$c_n x^n + c_{n-1} x^{n-1} + \cdots + c_1 x + c_0 \quad (c_n \neq 0)$$

The numbers $c_0, c_1, \ldots, c_n$ are called the ***coefficients*** of the polynomial. The coefficient c_n (which multiplies the highest power of x) is called the ***leading coefficient***, the term $c_n x^n$ is called the ***leading term***, and the coefficient c_0 is called the ***constant term***. Polynomials of degree 1, 2, 3, 4, and 5 are called ***linear***, ***quadratic***, ***cubic***, ***quartic***, and ***quintic***, respectively. For simplicity, general polynomials of low degree are often written without subscripts on the coefficients:

$$p(x) = a \qquad \boxed{\text{Constant polynomial}}$$
$$p(x) = ax + b \quad (a \neq 0) \qquad \boxed{\text{Linear polynomial}}$$
$$p(x) = ax^2 + bx + c \quad (a \neq 0) \qquad \boxed{\text{Quadratic polynomial}}$$
$$p(x) = ax^3 + bx^2 + cx + d \quad (a \neq 0) \qquad \boxed{\text{Cubic polynomial}}$$

When you attempt to factor a polynomial completely, one of three things can happen:

- You may be able to decompose the polynomial into distinct linear factors using only real numbers; for example,
$$x^3 + x^2 - 2x = x(x^2 + x - 2) = x(x - 1)(x + 2)$$

- You may be able to decompose the polynomial into linear factors using only real numbers, but some of the factors may be repeated; for example,
$$x^6 - 3x^4 + 2x^3 = x^3(x^3 - 3x + 2) = x^3(x - 1)^2(x + 2) \tag{1}$$

- You may be able to decompose the polynomial into linear and quadratic factors using only real numbers, but you may not be able to decompose the quadratic factors into linear factors using only real numbers (such quadratic factors are said to be ***irreducible*** over the real numbers); for example,
$$x^4 - 1 = (x^2 - 1)(x^2 + 1) = (x - 1)(x + 1)(x^2 + 1)$$
$$= (x - 1)(x + 1)(x - i)(x + i)$$

Here, the factor $x^2 + 1$ is irreducible over the real numbers.

In general, if $p(x)$ is a polynomial of degree n with leading coefficient a, and if complex numbers are allowed, then $p(x)$ can be factored as

$$p(x) = a(x - r_1)(x - r_2) \cdots (x - r_n) \qquad (2)$$

where $r_1, r_2, \ldots, r_n$ are called the **zeros** of $p(x)$ or the **roots** of the equation $p(x) = 0$, and (2) is called the **complete linear factorization** of $p(x)$. If some of the factors in (2) are repeated, then they can be combined; for example, if the first k factors are distinct and the rest are repetitions of the first k, then (2) can be expressed in the form

$$p(x) = a(x - r_1)^{m_1} (x - r_2)^{m_2} \cdots (x - r_k)^{m_k} \qquad (3)$$

where $r_1, r_2, \ldots, r_k$ are the *distinct* roots of $p(x) = 0$. The exponents $m_1, m_2, \ldots, m_k$ tell us how many times the various factors occur in the complete linear factorization; for example, in (3) the factor $(x - r_1)$ occurs m_1 times, the factor $(x - r_2)$ occurs m_2 times, and so forth. Some techniques for factoring polynomials are discussed later in this appendix. In general, if a factor $(x - r)$ occurs m times in the complete linear factorization of a polynomial, then we say that r is a root or zero of **multiplicity m**, and if $(x - r)$ has no repetitions (i.e., r has multiplicity 1), then we say that r is a **simple** root or zero. For example, it follows from (1) that the equation $x^6 - 3x^4 + 2x^3 = 0$ can be expressed as

$$x^3(x - 1)^2(x + 2) = 0 \qquad (4)$$

so this equation has three distinct roots—a root $x = 0$ of multiplicity 3, a root $x = 1$ of multiplicity 2, and a simple root $x = -2$.

Note that in (3) the multiplicities of the roots must add up to n, since $p(x)$ has degree n; that is,

$$m_1 + m_2 + \cdots + m_k = n$$

For example, in (4) the multiplicities add up to 6, which is the same as the degree of the polynomial.

It follows from (2) that a polynomial of degree n can have at most n distinct roots; if all of the roots are simple, then there will be *exactly n*, but if some are repeated, then there will be fewer than n. However, when counting the roots of a polynomial, it is standard practice to count multiplicities, since that convention allows us to say that a polynomial of degree n has n roots. For example, from (1) the six roots of the polynomial $p(x) = x^6 - 3x^4 + 2x^3$ are

$$r = 0, \ 0, \ 0, \ 1, \ 1, \ -2$$

In summary, we have the following important theorem.

C.1 **THEOREM** *If complex roots are allowed, and if roots are counted according to their multiplicities, then a polynomial of degree n has exactly n roots.*

■ THE REMAINDER THEOREM

When two positive integers are divided, the numerator can be expressed as the quotient plus the remainder over the divisor, where the remainder is less than the divisor. For example,

$$\tfrac{17}{5} = 3 + \tfrac{2}{5}$$

If we multiply this equation through by 5, we obtain

$$17 = 5 \cdot 3 + 2$$

which states that the *numerator is the divisor times the quotient plus the remainder*.

The following theorem, which we state without proof, is an analogous result for division of polynomials.

C.2   THEOREM   *If $p(x)$ and $s(x)$ are polynomials, and if $s(x)$ is not the zero polynomial, then $p(x)$ can be expressed as*

$$p(x) = s(x)q(x) + r(x)$$

where $q(x)$ and $r(x)$ are the quotient and remainder that result when $p(x)$ is divided by $s(x)$, and either $r(x)$ is the zero polynomial or the degree of $r(x)$ is less than the degree of $s(x)$.

In the special case where $p(x)$ is divided by a first-degree polynomial of the form $x - c$, the remainder must be some constant r, since it is either zero or has degree less than 1. Thus, Theorem C.2 implies that

$$p(x) = (x - c)q(x) + r$$

and this in turn implies that $p(c) = r$. In summary, we have the following theorem.

C.3   THEOREM (*Remainder Theorem*)   *If a polynomial $p(x)$ is divided by $x - c$, then the remainder is $p(c)$.*

▶ **Example 1**   According to the Remainder Theorem, the remainder on dividing

$$p(x) = 2x^3 + 3x^2 - 4x - 3$$

by $x + 4$ should be

$$p(-4) = 2(-4)^3 + 3(-4)^2 - 4(-4) - 3 = -67$$

Show that this is so.

Solution.   By long division

$$
\begin{array}{r}
2x^2 - 5x + 16 \\
x + 4\overline{\smash{\big)}\,2x^3 + 3x^2 - 4x - 3} \\
\underline{2x^3 + 8x^2} \\
-5x^2 - 4x \\
\underline{-5x^2 - 20x} \\
16x - 3 \\
\underline{16x + 64} \\
-67
\end{array}
$$

which shows that the remainder is -67.

Alternative Solution.   Because we are dividing by an expression of the form $x - c$ (where $c = -4$), we can use synthetic division rather than long division. The computations are

$$
\begin{array}{r|rrrr}
-4 & 2 & 3 & -4 & -3 \\
   &   & -8 & 20 & -64 \\
\hline
   & 2 & -5 & 16 & -67
\end{array}
$$

which again shows that the remainder is -67. ◄

■ THE FACTOR THEOREM

To *factor* a polynomial $p(x)$ is to write it as a product of lower-degree polynomials, called *factors* of $p(x)$. For $s(x)$ to be a factor of $p(x)$ there must be no remainder when $p(x)$ is divided by $s(x)$. For example, if $p(x)$ can be factored as

$$p(x) = s(x)q(x) \tag{5}$$

then

$$\frac{p(x)}{s(x)} = q(x) \tag{6}$$

so dividing $p(x)$ by $s(x)$ produces a quotient $q(x)$ with no remainder. Conversely, (6) implies (5), so $s(x)$ is a factor of $p(x)$ if there is no remainder when $p(x)$ is divided by $s(x)$.

In the special case where $x - c$ is a factor of $p(x)$, the polynomial $p(x)$ can be expressed as

$$p(x) = (x - c)q(x)$$

which implies that $p(c) = 0$. Conversely, if $p(c) = 0$, then the Remainder Theorem implies that $x - c$ is a factor of $p(x)$, since the remainder is 0 when $p(x)$ is divided by $x - c$. These results are summarized in the following theorem.

C.4   THEOREM (*Factor Theorem*)   *A polynomial $p(x)$ has a factor $x - c$ if and only if $p(c) = 0$.*

It follows from this theorem that the statements below say the same thing in different ways:

- $x - c$ is a factor of $p(x)$.
- $p(c) = 0$.
- c is a zero of $p(x)$.
- c is a root of the equation $p(x) = 0$.
- c is a solution of the equation $p(x) = 0$.
- c is an x-intercept of $y = p(x)$.

▶ **Example 2**   Confirm that $x - 1$ is a factor of

$$p(x) = x^3 - 3x^2 - 13x + 15$$

by dividing $x - 1$ into $p(x)$ and checking that the remainder is zero.

Solution.   By long division

$$
\begin{array}{r}
x^2 - 2x - 15 \\
x - 1 \overline{)\,x^3 - 3x^2 - 13x + 15} \\
\underline{x^3 - x^2} \phantom{{}-13x+15} \\
-2x^2 - 13x \\
\underline{-2x^2 + 2x} \\
-15x + 15 \\
\underline{-15x + 15} \\
0
\end{array}
$$

which shows that the remainder is zero.

Alternative Solution.   Because we are dividing by an expression of the form $x - c$, we can use synthetic division rather than long division. The computations are

$$
\begin{array}{r|rrrr}
1\rfloor & 1 & -3 & -13 & 15 \\
 & & 1 & -2 & -15 \\
\hline
 & 1 & -2 & -15 & 0
\end{array}
$$

which again confirms that the remainder is zero. ◄

■ **USING ONE FACTOR TO FIND OTHER FACTORS**

If $x - c$ is a factor of $p(x)$, and if $q(x) = p(x)/(x - c)$, then

$$p(x) = (x - c)q(x) \tag{7}$$

so that additional linear factors of $p(x)$ can be obtained by factoring the quotient $q(x)$.

▶ **Example 3**   Factor

$$p(x) = x^3 - 3x^2 - 13x + 15 \tag{8}$$

completely into linear factors.

Solution.   We showed in Example 2 that $x - 1$ is a factor of $p(x)$ and we also showed that $p(x)/(x - 1) = x^2 - 2x - 15$. Thus,

$$x^3 - 3x^2 - 13x + 15 = (x - 1)(x^2 - 2x - 15)$$

Factoring $x^2 - 2x - 15$ by inspection yields

$$x^3 - 3x^2 - 13x + 15 = (x - 1)(x - 5)(x + 3)$$

which is the complete linear factorization of $p(x)$. ◄

■ **METHODS FOR FINDING ROOTS**

A general quadratic equation $ax^2 + bx + c = 0$ can be solved by using the quadratic formula to express the solutions of the equation in terms of the coefficients. Versions of this formula were known since Babylonian times, and by the seventeenth century formulas had been obtained for solving general cubic and quartic equations. However, attempts to find formulas for the solutions of general fifth-degree equations and higher proved fruitless. The reason for this became clear in 1829 when the French mathematician Evariste Galois (1811–1832) proved that it is impossible to express the solutions of a general fifth-degree equation or higher in terms of its coefficients using algebraic operations.

Today, we have powerful computer programs for finding the zeros of specific polynomials. For example, it takes only seconds for a computer algebra system, such as *Mathematica* or *Maple*, to show that the zeros of the polynomial

$$p(x) = 10x^4 - 23x^3 - 10x^2 + 29x + 6 \tag{9}$$

are

$$x = -1, \quad x = -\tfrac{1}{5}, \quad x = \tfrac{3}{2}, \quad \text{and} \quad x = 2 \tag{10}$$

The algorithms that these programs use to find the integer and rational zeros of a polynomial, if any, are based on the following theorem, which is proved in advanced algebra courses.

C.5   THEOREM   *Suppose that*

$$p(x) = c_n x^n + c_{n-1} x^{n-1} + \cdots + c_1 x + c_0$$

is a polynomial with integer coefficients.

(a) *If r is an integer zero of $p(x)$, then r must be a divisor of the constant term c_0.*

(b) *If $r = a/b$ is a rational zero of $p(x)$ in which all common factors of a and b have been canceled, then a must be a divisor of the constant term c_0, and b must be a divisor of the leading coefficient c_n.*

For example, in (9) the constant term is 6 (which has divisors ± 1, ± 2, ± 3, and ± 6) and the leading coefficient is 10 (which has divisors ± 1, ± 2, ± 5, and ± 10). Thus, the only possible integer zeros of $p(x)$ are

$$\pm 1, \quad \pm 2, \quad \pm 3, \quad \pm 6$$

and the only possible noninteger rational zeros are

$$\pm \tfrac{1}{2}, \quad \pm \tfrac{1}{5}, \quad \pm \tfrac{1}{10}, \quad \pm \tfrac{2}{5}, \quad \pm \tfrac{3}{2}, \quad \pm \tfrac{3}{5}, \quad \pm \tfrac{3}{10}, \quad \pm \tfrac{6}{5}$$

Using a computer, it is a simple matter to evaluate $p(x)$ at each of the numbers in these lists to show that its only rational zeros are the numbers in (10).

▶ **Example 4**   Solve the equation $x^3 + 3x^2 - 7x - 21 = 0$.

Solution.   The solutions of the equation are the zeros of the polynomial

$$p(x) = x^3 + 3x^2 - 7x - 21$$

We will look for integer zeros first. All such zeros must divide the constant term, so the only possibilities are ± 1, ± 3, ± 7, and ± 21. Substituting these values into $p(x)$ (or using the method of Exercise 6) shows that $x = -3$ is an integer zero. This tells us that $x + 3$ is a factor of $p(x)$ and that $p(x)$ can be written as

$$x^3 + 3x^2 - 7x - 21 = (x + 3)q(x)$$

where $q(x)$ is the quotient that results when $x^3 + 3x^2 - 7x - 21$ is divided by $x + 3$. We leave it for you to perform the division and show that $q(x) = x^2 - 7$; hence,

$$x^3 + 3x^2 - 7x - 21 = (x + 3)(x^2 - 7) = (x + 3)(x + \sqrt{7})(x - \sqrt{7})$$

which tells us that the solutions of the given equation are $x = 3$, $x = \sqrt{7} \approx 2.65$, and $x = -\sqrt{7} \approx -2.65$. ◀

EXERCISE SET C   ⊂ CAS

1–2 Find the quotient $q(x)$ and the remainder $r(x)$ that result when $p(x)$ is divided by $s(x)$. ■

1. (a) $p(x) = x^4 + 3x^3 - 5x + 10$; $s(x) = x^2 - x + 2$
   (b) $p(x) = 6x^4 + 10x^2 + 5$; $s(x) = 3x^2 - 1$
   (c) $p(x) = x^5 + x^3 + 1$; $s(x) = x^2 + x$

2. (a) $p(x) = 2x^4 - 3x^3 + 5x^2 + 2x + 7$; $s(x) = x^2 - x + 1$
   (b) $p(x) = 2x^5 + 5x^4 - 4x^3 + 8x^2 + 1$; $s(x) = 2x^2 - x + 1$
   (c) $p(x) = 5x^6 + 4x^2 + 5$; $s(x) = x^3 + 1$

3–4 Use synthetic division to find the quotient $q(x)$ and the remainder $r(x)$ that result when $p(x)$ is divided by $s(x)$. ■

3. (a) $p(x) = 3x^3 - 4x - 1$; $s(x) = x - 2$
   (b) $p(x) = x^4 - 5x^2 + 4$; $s(x) = x + 5$
   (c) $p(x) = x^5 - 1$; $s(x) = x - 1$

4. (a) $p(x) = 2x^3 - x^2 - 2x + 1$; $s(x) = x - 1$
   (b) $p(x) = 2x^4 + 3x^3 - 17x^2 - 27x - 9$; $s(x) = x + 4$
   (c) $p(x) = x^7 + 1$; $s(x) = x - 1$

5. Let $p(x) = 2x^4 + x^3 - 3x^2 + x - 4$. Use synthetic division and the Remainder Theorem to find $p(0)$, $p(1)$, $p(-3)$, and $p(7)$.

6. Let $p(x)$ be the polynomial in Example 4. Use synthetic division and the Remainder Theorem to evaluate $p(x)$ at $x = \pm 1$, ± 3, ± 7, and ± 21.

7. Let $p(x) = x^3 + 4x^2 + x - 6$. Find a polynomial $q(x)$ and a constant r such that
(a) $p(x) = (x - 2)q(x) + r$
(b) $p(x) = (x + 1)q(x) + r$.

8. Let $p(x) = x^5 - 1$. Find a polynomial $q(x)$ and a constant r such that
(a) $p(x) = (x + 1)q(x) + r$
(b) $p(x) = (x - 1)q(x) + r$.

9. In each part, make a list of all possible candidates for the rational zeros of $p(x)$.
(a) $p(x) = x^7 + 3x^3 - x + 24$
(b) $p(x) = 3x^4 - 2x^2 + 7x - 10$
(c) $p(x) = x^{35} - 17$

10. Find all integer zeros of

$$p(x) = x^6 + 5x^5 - 16x^4 - 15x^3 - 12x^2 - 38x - 21$$

11–15 Factor the polynomials completely. ■

11. $p(x) = x^3 - 2x^2 - x + 2$

12. $p(x) = 3x^3 + x^2 - 12x - 4$

13. $p(x) = x^4 + 10x^3 + 36x^2 + 54x + 27$

14. $p(x) = 2x^4 + x^3 + 3x^2 + 3x - 9$

15. $p(x) = x^5 + 4x^4 - 4x^3 - 34x^2 - 45x - 18$

c **16.** For each of the factorizations that you obtained in Exercises 11–15, check your answer using a CAS.

17–21 Find all real solutions of the equations. ■

17. $x^3 + 3x^2 + 4x + 12 = 0$

18. $2x^3 - 5x^2 - 10x + 3 = 0$

19. $3x^4 + 14x^3 + 14x^2 - 8x - 8 = 0$

20. $2x^4 - x^3 - 14x^2 - 5x + 6 = 0$

21. $x^5 - 2x^4 - 6x^3 + 5x^2 + 8x + 12 = 0$

c **22.** For each of the equations you solved in Exercises 17–21, check your answer using a CAS.

23. Find all values of k for which $x - 1$ is a factor of the polynomial $p(x) = k^2 x^3 - 7kx + 10$.

24. Is $x + 3$ a factor of $x^7 + 2187$? Justify your answer.

c **25.** A 3 cm thick slice is cut from a cube, leaving a volume of 196 cm^3. Use a CAS to find the length of a side of the original cube.

26. (a) Show that there is no positive rational number that exceeds its cube by 1.
(b) Does there exist a real number that exceeds its cube by 1? Justify your answer.

27. Use the Factor Theorem to show each of the following.
(a) $x - y$ is a factor of $x^n - y^n$ for all positive integer values of n.
(b) $x + y$ is a factor of $x^n - y^n$ for all positive even integer values of n.
(c) $x + y$ is a factor of $x^n + y^n$ for all positive odd integer values of n.

D

SELECTED PROOFS

PROOFS OF BASIC LIMIT THEOREMS

An extensive excursion into proofs of limit theorems would be too time consuming to undertake, so we have selected a few proofs of results from Section 1.2 that illustrate some of the basic ideas.

D.1 **THEOREM** *Let a be any real number, let k be a constant, and suppose that* $\lim\limits_{x \to a} f(x) = L_1$ *and that* $\lim\limits_{x \to a} g(x) = L_2$. *Then:*

(a) $\lim\limits_{x \to a} k = k$

(b) $\lim\limits_{x \to a} [f(x) + g(x)] = \lim\limits_{x \to a} f(x) + \lim\limits_{x \to a} g(x) = L_1 + L_2$

(c) $\lim\limits_{x \to a} [f(x)g(x)] = \left(\lim\limits_{x \to a} f(x) \right) \left(\lim\limits_{x \to a} g(x) \right) = L_1 L_2$

PROOF (*a*)   We will apply Definition 1.4.1 with $f(x) = k$ and $L = k$. Thus, given $\epsilon > 0$, we must find a number $\delta > 0$ such that

$$|k - k| < \epsilon \quad \text{if} \quad 0 < |x - a| < \delta$$

or, equivalently,

$$0 < \epsilon \quad \text{if} \quad 0 < |x - a| < \delta$$

But the condition on the left side of this statement is *always* true, no matter how δ is chosen. Thus, any positive value for δ will suffice.

PROOF (*b*)   We must show that given $\epsilon > 0$ we can find a number $\delta > 0$ such that

$$|(f(x) + g(x)) - (L_1 + L_2)| < \epsilon \quad \text{if} \quad 0 < |x - a| < \delta \tag{1}$$

However, from the limits of f and g in the hypothesis of the theorem we can find numbers δ_1 and δ_2 such that

$$|f(x) - L_1| < \epsilon/2 \quad \text{if} \quad 0 < |x - a| < \delta_1$$

$$|g(x) - L_2| < \epsilon/2 \quad \text{if} \quad 0 < |x - a| < \delta_2$$

Moreover, the inequalities on the left sides of these statements *both* hold if we replace δ_1 and δ_2 by any positive number δ that is less than both δ_1 and δ_2. Thus, for any such δ it follows that

$$|f(x) - L_1| + |g(x) - L_2| < \epsilon \quad \text{if} \quad 0 < |x - a| < \delta \tag{2}$$

However, it follows from the triangle inequality [Theorem F.5 of Appendix F] that

$$|(f(x) + g(x)) - (L_1 + L_2)| = |(f(x) - L_1) + (g(x) - L_2)|$$
$$\leq |f(x) - L_1| + |g(x) - L_2|$$

so that (1) follows from (2).

PROOF (c) We must show that given $\epsilon > 0$ we can find a number $\delta > 0$ such that

$$|f(x)g(x) - L_1 L_2| < \epsilon \quad \text{if} \quad 0 < |x - a| < \delta \tag{3}$$

To find δ it will be helpful to express (3) in a different form. If we rewrite $f(x)$ and $g(x)$ as

$$f(x) = L_1 + (f(x) - L_1) \quad \text{and} \quad g(x) = L_2 + (g(x) - L_2)$$

then the inequality on the left side of (3) can be expressed as (verify)

$$|L_1(g(x) - L_2) + L_2(f(x) - L_1) + (f(x) - L_1)(g(x) - L_2)| < \epsilon \tag{4}$$

Since

$$\lim_{x \to a} f(x) = L_1 \quad \text{and} \quad \lim_{x \to a} g(x) = L_2$$

we can find positive numbers δ_1, δ_2, δ_3, and δ_4 such that

$$
\begin{array}{ll}
|f(x) - L_1| < \sqrt{\epsilon/3} & \text{if} \quad 0 < |x - a| < \delta_1 \\[2mm]
|f(x) - L_1| < \dfrac{\epsilon}{3(1 + |L_2|)} & \text{if} \quad 0 < |x - a| < \delta_2 \\[2mm]
|g(x) - L_2| < \sqrt{\epsilon/3} & \text{if} \quad 0 < |x - a| < \delta_3 \\[2mm]
|g(x) - L_2| < \dfrac{\epsilon}{3(1 + |L_1|)} & \text{if} \quad 0 < |x - a| < \delta_4
\end{array} \tag{5}
$$

Moreover, the inequalities on the left sides of these four statements *all* hold if we replace δ_1, δ_2, δ_3, and δ_4 by any positive number δ that is smaller than δ_1, δ_2, δ_3, and δ_4. Thus, for any such δ it follows with the help of the triangle inequality that

$$|L_1(g(x) - L_2) + L_2(f(x) - L_1) + (f(x) - L_1)(g(x) - L_2)|$$
$$\leq |L_1(g(x) - L_2)| + |L_2(f(x) - L_1)| + |(f(x) - L_1)(g(x) - L_2)|$$
$$= |L_1||g(x) - L_2| + |L_2||f(x) - L_1| + |f(x) - L_1||g(x) - L_2|$$
$$< |L_1|\frac{\epsilon}{3(1 + |L_1|)} + |L_2|\frac{\epsilon}{3(1 + |L_2|)} + \sqrt{\epsilon/3}\sqrt{\epsilon/3} \quad \boxed{\text{From (5)}}$$
$$= \frac{\epsilon}{3}\frac{|L_1|}{1 + |L_1|} + \frac{\epsilon}{3}\frac{|L_2|}{1 + |L_2|} + \frac{\epsilon}{3}$$
$$< \frac{\epsilon}{3} + \frac{\epsilon}{3} + \frac{\epsilon}{3} = \epsilon \quad \boxed{\text{Since } \frac{|L_1|}{1 + |L_1|} < 1 \text{ and } \frac{|L_2|}{1 + |L_2|} < 1}$$

> Do not be alarmed if the proof of part (c) seems difficult; it takes some experience with proofs of this type to develop a feel for choosing a valid δ. Your initial goal should be to understand the ideas and the computations.

which shows that (4) holds for the δ selected. ∎

▪ PROOF OF A BASIC CONTINUITY PROPERTY

Next we will prove Theorem 1.5.5 for two-sided limits.

D.2   THEOREM (*Theorem 1.5.5*)   *If $\lim_{x \to c} g(x) = L$ and if the function f is continuous at L, then $\lim_{x \to c} f(g(x)) = f(L)$. That is,*

$$\lim_{x \to c} f(g(x)) = f\left(\lim_{x \to c} g(x)\right)$$

PROOF We must show that given $\epsilon > 0$, we can find a number $\delta > 0$ such that

$$|f(g(x)) - f(L)| < \epsilon \quad \text{if} \quad 0 < |x - c| < \delta \tag{6}$$

Since f is continuous at L, we have

$$\lim_{u \to L} f(u) = f(L)$$

and hence we can find a number $\delta_1 > 0$ such that

$$|f(u) - f(L)| < \epsilon \quad \text{if} \quad |u - L| < \delta_1$$

In particular, if $u = g(x)$, then

$$|f(g(x)) - f(L)| < \epsilon \quad \text{if} \quad |g(x) - L| < \delta_1 \tag{7}$$

But $\lim_{x \to c} g(x) = L$, and hence there is a number $\delta > 0$ such that

$$|g(x) - L| < \delta_1 \quad \text{if} \quad 0 < |x - c| < \delta \tag{8}$$

Thus, if x satisfies the condition on the right side of statement (8), then it follows that $g(x)$ satisfies the condition on the right side of statement (7), and this implies that the condition on the left side of statement (6) is satisfied, completing the proof. ∎

■ PROOF OF THE CHAIN RULE
Next we will prove the chain rule (Theorem 2.6.1), but first we need a preliminary result.

D.3 THEOREM *If f is differentiable at x and if $y = f(x)$, then*

$$\Delta y = f'(x)\Delta x + \epsilon \Delta x$$

where $\epsilon \to 0$ as $\Delta x \to 0$ and $\epsilon = 0$ if $\Delta x = 0$.

PROOF Define

$$\epsilon = \begin{cases} \dfrac{f(x + \Delta x) - f(x)}{\Delta x} - f'(x) & \text{if } \Delta x \neq 0 \\[2ex] 0 & \text{if } \Delta x = 0 \end{cases} \tag{9}$$

If $\Delta x \neq 0$, it follows from (9) that

$$\epsilon \Delta x = [f(x + \Delta x) - f(x)] - f'(x)\Delta x \tag{10}$$

But

$$\Delta y = f(x + \Delta x) - f(x) \tag{11}$$

so (10) can be written as

$$\epsilon \Delta x = \Delta y - f'(x)\Delta x$$

or

$$\Delta y = f'(x)\Delta x + \epsilon \Delta x \tag{12}$$

If $\Delta x = 0$, then (12) still holds (why?), so (12) is valid for all values of Δx. It remains to show that $\epsilon \to 0$ as $\Delta x \to 0$. But this follows from the assumption that f is differentiable at x, since

$$\lim_{\Delta x \to 0} \epsilon = \lim_{\Delta x \to 0} \left[\frac{f(x + \Delta x) - f(x)}{\Delta x} - f'(x) \right] = f'(x) - f'(x) = 0 \quad ∎$$

We are now ready to prove the chain rule.

D.4 **THEOREM** (*Theorem 2.6.1*) *If g is differentiable at the point x and f is differentiable at the point g(x), then the composition f ∘ g is differentiable at the point x. Moreover, if y = f(g(x)) and u = g(x), then*

$$\frac{dy}{dx} = \frac{dy}{du} \cdot \frac{du}{dx}$$

PROOF Since g is differentiable at x and $u = g(x)$, it follows from Theorem D.3 that

$$\Delta u = g'(x)\Delta x + \epsilon_1 \Delta x \tag{13}$$

where $\epsilon_1 \to 0$ as $\Delta x \to 0$. And since $y = f(u)$ is differentiable at $u = g(x)$, it follows from Theorem D.3 that

$$\Delta y = f'(u)\Delta u + \epsilon_2 \Delta u \tag{14}$$

where $\epsilon_2 \to 0$ as $\Delta u \to 0$.

Factoring out the Δu in (14) and then substituting (13) yields

$$\Delta y = [f'(u) + \epsilon_2][g'(x)\Delta x + \epsilon_1 \Delta x]$$

or

$$\Delta y = [f'(u) + \epsilon_2][g'(x) + \epsilon_1]\Delta x$$

or if $\Delta x \neq 0$,

$$\frac{\Delta y}{\Delta x} = [f'(u) + \epsilon_2][g'(x) + \epsilon_1] \tag{15}$$

But (13) implies that $\Delta u \to 0$ as $\Delta x \to 0$, and hence $\epsilon_1 \to 0$ and $\epsilon_2 \to 0$ as $\Delta x \to 0$. Thus, from (15)

$$\lim_{\Delta x \to 0} \frac{\Delta y}{\Delta x} = f'(u)g'(x)$$

or

$$\frac{dy}{dx} = f'(u)g'(x) = \frac{dy}{du} \cdot \frac{du}{dx} \quad \blacksquare$$

■ PROOF THAT RELATIVE EXTREMA OCCUR AT CRITICAL POINTS

In this subsection we will prove Theorem 4.2.2, which states that the relative extrema of a function occur at critical points.

D.5 **THEOREM** (*Theorem 4.2.2*) *Suppose that f is a function defined on an open interval containing the point x_0. If f has a relative extremum at $x = x_0$, then $x = x_0$ is a critical point of f; that is, either $f'(x_0) = 0$ or f is not differentiable at x_0.*

PROOF Suppose that f has a relative maximum at x_0. There are two possibilities—either f is differentiable at x_0 or it is not. If it is not, then x_0 is a critical point for f and we are done. If f is differentiable at x_0, then we must show that $f'(x_0) = 0$. We will do this by showing that $f'(x_0) \geq 0$ and $f'(x_0) \leq 0$, from which it follows that $f'(x_0) = 0$. From the definition of a derivative we have

$$f'(x_0) = \lim_{h \to 0} \frac{f(x_0 + h) - f(x_0)}{h}$$

so that

$$f'(x_0) = \lim_{h \to 0^+} \frac{f(x_0 + h) - f(x_0)}{h} \tag{16}$$

and

$$f'(x_0) = \lim_{h \to 0^-} \frac{f(x_0 + h) - f(x_0)}{h} \tag{17}$$

Because f has a relative maximum at x_0, there is an open interval (a, b) containing x_0 in which $f(x) \leq f(x_0)$ for all x in (a, b).

Assume that h is sufficiently small so that $x_0 + h$ lies in the interval (a, b). Thus,

$$f(x_0 + h) \leq f(x_0) \quad \text{or equivalently} \quad f(x_0 + h) - f(x_0) \leq 0$$

Thus, if h is negative,

$$\frac{f(x_0 + h) - f(x_0)}{h} \geq 0 \tag{18}$$

and if h is positive,

$$\frac{f(x_0 + h) - f(x_0)}{h} \leq 0 \tag{19}$$

But an expression that never assumes negative values cannot approach a negative limit and an expression that never assumes positive values cannot approach a positive limit, so that

$$f'(x_0) = \lim_{h \to 0^-} \frac{f(x_0 + h) - f(x_0)}{h} \geq 0 \qquad \boxed{\text{From (17) and (18)}}$$

and

$$f'(x_0) = \lim_{h \to 0^+} \frac{f(x_0 + h) - f(x_0)}{h} \leq 0 \qquad \boxed{\text{From (16) and (19)}}$$

Since $f'(x_0) \geq 0$ and $f'(x_0) \leq 0$, it must be that $f'(x_0) = 0$.

A similar argument applies if f has a relative minimum at x_0. ■

■ PROOFS OF TWO SUMMATION FORMULAS

We will prove parts (a) and (b) of Theorem 5.4.2. The proof of part (c) is similar to that of part (b) and is omitted.

D.6 **THEOREM** (*Theorem 5.4.2*)

(a) $\displaystyle\sum_{k=1}^{n} k = 1 + 2 + \cdots + n = \frac{n(n+1)}{2}$

(b) $\displaystyle\sum_{k=1}^{n} k^2 = 1^2 + 2^2 + \cdots + n^2 = \frac{n(n+1)(2n+1)}{6}$

(c) $\displaystyle\sum_{k=1}^{n} k^3 = 1^3 + 2^3 + \cdots + n^3 = \left[\frac{n(n+1)}{2}\right]^2$

PROOF (a) Writing

$$\sum_{k=1}^{n} k$$

two ways, with summands in increasing order and in decreasing order, and then adding, we obtain

$$\sum_{k=1}^{n} k = \quad 1 \quad + \quad 2 \quad + \quad 3 \quad + \cdots + (n-2) + (n-1) + \quad n$$

$$\sum_{k=1}^{n} k = \quad n \quad + (n-1) + (n-2) + \cdots + \quad 3 \quad + \quad 2 \quad + \quad 1$$

$$2\sum_{k=1}^{n} k = (n+1) + (n+1) + (n+1) + \cdots + (n+1) + (n+1) + (n+1)$$

$$= n(n+1)$$

Thus,

$$\sum_{k=1}^{n} k = \frac{n(n+1)}{2}$$

PROOF (*b*)   Note that

$$(k+1)^3 - k^3 = k^3 + 3k^2 + 3k + 1 - k^3 = 3k^2 + 3k + 1$$

So,

$$\sum_{k=1}^{n}[(k+1)^3 - k^3] = \sum_{k=1}^{n}(3k^2 + 3k + 1) \qquad (20)$$

Writing out the left side of (20) with the index running *down* from $k = n$ to $k = 1$, we have

The sum in (21) is an example of a *telescoping sum*, since the cancellation of each of the two parts of an interior summand with parts of its neighboring summands allows the entire sum to collapse like a telescope.

$$\sum_{k=1}^{n}[(k+1)^3 - k^3] = [(n+1)^3 - n^3] + \cdots + [4^3 - 3^3] + [3^3 - 2^3] + [2^3 - 1^3]$$
$$= (n+1)^3 - 1 \qquad (21)$$

Combining (21) and (20), and expanding the right side of (20) by using Theorem 5.4.1 and part (*a*) of this theorem yields

$$(n+1)^3 - 1 = 3\sum_{k=1}^{n} k^2 + 3\sum_{k=1}^{n} k + \sum_{k=1}^{n} 1$$
$$= 3\sum_{k=1}^{n} k^2 + 3\frac{n(n+1)}{2} + n$$

So,

$$3\sum_{k=1}^{n} k^2 = [(n+1)^3 - 1] - 3\frac{n(n+1)}{2} - n$$
$$= (n+1)^3 - 3(n+1)\left(\frac{n}{2}\right) - (n+1)$$
$$= \frac{n+1}{2}[2(n+1)^2 - 3n - 2]$$
$$= \frac{n+1}{2}[2n^2 + n] = \frac{n(n+1)(2n+1)}{2}$$

Thus,

$$\sum_{k=1}^{n} k^2 = \frac{n(n+1)(2n+1)}{6} \qquad \blacksquare$$

■ **PROOF OF THE LIMIT COMPARISON TEST**

D.7   THEOREM (*Theorem 9.5.4*)   *Let $\sum a_k$ and $\sum b_k$ be series with positive terms and suppose that*

$$\rho = \lim_{k \to +\infty} \frac{a_k}{b_k}$$

If ρ is finite and $\rho > 0$, then the series both converge or both diverge.

PROOF   We need only show that $\sum b_k$ converges when $\sum a_k$ converges and that $\sum b_k$ diverges when $\sum a_k$ diverges, since the remaining cases are logical implications of these (why?). The idea of the proof is to apply the comparison test to $\sum a_k$ and suitable multiples of $\sum b_k$. For this purpose let ϵ be any positive number. Since

$$\rho = \lim_{k \to +\infty} \frac{a_k}{b_k}$$

it follows that eventually the terms in the sequence $\{a_k/b_k\}$ must be within ϵ units of ρ; that is, there is a positive integer K such that for $k \geq K$ we have

$$\rho - \epsilon < \frac{a_k}{b_k} < \rho + \epsilon$$

In particular, if we take $\epsilon = \rho/2$, then for $k \geq K$ we have

$$\frac{1}{2}\rho < \frac{a_k}{b_k} < \frac{3}{2}\rho \quad \text{or} \quad \frac{1}{2}\rho b_k < a_k < \frac{3}{2}\rho b_k$$

Thus, by the comparison test we can conclude that

$$\sum_{k=K}^{\infty} \frac{1}{2}\rho b_k \quad \text{converges if} \quad \sum_{k=K}^{\infty} a_k \quad \text{converges} \tag{22}$$

$$\sum_{k=K}^{\infty} \frac{3}{2}\rho b_k \quad \text{diverges if} \quad \sum_{k=K}^{\infty} a_k \quad \text{diverges} \tag{23}$$

But the convergence or divergence of a series is not affected by deleting finitely many terms or by multiplying the general term by a nonzero constant, so (22) and (23) imply that

$$\sum_{k=1}^{\infty} b_k \quad \text{converges if} \quad \sum_{k=1}^{\infty} a_k \quad \text{converges}$$

$$\sum_{k=1}^{\infty} b_k \quad \text{diverges if} \quad \sum_{k=1}^{\infty} a_k \quad \text{diverges} \quad \blacksquare$$

▉ PROOF OF THE RATIO TEST

D.8   THEOREM (*Theorem 9.5.5*)   *Let $\sum u_k$ be a series with positive terms and suppose that*

$$\rho = \lim_{k \to +\infty} \frac{u_{k+1}}{u_k}$$

(*a*)   *If $\rho < 1$, the series converges.*

(*b*)   *If $\rho > 1$ or $\rho = +\infty$, the series diverges.*

(*c*)   *If $\rho = 1$, the series may converge or diverge, so that another test must be tried.*

PROOF (*a*)   The number ρ must be nonnegative since it is the limit of u_{k+1}/u_k, which is positive for all k. In this part of the proof we assume that $\rho < 1$, so that $0 \leq \rho < 1$.

   We will prove convergence by showing that the terms of the given series are eventually less than the terms of a convergent geometric series. For this purpose, choose any real number r such that $0 < \rho < r < 1$. Since the limit of u_{k+1}/u_k is ρ, and $\rho < r$, the terms of the sequence $\{u_{k+1}/u_k\}$ must eventually be less than r. Thus, there is a positive integer K such that for $k \geq K$ we have

$$\frac{u_{k+1}}{u_k} < r \quad \text{or} \quad u_{k+1} < r u_k$$

This yields the inequalities

$$u_{K+1} < ru_K$$
$$u_{K+2} < ru_{K+1} < r^2 u_K$$
$$u_{K+3} < ru_{K+2} < r^3 u_K \tag{24}$$
$$u_{K+4} < ru_{K+3} < r^4 u_K$$
$$\vdots$$

But $0 < r < 1$, so

$$ru_K + r^2 u_K + r^3 u_K + \cdots$$

is a convergent geometric series. From the inequalities in (24) and the comparison test it follows that

$$u_{K+1} + u_{K+2} + u_{K+3} + \cdots$$

must also be a convergent series. Thus, $u_1 + u_2 + u_3 + \cdots + u_k + \cdots$ converges by Theorem 9.4.3(c).

PROOF (b) In this part we will prove divergence by showing that the limit of the general term is not zero. Since the limit of u_{k+1}/u_k is ρ and $\rho > 1$, the terms in the sequence $\{u_{k+1}/u_k\}$ must eventually be greater than 1. Thus, there is a positive integer K such that for $k \geq K$ we have

$$\frac{u_{k+1}}{u_k} > 1 \quad \text{or} \quad u_{k+1} > u_k$$

This yields the inequalities

$$u_{K+1} > u_K$$
$$u_{K+2} > u_{K+1} > u_K$$
$$u_{K+3} > u_{K+2} > u_K \tag{25}$$
$$u_{K+4} > u_{K+3} > u_K$$
$$\vdots$$

Since $u_K > 0$, it follows from the inequalities in (25) that $\lim_{k \to +\infty} u_k \neq 0$, and thus the series $u_1 + u_2 + \cdots + u_k + \cdots$ diverges by part (a) of Theorem 9.4.1. The proof in the case where $\rho = +\infty$ is omitted.

PROOF (c) The divergent harmonic series and the convergent p-series with $p = 2$ both have $\rho = 1$ (verify), so the ratio test does not distinguish between convergence and divergence when $\rho = 1$. ■

■ PROOF OF THE REMAINDER ESTIMATION THEOREM

> **D.9 THEOREM (*Theorem 9.7.4*)** *If the function f can be differentiated $n + 1$ times on an interval containing the number x_0, and if M is an upper bound for $|f^{(n+1)}(x)|$ on the interval, that is, $|f^{(n+1)}(x)| \leq M$ for all x in the interval, then*
>
> $$|R_n(x)| \leq \frac{M}{(n+1)!}|x - x_0|^{n+1}$$
>
> *for all x in the interval.*

PROOF We are assuming that f can be differentiated $n + 1$ times on an interval containing the number x_0 and that

$$|f^{(n+1)}(x)| \leq M \tag{26}$$

for all x in the interval. We want to show that

$$|R_n(x)| \leq \frac{M}{(n+1)!}|x - x_0|^{n+1} \tag{27}$$

for all x in the interval, where

$$R_n(x) = f(x) - \sum_{k=0}^{n} \frac{f^{(k)}(x_0)}{k!}(x - x_0)^k \tag{28}$$

In our proof we will need the following two properties of $R_n(x)$:

$$R_n(x_0) = R'_n(x_0) = \cdots = R_n^{(n)}(x_0) = 0 \tag{29}$$

$$R_n^{(n+1)}(x) = f^{(n+1)}(x) \quad \text{for all } x \text{ in the interval} \tag{30}$$

These properties can be obtained by analyzing what happens if the expression for $R_n(x)$ in Formula (28) is differentiated j times and x_0 is then substituted in that derivative. If $j < n$, then the jth derivative of the summation in Formula (28) consists of a constant term $f^{(j)}(x_0)$ plus terms involving powers of $x - x_0$ (verify). Thus, $R_n^{(j)}(x_0) = 0$ for $j < n$, which proves all but the last equation in (29). For the last equation, observe that the nth derivative of the summation in (28) is the constant $f^{(n)}(x_0)$, so $R_n^{(n)}(x_0) = 0$. Formula (30) follows from the observation that the $(n+1)$-st derivative of the summation in (28) is zero (why?).

Now to the main part of the proof. For simplicity we will give the proof for the case where $x \geq x_0$ and leave the case where $x < x_0$ for the reader. It follows from (26) and (30) that $|R_n^{(n+1)}(x)| \leq M$, and hence

$$-M \leq R_n^{(n+1)}(x) \leq M$$

Thus,

$$\int_{x_0}^{x} -M \, dt \leq \int_{x_0}^{x} R_n^{(n+1)}(t) \, dt \leq \int_{x_0}^{x} M \, dt \tag{31}$$

However, it follows from (29) that $R_n^{(n)}(x_0) = 0$, so

$$\int_{x_0}^{x} R_n^{(n+1)}(t) \, dt = R_n^{(n)}(t) \Big]_{x_0}^{x} = R_n^{(n)}(x)$$

Thus, performing the integrations in (31) we obtain the inequalities

$$-M(x - x_0) \leq R_n^{(n)}(x) \leq M(x - x_0)$$

Now we will integrate again. Replacing x by t in these inequalities, integrating from x_0 to x, and using $R_n^{(n-1)}(x_0) = 0$ yields

$$-\frac{M}{2}(x - x_0)^2 \leq R_n^{(n-1)}(x) \leq \frac{M}{2}(x - x_0)^2$$

If we keep repeating this process, then after $n + 1$ integrations we will obtain

$$-\frac{M}{(n+1)!}(x - x_0)^{n+1} \leq R_n(x) \leq \frac{M}{(n+1)!}(x - x_0)^{n+1}$$

which we can rewrite as

$$|R_n(x)| \leq \frac{M}{(n+1)!}(x - x_0)^{n+1}$$

This completes the proof of (27), since the absolute value signs can be omitted in that formula when $x \geq x_0$ (which is the case we are considering). ■

■ **PROOF OF THE EQUALITY OF MIXED PARTIALS**

D.10   THEOREM (*Theorem 13.3.2*)   *Let f be a function of two variables. If f_{xy} and f_{yx} are continuous on some open disk, then $f_{xy} = f_{yx}$ on that disk.*

PROOF   Suppose that f is a function of two variables with f_{xy} and f_{yx} both continuous on some open disk. Let (x, y) be a point in that disk and define the function

$$w(\Delta x, \Delta y) = f(x + \Delta x, y + \Delta y) - f(x + \Delta x, y) - f(x, y + \Delta y) + f(x, y)$$

Now fix y and Δy and let

$$g(x) = f(x, y + \Delta y) - f(x, y)$$

so that

$$w(\Delta x, \Delta y) = g(x + \Delta x) - g(x) \tag{32}$$

Since f is differentiable on an open disk containing (x, y), the function g will be differentiable on some interval containing x and $x + \Delta x$ for Δx small enough. The Mean-Value Theorem then applies to g on this interval, and thus there is a c between x and Δx with

$$g(x + \Delta x) - g(x) = g'(c)\Delta x$$

But

$$g'(c) = f_x(c, y + \Delta y) - f_x(c, y)$$

so from Equation (32)

$$w(\Delta x, \Delta y) = g(x + \Delta x) - g(x) = g'(c)\Delta x = (f_x(c, y + \Delta y) - f_x(c, y))\Delta x \tag{33}$$

Now let $h(y) = f_x(c, y)$. Since f_x is differentiable on an open disk containing (x, y), h will be differentiable on some interval containing y and $y + \Delta y$ for Δy small enough. Applying the Mean-Value Theorem to h on this interval gives a d between y and $y + \Delta y$ with

$$h(y + \Delta y) - h(y) = h'(d)\Delta y$$

But $h'(d) = f_{xy}(c, d)$, so by (33) and the definition of h we have

$$w(\Delta x, \Delta y) = (f_x(c, y + \Delta y) - f_x(c, y))\Delta x$$
$$= (h(y + \Delta y) - h(y))\Delta x = h'(d)\Delta y \Delta x$$
$$= f_{xy}(c, d)\Delta y \Delta x$$

and

$$f_{xy}(c, d) = \frac{w(\Delta x, \Delta y)}{\Delta y \Delta x} \tag{34}$$

Since c lies between x and Δx and d lies between y and Δy, (c, d) approaches (x, y) as $(\Delta x, \Delta y)$ approaches $(0, 0)$. It then follows from the continuity of f_{xy} and (34) that

$$f_{xy}(x, y) = \lim_{(\Delta x, \Delta y) \to (0,0)} f_{xy}(c, d) = \lim_{(\Delta x, \Delta y) \to (0,0)} \frac{w(\Delta x, \Delta y)}{\Delta y \Delta x}$$

In similar fashion to the above argument, it can be shown that

$$f_{yx}(x, y) = \lim_{(\Delta x, \Delta y) \to (0,0)} \frac{w(\Delta x, \Delta y)}{\Delta y \Delta x}$$

and the result follows. ■

■ PROOF OF THE TWO-VARIABLE CHAIN RULE FOR DERIVATIVES

> **D.11**   **THEOREM** (*Theorem 13.5.1*)   *If $x = x(t)$ and $y = y(t)$ are differentiable at t, and if $z = f(x, y)$ is differentiable at the point $(x(t), y(t))$, then $z = f(x(t), y(t))$ is differentiable at t and*
> $$\frac{dz}{dt} = \frac{\partial z}{\partial x}\frac{dx}{dt} + \frac{\partial z}{\partial y}\frac{dy}{dt}$$

PROOF Let Δx, Δy, and Δz denote the changes in x, y, and z, respectively, that correspond to a change of Δt in t. Then

$$\frac{dz}{dt} = \lim_{\Delta t \to 0} \frac{\Delta z}{\Delta t}, \quad \frac{dx}{dt} = \lim_{\Delta t \to 0} \frac{\Delta x}{\Delta t}, \quad \frac{dy}{dt} = \lim_{\Delta t \to 0} \frac{\Delta y}{\Delta t}$$

Since $f(x, y)$ is differentiable at $(x(t), y(t))$, it follows from (5) in Section 13.4 that

$$\Delta z = \frac{\partial z}{\partial x} \Delta x + \frac{\partial z}{\partial y} \Delta y + \epsilon(\Delta x, \Delta y)\sqrt{(\Delta x)^2 + (\Delta y)^2} \tag{35}$$

where the partial derivatives are evaluated at $(x(t), y(t))$ and where $\epsilon(\Delta x, \Delta y)$ satisfies $\epsilon(\Delta x, \Delta y) \to 0$ as $(\Delta x, \Delta y) \to (0, 0)$ and $\epsilon(0, 0) = 0$. Dividing both sides of (35) by Δt yields

$$\frac{\Delta z}{\Delta t} = \frac{\partial z}{\partial x} \frac{\Delta x}{\Delta t} + \frac{\partial z}{\partial y} \frac{\Delta y}{\Delta t} + \frac{\epsilon(\Delta x, \Delta y)\sqrt{(\Delta x)^2 + (\Delta y)^2}}{\Delta t} \tag{36}$$

Since

$$\lim_{\Delta t \to 0} \frac{\sqrt{(\Delta x)^2 + (\Delta y)^2}}{|\Delta t|} = \lim_{\Delta t \to 0} \sqrt{\left(\frac{\Delta x}{\Delta t}\right)^2 + \left(\frac{\Delta y}{\Delta t}\right)^2} = \sqrt{\left(\lim_{\Delta t \to 0} \frac{\Delta x}{\Delta t}\right)^2 + \left(\lim_{\Delta t \to 0} \frac{\Delta y}{\Delta t}\right)^2}$$

$$= \sqrt{\left(\frac{dx}{dt}\right)^2 + \left(\frac{dy}{dt}\right)^2}$$

we have

$$\lim_{\Delta t \to 0} \left| \frac{\epsilon(\Delta x, \Delta y)\sqrt{(\Delta x)^2 + (\Delta y)^2}}{\Delta t} \right| = \lim_{\Delta t \to 0} \frac{|\epsilon(\Delta x, \Delta y)|\sqrt{(\Delta x)^2 + (\Delta y)^2}}{|\Delta t|}$$

$$= \lim_{\Delta t \to 0} |\epsilon(\Delta x, \Delta y)| \cdot \lim_{\Delta t \to 0} \frac{\sqrt{(\Delta x)^2 + (\Delta y)^2}}{|\Delta t|}$$

$$= 0 \cdot \sqrt{\left(\frac{dx}{dt}\right)^2 + \left(\frac{dy}{dt}\right)^2} = 0$$

Therefore,

$$\lim_{\Delta t \to 0} \frac{\epsilon(\Delta x, \Delta y)\sqrt{(\Delta x)^2 + (\Delta y)^2}}{\Delta t} = 0$$

Taking the limit as $\Delta t \to 0$ of both sides of (36) then yields the equation

$$\frac{dz}{dt} = \frac{\partial z}{\partial x} \frac{dx}{dt} + \frac{\partial z}{\partial y} \frac{dy}{dt} \quad \blacksquare$$

ANSWERS TO
ODD-NUMBERED EXERCISES

▶ **Exercise Set 0.1 (Page 12)**

1. **(a)** $-2.9, -2.0, 2.35, 2.9$ **(b)** none **(c)** $y = 0$ **(d)** $-1.75 \le x \le$ 2.15 **(e)** $y_{max} = 2.8$ at $x = -2.6$; $y_{min} = -2.2$ at $x = 1.2$

3. **(a)** yes **(b)** yes **(c)** no **(d)** no

5. **(a)** 1999, about $47,700 **(b)** 1993, $41,600 **(c)** first year

7. **(a)** $-2; 10; 10; 25; 4; 27t^2 - 2$ **(b)** $0; 4; -4; 6; 2\sqrt{2}; f(3t) = 1/3t$ for $t > 1$ and $f(3t) = 6t$ for $t \le 1$

9. **(a)** domain: $x \ne 3$; range: $y \ne 0$ **(b)** domain: $x \ne 0$; range: $\{-1, 1\}$ **(c)** domain: $x \le -\sqrt{3}$ or $x \ge \sqrt{3}$; range: $y \ge 0$ **(d)** domain: $-\infty < x < +\infty$; range: $y \ge 2$ **(e)** domain: $x \ne (2n + \frac{1}{2})\pi, n = 0, \pm1, \pm2, \ldots$; range: $y \ge \frac{1}{2}$ **(f)** domain: $-2 \le x < 2$ or $x > 2$; range: $0 \le y < 2$ or $y > 2$

11. **(a)** no; births and deaths **(b)** decreases for 8 hours, takes a jump upward, and repeats

13.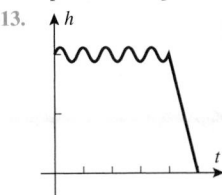

15. function; $y = \sqrt{25 - x^2}$

17. function; $y = \begin{cases} \sqrt{25 - x^2}, & -5 \le x \le 0 \\ -\sqrt{25 - x^2}, & 0 < x \le 5 \end{cases}$

19. False; for example, the graph of the function $f(x) = x^2 - 1$ crosses the x-axis at $x = \pm1$.

21. False; the range also includes 0.

23. **(a)** 2, 4 **(b)** none **(c)** $x \le 2; 4 \le x$ **(d)** $y_{min} = -1$; no maximum

25. $h = L(1 - \cos\theta)$

27. **(a)** $f(x) = \begin{cases} 2x + 1, & x < 0 \\ 4x + 1, & x \ge 0 \end{cases}$ **(b)** $g(x) = \begin{cases} 1 - 2x, & x < 0 \\ 1, & 0 \le x < 1 \\ 2x - 1, & x \ge 1 \end{cases}$

29. **(a)** $V = (8 - 2x)(15 - 2x)x$ **(b)** $0 < x < 4$ **(c)** $0 < V \le 90$, approximately

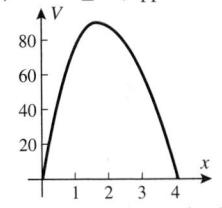

(d) V appears to be maximal for $x \approx 1.7$.

31. **(a)** $L = x + 2y$ **(b)** $L = x + 2000/x$ **(c)** $0 < x \le 100$ **(d)** $x \approx 45$ ft, $y \approx 22$ ft

33. **(a)** $r \approx 3.4, h \approx 13.7$ **(b)** taller **(c)** $r \approx 3.1$ cm, $h \approx 16.0$ cm, $C \approx 4.76$ cents

35. **(i)** $x = 1, -2$ **(ii)** $g(x) = x + 1$, all x

37. **(a)** $25°$F **(b)** $13°$F **(c)** $5°$F **39.** $15°$F

▶ **Exercise Set 0.2 (Page 24)**

1. **(a)** **(b)** **(c)** **(d)**

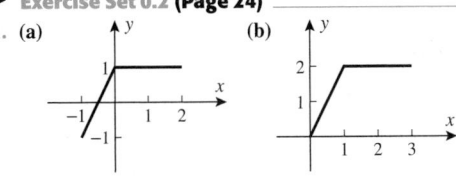

3. **(a)** **(b)** **(c)** **(d)**

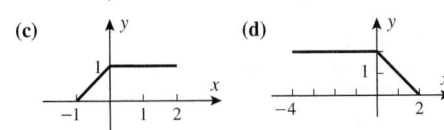

5. 7.

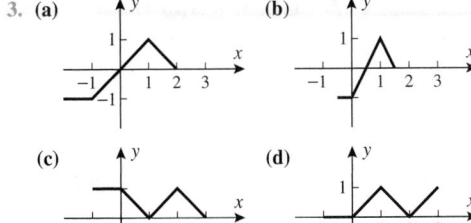

9. 11.

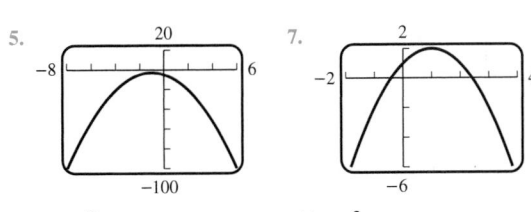

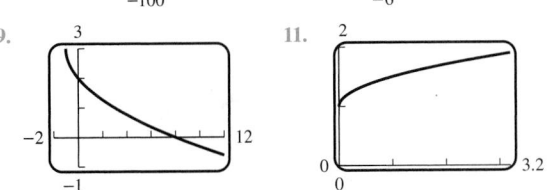

13.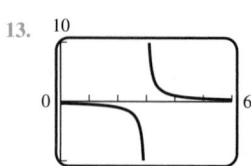

15.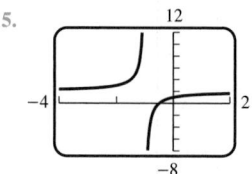

17.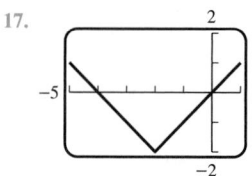

19.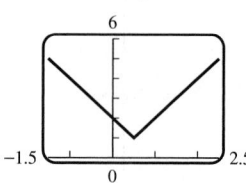

21.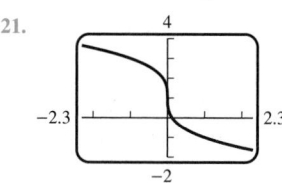

23.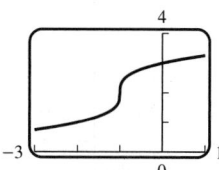

25. (a)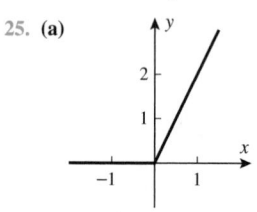

(b) $y = \begin{cases} 0, & x \le 0 \\ 2x, & x > 0 \end{cases}$

27. $3\sqrt{x-1}, x \ge 1; \sqrt{x-1}, x \ge 1; 2x - 2, x \ge 1; 2, x > 1$

29. (a) 3 **(b)** 9 **(c)** 2 **(d)** 2 **(e)** $\sqrt{2+h}$ **(f)** $(3+h)^3 + 1$

31. $1 - x, x \le 1; \sqrt{1-x^2}, |x| \le 1$

33. $\dfrac{1}{1-2x}, x \ne \dfrac{1}{2}, 1; -\dfrac{1}{2x} - \dfrac{1}{2}, x \ne 0, 1$

35. (a) $g(x) = \sqrt{x}, h(x) = x + 2$ **(b)** $g(x) = |x|, h(x) = x^2 - 3x + 5$

37. (a) $g(x) = x^2, h(x) = \sin x$ **(b)** $g(x) = 3/x, h(x) = 5 + \cos x$

39. (a) $g(x) = x^3, h(x) = 1 + \sin(x^2)$
(b) $g(x) = \sqrt{x}, h(x) = 1 - \sqrt[3]{x}$

Responses to True–False questions may be abridged to save space.

41. True; see Definition 0.2.1.

43. True; see Theorem 0.2.3 and the definition of even function that follows.

45.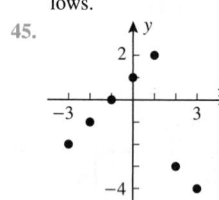

47.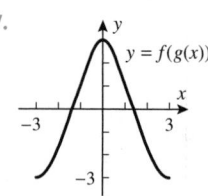

49. $\pm 1.5, \pm 2$ **51.** $6x + 3h, 3w + 3x$ **53.** $-\dfrac{1}{x(x+h)}, -\dfrac{1}{xw}$

55. f: neither, g: odd, h: even

57. (a) 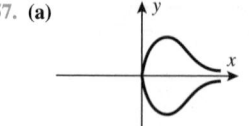 **(b)**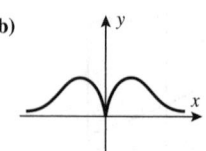

(c)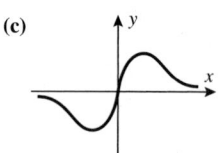

59. (a) even **(b)** odd **(c)** even **(d)** neither **(e)** odd **(f)** even

63. (a) y-axis
(b) origin
(c) x-axis, y-axis, origin

65.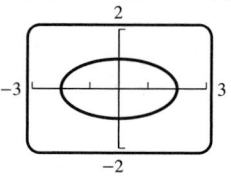

67.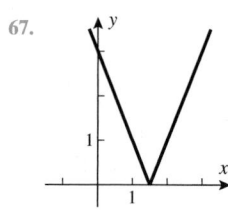

69. (a)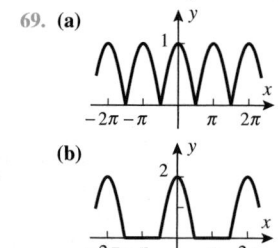
(b)

71. yes; $f(x) = x^k, g(x) = x^n$

▶ **Exercise Set 0.3 (Page 35)**

1. (a) $y = 3x + b$ **(c)**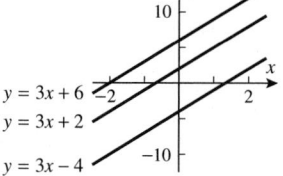
(b) $y = 3x + 6$

$y = 3x + 6$
$y = 3x + 2$
$y = 3x - 4$

3. (a) $y = mx + 2$ **(c)**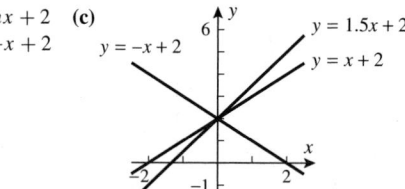
(b) $y = -x + 2$

$y = -x + 2$
$y = 1.5x + 2$
$y = x + 2$

5. $y = \pm\dfrac{9 - x_0 x}{\sqrt{9 - x_0^2}}$

7. 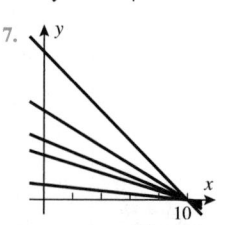 y-intercepts represent current value of item being depreciated.

9. (a) slope: -1 **(b)** y-intercept: $y = -1$

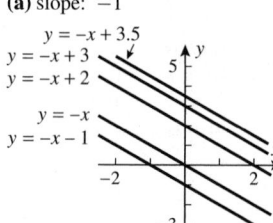

$y = -x + 3.5$
$y = -x + 3$
$y = -x + 2$
$y = -x$
$y = -x - 1$

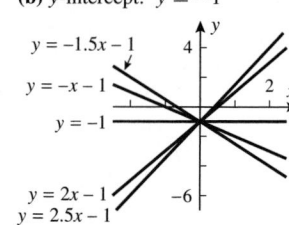

$y = -1.5x - 1$
$y = -x - 1$
$y = -1$
$y = 2x - 1$
$y = 2.5x - 1$

(c) pass through $(-4, 2)$

$y = -1.5(x + 4) + 2$

$y = -(x + 4) + 2$

$y = 2$

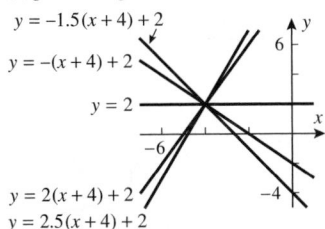

$y = 2(x + 4) + 2$
$y = 2.5(x + 4) + 2$

(d) x-intercept: $x = 1$

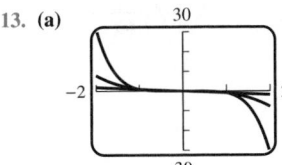

$y = 2(x - 1)$
$y = \frac{3}{2}(x - 1)$
$y = (x - 1)$

$y = -2(x - 1)$

$y = -3(x - 1)$

11. (a) VI
(b) IV
(c) III
(d) V
(e) I
(f) II

13. (a)

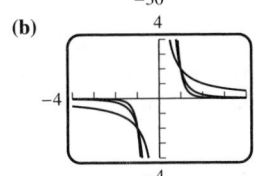

(b)

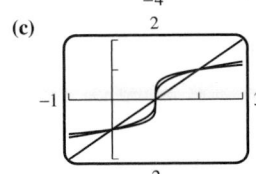

(c)

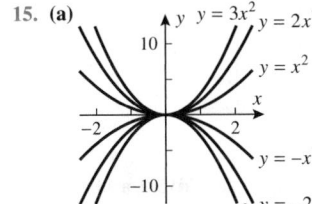

15. (a)

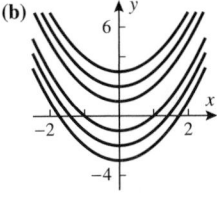

$y = 3x^2$ $y = 2x^2$

$y = x^2$

$y = -x^2$

$y = -3x^2$ $y = -2x^2$

(b)

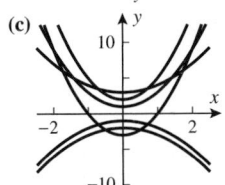

(c)

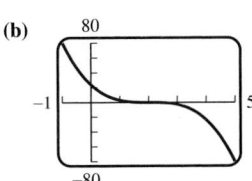

17. (a)

(b)

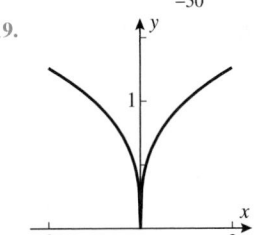

19.

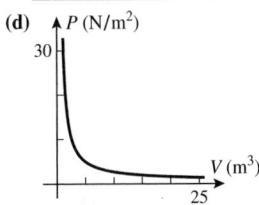

21. (a) newton-meters (N·m)   **(b)** 20 N·m

(c)

V (L)	0.25	0.5	1.0	1.5	2.0
P (N/m²)	80×10^3	40×10^3	20×10^3	13.3×10^3	10×10^3

(d)

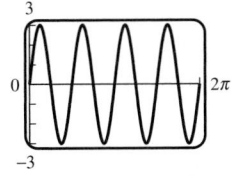

23. (a) $k = 0.000045$ N·m²
(b) 0.000005 N
(d) The force becomes infinite;
the force tends to zero.

(c)

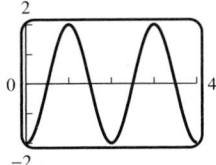

Responses to True–False questions may be abridged to save space.

25. True; see Figure 0.3.2(b).

27. False; the constant of proportionality is $2 \cdot 6 = 12$.

29. (a) II; $y = 1$, $x = -1, 2$ **(b)** I; $y = 0$, $x = -2, 3$ **(c)** IV; $y = 2$
(d) III; $y = 0$, $x = -2$

31. (a) $y = 3 \sin(x/2)$ **(b)** $y = 4 \cos 2x$ **(c)** $y = -5 \sin 4x$

33. (a) $y = \sin[x + (\pi/2)]$ **(b)** $y = 3 + 3 \sin(2x/9)$
(c) $y = 1 + 2 \sin\left(2x - \dfrac{\pi}{2}\right)$

35. (a) amplitude $= 3$, period $= \pi/2$ **(b)** amplitude $= 2$, period $= 2$

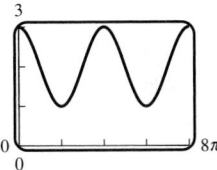

(c) amplitude $= 1$, period $= 4\pi$

37. $x = \dfrac{5\sqrt{13}}{2} \sin(2\pi t + \tan^{-1} \dfrac{1}{2\sqrt{3}})$

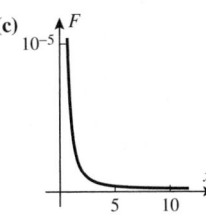

▶ **Exercise Set 0.4 (Page 48)**

1. **(a)** yes **(b)** no **(c)** yes **(d)** no
3. **(a)** yes **(b)** yes **(c)** no **(d)** yes **(e)** no **(f)** no
5. **(a)** yes **(b)** no
7. **(a)** $8, -1, 0$
   (b) $[-2, 2], [-8, 8]$
   (c)
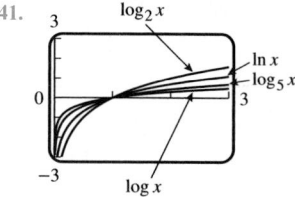
9. $\frac{1}{7}(x + 6)$
11. $\sqrt[3]{(x + 5)/3}$
13. $-\sqrt{3/x}$
15. $\begin{cases} (5/2) - x, & x > 1/2 \\ 1/x, & 0 < x \le 1/2 \end{cases}$
17. $x^{1/4} - 2$ for $x \ge 16$
19. $\frac{1}{2}(3 - x^2)$ for $x \le 0$

21. **(a)** $f^{-1}(x) = \dfrac{-b + \sqrt{b^2 - 4a(c - x)}}{2a}$
    (b) $f^{-1}(x) = \dfrac{-b - \sqrt{b^2 - 4a(c - x)}}{2a}$

23. **(a)** $y = (6.214 \times 10^{-4})x$ **(b)** $x = \dfrac{10^4}{6.214} y$
    (c) how many meters in y miles
25. **(b)** symmetric about the line $y = x$ 27. 10
Responses to True–False questions may be abridged to save space.
31. False; $f^{-1}(2) = 2$
33. True; see Theorem 0.4.3.
35. $\frac{4}{5}, \frac{3}{5}, \frac{3}{4}, \frac{5}{3}, \frac{5}{4}$
37. **(a)** $0 \le x \le \pi$ **(b)** $-1 \le x \le 1$ **(c)** $-\pi/2 < x < \pi/2$
    (d) $-\infty < x < +\infty$ 39. $\frac{24}{25}$
41. **(a)** $\dfrac{1}{\sqrt{1 + x^2}}$ **(b)** $\dfrac{\sqrt{1 - x^2}}{x}$ **(c)** $\dfrac{\sqrt{x^2 - 1}}{x}$ **(d)** $\dfrac{1}{\sqrt{x^2 - 1}}$
43. **(a)**
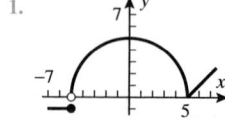
(b)

45. **(a)** 0.25545, error **(b)** $|x| \le \sin 1$
47. **(a)** cot$^{-1}(x)$ csc$^{-1}(x)$
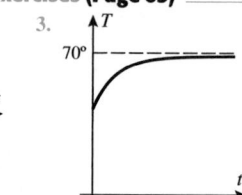
(b) cot$^{-1} x$: all x, $0 < y < \pi$
   csc$^{-1} x$: $|x| \ge 1$, $0 < |y| < \pi/2$
49. **(a)** 55.0° **(b)** 33.6° **(c)** 25.8° 51. **(a)** 21.1 hours **(b)** 2.9 hours
53. 29°

▶ **Exercise Set 0.5 (Page 61)**

1. **(a)** -4 **(b)** 4 **(c)** $\frac{1}{4}$ 3. **(a)** 2.9690 **(b)** 0.0341
5. **(a)** 4 **(b)** -5 **(c)** 1 **(d)** $\frac{1}{2}$ 7. **(a)** 1.3655 **(b)** -0.3011
9. **(a)** $2r + \dfrac{s}{2} + \dfrac{t}{2}$ **(b)** $s - 3r - t$
11. **(a)** $1 + \log x + \frac{1}{2}\log(x - 3)$ **(b)** $2\ln |x| + 3\ln \sin x - \frac{1}{2}\ln(x^2 + 1)$
13. $\log \frac{256}{3}$ 15. $\ln \dfrac{\sqrt[3]{x}(x + 1)^2}{\cos x}$ 17. 0.01 19. e^2 21. 4

23. $\sqrt{3/2}$ 25. $-\dfrac{\ln 3}{2 \ln 5}$ 27. $\frac{1}{3}\ln \frac{7}{2}$ 29. -2
31. **(a)** domain: $(-\infty, +\infty)$; range: $(-1, +\infty)$
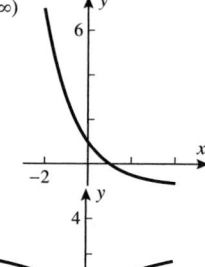
(b) domain: $x \ne 0$; range: $(-\infty, +\infty)$
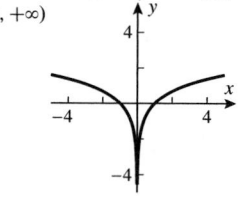
33. **(a)** domain: $x \ne 0$; range: $(-\infty, +\infty)$
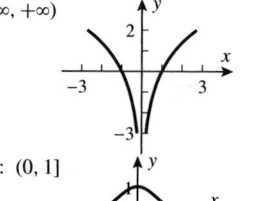
(b) domain: $(-\infty, +\infty)$; range: $(0, 1]$
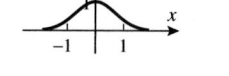

Responses to True–False questions may be abridged to save space.
35. False; exponential functions have constant base and variable exponent.
37. True; $\ln x = \log_e x$ 39. 2.8777, -0.3174
41.
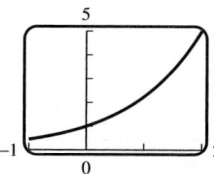
43. **(a)** no   **(d)** $y = (\sqrt{5})^x$
    (b) $y = 2^{x/4}$
    (c) $y = 2^{-x}$

45. $\log \frac{1}{2} < 0$, so $3 \log \frac{1}{2} < 2 \log \frac{1}{2}$ 47. 201 days
49. **(a)** 7.4, basic **(b)** 4.2, acidic **(c)** 6.4, acidic **(d)** 5.9, acidic
51. **(a)** 140 dB, damage **(b)** 120 dB, damage **(c)** 80 dB, no damage
    (d) 75 dB, no damage
53. ≈ 200 55. **(a)** $\approx 5 \times 10^{16}$ J **(b)** ≈ 0.67

▶ **Chapter 0 Review Exercises (Page 63)**

1.
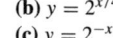
3.

5. (a) $C = 5x^2 + (64/x)$ (b) $x > 0$

7. (a) $V = (6 - 2x)(5 - x)x$ ft^3
   (b) $0 < x < 3$
   (c) 3.57 ft $\times$ 3.79 ft $\times$ 1.21 ft

9.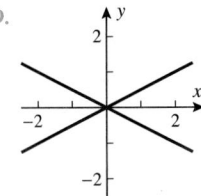

11.

x	-4	-3	-2	-1	0	1	2	3	4
$f(x)$	0	-1	2	1	3	-2	-3	4	-4
$g(x)$	3	2	1	-3	-1	-4	4	-2	0
$(f \circ g)(x)$	4	-3	-2	-1	1	0	-4	2	3
$(g \circ f)(x)$	-1	-3	4	-4	-2	1	2	0	3

13. $0, -2$ 15. $1/(2 - x^2)$, $x \neq \pm 1, \pm\sqrt{2}$

17. (a) odd   (b) even   (c) neither   (d) even

19. (a) circles of radius 1 centered on the parabola $y = x^2$
    (b) parabolas congruent to $y = x^2$ that open up with vertices on the
    line $y = x/2$

21. (a) 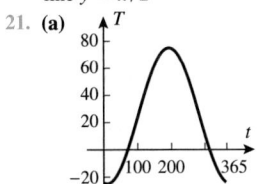   (b) January 11   (c) 122 days

23. A: $\left(-\frac{2}{3}\pi, 1 - \sqrt{3}\right)$; B: $\left(\frac{1}{3}\pi, 1 + \sqrt{3}\right)$; C: $\left(\frac{2}{3}\pi, 1 + \sqrt{3}\right)$;
    D: $\left(\frac{5}{3}\pi, 1 - \sqrt{3}\right)$

27. (a) $\frac{1}{2}(x + 1)^{1/3}$ (b) none   (c) $\frac{1}{2}\ln(x - 1)$ (d) $\dfrac{x + 2}{x - 1}$
    (e) $\dfrac{1}{2 + \sin^{-1} x}$ (f) $\tan\left(\dfrac{1}{3x} - \dfrac{1}{3}\right)$, $x < -\dfrac{2}{3\pi - 2}$ or $x > \dfrac{2}{3\pi + 2}$

29. (a) $\frac{33}{65}$ (b) $\frac{56}{65}$ 31. $\frac{10^{60}}{63360} \approx 1.6 \times 10^{55}$ miles   33. $15x + 2$

35. (a) 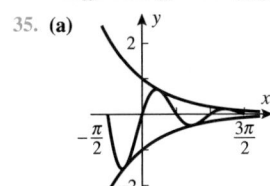   (b) $-\dfrac{\pi}{2}, 0, \dfrac{\pi}{2}, \pi, \dfrac{3\pi}{2}$; $-\dfrac{\pi}{4}, \dfrac{\pi}{4}, \dfrac{3\pi}{4}, \dfrac{5\pi}{4}$

37. (a) 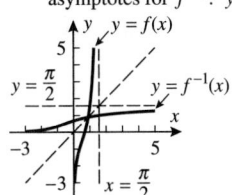   (b) about 10 years   (c) 220 sheep

39. (b) 3.654, 332105.108

41. (a) f is increasing   (b) asymptotes for f: $x = 0$ and $x = \pi/2$;
    asymptotes for f^{-1}: $y = 0$ (as $x \to -\infty$) and $y = \pi/2$ (as $x \to +\infty$)

▶ Exercise Set 1.1 **(Page 77)**

1. (a) 3   (b) 3   (c) 3   (d) 3

3. (a) -1 (b) 3   (c) does not exist   (d) 1

5. (a) 0   (b) 0   (c) 0   (d) 3   7. (a) $-\infty$ (b) $-\infty$ (c) $-\infty$ (d) 1

9. (a) 1   (b) $-\infty$ (c) does not exist   (d) -2

11.

x	-0.01	-0.001	-0.0001	0.0001	0.001	0.01
$f(x)$	0.99502	0.99950	0.99995	1.00005	1.00050	1.00502

The limit appears to be 1.

13. (a) $\frac{1}{3}$ (b) $+\infty$ (c) $-\infty$ 15. (a) 3   (b) does not exist

Responses to True–False questions may be abridged to save space.

17. False; see Example 6.

19. False; the one-sided limits must also be equal.

21. 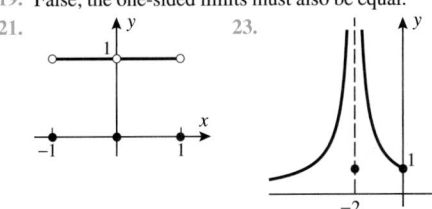   23.

31. (a) rest length   (b) 0. As speed approaches c, length shrinks to zero.

33. The limit should be 1.

25.   27. $y = -2x - 1$
      29. $y = 4x - 3$

▶ Exercise Set 1.2 **(Page 87)**

1. (a) -6 (b) 13   (c) -8 (d) 16   (e) 2   (f) $-\frac{1}{2}$

3. 6   5. $\frac{3}{4}$ 7. 4   9. $-\frac{4}{5}$ 11. -3 13. $\frac{3}{2}$ 15. $+\infty$

17. does not exist   19. $-\infty$ 21. $+\infty$ 23. does not exist   25. $+\infty$

27. $+\infty$ 29. 6   31. (a) 2   (b) 2   (c) 2

Responses to True–False questions may be abridged to save space.

33. True; this is Theorem 1.2.2(a).   35. False; see Example 9.   37. $\frac{1}{4}$

39. (a) 3   (b)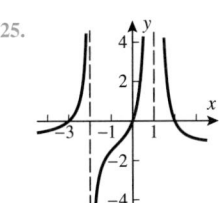

41. (a) Theorem 1.2.2(a) does not apply.
    (b) $\displaystyle\lim_{x \to 0^+}\left(\frac{1}{x} - \frac{1}{x^2}\right) = \lim_{x \to 0^+}\left(\frac{x - 1}{x^2}\right) = -\infty$ 43. $a = 2$

45. The left and/or right limits could be $\pm\infty$; or the limit could exist and
    equal any preassigned real number.

▶ Exercise Set 1.3 **(Page 96)**

1. (a) $-\infty$ (b) $+\infty$ 3. (a) 0   (b) -1

5. (a) -12 (b) 21   (c) -15 (d) 25   (e) 2   (f) $-\frac{3}{5}$ (g) 0
   (h) does not exist

7. (a)

x	0.1	0.01	0.001	0.0001	0.00001	0.000001
$f(x)$	1.471128	1.560797	1.569796	1.570696	1.570786	1.570795

The limit appears to be $\pi/2$.   (b) $\pi/2$

9. $-\infty$ **11.** $+\infty$ **13.** $\frac{3}{2}$ **15.** 0 **17.** 0 **19.** $-\infty$ **21.** $-\frac{1}{7}$

23. $\dfrac{-\sqrt[3]{5}}{2}$ **25.** $-\sqrt{5}$ **27.** $1/\sqrt{6}$ **29.** $\sqrt{3}$ **31.** 0 **33.** 1

35. 1 **37.** $-\infty$ **39.** e

Responses to True–False questions may be abridged to save space.

41. False; 1^∞ is an indeterminate form. The limit is e^2.

43. True; consider $f(x) = (\sin x)/x$.

45. $\lim\limits_{t \to +\infty} n(t) = +\infty$; $\lim\limits_{t \to +\infty} e(t) = c$ **47.** (a) $+\infty$ (b) -5

51. (a) no (b) yes; $\tan x$ and $\sec x$ at $x = n\pi + \pi/2$, and $\cot x$ and $\csc x$ at $x = n\pi$, $n = 0, \pm1, \pm2, \ldots$

55. $+\infty$ **57.** $+\infty$ **59.** 1 **61.** e

65. (a)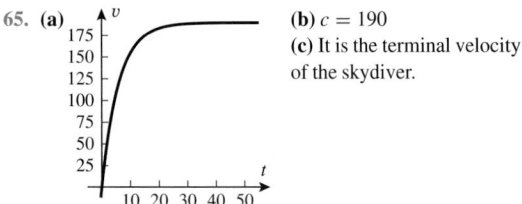
(b) $c = 190$
(c) It is the terminal velocity of the skydiver.

67. (a) e (c) e^a **69.** $x + 2$ **71.** $1 - x^2$ **73.** $\sin x$

▶ **Exercise Set 1.4 (Page 106)**

1. (a) $|x| < 0.1$ (b) $|x - 3| < 0.0025$ (c) $|x - 4| < 0.000125$

3. (a) $x_0 = 3.8025$, $x_1 = 4.2025$ (b) $\delta = 0.1975$

5. $\delta = 0.0442$ **7.** $\delta = 0.13$

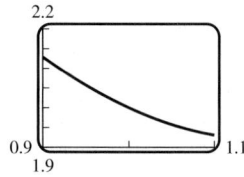

11. $|(3x - 5) - 1| = |3x - 6| = 3 \cdot |x - 2| < 3 \cdot \delta = \epsilon$

13. $\delta = 1$ **15.** $\delta = \frac{1}{3}\epsilon$ **17.** $\delta = \epsilon/2$ **19.** $\delta = \epsilon$ **21.** $\delta = \epsilon$

Responses to True–False questions may be abridged to save space.

23. True; $|f(x) - f(a)| = |m||x - a|$

25. True; constant functions

29. (b) 65 (c) $\epsilon/65$; 65; 65; $\epsilon/65$ **31.** $\delta = \min\left(1, \frac{1}{6}\epsilon\right)$

33. $\delta = \min(1, \epsilon/(1 + \epsilon))$ **35.** $\delta = 2\epsilon$

39. (a) $-\sqrt{\dfrac{1 - \epsilon}{\epsilon}}$; $\sqrt{\dfrac{1 - \epsilon}{\epsilon}}$ (b) $\sqrt{\dfrac{1 - \epsilon}{\epsilon}}$ (c) $-\sqrt{\dfrac{1 - \epsilon}{\epsilon}}$

41. 10 **43.** 999 **45.** -202 **47.** -57.5 **49.** $N = \dfrac{1}{\sqrt{\epsilon}}$

51. $N = -\dfrac{5}{2} - \dfrac{11}{2\epsilon}$ **53.** $N = (1 + 2/\epsilon)^2$

55. (a) $|x| < \frac{1}{10}$ (b) $|x - 1| < \frac{1}{1000}$
(c) $|x - 3| < \frac{1}{10\sqrt{10}}$ (d) $|x| < \frac{1}{10}$

57. $\delta = 1/\sqrt{M}$ **59.** $\delta = 1/M$ **61.** $\delta = 1/(-M)^{1/4}$ **63.** $\delta = \epsilon$

65. $\delta = \epsilon^2$ **67.** $\delta = \epsilon$ **69.** (a) $\delta = -1/M$ (b) $\delta = 1/M$

71. (a) $N = M - 1$ (b) $N = M - 1$

73. (a) 0.4 amps (b) about 0.39474 to 0.40541 amps (c) $3/(7.5 + \delta)$ to $3/(7.5 - \delta)$ (d) $\delta \approx 0.01870$ (e) current approaches $+\infty$

▶ **Exercise Set 1.5 (Page 118)**

1. (a) not continuous, $x = 2$ (b) not continuous, $x = 2$
(c) not continuous, $x = 2$ (d) continuous (e) continuous
(f) continuous

3. (a) not continuous, $x = 1, 3$ (b) continuous
(c) not continuous, $x = 1$ (d) continuous
(e) not continuous, $x = 3$ (f) continuous

5. (a) no (b) no (c) no (d) yes (e) yes (f) no (g) yes

7. (a) (b) (c) (d)

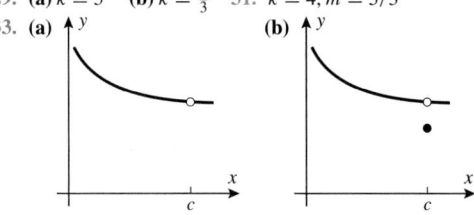

9. (a) (b) One second could cost you one dollar.

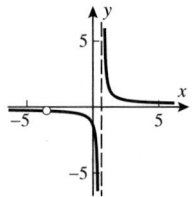

11. none **13.** none **15.** $-1/2, 0$ **17.** $-1, 0, 1$ **19.** none

21. none

Responses to True–False questions may be abridged to save space.

23. True; the composition of continuous functions is continuous.

25. False; let f and g be the functions in Exercise 6.

27. True; $f(x) = \sqrt{f(x)} \cdot \sqrt{f(x)}$

29. (a) $k = 5$ (b) $k = \frac{4}{3}$ **31.** $k = 4, m = 5/3$

33. (a) (b)

35. (a) $x = 0$, not removable (b) $x = -3$, removable
(c) $x = 2$, removable; $x = -2$, not removable

37. (a) $x = \frac{1}{2}$, not removable;
at $x = -3$, removable
(b) $(2x - 1)(x + 3)$

45. $f(x) = 1$ for $0 \le x < 1$, $f(x) = -1$ for $1 \le x \le 2$

49. $x = -1.25, x = 0.75$ **51.** $x = 2.24$

▶ **Exercise Set 1.6 (Page 125)**

1. none **3.** $x = n\pi, n = 0, \pm1, \pm2, \ldots$

5. $x = n\pi, n = 0, \pm1, \pm2, \ldots$

7. $2n\pi + (\pi/6), 2n\pi + (5\pi/6), n = 0, \pm1, \pm2, \ldots$

9. $\left[-\frac{1}{2}, \frac{1}{2}\right]$ **11.** $(0, 3)$ and $(3, +\infty)$ **13.** $(-\infty, -1]$ and $[1, +\infty)$

15. (a) $\sin x, x^3 + 7x + 1$ (b) $|x|, \sin x$ (c) $x^3, \cos x, x + 1$

17. 1 **19.** $-\pi/6$ **21.** 1 **23.** 3 **25.** $+\infty$ **27.** $\frac{7}{3}$

29. 0 **31.** 0 **33.** 1 **35.** 2 **37.** does not exist **39.** 0

41. (a)

x	4	4.5	4.9	5.1	5.5	6
$f(x)$	0.093497	0.100932	0.100842	0.098845	0.091319	0.076497

The limit appears to be $\frac{1}{10}$. **(b)** $\frac{1}{10}$

Responses to True–False questions may be abridged to save space.

43. True; use the Squeezing Theorem.

45. False; consider $f(x) = \tan^{-1} x$.

47. (a) Using degrees instead of radians   **(b)** $\pi/180$

49. 1   **51.** $k = \frac{1}{2}$ **53. (a)** 1   **(b)** 0   **(c)** 1

55. $-\pi$ **57.** $-\sqrt{2}$ **59.** 1   **61.** 5

63. $\lim_{x \to 0} \sin(1/x)$ does not exist

65. The limit is 0.

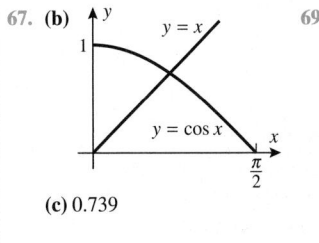

67. (b)

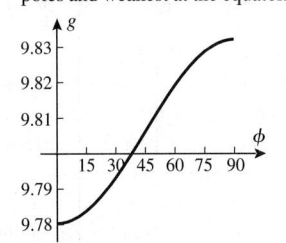

(c) 0.739

69. (a) Gravity is strongest at the poles and weakest at the equator.

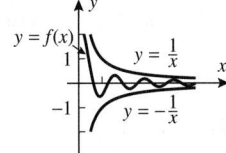

▶ **Chapter 1 Review Exercises (Page 128)**

1. (a) 1   **(b)** does not exist   **(c)** does not exist   **(d)** 1   **(e)** 3   **(f)** 0
   (g) 0   **(h)** 2   **(i)** $\frac{1}{2}$

3. (a) 0.405   **5.** 1   **7.** $-3/2$ **9.** $32/3$

11. (a) $y = 0$ **(b)** none   **(c)** $y = 2$ **13.** 1   **15.** $3 - k$ **17.** 0

19. e^{-3} **21.** \$2001.60, \$2009.66, \$2013.62, \$2013.75

23. (a) $2x/(x - 1)$ is one example.

25. (a) $\lim_{x \to 2} f(x) = 5$ **(b)** $\delta = 0.0045$

27. (a) $\delta = 0.0025$ **(b)** $\delta = 0.0025$ **(c)** $\delta = 1/9000$
   (Some larger values also work.)

31. (a) $-1, 1$ **(b)** none   **(c)** $-3, 0$ **33.** no; not continuous at $x = 2$

35. Consider $f(x) = x$ for $x \neq 0$, $f(0) = 1$, $a = -1$, $b = 1$, $k = 0$.

▶ **Chapter 1 Making Connections (Page 130)**

Where correct answers to a Making Connections exercise may vary, no answer is listed. Sample answers for these questions are available on the Book Companion Site.

4. (a) The circle through the origin with center $\left(0, \frac{1}{8}\right)$
   (b) The circle through the origin with center $\left(0, \frac{1}{2}\right)$
   (c) The circle does not exist.
   (d) The circle through the origin with center $\left(0, \frac{1}{2}\right)$
   (e) The circle through (0, 1) with center at the origin.
   (f) The circle through the origin with center $\left(0, \dfrac{1}{2g(0)}\right)$
   (g) The circle does not exist.

▶ **Exercise Set 2.1 (Page 140)**

1. (a) 4 m/s   **(b)**
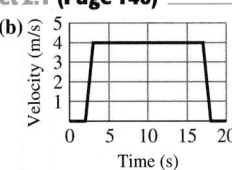

3. (a) 0 cm/s   **(b)** $t = 0$, $t = 2$, and $t = 4.2$ **(c)** maximum: $t = 1$;
   minimum: $t = 3$ **(d)** -7.5 cm/s

5. straight line with slope equal to the velocity

7. Answers may vary.   **9.** Answers may vary.

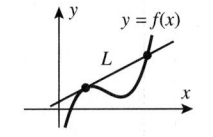
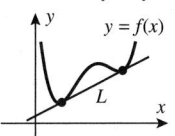

11. (a) 2   **(b)** 0   **(c)** $4x_0$
   (d)

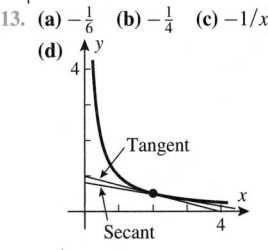

13. (a) $-\frac{1}{6}$ **(b)** $-\frac{1}{4}$ **(c)** $-1/x_0^2$
   (d)

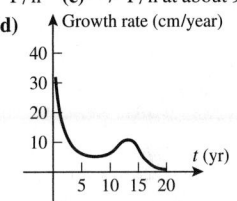

15. (a) $2x_0$ **(b)** -2 **17. (a)** $1 + \dfrac{1}{2\sqrt{x_0}}$ **(b)** $\frac{3}{2}$

Responses to True–False questions may be abridged to save space.

19. True; set $h = x - 1$, so $x = 1 + h$ and $h \to 0$ is equivalent to $x \to 1$.

21. False; velocity is a ratio of change in position to change in time.

23. (a) $72°$ F at about 4:30 P.M.   **(b)** $4°$F/h   **(c)** $-7°$F/h at about 9 P.M.

25. (a) first year   **(d)**
   (b) 6 cm/year
   (c) 10 cm/year at about age 14

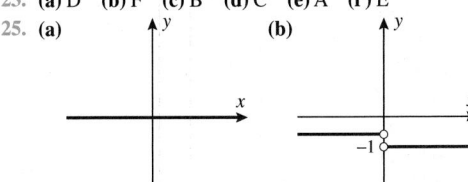

27. (a) 19,200 ft   **(b)** 480 ft/s   **(c)** 66.94 ft/s   **(d)** 1440 ft/s

---

▶ **Exercise Set 2.2 (Page 152)**

1. 2, 0, -2, -1 **5.**
3. (b) 3   **(c)** 3

7. $y = 5x - 16$
9. $4x$, $y = 4x - 2$
11. $3x^2$; $y = 0$

13. $\dfrac{1}{2\sqrt{x + 1}}$; $y = \frac{1}{6}x + \frac{5}{3}$ **15.** $-1/x^2$ **17.** $2x - 1$

19. $-1/(2x^{3/2})$ **21.** $8t + 1$

23. (a) D   **(b)** F   **(c)** B   **(d)** C   **(e)** A   **(f)** E

25. (a)   **(b)**

(c)

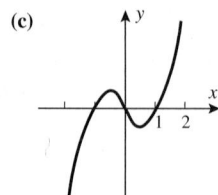

Responses to True–False questions may be abridged to save space.

27. False; $f'(a) = 0$ **29.** False; for example, $f(x) = |x|$

31. (a) $\sqrt{x}, 1$ **(b)** $x^2, 3$ **33.** -2

35. $y = -2x + 1$

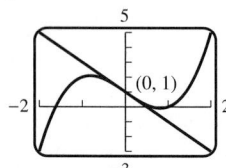

37. (b)

w	1.5	1.1	1.01	1.001	1.0001	1.00001
$[f(w) - f(1)]/(w - 1)$	1.6569	1.4355	1.3911	1.3868	1.3863	1.3863

39. (a) 0.04, 0.22, 0.88 **(b)** best: $\dfrac{f(2) - f(0)}{2 - 0}$; worst: $\dfrac{f(3) - f(1)}{3 - 1}$

41. (a) dollars per foot **(b)** the price per additional foot **(c)** positive **(d)** $1000

43. (a) $F \approx 200$ lb, $dF/d\theta \approx 50$ lb/rad **(b)** $\mu = 0.25$

45. (a) $T \approx 115°F$, $dT/dt \approx -3.35°F/min$ **(b)** $k = -0.084$

Exercise Set 2.3 (Page 161)

1. $28x^6$ **3.** $24x^7 + 2$ **5.** 0 **7.** $-\frac{1}{3}(7x^6 + 2)$

9. $-3x^{-4} - 7x^{-8}$ **11.** $24x^{-9} + (1/\sqrt{x})$

13. $f'(x) = ex^{e-1} - \dfrac{\sqrt{10}}{x^{(1+\sqrt{10})}}$

15. $3ax^2 + 2bx + c$ **17.** 7 **19.** $2t - 1$ **21.** 15 **23.** -8 **25.** 0

27. 0 **29.** $32t$ **31.** $3\pi r^2$

Responses to True–False questions may be abridged to save space.

33. True; apply the difference and constant multiple rules.

35. False; $\dfrac{d}{dx}[4f(x) + x^3]\Big|_{x=2} = [4f'(x) + 3x^2]\Big|_{x=2} = 32$

37. (a) $4\pi r^2$ **(b)** 100π **39.** $y = 5x + 17$

41. (a) $42x - 10$ **(b)** 24 **(c)** $2/x^3$ **(d)** $700x^3 - 96x$

43. (a) $-210x^{-8} + 60x^2$ **(b)** $-6x^{-4}$ **(c)** $6a$

45. (a) 0 **49.** $\left(1, \frac{5}{6}\right)\left(2, \frac{2}{3}\right)$
(b) 112
(c) 360

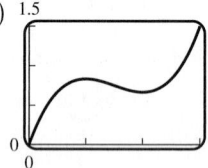

51. $y = 3x^2 - x - 2$ **53.** $x = \frac{1}{2}$

55. $(2 + \sqrt{3}, -6 - 4\sqrt{3}), (2 - \sqrt{3}, -6 + 4\sqrt{3})$

57. $-2x_0$ **61.** $-\dfrac{2GmM}{r^3}$ **63.** $f'(x) > 0$ for all $x \neq 0$

65. yes, 3

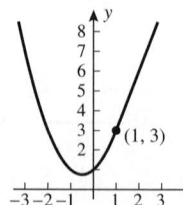

67. not differentiable at $x = 1$ **69. (a)** $x = \frac{2}{3}$ **(b)** $x = \pm 2$ **71. (b)** yes

73. (a) $n(n - 1)(n - 2) \cdots 1$ **(b)** 0 **(c)** $a_n n(n - 1)(n - 2) \cdots 1$

79. $-12/(2x + 1)^3$ **81.** $-2/(x + 1)^3$

Exercise Set 2.4 (Page 168)

1. $4x + 1$ **3.** $4x^3$ **5.** $18x^2 - \frac{3}{2}x + 12$

7. $-15x^{-2} - 14x^{-3} + 48x^{-4} + 32x^{-5}$ **9.** $3x^2$

11. $\dfrac{-3x^2 - 8x + 3}{(x^2 + 1)^2}$ **13.** $\dfrac{3x^2 - 8x}{(3x - 4)^2}$ **15.** $\dfrac{x^{3/2} + 10x^{1/2} + 4 - 3x^{-1/2}}{(x + 3)^2}$

17. $2(1 + x^{-1})(x^{-3} + 7) + (2x + 1)(-x^{-2})(x^{-3} + 7) +$
$(2x + 1)(1 + x^{-1})(-3x^{-4})$ **19.** $3(7x^6 + 2)(x^7 + 2x - 3)^2$

21. -29 **23.** 0 **25. (a)** $-\frac{37}{4}$ **(b)** $-\frac{23}{16}$

27. (a) 10 **(b)** 19 **(c)** 9 **(d)** -1 **29.** $-2 \pm \sqrt{3}$ **31.** none **33.** -2

37. $F''(x) = xf''(x) + 2f'(x)$

39. $R'(120) = 1800$; increasing the price by Δp dollars increases revenue by approximately $1800\Delta p$ dollars.

41. $f'(x) = -nx^{-n-1}$

Exercise Set 2.5 (Page 172)

1. $-4\sin x + 2\cos x$ **3.** $4x^2 \sin x - 8x \cos x$

5. $(1 + 5\sin x - 5\cos x)/(5 + \sin x)^2$ **7.** $\sec x \tan x - \sqrt{2} \sec^2 x$

9. $-4\csc x \cot x + \csc^2 x$ **11.** $\sec^3 x + \sec x \tan^2 x$ **13.** $-\dfrac{\csc x}{1 + \csc x}$

15. 0 **17.** $\dfrac{1}{(1 + x\tan x)^2}$ **19.** $-x\cos x - 2\sin x$

21. $-x\sin x + 5\cos x$ **23.** $-4\sin x \cos x$

25. (a) $y = x$ **(b)** $y = 2x - (\pi/2) + 1$ **(c)** $y = 2x + (\pi/2) - 1$

29. (a) $x = \pm\pi/2, \pm 3\pi/2$ **(b)** $x = -3\pi/2, \pi/2$
(c) no horizontal tangent line **(d)** $x = \pm 2\pi, \pm\pi, 0$

31. 0.087 ft/deg **33.** 1.75 m/deg

Responses to True–False questions may be abridged to save space.

35. False; by the product rule, $g'(x) = f(x)\cos x + f'(x)\sin x$.

37. True; $f(x) = (\sin x)/(\cos x) = \tan x$, so $f'(x) = \sec^2 x$.

39. $-\cos x$ **41.** 3, 7, 11, ...

43. (a) all x **(b)** all x **(c)** $x \neq (\pi/2) + n\pi, n = 0, \pm 1, \pm 2, \ldots$
(d) $x \neq n\pi, n = 0, \pm 1, \pm 2, \ldots$ **(e)** $x \neq (\pi/2) + n\pi, n = 0, \pm 1,$
$\pm 2, \ldots$ **(f)** $x \neq n\pi, n = 0, \pm 1, \pm 2, \ldots$ **(g)** $x \neq (2n + 1)\pi, n = 0,$
$\pm 1, \pm 2, \ldots$ **(h)** $x \neq n\pi/2, n = 0, \pm 1, \pm 2, \ldots$ **(i)** all x

Exercise Set 2.6 (Page 178)

1. 6 **3. (a)** $(2x - 3)^5, 10(2x - 3)^4$ **(b)** $2x^5 - 3, 10x^4$

5. (a) -7 **(b)** -8 **7.** $37(x^3 + 2x)^{36}(3x^2 + 2)$

9. $-2\left(x^3 - \dfrac{7}{x}\right)^{-3}\left(3x^2 + \dfrac{7}{x^2}\right)$ **11.** $\dfrac{24(1 - 3x)}{(3x^2 - 2x + 1)^4}$

13. $\dfrac{3}{4\sqrt{x}\sqrt{4 + 3\sqrt{x}}}$ **15.** $-\dfrac{2}{x^3}\cos\left(\dfrac{1}{x^2}\right)$ **17.** $-20\cos^4 x \sin x$

19. $-\dfrac{3}{\sqrt{x}}\cos(3\sqrt{x})\sin(3\sqrt{x})$ **21.** $28x^6 \sec^2(x^7)\tan(x^7)$

23. $-\dfrac{5\sin(5x)}{2\sqrt{\cos(5x)}}$

25. $-3[x + \csc(x^3 + 3)]^{-4}[1 - 3x^2\csc(x^3 + 3)\cot(x^3 + 3)]$

27. $10x^3 \sin 5x \cos 5x + 3x^2 \sin^2 5x$

29. $-x^3 \sec\left(\dfrac{1}{x}\right)\tan\left(\dfrac{1}{x}\right) + 5x^4 \sec\left(\dfrac{1}{x}\right)$

31. $\sin(\cos x)\sin x$ **33.** $-6\cos^2(\sin 2x)\sin(\sin 2x)\cos 2x$

35. $35(5x + 8)^6(1 - \sqrt{x})^6 - \dfrac{3}{\sqrt{x}}(5x + 8)^7(1 - \sqrt{x})^5$

37. $\dfrac{33(x - 5)^2}{(2x + 1)^4}$ **39.** $-\dfrac{2(2x + 3)^2(52x^2 + 96x + 3)}{(4x^2 - 1)^9}$

41. $5[x\sin 2x + \tan^4(x^7)]^4[2x\cos 2x + \sin 2x + 28x^6 \tan^3(x^7)\sec^2(x^7)]$

43. $y = -x$ **45.** $y = -1$ **47.** $y = 8\sqrt{\pi}x - 8\pi$ **49.** $y = \frac{7}{2}x - \frac{3}{2}$

51. $-25x\cos(5x) - 10\sin(5x) - 2\cos(2x)$ **53.** $4(1 - x)^{-3}$

55. $3\cot^2\theta\csc^2\theta$ **57.** $\pi(b - a)\sin 2\pi\omega$

59. (a)

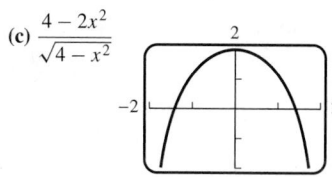

(c) $\dfrac{4 - 2x^2}{\sqrt{4 - x^2}}$

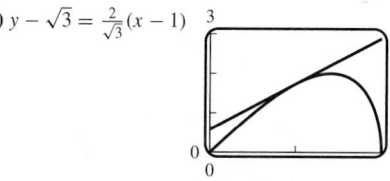

(d) $y - \sqrt{3} = \dfrac{2}{\sqrt{3}}(x - 1)$

Responses to True–False questions may be abridged to save space.

61. False; by the chain rule, $\dfrac{d}{dx}[\sqrt{y}] = \dfrac{1}{2\sqrt{y}} \cdot \dfrac{dy}{dx} = \dfrac{f'(x)}{2\sqrt{f(x)}}$.

63. False; by the chain rule, $dy/dx = (-\sin[g(x)]) \cdot g'(x)$.

65. (c) $f = 1/T$ **(d)** amplitude $= 0.6$ cm, $T = 2\pi/15$ seconds per oscillation, $f = 15/(2\pi)$ oscillations per second

67. $\dfrac{7}{24}\sqrt{6}$ **69. (a)** $10\,\text{lb/in}^2, -2\,\text{lb/in}^2/\text{mi}$ **(b)** $-0.6\,\text{lb/in}^2/\text{s}$

71. $\begin{cases} \cos x, & 0 < x < \pi \\ -\cos x, & -\pi < x < 0 \end{cases}$

73. (c) $-\dfrac{1}{x}\cos\dfrac{1}{x} + \sin\dfrac{1}{x}$ **(d)** limit as x goes to 0 does not exist

75. (a) 21 **(b)** -36 **77.** $1/(2x)$ **79.** $\frac{2}{3}x$ **83.** $f'(g(h(x)))g'(h(x))h'(x)$

▶ **Chapter 2 Review Exercises (Page 181)** _____

3. (a) $2x$ **(b)** 4 **5.** 58.75 ft/s **7. (a)** 13 mi/h **(b)** 7 mi/h

9. (a) $-2/\sqrt{9 - 4x}$ **(b)** $1/(x + 1)^2$

11. (a) $x = -2, -1, 1, 3$ **(b)** $(-\infty, -2), (-1, 1), (3, +\infty)$
(c) $(-2, -1), (1, 3)$ **(d)** 4

13. (a) 78 million people per year **(b)** 1.3% per year

15. (a) $x^2\cos x + 2x\sin x$ **(c)** $4x\cos x + (2 - x^2)\sin x$

17. (a) $(6x^2 + 8x - 17)/(3x + 2)^2$ **(c)** $118/(3x + 2)^3$

19. (a) 2000 gal/min **(b)** 2500 gal/min **21. (a)** 3.6 **(b)** -0.777778

23. $f(1) = 0, f'(1) = 5$ **25.** $y = -16x, y = -145x/4$

29. (a) $8x^7 - \dfrac{3}{2\sqrt{x}} - 15x^{-4}$ **(b)** $(2x + 1)^{100}(1030x^2 + 10x - 1414)$

31. (a) $\dfrac{(x - 1)(15x + 1)}{2\sqrt{3x + 1}}$ **(b)** $-3(3x + 1)^2(3x + 2)/x^7$

33. $x = -\frac{7}{2}, -\frac{1}{2}, 2$ **35.** $y = \pm 2x$

37. $x = n\pi \pm (\pi/4), n = 0, \pm 1, \pm 2, \ldots$ **39.** $y = -3x + (1 + 9\pi/4)$

41. (a) $40\sqrt{3}$ **(b)** 7500

▶ **Chapter 2 Making Connections (Page 184)** _____

Where correct answers to a Making Connections exercise may vary, no answer is listed. Sample answers for these questions are available on the Book Companion Site.

2. (c) $k = 2$ **(d)** $h'(x) = 0$

3. (b) $f' \cdot g \cdot h \cdot k + f \cdot g' \cdot h \cdot k + f \cdot g \cdot h' \cdot k + f \cdot g \cdot h \cdot k'$

4. (c) $\dfrac{f' \cdot g \cdot h - f \cdot g' \cdot h + f \cdot g \cdot h'}{g^2}$

▶ **Exercise Set 3.1 (Page 190)** _____

1. (a) $(6x^2 - y - 1)/x$ **(b)** $4x - 2/x^2$ **3.** $-\dfrac{x}{y}$ **5.** $\dfrac{1 - 2xy - 3y^3}{x^2 + 9xy^2}$

7. $\dfrac{-y^{3/2}}{x^{3/2}}$ **9.** $\dfrac{1 - 2xy^2\cos(x^2y^2)}{2x^2y\cos(x^2y^2)}$

11. $\dfrac{1 - 3y^2\tan^2(xy^2 + y)\sec^2(xy^2 + y)}{3(2xy + 1)\tan^2(xy^2 + y)\sec^2(xy^2 + y)}$ **13.** $-\dfrac{8}{9y^3}$ **15.** $\dfrac{2y}{x^2}$

17. $\dfrac{\sin y}{(1 + \cos y)^3}$ **19.** $-1/\sqrt{3}, 1/\sqrt{3}$

Responses to True–False questions may be abridged to save space.

21. False; the graph of f need only coincide with a portion of the graph of the equation in x and y.

23. False; the equation is equivalent to $x^2 = y^2$ and $y = |x|$ satisfies this equation.

25. $-15^{-3/4} \approx -0.1312$ **27.** $-\frac{9}{13}$

31. (a)

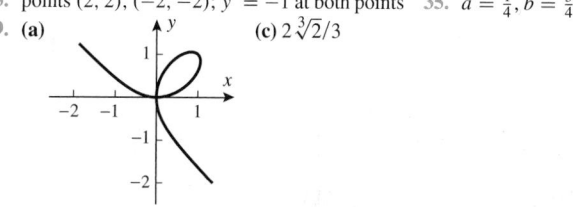

(c) $x = -y^2$ or $x = y^2 + 1$

33. points $(2, 2), (-2, -2); y' = -1$ at both points **35.** $a = \frac{1}{4}, b = \frac{5}{4}$

39. (a)

(c) $2\sqrt[3]{2}/3$

▶ **Exercise Set 3.2 (Page 195)** _____

1. $1/x$ **3.** $1/(1 + x)$ **5.** $2x/(x^2 - 1)$ **7.** $\dfrac{1 - x^2}{x(1 + x^2)}$ **9.** $2/x$

11. $\dfrac{1}{2x\sqrt{\ln x}}$ **13.** $1 + \ln x$ **15.** $2x\log_2(3 - 2x) - \dfrac{2x^2}{(\ln 2)(3 - 2x)}$

17. $\dfrac{2x(1 + \log x) - x/(\ln 10)}{(1 + \log x)^2}$ **19.** $1/(x\ln x)$ **21.** $2\csc 2x$

23. $-\dfrac{1}{x}\sin(\ln x)$ **25.** $2\cot x/(\ln 10)$ **27.** $\dfrac{3}{x - 1} + \dfrac{8x}{x^2 + 1}$

29. $-\tan x + \dfrac{3x}{4 - 3x^2}$

Responses to True–False questions may be abridged to save space.

31. True; $\lim\limits_{x \to 0^+}\dfrac{1}{x} = +\infty$ **33.** True; $1/x$ is an odd function.

35. $x\sqrt[3]{1 + x^2}\left[\dfrac{1}{x} + \dfrac{2x}{3(1 + x^2)}\right]$

37. $\dfrac{(x^2 - 8)^{1/3}\sqrt{x^3 + 1}}{x^6 - 7x + 5}\left[\dfrac{2x}{3(x^2 - 8)} + \dfrac{3x^2}{2(x^3 + 1)} - \dfrac{6x^5 - 7}{x^6 - 7x + 5}\right]$

39. (a) $-\dfrac{1}{x(\ln x)^2}$ **(b)** $-\dfrac{\ln 2}{x(\ln 2)^2}$

41. $y = ex - 2$ **43.** $y = -x/e$ **45. (a)** $y = x/e$ **47.** $A(w) = w/2$

51. $f(x) = \ln(x + 1)$ **53. (a)** 3 **(b)** -5 **55. (a)** 0 **(b)** $\sqrt{2}$

▶ **Exercise Set 3.3 (Page 201)** _____

1. (b) $\frac{1}{9}$ **3.** $-2/x^2$ **5. (a)** no **(b)** yes **(c)** yes **(d)** yes

7. $\dfrac{1}{15y^2 + 1}$ **9.** $\dfrac{1}{10y^4 + 3y^2}$ **13.** $f(x) + g(x), f(g(x))$

15. $7e^{7x}$ **17.** $x^2e^x(x + 3)$ **19.** $\dfrac{4}{(e^x + e^{-x})^2}$

21. $(x\sec^2 x + \tan x)e^{x\tan x}$ **23.** $(1 - 3e^{3x})e^{x - e^{3x}}$

25. $\dfrac{x - 1}{e^x - x}$ **27.** $2^x\ln 2$ **29.** $\pi^{\sin x}(\ln \pi)\cos x$

31. $(x^3 - 2x)^{\ln x}\left[\dfrac{3x^2 - 2}{x^3 - 2x}\ln x + \dfrac{1}{x}\ln(x^3 - 2x)\right]$

33. $(\ln x)^{\tan x}\left[\dfrac{\tan x}{x\ln x} + (\sec^2 x)\ln(\ln x)\right]$

35. $(\ln x)^{\ln x}\left[\dfrac{\ln(\ln x)}{x} + \dfrac{1}{x}\right]$ **37.** $3/\sqrt{1 - 9x^2}$

39. $-\dfrac{1}{|x|\sqrt{x^2-1}}$ **41.** $3x^2/(1+x^6)$ **43.** $-\dfrac{\sec^2 x}{\tan^2 x} = -\csc^2 x$

45. $\dfrac{e^x}{|x|\sqrt{x^2-1}} + e^x \sec^{-1} x$ **47.** 0   **49.** 0   **51.** $-\dfrac{1}{2\sqrt{x}(1+x)}$

Responses to True–False questions may be abridged to save space.

53. False; consider $y = Ae^x$.   **55.** True; use the chain rule.

59. $\dfrac{(3x^2 + \tan^{-1} y)(1+y^2)}{(1+y^2)e^y - x}$ **61. (b)** $1 - (\sqrt{3}/3)$

63. (b) $y = (88x - 89)/7$ **69.** $r = 1, K = 12$

71. 3   **73.** $\ln 10$ **75.** 12π

▶ **Exercise Set 3.4 (Page 208)**

1. (a) 6   **(b)** $-\frac{1}{3}$ **3. (a)** -2 **(b)** $6\sqrt{5}$

5. (b) $A = x^2$ **(c)** $\dfrac{dA}{dt} = 2x\dfrac{dx}{dt}$ **(d)** $12\ \text{ft}^2/\min$

7. (a) $\dfrac{dV}{dt} = \pi\left(r^2\dfrac{dh}{dt} + 2rh\dfrac{dr}{dt}\right)$ **(b)** $-20\pi\ \text{in}^3/\text{s}$; decreasing

9. (a) $\dfrac{d\theta}{dt} = \dfrac{\cos^2\theta}{x^2}\left(x\dfrac{dy}{dt} - y\dfrac{dx}{dt}\right)$ **(b)** $-\frac{5}{16}\ \text{rad/s}$; decreasing

11. $\dfrac{4\pi}{15}\ \text{in}^2/\min$ **13.** $\dfrac{1}{\sqrt{\pi}}\ \text{mi/h}$ **15.** $4860\pi\ \text{cm}^3/\min$ **17.** $\frac{5}{6}\ \text{ft/s}$

19. $\dfrac{125}{\sqrt{61}}\ \text{ft/s}$ **21.** 704 ft/s

23. (a) 500 mi, 1716 mi   **(b)** 1354 mi; 27.7 mi/min

25. $\dfrac{9}{20\pi}\ \text{ft/min}$ **27.** $125\pi\ \text{ft}^3/\min$ **29.** 250 mi/h

31. $\dfrac{36\sqrt{69}}{25}\ \text{ft/min}$ **33.** $\dfrac{8\pi}{5}\ \text{km/s}$ **35.** $600\sqrt{7}\ \text{mi/h}$

37. (a) $-\frac{60}{7}$ units per second   **(b)** falling   **39.** -4 units per second

41. $x = \pm\sqrt{\dfrac{-5+\sqrt{33}}{2}}$ **43.** 4.5 cm/s; away   **47.** $\dfrac{20}{9\pi}\ \text{cm/s}$

▶ **Exercise Set 3.5 (Page 217)**

1. (a) $f(x) \approx 1 + 3(x-1)$ **(b)** $f(1+\Delta x) \approx 1 + 3\Delta x$ **(c)** 1.06

3. (a) $1 + \frac{1}{2}x$, 0.95, 1.05   **17.** $|x| < 1.692$

(b)

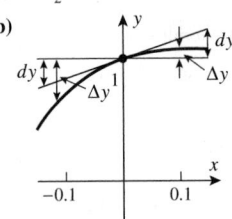

19. $|x| < 0.3158$ **21. (a)** 0.0174533   **(b)** $x_0 = 45°$ **(c)** 0.694765

23. 83.16   **25.** 8.0625   **27.** 8.9944   **29.** 0.1   **31.** 0.8573

33. 0.780398   **37. (a)** 4, 5   **(b)**

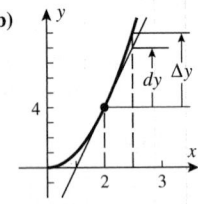

39. $3x^2\,dx, 3x^2\Delta x + 3x(\Delta x)^2 + (\Delta x)^3$

41. $(2x - 2)\,dx, 2x\Delta x + (\Delta x)^2 - 2\Delta x$

43. (a) $(12x^2 - 14x)\,dx$ **(b)** $(-x\sin x + \cos x)\,dx$

45. (a) $\dfrac{2 - 3x}{2\sqrt{1-x}}\,dx$ **(b)** $-17(1+x)^{-18}\,dx$

Responses to True–False questions may be abridged to save space.

47. False; $dy = (dy/dx)\,dx$ **49.** False; consider any linear function.

51. 0.0225   **53.** 0.0048   **55. (a)** $\pm 2\ \text{ft}^2$ **(b)** side: $\pm 1\%$; area: $\pm 2\%$

57. (a) opposite: ± 0.151 in; adjacent: ± 0.087 in

    (b) opposite: $\pm 3.0\%$; adjacent: $\pm 1.0\%$

59. $\pm 10\%$ **61.** $\pm 0.017\ \text{cm}^2$ **63.** $\pm 6\%$ **65.** $\pm 0.5\%$ **67.** $15\pi/2\ \text{cm}^3$

69. (a) $\alpha = 1.5 \times 10^{-5}/°\text{C}$ **(b)** 180.1 cm long

▶ **Exercise Set 3.6 (Page 226)**

1. (a) $\frac{2}{3}$ **(b)** $\frac{2}{3}$

Responses to True–False questions may be abridged to save space.

3. True; the expression $(\ln x)/x$ is undefined if $x \le 0$.

5. False; applying L'Hôpital's rule repeatedly shows that the limit is 0.

7. 1   **9.** 1   **11.** -1 **13.** 0   **15.** $-\infty$ **17.** 0   **19.** 2   **21.** 0

23. π **25.** $-\frac{5}{3}$ **27.** e^{-3} **29.** e^2 **31.** $e^{2/\pi}$ **33.** 0   **35.** $\frac{1}{2}$

37. $+\infty$ **39.** 1   **41.** 1   **43.** 1   **45.** 1   **47. (b)** 2

49. 0

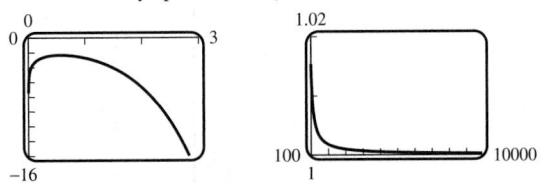

51. e^3

53. no horizontal asymptote   **55.** $y = 1$

57. (a) 0   **(b)** $+\infty$ **(c)** 0   **(d)** $-\infty$ **(e)** $+\infty$ **(f)** $-\infty$ **59.** 1

61. does not exist   **63.** Vt/L **67. (a)** no   **(b)** Both limits equal 0.

69. does not exist

▶ **Chapter 3 Review Exercises (Page 228)**

1. (a) $\dfrac{2 - 3x^2 - y}{x}$ **(b)** $-\dfrac{1}{x^2} - 2x$ **3.** $-\dfrac{y^2}{x^2}$

5. $\dfrac{y\sec(xy)\tan(xy)}{1 - x\sec(xy)\tan(xy)}$ **7.** $-\dfrac{21}{16y^3}$

9. $2/(2-\pi)$ **13.** $(\sqrt[3]{4}/3, \sqrt[3]{2}/3)$

15. $\dfrac{1}{x+1} + \dfrac{2}{x+2} - \dfrac{3}{x+3} - \dfrac{4}{x+4}$ **17.** $\dfrac{1}{x}$ **19.** $\dfrac{1}{3x(\ln x + 1)^{2/3}}$

21. $\dfrac{1}{(\ln 10)x\ln x}$ **23.** $\dfrac{3}{2x} + \dfrac{2x^3}{1+x^4}$ **25.** $2x$ **27.** $e^{\sqrt{x}}(2 + \sqrt{x})$

29. $\dfrac{2}{\pi(1+4x^2)}$ **31.** $e^x x^{(e^x)}\left(\ln x + \dfrac{1}{x}\right)$ **33.** $\dfrac{1}{|2x+1|\sqrt{x^2+x}}$

35. $\dfrac{x^3}{\sqrt{x^2+1}}\left(\dfrac{3}{x} - \dfrac{x}{x^2+1}\right)$

37. (b)

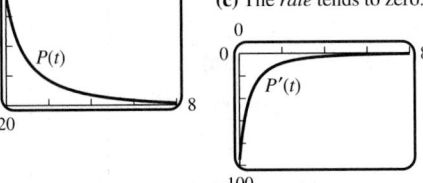

(d) curve must have a horizontal tangent line between $x = 1$ and $x = e$

(e) $x = 2$

39. e^2 **41.** $e^{1/e}$ **43.** No; for example, $f(x) = x^3$.   **45.** $\left(\frac{1}{3}, e\right)$

51. (a) 100

(b) The population tends to 19.
(c) The *rate* tends to zero.

53. $+\infty, +\infty$: yes; $+\infty, -\infty$: no; $-\infty, +\infty$: no; $-\infty, -\infty$: yes

55. $+\infty$ **57.** $\frac{1}{9}$ **59.** $500\pi\ \text{m}^2/\min$

61. (a) $-0.5, 1, 0.5$ **(b)** $\pi/4, 1, \pi/2$ **(c)** $3, -1.0$

63. (a) between 139.48 m and 144.55 m   **(c)** $|d\phi| \leq 0.98°$

▶ **Chapter 3 Making Connections (Page 230)**

Answers are provided in the Student Solutions Manual.

▶ **Exercise Set 4.1 (Page 241)**

1. (a) $f' > 0, f'' > 0$ **(b)** $f' > 0, f'' < 0$

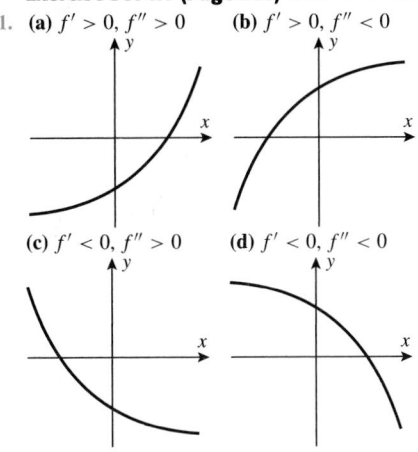

(c) $f' < 0, f'' > 0$ **(d)** $f' < 0, f'' < 0$

3. A: $dy/dx < 0, d^2y/dx^2 > 0$;   B: $dy/dx > 0, d^2y/dx^2 < 0$;
 C: $dy/dx < 0, d^2y/dx^2 < 0$ **5.** $x = -1, 0, 1, 2$

7. (a) $[4, 6]$ **(b)** $[1, 4], [6, 7]$ **(c)** $(1, 2), (3, 5)$ **(d)** $(2, 3), (5, 7)$
 (e) $x = 2, 3, 5$

9. (a) $[1, 3]$ **(b)** $(-\infty, 1], [3, +\infty)$ **(c)** $(-\infty, 2), (4, +\infty)$ **(d)** $(2, 4)$
 (e) $x = 2, 4$

Responses to True–False questions may be abridged to save space.

11. True; see definition of decreasing: $f(x_1) > f(x_2)$ whenever
 $0 \leq x_1 < x_2 \leq 2$.

13. False; for example, $f(x) = (x - 1)^3$ is increasing on $[0, 2]$ and
 $f'(1) = 0$.

15. (a) $[3/2, +\infty)$ **(b)** $(-\infty, 3/2]$ **(c)** $(-\infty, +\infty)$ **(d)** none **(e)** none

17. (a) $(-\infty, +\infty)$ **(b)** none **(c)** $(-1/2, +\infty)$ **(d)** $(-\infty, -1/2)$ **(e)** $-1/2$

19. (a) $[1, +\infty)$ **(b)** $(-\infty, 1]$ **(c)** $(-\infty, 0), (\frac{2}{3}, +\infty)$ **(d)** $(0, \frac{2}{3})$ **(e)** $0, \frac{2}{3}$

21. (a) $\left[\dfrac{3 - \sqrt{5}}{2}, \dfrac{3 + \sqrt{5}}{2}\right]$ **(b)** $\left(-\infty, \dfrac{3 - \sqrt{5}}{2}\right], \left[\dfrac{3 + \sqrt{5}}{2}, +\infty\right)$
 (c) $\left(0, \dfrac{4 - \sqrt{6}}{2}\right), \left(\dfrac{4 + \sqrt{6}}{2}, +\infty\right)$ **(d)** $(-\infty, 0), \left(\dfrac{4 - \sqrt{6}}{2}, \dfrac{4 + \sqrt{6}}{2}\right)$
 (e) $0, \dfrac{4 \pm \sqrt{6}}{2}$

23. (a) $[-1/2, +\infty)$ **(b)** $(-\infty, -1/2]$ **(c)** $(-2, 1)$
 (d) $(-\infty, -2), (1, +\infty)$ **(e)** $-2, 1$

25. (a) $[-1, 0], [1, +\infty)$ **(b)** $(-\infty, -1], [0, 1]$ **(c)** $(-\infty, 0), (0, +\infty)$
 (d) none **(e)** none

27. (a) $(-\infty, 0]$ **(b)** $[0, +\infty)$ **(c)** $(-\infty, -1), (1, +\infty)$
 (d) $(-1, 1)$ **(e)** $-1, 1$

29. (a) $[0, +\infty)$ **(b)** $(-\infty, 0]$ **(c)** $(-2, 2)$
 (d) $(-\infty, -2), (2, +\infty)$ **(e)** $-2, 2$

31. (a) $[0, +\infty)$ **(b)** $(-\infty, 0]$ **(c)** $\left(-\sqrt{\dfrac{1 + \sqrt{7}}{3}}, \sqrt{\dfrac{1 + \sqrt{7}}{3}}\right)$
 (d) $\left(-\infty, -\sqrt{\dfrac{1 + \sqrt{7}}{3}}\right), \left(\sqrt{\dfrac{1 + \sqrt{7}}{3}}, +\infty\right)$ **(e)** $\pm\sqrt{\dfrac{1 + \sqrt{7}}{3}}$

33. increasing: $[-\pi/4, 3\pi/4]$; decreasing: $[-\pi, -\pi/4], [3\pi/4, \pi]$;
 concave up: $(-3\pi/4, \pi/4)$; concave down: $(-\pi, -3\pi/4), (\pi/4, \pi)$;
 inflection points: $-3\pi/4, \pi/4$

35. increasing: none; decreasing: $(-\pi, \pi)$; concave up: $(-\pi, 0)$;
 concave down: $(0, \pi)$; inflection point: 0

37. increasing: $[-\pi, -3\pi/4], [-\pi/4, \pi/4], [3\pi/4, \pi]$; decreasing:
 $[-3\pi/4, -\pi/4], [\pi/4, 3\pi/4]$; concave up: $(-\pi/2, 0), (\pi/2, \pi)$;
 concave down: $(-\pi, -\pi/2), (0, \pi/2)$; inflection points: $0, \pm\pi/2$

39. (a)   **(b)**

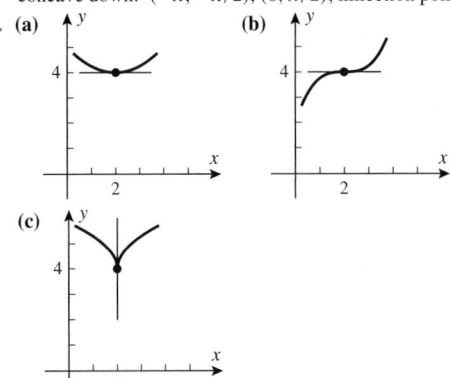

(c)

41. $1 + \frac{1}{3}x - \sqrt[3]{1 + x} \geq 0$ if $x > 0$ **43.** $x \geq \sin x$

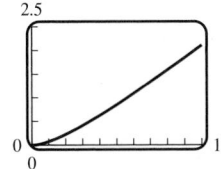 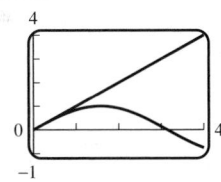

47.

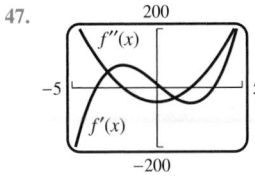

points of inflection at $x = -2, 2$;
concave up on $[-5, -2], [2, 5]$;
concave down on $[-2, 2]$;
increasing on $[-3.5829, 0.2513]$
 and $[3.3316, 5]$;
decreasing on $[-5, -3.5829]$,
 $[0.2513, 3.3316]$

49. $-2.464202, 0.662597, 2.701605$ **53. (a)** true **(b)** false

57. (c) inflection point $(1, 0)$; concave up on $(1, +\infty)$;
 concave down on $(-\infty, 1)$

63.   **65.**

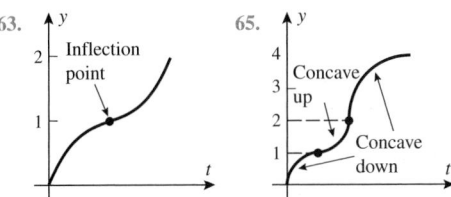

67. (a) $\dfrac{LAk}{(1 + A)^2}$ **69.** the eighth day

 (c) $\dfrac{1}{k}\ln A$

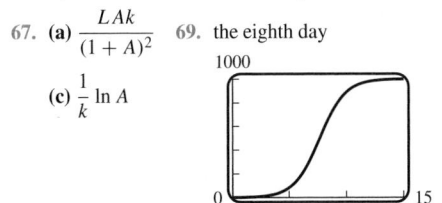

▶ **Exercise Set 4.2 (Page 252)**

1. **(a)** 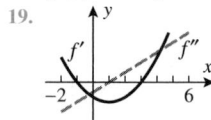   **(b)**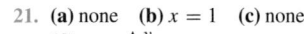

(c) 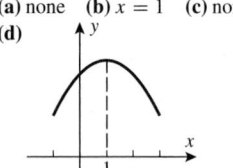   **(d)**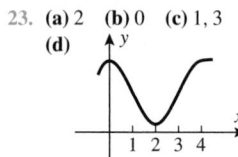

5. **(b)** nothing   **(c)** f has a relative minimum at $x = 1$,
g has no relative extremum at $x = 1$.

7. critical: $0, \pm\sqrt{2}$; stationary: $0, \pm\sqrt{2}$

9. critical: $-3, 1$; stationary: $-3, 1$ 11. critical: $0, \pm 5$; stationary: 0

13. critical: $n\pi/2$ for every integer n;
stationary: $n\pi + \pi/2$ for every integer n

Responses to True–False questions may be abridged to save space.

15. False; for example, $f(x) = (x - 1)^2(x - 1.5)$ has a relative maximum
at $x = 1$, but $f(2) = 0.5 > 0 = f(1)$.

17. False; to apply the second derivative test (Theorem 4.2.4) at $x = 1$,
$f'(1)$ must equal 0.

19.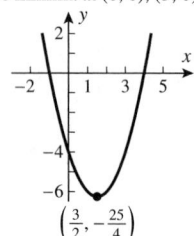

21. **(a)** none   **(b)** $x = 1$ **(c)** none
(d)

23. **(a)** 2   **(b)** 0   **(c)** 1, 3
(d)

25. 0 (neither), $\sqrt[3]{5}$ (min)   27. -2 (min), $2/3$ (max)   29. 0 (min)

31. -1 (min), 1 (max)   33. relative maximum at $(4/3, 19/3)$

35. relative maximum at $(\pi/4, 1)$; relative minimum at $(3\pi/4, -1)$

37. relative maximum at $(1, 1)$; relative minima at $(0, 0)$, $(2, 0)$

39. relative maximum at $(-1, 0)$; relative minimum at $(-3/5, -108/3125)$

41. relative maximum at $(-1, 1)$; relative minimum at $(0, 0)$

43. no relative extrema   45. relative minimum at $(0, \ln 2)$

47. relative minimum at $(-\ln 2, -1/4)$

49. relative maximum at $(3/2, 9/4)$; relative minima at $(0, 0)$, $(3, 0)$

51. intercepts: $(0, -4), (-1, 0), (4, 0)$;
stationary point: $(3/2, -25/4)$ (min);
inflection points: none

53. intercepts: $(0, 5)$, $\left(\dfrac{-7 \pm \sqrt{57}}{4}, 0\right)$, $(5, 0)$;
stationary points: $(-2, 49)$
(max), $(3, -76)$ (min);
inflection point: $(1/2, -27/2)$

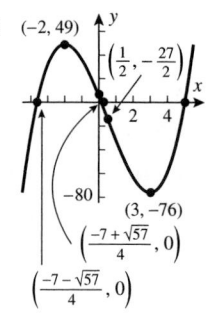

55. intercepts: $(-1, 0), (0, 0), (2, 0)$;
stationary points: $(-1, 0)$ (max),
$\left(\dfrac{1 - \sqrt{3}}{2}, \dfrac{9 - 6\sqrt{3}}{4}\right)$ (min),
$\left(\dfrac{1 + \sqrt{3}}{2}, \dfrac{9 + 6\sqrt{3}}{4}\right)$ (max);
inflection points: $\left(-\dfrac{1}{\sqrt{2}}, \dfrac{5}{4} - \sqrt{2}\right)$,
$\left(\dfrac{1}{\sqrt{2}}, \dfrac{5}{4} + \sqrt{2}\right)$,

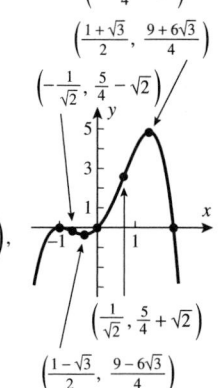

57. intercepts: $(0, -1), (-1, 0), (1, 0)$;
stationary points: $(-1/2, -27/16)$ (min),
$(1, 0)$ (neither);
inflection points: $(0, -1), (1, 0)$

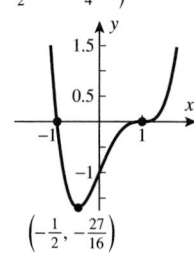

59. intercepts: $(-1, 0), (0, 0), (1, 0)$;
stationary points: $(-1, 0)$ (max),
$\left(-\dfrac{1}{\sqrt{5}}, -\dfrac{16}{25\sqrt{5}}\right)$ (min),
$\left(\dfrac{1}{\sqrt{5}}, \dfrac{16}{25\sqrt{5}}\right)$ (max), $(1, 0)$ (min);
inflection points: $\left(-\sqrt{\dfrac{3}{5}}, -\dfrac{4}{25}\sqrt{\dfrac{3}{5}}\right)$,
$(0, 0)$, $\left(\sqrt{\dfrac{3}{5}}, \dfrac{4}{25}\sqrt{\dfrac{3}{5}}\right)$

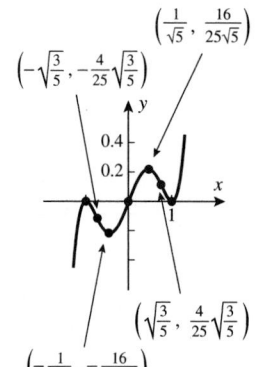

61. (a)

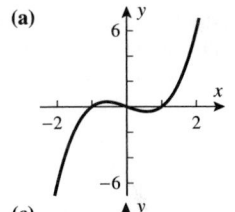

(b)

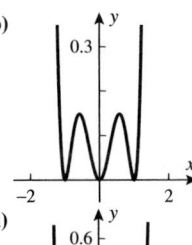

(c)

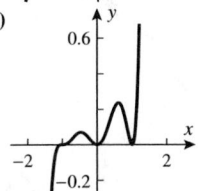

(d)

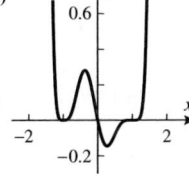

63. relative min of 0 at $x = \pi/2, \pi, 3\pi/2$;
relative max of 1 at $x = \pi/4, 3\pi/4,$
$5\pi/4, 7\pi/4$

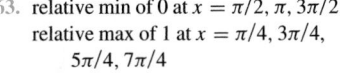

65. relative min of 0 at $x = \pi/2, 3\pi/2$;
relative max of 1 at $x = \pi$

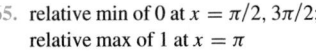

67. relative min of $-1/e$ at $x = 1/e$

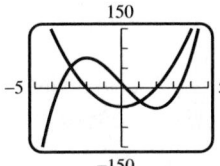

69. relative min of 0 at $x = 0$;
relative max of $1/e^2$ at $x = 1$

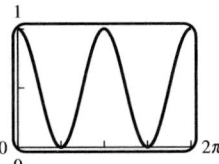

71. relative minima at $x = -3.58, 3.33$;
relative max at $x = 0.25$

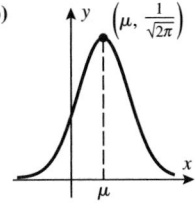

73. relative maximum at $x \approx -0.272$; relative minimum at $x \approx 0.224$
75. relative maximum at $x = 0$; relative minima at $x \approx \pm 0.618$
77. (a) 54   **(b)** 9
79. (b)

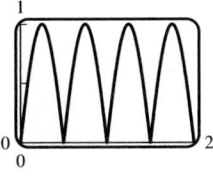

▶ **Exercise Set 4.3 (Page 264)**

1. stationary points: none;
inflection points: none;
asymptotes: $x = 4, y = -2$;
asymptote crossings: none

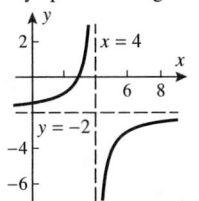

3. stationary points: none;
inflection point: $(0, 0)$;
asymptotes: $x = \pm 2, y = 0$;
asymptote crossings: $(0, 0)$

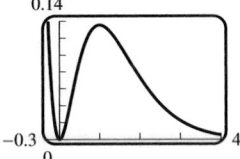

5. stationary point: $(0, 0)$;
inflection points: $\left(\pm\frac{2}{\sqrt{3}}, \frac{1}{4}\right)$;
asymptote: $y = 1$;
asymptote crossings: none

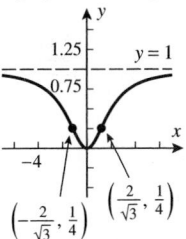

7. stationary point: $(0, -1)$;
inflection points: $(0, -1)$,
$\left(-\frac{1}{\sqrt[3]{2}}, -\frac{1}{3}\right)$;
asymptotes: $x = 1, y = 1$;
asymptote crossings: none

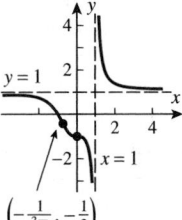

9. stationary point: $(4, 11/4)$;
inflection point: $(6, 25/9)$;
asymptotes: $x = 0, y = 3$;
asymptote crossing: $(2, 3)$

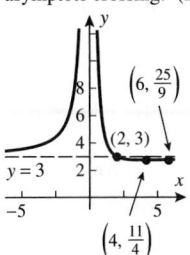

11. stationary point: $(-1/3, 0)$;
inflection point: $(-1, 1)$;
asymptotes: $x = 1, y = 9$;
asymptote crossing: $(1/3, 9)$

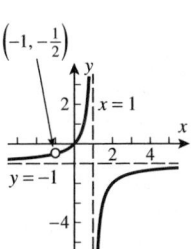

13. stationary points: none;
inflection points: none;
asymptotes: $x = 1, y = -1$;
asymptote crossings: none

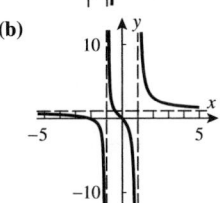

15. (a)

(b)

17.

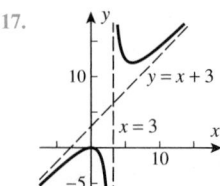

19. stationary point: $\left(-\frac{1}{\sqrt[3]{2}}, \frac{3}{2}\sqrt[3]{2}\right)$; $\left(-\frac{1}{\sqrt[3]{2}}, \frac{3}{2}\sqrt[3]{2}\right)$

inflection point: $(1, 0)$;
asymptotes: $y = x^2$, $x = 0$;
asymptote crossings: none

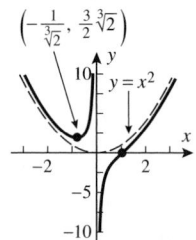

21. stationary points: $(-4, -27/2)$, $(2, 0)$;
inflection point: $(2, 0)$;
asymptotes: $x = 0$, $y = x - 6$;
asymptote crossing: $(2/3, -16/3)$

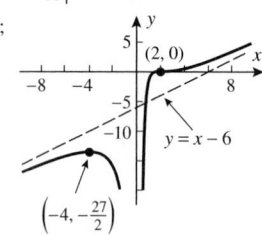

23. stationary points: $(-3, 23)$, $(0, -4)$;
inflection point: $(0, -4)$;
asymptotes: $x = -2$, $y = x^2 - 2x$;
asymptote crossings: none

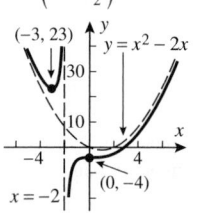

25. **(a)** VI   **(b)** I   **(c)** III   **(d)** V   **(e)** IV   **(f)** II

Responses to True–False questions may be abridged to save space.

27. True; if deg $P >$ deg Q, then $f(x)$ is unbounded as $x \to \pm\infty$; if deg $P <$ deg Q, then $f(x) \to 0$ as $x \to \pm\infty$.

29. False; for example, $f(x) = (x - 1)^{1/3}$ is continuous (with vertical tangent line) at $x = 1$, but $f'(x) = \dfrac{1}{3(x-1)^{2/3}}$ has a vertical asymptote at $x = 1$.

31. critical points: $(\pm 1/2, 0)$;   **33.** critical points: $(-1, 1)$, $(0, 0)$;
inflection points: none   inflection points: none

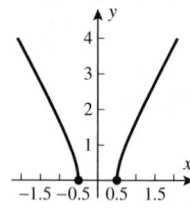 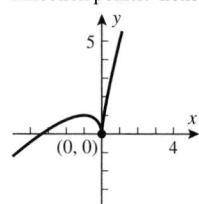

35. critical points: $(0, 0)$, $(1, 3)$; inflection points: $(0, 0)$, $(-2, -6\sqrt[3]{2})$.
It's hard to see all the important features in one graph, so two graphs are shown:

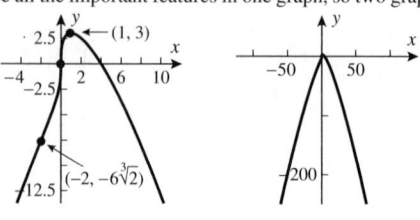

37. critical points: $(0, 4)$, $(1, 3)$;
inflection points: $(0, 4)$, $(8, 4)$

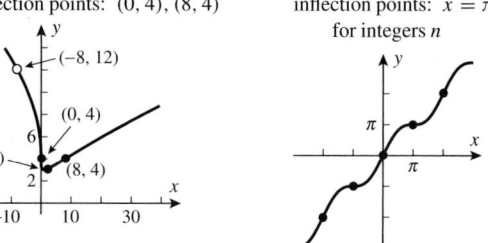

39. extrema: none;
inflection points: $x = \pi n$
for integers n

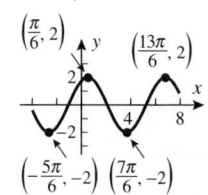

41. minima: $x = 7\pi/6 + 2\pi n$ for integers n; $\left(\frac{\pi}{6}, 2\right)$ $\left(\frac{13\pi}{6}, 2\right)$
maxima: $x = \pi/6 + 2\pi n$ for integers n;
inflection points: $x = 2\pi/3 + \pi n$
for integers n

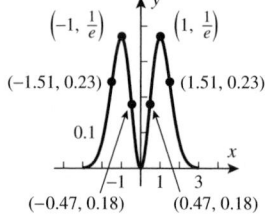

$\left(-\frac{5\pi}{6}, -2\right)$ $\left(\frac{7\pi}{6}, -2\right)$

43. relative minima: 1 at $x = \pi$; -1 at $x = 0, 2\pi$;
relative maxima: $5/4$ at $x = -2\pi/3, 2\pi/3, 4\pi/3, 8\pi/3$;
inflection points where $\cos x = \dfrac{-1 \pm \sqrt{33}}{8}$: $(-2.57, 1.13)$,
$(-0.94, 0.06)$, $(0.94, 0.06)$, $(2.57, 1.13)$, $(3.71, 1.13)$, $(5.35, 0.06)$,
$(7.22, 0.06)$, $(8.86, 1.13)$

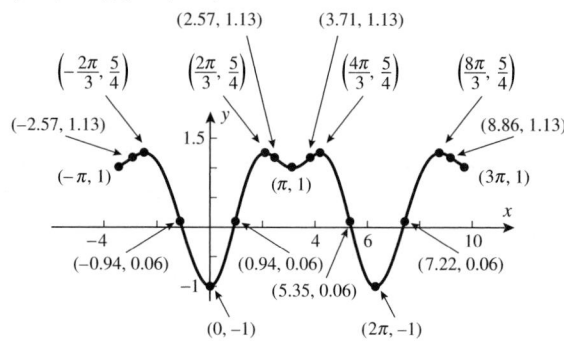

45. **(a)** $+\infty$, 0   **47.** **(a)** 0, $+\infty$
(b)   **(b)**

49. **(a)** 0, 0
(b) relative max $= 1/e$ at $x = \pm 1$; relative min $= 0$ at $x = 0$;
inflection points where $x = \pm\sqrt{\dfrac{5 \pm \sqrt{17}}{4}}$:
about $(\pm 0.47, 0.18)$, $(\pm 1.51, 0.23)$; asymptote: $y = 0$

51. (a) $-\infty, 0$
(b) relative max $= -e^2$
at $x = 2$;
no relative min;
no inflection points;
asymptotes: $y = 0, x = 1$

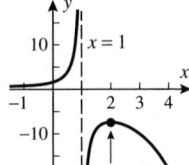

53. (a) $0, +\infty$
(b) critical points at $x = 0.2$;
relative min at $x = 0$,
relative max at $x = 2$;
points of inflection at $x = 2 \pm \sqrt{2}$;
horizontal asymptote $y = 0$
as $x \to +\infty$
$\lim\limits_{x \to -\infty} f(x) = +\infty$

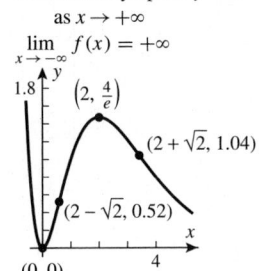

55. (a) $+\infty, 0$
(b)

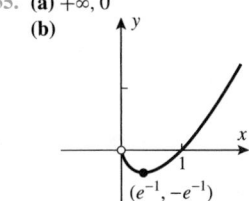

57. (a) $+\infty, 0$
(b)

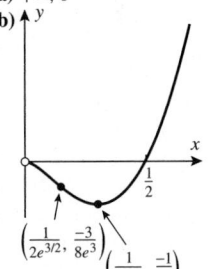

59. (a) $+\infty, 0$
(b) no relative max; relative min $= -\dfrac{3}{2e}$ at $x = e^{-3/2}$;
inflection point: $(e^{3/2}, 3e/2)$;
no asymptotes. It's hard to see all the important features in one graph,
so two graphs are shown:

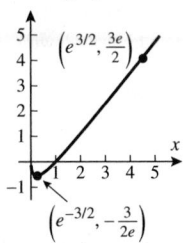

61. (a)

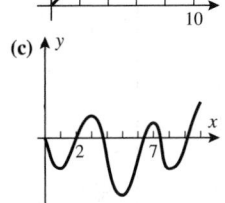

(b) relative max at $x = 1/b$;
inflection point at $x = 2/b$

63. (a) does not exist, 0
(b) $y = e^x$ and $y = e^x \cos x$ intersect for
$x = 2\pi n$, and $y = -e^x$ and $y = e^x \cos x$
intersect for $x = 2\pi n + \pi$,
for all integers n.

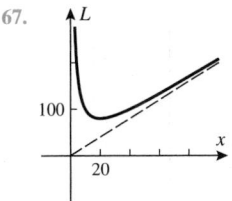

(c) Graphs for $a = 1$:

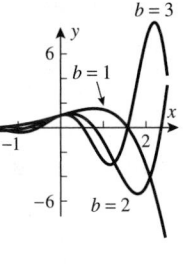

65. (a) $x = 1, 2.5, 3, 4$ (b) $(-\infty, 1], [2.5, 3]$
(c) relative max at $x = 1, 3$;
relative min at $x = 2.5$ (d) $x \approx 0.6, 1.9, 4$

67.

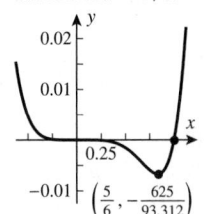

69. Graph misses zeros at $x = 0, 1$
and min at $x = 5/6$.

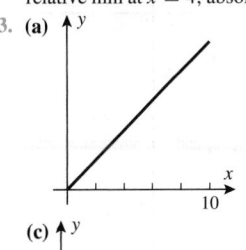

▶ **Exercise Set 4.4 (Page 272)**

1. relative maxima at $x = 2, 6$; absolute max at $x = 6$;
relative min at $x = 4$; absolute minima at $x = 0, 4$

3. (a)

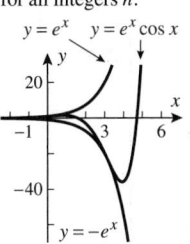

(b)

(c)

7. max $= 2$ at $x = 1, 2$;
min $= 1$ at $x = 3/2$
9. max $= 8$ at $x = 4$;
min $= -1$ at $x = 1$
11. maximum value $3/\sqrt{5}$ at $x = 1$;
minimum value $-3/\sqrt{5}$ at $x = -1$
13. max $= \sqrt{2} - \pi/4$ at $x = -\pi/4$;
min $= \pi/3 - \sqrt{3}$ at $x = \pi/3$
15. maximum value 17 at $x = -5$; minimum value 1 at $x = -3$.
Responses to True–False questions may be abridged to save space.
17. True; see the Extreme-Value Theorem (4.4.2).
19. True; see Theorem 4.4.3.
21. no maximum; min $= -9/4$ at $x = 1/2$
23. maximum value $f(1) = 1$; no minimum
25. no maximum or minimum
27. max $= -2 - 2\sqrt{2}$ at $x = -1 - \sqrt{2}$; no minimum
29. no maximum; min $= 0$ at $x = 0, 2$

31. maximum value 48 at $x = 8$;
minimum value 0 at $x = 0, 20$

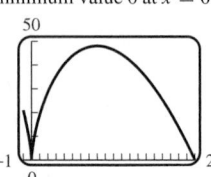

33. no maximum or minimum

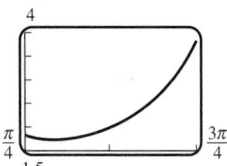

35. max $= 2\sqrt{2} + 1$ at $x = 3\pi/4$; min $= \sqrt{3}$ at $x = \pi/3$

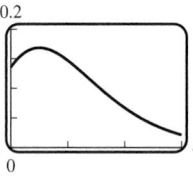

37. maximum value $\frac{27}{8}e^{-3}$ at $x = \frac{3}{2}$;
minimum value $64/e^8$ at $x = 4$

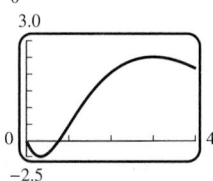

39. max $= 5 \ln 10 - 9$ at $x = 3$;
min $= 5 \ln(10/9) - 1$ at $x = 1/3$

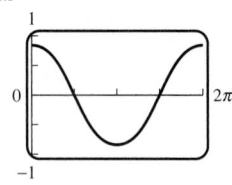

41. maximum value $\sin(1) \approx 0.84147$;
minimum value $-\sin(1) \approx -0.84147$

43. maximum value 2; minimum value $-\frac{1}{4}$
45. max $= 3$ at $x = 2n\pi$; min $= -3/2$ at $x = \pm 2\pi/3 + 2n\pi$
for any integer n **49.** 2, at $x = 1$
53. maximum $y = 4$ at $t = \pi, 3\pi$; minimum $y = 0$ at $t = 0, 2\pi$

▶ **Exercise Set 4.5 (Page 283)** _____

1. (a) 1 (b) $\frac{1}{2}$ **3.** 500 ft parallel to stream, 250 ft perpendicular
5. 500 ft ($3 fencing) × 750 ft ($2 fencing) **7.** 5 in × $\frac{12}{5}$ in
9. $10\sqrt{2} \times 10\sqrt{2}$ **11.** 80 ft ($1 fencing), 40 ft ($2 fencing)
15. maximum area is 108 when $x = 2$
17. maximum area is 144 when $x = 2$
19. 11,664 in^3 **21.** $\frac{200}{27}$ ft^3 **23.** base 10 cm square, height 20 cm
25. ends $\sqrt[3]{3V/4}$ units square, length $\frac{4}{3}\sqrt[3]{3V/4}$
27. height $= 2R/\sqrt{3}$, radius $= \sqrt{2/3}R$
31. height $=$ radius $= \sqrt[3]{500/\pi}$ cm **33.** $L/12$ by $L/12$ by $L/12$
35. height $= L/\sqrt{3}$, radius $= \sqrt{2/3}L$
37. height $= 2\sqrt[3]{75/\pi}$ cm, radius $= \sqrt{2}\sqrt[3]{75/\pi}$ cm
39. height $= 4R$, radius $= \sqrt{2}R$
41. $R(x) = 225x - 0.25x^2$; $R'(x) = 225 - 0.5x$; 450 tons
43. (a) 7000 units (b) yes (c) $15 **45.** 13,722 lb **47.** $3\sqrt{3}$
49. height $= r/\sqrt{2}$ **51.** $\left(\sqrt{2}, \frac{1}{2}\right)$ **53.** $\left(-1/\sqrt{3}, \frac{3}{4}\right)$
55. (a) π mi (b) $2\sin^{-1}(1/4)$ mi **57.** $4(1 + 2^{2/3})^{3/2}$ ft
59. 30 cm from the weaker source **61.** $\sqrt{24} = 2\sqrt{6}$ ft

▶ **Exercise Set 4.6 (Page 294)** _____

1. (a) positive, negative, slowing down
(b) positive, positive, speeding up
(c) negative, positive, slowing down
3. (a) left
(b) negative
(c) speeding up
(d) slowing down

5.

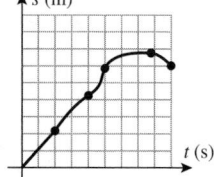

7.

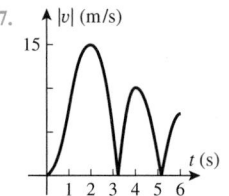
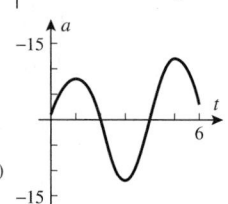

Responses to True–False questions may be abridged to save space.
9. False; a particle has positive velocity when its position versus time
graph is increasing; if that positive velocity is decreasing, the particle
would be slowing down.
11. False; acceleration is the derivative of velocity (with respect to time);
speed is the absolute value of velocity.
13. (a) 7.5 ft/s^2 (b) $t = 0$ s
15. (a)

t	s	v	a
1	0.71	0.56	-0.44
2	1	0	-0.62
3	0.71	-0.56	-0.44
4	0	-0.79	0
5	-0.71	-0.56	0.44

(b) stopped at $t = 2$;
moving right at $t = 1$;
moving left at $t = 3, 4, 5$
(c) speeding up at $t = 3$;
slowing down at $t = 1, 5$;
neither at $t = 2, 4$

17. (a) $v(t) = 3t^2 - 6t, a(t) = 6t - 6$
(b) $s(1) = -2$ ft, $v(1) = -3$ ft/s, $|v(1)| = 3$ ft/s, $a(1) = 0$ ft/s^2
(c) $t = 0, 2$ s (d) speeding up for $0 < t < 1$ and $2 < t$, slowing
down for $1 < t < 2$ (e) 58 ft
19. (a) $v(t) = 3\pi \sin(\pi t/3), a(t) = \pi^2 \cos(\pi t/3)$ (b) $s(1) = 9/2$ ft,
$v(1) = \text{speed} = 3\sqrt{3}\pi/2$ ft/s, $a(1) = \pi^2/2$ ft/s^2 (c) $t = 0$ s, 3 s
(d) speeding up: $0 < t < 1.5, 3 < t < 4.5$;
slowing down: $1.5 < t < 3, 4.5 < t < 5$ (e) 31.5 ft
21. (a) $v(t) = -\frac{1}{3}(t^2 - 6t + 8)e^{-t/3}, a(t) = \frac{1}{9}(t^2 - 12t + 26)e^{-t/3}$
(b) $s(1) = 9e^{-1/3}$ ft, $v(1) = -e^{-1/3}$ ft/s, speed $= e^{-1/3}$ ft/s, $a(1) =$
$\frac{5}{3}e^{-1/3}$ ft/s^2 (c) $t = 2$ s, 4 s
(d) speeding up: $2 < t < 6 - \sqrt{10}, 4 < t < 6 + \sqrt{10}$; slowing
down: $0 < t < 2, 6 - \sqrt{10} < t < 4, 6 + \sqrt{10} < t$
(e) $8 - 24e^{-2/3} + 48e^{-4/3} - 33e^{-5/3}$
23. (a) $\sqrt{5}$ (b) $\sqrt{5}/10$

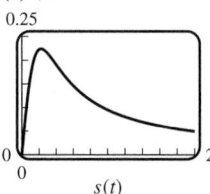
$s(t)$

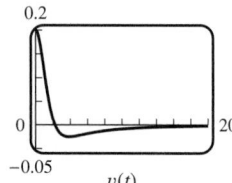
$v(t)$

(c) speeding up for $\sqrt{5} < t < \sqrt{15}$; slowing down for $0 < t < \sqrt{5}$ and $\sqrt{15} < t$

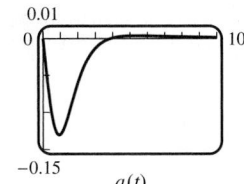

$a(t)$

25.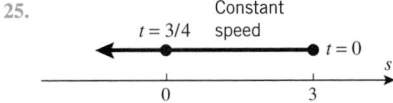

27.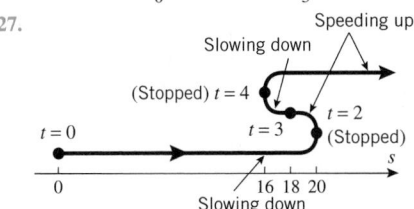

29.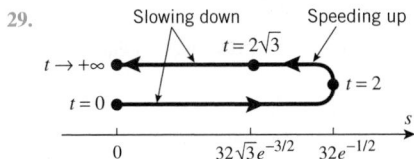

31.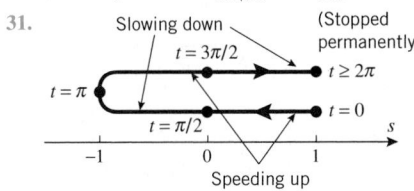

33. (a) 12 ft/s (b) $t = 2.2$ s, $s = -24.2$ ft
35. (a) $t = 2 \pm 1/\sqrt{3}$, $s = \ln 2$, $v = \pm\sqrt{3}$ (b) $t = 2$, $s = 0$, $a = 6$
37. (a) 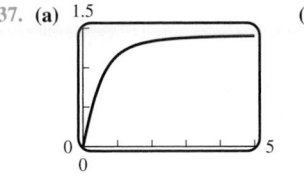 (b) $\sqrt{2}$

39. (b) $\frac{2}{3}$ unit (c) $0 \le t < 1$ and $t > 2$

▶ **Exercise Set 4.7 (Page 300)**

1. 1.414213562 3. 1.817120593 5. $x \approx 1.76929$
7. $x \approx 1.224439550$ 9. $x \approx -1.24962$ 11. $x \approx 1.02987$
13. $x \approx 4.493409458$ 15. $x \approx 0.68233$

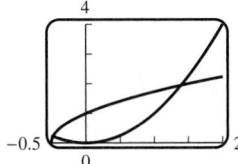

17. -0.474626618, 1.395336994 19. $x \approx 0.58853$ or 3.09636

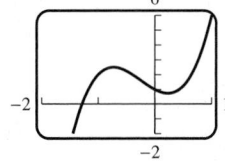

Responses to True–False questions may be abridged to save space.
21. True; $x = x_{n+1}$ is the x-intercept of the tangent line to $y = f(x)$ at $x = x_n$.
23. False; for example, if $f(x) = x(x - 3)^2$, Newton's Method fails (analogous to Figure 4.7.4) with $x_1 = 1$ and approximates the root $x = 3$ for $x_1 > 1$.
25. (b) 3.162277660 27. -4.098859132
29. $x = -1$ or $x \approx 0.17951$ 31. $(0.589754512, 0.347810385)$
33. (b) $\theta \approx 2.99156$ rad or 171° 35. -1.220744085, 0.724491959
37. $i = 0.053362$ or 5.33% 39. (a) The values do not converge.

▶ **Exercise Set 4.8 (Page 308)**

1. $c = 4$ 3. $c = \pi$ 5. $c = 1$ 7. $\frac{5}{4}$
9. (a) $[-2, 1]$
   (b) $c \approx -1.29$
   (c) -1.2885843

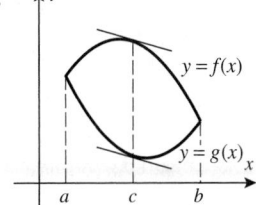

Responses to True–False questions may be abridged to save space.
11. False; Rolle's Theorem requires the additional hypothesis that f is differentiable on (a, b) and $f(a) = f(b) = 0$; see Example 2.
13. False; the Constant Difference Theorem applies to two functions with equal derivatives on an interval to conclude that the functions differ by a constant on the interval.
15. (b) $\tan x$ is not continuous on $[0, \pi]$. 25. $f(x) = xe^x - e^x + 2$
35. (b) $f(x) = \sin x$, $g(x) = \cos x$
37.   41. $a = 6$, $b = -3$

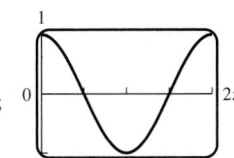

▶ **Chapter 4 Review Exercises (Page 310)**

1. (a) $f(x_1) < f(x_2)$; $f(x_1) > f(x_2)$; $f(x_1) = f(x_2)$
   (b) $f' > 0$; $f' < 0$; $f' = 0$
3. (a) $\left[\frac{5}{2}, +\infty\right)$ (b) $\left(-\infty, \frac{5}{2}\right)$ (c) $(-\infty, +\infty)$ (d) none (e) none
5. (a) $[0, +\infty)$ (b) $(-\infty, 0]$ (c) $(-\sqrt{2/3}, \sqrt{2/3})$
   (d) $(-\infty, -\sqrt{2/3})$, $(\sqrt{2/3}, +\infty)$ (e) $-\sqrt{2/3}$, $\sqrt{2/3}$
7. (a) $[-1, +\infty)$ (b) $(-\infty, -1]$ (c) $(-\infty, 0)$, $(2, +\infty)$
   (d) $(0, 2)$ (e) $0, 2$
9. (a) $(-\infty, 0]$ (b) $[0, +\infty)$ (c) $(-\infty, -1/\sqrt{2})$, $(1/\sqrt{2}, +\infty)$
   (d) $(-1/\sqrt{2}, 1/\sqrt{2})$ (e) $\pm 1/\sqrt{2}$
11. increasing on $[\pi, 2\pi]$;
    decreasing on $[0, \pi]$;
    concave up on $(\pi/2, 3\pi/2)$;
    concave down on $(0, \pi/2)$, $(3\pi/2, 2\pi)$;
    inflection points: $(\pi/2, 0)$, $(3\pi/2, 0)$

13. increasing on $[0, \pi/4]$, $[3\pi/4, \pi]$;
    decreasing on $[\pi/4, 3\pi/4]$;
    concave up on $(\pi/2, \pi)$;
    concave down on $(0, \pi/2)$;
    inflection point: $(\pi/2, 0)$

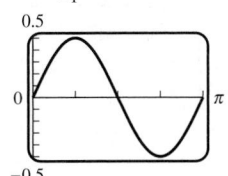

15. (a) 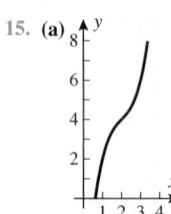 (b) 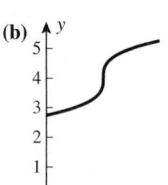 (c)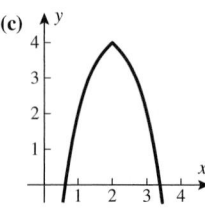

17. $-\dfrac{b}{2a} \le 0$ **19.** $x = -1$ **21.** (a) at an inflection point

25. (a) $x = \pm\sqrt{2}$ (stationary points) (b) $x = 0$ (stationary point)

27. (a) relative max at $x = 1$, relative min at $x = 7$, neither at $x = 0$
 (b) relative max at $x = \pi/2$, $3\pi/2$; relative min at $x = 7\pi/6$, $11\pi/6$
 (c) relative max at $x = 5$

29. $\lim\limits_{x \to -\infty} f(x) = +\infty$, $\lim\limits_{x \to +\infty} f(x) = +\infty$;
 relative min at $x = 0$;
 points of inflection at $x = \tfrac{1}{2}$, 1;
 no asymptotes

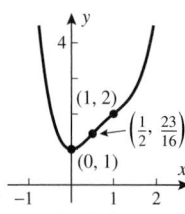

31. $\lim\limits_{x \to \pm\infty} f(x)$ does not exist; critical point at $x = 0$; relative min
 at $x = 0$; point of inflection when $1 + 4x^2 \tan(x^2 + 1) = 0$;
 vertical asymptotes at $x = \pm\sqrt{\pi\left(n + \tfrac{1}{2}\right) - 1}$, $n = 0, 1, 2, \ldots$

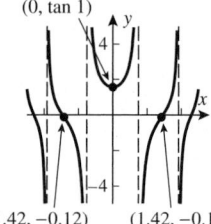

$(-1.42, -0.12)$ $(1.42, -0.12)$

33. critical points at $x = -5$, 0; relative max at $x = -5$, relative min at
 $x = 0$; points of inflection at $x \approx -7.26$, -1.44, 1.20; horizontal
 asymptote $y = 1$ for $x \to \pm\infty$

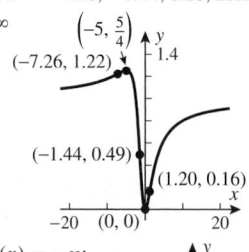

35. $\lim\limits_{x \to -\infty} f(x) = +\infty$, $\lim\limits_{x \to +\infty} f(x) = -\infty$;
 critical point at $x = 0$;
 no extrema;
 inflection point at $x = 0$
 (f changes concavity);
 no asymptotes

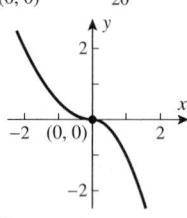

37. no relative extrema **39.** relative min of 0 at $x = 0$

41. relative min of 0 at $x = 0$ **43.** relative min of 0 at $x = 0$

45. (a) 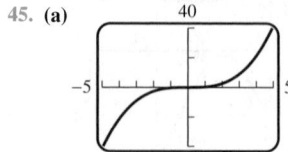 (b) relative max at $x = -\tfrac{1}{20}$;
 relative min at $x = \tfrac{1}{20}$

47. (a)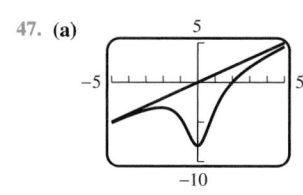

49. $f(x) = \dfrac{x^2 + x - 7}{3x^2 + x - 1}$, $x \ne \dfrac{1}{2}$

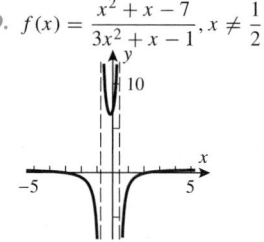

horizontal asymptote $y = 1/3$
vertical asymptotes at
$x = (-1 \pm \sqrt{13})/6$

(c) The finer details can be seen
when graphing over a much smaller
x-window.

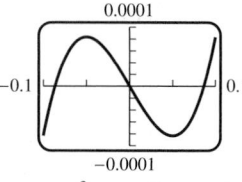

53. (a) true (b) false

55. (a) no max; min $= -13/4$ at $x = 3/2$ (b) no max or min
 (c) no max; min $m = e^2/4$ at $x = 2$
 (d) no max; min $m = e^{-1/e}$ at $x = 1/e$

57. (a) minimum value 0 for $x = \pm 1$; (b) max $= 1/2$ at $x = 1$;
 no maximum   min $= 0$ at $x = 0$

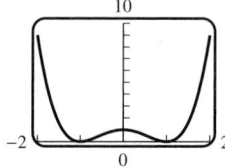

(c) maximum value 2 at $x = 0$; (d) maximum value
 minimum value $\sqrt{3}$ at $x = \pi/6$ $f(-2 - \sqrt{3}) \approx 0.84$;
 minimum value
 $f(-2 + \sqrt{3}) \approx -0.06$

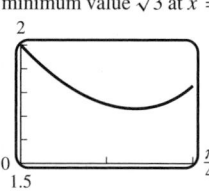 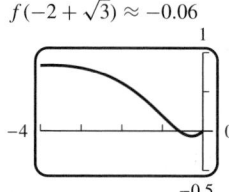

59. (a) 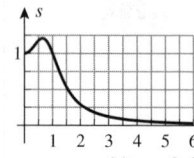 (b) minimum:
 $(-2.111985, -0.355116)$;
 maximum:
 $(0.372591, 2.012931)$

61. width $= 4\sqrt{2}$, height $= 3\sqrt{2}$ **63.** 2 in square

65. (a) yes (b) yes

67. (a) $v = -2\dfrac{t(t^4 + 2t^2 - 1)}{(t^4 + 1)^2}$, $a = 2\dfrac{3t^8 + 10t^6 - 12t^4 - 6t^2 + 1}{(t^4 + 1)^3}$

(b)

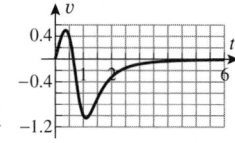 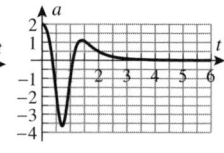

(c) $t \approx 0.64$, $s \approx 1.2$ (d) $0 \le t \le 0.64$

(e) speeding up when $0 \leq t < 0.36$ and $0.64 < t < 1.1$, otherwise slowing down **(f)** maximum speed ≈ 1.05 when $t \approx 1.10$

69. $x \approx -2.11491, 0.25410, 1.86081$

71. $x \approx -1.165373043$

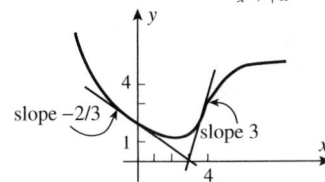

73. 249×10^6 km

75. **(a)** yes, $c = 0$ **(b)** no
(c) yes, $c = \sqrt{\pi/2}$

77. use Rolle's Theorem

▶ **Chapter 4 Making Connections (Page 314)**

Where correct answers to a Making Connections exercise may vary, no answer is listed. Sample answers for these questions are available on the Book Companion Site.

1. **(a)** no zeros **(b)** one **(c)** $\lim_{x \to +\infty} g'(x) = 0$

slope $-2/3$ / slope 3

2. **(a)** $(-2.2, 4)$, $(2, 1.2)$, $(4.2, 3)$
(b) critical numbers at $x = -5.1, -2, 0.2, 2$; local min at $x = -5.1, 2$; local max at $x = -2$; no extrema at $x = 0.2$; $f''(1) \approx -1.2$

3. $x = -4, 5$ 4. **(d)** $f(c) = 0$

6. **(a)** route (i): 10 s; route (iv): 10 s
(b) $2 \leq x \leq 5$; $\dfrac{4\sqrt{10}}{2.1} + \dfrac{5}{0.7} \approx 13.166$ s
(c) $0 \leq x \leq 2$; 10 s
(d) route (i) or (iv); 10 s

▶ **Exercise Set 5.1 (Page 321)**

1.
n	2	5	10	50	100
A_n	0.853553	0.749739	0.710509	0.676095	0.671463

3.
n	2	5	10	50	100
A_n	1.57080	1.93376	1.98352	1.99935	1.99984

5.
n	2	5	10	50	100
A_n	0.583333	0.645635	0.668771	0.688172	0.690653

7.
n	2	5	10	50	100
A_n	0.433013	0.659262	0.726130	0.774567	0.780106

9.
n	2	5	10	50	100
A_n	3.71828	2.85174	2.59327	2.39772	2.37398

11.
n	2	5	10	50	100
A_n	1.04720	0.75089	0.65781	0.58730	0.57894

13. $3(x-1)$ 15. $x(x+2)$ 17. $(x+3)(x-1)$

Responses to True–False questions may be abridged to save space.

19. False; the limit would be the area of the circle 4π.

21. True; this is the basis of the antiderivative method.

23. area $= A(6) - A(3)$ 27. $f(x) = 2x$; $a = 2$

▶ **Exercise Set 5.2 (Page 330)**

1. **(a)** $\displaystyle\int \frac{x}{\sqrt{1+x^2}}\,dx = \sqrt{1+x^2} + C$

(b) $\displaystyle\int (x+1)e^x\,dx = xe^x + C$

5. $\dfrac{d}{dx}\left[\sqrt{x^3+5}\right] = \dfrac{3x^2}{2\sqrt{x^3+5}}$, so $\displaystyle\int \dfrac{3x^2}{2\sqrt{x^3+5}}\,dx = \sqrt{x^3+5} + C$.

7. $\dfrac{d}{dx}[\sin(2\sqrt{x})] = \dfrac{\cos(2\sqrt{x})}{\sqrt{x}}$, so $\displaystyle\int \dfrac{\cos(2\sqrt{x})}{\sqrt{x}}\,dx = \sin(2\sqrt{x}) + C$.

9. **(a)** $(x^9/9) + C$ **(b)** $\frac{7}{12}x^{12/7} + C$ **(c)** $\frac{2}{9}x^{9/2} + C$

11. $\dfrac{5}{2}x^2 - \dfrac{1}{6x^4} + C$ 13. $-\dfrac{1}{2}x^{-2} - \dfrac{12}{5}x^{5/4} + \dfrac{8}{3}x^3 + C$

15. $(x^2/2) + (x^5/5) + C$ 17. $3x^{4/3} - \frac{12}{7}x^{7/3} + \frac{3}{10}x^{10/3} + C$

19. $\dfrac{x^2}{2} - \dfrac{2}{x} + \dfrac{1}{3x^3} + C$ 21. $2\ln|x| + 3e^x + C$

23. $-3\cos x - 2\tan x + C$ 25. $\tan x + \sec x + C$

27. $\tan\theta + C$ 29. $\sec x + C$ 31. $\theta - \cos\theta + C$

33. $\frac{1}{2}\sin^{-1}x - 3\tan^{-1}x + C$ 35. $\tan x - \sec x + C$

Responses to True–False questions may be abridged to save space.

37. True; this is Equations (1) and (2).

39. False; the initial condition is not satisfied since $y(0) = 2$.

41.

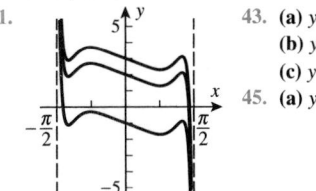

43. **(a)** $y(x) = \frac{3}{4}x^{4/3} + \frac{5}{4}$
(b) $y = -\cos t + t + 1 - \pi/3$
(c) $y(x) = \frac{2}{3}x^{3/2} + 2x^{1/2} - \frac{8}{3}$

45. **(a)** $y = 4e^x - 3$ **(b)** $y = \ln|t| + 5$

47. $s(t) = 16t^2 + 20$ 49. $s(t) = 2t^{3/2} - 15$

51. $f(x) = \frac{4}{15}x^{5/2} + C_1 x + C_2$ 53. $y = x^2 + x - 6$

55. $f(x) = \cos x + 1$ 57. $y = x^3 - 6x + 7$

59. **(a)** **(b)** **(c)** $f(x) = \dfrac{x^2}{2} - 1$

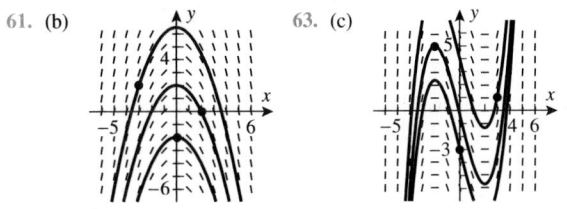

61. **(b)** 63. **(c)**

67. **(b)** $\pi/2$ 69. $\tan x - x + C$

71. **(a)** $\frac{1}{2}(x - \sin x) + C$ **(b)** $\frac{1}{2}(x + \sin x) + C$

73. $v = \dfrac{1087}{\sqrt{273}}T^{1/2}$ ft/s

▶ **Exercise Set 5.3 (Page 338)**

1. **(a)** $\dfrac{(x^2+1)^{24}}{24} + C$ **(b)** $-\dfrac{\cos^4 x}{4} + C$

3. **(a)** $\frac{1}{4}\tan(4x + 1) + C$ **(b)** $\frac{1}{6}(1 + 2y^2)^{3/2} + C$

5. **(a)** $-\frac{1}{2}\cot^2 x + C$ **(b)** $\frac{1}{10}(1 + \sin t)^{10} + C$

7. **(a)** $\frac{2}{7}(1 + x)^{7/2} - \frac{4}{5}(1 + x)^{5/2} + \frac{2}{3}(1 + x)^{3/2} + C$
(b) $-\cot(\sin x) + C$

9. **(a)** $\ln|\ln x| + C$ **(b)** $-\frac{1}{5}e^{-5x} + C$

11. (a) $\frac{1}{3}\tan^{-1}(x^3) + C$ (b) $\sin^{-1}(\ln x) + C$

15. $\frac{1}{40}(4x - 3)^{10} + C$ 17. $-\frac{1}{7}\cos 7x + C$ 19. $\frac{1}{4}\sec 4x + C$

21. $\frac{1}{2}e^{2x} + C$ 23. $\frac{1}{2}\sin^{-1}(2x) + C$ 25. $\frac{1}{21}(7t^2 + 12)^{3/2} + C$

27. $\dfrac{3}{2(1 - 2x)^2} + C$ 29. $-\dfrac{1}{40(5x^4 + 2)^2} + C$ 31. $e^{\sin x} + C$

33. $-\frac{1}{6}e^{-2x^3} + C$ 35. $\tan^{-1} e^x + C$ 37. $\frac{1}{5}\cos(5/x) + C$

39. $-\frac{1}{15}\cos^5 3t + C$ 41. $\frac{1}{2}\tan(x^2) + C$ 43. $-\frac{1}{6}(2 - \sin 4\theta)^{3/2} + C$

45. $\sin^{-1}(\tan x) + C$ 47. $\frac{1}{6}\sec^3 2x + C$ 49. $-e^{-x} + C$

51. $-e^{-2\sqrt{x}} + C$ 53. $\frac{1}{6}(2y + 1)^{3/2} - \frac{1}{2}(2y + 1)^{1/2} + C$

55. $-\frac{1}{2}\cos 2\theta + \frac{1}{6}\cos^3 2\theta + C$ 57. $t + \ln|t| + C$

59. $\int [\ln(e^x) + \ln(e^{-x})]\,dx = C$

61. (a) $\sin^{-1}\left(\frac{1}{3}x\right) + C$ (b) $\frac{1}{\sqrt{5}}\tan^{-1}\left(\frac{x}{\sqrt{5}}\right) + C$

   (c) $\dfrac{1}{\sqrt{\pi}}\sec^{-1}\left(\dfrac{x}{\sqrt{\pi}}\right) + C$

63. $\dfrac{1}{b}\dfrac{(a + bx)^{n+1}}{n + 1} + C$ 65. $\dfrac{1}{b(n + 1)}\sin^{n+1}(a + bx) + C$

67. (a) $\frac{1}{2}\sin^2 x + C_1$; $-\frac{1}{2}\cos^2 x + C_2$ (b) They differ by a constant.

69. $\frac{2}{15}(5x + 1)^{3/2} - \frac{158}{15}$ 71. $y = -\frac{1}{2}e^{2t} + \frac{13}{2}$

73. (a) $\sqrt{x^2 + 1} + C$ 75. $f(x) = \frac{2}{9}(3x + 1)^{3/2} + \frac{7}{9}$

(b)

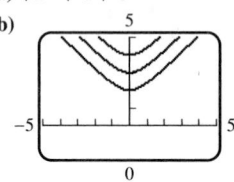

▶ **Exercise Set 5.4 (Page 350)**

1. (a) 36 (b) 55 (c) 40 (d) 6 (e) 11 (f) 0 3. $\sum_{k=1}^{10} k$ 5. $\sum_{k=1}^{10} 2k$

7. $\sum_{k=1}^{6}(-1)^{k+1}(2k - 1)$ 9. (a) $\sum_{k=1}^{50} 2k$ (b) $\sum_{k=1}^{50}(2k - 1)$ 11. 5050

13. 2870 15. 214,365 17. $\frac{3}{2}(n + 1)$ 19. $\frac{1}{4}(n - 1)^2$

Responses to True–False questions may be abridged to save space.

21. True; by parts (a) and (c) of Theorem 5.4.2.

23. False; consider $[a, b] = [-1, 0]$.

25. (a) $\left(2 + \frac{3}{n}\right)^4 \cdot \frac{3}{n}, \left(2 + \frac{6}{n}\right)^4 \cdot \frac{3}{n}, \left(2 + \frac{9}{n}\right)^4 \cdot \frac{3}{n}$,

   $\left(2 + \frac{3(n - 1)}{n}\right)^4 \cdot \frac{3}{n}, (2 + 3)^4 \cdot \frac{3}{n}$ (b) $\sum_{k=0}^{n-1}\left(2 + k \cdot \frac{3}{n}\right)^4 \frac{3}{n}$

27. (a) 46 (b) 52 (c) 58 29. (a) $\frac{\pi}{4}$ (b) 0 (c) $-\frac{\pi}{4}$

31. (a) 0.7188, 0.7058, 0.6982 (b) 0.6688, 0.6808, 0.6882
   (c) 0.6928, 0.6931, 0.6931

33. (a) 4.8841, 5.1156, 5.2488 (b) 5.6841, 5.5156, 5.4088
   (c) 5.3471, 5.3384, 5.3346

35. $\frac{15}{4}$ 37. 18 39. 320 41. $\frac{15}{4}$ 43. 18 45. 16 47. $\frac{1}{3}$ 49. 0

51. $\frac{2}{3}$ 53. (b) $\frac{1}{4}(b^4 - a^4)$

55. $\dfrac{n^2 + 2n}{4}$ if n is even; $\dfrac{(n + 1)^2}{4}$ if n is odd 57. $3^{17} - 3^4$ 59. $-\frac{399}{400}$

61. (b) $\frac{1}{2}$ 65. (a) yes (b) yes

▶ **Exercise Set 5.5 (Page 360)**

1. (a) $\frac{71}{6}$ (b) 2 3. (a) $-\frac{117}{16}$ (b) 3 5. $\displaystyle\int_{-1}^{2} x^2\,dx$

7. $\displaystyle\int_{-3}^{3} 4x(1 - 3x)\,dx$

9. (a) $\displaystyle\lim_{\max \Delta x_k \to 0} \sum_{k=1}^{n} 2x_k^* \Delta x_k$; $a = 1, b = 2$

   (b) $\displaystyle\lim_{\max \Delta x_k \to 0} \sum_{k=1}^{n} \frac{x_k^*}{x_k^* + 1}\Delta x_k$; $a = 0, b = 1$

13. (a) $A = \frac{9}{2}$ (b) $-A = -\frac{3}{2}$

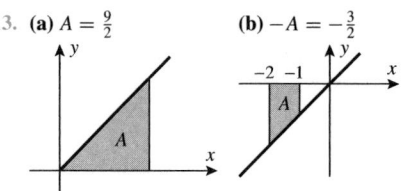

(c) $-A_1 + A_2 = \frac{15}{2}$ (d) $-A_1 + A_2 = 0$

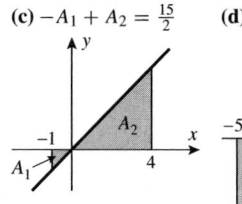 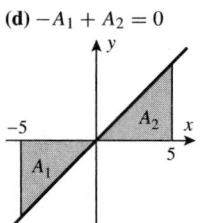

15. (a) $A = 10$ (b) $A_1 - A_2 = 0$ by symmetry

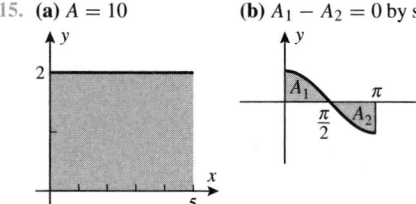

(c) $A_1 + A_2 = \frac{13}{2}$ (d) $\pi/2$ 17. (a) 2
   (b) 4
   (c) 10
   (d) 10

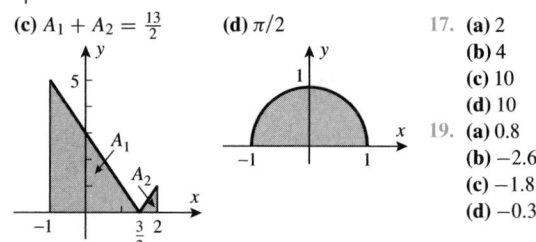

19. (a) 0.8
   (b) -2.6
   (c) -1.8
   (d) -0.3

21. -1 23. 3 25. -4 27. $(1 + \pi)/2$

Responses to True–False questions may be abridged to save space.

29. False; see Theorem 5.5.8(a).

31. False; consider $f(x) = x - 2$ on $[0, 3]$.

33. (a) negative (b) positive 37. $\frac{25}{2}\pi$ 39. $\frac{5}{2}$

45. (a) integrable (b) integrable (c) not integrable (d) integrable

▶ **Exercise Set 5.6 (Page 373)**

1. (a) $\int_0^2 (2 - x)\,dx = 2$ (b) $\int_{-1}^{1} 2\,dx = 4$ (c) $\int_1^3 (x + 1)\,dx = 6$

3. (a) $x^* = f(x^*) = 1$ (b) x^* is any point in $[-1, 1]$, $f(x^*) = 2$

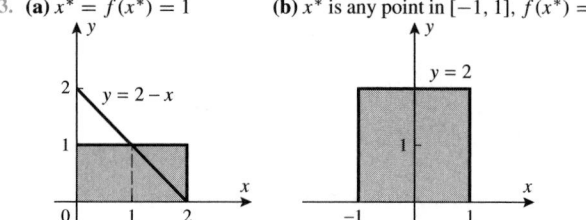

(c) $x^* = 2$, $f(x^*) = 3$

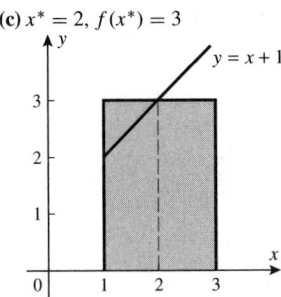

5. $\frac{65}{4}$ 7. 14   9. $\frac{3}{2}$ 11. (a) $\frac{4}{3}$ (b) -7 13. 48   15. 3   17. $\frac{845}{5}$
19. 0   21. $\sqrt{2}$ 23. $5e^3 - 10$ 25. $\pi/4$ 27. $\pi/12$ 29. -12
31. (a) 5/2   (b) $2 - \frac{\sqrt{2}}{2}$ 33. (a) $e + (1/e) - 2$ (b) 1

35. (a) $\frac{17}{6}$ (b) $F(x) = \begin{cases} \dfrac{x^2}{2}, & x \le 1 \\[2mm] \dfrac{x^3}{3} + \dfrac{1}{6}, & x > 1 \end{cases}$

Responses to True–False questions may be abridged to save space.
37. False; since $|x|$ is continuous, it has an antiderivative.
39. True; by the Fundamental Theorem of Calculus.
41. 0.6659; $\frac{2}{3}$ 43. 3.1060; $\dfrac{1}{\tan 1}$ 45. 12   47. $\frac{9}{2}$
49. area $= 1$ 51. area $= e + e^{-1} - 2$

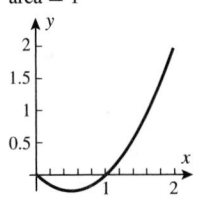   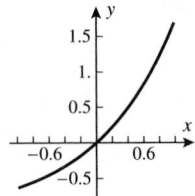

53. (b) degree mode, 0.93
55. (a) change in height from age 0 to age 10 years; inches
    (b) change in radius from time $t = 1$ s to time $t = 2$ s; centimeters
    (c) difference between speed of sound at $100°\,$F and at $32°\,$F; feet per
    second   (d) change in position from time t_1 to time t_2; centimeters
57. (a) $3x^2 - 3$ 59. (a) $\sin(x^2)$ (b) $e^{\sqrt{x}}$ 61. $-x \sec x$
63. (a) 0   (b) 5   (c) $\frac{4}{5}$
65. (a) $x = 3$ (b) increasing on $[3, +\infty)$, decreasing on $(-\infty, 3]$
    (c) concave up on $(-1, 7)$, concave down on $(-\infty, -1)$ and $(7, +\infty)$
67. (a) $(0, +\infty)$ (b) $x = 1$
69. (a) 120 gal   (b) 420 gal   (c) 2076.36 gal   71. 1

▶ **Exercise Set 5.7 (Page 382)**

1. (a) displacement $= 3$; distance $= 3$
   (b) displacement $= -3$; distance $= 3$
   (c) displacement $= -\frac{1}{2}$; distance $= \frac{3}{2}$
   (d) displacement $= \frac{3}{2}$; distance $= 2$
3. (a) 35.3 m/s   (b) 51.4 m/s   5. (a) $t^3 - t^2 + 1$ (b) $4t + 3 - \frac{1}{3}\sin 3t$
7. (a) $\frac{3}{2}t^2 + t - 4$ (b) $t + 1 - \ln t$
9. (a) displacement $= 1$ m; distance $= 1$ m
   (b) displacement $= -1$ m; distance $= 3$ m
11. (a) displacement $= \frac{9}{4}$ m; distance $= \frac{11}{4}$ m
    (b) displacement $= 2\sqrt{3} - 6$ m; distance $= 6 - 2\sqrt{3}$ m
13. 4, 13/3   15. 296/27, 296/27
17. (a) $s = 2/\pi$, $v = 1$, $|v| = 1$, $a = 0$
    (b) $s = \frac{1}{2}$, $v = -\frac{3}{2}$, $|v| = \frac{3}{2}$, $a = -3$ 19. $t \approx 1.27$ s

21.

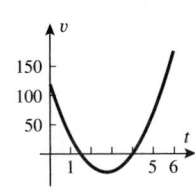   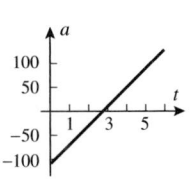

Responses to True–False questions may be abridged to save space.
23. True; if $a(t) = a_0$, then $v(t) = a_0 t + v_0$.
25. False; consider $v(t) = \sin t$ on $[0, 2\pi]$.
27. (a) 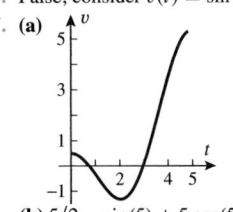   29. (a)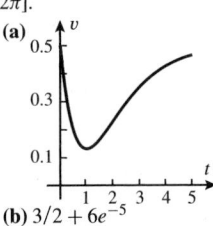

   (b) $5/2 - \sin(5) + 5\cos(5)$ (b) $3/2 + 6e^{-5}$

31. (a)   (b)

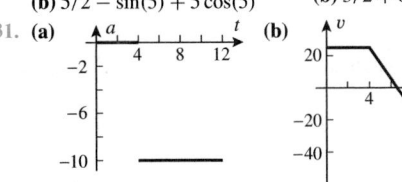

   (c) 120 cm, -20 cm   (d) 131.25 cm at $t = 6.5$ s
33. (a) $-\frac{121}{5}$ ft/s^2 (b) $\frac{70}{33}$ s   (c) $\frac{60}{11}$ s   35. 50 s, 5000 ft
37. (a) 16 ft/s, -48 ft/s   (b) 196 ft   (c) 112 ft/s
39. (a) 1 s   (b) $\frac{1}{2}$ s   41. (a) 6.122 s   (b) 183.7 m   (c) 6.122 s   (d) 60 m/s
43. (a) 5 s   (b) 272.5 m   (c) 10 s   (d) -49 m/s
    (e) 12.46 s   (f) 73.1 m/s   45. 113.42 ft/s

▶ **Exercise Set 5.8 (Page 388)**

1. (a) 4   (c) 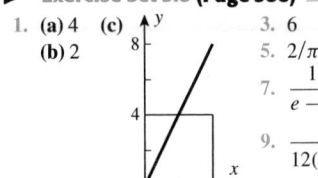   3. 6
   (b) 2   5. $2/\pi$
                                      7. $\dfrac{1}{e - 1}$
                                      9. $\dfrac{\pi}{12(\sqrt{3} - 1)}$

11. $\dfrac{1 - e^{-8}}{8}$ 13. (a) 5.28   (b) 4.305   (c) 4   15. (a) $-\frac{1}{6}$ (b) $\frac{1}{2}$
Responses to True–False questions may be abridged to save space.
19. False; let $g(x) = \cos x$; $f(x) = 0$ on $[0, 3\pi/2]$.
21. True; see Theorem 5.5.4(b).
23. (a) $\frac{263}{4}$ (b) 31   25. 1404π lb   27. 97 cars/min   31. 27

▶ **Exercise Set 5.9 (Page 394)**

1. (a) $\frac{1}{2} \int_1^5 u^3\, du$ (b) $\frac{3}{2} \int_9^{25} \sqrt{u}\, du$ (c) $\frac{1}{\pi} \int_{-\pi/2}^{\pi/2} \cos u\, du$
   (d) $\int_1^2 (u + 1)u^5\, du$ 3. (a) $\frac{1}{2} \int_{-1}^1 e^u\, du$ (b) $\int_1^2 u\, du$
5. 10   7. 0   9. $\frac{1192}{15}$ 11. $8 - (4\sqrt{2})$ 13. $-\frac{1}{48}$ 15. $\ln \frac{21}{13}$
17. $\pi/6$ 19. $25\pi/6$ 21. $\pi/8$ 23. $2/\pi$ m   25. 6   27. $\pi/18$
29. 2   31. $\frac{2}{3}(\sqrt{10} - 2\sqrt{2})$ 33. $2(\sqrt{7} - \sqrt{3})$ 35. 1   37. 0
39. $(\sqrt{3} - 1)/3$ 41. $\frac{106}{405}$ 43. $(\ln 3)/2$ 45. $\pi/(6\sqrt{3})$ 47. $\pi/9$
49. $\frac{23}{4480}$ 51. (a) $\frac{5}{3}$ (b) $\frac{5}{3}$ (c) $-\frac{1}{2}$ 55. $\approx 48{,}233{,}500{,}000$
57. (a) 0.45   (b) 0.461   59. $(\ln 7)/2$ 61. (a) $2/\pi$
65. (b) $\frac{3}{2}$ (c) $\pi/4$

▶ **Exercise Set 5.10 (Page 406)**

1. (a) 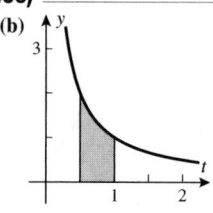 (b)

(c)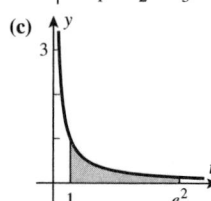

3. (a) 7 (b) −5 (c) −3 (d) 6

5. 1.603210678;

   magnitude of error is < 0.0063

7. (a) $x^{-1}, x > 0$ (b) $x^2, x \neq 0$ (c) $-x^2, -\infty < x < +\infty$
   (d) $-x, -\infty < x < +\infty$ (e) $x^3, x > 0$ (f) $\ln x + x, x > 0$
   (g) $x - \sqrt[3]{x}, -\infty < x < +\infty$ (h) $e^x/x, x > 0$

9. (a) $e^{\pi \ln 3}$ (b) $e^{\sqrt{2} \ln 2}$ 11. (a) $\sqrt{e}$ (b) e^2 13. $x^2 - x$

15. (a) $3/x$ (b) 1 17. (a) 0 (b) 0 (c) 1

Responses to True–False questions may be abridged to save space.

19. True; both equal $-\ln a$.

21. False; the integrand is unbounded on $[-1, e]$ and thus the integrand is undefined.

23. (a) $2x^3\sqrt{1+x^2}$ (b) $-\frac{2}{3}(x^2+1)^{3/2} + \frac{2}{5}(x^2+1)^{5/2} - \frac{4\sqrt{2}}{15}$

25. (a) $-\cos(x^3)$ (b) $-\tan^2 x$ 27. $-3\frac{3x-1}{9x^2+1} + 2x\frac{x^2-1}{x^4+1}$

29. (a) $3x^2 \sin^2(x^3) - 2x \sin^2(x^2)$ (b) $\frac{2}{1-x^2}$

31. (a) $F(0) = 0$, $F(3) = 0$, $F(5) = 6$, $F(7) = 6$, $F(10) = 3$
    (b) increasing on $\left[\frac{3}{2}, 6\right]$ and $\left[\frac{37}{4}, 10\right]$, decreasing on $\left[0, \frac{3}{2}\right]$ and $\left[6, \frac{37}{4}\right]$
    (c) maximum $\frac{15}{2}$ at $x = 6$, minimum $-\frac{9}{4}$ at $x = \frac{3}{2}$
    (d)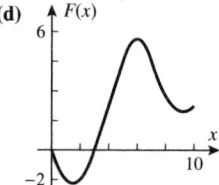

33. $F(x) = \begin{cases} (1-x^2)/2, & x < 0 \\ (1+x^2)/2, & x \geq 0 \end{cases}$ 35. $y(x) = x^2 + \ln x + 1$

37. $y(x) = \tan x + \cos x - (\sqrt{2}/2)$

39. $P(x) = P_0 + \int_0^x r(t)\,dt$ individuals 41. I is the derivative of II.

43. (a) $t = 3$ (b) $t = 1, 5$
    (c) $t = 5$ (d) $t = 3$
    (e) F is concave up on $\left(0, \frac{1}{2}\right)$ and $(2, 4)$,
    concave down on $\left(\frac{1}{2}, 2\right)$ and $(4, 5)$.

(f)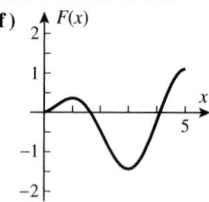

45. (a) relative maxima at $x = \pm\sqrt{4k+1}, k = 0, 1, \ldots$; relative minima
    at $x = \pm\sqrt{4k-1}, k = 1, 2, \ldots$
    (b) $x = \pm\sqrt{2k}, k = 1, 2, \ldots$, and at $x = 0$

47. $f(x) = 2e^{2x}, a = \ln 2$ 49. 0.06

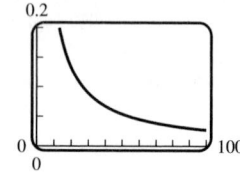

▶ **Chapter 5 Review Exercises (Page 408)**

1. $-\frac{1}{4x^2} + \frac{8}{3}x^{3/2} + C$ 3. $-4\cos x + 2\sin x + C$

5. $3x^{1/3} - 5e^x + C$ 7. $\tan^{-1} x + 2\sin^{-1} x + C$

9. (a) $y(x) = 2\sqrt{x} - \frac{2}{3}x^{3/2} - \frac{4}{3}$ (b) $y(x) = \sin x - 5e^x + 5$
   (c) $y(x) = \frac{5}{4} + \frac{3}{4}x^{4/3}$ (d) $y(x) = \frac{1}{2}e^{x^2} - \frac{1}{2}$

13. $\frac{1}{2}\sec^{-1}(x^2 - 1) + C$ 15. $\frac{1}{3}\sqrt{5 + 2\sin 3x} + C$

17. $-\frac{1}{3a}\frac{1}{ax^3+b} + C$

19. (a) $\sum_{k=0}^{14}(k+4)(k+1)$ (b) $\sum_{k=5}^{19}(k-1)(k-4)$

21. $\frac{32}{3}$ 23. 0.35122, 0.42054, 0.38650

27. (a) $\frac{3}{4}$ (b) $-\frac{3}{2}$ (c) $-\frac{35}{4}$ (d) −2 (e) not enough information
    (f) not enough information

29. (a) $2 + (\pi/2)$ (b) $\frac{1}{3}(10^{3/2} - 1) - \frac{9\pi}{4}$ (c) $\pi/8$

31. 48 33. $\frac{2}{3}$ 35. $\frac{3}{2} - \sec 1$ 37. $\frac{5}{2}$ 39. $\frac{52}{3}$ 41. $e^3 - e$

43. area $= \frac{1}{6}$ 45. $\frac{22}{3}$

47. (a) $x^3 + 1$

49. e^{x^2}

51. $|x - 1|$

53. $\frac{\cos x}{1 + \sin^3 x}$

57. (b) $\frac{\pi}{2}$; $\tan^{-1} x + \tan^{-1}\left(\frac{1}{x}\right) = \frac{\pi}{2}$

59. (a) $F(x)$ is 0 if $x = 1$, positive if $x > 1$, and negative if $x < 1$.
    (b) $F(x)$ is 0 if $x = -1$, positive if $-1 < x \leq 2$,
    and negative if $-2 \leq x < -1$.

61. (a) $\frac{4}{3}$ (b) $e - 1$ 63. $\frac{3}{10}$ 67. $\frac{1}{4}t^4 - \frac{2}{3}t^3 + t + 1$

69. $t^2 - 3t + 7$ 71. 12 m, 20 m 73. $\frac{1}{3}$ m, $\frac{10}{3} - 2\sqrt{2}$ m

75. displacement $= -6$ m; distance $= \frac{13}{2}$ m

77. (a) 2.2 s (b) 387.2 ft 79. $v_0/2$ ft/s 81. $\frac{121}{5}$ 83. $\frac{2}{3}$ 85. 0

87. $2 - 2/\sqrt{e}$ 89. (a) e^2 (b) $e^{1/3}$

▶ **Chapter 5 Making Connections (Page 412)**

Where correct answers to a Making Connections exercise may vary, no
answer is listed. Sample answers for these questions are available on the
Book Companion Site.

1. (b) $b^2 - a^2$ 2. 16/3 3. 12

4. (a) the sum for f is m times that for g
   (b) $m\int_0^1 g(x)\,dx = \int_0^m f(x)\,du$

5. (a) they are equal (b) $\int_2^3 g(x)\,dx = \int_4^9 f(u)\,du$

▶ **Exercise Set 6.1 (Page 419)**

1. 9/2 3. 1 5. (a) 4/3 (b) 4/3 7. 49/192 9. 1/2 11. $\sqrt{2}$

13. $\frac{1}{2}$ 15. $\pi - 1$ 17. 24 19. 37/12 21. $4\sqrt{2}$ 23. $\frac{1}{2}$

25. $\ln 2 - \frac{1}{2}$

Responses to True–False questions may be abridged to save space.

27. True; use area Formula (1) with $f(x) = g(x) + c$.

29. True; the integrand must assume both positive and negative values.
    By the Intermediate-Value Theorem, the integrand must be equal to 0
    somewhere in $[a, b]$.

31. $k \approx 0.9973$ 33. 9152/105 35. $9/\sqrt[3]{4}$

37. (a) 4/3 (b) $m = 2 - \sqrt[3]{4}$ 39. 1.180898334

41. 0.4814, 2.3639, 1.1897 43. 2.54270

45. racer 1's lead over racer 2 at time $t = 0$

47. **(a)** (area above graph of g and below graph of f) minus (area above graph of f and below graph of g)
   (b) area between graphs of f and g 49. $a^2/6$

▶ **Exercise Set 6.2 (Page 428)** _____

1. 8π 3. $13\pi/6$ 5. $(1 - \sqrt{2}/2)\pi$ 7. 8π 9. $32/5$ 11. $256\pi/3$
13. $2048\pi/15$ 15. 4π 17. $\pi^2/4$ 19. $3/5$ 21. 2π
23. $72\pi/5$ 25. $\dfrac{\pi}{2}(e^2 - 1)$

Responses to True–False questions may be abridged to save space.

27. False; see the solids associated with Exercises 9 and 10.
29. False; see Example 2 where the cross-sectional area is a linear function of x.

31. $4\pi ab^2/3$ 33. π 35. $\int_a^b \pi[f(x) - k]^2 \, dx$ 37. **(b)** $40\pi/3$
39. $648\pi/5$ 41. $\pi/2$ 43. $\pi/15$ 45. $40{,}000\pi$ ft^3 47. $1/30$
49. **(a)** $2\pi/3$ **(b)** $16/3$ **(c)** $4\sqrt{3}/3$ 51. 0.710172176 53. π
57. **(b)** left ≈ 11.157; right ≈ 11.771; $V \approx$ average $= 11.464$ cm^3
59. $V = \begin{cases} 3\pi h^2, & 0 \le h < 2 \\ \frac{1}{3}\pi(12h^2 - h^3 - 4), & 2 \le h \le 4 \end{cases}$ 61. $\frac{2}{3}r^3 \tan\theta$ 63. $16r^3/3$

▶ **Exercise Set 6.3 (Page 436)** _____

1. $15\pi/2$ 3. $\pi/3$ 5. $2\pi/5$ 7. 4π 9. $20\pi/3$ 11. $\pi \ln 2$ 13. $\pi/2$
15. $\pi/5$

Responses to True–False questions may be abridged to save space.

17. True; this is a restatement of Formula (1).
19. True; see Formula (2).
21. $2\pi e^2$ 23. 1.73680 25. **(a)** $7\pi/30$ **(b)** easier
27. **(a)** $\int_0^1 2\pi(1 - x)x \, dx$ **(b)** $\int_0^1 2\pi(1 + y)(1 - y) \, dy$
29. $7\pi/4$ 31. $\pi r^2 h/3$ 33. $V = \frac{4}{3}\pi(L/2)^3$ 35. $b = 1$

▶ **Exercise Set 6.4 (Page 441)** _____

1. $L = \sqrt{5}$ 3. $(85\sqrt{85} - 8)/243$ 5. $\frac{1}{27}(80\sqrt{10} - 13\sqrt{13})$ 7. $\frac{17}{6}$

Responses to True–False questions may be abridged to save space.

9. False; f' is undefined at the endpoints ± 1.
11. True; if $f(x) = mx + c$ over $[a, b]$, then $L = \sqrt{1 + m^2}(b - a)$, which is equal to the given sum.
13. $L = \ln(1 + \sqrt{2})$
15. **(a)**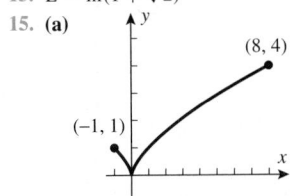
   (b) dy/dx does not exist at $x = 0$.
   (c) $L = (13\sqrt{13} + 80\sqrt{10} - 16)/27$

17. **(a)** They are mirror images across the line $y = x$.   **(b)** $\int_{1/2}^2 \sqrt{1 + 4x^2} \, dx, \int_{1/4}^4 \sqrt{1 + \frac{1}{4x}} \, dx$,
   $x = \sqrt{u}$ transforms the first integral into the second.
   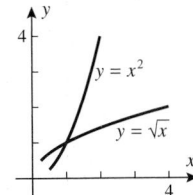
   (c) $\int_{1/4}^4 \sqrt{1 + \frac{1}{4y}} \, dy, \int_{1/2}^2 \sqrt{1 + 4y^2} \, dy$
   (d) $4.0724, 4.0716$
   (e) The first: Both are underestimates of the arc length, so the larger one is more accurate.
   (f) $4.0724, 4.0662$ **(g)** 4.0729

19. **(a)** They are mirror images across the line $y = x$.   **(b)** $\int_0^{\pi/3} \sqrt{1 + \sec^4 x} \, dx$,
   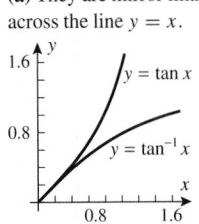
   $\int_0^{\sqrt{3}} \sqrt{1 + \frac{1}{(1 + x^2)^2}} \, dx$,
   $x = \tan^{-1} u$ transforms the first integral into the second.
   (c) $\int_0^{\sqrt{3}} \sqrt{1 + \frac{1}{(1 + y^2)^2}} \, dy$,
   $\int_0^{\pi/3} \sqrt{1 + \sec^4 y} \, dy$
   (d) $2.0566, 2.0567$

   (e) The second: Both are underestimates of the arc length, so the larger one is more accurate.   **(f)** $2.0509, 2.0571$ **(g)** 2.0570
23. $k = 1.83$ 25. 196.31 yards   27. $(2\sqrt{2} - 1)/3$
29. π 31. $L = \sqrt{2}(e^{\pi/2} - 1)$ 33. **(b)** 9.69 **(c)** 5.16 cm

▶ **Exercise Set 6.5 (Page 447)** _____

1. $35\pi\sqrt{2}$ 3. 8π 5. $40\pi\sqrt{82}$ 7. 24π 9. $16\pi/9$
11. $16{,}911\pi/1024$ 13. $2\pi[\sqrt{2} + \ln(\sqrt{2} + 1)]$ 15. $S \approx 22.94$

Responses to True–False questions may be abridged to save space.

17. True; use Formula (1) with $r_1 = 0, r_2 = r, l = \sqrt{r^2 + h^2}$.
19. True; the sum telescopes to the surface area of a cylinder.
21. 14.39 23. $S = \int_a^b 2\pi[f(x) + k]\sqrt{1 + [f'(x)]^2} \, dx$
33. $\dfrac{8}{3}\pi(17\sqrt{17} - 1)$ 35. $\dfrac{\pi}{24}(17\sqrt{17} - 1)$

▶ **Exercise Set 6.6 (Page 456)** _____

1. 7.5 ft·lb   3. $d = 7/4$ 5. 100 ft·lb   7. 160 J   9. 20 lb/ft

Responses to True–False questions may be abridged to save space.

11. False; the work done is the same.
13. True; joules   15. $47{,}385\pi$ ft·lb   17. $261{,}600$ J
19. **(a)** $926{,}640$ ft·lb   **(b)** hp of motor $= 0.468$ 21. $75{,}000$ ft·lb
23. $120{,}000$ ft·tons   25. **(a)** $2{,}400{,}000{,}000/x^2$ lb
   (b) $(9.6 \times 10^{10})/(x + 4000)^2$ lb   **(c)** 2.5344×10^{10} ft·lb
27. $v_f = 100$ m/s
29. **(a)** decreases of 4.5×10^{14} J   **(b)** ≈ 0.107 **(c)** ≈ 8.24 bombs

▶ **Exercise Set 6.7 (Page 465)** _____

1. **(a)** positive: m_2 is at the fulcrum, so it can be ignored; masses m_1 and m_3 are equidistant from position 5, but $m_1 < m_3$, so the beam will rotate clockwise.   **(b)** The fulcrum should be placed $\frac{50}{7}$ units to the right of m_1.
3. $\left(\frac{1}{2}, \frac{1}{2}\right)$ 5. $\left(1, \frac{1}{2}\right)$ 7. $\left(\frac{2}{3}, \frac{1}{3}\right)$ 9. $\left(\frac{5}{14}, \frac{38}{35}\right)$ 11. $\left(\frac{2}{3}, \frac{1}{3}\right)$
13. $\left(-\frac{1}{2}, 4\right)$ 15. $\left(\frac{1}{2}, \frac{8}{5}\right)$ 17. $\left(\frac{9}{20}, \frac{9}{20}\right)$ 19. $\left(\frac{49}{48}, \frac{7}{3} - \ln 2\right)$
23. $\frac{4}{3}; \left(\frac{3}{5}, \frac{3}{8}\right)$ 25. $3; \left(0, \frac{2}{3}\right)$ 27. $8; \left(\frac{\pi}{2}, \frac{\pi}{8}\right)$
29. $\ln 4 - 1; \left(\dfrac{4\ln 4 - 3}{4\ln 4 - 4}, \dfrac{(\ln 2)^2 + 1 - \ln 4}{\ln 4 - 1}\right)$

Responses to True–False questions may be abridged to save space.

31. True; use symmetry.   33. True; use symmetry.
35. $\left(\dfrac{2a}{3}, 0\right)$ 37. $(\bar{x}, \bar{y}) = \left(0, \dfrac{(a + 2b)c}{3(a + b)}\right)$
41. $2\pi^2 abk$ 43. $(a/3, b/3)$

▶ **Exercise Set 6.8 (Page 472)** _____

1. **(a)** $F = 31{,}200$ lb; $P = 312$ lb/ft^2
   (b) $F = 2{,}452{,}500$ N; $P = 98.1$ kPa
3. 499.2 lb   5. 8.175×10^5 N   7. $1{,}098{,}720$ N   9. yes
11. $\rho a^3/\sqrt{2}$ lb

Responses to True–False questions may be abridged to save space.

13. True; this is a consequence of inequalities (4).

15. False; by Equation (7) the force can be arbitrarily large for a fixed volume of water.

17. 63,648 lb   19. 9.81×10^9 N   21. (b) $80\rho_0$ lb/min

▶ **Exercise Set 6.9 (Page 482)**

1. (a) ≈ 10.0179 (b) ≈ 3.7622 (c) $15/17 \approx 0.8824$
   (d) ≈ -1.4436 (e) ≈ 1.7627 (f) ≈ 0.9730

3. (a) $\dfrac{4}{3}$ (b) $\dfrac{5}{4}$ (c) $\dfrac{312}{313}$ (d) $-\dfrac{63}{16}$

5.

	$\sinh x_0$	$\cosh x_0$	$\tanh x_0$	$\coth x_0$	$\operatorname{sech} x_0$	$\operatorname{csch} x_0$
(a)	2	$\sqrt{5}$	$2/\sqrt{5}$	$\sqrt{5}/2$	$1/\sqrt{5}$	$1/2$
(b)	3/4	5/4	3/5	5/3	4/5	4/3
(c)	4/3	5/3	4/5	5/4	3/5	3/4

9. $4\cosh(4x - 8)$ 11. $-\dfrac{1}{x}\operatorname{csch}^2(\ln x)$

13. $\dfrac{1}{x^2}\operatorname{csch}\left(\dfrac{1}{x}\right)\coth\left(\dfrac{1}{x}\right)$ 15. $\dfrac{2 + 5\cosh(5x)\sinh(5x)}{\sqrt{4x + \cosh^2(5x)}}$

17. $x^{5/2}\tanh(\sqrt{x})\operatorname{sech}^2(\sqrt{x}) + 3x^2\tanh^2(\sqrt{x})$

19. $\dfrac{1}{\sqrt{9 + x^2}}$ 21. $\dfrac{1}{(\cosh^{-1}x)\sqrt{x^2 - 1}}$ 23. $-\dfrac{(\tanh^{-1}x)^{-2}}{1 - x^2}$

25. $\dfrac{\sinh x}{|\sinh x|} = \begin{cases} 1, & x > 0 \\ -1, & x < 0 \end{cases}$ 27. $-\dfrac{e^x}{2x\sqrt{1 - x}} + e^x\operatorname{sech}^{-1}x$

29. $\frac{1}{7}\sinh^7 x + C$ 31. $\frac{2}{3}(\tanh x)^{3/2} + C$ 33. $\ln(\cosh x) + C$

35. $37/375$ 37. $\frac{1}{3}\sinh^{-1}3x + C$ 39. $-\operatorname{sech}^{-1}(e^x) + C$

41. $-\operatorname{csch}^{-1}|2x| + C$ 43. $\frac{1}{2}\ln 3$

Responses to True–False questions may be abridged to save space.

45. True; see Figure 6.9.1   47. True; $f(x) = \sinh x$

49. $16/9$ 51. 5π 53. $\frac{3}{4}$

55. (a) $+\infty$ (b) $-\infty$ (c) 1   (d) -1 (e) $+\infty$ (f) $+\infty$

63. $|u| < 1$: $\tanh^{-1}u + C$; $|u| > 1$: $\tanh^{-1}(1/u) + C$

65. (a) $\ln 2$ (b) $1/2$ 71. 405.9 ft

73. (a)

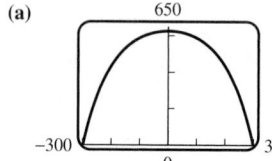

(b) 1480.2798 ft
(c) ± 283.6249 ft
(d) $82°$

75. (b) 14.44 m   (c) $15\ln 3 \approx 16.48$ m

▶ **Chapter 6 Review Exercises (Page 485)**

7. (a) $\int_a^b (f(x) - g(x))\,dx + \int_b^c (g(x) - f(x))\,dx + \int_c^d (f(x) - g(x))\,dx$ (b) 11/4

9. $4352\pi/105$ 11. $3/2 + \ln 4$ 13. 9   15. $\dfrac{\pi}{6}\left(65^{3/2} - 37^{3/2}\right)$

17. (a) $W = \frac{1}{16}$ J   (b) 5 m   19. $\left(\frac{8}{5}, 0\right)$

21. (a) $F = \int_0^1 \rho x 3\,dx$ N   (b) $F = \int_1^4 \rho(1 + x)2x\,dx$ lb/ft^2

(c) $F = \int_{-10}^0 9810|y|2\sqrt{\dfrac{125}{8}}(y + 10)\,dy$ N

▶ **Chapter 6 Making Connections (Page 487)**

Where correct answers to a Making Connections exercise may vary, no answer is listed. Sample answers for these questions are available on the Book Companion Site.

1. (a) πA_1 (b) $a = \dfrac{A_1}{2A_2}$ 2. 1,010,807 ft·lb   3. $\int_0^a 2\pi r f(r)\,dr$

▶ **Exercise Set 7.1 (Page 490)**

1. $-2(x - 2)^4 + C$ 3. $\frac{1}{2}\tan(x^2) + C$ 5. $-\frac{1}{3}\ln(2 + \cos 3x) + C$

7. $\cosh(e^x) + C$ 9. $e^{\tan x} + C$ 11. $-\frac{1}{30}\cos^6 5x + C$

13. $\ln(e^x + \sqrt{e^{2x} + 4}) + C$ 15. $2e^{\sqrt{x-1}} + C$ 17. $2\sinh\sqrt{x} + C$

19. $-\dfrac{2}{\ln 3}3^{-\sqrt{x}} + C$ 21. $\frac{1}{2}\coth\dfrac{2}{x} + C$ 23. $-\frac{1}{4}\ln\left|\dfrac{2 + e^{-x}}{2 - e^{-x}}\right| + C$

25. $\sin^{-1}(e^x) + C$ 27. $-\frac{1}{2}\cos(x^2) + C$ 29. $-\dfrac{1}{\ln 16}4^{-x^2} + C$

31. (a) $\frac{1}{2}\sin^2 x + C$ (b) $-\frac{1}{4}\cos 2x + C$

33. (b) $\ln\left|\tan\dfrac{x}{2}\right| + C$ (c) $\ln\left|\cot\left(\dfrac{\pi}{4} - \dfrac{x}{2}\right)\right| + C$

▶ **Exercise Set 7.2 (Page 498)**

1. $-e^{-2x}\left(\dfrac{x}{2} + \dfrac{1}{4}\right) + C$ 3. $x^2e^x - 2xe^x + 2e^x + C$

5. $-\frac{1}{3}x\cos 3x + \frac{1}{9}\sin 3x + C$ 7. $x^2\sin x + 2x\cos x - 2\sin x + C$

9. $\dfrac{x^2}{2}\ln x - \dfrac{x^2}{4} + C$ 11. $x(\ln x)^2 - 2x\ln x + 2x + C$

13. $x\ln(3x - 2) - x - \frac{2}{3}\ln(3x - 2) + C$ 15. $x\sin^{-1}x + \sqrt{1 - x^2} + C$

17. $x\tan^{-1}(3x) - \frac{1}{6}\ln(1 + 9x^2) + C$ 19. $\frac{1}{2}e^x(\sin x - \cos x) + C$

21. $(x/2)[\sin(\ln x) - \cos(\ln x)] + C$ 23. $x\tan x + \ln|\cos x| + C$

25. $\frac{1}{2}x^2e^{x^2} - \frac{1}{2}e^{x^2} + C$ 27. $\frac{1}{4}(3e^4 + 1)$ 29. $(2e^3 + 1)/9$

31. $3\ln 3 - 2$ 33. $\dfrac{5\pi}{6} - \sqrt{3} + 1$ 35. $-\pi/2$

37. $\dfrac{1}{3}\left(2\sqrt{3}\pi - \dfrac{\pi}{2} - 2 + \ln 2\right)$

Responses to True–False questions may be abridged to save space.

39. True; see the subsection "Guidelines for Integration by Parts."

41. False; e^x isn't a factor of the integrand.

43. $2(\sqrt{x} - 1)e^{\sqrt{x}} + C$ 47. $-(3x^2 + 5x + 7)e^{-x} + C$

49. $(4x^3 - 6x)\sin 2x - (2x^4 - 6x^2 + 3)\cos 2x + C$

51. $\dfrac{e^{ax}}{a^2 + b^2}(a\sin bx - b\cos bx) + C$ 53. (a) $\frac{1}{2}\sin^2 x + C$

55. (a) $A = 1$ (b) $V = \pi(e - 2)$ 57. $V = 2\pi^2$ 59. $\pi^3 - 6\pi$

61. (a) $-\frac{1}{4}\sin^3 x \cos x - \frac{3}{8}\sin x \cos x + \frac{3}{8}x + C$ (b) 8/15

65. (a) $\frac{1}{3}\tan^3 x - \tan x + x + C$ (b) $\frac{1}{3}\sec^2 x\tan x + \frac{2}{3}\tan x + C$
   (c) $x^3e^x - 3x^2e^x + 6xe^x - 6e^x + C$

69. $(x + 1)\ln(x + 1) - x + C$ 71. $\frac{1}{2}(x^2 + 1)\tan^{-1}x - \frac{1}{2}x + C$

▶ **Exercise Set 7.3 (Page 506)**

1. $-\frac{1}{4}\cos^4 x + C$ 3. $\dfrac{\theta}{2} - \dfrac{1}{20}\sin 10\theta + C$

5. $\dfrac{1}{3a}\cos^3 a\theta - \cos a\theta + C$ 7. $\dfrac{1}{2a}\sin^2 ax + C$

9. $\frac{1}{3}\sin^3 t - \frac{1}{5}\sin^5 t + C$ 11. $\frac{1}{8}x - \frac{1}{32}\sin 4x + C$

13. $-\frac{1}{10}\cos 5x + \frac{1}{2}\cos x + C$ 15. $-\frac{1}{3}\cos(3x/2) - \cos(x/2) + C$

17. $2/3$ 19. 0   21. $7/24$ 23. $\frac{1}{2}\tan(2x - 1) + C$

25. $\ln|\cos(e^{-x})| + C$ 27. $\frac{1}{4}\ln|\sec 4x + \tan 4x| + C$

29. $\frac{1}{3}\tan^3 x + C$ 31. $\frac{1}{16}\sec^4 4x + C$ 33. $\frac{1}{7}\sec^7 x - \frac{1}{5}\sec^5 x + C$

35. $\frac{1}{4}\sec^3 x\tan x - \frac{5}{8}\sec x\tan x + \frac{3}{8}\ln|\sec x + \tan x| + C$

37. $\frac{1}{3}\sec^3 t + C$ 39. $\tan x + \frac{1}{3}\tan^3 x + C$

41. $\frac{1}{8}\tan^2 4x + \frac{1}{4}\ln|\cos 4x| + C$ 43. $\frac{2}{3}\tan^{3/2}x + \frac{2}{7}\tan^{7/2}x + C$

45. $\dfrac{1}{2} - \dfrac{\pi}{8}$ 47. $-\frac{1}{2} + \ln 2$ 49. $-\frac{1}{5}\csc^5 x + \frac{1}{3}\csc^3 x + C$

51. $-\frac{1}{2}\csc^2 x - \ln|\sin x| + C$

Responses to True–False questions may be abridged to save space.

53. True; $\int \sin^5 x \cos^8 x\,dx = \int \sin x(1 - \cos^2 x)^2 \cos^8 x\,dx = -\int (1 - u^2)^2 u^8\,du = -\int (u^8 - 2u^{10} + u^{12})\,du$

55. False; use this identity to help evaluate integrals of the form $\int \sin mx \cos nx\,dx$.

59. $L = \ln(\sqrt{2} + 1)$ 61. $V = \pi/2$

67. $-\dfrac{1}{\sqrt{a^2+b^2}}\ln\left[\dfrac{\sqrt{a^2+b^2}+a\cos x-b\sin x}{a\sin x+b\cos x}\right]+C$

69. (a) $\frac{2}{3}$ (b) $3\pi/16$ (c) $\frac{8}{15}$ (d) $5\pi/32$

▶ **Exercise Set 7.4 (Page 513)**

1. $2\sin^{-1}(x/2)+\frac{1}{2}x\sqrt{4-x^2}+C$ 3. $8\sin^{-1}\left(\dfrac{x}{4}\right)-\dfrac{x\sqrt{16-x^2}}{2}+C$

5. $\frac{1}{16}\tan^{-1}(x/2)+\dfrac{x}{8(4+x^2)}+C$ 7. $\sqrt{x^2-9}-3\sec^{-1}(x/3)+C$

9. $-(x^2+2)\sqrt{1-x^2}+C$ 11. $\dfrac{\sqrt{9x^2-4}}{4x}+C$ 13. $\dfrac{x}{\sqrt{1-x^2}}+C$

15. $\ln\left|\sqrt{x^2-9}+x\right|+C$ 17. $\dfrac{-x}{9\sqrt{4x^2-9}}+C$

19. $\frac{1}{2}\sin^{-1}(e^x)+\frac{1}{2}e^x\sqrt{1-e^{2x}}+C$ 21. $2/3$ 23. $(\sqrt{3}-\sqrt{2})/2$

25. $\dfrac{10\sqrt{3}+18}{243}$

Responses to True–False questions may be abridged to save space.

27. True; with the restriction $-\pi/2\le\theta\le\pi/2$, this substitution gives $\sqrt{a^2-x^2}=a\cos\theta$ and $dx=a\cos\theta\,d\theta$.

29. False; use the substitution $x=a\sec\theta$ with $0\le\theta<\pi/2\,(x\ge a)$ or $\pi/2\le\theta<\pi\,(x\le-a)$.

31. $\frac{1}{2}\ln(x^2+4)+C$

33. $L=\sqrt{5}-\sqrt{2}+\ln\dfrac{2+2\sqrt{2}}{1+\sqrt{5}}$ 35. $S=\dfrac{\pi}{32}\left[18\sqrt{5}-\ln(2+\sqrt{5})\right]$

37. $\tan^{-1}(x-2)+C$ 39. $\sin^{-1}\left(\dfrac{x-1}{2}\right)+C$

41. $\ln(x-3+\sqrt{(x-3)^2+1})+C$

43. $2\sin^{-1}\left(\dfrac{x+1}{2}\right)+\frac{1}{2}(x+1)\sqrt{3-2x-x^2}+C$

45. $\dfrac{1}{\sqrt{10}}\tan^{-1}\sqrt{\frac{2}{5}}(x+1)+C$ 47. $\pi/6$

49. $u=\sin^2 x,\ \frac{1}{2}\displaystyle\int\sqrt{1-u^2}\,du$
$=\frac{1}{4}[\sin^2 x\sqrt{1-\sin^4 x}+\sin^{-1}(\sin^2 x)]+C$

51. (a) $\sinh^{-1}(x/3)+C$ (b) $\ln\left(\dfrac{\sqrt{x^2+9}}{3}+\dfrac{x}{3}\right)+C$

▶ **Exercise Set 7.5 (Page 521)**

1. $\dfrac{A}{x-3}+\dfrac{B}{x+4}$ 3. $\dfrac{A}{x}+\dfrac{B}{x^2}+\dfrac{C}{x-1}$

5. $\dfrac{A}{x}+\dfrac{B}{x^2}+\dfrac{C}{x^3}+\dfrac{Dx+E}{x^2+2}$ 7. $\dfrac{Ax+B}{x^2+5}+\dfrac{Cx+D}{(x^2+5)^2}$

9. $\frac{1}{5}\ln\left|\dfrac{x-4}{x+1}\right|+C$ 11. $\frac{5}{2}\ln|2x-1|+3\ln|x+4|+C$

13. $\ln\left|\dfrac{x(x+3)^2}{x-3}\right|+C$ 15. $\dfrac{x^2}{2}-3x+\ln|x+3|+C$

17. $3x+12\ln|x-2|-\dfrac{2}{x-2}+C$

19. $\ln|x^2-3x-10|+C$

21. $x+\dfrac{x^3}{3}+\ln\left|\dfrac{(x-1)^2(x+1)}{x^2}\right|+C$

23. $3\ln|x|-\ln|x-1|-\dfrac{5}{x-1}+C$

25. $\dfrac{2}{x-3}+\ln|x-3|+\ln|x+1|+C$

27. $\dfrac{2}{x+1}-\dfrac{1}{2(x+1)^2}+\ln|x+1|+C$

29. $-\frac{7}{34}\ln|4x-1|+\frac{6}{17}\ln(x^2+1)+\frac{3}{17}\tan^{-1}x+C$

31. $3\tan^{-1}x+\frac{1}{2}\ln(x^2+3)+C$

33. $\dfrac{x^2}{2}-2x+\frac{1}{2}\ln(x^2+1)+C$

Responses to True–False questions may be abridged to save space.

35. True; partial fractions rewrites proper rational functions $P(x)/Q(x)$ as a sum of terms of the form $\dfrac{A}{(Bx+C)^k}$ and/or $\dfrac{Dx+E}{(Fx^2+Gx+H)^k}$.

37. True; $\dfrac{2x+3}{x^2}=\dfrac{2x}{x^2}+\dfrac{3}{x^2}=\dfrac{2}{x}+\dfrac{3}{x^2}$.

39. $\frac{1}{6}\ln\left(\dfrac{1-\sin\theta}{5+\sin\theta}\right)+C$ 41. $e^x-2\tan^{-1}\left(\frac{1}{2}e^x\right)+C$

43. $V=\pi\left(\frac{19}{5}-\frac{9}{4}\ln 5\right)$ 45. $\dfrac{1}{\sqrt{2}}\tan^{-1}\left(\dfrac{x+1}{\sqrt{2}}\right)+\dfrac{1}{x^2+2x+3}+C$

47. $\frac{1}{8}\ln|x-1|-\frac{1}{5}\ln|x-2|+\frac{1}{12}\ln|x-3|-\frac{1}{120}\ln|x+3|+C$

▶ **Exercise Set 7.6 (Page 531)**

1. Formula (60): $\frac{4}{3}x+\frac{4}{9}\ln|3x-1|+C$

3. Formula (65): $\dfrac{1}{5}\ln\left|\dfrac{x}{5+2x}\right|+C$

5. Formula (102): $\frac{1}{5}(x-1)(2x+3)^{3/2}+C$

7. Formula (108): $\dfrac{1}{2}\ln\left|\dfrac{\sqrt{4-3x}-2}{\sqrt{4-3x}+2}\right|+C$

9. Formula (69): $\dfrac{1}{8}\ln\left|\dfrac{x+4}{x-4}\right|+C$

11. Formula (73): $\dfrac{x}{2}\sqrt{x^2-3}-\dfrac{3}{2}\ln|x+\sqrt{x^2-3}|+C$

13. Formula (95): $\dfrac{x}{2}\sqrt{x^2+4}-2\ln(x+\sqrt{x^2+4})+C$

15. Formula (74): $\dfrac{x}{2}\sqrt{9-x^2}+\dfrac{9}{2}\sin^{-1}\dfrac{x}{3}+C$

17. Formula (79): $\sqrt{4-x^2}-2\ln\left|\dfrac{2+\sqrt{4-x^2}}{x}\right|+C$

19. Formula (38): $-\dfrac{\sin 7x}{14}+\dfrac{1}{2}\sin x+C$

21. Formula (50): $\dfrac{x^4}{16}[4\ln x-1]+C$

23. Formula (42): $\dfrac{e^{-2x}}{13}[-2\sin(3x)-3\cos(3x)]+C$

25. Formula (62): $\dfrac{1}{2}\displaystyle\int\dfrac{u\,du}{(4-3u)^2}=\dfrac{1}{18}\left[\dfrac{4}{4-3e^{2x}}+\ln\left|4-3e^{2x}\right|\right]+C$

27. Formula (68): $\dfrac{2}{3}\displaystyle\int\dfrac{du}{u^2+4}=\dfrac{1}{3}\tan^{-1}\dfrac{3\sqrt{x}}{2}+C$

29. Formula (76): $\dfrac{1}{2}\displaystyle\int\dfrac{du}{\sqrt{u^2-9}}=\dfrac{1}{2}\ln|2x+\sqrt{4x^2-9}|+C$

31. Formula (81): $\dfrac{1}{4}\displaystyle\int\dfrac{u^2}{\sqrt{2-u^2}}\,du=-\dfrac{1}{4}x^2\sqrt{2-4x^4}$
$+\dfrac{1}{4}\sin^{-1}\left(\sqrt{2}x^2\right)+C$

33. Formula (26): $\displaystyle\int\sin^2 u\,du=\frac{1}{2}\ln x-\frac{1}{4}\sin(2\ln x)+C$

35. Formula (51): $\dfrac{1}{4}\displaystyle\int ue^u\,du=\frac{1}{4}(-2x-1)e^{-2x}+C$

37. $u=\sin 3x$, Formula (67): $\dfrac{1}{3}\displaystyle\int\dfrac{du}{u(u+1)^2}$
$=\dfrac{1}{3}\left(\dfrac{1}{\sin 3x+1}+\ln\left|\dfrac{\sin 3x}{\sin 3x+1}\right|\right)+C$

39. $u=4x^2$, Formula (70): $\dfrac{1}{8}\displaystyle\int\dfrac{du}{u^2-1}=\dfrac{1}{16}\ln\left|\dfrac{4x^2-1}{4x^2+1}\right|+C$

41. $u=2e^x$, Formula (74): $\dfrac{1}{2}\displaystyle\int\sqrt{3-u^2}\,du=\frac{1}{2}e^x\sqrt{3-4e^{2x}}$
$+\dfrac{3}{4}\sin^{-1}\left(\dfrac{2e^x}{\sqrt{3}}\right)+C$

43. $u=3x$, Formula (112): $\dfrac{1}{3}\displaystyle\int\sqrt{\frac{5}{3}u-u^2}\,du=\dfrac{18x-5}{36}\sqrt{5x-9x^2}$
$+\dfrac{25}{216}\sin^{-1}\left(\dfrac{18x-5}{5}\right)+C$

45. $u = 2x$, Formula (44): $\int u \sin u \, du = \sin 2x - 2x \cos 2x + C$

47. $u = -\sqrt{x}$, Formula (51): $2 \int u e^u \, du = -2(\sqrt{x}+1)e^{-\sqrt{x}} + C$

49. $x^2 + 6x - 7 = (x+3)^2 - 16$, $u = x + 3$, Formula (70):
$$\int \frac{du}{u^2 - 16} = \frac{1}{8} \ln \left| \frac{x-1}{x+7} \right| + C$$

51. $x^2 - 4x - 5 = (x-2)^2 - 9$, $u = x - 2$, Formula (77):
$$\int \frac{u+2}{\sqrt{9-u^2}} \, du = -\sqrt{5+4x-x^2} + 2\sin^{-1}\left(\frac{x-2}{3}\right) + C$$

53. $u = \sqrt{x-2}$, $\frac{2}{5}(x-2)^{5/2} + \frac{4}{3}(x-2)^{3/2} + C$

55. $u = \sqrt{x^3 + 1}$,
$$\frac{2}{3} \int u^2(u^2 - 1) \, du = \frac{2}{15}(x^3+1)^{5/2} - \frac{2}{9}(x^3+1)^{3/2} + C$$

57. $u = x^{1/3}$, $\int \frac{3u^2}{u^3 - u} \, du = \frac{3}{2} \ln |x^{2/3} - 1| + C$

59. $u = x^{1/4}$, $4 \int \frac{1}{u(1-u)} \, du = 4 \ln \frac{x^{1/4}}{|1 - x^{1/4}|} + C$

61. $u = x^{1/6}$,
$$6 \int \frac{u^3}{u-1} \, du = 2x^{1/2} + 3x^{1/3} + 6x^{1/6} + 6 \ln |x^{1/6} - 1| + C$$

63. $u = \sqrt{1 + x^2}$, $\int (u^2 - 1) \, du = \frac{1}{3}(1+x^2)^{3/2} - (1+x^2)^{1/2} + C$

65. $\int \dfrac{1}{1 + \dfrac{2u}{1+u^2} + \dfrac{1-u^2}{1+u^2}} \dfrac{2}{1+u^2} \, du = \int \dfrac{1}{u+1} \, du$
$$= \ln | \tan(x/2) + 1| + C$$

67. $\int \dfrac{d\theta}{1 - \cos\theta} = \int \dfrac{1}{u^2} \, du = -\cot(\theta/2) + C$

69. $\int \dfrac{1}{\dfrac{2u}{1+u^2} + \dfrac{2u}{1+u^2} \cdot \dfrac{1+u^2}{1-u^2}} \cdot \dfrac{2}{1+u^2} \, du = \int \dfrac{1-u^2}{2u} \, du$
$$= \frac{1}{2} \ln | \tan(x/2)| - \frac{1}{4} \tan^2(x/2) + C$$

71. $x = \dfrac{4e^2}{1 + e^2}$ 73. $A = 6 + \frac{25}{2} \sin^{-1} \frac{4}{5}$ 75. $A = \frac{1}{40} \ln 9$

77. $V = \pi(\pi - 2)$ 79. $V = 2\pi(1 - 4e^{-3})$

81. $L = \sqrt{65} + \frac{1}{8} \ln(8 + \sqrt{65})$ 83. $S = 2\pi \left[\sqrt{2} + \ln(1 + \sqrt{2}) \right]$

85.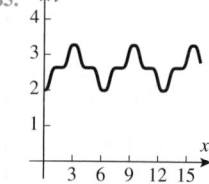

91. $\frac{1}{31} \cos^{31} x \sin^{31} x + C$

93. $-\frac{1}{9} \ln |1 + x^{-9}| + C$

▶ Exercise Set 7.7 (Page 544)

1. $\int_0^3 \sqrt{x+1} \, dx = \frac{14}{3} \approx 4.66667$
   (a) $M_{10} = 4.66760$; $|E_M| \approx 0.000933996$
   (b) $T_{10} = 4.66480$; $|E_T| \approx 0.00187099$
   (c) $S_{20} = 4.66667$; $|E_S| \approx 9.98365 \times 10^{-7}$

3. $\int_0^{\pi/2} \cos x \, dx = 1$
   (a) $M_{10} = 1.00103$; $|E_M| \approx 0.00102882$
   (b) $T_{10} = 0.997943$; $|E_T| \approx 0.00205701$
   (c) $S_{20} = 1.00000$; $|E_S| \approx 2.11547 \times 10^{-7}$

5. $\int_1^3 e^{-2x} \, dx = \frac{-1 + e^4}{2e^6} \approx 0.0664283$
   (a) $M_{10} = 0.0659875$; $|E_M| \approx 0.000440797$
   (b) $T_{10} = 0.0673116$; $|E_T| \approx 0.000883357$
   (c) $S_{20} = 0.0664289$; $|E_S| \approx 5.87673 \times 10^{-7}$

7. (a) $|E_M| \leq \dfrac{9}{3200} = 0.0028125$
   (b) $|E_T| \leq \dfrac{9}{1600} = 0.005625$
   (c) $|E_S| \leq \dfrac{81}{10,240,000} \approx 7.91016 \times 10^{-6}$

9. (a) $|E_M| \leq \dfrac{\pi^3}{19,200} \approx 0.00161491$
   (b) $|E_T| \leq \dfrac{\pi^3}{9600} \approx 0.00322982$
   (c) $|E_S| \leq \dfrac{\pi^5}{921,600,000} \approx 3.32053 \times 10^{-7}$

11. (a) $|E_M| \leq \dfrac{1}{75e^2} \approx 0.00180447$
    (b) $|E_T| \leq \dfrac{2}{75e^2} \approx 0.00360894$
    (c) $|E_S| \leq \dfrac{1}{56,250e^2} \approx 2.40596 \times 10^{-6}$

13. (a) $n = 24$ (b) $n = 34$ (c) $n = 8$

15. (a) $n = 13$ (b) $n = 18$ (c) $n = 4$

17. (a) $n = 43$ (b) $n = 61$ (c) $n = 8$

Responses to True–False questions may be abridged to save space.

19. False; T_n is the average of L_n and R_n.

21. False; $S_{50} = \frac{2}{3} M_{25} + \frac{1}{3} T_{25}$

23. $g(x) = \frac{1}{24} x^2 - \frac{3}{8} x + \frac{13}{12}$

25. $S_{10} = 1.49367$; $\int_{-1}^1 e^{-x^2} \, dx \approx 1.49365$

27. $S_{10} = 3.80678$; $\int_{-1}^2 x\sqrt{1+x^3} \, dx \approx 3.80554$

29. $S_{10} = 0.904524$; $\int_0^1 \cos x^2 \, dx \approx 0.904524$

31. (a) $M_{10} = 3.14243$; error $E_M \approx -0.000833331$
    (b) $T_{10} = 3.13993$; error $E_T \approx 0.00166666$
    (c) $S_{20} = 3.14159$; error $E_S \approx 6.20008 \times 10^{-10}$

33. $S_{14} = 0.693147984$, $|E_S| \approx 0.000000803 = 8.03 \times 10^{-7}$

35. $n = 116$ 39. 3.82019 41. 1071 ft   43. 37.9 mi   45. 9.3 L

47. (a) $\max |f''(x)| \approx 3.844880$ (b) $n = 18$ (c) 0.904741

49. (a) The maximum value of $|f^{(4)}(x)|$ is approximately 12.4282.
    (b) $n = 6$ (c) $S_6 = 0.983347$

▶ Exercise Set 7.8 (Page 554)

1. (a) improper; infinite discontinuity at $x = 3$ (b) not improper
   (c) improper; infinite discontinuity at $x = 0$
   (d) improper; infinite interval of integration
   (e) improper; infinite interval of integration and infinite discontinuity
   at $x = 1$ (f) not improper

3. $\frac{1}{2}$ 5. $\ln 2$ 7. $\frac{1}{2}$ 9. $-\frac{1}{4}$ 11. $\frac{1}{3}$ 13. divergent   15. 0

17. divergent   19. divergent   21. $\pi/2$ 23. 1   25. divergent

27. $\frac{9}{2}$ 29. divergent   31. $\pi/2$

Responses to True–False questions may be abridged to save space.

33. True; see Theorem 7.8.2 with $p = \frac{4}{3} > 1$.

35. False; the integrand $\dfrac{1}{x(x-3)}$ is continuous on [1, 2].

37. 2   39. 2   41. $\frac{1}{2}$

43. (a) 2.726585 (b) 2.804364 (c) 0.219384 (d) 0.504067 45. 12

47. -1 49. $\frac{1}{3}$ 51. (a) $V = \pi/2$ (b) $S = \pi[\sqrt{2} + \ln(1 + \sqrt{2})]$

53. (b) $1/e$ (c) It is convergent.   55. $V = \pi$

59. $\dfrac{2\pi N I}{kr} \left(1 - \dfrac{a}{\sqrt{r^2 + a^2}} \right)$

61. (b) 2.4×10^7 mi·lb   63. (a) $\dfrac{1}{s^2}$ (b) $\dfrac{2}{s^3}$ (c) $\dfrac{e^{-3s}}{s}$

67. (a) 1.047 71. 1.809

▶ **Chapter 7 Review Exercises (Page 557)**

1. $\frac{2}{27}(4+9x)^{3/2}+C$ 3. $-\frac{2}{3}\cos^{3/2}\theta+C$ 5. $\frac{1}{6}\tan^3(x^2)+C$

7. **(a)** $2\sin^{-1}(\sqrt{x/2})+C$; $-2\sin^{-1}(\sqrt{2-x}/\sqrt{2})+C$; $\sin^{-1}(x-1)+C$

9. $-xe^{-x}-e^{-x}+C$ 11. $x\ln(2x+3)-x+\frac{3}{2}\ln(2x+3)+C$

13. $(4x^4-12x^2+6)\sin(2x)+(8x^3-12x)\cos(2x)+C$

15. $\frac{1}{2}\theta-\frac{1}{20}\sin 10\theta+C$ 17. $-\frac{1}{6}\cos 3x+\frac{1}{2}\cos x+C$

19. $-\frac{1}{8}\sin^3(2x)\cos 2x-\frac{3}{16}\cos 2x\sin 2x+\frac{3}{8}x+C$

21. $\frac{9}{2}\sin^{-1}(x/3)-\frac{1}{2}x\sqrt{9-x^2}+C$ 23. $\ln|x+\sqrt{x^2-1}|+C$

25. $\dfrac{x\sqrt{x^2+9}}{2}-\dfrac{9\ln(|\sqrt{x^2+9}+x|)}{2}+C$ 27. $\frac{1}{5}\ln\left|\dfrac{x-1}{x+4}\right|+C$

29. $\frac{1}{2}x^2-2x+6\ln|x+2|+C$

31. $\ln|x+2|+\dfrac{4}{x+2}-\dfrac{2}{(x+2)^2}+C$

35. Formula (40): $-\dfrac{\cos 16x}{32}+\dfrac{\cos 2x}{4}+C$

37. Formula (113): $\frac{1}{24}(8x^2-2x-3)\sqrt{x-x^2}+\frac{1}{16}\sin^{-1}(2x-1)+C$

39. Formula (28): $\frac{1}{2}\tan 2x-x+C$

41. $\displaystyle\int_1^3\dfrac{1}{\sqrt{x+1}}=4-2\sqrt{2}\approx 1.17157$
    (a) $M_{10}=1.17138$; $|E_M|\approx 0.000190169$
    (b) $T_{10}=1.17195$; $|E_T|\approx 0.000380588$
    (c) $S_{20}=1.17157$; $|E_S|\approx 8.35151\times 10^{-8}$

43. **(a)** $|E_M|\le\dfrac{1}{1600\sqrt{2}}\approx 0.000441942$
    (b) $|E_T|\le\dfrac{1}{800\sqrt{2}}\approx 0.000883883$
    (c) $|E_S|\le\dfrac{7}{15{,}360{,}000\sqrt{2}}\approx 3.22249\times 10^{-7}$

45. **(a)** $n=22$ **(b)** $n=30$ **(c)** $n=6$ 47. 1   49. 6

51. e^{-1} 53. $a=\pi/2$ 55. $\dfrac{x}{3\sqrt{3+x^2}}+C$ 57. $\frac{5}{12}-\frac{1}{2}\ln 2$

59. $\frac{1}{6}\sin^3 2x-\frac{1}{10}\sin^5 2x+C$

61. $\frac{2}{13}e^{2x}\cos 3x+\frac{3}{13}e^{2x}\sin 3x+C$

63. $-\frac{1}{6}\ln|x-1|+\frac{1}{15}\ln|x+2|+\frac{1}{10}\ln|x-3|+C$

65. $4-\pi$ 67. $\ln\dfrac{\sqrt{e^x+1}-1}{\sqrt{e^x+1}+1}+C$ 69. $\dfrac{\pi}{12}+\dfrac{\sqrt{3}}{2}-1$

71. $\sqrt{x^2+2x+2}+2\ln(\sqrt{x^2+2x+2}+x+1)+C$ 73. $\dfrac{1}{2(a^2+1)}$

▶ **Chapter 7 Making Connections (Page 559)**

Where correct answers to a Making Connections exercise may vary, no answer is listed. Sample answers for these questions are available on the Book Companion Site.

3. **(a)** $\Gamma(1)=1$ **(c)** $\Gamma(2)=1$, $\Gamma(3)=2$, $\Gamma(4)=6$

5. **(b)** 1.37078 seconds

▶ **Exercise Set 8.1 (Page 566)**

3. **(a)** first order   **(b)** second order

Responses to True–False questions may be abridged to save space.

5. False; only first-order derivatives appear.

7. True; it is third order.

15. $y(x)=e^{-2x}-2e^x$ 17. $y(x)=2e^{2x}-2xe^{2x}$

19. $y(x)=\sin 2x+\cos 2x$ 21. $y(x)=-2x^2+2x+3$

23. $y(x)=2/(3-2x)$ 25. $y(x)=2/x^2$

27. **(a)** $\dfrac{dy}{dt}=ky^2$, $y(0)=y_0$ $(k>0)$
    (b) $\dfrac{dy}{dt}=-ky^2$, $y(0)=y_0$ $(k>0)$

29. **(a)** $\dfrac{ds}{dt}=\frac{1}{2}s$ **(b)** $\dfrac{d^2s}{dt^2}=2\dfrac{ds}{dt}$ 33. **(b)** $L/2$

▶ **Exercise Set 8.2 (Page 575)**

1. $y=Cx$ 3. $y=Ce^{-\sqrt{1+x^2}}-1$, $C\ne 0$

5. $2\ln|y|+y^2=e^x+C$ 7. $y=\ln(\sec x+C)$

9. $y=\dfrac{1}{1-C(\csc x-\cot x)}$, $y=0$

11. $y^2+\sin y=x^3+\pi^2$ 13. $y^2-2y=t^2+t+3$

15. **(a)**

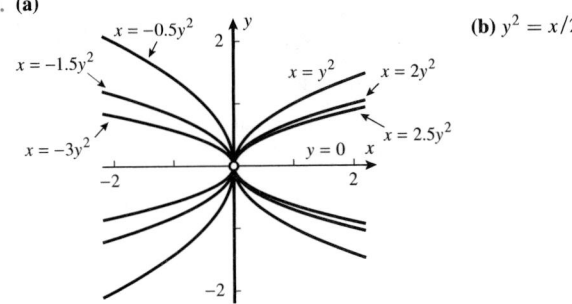

(b) $y^2=x/2$

17. $y=\dfrac{C}{\sqrt{x^2+4}}$

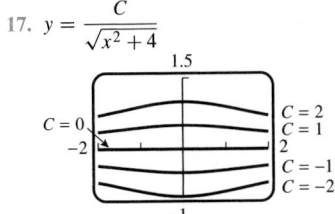

19. $x^3+y^3-3y=C$

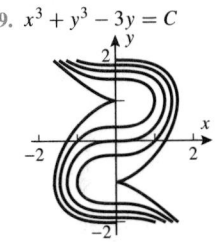

Responses to True–False questions may be abridged to save space.

21. True; since $\dfrac{1}{f(y)}\,dy=dx$.   23. True; since $\left(\frac{1}{2}\right)^5 32=1$.

27. $y=\ln\left(\dfrac{x^2}{2}-1\right)$

29. **(a)** $y'(t)=y(t)/50$, $y(0)=10{,}000$ **(b)** $y(t)=10{,}000e^{t/50}$
    (c) $50\ln 2\approx 34.66$ hr   **(d)** $50\ln(4.5)\approx 75.20$ hr

31. **(a)** $\dfrac{dy}{dt}=-ky$, $k\approx 0.1810$ **(b)** $y=5.0\times 10^7e^{-0.181t}$
    (c) $\approx 219{,}000$ atoms   **(d)** 12.72 days

33. $50\ln(100)\approx 230.26$ days   35. 3.30 days

39. **(b)** 70 years   **(c)** 20 years   **(d)** 7%

43. **(a)** no   **(b)** same, $r\%$ 45. **(b)** $\ln(2)/\ln(5/4)\approx 3.106$ hr

47. **(a)** \$1491.82   **(b)** \$4493.29   **(c)** 8.7 years

51. **(a)**

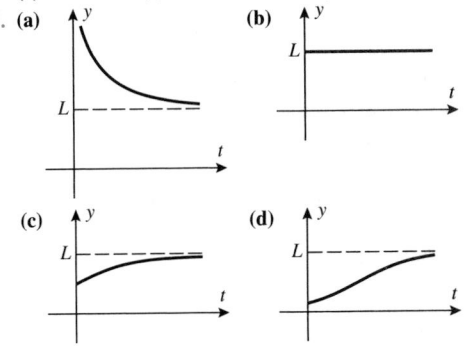

53. $y_0\approx 2$, $L\approx 8$, $k\approx 0.5493$

55. **(a)** $y_0=5$ **(b)** $L=12$ **(c)** $k=1$ **(d)** $t=0.3365$
    (e) $\dfrac{dy}{dt}=\frac{1}{2}y(12-y)$, $y(0)=5$

57. **(a)** $y=\dfrac{1000}{1+49e^{-0.115t}}$

(b)

t	0	1	2	3	4	5	6	7
y(t)	20	22	25	28	31	35	39	44

t	8	9	10	11	12	13	14
y(t)	49	54	61	67	75	83	93

(c)

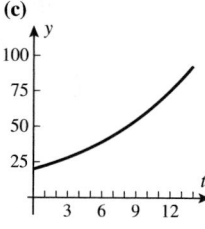

59. **(a)** $T = 21 + 74e^{-kt}$ **(b)** 6.22 min
61. **(a)** $v = c \ln \dfrac{m_0}{m_0 - kt} - gt$ **(b)** 3044 m/s
63. **(a)** $h \approx (2 - 0.003979t)^2$ **(b)** 8.4 min
65. **(a)** $v = 128/(4t + 1)$, $x = 32 \ln(4t + 1)$

▶ **Exercise Set 8.3 (Page 584)**

1. 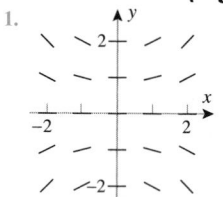   3.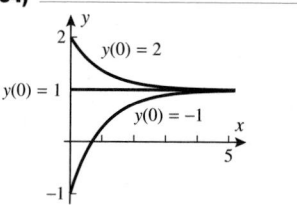

5. $y \to 1$ as $x \to +\infty$

7.

n	0	1	2	3	4	5	6	7	8
x_n	0	0.5	1	1.5	2	2.5	3	3.5	4
y_n	1.00	1.50	2.07	2.71	3.41	4.16	4.96	5.82	6.72

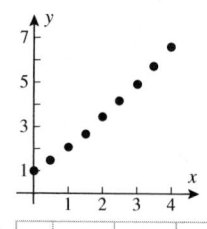

9.

n	0	1	2	3	4
t_n	0.00	0.50	1.00	1.50	2.00
y_n	1.00	1.27	1.42	1.49	1.53

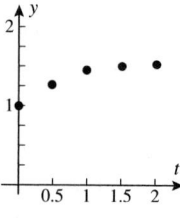

11. 0.62

Responses to True–False questions may be abridged to save space.
13. True; the derivative is positive.
15. True; $y = y_0$ is a solution if y_0 is a root of p.
17. **(b)** $y(1/2) = \sqrt{3}/2$ 19. **(b)** The x-intercept is $\ln 2$.
23. **(a)** $y' = \dfrac{2xy - y^3}{3xy^2 - x^2}$ **(c)** $xy^3 - x^2y = 2$
25. **(b)** $\lim\limits_{n \to +\infty} y_n = \lim\limits_{n \to +\infty} \left(\dfrac{n+1}{n}\right)^n = e$

▶ **Exercise Set 8.4 (Page 592)**

1. $y = e^{-3x} + Ce^{-4x}$ 3. $y = e^{-x} \sin(e^x) + Ce^{-x}$ 5. $y = \dfrac{C}{\sqrt{x^2 + 1}}$
7. $y = \dfrac{x}{2} + \dfrac{3}{2x}$ 9. $y = 4e^{x^2} - 1$

Responses to True–False questions may be abridged to save space.
11. False; $y = x^2$ is a solution to $dy/dx = 2x$, but $y + y = 2x^2$ is not.
13. True; it will approach the concentration of the entering fluid.

15. 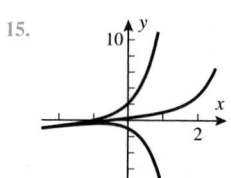   17. $\lim\limits_{x \to +\infty} y = \begin{cases} +\infty & \text{if } y_0 \geq 1/4 \\ -\infty, & \text{if } y_0 < 1/4 \end{cases}$

19. **(a)**

n	0	1	2	3	4	5
x_n	0	0.2	0.4	0.6	0.8	1.0
y_n	1	1.20	1.48	1.86	2.35	2.98

(b) $y = -(x + 1) + 2e^x$

x_n	0	0.2	0.4	0.6	0.8	1.0
$y(x_n)$	1	1.24	1.58	2.04	2.65	3.44
Absolute error	0	0.04	0.10	0.19	0.30	0.46
Percentage error	0	3	6	9	11	13

21. **(a)** $200 - 175e^{-t/25}$ oz   **(b)** 136 oz   23. 25 lb
27. **(a)** $I(t) = 2 - 2e^{-2t}$ A   **(b)** $I(t) \to 2$ A

▶ **Chapter 8 Review Exercises (Page 594)**
3. $y = \tan(x^3/3 + C)$ 5. $\ln|y| + y^2/2 = e^x + C$ and $y = 0$
7. $y^{-4} + 4\ln(x/y) = 1$
9. 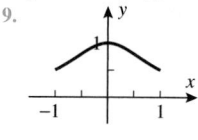   11.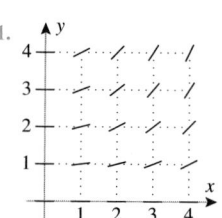

13.

n	0	1	2	3	4	5	6	7	8
x_n	0	0.5	1	1.5	2	2.5	3	3.5	4
y_n	1	1.50	2.11	2.84	3.68	4.64	5.72	6.91	8.23

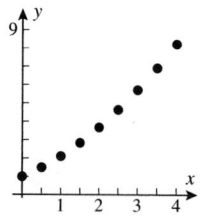

15. $y(1) \approx 1.00$

n	0	1	2	3	4	5
t_n	0	0.2	0.4	0.6	0.8	1.0
y_n	1.00	1.20	1.26	1.10	0.94	1.00

17. about 2000.6 years   19. $y = e^{-2x} + Ce^{-3x}$
21. $y = -1 + 4e^{x^2/2}$ 23. $y = 2 \operatorname{sech} x + \frac{1}{2}(x \operatorname{sech} x + \sinh x)$
25. **(a)** linear   **(b)** both   **(c)** separable   **(d)** neither   27. about 646 oz

▶ **Chapter 8 Making Connections (Page 595)**

Where correct answers to a Making Connections exercise may vary, no answer is listed. Sample answers for these questions are available on the Book Companion Site.

1. **(b)** $y = 2 - 3e^{-2x}$
3. **(a)** $du/dx = (f(u) - u)/x$ **(b)** $x^2 - 2xy - y^2 = C$

▶ **Exercise Set 9.1 (Page 605)**

1. (a) $\frac{1}{3^{n-1}}$ (b) $\frac{(-1)^{n-1}}{3^{n-1}}$ (c) $\frac{2n-1}{2n}$ (d) $\frac{n^2}{\pi^{1/(n+1)}}$
3. (a) 2, 0, 2, 0 (b) 1, −1, 1, −1 (c) $2(1+(-1)^n)$; $2+2\cos n\pi$
5. (a) The limit doesn't exist due to repeated oscillation between −1
   and 1. (b) −1; 1; −1; 1; −1 (c) no
7. $\frac{1}{3}, \frac{2}{4}, \frac{3}{5}, \frac{4}{6}, \frac{5}{7}$; converges, $\lim\limits_{n\to+\infty} \frac{n}{n+2} = 1$
9. 2, 2, 2, 2, 2; converges, $\lim\limits_{n\to+\infty} 2 = 2$
11. $\frac{\ln 1}{1}, \frac{\ln 2}{2}, \frac{\ln 3}{3}, \frac{\ln 4}{4}, \frac{\ln 5}{5}$; converges, $\lim\limits_{n\to+\infty} \frac{\ln n}{n} = 0$
13. 0, 2, 0, 2, 0; diverges 15. $-1, \frac{16}{9}, -\frac{54}{28}, \frac{128}{65}, -\frac{250}{126}$; diverges
17. $\frac{6}{2}, \frac{12}{8}, \frac{20}{18}, \frac{30}{32}, \frac{42}{50}$; converges, $\lim\limits_{n\to+\infty} \frac{1}{2}\left(1+\frac{1}{n}\right)\left(1+\frac{2}{n}\right) = \frac{1}{2}$
19. $e^{-1}, 4e^{-2}, 9e^{-3}, 16e^{-4}, 25e^{-5}$; converges, $\lim\limits_{n\to+\infty} n^2 e^{-n} = 0$
21. $2, \left(\frac{5}{3}\right)^2, \left(\frac{6}{4}\right)^3, \left(\frac{7}{5}\right)^4, \left(\frac{8}{6}\right)^5$; converges, $\lim\limits_{n\to+\infty}\left[\frac{n+3}{n+1}\right]^n = e^2$
23. $\left\{\frac{2n-1}{2n}\right\}_{n=1}^{+\infty}$; converges, $\lim\limits_{n\to+\infty} \frac{2n-1}{2n} = 1$
25. $\left\{(-1)^{n+1}\frac{1}{3^n}\right\}_{n=1}^{+\infty}$; converges, $\lim\limits_{n\to+\infty} (-1)^{n+1}\frac{1}{3^n} = 0$
27. $\left\{(-1)^{n+1}\left(\frac{1}{n}-\frac{1}{n+1}\right)\right\}_{n=1}^{+\infty}$;
   converges, $\lim\limits_{n\to+\infty} (-1)^{n+1}\left(\frac{1}{n}-\frac{1}{n+1}\right) = 0$
29. $\{\sqrt{n+1}-\sqrt{n+2}\}_{n=1}^{+\infty}$; converges, $\lim\limits_{n\to+\infty}(\sqrt{n+1}-\sqrt{n+2}) = 0$
Responses to True–False questions may be abridged to save space.
31. True; a sequence is a function whose domain is a set of integers.
33. False; for example, $\{(-1)^{n+1}\}$ diverges with terms that oscillate
   between 1 and −1. 35. The limit is 0.
37. for example, $\{(-1)^n\}_{n=1}^{+\infty}$ and $\{\sin(\pi n/2)+1/n\}_{n=1}^{+\infty}$
39. (a) 1, 2, 1, 4, 1, 6 (b) $a_n = \begin{cases} n, & n \text{ odd} \\ 1/2^n, & n \text{ even} \end{cases}$
   (c) $a_n = \begin{cases} 1/n, & n \text{ odd} \\ 1/(n+1); & n \text{ even} \end{cases}$
   (d) (a) diverges; (b) diverges; (c) $\lim\limits_{n\to+\infty} a_n = 0$
43. (a) $(0.5)^{2n}$ (c) $\lim\limits_{n\to+\infty} a_n = 0$ (d) $-1 \leq a_0 \leq 1$
45. (a)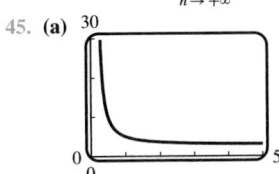
   (b) $\lim\limits_{n\to+\infty}(2^n+3^n)^{1/n} = 3$
49. (a) $N = 4$ (b) $N = 10$ (c) $N = 1000$

▶ **Exercise Set 9.2 (Page 613)**

1. strictly decreasing 3. strictly increasing 5. strictly decreasing
7. strictly increasing 9. strictly decreasing 11. strictly increasing
Responses to True–False questions may be abridged to save space.
13. True; $a_{n+1} - a_n > 0$ for all n is equivalent to $a_1 < a_2 < a_3 < \cdots <$
   $a_n < \cdots$.
15. False; for example, $\{(-1)^{n+1}\} = \{1, -1, 1, -1, \ldots\}$ is bounded but
   diverges.
17. strictly increasing 19. strictly increasing
21. eventually strictly increasing 23. eventually strictly increasing
25. Yes; the limit lies in the interval [1, 2].
27. (a) $\sqrt{2}, \sqrt{2+\sqrt{2}}, \sqrt{2+\sqrt{2+\sqrt{2}}}$ (e) $L = 2$

▶ **Exercise Set 9.3 (Page 621)**

1. (a) $2, \frac{12}{5}, \frac{62}{25}, \frac{312}{125}; \frac{5}{2}\left(1-\left(\frac{1}{5}\right)^n\right)$; $\lim\limits_{n\to+\infty} s_n = \frac{5}{2}$ (converges)
   (b) $\frac{1}{4}, \frac{3}{4}, \frac{7}{4}, \frac{15}{4}; -\frac{1}{4}(1-2^n)$; $\lim\limits_{n\to+\infty} s_n = +\infty$ (diverges)
   (c) $\frac{1}{6}, \frac{1}{4}, \frac{3}{10}, \frac{1}{3}; \frac{1}{2}-\frac{1}{n+2}$; $\lim\limits_{n\to+\infty} s_n = \frac{1}{2}$ (converges)
3. $\frac{4}{7}$ 5. 6 7. $\frac{1}{3}$ 9. $\frac{1}{6}$ 11. diverges 13. $\frac{448}{3}$
15. (a) Exercise 5 (b) Exercise 3 (c) Exercise 7 (d) Exercise 9
Responses to True–False questions may be abridged to save space.
17. False; an infinite series converges if its sequence of *partial sums*
   converges.
19. True; the sequence of partial sums $\{s_n\}$ for the harmonic series satisfies
   $s_{2^n} > \frac{n+1}{2}$, so this series diverges.
21. 1 23. $\frac{532}{99}$ 27. 70 m
29. (a) $S_n = -\ln(n+1)$; $\lim\limits_{n\to+\infty} S_n = -\infty$ (diverges)
   (b) $S_n = \sum\limits_{k=2}^{n+1}\left[\ln\frac{k-1}{k} - \ln\frac{k}{k+1}\right]$, $\lim\limits_{n\to+\infty} S_n = -\ln 2$
31. (a) converges for $|x| < 1$; $S = \frac{x}{1+x^2}$
   (b) converges for $|x| > 2$; $S = \frac{1}{x^2-2x}$
   (c) converges for $x > 0$; $S = \frac{1}{e^x-1}$
33. $a_n = \frac{1}{2^{n-1}}a_1 + \frac{1}{2^{n-1}} + \frac{1}{2^{n-2}} + \cdots + \frac{1}{2}$, $\lim\limits_{n\to+\infty} a_n = 1$

▶ **Exercise Set 9.4 (Page 629)**

1. (a) $\frac{4}{3}$ (b) $-\frac{3}{4}$
3. (a) $p = 3$, converges (b) $p = \frac{1}{2}$, diverges
   (c) $p = 1$, diverges (d) $p = \frac{2}{3}$, diverges
5. (a) diverges (b) diverges (c) diverges (d) no information
7. (a) diverges (b) converges
9. diverges 11. diverges 13. diverges 15. diverges 17. diverges
19. converges 21. diverges 23. converges 25. converges for $p > 1$
29. (a) diverges (b) diverges
Responses to True–False questions may be abridged to save space.
31. False; for example, $\sum\limits_{k=0}^{\infty} 2^{-k}$ converges to 2, but $\sum \frac{1}{2^{-k}} = \sum 2^k$
   diverges.
33. True; see Theorem 9.4.4.
35. (a) $(\pi^2/2) - (\pi^4/90)$ (b) $(\pi^2/6) - (5/4)$ (c) $\pi^4/90$
37. (d) $\frac{1}{11} < \frac{1}{6}\pi^2 - s_{10} < \frac{1}{10}$
39. (a) $\int_n^{+\infty} \frac{1}{x^4}\,dx = \frac{1}{3n^3}$; apply Exercise 36(b) (b) $n = 6$
   (c) $\frac{\pi^4}{90} \approx 1.08238$
41. converges

▶ **Exercise Set 9.5 (Page 636)**

1. (a) converges (b) diverges 5. converges 7. converges
9. diverges 11. converges 13. inconclusive 15. diverges
17. diverges 19. converges
Responses to True–False questions may be abridged to save space.
21. False; the limit comparison test uses a limit of the quotient of
   corresponding terms taken from two different sequences.
23. True; use the limit comparison test with the convergent series
   $\sum (1/k^2)$.
25. converges 27. converges 29. converges 31. converges
33. diverges 35. diverges 37. converges 39. converges
41. diverges 43. converges 45. converges 47. converges

49. $u_k = \dfrac{k!}{1 \cdot 3 \cdot 5 \cdots (2k-1)}$; $\rho = \lim\limits_{k \to +\infty} \dfrac{k+1}{2k+1} = \dfrac{1}{2}$; converges
51. **(a)** converges **(b)** diverges **53.** **(a)** converges

▶ **Exercise Set 9.6 (Page 646)**

3. diverges **5.** converges **7.** converges absolutely **9.** diverges
11. converges absolutely **13.** conditionally convergent **15.** divergent
17. conditionally convergent **19.** conditionally convergent
21. divergent **23.** conditionally convergent **25.** converges absolutely
27. converges absolutely
Responses to True–False questions may be abridged to save space.
29. False; an alternating series has terms that alternate between positive
and negative.
31. True; if a series converges but diverges absolutely, then it converges
conditionally.
33. $|\text{error}| < 0.125$ **35.** $|\text{error}| < 0.1$ **37.** $n = 9999$
39. $n = 39{,}999$ **41.** $|\text{error}| < 0.00074$; $s_{10} \approx 0.4995$; $S = 0.5$
43. 0.84 **45.** 0.41 **47.** **(c)** $n = 50$
49. **(a)** If $a_k = \dfrac{(-1)^k}{\sqrt{k}}$, then $\sum a_k$ converges and $\sum a_k^2$ diverges.

If $a_k = \dfrac{(-1)^k}{k}$, then $\sum a_k$ converges and $\sum a_k^2$ also converges.

(b) If $a_k = \dfrac{1}{k}$, then $\sum a_k^2$ converges and $\sum a_k$ diverges. If $a_k = \dfrac{1}{k^2}$,
then $\sum a_k^2$ converges and $\sum a_k$ also converges.

▶ **Exercise Set 9.7 (Page 657)**

1. **(a)** $1 - x + \frac{1}{2}x^2, 1 - x$ **(b)** $1 - \frac{1}{2}x^2, 1$
3. **(a)** $1 + \frac{1}{2}(x-1) - \frac{1}{8}(x-1)^2$ **(b)** 1.04875 **5.** 1.80397443
7. $p_0(x) = 1, p_1(x) = 1 - x, p_2(x) = 1 - x + \frac{1}{2}x^2,$

$p_3(x) = 1 - x + \frac{1}{2}x^2 - \frac{1}{3!}x^3,$

$p_4(x) = 1 - x + \frac{1}{2}x^2 - \frac{1}{3!}x^3 + \frac{1}{4!}x^4; \sum\limits_{k=0}^{n} \dfrac{(-1)^k}{k!}x^k$

9. $p_0(x) = 1, p_1(x) = 1, p_2(x) = 1 - \dfrac{\pi^2}{2!}x^2, p_3(x) = 1 - \dfrac{\pi^2}{2!}x^2,$

$p_4(x) = 1 - \dfrac{\pi^2}{2!}x^2 + \dfrac{\pi^4}{4!}x^4; \sum\limits_{k=0}^{\lfloor n/2 \rfloor} \dfrac{(-1)^k \pi^{2k}}{(2k)!}x^{2k}$ (See Exercise 70 of
Section 0.2.)

11. $p_0(x) = 0, p_1(x) = x, p_2(x) = x - \frac{1}{2}x^2, p_3(x) = x - \frac{1}{2}x^2 + \frac{1}{3}x^3,$

$p_4(x) = x - \frac{1}{2}x^2 + \frac{1}{3}x^3 - \frac{1}{4}x^4; \sum\limits_{k=1}^{n} \dfrac{(-1)^{k+1}}{k}x^k$

13. $p_0(x) = 1, p_1(x) = 1, p_2(x) = 1 + \dfrac{x^2}{2},$

$p_3(x) = 1 + \dfrac{x^2}{2}, p_4(x) = 1 + \dfrac{x^2}{2} + \dfrac{x^4}{4!}; \sum\limits_{k=0}^{\lfloor n/2 \rfloor} \dfrac{1}{(2k)!}x^{2k}$ (See Exercise 70 of Section 0.2.)

15. $p_0(x) = 0, p_1(x) = 0, p_2(x) = x^2, p_3(x) = x^2,$

$p_4(x) = x^2 - \frac{1}{6}x^4; \sum\limits_{k=0}^{\lfloor n/2 \rfloor - 1} \dfrac{(-1)^k}{(2k+1)!}x^{2k+2}$ (See Exercise 70 of Section 0.2.)

17. $p_0(x) = e, p_1(x) = e + e(x-1),$

$p_2(x) = e + e(x-1) + \dfrac{e}{2}(x-1)^2,$

$p_3(x) = e + e(x-1) + \dfrac{e}{2}(x-1)^2 + \dfrac{e}{3!}(x-1)^3,$

$p_4(x) = e + e(x-1) + \dfrac{e}{2}(x-1)^2 + \dfrac{e}{3!}(x-1)^3 + \dfrac{e}{4!}(x-1)^4;$

$\sum\limits_{k=0}^{n} \dfrac{e}{k!}(x-1)^k$

19. $p_0(x) = -1, p_1(x) = -1 - (x+1),$
$p_2(x) = -1 - (x+1) - (x+1)^2,$
$p_3(x) = -1 - (x+1) - (x+1)^2 - (x+1)^3,$
$p_4(x) = -1 - (x+1) - (x+1)^2 - (x+1)^3 - (x+1)^4;$
$\sum\limits_{k=0}^{n} (-1)(x+1)^k$

21. $p_0(x) = p_1(x) = 1, p_2(x) = p_3(x) = 1 - \dfrac{\pi^2}{2}\left(x - \dfrac{1}{2}\right)^2,$

$p_4(x) = 1 - \dfrac{\pi^2}{2}\left(x - \dfrac{1}{2}\right)^2 + \dfrac{\pi^4}{4!}\left(x - \dfrac{1}{2}\right)^4;$

$\sum\limits_{k=0}^{\lfloor n/2 \rfloor} \dfrac{(-1)^k \pi^{2k}}{(2k)!}\left(x - \dfrac{1}{2}\right)^{2k}$ (See Exercise 70 of Section 0.2.)

23. $p_0(x) = 0, p_1(x) = (x-1), p_2(x) = (x-1) - \frac{1}{2}(x-1)^2,$
$p_3(x) = (x-1) - \frac{1}{2}(x-1)^2 + \frac{1}{3}(x-1)^3,$
$p_4(x) = (x-1) - \frac{1}{2}(x-1)^2 + \frac{1}{3}(x-1)^3 - \frac{1}{4}(x-1)^4;$
$\sum\limits_{k=1}^{n} \dfrac{(-1)^{k-1}}{k}(x-1)^k$

25. **(a)** $p_3(x) = 1 + 2x - x^2 + x^3$
(b) $p_3(x) = 1 + 2(x-1) - (x-1)^2 + (x-1)^3$
27. $p_0(x) = 1, p_1(x) = 1 - 2x,$
$p_2(x) = 1 - 2x + 2x^2,$
$p_3(x) = 1 - 2x + 2x^2 - \frac{4}{3}x^3$

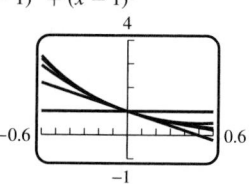

29. $p_0(x) = -1, p_2(x) = -1 + \frac{1}{2}(x - \pi)^2,$

$p_4(x) = -1 + \frac{1}{2}(x-\pi)^2 - \frac{1}{24}(x-\pi)^4,$

$p_6(x) = -1 + \frac{1}{2}(x-\pi)^2 - \frac{1}{24}(x-\pi)^4$

$\quad + \frac{1}{720}(x-\pi)^6$

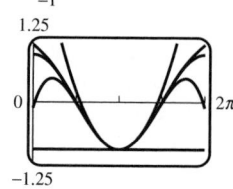

Responses to True–False questions may be abridged to save space.
31. True; $y = f(x_0) + f'(x_0)(x - x_0)$ is the first-degree Taylor
polynomial for f about $x = x_0$.
33. False; $p_6^{(4)}(x_0) = f^{(4)}(x_0)$ **35.** 1.64870 **37.** IV
39. **(a)**

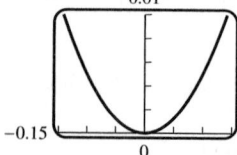

(b)

x	−1.000	−0.750	−0.500	−0.250	0.000	0.250	0.500	0.750	1.000
$f(x)$	0.431	0.506	0.619	0.781	1.000	1.281	1.615	1.977	2.320
$p_1(x)$	0.000	0.250	0.500	0.750	1.000	1.250	1.500	1.750	2.000
$p_2(x)$	0.500	0.531	0.625	0.781	1.000	1.281	1.625	2.031	2.500

(c) $|e^{\sin x} - (1 + x)| < 0.01$
for $-0.14 < x < 0.14$

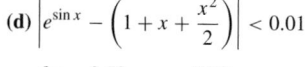

(d) $\left| e^{\sin x} - \left(1 + x + \dfrac{x^2}{2}\right)\right| < 0.01$

for $-0.50 < x < 0.50$

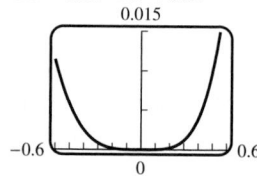

41. (a) $[0, 0.137]$ (b) 0.002

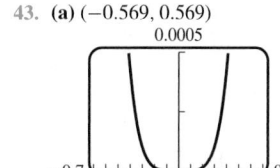

43. (a) $(-0.569, 0.569)$

45. $(-0.311, 0.311)$

Exercise Set 9.8 (Page 667)

1. $\displaystyle\sum_{k=0}^{\infty} \frac{(-1)^k}{k!} x^k$ **3.** $\displaystyle\sum_{k=0}^{\infty} \frac{(-1)^k \pi^{2k}}{(2k)!} x^{2k}$ **5.** $\displaystyle\sum_{k=1}^{\infty} \frac{(-1)^{k+1}}{k} x^k$

7. $\displaystyle\sum_{k=0}^{\infty} \frac{1}{(2k)!} x^{2k}$ **9.** $\displaystyle\sum_{k=0}^{\infty} \frac{(-1)^k}{(2k+1)!} x^{2k+2}$ **11.** $\displaystyle\sum_{k=0}^{\infty} \frac{e}{k!}(x-1)^k$

13. $\displaystyle\sum_{k=0}^{\infty}(-1)(x+1)^k$ **15.** $\displaystyle\sum_{k=0}^{\infty} \frac{(-1)^k \pi^{2k}}{(2k)!}\left(x-\frac{1}{2}\right)^{2k}$

17. $\displaystyle\sum_{k=1}^{\infty} \frac{(-1)^{k-1}}{k}(x-1)^k$ **19.** $-1 < x < 1;\ \dfrac{1}{1+x}$

21. $1 < x < 3;\ \dfrac{1}{3-x}$ **23.** (a) $-2 < x < 2$ (b) $f(0) = 1;\ f(1) = \frac{2}{3}$

Responses to True–False questions may be abridged to save space.

25. True; see Theorem 9.8.2(c).

27. True; the polynomial *is* the Maclaurin series and converges for all x.

29. $R = 1;\ [-1, 1)$ **31.** $R = +\infty;\ (-\infty, +\infty)$ **33.** $R = \frac{1}{5};\ \left[-\frac{1}{5}, \frac{1}{5}\right]$

35. $R = 1;\ [-1, 1]$ **37.** $R = 1;\ (-1, 1]$ **39.** $R = +\infty;\ (-\infty, +\infty)$

41. $R = 1;\ [-1, 1]$ **43.** $R = 1;\ (-2, 0]$ **45.** $R = \frac{4}{3};\ \left(-\frac{19}{3}, -\frac{11}{3}\right)$

47. $R = +\infty;\ (-\infty, +\infty)$ **49.** $(-\infty, +\infty)$ **55.** radius $= R$

61. (a) $n = 5;\ s_5 \approx 1.1026$ (b) $\zeta(3.7) \approx 1.10629$

Exercise Set 9.9 (Page 676)

3. 0.069756 **5.** 0.99500 **7.** 0.99619 **9.** 0.5208

11. (a) $\displaystyle\sum_{k=1}^{\infty} 2\frac{(1/9)^{2k-1}}{2k-1}$ (b) 0.223

13. (a) $0.4635;\ 0.3218$ (b) 3.1412 (c) no

15. (a) error $\leq 9 \times 10^{-8}$ (b)

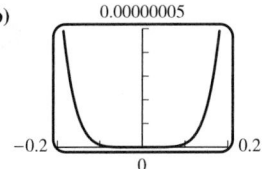

17. (a) $\displaystyle\sum_{k=0}^{\infty}(-1)^k x^k$ (b) $1 + \dfrac{x}{3} + \displaystyle\sum_{k=2}^{\infty}(-1)^{k-1}\frac{2\cdot 5\cdots(3k-4)}{3^k k!} x^k$

(c) $\displaystyle\sum_{k=0}^{\infty}(-1)^k \frac{(k+2)(k+1)}{2} x^k$ **23.** 23.406%

Exercise Set 9.10 (Page 686)

1. (a) $1 - x + x^2 - \cdots + (-1)^k x^k + \cdots;\ R = 1$

(b) $1 + x^2 + x^4 + \cdots + x^{2k} + \cdots;\ R = 1$

(c) $1 + 2x + 4x^2 + \cdots + 2^k x^k + \cdots;\ R = \frac{1}{2}$

(d) $\dfrac{1}{2} + \dfrac{1}{2^2} x + \dfrac{1}{2^3} x^2 + \cdots + \dfrac{1}{2^{k+1}} x^k + \cdots;\ R = 2$

3. (a) $(2 + x)^{-1/2} = \dfrac{1}{2^{1/2}} - \dfrac{1}{2^{5/2}} x + \dfrac{1\cdot 3}{2^{9/2}\cdot 2!} x^2 - \dfrac{1\cdot 3\cdot 5}{2^{13/2}\cdot 3!} x^3 + \cdots$

(b) $(1 - x^2)^{-2} = 1 + 2x^2 + 3x^4 + 4x^6 + \cdots$

5. (a) $2x - \dfrac{2^3}{3!} x^3 + \dfrac{2^5}{5!} x^5 - \dfrac{2^7}{7!} x^7 + \cdots;\ R = +\infty$

(b) $1 - 2x + 2x^2 - \dfrac{4}{3} x^3 + \cdots;\ R = +\infty$

(c) $1 + x^2 + \dfrac{1}{2!} x^4 + \dfrac{1}{3!} x^6 + \cdots;\ R = +\infty$

(d) $x^2 - \dfrac{\pi^2}{2} x^4 + \dfrac{\pi^4}{4!} x^6 - \dfrac{\pi^6}{6!} x^8 + \cdots;\ R = +\infty$

7. (a) $x^2 - 3x^3 + 9x^4 - 27x^5 + \cdots;\ R = \frac{1}{3}$

(b) $2x^2 + \dfrac{2^3}{3!} x^4 + \dfrac{2^5}{5!} x^6 + \dfrac{2^7}{7!} x^8 + \cdots;\ R = +\infty$

(c) $x - \dfrac{3}{2} x^3 + \dfrac{3}{8} x^5 + \dfrac{1}{16} x^7 + \cdots;\ R = 1$

9. (a) $x^2 - \dfrac{2^3}{4!} x^4 + \dfrac{2^5}{6!} x^6 - \dfrac{2^7}{8!} x^8 + \cdots$

(b) $12x^3 - 6x^6 + 4x^9 - 3x^{12} + \cdots$

11. (a) $1 - (x - 1) + (x - 1)^2 - \cdots + (-1)^k(x - 1)^k + \cdots$ (b) $(0, 2)$

13. (a) $x + x^2 + \dfrac{x^3}{3} - \dfrac{x^5}{30} + \cdots$ (b) $x - \dfrac{x^3}{24} + \dfrac{x^4}{24} - \dfrac{71}{1920} x^5 + \cdots$

15. (a) $1 + \frac{1}{2}x^2 + \frac{5}{24}x^4 + \frac{61}{720}x^6 + \cdots$ (b) $x - x^2 + \frac{1}{3}x^3 - \frac{1}{30}x^5 + \cdots$

19. $2 - 4x + 2x^2 - 4x^3 + 2x^4 + \cdots$

25. $[-1, 1];\ [-1, 1)$ **27.** (a) $\displaystyle\sum_{k=0}^{\infty} x^{2k+1}$ (b) $f^{(5)}(0) = 5!,\ f^{(6)}(0) = 0$

(c) $f^{(n)}(0) = n!c_n = \begin{cases} n! & \text{if } n \text{ odd} \\ 0 & \text{if } n \text{ even} \end{cases}$

29. (a) 1 (b) $-\frac{1}{3}$ **31.** 0.3103 **33.** 0.200

35. (a) $\displaystyle\sum_{k=0}^{\infty} \frac{x^{4k}}{k!};\ R = +\infty$ **37.** (a) $3/4$ (b) $\ln(4/3)$

39. (a) $x - \frac{1}{6}x^3 + \frac{3}{40}x^5 - \frac{5}{112}x^7 + \cdots$

(b) $x + \displaystyle\sum_{k=1}^{\infty}(-1)^k \frac{1\cdot 3\cdot 5\cdots(2k-1)}{2^k k!(2k+1)} x^{2k+1}$ (c) $R = 1$

41. (a) $y(t) = y_0 \displaystyle\sum_{k=0}^{\infty} \frac{(-1)^k(0.000121)^k t^k}{k!}$ (c) $0.9998790073\,y_0$

43. $2\pi\sqrt{\dfrac{L}{g}}\left(1 + \dfrac{k^2}{4} + \dfrac{9k^4}{64}\right)$

Chapter 9 Review Exercises (Page 689)

9. (a) true (b) sometimes false (c) sometimes false

(d) true (e) sometimes false (f) sometimes false

(g) false (h) sometimes false (i) true

(j) true (k) sometimes false (l) sometimes false

11. (a) $\left\{\dfrac{n+2}{(n+1)^2 - n^2}\right\}_{n=1}^{+\infty}$; converges, $\displaystyle\lim_{n\to+\infty} \frac{n+2}{(n+1)^2 - n^2} = \frac{1}{2}$

(b) $\left\{(-1)^{n+1}\dfrac{n}{2n+1}\right\}_{n=1}^{+\infty}$; diverges

15. (a) converges (b) converges **17.** (a) converges (b) diverges

19. (a) diverges (b) converges **21.** $\dfrac{1}{4\cdot 5^{99}}$

23. (a) 2 (b) diverges (c) $3/4$ (d) $\pi/4$ **25.** $p > 1$

29. (a) $p_0(x) = 1,\ p_1(x) = 1 - 7x,\ p_2(x) = 1 - 7x + 5x^2,$

$p_3(x) = 1 - 7x + 5x^2 + 4x^3,\ p_4(x) = 1 - 7x + 5x^2 + 4x^3$

33. (a) $e^2 - 1$ (b) 0 (c) $\cos e$ (d) $\frac{1}{3}$

37. (a) $x - \frac{2}{3}x^3 + \frac{2}{15}x^5 - \frac{4}{315}x^7$ (b) $x - \frac{2}{3}x^3 + \frac{2}{15}x^5 - \frac{4}{315}x^7$

Chapter 9 Making Connections (Page 691)

Where correct answers to a Making Connections exercise may vary, no answer is listed. Sample answers for these questions are available on the Book Companion Site.

1. (a) $\dfrac{a \sin \theta}{1 - \cos \theta}$ (b) $a \csc \theta$ (c) $a \cot \theta$

2. (a) $A = 1, B = -2$ (b) $s_n = 2 - \dfrac{2^{n+1}}{3^{n+1} - 2^{n+1}}; 2$

4. (a) $124.58 < d < 124.77$ (b) $1243 < s < 1424$

6. (b) $v(t) \approx v_0 - \left(\dfrac{cv_0}{m} + g\right)t + \dfrac{c^2}{2m^2}\left(v_0 + \dfrac{mg}{c}\right)t^2$

▶ **Exercise Set 10.1 (Page 700)**

1. (a) $y = x + 2 \ (-1 \le x \le 4)$

(c)

t	0	1	2	3	4	5
x	-1	0	1	2	3	4
y	1	2	3	4	5	6

(d)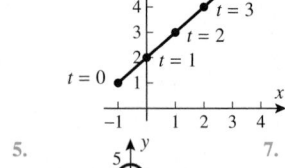

3.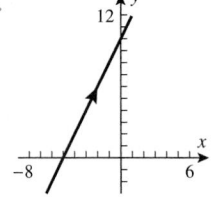

5.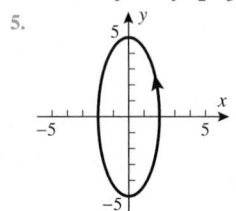

7.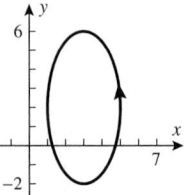

9.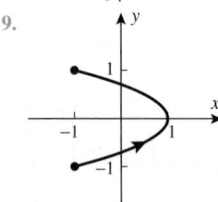

11.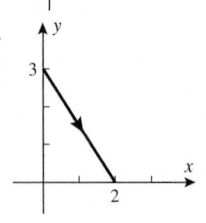

13. $x = 5 \cos t, y = -5 \sin t \ (0 \le t \le 2\pi)$ **15.** $x = 2, y = t$

17. $x = t^2, y = t \ (-1 \le t \le 1)$

19. (a)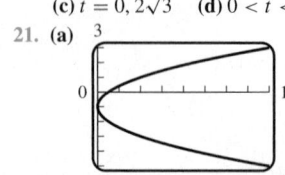

(b)

t	0	1	2	3	4	5
x	0	5.5	8	4.5	-8	-32.5
y	1	1.5	3	5.5	9	13.5

(c) $t = 0, 2\sqrt{3}$ (d) $0 < t < 2\sqrt{2}$ (e) $t = 2$

21. (a) 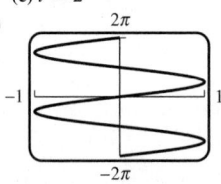 (b)

23. (a) IV (b) II (c) V (d) VI (e) III (f) I   **25.** (b) $\frac{1}{2}$ (c) $\frac{3}{4}$

27. (b) from (x_0, y_0) to (x_1, y_1)

(c) $x = 3 - 2(t - 1), y = -1 + 5(t - 1)$

29. 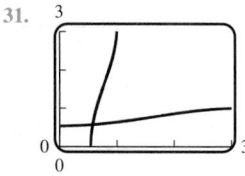 **31.**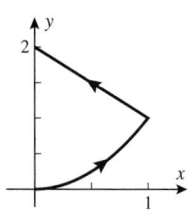

Responses to True–False questions may be abridged to save space.

33. False; $x = \sin t, y = \cos^2 t$ describe only the portion of the parabola $y = 1 - x^2$ with $-1 \le x \le 1$.

35. True; $\dfrac{dy}{dx} = \dfrac{dy/dt}{dx/dt} = \dfrac{12t^3 - 6t^2}{x'(t)}$ **37.**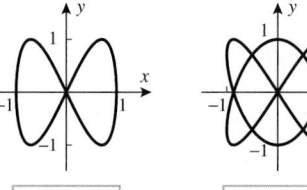

39. (a) $x = 4 \cos t, y = 3 \sin t$ (b) $x = -1 + 4\cos t, y = 2 + 3 \sin t$

41. $-4, 4$ **43.** both are positive **45.** $4, 4$ **47.** $2/\sqrt{3}, -1/(3\sqrt{3})$

49. $\sqrt{3}, 4$ **51.** $y = -e^{-2}x + 2e^{-1}$

53. (a) $0, \pi, 2\pi$ (b) $\pi/2, 3\pi/2$

55. (a)   (b) $y = -2x, y = 2x$

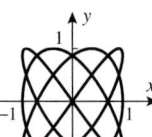 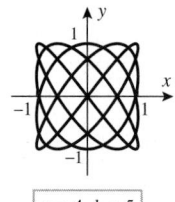

$a = 1, b = 2$ $a = 2, b = 3$

$a = 3, b = 4$ $a = 4, b = 5$

57. $y = 2x - 8, y = -2x + 8$ **59.**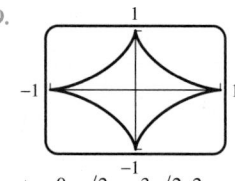

$t = 0, \pi/2, \pi, 3\pi/2, 2\pi$

61. (a) $\dfrac{dy}{dx} = \dfrac{3 \sin t}{1 - 3 \cos t}$ (b) $\theta \approx -0.4345$

63. (a) ellipses with fixed center, varying axes of symmetry

(b) ellipses with varying center, fixed shape, size, and orientation

(c) circles of radius 1 with centers on line $y = x - 1$

65. $\frac{1}{3}(5\sqrt{5} - 8)$ **67.** 3π **69.** $\dfrac{\sqrt{10}}{2}(e^2 - e^{-2})$

73. (b) $x = \cos t + \cos 2t, y = \sin t + \sin 2t$ (c) yes

75. $S = 49\pi$ **77.** $S = \sqrt{2}\pi$

▶ **Exercise Set 10.2 (Page 716)** _____

1.

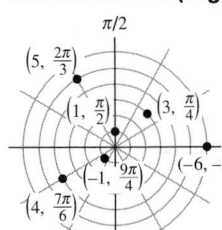

3. (a) $(3\sqrt{3}, 3)$
(b) $(-7/2, 7\sqrt{3}/2)$
(c) $(3\sqrt{3}, 3)$
(d) $(0, 0)$
(e) $(-7\sqrt{3}/2, 7/2)$
(f) $(-5, 0)$

5. (a) $(5, \pi), (5, -\pi)$ (b) $(4, 11\pi/6), (4, -\pi/6)$
(c) $(2, 3\pi/2), (2, -\pi/2)$ (d) $(8\sqrt{2}, 5\pi/4), (8\sqrt{2}, -3\pi/4)$
(e) $(6, 2\pi/3), (6, -4\pi/3)$ (f) $(\sqrt{2}, \pi/4), (\sqrt{2}, -7\pi/4)$

7. (a) $(5, 0.92730)$ (b) $(10, -0.92730)$ (c) $(1.27155, 2.47582)$

9. (a) circle (b) line (c) circle (d) line

11. (a) $r = 3\sec\theta$ (b) $r = \sqrt{7}$ (c) $r = -6\sin\theta$
(d) $r^2\cos\theta\sin\theta = 4/9$

13.

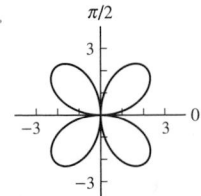

15.

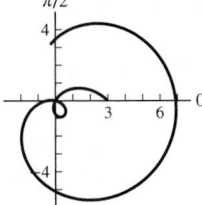

17. (a) $r = 5$ (b) $r = 6\cos\theta$ (c) $r = 1 - \cos\theta$

19. (a) $r = 3\sin 2\theta$ (b) $r = 3 + 2\sin\theta$ (c) $r^2 = 9\cos 2\theta$

21.

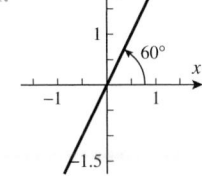

23.

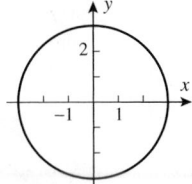

25.

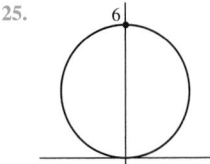

Circle

27.

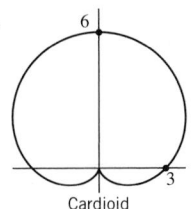

Cardioid

29.

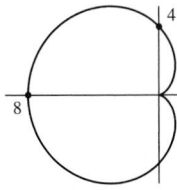

Cardioid

31.

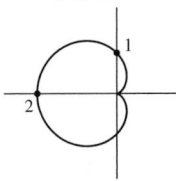

Cardioid

33.

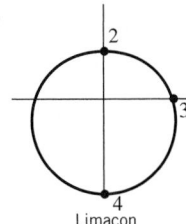

Limaçon

35.

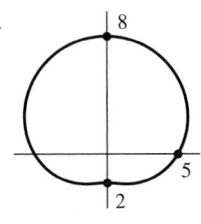

Limaçon

37.

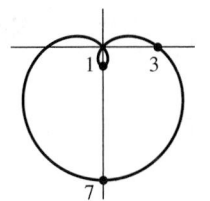

Limaçon

39.

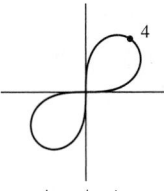

Lemniscate

41.

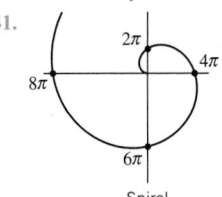

Spiral

43.

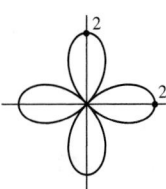

Four-petal rose

45.

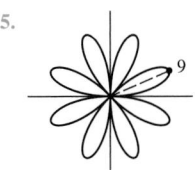

Eight-petal rose

Responses to True–False questions may be abridged to save space.

47. True; $\left(-1, \dfrac{\pi}{3}\right)$ describes the same point as $\left(1, \dfrac{\pi}{3} + \pi\right)$, which describes the same point as $\left(1, \dfrac{\pi}{3} + \pi - 2\pi\right) = \left(1, -\dfrac{2\pi}{3}\right)$.

49. False; $-1 < \sin 2\theta < 0$ for $\pi/2 < \theta < \pi$, so this portion of the graph is in the fourth quadrant.

51. $0 \le \theta \le 4\pi$

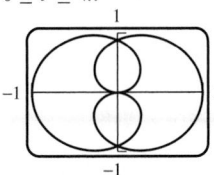

53. $0 \le \theta \le 8\pi$

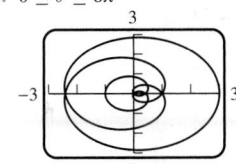

55. $0 \le \theta \le 5\pi$

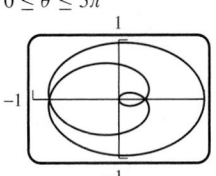

57. (a) $-4\pi < \theta < 4\pi$

61. (a)

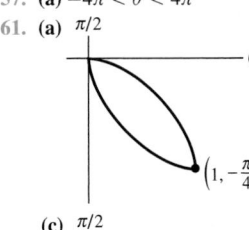

(b)

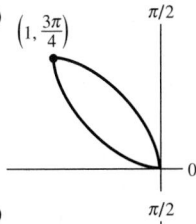

(c)

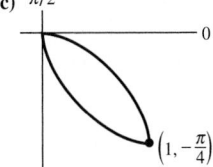

(d)

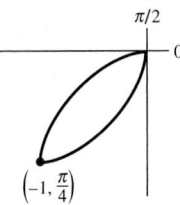

63. (a) $\pi/2$ **(b)** $\pi/2$

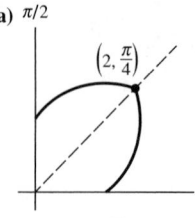

$\left(2, \frac{\pi}{4}\right)$

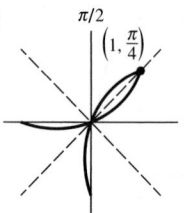

$\left(1, \frac{\pi}{4}\right)$

67. (a) $r = 1 + \dfrac{\sqrt{2}}{2}(\cos\theta + \sin\theta)$ **(b)** $r = 1 + \sin\theta$

   (c) $r = 1 - \cos\theta$ **(d)** $r = 1 - \dfrac{\sqrt{2}}{2}(\cos\theta + \sin\theta)$

69. $(3/2, \pi/3)$ **73.** $\sqrt{2}$

▶ **Exercise Set 10.3 (Page 726)**

1. $\sqrt{3}$ **3.** $\dfrac{\tan 2 - 2}{2\tan 2 + 1}$ **5.** $1/2$ **7.** $1, 0, -1$

9. horizontal: $(3a/2, \pi/3), (0, \pi), (3a/2, 5\pi/3)$;
   vertical: $(2a, 0), (a/2, 2\pi/3), (a/2, 4\pi/3)$

11. $(0, 0), (\sqrt{2}/4, \pi/4), (\sqrt{2}/4, 3\pi/4)$

13. $\pi/2$ **15.** $\pi/2$

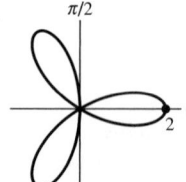

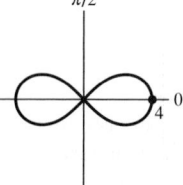

$\theta = \pi/2, \pm\pi/6$ $\theta = \pm\pi/4$

17.

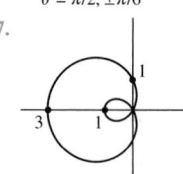

$\theta = \pm\pi/3$

19. $L = 2\pi a$ **21.** $L = 8a$

23. (b) ≈ 2.42

(c)

n	2	3	4	5	6	7
L	2.42211	2.22748	2.14461	2.10100	2.07501	2.05816

n	8	9	10	11	12	13	14
L	2.04656	2.03821	2.03199	2.02721	2.02346	2.02046	2.01802

n	15	16	17	18	19	20
L	2.01600	2.01431	2.01288	2.01167	2.01062	2.00971

25. (a) $\displaystyle\int_{\pi/2}^{\pi} \frac{1}{2}(1 - \cos\theta)^2 d\theta$ **(b)** $\displaystyle\int_{0}^{\pi/2} 2\cos^2\theta\, d\theta$

   (c) $\displaystyle\int_{0}^{\pi/2} \frac{1}{2}\sin^2 2\theta\, d\theta$ **(d)** $\displaystyle\int_{0}^{2\pi} \frac{1}{2}\theta^2 d\theta$

   (e) $\displaystyle\int_{-\pi/2}^{\pi/2} \frac{1}{2}(1 - \sin\theta)^2 d\theta$ **(f)** $\displaystyle\int_{0}^{\pi/4} \cos^2 2\theta\, d\theta$

27. (a) πa^2 **(b)** πa^2 **29.** 6π **31.** 4π **33.** $\pi - 3\sqrt{3}/2$

35. $\pi/2 - \frac{1}{4}$ **37.** $10\pi/3 - 4\sqrt{3}$ **39.** π **41.** $9\sqrt{3}/2 - \pi$

43. $(\pi + 3\sqrt{3})/4$ **45.** $\pi - 2$

Responses to True–False questions may be abridged to save space.

47. True; apply Theorem 10.3.1: $\left.\cos\dfrac{\theta}{2}\right|_{\theta=3\pi} = 0$ and $\left.\dfrac{dr}{d\theta}\right|_{\theta=3\pi} =$
   $\dfrac{1}{2} \neq 0$, so the line $\theta = 3\pi$ (the x-axis) is tangent to the curve at
   the origin.

49. False; the area of the sector is $\dfrac{\theta}{2\pi} \cdot \pi r^2 = \dfrac{1}{2}\theta r^2$.

51. (b) a^2 **(c)** $2\sqrt{3} - \dfrac{2\pi}{3}$ **53.** $8\pi^3 a^2$

59. $\pi/16$

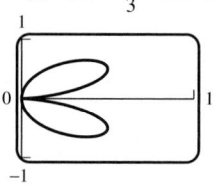

65. π^2

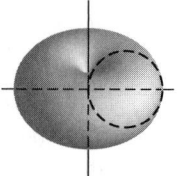

67. $32\pi/5$

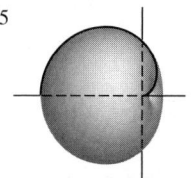

▶ **Exercise Set 10.4 (Page 744)**

1. (a) $x = y^2$ **(b)** $-3y = x^2$ **(c)** $\dfrac{x^2}{9} + \dfrac{y^2}{4} = 1$ **(d)** $\dfrac{x^2}{4} + \dfrac{y^2}{9} = 1$

   (e) $y^2 - x^2 = 1$ **(f)** $\dfrac{x^2}{4} - \dfrac{y^2}{4} = 1$

3. (a) focus: $(1, 0)$;   **(b)** focus: $(0, -2)$;
   vertex: $(0, 0)$;   vertex: $(0, 0)$;
   directrix: $x = -1$ directrix: $y = 2$

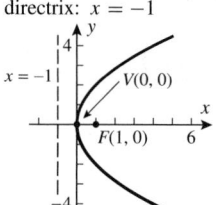

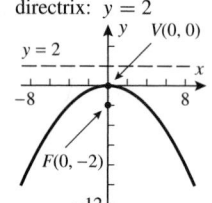

5. (a)   **(b)**

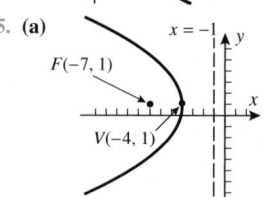

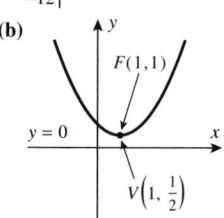

7. (a)   **(b)**

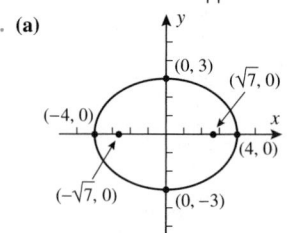

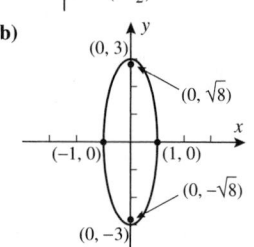

9. (a) $\dfrac{(x+3)^2}{16} + \dfrac{(y-5)^2}{4} = 1$

$c^2 = 16 - 4 = 12, c = 2\sqrt{3}$

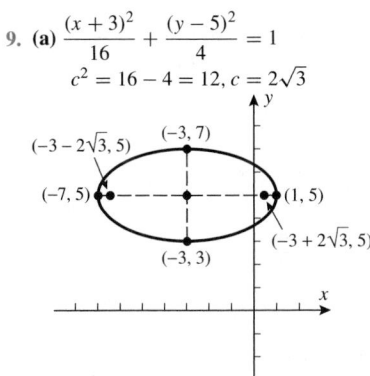

(b) $\dfrac{x^2}{4} + \dfrac{(y+2)^2}{9} = 1$

$c^2 = 9 - 4 = 5, c = 2\sqrt{5}$

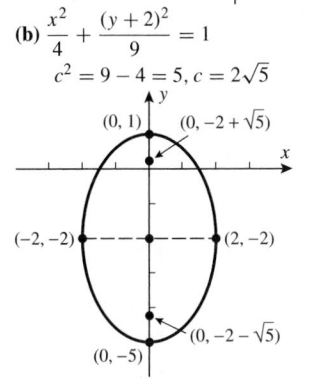

11. (a) vertices: $(\pm 4, 0)$;
foci: $(\pm 5, 0)$;
asymptotes: $y = \pm 3x/4$

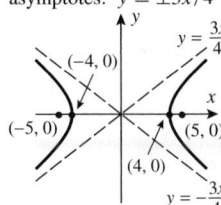

(b) vertices: $(0, \pm 2)$;
foci: $(0, \pm 2\sqrt{10})$;
asymptotes: $y = \pm x/3$

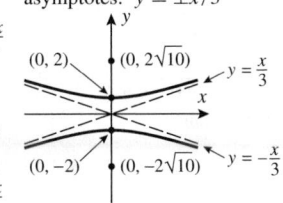

13. (a) $c^2 = 3 + 5 = 8, c = 2\sqrt{2}$

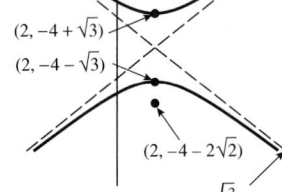

(b) $\dfrac{(x+1)^2}{1} - \dfrac{(y-3)^2}{2} = 1$

$c^2 = 1 + 2 = 3, c = \sqrt{3}$

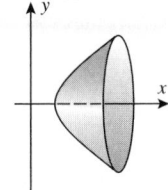

15. (a) $y^2 = 12x$ (b) $x^2 = -y$ 17. $y^2 = 2(x-1)$

19. (a) $\dfrac{x^2}{9} + \dfrac{y^2}{4} = 1$ (b) $\dfrac{x^2}{16} + \dfrac{y^2}{25} = 1$

21. (a) $\dfrac{x^2}{81/8} + \dfrac{y^2}{36} = 1$ (b) $\dfrac{(x+1)^2}{4} + \dfrac{(y-2)^2}{5} = 1$

23. (a) $\dfrac{x^2}{4} - \dfrac{y^2}{5} = 1$ (b) $\dfrac{y^2}{4} - \dfrac{x^2}{9} = 1$

25. (a) $\dfrac{y^2}{9} - \dfrac{x^2}{16} = 1, \dfrac{x^2}{16} - \dfrac{y^2}{9} = 1$ (b) $\dfrac{x^2}{9/5} - \dfrac{y^2}{36/5} = 1$

Responses to True–False questions may be abridged to save space.

27. False; the description matches a parabola.

29. False; the distance from the parabola's focus to its directrix is $2p$; see Figure 10.4.6.

31. (a) 16 ft   (b) $8\sqrt{3}$ ft   35. $\frac{1}{16}$ ft

39. $\frac{1}{32}(x-4)^2 + \frac{1}{36}(y-3)^2 = 1$

43. $L = D\sqrt{1 + p^2}, T = \frac{1}{2}pD$ 45. $(64.612, 200)$

47. (a) $V = \dfrac{\pi b^2}{3a^2}(b^2 - 2a^2)\sqrt{a^2 + b^2} + \dfrac{2}{3}ab^2\pi$

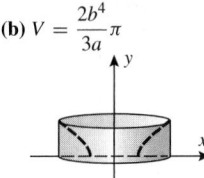

(b) $V = \dfrac{2b^4}{3a}\pi$

53. (a) $(x-1)^2 - 5(y+1)^2 = 5$, hyperbola
(b) $x^2 - 3(y+1)^2 = 0, x = \pm\sqrt{3}(y+1)$, two lines
(c) $4(x+2)^2 + 8(y+1)^2 = 4$, ellipse
(d) $3(x+2)^2 + (y+1)^2 = 0$, the point $(-2, -1)$ (degenerate case)
(e) $(x+4)^2 + 2y = 2$, parabola
(f) $5(x+4)^2 + 2y = -14$, parabola

▶ **Exercise Set 10.5 (Page 753)**

1. (a) $x' = -1 + 3\sqrt{3}$, $y' = 3 + \sqrt{3}$ 3. $y'^2 - x'^2 = 18$, hyperbola
   (b) $3x'^2 - y'^2 = 12$
   (c)

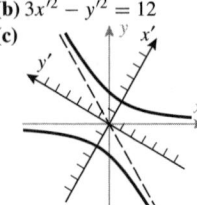 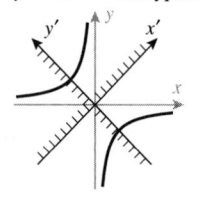

5. $\frac{1}{3}x'^2 - \frac{1}{2}y'^2 = 1$, hyperbola   7. $y' = x'^2$, parabola

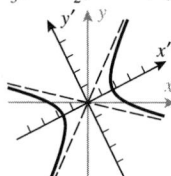 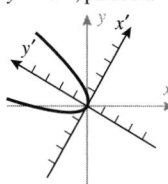

9. $y'^2 = 4(x' - 1)$, parabola   11. $\frac{1}{4}(x' + 1)^2 + y'^2 = 1$, ellipse

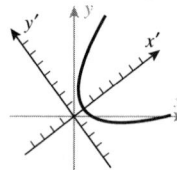 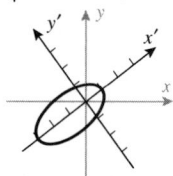

13. $x^2 + xy + y^2 = 3$
19. vertex: $(0, 0)$; focus: $(-1/\sqrt{2}, 1/\sqrt{2})$; directrix: $y = x - \sqrt{2}$
21. vertex: $(4/5, 3/5)$; focus: $(8/5, 6/5)$; directrix: $4x + 3y = 0$
23. foci: $\pm(4\sqrt{7}/5, 3\sqrt{7}/5)$; vertices: $\pm(16/5, 12/5)$;
    ends: $\pm(-9/5, 12/5)$
25. foci: $(1 - \sqrt{5}/2, -\sqrt{3} + \sqrt{15}/2)$, $(1 + \sqrt{5}/2, -\sqrt{3} - \sqrt{15}/2)$;
    vertices: $(-1/2, \sqrt{3}/2)$, $(5/2, -5\sqrt{3}/2)$;
    ends: $(1 + \sqrt{3}, 1 - \sqrt{3})$, $(1 - \sqrt{3}, -1 - \sqrt{3})$
27. foci: $\pm(\sqrt{15}, \sqrt{5})$; vertices: $\pm(2\sqrt{3}, 2)$;
    asymptotes: $y = \frac{5\sqrt{3} \pm 8}{11}x$
29. foci: $\left(-\frac{4}{\sqrt{5}} \pm 2\sqrt{\frac{13}{5}}, \frac{8}{\sqrt{5}} \pm \sqrt{\frac{13}{5}}\right)$;
    vertices: $(2/\sqrt{5}, 11/\sqrt{5})$, $(-2\sqrt{5}, \sqrt{5})$;
    asymptotes: $y = 7x/4 + 3\sqrt{5}$, $y = -x/8 + 3\sqrt{5}/2$

▶ **Exercise Set 10.6 (Page 761)**

1. (a) $e = 1, d = \frac{3}{2}$ (b) $e = \frac{1}{2}, d = 3$

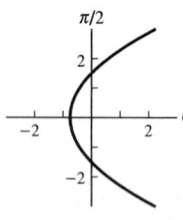 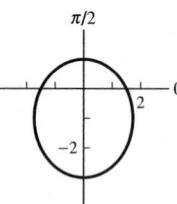

3. (a) parabola, opens up   (b) ellipse, directrix above the pole

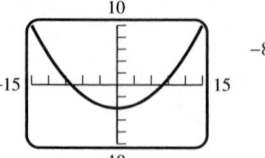

5. (a) $r = \dfrac{6}{4 + 3\cos\theta}$ (b) $r = \dfrac{1}{1 + \cos\theta}$ (c) $r = \dfrac{12}{3 + 4\sin\theta}$
7. (a) $r_0 = 2, r_1 = 6$; $\frac{1}{12}x^2 + \frac{1}{16}(y + 2)^2 = 1$
   (b) $r_0 = \frac{1}{3}, r_1 = 1$; $\frac{9}{4}\left(x - \frac{1}{3}\right)^2 + 3y^2 = 1$
9. (a) $r_0 = 1, r_1 = 3$; $(y - 2)^2 - \dfrac{x^2}{3} = 1$
   (b) $r_0 = 1, r_1 = 5$; $\dfrac{(x + 3)^2}{4} - \dfrac{y^2}{5} = 1$
11. (a) $r = \dfrac{12}{2 + \cos\theta}$ (b) $r = \dfrac{64}{25 - 15\sin\theta}$
13. $r = \dfrac{5\sqrt{2} + 5}{1 + \sqrt{2}\cos\theta}$ or $r = \dfrac{5\sqrt{2} - 5}{1 + \sqrt{2}\cos\theta}$
Responses to True–False questions may be abridged to save space.
19. True; the eccentricity e of an ellipse satisfies $0 < e < 1$ (Theorem 10.6.1).
21. False; eccentricity correlates to the "flatness" of an ellipse, which is independent of the distance between its foci.
23. (a) $T \approx 248$ yr
   (b) $r_0 \approx 4,449,675,000$ km, $r_1 \approx 7,400,325,000$ km
   (c) $r \approx \dfrac{37.05}{1 + 0.249\cos\theta}$ AU   (d)

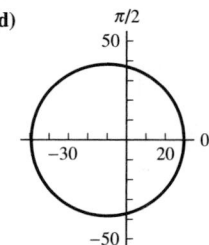

25. (a) $a \approx 178.26$ AU   (d)
   (b) $r_0 \approx 0.8735$ AU,
    $r_1 \approx 355.64$ AU
   (c) $r \approx \dfrac{1.74}{1 + 0.9951\cos\theta}$ AU

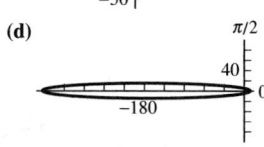

27. 563 km, 4286 km

▶ **Chapter 10 Review Exercises (Page 763)**

1. $x = \sqrt{2}\cos t$, $y = -\sqrt{2}\sin t$ $(0 \leq t \leq 3\pi/2)$ 3. (a) $-1/4, 1/4$
5. (a) $t = \pi/2 + n\pi$ for $n = 0, \pm1, \dots$ (b) $t = n\pi$ for $n = 0, \pm1, \dots$
7. (a) $(-4\sqrt{2}, -4\sqrt{2})$ (b) $(7/\sqrt{2}, -7/\sqrt{2})$ (c) $(4\sqrt{2}, 4\sqrt{2})$
   (d) $(5, 0)$ (e) $(0, -2)$ (f) $(0, 0)$
9. (a) $(5, 0.6435)$ (b) $(\sqrt{29}, 5.0929)$ (c) $(1.2716, 0.6658)$
11. (a) parabola   (b) hyperbola   (c) line   (d) circle
13.   15.   17.

 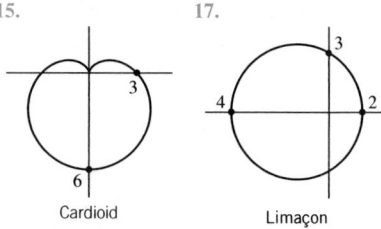

Line   Cardioid   Limaçon

19. (a) $-2, 1/4$ (b) $-3\sqrt{3}/4, 3\sqrt{3}/4$
21. (a) The top is traced from right to left as t goes from 0 to π. The bottom is traced from right to left as t goes from π to 2π, except for the loop, which is traced counterclockwise as t goes from $\pi + \sin^{-1}(1/4)$ to $2\pi - \sin^{-1}(1/4)$.   (b) $y = 1$
   (c) horizontal: $t = \pi/2, 3\pi/2$; vertical: $t = \pi + \sin^{-1}(1/\sqrt[3]{4})$, $2\pi - \sin^{-1}(1/\sqrt[3]{4})$
   (d) $r = 4 + \csc\theta$, $\theta = \pi + \sin^{-1}(1/4)$, $\theta = 2\pi - \sin^{-1}(1/4)$

23. $A = 6\pi$ 25. $A = \dfrac{5\pi}{12} - \dfrac{\sqrt{3}}{2}$ 27.

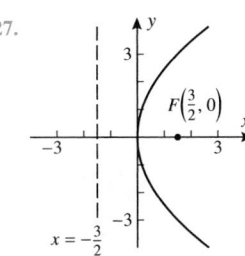

29.

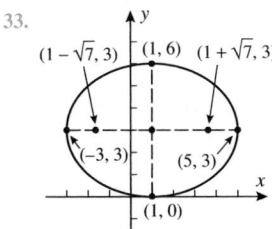

focus: $(9/4, -1)$;
vertex: $(4, -1)$;
directrix: $x = 23/4$

31.

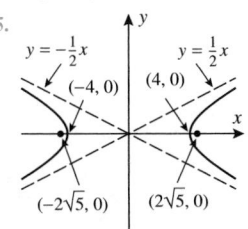

foci: $(0, \pm\sqrt{21})$;
vertices: $(0, \pm 5)$;
ends: $(\pm 2, 0)$

33.

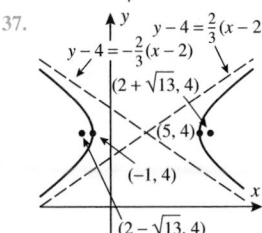

35.

37.

39. $x^2 = -16y$ 41. $y^2 - x^2 = 9$

43. **(b)** $x = \dfrac{v_0^2}{g} \sin\alpha\cos\alpha$; $y = y_0 + \dfrac{v_0^2 \sin^2\alpha}{2g}$

45. $\theta = \pi/4$; $5(y')^2 - (x')^2 = 6$; hyperbola

47. $\theta = \tan^{-1}(1/2)$; $y' = (x')^2$; parabola

49. **(a)** (i) ellipse;   (ii) right;   (iii) 1   **(b)** (i) hyperbola   (ii) left;
(iii) 1/3   **(c)** (i) parabola;   (ii) above;   (iii) 1/3   **(d)** (i) parabola;
(ii) below;   (iii) 3

51. **(a)** $\dfrac{(x+3)^2}{25} + \dfrac{(y-2)^2}{9} = 1$ **(b)** $(x+2)^2 = -8y$

(c) $\dfrac{(y-5)^2}{4} - 16(x+1)^2 = 1$

53. 15.86543959

▶ **Chapter 10 Making Connections (Page 766)**

Where correct answers to a Making Connections exercise may vary, no
answer is listed. Sample answers for these questions are available on the
Book Companion Site.

1. **(a)**

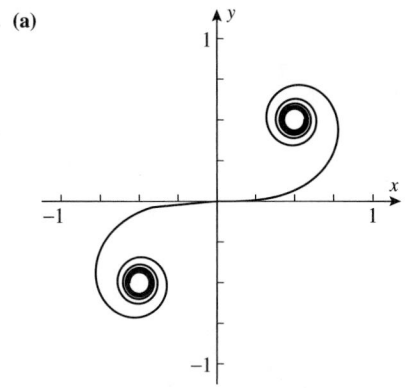

(c) $L = \displaystyle\int_{-1}^{1} \left[\cos^2\left(\dfrac{\pi t^2}{2}\right) + \sin^2\left(\dfrac{\pi t^2}{2}\right) \right] dt = 2$

2. **(a)** $P: (b\cos t, b\sin t)$;
$Q: (a\cos t, a\sin t)$;
$R: (a\cos t, b\sin t)$

▶ **Exercise Set 11.1 (Page 771)**

1. **(a)** $(0, 0, 0)$, $(3, 0, 0)$, $(3, 5, 0)$, $(0, 5, 0)$, $(0, 0, 4)$, $(3, 0, 4)$,
$(3, 5, 4)$, $(0, 5, 4)$
(b) $(0, 1, 0)$, $(4, 1, 0)$, $(4, 6, 0)$, $(0, 6, 0)$, $(0, 1, -2)$,
$(4, 1, -2)$, $(4, 6, -2)$, $(0, 6, -2)$

3. $(4, 2, -2)$, $(4, 2, 1)$, $(4, 1, 1)$, $(4, 1, -2)$, $(-6, 1, 1)$,
$(-6, 2, 1)$, $(-6, 2, -2)$, $(-6, 1, -2)$

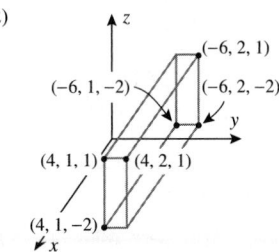

5. **(a)** point   **(b)** line parallel to the y-axis
(c) plane parallel to the yz-plane

9. radius $\sqrt{74}$, center $(2, 1, -4)$ 11. **(b)** $(2, 1, 6)$ **(c)** area 49

13. **(a)** $(x-1)^2 + y^2 + (z+1)^2 = 16$
(b) $(x+1)^2 + (y-3)^2 + (z-2)^2 = 14$
(c) $\left(x + \dfrac{1}{2}\right)^2 + (y-2)^2 + (z-2)^2 = \dfrac{5}{4}$

15. $(x-2)^2 + (y+1)^2 + (z+3)^2 = r^2$;
(a) $r^2 = 9$ **(b)** $r^2 = 1$ **(c)** $r^2 = 4$

Responses to True–False questions may be abridged to save space.

19. False; see Figure 11.1.6.

21. True; see Figure 11.1.3.

23. sphere, center $(-5, -2, -1)$, radius 7

25. sphere; center $\left(\dfrac{1}{2}, \dfrac{3}{4}, -\dfrac{5}{4}\right)$, radius $\dfrac{3\sqrt{6}}{4}$

27. no graph

29. **(a)**   **(b)**   **(c)**

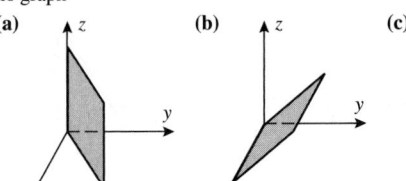
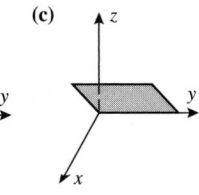

31. (a) 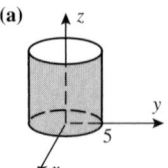 **(b)** 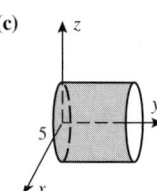 **(c)**

33. (a) $-2y + z = 0$ **(b)** $-2x + z = 0$ **(c)** $(x-1)^2 + (y-1)^2 = 1$
(d) $(x-1)^2 + (z-1)^2 = 1$

35. 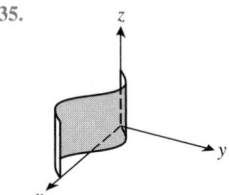 **37.**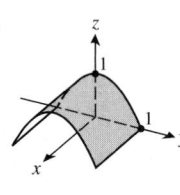

39. 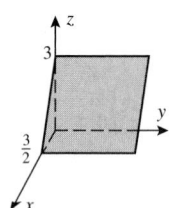 **41.**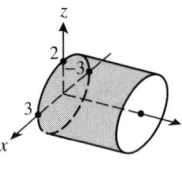

43.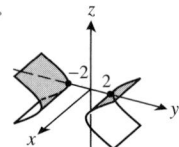

45.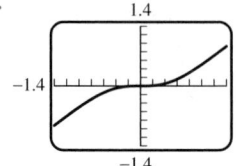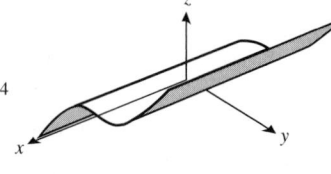

47. largest distance, $3 + \sqrt{6}$; smallest distance, $3 - \sqrt{6}$
49. all points outside the circular cylinder $(y+3)^2 + (z-2)^2 = 16$
51. $r = (2 - \sqrt{3})R$ **53. (b)** $y^2 + z^2 = e^{2x}$

▶ **Exercise Set 11.2 (Page 782)**

1. (a-c) 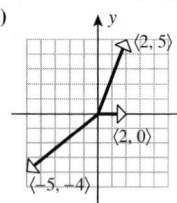 **(d-f)**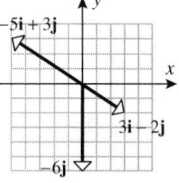

3. (a,b) 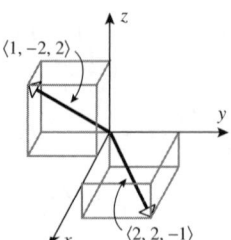 **(c,d)**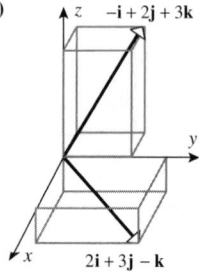

5. (a) $\langle 3, -4 \rangle$ **(b)** $\langle -2, -3, 4 \rangle$

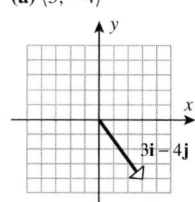 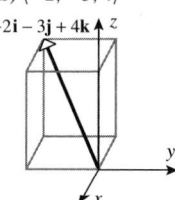

7. (a) $\langle -1, 3 \rangle$ **(b)** $\langle -7, 2 \rangle$ **(c)** $\langle -3, 6, 1 \rangle$
9. (a) $\langle 4, -4 \rangle$ **(b)** $\langle 8, -1, -3 \rangle$
11. (a) $-\mathbf{i} + 4\mathbf{j} - 2\mathbf{k}$ **(b)** $18\mathbf{i} + 12\mathbf{j} - 6\mathbf{k}$ **(c)** $-\mathbf{i} - 5\mathbf{j} - 2\mathbf{k}$
(d) $40\mathbf{i} - 4\mathbf{j} - 4\mathbf{k}$ **(e)** $-2\mathbf{i} - 16\mathbf{j} - 18\mathbf{k}$ **(f)** $-\mathbf{i} + 13\mathbf{j} - 2\mathbf{k}$
13. (a) $\sqrt{2}$ **(b)** $5\sqrt{2}$ **(c)** $\sqrt{21}$ **(d)** $\sqrt{14}$
15. (a) $2\sqrt{3}$ **(b)** $\sqrt{14} + \sqrt{2}$ **(c)** $2\sqrt{14} + 2\sqrt{2}$ **(d)** $2\sqrt{37}$
(e) $(1/\sqrt{6})\mathbf{i} + (1/\sqrt{6})\mathbf{j} - (2/\sqrt{6})\mathbf{k}$ **(f)** 1
Responses to True–False questions may be abridged to save space.
17. False; $\|\mathbf{i} + \mathbf{j}\| = \sqrt{2} \neq 1 + 1 = 2$
19. True; one in the same direction and one in the opposite direction.
21. (a) $(-1/\sqrt{17})\mathbf{i} + (4/\sqrt{17})\mathbf{j}$ **(b)** $(-3\mathbf{i} + 2\mathbf{j} - \mathbf{k})/\sqrt{14}$
(c) $(4\mathbf{i} + \mathbf{j} - \mathbf{k})/(3\sqrt{2})$
23. (a) $\langle -\frac{3}{2}, 2 \rangle$ **(b)** $\dfrac{1}{\sqrt{5}} \langle 7, 0, -6 \rangle$
25. (a) $\langle 3\sqrt{2}/2, 3\sqrt{2}/2 \rangle$ **(b)** $\langle 0, 2 \rangle$ **(c)** $\langle -5/2, 5\sqrt{3}/2 \rangle$ **(d)** $\langle -1, 0 \rangle$
27. $\langle (\sqrt{3} - \sqrt{2})/2, (1 + \sqrt{2})/2 \rangle$
29. (a) $\langle -2, 5 \rangle$ **(b)** $\langle 3, -8 \rangle$

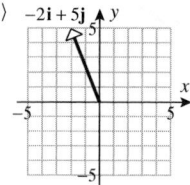 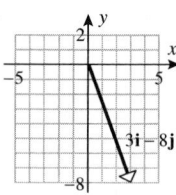

31. $\langle -\frac{2}{3}, 1 \rangle$ **33.** $\mathbf{u} = \frac{5}{7}\mathbf{i} + \frac{2}{7}\mathbf{j} + \frac{1}{7}\mathbf{k}$, $\mathbf{v} = \frac{8}{7}\mathbf{i} - \frac{1}{7}\mathbf{j} - \frac{4}{7}\mathbf{k}$
35. $\sqrt{5}, 3$ **37. (a)** $\pm\frac{5}{3}$ **(b)** 3
39. (a) $\langle 1/\sqrt{10}, 3/\sqrt{10} \rangle, \langle -1/\sqrt{10}, -3/\sqrt{10} \rangle$
(b) $\langle 1/\sqrt{2}, -1/\sqrt{2} \rangle, \langle -1/\sqrt{2}, 1/\sqrt{2} \rangle$ **(c)** $\pm\dfrac{1}{\sqrt{26}} \langle 5, 1 \rangle$
41. (a) the circle of radius 1 about the origin
(b) the closed disk of radius 1 about the origin
(c) all points outside the closed disk of radius 1 about the origin
43. (a) the (hollow) sphere of radius 1 about the origin
(b) the closed ball of radius 1 about the origin
(c) all points outside the closed ball of radius 1 about the origin
45. magnitude $= 30\sqrt{5}$ lb, $\theta \approx 26.57°$
47. magnitude ≈ 207.06 N, $\theta = 45°$
49. magnitude ≈ 94.995 N, $\theta \approx 28.28°$
51. magnitude ≈ 9.165 lb, angle $\approx -70.890°$
53. ≈ 183.02 lb, 224.13 lb
55. (a) $c_1 = -2$, $c_2 = 1$

▶ **Exercise Set 11.3 (Page 792)**
1. (a) -10; $\cos\theta = -1/\sqrt{5}$ **(b)** -3; $\cos\theta = -3/\sqrt{58}$
(c) 0; $\cos\theta = 0$ **(d)** -20; $\cos\theta = -20/(3\sqrt{70})$
3. (a) obtuse **(b)** acute **(c)** obtuse **(d)** orthogonal
5. $\sqrt{2}/2, 0, -\sqrt{2}/2, -1, -\sqrt{2}/2, 0, \sqrt{2}/2$
7. (a) vertex B **(b)** $82°, 60°, 38°$ **13.** $r = 7/5$
15. (a) $\alpha = \beta \approx 55°, \gamma \approx 125°$ **(b)** $\alpha \approx 48°, \beta \approx 132°, \gamma \approx 71°$
19. (a) $\approx 35°$ **(b)** $90°$
21. $64°, 41°, 60°$ **23.** $71°, 61°, 36°$

25. (a) $\left\langle \frac{2}{3}, \frac{4}{3}, \frac{4}{3} \right\rangle, \left\langle \frac{4}{3}, -\frac{7}{3}, \frac{5}{3} \right\rangle$

(b) $\left\langle -\frac{74}{49}, -\frac{111}{49}, \frac{222}{49} \right\rangle, \left\langle \frac{270}{49}, \frac{62}{49}, \frac{121}{49} \right\rangle$

27. (a) $\langle 1, 1 \rangle + \langle -4, 4 \rangle$ (b) $\left\langle 0, -\frac{8}{5}, \frac{4}{5} \right\rangle + \left\langle -2, \frac{13}{5}, \frac{26}{5} \right\rangle$

(c) $\mathbf{v} = \langle 1, 4, 1 \rangle$ is orthogonal to $\mathbf{b}$.

Responses to True–False questions may be abridged to save space.

29. True; $\mathbf{v} + \mathbf{w} = \mathbf{0}$ implies $0 = \mathbf{v} \cdot (\mathbf{v} + \mathbf{w}) = \|\mathbf{v}\|^2 \neq 0$, a contradiction.

31. True; see Equation (12).   **33.** $\sqrt{564/29}$ **35.** 169.8 N

37. $-5\sqrt{3}$ J   **45.** (a) $40°$ (b) $x \approx -0.682328$

▶ **Exercise Set 11.4 (Page 803)** _____

1. (a) $-\mathbf{j} + \mathbf{k}$ **3.** $\langle 7, 10, 9 \rangle$ **5.** $\langle -4, -6, -3 \rangle$

7. (a) $\langle -20, -67, -9 \rangle$ (b) $\langle -78, 52, -26 \rangle$

(c) $\langle 0, -56, -392 \rangle$ (d) $\langle 0, 56, 392 \rangle$

9. $\frac{1}{\sqrt{2}}, -\frac{1}{\sqrt{2}}, 0$ **11.** $\pm\frac{1}{\sqrt{6}}\langle 2, 1, 1 \rangle$

Responses to True–False questions may be abridged to save space.

13. True; see Theorem 11.4.5(c).

15. False; let $\mathbf{v} = \mathbf{u} = \mathbf{i}$ and let $\mathbf{w} = 2\mathbf{i}$.

17. $\sqrt{59}$ **19.** $\sqrt{374}/2$

21. 80   **23.** -3 **25.** 16   **27.** (a) yes   (b) yes   (c) no

29. (a) 9   (b) $\sqrt{122}$ (c) $\sin^{-1}\left(\frac{9}{14}\right)$

31. (a) $2\sqrt{141/29}$ (b) $6/\sqrt{5}$ **33.** $\frac{2}{3}$ **37.** $\theta = \pi/4$

39. (a) $10\sqrt{2}$ lb·ft, direction of rotation about P is counterclockwise looking along $\overrightarrow{PQ} \times \mathbf{F} = -10\mathbf{i} + 10\mathbf{k}$ toward its initial point

(b) 10 lb·ft, direction of rotation about P is counterclockwise looking along $-10\mathbf{i}$ toward its initial point

(c) 0 lb·ft, no rotation about P

41. ≈ 36.19 N·m   **45.** $-8\mathbf{i} - 20\mathbf{j} + 2\mathbf{k}, -8\mathbf{i} - 8\mathbf{k}$ **49.** 1.887850

▶ **Exercise Set 11.5 (Page 810)** _____

1. (a) $L_1: x = 1, y = t, L_2: x = t, y = 1, L_3: x = t, y = t$

(b) $L_1: x = 1, y = 1, z = t, L_2: x = t, y = 1, z = 1,$
$L_3: x = 1, y = t, z = 1, L_4: x = t, y = t, z = t$

3. (a) $x = 3 + 2t, y = -2 + 3t$; line segment: $0 \leq t \leq 1$

(b) $x = 5 - 3t, y = -2 + 6t, z = 1 + t$; line segment: $0 \leq t \leq 1$

5. (a) $x = 2 + t, y = -3 - 4t$ (b) $x = t, y = -t, z = 1 + t$

7. (a) $P(2, -1), \mathbf{v} = 4\mathbf{i} - \mathbf{j}$ (b) $P(-1, 2, 4), \mathbf{v} = 5\mathbf{i} + 7\mathbf{j} - 8\mathbf{k}$

9. (a) $\langle -3, 4 \rangle + t\langle 1, 5 \rangle$; $-3\mathbf{i} + 4\mathbf{j} + t(\mathbf{i} + 5\mathbf{j})$

(b) $\langle 2, -3, 0 \rangle + t\langle -1, 5, 1 \rangle$; $2\mathbf{i} - 3\mathbf{j} + t(-\mathbf{i} + 5\mathbf{j} + \mathbf{k})$

Responses to True–False questions may be abridged to save space.

11. False; the lines could be skew.

13. False; see part (b) of the solution to Example 3.

15. $x = -5 + 2t, y = 2 - 3t$ **17.** $x = 3 + 4t, y = -4 + 3t$

19. $x = -1 + 3t, y = 2 - 4t, z = 4 + t$

21. $x = -2 + 2t, y = -t, z = 5 + 2t$

23. (a) $x = 7$ (b) $y = \frac{7}{3}$ (c) $x = \frac{-1 \pm \sqrt{85}}{6}, y = \frac{43 \mp \sqrt{85}}{18}$

25. $(-2, 10, 0)$; $(-2, 0, -5)$; The line does not intersect the yz-plane.

27. $(0, 4, -2), (4, 0, 6)$ **29.** $(1, -1, 2)$ **33.** The lines are parallel.

35. The points do not lie on the same line.

39. $\langle x, y \rangle = \langle -1, 2 \rangle + t\langle 1, 1 \rangle$

41. the point $1/n$ of the way from $(-2, 0)$ to $(1, 3)$

43. the line segment joining the points $(1, 0)$ and $(-3, 6)$

45. $(5, 2)$ **47.** $2\sqrt{5}$ **49.** distance $= \sqrt{35/6}$

51. (a) $x = x_0 + (x_1 - x_0)t, y = y_0 + (y_1 - y_0)t, z = z_0 + (z_1 - z_0)t$

(b) $x = x_1 + at, y = y_1 + bt, z = z_1 + ct$

53. (b) $\langle x, y, z \rangle = \langle 1 + 2t, -3 + 4t, 5 + t \rangle$

55. (b) $84°$ (c) $x = 7 + t, y = -1, z = -2 + t$

57. $x = t, y = 2 + t, z = 1 - t$

59. (a) $\sqrt{17}$ cm   (b) 10   (d) $\sqrt{14}/2$ cm

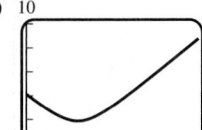

▶ **Exercise Set 11.6 (Page 819)** _____

1. $x = 3, y = 4, z = 5$ **3.** $x + 4y + 2z = 28$ **5.** $z = 0$

7. $x - y = 0$ **9.** $y + z = 1$ **11.** $2y - z = 1$

13. (a) parallel   (b) perpendicular   (c) neither

15. (a) parallel   (b) neither   (c) perpendicular

17. (a) point of intersection is $\left(\frac{5}{2}, \frac{5}{2}, \frac{5}{2} \right)$ (b) no intersection

19. $35°$

Responses to True–False questions may be abridged to save space.

21. True; each will be the negative of the other.

23. True; the direction vector of L must be orthogonal to both normal vectors.

25. $4x - 2y + 7z = 0$ **27.** $4x - 13y + 21z = -14$

29. $x + y - 3z = 6$ **31.** $x + 5y + 3z = -6$

33. $x + 2y + 4z = \frac{29}{2}$ **35.** $x = 5 - 2t, y = 5t, z = -2 + 11t$

37. $7x + y + 9z = 25$ **39.** yes

41. $x = -\frac{11}{7} - 23t, y = -\frac{12}{7} + t, z = -7t$

43. $\frac{5}{3}$ **45.** $5/\sqrt{54}$ **47.** $25/\sqrt{126}$

49. $(x - 2)^2 + (y - 1)^2 + (z + 3)^2 = \frac{121}{14}$ **51.** $5/\sqrt{12}$

▶ **Exercise Set 11.7 (Page 830)** _____

1. (a) elliptic paraboloid, $a = 2, b = 3$

(b) hyperbolic paraboloid, $a = 1, b = 5$

(c) hyperboloid of one sheet, $a = b = c = 4$

(d) circular cone, $a = b = 1$ (e) elliptic paraboloid, $a = 2, b = 1$

(f) hyperboloid of two sheets, $a = b = c = 1$

3. (a) $-z = x^2 + y^2$, circular paraboloid opening down the negative z-axis

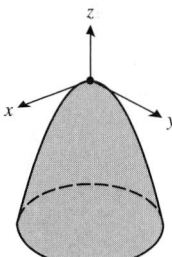

(b) $z = x^2 + y^2$, circular paraboloid, no change

(c) $z = x^2 + y^2$, circular paraboloid, no change

(d) $z = x^2 + y^2$, circular paraboloid, no change

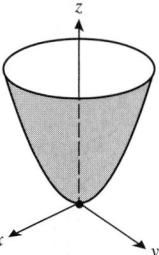

(e) $x = y^2 + z^2$, circular paraboloid opening along the positive x-axis

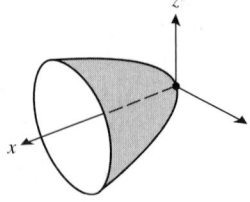

(f) $y = x^2 + z^2$, circular paraboloid opening along the positive y-axis

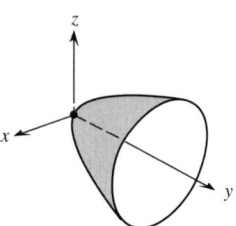

5. (a) hyperboloid of one sheet, axis is y-axis
   (b) hyperboloid of two sheets separated by yz-plane
   (c) elliptic paraboloid opening along the positive x-axis
   (d) elliptic cone with x-axis as axis
   (e) hyperbolic paraboloid straddling the x-axis
   (f) paraboloid opening along the negative y-axis

7. (a) $x = 0: \dfrac{y^2}{25} + \dfrac{z^2}{4} = 1$;
   $y = 0: \dfrac{x^2}{9} + \dfrac{z^2}{4} = 1$;
   $z = 0: \dfrac{x^2}{9} + \dfrac{y^2}{25} = 1$

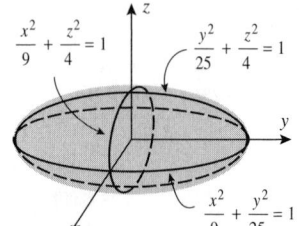

   (b) $x = 0: z = 4y^2$;
   $y = 0: z = x^2$;
   $z = 0: x = y = 0$

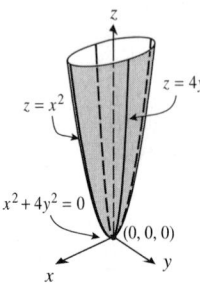

   (c) $x = 0: \dfrac{y^2}{16} - \dfrac{z^2}{4} = 1$;
   $y = 0: \dfrac{x^2}{9} - \dfrac{z^2}{4} = 1$;
   $z = 0: \dfrac{x^2}{9} + \dfrac{y^2}{16} = 1$

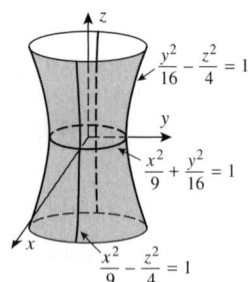

9. (a) $4x^2 + z^2 = 3$; ellipse   (b) $y^2 + z^2 = 3$; circle
   (c) $y^2 + z^2 = 20$; circle   (d) $9x^2 - y^2 = 20$; hyperbola
   (e) $z = 9x^2 + 16$; parabola   (f) $9x^2 + 4y^2 = 4$; ellipse

Responses to True–False questions may be abridged to save space.

11. False; "quadric" refers to second powers.

13. False; none of the cross sections need be circles.

15.
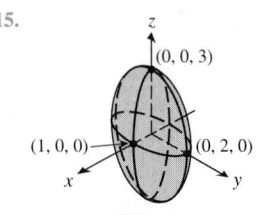
Ellipsoid

17.
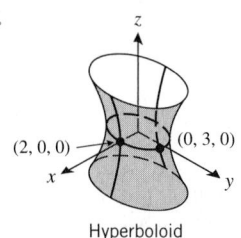
Hyperboloid of one sheet

19.
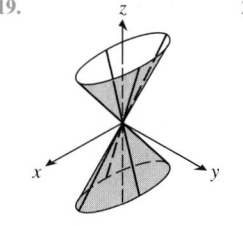
Elliptic cone

21.
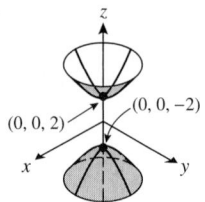
Hyperboloid of two sheets

23.
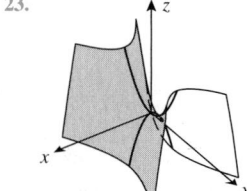
Hyperbolic paraboloid

25.
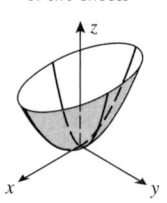
Elliptic paraboloid

27.
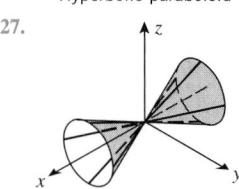
Circular cone

29.
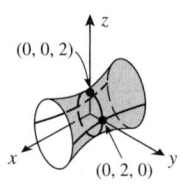
Hyperboloid of one sheet

31.
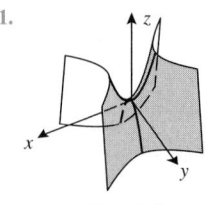
Hyperbolic paraboloid

33.
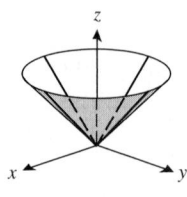

35.
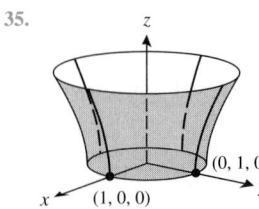

37.
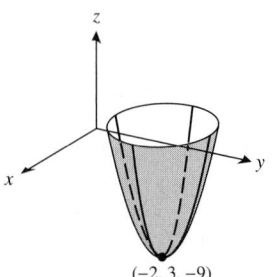
Circular paraboloid

39.

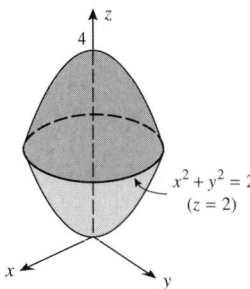

Ellipsoid

41. (a) $\dfrac{x^2}{9} + \dfrac{y^2}{4} = 1$ (b) $6, 4$ (c) $(\pm\sqrt{5}, 0, \sqrt{2})$
(d) The focal axis is parallel to the x-axis.

43. (a) $\dfrac{y^2}{4} - \dfrac{x^2}{4} = 1$ (b) $(0, \pm 2, 4)$ (c) $(0, \pm 2\sqrt{2}, 4)$
(d) The focal axis is parallel to the y-axis.

45. (a) $z + 4 = y^2$ (b) $(2, 0, -4)$ (c) $\left(2, 0, -\frac{15}{4}\right)$
(d) The focal axis is parallel to the z-axis.

47. circle of radius $\sqrt{2}$ in the plane $z = 2$, centered at $(0, 0, 2)$

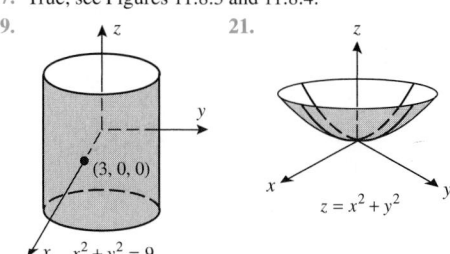

49. $y = 4(x^2 + z^2)$ **51.** $z = (x^2 + y^2)/4$ (circular paraboloid)

▶ **Exercise Set 11.8 (Page 837)** _____

1. (a) $(8, \pi/6, -4)$ (b) $(5\sqrt{2}, 3\pi/4, 6)$
(c) $(2, \pi/2, 0)$ (d) $(8, 5\pi/3, 6)$

3. (a) $(2\sqrt{3}, 2, 3)$ (b) $(-4\sqrt{2}, 4\sqrt{2}, -2)$
(c) $(5, 0, 4)$ (d) $(-7, 0, -9)$

5. (a) $(2\sqrt{2}, \pi/3, 3\pi/4)$ (b) $(2, 7\pi/4, \pi/4)$
(c) $(6, \pi/2, \pi/3)$ (d) $(10, 5\pi/6, \pi/2)$

7. (a) $(5\sqrt{6}/4, 5\sqrt{2}/4, 5\sqrt{2}/2)$ (b) $(7, 0, 0)$
(c) $(0, 0, 1)$ (d) $(0, -2, 0)$

9. (a) $(2\sqrt{3}, \pi/6, \pi/6)$ (b) $(\sqrt{2}, \pi/4, 3\pi/4)$
(c) $(2, 3\pi/4, \pi/2)$ (d) $(4\sqrt{3}, 1, 2\pi/3)$

11. (a) $(5\sqrt{3}/2, \pi/4, -5/2)$ (b) $(0, 7\pi/6, -1)$
(c) $(0, 0, 3)$ (d) $(4, \pi/6, 0)$

Responses to True–False questions may be abridged to save space.

15. True; see Figure 11.8.1b.

17. True; see Figures 11.8.3 and 11.8.4.

19.   **21.**

23.   **25.**

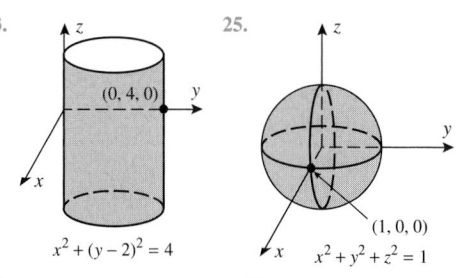

$x^2 + (y-2)^2 = 4$ $x^2 + y^2 + z^2 = 1$

27.   **29.**

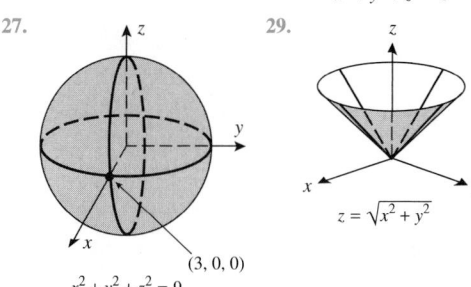

$x^2 + y^2 + z^2 = 9$ $z = \sqrt{x^2 + y^2}$

31.   **33.**

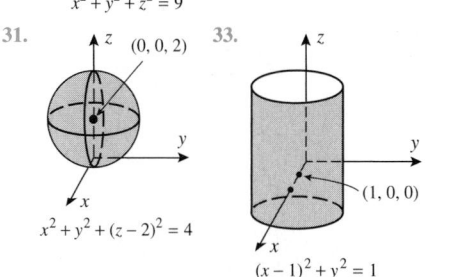

$x^2 + y^2 + (z-2)^2 = 4$ $(x-1)^2 + y^2 = 1$

35. (a) $z = 3$ (b) $\rho = 3\sec\phi$ **37.** (a) $z = 3r^2$ (b) $\rho = \frac{1}{3}\csc\phi\cot\phi$

39. (a) $r = 2$ (b) $\rho = 2\csc\phi$ **41.** (a) $r^2 + z^2 = 9$ (b) $\rho = 3$

43. (a) $2r\cos\theta + 3r\sin\theta + 4z = 1$
(b) $2\rho\sin\phi\cos\theta + 3\rho\sin\phi\sin\theta + 4\rho\cos\phi = 1$

45. (a) $r^2\cos^2\theta = 16 - z^2$ (b) $\rho^2(1 - \sin^2\phi\sin^2\theta) = 16$

47. all points on or above the paraboloid $z = x^2 + y^2$ that are also on or below the plane $z = 4$

49. all points on or between concentric spheres of radii 1 and 3 centered at the origin

51. spherical: $(4000, \pi/6, \pi/6)$; rectangular: $(1000\sqrt{3}, 1000, 2000\sqrt{3})$

53. (a) $(10, \pi/2, 1)$ (b) $(0, 10, 1)$ (c) $(\sqrt{101}, \pi/2, \tan^{-1} 10)$

▶ **Chapter 11 Review Exercises (Page 838)** _____

3. (b) $-1/2, \pm\sqrt{3}/2$ (d) true

5. (a) $r^2 = 16$ (b) $r^2 = 25$ (c) $r^2 = 9$

7. $(7, 5)$

9. (a) $-\frac{3}{4}$ (b) $\frac{1}{7}$ (c) $(48 \pm 25\sqrt{3})/11$ (d) $c = \frac{4}{3}$

13. 13 ft·lb   **15.** (a) $\sqrt{26}/2$ (b) $\sqrt{26}/3$

17. (a) 29   (b) $\dfrac{29}{\sqrt{65}}$ **19.** $x = 4 + t, \; y = 1 - t, \; z = 2$

21. $x + 5y - z - 2 = 0$ **23.** $a_1 a_2 + b_1 b_2 + c_1 c_2 = 0$

25. (a) hyperboloid of one sheet   (b) sphere   (c) circular cone

27. (a) $z = x^2 - y^2$ (b) $xz = 1$

29. (a) 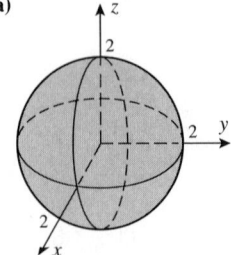 **(b)**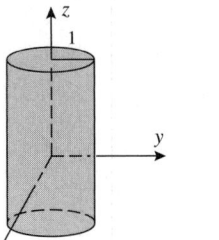

(c)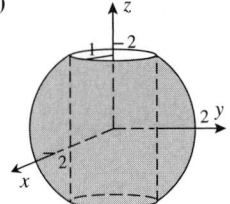

31. (a) 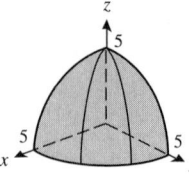 **(b)**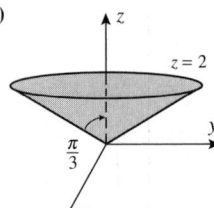

(c)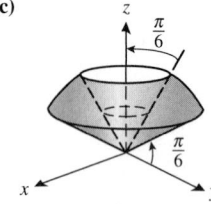

▶ **Chapter 11 Making Connections (Page 840)**

Answers are provided in the Student Solutions Manual.

▶ **Exercise Set 12.1 (Page 845)**

1. $(-\infty, +\infty)$; $\mathbf{r}(\pi) = -\mathbf{i} - 3\pi\mathbf{j}$ **3.** $[2, +\infty)$; $\mathbf{r}(3) = -\mathbf{i} - \ln 3\mathbf{j} + \mathbf{k}$

5. $\mathbf{r} = 3\cos t\mathbf{i} + (t + \sin t)\mathbf{j}$ **7.** $x = 3t^2$, $y = -2$

9. the line in 2-space through $(3, 0)$ with direction vector $\mathbf{a} = -2\mathbf{i} + 5\mathbf{j}$

11. the line in 3-space through the point $(0, -3, 1)$ and parallel to the vector $2\mathbf{i} + 3\mathbf{k}$

13. an ellipse centered at $(0, 0, 1)$ in the plane $z = 1$

15. (a) slope $-\frac{3}{2}$ **(b)** $\left(\frac{5}{2}, 0, \frac{3}{2}\right)$

17. (a) 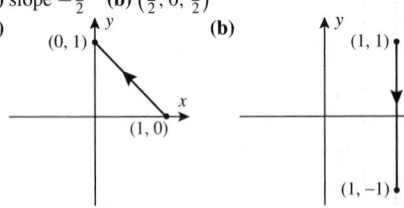 **(b)**

19. $\mathbf{r} = (1 - t)(3\mathbf{i} + 4\mathbf{j})$, $0 \le t \le 1$

21. $x = 2$ 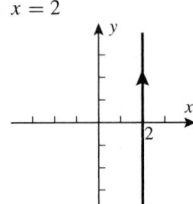 **23.** $(x - 1)^2 + (y - 3)^2 = 1$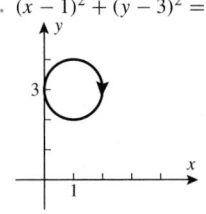

25. $x^2 - y^2 = 1$, $x \ge 1$ 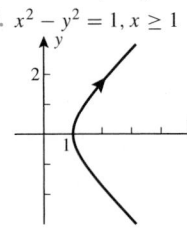 **27.**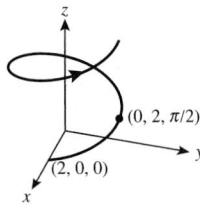

29.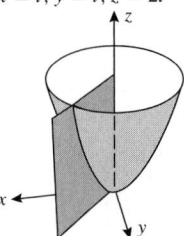

Responses to True–False questions may be abridged to save space.

31. False; the natural domain of a vector-valued function is the *intersection* of the domains of its component functions.

33. True; $\mathbf{r}(t) = (1 - t)\mathbf{r}_0 + t\mathbf{r}_1 \, (0 \le t \le 1)$ represents the line segment in 3-space that is traced from $\mathbf{r}_0$ to $\mathbf{r}_1$.

35. $x = t$, $y = t$, $z = 2t^2$

37. $\mathbf{r}(t) = t\mathbf{i} + t^2\mathbf{j} \pm \frac{1}{3}\sqrt{81 - 9t^2 - t^4}\mathbf{k}$ **43.** $c = 3/(2\pi)$

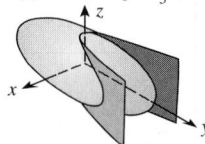

47. (a) III, since the curve is a subset of the plane $y = -x$
(b) IV, since only x is periodic in t and y, z increase without bound
(c) II, since all three components are periodic in t
(d) I, since the projection onto the yz-plane is a circle and the curve increases without bound in the x-direction

49. (a) $x = 3\cos t$, $y = 3\sin t$, $z = 9\cos^2 t$
(b)

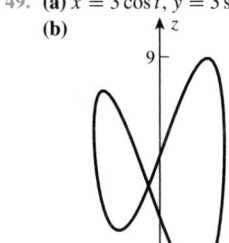

▶ **Exercise Set 12.2** (Page 856) _____

1. $\left(\frac{1}{3}, 0\right)$ 3. $2\mathbf{i} - 3\mathbf{j} + 4\mathbf{k}$ 5. (a) continuous   (b) not continuous
7.
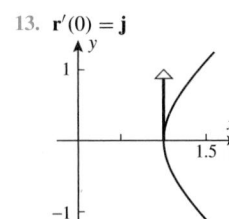
9. $(\sin t)\mathbf{j}$ 11. $\mathbf{r}'(2) = \langle 1, 4\rangle$

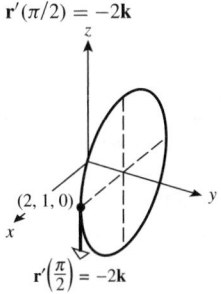

13. $\mathbf{r}'(0) = \mathbf{j}$

15. $\mathbf{r}'(\pi/2) = -2\mathbf{k}$

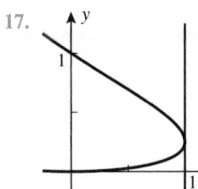

17.
19. $x = 1 + 2t$, $y = 2 - t$
21. $x = 1 - \sqrt{3}\pi t$, $y = \sqrt{3} + \pi t$, $z = 1 + 3t$
23. $\mathbf{r} = (-\mathbf{i} + 2\mathbf{j}) + t\left(2\mathbf{i} + \frac{3}{4}\mathbf{j}\right)$
25. $\mathbf{r} = (4\mathbf{i} + \mathbf{j}) + t(-4\mathbf{i} + \mathbf{j} + 4\mathbf{k})$
27. (a) $\mathbf{i} - \mathbf{j} + \mathbf{k}$ (b) $-\mathbf{i} + \mathbf{k}$ (c) 0
29. $7t^6$; $18t^5\mathbf{i} - 10t^4\mathbf{j}$
31. $3t\mathbf{i} + 2t^2\mathbf{j} + \mathbf{C}$

33. $-(\cos t)\mathbf{i} - (\sin t)\mathbf{j} + \mathbf{C}$ 35. $\mathbf{j}$ 37. $(5\sqrt{5} - 1)/3$
39. $\frac{52}{3}\mathbf{i} + 4\mathbf{j}$

Responses to True–False questions may be abridged to save space.

41. False; for example, $\mathbf{r}(t) = \langle t, |t|\rangle$ is continuous at $t = 0$, but the specified limit doesn't exist at $t = 0$.

43. True; see the definition of $\int_a^b \mathbf{r}(t)\,dt$.

45. $(t^2 + 1)\mathbf{i} + (t^3 - 1)\mathbf{j}$

47. $y(t) = \left(\frac{1}{2}t^2 + 2\right)\mathbf{i} + (e^t - 1)\mathbf{j}$

49. (a) $(-2, 4, 6)$ and $(1, 1, -3)$ (b) $76°, 71°$ 51. $68°$

▶ **Exercise Set 12.3** (Page 866) _____

1. smooth   3. not smooth, $\mathbf{r}'(1) = \mathbf{0}$ 5. $L = \frac{3}{2}$ 7. $L = e - e^{-1}$
9. $L = 28$ 11. $L = 2\pi\sqrt{10}$ 13. $\mathbf{r}'(\tau) = 4\mathbf{i} + 8(4\tau + 1)\mathbf{j}$
15. $\mathbf{r}'(\tau) = 2\tau e^{\tau^2}\mathbf{i} - 8te^{-\tau^2}\mathbf{j}$

Responses to True–False questions may be abridged to save space.

17. False; $\int_a^b \|\mathbf{r}'(t)\|\,dt$ is a scalar that represents the arc length of the curve in 2-space traced by $\mathbf{r}(t)$ from $t = a$ to $t = b$ (Theorem 12.3.1).

19. False; $\mathbf{r}'$ isn't defined at the point corresponding to the origin.
21. (a) $x = \frac{s}{\sqrt{2}}$, $y = \frac{s}{\sqrt{2}}$ (b) $x = y = z = \frac{s}{\sqrt{3}}$
23. (a) $x = 1 + \frac{s}{3}$, $y = 3 - \frac{2s}{3}$, $z = 4 + \frac{2s}{3}$ (b) $\left(\frac{28}{3}, -\frac{41}{3}, \frac{62}{3}\right)$
25. $x = 3 + \cos s$, $y = 2 + \sin s$, $0 \le s \le 2\pi$
27. $x = \frac{1}{3}[(3s + 1)^{2/3} - 1]^{3/2}$, $y = \frac{1}{2}[(3s + 1)^{2/3} - 1]$, $s \ge 0$
29. $x = \left(\frac{s}{\sqrt{2}} + 1\right)\cos\left[\ln\left(\frac{s}{\sqrt{2}} + 1\right)\right]$,
$y = \left(\frac{s}{\sqrt{2}} + 1\right)\sin\left[\ln\left(\frac{s}{\sqrt{2}} + 1\right)\right]$,
$0 \le s \le \sqrt{2}(e^{\pi/2} - 1)$
33. $x = 2a\cos^{-1}[1 - s/(4a)]$
$\qquad -2a(1 - [1 - s/(4a)]^2)^{1/2}(2[1 - s/(4a)]^2 - 1)$,
$y = \frac{s(8a - s)}{8a}$ for $0 \le s \le 8a$
35. (a) $9/2$ (b) $9 - 2\sqrt{6}$ 37. (a) $\sqrt{3}(1 - e^{-2})$ (b) $4\sqrt{5}$
39. (a) $g(\tau) = \pi(\tau)$ (b) $g(\tau) = \pi(1 - \tau)$ 41. 44 in
43. (a) $2t + \frac{1}{t}$ (b) $2t + \frac{1}{t}$ (c) $8 + \ln 3$

▶ **Exercise Set 12.4** (Page 872) _____

1. (a)   (b)

5. $\mathbf{T}(1) = \frac{2}{\sqrt{5}}\mathbf{i} + \frac{1}{\sqrt{5}}\mathbf{j}$, $\mathbf{N}(1) = \frac{1}{\sqrt{5}}\mathbf{i} - \frac{2}{\sqrt{5}}\mathbf{j}$
7. $\mathbf{T}\left(\frac{\pi}{3}\right) = -\frac{\sqrt{3}}{2}\mathbf{i} + \frac{1}{2}\mathbf{j}$, $\mathbf{N}\left(\frac{\pi}{3}\right) = -\frac{1}{2}\mathbf{i} - \frac{\sqrt{3}}{2}\mathbf{j}$
9. $\mathbf{T}\left(\frac{\pi}{2}\right) = -\frac{4}{\sqrt{17}}\mathbf{i} + \frac{1}{\sqrt{17}}\mathbf{k}$, $\mathbf{N}\left(\frac{\pi}{2}\right) = -\mathbf{j}$
11. $\mathbf{T}(0) = \frac{1}{\sqrt{3}}\mathbf{i} + \frac{1}{\sqrt{3}}\mathbf{j} + \frac{1}{\sqrt{3}}\mathbf{k}$, $\mathbf{N}(0) = -\frac{1}{\sqrt{2}}\mathbf{i} + \frac{1}{\sqrt{2}}\mathbf{j}$
13. $x = s$, $y = 1$ 15. $\mathbf{B} = \frac{4}{5}\cos t\mathbf{i} - \frac{4}{5}\sin t\mathbf{j} - \frac{3}{5}\mathbf{k}$ 17. $\mathbf{B} = -\mathbf{k}$
19. $\mathbf{T}\left(\frac{\pi}{4}\right) = \frac{\sqrt{2}}{2}(-\mathbf{i} + \mathbf{j})$, $\mathbf{N}\left(\frac{\pi}{4}\right) = -\frac{\sqrt{2}}{2}(\mathbf{i} + \mathbf{j})$,
$\mathbf{B}\left(\frac{\pi}{4}\right) = \mathbf{k}$; rectifying: $x + y = \sqrt{2}$; osculating: $z = 1$; normal: $-x + y = 0$

Responses to True–False questions may be abridged to save space.

21. False; $\mathbf{T}(t)$ points in the direction of increasing parameter but may not be orthogonal to $\mathbf{r}(t)$. For example, if $\mathbf{r}(t) = \langle t, t\rangle$, then $\mathbf{T}(t) = \langle 1/\sqrt{2}, 1/\sqrt{2}\rangle$ is parallel to $\mathbf{r}(t)$.

23. True; $\mathbf{T}(s) = \mathbf{r}'(s)$, the unit tangent vector, and $\mathbf{N}(s) = \frac{\mathbf{r}''(s)}{\|\mathbf{r}''(s)\|}$, the unit normal vector, are orthogonal, so $\mathbf{r}'(s)$ and $\mathbf{r}''(s)$ are orthogonal.

▶ **Exercise Set 12.5** (Page 879) _____

1. $\kappa \approx 2$ 3. (a) I is the curvature of II.   (b) I is the curvature of II.
5. $\frac{6}{|t|(4 + 9t^2)^{3/2}}$ 7. $\frac{12e^{2t}}{(9e^{6t} + e^{-2t})^{3/2}}$ 9. $\frac{4}{17}$ 11. $\frac{1}{2\cosh^2 t}$
13. $\kappa = \frac{2}{5}$, $\rho = \frac{5}{2}$ 15. $\kappa = \frac{\sqrt{2}}{3}$, $\rho = \frac{3\sqrt{2}}{2}$ 17. $\kappa = \frac{1}{4}$

Responses to True–False questions may be abridged to save space.

19. True; see Example 1: a circle of radius a has constant curvature $1/a$.
21. False; see Definition 12.5.1: the curvature of the graph of $\mathbf{r}(s)$ is $\|\mathbf{r}''(s)\|$, the length of $\mathbf{r}''(s)$.
25. 1   27. $\frac{e^{-1}}{(1 + e^{-2})^{3/2}}$ 29. $\frac{96}{125}$ 31. $\frac{1}{\sqrt{2}}$

33. (a)  **(b)**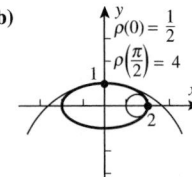

35.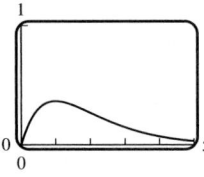

37. (a) $\kappa = \dfrac{|12x^2 - 4|}{[1 + (4x^3 - 4x)^2]^{3/2}}$ **(b)**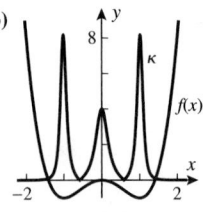

(c) $\rho = \frac{1}{4}$ for $x = 0$ and $\rho = \frac{1}{8}$ when $x = \pm 1$

41. $\dfrac{3}{2\sqrt{2}}$ **43.** $\frac{2}{3}$ **45.** $\rho = 2|p|$ **47.** $(3, 0), (-3, 0)$

51. (b) $\rho = \sqrt{2}$ **(c)**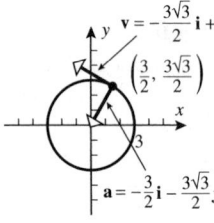

55. $a = \dfrac{1}{2r}$

63. $\tau = \dfrac{2}{(t^2 + 2)^2}$

65. $\tau = -\dfrac{\sqrt{2}}{(e^t + e^{-t})^2}$

▶ **Exercise Set 12.6 (Page 891)**

1. $\mathbf{v}(t) = -3 \sin t\,\mathbf{i} + 3 \cos t\,\mathbf{j}$
$\mathbf{a}(t) = -3 \cos t\,\mathbf{i} - 3 \sin t\,\mathbf{j}$
$\|\mathbf{v}(t)\| = 3$

3. $\mathbf{v}(t) = e^t\mathbf{i} - e^{-t}\mathbf{j}$
$\mathbf{a}(t) = e^t\mathbf{i} + e^{-t}\mathbf{j}$
$\|\mathbf{v}(t)\| = \sqrt{e^{2t} + e^{-2t}}$

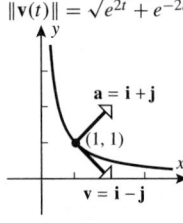

5. $\mathbf{v} = \mathbf{i} + \mathbf{j} + \mathbf{k}$, $\|\mathbf{v}\| = \sqrt{3}$, $\mathbf{a} = \mathbf{j} + 2\mathbf{k}$

7. $\mathbf{v} = -\sqrt{2}\mathbf{i} + \sqrt{2}\mathbf{j} + \mathbf{k}$, $\|\mathbf{v}\| = \sqrt{5}$, $\mathbf{a} = -\sqrt{2}\mathbf{i} - \sqrt{2}\mathbf{j}$

13. minimum speed $3\sqrt{2}$ when $\mathbf{r} = 24\mathbf{i} + 8\mathbf{j}$

15. (a) 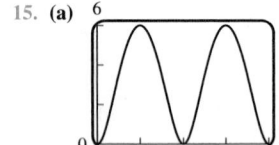 **(b)** maximum speed $= 6$, minimum speed $= 3$
(d) The maximum speed first occurs when $t = \pi/6$.

17. $\mathbf{v}(t) = (1 - \sin t)\mathbf{i} + (\cos t - 1)\mathbf{j}$;
$\mathbf{r}(t) = (t + \cos t - 1)\mathbf{i} + (\sin t - t + 1)\mathbf{j}$

19. $\mathbf{v}(t) = (1 - \cos t)\mathbf{i} + \sin t\,\mathbf{j} + e^t\mathbf{k}$;
$\mathbf{r}(t) = (t - \sin t - 1)\mathbf{i} + (1 - \cos t)\mathbf{j} + e^t\mathbf{k}$

21. $15°$ **23. (a)** $0.7\mathbf{i} + 2.7\mathbf{j} - 3.4\mathbf{k}$ **(b)** $\mathbf{r}_0 = -0.7\mathbf{i} - 2.9\mathbf{j} + 4.8\mathbf{k}$

25. $\Delta\mathbf{r} = 8\mathbf{i} + \frac{26}{3}\mathbf{j}$, $s = (13\sqrt{13} - 5\sqrt{5})/3$

27. $\Delta\mathbf{r} = 2\mathbf{i} - \frac{2}{3}\mathbf{j} + \sqrt{2}\ln 3\mathbf{k}$; $s = \frac{8}{3}$

31. (a) $a_T = 0$, $a_N = \sqrt{2}$ **(b)** $a_T\mathbf{T} = 0$, $a_N\mathbf{N} = \mathbf{i} + \mathbf{j}$ **(c)** $1/\sqrt{2}$

33. (a) $a_T = 2\sqrt{5}$, $a_N = 2\sqrt{5}$ **(b)** $a_T\mathbf{T} = 2\mathbf{i} + 4\mathbf{j}$, $a_N\mathbf{N} = 4\mathbf{i} - 2\mathbf{j}$
(c) $2/\sqrt{5}$

35. (a) $a_T = -7/\sqrt{6}$, $a_N = \sqrt{53/6}$
(b) $a_T\mathbf{T} = -\frac{7}{6}(\mathbf{i} - 2\mathbf{j} + \mathbf{k})$, $a_N\mathbf{N} = \frac{13}{6}\mathbf{i} + \frac{19}{3}\mathbf{j} + \frac{7}{6}\mathbf{k}$ **(c)** $\dfrac{\sqrt{53}}{6\sqrt{6}}$

37. $a_T = -3$, $a_N = 2$, $\mathbf{T} = -\mathbf{j}$, $\mathbf{N} = \mathbf{i}$ **39.** $-3/2$

41. $a_N = 8.41 \times 10^{10}$ km/s^2

43. $a_N = 18/(1 + 4x^2)^{3/2}$ **45.** $a_N = 0$

Responses to True–False questions may be abridged to save space.

47. True; the velocity and unit tangent vectors have the same direction, so are parallel.

49. False; in this case the velocity and acceleration vectors will be parallel, but they may have opposite direction.

53. ≈ 257.20 N

55. $40\sqrt{3}$ ft **57.** 800 ft/s **59.** $15°$ or $75°$ **61. (c)** ≈ 14.942 ft

63. (a) $\rho \approx 176.78$ m **(b)** $\frac{125}{4}$ m

65. (b) R is maximum when $\alpha = 45°$, maximum value v_0^2/g

67. (a) 2.62 s **(b)** 181.5 ft

69. (a) $v_0 \approx 83$ ft/s, $\alpha \approx 8°$ **(b)** 268.76 ft

▶ **Exercise Set 12.7 (Page 901)**

7. 7.75 km/s **9.** 10.88 km/s

11. (a) minimum distance $= 220{,}680$ mi,
maximum distance $= 246{,}960$ mi **(b)** 27.5 days

13. (a) 17,224 mi/h **(b)** $e \approx 0.071$, apogee altitude $= 819$ mi

▶ **Chapter 12 Review Exercises (Page 902)**

3. the circle of radius 3 in the xy-plane, with center at the origin

5. a parabola in the plane $x = -2$, vertex at $(-2, 0, -1)$, opening upward

11. $x = 1 + t$, $y = -t$, $z = t$ **13.** $(\sin t)\mathbf{i} - (\cos t)\mathbf{j} + \mathbf{C}$

15. $y(t) = \left(\frac{1}{3}t^3 + 1\right)\mathbf{i} + (t^2 + 1)\mathbf{j}$ **17.** 15/4

19. $\mathbf{r}(s) = \dfrac{s - 3}{3}\mathbf{i} + \dfrac{12 - 2s}{3}\mathbf{j} + \dfrac{9 + 2s}{3}\mathbf{k}$ **25.** 3/5 **27.** 0

29. (a) speed **(b)** distance traveled
(c) distance of the particle from the origin

33. (a) $\mathbf{r}(t) = \left(\frac{1}{6}t^4 + t\right)\mathbf{i} + \left(\frac{1}{2}t^2 + 2t\right)\mathbf{j} - \left(\frac{1}{4}\cos 2t + t - \frac{1}{4}\right)\mathbf{k}$
(b) 3.475 **35.** 10.65 km/s **37.** 24.78 ft

▶ **Chapter 12 Making Connections (Page 904)**

Where correct answers to a Making Connections exercise may vary, no answer is listed. Sample answers for these questions are available on the Book Companion Site.

1. (c) (i) $\mathbf{N} = \frac{1}{\sqrt{5}}\mathbf{i} - \frac{2}{\sqrt{5}}\mathbf{j}$ **(ii)** $\mathbf{N} = -\mathbf{j}$

2. (b) (i) $\mathbf{N} = -\sin t\,\mathbf{i} - \cos t\,\mathbf{j}$

(ii) $\mathbf{N} = \dfrac{-(4t + 18t^3)\mathbf{i} + (2 - 18t^4)\mathbf{j} + (6t + 12t^3)\mathbf{k}}{2\sqrt{81t^8 + 117t^6 + 54t^4 + 13t^2 + 1}}$

3. (c) $\kappa(s) \to +\infty$, so the spiral winds ever tighter.

4. semicircle: 53.479 ft; quarter-circle: 60.976 ft; point: 64.001 ft

▶ **Exercise Set 13.1 (Page 914)**

1. (a) 5 **(b)** 3 **(c)** 1 **(d)** -2 **(e)** $9a^3 + 1$ **(f)** $a^3b^2 - a^2b^3 + 1$

3. (a) $x^2 - y^2 + 3$ **(b)** $3x^3y^4 + 3$ **5.** $x^3e^{x^3(3y+1)}$

7. (a) $t^2 + 3t^{10}$ **(b)** 0 **(c)** 3076

9. (a) WCI $= 17.8°$F **(b)** WCI $= 22.6°$F

11. (a) 66% **(b)** 73.5% **(c)** 60.6%

13. (a) 19 **(b)** -9 **(c)** 3 **(d)** $a^6 + 3$ **(e)** $-t^8 + 3$
(f) $(a + b)(a - b)^2b^3 + 3$

15. $(y + 1)e^{x^2(y+1)z^2}$ **17. (a)** $80\sqrt{\pi}$ **(b)** $n(n + 1)/2$

19. 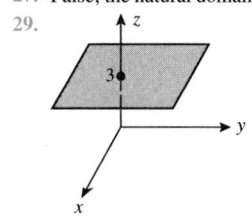   **21.**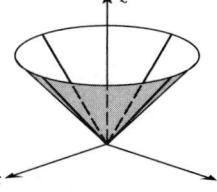

23. **(a)** all points above or on the line $y = -2$ **(b)** all points on or within the sphere $x^2 + y^2 + z^2 = 25$ **(c)** all points in 3-space

Responses to True–False questions may be abridged to save space.

25. True; the interval $[0, 1]$ is the intersection of the domains of $\sin^{-1} t$ and $\sqrt{t}$.

27. False; the natural domain is an infinite solid cylinder.

29. 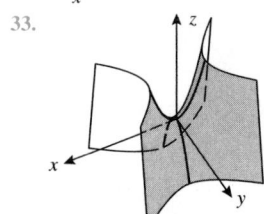   **31.**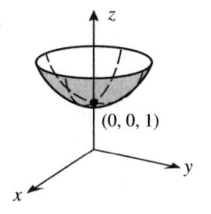

33. 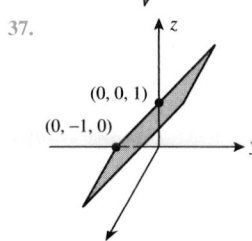   **35.**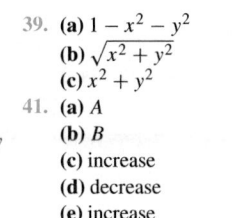

37. 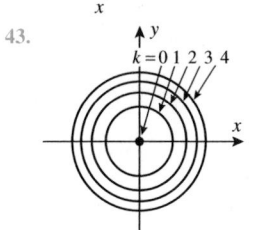   **39.** **(a)** $1 - x^2 - y^2$
(b) $\sqrt{x^2 + y^2}$
(c) $x^2 + y^2$

41. **(a)** A
(b) B
(c) increase
(d) decrease
(e) increase
(f) decrease

43. 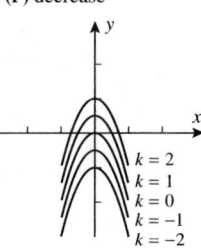   **45.**

47.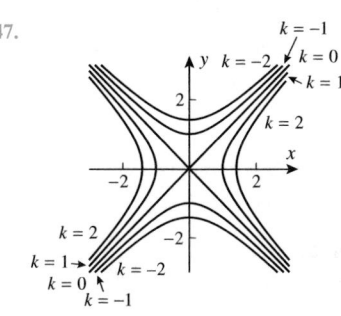

49. 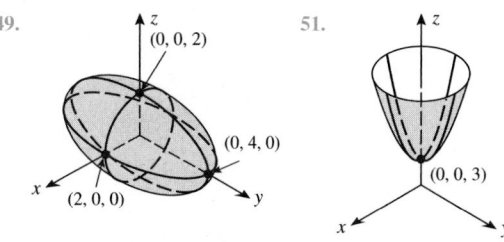   **51.**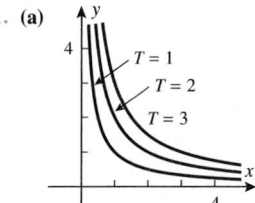

53. concentric spheres, common center at $(2, 0, 0)$

55. concentric cylinders, common axis the y-axis

57. **(a)** $x^2 - 2x^3 + 3xy = 0$ **(b)** $x^2 - 2x^3 + 3xy = 0$
(c) $x^2 - 2x^3 + 3xy = -18$

59. **(a)** $x^2 + y^2 - z = 5$ **(b)** $x^2 + y^2 - z = -2$ **(c)** $x^2 + y^2 - z = 0$

61. **(a)**   **(b)** the path $xy = 4$

63. **(a)**   **(b)**

65. **(a)**   **(b)**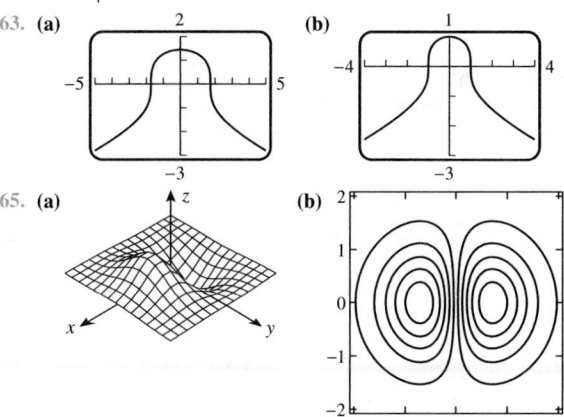

67. **(a)** The graph of g is the graph of f shifted one unit in the positive x-direction.
(b) The graph of g is the graph of f shifted one unit up the z-axis.
(c) The graph of g is the graph of f shifted one unit down the y-axis and then inverted with respect to the plane $z = 0$.

▶ **Exercise Set 13.2 (Page 925)**

1. 35   **3.** -8 **5.** 0

7. **(a)** along $x = 0$ limit does not exist
(b) along $x = 0$ limit does not exist

9. 1   **11.** 0   **13.** 0   **15.** limit does not exist   **17.** $\frac{8}{3}$ **19.** 0

21. limit does not exist   **23.** 0   **25.** 0   **27.** 0

Responses to True–False questions may be abridged to save space.

29. True; by the definition of open set.

31. False; let $f(x, y) = \begin{cases} 1, & x \le 0 \\ -1, & x > 0 \end{cases}$ and let $g(x, y) = -f(x, y)$.

33. **(a)** no   **(d)** no; yes   **37.** $-\pi/2$ **39.** no

41.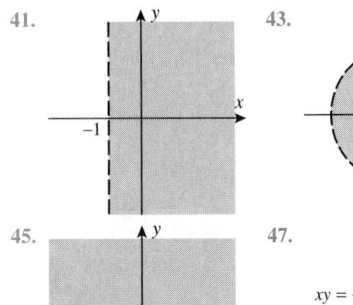

43.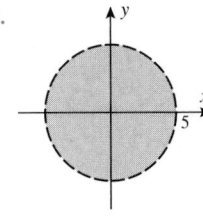

45.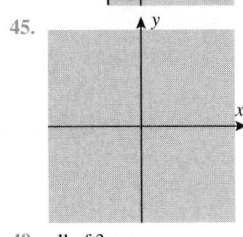

47.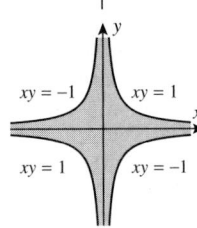

$xy = -1$ $xy = 1$

$xy = 1$ $xy = -1$

49. all of 3-space

51. all points not on the cylinder $x^2 + z^2 = 1$

▶ **Exercise Set 13.3 (Page 936)**

1. (a) $9x^2y^2$ (b) $6x^3y$ (c) $9y^2$ (d) $9x^2$ (e) $6y$ (f) $6x^3$ (g) 36 (h) 12

3. (a) $\frac{3}{8}$ (b) $\frac{1}{4}$ **5.** (a) $-4\cos 7$ (b) $2\cos 7$

7. $\partial z/\partial x = -4$; $\partial z/\partial y = \frac{1}{2}$ **9.** (a) 4.9 (b) 1.2

11. $z = f(x, y)$ has II as its graph, f_x has I as its graph, and f_y has III as its graph.

Responses to True–False questions may be abridged to save space.

13. True; on $y = 2$, $f(x, 2) = c$ is a constant function of x.

15. True; z must be a linear function of x and y.

17. $8xy^3e^{x^2y^3}$, $12x^2y^2e^{x^2y^3}$

19. $x^3/(y^{3/5} + x) + 3x^2\ln(1 + xy^{-3/5})$, $-\frac{3}{5}x^4/(y^{8/5} + xy)$

21. $-\dfrac{y(x^2 - y^2)}{(x^2 + y^2)^2}$, $\dfrac{x(x^2 - y^2)}{(x^2 + y^2)^2}$

23. $(3/2)x^2y(5x^2 - 7)(3x^5y - 7x^3y)^{-1/2}$

$(1/2)x^3(3x^2 - 7)(3x^5y - 7x^3y)^{-1/2}$

25. $\dfrac{y^{-1/2}}{y^2 + x^2}$, $-\dfrac{xy^{-3/2}}{y^2 + x^2} - \dfrac{3}{2}y^{-5/2}\tan^{-1}\left(\dfrac{x}{y}\right)$

27. $-\frac{4}{3}y^2\sec^2 x(y^2\tan x)^{-7/3}$, $-\frac{8}{3}y\tan x(y^2\tan x)^{-7/3}$

29. $-6, -21$ **31.** $1/\sqrt{17}, 8/\sqrt{17}$

33. (a) $2xy^4z^3 + y$ (b) $4x^2y^3z^3 + x$ (c) $3x^2y^4z^2 + 2z$ (d) $2y^4z^3 + y$ (e) $32z^3 + 1$ (f) 438

35. $2z/x$, z/y, $\ln(x^2y\cos z) - z\tan z$

37. $-y^2z^3/(1 + x^2y^4z^6)$, $-2xyz^3/(1 + x^2y^4z^6)$, $-3xy^2z^2/(1 + x^2y^4z^6)$

39. $yze^z\cos(xz)$, $e^z\sin(xz)$, $ye^z(\sin(xz) + x\cos(xz))$

41. $x/\sqrt{x^2 + y^2 + z^2}$, $y/\sqrt{x^2 + y^2 + z^2}$, $z/\sqrt{x^2 + y^2 + z^2}$

43. (a) e (b) $2e$ (c) e

45. (a) 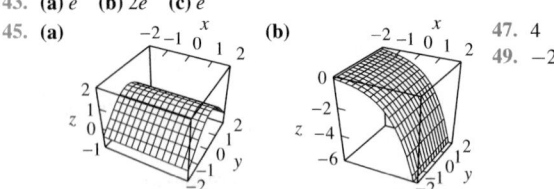 (b) **47.** 4 **49.** -2

51. (a) $\partial V/\partial r = 2\pi rh$ (b) $\partial V/\partial h = \pi r^2$ (c) 48π (d) 64π

53. (a) $\dfrac{1}{5}\dfrac{\text{lb}}{\text{in}^2\cdot\text{K}}$ (b) $-\dfrac{25}{8}\dfrac{\text{in}^5}{\text{lb}}$

55. (a) $\dfrac{\partial V}{\partial l} = 6$ (b) $\dfrac{\partial V}{\partial w} = 15$ (c) $\dfrac{\partial V}{\partial h} = 10$

59. (a) $\pm\sqrt{6}/4$ **61.** $-x/z$, $-y/z$

63. $-\dfrac{2x + yz^2\cos(xyz)}{xyz\cos(xyz) + \sin(xyz)}$; $-\dfrac{xz^2\cos(xyz)}{xyz\cos(xyz) + \sin(xyz)}$

65. $-x/w, -y/w, -z/w$

67. $-\dfrac{yzw\cos(xyz)}{2w + \sin(xyz)}, -\dfrac{xzw\cos(xyz)}{2w + \sin(xyz)}, -\dfrac{xyw\cos(xyz)}{2w + \cos(xyz)}$

69. $e^{x^2}, -e^{y^2}$

71. $f_x(x, y) = 2xy^3\sin(x^6y^9)$, $f_y(x, y) = 3x^2y^2\sin(x^6y^9)$

73. (a) $-\dfrac{\cos y}{4\sqrt{x^3}}$ (b) $-\sqrt{x}\cos y$ (c) $-\dfrac{1}{2\sqrt{x}}\sin y$ (d) $-\dfrac{1}{2\sqrt{x}}\sin y$

75. $-32y^3$ **77.** $-e^x\sin y$ **79.** $\dfrac{20}{(4x - 5y)^2}$ **81.** $\dfrac{2(x - y)}{(x + y)^3}$

83. (a) $\dfrac{\partial^3 f}{\partial x^3}$ (b) $\dfrac{\partial^3 f}{\partial y^2\partial x}$ (c) $\dfrac{\partial^4 f}{\partial x^2\partial y^2}$ (d) $\dfrac{\partial^4 f}{\partial y^3\partial x}$

85. (a) $30xy^4 - 4$ (b) $60x^2y^3$ (c) $60x^3y^2$

87. (a) -30 (b) -125 (c) 150

89. (a) $15x^2y^4z^7 + 2y$ (b) $35x^3y^4z^6 + 3y^2$ (c) $21x^2y^5z^6$ (d) $42x^3y^5z^5$ (e) $140x^3y^3z^6 + 6y$ (f) $30xy^4z^7$ (g) $105x^2y^4z^6$ (h) $210xy^4z^6$

97. $\dfrac{\partial f}{\partial v} = 8vw^3x^4y^5$, $\dfrac{\partial f}{\partial w} = 12v^2w^2x^4y^5$, $\dfrac{\partial f}{\partial x} = 16v^2w^3x^3y^5$, $\dfrac{\partial f}{\partial y} = 20v^2w^3x^4y^4$

99. $\dfrac{\partial f}{\partial v_1} = \dfrac{2v_1}{v_3^2 + v_4^2}$, $\dfrac{\partial f}{\partial v_2} = \dfrac{-2v_2}{v_3^2 + v_4^2}$, $\dfrac{\partial f}{\partial v_3} = \dfrac{-2v_3(v_1^2 - v_2^2)}{(v_3^2 + v_4^2)^2}$, $\dfrac{\partial f}{\partial v_4} = \dfrac{-2v_4(v_1^2 - v_2^2)}{(v_3^2 + v_4^2)^2}$

101. (a) 0 (b) 0 (c) 0 (d) 0 (e) $2(1 + yw)e^{yw}\sin z\cos z$ (f) $2xw(2 + yw)e^{yw}\sin z\cos z$

103. $-i\sin(x_1 + 2x_2 + \cdots + nx_n)$

105. (a) xy-plane, $12x^2 + 6x$ (b) $y \neq 0, -3x^2/y^2$

107. $f_x(2, -1) = 11$, $f_y(2, -1) = -8$

109. (b) does not exist if $y \neq 0$ and $x = -y$

▶ **Exercise Set 13.4 (Page 947)**

1. 5.04 **3.** 4.14 **9.** $dz = 7\,dx - 2\,dy$ **11.** $dz = 3x^2y^2\,dx + 2x^3y\,dy$

13. $dz = \dfrac{y}{1 + x^2y^2}\,dx + \dfrac{x}{1 + x^2y^2}\,dy$ **15.** $dw = 8\,dx - 3\,dy + 4\,dz$

17. $dw = 3x^2y^2z\,dx + 2x^3yz\,dy + x^3y^2\,dz$

19. $dw = \dfrac{yz}{1 + x^2y^2z^2}\,dx + \dfrac{xz}{1 + x^2y^2z^2}\,dy + \dfrac{xy}{1 + x^2y^2z^2}\,dz$

21. $df = 0.10$, $\Delta f = 0.1009$ **23.** $df = 0.03$, $\Delta f \approx 0.029412$

25. $df = 0.96$, $\Delta f \approx 0.97929$

Responses to True–False questions may be abridged to save space.

27. False; see the discussion at the beginning of this section.

29. True; see Theorems 13.4.3 and 13.4.4.

31. The increase in the area of the rectangle is given by the sum of the areas of the three small rectangles, and the total differential is given by the sum of the areas of the upper left and lower right rectangles.

33. (a) $L = \frac{1}{5} - \frac{4}{125}(x - 4) - \frac{3}{125}(y - 3)$ (b) 0.000176603

35. (a) $L = 0$ (b) 0.0024

37. (a) $L = 6 + 6(x - 1) + 3(y - 2) + 2(z - 3)$ (b) -0.000481

39. (a) $L = e + e(x - 1) - e(y + 1) - e(z + 1)$ (b) 0.01554

45. 0.5 **47.** $1, 1, -1, 2$ **49.** $(-1, 1)$ **51.** $(1, 0, 1)$ **53.** 8%

55. $r\%$ **57.** 0.3%

59. (a) $(r + s)\%$ (b) $(r + s)\%$ (c) $(2r + 3s)\%$ (d) $\left(3r + \dfrac{s}{2}\right)\%$

61. ≈ 39 ft^2

▶ **Exercise Set 13.5 (Page 956)**

1. $42t^{13}$ **3.** $3t^{-2}\sin(1/t)$ **5.** $-\frac{10}{3}t^{7/3}e^{1-t^{10/3}}$ **7.** $\dfrac{dw}{dt} = 165t^{32}$

9. $-2t\cos t^2$ **11.** 3264 **13.** 0

17. $24u^2v^2 - 16uv^3 - 2v + 3$, $16u^3v - 24u^2v^2 - 2u - 3$

19. $-\dfrac{2\sin u}{3\sin v}, -\dfrac{2\cos u\cos v}{3\sin^2 v}$ 21. $e^u, 0$

23. $3r^2\sin\theta\cos^2\theta - 4r^3\sin^3\theta\cos\theta,$
$\quad -2r^3\sin^2\theta\cos\theta + r^4\sin^4\theta + r^3\cos^3\theta - 3r^4\sin^2\theta\cos^2\theta$

25. $\dfrac{x^2+y^2}{4x^2y^3}, \dfrac{y^2-3x^2}{4xy^4}$ 27. $\dfrac{\partial z}{\partial r} = \dfrac{2r\cos^2\theta}{r^2\cos^2\theta+1}, \dfrac{\partial z}{\partial\theta} = \dfrac{-2r^2\cos\theta\sin\theta}{r^2\cos^2\theta+1}$

29. $\dfrac{dw}{d\rho} = 2\rho(4\sin^2\phi+\cos^2\phi), \dfrac{dw}{d\phi} = 6\rho^2\sin\phi\cos\phi, \dfrac{dw}{d\theta} = 0$

31. $-\pi$ 33. $\sqrt{3}e^{\sqrt{3}}, (2-4\sqrt{3})e^{\sqrt{3}}$

Responses to True–False questions may be abridged to save space.

35. False; the symbols ∂z and ∂x have no individual meaning.

37. False; consider $z = xy, x = t, y = t$.

39. $-\dfrac{2xy^3}{3x^2y^2-\sin y}$

41. $-\dfrac{ye^{xy}}{xe^{xy}+ye^y+e^y}$ 43. $\dfrac{2x+yz}{6yz-xy}, \dfrac{xz-3z^2}{6yz-xy}$

45. $\dfrac{ye^x}{15\cos 3z+3}, \dfrac{e^x}{15\cos 3z+3}$

59. $\dfrac{\partial w}{\partial\rho} = (\sin\phi\cos\theta)\dfrac{\partial w}{\partial x} + (\sin\phi\sin\theta)\dfrac{\partial w}{\partial y} + (\cos\phi)\dfrac{\partial w}{\partial z},$
$\dfrac{\partial w}{\partial\phi} = (\rho\cos\phi\cos\theta)\dfrac{\partial w}{\partial x} + (\rho\cos\phi\sin\theta)\dfrac{\partial w}{\partial y} - (\rho\sin\phi)\dfrac{\partial w}{\partial z},$
$\dfrac{\partial w}{\partial\theta} = -(\rho\sin\phi\sin\theta)\dfrac{\partial w}{\partial x} + (\rho\sin\phi\cos\theta)\dfrac{\partial w}{\partial y}$

63. (a) $\dfrac{dw}{dt} = \sum\limits_{i=1}^{4}\dfrac{\partial w}{\partial x_i}\dfrac{dx_i}{dt}$ (b) $\dfrac{\partial w}{\partial v_j} = \sum\limits_{i=1}^{4}\dfrac{\partial w}{\partial x_i}\dfrac{\partial x_i}{\partial v_j}, j = 1, 2, 3$

▶ **Exercise Set 13.6 (Page 968)**

1. $6\sqrt{2}$ 3. $-3/\sqrt{10}$ 5. -320 7. $-314/741$ 9. 0   11. $-8\sqrt{2}$

13. $\sqrt{2}/4$ 15. $72/\sqrt{14}$ 17. $-8/63$ 19. $1/2+\sqrt{3}/8$ 21. $2\sqrt{2}$

23. $1/\sqrt{5}$ 25. $-\frac{3}{2}e$ 27. $3/\sqrt{11}$ 29. (a) 5   (b) 10   (c) $-5\sqrt{5}$

31. III   33. $4\mathbf{i}-8\mathbf{j}$

35. $\nabla w = \dfrac{x}{x^2+y^2+z^2}\mathbf{i} + \dfrac{y}{x^2+y^2+z^2}\mathbf{j} + \dfrac{z}{x^2+y^2+z^2}\mathbf{k}$

37. $-36\mathbf{i}-12\mathbf{j}$ 39. $4(\mathbf{i}+\mathbf{j}+\mathbf{k})$

41.

43.

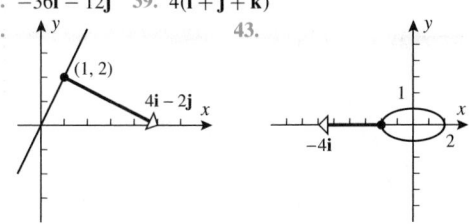

45. $\pm(-4\mathbf{i}+\mathbf{j})/\sqrt{17}$ 47. $\mathbf{u} = (3\mathbf{i}-2\mathbf{j})/\sqrt{13}, \|\nabla f(-1, 1)\| = 4\sqrt{13}$

49. $\mathbf{u} = (4\mathbf{i}-3\mathbf{j})/5, \|\nabla f(4, -3)\| = 1$ 51. $\dfrac{1}{\sqrt{2}}(\mathbf{i}-\mathbf{j}), 3\sqrt{2}$

53. $\dfrac{1}{\sqrt{2}}(-\mathbf{i}+\mathbf{j}), \dfrac{1}{\sqrt{2}}$

55. $\mathbf{u} = -(\mathbf{i}+3\mathbf{j})/\sqrt{10}, -\|\nabla f(-1, -3)\| = -2\sqrt{10}$

57. $\mathbf{u} = (3\mathbf{i}-\mathbf{j})/\sqrt{10}, -\|\nabla f(\pi/6, \pi/4)\| = -\sqrt{5}$

59. $(\mathbf{i}-11\mathbf{j}+12\mathbf{k})/\sqrt{266}, -\sqrt{266}$

Responses to True–False questions may be abridged to save space.

61. False; they are equal.   63. False; let $\mathbf{u} = \mathbf{i}$ and let $f(x, y) = y$.

65. $8/\sqrt{29}$

67. (a) $\approx 1/\sqrt{2}$
    (b)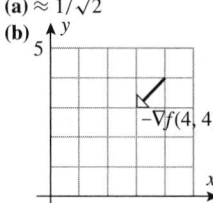

69. $9x^2+y^2 = 9$

71. $36/\sqrt{17}$

73. (a) $2e^{-\pi/2}\mathbf{i}$

75. $-\frac{5}{3}(2\mathbf{i}-\mathbf{j}-2\mathbf{k})$

81. $x(t) = e^{-8t}, y(t) = 4e^{-2t}$

83.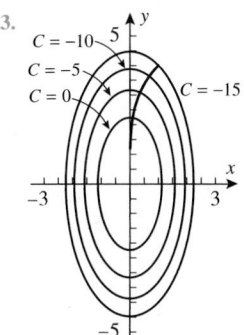

85. (a)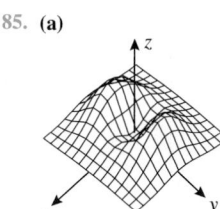

(c) $\nabla f = [2x - 2x(x^2+3y^2)]e^{-(x^2+y^2)}\mathbf{i}$
$\quad + [6y - 2y(x^2+3y^2)]e^{-(x^2+y^2)}\mathbf{j}$
(d) $x = y = 0$ or $x = 0, y = \pm 1$ or $x = \pm 1, y = 0$

▶ **Exercise Set 13.7 (Page 975)**

1. (a) $x+y+2z = 6$ (b) $x = 2+t, y = 2+t, z = 1+2t$
   (c) $35.26°$

3. tangent plane: $3x - 4z = -25$;
   normal line: $x = -3+(3t/4), y = 0, z = 4-t$

5. tangent plane: $48x - 14y - z = 64$;
   normal line: $x = 1+48t, y = -2-14t, z = 12-t$

7. tangent plane: $x - y - z = 0$;
   normal line: $x = 1+t, y = -t, z = 1-t$

9. tangent plane: $3y - z = -1$;
   normal line: $x = \pi/6, y = 3t, z = 1-t$

11. (a) all points on the x-axis or y-axis   (b) $(0, -2, -4)$

13. $\left(\frac{1}{2}, -2, -\frac{3}{4}\right)$ 15. (a) $(-2, 1, 5), (0, 3, 9)$ (b) $\dfrac{4}{3\sqrt{14}}, \dfrac{4}{\sqrt{222}}$

Responses to True–False questions may be abridged to save space.

17. False; they need only be parallel.

19. True; see Formula (15) of Section 13.4.

21. $\pm\dfrac{1}{\sqrt{365}}(\mathbf{i}-\mathbf{j}-19\mathbf{k})$ 25. $(1, 2/3, 2/3), (-1, -2/3, -2/3)$

27. $x = 1+8t, y = -1+5t, z = 2+6t$

29. $x = 3+4t, y = -3-4t, z = 4-3t$

▶ **Exercise Set 13.8 (Page 985)**

1. (a) minimum at $(2, -1)$, no maxima
   (b) maximum at $(0, 0)$, no minima   (c) no maxima or minima

3. minimum at $(3, -2)$, no maxima   5. relative minimum at $(0, 0)$

7. relative minimum at $(0, 0)$; saddle points at $(\pm 2, 1)$

9. saddle point at $(1, -2)$ 11. relative minimum at $(2, -1)$

13. relative minima at $(-1, -1)$ and $(1, 1)$ 15. saddle point at $(0, 0)$

17. no critical points   19. relative maximum at $(-1, 0)$

21. saddle point at $(0, 0)$;
    relative minima at $(1, 1)$
    and $(-1, -1)$

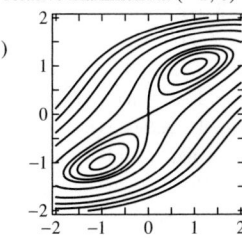

Responses to True–False questions may be abridged to save space.

23. False; let $f(x, y) = y$.

25. True; this follows from Theorem 13.8.6.

27. **(b)** relative minimum at $(0, 0)$

31. absolute maximum 0,
    absolute minimum -12

33. absolute maximum 3,
    absolute minimum -1

35. absolute maximum $\frac{33}{4}$,
    absolute minimum $-\frac{1}{4}$

37. $16, 16, 16$

39. maximum at $(1, 2, 2)$

41. $2a/\sqrt{3}, 2a/\sqrt{3}, 2a/\sqrt{3}$

43. length and width 2 ft, height 4 ft

45. **(a)** $x = 0$: minimum -3, maximum 0;
    $x = 1$: minimum 3, maximum $13/3$;
    $y = 0$: minimum 0, maximum 4;
    $y = 1$: minimum -3, maximum 3
    (b) $y = x$: minimum 0, maximum 3;
    $y = 1 - x$: maximum 4, minimum -3
    (c) minimum -3, maximum $13/3$

47. length and width $\sqrt[3]{2V}$, height $\sqrt[3]{2V}/2$ 51. $y = \frac{3}{4}x + \frac{19}{12}$

53. $y = 0.5x + 0.8$

55. **(a)** $y = 63.73 + 0.2565t$ **(b)**
    (c) about 84 years

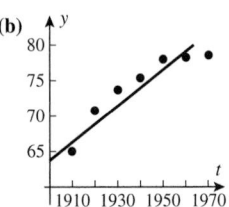

57. **(a)** $P = \dfrac{2798}{21} + \dfrac{171}{350}T$ **(b)**
    (c) $T \approx -272.7096°C$

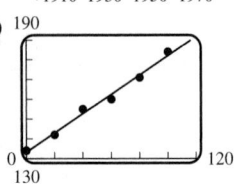

▶ **Exercise Set 13.9 (Page 996)**

1. **(a)** 4   3. **(a)**

    (c) maximum $\frac{101}{4}$,
    minimum -5

5. maximum $\sqrt{2}$ at $(-\sqrt{2}, -1)$ and $(\sqrt{2}, 1)$,
   minimum $-\sqrt{2}$ at $(-\sqrt{2}, 1)$ and $(\sqrt{2}, -1)$

7. maximum $\sqrt{2}$ at $(1/\sqrt{2}, 0)$, minimum $-\sqrt{2}$ at $(-1/\sqrt{2}, 0)$

9. maximum 6 at $\left(\frac{4}{3}, \frac{2}{3}, -\frac{4}{3}\right)$, minimum -6 at $\left(-\frac{4}{3}, -\frac{2}{3}, \frac{4}{3}\right)$

11. maximum is $1/(3\sqrt{3})$ at $(1/\sqrt{3}, 1/\sqrt{3}, 1/\sqrt{3})$,
    $(1/\sqrt{3}, -1/\sqrt{3}, -1/\sqrt{3})$, $(-1/\sqrt{3}, 1/\sqrt{3}, -1/\sqrt{3})$, and
    $(-1/\sqrt{3}, -1/\sqrt{3}, 1/\sqrt{3})$; minimum is $-1/(3\sqrt{3})$ at
    $(1/\sqrt{3}, 1/\sqrt{3}, -1/\sqrt{3})$, $(1/\sqrt{3}, -1/\sqrt{3}, 1/\sqrt{3})$,
    $(-1/\sqrt{3}, 1/\sqrt{3}, 1/\sqrt{3})$, and $(-1/\sqrt{3}, -1/\sqrt{3}, -1/\sqrt{3})$

Responses to True–False questions may be abridged to save space.

13. False; a Lagrange multiplier is a scalar.

15. False; we must solve three equations in three unknowns.

17. $\left(\frac{3}{10}, -\frac{3}{5}\right)$ 19. $\left(\frac{1}{6}, \frac{1}{3}, \frac{1}{6}\right)$

21. $(3, 6)$ is closest and $(-3, -6)$ is farthest   23. $5(\mathbf{i} + \mathbf{j} + \mathbf{k})/\sqrt{3}$

25. $9, 9, 9$ 27. $(\pm\sqrt{5}, 0, 0)$ 29. length and width 2 ft, height 4 ft

33. **(a)** $\alpha = \beta = \gamma = \pi/3$, maximum $1/8$
    (b)

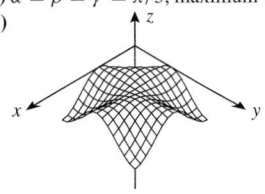

▶ **Chapter 13 Review Exercises (Page 997)**

1. **(a)** xy **(b)** $e^{r+s} \ln(rs)$

5. **(a)** not defined on line $y = x$ **(b)** not continuous

9. **(a)** 12 Pa/min   **(b)** 240 Pa/min

15. df (the differential of f) is an approximation for Δf (the change in f)

17. $dV = -0.06667$ m³; $\Delta V = -0.07267$ m³   19. 2

21. $\dfrac{-f_y^2 f_{xx} + 2 f_x f_y f_{xy} - f_x^2 f_{yz}}{f_y^3}$ 25. $\dfrac{7}{2} + \dfrac{4}{5} \ln 2$ 27. $-7/\sqrt{5}$

29. $(0, 0, 2), (1, 1, 1), (-1, -1, 1)$ 31. $\left(-\frac{1}{3}, -\frac{1}{2}, 2\right)$

33. relative minimum at $(15, -8)$

35. saddle point at $(0, 0)$, relative minimum at $(3, 9)$

37. absolute maximum of 4 at $(\pm 1, \pm 2)$, absolute minimum of 0 at
    $(\pm\sqrt{2}, 0)$ and $(0, \pm 2\sqrt{2})$

39. $I_1 : I_2 : I_3 = \dfrac{1}{R_1} : \dfrac{1}{R_2} : \dfrac{1}{R_3}$

41. **(a)** $\partial P/\partial L = c\alpha L^{\alpha-1} K^\beta$, $\partial P/\partial K = c\beta L^\alpha K^{\beta-1}$

▶ **Chapter 13 Making Connections (Page 999)**

Answers are provided in the Student Solutions Manual.

▶ **Exercise Set 14.1 (Page 1007)**

1. 7   3. 2   5. 2   7. 3   9. $1 - \ln 2$ 11. $\dfrac{1 - \ln 2}{2}$ 13. 0   15. $\frac{1}{3}$

17. **(a)** 37/4   **(b)** exact value = 28/3; differ by 1/12

19. $(1, 0, 4)$ 21.

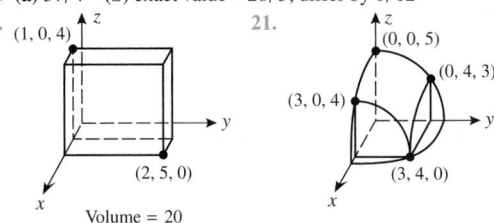

Volume = 20

Responses to True–False questions may be abridged to save space.

23. False; ΔA_k is the area of such a rectangular region.

25. False; $\displaystyle\iint\limits_{R} f(x, y)\, dA = \int_1^5 \int_2^4 f(x, y)\, dy\, dx$.

29. 19   31. 8   33. $\dfrac{1}{3\pi}$ 35. $1 - \dfrac{2}{\pi}$ 37. $\frac{14}{3}$ °C   39. 1.381737122

41. first integral equals $\frac{1}{2}$, second equals $-\frac{1}{2}$; no

▶ **Exercise Set 14.2 (Page 1015)**

1. $\frac{1}{40}$ 3. 9   5. $\dfrac{\pi}{2}$ 7. $\frac{1}{12}$

9. **(a)** $\displaystyle\int_0^2 \int_0^{x^2} f(x, y)\, dy\, dx$ **(b)** $\displaystyle\int_0^4 \int_{\sqrt{y}}^2 f(x, y)\, dx\, dy$

11. **(a)** $\displaystyle\int_1^2 \int_{-2x+5}^3 f(x, y)\, dy\, dx + \int_2^4 \int_1^3 f(x, y)\, dy\, dx +$
    $\displaystyle\int_4^5 \int_{2x-7}^3 f(x, y)\, dy\, dx$ **(b)** $\displaystyle\int_1^3 \int_{(5-y)/2}^{(y+7)/2} f(x, y)\, dx\, dy$

13. **(a)** $\frac{16}{3}$ **(b)** 38   15. 576   17. 0   19. $\dfrac{\sqrt{17} - 1}{2}$ 21. $\frac{50}{3}$

23. $-\frac{7}{60}$ **25.** $\dfrac{1-\cos 8}{3}$

27. (a)

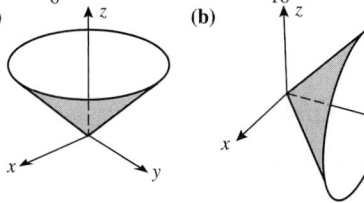

(b) $(-1.8414, 0.1586), (1.1462, 3.1462)$
(c) -0.4044
(d) -0.4044

29. $\sqrt{2}-1$ **31.** 32

Responses to True–False questions may be abridged to save space.

33. False; $\displaystyle\int_0^1\int_{x^2}^{2x} f(x,y)\,dy\,dx$ integrates $f(x,y)$ over the region between the graphs of $y=x^2$ and $y=2x$ for $0 \le x \le 1$ and results in a number, but $\displaystyle\int_{x^2}^{2x}\int_0^1 f(x,y)\,dx\,dy$ produces an expression involving x.

35. False; although R is symmetric across the x-axis, the integrand may not be.

37. 12   **39.** 27π **41.** 170   **43.** $\dfrac{27\pi}{2}$ **45.** $\dfrac{\pi}{2}$

47. $\displaystyle\int_0^{\sqrt{2}}\int_{y^2}^{2} f(x,y)\,dx\,dy$ **49.** $\displaystyle\int_1^{e^2}\int_{\ln x}^{2} f(x,y)\,dy\,dx$

51. $\displaystyle\int_0^{\pi/2}\int_0^{\sin x} f(x,y)\,dy\,dx$ **53.** $\dfrac{1-e^{-16}}{8}$ **55.** $\dfrac{e^8-1}{3}$

57. (a) 0   **(b)** $\tan 1$ **59.** 0   **61.** $\dfrac{\pi}{2}-\ln 2$ **63.** $\frac{2}{3}$°C   **65.** 0.676089

▶ **Exercise Set 14.3 (Page 1024)** _____

1. $\frac{1}{6}$ **3.** $\frac{2}{9}a^3$ **5.** 0   **7.** $\dfrac{3\pi}{2}$ **9.** $\dfrac{\pi}{16}$ **11.** $\displaystyle\int_{\pi/6}^{5\pi/6}\int_2^{4\sin\theta} f(r,\theta)r\,dr\,d\theta$

13. $8\displaystyle\int_0^{\pi/2}\int_1^3 r\sqrt{9-r^2}\,dr\,d\theta$ **15.** $2\displaystyle\int_0^{\pi/2}\int_0^{\cos\theta}(1-r^2)r\,dr\,d\theta$

17. $\dfrac{64\sqrt{2}}{3}\pi$ **19.** $\dfrac{5\pi}{32}$ **21.** $\dfrac{27\pi}{16}$ **23.** $(1-e^{-1})\pi$ **25.** $\dfrac{\pi}{8}\ln 5$ **27.** $\dfrac{\pi}{8}$

29. $\frac{16}{9}$ **31.** $\dfrac{\pi}{2}\left(1-\dfrac{1}{\sqrt{1+a^2}}\right)$ **33.** $\dfrac{\pi}{4}(\sqrt{5}-1)$

Responses to True–False questions may be abridged to save space.

35. True; the disk is given in polar coordinates by $0 \le r \le 2, 0 \le \theta \le 2\pi$.

37. False; the integrand is missing a factor of r:
$$\iint_R f(r,\theta)\,dA = \int_0^{\pi/2}\int_1^{2} f(r,\theta)r\,dr\,d\theta.$$

39. $\pi a^2 h$ **41.** $\dfrac{1}{5}+\dfrac{\pi}{2}$

43. (a) $\frac{4}{3}\pi a^2 c$ **(b)** $\approx 1.0831682 \times 10^{21}$ m³   **45.** $2a^2$

▶ **Exercise Set 14.4 (Page 1036)** _____

1. 6π **3.** $\dfrac{\sqrt{5}}{6}$ **5.** $\sqrt{2}\pi$ **7.** $\dfrac{(10\sqrt{10}-1)\pi}{18}$ **9.** 8π

11. (a)   **(b)**

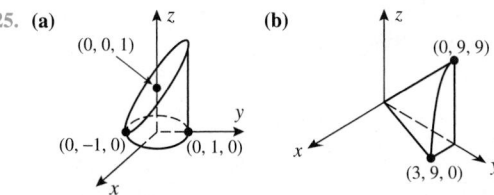

(c)

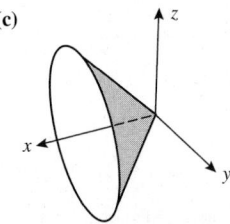

13. (a) $x=u, y=v, z=\frac{5}{2}+\frac{3}{2}u-2v$ **(b)** $x=u, y=v, z=u^2$
15. (a) $x=\sqrt{5}\cos u, y=\sqrt{5}\sin u, z=v; 0 \le u \le 2\pi, 0 \le v \le 1$
   (b) $x=2\cos u, y=v, z=2\sin u; 0 \le u \le 2\pi, 1 \le v \le 3$
17. $x=u, y=\sin u\cos v, z=\sin u\sin v$
19. $x=r\cos\theta, y=r\sin\theta, z=\dfrac{1}{1+r^2}$
21. $x=r\cos\theta, y=r\sin\theta, z=2r^2\cos\theta\sin\theta$
23. $x=r\cos\theta, y=r\sin\theta, z=\sqrt{9-r^2}; r \le \sqrt{5}$
25. $x=\dfrac{1}{2}\rho\cos\theta, y=\dfrac{1}{2}\rho\sin\theta, z=\dfrac{\sqrt{3}}{2}\rho$ **27.** $z=x-2y$; a plane
29. $(x/3)^2+(y/2)^2=1; 2 \le z \le 4$; part of an elliptic cylinder
31. $(x/3)^2+(y/4)^2=z^2; 0 \le z \le 1$; part of an elliptic cone
33. (a) $x=r\cos\theta, y=r\sin\theta, z=r, 0 \le r \le 2;$
   $x=u, y=v, z=\sqrt{u^2+v^2}, 0 \le u^2+v^2 \le 4$
35. (a) $0 \le u \le 3, 0 \le v \le \pi$ **(b)** $0 \le u \le 4, -\pi/2 \le v \le \pi/2$
37. (a) $0 \le \phi \le \pi/2, 0 \le \theta \le 2\pi$ **(b)** $0 \le \phi \le \pi, 0 \le \theta \le \pi$
39. $2x+4y-z=5$ **41.** $z=0$ **43.** $x-y+\dfrac{\sqrt{2}}{2}z=\dfrac{\pi\sqrt{2}}{8}$
45. $\dfrac{(17\sqrt{17}-5\sqrt{5})\pi}{6}$

Responses to True–False questions may be abridged to save space.

47. False; the surface area is $S=\displaystyle\iint_R \sqrt{[f_x(x,y)]^2+[f_y(x,y)]^2+1}\,dA.$

49. True; see the discussion preceding Definition 14.4.1.
51. $4\pi a^2$ **55.** $4\pi^2 ab$ **57.** 9.099
59. $(x/a)^2+(y/b)^2+(z/c)^2=1$; ellipsoid
61. $(x/a)^2+(y/b)^2-(z/c)^2=-1$; hyperboloid of two sheets

▶ **Exercise Set 14.5 (Page 1045)** _____

1. 8   **3.** $\frac{47}{3}$ **5.** $\frac{81}{5}$ **7.** $\frac{128}{15}$ **9.** $\pi(\pi-3)/2$ **11.** $\frac{1}{6}$ **13.** 9.425
15. 4   **17.** $\frac{256}{15}$

19. (a) $\displaystyle\int_{-1}^1\int_{-\sqrt{1-x^2}}^{\sqrt{1-x^2}}\int_{4x^2+y^2}^{4-3y^2} f(x,y,z)\,dz\,dy\,dx$

(b) $\displaystyle\int_{-1}^1\int_{-\sqrt{1-y^2}}^{\sqrt{1-y^2}}\int_{4x^2+y^2}^{4-3y^2} f(x,y,z)\,dz\,dx\,dy$

21. $4\displaystyle\int_0^1\int_0^{\sqrt{1-x^2}}\int_{4x^2+y^2}^{4-3y^2} dz\,dy\,dx$

23. $2\displaystyle\int_{-3}^3\int_0^{\frac{1}{3}\sqrt{9-x^2}}\int_0^{x+3} dz\,dy\,dx$

25. (a)   **(b)**

(c)

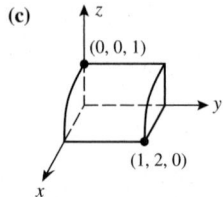

Responses to True–False questions may be abridged to save space.

27. True; apply Fubini's Theorem (Theorem 14.5.1).

29. False;

$$\iiint_G f(x, y, z)\, dV = \int_0^1 \int_0^{\sqrt{1-x^2}} \int_0^{\sqrt{1-x^2-y^2}} f(x, y, z)\, dz\, dy\, dx.$$

33. $\frac{3}{4}$ **35.** 3.291

37. (a) $\int_0^a \int_0^{b(1-x/a)} \int_0^{c(1-x/a-y/z)} dz\, dy\, dx$ is one example.

39. (a) $\int_0^2 \int_0^{\sqrt{4-x^2}} \int_0^5 f(x, y, z)\, dz\, dy\, dx$

(b) $\int_0^9 \int_0^{3-\sqrt{x}} \int_y^{3-\sqrt{x}} f(x, y, z)\, dz\, dy\, dx$

(c) $\int_0^2 \int_0^{4-x^2} \int_y^{8-y} f(x, y, z)\, dz\, dy\, dx$

▶ **Exercise Set 14.6 (Page 1056)**

1. $\frac{\pi}{4}$ **3.** $\frac{\pi}{16}$

5. The region is bounded by the xy-plane and the upper half of a sphere of radius 1 centered at the origin; $f(r, \theta, z) = z$.

7. The region is the portion of the first octant inside a sphere of radius 1 centered at the origin; $f(\rho, \theta, \phi) = \rho \cos \phi$.

9. $\frac{81\pi}{2}$ **11.** $\frac{152}{3}\pi + \frac{80}{3}\pi\sqrt{5}$ **13.** $\frac{64\pi}{3}$ **15.** $\frac{11\pi a^3}{3}$ **17.** $\frac{\pi a^6}{48}$

19. $\frac{32(2\sqrt{2}-1)\pi}{15}$

Responses to True–False questions may be abridged to save space.

21. False; the factor r^2 should be r [Formula (6)]:

$$\iiint_G f(x, y, z)\, dV = \iiint_{\substack{\text{appropriate} \\ \text{limits}}} f(r \cos \theta, r \sin \theta, z)r\, dz\, dr\, d\theta.$$

23. True; G is the spherical wedge bounded by the spheres $\rho = 1$ and $\rho = 3$, the half-planes $\theta = 0$ and $\theta = 2\pi$, and above the cone $\phi = \pi/4$, so

$$(\text{volume of } G) = \iiint_G dV = \int_0^{\pi/4} \int_0^{2\pi} \int_1^3 \rho^2 \sin \phi\, d\rho\, d\theta\, d\phi.$$

25. (a) $\frac{5}{2}(-8 + 3 \ln 3) \ln(\sqrt{5} - 2)$ **(b)** $f(x, y, z) = \frac{y^3}{x^3\sqrt{1+z^2}}$; G is the cylindrical wedge $1 \le r \le 4$, $\frac{\pi}{6} \le \theta \le \frac{\pi}{3}$, $-2 \le z \le 2$

27. $\frac{4\pi a^3}{3}$ **29.** $\frac{2(\sqrt{3}-1)\pi}{3}$

▶ **Exercise Set 14.7 (Page 1068)**

1. -17 **3.** $\cos(u - v)$ **5.** $x = \frac{2}{9}u + \frac{5}{9}v$, $y = -\frac{1}{9}u + \frac{2}{9}v$; $\frac{1}{9}$

7. $x = \frac{\sqrt{u+v}}{\sqrt{2}}$, $y = \frac{\sqrt{v-u}}{\sqrt{2}}$; $\frac{1}{4\sqrt{v^2-u^2}}$ **9.** 5   **11.** $\frac{1}{v}$

Responses to True–False questions may be abridged to save space.

13. False; $|\partial(x, y)/\partial(u, v)| = \|\partial\mathbf{r}/\partial u \times \partial\mathbf{r}/\partial v\|$; evaluating this at (u_0, v_0) gives the area of the indicated parallelogram.

15. False; $\partial(x, y)/\partial(r, \theta) = r$.

17.

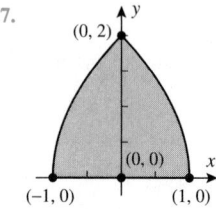

19.

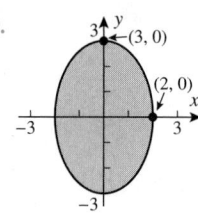

21. $\frac{3}{2}\ln 3$ **23.** $1 - \frac{1}{2}\sin 2$ **25.** 96π **27.** $\frac{\pi}{24}(1 - \cos 1)$ **29.** $\frac{192}{5}\pi$

31. $u = \begin{cases} \cot^{-1}(x/y), & y \ne 0 \\ 0, & y = 0 \text{ and } x > 0 \\ \pi, & y = 0 \text{ and } x < 0 \end{cases}$
$v = \sqrt{x^2 + y^2}$; other answers possible

33. $u = (3/7)x - (2/7)y$, $v = (-1/7)x + (3/7)y$; other answers possible

35. $\frac{1}{4}\ln\frac{5}{2}$

37. $\frac{1}{2}\left[\ln(\sqrt{2}+1) - \frac{\pi}{4}\right]$ **39.** $\frac{35}{256}$ **41.** $2\ln 3$ **45.** $21/8$

▶ **Exercise Set 14.8 (Page 1077)**

1. $M = \frac{13}{20}$, center of gravity $\left(\frac{190}{273}, \frac{6}{13}\right)$

3. $M = a^4/8$, center of gravity $(8a/15, 8a/15)$

5. $\left(\frac{1}{2}, \frac{1}{2}\right)$ **7.** $\left(\frac{1}{2}, \frac{1}{2}, \frac{1}{2}\right)$

Responses to True–False questions may be abridged to save space.

9. True; recall this from Section 6.7.

11. False; the center of gravity of the lamina is $(\bar{x}, \bar{y}) = (M_y/M, M_x/M)$, where M_y and M_x are the lamina's first moments about the y- and x-axes, respectively, and M is the mass of the lamina.

15. $\left(\frac{128}{105\pi}, \frac{128}{105\pi}\right)$ **17.** $\left(\frac{1}{4}, \frac{1}{4}, \frac{1}{4}\right)$ **19.** $\left(\frac{1}{2}, 0, \frac{3}{5}\right)$

21. $(3a/8, 3a/8, 3a/8)$

23. $M = a^4/2$, center of gravity $(a/3, a/2, a/2)$

25. $M = \frac{1}{6}$, center of gravity $\left(0, \frac{16}{35}, \frac{1}{2}\right)$ **27. (a)** $\left(\frac{5}{8}, \frac{5}{8}\right)$ **(b)** $\left(\frac{2}{3}, \frac{1}{2}\right)$

29. (1.177406, 0.353554, 0.231557)

31. $\frac{27\pi}{4}$ **33.** $\pi k a^4$ **35.** $\left(0, 0, \frac{7}{16\sqrt{2}-14}\right)$ **37.** $(3a/8, 3a/8, 3a/8)$

39. $(2-\sqrt{2})\pi/4$ **41.** $(0, 0, 8/15)$ **43.** $(0, 195/152, 0)$

47. $\frac{1}{2}\delta\pi a^4 h$ **49.** $\frac{1}{2}\delta\pi h(a_1^4 - a_1^4)$ **53.** $2\pi^2 abk$ **55.** $(a/3, b/3)$

▶ **Chapter 14 Review Exercises (Page 1080)**

3. (a) $\iint_R dA$ **(b)** $\iiint_G dV$ **(c)** $\iint_R \sqrt{1 + \left(\frac{\partial z}{\partial x}\right)^2 + \left(\frac{\partial z}{\partial y}\right)^2}\, dA$

5. $\int_0^1 \int_{1-\sqrt{1-y^2}}^{1+\sqrt{1-y^2}} f(x, y)\, dx\, dy$

7. (a) $a = 2, b = 1, c = 1, d = 2$ or $a = 1, b = 2, c = 2, d = 1$ **(b)** 3

9. $-\frac{1}{\sqrt{2\pi}}$ **13.**

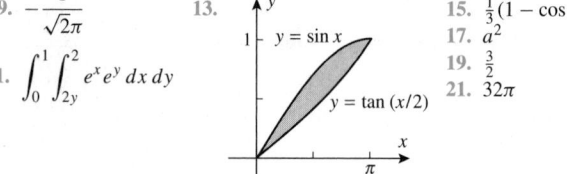

11. $\int_0^1 \int_{2y}^2 e^x e^y\, dx\, dy$

15. $\frac{1}{3}(1 - \cos 64)$ **17.** a^2 **19.** $\frac{3}{2}$ **21.** 32π

23. (a) $\int_0^{2\pi} \int_0^{\pi/3} \int_0^a \rho^4 \sin^3 \phi\, d\rho\, d\phi\, d\theta$

(b) $\int_0^{2\pi} \int_0^{\sqrt{3}a/2} \int_{r/\sqrt{3}}^{\sqrt{a^2-r^2}} r^3\, dz\, dr\, d\theta$

(c) $\int_{-\sqrt{3}a/2}^{\sqrt{3}a/2} \int_{-\sqrt{(3a^2/4)-x^2}}^{\sqrt{(3a^2/4)-x^2}} \int_{\sqrt{x^2+y^2}/\sqrt{3}}^{\sqrt{a^2-x^2-y^2}} (x^2 + y^2)\, dz\, dy\, dx$

25. $\frac{\pi a^3}{9}$ **27.** $\frac{1}{24}(26^{3/2} - 10^{3/2}) \approx 4.20632$ **29.** $2x + 4y - z = 5$

33. (a) $\dfrac{1}{2(u+w)}$ (b) $\frac{1}{2}(7\ln 7 - \ln 84, 375)$ **35.** $\left(\frac{8}{5}, 0\right)$
37. $(0, 0, h/4)$

▶ **Chapter 14 Making Connections (Page 1082)**

Where correct answers to a Making Connections exercise may vary, no answer is listed. Sample answers for these questions are available on the Book Companion Site.

1. (b) $\dfrac{\pi}{4}$ 3. (a) 1.173108605   (b) 1.173108605
4. (a) the sphere $0 \le x^2 + y^2 + z^2 \le 1$ (b) 4.934802202   (c) $\pi^2/2$
5. (b) 4.4506   6. $\frac{4}{35}\pi a^3$

▶ **Exercise Set 15.1 (Page 1092)**

1. (a) III   (b) IV   3. (a) true   (b) true   (c) true

5. 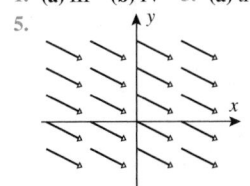   7.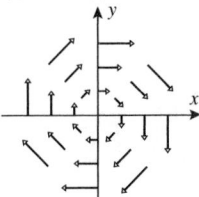

9.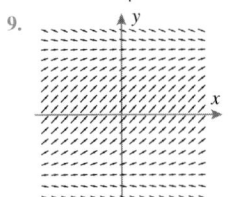

Responses to True–False questions may be abridged to save space.
11. False; the vector field has a nonzero **k**-component.
13. True; this is the curl of **F**.
15. (a) all x, y (b) all x, y 17. div $\mathbf{F} = 2x + y$, curl $\mathbf{F} = z\mathbf{i}$
19. div $\mathbf{F} = 0$, curl $\mathbf{F} = (40x^2z^4 - 12xy^3)\mathbf{i} + (14y^3z + 3y^4)\mathbf{j} - (16xz^5 + 21y^2z^2)\mathbf{k}$
21. div $\mathbf{F} = \dfrac{2}{\sqrt{x^2 + y^2 + z^2}}$, curl $\mathbf{F} = 0$ 23. $4x$ 25. 0
27. $(1 + y)\mathbf{i} + x\mathbf{j}$
39. $\nabla \cdot (k\mathbf{F}) = k\nabla \cdot \mathbf{F}$, $\nabla \cdot (\mathbf{F} + \mathbf{G}) = \nabla \cdot \mathbf{F} + \nabla \cdot \mathbf{G}$, $\nabla \cdot (\phi\mathbf{F}) = \phi\nabla \cdot \mathbf{F} + \nabla\phi \cdot \mathbf{F}$, $\nabla \cdot (\nabla \times \mathbf{F}) = 0$ 47. (b) $x^2 + y^2 = K$
49. $\dfrac{dy}{dx} = \dfrac{1}{x}$, $y = \ln x + K$

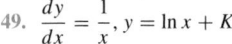

▶ **Exercise Set 15.2 (Page 1108)**

1. (a) 1   (b) 0   3. 16
7. (a) $-\frac{11}{108}\sqrt{10} - \frac{1}{36}\ln(\sqrt{10} - 3) - \frac{4}{27}$ (b) 0   (c) $-\frac{1}{2}$
9. (a) 3   (b) 3   (c) 3   (d) 3
Responses to True–False questions may be abridged to save space.
11. False; line integrals of functions are independent of the orientation of the curve.   13. True; this is Equation (26).
15. 2   17. $\frac{13}{20}$ 19. $1 - \pi$ 21. 3   23. $-1 - (\pi/4)$ 25. $1 - e^3$
27. (a) $\dfrac{63\sqrt{17}}{64} + \frac{1}{4}\ln(4 + \sqrt{17}) - \frac{1}{8}\ln\dfrac{\sqrt{17} + 1}{\sqrt{17} - 1} - \frac{1}{4}\ln(\sqrt{2} + 1) + \frac{1}{8}\ln\dfrac{\sqrt{2} + 1}{\sqrt{2} - 1}$ (b) $1/2 - \pi/4$

29. (a) -1 (b) -2 31. $\frac{5}{2}$ 33. 0   35. $1 - e^{-1}$ 37. $6\sqrt{3}$
39. $5k\tan^{-1} 3$ 41. $\frac{3}{5}$ 43. $\frac{27}{28}$ 45. $\frac{3}{4}$ 47. $\dfrac{17\sqrt{17} - 1}{4}$
49. (b) $S = \displaystyle\int_C z(t)\,dt$ (c) 4π 51. $\lambda = -12$

▶ **Exercise Set 15.3 (Page 1120)**

1. conservative, $\phi = \dfrac{x^2}{2} + \dfrac{y^2}{2} + K$ 3. not conservative
5. conservative, $\phi = x\cos y + y\sin x + K$
9. -6 11. $9e^2$ 13. 32   15. $W = -\frac{1}{2}$ 17. $W = 1 - e^{-1}$
Responses to True–False questions may be abridged to save space.
19. False; the integral must be 0 for *all* closed curves C.
21. True; if $\nabla\phi$ is constant, then ϕ must be a linear function.
23. $\ln 2 - 1$ 25. ≈ -0.307 27. no   33. $h(x) = Ce^x$
35. (a) $W = -\dfrac{1}{\sqrt{14}} + \dfrac{1}{\sqrt{16}}$ (b) $W = -\dfrac{1}{\sqrt{14}} + \dfrac{1}{\sqrt{6}}$ (c) $W = 0$

▶ **Exercise Set 15.4 (Page 1127)**

1. 0   3. 0   5. 0   7. 8π 9. -4 11. -1 13. 0
Responses to True–False questions may be abridged to save space.
15. False; Green's Theorem applies to closed curves.
17. True; the integral is the area of the region bounded by C.
19. (a) ≈ -3.550999378 (b) ≈ -0.269616482 21. $\frac{3}{8}a^2\pi$ 23. $\frac{1}{2}abt_0$
27. Formula (1) of Section 6.1   29. $\frac{250}{3}$ 31. $-3\pi a^2$ 33. $\left(\frac{8}{15}, \frac{8}{21}\right)$
35. $\left(0, \dfrac{4a}{3\pi}\right)$ 37. the circle $x^2 + y^2 = 1$ 39. 69

▶ **Exercise Set 15.5 (Page 1136)**

1. $\dfrac{15}{2}\pi\sqrt{2}$ 3. $\dfrac{\pi}{4}$ 5. $-\dfrac{\sqrt{2}}{2}$ 7. 9
Responses to True–False questions may be abridged to save space.
9. True; this follows from the definition.
11. False; the integral is the total mass of the lamina.
13. (b) $2\pi\left[1 - \sqrt{1 - r^2} + \dfrac{r^2}{2}\right] \to 3\pi$ as $r \to 1^-$
    (c) $\mathbf{r}(\phi, \theta) = \sin\phi\cos\theta\mathbf{i} + \sin\phi\sin\theta\mathbf{j} + \cos\phi\mathbf{k}$,
    $0 \le \theta \le 2\pi, 0 \le \phi \le \pi/2$;
    $\displaystyle\iint (1 + z)\,dS = \int_0^{2\pi}\int_0^{\pi/2}(1 + \cos\phi)\sin\phi\,d\phi\,d\theta = 3\pi$
17. (c) $4\pi/3$
19. (a) $\dfrac{\sqrt{29}}{16}\displaystyle\int_0^6\int_0^{(12-2x)/3} xy(12 - 2x - 3y)\,dy\,dx$
    (b) $\dfrac{\sqrt{29}}{4}\displaystyle\int_0^3\int_0^{(12-4z)/3} yz(12 - 3y - 4z)\,dy\,dz$
    (c) $\dfrac{\sqrt{29}}{9}\displaystyle\int_0^3\int_0^{6-2z} xz(12 - 2x - 4z)\,dx\,dz$
21. $\dfrac{18\sqrt{29}}{5}$
23. $\displaystyle\int_0^4\int_1^2 y^3z\sqrt{4y^2 + 1}\,dy\,dz$; $\dfrac{1}{2}\displaystyle\int_0^4\int_1^4 xz\sqrt{1 + 4x}\,dx\,dz$
25. $\dfrac{391\sqrt{17}}{15} - \dfrac{5\sqrt{5}}{3}$ 27. $\frac{4}{3}\pi\delta_0$ 29. $\frac{1}{4}(37\sqrt{37} - 1)$ 31. $M = \delta_0 S$
33. $(0, 0, 149/65)$ 35. $\dfrac{93}{\sqrt{10}}$ 37. $\dfrac{\pi}{4}$ 39. 57.895751

▶ **Exercise Set 15.6 (Page 1146)**

1. (a) zero   (b) zero   (c) positive   (d) negative   (e) zero   (f) zero
3. (a) positive   (b) zero   (c) positive   (d) zero   (e) positive   (f) zero
5. (a) $n = -\cos v\mathbf{i} - \sin v\mathbf{j}$ (b) inward   7. 2π 9. $\dfrac{14\pi}{3}$ 11. 0
13. 18π 15. $\frac{4}{9}$ 17. (a) 8   (b) 24   (c) 0

Responses to True–False questions may be abridged to save space.

19. False; the Möbius strip has no orientation.

21. False; the net volume can be zero because as much fluid passes through the surface in the negative direction as in the positive direction.

23. 3π 25. (a) $0 \, \text{m}^3/\text{s}$ (b) $0 \, \text{kg/s}$ 27. (b) $32/3$

29. (a) $4\pi a^{k+3}$ (b) $k = -3$ 31. $a = 2, 3$

▶ **Exercise Set 15.7 (Page 1157)** _____

1. 3   3. $\dfrac{4\pi}{3}$

Responses to True–False questions may be abridged to save space.

5. False; it equates a surface integral and a triple integral.

7. True; see subsection entitled Sources and Sinks.

9. 12   11. $3\pi a^2$ 13. 180π 15. $\dfrac{192\pi}{5}$ 17. $\dfrac{\pi}{2}$

19. $\dfrac{4608}{35}$ 21. 135π 33. no sources or sinks

35. sources at all points except the origin, no sinks   37. $\dfrac{7\pi}{4}$

▶ **Exercise Set 15.8 (Page 1164)** _____

1. $\frac{3}{2}$ 3. 0   5. 2π 7. 16π 9. 0   11. πa^2

Responses to True–False questions may be abridged to save space.

13. True; see Theorem 15.8.1.   15. False; the circulation is $\int_C \mathbf{F} \cdot \mathbf{T} \, ds$.

17. (a) $\frac{3}{2}$ (b) -1 (c) $-\dfrac{1}{\sqrt{2}}\mathbf{j} - \dfrac{1}{\sqrt{2}}\mathbf{k}$ 23. $-\dfrac{5\pi}{4}$

▶ **Chapter 15 Review Exercises (Page 1166)** _____

3. $\dfrac{1-x}{\sqrt{(1-x)^2 + (2-y)^2}}\mathbf{i} + \dfrac{2-y}{\sqrt{(1-x)^2 + (2-y)^2}}\mathbf{j}$ 5. $\mathbf{i} + \mathbf{j} + \mathbf{k}$

7. (a) $\displaystyle\int_a^b \left[f(x(t), y(t))\dfrac{dx}{dt} + g(x(t), y(t))\dfrac{dy}{dt} \right] dt$

(b) $\displaystyle\int_a^b f(x(t), y(t))\sqrt{x'(t)^2 + y'(t)^2} \, dt$

11. 0   13. $-7/2$ 17. (a) $h(x) = Cx^{-3/2}$ (b) $g(y) = C/y^3$

21. $A = \dfrac{1}{2}\displaystyle\int_\alpha^\beta r^2 \, d\theta$

23. $\displaystyle\iint_R f(x(u,v), y(u,v), z(u,v))\|r_u \times r_v\| \, du \, dv$ 25. yes   27. 2π

31. -8π 35. (a) conservative   (b) not conservative

▶ **Chapter 15 Making Connections (Page 1168)** _____

Answers are provided in the Student Solutions Manual.

▶ **Appendix A (Page A1)** _____

1. (e)   3. (b), (c)   5. $[-3, 3] \times [0, 5]$

7. $[-5, 14] \times [-60, 40]$ 9. $[-0.1, 0.1] \times [-3, 3]$

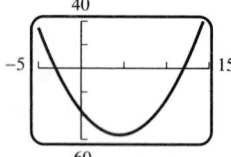

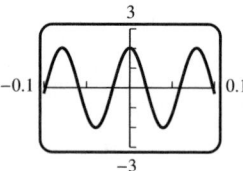

11. $[-400, 1050] \times [-1500000, 10000]$ 13. $[-2, 2] \times [-20, 20]$

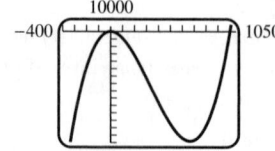

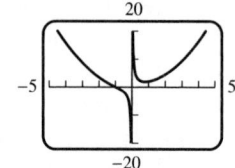

17. (a) $f(x) = \sqrt{16 - x^2}$ (b) $f(x) = -\sqrt{16 - x^2}$ (e) no

19. (a)

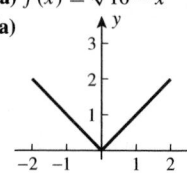

(b)

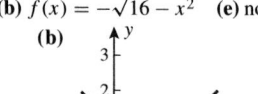

(c)

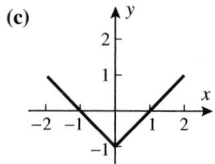

(d)

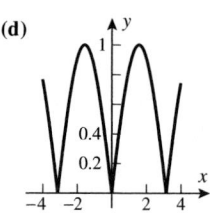

(e)

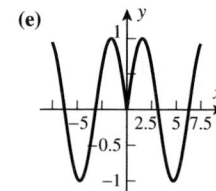

(f)

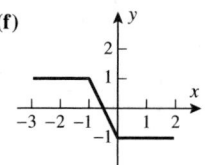

21.

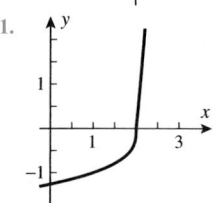

25. (a)

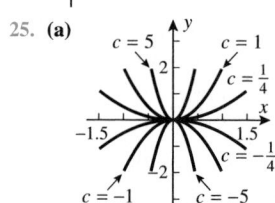

The graph is stretched in the vertical direction, and reflected across the x-axis if $c < 0$.

(b)

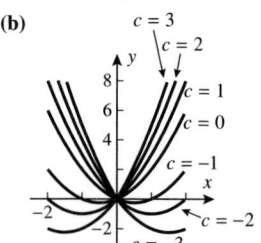

The graph is translated so its vertex is on the parabola $y = -x^2$.

(c)

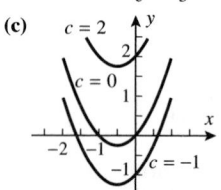

The graph is translated vertically.

27.

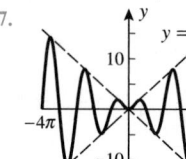

29. (a) 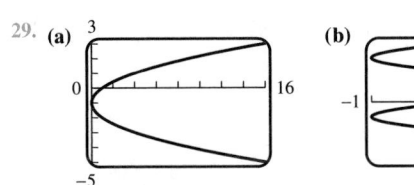   (b)

31. 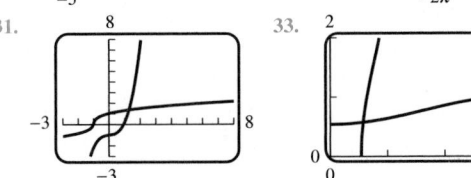   33.

35. (a) $x = 4\cos t, y = 3\sin t$ (b) $x = -1 + 4\cos t, y = 2 + 3\sin t$

▶ **Appendix B (Page A13)**

1. (a) $\frac{5}{12}\pi$ (b) $\frac{13}{6}\pi$ (c) $\frac{1}{9}\pi$ (d) $\frac{23}{30}\pi$

3. (a) $12°$ (b) $(270/\pi)°$ (c) $288°$ (d) $540°$

5.

	$\sin\theta$	$\cos\theta$	$\tan\theta$	$\csc\theta$	$\sec\theta$	$\cot\theta$
(a)	$\sqrt{21}/5$	$2/5$	$\sqrt{21}/2$	$5/\sqrt{21}$	$5/2$	$2/\sqrt{21}$
(b)	$3/4$	$\sqrt{7}/4$	$3/\sqrt{7}$	$4/3$	$4/\sqrt{7}$	$\sqrt{7}/3$
(c)	$3/\sqrt{10}$	$1/\sqrt{10}$	3	$\sqrt{10}/3$	$\sqrt{10}$	$1/3$

7. $\sin\theta = 3/\sqrt{10}, \cos\theta = 1/\sqrt{10}$ 9. $\tan\theta = \sqrt{21}/2, \csc\theta = 5/\sqrt{21}$

11. 1.8

13.

	θ	$\sin\theta$	$\cos\theta$	$\tan\theta$	$\csc\theta$	$\sec\theta$	$\cot\theta$
(a)	$225°$	$-1/\sqrt{2}$	$-1/\sqrt{2}$	1	$-\sqrt{2}$	$-\sqrt{2}$	1
(b)	$-210°$	$1/2$	$-\sqrt{3}/2$	$-1/\sqrt{3}$	2	$-2/\sqrt{3}$	$-\sqrt{3}$
(c)	$5\pi/3$	$-\sqrt{3}/2$	$1/2$	$-\sqrt{3}$	$-2/\sqrt{3}$	2	$-1/\sqrt{3}$
(d)	$-3\pi/2$	1	0	—	1	—	0

15.

	$\sin\theta$	$\cos\theta$	$\tan\theta$	$\csc\theta$	$\sec\theta$	$\cot\theta$
(a)	$4/5$	$3/5$	$4/3$	$5/4$	$5/3$	$3/4$
(b)	$-4/5$	$3/5$	$-4/3$	$-5/4$	$5/3$	$-3/4$
(c)	$1/2$	$-\sqrt{3}/2$	$-1/\sqrt{3}$	2	$-2/\sqrt{3}$	$-\sqrt{3}$
(d)	$-1/2$	$\sqrt{3}/2$	$-1/\sqrt{3}$	-2	$2/\sqrt{3}$	$-\sqrt{3}$
(e)	$1/\sqrt{2}$	$1/\sqrt{2}$	1	$\sqrt{2}$	$\sqrt{2}$	1
(f)	$1/\sqrt{2}$	$-1/\sqrt{2}$	-1	$\sqrt{2}$	$-\sqrt{2}$	-1

17. (a) 1.2679 (b) 3.5753

19.

	$\sin\theta$	$\cos\theta$	$\tan\theta$	$\csc\theta$	$\sec\theta$	$\cot\theta$
(a)	$a/3$	$\sqrt{9-a^2}/3$	$a/\sqrt{9-a^2}$	$3/a$	$3/\sqrt{9-a^2}$	$\sqrt{9-a^2}/a$
(b)	$a/\sqrt{a^2+25}$	$5/\sqrt{a^2+25}$	$a/5$	$\sqrt{a^2+25}/a$	$\sqrt{a^2+25}/5$	$5/a$
(c)	$\sqrt{a^2-1}/a$	$1/a$	$\sqrt{a^2-1}$	$a/\sqrt{a^2-1}$	a	$1/\sqrt{a^2-1}$

21. (a) $3\pi/4 \pm n\pi, n = 0, 1, 2, \ldots$
    (b) $\pi/3 \pm 2n\pi$ and $5\pi/3 \pm 2n\pi, n = 0, 1, 2, \ldots$
23. (a) $\pi/6 \pm n\pi, n = 0, 1, 2, \ldots$
    (b) $4\pi/3 \pm 2n\pi$ and $5\pi/3 \pm 2n\pi, n = 0, 1, 2, \ldots$
25. (a) $3\pi/4 \pm n\pi, n = 0, 1, 2, \ldots$
    (b) $\pi/6 \pm n\pi, n = 0, 1, 2, \ldots$
27. (a) $\pi/3 \pm 2n\pi$ and $2\pi/3 \pm 2n\pi, n = 0, 1, 2, \ldots$
    (b) $\pi/6 \pm 2n\pi$ and $11\pi/6 \pm 2n\pi, n = 0, 1, 2, \ldots$
29. $\sin\theta = 2/5, \cos\theta = -\sqrt{21}/5, \tan\theta = -2/\sqrt{21},$
    $\csc\theta = 5/2, \sec\theta = -5/\sqrt{21}, \cot\theta = -\sqrt{21}/2$
31. (a) $\theta = \pm n\pi, n = 0, 1, 2, \ldots$ (b) $\theta = \pi/2 \pm n\pi, n = 0, 1, 2, \ldots$
    (c) $\theta = \pm n\pi, n = 0, 1, 2, \ldots$ (d) $\theta = \pm n\pi, n = 0, 1, 2, \ldots$

(e) $\theta = \pi/2 \pm n\pi, n = 0, 1, 2, \ldots$ (f) $\theta = \pm n\pi, n = 0, 1, 2, \ldots$

33. (a) $2\pi/3$ cm   (b) $10\pi/3$ cm   35. $\frac{2}{5}$

37. (a) $\dfrac{2\pi - \theta}{2\pi}R$ (b) $\dfrac{\sqrt{4\pi\theta - \theta^2}}{2\pi}R$ 39. $\frac{21}{4}\sqrt{3}$ 41. 9.2 ft

43. $h = d(\tan\beta - \tan\alpha)$ 45. (a) $4\sqrt{5}/9$ (b) $-\frac{1}{9}$

47. $\sin 3\theta = 3\sin\theta\cos^2\theta - \sin^3\theta, \cos 3\theta = \cos^3\theta - 3\sin^2\theta\cos\theta$

61. (a) $\cos\theta$ (b) $-\sin\theta$ (c) $-\cos\theta$ (d) $\sin\theta$

69. (a) $153°$ (b) $45°$ (c) $117°$ (d) $89°$ 71. (a) $60°$ (b) $117°$

▶ **Appendix C (Page A27)**

1. (a) $q(x) = x^2 + 4x + 2, r(x) = -11x + 6$
   (b) $q(x) = 2x^2 + 4, r(x) = 9$
   (c) $q(x) = x^3 - x^2 + 2x - 2, r(x) = 2x + 1$
3. (a) $q(x) = 3x^2 + 6x + 8, r(x) = 15$
   (b) $q(x) = x^3 - 5x^2 + 20x - 100, r(x) = 504$
   (c) $q(x) = x^4 + x^3 + x^2 + x + 1, r(x) = 0$
5.

x	0	1	-3	7
$p(x)$	-4	-3	101	5001

7. (a) $q(x) = x^2 + 6x + 13, r = 20$ (b) $q(x) = x^2 + 3x - 2, r = -4$
9. (a) $\pm1, \pm2, \pm3, \pm4, \pm6, \pm8, \pm12, \pm24$
   (b) $\pm1, \pm2, \pm5, \pm10, \pm\frac{1}{3}, \pm\frac{2}{3}, \pm\frac{5}{3}, \pm\frac{10}{3}$ (c) $\pm1, \pm17$
11. $(x+1)(x-1)(x-2)$ 13. $(x+3)^3(x+1)$
15. $(x+3)(x+2)(x+1)^2(x-3)$ 17. -3 19. $-2, -\frac{2}{3}, -1 \pm \sqrt{3}$
21. $-2, 2, 3$ 23. $2, 5$ 25. 7 cm

INDEX